Who's Who in America

Biographical Reference Works Published by Marquis Who's Who

Who's Who Publications

Who's Who in America

Who's Who in America supplements:

Who's Who in America Index by Professional Area and Geographic Location

Who's Who in America College Alumni Directory

Who's Who in America Birthdate Index

Who Was Who in America

Historical Volume (1607-1896)

Volume I (1897-1942)

Volume II (1943-1950)

Volume III (1951-1960)

Volume IV (1961-1968)

Volume V (1969-1973)

Volume VI (1974-1976)

Volume VII (1977-1981)

Who Was Who in American History—Arts and Letters

Who Was Who in American History—The Military

Who Was Who in American History—Science and Technology

Who's Who in the World

Who's Who in the East

Who's Who in the Midwest

Who's Who in the South and Southwest

Who's Who in the West

Who's Who in American Law

Who's Who of American Women

Who's Who in Finance and Industry

Who's Who in Frontier Science and Technology

Who's Who in Religion

World Who's Who in Science

Directory of Women in Marquis Who's Who Publications

Marquis Who's Who Publications/Index to All Books 1984

Volume 1 Alphabetic

Volume 2 Geographic

Professional Publications

Directory of Medical Specialists

Marquis Who's Who Directory of Online Professionals

Marquis Who's Who Directory of Computer Graphics

Marquis Who's Who Directory of Professionals and Resources in Cancer

Marquis Who's Who Directory of Professionals and Resources in Rehabilitation

Database

Marquis Who's Who Database

Who's Who in America®

43rd edition
1984-1985
Volume 1

MARQUIS
Who's Who

Marquis Who's Who, Inc.
200 East Ohio Street
Chicago, Illinois 60611 U.S.A.

Library of Congress Catalog Card Number 4-16934
International Standard Book Number 0-8379-0-143-X
Product Code Number 030317

Distributed in Europe by
Thompson, Henry Limited
London Road
Sunningdale, Berks
SL5 OEP, England

Distributed in Asia by
United Publishers Services Ltd.
Kenkyu-Sha Bldg.
9, Kanda Surugadai 2-Chome
Chiyoda-Ku, Tokyo, Japan

Manufactured in the United States of America

Table of Contents

Preface

First published in 1899, *Who's Who in America* has become the standard of contemporary biography throughout the nation. The "Big Red Book" is known for its readily available store of life and career data on noteworthy individuals.

The book has grown from 8,602 names in the first edition to approximately 75,000 biographees in the forty-third edition. *Who's Who in America* includes outstanding individuals in Canada and Mexico as well as the United States. The growth of the directory attests to its success in reflecting demographic crosscurrents within American society and in profiling key men and women who influence the nation's development. In addition, this steady growth proves the success of *Who's Who in America* in carrying out the intent of its original publisher, A.N. Marquis. In 1898, when he recognized the need for an American biographical directory, Mr. Marquis declared that the guiding principle behind such a venture would be to chronicle the lives of individuals whose achievements and contributions to society made them subjects of widespread reference interest and inquiry. The forty-third edition continues to uphold that principle.

The current edition, published at the eighty-fifth anniversary of the first volume, marks a milestone in the history of *Who's Who in America*. Marquis Who's Who has long used computerized typesetting in the printing of its books. For the forty-third edition of *Who's Who in America*, sophisticated computer technology has been applied to the content of the sketches to provide an improved level of consistency in the definition and arrangement of information. The technology was used in order to create an online database of the sketches in *Who's Who in America*, enabling the user to obtain information about individuals with specifically defined traits, for example, architects living in the midwest who are older than fifty years of age. Such information, now available from Marquis Who's Who or on most personal computers or terminals through convenient telecommunications networks, provides additional access to the many biographical items in each sketch beyond searching for individuals by name.

The biographical sketches in the book, while written in the well-known *Who's Who in America* format, contained minor variations in style that had developed over many years. For example, creative works were sometimes listed as career activity and sometimes found near the end of the sketch as special achievements. In order to make computer analysis possible, the variables in the sketches, such as education, awards, creative works, and all the other topics of information covered, had to be defined consistently and placed uniformly in the same relative position in each sketch. While maintaining the traditional Who's Who style, some of the biographical sketches may have a new look. The improvement in consistency will continue with each edition, as the technology is successively applied.

The biographical data contained in the pages of *Who's Who in America* come from the best sources available—the biographees themselves, resulting in accurate and current biographical information. In the two years it takes to develop a single edition of *Who's Who in America*, many steps are taken. Potential biographees are identified by Marquis researchers and editors. Candidates are sent data forms and are invited to submit complete biographical and career information. These data are reviewed to confirm that candidates meet the stringent selection criteria. Sketches are then prepared and sent to biographees for prepublication checking.

In some cases where individuals fail to submit biographical data, Marquis staff members compile the information through independent research. Sketches compiled in this manner are denoted by the symbol *. For a small number of cases, where detailed biographical data were not available at publication, the editors have written brief sketches with current career information; these are indicated by the symbol §.

Ultimate selection is based on reference value. Individuals become eligible for listing by virtue of their positions and/or noteworthy achievements that have proved to be of significant value to society. An individual's desire to be listed is not sufficient reason for inclusion. Similarly, wealth or social position is not a criterion. Purchase of the book is never a factor in the selection of biographees.

To maintain its reputation for currentness and, at the same time, to adhere to space limitations, *Who's Who in America* undergoes meticulous review of selection criteria with each edition. Deletion of some names is inevitable; such deletion is not arbitrary. For example, if a biographee has retired from active participation in a career or public life, the sketch may be excluded. In large part, it is career development that determines inclusion or continuation.

To produce the most efficient reference source available, *Who's Who in America* provides several special features. First, the edition contains a cumulative Retiree Index of persons whose names were deleted from the forty-second or forty-third editions because they have retired from active work. This Index enables the user to locate the last published biographical sketch of each listee. Second, there is a Necrology of biographees whose sketches appeared in the forty-second edition and whose deaths were reported prior to the closing of this edition. The sketches have been removed from the book; complete biographical sketches of these individuals, including date of death and place of interment, will be included in the forthcoming Volume VIII of *Who Was Who in America*.

The third feature is an expanded listing of individuals whose sketches appear in one of the Marquis regional or topical directories. Included are *Who's Who in the East*, *Who's Who in the Midwest*, *Who's Who in the South and Southwest*, and *Who's Who in the West*, as well as *Who's Who in American Law*, *Who's Who of American Women*, *Who's Who in Finance and Industry*, and the first edition of *Who's Who in Frontier Science and Technology*. While some of these individuals are biographees in this edition, most are not. Thus, the reference potential of *Who's Who in America* is broadened by the listing of individuals found in the complementary Marquis volumes.

Finally, many of the sketches end with an italicized feature, "Thoughts on My Life." The statement is written by the biographee and reflects those principles, goals, ideals, and values that have been guidelines for success and high standards.

Putting together a reference source as comprehensive as *Who's Who in America* is a herculean challenge. Marquis Who's Who editors exercise diligent care in preparing each sketch for publication. Despite all precautions, however, errors do occasionally occur. Users of this directory are invited to draw the attention of the publisher to any such errors so that corrective measures can be taken in a subsequent edition.

Adele Hast, Ph.D.
Editor-in-Chief

Board of Advisors

Marquis Who's Who gratefully acknowledges the following distinguished individuals who have made themselves available for review, evaluation, and general comment with regard to the publication of the 43rd Edition of *Who's Who in America.* The advisors have enhanced the reference value of this edition by the nomination of outstanding individuals for inclusion. However, the Board of Advisors—either collectively or individually—is in no way responsible for the final selection of names appearing in this volume, nor does the Board of Advisors bear responsibility for the accuracy or comprehensiveness of the biographical information or other material contained herein.

Fred Basolo
Immediate Past President
American Chemical Society

Willard L. Boyd
President
Field Museum of Natural History

John M. Coady, D.D.S.
Executive Director
American Dental Association

Arlene Croce
Dance Critic
The New Yorker

Jean Dalrymple
Director
American National Theatre and Academy

Sherman R. Emery
Editorial Consultant
Interior Design

Milton Friedman
Senior Research Fellow
Hoover Institution on War, Revolution and Peace

Thomas H. Gonser
Executive Director
American Bar Association

Barbara Haskell
Curator
Whitney Museum of American Art

Townsend Hoopes
President
Association of American Publishers

Elizabeth T. Kennan
President
Mount Holyoke College

Robert W. Krauss
Executive Director
Federation of American Societies for Experimental Biology

James Levine
Music Director
Metropolitan Opera Association

Martin E. Marty
Professor
The Divinity School
The University of Chicago

David O. Meeker, Jr.
Architect and Planner
Former Executive Vice President
The American Institute of Architects

Margaret M. Mills
Executive Director
American Academy and Institute of Arts and Letters

Joseph Papp
Producer
New York Shakespeare Festival

Louis Rukeyser
Economic Commentator
Host, *Wall Street Week*

Marianne Scott
Director of Libraries
McGill University

Wilfrid J. Sheed
Author

Stuart Silver
Vice President Design Communications
Knoll International Inc.

John F. Sullivan
President and Publisher
National Journal

Lewis Thomas, M.D.
President Emeritus
Memorial Sloan-Kettering Cancer Center

Lawrence W. Towner
President and Librarian
The Newberry Library

James A. Van Allen
Chairman
Department of Physics
The University of Iowa

John W. Ward
President
American Council of Learned Societies

Robert Wedgeworth
Executive Director
American Library Association

Irwin Winkler
Motion Picture Producer
Chartoff-Winkler Productions, Inc.

Eugene Zwoyer
Consulting Engineer
Former President
American Association of Engineering Societies, Inc.

Standards of Admission

The foremost consideration in determining who will be admitted to the pages of *Who's Who in America* is the extent of an individual's reference interest. Reference value is based on either of two factors: 1) the position of responsibility held or 2) the level of significant achievement attained in a career of noteworthy activity. The majority of biographees qualify for admission on the basis of the first factor, a specific position of responsibility. Incumbency in the position makes the person someone of high reference interest. The factor of position includes the following categories:

1. High-ranking members of the legislative, executive, and judicial branches of the United States government. This group includes, for example, members of Congress, cabinet secretaries, chief administrators of selected federal agencies and commissions, and justices of the federal courts.
2. Military officers on active duty with the rank of major general or higher in the army, air force, and marine corps, and of rear admiral or higher in the navy.
3. Specified state government officials. Among them are governors, lieutenant governors, secretaries of state, attorneys general, treasurers, and other selected positions such as president of the state senate, the state university system administrator, and the chief state health officer. This standard includes officials of American territories.
4. Judges of state and territorial courts of the highest appellate jurisdiction.
5. High-level officials of principal cities, based on population. These officials include mayors, police chiefs, school superintendents, and other selected positions.
6. Leading government officials of Canada and Mexico. In Canada, this group includes, as examples, the prime minister, premiers of the provinces, ministers of departments of the federal government, and justices of the highest courts. Examples in the Mexican government are the president and cabinet secretaries of the national government.
7. Principal officers of major national and international businesses as defined by several quantitative criteria.
8. Ranking administrative officials of major universities and colleges. Some of the officers included in this category are president, provost, dean, and selected department heads.
9. Heads of leading philanthropic, cultural, educational, professional, and scientific institutions and associations. These institutions include, for example, selected foundations, museums, symphony orchestras, libraries, and research laboratories.
10. Selected members of honorary organizations such as the National Academy of Sciences, the National Academy of Design, and the Institute of Medicine. This group includes elected fellows of specified organizations, for example, the Royal Society of Canada and the American College of Trial Lawyers.
11. Chief ecclesiastics of the principal religious denominations.
12. Recipients of major national and international awards. A few examples are the Nobel and Pulitzer prizes, the Academy Award, and the American Institute of Architecture Gold Medal for Architecture.

Admission by the second factor—significant achievement—is based on the application of objective criteria established for each field. An artist whose works hang in major museums qualifies for admission for noteworthy accomplishment. The professor who has made important research contributions in his field is of reference interest because of his outstanding achievements. Qualitative standards determine eligibility for every field.

In many instances, there is considerable overlap between the two factors used for inclusion in *Who's Who in America*. For example, the head of a major library is in the book because of position, but reaching that responsibility also signifies important achievement. Similarly, a state governor not only holds a position that warrants inclusion; attaining that post also represents significant achievement in the political world. In both cases the reference value of the biographical sketch is significant. Whether the person has been selected because of position or as a mark of achievement, the biographee in *Who's Who in America* has noteworthy accomplishments beyond those of the vast majority of contemporaries.

Key to Information in this Directory

❶ **DAVIES, STEPHEN FRANCIS,** ❷ physics educator; ❸ b. Evanston, Ill., Oct. 8, 1930; ❹ s. Paul Harwell and Mary Louise (Ryan) D.; ❺ m. Elizabeth C. Swan, June 10, 1956; ❻ children: Robert Dwight, Mary Adele, William Fremont. ❼ B.S., Princeton U., 1953; Ph.D., MIT, 1959. ❽ Cert. safety profl., Mass. ❾ Research asst. radiation lab. physics dept. MIT, Cambridge, 1959-61; assoc. physicist Battelle Meml. Inst., Columbus, Ohio, 1961-64; asst. prof. physics Columbia U., N.Y.C., 1965-69, assoc. prof., 1969-75, prof. radiation physics, 1975—; vis. scientist Am. Inst. Physics, 1978; vis. prof. Rensselaer Poly. Inst., Troy, N.Y., 1981-82; chmn. commn. radiation physics Internat. Union Pure and Applied Physics, 1979-81; mem. Nat. Sci. Bd., 1982—. ❿ Editor: Radiation Testing Standards, 1976; contbr. articles to profl. jours. ⓫ Trustee Cornell U.; bd. dirs. Fairfield County chpt. Am. Cancer Soc., Greenwich Civic Orch. ⓬ Served with USN, 1948-49. ⓭ Recipient Research prize N.Y. Acad. Scis., 1980; fellow Sloan Found., 1974-76, Guggenheim Found., 1981. ⓮ Mem. AAAS, Am. Phys. Soc., Nat. Acad. Scis., Am. Nuclear Soc., Sigma Xi. ⓯ Republican. ⓰ Episcopalian. ⓱ Clubs: Down Town (N.Y.C.); Rolling Meadows Country. ⓲ Lodge: Masons ⓳ Home: 411 Wolf Pit Rd Greenwich CT 06830 ⓴ Office: Dept Physics Columbia U New York NY 10002

KEY

❶ Name
❷ Occupation
❸ Vital Statistics
❹ Parents
❺ Marriage
❻ Children
❼ Education
❽ Professional certifications
❾ Career
❿ Writings and creative works
⓫ Civic and political activities
⓬ Military record
⓭ Awards and fellowships
⓮ Professional and association memberships
⓯ Political affiliation
⓰ Religion
⓱ Clubs
⓲ Lodges
⓳ Home address
⓴ Office address

Table of Abbreviations

The following abbreviations and symbols are used in this book.

* Sketch was researched or updated by Marquis Who's Who editorial staff and has not been verified by the biographee.

§ Brief sketch with current career information was written by Marquis Who's Who editorial staff and has not been verified by the biographee.

A.A. Associate in Arts
AAAL American Academy of Arts and Letters
AAAS American Association for the Advancement of Science
AAHPER Alliance for Health, Physical Education and Recreation
AAU Amateur Athletic Union
AAUP American Association of University Professors
AAUW American Association of University Women
A.B. Arts, Bachelor of
AB Alberta
ABA American Bar Association
ABC American Broadcasting Company
AC Air Corps
acad. academy, academic
acct. accountant
acctg. accounting
ACDA Arms Control and Disarmament Agency
ACLU American Civil Liberties Union
ACP American College of Physicians
ACS American College of Surgeons
ADA American Dental Association
a.d.c. aide-de-camp
adj. adjunct, adjutant
adj. gen. adjutant general
adm. admiral
adminstr. administrator
adminstrn. administration
adminstrv. administrative
ADP automatic data processing
adv. advocate, advisory
advt. advertising
A.E. Agricultural Engineer (for degrees only)
A.E. and P. Ambassador Extraordinary and Plenipotentiary
AEC Atomic Energy Commission
aero. aeronautical, aeronautic
aerodyn. aerodynamic
AFB Air Force Base
AFL-CIO American Federation of Labor and Congress of Industrial Organizations
AFTRA American Federation TV and Radio Artists
agr. agriculture
agrl. agricultural
agt. agent
AGVA American Guild of Variety Artists
agy. agency
A&I Agricultural and Industrial
AIA American Institute of Architects
AIAA American Institute of Aeronautics and Astronautics
AID Agency for International Development
AIEE American Institute of Electrical Engineers
AIM American Institute of Management
AIME American Institute of Mining, Metallurgy, and Petroleum Engineers
AK Alaska
AL Alabama
ALA American Library Association
Ala. Alabama
alt. alternate
Alta. Alberta
A&M Agricultural and Mechanical
A.M. Arts, Master of
Am. American, America
AMA American Medical Association
A.M.E. African Methodist Episcopal
Amtrak National Railroad Passenger Corporation
AMVETS American Veterans of World War II, Korea, Vietnam
anat. anatomical
ann. annual
ANTA American National Theatre and Academy
anthrop. anthropological
AP Associated Press
APO Army Post Office
Apr. April
apptd. appointed
apt. apartment
AR Arkansas
ARC American Red Cross
archeol. archeological
archtl. architectural
Ariz. Arizona
Ark. Arkansas
ArtsD. Arts, Doctors of
arty. artillery
ASCAP American Society of Composers, Authors and Publishers
ASCE American Society of Civil Engineers
ASHRAE American Society of Heating, Refrigeration, and Air Conditioning Engineers
ASME American Society of Mechanical Engineers
assn. association
assoc. associate
asst. assistant
ASTM American Society for Testing and Materials
astron. astronomical
astrophys. astrophysical
ATSC Air Technical Service Command
AT&T American Telephone & Telegraph Company
atty. attorney
AUS Army of the United States
Aug. August
aux. auxiliary
Ave. Avenue
AVMA American Veterinary Medical Association
AZ Arizona

B. Bachelor
b. born
B.A. Bachelor of Arts
B.Agr. Bachelor of Agriculture
Balt. Baltimore
Bapt. Baptist
B. Arch. Bachelor of Architecture
B.A.S. Bachelor of Agricultural Science
B.B.A. Bachelor of Business Administration
BBC British Broadcasting Corporation
B.C., BC British Columbia
B.C.E. Bachelor of Civil Engineering
B.Chir. Bachelor of Surgery
B.C.L. Bachelor of Civil Law
B.C.S. Bachelor of Commercial Science
B.D. Bachelor of Divinity
bd. board
B.E. Bachelor of Education
B.E.E. Bachelor of Electrical Engineering
B.F.A. Bachelor of Fine Arts
bibl. biblical
bibliog. bibliographical
biog. biographical
biol. biological
B.J. Bachelor of Journalism
Bklyn. Brooklyn
B.L. Bachelor of Letters
bldg. building
B.L.S. Bachelor of Library Science
Blvd. Boulevard
bn. battalion
B.&O.R.R. Baltimore & Ohio Railroad
bot. botanical
B.P.E. Bachelor of Physical Education
br. branch
B.R.E. Bachelor of Religious Education
brig. gen. brigadier general
Brit. British, Brittanica
Bros. Brothers
B.S. Bachelor of Science
B.S.A. Bachelor of Agricultural Science
B.S.D. Bachelor of Didactic Science
B.S.T. Bachelor of Sacred Theology
B.Th. Bachelor of Theology
bull. bulletin
bur. bureau

bus. business
B.W.I. British West Indies

CA California
CAA Civil Aeronautics Administration
CAB Civil Aeronautics Board
Calif. California
C.Am. Central America
Can. Canada, Canadian
CAP Civil Air Patrol
capt. captain
CARE Cooperative American Relief Everywhere
Cath. Catholic
cav. cavalry
CBC Canadian Broadcasting Company
CBI China, Burma, India Theatre of Operations
CBS Columbia Broadcasting System
CCC Commodity Credit Corporation
CCNY City College of New York
CCU Cardiac Care Unit
CD Civil Defense
C.E. Corps of Engineers, Civil Engineer (in firm's name only or for degree)
cen. central (To be used for court system only)
CENTO Central Treaty Organization
CERN European Organization of Nuclear Research
cert. certificate, certification, certified
CETA Comprehensive Employment Training Act
CFL Canadian Football League
ch. church
Ch.D. Doctor of Chemistry
chem. chemical
Chem.E. Chemical Engineer
Chgo. Chicago
chirurg. chirurgical
chmn. chairman
chpt. chapter
CIA Central Intelligence Agency
CIC Counter Intelligence Corps
Cin. Cincinnati
cir. circuit
Cleve. Cleveland
climatol. climatological
clin. clinical
clk. clerk
C.L.U. Chartered Life Underwriter
C.M. Master in Surgery
C.&N.W.Ry. Chicago & Northwestern Railway
CO Colorado
Co. Company
COF Catholic Order of Foresters
C. of C. Chamber of Commerce
col. colonel.
coll. college
Colo. Colorado
com. committee
comd. commanded
comdg. commanding
comdr. commander
comdt. commandant
commd. commissioned
comml. commercial
commn. commission
commr. commissioner
condr. conductor
Conf. Conference
Congl. Congregational, Congressional
Conglist. Congregationalist
Conn. Connecticut
cons. consultant, consulting
consol. consolidated
constl. constitutional
constn. constitution
constrn. construction
contbd. contributed
contbg. contributing
contbn. contribution
contbr. contributor
Conv. Convention
coop. cooperative
CORDS Civil Operations and Revolutionary Development Support
CORE Congress of Racial Equality
corp. corporation, corporate
corr. correspondent, corresponding, correspondence
C.&O.Ry. Chesapeake & Ohio Railway
C.P.A. Certified Public Accountant
C.P.C.U. Chartered property and casualty underwriter
C.P.H. Certificate of Public Health
cpl. corporal
CPR Cardio-Pulmonary Resuscitation
C.P.Ry. Canadian Pacific Railway
C.S. Christian Science
C.S.B. Bachelor of Christian Science
CSC Civil Service Commission
C.S.D. Doctor of Christian Science
CT Connecticut
ct. court
ctr. center
CWS Chemical Warfare Service
C.Z. Canal Zone

d. daughter
D. Doctor
D.Agr. Doctor of Agriculture
DAR Daughters of the American Revolution
dau. daughter
DAV Disabled American Veterans
D.C., DC District of Columbia
D.C.L. Doctor of Civil Law
D.C.S. Doctor of Commercial Science
D.D. Doctor of Divinity
D.D.S. Doctor of Dental Surgery
DE Delaware
dec. deceased
Dec. December
def. defense
Del. Delaware
del. delegate, delegation
Dem. Democrat, Democratic
D.Eng. Doctor of Engineering
denom. denomination, denominational
dep. deputy
dept. department
dermatol. dermatological
desc. descendant
devel. development, developmental
D.F.A. Doctor of Fine Arts
D.F.C. Distinguished Flying Cross
D.H.L. Doctor of Hebrew Literature
dir. director
dist. district
distbg. distributing
distbn. distribution
distbr. distributor
disting. distinguished
div. division, divinity, divorce
D.Litt. Doctor of Literature
D.M.D. Doctor of Medical Dentistry
D.M.S. Doctor of Medical Science
D.O. Doctor of Osteopathy
D.P.H. Diploma in Public Health
D.R. Daughters of the Revolution
Dr. Drive, Doctor
D.R.E. Doctor of Religious Education
Dr.P.H. Doctor of Public Health, Doctor of Public Hygiene
D.S.C. Distinguished Service Cross
D.Sc. Doctor of Science
D.S.M. Distinguished Service Medal
D.S.T. Doctor of Sacred Theology
D.T.M. Doctor of Tropical Medicine
D.V.M. Doctor of Veterinary Medicine
D.V.S. Doctor of Veterinary Surgery

E. East
ea. eastern (use for court system only)
E. and P. Extraordinary and Plenipotentiary
Eccles. Ecclesiastical
ecol. ecological
econ. economic
ECOSOC Economic and Social Council (of the UN)
E.D. Doctor of Engineering
ed. educated
Ed.B. Bachelor of Education
Ed.D. Doctor of Education
edit. edition
Ed.M. Master of Education
edn. education
ednl. educational
EDP electronic data processing
Ed.S. Specialist in Education
E.E. Electrical Engineer (degree only)
E.E. and M.P. Envoy Extraordinary and Minister Plenipotentiary

EEC European Economic Community
EEG electroencephalogram
EEO Equal Employment Opportunity
EEOC Equal Employment Opportunity Commission
EKG electrocardiogram
E.Ger. German Democratic Republic
elec. electrical
electrochem. electrochemical
electrophys. electrophysical
elem. elementary
E.M. Engineer of Mines
ency. encyclopedia
Eng. England
engr. engineer
engring. engineering
entomol. entomological
environ. environmental
EPA Environmental Protection Agency
epidemiol. epidemiological
Episc. Episcopalian
ERA Equal Rights Amendment
ERDA Energy Research and Development Administration
ESEA Elementary and Secondary Education Act
ESL English as Second Language
ESSA Environmental Science Services Administration
ethnol. ethnological
ETO European Theatre of Operations
Evang. Evangelical
exam. examination, examining
exec. executive
exhbn. exhibition
expdn. expedition
expn. exposition
expt. experiment
exptl. experimental

F.A. Field Artillery
FAA Federal Aviation Administration
FAO Food and Agriculture Organization (of the UN)
FBI Federal Bureau of Investigation
FCA Farm Credit Administration
FCC Federal Communication Commission
FCDA Federal Civil Defense Administration
FDA Food and Drug Administration
FDIA Federal Deposit Insurance Administration
FDIC Federal Deposit Insurance Corporation
F.E. Forest Engineer
FEA Federal Energy Administration
Feb. February
fed. federal
fedn. federation
FERC Federal Energy Regulatory Commission
fgn. foreign
FHA Federal Housing Administration
fin. financial, finance
FL Florida
Fla. Florida
FMC Federal Maritime Commission
FOA Foreign Operations Administration
found. foundation
FPC Federal Power Commission
FPO Fleet Post Office
frat. fraternity
FRS Federal Reserve System
FSA Federal Security Agency
Ft. Fort
FTC Federal Trade Commission

G-1 (or other number) Division of General Staff
Ga., GA Georgia
GAO General Accounting Office
gastroent. gastroenterological
GATT General Agreement of Tariff and Trades
gen. general
geneal. genealogical
geod. geodetic
geog. geographic, geographical
geol. geological
geophys. geophysical
gerontol. gerontological
G.H.Q. General Headquarters
G.N. Ry. Great Northern Railway
gov. governor
govt. government
govtl. governmental
GPO Government Printing Office
grad. graduate, graduated
GSA General Services Administration
Gt. Great
GU Guam
gynecol. gynecological

hdqrs. headquarters
HEW Department of Health, Education and Welfare
H.H.D. Doctor of Humanities
HHFA Housing and Home Finance Agency
HHS Department of Health and Human Services
HI Hawaii
hist. historical, historic
H.M. Master of Humanics
homeo. homeopathic
hon. honorary, honorable
Ho. of Dels. House of Delegates
Ho. of Reps. House of Representatives
hort. horticultural
hosp. hospital
HUD Department of Housing and Urban Development
Hwy. Highway
hydrog. hydrographic

IA Iowa
IAEA International Atomic Energy Agency
IBM International Business Machines Corporation
IBRD International Bank for Reconstruction and Development
ICA International Cooperation Administration
ICC Interstate Commerce Commission
ICU Intensive Care Unit
ID Idaho
IEEE Institute of Electrical and Electronics Engineers
IFC International Finance Corporation
IGY International Geophysical Year
IL Illinois
Ill. Illinois
illus. illustrated
ILO International Labor Organization
IMF International Monetary Fund
IN Indiana
Inc. Incorporated
ind. independent
Ind. Indiana
Indpls. Indianapolis
indsl. industrial
inf. infantry
info. information
ins. insurance
insp. inspector
insp. gen. inspector general
inst. institute
instl. institutional
instn. institution
instr. instructor
instrn. instruction
intern. international
intro. introduction
IRE Institute of Radio Engineers
IRS Internal Revenue Service
ITT International Telephone & Telegraph Corporation

JAG Judge Advocate General
JAGC Judge Advocate General Corps
Jan. January
Jaycees Junior Chamber of Commerce
J.B. Jurum Baccolaureus
J.C.B. Juris Canoni Baccalaureus
J.C.D. Juris Canonici Doctor, Juris Civilis Doctor
J.C.L. Juris Canonici Licentiatus
J.D. Juris Doctor
j.g. junior grade
jour. journal
jr. junior
J.S.D. Juris Scientiae Doctor
J.U.D. Juris Utriusque Doctor
jud. judicial

Kans. Kansas

K.C. Knights of Columbus
K.P. Knights of Pythias
KS Kansas
K.T. Knight Templar
Ky., KY Kentucky

La., LA Louisiana
lab. laboratory
lang. language
laryngol. laryngological
LB Labrador
lectr. lecturer
legis. legislation, legislative
L.H.D. Doctor of Humane Letters
L.I. Long Island
lic. licensed, license
L.I.R.R. Long Island Railroad
lit. literary, literature
Litt.B. Bachelor of Letters
Litt.D. Doctor of Letters
LL.B. Bachelor of Laws
LL.D. Doctor of Laws
LL.M. Master of Laws
Ln. Lane
L.&N.R.R. Louisville & Nashville Railroad
L.S. Library Science (in degree)
lt. lieutenant
Ltd. Limited
Luth. Lutheran
LWV League of Women Voters

m. married
M. Master
M.A. Master of Arts
MA Massachusetts
mag. magazine
M.Agr. Master of Agriculture
maj. major
Man. Manitoba
Mar. March
M.Arch. Master in Architecture
Mass. Massachusetts
math. mathematics, mathematical
MATS Military Air Transport Service
M.B. Bachelor of Medicine
MB Manitoba
M.B.A. Master of Business Administration
MBS Mutual Broadcasting System
M.C. Medical Corps
M.C.E. Master of Civil Engineering
mcht. merchant
mcpl. municipal
M.C.S. Master of Commercial Science
M.D. Doctor of Medicine
Md, MD Maryland
M.Dip. Master in Diplomacy
mdse. merchandise
M.D.V. Doctor of Veterinary Medicine
M.E. Mechanical Engineer (degree only)
ME Maine
M.E.Ch. Methodist Episcopal Church
mech. mechanical
M.Ed. Master of Education
med. medical
M.E.E. Master of Electrical Engineering
mem. member
meml. memorial
merc. mercantile
met. metropolitan
metall. metallurgical
Met.E. Metallurgical Engineer
meteorol. meteorological
Meth. Methodist
Mex. Mexico
M.F. Master of Forestry
M.F.A. Master of Fine Arts
mfg. manufacturing
mfr. manufacturer
mgmt. management
mgr. manager
M.H.A. Master of Hospital Administration
M.I. Military Intelligence
MI Michigan
Mich. Michigan
micros. microscopic, microscopical
mid. middle (use for Court System only)
mil. military
Milw. Milwaukee
mineral. mineralogical
Minn. Minnesota
Miss. Mississippi
MIT Massachusetts Institute of Technology
mktg. marketing
M.L. Master of Laws
MLA Modern Language Association
M.L.D. Magister Legnum Diplomatic
M.Litt. Master of Literature
M.L.S. Master of Library Science
M.M.E. Master of Mechanical Engineering
MN Minnesota
mng. managing
Mo., MO Missouri
moblzn. mobilization
Mont. Montana
M.P. Member of Parliament
M.P.E. Master of Physical Education
M.P.H. Master of Public Health
M.P.L. Master of Patent Law
Mpls. Minneapolis
M.R.E. Master of Religious Education
M.S. Master of Science
MS, Ms. Mississippi
M.Sc. Master of Science
M.S.F. Master of Science of Forestry
M.S.T. Master of Sacred Theology
M.S.W. Master of Social Work
MT Montana
Mt. Mount
MTO Mediterranean Theatre of Operations
mus. museum, musical
Mus.B. Bachelor of Music
Mus.D. Doctor of Music
Mus.M. Master of Music
mut. mutual
mycol. mycological

N. North
NAACP National Association for the Advancement of Colored People
NACA National Advisory Committee for Aeronautics
NAD National Academy of Design
N.Am. North America
NAM National Association of Manufacturers
NAPA National Association of Performing Artists
NAREB National Association of Real Estate Boards
NARS National Archives and Record Service
NASA National Aeronautics and Space Administration
nat. national
NATO North Atlantic Treaty Organization
NATOUSA North African Theatre of Operations
nav. navigation
N.B., NB New Brunswick
NBC National Broadcasting Company
N.C., NC North Carolina
NCCJ National Conference of Christians and Jews
N.D., ND North Dakota
NDEA National Defense Education Act
NE Nebraska
NE Northeast
NEA National Education Association
Nebr. Nebraska
NEH National Endowment for Humanities
neurol. neurological
Nev. Nevada
NF Newfoundland
NFL National Football League
Nfld. Newfoundland
N.G. National Guard
N.H. NH New Hampshire
NHL National Hockey League
NIH National Institutes of Health
NIMH National Institute of Mental Health
N.J., NJ New Jersey
NLRB National Labor Relations Board
NM New Mexico
N.Mex. New Mexico
No. Northern
NOAA National Oceanographic and Atmospheric Administration
NORAD North America Air Defense
NOW National Organization for Women
Nov. November
N.P.Ry. Northern Pacific Railway
nr. near

NRC National Research Council
N.S., NS Nova Scotia
NSC National Security Council
NSF National Science Foundation
N.T. New Testament
NT Northwest Territories
numis. numismatic
NV Nevada
NW Northwest
N.W.T. Northwest Territories
N.Y., NY New York
N.Y.C. New York City
NYU New York University
N.Z. New Zealand

OAS Organization of American States
ob-gyn obstetrics-gynecology
obs. observatory
obstet. obstetrical
O.D. Doctor of Optometry
OECD Organization of European Cooperation and Development
OEEC Organization of European Economic Cooperation
OEO Office of Economic Opportunity
ofcl. official
OH Ohio
OK Oklahoma
Okla. Oklahoma
ON Ontario
Ont. Ontario
ophthal. ophthalmological
ops. operations
OR Oregon
orch. orchestra
Oreg. Oregon
orgn. organization
ornithol. ornithological
OSHA Occupational Safety and Health Administration
OSRD Office of Scientific Research and Development
OSS Office of Strategic Services
osteo. osteopathic
otol. otological
otolaryn. otolaryngological

Pa., PA Pennsylvania
P.A. Professional Association
paleontol. paleontological
path. pathological
P.C. Professional Corporation
PE Prince Edward Island
P.E.I. Prince Edward Island (text only)
PEN Poets, Playwrights, Editors, Essayists and Novelists (international association)
penol. penological
P.E.O. women's organization (full name not disclosed)
pfc. private first class
PHA Public Housing Administration
pharm. pharmaceutical
Pharm.D. Doctor of Pharmacy
Pharm. M. Master of Pharmacy
Ph.B. Bachelor of Philosophy
Ph.D. Doctor of Philosophy
Phila. Philadelphia
philharm. philharmonic
philol. philological
philos. philosophical
photog. photographic
phys. physical
physiol. physiological
Pitts. Pittsburgh
Pkwy. Parkway
Pl. Place
P.&L.E.R.R. Pittsburgh & Lake Erie Railroad
P.O. Post Office
PO Box Post Office Box
polit. political
poly. polytechnic, polytechnical
PQ Province of Quebec
P.R., PR Puerto Rico
prep. preparatory
pres. president
Presbyn. Presbyterian
presdl. presidential
prin. principal
proc. proceedings
prod. produced (play production)
prodn. production
prof. professor
profl. professional
prog. progressive
propr. proprietor
pros. atty. prosecuting attorney
pro tem pro tempore
PSRO Professional Services Review Organization
psychiat. psychiatric
psychol. psychological
PTA Parent-Teachers Association
ptnr. partner
PTO Pacific Theatre of Operations, Parent Teacher Organization
pub. publisher, publishing, published
pub. public
publ. publication
pvt. private

quar. quarterly
q.m. quartermaster
Q.M.C. Quartermaster Corps.
Que. Quebec

radiol. radiological
RAF Royal Air Force
RCA Radio Corporation of America
RCAF Royal Canadian Air Force
RD Rural Delivery
Rd. Road
REA Rural Electrification Administration
rec. recording
ref. reformed
regt. regiment
regtl. regimental
rehab. rehabilitation
rep. representative
Rep. Republican
Res. Reserve
ret. retired
rev. review, revised
RFC Reconstruction Finance Corporation
RFD Rural Free Delivery
rhinol. rhinological
R.I., RI Rhode Island
R.N. Registered Nurse
roentgenol. roentgenological
ROTC Reserve Officers Training Corps
R.R. Railroad
Ry. Railway

s. son
S. South
SAC Strategic Air Command
SALT Strategic Arms Limitation Talks
S.Am. South America
san. sanitary
SAR Sons of the American Revolution
Sask. Saskatchewan
savs. savings
S.B. Bachelor of Science
SBA Small Business Administration
S.C., SC South Carolina
SCAP Supreme Command Allies Pacific
Sc.B. Bachelor of Science
S.C.D. Doctor of Commercial Science
Sc.D. Doctor of Science
sch. school
sci. science, scientific
SCLC Southern Christian Leadership Conference
SCV Sons of Confederate Veterans
S.D., SD South Dakota
SE Southeast
SEATO Southeast Asia Treaty Organization
sec. secretary
SEC Securities and Exchange Commission
sect. section
seismol. seismological
sem. seminary
s.g. senior grade
sgt. sergeant
SHAEF Supreme Headquarters Allied Expeditionary Forces
SHAPE Supreme Headquarters Allied Powers in Europe
S.I. Staten Island
S.J. Society of Jesus (Jesuit)
S.J.D. Scientiae Juridicae Doctor
SK Saskatchewan
S.M. Master of Science
So. Southern

soc. society
sociol. sociological
S.P. Co. Southern Pacific Company
spl. special
splty. specialty
Sq. Square
sr. senior
S.R. Sons of the Revolution
SS Steamship
SSS Selective Service System
St. Saint, Street
sta. station
stats. statistics
statis. statistical
S.T.B. Bachelor of Sacred Theology
stblzn. stabilization
S.T.D. Doctor of Sacred Theology
subs. subsidiary
SUNY State University of New York
supr. supervisor
supt. superintendent
surg. surgical
SW Southwest

TAPPI Technical Association of Pulp and Paper Industry
Tb Tuberculosis
tchr. teacher
tech. technical, technology
technol. technological
Tel.&Tel. Telephone & Telegraph
temp. temporary
Tenn. Tennessee
Ter. Territory
Terr. Terrace
Tex. Texas
Th.D. Doctor of Theology
theol. theological
Th.M. Master of Theology
TN Tennessee
tng. training
topog. topographical
trans. transaction, transferred
transl. translation, translated
transp. transportation
treas. treasurer
TV television
TVA Tennessee Valley Authority
twp. township
TX Texas
typog. typographical

U. University
UAW United Auto Workers
UCLA University of California at Los Angeles
UDC United Daughters of the Confederacy
U.K. United Kingdom
UN United Nations
UNESCO United Nations Educational, Scientific and Cultural Organization
UNICEF United Nations International Children's Emergency Fund
univ. university
UNRRA United Nations Relief and Rehabilitation Administration
UPI United Press International
U.P.R.R. United Pacific Railroad
urol. urological
U.S. United States
U.S.A. United States of America
USAAF United States Army Air Force
USAF United States Air Force
USAFR United States Air Force Reserve
USAR United States Army Reserve
USCG United States Coast Guard
USCGR United States Coast Guard Reserve
USES United States Employment Service
USIA United States Information Agency
USMC United States Marine Corps
USMCR United States Marine Corps Reserve
USN United States Navy
USNG United States National Guard
USNR United States Naval Reserve
USO United Service Organizations
USPHS United States Public Health Service
USS United States Ship
USSR Union of the Soviet Socialist Republics
USV United States Volunteers
UT Utah

VA Veterans' Administration
Va., VA Virginia
vet. veteran, veterinary
VFW Veterans of Foreign Wars
V.I., VI Virgin Islands
vice pres. vice president
vis. visiting
VISTA Volunteers in Service to America
VITA Volunteers in Technical Service
vocat. vocational
vol. volunteer, volume
v.p. vice president
vs. versus
Vt., VT Vermont

W. West
WA Washington (state)
WAC Women's Army Corps
Wash. Washington (state)
WAVES Women's Reserve, U.S. Naval Reserve
WCTU Women's Christian Temperance Union
we. Western (use for court system only)
W. Ger. Germany, Federal Republic of
WHO World Health Organization
WI, Wis. Wisconsin
W.I. West Indies
WSB Wage Stabilization Board
WV West Virginia
W.Va. West Virginia
WY Wyoming
Wyo. Wyoming

YK Yukon Territory (for address)
YMCA Young Men's Christian Association
YMHA Young Men's Hebrew Association
YM & YWHA Young Men's and Young Women's Hebrew Association
Y.T. Yukon Territory
YWCA Young Women's Christian Association
yr. year

zool. zoological

Alphabetical Practices

Names are arranged alphabetically according to the surnames, and under identical surnames according to the first given name. If both surname and first given name are identical, names are arranged alphabetically according to the second given name. Where full names are identical, they are arranged in order of age—with the elder listed first.

Surnames, beginning with De, Des, Du, however capitalized or spaced, are recorded with the prefix preceding the surname and arranged alphabetically, under the letter D.

Surnames beginning with Mac and Mc are arranged alphabetically under M.

Surnames beginning with Saint or St. appear after names that begin Sains, and are arranged according to the second part of the name, e.g. St. Clair before Saint Dennis.

Surnames beginning with Van, Von or von are arranged alphabetically under letter V.

Compound hyphenated surnames are arranged according to the first member of the compound. Compound unhyphenated surnames are treated as hyphenated names.

Parentheses used in connection with a name indicate which part of the full name is usually deleted in common usage. Hence Abbott, W(illiam) Lewis indicates that the usual form of the given name is W. Lewis. In such a case, the parentheses are ignored in alphabetizing.

Who'sWho in America

AACH, HERBERT, painter; b. Cologne, Germany, Mar. 24, 1923; came to U.S., 1938, naturalized, 1942; s. Leo and Frieda (Schloss) A.; m. Doris Schein, Jan. 23, 1929; children—Christopher Jeffry, John Dennis. Student, Cologne Acad. Art, 1936-37, Pratt Inst., 1940-41, Stanford, 1942-43, Escuela de Pintura y Escultura, Mexico, 1948-50, Bklyn. Mus. Art Sch., 1946-48, 50-51. Tech. dir. Sargent Art Material Co., Inc., Hazleton, Pa., 1954-64; tchr. Bklyn. Mus. Art Sch., 1947-48, 50-51, Kingsbridge Community Center, 1951-53, Hazleton Art League, 1954-64, Queens Coll., 1965—, Scarsdale (N.Y.) Studio, 1965—, Pratt Inst., 1965—; chmn. dept. art. Queens Coll., 1976—; pres. Artists Tech. Research Inst., 1976—; lectr. Mem. standing com. artists materials U.S. Govt., 1962, then mem. standard practices com. Exhibited one-man shows including, Creative Gallery, 1952, 54, Stroudsburg Gallery, 1957, Art Direction Gallery, 1958, Evergart Mus., 1959, Landry Gallery, 1961, Pa. State U., 1962, Jacques Seligmann Gallery, 1964, 66, Hazelton Art League, 1964, Fischbach Gallery, 1966, Howard Wise Gallery, 1967, Martha Jackson Gallery, 1974, Albright Knox Mus., Buffalo, 1975, Allentown Art Mus., 1978, group shows include, Whitney Mus., Bklyn. Mus., numerous others; Author articles in field.; Contbg. editor: Color Engring, 1962—, Arts mag, 1966—. Served with AUS, World War II. Recipient 1st prize Creative Gallery, 1951; Hazelton Art League Annual, 1956, 63; Roberson Meml. Center Annual, 1959; numerous others. Mem. Artists Workshop Club, Intersoc. Color Council, Coll. Art Assn., Nat. Art Edn. Assn., Eastern Art Edn. Assn., Inst. Study of Art in Edn., U.S., N.Y. cacti and succulent socs., Color Forum (founding). Home: 523 E 14th St New York City NY 10009 Studio: 404 E 14th St New York City NY 10009 *At this point in my life I cannot think of having done something else different or better than my commitment of creating and teaching art. While this may sound like a conceited affirmation, it's intent is really a juxtaposition to human affairs as they exist today. It makes life worthwhile to me.*

AAGAARD, GEORGE NELSON, medical educator; b. Mpls., Aug. 16, 1913; s. George N. and Lucy T. (Nelson) A.; m. Lorna D. Docken, Aug. 26, 1939; children: Diane Louise, George Nelson, Richard Nelson, David Nelson, Steven Nelson. B.S., U. Minn., 1934, M.B., 1936, M.D., 1937. Intern Mpls. Gen. Hosp., 1936-37; successively fellow, instr., asst. prof. internal medicine U. Minn. Med. Sch., 1941-47, assoc. prof., dir. continuing med. edn., 1948-51; prof. medicine, dean Southwestern Med. Sch., U. Tex., 1952-54; dean U. Washington Sch. Medicine, 1954-64, prof. medicine, 1954-78, disting. prof. medicine and pharmacology, 1978—, head div. clin. pharmacology, 1964-79; mem. Nat. Adv. Council for Health Research Facilities USPHS, 1954-58; mem. nat. adv. heart council NIH, 1961-65; mem. spl. med. adv. group VA, 1970-74; chmn. bd. trustees Network for Continuing Med. Edn., 1966-78. Bd. dirs., editorial bd.: Western Jour. Medicine. Mem. Am. Heart Assn. (trustee), Assn. Am. Med. Colls. (pres. 1960-61), AMA (dir., chmn. com. continuing profl. edn. programs 1972), Pharm. Mfrs. Assn. Found. (mem. sci. adv. com. 1967-74), Am. Soc. Clin. Pharmacology and Therapeutics (pres. 1977, Flexner award 1983), N.Y. Acad. Scis., A.A.A.S., Washington, King County med. socs., Alpha Omega Alpha. Home: 3810 49th Ave NE Seattle WA 98105

AAKER, DAVID A., educator. B.S., M.I.T., 1960; M.S., Stanford U., 1967, Ph.D. (Ford Found. fellow), 1969. Cost engr., sales engr., product sales mgr. Tex. Instruments, Inc., 1960-65; asst. prof. Sch. Bus. Adminstrn., U. Calif., Berkeley, 1968-72, asso. prof., 1972-76, prof., 1976—, J. Gary Shansby prof. mktg. strategy, 1982—. Author: (with others) Modern Marketing, 1975, (with John G. Myers) Advertising Management: An Analytical Approach, 1975, 2d edit., 1982, (with George S. Day) Marketing Research; Editor: Consumerism: Search for the Consumer Interest, 1971, 4th edit., 1982, Multivariate Analysis in Marketing: Theory and Applications, 1971, Readings in Advertising Management, 1975, Strategic Market Management, 1984; asso. editor: Management Sci., 1971—; adv. editor mktg. field, John Wiley & Sons, Inc., 1973—; editorial bd.: Jour. Mktg. Research, 1969-77; contbr. over 50 articles to profl. jours. Recipient Spl. Merit award Thompson Gold Medal Competition, 1972; named One of Top 20 most cited mktg. scholars Ga. State study, 1972-75, One of 30 leaders in field of mktg. thought U. Wis., 1975. Mem. Am. Mktg. Assn., Tau Beta Pi. Home: 18 Eastwood Dr Orinda CA 94563 Office: Sch Bus Adminstrn U Calif Berkeley CA 94720

AARON, BENJAMIN, educator, arbitrator; b. Chgo., Sept. 2, 1915; s. Henry Jacob and Rose (Weinstein) A.; m. Eleanor Opsahl, May 24, 1941; children: Judith, Louise. A.B., U. Mich., 1937; LL.B., Harvard U., 1940; postgrad., U. Chgo., 1940-41. With Nat. War Labor Bd., 1942-45; mem. labor adv. com. to Supreme Comdr. Allied Powers, Tokyo, 1946; research asso. Inst. Indsl. Relations; lectr. labor law, dept. econs. UCLA, 1946-51, asso. dir., 1957-60, dir., 1960-75, prof. law, 1960—; Faculty mem. Salzburg (Austria) Seminar in Am. Studies, 1958, 67; arbitrator labor-mgmt. disputes, 1946—; pub. mem. WSB, Washington, 1951-52; mem. Statutory Arbitration Bd. in R.R. Dispute, 1963-64; chmn. Calif. Farm Labor Panel, 1965-66; mem. Nat. Commn. on Tech., Automation and Economic Progress, 1965-66; pub. mem. Adv. Council on Employee Welfare and Pension Benefit Plans, 1966-68; vis. prof. Harvard U., 1972, U. Mich., 1979; mem. pub. rev. bd. U.A.W., 1975—; mem. arbitration services adv. com. Fed. Mediation and Conciliation Service, 1974-82. Author: Legal Status of Employee Benefit Rights Under Private Pension Plans, 1961; Editor: The Employment Relation and The Law, 1957, Labor Courts and Grievance Settlement in Western Europe, 1970, Comparative Labor Law jour, 1979—; co-editor: Industrial Conflict: A Comparative Legal Survey, 1972; editorial bd., Internat. Labor Law Reps., 1974—. Fellow Center for Advanced Study in Behavioral Sciences, 1966-67; vis. fellow Clare Hall, Cambridge (Eng.) U., 1973; named First Southwestern Legal Found. Research Fellows' Disting. Scholar in Residence, 1971; first Howard W. Wissner Meml. Lectr. Tulane U., 1971; Phi Beta Kappa vis. scholar, 1978-79. Mem. Nat. Acad. Arbitrators (pres. 1962, bd. govs.), Am. Bar Assn. (sec. sect. labor relations law 1975-76), Indsl. Relations Research Assn. (exec. bd. 1965-68, pres. 1972), Am. Arbitration Assn. (mem. adv. council Los Angeles 1975-76, Disting. Service award 1981), AAUP, Internat. Soc. Labor Law and Sociol. Security (chmn. U.S. nat. com., internat. exec. com. 1967-83, v.p. N.Am. region 1982—). Home: 316 18th Street Santa Monica CA 90402 Office: UCLA Los Angeles CA 90024

AARON, BETSY, journalist; b. N.Y.C., Nov. 11, 1938; d. Bertram Henry and Evelyn (Horner) Siegeltuch; m. Richard Threlkeld, 1983. B.A., Am. U., 1960. Researcher, writer, field producer, reporter, corr. ABC News, Washington, N.Y.C., Chgo., 1960-76; network corr. CBS News, Atlanta, N.Y.C., 1976-80, NBC Mag., NBC News, N.Y.C., 1980-82; nightline corr. ABC News, N.Y.C., 1982—. Office: 7 W 66th St New York NY 10023

AARON, CHLOE WELLINGHAM, television executive; b. Santa Monica, Calif., Oct. 9, 1938; d. John Rufus and Grace (Lloyd) Wellingham; m. David Laurence Aaron, Aug. 11, 1962; 1 son, Timothy Wellingham. B.A., Occidental Coll., 1961; M.A., George Washington U., 1966. Free-lance journalist, 1965-70; dir. Public Media program Nat. Endowment for Arts, Washington, 1970-76; sr. v.p. programming Public Broadcasting Service, Washington, 1976-81; pres. Chloe Aaron Assocs., 1981—. Producer: TV film The Soldier's Tale, PBS, 1984. Mem. trustee com. on film Museum Modern Art, N.Y.C.; mem. film and video com. Whitney Mus. Am. Art; mem. nat. adv. bd. Center for the Book.; mem. bd. pub. devel. Corp. of N.Y.C., Stowe Sch., Ctr. Visual History, Nancy Hanks Ctr. Mem. Nat. Acad. TV Arts and Scis., Internat. Radio and TV Soc., Am. Women in Radio and TV.

AARON, DANIEL, educator, author; b. Chgo., Aug. 4, 1912; s. Henry J. and Rose (Weinstein) A.; m. Janet Summers, Aug. 25, 1937; children: Jonathan, James Summers, Paul Gaston. A.B., U. Mich., 1933; Ph.D., Harvard U., 1943; Litt.D. (hon.), Union Coll., 1967, U. Pa., 1976, Colby Coll., 1981. Asst. U. Mich., 1935-36; instr. Harvard U., 1936-39, prof. English, 1971—, Victor Thomas prof. emeritus dept. English and Am. lang. and lit., 1975; mem. faculty Smith Coll., 1939-71, prof. English, 1958-61, Mary Augusta Jordon prof., 1961-71, dir. Am. studies, 1948-71; vis. prof. Bennington Coll., 1950-51, U. Helsinki (Finland), 1951-52, U. Warsaw (Poland), 1962-63, MIT, fall 1965, Harvard U., 1971—, Brandeis U., spring 1983; Fulbright prof. U. Sussex (Eng.), 1968-69; summer lectr. Salzburg Seminar Am. Studies, 1949—, dir., 1956—; fellow Nat. Humanities Inst., Yale U., 1975-76; pres. Library of Am., 1979—. Author: Men of Good Hope, 1952, Writers on the Left, 1961, (with W. Miller and R. Hofstadter) The United States: The History of the Republic, 1957; Editor: (with Alfred Kazin) R.W. Emerson: A Modern Anthology, 1959, Paul E. More's Shelbourne Essays in American Literature, 1963, (with Robert Bendiner) The Strenuous Decade: A Social and Intellectual Record of the 1930's, 1970, The Unwritten War: American Writers and the Civil War, 1973. Guggenheim fellow, 1948; fellow Center Advanced Study Behavioral Scis., 1958-59. Mem. Am. Studies Assn. (pres. 1971-73). Home: 12 Farwell Pl Cambridge MA 02138

AARON, DANNY DOYLE, insurance company executive; b. Dallas, Apr. 10, 1948; s. Grady Franklin and Ruth Wannell (Painter) A. B.A. with high honors, N. Tex. State U., Denton, 1970; J.D., So. Methodist U., 1973. Bar: Tex. bar 1973. V.p., asso. gen. counsel Southland Life Ins. Co., Dallas, 1979—. Hatton W. Sumners scholar, 1970-73. Mem. Am., Dallas bar assns., State Bar Tex., Order of Coif. Home: 3525 Normandy Dallas TX 75205 Office: 1105 Southland Center Dallas TX 75201

AARON, HENRY, professional baseball team executive; b. Mobile, Ala., Feb. 5, 1934; s. Herbert and Estella A.; children: Gail, Hank, Lary, Gary (dec.), Dorinda; m. Billye Williams, Nov. 1973; 1 dau., Ceci. Ed. pub. schs. Former semi-pro baseball player; baseball player Milw. Braves (became Atlanta Braves 1966), 1954-74, now v.p. player devel.; with Milw. Brewers, 1975-76. Pres. No Greater Love, 1974; state chmn. Wis. Easter Seal Soc., 1975; nat. sports chmn. Nat. Easter Seal Soc., 1974; nat. chmn. Friends of Fisk for Athletics; organizer Hank Aaron Scholarship Fund, 1974; sponsor Hank Aaron Celebrity Bowling Tournament for Sickle Cell Anemia, 1972. Broke Babe Ruth record for career home runs by hitting 715th home run, Apr. 8, 1974. Address: Atlanta Braves Inc PO Box 4064 Atlanta GA 30302 *

AARON, HENRY, economics educator; b. Chgo., June 16, 1936; s. David and Betty (Cooper) A.; m. Ruth Kotell, May 5, 1963; children: Jeffrey, Melissa. A.B., U. Calif., Los Angeles, 1958; M.A., Harvard U., 1960, Ph.D., 1963. Asso. prof. econs. U. Md., 1967-75, prof., 1975-77, 79—; sr. fellow Brookings Instn., 1968-77, 78—; asst. sec. planning and evaluation HEW, Washington, 1977-78; sr. staff economist Pres's. Council Econ. Advisers, 1966-67; mem. Gov. Md. Council Econ. Advisers, 1968-75; vis. prof. econs. Harvard U., 1974; cons. govt. agys., 1967—; dir. Abt Assos.; chmn. Adv. Council on Social Security, 1978—; trustee Tchrs. Ins. and Annuity Assn., 1984—. Author: Who Pays the Property Tax?, 1974, Politics and the Professors, 1978, The Peculiar Problem of Taxing Life Insurance, 1983, The Economic Effects of Social Security, 1984, The Painful Prescription: Rationing Hospital Care, 1984. Mem. Am. Econ. Assn. (exec. com. 1978-81). Home: 1326 Hemlock St NW Washington DC 20012 Office: 1775 Massachusetts Ave NW Washington DC 20036

AARON, IRA EDWARD, educator; b. Jenkins County, Ga., July 9, 1919; s. Thomas William and Sally (Lane) A. A.B. in Journalism, U. Ga., 1941, M.Ed., 1947; Ph.D., U. Minn., 1954. Tchr., prin. Jenkins County Pub. Schs., 1941, 46-47; asst. prof. U. Ga., Athens, 1948-55, asso. prof., 1955-60, prof. edn., 1960-67, alumni found. distinguished prof., 1967—. Author (with others), Scott, Foresman reading and spelling series, 1967—; Contbr. articles and pamphlets on reading and spelling instrn. Served with USAAF, 1942-46. Gen. Edn. Bd. fellow, 1949-50. Mem. N.E.A. (life), Am. Psychol. Assn., Am. Ednl. Research Assn., Internat. Reading Assn. (pres. 1983-84), Phi Beta Kappa, Phi Kappa Phi, Phi Delta Kappa, Kappa Delta Pi. Home: 7 S Stratford Dr Athens GA 30605

AARON, M. ROBERT, elec. engr.; b. Phila., Aug. 21, 1922; s. Edward A. and Beatrice A.; m. Wilma Spiegelman, Nov. 18, 1944; children—Richard, James. B.S.E.E., U. Pa., 1949, M.S.E.E., 1951. Research engr. Franklin Inst. Research Labs., Phila., 1949-51; with Bell Telephone Labs. Inc., Murray Hill, N.J., 1951—, supr., 1954-68, dept. head, 1968—; lectr., tchr. in field. Mem. adv. com. Whippany (N.J.) Sch. Bd., 1950's. Contbr. articles to profl. jours; contbr. poems to tech. jours. Tutor NAACP Program, Red Bank, N.J., 1966-68. Served to lt. (j.g.) USCG, 1942-45. Fellow IEEE (mem. fin. bd. 1976-77, co-recipient Alexander Graham Bell medal 1978); mem. Nat. Acad. Engring., IEEE Circuits and Systems Soc. (asso. editor 1969-71, pres. 1973), IEEE Communications Soc. (chmn. awards bd. 1975-79, 80—). Patentee in field. Office: Bell Telephone Labs Inc Holmdel NJ 07733

AARONS, JULES, physicist; b. N.Y.C., Oct. 3, 1921; s. Joseph and Sadie (Gold) A.; m. Jeanette Lampert, 1944; children: Herbert Gene, Philip Ellis. B.S. in Edn., CCNY, 1942; M.A. in Sci., Boston U., 1949; Doctorate, U. Paris, 1954. Scientist Air Force Cambridge Research Lab., 1946-55; chief radio astronomy br. Air Force Geophysics Lab., Hanscom AFB, Mass., 1955-81; research prof. in astronomy and space sci. Boston U., 1981—. Editor Radio Astronomical Studies of the Atmosphere; contbr.articles to profl. jours. Served with USAAF, 1942-45. Recipient Disting. Civilian Service award USAF, 1969. Fellow IEEE (Harry Diamond award 1982, former chmn. Agard Panel Electromagnetic Propagation); mem. Am. Geophys. Union. Home: 46 Kingswood Rd Auburndale MA 02166 Office: Boston Univ Dept Astronomy 725 Commonwealth Boston MA 02215

AARONS, STUART HARRY, corporation executive, lawyer; b. Yonkers, N.Y., Sept. 15, 1910; s. Martin S. and Lillian (Geller) A.; m. Florence Josephson, Feb. 26, 1950; children: Barry M., Philip J. B.A. cum laude, City Coll. N.Y., 1929, LL.B., Harvard, 1932. Bar: N.Y. 1933, U.S. Supreme Ct. 1943. House counsel Warner Bros. Pictures, N.Y.C., 1932-53; house counsel, v.p. Stanley Warner Theatres, Inc., N.Y.C., 1953-67; sec. Glen Alden Corp., N.Y.C., 1968—, ILC Industries, Inc., Rapid-Am. Corp. Chmn. bd. dirs. Riverdale Jewish Center. Served to 1st lt., inf. AUS, 1943-46. Decorated Bronze Star medal, Army Commendation medal, Mil. Merit medal Republic Philippines. Mem. Am. Bar Assn., Assn. Bar City N.Y., Am. Soc. Corporate Secs., Phi Beta Kappa. Clubs: Men's (pres.), Harvard (N.Y.C.)). Home: 4525 Henry Hudson Pkwy New York NY 10471 Office: 888 7th Ave New York NY 10106 *I believe in the dignity of man. I believe in hard work and not doing things just to get by. Play every game according to the rules and don't cut corners.*

AARONSON, DAVID ERNEST, lawyer, educator; b. Washington, Sept. 19, 1940; s. Edward Allan and May (Rosett) A. B.A. in Econs, George Washington U., 1961, M.A., 1964, Ph.D., 1970; LL.B., Harvard U., 1964; LL.M. (E. Barrett Prettyman fellow), Georgetown U., 1965. Bar: D.C. bar 1965, Md. bar 1975, U.S. Supreme Ct. bar 1969. Research asst. Office of Commr., Bur. Labor Stats., U.S. Dept. Labor, Washington, 1961; staff atty. legal intern program Georgetown Grad. Law Center, Washington, 1964-65; research asso. patent research project dept. econs. George Washington U., Washington, 1966; asso. firm Aaronson and Aaronson, Washington, 1965-67, partner, 1967-70; mem. faculty Am. U. Law Sch., Washington, 1970—; prof. Sch. Justice, Coll. Public and Internat. Affairs, 1981—; dep. dir. Law and Policy Inst. abroad in, Jerusalem, Israel, summer, 1978; interim dir. clin. programs Md. Criminal Justice Clinic, 1971-73, founder prosecutor criminal litigation clinic, 1972; vis. prof. Law Sch. of Hebrew U., Jerusalem, summer, 1978; trustee Montgomery-Prince George's Continuing Legal Edn. Inst., 1983—. Author: Maryland Criminal Jury Instructions and Commentary, 1975, (with N.N. Kittrie and D. Saari) Alternatives to Conventional Criminal Adjudication: Guidebook for Planners and Practitioners, 1977, (with B. Hoff, P. Jaszi, N.N. Kittrie and D. Saari) The New Justice: Alternatives to Conventional Criminal Adjudication, 1977, (with C.T. Dienes and M.C. Musheno) Decriminalization of Public Drunkenness: Tracing the Implementation of a Public Policy, 1981, Public Policy and Police Discretion: Processes of Decriminalization, 1984; contbr. articles to legal and public policy jours. Mem. council Friendship Heights Village Council, 1979. Recipient Outstanding Community Service award, 1980; Named Outstanding Tchr. Am. U. Law Sch., 1978, 81; Pauline Ruyle Moore scholar in Pub. Law, 1983. Mem. Am. Bar Assn., Am. Trial Lawyers Assn., D.C. Bar Assn. (chmn. criminal code rev. com. 1971-73), Md. State Bar Assn., Montgomery County (Md.) Bar Assn., Am. Econ. Assn., Phi Beta Kappa, Omicron Delta Kappa, Delta Sigma Rho, Phi Delta Epsilon. Office: Myers Hall Room 205 American Univ Law School Mass and Nebraska Ave NW Washington DC 20016

AARONSON, HUBERT IRVING, metallurgical engineering educator; b. N.Y.C., July 10, 1924; s. Robert Benjamin and A. B.S., Carnegie Inst. Tech., (now Carnegie Mellon U.), 1948, M.S., Ph.D., 1954. Research metallurgist Metals Research Lab., Carnegie Inst. Tech., 1953-57; supr. phase transformation sect. dept. metallurgy, sci. research staff Ford Motor Co., Dearborn, Mich., 1958-72; sr. vis. fellow U. Manchester, 1972; prof. dept. metall. engring. Mich. Tech. U., Houghton, 1972-79; R.F. Mehl prof. Carnegie-Mellon U., 1979. Editor: Decomposition of Austenite by Diffusional Processes, 1962, Phase Transformations, 1970, Diffusion, 1972, Procs. of Internat. Conf. on Solid-Phase Transformations, 1983; contbr. numerous articles to profl. jours. Served to 1st lt. USAAF, 1943-46. Decorated Air medal with oak leaf cluster. Fellow Am. Soc. Metals (tech. div. bd. 1976-80, chmn. tech. div. bd. 1978-80, chmn. materials sci. div. 1976-78, Edgar C. Bain award Pitts. chpt. 1983); mem. AIME (Champion H. Mathewson Gold Medal 1968), Am. Soc. Metals, Metals Soc. (U.K.), Internat. Metall. Soc., Sigma Xi. Jewish. Home: 2 Bayard Rd Pittsburgh PA 15213 Office: Dept Metall Engring Carnegie Mellon U Pittsburgh PA 15213

AARONSON, ROBERT JAY, state official; b. Temple, Tex., June 8, 1942; s. Leonard and Ruth (Lader) A.; m. Louise Elaine Loia, June 6, 1967; children: Steven Bradford, Suzanne Denise. A.B., Brown U., 1964; M.Govtl. Adminstrn., Wharton Sch., U. Pa., 1965. Spl. asst. Southeastern Pa. Transp. Authority, Phila., 1965-67; transp. rep. Urban Mass Transp. Adminstrn., Washington, 1967-69; transp. adviser HUD, 1969-71; aviation adminstr. Md. Dept. Transp., Balt., 1972-78; asso. adminstr. for airports FAA, Washington, 1978-81; dir. aviation Port Authority of N.Y. and N.J., N.Y.C., 1981—; lectr. Center Spl. and Advanced Programs, Washington. Samuel S. Fels fellow, 1964-65. Mem. Nat. Assn. State Aviation Ofcls. (pres. 1978), Airport Operators Council Internat. (dir. 1977-78), Am. Assn. Airport Execs. Club: Wings (gov.). Home: 412 Redmond Rd South Orange NJ 07079 Office: Room 65W One World Trade Center New York NY 10048

AARONSON, STUART ALAN, cancer researcher; b. Mt. Clemens, Mich., Feb. 28, 1942; s. Michael and Frances (Leviant) A.; m. Gayle R. Ziff, Aug. 21, 1971; children: Lauren, David, Daniel. B.S., U. Calif.-Berkeley, 1962, M.S., 1965; M.D., U. Calif.-San Francisco, 1966. Staff assoc. viral carcinogenesis br. Nat. Cancer Inst., Bethesda, Md., 1967-69, sr. staff fellow, 1969-70, head molecular biology sect., 1970-77, chief lab. celluar and molecular biology, 1977—. Contbr. over 200 articles to profl. jours. Served with USPHS, 1967-70, 75—. Recipient Meritorious Service medal USPHS, 1982. Mem. Am. Assn. Cancer Research (Rhoads Meml. award 1982), Am. Soc. Microbiology,

AAAS, Fedn. Am. Socs. Exptl. Biology. Office: NCI Bldg 37 Room 1A07 Bethesda MD 20205

AARSLEFF, HANS, linguistics educator; b. Rungsted Kyst, Denmark; came to U.S., 1948, naturalized, 1964; s. Einar Faber and Inger (Lotz) A. B.A., U. Copenhagen, 1945; Ph.D., U. Minn., 1960. Instr. English U. Minn., 1952-56; instr. Princeton U., 1956-60, asst. prof., 1960-65, assoc. prof., 1965-72, prof., 1972—. Author: The Study of Language in England 1780-1860, 1967, From Locke to Saussure: Essays on the Study of Language and Intellectual History, 1982; assoc. editor: The Historiography of Linguistics; bd. editors: Jour. History Ideas, 1979—; contbr. articles to jours. and books. Jr. fellow Council of Humanities Princeton U., fall 1962; fellow Am. Council Learned Socs., 1964-65, 72-73, NEH, 1975-76. Mem. MLA, Linguistic Soc. Am., Lardomshistoriska Samfundet (Uppsala, Sweden), Leibniz Gesellschaft (Hanover, Germany), Société d'histoire et d'épistemologie des sciences du langage (Paris). Office: Dept English Princeton U Princeton NJ 08544

AASEN, LAWRENCE OBERT, orgn. exec.; b. Gardner, N.D., Dec. 5, 1922; s. Theodore and Clara Olina (Brenden) A.; m. Martha Ann McMullan, Nov. 25, 1954; children—David Lawrence, Susan Clare. Ph.B., U. N.D., 1947; M.S., Boston U., 1949. With McGraw Hill Publishing Co., N.Y.C., 1952-54; with N.Y. Life Ins. Co., 1954-67, asst. v.p., 1965-67; exec. sec. Better Vision Inst., N.Y.C., 1967—. Mem. Westport (Conn.) Democratic Town Com. Served with AUS, 1943-45. Mem. Public Relations Soc. Am., Am. Soc. Assn. Execs. Congregationalist. Home: 31 Ellery Ln Westport CT 06880 Office: 230 Park Ave New York NY 10017

ABADI, FRITZIE, artist, educator; b. Aleppo, Syria, Mar. 10, 1915; U.S., 1924; d. Matloub and Esther (Nahum) A.; m. Al Hidary, Feb. 11, 1934 (div. 1955); children: Annette Goldman, Esther Louise Friedberg (dec.); m. Lewis Ginsburg, Feb. 24, 1963. Student, Art Students League, 1947-48. Contbr. art data, Smithsonian Instn., Washington, 1980; exhibited group shows, Yeshiva U., N.Y.C., 1971-79, Whitney Mus. Am. Art, N.Y.C., Butler Art. Inst., ten one-woman shows. Recipient awards in media, oil painting, collage, assemblage. Mem. Am. Soc. Contemporary Artists (pres. 1971-73, dir., advisor), Nat. Assn. Women Artists, Artists Equity. Democrat. Jewish. Home: 201 W 70th St New York NY 10023 Office: Studio 41 Union Sq New York NY 10003

ABADIR, ADEL RAMSEY, physician; b. Cairo, Apr. 15, 1935; U.S., 1958, naturalized, 1966; s. Ramsey E. and Victoria S. (Shefik) A.; m. Dale M. Garlick, Dec. 21, 1969; children—Michelle Christine, Adel Ramsey, Tanya Irene, Edward Alan. M.D., Alexandria Med. Sch., 1957. Diplomate: Am. Bd. Anesthesiology. Intern Alexandria (Egypt) U. Hosp., 1957-58; rotating intern Misericordia Hosp., 1958-59; resident N.Y. U. Hosp., 1959-61; from clin. instr. to clin. prof. medicine N.Y. U., 1962-72; attending physician Univ. Hosp., N.Y.C., 1971—; acting dir., 1972; acting asso. dir. Bellevue Hosp., N.Y.C., 1972-73; dir. Brookdale Hosp. Med. Center, Bklyn., 1973—; prof. anesthesia N.Y. U. Med. Sch., 1972—. Contbr. articles to profl. jours. Fellow Am. Soc. Anesthesiologists, Am. Soc. Abdominal Surgeons, Soc. Neurosurg. Anesthesia and Neurologic Supportive Care, N.Y. Acad. Sci., N.Y. Acad. Medicine.; Mem. N.Y. State Soc. Anesthesiologists; mem. Am. Egyptian Soc., N.Y. County Med. Soc.; Mem. Am. Assn. French Speaking Health Profls., Soc. Regional Anesthesiologists, Internat. Assn. Study Pain, Soc. Cardiovascular Anesthesiologists, Internat. Anesthesia Research Soc., Am. Pain Soc., Eastern Pain Assn., AMA. Club: N.Y. Athletic. Home: 1045 Constable Dr Mamaroneck NY 10543 Office: Brookdale Hosp Center Brooklyn NY 11212

ABALIAN, ARBAK ARSHAK, structural engineer; b. Teheran, Iran, May 12, 1920; came to U.S., 1950, naturalized, 1955; s. Arshak M. and Anna (Khosrovian) A.; m. Suzanne Kadimian, Nov. 22, 1943; children: Arbak Anthony, Arline, Adriene, Alexandra. B.S.C., Am. Coll. Teheran, 1939; diploma engring. within industry, London, 1949. Registered profl. engr., Iran, N.Y., N.J., Conn., Mass., D.C., Calif., Nev., Ohio, Fla. Asst. chief engr. Societe Baziar, Teheran, 1940-41; engr. Anglo-Iranian Oil Co., Abadan, Iran, 1941-42, dep. supt., 1942-49; office engr. 3d Mil. Service, U.S. Army, 1945-46; dep. chief engr. Custom Engring. Co., N.Y.C., 1951-52; cons. engr., N.Y.C., 1952—, Newark, 1957—, Los Angeles, 1962—; sr. v.p., dir. structural and civil engring. Welton Becket Assocs., N.Y.C., Los Angeles, Houston, Atlanta, Chgo., San Francisco; dir. Iran Becket Cons., Marist Coll., Poughkeepsie, N.Y., 1952—. Designer: Cantiague Park Stadium, L.I., N.Y., Armenian Cathedral, N.Y.C., Champagniat Hall, Marist Coll. Recipient concrete industry award for best design and conception of concrete structure, Merit award Concrete Industry Bd., 1972, Silver prize L.I. Assn. Commerce and Industry, 1972. Fellow ASCE; mem. Am. Concrete Inst., Iranian Armenian Soc. (hon.). Democrat. Club: Presidential (N.Y.C.). Home: 47-27 243d St Douglaston NY 11362 Office: 360 Park Ave S New York NY 10010

ABARAY, RAYMOND F., food company executive; b. Pitts., Jan. 31, 1932; s. George and Susan A.; m. Clare M. Gombita, June 25, 1955; 1 child, Terry L. B.B.A., U. Pitts., 1953; M.B.A., Duquesne U., 1962. Div. controller Kroger co., 1964-70; controller food stores Kroger Co., Cin., 1970-72, v.p., controller, 1972-78, v.p. MIS, 1978—. Mem. adv. council Miami U., Oxford, Ohio, 1979-82; chmn. ann. fin. conf. Food Mktg. Inst., 1975; exec. cabinet United Appeal, Cin., 1977; pres. Ctr. Econ. Edn. Mem. Fin. Execs. Inst. Roman Catholic. Roman Catholic. Club: Bankers (Cin.). Home: 7950 E Galbraith Rd Cincinnati OH 45243 Office: Kroger Co 1014 Vine St Cincinnati OH 45201

ABATE, ERNEST NICHOLAS, state legislator; b. New Haven, Aug. 10, 1943; s. Nicholas Anthony and Rose Marie (Virgulto) A.; m. Barbara Zempel, June 16, 1966; children: Charles Porter, Edward Stockton. B.S. in Polit. Sci, Villanova (Pa.) U., 1965; LL.B., J.D., Notre Dame U., 1968. Bar: Conn. bar 1969. With firm Abate, Fox & Farrell, Stamford, Conn., 1972—; mem. Conn. Ho. of Reps., 1974—, chmn. judiciary com., 1977-78, speaker of house, 1979—. City committeeman City of Stamford, 1974-77; bd. dirs. Fed. Health Systems Agy., Inc., 1975-78, Community Return, Inc., Touch, Inc., Aid for the Retarded, Inc.; incorporator Stamford Hosp. Corp.; trustee Conn. Public TV and Radio.; bd. dirs. Alcoholism Council, Inc. Served to capt. USMCR, 1969-72. Named Young Man of Yr. and; recipient Disting. Service award Stamford Jaycees, 1976, Navy Achievement medal. Mem. Am. Bar Assn., Conn. Bar Assn., Stamford Bar Assn. Democrat. Home: 69 Old North Stamford Rd Stamford CT 06903 Office: 607 Bedford St Stamford CT 06901 also Ho of Reps Office of Speaker State Capitol Hartford CT 06115

ABBADO, CLAUDIO, conductor; b. Milan, Italy, June 26, 1933; s. Michelangelo A.; m. Gabriella Abbado. Grad. as pianist, Giuseppe Verdi Conservatory, Milan, 1955; student conducting, Hans Swarowsky, Vienna Acad. Music. Conducting debut with, Orch. Filarmonica, Trieste, 1958; operatic conducting debut, 1959; U.S. conducting debut with, N.Y. Philharm. Orch., 1963; music dir.: La Scala, Milan, 1968—; conducted: Don Carlo, Met. Opera Co., N.Y.C., 1968; permanent condr., Vienna Philharm. Orch., 1971—; prin. condr., London Symphony Orch., 1979; prin. guest condr., Chgo. Symphony Orch., 1982—; condr. major orchs., opera cos. in, U.S., Europe, Asia including Berlin, Salzburg, Edinburgh Festival, Berlin Deutsche Oper; musical dir., European Youth Orch., 1977— (Recipient Koussevitzky conducting prize 1958), European Youth Orch. (Mitropoulos prize 1963), European Youth Orch. (Diapason award, (several), European Youth Orch. (Grand Prix du Disque), European Youth Orch. (Deutscher Schallplatten Preis), European Youth Orch. (Edison prize), European Youth Orch. (Grammy award), European Youth Orch. (Mozart medal Mozart Gemeinde, Vienna 1973). Office: care Columbia Artisits Mgmt Inc 165 W 57th St New York NY 10019 *

ABBAMONT, JOSEPH PATRICK, financial executive; b. N.Y.C., July 19, 1921; s. James J. and Catharine (Gould) A.; m. Heidi Hoesli, May 25, 1946; children: Joseph, Gary, Heidi Jean, Richard. B.S. magna cum laude, N.Y. U., 1949. With A.S. Karasick & Co., C.P.A.s, N.Y.C., 1949-59; sec., treas. The Businessman's Funds Inc. (and predecessor corps.), N.Y.C., 1963-73; treas. Brookdale Investors Services, N.Y.C., 1968-72, First Investors Fund Group also First Investors Mgmt. Co., 1972-80, asst. treas., 1980—. Served with USAAF, 1942-45. Mem. N.Y. State Soc. C.P.A.s. Roman Catholic. Home: 45 Richford Rd Kendall Park NJ 08824 Office: 120 Wall St New York NY 10005

ABBATE, PAUL J., judge; b. N.Y.C., Mar. 28, 1919; s. Salvatore and Mary (Clemente) A.; m. Tamara Lookianov, Sept. 8, 1946; children—Michael, Paul, Greg (dec.), Maria. B.S., U.S. Mcht. Marine Acad., 1943; LL.B., St. Johns U., 1949; LL.M., Bklyn. Law Sch., 1952. Bar: U.S. Supreme Ct. bar 1956. Practiced law, N.Y.C., 1952-66, atty. gen., Guam, Agana, 1966-68; judge Island Ct., 1968-74; presiding judge Superior Ct. of Guam, 1974—; prof. law Coll. Guam; chmn. Jud. Council, 1979—, Bd. Law Examiners, 1979—. Ordained deacon Roman Catholic Ch. Served with USN. Decorated Bronze Star, Purple Heart. Office: Presiding Judge Superior Ct of Guam Judiciary Bldg Agana GU 96910

ABBE, ELFRIEDE MARTHA, sculptor, graphic artist; b. Washington, Feb. 6, 1919; d. Cleveland Jr. and Frieda (Dauer) A. Student, Art Inst. Chgo., 1937; B.F.A., Cornell U., 1940; postgrad., Syracuse U., 1947. Author and illustrator: books including The Plants of Virgil's Georgics, 1965; One-woman exhbns. include, Carnegie-Mellon U., 1962, 69, Cornell U., 1963, Trinity Coll., Hartford, 1964, Arts Club of Washington, 1972, Cornell Club of N.Y., 1977, Copley Soc. Boston, 1978, Woods-Gerry Gallery, R.I. Sch. Design, 1983; represented in permanent collections, Boston Mus. Fine Arts, Cin. Art Mus., Dumbarton Oaks, Washington, Houghton Library, Harvard U., Hunt Library, Carnegie-Mellon U., N.Y. Pub. Library, Rosenwald Collection Nat. Gallery; sculpture placed includes, Cornell U. Mann Library and Morrison Hall, McGill U., N.Y. Bot. Gardens, Hunt Library, Pitts., Pres.'s Office, Keene (N.H.) State Coll. Recipient Gold medals Pen and Brush, N.Y.C., 1964, Nat. Arts Club, 1970, Acad. Artists Assn., Springfield, Mass., 1976, Founders' Prize Pen and Brush, 1977; Bd. Dirs. award Salmagundi Club N.Y., 1978; Elliot Liskin award, 1979. Fellow Nat. Sculpture Soc.; mem. Nat. Soc. Mural Painters, Nat. Arts Club N.Y. Home: Applewood Manchester Center VT 05255

ABBE, GEORGE BANCROFT, author; b. Somers, Conn., Jan. 28, 1911; s. Harry Allen Grant and Aida (Kittredge) A.; m. Barbara Rossiter, Sept. 22, 1934. Student, Cushing Acad., 1928; B.A., U. N.H., 1933; M.A., U. Iowa, 1938. Tchr. lit., writing Mt. Holyoke Coll., Yale, Columbia, U. Iowa, U. Maine, U. Pitts., Wayne U., Springfield Coll., U. N.H.; staff writers confs. U. N.H., Idaho State Coll., Corpus Christi (Tex.) Fine Arts Colony, Wooster (Ohio) Coll., Western Mass., State of Maine, Cape Cod, others; co-dir. New Eng. Writers Conf., Suffield (Conn.) Acad.; faculty Tchrs. Coll. Conn., New Britain, 1955-57; asst. prof. English Russell Sage Coll., 1958-64, asso. prof. English, 1964-67, resident author, 1958-67; prof. humanities, writer-in-residence State U. Coll., Plattsburgh, N.Y.; dir. Champlain Writers Conf. Editorial bd.: Book Club for Poetry; adv. editor: Poetry Public; Author: Voices in the Square, 1938, Dreamer's Clay, 1940, Wait for These Things, 1940, Letter Home, 1945, Mr. Quill's Crusade, 1948, The Wide Plains Roar, 1954, Bird in the Mulberry, 1954, Poetry, the Great Therapy, 1956, The Incandescent Beast, 1957, The Winter House, 1957, One More Puritan, 1960; play The Adomatic Man, 1960; The Collected Poems of George Abbe, 1935-61, 1961, Stephen Vincent Benet on Writing, 1964, You and Contemporary Poetry: An Aid-to-Appreciation, 1964, The Larks, 1965, The Non-conformist, 1966, The Funeral, 1967, Shatter the Day, 1968, Yonderville, 1969, Dreams and Dissent, New Poems, 1961-70, 1971, Abbe and Benét, 1973, The Pigeon Lover (fiction-biography), 1981; Editor: Hill Wind, 1935; Contbr. short stories and poems to books, mags., lit. publs.; Recording artist, Folkways Corp., poems, Two hour rec. of poems, Library of Congress. Recipient Shelley Meml. award, 1956. Mem. Poetry Soc. Am.

ABBEN, PEER, architect; b. Copenhagen, Denmark, Sept. 8, 1916; came to U.S., 1963; s. George Valdemar and Ingeborg (Holm) A.; m. Pia Vilma Jorgensen, May 10, 1943 (div. 1962); children—Pia Lee, Mei Yin. Bldg. constrn. and engring. student, Coll. Tech. Soc. Copenhagen, 1935-38, Royal Acad. Fine Arts, Copenhagen, 1943. Certificate for skilled bricklayer, Copenhagen Guild and Trade Union, 1937; Registered profl. architect, Tanzania, Kenya, Hawaii, Wash. Prin. archtl. firm, Denmark, 1948, Tanganyika (now Tanzania), E. Africa, 1949-52, Kenya, E. Africa, 1952-63, self-employed architect, Honolulu, 1964—; instr. architecture Royal Coll., Nairobi, 1962, 63, U. Hawaii, 1967, 68; cons. architect Oceanic Properties, Inc. planning dept., Honolulu, 1968, 69. Prin. archtl. works in E. Africa include residences, farm houses, comml. offices and bank bldgs., med. tng. center, dormitories, hosp., chs., various pub. bldgs., schs. including Arya Girls' Sch, Nairobi (Gold medal in Architecture 1957), in Honolulu; prin. works include condominium apts., townhouses, garden houses and residences. Recipient Neuhausenske reward in architecture, 1944-45, Queen Alexandra of Eng. reward, 1946; Hielmstjerne-Rosencroneske Found. grantee, 1947. Fellow Acad. Assn. Danish Architects, Fedn. Danish Architects; mem. Fine Arts Soc. Denmark, AIA (corporate mem.), Honolulu Acad. Arts. Club: Adventurers (Honolulu). Address: 1650 Ala Moana Blvd Suite 1609 Honolulu HI 96815 *A smile costs nothing but gives much. It enriches those who receive it without making poorer those who give it. It takes but a moment, but the memory of it sometimes lasts forever. None is so rich that he/she can get along without it, and none is so poor but that he/she can be made rich by it. A smile creates happiness wherever we are.*

ABBERLEY, JOHN J., lawyer; b. Bklyn., Dec. 16, 1916; s. Lester Stokes and Mary Abigail (Lyon) A.; m. Mary Anna John; children—Lester Stokes II, Georgine M., Frederick C. A.B., Williams Coll., 1939; LL.B., U. Va., 1942. Bar: Va. bar 1942, N.Y. bar 1946. Since practiced, N.Y.C.; mem. Abberley, Kooiman, Marcellino, Clay, 1946—; Spl. asst. to dir. Office Econ. Affairs, Paris, FOA, 1953-54. Dir. Netherland-Am. Found.; Trustee Suffield (Conn.) Acad.; Pres. Clinton Hall Assn. Served as lt. USNR, 1942-46; ETO. Mem. Internat. Law Assn. (sec., treas. Am. br.), Am. Bar Assn., Assn. Bar City N.Y., Delta Kappa Epsilon, Phi Delta Phi. Episcopalian. Home: Stamford CT Office: 521 Fifth Ave New York NY 10017

ABBETT, ROBERT WILLIAM, cons. engr.; b. Jamesport, Mo., Dec. 23, 1902; s. Phillip Allen and Virginia Abbett A.; m. Ruth Virginia Bloomer, Oct. 1953; 1 son, Robert William. B.S., U. Mo., Rolla, 1927, C.E., 1933; M.S., Yale, 1932; Sc.D. (hon.), Gettysburg Coll., 1953. Surveyor, designer, engr. constrn. rys., municipal projects, bridges, bldgs. for (various pvt., govt. agys.), 1923-29; instr. dept. civil engring. Yale, 1929-33; asso. prof. civil engring. Union Coll., Schenectady, 1933-39; asso. Parsons, Klapp, Brinckerhoff & Douglas, also Waddell & Hardesty (cons. engrs.), N.Y.C., 1938-40; asst. prof. civil engring. Columbia, 1940-41; founding partner Tippetts Abbett McCarthy Stratton (engrs. and architects), N.Y.C., 1945—; Cons. engr. U.S., fgn. rys., hwys., bridges, port devel., harbor works, U.S. and fgn. mineral devel. projects. Author: Engineering Contracts and Specifications; Editor in chief: Am. Civil Engring. Practice; Contbr. articles to profl. mags. Served from lt. to comdr. C.E. USNR, 1941-45. Mem. Am. Soc. C.E., Am. Cons. Engrs. Council, Sigma Xi. Clubs: Yale, University, Anglers (N.Y.C.). Home: 2 Sutton Pl S New York NY 10022

ABBOT, EDWARD GEORGE, labor union executive; b. Edinburgh, Scotland, Jan. 18, 1936; emigrated to Can., 1957; s. Edward George and Cissie (Baird) A.; m. Iris Margret Thain, June 24, 1958. LL.B., LaSalle Extension U., Chgo., 1971; B.A. in Psychology, U. Waterloo, (Ont., Can.), 1983. Communication technician Can. Pacific Telecommunications, Montreal, Que., Can., 1958-66; officer United Telegraph Workers Union, 1966-71; asst. mgr. labor relations Can. Pacific Ry., Montreal, 1971-73; exec. sec. Can. Ry. Labour Assn., Ottawa, Ont., 1973—. Can. Labour Congress Nuffield travelling fellow, 1971. Office: Can Ry Labour Assn 513-130 Albert St Ottawa ON Canada K1P 5G4 *

ABBOT, QUINCY SEWALL, insurance executive; b. Wilkes-Barre, Pa., Apr. 24, 1932; s. Theodore S. and Alice (Howell) A.; m. Zelia Gillam, Jan. 12, 1957; children: Elizabeth, Susan, Rebecca, Jane. A.B., Williams Coll., 1954. Actuarial student Conn. Gen. Life Ins. Co., Hartford, 1954-55, 59-64, asst. actuary, 1964-67, assoc. actuary, 1967-70, dir. taxes, 1970-75, v.p., 1975-82, CIGNA, Phila., 1982—. Pres. Hartford Assn. Retarded Citizens, 1975-76, Conn. Assn. Retarded Citizens, 1981-83, Corp. Ind. Living, Hartford, 1980-81; bd. dirs. Nat. Assn. Retarded Citizens, 1977-80. Served to 1st lt. U.S. Army, 1955-58. Fellow Soc. Actuaries; mem. Tax Execs. Inst. (chpt. pres. 1970-71), Ins. Assn. Conn. (chmn. tax com. 1975-83), Am. Council Life Ins. (tax com.). Republican. Mem. United Ch. of Christ. Home: 52 Sunrise Hill Dr West Hartford CT 06107 Office: 750 Bloomfield Ave Hartford CT 06152

ABBOT, WILLIAM WRIGHT, educator; b. Louisville, Ga., May 20, 1922; s. William Wright and Lillian (Carswell) A.; m. Eleanor Pearre, Mar. 31, 1958; children—William Wright, John Pearre. Student, Davidson (N.C.) Coll., 1939-41; A.B., U. Ga., 1943; M.A., Duke, 1949, Ph.D., 1953. Tchr. Louisville Acad., 1946-47, McCallie Sch., 1951-52; from asst. prof. to prof. history Coll. William and Mary, 1953-58, 59-66; asso. prof. Northwestern U., 1958-59, Rice U., 1961-63; James Madison prof. history U. Va., 1966—; chmn. history dept. 1972-74. Author: The Royal Governors of Georgia, 1754-1775, 1957, The Colonial Origins of the United States, 1607-1763, 1975; Editor-in-chief: The Papers of George Washington, 1977—; Editor: Jour. So. History, 1961-63; book rev. editor: William and Mary Quar., 1955-61; editor, 1963-66. Served to lt. USNR, 1943-46. Mem. Inst. Early Am. History and Culture (council 1976-79), So. Hist. Assn. (exec. council 1978-81), Phi Beta Kappa. Home: 804 Rugby Road Charlottesville VA 22903

ABBOTT, ALVIN ARTHUR, publishing executive; b. Sidney, Ohio, Sept. 14, 1928; s. Roy Edward and Mildred Eileen (Filler) A.; m. Cora May Williams, June 24, 1949; children—Allan, Rima, Elinor, Laura. A.B., Wittenberg U., 1949; M.A., Ohio State U., 1964. With firm Cole-Layer-Trumble, real estate appraisal, Dayton, Ohio, 1949-51; v.p. William Exline Inc., Cleve., 1951-59; salesman Burroughs Corp., Columbus, 1959-62; instr. Central Mich. U., Mt. Pleasant, 1965-66; asst. prof. U. Wis.-Stevens Point, 1966-69; with Harper & Row Pubs., N.Y.C., 1969-81, editor-in-chief, 1973-77, assoc. pub., 1977-81; v.p. research and analysis Springer-Verlag, N.Y.C., 1981—. Mem. Alpha Tau Omega. Home: 25 Dogwood Circle Matawan NJ 07747 Office: 175 Fifth Ave New York NY 10022

ABBOTT, BERENICE, photographer; b. Springfield, Ohio, July 17, 1898; d. Charles E. and Alice (Bunn) A. Student, Ohio State U., 1917-18, student of journalism and sculpture, 1918-21, student of sculpture, 1921-23; also at, Kunstschule, Berlin, 1923. Photography asst. Man Ray, Paris, 1923-25; owner photog. studio, Paris, 1926-29, profl. portrait photographer; returned to, N.Y., 1929; specialized in documentary and portrait photography; photographer Fed. Arts Project, N.Y.C., 1930-39. Exhbns. include, Mus. Modern Art, N.Y.C., Smithsonian Instn., Washington, Marlborough Gallery, N.Y., Lunn Gallery, Washington, Bklyn. Mus., Art Inst. Chgo., Internat. Ctr. for Photography, N.Y.C., Vision Gallery, Boston, works represented in permanent collections, Mus. Modern Art, N.Y.C., Met. Mus. Art, N.Y.C., Mus. Fine Arts, Boston, Smithsonian Instn., Washington, Art Inst. Chgo., Mus. Fine Arts, Houston, San Francisco Mus. Art, Bibliothèque Nationale, Paris; books include Changing New York, 1939, Greenwich Village Today and Yesterday, 1949, A Portrait of Maine, 1968, Berenice Abbott Photographs, 1970, Guide to Better Photography, 1941, 53, The View Camera Made Simple, 1948, The World of Atget, 1964. Office: care Press Relations Horizon Press 156 Fifth Ave New York NY 10010 *

ABBOTT, BERNARD CYRIL, biology educator; b. E. Coker, Eng., Oct. 13, 1920; came to U.S., 1957, naturalized, 1977; s. Frederick B. and Daisy J. (Hawkins) A.; m. Doris Pontin, Oct. 14, 1944; 1 dau., Pauline. B.S., Univ. Coll., London, 1941, Ph.D. in Physiology, 1950. Lectr. biophysics and physiology Univ. Coll., 1946-53; prin. sci. officer Marine Biol. Assn., U.K., Plymouth, 1953-57; asso. prof. zoology UCLA, 1957-62; prof. biophysics and physiology, head div. biophysics U. Ill., Urbana, 1962-68; prof. biol. scis. U. So. Calif., 1968—, chmn. dept. biol. scis., 1968-82; instl. rep. Assn. Systematics Collections, 1972—. Contbr. articles to profl. jours. Bd. dirs. Allan Hancock Found., 1968-82. Served to maj. Brit. Army, 1942-46. Fellow Inst. Physics London, Royal Soc. Medicine; mem. Am. Heart Assn. (Distinguished Scientist award 1975), Internat. Soc. Toxicology (council 1972—), Soc. Gen. Physiology (council 1964-77), Orgn. Tropical Studies (council 1969-73), Physiol. Soc. London, Am. Physiol. Soc., Biophys. Soc. (council 1968-72), Soc. Exptl. Biology, Marine Biol. Assn., Am. Soc. Zoologists, Biomed. Engring. Soc., Sigma Xi. Episcopalian. Office: Dept Biol Scis Univ So Calif Los Angeles CA 90007

ABBOTT, CHARLES HOMER, ret. rope co. exec.; b. Houston, Dec. 29, 1909; s. Charles Howard and Lela (Hunt) A.; m. Jane Millikin, Apr. 5, 1940; children—Edwin Hunt, John Millikin, Betsy, Fred Hardy. Student. U. Nebr., 1928-29; A.B., Yale, 1932; LL.B., St. Lawrence U., 1938. Employed sales dept. U.S. Indsl. Alcohol Co., N.Y.C., 1932-33, Nat. Distillers Products Corp., 1933-42; O.P.A.; field operations officer Fuel Rationing div., 1942-43; asst. to adminstr. in charge of price bds. O.P.A., 1946-47; sp. sales rep. Gt. Lakes Steel Corp., 1947-49; Southeastern mgr. Gen. Plywood Corp., 1949-51, gen. sales mgr., 1951-52, v.p., 1952-55; sales mgr. panel and door div. Atlas Plywood Corp., gen. mgr., 1956-58; v.p. marketing Stylon Corp., Milford, Mass., 1958-62, dir., 1959-63, Samson Cordage Works, Boston, 1962-76, pres., 1963-75, chmn. bd., 1975-76, Samson Ocean Systems, Inc., 1976-79, ret., 1979; Pres., chmn. exec. com. Cordage Inst., 1977—. Served to lt. USN, 1943-46. Mem. Phi Delta Theta, Phi

Delta Phi. Club: Yale (N.Y.C.). Home: 156 Ridgeway Rd Weston MA 02193 Office: 99 High St Boston MA 02110

ABBOTT, DONALD PUTNAM, educator, marine biologist; b. Chgo., Oct. 14, 1920; s. Donald Putnam and Marion (Dummer) A.; m. Isabella Aiona, Mar. 3, 1943; 1 dau., Ann Kaiue. B.A., U. Hawaii, 1941; M.A., U. Calif. at Berkeley, 1948, Ph.D., 1950. Mem. faculty Stanford, 1950-82, prof. biology, 1963-82, prof. emeritus, 1982—; asst. dir. Hopkins Marine Sta., Stanford, 1962-66, asso. dir., 1966-82; Mem. Pacific Sci. Bd. Ifaluk Atoll Expdn., 1953, Hawaii-Philippines Sulu Sea Expdn., 1957, Galapagos Internat. Sci. Project, 1964; chief scientist TE VEGA Cruise 5, Indian Ocean, 1964, TE VEGA Cruise 18, Eastern Tropical Pacific, 1968, PROTEUS cruise 22, B.C., 1970; invertebrates adv. com. Smithsonian Oceanographic Sorting Center; vis. prof. West Indies Lab., St. Croix, V.I., 1973-75, 77. Author: (with others) Intertidal Invertebrates of the Central California Coast, 1954, (with M. Bates) Coral Island, 1958, (with others) Intertidal Invertebrates of California, 1980; Editorial bd.: The Veliger. Served with AUS, 1943-46. Recipient Dean's award for distinguished teaching, 1976, Lloyd W. Dinkelspiel award for outstanding service to undergrad. edn., 1982. Fellow AAAS, Calif. Acad. Scis.; mem. So. Calif. Acad. Scis., Am. Soc. Zoologists, Soc. Systematic Zoology, Western Soc. Naturalists. Democrat.

ABBOTT, DOUGLAS EUGENE, mechanical engineering educator; b. Glendale, Calif., Apr. 20, 1934; s. Richard Edward and Eva (Pogue) A.; m. Doris Bernice Newmark, Dec. 16, 1956; children: Sandra Lee, Jodi Frances, Shari Evalinis, Traci Bernice. B.M.E., Stanford U., 1956, M.M.E., 1957, Ph.D., 1961. Asst. head fluid mechanics sect. Vidya div. Itek Corp., Palo Alto, Calif., 1960-64; lectr. Stanford U., 1963-64; asso. prof. Purdue U., 1964-69, prof., 1969-77, dir. thermal scis. and propulsion center, 1972-77; prof., chmn. dept. mech. engring. and mechanics, dir. computer-aided design/computer-aided mfg. ednl. program Lehigh U., Bethlehem, Pa., 1977-83, vice provost for computing and info. services, 1983—; Staff cons. Midwest Applied Sci. Corp., Lafayette, Ind., 1964-72; energy controls div. Bendix Corp., South Bend, Ind., 1967-75, Westinghouse Research and Devel. Center, Pitts., 1970-75, ERDA, 1975-77; chmn. air breathing propulsion adv. com. Air Force Office of Sci. Research, 1973-83. Hon. research fellow Sci. Research Council, U.K., 1971-72. Fellow Am. Phys. Soc.; fellow AAAS; mem. Am. Inst. Aeronautics and Astronautics, ASME, N.Y. Acad. Scis., Pi Tau Sigma. Home: 1865 Cloverleaf St Bethlehem PA 18017 Office: Linderman Library Lehigh U Bethlehem PA 18015

ABBOTT, EDWARD LEROY, finance executive; b. Dayton, Ohio, Dec. 18, 1930; s. Roy Edward and Mildred Eileen (Filler) A.; m. Elizabeth Joan Grahame, June 8, 1957; children: Jay Edward, Julie Beth. A.B., Wittenberg U., 1952; postgrad., Ohio State U., 1952-53. With Northwestern Mut. Life Ins. Co., 1956-73, regional mgr., Washington, 1970-73; v.p. real estate Acacia Mut. Life Ins. Co., Washington, 1973-74, fin. v.p., 1974-76, fin. v.p., treas., 1976-78, exec. v.p., treas., 1978-83; dir., fin. v.p., treas. Acacia Nat. Life Ins. Co., 1974-82; exec. v.p. Westport Co., 1983—; chmn. bd. Acacia Fund Corp., 1975-79, Acacia Investment Mgmt. Co., 1975-79; dir. Westport Co. Mem. Friends of Kennedy Center. Served with U.S. Army, 1954-55. Mem. Mortgage Bankers Assn. Am., Washington Bd. Trade, Mortgage Bankers Assn. Met. D.C., Am. Council Life Ins., Internat. Platform Assn., Alpha Tau Omega. Republican. Home: 6605 Goldsboro Rd Falls Church VA 22042 Office: 830 Post Rd E Westport CT 06680

ABBOTT, EDWIN HUNT, chemistry educator; b. N.Y.C., Dec. 28, 1941; s. Charles Homer and Jane (Millikin) A.; m. Ann Quain, June 13, 1964; children: Corinne, Catherine. B.S., Tufts U., 1964; Ph.D., Tex. A&M U., 1969. Asst. prof. chemistry Hunter Coll., N.Y.C., 1970-73, assoc. prof., 1974-77; prof. chemistry Mont. State U., Bozeman, 1977—, head dept. chemistry, 1977—. Contbr. articles to profl. jours. Fellow N.Y. Acad. Scis.; mem. Am. Chem. Soc., Sigma Xi. Home: 3917 Sourdough Rd Bozeman MT 59715 Office: Dept Chemistry Mont State U Bozeman MT 59717

ABBOTT, GEORGE, playwright, producer; b. Forestville, N.Y., June 25, 1887; s. George Burwell and May (McLaury) A.; m. Ednah Levis, July 9, 1914 (dec. 1930); 1 dau., Judith Ann; m. Mary Sinclair, Apr. 1946. A.B., U. Rochester, 1911, H.H.D., 1961; postgrad., Harvard U., 1912; H.H.D., U. Miami, Fla., 1974. Became an actor, 1913; appeared, 48th St. Theatre, 1915; actor: The Queen's Enemy, 1916; asst. stage mgr.: Three Wise Fools, 1918; writer, dir. plays and films, 1919; co-author and dir.: plays including Love 'Em and Leave 'Em; dir. Broadway plays: Coquette; Four Walls, Three Men on a Horse, On Your Toes, The Boys From Syracuse, Best Foot Forward, Where's Charley?, A Tree Grows in Brooklyn, The Pajama Game, Damn Yankees, New Girl in Town, Chicago, Boy Meets Girl, Brother Rat, Room Service, What a Life, Primrose Path, Too Many Girls, Pal Joey, Kiss and Tell, On The Town, Billion Dollar Baby, High Button Shoes, Call Me Madam, Wonderful Town, Never Too Late, A Funny Thing Happened on the Way to the Forum, Take Her, She's Mine, Flora, The Red Menace, Fade Out-Fade In, Help Stamp Out Marriage, Agatha Sue, I Love You, How Now, Dow Jones, 1967, The Education of Hyman Kaplan, 1968, The Fig Leaves Are Falling, 1968, Three Men on a Horse, 1969, Norman, Is That You?, 1970, Not Now Darling, 1970, dir. others; revival (musical) On Your Toes, 1983; also dir. of: motion pictures Damn Yankees; Author: Try-Out, 1979. Co-recipient Pulitzer Prize for Fiorello, 1960; N.Y. Drama Critics Circle award, 1960; Tony award, 1955, 56, 60, 63; Donaldson award, 1946, 48, 53, 55; Lawrence Langner award, 1976; Handel medallion City of N.Y., 1976. Clubs: Coffee House, Dutch Treat (N.Y.C.); Indian Creek (Fla.) Country; Merriewold (N.Y.). Office: 1270 Ave of Americas New York NY 10020

ABBOTT, ISABELLA AIONA, biology educator; b. Hana, Maui, Hawaii, June 20, 1919; d. Loo Yuen and Annie Patsue (Chung) Aiona; m. Donald P. Abbott, Mar. 3, 1943; 1 dau., Ann Kaiue Abbott Conner. A.B., U. Hawaii, 1941; M.S., U. Mich., 1942; Ph.D., U. Calif., Berkeley, 1950. Prof. biology Stanford U., 1972-82; G.P. Wilder prof. botany U. Hawaii, 1978—; vis. research biologist and tchr., Japan and Chile. Author: (with G.J. Hollenberg) Marine Algae of California, 1976; contbr. articles to profl. jours. Co-recipient N.Y. Bot. Garden award for best book in botany, 1978. Mem. Internat. Phycological Soc. (treas. 1964-68), Western Soc. Naturalists (sec. 1962-64, pres. 1977), Phycological Soc. Am., Brit. Phycological Soc., Hawaiian Bot. Soc. Office: 3190 Maile Way Botany Dept Univ of Hawaii Honolulu HI 96822

ABBOTT, JEANNE MONTAGUE, newspaper editor; b. St. Louis, Oct. 9, 1944; d. Richard Thomas and Vesta (Spurgeon) Odell; m. Richard Montague, 1968 (div. 1973); m. Stanley Abbott, Mar. 16, 1975; children: Robson Powell, Ellen Eaton (dec.). B.A., B.J., U. Mo., 1967, M.A., 1969. Mem. staff Anchorage Daily News, 1969—, editor, 1971—; Alaska stringer Time mag., 1975—, People mag., 1975—; instr. journalism U. Alaska, 1974-81. Mem. Alaska Center for Environment. Mem. Phi Beta Kappa, Kappa Tau Alpha, Phi Sigma Iota. Club: Alaska Press. Home: 1417 F St Anchorage AK 99510 Office: 200 Potter Dr Anchorage AK 99510

ABBOTT, JOHN DAVID, clergyman, church official; b. Wyoming, Del., Sept. 29, 1922; s. John Wesley and Mary Mabel (Boggs) A.; m. Gladys Irene Kirkendall, July 22, 1943; children: John David, Kenneth Wayne. Th.B., United Wesleyan Coll., 1943; D.D. (hon.), Houghton Coll., 1969. Ordained to ministry The Wesleyan Ch., 1944; pastor in, Chestertown, Md., 1943, Richeyville and Bentleyville, Pa., 1944, Warren, Pa., 1945-49, Cambridge, Md., 1950-53; dist. supt. Delmarva dist. The Wesleyan Ch., Denton, Md., 1953-60, gen. sec. Sunday schs. and youth, Indpls., 1960-62; exec. dir. Pilgrim Pension Plan, 1960-62, gen. sec.-treas., 1962-66, gen. supt., 1966—, mem. bd. pensions, 1960-80; Mem. exec. com. World Methodist Council, 1971—, 1st vice chmn. Am. sect., 1976—, sec. Am. sect., 1982—; v.p. Wesleyan World Fellowship, 1976—, The Wesleyan Ch. Corp., 1976-80; mem. exec. com. Gen. Commn. Chaplains and Armed Forces Personnel, 1976-80; trustee United Wesleyan Coll. Editor: Sunday Sch. Advance, 1960, Pilgrim Youth News, 1960-62. Mem. Christian Holiness Assn. (pres. 1976-78), Nat. Assn. Evangelicals, Delta Epsilon Chi. Home: 1413 Glendale Dr Marion IN 46952 Office: Box 2000 Marion IN 46953

ABBOTT, JOHN SHELDON, law school administrator; b. Detroit, May 10, 1926; s. Arthur James and Florence E. (Allen) A.; m. Virginia H. Young, Aug. 13, 1976; children by previous marriage: Laura Kathryn, John Sheldon Jr. A.B., Kalamazoo Coll., 1950; J.D., Detroit Coll. Law, 1953, LL.D. (hon.); LL.M., U. Mich., 1954. Bar: Mich. 1954. Individual practice law, Detroit, 1954-59, prof. law, Detroit Coll. Law, 1959-70, asso. dean, 1970-72, dean, chief adminstrv. officer, 1972—; cons. Mich. Law Revision Commn., 1967; commr. State Bar Mich. Author: Organizing Small Business Enterprises, 1962. Served with USN, 1944-45. Fellow Am. Bar Found.; Mem. Am. Judicature Soc., Assn. Ind. Colls. and Univs. (exec. com.), Am. Bar Assn., Mich. Bar Assn., Detroit Bar Assn. Club: Detroit Athletic. Home: 32020 Franklin Rd Box 53 Franklin MI 48025 Office: 130 E Elizabeth St Detroit MI 48201

ABBOTT, LAWRENCE, author, economist; b. Cornwall, N.Y., July 9, 1902; s. Ernest Hamlin and May Louise (Kleberg) A.; m. Ann Sands Tatham, Oct. 22, 1932; children: Vaughan, Sarah Tatham, Pauline Sands (Mrs. Kenneth E. McMurtry); m. Marie Bohrn Lambert, Dec. 9, 1966. A.B. cum laude with honors in Music, Harvard U., 1924; A.M., Columbia U., 1945, Ph.D., 1951. Advt. writer, publicity writer and mgr. country inn, 1924-33; mem. writing staff program dept. NBC, 1934-42; mem. faculty Hotchkiss Sch., 1943-47; instr. econs. Columbia U., 1947-51; asso. prof. econs. Mt. Holyoke Coll., 1951-53, Union Coll., 1953-56, prof., 1956-68, prof. emeritus, 1968—, chmn. dept. econs., 1962-66; Fulbright lectr. Pierce Coll., Athens, Greece, 1966-67. Contbr. to: including a monthly music rev. column Rolls and Discs, 1925-28; contbg. editor: Time mag, 1942-43; Author: books Student's Workbooks and Teacher's Guide, 1936-41, Approach to Music, 1940, Listener's Book on Harmony, 1941, Quality and Competition, 1955, Economics and the Modern World, 1960, rev., 1967, World Federalism: What? Why? How?, 1975, rev. edit., 1982; song The Ghost of John McCrae, 1928. Chmn. publs. com. World Federalist Edn. Fund, 1973—; bd. dirs. World Federalists Assn., 1975—, exec. com., 1979—, sec., 1982; editor World Federalist, 1981—; del. Tokyo Congress, 1980, Netherlands Congress, 1983. Mem. Am. Econ. Assn., AAUP, Royal Econ. Soc. Club: Century. Home: 259 High Street Coventry CT 06238

ABBOTT, PHILIP, actor; b. Lincoln, Nebr., Mar. 20, 1924; s. John Merriam and Helen Abbott (Boggs) Alexander; m. Jane DuFrayne, Apr. 29, 1950; children—Denise, David, Nelson. Student, Pasadena Playhouse, 1942, Fordham U., 1950-51. Chmn. bd., 1962-65, 67-68, 70, pres., Nelson Co., TV. Hon. sheriff, Tarzana, Calif., 1970, hon. mayor, 1972-74. Broadway debut in: Harvest of Years, 1948; other Broadway plays include Detective Story, 1950, Springtime Folly, 1951, The Square Root of Wonderful, 1957, Two For The Seesaw, 1958; appeared in: motion pictures The Bachelor Party, 1957, The Invisible Boy, 1957, The Miracle of the White Stallions, 1962, Those Calloways, 1963, Sweet Bird of Youth, 1961, The Spiral Road, 1961, Hangar 18, 1980, Savanna Smiles, 1981; host-narrator: TV series The House on High St, 1959-60; co-star: FBI, 1965-74; adapted and directed for stage: Promises To Keep, 1965, The Web and the Rock, 1968; co-founder, Theatre West, Inc., 1962, Theatre West/Club Theatre, 1969; dir.: A Partridge in a Pear Tree, J.F.K. Center for Performing Arts, 1980; writer, producer dir.: Operation: Street Encounter, 1972; co-author, producer, dir. 9 films for, U.S. Dept. Justice Law Enforcement Assistance Adminstrn. and Nat. Edn. Inst., including, Under the Law Parts I and II, 1973; author, producer, dir.: 5 film series Learning Laws, 1982; writer, dir.: O Socrates, San Diego State U., 1976; dir.: A Partridge in a Pear Tree, Kennedy Center for Performing Arts, 1980; co-author, dir., host: 10 films Lessons in Living Parts I and II for, Walt Disney Ednl. Media Co., 1978-81; host-narrator: TV series Hidden Places, Public Broadcasting Service, Nebr. Ednl. Bd. govs., bd. dirs. Spastic Children's Found., Los Angeles; pres. United Cerebral Palsy/Spastic Children's Found., Los Angeles, 1981-82, chmn. bd., 1983-84. Served with USAAF, 1943-45. Decorated D.F.C., Air medal with three oak leaf clusters. Mem. Actors Equity Assn., Screen Actors Guild, Dirs. Guild Am., A.F.T.R.A., Cinema Circulus, Info. Film Producers Am., Nat. Acad. TV Arts and Scis., Airplane Owners and Pilots Assn., Am. Judicature Soc. Office: Nelson Co 5400 Shirley Ave Tarzana CA 91356

ABBOTT, PRESTON SARGENT, psychologist; b. Peabody, Mass., Nov. 26, 1922; s. George Warren and Dorothy Quincy (Kelley) A.; m. Barbara Mount Beattie, Aug. 27, 1947; children: Judith, David, Mark. A.B., Bates Coll., 1947; M.A., U. Hawaii, 1948; Ph.D., Brown U., 1953. Research psychologist U.S. Air Force Personnel Tng. Center, Sacramento, 1951-55; psychologist Human Resources Research Office, Washington and Columbus, Ga., 1955-60; dir. research Human Ecology Fund, N.Y.C., 1960-65, Washington, 1963-65; program dir. Center for Research in Social Scis., 1966-70; dir. research AM. Insts. for Research, Washington, 1970-75; pres. Abbott Assos., Inc., Alexandria, Va., 1975—; cons. Nat. Acad. Scis., NIMH, U.S. Army, U.S. Air Force.; Bd. dirs. Cathay Corp. Contbr. articles on tng. and stress adjustment to publs. Served with AUS, 1942-45. Decorated D.F.C., Purple Heart, Air medal; NIMH grantee, 1966-67. Fellow Am. Psychol. Assn.; mem. Sigma Xi. Home: 1305 Namassin Rd Alexandria VA 22308 Office: 801 N Pitt St Alexandria VA 22314

ABBOTT, REGINALD MAX, retired symphony orchestra executive; b. Bryson City, N.C., Apr. 11, 1926; s. Joseph Reginald and Carrie P. A.; m. Mary Haithecock, June 4, 1949; children: Leslie Anne, Reginald Max. B.S. in Chemistry, U. N.C., 1950, M.Ed., 1953, D.Ed., 1965. Tchr., prin. Winston-Salem (N.C.) schs., 1951-62; exec. sec. N.C. Sch. Bds. Assn., 1962-65; supt. Kinston (N.C.) city schs., 1965-69; asst. supt. N.C. Dept. Public Instrn., 1969-71; supt. Fayetteville (N.C.) city schs., 1971-80; pres. N.C. Symphony, Raleigh, 1980-82, ret., 1982. Served with USNR, 1944-46. Mem. Nat., N.C. edn. assns., Am. Assn. Sch. Adminstrs., Phi Delta Kappa. Democrat. Methodist. Office: Box 602 Bryson City NC 28713

ABBOTT, ROBERT DEAN, educational psychology educator; b. Twin Falls, Idaho, Dec. 19, 1946; s. Charles Dean and Billie June (Moore) A.; m. Sylvia Patricia Keim, Dec. 16, 1967; children: Danielle, Matthew. B.A., Calif. Western U., San Diego, 1967; M.S., U. Wash., 1968, Ph.D., 1970. Asst. prof., assoc. prof. Calif. State U.-Fullerton, 1970-75; asst. prof., prof. ednl. psychology U. Wash., Seattle, 1975—. Author: Elementary Multivariate Statistics, 1983; contbr. articles to profl. jours. Calif. State scholar, 1964-67; Elliott H. Wheeler scholar, 1964. Mem. Am. Psychol. Assn., Am. Ednl. Research Assn., Am. Stats. Assn., Psychometric Soc. Methodist. Office: Ednl Psychology DQ-12 U Wash Seattle WA 98195

ABBOTT, ROBERT TUCKER, zoologist, author; b. Watertown, Mass., Sept. 28, 1919; s. Charles M. and Frances (Tucker) A.; m. Mary Sisler, Feb. 18, 1946 (dec. 1964); children: Robert T., Carolyn T., Cynthia Douglas; m. Cecelia White, May 13, 1977. B.S., Harvard, 1942; M.S., George Washington U., 1953, Ph.D., 1955. Asso. curator Smithsonian Instn., Washington, 1946-54; curator Acad. Natural Scis. of Phila., 1955-69, also chmn. dept. mollusks, 1955-69; asst. dir. Del. Mus. of Natural History, 1970-77; pres. Am. Malacologists, Inc., Melbourne, Fla., 1977—; adj. prof. U. Del., 1973-79. Author: American Seashells, 1954, 2d edit., 1974, Introducing Seashells, 1955, Seashells of the World, 1962, 2d edit., 1982, How to Know the American Marine Shells, 1961, Kingdom of the Seashell, 1972, The Shell, (with H. Stix), 1968, Shells in Color, 1973, The Best of the Nautilus, 1976, Standard Catalog of Shells, (with R. Wagner) Compendium of Seashells, 1982. Served to lt. USNR, 1942-46. Recipient award of Excellence for Books Comml. Arts Mag., 1967, Certificate of award Smithsonian Instn., 1953. Fellow A.A.A.S.; mem. Am. Malacological Union (pres. 1959), Soc. Systematic Zoology (sec. 1956-59, council 1974-76), Malacological Soc. of Australia, Paleontol. Research Inst., Harvard Grad. Soc. Council. Home: 2208 S Colonial Dr Melbourne FL 32901-0328 Office: American Malacologists Inc PO Box 2255 Melbourne FL 32901-0328 *Giving more than you receive, helping those who would take from you, and maintaining integrity in the face of frustration and temptation are the self-generating avenues towards personal freedom and ultimate success.*

ABBOTT, ROY TWINING, JR., investment banker; b. Bklyn., Jan. 19, 1931; s. Roy T. and Mary I. (Bright) A.; m. Leigh Hinsie, Apr. 17, 1954; children—Ann, Kenneth VanHorn, William Hinsie. B.A., Dartmouth Coll., 1952, M.B.A., 1953; postgrad., N.Y. U. Grad. Sch. Bus., 1953-54. With Chase Manhattan Bank, 1953-66, v.p., dist. exec. charge Southwest area, 1964-66; sr. v.p. Gulf & Western Industries, Inc., N.Y.C., 1966-67, sr. v.p. finance, 1967-74; also dir.; pres. Assos. 1st Capital Corp., 1974-76, dir., 1969-76; mng. dir. corp. finance, dir. Drexel Burnham Lambert, Inc., N.Y.C., 1976—; dir. Centennial Capital Cash Mgmt. Trust; adviser Advanced Mgmt. Research, Inc. Mem. Amos Tuck Sch. Alumni Assn., Delta Upsilon. Club: Canoe Brook Country (Summit, N.J.). Home: 343 Long Hill Dr Short Hills NJ 07078 Office: 60 Broad St New York NY 10004

ABBOTT, STANLEY EUGENE, newspaper editor; b. Hutchinson, Kans., July 22, 1942; s. Harold Seth and Dorothy Elizabeth (Dicus) A.; m. Trudie Thomas, Apr. 13, 1962 (div.); 1 dau., April-Ambre Sara; m. Jeanne Odell, Mar. 16, 1975; children: Robson Powell, Ellen Eaton. B.A., Calif. State U., Los Angeles, 1965. Exec. editor Anchorage (Alaska) Daily News, 1965-82; City editor Columbian Missourian, 1982—; Instr. Anchorage Community Coll., summer 1972, Sch. Journalism, U. Mo., 1982—; mng. editor IRE Jour., 1983—. Mem. Alaska Press Club (chpt. pres. 1972), AP Mng. Editors Assn., Alaska Newspaper Assn. Office: Missourian PO Box 917 Columbia MO 65205

ABBOTT, THOMAS BENJAMIN, educator; b. Washington County, Pa., June 27; s. Thomas Rankin and Emma Elizabeth (Behling) A.; m. Lee M. Parsons, Dec. 29, 1945; children—John Parsons, Amy Parsons. B.A., Muskingum Coll., New Concord, Ohio, 1943; M.A., Case Western Res. U., 1947; Ph.D., U. Fla., 1957. Lectr. U. So. Calif., 1957-58; prof. speech Baylor U., 1958-63, U. Fla., 1963-78, chmn. dept. speech, 1978—; cons. Westinghouse Elec. Corp. Health Systems, 1978—. Bd. dirs. Fla. Easter Seal Soc., 1969—, Nat. Easter Seal Soc., 1978—. Served with AUS, 1942-45. Fellow Am. Speech-Lang.-Hearing Assn. (cert.; legis. council); mem. Council Exceptional Children, Speech Communication Assn., So. Speech Communication Assn., Fla. Lang.-Speech-Hearing Assn. (honors award), Fla. Speech Communication Assn. Democrat. Episcopalian. Club: U. Fla. Faculty (pres.). Office: 335 ASB University of Florida Gainesville FL 32611

ABBOTT, WILLIAM WALLACE, consumer products company executive; b. Dallas, June 21, 1931; s. William Royal and Mary Louise (Wallace) A.; m. Jan Voorheis, June 15, 1957; children: William Scott, Marna louise, Aubrey Jan, David Wallace. B.S., Davidson Coll., N.C., 1952; M.B.A., Harvard U., 1954. With Procter & Gamble Co., Cin., 1954—, v.p. staff ops., 1975-76, sr. v.p., 1976—. Gen. chmn. Cin. United Way campaign, 1977; pres. Cin. council Boy Scouts Am., 1973-75. Mem. NAM (trustee), Cin. C. of C. (v.p. 1979-81), Am. Enterprise Inst., Joint Council Econ. Edn. (exec. com.). Republican. Methodist. Clubs: Camargo, Queen City, Commonwealth. Home: 5125 Ivy Farm Cincinnati OH 45243 Office: Procter & Gamble Co 6th and Sycamore Sts Cincinnati OH 45202

ABBOTT, WILTON ROBERT, aerospace engineer; b. Campbell, Calif., Jan. 19, 1916; s. Ernest A. and Audrey (Keesling) A.; m. Pearl Honeychurch, Sept. 2, 1938; children: Wilton R., Mary Louise, Mark R. B.S., U. Calif.-Berkeley, 1937; postgrad., Stanford U., 1937-38; M.S., Iowa State U., 1942, Ph.D., 1945. Asst. Stanford U., 1937-38; engr. Remler Co., Ltd., San Francisco, 1938-39, Gen. Electric Co., 1939-40; asst. prof. to assoc. prof. Iowa State U., Ames, 1940-46; asst. prof. U. Calif.-Berkeley, 1946-51; research specialist N.Am. Aviation, Downey, Calif., 1951-57; sr. cons. engr. Lockheed Missiles and Space Co., Sunnyvale, Calif., 1957—, chief devel. engr. Agena spacecraft; asst. prof. San Jose State U., 1981—; prof. Chapman Coll., 1983—; program chmn. Reliability and Maintainability Symposium, 1970. Contbr. articles to profl. jours.; patentee in field. Trustee Linfield Coll., 1977—, chmn. vis. com. natural scis., 1980—. Recipient cert. of excellence Gemini Agena Taget Vehicle Program, 1966. Mem. IEEE (life sr.), Reliability Soc., Systems, Man and Cybernetics Soc. (sr.), Sigma Xi, Eta Kappa Nu, Tau Beta Pi. Baptist. Lodge: Masons. Home: 27899 Via Ventana Los Altos Hills CA 94022 Office: Bldg 538 6223 PO Box 504 Sunnyvale CA 94086 *A basic principle of System Theory may be interpreted as showing that a complex problem cannot be satisfied by a simple solution. Thus, since most real problems are complex, one should be suspicious of a simple solution to any problem. Certainly to understand the place of humans in the universe is to solve a complex problem. Therefore I find it impossible to believe that an understanding based entirely on Science or one based entirely on Religion can be correct.*

ABBOTT, WOODROW ACTON, air force officer; b. Eubank, Ky., Dec. 16, 1919; s. William Thomas and Susie Ellen (Gastineau) A.; m. Lois Marie Scobee, May 17, 1944; children: Woodrow Acton II, Celesta Ann, Teletha Gay. Student, Butler U., 1939-43; B.S., U. Md., 1955, postgrad., 1956; M.B.A., Golden State U., 1982. Commd. 2d lt. USAAF, 1943; advanced through grades to brig. gen. USAF, 1969; B-17 pilot, ETO, 1944-45; assigned Far East Air Force, 1950-52; with SAC, 1956-71; comdr. 92d Wing, 1966-67, 93d Wing, 1968-69, 307th Strategic Wing and 4258th Strategic Wing, Thailand, 1969-70, 42d Air Div., 1970-71; insp. gen. SAC, 1971-73; dir. intelligence J-2, also insp. gen. U.S., Readiness Command, MacDill AFB, Fla., 1973—. Decorated D.S.M. with oak leaf cluster, Legion of Merit with 2 oak leaf clusters, D.F.C., Meritorious Service medal, Air medal with 6 oak leaf clusters, Air Force Commendation medal with 2 oak leaf clusters, Army Commendation medal, Purple Heart; Supreme Command Forward badge 1st class, Thailand). Mem. Delta Sigma Pi. Clubs: Tampa (Fla.); Yacht and Country, Merced Golf and Country, Merced

Racquet. Home: 1192 Paseo Verde Merced CA 95340 *From the age of maturity I have considered INTEGRITY as the one indispensable quality a person must possess in order to achieve his or her life's goals, regardless of how lofty or humble those ambitions may be.*

ABBOUD, A. ROBERT, oil company executive; b. Boston, May 29, 1929; s. Alfred and Victoria (Karam) A.; m. Joan Grover, June 11, 1955; children: Robert, Jeanne Frances, Katherine Jane. B.S. cum laude, Harvard U., 1951, LL.B., 1956, M.B.A., 1958. Asst. cashier First Nat. Bank of Chgo., 1960-62, asst. v.p., 1962-64, v.p., 1964-69, sr. v.p., 1969-72, exec. v.p., 1972-73, vice chmn. bd., 1973-74, dep. chmn. bd., 1974-75, chmn. bd., 1975-80; pres., chief operating officer Occidental Petroleum Corp., Los Angeles, 1980—; dir. Hart Schaffner & Marx, Inland Steel Co. Served with USMCR, 1951-53. Mem. Los Angeles Area C. of C. (dir.). Clubs: Econ., Chicago, Comml., Barrington Hills Country. Office: Occidental Petroleum Corp 10889 Wilshire Blvd Los Angeles CA 90024

ABBOUD, FRANCOIS MITRY, physician, educator; b. Cairo, Egypt, Jan. 5, 1931; came to U.S., 1955, naturalized, 1963; s. Mitry Y. and Asma (Habac) A.; m. Doris Evelyn Khal, June 5, 1955; children—Mary Agnese, Susan Marie, Nancy Louise, Anthony Lawrence. Student, U. Cairo, 1948-52; M.B., B.Ch., Ein Chams U., 1955. Intern Demerdash Govt. Hosp., Cairo, 1955; resident Milw. County Hosp., 1955-58; Am. Heart Assn. research fellow cardiovascular labs. Marquette U., 1958-60; Am. Heart Assn. advanced research fellow U. Iowa, 1960-62, asst. prof., 1961-65, asso. prof. medicine, 1965-68, prof. medicine, 1968—, prof. physiology and biophysics, 1975—; dir. cardiovascular div., 1970-76, chmn. dept. internal medicine, 1976—, dir. cardiovascular center, 1974—; attending physician VA Hosp., Iowa City, 1963—, U. Iowa Hosps., 1961—; chmn. research rev. com. Nat. Heart, Lung and Blood Inst., 1978-80. Editor: Circulation Research, 1981—. Recipient European Traveling fellow French Govt., 1948; NIH career devel. awardee, 1962-71. Mem. Am. Soc. Clin. Investigation, Central Soc. for Clin. Research, Soc. Exptl. Biology and Medicine, A.C.P., AMA, Am. Fedn. Clin. Research (pres. 1971-72), Assn. Univ. Cardiologists, Assn. Profs. Medicine, Assn. Am. Physicians (treas. 1979—), Am. Physiol. Soc. (chmn. circulation group 1979-80, chmn. clin. physiology sect. 1979—), Am. Clin. and Climatological Assn., Am. Soc. Pharmacology and Exptl. Therapeutics (award exptl. therapeutics 1972), Sigma Xi. Research and publs. in cardiovascular physiology on neurohumoral control of circulation in man and animals. Home: 334 Highland Dr Iowa City IA 52240

ABBRECHT, PETER HERMAN, physiologist, educator; b. Toledo, Nov. 27, 1930; s. Hermann Richard and Paula Katherine (Schwenk) A.; m. Anne Patterson Lampman, Feb. 16, 1957; children—Elaine, Brian. B.S., Purdue U., 1952; M.S., U. Mich., 1953, Ph.D. in Chem. Engring, 1957, M.D., 1962. Diplomate: Am. Bd. Internal Medicine. Sr. chem. engr. Minn. Mining & Mfg. Co., Detroit, 1956-58; intern U. Calif. Hosp., Los Angeles, 1962-63; mem. faculty U. Mich. Med. Sch., Ann Arbor, 1963-80, prof. physiology, 1972-80, chmn. bioengring. program, 1972-77, prof. internal medicine, 1976-80; prof. internal medicine and physiology Uniformed Services U. of Health Scis., Bethesda, Md.; and cons. physician Walter Reed Army Med. Center, 1980—; guest scientist Naval Med. Research Inst., 1980—; resident in internal medicine U. Mich. Hosp., 1971-72, fellow in pulmonary disease, 1974-75; vis. prof. bioengring. U. Calif., San Diego, 1973; dir. physiology and biomed. engring. program NIGMS-NIH, 1977-78; cons. VA, NASA, Air Force Office Sci. Research, NIH, NSF; mem. nat. research resources advisory council, 1975-78. Editor in chief: Internat. Jour. Biomed. Engring, 1972-74; Editorial bd.: Jour. Biomechanics; editor-in-chief: Jour. Bioengring, 1979—; Contbr. articles to profl. jours. Recipient outstanding research award Mich. Heart Assn., 1960; research career devel. award NIH, 1969-73. Fellow ACP; mem. Biomed. Engring. Soc. (dir. 1970-72); Mem. Am. Physiol. Soc., Am. Thoracic Soc., Soc. Exptl. Biology and Medicine. Home: 2806 Spencer Rd Chevy Chase MD 20015

ABDELA, ANGELO SOLOMON, manufacturing company executive; b. Cairo, Egypt., Apr. 17, 1942; s. Victor and Renee A.; m. Catherine Marguerite Frisch, June 20, 1969; 1 dau., Daphne. B. Econs. and Stats., Hebrew U., Jerusalem, 1966; M.B.A., European Inst. Bus. Adminstrn., Fontainebleau, France, 1968. Asst. new bus. devel. CPC Europe, Brussels, 1968-70; mng. dir. CPC Kenya Ltd., Nairobi, 1970-73; fin. and adminstrn. dir. Besin ve Misir, Istanbul, Turkey, 1973-75; staff asst. CPC Internat., Englewood Cliffs, N.J., 1975-78, asst. treas., 1978-81, treas., 1981—; dir. Latin Am. Agribus. Devel. Corp. Mem. Nat. Assn. Bus Economists, Soc. Internat. Treasurers., Fin. Execs. Inst. Home: 115 Central Park W New York NY 10023 Office: Internat Plaza PO Box 8000 Englewood Cliffs NJ 07632

ABDEL-KHALIK, AHMED RASHAD, business educator; b. Meet-Ghamer, Egypt, May 30, 1940; came to U.S., 1964, naturalized, 1975; s. Mohamed Ahmed and Gamilah El-Morsey (Abdel-bary) Abdel-K.; m. Maria Eugenia, June 30, 1973; children: Jasmine, Catherine, Justin Christopher. B.Com. hon., Cairo U., 1961; M.B.A., Ind. U., 1965, A.M., 1966; Ph.D., U. Ill.-Urbana, 1972. Asst. prof. bus. Columbia U., N.Y.C., 1972-74, assoc. prof., 1974-75; assoc. prof. bus. adminstrn. Duke U., Durham, N.C., 1975-77; W.J. Matherly prof. acctg. U. Fla., Gainesville, 1977-80, grad. research prof., 1977-83, dir. Acctg. Research Ctr., 1977-83; Welden Powell prof. U. Ill.-Champaign, 1983—; vis. Winspear Found. prof. U. Alta., 1982-83. Author, editor several books; contbr. articles to acad. and profl. jours.; founding editor: Jour. Accounting Literature. Ernst & Ernst fellow, 1971-72. Mem. Am. Acctg. Assn. (doctoral fellow 1971-72, dir. research 1980-82), Am. Econ. Assn., Am. Inst. Decision Scis., Fin. Execs. Inst., Am. Fin. Assn., Beta Alpha Psi. Home: 1816 Old Maple Ln Savoy IL 61874 Office: 294 Commerce West U Ill Champaign IL 61820

ABDELLAH, FAYE GLENN, U.S. Public Health Service official; b. N.Y.C., Mar. 13, 1919; d. H.B. and Margaret (Glenn) A. R.N., Ann May Sch. Nursing, N.J., 1942; B.S., Tchrs. Coll., Columbia U., 1945, M.A., 1947, Ed.D., 1955; LL.D. (hon.), Case Western Res. U., 1967, Rutgers U., 1973, Sc.D., U. Akron, 1978, Cath. U. Am., 1981, Monmouth Coll., 1982, Eastern Mich U. Commd. officer USPHS, 1949, advanced through grades to dep. surgeon gen. (Navy rear adm.), 1970; chief nursing edn. br., div. nursing, 1949-59; chief research grants br. Bur. Health Manpower Edn., NIH, HEW, 1959-69; dir. Office Research Tng. Nat. Center for Health Services Research and Devel., Health Services Mental Health Adminstrn., 1969; asst. surgeon gen., chief nurse officer USPHS, Rockville, Md., 1970—; acting dep. dir. Nat. Center for Health Services Research and Devel., 1971, Bur. Health Services Research and Evaluation, Health Resources Adminstrn., 1973; dir. Office Long-Term Care, Office Asst. Sec. for Health, HEW, 1973—. Author: Effect of Nurse Staffing on Satisfactions with Nursing Care, 1959, Patient Centered Approaches to Nursing, 1960, Better Patient Care Through Nursing Research, 1965, 2d edit., 1979, Intensive Care, Concepts and Practices for Clinical Nurse Specialists, 1969, New Directions in Patient Centered Nursing, 1972; Contbr. articles to profl. jours. Recipient Mary Adelaide Nutting award, 1983. Charter fellow Am. Acad. Nursing (v.p.); mem. Am. Psychol. Assn., AAAS, Assn. Mil. Surgeons U.S., Sigma Theta Tau, Phi Lambda Theta. Home: 3713 Chanel Rd Annandale VA 22003 Office: Room 18-67 5600 Fishers Ln Rockville MD 20852

ABDELSAYED, GABRIEL H.A., clergyman; b. Minia, Egypt, Apr. 3, 1927; came to U.S., 1969; s. Ameen A. (now Friar Mathew) and Nazeera (Abdelsayed) Ghabour; m. Tahani M., Fed. 17, 1952; children: Wafaa, George, Wafeck, Lucy. B.A. in History, Cario U., 1948, M.A., Cairo U., 1955; Ph.D. in History with honors, Cario U., 1960; Ed.Dip., Ein Shams U., Egypt, 1950. Ordained to ministry Coptic Orthodox Ch. Prof. Tchrs. Tng. Inst., Cario, 1955-68; vis. prof. Middle East Ctr. U. Utah, Salt Lake City, 1969-70, Monterey Inst. Fgn. Studies, Calif., summer 1970; postdoctoral fellow Inst. Ecumenical and Cultural Research, Minn., 1970; rector, chief exec. Coptic Orthodox Ch. N.Y. and N.J., Jersey City, 1970—; asst. prof. St. John's U., N.Y.C., 1972-76; adj. assoc. prof. Grad. Inst. Coptic Studies, Cairo, 1964-69; mem. Oriental Orthodox Roman Catholic Com. on Christian Unity, N.Y.C., 1969—; mem. governing bd., chief exec. Coptic del. Nat. Council Chs., 1978—. Author: Egyptian Monasticism and Cenobitism, 1963, Rise of the Second Mamluk Dynasty, 1967 (award), St. Mark in Africa, 1968, Ten Years of History of Coptic Church, 1969. Recipient medal of Holy Cross Ethipian Patriarchate, Ethiopia, 1973. Office: Coptic Orthodox Ch 427 West Side Ave Jersey City NJ 07304 *

ABDNOR, JAMES, senator; b. Kennebec, S.D., Feb. 13, 1923; s. Samuel J. and Mary (Wehby) A. B.A. in Bus. Adminstrn., U. Nebr., 1945. Tchr., coach, Presho, S.D., 1946-48, farmer, rancher, Kennebec, 1945—; mem. 93d-96th Congresses from S.D.; U.S. senator, 1981—; Chmn. S.D. Young Republicans, 1953-55; mem. S.D. Senate, 1956-69, pres. pro-tem, 1967-68; lt. gov. S.D., 1969-70. Served with AUS. Mem. Kennebec Jr. C. of C. (past pres.), Am. Legion, S.D. Wheat Producers, S.D. Stockgrowers, S.D. Farmers Union, S.D. Farm Bur., Isaak Walton League, Sigma Chi. Clubs: Masons, Elks. Home: Kennebec SD 57544 Office: 309 Hart Senate Office Bldg Washington DC 20510

ABDUL-JABBAR, KAREEM (LEW ALCINDOR), professional basketball player; b. N.Y.C., Apr. 16, 1947; s. Ferdinand Lewis and Cora Alcindor. Grad., UCLA, 1969. Basketball player with Milw. Bucks, 1969-75, Los Angeles Lakers, 1975—. Appeared: on TV in Mannix, The Man from Atlantis; appeared in: movies The Fish that Saved Pittsburgh, 1979, Airplane, 1980. Named Rookie of Year, 1970; recipient Maurice Podoloff Cup, named Most Valuable Player NBA, 1971, 72, 74, 76, 77, 80; mem. NBA All-Star Team, 1970-84; named to NBA 35th Anniversary All-Time Team, 1980, NBA Rookie of Yr., 1970, NBA Playoff Most Valuable Player, 1971; mem. NBA Championship Team, 1971, 80, 82; NCAA Tournament Most Outstanding Player, 1967, 68, 69. Muslim. Became NBA all-time leading scorer, 1984. Address: care Los Angeles Lakers PO Box 10 Los Angeles CA 90306 *

ABEGG, MARTIN G., university president; b. Alliance, Nebr., Oct. 3, 1925; s. Frank and Mary Anna (Newberry) A.; m. Barbara Louise Chamberlain, June 29, 1946; children: Martin Gerald, Robert Miles. B.S. in Gen. Engring, Bradley U., 1947; M.S. in Civil Engring, U. Colo., 1951, Ph.D., Rensselaer Poly. Inst., 1960; LL.D. (hon.), Ill. Coll., 1982. Registered profl. engr., Ill.; registered land surveyor, Ill. Instr. engring. Bradley U., 1947-50, asst. prof., 1950-55, asso. prof., 1955-60, prof., 1960—, head dept. civil engring., 1960-63; dean Coll. Engring. and Tech., 1963-70, pres., 1971—; Engring. aide Ill. Div. Hwys., Dixon, 1946, civil engr., Peoria, Ill., 1948; park dist. engr., Peoria, 1953-55; cons. engr. Norman Porter & Assos., N.Y.C., 1956-57, 59. Served to lt. (j.g.) USNR, 1943-46. Recipient Putnam award Bradley U., 1961. Mem. Am. Soc. C.E., Am. Soc. Engring. Edn., Ill., Nat. socs. profl. engrs., Sigma Xi, Sigma Tau, Phi Kappa Phi, Omicron Delta Kappa, Lambda Chi Alpha, Tau Beta Pi, Chi Epsilon. Club: Rotarian (pres. 1971—). Home: 208 Wolf Rd Peoria IL 61614 Office: 1501 Bradley Ave Peoria IL 61625

ABEL, ALLEN JOEL, journalist; b. Bklyn., Jan. 31, 1950; s. Benjamin and Henrietta (Jacobson) A.; m. Linda Joy Deyo, Apr. 20, 1974. B.Sc. in Physics, Rensselaer Poly. Inst., Troy, N.Y., 1971. Sports reporter Troy Record, 1972-74, Albany (N.Y.) Times-Union, 1974-77; commentator Sta. WTRY, Troy, 1974-77, CFRB, Toronto, 1982—; sports columnist Globe and Mail, Toronto, Ont., Can., 1977-83, Peking corr., 1983—; commentator Sta. CFRB, Toronto, Ont., Can., 1982—. Author: But I Loved It Plenty Well, 1983. Recipient N.Y. State AP Writing award, 1972-75, Nat. Newspaper Can. award, 1979; winner Hearst Writing competition, 1975. Mem. Assn. Internat. de la Presse Sportive (dir.). Office: 444 Front St W Toronto M5V 2S9 Canada

ABEL, BRENT MAXWELL, lawyer; b. Washington, May 6, 1916; s. Charles and Susan Alice (Maxwell) A.; m. Corinne W. VanHorne, Nov. 2, 1973; children by previous marriage: Brent Maxwell, Molly D. A.B., Harvard, 1937, LL.B., 1940. Bar: N.Y. 1940, Calif. 1946. Assoc. Cravath, Swaine & Moore, N.Y.C., 1940-41; asso. firm McCutchen, Doyle, Brown & Enersen (and predecessor), San Francisco, 1946-54, partner, 1954—; vis. lectr. law U. Calif., 1955-60; dir. U.S. Trust Corp.; trustee U.S. Trust Co. N.Y., 1979—; Mem. overseers com. to visit Harvard Law Sch., 1967-68, chmn., 1977-82. Bd. dirs. San Francisco chpt. Am. Cancer Soc., 1957-63, pres., 1959-60; trustee Anna Head Sch., Oakland, Calif., 1962-71, Phillips Exeter Acad., Exeter, N.H., 1959-75, San Francisco Performing Arts Found., 1980—; bd. overseers Harvard U., 1975-81. Served with USNR, 1941-46; Capt. Res. Decorated Navy Cross, Navy Unit commendation ribbon. Mem. Phillips Exeter Acad. Gen. Alumni Assn. (pres. 1964-66), Bar Assn. San Francisco (pres. 1964), Am. Bar Assn., State Bar Calif. (bd. govs. 1972-75, pres. 1974-75), Harvard Law Sch. Assn. No. Calif. (pres. 1961), San Francisco Legal Aid Soc. (pres. 1967-68), Asso. Harvard Alumni (pres. 1971-72). Clubs: Bohemian, Bankers, Pacific Union (San Francisco); Harvard (N.Y.C.). Home: 1054 Chestnut St San Francisco CA 94109 Office: 3 Embarcadero Center San Francisco CA 94111

ABEL, CLARENCE, JR., lawyer; b. Indpls., Dec. 12, 1928; s. Clarence and Celeste G. (Stevens) A.; m. Marilyn Sue Warner, Mar. 24, 1951; children—Brian Dwight, Julie Beth. B.B.A., U. Toledo, 1950, J.D., 1958. Bar: Ohio bar 1959. Life underwriter Equitable Life of Iowa, 1950-51; salary payroll adminstr., asst. credit mgr., auditor, asst. to treas. DeVilbiss Co., 1951-61; since practiced in, Toledo; asso. Conn. Krause & Bowman, 1961; co-founder, gen. partner Bowman, Abel & Raitz (and predecessor firms), 1962-78; counsel for Johnson Estates, Moore Accounting & Tax, Lutton Dental Labs., McMahon Enterprises, Flintkote Co., Co-op. Tool Sales, Shinner's Meats, A & B Tool Co. Pres. McKinley PTA, 1965-67; Mem. Republican Workshops, 1962-64, Lucas County Rep. Club, also Ohio Rep. Finance Com., 1963-65; trustee YMCA. Served with USMCR, 1947-50. Mem. Am. Judicature Soc., ABA, Ohio Bar Assn., Lucas County Bar Assn., Toledo Bar Assn. (com. chmn.), Toledo Law Assn., Comml. Law League, Toledo Mus. Art, U. Toledo Alumni Assn., U. Toledo Law Alumni Assn. (dir., pres.), Sigma Alpha Epsilon, Delta Theta Phi. Mem. United Ch. Christ (deacon moderator). Clubs: Mason. Clubs, University of Toledo Tower, Exchange. Home: 818 Lakeview Dr Clarklake MI 49234 Office: 2509 Sylvania Ave Suite 12 Toledo OH 43613

ABEL, DEFOREST WILLIAMS, JR., insurance company executive; b. Providence, Apr. 14, 1929; s. DeForest Williams and Grace Isabel (Marshall) A.; children: DeForest Williams III, Diane Christine, Wendy Lee, Richard Ellsworth, Virginia Caroline. Student, Nichols Coll., Dudley, Mass., 1948-49, U. Miami, Fla., 1949-51. With Amica Mut. Ins. Co., 1951—, dir., 1965—, pres., 1968—, pres., chief exec. officer, 1971—; pres., dir. Amica Life Ins. Co.; chmn. bd. trustees Amica Pension Fund; pres., dir. Amica Services, Inc. Mem. corp. Women and Infants Hosp., R.I., Cranston (R.I.) Osteo. Gen. Hosp.; hon. trustee Bryant Coll., Smithfield, R.I.; bd. dirs. New Eng. Council; ex-officio bd. dirs. Meeting St. Sch.; alt. del. Nat. Easter Seal Soc.; trustee Nichols Coll.; mem. Naval War Coll. Found. Served with USAF, 1951. Mem. Alliance Am. Insurers (dir.), Am. Inst. Property and Liability Underwriters (trustee), Ins. Inst. Am. (trustee), Gen. Soc. Colonial Wars, R.I. Sch. Design Mus. (life mem.), Sigma Phi Upsilon. Clubs: Squantum, R.I. Country (Barrington); University, Turks Head, British Empire, Agawam (Providence); Boston Madison Sq. Garden, Sea Island (Ga.) Golf; University, River (Jacksonville, Fla.). Lodge: Adelphi. Office: 10 Weybosset St Providence RI 02940

ABEL, ELIE, reporter, broadcaster, educator; b. Montreal, Que., Can., Oct. 17, 1920; s. Jacob and Rose (Savetsky) A.; m. Corinne Adelaide Prevost, Jan. 28, 1946; children: Mark, Suzanne. B.A., McGill U., 1941, LL.D., 1971; M.S. in Journalism, Columbia U., 1942; LL.D., U. Western Ont., 1976. Reporter Windsor (Ont.) Star, 1941; asst. city editor Montreal Gazette, 1945-46; fgn. corr. N.Am. Newspaper Alliance, Berlin, 1946-47; UN corr. Overseas News Agy., 1947-49; also nat. corr. N.Y. Times, 1949-59; Washington bur. chief Detroit News, 1959-61; with NBC, 1961-69, chief London bur., 1965-67; diplomatic corr. NBC News, Washington, 1967-69; Godfrey Lowell Cabot prof., also dean Grad. Sch. Journalism, Columbia U., N.Y.C., 1969-79; Harry and Norman Chandler prof. Stanford U., 1979—; Bd. govs. Am. Stock Exchange, 1974-78. Author: The Missile Crisis, 1966, (with Marvin Kalb) Roots of Involvement, The U.S. in Asia 1784-1971, 1971, (with Averell Harriman) Special Envoy to Churchill and Stalin, 1941-46, 1975; editor: What's News: The Media in American Society, 1981. Recipient George Foster Peabody award for outstanding radio news, 1968; Overseas Press Club award for best interpretation of fgn. news, 1969. Mem. Council Fgn. Relations, Sigma Delta Chi. Club: Century (N.Y.C.). Address: Dept Communication Stanford Univ Stanford CA 94305

ABEL, HAROLD, university president; b. N.Y.C., July 31, 1926; s. Felix N. and Jennie (Schaefer) A.; m. Iris Tash, Jan. 30, 1949; children: Lawrence William, Matthew Robert. A.B., Syracuse U., 1949, M.A., 1951, Ph.D., 1958; D.Litt. (hon.). Tchr. advanced mentally retarded Syracuse (N.Y.) Pub. Schs., 1950-51; tchr. intermediate mentally retarded Rochester (N.Y.) Pub. Schs., 1951-52; asst. instr. Sch. Edn. Syracuse U., 1952-54, asst. instr. dept. psychology, 1954-56; assoc. prof. to prof. depts. psychology and home econs. and dir. child devel. lab. U. Nebr., 1956-65, chmn. dept. human devel., 1963-65; dir. div. psycho-ednl. studies, prof. edn. U. Oreg., 1965-68, assoc. dean, prof. ednl. psychology Coll. Edn., 1968-70; pres. Castleton State Coll., 1970-75, Central Mich. U., 1975—; Mem. Gov. Nebr. Commn. on Human Relations, 1963-65; vice chmn. Gov. Neb. Interagy. Com. on Mental Retardation, 1963-65; mem. mayor's com. on phys. handicapped, Lincoln, Nebr., 1963-65; mem. Gov. Oreg. Com. on Aging, 1967-68, Gov.'s Statewide Health Coordinating Council, Mich.; mem. nat. adv. com. Project Follow-Through, 1967-69. Served with AUS, 1945-46. Mem. AAAS, Am. Psychol. Assn., Soc. Research in Child Devel., Sigma Xi, Phi Delta Kappa. Home: 524 E Bellows St Mount Pleasant MI 48858 Office: Central Mich U Mount Pleasant MI 48859

ABEL, REUBEN, educator; b. N.Y.C., Nov. 25, 1911; s. Louis and Dora (Friedsell) A.; m. Marion Buchman, July 30, 1937; children—Richard L., Elizabeth F. A.B., Columbia U., 1929; J.D., N.Y. U., 1934; M.Social Sci., New Sch., 1941, Ph.D., 1952. Dept. store buyer, 1929-44, 46-48; faculty New Sch. for Social Research, N.Y.C., 1950—, adj. prof. philosophy, 1967—, chmn. humanities div., 1965-82, assoc. dean, 1972-74; Regional unit chief OPA, 1944-46; pres., treas. Atlas Bedspread Co., Inc., N.Y.C., 1948-61; Chmn. Conf. on Methods in Philosophy and Scis., 1966-68, sec.-treas., 1950-53. Author: The Pragmatic Humanism of F.C.S. Schiller, 1955, Man Is The Measure, 1976; also articles, revs. encys.; Editor: Humanistic Pragmatism, 1966. Mem. Am. Philos. Assn., Am. Assn. U. Profs., Philosophy of Sci. Assn., Internat. Assn. for Philosophy of Law and Social Philosophy, Am. Soc. for Aesthetics, Soc. Philosophy and Psychology, N.Y. Philos. Club. Home: 17 Monroe Ave Larchmont NY 10538 Office: 66 W 12th St New York NY 10011

ABEL, RICHARD FRANCIS, government official, air force officer; b. Akron, Ohio, Oct. 28, 1933; s. Frank William and Cecelia Marie (Kleinhenz) A.; m. Shirley Ann Voelcker, Nov. 10, 1956; children: Tamara D. Abel Mattson, Teresa M., Katrina L., Timothy L. B.S., U. Detroit, 1956; postgrad., Boston U., 1962. Commd. 2d lt. U.S. Air Force, 1956, advanced through grades to brig. gen., 1981; served chief combat news div. 7th Air Force, Republic of Vietnam, 1968-69; pub. affairs officer for commander-in-chief U.S. Pacific Command, 7th Air Force, Hawaii, 1969-72; dir. admissions liason office U.S. Air Force Acad., Colorado Springs, Colo., 1972-75; dir. pub. affairs Pacific Command, 1975-78; spl. asst. to Chmn. Joint Chief of Staff U.S. Air Force Acad., Washington, 1978-80; dir. pub. affairs Office Sec. of Air Force, Washington, 1980—. Contbr. articles to publs. Vice chmn. nat. bd. dirs. Fellowship of Christian Athletes, 1980; mem. Nat. Pub. Info. Com. USO, 1980. Decorated Bronze Star, Meritorious Service Medal with oak leaf cluster, Def. Superior Service Medal, Def. Meritorious Service Medal. Mem. Air Force Assn., Nat. Aero. Assn. (dir. 1980), Order of Daedalians. Office: Sec of Air Force Office Public Affairs Room 4D922 Pentagon Washington DC 20330

ABEL, ROBERT BERGER, science administrator; b. Providence, July 21, 1926; s. Abraham Lincoln and Betty Ruth (Berger) A.; m. Nancy Marilyn Klein, Oct. 4, 1953; Children: Alan Stewart, Deborah Jane. B.S., Brown U., 1947; M.E.A., George Washington U., 1962; Ph.D., Am. U., 1972. Chemist Woods Hole (Mass.) Oceanographic Instn., 1947-50; oceanographer U.S. Navy Hydrographic Office, Suitland, Md., 1950-55, asst. to dir., 1955-60; asst. research coordinator Office Naval Research, Washington, 1961-64; exec. sec. Interagy. Com. Oceanography, 1960-67; asst. exec. sec. Nat. Council Marine Resources and Engring. Devel., 1967-68; dir. Nat. Sea Grant Program, Dept. Commerce, 1968-77; asst. v.p. Tex. A&M U., 1977-78; v.p. N.J. Marine Scis. Consortium, Fort. Hancock, 1979-81, pres., 1981—; instr. oceanography USNR Officers Sch., 1960-65, Fairleigh Dickinson U., 1966—, U. Va., 1973—; instr. ocean mgmt. Rutgers U., 1980—; dir. Israel Oceanographic & Limnol. Research, Ltd., CEM, Inc. Pres. Cris-Mar Manor Civic Assn., 1957-61; Bd. dirs. Tantalon Civic Assn., 1973-74, Ctr. Ocean Law and Policy. Served with USNR, 1944-46. Recipient Superior Service award Navy Dept., 1963, Disting. Service award, 1967; Gold medal Dept. Commerce, 1973; Man of Year award Nat. Sea Grant Program, 1977; Disting. Alumnus award George Washington U., 1983; decorated Order Jules Richard (Monaco), 1951. Mem. Am. Chem. Soc., Research Soc. Am. (past pres. chpt.), Marine Tech. Soc. (pres. 1974-75), Am. Soc. Oceanography (pres. 1971-72), Gulf and Caribbean Fisheries Inst. (dir.). Jewish (v.p. congregation). Clubs: Cosmos, Admirals, Brown, Toastmasters (Washington). Home: 55 Queen Anne Dr Shrewsbury NJ 07701 Office: NJ Marine Scis Consortium Fort Hancock NJ 07732

ABEL, WILLARD EDWARD, agriculturist, cons.; b. Vancouver, Wash., Aug. 10, 1906; s. Charlie Edward and Julia (Wilson) A.; m.

Hazel Belle Shoemaker, Nov. 1, 1930; 1 son, David. A.A., Centralia Jr. Coll., 1927. With Western Internat. Hotels Co., 1925-71, successively room clk., asst. mgr., mgr., 1930-53, v.p., 1953-62, sr. v.p., 1963-71; pres., gen. mgr. Hotel Sir Francis Drake, San Francisco, 1947-59; exec. v.p. St. Francis Hotel Corp., 1959-61, pres., 1961-72; also dir.; pres. Internat. Western Hotels Ltd., 1965-71, Ellis O'Farrell Garage Corp., 1965-76; v.p. Western Internat. Mgmt. Co., Hoteles Biltmore de Guatemala; sr. v.p., dir. Western Internat. Hotels Co., to 1970; cons. in field; farmer, apple grower, Sebastopol, Calif. Served in AUS, 1941-46; lt. col. Q.M. Mem. Am. Hotel and Motel Assn. (pres. 1965, pres., dir. ednl. inst.), Calif. Hotel Assn. (past pres., dir.), San Francisco C. of C. (dir.). Home: 1659 16th Ave San Francisco CA 94122 also 615 Tilton Rd Sebastopol CA 95472

ABELE, HOMER E., judge; b. Wellston, Ohio, Nov. 21, 1916; s. Oscar and Margaret (Burke) A.; m. Addie Riggs, 1938; children: Terrell Ann, Peter Burke, Andy. LL.B., Ohio State U., 1953, J.D., 1970. Bar: Ohio 1954, U.S. Supreme Ct. 1954. Mem. CCC, 1935-36; with Anchor Hocking Glass Corp., Lancaster, Ohio; then Austin Powder Co., McArthur, Ohio, to 1941; patrolman Ohio State Hwy. Patrol, Van Wert, 1941-43, 46; solicitor McArthur; Vinton County rep. Ohio Gen. Assembly, 1949-52; asst. to campaign mgr. Sen. Robert A. Taft, Republican Nat. Conv., Chgo., 1952; legis. counsel Spl. Transp. Com., 1953-57; del. Rep. Nat. Conv., San Francisco, 1956; Rep. nominee for Congress, 10th Ohio Dist., 1958; mem. 88th Congress from 10th Dist. Ohio; judge 4th Dist. Ohio Ct. Appeals, 1967-77, presiding judge, 1977-78; chief justice Ct. Appeals Ohio, 1978; Past state dept. judge adv. Am. Legion Ohio; chmn. ct. sect. Am. Legion Buckeye Boy's State, 1969-79, pres., 1981, 82. Program chmn. McArthur Devel. Assn.; Vinton County trustee Southeastern Ohio Regional Council. Served with USAAF, 1943-46. Mem. Am. Legion (exec. officer to past state comdr.), Ohio, Vinton County bar assns., Ohio Bar Found. Clubs: McArthur Lions (past pres.), Soc. South Pole (life). Home: McArthur OH 45651 Office: 4th Appellate Dist McArthur OH 45651

ABELES, JAMES DAVID, manufacturing company executive; b. N.Y.C., Mar. 24, 1916; s. James A. and Williemene H. (Kirtl) A.; m. Elizabeth Brunet, Aug. 24, 1940 (dec. 1978); children: James B. and Elizabeth K. (twins); m. Mary E. Ballantyne, Dec. 11, 1982. Student, Stevens Inst. Tech., 1935-36, M.I.T., 1936-37. Tool and die apprentice Electrolux Co., 1934-35; erecting engr. U.S. Fire Protection Co., 1937-38; sales engr. Thomas F. Mason Co., 1938-39; time study engr. Waterbury Button Co., 1939-40; with Purolator, Inc., Rahway, N.J., 1940—, dir., 1954—, pres., 1955-70, chmn. exec. com., 1970-73; pres., dir. Interpace Corp., 1973-74, chmn. bd. dirs., 1974—; dir. Fidelity Union Bank N.A. Mem. Jockey Hollow Fish and Game Protective Assn., Chi Phi. Clubs: Somerset Hills Country (Bernardsville, N.J.); Bloomingrove Hunting and Fishing (Hawley, Pa.). Home: Beverly Dr Bernardsville NJ 07924

ABELES, JOSEPH CHARLES, business executive; b. N.Y.C., Jan. 6, 1915; s. Charles and Lucy (Koerner) A.; m. Sophia Weiner, Jan. 25, 1940; children: Lucille S., Nancy Jo (dec.), Barbara A. B.S., N.Y.U., 1935. Indsl. engr. Parker-Kalon, N.Y.C., 1935-36; chem. sales agt. Fasey & Bestoff, N.Y.C., 1936-53; v.p. sales, treas. Kawecki Chem. Co., N.Y.C., 1953-59, pres., 1958- 69; chmn. bd., chief exec. officer Kawecki Berylco Industries, Inc. (merger Kawecki Chem. Co. and The Beryllium Corp., 1968), N.Y.C., 1968-80, pres., 1977-80; vice chmn. Columbian Enterprises, Inc.; dir. Materials Research Corp., Orangeburg, N.Y., Electro-Metals Corp., Calif., Essex Chem. Corp., Clifton, N.J., Power Conversion, Inc., Elmwood Park, N.J., Consol. Beryllium Ltd., Milford-Haven, Wales. Mem. Am. Chem. Soc., Am. Soc. Metals, Engrs. Club, Chemists Club N.Y.C. Club: Elmwood Country (Westchester, N.Y.). Home: 1055 Bedford Rd Pleasantville NY 10570 Office: 100 Park Ave New York NY

ABELES, NORMAN, educator, psychologist; b. Vienna, Austria, Apr. 15, 1928; came to U.S., 1939, naturalized, 1944; s. Felix and Bertha (Gronich) A.; m. Jeanette Bueller, Apr. 14, 1957; children: Linda, Mark. B.A., NYU, 1949; M.A., U. Tex., 1952, Ph.D., 1958. Diplomate: Am. Bd. Profl. Psychology (Midwest regional bd. 1972-78, chmn. regional bd. 1975-77; nat. trustee 1975-77). Fellow in counseling U. Tex., Austin, 1956-57; instr. Mich. State U., East Lansing, 1957-59, asst. prof., 1959-64, asso. prof., 1964-67, prof. psychology, 1968—, dir. psychol. clinic, 1978—, co-dir. clin. tng., 1981—, asst. dir. counseling center, 1965-71; U.S. State Dept. ednl. exchange prof. U. Utrecht, Netherlands, 1969, vis. prof., 1975; cons. Peace Corps, 1965-69, Social Security/Disability Hearings, 1962—; mem. Mich. Commn. Cert. of Psychologists, 1962-77, chmn., 1966-68; mem. council Nat. Register Health Service Providers in Psychology, 1974—, vice chmn., 1975-80. Contbr. articles to profl. jours.; editor: Acad. Psychology Bull., 1978-82; cons. editor: Profl. Psychology: Research and Practice, 1979-81; editor, 1983—. Served with U.S. Army, 1954-56. Fulbright-Hays grantee, 1969. Fellow Am. Psychol. Assn. (council of reps. 1972-75, 77-79, policy and planning bd. 1975-79, chmn. 1976, rec. sec. 1980—); mem. Midwestern Psychol. Assn., Mich. Psychol. Assn. (legis. chmn. 1964-72, pres. 1971-72, Disting. Psychologist 1974), Sigma Xi. Home: 953 Rosewood St East Lansing MI 48823

ABELES, ROBERT HEINZ, biochemistry educator; b. Vienna, Austria, Jan. 14, 1926; came to U.S., 1939, naturalized, 1944; s. Ernest and Carolyn (Schwartz) A.; m. Barbara Anne Mincher, Sept. 20, 1948; children—Lisa Joy, Steven Leon. M.S., U. Chgo., 1950; Ph.D., U. Colo., 1955. Postdoctoral fellow Harvard, 1955-57; asst. prof. chemistry Ohio State U., 1957-60; asso. prof. biochemistry U. Mich., 1960-64; prof. biochemistry Brandeis U., Waltham, Mass., 1964—, chmn. dept. biochemistry, 1973—; Lectr. in field in, Am., Europe. Editorial bd.: Jour. Biol. Chemistry, 1968-72, Biochemistry, 1972—; Contbr. articles to profl. jours. Served with AUS, 1944-46. Mem. Am. Acad. Arts and Scis., Am. Chem. Soc., Am. Soc. Biol. Chemists, A.A.A.S., Nat. Acad. Sci. Research in mechanism of action of enzymes and co-enzymes, drug design. Named to Aron and Imre Tauber Chair of Biochemistry and Molecular Pharmacology, 1977. Home: 415 Ward St Newton Centre MA 02159 Office: Brandeis Univ Waltham MA 02154

ABELES, SIGMUND M., sculptor, printmaker; b. N.Y.C., Nov. 6, 1934; s. Samuel and Henrietta (Banner) A.; children: David Paul, Shoshanna Lynn, Maxwell Merck Abeles. Student, Pratt Inst., 1952-53, Art Students' League, summer 1954, Skowhegan Sch., (scholar), summers 1955-56, Bklyn. Mus. Sch., (Graphics scholar), 1956-57; A.B. in Art, U. S.C., 1955; M.F.A., Columbia U., 1957. Mem. faculty Swain Sch. Design, New Bedford, Mass., 1961-64; resident artist Wellesley (Mass.) Coll., 1964-69; asst. prof. art Boston U., 1969-70; prof. U. N.H., 1970—. Represented in permanent collections, including, Albert & Victoria Mus., London, Library of Congress, Washington, Mus. Modern Art, N.Y.C., Museo de Arte, Ponce, P.R., Phila. Mus. Art, Mus. Fine Art, Boston; vis. sculptor, Johnson Atelier, Tech. Inst. for Sculpture, 1977. Nat. Inst. Arts and Letters grantee, 1965; Nat. Council Arts and Humanities sabbatical grantee, 1966; Louis Comfort Tiffany Found. grantee, 1967; U. N.H. Grad. Sch. Sculpture grantee, 1973. Mem. Nat. Acad. Design (assoc., Leo Meisner prize 1983), Soc. Am. Graphic Artists. Office: Paul Creative Arts Center U NH Durham NH 03824 *I strive to observe life with a penetrating eye that I hope can go beyond surface reality to reveal psychological and visual truth, even magic.*

ABELL, DAVID ROBERT, lawyer; b. Raleigh, N.C., Nov. 24, 1934; s. De Witt Sterling and Edna Renilda (Doughty) A.; m. Elizabeth Ayres Phelps, Aug. 31, 1957; children: David Charles, Elizabeth Ann, Kimberly Sterling, Hilary Ayres, Glenn Bryan. B.A., Denison U., 1956; J.D. (Internat. fellow), Columbia U., 1963. Bar: Pa. 1963, Ill. 1973. Pvt. practice, Winnetka, Ill., 1974—; assoc. Ballard, Spahr, Andrews & Ingersoll, Phila., 1963-69; sec., counsel Hurst Performance, Inc., Warminster, Pa., 1969-70; sec., gen. counsel STP Corp., Des Plaines, Ill., 1970-72; v.p., sec., treas. Microcor, Inc., Winnetka, 1973-74. Author: Residential Real Estate Paralegal System, 1977,83. Bd. dirs. N. Shore Sr. Center, 1979—; trustee Chgo. chpt. Nat. Multiple Sclerosis Soc., 1979—. Served as aviator USMCR, 1956-60. Mem. ABA, Pa. Bar Assn., Ill. Bar Assn. (chmn. sect. mgmt. and econs. of practice law 1979-80), Chgo. Bar Assn., Omicron Delta Kappa. Episcopalian. Club: Winnetka Rotary (pres. 1977-78). Home: 466 Poplar St Winnetka IL 60093 Office: 799 Elm St Winnetka IL 60093

ABELL, MILLICENT DEMMIN, university library administration; b. Wichita, Kans., Feb. 15, 1934; d. Frederic Albert and Euphemia Millicent (Brown) Demmin; m. Julian Leo Abell, June 16, 1962; 1 son, Frederic Julian. B.A. in Psychology, Colo. Coll., 1956; M.A. in Personnel, Columbia U., 1958; M.L.S., SUNY, Albany, 1965; M.A. in Polit. Sci, U. Colo., 1969. Reference librarian U.S. Mil. Acad., West Point, N.Y., 1964-65, Penrose Public Library, Colorado Springs, Colo., 1966-68; asst. librarian Bus. Adminstrn. Library, U. Wash., Seattle, 1969-71, asst. dir. libraries, 1971-73; asso. dir. univ. libraries SUNY, Buffalo, 1973-76; univ. librarian U. Calif., San Diego, 1977—; bd. dirs. Center for Research Libraries, 1979—, vice-chair, 1983–84. Mem. editorial bd.: Jour. Acad. Librarianship, 1974-76; asso. editor: Library Research, 1978-82; contbr. articles to profl. jours. Mem. Assn. Coll. and Research Libraries (dir. 1976-78, 79—, pres. 1980-81), Assn. Research Libraries (dir. 1979—, pres. 1981-82), ALA (council 1983—). Office: Central Univ Library U Calif La Jolla CA 92093 *

ABELL, MURRAY RICHARDSON, pathologist; b. Aylmer, Ont., Can., Oct. 14, 1920; came to U.S., 1952, naturalized, 1958; s. Murray Clement and Alta May (Richardson) A.; m. Ruth Barbara Summers, May 1, 1944; children—David William, Catherine Mary, Michael James, Grant Gustan. M.D., U. Western Ont., 1944, Ph.D., 1951. Diplomate: Am. Bd. Pathology (trustee 1969—). Intern St. Michael's Hosp., Toronto, Ont., 1944-45; resident in medicine Westminster Hosp., London, Ont., 1946-47; fellow, sr. instr. depts. pathology and clin. pathology U. Western Ont., London, 1947-52; instr. pathology U. Mich., Ann Arbor, 1952-53, asst. prof., 1953-56, asso. prof., 1956-59, prof., 1959—. Served with M.C. Royal Can. Army, 1943-46. Mem. Internat. Acad. Pathology, Coll. Am. Pathologists, Am. Soc. Clin. Pathologists, Am. Assn. Pathologists, Arthur Purdy Stout Soc., AMA, Gynecologic Oncologists. Home: 3601 Hudson Ln Tampa FL 33618 Office: Am Bd Pathology 112 Lincoln Center 5401 W Kennedy Blvd Tampa FL 33623

ABELL, PAUL IRVING, educator; b. Pelham, Mass., July 24, 1923; s. Max F. and Virginia (Bennett) A.; m. Phyllis Killam, July 1, 1950 (div.); 1 dau., Susan E.; m. Frances Martindale, Aug. 30, 1980. B.S., U. N.H., 1948; Ph.D., U. Wis., 1951. Instr. U. R.I., Kingston, 1951-64, prof. chemistry, 1964—; Fulbright lectr., Egypt, 1965-66. Served with AUS, 1943-46. Recipient Petroleum Research Fund Internat. Research grants U. Wales, 1961-62, U. Bristol, 1969-70. Mem. Am. Chem. Soc., Chem. Soc. London, Geochem. Soc., Explorers Club, Sigma Xi, Phi Kappa Phi. Mem. research expdns. in paleontology of Omo River and Lake Rudolf regions of E. Africa sponsored by Nat. Geog. Soc., 1966. Home: Wolf Rock Rd Kingston RI 02881 Office: Dept Chemistry U RI Kingston RI 02881

ABELL, RICHARD BENDER, lawyer; b. Phila., Dec. 2, 1943; s. Ernest George and Charlotte Amelia (Bender) A.; m. Lucia del Carmen Lombana-Cadavid, Dec. 2, 1968; children: David, Christian, Rachel. B.A. in Internat. Affairs, George Washington U., 1966, J.D., 1974. Bar: Pa. 1974. Vol. Peace Corps, Columbia, 1967-69; assoc. Reilly & Fogwell, West Chester, Pa., 1974-80; asst. dist. atty., Chester Coutny, Pa., 1974-79; staff mem. U.S. Senator Richard Schweiker, Washington, 1979-80; dir. Office of Program Devel. Peace Corp., Washington, 1981-83; dep. asst. atty. gen. U.S. Dept. Justice, Washington, 1983—; mem. adj. faculty Del. Law Sch., Wilmington, 1975-77, West Chester State U., 1976. Chmn. Young Republicans of Pa., Harrisburg, 1976-78, Young Rep. Nat. Fedn., Washington, 1979-81; mem. exec. com. Rep. Nat. Com., Washington, 1979-81; nat. bd. dirs. Young Ams. for Freedom, Sterling, Va., 1979-83. Served with U.S. Army, 1969-71. Decorated Purple Heart; recipient Order of Scarlet award George Washington U., 1966. Mem. Chester County Bar Assn., Pa. Bar Assn. Episcopalian. Home: 8209 Chancery Ct Alexandria VA 22308 Office: Dept Justice Office of Justice Assistance Research and Statistics 633 Indiana Ave NW Washington DC 20531

ABELL, THOMAS HENRY, lawyer; b. Wharton, Tex., May 7, 1909; s. Thomas James and Lyda (Horton) A.; m. Frances Norris Wright, June 24, 1934; children—Madeleine (Mrs. Robert C. Wither), Alex G., Tom J. Student, Tex. A. and M. Coll., 1926-27; LL.B., Tex. U., 1933. Bar: Tex. bar 1933, U.S. Supreme Ct 1937. Practice in, Wharton, 1933—; county atty. Wharton County, 1937-40, county judge, 1943-46; Dir. Houston Lighting & Power Co.; Bd. dirs. Tex. Mid-Coastal Water Devel. Assn., Palacois, 1961-79. Trustee Wharton Sch. Dist., 1949-58, Runnells Fund, Bay City, Tex.; bd. dirs. Gulf Coast Med. Found., Wharton; pres. bd. trustees Wharton County Mus. Assn. Mem. Am. Simmental Assn. (trustee), Sigma Nu. Episcopalian. Home: 314 North Resident St Wharton TX 77488 Office: Box 746 Wharton TX 77488

ABELOFF, ABRAM JOSEPH, surgeon; b. N.Y.C., Mar. 19, 1900; s. Samuel and Rebecca Esther (Rogow) A.; m. Gertrude Theresa Kopsch, May 15, 1953; 1 son, Tobias Samuel. A.B., Columbia, 1922, M.D., 1926. Diplomate: Am. Bd. Surgery. Sub-surg. intern Presbyn. Hosp., N.Y.C., 1926-27; surg. intern Lenox Hill Hosp., 1927-29; research asst. Inst. Pathology U. Freiburg, Germany, 1929; surg. service Frankfurt U., Germany, U. Vienna, Austria, 1930; adj. surgeon Beth Israel Hosp., 1930-37; asso. surgeon Neurol. Hosp., N.Y.C., 1930-33; asst. adj. surgeon Lenox Hill Hosp., 1930-36, attending surgeon clinic, 1930-36, chief surgeon, 1936-42, adj. attending, 1936-46, asso. surgeon, 1946-54, attending surgeon, 1954-65, cons. surgeon, 1965—, charge service, 1971; surgeon Lexington Sch. for Deaf, 1947-68; asso. clin. prof. surgery N.Y. U., 1947—. Mem. exec. com., emeritus chmn. med. adv. bd. Am. Jewish Joint Distbn. Com.; adv. bd. Paul Baerwald Sch. Social Work, Paris.; Past pres., now treas., trustee Physicians Home; bd. visitors Watson Library Met. Mus. Art; trustee Columbia U., 1959-65. Served to col. M.C. AUS, 1942-46; hosp. comdr. 256th Sta. Hosp., 19th Field Hosp., 21st Sta. Hosp., 113th Gen. Hosp., Lawson Gen. Hosp.; surg. cons. Persian Gulf Command. Decorated Legion of Merit; Distinctive Service Cross of State of N.Y.; recipient Distinguished Service medal Columbia U. Alumni Fedn., 1963; Distinctive Achievement award Stuyvesant High Sch., 1965; Alumni Silver medal Coll. Phys. & Surg., 1969; Meritorious Service Unit citation Lawson Gen. Hosp. Fellow A.C.S., Brazilian Coll. Surgeons; mem. N.Y. Acad. Medicine, N.Y. Surg. Soc. (past council mem.), AMA, N.Y. State and County med. socs., Assn. Alumni Coll. Phys. and Surg. Columbia U. (pres. 1956-57), N.Y. Hist. Soc. (life). Club: Grolier (N.Y.C.). Home: 150 E 77th St New York NY 10021 Office: 130 E 77th St New York NY 10021

ABELSON, ALAN, editor, columnist; b. N.Y.C., Oct. 12, 1925; s. Harry Carl and Vivian (Finkelstein) A.; m. Virginia Eloise Peterson, Sept. 1, 1951; children—Justin Adams, Reed Vivian. B.S. in Chemistry and English, Coll. City N.Y., 1946; M.A. in Creative Writing, U. Iowa, 1947. Reporter N.Y. Jour. Am., N.Y.C., 1949-56, stock market columnist, 1952-56; with Barron's Mag., N.Y.C., 1956—, mng. editor, 1965-81, editor, 1981—; columnist Up & Down Wall St., 1966—. Office: 22 Cortlandt St New York NY 10007 *

ABELSON, HAROLD HERBERT, educator; b. N.Y.C., Sept. 25, 1904; s. Max and Jennie (Bernstein) A.; m. Lucie Bernard, Aug. 24, 1926; children: Jane Frances, Robert Bernard. Student, Townsend Harris Hall, 1917-20; B.E., CCNY, 1924; A.M., Columbia U., 1925, Ph.D., 1927. Registered psychologist, N.Y. State. Tutor dept. edn. CCNY, 1924-28, instr., 1928-35, asst. prof., 1935-42, asso. prof., 1942-48, prof., 1948-66, dean Sch. Edn., 1952-66, acting dean tchr. edn., 1966-67, prof. div. tchr. edn., 1967-74, prof., dean emeritus, 1974—; dir. ednl. clinic CCNY, 1941-52; sr. research asso. Human Interaction Research Inst., Los Angeles, 1974—; prof. U. Colo., summer 1938, Cornell U., summer 1949-50, Hunter Coll., summer 1952-58; vis. lectr. New Sch. Social Research, 1948-60, Lehman Coll., 1967-74; expert cons. adj. gen. office War Dept., summer 1944; pres. Interstate Tchr. Edn. Conf., 1962; chmn. adv. bd. Emeritus Coll., Santa Monica Coll., 1974-76, instr., 1977—. Author: Art of Educational Research; co-author: Putting Knowledge to Use; contbr.: articles to profl. jours. Recipient Townsend Harris medal City Coll. Alumni Assn., 1962. Fellow Am. Psychol. Assn., AAAS; mem. Am. Edn. Research Assn., Eastern, Western, N.Y. State psychol. assns., City Coll., Columbia Grad. alumni assns., Phi Beta Kappa, Kappa Delta Pi. Home: 914 Lincoln Blvd Santa Monica CA 90403

ABELSON, JOHN NORMAN, biology educator; b. Grand Coulee Dam, Wash., Oct. 19, 1938. B.S., Wash. State U., 1960; Ph.D., Johns Hopkins U., 1965; postgrad., Lb. Molecular Biology, Cambridge, Eng., 1965-68. Asst. prof. dept. chemistry U. Calif.-San Diego, 1968-73, assoc. prof., 1973-77, prof., 1977-82; prof. biology Calif. Inst. Tech., Pasadena, 1982—; founding bd. dirs. Agouron Inst. (La Jolla), Calif., 1979—. Exec. editor: Analytical Biochemistry, 1980—; mem. editorial bd.: Jour. Biol. Chemistry, 1981—; mem. editorial com., Ann. Rev. Inc., 1982—; contbr. numerous articles to profl. jours. Mem. Am. Soc. Biol. Chemists, Am. Chem. Soc., Am. Soc. Microbiology. Home: 805 S Madison Ave Pasadena CA 91106 Office: Calif Inst Tech Pasadena CA 91125

ABELSON, PHILIP HAUGE, physical chemist, institution executive; b. Tacoma, Apr. 27, 1913; s. Ole Andrew and Ellen (Hauge) A.; m. Neva Martin, Dec. 30, 1936; 1 dau., Ellen Hauge (Mrs. John C. Cherniavsky). B.S., Wash. State Coll., 1933; M.S., 1935; Ph.D., U. Calif., 1939; D.Sc., Yale, 1964, So. Meth. U., 1969, Tufts U., 1976, Duke U., 1981, U. Pitts., 1982; D.H.L., U. Puget Sound, 1968. Asst. physicist Carnegie Instn. of Washington, 1939-41; assoc. physicist Naval Research Lab., Washington, D.C., 1941-42, physicist, 1942-44, sr. physicist, 1944-45, prin. physicist, 1945; civilian in charge Naval Research Lab. br. Navy Yard, Phila., 1944-45; chmn. biophysics sect. dept. terrestrial magnetism Carnegie Instn., 1946-53; dir. Geophysics Lab., 1953-71, pres. of instn., 1971-78, trustee, 1978—; Chmn. com. on radiation cataracts NRC, 1949-57, sub-com. on shock, 1950-53, mem. plowshare adv. com., 1959-63; gen. adv. com. AEC, 1960-63; mem. biophysics and biophys. chemistry study sect. Nat. Inst. Arthritis and Metabolic Diseases, NIH, 1956-59, mem. phys. biology tng. grants com., 1958-60, bd. sci. counselors, 1960-63; cons. NASA, 1960-63; mem. Nat. Acad. Scis., 1959—, mem. council, 1977—, Inst. Medicine, 1973—. Author: Energy for Tomorrow, 1975; Mem. adv. bd.: Jour. Nat. Cancer Inst, 1947-52; editor: Researches in Geochemistry, 1959, Vol. 2, 1967, Energy: Use, Conservation and Supply, 1974, Food: Politics, Economics, Nutrition, and Research, 1975, Materials: Renewable and Nonrenewable, 1976, Electronics: The Continuing Revolution, 1977; co-editor: Jour. Geophys. Research, 1959-65; editor: Science, 1962—; Contbr. articles to sci. jours. Recipient Disting. Civilian Service medal, 1945, ann. award phys. sci. Washington Acad. Sci., 1950, Distinguished Alumnus award Wash. State U., 1962; Hillebrand award Chem. Soc. Washington, 1962; Modern Medicine award, 1967; Mellon award Carnegie-Mellon U., 1970; Joseph Priestley award Dickinson Coll., 1973; Sci. Achievement award A.M.A., 1974; Hon. Scroll award D.C. Inst. Chemists, 1976; Kalinga prize UNESCO, 1972. Fellow Am. Phys. Soc., Geol. Soc. Am., Mineral. Soc. Am., Geol. Soc. Washington, Am. Acad. Arts and Scis.; mem. Am. Nuclear Soc., Seismol. Soc. Am., Internat. Union Geol. Scis. (pres. 1972-76), Brit. Biochem. Soc., Brit. Mineral. Soc., Am. Chem. Soc., Am. Philos. Soc., Soc. Am. Bacteriologists, Am. Geophys. Union (pres. 1972-74), Am. Assn. Petroleum Geologists, Geochemical Soc., Washington Acad. Scis., Biophysical Soc., Philos. Soc. Washington, Phi Beta Kappa (senator-at-large 1972—), Sigma Xi. Club: Cosmos (pres. 1972). Home: 4244 50th St NW Washington DC 20016 Office: 1515 Massachusetts Ave NW Washington DC 20005

ABELSON, RAZIEL ALTER, educator; b. N.Y.C., June 24, 1921; s. Alter and Anna (Schwartz) A.; m. Ulrike Koenigsfeld, Aug. 24, 1947 (div.); 1 son, Gabriel; m. Marie-Louise Friquegnon, 1973; 1 dau., Maris. Student, Bklyn. Coll., 1938-40; M.A., U. Chgo., 1950; Ph.D., N.Y.U., 1957. Instr. philosophy Hunter Coll., N.Y.C., 1950-52; prof. philosophy N.Y.U., 1953—; vis. prof. Columbia U., 1962, U. Hawaii, 1965, SUNY at Buffalo, 1967, U. Calif. at San Diego, 1970; vis. scholar Inst. Advanced Studies Behavioral Scis., Stanford, 1965. Author: Ethics and Metaethics, 1963, Ethics for Modern Life, 1975, Persons, 1977, The Philosophical Imagination, 1977; contbr. articles to profl. jours. Served with U.S. Maritime Service, 1941-46. Am. Council Learned Socs. research grantee, 1968. Mem. Am. Assn. U. Profs., Am. Philos. Assn. Home: 110 Bleecker St New York NY 10012 *Principles: Don't be afraid to be wrong; respect other persons.*

ABELSON, ROBERT PAUL, educator; b. N.Y.C., Sept. 12, 1928; s. Miles Arthur and Margaret (Coble) A.; m. Willa Dinwoodie, June 11, 1955; children—John, William. B.S., Mass. Inst. Tech., 1948, M.S., 1950; Ph.D., Princeton, 1953. Psychometric fellow Princeton, 1950-52; mem. faculty Yale U., 1952—, prof., 1963—, now Eugene Higgins prof. psychology; dir. Simulmatics Corp., 1961-67. Co-author: Candidates, Issues and Strategies, 1965, Theories of Cognitive Consistency, 1968, Scripts, Plans, Goals and Understanding, 1977. Fellow Center Advanced Study Behavioral Scis., 1957-58, 65-66. Fellow Am. Psychol. Assn., Am. Statis. Assn., Am. Acad. Arts and Scis. Home: 827 Whitney Ave New Haven CT 06511

ABELT, RALPH WILLIAM, banker; b. Elmhurst, Ill., Feb. 16, 1929; s. P. Alfred and Clara S. (Springhorn) A.; m. Patricia Mitchell, Feb. 2, 1952; children: Susan E., Christopher M., Leslie A. B.S., U. Colo., 1952; M.B.A., Ind. U., 1953. Acct. Marion Hutchinson, C.P.A., Denver, 1952; v.p. comml. banking Continental Ill., Chgo., 1953-77; pres., chief exec. officer, dir. Bank One of Northeastern Ohio, NA, Painesville, 1977-83; chmn., chief exec. officer Bank One Cleve., NA, 1983—. Past pres., mem. exec. bd. Northeast Ohio council Boy Scouts Am., Painesville, 1981; bd. dirs. United Way of Lake County, Inc., Painesville, 1981; chmn. Lake County, U.S. Savs. Bond Div., 1982—, Lakeland Community Coll. Found., Mentor, Ohio, 1981; trustee Holden Arboretum, Kirtland, Ohio, 1982, Episcopal Diocese of Ohio. Served with USMC, 1946-48. Mem. Robert Morris Assoc., Am. Bankers Assn., Ohio Bankers Assn. Clubs: Firestone Country, Cleve.

Treasurers, Kirtland (Ohio) Country, Madison (Ohio) Country. Home: 321 Barrington Ridge Painesville OH 44077 Office: Bank One Cleve 30 South Park Pl Painesville OH 44077

ABELY, JOSEPH FRANCIS, JR., manufacturing company executive; b. Boston, Jan. 22, 1929; s. Joseph Francis and Nora G. (Coffey) A.; m. Brenda Conlon, Aug. 24, 1957; children: James Christopher, Karen Marie. B.S., Boston Coll., 1950; M.B.A., Harvard U., 1952, J.D., 1956. Bar: Mass. bar 1956. With W.R. Grace & Co., 1956-63; gen. mgr. Cryovac Equipment div., 1962-63; with Gen. Foods Corp., 1963-77, exec. v.p., 1972-74, dir., 1973-77, vice chmn., 1974-77; exec. v.p. R.J. Reynolds Industries, Winston-Salem, N.C., 1977-79, vice chmn. bd., dir., chmn. fin. com., 1979—; dir. Stauffer Chem. Co., NCNB Corp., Burlington Industries, Inc., Richardson-Vicks, Inc. Bd. govs. Nat. ARC; trustee Boston Coll., Southeastern Center for Contemporary Art. Served with USAF, 1952-53. Mem. Council Fin. Execs. (past chmn.), Internat. Econ. Policy Assn., Council Fgn. Relations. Home: 2866 Merry Acres Ln Winston-Salem NC 27106 Office: World Hdqrs Bldg Winston-Salem NC 27102

ABERASTAIN, JOSE MANUEL, ballet master; b. San Luis, Argentina, May 14, 1938; came to U.S., 1970; s. Ladislao and Margarita Maria (Quiroga) A. Student, U. Buenos Aires, Teatro Colon. Mem. faculty Washington Sch. Ballet, 1970-72, Pa. Ballet Sch., 1972-74, Va. Intermont Coll., 1974-76; asst. prof. ballet Dallas Ballet Acad., So. Methodist U., 1981—; guest tchr., master classes U.S. and abroad; choreographer, 1971. Dancer, Teatro Colon ballet co., 1959-62, Nat. Ballet Cuba, 1962-64, Classical Ballet Mex., 1964-66, Chilean Nat. Ballet, 1966-68, Stuttgart (W. Ger.) Ballet, 1968-70; ballet master, Ohio Ballet, 1976-81; prin. works include Divergence, performed by Washington Ballet and, Bristol Concert Ballet, Children's Games, Bristol Concert Ballet. Office: Dance Div So Methodist U Dallas TX 75275 *Teaching is an act of love, that requires knowledge, generosity and total committment.*

ABERCROMBIE, JOHN BUFORD, lawyer; b. Houston, Oct. 26, 1926; s. Bolling Anderson and Maude (Gilchreas) A.; m. Virginia Townsend, Apr. 1, 1950; children: John B., Virginia Lee, Gilchreas. B.S. in M.E., Rice U., 1948; LL.B., U. Tex.-Austin, 1951. Bar: Tex. 1980, U.S. Dist. Ct. (so. dist.) Tex. 1951, U.S. Dist. Ct. (ea. dist.) Tex. 1976, U.S. Dist. Ct. (we. dist.) Tex. 1976, U.S. Ct. Appeals (5th and 11th cirs.) 1981, U.S. Supreme Ct. 1973. Jr. engr. Cameron Iron Works, Houston, 1947-48; assoc. Baker & Botts, Houston, 1948-63, ptnr., 1963—. Served to lt. (j.g.) USN, 1944-46. Mem. ABA, Tex. Bar Assn., Houston Bar Assn. Republican. Episcopalian. Club: Houston Country. Office: Baker & Botts 3000 One Shell Plaza Houston TX 77002

ABERCROMBIE, LEE ROY, JR., financial executive; b. San Francisco, Aug. 26, 1929; s. Lee R. and Cora May (Maaske) A.; m. Mary Katherine Kinney, Aug. 22, 1980; 1 son, John David. B.A., Stanford U., 1950, M.B.A., 1952. Asst. controller, asst. treas. FMC Corp., 1955-73; v.p. fin., treas. Morrison Knudsen Co. Inc., Boise, Idaho, 1973—; dir. First Idaho Corp. Chmn. finance com., bd. dirs. Blue Cross Idaho; bd. dirs., past pres. Boise Family YMCA; vice chmn. State of Idaho Endowment Funds Investment Bd.; bd. dirs., past treas. ARC, bd. dirs., treas. Regional Blood Center; bd. dirs. Ada County United Way; trustee, chmn. fin. com. Coll. of Idaho; mem. adv. council Boise State U. Sch. Bus. Served as supply officer USNR, 1952-55. Mem. Fin. Execs. Inst., Nat. Assn. Accts., Stanford U. Bus. Sch. Alumni Assn., So. Idaho Sailing Assn., Boise C. of C. (dir.), Phi Beta Kappa. Republican. Office: PO Box 7808 Boise ID 83729

ABERLE, DAVID FRIEND, anthropologist, educator; b. St. Paul, Nov. 23, 1918; s. David Winfield and Lisette (Friend) A.; m. Eleanor Kathleen Gough, Sept. 5, 1955; 1, son. A.B. summa cum laude, Harvard U., 1940; Ph.D. in Anthropology, Columbia U., 1950; postgrad., U. N.Mex., summers 1938-40, No. Ariz. U., summers 1971, 73, Harvard U., 1946-47. Instr. dept. social relations Harvard U., Cambridge, Mass., 1947-50, research assoc. Sch. Pub. Health, 1948-50; vis. assoc. prof. Page Sch., Johns Hopkins U., Balt., 1950-52; assoc. prof., then prof. dept. sociology and dept. anthropology U. Mich., Ann Arbor, 1952-60; fellow Ctr. Advanced Study in Behavioral Scis., Stanford, Calif., 1955-56; Simon vis. prof. and hon. research assoc. dept. social anthropology Manchester U., Eng., 1960-61; prof., chmn. dept. anthropology Brandeis U., Waltham, Mass., 1961-63; prof. dept. anthropology U. Oreg., Eugene, 1963-67; prof. dept. anthropology and sociology U. B.C., Vancouver, Can., 1967-84, prof. emeritus, 1984—; cons. Inst. Devel. Anthropology, Inc., Binghamton, N.Y., 1978-79; cons. to attys. Navajo Tribe, 1976-77. Author: The Peyote Religion Among the Navaho, 1966, (with Isidore Dyen) Lexical Reconstruction, the Case of the Proto-Athapaskan Kinship System, 1974; contbr. articles on social anthropology and Navaho Indians to scholarly jour.; rev. editor: Am. Anthropologist, 1952-55. Served with U.S. Army, 1942-46. Recipient Social Sci. Research Council Demobilization award, 1946; Harvard U. Nat. scholar; NIMH grantee; USPHS grantee; Wenner-Gren Found. grantee, 1954-63; NSF grantee, 1965-72; Can. Council grantee, 1969-77; Social Scis. and Humanities Research Council Can., 1978-80, 84-86. Fellow Am. Anthrop. Assn.; mem. Royal Anthrop. Inst. Great Britain and Ireland, Am. Sociol. Assn., Soc. Applied Anthropology, Am. Ethnol. Assn., Can. Ethnol. Assn., Can. Sociology and Anthropology Assn. Jewish. Am. family, kinship relations in Mongols of Manchuria, Navajo Indians and research religion and econ. devel. of various pre-indslcultures. Home: 4518 Marine Dr West Vancouver BC Canada V7W 2N9 Office: Univ BC Anthropology Dept 6303 NW Marine Dr Vancouver BC Canada V6T 2B2

ABERNATHY, FREDERICK H., mechanical engineering educator; b. Denver, June 30, 1930; s. Henry James and Irene Sarah (Lehman) A.; m. AnnaMaria Herbert, June 18, 1961; children: Sarah, Marian, Pauline. B.S. in Mech. Engring., Newark Coll. Engring., 1951; postgrad., Oak Ridge Sch. Reactor Tech., 1952; S.M., Harvard U., 1954, Ph.D., 1959. Gordon McKay prof. mech. engring. Harvard U., Cambridge, Mass., 1963-72, 74—; dir. engring. div. NSF, Washington, 1972-73, dir. energy-realted research, 1973-74. Fellow Am. Acad. Arts and Scis.; mem. ASME, Am. Soc. Engring. Edn., Am. Phys. Soc. Home: 45 Islington Rd Auburndale MA 02166 Office: Harvard Univ Pierce Hall 40 Oxford St Cambridge MA 02138

ABERNATHY, JACK HARVEY, retired petroleum company executive; b. Shawnee, Okla., June 10, 1911; s. George Carl and Carrie (Howell) A.; m. Mary Ann Staig, June 13, 1932 (div. dec); children: Jack Harvey, Carrilee Abernathy Bell; m. Virginia Watson, Dec. 21, 1974. B.S. in Petroleum Engring, U. Okla., 1933. Petroleum engr. Sinclair Oil & Gas Co., 1933-34; chief engr., gen. prodn. supt. Sunray DX OIL Co., Tulsa, Okla., 1935-45; pres. Seneca Oil Co., Oklahoma City, 1959-65, Post Oak Oil Co., 1966-72; chmn. exec. com., dir. Entex, Inc., Houston, 1972—; pres., chmn. dir. Big Chief Drilling Co., Oklahoma City, 1946-82; dir. Entex Petroleum, Inc., Houston, Entex Coal Co., Hinderliter Industries; dir., mem. exec. com. Liberty Nat. Bank & Trust Co., Oklahoma City, 1967—; adv. dir., mem. exec. com. Southwestern Bank & Trust Co., Oklahoma City, 1964—; mem., past chmn. Nat. Petroleum Council, 1957-83. Contbr. numerous tech. articles to profl. jours. Bd. dirs. Oklahoma City Zool. Soc.; trustee U. Okla. Found., Oklahoma City Community Found. Recipient numerous awards.; elected to Okla. State Hall of Fame, 1971. Mem. Mid-Continent Oil and Gas Assn. (dir.), Am. Petroleum Inst. (dir., exec. com. 1964-83), Oklahoma City C. of C. (dir.), All-Am. Wildcatters, Nat. Soc. Profl. Engrs., Soc. Petroleum Engrs., Sigma Tau, Tau Beta Pi, Pi Epsilon Tau, Beta Gamma Sigma. Presbyterian. Clubs: Men's Dinner, Petroleum (Oklahoma City); Ramada (Houston); Oklahoma City Golf and Country; Avandaro Golf (Valle de Bravo, Mexico). Home: 2303 NW Grand Blvd Oklahoma City OK 73113 Office: 601 NE 63d St PO Box 14837 Oklahoma City OK 73113

ABERNATHY, JAMES LOGAN, broadcasting executive; b. Kansas City, Mo., Jan. 23, 1941; s. James Logan and Caryl (Nicolson) A.; m. Kevin Kearns McLean, Sept. 12, 1981; 1 dau., Nell Logan. Ed., Hackley Sch., 1959, Brown U. Dir. corp. info., asso. dir. investor relations CBS, N.Y.C., 1967-72; v.p. investor relations Warner Communications, Inc., N.Y.C., 1972-74, ABC, Inc., 1974-77, v.p. corp. relations, 1977-79, v.p. corp. affairs, 1979—. Served with USMCR, 1959-65. Mem. Investor Relations Assn. (pres., exec. com.), Nat. Investor Relations Inst. Clubs: Knickerbocker, Doubles, Rockaway Hunting. Home: 40 Central Park S New York NY 10019 Office: ABC 1330 Ave of Americas New York NY 10019

ABERNATHY, JOHN DANIEL, III, accounting firm executive; b. Miami, Fla., May 2, 1937; s. John D. and Elsie (Sander) A.; m. Alice J. Paul, Oct. 29, 1976. B.B.A., Emory U., 1959. C.P.A., Ga. Audit staff to mgr. Arthur Anderson & Co., Atlanta, 1959-71; audit ptnr. to ptnr. in charge Seidman & Seidman, Hight Point, N.C., 1971-73, dir. acctg. and auditing, High Point, Atlanta, 1973-75, ptnr. in charge, N.Y.C., 1975-82; asst. to mng. ptnr. Seidman & Sidman, High Point, N.Y.C., 1979-83; mng. ptnr. Seidman & Seidman, High Point, 1983—. Recipient Outstanding Profl. Achievement award Am. Jewish Congress (accts., bankers, factors div.), 1981. Mem. Am. Inst. C.P.A.s (council 1983), Nat. Assn. Accts., N.Y. State Soc. C.P.A.s (bd. dirs. 1982, exec. com. 1983), Beta Alpha Psi. Republican. Baptist. Office: Seidman & Seidman 15 Columbus Circle New York NY 10023

ABERNATHY, JOSEPH DUNCAN, data processing executive; b. Charlotte, N.C., May 25, 1944; s. Joel Leander and Carma Blaine (Arrowood) A.; m. Phyllis Kay Weaver, Sept. 29, 1979; children by previous marriage: Jimmy, Sharon, Dean. Assoc. in Communications, Devry Tech. Inst., 1963; B.S., U. N.C.-Charlotte, 1970. Broadcast engr. Jefferson-Pilot Broadcasting Co., Charlotte, 1970-73; mgr. data processing Jeffesn Data Power Co., Charlotte, 1973—; pres. Freedom Automotive, Inc., Charlotte, 1979—; tchr. Central Piedmont Community Coll., Charlotte, 1973-74, Belmont Abbey Coll., N.C., 1977-78. Recipient Sigma Chi award, 1970. Mem. Carolina Honeywell User's Group, IBM Gen. Systems Users Group, Data Processing Mgmt. Assn. (pres. Charlotte chpt.). Home: 5601 Sardis Rd Charlotte NC 28211 Office: 501 Archdale Dr Charlotte NC 28210

ABERNATHY, K. BROOKS, manufacturing company executive; b. Missoula, Mont., Aug. 30, 1918; s. Austin Irwin and Evelyn (Thompson) A.; m. Susan Koskinen, Mar. 7, 1942; children: Lynn Abernathy Stokoe, Gail Abernathy Dickrell, Kenneth Brooks. B.A., Northwestern U., 1941; postgrad., Harvard Bus. Sch., 1967. With Gen. Electric Co., 1941-62; treas. Brunswick Corp., Skokie, Ill., 1962-69, v.p., 1969-72, pres., chief operating officer, 1972-83, chmn., 1976-83, chief exec. officer, 1976-82, pres. internat. div., 1968-69, pres. Kiekhaefer Mercury div., 1969-72, now dir.; dir. Am. Nat. Bank, Heller Internat., NICOR, Inc., Stone Container Corp. Office: Brunswick Corp One Brunswick Plaza Skokie IL 60077

ABERNATHY, MABRA GLENN, political science educator; b. Birmingham, Ala., Nov. 25, 1921; s. James Robert and Lynia Esther (Vines) A.; m. Nancy Katherine Perry, Sept. 6, 1949; children: M. Glenn, T. Duncan, Richard C. B.S., Birmingham-So. Coll., 1942; M.A., U. Ala., 1947; Ph.D., U. Wis., 1953. Asst. city mgr. Mountain Brook, Ala., 1947-48; instr. polit. sci. U. Ala., 1948-49; mem. faculty dept. polit. sci. U. S.C., Columbia, 1951—, Olin D. Johnston prof. polit. sci., 1977—; vis. asst. prof. U. Wis., 1959-60; vis. prof. U. Southampton (Eng.), 1982. Author The Right of Assembly and Association, 1961, 2d edit., 1981, Civil Liberties Under the Constitution, 3d edit, 1977. Served with USAF, 1942-46. Mem. So. Polit. Sci. Assn., Am. Polit. Sci. Assn. Methodist. Club: Kosmos (Columbia). Home: 41 Dinwood Circle Columbia SC 29204 Office: Dept Govt and Internat Studies U SC Columbia SC 29208

ABERNATHY, RALPH DAVID, clergyman; b. Linden, Ala., Mar. 11, 1926; s. W.L. and Louivery (Bell) A.; m. Juanita Odessa Jones, Aug. 31, 1952; children: Juandalynn Ralpheda, Donzaleigh Avis, Ralph David III, Kwame Luthuli. B.S., Ala. State Coll., 1950; M.A. in Sociology, Atlanta U., 1951; LL.D., Allen U., S.C., 1960, Southampton Coll., L.I. U., 1969, Ala. State U., Montgomery, 1974; D.D. (hon.), Morehouse Coll., 1971, Kalamazoo Coll., 1978. Personnel counselor, instr. social sci. Ala. State Coll., 1951; ordained to ministry Bapt. Ch., 1948; pastor First Bapt. Ch., Montgomery, Ala., 1951-61, West Hunter St. Bapt. Ch., Atlanta, 1961—. Organizer Montgomery Improvement Assn., 1955; initiator bus. boycott, Montgomery, 1955, an organizer, 1957; since financial sec.-treas. So. Christian Leadership Conf., v.p at large, then pres., 1968-77; leader Poor People's Campaign, Resurrection City, Washington, 1968; chmn. Commn. on Racism and Apartheid; addressed UN, 1971; Mem. Atlanta Ministers Union; organizer, chmn. Operation Breadbasket, Atlanta; mem. adv. com. Congress Racial Equality; participant World Peace Council Presdl. Com. Meeting, Santiago, Chile, 1972; Active local ARC, Am. Cancer Soc., YMCA. Recipient Peace medal German Democratic Republic, 1971. Mem. NAACP, Kappa Alpha Psi, Phi Delta Kappa. Club: Mason (32 deg.). Home and ch. dynamited, 1957. Office: 1040 Gordon St SW Atlanta GA 30310 *

ABERNATHY, ROBERT SHIELDS, med. educator; b. Gastonia, N.C., Nov. 18, 1923; s. Thomas Jackson and Emma Frances (Glenn) A.; m. Rosalind Gower Smith, Apr. 2, 1949; children—Robert S., David S., Susan G., Thomas G., Douglas L. Student, Davidson Coll., 1941-43, Mass. Inst. Tech., 1943-44, Yale, 1944; B.S., Duke, (Borden undergrad. grantee), 1949; M.D., 1949; Ph.D., U. Minn., 1957. Diplomate: Am. Bd. Internal Medicine. Intern U. Minn., 1949-50, fellow in medicine, 1950-51, 53-54, research fellow, 1954-55, instr. medicine, microbiology and lab. medicine, 1955-57; asst. prof. medicine and microbiology U. Ark. Med. Center, Little Rock, 1957-60, asso. prof., 1960-66, prof., 1966—, chmn. dept. medicine, 1967-76, dir. infectious diseases, 1976—; cons. VA Hosp., Little Rock.; Mem. regional adv. group Ark. Regional Med. Program, 1966—; panel mem. NRC, 1966-68; mem. com. Nat. Heart and Lung Inst., 1970-72; cons. USPHS, 1966—. Editorial cons., various med. jours. Served with M.C. AUS, 1943-45, 51-53. A.C.P. fellow, 1954-55. Fellow A.C.P. (gov. 1971—); mem. Am. Thoracic Soc., Infectious Disease Soc., Assn. Profs. Medicine, Sigma Xi, Alpha Omega Alpha. Research brucellosis, bacterial endotoxins, autoimmunity in neurologic diseases, other. Home: 230 Kingsrow Dr Little Rock AR 72207

ABERNETHY, GEORGE LAWRENCE, educator; b. West Orange, N.J., Aug. 23, 1910; s. John and Lydia (Johnson) A.; m. Helen Sarah McLandress, Aug. 25, 1936; children: Robert John, Jean Helen (Mrs. Thomas H. Poston). A.B., Bucknell U., 1932; M.A., Oberlin Coll., 1933; Ph.D., U. Mich., 1936. Prof. philosophy Culver-Stockton Coll., Canton, Mo., 1936-40; prof. philosophy and psychology U. S.D., Vermillion, 1940-46; prof. philosophy Davidson (N.C.) Coll., 1946—, Richardson prof., 1967—, Dana prof., 1974—, emeritus, 1976—; vis. prof. Coll. Charleston (S.C.), summer 1951; mem. faculty U. N.C. at Charlotte, part-time, 1947-48, Barber-Scotia Coll., Concord, N.C., 1951-52; mem. regional selection com. Woodrow Wilson Fellowships Found., 1960-62; Ford Found. Faculty fellow Columbia, 1952-53, Cooperative Humanities program fellow U. N.C.-Duke, 1967-68. Author: Pakistan- A Selected Annotated Bibliography, 1957, 60, 68, 74, The Idea of Equality, 1959, Living Wisdom from the World's Relgions, 1965, (with T.A. Langford) Philosophy of Religion, 1963, 68, History of Philosophy, 1965, Introduction to Western Philosophy, 1970; Contbg. editor: Presbyn. Outlook, 1963-75. Recipient Thomas Jefferson award McConnell Found., 1962, Bucknell U. Alumni medal, 1969. Mem. N.C. Philos. Soc. (pres. 1951-52), AAUP, Am. Philos. Assn., So. Soc. Philosophy and Psychology, Assn. Asian Studies, Philosophy Discussion Club Charlotte. Democrat. Presbyn. Home: 100 Hillside Dr Davidson NC 28036

ABERSFELLER, HEINZ ANDREW, real estate executive; b. Frankfurt am Main, Germany, Apr. 23, 1920; came to U.S., 1922, naturalized, 1941; s. Frank and Anna (Friedel) A.; m. Margaret Sturdivant, Feb. 1, 1942; 1 dau., Gretchen Anne Abersfeller Schmidt; m. Peggy Beckett Harlan, Apr. 21, 1973. Student, U. Md., Am. U., also LaSalle Extension U. With U.S. Govt., 1944; asst. post quartermaster Heidelberg (Germany) Mil. Post., 1947-49; chief supply and logistics Office Q.M.G., Heidelberg, 1949-52, dep. asst. quartermaster gen. clothing and textile material, Washington, 1952-57; regional dir. fed. supply service GSA, Washington, 1957-61, regional adminstr. region 10, Seattle, 1961-62, regional adminstr. region 3, Washington, 1962-64, commr. fed. supply service, 1964—; pres., chief exec. officer Eastern Realty Investment Corp., 1983—; dir. gen. services Corp. for Pub. Broadcasting, 1971—; pres. L'Enfant Plaza Corp, 1972—; chmn. Pres.'s Com. Blind Made Products. Recipient Meritorious Service medal (2) Dept. Army; Disting. Service award GSA; Exceptional Service award GSA. Mem. Def. Supply Assn. (nat. v.p. 1967-70, gov), Armed Forces Mgmt. Assn. (gov.). Clubs: KC, Elks. Home: 49 Montgomery Ln Port Ludlow WA 98365 Office: 490 L'Enfant Plaza East SW Washington DC 20024

ABETTI, PIER ANTONIO, management of technology educator, consulting engineer; b. Florence, Italy, Feb. 7, 1921; came to U.S., 1946; s. Georgio and Anna (Garino) A.; m. Elizabeth Burr Nelson, June 11, 1948; children: George E., Frank A. Student, Poly. Inst., Turin, Italy, 1940-44; Dr. indsl. Engring., U. Pisa, Italy, 1945; M.S. in Elec. Engring., Ill. Inst. Tech., Chgo., 1948, Ph.D., 1953. Registered profl. engr., Mass. Advanced devel. engr. Gen. Electric Co., Pittsfield, Mass., 1948-56, mgr. Project EHV, 1957-62, mgr. pvt. telephone systems, Lynchburg, Va., 1971-73, mgr. Europe strategic planning, Brussels, 1974-79, cons.research and devel., Schenectady, N.Y., 1980-81; dep. gen. mgr. UNIVAC-Europe, Lusanne, Switzerland, 1963-64; prof. mgmt. of tech. Rensselaer Poly. Inst., Troy, N.Y., 1982—, adj. prof., 1951-52; non-resident instr. MIT, 1950-51; adj. prof. Berrkshire Community Coll., Pittsfield, 1958-60; cons. Tech. Assessment Group, Schenetady, N.Y., 1980—. Contbr. articles to profl. jours. Pres. Berkshire Mycological Soc., Pittsfield, 1954-59, Berkshire Film Soc., Pittsfield, 1955-58. Recipient Coffin award Gen. Electric Co., 1952, Internat. prize Montefiore Inst., 1953, Recognition award Italian Hist. Soc. Am., 1953. Fellow IEEE (chmn. Volta scholarship 1961-66, mem. awards bd. 1984); mem. Eta Kappa Nu (Recognition award 1953), Tau Beta Pi. Office: Rensselaer Poly Inst Sch Mgmt Troy NY 12181 *In my life I have always tried to learn from my predecessors in science and technology and innovate based on their teaching and my original thinking.*

ABHAU, WILLIAM CONRAD, operations analyst, retired naval officer; b. Baltimore County, Md., Apr. 5, 1912; s. William Conrad and Gertrude (Lewis); m. Harriet Elliot Sanders, Oct. 17, 1942; children: Elliot, Marcy. B.S., U.S. Naval Acad., 1935; M.S., Naval Postgrad. Sch., 1956; grad., Naval War Coll., 1957. Commd. USN, advanced through grades to rear adm., 1964; gunnery officer USS New Jersey, World War II; asso. with Navy Research and Devel. effort, 1945-70,; comdr. U.S.S. E. A. Greene, 1947-48, Escort Squadron 16, 1953-54, U.S.S. Waccamaw, 1957-58, U.S.S. Helena, 1961-62, Cruiser-Destroyer Flotilla Four, 1965, Manned Spacecraft Recovery Force, Atlantic, 1966-67, Anti-Submarine Warfare Systems Project, Washington, 1967-70, ret., 1970; with Inst. for Def. Analyses, 1970—. Author mil. studies. Decorated Legion of Merit, Bronze Star medal. Mem. Ops. Research Soc. Am., Mil. Order World Wars. Clubs: Annapolis Yacht; Army and Navy (Washington). Home: 201 Scott Circle Annapolis MD 21401 Office: 1801 N Beauregard St Alexandria VA *Most achievement is the product of a sense of responsibility.*

ABISH, CECILE, artist; b. N.Y.C.; m. Walter Abish. B.F.A., Bklyn. Coll., 1953. Instr. art Queens Coll.; vis. artist U. Mass, Amherst, Cooper Union, Harvard U. Exhibitor one-woman shows, Newark Coll. Engring., 1968, Inst. Contemporary Art, Boston, 1974, U. Md., 1975, Alessandra Gallery, N.Y.C., 1977, Wright State U., Dayton, Ohio, 1978, Carpenter Ctr., Cambridge, Mass., 1979, Anderson Gallery, Va. Commonwealth U., Richmond, 1981, SUNY-Stony-Brook, 1982, group exhbns., Detroit Inst. Art, 1969, Aldrich Mus. Art, 1971, 10 Bleecker St., N.Y.C., 1972, Lakeview Ctr. Arts, Peoria. Ill., Bykert Gallery, N.Y.C., 1971-74, Michael Walls Gallery, N.Y.C., 1975, Fine Arts Bldg. Gallery, N.Y.C., 1976, Mus. Modern Art, N.Y.C., Hudson River Mus., 1979, Atlanta Arts Festival, 1980, New Mus., N.Y.C, 1980, 81, Kuntsgebaude, Stuttgart, W. Germany, 1981, numerous commns.; represented in permanent collections; contbr. art jours. Nat. Endowment Arts fellow, 1975, 77, 80; CAPS fellow, 1975. Mem. Coll. Art Assn., Women's Caucus for Art. Office: PO Box 485 Cooper Station 4th Ave New York NY 10276

ABKOWITZ, MARTIN AARON, educator; b. Revere, Mass., Sept. 19, 1918; s. Max and Annie (Weise) A.; m. Davette Eisenstein, Mar. 9, 1947; children—Janis Lynne, Mark David, Suzanne Jill. S.B. in Naval Architecture, Mass. Inst. Tech., 1940; A.M. in Physics, Harvard, 1949, Ph.D., 1953. Naval architect David Taylor Model Basin, 1940-42, physicist, 1946-49; faculty Mass. Inst. Tech., 1949—, prof. naval architecture, 1959—; Cons. engr., 1949—, Fulbright lectr., Denmark, 1962-63, France, 1971-72, Israel, 1979. Served to capt. AUS, 1942-46. Mem. Soc. Naval Architects and Marine Engrs., Sigma Xi. Home: 28 Peacock Farm Rd Lexington MA 02173 Office: Dept Ocean Engring Mass Inst Technology Cambridge MA 02139

ABLIN, RICHARD JOEL, immunologist; b. Chgo., May 15, 1940; s. Robert Benjamin and Minnie Edith (Gordon) A.; m. Linda Lee Lutwack; 1 son, Michael David. A.B., Lake Forest Coll., 1962; Ph.D. in Microbiology, SUNY-Buffalo, 1967. Grad. asst. dept. biology SUNY-Buffalo, 1963-65, research asst., summer 1963, research fellow, 1965-66; USPHS postdoctoral fellow dept. microbiology Sch. Medicine, lectr., lab instr., 1966-68; instr., research asst. Rosary Hill Coll., 1965-66; research cons. program med. edn. AID, Paraguay, 1968; dir. div. immunology Millard Fillmore Hosp., Buffalo, 1968-70; head sect. immunology, renal unit Meml. Hosp. of Springfield, 1970-73; dir. sect. immunobiology div. urology dept. surgery Cook County Hosp. and Hektoen Inst. for Med. Research, Chgo., 1973-75, sr. sci. officer div. immunology, 1976-83; sr. mem. sci. staff, clin. immunologist Cook County Hosp., 1973-75; asst. prof. medicine So. Ill. U., 1971-73; assoc. prof. microbiology Univ. Health Sci. (Chgo. Med. Sch.), 1973-74; research assoc. prof. urology, dir. immunology unit dept. urology Health Scis. Ctr., SUNY-Stony Brook, 1983—.

Editor: Allergologia et Immunopathologia, 1974—; contbg. editor: Current Perspective in Allergology and Immunopathology, 1974—, Allergologia et Immunopathologia Seminars in Immunopathology and Oncology, Ill. Med. Jour., 1975—; adv. editor: Jour. Cancer, 1976—; assoc. editor: Low Temperature Medicine, 1975—; mem. internat. editorial staff: Medikon, 1974—; mem. editorial bd.: Immunology and Allergy Practice, 1979—, Am. Jour. Reproductive Immunology, 1980; mem. sci. bd.: Tumor Diagnostik and Therapie, 1980; contbr. numerous articles to profl jours. and texts. Chief Sangamo Nation Y-Indian Guides, Springfield, 1972-73; mgr. Skokie Indians' Boys' Baseball, Ill., 1973-74, 77, 80, 81, bd. dirs., Ill., 1979-83, exec. v.p., Ill., 1981-82; cubmaster N.W. Suburban council Boy Scouts Am., 1974-78; asst. scoutmaster N.W. Suburban council Boy Scouts Am, 1975-77. Recipient Nat. Pres. Leader's Dist. Boy Scouts Am., 1975; named Cubmaster of Yr. Boy Scouts Am., 1977. Fellow Am. Assn. Clin. Immunology, Allergy, Am. Coll. Cryosurgery (adv. bd.); mem. Am. Assn. Cancer Research, AAAS, Am. Assn. Immunologists, Chgo. Assn. Immunologists, Am. Fedn. Clin. Research, Am. Soc. Immunology of Reprodn., Am. Soc. Microbiology, Brit. Assn. Surg. Oncology, Buffalo Collegium Immunology, Internat. Soc. Andrology, Internat. Soc. Chronobiology, Internat. Soc. Cryosurgery (hon. life pres.), Internat. Soc. Immunology Reprodn., Japan Soc. Low Temperature Medicine, N.Y. Acad. Scis., Reticuloendothelial Soc., Soc. Cryobiology, Soc. Protozoologists, Soc. Study Reprodn., Soc. Exptl. Biology and Medicine, Transplantation Soc., Nat. Registry Microbiologist (cert. specialist in pub. health and med. lab. microbiology), Cryoimmunotherapeutic Study Group (chmn.), Group d'Etudes de la Cryochirurgie (co-chmn. cryoimmunology sect.), Sigma Xi. Office: Immunology Unit Dept Urology Health Scis Ctr SUNY Stony Brook NY 11794

ABLON, RALPH E., industrial company executive; b. 1916. Student, Ohio State U., 1939. With Luria Bros. & Co., 1939-62, exec. v.p., 1948-55, pres., 1955-62, dir., 1962—; chmn., chief exec. officer Ogden Corp., N.Y.C., 1962—, pres., dir., 1972—. Served with USNR, World War II. Office: Ogden Corp 277 Park Ave New York NY 10172 *

ABNEE, A. VICTOR, JR., association executive; b. Lexington, Ky., June 12, 1923; s. A. Victor and Irene Sarah (Brogle) A.; m. Doris Heuck, Dec. 28, 1946; children: Janice Lee Abnee Williams, A. Victor, III. B.A., U. Cin., 1948. With U.S. Gypsum Co., 1948-63, dir. advt. and promotion, Chgo., 1961-63; with Gypsum Assn., Evanston, Ill., 1963—, exec. v.p., 1965—. Served to capt. C.E. AUS, 1943-46. Named Constrn. Industry Man of Yr. Wall and Ceiling Industries Assn., 1980. Mem. Nat. Inst. Bldg. Scis., ASTM, Nat. Safety Council, Am. Soc. Assn. Execs., Assn. Econ. Council Chgo., Sigma Chi. Clubs: Les Cheneaux Yacht (dir.); Foundation (dir.), University (Chgo.) (pres.); University (Evanston) (dir.); Skokie Country (Glencoe, Ill.); Gyro Internat., Shriners. Home: 788 Lincoln Ave Winnetka IL 66093 Office: 1603 Orrington Ave Evanston IL 60201

ABNEY, FREDERICK SHERWOOD, lawyer; b. Brownwood, Tex., Dec. 2, 1919; s. DeWitt Fleetwood and Margaret (Lyles) A.; m. Jeanne Elizabeth Larson, Feb. 28, 1942; children: Stephen Frederick, James Lorntz. B.A., U. Tex., Austin, 1942, LL.B., 1947. Bar: Tex. bar 1947, U.S. Supreme Ct. bar 1963. Pvt. practice, Brownwood, 1948-49, Dallas, 1949—. Served with USAAF, 1942-45. Mem. Am., Dallas bar assns., State Bar Tex., Am. Judicature Soc., Southwestern Legal Found., Dallas Bar Found., Tex. Bar Found. (life fellow), Delta Tau Delta, Phi Delta Phi. Mem. Sch. of Christianity. Home: 6730 Orchid Ln Dallas TX 75230 Office: 5952 Royal Ln Suite 264 Dallas TX 75230

ABOOD, LEO GEORGE, educator; b. Erie, Pa., Jan. 15, 1922; s. George E. and Sara (Muffet) A.; m. Lois Wuchner, Sept. 25, 1947; children: George T., Mary E. B.S., Ohio State U., 1943; Ph.D., U. Chgo., 1950. Instr. physiology U. Chgo., 1950-52; asso. prof. biochemistry U. Ill., Chgo., 1954-63, prof., 1963-65; prof. brain research and biochemistry U. Rochester, N.Y., 1965—; mem. biomed. research com. Nat. Inst. Drug Abuse; mem. com. on anticholinergics Nat. Acad. Sci., 1981—; Trustee Brain Research Found. U. Chgo.; bd. sci. dirs. Huxley Research Inst. Editorial bd.: Psychopharmacology Communications, 1974—, Jour. Neurosci. Research, 1974—; Contbr. numerous articles to profl. jours. Served with USNR, 1943-46. Mem. Am. Chem. Soc., Am. Physiol. Soc., Soc. Neurosci., Am. Soc. Neurochemistry. Patentee pharms. Home: 45 Crandon Way Rochester NY 14618 Office: Center for Brain Research U Rochester Med Center Rochester NY 14642

ABOUREZK, JAMES G., lawyer, former U.S. senator; b. Wood, S.D., Feb. 24, 1931; m. Margaret Bethea; children: Charles Thomas, Nikki June, Paul Edwin. B.S. in Civil Engring., S.D. Sch. Mines, 1961; J.D., U. S.D., 1966. Bar: S.D., D.C., U.S. Supreme Ct. Former ptnr. LaFleur & Abourezk, Rapid City, S.D.; mem. 92d Congress from 2d S.D. dist.; mem. U.S. Senate, 1973-78; mem. com. energy and natural resources, com. judiciary, com. budget, chmn. select com. on Indian affairs; mem. firm Abourezk, Sobol & Trister, Washington, 1979—. Served with USN, 1948-52. Democrat. Office: 21 DuPont Circle Suite 400 Washington DC 20036

ABPLANALP, GLEN HAROLD, civil engineer; b. Youngsville, N.Y., Nov. 9, 1914; s. William P. and Elizabeth (Tremper) A.; m. Marion Clark, Sept. 5, 1937; children: Diane Abplanalp Guinurule, Jeffrey. C.E., Rensselaer Poly. Inst., 1936; J.D., Fordham U., 1943. Bar: N.Y. bar 1943; Registered profl. engr., N.Y., N.J., Conn., Pa., Fla., Tenn., Ga., Mich., Wis., Tex., Md., N.C. Asst. dist. mgr. Wallace & Tiernan Co. Inc., Newark, 1936-43; sec-treas. Glenwal Co., Inc., Ridgewood, N.J., 1946-47; cons. engr. Havens & Emerson, Inc., N.Y.C. and Saddle Brook, N.J., 1947—, prin. engr., 1955-59, gen. partner, 1959-70, vice chmn., 1970-77, v.p., 1977-80, staff cons., 1980—; lectr. in field; head coop. research project on upper Passaic River, 1965—; cons. N.J. Commr. Health, 1964—. Contbr. articles to profl. jours.; legal editor: The Specifier, 1960—. Dir. Met. Youth for Christ. Served as lt. comdr. USNR, 1943-46. Recipient Pres's. plaque Constrn. Specifications Inst., 1963, 64, 67, 77. Fellow Constrn. Specifications Inst. (pres. 1960-61), ASCE (life), Am. Cons. Engrs. Council (chmn. contract documents com.); mem. Nat. Soc. Profl. Engrs. (past com. chmn.), Am. Arbitration Assn. (nat. panel), Am. Water Works Assn. (engring. and constrn. div., tech. and profl. council), Water Pollution Control Fedn., Am. Acad. Environ. Engrs. (diplomate, trustee), VFW, Pi Kappa Alpha. Presbyterian. Lodges: Masons; Shriners. Home: 539 Grove St Ridgewood NJ 07450 Office: 299 Market St Saddle Brook NJ 07662

ABRAHAM, GEORGE, research physicist, engineer; b. N.Y.C., July 15, 1918; s. Herbert and Dorothy (Jacoby) A.; m. Hilda Mary Wenz, Aug. 26, 1944; children: Edward H., Dorothy J., Anne H., Alice J. Sc.B., Brown U., 1940; S.M., Harvard U., 1942; Ph.D., U. Md., 1972; postgrad., MIT, George Washington U. Registered profl. engr., D.C. Chmn. bd., pres. bd. Intercollegiate Broadcasting System, N.Y., 1941—; radio engr. RCA, Camden, N.J., 1941; with Naval Research Lab., Washington, 1942—, head sci. edn., head exptl. devices and microelectronics sects., 1945-69, head systems applications Office of Dir. Research, 1969-75, research physicist Office Research and Tech. Applications, cons., 1975—; lectr. U. Md., 1945-52, George Washington U., 1952-67, Am. U., 1979; indsl. cons.; mem. Bd. Registration Profl. Engrs. Contbr. chpts. to books, articles to profl. jours. Chmn. bd. Canterbury Sch., Accokeek, Md.; mem. schs. and scholarships com. Harvard U.; active PTA, Boy Scouts Am. Served to capt. USNR, World War II. Recipient Group Achievement award Fleet Ballistic Missile Program U.S. Navy, 1963; Edison award Naval Research Lab., 1971; Navy Research Publ. award, 1974; Patent awards, 1959-75; D.C. Sci. citation, 1982; others. Fellow IEEE (Harry Diamond award 1981, Centennial award 1984), Washington Acad. Scis. (pres. 1974-75), N.Y. Acad. Scis., AAAS; Mem. Am. Phys. Soc., Am. Assn. Physics Tchrs., Am. Soc. Naval Engrs., Washington Soc. Engrs. (pres. 1974, award 1981), Philos. Soc. Washington, AAUP, Sierra Club, Sigma Xi, Sigma Pi Sigma, Tau Beta Pi, Sigma Tau, Eta Kappa Nu, Iota Beta Sigma. Clubs: Cosmos, Harvard (Washington); Appalachian Mountain (Boston); Sierra (San Francisco). Patentee in field. Home: 3107 Westover Dr SE Washington DC 20020 Office: Naval Research Lab Washington DC 20375

ABRAHAM, HENRY JULIAN, political science educator; b. Offenbach am Main, Germany, Aug. 25, 1921; s. Fredrick and Louise (Kullmann) A.; m. Mildred Kosches, Apr. 13, 1954; children: Philip F., Peter D. A.B. summa cum laude, Kenyon Coll., Gambier, Ohio, 1948, L.H.D., 1972; M.A., Columbia, 1949; Ph.D., U. Pa., 1952; LL.D. hon., U. Hartford, 1982, Knox Coll., 1982. Mem. faculty U. Pa., 1949-72, prof. polit. sci., 1962-72; Doherty prof. govt. and fgn. affairs U. Va., 1971-78, James Hart prof., 1978—; vis. prof. Swarthmore Coll., CCNY, univs. Colo., Columbia, Copenhagen, Stockholm, Aarhus, Lund, Göteborg, Oslo, Helsinki, Uppsala and Amsterdam; cons. in field 1956; Fulbright prof., Denmark, 1959-60. Author: Compulsory Voting, 1955, Government as Entrepreneur, 1956, Courts and Judges, 1959, Elements of Democratic Government, 1964, Essentials of National Government, 1971; author: Justices and Presidents, 1984; Author: The Judiciary, 1980, The Judicial Process, 1980; author: American Democracy, 1982; Author: Freedom and the Court, 1982; author: The Judiciary, 1983. Mem. com. on non-discrimination Phila. Bd. Edn., 1962; Mem. vis. com. on govt. Lehigh U., 1967—; trustee fedn. Jewish Agencies Greater Phila., 1970-72. Recipient award excellence undergrad. teaching U. Pa., 1959, 67, recipient U. Va., 1978; recipient Thomas Jefferson award U. Va., 1983; Nat. Endowment for Humanities fellow, 1975, 76, 78, 80, 81; NSF fellow, 1965; fellow Am. Philos. Soc., 1961-67, 79; Earhurt fellow, 1984. Mem. Fellows in Am. Studies (pres. 1966), Am. Polit. Sci. Assn. (v.p. 1980-82), Am. Acad. Polit. and Social Sci., Raven Soc., Law and Soc. Assn., Am. Soc. for Legal History, Met. Opera Guild, Phi Beta Kappa (vis. scholar 1970-71). Clubs: Greencroft (Charlottesville, Va.); Z, Imp (U. Va.); Franklin Inn (Phila.),. Home: 906 Fendall Terr Charlottesville VA 22903 Office: 232 Cabell Hall Univ Va Charlottesville VA 22903 *Basically-a commitment to hard work; to discipline; to a maintenance of a sense of humor; to a rejection of pompousness and egomania; to a resolute embrace of merit. Above all, an abiding faith in drawing the line between the rights and obligations of individuals and those of society without which the democratic process can neither work nor survive.*

ABRAHAM, LEROY, cattle brokerage firm executive, analyst; b. Memphis, Dec. 17, 1933; s. George G. and Celia Gold; m. Patricia Goodman, June 17, 1956; children: Leigh Abraham May, Kenneth G. D.V.M., U. Ill., 1957. Gen. practice vet.medicine, Memphis, 1957-63; pres. Dixie Nat. Stockyards, Memphis, 1963-83; market analyst, commodity broker Heinold Commodities, Inc., Stuart, Fla., 1983—, named to presidents council, 1983—; dir. certified markets Nat. Livestock Dealers. Contbr. articles, Am. Journal of Vet. Medicine. Named Man of Yr. Nat. Livestock Dealers Assn., 1975. Mem. Tenn. Vet. Med. Assn., AVMA. Republican. Jewish. Clubs:, Stuart Rotary. Lodges: Memphis Rotary; Stuart Rotary;. Home: 2821 E Ocean Stuart FL 33457 Office: Dixie Nat Stockyards 1460 Warford St Memphis TN 38108

ABRAHAM, PAUL LESLIE, banker; b. Andover, S.D., Mar. 1, 1921; s. Paul Leo and Mary Cecila (Langhammer) A.; m. Mary Carolyn Beeve, Jan. 9, 1946; 1 son, Thomas Richard. Student, U. Mo., 1941-43; B.S., Rockhurst Coll., 1948. Asst. trust officer First Nat. Bank, Kansas City, Mo., 1955-60, trust officer, 1960-63, v.p., 1963-67, sr. v.p., 1967—. Mem. Greater Kansas City Clearing House Assn.; Chmn. adminstrn. com. Rockhurst Coll., 1960, hon. dir., 1971—; mem. gift and bequest com. Avila Coll., 1970—; hon. bd. dirs. Bapt. Meml. Hosp., Kansas City, Mo.; chmn. bd. Payment and Telecommunications Cooporation. Served with USAAF, 1943-45. Decorated Air medal with 2 bronze clusters, D.F.C. Mem. Am., Mo. bankers assns., Am. Inst. Banking. Home: 5311 Chadwick St Shawnee Mission KS 66205 Office: 14 W 10th St Kansas City MO 64105

ABRAHAM, WILLARD, educator; b. Chgo., May 18, 1916; s. Edward and Sadie (Weiss) A.; m. Shirley Dale Wiener, June 13, 1948; children—Edward, Andrew, Amy Rebecca. B.S., Ill. Inst. Tech., 1940; M.Ed., Chgo. Tchrs. Coll., 1942; Ph.D., Northwestern U., 1950. With Postal Telegraph Co., Chgo., 1935-39, Roosevelt U., 1946-53; mem. faculty Coll. Edn., Ariz. State U., Tempe, 1953—, now prof. dept. spl. edn.; Cons. numerous orgns.; ednl. collaborator Coronet Films, Grolier Ednl. Services.; Asso. editor Exceptional Children mag. Author: Your Post-War Career, 1945, Get the Job, 1946, A Guide for the Study of Exceptional Children, 1956, A Look at Reading, 1957, Barbara-A Prologue, 1958, Common Sense about Gifted Children, 1958, The Slow Learner, 1964, A Time for Teaching, 1964, A Study of the Devereux Found, 1970, Living With Preschoolers, 1976, A Dictionary of Special Education Terms, 1980, You Always Lag One Child Behind, 1980; Editor: The Preparation of B(ur.) (of) I(ndian) A(ffairs) Teacher and Dormitory Aides, 1968; Author: weekly column Our Children; monthly article Parent Talk; Contbr. profl. jours. Served with AUS, 1942-46. Recipient Faculty Achievement award Ariz. State U., 1965. Mem. Council Exceptional Children, Am. Assn. U. Profs., Phi Delta Kappa. Home: 6402 E Chaparral Rd Scottsdale AZ 85253 Office: Coll Edn Ariz State Univ Tempe AZ 85287 *My goals are to keep my family healthy and satisfied, to make a living, to perform services for others, to have time for reading, movies, socializing, and keeping on top of my profession, and to write regularly for publication.*

ABRAHAMS, JOHN HAMBLETON, life insurance company executive; b. Topeka, Aug. 10, 1913; s. John Vanneman and Meliora Clarkson (Hambleton) A.; m. Julia Laval Jencks, Apr. 30, 1938; 1 dau., Julia Louise (Mrs. Russell T. Dowell). Ph.B., U. Chgo., 1935; D.B.A. (hon.), Washburn U., Topeka, 1978. With Security Benefit Life Ins. Co., Topeka, 1935—, exec. v.p., 1953-54, pres., chmn. bd., 1954-75, chmn. bd., chief exec. officer, 1975-78, chmn. bd., 1978—; dir. First Nat. Bank Topeka, Capitol Fed. Savs. & Loan Assn., Topeka, Kans. Devel. Credit Corp., Didde-Glaser Inc., Emporia, Kans., Kans. Venture Capital Inc. Trustee Menninger Found. Served to lt. USNR, 1942-45. Mem. Kan. Assn. Commerce and Industry (pres. 1970), Greater Topeka C. of C. (pres. 1950), Chi Psi. Clubs: Topeka Country; Kansas City (Mo.). Home: 24 Pepper Tree Ln Topeka KS 66611 Office: 700 Harrison St Topeka KS 66636

ABRAHAMS, ROBERT DAVID, lawyer, author; b. Phila., Sept. 24, 1905; s. William and Anne (David) A.; m. Florence Kohn, Nov. 21, 1929 (dec. Sept. 23, 1975); children: Richard Irving, Roger David, Marjorie (Mrs. Clifford Slavin); m. Jane Sunstein Freedman, Jan. 27, 1977. LL.B., Dickinson Sch. Law, 1925, LL.D., 1973. Bar: Pa. bar 1925. Sec. to commr. gen. to Europe for Sesqui-Centennial Expn., 1925; asst. city solicitor, 1927-32; editor Independent (weekly), 1932; consul at Phila. for Dominican Republic, 1931-62; asst. chief counsel Legal Aid Soc. Phila., 1933-50, chief counsel, 1950-73; now partner Abrahams & Loewenstein.; Faculty law Temple U.; exec. dir. Community Legal Service, 1966-67. Author: verse Come Forward, 1928, New Tavern Tales; fiction, 1930, (with M.J. Meyer) Handbook of Pennsylvania Collection Practice, 1931, The Pot Bellied Gods; verse, 1932, Death After Lunch; novel, 1941, Death in 1-2-3, 1942, Three Dozen; verse, 1945, Mr. Benjamin's Sword, 1948, Room for a Son; novel, 1951, The Commodore, 1954, The Uncommon Soldier, 1958, Sound of Bow Bells, 1962, Humphrey's Ride, 1964, The Bonus of Redonda, 1967, Beginnings, 1975, The Daddy's Ear, 1980; Contbr. verse, prose to, Sat. Eve. Post, Esquire, Story, other mags.; contbr. profl. articles to law jours. Bd. dirs. Pa. Prison Soc., pres., 1968-72; bd. dirs., trustee Dickinson Sch. Law.; pres. Community Health Center, 1945-52, Jewish Family Service, 1951-54; mem. expert com. on Low Cost Legal Service, Am. Bar Survey of Legal Profession.; founder Horatio Nelson Free Mus., Nevis. Decorated Order of Duarte, 1945, Order of Christopher Columbus, 1957; Dominican Republic). Mem. Nat. Legal Aid Assn. (v.p. 1957, Reginald Heber Smith award 1962), Internat. Bar Assn., ABA, Pa. Bar Assn., Phila. Bar Assn. (chmn. com. on pub. service 1961-62, com. censors 1962-65, Fidelity Bank award 1972), Tau Epsilon Rho. Democrat. Jewish. Clubs: Mason., Locust, Franklin Inn. Founder, Phila. Neighborhood Law Office Plan, 1st successful legal service plan for persons in middle income group, 1939. Morning Star Fig Tree Nevis West Indies Office: Land Title Bldg Philadelphia PA 19110 *Life is adventure-one must embrace it with love.*

ABRAHAMS, VIVIAN CECIL, physiology educator; b. London, Eng., Oct. 19, 1927; emigrated to Can., 1963; s. Woolf S. and Eva (Shirotta) A.; m. Pamela Dance, Sept. 10, 1955; children: Graham, Mark, Carolyn, Jennifer. B.Sc., Edinburgh (Scotland) U., 1952, Ph.D., 1955, D.Sc., 1978. Asst., also lectr. physiology Edinburgh U., 1952-55; instr. U. Pa., Phila., 1955-56; scientist Nat. Inst. Med. Research, London, 1956-63; assoc. prof. Queen's U., Kingston, Ont., Can., 1963-67, prof., 1967—, head dept., 1976—; Chmn. bd. dirs. Ont. Grad. Study Programme, 1977-78. Contbr. articles to profl. jours. Served with Royal Arty., 1945-48. Fulbright fellow, 1955-56; Beit Meml. fellow, 1956-59. Mem. Soc. Neurosci., Assn. of Sci., Engring. and Tech. Community of Can. (pres. 1979-80), Physiol. Soc., Canadian Physiol. Assn. (pres. 1983-84), Am. Physiol. Soc., Internat. Assn. Study of Pain, Can. Assn. Neurosci. (pres. 1981-82), Internat. Brain Research Orgn. Home: 259 Fairway Hills Crescent Kingston ON Canada

ABRAHAMS, WILLIAM MILLER, editor, author; b. Boston, Jan. 23, 1919; s. Louis and Wilhelmina (Miller) A. B.A., Harvard U., 1941. Editor Atlantic Monthly Press, Boston, 1955-77; contbg. editor Atlantic Monthly, 1968-79, Inquiry mag., 1978—; sr. editor (West Coast) Holt, Rinehart & Winston, N.Y.C., 1977-84, E.P. Dutton, 1984—; editor O. Henry Awards ann. vols., 1967—. Author: Interval in Carolina, 1945, By the Beautiful Sea, 1947, Imperial Waltz, 1954, Children of Capricorn, 1963, (with Peter Stansky) Journey to the Frontier, 1966, The Unknown Orwell, 1972, Orwell: The Transformation, 1979. Served with AUS, 1942-45. Home: 375 Pinehill Rd Hillsborough CA 94010 Office: care EP Dutton 2 Park Ave New York NY 10016

ABRAHAMSEN, DAVID, psychiatrist, psychoanalyst, author; b. Trondheim, Norway, June 23, 1903; came to U.S., 1940, naturalized, 1946; s. Salomon and Marie (Fischer) A.; m. Lova Katz, May 5, 1932; children: Inger Abrahamsen Elliott, Anne-Marie Abrahamsen Foltz. M.D., Royal Frederick U., Oslo, 1929; postgrad., Tavistock Clinic and Nat. Hosp., London, London Sch. Econs., 1936-37; M.D., SUNY, 1943. Diplomate: Am. Bd. Psychiatry and Neurology. Dist. pub. health officer, pvt. practice medicine, Norway, 1929-31; intern Royal Norwegian Clinics, Oslo U., 1931-32; resident, asst. physician neurology and psychiatry Psychiat. Clinic, Oslo, 1932-36; dir., supr. Children's Home, Oslo, 1934-36; psychiatrist Dept. Justice, Oslo, 1938-40, St. Elizabeth's Hosp., Washington, 1940-41, Ill. State Penitentiary, 1941-42; research asso. psychiatry Menninger Clinic, Southard Sch., Topeka, 1942-43; psychiatrist Bellevue Hosp., 1943-44; research asso. dept. psychiatry Columbia U., 1944-53, research dir. child guidance and mental hygiene, 1950-53; dir. research, treatment behavior disorders in children Psychiat. Inst., N.Y.C., 1944-48; dir. sci. research N.Y. State Dept. Mental Hygiene, 1948-52, cons., 1955-65; vis. prof. grad. faculty polit. and social sci. New Sch. for Social Research, 1959-61; research psychiat. cons. dept. psychiatry Roosevelt Hosp., N.Y.C., 1968—; organizer, dir. Psychiat. Forum, Inc., 1946—; mem. bd. Home Adv. Council, Home Term Ct., N.Y.C., 1953—; mem. bd., adv. bd. Mus. Therapy Orgn., 1954—; mem. N.Y. Gov s Com to Propose New Legislation on Definition Legal Insanity, 1957—; bd. overseers Lemberg Center for Study of Violence, Brandeis U. Author: I am a Jew (in Norwegian), 1935, Crime and the Human Mind, 1944, Men, Mind and Power, 1945, The Mind and Death of a Genius, 1946, Report on Study of 102 Sex Offenders at Sing Sing Prison as Submitted to Governor Thomas E. Dewey, 1950, Who Are the Guilty?-A Study of Education and Crime, 1962, The Road to Emotional Maturity, 1958, The Psychology of Crime, 1960, The Emotional Care of Your Child, 1969, Our Violent Society, 1970, The Murdering Mind, 1973, Nixon vs. Nixon: An Emotional Tragedy, 1977, The Mind of the Accused: A Psychiatrist in the Courtroom; also numerous reports.; contbr. articles to sci., med. jours. Served with Norwegian Army, 1940. Fellow AMA, Am. Psychiat. Assn., N.Y. Acad. Medicine; mem. Norwegian Med. Assn., N.Y. County Med. Soc., Am. Soc. Criminology, N.Y. Soc. Clin. Psychiatry, Am. Coll. Psychoanalysts, Authors League, PEN. Address: 1035 Fifth Ave New York NY 10028

ABRAHAMSEN, SAMUEL, Judaic studies educator; b. Trondheim, Norway, Oct. 28, 1917; came to U.S., 1940, naturalized, 1948; s. Solomon and Miriam (Fischer) A.; m. Minerva S. Passman, June 8, 1947; children: Joy S. Abrahamsen Land, Judith. A.B., M.A., U. Oslo, 1939; postgrad., U. Calif., Berkeley, 1940-41, Cambridge U., 1943; Ph.D. (Agnes Brown Leach fellow), New Sch., N.Y.C., 1955, Hebrew Union Coll., 1957, Cornell U., 1962. U.S. coordinator of info. Short Wave Research, Inc., N.Y.C., 1941-42; instr. Royal Norwegian Free Forces in Can., U.K. and Norway, 1942-45, Trondheim Katedralskole, Norway, 1945-46; instr. Norwegian and social studies Bay Ridge High Sch., Bklyn., 1951-63; asst. prof. edn. Bklyn. Coll., 1963-69, assoc. prof., 1970-73, prof. Judaic studies, 1973—, acting chmn. dept. Judaic studies, 1971-72, dep. chmn., 1972-75, chmn., 1975-80, faculty coordinator Judaic studies program, 1970—; instr. Norwegian CCNY, 1954-58, Internat. Summer Sch., U. Oslo, 1959; instr. contemporary civilization and econs. Bronx Community Coll., 1960-63; vis. assoc. prof. Cornell U., summer 1967, NYU, 1967-68; dir. grad. travel seminar in comparative and internat. edn. Queens Coll., summers 1969, 70; mem. faculty seminar Leo Baeck Inst., N.Y.C., 1976—, sec., 1977-82, adv. bd., 1978—; participant Ibsen Sesquicentennial Symposium, N.Y.C., 1977-78; research asso. UNESCO, 1967-69; cons. N.Y.C. Bd. Jewish Edn., 1956-71. Author: Sweden's Foreign Policy, 1957, Say It in Norwegian, 1957; Assoc. editor: Western European Education, 1968-72; contbg. editor: Edn. News and Notes, 1968-71, The Comprehensive History of the Holocaust (Yad Vashem); contbr. articles to scholarly jours. Mem. nat. gov. council Am. Jewish Congress, 1973—, v.p. Bklyn. div., 1975—, chmn. commn. Jewish affairs, 1977-80, co-chmn. com. on Jewish life and culture, 1980—; mem. acad. com. World Jewish Congress, 1979—; mem. adv. bd. Met. N.Y. Commn. on Tchr. Edn. and Profl. Standards, 1966-70; mem. staff religious sch. Temple Beth Emeth, 1952-57; mem. faculty Congregation Beth Elohim, Bklyn., 1956-61; sec. Center for Migratory Studies, Bklyn. Coll., 1965-76; mem. com. on planning and ednl.

policy, 1972-74; sec. Tribute to Danes, Inc., 1968-72, Norwegian Immigration Sesquicentennial Commn., 1973-75; mem. adv. bd. study-abroad program CUNY, 1968-70; now chmn. adv. council Scandinavian Seminars, Center European Studies; chmn. acad. com. Scandinavia Today, Am.-Scandinavian Found., 1981—; trustee Conservative Synagogue Fifth Ave., N.Y.C., 1967-80; dir. Bklyn. Coll. Summer Inst. in Israel, 1971-72, 73-74; adviser to academic council Am. Colls. Jerusalem, 1967-72; participant Ann. Am. Israeli Dialogue, Jerusalem, 1973, 77, 80; chmn. Kallah session Hillel Found., Bklyn. Coll., 1978-81. Decorated King Haakon VII Meml. medal, Royal Norwegian St. Olav medal, Norway; recipient Nat. Hillel Gold Key, 1970; hon. citation Alumni Assn. New Sch., 1971; scroll of honor State of Israel Bonds, 1975; award Ind. Jewish Student Union, Bklyn. Coll., 1978; honoree Salute to Scholars CUNY, 1982; Jewish Commn. on Edn. fellow, Israel, summer 1964; CUNY research award, 1975-76; fellow Meml. Found. for Jewish Culture, 1975-76, 81-82; Am. Council Learned Socs. grantee, 1981; Royal Norwegian Ministry grantee, 1981; NEH research grantee, 1982-83; N.Y. Council Humanities grantee, 1982-83. Mem. Norseman's League (advisory bd. 1954-60, dir. 1968-77, v.p. 1978-80), Am. Scandinavian Found. (chmn. library and info. com. 1965—, pres. N.Y. chpt. 1979-81), Doctorate Assn. N.Y. Educators (editor Lux et Veritas 1959-61), Soc. for Advancement Scandinavian Study, Ibsen Soc. Am. (sec. 1978—), Faculty Hillel Assn. (past pres.), AAUP, Am. Econs. Assn., Assn. Supervision and Curriculum Devel., NEA, Comparative Edn. Soc., History Edn. Soc., Modern Lang. Assn., N.Y. Soc. Exptl. Study Edn., Norwegian-Am. Hist. Assn. (exec. bd. 1981—), Am.-Jewish Hist. Soc., Nat. Assn. Temple Educators, Assn. Jewish Studies, Am. Acad. Jewish Research, Univ. Centers for Rational Alternatives (chpt. pres. 1969-70), World Union Jewish Studies, Conf. Jewish Social Studies, Am. Acad. Com. for Peace in Middle East, Nat. Council Jewish Edn., Am. Friends Hebrew U. Home: 4 Washington Square Village New York NY 10012 Office: Bklyn Coll Dept Judaic Studies Brooklyn NY 11210

ABRAHAMSON, JAMES ALAN, air force officer; b. Williston, N.D., May 19, 1933; s. Norval S. and Thelma B. (Helle) A.; m. Barbara Jean Northcott, Nov. 7, 1959; children: Kelly Anne, James A. B.S. in Aero. Engring., MIT, 1955; M.S. in Aerospace Engring., U. Okla., 1961. Commd. 2d lt. U.S. Air Force, 1955, advanced through grades to maj. gen., 1978, flight instr., Bryan AFB, Tex., 1957-59, spacecraft project officer Vela nuclear detection saltellite program, Los Angeles AF Sta., 1961-64; figher pilot Tactical Air Command, 1964; astronaut USAF Manned Orbiting Lab., 1967-69; mem. staff NACS, Exec. Office of Pres., 1969-71; program dir. Maverick Program, 1971-73; comdr. 495th text wing U.S. Air Force, Wright Patterson AFB, Ohio, 1973-74; insp. gen. Air Force Systems Command, 1974-76; system program dir., multinat. F-16 program U.S. Air Force, 1976—. Decorated D.S.M., Legion of Merit with one cluster, Air medal with cluster, Meritorious Service medal; recipient award Daedalian Weapon System Mgmt. Assn., Aerospace Power award Air Force Assn., Dayton. Home: 610 Young Dr Wright Patterson AFB OH 45433 Office: ASD-YP Wright Patterson AFB OH 45433

ABRAHAMSON, SHIRLEY SCHLANGER, justice Supreme Court Wisconsin; b. N.Y.C., Dec. 17, 1933; d. Leo and Ceil (Sauerteig) Schlanger; m. Seymour Abrahamson, Aug. 26, 1953; 1 son, Daniel Nathan. A.B., NYU, 1953; J.D., Ind. U., 1956; S.J.D., U. Wis., 1962. Bar: Wis. 1962. Asst. dir. Legis. Drafting Research Fund, Columbia U. Law Sch., 1957-60; since practiced in Madison; mem. firm Lafollette, Sinykin, Anderson & Abrahamson, 1962-76; justice Supreme Ct. Wis., Madison, 1976—; prof. U. Wis. Sch. Law, 1966—; Mem. Wis. Bd. Bar Commrs.; mem. adv. bd. Nat. Inst. Justice, U.S. Dept. Justice, 1980—; mem. Mayor's Adv. Com., Madison, 1968-70, Gov.'s Study Com. on Jud. Orgn., 1970-72; bd. visitors Ind. U. Sch. Law, 1972—; Bd. dirs. League Women Voters, Madison, 1963-65; Union council Wis. Union, U. Wis., 1970-71. Editor: Constitutions of the United States (National and State) 2 vols, 1962. Bd. dirs. Wis. Civil Liberties Union, 1968-72, chmn. Capital Area chpt., 1969. Mem. Am. Bar Assn. (council, sect. of legal edn. and admissions to the bar 1976—, mem. commn. on undergrad. edn. in law and the humanities 1978-79), Wis. Bar Assn., Dane County Bar Assn., Am. Law Inst., Order of Coif, Phi Beta Kappa. Office: State Capitol Rm 231E Madison WI 53702 *

ABRAHAMSON, STEPHEN, educator; b. Phila., Jan. 24, 1921; s. Philip and Hettie (Gillis) A.; m. Evelyn May Gager, Aug. 2, 1948; children: Philip Gager, David Lee. B.S. in Edn, Temple U., Phila., 1942, Ed.M., 1948; Ph.D., N.Y. U., 1951. High sch. tchr. in, Pa., 1942-43, 46-48; instr. secondary edn. Temple U., 1948-49; research asst. N.Y. U., 1949-51; field worker Bur. Intercultural Edn.-Yale U., 1951-52; mem. faculty U. Buffalo, 1952-63, prof. edn., 1959-63; dir. Ednl. Research Center, 1953-58; prof., chmn. dept. med. edn., dir. div. research in med. edn. U. So. Calif., 1963—; vis. prof. edn. Stanford U. Med. Sch., 1959-60; vis. prof. surgery U. Adelaide, Australia, 1974; mem.-at-large Nat. Bd. Med. Examiners, 1971-81; cons. in field. Co-author: Teaching and Learning in Medical Schools, 1961; Editorial bd.: Jour. Med. Edn, 1974-82. Served with USAAF, 1943-46. Mem. Am. Ednl. Research Assn., Assn. Am. Med. Colls., Phi Delta Kappa. Co-inventor computer-controlled patient simulator. Home: 1806 Fletcher St South Pasadena CA 91030 Office: 2025 Zonal Ave Los Angeles CA 90033

ABRAM, JOHN CHARLES, utilities company executive; b. Des Moines, Sept. 1, 1920; s. John C. and Mary (Jones) A.; m. Dorothy Buettner, Dec. 28, 1946; children: James Morgan, Susan Diane. Student, Glendale Coll., 1938-40; B.S. in Engring, UCLA, 1948. With Pacific Lighting Service Co., 1959-71; with So. Calif. Gas Co., 1951-57, 71—, sr. v.p., Angeles, 1974-81, vice chmn., 1980-81, chmn. bd., chief exec. officer, 1981—. Mgr. indsl. devel. Los Angeles C. of C., 1957-59; Bd. dirs. Los Angeles Central City Assn., 1974—, Hollywood Presbyn. Hosp. Found.; trustee Calif. Mus. Sci. and Industry Found. Served with USAAF, 1943-46. Mem. Pacific Coast Gas Assn. (dir. 1973-80, chmn. 1980-81), Am. Gas Assn. (dir. 1981—), Gas Research Inst. (dir. 1980, vice chmn. 1981-83, chmn. 1983-85), UCLA Alumni Assn., U. Calif. at Berkeley Alumni Assn. Republican. Congregationalist. Clubs: Calif., Los Angeles, Oakmont Country. Office: 810 S Flower St Los Angeles CA 90017

ABRAM, MORRIS BERTHOLD, lawyer, former university president; b. Fitzgerald, Ga., June 19, 1918; s. Sam and Irene (Cohen) A.; m. Jane Maguire, Dec. 23, 1943 (div. 1974); children: Ruth, Ann, Morris Berthold, Jonathan Adam, Joshua Anthony; m. Carlyn Feldman Fisher, Jan. 25, 1975. A.B. summa cum laude, U. Ga., 1938; J.D., U. Chgo., 1940; B.A. (Rhodes scholar), Oxford U., 1948, M.A., 1953; LL.D., Davidson Coll., 1972, Yeshiva U., 1975. Partner Paul, Weiss, Rifkind, Wharton & Garrison, N.Y.C., 1962-68; pres. Brandeis Univ., Waltham, Mass., 1968-70; partner law firm Paul, Weiss, Rifkind, Wharton & Garrison, N.Y.C., 1970—; Pros. staff Internat. Mil. Tribunal, Nurnberg, Germany, 1946; asst. to dir. Com. for Marshall Plan, 1948; regional counsel WSB; gen. counsel Peace Corps, 1961; mem. subcom. on prevention of discrimination and protection of minorities UN, 1963-65; U.S. rep. UN Commn. Human Rights, 1965-68; co-chmn. planning conf. White House Conf. on Civil Rights, 1965; mem. exec. com. President's Nat. Com. Community Relations, 1964-68; chmn. Moreland Act Commn. on Nursing Homes and Residential Facilities, 1975-76, Pres.'s Commn. for Study of Ethics in Medicine and Biomed. and Behavioral Research, 1979-83; vice chmn. U.S. Commn. Civil Rights, 1984—; lectr. Oxford U. (Eng.). Author: The Day is Short, 1982; co-author: How to Stop Violence in Your Community, 1950. Pres. Family Serv. Soc. of, Fulton, DeKalb, Cobb counties, 1957-59; chmn. Atlanta Citizens Crime Com., 1958-60; nat. pres. Am. Jewish Com., 1963-68; Bd. dirs. 20th Century Fund; pres. Field Found., 1965—; bd. dirs. Morehouse Coll., Inst. Internat. Edn., Council Fgn. Relations; trustee Weizmann Inst. Sci., 1966—, Sarah Lawrence Coll., 1971-74, Inst. Internat. Edn., 1969-74; chmn. United Negro Coll. Fund, 1970-79; chmn. bd. Benjamin N. Cardozo Law Sch., Yeshiva U., 1976-79; mem. Nat. Adv. Council Econ. Opportunity, 1967-68. Served to maj. USAAF, 1941-45. Decorated Legion of Merit, 1946. Fellow (hon.), Pembroke Coll., Oxford U., Am. Coll. Trial Lawyers; mem. Lawyers Club Atlanta, N.Y. State, Am., Ga., Atlanta bar assns., Assn. Bar City N.Y., Phi Beta Kappa, Omicron Delta Kappa, Phi Kappa Phi. Home: 15 W 81st St New York NY 10024 Office: 1121 Vermont Ave NW Washington DC 20425

ABRAM, PRUDENCE BEATTY, bankruptcy judge; b. Kingston, R.I., Nov. 19, 1942; d. Kenneth Orion and Mary Catharine (Carter) Beatty; m. Sam Laud Abram, Dec. 21, 1968; 1 dau., Andrea Beatty. B.A., U. Mich., 1964, J.D. cum laude, 1968. Bar: Mich. 1969, N.Y. 1971, U.S. Dist. Ct. for so. dist. N.Y. 1972, U.S. Dist. Ct. for eastern div. N.Y. 1972, U.S. Ct. Appeals for 2d circuit 1972, U.S. Supreme Ct. 1979. Assoc. firm Breed Abbott & Morgan, N.Y.C., 1970-72, Weil Gotshal & Manges, 1972-78, Krause, Hirsch & Gross, 1978-79; ptnr. firm Stroock & Stroock & Lavan, N.Y.C., 1980-82; judge U.S. Bankruptcy Ct. for So. Dist. N.Y., N.Y.C., 1982—. Mem. ABA (bus. bankruptcy com. 1976—), Assn. Bar City N.Y. Home: 200 E 57th St New York NY 10022 Office: US Banruptcy Ct 40 Foley Sq New York NY 10007

ABRAMOFF, PETER, biology educator; b. Montreal, Que., Can., Dec. 28, 1927; came to U.S., 1950, naturalized, 1958; s. William and Dora Ann (Sherman) A.; m. Therese J. Trzcinko, June 6, 1953; children—Mark Kevin, Ann Marie, Monica Marie, Kathryn Mary, Bonnie Marie, Phillip Daniel. B.Sc., U. Western Ont., 1950; M.Sc., U. Detroit, 1952; Ph.D., U. Wis., 1955. Teaching asst. biology Assumption Coll., 1948-50, U. Detroit, 1950-52; instr. biology Marquette U., Milw., 1955-59, asst. prof., 1959-62, asso. prof., 1962-67, summer chmn. dept., 1963, 64, asst. chmn., 1964-65, chmn., 1965—, prof., 1967—; asso. dir. biology sect. NSF In-service Inst. Sci. and Math., 1961-62, Wehr Disting. prof. biology, 1978—; clin. prof. immunology Med. Coll., Wis., 1972—; guest scholar Kans. State U., 1962. Author: (with Thomson) Laboratory Outlines in Biology, 1963, Teacher's Handbook for Laboratory Outlines in Biology, 1963, (wth Thomson) An Experimental Approach to Biology, 1966, (with Thomson) Teacher's Handbook for an Experimental Approach to Biology, 1966, Laboratory Studies in Animal Biology, 1966, Teacher's Handbook for Laboratory Studies in Animal Biology, 1966, Investigations of Cells Organisms, 1968, Teacher's Manual for Investigations of Cells and Organisms, 1968, (with LaVia) Biology of the Immune Response, 1970, (with Thomson) Laboratory Outlines in Biology II, 1972, Laboratory Manual: Biology and Man, 1975, An Experimental Approach to Biology, 2d edit., 1976, Laboratory Outlines in Zoology, 1978, Laboratory Outlines in Biology III, 1982; Contbr articles to profl. jours. Recipient biol. scis. proficiency award Assumption Coll., 1950; Wis. Alumni Research Found. fellow, 1952-54; USPHS fellow U. Wis., 1954-55. Mem. Am. Assn. Immunologists, Am. Inst. Biol. Scis., Am. Inst. Zoologists (sec. div. comparative immunology), Reticuloendothelial Soc. (pres. 1980), Internt. Union Reticuloendothelial Socs. (sec. 1977—), Soc. Exptl. Biology and Medicine, Sigma Xi. Home: 18200 Chevy Chase Dr Brookfield WI 53005 Office: Biology Dept Marquette U Milwaukee WI 53233

ABRAMOVICE, BEN, hospital administrator; b. Chgo., Dec. 12, 1932; s. Norman Wolfe and Rose (Kushner) A. A.B. in Zoology, U. Calif.-Berkeley, 1954; M.B.A. in Hosp. Adminstrn., U. Chgo., 1960. Adminstrv. asst. Ohio State U. Med. Ctr., Columbus, 1959-61; asst. dir. Jewish Home for Aged, San Francisco, 1961-66; adminstr. Parkland Convalescent Hosp., San Leandro, Calif., 1966-69; dir. planning and devel. Jewish Welfare Fedn., Oakland, Calif., 1969-71; exec. dir. Home for Jewish Parents, Oakland, 1971-81; exec. adminstr. Laguna Honda Hosp., San Francisco, 1981—; mem. White House Conf. on Aging; instr. Golden Gate U.; lectr.; mem. Jewish Commn. on Aging., Bd. Examiners Nursing Home Adminstrs. State of Calif., numerous panels on long term care. Contbr. articles to profl. jours.; author video and films. Bd. dirs. Berkeley Law Found.; bd. dirs City Art Celebration, San Francisco. Served with U.S. Army, 1956-58. Mem. Am. Assn. Homes for Aging (ho. of dels.), Western Gerontol. Soc. (Past chmn. pub. policy and legis. action com.), Calif. Assn. Homes for Aging (pres. 1975-77, Pres.'s award of merit 1980), Am. Hosp. Assn., Gerontol. Soc., Nat. Assn. Jewish Homes for Aging (dir., chmn. seminar). Office: Laguna Honda Hosp 375 Laguna Honda Blvd San Francisco CA 94116

ABRAMOVITZ, MAX, architect; b. Chgo., May 23, 1908; s. Benjamin and Sophia (Maimon) A.; m. Anne Marie Causey, Sept. 4, 1937 (div.); children: Michael John, Katherine Paul; m. Anita Zeltner Brooks, Feb. 29, 1964. B.S., U. Ill., 1929; M.S., Columbia U., 1931; postgrad., Ecole des Beaux Arts, 1932-34; D.F.A. (hon.), U. Pitts., 1961, U. Ill., 1970. Partner firm Harrison & Abramovitz, architects, 1945-76, Abramovitz-Harris-Kingsland, architects, N.Y.C., 1976—; asso. prof. Yale U. Sch. Fine Arts, 1939-42; dep. dir. UN Hdqrs. Planning Office, 1947-52; Cons. Brandeis U., U. Pitts. Prin. works include U.S. Steel Bldg, Pitts., Nationwide Ins, Columbus, Ohio, Assembly Hall and Krannert Center Performing Arts, U. Ill.-Urbana; chapels Brandeis U; major campus devel. La Banque Rothschild, Paris, France, Groupe des Assurances Nationales, LaDefense, France. Trustee Mt. Sinai Med. Center, N.Y.C. Served with C.E. AUS, 1942-45; col., 1950-52; spl. asst. to asst. sec. air force, Mar. 1952-July 1952. Recipient Legion of Merit fellow Brandeis U., 1963; Achievement award U. Ill. Alumni Assn., 1963. Fellow AIA; mem. Am. Soc. C.E., Regional Plan Assn. (chmn. bd. 1966-68, dir. 1968—), Archtl. League N.Y., N.Y. Bldg. Congress (gov. 1957-64). Club: Century Assn. (N.Y.C.). Home: 930 Fifth Ave New York NY 10021 Office: 630 Fifth Ave New York NY 10111

ABRAMOVITZ, MOSES, economist, educator; b. Bklyn., Jan. 1, 1912; s. Nathan and Betty (Goldenberg) A.; m. Carrie Glasser, June 23, 1937; 1 son, Joel Nathan. A.B., Harvard, 1932; Ph.D., Columbia, 1939. Instr. Harvard, 1936-38; mem. research staff Nat. Bur. Econ. Research, 1938-69; lectr. Columbia, 1940-42, 46-48; prof. econs. Stanford, 1948—, Coe prof. Am. econ. history, exec. head dept. econs., 1963-65, 71-74; vis. prof. U. Pa., 1955; prin. economist WPB, 1942, OSS, 1943-44; econ. adviser to U.S. rep. on Allied Commn. on Reparations, 1945-46, to sec.-gen. Orgn. for Econ. Coop. and Devel., 1962-63; vis. fellow All Souls Coll., Oxford, Eng., 1968. Author: Price Theory for a Changing Economy, 1939, Inventories and Business Cycles, 1950, (with Vera Eliasberg) The Growth of Public Employment in Great Britain, 1957; also articles.; Editor: Capital Formation and Economic Growth, 1955; mng. editor: Jour. Econ. Lit., 1981—. Served as lt. AUS, 1944-45. Fellow Am. Acad. Arts and Sciences; Distinguished fellow Am. Econ. Assn. (pres. 1980), Am. Statis. Assn.; mem. Am. Econ. History Assn., Phi Beta Kappa. Home: 762 Dolores St Stanford CA 94305 Office: Stanford University Stanford CA 94305

ABRAMOWICZ, ALFRED L., bishop; b. Chgo., Jan. 27, 1919. Ed., St. Mary Sem., Mundelein; J.C.L., Gregorian U., Rome. Ordained priest Roman Catholic Ch., 1943; papal chamberlain, very rev. msgr. and officialis Chgo. Archdiocesan Ct. when named titular bishop of paestum and aux. of Chgo., 1968, consecrated bishop, 1968. Home: 4327 S Richmond Ave Chicago IL 60632

ABRAMOWITZ, MORTON I., ambassador; b. Lakewood, N.J., Jan. 20, 1933; s. Mendel and Dora (Smith) A.; m. Sheppie Glass, Sept. 13, 1959; children: Michael, Rachel. B.A., Stanford U.; M.A., Harvard U., 1955. Joined U.S. Fgn. Service, 1960; 3d sec., vice consul, Taipei, Formosa, 1960-62; with Fgn. Area and Lang. Tng. Center, Taichung, Taiwan, 1962-63; consul, polit. officer, Hong Kong, 1963-66; assigned Bur. Econ. Affairs, 1966-68; Sr. Inter dept. Group, 1968-69; spl. asst. under-sec. state, 1969-71; research asso. Inst. for Strategic Studies, 1971; asst. to sec. of def., 1972-73; polit. adviser to Comdr.-in-Chief Pacific, 1973-78; also dep. asst. sec. def. for Inter-Am., E. Asia and Pacific, 1974-78, ambassador to, Bangkok, Thailand, 1978-83, U.S. rep. to Mutual and Balanced Force Reduction Negotiations, Vienna, 1983—. Author: (with Richard Moorsteen) Remaking China Policy, 1972, Moving the Glacier, the Two Koreas and the Powers, 1972, East Asian Actors and Issues; contbr. articles aspects Taiwan's econ. growth. Served with AUS, 1957. Recipient Disting. Public Service award Dept. Def., 1976, Sec. Def. Disting. Service award, 1978; Joseph C. Wilson award, 1980; Pres's award for disting. fed. service, 1981. Mem. Phi Beta Kappa. Home: 5026 Klingle St NW Washington DC 20016 Office: US MBFR Delegation 11 Obersteinergasse Vienna Austria

ABRAMS, BERNARD WILLIAM, construction, manufacturing property development company executive; b. West Palm Beach, Fla., Jan. 21, 1925; s. Alfred Robert and Sara Lee (Kaufman) A.; m. Susan Miller Block, Oct. 23, 1955; children: David Louis, Janet Beth, Judith Frances. B.S., U.S. Mil. Acad., 1947. With Abrams Industries, Inc., Atlanta, 1953—, chmn. bd., chief exec. officer, 1971—; dir. Bank South Corp., Atlanta. Nat. keynote speaker ARC campaign, 1953; chmn. appointments com. Armed Forces Acads., 5th Congressional Dist. of Ga., 1968-70; bd. dirs. Hank Aaron Scholarship Fund, 1974-76; co-chmn. Atlanta Com. for Devel. U.S. Army Inf. Mus., Ft. Benning, Ga., 1976; gen. chmn. United Way campaign, 1975-76; pres. Atlanta Area council Boy Scouts Am., 1977-79; active USO Council Greater Atlanta, 1979; mem. adv. com. Ga. Tech. Inst. Coll. Indsl. Mgmt., 1978; active Jewish Welfare Fedn., 1975-78; civilian aide to Sec. of Army, 1978—; mem. Ga. Gov.'s Edn. Commn., chmn. definition com., 1983-84; trustee West Point Cadet Jewish Chapel, 1966—. Served to capt. U.S. Army, 1947-53; Korea. Decorated Silver Star, Bronze Star with V, Purple Heart with oak leaf cluster, Combat Infantry badge; recipient Silver Beaver award Boy Scouts Am., 1972; Disting. Service award United Way, 1975; USO World Bd. Govs. award, 1984. Mem. Assn. U.S. Army (pres. 3d region 1966-67, cert. of appreciation 1965, citation 1978), Ga. Bus. and Industry Assn. (Appreciation award 1972), Assn. for Corp. Growth (pres. 1981), Concerned Businessmen's Forum, West Point Soc. of Atlanta (pres. 1959-62), Assn. Grads. U.S. Mil. Acad. (trustee 1959-62), Phi Eta Sigma. Republican. Clubs: Commerce, Standard, B'nai B'rith (Outstanding Lodge Pres. citation 1972). Office: Abrams Industries Inc PO Box 76600 Atlanta GA 30328

ABRAMS, BURT JAY, lawyer; b. Bklyn., Oct. 21, 1934; s. Samuel W. and Beatrice (Blick) A.; m. Fern Broida, Jan. 7, 1960; children: Janis Claire, Alison Sloan. A.B., Princeton U., 1955; J.D., Harvard U., 1958. Bar: N.Y. 1959, D.C. 1962, U.S. Supreme Ct. 1962, U.S. Tax Ct. 1963. Atty., advisor Tax Ct. of U.S., Washington, 1958-60; atty. U.S. Dept. Justice, Washington, 1960-62; assoc. firm Milbank, Tweed, Hadley & McCloy, N.Y.C., 1962-68, ptnr., 1969—. Contbr. articles to profl. jours. Trustee Orange Valley Social Settlement, West Orange, N.J., 1972—, pres., West Orange, N.J., 1978-80. Mem. ABA, N.Y. Bar Assn. (tax sect. exec. com. 1973-74), Bar Assn. City N.Y., Harvard Law Sch. Assn. N.Y.C., Princeton Alumni Assn. Essex County. Jewish. Clubs: Knoll Country, Wall St. Office: 1 Chase Manhattan Plaza New York NY 10005

ABRAMS, EDWARD MARVIN, construction company executive; b. South Bend, Ind., Mar. 13, 1927; s. Alfred Robert and Sara Lee (Kaufman) A.; m. Ann Uhry, Oct. 11, 1953; children: Alan Ralph, Laurie, James Andrew. Student, Ga. Inst. Tech., 1947-48; B.S. cum laude, U. Notre Dame, 1950; grad., Naval Officer Candidate Sch., 1951. Pres. Abrams Industries, Inc., Atlanta, 1953—, also dir.; chmn. bd. Fin. Properties Developers, Inc.; mem. faculty Univ. of Shopping Centers. Mem. interreligious affairs com. Am. Jewish Com., 1969—, chmn. Atlanta chpt., 1971-73, mem. nat. task force on social club discrimination; mem. adv. council Coll. Arts and Letters, U. Notre Dame, 1972—, chmn., 1977-78; co-chmn. Ga. region NCCJ, 1977—; active United Way Metro Atlanta. Served with USN, 1945-47, 50-52. Mem. Internat. Council Shopping Centers, Urban Land Inst., Ga. Engring. Soc., Atlanta C. of C. (chmn. aviation task force com. 1981), Notre Dame Alumni Assn. Clubs: Rotary; Commerce, Notre Dame (Atlanta). Home: 3770 Paces Ferry Rd Atlanta GA 30327 Office: 5775-A Glenridge Dr Suite 205 Atlanta GA 30328

ABRAMS, ELLIOTT, government official; b. N.Y.C., Jan. 24, 1948; s. Joseph and Mildred (Kauder) A.; m. Rachel Decter, Mar. 9, 1980; children: Jacob, Sarah. B.A., Harvard U., 1969, J.D., 1973; M.S. in Econs, London Sch. Econs., 1970. Bar: N.Y. bar 1974, D.C. bar 1979. Atty. Breed, Abbott & Morgan, N.Y.C., 1974-75; asst. counsel U.S. Senate Permanent Subcom. on Investigations, Washington, 1975; spl. counsel Sen. Henry M. Jackson, 1975-76, Sen. Daniel P. Moynihan, 1977-78, chief of staff, 1978-79; atty. Verner, Liipfert, Bernhard & McPherson, Washington, 1979-80; asst. sec. for internat. orgn. affairs U.S. Dept. State, Washington, 1981, asst. sec. for human rights and humanitarian affairs, 1981—. Mem. Am. Jewish Com. Mem. Council Fgn. Relations. Office: Dept State Rm 7802 Washington DC 20520

ABRAMS, EUGENE BERNARD, cons.; b. Trenton, N.J., Oct. 10, 1919; s. Herman and Sarah (Hirschson) A.; m. Monique Leiba, Apr. 28, 1950; children—Monique, Segal, Jacqueline Segal. Student, U. So. Calif., 1946-47, U. Paris, France, 1947-48; B.A., U. Md., 1956. Joined U.S. Fgn. Service, 1948; assigned Embassy, Paris, 1948-51, ECA mission to, France, 1951-52, ECA office spl. rep., Paris, 1952-58; with Office African Affairs, ICA, Washington, 1958-61; dep. dir. AID mission to, Guinea, Conakry, 1961-63, AID affairs officer, Abidjan, Ivory Coast, 1963-65; chief tech. assistance policies div. OECD, Paris, 1965-67, head econ. devel. div., 1967-68; dir. tech. assistance Orgn. for Rehab. Through Tng., 1968-79; cons. internat. econ. affairs, 1980—; gen. mgr. Action for Devel. Internat., 1981—. Served to 2d lt. USAAF, 1939-45. Mem. Soc. Internat. Devel. (vice chmn. Swiss chpt.), Internat. Council Voluntary Agys. (treas. governing bd., chmn. econ. and social devel. commn.). Home: 41 Chemin de Planta 1223 Cologny Switzerland

ABRAMS, FLOYD, lawyer; b. N.Y.C., July 9, 1936; s. Isadore and Rae (Eberlin) A.; m. Efrat Surasky, Dec. 25, 1963; children: Daniel, Ronnie. B.A., Cornell U., 1956; LL.B., Yale U., 1960. Bar: N.Y. 1961. Research asst. dept. politics Princeton U., 1960-61; law clk. to Paul Leahy U.S. Dist. Ct., Wilmington, Del., 1961-63; assoc. firm Cahill Gordon & Reindel, N.Y.C., 1963-70, ptnr., 1970—; vis. lectr. Yale U., 1974-79; assoc. in journalism Grad. Sch. Journalism, Columbia U., 1980; lectr. Law Sch., Columbia U., 1981—. Mem. bd editors: N.Y. Law Jour., 1983—. Bd. dirs. Mexican Am. Legal Def. and Ednl. Fund, Dalton Sch., 1978-81, Ams. Watch, 1982-83, Dalton Sch., 1978-84; v.p. Dalton Sch., 1982-83; bd. dirs. media and soc. seminars, 1980—, vice chmn., 1983—. Mem. ABA (chmn. rights of expression com. individual rights sect. 1976-79, Ross essay prize 1967, chmn. freedom of speech and press com. litigation sect. 1977-79, mem. forum com. 1979-80, amicus curiae com. 1980-82), Assn. Bar City N.Y. (comml. law com. 1978-82). Home: 1136 Fifth Ave New York NY 10028 Office: 80 Pine St New York NY 10005

ABRAMS, HERBERT KERMAN, physician, educator; b. Chgo., 1913. B.S., Northwestern U.; M.D., M.S., U. Ill., 1940; M.P.H., Johns Hopkins, 1947. Intern Cook County Hosp., Chgo., 1940-41; chief Bur. of Adult Health, Calif. Health Dept., 1947-52; dir. Chgo. Union Health Service, 1953-66; dir. dept. community medicine Chgo. Med. Sch.-Mt. Sinai Hosp., Chgo., 1966-68; prof., head dept. family community medicine U. Ariz., Tucson, 1968-78; dir. Ariz. Center for Occupational Safety and Health, 1978—. Served with USPHS. Mem. AMA, Am. Public Health Assn. (v.p. 1981-82), Assn. Tchrs. Preventive Medicine, Am. Occupational Med. Assn. Office: Ariz Center Occupational Safety and Health Ariz Health Scis Center U Ariz Tucson AZ 85724

ABRAMS, HERBERT LEROY, radiologist, educator; b. N.Y.C., Aug. 16, 1920; s. Morris and Freda (Sugarman) A.; m. Marilyn Spitz, Mar. 23, 1943; children: Nancy, John. B.A., Cornell U., 1941; M.D., State U. Medicine, N.Y., 1946. Diplomate: Am. Bd. Radiology. Intern L.I. Coll. Hosp., 1946-47; resident in internal medicine Montefiore Hosp., Bronx, N.Y., 1947-48; resident in radiology Stanford U. Hosp., 1948-51; practice medicine specializing in radiology Stanford, Calif., 1951-67; faculty Sch. Medicine Stanford, 1951-67, dir. div. diagnostic roentgenology, 1961-67, prof. radiology, 1962-67; Philip H. Cook prof. radiology Harvard U., 1967-80, chmn. dept. radiology, 1967-80; radiologist-in-chief Peter Bent Brigham Hosp., Boston, 1967-80; chmn. dept. radiology Brigham and Women's Hosp., Boston, 1981—; radiologist-in-chief Sidney Farber Cancer Inst., Boston, 1974—; R.H. Nimmo vis. prof. U. Adelaide, Australia; mem. radiation study sect. NIH, 1962-66; cons. to hosps., profl. socs. Author: (with others) Congenital Heart Disease, 1965; Coronary Arteriography: A Practical Approach, 1983; Editor: Angiography, 1961, 3d edit., 1983, Investigative Radiology; editor-in-chief: Cardiovascular and Interventional Radiology Postgrad. Radiology; Contbr. (with others) articles to profl. jours. Nat. Cancer Inst. fellow, 1950; Spl. Research fellow Nat. Heart Inst., 1960, 73-74; David M. Gould Meml. lectr. Johns Hopkins, 1964; William R. Whitman Meml. lectr., 1968; Leo G. Rigler lectr. Tel-Aviv U., 1969; Holmes lectr. New Eng. Roentgen Ray Soc., Boston, 1970; Ross Golden lectr. N.Y. Roentgen Ray Soc., N.Y.C., 1971; Stauffer Meml. lectr. Phila. Roentgen Ray Soc., 1971; J.M.T. Finney Fund lectr. Md. Radiol. Soc., Ocean City, 1972; Aubrey Hampton lectr. Mass. Gen. Hosp., Boston, 1974; Kirklin-Weber lectr. Mayo Clinic, 1974; Crookshank lectr. Royal Coll. Radiology, 1980; W.H. Herbert lectr. U. Calif.; Caldwell lectr. Am. Roentgen Ray Soc., 1982; Percy lectr. McMaster Med. Sch., 1983; Henry J. Kaiser sr. fellow Center for Advanced Study in Behavioral Sci., 1980-81. Hon. fellow Royal Coll. Radiology; mem. Assn. Univ. Radiologists (Gold medal 1984), Inst. Medicine, Am. Coll. Radiology, Am. Heart Assn., Am. Soc. Nephrology, Radiol. Soc. N.Am., N.Am. Soc. Cardiac Radiology (pres. 1979-80), Soc. Cardiovascular Radiology, Mass. Radiologic Soc., Soc. Chmn. Acad. Radiology Depts. (pres. 1970-71), Phi Beta Kappa, Alpha Omega Alpha. Home: 433 Walnut St Brookline MA 02146 Office: Harvard Med Sch Boston MA 02115

ABRAMS, IRWIN, emeritus history educator; b. San Francisco, Feb. 24, 1914; s. J. Lewis and Belle (Newman) A.; m. Freda Webster Morrill, June 30, 1939; children: David Morrill, Carol Webster (Mrs. Veijo Abrams-Reis), James Lawrence. A.B. with great distinction, Stanford, 1934; A.M., Harvard, 1935; Ph.D., Harvard U., 1938. Instr. history Stanford U., 1938-43; personnel officer, dir. fgn. service tng. Am. Friends Service Com., 1943-46; dir. Quaker Overseas Work Camps, 1946-47; mem. faculty Antioch Coll., 1947-79, prof. history, 1951-79, chmn., dept., 1949-60, 64-66; Disting. Univ. prof. Antioch U., 1979-81, Disting. Univ. prof. emeritus, 1981—; specialist Dept. State exchange program, Germany, 1953; chmn. internat. student seminars Am. Friends Service Com., Europe, summers 1956, 57, 64; ednl. dir. shipboard programs Council Student Travel, summers 1956-64; Fulbright lectr. U. Cologne, Germany, 1961; dir. Yugoslav seminar Great Lakes Colls. Assn., summers 1965-67, 69-70, 72, co-dir., Poland, 1974, Task Force on Internat. Edn., Internat. City Mgmt. Assn., 1976; adv. council grad. fellowship program Danforth Found., 1969-72; cons. on internat. edn. U.S. Office Edn., Inst. Internat. Edn.; bd. dirs. Council Internat. Ednl. Exchange, 1969-73; co-ordinator internat. programs Great Lakes Coll. Assn., 1967-73, dir. European term on comparative urban studies, 1972-75; Sheldon Traveling fellow Harvard, 1936-37. Author: (with others) History of World Civilization, 1957, Study Abroad, 1960, Journey Through a Wall: A Quaker Mission to Divided Germany, 1964, (with David Arnold) The American College and International Education, 1967; Bd. editors: Antioch Rev, 1955-71. Mem. Internat. Studies Assn., Conf. on Peace Research in History (council 1978-79), Soc. Values in Higher Edn. (postdoctoral fellow 1951), Internat. Soc. Ednl., Cultural and Sci. Interchange (v.p. 1976-78, pres. 1978-82), Phi Beta Kappa., Soc. of Friends. Home: 913 Xenia Ave Yellow Springs OH 45387

ABRAMS, JULES CLINTON, psychologist; b. Phila., June 4, 1927; s. Abraham and Sara (Rubinoff) A.; m. Ellen Shuman, Aug. 7, 1955; children—Richard, Robbi, Larry, Nancy. Student, La Salle Coll., 1944-45; A.B., Temple U., 1948, M.A., 1949, Ph.D., 1955, U. Toronto, 1949-50. Psychologist Sklar Sch., Phila., 1956-60; dir. Reading Improvement Inst., Pa., 1955-64; prof. psychiatry, head sect. psychology, dir. Inst. for Learning; dir. grad. edn. in psychology Hahnemann Med. Coll., Phila., 1968—; prof. Johns Hopkins, 1975—. Author: Diagnosis, Correction, and Prevention of Reading Disabilities; Contbr. numerous articles to profl. jours. Pres. Parkway Day Sch., Phila., 1966-76. Fellow Am. Psychol. Assn.; mem. Assn. for Child Psychoanalysis, AAAS, Internat. Reading Assn., N.Y. Acad. Sci., Council for Exceptional Children, Sigma Xi. Home: 1505 Paper Mill Rd Philadelphia PA 19118 Office: 230 N Broad St Philadelphia PA 19102

ABRAMS, LEE NORMAN, lawyer; b. Chgo., Feb. 28, 1935; s. Saul E. and Evelyn (Cohen) A.; m. Myrna Parker, Dec. 26, 1965; 1 dau., Elana Shira. A.B., U. Mich., 1951, J.D., 1957. Bar: Ill. 1957, U.S. Tax Ct. 1972, U.S. Supreme Ct. 1961. Assoc. firm Mayer, Brown & Platt and predecessors, Chgo., 1957-66, ptnr., 1966—. Mem. visitors com. U. Mich. Law Sch., 1970—; bd. assocs. Nat. Coll. Edn., Chgo., 1973—. Recipient gold medal Am. Inst. C.P.A.s, 1958. Mem. ABA (council antitrust sect. 1975-77, fin. officer antirtrust sect. 1977-81, chmn. FTC com. 1972-75, forum com on franchising 1981—), Chgo. Bar Assn. (antitrust law com. 1970—), U.S. C. of C. (antitrust and trade regulation com. 1974-80). Home: 2315 Meadow Dr S Wilmette Il 60091 Office: Mayer Brown & Platt 231 S LaSalle St Chicago IL 60604

ABRAMS, MEYER HOWARD, educator; b. Long Branch, N.J., July 23, 1912; s. Joseph and Sarah (Shanes) A.; m. Ruth Gaynes, Sept. 1, 1937; children: Jane, Judith. A.B., Harvard U., 1934, M.A., 1937, Ph.D., 1940; postgrad. (Henry fellow), Cambridge (Eng.) U., 1934-35; D.H.L. (hon.), U. Rochester, 1978, Northwestern U., 1981, U. Chgo., 1982. Instr. Harvard, 1938-42; research asso. psycho-acoustic lab. Harvard U., 1942-45; asst. prof. English, Cornell U., Ithaca, N.Y., 1945-47, asso. prof., 1947-53, prof., 1953-60, Frederic J. Whiton prof. English,, 1960-73, Class of 1916 prof. English, 1973—; adv. editor W.W. Norton & Co., Inc., 1961—; bd. editors various Cornell publs. Hon. sr. fellow Sch. Criticism and Theory, Northwestern U.; Fulbright lectr. Royal U. Malta, Cambridge U., 1953; Roache lectr. U. Ind., 1963; Alexander lectr. U. Toronto, 1964; Ewing lectures UCLA, 1975; Cecil Green lectr. U. B.C., 1980; Mem. founders group Nat. Humanities Center; mem. council of scholars Library of Congress, 1980—, chmn. counci of scholars, 1984. Author: The Milk of Paradise, 1934, 2d edit., 1970, The Mirror and the Lamp: Romantic Theory and the Critical Tradition, 1953, A Glossary of Literary Terms, 1957, 4th edit., 1981, Natural Supernaturalism: Tradition and Revolution in Romantic Literature, 1971, The Correspondent Breeze: Essays on English Romanticism, 1984, also publs. on mil. communications; editor: The Poetry of Pope, 1954; Editor: Literature and Belief, 1958, The Romantic Poets: Modern Essays in Criticism, 1960, rev. edit., 1975, The Norton Anthology of English Literature, 1962, 4th edit., 1979, Wordsworth: A Collection of Critical Essays, 1972, (with others) Wordsworth's Prelude: Norton Critical Edition, 1979. Recipient Christian Gauss prize Phi Beta Kappa, 1954, James Russell Lowell prize, 1971, Am. Acad. award humanistic studies, 1984; Rockefeller fellow, 1946; Ford fellow, 1952; Guggenheim fellow, 1958, 60-61; fellow Center for Advanced Study in the Behavioral Scis. Stanford U., 1967-68; vis. fellow All Soul's Coll., Oxford, 1977. Mem. AAUP, MLA (exec. council 1961-64), Am. Acad. Arts and Scis., Am. Philos. Soc., Phi Beta Kappa, Sigma Xi. Home: 512 Highland Rd Ithaca NY 14850

ABRAMS, MUHAL RICHARD, pianist, composer; b. Chgo., Sept. 19, 1930. Student, Chgo. Music Coll. Profl. debut, 1948; writer music for, King Fleming Band, 1950; pianist, arranger, composer, MJT plus 3, 1955; formed big band, The Exptl. Band, 1961; founder: Assn. Advancement Creative Music, Chgo., 1965; accompanist, Art Ensemble Chgo., Anthony Braxton; compositions include The Bird Song; albums include Creative Construction Company, Blues Forever, Mama & Daddy, 1 = OQA + 19, Rejoicing with the Light, Sightsong, Spihumonesty. Recipient Poll award Down Beat Critics, 1974. Address: care Press Relations Black Saint Label Rounder Records Corp 186 Willow Ave Somerville MA 10019 *

ABRAMS, NORMAN, legal educator; b. Chgo., July 7, 1933; s. Harry A. and Gertrude (Dick) A.; m. Toshka Alster, 1977; children: Marshall David, Julie, Hanna. A.B., U. Chgo., 1952, J.D., 1955. Bar: Ill. 1956. Asso.-in-law Columbia U. Law Sch., 1955-57; research asso. Harvard Law Sch., 1957-59; sec. Harvard-Brandeis Coop. Research for Israel's Legal Devel., 1957-58, dir., 1959; mem. faculty Law Sch. UCLA, 1959—, prof. law, 1964—, co-dir. Ctr. for Internat. and Strategic Studies, 1982-83; vis. prof. Hebrew U., 1969-70, Bar Ilan U., 1970-71, spring 1978, U. So. Calif., summer 1972, spring 1973, Stanford U., fall 1977, U. Calif. at Berkeley, fall 1977, Loyola U., Los Angeles, summers 1974, 75, 76, 79; spl. asst. to U.S. atty. gen., also prof.-in-residence criminal div. Dept. Justice, 1966-67; reporter for So. Calif. indigent accused persons study Am. Bar Found., 1963; cons. Gov. Calif. Commn. Los Angeles Riots, 1965; Pres.'s. Commn. Law Enforcement and Adminstrn. Justice, 1966-67, Nat. Commn. on Reform of Fed. Criminal Laws, 1967-69, Rand Corp., 1968-74, Center for Adminstrv. Justice, Am. Bar Assn., 1973-77, Nat. Adv. Commn. on Criminal Justice Standards, Organized Crime Task Force, 1976; spl. hearing officer, conscientious objector cases U.S. Dept. Justice, 1967-68. Chmn. Jewish Conciliation Bd., Los Angeles, 1975-81; bd. dirs. Bet Tzedek Los Angeles Hillel Council.; chmn. So. Calif. region Am. Profs. for Peace in Middle East, 1981-83. Mem. Phi Beta Kappa. Office: 405 Hilgard Ave Los Angeles CA 90024

ABRAMS, PHILIP, U.S. government official; b. Boston, Nov. 13, 1939; s. Julius and Eva (Hodess) A.; m. Rosalyn Merle Heifetz, Aug. 23, 1970; children: Mark Solomon, Jonathan Samuel, Daniel Jason. B.A., Williams Coll., 1961. Supt., project mgr. Poley-Abrams Corp., Brookline, Mass., 1961, 1965-66; ptnr., treas. Abreen Corp., Brookline, Mass., 1966-81; gen. dep. asst. sec. HUD, Washington, 1981, asst. sec. for housing and fed. housing commr., 1982-83, under sec., 1983—. Mem. local bd. SSS, Brookline, Mass, 1970-74; mem. Brookline Redevel. Authority, 1971-74, Gov. Sargeant's Adv. Com. on Constrn., Mass., 1971-72; chmn. Ward 5 Republican Com., Newton, Mass, 1979-81. Served to lt. USNR, 1961-65. Recipient Men Who Made Marks in the Constrn. Industry award Engring. News-Record mag., 1975, 76. Mem. Associated Builders and Contractors (pres. 1975), Nat. Constrn. Industry Council (chmn. 1976-77), Associated Gen. Contractors, Am. Inst. Constructors. D.D.D. Jewish. Lodges: B'nai B'rith; Masons. Home: 3219 Macomb St NW Washington DC 20008 Office: Dept HUD 451 7th St SW Washington DC 20410

ABRAMS, RICHARD LEE, physicist; b. Cleve., Apr. 20, 1941; s. Morris S. and Corinne (Tobias) A.; m. Jack Shack, Aug. 12, 1962; children: Elizabeth, Laura. B. Engring. Physics, Cornell U., Ithaca, N.Y., 1964, Ph.D., 1968. Mem. tech. staff Bell Telephone Labs., Whippany, N.J., 1968-71; sect. head Hughes Research Labs., Malibu, Calif., 1971-75, dept. mgr., 1975-83; chief scientist Space and Communications group Hughes Aircraft Co., El Segundo, Calif., 1983—; program co-chmn. Conf. on Laser Engring. and Applications, Washington, 1979; chmn. Conf. on Lasers and Electro-Optics, Phoenix, 1982. Assoc. editor: Optics Letters, 1979-82; patentee in field. Fellow IEEE (assoc. editor Jour. Quantum Electronics 1980-83), Optical Soc. Am. (bd. dirs. 1982—); mem. IEEE Quantum Electronics and Applications Soc. (adminstrve. com. 1980-83, v.p. 1982, pres. 1983), Tau Beta Pi, Phi Kappa Phi. Club: Riviera Country (Pacific Palisdades, Calif.). Home: 922 Enchanted Way Pacific Palisades CA 90272 Office: Hughes Aircraft Co PO Box 92919 Bldg S50 Los Angeles CA 90009

ABRAMS, RICHARD MARTIN, historian; b. Bklyn., July 12, 1932; s. Nathan and Ida (Levine) A.; m. Marcia Lee Ash, Aug. 14, 1960; children: Laura Susan, Robert Samuel, Jennifer Sharon. B.A., Columbia U., 1953, M.A., 1955, Ph.D., 1962. Instr., lectr. history Columbia U., 1957-60; instr. history U. Calif., Berkeley, 1961-62, asst. prof., 1962-66, asso. prof., 1966-72, prof., 1972—; Fulbright prof. history London Sch. Econs. and Polit. Sci., 1968, U. London, 1968-69; NEH fellow, 1972-73, dir. summer seminar for coll. tchrs., 1977, 79, 81, 84; Social Sci. Research Council fellow, 1960-61, 64-65. Author: Conservatism in a Progressive Era, 1964, (with Lawrence W. Levine) The Shaping of Twentieth Century America, 1967, rev. edit., 1971, (with Leuchtenburg et al) The Unfinished Century, 1973, The Issue of Federal Regulation, 1963, The Burdens of Progress, 1978; contbr. articles to profl. publs.; Editorial bd.: Revs. in Am. History. Mem. Am. Hist. Assn., Orgn. Am. Historians, Econ. History Assn., Am. Soc. Legal History, Newcomen Soc. N.Am. (hon.), World Affairs Council. Home: 422 Michigan Ave Berkeley CA 94707

ABRAMS, ROBERT, state official; b. Bronx, N.Y., July 4, 1938; s. Benjamin and Dorothy A.; m. Diane B. Schulder, Sept. 15, 1974; 1 dau., Rachel Schulder. B.A., Columbia U., 1960; J.D., N.Y. U., 1963; LL.D. (hon.), Hofstra U., 1979. Mem. N.Y. State Assembly, 1965-69; pres. Borough of Bronx, 1970-78; atty. gen. State of N.Y., 1979—. Recipient Benjamin Cardozo award for legal excellence Jewish Lawyers Guild, 1979, Interfaith award Council of Chs. of N.Y.C.; recipient Brotherhood award B'nai B'rith, Man of Yr. award NAACP, Alumni Achievement award NYU Sch. Law. Mem. Assn. Bar City of N.Y., Bronx County Bar Assn., Nat. Assn. Attys. Gen. (chairperson environ. protection com.), N.Y. Civil Liberties Union., Northeastern Regional Conf. Attys. Gen. (past chairperson). Democrat. Office: 2 World Trade Center New York NY 10047

ABRAMS, RUTH I., state justice; b. Boston, Dec. 26, 1930; d. Samuel and Matilda B. and A. B.A., Radcliffe Coll., 1953; LL.B., Harvard U., 1956; hon. degree, Mt. Holyoke Coll., 1977, Suffolk U., 1977, New Eng. Sch. Law, 1978. Bar: Mass. 1957. Partner firm Abrams, Abrams & Abrams, Boston, 1957-60; asst. dist. atty., Middlesex County, Mass., 1961-69, asst. atty. gen. Mass., chief appellate sect. criminal div., 1969-71; spl. counsel Supreme Jud. Ct. Mass., 1971-72; asso. justice Superior Ct. Commonwealth of Mass., 1972-77, Supreme Jud. Ct. Mass., Boston, 1977—; mem. Gov.'s Commn. on Child Abuse, 1970-71, Mass. Law Revision Commn. Proposed Criminal Code for Mass., 1969-71; trustee Radcliffe Coll., from 1981. Editor: Handbook for Law Enforcement Officers, 1969-71. Recipient Radcliffe Coll. Achievement award, 1976, Radcliffe Grad. Soc. medal, 1977. Mem. ABA (com. on proposed fed. code from 1977), Mass. Bar Assn., Am. Law Inst., Am. Judicature Soc. (dir. 1978), Am. Judges Assn., Mass. Assn. Women Lawyers. Office: Supreme Judicial Ct 1300 New Courthouse Boston MA 02108 *

ABRAMS, SAMUEL K., lawyer; b. Phila., May 31, 1913; s. Maurice and Mary (Hockstein) A.; m. Sylvia Lester, June 19, 1949; 1 son, Richard K. B.A., U. Okla., 1933, LL.B., 1936; postgrad., Wharton Sch., U. Pa. Bar: Okla. 1936, D.C. 1949. Asst. county atty., Logan County, Okla., 1937-41, atty. civil div. Dept. Justice, 1947-49; asst. U.S. atty. D.C., 1949-50; acting asst. gen. counsel Econ. Stblzn. Agy., 1950; chief merger and clearance sect., antitrust div. Dept. Justice, 1951-52; partner firm Morison, Murphy, Abrams & Haddock (and predecessors), Washington, 1952-79, Baker & Hostetler, 1979—; adv. bd. antitrust and trade regulation report Bur. Nat. Affairs; lectr. Fed. Publns., Inc. Served to capt. AUS, 1942-46. Mem. Am. Bar Assn., D.C. Bar Assn., Okla. Bar Assn., Phi Beta Kappa, Order of Coif. Club: Internat. (Washington). Home: 5828 Lenox Rd Bethesda MD 20817 Office: 818 Connecticut Ave NW Washington DC 20006

ABRAMS, TALBERT, aviator, photogrammetrist, instrument manufacturer, scientific consultant and explorer; b. Tekonsha, Mich., Aug 17, 1895; s. William Blodgett and Sarah Elizabeth (Bruner) A.; m. Leota Fry, Jan. 15, 1923 (dec. Feb. 1978). Student, U.S. Naval Aero. Sch., Pensacola, Fla., 1917; D.Sc. (hon.), Mich. Coll. Mining and Tech., 1952, D.Eng., Mich. State U., 1961, LL.D., Western Mich. U., 1971. U.S. transport pilot signed by Orville Wright, Air Mail Service, 192O, Mich. Aero. Service Corp., 1921; v.p. Mich. Airways, 1922; pres. Abrams Aerial Survey Corp., 1923-58, chmn. bd. dirs., 1958—; pres. Abrams Aircraft Corp., 1936-44, Abrams Instrument Corp. (merged with Curtiss-Wright Corp.), 1961), 1937-61, Airlandia, Inc., 1954—, Aerial Explorers Corp., 1961—; chmn. bd. Abrams Aerial Survey Corp.; sci. cons. Curtiss- Wright Corp.; founder Abrams Research & Test Center, Mich., 1955; mapped, Isle Royale, 1929; large areas for U.S. Govt., 1917—, P.R., 1935-37, Dominican Republic, W.I., 1940-41, Cuba, 1935-44, Liberian Survey Firestone Plantations Co.; mem. U.S. Navy-NSF Operation Deep Freeze, 1963-67; numerous aerial surveys fgn. countries; del. sev. internat. congresses; served in civilian capacity for USMC, U.S. Army, USAF, USN.; Pres. Talbert & Leota Abrams Found., 1960—. Author: The Essentials of Aerial Surveys and Photo Interpretation (used as textbook USMC, Army and Navy). Donor Talbert Abrams award, Am. Soc. Photogrammetry, 1944—; donor Talbert and Leota Abrams Planetarium to Mich. State U., 1961, Meridian-Base Line Surveyors Park (hist. site) to State of Mich., 1967; donated Stratoplane Explorer to Nat. Air Mus., Smithsonian Instn., Washington. Served with aviation sect. USMC, 1917-19; Served with aviation sect. U.S. Army AC Res., 1924-34. Recipient Civilian Service award U.S. Army; Order Arctic Realm USAF, Alaska; Hon. Centennial award Mich. State U., 1955; Community Service award City of Lansing, Mich., 1962; Order of Magellan Circumnavigators Club, 1963; apptd. indsl. ambassador State Mich., 1958; named to OX-5 Aviation Hall of Fame, 1972; Antartic mountain named Abrams Mountain, 1966. Mem. NAM (nuclear energy com.), ASCE, Mich. Soc. Civil Engrs. (hon.), Am. Soc. Photogrammetry (pres. 1951, hon. life mem.), Mich. Engring. Soc. (hon.), Detroit Soc. Engrs., Mich. Soc. Profl. Engrs. (hon.), Am. Congress Surveying and Mapping (hon), Soc. of South Pole, Australian Inst. Cartographers, Quiet Birdmen, Soc. Am. Mil. Engrs., Am. Ordnance Assn. (past v.p.), Am. Legion, VFW, First Marine Aviation Force Vets. Assn., Last Man Pioneer Air Mail Club, Chi Epsilon (hon.), Pi Tau Sigma (hon.), Tau Beta Pi (hon). Clubs: Masons, Rotary, Explorers, Wings (N.Y.C.); Lansing Engrs., City (dir.), Lansing Country, Circumnavigators. Inventor Abrams Contour Finder, 1929, Abrams Stratoplane Explorer, 1938, 16 mm. gun camera, radar cameras, Army steroscopes, intervalometers, photogrammetric computers. Flights around the World, 1948, 58, 59, 61, 63, 66, 68, 77; visited 96 countries since World War II, South Pole, 45, 64, 66; transport pilot. Office: 124 N Larch St Lansing MI 48910 *

ABRAMS, WARREN ELLIOTT, mktg. exec.; b. Bklyn., Oct. 27, 1928; s. Joseph D. and Ann (Weidenbaum) A.; m. Roberta Nathanson, Aug. 26, 1952; children—Alan, Michael, Carolyn. B.S., Va. Poly. Inst., 1950; postgrad., U. Maine, 1952-53. Indsl. engr. Lewyt Corp., Bklyn., 1950-52; with Hudson Pulp & Paper Corp., N.Y.C., 1953-79, sr. v.p. indsl. products, 1970-73, exec. v.p., 1973-79; chmn. bd., chief exec. officer Am. Israel Investors Ltd.; pres. Warren Elliott Assos.; product devel. and mktg.; dir. Ampal, Am.-Israel Corp. Chmn. L.I. unit United Jewish Appeal, 1969-74; chm. joint purchasing com. Fedn. Jewish Philanthropies, 1971-76; chmn. organizing com. U.S. team, 11th Maccabiah Games, Israel, 1981. Home: 860 UN Plaza New York NY 10017 Office: 823 UN Plaza New York NY 10017

ABRAMSON, ARNOLD ERNEST, publisher; b. N.Y.C., Oct. 12, 1914; s. Henry and Libbie (Tunick) A.; m. Doris T. Waters, Nov. 24, 1935; children—Peter, Laurie. Student pub. schs. With Macfadden Publs., Inc., N.Y.C. and; Trenton, N.J., 1935-37, traveling supr. Midwest states, 1937-39; v.p. Farrell Pub. Corp., 1939-41; organized Universal Pub. & Distbg. Corp., N.Y.C., 1947, pres., chmn. bd., 1947—; pres. Sports Underwriters Inc., Dallas; chmn. bd. Seraphim Pub. Group, Inc.; founder Universal-Tandem Pub. Co., Ltd., London; founding pub. Ski mag., Golf mag., Family Handyman mag.; pub. Mgmt. Info. Weekly, Award House Books, Award Books. Served from pvt. to capt., inf. N.Y. N.G., 1942-47. Mem. Golf Writers Assn., Ski Writers Assn., 71st Inf. Vets. Assn. Clubs: Lake Isle Golf, Sun Valley Ski, Overseas Press, Overseas Yacht. Home: Laurel Hill Dr Pleasantville NY 10570 Office: 720 White Plains Rd Eastchester Scarsdale PO NY 10583

ABRAMSON, DAVID IRVIN, physician, educator; b. N.Y.C., Oct. 14, 1905; s. Aaron and Anna (Oschrin) A.; m. Louise Felson, Aug. 17, 1940; children—Julie Syril, Marian Beth. Student, Coll. City N.Y., 1922-23, Columbia, 1923-24; M.D., L.I. Coll. Medicine, 1929. Diplomate: Am. Bd. Internal Medicine, sub-specialty cardiovascular disease. Intern Bushwick Hosp., Bklyn., 1929-30; pvt. practice peripheral vascular disease, Chgo., 1946-75; instr. physiology L.I. Coll. Medicine, 1930-36; dir. cardiovascular research May Inst. Med. Research, Cin., 1938-42; asst. prof. medicine U. Ill., 1946-54, asso. prof., 1954-55, prof. dept. medicine, prof., head dept. phys. medicine and rehab., 1955-72, prof. emeritus dept. phys. medicine and rehab., 1972—; cons. Hines and West Side VA Hosp.; sr. attending physician Michael Reese Mt. Sinai hosps., Chgo., 1954—. Author: Vascular Responses in Extremities of Man in Health and Disease, 1944,

Diagnosis and Treatment of Peripheral Vascular Disorders, 1956, Circulation in the Extremities, 1967, Vascular Disorders of the Extremities, 1974, Circulatory Diseases of the Limbs: A Primer, 1978, Self-assessment of Current Knowledge in Peripheral Vascular Disorders, 1980, Vascular Problems in Musculoskeletal Disorders of the Limbs, 1981; Editor: Blood Vessels and Lymphatics, 1962; Contbr. articles med. jours. Served to maj. M.C., AUS, 1942-46. Fellow A.C.P., Am. Heart Assn.; mem. Am. Physiol. Soc., Central Soc. Clin. Research, Am. Soc. Clin. Investigation, Chgo. Med. Soc., Chgo. Soc. Internal Medicine, Sigma Xi. Home: 916 N Oak Park Ave Oak Park IL

ABRAMSON, HYMAN NORMAN, engring. and sci. research exec.; b. San Antonio, Mar. 4, 1926; s. Nathan and Pearl (Westerman) A.; m. Idelle Rebecca Ringel, Apr. 20, 1947; children— Phillip David, Mark Donald. B.S.M.E., Stanford U., 1950, M.S. in Engring. Mechanics, 1951; Ph.D. in Engring. Mechanics (So. Fellowship Fund fellow), U. Tex., Austin, 1956. Engr. U.S. Naval Air Missile Test Center, Point Mugu, Calif., 1947-48; project engr. Chance Vought Aircraft Co., Dallas, 1951-52; asso. prof. aero. engring. Tex. A&M U., 1952-55; sect. mgr., dept. dir. S.W. Research Inst., San Antonio, 1956-72, v.p. div. engring. scis., 1972—; mem. research adv. com. USCG; adv. panel engring. mechanics NSF; com. U.S. Dept. Commerce. Author: An Introduction to the Dynamics of Airplanes, 1958, reprinted, 1971; contbr. numerous articles to profl. publs.; editor: (with others) Applied Mechanics Surveys, 1966, The Dynamic Behavior of Liquids in Moving Containers, 1966; asso. editor: Applied Mechanics Revs, 1954—; editorial adv. bd.: Jour. Computers and Structures, 1970—, Aeros. and Astronautics, 1975—. Mem. Greater San Antonio C. of C., and City of San Antonio Market Sq. Adv. Com., 1973-77; mem. U.S. Bicentennial Com. of San Antonio, 1975-76. Served with USN, 1943-45. Mem. AIAA (Disting. Service award 1973, dir.), ASME (v.p.; hon.), Nat. Acad. Engring., Soc. Naval Architects and Marine Engrs., AAAS, Sigma Xi. Republican. Jewish. Home: 1511 Spanish Oaks Dr San Antonio TX 78213 Office: 6220 Culebra Rd San Antonio TX 78284

ABRAMSON, MARTIN, author, journalist; b. Bklyn., Jan. 25, 1921; s. Jacob and Bessie (Horwitz) A.; m. Marcia Zagon, May 9, 1948; children: Barry, Jill. B.B.A., CCNY, 1940; postgrad., Columbia U. Sch. Journalism, 1941, U. Calif., 1942. Syndicated feature writer; feature writer N.Y. Herald-Tribune, N.Y.C., 1958-67; TV writer; instr. mag. writing Nassau Community Coll.; also Congl. press sec.; pub. affairs dir. L.I. Planning Commn., 1974-79. Author: The Real Al Jolson, 1956, The Barney Ross Story (Monkey on My Back), 1959, The Padre of Guadalcanal Story, 1964, Hollywood Surgeon, 1969, Forgotton Fortunes, 1973, The Trial of Chaplain Jensen, 1976, Consumer's Guide to Travel Agencies, 1979; contbr.: articles to various mags. including Reader's Digest, Esquire, Parade, Good Housekeeping, Cosmopolitan. Trustee Peninsula Pub. Library. Served with U.S. Army; World War II. Decorated Bronze Star for outstanding service as corr.; recipient best mag. article award Writers Alliance, 1975, Best Sports Stories award Citadel Press, 1971, award for community services Kiwanis, 1978. Mem. Am. Soc. Journalists and Authors (charter). Club: Overseas Press. Office: 827 Peninsula Blvd Woodmere NY 11598

ABRAMSON, MAXWELL, physician; b. N.Y.C., July 22, 1935; s. Sidney and Esther (Ochs) A.; m. Marcia Mangulies, June 22, 1958; children—Rebecca, Stuart, Deborah. B.A., Wesleyan U., Middletown, Conn., 1957; M.D., Albany (N.Y.) Med. Coll., 1961. Intern Strong Meml. Hosp., Rochester, N.Y., 1961-62, resident, 1962-63; resident in otolaryngology Mass. Eye and Ear Infirmary, Boston, 1965-68; fellow in medicine Mass. Gen. Hosp., Boston, 1968-70; asst. prof., then asso. prof. otolarygnology and maxillofacial surgery U. Iowa Med. Sch., 1970-77; prof. otolaryngology, chmn. dept. Columbia U. Coll. Phys. and Surg., 1977—. Author editor papers in field. Served to capt. M.C., USAF, 1963-65. Spl. research fellow NIH, 1963-64. Mem. A.C.S., AMA, Soc. U. Otolaryngologists, Am. Acad. Otolaryngology, Head and Neck Surgery, Am. Otol. Assn., Trilogical Soc., Assn. Research in Otolaryngology. Jewish. Home: 23 Sisson Terr Tenafly NJ 07670 Office: 630 W 168th St New York NY 10032

ABRAMSON, MORRIE KAPLAN, electronics executive; b. Houston, Dec. 28, 1934; s. Albert and Pearl (Kaplan) A.; m. Rolaine Segal, July 1, 1962; children: Karen Hope, Beth Ellen. B.B.A., U. Tex., 1954; postgrad., U. Houston, 1956. With Sterling Electronics Corp., Houston, 1954-73, v.p., sec., 1961-68, exec. v.p., dir., 1968-73; pres., dir. Kann-Ellert Electronics, Balt., 1970-73, Meridian Electronics, Richmond, Va., 1970-73; pres. Kent Electronics Corp., Houston, 1973-77, chmn. bd., 1973—. Mem. Houston C. of C., Nat. Electronic Distbrs. Assn., Phi Sigma Delta. Jewish. Club: Westwood Country. Home: 2210 Amberly Ct Houston TX 77063 Office: 5604 Bonhomme Rd Houston TX 77036

ABRAMSON, NORMAN, educator; b. Boston, Apr. 1, 1932; s. Edward and Esther (Voslavsky) A.; m. Joan Freulich, July 4, 1954; children—Mark David, Carin Lynn. A.B., Harvard U., 1953; M.A., UCLA, 1955; Ph.D., Stanford U., 1958. Asst. prof. Stanford (Calif.) U., from 1958, asso. prof., to 1965; vis. prof. U. Calif., Berkeley, 1965, Harvard U., Cambridge, Mass., 1965-66; prof. U. Hawaii, Honolulu, 1966—; vis. prof. M.I.T., 1981-82; chmn. bd. Tech. Edn. Assos., Sydney, Australia; dir. Public Service Satellite Consortium, Washington, Pacific Telecommunications Council; cons. Internat. Telecommunications Union, Geneva. Author: Information Theory and Coding, 1963; co-editor: Computer Communication Networks, 1973. Mem. IEEE. Patentee in field. Home: 3044 Kiele Ave Honolulu HI 96815 Office: Dept Elec Engring Univ Hawaii Honolulu HI 96822

ABRAVANEL, MAURICE, musical director; b. Salonica, Greece, Jan. 6, 1903; came to U.S., 1936; s. Edouard and Rachel (Bitty) A.; m. Lucy Carasso, 1947. Ed., Gymnasium, Lausanne, Switzerland, 1917-19, U. Lausanne, 1919-21, U. Zurich, 1921-22; LL.D., U. Utah, State U., Westminster Coll. Began as orch. condr., 1924; has conducted leading symphony orchs. in, U.S., Europe, Australia; condr., Met. Opera, N.Y.; Kurt Weill premieres Seven Deadly Sins, 1933; Knickerbocker Holiday, 1938, Lady in the Dark, 1940, One Touch of Venus, 1943, Street Scene, 1946, Regina, 1949, Utah Symphony Orch., 1947-79; mus. dir., Acad. of the West, Santa Barbara, Calif.; acting mus. dir., Berkshire Music Ctr., Tanglewood, Mass., 1982; now artist-in-residence, Berkshire Music Ctr., Tanglewood, Mass.; condr. numerous rec. premieres: 1st studio recs. Mahler—Symphony No. 7 and No. 8; condr. complete orchestral works of Mahler, Brahms, Tchaikovsky and Grieg. Recipient Antoinette Perry award, 1950; Kilenyi Mahler medal, 1965; Ditson Condr.'s award, 1971; Gold Baton award Am. Symphony Orch. League, 1981. Hon. mem. Internat. Gustav Mahler Soc. Concert Hall named in his honor. Home: 123 W S Temple Salt Lake City UT 84101

ABROMS, EDWARD MACKIN, motion picture company executive; b. Los Angeles, May 6, 1935; s. George and Marjorie (McQuire) A.; m. Colleen Johnson, Nov. 23, 1958; children: Edward R., Lynne, Cindy. Student, Hollywood Profl. Sch., 1950-53, U. So. Calif., 1953-55. Film editor Banner Productions, Hollywood, Calif., 1966-68; dialogue dir. Universal City Studios, Calif., 1961-65, film editor, 1968-73, film dir., 1971; prin. E.M.A. Enterprises, Inc., Thousand Oaks, Calif.; producer segments numerous TV programs. Asst. scoutmaster Boy Scouts Am., 1974-75. Recipient Emmy award for outstanding film editing, 1970, 71, Acad. award nomination for film editing for Blue Thunder, 1983. Mem. Dirs. Guild Am., Acad. TV Arts and Scis., Acad. Motion Picture Arts and Scis., Soc. Motion Picture and TV Engrs., Am. Cinema Editors, Inc., Motion Picture Editors Guild. Home: 1866 Marlowe St Thousand Oaks CA 91360 Office: EMA Enterprises Inc 1866 Marlowe St Thousand Oaks CA 91360

ABSHIRE, DAVID MANKER, government official, educational administrator; b. Chattanooga, Apr. 11, 1926; s. James Ernest and Phyllis (Patten) A.; m. Carolyn Lamar Sample, Sept. 7, 1957; children: Lupton Patten, Anna Lamar, Mary Lee Sample, Phyllis Anderson, Carolyn. Student, U. Chattanooga, 1945; B.S., U.S. Mil. Acad., 1951; Ph.D., Georgetown U., 1959. Mem. minority staff U.S. Ho. Reps., 1958-60; dir. spl. projects Am. Enterprise Inst., Washington, 1961-62; exec. dir. Center Strategic and Internat. Studies, Georgetown U., 1962-70, 73—, chmn., 1973-82, pres., 1982-83; ambassador, U.S. permanent rep. North Atlantic Council, 1983—; asst. sec. state for congl. relations, 1970-73; presdl. appointee Congl. Commn. on Orgn. of Govt. for Conduct of Fgn. Policy, 1973-75; chmn. U.S. Bd. for Internat. Broadcasting, 1974-77; dir. nat. security group Transition Office of Pres.-Elect Reagan, 1980-81. Author: (with others) Detente, 1965, Vietnam Legacy, 1976, The South Rejects a Prophet: The Life of Senator D.M. Key, 1967, International Broadcasting: A New Dimension of Western Diplomacy, 1976, Foreign Policy Makers: President vs. Congress, 1979; editor: National Security, 1963, Portuguese Africa, 1969, Research Resources for the Seventies, 1971, The Growing Power of Congress, 1981; co-editor: Washington Quar., 1977-83. Mem. adv. bd. Naval War Coll., 1975-79; vice-chmn. bd. Youth for Understanding, 1979-80; trustee Baylor Sch., 1980—; mem. Pres.'s Fgn. Intelligence Adv. Bd., 1981-83. Served with AUS, 1945-46; to 1st lt., 1951-56; capt. Res. ret. Decorated Bronze Star medal with oak leaf cluster, with V for Valor, V commendation ribbon with metal pendant; Order of Crown (Belgium).; recipient John Carroll award. Mem. Council Fgn. Relations, Am. Acad. Polit. and Social Scis., Internat. Inst. Strategic Studies, Gold Key Soc., Phi Alpha Theta. Republican. Episcopalian. Clubs: Internat., Alfalfa, Metropolitan (Washington); Metropolitan (N.Y.C.). Home: 311 S St Asaph St Alexandria VA 22314 Office: US Mission to NATO APO New York NY 09667

ABTS, HENRY WILLIAM, banker; b. Columbus, Nebr., July 3, 1918; s. Matthew C. and Irene (Xanders) A.; m. Virginia Lung, Nov. 7, 1942; children: Bruce M., Susan A. (Mrs. J. Farnham). B.S., Butler U., 1941. Asst. mgr. indsl. relations Union Carbide Co., Kokomo, Ind., 1945-54, personnel mgr., N.Y.C., 1954-56, dir. indsl. relations, South Charleston, W.Va., 1956-60; v.p. personnel Cummins Engine Co., Inc., Columbus, Ind., 1960-68, v.p. adminstrn., sec., 1968-82, ret., 1982; v.p. Columbus Bank and Trust, 1982—; dir. Arkwright-Boston Ins. Co.; mem. regional adv. bd. Liberty Mut. Ins. Co. Served to capt. USAAF, 1941-45. Named Outstanding Young Man Kokomo Jr. C. of C., 1951, Boss of Year Columbus Jr. C. of C., 1963. Mem. Ind. C. of C., Ind. Golf Assn. (past pres., dir.), Phi Delta Theta. Mem. Christian Ch. Clubs: Otter Creek Golf (past pres.), Harrison Lakes Country (past pres.); Columbus Rotary (past pres.)). Home: 9544 W Raintree Dr S Columbus IN 47201 Office: 5th St and Washington Sts Columbus IN 47201

ABULARACH, RODOLFO MARCO ANTONIO, artist; b. Guatemala City, Jan. 7, 1933; U.S., 1959; s. Encarnacion and Maria Estala A.; m. Barbara Jane Berlind, Mar. 30, 1961; children: Marco Antonio, Gabriel Eduardo. 56 one-man shows, 1947—; exhibits include graphics IV Internat. Exhbn., Pratt Inst., N.Y.C., 1971; Biennial Pan-Am. Graphics, Cali, Colombia, 1970, Latinam. Exhbn., Caracas, 1967 (recipient 1st prize drawings-graphics), Arte Actual Am. y Espana, Madrid, 1963 (1st prize drawing). Fellow Guggenheim Found., 1959-60,61, Bellas Artes-Guatemala Art Student's League, 1959, Pan Am. Union Pratt Graphic Ctr., 1962-64, Tamarind Lithographic Workshop, Los Angeles, 1966; recipient Merit award spl. edit. print Internat. Biennial, San Francisco, 1980. Home: 14 W 17th St New York NY 10011

ABU-LUGHOD, JANET LOUISE, sociologist; b. Newark, Aug. 3, 1928; d. Irving O. and Tessie Lippman; m. Ibrahim Abu-Lughod, Dec. 8, 1950; children: Lila, Mariam, Deena, Jawad. B.A., U. Chgo., 1947, M.A., 1950; Ph.D. (NSF fellow), U. Mass., 1966. Dir. research Am. Soc. Planning Ofcls., 1950-52; sociologist-cons. Am. Council to Improve Our Neighborhoods, 1953-57; asst. prof. sociology Am. U., Cairo, 1958-60, Smith Coll., 1963-66; assoc. prof. Northwestern U., Evanston, Ill., 1967-71, prof. sociology, urban affairs, 1971—, dir. comparative urban studies program, 1974—; cons. to UN, 1971—, UNESCO, 1979-80. Author: (with Nelson Foote, others) Housing Choices and Constraints, 1960, Cairo - 1001 Years of the City Victorious, 1971, Third World Urbanization, 1977, Rabat: Urban Apartheid in Morocco, 1980; contbr. chpts. to books, articles, revs. to profl. jours.; (with Nelson Foote, others) also monographs. Rabat: Urban Apartheid in Morocco. Radcliffe Inst. Scholar, 1963-64; Ford faculty fellow, 1971-72; Guggenheim fellow, 1976-77; NEH fellow, 1977-78. Mem. Internat. Sociol. Assn., Am. Sociol. Assn. (com. on world sociology), Social Sci. History Assn., Chgo. Council on Fgn. Relations (dir. 1973-76), Social Sci. Research Council (com. on Near East 1973-75), Phi Beta Kappa. Office: Dept Sociology Northwestern Univ Evanston IL 60201

ABZUG, BELLA SAVITZKY, lawyer, former congresswoman; b. N.Y.C., July 24, 1920; d. Emanuel and Esther Savitzky; m. Maurice M. Abzug, June 4, 1944; children: Eve Gail, Isobel Jo. B.A., Hunter Coll., 1942; LL.B., Columbia U., 1947; hon. degree, Hunter Coll., Hobart Coll., Manhattanville Coll. Bar: N.Y. 1947. Practice in N.Y.C., 1944-70, 80—; legislative dir. Women Strike for Peace, 1961-70; mem. 92d congress from 19th Dist. N.Y., 93d-94th congresses from 20th Dist. N.Y.; Presiding officer Nat. Commn. on Observance of Internat. Women's Year, 1977; presided Nat. Women's Conf., Houston, 1977; co-chmn. Pres.'s Nat. Adv. Com. for Women, 1978; cable news commentator; speaker numerous coll. campuses. Editor: Columbia Law Rev.; author: Bella! Ms. Abzug Goes to Washington, 1972, Gender Gap: Bella Abzug's Guide to Political Power for American Women, 1984. Mem. Women Strike for Peace, Nat. Urban League, NOW, Nat. Women's Polit. Caucus, Hadassah, ACLU, Women U.S.A. (pres.), UN Assn. U.S., Ams. for Democratic Action (v.p.), B'nai B'rith. *

ACCARDO, SALVATORE FRANCIS, trust company executive; b. Newark, Dec. 30, 1937; s. Settimo and Teresa (Mineo) A. B.E.E., Cornell U., 1961; M.B.A. with distinction, NYU, 1963. Bus. planner, market researcher Gen. Electric Co., N.Y.C., 1963-67; v.p. research William D. Witter, Inc., N.Y.C., 1969-76, Drexel Burnham Lambert Group, 1976-77, Kidder, Peabody & Co., 1977-79, Shearson Loeb Rhoades, Inc., 1979-80; v.p. investment banking Shearson-Am. Express, Inc., N.Y.C., 1981-83; v.p. venture capital investments Mfrs. Hanover Trust Co., N.Y.C., 1983—. Bd. dirs. N.Y. Harp Ensemble; vol. N.Y. Philharm. Served with USAF, 1968. Named Instl. Investor All-Star Analyst, 1975-76, 78. Mem. N.Y. Elec. and Electronics Analysts Group, N.Y. Soc. Security Analysts. Clubs: University, Met. Opera. Home: 400 Central Park W Apt 15C New York NY 10025 Office: Mfrs Hanover Trust Co 600 Fifth Ave New York NY 10020

ACCETTURA, GUY, manufacturing company executive; b. Ceglie del Campo, Italy, Feb. 23, 1919; came to U.S., 1928; s. Vito L. and Maria (Roppo) A.; m. Mabel G. Blindell, May 11, 1946; children—Raymond V., Paul G., Carl J., Janet Rosalie, Linda Margaret. Student, Ill. Inst. Tech., 1936-38; B.S. cum laude in Commerce, De Paul U., 1948. With Western Electric Co., 1936-66, dir. orgn. planning, 1964-65, v.p., 1965-66; v.p., gen mgr. Bell Telephone Labs., Murray Hill, N.J., 1966-69; v.p. mfg. Western Electric Co., Newark, 1969-76, exec. v.p., 1976-79, sr. exec. v.p., 1979-82; also dir.; dir. Sandia Corp., 1966-69, 76—, Teletype Corp., 1969—. Acting Co. Mem. Columbus Water Planning Commn., 1963-64; Bd. dirs., pres. YM/YWCA of Newark and Vicinity, 1973-74; trustee, exec. com. N.J. Symphony Orch.; trustee, exec. com., sec. N.J. Symphony Hall; trustee Western Electric Fund, 1971-76, Rutgers U. Found., 1977-78, Bucknell U., 1981—. Served with AUS, 1942-46; ETO. Decorated Bronze Star. Mem. NAM, Columbus C. of C. (dir. 1963-64), Pi Gamma Mu. Club: Rotarian. Home: 467 Carlton Rd Wyckoff NJ 07481 Office: Western Electric Co 222 Broadway New York NY 10038

ACCONCI, VITO (HANNIBAL), conceptual artist; b. Bronx, N.Y., Jan. 24, 1940; s. Amilcare Privato and Catherine (Colombo) A. A.B., Holy Cross Coll., Worcester, Mass., 1962; M.F.A., U. Iowa, 1964. Mem. faculty Sch. Visual Arts, N.Y.C., 1968-71, 77, N.S. Coll. Art and Design, Halifax, 1971-72, 78, Calif. Inst. Art and Design, Valencia, 1976. Author: Pulse: From my Mother, Multiplicata, 1972, Ten-Point Plan for Video, Video Art, 1976, Think/Leap/Rethink/Fall, 1977; contbr.: Conceptual Art, 1972, featured in issue of Avalanche mag., 1972; One-man exhbns. include, John Gibson Gallery, N.Y.C., 1971, Sonnabend Gallery, N.Y.C., 1972, 73, 75, 76, 77, Galeria Schema, Florence, Italy, 1973, Galeria A. Castelli, Milan, Italy, 1974, Modern Art Agency, Naples, Italy, 1977, Wright State U., Dayton, Ohio, 1976, Centre d'Art Contemporain, Geneva, Switzerland, Mus. Contemporary Art, Chgo., 1980, U. Mass., 1982, group exhbns. include, Documenta V, Kassel, Germany, 1972, Contemporanea, Rome, 1973, Mus. Modern Art, N.Y.C., 1976, Venice Biennale, Whitney Biennial, N.Y.C., 1977, Documenta VI, Kassel, Inst. Contemporary Art, U. Pa., 1980, Whitney Mus. Am. Art, N.Y.C., 1981, Kunsthaus, Zurich, Switzerland, Padighione d'Arte Contemporaine, Milan, Italy, Mus. Contemporary Art, Chgo., Crown Point Gallery, Oalkland, Calif., Weatherspoon Gallery, U. N.C.-Greensboro, Hirschhorn Mus., N.Y.C., High Mus. Art, Atlanta, 1982, Centre d'Art Contemporaine, Geneva, Stedlijk Mus., Amsterdam, Mus. d'Art Contemporaine, Toronto, Ont., Can. Grantee N.Y. State Council, 1976, Nat. Endowment Arts, 1976. Office: care Max Protetch 37 W 57th St New York NY 10019 *

ACCORSI, ERNEST WILLIAM, JR., professional football manager; b. Hershey, Pa., Oct. 29, 1941; s. Ernest William and Mary Doris (Nardi) A.; m. Judy Ann Nangle, Sept. 9, 1967; children: Michael Ryan, Sherlyn Paige, Patrick Vincent. B.A., Wake Forest U., 1963. Sportswriter Phila. Inquirer, 1966-69; sports info. dept. Pa. State U., University Park, 1969-70; pub. relations dir. Balt. Colts., Balt., 1970-75, asst. gen. mgr., Owings Mills, Md., 1977-82, gen. mgr., 1982—; mem. commrs. staff NFL, N.Y.C., 1975-77. Bd. dirs. Nat. Football Found., N.Y.C., 1983. Served with U.S. Army N.G., 1964. Recipient Columbia award Italian-Am. Orgns. Md, Balt., 1982; named Grand Marshall Conv. Council Colts' Corrals, 1983. Mem. Advt. Club Balt. (bd. dirs. 1978—). Roman Catholic. Office: Balt Colts Football Club 11001 Bonita Ave Owings Mills MD 21117

ACCURSO, ANTHONY, artist; b. Bklyn., Apr. 5, 1940; s. Carl Joseph and Mary Civita (Iannella) A. Student, Bklyn. Mus. Art Sch., 1950-52, Sch. Art and Design, N.Y.C., 1954-57, Pratt Inst., 1961-69, Sch. Visual Arts, N.Y.C., 1977. Exhibited group show, Bronx Mus. Arts in Cooperation with Met. Mus. Art, N.Y.C., 1972, Notre Dame U. Law Sch., 1973, Harbor Gallery, L.I., N.Y., 1975, Syracuse U., 1976, Huntsville Mus. Art, Ala., Galerie Mouffe, Paris, 1978, Galerie Vallombreuse, Biarritz, France, 1977; illustrator: Sci. Digest mag., N.Y.C., 1960-67; illustrator-corr., trial-courtroom-news media artist: ABC-TV World News Tonight, Washington, N.Y.C., Chgo. and Atlanta, 1969—, WABC-TV Eyewitness News, N.Y.C., 1969—, Nightline ABC-TV News, N.Y.C., 1980, Cable News Network, N.Y. bur., 1980, MacNeil-Lehrer Report, PBS-TV, 1979; illustrator: Newsweek mag., 1974—; TV program ABC-TV series Close up, 1980; artist-actor: TV series All My Children, 1979; illustrator: book Man's Contact with UFO's, 1974; motion picture Mysteries From Beyond Earth, 1975. Recipient Gold medal Accademia Italia delle Arti del Lavoro, Parma, Italy, 1980. Address: 5309 7th Ave Brooklyn NY 11220

ACHENBACH, JAN DREWES, engineering scientist, educator; b. Leeuwarden, Netherlands, Aug. 20, 1935; came to U.S., 1959, naturalized, 1978; s. Johannes and Elizabeth (Schipper) A.; m. Marcia Graham Fee, July 15, 1961. Kand. Ir., Delft U. Tech., 1959; Ph.D., Stanford U., 1962. Preceptor Columbia U., 1962-63; asst. prof. Northwestern U., Evanston, Ill., 1963, assoc. prof., 1966-69, prof. dept. civil engring., 1969—, Walter P. Murphy prof. civil engring. and applied math., 1981—; vis. assoc. prof. U. Calif., San Diego, 1969; vis. prof. Tech. U. Delft, 1970-71; cons. Argonne Nat. Labs., 1975—; prof. Huazhong Inst. Sci. and Tech., 1981; mem. at large U.S. Nat. Com. Theoretical and Applied Mechanics, 1972-78. Author: Wave Propagation in Elastic Solids, 1973, A Theory of Elasticity with Microstructure for Directionally Reinforced Composites, 1975, (with A.K. Gankson and H. McMaken) Ray Methods for Waves in Electric Solids, 1982; editor: (with J. Miklowitz) Modern Problems in Elastic Wave Propagation, 1978; editor-in-chief: Wave Motion, 1979—. Recipient award C. Gelderman Found., 1970, C.W. McGraw Research award Am. Soc. Engring. Edn., 1975. Fellow Am. Acad. Mechanics (pres. 1978-79), ASME; mem. Am. Geophys. Union, AIAA., U.S. Nat. Acad. Engring. Home: 574 Ingleside Park Evanston IL 60201 Office: Dept Civil Engring Northwestern U Evanston IL 60201

ACHENBAUM, ALVIN ALLEN, business executive; b. N.Y.C., Dec. 11, 1925; s. Benjamin and Dora (Dworin) A.; m. Barbara Ann Greenwald, June 24, 1951; children: Jonathan Peter, Lisa Jane, Martha Beth. B.S., UCLA, 1950; M.S., Columbia, 1951. Mgr. market research McCann-Erickson, N.Y.C., 1951-57; exec. v.p., sec., dir. Grey Advt., Inc., N.Y.C., 1957-71; exec. v.p. J. Walter Thompson Co., 1971-74; chmn. bd. Canter, Achenbaum, Assocs., Inc., N.Y.C., 1974—. Mem. Citizens Adv. Com. of Irvington, 1970—; mem. Middle Eastern affairs com. Anti-Defamation League; adv. com. Assn. Consumer Research.; Trustee Marketing Sci. Inst. Served with USAAF, 1944-46. Mem. Market Research Council N.Y., Copy Research Council N.Y., Am. Marketing Assn., Am. Econ. Assn., Am. Statis. Assn., Assn. Pub. Opinion Research, Beta Gamma Sigma. Home: 34 Mallard Rise Irvington NY 10533 Office: 950 3d Ave New York City NY 10022

ACHEPOHL, KEITH ANDEN, artist; b. Chgo., 1934; s. Harry F. and Virginia (Peteranden) A.; m. Patricia Ray; children—Adam, Jared, Johanna. B.A. (Honnold fellow 1956), Knox Coll., Galesburg, Ill., 1956; M.F.A. (grad. scholar 1959-60), U. Iowa, 1960. Instr. U. Iowa, 1962, 64-67; asst. prof. art, gallery dir. Hope Coll., Holland, Mich., 1967-69; artist-in-residence Pacific Lutheran U., Tacoma, Wash., 1969-70, assoc. prof., gallery dir., 1971; vis. artist printmaking U. Iowa, 1972-73, mem. faculty, 1973—, prof. art, 1981—. One-man exhbns. include, Achenbacnbach Found. Graphic Arts, San Francisco, 1975, Am. Cultural Center, Cairo, 1979, Des Moines Arts Center, Mus. Fine

Arts Salt Lake City, 1980, Art Inst. Chgo., 1981, Nat. Mus. Am. Art, 1982; executed watercolor series Egypt Day and Night, 1977—; suite or mezzotints Mura-I-XV, 1978-81; illustrator books, 1962—. Recipient Gold medal Mediterranean Biennale, 1982; Grantee USIA, 1963, 77, Tiffany Found., 1965, Shell Oil Co., 1971, U. Iowa, 1976, USIS, 1977; Fulbright-Hays fellow, 1978-79. Home: 630 W Park Rd Iowa City IA 52240 Office: U Iowa Iowa City IA 52242

ACHESON, ALLEN MORROW, consulting engineer; b. Tanta, Egypt, June 12, 1926; s. Samuel Irvine and Hazel Lenore (Welker) A.; m. Mary Jean Baird, Aug. 5, 1950 (div. May 1978); children: Rebecca R., Jennifer E., Scott A., Jon M.; m. Ruthann Ivy, Nov. 3, 1979 (div. June 1980). B.S. in Mech. Engring, Iowa State U., 1950. Registered profl. engr., Mo., Iowa, Mich., Kans. Sta. supt. Iowa Pub. Service Co., Carroll, 1950-54; engr. Proctor & Gamble Co., 1954-55, Iowa-Ill. Gas & Electric Co., 1955-56; mgr. City Power & Light Co., Independence, Mo., 1956-60; mgmt. adviser Yanhee Electricity Authority, Bangkok, Thailand, 1960-63; exec. v.p. Black & Veatch Internat., Kansas City, Mo., 1964-73, pres., 1973—; gen. partner Black & Veatch, 1974-75, exec. partner, 1975—. Trustee Tarkio (Mo.) Coll., 1964-77, chmn., 1975-77; elder Trinity and Rolling Hills United Presbyn. Ch. Served with USNR, 1944-46. Recipient Profl. Achievement citation Coll. Engring., Iowa State U., 1976. Fellow Am. Cons. Engrs. Council (chmn. internat. engring. div.); mem. ASME, Nat., Mo. socs. profl. engrs., Soc. Am. Mil. Engrs. Home: 4421 W 111th Terr Leawood KS 66211 Office: 1500 Meadow Lake Pkwy Kansas City MO 64114

ACHESON, DAVID CAMPION, lawyer; b. Washington, Nov. 4, 1921; s. Dean G. and Alice (Stanley) A.; m. Patricia Castles, May 1, 1943; children: Eleanor Dean, David Campion, Peter Wesley. B.A., Yale U., 1942; LL.B., Harvard U., 1948. Bar: D.C., Pa., U.S. Supreme Ct. With Office Gen. Counsel AEC, 1948-49; with firm Covington & Burling, Washington, 1950-61, mem. firm, 1958-61; U.S. atty. for D.C., 1961-65, spl. asst. to sec. treasury, 1965-67; v.p., sr. v.p., gen. counsel Communications Satellite Corp., 1967-74; partner Jones, Day, Reavis & Pogue, Washington, 1974-78, Drinker Biddle & Reath, Phila. and Washington, 1978—. Author: (with others) Effective Washington Representation, 1983; editor: This Vast External Realm, 1973, (with David McLellan) Among Friends, 1980. Trustee Internat. Econ. Studies Inst.; bd. regents, mem. exec. com. Smithsonian Instn.; bd. dirs. Atlantic Council U.S.; bd. dirs., exec. com. Com. on Present Danger. Episcopalian. Clubs: Metropolitan, Alibi (Washington); Century Assn. (N.Y.C.). Home: 3101 Garfield St NW Washington DC 20008 also South Yarmouth MA 02664 Office: 1752 N St Suite 500 Washington DC 20036

ACHESON, JOHN SIDNEY, insurance executive; b. Boissevain, Man., Can., Apr. 12, 1922; s. Sidney Richards and Margaret Bell (Scott) A.; m. Frances Marjorie Matkin, July 7, 1945; children: Kathleen Joan Acheson Troost, Robert John, Douglas Scott, Gail Marion. B.Commerce with honors, U. Man., 1951. Clk., teller Royal Bank of Can., Winnipeg, Man., 1939-45, asst. acct., 1945-46; with Dominion Life Ins. Co., Waterloo, Ont., Can., 1951—, supt. agys., 1962-64, asst. dir. agys., 1964-65, v.p., dir. agys., 1965-70, exec. v.p., 1970, pres., 1971—, also dir.; dir. Lincoln Nat. Life Ins. Co., Ft. Wayne, Ind., Gray Coach Lines, Ltd., Toronto, Ont., Waterloo Ins. Co., Island Life Ins. Co., Kingston, Jamaica. Bd. govs. Wilfred Laurier U., 1975-80; bd. dirs. Kitchener-Waterloo YMCA. Served with RCAF, 1941-45. Mem. Soc. Actuaries, Can. Inst. Actuaries, Can. Life and Health Ins. Assn., Internat. Congress Actuaries. Clubs: Westmount Golf and Country (dir. 1972-77), Kitchener Rotary (dir. 1981—). Office: Dominion Life Assurance Co Waterloo ON N2J 4C6 Canada *

ACHESON, LOUIS KRUZAN, JR., aerospace engineer; b. Brazil, Ind., Apr. 2, 1926; s. Louis Kruzan and Irene Ruth (Morrison) A.; m. Hyla Armstrong Cook, July 12, 1958; children: Mary Ruth, William Louis. B.S. in E.E., Case Inst. Tech., 1946; Ph.D. in Theoretical Physics, MIT, 1950. Mem. tech. staff Hughes Aircraft Co., Los Angeles, 1950—, sr. scientist systems labs space and communications group, 1960; with Inst. Def. Analyses, Washington, 1958-59. Contbr.: articles to profl. pubs. Mem. Soc. Gen. Systems Research, Am. Phys. Soc., Am. Geophys. Union, AIAA, Brit. Interplanetary Soc., AAAS, Mensa, Sigma Xi, Tau Beta Pi, Eta Kappa Nu, Theta Tau, Sigma Chi, Worldview Exploration Seminar, Unity-in-Diversity Council, Bertrand Russell Soc. Home: 17721 Marcello Pl Encino CA 91316 Office: Hughes Aircraft Co PO Box 92919 Los Angeles CA 90009

ACHESON, ROY MALCOLM, educator, epidemiologist; b. Belfast, Ireland, Aug. 18, 1921; emigrated to U.S., 1962, naturalized, 1968; s. Malcolm King and Dorothy (Rennoldson) A.; m. Fiona Marigo O'Brien, Mar. 16, 1950; children: Malcolm O'Brien, Vincent Rennoldson, Marigo Fiona. B.A., Trinity Coll., Dublin, Ireland, 1945, M.A., 1949, Sc.D., 1962; B.A., U. Oxford, Eng., 1948, M.A., 1951, B.M., B.Ch., 1951, D.M., 1954; M.A. (hon.), Yale, 1964; M.D., Sc.D., U. Cambridge, Eng., 1976. Intern, then resident internal medicine Radcliffe Infirmary, Oxford, 1951-55; lectr. social medicine U. Dublin (Ireland), 1955-59; reader social and preventive medicine U. London, Eng., 1959-62; mem. faculty Yale Sch. Medicine, 1962-75, prof. epidemiology, 1964-72; fellow Jonathan Edwards Coll., 1966-75; dir. Center for Tng. in Community Medicine, London (Eng.) Sch. Hygiene and Tropical Medicine, 1972-76; prof. health services studies U. London, 1974-76; prof. community medicine U. Cambridge, Eng., 1976—; professorial fellow Churchill Coll., 1976—; R. Samuel McLaughlin vis. prof. in residence Med. Sch. McMaster U., Hamilton, Ont., Can., 1976-77; Mem. expert com. health statistics WHO, 1966; cons., tech. adviser epidemiology and med. edn. Pan-Am. Health Orgn., in Peru, Venezuela, P.R. and; Argentina, India and Colombia, 1964—; cons. med. edn. AID, East Pakistan, 1963; cons. epidemiology NIH, 1963-72; mem. nat. adv. com. thrombosis Nat. Heart Inst., 1968-70; mem. epidemiology study sect. Nat. Inst. Gen. Med. Scis., 1970-72; cons. epidemiology WHO, Europe, 1973, adv. health services research, Geneva, 1978—; mem. Gen. Med. Council, 1979—, exec. com., edn. com., 1979—. Contbr. articles to profl. jours.; Editor: Comparability in International Epidemiology, 1965, Seminars in Community Medicine, Vol. 1, 1976, Vol. 2, 1977; asst. editor: Jour. Epidemiology and Community Health, 1977—. Served with Brit. Army, 1940-45. Rockefeller traveling fellow medicine, 1955-56; Commonwealth Fund traveling fellow, 1968-69; fellow Trinity Coll., Dublin, 1957-59. Fellow Royal Coll. Physicians (Eng.); mem. Am. Heart Assn. (fellow epidemiological council), Internat. Epidemiol. Assn. (council 1964-74, gen. sec. 1964-68, ednl. sec. 1968-74). Office: Addenbrooke's Hosp Hills Rd Cambridge CB2 2QQ England

ACHILLES, THEODORE CARTER, former govt. ofcl.; b. Rochester, N.Y., Dec. 29, 1905; s. Henry Lawrence and Gertrude (Strong) A.; m. Marian Field, June 4, 1933; children—Marian Achilles Smith, Theodore Carter, Daphne, Stephen. A.B., Stanford U., 1925; student, Yale, 1926-28. Newspaper work, in Calif. and, Japan, 1928-31, vice-consul, Havana, 1932, Rome, 1933; assigned to Dept. State, 1935; sec. Am. embassy, London, 1939; chargé d'affaires ad interim near govts., of Poland, Belgium, Netherlands and Norway, 1940-41; assigned Dept. State, Washington, 1941; asst. chief Div. Brit. Commonwealth Affairs, 1944, chief, 1944; 1st sec. Am. embassy, London, 1945, Brussels, 1946; dir. Western European Affairs, 1947; U.S. vice dep. North Atlantic Council, London, 1950; minister, Paris, 1952, Am. ambassador to Peru, 1956-60, counselor Dept. State, Washington, 1960; spl. asst. to sec. of state, dir. Operations Center, 1961-62; cons. NASA, 1963-68; vice chmn. Atlantic Council U.S., Internat. Mgmt. and Devel. Inst.; Mem. U.S. del. ILO Conf., 1941, UN Conf. on Food and Agr., 1943, UN Conf. on Internat. Orgn., San Francisco, 1945, Council Fgn. Ministers, London, 1945; first session UN Assembly, London, 1946, 2d session, N.Y., 1947, Paris Conf., 1946, North Atlantic Pact Negotiations, 1948-49, NATO, 195O-52, 6O, CENTO, SEATO; and Colombo Plan Confs., 1960; Bd. govs. Atlantic Inst., Paris, 1969-73. Co-editor: Atlantic Community Quar, 1963-75. Mem. Beta Theta Pi. Clubs: Alibi, Met., Chevy Chase (Washington); Yale, Brook (N.Y.C.). Home: 2855 Woodland Dr NW Washington DC 20008 *The essence of negotiation is finding mutuality of interest.*

ACHINSTEIN, ASHER, economist; b. N.Y.C., Dec. 6, 1900; s. Hyman and Fanny (Horowitz) A.; m. Betty Comras, Aug. 27, 1931 (dec. Oct. 1964); 1 son, Peter; m. Martha Lantner, Apr. 3, 1966. B.S., Coll. City N.Y., 1922; M.A., Columbia, 1924, Ph.D., 1927. Tchr. econs. Eastern Dist. High Sch., Bklyn., 1924-26; sr. investigator econ. research Personnel Classification Bd., Washington, 1928-29; mem. research staff Nat. Indsl. Conf. Bd., N.Y.C., 1929-30; asst. dir. N.Y., State Housing Bd., 1930-36; asst. dir. research U.S. Housing Authority, 1938-40; lectr. econs., Columbia, 1940-42; chief constrn. and planning sect. WPB, Washington, 1941-45; prof. Biarritz (France) Am. U., 1945-46; sr. specialist Legis. Reference Service, Library Congress, Washington, 1949-70; economist Council Econ. Advisers, 1953-55, U.S. Senate Banking and Currency Commn., 1955-58, Social Sci. Research Council Research Council fellow, 1927-28. Author: Buying Power of Labor and Post War Cycles, 1927, Introduction to Business Cycles, 1950, Institutional Investors and the Stock Market, 1956, Federal Reserve Policy and Economic Stability, 1958, Congress and American Housing, 1968, Inflation and Interrest Rates, 1970; Contbr. to American Economic History, 1961. Rockefeller Found. grantee U.S. housing study, 1933-34. Mem. Am. Econ. Assn. Home: 8504 Meadowlark Ln Bethesda MD 20817

ACHINSTEIN, PETER JACOB, educator, philosopher; b. N.Y.C., June 30, 1935; s. Asher and Betty (Comras) A.; m. Merle Ann Beck, Sept. 7, 1957; children: Jonathan, Sharon, Betty. A.B., Harvard, 1956, A.M., 1958, Ph.D., 1961; postgrad. (Knox Traveling fellow), Oxford U., Eng., 1959-60. Asst. prof. U. Iowa, Iowa City, 1961-62; asst. prof. philosophy Johns Hopkins, Balt., 1962-64, asso. prof., 1964-68, prof., 1968—, chmn. dept. philosophy, 1968-77; vis. prof. M.I.T., Cambridge, 1965-66, Stanford (Calif.) U., 1967, City U. N.Y., 1973; mem. adv. panel NSF, 1968-70, 79-81; Lady Davis vis. prof. Hebrew U., Jerusalem, spring 1976. Author: Concepts of Science, 1968, Law and Explanation, 1971, The Nature of Explanation, 1983; Editor: (with Stephen Barker) The Legacy of Logical Positivism, 1969, The Concept of Evidence, 1983; Editorial bd.: Philosophy of Science, 1973. Guggenheim fellow, 1966-67. Mem. Philosophy of Sci. Assn. (bd. govs.), Internat. Union History and Philosophy (del. U.S. 1967-73, 79—), Phi Beta Kappa. Office: Dept Philosophy Johns Hopkins U Baltimore MD 21218

ACHORN, ROBERT COMEY, newspaper publisher; b. Westboro, Mass., Mar. 31, 1922; s. Edward Welt and Mabel (Comey) A.; m. Jean Mary Berlo, Sept. 23, 1950 (dec. 1980); children: Nancy Louise (Mrs. Eric Engberg), Susan Jean, Edward Christopher, Judith Joyce, Carole Lee.; m. Ann Bouvier, Aug. 20, 1982. A.B., Brown U., 1943. Reporter Worcester (Mass.) Telegram, 1946-53; editorial writer Evening Gazette, Worcester, 1953-60, mng. editor, 1964-67; editor editorial pages Worcester Telegram & Gazette, 1964-67, assoc. editor, 1967-70, editor, 1970-73, v.p., editor, 1973-81, assoc. pub., exec. v.p., 1981-82, pub., 1982—; dir. AP, State Mut. Securities, Inc., Enterprise-Sun Inc.; trustee Worcester County Instn. for Savs.; Mem. newspaper adv. bd. UPI, 1974-78. Pres. United Way of Central Mass., Worcester, 1973-75; v.p. The Meml. Hosp., Worcester, 1976; vice chmn. Central Mass. chpt. ARC, 1976-84, chmn., 1984—; media chmn. Mass. Bar-Press Com., 1976-77; chmn. trustees Worcester Found. Exptl. Biology, 1984—. Served with USNR, 1943-46. Fellow Acad. New Eng. Journalists; mem. U.P.I. New Eng. Newspaper Editors (pres. 1969), Am. Soc. Newspaper Editors, New Eng. Soc. Newspaper Editors (pres. 1968), New Eng. AP News Exec. Assn. (pres. 1971), Am. Antiquarian Soc., Phi Beta Kappa, Sigma Delta Chi. Clubs: Worcester, Worcester Econ. (pres. 1975), Bohemian, Tatnuck Country, Nat. Press. Lodge: Rotary. Office: 20 Franklin St Worcester MA 01613

ACHTERT, WALTER SCOTT, publisher; b. Yeadon, Pa., May 23, 1943; s. Alfred Carl Robert and Geraldine (Schollenberger) A. A.B., Drew U., 1965; M.A., NYU, 1966, Ph.D., 1972. Asst. to exec. dir. MLA, N.Y.C., 1967-72, dir. book publs. and research programs, 1972—; mem. selection jury Commonwealth Award for Lit., 1980—. Author: (with Joseph Gibaldi) MLA Handbook for Writers of Research Papers, Theses and Dissertation, 1977; editor: MLA Abstracts, 1970-74. Mem. MLA. Home: 166 Bank St New York NY 10014 Office: MLA 62 Fifth Ave New York NY 10011

ACITO, DANIEL JOSEPH, interior designer; b. Cin., May 18, 1918; s. Domenic and Carmella (DeRosa) A.; m. Bette Lou Arnold, Sept. 3, 1955; children—Marc Arnold, Brian Ashley, Dorian Leigh. Student, Cin. Art Acad., 1933-36, U. Cin., 1937-63. Interior and display designer Cin. dept. stores, 1939-42; partner Venito Studios, Cin., 1947-51; propr. Dan Acito Interiors, Cin., 1951-68, Dan Acito & Assos., Orlando, Fla., 1968-73; pres. Interior Design Consultants, Inc., Winter Park, Fla., 1973—; mem. Cin. Design Adv. Bd., 1963-66. Painter large hist. murals; crafter metal sculptures; interior design cons. and restorer, San Juan Hotel, Orlando; original artist and restorer, N.W. Territory mural at Miami U. campus, Hamilton, Ohio.; Author articles. Bd. dirs., exec. Christian Service Center, Orlando, 1973; chmn. Greater Cin. Neighborhood Assn., 1965-67; bd. dirs. Cin. Better Housing League, 1964-66; exec. con. Maitland (Fla.) Goals Planning Com., 1968-71; pres. Winter Park Council Chs., 1972-73; mem. Orlando Catholic Diocesan Ecumenical Commn., 1973-77, Orlando Area Christian-Jewish Dialogue, 1975-77; co-chmn. Orlando Historic Preservation Com., 1972-76. Served with AUS, 1942-46; PTO, ETO. Recipient Nat. Community Service award Nat. Soc. Interior Designers-A.I.D., 1974. Fellow Am. Soc. Interior Designers (sec 1968, mem., nat. dir., chmn. Fla. chpt. ednl. com.). Republican. Roman Catholic. Home: 176 Balfour Dr Winter Park FL 32792 Office: 132 E New England Ave Winter Park FL 32789 *A well known biblical quotation calls attention to a sad commentary on the quality and quantity of the individual's efforts throughout time. It reads: "The days of man are like grass, they blossom as flowers in the field; when the wind comes by they are gone, never more to be known in that place." It is a loss that the latent talents in every person cannot be uncovered, developed and put to good use, so that everyone would be a candidate for Who's Who. A man should not be as a flower at the mercy of the passing wind. He should be able to leave his mark and thereby contribute to and advance the quality of life in this world.*

ACKELL, EDMUND FERRIS, univ. pres.; b. Danbury, Conn., Nov. 29, 1925; s. Ferris M. and Barbara (Elias) A.; m. Carole M. Pryde, June 4, 1969. B.S., Holy Cross Coll., Worcester, Mass., 1949; D.M.D., Tufts U., 1953; M.D., Case Western Res. U., 1962; postgrad., U. Pa., 1955-57. Intern Bellevue Hosp., N.Y.C.; resident Meadowbrook Hosp.; practice medicine, specializing in oral and maxillofacial surgery; prof. medicine and dentistry U. Fla. Med. and Dental Sch., 1966-69; dean Sch. Dentistry, 1966-69, univ. v.p. health affairs, 1969-74; v.p. health affairs U. So. Calif., 1974-78; pres. Va. Commonwealth U., Richmond, 1978—; dir. Whittaker Corp., United Va. Bank. Served with USNR, 1943-46. Mem. AMA, ADA, Soc. Health and Human Values, Am. Public Health Assn., Va. Med. Assn., Va. Dental Assn., Richmond C. of C. (dir.). Clubs: Commonwealth, Country of Va. Home: 4700 Charmian Rd Richmond VA 23226 Office: 910 W Franklin St Richmond VA 23284

ACKER, ARTHUR MALCOLM, glass company executive; b. Allston, Mass., May 11, 1930; s. Robert Henry and Irene Agnes (Reed) A.; m. Barbara Arabelle Rundlett, Dec. 19, 1953; 1 son, John Arthur. B.B.A., Northwestern U., 1955; postgrad., U. Tenn., 1973. Estimator contract sales, contract mgr. Pitts. Plat. Glass Co., Boston, 1951-56; from dist. mgr. to v.p. sales and mktg. ASG Ind., Kingsport, Tenn., 1956-75; pres., dir. Shatterproof Glass Corp., Detroit, 1975-79; chmn., chief exec. officer Enhanced Glass Corp., Waco, Tex., 1979—. Dir. Flat Glass Energy Conservation Comm., 1974-76; Bd. dirs. Kingsport, Tenn. United Fund, 1973-74, Holston Valley Community Hosp., 1974-75; bd. govs. exec. devel. program U. Tenn., 1973-76. Served with USAF, 1948-49, 50-51. Mem. Nat. Glass Dealers Assn., Laminators Safety Glass Assn. (pres. 1977-78). Republican. Presbyterian. Clubs: Lakewood Tennis, Elks. Home: 3507 Greenleaf Dr Waco TX 76710 Office: 2901 Marlin Hwy 6 Waco TX 76705

ACKER, C. EDWARD, airline executive; b. 1929. B.A. in Econs. and Psychology, So. Meth. U., 1950. Pres., chief operating officer Braniff Airways Inc., 1965-75; pres. Transway Internat. Corp., 1975-76, Gulf United Corp., 1976-77; chmn., chief exec. officer Air Fla., 1977-81, Pan Am. World Airways Inc., N.Y.C., 1981—, pres., chief operating officer, 1982—, dir.; dir. Gulf United Corp., Intercontinental Hotels Corp. Office: Pan Am World Airways 200 Park Ave New York NY 10166

ACKER, DUANE CALVIN, university president; b. Atlantic, Iowa, Mar. 13, 1931; s. Clayton and Ruth (Kimball) A.; m. Shirley Hansen, Mar. 23, 1952; children: Diane Jean, LuAnn Fay. B.S., Iowa State U., 1952, M.S., 1953; Ph.D., Okla. State U., 1957. Instr. animal husbandry Okla. State U., 1953-55; mem. faculty Iowa State U., 1955-62, asso. prof. animal sci., asso. prof. charge farm operation curriculum, 1958-62; assoc. dean agr., dir. resident instrn. Kans. State U., Manhattan, 1962-66; dean agr. and biol. scis., dir. agrl. expt. sta. S.D. State U., Brookings, 1966-74; dir. Coop. Extension Service, 1971-74; vice chancellor Inst. Agrl. and Natural Resources, U. Nebr., Lincoln, 1974-75; pres. Kans. State U., Manhattan, 1975—; dir. Fed. Res. Bank of Kansas City, Kansas Power and Light Co., Gas Service Co.; Cons. Schering Corp., 1959-60; curriculum planning cons., Argentina, AID, 1961; mem. U.S. team for rev. Marshall plan aid to W. Germany, 1967; co-chmn. USA expt. sta. task force on quality of the environment, 1967-68; del. to OECD conf. higher edn. agr., Paris, 1970; chmn. North Central Intercoll. Athletic Conf., 1971-72; mem. S.D. Commn. on Exec. Reorgn., 1971-72. Author: Animal Science and Industry, 1963, 71, 83. Named Prof. of Year Iowa State U. Agr., 1959; recipient Tall Corn award for acad. advising Iowa State U., 1962. Mem. Am. Soc. Animal Sci., AAAS (chmn. agr. sect. 1982-83), Farm House Frat., Nat. Assn. State Univs. and Land-Grant Colls. (chmn. div. agr. 1970-71, exec. com. 1983—), Newcomen Soc., Sigma Xi, Alpha Zeta, Gamma Sigma Delta (internat. pres. 1974-76), Phi Kappa Phi. Presbyn. Club: Mason. Home: 100 Wilson Ct Manhattan KS 66506

ACKER, GARY LEWIS, broadcasting executive; b. Springfield, Mo., July 13, 1933; s. John Wesley and Lois Marguerite (Van Hall) A.; m. Janet Faye Nida, Dec. 30, 1976; children: Mark Lewis, Melissa Lois, Gay Louise. Grad. public schs., 1950. Pres. Queen City Broadcasting Co., Springfield, 1970—; owner, pres. Good News Broadcasting Co., WROS-AM, Jacksonville, Fla., KWAS, Amarillo, Tex., KEPT-FM, Shreveport, La., KLFJ, Springfield, KRIZ, Roswell, N.Mex., KFIX-FM, Laredo, Tex., KKOL and KELP, El Paso, Tex. Mem. Nat. and Religious Broadcasters. Home: Route 5 PO Box 15 Yukon OK 73099

ACKER, JOSEPH EDINGTON, JR., cardiologist; b. Knoxville, Tenn., Oct. 19, 1918; s. Joseph Edwan and Kate Loubelle (Edington) A.; m. Elizabeth Chase Gutch, Nov. 14, 1942; children: Joseph Edington III, Judith Ann Acker Mitchell, Julia Chase Acker Van Mol, John Howard, Janet Sue. B.S., U. Tenn., 1941, M.D., 1941. Diplomate: Am. Bd. Internal Medicine. Intern Kansas City Gen. Hosp., 1941-42; resident Cleve. City Hosp., 1946-48; pvt. practice internal medicine, Knoxville, 1948-55, cardiology, 1955—; mem. Knoxville Cardiovascular Group, 1962—; dir. cardiac rehab. outpatient programs U. Tenn. Meml. Hosp., St. Mary's Meml. Hosp., Ft. Sanders Presbyn. Hosp., 1977—; prof. clin. medicine Meml. Research Center and Hosp. U. Tenn., 1957—, chief cardiac work evaluation clinic, 1956-72, Knoxville Gen. Hosp., 1948-56. Author: (with Erb and Mann) Physicians Handbook for Evaluation of Cardiovascular and Physical Fitness, 1970; Editor: Newsletter Internat. Soc. Cardiology, 1972-80. Served to lt. comdr. USNR, 1942-46. Fellow A.C.P., Council Clin. Cardiology Am. Heart Assn., Am. Coll. Cardiology; mem. East Tenn. Heart Assn. (pres. 1956), Tenn. Heart Assn. (pres. 1961-63), Internat. Soc. Cardiology (rehab. council 1968-79). Home: 1307 Weisgarber Rd Knoxville TN 37919 Office: 1928 Alcoa Hwy Knoxville TN 37920

ACKER, NATHANIEL HULL, educational administrator; b. Manistee, Mich., July 29, 1927; s. Carmon M. and Cathryn (Keiser) A.; m. Mary Anne Brawley, June 6, 1951; children: Kristan, Nathaniel Hull Jr., Amy. B.S. in Bus. Adminstrn., Miami U., Oxford, Ohio, 1951. Sales rep. Proctor and Gamble Co., 1951-52, Peninsular Steel Co., Dayton, Ohio, 1952-53; with Mutschler Bros. Co., Nappanee, Ind., 1953-70; v.p. Mutschler Midwest, Inc., Chgo., 1963-68; regional mgr. Ohio-Ky.-Mich., 1968-70; dir. Am. Peace Corps Office Vol. Placement Midwest Region, Chgo., 1970-71; asso. dir. Northern region, New Delhi, India, 1971-72, exec. officer, 1972-73; dir. estate planning St. Lawrence U., Canton, N.Y., 1973-78; v.p. instl. devel. Hampden-Sydney (Va.) Coll., 1978-84; dir. devel. Episcopal High Sch., Alexandria, Va., 1984—. Park commr., Lake Bluff, Ill., 1965-68, pres., 1967-68; mem. Citizen's Com. for Lake Forest-Lake Bluff High Sch., 1966, Sch. Caucus, 1963-64, Village Bd. Caucus, 1966-68, Citizens' Com. for Rockland Park, 1964; chmn. Lake Bluff United Fund, 1962-63. Mem. Sigma Alpha Epsilon. Home: 1200 N Quaker Ln Alexandria VA 22302 also Pilgrim Sta Frankfort MI 49635

ACKER, ROBERT FLINT, microbiologist; b. Chgo., Aug. 24, 1920; s. Robert Booth and Mary (Flint) A.; m. Phyllis Catharine Fry, Jan. 2, 1948; children: Catharine Elizabeth, Barbara Fenner, Robert Macdonald, James Christopher. B.A., Ind. U., 1942, M.A., 1948; Ph.D., Rutgers U., 1953. Asst. prof. Iowa State U., Ames, 1954-59; asst. chief cancer chemotherapy dept., chief quality control dept. Microbiol. Assos., Inc., Bethesda, Md., 1959-61, chief dept. cell and media prodn., 1961-62; dir. microbiology program Office of Naval Research, Dept. Navy, Washington, 1962-69; dir. fed. program devel., asst. dean faculties for research, prof. biol. scis. Northwestern U., Evanston, Ill., 1969-74; exec. dir. Am. Soc. Microbiology, Washington, 1974-81, Nat. Fedn. Infectious Disease, Chevy Chase, Md., 1981—. Author: (with R.R. Jennings) The Protistan Kingdom, 1970; editor: Proc. 24th Internat. Congress on Marine Corrosion and Fouling, 1972; editorial bd.: Applied Microbiology, 1962-73. Chmn. urban ministry com. Nat. Presbyn. Ch., Washington, 1978, chmn. mission com., Washington, 1978, 79; v.p. bd. dirs. Iona House Center for the Elderly, Washington, 1978-79, pres., 1979-81; trustee Massanetta Conf. Ctr.,

1983—. Served with USNR, 1942-46. Fellow Am. Acad. Microbiology; mem. Soc. Indsl. Microbiology, Soc. Gen. Microbiology (U.K.), Am. Inst. Biol. Scis., Inter-Soc. Council Biology and Medicine, Council Engring. and Sci. Soc. Execs., Am. Soc. Assn. Execs. Club: Cosmos. Home: 4 E Lenox St Chevy Chase MD 20815 Office: 5530 Wisconsin Ave Chevy Chase MD 20815

ACKERLY, ROBERT SAUNDERS, JR., educator; b. N.Y.C., Oct. 7, 1929; s. Robert Saunders and Pauline Whipple (Morgan) A.; m. Linda M. Loucks, June 18, 1955; children: Donald Houston, Wendy Saunders. Student, Cornell U., 1947-49; B.A., Coll. of Wooster, 1952; A.M., Colgate U., 1959; Ed.D., Ind. U., 1963. Freshman advisor Colgate U., Hamilton, N.Y., 1952-54; asst. dean students Ill. Inst. Tech., Chgo., 1958-60; counselor grad. div. Sch. Edn., Ind. U., Bloomington, 1960-63; asst. to v.p. for acad. affairs, San Diego State U., 1963-70, assoc. dean acad. planning, 1970-74; assoc. dean Univ. Coll., 1974-76, prof. edn., 1976—. Served with USAF, 1955-58; to lt. col. USAFR. Mem. Adult Edn. Assn., Calif. State Employees Assn., Air Force Assn., Nat. Acad. Advising Assn., Res. Officers Assn., Ret. Officers Assn., Phi Delta Kappa. Republican. Home: 9206 Shirley Ct La Mesa CA 92041 Office: San Diego State U San Diego CA 92182

ACKERMAN, ARTHUR WALDRON, JR., mfg. co. exec.; b. Ypsilanti, Mich., July 11, 1925; s. Arthur Waldron and Edith (Marsh) A.; m. Carolyn Gordon, June 12, 1948; children—Gwendolyn Ackerman Hansen, Arthur Waldron, III, Stephen Gordon, John Erichsen, Cynthia. B.S., U. Mich., 1950, M.B.A., 1951. C.P.A., Mich. Mgmt. engr., then staff accountant Ernst & Whinney, C.P.A.'s, Detroit, 1951-57; with Huck Mfg. Co., aerospace and fastening systems mfrs., Detroit, 1957—, v.p. fin., 1975-77, pres., 1977—; v.p., group exec. Fed. Mogul Corp., 1980—; dir. Brass-Craft Mfg. Co., Detroit. Trustee Boys and Girls Clubs Met., Detroit, 1979—. Served as ensign USNR, 1943-45. Mem. Fin. Execs. Inst., Indsl. Fasteners Inst. Clubs: Detroit Athletic, Detroit, Newport-Irvine Rotary (div.), Balboa Bay Yacht, Dana Point Yacht. Address: 6 Thomas Irvine CA 92714

ACKERMAN, BETTYE LOUISE (MRS. SAM JAFFE), actress; b. Cottageville, S.C., Feb. 28, 1928; d. Clarence Kilgo and Mary Mildred (Baker) A.; m. Sam Jaffe, June 7, 1956. B.A., Columbia U., 1954; student, Otis Art Inst., 1964-68, Theatre Wing, N.Y.C., 1954-56, Stella Adler Sch., 1956-58. Stage appearances Pheelie in No 'count Boy, 1954, Elmire in Tartuffe, 1955, 56, Antigone, 1956, tour of The Lark, 1956-57, Portia in Merchant of Venice, Dickinson (N.D.) State Coll., 1971; films Face of Fire, 1958, Rascal, 1969; TV movies Companions in Nightmare, 1968, Heat of Anger, 1971, Murder or Mercy, 1974, The Feather and Father Gang, 1977, The Yeagers, 1979; TV Confessions of a Married Man, 1982; others; appeared as Maggie Graham: TV movies on Ben Casey TV series, 1961-66; as Anne Frazier in: TV series Bracken's World; numerous guest appearances Good Morning America; numerous others; tchr. body movement, Lucy Feagin Sch. Drama, N.Y.C., 1953, recorded, Salome and School for Scandal; lectr., demonstrator ethnic dances, Louise Gifford Pantomime classes Columbia U., 1954-56; one-woman art shows, Erskine Coll., Due West, S.C., 1970, 76, Lambert Gallery, Los Angeles, 1970, Monterey Peninsula Mus. of Art, 1980, Drew U., 1982, U.S. Internat. U., group show, Gallery 8, Claremont, Calif., 1976, Galleria Beretich, Claremont, Calif., 1981. West Coast campaign chmn. Muscular Dystrophy Assn., 1963-69; sec., bd. dirs. Hollywood Motion Picture and TV Mus. First woman grand marshall I Am An American and Constitution Day Parade, Balt., 1972. Home: 302 N Alpine Dr Beverly Hills CA 90210 Office: care Sue Goldin Talent Agy 119 N San Vicente Blvd Beverly Hills CA 90211

ACKERMAN, BRUCE ARNOLD, lawyer, educator; b. N.Y.C., Aug. 19, 1943; s. Nathan and Jean (Rosenberg) A.; m. Susan Gould Rose, May 27, 1967; children—Sybil Rose, John Mill. B.A. summa cum laude, Harvard U., 1964; LL.B. with honors, Yale U., 1967. Bar: Pa. 1970. Law clk. U.S. Ct. Appeals, 1967-68; to Justice John M. Harlan U.S. Supreme Ct., 1968-69; prof. law and public policy analysis U. Pa., 1969-74; prof. law, Yale U., 1974-82; Beekman prof. law and philosophy Columbia U., 1982—. Author: Private Property and the Constitution, 1977, Social Justice in the Liberal State, 1980 (Gavel award ABA), (with Hassler) Clean Coal/Dirty Air, 1981, Reconstructing American Law, 1984, (with others) The Uncertain Search for Environmental Quality, 1974 (Henderson prize Harvard Law Sch.). Office: 435 W 116th St New York NY 10027

ACKERMAN, EUGENE, biophysics educator; b. Bklyn., July 8, 1920; s. Saul Benton and Dorothy (Salwen) A.; m. Dorothy Hopkirk, June 5, 1943; children—Francis H., Emmanuel T., Amy R. Ackerman de Canésie. B.A., Swarthmore Coll., 1941; Sc.M., Brown U., 1943; Ph.D., U. Wis., 1949; postgrad., U. Pa., 1949-51, fellow, 1957-58. Instr. Brown U., 1943; from asst. prof. to prof. biophysics Pa. State U., 1951-60; mem. faculty U. Minn. Mayo Grad. Sch. Medicine, 1960-67, prof. biophysics, 1965—; staff cons. biophysics Mayo Found. and Mayo Clinic, 1960-67; Hill Family Found. prof. biomed. computing, prof. biometry also computer scis. U. Minn., Mpls., 1967-79, dir. div. health computer sci., 1969-79, prof. dept. lab. medicine, 1969—; dir. computer facility Mayo Found., 1964-65; Cons. bioacoustics USAF, 1957-62; mem. epidemiology and biometry tng. com. NIH, 1963-67, spl. study sect. ultrasonic applications, 1965-67, spl. study sect. lab. med. scis., 1967-69, computer and biomath. sci. study sect., 1969-73. Author: Biophysical Science, 1962, 2d edit; (with L. Ellis and L. Williams), 2d edit., 1979; Author: (with L. Gatewood) Math Models in the Health Sciences, 1979; editor: Biophys. Jour., 1983—; Author also articles, tech. reports, chpts. in books. Research grantee Am. Cancer Soc., 1953-56; NSF, 1958-64; NIH, 1954—. Mem. A.A.A.S., Biophys. Soc., Am. Physiol. Soc., N.Y., Minn. acads. sci., Assn. Computing Machinery, Soc. Math. Biology, IEEE, Phi Beta Kappa, Sigma Xi, Gamma Alpha. Mem. Soc. of Friends. Home: 11301 Park Ridge Dr W Minnetonka MN 55343 Office: Box 511 Mayo Meml Bldg U Minn 420 Delaware St SE Minneapolis MN 55455

ACKERMAN, GARY L., congressman; b. Bklyn., Nov. 19, 1942; s. Max and Eva (Barnett) A.; m. Rita Tewel, May 27, 1967; children: Lauren Meredith, Corey Brian, Ari David. B.A., Queens Coll., 1965. Owner, mgr. newspaper firm, Flushing, N.Y., 1970—, advt. agy., 1972—; mem. N.Y. Senate, 1979—, 98th Congress. Mem. Queens Coll. Alumni Assn. Democrat. Club: B'nai B'rith. Office: Room 1631 Longworth House Office Bldg Washington DC 20515 *

ACKERMAN, GERALD MARTIN, art educator; b. Alameda, Calif., Aug. 21, 1928; s. Alois M. and Eva L. (Sadler) A. B.A., U. Calif.-Berkeley, 1952; postgrad., U. Munich, W.Ger., 1955-58; Ph.D., Princeton U., 1964. Instr. Bryn Mawr Coll., Pa., 1960-64; asst. prof. Stanford U., Calif., 1964-70; assoc. prof. dept. art Pomona Coll., Claremont, Calif., 1970-75, prof., 1975—, chmn. dept. art, 1972-82; Fulbright prof. U. Leningrad, 1980. Author: exhbn. catalogue Gerome, 1972; contbr. articles to profl. jours.; playwright: Family and Friends, 1979, The Surfer, 1981. Mem. Coll. Art Assn., Deutsche Verein fur Kunstgeschichte, Societe de l'histoire de l'art francaise. Democrat. Club: Black and White Men Together. Home: 360 S Mills Ave Claremont CA 91711 Office: Dept Art Pomona Coll Claremont CA 91711

ACKERMAN, HAROLD A., judge. Student, Seton Hall U., 1945-46, 48; LL.B., Rutgers U., 1951. Bar: N.J. 1951. Adminstrv. asst. to Commr. of Labor and Industry, State of N.J., 1955-56; judge of compensation State of N.J., 1956-62, supervising judge of compensation, 1962-65; judge Union County Dist. Ct., 1965-70, presiding judge, 1966-70; judge Union County Ct., 1970-73, Superior Ct. law div., 1973-75, Superior Ct. Chancery div., 1975-79, U.S. Dist. Ct., Dist. of N.J., 1980—; mem. Supreme Ct. Com. on Revision of Rules, 1967; chmn. Supreme Ct. Com. on County Dist. Cts., 1968; mem. faculty Nat. Jud. Coll., 1978. Office: US Dist Ct US Post Office and Courthouse 402 E State St PO Box 1688 Trenton NJ 08605 *

ACKERMAN, HARRY S., motion picture co. exec.; b. Albany, N.Y., Nov. 17, 1912; s. Harold and Ann (Flannery) A.; m. Elinor Donahue, Apr. 21, 1961; children—Brian, Peter, James, Christopher; children by previous marriage—Susan, Stephen. A.B., Dartmouth, 1935. Freelance writer and actor, 1935-36; radio dir. Young & Rubicam, N.Y.C., 1936-42, radio prodn. head, 1942-45, v.p. charge radio programs, 1945; exec. producer CBS, N.Y.C., 1948, dir. network programs, Hollywood, Calif., 1948, v.p., dir. TV and radio, 1949-51, v.p. charge TV, 1951-55; exec. dir. spl. prodns. CBS-TV, 1956-57; pres. Ticonderoga Prodns., ind. producer TV, 1957-58; v.p., exec. producer Screen Gems Pictures Corp. div. Columbia Pictures Industries, Inc., 1958-73; head Harry Ackerman Prodns.; v.p. Capitol Pictures, Inc., Hollywood; spl. radio cons. U.S. Treasury, 1944-46. Bd. dirs. TV Acad. Found.; trustee, mem. exec. com. Motion Picture Relief Fund. Mem. Acad. TV Arts and Scis. (past pres. Los Angeles, past nat. pres.), Manuscripts Soc. (charter, dir.), Am. Arbitration Assn. Club: Dartmouth So. Calif. Home: 4525 Lemp Ave North Hollywood CA 91602 Office: 315 S Beverly Dr Beverly Hills CA 90212

ACKERMAN, HELEN PAGE, librarian, educator; b. Evanston, Ill., June 30, 1912; d. John Bernard and Florence Page (Jarvis). B.A., Agnes Scott Coll., Decatur, Ga., 1933; B.L.S., U. N.C., 1940. Cataloger Columbia Theol. Sem., 1942-43; post librarian U.S. Army, Aberdeen Proving Ground, Md., 1943-45; asst. librarian Union Theol. Sem., Richmond, Va., 1945-49; reference librarian UCLA, 1949-54, asst. univ. librarian, 1954-65, asso. univ. librarian, 1965-73, univ. librarian, 1973-77, prof. Sch. Info. and Library Sci., 1973-77, 82, 83; vis. prof. Sch. Librarianship, U. Calif., Berkeley, 1978, 80. Recipient Disting. Alumni award U. N.C., 1973; award of distinction in library sci. U. Calif. at Los Angeles Alumnae Assn., 1977. Mem. Am., Calif. library assns., AAUW (Status of Women award 1973), Council on Library Resources (bd. mem. 1975—). Home: 310 20th St Santa Monica CA 90402 Office: 405 Hilgard Ave Los Angeles CA 90024

ACKERMAN, HERBERT, security dealer and broker; b. N.Y.C., May 30, 1929; s. Harry and Florence (Levy) A.; m. Caryl Bindler, Apr. 29, 1956; children: Lynn, Joyce, Marcia. B.S., Hofstra U., 1950. C.P.A., N.Y. Acct. Fields Fischgrund Aerenson, N.Y.C., 1952-58; ptnr. Glickenhaus & Co., N.Y.C., 1958—. Served with U.S. Armed Forces, 1950-52. Mem. N.Y. Stock Exchange. Home: 512 Ross Pl Oceanside NY 11572 Office: Glickenhaus & Co 6 E 43d St New York NY 10017

ACKERMAN, JACK ROSSIN, investment banker; b. N.Y.C., Feb. 8, 1931; s. Robert M. and Florence (Rossin) A.; m. Dana Lowenthal, Nov. 29, 1974; children: Ellen, Jay, Robin, Bradley. B.A., Harvard U., 1953, M.B.A., 1955. With Bache Halsey Stuart Shields, Inc., N.Y.C., 1955-80; mng. dir. Drexel Burnham Lambert, Inc., N.Y.C., 1980—; dir. Mich. Gen. Corp., Dallas, Kinney Systems Inc., N.Y.C. Trustee Jewish Bd. Family and Children's Services, 1980; bd. dirs. Jewish Found. Edn. Women, 1980. Clubs: Century, Country (Purchase, N.Y.). Office: 55 Broad St New York City NY 10004

ACKERMAN, JAMES NILS, lawyer; b. Pleasant Dale, Nebr., Mar. 16, 1912; s. Albert Ferdinand and Irma Marie (Berlet) A.; m. Jean Caroline Doty, Aug. 8, 1939; children: Thomas Richard, Mary Alice. A.B., Nebr. Wesleyan U., 1933, LL.D., 1975; LL.B., Harvard U., 1938. Bar: Nebr. 1938. Practice of law Davis & Stubbs, 1938-41, Davis, Stubbs & Ackerman, 1941-42, Peterson & Devoe, 1947-48; ptnr. Peterson, Devoe & Ackerman, 1948-52, Peterson & Ackerman, Lincoln, Nebr., 1952-77, Pierson, Ackerman, Fichett, Akin & Hunzeker, 1977—; with FBI, 1942-47; asst. gen. counsel Bankers Life Ins. Co., Nebr., 1947-55, gen. counsel, 1955-77, v.p., 1960-77, trustee, 1957-77; U.S. magistrate Dist. Nebr., Lincoln, 1979-81; dir. Farmers Mut. Ins. Co., Gateway Bank, 1971—, chmn. bd., 1975-83; sec., gen. counsel Nebr. Ins. Fedn., 1978—. Bd. dirs. Lincoln Community Chest, 1965-68, chmn. bd., 1967-68; bd. dirs. Lincoln Community Council, 1950-65, County-City Implementation Commn., 1974, Lancaster County Child Guidance Clinic, 1946-54, Lincoln Symphony. Orch. Assn., 1965-72; Chmn. Lancaster County Rep. Party, 1950; del. Rep. county and state convs.; mem. Pres.'s Adv. Com. for J.F. Kennedy Center for Performing Arts, 1970-77, Nebr. Coordinating Commn. for Post-Secondary Edn., 1977-82; bd. govs. Nebr. Wesleyan U., 1964—, chmn., 1964-76. Mem. Nebr. Bar Assn. (v.p. 1942), Lincoln Bar Assn. (pres. 1957), Assn. Life Ins. Counsel (pres. 1969-70), Am. Life Conv. (chmn. legal sect. 1960), Nebr. Ins. Fedn. (pres. 1970-73), Lincoln C. of C. (dir. 1968-70). Presbyterian. Clubs: Mason, Shriner, Jester, Lincoln Country, Nebraska (Lincoln). Home: 6920 Sumner St Lincoln NE 65806 Office: 530 S 13th St Suite B Lincoln NE 68508

ACKERMAN, JAMES SLOSS, fine arts educator; b. San Francisco, Nov. 8, 1919; s. Lloyd S. and Louise (Sloss) A.; m. Mildred Rosenbaum, Apr. 11, 1947; children: Anne, Anthony, Sarah. A.B., Yale U., 1941; M.A., N.Y. U., 1947, Ph.D., 1952; L.H.D., Kenyon Coll., 1961; D.F.A., Md. Inst., 1972, Mass. Coll. Art, 1984; L.H.D., U. Md., 1976. Part-time instr. Yale, 1946-48; research fellow Am. Acad. in Rome, 1949-52; asst. prof. then prof. U. Calif., 1952-60; editor in chief Art Bull., 1956-60; prof. fine arts Harvard U., 1960—, chmn. dept. fine arts, 1963-68, 82—; Slade prof. fine art, fellow King's Coll., Cambridge U., 1969-70; Vis. fellow Council Humanities, Princeton, 1960-61; fellow Am. Council Learned Socs., 1964-65; pres. Univ. Film Study Center, 1967-68; Sr. fellow Nat. Endowment Humanities, 1974-75; Trustee Am. Acad. in Rome. Author: The Cortile del Belvedere, 1954, The Architecture of Michelangelo, 1961 (winner Alice D. Hitchcock award Soc. Archtl. Historians 1961, Charles R. Morey award 1963), (with Rhys Carpenter) Art and Archaeology, 1963, Palladio, 1967, Palladio's Villas, 1967; (with Kathleen Weil-Garris) films Looking for Renaissance Rome, 1975, Palladio the Architect and His Influence in America; Contbr. to 17th Century Sci. and the Arts, 1961. Trustee The Artists Found., pres., 1977-79; mem. council of scholars Library of Congress, 1980-82. Recipient medal for service in art edn. Nat. Gallery Art, 1966; Centennial citation U. Calif., 1968. Fellow Am. Acad. Arts and Scis., Accademia Olimpica (corr.), Brit. Acad. (corr.), Royal Acad. Arts and Scis. Uppsala (corr.), Royal Soc. for Encouragement of Arts; mem. Soc. Archtl. Historians, Coll. Art Assn., Renaissance Soc. Am. Home: 12 Coolidge Hill Rd Cambridge MA 02138 Office: Fogg Museum Harvard U Cambridge MA 02138

ACKERMAN, JAMES WALDO, judge; b. Jacksonville, Fla., Jan. 1, 1926; s. James Waldo and Mary (Mundee) A.; m. Doris Ann Bivin, July 3, 1952; children: James Waldo III, Anne Francis, Philip William. B.S., Marquette U., 1947, J.D., 1949. Bar: Ill. 1949. Practiced, in Springfield, Ill., 1949-71, state's atty., Sangamon County, Ill., 1956-60; corp. counsel City of Springfield, 1960-62; asst. state treas. State of Ill., 1962-64, chief dep. atty. gen., 1970-71; atty. Springfield Election Commn., 1964-68; asso. gen. counsel Ill. Municipal League, 1966-68; formerly judge Ill. Circuit Ct., 7th circuit, Springfield; now judge U.S. Dist. Ct. Central Dist. Ill., Springfield, chief judge, 1982—; adj. prof. dept. med. humanities So. Ill. U.; apptd. mem. Jud. Conf. Com. on Operation of Jury System, 1981. Contbr.: article Jour. Legal Medicine. Served with USNR, 1944-46, 52-54. Home: 25 Interlacken Springfield IL 62704 Office: PO Box 315 Springfield IL 62705

ACKERMAN, JOHN HENRY, health services consultant, physician; b. Fond du Lac, Wis., Feb. 27, 1925; s. Henry Theodore and Clara Frances (Voss) A.; m. Eugenia Ellen Mulligan, May 22, 1948; children: H. John, Mary, Lisa, Paul. Student, Cornell U., 1943-44, Ind. U., 1944; M.D., Marquette U., 1948; M.P.H., Johns Hopkins U., 1955. Intern St. Agnes Hosp., Fond du Lac, 1948-49; family practice medicine, Clarksville, Iowa, 1949-51; commd. officer USPHS, 1951-70; dep. chief tng. program Center Disease Control, Atlanta, 1970, ret. as med. dir., 1970; dep. dir. Ohio Dept. Health, Columbus, 1971-75, dir., 1975-83; clin. prof. preventive medicine Ohio State U.; cons. WHO. Served with AUS, 1943-46. Fellow Am. Pub. Health Assn., Am. Coll. Preventive Medicine, Royal Soc. Health; mem. Commd. Officers Assn., Ohio Med. Assn., Columbus Acad. Medicine, Alpha Kappa Kappa. Roman Catholic. Clubs: Assn. Ohio Commodores; Athletic (Columbus). Home: 4183 Reedbury Ln Columbus OH 43220 Office: 2941 Kenny Rd Columbus OH 43221

ACKERMAN, LENNIS CAMPBELL, consultant; b. Los Angeles, July 28, 1917; s. Lennis Howard and Ethel (Campbell) A.; m. Barbara Bohlken, July 27, 1941; children: Nancy (Mrs. Michael H. Burnaugh), Janet (Mrs. Robert W. Lesser), John, Barbara, George. A.B., UCLA, 1940. With Texaco, Los Angeles, 1940-43, Schenley Distillers, San Francisco, 1945-48; merchandiser Richfield Oil Corp., San Francisco, 1949-52; sales rep. Walker Mfg. Co., 1952-56, mktg. adminstr., 1956-58; v.p., gen. mgr. Can. subs. Galt Metal Industries, 1958-63, v.p. internat. ops. parent co., 1963-65, v.p. mktg., 1965, pres., 1966-68; pres., chief exec. officer Newport News Shipbldg. and Dry Dock Co., 1969-73; exec. v.p. Tenneco, Inc., 1972-73; group v.p. Questor Corp., 1973-78; assoc. dean Sch. Bus. Adminstrn., Coll. William and Mary, Williamsburg, Va., 1978-83; dir. Mid Am. Industries, Inc., Norfolk Shipbldg. & Dry Dock Corp. Sec. Va. Port Authority, 1971-73; mem. Sch. Bus. Adminstrn. Sponsors, Inc., Coll. William and Mary, 1970-79, chmn., 1970-72. Served with USAAF, 1943-45. Mem. Soc. Automotive Engrs., Beta Gamma Sigma (hon.), Alpha Sigma Phi. Episcopalian. Clubs: Met. (Washington); Pine Valley, James River Country. Office: PO Box 313 Williamsburg VA 23185

ACKERMAN, MARSHALL, publishing company executive; b. N.Y.C., Jan. 22, 1925; s. Albert and Beatrice (Munstuk) A.; m. Carol Lipman, June 8, 1948; children: Stark, Scott, A. Marc. A.B., Harvard U., 1949; M.S. in Journalism, Northwestern U., 1950. Dir. employee relations Gimbel Bros., N.Y.C., 1950-51; account exec. Leonard Wolf & Assos. (advt. agy.), N.Y.C., 1951-54; with Rodale Press, Inc., 1954—, exec. v.p., 1967—, vice chmn. bd., 1978—; pub. Prevention mag., 1977—, Theatre Crafts mag., 1967—. Pres. bd. assos. Cedar Crest Coll., Allentown, Pa., 1976-78, trustee, Allentown, Pa., 1983—; pres. Pa. Stage Co., Allentown, 1978-80. Served with U.S. Army, 1943-46. Decorated Bronze Star, Purple Heart. Club: Harvard (N.Y.C.). Home: 2250 Lehigh Pkwy N Allentown PA 18103 Office: Rodale Press Inc 33 E Minor St Emmaus PA 18049

ACKERMAN, ORA RAY, hosp. supt.; b. Mapleton, Minn., Jan. 13, 1931; s. Ora R. and Minnie T. (Quam) A.; m. Barbara Singley, Mar. 25, 1951; children—Bruce, David, Cindy. B.S. with distinction, U. Minn., 1953; M.Ed., 1955; M.Ed. certificate dir. recreation, Ind. U., 1961; Ed.D., 1963, N.Y. U., 1966; grad. exec. devel. program, Ind. U., 1968. Mental health coordinator in, Calif., Md. and, Ind., 1953-63; dir. edn. and activity therapy Ind. Dept. Mental Health, 1963-66; supt. Ft. Wayne (Ind.) State Hosp. and Tng. Center, 1966—; Vis. prof. psychology Ind. U. (Purdue-Ft. Wayne campus), 1967—; Mem. adv. council title IV-A, Ind. State Library, 1968—; mem. gov.'s tech. planning com. for devel. plans for Correction Center, 1970—; mem. Ind. Mental Health-Mental Retardation Commn., 1970—, Gov.'s Com. to Study Mental Health Laws. Contbr. to profl. jours. Mem. Nat. Recreation Assn. (dist. adv. com. 1965-68), Nat. Therapeutic Recreation Soc. (div. 1966-69), Am. Soc. Mental Hosp. Bus. Adminstrs., Am. Soc. Mental Deficiency, Am. Cancer Soc. (mem. nat. house dels., bd. dirs. Ind. div.), Am. Recreation Soc., Ind. Park and Recreation Assn. Methodist (chmn. bd. 1967, mem. commn. social concerns 1958-69). Club: Kiwanian. Office: 4900 Saint Joe Rd Fort Wayne IN 46815 802 Northwood Blvd Fort Wayne IN 46805

ACKERMAN, PHILIP CHARLES, utility executive; b. Kenmore, N.Y., Feb. 14, 1944; s. Harold Lewis and Marion (Ehrhardt) A.; m. Nancy Margaret Weig, Sept. 11, 1967; children—David Philip, Kathryn Elizabeth. B.S., SUNY, Buffalo, 1965; LL.B., Harvard U., 1968. Bar: N.Y. bar 1968. Atty. Iroquois Gas Corp., Buffalo, 1968-74; asst. sec. Nat. Fuel Gas Distbn. Corp., Buffalo, 1974-75, sec., 1975—, gen. counsel, 1976—; v.p. Seneca Resources Corp., Nat. Fuel Gas Co., 1980—. Mem. Orchard Park (N.Y.) Planning Bd., 1972-78, chmn., 1977-78; mem. council Canisius Coll. Sch. Bus. Adminstr. Mem. Am. Bar Assn., N.Y. State Bar Assn., Erie County Bar Assn., Niagara Frontier Corp. Counsel Assn. (chmn. audit com. 1979-81), Am. Gas Assn. (chmn. ins. com. 1974-76), Audubon Soc., Sierra Club., Buffalo Soc. Natural Scis. (bd. mgrs.). Republican. Club: Sitzmarker Ski (dir.). Office: 10 Lafayette Sq Buffalo NY 14203

ACKERMAN, RAYMOND BASIL, advertising agency executive; b. Pitts., Aug. 7, 1922; s. Charles Raymond and Teresa Jane (Grasinger) A.; m. Lucille Frances Flanagan, June 14, 1948; children: Patricia Ackerman Conley, Annie, Ray, Susie Ackerman Fuller, Mark, Amy Lou. B.S., Oklahoma City U., 1951. Mem. display advt. staff Okla. Pub. Co., Oklahoma City, 1947-52; account exec. Knox-Ackerman Advt., Oklahoma City, 1952-53; pres. Ackerman Assos., Oklahoma City, 1954-74; chmn. bd. Ackerman & McQueen, Inc., Oklahoma City, Tulsa and Dallas, 1975—; dir. Founders Bank & Trust Co. Author: Tomorrow Belongs to Oklahoma, 1964. Pres., gen. chmn. Oklahoma City United Appeal, 1964-66; chmn. Oklahoma City Salvation Army, 1968; pres. Oklahoma City Better Bus. Bur., 1966; gen. chmn. Nat. Finals Rodeo Oklahoma City, 1965—; bd. dirs. Jr. Achievement, Oklahoma City, Okla. Water Found.; lay adv. bd. St. Anthony Hosp.; trustee, pres. Omniplex Sci. Mus., Oklahoma City, 1979-80; trustee Oklahoma City Youth Park. Served with USN, 1942-47; rear adm. ret. USNR. Decorated Meritorious Service medal. Disting. Pub. Service medal; named Outstanding Grad. Oklahoma City U., 1964; recipient Silver medal Am. Advt. Fedn., 1982. Mem. Naval Res. Assn. (nat. pres. 1969-71), Navy League (nat. dir. 1972-76, pres. Okla. chpt. 1974-76), Oklahoma City C. of C. (dir.), Oklahoma City Advt. Club (pres. 1963-64). Home: 12905 Laurel Valley Ct Oklahoma City OK 73142 Office: 5708 Mosteller Dr Oklahoma City OK 73112

ACKERMAN, ROBERT KILGO, college dean, historian; b. Williston, S.C., Oct. 26, 1933; s. Clarence Kilgo and Mary Mildred (Baker) A.; m. May Morgan, Jan. 28, 1956; children: Mark, Roxanne, Bettye. A.B., U. S.C., 1956, M.A., 1961, Ph.D., 1965; postdoctoral, Harvard Inst. Ednl. Mgmt., 1975. Archivist S.C. Archives, Columbia, 1962-63; from asst. prof. to prof. history Erskine Coll., 1963-71, v.p. for acad. affairs, 1971-75; dean Coll. Liberal Arts, Drew U., 1975—; Cons. Charleston County (S.C.) Schs., Charleston, 1969-75; lectr. and writer on Am. South. Author: filmstrip series The History of South Carolina, 1969; author: South Carolina Colonial Land Policies, 1976; co-editor: Perspectives on South Carolina, 1973. Chmn. com. publs. S.C.

Tricentennial, 1970; v.p. Christian Action Council, 1972-75; mem. Christian-Jewish Com. for S.C.; bd. dirs. Abbeville County (S.C.) Mental Health Commn.; pres. bd. trustees Colonial Symphony, Madison, N.J., 1983—. Served to capt. USMC, 1956-59. Mem. So. Assn. Colls. and Schs. (chmn. coms. accreditation 1971—), Middle States Assn. Schs., N.J. Assn. Colls. and Univs. (dir.), Am. Assn. Higher Edn., S.C. Hist. Assn., Phi Beta Kappa (v.p. area 1975, chpt. pres.), Omicron Delta Kappa. Methodist.

ACKERMAN, SANFORD SELIG, fin. exec.; b. Phila., Mar. 3, 1932; s. Leon F. and Laura (Axelman) A.; m. Amy Ruth Gleicher, July 5, 1969; children—Timothy Leon, Peter Milgram, Daniel Aaron. B.M.E., U. Del., 1953; M.S., Cornell U., 1958. Mech. engr. Westinghouse Electric Corp., Lester, Pa., 1953-54; prin. Touche Ross & Co., N.Y.C., 1958-73; sr. v.p. fin. Needham, Harper & Steers, Inc., N.Y.C., 1974-79; sr. v.p. fin. and adminstrn. Syska & Hennessy, Inc., N.Y.C., 1979—. Mem. bd. edn. Byram Hills (N.Y.) Sch. Dist., 1977. Served with AUS, 1953-55. Cornell U. jr. fellow, 1956. Address: 3 Mead Rd Armonk NY 10504

ACKERMAN, TREDA STERN, investment research company executive; b. N.Y.C., Mar. 17, 1947; d. Alfred S. and Gertrude (Scher) Stern; m. Kenneth Jay Ackerman, Nov. 4, 1972 (div. 1980). B.A. in Polit. Sci., CUNY, 1968. Analyst mcpl. bond research Dun & Bradstreet Inc., N.Y.C., 1968-71, sr. analyst mcpl. bond research, 1971-73; asst. v.p. analyst mcpl. bond research Moody's Investors Service Inc., N.Y.C., 1973-75, v.p. assoc. dir., 1975-79, sr. v.p.,dir mcpl. bond dept., 1979-81, exec. v.p.,dir. mcpl. bond dept., 1981—. Mem. Mcpl. Forum of N.Y., Soc. Mcpl. Analysts, Fin. Women's Assn., Women's Econ. Roundtable, Mcpl. Analysts Group N.Y., Mcpl. Fin. Officers Assn. Democrat. Home: 315 E 86th St New York NY 10028 Office: 99 Church St New York NY 10007

ACKERMAN, WESLEY ARDMORE, chem. co. exec.; b. Elizabeth, N.J., Apr. 29, 1921; s. Harry and Maude (Peterson) A.; m. Jacqueline R. Henning, Sept. 11, 1948; 1 son, Michael D. Student, U. Ariz., 1939-42; M.B.A., Harvard, 1943. With U.S. Borax & Chem. Corp. (and predecessors), Los Angeles, 1947—, sec., 1957—. Served with AUS, 1943-46. Home: 26119 Basswood Ave Rancho Palos Verdes CA 90274 Office: 3075 Wilshire Blvd Los Angeles CA 90010

ACKERMANN, WILLIAM CARL, cons. engr., educator; b. Sheboygan, Wis., Oct. 7, 1913; s. William H. and Frances E. (Shermer) A.; m. Margaret A. Koepsell, May 6, 1942; children—William C., Nancy A., Arthur J. Student, Lawrence Coll., 1930-32; B.S. in C.E. with honors, U. Wis., 1935; D.Sc., Northwestern U., 1970, So. Ill. U., 1971. Constrn. engr. Kimberly-Clark Corp., 1935; hydraulic engr. water control planning dept. TVA, 1935-54; head watershed hydrology sect. U.S. Dept. Agr., 1954-56; chief Ill. Water Survey, 1956-79; adj. prof. civil engring. U. Ill., 1980—; adviser office sci. and tech. Exec. Office Pres., Washington, 1963-64; Mem. basin com. Fed. Inter-Agy. on Rivers, 1948-56, chmn. sedimentation com., 1955-56; mem. President's Water Resources Policy Commn., 1950; presdl. adv. com. Water Resources Policy, 1955. Recipient Distinguished Service citation U. Wis., 1964; Lincoln Acad. medal, 1967; Horton medal, 1980. Fellow Am. Geophys. Union (pres. 1966-68); mem. Nat. Acad. Engring. (council 1972-75), NRC (nat. adv. com. on oceans and atmosphere 1974-77), Internat. Assn. Sci. Hydrology (v.p. 1967-71, pres. 1971), Ill. Acad. Sci., Am. Soc. C.E. (Collingwood award 1944, chmn. hydraulics div. 1966-67, dir. 1971-74), Am. Water Resources Assn. (hon.), Am. Water Works Assn. (hon.), Sigma Xi, Chi Epsilon, Tau Beta Pi. Presbyn. (deacon 1950-53, elder 1962-65). Club: Cosmos (Washington). Home: 701 Hamilton Dr Champaign IL 61820 Office: U Ill Urbana IL 61801

ACKLEY, (HUGH) GARDNER, economist, educator; b. Indpls., June 30, 1915; s. Hugh M. and Margaret (McKenzie) A.; m. Bonnie A. Lowry, Sept. 18, 1937; children: David A., Donald G. A.B., Western Mich. U., 1936, LL.D., 1964; A.M., U. Mich., 1937, Ph.D., 1940; LL.D., Kalamazoo Coll., 1967. Instr. econs. Ohio State U., 1939-40, U. Mich., 1940-41; with OPA, Washington, 1941-43, 1944-46, OSS, 1943-44; asst. prof. U. Mich., 1946-47, asso. prof., 1947-52, prof., 1952-68, chmn. dept., 1955-61, Adams Disting. Univ. prof. polit. economy, 1969-84, emeritus, 1984—; asst. dir. OPS, Washington, 1951-52; mem. President's Council Econ. Advisers, 1962-68, chmn., 1964-68; U.S. ambassador to Italy, 1968-69, mem. or chmn. U.S. del. to meetings various internat. orgns., 1964-68; vis. prof. UCLA, summer 1950; cons. Econ. Stablzn. Agy., Washington, 1950, Dept. Army, 1961, Baker, Weeks and Co., Inc., N.Y.C., 1969-74; mem. asso. staff The Brookings Instn., 1977-79; mem. Trilateral Commn., 1977-83, Adv. Council on Social Security, 1978-80, Dem. Policy Council, chmn. econ. affairs com., 1969-72; bd. dirs. Social Sci. Research Council, 1959-62, Nat. Bur. Econ. Research, 1971-80, Joint Council on Econ. Edn., 1971-77; dir. Banco di Roma, Chgo., 1973—; mem. research adv. com. Com. on Econ. Devel., 1979-82. Author: Macroeconomic Theory, 1961, Stemming World Inflation, 1971, Macroeconomics: Theory and Policy, 1978; contbr. articles to profl. jours., revs.; bd. editors: Am. Econ. Rev., 1953-56; columnist: Dun's, 1971—. Fulbright scholar, 1956-57; Ford Found. Faculty research fellow, 1961-62; decorated cavaliere del Gran Croce, Italy, 1969; recipient Disting. Alumnus award Western Mich. U., 1970; Disting. Faculty Achievement award U. Mich., 1976. Fellow Am. Acad. Arts and Scis. (membership com. 1978-80); mem. Am. Philos. Soc., Am. Econ. Assn. (v.p. 1963, pres. 1982), Mich. Acad. Sci., Nat. Economists Club, Kappa Delta Pi, Tau Kappa Alpha, Phi Kappa Phi. Home: 907 Berkshire Rd Ann Arbor MI 48104 Office: Dept Econs Univ Mich Ann Arbor MI 48104

ACKLEY, ROGER KURTH, consultant; b. Schenectady, Nov. 10, 1914; s. Frederic Stacy and Frances Adelaide (Jackson) A.; m. Rita Evelyn Senior, Nov. 10, 1958; children: Jane (Mrs. Wayne Stratton), Frederic, John, Evelyn, Paul. Student, UCLA, 1934; A.B., U. Redlands, 1937; postgrad., Eastern Bapt. Theol. Sem., 1938, U. So. Calif., 1939. Ordained to ministry Baptist Ch., 1943; minister edn. Wilshire Presbyn. Ch., Los Angeles, 1938-39, First Friends Ch., Whittier, Calif., 1939-41, First Bapt. Ch., Portland, Oreg., 1941-42; dir. Christian edn. So. Calif. Bapt. Conv., Los Angeles, 1942-44; minister First Bapt. Ch., Grand Junction, Colo., 1944-45; sr. relocation officer War Relocation Authority, U.S. Dept. Interior, 1945-46; team dir., head resettlement Land Neidersachen, Germany, UNRRA, 1946-49, IRO, 1949-51; program officer U.S. Tech. Mission, Cairo, Egypt, 1952-55; cons. evacuation refugees French, Vietnamese govts. U.S. State Dept., 1955-56, dir. escapee program western Europe, 1956-60, consul, Salzburg, Austria, 1960-61; exec. dir. devel. and pub. relations project HOPE, Washington, 1962; midwest regional mgr. K.L.M. Royal Dutch Airlines, Chgo., 1962-72; dir. program Ind., ACTION, Indpls., 1972-73; pres. Am. Leprosy Missions, N.J., 1974-81; cons. Leonard Wood Meml., Am. Leprosy Found., 1981—; mem. adv. bd. Damien-Dutton Soc. for Leprosy Aid. Recipient Disting. Service award U. Redlands, 75th Celebration medallion U. Redlands. Mem. Order St. Lazarus of Jerusalem (hon., comdr.), Internat. Leprosy Assn. Home: 430 Ridgewood Ave Glen Ridge NJ 07028 Office: 616 Bedford Ave Bellmore NY 11710 *It is my conviction that the satisfying life is one of service to others. The degree of satisfaction lies in the degree of self-denial.*

ACKMAN, MILTON ROY, lawyer; b. N.Y.C., July 17, 1932; m. Carmela Suckow, July 14, 1959; children: David M., Daniel L. B.B.A., CCNY, 1953; LL.B, Columbia U., 1958. Bar: N.Y. 1958. Assoc. firm Fried, Frank, Harris, Shriver & Jacobson, N.Y., 1959-66, ptnr., N.Y.C., 1967—; law sec. Judge William B. Herlands, U.S. Dist. Ct. (so.dist.), N.Y., 1958-59. Served with U.S. Army, 1953-55. Mem. Assn. Bar City N.Y. Home: 505 Laguardia Pl New York NY 10012 Office: 1 New York Plaza New York NY 10004

ACKMANN, LOWELL EUGENE, electric engineer; b. Elgin, Ill., July 2, 1923; s. Henry C. and Matilda (Rineck) A.; m. Dorothy Collier, July 26, 1948; children: Robert, Lee, Barbara. B.S.E.E., U. Ill., 1944. Engr. Allis-Chalmers Mfg. Co., Milw., 1946-48, sales engr., Chgo., 1948-52, Peoria, Ill., 1952-54; v.p. Roland Constrn. Co., Dallas, 1954-56; elec. engr. Sargent & Lundy, Chgo., 1956-68, ptnr., 1966, mgr. electric dept., 1968-76, dir. services, 1976-84, sr. ptnr., 1984—. Served with USN, 1943-46. Recipient Disting. Alumnus award Elec. Engring. Alumni Assn., U. Ill., 1979. Mem. Atomic Indsl. Forum, Western Soc. Engrs., Ill. Soc. Profl. Engrs., IEEE, Nat. Soc. Profl. Engrs. Clubs: Inverness Golf, Chgo. Athletic Assn. Home: 200 Dover Circle Inverness IL 60067 Office: 55 E Monroe St Chicago IL 60603

ACKOFF, RUSSELL LINCOLN, systems sciences educator; b. Phila., Feb. 12, 1919; s. Jack and Fannie (Weitz) A.; m. Alexandra Makar, July 17, 1949; children: Alan W., Karen B., Karla S. B.Arch., U. Pa., 1941, Ph.D., 1947; D.Sc., U. Lancaster, 1967. Asst. instr. philosophy U. Pa., Phila., 1941-42, 46-47, prof. systems scis., 1964—, chmn. dept. statistics and operations research, 1964-66, chmn., 1964-69, dir., 1964-67, 69-70, chmn. social systems scis. unit, 1974-78, chmn., 1970-74, 76-79; asst. prof. philosophy and math. Wayne U., Detroit, 1947-51; asso. prof., prof. operations research Case Inst. Tech., Cleve., 1951-64; Methodological cons. U.S. Bur. Census, 1950-51; cons. Eastern Airlines, Emerson Electric Co., Gen. Foods Co., Mobil Oil Co., Nat. Acad. Scis., Nat. U. Mexico, Sci. and Tech. Research Council, Turkey, Western Electric Co.; dir. Mantua Indsl. Devel. Corp. Author: (with C.W. Churchman) Psychologistics, 1946, Methods of Inquiry, 1950, (with C.W. Churchman and M. Wax) Measurement of Consumer Interest, 1947, The Design of Social Research, 1953, (with C.W. Churchman and E.L. Arnoff) Introduction to Operations Research, 1957, Progress in Operations Research, I, 1961, Scientific Method, 1962, (with P. Rivett) A Manager's Guide to Operations Research, 1963, (with M. Sasieni) Fundamentals of Operations Research, 1968, A Concept of Corporate Planning, 1970, (with F.E. Emery) On Purposeful Systems, 1972, Redesigning The Future, 1974, (with T.A. Cowan et al) Designing a National Scientific and Technological Communication System, 1976, The Art of Problem Solving, 1978, Creating the Corporate Future, 1981; Editor: Management Science, 1965-70, Systems and Mgmt. Ann, 1974, The SCATT Report, 1976; asso. editor: Operations Research, 1953-65, Conflict Resolution, 1964-70; book rev. editor: Philosophy of Science, 1947-53; mem. abstracting staff: Biological Abstracts, 1950-51; adv. editor mgmt. sci., John Wiley & Sons, 1964—; mem. adv. bd.: Mathematical Spectrum, 1968—; mem. editorial bd.: Management Decision, 1968—; editorial asso.: European Jour. Operational Research; Contbr. articles profl. jours. Mem. Young Gt. Soc., Phila. Served to 1st lt. AUS, 1942-46. Fellow Am. Statis. Assn., Operations Research Soc. Am. (v.p., pres. 1956-57); mem. Inst. Mgmt. Scis. (v.p. 1965), Operational Research Soc. (U.K.) (Silver medal 1971), Soc. Gen. Systems Research, Operational Research Soc. India, Peace Research Soc., Sigma Xi, Tau Sigma Delta. Home: 1940 Lombard St Philadelphia PA 19146 Office: Wharton Sch U Pa Philadelphia PA 19104

ACOSTA, RAYMOND LUIS, judge; b. N.Y.C., May 31, 1925; s. Ramon J. and Carmen J. (Acha-Jimenez) Acosta-C.; m. Marie Hatcher, Nov. 2, 1957; children: Regina, Gregory, Ann Marie. Student, Princeton U., 1948; J.D., Rutgers U., 1951. Spl. agt. FBI, San Diego, Washington, Miami, Fla., 1954-58; asst. U.S. atty., San Juan, P.R., 1958-61, individual practice law, 1961-67; trust officer Banco Credito y Ahorro Ponceno, San Juan, 1967-80; U.S. atty. Dist. P.R., Hato Rey, 1980-82; judge U.S. Dist. Ct. P.R., San Juan, 1982—; Alt. del. U.S.-P.R. Commn. on Status, 1962-63; mem. Gov.'s Spl. Com. to Study Structure and Orgn. Police Dept., P.R., 1969. Contbr. articles to profl. jours. Pres. United Fund, P.R., 1979. Served with USN, 1943-46. Recipient Meritorious Service certificate, 1976; Recipient Merit certificate Mayor San Juan, 1973. Mem. Fed. Bar Assn. (pres., P.R. 1967), P.R. Bankers Assn. (chmn. trust div. 1971, 75, 77), P.R. Bar Assn., Soc. Former Spl. Agts. FBI, Bergen County (N.J.) Bar Assn. Roman Catholic. Club: Rotary (San Juan). Office: Post Office and Courthouse Bldg Old San Juan PR 00904

ACRET, JAMES ELVERO, lawyer; b. Mpls., Dec. 19, 1930; s. Eugene Simpson and Marian Campbell (McMillan) A.; m. Gretchen Logan Jones, Jan. 19, 1957; children: Douglas Howard, Craig Stephen, Clayton Stuart, Darryl Scott, Amanda Sue, James Elvero. Student, Stanford, 1948-49; B.A., UCLA, 1951, B. Laws, 1957. Bar: Calif. 1957. Since practiced, Los Angeles; asso. firm Monteleone & McCrory, Los Angeles, 1957-58; partner firm Acret & Perrochet, Los Angeles, 1958-83, Law Offices of James Acret, Santa Monica, Calif., 1983—; nat. panel arbitrators Am. Arbitration Assn., 1963—, bd. dirs., 1980—; Spl. counsel Calif. Building Industry Assn., 1963—; gen. counsel Bldg. Industry Assn. So. Calif. Inc., 1963—. Author: California Construction Law Manual, 1969, Attorney's Guide to California Construction Contracts and Disputes, 1976, Architects and Engineers, Their Professional Responsibilities, 1977; prin. cons.: Calif. Mechanics Liens, 1972. Bd. mgrs. Camp br. Los Angeles Met. YMCA, 1974—. Served with USAF, 1951-53. Home: 530 Alma Real Dr Pacific Pallisades CA Office: 401 Wilshire Blvd Santa Monica CA 90401

ACRIVOS, ANDREAS, chem. engr., educator; b. Athens, Greece, June 13, 1928; came to U.S., 1947, naturalized, 1962; s. Athanasios and Anna (Besi) A.; m. Juana Vivo, Sept. 1, 1956. B.S. in Chem. Engring, Syracuse U., 1950; M.S., U. Minn., 1951, Ph.D., 1954. Instr., asst. prof., asso. prof. U. Calif., Berkeley, 1954-62; prof. chem. engring. Stanford U., 1962—. Contbr. tech. articles to profl. jours. Guggenheim fellow, 1959, 76. Mem. Am. Inst. Chem. Engrs. (Profl. Progress award), Am. Chem. Soc., Am. Phys. Soc., Soc. Rheology, Nat. Acad. Engring. Office: Dept Chem Engring Stanford U Stanford CA 94305

ACTON, DAVID, lawyer; b. Phila., Feb. 13, 1933; s. Kenneth Davis and Mary (Musselman) A.; m. Barbara Ann Sullivan, June 18, 1955; children—Lauren Doane, Paul Bodine; m. Jane Thomas Young, June 24, 1978. Grad., Episcopal Acad., 1951; A.B., Yale, 1955; J.D., U. Pa., 1960. Assoc. Krusen, Evans & Byrne, Phila., 1960-63; asst. sec., asst. gen. counsel Leeds & Northrup Co., Phila., 1963-65, sec., gen. counsel, North Wales, Pa., 1965-71; v.p., gen. counsel K.S. Sweet Assos., King of Prussia, Pa., 1971-75; practice in, Bryn Mawr, Pa., 1975-77; v.p. Crockett Mortgage Co., Valley Forge, Pa.; gen. mgr. Hershey's Mill, 1977-82; exec. v.p. Ultec, Inc., Exton, Pa., 1982—. Served as lt. (j.g.) USNR, 1955-57. Mem. Am., Pa., Phila. bar assns., Colonial Soc. Pa., Mensa. Clubs: Union League, Philadelphia Country, Merion Cricket, Yale (Phila.). Home: 401 Mulberry Ln Haverford PA 19041 Office: 964 E Swedesford Rd PO Box 389 Exton PA 19341

ACTON, NORMAN, health organization executive; b. Denver, Oct. 29, 1918; s. Norman Erwin and Mildred (Welch) A.; m. Katherine E. Brown, June 9, 1946; 1 dau., Mary Ann. B.S. in Journalism, U. Ill., 1939; D.Sc. (hon.), L.I. U., 1973. Engaged in advt. and pub. relations, 1939-43; chief econs. and labor sect. Gifu Mil. Govt. Team, Japan, 1947-49; exec. dir. U.S. Com. Resettlement Physically Disabled, 1950-51; asst. sec. gen. Internat. Soc. Welfare Cripples, 1951-54; exec. dir. U.S. com. for UNICEF, 1954-59, bd. dirs., 1967-69; dep. sec. gen. World Vets. Fedn., 1959-61, sec. gen., 1961-67, Rehab. Internat., N.Y.C., 1967—; Chmn. non-govtl. organ com. UNICEF, 1952-54, cons., 1957; chmn. conf. group U.S. orgns. for UN, 1958; pres. Internat. Working Group on Sports for Disabled, 1961-64; mem. Pres.'s Com. Employment Handicapped, 1952-57, 63—; chmn. Conf. World Orgns. Interested in Handicapped, 1964-67, 69—; pres. Internat. Sports Orgn. for Disabled, 1965-66; adv. bd. rehab. and edn. program Ptnrs. of The Ams., 1970—; cons. UN, 1981—. Author: Rehabilitation of the Physically Handicapped, 1953. Bd. dirs. Inst. de la Vie, 1961-67. Served to capt. AUS, 1943-47. Mem. Soc. Internat. Devel., Phi Gamma Delta. Home: Route 5 Box 518 Gloucester VA 23061 Office: 432 Park Ave S New York NY 10016

ACUFF, ROY CLAXTON, singer, fiddler, bandleader; b. Maynardville, Tenn., Sept. 15, 1903; s. Neill and Ida (Carr) A.; m. Mildred Louise Douglas, Dec. 25, 1936; 1 son, Roy Neil. Ed. pub. schs., Knoxville, Tenn. Co-owner Acuff-Rose Pub. Co., Hickory Records. Profl. singer, musician, Doc Hower's Medicine Show; then performer with his band The Crazy Tennesseans (name later Smoky Mountain Boys), Sta. WNOK, Knoxville, Tenn.; rec. artist, Columbia Records, 1936; Mem., Grand Ole Opry radio program, from 1938; 1st appearance with Smoky Mountain Boys on Grand Ole Opry, 1938; appeared with, Grand Ole Opry, 1938—; played with his band in motion pictures during, 1940s; songs include The Precious Jewel, Great Speckled Bird, Wabash Cannonball, Wreck on the Highway, Night Train to Memphis, Beneath the Lonely Mountain of Clay; yearly tours for, U.S.O., 1949-71. Named to Country Music Hall of Fame, 1962. Nominee for gov. Tenn., 1948. *

ACUÑA, HÉCTOR R., health organization consultant; b. Cananea, Sonora, Mexico, Sept. 24, 1921; s. José and Bertha (Monteverde) A.; m. Beatriz Dolores Hallatt de Acuña, Oct. 5, 1946; children: Beatriz, Bertha, Lourdes, Lidia, Lisette. M.D. Faculty of Medicine, U. Mex., 1947; M.P.H., Yale U., 1951. Epidemiologist, then med. dir. Office for Inter-Am. Coop. in Public Health, Ministry of Health and Welfare, Mex., 1947-54; chief med. adviser Pan Am. Sanitary Bur., Dominican Republic, El Salvador, Guatemala, 1954-62; vis. prof. preventive medicine and public health U. Santo Domingo, 1954-57, U. P.R., 1955-56, U. El Salvador, 1957-58, U. Guatemala, 1958-62; rep., chief med. advisor WHO, Regional Office for Eastern Mediterranean, Pakistan, 1962-64; dir. internat. affairs Ministry Health and Welfare, Mexico, 1971-74; dir. Pan Am. Sanitary Bur., 1975-83; vis. prof. Sch. Public Health, John Hopkins U., 1975, Yale U., 1976. Contbr. articles to med. jours. Decorated by govts. of Dominican Republic, Guatemala, Costa Rica, Venezuela, Bolivia and Spain. Mem. Am. Public Health Assn., Internat. Health Soc., Mex. Soc. Public Health, Internat. Health Resource Consortium, Internat. Coll. Surgeons (hon.), ADA (hon.), Yale U. Alumni Assn. Home: 25 Fuente de los Carretones Lomas de las Palmas HuixquilucanMexico 52760 Office: PO Box 105-34 Mexico DFMexico

ACZEL, JANOS DEZSO, mathematics educator; b. Budapest, Hungary, Dec. 26, 1924; s. Dezso and Iren (Adler) A.; m. Susan Kende, Dec. 14, 1946; children: Catherina, Julie. M.A., U. Budapest, 1947, Ph.D., 1947; Habil., Hungarian Acad. Sci., 1952, D.Sc., 1957. Faculty U. Szeged, Hungary, 1948-50; prof. math. Tech. U., Miskolc, 1950-52, U. Debrecen, Hungary, 1952-65, U. Waterloo, Ont., Can., 1965—, disting. prof., 1969—; vis. prof. U. Fla., Gainesville, 1963-64, 81, Stanford U., 1964, U. Koln, Germany, 1965, U. Giessen, 1966, 70, Ruhr U., Bochum, Germany, 1968, Ist. Naz. Alta Matematica, Rome, 1971, Monash U., Clayton, Victoria, Australia, 1972, Ahmadu Bello U., Zaria, Nigeria, 1975-76, U. Lecce, Italy, 1976, Calif. Inst. Tech., 1978, U. Ariz., 1978, Karl-Franzens U., Graz, Austria, 1979, Okayama U. (Japan), 1984. Author: (with S. Golab) Funktionalgleichungen der Theorie der geometrischen Objekte, 1960, Vorlesungen uber Funktionalgleichungen und ihre Anwendungen, 1961, Ein Blick auf Funktionalgleichungen und ihre Anwendungen, 1962, Lectures on Functional Equations and Their Applications, 1966, On Applications and Theory of Functional Equations, 1969, (with Z. Daroczy) Measures of Information and Their Characterisations, 1975; also numerous articles. Recipient M. Beke award J. Bolyai Math. Soc., 1961, Hungarian Acad. Scis. award, 1962. Fellow Royal Soc. Can.; mem. Can. Math. Soc., Am. Math. Soc., N.Y. Acad. Sci., Osterreichische Mathematische Gesellschaft. Initiated modern theory of functional equations; gave gen. theorems and applications in geometry, econs., probability, and info. theory; theories of mean values and measurement, ordered and continuous groups, semi-groups, quasi-groups, and webs. Office: Centre for Info Theory Faculty of Math U Waterloo Waterloo ON Canada N2L 3G1

ADAIR, CHARLES E., medical products distribution company executive; b. Birmingham, Ala., Dec. 26, 1947; s. Charles Watkins and Martha Edd (Chisenball) A.; m. Alice Virginia Barker, Jan. 31, 1970; children: Charles Thomas, Emily Elizabeth. Student, Vanderbilt U., 1966; B.S. in Acctg., U. Ala.-Tuscaloosa, 1970. C.P.A. Sr. acct. Haskins & Sells, Brimingham, 1970-73; chief fin. officer Durr-Fillauer Med. Inc., Montgomery, Ala., 1973-77, exec. v.p., 1977-81, pres., chief operating officer, 1981—. Served to sgt. U.S. Army, 1970. Mem. Fin. Execs. Inst., Am. Inst. C.P.A.'s, Ala. Soc. C.P.A.'s. Home: 2431 Hermitage Dr Montgomery AL 36111 Office: Durr Fillauer Med Inc 218 Commerce St Montgomery AL 36192

ADAIR, CHARLES ROBERT, JR., lawyer; b. Narrows, Va., Sept. 29, 1914; s. Charles Robert and Margaret (Davis) A.; m. Lillian Adele Duffee, Sept. 19, 1942. B.S., U. Ala., 1942, LL.B., 1948, J.D., 1969. Bar: Ala. bar 1948. Since practiced in, Dadeville, solicitor, Tallapoosa County, 1955-73; vice chmn. Ala. Securities Commn., 1969-71; commr., mem. exec. com. Ala. State Bar, v.p., 1982-83; v.p., dir. Dadeville Industries, Inc., Dadeville Lumber Co., Inc.; dir. Bank of Dadeville. Chmn. Dadeville One Drive, 1960; chmn. Horseshoe Bend Regional Library, 1960-65; mem., sec. planning commn. City of Dadeville, 1965-80; hon. life mem. Bethel Vol. Fire Dept. and Rescue Service, Jackson's Gap Vol. Fire Dept. and Rescue Service; trustee Ala. Law Inst., Ala. Bar Found. Served as officer USAAF, World War II. Mem. Am. Judicature Soc., Am. bar assn., Ala. bar assn., Tallapoosa County bar assn., 5th Circuit bar assn. (pres.), Farrah Law Soc. (trustee), V.F.W., Am. Legion, Newcomen Soc., Air Force Assn., E. Ala. Peace Officers Assn. (hon. life), Scabbard and Blade, Omicron Delta Kappa, Delta Tau Delta, Phi Alpha Delta. Democrat. Presbyn. Clubs: Mason, Kiwanian (dist. lt.-gov. 1980-81), The Club, Relay House, Downtown, Willow Point Golf and Country, Still Waters, Quarterback (past capt.). Home: Duffee's Hill Dadeville AL 36853 Office: 204 Broadnax St Dadeville AL 36853

ADAIR, CHARLES WATKINS, coal company executive; b. Dora, Ala., July 20, 1923; s. William Fred and Esther (Watkins) A.; m. Martha Edd Chisenhall, Mar. 21, 1947; children: Charles Edward, Marcia Diane, William Gregg. Controller Woodward Co., Ala., 1948-66, v.p. fin., 1966-71, pres., 1971-77; group v.p. Mead Corp., Dayton, Ohio, 1971-78; pres. Mulla Cotl Co., Woodward, 1978-82; asst. to chief exec. officer Drummond Co., Jasper, Ala., 1982—; dir. Central Bank, Birmingham, Ala., 1972-77. Bd. dirs. Bessemer C. of C., Ala., Met. Devel. Bd., Birmingham, 1981-83, Assoc. Industries Ala., 1972-

83; pres. Regional Council Alcoholism, Birmingham, 1982-83. Served with USAF, 1943-46. Mem. Fin. Execs. Inst. (pres. chpt. 1970-71), Nat. Assn. Accts. (pres. chpt. 1972-73). Presbyterian. Clubs: Shoal Creek, The Club of Birmingham. Home: 2133 Viking Circle Birmingham AL 35216 Office: Drummong Co PO Box 1549 Jasper AL 35216

ADAIR, JOHN DOUGLAS, tool manufacturer; b. Ardmore, Pa., May 24, 1920; s. Herbert J., Sr. and Margaret (Douglas) A.; m. Barbara Whitaker, July 23, 1940; children: John Douglas, Richard Herbert; m. Peggy Sawyer, Oct. 10, 1977. Student, Dartmouth Coll., 1938-39, George Washington U., 1940. Chief estimator Kieckhefer Container Corp., Camden, N.J., 1939-41; insp. N.Y. Shipbldg. Corp., N.Y.C., 1941-42; exec. asst. Kent-Moore Corp., Warren, Mich., 1946-47, pres., dir., 1947-82, chmn., dir., 1982—; dir. Douglas & Lomason Co., Robinair Mfg. Corp., Pyles Industries, Inc., Maynard Mfg. Co., Kent-Moore Stamping & Fabricating Co., Standard Composite Die Co., Norbrook, Inc., Kent-Moore U.K., Ltd., Eng., Kent-Moore (Europe) A.G. (Switzerland). Chmn. bd. dirs. Kidney Found., Mich., 1956—; bd. dirs. Nat. Kidney Found., 1956-65; v.p., bd. dirs. Mich. United Fund, 1964-73; trustee Village of Grosse Pointe Shores, Mich., 1952-55; Trustee Kent-Moore Found., 1954—; bd. dirs. Goodwill Industries Mich., 1951-64. Served from pvt. to 1st lt. AUS, 1943-46. Clubs: Country, Econ. (Detroit); Bloomfield Hills (Mich.) Country; Pine Valley Golf (Clementon, N.J.); Jupiter (Fla.) Hills; Seminole Golf (N. Palm Beach, Fla.); The Hundred. Home: 21 Waverly Ln Grosse Pointe Farms MI 48236 Office: Kent-Moore Corp 28635 Mound Rd Warren MI 48092

ADAIR, RED (PAUL NEAL ADAIR), oil well problem control specialist; b. 1915; married; 1 son. Worked in oil well fire and gusher control with Myron Kinley, 1939-59; with E. Matthews, A. Hansen Red Adair Oil Well Fires & Blowouts Control Co., Houston, 1959—. Office: Red Adair Oil Well Fires & Blowouts Control Co 8705 Katy Freeway Houston TX 77024 *

ADAM, HELEN, poet; b. Glasgow, Scotland, Dec. 2, 1909; came to U.S., 1939, naturalized, 1947; d. William A. and Isabella Dunn. Author: poetry Ballads, 1964, Selected Poems and Ballads, 1964, Turn Again to Me, 1977, Gone Sailing, 1980; musical comedy San Francisco's Burning, 1962, also reprint with music, 1983; witch stories Ghosts and Grinning Shadows, 1979; Songs and Music, 1983. Home: 223 E 82nd St New York NY 10028

ADAM, JOHN, JR., insurance company executive; b. Braintree, Mass., Dec. 14, 1914; s. John and Harriet E. (Hubley) A.; m. Ruth E. Maddock, Dec. 27, 1945. A.B., Oberlin Coll., 1937; LL.D., Clark U., 1974. Underwriter Glens Falls Ins. Co., 1938-39, mgr. inland marine dept., 1939-40; with Central Mut. Ins. Co., 1940-60, v.p., 1957-60, Worcester Mut. Ins. Co., 1960, pres., 1960-79; also dir. pres., dir. Hanover Ins. Cos., 1969-79, dir. and pres. emeritus, 1979—; pres. Heald, Inc., 1979—; dir. Citizens Ins. Co. Am., Beacon Mut. Indemnity Co., Am. Select Risk Ins. Co., Shawmut Worcester County Bank, Marine Office of Am. Corp., Sharfman's, Worcester; mem. adv. com. Mich. Investment Fund. Author: More Sales for You, 1949, also articles. Vice chmn. Mass. Bd. Higher Edn., 1974-77, chmn., 1972-74, 77; v.p., trustee Worcester Art Mus.; chmn. Worcester County Music Assn. Mem. Worcester C. of C. (past pres., dir.), C.P.C.U. Soc. (nat. pres. 1967, dir.), Worcester Econ. Club (past pres.), Boston Sales Execs. Club (past pres.). Office: 440 Lincoln St Worcester MA 01605

ADAM, PAUL JAMES, engineering company executive, mechanical engineer; b. Kansas City, Mo., Oct. 26, 1934; s. Paul James and Adrienne (Zimmerman) A.; m. Barbara Ann Mills, Dec. 18, 1956; children: Paul James, Blair Dodderidge, Matthew Mills. B.S. in Mech. Engring., U. Kans., 1956. Registered profl. engr., 14 states. Mech. engr. Black & Veatch, Cons. Engrs., Kansas City, Mo., 1956, 59-74, ptnr. asst. head power div., 1975-78, exec. ptnr., head power div., 1978—; dir. First Continental Bank & Trust Co. Mem. engring. adv. bd. U. Kans., 1982—. Served to 1st lt. USAF, 1956-59. Mem. Nat. Soc. Profl. Engrs., Mo. Soc. Profl. Engrs., ASME, Am. Nuclear Soc., Atomic Indsl. Forum, Tau Beta Pi, Sigma Tau, Pi Tau Sigma, Omicron Delta Kappa, Alpha Tau Omega. Episcopalian. Clubs: Mission Hills Country, Saddle and Sirloin. Office: Black & Veatch 1500 Meadow Lake Pkwy Kansas City MO 64114

ADAMANY, DAVID WALTER, university administrator; b. Janesville, Wis., Sept. 23, 1936; s. Walter Joseph and Dora Marie (Mutter) A. A.B., Harvard U., 1958, J.D., 1961; M.S., U. Wis., Madison, 1963, Ph.D., 1967. Bar: Wis. bar 1961. Asst. to atty. gen., Wis., 1961-63; exec. pardon counsel State of Wis., 1963; commr. Wis. Public Service Commn., 1963-65; instr. polit. sci. Wis. State U., Whitewater, 1965-67; asst. prof., then asso. prof. Wesleyan U., Middletown, Conn., 1967-72, dean coll., 1969-71; asso. prof., then prof. polit. sci. U. Wis., Madison, 1972-77; sec. of revenue State of Wis., 1974-76; v.p. acad. affairs Calif. State U., Long Beach, 1977-80, U. Md., 1980-82; pres. Wayne State U., 1982—; chmn. Wis. Council Criminal Justice, 1973-75; mem. Wis. Elections Bd., 1974-77, chmn., 1976-77. Author: Financing Politics, 1969, Campaign Finance in America, 1972, Borzoi Reader in American Politics, 1972; co-author: American Government: Democracy and Liberty in Balance, 1975, Political Money, 1975; editorial bd.: Social Sci. Quarterly, 1973—, State and Local Govt. Rev, 1974—; contbr. articles to profl. jours. Bd. dirs. Detroit Symphony Orch., Detroit Med. Ctr., United Found., Met. Center High Tech., Mich. High Tech. Task Force; mem. profl. practices com. Detroit Inst. Art; Mem. Mich. Gov.'s Commn. Jobs and Econ. Devel. Mem. Am. Polit. Sci. Assn., ACLU, State Bar Wis. Democrat. Office: Office of Pres Wayne State U Detroit MI 48202

ADAMCZEWSKI, ZYGMUNT, philosophy educator; b. Bydgoszcz, Poland, May 27, 1921; s. Stanislaw and Izabella (Gouth) A.; m. Melanie Hafele, Mar. 15, 1951; children: Eva D., Jan Z. Student, U. Innsbruck, Austria, 1945-46; B.A. with honours, U. London, 1947-51; A.M., Columbia U., 1952; Ph.D., Harvard U., 1955. Asst. Harvard U., 1954; instr. L.I. U., 1955; asst. prof. philosophy Mont. State U., 1956-62; asso. prof. U. Waterloo, Can., 1962-67, prof., 1967-69, Brock U., St. Catharines, Ont., 1969—. Author: The Tragic Protest, 1964, Kant's Existential Thought, 1969, The Question of Ethics in Our Time, 1983; Contbr. articles to profl. jours. Served with Polish Army, 1938-39. Mem. Am., Canadian philos. assns., Soc. Phenomenology and Existential Philosophy. Home: 27 Royal York Rd St Catharines ON Canada

ADAMIAN, GREGORY H., college president; b. Somerville, Mass., Sept. 17, 1926; s. Adam K. and Sandy (Martin) A.; m. June Mouradian, July 6, 1958 (dec. Jan. 1967); children: Douglas, Daniel; m. Deborah Murdza, Jan. 1, 1978. A.B., Harvard, 1947; then M.P.A.; J.D., Boston U., 1951. Bar: Mass. 1951. Since practiced in, Cambridge; lectr. law and econs. Suffolk U., 1953-54; prof. law Bentley Coll., Waltham, Mass., 1955-67, chmn. dept. law, 1968-70, pres. coll., 1970—; lectr. real estate law Am. Savs. and Loan Inst.; bd. dirs. College Student Loan Authority; Trustee Bentley Coll., Waltham Hosp.; bd. dirs. Nat. Assn. Armenian Studies and Research, Inc., Armenian Gen. Benevolent Union., Mass. Higher Edn. Assistance Corp. Served as lt. USN. Recipient Boyan humanities award Armenian Students Assn., 1973. Mem. Assn. Ind. Colls. and Univs. Mass. (treas.), Am. Bus. Law Assn., Am., Mass., Boston bar assns., Sigma Chi. Mem. Armenian Apostolic Ch. Clubs: Mason, Shriner, Oakley Country (Belmont, Mass.); Algonquin (Boston). Home: 121 Forest St Waltham MA 02154

ADAMOVICH, SHIRLEY GRAY, librarian; b. Pepperell, Mass., May 8, 1927; d. Willard Ellsworth and Carrie (Shattuck) Gray; m. Frank Walter Adamovich, Aug. 31, 1960; children: Carrie Rose, Elizabeth Maude. B.A., U. N.H., 1954; M.S., Simmons Coll., Boston, 1955. Cons. Vt. State Library, Montpelier, 1955-58; head cataloger Bentley Coll., Waltham, Mass., 1958-60; tchr. U. N.H. System, Durham, 1965-79; asst. state librarian N.H. State Library, Concord, 1979-81, state librarian, 1981—. Editor: A Reader in Library Technology, 1975. Served in USAF, 1949-53. Mem. AlA, New Eng. Library Assn., Chief Officers of State Library Agys., N.H. Library Assn., N.H. Library Trustees Assn., N.H. Ednl. Media Assn. Office: NH Office Library 20 Park St Concord NH 03301

ADAMS, ALBERT WILLIE, JR., soft drink co. ofcl.; b. Detroit, Nov. 22, 1948; s. Albert Willie and Goldie Inez (Davis) A.; m. Linda Maureen North, Sept. 2, 1972; children—Nichole Leahna, Albert Willie III, Melanie Rachel. B.A. in Elementary Edn, Harris Tchrs. Coll., St. Louis, 1970; M.B.A., So. Ill. U., Edwardsville, 1974. Recreation leader City of St. Louis, 1967-69; recreation supr. Mo. Hills Home for Boys, 1969-70; tchr. spl. edn. St. Louis Bd. Edn., 1968-71; personnel asst. Equal Opportunity Adminstrn., Seven-Up Co., St. Louis, 1971-75, corporate equal opportunity adminstr., 1975-80, sr. employee relations adminstr., 1980-81, personnel mgr., 1981-82, mgr. indsl. relations, 1982—; residence counselor Magdala Found., halfway house, 1971-77. Community-at-large mem. Affirmative Action Commn. Minorities, St. Louis U., 1974-76; chmn. St. Louis corporate solicitation United Negro Coll. Fund, 1972; mem. adv. com. Statewide Job Placement Service, 1979—, Project Search, 1980—. St. Louis Post-Dispatch scholar, 1971; Parsons-Blewett Meml. scholar tchrs., 1971; recipient Jr. Achievement scholarship award, 1966, St. Louis Sales and Mktg. Execs. award, 1966, St. Louis Sentinel achiever award, 1980. Mem. St. Louis Indsl. Relations Assn., Assn. M.B.A. Execs., Kappa Alpha Psi. Baptist. Home: 2331 Albion Pl Saint Louis MO 63104 Office: 555 McDonnell Blvd Hazelwood MO 63042

ADAMS, ALFRED HUGH, college president; b. Punta Gorda, Fla., Mar. 8, 1928; s. Alfred and Irene (Gatewood) A.; m. Joyce Morgan, Nov. 10, 1954; children: Joy, Al, Paul. A.A., U. Fla., 1948; B.S., Fla. State U., 1950, M.S., 1956, Ed.D., 1962; L.H.D., Fla. Atlantic U., 1972. Asst. coach varsity football Fla. State U., 1955-58, asst. dir. housing, instr. edn., 1958-62, asst. dean men, asst. prof. edn., 1962-64; supt. pub. instrn. Charlotte County, Fla., 1965-68; pres. Broward Community Coll., Ft. Lauderdale, Fla., 1968—; bd. dirs. Am. Council on Edn.; vis. lectr. in higher edn. Inst. Higher Edn., U. Fla.; also mem. com. on internat. edn. relations, com. on mil-higher edn. relations; mem. adv. com. Inst. Internat. Edn.; dir. Sun Bank/South Fla., N.A.; Vice chmn. Gov. Fla. Commn. Quality Edn., 1968-70; mem. Gov.'s Adv. Com. Edn., 1966-70; mem. regional council Southeastern Edn. Corp., 1966-69; mem. commn. adminstrv. affairs Am. Council on Edn., 1973; pres. Pub. Instns. Higher Learning in So. States, 1975; mem. adv. com. Joint Council on Econ. Edn.; chmn. AACJC Internat./Intercultural Consortium, S.E. Fla. Ednl. Consortium; chmn. council pres. Fla. Community Colls.; Trustee South Fla. Edn. Center, Pub. Service TV. Mem. editorial bd., Soc. for Coll. and Univ. Planning. Pres. United Way, 1973; bd. dirs. local chpt. ARC, 1971; bd. dirs. local State U. Sports Hall of Fame.; bd. dirs. Opera Guild, Ft. Lauderdale, Fla., pres., Ft. Lauderdale, Fla., 1983-85. Served to comdr. USNR, 1945-46, 52-55. Decorated; knight Internat. Constantinian Order, 1971; recipient Liberty Bell award, 1975; named patriot Fla. Bicentennial Commn.; Patriot award Freedoms Found.; disting. alumnus award Fla. State U.; cert. of recognition Fla. Ho. of Reps. Mem. Fla. Tchr. Edn. Adv. Council, Fla. Edn. Council Ethics Com. Sch. Adminstrs., Am. Assn. Sch. Adminstrs., Ft. Lauderdale C. of C. (v.p.), Profl. Practices Commn., Fla. Assn. Colls. and Univs. (pres. 1975), Naval Res. Assn., Res. Officers Assn., U.S. Naval Inst. (life), Broward Minutemen (pres.), Fla. Inter-agy. Law Enforcement Planning Council, Omicron Delta Kappa, Phi Theta Kappa. Methodist. Clubs: Kiwanian., Gulfstream Sailing, Fort Lauderdale.; Tower (gov.) (1983—). Home: 105 N Victoria Park Rd Fort Lauderdale FL 33301

ADAMS, ALFRED JOHN, public affairs consultant; b. Liverpool, Eng., Nov. 22, 1931; came to U.S., 1962, naturalized, 1971; s. Wilfrid and Francine Sophia (Bertrand) A.; m. Vibeke Dinsen, June 3, 1963 (div. 1975); m. Judith Ann Duff, Oct. 15, 1978; 1 dau., Caroline Louise. Corr. London Daily Telegraph, 1952-56; editor, bur. chief, asst. dir. news Radio Free Europe, Bonn and Munich, W.Ger., 1956-62; Africa corr. ABC News, 1963; writer CBS News, N.Y.C., 1964-70; dir. pub. affairs U.S. Price Commn., Washington, 1972-73; pres. John Adams Assocs., Inc., Washington, 1973—. Author: (with J.M. Burke) Civil Rights: A Current Guide to the People, Organizations and Events, 1970; editor: Energy Policy: Industry Perspectives, 1975. Bd. dirs. Psychiat. Inst. Found., Washington, 1974-79; exec. dir. Environ. Industry Council, 1975-80; mem. adv. bd. Gaullaudet Coll. for Deaf, Washington, 1977-79. Served to lt. King's Shropshire Light Inf., 1951-52; Korea. Recipient Disting. Service award U.S. Price Commn., 1973. Mem. Inst. Journalists, Pub. Relations Soc. Am. (Silver anvil award 1978). Clubs: Overseas Press (N.Y.C.); Nat. Press; Kenwood (Washington); Severn River Yacht (Annapolis, Md.). Home: 3015 44th St NW Washington DC 20016 Office: 1825 K St NW Washington DC 20006

ADAMS, ALGALEE POOL, college dean, art educator; b. Columbia, Mo., Nov. 6, 1919; d. William I. and Anna Ethelene (Dunning) Pool; 1 dau., Judith Dean Adams. B.S. in Art and English, U. Mo., 1941, M.A., 1951; Ed.D. in Fine Arts and Art Edn, Pa. State U., 1960. Tchr. art Cuba (Mo.) High Sch., 1941-42, Hickman High Sch., Columbia, 1942-43; art specialist elementary schs., St. Joseph, Mo., 1943-45; tchr. art St. Clair (Mo.) High Sch., 1946-49; pub. sch. art supr., Webb City, Mo., 1949-51; instr. dept. of art St. Cloud (Minn.) State Coll., 1951-58, asst. prof., 1958-60, asso. prof., 1960-63, prof., 1963-64, chmn. dept. art, 1959-64; prof. art edn. Mass. Coll. Art, Boston, 1964-77, also chmn. div. of edn., 1967-70, dir. tchr. placement, 1964-70, dir. grad. programs in edn., 1970-77; chmn. grad. council, 1970-74; dean Firelands Coll. Bowling Green State U., Huron, Ohio, 1977—; mem. gov.'s adv. commn. on edn. in arts, 1958, 67; asso. dir. Project Renewal Mass. State Coll. System, 1974-76; art curriculum cons. to numerous pub. schs. in, Minn., 1951-64; art cons. to Minn. Ins. Info. Center, 1960-62; chmn. Eastern Arts Student Conf., N.Y.C., 1968; participant Internat. Conf., Notre Dame U., 1968; field reader HEW, 1966-70. Recipient Distinguished Alumni award U. Mo., 1968. Mem. Nat. Art Edn. Assn. (faculty adviser 1965-69, chmn. student conf. 1969, seminar chmn. conf. 1967, speaker nat. conv. 1961, 66, 67, life mem.), AAUW, Mass. State Coll. Assn., Eastern Arts Assn. (speaker conv. 1966), Sigma Pi Alpha, Phi Delta Kappa, Delta Phi Delta, Kappa Pi, Delta Kappa Gamma. Club: Zonta. Office: 901 Rye Beach Rd Huron OH 44839 *Early in my teaching career, I was conscious of the differences between creative teaching and other more traditional philosophies and methods. This awareness and concern led to the development of my professional goal "to have a broad impact on improving the quality of teaching."*

ADAMS, ALICE, writer; b. Fredericksburg, Va., Aug. 14, 1926; d. Nicholson Barney and Agatha Erskine (Boyd) A.; 1 son, Peter Adams Linenthal. A.B., Radcliffe Coll., 1946. Author: novels Careless Love, 1966; (novels) Families and Surviviors, 1975, Listening to Billie, 1978, Rich Rewards, 1980, Superior Women, 1984; (short story collections) Beautiful Girl, 1979; To See You Again, 1982; contbr. short stories to: New Yorker, others. Mem. PEN. Democratic Socialist. Office: care Press Relations Alfred A Knopf Inc 201 E 50th St New York NY 10022

ADAMS, ALICE PATRICIA, sculptor; b. N.Y.C., Nov. 16, 1930; d. Charles P. and Loretto G. (Tobin) A.; m. William D. Gordy, Feb. 7, 1969; 1 dau., Katherine Adams Gordy. Student, Adelphi Coll., 1948-50; B.F.A., Columbia U., 1953; postgrad. (French Govt. fellow), 1953-54, L'Ecole Nat d'Art Decoratif, Aubusson, France, 1953-54. Lectr. Manhattanville Coll., Purchase, N.Y., 1960-79; instr. sculpture Sch. Visual Arts, 1980-84. One-man shows, N.Y.C., 1972, 74, 75, Hall Bromm Gallery, N.Y.C., 1979, 80, group shows include, Whitney Museum Am. Art, N.Y.C., 1971, 73, Indpls. Mus. Art, 1974, Nassau County Mus. Fine Arts, Roslyn, N.Y., 1977, Wave Hill, Riverdale, N.Y., 1979; represented in permanent collections, Weatherspoon Gallery U. N.C., Greensboro, U. Nebr., L'Ecole Nat d'Art Decoratif, Everson Mus., Syracuse, N.Y., Haags Gemetemuseum, The Hague, Netherlands. Creative Artists Pub. Service grantee, 1973-74, 76-77; Nat. Endowment for Arts Artists grantee, 1978-79; Guggenheim fellow, 1981-82. Home: 55 Walker St New York NY 10013

ADAMS, ALVIN PHILIP, aviation management consultant; b. Grand Junction, Colo., Dec. 29, 1905; s. Orson and Letty (Low) A.; m. Elizabeth Miller, May 29, 1929 (div. 1946); children: Nathan, Edith Low, Alvin; m. Shirley Ward, June 30, 1951; 1 dau., Helen Ward. Ph.B., Yale U., 1927. Aviation editor Wall St. Jour., N.Y.C., 1927-29; v.p. Aero Industries, Inc., 1929-34, Nat. Aviation Corp., 1930-34; pres. Western Air Lines (formerly Western Air Express Corp.), Los Angeles, 1934-40, Seaboard Airways, Inc., N.Y.C., 1940-43; v.p. Fairchild Engine & Airplane Corp., N.Y.C., 1942-45; owner Alvin P. Adams & Assocs., Los Angeles, 1944; v.p. Pan Am. World Airways, N.Y.C., 1951-70; aviation mgmt. cons., 1970; pres., chmn. Airbus Industries N.Am., 1974-77. Past mem. exec. com. Nat. Football Found., Internat. Center, N.Y.C.; former trustee Nat. Art Mus. of Sport. Episcopalian. Clubs: Sky (hon., past pres., now dir.), Madison Square Garden, Deepdale Golf, Yale (past council), Conquistadores del Cielo (life, charter), Boone and Crockett (N.Y.C.)). Home and Office: 930 Fifth Ave New York NY 10021

ADAMS, ALVIN PHILIP, JR., ambassador, lawyer; b. N.Y.C., Aug. 29, 1942; s. Alvin P. and Elizabeth (Miller) A.; m. Mai-Ann Nguyen, Jan. 27, 1973; children: Tung T., Lex N. B.A., Yale U., 1964; J.D., Vanderbilt U., 1967. Bar: N.Y., D.C. Staff mem. Nat. Security Council, Washington, 1972-74; spl. asst. to Sec. of State U.S. Dept. of State, Washington, 1974-76, dep. dir. Office of Bus. Practices, 1977-79, dir. secretariat staff, 1981, dep. exec. sec., 1981-83, ambassador to Republic of Djibouti, 1983—. Recipient Meritorious Honor award USAID, 1970; reipient Meritorius Honor award U.S. Dept. of State, Washington, 1972. Mem. N.Y. State Bar Assn., D.C. Bar Assn., U.S. Fgn. Service Assn. Roman Catholic. Clubs: Yale (N.Y.C.); International (Washington). Office: Am Embassy-Kjibouti care Dept State Washington DC 20520

ADAMS, ANDREW JOSEPH, army officer; b. Rose Hill, Ala., Aug. 29, 1909; s. Alfred E. and Eunice (Clements) A.; m. DeLellis Frances Shramek, Oct. 25, 1934; children—Carol (Mrs. Charles E. Lucier), Andrew Joseph, Elizabeth (Mrs. Ronald W. Robison). B.S., U.S. Mil. Acad., 1931; grad., Inf. Sch., 1938, Command and Gen. Staff Coll., 1942, Air Command and Gen. Staff Sch., 1946, Indsl. Coll. Armed Forces, 1953. Commd. 2d lt. U.S. Army, 1931, advanced through grades to maj. gen., 1956; chief staff, combat comdr. 7th Armored Div., ETO, 1944-45; instr. Air Command Staff Coll., 1946-49; adviser Peruvian Army, 1950-52; chief mgmt. div. Office Comptroller, U.S. Army, 1953; comdr. 23d Inf. Regt., also sr. adviser to comdg. gen. 2d Republic of Korea Army, 1954-55; dir. personnel, also dir. supply operations Office Dep. Chief Staff for Logistics, Dept. Army, 1955-59; dep. chief staff for logistics Hdqtrs. U.S. Army, Europe, 1959-61; dep. comdg. gen. 7th U.S. Army; also comdg. gen. 7th U.S. Support Command and Mobile Land Force, Allied Forces Europe, 1961-62; comdg. gen. XIX U.S. Army Corps, 1962-63; dep. chief staff logistics Hdqrs. U.S. Army Pacific, 1963-66, U.S. Continental Army Command, 1966-67; chief exec. and sec. Am. Battle Monuments Commn., Washington, 1967—; dir. Fort Rucker Nat. Bank.; Director Army Stock Fund, 1957-59, U.S. Army Pacific Stock Fund, 1963-66, U.S. Army CONARC Stock Fund, 1966; chmn. bd. dirs. Pacific Army-Air Force Exchange System, 1964-66. Decorated D.S.M., Silver Star, Legion of Merit with oak leaf cluster, Bronze Star, Army Commendation medal with oak leaf cluster; Legion of Honor; Croix de Guerre with palm, France; Ulchi medal with gold star, Korea; Mil. Order Ayachucho, Peru). Home: 3412 Chiswick Ct Silver Spring MD 20906 Office: Am Battle Monuments Commn Washington DC 20314

ADAMS, ANDREW STANFORD, govt. ofcl.; b. San Francisco, July 8, 1922; s. Edward Lewis and Jane Eva (Kurowsky) A.; m. Anke Peters, Oct. 2, 1967; children—Anya, Arva. Ed.D., U. Calif. at Berkeley, 1954. Dep. dir. edn. and rehab. VA (and other fed. govt. posts), 1964-70, 73-74; supt. schs., prin., tchr. in, Mo., Nev. and, Calif., 1951-64, 70-73, profl. baseball player, 1945-50, univ. prof. several colls. and univs., 1955—; U.S. commr. Rehab. Services Adminstrn., Washington, 1974-77; spl. asst. Office of Sec., Dept. of Interior, Washington, 1977—. Contbr. articles to profl. jours. Served with USAAF, 1942-45. Recipient numerous awards for pub. service. Mem. Am. Assn. Sch. Adminstrs., Nat. Rehab. Assn., others. Home: 1600 S Joyce St Apt B-409 Arlington VA 22202 Office: Office of Sec Dept Interior Washington DC 20240

ADAMS, ARLIN MARVIN, judge; b. Phila., Apr. 16, 1921; s. Aaron M. and Mathilda (Landau) A.; m. Neysa Cristol, Nov. 10, 1942; children—Carol (Mrs. Howard Kirshner), Judith A., Jane C. B.S. in Econs, Temple U., 1941; LL.B., U. Pa., 1947, M.A., 1950, D.H.L., 1964; D.Sc., Phila. Coll., 1965; LL.D., Phila. Coll. Textiles, 1966. Bar: Pa. bar 1947. Law clk. Chief Justice Horace Stern, Pa. Supreme Ct., 1947; asso. firm Schnader, Harrison, Segal & Lewis, Phila., 1947-50, sr. partner, 1950-63, 66-69; sec. pub. welfare Commonwealth of Pa., 1963-66; judge U.S. Ct. Appeals 3d Circuit, Phila., 1969—; instr. Am. Inst. Banking, Phila., 1948-50; lectr. fed. practice Law Sch., U. Pa., Phila., 1952-56, constl. law, 1972—. Vice pres. Fed. Jewish Agys., 1969-71, mem. exec. com. and cabinet, 1969—; v.p. Albert Einstein Med. Center, Phila., 1970—; Chmn. bd dirs. Moss Rehab. Hosp., Phila., Fels Inst. Govt., Phila., Sch. Social Work, Bryn Mawr (Pa.) Coll., Diagnostic and Rehab. Center, Phila., 1971-72; trustee U. Pa. Law Sch., Hebrew Union Coll., Cin., German Marshall Meml. Fund, Lewis H. Stevens Trust, Bryn Mawr Coll., Med. Coll. Pa., 1907 Found.; bd. overseers Wharton Sch., U. Pa., Columbia U. Center for Law and Econ. Studies, U. Pa. Inst. for Law and Econs., William Penn Found. Served as lt. USNR, 1942-46; PTO. Recipient Disting. Service award, 1981, Justice award, 1982. Mem. Am. Law Inst., Am. Bar Found., Am. Bar Assn. (del. ho. of dels. 1966-67, 75-78, chmn. trade assn. com.), Pa. Bar Assn. (del. ho. of dels. 1967-71), Phila. Bar Assn. (chancellor 1967), Am. Judicature Soc. (pres. 1975-77), Am. Philos. Soc. (sec. 1980—), Order of Coif, Beta Gamma Sigma. Clubs: Mason (32 deg.),

Phila., Midday, Locust, Union League, Sunday Breakfast, Legal, Junior Legal, Sociolegal (Phila.). Home: 3006 Foxx Ln Philadelphia PA 19144 Office: US Courthouse Philadelphia PA 19106

ADAMS, ARTHUR EUGENE, university administrator; b. Indianola, Iowa, Apr. 11, 1917; s. Arthur Henry and Armenia (James) A.; m. Ouida Janet Steckelberg, Aug. 9, 1942; children: Russell James, Joan Catherine. B.A., U. Nebr., 1942; Ph.D., Cornell U., 1951, Harvard, 1954-55. Prof. history Mich. State U., 1951-70, chmn. Russian and Eastern European studies program, 1963-70; prof. history, dean Coll. Humanities, Ohio State U., 1970-77, prof. history, asso. provost, 1977-78, vice provost, 1978-82; cons. on Soviet Union affairs Radio Free Europe, 1961-63, Nat. Endowment for Humanities, 1966-70; bd. dirs. Midwest Univs. Consortium for Internat. Activities, 1977-83; mem. commn. on accreditation Am. Council Edn., 1978-82; mem. adv. group on adult edn. Coll. Bd., 1980-82. Author: An Historical Atlas of Russia and East Europe, 1967, Bolsheviks in the Ukraine (Borden award Hoover Inst. and Library 1963), Men Versus Systems: Agriculture in the USSR, Poland and Czechoslovakia, 1971, Stalin and his Times, 1972. Mem. Commn. for a Greater Columbus, 1979—, Radio Free Europe/Radio Liberty Bd., 1978-82. Served to maj. AUS, 1942-46. Social Sci. Research Council grantee, 1956; Carnegie Corp. Inter-Univ. travel grantee to USSR, 1957; recipient Outstanding Prof. award Mich. State U., 1959. Mem. Am. Hist. Assn., Mich. Acad. Arts and Scis. (chmn. Russian studies sect. 1960-61, 65-66), Am. Assn. Advancement Slavic Studies (bd. Midwest Slavic Conf. 1968-69), Phi Beta Kappa, Phi Kappa Phi, Delta Tau Kappa. Home: 2106 W Lane Ave Columbus OH 43221

ADAMS, ARTHUR HARVEY, consultant, retired marine corps officer; b. Jasper, Minn., Apr. 16, 1915; s. Arthur Harvey and Millie (Davison) A.; m. Kathleen L. Watson, Nov. 29, 1939; children—Frederick A., Kathleen (Mrs. Joseph A. Baczko, Jr.), Melissa J. (Mrs. Neal Tully), Judith A. Zimmermann. B.B.A., U. Minn., 1938. Enlisted in USMCR, 1936, apptd. marine aviation cadet, 1938; designated naval aviator and commd. 2d lt. USMC, 1939, advanced through ranks to maj. gen., 1967; aviator, World War II, PTO; grad. Navy Test Pilot Tng. Sch., Patuxent River, Md., 1950; stationed, Korea, 1952-53; staff officer Hdqrs. U.S. European Command, Paris, France, 1959-62; dir. information Hdqrs. USMC, Washington, 1963-66; comdg. gen. 4th Marine Air Wing, 1966-68, 3d Marine Air Wing, 1968-69; sr. mem. UN Command Mil. Armistice Commn., Seoul and Panmunjom, Korea, 1969-70; dep. comdg. gen. Fleet Marine Force, Pacific, 1970-72; dep. chief of staff Atlantic Command, 1972-75; ret., 1975; office adminstr. law firm Willcox, Savage, Lawrence, Dickson & Spindle, P.C., Norfolk, Va., until 1983, ret., 1983. Decorated Legion of Merit with 3 gold stars, D.F.C. with four oak leaf clusters, Bronze Star with combat V and gold star, Air medal with fourteen oak leaf clusters, Meritorious Service medal; Order of Nat. Security Merit 3d class Republic of Korea). Address: 7404 Cortlandt Pl Norfolk VA 23505

ADAMS, AUGUSTUS ETHRIDGE, tire company executive; b. Columbus, Ga., Oct. 1, 1931; s. Augustus E. and Mary Lee (Tyson) A.; m. Patricia Ann Pointer, July 12, 1954; children: Deborah, Elizabeth, A.E. III, Peter, Lauralee. B.S., Auburn U., 1952, B.A., 1952; diploma, Northwestern U., 1978. Vice-pres. fin. Firestone Argentina, Buenos Aires, 1964-69, Firestone Brazil, Sao Paulo, 1969-71; asst. to pres. Firestone Internat. Co, Akron, Ohio, 1971-73; pres., mng. dir. Firestone Venezuela, Valencia, 1973-74, Firestone Argentiana, Buenos Aires, 1974-75, Firestone Australia, Sydney, 1975-76; v.p. Latin Am. Firestone Internat.Co., Akron, 1976-80; pres., chief exec. officer Gen. Tire Can. Ltd., Barrie, Ont., 1980—, dir., 1982—; v.p., area dir. Latin Am. Gen. Tire Internat. Co., 1984—; dir. Gen. Popo, S.A. Mex., Ecuador Rubber Co. Bd. dirs. Lincoln Sch., Buenos Aires, 1974-75, Am. Sch., Valencia, 1973-74; assoc. Smithsonian Instn., Washington, 1976. Served with U.S. Army, 1954-56. Mem. Rubber Mfrs. Assn. (bd. dirs. Toronto 1980—, bd. dirs. Argentina 1974-75, pres. Venezuela 1974), Am. Mgmt. Assn., Nat. Fgn. Trade Council, Am. C. of C., Confederate Meml. Lit. Soc., United Sons Confederate Vets., Delta Sigma Pi. Clubs: Kempenfeldt Bay Yacht (Barrie); Chalputepec Golf (Mex.). Home: 120 Overwood Rd Akron OH 44313 Office: Gen Tire Internat One General St Akron OH 44329

ADAMS, BENJAMIN RAIFORD, packing co. exec.; b. Deland, Fla., Sept. 25, 1926; s. Benjamin Walker and Emma (Bennett) A.; Apr. 19, 1952; children—June Leigh, Benjamin Raiford, William Wright. B.S., Stetson U., 1949; postgrad., So. Coll., 1952. Acct. Clinton Foods, Inc., Dunedin, Fla., 1949-52; gen. mgr., then exec. v.p. West Coast Pazco Packing Co., Dade City, Fla., 1952-68; pres., chmn. bd. Adams Packing Assn., Inc., Auburndale, Fla., 1968—; chmn. bd. R.C. Bottlers Fla.; dir. Cypress Garden, 1st Nat. Bank, Bank of Pasco, Texsun Corp. (others.). Chmn. bd. Bartow (Fla.) Gen. Hosp.; vice chmn. bd. dirs. Winter Haven (Fla.) Hosp. Served with USAAF, World War II; PTO. Democrat. Methodist. Clubs: Winter Haven Country, Fla., Masons; Shriners (Tampa). Office: 625 Bridgers Ave Auburndale FL 33823

ADAMS, BERNARD SCHRODER, college president; b. Lancaster, Pa., July 20, 1928; s. Martin Ray and Charlotte (Schroder) A.; m. Natalie Virginia Stout, June 2, 1951; children: Deborah Rowland, David Schroder. B.A., Princeton, 1950; M.A., Yale, 1951; Ph.D., U. Pitts., 1964; LL.D. (hon.), Lawrence U., 1967. Asst. dir. admissions, instr. English Princeton, 1953-57; dir. admissions and student aid U. Pitts., 1957-60, spl. asst. to chancellor, 1960-64; dean students, lectr. English Oberlin (Ohio) Coll., 1964-66; pres. Ripon (Wis.) Coll., 1966—; dir. Wis. Power & Light Co., Newton Income and Growth Funds, Inc.; cons., examiner, exec. commr. Commn. on Instns. Higher Edn., North Central Assn. Colls. and Secondary Schs., 1972—; Bd. dirs. Asso. Colls. Midwest, 1966—, chmn., 1973-75. Author articles. Served to 1st lt. USAF, 1951-53. Woodrow Wilson fellow, 1951. Mem. Modern Lang. Assn., Wis. Assn. Ind. Colls. and Univs. (dir. 1966—, pres. 1969-71, 83—), Wis. Found. Ind. Colls. and Univs. (pres. 1973-75), Omicron Delta Kappa. Home: 1 Merriman Ln Ripon WI 54971

ADAMS, BROOKE, actress; b. N.Y.C., Feb. 8, 1949. Student, High Sch. Performing Arts, N.Y.C., Inst. Am. Ballet, Lee Strasberg. Actress appearing in: films including Days of Heaven, 1978, Invasion of the Bodysnatchers, 1978, A Man, A Woman and A Bank, 1979, Cuba, 1979, Shock Waves, 1980, Tell Me a Riddle, 1980; TV shows including Murder on Flight 502, James Dean, Portrait of a Friend, The Last of the Belles, The Lords of Flatbush, The Daughter of Joshua Cabe. Care Phil Gersh Agy Inc 222 N Canon Dr Beverly Hills CA 90210 *

ADAMS, CAROLYN ETHEL, dancer; b. N.Y.C., Aug. 16, 1943; d. Julius J. and Olive L. (Arnold) A. Certificate, Schola Cantorum, France, 1964; B.A., Sarah Lawrence Coll., 1965. Guest tchr. regional cos., colls., including Sarah Lawrence Coll.; co-dir. Harlem Dance Studio, 1970—; With Ballets Contemporains, France, 1963-64; prin. dancer Paul Taylor Co., N.Y.C., 1965—, prin. dancer yearly U.S. and world tours including TV appearances with co., 1965-82, master tchr., 1965-82; guest artist Paul Taylor's Aureole with Nureyev and Friends Uris Theatre, N.Y.C., 1974; guest artist Jacob's Pillow, 1975; cons. Nat. Endowment for Arts; Pres. Harlem Dance Found., 1973—; vice-chmn. dance panel N.Y. State Council on Arts. Creator: story for musical Santa Claus and the Unicorn, 1973; performances include: Santa Claus and the Unicorn, 1976-82; choreographer: N.Y. World's Fair, 1964, R.I. Dance Repertory Co., 1974, Santa Claus and the Unicorn, 1976-81; contbr. articles on dance and housing preservation to publs. Co-founder, chmn. Central Harlem Brownstone Preservation Com., 1970—; trustee Sarah Lawrence Coll., mem. alumni bd. at large, 1975-77; mem. Real Estate Bd. of N.Y. State. Recipient Mademoiselle mag. merit award, 1968; named Dancer of Month Dance Mag., 1970, Outstanding Career Woman Glamour Mag., 1973. Mem. Sarah Lawrence Coll. Alumnae Assn. (dir. 1972-75). Episcopalian. Home: 144 W 121st St New York NY 10027 Office: 550 Broadway New York NY 10012 *I seek for myself what I wish for all individuals: to be entrusted with my abilities, thereby rendered free to function.*

ADAMS, CHARLES FRANCIS, business executive; b. Boston, May 2, 1910; s. Charles F. and Frances (Lovering) A.; m. Margaret Stockton, June 16, 1934 (dec. 1972); children: Abigail (Mrs. James C. Manny), Alison (Mrs. Alison Robinson), Timothy; m. Beatrice D. Penati, Oct. 1973. Student, St. Mark's Sch., Southboro, Mass., 1922-28; A.B., Harvard U., 1932; D.B.A., Suffolk U., 1953, Northeastern U., 1959; LL.D., Bates Coll., 1960. Asso. with Jackson & Curtis (investment bankers), Boston, 1934-37, partner, 1937-42, 1942-47; exec. v.p. Raytheon Co., Waltham, Mass., 1947-48, pres., 1948-60, 62-64, chmn. bd., 1960-62, 64-75, chmn. finance com., 1975—, also dir. Chmn. bd. trustees Woods Hole Oceanographic Inst.; trustee Cotting Sch. Crippled Children of Boston, Childrens Hosp. Med. Center. Served with USNR, 1940-46; comd. vessels; Atlantic and Pacific Theatres; released to inactive duty as comdr. Fellow Am. Acad. Arts and Scis. Clubs: Somerset, Brook, The Country, New York Yacht, Cruising of America. Home: 195 Dedham St Dover MA 02030 Office: Raytheon Co 141 Spring St Lexington MA 02173

ADAMS, CHARLES FRANCIS, advertising association executive; b. Detroit, Sept. 26, 1927; s. James R. and Bertha C. (DeChant) A.; m. Helen R. Harrell, Nov. 12, 1949; children: Charles Francis, Amy Ann, James Randolph, Patricia Duncan. B.A., U. Mich., 1948; postgrad., U. Calif., Berkeley, 1949. With D'Arcy-MacManus & Masius, Inc., 1947-80, exec. v.p., dir., 1970-76, pres., chief operating officer, 1976-80; exec. v.p., dir. Washington Office, Am. Assn. Advt. Agys., 1980—; chmn., dir. Wajim Corp., Detroit; past mem. steering com. Nat. Advt. Rev. Bd.; mem. mktg. com. U.S. Info. Agy. Author: Common Sense in Advertising, 1965. Memexec. com. Oakland Univ. Mem. Am. Assn. Advt. Agys. (dir., mem. govt. relations com.), Advt. Fedn. Am. (past dir.), Nat. Outdoor Advt. Bur. (past chmn.), Theta Chi, Alpha Delta Sigma (hon.). Republican. Roman Catholic. Clubs: Olympic Country, Bloomfield Hills Country; Renaissance (Detroit); Nat. Golf Links Am. (Southampton, L.I.); Olympic (San Francisco). Home: 3265 O St NW Washington DC 20007 also 6139 Dakota Circle Birmingham MI 48010 also 2240 Hyde St San Francisco CA 94109 Office: 1899 L St NW Suite 700 Washington DC 20036

ADAMS, CHARLES J., former corporation executive, retired air force officer; b. Beaver Dam, Utah, Aug. 22, 1921; s. Arthur Walter and Mary Elizabeth (Ericksen) A.; m. Virginia Lee Polk, May 3, 1944; children: Mary Keen, Charles J. Student, U. Utah, 1939-41; B.S. in Edn, U. Omaha, 1958. Commd. 2d lt. USAAF, 1943; advanced through grades to brig. gen. USAF, 1971; mem. Ronne Antarctic Expdn., 1947-48; comdr. 44th Strategic Missile Wing, Ellsworth AFB, S.D., 1969-70, comdr. 821st Strategic Aerospace Div., 1970-71; with Hdqrs. USAF, Washington, 1962-67, 1971-73; ret., 1973; mgr. field offices GTE Sylvania, Vanderberg AFB, Calif.; and Grand Forks AFB, N.D., 1974-76, asst. gen. mgr. communications system div., Needham, Mass., 1976-80; mgr. field office Vandenberg AFB, Calif., 1980—. Decorated D.S.M., Legion of Merit, D.F.C., Air medal, Air Force Commendation medal. Mem. Order of Daedalians, Sigma Nu. Clubs: Rotarian., Explorers (N.Y.C.). Home: 302 Wisteria Santa Maria CA 93455

ADAMS, CHARLES JAIRUS, lawyer; b. Randolph, Vt., Feb. 17, 1917; s. Charles B. and Jeanette E. (Metzger) A.; m. Mary E. Tobey, July 5, 1942; children: Mary Jean, Carol Ann. B.S. in Elec. Engring, Norwich U., 1939; LL.B., Boston U., 1951. Bar: Vt. 1951. Student engr. Gen. Electric Co., also New Eng. Power Co., 1939-41; plant supt. Demeritt Co., Waterbury, Vt., 1946-48; practiced in, Montpelier and Waterbury, 1951—; partner firm Adams, Darby & Laundon, 1980—; atty. gen., Vt., 1962-63; Chmn. State of Vt. Legis. Apportionment Bd., 1972-80; mem. adv. com. on civil rules Vt. Supreme Ct., 1971-82. Trustee Village Waterbury, 1956-57, pres., 1958; moderator Town Waterbury, 1961; Mem. Waterbury Pub. Library Assn., 1961—. Served with AUS, 1941-46. Mem. ABA, Vt. Bar Assn. (treas. 1951-55), Washington County Bar Assn. (pres. 1966-67), Am. Judicature Soc., Am. Legion, Norwich U. Gen. Alumni Assn. (pres. 1960-61). Republican. Conglist. Clubs: Mason, Shriner, Rotarian. Home: 11 Swasey Ct Waterbury VT 05676 Office: 12 S Main St Waterbury VT 05676

ADAMS, CHARLES LYNFORD, educator; b. Joliet, Ill., May 11, 1929; s. Charles Lynford and Eloise A. (Henault) A.; m. Joan Marie Johnson, June 6, 1953; children—Rebecca Lynn, Stephen Thomas. B.A., Mich. State U., 1951; M.A., U. Ill., 1952; Ph.D., U. Oreg., 1959. Instr. English U. Ore., 1959-60; asst. prof. U. Nev., Las Vegas, 1960-65, asso. prof., 1965-67, prof. English, 1967—; Las Vegas rep. U. Nev. System Grad. Sch., 1964-66, coordinator grad. studies, 1966-68, dean grad. studies, 1968-71. Mem. adv. com. Univ. Mus. Soc. Served with AUS, 1954-56. Mem. Modern Lang. Assn., Nat., Nev., So. Nev. councils tchrs. English, Rocky Mountain Modern Lang. Assn., Conf. Coll. Composition and Communication, Philol. Assn. Pacific Coast, Nat. Soc. Profs., Phi Kappa Phi. Home: 1921 E St Louis Las Vegas NV 89104 Office: 4505 S Maryland Pkwy Las Vegas NV 89154

ADAMS, CHRISTOPHER STEVE, JR., former air force officer, scientific laboratory official; b. Shreveport, La., July 8, 1930; s. Christopher Steve and Armenda Lee (Tanner) A.; m. Mary Alene Mitchell, Aug. 22, 1953; children: Cynthia, Charlotte, Cheri, Christopher III. A.S., Tarleton State U., 1950; B.S., East Tex. State U., 1952. Commd. U.S. Air Force, 1952, advanced through grades to maj. gen., 1979; B-36 pilot 95th Bombardment Wing, Biggs AFB, Tex., 1954-59, Ramey AFB, P.R.; B-52G pilot with 72nd Bombardment Wing, 1959-63; missile combat crew comdr. 44th Strategic Missil Wing, Ellsworth, AFB, S.D., 1963-66; chief ops. and tng. 388th Combat Support Group, 388th Tactical Fighter Wing, Korat Royal Thai AFB, Thailand, 1966-67; action officer for ops. and plans directorate J-3, Headquarters Joint Task Force 8, Sandia Base, N.Mex., 1967-70; dir. plans and policy J-5, Def. Nuclear Agy., Washington, 1970-73; vice comdr., then comdr. 90th Strategic Missile Wing, 1973-75; comdr. 12th Air Div., 1975-78; dep. chief staff, ops. plans Hdqrs. SAC; and dep. dir. for, Single Integrated Operational Plan of Joint Strategic Target Planning Staff, Offutt AFB, Nebr., 1979-82; ret., 1982; assoc. dir. U. Calif. Los Alamos Nat. Lab., 1982—. Contbr. articles to profl. jours. Bd. dirs. ARC, 1976-78, Mid-Am. Council Boy Scouts Am., 1976-81. Decorated D.S.M., Def. Superior Service medal, Legion of Merit, Air Force Commendation medal. Presbyterian. Home: 2030 Rio Bravo Los Alamos NM 87545 Office: ADTS Los Alamos NM 87545 *America the beautiful. I have dedicated my life through service to preserve our freedom. There is no better place on earth—I know, I've been there.*

ADAMS, CLINTON, painter, educator; b. Glendale, Calif., Dec. 11, 1918; s. Merritt Cooley and Effie (Mackenzie) A.; m. Mary Elizabeth Atchison, Jan. 9, 1943; 1 son, Michael Gerald. Ed.B., U. Calif. at Los Angeles, 1940, M.A., 1942. Instr. art U. Calif. at Los Angeles, 1946-48, asst. prof., 1948-54; prof. art, head dept. U. Ky.; also dir. Art Gallery, 1954-57; prof. art, head dept. U. Fla., 1957-61; dean Coll. Fine Arts, U. N.Mex., Albuquerque, 1961-76, asso. provost, dean faculties, 1976-77; dir. Tamarind Inst., 1970—; asso. dir. Tamarind Lithography Workshop, Los Angeles, 1960-61, program cons., 1961-70. Represented in collections, Bklyn. Mus., Art. Inst. Chgo., Pasasdena Art. Mus., Grunwald Center Graphic Arts, Mus. Modern Art, Los Angeles County Art Mus., and others; Author: (with Garo Antreasian) The Tamarind Book of Lithography: Art and Techniques, 1970, Fritz Scholder: Lithographs, 1975, American Lithographers, 1900-1960: The Artists and Their Printers, 1983; Editor: The Tamarind Papers, 1974—. Mem. Coll. Art Assn. (program chmn. 1963), Nat. Council Fine Arts Deans (chmn. 1965-67), Mid-Am. Coll. Art Assn. (pres. 1973). Home: 1917 Morningside Dr NE Albuquerque NM 87110

ADAMS, DAVID EARL, publishing company executive; b. Columbus, Ohio, May 28, 1948; s. Robert Earl and Helen (Beresh) A.; m. Maurean Burritt, May 11, 1968; children: David, Andrew, Aimee, Michael, Joseph. B.S., U. Tenn., 1970. Staff acct. Arthur Andersen & Co., N.Y.C., 1970-71; controller Charles C. Ervin Co., Charlotte, N.C., 1971-77, The Mother Earth News, Inc., Hendersonville, N.C., 1977-80, pres., 1980. Office: PO Box 70 Hendersonville NC 28791

ADAMS, DAVID KENNETH, exporter; b. Kalamazoo, Feb. 20, 1935; s. H. Kenneth and Dorothy (Lawrence) A.; m. Mina Jean Hoag, Mar. 31, 1956; 1 dau., Martha Lynn. B.A., Western Mich. U., 1957; M.S., S.D. State U., 1959; Ph.D., Ind. U., 1962. Asst. prof. history Am. U. in Cairo, 1962-65; asst. prof., asso. prof. history Beloit (Wis.) Coll., 1965-76, dir. Porter Scholars div., 1972-73, dean of coll., 1973-76; v.p., acad. dean Olivet (Mich.) Coll., 1976-82; pres. Island Exporters, dir. Gerona, Ltd., 1982—. Mem. World Trade Council. Home: 2701 NE 56th Ct Fort Lauderdale FL 33308

ADAMS, DEWEY ALLEN, vocational educator; b. Fuquay Springs, N.C., Apr. 29, 1931; s. Roy A. and Eva A. (Champion) A. B.S., N.C. State U., 1954, M.S., 1958; Ed. D. in Adminstrn. and Supervision, U. Fla., 1966. Tchr., prin. Kenly Pine Forest Sch., N.C., 1954-60; supr. Dept. of State, Raleigh, N.C., 1960-62; dean Rockingham Community Coll., Reidsville, N.C., 1964-66; assoc. prof. N.C. State U., 1966-71; prof., dir. Va. Poly. Inst. and State U., Blacksburg, 1971-76; prof., chmn. dept. comprehensive vocat. edn. Ohio State U., Columbus, 1976—; cons., trainer Effective Leadership Devel. Assn., 1978—. Editor (with others) Vocational Education in America, 1983; contbr. chpts. in books. Recipient plaque Univ. Indsl. Arts Assn., Blacksburg, 1967, cert. Nat. Personnel Devel. Group., 1979. Mem. Adult Edn. Assn. (pres. 1969-71), Personnel Devel. Assn. (pres. 1982-84), Phi Delta Kappa, Omicron Tau Theta. Home: 895 Kenwyn Ct Columbus OH 43220 Office: Comprehensive Vocational Education 1960 Kenny Rd Columbus OH 43210

ADAMS, DONALD KENDRICK, comparative education educator, writer; b. North Berwick, Maine, Feb. 21, 1925; s. Howard Franklin and Amy Frances (Welch) A.; m. Janet Sue Cabe, Sept. 1, 1960; children: Lance Howard, Amy Louise. B.A., U. N.H., 1949; M.A., U. Conn., 1954, Ph.D., 1956. Asst. prof. George Peabody Coll., 1958-60; assoc. pof. edn. Syracuse U., 1961-63, chmn. culturals found. of edn., 1964-70; chmn. div. edn. studies U. Pitts., 1971-74, prof. ednl. planning, 1975—; scholar in residence East-West Ctr., Honolulu, 1965-66; cons. USAID, 1957-58, Ford Found., UNESCO, Peace Corps. Author: Patterns of Education in Contemporary Societies, 1964 (NEA Book Distinction 1964), Patterns of Education In Contemporary Societies, 1964 (Pi Lambda Theta Nat. Book award 1975), Education and Modernization in Asia: A Systems Analysis, 1970, Education and Social Change in Modern America, 1975; cons. editor, David McKay Co., 1970-80. Served to lst lt. USAF, 1945, 51-52. Recipient Outstanding Faculty award Grad. Sch. Edn. U. Pitts., 1977. Mem. comparative and Internat. Edn. Soc. (pres. 1965), Internat. Soc. Edn. Planners (pres. 1974), Am. dnl. Studies Assn. (dir. 1978). Democrat. Club: Pitts. Road Runners. Home: 1106 Gilcrest Dr Pittsburgh PA 15235 Office: Internat & Devel Edn Program Univ Pitts 5A01 Forbes Quadrangle Pittsburgh PA 15260

ADAMS, DOUGLASS FRANKLIN, radiologist, educator; b. Lewiston, Maine, Aug. 5, 1935; s. Shirah Devoy and Olive (Colburn) A.; m. Eleanor Pohleven, Aug. 15, 1954; children: Stanford, Jennifer, Jason. B.A., Stetson U., 1957; B.S., Wake Forest Coll., Winston-Salem, N.C., 1957; M.D., Bowman Gray Sch. Medicine, Winston-Salem, 1960; S.M. (Sloan fellow), M.I.T., 1974. Intern Phila. Gen. Hosp., 1960, resident in radiology, 1960-61; resident in radiology, then fellow Am. Cancer Soc., Stanford U. Hosp., 1963-66; radiologist Peter Bent Brigham Hosp., Boston, 1967-79, Brigham and Women's Hosp., Boston, 1981—; instr. Stanford U. Med. Sch., 1966-67; mem. faculty Harvard U. Med. Sch., 1967-79, 81—, assoc. prof. radiology, 1976-82, prof. radiology, 1982—; prof. radiology, chmn. dept. U. Mich. Med. Sch., 1979-81. Mem. editorial bds. profl. jours. Served as capt. M.C. USAF, 1961-63. James Picker Found. scholar, 1967-70. Mem. Am. Coll. Radiology, Assn. Univ. Radiologists, Radiol. Soc. N. Am., Alpha Omega Alpha. Home: 9 Riverview Terr Dover MA 02030 Office: 75 Francis St Boston MA 02115

ADAMS, EARL WILLIAM, JR., economics educator; b. Lansing, Mich., Nov. 13, 1937; s. Earl William and V. Crystal (Woodruff) A.; m. Barbara Joan Charlton, Aug. 4, 1964; children: Earl William, III, Nicholas Charlton. B.A., U. Mich., 1959; Ph.D., Mass. Inst. Tech., 1971. Asst. prof. econs. Amherst Coll., 1963-66, U. Pitts., 1966-72; Andrew Wells Robertson prof. econs. Allegheny Coll., Meadville, Pa., 1972—; vis. asst. prof. U. Mass., 1966; research dir. bus. taxation Pa. Tax Commn., 1979-81; mem. adv. council Pa. Blue Shield, 1980-82, mem. corp., 1982—. Contbr. to profl. publs. Woodrow Wilson fellow, 1959. Mem. Am. Econs. Assn., Pa. Conf. Economists, Phi Beta Kappa, Phi Kappa Phi. Home: 311 Meadow St Meadville PA 16335 Office: Dept Econs Allegheny Coll Meadville PA 16335:

ADAMS, EDIE, actress, TV entertainer; b. Kingston, Pa., Apr. 16, 1929; d. Sheldon A. and Ada (Adams) Enke; m. Ernie Kovacs, Sept. 12, 1955 (dec.); 1 dau., Mia Susan (dec.).; m. Marty Mills, 1964 (div. 1972); 1 son, Joshua Dylan; m. Pete Candoli, 1972 (separated 1979), 1972. Student, Julliard Sch. Music, 1945-50, Columbia Sch. Dramatic Arts, 1949-50. Played in: Wonderful Town, 1952-53 (Donaldson award best debut actress, best supporting actress), Lil Abner, 1956-57 (Antoinette Perry award best featured actress); actress series TV variety shows, ABC; appeared stage show, Las Vegas; co-star: film Call Me Bwana, 1963; opera debut in: La Perichole, Seattle Opera Co., 1972. Recipient Comml. Spokeswoman of Year award.

ADAMS, EDWARD BEVERLE, electronics company executive; b. N.Y.C., Jan. 31, 1939; s. Clarence Lancelot and Erna Clarica (Larier) A.; m. Mary Louise Johnson, Nov. 21, 1964; children: Jennifer, Edward, Michelle. B. Indsl. Engring., N.Y. U., 1959; postgrad., U. Vt., 1968-69; Sloan fellow, Stanford, 1974. Buying mgr., product ind. engrs. mgr. IBM Corp., Burlington, Vt., 1964-69, adminstrv. asst. to v.p. mfg., Armonk, N.Y., 1969-70, ops. mgr., Boulder, Colo., 1970-73, mfg. mgr., Boulder, 1974-75, plant mgr., Austin, Tex., 1975-80, dir. site ops., 1980—; adv. dir. Community Nat. Bank, Austin.; Exec. in residence U. Colo., 1973. Bd. dirs. Austin Area Urban League, Brackenridge Hosp., 1978-80; mem. adv. bd. Stanford Sloan. Home:

7308 Valburn Dr Austin TX 78731 Office: 11400 Burnet Rd Austin TX 78759

ADAMS, EDWARD FRANKLIN, business brokerage and services company executive; b. Washington, Oct. 15, 1936; s. Albert Edward and Mary Alverta (Steele) A.; m. Roberta Ellen Tilley, Oct. 24, 1964; children: Christine, Brian, Heather. B.S. in Chem. Engring, U. Md., 1958, Ph.D., Rennselaer Poly. Inst., 1962. Research scientist Corning Glass Works, N.Y., 1962-68, supr. lighting products div., 1968-70, mgr. engring., advanced product plant, 1971-73; mgr. Corstar Products, 1973-77; dir. research and devel. Anchor Hocking Corp., Lancaster, Ohio, 1977-79, v.p. research and engring., 1979-83; pres. Mid Atlantic Bus. Investment Group, 1983—. Cons. Jr. Achievement, 1981. Named Boss of Year Profl. Secs. Internat., 1981. Mem. Am. Ceramic Soc., Am. Inst. Chem. Engrs., Am. Chem. Soc. Republican. Patentee in field. Home: 7104 Greenvale Pkwy Hyattsville MD 20784

ADAMS, EDWARD THOMAS (EDDIE), photographer; b. New Kensington, Pa., June 12, 1933; s. Edward I. and Adelaide (Suprano) A.; children: Susan Ann, Edward II, Amy Marie. Grad., New Kensington High Sch., 1951. Staff photographer New Kensington Daily Dispatch, 1950-58, Battle Creek, Mich.; Enquirer & News, 1958, Phila. Eve. Bull., 1958-62, A.P., 1962-72, Time mag., 1972-76; spl. corr. A.P., 1976-80; free-lance photographer, 1980—; prof. emeritus Daytona Beach Community Coll. (Fla.), 1984; lectr. in field, 1959—. Served with USMC, 1951-54. Recipient Pulitzer prize in photography, 1969; Grand prize World Press Photography, 1969; 1st pl. award, 1972; named 3d place World Photo Reporter, 1969; 2d place World Photo Reporter, 1970; recipient Sigma Delta Chi award, 1969, 78, 80, several Overseas Press Club Am. awards, 1969, 74, George Polk Meml. award, 1969, 78, 79, Nat. Press Photographer award, 1969; 1st place A.P. Mng. Editors, 1968, 79; Best Pictures in Book or Mag. award Overseas Press Club, 1975; named Photographer of Year N.Y. Press Photographers, 1966, 67, 70, 72; Middle Atlantic States, 1958, 59; Phila. Art Dirs. award, 1961; Nat. Headliners award, 1973; World Press Photo award, 1974, 75, 78, 82, 83, 84; Mag. Photographer of Yr. U. Mo.-Nat. Press Photographers Assn., 1975; Joseph Sprague Meml. award Nat. Press Photographers Assn., 1976; Silver Prix award Japan Advt. Assn., 1978; Robert Capa Meml. award, 1978; Am. Soc. Mag. Photographers Ann. award, 1980; W. Ger. Photokina award, 1978; others. Office: 435 W 57 St New York NY 10019 *I always hope that everytime I squeeze the shutter on my camera and once the photographs are published—that something good will happen to the subjects portrayed—or their cause.*

ADAMS, EDWIN MELVILLE, former foreign service officer, author, lecturer; b. Gridley, Ill., Sept. 28, 1914; s. Edwin Melville and Crystal (Montgomery) A. A.B., U. Ill., 1936, LL.B., 1939; postgrad., The Hague Acad. Internat. Law, summer 1951. Bar: Ill. 1939. Atty. State Farm Ins. Cos., Bloomington, Ill., 1939-42; officer charge Brazil area World Trade intelligence div., State Dept., Washington, 1942-43, negotiator German external assets agreements with neutral countries, 1946-48; successively assigned by State Dept. to, London, Paris, Bern and Frankfort; as U.S. negotiator at internat. econ. confs., 1948-50; econ. attache Am. embassy, The Hague, 1950-52; charge Italian econ. affairs State Dept., 1952-55; dep. chief mut. def. affairs, 2d sec. Am. embassy, Rome, Italy, 1955-58, chief mut. def. affairs, 1st sec., 1958-61; officer in charge econ. affairs for N. Africa Dept. State, 1961-64, career mgmt. officer, 1964-65; spl. asst. to dep. under sec. state, 1965-67; asso. dean Fgn. Service Inst., 1967-68; cons. Dept. State, 1968-72. Host: radio show Passport, WAMU, 1972—; author-narrator, NBC-TV show, Venice, My Love, 1972; pub. broadcasting The Social Responsibility of Business; radio shows My Beloved Italy; star, CBS-TV show, The Empty Frame, 1973; Appeared in: films The Last Detail, 1974, Airport, 1975, Three Days of the Condor, 1975, Franklin and Eleanor, The Other Side of Midnight, Company, The Seduction of Joe Tynan, Justice for All, First Monday in October. U.S. del. Conf. of African States on Devel. of Edn. in Africa, 1961. Served to lt. (j.g.) USNR, 1943-46; PTO. Decorated cavaliere ufficiale Order of Merit of Italian Republic. Mem. Screen Actors Guild, AFTRA, Actors Equity, Phi Delta Phi, Phi Kappa Sigma. Espicopalian. Club: Mason. (Washington). Home: 2540 Massachusetts Ave NW Washington DC 20008 *Each individual must find himself, his own assets, his own liabilities, his own ambitions, and cast aside the chains of his environment which may limit him to a particular business or profession. Try new types of work. Test your creativity. Only then, using the particular gifts which the Lord has given, will one achieve satisfaction.*

ADAMS, ELIE MAYNARD, philosophy educator; b. Clarkton, Va., Dec. 29, 1919; s. Wade Hampton and Bessie (Callaway) A.; m. Phyllis Margaret Stevenson, Dec. 22, 1942; children: Steven Maynard, Jill Elaine. B.A., U. Richmond, 1941, M.A., 1944; B.D., Colgate-Rochester Div. Sch., 1944; M.A. (Colgate-Rochester grad. scholar),. Teaching fellow Harvard U., 1946-47; asst. prof. philosophy Ohio U., 1947-48; asst. prof. U. N.C., 1948-53, asso. prof., 1953-58, prof., 1958-71, Kenan prof., 1971—, chmn. dept. philosophy, 1960-65, chmn. faculty, 1976-79, chmn. Program in Humanities for Study of Human Values; vis. prof. U. So. Calif., 1966, SUNY, 1971, U. Calgary (Alta., Can.), 1977; dir. Curriculum on Peace, War and Def., 1970-72; Adv. com. Nat. Humanities Center; mem. N.C. Humanities Com., N.C. Gov.'s Task Force on Sci. and Tech. Author: The Fundamentals of General Logic, 1954, Logic Problems, 1954, (with others) The Language of Value, 1957, Ethical Naturalism and the Modern World View, 1960, Philosophy and the Modern Mind, 1975, (with others) The Idea of America, 1977; also articles in philos. jours.; editor: Categorical Analysis: Selected Essays of Everett W. Hall on Philosophy, Value, Knowledge and Mind, 1964; Editor: Commonsense Realism, 1966. Recipient Thomas Jefferson award, 1971, Outstanding Educator of Am. award, 1971. Mem. Mind Assn., Am. Philos. Assn. (mem. exec. com. Eastern div. 1961-64, chmn. program com. 1965), N.C. Philos. Soc. (past pres.), So. Soc. Philosophy and Psychology (exec. council 1963-66, pres. 1968-69), Am. Assn. Advancement of Humanities. Home: 813 Old Mill Rd Chapel Hill NC 27514

ADAMS, EVA BERTRAND, management consultant; b. Wonder, Nev.; d. Verner Lauer and Cora (Varble) A. B.A., U. Nev.; M.A., Columbia, 1937; LL.B., Washington Coll. Law, 1948; LL.M., George Washington U., 1950; LL.D., U. Portland, 1966, U. Nev., 1967; J.D., Am. U., 1969. Bar: Nev. and D.C. bars 1950. Tchr. Las Vegas High Sch.; asst. dean Women, instr. English U. Nev., 1937-40; administrv. asst. to Sen. Pat McCarran, 1940-54, Sen. Ernest Brown, 1954, Sen. Alan Bible, 1954-61; dir. Bur. of Mint, Washington, 1961-69; mgmt. cons., 1969—; dir. Fund Mgmt. Co. Omaha, Teletrip Co.; Mem. Commn. on White House Fellows, 1970-73; mem. adv. com. on rights and responsibilities of women Sec. HEW, 1974-76; mem. nat. bd. Med. Coll. Pa. Mem. Washoe and St. Mary's Hosp. Guild; bd. dirs. Politecnic U.P.R. Mem. Am., Fed., Nev., D.C. bar assns., Nat. Exec. Secs. Assn. (hon.), Am. Women in Radio and TV, Reno C. of C., Senate Secs. Assn. (pres. 1943-44), Bus. and Profl. Women Assn., Cap and Scroll, Kappa Alpha Theta, Kappa Phi, Kappa Delta Pi. Clubs: Am. Newspaper Women's, Soroptomist, 1925 F Street. Home: 701 Skyline Blvd Reno NV 89509 *With all the competition in this world, any person, male or female, must be willing to do one thing to succeed - and that is WORK HARD. I have never felt the long arm of discrimination because I was a woman, sometimes in a man's job. I feel this is true because I knew, when I took any such job, that I had to "work like a man," while retaining my femininity, but never "over-using" it.*

ADAMS, EVERETT MERLE, sociologist, educator; b. Spencer, Iowa, Dec. 27, 1920; s. Everett Merle and Irma (Beatty) A.; m. J. Clare, June 2, 1943; children—Clare, Douglas, Samuel. A.B., Doane Coll., 1942; M.A., Harvard, 1960, Ph.D., 1963. Instr. sociology Syracuse U., 1950-57; asst. prof. U. N.D., 1957-58; asst. prof. to prof. sociology U. Colo., 1958—, chmn. dept., 1966-70, 76-78; Dir. Responsive Environments Found., Hamden, Conn., 1967—. Served with USAAF, 1942-46. Mem. Am. Sociol. Assn. Home: 907 12th St Boulder CO 80302

ADAMS, FAY, educator; b. Dinuba, Calif.; d. Samuel K. and Lulu J. (Harper) Greene; m. William Douglas Adams, Nov. 1, 1924; 1 dau., Marilinda; m. Ernest W. Tiegs, Sept. 1, 1949; m. William S. Noblitt, Mar. 31, 1984. A.B., U. So. Calif., 1926, A.M., 1929; Ph.D., Columbia U., 1934. Elementary tchr. pub. schs., Los Angeles, 1924-26, secondary tchr., 1926-29; tng. tchr. U. Calif., Los Angeles, 1929; instr. edn. U. So. Calif., 1929-34, asst. prof. edn., also dir. elementary tchr. tng., 1934-40, asso. prof. edn., 1940-46, prof. edn., 1946—. Author: Initiating an Activity Program into a Public School, 1934, Educating America's Children: Elementary School Curriculum and Method, 1954; Co-author: Teaching the Bright Pupil, 1928, Man-The Nature Tamer, 1941, Teaching Children to Read, 1949, Story of Nations, 1952, The Problems of Education, 1938; Editor: (with Ernest W. Tiegs) Tiegs-Adams Social Studies Series (Books 1-9), 1949, 54, 56, 58, 60, 65, 68, 75-79, 83, Teaching the Social Studies, 1959, 65, California: Your State, 1983. Mem. Phi Beta Kappa, Kappa Delta, Pi Lambda Theta, Delta Kappa Gamma (Calif. treas. 1937-38). Home: 5825 Green Oak Dr Los Angeles CA 90068

ADAMS, FLOYD CECIL, JR., army officer; b. Athens, Ga., Oct. 4, 1930; s. Floyd Cecil and Louise (Ivey) A.; m. Sally Ann Hart, Dec. 27, 1958; children: Susie Jane, Floyd Cecil, Edward Hart. B.S., Disting. Mil. Grad., (The Citadel), 1952; grad., U.S. Army Command and Gen. Staff Coll., 1963, Nat. War Coll., 1971; M.S. in Internat. Affairs, George Washington U., 1971. Commd. 2d. lt. U.S. Army, 1952, advanced through grades to brig. gen., comdr. batteries, Europe and Korea, Europe and Vietnam, comdr. 3d Armored Div. Artillery, instr. Field Artillery Sch., tactical officer U.S. Mil. Acad., mem. staff Pentagon, Washington, mem. staff NATO, dep. comdg. gen. recruiting command, comdr. First ROTC Region, Ft. Bragg, N.C., 1979—. Author: A Case for the Draft in the 1970's, 1971. Decorated Silver Star; decrated Legion of Merit; winner Douglas MacArthur award as nat. outstanding ROTC grad., 1952. Mem. Assn. U.S. Army, The Citadel, Scabbard and Blade (hon.). Episcopalian. Home: 5 Hoyle Plaza Fort Bragg NC 28307 Office: First ROTC Region Fort Bragg NC 28307

ADAMS, F(RANCIS) GERARD, economist, educator; b. Apr. 28, 1929; s. Walter and Margot A.; m. Courtney Sherbrooke, June 13, 1953; children: Leslie, Colin, Loren, Mark. B.A., U. Mich., 1949, M.A., 1951, Ph.D., 1956. Instr. dept. econs. U. Mich., Ann Arbor, 1952-56; economist Calif. Tex. Oil Corp., N.Y.C., 1956-59; cons. economist, mgr. gen. econs. dept. Compagnie Francaise des Petroles, N.Y.C. and Paris, 1959-61; mem. faculty U. Pa., Phila., 1961—, prof. econs. and fin., 1971—; dir. Econs. Research Unit, 1961—; sec., sr. cons. Wharton EFa, Inc., Phila., 1969—. Author: (with others) An Econometric Analysis of International Trade, 1969, (with J.R. Behrman) Econometric Models of World Agricultural Commodity Markets, 1976, Commodity Exports and Economic Development, 1982; editor: (with S.A. Klein) Stabilizing World Commodity Markets—Analysis, Practice and Policy, 1978; Author: (with L.R. Klein) Industrial Policies for Growth and Competitiveness, 1983; editor: (with Bert Hickman) Global Econometrics, 1983. Home: 105 W Ivywood Ln Radnor PA 19087 Office: Univ of Pa Dept Econs 3718 Locust Walk Philadelphia PA 19104

ADAMS, FRANCIS L(EE), engineer; b. Talladega, Ala., June 28, 1906; s. Samuel Robert and Margaretta (Hinton) A.; m. Lucy Gray Gibson, June 4, 1938; children: Virginia Gibson (Mrs. Marx Holder), Ann Fairfax (Mrs. George Gerald Marburger, Jr.). B.S.C.E., U. N.C., 1929; postgrad. in Water Power Engring, Lowell Inst., MIT, 1930. Student engr. So. Ry., 1927-28; structural designer Stone & Webster Engring. Corp., 1929-31; asst. engr. Office Mcpl. Architect D.C., 1931-32, Public Utilities Commn. D.C., 1932-33; engr. investigator Public Works Adminstrn., Washington, 1933; with FPC, 1934-62, asso. engr. nat. power survey, 1934-36; hydraulic engr. Denver regional office, 1936-38, sr. engr., asst. regional dir., 1938-41; regional adminstr. Ft. Worth regional office, 1941-45; asst. chief Bur. Power, Washington, 1945-51, chief, 1951-62; also chief engr. Fed. Power Commn., 1958-62; asst. v.p. Pacific Power & Light Co., 1964-71; cons. engr., 1971—; asso. Overseas Adv. Assos., Inc., 1975—; Mem. Internat. Joint Commn., U.S. and Can., 1958-62, Niagara Bd. Control, St. Lawrence River Bd. Control, St. Lawrence River Joint Bd. Engrs., Passamaquoddy Engring. Bd.; ofcl. U.S. dels. World Power Conf. and Internat. Congress on Large Dams, New Delhi, 1951, Internat. Assn. Hydraulic Research, Bombay, 1951, Internat. Conf. Large Electric High-Tension Systems (CIGRE), Paris, 1952; chmn. U.S. del. World Power Conf., Belgrade, Yugoslavia, 1957, U.S. dels. World Power Conf., Montreal, Can., 1958, U.S. del. World Power Conf., Madrid, 1960; chmn. U.S. nat. com. World Power Conf. (now World Energy Conf.), 1960, 61. Mem.; Fellow ASCE (life); mem. Washington Soc. Engrs. (life), Phi Beta Kappa, Tau Beta Pi, Phi Kappa Sigma. Episcopalian. Club: Cosmos (Washington). Home: 3900 Watson Pl NW Washington DC 20016

ADAMS, FRED, JR., food company executive; b. 1931. B.S., Miss. So. Coll., 1954. With Ralston Purina Feed Co., 1954-57, Adams Enterprises, Inc., 1957-61, Adams Egg Farms Inc., 1957-61, Adams Enterprise, Inc. (merger become Adams Foods, Inc.), from 1964; chmn. bd., chief exec. officer Cal-Maine Foods, Inc., Jackson, Miss. Address: Cal-Maine Foods Inc 3320 Woodrow Wilson Ave Jackson MS 39207 *

ADAMS, GEORGE JOHN, utility executive; b. Shoe Cove, Nfld., Can., Apr. 8, 1924; s. Cecil Arthur and Sophia (Mercer) A. Student, Tufts U., 1943-46. Acct. R. Pike, Ltd., 1947-50; mgr. S.W. Coop. Ltd., 1950-52; salesman D.H. Goose Ltd., 1952-55; with Nfld. Light & Power Co. Ltd., St. John's, 1955—, asst. sec.-treas., then treas., 1962-80, dir. fin., 1980-82, v.p. fin., 1982—; chmn. bus. course adv. com. Nfld. Coll. Trades and Tech. Mem. Sci. Mgmt. Accts. Can., Fin. Execs. Inst. Can. Home: Shoe Cove Box 8752 St John's NF A1B 1K1 Canada Office: 55 Kenmount Rd St John's NF A1B 3P6 Canada

ADAMS, GEORGIA S., educator; b. Ortonville, Minn., May 23, 1913; d. John Frederick and Ella (Merry) Wein; m. Joseph John Adams, Sept. 7, 1946; children—Margaret (Mrs. Lawrence Cross), Jo-Ann, Joseph, Mary. A.B., U. So. Calif., 1933, M.S., 1935, Ph.D., 1941; postdoctoral student, U. Chgo., 1941, Claremont Grad. Sch., 1952-53. Research asst., research dir. Pasadena City Schs., 1936-51; instr. Muir Coll., 1951-52, 53-54; lectr. Claremont Grad. Sch., 1953-63; prof. edn. Calif. State U. at Los Angeles, 1954—; assessment coordinator Nat. Dissemination and Assessment Center, ESEA, Title VII; vis. prof. U. Hawaii, summer 1959, 67; dir. evaluation teaching team project Ford Found., 1957-58, coordinator ednl. founds., 1964-66; cons. Project Teach, Office Edn. Project A Reading Program for Mexican-Am. Children, Orientation and Mobility Skills for the Blind. Author: Exploring the World of Work, 1937, Evaluating Group Guidance Work in Secondary Schools, 1945, California Test in Social and Related Sciences, 1947, 54, Measurement and Evaluation for the Elementary School Teacher, 1954, Measurement and Evaluation for the Secondary School Teacher, 1956, Social Relationships in the Classroom, 1958, California Survey Tests, 1958, Measurement and Evaluation in Education and Psychology, 1964, Spanish edit., 1970. Recipient Outstanding Prof. award Cal. State U., 1969. Fellow Am. Psychol. Assn., mem. Am. Ednl. Research Assn., AAAS (mem. council 1971), Internat. Council Psychologists (sec.-gen.), Phi Beta Kappa, Pi Lambda Theta (nat. pres. 1970-73). Home: 2772 N Lake Ave Altadena CA 91001 Office: 5151 State University Dr Los Angeles CA 90032

ADAMS, HAROLD LYNN, architect; b. Palmer, Tex., May 15, 1939; s. Charles Roy and Lola (Beck) A.; m. Janice Lindhurst, Aug. 29, 1963; children: Harold Lynn, Abigail, Ashley, Sam. B.S. in Architecture, Tex. A&M U., 1962. Registered architect 30 states. Draftsman Pratt Box Henderson, Dallas, 1960; intern William B. Tabler & Assocs., N.Y.C., 1961, 62-67; architect John Carl Warnecke & Assocs., Washington, 1962-66, RTKL Assocs., Inc., Balt., 1967—; assoc. prof. part-time U. Md., College Park, 1971-75. Contbg. author: Current Techniques in Architectural Practice. Chmn. archtl. div. United Fund Drive, 1972; pres. Balt. Promotion Council, 1975-76; mem. task force on econ. devel. Balt. C. of C., 1975; exec. com. Mt. Washigton Country Sch. for Boys, 1976-77; bd. mgrs. Black Rock YMCA, 1971; vice chmn. GBC Found.; mem. Greater Balt. Com. on Edn., 1977-80, Com. on Planning, 1980-82; bd. dirs. Greater Balt. Com., 1983—; mem. Tex. A&M Devel. Council, 1982. Recipient Featherlite Design award Tex. A&M U., 1962, Davidson Design award Tex. A&M U., 1962, Alpha Rho Chi medal, 1962. Fellow AIA (pres. 1973-74); mem. Urban Land Inst. Democrat. Baptist. Clubs: Internat. (Washington); Dallas; Center (Balt.). Home: 1601 The Terraces Baltimore MD 21209

ADAMS, HAZARD SIMEON, educator, author; b. Cleve., Feb. 15, 1926; s. Robert Simeon and Mary (Thurness) A.; m. Diana White, Sept. 17, 1949; children: Charles Simeon, Perry White. A.B., Princeton, 1948; M.A., U. Wash., 1949, Ph.D., 1953. Instr. English Cornell U., 1952-56; asst. prof. U. Tex., 1956-59; vis. asso. prof. Washington U., St. Louis, 1959; from asso. prof. to prof. Mich. State U., 1959-64; Fulbright lectr. U. Dublin, 1962-63; prof. U. Calif. at Irvine, 1964—, founding chmn. English dept., 1964-69; dean Sch. Humanities, 1970-72, vice chancellor acad. affairs, 1972-74; co-dir. Sch. Criticism and Theory, 1975-77; sr. fellow, 1975—; prof. English and comparative lit. U. Wash., 1977—. Mem.: editorial bd. Epoch, 1954-56, Tex. Studies Lit. and Lang, 1957-68, Studies in Romanticism, 1966—, Blake Studies, 1969—, Modern Lang. Quar, 1977—; author: Poems by Robert Simeon Adams, 1952; Author: Blake and Yeats: The Contrary Vision, 2d edit., 1969, The Contexts of Poetry, 1963, William Blake: A Reading of the Shorter Poems, 1963, Poetry: An Introductory Anthology, 1968, The Horses of Instruction, 1968, Fiction as Process, 1968, The Interests of Criticism, 1969, William Blake: Jerusalem, Selected Poems and Prose, 1970, The Truth About Dragons, 1971, Critical Theory Since Plato, 1971, Lady Gregory, 1973, The Academic Tribes, 1976, Philosophy of the Literary Symbolic, 1983, Joyce Cary's Trilogies, 1983. Served to 1st lt. USMCR, 1943-45, 51. Guggenheim fellow, 1974-75. Mem. Modern Lang. Assn., Philol. Assn. Pacific Coast, Am. Soc. Aesthetics, Am. Com. for Irish Studies, Phi Beta Kappa. Home: 3930 NE 157th Pl Seattle WA 98155 Office: Dept English U Wash Seattle WA 98195

ADAMS, J. STACY, psychologist; b. Brussels, Belgium, Mar. 16, 1925; s. Charles Stacy and Simonne (Herrman) A.; m. Antoinette Hamilton, Feb. 14, 1952 (div.); children: Michele, Erica. B.A., U. Miss., 1948; M.A., U. N.C., 1955, Ph.D., 1957. Dep. chief Attitude Research br. U.S. Army, Europe, 1948-53; asst. prof. Stanford U., Palo Alto, Calif., 1957-60; cons. Gen. Electric Co., N.Y.C., 1960-67; adj. asso. prof. Columbia U., 1962-67; R.J. Reynolds prof. U. N.C., Chapel Hill, 1967—; advisor behavioral research panel Gen. Electric Co., 1967-70; Mem. research com. NSF, 1968-69; mem. adv. com. Center for Creative Leadership, 1968-71. Author: (with D. Katz and R.L. Kahn) The Study of Organizations, 1980; others; contbr. articles to profl. jours. Served with U.S. Navy, 1942-46. Recipient Carolina Psychology Disting. Alumnus award U. N.C., 1977, Rendleman Doctoral Teaching award, 1980; Gen. Electric Co. grantee, 1967-69; NSF grantee, 1972-76. Mem. Am. Psychol. Assn., Acad. Mgmt. Office: U North Carolina Carroll Hall Chapel Hill NC 27514

ADAMS, JACK ASHTON, psychology educator; b. Davenport, Iowa, Aug. 3, 1922; s. Alonzo Theodore and Florence Emma (Gromoll) A.; m. Marjorie Ruth McGuire, Aug. 12, 1946 (div. 1982); children: Samuel Ashton, Sarah Lee. B.A., U. Iowa, 1948, M.A., 1950, Ph.D., 1951. Research psychologist USAF Personnel and Tng. Research Center, 1951-57; prof. psychology U. Ill., 1957—; liaison scientist U.S. Office of Naval Research, London, 1977-78; asso. mem. Center for Advanced Study, U. Ill., 1970-71. Author: Human Memory, 1967, Learning and Memory: An Introduction, 1976, rev. edit., 1980. Served with inf. AUS, 1943-45; ETO. Decorated Bronze Star medal; recipient F.V. Taylor award for outstanding contbns. to engring. psychology Soc. Engring. Psychologists.; Fulbright research scholar, Netherlands, 1963-64. Fellow Am. Psychol. Assn., Human Factors Soc.; mem. Psychonomic Soc. Home: 2120 Harbortown Circle Champaign IL 61821

ADAMS, JAMES BLACKBURN, state govt. ofcl., former fed. govt. ofcl., lawyer; b. Corsicana, Tex., Dec. 21, 1926; s. Lynn and Florence (Blackburn) A.; m. Ione Winistorfer, Sept. 3, 1955; children—James Blackburn, Elizabeth, Martha. Student, La. State U., 1944, Yale U., 1944-45; B.A., Baylor U., 1950, LL.B., 1949, J.D., 1969. Bar: Tex. bar 1949, U.S. Supreme Ct. bar 1965. Asst. county atty. Limestone County, Tex., 1950; mem. Tex. Ho. of Reps., 1951; spl. agt. FBI, Seattle and San Francisco offices, 1951-53, supervisory spl. agt., 1953-59, asst. spl. agt. in charge, 1959-61, asst. chief personnel sect., 1961-65, chief personnel sect., 1965-71, exec. asst. to asst. to dir. adminstrn., Washington, 1971-72, spl. agt. in charge, San Antonio (Tex.) div., 1972-74; asst. dir., head Office of Planning and Evaluation, Washington, 1974, asst. to dir., 1974-78, asso. dir., 1978-79, ret., 1979; exec. dir. criminal justice div. Gov.'s Office, State of Tex., 1979-80; dir. Dept. Public Safety, 1980—; guest lectr. various U.S. and fgn. law enforcement, intelligence and bus. groups, 1974-79. Served with U.S. Army, 1945-46; PTO. Recipient numerous govt. achievement awards, 1953-79, Atty. Gen.'s award for Disting. Service, 1978; Nat. Intelligence Disting. Service medal, 1979. Mem. U.S. Supreme Ct. Bar, Tex. Bar Assn., Internat. Chiefs of Police Assn., Tex. Police Assn., Tex. Sheriff's Assn. Presbyterian. Club: Masons. Office: 5805 N Lamar Blvd Austin TX 78773

ADAMS, JAMES NORMAN, microbiologist; b. Bklyn., Nov. 4, 1932; s. James Thomas and Anna Gertrude (Feldzaman) A.; m. Margie Beatrice McDaniel, Sept. 6, 1955; children—Bruce E., Leah E., Connie J., Thomas M. B.S., U. Ky., 1954; Ph.D., U. Ga., 1961. Research asst. Okla. State U., Stillwater, 1955-56; research fellow U. Ga., Athens, 1959-62, asst. prof., 1962-63; mem. faculty U. S.D., Vermillion, 1963-75, asst. prof., 1963-67, asso. prof., 1967-71, prof. microbiology, 1971-75, acting chmn., 1970-71; prof., coordinator med. microbiology Sch. Medicine U. S.C., Columbia, 1975-79; pres. Micros Cons., 1979—; vis.

prof. Med. Coll. Ga., 1972, Universidad de los Andes, Merida, Venezuela, 1974, Universidad Nacional Autonoma de Mexico, 1975; adj. prof. biology U.S.C.-Beaufort, 1982; cons. on research Polish Acad. Sci., Wroclaw, Poland, 1976. Cons. editor: The Aquarium Jour, 1961-66; assoc. editor: Biology of Actinomycetes and Related Organisms, 1975—; adv. com.: Bergey's Manual of Determinative Bacteriology, 1966-70; review: Indsl. Microbial Genetics; mem. editorial bd.: Jour. Bacteriology, 1973-79; invited reviewer: Internat. Jour. Systematic Bacteriology, 1969, Canadian Jour. Microbiology, 1972—; contbr. articles to profl. jours. Served with U.S. Army, 1957-61. USPHS career devel. awardee, 1966-75. Fellow Am. Acad. Microbiology; mem. AAAS, Am. Soc. Microbiology, Soc. for Gen. Microbiology, Soc. for Indsl. Microbiology, Genetics Soc. Am., Sigma Xi, Phi Kappa Phi, Tau Kappa Epsilon (U.S.D. chpt. advisor 1967-70). Club: Am. Radio Relay League. Developer conjugation system in bacterial genus Nocardia. Home: 1611 Aster St Beaufort SC 29902 Office: PO Box 1366 Beaufort SC 29902

ADAMS, JAMES THOMAS, surgeon; b. Rochester, N.Y., Mar. 28, 1930; s. Thomas and Sarah A.; m. Jacqueline K. Stemmler, July 7, 1952; children—Pamela, Mark, Sari Lynn. A.B., Washington U., St. Louis, 1951, M.D., 1955. Intern, then resident in surgery Barnes Hosp., St. Louis, 1955-60; mem. faculty U. Rochester Med. Sch., 1962—, prof. surgery, 1977—. Author papers in field, chpts. in books. Served as officer M.C. USAR, 1960-62. Mem. Am. Surg. Assn., Soc. Internat. de Chirurgie, Soc. U. Surgeons, Central Surg. Assn., Soc. Vascular Surgery, Am. Gastroenterol. Assn., Soc. Surgery Alimentary Tract, Am. Assn. Surgery Trauma, Phi Beta Kappa, Sigma Xi, Alpha Omega Alpha. Club: Oak Hill Country (Rochester). Co-designer inferior vena cava clip. Office: 601 Elmwood Ave Rochester NY 14642

ADAMS, JOEY, comedian, author; b. N.Y.C., Jan. 6, 1911; s. Nathan and Ida (Chonin) Abramowitz; m. Cindy Heller, Feb. 14, 1952. Student, Coll. City, N.Y., 1931, 1952, Columbia, 1950, N.Y.U., 1959, L.I. U., Chung-Aug U., Korea; Ph.D., Fu-Jen U., Taipei, Taiwan. Nightclub and vaudeville entertainer, throughout U.S., 1930—; motion pictures include Ringside, 1945, Singing in the Dark; also producer, 1956; theatrical appearances include The Gazebo, 1959, Guys and Dolls, 1960; radio-TV programs include Sez Who, 1958, Person to Person, 1959, Joey Adams Show, 1956-58, Gags to Riches, 1958; also guest appearances, also radio show for, WEVD Syndicate, recordings for, Coral Records, MGM, Roulette Records, State Dept. rep. to entertain soldiers around world, 1958, Pres.'s goodwill ambassador; syndicated columnist Strictly for Laughs, N.Y. Post.; Author: From Gags to Riches (entire proceeds given to Damon Runyon Cancer Fund), 1946, The Curtain Never Falls, 1949, Strictly For Laughs, 1955, Joey Adams Joke Book, 1952, Joke Dictionary, 1961, Round the World Joke Book, 1964, Cindy and I, 1957, It Takes One to Know One, 1959, On the Road for Uncle Sam, 1963, L.B.J.'s Texas Laughs, 1964, The Borscht Belt, Ency. of Humor, Son of Encyclopedia of Humor, 1971, Laugh Your Calories Away, 1971, The God Bit, 1973, Speakers Bible of Humor, 1973, Joey Adams Ethnic Humor, Here's to the Friars, Joey Adams Joke Diary, 1979, Brother Billy the Pain from Plains, 1979, Strictly for Laughs, 1981, Live Longer Through Laughter, 1984; also mysteries. Dir. Central State Bank.; Dep. commr. N.Y.C. Youth Bd., chmn. entertainment com. for youth, 1959—; commr. youth, N.Y.C.; del. Allied Entertainment Unions, 1959—; bd. dirs. Theatre Authority, 1959—; chmn. spl. events com. March of Dimes, 1955; pres. Am. Guild Variety Artists, 1959—; pres. retirement found., chmn. youth fund; pres. Actors Youth Fund, Sr. Citizens of Am. Fund; personal rep. of Pres. U.S. as entertainer to, Asia, Africa, 1961. Named Man of Year March of Dimes, 1958, City of Hope, 1959, N.Y.C. Police Dept., 1960; recipient Humanitarian awards Yiddish Theatrical Alliance, 1960, Am. Cancer Soc., 1952, Crusade for Freedom, 1956; Pope's Medal, 1971; honored by Israeli Govt. for work in United Jewish Appeal and Israel Bond drives, 1952; also numerous citations Am. Guild Variety Artists created; Joey Awards for talent in variety field, 1960. Mem. Screen Actors Guild, A.F.T.R.A., Actors Equity Assn. Home: 1050 Fifth Ave New York NY 10028 Office: 160 W 46th St New York NY 10036 *As the "adopted son" and protege of the late mayor of New York City, Fiorello LaGuardia, I have always lived by his words to me when I was 6 years old: "Don't worry about people knowing you, make yourself worth knowing," and by the words of Mary Baker Eddy: "A dose of joy is a spiritual cure."*

ADAMS, JOHN, utility executive; b. Paget, Bermuda, Feb. 23, 1922; came to U.S., 1945; s. Henry Coolidge and Louise (Scarritt) A.; m. Ellen Noonan, Feb. 21, 1948; children: Ann Scarritt, Mary Minturn. B.S., Columbia U. Sch. Bus., 1950. Chartered fin. analyst. Asst. to v.p. fin. West Penn Electric Co., N.Y.C., 1950-57; fin. analyst Burns & Roe, Inc., N.Y.C., 1957-58; asst. sec., asst. treas. Middle South Utilities, N.Y.C., 1958-63; v.p. Kidder Peabody & Co. Inc., N.Y.C., 1963-72; sr. v.p.-fin Allegheny Power System Inc., N.Y.C., 1972—; dir. West Penn Power Co., Monongahela Power Co., Potomac Edison Co., Ohio Valley Electric Co. Served with USN, 1944-46; PTO. Mem. N.Y. Soc. Sercurity Analysts. Republican. Clubs: Rumson Country, Seabright Beach (N.J.); Board Room (N.Y.C.).

ADAMS, JOHN ALLAN STEWART, educator, geochemist; b. Independence, Mo., Nov. 1, 1926; s. George Carroll and Eva (Stewart) A.; m. Anne Donchin, Apr. 8, 1949 (div. 1973); children—Joanne Athena, John Allan Stewart, David Donchin, Christopher Barth. Ph.B., U. Chgo., 1946, B.S., 1948, M.S., 1949, Ph.D., 1951. Project asso., lectr. geochemistry U. Wis., 1951-54; mem. faculty Rice U., 1954—, prof. geology, 1960—, chmn. dept., 1965-71. Am. exec. editor: Geochimica et Cosmochimica Acta, 1960-66; Author: (with John J.W. Rogers) Fundamentals of Geology, 1966; Editor: (with W.M. Lowder) The Natural Radiation Environment, 1964, 73. Served with USNR, 1945-46. NSF sr. postdoctoral fellow, 1960. Fellow Am. Inst. Chemists, Geol. Soc. Am., Sigma Xi; mem. Geochem. Soc., Am. Chem. Soc., Am. Assn. Petroleum Geologists (Disting. lectr. 1955). Research in geochemistry, geochronology, revised geol. time scale, new methods of exploring for nuclear fuels, environmental geology, nuclear power plant siting and monitoring, lunar radioactivity, atmospheric carbon dioxide. Office: Dept Geology Rice Univ Houston TX 77001

ADAMS, JOHN BERRY, educator; b. Millville, N.J., Apr. 8, 1920; s. William Payne and Edith (Berry) A.; m. Polly-Betts Goslin, Oct. 11, 1947; children—Mark David, Jane Elizabeth. A.B., U. Calif. at Berkeley, 1953; M.S., U. Wis., 1954, Ph.D., 1957. European sales mgr. Wheaton Glass Co., Millville, N.J., 1946-49; broker Harris Realty, Wildwood, N.J., 1949-51; asst. prof. Mich. State U., 1957-58; reporter, copy editor Wis. State Jour., 1955-58; mem. faculty U. N.C., 1958—, prof. journalism, 1964—, dean Sch. Journalism, 1969-79; mem. exec. com. Am. Assn. Schs. and Depts. of Journalism, 1973-76, pres., 1975-76; cons., lectr. in field. Contbr. profl. jours. Served to capt. USAAF, 1942-46; lt. col. Res. ret., 1980. Mem. Assn. Edn. Journalism (exec. com. 1968-70), Am. Council Edn. Journalism (chmn. accrediting com. 1976-79), Internat. Assn. Mass Communication Research (exec. com. 1966-70), Am. Press Inst. (so. regional adv. bd. 1978—), Phi Beta Kappa, Phi Kappa Phi. Home: 1 Chatham Ln Estes Hills Chapel Hill NC 27514

ADAMS, JOHN COOLIDGE, composer, conductor; b. Worcester, Mass., Feb. 15, 1947; s. Carl John and Elinore Mary (Coolidge) A. Studied with Leon Kirchner, Earl Kim, Roger Sessions, and Mario di Beneventura, Harvard U., A.B. magna cum laude, 1969, M.A., 1971. Artistic advisor, San Francisco Symphony Orch., 1978—; also composer-in-residence, San Francisco Symphony Orch.; dir., New Music Ensemble, from 1972; faculty mem., San Francisco Conservatory, 1972—; composer-in-residence, Marlboro Festival, 1970; musical compositions include Electric Wake, 1968, Heavy Metal, 1971, Hocky Seen, 1972, American Standard, 1973, Mary Lou: A Routine, 1973, Kataadn, 1973, Onyx, 1976, Etudes and a continuum, 1976, Phrygian Gates, 1977, Shaker Loops, 1978; Onyx, Grounding, Sermon, Strident Bands, Wave-makers, 1978; musical compositions include Common Tones, 1979, Harmonium, 1980. Address: San Francisco Symphony Davies Hall San Francisco CA 94102 *

ADAMS, JOHN EVI, psychiatrist, educator; b. Durham, N.C., May 23, 1937; s. Joseph Edison and Katherine Carter (Smith) A.; m. Ann C. Absalom, Apr. 17, 1965; children—Christopher Dylan, Gregory Carter. B.A., Swarthmore Coll., 1959; M.D., Cornell U., 1964. Diplomate: Am. Bd. Psychiatry and Neurology. Intern Vanderbilt U. Hosp., Nashville, 1964-65; resident, research fellow in psychiatry Stanford (Calif.) Med. Center, 1965-68; spl. asst. to dir. NIMH, Bethesda, Md., 1968-69, asso. dir. div. manpower and tng., 1969-70, mem. exptl. and spl. tng. rev. com., Rockville, Md., 1979—; asst. prof. psychiatry Stanford U. Sch. Medicine, 1970-74; prof., chmn. dept. psychiatry U. Fla. Coll. Medicine, Gainesville, 1974—; mem. tng. rev. com. Nat. Inst. on Alcoholism and Alcohol Abuse, Rockville, Md., 1971-75; chmn., 1974-75; chmn. nat. adv. com. Nat. Center on Alcohol Edn., Arlington, Va., 1974-75; mem. Fla. Gov.'s Adv. Council on Mental Health, 1975, Fla. Mental Health Program Office Adv. Council, 1975—; cons. VA Med. Center, Gainesville, 1974—; psychiatrist in chief Shands Teaching Hosp., Gainesville, 1974—. Editor: (with G. Coelho and D. Hamburg) Coping and Adaptation, 1974. Served to surgeon USPHS, 1968-70. Mem. AAAS, Am. Psychiat. Assn., Am. Psychosomatic Soc., Am. Coll. Psychiatrists, So. Psychiat. Assn., Group Advancement Psychiatry. Home: 2834 NW 31st Terr Gainesville FL 32605 Office: Dept Psychiatry Box J256 Univ Fla Gainesville FL 32610

ADAMS, JOHN FRANKLIN, economist, educator; b. Tacoma, June 1, 1919; s. Eugene Franklin and Daisy Mabel (Danielson) A.; m. D. Louise Williams, Oct. 7, 1944; children—John Franklin, William Robert. B.A., Linfield Coll., 1940; M.A., Coll. Puget Sound, 1942; Ph.D. (fellow Huebner, Harrison founds.), U. Pa., 1949. Teaching fellow Coll. Puget Sound, Tacoma, 1940-42; fiscal analyst U.S. Bur. Budget, 1943-45; instr. Sch. Bus. and Pub. Adminstrn., Temple U., 1946-48, asst. prof., 1948-51, assoc. prof., 1951-55, prof. econs., 1955-71; dir. Bur. Econ. and Bus. Research, 1949-62, on leave, 1957-58, asst. v.p. charge research, 1958-66, asst. v.p. for fin. affairs, asst. treas., 1966-71; prof. ins., dir. Center for Ins. Research; dir. ins. and fringe benefit programs Ga. State U., 1971—, chmn. Regents' com. fringe benefits, 1979—; assoc. dean adminstrn. and research Coll. Bus. Adminstrn., 1979—; project adminstr., researcher (with others) U.S. Dept. Labor Study Labor Markets in the Rural South: A Study Based on Four Rural Southern Counties, 1977; lectr. Wharton Grad. Sch., U. Pa., 1955-59; Mem. employer accounts review bd. Pa. Bur. Employment Security, 1955-57, exec. dir., 1957-58; Del. div. on aging Phila. Health and Welfare Council; mem. Ga. Gov.'s Med. Malpractice Adv. Council, 1975—; Pub. mem. bur. employment security Dept. Labor and Industry, Pa. Adv. Council, 1951-57; all industry exams. com. Commonwealth Pa. Ins. Commn., 1958-63; Fellow Gerontol. Soc.; mem. Greater Phila.-Del.-S. Jersey Research Councils, 1955-71; mem. econ. studies adv. com. Pa. Planning Bd., 1962; chmn. population sub-com. Phila. area com. White House Conf. on Aging, 1960-61. Co-author: An Introduction to Modern Economics, 1951; author: Risk Management and Insurance Guidelines for Higher Education, 1972, (with Aiken and Hall) Liability-Legal Liabilities in Higher Education, Their Scope and Management, 1976, (with others) Employment, Income and Welfare in the Rural South, 1977; Gen. editor, contbr. unemployment compensation systems studies in Pa., Minn., N.D., Ga., Wyo., econ. resources and devels. studies S.E. Pa. and Eastwick, Pa.; Author: (with Rungeling et al) Employment, Income, and Welfare in the Rural South, 1977, (with Larry D. Gaunt) Policy Perspectives and Underwriting Information Techniques, 1978, Survey of the Insurance Distribution System, 1979; editor: Proc. Joint Conferences on Problems of Making a Living while Growing Old, 1952, 53, 54, also Econs. and Bus. Bull, Experience Rating In Unemployment Compensation to Pa, 1959, Temple U. Bur. Econ. and Bus. Research; editor, contbr. monographs, univ. publs., tech. jours., govtl. pubs.; project dir., editor: Older Worker Study, Phila. area, 5 vols, 1958; others. Bd. govs. Ins. Hall Fame, 1966—; bd. dirs., mem. exec. com. Internat. Ins. Seminar, 1965—. Mem. Nat. Assn. Coll. and Univ. Bus. Officers (mem. com. on govtl. relations 1971-77, personnel and risk mgmt. and ins. com.), Am. Econ. Assn., Am. Risk and Ins. Assn. (chmn. research com. 1958-65, v.p. 1964-65, pres. 1965-66), Nat. Council U. Research Adminstrs. (sec.-treas. 1963-69, v.p. 1969-71, pres. 1971-73, exec. com. 1963-73), Phila. C. of C. (asso. chmn. manpower task force, mem. nat. commn. econ. security), Nat. Council Adminstrv. Research, Nat. Commn. Ins. Terminology (mem., editor social ins. com.), Univ. Risk and Ins. Mgmt. Assn. Home: 2970 Rockingham Dr NW Atlanta GA 30327

ADAMS, JOHN HAMILTON, lawyer; b. N.Y.C., Feb. 15, 1936; s. John and Barbara (Johnston) A.; m. Patricia Brandon Smith, Sept. 30, 1963; children: Katherine L., John H., Ramsay W. B.A., Mich. State U., 1959; LL.B., Duke U., 1962. Bar: N.Y. 1963. Atty. Cadwalader, Wickersham & Taft, N.Y.C., 1962-65; asst. U.S. atty. So. Dist. N.Y., N.Y.C., 1965-69; exec. dir. Nat. Resources Def. Council, Inc., N.Y.C., 1970—; adj. prof. law NYU Sch. Law, 1974—; pres. Open Space Inst., N.Y.C., 1979—. Bd. dirs. Council for Pub. Interest Law, Washington, 1977-83, Catskill Ctr. for Conservation, Arkville, N.Y., 1974—, League of Conservation Voters, Washington, 1982—, Hudson River Found. Sci. and Environ. Research, Inc., 1981—, N.Y. Lawyers Alliance for Nuclear Arms Control, 1982—. Club: Coffee House. Home: RD 1 Garrison NY 12776 Office: Natural Resources Def Council Inc 122 E 42d St 45th Floor New York NY 10168

ADAMS, JOHN HANLY, editor, writer, consultant; b. Sikeston, Mo., Nov. 2, 1918; s. Laurence B. and Mary B. (O'Connell) A.; m. Helen Lorraine Pollard, Apr. 18, 1942; children: John Bruce, Barbara Alison, Lawrence Kirby. B.A. in Econs.; B.J., U. Mo., 1940. Reporter Eugene (Oreg.) Daily News, 1940; mem. news staff U.S. News & World Report, Washington, 1940-79, asso. exec. editor, 1968-70, mng. editor, 1970-76, exec. editor, 1976-79, dir., 1973-79; contbg. editor Nation's Bus. mag., 1981-82; editorial cons. Ernst & Whinney, 1980-82, Tax Found., Inc., 1983—; dir. Design Data Systems, Inc., Washington Writers Service, Inc. Served with USNR, 1943-46. Mem. White House Corrs. Assn., Sigma Delta Chi. Clubs: National Press, International (Washington). Home and Office: 3700 N Edison St Arlington VA 22207

ADAMS, JOHN JOSEPH, lawyer; b. Marshalltown, Iowa, June 25, 1916; s. Thomas Edward and Susan (Watson) A.; m. Virginia McCabe, Sept. 21, 1940; children: John Thomas, James McCabe, Ann Virginia. B.A., U. Mich., 1938, J.D., 1940. Bar: Iowa 1940, Ohio 1942, U.S. Dist. Ct. (no. dist.) Ohio 1942, U.S. Ct. Appeals (6th cir.) 1947, U.S. Supreme Ct. 1948. Law clk. to justice U.S. Supreme Ct., Washington, 1940-41; assoc., then ptnr. Squire, Sanders & Dempsey, Cleve., 1941—; dir. Dresser Industries, Dallas; officer, dir. Columbus Auto Parts Co., Ohio, A.E. Ehrke & Co., Cleve. Contbr. articles to legal publs. Served to capt. JAGD U.S. Army, 1943-46; ETO. Mem. ABA, Cleve. Bar Assn., Cuyahoga County Bar Assn., Ohio Bar Assn., Indsl. Relations Research Assn. Republican. Clubs: Union, Westwood Country; Ct. Nisi Prius (Cleve.). Office: Squire Sanders & Dempsey 1800 Huntington Bldg Cleveland OH 44115

ADAMS, JOHN L., banker; b. 1944. B.B.A., U. Tex., 1966, J.D., 1969. Asst. v.p., mgr. met. div. Tex. Commerce Bank N.Am., Houston, 1973-74, v.p., 1974-75, sr. v.p., mgr. met. div., 1975-77, mgr. nat. div., 1977-82, exec. v.p., 1982—, dir. Office: Tex Commerce Bank N Am 712 Main St Houston TX 77002 *

ADAMS, JOHN MARSHALL, lawyer; b. Columbus, Ohio, Dec. 6, 1930; s. H.F. and Ada Margaret (Gregg) A.; m. Janet Hawk, June 28, 1952; children: John Marshall, Susan Lynn, William Alfred. B.A., Ohio State U., 1952; J.D. summa cum laude, 1954. Bar: Ohio 1954. Mem. firm Cowan & Adams, Columbus, 1954-55; asst. city atty. City of Columbus, 1955-56; mem. firm Knepper, White, Richards & Miller, 1956-63; practiced in, Columbus, 1963-74; partner firm Porter, Wright, Morris & Arthur, Columbus, 1975—; dir. Ohio Bar Liability Ins. Co.; Trustee Ohio Legal Center Inst., 1976-81, Ohio Lawpac, 1980—. Fellow Am. Coll. Trial Lawyers, Am. Bar Found., Ohio Bar Found. (trustee 1975—); mem. ABA, Ohio Bar Assn. (exec. com. 1975-80, fellow, pres. 1978-79); mem. Columbus Bar Assn. (gov. 1970-76), Dayton Bar Assn. (pres. 1974-75), Lawyers Club (pres. 1968-69), Order of Attorneys, Delta Upsilon, Phi Delta Phi. Republican. Clubs: Masons, Athletic, Scioto Country. Home: 3921 Lytham Ct Apt. 14 Columbus OH 43220 Office: 37 W Broad St Columbus OH 43215

ADAMS, JOHN QUINCY, insurance company executive; b. Dover, Mass., Dec. 24, 1922; s. Arthur and Margery (Lee) A.; m. Nancy Motley, Feb. 1, 1947; children: Nancy Barton, John Quincy, Margery Lee, Benjamin Crowninshield. Student, St. Paul's Sch., 1941; A.B., Harvard U., 1945. With John Hancock Mut. Ins. Co., 1947—, 2d v.p., 1961-65, v.p., 1965-68, sr. v.p., 1968—; dir., chmn. John Hancock Venture Capital Mgmt., Inc.; dir. Zurn Industries, John Hancock Growth Fund, John Hancock Advisers, Inc., John Hancock U.S. Govt. Securities Fund, John Hancock Investors, John Hancock Income Securities, Mass. Bus Devel. Corp., Independence Investment Assocs., Tucker Anthony Holding Corp.; trustee John Hancock Tax-Exempt Trust, Provident Instn. for Savs., Real Estate Investment Trust, John Hancock Cash Mgmt. Trust. Mem. com. on univ. resources Harvard; bd. dirs. New Eng. Historic Seaport; mem. corp. Mus. of Sci.; bd. overseers Boston Symphony Orch. Home: 17 Wilsondale St Dover MA 02030 Office: John Hancock Mutual Life Ins Co John Hancock Pl PO Box 111 Boston MA 02117

ADAMS, JOHN R., educator; b. Cin., July 22, 1900; s. Thomas and Margaret (Morse) A.; m. Jane Ford, June 26, 1923. A.B., U. Mich., 1920, M.A., 1922; Ph.D., U. So. Calif., 1940. Instr. rhetoric U. Mich., 1920-25; asso. in English U. Wash., 1925-28; with San Diego State U., 1928—, prof. English, 1940, chmn. div. langs. and lit., 1946-56, chmn. div. of humanities, 1956-68, univ. archivist, 1968—; vis. prof. summers Ala. Poly Inst., 1925, U. So. Calif., 1940, San Francisco State Coll., 1948. Author: Harriet Beecher Stowe, 1963, Books and Authors of San Diego, 1966, Regional Sketches of H.B. Stowe, 1972, Edward Everett Hale, 1977. Mem. Modern Lang. Assn., Am. Assn. U. Profs., Philol. Assn. Pacific Coast, San Diego County Hist. Soc., Phi Beta Kappa. Club: University (San Diego). Home: 4131 Marlborough Ave San Diego CA 92105 Office: John R Adams Humanities Bldg San Diego State U San Diego CA 92182

ADAMS, JOHN RICHARD, educator, physician; b. Eureka, Calif., Jan. 6, 1918; s. Frank R. and Katherine (Odenbaugh) A.; m. Patricia Harrigan, Sept. 12, 1968. Student Northwestern U, 1935-39; M.D., C.M., McGill U., 1943. Intern Montreal (Que.) Gen. Hosp., 1943; resident Winter VA Hosp., 1946-49; fellow Menninger Sch. Psychiatry, Topeka, 1946-49; staff psychiatrist Menninger Found., 1949-54, dir. admissions, 1953-54; prof. psychiatry and neurology Northwestern U., Chgo., 1954-80, prof. psychiatry and behavioral sci., 1980—; chief psychiatry Passavant Meml. Hosp., Chgo., 1954-71; dir. clin. services and tng. Northwestern Meml. Hosp., Chgo., 1972-75; dir. div. of attending staff Inst. Psychiatry, 1976—. Served to capt. M.C. AUS, 1943-46. Fellow Am. Psychiat. Assn.; mem. Ill. Psychiat. Soc. (pres. 1963-64). Home: 561 Cherry St Winnetka IL 60093 Office: 707 N Fairbanks Ct Chicago IL 60611

ADAMS, JOHN ROBERT, librarian; b. Plainview, Tex., Feb. 14, 1938; s. Jesse Benjamin and Mary Ruth (Caddel) A.; m. Jane Merrick Grant, July 24, 1960; 1 dau., Susan Ann. B.A., Baylor U., 1960; B.D., Southwestern Bapt. Theol. Sem., 1963; M.A., U. Chgo., 1968. Asst. circulation librarian U. Chgo., 1965-68; asst. to dir. libraries Washington U., St. Louis, 1968-70, asst. dir. for reader services, 1970-72, asst. univ. librarian, 1972-73; asso. univ. librarian U. Ariz., Tucson, 1973-79; librarian Wesleyan U., Middletown, Conn., 1979—. Mem. ALA, Conn. Library Assn. Congregationalist. Home: 33 Mansfield Terr Middletown CT 06457 Office: Olin Library Wesleyan Univ Middletown CT 06457

ADAMS, JOHN WILLIAM, diversified manufacturing corporation executive; b. Ottawa, Ont., Canada, June 17, 1924; m. Katheleen Adams, Apr. 18, 1953; children: Peter, Paul, Annmarie. Wirh EMCO Ltd., london, ont., Canada, 1950—, comptroller, London, Ont., Canada, from 1950, exec. v.p., treas., 1970-78, pres., chief exec. officer, 1976—, dir., 1956—. Bd. dirs. London Cancer Soc.; chmn. bd. dirs. St. Joseph's Hosp. London; mem.adv. bd. U. Western Ont. Sch. Bus. Adminstrn.; chmn. Spl. Com. to Examining Role of Auditor (Adams Report 1978); mem. Accts. Internat. Study Group, 1973-76, chmn., 1976. Decorated Queen's Silver Jubilee medal, 1977, knight comdr. Order St. Sylvestre, 1978. Mem. Can. Inst. Chartered Accts. (pres. 1978-79). Clubs: London, London Hunt and Country, Toronto. Office: EMCO Ltd 1108 Dundas St E London ON Canada N6A 4N7 *

ADAMS, JON QUINCY, banker; b. Mobile, Ala., June 1, 1925; s. Samuel Boyd and Dora Willie (Williams) A.; m. Eran Jobe, Nov. 26, 1952; children: Laura Adams Ezell, Samuel Russell. B.S., U. Ala., 1949, LL.B., 1950. Bar: Ala. 1950. Practice law, Mobile, 1950-51; trust officer First Nat. Bank of MObile, 1951-74; sr. exec. v.p. First Nat. Bank of Mobile, 1974-82, pres., chief exec. officer, 1982; chmn. bd. First Nat. Bnk of Mobile, 1982—; pres. First Bancgroup-Ala. Inc.; dir. Alco Land & Timber Co., Mobile, Loyal Am. life Ins. co., MWS Land Co. Chmn. Assoc. Industries Ala., 1982-83; bd. dirs. ARC, Mobile, Mobile United, Boy Scouts Am., Mobile Community Found.; chmn Springhill Meml. Hosp., Mobile. Serve to lt. j.g. USN, 1943-46. Mem. Mobile Area C. of C. (dir.). Am. Baptist. Clubs: Country of Mobile; Athelstan (Mobile); Lakewood Golf. Home: 58 Clarise Circle Mobile AL 36608 Office: First Nat Bank of Mobile 31 N Royal St PO Drawer 1467 Mobile AL 36621

ADAMS, JOSEPH ELKAN, automotive manufacturing consultant; b. Cleve., Feb. 26, 1913; s. Samuel A. and Dorothy (Berkson) A.; m. Eleanore Ture, Aug. 30, 1940; children: Stephen Eric, Gail M. B.S., Carnegie Inst. Tech., 1934. Asst. to pres. Garland Co., Cleve., 1934-38; gen. mgr. Internat. Molded Plastics, 1938-41; dir. material control White Motor Corp. (formerly White Motor Co.), Cleve., 1945-50, dir. purchasing and planning, 1950-55, gen. mgr. mfg., 1955, v.p., 1956-59, exec. v.p., 1959-72; now cons. and investor; chmn. bd. Gen. Computer Corp., Macedonia, Ohio, 1977—; dir. Am. Switchgear Corp., Canton, Ohio, chmn. exec. com., 1982—; spl. asst. for prodn. to v.p. ops. WPB, Washington, 1941-44. Trustee, v.p. Cleve. Playhouse. Mem. Soc. Automotive Engrs., Mus. Arts Assn. Cleve. (trustee, exec. com., treas. 1982), Pi Tau Sigma (v.p.), Pi Delta Epsilon, Beta Sigma Rho. Clubs: Mid-Day, Cleve. City, Oakwood, Clevelander, Republic, Sharon. Home: 3031 Manchester Rd Shaker Heights OH 44122 *I believe very strongly that a person should say what he thinks and not deceive himself or anyone else. Very few people accept the fact that success is not only a question of ability but also being at the right place at the right time.*

ADAMS, JOSEPH PETER, retired lawyer, consultant; b. Seattle, Nov. 15, 1907; s. Joseph and Selma Margaret (Peterson) A.; m. Margaret Bare Adams, Jan. 13, 1940; 1 dau., Janis Margaret. A.B., U. Wash., 1928, J.D., 1932; grad. naval aviator, U.S. Naval Air Sta., Pensacola, Fla., 1930. Bar: Wash. 1932, D.C. 1953. Practiced, Seattle, 1932-40; dir. aeros. State of Wash., 1946-49; mem. CAB, 1951-56, vice chmn., 1955-56; aviation cons. Senate Commerce Com.; Mem. NACA, 1952-56; exec. dir., gen. counsel Assn. Local Transport Airlines, Washington, 1957-73, fed. affairs counsel, 1973-80. Charter mem. Nat. Capital Democratic Club. Served as capt. USMCR, 1929-40; released from World War II as col. Res. aviation, 1946; promoted to brig. gen., 1959. Decorated Combat Legion of Merit. Mem. USMC Res. Officers Assn. (life), Marine Corps League, Nat. Aero. Assn. (Elder Statesman of Aviation 1984), Legion of Honor of Order of DeMolay, Sigma Alpha Epsilon, Phi Delta Phi. Democrat. Clubs: Cosmos, Aero (Washington) (pres. 1962); National Aviation (award for achievement 1970); Wings (N.Y.C.); Executive, Army-Navy., Pensacola Country (Fla.). Home: 1004 Harbourview Circle Pensacola FL 32507 *First enjoyed entire series of Horatio Alger struggles entitled "Slow But Sure," and then an active political life as a Democrat imbued with the basic philosophy of "the greatest good for the greatest number."*

ADAMS, KENNETH STANLEY, JR., energy company executive, football executive; b. Bartlesville, Okla., Jan. 3, 1923; s. Kenneth Stanley and Blanch (Keeler) A.; m. Nancy Neville, Oct. 26, 1946; children—Susan (Mrs. Thomas S. Smith), Amy, Kenneth Stanley III. Student, Menlo Coll., 1940-41, U. Kans., 1941-44. Chmn. bd. Adams Resources & Energy, Inc., Houston; v.p. Travel House of Houston; owner Bud Adams Ranches, KSA Industries, Inc., Houston Oilers, Inc., River Garden Farms, Southwest Lincoln-Mercury, Inc., Southwest Motor Leasing; adv. dir. First City Nat. Bank Houston, Am. Bank & Trust Co. Houston. Mem. exec. bd. Sam Houston Area council Boy Scouts Am.; trustee Profl. Football Hall Fame. Served with USNR, 1943-46. Named Houston Salesman of Year, 1960, Mr. Sportsman of 1961, Westerner of Year, 1969. Mem. Tex. Ind. Producers and Royalty Owners Assn., Ind. Petroleum Assn., Am., Houston Assn. Petroleum Landmen, Houston Geol. Soc., Sigma Chi (named Significant Sig 1963). Clubs: River Oaks Country, Houston, Petroleum, 100 of Houston. Office: PO Box 844 Houston TX 77001

ADAMS, LANE WEBSTER, association executive; b. Logan, Utah, July 3, 1915; s. Orval W. and Luella (Nebeker) A.; m. Elaine Evans, Sept. 1, 1937; children—Victoria, Anthony L. Student, U. Utah, 1931-33, Grad. Sch. Banking Rutgers U., 1938-40. Banker, Salt Lake City, 1936-49; v.p., mem. exec. com. Zions 1st Nat. Bank, j4Salt Lake City, 1949-59; dir. Paul Revere Investors; Bd. dirs. Am. Cancer Soc., 1948-59, treas., 1953-59, exec. v.p., 1959—. Mem. Nat. Adv. Cancer Council, 1957-58, Nat. Adv. Allergy and Infectious Diseases Council, 1966-68; state dir. SSS Mo. Bd. regents Grad. Sch. Banking Rutgers U. Clubs: Alta (Salt Lake City); Country (New Canaan, Conn.). Office: Am Cancer Soc 777 3d Ave New York NY 10017 *

ADAMS, LARRY LEE, manufacturing company executive; b. Charlotte, Mich., Jan. 8, 1938; s. Donald Lyle and Mildred Marie (Keith) A.; m. Sharon Colleen Housler, Oct. 2, 1960; children: James F., Katherine E., Sarah M. B.S., Western Mich. U., 1963. Plant engr. Eaton Corp., Battle Creek, Mich., 1965-66, quality control mgr., 1966-70, engring. mgr., 1970-72, plant mgr., Sanford, N.C., 1972-77, div. mgr., Brazil, 1977-81; div. pres. Abex Corp., Winchester, Va., 1981—; dir. Eaton Corp., Brazil, 1977-81. Bd. dirs. United Fund, Winchester, 1983—; vice chmn. Lord Fairfax Community Coll. Found., 1983—; mem. Shenandoah Coll. Pres.'s Council, Winchester, 1983—; twp. trustee Battle Creek Twp., 1972. Boys Club of Am. fellow, 1981-83. Mem. Soc. Automotive Engrs. Republican. Club: Rotary. Home: 609 Bellview Ave Winchester VA 22601 Office: Abex Corp 2410 Papermill Rd Winchester VA 22601

ADAMS, LEONARD C., electrical engineering educator; b. Saluda, S.C., Nov. 7, 1921; s. James P. and Amelia Ann (Minnick) A.; m. Rachel Adams, June 18, 1945; children: James P., Richard C., Ann S. B.S. in Elec. Engring, Clemson Coll., 1943, M.S., Okla. State U., 1950; Ph.D. in Elec. Engring. and Physics, U. Fla., 1953. Registered profl. engr., La., S.C. From instr. to prof. elec. engring. Clemson Coll., 1946-58; dir. Engring. Expt. Sta., 1959-61; exptl. reactor physicist Savannah River Lab., 1958-59; now prof. elec. engring. La. State U.; Past pres. Southeastern Center for Elec. Engring. Edn. Served to 1st lt. Signal Corps AUS, 1943-46. Mem. Am. Soc. Engring. Edn., IEEE (past chmn. Baton Rouge sect.), Baton Rouge Council Engring. and Sci. Socs. (pres. 1965-66), Sigma Xi, Tau Beta Pi, Phi Kappa Phi, Eta Kappa Nu. Home: 12123 N Lakeview Dr Baton Rouge LA 70810

ADAMS, LESLIE BUNN, JR., publishing company executive; b. Phila., Mar. 22, 1932; s. Leslie Bunn and Winifred (Green) A.; m. Ethel M. Lane, July 24, 1958; 1 dau., Amanda. A.B., U. N.C., 1952, postgrad. in English lit. (Univ. fellow), 1955; M.A., Columbia U., 1955; J.D., Cumberland Law Sch., 1971; LL.D., William Penn Coll., 1983. Bar: Ala. bar 1971. Pres. Les Adams & Assos., Inc., Orlando, Fla., 1959-62; advt. dir. State of Fla., Tallahassee, 1962-63; v.p. Rose Printing Co., Tallahassee, 1963-65, Oxmoor House, Inc., Birmingham, 1965-77; pres. Gryphon Edits., Inc., Birmingham, Ala., 1977—. Served with U.S. Army, 1952-54. Recipient Carey-Thomas award for distinguished pub. Pub.'s Weekly mag., 1974. Mem. ABA, Ala. Bar Assn. Democrat. Episcopalian. Club: The Club (Birmingham). Home: 3840 Brook Hollow Ln Birmingham AL 35243 Office: PO Box 76108 Birmingham AL 35223

ADAMS, MAC CARTER, government official; b. Gretna, Va., Jan. 3, 1925; s. Neville Lamont and Selma Brough (Woodson) A.; m. Jane Krist, Feb. 27, 1946 (div. 1978); children: Kimberly Sue (Mrs. John F. Baaumann), Christopher Carter, Kyle Elizabeth; m. 2d Hazelgene Butler, 1978. Student, U. Va., 1943-44; B.S. in Mech. Engring., Cornell U., 1946, M. Aero. Engring., 1949, Ph.D., 1953. Engr. Ingersoll Rand Co., 1946, NACA, 1946-47, 49-51; design specialist Douglas Airplane Co., 1953-55; dep. dir. Avco-Everett Research Lab., 1955-60, v.p., tech. dir. research and devel. div., Avco, 1960-65; assoc. adminstr. Office Advanced Research and Tech., NASA, 1965-68; v.p., dep. group exec. Avco Govt. Products Group, 1968-71, v.p., gen. mgr. Avco Systems div., 1971-75, v.p., group exec. Avco Research and Systems Group, 1975-82; dep. undersec. tactical warfare programs Dept. Def., 1982—; mem. spl. ind. adv. com. missile and spacecraft aerodynamics NASA, 1959-62, chmn. spl. adv. com. missile and space vehicle aerodynamics, 1962-65; mem. mech. engring. vis. com. MIT, 1967-73. Served with USNR, 1943-46. Recipient Exceptional Service medal NASA, 1968. Fellow AIAA (chmn. com. vehicle reentry 1963-64, bd. dirs. 1965-67, 70-72); mem. Sigma XI, Tau Beta Pi. Clubs: Nat. Space (gov. 1971—), Army-Navy. Office: The Pentagon Room 3E-1044 Washington DC 20301 *

ADAMS, MARGARET BERNICE, museum official; b. Toronto, Ont., Can., Apr. 29, 1936; came to U.S., 1948, naturalized, 1952; d. Robert Russell and Kathleen Olive (Buffin) A.; m. Alberto Enrique Sánchez-Quiñonez, Nov. 30, 1956 (div. 1960). A.A. (Deans scholar), Monterey (Calif.) Peninsula Coll., 1969, B.A., San Jose (Calif.) State U., 1971, M.A., U. Utah, 1972. Curator ethnic arts Civic Art Gallery, San Jose, 1971; staff asst. Utah Mus. Fine Arts, Salt Lake City, 1972; lectr./curator Coll. Seven, U. Calif., Santa Cruz, 1972-74; part-time educator Cabrillo Coll., Aptos, Calif., 1973, Monterey Peninsula Coll., 1973—; dir. U.S. Army Mus., Presidio of Monterey, 1974-83; chief. mus. br. Ft. Ord Mil. Complex, 1983—; Guest curator Am. Indian arts Monterey Peninsula Mus. Art, 1975—. Author: Indian Tribes of North America and Chronology of World Events in Prehistoric Pueblo Times, 1975, Historic Old Monterey, 1976; Contbg. editor: Indian Am; Contbr. articles to jours. Mem. native Am. adv. panel AAAS, Washington, 1972-78; mem. rev. and adv. com. Project Media, Nat. Indian Edn. Assn., Mpls., 1973-78; working mem. Program for Tng. Am. Indian Counsellors in Alcoholism Counselling and Rehab. Programs, 1972-74. Grad. fellow U. Utah, 1972. Mem. Am. Anthrop. Assn., Am. Assn. Museums, Soc. for Applied Anthropology, Soc. Am. Archeology, Am. Ethnol. Soc., Nat., Calif., Indian edn. assns. Home: 363 Hillcrest Ave Pacific Grove CA 93950 Office: Museum Branch DPT Fort Ord CA 93941

ADAMS, MARK, artist; b. Ft. Plain, N.Y., Oct. 27, 1925; s. Earl D. and Edith (Wohlgemuth) A.; m. Beth Van Hoesen, Sept. 12, 1953. Student, Syracuse U., 1943-46, Hans Hofmann Sch. Fine Arts, 1946, 48, Jean Lurcat, 1955. Instr. San Francisco Art Inst., 1961; panelist Internat. Symposium on Tapestry, San Francisco, 1976; disting. vis. prof. U. Calif. at Davis, 1978. Painter in residence, Am. Acad. in Rome, 1963; One-man shows include, deYoung Mus., San Francisco, 1959, Portland (Oreg.) Mus., 1961, Calif. Palace of Legion of Honor, San Francisco, retrospective, 1970, San Francisco Mus. Modern Art, 1962, French & Co., N.Y.C., 1964, John Berggruen Gallery, San Francisco, 1978, 80, 82, Graham Modern, N.Y.C., 1981, 84; exhibited in numerous group shows, including, Mus. Contemporary Crafts, N.Y.C., 1957, 58, 62, 65, Mus. Contemporary Crafts, Dallas Mus., 1958, Internat. Biennial of Tapestry, Lausanne, Switzerland, 1962, 65, St. Louis Art Mus., 1964, Norfolk Mus., 1966; represented in permanent collections, San Francisco Mus. Modern Art, Dallas Mus. Fine Arts, Chase Manhattan Bank, N.Y.C., San Francisco Pub. Library, Legion of Honor Mus., San Francisco; maj. archtl. commns. include tapestries, Bank of Calif., San Francisco, Weyerhauser Co., Tacoma, Wash., Fairmont Hotel, Dallas, San Francisco Internat. Airport, stained glass, Temple Emanu-el, San Francisco, St. Thomas More Cath. Ch., San Francisco, St. Andrews Episcopal Ch., Saratoga, Calif. Address: care John Berggruen Gallery 228 Grant Ave San Francisco CA 94108

ADAMS, MASON, actor; b. N.Y.C., Feb. 26, 1919; m. Margot Adams; children: Betsy, Bil. M.A. in Theater Arts, U. Wis. Instr. Neighborhood Playhouse, N.Y.C. Title role in: radio serial Pepper Young's Family, 1946-60; Broadway stage debut in: play Get Away Old Man; other stage appearances include The Shortchanged Review; appeared in: TV series Lou Grant, 1979-82 (Emmy nominee 1979, 80); current TV appearances include: PBS Freedom to Speak, Solomon Northrup's Odyssey; voice in numerous TV commercials. Mem. Players, Ensemble Studio Theater, Phi Kappa Phi, Delta Sigma Rho.

ADAMS, OSCAR WILLIAM, state justice; b. Birmingham, Ala., Feb. 7, 1925; s. Oscar William and Ella Virginia (Eaton) A.; m. Willa Ingersoll, Dec. 25, 1949 (dec.); children: Oscar William, III, Gail Ingersoll Adams Harden, Frank T. A.B., Talladega (Ala.) Coll., 1944; LL.B., Howard U., 1947. Bar: Ala. bar. Practice in, Birmingham, 1947-80; partner firm Adams & Adams, 1980; asso. justice Supreme Ct. Ala., 1980—; past instr. Miles Coll. Sch. Law; bd. dirs. Lawyers Com. Civil Rights Under Law. Recipient Winner's award Talladega Coll.; award EEO Commn. Mem. Ala. Law Inst., Ala. Lawyers Assn. (award for outstanding public and profl. service), Nat. Bar Assn. (jud. council), Am. Trial Lawyers Assn., Omega Psi Phi, Phi Beta Boule. Democrat. Methodist. Clubs: Shriners, Elks. Home: 3531 Carter Hill Rd Montgomery AL 36111 Office: PO Box 218 Montgomery AL 36101

ADAMS, PARK, III (PEPPER ADAMS), musician; b. Highland Park, Mich., Oct. 8, 1930; s. Park II and Cleo (Coyle) A.; m. Claudette Nadra, Feb. 14, 1976; 1 stepson, Dylan Foster Hill. Student, Wayne State U., 1948-50. Pres. Excerent Music (music pubs.). Profl. baritone saxophonist/clarinetist, 1944—, appearances with, Stan Kenton, Theolonious Monk, Benny Goodman, Dizzy Gillespie, others; co-leader, Quintet with Donald Byrd, 1958-62; rec. artist for, Blue Note, Spotlight, ENJA records; with, Thad Jones-Mel Lewis Orch., 1966-77; albums include, Encounter!, Ephemera, 1973, Reflectory, 1978, Urban Dreams, 1981. Served with AUS, 1951-53; Korea. Recipient New Star award Down Beat mag., 1957; Talent Deserving of Wider Recognition award Down Beat mag., 1967; All-Star's All-Star award Playboy mag., 1975; winner Down Beat Critic's Poll, 1979, 80, 81. Mem. Nat. Acad. Rec. Arts and Scis. (gov. 1978-82), ASCAP. *

ADAMS, PAT, artist, educator; b. Stockton, Calif., July 8, 1928; d. Roy Alanson and Minerva Matilda (Smith) A.; m. Vincent John Longo, Apr.21, 1951 (div.); children: Matthew Adams, Jason Rice; m. R. Arnold Ricks III, June 24, 1972. B.A., U. Calif.-Berkeley, 1949; student, Calif. Coll. Arts and Crafts, 1945, Chgo. Art Inst., 1947, Bklyn. Mus. Art Sch., 1950-51. Mem. art faculty Bennington Coll., Vt., 1964—; vis. critic of painting Yale U., New Haven, Conn., 1971-72, 76, 79, 82-83; vis. lectr. Queens Coll., N.Y.C., 1972; vis. artist U. Iowa, 1976, U. N. Mex., 1978, U. Western Ky., 1978, Columbia U., 1979; trustee Vt. Council for Arts, 1977-81. One-woman shows, Rutgers U. Art Mus., 1978, Contemporary Art Ctr., Cin., 1979, Columbus Mus. Art and Sci., S.C., 1982, Va. Commonwealth U.; exhibited in group shows, Montclair Art Mus., N.J., Berkshire Mus., Pittsfield, Mass., 1981, Boston Mus. Fine Arts., 1982, Mus. Fine Arts, Houston, U. Hawaii-Hilo, 1983, Lehigh U., Chrysler Mus., Norfolk, Va., Am. Acad. and Inst. Arts and Letters; contbr. articles to profl. jours. Bd. dirs Yaddo Found., 1972—. Recipient award Nat. Council for Arts, 1968, Disting. Teaching of Art award Coll. Art Assn. Am., 1984; Fulbright scholar, 1956; grantee Yaddo Found., 1954, 64, 69, 70, McDowell Colony, 1968, 72, Nat. Endowment Arts, 1976. Mem. Phi Beta Kappa, Delta Epsilon. Home: 370 Elm St Bennington VT 05201

ADAMS, PAUL WINFREY, lawyer, business executive; b. Ozark, Ark., July 10, 1913; s. Robert Montague and Myrtle (Johnson) A.; m. Louise Forbes Barnes, Mar. 21, 1942; children: Sally B. (Mrs. T. V. O'Connor), Thomas Fuller, Edward Montague. B.S., Trinity Coll., Hartford, Conn., 1935; LL.B., Yale, 1938. Bar: Conn. 1938, N.Y. 1964. Practiced in, Hartford, 1938-42, 45-50, New Haven, 1958-64, N.Y.C., 1964-72, Greenwich and Darien, Conn., 1972-84; pres. Montague & Co., 1981—; counsel Mfrs. Assn. Conn., 1939-42; pres. The Norden Labs. Corp., 1949-55; chmn. bd. Mut. Assurance Co., 1951—, Norden-Ketay Corp., N.Y.C., 1956-58; dir. Abbott Ball Co., Internat. Forecasting Corp., Effex Mgmt., Currency Mgmt. of Greenwich, Hedging Co.; asst. dean Yale Law Sch., 1956-58. Pres. Pope-Brooks Found.; Chmn., trustee Avon Old Farms Sch., 1948-52; trustee Trinity Coll., 1958-64, St. Margaret's Sch., 1967-71; founding trustee Southborough Sch., 1971-74; trustee Stone Found., Atlantic Round, Inc. Served as lt. USNR, 1942-45. Clubs: Country (Fairfield, Conn.); N.Y. Yacht, India House (N.Y.C.); Cruising of America, Royal Scandinavian Yacht, Royal Bermuda, Indian Harbour. PO Box 936 Southport CT 06490

ADAMS, PEPPER *See* **ADAMS, PARK, III**

ADAMS, PERRY RONALD, coll. adminstr.; b. Parkersburg, W.Va., Sept. 16, 1921; s. Russell Douglas and Beulah Grace (Cunningham) A.; m. Ann Mallory Gillespie, Dec. 25, 1943; children—Suzanne Adams Markwell, Sally. A.B., U. Ky., 1943, M.A., 1948; Ed.D., U. Fla., 1965. Instr. U. Ky., 1948-53; dir. music; U. Fla., 1953-65; dean instruction Polk Jr. Coll., Winter Haven, Fla., 1965-69; provost No. Va. Community Coll., Annandale, 1969-70; pres. Paul D. Camp Community Coll., Franklin, Va., 1970-79; vice chancellor Va. Community Coll. System, Richmond, 1979—; dir. United Va. Bank. Trustee Southampton Meml. Hosp. Served with U.S. Navy, 1942-47. Kellogg fellow, 1963-65. Mem. Assn. Supervision and Curriculum Devel., Am. Assn. Higher Edn., Am. Vocat. Assn., Phi Mu Alpha (nat. councilman), Phi Delta Kappa, Kappa Delta Pi. Clubs: Rotary Internat., Cypress Cove Country. Home: 10811 Whitaker Woods Rd Richmond VA 23233 Office: Monroe Bldg N 14th St Richmond VA 23212

ADAMS, PETER FREDERICK, civil engineer, educator; b. Halifax, N.S., Can.; m. Barbara Adams, Oct. 11, 1957; 3 sons. B.Eng., N.S. Tech. Coll., 1958, M.Engr., 1961; Ph.D., Lehigh U., 1966. With Internat. Nickel Co. Can., 1958-59, Dominion Bridge Co., 1974-75; mem. faculty U. Alta., Edmonton, 1960—, prof. civil engring., 1971—; dean Faculty of Engring., 1976-84; pres. Ctr. for Frontier Engring. Research, 1984—; lectr. in field. Author: (Krentz & Kulak) Canadian Structural Steel Design, 1973, (Krewtz & Kulak) Limit States Design in Structural Steel, 1977. Past pres. Aspen Gardens Community League. Mem. Can. Soc. Civil Engring., ASCE, Internat. Assn. Bridge and Structural Engring., Can. Standards Assn. Club: Toastmasters (past pres.). Office: U Alta Faculty of Engring 5-1 Mech Engring Bldg Edmonton AB T6G 2G8 Canada

ADAMS, PHELPS HAVILAND, former public relations executive; b. Boston, Dec. 14, 1902; s. Henry Ethelbert and Mary Aurora (Haviland) A.; m. Ruth E. Hollinger, June 18, 1928. Student, U. Colo., 1919-22; B.Litt., Columbia U., 1924, 1924, London Sch. of Econs., 1924, The Sorbonne, Paris, France, 1925. Columbia corr. N.Y. Herald, 1923; joined staff of N.Y. Sun; as reporter, 1926, Washington corr., 1929-50; war corr. aboard U.S.S. Enterprise, off Japan, April 1945; spl. asst. to asst. to chmn. U.S. Steel Corp., 1950-55, exec. dir. public relations and asst. to chmn., 1955-57, v.p. public relations, 1957-63, adminstrv. v.p. public relations, 1964-67; Pres. Litchfield Park (Ariz.) Library Assn., 1970-71. Bd. dirs. Ch. at Litchfield Park (Ariz.), 1984—. Recipient Freedoms Found. Honor award, 1950; Gold Plate award Am. Acad. Achievement, 1967. Mem. Pub. Relations Seminar (chmn. 1959-60), Sigma Delta Chi. Clubs: Alfalfa, Gridiron (pres. 1948), Nat. Press (Washington); Wigwam Golf and Country (Litchfield Park, Ariz.). Sent to Palestine, Trans-Jordan, Syria and Lebanon to do spl. series entitled The Truth About Palestine, Oct.-Dec. 1937. Address: PO Box 881 Litchfield Park AZ 85340

ADAMS, PHILIP, lawyer; b. Los Angeles, July 18, 1905; s. Thaddeus Lafayette and Lena (Kelly) A.; m. Alice Rahman, 1933; children—Stephen, Judith, Deborah, Kate; m. Elaine Margaret Anderson, 1968. Student, Pomona Coll., 1924-27; J.D., Hastings Coll. Law, U. Calif., 1938; LL.D. (hon.), Ch. Div. Sch. of Pacific, Berkeley, Calif., 1965. Bar: Calif. bar 1938. Purser Panama Mail S.S. Line, 1928-29; profl. investigator, 1930-38, individual practice law, San Francisco, 1938—; atty. U.S. Govt., 1942-46; instr. domestic relations Golden Gate Law Sch., 1971-72. Author: Adoption Practice in California, 1956. Dir. Children's Protective Soc., 1939-44, United Cerebral Palsy Assn., San Francisco, 1952-72, Assn. for Mental Health, San Francisco, 1952—, United Bay Area Crusade, 1955-61, United Community Fund, San Francisco, 1957-62, San Francisco State Coll., 1964-69, Am. Democratic Action; trustee Ch. Div. Sch. of Pacific, 1951-76; nat. v.p. Episcopal Evang. Fellowship, 1952-61; chancellor Episcopal Diocese of Calif., 1960-67; dep. Episcopal Gen. Conv., 1946-70; pres. bd. trustees Grad. Theol. Union, Berkeley, 1963-66. Fellow Am. Acad. Matrimonial Lawyers (dir. No. Calif. chpt. 1968—); mem. ABA (chmn. com. on adoption, family law sect. 1959-60), Calif., San Francisco bar assns., Lawyers Club San Francisco (gov. 1956), Am. Acad. Polit. and Social Sci., San Francisco Symphony Assn., Soc. Genealogists (London). Clubs: Villa Taverna, Commonwealth. Home: 2170 Jackson St San Francisco CA 94115 Office: 220 Montgomery St San Francisco CA 94104

ADAMS, PHOEBE-LOU, journalist; b. Hartford, Conn., Dec. 18, 1918; d. Harold Irving and Alice (Burlingame) A. A.B. cum laude, Radcliffe Coll., 1939. Reporter Hartford Courant, 1942-45; with editorial staff Atlantic Monthly, Boston, 1945—. Author: A Rough Map of Greece, 1965. Office: 8 Arlington St Boston MA 02116

ADAMS, RALPH EDWIN, physician; b. Caldwell, Idaho, May 30, 1930; s. Edwin E. and Ruth (Shawver) A.; m. Patricia Anne Wessels, Sept. 27, 1958; children—Julie, Erik, Laurie. B.Th., N.W. Christian Coll., 1952; B.S., U. Oreg., 1954, M.D., 1956; M.B.A., U. Chgo., 1961. Intern Gorgas Hosp., Ancon, C.Z., 1956-57; resident surgery Mayo Found., 1957-59; asst. sec. Council Med. Edn. and Hosps., A.M.A., Chgo., 1960-62; med. dir. St. Joseph's Hosp., Victoria, B.C., 1962-66; exec. v.p. adminstrn. Presbyn.-St. Luke's Hosp., Chgo., 1966-68; exec. dir. So. Nev. Meml. Hosp., Las Vegas, 1968-69; resident radiology U. Okla. Med. Center, 1969-72; pvt. practice medicine, specializing in diagnostic radiology, Oklahoma City, 1972—; cons. Health, Edn. and Welfare, Health Services and Mental Health Adminstrn. Mem. Nev. Comprehensive Health Planning Council, 1968-69. Mem. Am. Hosp. Assn., Am. Protestant Hosp. Assn. (trustee, chmn. Council on Assn. Devel.), Am. Coll. Hosp. Adminstrs. Home: 1515 NW 35th St Oklahoma City OK 73118

ADAMS, RALPH WYATT, SR., university president, lawyer; b. Samson, Ala., June 4, 1915; s. Alfred E. and Eunice M. (Clements) A.; m. Dorothy Kelly, Sept. 5, 1942; children: Ralph Wyatt, Kelly Clements (Mrs. James B. Allen, Jr.), Samuel. A.B., Birmingham-So. Coll., 1937; LL.B., U. Ala., 1940, LL.D., 1965, J.D., 1969; postgrad., U. Colo., 1958, George Washington U., 1960, Princeton U., 1966, Harvard U., 1981, Jesus Coll., Oxford U., 1983. Bar: Ala. 1940, U.S. Supreme Ct. 1940. Atty., dep. supt. Ala. Dept. Ins., 1945-46; judge, Tuscaloosa, Ala., 1946-47; founder Acad. Life Ins. Co., Denver, 1957; tchr. life ins. U. Colo.; dep. dean, acting dean Air Force Law Sch., Air U.; pres. Troy (Ala.) State U., 1964—; dir. Bankers Credit Life Ins. Co., Adams Life Ins. Co., South Trust Bank, First Ala. Bank of Troy. Former mem., chmn. State Personnel Bd. Ala., State Ins. Bd. Ala.; chmn. Ala. Oil and Gas Bd., Presdl. Clemency Bd.; commr. Edn. Commn. of States; past Ala. dir. Selective Service; past pres. Assn. Ala. Coll. and U. Pres.'s and Adminstrs., Gulf South Conf.; trustee, vice chmn. Lyman Ward Mil. Acad., Camp Hill, Ala.; bd. dirs. Pike Manor Nursing Home. Served to capt. USAAF, 1941-45; maj. gen. Res.; maj. gen. also Ala. Air N.G. Recipient Silver Beaver award Boy Scouts Am.; Alumnus of Year award Birmingham-So. Coll., 1978;

named to Ala. Acad. Honor, 1977, ICMS Newspaper Carrier Hall of Fame, 1979; Man of Yr., Troy, 1968, 75; First Citizen of Area C. of C., Algernon Sydney Sullivan, 1982. Mem. English Speaking Union (former nat. bd. dirs.), Am. Legion (state comdr. 1977-78), Mortar Bd., Phi Alpha Delta, Kappa Delta Pi, Pi Delta Phi, Kappa Phi Kappa, Phi Kappa Phi, Lambda Chi Alpha, Omicron Delta Kappa, Pi Tau Chi. Methodist. Clubs: Mason, Rotarian., Alexandria Civitan (past pres.), Army-Navy Country (Alexandria, Va.); Montgomery (Ala.) Country, Troy Country.; Met. (Washington). Home: President's Mansion Troy State U Troy AL 36081

ADAMS, RANALD TREVOR, JR., cons., retired air force officer; b. Ft. Sill, Okla., Mar. 7, 1925; s. Ranald Trevor and Mary (King) A.; m. Jeannette Malloy Chichester, May 3, 1947; children: Ranald T. III, Mary M., Jeannette M. Student, Va. Poly. Inst., 1941-43; B.S., U.S. Mil. Acad., 1946; M.S., George Washington U., 1966. Commd. 2d lt. USAF, 1946, advanced through grades to lt. gen., 1978; served in Korean conflict, 1950-51, Vietnam, 1968-69, comdr. 408 Fighter Group, 1969-71; asst. dep. chief staff ops. N.Am. Air Def. Command, Hdqrs. NORAD, 1971-73; comdr. 26 N.Am. Air Def. Command Region/Air Div., Luke AFB, Ariz., 1973-74; dep. insp. gen. inspection and safety Norton AFB, Calif., 1974-77; dir. InterAm. Def. Coll., Ft. McNair, D.C., 1977-78; chmn. Interam. Def. Bd., Washington, 1978-81, ret., 1981; cons., 1981—. Decorated Legion of Merit, Meritorious Service medal, D.S.M., D.F.C., Air medal. Mem. Air Force Assn., Order Daedalians (flight capt. 1973). Home and Office: 1002 Emerald Dr Alexandria VA 22308

ADAMS, RICHARD DONALD, ret. naval res. officer, export exec.; b. Ambridge, Pa., June 14, 1909; s. Arthur David and Mary May (Patterson) A.; m. Lorene M. Hoffer, Nov. 19, 1950; children—David Byron, April Annette. B.S. in Mech. and Elec. Engring, U.S. Naval Acad., 1932. Registered profl. engr., Calif. Commd. ensign U.S. Navy, 1932; active duty, 1932-37, 41-46; mem. Res., 1937-41, 46-69; advanced through grades to rear adm., 1963, rep. of comdt. 12th Naval Dist., 1964-66, dep. comdr. Wester Sea Frontier, 1966-69; ret. With Superior Diesel Engine Co., 1937-41; owner, mgr. Overseas Indsl. Services (exporters machinery and indsl. supplies), San Francisco, 1952—, R.D. Adams Co. (mfrs. agts.), 1946—. Decorated Army Distinguished Unit citation, Navy Res. medal with 3 bronze stars, other campaign and area ribbons. Mem. Am. Soc. M.E., Navy League U.S., Naval Reserve Assn., U.S. Naval Acad. Found., Res. Officers Assn. U.S., U.S. Naval Inst., U.S. Naval Acad. Alumni Assn. Club: Mason (32 deg.). Home: 495 Redwood Ave San Bruno CA 94066 Office: 681 Market St San Francisco CA 94105

ADAMS, RICHARD E., diversified heavy industry manufacturing company executive. Exec. v.p. aerospace Gen. Dynamic Corp. Office: Pierre Laclede Ctr St. Louis MO 63105§

ADAMS, RICHARD GEORGE, author; b. Newbury, Berkshire, Eng., May 9, 1920; s. Evelyn George Beadon and Lilian Rosa (Button); m. Elizabeth Acland, Sept. 26, 1949; children: Juliet Vera Lucy, Rosamond Elizabeth. M.A., Oxford U., 1948. Author: Watership Down, Shardik, The Plague Dogs, The Girl in a Swing, The Unbroken Web, Nature Through the Seasons, Nature Day and Night, Voyage Through the Antarctic, The Ship's Cat, The Tyger Voyage. Served with Brit. Army, 1940-46. Recipient Carnegie medal, 1972, Guardian award for children's lit., 1972. Fellow Royal Soc. Lit.; mem. Royal Soc. for Prevention of Cruelty to Animals (former pres.). Mem. Ch. of Eng. Clubs: Marylebone Cricket., Savile. Address: 26 Church St Whitchurch Hampshire UK

ADAMS, RICHARD LEON, banker; b. Scottsbluff, Nebr., July 19, 1921; s. Clyde Charles and Elizabeth (Sullvain) A.; m. Mildred Catherine Moody, Oct. 29, 1945; children— Janine Elaine, Richard Leon, Nancy Sue, Charles Clyde III, Donna Jo. Student, Okla. A. and M. Coll., 1940; diploma, Grad. Sch. Banking of South, La. State U., 1963. Clk. Scottsbluff Nat. Bank, 1937-41; with First Nat. Bank Palm Beach, Fla., 1947-78, sr. v.p., 1965-68, exec. v.p., 1968-79; vice chmn. bd., pres. Palm Beach Mall Bank, W. Palm Beach, Fla., 1970—. Treas. Palm Beach County Council P.T.A., 1965-66; Bd. dirs. Fla. Bankers Assn. Ednl. Found., chmn., 1971-72, v.p., 1977-78, pres., 1979-80; bd. dirs. Palm Beach County Heart Assn., pres., 1975-76; bd. dirs. Palm Beach County Comprehensive Community Mental Health Center; adv. bd. Palm Beach County Salvation Army. Served to maj. USAAF, 1941-46; Served to maj. USAF, 1951-53; ETO; Served to maj. USAF; Korea. Decorated D.F.C., Air medal with oak leaf cluster. Mem. Am. Bankers Assn. (exec. com. real estate and housing div. 1972-75, governing council 1980-83), Fla. Bankers Assn. (chmn. mortgage div. 1968-69, mem. comml. credit com. 1969—, chmn. credit div. 1972-73, v.p. 1978-79, pres. 1979-80), Palm Beach County Bankers Assn. (pres. 1977-78), Homebuilders Soc. Real Estate Appraisers, Air Force Assn., Navy League, Assn. Gen. Contractors., Methodist (mem. ch. bd., trustee 1960), Palm Beach C. of C. (dir. 1970—), West Palm Beach C. of C. (dir. 1978—, v.p. 1979-80, pres. 1980-81). Clubs: Sailfish (Miami) (bd. govs. 1970—, pres. 1981—); Bankers (Miami); Flying Alligators, Quiet Birdmen, Islanders, Tuscawilla, Poinciana (Palm Beach). Home: 3101 Embassy Dr West Palm Beach FL 33401 Office: Mall Bank 151 Worth Ave Palm Beach FL 33480

ADAMS, RICHARD MILLER, airlines exec.; b. Orange, N.J., Apr. 15, 1919; s. Ray Russell and Zoa (Miller) A.; m. Annabel VanWinkle, June 20, 1942; children: Annabel, Elisabeth, Christopher. B.S. in Aero. Engring, U. Mich., 1940; E.D., UCLA, 1968. With Pan Am. World Airways, 1940-62, mgr. maintenance, overseas div., 1957-62; with Continental Air Lines, Inc., 1962—, sr. v.p. operating and tech. services, Los Angeles, 1965-75, exec. v.p. operating and tech. services, 1975-82, sr. v.p., 1983—, also dir., 1967-69, 72-83. Mem. Soc. Automotive Engrs., Conquistadores del Cielo, Tau Beta Pi, Delta Upsilon. Club: Lakeside Golf (Hollywood, Calif.). Office: Continental Airlines Inc Los Angeles Internat Airport Los Angeles CA 90009

ADAMS, RICHARD NEWBOLD, anthropologist, educator; b. Ann Arbor, Mich., Aug. 4, 1924; s. Randolph Greenfield and Helen Constance (Spiller) A.; m. Betty Virginia Hannstein, Nov 4, 1951; children: Walter Randolph, Tani Marilena, Gina Constance. A.B., U. Mich., 1947; M.A., Yale U., 1949, Ph.D., 1951. Ethologist Inst. Social Anthropology Smithsonian Instn., Guatemala City, 1950-51; specialist grantee State Dept., 1951-52; scientist WHO, Guatemala City, 1953-56; prof. sociology and anthropology Mich. State U., 1956-62; vis. prof. anthropology U. Calif., Berkeley, 1960-61; prof. anthropology, 1962—; asst. dir. Inst. Latin Am. Studies, U. Tex., Austin, 1962-67, chmn. dept. anthropology, 1964-67; program cons. Latin Am. div. Ford Found., 1967-78; vis. research prof. Research Sch. for Social Sci., Australian Nat. U., Canberra, 1980; vis. prof. Fed. U. Rio de Janeiro, 1970, Spanish Am. U., Mexico, 1974, 78, Nat. Inst. Anthropology and History, 1975, 76, U. São Paulo, Brazil, 1978. Author: Home Made Poems, 1934, Cultural Surveys of Panama-Nicaragua-Guatemala-El Salvador-Honduras, 1957, A Community in the Andes, 1959, Introduccion a la antropologia Aplicada, 1964, Second Sowing, Power and Secondary Development in Latin America, 1967, Crucifixion by Power, Essays in the National Social Structure of Guatemala, 1944-66, 1970, Energy and Structure: A Theory of Social Power, 1975, La red de expansion humana, 1978, Paradoxical Harvest: Energy and Explanation in British History, 1870-1914, 1982; Co-author: United States University Cooperation in Latin America, 1960, Responsibilities of the Foreign Scholar to the Local Scholarly Community, 1969; Co-editor: Human Organization Research, 1960, Contemporary Cultures and Societies of Latin America, 1964, The Anthropology of Power, 1977. Served to lt. (j.g.) USNR, 1943-46. Fellow Center for Advanced Studies in Behavioral Scis., 1977-78; Guggenheim fellow, 1974. Fellow Am. Anthrop. Soc. (exec. bd. 1970-72, pres. 1976-77), A.A.A.S. (v.p., sect. chmn. 1972-73); mem. Latin Am. Studies Assn. (pres. 1967-68), Soc. Applied Anthropology (pres. 1962-63), Am. Ethnol. Soc., Sigma Xi. Office: Dept Anthropology U Tex Austin TX 78712

ADAMS, RICHARD TOWSLEY, college vice-president; b. Chgo., July 15, 1921; s. Ralph Ephraim and IdaBelle (Towsley) A.; m. Joan Burridge, Nov. 2, 1963 (dec. May 1977); children: James Towsley, Michael Ralph; m. Joan Bisceglia Barkley, Oct. 27, 1978 (div. 1984). B.S., Purdue U., 1942, Ph.D., 1965. Disposal officer U.S. Dept. State, Brazil, India, 1943-46; v.p. Indamer Corp., Inc., 1946-69, pres., 1958-69; chmn. Indamer Afghan Industries, Inc., Afghanistan, 1960-69; asst. prof. U. Nev., 1963-65; prof., dir. Bus. Research and Service Inst.; dir. State Tech. Services Program, Western Mich. U., Kalamazoo, 1965-69; dean Sch. Bus., Ferris State Coll., Big Rapids, Mich., 1969-72; pres. Community Coll. Beaver County, Monaca, Pa., 1972-80; Cecil Walker disting. prof. fin., dean Coll. of Bus.; provost U. Charleston, W.Va., 1980-81, v.p., 1981—; chmn. bd. Devel. Cons., Inc., Cin., 1960-66; Chmn. Pa. Commn. Community Colls., 1976-77; mem. exec. com. Pa. Assn. Colls. and Univs., 1976-77; mem. Pa. 1202 Commn., 1976-77; mem. adv. com. Pa. Bd. Edn., 1976-77. Active Jr. Achievement; mem. Tippecanoe County (Ind.) Bd. Aviation Commrs., 1954-59, West Lafayette (Ind.) Bd. Sch. Trustees, 1959-63; v.p., dir. Mich. Found. Ednl.-Indsl. Cooperation, 1968-69. Mem. Am. Finance Assn., Ind. Soc. Chgo., Aircraft Owners and Pilots Assn., Phi Delta Theta, Alpha Kappa Psi. Methodist. Club: Rotarian (internat. dist. gov. 1978-79). Home: 5320 Stoneybrook Rd Charleston WV 25313

ADAMS, RICHEY DARELL, broadcast journalist; b. Mpls., Nov. 30, 1942; s. Richey Harry and Carol Iva (Butler) A. B.A. in Journalism, U. Minn., Mpls., 1965; postgrad. in journalism, Am. U., 1966-67. News corr. Sta.-WTOP, Washington, 1969-71; news editor Nat. Public Radio Network, Washington, 1971-74; asst. news dir. Sta.-WTOP-TV, Washington, 1974-76; editorial dir. Sta.-WDVM-TV, Washington, 1976—; adj. instr. Howard U. Sch. Communications, 1976-77. Writer/editor, USIA Voice of Am., Washington, 1965-69. Vol. emergency med. technician George Washington U. Hosp.; vol. instr. Md. Fire/Rescue Inst., U. Md.; media cons. U.S. Fire Adminstrn.; mem. Bethesda-Chevy Chase Rescue Squad. Recipient award for TV editorializing Chesapeake AP, 1975, 77, Editorial award Va. AP, 1977, Disting. Service award Sigma Delta Chi, 1977. Mem. Radio TV News Dirs. Assn. (Regional award for editorial commentary 1978), Nat. Broadcast Editorial Assn. (dir. 1977—, Editorial Excellence award 1978), Nat. Acad. TV Arts and Scis. (Emmy award for Washington Community service 1979), Nat. Assn. Emergency Med. Technicians, Nat. Registry Emergency Med. Technicians. Club: Capital Press (Washington). Office: 4001 Brandywine St NW Washington DC 20016

ADAMS, ROB L., oil company executive. Grad. in petroleum entring., Tex. A&M U. With Conoco, Inc., Stamford, Conn., 1946—, roustabout, N. Mex., 1946-52, dist. supt. prodn., Ponca City, Okla., 1952-55, div. supt., Roswell, N. Mex., 1955-59; mgr. prodn. marine regulation, then exec. v.p Hudson's Bay Oil & Gas Co., Ltd., 1959-66; mgr. prodn. dept. Conoco, Inc., 1966-74, v.p., gen. mgr. prodn., 1974-75, exec. v.p. worldwide petroleum prodn., 1975-80, group exec. v.p. exploration, prodn. and petroleum ops., 1980—, mem. exec. com., dir., 1981—. Office: Conoco Inc High Ridge Park Stamford CT 06904 *

ADAMS, ROBERT ALLAN, architect, environmental planner, facilities planner; b. N.Y.C., Mar. 27, 1929; s. George Allan and Carolyn J. (Witte) A. Diploma in Bldg. Constrn., SUNY, Farmingdale, 1949, Asso. in Applied Sci., Constrn. Tech., 1957; B.Arch., Pratt Inst., 1958. Job capt. Paul Thiry, Architect, Seattle, 1959-63; prin. Architects Workshop, Seattle, 1963-65; v.p. HNTB Inc., P.S. Robert A. Adams A.I.A., 1973-78; prin. RAA Robert A. Adams Facilities Planning Cons., 1978—. Designer-draftsman, Harrison & Abramovitz, Architects, N.Y.C., 1958-59; chief architect, Frankfurter & Assos., cons. engrs., Seattle, 1965-68; asso. architect, Sverdrup & Parcel & Assos., Inc., cons. engrs., Seattle, 1968-72; sr. architect, environmental planner, Howard Needles Tammen & Bergendoff, architects, engrs., planners, Seattle, 1972-73; Important works include Seattle Center Coliseum Design of Fixed and Mobile Stadium Seating, 1963, Design of The Flexible House, Seattle, 1964, Weyerhaeuser Co. Region Hdqrs., Springfield, Oreg., 1974, Bellevue (Wash.) Athletic Club, 1975; nat. design program customer service centers U.S., Weyerhaeuser Co., 1976; nat. design program customer service centers U.S., Weyerhaeuser Pulp and Paper Mill Complex, Columbus, Miss., 1980, distbn. ctr. hist. preservation project Weyerhaeuser Co., Balt., 1981. Served with C.E., AUS, 1951-52. Recipient Authority Low Cost Housing Design Competition award Seattle chapt. A.I.A., 1957; Home of the Month Design award, 1964. Presbyterian. Home: 3827 Cascadia Ave S Seattle WA 98118 Office: 9805 S 248th St Suite A31 Kent WA 98031

ADAMS, ROBERT FRANKLIN, lawyer; b. Jackson, Ala., July 10, 1907; s. David and Lucy (Lee) A.; m. Margaret Crossley, June 30, 1939; children: Robert Franklin, Mary Elizabeth Adams Perry, Laura Adams Phillips. A.B., U. Ala., 1927, LL.B., 1937. Bar: Ala. bar 1937. Officer and dir. Jackson Bank & Trust Co., 1927-34; since practiced law in, Mobile; mem. firm Johnstone, Adams, May, Howard & Hill, and predecessors, 1937—, ptnr., 1942—; dir. Title Ins. Co., Lerio Corp., So. Elec. & Pipefitting Corp. Past pres. Council of Social Agys.; past pres. Mobile Opera Guild; trustee Mobile Infirmary; mem. Adminstrv. Conf. of U.S., 1973-76. Served with AUS, 1944-45; ETO. Recipient Algernon Sidney Sullivan award. Mem. ABA, Ala. Bar Assn., Mobile Bar Assn. (past pres.), Internat. Soc. Barristers, Farrah Order Jurisprudence (pres. 1975-76), Soc. Hosp. Attys. of Am. Hosp. Assn., Mobile Area C. of C. (past treas., dir.), Omicron Delta Kappa, Sigma Chi. Baptist. Clubs: Kiwanis, Mobile Country, Bienville (past gov.). Home: 253 Island Ct Mobile AL 36606 Office: Mchts Nat Bank Bldg Annex Mobile AL 36602 *I have rarely succeeded in reaching my objectives, but I have tried to keep abreast of the times; to be fair; to be understanding; to be right in making decisions, and to stand by them; to actively participate in worthwhile civic endeavors, so as to be a useful citizen; to avoid the limelight; to be a good Christian; and to share my blessings, both material and spiritual.*

ADAMS, ROBERT HICKMAN, photographer; b. Orange, N.J., May 8, 1937; s. J. Ross and Lois (Hickman) A.; m. Kerstin Margarita Mornestam, June 11, 1960. B.A., U. Redlands, 1959; Ph.D. in English, U. So. Calif., 1965. Lectr., asst. prof. English Colo. Coll., Colorado Springs, 1962-70; ind. photographer, Longmont, Colo., 1970—. Exhibited one-man shows, Mus. Modern Art, 1971, 79, Denver Art Mus., 1978, Castelli Graphics, N.Y.C., 1979, Phila. Mus. Art, 1981, Milw. Art Mus., 1983; Author: The New West, 1974, Denver, 1977, Prairie, 1978, From the Missouri West, 1980, Beauty in Photography, 1981. Recipient award of merit Am. Assn. State and Local History, 1975; Guggenheim Meml. Found. fellow, 1973, 80; Nat. Endowment for Arts photography fellow, 1973, 78. Home: 326 Lincoln St Longmont CO 80501

ADAMS, ROBERT MCCORMICK, anthropologist, university official; b. Chgo., July 23, 1926; s. Robert McCormick and Janet (Lawrence) A.; m. Ruth Salzman Skinner, July 24, 1953; 1 dau., Megan. Ph.B., U. Chgo., 1947, M.A., 1952, Ph.D., 1956. Archaeol. field tng. in, Jarmo, Iraq, 1950-51, Yucatan, Mexico, 1953, field studies history irrigation and urban settlement, Iraq, Saudi Arabia, and, Iran, 1956—, reconnaissance and excavation ancient Mayan settlement patterns, Chiapas, Mexico, 1958-61; mem. faculty and staff Oriental Inst. U. Chgo., 1955—; asso prof. Oriental Inst., 1961-62, prof. Oriental Inst., 1962—, dir. Oriental Inst., 1962-68, 81-83, dean div. social scis., 1970-74, 79-80, provost, 1982—; resident dir. Baghdad Sch., Am. Schs. Oriental Research, 1968-69; chmn. assembly behavioral and social scis. NRC, 1972-76. Author: Land Behind Baghdad, 1965, The Evolution of Urban Society, 1966, (with H.J. Nissen) The Uruk Countryside, 1972, Heartland of Cities, 1981; Editor: (with C. H. Kraeling) City Invincible: A Symposium on Urbanization and Cultural Development in the Ancient Near East, 1960, (with C.S. Schelling) Corners of a Foreign Field, 1979, (with N.J. Smelser and D.J. Treiman) Behavioral and Social Science Research: A National Resource, 1982. Trustee Nat. Humanities Center, 1976-83, Russell Sage Found., 1978—. Served with USNR, 1944-46. Fellow Am. Acad. Arts and Scis., Middle East Studies Assn., Iraqi Acad. (asso.), AAAS, Am. Anthrop. Assn., mem. Soc. Am. Archaeology, German Archaeol. Inst., Nat. Acad. Scis., Am. Philos. Soc., Sigma Xi. Office: U Chgo 5801 S Ellis Ave Room 502 Chicago IL 60637

ADAMS, ROBERT MCLEAN, manufacturing company executive; b. Hibbing, Minn., Aug. 4, 1922; s. John William and Julia (Straub) A.; m. Carol Margaret Johnson, Sept. 4, 1943; children: Margaret, William, Carl, John Adams. A.A.S., Blackburn Coll., 1941, D.Sc., 1971; B.S., U. Ill., 1943, M.S., 1944, Ph.D., 1949. With 3M, St. Paul, 1949—, tech. dir., 1958-68, gen. mgr. new bus. ventures div., 1968-69, v.p. research and devel., 1969-81, sr. v.p. tech. services, 1981—, also dir.; dir. The Toro Co., Mpls., Grace Co. Chmn. exploring Indianhead council Boy Scouts Am., 1972; mem. adv. council Inst. Tech., U. Minn., 1971. Served to lt. (j.g.) USNR, 1944-49. Mem. Ind. Research Inst. Presbyterian. Home: 10426 Ideal Ave N White Bear Lake MN 55110 Office: 3M 3M Center Saint Paul MN 55144

ADAMS, ROBERT PARDEE, educator; b. Detroit, Apr. 21, 1910; s. William Henry and Florence (Gossard) A.; m. Roberta England, Oct. 8, 1932 (div. May 1960); children—Robert William, Claire Wentworth; m. Marjorie West Ford, June 10, 1961 (dec. Feb. 13, 1980). B.A., Oberlin Coll., 1931; Ph.D., U. Chgo., 1937. Instr. English Cornell U., Ithaca, N.Y., 1936, Parsons Coll., Fairfield, Iowa, 1936-37; instr., asst. prof., asso. prof. Mich. State U., East Lansing, 1937-47; asso. prof. U. Wash., Seattle, 1947-66, prof. English lit., 1966—; Editorial cons. Duke U. Press, Northwestern U. Press, 1967-68. Contbr. articles to profl. jours., books. Folger Shakespeare Library fellow, 1958; sr. fellow, 1971-72; Newberry Library sr. fellow, 1964-65. Mem. Modern Lang. Assn. Am., Renaissance Soc. Am., Philol. Assn. Pacific Coast, A.A.U.P., A.C.L.U. Unitarian. Clubs: Caxton (Chgo.); Queen City Yacht (Seattle). Home: 3180 NE 82d St Seattle WA 98115

ADAMS, ROBERT VINCENT, business equipment company executive; b. Hammond, Ind., Dec. 27, 1931; s. Vincent Charles and Mary Ann (Cison) A.; m. Marybelle Brewster, Apr. 6, 1959; children: Leslie Jean, Julie Ann, Robert Vincent. B.S.M.E., Purdue U., 1954; M.B.A., U. Chgo., 1960. Mktg. mgr. Bunker Ramo, Canoga Park, Calif., 1961-65, Sci. Data Systems, Santa Monica, Calif., 1965-68; dir. mktg. ops. Data Systems Div., El Segundo, Calif., 1968-73, v.p. mktg., 1973-77; pres. Printing Systems Group, El Segundo, 1977-83; group v.p. Systems Group, El Segundo, 1983—; dir. Wed Bush Corp., Los Angeles. Inventor control systems. Recipient Disting. Engring. award Purdue U., 1983. Republican. Presbyterian. Home: 1103 Via Curva Palos Verdes Estates CA 90274 Office: Xerox Corp 101 Continental Blvd El Segundo CA 90245

ADAMS, ROBERT WAUGH, JR., banker; b. Johnstown, Pa., Oct. 26, 1936; s. Robert Waugh and Mary Louise (Pyle) A.; m. Karen Elizabeth Day, June 13, 1964; children: Robert Waugh, Tara Anne. B.S. in Accounting, Pa. State U., 1958; M.B.A., U. Louisville, 1967; grad., Stonier Sch. Banking, 1967. Teller Cambria Savs. & Loan Assn., Johnstown, summers 1955, 56, 57, Johnstown Bank and Trust Co., summer 1958; with Citizens Fidelity Bank and Trust Co., Louisville, 1959—, asst. cashier, from 1961, asst. v.p., 1964, comptroller, 1967-69, v.p., 1969—; dir. fin. Ky. Housing Corp., 1977-79, dep. dir., dir. fin., 1979—; tchr. U. Louisville, 1972—. Active local United Fund, Louisville Fund, Parkhill Community Center. Served to capt. AUS, 1958-59. Mem. Planning Execs. Inst. (pres. 1969-70), Bank Adminstrn. Inst. (chpt. pres. 1973—), Am. Inst. Banking, Financial Execs. Inst. (chpt. pres. 1972-73, chmn. North Central regional conv. 1976), Theta Chi (treas., v.p. 1956-58), Delta Sigma Rho, Delta Sigma Pi, Scabbard and Blade, Skull and Bones. Roman Catholic. Club: Toastmasters (past club pres., area gov. 1967-68). Home: 4410 Deepwood Dr Louisville KY 40222 Office: 1231 Louisville Rd Frankfort KY 40601

ADAMS, RONALD L., rubber company executive; b. Jamestown, N.Y., July 31, 1934; s. Milford Lynn and Bessie (Peterson) A.; m. Janet, Feb. 23, 1957; children: Michael, Hannah, John. A.B., Ohio U., 1956. V.p. and gen. mgr. Paperboard Products, Lynchburg, Va., 1974-77, pres. and gen. mgr., Dayton, Ohio, 1977-80, Murray Rubber Co., Houston, 1980—. Club: University (Houston). Home: 12566 Westerley Ln Houston TX 77077 Office: Murry Rubber Co 5229 Langfield Houston TX 77040

ADAMS, RUSSELL B(AIRD), corporate executive; b. Wheeling, W.Va., Dec. 28, 1910; s. Russell Updegraff and Daisy Dell (Hilton) A.; m. Frances Esther Nordin, Oct. 27, 1935; children: Russell Baird, Richard Alan, Marilyn (Mrs. Joseph H. Felter, Jr.), David Anthony. Student, Elliott Bus. Coll., Wheeling, 1926, Bethany Coll., 1926-27, U. Ky., 1927. Office mgr. Bradford Supply Co.; and clerk John J. McKay, Sistersville, W.Va., 1927-30; various positions in office of chief post office insp. Post Office Dept., 1930-36, apptd. post office insp., 1936; trans. to CAA (later CAB), 1939, serving in various capacities in econ. bur., apptd. dir., 1945, mem., 1948; Rep. interdept. adv. com. on surplus aircraft disposal, 1944-46; tech. adviser U.S. delegation Internat. Civil Aviation Conf., Chgo., 1944, 1st Interim Assembly, Provisional Internat. Civil Aviation Orgn., Montreal, Can., 1946; mem. U.S. Sect. Com. of Internat. Tech. Aerial Legal Experts, 1946; chmn. econ. div. Air Coordinating Com., 1946-50; alternate rep. CAB, 1946-50; mem. Internat. Civil Aviation Orgn. Panel, 1947-50; alternate del. U.S. delegation First Assembly Internat. Civil Aviation Orgn., Montreal, Can., 1947; del. U.S. delegation commn. on multilateral agreement on comml. air rights in Internat. Air Transport, Geneva, Switzerland, 1947; chmn. U.S. delegation 2d Assembly Internat. Civil Aviation Orgn., Geneva, Switzerland, 1948; signing on behalf of U.S. in accordance with powers given by the pres. Conv. of Internat. Recognition of Rights in Aircraft, 1948; chmn. (U.S. delegation Peruvian negotiations), 1948, 1949, 1950, 1951, 4th Assembly Internat. Civil Aviation Orgn., 1950, U.S.-French Negotiation, Paris, 1951; spl. asst. to Sec. State, 1951; v.p. Pan Am. World Airways, 1951-72. Chmn. Davies Meml. Com. Decorated Grand Official Merit Ordem Soberana Vera Cruz, (Brazil). Mem. Sigma Nu. Democrat. Unitarian. Clubs: Metropolitan, National Aviation (v.p. 1955-65), Circus Saints & Sinners (bd. govs.), Aero (pres. 1960), Congressional Country, International (bd. govs. 1962—); International (Washington) (sec.

1966-84, pres. 1984—), Burning Tree.). Home: 9120 Harrington Dr Potomac MD 20854 Office: Third Floor 1801 K St NW Washington DC 20006

ADAMS, SAMUEL CLIFFORD, JR., ret. fgn. service officer; b. Waco, Tex., Aug. 15, 1920; s. Samuel Clifford and Sarah Catherine (Roberts) A.; m. Evelyn Baker Adams. B.A., Fisk U., 1940, M.A. (Social Sci. fellow), 1947; Ph.D. (John Hay Whitney Found. fellow), U. Chgo., 1952; postdoctoral student, London Sch. Econs. and Polit. Sci., Sch. Oriental and African Studies, also Maxwell Sch. of Syracuse U., 1957. Machinist trainee Norfolk (Va.) Navy Yard, 1942-44; research and teaching asst. grad. dept. Fisk U., 1946-47; dir. Marion Coop. Center, Am. Missionary Assn., 1947-50; research asst., com. on edn., tng. and research race relations, div. social scis. U. Chgo., 1950-51; mass edn. specialist U.S. Spl. Tech. and Econ. Mission to Asso. States Indo-China, 1952-54; acting chief edn. div. USOM, Saigon, Vietnam, 1954-55, chief edn. and community devel. divs., Phnom Penh, Cambodia, 1955-57; chief edn. adviser Office ICA Rep., Am. Consulate Gen., Lagos, Nigeria, 1958-61; rep. AID, Republic of Mali, Africa, 1961, dir. mission, 1962-64; mem. sr. seminar fgn. policy Fgn. Service Inst., Dept. State, Washington, 1964-65; dir. U.S. AID mission to Morocco, Rabat, 1965-68; U.S. ambassador to Niger, 1968-69; asst. adminstr. AID, Bur. for Africa, Dept. State, Washington, 1969-75, ret., 1975; pres. Adams & Co. Internat., Houston, 1975—; U.S. rep. 5th Spl. Session UN Gen. Assembly, 1965; adv. com. sci. and tech. devel. Office Sci. and Tech. Policy, Exec. Office of Pres., 1978; econ. devel. adv. panel World Bank, 1977-78; mem. Dist. Export Council, Dept. Commerce, Houston; project dir. AID African Research Study, 1976-77; mem. adv. com. on the Sahel Nat. Acad. Scis., 1978-81; mem. U.S. Adv. Group on Zimbabwe, 1980-81; mem. U.S. del. UN Conf. on Sci. and Tech. for Devel., 1979; mem. program planning com. 3d Biennial Woodlands Conf. on Growth Policies, U. Houston, 1978. Author articles on race and cultural relations, problems of econ. devel. in least developed nations, devel. adminstrn. Alumni trustee Fisk U., Nashville, 1978—. Served as chaplain's asst. AUS, 1944-46. Nominated William A. Jump Meml. award, 1954; recipient Arthur S. Flemming award, 1957, certificate meritorious service USAAF, 1946, Rockefeller Pub. Service award, 1972, Ralph Bunche award, 1972, Distinguished Honor award AID, 1972. Asso. fellow Royal Anthrop. Inst.; mem. Am. Sociol. Soc., U.S. C. of C. (econ. coms., mem. subcom. on internat. econ. policy 1977-80, mem. spl. task force on Africa 1979, 80), Houston C. of C. (internat. bus. com. 1978), Houston World Trade Assn. (dir. 1980), Alpha Phi Alpha. Home and Office: 3226 N MacGregor Way Houston TX 77004

ADAMS, SEIBERT GRUBER, JR., publisher; b. New Haven, Oct. 12, 1934; s. Seibert Gruber and Norma (Merz) A.; m. Gail G. Bone, June 11, 1957 (div. 1974); children: Sharon G., Sheryl G.; m. Ruth C. Adams, Sept. 28, 1975. B.A., Yale U., 1957. Exec. editor Holt-Dryden, Chgo., 1972-75; v.p. EBS-Dryden, Chgo., 1972-75, CBS Pub., N.Y.C., 1975-77, Random House, 1977—. Served to capt. USAF, 1957-61. Addres: 429 E 52d St Apt 22C New York NY 10022 Office: Coll Div Random House Inc 201 E 50th St New York NY 10022

ADAMS, SHERMAN, former gov. N.H.; b. East Dover, Vt., Jan. 8, 1899; s. Clyde H. and Winnie Marion (Sherman) A.; m. Rachel Leona White, July 28, 1923; children—Marion (Mrs. William Freese), Jean (Mrs. William M. Hallager), Sarah, Samuel. A.B., Dartmouth Coll., 1920, A.M., 1940; LL.D., U. N.H., 1950; D.C.L., New Eng. Coll., 1951; LL.D., Coll., St. Lawrence U., 1954, Center Coll., Ky., 1955, U. Maine, Middlebury Coll., 1957. Treas. Black River Lumber Co. Vt., 1921-22; mgr., timberland and lumber operations The Parker-Young Co., Lincoln, N.H., 1928-45; former dir. Pemigewasset R.R., Concord; pres. Loon Mountain Recreation Corp., 1966-79, chmn. bd., 1980—; mem. N.H. Ho. of Reps., 1941-44, chmn. com. on labor, 1941-42, speaker of house, 1943-44; mem. 79th Congress, 1945-47, 2d N.H. Dist.; gov. N.H., 1949-53; asst. to Pres. U.S., 1953-58; Chmn. Conf. N.E. Govs., 1951-52. Author: First Hand Report, 1961; also articles in Life; other mags.; Lectr. Pres. White Mountain Center for Music and Arts; chmn. Mt. Washington Commn., 1971—; Dir. (life) Northeastern Lumber Mfrs. Assn. Del. Rep. Nat. Conv., 1944, 52; Eisenhower floor leader 1952 conv. Served with USMCR, 1918. Recipient N.H. Outstanding Citizen of Year award Boy Scouts Am. Mem. (sr.) Soc. Am. Foresters, S.A.R. (N.H. soc.), Sigma Alpha Epsilon. Republican. Club: Mason (33rd deg.). Address: Pollard Rd Lincoln NH 03251

ADAMS, STANLEY, lyricist; b. N.Y.C., August 14, 1907; s. Henry Charles and Nan (Josephs) A.; m. Janice Schwarts, Sept. 28, 1940 (div.); 1 dau., Barbara Paula; m. Bernice Halperin. LL.B., N.Y. U., 1929. Mem. adv. bd. Am. Fedn. Musicians, Nat. Cultural Center, Washington, Kennedy Cultural Center; mem. adminstrv. council Confedn. Internat. Performing Rights Socs. Author of: lyrics for There Are Such Things, What A Diff'rence A Day Made, Little Old Lady, La Cucaracha; many others; contributed: songs to Duel in the Sun, Strategic Air Command (motion pictures); others. Bd. dirs. Braille Inst.; trustee Great Neck Symphony Assn. Recipient Presdl. citation Nat. Fedn. Music Clubs, 1961; Gold medal Phila. Club Printing House Craftsmen; Vet. Hosp. Radio and TV Guild award, 1964; Medal of Honor Nat. Arts Club, 1965; named hon. citizen State of Tenn., 1966. Mem. Country Music Assn. (v.p.), Am. Guild Authors and Composers (v.p. 1943-44), ASCAP (dir. 1944—, pres. 1953-80), Nat. Music Council (v.p.), Confedn. Internat. Des Societes D'Auteurs et Compositeurs (mem. exec. bur. 1976-78, pres. 1978-80), Delta Beta Phi. Clubs: Friars, Alfalfa (Washington). Home: 3 Orchard Ln Kings Point NY 11024 Office: ASCAP Bldg 1 Lincoln Plaza New York NY 10023

ADAMS, THEODORE LIONEL, clergyman; b. Bangor, Maine, Feb. 23, 1915; s. Raphael and Ida (Tomchin) A.; m. Bernice Nemetski, Jan. 11, 1938; children: Lawrence Myron, Howard Joseph, Sivia Esther, Myril Ita. B.A., Yeshiva U., 1936, M.S., 1960, Ph.D., 1962; Rabbi, Rabbi Isaac Elchanan Theol. Sem., 1937; postgrad., Columbia, 1944-47. Rabbi Congregation Mt. Sinai, Jersey City, 1938-53; rabbi Congregation Ohab Zedek, N.Y.C., 1953-74, rabbi emeritus, 1974—; asst. to pres., asst. prof. edn. Touro Coll., N.Y.C., 1974—; Pres. Rabbinical Council N.J., 1939-52; now hon. pres.; financial sec. Rabbinical Council of Am., 1948-50, v.p., 1950-52, pres., 1952-54; now hon. pres.; v.p. Synagogue Council of Am., 1955-57, pres., 1957-59, hon. pres., 1959—, mem. exec. bd., 1949—; also chmn. internat. affairs com.; nat. vice chmn. Nat. Council of Hapoel Hamizrachi, 1952—. Editor: Sermon Manual of Rabbinical Council of America, 1948; Contbr.: Jewish Life. Mem. OPA, 1941-46; mem. Jersey City Planning Commn., 1946-51, Civil Rights Commn., 1950-53; cons. to Gov. of N.J. on N.J. Youth Conf., 1947-50; del., cons. Mid- Century White House Conf. on Children and Youth, 1950; mem. dirs. Jewish Welfare Bd.; and rep. to U.S. Mission to UN; mem. Nat. Community Relations Adv. Com., Pres.'s People to People Com., 1957—, Pres.'s Com. for Internat. Econ. Growth, 1958—; del. White House Conf. on Children and Youth, 1960—; mem. Stryker's Bay Community Council, Manhattan.; Bd. dirs. Commn. on Conf. on Jewish Material Claims Against Germany; chmn. Nat. Exploratory Com. on Jewish Unity.; Del. World Zionist Congress, Jerusalem, 1956. Recipient Mordecai Ben David award Yeshiva U., 1950. Mem. Am. Sociol. Soc., Am. Acad. Polit. and Social Sci. Home: 12 Garden Ct Far Rockaway NY 11691 Office: 30 W 44 St New York NY 10036 *I recognize that many successes occur by chance. However it is my conviction that hard work, devotion to one's task and setting high ideals, play a major part in achieving any measure of success. Once I undertook something I didn't let anything sway me from carrying it to fruition. I never undertook anything in which I didn't believe strongly, and therefore made it something personal. One sometimes makes more enemies than friends with such a rigid approach, but the joy of accomplishment and the few real friends, make it worthwhile.*

ADAMS, THOMAS BROOKS, advertising executive; b. Detroit, Sept. 16, 1919; s. Andrew S. and Louise A. (Brooks) A.; m. Mary E. Bryant, Mar. 22, 1945; children: Janis E., Julie A., Kathleen M. B.A., Wayne State U., 1944. With Campbell-Ewald Co., Detroit, 1945—, chmn. bd., 1968—; dir. McLouth Steel Corp. Vice pres. United Found.; chmn. Wayne County Stadium Authority.; Trustee Children's Hosp. Mich., Menninger Found.; bd. dirs. Wayne State U. Alumni Fund. Served from ensign to lt. comdr. USNR, 1941-45; lt. comdr. Res. Decorated Navy Cross, D.F.C., Air medal, Presdl. Unit citation; named Outstanding Young Advt. Man of Year N.Y. Assn. Advt. Men and Women, 1955. Mem. Advt. Council (chmn., dir.). Home: 4315 Wabeek Lake Dr Bloomfield Hills MI 48013 Office: 30400 Van Dyke Ave Warren MI 48093

ADAMS, THOMAS MERRITT, lawyer; b. St. Louis, Sept. 27, 1935; s. Galen Edward and Chloe (Merritt) A.; m. Sarah McCardell Davis, June 6, 1959; children: Mark Merritt, John Harrison, William Shields, Thomas Bondurant. A.B., Washington U., St. Louis, 1956, J.D., 1960; postgrad., London Sch. Econs., 1957; LL.M., George Washington U., 1966. Bar: Mo. 1960, Calif. 1971. Atty. SEC, Washington, 1964-66; asst. dir., asst. gen. counsel Investment Bankers Assn., Washington, 1966-68; mem. Clabaugh & Adams. Author: State and Local Pension Funds, 1968; Contbr. articles to profl. jours. Chmn. Salina (Kans.) Community Ambassador program, 1961. Served to capt. USAF, 1960-63. Decorated Air Force Commendation medal. Mem. Fed. Bar assn., Phi Beta Kappa. Episcopalian. Office: Century Park Ctr 9911 W Pico Blvd Suite 620 Los Angeles CA 90035

ADAMS, WALTER, economist, educator; b. Vienna, Austria, Aug. 27, 1922; s. Edward and Ilona (Schildkraut) A.; m. Pauline Gordon, Aug. 23, 1943; 1 son, William James. B.A. magna cum laude, Bklyn. Coll., 1942; M.A., Yale U., 1946, Ph.D., 1947; LL.D. (hon.), Central Mich. U., 1973, Mich. State U., 1979. Instr. econs. Yale U., 1945-47; mem. faculty Mich. State U., East Lansing, 1947—, pres., 1969-70, disting. univ. prof. econs., 1970—; mem. U.S. Atty. Gen.'s Nat. Com. Study Antitrust Laws, 1953-55; vis. prof. Salzburg Seminar (Austria), 1959, U. Grenoble (France), 1966, Falkenstein Seminar (Ger.), 1972, U. Paris, 1982. Author: Monopoly in America, 1955, From Mainstreet to the Left Bank, 1959, Is the World Our Campus?, 1960, The Brain Drain, 1968, The Structure of American Industry, 6th edit, 1982, The Test, 1971; also articles. Mem. U.S. Adv. Commn. Internat. Ednl. and Cultural Affairs, 1961-69. Served with AUS, 1943-45. Decorated Bronze Star; recipient Adam Smith Gold medal econs., 1942; Ford Found. fellow, 1953. Mem. Am. Econ. Assn., NAACP, Assn. Social Econs. (pres. 1980-81), AAUP (pres. 1972-74), Midwest Econ. Assn. (pres. 1979-80), Delta Sigma Pi. Democrat. Clubs: Yale Western Mich., Harvard Central Mich. Home: 928 Lantern Hill Dr East Lansing MI 48823 *A sound game plan requires that you start from where you are, not from where you would like to be.*

ADAMS, WARREN SANFORD, 2D, retired food company executive, lawyer; b. Cleve., Sept. 4, 1910; s. Otis Howard and Hermine (Weis) A. A.B., Princeton, 1930; LL.B., Harvard, 1934; J.S.D., N.Y.U., 1941. Bar: N.Y. 1935. Pvt. practice, N.Y.C., 1934-40; gen. counsel chems. div. WPB, 1941; with CPC Internat. Inc. (formerly Corn Products Co.), 1946-76, gen. counsel, 1960-72, v.p., 1962-72, sr. v.p., gen. counsel, dir., 1972-76. Bd. dirs. Washington Sq. Fund, N.Y.C.; trustee, gen. counsel Whitehall Found., Inc. Served to maj. USMCR, 1942-46. Mem. ABA, Internat. Bar Assn. Episcopalian. Clubs: Racquet and Tennis, Met. Opera, Princeton (N.Y.C.); Ekwanok Golf (Manchester, Vt.); Nassau (Princeton, N.J.); Black Hall (Old Lyme, Conn.); Fisher's Island (N.Y.); Am. Soc. of Order of St. John; Royal and Ancient Golf (St. Andrews, Scotland); Honorable Co. Edinburgh Golfers (Gullane, Scotland); Boodle's (London, Eng.); Royal St. George's Golf (Sandwich, Eng.); Union (N.Y.C.). Home: 3021 Segovia Coral Gables FL 33134 care Thompson 680 Fifth Ave. New York NY 10019

ADAMS, WAYNE VERDUN, pediatric psychologist; b. Rhinebeck, N.Y., Feb. 24, 1945; s. John Joseph and Lorena Pearl (Munroe) A.; m. Nora Lee Swindler, June 12, 1971; children: Jennifer, Elizabeth. B.A., Houghton Coll., 1966; M.A. Inst. Child health and Human Devel. fellow, Syracuse U., 1969, Ph.D., 1970; postgrad., U. N.C., 1975. Asst. prof. Colgate U., Hamilton, N.Y., 1970-75; chief psychologist Alfred I. DuPont Inst., Wilmington, Del., 1976—; mem. Del. Bd. Licensure in Psychology, 1983—. Contbr. articles to profl. jours. Mem. Soc. Pediatric Psychology, Am. Psychol. Assn., Del. Psychol. Assn. (exec. com. 1979-82, pres. 1981-82), Am. Assn. for Behavior Therapy, Soc. for Behavioral Medicine, Soc. for Research in Child Devel. Office: Alfred I DuPont Inst PO Box 269 Wilmington DE 19899

ADAMS, WILLIAM CHARLES, manufacturing company executive; b. Reynoldsville, Pa., 1923; married. B.S., UCLA, 1950. With Federal-Mogul Corp., Southfield, Mich., 1950; various positions Arrowhead Products div. Federal-Mogul Corp., Southfield, Mich., 1950-60; gen. mfr. microtech. div. Federal-Mogul Corp., Southfield, Mich., 1960-65, gen. mgr. Arrowhead products div, 1965-68; gen. mgr. Nat. Seal div. Fedearl-Mogul Corp., Southfield, Mich, 1968-71; group mgr. rubber and plastics group Federal-Mogul Corp., Southfield, Mich., 1971-72, group mgr. products group, 1973-76, exec. v.p., 1976-77, pres., chief operating officer, 1977—. Office: Federal-Mogul Corp 26455 Northwestern Southfield MI 48076 *

ADAMS, WILLIAM EUGENE, chemical company executive; b. Mt. Vernon, Ohio, Oct. 18, 1930; s. Elmer William and Crystine Merle (Reichert) A.; m. Helen Virginia Drollinger, Aug. 29, 1953; children: Eric William, Barbara Ann. B.M.E., Ohio State U., 1955. Registered profl. engr., Ohio. Engr. Ethyl Corp., San Bernardino, Calif., 1955-58, project engr., Ferndale, Mich., 1958-67, product applications engr., 1967-70, research advisor, 1970-74, dir. auto research, 1974-76, mgr. Detroit research labs., 1976—. Contbr. articles to profl. jours. Mem. Soc. Automotive Engrs. (Horning Meml. award 1964), Detroit Engring. Soc. Presbyterian. Club: Recess. Home: 4306 Arlington Dr Royal Oak MI 48072 Office: Ethyl Corp 1600 W Eight Mile Rd Ferndale MI 48220

ADAMS, WILLIAM HENSLEY, educator; b. Nashville, Aug. 14, 1929; s. William Hensley and Mary Pauline (Vaughn) A.; children: Deska Lee, Norma Dee, Anita Rice, Patricia Lynn. A.B., U. Tenn., 1951; postgrad., U. Okla., 1951, Tulane U., 1953-54; M.S., La. State U., 1956; Ph.D., Auburn U., 1959. Grad. research asst. Auburn U., 1956-59; sr. research biologist Tenn. Game and Fish Commn., 1959-60; chmn. dept. biology, prof. biology Tenn. Wesleyan Coll., 1960-64; dean Coll. Arts and Scis.; prof. biology Tenn. Technol. U., Cookeville, 1964-66; with div. pre-coll. edn. in sci. NSF, 1966-68, div. undergrad. edn. in sci., 1969-73, div. higher edn. in sci., 1973-75, div. sci. edn. devel. and research, 1975-77, div. sci. improvement, 1977-81; cons.,, 1981—; mem. NSF Research Participation for Coll. Tchrs. Highlands Biol. Sta., 1961, NSF Summer Inst. Radiation Biology Oak Ridge Inst. Nuclear Studies, 1961, NSF Summer Inst. Comparative Anatomy Harvard, 1962, NSF Summer Inst. Marine Biology Duke Marine Lab., 1963, NSF-Tenn. Acad. Sci. Vis. Scientist Program, 1962-66; dir. NSF Coop. Coll.- Sch. Sci. Program, 1963-65; mem. Commn. Undergrad. Edn. in Biol. Scis. Southeastern Regional Conf., 1965, Advanced Placement Reader in Biology, 1965; Oak Ridge Inst. Nuclear Scis. Radiation Biology Conf., 1965. Served to lt. col. Med. Service Corps USAF, 1951-53, 68-69. Recipient Sigma Xi-Research Engring. Soc. Am. grant-in-aid, 1960-61, Tenn. Wesleyan Coll. Faculty award, 1962, Tenn. Technol. U. faculty research grant, 1966. Fellow Explorers Club; mem. AAAS, Am. Soc. Mammalogists (honorarium 1959), Am. Ornithologists Union, Cooper, Wilson ornithol. socs., Ecol. Soc. Am., Wildlife Soc. Home: Route 2 Catlett VA 22019 Office: PO Box 8 Manassas VA 22110 *Increasingly, people in positions of responsibility are abdicating their concomitant role as respected leaders and thereby failing to set good examples for young people to follow, especially at a time when they need high standards for self-emulation. Therefore I challenge young people to set forceful leadership as their highest personal goal in life and remember, as I have, that attainment of this goal will require the stamina necessary to remount their white chargers each time and no matter how often they are unseated.*

ADAMS, WILLIAM HESTER, III, lawyer; b. Jacksonville, Fla., May 8, 1926; s. William H. and Florence (Vought) A.; m. Carlie M. Collins, Mar. 30, 1967; children: David Barth, William Hester IV, Nancy Lynn, Laura Kurz, Amelia. A.B., Duke U., 1947, LL.B., 1950. Bar: Fla. 1950. Since practiced in, Fla.; ptnr. Mahoney, Hadlow & Adams, 1962—; Commr. uniform laws State of Fla., 1967—; sec., mem. exec. com. Nat. Conf. Commrs. Uniform State Laws, 1976-79; v.p., bd. dirs. Jacksonville Marine Inst.; bd. dirs. Associated Marine Inst., 1975—, chmn., 1977-79; trustee Jacksonville U.; mem. adv. com. Law and Econs. Center; mem. com. visitors U. Miami Law Sch. Served to lt. USNR, 1944-46, 51-52. Mem. ABA, Jacksonville Bar Assn., Fla. Bar, Mont Pelerin Soc., Order of Coif, Chi Phi. Office: Barnett Nat Bank Bldg Jacksonville FL 32201

ADAMS, WILLIAM JACKSON, JR., lawyer; b. Carthage, N.C., Sept. 15, 1908; s. William Jackson and Florence (Wall) A.; m. Elizabeth Whitehead, May 1, 1937; children—Elizabeth Whitehead (Mrs. R. Edward Morrissett, Jr.), William Jackson III. Student, Woodberry Forest Sch., Orange, Va.; A.B., U. N.C., 1930, J.D., 1933. Bar: N.C. bar 1932. Practice in, Rocky Mount, 1933- 39; chief div. legislative drafting and codification of statutes N.C. Dept. Justice, 1939-41; an asst. atty. gen., N.C., 1941-45, practice in, Greensboro, 1945—; Mem. steering com. to establish N.C. Constl. Study Commn., 1968-69; chmn. Spl. Liaison Tax Com. for S.E. Region, 1974. Student editor in chief: N.C. Law Rev, 1933; Contbr. profl. jours., yachting mags. Mem. Am. Bar Assn., N.C. Bar Assn. (pres. 1968-69), Greensboro Bar Assn. (pres. 1957-58), Am. Judicature Soc., Am. Coll. Probate Counsel, Nat. Conf. Bar Presidents, Phi Beta Kappa, Order of Coif, Phi Delta Phi. Democrat. Methodist. Clubs: Greensboro Country; Carolina Sailing (Henderson, N.C.) (charter, 1st commodore; Robinson cup 1959); Lake Norman Yacht (Mooresville, N.C.) (charter); Pamlico Sailing (Washington)). Home: 615 Woodland Dr Greensboro NC 27408 Office: One Southern Life Center Greensboro NC 27402

ADAMS, WILLIAM JOHN, JR., mech. engr.; b. Riverdale, Calif., Feb. 9, 1917; s. William John and Florence (Dodini) A.; m. Marijane E. Leishman, Dec. 26, 1939; children—W. Michael, John P. B.S., U. Santa Clara, 1937. Registered profl. mech. engr., agrl. engr., Calif. Design and project engr. Gen. Electric Co., Schenectady, 1937-45; project engr. FMC Corp., San Jose, Calif., 1946-47; chief engr. Bolens div., Port Washington, Wis., 1947-53; asst. gen. mgr. Central Engring. Labs., Santa Clara, 1953-71, dir. planning and ventures, advanced products div., 1971-76, mgr. new bus. ventures, 1976-80, cons. to mgmt., 1980—. Chmn. Santa Clara United Fund drive, 1967, Santa Clara Indsl. Citizens Bd., 1965-66; Bd. dirs. Santa Clara County council Boy Scouts Am., Santa Clara Valley Sci. Fair, Eagle Scout Assn. Fellow Am. Soc. Agrl. Engrs. (dir. Pacific Coast region); mem. ASME, Soc. Automotive Engrs., Joint Council Sci. and Math. Edn., Tau Beta Pi. Patentee in field U.S., Can., numerous fgn. countries. Home and Office: 774 Bellerose Dr San Jose CA 95128

ADAMS, WILLIAM LEROY, petroleum company executive; b. Clay Center, Kans., May 23, 1929; s. Glenn Cook and Elizabeth (Osenbaugh) A.; m. Betty Ann Froehlich, Aug. 29, 1954; children: Glenn A., Craig W., Drew H., Kenneth P. B.S., U. Kans., 1951; M.S., UCLA, 1956; A.M.P., U. Va., 1970. Cert. petroleum geologist. With Amoco Prodn. Co., 1956-81; v.p. exploration Amoco Prodn., Chgo., 1975-79, regional v.p., New Orleans, 1979-81; pres., chief operating officer Champlin Petroleum Co., Ft. Worth, 1981—. Dir. (1st Nat. Bank of Ft. Worth). Adv. council Boy Scouts Am., Irving, Tex.; trustee Tex. Christian U.; adv. council Engring. Found. U. Tex., Austin; dir. North Tex. Commn. Family Services Assn. Served to lt. USN, 1951-54; Korea. Recipient Best Tech. Paper award Am. Assn. Petroleum Geologists, 1963. Mem. Am. Petroleum Inst., Am. Assn. Petroleum Geologists, Mid-Continent Oil and Gas Assn. Republican. Clubs: Fort Worth Wildcatters (vice chmn.); Shady Oaks Country (Fort Worth); Petroleum, Century II. Home: 4404 Ridgehaven Rd Fort Worth TX 76116 Office: Champlin Petroleum Co 5301 Camp Bowie Blvd Fort Worth TX 76101

ADAMS, WILLIAM MANSFIELD, educator; b. Kissimmee, Fla., Feb. 19, 1932; s. Shirah Devoy and Olive (Goding) A.; m. Roberta Kay Blackwell, July 23, 1955; children: William Mansfield, Johnathan Blackwell, Christopher Daniel; m. Naoko Nakashizuka, 1976; children: Henele Iitaka, Alden Fernald. A.B. (Univ. scholar), U. Chgo., 1951; B.A., U. Calif., 1953; M.S. (Gulf scholar), St. Louis U., 1955, Ph.D., 1957; M.B.A., Santa Clara U., 1964; postgrad., M.I.T., 1967-70. Instrument man Shell Oil Co., Merced, Calif., 1953; geophys. trainee Stanolind Oil Co., New Orleans, 1953, Western Geophys. Co., Rankin, Tex., 1954; tech. officer Govt. Can., Ottawa, 1956; chief seismologist Geotech Corp., Laramie, Wyo., 1957-59; program tech. dir. U. Calif., Livermore, 1959-62; pres. Planetary Scis., Inc., Santa Clara, Calif., 1962-64; geophysicist U. Hawaii, Honolulu, 1964—; also prof. geophysics; exchange prof. Ind. U., Bloomington, 1975-76; UNESCO expert seismology Internat. Inst. Seismology and Earthquake Engring., Bldg. Research Inst., Tokyo, 1971-72; vis. fellow Co-op. Inst. Research in Environ. Scis., U. Colo., Boulder, 1970-71; research oceanographer Atlantic Marine and Environ. Lab., NOAA, Miami, Fla., 1979-80; cons. Del E. Webb, Kahuku Point, Oahu, Hawaii, 1969, Oceanic Properties, Lanai City, Lanai, Hawaii, 1969, C. Brewer Co., Punaluu, Hawaii, 1970, 74. Contbr. numerous articles to profl. jours. Fulbright grantee, 1956-57; NATO grantee Internat. Inst. Geothermal Research, Pisa, Italy, 1973. Mem. Am. Geophys. Union, Geol. Soc. Am., Seismol. Soc. Am. (editor Bull 1962-65), Acoustical Soc. Am., Soc. Exploration Geophysicists, AAUP, European Assn. Exploration Geophysicists, Tsunami Soc. (founder), Sigma Xi. Patentee in field. Office: 2525 Correa Rd Honolulu HI 96822

ADAMS, WILLIAM ROGER, historian; b. Mpls., Nov. 4, 1935; s. Jacob Anthony and Clara Louise (Jordan) A.; m. LaVonne May Turgeon, June 24, 1961; children: James Jacob, April Louise. B.A., U. Minn., 1961, M.A., 1967; Ph.D., Fla. State U., 1974. Analyst USIS, 1964-69; asst. prof. history Fla. State U., 1972-75; exec. dir. Fla. Bicentennial Commn., 1975-77; dir. Historic St. Augustine (Fla.) Preservation Bd., 1977—; prin. cons. Historic Properties Assos.; bd.

dirs. Fla. Trust Historic Preservation, 1979-81, Fla. Hist. Soc., 1980—. Served with AUS, 1955-57. Office: Box 1987 St Augustine Fl 32084

ADAMS, WILLIAM WHITE, manufacturing company executive; b. Dubuque, Iowa, May 14, 1934; s. Waldo and Therese (White) A.; m. Susan Joanne Cole, Dec. 29, 1956; children: Nancy, Sara, Mark, Catherine. B.S. in Indsl. Adminstrn., 1956. With Armstrong World Industries, Inc., Lancaster, Pa., 1956—, gen. sales mgr. residential ceiling systems div., 1975-80, group v.p. bldg. products ops., 1981, exec. v.p., 1982—. Mem. adv. bd. Lancaster-Lebanon council Boy Scouts Am., 1970—; bd. dirs. United Way Lancaster County, (Pa.), 1977-82; pres. Lancaster Symphony Assn., 1983—. Recipient Silver Beaver award Boy Scouts Am., 1979. Mem. Pa. C. of C. (dir.). Club: Lancaster Country (dir. 1978—). Office: Armstrong World Industries Inc Liberty and Charlotte Sts Lancaster PA 17604

ADAMSON, OSCAR CHARLES, II, lawyer; b. St. Paul, June 9, 1924; s. Oscar Charles and Dorothy M. (Garlock) A.; m. Mary Rae Josephson, Oct. 1, 1977. B.S.L., U. Minn., 1949, J.D., 1951. Bar: Minn. 1951, U.S. Supreme Ct 1960. Since practiced in Mpls.; partner Meagher, Geer, Markham, Anderson, Adamson, Flaskamp & Brennan, 1960—; adj. prof. law U. Minn. Law Sch., 1962-63, prof. law, 1963-66; mem. Minn. Supreme Ct. Adv. Com., 1965—. Author: (with James L. Hetland, Jr.) Minnesota Practice, Civil Rules Annotated, 1970. Served with USAAF, 1942-45. Decorated D.F.C., Purple Heart, Air medal. Mem. Am., Minn., Hennepin County bar assns. Clubs: Pool and Yacht, North Oaks Golf (St. Paul). Home: 14 Evergreen Rd North Oaks Saint Paul MN 55110 Office: 2250 IDS Center Minneapolis MN 55402

ADAMSON, RICHARD HENRY, biochemist; b. Council Bluffs, Iowa, Aug. 9, 1937; s. Holger Nels and Mary Carolyn (Dengle) A.; m. Charlene Denham, Oct. 25, 1963; children: Kristin, Kara. B.A., Drake U., 1957; M.S., State U. Iowa, 1959, Ph.D., 1961; M.A., George Washington U., 1968. Fellow State U. Iowa Coll. Medicine, Iowa City, 1958-61; commd. officer USPHS, NIH, Bethesda, Md., 1961-63; sr. investigator lab. chem. pharmacology Nat. Cancer Inst., Bethesda, Md., 1963-69, head pharmacology and exptl. therapeutics sec., 1969-73, acting chief lab., 1973-76, chief lab., 1976-81, div. dir., 1981—; lectr. physiology George Washington U., Washington, 1963-70; Fulbright vis. scientist St. Mary's Hosp. Med. Sch., London, 1965-66; sr. policy analyst Office Sci. and Tech. Policy Exec. Office of Pres., 1979-80. Author: numerous publs. in field; editorial bd.: Cancer Chemotherapy Reports, 1973-76, Xenobiotical, 1974—, Cancer Research, 1980—. Recipient USPHS Superior Service award, 1976, 82, Spl. Achievement award EEO, 1982. Mem. AAAS, Am. Assn. Cancer Research, N.Y. Acad. Sci., Iowa Acad. Sci., Biochem. Soc., Am. Soc. Pharmacology and Exptl. Therapeutics, Toxicology Soc., Am. Soc. Internat. Law, Acad. Polit. Sci., Internat. Assn. Comparative Research Leukemia. Office: NIH Bldg 31 11A03 Nat Cancer Inst Bethesda MD 20205

ADAMSON, TERRENCE BURDETT, lawyer; b. Floyd County, Ga., Nov. 13, 1946; s. Sollie Burdett and Lois Antoinette (Rogers) A.; 1 son, Terrence Morgan. B.A., Emory U., 1968, J.D. with distinction, 1973. Bar: Ga., D.C., U.S. Supreme Ct. Reporter Atlanta Constn., 1968-70; law clk. to Judge Griffin B. Bell U.S. Ct. Appeals, 5th Jud. Circuit, 1973-74; asso. firm Hansell & Post, Atlanta and Washington, 1974-77, partner, 1979—; Henry Luce scholar Ishii Law Office, Tokyo, 1975-76; spl. asst. to Atty. Gen. U.S. and dir. Office Public Affairs Dept. Justice, Washington, 1977-79. Contbr. articles to newspapers, mags. and law revs. Served with U.S. Army, 1969-73. Kennedy fellow Inst. Politics, Harvard U., 1979. Mem. Am. Bar Assn., Ga. Bar Assn., D.C. Bar Assn., Order of Coif, Order of Barristers, Omicron Delta Kappa. Democrat. Office: Hansell & Post 3300 First National Bank Tower Atlanta GA 30303

ADASKIN, MURRAY, composer; b. Toronto, Ont., Can., Mar. 28, 1906; s. Samuel and Nisha (Perstnyov) A.; m. Frances James, July 16, 1931. LL.D. (hon.), U. Lethbridge, Alta., Can., 1970, D.Mus., Brandon U., 1972, U. Windsor, Ont., 1972, U. Victoria, B.C., 1984, LL.D., U. Sask., Saskatoon, 1984. Prof. music, head dept. U. Sask., Saskatoon, 1952-66. Composer-in-residence, 1966-73; composer: opera Warden of the Plains; numerous orchestral and chamber works, works recorded on Columbia Records, RCA, others. Mem. Can. Council, 1966-69. Can. Council, fellow, 1960; named Saskatoon Citizen of Yr.; decorated officer Order of Can. Mem. Can. League Composers. Club: Arts and Letters Club (Toronto.).

ADATO, PERRY MILLER, documentary producer director; b. Yonkers, N.Y., Dec. 22; d. Perry and Ida (Block) Miller; m. Neil M. Adato, Sept. 11, 1955; children: Laurie, Michelle. Student, Marshalov Sch. Drama, N.Y.C., New Sch. Social Research; L.H.D. hon., Ill. Wesleyan U., 1984. Organizer, dir. Film Adv. Ctr., N.Y.C., 1952-55; film research coordinator CBS-TV, N.Y.C., 1955-64; assoc. producer NET (became WNET Thirteen, Pub. Broadcasting System 1972, N.Y.C., 1964-68, producer dir., 1968—; lectr. Fairfield U., Conn., 1974-75; guest lectr. on film, 1970—; mem. film award jury Am. Film Inst., Beverly Hills, Calif., 1974; judge film award Creative Artists Pub. Service, N.Y.C., 1976; chmn. UN Women in the Arts Com., 1976-77. Producer, dir.: TV documentary films including Dylan Thomas—The World I Breathe, 1968 (Emmy award for outstanding achievement in cultural documentary 1968), Gertrude Stein: When This You See, Remember Me, 1970 (Montreal Festival Diplome d'Excellence 1970, Am. Film Festival Blue Ribbon award 1970), The Great Radio Comedians, 1972 (Am. Film Festival Red Ribbon award 1975), An Eames Celebration—Several Worlds of Charles and Ray Eames, 1973 (Chgo. Internat. Film Festival Silver Hugo award 1973, Am. Film Festival Red Ribbon award 1973), Mary Cassatt—Impressionist From Philadelphia, 1974 (Women in Communication Clarion award 1974), Georgia O'Keeffe, 1977 (dirs. Guild Am. award for documentary achievement 1977, NCCJ Christopher award 1978, Com. for Internat. Events Golden Eagle award 1978, Women in Communications Clarion award 1978), Frankenthaler—Toward a New Climate, 1978 (Am. Film Festival Blue Ribbon award in fine arts 1979), Picasso—A Painter's Diary, 1980 (Dirs. Guild Am. award for directorial achievement in TV 1980, Alfred I. DuPont-Columbia U. award for excellence in broadcast journalism 1980, Com. for Internat. Events Golden Eagle award 1980, Am. Film Festival Blue Ribbon award in fine arts 1980, Internat. Festival of Films and Art First prize for Best Biography of an Artist 1981), Carl Sandburg—Echoes and Silences, 1982 (Women in Communication Matrix award 1982, Dirs. Guild Am. award for Achievement in TV documentary 1983). Hon. bd. dirs. Weston-Westport Arts Council, Westport, Conn., 1981-84. Poynter fellow Yale U., 1976; NEH grantee, 1980, 83. Mem. Dirs. Guild Am., Nat. Acad. TV Arts and Scis., Women in Film, Women in Communications. Office: WNET Thirteen 356 W 58th St New York NY 10019 *

ADAWI, IBRAHIM HASAN, educator; b. Palestine, Apr. 18, 1930; U.S., 1951, naturalized, 1961; s. Hasan and Dabella (Miari) A.; m. Gertrud Obert, Aug. 25, 1956; children: Omar, Nadia, Yasmin, Rhonda. B.S. in Engring. Physics, Washington U., St. Louis, 1953, Ph.D., Cornell U., 1957. Research physicist RCA Labs., Princeton, N.J., 1956-60; research cons. Battelle Meml. Inst., Columbus, Ohio, 1960-68; adj. prof. elec. engring. Ohio State U., 1965-68; prof. physics U. Mo., Rolla, 1968—; Fulbright lectr., Rabat, Morocco, 1982; vis. prof. U. Hamburg, W.Ger., winter 1977, Sch. Math. and Physics, U. East Anglia, Norwich, Eng., fall 1982; sr. scientist Motorola, Phoenix, summer 1979; vis. scientist Internat. Ctr. Theoretical Physics, Trieste, Italy, summer 1982. Jr. fellow Cornell U., 1953-54; J. McMullen scholar, 1954-55; Sigma Xi fellow, 1955-56. Mem. Am. Phys. Soc. Home: Route 4 Box 162 Rolla MO 65401 Office: Dept Physics U Mo-Rolla Rolla MO 65401 *Goals in science, and perhaps in life, are seldom reached; they are only approached asymptotically. The higher we soar the more dazzling is the panorama, but the wider is the horizon, and the frontiers of knowledge keep expanding.*

ADCOCK, DAVID FILMORE, radiologist, educator; b. Columbia, S.C., Sept. 19, 1938; s. David Filmore and Eloise (Daniel) A. B.S., U. S.C., 1958; M.D., Med. Coll. S.C., 1962. Diplomate: Am. Bd. Radiology, Am. Bd. Nuclear Medicine. Asst. prof. radiology U. N.C.-Chapel Hill, 1970-72; assoc. prof. U. U.C.-Chapel Hill, 1972-73; assoc. dir. nuclear medicine Crawford Long Hosp., Atlanta, 1973-74; dir. nuclear medicine Richard Meml. Hosp., Columbia, 1974-79; prof., chmn. dept. radiology U. S.C.-Columbia, 1979—; cons. in field. Contbr. articles to profl. jours. Served as capt. U.S. Army, 1963-66. Mem. Am. Coll. Radiology, Am. Coll. Nuclear Physicians, Radiol. Soc. N.Am., Assn. Univ. Radiologists, Soc. Chairmen Acad. Radiology Depts., Alpha Omega Alpha. Office: U SC Sch Medicine Dept Radiology Columbia SC 29208 *

ADCOCK, WILLIS ALFRED, electronics company executive; b. St. Johns, Que., Can., Nov. 25, 1922; came to U.S., 1936, naturalized, 1944; s. William Arthur and Luella (White) A.; m. Sara McCoy Whiddon, Dec. 28, 1970; children by previous marriage: William John, Robert Charles, Edward James, Margaret Eleanor Adcock Boshart. B.S. cum laude, Hobart Coll., 1943; Ph.D., Brown U., 1948; M.L.A., So. Meth. U., 1975. Mem. staff Woods Hole (Mass.) Oceanographic Inst., 1943-44; mem. tech. staff Clinton Labs., Oak Ridge, 1944-46, Stanolind Oil & Gas Co., Tulsa, 1948-53; mgr. devel. dept., mgr. integrated circuits dept. Tex. Instruments, Inc., Dallas, 1953-64; tech. dir. Sperry Semicondr., Norwalk, Conn., 1964-65; mgr. advanced planning, tech. devel. areas Tex. Instruments Inc., Dallas, 1965-75, asst. v.p. consumer products activity, 1975-78, prin. fellow, asst. v.p. corp. research devel. and engring., 1978-82, v.p. corp. staff, 1982—. Contbr. articles to profl. jours. Fellow IEEE, AAAS; mem. Nat. Acad. Engring., Am. Chem. Soc., Phi Beta Kappa, Sigma Xi. Episcopalian. Patentee in field. Home: 5409 Castlewood Rd Dallas TX 75229 Office: MS 271 PO Box 225474 Dallas TX 75265

ADDABBO, JOSEPH PATRICK, congressman; b. Queens County, N.Y., Mar. 17, 1925; s. Dominick and Anna (Polizzo) A.; m. Grace Salamone, June 12, 1949; children—Dominic, Dina, Joseph. Student, Coll. City N.Y., 1942-44; LL.B., St. John's Law Sch., 1946. Bar: N.Y. 1947. Practice law, Ozone Park, 1948—; mem. 87th Congress, 5th Dist., N.Y., 88th-97th Congresses from 7th Dist. N.Y., 98th Congress from 6th dist. N.Y. Mem. bldg. com. Ozone Park Jewish Center; regional chmn. Bishop's Diocesan Drive for High Sch. and Old Age Home; past pres. Ferrini Welfare League of Cath. Charities. Mem. Ozone Park Men's Assn. (past pres.), Queen's County Bar Assn. Democrat. Club: Kiwanian. Home: 132-43 86th St Ozone Park NY 11417 Office: 96-11 101st Ave Ozone Park NY 11417 also House Office Washington DC 20515 *I have always tried to keep in mind the fact that I serve at the pleasure of my constituents and that their well-being comes before the furtherance of my own career.*

ADDAMS, CHARLES SAMUEL, cartoonist; b. Westfield N.J., Jan. 7, 1912; s. Charles Huey and Grace M. (Spear) A.; m. Barbara Day, May 29, 1943 (div. Oct. 1951); m. Barbara Barb, Dec. 1, 1954 (div. 1956); m. Marilyn Matthews, May 31, 1980. Student, Colgate U., 1929-30, U. Pa., 1930-31, Grand Central Sch. Art, N.Y.C., 1931-32; D.F.A. (hon.), U. Pa., 1980. Exhibited in, Fogg Art Mus., R.I., Sch. Design, Mus. City N.Y., 1956, Pa. U. Mus., 1957, Met. Mus. Art, war exhbn., print exhbn.; cartoons appeared in New Yorker, 1935; TV show The Addams Family based on original cartoon characters; drawings in biennial New Yorker Album and The New Yorker War Album, 1942, Mus. Modern Art, N.Y.C.; Author: Drawn & Quartered, 1942, Addams and Evil, 1947, Monster Rally, 1950, Home Bodies, 1954, Nightcrawlers, 1957, Dear Dead Days, 1959, Black Maria, 1960, The Groaning Board, 1964, The Charles Addams Mother Goose, 1967, My Crowd, 1970, Monster Rally, 1975, Favorite Haunts, 1976, Creature Comforts, 1981. Served with AUS, 1943-46. Recipient Humor award Yale Record, 1954, spl. award Mystery Writers Am., 1961. Clubs: Coffee House, Vintage Car Club of Am., Armor and Arms. Address: care New Yorker Mag 25 W 43d St New York NY 10036

ADDELSON, KATHRYN PYNE, philosophy educator, writer; b. Providence, Apr. 22, 1932; d. Joseph Abraham and Catherine (Newton) Etchells; m. Terence Parsons, June 10, 1967 (div.); children: Catherine Casey Pyne, Shawn Pyne; m. 2d Richard Ullman Addelson, Oct. 31, 1980. A.B., Ind. U., 1961; Ph.D., Stanford U., 1968. Lectr. Bryn Mawr Coll., (Pa.), 1965-66, CCNY, N.Y.C., 1966-67; asst. prof. philosophy U. Ill., Chgo., 1967-72; prof. philosophy Smith Coll., Northampton, Mass., 1972—; assoc. editor Feminist Studies. Contbr. writings to anthologies and jours. Nat. Endowment for Humanities grantee, 1978-79; Nat. Endowment for Humanities fellow, 1978-79. Mem. Soc. for Women in Philosophy. Office: Smith College Northampton MA 01060

ADDERLEY, TERENCE E., corporate executive. Pres. Kelly Services, Inc., Troy, Mich. Office: Kelly Services Inc 999 W Big Beaver Rd Troy MI 48084§

ADDINGTON, KEENE HARWOOD, banker; b. Chgo., May 28, 1932; s. James Rol and Sarah Stires (Wood) A.; m. Constance Goldsmith, Nov. 16, 1968; children: Sarah Lee, Keene Harwood, II, Leslie, Margo, Pamela, Elinor, Brooks. B.A., Amherst Coll., 1954; postgrad., U. Chgo. Bus. Sch. Vice pres. mktg. Miehle Goss Dexter Inc., Chgo., 1959-72; pres. Pandrick Press Midwest Inc., Chgo., 1972-75; adminstrv. v.p., then exec. v.p. Am. Nat. Bank & Trust Co., Chgo., 1975-78, pres., 1978—; also dir.; sr. v.p., dir. Walter E. Heller Internat. Adv. group Opportunities Industrialization Center, Chgo.; treas. Met. Housing and Planning Council, Chgo.; adv. bd. Center Sports Medicine; trustee Glenwood (Ill.) Sch. Boys. Served to capt. USAF, 1954-58. Mem. Am. Bankers Assn., Assn. Res. City Bankers, Robert Morris Assos., Ill. Bankers Assn. Republican. Episcopalian. Clubs: Shoreacreas, Chicago, Economic, Onwentsia. Office: Am Nat Bank 33 N LaSalle St Chicago IL 60602

ADDINGTON, WHITNEY WOOD, physician; b. Chgo., Aug. 23, 1935; s. James Rol and Sarah Wood (Armour) A.; m. Ada Johnson Forgan, July 20, 1957; children: Joan, Sarah, Hilary, Anne. A.B., Princeton U., 1957; M.D., Northwestern U., 1961; M.S., Okla. U., 1967. Diplomate: Am. Bd. Internal Medicine. Intern Northwestern Meml. Hosp., Chgo., 1961-62, resident in internal medicine, 1962-65; prof. dept. medicine U Chgo., 1979—, head pulmonary sect., 1979, pres. med. staff, 1983—. Co-author: books in field, including Tuberculosis: Discussions in Patient Management, 1979; author, co-author numerous articles in field of pulmonary medicine. Served to lt. comdr. USPHS, 1965-67. Mem. A.C.P., Am. Thoracic Soc. Episcopalian. Clubs: Glenview, Misquamicut. Office: Dept Medicine U Chgo Box 75 950 E 59th St Chicago IL 60637

ADDIS, LAIRD CLARK, JR., philosopher, educator; b. Bath, N.Y., Mar. 25, 1937; s. Laird Clark and Dora Ersel (Webber) A.; m. Patricia Karen Peterson, Dec. 20, 1962; children—Kristin, Karin. B.A., U. Iowa, 1959, Ph.D., 1964; M.A. (Woodrow Wilson fellow), Brown U., 1960. Instr. U. Iowa, Iowa City, 1963-64, asst. prof., 1964-68, asso. prof., 1968-74, prof. philosophy, 1974—, also chmn. dept. philosophy.; Sr. Fulbright lectr. State U. Groningen, Netherlands, 1970-71. Author: (with Douglas Lewis) Moore and Ryle: Two Ontologists, 1965, The Logic of Society, 1975; contbr. articles to profl. jours. Mem. Am. Philos. Assn., Philosophy of Sci. Assn. Home: 20 W Park Rd Iowa City IA 52240 Office: Dept Philosophy U Iowa Iowa City IA 52242

ADDISON, ANTHONY, opera director and conductor; b. Bournemouth, Hants., Eng., Sept. 28, 1926; came to U.S., 1962; s. George Gillespie Lancelot and Tui Blackborne; m. Jane Grenville Cooper, June 19, 1954; children—Mark David, Jacqueline Grenville, Vivien Beatrice, Emily Catherine Tui. Student, Royal Acad. Music, 1943-45, 48. Mem. faculty U. Tex., Austin, 1981; dir. music Univ. Coll., London, 1949-52, 60-62; chorus master, condr. Carl Rosa Opera Co., 1952-59; free-lance condr. for ballet, musicals, opera, London and Europe, 1959-62; assoc. dir. Goldovsky Opera Inst., 1962-64; condr. Univ. Circle Youth Orch., Cleve., 1968-75; chmn. opera theater dept. Cleve. Inst. Music, 1964-81; radio reviewer of opera sta. WCLV. Contbr. articles on opera to local and nat. publs. Served to lt. Royal Army, 1945-48. Mem. Central Opera Service Nat. Opera Assn. (dir.), Met. Guild, Pi Kappa Lambda. Episcopalian. Home: 1306 Garner Austin TX 78704

ADDISON, FRANCIS GIRAULT, III, banker; b. Washington, Jan. 7, 1924; s. Francis Girault, Jr. and Alice Oden (Roberts) A.; m. Sherrard Coleman Marthinson, June 16, 1949; children—Christopher, Mary-Sherrard, Caroline, Elisabeth, Francis IV, Ann. Ed., St. Albans Sch., Washington, 1936-42; B.S., Washington and Lee U., 1942-46; LL.B., George Washington U., 1952. Vice pres. Equitable Savs. and Loan, Washington, 1947-60; v.p. First Am. Bank NA, Washington, 1960-66, sr. v.p., 1966-69, pres., 1970-74, chmn. bd., 1974—, also dir.; Chmn. Washington Heart Fund, 1971; mem. Washington Monument Assn., 1970—; Bd. dirs. Research Found. Washington Hosp. Center; adv. bd. Hollins Coll. Served with USNR, 1943-46. Mem. Washington Bd. Trade, Am. Bankers Assn. (governing council 1974), Res. City Bankers Assn., D.C. Bankers Assn. (pres. 1969-70), Soc. Cincinnati, U.S. C. of C. (com. on banking and monetary policies), Phi Delta Theta. Episcopalian (vestryman). Clubs: Chevy Chase (Md.); Metropolitan (dir.), Alibi, Alfalfa (Washington). Home: 1525 29th St NW Washington DC 20007 Office: 1st American Nat Bank 15th and H Sts NW Washington DC 20005

ADDISON, HERBERT JOHN, publishing executive; b. Berkeley, Calif., Nov. 21, 1932; s. Herbert and Clara Virginia (Mason) A.; m. Geraldyne Elaine Harvey, Aug. 17, 1957; children: Bradley Thomas, Gregory James. B.A., U. Calif.-Berkeley, 1958; M.A., NYU, 1959. Office-personnel mgr. Thomas Y. Corwell Co., N.Y.C., 1958-65; editor-in-chief coll. dept. Holt, Rinehart & Winston, Inc., N.Y.C., 1965-70; v.p., gen. mgr. coll. dept. Thomas Y. Crowell Co., N.Y.C., 1970-74; exec. editor coll. dept. John wiley & Sons, Inc., N.Y.C., 1974-78; gen. mgr. coll. dept. Oxford U. Press, Inc., N.Y.C., 1978-82, v.p., exec. editor, 1982—; adj. lectr. NYU, 1977-83. Author: Books and Bucks: The Business of College Textbook Publishing, 1980. Trustee Adult Sch. Montclair, N.J., 1976-80; mem. Civic Conf. Com., Glen Ridge, N.J., 1974-77. Served with U.S. Army, 1953-55. Mem. Am. Econ. Assn. Home: 46 Sherman Ave Glen Ridge NJ 07028 Office: Oxford Univ Press Inc 200 Madison Ave New York NY 10016

ADDISON, WALTER JOHN, transportation engineer; b. N.Y.C., June 6, 1926; s. Alvin Jack and Dorothy Beatrice (Alexander) A.; m. Anne Clemens, June 28, 1949; children: Deborah G., David L. B.C.E., CCNY, 1949. Registered profl. engr., N.Y., Md. Traffic engring. cons. Assn. Casualty & Surety Cos., N.Y.C., 1954-56; assoc. traffic engr. Wilbur Smith & Assocs., New Haven, 1956-57; county traffic engr. Baltimore County, Md., 1957-63; dep. chief engr. Md. Rds. Commn., Balt., 1963-69; gen. mgr. Met. Transit Authority of Balt., 1969-71; adminstr. Mass Transit Adminstr. of Md., Balt., 1971-79; exec. dir. Met. Transit Authority, Houston, 1979-81; projects mgr. Daniel, Mann, Johnson & Menden hall, 1982—; guest lectr. Cath. U. Am., 1966-67; chmn. bd. Transit Devel. Corp., 1974-77; instr. Johns Hopkins U., Balt., 1974-79; mem. nat. com. on tunneling tech. Nat. Acad. Sci., 1976-78. Served with USNR, 1944-46. Fellow Inst. Transp. Engrs. (pres. sect. 1965-66); mem. Am. Pub. Works Assn., Am. Pub. Transit Assn. (dir.). Home: 6349 Red Cedar Pl Baltimore MD 21209

ADDLESTONE, NATHAN SIDNEY, metals company executive; b. Charleston, S.C., Jan. 16, 1913; s. Abram and Rachel (Lader) A.; m. Marlene Kronsberg, Apr. 27, 1982; children by previous marriage: Carole Anita, Susan Lader. Grad. pub. high sch. With Sumter Iron & Metal Co., S.C., 1932-45, pres., 1938-45; founding pres. Addlestone & Co., Sumter, 1945-66, Addlestone Steel Corp., 1945-66; founder, chmn. bd. Steelmet, Inc., Charleston, 1961-73; chmn. bd. Steelmet Far East Corp., 1969-73, also Metals Processing Co., Providence; dir. L.L. Cohen Co., Inc., Philip L. Buxton, Inc., Tidewater Terminal, Inc., Utility Survey Corp., to 1973; pres. Columbia Steel & Metal Co., 1951—; pres., treas., dir. Metro Iron & Metal Corp., 1964-73; founder, chmn. bd., pres. Addlestone Internat. Corp., Charleston, 1973—, Addlestone Export Corp., 1974—, Automotive Recycling Corp., 1975—, East Coast Export Corp., 1975—; founder, pres., chmn. bd. Raw Materials Corp., 1969—; Mem. fgn. trade com. Inst. Scrap Iron and Steel, 1965—, vice chmn., 1970-71. Mem., del. Bur. Internat. de la Recuperation, 1973—; Bd. dirs. Jewish Community Center, Charleston; pres. Addlestone Hebrew Acad. Trust, 1976—; mem. Trident Area Commn. for Tech. Edn., 1976—, chmn. bd., 1981—. Mem. C. of C. Sumter (past pres.), Nat. Assn. Secondary Materials (past bd. dirs.), Inst. Scrap Iron and Steel (past bd. dirs.). Jewish. Clubs: Rotarian, Elk, Mason, Shriner. Home: Apt 10BC Dockside 330 Concord St Charleston SC 29402 Office: 8 Cumberland St PO Box 979 Charleston SC 29402

ADDUCI, VINCENT JAMES, assn. exec.; b. Oriolo, Italy, Mar. 1, 1920; s. George and Maria Frances (Panno) A.; m. Kathleen M. Barron, Nov. 23, 1946; children—Vincent James II, Dawn Maria, Lisa Anne. Student, U. Hawaii, 1939-41, Detroit Inst. Tech., 1948-49, Detroit Coll. Law, 1949-50, George Washington U., 1951, U. Mich., 1957. Enlisted as pvt. USAAF, 1939; advanced through grades to col. USAF, 1954; fighter, bomber pilot; insp. gen.; dep. dir. Office Legislative Liason; ret., 1960; v.p., then sr. v.p. Aerospace Industries Assn., 1960-70; pres. Electronics Industries Assn., Washington, 1970-77; pres., chief exec. officer Motor Vehicle Mfrs. Assn. U.S., Inc., 1977—; pres., chmn. bd. AV-SPA Corp., Washington, 1965-69; v.p. Aero Center, Washington, 1965-67. Author: Executive Development, 1950. Decorated Legion of Merit with oak leaf cluster, D.F.C., Air medal with 7 clusters, Purple Heart, Bronze Star. Mem. Am. Soc. Assn. Execs. (dir.), Internat. Rd. Fedn. (dir.), Bur. Permanent International des Constructeurs d'Automobiles (pres.), Hwy. Users Fedn. for Safety and Mobility (dir.), Nat. Safety Council (dir.), Nat. Quill and Scroll. Clubs: Internat., Army and Navy (Washington) (dir. 1976-77); Toastmasters (Arlington, Va.) (pres.); Recess (Detroit); Fauquier Springs Country (Warrenton, Va.). Home: 6419 Waterway Dr Falls Church VA 22044 Office: 1909 K St NW Washington DC 20006

ADDY, FREDERICK SEALE, oil company executive; b. Boston, Jan. 1, 1932; s. William R. and Edith (Seale) A.; m. Joyce Marilyn Marshall, Mar. 26, 1954; children: Deborah, William, Brian. B.A., Mich. State U., 1953, M.B.A., 1957. With Standard Oil Co., Ind.; (and its subsidiaries), 1957—, fin. analyst, 1957-61; econs. supr. Amoco Prodn. Co., 1962-67, acquisition mgr., 1968-71; treas. Am. Oil Co., Chgo., 1971-72; mgr. financial planning Standard Oil, 1972-73; v.p. adminstrn. Amoco Prodn. Co., 1973-75; gen. mgr. corp. planning Standard Oil, 1975-77, treas., 1978-81, v.p. fin. ops., 1981-83, v.p. fin., 1983—. Served with USAF, 1954-56. Mem. Soc. Petroleum Engrs. Home: 1230 Loch Ln Lake Forest IL 60045 Office: 200 E Randolph Dr Chicago IL 60601

ADDY, GEORGE ARTHUR, judge; b. Ottawa, Ont., Can., Sept. 28, 1915; s. Frederick W. and Clorida Richer (de la Fleche) A.; m. Joyce Rose Sylvia Head, Apr. 1942; children—Paul, Clive, Nicole Addy Scoane, Vincent, George. B.A., Ottawa U., 1937; grad., Osgoode Hall Law Sch., Can., 1940. Bar: Ont. bar 1942. Partner firm Vincent and Addy, Ottawa, 1945-55, Vincent, Addy and Carbonneau, 1955-60, sr. partner, 1960-67; mem. Ct. Martial Appeal Bd., 1953-59; justice Supreme Ct., Ont., Toronto, 1967-73, Fed. Ct. of Can., Ottawa, 1973—, Court Martial Appeal Ct., 1974—. Founding mem. Le Cercle Universitaire d'Ottawa, 1957, hon. life mem., 1968—, pres., 1965-66. Served to lt. col. Canadian Army, 1940-45. Hon. gov. Ottawa U., 1970—. Mem. Royal Canadian Armoured Corps Assn. (life: pres. 1957-58), Royal Canadian Mil. Inst. Club: Le Cercle de la Place d'Armes (Montreal). Office: Supreme Court of Canada Bldg Wellington St Ottawa ON K1A 0H9 Canada *

ADE, ERWIN JEROME, business exec.; b. Norwalk, Conn., Dec. 1, 1908; s. William and Flora (Loweth) A.; m. Mary Jane Carroll, Aug. 13, 1949; children—Jerome Carroll, James Loweth John. B.S., Washington and Lee U., 1932. Mem. firm Tamblyn & Tamblyn (fund raising), N.Y.C., 1936-38; nat. fund raising dir., commerce and industry div. Brit. Relief Soc., 1939; dir. fund raising Greater N.Y. Com. Commerce and Industry, Red Cross and United Service Orgns.; War Fund Campaigns, 1941-43; asso. dir. John Price Jones Corp., N.Y.C., 1945-47; nat. campaign dir. Planned Parenthood Fedn. Am., 1947-48, Am. Heart Assn., 1948-49; adminstrv. dir. Citizens Com. for Hoover Report, 1949-52; fund raising dir. Nat. Fund for Med. Edn., 1952-56; pres. Ade & Bliss, Inc., pub. relations counsellors, 1956-57, E. J. Ade & Co., Inc., N.Y.C., 1957-61, 63—; v.p., dir. pub. relations Fuller & Smith & Ross, Inc., N.Y.C., 1961-63; pres. Pointmakers, Inc., Betty Blue Art Centers, Inc.; v.p. Mktg. Innovations, Inc., 1970—; pres. Satellite Mktg. Assos., 1972—; chmn. bd. Genie Meals, Inc., 1971—; v.p. Universal Sports Publs., 1979—; pres. Internat. Coffee, 1977. Bd. dirs. Westchester County Multiple Sclerosis Soc., 1976; exec. v.p. Charles A. Lindbergh Meml. Fund; fund raising counsellor Nat. Planning Assn.; sec. Com. Am. Industry; chmn. 1960 campaign; trustee Hudson River Speech Center; bd. dirs. Fertility Research Fedn.; asst. to chmn. Eastern div. Am. Liberty League, 1935, exec. sec. Bronx and Richmond Counties, N.Y.C., 1940; exec. sec. United Rep. Fin. Com., 1940; dir. Textiles Go to War celebration, Spartanburg, S.C., 1943; asst. admissions officer UN Conf., San Francisco, 1945; bd. counsellors Council on Pub. Relations, Inc. Served with AUS, 1943-45. Mem. Pub. Relations Soc. Am., Assos. Engr. Corps, Co. K. Vets, 7th Regt. N.Y., Pi Kappa Phi. Republican. Clubs: Univ., Sleepy Hollow Country (N.Y.C.); North Palm Beach Country, Explorers. Home: 1208 Marine Way North Palm Beach FL 33408

ADEL, ARTHUR, physicist; b. Bklyn., Nov. 22, 1908; s. Morris and Jenny (Schrieber) A.; m. Catherine Emelia Backus, Sept. 11, 1935. A.B., U. Mich., 1931, Ph.D., 1933. Research asso. Lowell Obs., U. Mich., 1933-35; astrophysicist Lowell Obs., Flagstaff, Ariz., 1936-42; asst. prof. physics U. Mich., 1942-46, asst. prof. astronomy, 1946-48; prof. physics, also dir. Atmospheric Research Obs., No. Ariz. U., Flagstaff, 1948-76; now prof. emeritus; research fellow physics, instr. astronomy Johns Hopkins U., 1935-36; leader TWA eclipse expdn., Island of Ceylon, June, 1955. Contbr. to sci. jours. on astron. discoveries.; pub. hypothesis regarding origin of periodic phenomena, 1983. Fellow Am. Phys. Soc., Am. Astron. Soc., Internat. Astron. Union, Explorers Club; mem. Johns Hopkins U. Soc. Scholars, Phi Beta Kappa, Sigma Xi. Has specialized in study of planetary atmospheres and infrared spectroscopy of solar system. Prepared 1st definitive prismatic and grating maps of solar-telluric spectrum 7-14 microns, 1934-42; discovered strong Non-Rayleigh atmospheric infrared scattering, 1949; discovered atmospheric N2O and atmospheric HDO, 1939; discovered 20-micron window in earth's atmosphere, 1942; also determined temperature and location of the atmospheric nitrous oxide layer, 1949-50; demonstrated relationship of atmospheric nitrous oxide to the Nitrogen Cycle, 1951; origin atmospheric N2O, 1946-51; discovered periodic phenomena in stratosphere, 1956. Home: PO Box 942 Flagstaff AZ 86002

ADEL, JUDITH, graphic designer; b. Bronx, N.Y., Aug. 8, 1945; d. Seymour and Suzanne (Glaser) A.; m. Tony Savage, Mar. 1, 1978. B.A., CCNY, 1970. Editorial asst. Machinery mag., N.Y.C., 1963-65, asst. editor, 1965-66, asso. editor, 1966-67, mng. editor, 1967-72; prodn. mgr. World mag., 1972-73; art. dir. Saturday Rev./World, Inc., N.Y.C., 1973-77; asso. art dir. Bus. Week mag., 1977; founder, creative dir. Savage Group, design studio, 1979—; design cons.; art dir. Entermedia Theater, N.Y.C., 1978; guest lectr. Parsons Sch. Design. Designer: jacket, interior pages How to Look at Dance; Great Male Dancers of the Ballet, The King's Ballet Master: A Biography of August Bournonville, Alicia Alonso and the Cuban National Ballet, Twentieth Century Theater; designer: jacket Ballet Guide, 1979, Teleprompter Ann. Report, 1982, 1983 Party Book; advt. material for CBS, others. Recipient Design awards Creativity competitions, 1973, 74, 76, 76, 78, 79, award The 1975 One Show, Art Dirs. Club, 1975; winner competition Soc. Publ. Designers, 1975, 78, Soc. Illustrators Los Angeles, 1976; Desi awards Graphics: USA and Graphics: N.Y., 1978, 79; Blue Ribbon Ency. of Awards, 1979. Mem. Unicorn Repertory Co. N.Y.C. (founding), ACLU, Common Cause, Friends of the Earth, Smithsonian Assos. Democrat. Jewish. Home: 142 E 16th St New York NY 10003 Office: J Adel-Graphix/Savage Group 142 E 16th St New York NY 10003

ADELBERGER, ERIC GEORGE, physicist; b. Bryn Mawr, Pa., June 26, 1938; s. Erwin George and Emma Marie (Zeschky) A.; m. Audra Elizabeth Browman, Aug. 21, 1961; children: Karen Emma, Kurt Ludvig. B.S. with honors, Calif. Inst. Tech., 1960, Ph.D., 1967. Research asso. Stanford U., 1968-69; asst. prof. physics Princeton U., 1969-71; asst.prof. physics U. Wash., Seattle, 1971-72, assoc. prof., 1972-75, prof., 1975—. Assoc. editor: Phys. Rev. Letters, 1978—. NSF fellow, 1960-64; hon. Woodrow Wilson fellow, 1960-61; Guggenheim Found. fellow, 1981-82; Humboldt fellow, 1981-82; A.P. Sloan Found. fellow, 1971-76. Fellow Am. Phys. Soc. Asso. Office: Dept Physics FM-15 U Wash Seattle WA 98195

ADELIZZI, ROBERT FREDERICK, savings and loan executive; b. Phila., Feb. 9, 1935; s. Alfred Frederick and Natalie Marie (Vilotti) A.; m. Thomasine Starr Lane, Dec. 22, 1959; children—Mary Lee, Judith Anne, James Frederick. A.B., Dartmouth, 1957; J.D., U. San Diego, 1963. Bar: Calif. bar 1964. Pres., chief operating officer, dir. Home Fed. Savs. & Loan Assn., San Diego, 1981—; pres., chief exec. officer Pioneer Fed. Savs. & Loan Assn., Honolulu; pres. Conf. Fed. Savs. and Loan Assns.; dir. Doroado Growth Industries. Trustee Children's Hosp. and Health Center; chmn. bd. visitors U. San Diego Sch. Law. Served to capt. USMC, 1958-63. Mem. Am. Bar Assn., Calif. Bar Assn., San Diego County Bar Assn., Barristers of San Diego, Psi Upsilon, Phi Delta Phi. Republican. Roman Catholic. Clubs: Kona Kai, San Diego Tennis and Racquet, San Diego Yacht, Univ. Office: 701 Broadway San Diego CA 92101

ADELL, HIRSCH, lawyer; b. Novogrodek, Poland, Mar. 11, 1931; s. Nathan and Nachama (Wager) A.; m. Judith Audrey Fuss, Feb. 8, 1963; children—Jeremiah, Nikolas, Balthasar, Valentine. Student, City Coll. N.Y., 1949-52; B.A., U. Calif. at Los Angeles, 1955, LL.B., 1963. Bar: Cal. bar 1963. Adminstrv. asst. to State Senator Richard Richards, 1956-60; partner law firm Warren & Adell, Los Angeles, 1963-75; mem. Reich, Adell & Crost (PLC), Los Angeles, 1975—. Adv. bd. Fifth St. Studio Theatre. Served with AUS, 1953-55. Home: 545 S Norton Ave Los Angeles CA 90020 Office: 501 Shatto Pl Los Angeles CA 90020

ADELMAN, ALBERT HARRY, research and development executive; b. N.Y.C., Dec. 17, 1930; s. Paul and Esther (Wolfson) A.; m. Myra E. Burt, June 8, 1952; children: Karen, Peter. B.S., Bklyn. Coll., 1951; Ph.D., Poly. Inst. Bklyn., 1956; grad., Exec. Devel. Program, Cornell U., 1978. Research asso. physics N.Y. U., 1956-60; mem. staff Columbus (Ohio) div. Battelle Meml. Inst., 1960—, sect. mgr., then dept. mgr., 1971-79, asso. dir., 1979—; responsible for research ops. at Battelle Columbus Lab., Battelle New Eng. Marine Research Lab., Duxbury, Mass. and C.F. Kettering Lab., Yellow Springs, Ohio. Author. Trustee Mid-Ohio Health Planning Fedn., 1980—. Served with AUS, 1956-57. Fellow Eastman Kodak Co., 1956, NSF, 1958. Fellow AAAS; mem. Sigma Xi. Patentee in field. Home: 90 W Jeffrey Pl Columbus OH 43214 Office: 505 King Ave Columbus OH 43201

ADELMAN, IRMA GLICMAN, economics educator; b. Cernowitz, Rumania, Mar. 14, 1930; came to U.S., 1949, naturalized, 1955; d. Jacob Max and Raissa (Ettinger) Glicman; m. Frank L. Adelman, Aug. 16, 1950 (div. 1979); 1 son, Alexander. B.S., U. Calif., Berkeley, 1950, M.A., 1951, Ph.D., 1955. Teaching asso. U. Calif., Berkeley, 1955-56, instr., 1956-57, lectr. with rank asst. prof., 1957-58; vis. asst. prof. Mills Coll., 1958-59; acting asst. prof. Stanford, 1959-61, asst. prof., 1961-62; asso. prof. Johns Hopkins, Balt., 1962-65; prof. econs. Northwestern U., Evanston, Ill., 1966-72, U. Md., 1972-78; prof. econs. and agrl. econs. U. Calif. at Berkeley, 1979—; cons. div. indsl. devel. UN, 1962-63, AID, U.S. Dept. State, Washington, 1963—, Internat. Bank Reconstrn. and Devel., 1968—, ILO, Geneva, 1973—. Author: Theories of Economic Growth and Development, 1961, (with A. Pepelasis and L. Mears) Economic Development: Analysis and Case Studies, 1961, (with Eric Thorbecke) The Theory and Design of Economic Development, 1966, (with C.T. Morris) Society, Politics and Economic Development—A Quantitative Approach, 1967, Practical Approaches to Development Planning-Korea's Second Five Year Plan, 1969, Economic Development and Social Equity in Developing Countries, 1973, (with Sherman Robinson) Planning for Income Distribution, 1977. Fellow Center Advanced Study Behavioral Scis., 1970-71. Fellow Am. Acad. Arts and Scis., Econometric Soc.; mem. Social Sci. Assembly, Nat. Acad. Scis., Am. Econ. Assn. (mem. exec. com., v.p. 1969—), Social Sci. Research Council (dir.-at-large), Comparative Econ. Assn. (exec. com.), Am. Statis. Assn. Office: Dept Agr and Natural Resources Univ Calif Berkeley CA 94720

ADELMAN, KENNETH LEE, government official, political scientist; b. Chgo., June 9, 1946; s. Harry and Corinne (Unger) A.; m. Carol Craigle, Aug. 29, 1971; children: Jessica Craigle, Jocelyn Craigle. B.A., Grinnell Coll., 1968; M.A., Georgetown U., 1969, Ph.D., 1975. With U.S. Dept. Commerce, Washington, 1968-70; spl. asst. VISTA, Washington, 1970-72; liason officer AID, Washington, 1975-76; asst. to Sec. Def., Washington, 1976-77; sr. polit. scientist Stanford Research Inst., Arlington, Va., 1977-81; ambassador, dep. permanent rep. U.S. Mission to the UN, N.Y.C., 1981-83; dir. ACDA, Washington, 1983—; instr. Shakespeare Georgetown U., 1977-79. Contbr. numerous articles to profl. jours., newspapers and mags. Mem. exec. bd. Com. Present Danger, 1979. Jewish. Office: Arms Control & Disarmament Agency 320 21st St NW Washington DC 20451

ADELMAN, WILLIAM JOHN, educator; b. Chgo., July 26, 1932; s. William Sidney and Annie Teresa (Goan) A.; m. Nora Jill Walters, June 26, 1952; children: Michelle, Marguerite, Marc, Michael, Jessica. Student, Lafayette Coll., 1952; B.A., Elmhurst Coll., 1956; M.A., U. Chgo., 1964. Tchr. Whitecross Sch., Hereford, Eng., 1956-57, Jefferson Sch., Berwyn, Ill., 1957-60, Morton High Sch., Berwyn, 1960-66; mem. faculty dept. labor and indsl. relations U. Ill., Chgo., 1966—, prof., 1978—; coordinator Chgo. Labor Edn. Program, 1981—. Author: Touring Pullman, 1972, Haymarket Revisited, 1976, Pilsen and the West Side, 1981; writer: film Packingtown U.S.A., 1968; narrator: Palace Cars and Paradise: Pullman's Model Town, 1983. Bd. dirs. Chgo. Regional Blood Program, 1977-80; mem. Ill. State Employent Security Adv. Bd., 1974-75; Democratic candidate U.S. Ho. of Reps. from 14th dist. Ill., 1970. Ill. Humanities Council grantee, 1977; German Marshall Fund U.S. grantee, 1977. Mem. Ill. Labor History (founding mem., v.p.), Am. Fedn. Tchrs. Unitarian. Home: 408 S Austin Blvd Oak Park IL 60304 Office: Box 4348 U Ill Chicago IL 60680

ADELMAN, WILLIAM JOSEPH, JR., biophysics educator; b. Mt. Vernon, N.Y., Jan. 29, 1928; s. William Joseph and Helen Emma (Carlock) A.; m. Jean Alma Mayo, Sept. 3, 1951; children: Everett M., John W., Willa J. B.S. (N.Y. State scholar), Fordham U., 1950; M.S., U. Vt., 1952; Ph.D. (Univ. fellow), U. Rochester, N.Y., 1955. Aviation physiologist Sch. Aviation Medicine, Randolph AFB, Tex., 1955-56; instr., then asst. prof. physiology U. Buffalo Med. Sch., 1956-59; neurophysiologist Nat. Inst. Neurol. Diseases and Blindness, NIH, Bethesda, Md., 1959-62; asso. prof., then prof. physiology U. Md. Med. Sch., 1962-71, dir. physiology tng. program, 1963-71; dir. excitable membrane tng. program Marine Biol. Lab., Woods Hole, Mass., 1968-71, trustee, 1971-74; chief lab. biophysics NINCDS, NIH, 1971—; vis. scientist Cambridge (Eng.) U., 1960. Editor: Biophysics and Physiology of Excitable Membranes, 1971, The Biophysical Approach to Excitable Systems, 1981, Structure and Functions in Excitable Cells, 1983; Contbr. articles to profl. jours. NIH spl. fellow, 1969-70. Fellow AAAS; mem. Am. Physiol. Soc., Biophys. Soc., Soc. Gen. Physiologists, N.Y.Acad.Scis., Soc. for Neurosci. Office: LB NINCDS NIH Marine Biol Lab Woods Hole MA 02543

ADELMANN, FREDERICK JOSEPH, philosophy educator; b. Norwood, Mass., Feb. 18, 1915; s. Frederick Michael and Helen Margaret (Casey) A. A.B., Boston Coll., 1937, M.A., 1942; S.T.L., Weston Coll., 1948; Ph.D., St. Louis U., 1955. Entered Soc. of Jesus; ordained priest Roman Catholic Ch., 1947; instr. math. and physics Army Specialized Tng. Program, Boston Coll., 1942-44, asst. prof. philosophy, 1955-68, asso. prof. philosophy, 1968-70, prof., 1970—; chmn. dept., 1955-65; ascetical theology Exerzitienhaus Rottmannshohe, Germany, 1949-50; teaching fellow philosophy, St. Louis U., 1950-54; lectr. philosophy Weston (Mass.) Coll. Author: From Dialogue to Epilogue, 1968, (with others) Guide to Marxist Philosophy, 1972; Editor: Demythologizing Marxism, 1969, Authority, 1974, Philosophical Investigation in the USSR, 1975, Philosophy in the USSR Revisted, 1977, Contemporary Chinese Philosophy, 1982; Editor in chief: The Quest for the Absolute, 1966. Mem. AAUP, Am. Philos. Assn., Jesuit Philos. Assn., Realist Soc. Address: Boston College Chestnut Hill MA 02167

ADELMANN, HOWARD BERNHARDT, educator; b. Buffalo, May 8, 1898; s. Charles Michael and Louise Henrietta (Kohler) A.; m. Dorothy May Schullian, July 6, 1978. A.B., Cornell U., 1920, A.M., 1922, Ph.D., 1924; student, U. Freiburg, Germany, 1927; Sc.D. honoris causa, Ohio State U., 1962, M.D., U. Bologna, Italy, 1972. Asst. histology and embryology Cornell U., 1919-21, instr., 1921-25, asst. prof., 1925-37, prof., 1937—, chmn. dept. zoology, 1944-59, faculty rep. bd. trustees, 1947-51. Author: The Embryological Treatises of Hieronymus Fabricius (Crofts prize Cornell U. Press 1942), Marcello Malpighi and the Evolution of Embryology, 5 vols, (Pfizer award History of Science Soc. 1966); editor: The Correspondence of Marcello Malpighi, 5 vols, 1975; Asso. editor: Jour. Morphology, 1948-51; Contbr. sci. papers to profl. jours. NRC fellow biol. sci., 1927-28; Recipient Galileo Galilei prize U. Pisa, Italy, 1972; decorated Order Star Italian Solidarity, Italy, 1962; hon. citizenship Crevalcore, Italy, 1977. Fellow Institut Internat. d'Embryologie (Amsterdam); mem. Am. Assn. Anatomists, Am. Soc. Zoologists, Hist. Sci. Soc., Am. Assn. History Medicine (William H. Welch medal 1967), Internat. Acad. History Medicine, Phi Beta Kappa, Sigma Xi, Phi Kappa Phi. Republican. Lutheran. Home: 400 Triphammer Rd Apt L-1 Ithaca NY 14850

ADELS, ROBERT MITCHELL, journalist; b. Bklyn., June 5, 1948; s. Seymour I. and Regina (Cohan) A. B.A., U. Pa., 1969, M.A., 1971. Program dir. radio sta. WXPN, Phila., 1966-67; profl. rep. Jobete Music Pub. Co., N.Y.C., 1973; research asst. Annenberg Sch., 1970-71; freelance advt. copywriter, 1975—; buyer Los Angeles br. ABC Records & Tapes, 1976-77; dir. editorial services Gribbitt, 1977—; co-dir., co-founder (Musicsearch), 1977—. Writer-producer, Repertoire Theatre of the Air, WXPN-FM, Phila., 1968-69; contbg. editor: Friday Morning Quarterback, Phila., 1970-72; editor: Cash Box, N.Y.C., 1971-73; Music critic, Phila. Daily News, 1969-71; free-lance music critic, 1970—; revs. editor: Record World, 1973-75; Contbr. articles to profl. jours. Mem. NARAS. Home: 9000 Cynthia St Los Angeles CA 90069 Office: 5419 Sunset Blvd Los Angeles CA 90027

ADELSMAN, H(ARRIETTE) JEAN, editor; b. Indpls., Oct. 21, 1944; d. Joe and Beatrice Irene (Samuel) A. B.S.J., Northwestern U., 1966, M.S.J., 1967. Copy editor: Chgo. Sun-Times, 1967-75; fin. news editor, 1975-77; entertainment editor, 1977-80; asst. mng. editor/features, 1980—. Mem. Kappa Tau Alpha. Office: Chgo Sun-Times 401 N Wabash Ave Chicago IL 60611

ADELSON, HOWARD LAURENCE, history educator; b. Bklyn., July 16, 1925; s. Moses Hirsch and Esther (Finkelstein) A.; m. Helen Ruth Gottesman, Aug. 17, 1958 (div. 1970); children: Mark Hirsch, Sarah Phoebe. B.A., NYU, 1945; M.A., Columbia U., 1948, Princeton U., 1950, Ph.D., 1952. Instr. Princeton, 1952; instr. U. Ala., 1952; vis. lectr. Kyungsanbukto U., Taegu, Korea, 1953; prof. Coll. City N.Y., 1954—, chmn. dept. history, 1969-72; instr. N.Y. U., 1957-58; dir. Summer Seminar in Econ. History, 1960; exec. officer Ph.D. Program in History, City U., N.Y., 1966-69; dir. Univ. Centers for Rational Alternatives, Nat. Commn. on Am. Fgn. Policy.; Dir. studies Summer Seminar in Numismatics, 1954-69. Author: Light Weight Solidi and Byzantine Trade in the Sixth and Seventh Centuries, 1957, History of the American Numismatic Society, 1958, Medieval Commerce, 1962, (with George L. Kustas) A Bronze Hoard of the Period of Leo I, 1962, (with Robert Baker) The Oath of Purgation of Pope Leo III, Traditio VIII, 1952, The Holy Lance and the Hereditary German Monarchy, The Art Bulletin, 1966; Editorial bd.: American Zionist, 1969-74, Studies in Medieval and Renaissance History, 1963-69; editor, 1969-72. Trustee, chmn. acad. council Am. Friends Hebrew U., v.p., 1981; chmn. nat. council United Zionist Revisionists of Am.; mem. exec. com. Am. Zionist Fedn., 1981; bd. dirs. Nat. Com. on Am. Fgn. Policy, Brookdale Hosp. Med. Center; bd. govs. Bklyn. Jewish Center; v.p. Am. Friends Hebrew U.; asso. mem. bd. govs. Hebrew U., 1980, bd. overseers Rothberg Sch. for Overseas Students. Served with AUS, 1947-48; Served with USAF, 1952-54. Newell fellow, 1951; Volker Fund research grantee, 1960; recipient Jabotinsky Centennial medal, 1980. Fellow Am. Numismatic Soc.; mem. Am. Hist. Assn., Archaeol. Inst. Am., Am. Philol. Assn., Medieval Acad. Am., Jewish Publ. Soc. Am. (publ. com.), Zionist Orgn. Am. Clubs: Princeton, Men's Faculty Club Columbia U. (N.Y.C.). Home: 135 Eastern Pkwy Brooklyn NY 11238

ADELSON, MARVIN, educator; b. Bklyn., May 29, 1926; s. Isidore and Mollie (Gassner) A.; m. Ellen Arendale Denham, Apr. 1, 1961 (div. Apr. 18, 1975); 1 son, David William; m. Yolande Hargrave Chambers, Aug. 11, 1979. Student, Bklyn. Coll., 1942-43, Harvard U., 1943-44; B.S., Va. Poly. Inst., 1947; A.M., U. Ill., 1950; Ph.D. (Univ. fellow), U. Ill., 1952. Asst. prof. psychology, research assoc. aviation psychology lab. U. Ill. at Urbana, 1952-55; mgr. command control and infor. systems dept. Hughes Aircraft Co., Los Angeles and Fullerton, Calif., 1955-61; prin. scientist System Devel. Corp., Santa Monica, Calif., 1961-69; on leave as exec. dir. com. utlzn. sci. and engring. manpower Nat. Acad. Scis., 1963-64; co-founder, v.p., dir. Info. Transfer Corp., Santa Monica, 1969-70; lectr. architecture and urban design Sch. Architecture and Urban Planning, UCLA, 1969-70, prof., 1970—; also dir. Creative Problem Solving Program, 1971-76; dir. Urban Innovations Group, Los Angeles, 1971-72, 77—; Cons. planning, manpower, systems devel., edn. to firms, govt. agys., univs., founds., non-profit orgns.; founder, mem. adv. bd. Inst. for the Future, Menlo Park, Calif., 1969—; Mem. study group on alternatives Los Angeles Goals Project, 1969; program mgr. Calif. Gov.'s Commn. on Los Angeles Riots, 1965; mem. Los Angeles regional task force on corrections Calif. Council Criminal Justice, 1968-71; mem. study group on an Inst. for Applied Sci. and Social change in a Rural Area, Nat. Acad. Scis., 1969-71. Contbr. articles profl. jours.; Mem. editorial bd.: Jour. Systems Engring, 1970—, Technol. Forecasting and Social Change, 1969—, Education and Urban Soc, 1970—, Instructional Sci, 1971—, Jour. Edn. Tech, 1971—, The Info. Soc, 1980—. Bd. dirs., pres. Family Service, Los Angeles, 1967-74. Served with AUS, 1944-46. Mem. A.A.A.S., Sigma Xi. Home: 228 Monte Grigio Dr Pacific Palisades CA 90272 Office: Grad Sch. Architecture and Urban Planning U Calif Los Angeles CA 90024

ADELSON, MERVYN LEE, film production executive; b. Los Angeles, Oct. 23, 1929; s. Nathan and Pearl (Schwarzman) A.; m. Gail Kenaston, 1974; children from previous marriage: Ellen, Gary, Andrew. Ed., Menlo Park Jr. Coll. Pres. Market Town Builders, Las Vegas, 1957-63; partner Paradise Builders, Las Vegas, 1958-60; pres. Paradise Devel. Co., Las Vegas, from 1960; v.p. Realty Holdings, Inc., Las Vegas, from 1976; pres. Rancho La Costa, Inc., Carlsbad, from 1963; chmn. bd. Lorimar Prodns., Inc., Culver City, Calif., 1967—. Mem. Am. Film Inst., Acad. Motion Pictures. Clubs: La Costa Country, Las Vegas Country. *

ADELSTEIN, S(TANLEY) JAMES, physician, educator; b. N.Y.C., Jan. 24, 1928; s. George and Belle (Schild) A.; m. Mary Charlesworth Taylor, Sept. 20, 1957; children—Joseph Burrows, Elizabeth Dunster. B.S., M.I.T., 1949, M.S., 1949, Ph.D. in Biophysics (Nat. Found. fellow), 1957; M.D., Harvard U., 1953. Med. house officer Peter Bent Brigham Hosp., Boston, 1953-54, sr. asst. resident physician, 1957-58, chief resident, 1959-60; fellow Howard Hughes Med. Inst., 1957-58,

Henry A. and Camilus Christian fellow, 1959-60; Moseley Traveling fellow Harvard U., 1958-59; instr. anatomy Harvard Med. Sch., 1961-65, asst. prof., 1965-68, asso. prof. radiology, 1968-72, prof., 1972—, dean for acad. programs, 1978—; mem. Nat. Council for Radiation Protection Measurements, 1978—, dir., 1980—; cons. Med. Found. fellow, 1960-63. Mem. editorial bd.: Investigative Radiology, 1972-80, Postgrad. Radiology; asso. editor: Jour. Nuclear Medicine, 1975-81; contbr. articles to profl. jours. Trustee Am. Bd. Nuclear Medicine, 1972-78, sec., 1975-78. NIH Career Devel. awardee, 1965-68; Fogarty Sr. Internat. fellow, 1976. Mem. Am. Chem. Soc., Biophys. Soc., Assn. for Radiation Research, Radiation Research Soc. (councillor 1975-78), Soc. Nuclear Medicine (trustee 1970-74), Am. Coll. Nuclear Physicians, Boylston Med. Soc., Sigma Xi, Tau Beta Pi, Alpha Omega Alpha. Office: Harvard Med Sch 25 Shattuck St Boston MA 02215

ADEN, ARTHUR LAVERNE, office systems company executive; b. Ford County, Ill., Feb. 1, 1924; s. Johann Franzen and Ida Magda (Hafermann) A.; m. Leona A. Hoff, June 21, 1944; children: Donald A., Charles R., Sherry L., Gary D. Student, No. Ill. State Coll., 1941-43, U. Mich. and Air Force Tech. Tng. Commd., 1943-44; M.A., Harvard U., 1948, M.E.S., 1949, Ph.D., 1950. Sect. head Cambridge Research Center, 1950-53; asst. lab. mgr., engring. mgr. Sylvania Electric Procuts, 1953-58; with Motorola, Inc., 1958-63, Xerox Corp., Dallas, 1963—; now mgr. central engring. Office Products div. Contbr. in field. Served with AC U.S. Army, 1943-46. NRC fellow, 1948-50. Fellow IEEE (ann. award Phoenix sect. 1963); mem. Am. Phys. Soc., Am. Mgmt. Assn., Sigma Xi, Sigma Zeta. Lutheran. Office: 1341 W Mockingbird Ln Dallas TX 75247 *

ADER, RICHARD H., financial services executive; b. N.Y.C., Mar. 28, 1942; s. Nathan and Etta (Schecter) A.; m. Pamela Bennett, Jan. 2, 1965; children: Jason, Jennifer. B.S., U. Vt., 1963; postgrad., Pace U., 1966. Trust officer Chem. Bank, N.Y.C.; sr. exec. v.p. Integrated Resources, Inc., N.Y.C., 1971—; pres. Am. Property Investors, N.Y.C., 1978—; chmn. bd. Vista Properties, 1983—. Vice chmn. Manhattan div. Israel Bonds, 1982—. Served with Army N.G., 1963-69. Home: Brookwillows Woodland Rd Harrison NY 10528 Office: Integrated Resources Inc 666 3rd Ave New York NY 10017

ADER, ROBERT, psychologist, educator; b. N.Y.C., Feb. 20, 1932; s. Nathan and Mae (Levine) A.; m. Gayle Simon, June 2, 1957; children: Deborah, Janet, Norine, Leslie. B.S., Tulane U., 1953; Ph.D., Cornell U., 1957. Mem. faculty U. Rochester (N.Y.) Sch. Medicine and Dentistry, 1957—, prof. psychiatry and psychology, 1968—, prof. medicine, 1982—, George L. Engel prof. psychosocial medicine, 1983—, dir. div. behavioral and psychosocial medicine, 1982—; vis. prof. Rudolf Magnus Inst. Pharmacology, U. Utrecht (Netherlands) Med. Faculty, 1970-71; bd. dirs. Am. Inst. Stress, 1981—; adv. bd. Inst. Advancement Health, 1982—. Author numerous papers in field.; editor Psychoneuromunnology, 1981; editorial bd. profl. jours. Recipient Research Career Devel. award USPHS, 1964-69, Research Scientist award, 1969-84. Mem. Am. Psychosomatic Soc. (pres. 1979-80), Internat. Soc. Devel. Psychobiology (pres. 1981-82), Am. Psychol. Assn., Psychonomic Soc., Acad. Behavioral Medicine Research, AAUP, Eastern Psychol. Assn. Office: Dept Psychiatry U Rochester Med Center Rochester NY 14642

ADERHOLD, VICTOR WAYNE, broadcasting station executive; b. North Augusta, S.C., Mar. 28, 1941; s. Harvey Jordon and Vivian (Washington) A.; m. Barbara Jane Flowers, Sept. 25, 1971; 1 dau., Amy Blair. A.B.J., U. Ga., 1964. Sales rep. Sta. WPLO, Atlanta, 1968-74; sales mgr. Sta. WKLS, Atlanta, 1974-78; gen. mgr. Sta. WAIV, Jacksonville, Fla., 1979; gen. mgr., v.p. Sta. WFYV-FM, Jacksonville, 1980—. Served with U.S. Army, 1966-68. Decorated Bronze Star. Mem. Jacksonville Advt. Fedn. (dir.), Nat. Assn. Rec. Arts and Scis. (dir.), Di Gamma Kappa (past pres.), Sigma Delta Chi. Baptist. Home: 4308 Sage Oak Ct Jacksonville FL 32211 Office: 9090 Hogan Rd Jacksonville FL 32216

ADERS, ROBERT O., food co. exec.; b. Bridgeton, Ind., Apr. 21, 1927; s. Oral M. and Frieda (Howell) A.; m. Tabitha Simpson, Aug. 1975. B.S., Miami U., 1947; J.D., Ind. U., 1951. Bar: Ind. bar 1951, Ohio bar 1958, D.C. bar 1974. Teaching fellow Ind. U., 1951-52; trial atty. U.S. Dept. Justice, 1954-57; with Kroger Co., 1957—, gen. counsel, 1962-68, v.p., 1964-70, chmn. bd., 1970-74; also dir.; under sec. U.S. Dept. Labor, 1975-76; pres. Food Mktg. Inst., 1976—. Served with USNR, 1944-46, 52-54. Office: 1750 K St NW Washington DC 20006

ADIKES, PARK THOMAS, banker, lawyer; b. N.Y.C., Apr. 18, 1931; s. John and Ann (Linz) A.; m. Maryedith Anderson, Aug. 9, 1952; 1 dau., Patricia. B.S.S., Georgetown U., 1953; LL.B., N.Y. U., 1957. Bar: N.Y. 1958. With Williamsburgh Savs. Bank, Bklyn., 1953-54; with Jamaica Savs. Bank, Lynbrook, N.Y., 1954—, exec. v.p., 1965-67, pres., 1967-73, chmn. bd., 1973—, also trustee. Mem. bd. mgrs. Central Queens YMCA., Queens C. of C. (v.p., dir.). Roman Catholic. Clubs: Wheatley Hills Golf, Lawrence Beach, Village Bath, Manhasset Bay Yacht. Home: 87 Robbins Dr East Williston NY 11596 Office: 303 Merrick Rd Lynbrook NY 11564

ADISMAN, I. KENNETH, dentist; b. N.Y.C., Aug. 3, 1919; s. Joseph and Frances (Gertz) A.; m. Joan Sugarman, Aug. 27, 1957; children: Leslie, Kathryn. Student, Mich. State Coll., 1935-37; D.D.S., U. Buffalo, 1940; M.S., N.Y. U., 1960. Diplomate: Am. Bd. Prosthodontics (examiner; pres. 1980). Attending dentist N.Y. U. Med. Center, U. Hosp., N.Y.C., 1960-78; prof. dept. removable prosthodontics, dir. maxillofacial prosthetics Dental Center, 1978—, chmn. dept., 1978—; attending dentist Meml. Hosp., N.Y.C., 1976-78; pres. Greater N.Y. Acad. Prosthodontics Research Found., 1980; pres., dir. Internat. Circuit Courses, Inc. of Am. Prosthodontic Soc. Sect. editor: Jour. Prosthetic Dentistry, 1975-78. Served to maj. Dental Corps, U.S. Army, 1942-46. Fellow Acad. Denture Prosthetics, Acad. Maxillofacial Prosthetics; mem. Am. Coll. Dentists, Internat. Coll. Dentists, Greater N.Y. Acad. Prosthodontics, N.Y. Acad. Dentistry, N.Y. Acad. Sci. Clubs: Harmonie, Century. Office: 100 Central Park S New York NY 10019 *Life is an adventure with a beginning and an end. How we live it is our decision. What happens in life may not be by choice. The essence of life is achievement of one's goals—to succeed over obstacles and disappointments by the inner qualities of determination, persistence and faith. The grace of life is helping our fellow man.*

ADKERSON, J(OSEPH) CARSON, retired mining engineer; b. Lynchburg, Va., Feb. 10, 1892; s. Alonza Thomas and Lizzie Lillian (Carson) A.; m. Anne Winfield Clower, Mar. 11, 1961. Registered profl. mining engr., Va., D.C. Asst. engr. Piedmont-Manganese Corp., Lynchburg, 1912-13, Oxford Mining & Manganese Corp., 1913-14; engr., mgr. Powells Fort Manganese Mines, Woodstock, Va., 1915-19; v.p., engr. mgr. Hy-Grade Manganese Co., Woodstock, 1919-36; v.p., engr. Hy-Grade Manganese Prodn. & Sales Corp., Woodstock, 1929-32, Nat. Metals Corp., Damascus, Va., 1940-42; pres. Raw Materials Nat. Council, 1936-68; cons. engr. Cuban Am. Manganese Corp., N.Y.C., 1940-45. Chmn. Joint Conf. of Unfair Russian Competition, 1930-33; Mem. session Woodstock Presbyterian Ch., 1978-80. Recipient Outstanding Citizen award Woodstock C. of C., 1979. Mem. Am. Manganese Producers Assn. (pres. 1927-62). Clubs: Masons, Shriners, Rotary. Engaged in investigation and research work, manganese, tungsten, other strategic minerals. Home: 302 N Main St Woodstock VA 22664

ADKINS, ARTHUR WILLIAM HOPE, humanities educator; b. Leicester, Eng., Oct. 17, 1929; s. Archibald Arthur and Nora (Hope) A.; m. Elizabeth Mary Cullingford, Sept. 16, 1961; children—Matthew, Deborah. B.A., Oxford U., 1952, M.A., 1955, D.Phil., 1957. Asst. in humanities U. Glasgow, Scotland, 1954-56; lectr. Greek Bedford Coll., U. London, 1956-61; fellow in classical langs. and lit. Exeter Coll., Oxford U., 1961-65; prof. classics U. Reading, Eng., 1965-74; successively Edward Olson prof. Greek, prof. philosophy and early Christian lit. U. Chgo., 1974—; sr. vis. fellow Soc. Humanities, Cornell U., 1969-70. Author: books in field including Merit and Responsibility: A Study in Greek Values, 1960, From the Many to the One, 1970, Moral Values and Political Behavior in Ancient Greece, 1972. Mem. Am. Philological Assn., Classical Assn. Gt. Britain, Soc. Promotion of Hellenic Studies., Am. Philos. Assn. Home: 5416 S University Ave Chicago IL 60615 Office: Classics Dept Univ Chicago 1050 E 59th St Chicago IL 60637

ADKINS, DOUG, professional sports team executive, lawyer. V.p., counsel The Dallas Mavericks, Nat. Basketball Assn. Office: The Dallas Mavericks Reunion Arena 777 Sports St Dallas TX 75207§

ADKINS, HOWARD EUGENE, aluminum co. exec.; b. Depoy, Ky., Oct. 4, 1912; s. Elmer Eugene and Mattie Luvenia (Merrill) A.; m. Wilma Lucille Jenkins, Sept. 18, 1937; children—Howard Eugene Jr., Michael Ray, Wilma Carol, Martha Lee. B.A., Western Ky. State U., 1940; M.S., U. Wis., 1950. Tchr. pub. schs., Ky., 1934-42; asst. prof. to asso. prof. U. Wis., 1947-57; welding engr., then mgr. welding engring. tech. services Kaiser Aluminum and Chem. Sales, Inc., Rosemont, Ill., 1957-74, asst. dir. field tech. operations, 1974-77; pres. Howard E. Adkins and Assos. Inc., welding engring. firm, Park Ridge, Ill., 1978—; cons., lectr. in field. Contbr. articles to profl. lit. Served with USAAF, AUS, 1943-45. Recipient Bronze medallion and certificate Lincoln Arc Welding Found., 1953, Tech. Services Engring. award of Merit Kaiser Aluminum, 1969. Mem. Am. Welding Soc. (hon., Howard E. Adkins' Instr. Mem. award 1964, Meritorious certificate 1967, Lincoln Gold medal 1963, certificate Madison sect. 1966, Nat. Meritorious certificate and award 1974, dir. 1970-73, 76—, dir. aluminum assn. welding and joining com. 1970-71, 73), Am. Soc. Metals, Phi Delta Kappa. Republican. Methodist. Club: Mason. Home and office: 424 N Ashland Park Ridge IL 60068 *As a teacher, college professor and welding engineer, I have strived to fulfill my professional responsibilities with integrity, conscientiousness and perseverance - and with one more trait - enthusiasm. I have learned that perseverance can lag without enthusiasm. To always maintain a healthy enthusiastic spirit has not been easy. There have been many times in my professional life when I have had to stop - evaluate my personal outlook - and regenerate this most important ingredient. For without this, a most important assignment can be boring, dull, nothing. With it, the most mediocre task can be an enjoyable and rewarding experience.*

ADKINS, JOHN NATHANIEL, geophysicist; b. Spokane, Wash., July 23, 1911; s. John Dauford and Martha Ellen (Cabbage) A.; m. Katherine Owen Jackson, May 17, 1941. Student, Stanford, 1927-28, Sacramento Jr. Coll., 1930-32; A.B in Physics, U. Calif., 1936; Ph.D. in Seismology (U. fellow 1936-38), 1939, Mass. Inst. Tech., 1939-41. Staff div. war research Columbia, 1941-45; supervising engr. antennas Airborne Instruments Lab., Inc., N.Y.C., 1945-46; asst. prof. geophysics Mass. Inst. Tech., 1946-48; head geophysics br. Office Naval Research, 1948-49; dir. earth scis. div., 1949-58, dep. sci. dir., 1954-58, asso. research dir., 1958-59, asst. chief scientist, 1959-72; Chmn. div. earth scis. NRC, 1958-60. Fellow Geol. Soc. Am., A.A.A.S.; mem. Phi Beta Kappa, Sigma Xi, Theta Tau. Club: Talbot Country. Home: Martingham PO Box 757 St Michaels MD 21663

ADKISSON, PERRY LEE, university official; b. Hickman, Ark., Mar. 11, 1929; s. Robert Louise and Imogene (Perry) A.; m. Frances Rozelle, Dec. 29, 1956; 1 dau., Jean Amanda. B.S., U. Ark., 1950, M.S., 1954; Ph.D. in Entomology, Kans. State U., 1956. Asst. prof. entomology U. Mo., 1956-58; asso. prof. Tex. A&M U., 1958-63, prof., 1963—; Disting. prof. entomology, 1979—, head dept. entomology, 1967—, v.p. for agr. and renewable resources, 1978-80, dep. chancellor for agr., 1980-83, dep. chancellor, 1983—; cons. Internat. AEC, Vienna, 1969-74; Chmn. sci. adv. panel Gov. Tex. on Agrl. Chems., 1970-72; chmn. Tex. Pesticide Adv. Com., 1971—; mem. panel experts on integrated pest control UN/FAO, Rome, 1971—; mem. Structural Pest Control Bd., Tex., 1971-78, NRC World Food and Nutrition Study Team, 1977; chmn. com. biology pest species NRC, 1974; mem. environ. studies bd., study group problems pest control Nat. Acad. Sci.-NRC, 1972—; mem. vis. group Internat. Center Insect Physiology and Ecology, Nairobi, Kenya, 1974-75; mem. U.S. directorate UNESCO Man and the Biosphere Program, 1975—. Mem.: editorial com. Ann. Rev. Entomology, 1973—; contr. articles to profl. jours. Served with M.C. AUS, 1951-53. Recipient Alexander Von Humboldt award, 1980; Disting. Alumnus award Kans. State U., 1980; USPHS postdoctoral fellow Harvard U., 1963-64. Fellow AAAS; mem. Entomol. Soc. Am. (governing bd. 1971-79, pres. 1974, Bussart Meml. award 1967), Kans. Entomol. Soc., Internat. Orgn. Biol. Control, Am. Registry Profl. Entomologists (governing council 1976-78, pres. 1977), Nat. Acad. Scis., Phi Kappa Phi, Sigma Xi.

ADKISSON, RICHARD BLANKS, state supreme ct. justice; b. Little Rock, Ark., Oct. 12, 1932; s. Sam E. and Kathleen (Blanks) A.; m. Lila Matthews, Dec. 27, 1955; m. Virginia Ledbetter, Dec. 5, 1959; children—Lila Somers, Virginia Sheb, Katherine Sterling; m. Katheryn P. Johnson, May 21, 1975. B.S. in Bus. Adminstrn, U. Ark., 1957; LL.B., 1959; grad., Nat. Coll. Judiciary, 1970, Inst. Jud. Adminstrn. N.Y. U., 1981. Bar: Ark. bar 1959. Chief asst. atty. gen. State of Ark., 1963-66; pros. atty. 6th Judicial Dist., Little Rock, 1967-70, circuit ct. judge, Ark., 1971-81; chief justice Ark. Supreme Ct., 1981—. Served with USAF, 1951-54. Mem. ABA, Ark. Bar Assn., Pulaski County Bar Assn., Am. Judges Assn., Nat. Dist. Pros. Attys. Assn. (dir. 1967, 68), Ark. Pros. Attys. Assn. (pres. 1969, 70), Am. Legion, Sigma Alpha Epsilon, Delta Theta Phi. Democrat. Baptist. Club: Lions. Office: Justice Bldg Little Rock AR 72201

ADLER, AARON, advertising agency executive; b. Chgo., Jan. 31, 1917; s. Abraham and Rachel A.; m. Alice Gamberg, Aug. 10, 1941; children: Michael L., Allan J., Jody R. Student bus., Northwestern U., 1932-36. Copywriter Salem N. Baskin Advt. Agy., Chgo., 1937-40, Gourfain Cobb Advt. Agy., 1941-43; copywriter-account exec. William Hart Adler Advt. Agy., Chgo., 1946-49; copywriter, account exec. Olian Advt. Agy., Chgo., 1949-53; v.p. Gourfain-Loeff & Adler Advt. Agy., Chgo., 1953-66; exec. v.p., partner Stone & Adler Advt. Agy., Chgo., 1966-77, pres., 1977—; pres. Adler Corp., Chgo., 1966—; sec. Discovery House, mail order catalog co., Irvine, Calif., 1973-79; chmn. Bull. Atomic Scientists, Chgo., 1976—. Pres. North Shore Sch. of Jewish Studies, Evanston, 1964-66; bd. dirs. Albert Einstein Peace Prize Found., 1980; trustee Spertus Coll. Judaica. Served with M.C. U.S. Army, 1943-46. Mem. Direct Mail Mktg. Assn., Catalog Mailers Council, Chgo. Advt. Club, Am. Soc. Technion, Sierra Club, Exec. Service Corps. Office: 2834 Birchwood Wilmette IL 60091

ADLER, ARTHUR M., JR., management and chemical company executive; b. Chgo., Jan. 14, 1917; s. Arthur M. and Alma A.; m. Joan Greenebaum, Aug. 30, 1940; children: Jamie E., Wendy J., A. Michael. Student, Dartmouth Coll., 1935-38; B.S., Northwestern U., 1939. With Helene Curtis Industries, Inc., Chgo., 1940-73, v.p., 1956-66, exec. v.p., 1966-67, also dir., pres., 1967-73; pres. Arthur M. Adler & Co., Northfield, Ill., 1973—; dir. Groveland Health Services, 1982—. Mem. budget com. Community Fund Met. Chgo., 1970—, mem. central rev. com., 1968—, chmn. allocations com., vice chmn. agy. services com., 1970-76; Pres. bd. trustees Highland Park (Ill.) Hosp. Found., 1962-68, life trustee, 1968—. Home: 2385 Egandale Rd Highland Park IL 60035 Office: 550 Frontage Rd Northfield IL 60093

ADLER, DAVID, physicist; b. Bronx, N.Y., Apr. 13, 1935; s. Saul and Betty (Kopelman) A.; m. Alice Joan Salzman, June 8, 1958; children: Kyle, Andrew, Carrie. B.S., Rensselaer Poly. Inst., 1956; A.M. (Leeds and Northrup fellow), Harvard U., 1958; Ph.D. (NSF Coop. Grad. fellow), Harvard U., 1964. Research assoc. U.K. Atomic Energy Research Establishment, Harwell, Eng., 1964-65; research assoc. MIT, 1965-67, asst. prof. elec. engring., 1967-69, assoc. prof., 1969-75, prof., 1975—; lectr. Franco-Russian Summer Sch., Montpellier, France, 1971, Queen's U., 1974, Latin Am. Summer Sch., Venezuela, 1976, U. Campinas, Brazil, 1976, McMaster U., 1977, U. N.C., 1979, NATO, 1979, Kyoto (Japan) Summer Inst., 1980, U. Montreal, 1981, Caracas, Venezuela, 1982, U.N.C.C., 1983; chmn. Solar Photovoltaic Panel, Solar Energy Workshop, 1975; mem. com. basic research NRC, 1973-76; mem. organizing com. Internat. Symposium on Electronic Properties of Oxides, 1974, 6th Joint U.S.-USSR Symposium on Theory of Condensed Matter, 1976; co-chmn. 8th Internat. Conf. on Amorphous and Liquid Semiconductors, 1978; chmn. 1st Workshop on Threshold Switching, 1980; mem. external rev. com. NSF-MRL program Purdue U., 1978-81; chmn. SPIE Conf. Photorotaics for Solar Energy Applications, 1983. Author: Amorphous Semiconductors, 1971, Tokei Rikigaku oyobi Netsu Rikigaku, 1983; editor: Sci. and Tech. in Non-Crystalline Semicondrs., 1982; Editorial bd.: Jour. Nonmetals, 1971-76, Semicondrs. and Insulators, 1976—, Jour. Applied Physics, 1979—, Applied Physics Letters, 1979—; regional editor: Jour. Non-Crystalline Solids, 1981—; assoc. editor: Materials Research Bull., 1983—. Treas. Community Nursery Sch., Lexington, Mass., 1971-73, Maria Hastings PTA, Lexington, 1974-75. Recipient McKinney prize Rensselaer Poly. Inst., 1954, Gold medal Soc. Actuaries, 1955. Fellow Am. Phys. Soc. (exec. com. div. solid state physics), Am. Phy. Soc. (chmn. program com. conf. Defects in Amorphous Materials 1984); mem. IEEE (sr.), Am. Vacuum Soc. (sr.). Home: 10 Nickerson Rd Lexington MA 02173 Office: 77 Massachusetts Ave Room 13 3050 Cambridge MA 02139

ADLER, FRANCIS HEED, retired medical educator; b. Phila., Feb. 4, 1895; s. Lewis H. and Emma Augusta (Heed) A.; m. Emily Anne MacDonald, July 7, 1970; children by previous marriage: Jeanne Morris Adler Scott, Lynn. A.B., U. Pa., 1916, M.S., 1918, M.D., 1919. Diplomate: Am. Bd. Ophthalmology (sec.-treas.). Intern Hosp. U. Pa., 1919-21; mem. faculty U. Pa. Med. Sch., 1921-77, prof. ophthalmology, 1937-60, emeritus, 1960-77. Author: Physiology of the Eye, 1950, Text Book of Ophthalmology, 1941; cons. editor: Jour. Ophthalmology, 1960-65. Served with U.S. Army, World War I. Recipient Lucian Howe medal U. Buffalo, 1960, Proctor medal Assn. Research Ophthalmology, 1967. Mem. Am. Opthal. Soc. (Howe medal 1951), AMA (medal ophthalmology 1959, editor-in-chief), Archives Ophthalmology (1950-60), Am. Acad. Ophthalmology and Otolaryngology (pres. 1969). Clubs: Union League, Cricket (Phila.). Home: 8870 Towanda St Philadelphia PA 19118

ADLER, FRED PETER, electronics company executive; b. Vienna, Austria, Mar. 29, 1925; came to U.S., 1942, naturalized, 1947; s. Michael and Ellida (Bronner) A.; m. Christine Austin, 1971; children: Michael Steven, Andrew David. B.E.E. with honors, UCLA, 1945; M.E.E. (Charles A. Coffin fellow), Calif. Inst. Tech., 1948; Ph.D. magna cum laude, Calif. Inst. Tech., 1950. Elec. engr. Gen. Electric Co. Research and Cons. Labs., 1945-47; project engr. Jet Propulsion Lab., 1950; with Hughes Aircraft Co., 1950-70, sr. staff physicist, dept. mgr., 1954-57, mgr. advanced planning, 1957-59, dir. advanced projects labs., 1959-61, v.p., mgr. space systems div., 1961-66, v.p., asst. group exec., 1966-70; pres. Nadgeco Ltd., 1970-72, chmn. bd., 1973—; v.p., group exec. aerospace groups Hughes Aircraft Co., 1973-81, sr. v.p., pres. electro-optical and data systems group, 1981—; dir. Thomas Jefferson Research Ctr., 1973—. Co-author: text Guided Missile Engineering, 1959; also articles tech. jours. Fellow Am. Inst. Aeros. and Astronautics; mem. N.Y. Acad. Scis., Sigma Xi, Tau Beta Pi.

ADLER, FREDA SCHAFFER (MRS. G. O. W. MUELLER), criminologist, educator; b. Phila., Nov. 21, 1934; d. David and Lucia G. (de Wolfson) Schaffer; children by previous marriage: Mark, Jill, Nancy. B.A., U. Pa., 1956, M.A., 1968, Ph.D. (fellow), 1971. Instr. dept. psychiatry Temple U., Phila., 1971; research coordinator Addiction Scis. Center, 1971-72; research dir. sect. on drug and alcohol abuse Med. Coll. Pa., 1972-74, asst. prof. psychiatry, 1972-74; asso. prof. criminal justice Rutgers U., Newark, 1974-79, prof., 1979—; cons. on female criminality UN, 1975—; vis. fellow Yale U., 1976; cons. to Nat. Commn. on Marijuana and Drug Abuse, 1972-73, N.Y. U. Sch. Law, 1972-74; mem. faculty Nat. Jud. Coll., U. Nev., 1973—, Nat. Coll. Criminal Def. Lawyers and Public Defenders U. Houston, 1975; Mem. adv. com. Gen. Fedn. Women's Clubs, 1975-77; UN rep. Internat. Prisoner Aid Assn., 1973-75, Internat. Soc. Social Def.; sec. bd. dirs. Inst. for Continuous Study of Man, 1974-77, v.p., 1977—; UN rep. Internat. Assn. Social Def. Author: Sisters in Crime, 1975, The Incidence of Female Criminality in the Contemporary World, 1981, Nations Not Obsessed with Crime, 1983; co-author: A Systems Approach to Drug Treatment, 1975, Medical Lollypop, Junkie Insuline, or What?, The Criminology of Deviant Women, 1978; contbr. numerous articles in criminology and psychiatry to profl. jours.; editorial bd.: Criminology, 1971-73, Jour. Criminal Law and Criminology, 1982—; co-editor: Politics, Crime and the International Scene, 1972, Revue Internationale de Droit Penal, 1974; assoc. editor: LAE Jour., 1977—; cons. editor: Jour. Criminal Law and Criminology. Recipient (with G.O.W. Mueller) Beccaria medal in Gold Deutsche Kriminologische Gesellschaft, 1979. Mem. Am. Soc. Criminology (Herbert Bloch award 1972), Am. Sociol. Assn., Internat. Assn. Penal Law, U. Pa. Alumnae Assn (dir. 1974-77), Chi Omega (award 1956). Home: 30 Waterside Plaza New York NY 10010 Office: Sch Criminal Justice Rutgers U 15 Washington St Newark NJ

ADLER, FREDERICK RICHARD, lawyer, venture capitalist; b. N.Y.C., Apr. 4, 1925; s. Samuel and Rose (Axelrod) A.; m. Elsie Levite, June 26, 1949; children: Barbara Ilene, James Richard, Susan Ruth Ashley, Elizabeth Anne. B.A., Bklyn. Coll., 1948; J.D. magna cum laude, Harvard U., 1951. Bar: N.Y. 1952. Mem. firm Reavis & McGrath, N.Y.C., 1951—, partner, 1959—; dir., chmn. exec. com. Data Gen. Corp., Westbo, Mass., 1968—; mng. partner VENAD Assocs., VENAD II Assocs.; pres. Am. Venture Mgmt., Inc., Adler & Co.; chmn. Bio-Tech. Gen. Corp., N.Y.C., BRL Corp., Bethesda, Md., Daisy Systems Corp., Sunnyvale, Calif., Lexidata, Inc., Billerica, Mass.; dir. Scitex Corp. Ltd., Herzlia, Israel, Intermedics, Inc., Freeport, Tex. Trustee Tchrs. Ins. and Annuity Assn., 1977—; bd. overseers Meml. Sloan-Kettering Cancer Ctr. Served with U.S. Army, 1943-45. Mem. Nat. Venture Capital Assn. Clubs: University, West Side Tennis, Boardroom, Harvard. Office: 345 Park Ave New York NY 10154

ADLER, GERALD, lawyer; b. N.Y.C., Mar. 9, 1924; s. Albert and May (Stark) A.; m. Florence Cates, Mar. 28, 1948; children: Nancy Ann, Steven Jay, Wendy Sue, Amy Belle. B.S., M.A., Syracuse U., 1946-48; J.D., Yale, 1952. Bar: N.Y. bar 1952. Instr. Syracuse U.; also program dir. radio sta. WNDR, 1948-49; with firm Mudge, Stern, Williams & Tucker, N.Y.C., 1952-53; with NBC, 1953-73, dir. internat. enterprises, 1966-68, pres. enterprises div., 1968-73; ptnr firm Finley, Kumble, Wagner, Heine & Underberg, 1973-77; v.p., gen. counsel Penthouse Internat., Ltd., 1977-78; corp. counsel Playboy Enterprises, Inc., Chgo., 1978-82; mng. dir. Viacom Internat. Ltd., London, 1982—; dir. United Telecaster Sydney. Ltd. Author: Persuasion in the Political Campaign of, 1948, 1949; Editorial bd.: TV Quar. Trustee faculty Scarsdale Adult Sch. Served with AUS, 1942-46. Decorated Combat Infantryman's Badge, Bronze Star; recipient citation significant achievement internat. broadcasting Syracuse U., 1966. Mem. Nat. Acad. TV Arts and Scis., Internat. Radio and TV Soc., Newcomen Soc. N.Am. Home: 6 Molyneux St London WI England Office: 40 Conduit St London WI England

ADLER, JACOB HENRY, educator; b. Evansville, Ind., Mar. 26, 1919; s. Hiram J. and Jessica (Oberndorfer) A.; m. Emily Carolyn Rowe, June 1, 1952 (dec. d. 1978); children—Jennifer Brooke, James Rowe. B.A., U. Fla., 1939, M.A., 1947; A.M., Harvard U., 1948, Ph.D., 1951. Mem. faculty U. Ky., 1949-50, 51-69, prof. English, 1965-69, chmn. dept., 1964-69; prof. English Purdue U., 1969—, head dept., 1969-81; Fulbright lectr. Am. lit. univs. Delhi and Lucknow, India, 1960-61. Author: The Reach of Art: a Study in the Prosody of Pope, 1964, Lillian Hellman, 1969, also articles, chpts. in books. Served with AUS, 1942-46; CBI. Decorated Bronze Star. Mem. Modern Lang. Assn., Midwest Modern Lang. Assn., Nat. Council Tchrs. English, AAUP. Presbyterian. Home: 1523 Summit Dr West Lafayette IN 47906 Office: Dept English Purdue U Lafayette IN 47907

ADLER, JAMES BARRON, publisher; b. N.Y.C., Mar. 8, 1932; s. George G. and Mollie (Barron) A.; m. Esthy Lehmann, June 26, 1956; children: Laura Frances, Eric Stephen. A.B. magna cum laude, Harvard U., 1953. With NBC, N.Y.C., 1956-57, R.R. Bowker Co., 1957-61, Random House, Inc., 1961-64, G.P. Putnam's Sons, 1964-67; founder James B. Adler, Inc., 1967; founder, pres., chmn. Congressional Info. Service, Inc., Washington, 1969-81; mng. partner Adler Assos., 1981—; pres. Adler & Adler Pubs., 1983—; chmn. Greenwood Press, Inc., 1976-79; mem. U.S. Nat. Advisory Commn. Internat. Documentation Fedn., 1972-73. Served with U.S. Army, 1954-55. Recipient Profl. award Spl. Libraries Assn., 1972; Product of Yr. award Info. Industry Assn., 1971, 76. Mem. ALA, Am. Soc. Info. Sci. Clubs: Cosmos, Nat. Press. Home: 6925 Armat Dr Bethesda MD 20817 Office: 4550 Montgomery Ave Bethesda MD 20817

ADLER, JEROME WILLIAM, wine co. exec.; b. Jersey City, Mar. 26, 1931; s. William Henry and Edythe (Bukin) A.; m. Elaine Bader, Aug. 25, 1957; children—Mathew, Alison. B.A., Rutgers U., 1956. Vice pres. McCann Erickson Advt., N.Y.C., Chgo., 1960-66; v.p. mktg. and sales Barton Brands, Chgo., 1966-72, Heublein, Inc., Hartford, Conn., 1972-73; group v.p. STP, Ft. Lauderdale, Fla., 1973-74; pres. Montebello Co., Balt., 1974-76, Mogen David Wine Corp., Chgo., 1976—. Served with U.S. Army, 1951-54. Decorated Commendation medal, Combat Inf. badge. Office: 444 N Michigan Ave Suite 3000 Chicago IL 60611

ADLER, JULIUS, biologist, biochemist, educator; b. Edelfingen, Germany, Apr. 30, 1930; came to U.S., 1938, naturalized, 1943; s. Adolf and Irma (Stern) A.; m. Hildegard Wohl, Oct. 15, 1963; children: David Paul, Jean Susan. A.B., Harvard U., 1952; M.S., U. Wis., 1954, Ph.D., 1957; Postdoctoral fellow, Washington U., St. Louis, 1957-59, Stanford U., 1959-60. Asst. prof. biochemistry and genetics U. Wis., Madison, 1960-63, asso. prof., 1963-66, prof., 1966—, Edwin Bret Hart prof. biochemistry and genetics, 1972—, Steenbock prof. microbiol. scis., 1982—. Research, publs. in field. Mem. Am. Acad. Arts and Scis., Nat. Acad. Scis. Jewish. Home: 1234 Wellesley Rd Madison WI 53705 Office: Dept Biochemistry U Wis Madison WI 53706

ADLER, LARRY, executive; b. Frankfort, Ind., Dec. 18, 1938; s. Leon Sidney and Roslyn Jane (Woolf) A.; m. Ruthlee Figlure, Oct. 9, 1960; children: Laurie Kaye, Mark Allan, Joy Ellen. B.S. in Mktg. and Journalism, Ind. U., 1960. Asst. circulation and promotion mgr. McCall Corp., 1960-61; circulation and promotion mgr. Bartell-Media, Inc., 1961-63; sales promotion mgr. Golden Press, Inc., 1963-64; audio-visual dir., licensing mdse. dir., periodical publs. dir., advt. sales and mktg. dir. periodical div. Western Pub. Co., N.Y.C., 1964-74; v.p., pub., dir., treas. Washingtonian mag. and books Washington Mag., Inc., 1974-79; pres. Am. Program Bur., 1980; communications cons., 1980; pres., chmn. Adler Enterprises Ltd., 1981—, Adler Video Mktg., Ltd.; pres. Bergen Cablevision, Inc., Bergen County, N.J., 1970-72; asso. profl. lectr. Publs. Specialists program George Washington U., 1977-79. Creator, host: TV show Toy Fair News, 1968-73. Pres. Englewood (N.J.) Jaycees, 1965-66; mem. bd. edn. High Sch. Planning Com., Tenafly, N.J., 1969; program chmn. Tenafly Action Conf. on Edn., 1969; exec. bd. Maughan Sch. P.T.A., Tenafly, 1968-70; mem. steering com., long range planning com. Tenafly Bd. Edn., 1971-72; chmn. Tenafly Citizens Communications Com., 1971-72, Tenafly Townwide Com., 1972-73; chmn. bd. dirs. Capital Children's Mus., 1977-83; Bd. dirs. Englewood Boys Club, 1967-69. Mem. City and Regional Mag. Assn. (founder, pres., treas.), Ind. U. Alumni Assn., Alpha Delta Sigma, Zeta Beta Tau (v.p. 1960). Home: 8209 Wahly Dr Bethesda MD 20817 Office: 6804 Poplar Pl McLean VA 22101

ADLER, LAWRENCE, mining engineering educator; b. N.Y.C., June 6, 1923; s. Bertram and Serena (Katz) A.; m. Joan M. Anderson, June 29, 1957; children: Charles, Lauri Jo, Albert. A.B., NYU, 1946; B.S., Columbia U., 1949; M.S., U. Utah, 1953; Ph.D., U. Ill., 1964. Jr. engr. N.Am. Aviation Co., Los Angeles, 1951; asst. civil engr. City Los Angeles, 1952-55; asst. prof. mining engrng. U. Mo., Rolla, 1955-56, Lehigh U., Bethlehem, Pa., 1956-58, Mich. Technol. U., Houghton, 1958-61; assoc. prof. mining engrng. Va. Poly. Inst. and State U., Blacksburg, 1963-69, prof., 1969-78, pres. engrng. faculty orgn., mem. faculty senate, 1977-78; prof. mining engrng. W.Va. U., Morgantown, 1978—; cons. Rand Corp., Calumet & Hecla Co., Freeport Mining Co., Nat. Gypsum Co., U.S. Gypsum Co., Va. Coal and Coke Co., Singer Co., Pittston Co., U.S. Steel Co., Clinchfield Coal Co. Author: Excavation and Materials Handling, Ground Control in Bedded Formations; Contbr. articles to profl. jours.; Coordinating editor, contbr.: Mining Engrng. Handbook. Served with USAAF, 1943-45. Decorated Air medal, Purple Heart with one oak leaf cluster. Mem. ASCE, AIME, Sigma Xi. Presbyterian. Patentee field roof support device. Home: 1425 Dogwood Ave Morgantown WV 26505

ADLER, LEE, artist, educator, marketing executive; b. N.Y.C., May 22, 1926; s. Isidore and Anne (Blasser) A.; m. Florence Blumenkrantz, Dec. 28, 1956; 1 son, Derek Jonathan Tristan. B.A., Syracuse U., 1948; M.B.A., N.Y. U., 1960. Research account exec. Amos Parrish & Co., N.Y.C., 1954-56; dir. mktg. Lewin, Williams & Saylor, Inc., N.Y.C., 1956-57; with Interpub. Group Cos., Inc., N.Y.C., 1958-68; client service dir. Marplan, 1958-63; market devel. McCann-Erickson, Inc., N.Y.C., 1963-64; v.p. research and planning Pritchard, Wood, Inc., N.Y.C., 1964-65; v.p. mktg. services McCann-ITSM, Inc., N.Y.C., 1966-67; dir. research Market Planning Corp., N.Y.C., 1967-68; pres. Flouton, Adler & Assos., N.Y.C., 1969-70; dir. mktg. research RCA Corp., N.Y.C., 1970-74; prof. mktg. Fairleigh Dickinson U., Madison, N.J., 1974-80; partner Machlin-Adler Realty Co., Bklyn., 1978—; guest lectr. Columbia, Emory U., N.Y. U., U. Conn., St. John's U.; Bd. govs., v.p., chmn. research com. Bklyn. Heights Assn.; trustee Mktg. Communications Research Center. Author; editor: Attitude Research at Sea, 1966, Plotting Marketing Strategy, 1967, Attitude Research on the Rocks, 1968, Managing the Marketing Research Function, 1977; also articles; contbg. author, Modern Marketing Strategy, 1964, Handbook Modern Marketing, 1970, others.; one man shows include, Ruth White Gallery, N.Y.C., 1968, Salpeter Gallery, N.Y.C., 1967, N.Y.C. Community Coll., N.Y. U., 1972, New Bertha Schaefer Gallery, N.Y.C., 1973, 74, Hagley Mus., Wilmington, Del., 1974, Mickelson Gallery, Washington, 1975, Norton Gallery, St. Louis, 1974, Fairleigh Dickinson U., 1975, John Leech Gallery, Auckland, New Zealand, Poster Place, N.Y.C., Poster Place, Dallas, Canterbury Soc. Arts, Christ Church, New Zealand, 1975, Pub. Art Gallery, Dunedin, New Zealand, Waikato Art Gallery, Hamilton, New Zealand, Terrain Gallery, N.Y.C., Warwick (Eng.) Gallery, 1976, L.I. U., Bklyn., Kingpitcher Gallery, Pitts., Graham Gallery, N.Y.C., Instituto de Cultura His panica, Madrid, Spain, Mus. Modern Art, Mexico City, Universidad Autonoma de Nuevo Leon, Monterrey, Mex., Galeria de Arte, Saltillo, Mexico, Unidad de la Ciudadela, Monterrey, U. Monterrey, Instituto Tecnologico, Monterrey, USIA, Monterrey, Mus. Art, Torreon, Mexico, Albert White Gallery, Toronto, Ont., 1977, Centro de Arte Moderno, Guadalajara, Mexico, numerous others latest including, Mint Mus. Art, Charlotte, N.C., 1978, Heritage Found. Mus., 1978-79, Aldrich Mus. Contemporary Art, 1979, Gertrud Dorn Gallery, Stuttgart, W. Ger., Ulrich Mus. Art, Wichita, Kans. U., 1980; exhibited in group shows, Museo de Arte Contemporaneo, Bogota, Colombia, Whitney Mus. Am. Art, N.Y.C., State U. N.Y., Rochester, Bklyn. Mus., Am. Acad., Mus. Modern Art, Saõ Paulo, Brazil, N.A.D., Soc. Am. Graphic Artists, Fine Arts, Springfield, Mass., New Eng. Exhbn., Butler Inst. Am. Art, Youngstown, Ohio, numerous others; represented in many permanent collections including, Whitney Mus. Am. Art, Met. Mus. Art, Brit. Mus., Art Inst. Chgo., Corcoran Gallery, Washington, Fogg Art Mus., Harvard, Mus. Contemporary Art, São Paulo, Brazil, Bklyn. Mus., Seattle Art Mus., Albion (Mich.) Coll., Andrew Dickson White Mus. Art, Ithaca, N.Y., kButler Inst. Am. Art, Indpls. Mus. Art, Columbia Tchrs. Coll., Cin. Art Mus., N.Y. U., N.Y.C., Community Coll., Jersey City Mus., DeCordova Mus., Lincoln, Mass., Syracuse Art Mus., Ithaca Art Mus., Detroit Inst. Art, Mus. Modern Art, Sao Paulo, Mus. Fine Arts, Montreal, Phila. Mus. Art, Municipal Art Gallery, Dublin, Ireland, Hagley Mus., Wilmington, Del. Art Mus., Wilmington, Art Gallery Ont., Toronto, Auckland Art Mus., Fairleigh Dickinson U., Madison, N.J., L.I. U., Bklyn., Printmakers Workshop Collection, N.Y.C., Wichita State U., Larry Aldrich Mus., Ridgefield, Conn., Colgate U., Munson-Williams-Proctor Inst., Utica, N.Y., N.Y. Pub. Library, Instituto de Cultura Hispanica, Madrid, Edwin A. Ulrich Mus. Art, Wichita, Kans., Nat. Acad. Health and Safety, Beckley, W.Va., Civic Mus., Udine, Italy, Neuberger Mus., Pratt Graphics Center, SUNY, Purchase, Weatherspoon Art Gallery at U. N.C., Mint Mus. Art, Charlotte, N.C., USIA. Recipient Burndy Corp. award, 1969; Grumbacher award, 1968; Purchase award Soc. Am. Graphic Artists, 1979; won Childe Hassam Fund competition, 1969. Mem. Am. Mktg. Assn. (v.p. 1970-71, dir. 1968-70, chmn. attitude research com. 1963-65), Am. Assn. Pub. Opinion Research, Am. Sociol. Assn., N.Y. U. Grad. Sch. Bus. Adminstrn. Alumni Assn. (dir. 1964-67). Home: 168 Clinton St Brooklyn NY 11201 Lime Kiln Farm West Coxsackie NY 12192 Office: 168 Clinton St Brooklyn NY 11201

ADLER, MORTIMER JEROME, author; b. N.Y.C., Dec. 28, 1902; s. Ignatz and Clarissa (Manheim) A.; m. Caroline Sage Pring, 1963. Ph.D., Columbia U., 1928; B.A., Columbia Coll., 1983. Instr. Columbia U., 1923-30; asst. dir. People's Inst., N.Y.C., 1927-29; assoc. prof. philosophy of law U. Chgo., 1930-42, prof., 1942-52; dir. Inst. for Philos. Research, 1952—; pres. San Francisco Prodns., Inc., 1954—; dir. editorial planning 15th edit. Ency. Brit., 1966—, chmn. bd. editors, 1974—; Vis. lectr. St. John's Coll., Md., 1937—. Author: Dialectic, 1927, (with Jerome Michael) Crime Law and Social Science, 1933, (with Maude Phelps Hutchins) Diagrammatics, 1935, Art and Prudence, 1937, What Man Has Made of Man, 1938, St. Thomas and the Gentiles, 1938, How To Read a Book, 1940, (with Charles Van Doren) How To Read a Book, rev. edit., 1972, Problems for Thomists, The Problems of Species, 1940, A Dialectic of Morals, 1941, How To Think About War and Peace, 1944, (with Louis Kelso) The Capitalist Manifesto, 1958, The New Capitalists, 1961, (with Milton Mayer) The Revolution in Education, 1958, The Idea of Freedom, Vol. I, 1958, Vol. II, 1961, Great Ideas from the Great Books, 1961, The Conditions of Philosophy, 1965, The Difference of Man and the Difference It Makes, 1967, The Common Sense of Politics, 1971, (with William Gorman) The American Testament, 1975, Some Questions About Language, 1976, Philosopher at Large, 1977, Reforming Education, 1977, Aristotle for Everybody, 1978, How to Think About God, 1980, Six Great Ideas, 1981, The Angels and Us, 1982, The Paideia Proposal, 1983, Paideia Problems and Possibilities, 1983, How to Speak and How to Listen, 1983, A Vision of the Future, 1984; Editor: (with Charles Van Doren) Great Treasury of Western Thought, 1977; Assoc. editor: Great Books of the Western World, 1945—, Syntopicon, 1952; gen. editor: The Idea of Happiness, The Idea of Justice, The Idea of Love, The Idea of Progress, 1967; editor-in-chief: The Annals of America, 20 vols, 1968. Mem. Am., Am. Catholic philos. assns. Home: 1320 N State Pkwy Chicago IL 60610 Office: Inst for Philos Research 101 E Ontario St Chicago IL 60611

ADLER, NORMAN ABNER, lawyer, broadcasting and advt. exec.; b. N.Y.C., Oct. 8, 1909; s. Isaac Julius and Anna (Bluestein) A.; m. Leona Kleban, June 28, 1934; children—John Robert, Louise Rachel. B.A., N.Y. U., 1930; LL.B., Yale, 1933. Bar: N.Y. bar 1933. Asso. mem. firm Rosenberg, Goldmark & Colin, N.Y.C., 1933-38; spl. asst. to U.S. atty. gen., anti-trust div. Dept. Justice, 1938-45; asst. gen. atty. RCA, 1945-48; gen. atty. Columbia Records, 1948-55; v.p. charge Columbia Record Club, 1955-60; exec. v.p. Columbia Records (div. CBS), 1960-66; v.p., gen. mgr. CBS Ednl. Services Div., 1966-67; v.p., gen. exec. CBS, Inc., 1967-71; chmn. exec. com. Wunderman Ricotta & Kline, 1971-74. Mng. editor: Yale Law Jour, 1932-33. Mem. Riverside Pub. Health Com. Recipient Cullen prize for excellence in legal scholarship Yale, 1931. Mem. Am. Civil Liberties Union (acad. freedom com.), Fed. Bar Assn., Assn. Bar City N.Y., Order of Coif, Am. Arbitration Assn. (nat. panel arbitrators), Phi Beta Kappa Assos., Tau Kappa Alpha. Clubs: Players, City Athletic (N.Y.C.). Home: 2214 Caminito Castillo LaJolla CA 92037

ADLER, PETER HERMAN, conductor; b. Jablonec, Czechoslovakia, Dec. 2, 1899; came to U.S., 1938, naturalized, 1944; s. Bertold and Rinda A.; m. Helen George, Sept. 25, 1954. Student, Conservatory Music, Prague, Czechoslovakia. Dir. road co. Carmen Columbia Artists, 1944-45, cons., 1945-46; dir. Juilliard Am. Opera Ctr., 1971-82. Condr., Jablonec, Brno and Tepilce, Czechoslovakia, 1923-26, Bremen and Darmstadt, Germany, 1929-33; guest condr., Moscow, Leningrad and Kiev, Russia, 1933-36, Czechoslovakia, 1936-38; Am. debut N.Y. Philharmonic, 1939; guest condr. symphonies, operas, U.S., 1940-48; staged and conducted: musical sequences The Great Caruso; music and artisic dir., NBC Opera Co., 1949-59; music dir., Balt. Symphony Orch., 1959-67; spl. music cons., Nat. Ednl. TV, from 1967; music and artistic dir., WNET/13 Opera Theater, 1969—; guest condr., Met. Opera, 1972, 74; Contbr. to: Saturday Rev. Office: Juilliard Sch Lincoln Center New York NY 10023

ADLER, PHILIP, osteo. physician; b. N.Y.C., Jan. 2, 1925; s. Willie and Ethel (Zichler) A.; m. Ethel Kugler, Sept. 23, 1948; 1 dau., Deborah. B.S., N.Y. U., 1944; D.O., Phila. Coll. Osteo. Medicine, 1947. Diplomate: Nat. Bd. Osteo. Medicine and Surgery, Am. Osteo. Bd. Obstetrics and Gynecology. Intern Detroit Osteo. Hosp., 1947-48, resident obstetrics and gynecology, 1948-50, mem. profl. staff, 1950-72, sec. intern/resident tng. com., 1960-63, chmn. dept. obstetrics and gynecology, 1964-67; practice osteo. medicine specializing in obstetrics and gynecology, Farmington, Mich., 1950—; med. dir., dir. med. edn. Zieger/Botsford Osteo. Hosp., 1970-76, med. dir., 1970—; clin. prof. obstetrics and gynecology Mich. State U., Coll. Osteo. Medicine; cons. MIST Program.; Bd. dirs. Blue Shield of Mich., 1963-69; mem. adv. com. for teaching hosps. for social security studies HEW; mem. Mich. adv. com. Third Nat. Cancer Survey, Fed. Govt.; apptd. by gov. to Mich. State Health Coordinating Com., 1980-83. Contbr. articles to med. jours. Recipient Walter F. Patenge medal of pub. service Mich. Coll. Osteo. Medicine at Mich. State U., 1973, Medal of Pub. Service Ohio U. Coll. Osteo. Medicine, 1977, medal of Pub. Service Okla. Coll. Osteo. Medicine and Surgery, 1977. Fellow Am. Coll. Osteo. Obstetricians and Gynecologists; mem. Am. Osteo. Assn. (trustee 1968—, pres. 1977-78, chmn. dept. ednl. affairs 1976—), Mich. Assn. Osteo. Physicians and Surgeons (trustee 1963-68, pres. 1966-67), Wayne County Assn. Osteo. Physicians and Surgeons (trustee 1955-64, pres. 1961-62), Detroit Cancer Club, Am., Mich. assns. osteo. dirs. med. edn., Am., Mich. assns. for hosp. med. ecn., Mich. Assn. Regional Med. Programs (profl. adv. com.). Clubs: B'nai B'rith; Carlton (Chgo.). Home: 31020 McKinney Dr Franklin MI 48025 Office: 31020 McKinney Dr Franklin MI 48025

ADLER, RAYMOND H(ENRY), photojournalist; b. Dallas, June 12, 1942; s. Lee E. and Mable L. (Beach) A.; m. Mary Ann Brown, Sept. 1, 1962; 1 dau., Terrie Lynn. B.S., E. Tex. State U., 1968. Univ. photographer E. Tex. State U., 1968; staff photographer Austin (Tex.) Am. Statesman, 1969, Dallas Times Herald, 1970-73, asst. picture editor, 1973-74, chief photographer, 1974-78, dir. photography, 1978-83, graphics dir., 1983-84, asst. mng. editor, 1984—; mem. bd. advs. N. Tex. State U. journalism dept., 1979-81. Recipient awards AP, UPI, Sigma Delta Chi, Nat. Press Photographers Assn., U. Mo. Mem. Nat. Press Photographers Assn. Office: Dallas Times Herald Photo Dept 1101 Pacific Ave Dallas TX 75202

ADLER, RICHARD, composer-lyricist; b. N.Y.C., Aug. 3, 1921; s. Clarence and Elsa (Richard) A.; children by previous marriage: Andrew H., Christopher E. A.B., U. N.C., 1943. Mem. advt. dept. Celanese Corp. Am., 1946-50; White House cons. on the arts, 1965-69; Cons. on arts gov. N.C. Adv. bd. Inst. Outdoor Drama, 1968—, N.C. Performing School Arts, 1963—. Collaborator (with Jerry Ross); on scores for musicals John Murray Anderson's Almanac, 1953, Pajama Game, 1954; composer: score musical Damn Yankees, 1955, Kwamina, 1961; TV prodns. Little Woman, 1958, Gift of the Magi, 1958; produced and staged: White House Press Corrs. and Photographers show for Pres. Kennedy and Prime Minister MacMillan, 1962, N.Y.'s Birthday Salute for Kennedy, 1962, Inaugural Anniversary Salute to Pres. Kennedy, 1963, Salutes to Pres. Johnson, 1964, Inaugural Gala for Pres. Lyndon Johnson, 1965; producer, composer, lyricist: ABC-TV Stage 67 Musical Olympus 7-0000, fall 1966; composer, lyricist: A Mother's Kisses, 1968; co-producer: revival Pajama Game, 1973; producer: Rex, 1976; co-producer-composer: Music Is, 1976; composer, recorded Wilderness Suite, 1983; (Recipient Antoinette Perry award, Donaldson award, Variety Critics Poll for Pajama Game 1954, Damn Yankees 1955, Antoinette Perry nomination Kwamina 1962, Pulitzer Prize nomination Retrospectrum 1980, Yellowstone Overture 1981). Trustee John F. Kennedy Center for Performing Arts, 1964-77, exec. com., 1975-77; bd. dirs. New Dramatists, 1974—, Nat. Hypertension Assn., 1977—. Served to lt. (j.g.) USNR, 1943-46. Mem. Dramatists Guild (exec. council 1958-68), Am. Guild Authors and Composers (exec. council 1962), ASCAP (dir. chmn. exec. com.), ANTA (bd. dirs., exec. com.). Address: 8 E 83d St New York NY 10028 *I have turned my potentialities from the theatre (this year) to the concert-ballet field. I have written my first "serious" work, Memory of a Childhood, premiered in Detroit by the Detroit Symphony Oct. 6, 1978. It has since been performed in many different cities by the regional symphony orchestras. My second commission, "Retrospectrum," was premiered July 1979 at Carnegie Hall by the Soviet Emigré Chamber Orchestra. In May, 1980, "Yellowstone" for brass quartet and quintet was premiered in New York. "Yellowstone Overture" was commissioned for the American Philharmonic and was premiered at Carnegie Hall, Nov. 2, 1980. I am currently completing a new piece identifying the sounds of the instruments of the orchestra, for the uninitiated. I find these new kinds of endeavours (and the reception to them) to be uplifting.*

ADLER, RICHARD BROOKS, educator, electrical engineer; b. N.Y.C., May 9, 1922; s. Arthur H. and Florence (Brooks) A.; m. Dorothy Gordon, May 31, 1951; children: Gordon, Nicholas, Lucas. Student, Harvard, 1939-41; S.B., Mass. Inst. Tech., 1943, Sc.D., 1949. Mem. Faculty Mass. Inst. Tech., 1949—, prof. elec. engring., 1959—, asso. head elec. engring., 1978—, Cecil and Ida Green prof., 1974-76; research asst. Research Lab. Electronics, 1946-56; group leader solid state and transistor group Lincoln Labs., 1951-53; asso. Center Materials Scis. and Engring., 1963-74; cons. in field, 1952—. Author: (with S.J. Fricker) Notes on the Flow Scheduled Air Traffic, 1954, (with H.A. Haus) Limitations on Noise Performance of Linear Amplifiers, 1956, Circuit Theory of Linear Noisy Networks, 1959, (with others) Electromagnetic Fields, Energy and Forces, 1960, Electromagnetic Energy Transmission and Radiation, 1960, Introduction to Semiconductor Physics, 1964, Multistage Transistor Circuits, 1965, Electronic Conduction in Solids, 1967; also tech. papers, ednl. films. Served with USNR, 1944-46. Recipient Sloan teaching award Mass. Inst. Tech., 1955, 56; Premium award Royal Aero. Soc., 1955. Fellow Am. Acad. Arts and Scis., IEEE; mem. Sigma Xi, Eta Kappa Nu, Tau Beta Pi. Office: Dept Elec Engring and Computer Sci Room 38-409 Mass Inst Tech Cambridge MA 02139

ADLER, ROBERT, electronics engineer; b. Vienna, Austria, Dec. 4, 1913; came to U.S., 1940, naturalized, 1945; s. Max and Jenny (Herzmark) A.; m. Mary F. Buehl, 1946. Ph.D. in Physics, U. Vienna, 1937. Asst. to patent atty., Vienna, 1937-38; lab. Sci. Acoustics, Ltd., London, Eng., 1939-40, Asso. Research, Inc., Chgo., 1940-41; research group Zenith Radio Corp., Chgo., 1941-52, asso. dir. research, 1952-63, v.p., 1959-77, dir. research, 1963-77, EXTEL Corp., Northbrook, Ill., 1978-79, v.p. research, 1979-82; tech. cons. Zenith Corp., 1982—. Contbr. numerous articles profl. publs. Fellow IEEE (Edison medal 1980); mem. Nat. Acad. Engring. Developed various electron beam tubes for frequency modulation transmitters, for TV receivers, electron beam parametric amplifier; pioneer ultrasonic remote control for TV, ultrasonic light deflection for laser projection TV. Home: 327 Latrobe Ave Northfield IL 60093 Office: Zenith Ctr 1000 Milwaukee Ave Glenview IL 60025

ADLER, SAMUEL HANS, conductor; b. Mannheim, Ger., Mar. 4, 1928; came to U.S., 1939, naturalized, 1945; s. Hugo Chaim and Selma (Rothschild) A.; m. Carol Ellen Stalker, Feb. 14, 1960; children: Deborah Ruth, Naomi Leah. B.Mus., Boston U., 1948; M.A., Harvard

U., 1950; D.Mus. (hon.), So. Methodist U., 1969, D.F.A., Wake Forest U. Music dir. Temple Emanu-El, Dallas, 1953-66; prof. composition N. Tex. State U., Denton, 1957-66; Eastern regional dir. contemporary music project Ford Found., 1966-70; prof. composition Eastman Sch. Music, U. Rochester, N.Y., 1966—; hon. prof. U. Wales, Cardiff, 1984-89; lectr., condr. throughout world. Condr., Dallas Chorale, (1954-57), Dallas Lyric Theatre, (1955-59); composer 5 symphonies, 4 operas, 7 string quartets, sonatas for piano, violin (3), cello, flute, viola, concertos for flute, organ, violin and viola, piano, also for orch. and band, chamber and choral works, songs.; Author: Choral Conducting, 1971, Sight Singing, 1979, The Study of Orchestration, 1982. Served with AUS, 1950-52. Grantee Nat. Endowment Arts, Ford Found., Rockefeller Found.; recipient 6 1st prizes Tex. Composers Contest, Charles Ives award, 1965, ASCAP awards, 1960—, Lillian Fairchild award, 1968, Deems Taylor award, 1983; Guggenheim fellow, 1984-85. Mem. Music Educators Nat. Conf., Music Tchrs. Nat. Assn., ASCAP, Phi Mu Alpha Sinfonia. Jewish. Home: 54 Railroad Mills Rd Pittsford NY 14534 Office: 26 Gibbs St Rochester NY 14604

ADLER, SELIG, history educator; b. Balt., Jan. 22, 1909; s. Joseph G. and Della (Rubenstein) A.; m. Janet M. Sukernek, Aug. 26, 1936; children: Ellen Adler Krantz, Joseph G. B.A., U. Buffalo, 1931; M.A., U. Ill., 1932, Ph.D., 1934. Tchr. high schs., Buffalo, 1934-47; lectr. history SUNY-Buffalo (formerly U. Buffalo), 1941—, prof. history, 1952—, Samuel P. Capen prof. Am History, 1959-75, Disting. Service prof., 1975-80, Disting. prof. emeritus, 1980—; vis. prof. Cornell U., summer 1951, spring 1959, U. Rochester, 1952-53; historian, archivist Jewish Fedn. Greater Buffalo, 1980—. Author: The Isolationist Impulse, 1957, (with T.E. Connolly) From Ararat to Suburbia, 1960, The Uncertain Giant, 1921-41, 1965; also profl. articles.; contbg. editor: Judaism, 1956—. Mem. N.Y. State Kosher Law Adv. Bd., 1952-79. Mem. Am. Jewish Hist. Soc. (hon. life mem. exec. council), Phi Beta Kappa. Home: 352 Getzville Rd Buffalo NY 14226

ADLER, STEPHEN FRED, chemical company executive; b. Berlin, 1930; U.S., 1940, naturalized, 1945; s. Alfred Max and Ilse Johanna (Liepmann) A.; m. Judith Regina Weinberg, Dec. 23, 1951; children: Deborah Jeanne, Barbara Gail. B.S. in Chemistry (Sidney Hillman scholar), Roosevelt U., Chgo., 1951, M.S., Northwestern U., 1953, Ph.D. in Organic Chemistry (Sinclair fellow), 1953-54), 1954. From research chemist to group leader Am. Cyanamid Co., Stamford, Conn., 1954-69; with Stauffer Chem. Co., Dobbs Ferry, N.Y., 1969—, mgr. chems. dept., then asst. center dir., 1970-79, dir., 1979—. Author articles in field. Pres. Brookside Community Assn., 1963-65; fin. sec. Temple Shalom, Norwalk, Conn., 1968-69; sec. Jewish Fedn. Greater Norwalk, 1979-80, 1st v.p., 1980-81. Recipient award Phila. Patent Lawyers Assn., 1980. Mem. Am. Chem. Soc., N.Y. Acad. Scis. Home: 16 Grey Hollow Rd Norwalk CT 06850 Office: Stauffer Chem Co Livingston Ave Dobbs Ferry NY 10522 *I am convinced that people can alter their behavior to achieve more, given proper information and guidance. Secondly, I also insist on being involved and active if I decide to join any group or organization. These beliefs have helped to shape my approach to dealing with others in the organization and community in which I operate.*

ADLER, STEPHEN LOUIS, physicist; b. N.Y.C., Nov. 30, 1939; s. Irving and Ruth (Relis) A.; children: Jessica Wendy, Victoria Stephanie, Anthony Curtis. A.B. summa cum laude, Harvard U., 1961; Ph.D., Princeton U., 1964. Jr. fellow Soc. of Fellows Harvard U., 1964-66; research asso. Calif. Inst. Tech., 1966; mem. Inst. for Advanced Study, Princeton U., N.J., 1966-69; prof. Sch. Natural Scis., Inst. for Advanced Study, 1969-79, N.J. Albert Einstein prof., 1979—; vis. lectr. dept. physics Princeton U., 1969—; cons. in field. Author: (with R.F. Dashen) Current Algebras, 1968; contbr. articles to profl. jours. Fellow Am. Acad. Arts and Scis., Am. Phys. Soc.; mem. Nat. Acad. Scis., Phi Beta Kappa, Sigma Xi. Home: 287A Nassau St Princeton NJ 08540 Office: Inst for Advanced Study Princeton NJ 08540

ADLUM, MERLE DANIEL, union official; b. Friday Harbor, Wash., Feb. 21, 1919; s. Jack Daniel and Anna Ruth (Barene) A.; m. Virginia L. Schultz, Mar. 8, 1940; children: Virginia (Mrs. Clifford Houser), Joan (Mrs. James Chandler), Judy (Mrs. Del Blanks), Merle Daniel (dec.), Jacquelyn Stropple, John E. (dec.), Cynthia A. Larsen. Grad. high sch. Ofcl. Masters, Mates and Pilots Union, 1954-65; ofcl. Inland Boatmen's Union of the Pacific, Seattle, 1954-79, pres., 1967-79; v.p. Seafarers Internat. Union N. Am., 1969-79; trustee Puget Sound Maritime Trades Dept., 1961—, v.p., 1976-78, pres., 1978—, North by Northwest Adventureres, Inc., Seattle, 1969-72, Northwest Marine Tng. Program; Mem. Port Seattle Commn., 1963—, pres., 1967, 71, 75, 80; mem. Wash. Canal Commn., 1965—; now chmn.; mem. Mayor's Maritime Adv. Com., 1956—, chmn., 1970—; mem. statewide task force Alternatives for Washington; sec. Seattle King County Econ. Devel. Adv. Com., 1972—; now chmn.; chmn. Econ. Devel. Adv. Com., Marine Firemen Protection Working Com.; bd. dirs. Econ. Devel. Dist. Central Puget Sound, Econ. Devel. Council, Evergreen Safety Council, ARC, Council for Washington's Future, Downtown Coordinating Com., Washington State Trade Fair, Seattle Opportunities Industrialization Council. Trustee Nat. Multiple Sclerosis Soc., 1967—, Coast Guard Mus. N.W. Served with U.S. Navy, 1937-39. Named Maritime Man of Year Puget Sound Maritime Press Assn., 1972; recipient Outstanding Citizen award Muny League, 1967. Mem. Wash. Pub. Ports Assn., Pacific Coast Assn. Port Authorities (dir. 1964—), Northwest Waterways Assn., Seattle C. of C. (trustee 1971—, mem. exec. com.), Navy League, Japan Am. Soc., World Affairs Council, Puget Sound Maritime Hist. Soc. Clubs: Propeller Club, China Club. Home: 3707 35th Ave SW Seattle WA 98136 Office: Norton Bldg Seattle WA 98104

ADOLFO (ADOLFO SARDINA), fashion designer; b. Cardones, Cuba, Feb. 15, 1933. Began career as apprentice to, Balenciaga hat Salon, Paris, France, from 1950; with Bergdorf Goodman; chief designer, Emme Millinery, 1954-62; owner, designer fashion salon, Adolfo, Inc., N.Y.C., 1962—; also designer, Adolfo Men's Wear, Adolfo fragrance for Frances Denny. (Recipient Neiman-Marcus award), Adolfo fragrance for Frances Denny. (Coty award for innovative technique of making shaped hats without wiring or inner stuffing 1955), Adolfo fragrance for Frances Denny. (Coty award for a complete costume line 1969). Mem. Fashion Designers Am. (council) *

ADOMIAN, GEORGE, educator; b. Buffalo, Mar. 21, 1922; s. Haig and Rose (Harutunian) A.; m. Corinne Hodgson, Dec. 23, 1956; children: Haig, Diane, Laura, Aram. B.S., M.S., U. Mich.; postgrad., Calif. Inst. Tech.; Ph.D., UCLA, 1963. Sr. scientist Hughes Aircraft Co., 1953-64; prof. engring. research, prof. math. Pa. State U., 1964-66; Distinguished prof., David C. Barrow prof. math. U. Ga., 1966—; dir. Center for Applied Math., 1976—; cons. applied math., aerospace problems, systems theory; cons. Nat. Acad. Sci., Naval Studies Bd. Editor: Applied Stochastic Processes, 1980; Author: Stochastic Systems, 1983; Assoc. editor: Jour. Math. Analysis and Application; cons. editor transls. and publs. in applied mathematics and physics, linear and nonlinear stochastic dynamical systems. Served as lt. (j.g.) USNR. NASA grantee, 1970, 71; Sloan Found. grantee, 1975, 76, 77; NSF grantee, 1979, 80. Fellow AAAS; mem. Am. Math. Soc., Am. Phys. Soc., IEEE, Soc. Indsl. and Applied Math., Sigma Xi, Sigma Pi Sigma, Tau Beta Pi, Eta Kappa Nu. Home: 155 Clyde Rd Athens GA 30605 Office: Center for Applied Math Tucker Hall U Ga Athens GA 30602

ADORJAN, J(ULIUS) JOE, electric company executive; b. Duarte, Calif., Dec. 18, 1938; s. Joseph Julius and Julia Frances (Fuzerry) A.; m. Dianna Susan Schaeffer, May 25, 1963; children: Michelle, Michael, Joelle. Student, San Diego Jr. Coll., 1957-59; B.S.C., St. Louis U., 1963, M.S.C., 1967. With Century Electric Co., St. Louis, 1959-60, Chrysler Corp., 1963-65, Vickers div. Sperry Rand, 1965-68; sr. v.p. corp. devel. Emerson Electric Co., St. Louis, 1968—. Served to lt. USN, 1957-63. Office: Emerson Electric Co 8000 W Florissant Saint Louis MO 63136

ADOVASIO, JAMES M., archaeologist, educator; b. Youngstown, Ohio, Feb. 17, 1944; s. James A. and Lena Mary (Kicula) A.; m. Rhonda Andrews, Apr. 1, 1978. B.A. in Anthropology, magna cum laude, U. Ariz., 1965, postgrad, 1965-66; Ph.D. in Anthropology (NDEA fellow), U. Utah, 1970; D.Sc. (hon.), Washington and Jefferson Coll., 1983. Asst. prof. anthropology Youngstown State U., 1970-71; asst. prof. anthropology U. Pitts., 1972-75; asso. prof. Latin Am. studies, 1972—, asso. prof. anthropology, 1976-79, prof., 1979—, dir. cultural resource mgmt. program, 1976—; adj. asso. prof. anthropology Youngstown U., 1976-78; research asso. Smithsonian Instn., 1974—, Carnegie Mus., 1978—; dir. numerous archeol. surveys and excavations in Cyprus, Mex. and various midwestern and eastern regions of U.S.; dir. various archeol. material analysis from excavations. Contbr. numerous articles and studies on prehistoric N. Am. archaeology and social anthropology to scholarly jours., also book revs. Grantee Nat. Geog. Soc.; NSF; Baron Found.; Meadowcroft Found.; U. Pitts.; others; cert. Acad. Achievement Smithsonian Instn., 1972. Fellow Am. Anthrop. Assn.; mem. Soc. Am. Archaeology, Soc. Pa. Archaeology, Ohio Archaeol. Council, Am. Quaternary Assn., N.Y. Acad. Scis., AAAS, Phi Beta Kappa, Sigma Xi, Phi Eta Sigma. Roman Catholic. Office: Dept Anthropology Univ Pittsburgh Pittsburgh PA 15260 *To most Americans, "success" is inextricably interlinked with competition. I have always conducted myself in accord with a single principle. If you wish to be successful at anything, you compete only with yourself. If you excel or actually are "the best" at anything, you have succeeded only in mastering yourself.*

ADREON, HARRY BARNES, architect; b. Norfolk, Va., July 18, 1929; s. Harry Barnes and Helen Rae (Medairy) A.; m. Beatrice Marie Rice, Dec. 27, 1952. B.S., Va. Poly. Inst. and State U., 1950, M.S., 1952; student, Internat. Law Sch., 1977-78. Registered architect, Va., Md. Prin. archtl. firm Cross & Adreon, Washington, 1961—. Mem. Washington Episcopal Diocesan Archtl. Commn., 1966—; Bd. dirs. Arlington YMCA, 1982—. Served as capt. USMCR, 1952-54. Recipient Design award Nat. Assn. Home Builders, 1965-66; award for architecture Washington Bd. Trade, 1965; Design award Bethesda-Chevy Chase C. of C., 1966, 67; Nat. Honor award Am. Inst. Steel Constrn., 1968. Mem. AIA (corporate mem., House and Home award 1966, 67, Honor award Middle Atlantic region 1967, Nat. Honor award 1968, commr./dir. D.C. Met. chpt. 1976-78, chmn. mcpl. procedures com. D.C. Met. chpt. 1975), Washington Bldg. Congress, Constrn. Specifications Inst. (profl. mem., pres. D.C. chpt. 1972-74, chmn. region, 2 awards com., Pres.'s plaque 1975, cert. specifications writer, continuing edn. coordinator 1980—), Arlington County C. of C., Tau Sigma Delta. Episcopalian (vestryman 1961-63, 67-69, 71-73). Club: Kiwanis. (pres. 1983-84). Home: 4524 N 19th Rd Arlington VA 22207 Office: 950 N Glebe Rd Suite 140 Arlington VA 22203

ADRI *See* **STECKLING, ADRIENNE**

ADRIAN, BARBARA (MRS. FRANKLIN C. TRAMUTOLA), artist; b. N.Y.C., July 25, 1931; d. Allen Isaac and Mildred (Brown) A.; m. Franklin C. Tramutola, July 26, 1972. Student, Art Students League, 1947-54, Hunter Coll., 1951, Columbia Sch. Gen. Study, 1952-54. Art cons. Doyle-Dane-Bernbach, advt. agy., 1960, A.H. Macy, N.Y.C., 1960-61, Saks Fifth Avenue, 1960, Black, Starr & Gorham, 1960; instr. art workshop, Jamaica, N.Y., 1958-59, pvt. tchr. art, 1960—; instr. Art Students League, N.Y. One man shows, G. Gallery, 1957, G. Gallery, San Juan, P.R., 1951, Grippi Gallery, N.Y.C., 1963, Banfer Gallery, N.Y.C., 1966, Eileen Kuhlik Gallery, 1973; exhibited in group shows, G. Gallery, 1955-59, City Center Gallery, N.Y.C., 1954, N.Y.C. Festival, 1957, Portland (Maine) Mus., 1958, Workshop Gallery, N.Y.C., 1959, Grippi Gallery, 1960-63, Lane Gallery, Calif., 1962-63, Mus. Gallery, Lubbock, Tex., The Gallery, Norwalk, Ohio, 1962, Gallery 777, Plainview, L.I., N.Y., 1963, NAD, 1963, 81, Butler Art Inst., Youngstown, Ohio, 1963, Gallery Modern Art, N.Y.C., 1969, Child Hassam Fund Purchase Exhbn., N.Y.C., 1968, Orr's Gallery, San Diego, Pa. Acad. Fine Arts, Phila., 1980, Art Students League, N.Y.C., 1982, Norman A. Eppink Art Gallery, Emporia State U. (Kans.), 1983, Capricorn Gallery, Washington, Kenmore Gallery, Phila., Whitney Mus. Am. Art, Albrecht Art Mus; represented in permanent collections, Grippi Gallery, Summer Found., Butler Inst., McMay Mus., U. So. Ill., San Antonio, Corcoran Gallery, Washington; also pvt. collections in, U.S., P.R., Mex.; Recipient (Benjamin Altman prize 1968). Mem. Artists Equity of N.Y., Art Students League N.Y. (life), Pen and Brush (Dorothy Lapham Ferriss award 1983). Address: 420 E 64th St New York City NY 10021 *I want to paint the magic of man, and that magic, both real and phantasmagorical, by which he lives and feels. Art to me is more than a profession, it is the expression of all life.*

ADRIAN, CHARLES RAYMOND, political science educator; b. Portland, Oreg., Mar. 12, 1922; s. Harry Raymond and Helen K. (Petersen) A.; m. Audrey Jean Nelson, Apr. 2, 1946; children: Kristin, Nelson. B.A., Cornell (Iowa) Coll., 1947, LL.D., 1973; M.A., U. Minn., 1948, Ph.D., 1950; postdoctoral fellow, U. Copenhagen, Denmark, 1954-55. Instr., then asst. prof. govt. Wayne State U., 1949-55; from asst. prof. to prof. polit. sci. Mich. State U., 1955-66, chmn. dept., 1963-66; dir. Inst. Community Devel., 1958-63; prof. polit. sci. U. Calif., Riverside, 1966—, chmn. dept., 1966-70, acad. asst. to v.p. acad. affairs, 1973-74; cons. fed., state and local govt. ABC; research cons. Mich. Constl. Conv., 1961-62; Adminstrv. asst. to gov. Mich., 1956-57; mem. Meridian Twp. (Mich.) Planning Commn., 1957-60. Author: (with O. P. Williams) Four Cities: A Comparative Study in Community Politics, 1963, State and Local Governments, 2d edit., 1967, 3d edit., 1971, 4th edit., 1976, (with Charles Press) American Political Process, 1965, 2d. edit., 1969, Governing Urban America, 4th edit., 1972, 5th edit., 1977, American Politics Reappraised, 1974, (with E.S. Griffith) History of American City Government 1775-1870, 1976; also articles. Mem. Riverside Environ. Protection Commn., 1976-78. Served with USAAF, 1943-46; PTO. Faculty fellow Fund Advancement Edn., 1944-55.; Mem. Am. Polit. Sci. Assn., Am. Soc. Pub. Adminstrn., Phi Beta Kappa. Office: Dept Polit Sci U Calif Riverside CA 92521

ADRIAN, DONNA JEAN, librarian; b. Morden, Man., Can., Aug. 28, 1940; d. William Gordon and Dorothy Jean (Gregory) Frazer; m. James Ross Adrian, July 17, 1965. B.A., Brandon (Man.) Coll., 1962; B.L.S., McGill U., Montreal, 1963, M.L.S., 1969; tutor's cert., Laubach Literacy Can., 1982. Librarian Laurenvale Sch. Bd., Rosemere, Que., 1963-66; librarian, then library coordinator Rosemere High Sch., 1966-74; library coordinator North Island Regional Sch. Bd., Laval, Que., 1974-79; pedagogical cons. LaurenVal Sch. Bd., Laval, 1979—, now also literacy tutor; lectr. Concordia U., Montreal; mem. Laval Mayor's Library Com., 1975—. Mem. ALA, Canadian Library Assn., Internat. Assn. Sch. Librarians, Que. Assn. Sch. Librarians, Que. Sch. Library Assn., Corp. Profl. Librarians Que. Home: 194 Roi du Nord Ste Rose Laval PQ H7L 1W5 Canada Office: 530 Northcote Rd Rosemere PQ J7A 1Y2 Canada

ADRIANI, JOHN, physician, emeritus educator; b. Bridgeport, Conn., Dec. 2, 1907; s. Nicola and Lucia (Caseria) A.; m. Eleanor Anderson, Dec. 1936 (div. Feb. 1947); 1 son, John Nicholas; m. Irene Miller, Sept. 7, 1953. A.B., Columbia U., 1930, M.D., 1934. Diplomate: Am. Bd. Anesthesiology, (dir. 1960-72, chmn. exams. com. 1963-, pres. 1967-68). Intern surgery French Hosp., N.Y.C., 1934-36; resident anesthesiology Bellevue Hosp., N.Y.C., 1936-37; fellow N.Y.U., 1937-39, instr. anesthesiology dept. surgery, 1939-41; asst., then asso. clin. prof. surgery La. State U. Sch. Medicine, 1941-54, clin. prof. surgery and pharmacology, 1954; asst. prof., later asso. prof. anesthesiology Loyola Sch. Dentistry, New Orleans, 1945-56, prof. gen. anesthesiology, 1956-71; prof. surgery Tulane U., 1947-75, emeritus, 1975—; prof. anesthesiology La. State Med. Center, 1975—; dir. dept. anesthesiology Charity Hosp., 1941-75, emeritus dir., 1975—; dir. dept. inhalation therapy, 1941-69, dir. blood plasma bank, 1944-70, asst. dir., 1960-64; clin. prof. oral surgery Sch. Dentistry, La. State U., 1971—; assoc. dir. Charity Hosp., 1966-76, center chmn. regional med. program, 1967-70; cons. anesthesiologist Flint-Goodridge, VA, USPHS, Ochsner Found. hosps., Hotel Dieu, New Orleans; cons. anesthesiology, pharmacology and medico-legal problems La. Health and Human Resources Adminstrn., 1975-82; cons. to Touro Infirmary, New Orleans,; mem. adv. com. div. investigational drugs FDA, 1963-65, 72—, chmn. adv. com. on anesthetic and respiratory drugs, 1968-70, mem. adv. panel topical analgesics over-the-counter drugs, 1972-78, mem. adv. panel oral cavity preparations, 1974-80, cons. consumer protection div., 1980—; cons. FTC; mem. founders group expansion program Holy Cross Coll., 1963; mem. revision com., chmn. com. on anesthesia, subcom. on scope U.S. Pharmacopoeia, 1960-70; mem. U.S. Pharmacopeal Conv., 1970—, Nat. Formulary Admissions Com., 1970—. Author: Pharmacology of Anesthetic Drugs, rev. edit, 1970, Chemistry of Anesthesia, 1946, Techniques and Procedures of Anesthesia, 3d edit., 1964, Nerve Blocks, 1954, Selection of Anesthesia, 1955, General Anesthesiology For Students and Practitioners of Dentistry, 1958, The Recovery Room, 1958, Chemistry and Physics of Anesthesia, 1962, Appraisal-Current Concepts Anesthesiology (Mosby), Vol. 1, 1961, Vol. 2, 1964, Vol. 3, 1966, Vol. 4, 1969, Revision of Labat's Region Anesthesia, 1967, also numerous scientific and med. papers.; Editor: American Lecture Series in Anesthesiology; cons. editor: The Resident G. P. Survey Anesthesiology; editor: Anesthesiology, 1958-67; cons. editor: Dorland's Illustrated Med. Dictionary, 1969—, Internat. Corr. Soc. Anesthesiology. Bd. dirs. Cancer Soc., New Orleans; mem. Met. Action Com. of New Orleans, Public Affairs Research Council, Bur. of Govtl. Research of La., Italian-Am. Culture Center, Piazza Italiana, New Orleans.; trustee, mem. acad. bd. St. George's U. Med. Ctr., Granada, W.I. Named hon. col. staff Gov. La., 1965; hon. dep. atty. gen. State of La., 1980; hon. dep. Sheriff La Fourche Parish, 1980; recipient Distinguished Service award Am. Soc. Anesthesiologists, 1949, Internat. Anesthesiology Research Soc., 1957; Guedel medal for anesthesiology, 1959; Gold medal Assn. Alumni Coll. Physicians and Surgeons, Columbia, 1967; silver medal for achievements in medicine Columbia U. Sch. Medicine; Ralph M. Waters award internat. achievements in anesthesiology, 1968; decorated knight comdr. Order of Merit, Italy, 1969; named Nat. Italian Am. of Year, 1969; recipient Hon. Alumnus award Tulane Sch. Medicine, 12, Cert. of Honor Library of Congress, 1973; Monte M. Lemann award La. Civil Service League, 1975; named hon. senator La. Legislature, 1975, hon. atty. gen. State of La., 1980; recipient William McQuiston award Ill. Soc. Anesthesiology, 1982, NYU Med. Coll. Alumni award, 1982. Fellow Am. Soc. Clin. Pharm. and Chemotherapy, Am. Soc. Clin. Pharm. and Thera., Am. Coll. Anesthesiologists (gov. 1944-50, 56-60); mem. Am. Heart Assn., Assn. Colonic Surgeons, AAAS, Soc. Exptl. Biology and Medicine, So. Soc. Clinical Research, Internat. Anesthesia Research Soc., NRC, Columbia U. Alumni Assn., Am. Hosp. Assn., Assn. Univ. Anesthesiologists (pres. 1955), Assn. Univ. Anesthesiology Departmental Chmn., AMA (mem. council on drugs 1964-72, vice chmn. 1967, chmn. 1967-71), Internat. Soc. Comprehensive Medicine, Am. Soc. Anesthesiologists, La. Soc. Anesthesiologists (pres. 1950), New Orleans Soc. Anesthesiology (hon. mem. 1982), So. Soc. Anesthesiologists (pres. 1952—, cert. of recognition 1975), Acad. Anesthesiology (v.p., exec. com., citation of merit 1982), Cuban Soc. Anesthesiologists (hon.), Venezuelan Soc. Anesthesiologists (hon.), So. Med. Assn., Southeastern Surg. Congress, Am. Soc. Regional Anesthesia (hon.), History of Anesthesiology Soc. (hon.), Am. Soc. Regional Anesthesia (Easton Labat award 1980), History of Medicine Club, Am. Coll. Angiology, Am. Surg. Assn., Mexican Soc. Anesthesiology (hon. pres. 1954), La. Thoracic Soc., Yucatan Soc. Anesthesiology (hon. pres. 1966), Philippines Acad. Anesthesiology, Alton Ochsner Med. Found. Soc. (advisor), John Jay Assocs. Columbia Coll., Samuel Bard Assocs. of Columbia U. Coll. Physicians and Surgeons, Civil Service League La. (dir.), Assn. Wild-life and Fisheries of La., Sigma Xi, Alpha Omega Alpha. Clubs: Thoracophilis Horse Shoe, Century (Phys. and Surg.), Columbia University Alumni of New Orleans, 1834 of Tulane U. Home: 67 N Park Pl New Orleans LA 70124 Office: Charity Hospital New Orleans LA 70140

ADUJA, PETER AQUINO, lawyer, business executive; b. Vigan, Philippines, Oct. 19, 1920; came to U.S., 1927, naturalized, 1944; s. Dionicio and Francisca (Aquino) A.; m. Melodie Cabalona, July 31, 1949; children—Jay, Rebecca. B.A., U. Hawaii, 1944; J.D., Boston U., 1951. Bar: Hawaii bar 1953. Individual practice law, Hilo, Hawaii, 1953-60, Honolulu, from 1960; dep. atty. gen. State of Hawaii, 1957-60; judge Hawaii Dist. Ct., 1960-62; prin. broker AAP Realty, Inc., Honolulu, 1970—; pres. Aduja Corp., Las Vegas, Nev., 1972—, Travel-Air Internat., Honolulu, 1975—; mem. Hawaii Ho. of Reps., 1954-56, 67-74; del. Hawaii Constl. Conv., 1968; sec.-treas. Melodie Aduja, Inc., 1979—. Troop committeeman Aloha council Boy Scouts Am., 1959—; active ARC; bd. dirs. Salvation Army Adult Rehab. Center, Honolulu, 1965—, Goodwill Industries, Honolulu, 1972. Served with U.S. Army, 1944-46. Mem. Bar Assn. Hawaii, Hawaii Bd. Realtors. Democrat. Methodist. Home: 49 Niniko Pl Honolulu HI 96817 Office: 2046 N King St Honolulu HI 96819

AECK, RICHARD LEON, architect; b. Council Bluffs, Iowa, Feb. 26, 1912. Student, Morningside Coll., Sioux City, 1929-31; B.Arch., Ga. Sch. Tech., 1936. Chief Designer Ft. Ley & Co., Bogota, Colombia, 1937-38; pvt. practice, Atlanta, 1938-42; chief architect Pan Am. Airways (Brazilian Dist.), 1942-43; organized Aeck Assos., Atlanta, 1944; pres. Aeck Assos., Inc. (architects), 1962—; Cons. U.S. Overseas Mission to Cambodia, 1963; design critic Ga. Inst. Tech., Syracuse U., Cornell U., Tuskegee Inst.; Mem. adv. com. Atlanta Rapid Transit Authority; preceptor Rice U. Prin. works include H. Grady High Sch. Football Stadium, Atlanta, 1948, Alexander Memorial Basketball Coliseum, Ga. Tech., 1956, Peachtree House Apts, Atlanta, 1958, Holy Family Hosp, Atlanta, 1964, IBM Office Bldg, Tampa, 1965, Jamaica Citizens Bank, Kingston, 1968, Research Center, Lockheed Aircraft Co, Marietta, Ga., 1969, Grad. Studies Research Center, U. Ga., 1969, DeSoto-Hilton Hotel, Savannah, Ga., 1969, C & S Nat. Bank and Office Bldg, Atlanta, 1969, Floyd County Jr. Coll, Rome, Ga., 1970, Classroom Bldg. and Open Plaza, Ga. State U., 1971, Married Student Housing and Main Library Annex, U. Ga., 1972, Carter G. Woodson Elementary Sch, Atlanta, 1974, Banks-Jackson-Commerce Hosp, Commerce, Ga., 1974-75, Our Lady of Perpetual Help Free Cancer Home, Atlanta, 1974, N.W. Ga. Regional Hosp. Service Center, Rome,

Ga., 1975, Central Energy Plant Capitol Hill, Atlanta, 1976, Vocat. Agr. Sch, Elim. Jamaica, 1976, Grant St. Transit Sta, Atlanta, 1976, Twin Office Towers, Capitol Hill, Atlanta, 1976, Saudi Arabia Armed Forces Signal Center and Sch, Taif, 1979. Recipient various archtl. awards for excellence; Ivan Allen Sr. trophy, 1972.; fellow for design AIA, 1961. Home: 2200 W Wesley Rd NW Atlanta GA 30327

AEGERTER, ERNEST, pathologist, educator; b. Randolph, Nebr., Jan. 4, 1906; s. Ernest Alfred and Jessie (Dorman) A. A.B., Yankton Coll., 1928; B.S., U. S.D., 1929; M.D., U. Pa., 1932. Intern United Hosp., Westchester, N.Y., 1932-34; resident pathology Willard Parker Hosp., N.Y.C., 1935; fellow pathology Temple U. Med. Center, 1936, mem. faculty, 1936—, prof. pathology, 1945—, dir. dept., 1945-68, dir. emeritus, 1968—; lectr. orthopedic pathology U. Pa. Sch. Medicine, 1950—; vis. lectr. Med. Sch., U. Calif. at San Diego; cons. Phila. Gen. Hosp., Frankford Hosp., VA Hosp., U.S. Naval Hosp., Shriners Hosp.; Crippled Children (all Phila.), A. I. duPont Inst., Wilmington, Pa. Hosp. Crippled Children, Elizabethtown. Author: (with John Kirkpatrick) Orthopedic Diseases, 1958-75, Understanding Your Body, 1978, Save Your Heart, 1981. Mem. Am. Acad. Orthopedic Surgery (hon.), Internat. Skeletal Soc. (hon.), Am. Assn. Pathologists and Bacteriologists, Coll. Am. Pathologists. Home: 294 Bristol Rd Chalfont PA 18914

AESCHBACHER, WILLIAM DRIVER, historian; b. Tonganoxie, Kans., Jan. 12, 1919; s. Joseph Edmund and Annie Rose (Driver) A.; m. Flavia Ann Tharp, Dec. 20, 1944; children—William Richard, Robert David, Steven John. B.S., U. Neb., 1940, M.A., 1946, Ph.D., 1948. Asso. prof. history Murray (Ky.) State Coll., 1948-56; dir. Nebr. Hist. Soc., Lincoln, 1956-63, Eisenhower Library, Abilene, Kans., 1963-66; asso. prof. history U. Utah, 1966-68; head dept. history U. Cin., 1968—, univ. archivist, 1972—; Mem. adv. bd. Nat. Archives. Editor: Nebr. History, 1956-63. Served to 1st lt. AUS, 1942-45. Mem. Am., So., Western hist. assns., Orgn. Am. Historians (sec.-treas. 1956-70, treas. 1970), Agrl. History Soc., Am. Assn. State and Local History, Soc. Am. Archivists. Presbyn. Home: 8462 Foxcroft Dr Cincinnati OH 45231

AFFELDT, JOHN ELLSWORTH, physician; b. Lansing, Mich., May 26, 1918; s. John Ferdin and Pearl Heald (Gardner) A.; m. Nancy Faye Spomer, Sept. 2, 1942; children—John C., Elizabeth Affeldt Westberg, Cindy L. B.S., Andrews U., Berrien Springs, Mich., 1939; M.D., Loma Linda (Calif.) U., 1944. Intern Detroit Gen. Hosp., 1943-44; resident in internal medicine White Meml. Hosp., Los Angeles, 1946-49; fellow in pulmonary physiology Harvard Sch. Pub. Health, 1949-51; med. dir. Rancho Los Amigos Hosp., Downey, Calif., 1956-64, Los Angeles County Dept. Hosps., 1964-72, Los Angeles County Dept. Health Services, 1972-77; pres. Joint Commn. Accreditation Hosps., Chgo., 1977—. Served with AUS, 1944-47. Mem. AMA, A.C.P., Am. Congress Rehab. Medicine, Inst. Medicine, Western Soc. Clin. Research, Ill. Med. Assn., Chgo. Med. Soc. Home: 175 E Delaware Pl Chicago IL 60611 Office: 875 N Michigan Ave Chicago IL 60611

AFFLECK, JAMES G., chemical company executive; b. 1923; (married). B.A., Princeton, 1946; Ph.D., 1949. With Am. Cyanamid Co., 1947-84; research chemist, chemist, tech. rep., mgr. N.Y.C. New Products Office, 1947-57, mgr. rubber chem. dept., 1957-61, asst. gen. mgr. comml. devel. div., 1961-64, asst. gen. mgr. consumer products, 1964-65, asst. gen. mgr. internat. divs., 1965-67, gen. mgr. agrl. div., 1967-71, corporate v.p., 1971-72, pres., 1972-76, chmn., pres., chief exec., 1976-82, chmn., from 1983; dir. Potlatch Corp., N.J. Bell., Prudential Ins. Co.; Trustee Found. of Univ. Medicine and Dentistry, N.J., Am. Enterprise Inst., Joint Council Econ. Edn., Fairleigh Dickinson U.; bd. dirs. Mem. NAM (dir.), Pharm. Mfrs. Assn. (chmn.). Office: American Cyanamid Co Wayne NJ 07470

AFFLECK, MARILYN, sociology educator; b. Logan, Utah, July 1, 1932; d. Clark B. and Velda (Bryson) A.; children: Michelle Alisa, Kimberly Kay. B.A., U. Okla., 1954; M.A., Brigham Young U., 1957; Ph.D., UCLA, 1966. Instr., Central State Coll., Edmond, Okla., 1958-60; asst. prof. Fla. State U., Tallahassee, 1966-68; asst. prof. sociology U. Okla., Norman, 1968-70, asso. prof., 1971—, interim dean Grad. Coll., 1978-79, asst. dean, 1976-82. Recipient AMOCO Good Teaching award U. Okla., 1974. Mem. Am. Sociol. Assn., Okla. Sociol. Assn. (pres. 1974-75), South Central Women's Studies Assn. (treas. 1979-83). Democrat. Mormon. Home: 6395 Corky Dr Norman OK 73071 Office: Univ Okla 1000 Asp Ave Norman OK 73019

AFFLECK, RAYMOND TAIT, architect, educator; b. Penticton, B.C., Can., Nov. 20, 1922; s. John Earnest and Barbara (Tait) A.; m. Betty Ann Henley, Sept. 16, 1952; children: Graham (dec.), Neil, Jane, Gavin, Ewan. B.Arch., McGill U., 1947; postgrad., Eidgenossische Technische Hochschule, Zurich, Switzerland, 1948; LL.D., U. Calgary, 1972; Dr. Tech. hon., N.S. Tech. U., 1976. Asst. architect McDougall, Smith, Fleming, Montreal, Que., Can., 1948-49, Vincent Rother Assocs., Montreal, 1950-52; architect, prin. Affleck Desbarats Dimakopoulos Lebensold Sise, Montreal, 1952-70, Arcop Assocs., 1970—; asst. prof. McGill U., Montreal, 1954-58, vis. prof., 1960—; design cons. Nat. Capital Commn., Ottawa, Ont., Can., 1965-75, Wascana Centre Authority, Regina, Can., 1979—; mem. archtal. design com. City of Dorval, Can., 1960-62; mem. explorations jury Can. Council, Ottawa, 1970-76. Prin. works include: Place Bonaventure, 1968 (Massey medal 1972), Stpehen Leacock Bldg., 1966 (Massey medal 1972), Arts and Culture Centre, 1967, Market Sq., 1983, Maison Alcan, 1983. Recipient Can. Centennial medal Govt. of Can., 1967, Aga Kahn award for architecture, 1980. Fellow Royal Archtl. Inst. Can.; mem. Royal Can. Acad. (academician), Order of Architects of Que. (medal of honor 1983), Ont. Assn. Architects, Assn. Architects N.Y., Assn. Architects Calif. Clubs: Faculty (McGill U.); Mt. Royal Tennis (Montreal). Home: 16 St George's Pl Westmount Quebec PQ Canada H3Y 2L3 Office: Arcop Assocs 1440 St Catherine St W Suite 1025 Montreal PQ Canada H3G 1R8 *In my working life my main commitment is to the art of architecture,— stressing multi-sensual experience of space, by people in motion, rather than concern for form as an object. I am also concerned with the social aspects of the art—the process of decision-making involving clients, builders and designers, and the key role of imagination in this process. I have particular interest in pedestrian movements, mixed-use projects, and the challenge of Northern cities.*

AFFRONTI, LEWIS FRANCIS, microbiologist, educator; b. Rochester, N.Y., Aug. 12, 1928; s. John and Mary (Least) A.; m. Aileen Ledford, June 2, 1956; children—John, Lewis, Mary Louise, Eileen. B.A., U. Buffalo, 1950, M.A., 1951; Ph.D., Duke, 1958. Research asso. Buffalo VA Hosp., 1951-52, Roswell Meml. Cancer Inst., 1954; research asso. in Tb Henry Phipps Inst. U. Pa., 1957-58; asst. prof. George Washington U. Sch. Medicine, Washington, 1962-65, asso. prof., 1965-72, prof. microbiology, 1972—, chmn. dept. microbiology, 1973—; Cons. AVCO Research Corp., VA Hosp., Martinsburg, W.Va., VA Hosp. Center, Wilmington, Del.; U.S. rep. WHO Conf. on Skin Test Antigens and Vaccines, Geneva, 1966; Mem. med. adv. bd. VA, Wilmington, Del. Commd. officer USPHS, 1958-62; Served with USAF, 1952-54. NIH Spl. fellow, 1969; Nat. Tb fellow for Internat. Conf. on Tb, Moscow, 1971, Tokyo, 1973; Recipient WHO Exchange Research Workers award, 1970; interacad. exchange program award Nat. Acad. Sci., 1980. Mem. Am. Soc. Microbiology, Am. Acad. Microbiology, Am. Assn. for Immunologists, Reticuloendothelial Soc., Am. Thoracic Soc., Assembly on Microbiologists and Immunologists (sec. 1971-72), Assn. Med. Sch. Microbiology Chairmen (sec.-treas. 1976—), Wash. Acad. Sci. Clubs: K.C.; Toastmasters Internat. (Atlanta). Office: Dept Microbiology George Washington U Med Center 2300 Eye St Washington DC 20037

AGARWAL, PAUL DHARAM, electrical engineer, manufacturing company executive; b. Ambala, India, Jan. 21, 1924; came to U.S., 1947, naturalized, 1959; s. Dina Nath and Sherbati Honi A.; m. Mary M. Glenn, Dec. 22, 1951; children—Rani Lisa, Karen Lee, Paul Douglas, Deborah Anne. B.S.E.E. with honors, Benares Hindu U., 1944, M.E., 1944; M.S.E.E., Ill. Inst. Tech., 1949; Ph.D., Bklyn. Poly. Inst., 1958. Asst. prof. elec. engring. Bklyn. Poly. Inst., 1951-57; prof. elec. engring. U. Mass., 1957-61; head electric power and propulsion Gen. Motors Defense Labs., Santa Barbara, Calif., 1961-66; head elec. engring. dept. Gen. Motors Research Labs., Warren, Mich., 1966—; cons. to Gen. Electric Co., 1954-61; mem. adv. coms. NSF and Dept. Commerce, 1958-67. Contbr. papers to profl. publs. and confs. Recipient prize paper awards Am. Inst. Elec. Engrs., 1960, 62; NSF grantee, 1960. Fellow IEEE (vice chmn. ednl. activities bd. 1975-77, chmn. induction motor com. 1976); mem. Soc. Automotive Engrs. (exec. com. passenger car activity 1970), Sigma Xi (award 1960, various paper awards). Clubs: Cranbrook, Tennis. Patentee. Home: 773 Kirts St Troy MI 48084 Office: General Motors Research Labs Warren MI 48090

AGATA, BURTON C., lawyer, educator; b. N.Y.C., Feb. 7, 1928; s. Max and Augusta (Steger) A.; m. Dale S. Granirer, Dec. 24, 1955; children: Seth Hugh, Abby Fran. A.B., U. Mich., 1947, J.D., 1950; LL.M. in Trade Regulation (Food Law fellow), N.Y. U., 1951. Bar: N.Y. bar 1951. Counsel div. N.Y. State Banking Dept., 1955-59; ptnr. firm Burstein & Agata, Mineola and N.Y.C., 1959-61; prof. Mont. U., 1961-62, N.Mex. U., 1962-63, Houston U., 1963-69; counsel Nat. Commn. on Reform Fed. Criminal Laws, 1968-70; prof. law Hofstra U., 1970—, Max Schmertz Disting. Prof. Law, 1982—; faculty Nat. Inst. Trial Advocacy, 1977-81; dir. NE Regional Program, 1981—; spl. counsel N.Y. State Senate Minority; cons. Fed. Jud. Center, 1972, Inst. Jud. Adminstrn., 1973, HEW, 1971, White House Spl. Action Office Drug Abuse Prevention, 1973; Chmn. N.Y. State Task Force, Standards and Goals for Prosecution and Def., 1977-79; cons. Adv. Com. on Qualifications of Counsel, 2d Circuit, 1977; bd. dirs. Nassau Economic Opportunity Commn., 1972-73. Contbr. articles to law jours. Served with JAGC U.S. Army, 1951-54. Fellow U. Wis., 1963. Mem. Am. Law Inst., Am. Bar Assn., N.Y. State Bar Assn., Assn. Bar City N.Y., Fed. Jud. Council, Assn. Am. Law Schs. (chmn. criminal law sect. 1973). Home: 523 N Brookside Ave Freeport NY 11520 Office: Hofstra U Sch Law Hempstead NY 11550

AGATHOS, LOUIS JOHN, manufacturing company executive; b. Brigaton, Mass., Jan. 8, 1933; s. John Agnelo and Evelyn Elnora A.; m. Barbara Strauther Evans, Oct. 17, 1953; children—Debra Lynn, John Arthur. B.S. with high distinction in Chem. Engring, U. Maine, 1960, M.S. in Chem. Engring, 1961; M.B.A. with high distinction, Harvard U., 1965. Vice pres. ops. Brighams, Inc., Arlington, Mass., 1967-69; dir. fast food ops. Skychefs, Inc., N.Y.C., 1969-70; v.p., gen. mgr. Crimsco, Inc., Kansas City, Mo., 1970-74; corp. v.p. Sunbeam Corp., Oak Brook, Ill., 1976-80; group pres. Sunbeam Mgmt. Services, Oak Brook, 1976-80; pres. Market Forge Co., Everett, Mass., 1980—. Served with USN, 1949-53; Korea. Recipient Ober award, 1959, Hovey award, 1958, Goldman award, 1959; NSF fellow, 1960-61; Wesley Travis fellow, 1964-65. Mem. Am. Inst. Chem. Engrs., Nat. Assn. Food Equipment Mfrs., Nat. Restaurant Assn., Phi Kappa Phi, Tau Beta Pi. Club: Harvard Bus. Sch. Office: Market Forge Co 35 Garvey St Everett MA 02149 *

AGEE, WARREN KENDALL, journalism educator; b. Sherman, Tex., Oct. 23, 1916; s. Frederic M. and Minnie E. (Logsdon) A.; m. Edda Robbins, June 1, 1941; children: Kim Kathleen Agee Stimpert, Robyn Kendall Agee McIntosh. B.A. cum laude, Tex. Christian U., 1937; M.A., U. Minn., 1949, Ph.D., 1955. Mem. editorial staff Ft. Worth Star-Telegram, 1937-48; instr. journalism Tex. Christian U., 1948-50, asst. prof., 1950-55, asso. prof., 1955-57, prof., 1957-58, chmn. dept., 1950-58, faculty adviser student publs., 1949-58; prof. journalism, dean sch. journalism W.Va U., 1958-60; mem. ednl. adv. com. WJPB-TV, Fairmont and Weston, W.Va., 1959-60; nat. exec. officer Soc. Profl. Journalists, Sigma Delta Chi, 1960-62; prof. journalism, dean Evening Coll., Tex. Christian U., Ft. Worth, 1962-65; dean William Allen White Sch. Journalism, U. Kans., Lawrence, 1965-69, Henry W. Grady Sch. Journalism and Mass Communication U. Ga., 1969-75, prof. journalism, 1975—; vis. scholar U. Tex., fall 1975; copy editor Atlanta Constn., summer 1977; Pub. info. specialist USCG Res. Hdqrs., 1944-45; Mem. adv. screening com. journalism, com. internat. exchange of persons Conf. Bd. of Asso. Research Councils, Washington, 1958-62; mem. Am. Council on Edn. for Journalism and Mass Communication, 1958-60, 65-67; mem. accrediting com. Am. Council on Edn. for Journalism, 1969-76, vice chmn., 1973-74, chmn., 1974-76, chmn. appeals bd., 1977, 79, 81, 83; Mng. dir. William Allen White Found., 1965-69, trustee, 1970—; mng. dir. George Foster Peabody Radio and TV awards, 1969-75, Sigma Delta Chi Nat. Journalism Awards, 1960-62. Author: (with Edwin Emery and Phillip H. Ault) Introduction to Mass Communications, 1960, rev. edit., 1965, 70, 73, 76, 79, 82, Reporting and Writing the News, 1983; also articles.; Editor: The Press and the Public Interest, 1968, Mass Media In A Free Society, 1969, (with Emery and Ault) Perspectives on Mass Communications, 1982; Asso. editor, bus. mgr.: The Quill, 1960-62; press rev. columnist, contbg. editor, 1977—; adv. editorial bd.: Journalism Quar, 1955-60. Mem. Athens (Ga.) Internat. Relations Community Council, pres., 1980-82; pres. Friends of Mus. Art U. Ga., 1974-75; mem. Howard Blakeslee Media Awards judging com. Am. Heart Assn., 1976—, chmn. judging com., 1980—. Recipient Journalism award Fort Worth Press, 1936; Outstanding News Writing award Ft. Worth Profl. chpt. Sigma Delta Chi, 1946; Carl Towley award Journalism Edn. Assn., 1969; Outstanding Achievement award U. Minn., 1973; Wells Meml. key Sigma Delta Chi, 1978; Fulbright grantee to Portugal, 1982. Mem. Assn. Edn. in Journalism (pres. 1958), Am. Soc. Journalism Sch. Adminstrs. (pres. 1956), Am. Studies Assn., Southwestern Journalism Congress (sec. 1957-58), Internat. Press Inst., Sigma Delta Chi (pres. Fort Worth profl. chpt. 1954-55, sec. Tex. 1957-58, nat. v.p. campus chpt. affairs 1966-69, 78-79, leader council 1982—, v.p. N.E. Ga. profl. chpt. 1978-79, pres. 1979-80), So. Center Internat. Studies, Kappa Tau Alpha, Alpha Chi, Phi Kappa Sigma, Alpha Sigma Lambda. Methodist. Club: Gridiron (Ft. Worth). Lodge: Rotary. Home: 130 Highland Dr Athens GA 30606 Office: Henry W Grady Sch Journalism and Mass Communication U Ga Athens GA 30602 *One abiding goal has been to spread and deepen public understanding of the fundamentals of our democratic society as embodied in the Bill of Rights in general and the First Amendment in particular. That public understanding has been seriously eroded in recent years. Only through a renewed, vastly broadened national effort to teach these principles in our schools and other social institutions, and through the media of mass communication, will this erosion be halted and our nation, as we have known it, survive.*

AGEE, WILLIAM M., manufacturing executive; b. Boise, Idaho, Jan. 5, 1938; s. Harold J. and Suzanne (McReynolds). Student, Stanford U., 1956-57; A.A., Boise Jr. Coll., 1958; B.S. with high honors, U. Idaho, 1960; M.B.A. with distinction, Harvard U., 1963; D.Sc. in Indsl. Mgmt. (hon.), Lawrence Inst. Tech., 1977, Nathaniel Hawthorne Coll., 1977; D.C.S., Eastern Mich. U., 1978; LL.D. (hon.), U. Detroit, 1980; D.B.A. (hon.), Bryant Coll., R.I., 1980, Cleary Coll., Mich., 1980. Various positions Boise Cascade Corp., 1963-72, sr. v.p., chief fin. officer, 1969-72; exec. v.p., chief fin. officer The Bendix Corp., Southfield, Mich., 1972-76, pres., 1976-79, chief operating officer, 1976-77, chmn. bd., pres., chief exec. officer, 1977-83, pres., 1977-81, also dir., Allied Corp., Morristown, N.J., 1983; chmn., chief exec. officer Semper Enterprises, Inc., Osterville, Mass., 1983—; chmn. Uniform Software Systems, Inc., Santa Barbara, Calif., 1984—; dir. Gen. Foods Corp., Equitable Life Assurance Soc. U.S., Morrison-Knudsen Co. Inc., Dow Jones & Co., Inc., ASARCO, Inc.; chmn. Pres.'s Indsl. Adv. Subcom. Econ. and Trade Policy, 1978-79; bd. dirs. United Found., Nat. Council for U.S.-China Trade; mem. Harvard Bus. Sch. Assocs., Detroit Renaissance, Inc., Detroit Econ. Growth Corp. Trustee Urban Inst., Citizens Research Council Mich., Cranbrook Ednl. Community; chmn. Gov.'s Higher Edn. Capital Investment Adv. Com., 1979. Recipient Disting. Alumnus award Boise State U., 1972, Harvard Bus. Sch. Alumni Achievement award, 1977; named to U. Idaho Hall of Fame, 1978. Mem. Am. Inst. C.P.A.s, Idaho Soc. C.P.A.s, Mich. Assn. C.P.A.s, Council Fgn. Relations, Brit.-N.Am. Com., Conf. Bd., Bus. Roundtable, Phi Kappa Phi. Republican. Presbyterian. Clubs: Arid (Boise); Economic (dir.), Renaissance (Detroit)). Office: Semper Enterprises PO Box 2001 Osterville MA 02655 *

AGGARWAL, JAGDISHKUMAR KESHORAM, electrical engineer; b. Amritsar, India, Nov. 19, 1936; came to U.S., 1960, naturalized, 1972; s. K.J. and H.K. A.; m. S.K. Seth, July 10, 1965; children: Rajni, Malini. B.Sc., U. Bombay, 1957; B.Engring., U. Liverpool, Eng., 1960; M.S., U. Ill., Urbana, 1961, Ph.D., 1964. Mem. faculty U. Tex., Austin, 1964—, prof. elec. engring. and computer scis., 1972—, John J. McKetta energy prof., 1981—; vis. prof. U. Calif., Berkeley, 1969-70, Brown U., 1968. Editor: Digital Signal Processing, 1979, Deconvolution of Seismic Data; co-editor: Computer Methods in Image Analysis, 1977. Fellow IEEE; mem. Computer Soc. (chmn. confs., workshops), Pattern Recognition Soc. (Best Paper award 1975, asso. editor jour. 1978), Eta Kappa Nu. Club: Austin Yacht. Office: Dept Elec Engring U Tex Austin TX 78712

AGGARWAL, SUNDAR L(AL), rubber company executive; b. India, Oct. 15, 1922; came to U.S., 1945, naturalized, 1956; s. Basheshar Dyal and Bhagti (Devi) A.; m. Eleanor Weller, July 23, 1948; children: Vijay, Leila, Sheila. M.S. with honors, Punjab U., Lahore, India, 1943; Ph.D. in Chemistry and Chem. Engring, Cornell U., 1949. Sci. officer Nat. Chem. Lab., Poona, India, 1950-52; sr. scientist, sect. chief Olin Mathieson Chem. Corp., New Haven, Conn., 1952-57; head chem. physics research Gen. Tire & Rubber Co., Akron, Ohio, 1957-62, mgr. basic and materials research, mgr. tech. services, 1962-75, v.p., dir. research div., 1975—; lectr. at univs., U.S., Europe; Sci. Research Council (UK) fellow Imperial Coll., London U., 1975; chmn. Gordon Research Conf. on Elastomers, 1969. Contbr. articles on polymer sci. and tech. to profl. jours.; editor: Block Polymers, 1970. Fellow Plastics and Rubber Inst. (UK).; Mem. Am. Chem. Soc. (chmn. editorial bds. Rubber Rev., Rubber Div. 1975-79), Indsl. Research Inst., Dirs. Indsl. Research, Am. Phys. Soc., N.Y. Acad. Scis. Unitarian. Patentee synthetic rubbers. Office: One General St Akron OH 44329

AGGER, DONALD GEORGE, international technical transfer company executive; b. N.Y.C., Dec. 21, 1928; s. Oliver P. and Rose (Singer) A.; m. Susan Agger; children: David, Samuel, Marc, April. B.A. in Polit. Sci. with highest honors, Williams Coll., 1948; J.D., Yale, 1951. Bar: Conn. 1951, D.C. 1952. Practiced in, New Haven, 1951; atty. U.S. Govt., 1952-54; U.S. del. infrastructure com. NATO, 1954-58; pres. Am. Nord Aviation, Inc., Washington, 1959-67; asst. sec. U.S. Dept. Transp., Washington, 1967-69; dir. Panama Canal Co., 1967-69; pres. DGA Internat., Inc., Washington, 1969—; lectr. bus. math. Quinnipiac Coll., 1950-51, New Haven.; Mem. U.S. Citizens Com. on NATO, 1961-62, Pres.'s Task Force on Telecommunications, 1967-69, Pres.'s Commn. on Travel, 1968-69; chmn. U.S. del. 16th UN ICAO Gen. Assembly, 1968; Bd. dirs. Atlantic Council U.S., 1963—, Franki Found. Co., 1978—. Democrat. Clubs: Chequesset Yacht and Country (Wellfleet, Mass.); Internat., Wings, Nat. Aviation (Washington). Home: 2204 Decatur Pl NW Washington DC 20008 Office: care DGA Internat Inc 1225 19th St NW Washington DC 20036

AGGREY, ORISON RUDOLPH, foreign service officer; b. Salisbury, N.C., July 24, 1926; s. J.E. Kwegyir and Rose Rudolph (Douglass) A.; m. Francoise Fratacci, Nov. 5, 1966; 1 dau., Roxane Rose. B.S., Hampton Inst., 1946; M.S., Syracuse U., 1948; fellow Center for Internat. Affairs, Harvard U., 1964-65; LL.D. (hon.), Livingstone Coll., 1977. Publicity asst. United Negro Coll. Fund, 1947, 50; reporter Cleve. Call and Post, 1948-49; corr. Chgo. Defender, 1949; info. officer, vice consul Am. Consulate Gen., Lagos, Nigeria, 1951-53; asst. dir. USIS, Lille, France, 1953-54; asst. cultural affairs officer Am. embassy, Paris, 1954-57; dir. USIS Cultural Ctr., Paris, 1957-60; dep. pub. affairs adviser for Africa Dept. State, 1961-64; acting chief French br. Voice of Am., 1965; 1st sec., dep. pub. affairs officer Am. embassy, Kinshasa, Democratic Republic of Congo (now Zaire), 1966-68; program mgr. Motion Picture and TV Service, USIA, 1968-70; dir. West African affairs Dept. State, 1970-73; A.E. and P. to Gambia and Senegal, 1973-77, A.E. and P. to Romania, Bucharest, 1977-81; Dept. State fgn. affairs sr. fellow, research prof. diplomacy Georgetown U., Washington, 1981-83. Recipient USIA Meritorious Service award, 1955, Superior Service award, 1960, Hampton Inst. Alumni award, 1961; grand officer Senegalese Nat. Order of the Lion, 1977. Mem. Soc. Prodigal Sons State of N.C., Academie du Jazz Paris (hon.), Alpha Phi Alpha, Sigma Delta Chi, Alpha Kappa Mu. Club: Federal City. Home: 1257 Delaware Ave SW Washington DC 20024 Office: care Fgn Service Mail Room Dept State Washington DC 20520

AGHAJANIAN, GEORGE KEVORK, neuropharmacologist; b. Beirut, Apr. 14, 1932; s. Ghevont M. and Araxi (Movsessian) A. (parents Am. citizens); m. Anne Elaine Hammond, Jan. 10, 1959; children—Michael, Andrew, Carol, Laura. A.B., Cornell U., 1954; M.D., Yale, 1958. Intern Jackson Meml. Hosp., Miami, Fla., 1958-59; resident in psychiatry Yale U., New Haven, 1959-63, postdoctoral fellow psychiatry, 1961-63, asst. prof. psychiatry, 1965-68, asso. prof., 1968-70, asso. prof. psychiatry and pharmacology, 1970-74, prof., 1974—; mem. grant rev. coms. NIMH, 1968-71, 72-76. Contbr. articles to profl. jours. NIMH grantee, 1965-70, 70-75, 75—. Mem. Soc. for Neurosci., Am. Coll. Neuropsychopharmacology (Efron award 1975), Am. Soc. Pharmacology and Exptl. Therapeutics. Office: 34 Park St New Haven CT 06508

AGHAYAN, RAY(MOND) G., costume designer, TV producer; b. Teheran, Iran, July 29, 1934; came to U.S., 1952, naturalized, 1957; s. Hain and Jasmin (Frendian) A. B.A., U. Calif., Los Angeles. Costume designer for: films The Art of Love, 1964, Do Not Disturb, 1964, Our Man Flint, 1965, Glass Bottom Boat, 1965, In Like Flint, 1965, Caprice, 1966, Dr. Doolittle, 1967, Gaily, Gaily, 1969, Hannie Caluder, 1971, (with Bob Mackie) Ladys Sings the Blues, 1972, Funny Lady, 1975; designer: TV shows Judy Garland Show, 1963, Dick Van Dyke spl, 1963, Royal Follies of 1933, 1967, Robin Hood, 1966, Carol Channing and 101 Men, 1967, Carol Channing and Pearl Bailey on

Broadway, 1968, Leslie Uggams Show, 1969, Jim Nabors Show, 1970-71, Acad. Awards telecast, 1968, NBC Follies, 1973, Lily, 1975, Smothers Bros. Show, 1975, Lola, 1976, (with Bob Mackie) It's Greek to Me, 1964, Alice Through the Looking Glass, 1967, Carol Channing Presents the Seven Deadly Sins, 1968, Acad. Awards telecasts, 1971, 72, 75; theatrical prodn. Catch My Soul, 1966, Applause, 1969, (with Bob Mackie) On The Town, 1971, Lorelei, 1972; dir.: shows Little Mary Sunshine, The Lady's Not for Burning, Darkness at Noon, Candida, Paint Your Wagon, Brigadoon, Kismet, Caesar and Cleopatra; others; produced for: TV The Am. Fashion Awards, 1976, The Diahann Carroll Shows, 1976; also various nightclub acts. (Recipient Bronze medal French Bd. Trade 1967, Prestige award French Lace Industry 1967, Costume Designers Guild award 1968, All Am. Press Assos. award 1969, PAM award Phoenix Art Mus. 1970, Costume Designers Guild award 1967, Emmy award Nat. Acad. TV Arts and Scis. 1967). Democrat. 51 W 52d St New York NY 10019 *

AGHIORGOUSSIS, MAXIMOS DEMETRIOS, bishop; b. Callimassia, Chios, Greece, Mar. 5, 1935; s. Evanghelos G. and Lemonia G. (Rythianou) A. Licentiate,, Patriarchal Sch. Theology, Halki, 1957; Baccalaureate,, U. Louvain, Belgium, 1964, Th.D.,, 1964. Ordained to ministry Greek Orthodox Ch., 1957; chaplain U. Louvain, 1957-64; pastor chs., Brussels, Rome, Brookline, Mass., Manchester and Newport, N.H., 1960-78; observer-del. II Vatican Council, 1964-65; chaplain Holy Cross Sem., Brookline, 1967-76; prof. systematic theology Holy Cross Sch. Theology, Brookline, 1967-79, Christ Savior Sem., Johnstown, Pa., from 1979; bishop Greek Orthodox Diocese Pitts., from 1979; mem. Orthodox-Roman Cath. Consultation, from 1967; v.p. Nat. Council Chs. Christ U.S., 1979-81; ecumenical officer Greek Orthodox Archdiocese N. and S. Am., 1978-79, chmn. synodal coms. ecumenical affairs, spiritual renewal and youth, from 1979. Author articles in field. Mem. Orthodox Theol. Soc. Am., AAUP, Christian Assos. Pitts., Pa. Council Chs., W.Va. Council Chs., Helicon Cultural Soc. Address: 5201 Ellsworth Ave Pittsburgh PA 15232 *My ministry is such that it requires a total commitment to its goals, but first of all a total commitment to Christ. In my childhood, I was fortunate to be guided by excellent parents and grandparents, who gave me not only the necessary security and stability, but also the inspiration to imitate their personal commitment to the Lord. I fully trust in the grace of the Lord, but I also have always accepted my responsibility for everything I have done.* *

AGISIM, PHILIP, advertising company executive; b. Newark, Jan. 12, 1919; s. Isidore and Jennie (Socket) A.; m. Blanche Tedlow, June 14, 1942; children: Leslie Wayne, Elliot Steven. B.S., Rutgers U., 1941; M.B.A., N.Y. U., 1949. Asst. market research dir. Crowell-Collier Pub. Co., N.Y.C., 1945-49; asso. market research dir. Cowles Pub. Co., N.Y.C., 949-54; research and planning dir. J.B. Williams Co., N.Y.C., 1954-59, v.p., advt. dir., 1970-71; research dir. Parkson Advt. Agy., N.Y.C., 1959-63, v.p., 1963-69, exec. v.p., 1971-72, vice chmn., 1972-77, pres., 1978—, chief exec. officer, 1980-84, also dir.; vice chmn. Ohlmeyer Advt., 1984. Contbr. articles in field to profl. jours. Mem. Internat. Radio and TV Soc., Nat. Acad. TV Arts and Scis., Am. Mktg. Assn., Advt. Agency Fin. Mgmt. Group, Assn. Nat. Advertisers. Jewish. Clubs: Friars, Fairmount Country. Home: 650 Park Ave New York NY 10021 Office: 9 W 57th St New York NY 10019

AGLE, CHARLES KLEMM, architect, city planner; b. Bloomington, Ill., Oct. 19, 1906; s. Charles F. and Clara (Klemm) A.; (div.)children: Charles H., Kenneth C., Alan P.; m. Jo Ann Sayers, June 22, 1968. Grad., Choate Sch., 1923-25; A.B., Princeton U., 1929, M.F.A., 1931; student, Am. Sch., Fontainebleau, France, 1931. Asso. Henry Wright, Sr. (city planner), N.Y.C., 1931-34; dir. planning Fed. Pub. Housing Authority, 1934-43, Harrison, Ballard & Allen, N.Y.C., 1946-52; propr. own firm in city planning and architecture, Princeton, N.J., 1953—; mem. faculty community planning U. Pa., 1953-54; Princeton Grad. Sch., 1956-66. Editor, contbr.: Rehousing Urban America, 1934, An Approach to Urban Planning, 1953; Author: Zoning, 1965, Community Appearance, 1969, Planned Residential Neighborhoods, 1970, The Energy Crisis and Community Planning, 1974. Served with USNR, 1943-46. Recipient, 1968; Design award U.S. Dept. Housing and Urban Devel. Fellow AIA; mem. Am. Inst. Certified Planners, Am. Planning Assn., Regional Plan Assn. N.Y., Lambda Alpha. Home: 247 Elm Rd Princeton NJ 08540 Office: 10 Nassau St Princeton NJ 08540

AGLER, DAVID, conductor; b. South Bend, Ind., Apr. 12, 1947; s. Wave Bloom and Doris (Sheeler) A. B.Music, Westminister Choir Coll., Princeton, N.J., 1965-70; postgrad., Phila. Coll. Performing Arts, 1973-75. Mem. faculty Westminster Choir Coll., 1970-72, Acad. Vocal Arts, Phila., 1970-72, Phila. Coll. Performing Arts, 1973-75; adminstrv. dir. Spoleto Festival, 1974-75, gen. mgr., asso. music dir., 1975-76; mem. faculty San Francisco Conservatory Music, 1980—; dir. Am. Opera Project. Music dir., Syracuse Opera Theatre, 1978-79; music supr., resident condr., San Francisco Opera, 1979—. Named Exxon Arts-Endowment condr., 1979. Office: San Francisco Opera War Memorial Opera House San Francisco CA 94101

AGNEW, ALLEN FRANCIS, geologist; b. Ogden, Ill., Aug. 24, 1918; s. Theodore Lee and Agnes Nona (Faris) A.; m. Frances Marie Keiffer, Sept. 5, 1946; children: Allen Bruce, Lawrence Paul, Leslie Crae, Heather Lee. A.B. with highest honors in Geology, U. Ill., 1940, M.S., 1942; Ph.D., Stanford, 1949. Cert. geologist, Ind. Geologist Ill. Geol. Survey, 1939-42, U.S. Geol. Survey, 1942-55; asst. prof. geology U. Ala., 1948-49; asso. prof. geology U. S.D., 1955-57, prof., 1957-63; dir. S.D. Geol. Survey, 1957-63; prof. geology, dir. Water Resources Research Center, Indiana U., Bloomington, 1963-69; dir. Wash. Water Research Center; also prof. geology Wash. State U., 1969-74; sr. specialist environ. policy Congl. Research Service, Library of Congress, 1974-81; geol. cons., 1981—; prof. geology Oreg. State U., 1980—. Recipient Robert Peele award Am. Inst. Mining Engrs., 1958. Mem. Am. Inst. Profl. Geologists, Am. Geol. Inst., Nat. Water Well Assn., Assn. Engring. Geologists, Geol. Soc. Am., Soc. Mining Engrs. of Am., Inst. Mining, Metall. and Petroleum Engrs., A.A.A.S., Soc. Econ. Geologists, Soc. Environmental Geochemistry and Health, Phi Beta Kappa, Sigma Xi. Home: 3660 NW Roosevelt Dr Corvallis OR 97330

AGNEW, ARNOLD HARVEY, public affairs consultant; b. Toronto, Ont., Can., May 22, 1925; s. G. Harvey and Helen (Smith) A.; m. Flora Jane Mulligan, Aug. 9, 1952; children: John, Sarah, David, Elizabeth. B.A., U. Toronto, 1948, M.A., 1950. Reporter Halifax (N.S., Can.) Chronicle Herald, 1948, The Canadian Press, Halifax, 1949; reporter, editor Western Morning News, Plymouth, Eng., 1950; reporter London (Eng.) Daily Express, 1951, United Press, London, 1951-53, The Telegram, Toronto, 1953; editor in chief Sherbrooke (Que., Can.) Daily Record, 1957-60; mng. editor Toronto Telegram, 1960-64, exec. editor, 1964-70, v.p., editor-in-chief, 1970-71; gen. mgr. pub. affairs Toronto Dominion Bank, 1971-81. Councilor Village of Sturgeon Point, Ont.; Bd. dirs. St. John's Convalescent Hosp. Served with RCAF, 1944-45. Home: 87 Woodlawn Ave W Toronto ON Canada M4V 1G6

AGNEW, BRUCE ANDRAS, journalist; b. N.Y.C., Nov. 9, 1934; s. Clark Mansfield and Gloria (Bugyi) A.; m. Patricia F. Platt., Apr. 27, 1968; 1 dau., Eleanor Jean. B.A., Yale U., 1957. Reporter, Bridgeport (Conn.) Telegram, 1957-58, UPI, 1958-64; Washington corr. N.Y. Post, 1964-65; reporter McGraw-Hill World News (Business Week and other mags.), 1965—, Washington bur., chief congl. corr., 1976-77, econ. news editor Business Week, 1978—. Editor Washington Outlook page, 1970-76. Home: 3411 Turner Ln Chevy Chase MD 20015 Office: Nat Press Bldg Washington DC 20045

AGNEW, FRANKLIN ERNEST, III, food co. exec.; b. St. Louis, Apr. 13, 1934; s. Frank Ernest, Jr. and Susanne (Kohlsaat) A.; m. Dorothy Powning, Feb. 17, 1962; children—Carolyn W., Timothy S., Jennifer S. A.B. in Econs, Princeton, 1956; M.B.A., Harvard, 1958. C.P.A., 1961. With First Nat. Bank Chgo., 1958-62, loan officer, 1960-62; with Rockwell Mfg. Co., 1963-71, controller, 1963-66, v.p. mfg. power tool div., 1967-68, v.p. mfg. valve div., 1968-69, v.p. finance, 1969-71; sr. v.p., dir. H.J. Heinz Co., Pitts., 1971—, chief fin. officer, 1971-73, group exec., 1973—; Bd. dirs. Council of Americas, N.Y.C., St. Margaret Meml. Hosp., Pitts.; charter trustee Princeton U. Served with AUS, 1959. Mem. Am. Inst., C.P.A.'s, Council Internat. Execs. (conf. bd.). Clubs: Duquesne, Fox Chapel Golf (Pitts.). Home: 170 Forest Dr Pittsburgh PA 15238 Office: PO Box 57 Pittsburgh PA 15230

AGNEW, HAROLD MELVIN, physicist; b. Denver, Mar. 28, 1921; s. Sam E. and Augusta (Jacobs) A.; m. Beverly Jackson, May 2, 1942; children: Nancy E. Agnew Owens, John S. A.B., U. Denver, 1942; M.S., U. Chgo., 1948, Ph.D., 1949. With Los Alamos Sci. Lab., 1943-46, alt. div. leader, 1949-61, leader weapons div., 1964-70, dir., 1970-79; pres. GA Techs. Inc., San Diego, 1979—, Blaws Corp., 1967-72; sci. adviser Supreme Allied Comdr. in Europe, Paris, France, 1961-64; Chmn. Army Sci. Adv. Panel, 1965-70, mem., 1970-74; mem. aircraft panel Pres.'s Sci. Adv. Com., 1965-73; mem. USAF Sci. Adv. Bd., 1957-69, Def. Sci. Bd., 1965-70, Gov. N.Mex. Radiation Adv. Council, 1959-61; sec. N.Mex. Health and Social Services, 1971-73; chmn. gen. adv. com. ACDA, 1974-77, mem., 1977-81; mem. aerospace safety adv. panel NASA, 1968-74; mem. U.S. Army Sci. Bd., 1978-80, White House Sci. Council, 1982—. Mem. council engring. NRC, 1978-82, trustee council engring., 1982—; Mem. Los Alamos Bd. Ednl. Trustees, 1950-55, pres., 1955; mem. Woodrow Wilson Nat. Fellowship Found., 1973—; Mem. N.Mex. Senate, 1955-61; sec. N.Mex. Legis. Council, 1957-61; chmn. N.Mex. Senate Corp. Commn., 1957-61; bd. dirs. Fedn. Rocky Mountain States, Inc., 975-77. Recipient Ernest Orlando Lawrence award AEC, 1966; Enrico Fermi award Dept. Energy, 1978. Fellow Am. Phys. Soc., AAAS; mem. Nat. Acad. Scis., Nat. Acad. Engring. (Assembly of Engring.), Council on Fgn. Relations, Phi Beta Kappa, Sigma Xi, Omicron Delta Kappa. Home: 322 Punta Baja Solana Beach CA 92075 Office: PO Box 81608 San Diego CA 92138

AGNEW, JAMES BLANCHARD, financial consultant; b. Bklyn., Nov.4, 1915; s. John Paterson and Roberta (Blanchard) A.; m. Virginia Kerwin, Jan. 28, 1943; children: Nancy (Mrs. Nancy Wimmers), John R. Grad., Am. Inst. Banking, 1952; Stonier Grad. Sch. Banking, Rutgers U., 1960. With Chase Nat. Bank, N.Y.C., 1933-37, Mfrs. Trust Co., 1937-58; with Franklin Nat. Bank, Mineola, N.Y., 1958-68, sr. v.p., 1966-68, Security Nat. Bank, Huntington, N.Y., 1968-75; sr. v.p., chief lending officer Nassau Trust Co., Glen Cove, N.Y., 1975-76; gen. mgr., controller Kroll, Edelman, Elser & Wilson, N.Y.C., 1977-78; sr. v.p. Union Chelsea Nat. Bank, N.Y.C., 1978-83; fin. cons., 1983—. Mem. Harbour Green Civic Assn., 1960—. Served with USAAF, 1941-45. Mem. Robert Morris Assos., N.Y. Credit and Financial Mgmt. Assn., Commerce and Industry Assn. N.Y. (council 1964—). Clubs: Old Westbury (N.Y.); Golf and Country (bd. govs. 1964-76, treas. 1967-76. Home: 110 Fairfax Rd Massapequa NY 11758 Office: 500 Brush Hollow Rd Westbury NY 11590

AGNEW, JAMES KEMPER, advertising agency executive; b. Parkersburg, W.Va., May 10, 1939; s. James Pugh and Elinor Mary (Kemper) A.; m. Ann Haughey, Sept. 15, 1962; children: Scott Kemper, Steven James, Derek John. B.B.A., U. Mich., 1961; M.B.A., U. Calif., Berkeley, 1962; postgrad. spl. bus. studies, U. Oslo. With J. Walter Thompson, N.Y.C. and Paris, 1962-73, account exec., 1962-67, chmn. mgmt. com., Paris, 1967-70, v.p., mgmt. supr, N.Y.C., 1970-73; exec. v.p. J. Walter Thompson Co., head JWT/West, San Francisco, 1982—; sr. v.p., group account dir. McCann Erickson, Inc., N.Y.C., 1972-76, exec. v.p., gen. mgr., Los Angeles, 1976-82, pres., chief exec. officer, N.Y.C., 1982. Mem. U. Mich. Alumnae Club N.Y., U. Calif. Berkeley Alumnae Club. Address: J Walter Thompson Co Four Embarcadero Ctr Suite 900 San Francisco CA 94111 *

AGNEW, SPIRO THEODORE, internat. trade cons., former vice pres. U.S.; b. Balt., Nov. 9, 1918; s. Theodore S. and Margaret (Akers) A.; m. Elinor Isabel Judefind, May 27, 1942; children—James Rand, Pamela Lee, Susan Scott, Elinor Kimberly. Student, Johns Hopkins U.; LL.B., U. Balt.; LL.D., U. Md., Morgan State Coll., Ohio State U., Loyola U., Balt., Drexel U. Bar: Md. bar. Former claims adjuster Lumbermens Mut. Casualty Co.; then personnel dir. Schreiber Food Stores; formerly engaged pvt. practice law, Balt. and Baltimore County; then mem. firm Karl F. Steinmann; chmn. Baltimore County Bd. Appeals, 1958-61; exec. Baltimore County, 1962-66; gov., Md., 1967-69, vicé pres., U.S., 1969-73, resigned, 1973; cons. Pathlite, Inc., Crofton, Md.; now internat. trade cons. Calif.; Chmn. transp. com. Nat. Assn. Counties, 1963. Author: Canfield Decision, 1976, Go Quietly... Or Else, 1980. Served as officer AUS, 1941-45, 51. Decorated Bronze Star. Mem. Md., Baltimore County bar assns. Republican. Episcopalian. Clubs: Kiwanis, Whitemarsh Tennis and Recreation Center (Bowie, Md.) *

AGNEW, THEODORE LEE, JR., historian, eduçator; b. Ogden, Ill., Dec. 21, 1916; s. Theodore Lee and Agnes (Faris) A.; m. Jeanne Starrett LeCaine, Dec. 25, 1942; children: Theodore (dec.), Theodore Lee III, Susan Elizabeth (Mrs. Tom Balestreri), Hugh LeCaine, Peter Wallace, Marion Jeanne (Mrs. Robert Staab, Jr.). B.A., U. Ill., 1937, M.A., 1938; A.M., Harvard U., 1939, Ph.D., 1954. Grad. research asst. U. Ill., 1938; asst prof. history Okla. State U., Stillwater, 1947-54, asso. prof., 1954-60, prof., 1960—; vis. prof. history Emory U., summer 1964, 1966-67; Mem. World Meth. Council, 1976-81, exec. com., 1981—; mem. United Meth. Gen. Conf. and Jurisdictional Conf., 1976, 80; mem. gen. commn. on archives and history, commn. to study ministry, commn. on Christian unity and interreligious concerns United Meth. Ch.; mem. bds. S. Central Jurisdiction and Okla. Ann. Conf., del. from Okla., 1976, 80, 84; mem. joint adminstrv. bd. Meth. Theol. Sch. in Ohio and United Theol. Sem.; lay consultation council St. Paul Sch. Theology; bd. dirs. Frances E. Willard Home, Tulsa. Author: The South Central Jurisdiction, 1973; contbr. articles to profl. jours. Served from ensign to lt. USNR, 1942-46; comdr. Res. ret. Mem. Am. Hist. Assn., Orgn. Am. Historians, So. Hist. Assn., Am. Soc. Ch. History, Am. Studies Assn., Midcontinent Am. Studies Assn. (exec. bd. 1966-67, 74-76, 78-80, v.p. 1981, pres. 1982), Okla., Ill. hist. socs., AAUP (mem. council 1960-63), Phi Beta Kappa, Phi Kappa Phi, Phi Alpha Theta, Alpha Kappa Lambda, Omicron Delta Kappa. Democrat. Home: 1216 N Lincoln St Stillwater OK 74074

AGNEW, WILLIAM GEORGE, mech. engr., engring. lab. adminstr.; b. Oak Park, Ill., Jan. 12, 1926; s. Dupre L. and Marion S. (Roberts) A.; m. Norma Jean Light, Mar. 9, 1957; children—Brian R., Daniel D., Dalen W. B.S. in Mech. Engring, Purdue U., 1948, M.S., 1950, Ph.D., 1952. Research engr. Project Squid, U.S. Navy, Purdue U., 1948-50; with General Motors Research Labs., Warren, Mich., 1952—, dept. head fuels and lubricants, 1967-70, dept. head emissions research, 1970-71, tech. dir., 1971—. Contbr. articles to profl. jours. Served with Manhattan Dist. U.S. Army, 1944-46. Mem. Soc. Automotive Engrs. (Horning Meml. award 1960), ASME, Combustion Inst. (bd. dirs. 1960-76), Nat. Acad. Engring., AAAS, Engring. Soc. Detroit, Sigma Xi. Home: 3450 31 Mile Rd Romeo MI 48065 Office: Research Laboratories General Motors Technical Center Warren MI 48090

AGNICH, RICHARD JOHN, company executive, lawyer; b. Eveleth, Minn., Aug. 24, 1943; s. Frederick J. and Ruth H. (Welton) A.; m. Victoria Webb Trescher, Apr. 19, 1969; children: Robert Frederick, Michael McCord, Jonathon Welton. A.B. in Econs., Stanford U., 1965; J.D., U. Tex., 1969. Bar: Tex. 1969. Legis. asst., legal counsel to John G. Tower U.S Senate, 1969-70; adminstrv. asst. to John G. Tower U.S. Senate, 1971-72; asst. counsel Tex. Instruments Inc., Dallas, 1973-78, asst. gen. counsel, 1978-82, v.p., sec., gen. counsel, 1982—. Bd. dirs. Tex. Assn. Taxpayers, Tex. Lyceum; mem. adv. council Sch. Social Scis., U. Tex.-Dallas, Dallas Assembly. Mem. ABA, Tex. Bar Assn., Assn. Gen. Counsel, Am. Soc. Corp. Secs., Southwestern Legal Found. (adv. bd. Internat. and Comparative Law Ctr.). Republican. Presbyterian. Home: 4934 Crooked Ln Dallas TX 75229 Office: Tex Instruments Inc PO Box 225474 MS 241 Dallas TX 75265

AGOSIN, MOISES KANKOLSKY, educator; b. Marseilles, France, Dec. 1, 1922; came to U.S., 1968, naturalized, 1973; s. Abraham W. and Rachel S. (Kankolsky) A.; m. Frida Halpern, June 19, 1948; children—Cynthia Regina, Marjorie Stella, Mario Daniel. M.D., U. Chile, 1948. Intern Salvador Hosp., Santiago, Chile, 1946, resident parasitology and med. entomology, 1948; Rockefeller Found. fellow NIH, Bethesda, Md., 1952-54, research asso., 1955; head biochemistry sect., dept. parasitology U. Chile, 1957-59, chmn. dept. chemistry, prof. chemistry, 1960-67; research prof. zoology U. Ga., Athens, 1968—; vis. prof. U. Calif., Berkeley, 1960, U. London, 1964; cons. in field. Contbg. author: The Physiology of Insecta, 1974; editorial bd.: Exptl. Parasitology, 1967-73; contbr. articles to profl. jours. Grantee USPHS, 1958—, WHO, 1963-67, Wellcome Trust, 1966, NSF, 1974, U.S.-Israel bi-nat. Sci. Found., 1976. Fellow Am. Acad. Microbiology; mem. Am. Soc. Biol. Chemists, Biochem. Soc. (London), AAAS, N.Y. Acad. Scis., Am. Soc. Parasitology, Chilean Acad. Scis. Home: 177 Deertree Dr Athens GA 30605 Office: 173 Riverbend Research Labs Univ of Georgia Athens GA 30602 *Perhaps the most important driving force in my career has always been the need to find out not how phenomena occur but why. This has been coupled to my belief that there are only two types of research, good and bad, regardless of whether they are considered basic or applied.*

AGOSTA, KARIN ENGSTROM, book club dir.; b. New Haven, Jan. 25, 1936; d. Howard Theodore and Karin (Ekblom) Engstrom; m. William Carleton Agosta, July 2, 1958; children—Jennifer Ellen, Christopher William. B.A., Wellesley Coll., 1958. Freelance editor, N.Y.C., 1968-73; asst. to editor natural sci. Appleton-Century-Crofts, N.Y.C., 1969-71; staff editor Tchrs. Coll. Press, N.Y.C., 1971-72, mng. editor, 1972-76; dir. Young Parents Book Club, 1977—; Instr. Book Club, 1981—. Home: 32 Washington Sq New York NY 10011

AGOSTA, VITO, aerospace engineering educator; b. N.Y.C., July 26, 1923; s. John and Elizabeth (Alvares) A.; m. Mary Frago, Aug. 9, 1952; children: John Diana, Charles. M.S. in Engring, U. Mich., 1949; Ph.D., Columbia, 1959. Registered profl. engr., N.Y. Thermodynamicist DeLaval Steam Turbine Co., 1946-47; mem. faculty Poly. Inst. of N.Y., Bklyn., 1950—, prof. mech. and aerospace engring., 1962—; pres. Propulsion Scis., Inc., Huntington, N.Y., 1966-75, Fuels Systems Design Corp., Huntington, 1975—. Served with AUS, 1943-45. Mem. AIAA, Combustion Inst., ASME, Sigma Xi, Tau Beta Pi. Research on combustion stability in rocket motors; supersonic combustion of two phase systems; air and thermal pollution; heat transfer analysis in reacting fuels; inventor non-miscible liquid emulsifier, modulating oil burner; design and mfr. of modulating fuel emulsifier systems for engines and boilers. Home: 42 Cherry Ln Huntington NY 11743 Office: Fuels Systems Design Corp Huntington NY

AGOSTA, WILLIAM CARLETON, chemist, educator; b. Dallas, Jan. 1, 1933; s. Angelo N. and Helen Carleton (Jones) A.; m. Karin Solveig Engstrom, July 2, 1958; children—Jennifer Ellen, Christopher William. B.A., Rice Inst., 1954; A.M., Harvard U., 1955, Ph.D., 1957. NRC postdoctoral fellow Oxford (Eng.) U., 1957-58; Pfizer postdoctoral fellow U. Ill., Urbana, 1958-59; asst. prof. U. Calif., Berkeley, 1959-61; liaison scientist U.S. Navy, Frankfurt, Germany, 1961-63; asst. prof. Rockefeller U., 1963-67, asso. prof., 1967-74, prof., 1974—; cons. in field; officer, dir. Chiron Press, Inc. Contbr. articles to profl. jours. John Angus Erskine fellow, U. Canterbury (N.Z.), 1981—. Mem. Am. Chem. Soc., Chem. Soc. London, Interam. Photochem. Soc., Am. Soc. Photobiology, Phi Beta Kappa, Sigma Xi. Home: 32 Washington Sq New York NY 10011 Office: Rockefeller U 1230 York Ave New York NY 10021

AGRANOFF, BERNARD WILLIAM, educator, biochemist; b. Detroit, June 26, 1926; s. William and Phyllis (Pelavin) A.; m. Raquel Betty Schwartz, Sept. 1, 1957; children: William, Adam. M.D., Wayne State U., 1950; B.S., U. Mich., 1954. Intern Robert Packer Hosp., Sayre, Pa., 1950-51; biochemist Nat. Inst. Neurol. Diseases and Blindness, 1954-60; vis. scientist Max Planck Inst. Zellchemie, Munich, Germany, 1958-59; surgeon USPHS, 1954-60; mem. faculty U. Mich., Ann Arbor, 1960—, prof. biochemistry, 1965—; research biochemist Mental Health Research Inst., 1960—, asso. dir., 1977—; vis. scientist Nat. Inst. for Med. Research, Mill Hill, Eng., 1974-75; cons. pharm. industry, govt. Contbr. articles to profl. jours. Mem. Am. Soc. Biol. Chemist, Am. Chem. Soc., AAAS, Internat. Neurochem. Soc., Am. Soc. Neurochemistry (pres. 1973-75), Soc. for Neurosci. Research in brain lipids, biochem. basis of learning, memory and regeneration in the nervous system. Home: 2960 Overridge Dr Ann Arbor MI 48104 Office: Neurosci Lab Univ Mich 1103 E Huron St Ann Arbor MI 48109

AGRES, STUART JEROME, business executive; b. Chgo., June 16, 1945; s. Morris A. and Lee (Frank) A.; m. Patricia Meyer, Mar. 29, 1971; 1 dau., Jori. B.S., Ill. Inst. Tech., 1967; M.S., Mich. State U., 1968, Ph.D., 1971. Vice pres., group research dir. Leo Burnett U.S.A., Chgo., 1970-79; v.p. market devel. Adolph Coors Co., Golden, Colo., 1979-82; exec. v.p. The Marchalk Co., Inc., N.Y.C., 1982—. Mem. Am. Psychol. Assn. Office: Marschalk Co Inc 1345 Ave of Americans New York NY 10105

AGUIAR, ADAM MARTIN, chemist, educator; b. Newark, Aug. 11, 1929; s. Joaquim Ramahlo and Emilea Andrada (Nunes) A.; m. Laura E. Brand, Sept. 2, 1980; children: Justine Diane, David Laurence. B.S., Fairleigh Dickinson U., 1955; M.A., Columbia U., 1957, Ph.D., 1960. Chemist Otto B. May, Newark, 1948-55; asst. prof. Fairleigh Dickinson U., Rutherford, N.J., 1959-63; asst. prof. chemistry Tulane U., New Orleans, 1963-65, assoc. prof., 1965-67, prof., 1967-72; head dept. chemistry Newcomb Coll. div., 1970; dean grad. and research programs William Paterson Coll., Wayne, N.J., 1972-73; research prof. Rutgers U., Newark, 1973-75; prof. chemistry Fairleigh Dickinson U., Madison, N.J., 1975—; pres. Seltox Corp., N.J., 1980—; vice-chmn. Seltox Internat. Corp., Nev., 1981—; cons. chem. firms in, La. and N.J.

Contbr. articles to profl. jours. Union Carbide fellow, 1957; NIH fellow, 1959; recipient other grants. Mem. AAUP, Am. Chem. Soc., AAAS, Brit. Chem. Soc., N.Y. Acad. Sci., Center for Profl. Advancement, N.J. Acad. Sci., Am. Inst. Chemists, Oral Health Research Center, Am. Assn. Cons. Chemists and Chem. Engrs., Sigma Xi, Phi Lambda Epsilon, Phi Omega Epsilon. Home: 530 Valley Rd 2-P Upper Montclair NJ 07043 Office: 285 Madison Ave Fairleigh Dickinson U Madison NJ 07940

AGUILAR, FRANCIS JOSEPH, educator; b. N.Y.C., Aug. 19, 1932; s. Francisco and Maria Cecilia (Wagner) A.; m. Gillian Mary Crawford, May 25, 1964; children: Bruce Crawford, John Francis, Kim Marie, Anne-Marie. B.E.E., Rensselaer Poly. Inst., Troy, N.Y., 1954; M.B.A., Harvard U., 1959, D.B.A., 1965. Controller, No. Research and Engring. Corp., 1958; mem. faculty Harvard U. Bus. Sch., 1965—, prof. bus. adminstrn., 1971—; faculty chmn. internat. tchrs. program, 1969-73, chmn. sr. mgrs. program, 1972-74, mgmt. cons.; dir. Bowater Inc., Internat. Adoption Inc. Author: Scanning the Business Environment, 1967; co-author: European Problems in General Management, 1965. Served to lt. USNR, 1954-57. Home: 5 Somerset St Belmont MA 02178 Office: Morgan Hall 211 Harvard Bus Sch Boston MA 02163

AGUILAR, ROBERT P., U.S. district judge; b. Madera, Calif., Apr. 15, 1931. B.A., U. Calif., Berkeley, 1954; J.D., Hastings Coll. Law, San Francisco, 1958. Bar: Calif. 1960, U.S. Supreme Ct. 1966. Partner Aguilar & Edwards, San Jose, Calif., from 1960; judge U.S. Dist. Ct., No. Dist. Calif., San Francisco, 1980—; Mem. Regional Criminal Justice Planning Bd., from 1974; chmn. Santa Clara County (Calif.) Juvenile Justice Commn., 1975; mem. Santa Clara County Drug Abuse Task Force, 1974. Mem. Calif. Trial Lawyers Assn., Santa Clara County Criminal Trial Lawyers Assn., Am. Bar Assn., Calif. Bar Assn., Santa Clara County Bar Assn. (pres. 1972). Office: 450 Golden Gate Ave San Francisco CA 94102 *

AGUILERA, DONNA CONANT, psychologist, researcher; b. Kinmundy, Ill.; d. Charles E. and Daisy L. (Frost) Conant; m. George Limon Aguilera, Feb. 17, 1948; children: Bruce Allen, Craig Steven. R.N., Gordon Keller Sch. Nursing, 1947; B.S., UCLA, 1963, M.S., 1965; Ph.D., U. So. Calif., 1974. Teaching asst. UCLA, 1965, grad. research asst., 1965-66; prof. Calif. State U., Los Angeles, 1966-81; cons. crisis intervention Didi Hirsch Community Mental Health Ctr., Los Angeles, 1967; mem. Def. Adv. Com. Women in the Services, 1978-82; originator, project dir. Project Link Lab. Ind. Nursing Knowledge Calif. State U. Author: Crisis Intervention: Theory and Methodology, 1974, 4th edit. 1978, pub. in seven langs., Review of Psychiatric Nursing, 1977, 7th edit. 1978; contbr. articles to profl. publs. NIH fellow, 1972-75. Fellow Am. Acad. Nursing (sec. 1976-77, pres. 1977-78), Acad. Psychiat. Nurse Specialists, Internat. Acad. Eclectic Psychotherapists; mem. Am. Nurses Assn., Faculty Women's Assn., Am. Psychol. Assn., Calif. Psychol. Assn., AAUP, Alpha Tau Delta, Sigma Theta Tau. Home: 3924 Dixie Canyon Ave Sherman Oaks CA 91423 Office: 450 North Dr Suite 210 Beverly Hills CA 90210

AGUS, JACOB BERNARD, clergyman; b. Swislocz, Poland, Nov. 8, 1911; came to U.S., 1927, naturalized, 1929; s. Judah Leib and Bela (Bereznitsky) A.; m. Miriam Shore, June 16, 1940; children—Zalman, Edna (Mrs. Lawrence Povich), Robert, Deborah (Mrs. Robert Kleinman). A.B., Yeshiva U., 1933; A.M., Harvard U., 1938, Ph.D., 1939. Ordained rabbi, 1935; rabbi Temple Ashkenaz, Cambridge, Mass., 1935-39, Agudas Achim North Shore, Chgo., 1939-41; Beth Abraham Agudas, Dayton, Ohio, 1942-50, Beth El Congregation, Balt., 1950—; adj. prof. religion, history of Jewish thought Temple U., 1968-71; prof. Rabbinic Judaism reconstructionist Rabbinical Coll., 1969-71; vis. prof. modern Jewish philosophy Dropsie U., 1971—; Bd. dirs. Balt. br. NCCJ, Balt. br.; Am. Jewish Com., Balt. Asso. Jewish Charities and Welfare Fund; bd. regents Morgan State U., 1976—. Author: Modern Philosophies of Judaism, 1940, Guideposts in Modern Judaism, 1954, Banner of Jerusalem, 1946, The Evolution of Jewish Thought, 1959, The Meaning of Jewish History, 2 vols, 1963, The Vision and the Way, 1966, Dialogue and Tradition, 1971, Jewish Identity in an Age of Ideologies, 1978, The Jewish Quest, 1983; Mem. bd. editors Judaism quarterly, 1950—; cons. editor for: works on Judaism, Jewish history Ency. Britannica, 1957-68. Mem. Rabbinical Assembly Am., United Synagogues Am. Club: B'nai B'rith (nat. urban commn.). Home: 6317 Park Heights Ave Baltimore MD 21215 Office: 8101 Park Heights Ave Baltimore MD 21208 *To understand and to overcome the roots of hate was my ambition from earliest childhood. I am most impressed by the ambivalence of ideals, virtues and the loyalties of faith. We seek to build the Kingdom of God in the hearts of people and in society. But for every rainbow there is a dark cloud. The lights that lure us on bring darkness and dismay in the course of time, as well as the joy and the glory of fulfillment and redemption.*

AGUSTA, BENJAMIN J., computer co. exec.; b. Bklyn., July 1, 1931; s. Michael and Stephanie (Gallo) A.; m. Josephine Galante, Aug. 30, 1953; children—Michael, Stephanie, Joseph. B.S.E.E., M.I.T., 1952, M.S. in Elec. Engring, 1954; D.Eng., Syracuse U., 1964. Functional mgr. advanced solid state monolithic device research IBM Corp., Burlington, Vt., 1967-77, exec. mgr. gen. tech. devel., 1977-78, exec. mgr. div. tech. devel. staff, 1978—; instr. M.I.T., 1952-54. Mem. adv. bd.: IBM Jour. Research and Devel, 1974—; contbr. articles to profl. jours. Coordinator Burlington Internat. Games, 1977—. Served to 1st lt. USAR, 1952-54. Fellow IEEE; mem. Sigma Xi, Tau Beta Pi, Eta Kappa Nu. Roman Catholic. Clubs: Burlington Country, Elks. Home: 92 Oakcrest Dr Burlington VT 05401 Office: IBM River Rd Essex Junction VT 05452

AGUZZI-BARBAGLI, DANILO LORENZO, educator; b. Arezzo, Italy, Aug. 1, 1924; came to U.S., 1950; s. Guglielmo and Marianna (Barbagli) Aguzzi-B. Dottore in Lettere, U. Florence (Italy), 1949; Ph.D., Columbia U., 1959. Instr., asst. U. Chgo., 1959-64; asso. prof. Tulane U., New Orleans, 1964-71; prof. U. B.C., Vancouver, 1971—; Mem. Fulbright-Hayes final scholarship com., 1970—; adviser on scholarship application Can. Council, 1972-75. Author: Critical Edition of Della Poetica of Francesco Patrizi, 3 vols, 1969, 70, 71, 72, Critical Edition of Francesco Patrizi's Lettere ed opuscoli inediti, 1975; contbr. articles in field to profl. jours. Newberry Library fellow, Chgo., 1974; Folger Shakespeare Library fellow, Washington, 1975. Fellow Am. Philos. Soc.; mem. Newberry Library Assn., Dante Soc. Am., Italian Honor Soc. (regional rep.), Accademia Petrarca, Medieval Soc. Am., Renaissance Soc. Am., Modern Lang. Assn., AAUP, Am. Assn. Tchrs. Italian. Home: 485 Walsh Rd Atherton CA 94025 Office: University of British Columbia Vancouver BC V6T 1W5 Canada *Humanistic learning is a guiding light and an ever expanding process. Acquiring humanistic learning, inspiring love of it in others and sharing it with others, is, in fact, one of the better ways to serve society by defending some of the highest ideals of mankind.*

AHALT, J(OSHUA) DAWSON, agricultural economist, government official; b. Middletown, Md., Mar. 20, 1936; s. J. Guy and Helen Katherine (Gaver) A.; m. Harriet Ann Gernand, Nov. 9, 1963; children: Jonathan Dawson, Carol Leslie. B.S., U. Md., 1958; M.A., Am. U., 1966; postgrad., George Washington U., 1966-68. Br. rep. Sinclair Refining Co., Frederick, Md., 1959-62; agrl. economist U.S. Dept. Agr., Washington, 1962-71, sr. staff economist, 1973-77, chmn. World Agr. Outlook Bd., 1977-81, dep. asst. sec., 1981—; dep. assoc. dir. econ. policy Cost of Living Council, Washington, 1971-73. Author: (with Marvin Kosters) Controls and Inflation, 1975. Served with U.S. Army, 1958-59. Named Meritorious Exec. Pres., of U.S., 1980; recipient cert. of merit Price Commn., 1972, Cost of Living Council, 1972. Mem. Am. Agrl. Econs. Assn., Econs. Luncheon Group (chmn. 1979), Alpha Zeta, Omicron Delta Epsilon, Md. Grape Growers Assn. Home: 1811 N Jefferson St Arlington VA 22205 Office: Dept of Agriculture 14th and Independence Ave SW Washington DC 20250

AHART, JAN FREDRICK, engring. and constrn. co. exec.; b. U.S.A., May 13, 1941; s. Frank Lyle and Deloris Ruth (Solum) A.; m. Patricia Louise Heffner, Sept. 1, 1962; children—Erik Christopher, Wendy Kristine. B.B.A., Tex. A&M U., 1962; M.B.A., Harvard U., 1971. Bar: C.P.A., Va., Tex. Comml. auditor Arthur Andersen & Co., Houston, 1962-66; asst. controller Esso Standard Eastern (Far East), Tokyo, 1966-69; asst. v.p. Reynolds Metals Co., Richmond, Va., 1971-79; treas. Raymond Internat., Inc., Houston, 1979—. Mem. editorial bd.: Va. Acct, 1976-79. Served to capt., inf. AUS, 1963-65. Mem. Am. Inst. C.P.A.'s, Tex. C.P.A.'s, Am. Acctg. Assn. Home: 16307 N Greenfield Dr Spring TX 77373 Office: PO Box 27456 Houston TX 77027

AHEARN, JAMES, newspaper editor; b. S. Bend, Ind., Dec. 26, 1931; s. Francis T. and Loretto (Lorden) A.; m. Mary Ann Boesch, June 7, 1954; children—Michael James, Mary Elizabeth, Sarah Katharine, Margaret Ann. B.A., Amherst Coll., 1953; Nieman fellow, Harvard U., 1970-71. Reporter UPI, Boston, Newark and Trenton, N.J., 1957-61; state house corr. The Record, Hackensack, N.J., 1961-65, editorial writer, then editor editorial page, 1965-77, mng. editor, 1977—. Served with USNR, 1953-57. Recipient awards for editorial writing N.J. Press Assn., 1976, opinion sect. editing, 1974; award commentary Soc. Silurians, 1975. Mem. Am. Soc. Newspaper Editors. Home: 386 Spring Ave Ridgewood NJ 07450 Office: 150 River St Hackensack NJ 07602

AHEARNE, JOHN FRANCIS, govt. ofcl.; b. New Britain, Conn., June 14, 1934; s. Daniel Paul and Balbena Marian (Baloski) A.; m. Barbara Helen Drezek, June 19, 1956; children—Thomas, Paul, Mary Ann, Robert, Patricia. B. Engring. Physics Cornell U, 1957; M.S. in Physics, 1958; M.A., Princeton U., 1963, Ph.D., 1966. Nuclear weapons analyst USAF, 1959-61; asso. prof. physics USAF Acad., 1964-69; adj. prof. U. Colo., 1966-69; lectr. Colo. Coll., 1966-69; analyst Office Asst. Sec. Def. for Systems Analysis, 1969-70, dir. tactical air, 1970-72; dep. asst. sec. def. for gen. purpose programs, 1972-74, prin. dep. sec. def. manpower and res. affairs, 1974-76; staff White House Energy Office, 1977; dep. asst. sec. Dept. Energy, 1978; commr. U.S. Nuclear Regulatory Commn., 1978—, chmn., 1979-81. Bd. dirs. Woodstock Theol. Center, chmn., 1980—. Served with USAF, 1959-70. Gen. Electric Coffin fellow, 1957-58; recipient Dept. Def. Disting. Civilian Service medal and bronze palm, Sec. Def. Meritorious Service medal; named Boss of Year D.C. chpt. Nat. Secs. Assn., 1976. Mem. Am. Phys. Soc. Democrat. Roman Catholic. Office: 1717 H St Washington DC 20555

AHENAKEW, DAVID FREDERICK, national Indian Chief; b. Sandy Lake, Sask., Can., July 28, 1933; s. Edwin and Edith (Peekeekoot) A.; m. Grace, Dec. 18, 1951; children: Frederick, Shirley, Janet, Gregory, Ronald. Student, Sask. Pub. Schs.; LL.D. hon., U. Regina (Sask.), 1978. Tng. officer Govt. of Sask., Regina, 1967-68; chief Fedn. Sask. Indians, 1968-78; nat. chief Assembly of 1st Nations, Ottawa, 1982—; cons. Govt. of Sask., 1978-82. Served to sgt. Can. Army, 1951-67. Decorated Order of Can., 1979. Mem. Anglican Ch. of Can. Home: Gen Delivery Shell Lake SK Canada Office: Assembly of 1st Nations 222 Queen St Ottawa ON Canada K1P 5V9

AHERN, JAMES FRANCIS, insurance crime prevention institute administrator; b. New Haven, Jan. 24, 1932; s. James Patrick and Mary (Walsh) A.; m. Janet Margaret Wyatt, Feb. 14, 1952; children: Susan Eileen, Mary Elizabeth. Student, St. Thomas Sem., 1949-50, Gonzaga U., 1950-52; A.A., U. New Haven, 1962, B.B.A., 1964. Patrolman New haven Police Dept., 1954-62; sgt. New Haven Police Dept., 1962-67, lt., 1967-68, chief of police, 1968-71; dir. Ins. Crime Prevention Inst., Westport, Conn., 1971—; law enforement cons. Dept. Justice; mem. Pres.'s Commn. Campus Unrest, 1970. Author: Police in Trouble: Our Frightening Crisis in Law Enforcement, 1972. Mem. Democratic Nat. Policy Council, 1971-72; mem. security adv. com. Dem. Nat. Com., 1972; mem. adv. commn. spl. com. youth edn. for citizenship ABA, 1972-73; bd. dirs. Inst. Effective Criminal Justice, Lower East Side Action Project, N.Y.C. Mem. Am. Soc. Assn. Execs. Roman Catholic. Home: 223 Canner St New Haven CT 06511 Office: Ins Crime Prevention Inst 15 Franklin St Westport CT 06880

AHERN, JOSEPH EDWARD, wholesale grocery executive; b. Chgo., Aug. 3, 1926; s. James F. and Loretta (Bradley) A.; m. Celeste M. Sweeney, Nov. 3, 1951; children: Jean, Judith, Holly, Helen. B.S., Northwestern U., 1946, M.B.A., 1953. Pres. chief exec. officer United Grocers, Inc., Portland, Oreg., 1974-83; pres., chief exec. officer Spartan Stores, Inc., Grand Rapids, Mich., 1983—. Served to lt. j.g. USNR, 1944-47; PTO. Mem. Nat. Grocers Assn. (dir. 1981—). Office: Box 8700 Grand Rapids MI 49508

AHERN, PATRICK V., bishop; b. N.Y.C., Mar. 8, 1919. Student, Manhattan Coll., Cathedral Coll., N.Y.C., St. Joseph's Sem., N.Y.; mem., St. Louis U.; student, Notre Dame U. Ordained priest Roman Catholic Ch., 1945; ordained titular bishop of Maicra and aux. bishop, N.Y.C., 1970—. Office: 30 Manor Rd West Brighton Staten Island NY 10310 *

AHERN, ROBERT A(DAIR), database publishing company executive; b. Oklahoma City, June 1, 1948; s. Bernard Alfred and Patricia (McCabe) A.; children: Dawn Kimberly, Traci Robin. B.S. in History, U. Oreg., 1970. Intern U.S. Ho. of Reps., Washington, 1970; con-founder Capitol Services, Inc.(became div. TBITG 1981), Washington, 1972; v.p. Capitol Services, Inc. (became div. TBITG 1981), Washington, 1972-81, v.p. adminstrn., 1981-82, gen. mgr., 1982—. Mem. Info. Industry Assn. Democrat. Roman Catholic. Office: Capitol Services Inc 415 2d St NE Washington DC 20002

AHERN, TERRENCE SEAN, oil and gas company executive; b. Halifax, N.S., Can., Aug. 30, 1940; m. Donna Bruce, Aug. 22, 1964; children: Stephen, Kelly, Michaeline. B.Sc., St. Mary's U., 1963; M.B.A., Queen's U., 1966. Supr. mktg. and planning Merc. Bank, Montreal, Que., Can., 1971-72, chief acct., 1972-73, gen. mgr. and chief acct., 1973-75, sr. v.p. adminstrn., 1975-81; v.p. fin. Canterra Energy Ltd., Calgary, Alta., Can., 1981—; dir. Canshore Exploration Ltd., Calgary, Canterra Coal Inc., Pitts., Canterra Enterprises Inc., Penmore S.A., Fribourg, Switzerland, Westace B.V., Amsterdam, Netherlands. Home: 4331 Coronation Dr SW Calgary AB Canada T2S 1M3 Office: Canterra Energy Ltd 605 5th Ave SW Calgary AB Canada T2P 3H5

AHLBERG, CLARK DAVID, educator, former university president; b. Wichita, Kans., May 23, 1918; s. Grant and Sue McGuire A.; m. Rowena Osborn, Aug. 8, 1941; children: Val Jeanne, Thomas G., John C. A.B., U. Wichita, 1939; M.A., Syracuse U., 1942, Ph.D., 1951, LL.D., 1969. Grad. fellow, instr. polit. sci. Syracuse U., 1940-42, research dir. Washington Office, 1948-51, asst. dean Coll. Engring., 1951-54, asst. prof., 1951-54, v.p. adminstrn. and research, 1959-68, prof. polit. sci., Maxwell Citizenship and pub. Affairs, 1959-68; personnel asst. Panama Canal, 1942-43; mem. staff adminstrv. mgmt. div. VA, 1946-47; mem. staff. President's Sci. Research Bd., Washington, 1947; personnel researcher Nat. Bur. Standards, Washington, 1947-48; dep. dir. N.Y. State Budget Div., Albany, 1954-57, dir. budget, 1957-59; 1st dept. controller N.Y. State Dept. Audit and Control, Albany, 1959; pres. Syracuse U. Research Corp., 1959-68, Syracuse U. Press, 1959-68, Wichita State U., 1968-83, Univ. prof., 1983—; dir. 4th Nat. Bank & Trust Co., Whicita, Coleman Co. Inc. Author: (with John C. Honey) Attitudes of Scientists and Engineers About Their Government, 1950; editor: Agency and Departmental Statements on Research and Development Administration, 1947; contbr. articles to ednl. jours. Bd. dirs. Wichita Sedgwick Devel. Commn., Kans. Region NCCJ; NIH. Served with AUS, 1944-46. Mem. Am. Assn. State Colls. and Univs., Am. Council on Edn., Assn. Urban Univs., Inst. Internat. Edn., Inst. Logopedics. (trustee), Kans. Assn. Colls. and Univs., Nat. Council for Tchr. Accreditation, N. Central Assn. Colls. and Secondary Schs., Wichita State U. Library Assocs., Phi Eta Sigma, Phi Kappa Phi. Club: Wichita Books and Authors. Home: 224 N Belmont St Wichita KS 67208 Office: Wichita State U 1845 Fairmount St Box 145 Wichita KS 67208

AHLBERG, JOHN HAROLD, educator, mathematician; b. Middletown, Conn., Dec. 10, 1927; s. John Ludwig and Olga (Anderson) A. B.A., Yale U., 1950, M.A. in Mathematics, 1954, Ph.D., 1956; M.A. in Physics, Wesleyan U., 1952. Chief math. analysis United Aircraft Research Labs., East Hartford, Conn., 1956-68; prof. applied math. Brown U., 1968-83, prof. emeritus, 1983—; cons. math. and computer software devel., 1983—; vis. lectr. Soc. Indsl. and Applied Math., 1969-71; grad. lectr. Trinity Coll., 1959-68. Author: (with E.N. Nilson and J.L. Walsh) Theory of Splines and Their Application, 1967, Spli-sonf.-a CAD-CAM Computer Program Based on A-surfaces, 1983; Contbr. articles to profl. jours. Mem. Am. Math. Assn., Am. Math. Soc., Sigma Xi. Home and office: Deepwood Dr Amston CT 06231

AHLBRAND, RUSSELL LOWELL, JR., consulting engineering company executive; b. Fairfield, Ohio, Mar. 29, 1924; s. Russell Lowell and Alma Mae (Fleming) A.; m. Anne Ledbetter, Aug. 26, 1950; children: Thomas, Jane. B.S. in Elec. Engring., U. Cin., 1948. Design engr. Wente Electric Constrn. Co., Hamilton, Ohio, 1948-50; with A.M. Kinney, Inc., Cin., 1950—, asst. to pres., 1955-60, v.p., 1960-70, pres., 1970-81, vice chmn. bd., 1981—. Pres. Herman Schneider Found.; trustee Indian Hill Hist. Mus. Assn. Served with U.S. Army, 1943-46. Mem. IEEE. Clubs: Kenwood Country, Queen City, Indian Hill, Indoor Tennis. Lodge: Masons. Home: 8335 Old Stable Rd Cincinnati OH 45243 Office: A M Kinneny Inc 2900 Vernon Pl Cincinnati OH 45219

AHLBRANDT, ROGER SHERIDAN, business executive; b. Middletown, Ohio, Apr. 4, 1912; s. G.F. Ahlabrandt and Jeanette Helen (Jones) A.; m. Virginia C. Witherow, Apr. 13, 1940; children: Roger Sheridan, Virginia Crossan Warrick. B.S., U.S. Naval Acad., 1934. Student observer Allegheny Steel Corp., 1938, dist. mgr., 1939-42, 45-48, asst. mgr. cutting tools, 1948, mgr. stainless bar sales, 1950, treas., 1951-65, v.p., asst. to pres., 1965-66, exec. v.p., 1966-67, pres., 1967-72; corp. became Allegheny Ludlum Industries, 1970, chief exec. officer, 1968-76, chmn. bd., 1972-77, now chmn. exec. com., dir.; dir. Mellon Nat. Corp., Equitable Gas Co., Regional Indsl. Devel. Corp., Hammermill Paper Co. Trustee Shadyside Hosp.; chmn. bd. trustees U. Pitts.; bd. dirs., mem. exec. com. Allegheny Conf. on Community Devel. Served to lt. comdr. USNR, 1942-45. Mem. Am. Iron and Steel Inst. (past dir.), Pa. Soc., Pitts. C. of C. (dir.). Clubs: Fox Chapel Golf, Duquesne (Pitts.); Rolling Rock (Ligonier, Pa.); Laurel Valley Golf (Pitts.); Twenty-Nine Links (N.Y.C.). Home: 9 Edgewood Rd Fox Chapel Pittsburgh PA 15215 Office: Oliver Bldg Pittsburgh PA 15222

AHLEM, LLOYD HAROLD, retirement center executive; b. Moose Lake, Minn., Nov. 7, 1929; s. Harold Edward and Agnes (Carlson) A.; m. Anne T. Jensen, Dec. 29, 1952; children: Ted, Dan, Mary Jo, Carol, Aileen. A.A., North Park Coll., 1948; A.B., San Jose State Coll., 1952, M.A., 1955; Ed.D., U. So. Calif., 1962. Licensed psychologist, Calif. Tchr. retarded children Fresno County (Calif.) Pub. Schs., 1953-54; psychologist Baldwin Park (Calif.) Sch. Dist., 1955-62; prof. psychology Stanislaus State Coll., Turlock, Calif., 1962-70; pres. North Park Coll., Chgo., 1970-79, dir., 1966-70; exec. dir. Covenant Village Retirement Center, Turlock, 1979—. Author: Do I Have To Be Me, 1974, How to Cope: Managing Change, Crisis and Conflict, 1978, Help For the Families of the Mentally Ill, 1983; Columnist: Covenent Companion, 1972—. Decorated comdr. Order of Polar Star Sweden; recipient Disting. Alumnus award North Park Coll., 1966. Mem. Assn. Colls. Ill. (vice chmn. 1975-79). Mem. Covenant Ch. Home: 1165 La Sombra Turlock CA 95380 Office: 2125 N Olive Turlock CA 95380

AHLERS, ELEANOR EMILY, emeritus educator, librarian; b. Seattle, May 16, 1911; d. Francis Richard and Elizabeth Frances (Prior) A. A.B., U. Wash., 1932, M.A., 1957; B.S. in L.S, U. Denver, 1942; student, U. Calif., summer 1948. Tchr., librarian, South Bend, Wash., 1932-36, Mt. Vernon, 1936-42, high sch. librarian, Everett, Wash., 1942-53, also supr. sch. libraries, 1952-53; asst. prof. library sci., sch. edn. U. Oreg., 1953-57; exec. sec. Am. Assn. Sch. Librarians (div. ALA), 1957-61; supr. library services Wash. Dept. Pub. Instrn., Olympia, 1961-66; asso. prof. Sch. Librarianship. U. Wash., 1966-70, prof., 1970-76, emeritus, 1976—; instr. tchr.-librarian courses U. Wyo., summers, 1945, 46, San Jose State Coll., summers 1947, 52; asst. dir. workshop for sch. librarians Central Wash. Coll. Edn., summer 1951; coordinator workshop for sch. librarians U. Oreg., summer 1956; dir. sch. librarians workshop Kans. State Tchrs. Coll., summer 1964. Contbr. articles library, edn. periodicals; editor bulls. in field. Mem. Am. Assn. Sch. Librarians (pres. 1965-66), ALA, Wash. Sch. Library Assn., Phi Beta Kappa, Pi Lambda Theta, Mortar Board, Kappa Delta. Episcopalian. Office: School Librarianships U Wash Seattle WA 98195

AHLERS, ROLF WILLI, philosopher, theologian; b. Hamburg, Ger., June 22, 1936; came to U.S., 1966; s. Arthur W. and Ilse F. (Freund) A.; m. Luise Kuse, July 1965; children: Christoph Matthias, Marcus Andreas. B.A., Drew U., 1958; M.Div., Princeton Theol. Sem., 1961; Dr. Theol., Universitat Hamburg, 1966. Asst. prof. Theology Seminar Fur Systematische Theologie and Sozialethik, Hamburg Universitat, W. Ger., 1962-66; asst. prof. religion Ill. Coll., Jacksonville, 1966-72; Reynolds prof. philosophy and religion Russell Sage Coll., Troy, N.Y., 1973—. NEH grantee, 1972-73; Soc. for Health and Human Values grantee, 1975. Mem. Hegel Soc. Am., Am. Acad. Religion, Soc. for Phenomenology and Existential Philosophy, Internat. Soc. Philosophy and Lit., Nietzche Soc. N. Am., Internat. Soc. for Comparative Study of Civilization, Am. Philos. Soc. Presbyterian. Home: 3 Academy Rd Albany NY 12208 Office: Philosoph Dept Russell Sage Coll Troy NY 12180

AHLERT, ROBERT CHRISTIAN, educator; b. N.Y.C., Jan. 22, 1932; s. Christian William and Elma Adelaide (Wessel) A.; m. Barbara Grace Aldrich, June 5, 1954; children—Christi Ann, William King, Michael David. B.Chem. Engring., Poly. Inst. Bklyn., 1952; M.S., U. Calif. at Los Angeles, 1958; Ph.D. (N.Am. Aviation fellow), Lehigh U., 1964. Registered profl. engr., N.J. Jr. engr. chem. constrn. div. Am. Cyanamid Co., Linden, N.J., 1951, jr. chem. engr., Bound Brook, N.J.,

1952-54; research engr. (Rocketdyne div.); N.Am. Aviation, Inc., Canoga Park, Calif., 1954-56, sr. research engr., 1956-58, engring. supr., 1958-62, sr. tech. specialist, 1962-64, research group leader, 1964; asso. prof. Rutgers U., 1964-69, prof. chem. and biochem. engring., 1970—; exec. dir. Bur. Engring. Research, 1970-81. Contbr. numerous articles profl. jours. Mem. White Twp. (Warren County) Bd. Edn., 1967—, v.p., 1969, 78, pres., 1970, 79; mem. county and regional health planning councils. Fellow Am. Inst. Chemists; mem. Am. Inst. Chem. Engrs. (mem. or chmn. various coms.), Am. Soc. Engring. Edn., Nat. Soc. Profl. Engrs., Sigma Xi, Tau Beta Pi, Phi Lambda Upsilon. Home: PO Box 27 Buttzville NJ 07829

AHLFORS, LARS VALERIAN, mathematician, educator; b. Helsingfors, Finland, Apr. 18, 1907; s. Karl Axel and Sieva (Helander) A.; m. Erna Lehnert, June 22, 1933; children—Cynthia, Vanessa, Caroline. Ph.D., LL.D., Boston Coll., 1951; Sc.D., London U., 1978. Adj. math. U. Helsingfors, 1932-35, prof., 1938-44; asst. prof. math. Harvard, 1935-38; prof. U. Zurich, 1944-46; asso. prof. Harvard, 1946, prof. math., 1946—, named W.C. Graustein prof., 1964—, chmn. math. dept., 1948-50. Author: Complex Analysis, 1953; Contbr. papers on conformal mapping, Riemann surfaces, other brs. Theory of Function of a Complex Variable to profl. lit. Recipient Field's medal for math. research Internat. Congress of Mathematicians, Oslo, 1936, Wolf prize for Math., 1981. Mem. Am. Math. Soc., Am. Math. Assn., Societas Scientiarum Fennica, Academia Scientarum Fennica, Swedish Royal, Nat. acads. sci. Club: Faculty (Harvard). Home: 160 Commonwealth Ave Boston MA 02116 Office: Harvard Cambridge MA 02138

AHLGREN, GILBERT HAROLD, agronomist; b. South St. Paul, Dec. 25, 1913; s. Carl Oscar and Hilda Christina (Peterson) A.; m. Mildred Elizabeth Wyers, Sept. 11, 1943; children—Lynn, Alice, William. S.B., U. Wis., 1936; S.M., Rutgers U., Ph.D., 1941. Asst. agronomy U. Wis., 1936-37; asst. agronomy Rutgers U., 1937-38, instr. agronomy, 1939-41, asst. agronomist N.J. agrl. expt. sta., 1941-42, asso. agronomist, asso. prof., 1942-43, chmn. farm crops dept., prof., 1943—; agt. U.S. Dept. Agr., 1938-39; dir. Farmers State Bank, Frederic, Wis., 1974—; Pres. Northeastern Weed Control Conf., 1947, 48; agronomist Internat. Devel. Services, Nigeria, 1957, agrl. edn. adviser, Burma, 1961-62; agronomist U.S. AID, South Vietnam, 1962-66, dep. asst. dir. agr., 1966-67; chief of party IRI Research Inst., Rio di Janeiro, 1967-70; agrl. cons., 1970—, coordinator river project, Burnett County, Wis., 1976—. Author: Practical Field Crop Production for the Northeast, 1947, rev. edit. 1952, Forage Crops, 1949, rev. edit. 1956, Principles of Weed Control, 1951, Grassland Farming, 1955. Trustee Frederic Municipal Hosp., 1975—. Mem. Am. Soc. Agronomy, Genetics Soc. Am., Sigma Xi (sec. Rutgers chpt. 1945-46), Delta Theta Sigma. Republican. Presbyn. Home: Route 1 Box 276 Danbury WI 54830

AHLSCHIER, JOSEPH BAILEY, hospital adminstrator; b. Houston, Nov. 8, 1928; s. Joseph Bailey and Claris lydia (Rogers) A.; m. Concetta Theresa Malzone, Sept. 2, 1950; children: Elizabeth Ann, Lucy Ann. B.S. in Applied Sci., Richmond Profl. Inst., Coll. William and Mary, 1954; cert. in phys. therapy, Med. Coll Va., 1954; M.H.A., Med. Coll. Va., 1960. Asst. adminstr. Med. Coll. Va., Richmond, 1960-61; adminstr. Sheltering Arms Hosp., Richmond, 196-62, John Randolph Hosp., Hopewell, Va., 1962-64; pres. Milford Meml. Hosp., Del., 1964—; mem. Del. Med. Malpractice Commn., 1975-76, Del. Statewide Health Coordinating Council, 1977—; bd. govs. Middle Atlantic Health Congress, 1978—, chmn. bd. govs., 1981-82. Bd. dirs. Blood Bank Del., 1966-68, Children's Bur. Del., 1975-80; mem. Del. Tech. and Community Coll. Nursing Adv. Council, 1973—. Served with U.S. Army, 1946-48. Mem. Am. Hosp. Assn. (ho. of dels., regional adv. bd. 1969—), Assn. Def. Hosps. (pres. 1966-68, 77-78, 82, sec. treas. 1980). Office: Milford Meml Hosp Clarke Ave Milford DE 19963

AHLSCHWEDE, ARTHUR MARTIN, church ednl. ofcl.; b. Seward, Nebr., Dec. 5, 1914; s. Herman F. and Elizabeth (Birky) A.; m. Marie S. Spomer, Nov. 27, 1942; children—Carol, Kathleen, Nancy. B.S. in Edn, Concordia Tchrs. Coll., Seward, 1941, Litt.D., 1962; M.A., U. Minn., 1949; L.H.D., Concordia, Bronxville, 1980, LL.D., 1980. Prin. Luth. elementary schs., Hepler, Kans., 1935-37, Gillett, Ark., 1937-40, Mpls., 1942-49; prin. Concordia High Sch., St. Paul, 1949-53; acad. dean Concordia Coll., St. Paul, 1953-56; asst. exec. sec. bd. higher edn. Luth. Ch.-Mo. Synod, St. Louis, 1956-61, exec. sec., 1961—, chmn. div. higher edn., 1962-80; with Concordia, Austin, 1981—; mem. div. edn. Luth. Council U.S., 1966—. Recipient Christus Primus award Concordia Coll., Ann Arbor, Mich., 1965. Mem. Minn. Pvt. Sch. League, Luth. Edn. Assn., Internat. Walther League, Luth. Laymen's League, Gamma Sigma Delta, Phi Delta Kappa. Democrat. Home: 10105 Willfield Dr Austin TX 78753 Office: 3400 Interstate 35 North Austin TX 78705

AHLSTROM, BJORN, automotive manufacturing company executive; b. Stockholm, Sweden, Nov. 3, 1933; s. Stig John and Elsa Maria (Hesselman) A.; children: Monica, Lars, Annika. M.B.A., U. Gothenburg, Sweden, 1956; postgrad., Law Sch., U. Stockholm, 1958. Vice pres. data processing div. IBM Sweden, Stockholm, 1956-68; dir. mktg. AB Volvo, Gothenburg, 1968-72; pres. Volvo of Am. Corp., Rockleigh, N.J., 1972—; pres., chmn. Volvo Can. Ltd., Toronto, 1972—; dir. Volvo Penta AB, Congoleum Corp., United Jersey Bank. Bd. dirs. Swedish Export Promotion Council; mem. internat. adv. council Columbia U. Mem. Automobile Importers Am. (dir.), Motor Vehicles Mfrs. Assn. (dir.), Swedish-Am. C. of C. (chmn.). Office: Rockleigh Indsl Park Rockleigh NJ 07647

AHLSTROM, RONALD GUSTIN, artist; b. Chgo., Jan. 17, 1922; s. Frederick Karl and Gertrude (Gustin) A.; m. Nancy Costa; 1 son, Arn Gustin. Ed., U. Chgo., Art Inst. Chgo.; B.F.A., 1955. Asst. dir. McCormick Pl. Gallery, 1960-63; dir. Tacoma Art Mus., 1963—. One-man shows include, Barat Coll., Lake Forest, Ill., 1958, Blackhawk Restaurant, Chgo., 1961, collages at, Main St. Galleries, Chgo., 1969, J. Faulkner Galleries, Chgo., 1970, 71, Spiesberger Gallery, Skokie, Ill., 1975, Zriny-Hayes Gallery, Chgo., 1978, group shows include, Chgo. and Vicinity Ann., Art Inst. Chgo., 1955, 56, 59, 61, 62, 64, other shows at, Art Inst., 1957, 58, Inst. Jewish Studies, 1956, 1020 Art Center, 1957, Navy Pier, 1957, 58, Old Town Art Center, 1959, B.C. Holland Gallery, 1961, McCormick Pl. Art Gallery, 1961, 62, 63, Hyde Park (Ill.) Art Center, 1963, Studio 22, 1970, Studio 22, all Chgo., C. McNider Mus., Mason City, Iowa, 1971, Touchstone Gallery, N.Y.C., 1973; exhibited in, Chgo. Artists European Tour Exhibit, USIA, 1957-59, Festival of Fine Arts, Lake Forest, 1958, Soc. of Four Arts Exhibit, West Palm Beach, Fla., 1959, E. Mich. Coll. at Ypsilanti, 1960, Corcoran Gallery Art, Washington, 1961, Tacoma Art Mus., 1963, 5 Abstractionists, Main St. Galleries, 1968; represented in permanent collections, Tacoma Art Mus., Barat Coll. Gallery, Gutenberg Mus., Mainz, Germany, Art Inst. Chgo., Blue Cross, Chgo., Atlantic-Richfield, Chgo., Ill. Bell Telephone, Container Corp. Am., Chgo., also in numerous pvt. collections; work represented in: book Collage and Found. Art (Meilach and Ten Hoor), 1964, Collage and Assemblage, Trend and Techniques (Meilach and Ten Hoor), 1973. Served with U.S. Army, 1942-46. Recipient Clyde M. Carr prize for painting, 1955, Alumni of Sch. Art Inst. prize, 1959, Jane Broadus Clark prize, 1958; both Nvay Pier; Abel Fagan prize Festival Fine Arts, Lake Forest, 1958; Ford Found. purchase prize Seattle Art Mus., 1964. Represented in The Art of Collage (Gerald F. Brommer Davis) 1978. Home: 121 W Park Dr Lombard IL 60148

AHMAD, EQBAL, political scientist; b. Irki-Bihar, India, Dec. 30, 1931; s. Malik Ataur and Khatoon Ismail Rahman; m. Julie Sal Diamond, Oct. 25, 1969; 1 dau., Dohra Khadija. B.A., Punjab U., 1951, M.A., 1953; Ph.D., Princeton U., 1965. Lectr. Pakistan Mil. Acad., 1954-56, Forman Christian Coll., Lahore, Pakistan, 1956-57; asst. prof. Cornell U., 1965-68; fellow Adlai Stevenson Inst., Chgo., 1969-73; sr. fellow Inst. Policy Studies, Washington, 1974—; prof. Hampshire Coll., Amherst, Mass.; Mem. planning bd. Transnat. Inst., Amsterdam. Editorial bd.: Race and Class, 19—, L'Economiste du Tiers Monde, Afrique-Asie; adv. bd.: Arab Studies Quar; Contbr. articles to jours. and anthologies. Mem. nat. council Nat. Emergency Civil Liberties Com., N.Y. Rockefeller Found. fellow. Home: 215 W 92d St New York NY 10025 Office: 1901 Q St NW Washington DC 20009 also Paulus Potterstraat 20 1071 DA Amsterdam Holland

AHMAD, SHAIR, mathematics educator; b. Kabul, Afghanistan, June 19, 1935; s. and Mirand Fatima A.; m. Carol Fulton, Aug. 19, 1974; children: Taj M., Soraya, Schaud. B.S., U. Utah, 1960, M.S., 1962; Ph.D., Case Western Res. U., 1968. Instr. S.D. State U., 1962-64; asst. prof. U. N.D., 1965-66; instr. Case Western Res. U., 1966-68; mem. faculty Okla. State U., Stillwater, 1968-80, prof. math, 1975-78, chmn. dept., 1978-79; prof., chmn. dept. U. Miami, Coral Gables, Fla., 1980—. Co-editor: Differential Equations; contbr. articles to profl. jours. NSF grantee Colombia, 1977, 81, Chile, 1983; travel grantee, Helsinki, 1978. Mem. Soc. Indsl. and Applied Math, Am. Math. Soc. Office: Dept Math U Miami Coral Gables FL 33124

AHMAD, SHARON ERDKAMP, foreign service officer; b. Omaha, Dec. 20, 1933; d. Walter Edward and Lasca Gertrude (Arthur) Erdkamp; m. Syed Sajjad Ahmad, May 1, 1970 (dec.); children: Marya Syeda, Sameena Syeda. B.A., U. Omaha, 1955; M.A., Northwestern U., 1956. With Bur. Econ. Affairs, Dept. State, 1956-58, commd. fgn. service officer, 1958; assigned Am. embassy, Rome, 1958-60, Am. consulate gen., Curaçao, 1960-62, Dept. State (Can. afairs), 1963-66, Am. embassy, Rawalpindi, Pakistan, 1966-70, Dept. State for internat. trade policy, Washington, 1975-78, office dir., 1977-78, dep. asst. sec. for European affairs, 1978-83, staff econ. adv. Commn. on Security and Econ. Assistance, 1983—. Home: 3532 Appleton St NW Washington DC 20008 Office: Dept State 1801 K St NW Suite 921 Washington DC 20006

AHMANN, JOHN STANLEY, educator; b. Struble, Iowa, Oct. 17, 1921; s. Henry Frank and Philomena (Wictor) A.; m. Nancy Ellen Cain, Dec. 27, 1975; children—Sandi Ann, Sheri Kay, Gregory Steven, Shelly Joan. B.A., Trinity Coll., 1943; B.S., Iowa State U., 1947, M.S., 1949, Ph.D., 1951. Instr. profl. studies Iowa State U., 1949-51; asst. prof. div. ednl. psychology and psychol. measurement Cornell U., 1951-54, asso. prof., 1954-58, prof., 1958-60; prof. psychology Colo. State U., 1960-75; also asso. dir. Human Factors Research Lab., 1969-75, asst. to pres., 1961-64, head dept. psychology, 1962-64, acad. v.p., 1964-69; prof. edn. and psychology Iowa State U., Ames, 1975—, disting. prof. edn., 1981—, chmn. dept. profl. studies, 1975—; adj. prof. psychology and edn. U. Denver, 1971-76; vis. prof. Colo. State U., 1951, Wash. State U., 1960, Western Wash. U., 1970; Cons. research programs U.S. Dept. of Edn.; cons. for evalu. of ednl. programs in Colo., N.Y., La., Tex., Ark., Hawaii, Ga., Ariz., Ohio, Minn., Iowa; project dir. Nat. Assessment of Ednl. Progress, 1971-75; dir. various fed. and state sponsored research projects; honor lectr. Mid-Am. State U. Assn., 1976-77. Author: Statistical Methods in Educational and Psychological Research, 1954, Evaluating Student Progress, 6th edit, 1981, Evaluating Elementary School Pupils, 1960, Testing Student Achievements and Aptitudes, 1962, Measuring and Evaluating Educational Achievement, 2d edit, 1975, How Much Are Our Young People Learning?, 1976, Needs Assessment for Program Planning in Vocational Education, 1979, Academic Achievements of Young Americans, 1983; assoc. editor: Ednl. Studies, 1975-79. Served with USNR, 1943-46; PTO. Recipient Laureate award Iowa State U., 1975. Fellow AAAS, Am. Psychol. Assn.; mem. Am. Ednl. Research Assn., Nat. Council on Measurement in Edn., Sigma Xi, Phi Kappa Phi, Phi Delta Kappa, Phi Lambda Upsilon, Alpha Chi Sigma, Psi Chi. Home: 900 South Dakota Ave Apt B4 Ames IA 50010 Office: N 243 Quadrangle Iowa State Univ Ames IA 50011

AHMANN, MATHEW HALL, social action organization administrator; b. St. Cloud, Minn., Sept. 10, 1931; s. Norbert T. and Chlotilda (Hall) A.; m. Margaret Cunningham, Sept. 18, 1954; children: Elizabeth, Thomas, Teresa, Timothy, Ruth, Katherine. B.A., St. John's U., 1952; postgrad., U. Chgo., 1953-54. Social worker Chgo. Dept. Welfare, 1954-56; bus. and circulation mgr. Today mag., 1956-57; field rep. Catholic Interracial Council, Chgo., 1957-59, asst. and acting dir., 1959-60; exec. dir. Nat. Cath. Conf. Interracial Justice, 1959-68, Commn. on Ch. and Society, Archdiocese San Antonio, 1969-73; asso. dir. for govtl. relations Nat. Conf. Cath. Charities, 1973—; organizer, exec. sec. Nat. Conf. Religion and Race, 1962-63. Editor: The New Negro, 1961, Race: Challenge to Religion, 1963, (with Margaret Roach) The Church and the Urban Racial Crisis; Editorial bd.: Integrated Edn. Nat. exec. bd. Workers Def. League; adv. bd. Law Students Civil Rights Research Council. Mem. Am. Civil Liberties Union. Office: 1346 Connecticut Ave NW Washington DC 20036

AHMANSON, WILLIAM HAYDEN, savings and loan and insurance holding company executive; b. Omaha, Oct. 12, 1925; s. Hayden W. and Aimee (Talbod) A.; m. Gloria June Gamble, July 10, 1964; children: Mary Jane, Patricia Ann, Amy Catherine, Dorothy, Joanne, Kimberly. B.S., UCLA, 1950; LL.D., Creighton U., 1972. With H. F. Ahmanson & Co., Los Angeles, 1950—, chief exec. officer, 1969-84, chmn. bd., 1969—; Pres. Nat. Am. Ins. Co., Omaha, 1966—, chmn., 1975—, Home Savings & Loan Assn., 1969-84, Stuyvesant Ins. Group, Allentown, Pa., 1974—, Nat. Am. Ins. Co., Calif. Mem. Founders of Music Center, Los Angeles.; Bd. dirs. Hosp. of Good Samaritan; trustee, v.p. Ahmanson Found., Los Angeles, 1952—; trustee Greater Los Angeles Zoo Assn., Los Angeles County Museum Art, Calif. Inst. Arts. Served with USN. Clubs: Wilshire Country, Chevalier Du Tastevin, Jonathan. Office: 3731 Wilshire Blvd Los Angeles CA 90010 *

AHMED, KHALIL, scientist, educator; b. Lahore, Pakistan, Nov. 30, 1934; came to U.S., 1960, naturalized, 1965; s. Abdul and Ghulam (Sughra) Haq; m. Ritva Helena Veikkamo, June 27, 1969; children: Karim, Rehana. B.S. with honors, Panjab U., Pakistan, 1954, M.S., 1955; Ph.D., McGill U., Montreal, Can., 1960. Research asso. Wistar Inst., Phila., 1960-63; asst. prof. metabolic research Chgo. Med. Sch., 1963-67; mem. sr. staff Nat. Cancer Inst., Balt., 1967-71; research biochemist, chief toxicology research lab. VA Med. Center, Mpls., 1971—; asso. prof. lab. medicine and pathology U. Minn., Mpls., 1973-77, prof., 1977—; research career scientist VA Med. Research Service, 1978—; mem. pathology study sect. NIH, 1978-81; vis. scientist Lab. of Physiology, Helsinki, Finland, 1962; vis. lectr. Chgo. Med. Sch., 1968-69. Contbr. articles to profl. jours.; bd. consultants: Jour. Urology, 1981—. Named outstanding citizen Met. Chgo. Citizenship Council, 1966. Mem. Am. Soc. Pharm. and Exptl. Therapeutics, AAAS, Biochem. Soc. of London, Am. Soc. Biol. Chemists, Endocrine Soc., Sigma Xi. Office: Mpls VA Med Center 54th St and 48th Ave S Minneapolis MN 55417

AHNER, ALFRED FREDRICK, national guard officer; b. Huntington, Ind., Nov. 12, 1921; s. Ray C. and Kathryn (Stern) A.; m. Betty Young, May 3, 1944; children: Mark, Michael. B.A., Ind. Central U., 1947; M.S., Butler U., 1951. Joined Army N.G., 1947, advanced through grades to maj. gen., 1974; adj. gen. Ind. Army N.G., Indpls., 1960, 72—. Chmn., Easter Seals, Ind., 1975-76. Served with U.S. Army, World War II; ETO. Mem. N.G. Assn. Ind. (pres. 1965-66), Adjs. Gen. Assn. U.S. (pres. 1979-80), Am. Legion. Home: 3719 Lorrain Rd Indianapolis IN 46220 Office: Adjutant Gen's Office PO Box 41326 Indianapolis IN 46241

AHRENS, EDWARD HAMBLIN, JR., physician; b. Chgo., May 21, 1915; s. Edward Hamblin and Pauline (Forsyth) A.; m. Gertrude A. Fobes, Sept. 12, 1940; children: Sandra H., Peter Forsyth, Burgess. Grad., Hotchkiss Sch., 1933; B.S. magna cum laude, Harvard, 1937; M.D. cum laude, Harvard, 1941; Dr. Medicine honoris causa, U. Lund (Sweden), 1976. Diplomate: Am. Bd. Pediatrics. Intern Babies Hosp. of N.Y., 1942-43, chief resident, 1951-52; research asst. Rockefeller U., 1946-49, assoc., 1952-58, assoc. prof., 1958-60, prof., 1960—; Sr. fellow NRC and Nat. Found. Infantile Paralysis, 1949-52; mem. metabolism study sect. USPHS, 1956-61, chmn., 1959-61; founder Jour. Lipid Research, 1958, editor, 1963-69; pres. Lipid Research, Inc., 1963-74; mem. bd. sci. counselors National Heart Inst., 1963-67; sci. adv. com. New Eng. Regional Primate Center, 1963-69; mem. Stouffer Prize selection com., 1966-69; chmn. diet-heart rev. panel Nat. Heart Inst., 1967-68; mem. gen. clin. research centers com. NIH, 1970-74; mem. sci. adv. bd. Ernst Klenk Found., West Germany, 1975-80, bd. dirs., 1980—; adv. panel Population Council, 1980—. Mem. exec. bd. Regional Plan Assn., 1973-77, bd. dirs., 1979-82; pres. Onteora Arboretum, 1977—; bd. mgrs. N.Y. Bot. Garden, 1981—. Recipient Research Achievement award Am. Heart Assn., 1978. Mem. Nat. Acad. Scis., Am. Soc. Biol. Chemists, Assn. Am. Physicians, Am. Soc. Clin. Investigation, Phi Beta Kappa. Club: Century. Home: 125 Park Ave Bronxville NY 10708 Office: Rockefeller U 66th St and York Ave New York NY 10021

AHRENS, KENT, museum director, art historian; b. Martinsburg, W. Va.; s. Fred E. and Mary C. (Routzahn) A. A.B., Dartmouth Coll., 1961; M.A., U. Md., 1966; Ph.D., U. Del., 1972. Mem. faculty Fla. State U., Tallahassee, 1971-74, Randolph-Macon Woman's Coll., Lynchburg, Va., 1974-77; mem. curatorial staff Wadsworth Atheneum, Hartford, Conn., 1977-78; mem. faculty Georgetown U., Washington, 1979-82; dir. Everhart Mus., Scranton, Pa., 1982—; mem. task force on art activities Lynchburg Bicentennial Commn., 1975-76; project evaluator Md. Com. Humanities, 1980-82; adv. panel The Lucan Ctr., Scranton, Pa., 1983—. Author: (with others) Rembrandt in the National Gallery of Art, 1969; contbg. author: Wadsworth Atheneum Paintings: The Netherlands and German-speaking Countries, 1969 1978; contbr. articles on Am. art history profl. jours. Served as 1st lt. U.S. Army, 1962-64. Recipient grant-in-aid The Am. Philos. Soc., 1975; Samuel H. Kress fellow Nat. Gallery of Art, 1968-69; Chester Dale fellow Nat. Gallery of Art, 1970-71; NEH fellow, 1973-74. Mem. Coll. Art Assn., Am. Assn. Museums. Office: Everhart Museum Nay Aug Park Scranton PA 18510

AHRENS, THOMAS H., educator; b. N.Y.C., Oct. 25, 1919. B.A. magna cum laude, U. Buffalo, 1938; J.D., Harvard, 1941, N.Y.C. Tech. Coll., 1953. Bar: N.Y. bar 1946. Dir. Edward F. Gallaher Prodns., 1946—; lectr. wines and beverages N.Y.C. Tech. Coll., 1956-69; now prof., dir. program study abroad in France dept. hotel and restaurant mgmt.; dir. research, security analyst Templeton, Dobbrow and Vance, 1962-64; pres. Chef Phillip, Inc., 1956-69. Author radio and TV scripts on wines, gastronomy and music, 1946—. Served to 2d lt. AUS, 1942-45. Decorated officer Chaine des Rotisseurs; Confrerie Saint Etienne d'Alsace; Chevaliers du Tastevin; Commanderie des Cordons Bleus de France; Commanderie de Bordeaux; Medaille de la Ville de Paris, 1976. Mem. N.Y. Soc. Security Analysts, Cercle Interallie (Paris), AAUP, Phi Beta Kappa. Clubs: Harvard, Paris-American, Met., Met. Opera (N.Y.C.); Travellers (Paris). Home: 333 E 69th St New York NY 10021 Office: 300 Jay St Brooklyn NY 11201

AHRENS, WILLIAM HENRY, architect; b. N.Y.C., May 12, 1925; s. John Karl and Sophie (Hashage) A.; m. Joyce Nolan, Mar. 27, 1951. Student, R.I. Sch. Design, 1946; A.B. in Architecture, Princeton U., 1950, M.F.A., 1953; postgrad., Tehran U., 1960. Chief architect Litchfield, Whiting, Bowne, Iran, 1958-61, Rome, 1961-64; dir. internat. ops. Whiting Assos., Rome, 1964-67; architect William H. Ahrens, AIA, Rome, Italy. Prin. archtl. works include ITT Sheraton Hotel, Tunisia, 1971, 83, Aerhotel, Dakar, Senegal, Salalah Hotel, Sultanate of Oman, Esso hotels, Bordeaux, France, Bologna, Italy, Marriott Hotel, Tehran, Iran, New Uaddan Hotel, Tripoli, Libya, Faberge Plant, Italy, Quisisana Hotel, Capri. Mem. joint planning com. English-Speaking Chs., Rome, 1978-79. Served with USAAF, World War II; PTO. Recipient Book award AIA, 1953, Pub. Service award Tehran Lions Club, 1961. Mem. AIA, Nat. Council Archtl. Registration Bds., N.Y. State Assn. Architects. Clubs: Princeton (N.Y.C.); American, Circolo del Golf (Rome). Office: 3 Piazza Remuria Rome Italy 00153

AHRENSFELD, THOMAS FREDERICK, lawyer; b. Bklyn., June 30, 1923; s. Frederick Herman and Madeline Florence (Moffett) A.; m. Joan Ann McGowan, Mar. 17, 1944; 1 son, Thomas Frederick. A.B., Bklyn. Coll., 1948; LL.B., Columbia, 1948. Bar: N.Y. bar 1948. Asso., then partner Conboy, Hewitt, O'Brien & Boardman, N.Y.C., 1948-58; sec., asso. gen. counsel Philip Morris Inc., N.Y.C., 1959-70, v.p., gen. counsel, 1970-76, sr. v.p., gen. counsel, 1976—, also dir.; dir. Mission Viejo Co., 1970—, Miller Brewing Co., 1978—, Seven-Up Co., 1978—. Trustee Trinity-Pawling Sch. Corp. Served to 1st lt. USAAF, 1942-45. Decorated D.F.C. with clusters, Air medal with clusters. Mem. Assn. Bar City N.Y., Am. Bar Assn. Presbyn. (elder). Club: New York (Athletic.). Home: 85 Nannahagan Rd Pleasantville NY 10570 Office: 120 Park Ave New York NY 10017

AIBEL, HOWARD JAMES, diversified industry executive, lawyer; b. N.Y.C., Mar. 24, 1929; s. David and Anne (Fishman) A.; m. Katherine Walter Webster, June 6, 1952; children—David Webster, Daniel Walter, Jonathan Brown. A.B. magna cum laude, Harvard U., 1950, LL.B. cum laude, 1951. Bar: N.Y. bar 1952. Asso. firm White & Case, N.Y.C., 1952-57; with Gen. Electric Co., 1957-64, litigation counsel, 1960-64; with ITT, 1964—, sr. v.p., gen. counsel; dir. ITT World Communications, ITT Continental Baking Co., Internat. Standard Electric Co., The Sheraton Corp. Home: 21 Berkely Rd Westport CT 06880 Office: 320 Park Ave New York NY 10022

AIDINOFF, M(ERTON) BERNARD, lawyer; b. Newport, R.I., Feb. 2, 1929; s. Simon and Esther (Miller) A.; m. Celia Spiro, May 30, 1956; children: Seth G., Gail M. B.A., U. Mich., 1950; LL.B., Harvard U., 1953. Bar: N.Y. 1954. Law clk. to Judge Learned Hand, U.S. Ct. of Appeals, N.Y.C., 1955-56; with firm Sullivan & Cromwell, N.Y.C., 1956-63, partner, 1963-; dir. Gibbs & Cox, Inc., Goody Products, Inc.; Trustee Spence Sch., 1971-79; adv. com. Gibbs Bros. Fedn.; vis. com. Harvard U. Law Sch., 1976-82; adv. com. to IRS commr., 1979-80. Editor-in-chief: The Tax Lawyer, 1974-77. Served as 1st lt. JACC AUS, 1953-55. Mem. Am. Bar Assn. (vice chmn. sect. taxation 1974-

77, chmn.-elect 1981-82, chmn. 1982-83), N.Y. State Bar Assn., Assn. Bar City N.Y. (exec. com. 1974-78, chmn. exec. com. 1977-78, v.p. 1978-79, chmn. taxation com. 1979-81), Am. Law Inst. (fed. income tax project), Council Fgn. Relations, India Ho., Confrerie des Chevaliers du Tastevin, Commanderie de Bordeaux, Phi Beta Kappa. Home: 1120 5th Ave New York NY 10028 Office: 125 Broad St New York NY 10004

AIDMAN, CHARLES, actor, writer, director; b. Indpls., Jan. 31; s. George and Etta (Kwitny) A.; m. Betty Hyatt Linton. B.A., Ind. U., 1947; grad., Neighborhood Playhouse, N.Y.C., 1951. Star, dir., lyricist, adaptor: Spoon River Anthology, Broadway; starred in: show Zoot Suit, N.Y.C. and Los Angeles; off-Broadway show Career; nat. co. After the Fall; films include: Zoot Suit, Kotch; TV appearances include: MASH, Magnum P.I., Quincy; TV movies include: The Picture of Dorian Gray, Red Badge of Courage, Amelia Earhart; other stage roles include: Marc Anthony in Julius Caesar, N.Y. Shakespeare Festival, Thesus in The Cretan Woman, Macduff in Macbeth. Served to lt. (j.g.) USN, 1943-46. Recipient Emmy nomination for adaptation of CBS-TV spl. of Spoon River Anthology, 1969-70. Mem. Acad. Motion Picture Arts and Scis., Dirs. Guild Am., Screen Actors Guild, AFTRA, Actors' Equity, ASCAP, The Magic Castle (asso.). Club: Malibu Tennis. Home: 525 N Palm Dr Beverly Hills CA 90210

AIGNER, DENNIS JOHN, economics educator, consultant; b. Los Angeles, Sept. 27, 1937; s. Herbert Lewis and Della Geraldine (Balasek) A.; m. Vernita Lynne White, Dec. 22, 1957 (div. May 1977); children: Mitchell A., Annette N., Anita L., Angela D. B.S., U. Calif.-Berkeley, 1959, M.A., 1962, Ph.D., 1963. Asst. prof. econs. U. Ill., Urbana, 1962-67; from assoc. prof. to prof. U. Wis., Madison, 1967-76; prof., chmn. dept. econs. U. So. Calif., Los Angeles, 1976—; pres. Dennis Aigner Inc., Los Angeles, 1978—; dir. Live Wires Inc., Los Angeles. Author: Introduction to Statistical Decision Making, 1968, Basic Econometrics, 1971; editor: Latent Variables in Socio-Economic Models, 1977. Fulbright fellow, Belgium, 1970, 71; Fulgright fellow, Israel, 1983; NSF grantee, 1968-70, 70-72, 73-76, 79-81. Fellow Econometric Soc.; mem. Am. Statis. Assn., Am. Econ. Assn. Office: Dept Econs U So Calif University Park CA 90089

AIKAWA, JERRY KAZUO, physician, educator; b. Stockton, Calif., Aug. 24, 1921; s. Genmatsu and Shizuko (Yamamoto) A.; m. Chitose Aihara, Sept. 20, 1944; 1 son, Ronald K. A.B., U. Calif., 1942; M.D., Wake Forest Coll., 1945. Intern, asst. resident N.C. Baptist Hosp., 1945-47; NRC fellow in med. scis. U. Calif. Med. Sch., 1947-48; NRC, AEC postdoctoral fellow in med. scis. Bowman Gray Sch. Medicine, 1948-50, instr. internal medicine, 1950-53, asst. prof., 1953; established investigator Am. Heart Assn., 1952-58; exec. officer lab. service Univ. Hosps., 1958-61, dir. lab. services, 1961-83, dir. allied health program, 1969—, pres. med. bd.; assoc. dean clin. affairs asst. prof. U. Colo. Sch. Medicine, 1953- 60, asso. prof. medicine, 1960-67, prof., 1967—, prof. biometrics, 1974—, assoc. dean clin. affairs, 1974—; Pres. Med. bd. Univ. Hosps. Fellow ACP, Am. Coll. Nutrition; mem. Western Soc. Clin. Research, So. Soc. Clin. Research, Soc. Exptl. Biology and Medicine, Am. Fedn. Clin. Research, AAAS, Central Soc. Clin. Research, AMA, Assn. Am. Med. Colls., Phi Beta Kappa, Sigma Xi, Alpha Omega Alpha. Home: 619 S Poplar Way Denver CO 80224 Office: 4200 E 9th Ave Denver CO 80262

AIKAWA, MASAMICHI, pathologist; b. Kagoshima-Ken, Japan, Sept. 24, 1931; came to U.S., 1959, naturalized, 1973; s. Michiai and Aya (Hayashi) A.; m. Hiroko Ejiri, Dec. 28, 1968; children—Keiko, Taro. M.D., Kyoto U., 1958; D.Sc., 1965; M.S., Georgetown U., 1963. Diplomate: Am. Bd. Pathology. Intern Doctors Hosp., Washington, 1959-60; resident in pathology Georgetown U. Hosp., 1960-64; asso. pathologist Walter Reed Army Inst. Research, Washington, 1964-68; mem. faculty Case Western Res. U. Med. Sch., Cleve., 1968—, prof. pathology, 1974—; cons. electron microscopy Mt. Sinai Hosp., Cleve.; cons. renal pathology VA Hosp., Cleve.; prin. Japanese Lang. Sch., Cleve., 1977. Author: Intracellular Parasitic Protozoa, 1974, The Renal Biopsy: Clinical Pathological Correlations, 1980, also articles, chpts. in books.; Editorial bd.: Exptl. Parasitology, 1973—. Sr. internat. fellow USPHS, 1975; recipient Research Career Devel. award, 1970-75; research grantee, 1969—; commendation for performance U.S. Army, 1968. Mem. Am. Assn. Pathology, Am. Soc. Cell Biology, Internat. Acad. Pathology, Am. Soc. Tropical Hygiene and Medicine, Soc. Protozoology, Am. Soc. Parasitology, AAAS. Club: Cosmos (Washington). Home: 2249 Woodmere Dr Cleveland Heights OH 44106 Office: Inst Pathology Case Western Res Univ Medical Sch Cleveland OH 44106

AIKEN, LINDA HARMAN, foundation executive; b. Roanoke, Va., July 29, 1943; d. William Jordan and Betty Philips (Warner) Harman; married; children: June Elizabeth, Alan James. B.S. in Nursing, U. Fla., 1964, M.Nursing, 1966; Ph.D. in Sociology, U. Tex., 1973. Nurse, U. Fla. Med. Center, Gainesville, 1964-65; instr. Coll. Nursing, U. Fla., Gainesville, 1966-67, Sch. of Nursing, U. Mo., Columbia, 1967-70, clin. nurse specialist, 1967-70; program officer Robert Wood Johnson Found., Princeton, N.J., 1974-76, dir. research, 1976-79, asst. v.p., 1979-81, v.p., 1981—. Asso. editor: Jour. Health and Social Behavior, 1979-81; editorial bd.: Evaluation Quar., 1979-80, Med. Care, 1983—, Health and Med. Care Services Rev., 1979-81; author: Nursing in the 1980s, 1982, Health Policy and Nursing Practice, 1981; contbr. articles to profl. jours. Mem. Adv. Council Social Security, 1982-83. NIH Nurse Scientist fellow, 1970-73; NIH fellow, 1965-66. Mem. Inst. Medicine, Nat. Acad. Scis., Am. Acad. Nursing (pres. 1979-80), Am. Sociol. Assn. (chair med. sociology sect. 1983-84), Council Nurse Researchers, Am. Nurses Assn., Sigma Theta Tau, Phi Kappa Phi. Home: 242 Prospect Ave Princeton NJ 08540 Office: PO Box 2316 Princeton NJ 08540

AIKEN, ROBERT MCCUTCHEN, chemical company executive; b. ashington, Pa., Nov. 8, 1930; s. Robert Wilson and Helen (McCutchen) A.; m. Brenda Jean Ashton, Nov. 6, 1957; children: Jennifer Ann, Robert Ashton. B.S. in M.E., Case Inst. Tech., cleve. With E I. duPont Co., 1952—; planning mgr. plastics dept. E.I. duPont Co., Wilmington, Del., 1967-69, dist. sales mgr., Atlanta, 1969-70, asst. plant mgr., Victoria, Tex., 1970-71, mgr. polymer intermediates ops., Cape Fear, N.C., 1971-74, dir. Caustic-Chlorine div., Wilmington, 1974-75; asst. dir. Latin Am. div. E.I. duPont, Wilmington, 1975-81; dir. E.I. duPont Co., Wilmington, 1975-78, gen. mgr. internat. dept., 1978-81, v.p. internat., Wilmington, 1981—; dir. Du Pont Can. Inc.; bd. govs. Adela Investment Co.,SA. Served to lt. j.g. USN, 1955-58. Mem. World Affairs Council, U.S.-Mexico C. of C., Spain-U.S. C. of C., U.S.-German Democrat Republic Trade & Econ. Council. Republican. Club: Rodney Square (Wilmington). Home: 1225 Birmingham Rd West Chester PA 19380 Office: E I duPont de Nemours & Co 1007 Market St Wilmington DE 19898

AIKEN, WILLIAM, accountant; b. N.Y.C., Mar. 11, 1934; s. Eugene and Ida Lee (Brown) A.; m. Dorothy Harris, Oct. 9, 1954; children—Adrienne Doreen, William, Candice Deanna, Nicole Ophelia, Sharla Dorothy. B.B.A., Baruch Coll., 1963, M.B.A., 1970. C.P.A., N.Y. Ins. examiner N.Y. State Ins. Dept., N.Y.C., 1963-67; sr. accountant Arthur Young & Co., N.Y.C., 1967-72; partner Aiken & Wilson (C.P.A.s), N.Y.C., 1972-78; asst. dep. commr. for budget control N.Y.C. Human Resources Adminstrn., 1978-80; partner Main Hurdman (C.P.A.s), N.Y.C., 1980—; Mem. N.Y. State Bd. Pub. Accountancy, 1974—; Adj. prof. accountancy Medgar Evers Coll., 1973-74. Author: The Black Experience in Large Public Accounting Firms, 1971. Mem. adv. bd. Borough of Manhattan Community Coll., 1973—; bd. dirs. Westchester Minority Bus. Assistance Orgn., Inc., 1973—, Negro Ensemble Co., 1982—; mem. adv. council N.C. Central U., Bus., 1970-72; mem. Nat. Urban League Black Exec. Exchange Program, 1969—; Bd. dirs. Ethical-Fieldston Fund; trustee Studio Mus., in Harlem, 1974; treas. Bucks for Books, Inc. Yonkers Library, 1976—; mem. budget adv. com. City of Yonkers, 1976—. Served with USMC, 1953-56. Recipient Achievement award Nat. Assn. Black Accountants, 1975, Jackson State Coll. chpt., 1973; Achievement medal Nat. Assn. Negro Bus. and Profl. Womens Club, 1973; Distinguished Service award Harlem Preparatory Sch., 1971. Mem. Nat. Assn. Black Accountants (co-founder, pres. 1971-73, dir. 1971—, lit. award N.Y.C. chpt. 1983), Am. Inst. C.P.A.s (com. on minority recruitment 1973—, council 1975-78), N.Y. State Soc. C.P.A.s., Nat. Assn. Minority C.P.A. Firms, 100 Black Men (asst. treas., bd. dirs. 1983—), Nat. Assn. State Bds. of Accountancy, Accountants Club Am., Assn. Govt. Accountants, Mcpl. Fin. Officers Assn. Home: 5640 Netherland Ave Riverdale NY 10471 Office: Main Hurdman 55 E 52d St New York NY 10055 *As we strive to excell at a particular vocation, we should make every effort to prepare well, for it is better to be prepared and not called, than to be called and found unprepared.*

AIKEN, WILLIAM STRAUSS, JR., aeronautical engineer; b. Elizabeth, N.J., Nov. 11, 1920; s. William Strauss and Amy Ramsey (Mack) A.; m. Aileen Louise Saum, June 10, 1944; children: William Strauss, Frances Ann Aiken Mitchell, David A. Aero. Engr., Rensselaer Poly. Inst., Troy, N.Y., 1942. With NASA, 1942—, dir. transp. tech., then dir. aerodynamic and vehicle systems, Washington, 1974-79; chief engr., dir. aero. systems div. Office Aeros. and Space Tech., 1979—; chmn. flight mechanics panel Adv. Group Aerospace Research and Devel., NATO, 1965-67. Author numerous papers in. aeros. Recipient Exceptional Service medal NASA, 1975, rank of Presdl. Meritorious Exec., 1981. Fellow Royal Aero. Soc. Republican. Home: 2918 Blueberry Ln Bowie MD 20715 Office: NASA Washington DC 20546

AIKENS, C(LYDE) MELVIN, anthropology educator, archaeologist; b. Ogden, Utah, July 13, 1938; s. Clyde Walter and Claudia Elena (Brown) A.; m. Alice Hiroko Endo, Mar. 23, 1963; children: Barton Hiroyuki, Quinn Yoshihisa. A.S., Weber Coll., 1958; B.A., U. Utah, 1960; M.A., U. Chgo., 1962, Ph.D., 1966. Curator U. Utah Mus. Anthropology, Salt Lake City, 1963-66; asst. prof. U. Nev.-Reno, 1966-68, U. Oreg., Eugene, 1968-72, assoc. prof., 1972-78, prof. anthropology, 1978—. Author: Fremont Relationships, 1966, Hogup Cave, 1970; co-author: Prehistory of Japan, 1982; editor: Archaeological Studies, 1975. NSF research grantee, 1970, 78-80; NSF Sci. Faculty fellow Kyoto U., Japan, 1971-72; Japan Found. research fellow Kyoto U., 1977-78. Fellow Am. Anthrop. Assn., AAAS; mem. Soc. for Am. Archaeology. Home: 3470 McMillan St Eugene OR 97405 Office: Dept Anthropology U Oregon Eugene OR 97403

AIKENS, JOAN DEACON, govt. ofcl.; b. Lansdowne, Pa., May 1, 1928; d. Robert Wallace and Bessie (Crook) Deacon; m. Donald R. Aikens (div.); 1 son, Donald R. B.A., Ursinus Coll., 1950, LL.D. (hon.), 1979. Fashion cons. Park Ave. Shop, Swarthmore, Pa., 1971-73; v.p. Lew Hodges Communications, Inc., Valley Forge, Pa., 1974-75; mem. Fed. Election Commn., Washington, 1975—, vice chmn., 1977-78, chmn., 1978-79; Chmn. women's div. Washington conf. Republican Nat. Com., 1966; hospitality chmn. Pa. del. Rep. Nat. Conf., 1968, alt.-at-large, 1972; bd. dirs. Nat. Fedn. Rep. Women, 1972-75; active Pa. Council Rep. Women, 1960-74, pres., 1972-74; co-chmn. Women for McCorkle-Williams, Pa. Rep. State Com., 1970; mem. exec. com. Pa. Rep. State Com., 1972-74, elected mem., 1974; vice chmn. Citizens for Nixon-Agnew, Delaware County (Pa.) Rep. Party, 1968, Com. to Re-Elect the Pres., 1972; precinct committeewoman Swarthmore (Pa.) Rep. Party, 1960-75; pres. Swarthmore Council Rep. Women, 1970-72; chmn. various campaigns Swarthmore Rep. Hdqrs., 1960-74. Active Swarthmore Presbyn. Ch., 1955-64; bd. dirs. Women's Assn., 1956-60; active Riddle Meml. Hosp., Delaware County, Pa., 1958-74; pres. Women's Bd. Asso. Auxs., 1970-72; mem. Women's bd. Women's Med. Coll., Phila., 1978—. Office: 1325 K St NW Washington DC 20463

AIKMAN, JOHN EDGAR, lawyer, engr.; b. Brockway, Pa., Jan. 1, 1919; s. Charles E. and Lena (Smith) A.; m. Barbara C. Curry, Jan. 19, 1951; children—Nancy, Rebecca, John M. B.S., Pa. State U., 1940; J.D., U. Pitts., 1948. Bar: Pa. bar 1949. Fuel and power engr. U.S. Steel, Pitts., 1940-42; practice in, Brookville, Pa., 1948-68; v.p. Brockway Glass Co., Inc., Pa., 1968-77, gen. counsel, 1968—, sr. v.p., 1977—, corp. affairs, 1978—; pres. subs. Crown Airways, Inc.; dir. Unibank, Brookville, Pa. Served to maj. USAAF, 1942-46. Mem. Pa., Jefferson County bar assns. Home: Northview Dr Brookville PA Office: McCullough Ave Brockway PA 15825

AILES, ROGER EUGENE, production company executive; b. Warren, Ohio, May 15, 1940; s. Robert Eugene and Donna Marie (Cunningham) A. B.F.A., Ohio U., 1962. Assoc. dir. TV sta. KYW-TV, Cleve., 1962-63, producer, dir., 1963-65; producer Mike Douglas Show Westinghouse Broadcasting Corp., Phila., 1965-67, exec. producer, 1967-68; exec. producer TV for Richard M. Nixon, 1968; pres. Ailes Communications, Inc., N.Y.C., 1969—; exec. v.p. TV News Inc., N.Y.C., 1975-76; cons. WCBS-TV, 1978—; communications cons. to polit. and bus. leaders. Producer: Broadway musical Mother Earth, 1972; play Hot-L Baltimore, 1973-76; exec. producer, dir.: TV spl. The Last Frontier, 1974; producer, dir.: Fellini: Wizards, Clowns and Honest Liars (Emmy nominee 1977). Recipient 2 Emmy awards for Mike Douglas Show Nat. Assn. TV Arts and Scis., 1967, 68; award for Shakespeare prodn. Fine Arts Mag., 1964; Liberty Bell award Advt. Alliance of Phila., 1971; Commendation award for contbn. to communications Ohio U., 1972; 4 Obie awards for Hot-L Baltimore, 1973. Mem. Dirs. Guild Am., A.F.T.R.A., Radio/TV News Dirs. Assn. Office: 456 W 43d St New York NY 10036

AILES, STEPHEN, lawyer; b. Romney, W.Va., Mar. 25, 1912; s. Eugene Elliot and Sallie (Cornwell) A.; m. Helen Wales, June 24, 1939; children—Hester A. Nettles, Stephen Cornwell, Walter Brady, Richard Arvine. A.B., Princeton U., 1933; LL.B., W.Va. U., 1936. Bar: W.Va. bar 1936, D.C. bar 1946. Asst. prof. law W.Va. U., 1937-40; practice in, Martinsburg, W.Va., 1936-37, 40-42; mem. legal staff OPA, 1942-46, asst. gen. counsel consumer goods price div., 1945-46; counsel U.S. Econ. Mission to Greece, 1947; partner Steptoe & Johnson, 1948-61, 65-70, 77—; under sec. Army, 1961-64, sec., 1964-65; pres. Assn. Am. Railroads, 1971-77; mem. Pres.'s Fgn. Intelligence Adv. Bd., 1976-77, Intelligence Oversight Bd., 1976-77; dir. Riggs Nat. Bank, Washington. Former trustee Princeton U., Episcopal High Sch. Mem. Bar Assn. D.C., Am., Fed. bar assns., D.C. Bar, W.Va. Bar. Clubs: Chevy Chase (Md.); Burning Tree (Bethesda, Md.); Metropolitan, International, Alfalfa, Alibi, 1925 F St. (Washington). Home: 4521 Wetherill Rd Westmoreland Hills Bethesda MD 20816 Office: 1250 Connecticut Ave Washington DC 20036

AILEY, ALVIN, choreographer; b. Rogers, Tex., Jan. 5, 1931; s. Alvin and Lula E. (Cliff) A. Student, U. Calif. at Los Angeles, 1949-50, Los Angeles City Coll., 1950-51, San Francisco State Coll., 1952-53, Lester Horton Dance Theater, Los Angeles, 1949-51, 53; with, Hanya Holm, N.Y.C., 1954-55, Martha Graham, 1956, others; acting student with, Stella Adler, 1960-62; with, Milton Katselas, 1961, Princeton U., Bard Coll., Adelphi U., Cedar Crest Coll. Choreographer, Lester Horton Dance Theater, 1953—; formed, Alvin Ailey Am. Dance Theater, 1958; now artistic dir.; performed numerous festivals, 1959—, Australian, S.E. Asian tour, 1962, World Festival Negro Arts, Dakar, Senegal, 1966, World Festival Negro Arts, E. and W. Africa, 1967, World Festival Negro Arts, Russia, 1970, world tour, 1977, S. Am., 1978, 81; actor, 1961—; choreographer, dancer TV, 1954—, also motion pictures; performances include The Carefree Tree, 1956, Sing Man Sing, 1956, Show Boat, 1957, Jamaica, 1957, Call Me by My Rightful Name, Tiger Tiger Burning Bright, Talking To You; choreographed: musicals African Holiday; operas Leonard Bernstein's Mass; spls. for TV including Solo for Mingus, 1979, Memoria, 1979; spl. co. performances include inaugural eve gala for Pres, 1977, White House State Dinner, 1978, King of Morocco in Marrakesh, 1979; created numerous maj. works for co., also for Joffrey Ballet, Harkness Ballet, Am. Ballet Theater, Bat-Dor, Ballet Internat. de Caracas, Paris Opera Ballet, After Ballet co. Recipient Springarn medal, 1976, Mayor's Award of Art and Culture, 1977; Capezio award, 1978; UN Peace Medal. Address: Alvin Ailey Am Dance Theater 1515 Broadway New York NY 10036

AILLONI-CHARAS, DAN, business executive; b. Ploiesti, Rumania, May 22, 1930; came to U.S., 1950, naturalized, 1960; s. Max and Felicia (Lupescu) Charas; m. Miriam C. Taytelbaum, Oct 8, 1957; children—Ethan Benjamin, Orrin, Adam. A.B. with honors, U. Calif., Berkeley, 1952, M.A., 1953; M.A. Coro Found. fellow, 1953; Ph.D. (Univ. honors scholar), N.Y.U., 1968. Project dir. Marplan div. Communications Affiliates, Inc., N.Y.C., 1958-60; supr. advt. studies NBC, N.Y.C., 1960-62; dir. consumer and communications research Forbes Research, Inc., N.Y.C., 1962; mgr. market research Chesebrough-Pond's, Inc., N.Y.C., 1963-64, new products mgr., 1964-68, mgr. internat. mktg. services dept., 1968-69; pres. Stratmar Systems, Inc., N.Y.C., 1969—; asst., then prof. mktg. Pace U., 1963—. Editor: Mktg. Rev, 1960-63, Proc. 1st Ann. Conf. on Research Design, 1964, New Directions in Research Design, 2d Conf, 1965, Planning, 1968-71; Bd. editors: Jour. Consumer Marketing, 1982—. Trustee Inst. Advanced Mktg. Studies, 1965-66; bd. dirs. Young Men's Bd. Trade, 1960-63, N.Y. State Jr. C. of C., 1962, Philharmonic Symphony of Westchester, 1977-80; bd. advisers Ad Expo, 1978. Mem. Am. Mktg. Assn. (pres. N.Y. chpt. 1965-66, nat. v.p. 1970-71), Promotion Mktg. Assn. Am. (dir. 1978—, chmn. edn. com. 1979-81), N.Am. Soc. Corp. Planning (dir. 1970-72), Inst. of Dirs. (London), AAUP, Sigma Delta Chi, Phi Sigma Alpha. Clubs: Canadian, Met. Home: Woodland Dr Rye Brook NY 10573 Office: 385 Madison Ave New York NY 10017:

AINBINDER, SEYMOUR, real estate developer; b. Bklyn., July 10, 1928; s. Max Z. and Sonia (Alterman) A.; m. Rose B. Cooper, Jan. 14, 1951; children—Michael, Jonathan. Student, Upsala Coll., 1955, Rutgers U., 1956. Pres. Almart/J.B. Hunter div. Allied Stores Corp., 1962-72; v.p. Allied Stores, 1968-72, Arlen Shopping Centers, Chattanooga, 1972-77; founder Ainbinder Assos., Houston, 1977—. Active Nat. Conf. Christians and Jews, Boy Scouts Am., Friends of Tel Aviv U. Mem. Internat. Council Shopping Centers. Club: Westwood Country (Houston). Home: 11919 Longleaf Ln Houston TX 77024 Office: Ainbinder Assos 5850 San Felipe St Houston TX 77057

AINSLIE, MICHAEL LEWIS, organization executive; b. Johnson City, Tenn., May 12, 1943; s. George Lewis and Jean Clare (Waddell) A.; m. Lucy Scardino, Dec. 11, 1971; 1 son, Michael Loren, stepchildren: Katherine, Robbie Ann, Liza. B.A., Vanderbilt U., 1965; M.B.A., Harvard U., 1968. Assoc. McKinsey & Co., N.Y.C., 1968-71; pres. Palmas Del Mar, P.R., 1971-75; sr. v.p., chief operating officer N-Ren Corp., Cin., 1975-80; pres. Nat. Trust for Historic Preservation, Washington, 1980—; mem. policy panel for design arts Nat. Endowment for Arts, Washington, 1983; dir. Guest Services, Inc., Washington, 1981—. Bd. overseers U. Pa. Grad. Sch. Fine Arts, Phila., 1982—; mem. exec. council Harvard Bus. Sch., 1982—; bd. dirs. Nat. Bldg. Mus., Washington, 1982—; mem. alumni bd. Vanderbilt U., 1983—. Corning Found. fellow, 1965-66. Clubs: Metropolitan; F St. (Washington). Office: National Trust for Historic Preservation 1785 Massachusetts Ave NW Washington DC 20036

AINSWORTH, MARY DINSMORE SALTER, psychologist, educator; b. Glendale, Ohio, Dec. 1, 1913; d. Charles Morgan and Mary (Hoover) Salter; m. Leonard H. Ainsworth, June 10, 1950 (div. Aug. 1960). B.A., U. Toronto, 1935, M.A., 1936, Ph.D., 1939. Bar: Diplomate Am. Bd. Profl. Psychology. With U. Toronto, 1935-42; cons. to dir. personnel selection, maj. Can. Women's Army Corps, 1942-45; supt. Women's rehab. Dept. Vets. Affairs, Can., 1945-46; asst. prof. dept. psychology U. Toronto, 1946-50; sr. research psychologist Tavistock Clinic, London, 1950-54; sr. research fellow E. African Inst. Social Research, Kampala., Uganda., 1954-55; asso. prof. psychology Johns Hopkins U., 1956-63, prof. psychology, 1963-75, U. Va., Charlottesville, 1975—; fellow Center Advanced Studies, 1975-77; clin. psychologist Sheppard and Enoch Pratt Hosp., 1956-61; Fellow Center Advanced Study Behavioral Scis., 1967-68. Author: (with A.W. Ham) Doctor in the Making, 1942, (with B. Klopfer, W. Klopfer, R.R. Holt) Developments in the Rorschach Technique, 1954, (with L.H. Ainsworth) Measuring Security in Personal Adjustment, 1958, Infancy in Uganda, 1967, (with M.C. Blehar, E. Waters, S. Wall) Patterns of Attachment. Fellow Am. Psychol. Assn.; mem. Brit. Psychol. Soc., Soc. Research in Child Devel., Phi Beta Kappa. Home: 920 Rosser Ln Charlottesville VA 22903

AINSWORTH, OSCAR RICHARD, educator; b. Vicksburg, Miss., July 28, 1922; s. Richard Henry and Harriet (Henley) A.; m. Edith Josephine Wetzel, Dec. 20, 1947. A.A., Hinds Jr. Coll., 1945; B.A., U. Miss., 1946, M.A., 1946; Ph.D., U. Calif. at Berkeley, 1951. Prof. math. U. Ala., 1950—; summer employment Redstone Arsenal, ARGMA, ABMA George C. Marshall Space Flight Center, Huntsville, Ala., 1953-62; research engr. Douglas Aircraft, Long Beach, Cal., summer 1956; applied physicist Boeing Airplane Co., Seattle, summer 1957; cons. G.C. Marshall Space Flight Center, 1962-63, research contract, 1963-64; research contracts NASA, 1965—. Contbr. articles to profl. jours. NASA-ASEE fellow, 1982, 83. Mem. Am. Math. Soc., SIAM, Sigma Xi, Pi Mu Epsilon (hon.), Sigma Pi Sigma (hon.), Phi Kappa Psi. Home: 3102 30th St Northport AL 35476

AINSWORTH-LAND, GEORGE THOMAS, philosopher, author, educator; b. Hot Springs, Ark., Feb. 27, 1933; s. George Thomas Lock and Mary Elizabeth L; m. Jo A. Gunn, 1957 (dec. 1969); children—Robert E., Thomas G., Patrick A.; m. Vaune E. Ainsworth, Dec. 23, 1978. Student, Millsaps Coll., 1952-54, U. Veracruz, Mexico, 1957-59; Ph.D., Sussex Inst. Tech., Eng., 1967,. Program dir. Woodall TV Stas. of Ga., Columbus, 1951-52; ops. mgr. Lamar Broadcasting, Jackson, Miss., 1952-54; anthrop. research Cora, Huichole and Yaqui tribes, Latin Am., Mexico, 1955-60; dir. gen. Television del Norte (NBC), Mexico, 1960-62; v.p. Roman Corp., St. Louis, 1962-64; chmn. Transolve Inc., Cambridge, Mass.; and St. Petersburg, Fla., 1964-68; chief exec., chmn. Innotek Corp., N.Y.C.; also pres. Hal Roach Studios, Los Angeles and N.Y.C., 1969-71; chmn. emeritus, partner Turtle Bay Inst., N.Y.C., 1971-80; vice chmn. Wilson Learning Corp., Mpls., 1980—; pres. Inst. Transformational Research, Honolulu and Buffalo, 1980—; prof. Mankato State U., 1973-74; dir. Centre for Applied Creativity, Balt., Agapi Clinic, N.Y., Motivation Scis., Inc.,

N.Y.C., Inst. Fundamental and Holistic Research, Buffalo; trustee Forest Inst. Profl. Psychology, Des Plaines, Ill.; cons.-in-residence Synplex Inc., N.Y.C., AT&T, Iowa Pub. Service Corp., Forest Hosp., Des Plaines, Social Systems Inc., Chapel Hill, N.C., Children's Hosp., Nat. Med. Center, Washington; Mem. Nat. Action Com. on Drug Edn., 1974-75; co-chmn. Syncon Conf., So. Ill. U., 1972-74; keynoter Emerging Trends in Edn. Conf., Minn., 1974, 75, Bicentennial Conf. on Limits to Growth, So. Ill. U., 1976, No. States Power Conf., 1975, U.S. Office of Edn., Nat. Conf. Improvements in Edn., 1979, World Conf. on Gifted, 1977, S.W. Conf. on Arts, 1977, World Symposium on Humanity, 1979, Internat. Conf. Internal Auditors, 1977, Four Corners Conf. on Arts, 1977, Chautaugua Inst., 1977, 78, Conf. Am. Art Tchrs. Assn., 1979, Internat. Conf. on Gifted, 1982, others; keynoter, co-chmn. com. on society World Conf. Peace and Poverty, St. Joseph's U., Phila., 1968; mem. Nat. Security Seminar, U.S. Dept. Def., 1975; cons., keynoter corp. policy seminars The Bell System, AT&T, 1978, 79; mem. faculty Edison Electric Grad. Mgmt. Inst., 1972-78; artist-in-residence Acad. Visual and Performing Arts, Buffalo; lectr., seminarian in transformation theory, strategic planning and interdisciplinary research Menninger Found.; lectr., seminarian in transformation theory and interdisciplinary research U. Ga., Emory U., Waterloo (Can.) U., Office of Sec. HEW, Jamestown (N.Y.) Coll., Hofstra U., U.S. Office Edn., Calif. Dept. Edn., St. Louis U., Coll. William and Mary, Webster Coll., St. Louis, Wash. State Dept. Edn., U. Ky., So. Ill. U., St. John's U., Harvard U., U. South Fla., Mass. Inst. Tech., U. Veracruz, Children's Hosp. D.C., Gov.'s Sch. N.C., Scottsdale (Ariz.) Center Arts, Humbolt U., East Berlin, AAAS, others; advanced faculty Creative Problem Solving Inst., SUNY, 1965-, S. Conn. Coll.; distinguished lectr. Northwestern State U., La., State U. Coll. N.Y., Coll. of the Lakes, Ill.; cons. govt., industry and instns. in U.S. and abroad. Author: Innovation Systems, 1967, Innovation Technology, 1968, Four Faces of Poverty, 1968, (as George T.L. Land) Grow or Die: The Unifying Principle of Transformation, 1973, Creative Alternatives and Decision Making, 1974, The Opportunity Book, 1980, (with Vaune E. Ainsworth-Land) Forward to Basics; contbr. to profl. jours. and gen. mags. Trustee Am. Excellence Found., Washington. Recipient Community Leader Am. award Am. Biog. Inst., 1972-74; Internat. Community Service award Inst. Internat. Biography, London, 1978. Fellow N.Y. Acad. Scis.; mem. AAAS, Soc. Gen. Systems Research, Soc. Study Gen. Process (founding dir.), Am. Soc. Cybernetics (past v.p.), Creative Edn. Found. (colleague), Soc. Am. Value Engrs. (past dir.), World Future Soc., Internat. Platform Assn., Com. for Future (colleague), Authors Guild, Authors League Am., Life Expansion Network (Can.), Oceanic Soc. Club: Lambs (N.Y.C.). Research on interdisciplinary unification. Discovered prins. of transformation theory. Home: 1400 Lincoln Ave Minneapolis MN 55403 1314 Williams Ave Natchitoches LA 71457 Office: 6950 Washington Ave S Eden Prairie MN 55344 *I was fortunate enough in my youth to experience and learn what has been the most important idea and principle in my life, the natural law of enrichment through diversity. This concept means that change and growth come about more by combining differentnesses than by adding likenesses. As in the biological world, where such behavior produces the vitality of hybrids, and as in chemistry, where the co-valent bonds of carbon make life possible, in human life we can also benefit immeasurably from using our differences as a creative way to grow anew. Thus, we can evolve beyond polarizations such as nationalism, racism, sexism, institutionalism and other obstacles that separate us and stunt our ability to realise the full community of Man.*

AIRD, JOHN BLACK, lawyer, lieutenant governor Ontario; b. Toronto, Ont., Can., May 5, 1923; s. Hugo Reston and May (Black) A.; m. Lucille Jane Housser, July 27, 1944; children: Lucille Elizabeth Aird Menear, Jane Victor Aird Blackmore, Hugh Housser, Katherine Black. B.A., U. Toronto, 1946; LL.B., Osgoode Hall Law Sch.; LL.D. (hon.), Wilfred Laurier U., 1975, Royal Mil. Coll. Can., 1980, U. Western Ont., 1983. Bar: Ont. 1949, created queen's counsel, 1960. Assoc. Wilton & Edison, 1949-53; ptnr. Edison, Aird & Berlis, 1953-74, Aird, Zimmerman & Berlis, 1974-78, Aird & Berlis, Toronto, 1978—; chancellor Wilfred Laurier U., 1977—; mem. Senate of Can., 1964-74; lt. gov. Ont., 1980—; chmn. Can. sect. Can.-U.S. Permanent Joint Bd. Def., 1971-79; mem. Com. of Nine, N. Atlantic Assembly, 1973; chmn. Inst. Research on Public Policy, 1974—; mem. Senate of Can., 1964-74. Hon. counsel St. Paul's Anglican Ch., Toronto. Served as lt. Royal Can. Navy, 1942-45, capt. Can. Armed Forces Res., 1981; hon. col. 49th Field Regt., Royal Can. Army, 1983. Decorated officer Order Can.; knight of grace Order St. John of Jerusalem; Knight comdr. Order of St. Lazarus of Jerusalem. Mem. Naval Officers Assns. Can. (hon. pres.), Alpha Delta Phi. Anglican. Clubs: York, Toronto, Toronto Golf, Granite. Home: 2 Glenallan Rd Toronto ON Canada M4N 1G7 Office: Queen's Park/Legis Bldg Toronto ON Canada M7A 1A1

AIRD, KENNETH, banker; b. Detroit, June 13, 1925; s. David and Laura (Strang) A.; m. Jean Rodda, May 1, 1948; children—Nancy, David, Brian. B.B.A., U. Detroit, 1957; grad., Advanced Mgmt. Program, Harvard, 1965. With Mfrs. Nat. Bank Detroit, 1942—, exec. v.p., 1970-73, vice chmn. bd., 1973—. Served with AUS; 1943-46. Mem. Financial Execs. Inst., Bank Adminstrn. Inst. Clubs: Detroit, Harvard Business of Detroit, Detroit Athletic. Home: 37735 River Bend Farmington Hills MI 48024 Office: Mfrs Bank Tower Renaissance Center Detroit MI 48243

AIREY, JOHN RICHARD, scientific company executive; b. Wakefield, United Kingdom, May 17, 1940; came to U.S., 1964, naturalized, 1970; s. Jack N. and May (Mills) A.; m. Edna Sharpe, Sept. 2, 1961; children: John M., David C., James M. B.A., Cambridge U., 1961, M.A., 1971; Ph.D., Toronto U., 1964; postgrad. (fellow), Brown U., 1964-65. Prin. research scientist Avco Everett Research Lab., Mass., 1965-70; head laser physics br. U.S. Naval Research Lab., Washington, 1972-76; asst. dir. Office of Laser Fusion, U.S. Dept. Energy, 1976-78; dir. directed energy program, office of under sec. for research and engring. U.S. Dept. Def., Washington, 1978-82; v.p. Sci. Applications Inc., 1982—. Contbr. articles to profl. jours. NRC fellow, 1961-64; Ramsay fellow, 1970-71; recipient Crozier prize Am. Def. Preparedness Assn., 1981. Patentee supersonic flow gaseous chem. laser, 1971. Home: 1203 Azalea Dr Rockville MD 20850

AIRINGTON, HAROLD L., forest products company executive; b. Rockingham, N.C., Nov. 30, 1927; s. Clarence L. and Etta (Ross) A.; m. Joyce M. Pendergast, June 6, 1950; children: Karen, Deborah, Russell, James. Student, Balt. City Coll., Anne Arundel Coll., Balt. Salesman Ga. Pacific Corp., Charlotte, N.C., 1954-60; br. mgr. distbn. div. G-P Corp., Richmond, Va., 1960-70, regional mgr. distbn. div., Landover, Md., 1970-78; v.p. wood products sales Ga.-Pacific Corp., Atlanta, 1978—. *

AIRIS, THOMAS FERGRIEVE, cons. engr.; b. Eau Claire, Wis., May 2, 1906; s. Adam J. and Edna (Thomas) A.; m. Marcia M. Morse, Oct. 24, 1953; children—Susan, John, Janet. Student, Carroll Coll., Waukesha, Wis., 1924-25; B.S. in Civil Engring, U. Wis., 1929, 1956. Registered profl. engr., Wis., D.C. With Corps Engrs., 1929-59; constrn. engr. charge U.S. portion St. Lawrence Seaway, 1954-59; dep. dir. D.C. Dept. Hwys. and Traffic, 1959-63, dir., 1963-75; ret., 1975; cons. engr. on airport and hwy. constrn. in Iran and Washington Tippetts Abbett McCarthy Stratton, Washington, 1975—. Served to col., C.E. AUS, 1942-47, 50-53. Decorated Army Commendation medal; named one of top ten pub. works men of year Am. Pub. Works Assn., 1967, Greater Washington Area Engr. of Year by Engring. Socs., Greater Washington, 1966; Distinguished Service citation for contbns. to engring. U. Wis., 1977. Mem. Soc. Am. Mil. Engrs., Am. Soc. C.E., Am. Assn. State Hwy. and Transp. Ofcls. (pres. 1972-73), Am. Road Builders Assn. (bd. dirs. 1966-68), Assn. Hwy. Ofcls. N. Atlantic States (pres. 1966-67), Sigma Phi Epsilon. Home: 10119 Gary Rd Potomac MD 20854 Office: 1101 15th St NW Washington DC 20005

AIRTH, MISKIT, TV programming executive; b. Live Oak, Pa., May 29, 1939; d. George Edward and Dorothy A. A.B., Randolph-Macon Woman's Coll., 1961; M.A., Dallas Theatre Ctr., Baylor U., 1963. Mem. repertory theater, tchr.-dir. Children's Theater Dallas Theater Ctr., 1961-63; with touring children's theater Nat. Theater Co., 1963-64; with Phoenix Theater, 1964-69, Am. Place Theater, 1964-69, Shakespeare-in-the-Park, N.Y.C., 1964-69; producer Sta. WPIX-TV, N.Y.C., 1969-75; assoc. producer Good Morning America ABC-TV, N.Y.C., 1975-76; producer A Woman Is—With Bess Myerson Sta. WCBS-TV, N.Y.C., 1976-77; exec. producer Sta. WABC-TV, N.Y.C., 1977-80; dir. program devel. for East Coast Viacom Enterprises, N.Y.C., 1980-81; dir. programming and studio ops. Warner Amex Cable Communications, 1981—; vis. scholar Boston U. Communications Inst.; lectr. Womanschool, N.Y.C., Randolph-Macon Woman's Coll., Lynchburg, Va., New Sch. for Social Research, N.Y.C., Inst. New Cinema Artist. Producer: weekly film documentary New York Closeup, Sta. WPIX-TV, 8 N.Y. areas, 1969-73 (Emmy awards, 2 personal awards); documentary series WABC Spl. Reports, 1977-80; WABC You! show (Emmy for pilot show); instant spl. Life Was Worth Living, WABC, N.Y.C.; You Can't Get There From Here (Emmy), The Town That Build N.Y. (Emmy), Elvis-Love Him Tender with Joel Siegel (Emmy); (on location) prodns. Studio 30, QUBE Cable; Cincinnati Alive (Emmy), Swordquest (Ace award), (others). Mem. adv. com. So. Ohio Coll.; mem. planning com. Nat. Cancer Communications Conf., Houston. Recipient 2 Silver medals Internat. Film Festival, N.Y.C., 1979, 80, Emmy award for outstanding documentary, 1971, 72, 80, Emmy award for outstanding mag., 1980, Emmy award for outstanding entertainment, 1980, 2 awards of excellence Communications Excellence for Black Audiences, 1979, 80, Bd. Govs. award Nat. Acad. TV arts and Scis., 1983, award Nat. Cable TV Assn., 1982, 4 nominations 1983 Ace Awards, 1983 Emmy Awards. Mem. Nat. Acad. TV Arts and Scis. (gov. N.Y.C. chpt.), Am. Women in Radio and TV (dir. N.Y.C. chpt.), Women in Cable (founder, 1st pres. Cin. Tri-State chpt.), Phi Beta Kappa. Office: Warner Amex Cable Communications 11252 Cornell Park Dr Cincinnati OH 45242 *The secret of my sucess? Nobody ever told me I couldn't do or be anything I wanted. Also, I have insatiable curiosity about life.*

AISSEN, MICHAEL ISRAEL, mathematics educator; b. Istanbul, Turkey, Jan. 16, 1921; came to U.S., 1922, naturalized, 1943; s. Oscar Ansil and Judith (Cohen) A.; m. Mildred Davis, Apr. 17, 1944; children: Judith, Louis Claire. Student, Cooper Union Sch. Engring., 1938-41; B.S., CCNY, 1947; Ph.D., Stanford U., 1951. Research scientist radiation lab. Johns Hopkins U., 1951-60; assoc. prof. Fordham U., N.Y.C., 1961-64, prof. math., 1964-70; prof., chmn. dept. math. Newark Coll. Arts and Scis.-Rutgers U., Newark, 1970—; vis. prof. Syracuse U., spring 1977; cons. aerospace research labs. Air Force Dept., Dayton, Ohio, 1967-68; tchr. AID, Pakistan, 1967, 70; mem. Courant Inst. Math., 1960. Served with AUS, 1943-46. Mem. N.Y. Acad. Scis. (chmn. math. sect. 1970—, mem. conf. com. 1976-78), Soc. Indsl. and Applied Math. (chmn. Balt. sect. 1957), Am. Math. Soc., Math. Assn. Am. (new ideas com. 1976-78, bd. govs. 1979-82). Home: 248 North Ave W Cranford NJ 07016 Office: Math Dept Newark Coll Arts and Scis Rutgers U Newark NJ 07102

AITAY, VICTOR, violinist; b. Budapest, Hungary; came to U.S., 1946, naturalized, 1952; s. Sigmund and Irma (Fazekas) A.; m. Eva Vera Kellner, Nov. 17, 1946; 1 dau., Ava Georgianna. Pvt. study with father; entered, Royal Acad. Music at age 7; studied with, Bela Bartok, Ernest von Dohnanyi, Leo Weiner, Zoltan Kodaly; artist diploma, Franz Liszt Royal Acad. Music, Budapest, 1939. Prof. First Internat. String Congress; prof. violin DePaul U., Chgo., 1962—. Organizer, leader, Aitay String Quartet; on tour, Europe, recitals; also soloist symphony orchestras; concert master, Met. Opera Assn., N.Y.C., 1948-54; co-concertmaster, Chgo. Symphony Orch., 1954—; leader, Chgo. Symphony String Quartet; condr., music dir., Lake Forest (Ill.) Symphony Orch. Numerous performances Casals Festival at invitation of Pablo Casals. Office: Chicago Symphony Assn 220 S Michigan Ave Chicago IL 60604 *

AITKEN, HUGH GEORGE JEFFREY, economics educator; b. Deal, Eng., Oct. 12, 1922; came to U.S., 1948, naturalized, 1957; s. George Jeffrey and Ellen (Hughes) A.; m. Janice Hunter, July 9, 1955; 1 dau., Ellen Bradshaw. M.A., St. Andrews U., 1947, U. Toronto, 1948; Ph.D., Harvard U., 1951. Research fellow Harvard, 1951-55; from instr. to prof. econs. U. Calif. at Riverside, 1955-65; George D. Olds prof. econs. Amherst Coll., 1965—; Claude Bissell prof. U. Toronto (Ont., Can.), 1975. Author: The Welland Canal Company, 1954, Canadian Economic History, 1956, Taylorism at Watertown Arsenal, 1960, American Capital and Canadian Resources, 1961, Syntony and Spark — The Origins of Radio, 1976; Editor: Jour. Econ. History, 1966-69. Served with RAF, 1942-46. Guggenheim fellow, 1973-74; Nat. Endowment for Humanities fellow, 1978-79. Mem. Econ. History Assn., Soc. History Tech. Home: 155 Amity St Amherst MA 01002

AJAY, ABE, artist; b. Altoona, Pa., Mar. 24, 1919; s. William and Mary (Simmons) A.; m. Betty Raymond, Dec. 16, 1947; children—Alexander, Stephen, Robin. Student, public schs., Altoona. With WPA Fed. Art Project, 1939; staff artist newspaper PM, 1942-44; free lance artist for New York Times, Fortune, Sports Illustrated, other publs., 1946-64; prof. visual arts SUNY, Purchase, 1973—. Exhibited in one-man shows in, N.Y.C., Los Angeles, others, 1964—; represented in permanent collections, Met. Mus. Art, N.Y.C., Solomon R. Guggenheim Mus., N.Y.C., Hirshhorn Mus. and Sculpture Garden, Washington, others. Served with inf. AUS, 1944-45. SUNY faculty research fellow, 1979. Home: Walnut Hill Rd Bethel CT 06801 *The studio is my workshop and cathedral. No sanity exists outside its walls and no order but that which comes from my hand each day.*

AJEMIAN, ROBERT MYRON, journalist; b. Boston, July 8, 1925; s. Shahin and Rose (Takvorian) A.; m. Ruth MacCrellish, Sept. 6, 1952; children—Robert and Katharine (twins), Peter; m. Elizabeth Patterson, Nov. 27, 1959; children—David John and Andrew Howell. A.B., Harvard U., 1949. Sportswriter Boston Evening Am., 1948-51; reporter Life mag., N.Y.C., 1952-54; corr. Time, Life mags., Denver, 1954-56; asst. nat. affairs editor Life mag., N.Y.C., 1957-59; bur. chief Time-Life, Chgo., 1959-61; chief European bur. Life, Paris, France, 1961-63, polit. editor, N.Y.C., 1963-67, asst. mng. editor, 1968-72; corp. affairs Time, Inc., 1972-74; nat. polit. corr. Time Mag., 1974-77, Washington bur. chief, 1978—. Served to lt. (j.g.) USNR, World War II; PTO. Mem. Sigma Delta Chi. Clubs: Harvard Lake Shore (Chgo.); Millbrook (N.Y.); Golf and Tennis, Fed. City. Home: 2500 Massachusetts Ave NW Washington DC 20008 Office: 888 16th St NW Washington DC 20006

AJL, SAMUEL JACOB, microbiologist, biochemist; b. Poland, Nov. 15, 1923; came to U.S., 1939, naturalized, 1943; s. Joseph and Celia (Hertz) A.; m. Adele Davis, Sept. 15, 1946; children—Stephen Ira, Diane Francis, Leslie Judith. B.A., Bklyn. Coll., 1945; Ph.D., Iowa State Coll., 1949; L.H.D. (hon.), Dropsie U. Asst. prof. bacteriology Washington U. Sch. Medicine, St. Louis, 1949-52; on leave with Rockefeller U., 1951; chief microbiol. chemistry sect. Walter Reed Army Inst. Research, 1952-56, asst. chief dept. bacteriology, 1956-58; prof., dir. metabolic biology NSF, 1959-60; dir. research Albert Einstein Med. Center, Phila., 1960-71, Nat. Found.-March of Dimes, White Plains, N.Y., 1971-73, v.p. for research, 1973—; prof. dept. biology Temple U., 1960-71; research prof. microbiology Sch. Medicine, 1960-71; Mem. metabolic biology panel NSF, 1959—; Chmn. exec. bd., bd. govs. Dropsie U. Hebrew and Cognate Studies, Phila., 1966, acting pres., 1966-67. Contbr. articles profl. jours., papers.; Editor: Microbial Toxins, 1970, Archives of Biochemistry and Biophysics, 1969. Bd. dirs. Am. Jewish Com., Nat. Found. Jewish Culture. Recipient commendation for superior service U.S. Army, 1955; NSF sr. postdoctorate fellow, Jerusalem, Israel, Oxford, Eng., 1958; recipient Alumus Honors award for outstanding scientific achievements Bklyn. Coll., 1964. Fellow N.Y. Acad. Sci., Biochem. Soc. (Eng.); mem. Soc. Biol. Chemists Am., Soc. Microbiology, Soc. Exptl. Biology and Medicine, Am. Acad. Microbiology, Jewish Publ. Soc. Am. (v.p. 1969, dir.), Sigma Xi. Home: 2296 Bryn Mawr Ave Philadelphia PA 19131 Office: National Foundation-March of Dimes 1275 Mamaroneck Ave White Plains NY 10605

AJZENBERG-SELOVE, FAY, educator, physicist; b. Berlin, Germany, Feb. 13, 1926; came to U.S., 1940, naturalized, 1946; d. Mojzesz A. and Olga (Naiditch) Ajzenberg; m. Walter Selove, Dec. 18, 1955. B.S. in Engring, U. Mich., 1946; M.S., U. Wis., 1949, Ph.D., 1952. Research fellow Calif. Inst. Tech., 1952, 54; lectr. Smith Coll., 1952-53; cons., fellow Mass. Inst. Tech., 1952-53; from asst. prof. to asso. prof. Boston U., 1953-57; mem. faculty Haverford Coll., 1957-70, prof. physics, 1962-70, acting chmn. dept. physics, 1967-69; research prof. U. Pa., 1970-73, prof. physics, 1973—; vis. asst. prof. Columbia, summer 1955, Nat. U. Mexico, summer 1955; lectr. U. Pa., 1957; cons. in field, 1962-63; vis. asso. Calif. Inst. Tech., 1973-74; Exec. sec. com. physics faculties in colls. Am. Inst. Physics, 1962-65, mem. adv. com. manpower, 1963-68, adv. com. vis. scientists program, 1963-67; commr. Commn. on Coll. Physics, 1968-71; exec. sec. ad hoc panel on nuclear data compilations Nat. Acad. Scis.-NRC, 1971-75; mem. Commn. on Nuclear Physics, Internat. Union Pure and Applied Physics, 1972-78; Chmn. 1978; mem. U.S. delegation low energy nuclear physics to USSR, AEC, 1966; mem. Distinguished Faculty Awards Commn. Commonwealth of Pa., 1976; mem. nuclear sci. adv. com. Dept Energy-NSF, 1977-80; mem. numerical data adv. bd., assembly math. and phys. scis. NRC, 1977-79. Editor: Nuclear Spectroscopy, vol. A and B, 1960; bd. editors: Phys. Rev. C, 1981—. Smith-Mundt fellow, 1955; Guggenheim fellow, 1965-66. Fellow Am. Phys. Soc. (chmn. div. nuclear physics 1973-74), AAAS (governing council 1974-80, com. on council affairs 1977, 78); mem. Am. Inst. Physics (com. on public edn. and info. 1980—), AAUP, Phi Beta Kappa, Sigma XI (nat. lectr. 1973-74). Home: 118 Cherry Ln Wynnewood PA 19096 Office: U Pa Philadelphia PA 19104

AKAISHI, TADASHI, publishing co. exec.; b. Sendai, Japan, Jan. 22, 1925; came to U.S., 1949, naturalized, 1961; s. Yoshiaki and Yasu (Yamamoto) A.; m. Amy Nagata, Jan. 29, 1955; children—Carolyn Keiko, Janet Akemi. B.D., San Francisco Theol. Sem., 1950, Th.M., 1951, Th.D., 1957. Ordained to ministry Presbyn. Ch., 1953; pastor Christ Presbyn. Ch., Los Angeles, 1957-61; asso. editor John Knox Press, Richmond, Va., 1961-66, editor, 1966-67, editor-mgr., 1967-69; asst. pub. Harper & Row Pubs., Inc., N.Y.C., 1969-70, v.p., pub., 1970-73, group v.p., pub., 1973-76; v.p., pub. Barnes & Noble Books, 1971-76; v.p., dir. Kodansha Internat. U.S.A., 1977—. Author: Annotated Bibliography of New Testament Literature (1925-1955), 1955. Home: 8 Knollwood Rd Eastchester NY 10707 Office: 10 E 53d St New York NY 10022

AKAKA, DANIEL KAHIKINA, congressman; b. Honolulu, Sept. 11, 1924; s. Kahikina and Annie (Kahoa) A.; m. Mary Mildred Chong, May 22, 1948; children: Millannie, Daniel, Gerard, Alan, Nicholas. Grad., U. Hawaii, postgrad., 1966. Tchr. schs. in Hawaii, 1953-60; vice prin., then prin. Ewa Beach Elementary Sch., Honolulu, 1960-64; prin. Pohakea Elementary Sch., 1964-65, Kaneohe Elementary Sch., 1965-68; program specialist Hawaii Compensatory Edn., 1968-71; dir. Hawaii OEO, 1971-74; spl. asst. human resources Office Gov. Hawaii, 1975-76; mem. 95th-98th Congresses from Hawaii; chmn. Hawaii Prins. Conf. Bd. dirs. Hanahauoli Sch.; mem. Act 4 Ednl. Adv. Council, Library Adv. Council.; Trustee Kawaiahao Congl. Ch. Served with U.S. Army, 1945-47. Life mem. NEA; mem. Musicians Assn. Hawaii. Democrat. Address: 1007 Longworth Office Building Washington DC 20515

AKASOFU, SYUN-ICHI, geophysicist; b. Nagano-Ken, Japan, Dec. 4, 1930; came to U.S., 1958; s. Shigenori and Kumiko (Koike) A.; m. Emiko Endo, Sept. 25, 1961; children: Ken-Ichi, Keiko. B.S., Tohoku U., 1953, M.S., 1957; Ph.D., U. Alaska, 1961. Sr. research asst. Nagasaki U., 1953-55; research asst. Geophys. Inst., U. Alaska, 1958-61, mem. faculty, 1961—, prof. geophysics, 1964—. Author: Polar and Magnetospheric Substorms (Russian edit. 1971), 1968, The Aurora: A Discharge Phenomenon Surrounding the Earth (in Japanese), 1975, Physics of Magnetospheric Substorms, 1977, Aurora Borealis: The Amazing Northern Lights (Japanese edit. 1981), 1979; co-author: Sydney Chapman, Eighty, 1968, Solar-Terrestrial Physics (Russian edit. 1974); editor: Dynamics of the Magnetosphere, 1979; co-editor: Physics of Auroral Arc Formation, 1980—; editorial bd.: Planet and Earth Sci; co-editor: Space Sci. Revs. Recipient Chapman medal Royal Astron. Soc., 1976, award Japan Acad., 1977; named Disting. Alumnus U. Alaska, 1980. Fellow Am. Geophys. Union (John Adam Fleming medal 1979); mem. AAAS, Sigma Xi. *As a researcher of earth sciences, I feel that an artist and a scientist have something very much in common. Both watch carefully a natural object such as the aurora, a glacier, migrating birds, the Arctic Ocean, etc., and abstract whatever they feel the most essential part from the object. Then, an artist paints his abstraction on a canvas, while a scientist puts his abstraction into the form of equations.*

AKCASU, ZIYAEDDIN AHMET, nuclear engineer, educator; b. Aydin, Turkey, Aug. 26, 1924; s. Osman Nuri and Faika (Egel) A.; m. Melahat Turksal, July 16, 1954; children: Nur, Feza, Aydin. B.S., M.S., Tech. U. Istanbul, 1948; Ph.D., U. Mich., 1963. Asst. prof., then asso. prof. Tech. U. Istanbul, 1948-58; resident research asso. Argonne (Ill.) Nat. Lab., 1959-61; mem. faculty U. Mich., Ann Arbor, 1963—, prof. nuclear engring., 1968—. Co-author: Mathematical Methods in Nuclear Reactor Dynamics, 1971; Contbr. articles on statis. physics, reactor dynamics, reactor noise and polymer solution dynamic to profl. jours. Fellow Am. Nuclear Soc. (Distinguished Service award 1965, Outstanding Teaching award in engring. 1982); mem. Am. Phys. Soc., Turkish Phys. Soc., Sigma Xi. Home: 2820 Pebble Creek Ann Arbor MI 48104

AKE, JOHN NOTLEY, investment services executive, lawyer; b. Camden, N.J., July 27, 1941; s. John Notley and Martha (Loughry) A.; m. Rosmarie Fluckiger, Aug. 25, 1971; 1 dau., Christine. B.S., Columbia Coll., 1963; LL.B., U. Pa., 1966. Bar: D.C. 1967, Tex. 1978, U.S. Supreme Ct. 1970. Atty. SEC, Washington, 1966-72; ptnr. Rollison & Schaumberg, Washington, 1972-74; asst. gen. counsel

Investment Co. Inst., Washington, 1974-76; sr. v.p., gen. counsel Am. Capital Corp., Inc., Houston, 1977—. Mem. ABA, Tex. Bar Assn. Home: 3124 Amherst St Houston TX 77005 Office: Am Capital Corp Inc 2777 Allen Pkwy Suite R1010 Houston TX 77253

AKENSON, DONALD HARMAN, historian, educator; b. Mpls., May 22, 1941; s. Donald Nels and Fern L. (Harman) A. B.A., Yale U., 1962; Ph.D., Harvard U., 1967. Allston Burr sr. tutor Dunster House, Harvard U., 1966-67; asst. prof. history, asst. dean Yale Coll., 1967-70; asso. prof. history Queens U., Kingston, Ont., Can., 1970-74, prof., 1974—; hon. research fellow Queens U., Belfast, 1976-77; hon. prof. edn. Trinity Coll., Dublin, 1976-77; owner, pub. Langdale Press. Author: The Irish Education Experiment: The National System of Education in the Nineteenth Century, 1970, The Church of Ireland: Ecclesiastical Reform and Revolution 1800-1885, 1971, Education and Enmity: The Control of Schooling in Northern Ireland 1920-50, 1973, The United States and Ireland, 1973, A Mirror to Kathleen's Face: Education in Independent Ireland 1922-60, 1975, Local Poets and Social History: James Orr, Bard of Ballycarry, 1977, Between Two Revolutions: Islandmagee, County Antrim, 1798-1920, 1979, The Lazar House Notebooks, 1981, A Protestant in Purgatory: Richard Whately, Archbishop of Dublin, 1981; Editor: Canadian Papers in Rural History, 1978—. Recipient Can. Council research awards, 1974-83, Am. Council Learned Socs. research award, 1976-77. Fellow Royal Soc. Can., Royal Soc. Arts (U.K.); mem. Am. Conf. Irish Studies, Phi Beta Kappa. Clubs: Yale (N.Y.C.); County Antrim Yacht (N. Ireland). Office: Dept History Queens U Kingston ON K7L 3N6 Canada

AKER, J. CALVIN, associate justice state supreme court; b. 1939. B.S., Eastern Ky. U.; J.D., U. Tenn. Bar: Ky. 1970. Sole practice, Vico, Ky., until 1976; ptnr. Aker & Rogers, Somerset, 1976-78; judge Ky. 28th Dist. Ct., Somerset, Ky, 1978-80; assoc. justice Ky. Supreme Ct., Frankfurt, 1980—. Office: Ky Supreme Ct Capitol Bldg Frankfurt KY 40601 *

AKERS, ALBERT BAYLISS, army officer; b. Nashville, Nov. 12, 1928; s. Frank and Mary Bayliss (House) A.; m. Mary Louise Cole, Jan. 19, 1957; children—Frank E., Martha Cole. Student, Georgetown U., 1946-47; B.S., U.S. Mil. Acad., 1951; M.A. in Internat. Relations, Am. U., 1965; M.S. in Bus. Adminstrn, George Washington U., 1970; disting. grad., Indsl. Coll. Armed Forces, 1970; grad. advanced mgmt. course, U. So. Calif., 1974. Commd. 2d lt. U.S. Army, 1951, advanced through grades to maj. gen., 1978; service in, Vietnam, Germany, Italy and Thailand; dir. materiel plans and programs Office Dep. Chief Staff Research, Devel. and Acquisition, Hdqrs. U.S. Army, 1978-81; comdr. U.S. Army Tng. Center, Ft. Jackson, S.C., 1981—. Decorated Legion of Merit with oak leaf cluster, Bronze Star with V device, Army Commendation medal, Parachutist badge; Cross of Gallantry with palm (S.Vietnam).; named Ambassador of Yr. City of Columbia, S.C., 1983. Mem. Assn. U.S. Army, F.A. Assn., Assn. Grad. U.S. Mil. Acad. Episcopalian. Office: Comdg Gen US Army Tng Center and Ft Jackson Fort Jackson SC 29207

AKERS, JOHN FELLOWS, business executive; b. Boston, Dec. 28, 1934; s. Kenneth Fellows and Mary Joan (Reed) A.; m. Susan Davis, Apr. 16, 1960; children: Scott, Pamela, Ann. B.S., Yale U., 1956. With IBM Corp., Armonk, N.Y., 1960—, v.p., asst. group exec., 1976-78, v.p., group exec., 1978-82, sr. v.p., group exec., 1982-83, pres., 1983—, dir. Mem. adv. bd. Yale Sch. Orgn. and Mgmt. Served to lt. USNR, 1956-60. Office: IBM Corp Old Orchard Rd Armonk NY 10504

AKERS, JOHN MCCORKLE, trucking co. exec.; b. Maysville, Ky., Apr. 5, 1907; s. William Wirt and Elizabeth (Scott) A.; m. Dorothy Amanda Dozier, Feb. 14, 1945; children—Mildred Elizabeth, Dorothy Joanne, Mary Kathleen. A.B. in Econs, Davidson Coll., 1928, LL.D. (hon.), 1978; M.A. in Econs, U. N.C. at Chapel Hill, 1932; grad. student, Duke, 1933, Princeton, 1934. Asst. dir. WPA, Washington, 1935-37; v.p., gen. mgr. Akers Motor Lines, Inc., Gastonia, N.C., 1937-55, pres., 1955-72, A. & W. Realty Co., Gastonia, 1949-78, Akers Realty & Sales Co., Inc., Atlanta, 1950-72, Akers Center Hardware & Supply, Inc., Gastonia, 1955-79, A&W Rentals, Inc., 1958-69; mng. partner A. and W. Investment Co., 1977—; partner Akers Sales Co., Gastonia, N.C., 1948-72; mem. N.C. adv. bd. Liberty Mut. Ins. Co., Charlotte, 1961—. Mem. N.C. Bd. Conservation and Devel., 1960-68; pres. N.C. Indsl. Devel. Found., 1962, bd. dirs., 1963-65; chmn. Davidson Coll. Alumni Fund, 1955-57; Pres. Akers Found., 1955—; adv. bd. Transp. Center, Northwestern U., 1961-66; bd. visitors Davidson Coll., 1957—; trustee Queens Coll., Charlotte, 1947—; bd. dirs. N.C. Citizens Assn., 1961-77. Mem. Am. Trucking Assn. (bd. govs. regular common carrier conf. 1959-75, v.p. N.C. 1945-54, chmn. indsl. relations com. 1962-63, mem. exec. com. 1945—, nat. treas. 1954-62, 1st v.p. 1962-63, pres. 1963-64, chmn. bd. 1964-65), N.C. Motors Carriers Assn. (bd. mem. 1940—, pres. 1962-63), Transp. Assn. Am. (bd. dirs. 1962-72), Carolina Transp. Assn. (pres. 1940-60), Davidson Coll. Alumni Assn. (pres. 1957-58), U.S., Gastonia chambers commerce, Phi Beta Kappa, Pi Kappa Alpha. Presbyn. (chmn. deacons 1962, elder 1968—). Clubs: Gaston Country; Ponte Vedra (Fla.); Masons, Shriner. Home: 1102 Belvedere Ave Gastonia NC 28052 Office: PO Box 2726 Gastonia NC 28052

AKERS, TOM, JR., raw cotton broker, consultant; b. Woodford, Okla., May 1, 1919; s. George Tom and Sadie Dean (Jones) A.; m. Eleanor Hoskins, Dec. 23, 1971; children: Tom, Alyce, Peggy, John. B.S., Okla. A&M Coll., 1946; postgrad., Stanford U., 1966. Cotton classer Chickasha Cotton Oil Co., (Okla.), 1936-41; exec. v.p. Calcot. Ltd., Bakersfield, Calif., 1946-80; owner, ptnr. Tom Akers-Cotton, Bakersfield, 1980—; cons. Algodonerr Comercial Mexicana, 1980—, Central Cooperativa Nacional, Asuncion, Paraguay, 1982, Cooperativa Agropecuatrir, Tegucigal, Paraguay, 1983, Algodonerr Del Sun, Honduras, 1983. Campaign chmn. 18th Congl. Dist. Jimmy Carter for Pres., 1976-80, Kern County for Tom Bradley for Gov., 1982; mem. Kern County Democratic Central Com, 1978—. Served to maj. inf. AUS, 1941-46; PTO. Named Rotarian of Yr. East Bakersfield Rotary, 1974. Mem. Nat. Cotton Mktg. Study Group of U.S. Congress, Nat. Cotton Adv. Com. Democrat. Congregationalist. Club: Bakersfield Trade (dir. 1960-70). Lodge: East Bakersfield Rotary. Home: 4 Green Fair Ct Bakersfield CA 93309 Office: Tom Akers-Cotton 1716 Oak St Room 5 Bakersfield CA 93301

AKERS, WILLIAM WALTER, educator; b. Panola County, Tex., Dec. 31, 1922; s. Oscar Walter and Lela (Malone) A.; m. Nancy Tressel, Mar. 1, 1947; children—Susan Elaine, Carol Lorraine. B.S., Tex. Tech. Coll., 1943; M.S., U. Tex., 1944; Ph.D., U. Mich., 1951. With Atlantic Refining Co., 1947; mem. faculty Rice U., 1947—, prof. chem. engring., 1956—, chmn. dept., 1955-66; dir. Bio-Med. Engring., Lab., 1963-69, asst. to pres. univ., 1973-74, dir. univ. relations, 1974, v.p. for external affairs, 1975-80, v.p. adminstrn., 1980—; cons. chem. industries, 1947-65; Mem. council Oak Ridge Inst. Nuclear Studies, 1958-63, vice chmn., 1962, bd. dirs., 1963-69; tech. adviser to Yugoslavia, 1962; mem. U.S.-Afghanistan Ednl. Consortium, 1963-70; research project dir. Baylor Coll. Medicine, 1965-70; mem. biomed. engring. fellowship com. NIH, 1967-70; mem. Sec.'s Adv. Council for Coal Mine Health Research, 1970-71; mem. adv. council Nat. Inst. Occupational Safety and Health, 1971-73; mem. adv. com. on nuclear energy Tex. Energy and Natural Resources Adv. Council, 1980—. Author papers in field. Trustee St. Luke's Hosp., Houston, 1975-79; bd. dirs. S. Main Center Assn., 1976—. Served with C.E. AUS, 1941-43. Recipient Distinguished Engring. Alumnus award Tex. Tech U., 1967, Distinguished Alumnus award, 1968. Mem. AAAS, Am. Chem. Soc., Am. Inst. Chem. Engrs. (Best Fundamental Paper award 1967, Distinguished lectr. 1969), Am. Soc. Artificial Organs, Council on Fgn. Relations, Houston Philos. Soc., Sigma Xi, Tau Beta Pi. Episcopalian. Home: 5214 Green Tree Rd Houston TX 77056

AKESSON, NORMAN BERNDT, agrl. engr.; b. Grandin, N.D., June 12, 1914; s. Joseph Berndt and Jennie (Nonthene) A.; m. Margaret Blasing, Dec. 14, 1946; children—Thomas Ryan, Judith Elizabeth. B.S. in Agrl. Engring, N.D. State U., 1940, M.S., U. Idaho, 1942. Research fellow U. Idaho, 1940-42; physicist U.S. Navy, Bremerton, Wash., 1942-47; asst. prof. agrl. engring. U. Calif., Davis, 1947-56, asso. prof., 1956-62, prof., 1962—, agrl. meteorologist, 1977—; cons. Israel, 1968, Japan, 1980; Fulbright fellow, Eng. and East Africa, 1957-58; chmn. expert com. on vector control equipment WHO. Author: The Use of Aircraft in Agriculture, 1974, Pesticide Application Equipment and Techniques, 1979, Aircraft Use for Mosquito Control, 1981. Recipient research and devel. award FAO, 1973-74, WHO, 1978. Fellow Am. Soc. Agrl. Engrs. (chmn. Pacific region 1965, dir. 1972-74); mem. Entomol. Soc. Am., Weed Sci. Soc. Am. (editorial bd. 1968-70), Internat. Agrl. Aviation Assn., Brit. Soc. Agrl. Engring. Republican. Club: Farmers (London). Home: 748 Elmwood Dr Davis CA 95616 Office: Agrl Engring Dept U Calif Davis CA 95616

AKHTER, MOHAMMAD NASIR, physician, public health administrator; b. Jullandur, Punjab, India, June 6, 1944; came to U.S., 1970, naturalized, 1975; s. Mohammad and Fazal (Bibi) Sharif; m. Jeanette E. Easton, Sept. 26, 1970; 1 dau., Sarah. F.Sc., Govt. Coll. Lahore, Pakistan, 1962; M.B.B.S., King Edwards Med. Coll., Lahore, Pakistan, 1967; M.P.H., Johns Hopkins U., 1973. Diplomate: Am. Bd. Preventive Medicine. Resident and fellow Mt. Sinai Med. Sch., N.Y.C., 1973-76; chief div. emergency med. service Ill. Dept. Pub. Health, Springfield, Ill., 1976-78, Mich. Dept. Pub. Health, Lansing, 1978-80; dir. health State of Mo., Jefferson City, 1980-82, dep. dir. med. affairs, 1982—; cons. Mo. State Cancer Com., 1982-83, St. Joseph State Hosp., 1983; mem. rev. panel Ednl. Commn. for Fgn. Med. Grads., Phila., 1981—. Fellow Am. Coll. Preventive Medicine, Am. Coll. Internat. Physicians (pres. 1978, 79, 80); mem. AMA (vice-chmn. resident physician sect. 1975, 76, 77), Am. Coll. Emergency Physicians, Islamic Med. Assn. Home: 2400 Lynnwood Dr Columbia MO 65102 Office: State Dept Mental Health 2002 Missouri Blvd Jefferson City MO 65102

AKI, KEIITI, seismologist, educator; b. Tokyo, Japan, Mar. 3, 1930; came to U.S., 1966, naturalized, 1976; s. Koichi and Humiko (Kojima) A.; m. Haruko Uyeda, Mar. 25, 1956; children: Shota, Zenta. B.S., U. Tokyo, 1952, Ph.D., 1958. Research fellow Calif. Inst. Tech., 1958-60, vis. prof., 1963; instr. Internat. Inst. Seismology and Earthquake Engring., 1961-62; asso. prof. U. Tokyo, 1964-66; prof. geophysics MIT, Cambridge, 1966—, R.R. Shrock prof. earth and planetary scis., 1982—; vis. prof. U. Chile, 1970, 72, U. Paris, 1983; WAE geophysicist U.S. Geol. Survey, 1967-75; vis. scientist Royal Norwegian Council for Sci. and Indsl. Research, 1974; cons. Sandia Corp., 1976—; vis. scientist Los Alamos Sci. Labs., U. Calif., 1977—; cons. Del Mar Assos., 1977-78, Nuclear Regulatory Commn., 1978, UN, 1979, Time-Life, Inc., 1980-81, NSF, 1981—; vis. scientist Japan Soc. Promotion of Sci., 1978; chmn. com. on seismology Nat. Acad. Sci., 1978-79; Disting. vis. prof. U. Alaska, 1981; Mem. Nat. Council for Earthquake Prediction Evaluation, 1980—. Author: Stochastic Phenomena in Physics, 1956, Quantitative Seismology: Theory and Methods, Vols. I and II, 1980; editor-in-chief: Pure and Applied Geophysics; Mem. editorial com.: Tectonophysics, 1974—; assoc. editor: Geophys. Research Letters, 1977-82; adv. editor: Jour. Physics of Earth and Planetary Interiors. Fulbright postdoctoral fellow, 1958-60. Fellow Am. Acad. Arts and Scis.; mem. Nat. Acad. Scis., Am. Geophys. Union (mem. com. fellows 1975-76, pres. seismology sect. 1980), Seismological Socs. Am. (dir. 1971-74, v.p. 1978, pres. 1979), Japan), Royal Astron. Soc. Home: 56 Park Ln Newton MA 02159 Office: 77 Massachusetts Ave Cambridge MA 02139

AKIN, EWEN MARION, JR., coll. pres.; b. Chgo., June 28, 1930; s. Ewen M. and Ida V. (Pillow) A.; m. Doris M. Lowery; children—Helen V., Alva S. B.S., U. Ill., 1951; M.S., DePaul U., 1958; Ed.D., Nova U., 1977. Asst. prof. physics Wilson Jr. Coll., 1963-70; v.p. acad. affairs Kennedy-King Coll., 1970-73, pres., 1976—, Malcolm X Coll., 1973-76; cons. Race Desegregation Inst., Northeastern Ill. U.; panelist Issues Unlimited, Sta. WGN-TV, 1979, Face to Face, Sta. WLS-TV, 1979. Bd. dirs. Greater Lawndale Conservation Commn., 1973-76; v.p. bd. dirs. Schwab Rehab. Hosp., Chgo., 1975—; mem. State Senator Newhouse's Ednl. Adv. Com., 1979. Served with USMC, 1951-53; Korea. Recipient Alumni award DePaul U.; Affirmative Action award Breadbasket Comml. Assn.; Citation of Merit Sta. WAIT; Edn. award El Centro De La Causa. Mem. Am. Assn. Community and Jr. Colls. (v.p. N. Central region Council on Black Am. Affairs), Council Ill. Public Community Coll. Pres's. Clubs: City of Chgo., Chgo. Physics. Office: 6800 S Wentworth Ave Chicago IL 60621

AKIN, WALLACE ELMUS, geographer; b. Murphysboro, Ill., May 18, 1923; s. Samuel Elmus and Sarah Elizabeth (Lindsay) A.; m. Peggy Jean Holt, June 11, 1948; children—Dianna Jean, David Wallace. B.A., So. Ill. U., 1948; student, U. Mich., 1943-44; M.A., Ind. U., 1949; Ph.D., Northwestern U., 1952. Field investigations in Mexico, 1948; instr. phys. geography Northwestern U., 1950-52; field team chief Rural Land Classification Program for P.R., 1950-51; instr. geography Austin Peay State Coll., summer 1952; instr. U. Ill., Navy Pier Chgo., 1952-53; mem. faculty Drake U., 1953—, prof. geography and geology, 1962—, head dept., 1953—; cons., geologist Iowa Natural Resources Council, summers 1954-61; cons., editor Iowa State Water Plan, 1978; Fulbright research scholar Inst. Geography, U. Copenhagen, 1961-62. Editor, contbr. to bulls. Served to lt. (j.g.) USNR, 1943-46. Mem. Assn. Am. Geographers (chmn. West Lakes div. 1967), Arctic Inst. N.Am., Royal Danish Geog. Soc., Soil Conservation Soc. Am. (chmn. internat. relations com. 1963, mem. nat. scholarship com. 1973—, ofcl. rep. XIX Internat. Geog. Congress, Stockholm 1960). Home: 5800 Pleasant Dr Des Moines IA 50312

AKINAKA, ASA MASAYOSHI, lawyer; b. Honolulu, Jan. 19, 1938; s. Arthur Yoshinori and Misako (Miyoshi) A.; m. Betsy Yoshie Kurata, Oct. 7, 1967; children—David Asa Yoshio, Sarah Elizabeth Sachie. B.A. magna cum laude, Yale U., 1959; postgrad. (Rotary Found. fellow), Trinity Coll., Oxford U., 1959-60, Yale Law Sch., 1960-61; LL.B., Stanford Law Sch., 1964. Bar: Hawaii bar 1964. Research asst. U.S. Senator Oren Long, Washington, 1961-62; pvt. practice law, Honolulu, 1964—. V.p. YMCA, 1974—; bd. visitors Stanford Law Sch., 1971-74. Mem. Am. Bar Assn., Hawaii State Bar Assn. (pres. 1977), Nat. Conf. Bar Presidents. Democrat. Episcopalian. Club: Pacific. Address: PO Box 1035 Honolulu HI 96808

AKINS, CLAUDE, actor; b. Nelson, Ga.; m. Theresa Fairfield, 1952. B.S., Northwestern U. Salesman, Ind. With, Barter Theatre; appeared: in play The Rose Tattoo, N.Y.C.; several seasons with touring cos.; film appearances include From Here to Eternity, 1953, The Caine Mutiny, 1954, Onionhead, 1958, Rio Bravo, 1959, The Sea Chase, 1965, Johnny Concho, 1956, The Defiant Ones, 1958, Porgy and Bess, 1959, Inherit the Wind, 1960, How the West Was Won, 1962, The Killers, 1964, Ride Beyond Vengeance, 1966, Return of the Seven, 1966, Waterhole No. 3, 1967, The Devil's Brigade, 1968, Flap, 1970, Skyjacked, 1972, The Great Bank Robbery, 1969, Tentacles, 1977, The Timber Tramps, 1977; TV series Movin' On, 1974-76, Nashville 99, 1977, B.J. and the Bear, 1979, Sheriff Lobo, 1979-81; other TV appearances include The Last Rodeo; TV dramatic spl. Eric, 1975; TV movies Kiss Me, Kill Me, 1976, Tarantulas: The Deadly Cargo, 1977, Bus Stop, 1982. Office: care William Morris Agy Inc 151 El Camino Dr Beverly Hills CA 90212 *

AKINS, ZANE VERNON, association executive; b. Bethel, Kans., Apr. 13, 1940; s. Gerald Vernon and Vesta Jean (Rutherford) A.; m. Kay Ellen Cowan, Aug. 17, 1963; children: Michael Scott, Deborah Lynn, Christine Sue. B.S. in Agr, U. Mo., 1962. Farmer, 1962-64; service technician No. Ohio Breeders Assn., Tiffin, 1964-66; program dir. Holstein Assn. Am., Brattleboro, Vt., 1966-73, mgr. sire devel. service, 1973-77, adminstrv. asst., 1977-78, chief exec. officer, 1978—; exec. v.p. Holstein-Friesian Services, Inc., Brattleboro, 1978—. Bd. dirs. Windham County United Way, 1980—; corporator, chmn. pub. relations com. Brattleboro Meml. Hosp., 1982-83. Sears & Roebuck scholar; Freshman Curators scholar; Borden's scholar U. Mo., 1958-59; Sophomore Curators scholar; Campus Chest scholar, 1959-60; Am. Guernsey Cattle Club scholar, 1958-60. Mem. Purebred Dairy Cattle Assn. (dir. 1978), Nat. Soc. Livestock Records Assn. (v.p. 1982-84), Brattleboro C. of C. (dir. 1979-81), Alpha Gamma Rho (regional v.p.). Congregationalist. Home: PO Box 156 Newfane VT 05345 Office: 1 S Main St Brattleboro VT 05301

AKIYAMA, KAZUYOSHI, condr.; b. Tokyo, 1941. Grad. piano and conducting, Toho Sch. Music, 1963. Conducting debut, Tokyo Symphony Orch., 1964; permanent condr., music dir., 1964—; prin. guest condr., Osaka Philharm., 1965—; asst. condr., Toronto (Ont., Can.) Symphony, 1968-69; resident condr., music dir., Vancouver (B.C., Can.)Symphony Orch., 1972—; music dir., Am. Symphony Orch.; guest condr. numerous orchs. throughout world. Recipient Torii prize, 1974 *

AKIYOSHI, TOSHIKO, jazz composer, pianist, bandleader; b. Ryoyo, Manchuria, Dec. 12, 1929; d. Tatsuro and Shigeko (Hiraike) A.; m. Lewis Tabackin, Nov. 11, 1969; 1 child, Monday Michiru. Grad., Berklee Coll. Music, Boston. Founder pianist trio, 1953-70; appear throughout U.S., Europe, Japan; founder, leader, composer-arranger, Toshiko Akiyoshi/Lew Tabackin Big Band, 1972—; albums include Long Yellow Road, 1976 (named Best Jazz Album of Yr., Stereo Rev.), Insights, 1978. Named Best Arranger, Best Band by Downbeat Poll, 1978, 79 *

AKOS, FRANCIS, violinist; b. Budapest, Hungary, Mar. 30, 1922; came to U.S., 1954; s. Karoly and Rose (Reti) Weinberg; m. Phyllis Malvin Sommers, June 7, 1981; children from previous marriage—Katherine Elizabeth, Judith Margaret. Baccalaureate, Budapest, 1941; M.A., Franz Liszt Acad. Music, Budapest, 1940, Ph.D., 1941. Concertmaster, Budapest Symphony Orch., 1945-46, Royal Opera and Philharmonic Soc., Budapest, 1947-48, Gothenburg (Sweden) Symphony Orch., 1948-50, Municipal Opera, West Berlin, Ger., 1950-54, Mpls. Symphony Orch., 1954; asst. concertmaster, Chgo. Symphony Orch., 1955—; performed, Salzburg Festival, 1948, Scandinavian Festival, Helsinki, Finland, 1950, Berlin Festival, 1951, Prades Festival, 1953, Bergen Festival, 1962, Vienna Festival; founder, condr., Chgo. Strings, chamber orch., 1961; condr., Fox River Valley Symphony, Aurora, Ill., 1965-73, Chicago Heights (Ill.) Symphony, 1975-79, Highland Park Strings, 1979. Prizewinner Hubay competition, Budapest, 1939, Remenyi competition, Budapest, 1939. Home: 1310 Maple Ave Evanston IL 60201 Office: 220 S Michigan Ave Chicago IL 60604

AKSYONOV, VASSILY PAVLOVICH, author; b. Kazan, Russia, Aug. 20, 1932; came to U.S., 1980; s. Pavel Vassilievich and Eugenia Solomonovna (Ginzburg) A.; m. Maya Zmeul, May 30, 1980; 1 son, Alex. M.D., Leningrad Med. Inst., 1956. Intern Moscow Inst. for Tb Study, 1957-60. Author: novels Colleagues, 1960, The Ticket to the Stars, 1961, The Oranges From Morocco, 1963, It's Time, My Friend, 1964, Love to Electricity, 1972, Research of Genre, 1978, The Steel Gird, 1978, The Small Golden Piece of Iron, 1979, The Burn, 1980, The Crimean Island, 1981, The Rendezvous, 1981, The Paperscape, 1983. Fellow Kennan Inst. Advanced Russian Study, 1981—; Wilson Center fellow, 1982—. Mem. French P.E.N., Sweden P.E.N., Denmark P.E.N. Christian Orthodox. Office: Goucher Coll Towson MD 21204

AKUTAGAWA, DONALD, psychologist, educator; b. Grace, Idaho, June 7, 1923; s. Fred T. and Shizue (Oyama) A.; children by previous marriage: Trina Bortko, Murray, Doran. M.A., U. Chgo., 1951; Ph.D., U. Pitts., 1956. Group counselor Orthogenic Sch., U. Chgo., 1951-52; clin. psychologist Inst. Pa. Hosp., Phila., 1959-67; pvt. practice, Phila., 1957—, Bellevue, Wash., 1968—; chief community services Eastside Community Mental Health Center, Bellevue, 1968-72; clin. prof. psychology U. Wash., Seattle, 1974—. Served with AUS, 1944-46. Fellow Am. Orthopsychiat. Assn.; mem. Am. Psychol. Assn., Am. Assn. Marriage and Family Therapy., Wash. Assn. Marriage and Family Therapy (pres. 1982-83). Office: 1621 114th Ave SE Arbor Bldg Suite 118 Bellefield Office Park Bellevue WA 98004 *Ideal: To so live my life that the world is better for my having been a part of it.*

ALADJEM, SILVIO, obstetrician and gynecologist, educator; b. Bucharest, Romania, June 16, 1928; came to U.S., 1964, naturalized, 1969; s. Nahman and Lea (Campus) A.; m. Sonia Goldberg, Mar. 29, 1952; children—Vivien, Norman. M.D. summa cum laude, U. Uruguay, 1961. Diplomate: Am. Bd. Obstetrics and Gynecology; cert. subsplty. in maternal-fetal medicine. Intern Uruguay Pub. Health Service, Montevideo, 1961-62; resident in obstetrics and gynecology U. Uruguay, 1962-63, Cleve. Met. Gen. Hosp., 1964-67; fellow in obstetrics and gynecology Western Res. U., 1967, asst. prof., attending obstetrician and gynecologist, 1969-74; instr. Med. Coll. Ga., 1967-68, asst. prof., 1968-69; asso. prof. U. Ill., Chgo., 1975-76, prof., 1976-78, head div. perinatal medicine, 1976-78; prof., chmn. dept. obstetrics and gynecology Stritch Sch. Medicine, Loyola U., Chgo., 1978—; practice medicine specializing in obstetrics and gynecology, Chgo.; cons. Nat. Found. March of Dimes, Cleve., Chgo. Author: Risks in the Practice of Modern Obstetrics, 1972, 75, (with Audrey Brown) Clinical Perinatology, 1975, 79, Perinatal Intensive Care, 1976, Obstetrical Practice, 1980; contbr. articles to med. jours. Mem. Am. Coll. Obstetricians and Gynecologists (E. McDowell award 1967), Am. Fertility Soc. (C. Hartman award 1968), Soc. Gynecologic Investigation, Am. Soc. Anatomists, N.Y. Acad. Scis., Chgo. Gynecol. Soc., Chgo. Med. Soc., AMA, Ill. Med. Assn., Perinatal Group of Ill. (pres. 1976), Am. Assn. Maternal Neonatal Health (pres. 1978—). Home: 175 E Delaware Pl Chicago IL 60611 Office: 2160 S 1st Ave Maywood IL 60153

ALAIMO, ANTHONY A., judge; b. 1920. A.B., Ohio No. U.; J.D., Emory U. Bar: Ga. 1948. Now chief judge U.S. Dist. Ct. So. Dist. Ga., Brunswick. Office: US District Court PO Box 944 Brunswick GA 31521 *

ALAJALOV, CONSTANTIN, artist; b. Rostov on the Don, Russia, Nov. 18, 1900; came to U.S., 1923, naturalized, 1928; s. Ivan and Izabella (Avramov) A. Student, Gymnasium, Rostov, 1912-17, U. of

Petrograd, 1917. Teacher, lectr. Archipenko's L'Ecole d'Art, Phoenix Art Inst., etc. 1st participation in exhbn., 1916; drafted by Soviet Govt. as artist to paint murals, portraits, posters, 1920; sent to Persia, 1921; left Russia for Constantinople; painted murals in, U.S., 1923; with, The New Yorker, since 1926; worked on, Vanity Fair, Vogue, Town and Country, Fortune, Life, and others, covers, Saturday Evening Post, 1945; painted murals for, S.S. America, also, Sherry-Netherland Hotel; one-man shows, Hollywood, 1936, N.Y.C., 1942, Dallas, 1951, Art Mus., Wichita, Kan., 1972, paintings in, Dallas Art Mus., Bklyn. Mus., Mus. Modern Art, Phila. Mus. of Fine Arts, Mus. of City of N.Y., Library of Congress, Boston U., and others; painter: numerous portraits including Duke and Duchess of Windsor, John Sherman Cooper Angier Biddle Duke, others, 1964; The Constantin Alajalov Manuscript Collection established at, The Archives of Am. Art, Smithsonian Instn., 1980; illustrated: books George Gershwin Song Book, 1932, Our Hearts Were Young and Gay, by Cornelia Otis Skinner, 1942, Cinderella, by Alice Duer Miller, 1943, Conversation Pieces, A Collection of Alajalov's Paintings and Drawings, text by Janet Flanner, 1942. Office: 140 W 57th St New York NY 10019

ALALA, JOSEPH BASIL, JR., lawyer, accountant; b. Aleppo, Syria, Apr. 29, 1933; s. Joseph Basil and Waheda (Tall) A.; m. Nell Powers, Dec. 19, 1954; children: Sharon J., Tracy M., Joseph B. B.S. in Bus. Adminstrn., U. N.C., 1957, J.D. cum laude, 1959. Bar: N.C. 1959. Acct. Arthur Andersen & Co., Charlotte, N.C., 1959-62; pres. Garland & Alala, P.A., Gastonia, N.C., 1963—; lectr. various profl. assns. Contbr. articles to profl. jours. Bd. dirs. Garrison Community Found., Belmont Abbey Coll.; past mem. trustees, chmn. fin. com. St. Michael's Catholic Ch.; pres. Jaycees, 1964. Served with M.P. U.S. Army, 1954-55; Korea. Mem. Am. Judicature Soc., ABA, Am. Assn. Atty.-C.P.A.'s, N.C. Bar Assn., Gaston County Bar Assn., Am. Inst. C.P.A.'s, N.C. Assn. C.P.A.'s, Nat. Assn. Accts. Club: Gaston Country. Lodges: Knights of Malta; Rotary(Gastonia) (dir.). Home: 1216 South St Gastonia NC 28052 Office: 192 South St Gastonia NC 28052 *I believe everyone has four areas of responsibility in life: to his family, his church, his job and his community. My goal in life is to serve these areas with dignity and charity.*

ALAR, JOHN, tobacco company executive. Pres., chief exec. officer Brown & Williamson Tobacco Corp., Louisville. Office: Brown & Williamson Tobacco Corp 1600 W Hill St Louisville KY 40232 *

ALARY, JACQUES, social service educator; b. St. Augustin, Deux-Montagne, Que., Can., Nov. 29, 1932; s. Charles-Auguste and Melina (Gravel) A.; m. Simone Desrochers, Aug. 17, 1957; children: Claire, Lucie, Antoine. B.A., U. Montreal, 1953; M.A., 2, 1960; B.S.W., U. Ottawa, 1957; Ph.D., Tulane U., 1968. Cert. profl. social worker, Can. Social worker Family Social Service, Montreal, Que., 1958-63; prof. U. Monteal, 1963-83; dir. social service Family Social Service, 1979—; cons. Ministry of Social Affairs, Quebec, Que., 1968-70, Health and Welfare Can., Ottawa, Ont., Can., 1972-79; pres. Family Service Can., Ottawa, 1982—; founder, dir. research group Network Intervention, 1979; founder, dir. Social Policy Analysis, 1982; founder, pres. Social Service Agy.-Yough Consultation Bur., 1971. Founder, editor: jour. Intervention, 1969. Vice pres. Can. Assn. of Schs. of Social Work, Ottawa, 1973-74; pres. CLSC Cote-des Neiges, Montreal, 1976-78; mem. com. on social work Council of Univs., Quebec, 1979-82. Health and Welfare Can. fellow, 1964-66; grantee Social Scis. Research Council, 1975-76, Ministry of Social Affairs, 1979-80, Health and Welfare Can., 1980-83. Mem. Council Social Work Edn., Internat. Fedn. Social Workers (chmn. symposium com. Geneva 1983-84). Home: 4965 Connaught Ave Montreal PQ Canada H4V 1X4 Office: U Montreal PO Box 6128 Succursale A Montreal PQ Canada H3C 3J7

ALATIS, JAMES EFSTATHIOS, university dean; b. Weirton, W.Va., July 13, 1926; s. Efstathios and Vasiliki (Galanoudis) A.; m. Penelope Mastorides, Dec. 30, 1951; children: William, Stephen, Anthony. B.A., W.Va. U., 1948; M.A., Ohio State U., 1953; Ph.D., 1966. Fulbright lectr. English U., Athens, 1955-57; English testing and teaching specialist Dept. State, 1959-61; specialist for lang. research U.S. Office Edn., 1961-65, chief lang. sect., 1965-66; asso. dean Sch. Langs. and Linguistics, Georgetown U., Washington, 1966-73, dean, 1973—, asso. prof. linguistics, 1966-75, prof., 1975—; exec. sec. Tchrs. of English to Speakers of Other Langs., 1966-82, exec. dir., 1982—; pres. Joint Nat. Com. for Langs., 1981—; Mem. adv. council ERIC Clearinghouse on Linguistics, 1966-71, 73—; bd. dirs. CONPASS, 1966-70. Editor: Studies in Honor of Albert H. Marckwardt, 1972, (with Kristie Twaddell) English as a Second Language in Bilingual Education, 1976, (with Ruth Crymes) Human Factors in ESL, 1977, (with Gerli and Brod) Language in American Life, 1978, Internat. Dimensions of Bilingual Education, 1978, (with G. R. Tucker) Language in Public Life, 1979, Current Issues in Bilingual Education, 1980, (with others) The Second Language Classroom: Directions for the 1980s, 1981, Applied Linguistics and the Preparation of Second Language Teachers: Toward a Rationale, 1983; contbr. articles to profl. jours. Served with USNR, 1944-46. Recipient Mary Glide Goethe prize Am. Name Soc., 1954; Am. Council Learned Socs. summer study grantee in linguistics U. Mich., 1954. Mem. Am. Council on Teaching Fgn. Langs. Linguistic Soc. Am. (del. 1966-69), Nat. Council Tchrs. English, MLA, Nat. Assn. Fgn. Student Affairs (dir. 1965-66), Fedn. Internationale des Professeurs de Langues Vivantes (exec. com.), Phi Beta Kappa. Home: 5108 Sutton Pl Alexandria VA 22304 Office: Sch Langs and Linguistics Georgetown U Washington DC 20057

ALATKIN, MURRAY, wholesale paint company executive; b. N.Y.C., June 6, 1905; s. Hyman Noah and Rose (Goldman) Slatkin; m. Lillian Selsky, June 19, 1938; children: Joan, Robert. A.B., Johns Hopkins U., 1925; J.D., U. Md.-Balt., 1929. Bar: Md. 1932. With Felmor Corp., Balt., 1925—, pres., 1946—. Mem. Nat. Paint Distbrs. (pres. 1968-69), AFTRA, Md. Bar Assn. Clubs: Saints & Sinners (dir.); B'nai B'rith (recipient ann. Menorah award 1969), Zionist Orgn. Am. (hon. nat. v.p. 1980-1st Judge Simon E. Sobeloff award 1973), Zionist Orgn. Am. (hon. pres.). Home: Edmar Rd. Stevenson MD 21153 Office: Felmor Corp. 2020 Hollins Ferry Rd Baltimore MD 21153

AL-ATRAQCHI, MOHAMMED ALI, United Nations official, economic statistician; b. Iraq, Feb. 2, 1933; came to U.S., 1967; s. Mohammed S. and Zainab (Ahmed) Al-A.; m. Anne Delysia Sherman, Aug. 7, 1962; children: Waleed, Faris. B.S. in Math., Raghdad U., 1957; diploma in econ. statis., Bristol U., Eng., 1961, M.A., 1963; Ph.D. in Econ. Statis., London U., 1966. Tchr. math. Markaziah Intermediate Sch., Mosul, Iraq, 1957-58, Gharbiah Modern Intermediate Sch., Baghdad, 1958-60; asst. dir. Central Bank of Iraq, 1966; prof. Col 1. Econs. and Polit. Sci., Baghdad U., 1966-67; statistician dept. econ. and social affairs UN, N.Y.C., 1967-73, cons. to Security Council Com., 1973-79, sr. prolit. affairs officer, 1980—; statis and nat. account expert Arab Inst. for Econ. and Social Planning, Kuwait, 1972-73; adj. assoc. prof. statis. grad. div. Iona Coll., New Rochelle, N.Y., 1969-70; adj. prof. econ. statis C.W. Post Ctr., L.I. U., Greenvale, N.Y., 1975—. Author: The Application Means of Statistical Methods (in Arabic), 1980; contbr. (articles on internat. trade and econs. to profl. jours.). Mem. Am. Econ. Assn., N.Y. Educators Assn., Iraqui Econ. Assn., Royal Statis. Soc. (London). Home: 186-12 Midland Pkwy Jamaica Estates NY 11432 Office: UN Room 3540D Box 20 Grand Central PO New York NY 10017

ALAZRAKI, JAIME, Romance languages educator; b. La Rioja, Argentina, Jan. 26, 1934; came to U.S., 1962, naturalized, 1971; s. Leon and Clara A. (Bolomo) A.; children: Daphne G., Adina L. B.A., Hebrew U., Jerusalem, 1962; M.A., Columbia U., 1964, Ph.D., 1967. Instr. Columbia U., N.Y.C., 1964-67; asst. prof. U. Calif.-San Diego, 1967-68, assoc. prof., 1968-71, prof., 1971-77; prof. dept. romance langs. Harvard U., Cambridge, Mass., 1977—; vis. prof. U. Wis., 1972, UCLA, 1975-76; spl. advisor Guggenheim Found., 1981, 82. Author: Poetica y Poesia de P. Neruda, 1965, La prosa narrative de J.L. Borges, 1968, 74, 84, En busca del unicornio: Los cuentos de J. Cortazar, 1983; editor: (with I. Ivask) The Final Island: The Fiction of J. cortazar, 1978, J.L. Borges: el escritor y la critica, 1976. Recipient Nieto gold medal Argentina, 1970; NEH fellow, 1976; Guggenheim Found. fellow, 1971-72, 82-83. Mem. MLA, Internat. Inst. Ibero-Am. Lit., Am. Assn. Tchrs. Spanish and Portuguese (Huntington prize 1964). Home: 324-D Harvard St Cambridge MA 02139 Office: Dept Romance Langs Boylston Hall Harvard U Cambridge MA 02138

ALBANESE, LICIA, operatic soprano; b. Bari, Italy, July 22, 1913; d. Michele and Maria (Rugusa) A.; m. Joseph Gimma, Apr. 7, 1945. Studied voice under, Giuseppina R. Baldassare Tedeschi, Milan, Italy, 1932-35; LL.D., Seton Hall U.; L.H.D., Manhattan Coll., Fairfield (Conn.) U., Caldwell (N.J.) Coll., Marymount Manhattan Coll.; Mus.D. cum laude, St. Peters U., Jersey City; D.F.A., Siena Coll., Loudonville, N.Y.; hon. degree, Montclair State Coll. Adv. council 3d St. Music Sch. Settlement; trustee Bagby Music Lovers Found., N.Y.C.; chmn. Puccini Found., N.Y.C. Winner nat. singing contest, Italy, 1935; made an unexpected debut in role of: Madame Butterfly, Milan, Italy, 1934, (when the leading soprano became ill) Madame Butterfly, formal debut at, Royal Theater, Parma, Italy; in role of Madame Butterfly, Dec. 19, 1935; made: (with Beniamino Gigli) records of La Boheme, 1939; sang at concert in honor of Sir Neville Chamberlin and Lord Halifax, Rome, 1939, Covent Garden for the Festival of King George VI; made debut at, Met. Opera House, N.Y.C., in, Madame Butterfly and La Traviata, 1940. Decorated lady grand cross Order Holy Sepulchre. Sang at inauguration of Vatican City radio sta. and was decorated by Pope Pius XI. Home: 800 Park Av New York City NY 10021 *As stairs are not meant for standing or resting, but for reaching a higher level, so must you see in the early steps of your education their upward thrust toward the beauties of life's future, with the challenges and opportunities which await you at the top, if only you do not rest in reflection upon the past, but, looking daringly ahead, keep climbing and, through education, reap the golden harvest of your dreams.*

ALBECK, ANDY, motion picture co. exec.; b. Russia, Sept. 25, 1921. Began career with Columbia Pictures, 1939; with Central Motion Picture Exchange, 1947, Eagle Lion Classics, Inc., 1949, United Artist Corp., 1951—, asst. treas., 1970; v.p. United Artists and United Artists Broadcasting, 1972-73; pres. United Artists Broadcasting, 1973, sr. v.p. ops., 1976-78, pres., chief exec. officer, 1978-80, chmn. bd., 1980—. Address: care United Artists Corp 729 7th Ave New York NY 10019 *

ALBECK, STAN, basketball coach; b. Fairbury, Ill., May 17, 1931; s. Charles F. and Ruby M. A.; m. Phyllis Mann, Dec. 11, 1952; children: Gary, Sheree, Jon, and Roger (twins). Julie. B.A., Bradley U., 1955; M.A., Mich. State U., 1957. Coach Adrian Coll., No Mich. U., Denver U.; coach profl. team Denver, New Jersey; asst. coach profl. team San Diego; asst. coach Ky. Colonels, Los Angeles Lakers; head coach Cleve. Cavaliers, San Antonio Spurs, New Jersey Nets. Author Coaching Better Basketball. Served with U.S. Army, 1952-54. Named to No. Mich. Hall of Fame, 1979, Bradley U. Hall of Fame, 1981. Mem. Nat. Assn. Basketball Coaches. Lutheran. Office: PO Box 520 San Antonio TX 78292

ALBEE, ARDEN LEROY, educator, geologist; b. Port Huron, Mich., May 28, 1928; s. Emery A. and Mildred (Tool) A.; m. Charleen H. Ettenheim, 1978; children: Janet, Margaret, Carol, Kathy, James, Ginger, Mary, George. B.A., Harvard, 1950, M.A., 1951, Ph.D., 1957. Geologist U.S. Geol. Survey, 1950-59; prof. geology Calif. Inst. Tech., 1959—; chief scientist Jet Propulsion Lab., 1978—; Cons. in field, 1950; chmn. lunar sci. rev. panel NASA, 1972-77, mem. space sci. adv. com., 1976-80. Asso. editor: Jour. Geophys. Research, 1976—, Ann. Rev. Earth Space Scis, 1978—; contbr. numerous articles to profl. jours. Recipient Exceptional Sci. Achievement medal NASA, 1976. Fellow Mineral. Soc. Am. (asso. editor Am. Mineralogist 1972-76), Geol. Soc. Am. (asso. editor bull. 1972—), Geochem. Soc., Am. Geophys. Union. Home: 2040 Midlothian Dr Altadena CA 91001

ALBEE, EDWARD FRANKLIN, author, playwright; b. Mar. 12, 1928. Com. chmn. Brandeis U. Creative Arts Awards, 1983, 84. Plays written include The Zoo Story, 1958, The Death of Bessie Smith, 1959, The Sandbox, 1959, The American Dream, 1960, Who's Afraid of Virginia Woolf?, 1961-62, The Ballad of the Sad Cafe (adaption of Carson McCullers' novella), 1963, Tiny Alice, 1964, Malcolm, 1966, A Delicate Balance, 1966 (Pulitzer Prize winner 1967), Everything in the Garden, 1968, Box, Quotations from Chariman Mao, 1970, All Over, 1971, Seascape, 1975, Counting the Ways, 1976, Listening, 1977, The Man Who Had Three Arms, 1983, The Lady from DuBuque, 1978-79; adaptation of Lolita (Nabokov), 1980. Pres. Edward F. Albee Found. Recipient Pulitzer prize, 1967, 75; Gold medal in Drama Am. Acad. and Inst. Arts and Letters, 1980. Mem. Nat. Inst. Arts and Letters. *

ALBERDING, CHARLES HOWARD, petroleum and hotel executive; b. Cleyville, N.Y., Mar. 5, 1901; s. Charles and Doris (Roberts) A.; m. Bethine Wolverton, May 2, 1930; children: Beth Ann, Mary Katherine, Melissa Linda. E.E., Cornell U., 1923. Lab. asst., draftsman, operator Producers & Refiners Corp., Parco, Wyo., 1923-25; engr., cracking plant supt. Imperial Refineries, Ardmore, Okla., also Eldorado, Ark., 1925-27; head fgn. operating dept. Universal Oil Products Co., London, Eng., Ploesti, Roumania, Rangoon, Burma, Venice, Italy, 1927-33, head operating, service depts., Chgo. hdqrs., 1933-42; pres., dir. Paradise Inn, Inc., Jokake Inn, Inc., Vinoy Park Hotel Co., Holiday Hotel Corp., Alsonett Hotels, Sabine Irrigation Co., Sabine Canal Co., Tides Hotel Corp., Harmony Oil Corp., London Square Corp., Petroleum Spltys., Lincoln Lodge Corp., Peabody Hotel Corp., Memphis, Hermitage Hotel Co., Nashville, Royal Palms Inn, Inc., Torrey Pines Inn, La Jolla, Calif., Charleston First Corp.; Petroleum cons. WPB, 1942-43; dist. dir. petroleum refining Petroleum Adminstrn. for War, 1943-45. Mem. Scorpion. Republican. Conglist. Clubs: Valley (Phoenix); Kenilworth, Cornell (Chgo.); Sunset Country, Bath (St. Petersburg, Fla.); Tides Country (pres., dir.). Home: 99 Tudor Pl Kenilworth IL 60043 Office: 9 E Huron Chicago IL 60611

ALBERG, MILDRED FREED, film and TV producer-writer; b. Montreal, Que., Can., Jan. 15, 1921; d. Harry and Florence (Goldstein) Freed; m. Somer Alberg, Jan. 28, 1940 (dec.). Grad., high sch. Assoc. producer N.Y.C. Radio, 1940-43; writer radio shows AFL-CIO Community Services Com., N.Y.C., 1944-46; dri. info. CARE, Inc., N.Y.C., 1947-51; lectr. univs. Producer: Hallmark Hall of Fame, N.Y.C., 1953-60; TV series Our Am. Heritage, assoc. with Am. Heritage mag., N.Y.C., 1961-62; Broadway show Little Moon of Alban, 1961; film Hot Millions, 1968; film series on Bibl. archaeology, ABC-TV, 1972-75; producer, co-dir., co-writer: PBS documentary The Royal Archieves of Ebla, 1981; contbr. articles, N.Y. Post. Trustee Am. schs. Oriental Research; bd. dirs. Holy Land Conservation Fund. Recipient numerous awrds for radio, TV and film prodns.; NEH grantee, 1978-80. Mem. Am. Inst. Archeology, Writers Guild-East, Nat. Acad Tv Arts and Scis. (past gov.). Home: 6 New St Apt 2F East Norwalk CT 06855

ALBERGER, WILLIAM RELPH, lawyer, government official; b. Portland, Oreg., Oct. 11, 1945; s. Relph Griffin and Ferne (Ahlstrom) A.; m. Patricia Ann La Salle, June 2, 1971; 1 son, Eric Griffin. B.A., Willamette U., 1967; M.B.A., U. Iowa, 1971; J.D., Georgetown U., 1973. Bar: D.C. 1974. Legis. asst. U.S. Rep. Al Ullman, Washington, 1972-75, adminstrv. asst., 1975-77, House Com. on Ways and Means, 1977; mem. U.S. Internat. Trade Commn., Washington, 1977-82, vice-chmn., 1978-80, chmn., 1980-82. Mem. ABA (standing com. customs law 1983-84), D.C. Bar Assn., Internat. Bar Assn. Democrat. Office: Garvey, Shubert, Adams and Barer 100 Potomac St NW 5th Floor Washington DC 20007 *

ALBERS, ANNI, artist, textile designer; b. Berlin, Germany, June 12, 1899; came to U.S., 1933, naturalized, 1937; d. Siegfried and Toni (Ullstein) Fleischmann (changed name to Farman); m. Josef Albers, 1925. Student, Bauhaus in Weimar, 1922; diploma, Bauhaus Dessau, 1930; D.F.A. (h.c.), Md. Inst. Coll. of Art, 1972; LL.D., York U.; D.F.A. (hon.), Phila. Coll. Art, 1976, U. Hartford, 1979. Asst. prof. art Black Mountain (N.C.) Coll., 1933-49; lectr. Minn. Sch. Art, R.I. Sch. Design, San Francisco Mus. Art, Carnegie Inst. Tech., Phila. Mus. Coll. Art, U. Hawaii, Contemporary Art Mus., Houston, Rice Inst., Yale. Free lance work, Dessau and Berlin, 1930-33; free lance work, New Haven, 1950—, one-man shows include, Mus. Modern Art, 1949, Hartford (Conn.) Atheneum, 1953, Honolulu Acad., 1954, Mass. Inst. Tech., 1959, Carnegie Inst. Tech., Balt. Mus. Art, Yale Art Gallery, 1960, Contemporary Arts Mus., Houston, Kunstmuseum, Dusseldorf, Germany, 1975, Bauhaus-Archiv, Berlin, Bklyn. Mus., 1977; work represented in permanent collections, Mus. Modern Art, Met. Mus. Art, Art Inst. Chgo., Victoria and Albert Mus., London, Eng., Busch-Reisinger Mus. at Harvard, Balt. Mus. Art, Mus. Cranbrook Acad. Art, Currier Gallery Art, Bauhaus-Archiv, Jewish Mus., N.Y., Kunstgewerbemuseum der Staat Zurich, Kunsthalle Nürnberg (Ger.), Art Gallery Ont., Ft. Worth Art Mus., St. Louis Art Mus., Wadsworth Atheneum, Yale U., others, also pvt. collections; Author: Anni Albers: on Designing, 3d edit, 1971, Anni Albers: on Weaving, 1965, 2d edit., 1972, Anni Albers: pre-Columbian Mexican Miniatures, 1970, also articles. Recipient medal in craftsmanship A.I.A., 1961; citation Phila. Mus. Coll. Art, 1962; Gold medal Am. Crafts Council, 1981; Tamarind Lithography Workshop Fellow, 1964.

ALBERS, HENRY, astronomer, educator; b. Andover, Mass., Nov. 17, 1925; s. Henry F. and Edna (Oliver) A.; m. Wilma Clarice Smith, Mar. 17, 1950; children—Catherine Helen, Christina Edna, Henry Peter. A.B., Harvard, 1950; M.A., U. Minn., 1952; Ph.D., Case Inst. Tech., 1956. Instr. astronomy U. Minn., 1953-55; instr. astronomy Case Inst. Tech., 1955-56; asst. prof. astronomy Butler U., 1956-58, Vassar Coll., Poughkeepsie, N.Y., 1958-61, asso. prof., 1961-68, prof., 1968—. Author: Infrared Studies of the Southern Milky Way I and II; co-author: An Atlas of Identification Charts for Large Proper Motion Stars. Served with USAAF, 1943-46. NSF Sci. Faculty fellow, 1965. Mem. Am. Astron. Soc., AAAS, Am. Assn. U. Profs., Sigma Xi. Address: Vassar Coll Poughkeepsie NY 12601

ALBERS, JOHN RICHARD, soft drink company executive; b. Mpls., Oct. 5, 1931; s. Raymond A. and Lillian (Sharp) A.; m. Carol Jean Heines, Feb. 8, 1964; children: Scott Alan, Wendy Jean. B.A. in Econs., U. Minn., 1957. Sales rep. Minn. Mining, Chgo., 1957-59; account exec. Campbell-Mithun, Mpls., 1959-64; v.p. Grant Advt., Dallas, 1965; account supr. Knox-Reeves, Mpls., 1966-69; co-founder Zapata Foods, Mpls., 1969-71; v.p. Dr. Pepper, Dallas, 1971-81; pres. Dr. Pepper U.S.A., Dallas, 1983—; dir. Central Life Assurance Co., Des Moines. Mem. adv. bd. U. Dallas, 1981-83. Served to 1st. U.S. Army, 1954-56. Clubs: Bent Tree, DAC County, Chaparral (Dallas). Home: 7231 Tangleglen Dr Dallas TX 75240 Office: Dr Pepper Co 5523 E Mockingbird Ln Dallas TX 75206

ALBERSHEIM, PETER, biology educator; b. N.Y.C., Mar. 30, 1934; s. Walter Julius and Alberta (Green) A.; m. Joyce Elizabeth Johnson, June 9, 1958; children—Renee, Jim, Stephi. B.S., Cornell U., 1956; Ph.D., Calif. Inst. Tech., 1959. NSF postdoctoral research fellow Swiss Fed. inst. Tech., Zurich, Switzerland, 1959; instr. biology Harvard, Cambridge, Mass., 1960-61, asst. prof., 1961-64; asso. prof. biochemistry, dept. chemistry U. Colo., Boulder, 1964-67, prof., 1967—, also prof. molecular, cellular, developmental biology, 1970—; Faculty Research lectr. U. Colo. Council on Research and Creative Work, 1980; Storrer Life Scis. lectr. U. Calif., Davis, 1977; Dupont lectr. Tex. A. and M. U., 1978; vis. prof. U. Tex., 1978; cons. Montsanto Agrl. Chems., 1976—, Celanese Corp., 1981—, Weyerhauser Co., 1981—, Salk Inst. Biotech. Indsl. Assos., 1981—. Author: (with others) Twenty-six Afternoons of Biology - An Introductory Lab Manual, 1966; Contbr. articles to profl. jours.; mem. editorial bds.: Plant Physiology, Phytopathology, Jour. Biol. Chemistry; referee other jours. Recipient Robert L. Stearns award for contbns. to progress U. Colo., 1979; NIH grantee, 1960-65; NSF grantee, 1966-67, 71—; AEC-ERDA-Dept. Energy grantee, 1964—; Herman Frasch Found. grantee, 1972-77; Rockefeller Found. grantee, 1975—; USDA grantee, 1975—. Fellow AAAS; Mem. Am. Chem. Soc., Am. Soc. Biol. Chemists, Am. Soc. Plant Physiology (mem. exec. com. 1978—, Charles A. Shull award 1973), The Biochem. Soc., Am. Phytopathol. Soc., Sigma Xi, others. Home: 1440 Bellevue Dr Boulder CO 80302 Office: Dept Chemistry Box 215 U Colo Boulder CO 80309

ALBERT, ALFRED GERHARDT, retired government official, labor relations arbitrator; b. Burgstadt, Germany, June 25, 1920; came to U.S., 1923, naturalized, 1939; s. Rudolf and Franciska (Fischer) A.; m. Maria Julia Berger, Mar. 24, 1947; children—Diana (Mrs. Michael Moran), Christopher, Mark. Student, Seton Hall U., 1947-49; J.D., Rutgers U., 1951. Bar: Fed. Dist. Ct. bar 1951, D.C. Ct. Appeals bar 1952. With Dept. Labor, Washington, 1952—, dep. asso. solicitor for manpower, 1969-70; dep. assoc. solicitor for labor relations and civil rights, 1967-69, dep. solicitor dept., 1970—; rep. sec. labor to U.S.-Mexican Apellate Tribunal Adjudication contract disputes U.S. employers and Mexican workers, 1956-64; to Nat. Commn. State Workmen's Compensation Laws, 1971-72; labor relations arbitrator. Editor: Rutgers Law Rev, 1950-51. Chmn. Benefits Rev. Bd. Served with AAC, 1941-47; ETO; lt. col. USAF Res. ret. Mem. Fed. Bar Assn. (vice chmn. labor law com.), Isaac Walton League, Delta Theta Phi. Home and office:: 7822 E Beryl Ave Scottsdale AZ 85258

ALBERT, CALVIN, sculptor; b. Grand Rapids, Mich., Nov. 19, 1918; s. Philip and Ethel (Schlacht) A.; m. Martha Neff, Dec. 25, 1941; 1 dau., Jill. Student, Art Inst., Chgo., 1936-37, Inst. Design, Chgo., 1937-39. Mem. faculty N.Y.U., 1949-51, Bklyn. Coll., 1948-49, Inst. Design, Chgo., 1942-47; prof. art Pratt Inst., Bklyn., 1950—, head grad. sculpture program, 1960—. Exhibited in one man shows at, Theobald Gallery, Chgo., 1941, Grand Rapids Art Gallery, 1943, 48, Puma Gallery, N.Y.C., 1944, Art Inst., Chgo., 1945, California Palace of Legion of Honor, San Francisco, 1947; exhibited in one man shows at, Laurel Gallery, N.Y.C., 1950, Light Gallery, Southampton, N.Y., 1981, Phoenix Gallery, Washington, 1982, Ingberg Gallery, N.Y.C., 1983, Bologna-Londi Gallery, East Hampton, N.Y.; exhibited in traveling show, Des Moines Art Center; U. Mich., Grand Rapids Art

Gallery, Mich. State U., 1957, Grace Borgenicht Gallery, N.Y.C., 1952, 54, 56, 57, Stable Gallery, N.Y.C., 1959, 64, Jewish Mus., N.Y.C., 1960, Galleria George Lester, Rome, Italy, 1962, Landmark Gallery, N.Y.C., 1974, 77, Benson Gallery, Bridgehampton, N.Y., 1975; exhibited in retrospective, Guild Hall Mus., East Hampton, N.Y., 1979, group shows at, Houston Mus. Fine Arts, 1958-59, Addison Gallery, 1959, Galerie Claude Bernard, Paris, 1961, Art Inst. Chgo., 1962, Sculpture Biennale, Cararra, Italy, Pa. Acad., Phila., 1963, FAR Gallery, N.Y.C., 1964, Whitney Mus., 1954-57, 60, 62, 64, U. Ill., 1965; rep. permanent collections, Whitney Mus., Bklyn. Mus., Art Inst. Chgo., Detroit Inst. Arts, Met. Mus., Jewish Mus., U. Nebr., Chrysler Mus. Art, Wm. Rockhill Nelson Gallery Art.; Author: (with D.G. Seckler) Figure Drawing Comes to Life, 1957. Recipient Haass prize Detroit Inst. Arts, 1944, Forst award for sculpture Audubon Artists Annual, 1954, Anonymous Prize for sculpture Audubon Annual, 1957, Fulbright Advanced Research grant, Italy, 1961-62, Tiffany grant, 1963, 65, Guggenheim fellowship, 1966, Am. Inst. Arts and Letters award, 1975. Home: 325 W 16th St New York NY 10011

ALBERT, DANIEL MYRON, ophthalmologist, educator; b. Newark, Dec. 19, 1936; s. Maurice I. and Flora A.; m. Eleanor Kagle, June 26, 1960; children: B. Steven, Michael. B.S., Franklin and Marshall Coll., 1958; M.D., U. Pa., 1962; M.A. (hon.), Harvard U., 1976. Diplomate: Am. Bd. Ophthalmology. Intern Hosp. U. Pa., 1962-63, resident, 1963-66; surgeon USPHS, 1966-68; NIH spl. fellow in ophthalmic pathology Armed Forces Inst. Pathology, 1968-69; practice medicine specializing in ophthalmology, Boston, 1976—; asso. surgeon Mass. Eye and Ear Infirmary, 1976—, dir. eye pathology lab., 1979—; asst. prof. ophthalmology Yale U. Sch. Medicine, 1969-70, asso. prof., 1970-75, prof., 1975-76; prof. ophthalmic pathology Harvard U. Med. Sch., 1976—; cons. Peter Bent Brigham Hosp. Author: (with Scheie) Textbook of Ophthalmology, 9th edit., 1977, Jaeger's Atlas of Ophthalmology, 1972, Foundations of Ophthalmic Pathology, 1979; Contbr. articles to med. jours. Recipient Friedenwald award, 1981; William and Mary Greve scholar, 1978—. Fellow ACS; mem. Am. Assn. Ophthalmic Pathology. Jewish. Home: 36 Ledgewood Rd Weston MA 02193 Office: Mass Eye and Ear Infirmary 243 Charles St Boston MA 02114

ALBERT, EDDIE (EDWARD ALBERT HEIMBERGER), actor; b. Rock Island, Ill., Apr. 22, 1908; s. Frank and Julia (Jones) Heimberger; m. Maria Margarita Guadelupe Teresa Estella Bolado Castilla y O'Donnell (profl. name Margo); children: Edward, Maria. Student, U. Minn., 1927-29. With singing trio, Mpls., 1930; then, St. Louis, Cin., to N.Y.C., 1935; for: radio show Grace and Eddie; acted in Broadway version: No Hard Feelings, 1973; organized: for making ednl. films Eddie Albert Prodns, 1945, subjects such as sex edn., labor-mgmt. relations, desegregation, med. topics; appeared in: motion pictures including Teahouse of August Moon, 1956, Miracle of the White Stallions, 1963, Brother Rat, Carrie, 1976, Roman Holiday (nominated for Acad. award 1955), Oklahoma, 1955, Sun Also Rises, 1957, Roots of Heaven, 1958, Attack, 1958, Longest Day, 1962, Captain Newman, 1964, The Heartbreak Kid, 1972 (Academy award nominee), The Longest Yard, 1974, Escape to Witch Mountain, 1975, Yes, Giorgio, 1981; toured night-club act with wife, 1954; star of: TV series Green Acres, 1965-71, Switch, 1975-78; TV appearances include: Studio One, 1948-57, The Outer Limits, Show of Shows; Broadway appearances in: O, Evening Star, Brother Rat, Room Service, Boys from Syracuse, Miss Liberty, Music Man; appeared with: Circus Moderno, Mexico, 1941, Hagenbeck Circus, Europe, 1965, San Francisco Opera, 1982; conducted lecture tour on ecology, 1969-70; concert tour. Padrino, Plaza de la Raza. Participant World Hunger Conf., Rome, 1974; dir. U.S. Commn. on Refugees; bd. dirs. Film Council; trustee Nat. Recreation and Parks Assn., Alaska-Pacific U., Nat. Arbor Day Found.; nat. conservation chmn. Boy Scouts Am.; bd. dirs. solar lobby, mem. consumer adv. bd. Dept. Energy, Washington; chmn. Eddie Albert World Trees Found. Am. Recipient Nat. Film Critics award, 1972. Club: Bohemian (San Francisco). Address: care Internat Creative Mgmt 8899 Beverly Blvd Los Angeles CA 90048

ALBERT, EDWARD, actor, photographer; b. Feb. 20, 1951; s. Eddie A. and Margo. Student, U. Calif. at Los Angeles; Merit scholar, Oxford U. Appeared in: films Butterflies are Free, 1972, Forty Carats, 1973, Midway, 1976, The Domino Principle, 1977, The Greek Tycoon, 1978, The Day the World Ended, 1980; prodn. asst.: Patton, 1970; appeared in: TV films Death Cruise, 1974, Killer Bees, 1974, Black Beauty; series, 1978; TV appearances include Gibbsville, Orson Welles' Great Mysteries, Kung Fu, Medical Story, The Rookies, Police Story, Ellery Queen. 445 Park Ave New York NY 10022 *

ALBERT, ETHEL MARY, anthropology educator; b. New Britain, Conn., Mar. 28, 1918; d. Zundel and Dorothy (Eisenstadt) Sokolsky. B.A., Bklyn. Coll., 1942; M.A., Columbia, 1947; Ph.D., U. Wis., 1949. Instr. philosophy Bklyn. Coll., 1946-47, U. Wis., 1947-49, Syracuse U., 1949-52; prof. speech U. Calif. at Berkeley, 1958-66; prof. anthropology Northwestern U., 1966—, chmn. dept., 1972-73; inactive, 1977—; research asso. Harvard U. Lab. Social Relations, 1953-55; Ford Found. Overseas fellow, Africa, 1955-57; asst. dir. NSF Project on teaching anthropology, 1961; Social Sci. Research Council faculty research fellow, 1962. Author: (With Peterfreund and Denise) Great Traditions in Ethics, rev. edit, 1979, (with Kluckhohn) A Selected Bibliography on Values, Ethics and Esthetics, 1959, (with Mandelbaum and Lasker) Teaching of Anthropology, 1963, (with Vogt) The People of Rimrock, 1966; Contbr. articles profl. jours. NSF Sr. postdoctoral fellow, 1965-66. Fellow Am. Anthrop. Assn. Address: 420 Beach Rd Apt 503 Sarasota FL 33581

ALBERT, GERALD, mfg. co. exec.; b. Bklyn., Feb. 13, 1925; s. Barney and Minnie A.; m. Evelyn Kriegshan, July 4, 1948; children—Bruce M., Steven A. B.E.E., CCNY, 1948; postgrad., Poly. Inst. Bklyn. With EDO Corp. (sonar mfrs.), College Point, N.Y., 1948—, pres. indsl. and govt. products group, 1978-80, pres., chief operating officer, 1980—, also dir. Mem. Nat. Security Indsl. Assn. (trustee), Acoustical Soc. Am., Am. Def. Preparedness Assn., Am. Helicopter Soc., Am. Soc. Naval Engrs., NAM, Naval War Coll. Found., Soc. Naval Architects and Marine Engrs., U.S. Naval Inst., Flushing (N.Y.) C. of C. Address: EDO Corp 14-04 111th St College Point NY 11356

ALBERT, LEO N., publishing company executive; b. St. Agatha, Maine, Oct. 9, 1920; s. Felix Nicholas and Azilda (Michaud) A.; m. Virginia Martha Coffey, June 1, 1946. Student, Pace Coll., NYU. With Prentice-Hall, Inc., 1946—, now v.p., dir.; chmn. bd. Prentice-Hall Internat., Prentice-Hall Japan, Inc., Internat. Book Distbrs., London; dir. Prentice-Hall India Put. Ltd.; chmn. bd. Prentice-Hall Of Australia Ptg. Ltd.; chmn. adv. panel on copyright Dept. Stat. Mem. exec. com. Englewood Hosp. Served with USNCR, 1942-46; PTO. Mem. Assn. Am. Pubs. (bd. dirs., mem. exec. com., mem. internat. copywright com., chmn. Washington liaison com., chmn. postal com.). Home: 511 Grandview Terr Leonia NJ 07605 Office: Prentice-Hall Inc Englewood Cliffs NJ 07632

ALBERT, MARV, television station director, sportscaster; b. N.Y.C., June 12, 1943; s. Max and Alida (Kahn) A.; m. Benita Caress, Aug. 15, 1965; children: Kenny, Jackie, Denise, Brian. Student, Syracuse U., 1960-63; B.S. in Journalism, NYU, 1964. Announcer Sta. WOLF, Syracuse, N.Y., 1961-64; sports dir. Sta. WHN, N.Y.C., 1967-73; announcer N.Y. Knicks basketball team, 1967—, N.Y. Rangers hockey team, 1967—; basketball, football and boxing announcer NBC Sports Network, 1977—; sports dir. Sta. WNBC-TV, N.Y.C., 1974—. Author: Yes - a guide to Sportscasting, 1981, Marv Albert's Quiz Book, 1976, Krazy About the Knicks, 1970. Named Sports Personality of Yr. Spl. Olympics, N.Y.C., 1983. Mem. Nat. Sportscaster and Sportswriters Assn. (Sportscaster of Yr. 1971-84), Internat. Boxing Writers Assn. Lodge: B'nai B'rith. Office: NBC Sports Room 720F 30 Rockefeller Plaza New York NY 10020

ALBERT, ROBERT BERTRAND, chemical executive; b. N.Y.C., June 15, 1932; s. Sylvester and Anna (Kraus) A.; m. Audrey Miller, Feb. 17, 1963; children: Susan Beth, Randi Michelle. B.B.A., CCNY, 1952; LL.B., NYU, 1955. Bar: N.Y. 1955. Sr. staff auditor S.D. Leidesdorf & Co. (C.P.A.s), 1956-59; mem. tax staff Eisner & Lubin (C.P.A.s), 1959-60; tax mgr. Nat. Starch & Chem. Corp., N.Y.C., 1960-62, chief acct., 1962-64, asst. controller, 1964-66, asst. treas., 1965-70, controller, 1966-76, treas., 1970—, v.p., 1976-79, v.p. fin., 1979—, dir., 1983—. Mem. N.Y. Bar Assn., Financial Execs. Inst., N.Y. Soc. C.P.A.s. Home: 8 Torrance Dr Livingston NJ 07039 Office: 10 Finderne Ave Bridgewater NJ

ALBERT, ROBERT HARTMAN, mag. editor; b. Hershey, Pa., June 18, 1924; s. Thomas Warren and Hazel Noreen (Hartman) A. B.A., Pa. State U., 1948; M.A., Stanford, 1950; postgrad., U. N.C., 1950-52. With New Yorker mag., 1956-58, Newsweek mag., 1959-61; Sunday editor N.Y. Herald Tribune, 1961-63; editorial dir. McCall's Corp., 1963-64; editor, exec. v.p. Sales & Mktg. Mgmt. mag., N.Y.C., 1964—; corp. v.p. Bill Communications, 1972—; pres. Oley Furnace Vineyards, 1978—. Bd. dirs. Friends of Theatre and Music Collection, Mus. City N.Y. Served with USN, 1943-46, 50-51. Mem. Sales Exec. Club N.Y., Advt. Research Found., Am. Mktg. Assn., Am. Soc. Bus. Press Editors, Am. Soc. Mag. Editors, Pa. State Alumni Assn., ACLU. Clubs: Overseas Press; Wyomissing (Reading). Home: 10 Park Ave New York NY 10016 Office: 633 3d Ave New York NY 10017

ALBERTS, EUNICE DOROTHY, contralto; b. Boston, Nov. 27, 1922; d. Emanuel Victor and Adelle Rachel (Shalit) A.; m. Dean E. Nicholson, July 10, 1948; children: Adelle, Emily, Martha. Mus.B., New Eng. Conservatory Music, 1967. Mem. faculty Boston U., Lowell U. Debut as alto soloist in: Beethoven's 9th Symphony at, Tanglewood Festival, 1946, solo appearances, with orchs., including, Boston Symphony, Phila. Symphony Orch., Nat. Symphony Orch. of Washington, Mpls. Symphony Orch., N.Y. Philharmonic Orch., numerous festival appearances, including, Saratoga, Aspen, Bethlehem, Wolf Trap., Central City (Colo.); appeared with opera cos., Chgo. Lyric Opera, Houston Opera, Washington Opera, N.Y.C. Opera, New Orleans Opera; leading contralto, Opera Co., Boston, 1958—; appeared as Suzuki in: Madame Butterfly; as Dame Quickly in: Falstaff; appeared in: first Am. staged performances of War and Peace; rec. artist. Mem. Nat. Assn. Tchrs. Singing, Am. Guild Musical Artists, Sigma Alpha Iota. Office: Opera Co Boston 539 Washington St Boston MA 02111 *Looking back over the years, I consider myself to have been blessed indeed in being able to pursue the joyful art of singing. The work has been challenging and difficult, but the rewards are great in so many ways, and one of the most fulfilling is in bringing happiness and enjoyment to others.* *

ALBERTS, ROBERT C., author; b. July 15, 1907; s. William Edward and Leonora (Carman) A.; m. Zita Doberneck, 1932. B.A., U. Pitts., M.A., 1931. Editorial staff Bull.-Index mag., 1938-42, editor, 1940-42; with Ketchum, MacLeod & Grove, Inc., Pitts., 1942-43, 48-69, v.p., 1956-69; contbg. editor Am. Heritage mag., 1970-77. Author: The Most Extraordinary Adventures of Major Robert Stobo, 1965 (Soc. Colonial Wars award), The Golden Voyage: The Life and Times of William Bingham, 1752-1804, 1969, The Good Provider-H.J. Heinz and His 57 Varieties, 1973, A Charming Field for an Encounter - George Washington's Fort Necessity, 1976, George Rogers Clark and the Winning of the Old Northwest, 1976, Benjamin West: A Biography, 1978 (Christophers award), The Shaping of the Point, a History of the Pittsburgh Renaissance, 1980; editor: Records of North American Big Game, 1971. Served as editor Info. and Edn. Bull. AUS, 1946-48; Germany. Recipient Forbes medal Point Park Mus., 1981, Letterman of Distinction U. Pitts., 1981. Mem. Hist. Soc. of Western Pa. (sec., exec. com.), Authors Guild, Pa. Hist. Assn., Friends of U. Pitts. Libraries (bd. dirs.). Address: 99 Gladstone Rd Pittsburgh PA 15217

ALBERTSON, DAVID EDWIN, banker; b. Evanston, Ill., Mar. 7, 1937; s. Walter S. and Frances M. (Coon) A.; m. Carol E. Coolidge, Sept. 16, 1961; children: Robert Coolidge, David Stanley. B.S. in Bus. Adminstrn., Miami U., Ohio, 1959, M.A. in Econs., 1961. Vice pres. No. Trust Co., Chgo., 1961-71; pres., chief exec. officer State Nat. Bank, Evanston, 1971—. Vice pres. Evanston Hist. Soc., 1982-83; v.p., dir. Evanston C. of C., 1982-83; v.p. Evanston YMCA, 1982-83. Served with Ill. N.G., 1961-67. Mem. Bankers Club of Chgo. (exec. com.), Econ. Club of Chgo., Phi Beta Kappa. Republican. Congregationalist. Club: University. Home: 416 Elder Ln Winnetka IL 60093 Office: 1603 Orrington Ave Evanston IL 60204

ALBERTSON, DEAN, history educator; b. Denver, Aug. 22, 1920; s. George Howard and Vinnie (Robinson) A.; m. Johnnie Leinbach, Mar. 6, 1954 (div. Dec. 1968); children—Mark Nevins, Constant Kathryn. B.A., U. Calif. at Berkeley, 1942, M.A., 1947; Ph.D., Columbia, 1955. Asst. dir, oral history project Columbia, 1948-55; exec. asst. Com. Internat. Exchange Persons, 1956-59; instr. history Bklyn. Coll., 1959-61, asst. prof. history, 1961-64, asso. prof. history, 1965; prof. history U. Mass., Amherst, 1965—; dir. NDEA Insts. History, 1966, 67, 68. Author: Roosevelt's Farmer, 1961, Eisenhower as President, 1963, (with Howard H. Quint and Milton Cantor) Main Problems in American History, 1964, rev. edits., 1968, 72, 78, Am. History Visually, 1969, Rebels or Revolutionaries, Student Movements of the 1960's, 1975. Served to lt. (j.g.) USNR, 1943-45. Decorated Air medal with 3 clusters; recipient Research grant Am. Council Learned Socs., Social Sci. Research Council, Am. Philos. Soc., 1962-64. Mem. Am. Hist. Assn., Orgn. Am. Historians, Oral History Assn. (sec. 1968-69). Democrat. Office: Dept History U Mass Amherst MA 01002

ALBERTSON, FRED W(OODWARD), retired lawyer, radio engineer; b. Fairgrove, Mich., Sept. 29, 1908; s. Charles Elton Eugene and Helen Louise (Woodward) A.; m. Catherine Frances Dolan, June 10, 1942; children: Fred Woodward, Helen Dolan. A.B. U. Mich, 1931; J.D., 1934. Bar: Mich. 1934, D.C. 1935; Registered profl. elec.-communications engr., D.C. Engineered constrn. and operation several broadcast and radio telegraph stas., 1925-27; radio equipped and handled communications with remote meterol. expdns. and stas. U. Mich., 1927-34; gen. law practice, 1935-80, radio and communications legal counsel for radio, television, telegraph, telephone and broadcast cos. and stas., 1935-80; partner Dow, Lohnes & Albertson (specializing in communications, radio and air law), Washington, 1944-80; lic. radio operator, 1924-; licensee amateur radio sta. W4BD. Trustee, bd. dirs. Delta Theta Phi Found., 1945-46; trustee Legal Aid Soc. D.C., 1970-72. Life fellow Am. Bar Found., Radio Club Am.; mem. IEEE (sr. life mem.; chmn. Washington sect. 1946-47, mem. adminstrv. com. 1943-72, bd. editors proc. 1946-54), Broadcast Pioneers, World Peace Through Law Center (central planning com. 1966-72), Fed. Communications (pres. 1953-54), ABA (ho. dels. 1953-54, chmn. standing com. on communications 1957-58), D.C. Bar Assn., Armed Forces Communications and Electronics Assn. (Disting. life mem.), Delta Theta Phi (emeritus). Clubs: Washington Engrs. (co-founder, life mem.), Washington Radio (past pres.), Congressional Country (Washington) (hon. life); Key Biscayne (Fla.) Yacht; U. Mich. Radio (Ann Arbor) (co-founder, past pres.). Home: 310 Harbor Dr Key Biscayne FL 33149 Office: 1225 Connecticut Ave Washington DC 20036

ALBERTY, ROBERT ARNOLD, educator; b. Winfield, Kans., June 21, 1921; s. Luman Harvey and Mattie (Arnold) A.; m. Lillian Jane Wind, May 22, 1944; children—Nancy Lou, Steven Charles, Catherine Ann. B.S., U. Nebr., 1943, M.S., 1944, D.Sc., 1967; Ph.D., U. Wis., 1947; D.Sc., Lawrence U., 1967. Engaged in research blood plasma fractionation for U.S. Govt., 1944-46; mem. faculty U. Wis., 1947-67, prof. chemistry, 1955-67, assoc. dean letters and sci., 1961-63, dean, 1963-67, Sch. Sci., Mass. Inst. Tech., 1967-72; cons. NSF, 1958-83, NIH, 1962-72; chmn. commn. on human resources NRC, 1974-77; dir. Colt Industries, 1978—, Inst. for Def. Analysis, 1980—. Co-Author: Physical Chemistry, 6th edit, 1983, Experimental Physical Chemistry, 3d edit., 1970. Guggenheim fellow Calif. Inst. Tech., 1950-51; recipient Eli Lilly award biol. chemistry, 1955. Fellow AAAS; mem. Am. Chem. Soc. (chmn. com. on chemistry and public affairs 1978-80), Am. Soc. Biol. Chemists, Nat. Acad. Sci., Inst. Medicine, Am. Acad. Arts and Scis., Phi Beta Kappa, Sigma Xi. Home: 7 Old Dee Rd Cambridge MA 02138

ALBINO, GEORGE ROBERT, mining and steel company executive; b. Boston, Feb. 1929; m. Julianne E. Albino; children: William, Robert, George. A.B., Columbia U., 1950; M.B.A., Harvard Bus. Sch., 1954. Chmn., chief exec. officer, dir. Rio Algom Ltd.; Chmn., chief exec. officer Lornex Mining Corp. Ltd.; dir. Confedn. Life Ins. Co., Barclays Bank of Can., Rio Tinto-Zinc Corp. P.L.C.; Rossing Uranium Ltd., Consumers' Gas Co. Ltd. Served to capt. USMC, 1950-52. Clubs: Toronto, Nat., Mississauga Golf and Country. Office: 120 Adelaide St W Toronto 1 ON Canada

ALBOSTA, DONALD JOSEPH, congressman; b. Saginaw, Mich., Dec. 5, 1925; s. Paul John and Laura (Bennett) A.; m. Dorothy Ankoviak, Feb. 10, 1951; children: Christine, Paul. Farmer, owner Misteguay Farms, Saginaw; mem. Mich. Ho. of Reps., 96th-98th Congresses from 10th Mich. Dist.; pres. Prairie Farms Coop. Commr., Saginaw County; asso. dir. Saginaw County Soil Conservation Dist. Served with USNR, World War II. Named Outstanding Young Farmer of Yr., Jaycees, 1960. Mem. Nat. Beet Growers Assn., Nat. Fedn. Beet Growers, St. Charles C. of C. Democrat. Roman Catholic. Club: Lions. Office: 1434 Longworth House Office Bldg Washington DC 20515

ALBOSTA, RICHARD FRANCIS, engineering and construction company executive; b. Pitts., Apr. 13, 1936; s. Chester Anthony and Mary Regina (Arnani) A.; m. Barbara A. Barnes, Dec. 28, 1956 (div. 1967); children: David, Daniel; m. Kathleen Ann McKay, Feb. 15, 1969. B.B.A. in Acctg. Fin., U. Pitts., 1961; M.B.A., Duquesne U., 1966. C.P.A., Pa., N.Y. Mgr. Deloitte Haskins & Sells, Pitts., 1961-66; controller Rust Engring. Co., Pitts., 1966-70; dir. fin. Boise Cascade Corp., N.Y.C., 1970-72; v.p. fin. Ebasco Services Inc., N.Y.C., 1972-76, exec. v.p. fin. and adminstrn., 1976-82, group v.p., 1982—; dir. Ebanal CV SA, Mexico City, 1980—, VSL Corp., Los Gatos, Calif., 1980—; chmn., dir. Ebasco Constructors Inc., Lyndhurst, N.J., 1983—, Ebasco Plant Services Inc., Houston, 1983—. Home: 62 Sherwood Dr New Providence NJ 17974 Office: Ebasco Services Inc Two World Trade Ctr New York NY 10048

ALBRECHT, ARTHUR JOHN, advertising agency executive;; b. Woodhaven, N.Y., June 11, 1931; s. Charles Arthur and Anna (Klingner) A.; m. Sandi Edith Roberson, May 14, 1952; 1 dau., Sheryl Lyn. B.A. cum laude, Fla. State U., 1957. Successively salesman, sales promotion mgr., product mgr. Vick Chem. Co., 1958-63; group product mgr. Whitehall Labs., 1963-65; v.p. marketing J.B. Williams Inc., 1965-66; v.p., then sr. v.p. marketing Mitchum-Thayer div. Revlon, 1966-71; sr. v.p., mgmt. supr. William Esty Co. Inc., N.Y.C., 1971-81; pres. Petersen-Albrecht, Inc., 1981—; adj. asst. prof. Pace U., N.Y.C., 1976—; dir. Brand Acceleration Inc., Damon Therapeutics Inc.; lectr., cons. in field. Author: Magic Town, U.S.A, 1978; contbr.: articles to profl. jours. Ency. of Advt. Pres. Villard Hill Assn., 1973-74. Served with USMC, 1950-55. Mem. Pharm. Advt. Club, Nat. Writers Club, Proprietary Assn., Fla. State U. Alumni Assn., Internat. Platform Assn., Phi Beta Kappa, Phi Kappa Phi, Phi Eta Sigma, Alpha Delta Sigma (past chpt. pres., Outstanding Service award 1957). Republican. Unitarian. Clubs: Indian Springs Country, Century. Home: 144 Judson Ave Dobbs Ferry NY 10522 Office: 77 W 55th St New York NY 10019

ALBRECHT, FELIX ROBERT, mathematics educator; b. Cernauti, Bucovina, Romania, Apr. 19, 1925; came to U.S., 1964; s. Leo and Ietti (Ebner) A.; m. Isidora Wiegler, Dec. 17, 1947. Diploma in math., U. Bucharest, 1951. Research fellow, sr. research fellow Inst. Math., Rumanian Acad., Bucharest, 1951-63; assoc. prof. to prof. Wesleyan U., Middletown, Conn., 1964-68; prof. math. U. Ill., Urbana, 1968—. Contbr. articles to profl. jours., 1975. Mem. Am. Math. Soc., Math. Assn. Am. Address: Univ Ill 1409 W Green St Urbana IL 61801

ALBRECHT, FREDERICK IVAN, retail executive; b. Akron, Ohio, June 11, 1917; s. Ivan Willard and Ferm Llewelyn (Heathman) A.; m. Francia Adelaide Holliday, Dec. 11, 1941; children: Heather, Ivan Holliday, Frederick Steven, Gwyneth, Tatiana, Monica. B.A., Colgate U., 1940; LL.B., U. Akron, 1951. Bar: Ohio. Pres. Fred W. Albrecht Grocery Co., Akron, 1959-82, chmn. bd., 1982—; pres. Albrecht, Inc., 1976—; v.p. Kaase Baking Co., 1974—; dir. Ruhlin Constrn. Co., Firestone Bank. Chmn. Little Hoover Commn. for Study Summit County Govt., 1967-69, Akron Area Devel. Com., 1964-65, Community Improvement Corp. for Summit, Medina and Portage Counties, 1966-74, Akron Sesquicentennial, 1974-75; bd. dirs. U. Akron, 1961-67, chmn., 1967-70; chmn. Devel. Found., 1975—; pres. U. Akron Hilltoppers Club, 1970-71; bd. dirs. Children's Hosp., Akron, 1960—; trustee Akron United Way, 1961-66; vice chmn. Akron Bicentennial, 1976; gen. campaign chmn. Akron United Way/ ARC campaign, 1977. Served with U.S. Army, World War II. Recipient Alumni Hon. award U. Akron, 1972; Distinguished Exec. of Year award, 1975; award Sales/Mktg. Execs. Assn., Akron, 1976; recipient Meritorious Service award U. Akron Varsity Assn., 1980, award Acme-Click 40 Yr. Club, 1980; named Citizen of Yr., 1978. Clubs: Cascade (past dir.), Portage Country.). Lodge: Rotary. Address: 2700 Gilchrist Rd Akron OH 44305

ALBRECHT, HAROLD L., metals co. exec.; b. Portsmouth, Ohio, Dec. 9, 1921; s. Henry J. and Mary M. (Stoll) A.; m. Ruby V. Vaughan, Mar. 17, 1945; children—Elizabeth Ann, Linda Susan. B.Sc., Ohio State U., 1948; postgrad., Western Res. U., 1951-52. C.P.A., Ohio. Supervising accountant Ernst & Ernst, 1948-59; sec., treas. Faultless Rubber Co., Ashland, Ohio, 1959-66; controller Reynolds Metals Co., Richmond, Va., 1966—, v.p. supply and distbn., 1974—. Served with USAAF, 1942-46. Mem. Am. Inst. C.P.A., Ohio Soc. C.P.A., Beta Alpha Psi. Home: 200 Doverland Rd Richmond VA 23229 Office: 6601 W Broad St Richmond VA 23261

ALBRECHT, PAUL ABRAHAM, college dean; b. Newton, Kans., Dec. 9, 1922; s. Abraham and Lena (Ratzlaff) A.; m. Bernice Hertha Goertz, June 29, 1947; children: Patricia Kay (Mrs. Stanley Senner), Jeanne Elizabeth. B.A., Bethel Coll., 1947; M.A., U. Chgo., 1949, Ph.D., 1953. Survey dir. Nejelski & Co. Inc. (Mgmt. Counsels), N.Y.C., 1951-53; dir. communication projects Indsl. Relations Center U. Chgo., 1953-55; asst. prof. psychology Whittier (Calif.) Coll., 1955-57; asso. prof. psychology Claremont Men's Coll. and Claremont Grad. Sch., Calif., 1957-62, prof., 1962-68; prof., chmn. grad. faculty in bus. econs. Claremont (Calif.) Grad. Sch., 1968-71, dean grad. sch., 1972-82, v.p., 1980-82, exec. v.p., exec. dean, 1982—; mgmt. cons. to industry, 1951—; dir. Grad. Record Exams. Bd. Contbr. articles profl. jours. Mem. president's council advisers Bethel Coll. Mem. Am., Western psychol. assns., Nat. Council Univ. Research Adminstrs., Council Grad. Schs. U.S. (dir., chmn. 1980-81), Western Assn. Grad. Schs. (pres.), Western Assn. Schs. and Colls. (sr. accrediting commn.), AAAS, Sigma Xi. Home: 645 W 10th St Claremont CA 91711

ALBRECHT, RICHARD RAYMOND, airplane manufacturing company executive, lawyer; b. Storm Lake, Iowa, Aug. 29, 1932; s. Arnold Louis and Catherine Dorothea (Boettcher) A.; m. Constance Marie Berg, June 16, 1957; children: John Justin, Carl Arnold, Richard Louis, Henry Berg. B.A., U. Iowa, 1958, J.D. with highest honors, 1961. Bar: Wash. 1961. Assoc. firm Perkins, Coie, Stone, Olsen & Williams, Seattle, 1961-67, ptnr., 1968-74; gen. counsel U.S. Dept. Treasury, Washington, 1974-76; v.p., gen. counsel, sec. Boeing Co., Seattle, 1976-81, v.p. fin., contracts and internat. bus., 1981-83, v.p., gen. mgr. 747 div., 1983—. Trustee Wash. Mut. Savs. Bank. Served with AUS, 1955-58. Recipient Outstanding Citizen of Yr. award Seattle-King County Municipal League, 1968-69. Mem. Am., Wash. State, Seattle-King County bar assns., Am. Judicature Soc., Order of Coif, Sigma Nu, Omicron Delta Kappa, Phi Delta Phi. Club: Rainier (Seattle). Home: 1940 Shenandoah Dr E Seattle WA 98112 Office: Boeing Co PO Box 3707 M/S OA-06 Seattle WA 98124

ALBRECHT, RONALD FRANK, anesthesiologist; b. Chgo., Apr. 17, 1937; s. Frank William and Mabel Dorothy (Cassens) A.; m. Joyce Yvonne Burchfield, June 27, 1962; children: Ronald Frank II, Mark Burchfield, Meredith Ann. A.B., U. Ill., 1958, B.S., 1959, M.D., 1961. Diplomate: Am. Bd. Anesthesiology. Intern Cin. Gen. Hosp., 1961-62; resident in anesthesiology U. Ill. Research and Ednl. Hosp., Chgo., 1962-64, attending physician, 1966-73; clin. assoc. NIH, Bethesda, Md., 1964-66; practice medicine specializing in anesthesiology, Chgo., 1966—; mem. staff Michael Reese Med. Center, Chgo., chmn. dept. anesthesiology, 1971—; asst. prof. anesthesiology U. Ill., Chgo., 1966-70, clin. asso. prof., 1970-73; prof. anesthesiology U. Chgo., 1973-78, clin. prof. anesthesiology, 1978—. Contbr. articles to profl. jours. Served to lt. comdr. USPHS, 1964-66. Fellow Am. Coll. Anesthesiologists; mem. AMA, Ill. State Med. Soc., Chgo. Med. Soc., Am. Soc. Anesthesiologists, Ill. Soc. Anesthesiologists (pres. 1980-81), Chgo. Soc. Anesthesiologists, Internat. Anesthesia Research Soc., Assn. Anaesthetists Gt. Britain and Ireland, Am. Physiol. Soc. Presbyterian. Home: 28 Salem Ln Evanston IL 60203 Office: Dept Anesthesiology Michael Reese Medical Center Chicago IL 60616

ALBRIGHT, ARCHIE EARL, JR., investment banker; b. Akron, Ohio, Aug. 21, 1920; s. Archie E. and Hazel (Beard) A.; children: John, Anne, Catherine. A.B. magna cum laude, Wittenberg Coll., 1942; LL.B., J.D., Yale U., 1948. Bar: N.Y. 1948. Mem. firm Patterson, Belknap & Webb, 1948-53; asst. to pres. Stauffer Chem. Co., N.Y.C., 1953, v.p., 1958-65, exec. v.p., 1965-68; partner Kuhn Loeb & Co., N.Y.C., 1968-69; pres., chief exec. officer Glore Forgan Staats, Inc., 1969-70, Loeb Rhoades & Co., 1971; chmn. bd., chief exec. officer Drexel Firestone, Inc., 1972-73; vice chmn. bd., chmn. fin. com. Drexel Burnham Lambert Inc., 1973-78, sr. adv., 1979—; chmn. bd., dir. Transp. Equipment Corp., 1978-80; chmn. bd. GVC Corp., 1980—; dir. Grumman Corp., Anderson Devel. Co.; vis. prof., mem. adv. council Johns Hopkins U. Sch. Advanced Internat. Studies. Trustee Legal Aid Soc., Nat. Repertory Theater; mem. adv. council Hampshire Coll.; bd. dirs. Fgn. Policy Assn., Police Athletic League, Yale U. Law Sch. Fund; mem. N.Y. Philharmonic Soc.; mem. pres.'s council Kirkland Coll. Served to lt. USNR, 1942-46. Woodrow Wilson vis. fellow. Mem. Assn. Bar City N.Y., Council on Fgn. Relations, Fgn. Policy Assn. (pres., chief exec. officer 1983—), Pilgrims Soc. Clubs: Bond, Yale, Recess, Links (N.Y.C.); Bedford (N.Y.); Golf and Tennis, Pine Valley Golf; Nat. Golf (Southampton). Home: 625 Park Ave St New York NY 10021 also 46 Mountain Spring Rd Farmington CT 06032 Office: 205 Lexington Ave New York NY 10016

ALBRIGHT, GEORGE FRANKLIN, former life ins. co. exec.; b. Belmont, N.C., Sept. 13, 1916; s. Claude Lee and Minnie (Tate) A.; m. Dorothy Severs, June 25, 1938; children—Dorothy Jane, Claudia Ann, George Franklin. Grad., Davidson Coll., 1937, Advanced Mgmt. Program Harvard, 1956. Agt. Union Central Life Ins. Co., 1938-39; with Life Ins. Co. Va., Richmond, 1939-71, asst. to pres., 1956-57, v.p. charge agencies, 1957-61, sr. v.p., 1961-71, dir., 1960-71; ins. cons., 1971—; vice chmn. Harford Mut. Ins. Co.; dir. Bank of Va. Served to 1st lt AUS, 1943-46. Presbyn. Clubs: Mason., Commonwealth, Country of Va. Home: Berkshire Rd Richmond VA 23221

ALBRIGHT, HARRY WESLEY, JR., banker; b. Albany, N.Y., Mar. 19, 1925; s. Harry Wesley and Ruth Agnes (Kerwin) A.; m. Joan Diekman, June 27, 1953; children—Mary Kimberly, Deborah V., Harry Wesley, III, Peter D., Joan Kerwin, John D. B.A., Yale U., 1949; LL.B., Cornell U., 1952. Bar: N.Y. State bar 1954. With firm DeGraff, Foy, Conway & Holt-Harris, Albany, 1964-67; dep. sec. to gov. N.Y. State, 1967-68, dep. sec., appointments officer, 1968-70, exec. asst. to gov., 1970-72, supt. banks, 1972-74; spl. counsel to Vice Pres. Nelson A. Rockefeller, 1974-75; pres.; chief operating officer, trustee Dime Savs. Bank N.Y., Bklyn., 1975-81; pres. Thrift Instns. Adv. Council Fed. Res. Bd., 1983—. Bd. editors: N.Y. Law Jour, 1974. Bd. dirs. Bodman Found., Pratt Inst., Bklyn.; mem. regional panel selection White House Fellows; chmn. bd. Marymount Coll.; greater N.Y. adv. bd. Salvation Army. Served with AUS, 1943-46. Mem. Am., N.Y. State bar assns. Clubs: University (N.Y.C.); Sleepy Hollow Country (Scarborough-on-Hudson, N.Y.); Stockbridge (Mass.) Golf. Home: 567 Bedford Rd North Tarrytown NY 10591 Office: 589 Fifth Ave New York NY 10017

ALBRIGHT, HUGH NORTON, educator; b. Jerusalem, Palestine, Feb. 27, 1928; s. William Foxwell and Ruth (Norton) A. B.A., Catholic U., 1950; M.A., U. Pa., 1953, Ph.D., 1959. Instr. math. LaSalle Coll., Phila., 1951-58, asst. prof., 1958-65, asso. prof., 1965-70, prof., 1970—, chmn. dept., 1964-70, acting dean faculty arts and scis., 1970-72, dean, 1972-76. Mem. Am. Math. Soc., Math. Assn. Am., AAUP, Phi Beta Kappa, Sigma Xi. Roman Catholic. Home: 7018 Boyer St Philadelphia PA 19119

ALBRIGHT, JACK LAWRENCE, educator; b. San Francisco, Mar. 14, 1930; s. George Clement and Elizabeth Ann (Murphy) A.; m. Lorraine Aylmer Hughes, Aug. 17, 1957; children: Maryann Aylmer, Amy Elizabeth. B.S., Calif. State Poly. U., 1952; M.S., Wash. State U., 1954, Ph.D., 1957. Research asst. Wash. State U., 1952-54, 55-57, acting instr., 1954-55; instr. Calif. State Poly. U., 1955, 57-59; asst. prof. U. Ill., Urbana, 1959-63; mem. faculty Purdue U., 1963—, prof. animal sci. Sch. Agr., 1966—, prof. animal mgmt. and behavior Sch. Vet. Medicine, 1974—; mem. Ctr. Applied Ethology and Human/Animal Interactions Purdue U., 1982—; vis. prof. U. Reading, Eng., 1977-78, Dairy Shrine, Ft. Atkinson, Wis., 1958—; cons., lectr. in field. Author papers, revs., chpts. and books; reviewer sci. jours., NSF. Vestryman St. John's Episcopal Ch., West Lafayette, 1979-82; bellringer Salvation Army, 1964—. Fulbright scholar, N.Z., 1971-72; NSF grantee, summer 1964. Fellow AAAS, Ind. Acad. Sci.; mem. Am. Dairy Sci. Assn. (sec. 1972-73, chmn. prodn. council 1973-74), Animal Behavior Soc. (charter), Am. Soc. Animal Sci. (chmn. animal behavior com. 1970, 76, 85), Am. Soc. Vet. Ethology (charter), Soc. Vet. Ethology, Chillingham Wild Cattle Assn. (life), Commn. Farm Animal Care, Inc. (sec.-treas. 1981—), Soc. Study Ethics and Animals, Scientist's Center Animal Welfare (corr.), Blue Key, Sigma Xi, Alpha Zeta, Gamma Sigma Delta, Farm House. Republican. Episcopalian. Clubs: Kiwanis (pres. Lafayette 1969-70, sec. found. 1976-77. Home: 188 Blueberry Ln West Lafayette IN 47906 Office: Purdue U West Lafayette IN 47907

ALBRIGHT, JOSEPH MEDILL PATTERSON, newspaperman; b. New Orleans, Apr. 3, 1937; adopted by Ivan Albright, 1953 and Reeve; children: Anne Korbel, Alice Patterson, Katharine Medill. B.A., Williams Coll., 1958. Reporter Denver Post, summers 1956, 57, Chgo. Sun Times, 1958-61; with Newsday, 1961-71, chief Washington bur., 1969-71, dir., 1963-71; Washington corr. San Francisco Chronicle; also contbr. to N.Y. Times Mag., 1972-75; Washington corr. Cox Newspapers, 1976-82, chief fgn. correspondent, 1983—; legis. asst. to Senator Edmund S. Muskie, 1971-72. Author: What Makes Spiro Run?, 1972. Chmn. Alicia Patterson Found. Recipient Sigma Delta Chi award for disting. Washington reporting, 1979, 81; Nat. Press Club award for interpretive reporting, 1980; Scripps-Howard Found. citation for outstanding public service, 1979; Headliner award for investigative reporting, 1979, Raymond Clapper award for Disting. Washington Correspondence, 1982, Investigative Reporters and Editors award, 1982. Mem. Phi Beta Kappa. Clubs: Nat. Press, Federal City (Washington). Office: Piazza Grazioli 5 Rome Italy 00186

ALBRIGHT, JUSTIN W., lawyer; b. Lisbon, Iowa, Oct. 14, 1908; m. Mildred Carlton, 1935; 1 son, Carlton J. B.S.C., U. Iowa, 1931, J.D., 1933. Bar: Iowa bar 1933. Now mem. firm Simmons, Perrine, Albright & Ellwood, Cedar Rapids. Editor: Iowa Law Rev, 1932-33. Trustee YMCA of Met. Cedar Rapids. Served with AUS, World War II. Mem. Am., Iowa, Linn County bar assns., Cedar Rapids C. of C., Phi Delta Phi. Clubs: Mason (Shriner), Rotarian., Cedar Rapids Country, Pickwick (Cedar Rapids). Office: 12th Floor Mchts Nat Bank Bldg Cedar Rapids IA 52401

ALBRIGHT, LOLA (JEAN ALBRIGHT), actress; b. Akron, Ohio, July 20, 1924; d. John Paul and Marian Alma A. Student pub. schs., Akron. Actress numerous films and TV shows; films include Easter Parade, 1948, Champion, 1949, Girl From Jones Beach, 1948, Tulsa, 1949, Good Humor Man, 1950, When You're Smiling, 1950, Arctic Flight, 1952, Magnificent Matador, 1955, Tender Trap, 1956, Kid Galahad, 1962, Joy House, 1964, Lord Love a Duck, 1966, Where Were You When the Lights Went Out?, 1968, The Impossible Years, 1968, The Money Jungle, 1968, A Cold Wind in August, 1961, The Way West, 1967; appeared on: TV series Peter Gunn, 1958-61; guest star numerous TV shows. (Recipient Berlin Film Festival award for best performance (The Silver Bear) in film Lord Love A Duck 1966). Mem. Screen Actors Guild, AFTRA. Office: c/o J Carter Gibson Agy 9000 Sunset Blvd Los Angeles CA 90069

ALBRIGHT, LYLE FREDERICK, chemical engineering educator; b. Bay City, Mich., May 3, 1921; s. William Edward and Isabella (Sidebotham) A.; m. Jeanette Van Belle, Mar. 4, 1950; children: Christine, Diane. B.S. in Chem. Engring, U. Mich., 1943, M.S., 1944, Ph.D., 1950. Lab. technician Dow Chem. Co., Midland, Mich., 1939-41; chem. engr. E.I. duPont de Nemours & Co., Hanford, Wash., 1944-46; research chem. engr. Colgate-Palmolive Co., Jersey City, 1950-51; asst. prof. U. Okla., Norman, 1951-54, assoc. prof., 1954-55, Purdue U., West Layette, Ind., 1955-58, prof. chem. engring., 1958—; cons. to numerous chem. petroleum cos., 1960—. Author: Industrial and Laboratory Pyrolyses, 1976, Industrial and Laboratory Alkylations, 1977, Coke Formation on Metals, 1982, Pyrolysis: Theory and Industrial Practice, 1983; mem. editorial adv. bd.: Ency. Chem. Processing and Design; contbr. articles to various publs. Recipient Shreve prize Purdue U., 1960, 70. Fellow Am. Inst. Chem. Engrs. (dir. 1982—); mem. Am. Chem. Soc., Internat. Brotherhood Magicians, Sigma Xi, Tau Beta Pi. Methodist. Home: 4773N 250W West Lafayette IN 47906 Office: Sch of Chem Engring Purdue U West Lafayette IN 47907

ALBRIGHT, MADELEINE, political scientist; b. Prague, Czechoslovakia, May 15, 1937; d. Josef and Anna (Speeglova) Korbel; m. Joseph Medill Patterson Albright, June 11, 1959 (div. 1983); children: Anne Korbel, Alice Patterson, Katharine Medill. B.A. with honors, Wellesley Coll., 1959; M.A., Columbia U., 1968; cert., Russian Inst., 1968, Ph.D., 1976. Reporter Rolla Daily News, Mo., 1959; with pub. relations dept. Ency. Brit., 1960; Washington coordinator Maine for Muskie, 1975-76; chief legis. asst. to U.S. Senator Muskie, 1976-78; mem. staff in charge congl. liason NSC, 1978-81; fellow Woodrow Wilson Internat. Ctr. for Scholars, Washington, 1981-82; William H. Donner research prof. internat. affairs, dir. women in fgn. service Sch. Fgn. Service, Georgetown U., 1982—, sr. fellow in Soviet and Eastern European Affairs Ctr. for Strategic and Internat. Studies,, 1981. Author: Poland: The Role of the Press in Political Change, 1983; contbr. articles to profl. jours., chpts. to books. Bd. dirs. Beauvoir Sch., Washington, 1968-76, chmn., Washington, 1972-76; mem. exec. com. Chpt. of Washington Cathedral, 1972-76, mem., 1978-83; trustee Black Student Fund, 1969-78, 82—; mem. exec. com. D.C. Citizens for Better Pub. Edn., 1975-76; trustee Democratic Forum, 1976-78; bd. dirs. Washington Urban League, 1982—; trustee Williams Coll., 1978-82, Wellesley Coll., 1983—; chmn. fgn. relations task force, polit. action com. Woman's Nat. Dem. Club, 1975-76; Dem. campaign aide U.S. senator Mondale, 1972, U.S. senator Stevenson, 1975; fgn. policy coordinator Mondale for Pres. Campaign, 1984. Mem. Council Fgn. Relations, Am. Polit. Sci. Assn., Czeckoslovak Soc. Arts and Scis. Am., Atlantic Council U.S. (dir.), Am. Assn. for Advancement Slavic Studies, Nat. Dem. Inst. for Internat. Affairs (vice chmn.). Office: Sch Fgn Service Georgetown Univ Washington DC 20007

ALBRIGHT, PENROSE LUCAS, lawyer; b. Arkansas City, Kans., Feb. 10, 1925; s. Penrose Strong and Mary (Lucas) A.; m. Caridad Carballo, Dec. 15, 1951; children: Penrose C., Luis C., Eric S. B.S., U.S. Mcht. Marine Acad., 1946; B.A., Southwestern Coll., 1949; J.D., George Washington U., 1949. Bar: Kans. 1949, D.C. 1949, Ill. 1966, Va. 1968. Marine engr. Gulf Oil Corp., Port of N.Y., 1946-48; legis. asst. to U.S. senator from Kans., 1949; entered U.S. Navy as lt. (j.g.), 1949; served in U.S.S. Coral Sea, 1949-51; lt. Office Judge Adv. Gen., 1951-56; assoc. firm Ansell and Ansell, Washington, 1957; partner firm Mason, Mason & Albright, Washington, 1958-64, sr. partner, 1964—; counsel Navy-Maritime Adminstrn. Planning and Policy Group. Contbr. articles to profl. jours. Rear adm. JAGC, USNR; former dir. Naval Res. Law Programs. Decorated Legion of Merit; recipient Meritorious Service and Outstanding Profl. Achievement awards U.S. Mcht. Marine Acad. Mem. Am. Bar Assn. (mem. standing com. on lawyers in armed forces), Fed. Bar Assn., Va. Bar Assn., Arlington Bar Assn., Bar Assn. D.C., Judge Adv. Assn. (dir.), Am. Patent Law Assn., Res. Officers Assn., Naval Res. Assn. (mem. exec. com.), U.S. Mcht. Marine Acad. Alumni Assn., Naval War Coll. Found., Soc. Naval Engrs. Republican. Episcopalian. Club: Army-Navy Country. Patentee in transp. field. Home: 1523 Woodacre Dr McLean VA 22101 Office: 2306 S Eads St Arlington VA 22202: *You ask, "What is success?" There are many measures. No one is 100% success or failure. A measure I use for myself is completing important tasks so I can answer "Yes" to "Did you do your best?" Five gauges I try to apply for in myself and others, each being a mosaic of many characteristics, are: Integrity, Performance, Reliability, Attitude and Appearance—always, always understanding nobody is perfect, everyone stumbles and falls on occasion.*

ALBRIGHT, RAYMOND JACOB, govt. ofcl.; b. Reading, Pa., Apr. 7, 1929; s. Raymond Wolf and Catherine (Sherr) A.; m. Ruthmarie Reich, Sept. 13, 1952; children—Raymond Jacob, David Reich. B.A., Yale, 1951; Fulbright scholar, U. Vienna, Austria, 1951-52; M.A., Harvard, 1954, Ph.D.; in Polit. Sci., 1961. Fgn. affairs officer (Nat. Security Council affairs and policy planning) Office Asst. Sec. Def. (Internat. Security Affairs), 1954-61; with Office Asst. Sec. State (European affairs), 1961-62; nat. security affairs adviser Treasury Dept., 1962-67; asst. to sec. treasury (Nat. Security Affairs) Office Sec. Treasury, 1967-69; counselor for econ. affairs Am. embassy, Belgrade, Yugoslavia, 1969-72; fgn. service res. officer Dept. State, 1969-73; v.p. Export-Import Bank U.S., 1973—; Lectr. Yale, 1959, George Washington U., 1960. Author: (with others) Forging a New Sword, 1958. Mem. Kensington (Md.) Civic Assn., 1958-60; Bd. dirs. Fgn. Policy Discussion Group, Washington. Club: Yale (Washington) (bd. dirs., chmn. Yale and govt. com. 1966-69). Home: 3609 Dunlop St Chevy Chase MD 20815 Office: Export-Import Bank US Washington DC 20571

ALBRIGHT, ROBERT LEWIS, university president, consultant; b. Phila., Dec. 2, 1944; s. Robert Lindsay A. and Winifred (Alexander) Bannister Albright; m. Linda Diane Pittman, Feb. 24, 1968; children: Keia Lorriane, Lance Robert. A.B., Lincoln U., 1966; M.A., Tufts U., 1972; Ph.D., Kent State U., 1978. Dir admissions Lincoln U., Lincoln University, Pa., 1969-71, v.p., 1972-76; dir. Morton Consortium, R.R. Morton Meml. Inst., Washington, 1977-79; spl. asst. to asst. sec. U.S. Dept. Edn., Washington, 1979-81; vice chancellor U. N.C., Charlotte, 1981-83; pres. Johnson C. Smith U., Charlotte, 1983—; cons. U.S. Office Edn., Washington, 1970-79, Pa. Dept. Edn., Harrisburg, 1972-79, Research Triangle Inst., Research Triangle Park, N.C., 1982—; instr. Harvard U. Summer Inst., Cambridge, Mass., 1970—. Author: Moton Guide to Historically Black Colleges, 1978; editor: Student Services: Issues, Problems and Opportunites jour., 1983. Bd. dirs. United Family Services, Charlotte, 1982, Urban League, Charlotte, 1983; bd. visitors U. N.C., Charlotte, 1983. Recipient Sec.'s Cert. of Appreciation U.S. Dept. Edn., 1981. Mem. Am. Assn. Higher Edn., Nat. Assn. Equal Opportunity, Acad. Affairs Adminstrs. (v.p. 1974-76), Nat. Assn. Student Personnel Adminstrs., Nat. Assn. Personnel Workers (v.p. 1975-76). Democrat. Baptist. Lodge: Rotary. Home: 1723 Washington Ave Charlotte NC 28216 Office: Johnson C Smith U 100 Beatties Ford Rd Charlotte NC 28216

ALBRITTON, CLAUDE CARROLL, JR., geologist, educator; b. Corsicana, Tex., Apr. 7, 1913; s. Claude C. and Iris (Stapleton) A.; m. Jane Christman, Aug. 5, 1944; children: Jane DeHart, Claude C., Elizabeth Ann. A.B., B.S., So. Meth. U., 1933; A.M., Harvard U., 1934, Ph.D. (J.B. Woodworth fellow 1935-36), 1936. From instr. to asso. prof. geology So. Methodist U., 1936-47, prof., 1947-78, dean faculty Coll. Arts and Scis., 1952-57, dean Grad. Sch., 1957-71, vice provost for library devel., 1971-73, W.B. Hamilton prof. geology, dean libraries, 1973-78; sr. scientist Inst. Study of Earth and Man, 1978—; chmn. bd. publs. Colophon, 1968-78, exec. sec., 1971-78; dir. Grad. Research Center, Inc., 1961-64, Sci. Info. Inst., 1964-72; geologist U.S. Geol. Survey, 1942-49; Rosenbach fellow in bibliography U. Pa., 1969-70; cons. NSF, 1977-80; mem. U.S. Nat. Com. History of Geology, chmn., 1980-81; corr. mem. Internat. Com. History of Geol. Scis., 1972. Author: The Abyss of Time, 1980; co-author: The Midland Discovery, 1955, Guidelines and Standards for the Education of Secondary School Teachers of Science and Mathematics, 1971, The Prehistory of Nubia, 1968; editor and co-author: The Fabric of Geology, 1964, Uniformity and Simplicity, 1965, Filosofía de la Geologia, 1970, Philosophy of Geohistory, 1975; editor: Jour. Grad. Research Center, 1960-70; adv. editor for geology: Arno Press, 1976-80; contbr. articles to: Ency. Brit. Chmn. scholarship selection com. Chance Vought Aircraft Corp., 1955-63; mem. com. geosci. amd man Internat. Union Geol. Socs., U. Cambridge, Eng., 1971; mem. exec. com. John E. Owens Found.; trustee E. de Golyer Found. Recipient DeWitt medal, 1933. Mem. Dallas Council World Affairs (past dir.), AAAS (v.p. 1968, mem. philosophy of sci. and math. edn. 1970), Geol. Soc. Am. (councilor 1957-69, chmn. joint tech. program com. 1973, chmn. div. history of geology 1976-77, chmn. div. archeol. geology 1982-83, award 1983), Paleontol. Soc. (councillor 1956-62), Am. Assn. Petroleum Geologists, Am. Geol. Inst. (chmn. liberal arts panel 1963-66), Soc. Econ. Paleontologists and Mineralogists, Tex. Acad. Sci., Philos. Soc. Tex., Phi Beta Kappa, Sigma Xi (com. on lectureships 1976-82). Methodist. Clubs: Critic, Cadence, Cosmos. Home: 3436 University Blvd Dallas TX 75205

ALBRITTON, ROBERT SANFORD, life ins. exec.; b. St. Paul, Feb. 19, 1914; s. Elmer Sanford and Mary (Bierer) A.; m. Helen Richards, Mar. 14, 1938; children—David Richards, Robert Rapp. B.S., Northwestern U., 1935; M.B.A., U. Pa., 1937; C.L.U., 1947. Agy. supr. Minn. Mut. Life Ins. Co., Mpls., 1937-40; agt. Provident Mut. Life Ins. Co., Phila., Los Angeles, 1940—; pres. Albritton, Frank & Co., 1961—; chmn. ins. ops. com. Empire Gen. Life Ins. Co., 1963-78; pres. Million Dollar Round Table of Nat. Assn. Life Underwriters, 1960, Million Dollar Round Table Found., 1962-64. Mem. Phi Delta Theta. Club: Rancho Bernardo Golf. Home: 11972 Adorno Pl San Diego CA 92128 also Honokeana Cove Lahaina Maui HI Office: 1100 Wilshire Blvd Santa Monica CA 90403

ALBRITTON, ROGERS GARLAND, philosophy educator; b. Columbus, Ohio, Aug. 15, 1923; s. Errett Cyril and Rietta (Garland) A. Student, Swarthmore Coll., 1939-41; A.B., St. John's Coll., Annapolis, 1948; M.A. in Philosophy, Princeton U., 1952, Ph.D., 1955. Faculty asso. St. John's Coll., 1948-49; part-time instr. N.J. Coll. Women, 1952-53, also Princeton U.; instr. Sage Sch. Philosophy, Cornell U., 1953-56; mem. faculty Harvard, 1956-73, prof. philosophy, after 1962, chmn. com. higher degrees history and philosophy religion, 1960-62, chmn. dept. philosophy, 1963-70; prof. philosophy UCLA, 1973—, chmn. dept., 1979-81. Served with USAAF, 1943-46. Fellow Am. Acad. Arts and Scis.; mem. Am. Philos. Assn. (v.p. Pacific div. 1983-84). Office: Dept Philosophy U Calif Los Angeles 405 Hilgard Ave Los Angeles CA 90024

ALBRITTON, WILLIAM HAROLD, III, lawyer; b. Andalusia, Ala., Dec. 19, 1936; s. Robert Bynum and Carrie (Veal) A.; m. Jane Rollins Howard, June 2, 1958; children: William Harold IV, Benjamin Howard, Thomas Bynum. A.B., U. Ala., 1959, LL.B., 1960. Bar: Ala. 1960. Assoc. firm Albrittons & Rankin, Andalusia, 1962-66, partner, 1966-76; partner firm Albrittons & Givhan, Andalusia, 1976—; dir. TV Cable Co., Andalusia, Comml. Bank Andalusia. Pres. bd. Trustees Community Hosp. Andalusia; bd. dirs. Ala. Law Sch. Found., Ala. Law Inst.; mem. exec. com. Ala. Republican Party, 1967-78; chmn. Covington County Rep. Party, 1967—; trustee, elder 1st Presbyn. Ch.,

Andalusia. Served to capt. AUS, 1960-62. Mem. ABA, Covington County Bar Assn. (pres. 1973), Ala. State Bar (commr. 1981—, disciplinary commn. 1981—), Andalusia C. of C. (pres. 1967-68), Nat. Assn. R.R. Trial Counsel, Am. Judicature Soc., Ala. Def. Lawyers Assn. (pres. 1976-77), Internat. Assn. Ins. Counsel, Trial Attys. Am., Assn. Ins. Attys., Phi Beta Kappa, Phi Delta Phi, Omicron Delta Kappa, Alpha Tau Omega. Clubs: Rotary (pres. 1979), Andalusia Country (pres. 1977). Home: 730 Albritton Rd Andalusia AL 36420 Office: 109 Opp Ave Andalusia AL 36420

ALBUQUERQUE, LITA, artist; b. Santa Monica, Calif., Jan. 3, 1946; d. Mauriceo Yaeche and Ferida (Hayat) A.; m. Stephen Hecht Kahn, Jan., 1972 (div.); children: Isabelle, Jasmine. B.A. cum laude, UCLA, 1968; student, Otis Art Inst., 1971-72. Tchr. Claremont Grad. Coll., U. Calif., Santa Barbara, Otis/Parsons Sch., Los Angeles. Work exhibited nationally various group and solo shows including, Janus Gallery, Venice, Calif., San Francisco Mus. Modern Art, 1982, Hirshhorn Mus., Washington, 1981, Washington Monument, 1980, works included in numerous public and pvt. collections; Works include Première Lumière, 1974, Moments, 1976, Four Part Pieces, 1977, Materia Prima, 1979, Axis Mundi, Double Reflective, Abhasa; also outdoor installations. Nat. Endowment Arts fellow, 1975; NEA Art in Pub. Places grantee, 1983. Mem. Los Angeles Inst. Contemporary Arts. Studio: 305 Boyd St Los Angeles CA 90013

ALCALAY, ALBERT S., artist, educator; b. Paris, Aug. 11, 1917; U.S., 1951, naturalized, 1956; s. Samuel and Lepa (Afar) A.; m. Vera Eshenazi, Nov. 11, 1950; children: Leor, Ammiel. Student in Paris, Rome. Lectr. design Carpenter Center, Harvard U., 1960—. One man shows, De Cordova and Dana Mus., Lincoln, Mass., 1968, Visconti Gallery, Boston, 1983, others, retrospective, Carpenter Ctr., Harvard U., 1982, group shows, Inst. Contemporary Art, Boston, 1960, Venice (Italy) Biennale, Mus. Modern Art., 1955, Whitney Mus. Am. Art, 1956, 58, 60, U. Ill., Urbana, Pa. Acad. Fine Arts, 1960, represented permanent collections, Mus. Modern Art, N.Y.C., Boston Mus. Fine Arts, Fogg Art Mus., DeCordova and Dana Mus., Phillips Acad., Mus. Am. Art, Brandeis U. Rose Art Mus., U. Mass. Mus., Wellesley Coll. Mus., Colby Coll. Mus., Smith Coll., Rome Mus. Modern Art, U. Rome. Guggenheim fellow, 1959-60; recipient prize Boston Arts Festival, 1960. Home: 66 Powell St Brookline MA 02146 Office: Carpenter Center for Visual Arts Harvard U Cambridge MA 01238

ALCARAZ FIGUEROA, ESTANISLAO, clergyman; b. Patzcuaro, Michoacan, Mex., Oct. 23, 1918; s. Estanislao Alcaraz and Rafaela (Figueroa). Humanidades, Morelia Sem., 1937; Filosofía y Teología, Montezuma Sem., N.Mex., 1943. Ordained priest Roman Catholic Ch., 1942, consecrated bishop, 1959; bishop of Matamoros, Tamaulipas, 1959-68, San Luis Potosí, 1968-72, Morelia, Michoacan, archbishop of, Morelia, 1972—. Office: Apartado 17 Morelia Michoacan Mexico

ALCHIAN, ARMEN ALBERT, economics educator; b. Fresno, Calif., Apr. 12, 1914; s. Alex H. and Lily (Normart) A.; m. Pauline Crouse, Sept. 30, 1939; children: Arline (Mrs. Carlton Hoel), Allen. Student, Fresno State Coll., 1932-34; A.B., Stanford, 1936, Ph.D. in Econs., 1944. Asst. prof. U. Oreg., 1942; faculty UCLA, prof. econs., 1958—; Cons. Rand Corp., 1947-62; Pres. Found. for Research in Edn. and Econs.; trustee Internat. Inst. Econ. Affairs, Pacific Acad. Advanced Studies. Author: University Economics, 4th edit., 1971, Exchange and Production, 1969, 3d edit., 1977; Contbr. articles to profl. jours. Served to capt. USAAF, 1942-46. Mem. Mt. Pelerin Soc. Home: 3113 Colby St Los Angeles CA 90066

ALCINDOR, LEW *See* **ABDUL-JABBAR, KAREEM**

ALCOCK, NORMAN ZINKAN, research physicist; b. Edmonton, Alta., Can., May 29, 1918; s. Joseph Benjamin and Edith Alma (Zinkan) A.; m. Patricia Christian Sinclair Hunter, June 29, 1948; children: Stephen, Christopher, David, Nancy. B.Sc. in Elec. Engring, Queens U., 1940, M.S., Calif. Inst. Tech., 1941; Ph.D. in Physics, McGill U., 1946. Research engr. Nat. Research Council Can., 1941-43, Telecommunications Research Estab., Great Malvern, Eng., 1943-45; research physicist McGill Univ., 1943-45; asst. research physicist Atomic Energy Can., Ltd., 1946-50; v.p., dir. Isotope Products, Ltd., Oakville, Ont., 1950-57; gen. mgr. Isotopes Products div. Canadian Curtis-Wright, Ltd., 1957-58, dir. engring., 1958-59; cons. engr., 1960, self employed peace research, 1960-61; pres., dir. Canadian Peace Research Inst., 1962—. Served with RCAF, 1941-45. Mem. Sigma Xi. Home: PO Box 37 Port Credit ON L5G 4L5 Canada Office: Box 2308 Gryffin Lodge Huntsville ON P0A 1K0 Canada

ALCORN, DAVID STEWART, chemical company executive; b. Phila., June 1, 1923; s. David and Emily (Stewart) A.; m. Winifred Edsal, Mar. 20, 1948; children: Winifred L., David E., Charles S., Richard E. B.S. in Chem. Engring., U. Pa., 1943. Dir. mktg. Union Carbide Corp., N.Y.C., 1943-69; exec. v.p. J.T. Baker Chem. Co., Easton, Pa., 1969-73; pres. Dyes & Chem. Div., Crompton & Knowles, Reading, Pa., 1973—. Served to lt. (j.g.) USN, 1944-46. Mem. Comml. Devel. Orgn. (dir. 1978-81), Am. Chem. Soc. (chem. mktg. and econs. sect.). Home: RD 2 PO Box 1469 Mohnton PA 19540 Office: Crompton and Knowles Corp Love Rd Green Hills PA 19603

ALCORN, GORDON DEE, emeritus educator; b. Olympia, Wash., Apr. 6, 1907; s. John H. and Rachel (Austin) A.; m. Rowena Lung, Aug. 8, 1935; 1 dau., Patricia (Mrs. Jack Peterson). B.S., Coll. of Puget Sound, 1930; M.S., U. Wash., 1933, Ph.D., 1935. Instr. biology Coll. Puget Sound, 1930-35; asst. prof. botany U. Idaho, 1935-37; v.p., head biology Grays Harbor Coll., 1937-43, pres., 1945-46; asst. prof. U. Puget Sound, Tacoma, summers 1930-45, asso. prof. biology, 1946, prof., 1947-72, emeritus, 1972—, chmn. dept. biology, 1951-72, dir. grad. studies, 1970-74; Regester lectr., 1968; with War Manpower Commn. Div. Edn., 1943-45. Author: Northwest Birds-Distribution and Eggs, 1978, Silent Wings, 1982; Editor-in-chief: Murrelet, 1951-76; Contbr. articles to profl. jours. Mem. White House Conf. on Natural Beauty, 1965, Gov.'s Task Force, Tacoma Civic Arts, 1968-71; chmn. Wash. State Natural Preserve Adv. Com., 1971-83; mem. Pierce County Shoreline Adv. Com., 1971-77; dir. Puget Sound Mus. Natural History, 1951-72, 78—. Recipient Distinguished Service awards Nat. Park Service, 1975, Tobin Appreciation award, 1979. Mem. Izaak Walton League Am. (Conservationist of Year, Puget Sound chpt. 1969, dir. 1965-68), Nature Conservancy (gov. 1963-66, pres. chpt. 1975—, Oak Leaf award 1977, Gov. Emeritus award 1978), Cooper Ornithol. Soc., Am. Ornithol. Union, Pacific N.W. Bird and Mammal Soc. (pres. 1965-67), Am. Assn. U. Profs., Sigma Xi, Pi Gamma Mu, Phi Sigma. Republican. Baptist. Home: 3806 N 24th St Tacoma WA 98406 *Three major principles: To acquaint students with the uniqueness of life activities and to bring students to a reverence for life; to point up to students the constancy of aesthetics in and out of the sciences; to bring to students the knowledge of the intimate relationships among the sciences and social studies and humanities.*

ALCORN, HOWARD WELLS, state ofcl.; b. Suffield, Conn., May 14, 1901; s. Hugh M. and Cora Terry (Wells) A.; m. Bertha Eloise Pinney, Oct. 28, 1927; children—Carolyn Hatheway, Elizabeth Wells, Dorcas Terry. A.B., Dartmouth, 1923; student, Harvard Law Sch., Yale Law Sch. Bar: Conn. bar 1926. Judge Suffield Town Ct., 1929-43; exec. sec. to Gov. Conn., 1943; judge Superior Ct. Conn., 1943-59, chief judge, 1959-61; justice Supreme Ct. Conn., 1961-70, chief justice, 1970-71, state referee, 1971—; Dir. First Nat. Bank of Suffield, 1928-51, v.p., 1934-51; Chmn. zoning commn. Suffield, 1928-43; Mem. Conn. Ho. Reps., 1927-29, 31, speaker, 1931, floor leader Conn. Senate, 1933; chmn. Republican Town Com., Suffield, 1928-33; alternate del.-at-large Rep. Nat. Conv., 1932. Mem. ABA, Conn. Bar Assn., Hartford County Bar Assn. (treas. 1934-36), S.A.R., Sons Union Vets., Antiquarian and Landmarks Soc. (pres. 1936-40), Suffield Grange. Conglist. Clubs: Mason., Hartford. Home: 338 S Main St Suffield CT 06078 Office: State Library and Supreme Court Bldg Hartford CT 06103

ALCORN, HUGH MEADE, JR., lawyer, former chairman Republican National Committee; b. Suffield, Conn., Oct. 20, 1907; s. Hugh M. and Cora Terry (Wells) A.; m. Janet Hoffer, Oct. 21, 1933 (dec.); children: Thomas Glenn (dec.), Janet Eileen; m. Marcia Powell, Apr. 14, 1955. A.B., Dartmouth, 1930; LL.B., Yale, 1933; LL.D., U. Hartford, 1974. Bar: Conn. bar 1933. Ptnr. Alcorn, Bakewell & Smith (now Tyler, Cooper & Alcorn), Hartford, 1933—; asst. state's atty., Hartford County, 1935-42, state's atty., 1942-48; dir. United Bank & Trust Co., Hartford.; Mem. Conn. Ho. of Reps., 1937, 39, Rep. floor leader, 1939, speaker, 1941; chmn. Suffield Rep. Town Com., 1938-53; mem. Conn. Rep. State Central Com., 1948-57; del. Rep. Nat. Conv., 1940, 48, 52, 56, 60, alternate, 1944, vice chmn. arrangements com., 1956; mem. Rep. Nat. Com. from Conn., 1953-61, vice chmn., 1956-57, chmn., 1957-59, gen. counsel, 1960-61; Rep. floor leader constl. conv., 1965. Mem. Am. Coll. Trial Lawyers, ABA, Conn. Bar Assn. (pres. 1950-51), Hartford County Bar Assn., Sons Union Vets., Conn. Soc. S.A.R., Suffield Grange, Apollo Lodge, Phi Beta Kappa. Republican. Conglist. Clubs: Mason., Elk., Anglers (N.Y.C.); Rotary (Hartford) (pres. 1949-50). Home: 49 Russell Ave Suffield CT 06078 Office: 1 American Row Hartford CT 06103

ALCOTT, AMY STRUM, professional golfer; b. Kansas City, Mo., Feb. 22, 1956; d. Eugene Yale and Leatrice (Strum) A. Profl. golfer Ladies Profl. Golf Assn., 1975—; dir. Women's Golf Devel. Elizabeth Arden, Inc.; asst. golf coach UCLA Women's Golf Team; host Amy Alcott Golf Classic for Multiple Sclerosis Soc., 1980—. Named Rookie of Year Ladies Profl. Golf Assn., 1975, Player of Yr. Ladies Profl. Golf Assn., 1980; Player of Year Golf mag., 1980; named Jewish Athlete of Year, 1980; recipient Seagrams Seven Crown of Sports award, 1980, Vare Trophy, 1980. Winner, U.S. Golf Assn. Jr. Girl's Title, 1973; winner 21 profl. titles including Can. Open-Peter Jackson Classic, 1979, Women's U.S. Open, 1980, Nabisco-Dinah Shore Invitational, 1980. Address: Little Women Enterprises Inc PO Box 956 Pacific Palisades CA 90272

ALCOTT, JAMES ARTHUR, communications executive; b. Stillwater, Okla., Oct. 24, 1930; s. Arthur Bernard and Dorothy Laura (Hopkins) A.; m. Marilynn Hill, June 14, 1952; children—David, Thomas, Tobin, Anne. B.S. in Econs, Okla. State U., 1952; M.B.A., Stanford U., 1956. Credit analyst Republic Nat. Bank, Dallas, 1956-58; dir. econs. and mgmt. scis. Midwest Research Inst., Kansas City, Mo., 1958-69, trustee, 1969—; v.p. Heald, Hobson & Assos., N.Y.C., 1969-71; gen. mgr. Minn. Exptl. City Project, Mpls., 1971-74; pres., pub. Harper's mag., N.Y.C., 1975-80; v.p. Cowles Media Co., 1978—; Adv. com. AIA Research Corp., 1977-78; adv. bd. Carnegie-Mellon Inst. Research, 1975—; mem. commn. ecumenical missions and relations and program agy. United Presbyn. Ch., 1964-74; exec. com. Urban Coalition Greater Kansas City, Mo., 1968-69, Jackson County (Mo.) Govtl. Reorgn. Commn., 1968-69; chmn. research conf. Engring. Found., 1964-65; cons. Citizens Conf. on State Legislatures, 1971-72, Nat. Council Juvenile Ct. Judges, 1971-72. Served to 1st lt. USAF, 1952-54. Recipient Disting. Alumnus award Okla. State U., 1978; Named to Coll. Bus. Adminstrn. Hall of Fame, Okla. State U., 1978. Mem. Phi Delta Theta, Phi Kappa Phi, Beta Gamma Sigma. Office: 329 Portland Ave Minneapolis MN 55415

ALCOTT, JOHN, cinematographer; b. Eng. Films include The Shining, A Clockwork Orange, Barry Lyndon (Acad. award 1975), March or Die, Who Is Killing the Great Chefs of Europe?, Terror Train. Care American Soc Cinematographers 1782 N Orange Dr Hollywood CA 90028 *

ALDA, ALAN, actor; b. N.Y.C., Jan. 28, 1936; s. Robert and Joan (Browne) A.; m. Arlene Weiss. B.S., Fordham U., 1956. Tchr. Compass Sch. Improvisation. Performed with, Second City, 1963; Broadway appearances include The Apple Tree (Tony award nominee); motion pictures include Gone Are the Days, 1963, The Moonshine War, Paper Lion, 1968, Jenny, 1970, The Mephisto Waltz, 1971, The Extraordinary Seaman, 1968, The Moonshine War, 1970, To Kill a Clown, 1972, California Suite, 1978, Same Time, Next Year, 1978; appeared on TV in The Glass House, 1972, Marlo Thomas and Friends in Free to be... You and Me, 1974, 6 Rms Riv Vu, 1974, Tune in America, 1975; others; star: TV series M*A*S*H, 1972—; appeared in: TV film Kill Me If You Can, 1977; creator: TV series We'll Get By, CBS-TV, 1975; appeared in films: California Suite, 1978, Same Time Next Year, 1978; writer screenplay, actor: The Seduction of Joe Tynan, 1979; actor, writer, dir. film: The Four Seasons, 1981; Recipient (Theatre World award for Fair Game for Lovers, 2 Emmy awards for best actor in comedy series for M*A*S*H.). Office: care Martin Bregman Prodns 100 Universal City Plaza Universal City CA 91608 *

ALDEN, DOUGLAS WILLIAM, educator; b. Washington, Sept. 11, 1912; s. Alanson G. and Grace Anderson (Hunt) A.; m. Martha Seaver Bowditch, Sept. 11, 1937; children: Claire Douglas (Mrs. Dennis C. Drehmel), Barbara Bowditch (Mrs. Richard C. Giangiulio). A.B., Dartmouth Coll., 1933; A.M., Brown U., 1934, Ph.D., 1938; student, U. Paris, France, 1931-32, 35-36. Grad. asst. Brown U., 1936-38; instr. French, Tex. Tech. Coll., 1938-41, asst. prof., 1942; instr. French Amherst Coll., 1941-42; from instr. to assoc. prof. French, Princeton, 1945-61; prof. French, head dept. fgn. langs. U. Md., 1961-64; prof. French, chmn. dept. modern langs. U. Va., 1964-71, prof. French, 1971-83, prof. emeritus, 1983—, chmn. dept. Romance langs., 1966-71, acting chmn. dept. French, 1982-83; chmn. adv. council Sweet Briar Jr. Year in France, 1950-83. Author: Marcel Proust and his French Critics, 1940, 2d edit., 1973, Introduction to French Masterpieces, 1948, Cortina's French in 20 Lessons, 1950, Premier Manuel, 1954, Jacques de Lacretelle, an intellectual itinerary, 1958, (with André Maman) Grammaire et Style, 1967, Marcel Proust's Grasset Proofs: Commentary and Variants, 1978, Columbia Dictionary of Modern European Literature, French editor, 1980; Gen. editor: French XX Bibliography, 1949—; rev. editor: French Rev, 1964-71; editor vol. 7 (XX Century): (with R.A. Brooks) Critical Bibliography of French Literature, 1980; editor: (Vol. VI) The Twentieth Century, 1980; mem. editorial bd.: South Atlantic Rev, 1980—; corr.: Revue d'Histoire Littéraire de la France, 1980—. Served to capt. USAAF, 1942-45. Decorated Bronze Star; Croix de Guerre; officier de l'Ordre des Palmes Académiques, France). Mem. Modern Lang. Assn., Am. Assn. Tchrs. French (exec. council 1968-71, nat. pres. 1972-76), South Atlantic Modern Lang. Assn. (pres. Assn. Depts. Fgn. Langs. 1969-70), Assn. Internat. des Etudes Françaises, Société des Professeurs Français en Amérique, Alden Kindred Soc., Alpha Sigma Phi. Clubs: Appalachian Mountain; Country of Torrington (Conn.). Home: 1880 Westview Rd Charlottesville VA 22903 also Torrington Rd Goshen CT 06756

ALDEN, RAYMOND MACDONALD, former utility company executive, consultant; b. Palo Alto, Calif., Nov. 17, 1921; s. Raymond Macdonald and Barbara (Hitt) A.; m. Sara Wills, Aug. 30, 1946; children—David Wills, Merritt Ann (Mrs. D. Howard Booster), John Lee. A.B. in Engring, Stanford, 1944. Registered profl. engr., Hawaii, Kans. Engr. Western Union Telegraph Co., 1946-50; engr. Hawaiian Telephone Co., Honolulu, 1951-62, v.p., 1962-64; exec. v.p. United Telecommunications, Inc., Kansas City, Mo., 1964-73, pres., 1973-81, vice chmn., 1981-83, also dir., cons., 1983—; dir. C.J. Patterson Co., United Mo. Bank Kansas City. Served with USNR, 1944-46. Mem. IEEE (sr.), Nat. Soc. Profl. Engrs. Home: 4550 Warwick Blvd Kansas City MO 64111 Office: 4200 Somerset Dr Suite 210 Prairie Village KS 66208

ALDEN, VERNON ROGER, financial exec.; b. Chgo., Apr. 7, 1923; s. Arvid W. and Hildur Pauline (Johnson) A.; m. Marion Frances Parson, Aug. 18, 1951; children—Robert Parson, Anne Elizabeth, James Malcolm, David Douglas. A.B. magna cum laude, Brown U., 1945, LL.D., 1964; M.B.A., Harvard, 1950; LL.D., Emerson Coll., 1957, Ohio Wesleyan U., 1964, R.I. Coll., 1965, William Jewell Coll., 1965, Loyola U., 1966, Wilberforce U., Ottawa U., 1970, Babson Coll., 1972; L.H.D., North Park Coll., 1965; Lit.D., Ohio U., 1969; D.P.S., Bowling Green U., 1969; Litt.D., Bethany Coll., 1970. Admission officer Brown U., 1946-48; asst. dir. admissions Northwestern U., 1950-51; dir. financial aid Harvard Grad Sch. Bus. Adminstrn., asso. dean faculty, 1951-61; pres. Ohio U., Athens, 1962-69; chmn. bd., chmn. exec. com. Boston Co. and subsidiary Boston Safe Deposit & Trust Co., 1969-78; also dir.; chmn. Mass. Bus. Devel. Council, 1978—; Ednl. dir. U. Hawaii Advanced Mgmt. Program, summer 1960, Keio U. Advanced Mgmt. Program, Tokyo, summers 1960-61; mem. exec. com., dir. Mead Corp., Digital Equipment Corp., McGraw Hill Corp., Colgate-Palmolive Corp.; dir. ARA Services, Inc., Augat, Inc. Chmn. Pres.' Task Force to plan Job Corps program; vis. com. Harvard Grad. Sch. Edn.; chmn. Mass. Council on Arts and Humanities; trustee, mem. exec. com. Boston Symphony Orch.; chmn. arts facilities com. M.I.T.; adv. com. U.S. Japan Friendship Commn.; bd. visitors Fletcher Sch. Law and Diplomacy; trustee mem. exec. com. Brown U.; trustee Mus. Sci., Boston; chmn. finance com., trustee French Library, Boston; overseer Mus. Fine Arts, Boston. Served to lt. USNR, 1943-46. Recipient Gov.'s award State Ohio, 1969; Founder's citation Ohio U., 1969; Bus. Statesman award Harvard Grad. Sch. Bus., 1975. Mem. Assn. Japan-Am. Socs (vice chmn.), Japan Soc. of Boston (pres.), Phi Beta Kappa, Phi Kappa Phi, Phi Delta Theta, Beta Gamma Sigma, Omicron Delta Kappa. Episcopalian. Clubs: Somerset (Boston); Edgartown Yacht (Martha's Vineyard); Country (Brookline). Home: 37 Warren St Brookline MA 02146

ALDER, BERNI JULIAN, physicist; b. Duisburg, Ger., Sept. 9, 1925; came to U.S., 1941, naturalized, 1944; s. Ludwig and Ottilie (Gottschalk) A.; m. Esther Berger, Dec. 28, 1956; children—Kenneth, Daniel, Janet. B.S., U. Calif., Berkeley, 1947, M.S., 1948; Ph.D., Calif. Inst. Tech., 1951. Instr. chemistry U. Calif., Berkeley, 1951-54; theoretical physicist Lawrence Livermore Lab., Livermore, Calif., 1955—; van der Waals prof. U. Amsterdam, Netherlands, 1971; prof. associé U. Paris, 1972. Author: Methods of Computational Physics, 1963; editor: Jour. Computational Physics, 1966—. Served with USN, 1944-46. Guggenheim fellow, 1954-55; NSF sr. postdoctoral fellow, 1963-64. Fellow Am. Phys. Soc.; mem. Nat. Acad. Scis., Am. Chem. Soc. Republican. Jewish. Office: PO Box 808 Lawrence Livermore Lab Livermore CA 94550

ALDER, EDWIN FRANCIS, chem. co. exec.; b. Hugo, Okla., Sept. 1, 1927; s. Joseph B. and Mary Frances (Alder) A.; m. Ann Ruth Wilson, Feb. 10, 1951; children—Gwendolyn Ann, Jan Allison, Martha Ellen, Steven Edwin. B.S., U. Okla., 1951, Ph.D., 1956; M.S. (Wychwood fellow), U. Chgo., 1952; Fulbright fellow, U. Bergen, Norway, 1953-54. Instr. Ark. State Coll., Jonesboro, 1953, U. Okla., 1955, U. Ark., Fayetteville, 1955-57; with Eli Lilly & Co., Indpls., 1957—, v.p. agrl. research and devel., 1969—, v.p. research labs., 1973—, dir., 1978—; mem. com. persistent pesticides Nat. Acad. Sci./NRC, 1968; mem. commn. on pesticides HEW, 1969. Contbr. articles to profl. jours. Served with USN, 1945-48. Mem. AAAS, Weed Sci. Soc. Am., Phi Beta Kappa, Sigma Xi. Research on dinitroaniline herbicides. Home: 10140 E Troy Ave Indianapolis IN 46239 Office: PO Box 708 Greenfield IN 46140

ALDER, JONATHAN R., mktg. exec.; b. Akron, Ohio, Mar. 12, 1922; m. Reta Biehle; 6 children. Grad., Denison U., 1947. With E. Clare Weber Agy., New Eng. Life, Cleve., 1947—, supr., 1953-58, asst. gen. agt., 1958-63, asso. gen. agt., 1963-69, partner, gen. agt., 1969-72, gen. agt., 1972-76, exec. v.p. home office, Boston, 1976—, dir., 1976—. Served to 1st lt. U.S. Army; ETO. Mem. (Assn. C.L.U.s, pres. Cleve. chpt.), Cleve. Life Underwriters (dir.), Cleve. Estate Planning Council (pres.). Office: New Eng Mut Life Ins Co 501 Boylston St Boston MA 02117

ALDERFER, CLAYTON PAUL, organizational psychologist, educator, consultant, administractor; b. Sellersville, Pa., Sept. 1, 1940; s. Joseph Paul and Ruth Althea (Buck) A.; m. Charleen Judith Frankenfield, July 14, 1962; children: Kate, Benjamin. B.S. with high honors, Yale U., 1962, Ph.D., 1966. Cert. Am. Bd. Profl. Psychology; cert. Internat. Cons. Asst. prof. Cornell U., Ithaca, N.Y., 1966-68, Yale U., New Haven, 1968-70, assoc. prof., 1970-78; prof. Sch. Orgn. Mgmt., Yale U., New Haven, 1978—, assoc. dean, 1982—. Author: Existence, Relatedness and Growth, 1972, Learning from Changing, 1975; contbr. articles to profl. jours.; bd. editors: Jour. Applied Behavioral Sci., 1978—; editor: Advances in Experiential Social Processes, vol. 1, 1978, Advances in Experiential Social Processes, vol. 2, 1980. Bd. dirs. NTL Inst., Arlington, Va., 1975-78. Grantee Office Naval Research, 1970-74, 79-80, 82—; recipient Cattell award, 1972, McGregor award, 1979. Fellow Am. Psychol. Assn., Soc. Applied Anthropology; mem. Sigma Xi, Tau Beta Pi. Democrat. Lutheran. Home: 14 Ann Dr Bethany CT 06525 Office: Yale Sch Orgn and Mgmt 52 Hillhouse Ave New Haven CT 06520

ALDERMAN, BISSELL, architect; b. Holyoke, Mass., Sept. 19, 1912; s. George P. B. and Hortense B. (Goslee) A.; m. Mary Evelyn Compton, Nov. 16, 1935; children: Jean Compton Alderman Hazen, Mary Evelyn Alderman Lord, Sarah Holly Alderman McLellan. B.Arch., MIT, 1935, M.Arch., 1937, traveling fellow, 1937-38. Registered architect, N.H.; cert. Nat. Council Archtl. Registration Bds. Mem. faculty MIT, 1938, 41-43, U. Wash., 1939-41; ptnr. Alderman & Mac Neish, 1951-78; Trustee Williston Acad., 1952-68, Vanguard Savs. Bank, Holyoke, 1953-78. Important works include, Weymouth (Mass.) Library, Medford (Mass.) Library, Community Savs. Bank, Holyoke, Vanguard Savings Bank, Holyoke, Northampton (Mass.) Inst. for Savs., Mohawk Trail Regional High Sch., Buckland, Mass., Amherst Jr, Amherst (Mass.), Nonotuck (Mass.) Savs. Bank, Lunt Silversmiths Office Bldg., Greenfield, Mass., 1969, Minnechaug High Sch., Wilbraham, Mass., Algonquin High Sch., Northboro, Mass., Assabet Regional Vocat. Tech. High Sch., Marlboro, Mass., Thorton W. Burgess Intermediate Sch., Hampden, Mass., Westfield (Mass.) High Sch., Dudley/Charlton (Mass.), Regional High Sch. North Shore Regional Vocat. Tech. High Sch., St. Stanislaus Sch., Chicopee, Mass. Served with USAAF, 1943-45. Recipient 5th prize William and Mary Festival Theater Competition, 1938; Hon. mention Smithsonian Art Gallery Competition, 1939; RCD Medal of Freedom.

Fellow AIA (past pres. Western Mass. chpt.); mem. Mass. Assn. Architects (past pres.), Boston Soc. Architects, Tau Sigma Delta, Kappa Sigma. Congregationalist. Clubs: Rotary, Dublin, Thorndike. Jaffrey Center NH 03454

ALDERMAN, JAMES E(LLIOTT), justice Supreme Court Florida; b. Ft. Pierce, Fla., Nov. 1, 1936; s. B.E. and Frances (Allen) A.; m. Jennie I. Thompson, Mar. 3, 1961; 1 son, James Allen. B.A., U. Fla., 1958, LL.B., 1961. Bar: Fla. 1961. Practiced in Ft. Pierce, Fla., 1961-71; county judge St. Lucie County (Fla.) Ct., 1971-72; circuit judge 19th Jud. Circuit Ct. of Fla., 1973-76; appellate judge 4th Dist. Ct. Appeal Fla., 1976-78; justice Fla. Supreme Ct., Tallahassee, 1978—, now chief justice. Mem. Fla. Bar. Episcopalian. Office: Supreme Ct Bldg Tallahassee FL 32304 *

ALDERMAN, JOHN PERRY, lawyer; b. Mt. Airy, N.C., July 22, 1935; s. John and Elizabeth (Perry) A.; m. Marion Elizabeth Allen, Aug. 4, 1956; children: John Owen, Nancy Greene. B.A., Emory and Henry Coll., 1955; LL.B., U. Va., 1958. Bar: Va. 1958. Ptnr. Alderman & Alderman, Hillsbille, Va., 1958-81; U.S. atty. Western Dist. Va., Roanoke, 1981—; Commonwealth atty. (Va. prosecutor), Hillsbille, 1963-81. Author 1850 Census Annotated: Carroll County, Va., 1979. Rector Radford U., Va., 1980-82, bd. visitors, Va., 1974-82. Mem. Nat. Dist. Atty. Assn., Va. Commonwealth Atty. Assn., Order of Coif. Republican. Presbyterian. Lodge: Rotary (past pres.). Home: 3324 Penn Forest Blvd Roanoke VA 24018 Office: US Atty's Office Box 1709 Roanoke VA 24008

ALDERMAN, LOUIS CLEVELAND, JR., college president; b. Douglas, Ga., Aug. 12, 1924; s. Louis Cleveland and Minnis Amelia (Wooten) A.; m. Anne Augusta Whipple, Dec. 31, 1952; children: Amelia Anne, Louis Cleveland III, Fielding Dillard, Jonathan Augustus. A.A., South Ga. Coll., 1942; A.B., Emory U., 1946; M.S., U. Ga., 1949; postgrad., Columbia U., summers 1951-54; Ed.D. (Ford Found. fellow), Auburn U., 1959; postgrad. Pres.'s Inst., Harvard U., 1965; postgrad. TransAtlantic Inst., Oxford U., 1982-84. USPHS grad. research asst. U. Ga., 1948-49; instr. biology Rome Center, 1949-50; dir., asst. prof. biology Savannah Center, 1950-51, Rome Center, 1951-56, Columbus Center, 1956-59; dir. Henderson Coll., U. Ky., 1959-64; pres. Middle Ga. Coll., Cochran, 1964—; Trustee Middle Ga. Coll. Found., pres., 1982-84; mem. adv. council Univ. System of Ga., 1964—; bd. dirs. Bleckley County Hosp. Authority, 1969-79, Cochran Community House, 1964-79; trustee Ga. Rotary Student Fund, 1975-78, 81-84; chmn. Cochran-Bleckley Bicentennial Com.; pres. Bleckley-Cochran Bicentennial Celebration, Inc.; chmn. 8th dist. Ga. State C. of C. Travel Council; dist. chmn. Rotary Found.; lt. col., aide-de-camp Gov.'s Staff State of Ga. Author: Focus on Change, 1964, Fifty Years as Middle Georgia College, 1967, Education in the American Colonies, 1971, History of Old Richland Church, 1972, Signers of the Declaration of Independence, 1974, The Sureties for Magna Charta, 1980; Contbr. articles to profl. jours. Served to sgt. U.S. Army, 1942-46; PTO. Recipient Good Citizenship award Civitan Club, 1955, Club Service award Rotary Internat., 1968-69, Outstanding Rotarian award, 1976; Paul Harris fellow Rotary Club. Mem. Am. Assn. Jr. and Community Coll. Pres.'s Acad., Assn. Higher Edn., Ga. Hist. Soc., Nat. Hist. Soc., Ga. Geneal. Soc., SAR, Order Ky. Cols., NEA, Ga. Assn. Colls. (bd. dirs., v.p. 1981-82, pres. 1982-83), Ga. Assn. Educators, Ga. Assn. Jr. Colls. (exec. com. 1967-70, pres. 1968-69), Pulaski Hist. Commn. (v.p., bd. dirs. 1976-80), Ga. Heart Assn. (12th dist. chmn. and cabinet mem. 1976-81), Cochran-Bleckley C. of C. (1st v.p., dir., v.p.), SAR (Kendall award 1980), Ga. Soc. SAR (bd. mgrs. 1979-82, v.p. 1981-82, pres. 1983-84), Middle Ga. chpt. SAR (organizing pres. 1979-80, pres. 1980-83), Magna Charta Barons, Descs. Order Knights of Garter, Descs. of Founders of Hartford Order Founders and Patriots Am., Soc. Friends St. George's Chapel, Order of Washington, Plantagenet Soc., Order of Crown, Ams. of Royal Descent, Ancient and Honorable Arty. Co. of Mass., Phi Delta Kappa, Phi Theta Kappa, Gamma Beta Phi, Sigma Nu, Phi Beta Lambda, others. Democrat. Baptist (deacon, chmn. bd. deacons 1982-83). Clubs: Rotary (bd. dirs. 1965-69, pres. 1967-68), Rotary (gov. dist. 692 1976-77), Uchee Trail Country, Statesman. Home: 502 Old Chester Rd Cochran GA 31014 Office: 101 Sanford Hall Middle GA Coll Cochran GA 31014 *I have found that the way to be happiest is to seek and find how best to serve—both God and fellow man.*

ALDERSON, WILLIAM THOMAS, museum director; b. Schenectady, May 8, 1926; s. William Thomas and Helen Martha (Knowlton) A.; m. Sylvia Caldwell Farrell, Sept. 14, 1953; children: William Thomas III, Virginia Ann, Rebecca Louise. A.B., Colgate U., 1947; student, Howard Coll., 1944-45, Tulane U., 1945-46; M.A., Vanderbilt U., 1949, Ph.D., 1952. Sr. archivist Tenn. State Library and Archives, 1952-57, asst. state librarian and archivist, 1959-61; exec. sec. Tenn. Hist. Commn., 1957-61, state librarian and archivist, chmn. commn., 1961-64; dir. Am. Assn. State and Local History; editor History News, Nashville, 1964-78; prof., dir. mus. studies William Watson Harrington Disting.; lectr. in history U. Del., Newark, 1978-82; dir. Margaret Woodbury Strong Mus., Rochester, N.Y., 1982—; asst. editor Tennessee Hist. Quar., 1953, assoc. editor, 1954-55, editor, 1956-65; editor 1956-65.; Adv. com. Library of Congress Nat. Union Catalog Manuscript Collections, 1965-70; adv. com. hist. socs. and humanistic mus. NEH, 1966; mus. adv. panel Nat. Endowment Arts, 1972-75, co-chmn., 1974-75; adv. com. Historic Am. Bldgs. Survey, 1967-71; mem. Nat. Museum Act adv. council Smithsonian Instn., 1971-76; instr. extension div. U. Tenn., 1954-61; vis. asst. prof. history Vanderbilt U., 1955-56, adj. prof., 1973-78; dir. Am. Heritage Pub. Co., 1965-78; mem. Hist. Commn. Met. Nashville and Davidson County, 1966-70; trustee Sleepy Hollow Restorations, 1981—. Author: Tennessee Historical Markers, 1958, (with R.H. White) A Guide to the Study and Reading of Tennessee History, 1959, (with R.M. McBride) Tennessee Historical Markers, 1962, (with H.G. Thomas) Historic Sites in Tennessee, 1963, Tennessee, A Student's Guide to Localized History, 1966, (with Shirley P. Low) Interpretation of Historic Sites, 1976; co-editor: Landmarks of Tennessee History, 1965; editor: American Issues, 1976; contbr. to encys., profl. jours. Served with USNR, 1943-46. Fellow Soc. Am. Achivists (council 1963-67); mem. Am. Assn. State and Local History (council 1959-64), Am. Records Mgmt. Assn. (pres. S.E. chpt. 1963-64), Tenn. Assn. Mus. (pres. 1965-67), Assn. Preservation Tenn. Antiquities (trustee 1964-71), Colgate U. Alumni Assn. (pres. Tenn. chpt. 1962-66), Nashville Rose Soc. (pres. 1963), So. Hist. Assn., Orgn. Am. Historians, Tenn. Hist. Soc. (v.p. 1969-71), Am. Assn. Mus. (chmn. accreditation commn. 1970-73, mem. exec. com. 1978-80), Northeast Museums Conf. (v.p. 1978-80, pres. 1980-82). Republican. Methodist. Home: 6 Spruce Ct Pittsford NY 14534 Office: Margaret Woodbury Strong Mus One Manhattan Sq Rochester NY 14607

ALDISERT, RUGGERO JOHN, U.S. circuit judge; b. Carnegie, Pa., Nov. 10, 1919; s. John S. and Elizabeth (Magnacca) A.; m. Agatha Maria DeLacio, Oct. 4, 1952; children—Lisa Maria, Robert, Gregory. B.A., U. Pitts., 1941, J.D., 1947. Bar: Pa. bar 1947. Gen. practice law, Pitts., 1947-61; judge Ct. Common Pleas., Allegheny County, 1961-68, 3d U.S. Circuit Ct. Appeals, 1968—; adj. prof. law U. Pitts. Sch. Law, 1964—; faculty Appellate Judges Seminar, N.Y.U., 1971—, asso. dir., 1979—; lectr. internat. seminar legal medicine U. Rome, 1965, Law Soc. London, 1967, Internat. seminar comparative law, Rome, 1971; chmn. Fed. Appellate Judges Seminar; bd. dirs. Fed. Jud. Center, Washington, 1974-79; mem. Pa. Civil Procedural Rules Com., 1965—, Jud. Conf. Com. on Adminstrn. Criminal Law, 1971-77; chmn. adv. com. on bankruptcy rules Jud. Conf. U.S., 1979—; lectr. univs. in U.S. and abroad. Author: Il Ritorno al Paese, 1966-67, The Judicial Process, Readings, Materials and Cases, 1976. Allegheny dist. chmn. Multiple Sclerosis Soc., 1961-68; pres. Italian Sons and Daus. Am. Cultural Heritage Found., 1965-68; Trustee U. Pitts., 1968—; chmn. bd. visitors Pitts. Sch. Law, 1978—. Served to maj. USMCR, 1942-46. Recipient Outstanding Merit award Allegheny County Acad. Trial Lawyers, 1964. Fellow Internat. Acad. Law and Sci., Am. Coll. Legal Medicine; mem. Inst. Jud. Adminstrn., Am. Law Inst., Pitts. Legal Med. Inst., Italian Sons and Daus. of Am. (pres. 1954-68), Italian Sons and Daus. Am. Fraternal Assn. (nat. pres. 1960-68), Phi Beta Kappa, Phi Alpha Delta, Omicron Delta Kappa. Democrat. Roman Catholic. Home: 1000 Grandview Ave Pittsburgh PA 15211 Office: 831 Federal Bldg Liberty Ave Pittsburgh PA 15222

ALDREDGE, THEONI VACHLIOTIS, costume designer; b. Athens, Greece, Aug. 22, 1932; d. Gen. Athanasios and Meropi (Gregoriades) Vachliotis; m. Thomas E. Aldredge, Dec. 10, 1953. Student, Am. Sch., Athens, Athens, 1949-53, Goodman Theatre, Chgo. Mem. design staff Goodman Theatre, 1951-53; head designer N.Y. Shakespeare Festival, 1962—. Designer numerous Broadway and off Broadway shows, ballet, opera, television spls.; films include: You're a Big Boy Now, The Great Gatsby (Brit. Motion Picture Acad. award 1976), Network, The Rose, Monsignore; films include Ghostbusters; Broadway shows include: A Chorus Line (Theatre World award 1976), Annie (Antoinette Perry award 1977), Barnum (Antoinette Perry award 1979), Dream Girls, Woman of the Year, La Cage Aux Folles (Tony award 1984), 42nd Street; Broadway shows include The Rink; creator: Jane Fonda Workouts Fashion Line. Recipient Obie award for Distinguished Service to Off Broadway Theatre Village Voice, Maharam award for Peer Gynt; numerous Drama Desk and Critics awards. Mem. United Scenic Artists, Costume Designers Guild, Acad. Motion Picture Arts Scis. (Oscar award Great Gatsby 1975). Office: 890 Broadway New York NY 10003 *

ALDRICH, ALEXANDER, lawyer; b. N.Y.C., Mar. 14, 1928; s. Winthrop Williams and Harriet (Alexander) A.; m. Elizabeth Bayard Hollins, Aug. 11, 1951 (div.); children—Elizabeth, Winthrop, Amanda, Alexander; m. Phyllis W. Watts, July 28, 1971; children—William, Sarah. A.B., Harvard, 1950, LL.B., 1953; M. Pub. Adminstrn., N.Y. U., 1960. Bar: N.Y. bar 1955. Practiced, N.Y.C., 1955-56; sec. N.Y.C. Police Dept., 1956-58, dep. commr. charge youth program, 1958-60; dir. N.Y. State Div. Youth, Albany, 1960-63; exec. asst. to gov. State of N.Y., Albany, 1963-66; exec. dir. Hudson River Valley Commn., 1966-69; pres. L.I.U., 1969-71; commr. Parks and Recreation State N.Y., Albany, 1971-75; atty. firm Helm, Shapiro, Ayers, Anito & Aldrich, Saratoga Springs, N.Y., 1975—; pres. Aldrich Mgmt., Inc., 1979—. Trustee Am. U., Cairo, Egypt, Yaddo; chmn. Nat. Adv. Council on Historic Preservation, 1981—. Mem. N.Y. Zool. Soc. (trustee). Home: 104 Union Ave Saratoga Springs NY 12866 Office: 493 Broadway Saratoga Springs NY 12866

ALDRICH, ANN, federal judge; b. Providence, R.I., June 28, 1927; d. Allie C. and Ethel M. (Carrier) A.; m. Chester Aldrich, 1960 (dec.); children—Martin, William; children by previous marriage—James, Allen. B.A.; cum laude, Columbia U., 1948; LL.B. cum laude, N.Y. U., 1950, LL.M., 1964, S.J.D. Bar: D.C. bar, N.Y. bar 1952, Conn. bar 1966, Ohio bar 1973, Supreme Ct. bar 1956. Research asst. to mem. faculty N.Y. U. Sch. Law; asso. firm Samuel Nakasian, Washington, 1952-53; mem. gen. counsel's staff FCC, Washington, 1953-60; U.S. del. to Internat. Radio Conf., Geneva, 1959; practice law, Darien, Conn.; asso. prof. law Cleve. State U., 1968-71, prof., 1971-80; also chmn. curriculum com.; now U.S. Dist. Ct.; judge No. Dist. Ohio, Cleve.; bd. govs. Citizens' Communications Center, Inc., Washington; mem. litigation com.; guest lectr. Calif. Inst. Tech., Pasadena, summer 1971. Mem. Fed. Bar Assn., Nat. Assn. of Women Judges, Fed. Communications Bar Assn. Episcopalian. Office: 212 US Courthouse Cleveland OH 44114 *

ALDRICH, BAILEY, judge; b. Boston, Apr. 23, 1907; s. Talbot and Eleanor (Little) A.; m. Elizabeth Perkins, Aug. 13, 1932; children: Jonathan, David. A.B., Harvard U., 1928, LL.B., 1932. Bar: Mass. 1932. With Choate, Hall Hall & Stewart, Boston, 1932-54; judge U.S. Dist. Ct. Mass., 1954-59, U.S. Ct. Appeals, 1959-64, chief judge, 1965-72, now sr. judge. Mem. Am. Law Inst., Am. Acad. Arts and Scis., Soc. of Cin. Office: US Courthouse Rm 1634 Boston MA 02109 *

ALDRICH, CLARENCE KNIGHT, physician, educator; b. Chgo., Apr. 12, 1914; s. L. Sherman and Bessie A. (Knight) A.; m. Julie H. Murphy, Feb. 4, 1942; children—Carol K., Michael S., Thomas K., Robert F. B.A., Wesleyan U., 1935; M.D., Northwestern U., 1940. Faculty U. Minn. Med. Sch., 1947-55, asst. prof., 1947-52, asso. prof., 1952-55; prof. psychiatry U. Chgo. Sch. Medicine, 1955-70, chmn. dept. psychiatry, 1955-64; vis. prof. psychiatry U. Edinburgh, 1963-64; prof., chmn. dept. N.J. Med. Sch., Newark, 1970-73; prof. psychiatry Sch. Medicine, U. Va., Charlottesville, 1973-77, prof. psychiatry and family practice, 1977—; mem. Center Advanced Studies, 1981—; dir. Blue Ridge Mental Health Center, 1973-75. Author: Psychiatry for the Family Physician, 1955, Introduction to Dynamic Psychiatry, 1966, (with C. Nighswonger) A Casebook for Pastoral Counseling, 1968. Served from asst. surgeon to surgeon USPHS, 1940-46. Fellow Am. Coll. Psychiatrists, Am. Orthopsychiat. Assn., Am. Psychiat. Assn.; mem. Group for Advancement Psychiatry. Home: 905 Cottage Ln Charlottesville VA 22903 Office: Box 269 U Va Med Center Charlottesville VA 22908

ALDRICH, DANIEL GASKILL, JR., university chancellor; b. Northwood, N.H., July 12, 1918; s. Daniel Gaskill and Marian (Farnum) A.; m. Jean Hamilton, Aug. 23, 1941; children: Daniel Gaskill III, Elizabeth, Stuart Hamilton. B.S., U.R.I., 1939, D. Sc. (hon.), 1960; M.S., U. Ariz., 1941; Ph.D., U. Wis., 1943, D.Sc. (hon.), 1982; D.H.L., U. Redlands, Chapman Coll. Research chemist U. Calif. Citrus Expt. Sta., Riverside, 1943-55; chmn. dept. soils and plant nutrition U. Calif., Davis and Berkeley, 1955-59, univ. dean agr., Berkeley, 1959-62, now chancellor, Irvine; dir. Pacific Mut. Co. Mem. exec. bd. Orange County council Boy Scouts Am.; bd. dirs. Big Brothers Orange County, SRI Internat., Internat. Vol. Services; trustee Pacific Sch. Religion. Served as maj., inf. AUS; lt. col. Res. Mem. AAAS (past pres. Pacific div.), Western Soc. Soil Sci. (pres.), Am. Soc. Agronomy (dir.), Nat. Acad. Scis. (agrl. edn. policy com., commn. on edn. in agr. and nat. resources), Nat. Assn. State Univs. and Land-Grant Colls., Soil Conservation Soc., Soil Sci. Soc. Am., Am. Soc. Hort. Sci. Mem. United Ch. Christ.

ALDRICH, FRANK NATHAN, banker; b. Jackson, Mich., June 8, 1923; s. Frank Nathan and Marion (Butterfield) A.; m. Edna Dora DeJan, Nov. 21, 1956; children: Marion Dolores, Clinton Pershing. Student, U. Md., summer 1943; A.B. in Govt, Dartmouth Coll., 1948; postgrad., Harvard U., summer 1948. Sub-mgr. First Nat. Bank of Boston, Havana, Cuba, 1949-60, Rio de Janeiro, Brazil, 1961-62, sub-mgr., Sao Paulo, Brazil, 1963-64, mgr., 1965, exec. mgr., 1966; v.p. Brazilian brs., 1966-69, v.p. overseas ops., Boston, 1969-70; v.p. Latin Am.-Asia-Africa-Middle East div., Boston, 1970-73; sr. v.p. Latin Am. div., Boston, 1973—; pres., dir. Caribbean Am. Service Investment & Finance Co., Georgetown, Cayman Island; exec. v.p., dir. Boston Overseas Financial Corp., Boston; chmn. bd. Bank of Boston Trust Co. (Bahamas) Ltd., Nassau; dir. Corporacion Financiera Boston, La Paz, Bolivia, Banco de Boston Dominicano S.A., Santo Domingo, Dominican Republic, Corporacion Internacional de Boston S.A., San Jose, Costa Rica, Sociedad Anonima Servicios e Inversiones, Buenos Aires, Boston S.A. Administracao e Empreendimentos, Sao Paulo, Brazil, Arrendadora Industrial Venezolana C.A., Caracas, Venezuela, Boston Internat. Fin. Corp., Curacao, Netherlands Antilles, Bank of Boston Internat., N.Y.C., Los Angeles and Miami., Banco Latino americano de Exportaciones, Panama City, Panama. Bd. dirs. Latin Am. scholarship program Am. Univs., Cambridge, Mass. Served with USAAF, 1943-46. Decorated Air medal with 4 oak leaf clusters, D.F.C., U.S.; Medalha Marechal Candido Mariano da Silva Rondon, Brazil). Asso. fellow Brit. Interplanetary Soc.; mem. Air Force Assn., Res. Officers Assn., Inst. Nav., Royal Astron. Soc. Canada, Md. Hist. Soc., Am. C. of C. Rio de Janeiro, Am. C. of C. Sao Paulo, Sphinx Soc., Beta Theta Pi. Clubs: Mason (Shriner), International (Washington); Harvard (Boston); Dartmouth College, Yale (N.Y.C.); American (Miami, Fla.); Wellesley (Mass.) Country. Home: 13 Indian Spring Rd Dover MA 02030 Office: 100 Federal St Boston MA 02106

ALDRICH, HULBERT (STRATTON ALDRICH), banker; b. Fall River, Mass., Apr. 3, 1907; s. Stanley Alden and Jane Stratton (Pratt) A.; m. Amy Durfee, Jan. 19, 1934; children: Ann, Jane Stratton. Ph.B., Yale U., 1930. With New York Trust Co., N.Y.C., 1930-59, asst. treas., 1939-43, v.p., 1943-52, pres., dir., 1952-59; vice chmn., dir. Chem. Bank, 1959-72; chmn. Hill Samuel Inc., N.Y.C., 1972—; dir. C.T. Wilson Co., Ametek, Inc.; hon. dir., mem. exec. com. IBM World Trade Corp.; dir. Nat. Distillers & Chem. Corp.; hon. trustee Empire Savs. Bank, N.Y.C.; hon. dir. Commonwealth Fund; mem. internat. adv. bd. Chem. Bank.; Trustee Presbyn. Hosp. Clubs: Century, Yale, River, Links, Links Golf. Home: 1088 Park Ave New York NY 10028 Office: 375 Park Ave New York NY 10022

ALDRICH, NELSON WILMARTH, architect; b. N.Y.C., Apr. 6, 1911; s. William Truman and Dorothea (Davenport) A.; m. Eleanor Tweed (div.); 1 son, Nelson Wilmarth; m. Frances Turner, Nov. 9, 1940; children—Frances D. Maher, Abigail Cheever, Rosalie C. West. A.B., Harvard, 1934, M.Arch., 1938; L.H.D. (hon.), Tufts U., 1956; LL.D., Emerson Coll., 1962. Designer Harrison & Abramoviz, 1939-40; project planner U.S. Housing Authority, 1940-42; partner Campbell, Aldrich & Nulty, Boston, 1947-74; pres. Aldrich, Pounder & Assos., Inc., Boston, 1974—; cons. architect Dartmouth, Bradford Jr. Coll., Phillips Exeter Acad.; asso. architect Boton City Hall; architect, developer Portsmouth (N.H.) Urban Renewal Project.; Co-founder, chmn. Boston Arts Festival, 1952-64; dir. Boston Archtl. Center, 1968-72; chmn. Boston Art Commn., 1955-75; mem. Planning Bd. Town of Marblehead, Mass., 1979—; pres. Inst. Contemporary Art, 1947-60, trustee, 1960-64; mem. archtl. design adv. com. Boston Redevel. Authority, Boston, 1959—; mem. Mass. Bd. Regional Community Colls., 1961-72; trustee Boston Mus. of Fine Arts, 1954—, Radcliffe Coll., 1957-71, vice chmn., 1961-66; v.p. Met. Boston Arts Center, 1958-60, pres., 1960-63; bd. dirs. New Eng. Hist. Seaport, 1977—. Served as lt. comdr. USNR, 1942-46; charge combat aircraft service units; Pacific. Fellow AIA, Am. Acad. Arts and Scis.; mem. Boston Soc. Architects, Mass. Assn. Architects (dir. 1950-58), Harvard Alumni Assn. (dir. 1962-65). Club: Tavern (Boston). Home: Peach's Point Marblehead MA 01945

ALDRICH, PATRICIA ANNE RICHARDSON, editor; b. St. Paul, Apr. 6, 1926; d. James Calvin and Anna Catherine (Eskra) Richardson; m. Edwin Chauncey Aldrich, July 31, 1948; 1 son, Mason Calvin. Student, Stout Inst., 1944-45; B.S. in Journalism; scholar, Northwestern U., 1948. Editor Child's World News, The Child's World, Inc., Chgo., 1952-57; asso. editor Home Life mag. Advt. Div., Inc., Chgo., 1957-71, editor, 1971—. Mem. steering com., publicity chmn. Evanston Urban League, 1961-64; Mem. Women in Communications, Inc. Democrat. Office: Advt Div Inc 111 E Wacker Dr Chicago IL 60601

ALDRICH, RICHARD JOHN, agronomist; b. Fairgrove, Mich., Apr. 16, 1925; s. George and Eva Ann (Misner) A.; m. June Ellen Ellison, Apr. 3, 1943; children: Judith Allman, Sharon Sneed, Jeffrey. B.S., Mich. State U., 1948; Ph.D., Ohio State U., 1950. Agronomist U.S. Dept. Agr., North Brunswick, N.J., 1950-57; asst. dir. Agr. Exptl. Sta., Mich. State U., East Lansing, 1957-64; assoc. dir., dean agr. exptl. sta. U. Mo., Columbia, 1964-76; adminstr. CSRS, U.S. Dept. Agr., Washington, 1976-78; prof. agronomy U. Mo., Columbia, 1978-81; research agronomist, prof. SEA-ARS, Dept. Agr.-U. Mo., 1981—; cons. OTA, U.S. Congress, 1979, The Standard Oil Co., 1983; mem. adv. com. Fed. Assistance Rev., 1970-71; pres. Agr. Research Inst., 1974-75. Author: Weed Crop Ecology, 1983; contbr. articles to profl. jours. Served to 1st lt. USAAF, 1943-46. Mem. Weed Sci. Soc. Am., Am. Soc. Agronomy (dir. 1949-50), Agrl. Research Inst. (pres. 1974-75), Nat. Assn. State Univs. and Land Grant Colls. Home: 1715 Woodrail Ave Columbia MO 65201 Office: SEA-ARS USDA Columbia MO 65211

ALDRICH, RICHARD ORTH, ins. co. exec.; b. Cambridge, Mass., Feb. 13, 1921; s. Harold Jere and Hazel M. (Orth) A.; m. Lois Anne McKenney, Oct. 16, 1946; children: Hope A., Richard H., Caleb F. B.S., Harvard U., 1942, LL.B., 1948; grad., Advanced Mgmt. Program, 1967. Bar: Mass. bar 1948. Asso. firm Tyler & Reynolds, Boston, 1948-55; asst. counsel John Hancock, Boston, 1955-59, asso. counsel, 1959-66, counsel, 1966—, v.p., 1970—. Mem. Wellesley (Mass.) Town Meeting, 1955-82; mem. Wellesley Bd. Appeal, 1955-74, chmn., 1965-74. Served with USN, 1942-46. Mem. ABA, Am. Council Life Ins., Mass. Bar Assn., Boston Bar Assn., Assn. Life Ins. Counsel. Republican. Roman Catholic. Clubs: Univ. (Boston); Wellesley Country. Home: 26 Lathrop Rd Wellesley MA 02181 Office: John Hancock Pl Boston MA 02117

ALDRICH, ROBERT, motion picture director, producer; b. Cranston, R.I., 1918; children: Adell Aldrich, William, Alida Aldrich Shaffer, Kelly. Student, U. Va. Pres. Assocs. & Aldrich Co., Inc., Aldrich Studios, Los Angeles. TV shows include The Doctor, China Smith; dir.: films Big Leaguer, Apache, Vera Cruz, Autumn Leaves, Ten Seconds to Hell, Angry Hills, Last Sunset, What Ever Happened to Baby Jane?, 4 for Texas, Hush. . .Hush Sweet Charlotte, Flight of the Phoenix, Dirty Dozen, Hustle, Emporer of the North, The Longest Yard, Twilight's Last Gleaming, Choirboys, No-Knife; producer, dir.: World for Ranson; dir.: Kiss Me Deadly, The Big Knife, Attack!, The Legend of Lylah Clare, The Killing of Sister George, Too Late the Hero; producer,dir.: The Grissom Gang; producer, dir. The Frisco Kid, 1979. Mem. Dirs. Guild Am. (pres.). Home: 901 S Longwood Ave Los Angeles CA 90019 Office: Aldrich Co 606 N Larchmont Blvd Suite 209 Los Angeles CA 90004

ALDRICH, ROBERT ADAMS, agrl. engr.; b. Veteran Twp., N.Y., Apr. 25, 1924; s. Luman Woodbridge and Mabel Hastings (Gibbs) A.; m. Roberta Ann Bowlby, Aug. 27, 1946; children—Susan Carol, Gail Jessica, Kathleen Lois, Margaret Louise. B.S. in Agrl. Engring, Wash. State U., 1950, M.S., 1952; Ph.D., Mich. State U., 1958. Instr., then asso. prof. agrl. engring. Wash. State U., 1951-58; asso. prof. U. Ky., 1958-59, Mich. State U., 1959-62; asso. prof., then prof. Pa. State U., 1962-79; prof. agrl. engring., head dept. U. Conn., Storrs, 1979—. Author papers in field. Served with C.E. AUS, 1942-46. Mem. Am. Soc. Agrl. Engrs., Nat. Soc. Profl. Engrs., ASHRAE. Home: 295

Wormwood Hill Rd Mansfield Center CT 06250 Office: Agrl Engring Dept U-15 U Conn Storrs CT 06268

ALDRICH, ROBERT ANDERSON, physician; b. Evanston, Ill., 1917; m. Marjorie Duttenhofer, 1940; children: Robert Anderson, Stephen M., Frederick G. M.D., Northwestern U., 1944. Diplomate: Am. Bd. Pediatrics, 1951. Intern Evanston Hosp., 1943-44; resident pediatrics U. Minn. Hosps., 1946-48, sr. fellow pediatrics, 1948-49; instr. pediatrics U. Minn. Grad. Sch., 1951; assoc. staff Mayo Clinic, Rochester, Minn., 1949-50, cons. pediatrics, 1950—; asst. prof. pediatrics U. Oreg. Med. Sch., 1951-53, assoc. prof., 1953-56; prof. pediatrics U. Wash., Seattle, 1956-63, 64-70, chmn. dept., 1956-62, head div. human ecology dept. pediatrics, 1967-70, dir. health resources study center, 1966-70; v.p. health affairs U. Colo., Denver, 1970-75, prof. preventive medicine and comprehensive health care, prof. pediatrics Sch. Medicine, 1970-81, emeritus, 1981—, prof. anthropology, 1978-81, emeritus, 1981—; clin. prof. pediatrics U. Wash., 1980—, affiliate prof., 1982—. Dir. Nat. Inst. Child Health and Human Devel., NIH, Bethesda, Md., 1963-64; Mem. Pres.'s Com. on Mental Retardation, 1966-71, vice chmn., 1966-71; chmn. Gov.'s Council on Mental Health and Mental Retardation, 1968-70. Served to lt. (s.g.) M.C. USNR, 1944-46. Mem. King County Med. Soc., North Pacific Pediatric Soc., Soc. Pediatric Research, Am. Acad. Pediatrics, Am. Pediatrics Soc., Internat. Assn. Child Ecology (pres. 1982). Address: 5101 NE 41st St Seattle WA 98105

ALDRICH, THOMAS ALBERT, brewing exec., former air force officer; b. Rosebud, Tex., Nov. 30, 1923; s. John Albert and Georgia Opal (Hilliard) A.; m. Virginia Elaine Peterson, Mar. 1, 1944; children—Sharon Aldrich Lingus, Pamela Aldrich Williams, Thomas Charles. Student, Tex. A. and M. U., 1942-43, U. Chgo., 1943-44; B.A. in Math, George Washington U., 1961; M.S. in Bus. Adminstrn, George Washington U., 1968. Commd. 2d lt. USAAF, 1944; advanced through grades to maj. gen. USAF, 1974; pilot, meteorologist, 1943-57; dep. dir. air operations Air Weather Service, Washington, 1957-60; student Air War Coll., 1960-61; comdr. 57th Weather Reconnaissance Squadron, Melbourne, Australia, 1962-65; chief, mil. employment div. Air Command and Staff Coll., 1965-68; dir. war plans Hdqrs. Mil. Airlift Command, Scott AFB, Ill., 1968-69; comdr. 9th Weather Reconnaissance Wing, McClellan AFB, Calif., 1969-70; vice comdr. USAF Air Weather Service, Scott AFB, Ill., 1970-71, comdr., 1973-74, U.S. Forces Azores, Portugal, 1971-73; dep. chief of staff, plans Hdqrs. Mil. Airlift Command, 1974-75; comdr. 22d Air Force, Travis AFB, Calif., 1975-78; v.p., corp. rep. Anheuser-Busch, Inc., Sacramento, 1978—. Decorated D.S.M., Legion of Merit with oak leaf cluster, Meritorious Service medal. Mem. Nat. Honor Soc., U.S. Brewers Assn., Calif. Mfrs. Assn. (dir.), Calif. C. of C., Phi Theta Kappa. Republican. Presbyterian. Home: 1355 Commons Dr Sacramento CA 95825 Office: Anheuser-Busch Inc 1451 River Park Dr Suite 126 Sacramento CA 95815

ALDRICH, VIRGIL CHARLES, educator; b. Narsingpur, India, Sept. 13, 1903; s. Floyd Clemet and Ann (Hanley) A.; m. Louise Hafliger, Sept. 3, 1927; 1 son, David Virgil. B.A., Ohio Wesleyan U., 1925, L.H.D. (hon.), 1963; student, Oxford U., 1926-27; Diplome d'Etudes Superieures de Philosophie, La Sorbonne, 1928; Ph.D., U. Calif. at Berkeley, 1931; L.H.D., Kenyon Coll., 1972. Instr., asst. prof. Rice Inst., 1931-42; vis. prof. Columbia, 1942-46; prof. philosophy Kenyon Coll., 1946-65; vis. prof. Brown U., 1962-63; prof. U. N.C., 1965-72, U. Utah, Salt Lake City, 1972—; Dir. Kyoto Am. Studies Inst., Japan. Author: Philosophy of Art, 1963; Contbr.: Readings in Philosophical Analysis, 1951, Reflections on Art, 1958, Faith and the Philosophers, 1962, Religious Experience and Truth, 1961, World Perspectives in Philosophy, 1967, Gilbert Ryle Symposium Proceedings, 1972. Sterling fellow Yale, 1931-32. Mem. Am. Philos. Assn. (pres.), Am. Soc. Aesthetics (trustee, pres.), So. Soc. Philosophy and Psychology. Home: 450 Northmont Way Salt Lake City UT 84103 *Whenever my hands or my head were doing something really worthwhile, I have had the impression that I was not the agent or the author. Something bigger and better than my little, precise, catalogued self was at work in and through me. The art of good living is the art of making room within oneself for whatever that greater thing is, call it what you like.*

ALDRIDGE, ALFRED OWEN, educator; b. Buffalo, Dec. 16, 1915; s. Albert and Jane (Ette) A.; m. Mary Hennen Dellinger, May 18, 1941 (div. 1956); 1 dau., Cecily (Mrs. John Ward); m. Adriana Garcia Davila, June 7, 1963. B.S. in Edn, Ind. U., 1937; M.A., U. Ga., 1938; Ph.D., Duke, 1942; D.U.P., U. Paris, France, 1955. Prof. comparative lit. U. Buffalo, 1942-47, U. Md., 1947-67, U. Ill., 1967—; Fulbright prof., France, 1953, Smith-Mundt prof., Brazil, 1957; vis. prof. Nihon U., Japan, 1976, 82, Kuwait U., 1983. Author: Franklin and His French Contemporaries, 1957, Man of Reason: Life of Thomas Paine, 1959, Jonathan Edwards, 1964, Benjamin Franklin: Philosopher and Man, 1965, Benjamin Franklin and Nature's God, 1967, Comparative Literature: Matter and Method, 1969, The Ibero-American Enlightenment, 1971, Voltaire and the Century of Light, 1975, Hikadu Bungaku: Comparative Literature East and West, 1979, Early American Literature: A Comparatist Approach, 1982; Editor: Comparative Lit. Studies, 1963—; Adv. editor: Eighteenth Century Life. NEH, 1973-74. Mem. Am. Comparative Lit. Assn. (adv. bd. 1965-71, 74—, v.p. 1977-80, pres. 1980-83), Internat. Comparative Lit. Assn. (adv. bd. 1970—), Am. Soc. 18th Century Studies (adv. bd. 1968-75). Home: 101 E Chalmers St Champaign IL 61820 Office: U Ill Modern Lang Bldg Urbana IL 61801

ALDRIDGE, EDWARD C., JR., government official; b. Houston, Aug. 18, 1938. B.S., Tex. A & M U., 1960; M.S., Ga. Inst. Tech., 1962. Mgr. missile and space div. Douglas Aircraft Co., Santa Monica, Calif., 1962-67, Washington, 1962-67; dir. strategic def. div. Dept. Def., 1967-72, dep. asst. sec. for strategic programs, 1974-76; dir. planning and evaluation Office of Sec. Def., 1976-77; sr. mgr. LTV Aerospace Corp., Dallas, 1972-73; sr. mgmt. assoc. Office Mgmt. and Budget, Washington, 1973-74; v.p. Strategic Systems Group System Planning Corp., Arlington, Va., 1977-81; undersec. Dept. Air Force, 1981—; advisor Strategic Arms Limitation Talks, Helsinki and Vienna. Office: Pentagon Washington DC 20330 *

ALDRIDGE, GORDON JAMES, social work educator; b. Toronto, Ont., Can., Oct. 19, 1916; came to U.S., 1950, naturalized, 1956; s. Eugene Froyard and Alicia (Jourdan) A.; m. Gladys Chapman, June 21, 1941; 1 son, Ronald Gordon. B.A., U. Toronto, 1938, diploma in social work, 1939, M.A., 1948, M. Social Work, 1949; Ph.D., U. Mich., 1955, U. London, 1963. Caseworker Family Agy., Toronto, 1939-41, case supr., 1946-50; asst. exec. dir., 1949-50; Lectr. U. Toronto, 1946-50; asso. prof. social work, dir. Human Relations Inst., Fla. State U., 1950-52; asso. prof. social work Mich. State U., 1952-57, prof., 1957-78; dir. Sch. Social Work, 1959-66; prof. social work Ariz. State U., 1978—. Author: Social Welfare and the Aged, 1959, Social Issues and Psychiatric Social Work Practice, 1959, (with J. Kaplan) Social Welfare of the Aging, 1962, (with Earl J. McGrath) Liberal Education and Social Work, 1965, Undergraduate Social Work Education, 1972; Contbr. to, Florida State University Studies, 1952, (with Earl J. McGrath) Living in the Later Years, 1952, Education for Later Maturity, 1954, Aging is Everyone's Concern, 1957, Undergraduate Social Work Education and the Needs of the Work Incentive Program, 1972, Aging and Communication, 1976, also articles profl. jours. Active state, nat., internat. health and welfare orgns. Served from 2d lt. to maj. Canadian Army, 1941-46; ETO. Mem. Council on Social Work Edn., Nat. Assn. Social Workers, Gerontological Soc., Internat. Assn. Gerontology, Canadian Assn. on Gerontology. Home: 7709 E Sheridan Scottsdale AZ 85257

ALDRIDGE, JOHN WATSON, educator, author; b. Sioux City, Iowa, Sept. 26, 1922; s. Walter Copher and Nell (Watson) A.; m. Leslie Felker, Dec. 10, 1954 (div. June 1968); 1 son, Geoffrey; children by previous marriages: Henry, Stephen, Leslie, Jeremy; m. Alexandra Bertash, July 13, 1968 (div. Dec. 1982). Student, U. Chattanooga, 1940-43; fellow, Breadloaf Sch. English, summer 1942; B.A., U. Calif.-Berkeley, 1947. Lectr. English U. Vt., 1948-50, asst. prof., 1950-53, 54-55; lectr. Christian Gauss Seminars Criticism, Princeton, 1953-54; mem. lit. faculty Sarah Lawrence Coll., also New Sch. Social Research, 1957; prof. English Queens Coll., 1957; Berg prof. English N.Y.U., 1958; Fulbright lectr. U. Munich, Germany, 1958-59; writer-in-residence Hollins Coll., 1960-62; Fulbright lectr. U. Copenhagen, Denmark, 1962-63; prof. English U. Mich., 1964—; book critic N.Y. Herald Tribune Book Week, 1965-66, Saturday Review, 1970—; Staff Bread Loaf Writers Conf., 1966-69; chief regional judge Book-of-the Month Writing Fellowship Program, 1966-67; spl. adviser for Am. studies U.S. embassy, Germany, 1972-73. Author: After the Lost Generation, 1951, Critiques and Essays on Modern Fiction, 1952, In Search of Heresy, 1956, The Party at Cranton, 1960, Time to Murder and Create, 1966, In the Country of the Young, 1970, The Devil in the Fire, 1972, The American Novel and the Way We Live Now, 1983; also articles.; Editor: Selected Stories by P.G. Wodehouse, 1958. Served with AUS, 1943-45; ETO. Decorated Bronze Star medal; Rockefeller Humanities fellow, 1976-77. Mem. Authors Guild and League of Am., MLA, Nat. Book Critics Circle, P.E.N. Home: 1050 Wall St Ann Arbor MI 48105

ALDRIDGE, MARY HENNEN DELLINGER, chemistry educator; b. Brownstown, Ark., Jan. 11, 1919; d. Bonnie and Sadie B. (Reeves) Dellinger; m. Alfred Owen Aldridge, May 18, 1941 (dec. div. 1956); 1 dau., Cecily Joan (Mrs. John P. Ward, Jr.). B.S. in Chemistry, U. Ga., 1939; M.A., Duke, 1941; Ph.D. in Biochemistry, Georgetown U., 1954. Chemist E.I. duPont de Nemours & Co., 1941-47; asst. prof. U. Md., 1947-55; asso. prof. Am. U., 1955-62, prof. chemistry, 1962—, chmn. dept. chemistry, 1979—; pres. Chemco, Inc., 1962-65, Aldridges & Assos. & Co., Inc., 1965-76. Recipient Service award Washington chpt. Alpha Chi Sigma, 1977; Research grantee USPHS, 1967-68, Surgeon Gen.'s Office, U.S. Army, 1961-64, 66-69; Eve. Star faculty research grantee, 1961; research grantee Office Water Resources, 1975-76, Office Naval Research, 1976-78, U.S. Army, 1976-79. Mem. Am. Chem. Soc. (com. on chemistry and pub. affairs 1971-74), Washington Acad. Scis. (chmn. teaching sci. panel for Sci. Achievement awards 1969-71, gen. chmn. 1972-74, sec. 1974-75, treas. 1976-77, pres. 1978-79), Chem. Soc. Washington (chmn. nat. com. women's activities 1962, chmn. organic topical group 1962-63, bd. mgrs. 1962-66, sec. 1967-68, councilor 1967-69, 71-77, pres. 1970, Charles L. Gordon Meml. award 1981), AAAS, AAUP, Am. Inst. Chemists (chmn. honor scroll com. Washington sect. 1974-75, Honor Scroll award 1982), Washington Philos. Soc., Washington Chromatography Discussion Group (bd. govs. 1966-79, pres. 1974-75), Sigma Xi, Sigma Delta Epsilon, Iota Sigma Pi. Home: 2930 45th St NW Washington DC 20016

ALDRIDGE, ROBERT BRUCE, accountant; b. Groveport, Ohio, May 4, 1939; s. Hollis Kuhn and Clairbelle Mae (Smith) A.; m. Carolyn Ann Mekush, Dec. 20, 1962; children: Cynthia Ann, Deborah Kay. B.S., Ohio State U., 1962; M.B.A., U. So. Calif., 1965. C.P.A., Calif. Assoc. controller Bullocks, Los Angeles, 1967-73; controller Bullock's North, Menlo Park, Calif., 1973-74; v.p. Famous Barr, St. Louis, 1974-80, May Dept. Stores, 1980—. Fund raiser YMCA, St. Louis, 1975—; trustee Fox Creek Valley Assn., Pacific, Mo., 1978-82. Served with U.S. Army, 1962. Mem. Retail Controllers (vice chmn. 1971-72, 73-74). Republican. Lutheran. Home: 18600 Vixen Dr Pacific MO 63069 Office: 611 Olive St Saint Louis MO 63101

ALDRIN, EDWIN EUGENE, JR.(BUZZ), former astronaut, science consultant; b. Montclair, N.J., Jan. 20, 1930; children: James Michael, Janice Ross, Andrew John. B.S., U.S. Mil. Acad., 1951; Sc.D. in Astronautics, MIT, 1963; Sc.D. (hon.), Gustavus Adolphus Coll., 1967, Clark U., 1969, U. Portland, 1970, St. Peter's Coll., 1970; Litt.D. (hon.), Montclair State Coll., 1969; D.Hum. (hon.), Seton Hall U., 1970. Commd. officer USAF, 1951, advanced through grades to col.; served as fighter pilot in Korea, 1953; pilot Gemini XII orbital rendezvous space flight, Nov. 11-15, 1966; lunar module pilot on first manned lunar landing Apollo XI; comdr. Aerospace Research Pilots Sch., Edwards AFB, Calif., 1971-72; now sci. cons. Beverly Hills Oil Co., Los Angeles. Author: Return to Earth, 1973. Decorated D.S.M., Legion of Merit, D.F.C. with oak leaf cluster, Air medal with 2 oak leaf clusters; recipient numerous awards including Presdl. medal of Freedom, 1969. Fellow AIAA; mem. Soc. Exptl. Test Pilots, Royal Aero. Soc. (hon.), Sea Space Symposium; charter Internat. Acad. Astronautics (corr.), Sigma Xi, Tau Beta Pi. Club: Masons (33 deg). Established record over 7 hours and 52 minutes outside spacecraft in extravehicular activity. Office: Beverly Hills Oil Co One Century Plaza Suite 1760 2029 Century Park E Los Angeles CA 90067 *

ALEGI, PETER CLAUDE, lawyer; b. New Haven, Conn., July 26, 1935; s. Claude D. and Margaret (Lettieri) A.; m. Nicoletta Barbaritos, Dec. 16, 1961; children: Gregory, Daniel, Peter. B.A. cum laude, Yale U., 1956, LL.B., 1959; postgrad. Fulbright scholar, U. Rome, Italy, 1959-60. Bar: Conn. 1959, R.I. 1962, Ill. 1965, U.S. Supreme Ct. 1965. Assoc. Hinckley, Allen, Salisbury Parsons and predecessors, Providence, R.I., Conn., 1961-64, ptnr., Chgo., 1964-65, Milan and Rome, 1965-66, 1967—; vis. lectr. Temple U. Law Sch., Phila., 1980-81, Yale U. Law Sch., New Haven, 1981—. Author: Italian Income Taxation, 1974; contbr. articles to profl. jours. Chmn. Democrats Abroad-Italy, 1976—; commr. Fulbright Commn., Rome, 1979—. Mem. Yale Alumni Assn. (dir. 1970-79), ABA, Italian Assn. Tax Advisors. Roman Catholic. Club: Tennis Parioli (Rome). Office: Hinckley Allen Salisbury Parsons Via Venti Settembre 1 Rome Italy 00187

ALEO, JOSEPH JOHN, scientist, educator; b. Wilkes-Barre, Pa., Oct. 8, 1925; s. Vincent and Martha (Lupino) A.; m. Fannie Ocuto, Aug. 28, 1949; children—Joseph John, James Robert. B.S., Bucknell U., 1948; D.D.S., Temple U., 1953; Ph.D., U. Rochester, 1965. Dental surgeon USPHS, 1953-54; pvt. practice dentistry, Meshoppen, Pa., 1954-60; research fellow U. Rochester, 1960-65; asso. prof., chmn. dept. pathology Temple U., 1965-67, prof., chmn. dept., 1967-70, dean advanced edn. and research, 1970—; cons. NIH. Contbr. articles sci. jours. Served with AUS, 1943-46. Mem. Am. Soc. Exptl. Pathology, Internat. Assn. Dental Research, Pathology Soc. Phila., Omicron Kappa Upsilon. Office: 3223 N Broad St Philadelphia PA 19140

ALESSANDRONI, VENAN JOSEPH, lawyer; b. N.Y.C., Mar. 1, 1915; s. Anthony P. and Andromeda (Rossini) A.; m. Alice Shaughnessy, Feb. 2, 1949; m. Adelle Lincoln, Mar. 10, 1974. A.B., Columbia U., 1937, J.D., 1939. Bar: N.Y. 1941, also, Supreme Ct. of Korea 1946. Announcer CBS Artists Service, Inc., 1940; U.S. atty. Bd. Econ. Warfare, 1942; mem. U.S. Fgn. Econ. Adminstrn. Mission, Belgian Congo, 1943; with Wormser, Kiely, Alessandroni, Hyde & McCann (and predecessor firm), N.Y.C., 1946—, sr. partner, 1959—; Legal officer Mil. Govt. Korea, 1945-46; legal adviser to provincial gov. Kyunggi-Do, Korea, 1946; chief provost judge, City of Seoul, 1946; adj. prof., law sch. U. Miami, 1974—; lectr. various tax insts., univs., profl. assns. Author: The Executor, 1963, Applied Estate Planning, 1963, also articles.; Departmental editor: Jour. Taxation, 1955-56. Recipient U.S. Army Commendation award, 1946; regional award N.Y. Times, 1932; Curtis medal Columbia, 1936. Mem. Assn. Bar City N.Y. Club: Union League. Home: Eggleston Ln Old Greenwich CT 06870 Office: 100 Park Ave New York NY 10017

ALEVIZOS, SUSAN BAMBERGER, lawyer, santouri player, author; b. N.Y.C., May 19, 1936; d. L. Richard and Helen (Thatcher) Bamberger; m. Theodore George Alevizos, May 6, 1960; children—Gregory, L. Richard, Theodore. B.A., Smith Coll., 1958; postgrad., Columbia, 1959-60, Women's Lyceum, Athens, Greece, 1967-68; Master classes with, Maestro Yannis Jovenos, Naxos, Greece, 1967-74; J.D., Suffolk U., 1978. Bar: Mass. bar 1978, Fed. bar 1979. Atty. firm Alevizos & Alevizos, Boston, 1978—; Cons. Greek div. MGM Records; rec. div. Nat. Geog. Soc. Santouri player, 1967—, performed concerts, UN, N.Y.C., 1969, Am. embassy, Athens, 1968, Boston Mus. Fine Arts, 1972, Gardiner Mus., Boston, 1971, also in, Gardiner Mus., Phila., Milw. and Detroit, field work, Nat. Folklore Archives of Greece, 1956—; recs. include Songs of Greece, 1960, Folksongs of Greece, 1961, Greek Folksongs, 1969, Poetry and Song, 1973, Traditional Songs and Dances of Greece and the Grecian Islands, 1978; Author: Folksongs of Greece, 1968; legal columnist Hellenic Chronicle, Boston, 1979—; contbr. articles to profl. publs. Mem. Am. Bar Assn., Mass. Bar Assn., Boston Bar Assn., Assn. Trial Lawyers Am., Am. Folklore Soc. Office: 43 Kingston St Boston MA 02111

ALEVIZOS, THEODORE GEORGE, lawyer, singer, author; b. Milw., Feb. 7, 1926; s. Gregory and Mary (Passaris) A.; m. Susan Thatcher Bamberger, May 6, 1960; children: Gregory, L. Richard, Theodore. Ph.B., Marquette U., 1950; postgrad., Juilliard Sch. Music, 1950-51; M.S., Columbia U., 1957; J.D., Suffolk U., 1966. Bar: Mass. 1974, Fed. 1975, U.S. Supreme Ct. 1980. Mem. sales staff McKesson & Robbins, Milw., 1952-56; asst. cataloger N.Y. U. Med. Library, N.Y.C., 1956-57; asst. circulation librarian Widener Library, Harvard, 1957-61; asst. librarian Lamont Library, 1961-64, dir., 1964-74; mem. faculty Harvard U., 1966-74, lectr. modern Greek, 1969-73, lectr. voice, 1972-74, assoc. univ. librarian for pub. services, 1966-74; practiced in Boston, 1974—; mem. Alevizos & Alevizos, 1978—; instr. modern Greek, The Voice in Performance Cambridge Adult Center, 1972—; nat. and internat. concertizing.; Cons. MGM Records, Inc., 1965-71; Orgn. for Social and Tech. Innovation, Inc., Cambridge, 1968-70; mus. cons. Nat. Geographic, 1971-73; Bd. dirs. Harvard Coop., 1973-74; mem. corp. Cambridge Center Adult Edn. Author: Folksongs of Greece, 1968; legal columnist: Hellenic Chronicle, Boston, 1979—; Recordings include: Folksingers Round Harvard Square, 1959, Songs of Greece, 1960, Folksongs of Greece, 1961, Greek Folksongs, 1969, Poetry and Song, 1973, Traditional Songs and Dances of Greece and the Grecian Islands, 1978. Trustee Dexter Sch., 1976—, v.p. bd. trustees, 1980—. Served with USNR, 1944-46; PTO. Decorated Bronze Star.; Hon. assoc. Center for Neo-Hellenic Studies, U. Tex. at Austin, 1967—. Mem. Am., Mass., Boston bar assns., Mass. Acad. Trial Attys., ALA, Am. Folklore Soc., Modern Greek Studies Assn., Inst. Byzantine and Modern Greek Studies (hon.). Office: 43 Kingston St Boston MA 02111

ALEXANDER, ALEC PETER, educator, univ. adminstr.; b. San Francisco, Sept. 21, 1923; s. Peter and Athena (Vrionis) Zacharatos; m. Lesley Jones, Feb. 28, 1953; children—Jane, Peter. B.A., U. Calif., Berkeley, 1949, Ph.D., 1957. Asst. prof. Northwestern U., Evanston, Ill., 1957-59; asst. prof. econs. U. Calif., Santa Barbara, 1960-65, asso. prof., 1965-69, prof., 1969—; dean Coll. Letters and Sci., 1971-73, vice chancellor for acad. affairs, 1973-78, acting chancellor, 1977; sr. research analyst Greek Center for Econ. Research, 1963-64. Contbr. articles to profl. jours. Bd. dirs. Goleta Valley Hosp. Served with Nat. Groups of Greek Guerillas, 1944-45. Ford Found. fellow, 1954-56; Social Sci. Research Council fellow, 1959-60. Mem. Am. Econ. Assn. Home: 605 San Roque St Santa Barbara CA 93105

ALEXANDER, ANDREW LAMAR, governor of Tennessee; b. Knoxville, Tenn., July 3, 1940; s. Andrew Lamar and Genevra Floreine (Rankin) A.; m. Leslee Kathryn Buhler, Jan. 4, 1969; children: Drew, Leslee, Kathryn, Will. B.A., Vanderbilt U., 1962; J.D., NYU, 1965. Bar: La., Tenn. Law clk. Judge John Minor Wisdom 5th Circuit Ct. Appeals, New Orleans; assoc. firm Fowler, Rountree, Fowler & Robertson, Knoxville, 1965; legis. asst. to Senator Howard Baker, 1967-68; exec. asst. to Bryce Harlow, White House Congl. Liaison Office, 1969-70; ptnr. firm Dearborn and Ewing, Nashville, 1971-78; gov. State of Tenn., Nashville, 1978—; Chmn. Appalachian Regional Commn., 1980-81; vice chmn. Adv. Commn. on Intergovtl. Relations; mem. President's Task Force on Federalism; chmn. Nat. Gov.'s Assn. Com. on Exec. Mgmt. and Fiscal Affairs; mgr. Winfield Dunn for Gov. Campaign, 1970, chief transition, 1970-71; candidate, Republican nominee for gov. of Tenn., 1974. N.Y. U. Law Sch. Root-Tilden scholar. Mem. Phi Beta Kappa. Republican. Presbyterian. Office: State Capitol 1st Floor Nashville TN 37219 *

ALEXANDER, ARVIN J., lawyer; b. Lethbridge, Alta., Can., May 10, 1909; s. John M. and Lona (Ledford) A.; m. Anne Lawrie Valentine, Aug. 4, 1934; 1 son, Donald V. LL.B., Ohio State U., 1936, J.D., 1970. Bar: Ohio bar 1966. Partner firm Alexander, Ebinger, Fisher, McAlister & Lawrence, Columbus, 1946—. Mem. Columbus City Council, 1939-43, pres., 1943; mem. Met. Airport Com., 1956-63; chmn. trustees Columbus Better Bus. Bur. Central Ohio, 1958-61; pres. Citizens Research, Inc., 1962-64, chmn. bd., 1964-66; mem. Downtown Area Commn. Bd., 1965-75, life trustee, 1976—; trustee, vice chmn. trustees, chmn. exec. com. Mut. Investing Found., Columbus; trustee Columbus Sinking Fund, 1953-64, pres., 1957-58. Mem. Am., Ohio State, Columbus bar assns., Navy League (judge advocate 1963). Home: 3725 Olentangy Blvd Columbus OH 43214 Office: 17 S High St Columbus OH 43215

ALEXANDER, BENJAMIN HAROLD, government official; b. Roberta, Ga., Oct. 18, 1921; s. Bush Monoah and Annie Willie (Flowers) A.; m. Mary Ellen Spurlock, Mar. 21, 1948; children: Drew Wilson, Dawn Criket. B.A., U. Cin., 1943; M.S., Bradley U., Peoria, Ill., 1950; Ph.D., Georgetown U., 1957. Adminstr. new health career projects Nat. Center for Health Services Research and Devel., Rockville, Md., 1968-71; acting chief gen. research support br. div. research resources NIH, Bethesda, Md., 1971-74; pres. Chgo. State U., from 1974; then pres. U. of D.C.; dep. asst. sec. Dept. Edn., Washington, 1984—; Fellow Acad. of Sci., Washington, 1966—; chmn. research adv. council Water Resources Center, Washington Tech. Inst., 1973-74; chmn. Nelson Com. Workshop, 1973, D.C. Commn. on Arts and Humanities, 1974; mem. adv. com. NSF, 1977; mem. Washington Bd. Edn., 1966-69; 2d v.p. D.C. Fedn. Civic Assns., 1970-71, pres., 1972-73; mem. Howard U. Commn. on Sch. of Edn., 1973; trustee Washington Tchrs. Coll.; bd. dirs. Bradley U., 1980; non-lawyer mem. bd. dirs. Am. Judicature Soc., 1980. Contbr. articles to profl. jours. Served with AUS, 1943-47; to maj. Res., 1947-65. Recipient certificate of achievement Dept. of Army, 1967; medal for service to youth D.C. YMCA, 1974; Ann. Alumni Achievement award Georgetown U., 1974, Bradley U., 1977; certificate for distinguished pub. service Washington City Govt., 1974; resolution of appreciation D.C. City Council, 1974; Achiever's award Chgo./South C. of C.,

1976; Walter Reuther Humanitarian award, 1978; Internat. Educators award Sigma Gamma Rho, 1978; Outstanding Educators award Am. Tobacco Co., 1978. Mem. Chem. Soc. Washington (chmn. symposium on pollution 1970, program chmn. 1971, certificate of appreciation 1970), Am. Chem. Soc. (Community Service award 1967), D.C. Congress Parents and Tchrs.; mem. ABA (nat. non-lawyer mem. accreditation com.); life Alpha Phi Alpha (Disting. Educator plaque). Patentee in field. Office: Dept Edn ROB-C 400 Maryland Ave SW Washington DC 20202

ALEXANDER, CARL ALBERT, ceramic engr.; b. Chillicothe, Ohio, Nov. 22, 1928; s. Carl B. and Helen E. A.; m. Dolores J Herstenstein, Sept. 4, 1954; children—Carla C., David A. B.S., Ohio U., 1953, M.S., 1956; Ph.D., Ohio State U., 1961. Mem. staff Battelle Columbus Labs., 1956—, research leader, 1974—, mgr. physico-chem. systems, 1976—; mem. faculty Ohio State U., 1963—, prof. ceramic and nuclear engring., 1977—. Author. Served to lt. (j.g.) USNR, 1951-54. Recipient Merit award NASA, 1971, citations Dept. Energy, AEC, ERDA. Mem. Am. Soc. Mass Spectrometry, Keramos, Sigma Xi. Patentee in field. Home: 4249 Haughn Rd Grove City OH 43123 Office: 505 King Ave Columbus OH 43201

ALEXANDER, CECIL ABRAHAM, architect; b. Atlanta, Mar. 14, 1918; s. Cecil Abraham and Julia (Moses) A.; m. Hermione Weil, Jan. 20, 1943; children: Therese, Judith, Douglas. Student, Ga. Inst. Tech., 1936; A.B., Yale, 1940, Mass. Inst. Tech., 1941; M. Arch., Harvard, 1947. Partner Alexander & Rothschild (architects), Atlanta, 1949-58; chmn. bd. Finch, Alexander, Barnes, Rothschild & Paschal, Architects and Engrs., Inc., Atlanta, 1958—; chmn. bd. A.S.D. Inc.; interior design service; architect Ga. Power Bldg., 1st Nat. Bank, both Atlanta, Cin. Riverfront Stadium, Coca-Cola Internat. Hdqrs., Sci. Atlanta Hdqrs. U.S. Pavilion Expo '82, So. Bell Hdqrs.; Chmn. Atlanta Citizens Adv. Com. Urban Renewal, 1958-60; vice chmn. Atlanta Met. Planning Commn., 1962—; chmn. Ga. Fgn. Trade Zone Corp. Past vice chmn. Community Council, Atlanta, Ga.; Mem. Mayor's Adv. Com. Race Relations, Nat. Citizens Com. Community Relations; chmn. Atlanta chpt. Am. Jewish Com., 1963; chmn. housing resources com. City of Atlanta; past chmn. com. Yale Sch. Architecture; pres., founder Resurgens Atlanta; v.p. Atlanta Symphony Orch.; Mem. Yale Nat. Alumni Bd., 1963; bd. dirs., exec. com. Clark Coll.; past bd. dirs. Marist High Sch., Atlanta. Served to lt. col. USMCR, World War II. Decorated Air medal, D.F.C.; Recipient Brotherhood award NCCJ, 1973; Archdiocesan Medal of St. Paul, 1980. Fellow AIA (pres. Ga. 1957, Ivan Allen award); mem. Atlanta C. of C. (dir.). Home: 2322 Mt Paran Rd Atlanta GA 30327 Office: Suite 1400 Equitable Bldg 100 Peachtree St NW Atlanta GA 30303

ALEXANDER, CHARLES THOMAS, journalism educator; b. Mpls., Sept. 21, 1928; s. Charles Thomas and Mary (Stinson) A.; m. Elizabeth Jean Brown, Dec. 29, 1951; children: Elizabeth Stinson, Lucy Bruce. A.B., Duke, 1950; student, Boston U. Sch. Theology, 1953-55; M.S. in Journalism, Columbia, 1956. With Stinson Bros. Dry Goods Co., Mt. Vernon, Ind., 1950-51, Washington Star, 1956-61; mng. editor Wilmington (Del.) Morning News, 1961-63, Wilmington Morning News and Eve. Jour., 1963-66, Dayton (Ohio) Jour. Herald, 1966-68, editor, 1968-71, editor and pub., 1971-75; asst. dean, prof. Medill Sch. Journalism, Northwestern U., 1975—. Served with AUS, 1951-53. Mem. Sigma Delta Chi, Phi Kappa Psi. Presbyn. Home: 1312 Knox Pl Alexandria VA 22304 Office: 1333 F St NW Washington DC 20004

ALEXANDER, CHARLES WYLIE, marketing executive; b. Orange, N.J., Nov. 22, 1939; s. Charles Wylie and Evelyn (Sinclair) A.; 1 son, Jeffrey Sinclair. B.S., A.B. in Econs., Lafayette Coll., 1962. Vice pres. Young & Rubicam, Inc., N.Y.C., 1972-79, sr. v.p., 1980-82; ptnr. Venture Mktg. Internat., Summit, N.J., 1983—. Served as 1st lt. Inf. U.S. Army, 1962-64. Republican. Presbyterian. Clubs: Yale (N.Y.C.); Queen City (Cin.). Address: 200 Kent Place Blvd Summit NJ 07901

ALEXANDER, CLIFFORD L., JR., management consultant, lawyer, former secretary of army; b. N.Y.C., Sept. 21, 1933; s. Clifford L. and Edith (McAllister) A.; m. Adele Logan, July 11, 1959; children—Elizabeth, Mark Clifford. A.B. cum laude, Harvard, 1955; LL.B., Yale U., 1958; LL.D. (hon.), Malcolm X Coll., 1972, Morgan State U., 1978, Wake Forest U., 1978, U. Md., 1980, Atlanta U., 1982. Bar: N.Y. 1960, U.S. Supreme Ct 1960, D.C. 1960. Asst. to dist. atty., N.Y. County, 1959-61; exec. dir. Manhattanville Hamilton Grange (neighborhood conservation project), 1961-62; exec. program dir. HARYOU, Inc., 1962-63, also pvt. practice law, N.Y.C., 1962-63; mem. staff Nat. Security Council, 1963- 64; dep. spl. asst. to Pres. Johnson, 1964-65, assoc. spl. counsel, 1965-66, dep. spl. counsel, 1966-67; chmn. Equal Employment Opportunity Commn., 1967-69; partner firm Arnold & Porter, 1969-75, Verner, Liipfert, Bernhard, McPherson & Alexander, 1975-76; sec. army, 1977-80; pres. Alexander & Assocs., Inc. (cons.), Washington, 1981—; dir. Pa. Power & Light Co., Dreyfus Third Century Fund., Dreyfus Gen. Money Market Fund, Dreyfus Common Stock Fund, Dreyfus Govt. Securities Fund, Dreyfus Tax Exempt Fund, MCI Corp.; adj. prof. Georgetown U.; prof. Howard U., Washington.; Mem. Pres.'s Commn. on Income Maintenance Programs, 1967-68; Pres.'s spl. ambassador to the Independence of Swaziland, 1968; mem. Pres.' Commn. for Observation Human Rights Yr., 1968; bd. dirs. Mex.-Am. Legal Def. and Ednl. Fund, NAACP Legal Def. and Ednl. Fund; bd. overseers Harvard U., 1969-75; trustee Atlanta U. Host, co-producer: TV program Cliff Alexander: Black on White, 1971-74. Served with AUS, 1958-59. Named hon. citizen, Kansas City, Mo., 1965; recipient Ames award Harvard, 1955; Frederick Douglass award, 1970; Outstanding Civilian Service award Dept. Army, 1980; Disting. Public Service award Dept. Def., 1981; others. Mem. Am., D.C. bar assns. Club: Reveille (N.Y.C.) (Annual Outstanding Achievement award 1966). Home: 512 A St SE Washington DC 20003 Office: 400 C St NE Washington DC 20002

ALEXANDER, DENISE, actress, photography journalist, writer; b. L.I., N.Y., Nov. 11, 1945; d. Alec and Helen Madeleine (Rowe) A. Student, UCLA, 1965. Freelance TV, radio, film and stage performer, 1953-67; appeared: Broadway prodn. Children's Hour, 1955, Crime in the Streets, 1960; film Under the Yum Yum Tree, 1965; TV series The Virginian, 1962-67; played role of Susan Martin on NBC-TV's: Days of Our Lives serial, 1967-73; plays role of Dr. Lesley Webber, ABC-TV's: Gen. Hospital, 1973—; photo journalist; contbr. to: nat. mags. including Jack and Jill. Recipient Ann. Readers' Poll award for Best Actress, Daytime TV mag. (3). Mem. Screen Actors Guild, AFTRA, Actors Equity Assn., Hollywood Acad. TV Arts and Scis., Actors and Others for Animals, Cousteau Soc., Fund for Animals, Neighbors of Watts, Filmex Film Soc., Wild Horse Organized Assistance, Pi Beta Phi, Zeta Phi Eta. Address: care Creative Artists Agy Inc 1888 Century Park E Suite 1400 Los Angeles CA 90067 *

ALEXANDER, DENTON EUGENE, educator; b. Potomac, Ill., Dec. 18, 1917; s. Jesse and Mary (Selsor) A.; m. Elizabeth Dale Bowman, Nov. 4, 1943. Student, Ill. State U., 1935-37; B.S., U. Ill., 1941, Ph.D., 1950. Tchr. elem. schs., Vermilion County, Ill., 1935-37; instr. U.S. Air Corps, Chanute Field, Rantoul, Ill., 1941-42, Lincoln (Nebr.) Air Base, 1942-43; prodn. supr. Manhattan Project, Oak Ridge, 1943-47; research asst. U. Ill., 1947-51, prof. plant breeding dept. agronomy, 1961—; cons. in field. Recipient Paul A Funk award U. Ill., 1971. Mem. Crop Sci. Soc. Am., Am. Soc. Agronomy (Crop Sci. award 1970), Soviet Acad. Agrl. Scis. (fgn.), Assn. Genetic Socs. Yugoslavia, Phi Kappa Phi. Home: 701 W Pennsylvania Ave Urbana IL 61801 Office: Dept Agronomy U Ill 1102 S Goodwin Ave Urbana IL 61801

ALEXANDER, DONALD CRICHTON, lawyer; b. Pine Bluff, Ark., May 22, 1921; s. William Crichton and Ella Temple (Fox) A.; m. Margaret Louise Savage, Oct. 9, 1946; children: Robert C., James M. B.A. with honors, Yale U., 1942; LL.B. magna cum laude, Harvard U., 1948; LL.D., St. Thomas Inst., 1975. Bar: D.C. 1949, Ohio 1954, N.Y. 1978. Assoc. Covington & Burling, Washington, 1948-54, Taft, Stettinius & Hollister, Cin., 1954-56, ptnr., 1956-66, Dinsmore, Shohl, Coates & Deupree, Cin., 1966-73; commr. IRS, 1973-77; mem. Commn. on Fed. Paperwork, 1975-77; ptnr. Olwine, Connelly, Chase, O'Donnell & Weyher, N.Y.C., Washington, 1977-79, Morgan, Lewis & Bockius, N.Y.C. and Washington, 1979—; mem. adv. group to commr. IRS, 1969-70; cons. Treasury Dept., 1970-72; mem. adv. bd. NYU Tax Inst., 1969-73, 77—, Tax Mgmt., Inc., 1968-73, 77—; co-chmn. bd. advs. NYU/IRS Continuing Profl. Edn. Program. Author: The Arkansas Plantation, 1943; also articles on fed. taxation. Served to capt. AUS, 1942-45. Decorated Silver Star, Bronze Star. Mem. ABA (vice chmn. taxation sect. 1967-68), Am. Law Inst. (tax adv. group), U.S. C. of C. (taxation com. 1977—). Clubs: Cin. Country; Chevy Chase (Md.); Metropolitan (Washington); Nantucket Yacht (Mass.); Mill Reef (Antigua, B.W.I.); Yale of N.Y. Home: 2801 New Mexico Ave NW Washington DC 20007 Office: 1800 M St NW Washington DC 20036

ALEXANDER, DUANE FREDERICK, pediatrician, research administrator; b. Balt., Aug. 11, 1940; s. Fred Lucas and Christiana H. (Shawacre) A.; m. Marianne Ellis, June 23, 1963; children: Keith Duane, Kristin Marianne. B.S., Pa. State U., 1962; M.D., Johns Hopkins U., 1966. Diplomate: Am. Bd. Pediatrics. Intern Johns Hopkins Hosp., Balt., 1966-67, resident, 1967-68, fellow, 1970-71; commd. officer USPHS, 1968—, now capt.; clin. assoc. Nat. Inst. Child Health and Human Devel., NIH, Bethesda, Md., 1968-70, asst. to sci. dir., 1971-74, asst. to dir., 1978-82, dep. dir., 1982—; staff pediatrician Nat. Commn. for Protection of Human Subjects of Research, Bethesda, 1974-78. Contbr. articles to profl. jours. Recipient Commendation medal USPHS, 1970. Fellow Am. Acad. Pediatrics, Soc. Devel. Pediatrics. Methodist. Home: 4713 Manor Ln Ellicott City MD 21043 Office: NIH 9000 Rockville Pike Bethesda MD 20205

ALEXANDER, EBEN, JR., neurological surgeon; b. Knoxville, Tenn., Sept. 14, 1913; s. Eben and Elizabeth (MacMath) A.; m. Elizabeth West, Oct. 8, 1942; children: Jean Alexander Mortimer, Eben III, Elizabeth MacMath, Phyllis. A.B., U. N.C., 1935; M.D. cum laude, Harvard U., 1939. Diplomate: Am. Bd. Neurol. Surgery. Intern Peter Bent Brigham Hosp., also Children's Hosp., Boston, 1939-41, resident in neurosurgery, 1947-48, Children's Hosp., 1941-42; surg. fellow Harvard U. Med. Sch.; neurosurg. fellow Children's Hosp.; also jr. asso. neurosurgery Peter Bent Brigham Hosp., 1946-47; asst. in surgery Harvard U. Med. Sch., 1947-48; resident in neurosurgery Toronto (Ont., Can.) Gen. Hosp., 1948-49; mem. faculty Bowman Gray Sch. Medicine, Wake Forest U., Winston-Salem, N.C., 1949—, prof. neurosurgery, 1954—, head sect. neurosurgery, 1949-78; chief profl. services N.C. Bapt. Hosp., Winston-Salem, 1953-73, mem. staff, 1949—; bd. sci. counselors Nat. Inst. Neurol. Disease and Blindness, 1961-64, mem. program project com., 1967-71, mem. neurol. sci. research com., 1962-66; adv. com. Clin. Info. Center, 1972—; mem. brain tumor study group Nat. Cancer Inst., 1968-81; past pres. United Med. Research Found., N.C.; mem. joint adminstrv. bd. N.C. Bapt. Hosp.-Bowman Gray Med. Sch., 1972—; mem. Nat. Bd. Med. Examiners, 1980—, liaison com. med. edn., 1981—. Author numerous articles in field.; Editorial bd.: Jour. Neurosurgery, 1961-70; chmn., 1969-70; assoc. editor: Surg. Neurology. Trustee Centenary United Meth. Ch., Winston-Salem; permanent pres. Harvard U. Med. Sch. Class 1939. Served to maj. M.C. AUS, 1942-46. Decorated Bronze Star. Fellow A.C.S. (v.p. 1976-77); mem. Am. Acad. Neurol. Surgeons (sec.-treas. 1953-57, v.p. 1962-63, pres. 1980-81), Am. Acad. Neurology (asso.), AAAS, Harvey Cushing Soc. (pres. 1966), AMA (chmn. sect. council neurosurgery 1969-74, del. interspltly. adv. bd. 1971-81, vice chmn. interspltly. adv. bd. 1976-78, chmn. 1979-80, mem. council on med. edn. 1978—), Am. Assn. Neurol. Surgeons, Harvard Med. Alumni Assn. (pres. 1980-81), N.C. Surg. Assn., Assn. Research Nervous and Mental Disease, Mass., Forsyth County, N.C. med. socs., Neurosurg. Soc. Am., Council Med. Splty. Socs. (alt. del. 1976-77), Congress Neurol. Surgeons (hon.), Neurosurg. Travel Club, N.C., So. neurosurg. socs., Soc. Neurol. Surgery (pres. 1972-73), Deutsche Gesselschaft für Neurochirurgie (corr.), Alpha Omega Alpha, Nu Sigma Nu, Sigma Alpha Epsilon. Methodist. Clubs: Rotary (Winston-Salem) (past pres.); Torch, Old Town, Forsyth Assembly (pres. 1977). Home: 1941 Georgia Ave Winston-Salem NC 27104 Office: 300 S Hawthorne Rd Winston-Salem NC 27103

ALEXANDER, EDWARD LAWSON, physical chemist, educator; b. Lewiston, Maine, Oct. 22, 1925; s. Irving Edward and Sarah (Drew) A.; children: Bruce E., Steven M., Jeffrey D., Beth L. B.S., U. Maine, 1950, M.S., 1951; Ph.D. in Phys. Chemistry, Vanderbilt U., 1955. Research asso. nuclear and radiation chemistry Knolls Atomic Power Lab., Gen. Electric Co., 1955-57; asso. prof., asst. dir. reactor project, radiation safety officer Ga. Inst. Tech., 1957-58; mgr. radiol. scis., indsl. reactor labs. Columbia U., 1958-62; prof., dir. radiation sci. center Rutgers U., 1962-67; prof. radiol. scis., dean Grad. Sch., Lowell Tech. Inst., 1967-76; dean research, dir. U. Lowell Research Found., 1976-80; prof., coordinator radiol. scis. program U. Lowell, 1980—; chmn. Conf. Radiol. Health, 1964-65. Mem. Health Physics Soc. (pres. Greater N.Y. chpt. 1962). Office: 110 Pinanski Center U Lowell Physics Dept Lowell MA 01854

ALEXANDER, EDWARD RUSSELL, disease research administrator; b. Chgo., June 15, 1928; s. Russell Green and Ethelyn Satterlee (Abel) A. Ph.B., U. Chgo., 1948, B.S., 1950, M.D., 1953. Intern Cin. Gen. Hosp.; chief surveillance sect. Communicable Disease Center, Atlanta, 1955-57, 59-60; resident, instr. dept. pediatrics U. Chgo., 1954-55, 57-59; asst. prof. dept. preventive medicine and dept. pediatrics U. Wash., Seattle, 1961-65, asso. prof., 1965-69, prof., 1969-79, chmn. dept. epidemiology, 1970-75; prof. dept. pediatrics U. Ariz., Tucson, 1979-83; dir. research br., venereal diseases control div. Centers for Disease Control, Atlanta, 1983—. Contbr. articles to profl. jours. Markle scholar, 1962-67. Mem. Am. Acad. Pediatrics, Am. Pediatric Soc., Am. Pub. Health Assn., Assn. Tchrs. Preventive Medicine, Am. Epidemiol. Soc., Soc. Epidemiol. Research, Internat. Epidemiol. Soc., King County Med. Soc. Office: Research Br. Venereal Disease Control Div Centers for Disease Control Atlanta GA 30333

ALEXANDER, GEORGE F., writer; b. Bklyn., July 17, 1934; s. George E. and Justine E. (O'Malley) A.; m. Daryl P. Orians, Feb. 1969; children—Meghan, Scott; children by previous marriage—Donna, Geraldine. B.S. in Journalism, Fordham U., 1956. With Aviation Week mag. McGraw-Hill, 1960-67, Cape Canaveral bur. chief, 1962-67; with Newsweek mag., 1967-72, sci. editor, 1968-72; sci. writer Los Angeles Times, 1972—. Served with USAF, 1957-60. Recipient AAAS/Westinghouse Sci. Writing award, 1974. Mem. Nat. Assn. Sci. Writers (pres. 1976-78). Office: Los Angeles Times Times Mirror Sq Los Angeles CA 90053

ALEXANDER, GEORGE JONATHON, university dean, legal educator; b. Berlin, Germany, Mar. 8, 1931; s. Walter and Sylvia (Grill) A.; m. Katharine Violet Sziklai, Sept. 6, 1958; children: Susan Katina, George Jonathon II. A.B. with maj. honors, U. Pa., 1953, J.D. cum laude, 1959; LL.M., Yale U., 1965, J.S.D., 1969. Bar: Ill. 1960, N.Y. 1961, Calif. 1974. Instr. law, Bigelow fellow U. Chgo., 1959-60; instr. internat. relations Naval Res. Officers Sch., Forrest Park, Ill., 1959-60; prof. law Syracuse U. Coll. Law, 1960-70, assoc. dean, 1968-69; vis. prof. law U. So. Calif., 1963; prof. law, dean U. Santa Clara (Calif.) Law Sch., 1970—; cons. in field. Author: Civil Rights, U.S.A., Public Schools, 1963, Honesty and Competition, 1967, Jury Instructing on Medical Issues, 1966, Cases and Materials on Space Law, 1971, The Aged and the Need for Surrogate Management, 1972, Commercial Torts, 1973, U.S. Antitrust Laws, 1980, also articles, chpts. in books, one film. Dir. Domestic and Internat. Bus. Problems Honors Clinic, Syracuse U., 1966-69, Regulations in Space Project, 1968-70; ednl. cons. Comptroller Gen., U.S., 1977—; dir., mem. exec. com. U.S. assn. Internat. Inst. Space Laws, 1968-83, Nat. Sr. Citizens Law Center, 1983—; co-founder Am. Assn. Abolition Involuntary Mental Hospitalization, 1970, dir., 1970—. Served with USN, 1953-56. U.S. Navy scholar U. Pa., 1949-52; Law Boards scholar, 1956-59; Sterling fellow Yale, 1964-65; recipient Ralph E. Kharas Civil Liberties award, 1970. Mem. ABA (Commn. on Legal Problems of Elderly), N.Y. State Bar Assn., Calif. Bar Assn. (first chmn. com. legal problems of aging), Assn. Am. Law Schs., Soc. Am. Law Tchrs. (dir., pres. 1979), AAUP (chpt. pres. 1962), N.Y. Civil Liberties Union (chpt. pres. 1965, dir., v.p. 1966-70), Am. Acad. Polit. and Social Sci., Order of Coif, Justinian Honor Soc., Phi Alpha Delta (chpt. faculty adviser 1967-70). Home: 11600 Summit Wood Rd Los Altos Hills CA 94022 Office: Univ Santa Clara Santa Clara CA 95053 *I think a primary purpose of law is the protection of individual rights. That requires disproportionate attention to the interests of groups not in the mainstream of our society.*

ALEXANDER, HAROLD, bioengineer, educator; b. N.Y.C., Nov. 12, 1940; s. Jack and Freda (Koltun) A.; m. Sheila M. Eisner, Dec. 20, 1964; children: Robin, Andrea. B.S., NYU, 1962, M.S., 1963, Ph.D., 1967. Asst. research scientist NYU, Bronx, 1966-67, assoc. research scientist, 1967-68; asst. prof. Stevens Inst. Tech., Hoboken, N.J., 1968-71, assoc. prof., 1971-77, co-dir. med. engring. lab., 1973-77, head lab. balloon tech., 1968-74; assoc. prof. dept. surgery, dir. G.L. Schultz Labs. for Orthopedic Research N.J. Med. Sch., Newark, 1977-81, prof., 1981—; lectr. in pediatrics Mt. Sinai Sch. of Medicine, N.Y.C., 1975-77; cons. Johnson & Johnson Research Labs., New Brunswick, N.J., 1975-76; vis. prof. Coll. Engring., Rutgers U., 1975-76; adv. on fabricatio of balloons USAF, 1968-74; v.p. C.A.S., Inc., 1974-78, pres., 1978—. Contbr. articles to profl. jours., chpts. to books; researcher cardiovascular and orthopedic bioengring. Mem. ASME, Soc. Biomaterials, N.J. Orthopedic Soc., Orthopedic Research Soc., ASTM. Instrumental in development of new system for measurement of infant blood pressure and absorbable composites for orthopedic implant use. Home: 47 Elmwood Pl Shore Hills NJ 07078 Office: Sect Orthopaedic Surgery NJ Med Sch 100 Bergen St G-574 Newark NJ 07103

ALEXANDER, HERBERT E., political scientist; b. Waterbury, Conn., Dec. 21, 1927; s. Nathan and Pearl (Shub) A.; m. Nancy Frances Greenfield, Dec. 5, 1953; children: Michael David, Andrew Steven, Kenneth Bruce. B.A., U. N.C., 1949; M.A., U. Conn., 1951; Ph.D., Yale U., 1958. Asso. dir. adminstrn. officer money in politics research project U. N.C. at Chapel Hill, 1954-55; instr. Princeton U., 1956-58; dir. Citizens' Research Found., Princeton, 1958—; prof. polit. sci. U. So. Calif., 1978—; exec. dir. Pres.'s Com. on Campaign Costs, Washington, 1961-62; cons. Pres. U.S., 1962-64, House Adminstrn. Com., 1966-67, Comptroller Gen. U.S. and Office Fed. Elections at GAO, 1972-73, Senate Select Com. on Presdl. Campaign Activities, 1973—; vis. lectr. Princeton U., 1965, U. Pa., Phila., 1967-68, Yale U., 1977; cons. N.J. Election Law Enforcement Commn., 1973-78, N.Y. State Bd. Elections, 1974-76, Ill. Bd. Elections, 1974-75, others. Author: Studies in Money in Politics, vol. 1, 1965, vol. 2, 1970, vol. 3, 1974; editor: Money in Politics, 1972, Financing the 1976 Election, 1979, Financing the 1980 Election, 1983, Financing Politics, 1976, 2d edit., 1980, 3d edit., 1984, Campaign Money, 1976. Served with AUS, 1946-47. Mem. Am. Polit. Sci. Assn., Nat. Mcpl. League, Pi Sigma Alpha. Home: 10210 Autumn Leaf Circle Los Angeles CA 90077 Office: Univ So Calif Research Annex 3716 S Hope St Los Angeles CA 90007

ALEXANDER, HOLMES, ret. journalist; b. Parkersburg, W.Va., Jan. 29, 1906; s. Charles Butler and Margaret (Moss) A.; m. Mary Barksdale, June 24, 1933 (dec.); children: Hunter Holmes, Peter Barksdale, Mary Madge Alexander Dufour; m. Rosalind H. White, Nov. 3, 1978. B.A., Princeton U., 1928; postgrad, Trinity Coll., Cambridge, Eng., 1928-29; Litt.D., Salem (W.Va.) Coll., 1971. Mem. Md. Gen. Assembly, 1931-35; syndicated columnist McNaught Syndicate, N.Y.C., 1947-81, ret., 1981. Author: American Talleyrand: Life of Martin Van Buren, 1935, The Proud Pretender: Life of Aaron Burr, 1937, American Nabob, 1939, Dust in the Afternoon, 1940, Selina, 1942, Tomorrow's Air Age, 1953, The Famous Five, 1958, Shall Do No Murder, 1959, West of Washington, 1962, The Equivocal Men, 1964, The Spirit of '76, 1966, Between the Stirrup and the Ground, 1967, Pen and Politics, 1970, With Friends Possess'd, 1970, To Covet Honor: Life of Alexander Hamilton, The Hidden Years of Stonewall Jackson, 1981, Never Lose a War, 1983. Served with Md. N.G., 1941-42; maj. USAAF, 1942-45. Recipient George Washington Honor medal Freedoms Found. at Valley Forge, 1973; decorated Army Air medal. Mem. Soc. Lees Va., Soc. Cin., Overseas Writers Assn., Sigma Delta Chi. Episcopalian. Clubs: 1925 F St, National Press, Metropolitan (Washington). Home: 922 25th St NW Washington DC 20037

ALEXANDER, JAMES ALLEN, thoracic and cardiovascular surgeon, educator; b. Charlotte, N.C., May 8, 1940; s. Leon George and Virginia Grace (Young) A.; m. Catherine Ann Wellington, June 12, 1965; children: Kelly, Katie, Kimberly. B.S., Davidson Coll., 1962; M.D., Duke U., 1966. Diplomate: Am. Bd. Surgery, Am. Bd. Thoracic Surgery. Thoracic resident Duke U., Durham, N.C., 1976; asst. chief thoracic surgery service Wilford Hall-USAF Med. Ctr., 1975-76; clin. instr. U. Tex., San Antonio, 1974-76; asst. prof. surgery U. Pa., Phila., 1976-77; assoc. chief thoracic surgery Children's Hosp., Phila., 1976-77; assoc. prof., div. chief thoracic and cardiovascular surgery U. Fla., Gainesville, 1977-81, prof., div. chief, 1981—; program dir. Thoracic Surgery Dir.'s Assn., Gainesville, 1977—. Served to 1t. col. USAF, 1974-76. Recipient Phyusicians Recognition award AMA, 1980, Scientific award ACA, 1981, 82. Fellow Am. Coll. Cardiology, Am. Coll. Chest Physicians, ACS; mem. Thoracic Surg. Assn., Thoracic Surgery Dirs. Assn., Fla. Soc. Thoacic and Cardiovascular Surgeons (pres.). Presbyterian. Club: Gainesville Gold and Country. Home: 6200 SW 36th Way Gainesville FL 32608 Office: Div Thoracic and Cardiovascular Surgery U Fla Coll Medicine PO Box J286 Gainesville FL 32610

ALEXANDER, JAMES CREW, mathematics educator; b. Zanesville, Ohio, Mar. 22, 1942; s. James E. and Jean (Crew) A.; m. Rosemary Keene, Apr. 1, 1972; children: Stacey, Blythe. B.A., Johns Hopkins U., 1964, Ph.D., 1968. Instr. Johns Hopkins U., Balt., 1967-69; research assoc. U. Md., College Park, 1969-70, asst. prof. math., 1970-73, assoc. prof., 1973-79, prof., 1979—. Mem. Am. Math. Soc., Soc. Indsl. and Applied Math. Office: Dept Math Univ Md College Park MD 21043

ALEXANDER, JAMES ECKERT, editor; b. Zanesville, Ohio, Sept. 4, 1913; s. James Rufus and Nellie (Hunter) A.; m. Jean Kathryn Crew, July 1, 1940; children: James C., Jean (Mrs. Joseph D. Small III), John R. A.B., Washington and Jefferson Coll., 1935. Reporter Akron (Ohio) Beacon Jour., 1937, 47-48, Pitts. Press, 1937-38; editor Zanesville News, 1939-42; Sunday editor Mpls. Star-Jour. and Tribune, 1942-45; pub. relations exec. Minn. and Ont. Paper Co., Mpls., 1946; writer, editor Pitts. Post-Gazette, 1949-65, city editor, 1965-72, asst. mng. editor, 1972-73, mng. editor, 1973-79, asst. to pub., 1979—, book editor, 1950—; prof. U. Pitts., 1963-65; book critic sta. KDKA-TV, Pitts., 1963-67. Mem. Beta Theta Pi (dist. chief 1942-46). Democrat. Presbyn. Club: Montour Heights Country (Pitts.). Home: 633 Rock Springs Rd Pittsburgh PA 15228 Office: 50 Blvd of Allies Pittsburgh PA 15222

ALEXANDER, JAMES HENRY, insurance broker, state official; b. McKenzie, Tenn., Jan. 2, 1922; s. E. Marvin and Lillis (McElroy) A.; m. Lola Diuguid Chesnut, Dec. 21, 1945; children: Anne Elizabeth, James Henry, Jean. Student, Bethel Coll., 1939-41; B.S. in Bus. Adminstrn, U. Tenn., 1943. In gen. ins. bus., McKenzie, 1946—; treas. State of Tenn., Nashville, 1963-67; gov.'s staff dir. for indsl. devel., 1967-71; exec. dir. Insurors of Tenn., 1971—; dir. McKenzie Banking Co.; Mem. McKenzie Sch. Bd., 1947-64; pres. Tenn. Sch. Bd. Assn., 1961; chmn. Tenn. Heart Fund, 1963-64. Sec. Tenn. Bd. Elections, 1953-62; campaign mgr. Gov. Frank Clement for gov., 1962, for U.S. Senate, 1964; alternate del. Dem. Nat. Conv., 1956, 64, 68; mem. bus. council Bethel Coll.; mem. athletic bd. U. Tenn., Knoxville.; Trustee Lambuth Coll., Jackson, Tenn., 1967-75; pres. Tenn. Sports Hall of Fame, 1975. Served to lt. (j.g.) USNR, 1943-46. Mem. Insurors of Tenn. (v.p.), Tenn. Assn. Execs. (pres.), Am. Legion (dist. comdr. 1950, V.F.W.). Methodist. Clubs: Elk, Rotarian., Richland Country, Nashville City (Nashville). Home: 719 N Stonewall St McKenzie TN 38201 Office: PO Box 249 McKenzie TN 38201 also 174 N Main McKenzie TN 38201 also Suite 1412 Parkway Towers Nashville TN 37219

ALEXANDER, JAMES MARSHALL, JR., architect; b. Chattanooga, Apr. 11, 1921; s. James Marshall and Ruth (Slocum) A.; m. Alice Jane Chenoweth, Apr. 3, 1943; children—Carolyn Alexander Madison, Susan Alexander Davis, Richard M. B.S. in Architecture, U. Cin., 1943. Design planner Raymond Loewy Assocs., N.Y.C., 1942, 46-47; mem. faculty U. Cin., 1947—, prof. indsl. design, 1961—, head dept., 1963-76; dir. Design Research Collaborative, 1964-75, asso. dean, 1975—; pvt. practice architecture and design, Cin., 1952—; invited seminar lectr., USSR, 1976, East Ger., 1978. Author govt. contract reports on light-weight expandable air-transportable shelter systems. Bd. dirs. Charter Com. Cin. and Hamilton County, 1967-73. Served to 1st lt. CAC AUS, 1943-46. Grantee Kaufmann Found., 1973, NEA, 1972, 75. Fellow Indsl. Designers Soc. Am. (v.p. 1973-74, sec. 1975-77); mem. Am. Soc. Indsl. Designers, Indsl. Design Edn. Assn. (pres. 1961-63), Nat. Assn. Schs. Art. Democrat. Unitarian. Clubs: Cin. Torch (pres. 1960-61), Cin. Faculty (gov. 1977). Home: 124 Congress Run Rd Wyoming OH 45215 Office: College Design Architecture and Art University of Cincinnati Cincinnati OH 45221

ALEXANDER, JANE, actress; b. Boston, Oct. 28, 1939; d. Thomas Bartlett and Ruth (Pearson) Quigley; m. Robert Alexander, July 23, 1962 (div. 1969); 1 son, Jason; m. Edwin Sherin, Mar. 29, 1975. Student, Sarah Lawrence Coll., 1957-59, U. Edinburgh, 1959-60. Appeared prodns., Charles Playhouse Boston, 1964-65, Arena Stage, Washington, 1965-68, 70—, Am. Shakespeare Festival; plays include Major Barbara, Stratford, Conn., summers 1971-72; Broadway prodns. include Great White Hope, 1968-69 (Tony award, Drama Desk award, Theatre World award), 6 Rms Riv Vu, 1972-73, Find Your Way Home, 1974, Hamlet, 1975, The Heiress, 1976, First Monday in October, 1978, Goodbye Fidel, 1980, Monday After the Miracle, 1982; also appeared in plays The Time of Your Life, Plumstead Playhouse, Washington and Los Angeles, Present Laughter, 1975, The Master Builder, 1977, Losing Time, 1980, Antony and Cleopatra, 1981, Hedda Gobler, 1981; appeared in films Great White Hope, 1969, A Gunfight, 1970, The New Centurions, 1972, All the President's Men, 1976, The Betsy, 1978, Kramer vs. Kramer, 1979, Brubaker, 1980, Night Crossing, 1981, Testament, 1983; appeared in TV films Welcome Home Johny Bristol, 1971, Miracle on 34th St, 1973, Death Be Not Proud, 1974, Eleanor and Franklin, 1976, Eleanor and Franklin: The White House Years, 1977 (TV Critics Circle award), Lovey, 1977, A Question of Love, 1978, Playing For Time, 1980 (Emmy award), Calamity Jane: The Diary of a Frontier Woman, 1981, Dear Liar, 1981, Kennedy's Children, 1981; appeared in TV spl. A Circle of Children, 1977 (Recipient Antoinette Perry award 1969), Calamity Jane, 1984; author: (with Greta Jacobs) The Bluefish Cookbook, 1979-83; translator: (with Sam Engelstad) The Master Builder (Henrik Ibsen), 1978. Recipient Achievement in Dramatic Arts award St. Botolph Club, 1979, Israel Cultural award, 1982. Office: care William Morris Agy 1350 Ave of the Americas New York NY 10019

ALEXANDER, JOHN DAVID, JR., college president; b. Springfield, Tenn., Oct. 18, 1932; s. John David and Mary Agnes (McKinnon) A.; m. Catharine Coleman, Aug. 26, 1956; children: Catharine McKinnon, John David III, Julia Mary. B.A., Southwestern at Memphis, 1953; student, Louisville Presbyn. Theol. Sem., 1953-54; D.Phil. (Rhodes Scholar), Oxford (Eng.) U., 1957; LL.D., U. So. Calif., Occidental Coll., 1970, Centre Coll. of Ky., 1971; L.H.D., Loyola Marymount U., 1983. Assoc. prof. San Francisco Theol. Sem., 1957-65; pres. Southwestern at Memphis, 1965-69, Pomona Coll., Claremont, Calif., 1969—; Am. sec. Rhodes Scholarship Trust, 1981—; mem. commn. liberal learning Assn. Am. Colls., 1966-69, 1971-74; mem. commn. colls. So. Assn. Colls. and Schs., 1966-69; mem. Nat. Commn. on Acad. Tenure, 1971-72; dir. Gt. Western Fin. Corp.; Bd. dirs. Community TV of So. Calif., Louisville Presbyn. Theol. Sem., 1966-69; trustee Tchrs. Ins. and Annuity Assn., 1970—, Woodrow Wilson Nat. Fellowship Found., 1978—; bd. dirs. Am. Council on Edn., 1981—. Mem. Am. Oriental Soc., Soc. Bib. Lit., Soc. Religion in Higher Edn., Phi Beta Kappa Alumni in So. Calif. (pres. 1974-76), Omicron Delta Kappa, Sigma Nu. Clubs: Century (N.Y.C.); University, Calif. (Los Angeles); Bohemian (San Francisco).

ALEXANDER, JOHN DAVIS, lawyer; b. Holland Island, Md., May 10, 1899; s. Harvey George and Nancy Harper (Sheetz) A.; m. Mildred Lillian Ebelein, Nov. 2, 1946; children—Dorothy (Mrs. Joseph David Watson), John Davis. Now sr. partner firm Constable, Alexander, Daneker & Skeen; Balt. Instr. Law Sch. U. Balt., 1928-73. Served with USMCR, World War I. Clubs: Engineering, Barristers. Home: 11505 Manor Rd Glenarm MD 21057 Office: 1000 Maryland Trust Bldg Calvert and Redwood Sts Baltimore MD 21202

ALEXANDER, JOHN FRANK, tenor; b. Meridian, Miss.; s. Charles Curtis and Eva (Ogburn) A.; m. Sue Travis, Aug. 10, 1952; 1 dau., Cindy Sue. Student, Duke U., 1941-43; B.Mus., Cin. Conservatory Music, 1949; D.Performing Arts, U. Cin., 1968. Disting. prof. voice and opera U. Cin., 1974—. Tenor with, NBC TV Opera, 1956-59, N.Y.C. Opera, 1957-61; leading tenor, Met. Opera Co., 1961—; leading tenor with, Phila. Lyric Opera, Pitts. Opera, Ft. Worth Opera, New Orleans Opera, Vancouver (B.C., Can.) Opera, Vienna Staatsoper, Covent Garden, London, Vienna Volksoper, San Francisco Opera, Opera Co. Boston, Chgo. Lyric Opera, Houston Grand Opera, others; recording artist for, RCA Victor, Columbia, London records. Served with USAAF, 1944-46. Mem. Am. Guild Musical Artists (gov.). Congregationalist. Clubs: Dutch Treat (N.Y.C.); Manhasset Bay Yacht. Office: Columbia Artists Mgmt 165 W 57th St New York NY 10019 *

ALEXANDER, JOHN HARVEY, clergyman, former church association executive; b. Boston, Oct. 19, 1919; s. John and Elizabeth (Coffin) A.; m. Donna Eloise Estabrooke, June 27, 1943; children—John Kenneth, Karen Jean (Mrs. Thomas F. Hoffman), Margaret Jane, Elizabeth Ann. A.B., Bowdoin Coll., 1948; M.Div., Bangor Theol. Sem., 1951; D.D., Piedmont Coll., 1970. Ordained to ministry Congl. Ch., 1948, minister, Winthrop, Maine, 1943-49, Galewood Community Ch., Chgo., 1949-56; asso. minister 1st Congl. Ch., Wauwatosa, Wis., 1956-62, minister, Marshalltown, Iowa, 1962-67; moderator organizational meeting Nat. Assn. Congl. Christian Chs., Detroit, 1955, chmn. exec. com., 1960-61, asso. exec. sec., 1967-69, exec. sec., 1969-75; minister Congl. Ch., Sun City, Ariz., 1976—; Del. Internat. Congl. Council, Rotterdam, Holland, 1962; supr. Nat. Pilgrim Fellowship Youth Work-camp to Greece, 1964; pres. Marshall County (Iowa) Council Chs., 1965-66; sec.-treas., bd. dirs. Com. for Continuation of Congl. Christian Chs., 1962—; adminstrv. visitor to World-Wide overseas missions, 1969; pres. Sun City Area Ministers Assn., 1978-80; Chmn. 36th ward Citizens' Adv. Council, Chgo., 1954-56. Co-pres.: Internat. Congl. Fellowship, 1975-79; mem. exec. com., 1975—. Republican. Clubs: Rotarian (bd. dirs. 1964-67), Mason (32 deg.). Active nat., internat. efforts to preserve free chs. as expressed in policy, practices of Cong. Christian Chs. Home: 10701 Garnette Dr Sun City AZ 85373 Office: 18401 99th Ave PO Box 1596 Sun City AZ 85372

ALEXANDER, JOHN HEALD, lawyer; b. Denver, Nov. 15, 1904; s. Harry Heald and Margaret (McGowan) A.; m. Edna Perkins, Aug. 28, 1926; children: John Heald, Judith, Anne. A.B., Yale, 1926, LL.B., 1928. Bar: N.Y. 1929, N.J. 1943, D.C. 1966. Sr. ptnr. firm Mudge Rose Guthrie Alexander & Ferdon, N.Y.C.; dir. Straight Enterprises, Inc.; Chmn. Pres.'s Task Force on Bus. Tax, 1969-70. Mem. Am., N.Y. State bar assns., Assn. Bar City N.Y., Am. Law Inst. Clubs: Down Town Assn., Yale (N.Y.C.); Baltusrol Golf (Springfield, N.J.). Home: 1 Beekman Pl New York NY 10022 Office: 20 Broad St New York NY 10005

ALEXANDER, JOHN MACMILLAN, JR., chemistry educator; b. Columbia, Mo., Aug. 17, 1931; s. John Macmillan and Victoria (Holladay) A.; m. Betty Jo Linton, Aug. 1, 1953; children—Mary Jo, John Macmillan III, Frank Linton, James Holladay. B.S., Davidson Coll., 1953; Ph.D., Mass. Inst. Tech., 1956. Research asso. Mass. Inst. Tech., 1956-57; research chemist Lawrence Radiation Lab., Berkeley, Calif., 1957-63; asso. prof. chemistry State U. N.Y. at Stony Brook, 1963-67, prof., 1968—, chmn. dept., 1970-72; AEC-ERDA, Dept. Energy researcher, 1964—; research collaborator Brookhaven Nat. Lab., 1964—; chmn. Gordon Research Conf. on Nuclear Chemistry, 1966; mem. exec. com. Berkeley Superhilac Accelerator, 1975-78; vis. scientist Centre d'Etudes Nucléaire, Bordeaux, France, 1974; vis. prof. Centre d'Etudes Nucleaires de Bordeaux-Gradignan and Institut de Physique Nucléaire, Orsay, France, 1978; program adv. com. Tandem Van De Graaff Accelerator, Brookhaven Nat. Lab., 1977—. Assoc. editor: Am. Chem. Soc. Monographs, 1968-69; Contbr. articles to profl. jours. Dupont teaching fellow, 1955-56; Sloan fellow, 1964-67; Guggenheim fellow Laboratoire de Chimie Nucléaire, Orsay, France, 1969-70. Mem. Am. Chem. Soc., Am. Phys. Soc., Phi Beta Kappa. Democrat. Club: Midget Ocean Racing (L.I. Sound champion 1973-75). Research on radioactivity, high-energy nuclear reactions: fission, spallation, and fragmentation; heavy ion reactions: elastic scattering, complete fusion and reaction cross sects., energy and spin dissipation, evaporative deexcitation. Home: 14 Highwood Rd Setauket NY 11733 Office: Dept Chemistry State Univ New York Stony Brook NY 11794

ALEXANDER, JOSEPH KUNKLE, JR., physicist; b. Staunton, Va., Jan. 9, 1940; s. Joseph Kunkle and Charlotte (Harper) A.; m. Diana Lenore Titolo, Sept. 22, 1962; children—Kathryn, Stephen, David. B.S. in Physics, Coll. William and Mary, 1960, M.A., 1962. Physicist Nat. Bur. Standards, 1960; research asst. Coll. William and Mary, 1960-62; physicist Goddard Space Flight Center, NASA, Greenbelt, Md., 1962—, head planetary magnetospheres br., 1976—; vis. scientist U. Colo., 1973-74. Contbr. articles to sci. and tech. jours. Mem. Am. Geophys. Union, Internat. Union Radio Sci., Internat. Astron. Union. Office: NASA Goddard Space Flight Center Code 695 Greenbelt MD 20771

ALEXANDER, JUDD HARRIS, paper company executive; b. Owatonna, Minn., Mar. 23, 1925; s. Mark Hastings and Veta Enola (Harris) A.; m. Theo Mary Paltzer, May 19, 1956; children: Morah Lee, Duncan McIndoe, Todd Stewart. B.A., Carleton Coll., 1949; postgrad. in bus, Harvard U., 1967. Co-founder Nu-Bilt Co., Owatonna, dir., 1942-71; sec. in pres.'s office, salesman Marathon Corp., Rothschild, Wis., 1949-57; with Am. Can Co., Greenwich, Conn., 1957—, v.p., gen. mgr. spl. products packaging, 1972-73, sr. v.p. group exec. packaging, 1974-75, sr. v.p. office of chmn., 1975-81, exec. v.p. paper sector, 1981-82; exec. v.p. James River Corp., Norwalk, Conn, 1982—; chmn. Paperboard Packaging Council, 1976-78, Can Mfrs. Inst., 1978-80, Solid Waste Council of Paper Industry, 1977—; adj. prof. environ. sci. SUNY, Syracuse, 1979—. Contbr. articles to profl. and bus. jours., including Wall Street Jour., N.Y. Times, Industry Week. Trustee Carleton Coll., 1973—, Am. Shakespeare Theater, 1980-82; bd. dirs. New Eng. Legal Found., 1979-82, Keep Am. Beautiful, 1980—. Served with U.S. Army, 1943-46. Decorated Combat Inf. badge; Woodrow Wilson vis. fellow, 1975—. Mem. Conn. Bus. and Industry Assn. (dir. 1976-80). Republican. Congregationalist. Clubs: Country (Darien, Conn.); North Shore Golf (Menasha, Wis.). Home: 2 Woods End Rd Darien CT 06820 Office: James River Corp 800 Connecticut Ave Norwalk CT 06854

ALEXANDER, JUDITH ANN, bank cons.; b. Fort Sill, Okla., Oct. 14, 1940; d. James Buchanan and Gerry Lee (Gibbs) Permenter; m. Robert Miles Turner, Oct. 28, 1962 (div. 1972); m. Clarence Withers Alexander, Dec. 19, 1975. Student, U. Okla., 1958-59; B.A. in English, U. Tulsa, 1962; M.B.A., U. Okla., 1969; postgrad., U. St. Thomas, 1975-78. Asst. cashier So. Nat. Bank of Houston, 1971-73, asst. controller, 1973-74, asst. v.p. and asst. controller, 1974, v.p., controller, 1974-77, sr. v.p., controller, 1977-79; cons., 1979—. Mem. Houston Mus. Fine Arts, Houston Bot. Soc., NOW, Nat. Wildlife Fedn., Nat. Audubon Soc., Am. Soc. Women Accts., Tex. Bankers Assn. (asso.), Beta Gamma Sigma, Gamma Phi Beta. Republican. Office: 7715 Burning Hills Houston TX 77071 *Learning, discipline, and independence are my goals and the major contributors to my success in business and personal life.*

ALEXANDER, KENNETH LEWIS, editorial cartoonist; b. Gridley, Calif., June 16, 1924; s. Zareh and Rose (Affolter) A.; m. Dariel A. Hereford, July 15, 1949; children: Mark Kenneth, Stephen Scott, Peter Neil. Student, U. Calif. at Berkeley, 1942-43, Rutgers U., 1943-44, Calif. Coll. Arts and Crafts, 1946-47. Free-lance comml. artist, 1947-58; editor Pictorial Living mag., San Francisco Examiner, 1958-63; Sunday art dir., 1963-66; syndicated editorial cartoonist with Copley News Service, 1966—; TV editorial cartoonist, sta. KGO-TV, 1968-69; Author: (with Andrew Curtin) A Gallery of Great Americans. Served with AUS, 1943-46. Mem. Nat. Cartoonists Soc., Soc. Am. Editorial Cartoonists, Am. Newspaper Guild, A.F.T.R.A., Kappa Alpha. Home: 1182 Glen Rd Lafayette CA 94549 Office: 110 5th St San Francisco CA 94103 *As a relatively successful member of a profession whose sine qua non is the ability to come up with an endless supply of interesting, original ideas, I assign myself no credit whatever for having that ability. It is a God-given talent, and it is to Him I turn for the inspiration, the comfort, and the reassurance that He so generously and lovingly provides. And it is to Him I give my daily thanks.*

ALEXANDER, LAMAR, governor of Tennessee; b. Knox County, Tenn., July 3, 1940; s. Andrew Lamar and Flo A.; m. Leslee Kathryn Buhler, Jan. 4, 1969; children—Drew, Leslee, Kathryn, Will. B.A., Vanderbilt U., 1962; J.D., N.Y. U., 1965. Mem. firm Fowler, Rountree, Fowler and Robertson, 1965; law clk. Hon. John Minor Wisdom, U.S. Ct. Appeals, New Orleans; campaign coordinator U.S. Senator Howard Baker, 1966; legis. asst. to Sen. Baker, 1967-69; exec. asst. White House Office Congl. Relations, Washington, 1969-70; mgr. gubernatorial campaign of Winfield Dunn, 1970; transition coordinator for Gov. Dunn; mem. firm Dearborn and Ewing, Nashville, 1971-78; candidate for gov. of Tenn., 1974; spl. counsel to U.S. Senate Minority Leader Howard Baker, 1977; gov. of Tenn., 1979—; Founder, co-chmn. Tenn. Citizens for Revenue Sharing, 1971; founder, 1st chmn. Tenn. Council on Crime and Delinquency, 1973; chmn. Appalachian Regional Commn., 1980; vice chmn. Adv. Commn. on Intergovtl. Relations, 1981; mem. Pres.'s Task Force on Federalism., 1981. Polit. commentator, Nashville television sta., 1975-77. Mem. Nat. Gov.'s Assn. (chmn. com. on exec. mgmt. and fiscal affairs 1981), Phi Beta Kappa. Republican. Presbyterian. Office: Office of Governor State Capitol Nashville TN 37219

ALEXANDER, LANDON VELTMANN, insurance company executive; b. Houston, Sept. 18, 1929; s. John Lake, Jr. and Alece Eda (Veltmann) A.; m. Charlean Frances Gajewsky, Apr. 16, 1950; children: Keith, Mary, Sherry. B.A., Rice U., Houston, 1951. With Cravens, Dargan & Co., Houston, 1951-72, v.p. mktg., 1969-72; gen. mgr. Dallas service center St. Paul Fire & Marine Ins. Co., 1972-76, v.p. personal lines underwriting, St. Paul, 1976-78, sr. v.p. mktg., 1978—, also dir.; dir. Nat. Ins. Wholesalers, Surplus Lines (Ins. Co.); dirs. Tex. Joint Underwriting Assn., 1975; mem. Tex. Med. Malpractice Study Commn., 1975. Republican. Episcopalian. Home: 3725 S Hills Way Eagan MN 55123 Office: 385 Washington St Saint Paul MN 55102

ALEXANDER, LENORA COLE, government official; b. Buffalo, Mar. 9, 1935; d. John L. and Susie (Stamper) Cole; m. T.M. Alexander, June 22, 1976. B.S., SUNY-Buffalo, 1957, M.Ed., 1969, Ph.D., 1974. Vice pres. student life Am. U., Washington, 1974-77; vice pres. student affairs U. D.C., 1978-81; dir. Women's Bureau Dept. Labor, Washington, 1981—. Bd. dirs. D.C. Rental Accommodations Commn., 1978-79, Legal Aid Soc., Washington, 1975-77; trustee Wider Opportunities for Women, 1975-77. SUNY grad. fellow, 1968; named Disting. Alumnus SUNY-Buffalo, 1983. Mem. Delta Sigma Theta. Republican. Home: 3020 brandywine St NM Washington DC 20008 Office: Dept Labor Women's Bureau 200 Constitution Ave NW Washington DC 20210

ALEXANDER, LEWIS MCELWAIN, geographer, educator; b. Summit, N.J., June 15, 1921; s. Harry Louis and Laura (Stryker) A.; m. Jacqueline Peterson, Dec. 30, 1950; children: Louise Anne, Lance Stryker. A.B., Middlebury (Vt.) Coll., 1942; M.A., Clark U., 1948, Ph.D., 1949. Instr. geography Hunter Coll., 1949-50; asst. prof. geography Harpur Coll., State U. N.Y., 1950-57, asso. prof., 1957-60; prof. geography U. R.I., Kingston, 1960-80, 83—, chmn. dept., 1960-80, dir., 1968-80, 1983—; Cons. State Dept., 1963—; dir. Office of Geographer, 1980-83; exec. dir. Law of Sea Inst., 1965-73; mem. ocean affairs adv. com. Dept. State, 1973-80; dep. dir. Pres.'s Commn. on Marine Sci., Engring. and Resources, 1967-68; cons. Nat. Council for Marine Resources and Engring. Devel., 1969-70; mem. adv. com. on law of sea Interagy. Law of Sea Task Force, 1973-80; mem. ocean policy com., ocean affairs bd. NRC, 1973-76. Author: World Political Patterns, 2d edit, 1963, Offshore Geography of Northwestern Europe, 2d edit, 1966, The Northeastern United States, 1966, 2d edit., 1976, Regional Cooperation in Marine Science, 1979; mem. editorial bd.: Ocean Devel. and Internat. Law Jour, 1973—, Ocean Mgmt, 1973—, Marine Policy, 1976—. Served with USAAF, 1942-46. Recipient Annual award Sea Grant Assn., 1979; Office Naval Research grantee, 1958, 62, 66, 76. Mem. Assn. Am. Geographers (Honors award 1980), Am. Geog. Soc., Am. Soc. Internat. Law, Marine Tech. Soc. Club: Cosmos. Home: 28 Beech Hill Rd Peace Dale RI 02879 Office: Washburn Hall U RI Kingston RI 02881

ALEXANDER, LLOYD CHUDLEY, author; b. Phila., Jan. 30, 1924; s. Alan Audley and Edna (Chudley) A.; m. Janine Denni, Jan. 8, 1946; 1 dau., Madeleine (Mrs. Zohair Khalil). Student, West Chester (Pa.) State Coll., 1942, Lafayette Coll., 1943, U. Paris, 1946. Free-lance writer and translator, 1946—, cartoonist, pianist, advt. writer, mag. editor, 1948—; author-in-residence Temple U., 1970. Author: And Let The Credit Go, 1955, My Five Tigers, 1956, Janine is French, 1958, August Bondi, 1958 (Isaac Siegel Meml. award 1959), My Love Affair with Music, 1960, Aaron Lopez, 1960, Time Cat, 1963, Fifty Years in the Doghouse, 1964, (with Dr. Louis J. Camuti) Park Avenue Vet, 1962, The Book of Three, 1964 (A.L.A. notable book 1964), The Black Cauldron, 1965 (A.L.A. notable book 1965), Coll and His White Pig, 1965, The Castle of Llyr, 1966 (A.L.A. notable book 1966), Taran Wanderer, 1967, The Truthful Harp, 1967, The High King, 1968 (Newbery medal 1969), The Marvelous Misadventures of Sebastian, 1970 (Nat. Book award 1971), The King's Fountain, 1971, The Four Donkeys, 1972, The Foundling, 1973 (A.L.A. notable book 1973), The Cat Who Wished to be a Man, 1973 (A.L.A. notable book), The Wizard in the Tree, 1975, The Town Cats, 1977 (ALA notable book 1977), The First Two Lives of Lukas-Kasha, 1978, Westmark, 1981 (Am. Book award 1982), The Kestrel, 1982, The Beggar Queen, 1984; Translator from French: (Paul Eluard) Selected Writings, 1950, (Jean-Paul Sartre) The Wall, 1951, Nausea, 1953, (Paul Vialar) The Sea Rose, 1951. Bd. dirs. Carpenter Lane Chamber Music Soc., Phila. Served with AUS, World War II. Mem. Authors League Am., P.E.N. Address: 1005 Drexel Ave Drexel Hill PA 19026

ALEXANDER, MARTIN, educator, researcher; b. Newark, Feb. 4, 1930; s. Meyer and Sarah (Rubinstein) A.; m. Renee Rafaela Wulf, Aug. 26, 1951; children: Miriam H., stanley W. B.S., Rutgers U., 1951; M.S., U. Wis., 1953, Ph.D., 1955. Asst. prof. agronomy Cornell U., Ithaca, N.Y., from 1955, now L.H. Bailey prof; advisor agys. fed. govt., Washington, 1965—; advisor UN agys., Kenya, France, Italy, 1963—; mem. coms. Nat. Acad. Sci., Washington, 1971—; cons. Author: Microbial Ecology, 1971, Introduction to Soil Microbiology, 1977; editor: Advances in Microbial Ecology, 5 vols., 1977-81. Recipient Indsl. Research 100 award, 1968, Fisher award Am. Soc. Microbiology, 1980. Fellow Am. Acad. Microbiology, AAAS, Am. Soc. Agronomy (Soil Sci. award 1964). Home: 301 Winthrop Dr Ithaca NY 14853 Office: Cornell U Ithaca NY 14853

ALEXANDER, MAURICE MYRON, forestry educator emeritus; b. S. Onondaga, N.Y., Dec. 18, 1917; s. Myron Lucius and Etta May (Fenner) A.; m. Annette Reina Blain, Aug. 2, 1943; children—Ralph John, Richard Maurice, Robert Alan. B.S., N.Y. State Coll. Forestry, 1940; M.S., U. Conn., 1942; Ph.D., State U. Coll. Forestry, Syracuse,

N.Y., 1950. Fish and wildlife biologist Conn. Bd. Fish and Game, summers 1941, 42, 45-46; instr. forestry and wildlife mgmt. U. Conn., 1946-47; mem. faculty State U. Coll. Forestry, Syracuse, 1949—, prof. forest zoology, 1965-83, prof. emeritus, 1983—, chmn. dept., 1965-77; adviser N.Y. State Fish and Wildlife Mgmt. Bd., 1964-83; mem. N.Y. State Freshwater Wetlands Appeals Bd., 1976—. Served to capt. AUS, 1942-46; ETO. Decorated Bronze Star. Fellow A.A.A.S.; mem. Am. Soc. Mammologists (life), Wildlife Soc., Ecol. Soc. Am., Am. Inst. Biol. Scis., Soc. Study Amphibians and Reptiles, Sigma Xi. Home: 4039 Tanner Rd RD 2 Syracuse NY 13215 *Life is a brief opportunity that each of us is given to make this world a better place for others that follow. By better we obviously think in terms of economic, social, and religious well being; but above this we should consider the stability of the environment, as it naturally exists and as it is occupied and used by man. If I have been successful in my career it is because I helped others, students and colleagues, to be successful and their success has reflected me in good light.*

ALEXANDER, MELTON LEE, lawyer; b. Chester, Pa., Jan. 4, 1927; s. Richard Lincoln and Marie (Owens) A.; m. Beverly Ann Lankford, Apr. 18, 1969. B.A. in History, U. Ala., 1950, LL.B., 1954. Bar: Ala. 1954, U.S. Dist. Ct. for No. Dist. Ala 1954, U.S. Ct. Appeals (5th cir.) 1954, U.S. Supreme Ct. 1954, U.S. Dist. Ct. (we. dist.) Tenn. 1982, U.S. Dist. Ct. (mid. dist.) Ala. 1982, U.S. Ct. Appeals (6th and 11th cirs.) 1982. Spl. agt. FBI, Cleve., 1954-55, Washington, 1955-58, spl. agt., supr., Birmingham, Ala., 1958-66; criminal prosecutor, asst. U.S. atty. No. Dist. Ala., Birmingham, 1966—, 1st asst., 1970-73, chief prosecutor, 1977-82, ret., 1982; mem. firm Collins and Alexander, 1982—; Nat. adv. bd. Am. Security Council. Mem. editorial bd.: Ala. Law Rev, 1951, 53-54. Served to sgt. paratroops, World War II; capt. AUS, 1951-53; Korea. Decorated Bronze star, Combat Inf. Badge; recipient Atty. Gen.'s award, 1970, 82, U.S. Secret Service honor award, 1982. Mem. Farrah Order Jurisprudence, Nat. Criminal Def. Lawyers Assn., Ala. Criminal Def. Lawyers Assn., Assn. Trial Lawyers Am., Phi Beta Kappa. Home: 2044 Cedarcrest Dr Birmingham AL 35214 Office: Collins and Alexander Suite 1044 Park Place Tower Birmingham AL 35203

ALEXANDER, MYRL EARLY, criminal justice educator; b. Dayton, Ohio, Aug. 23, 1909; s. John Lester and Florence (Early) A.; m. Lorene Shoemaker, Jan. 18, 1934; children: Nancy (Mrs. Robert B. Hibbs), John Alexander. A.B., Manchester Coll., 1930, LL.D., 1956; LL.D., Pacific Luth. U., 1966; L.H.D., Susquehanna U., 1972. Warden's asst. U.S. Penitentiary, Atlanta, 1931; parole exec. U.S. Bd. Parole, Washington, 1937-40; assoc. warden U.S. Penitentiary, Lewisburg, Pa., 1940-43; warden Fed. Correctional Instn., Danbury, Conn., 1943-45; chief prisons Mil. Govt. for Germany, 1945-46; asst. dir. Bur. Prisons, Dept. Justice, Washington, 1947-61, dir., 1964-70; prof. correctional adminstrn., dir. Center for Study Crime, Delinquency and Corrections, So. Ill. U., Carbondale, 1961-64, 70-73; prof. criminal justice U. Fla., Gainesville, 1974—; U.S. rep., vice chmn. delegation UN Congress on Prevention Crime and Treatment of Offenders, Stockholm, 1965, Kyoto, Japan, 1970; U.S. corr. sect. on social def. UN; spl. cons. various state correctional systems. Author: Jail Administration, 1957. Mem. exec. bd. Ill. Synod, Luth. Ch. in Am., 1961-64, mem. bd. social ministry, 1966-72; mem. bd. social ministry Mission in N.Am., 1972-80. Recipient Pres.'s award for distinguished fed. service, 1967. Mem. Am. Correctional Assn. (pres. 1956), Osborne Assn. Democrat. Home: 1717 NW 23d Ave Apt 2B Gainesville FL 32605 *Respect for human dignity in prisons was hard to find when I began my work there. Human behavioral sciences were rarely used. Public esteem for those who worked in prisons was non-existent. Rehabilitation, change in human behavior, was only a rhetorical goal. Now the necessity for vast change has produced a national ferment involving government, universities and industry.*

ALEXANDER, NORMAN E., chemical executive; b. N.Y.C., 1914; m. Marjorie Wulf; four children. A.B., Columbia U., 1934, LL.B., 1936. Chmn. bd., chief exec. officer Sun Chem. Corp., N.Y.C., 1957—; chmn. bd. Chromalloy Am. Corp., St. Louis, 1980—, chief exec. officer, 1982—; dir. Kidde & Co., Inc.; Past chmn. bd. trustees N.Y. Med. Coll./Flower-Fifth Ave. Hosps.; trustee Rockefeller U. Council. Mem. NAM (trustee), Conf. Bd., Chief Execs. Forum (dir.). Address: 200 Park Ave New York NY 10166

ALEXANDER, NORMAN JAMES, investment consultant; b. Regina, Sask., Can., Feb. 9, 1909; s. Robert Merrillees and Catherine (Clarke) A.; m. Juanita Yvonne Denny, Apr. 25, 1944. Former v.p. James Richardson & Sons, Ltd., Winnipeg, Man., Can.; also mng. partner Richardson Securities of Can.; now investment cons.; dir. Dome Petroleums Ltd., Continental Ill. (Can.) Ltd. Clubs: Vancouver, Capilano Golf and Country (Vancouver); St. Charles Golf and Country, Winter, Manitoba, Squash Racquet (Winnipeg). Home: 85 Yale Ave Winnipeg MB R3M 0K9 Canada Office: 2410 Richardson Bldg 1 Lombard Pl Winnipeg MB R3B 0X3 Canada

ALEXANDER, PETER ALBERT, banker; b. Shreveport, Feb. 24, 1942; s. Edward P. and Nicole M. (Ducrot) A.; m. Margaret Hickman Powell; children—Corinne Eve Nicole, Marc Edward Drake. B.A., Hautes Etudes Commerciales, Paris, 1964; M.B.A., Wharton Sch., U. Pa., 1966. With Chem. Bank, N.Y.C., 1971—, regional v.p. N. Asia, Tokyo, 1977, sr. v.p. multinat. group, N.Y.C., 1981—. Home: 80 Prospect Hill Ave Summit NJ 07901 Office: 277 Park Ave New York City NY 10172

ALEXANDER, RAYMOND STANLEY, medical center exec.; b. Bklyn., Nov. 9, 1931; s. Israel and Rose A.; m. Rosalie David, July 4, 1960; children—Marian, Jerry, Karen. A.B., Dartmouth Coll., 1953; M.B.A., Amos Tuck Sch., 1954; M.S., Columbia U., 1956. Asst. commr. health, N.Y.C., 1966-68; adminstr. Montefiore Hosp., Bronx, N.Y., 1968-70; exec. v.p. Mt. Sinai Med. Center, Milw., 1970-76; pres., chief exec. officer Albert Einstein Med. Center, Phila., 1976—; adj. asst. prof. Columbia U., 1975—; adj. prof. Wharton Sch., U. Pa., 1977—. Contbr. articles to profl. jours. Served with USAF, 1956-59. Fellow Am. Coll. Hosp. Adminstrs., Am. Public Health Assn. Office: Albert Einstein Med Center York and Tabor Rds Philadelphia PA 19141

ALEXANDER, ROBERT JACKSON, economist, educator; b. Canton, Ohio, Nov. 26, 1918; s. Ralph S. and Ruth (Jackson) A.; m. Joan O. Powell, Mar. 26, 1949; children: Anthony, Margaret. B.A., Columbia U., 1940; M.A., Columnbia U., 1941; Ph.D., Columbia U., 1950. Asst. economist Bd. Econ. Warfare, 1942, Office Inter-Am. Affairs, 1945-46; mem. faculty Rutgers U., 1947—, prof. econs., 1961—; mem. Latin Am. Task Force, 1960-61. Author: (27 books) books including Juan Domingo Peron: A History, 1979, Romulo Betancourt and the Transformation of Venezuela, 1982, Bolivia: Past, Present and Future of its Policies, 1982. Mem. nat. bd. League Indsl. Democracy, 1955—; mem. nat. exec. com. Socialist Party-Social Dem. Fedn., 1957-66. Served with USAAF, 1942-45. Decorated officer Order Condor of the Andes Bolivia. Mem. Am. Econ. Assn., Latin Am. Studies Assn., Middle Atlantic Council Latin Am. Studies, Council Fgn. Relations, Internat. Assn. Democracy and Freedom (chmn. N.Am. com. 1970), Phi Gamma Delta. Home: 944 River Rd Piscataway NJ 08854 Office: Rutgers U New Brunswick NJ 08903 *I have sought to extend the bounds of knowledge through research and writing, and to pass on to my children and students not only what I have learned, but also, hopefully, some idea of how to behave in a civilized manner.*

ALEXANDER, ROSEMARY ELIZABETH, editor; b. Dansville, N.Y., Feb. 27, 1926; d. Raymond John and Elizabeth Emma (Lang) Sahrle; m. Frank Alexander, May 15, 1965; 1 son, Frank William III. B.A., Hartwick Coll., 1946; M.S., SUNY- Geneseo, 1956. Tchr. Central Sch., Andes, N.Y., 1946-47; editorial asst. Instr. mag., Dansville, 1947-52, asst. editor, 1952-61, features editor, 1961-66, prodn. editor, 1966-72, mng. editor, 1972, exec. editor, 1972-76, adminstrv. editor, 1976-79, editorial dir., instr. curriculum materials, 1979-82; asst. sec. Instr. Publs. Inc., Dansville, 1974-82; free lance writer, editor, cons., 1982—. Mem. Nat. Assn. Elem. Sch. Prins., Internat. Reading Assn., Assn. Supervision and Curriculum Devel., Nat. Council Tchrs. English, Ednl. Press Assn., Order Eastern Star. Republican. Lutheran. Address: 4 Sterner Rd Dansville NY 14437 Office: Instr Publs Inc 7 Bank Dansville NY 14437

ALEXANDER, ROY, public relations executive, editor; b. Asheville, N.C., Feb. 3, 1928; s. William Roy and Ruth (Upshaw) A. Ph.B., Northwestern U., 1954. Mng. editor Daily Northwestern, 1951-52; asso. editor Food Retailing, 1951-55; dir. pub. relations Mid-States Corp., 1952-53; editor Splty. Salesman, 1953-56, Mobile Homes mag., 1953-54; account exec. Philip Lesly Co., 1956-58, v.p., 1958-62; pres. Alexander Co., N.Y.C., 1962—; editor Mktg. Times, 1970—, Readout, 1974-75, Lowenbrau Letter; mgr. New York product publicity activities for Wurlitzer Co.; public relations counsel Grad. Sch. Sales Mgmt. and Mktg., Lincoln Logs Ltd.; condr. course in public relations and mktg. New Sch., 1971; cons. to The Maleck Group, Rockwood Products, Flam-X, Better Advantage, Inc.; dir. consumer edn. program Youth for Fed. Union, Washington; counselor Info. Industry Assn., Bethesda, Md., Environment Info. Center, N.Y.C., A. William Smyth Assos., Ross, Calif., River City Furnace Ltd., Mason City, Iowa, Phoenix Co., Asheville, N.C. Writer, exec. producer: color motion picture The Greening of Augusta, 1973; dir.: public edn. program Iron Mountain Stoneware; creator state-wide edn. program, W.Va. Coal Assn.; designer, creator communications and promotion program, Singer Bus. Machines; dir. nationwide public edn. program, Nat. Pest Control Assn.; creator underdog communications program, Minerals Edn. Council, new research concept, Youth Data Service; Author: Direct Salesman's Handbook, 1958, Duke Medical Center's Ricer's Guide, 1975, Mehdi: Story of Metlife's Top Salesman, 1977, Secrets of Closing Sales, 1981; co-author: Climbing the Corporate Matterhorn, 1984. Served with AUS, 1946-49; feature editor Armed Forces Press Service, 1948-49. Mem. Sales and Mktg. Execs. Internat. (public relations counsel), Am. Footwear Mfrs. Assn. (editor Jour. Footwear Mgmt.), Pi Sigma Epsilon. Address: 239 E 32d St New York NY 10016 *My guiding principles: (1) Do something even if it's wrong - percentages favor the activist. (2) Don't waste words or time—both are in finite supply. (3) All generalizations are false—including these. (4) Assume most people will fail their responsibilities and plan accordingly. (5) Anything worth doing is worth doing to excess. (6) Avoid all medication; solve health problem with diet and exercies. (7) Never forget: The free market system made it all possible.*

ALEXANDER, SANDER PETER, cosmetic company executive; b. Bklyn., Nov. 12, 1929; (married). Ed., Bklyn. Coll. Vice pres. fin. Champion Internat. Co., 1969-71, sr. v.p. fin., chief fin. officer, 1971-75; also dir.; sr. v.p. fin., chief fin. officer Revlon Inc., N.Y.C., 1975—, also dir., mem. exec. com.; sr. exec. v.p., dir. Londontown Mfg. Co., Balt. Bd. dirs. Bklyn. Coll. Found. Mem. NAM (audit com.). Office: 767 Fifth Ave New York NY 10022

ALEXANDER, SHANA, journalist, author, lectr.; b. N.Y.C., Oct. 6, 1925; d. Milton and Cecelia (Rubenstein) Ager; m. Stephen Alexander, 1951 (div.); 1 dau., Katherine. Student, Vassar Coll., 1942-45. With PM, 1944-46, Harper's Bazaar, 1946-47; with Flair, 1950; reporter Life mag., 1951-61, staff writer, 1961-64; writer twice monthly column The Feminine Eye, 1964-69; editor McCall's mag., N.Y.C., 1969-71; v.p. Norton Simon Communications, Inc., 1971-72; radio and TV commentator Spectrum CBS News, 1971-72; columnist, contbg. editor Newsweek, 1972-75; commentator CBS 60 Minutes, 1975-79; Bd. dirs. Am. Film Inst. Author: The Feminine Eye, 1970, Shana Alexander's State-by-State Guide to Women's Legal Rights, 1975, Talking Woman, 1976, Anyone's Daughter, 1979, Appearance of Evil: The Trial of Patty Hearst. Recipient Sigma Delta Chi and U. So. Cal. Nat. Journalism award, 1965, Los Angeles Times Woman of Year award, 1967, Golden Pen award Am. Newspaper Womens Club, 1969, Front Page award Newswomen's Club N.Y., 1973, Matrix award N.Y. Women in Communications, 1973-74, Spirit of Achievement award Albert Einstein Coll. Med., 1976; Creative Arts award Nat. Women's div. Am. Jewish Congress. Office: 444 Madison Ave New York NY 10022 *

ALEXANDER, SYDENHAM BENONI, physician, educator; b. Charlotte, N.C., May 28, 1919; s. Thomas Willis and Alice Winston (Spruill) A.; m. Frances Huger Allison, Oct. 28, 1944; children: Susan Alexander Yates, Sydenham Benoni, Frank Spruill, Frances Huger Alexander Cade. A.B., U. N.C., 1941, cert. Sch. Medicine, 1943; M.D., Med. Coll. Va., Richmond, 1944. Diplomate: Am. Bd. Internal Medicine. Intern U.S. Naval Hosp., Bethesda, Md., 1944-45; asst. physician, instr. U. N.C., 1946-53, asso. physician, asst. prof., 1955-56, asst. adminstr. div. health affairs, 1956-65, fellow Exec. Program Sch. Bus. Adminstrn., 1964-65; chief resident, instr. Med. Coll. Va., Richmond, 1947-49; vis. scientist NIH, Bethesda, Md., 1962-63; dir. Student Health Service U. Ala., University, 1966-79, prof. and physician, 1966—; cons. USPHS, 1963-66, VA Hosp., Tuscaloosa, 1973-78. Bd. dirs. N.C. Home for Aging, Southern Pines, 1963-65; trustee St. Marys Jr. Coll., Raleigh, N.C., 1963-65; bd. visitors Kanuga Confs., Hendersonville, N.C., 1979—. Served from lt. (j.g.) to comdr. M.C., USNR, 1944-46, 53-55; PTO. Fellow ACP (life), Am. Coll. Health Assn. (mem. council 1969—, v.p. 1969-70); mem. Delta Kappa Epsilon, Phi Chi, Alpha Omega Alpha. Episcopalian. Club: Indian Hills Country (Tuscaloosa). Home: 1027 Indian Hills Dr Tuscaloosa AL 35406 Office: PO Box Y University Health Service University Tuscaloosa AL 35486

ALEXANDER, THEODORE MARTIN, insurance and real estate consultant; b. Montgomery, Ala., Mar. 7, 1909; s. James H. and Hattie (Hamilton) A.; m. Dorothy Hudson, Aug. 31, 1931 (dec.); children: Theodore Martin (dec.), Alvia Elizabeth, Dorothy Gwendolyn; m. Lenora Cole, June 22, 1975. B.A. in Bus. Adminstrn. with honors, Morehouse Coll., 1931, LL.D., 1970. Founder, 1931; since pres. Alexander & Co., Inc. (gen. ins. agy.), Atlanta; chmn. bd. Alexander and Assocs., Inc.; founder, 1949; former exec. v.p. Southeastern Fidelity Fire Ins. Co., Atlanta; pres., treas. University Plaza Apts., Inc.; sec., dir., exec. com. Mut. Fed. Savs. & Loan Assn., Atlanta, 1932-68; partner Met. Atlanta Rapid Transit Authority Ins. Mgrs.; vice chmn., mem. exec. and finance coms. Atlanta Univ. Center Corp.; mem. Met. Washington Bd. Trade, 1977—; presdl. appointee with Senate confirmation to bd. dirs. African Devel. Found.; mem. Inner Circle Senatorial Com. U.S.A.; adj. prof. ins. Howard U., Washington. Fed. jury commr. No. Dist. Ga.; trustee Atlanta Community Chest; sec. bd. trustees Morehouse Coll.; bd. dirs. Butler St. YMCA, Atlanta, 1958—, mem. race relations com., internat. com., del. world council, 1961; mem. nat. bd.; bd. dirs. Boys' Club Greater Washington; mem. citizens adv. com., chmn. relocation com. Atlanta Urban Renewal; mem. better housing commn.; mem. housing appeal bd., vice chmn. ethics bd. City Atlanta; mem. nat. citizens com. for community relations Dept. Commerce, 1964; mem. adv. com. Met. Planning Commn. Atlanta; asst. treas. Atlanta Community Chest; mem. Atlanta Community relations; pres. Sr. Citizens Met. Atlanta, 1968-69; candidate Atlanta City Council, 1957; candidate for Ga. State Senate, 1962. Mem. NAACP, Urban League, Atlanta C. of C., Alpha Phi Alpha, Sigma Pi Phi, Delta Sigma Rho. Republican. Baptist. Clubs: Masons, Shriners, Commerce (Atlanta); Capitol Hill Republican (Washington). Home: 3020 Brandywine St NW Washington DC 20008 also George Town Exec Park PO Box 76677 Atlanta GA 30328 Office: 1729 Wisconsin Ave NW Washington DC 20007 *One must contribute to the growth and development of the community which has contributed to his success. Equal opportunity carries with it equal responsibility. One must never go to the banquet table with only an appetite.*

ALEXANDER, THERON, psychologist, writer, consultant; s. Theron and Mary Helen (Jones) A.; m. Marie Bailey; children: Thomas, Mary. Ph.D., U. Chgo., 1949. Asst. prof. psychology Fla. State U., 1949-54; dir. Mental Health Clinic, 1954-57; asso. prof. psychology in pediatrics U. Iowa, to 1965; prof. psychology in pediatrics U. Miami (Fla.), 1965-66; research prof. Community Studies Center of Temple U., Phila., 1966-68; dir. Child Devel. Research Center, 1966-69; pres. Alexander Assocs., 1980—; lectr., Sao Paulo, Brazil, 1977. Author: Psychotherapy in Our Society, 1963, Children and Adolescents, 1969, Human Development in an Urban Age, 1973, El Desarrollo Humano en la Epoca del Urbanismo, 1978, (with others) Developmental Psychology, 1980. Served with USNR, World War II; PTO. Recipient cert. Gov. State of Sao Paulo (Brazil), 1977; Legion of Honor, 1979. Fellow Am. Psychol. Assn.; mem. Eastern Psychol. Assn., Soc. Research in Child Devel., Soc. Pediatric Psychology, Pa. Psychol. Assn., Sigma Xi. Office: 270 Aldrin Dr Ambler PA 19002

ALEXANDER, THOMAS BENJAMIN, educator; b. Nashville, July 23, 1918; s. Thomas Benjamin and Mary Christine (Sanders) A.; m. Elise Hadley Pritchett, June 16, 1941; children: Wynne Hadley Alexander Guy, Elaine Elliston Alexander Gates, Pope Alexander Norris. A.B., Vanderbilt U., 1939, M.A., 1940, Ph.D., 1947. From asst. prof. to assoc. prof. history Clemson U., S.S., 1946-49; prof., chmn. div. social scis. Ga. So. U., Statesboro, 1949-57; from assoc. prof. to prof. history U. Ala., Tuscallosa, 1957-69; prof. history U. Mo., Columbia, 1969—, Middlebush prof. history, 1979-82. Author: Political Reconstruction in Tennessee, 1950, Thomas A.R. Nelson of East Tennessee, 1956, Sectional Stress and Party Strength, 1836-1860, 1967, The Anatomy of the Confederate Congress, 1972 (Sydnor award 1973, Jefferson Davis award 1972). Served to lt. USNR, 1943-46; ETO. Fellow Guggenheim Found., 1955-56; grantee Social Sci. Research Council, 1947, 67-68; fellow Inst. So. History, 1968-69. Mem. So. Hist. Assn. (pres. 1980), Am. Hist. Assn., AAUP, Orgn. Am. History, Social Sci. History Assn., S.C. Hist. Assn. (pres. 1958). Home: 2606 Summit Rd Columbia MD 65201 Office: Univ Mo Dept History Columbia MD 65211

ALEXANDER, THOMAS EDWARD, retail exec.; b. Los Angeles, July 11, 1931; s. Edward Clifton and Ruth Ethlyn (Massey) A.; 1 dau., Ann. B.A. in Polit. Sci, U. Colo., 1953. Sr. advt. planner Marshall Field & Co., Chgo., 1957-61; v.p. sales promotion Joske's, Houston, 1961-68; v.p. mktg. and sales promotion The Bon Marche, Seattle, 1968-70; sr. v.p. sales promotion Neiman-Marcus, Dallas, 1970-78, exec. v.p. mktg. and sales promotion, 1980—. Bd. dirs. Panhandle Plains Hist. Mus., Canyon, Tex. Served to capt. USAF, 1953-56. Mem. Am. Chianina Assn., Tex. Longhorn Breeders Assn., Tex. and Southwestern Cattle Raisers Assn., Sigma Alpha Epsilon. Address: 1618 Main St Dallas TX 75201

ALEXANDER, WELBORN EXCELL, JR., railroad executive; b. Lenoir, N.C., Feb. 12, 1941; s. Welborn Excell and Nancy Ellen (Thompson) A.; m. Patricia Carson Hutchins, June 8, 1963; children: Welborn Excell, III, Lucinda Carson. B.A., Duke U., 1963; postgrad., Baruch Sch. Bus. Adminstrn., CCNY. With sales dept. So. Ry. System, 1963-67; industry planning analyst N.Y. Central R.R., 1967-69; industry planning analyst, mgr. mktg., dir. mktg., asst. v.p. mktg., then v.p. mktg. Penn Central Transp. Co., to 1974-76; v.p. sales and mktg. planning Seaboard Coast Line/Louisville & Nashville R.R., 1976-78; sr. v.p. sales and mktg. Seaboard Coast Line Industries, Jacksonville, Fla., 1978-79, exec. v.p. sales and mktg., 1980—; dir. Seaboard Coast Line R.R. Co., Flagship Banks, Inc., Louisville & Nashville R.R. Co. Mem. Nat. Freight Transp. Assn., Am. Soc. Traffic and Transp., Fla. C. of C. (past dir.), Phi Beta Kappa, Phi Delta Theta. Presbyterian. Clubs: Rotary, River, San Jose Country., Tournament Players. Office: 500 Water St Jacksonville FL 32202

ALEXANDER, WILLIAM BROOKS, lawyer, state senator; b. Boyle, Miss., Dec. 23, 1921; s. William Brooks and Vivien (Beaver) A.; m. Belle McDonald, Mar. 12, 1950; children—Brooks, Becky, John, Jason, Grace. Student, Miss. Coll., 1940-42; LL.B., U. Miss., 1948. Bar: Miss. 1948. Partner firm Alexander, Johnston & Alexander, Cleveland, 1948—; mem. Miss. Senate, 1960—. Now pres. pro tem.; Past pres. Miss. Heart Assn.; bd. dirs. Miss. Coll. Served with AUS, 1942-46. Mem. Miss. Bar Assn. (Outstanding Legislator), Bolivar County Bar Assn., Am. Legion, VFW (past dep. comdr.). Baptist. Club: Exchange. Lodge: Masons. Office: PO Drawer J Cleveland MS 38732

ALEXANDER, WILLIAM HENRY, lawyer; b. Thomson, Ill., Nov. 16, 1902; s. Cyrus Hall and Mary Letitia (Livingston) A.; m. Jane Ashcraft, Dec. 22, 1934; children: Willa Jane, William Raymond, David Risdon, Sarah Susan and Peter Llewellyn (twins), Edwin Michael, James Livingston. B.S., Knox Coll., 1926; postgrad., U. Chgo. Law Sch., 1926-29. Bar: Ill. bar 1930. Law clk. to sr. judge U.S. Circuit Ct. Appeals, 1930-35; with firm Ashcraft & Ashcraft, Chgo., 1935-82, mem., 1936-82, Alexander & Alexander, 1982—. Trustee Village of Wilmette, Ill., 1941-45, pres., 1945-53; hon. mem. Wilmette Hist. Commn.; Bd. dirs., pres. Eleanor Assn.; trustee, pres. Chgo. Wesley Meml. Hosp.; trustee Northwestern U. Citizen fellow Inst. Medicine Chgo. Mem. ABA, Ill. Bar Assn., Chgo. Bar Assn. (pres. 1960-61), Chgo. Hist. Soc. (life), Chgo. Natural History Mus. (life), Scabbard and Blade, Phi Alpha Delta, Lambda Chi Alpha. Republican. Methodist. Clubs: Rotarian., Indian Hill (Winnetka); Law (Chgo.); Wilmette Curling. Home: 1025 Mohawk Rd Wilmette IL 60091

ALEXANDER, WILLIAM HENRY, judge; b. Macon, Ga., Dec. 10, 1930; s. William Henry and Lenora Elizabeth (Wilburn) A.; 1 dau., Jill Marie. B.S., Ft. Valley (Ga.) State Coll., 1951; J.D., U. Mich., 1956; LL.M., Georgetown U., 1961. Bar: Ga, Mich. 1957, U.S. Supreme Ct. 1969. Practiced law, Atlanta, 1963-75; judge City Ct. of Atlanta, 1975-76, Criminal Ct. Fulton County, 1976-77, State Ct. Fulton County, 1977—; Mem. Ga. Ho. of Reps., 1966-75; mem. Fulton County (Ga.) Democratic Exec. Com., 1968-75, Ga. Dem. Exec. Com., 1966-69; alt. del. Dem. Nat. Conv., 1968. Pres. Atlanta Legal Aid Soc., 1973. Served with AUS, 1951-53. Mem. Am., Ga., Atlanta, Nat., Gate City bar assns., Am. Judicature Soc., Am. Judges Assn., ACLU (state pres. 1968-69, Beta Gamma Sigma.). Clubs: Atlanta Lawyers, Old Warhorse Lawyers, Kiwanis, Resurgens (Atlanta). Home: 4540 Birdie Ln SW Atlanta GA 30331 Office: 160 Pryor St SW Atlanta GA 30303

ALEXANDER, WILLIAM HERBERT, construction company executive, former army officer; b. Harrisburg, Pa., Apr. 17, 1941; s. Wallace Hale and Jeannette Kauffman (Hackenberger) A.; m. Marion Elizabeth Carey, Nov. 30, 1963; children: Charles, Elizabeth, Robert, Kathryn. B.S., U.S. Mil. Acad., 1963; M.B.A., U. Pitts., 1969. Registered profl. engr., Pa. Commd. 2d lt. U.S. Army, 1963, advanced through grades to capt., 1968; platoon leader, co. comdr., Kitzingen, Germany, 1963-66; capt., co. comdr. Officer Candidate Regiment, Ft. Belvoir, Va., 1966-67; staff officer, engr. constrn. battalion, Cu Chi, Vietnam, 1968, resigned, 1968; project mgr. H.B. Alexander & Son, Inc., Harrisburg, 1970-77, pres., 1977—; dir. Commonwealth Nat. Bank, Mchts. & Businessmen's Mut. Ins. Co. Bd. dirs. AAA Central Penn Auto Club, Polyclinic Med. Ctr.; pres. Tri County United Way, 1979-80, Ams. for Competitive Enterprise System, 1981-82. Decorated Bronze Star. Mem. Pa. Soc. Profl. Engrs., ASCE, Harrisburg C. of C. (dir., chmn. 1982-83), Beta Gamma Sigma. Republican. Presbyterian (elder). Club: Harrisburg Rotary (pres. 1981-82). Home: 16 Wagner St Hummelstown PA 17036 Office: 315 Vaughn St Harrisburg PA 17105

ALEXANDER, WILLIAM OLIN, real estate company executive; b. Lexington, Ky., Aug. 2, 1939; s. Elby Olin and Louise (Watson) A.; m. Yvonne Davis, Jan. 26, 1961; children: Keith Davis, Hope. B.S., U. Ky., 1961. C.P.A., Fla. Auditor Ring, Mahony & Arner (C.P.A.s), Miami, Fla., 1961-62, sr. auditor, 1964-66; v.p., treas. Seabird Industries, Miami, 1966-70, exec. v.p., 1970-73; controller Belcher Oil Co., Miami, 1973-75, treas., 1976-83; sr. v.p., treas. Mitchell Co., Mobile, Ala., 1983—. Served to 1st lt. AUS, 1962-64. Mem. Am. Inst. C.P.A.s, Ala. Inst. C.P.A.s, Exec. Assn. Greater Miami, Porsche Club Am., Beta Alpha Psi, Delta Sigma Pi, Delta Tau Delta. Republican. Clubs: Miami Shores Country, Bath, Bankers, Porsche of Am. Home: 1150 Chimney Top Dr W Mobile AL 36609 Office: 1st Southern Tower Bldg Mobile AL 36608

ALEXANDER, WILLIAM OWEN, savings and loan executive; b. Oklahoma City, Jan. 5, 1924; s. John Delmer and Flossie Belle (Beaty) A.; m. Katherine I. McMillan, Aug. 23, 1947; children: John Delmer II, James M. Student, U. Okla., 1941, U. Miss., 1943; B.S., Oklahoma City U., 1948. Pres. Ins., Inc., 1946-60; exec. v.p., mgr. trust dept. First Nat. Bank & Trust Co., Oklahoma City, 1961-75; pres. Continental Fed. Savs. & Loan Assn., Oklahoma City, 1975—, also dir.; mem. Oklahoma City br. Fed. Res. Bank of Kansas City; dir. 1st Life Assurance Co., Oklahoma City, Am. First Corp., Oklahoma City. Past treas. City of Nichols Hills, Okla.; Bd. dirs., past chmn. Salvation Army. Mem. Oklahoma City Retailers Assn. (bd. dirs.); Mem. Kappa Alpha. Clubs: Masons; Men's Dinner (Oklahoma City) (dir., pres.). Home: PO Box 838 Oklahoma City OK 73101

ALEXANDER, WILLIAM POWELL, electronics co. exec.; b. Buffalo, June 16, 1934; s. James Nelson and Helen (Johnston) A.; m. Eunice Gail Elwood, May 8, 1981; 1 dau., Christine Bray. B.A., Gettysburg Coll., 1956; postgrad., Temple U., 1960-62. With Aetna Casualty & Surety Co., 1956-57; with RCA Corp., N.Y.C., 1960—, sr. asst. sec., 1973-78, sec., 1978—; sec. NBC, Hertz Corp., RCA Communications, Coronet Industries. Served to 1st lt. USAAF, 1957-59. Mem. Am. Soc. Corp. Secs., Phi Kappa Psi. Office: RCA 30 Rockefeller Plaza New York NY 10020

ALEXANDER, WILLIAM VOLLIE, JR., Congressman; b. Memphis, Jan. 16, 1934; 1 dau., Alyse Haven. B.A. in Polit. Sci., Southwestern at Memphis, 1957; LL.B., Vanderbilt U., 1960. Bar: Tenn. and Ark. 1960; cert. aquanaut NOAA. Legal research asst. Fed. Judge Marion Boyd, Memphis, 1960-61; asso. Montedonico, Boone, Gilliland, Heiskell & Loch, 1961-63; partner Swift & Alexander, Osceola, Ark., 1963-68; mem. 91st-98th Congresses 1st Ark. Dist.; chief dep. majority whip, mem. appropriations com.; sec. Export Task Force; past mem. Ark. Waterways Commn.; mem. Pres.'s Export Council; former mem. Nat. Alcohol Fuels Commn.; bd. dirs. Am. Oceanic Orgn. Mem. Democratic Party Steering and Policy Com.; mem. Dem. Congl. Campaign Com.; chmn. 1st Congl. Dist. Dem. Caucus. Served with AUS, 1951-53. Mem. Kappa Sigma, Phi Delta Phi. Episcopalian. Address: 203 Cannon House Office Bldg Washington DC 20515 *

ALEXANDER, WILLIS WALTER, trust company executive; b. Trenton, Mo., Jan. 2, 1919; s. Willis W. and Ethel Claire (Newmeyer) A.; m. Doris Vosburg, June 20, 1942 (div. May 1975); children: Eric Willis, Barbara Louise Alexander, Patricia Ann Alexander; m. Sandra Skidmore, Oct. 1975; children: Margaret Claire, Mary Katherine. B.A., U. Mo., 1940; M.B.A., U. Pa., 1941. Asst. sec. to exec. v.p. Trenton Trust Co., 1947-60, pres., 1960-74, chmn. bd., 1974—; pres. state bank div. Am. Bankers Assn., Washington, 1966-67, v.p., 1967-68, pres., 1968-69, exec. v.p., 1969—; co-pub. Trenton Republican Times, 1963—; exec. v.p. Internat. Monetary Conf., 1971—. Served to lt. comdr. USNR, 1941-47. Mem. Mo. Bankers Assn. (pres. 1959-60). Clubs: Metropolitan, Internat. (Washington). Home: 12118 Quorn Ln Reston VA 22091 Office: Am Bankers Assn 1120 Connecticut Ave NW Washington DC 20036

ALEXANDERSON, GERALD LEE, mathematician; b. Caldwell, Idaho, Nov. 13, 1933; s. Albert William and Alvina (Gertlar) A. B.A., U. Oreg., 1955; M.S., Stanford U., 1958. Instr. math. U. Santa Clara, Calif., 1958-62, asst. prof., 1962-68, coordinator honors program, 1965-67, asso. prof., 1968-72, prof., 1972—, Michael and Elizabeth Valeriote prof., 1979—, chmn. dept., 1967—, dir. Div. Math. and Natural Scis., 1981—; lectr. Stanford U., summers 1958, 59, U. Geneva, 1964-65; asso. dir. William Lowell Putnam Math. Competition, 1975—. Author: (with A.P. Hillman) Functional Trigonometry, 1961, rev. edit., 1971, Algebra and Trigonometry, 1963, Algebra Through Problem Solving, 1966, First Undergraduate Course in Abstract Algebra, 1973, rev. edit., 1978; asso. editor: Two-Year College Mathematics Jour., 1979—, Am. Math. Monthly 1983—; contbr. articles to math. jours. Trustee U. Santa Clara, 1979—. Recipient Pres.'s Spl. Recognition award U. Santa Clara, 1978. Mem. Am. Math. Soc., Math. Assn. Am. (sec.-treas. No. Calif. sect. 1967-70, chmn. 1971-72, nat. bd. govs. 1975-78, com. on undergrad. program in math. 1977—, com. on Dolciani Math. Exposition series 1977—), Math Assn. Am. (bd. cons. 1982—), Fibonacci Assn. (pres. 1980—), Phi Beta Kappa, Sigma Xi, Pi Mu Epsilon, Pi Delta Phi, Phi Eta Sigma. Home: 1133 Highland Ave Santa Clara CA 95050

ALEXANIAN, RAYMOND, hematologist; b. N.Y.C., June 8, 1932; s. Hagop and Eleeza (Bynderian) A.; m. Lois Abbott, Jan. 16, 1960; 1 dau., Jane. B.A. with highest honors, Dartmouth Coll., 1952; M.D., Harvard U., 1955. Diplomate: Am. Bd. Internal Medicine. Intern King County Hosp., Seattle, 1955-56; successively asst. resident in medicine, research fellow in hematology, instr. medicine U. Wash. Med. Sch., 1958-64; mem. faculty U. Tex. M.D. Anderson Hosp., Houston, 1964—, prof. medicine, alternate head dept., 1975—. Contbr. numerous articles on myeloma and related disorders to med. jours. Served as capt. M.C. AUS, 1956-58. Mem. Am. Soc. Hematology, AMA, Tex. Med. Assn. Home: 4082 Breakwood Dr Houston TX 77025 Office: Dept Medicine MD Anderson Hosp 6723 Bertner St Houston TX 77030

ALEXEFF, IGOR, educator; b. Pitts., Jan. 5, 1931; s. Alexander and Tamara (Tchirkow) A.; m. Anne L. Fabina, Feb. 4, 1954; children: Alexander, Helen. B.A., Harvard U., 1952; M.S., U. Wis., 1955, Ph.D., 1959. Registered profl. engr., Tenn. Research engr. Westinghouse Corp., Pitts., 1952-53; NSF postdoctoral fellow U. Zurich, Switzerland, 1959-60; group leader controlled thermonuclear fusion Oak Ridge Nat. Lab., 1960-71; prof. elec. engring. U. Tenn., 1971—; vis. prof. Inst. Plasma Physics, Nagoya, Japan, 1973, Phys. research Lab., Ahmedabad, India, 1975; physics dept. U. Natal, Durban, S. Africa, 1976; vis. prof. Universidade Federal Fluminense Niteroi, Brazil, 1978; organizer Plasma Physics Workshop, U.S. and, India, 1976; chmn. Gordon Research Conf. on Plasma Physics, 1974; v.p. So. Appalachian Sci. and Engring. Fair. Contbr. articles to profl. jours. Fellow Am. Phys. Soc. (sec.-treas. div. plasma physics), IEEE (asso. editor Transactions on Plasma Sci.; organizer 1st Internat. Conf. on Plasma Sci. 1974, former pres. Oak Ridge chpt.); mem. Nuclear and Plasma Sci. Soc. of IEEE (v.p.). Home: 2790 Turnpike Oak Ridge TN 37830 Office: Ferris Hall U Tenn Knoxville TN 37916 also 1907 Holston River Rd Knoxville TN 37914

ALEXION, JOHN COULON, university dean, educator, corporate director, consultant; b. N.Y.C., Jan. 2, 1916; s. Alexander John and Madeleine C. (Coulon) A.; m. Grace E. Bunn, Oct. 15, 1938; 1 dau., Karen Alexion Scheidt. Student, Poly. Inst. N.Y., 1937-41; B.Sc. in Mgmt., NYU, 1945, M.B.A., 1945, Ph.D., 1964. Vice pres. corporate devel. Liggett Drug Co., Stamford, Conn., 1956-59; pres. Gens, Jarboe, Inc., N.Y.C., 1959-61; v.p. adminstrn. Va. Metal Products, Inc., Orange, 1961-63; chmn. dept. fin. and law Adelphi U., Garden City, N.Y., 1963-66; v.p. bus. and career-oriented programs, dean Coll. Bus. Adminstrn. St. John's U., Jamaica, N.Y., 1966—; cons. Irvin Industries, Inc., N.Y.C., 1964-82, dir., 1964-80; chmn. bd. State-Wide Ins. Co., Great Neck, N.Y., 1966—; dir. spl. projects Va. Metal Industries, Inc., Orage, 1983—; pres. Alexion & Assocs., mgmt. cons., Glen Oaks, N.Y., 1973—; cons. Mobil Oil Corp., N.Y.C., 1972—. Pres. Am. Hellenic Inst., Washington, 1982. Served to capt. Supply Corps USNR, 1949-76; to rear adm. N.Y. Naval Militia, 1981—. Decorated Navy Commendation medal, Joint Service Commendation medal, medal for Disting. Civilian Service Dept. Army, 1982, Pres.'s medal St. John's U., 1977. Mem. ASME (sr.), Soc. Am. Mil. Engrs., Naval Res. Assn. (chpt. v.p. adminstrn. 1981—), Naval Order U.S., Mil. Order World Wars, Vets. 7th Regt. (life), Beta Gamma Sigma. Republican. Office: St John's U Jamaica NY 11439

ALEXIS, MARCUS, economics educator; b. N.Y.C., Feb. 26, 1932; 3 children. B.A., Bklyn. Coll., 1953; M.A. (Univ. scholar, Hinman fellow), Mich. State U., 1954; Ph.D. (Univ. fellow), U. Minn., 1959. Instr. econs. U. Minn., 1954-57; asst. prof. econs. and mktg. Macalester Coll., 1957-60; asso. prof. mktg. DePaul U., 1960-62; asso. prof. to prof. bus. adminstrn. U. Rochester, 1962-70; prof. econs. Northwestern U., Evanston, Ill., 1970—, chmn., 1976-79, 82—, dir. summer program in econs. for minority students, 1974-79; vis. prof. U. Calif. at Berkeley, 1969-71; vis. scholar Ford Found.; fellow Grad. Sch. Bus., Harvard, 1961-62; vis. asso. prof. U. Minn., 1962, 65. Bd. dirs. Operation Push (People United to Save Humanity), 1971-73; commr. Interstate Commerce Commn., 1979-80, vice chmn., 1981, acting chmn., 1981. Recipient Outstanding Achievement award U. Minn., 1981. Mem. Am. Econ. Assn. (mem. com. to increase supply of minority economists 1971—, chmn. 1974—, mem. com. on honors and awards 1972-78, mem. nominating com. 1981-82), Am. Mktg. Assn. (dir. 1968-70), Caucus Black Economists (chmn. 1969-71, steering com. 1969-73, 75-76), Nat. Econ. Assn. (steering com. 1976—, Samuel Z. Westerfield award 1979). Office: Coll Arts and Scis Northwestern U Evanston IL 60201

ALEXY, R. JAMES, manufacturing company executive; b. Washington, Pa., Oct. 24, 1940; s. Robert J. and Julia S. (Stevens) A.; m. Sue Anne Snyder, Sept. 1, 1962; children: Brooke Elizabeth, Jennifer Paige. B.A., Cornell U., 1962, M.B.A., 1964. Indsl. sales mgr. Scott Paper Co., Phila., 1964-67; div. mktg./sales mgr. Brown Co., Gulf & Western Industries, Kalamazoo, 1968-71, div. gen. mgr., N.Y.C., 1971-73, group v.p., gen. mgr., Eau Claire, Wis., 1973-79; exec. v.p. Pope & Talbot, Inc., Eau Claire, 1980-81, Ft. Howard Paper Co., Green Bay, Wis., 1981—; dir. First Wis. Nat. Bank, Eau Claire. Chmn. United Way, Eau Claire, 1981; bd. dirs. Eau Claire YMCA; bd. advisers U. Wis., Stout, U. Wis.-Eau Claire Found. Mem. Am. Paper Inst. (past pres. tissue div.). Republican. Clubs: Saucon Valley Country (Bethlehem, Pa.); N.Y. Athletic, Cornell (N.Y.C.); Oneida Country (Green Bay). Home: 4494 Seminole Trail Green Bay WI 54303 Office: PO Box 130 Green Bay WI 54303

ALFANGE, DEAN, lawyer; b. Constantinople, Dec. 2, 1900; U.S., 1901; m. Thalia Perry, Aug. 11, 1929; children—Whitman, Dean. A.B., Hamilton Coll., 1922; LL.B., Columbia U., 1925. Bar: N.Y, U.S. Supreme Ct. 1925. Since practiced in, N.Y.C.; Chmn. N.Y.C. Appeals Bd. 6, Enemy Alien Hearing Bd. So. Dist. N.Y.; mem. N.Y. State Bd. Inquiry in Longshore Industry; founder Legion for Am. Unity, 1940; mem. exec. com. Citizens for Victory; dir. Better Understanding Found. for Religious and Racial Tolerance, Greek War Relief Assn.; nat. chmn. Emergency Com. to Save Jewish People of Europe; chmn. N.Y. State Quarter Horse Racing Commn., 1971—, Am. Christian Palestine Com. of Greater N.Y.; Chmn. Fgn. Lang. Speakers Bur. Dem. Presdl. Campaign Com., 1940; Dem. candidate for Congress 17th N.Y. Dist., 1941; nominated for gov. N.Y., Am. Labor Party, 1942; chmn. Liberal and Labor Com. which founded Liberal party State of N.Y., 1944, Israel Anniversary Celebration Com., 1949. Author: This Week mag. and Reader's Digest The Horse Racing Industry, 1976. Trustee Fashion Inst. Tech., N.Y., United Greek Orthodox Charities, Archdiocesan Greek Cathedral of Holy Trinity, N.Y.; pres. LaGuardia Meml. Settlement House. Recipient Freedom Found. Award, 1960; Theodore Roosevelt Meml. award for non-fiction book The Supreme Court and the National Will, 1937; Donor scholarship endowments Hamilton Coll. to promote democratic govt. and religious understanding. Mem. Nat. Inst. Social Scis., Am. Acad. Polit. and Social Sci., UN Assn. (dir.), NAACP, Am., N.Y. bar assns., Am. Legion, Nat. Inst. Social Scis., Am. Hellenic Congress (nat. chmn.), Order of Ahepa (past nat. pres.), Am. Quarter Horse Assn. (racing com.), Grand St. Boys Assn., United Hunts Assn., Phi Beta Kappa, Pi Delta Epsilon, Delta Sigma Rho. Clubs: Mason., Elk., Turf and Field, Economic of N.Y., Circus Saints and Sinners; Governor's (N.Y.) (exec. com.). Home: 65 Central Park W New York NY 10023 Office: 9 E 40th St New York NY 10016 *I do not choose to be a common man. It is my right to be uncommon—if I can. I seek opportunity—not security. I do not wish to be a kept citizen, humbled and dulled by having the state look after me. I want to take the calculated risk; to dream and to build, to fail and to succeed. I refuse to barter incentive for a dole. I prefer the challenges of life to the guaranteed existence; the thrill of fulfillment to the stale calm of utopia. I will not trade freedom for beneficence nor my dignity for a handout. I will never cower before any master nor bend to any threat. It is my heritage to stand erect, proud and unafraid; to think and act for myself, enjoy the benefit of my creations and to face the world boldly and say, this I have done. All this is what it means to be an American.*

ALFANGE, DEAN, JR., political science educator; b. N.Y.C., May 6, 1930; s. Dean and Thalia (Perry) A.; m. Barbara Jean Vance, June 6, 1959. A.B., Hamilton Coll., 1950; M.A., U. Colo., 1960; Ph.D., Cornell U., 1967. Instr., then asst. prof. govt. Lafayette Coll., Easton, Pa., 1963-67; from asst. prof. to assoc. prof. polit. sci. U. Mass., Amherst, 1967-75, prof., 1975—; dean Faculty Social and Behavioral Scis., 1970-75, acting vice chancellor for acad. affairs, 1975-76, 83—; vis. scholar Yale Law Sch., 1977-78. Served to 1st lt. USAF, 1952-57. Home: 5 Montague Rd Leverett MA 01054 Office: Dept Polit Sci U Mass Amherst MA 01003

ALFANO, BLAISE FRANCIS, surgeon; b. Boston, Sept. 14, 1923; s. Frank and Frances M. (Palopolli) A.; m. Virginia Forte, Sept. 19, 1953; children—Blaise Francis (dec.), Kathryn, Mark, Stephen, Paul. A.B., Harvard U., 1946; M.D., Tufts U., 1950. Intern Cambridge City Hosp., 1950-51, resident in surgery, 1951-54, mem. teaching staff, 1954-64, mem. surg. staff, 1954-64; practice medicine specializing in surgery, Melrose, Mass., 1954—; mem. surg. staff Melrose-Wakefield (Mass.) Hosp., 1954—, Winchester (Mass.) Hosp., 1954—, New Eng. Meml. Hosp., Stoneham, Mass., 1954-79; dir. Bay Bank Middlesex; exec. sec. Am. Soc. Abdominal Surgeons, 1959—; dir. publs. Jour. of Abdominal Surgery. Author textbooks. Served with USNR, 1943-46. Fellow Am. Geriatrics Soc.; mem. AMA, Mass. Med. Soc., Middlesex East Dist. Med. Soc., Am. Coll. Gastroenterology, AAAS, Assn. Med. and Allied Publs., Inst. Advancement of Med. Communication, Am. Med. Writers Assn., Med. Soc. Execs. Assn., Am. Med. Soc. Vienna, Profl. Conv. Mgmt. Assn., Am. Assn. Med. Soc. Execs., Phi Beta Pi. Home: 22 Everett Ave Winchester MA 01890 Office: 675 Main St Melrose MA 02176

ALFANO, CHARLES THOMAS, lawyer; b. Suffield, Conn., June 21, 1920; s. Dominick and Rosina (Dimartin) A.; m. Mary Ann Sinatro, Nov. 13, 1954; children: Diane Elizabeth, Andrea Rose, Charles Thomas, Susan. Student, Ill. Coll., 1939-40; B.A. cum laude, U. Conn., 1943; LL.B., J.D., U. Mich., 1948. Bar: Conn. 1948. Since practiced in, Hartford; partner firm Alfano & Halloran; judge Town Ct. of Suffield, 1949-51, 55-59; mem. Conn. Senate, 1959-77, asst. majority leader, 1966, pres. pro tem, 1967-73, minority leader, 1973-75, v.p. pro tem, 1975-77; corp. counsel, Town of Suffield, 1977—; dir., chmn. bd. Suffield Savs. Bank; dir. Conn. Water Co. Bd. dirs. Conn. Pub. TV. Served with USNR, 1942-47; ETO. Mem. Am., Conn., Hartford County bar assns., Am. Trial Lawyers Assn., Conn. Trial Lawyers Assn. (dir.). Club: K.C. Home: 50 Marbern Dr Suffield CT 06078 Office: 89 Oak St Hartford CT 06103 also 53 Mountain Rd Suffield CT 06078

ALFERS, GERALD JUNIOR, banker; b. Axtell, Kans., Dec. 12, 1931; s. Joseph Gerald and Olive (Gates) A.; m. Barbara Ruth Small, Aug. 20, 1955; children: Jerilyn, Joseph, Jean, John, James, Jennifer, Jeffrey. Grad. certificate, Am. Inst. Banking, 1964, Pacific Coast Banking Sch., 1967, Nat. Comml. Lending Grad. Sch., U. Okla., 1976. Cert. comml. lender. With Pacific Nat. Bank, Seattle, 1949-80, asst. v.p., 1961-63, v.p., cashier, 1963-72, v.p., mgr. Univ. br., 1972-74, v.p., regional mgr., 1974-76, sr. v.p., 1976-81; exec. v.p. First Interstate Bank of Wash., 1981—; Instr. Seattle Community Coll., Shoreline Community Coll.; pres., dir. Seafair Fund, 1982-83. Bd. govs. YMCA, 1972-75, chmn., 1974-75; bd. dirs. Seafair, 1979—, pres., 1981-82. Mem. Acad. Certified Adminstrv. Mgrs., Wash. Bankers Assn. (chmn. bank operations com. 1967-69), Adminstrv. Mgmt. Soc. (dir. 1972-74), Clearing House Assn. Seattle (chmn. bank operations com. 1969-72), Am. Inst. Banking (sec., dir. 1956-61). Roman Catholic. Clubs: Rotarian., Wash. Athletic, Broadmoor Golf (Seattle); Rainier. Home: 9358 California Av SW Seattle WA 98136 Office: Financial Center Seattle WA 98111

ALFIDI, RALPH JOSEPH, radiologist, educator; b. Rome, Italy, Apr. 20, 1932; s. Lucas and Angeline (Panella) A.; m. Rose Ester Senesac, Sept. 3, 1956; children: Sue, Lisa, Christine, Catherine, Mary, John. A.B., Ripon (Wis.) Coll., 1955; M.D., Marquette U., Milw., 1959. Intern Oakwood Hosp., Dearborn, Mich., 1959-60; resident, chief resident, A.C.S. fellow U. Va., 1960-63; practice medicine, specializing in radiology, Cleve., 1965—; staff mem. Cleve. Clinic, 1965-78, head dept. hosp. radiology, 1968-78; dir. dept. radiology Univ. Hosps., Cleve.; cons. VA Hosp., Hillcrest Hosp., Cleve.; chmn. dept. radiology Case Western Res. U. Sch. Medicine, 1978—; Chmn. staff Cleve. Clinic Found., 1975-76. Author: Complications and Legal Implications of Special Procedures, 1972, Computed Tomography of the Human Body: An Atlas of Normal Anatomy, 1977; Editor: Whole Body Computed Tomography, 1977; Contbr. articles to radiology jours. Served to capt., M.C. U.S. Army Res., 1963-65. Picker Found. grantee, 1969-70; NRC grantee, 1969-70. Fellow Am. Coll. Radiology; mem. AMA, Radiol. Soc. N. Am., Am. Roentgen Ray Soc., Am. Heart Assn., Soc. Cardiovascular Radiology, Soc. Gastrointestinal Radiology, Soc. Computed Body Tomography (pres. 1977-78), Eastern Radiol. Soc., Ohio Radiol. Soc., Cleve. Radiol. Soc. (pres. 1976-77). Roman Catholic. Clubs: Hillbrook, Chagrin Valley Racquet., Kirtland Country. Home: 742 Coy Ln Chagrin Falls OH 44022 Office: Case Western Res U Dept Radiology 2074 Abington Rd Cleveland OH 44106

ALFIERI, JOHN JOSEPH, Spanish educator; b. Central Nyack, N.Y., Jan. 25, 1917; s. Giovanni N. and Assunta (Padrone) A.; m. Graciela Andrade, Aug. 20, 1960. B.A., U. Southwestern La., 1950; M.A. in Romance Langs, U. Iowa, 1952; Ph.D. in Spanish, U. Iowa, 1957; postgrad., U. Madrid, 1963-64, Italian U. for Foreigners, Perugia, summers 1963, 74, U. Wis., 1977; M.A. (hon.), Lawrence U., 1982. Wollpert prof. Spanish, chmn. Spanish dept. Lawrence U., Appleton, Wis., 1954-82, prof. emeritus, 1982—. Contbr. articles and reviews to profl. publs. Mem. MLA, Am. Assn. Tchrs. of Spanish, Am. Assn. Tchrs. of Italian, Cervantes Soc. Am. Home: 803 E Alton St Appleton WI 54911

ALFIN-SLATER, ROSLYN BERNIECE, biochemist, nutritionist, educator; b. Bklyn., July 28, 1916; d. Sam and Lillian (Rubinsky) Alfin; m. Grant G. Slater, July 30, 1948. B.A., Bklyn. Coll., 1936; A.M., Columbia, 1942, Ph.D., 1946. Asst. in charge lecture div., chemistry dept. Bklyn. Coll., 1938-43, tutor gen. inorganic chemistry, 1943, instr. inorganic chemistry, qualitative analysis, evenings 1946-48; asst. instr. inorganic chemistry, exptl. phys. chemistry, food analysis Columbia, 1943-45; research fellow Corn Industries Research Found., 1945-46; instr. biochemistry N.Y. U. Coll. Dentistry, 1945-46; research chemist indsl. enzymes Takamine Labs., Clifton, N.J., 1946-47; research fellow Sloan Kettering Inst. Cancer Research, 1947-48; research asso. dept. biochemistry and nutrition U. So. Calif. Sch. Medicine, 1948-52, vis. asst. prof., 1952-56, vis. asso. prof., 1956-59; asso. prof. nutrition U. Calif., Los Angeles, 1959-65, prof., 1965—, prof. biol. chemistry, 1971—; div. head, environ. and nutritional sci. Sch. Pub. Health, 1969-77; Mem. nutrition study sect. NIH, 1968-72; mem. com. for dietary allowances, food and nutrition bd. NRC, 1970-74, mem. nat. com., internat. union nutritional scis., 1974—, mem. food and nutrition bd., 1975-81, vice chmn., 1978-79. Editor: (with D. Kritchevsky) Human Nutrition—A Comprehensive Treatise, 5 vols., 1980; Contbr. to sci. books, jours.; Editorial bd.: jour. Nutrition, 1966-70, Advances in Lipid Research, 1970-74, Am. Jour. Clin. Nutrition, 1975-78; Assoc. editor: Lipids, 1972-78, AGE, Jour. Am. Aging Assn, 1977—, Nutrition and the M.D, 1974—, Drug-Nutrient Interactions, 1980—. Fellow AAAS, Am. Heart Assn. (council on arteriosclerosis), Am. Pub. Health Assn.; mem. N.Y. Acad. Scis., Am. Soc. Biol. Chemists, Am. Inst. Nutrition (Osborne and Mendel award 1970, Borden award 1981), Soc. Exptl. Biology and Medicine, Am. Oil Chemists Soc., Am. Inst. Nutrition (treas. 1977-80), Soc. Nutrition Edn. (pres. 1978-79), Internat. Soc. Cardiology, Am. Dietetic Assn. (hon.), Sigma Xi, Phi Sigma, Iota Sigma Pi, Omicron Nu (hon.). Home: 986 Somera Rd Los Angeles CA 90077

ALFONSO, ANTONIO ESCOLAR, surgeon; b. Manila, Philippines, Nov. 25, 1943; came to U.S., 1968, naturalized, 1978; s. Ricardo Lagdameo and Marita (Escolar) Alfonso; m. Teresita Nazereno, Apr. 25, 1970; children: Margaretta, Roberto. A.B. cum laude, Ateneo U., 1963, M.D., U. Philippines, 1968. Diplomate: Am. Bd. Surgery. Intern U. Philippines-Philippine Gen. Hosp., 1968; instr. surgery Temple U., Phila., 1968-72; sr. fellow surg. oncology Univ. Med. Ctr., N.Y.C., 1972-74; dir. head and neck surgery service Downtown State Med. Ctr., Bklyn., 1974—, assoc. dir. div. surg. oncology, 1974—, asst. prof. surgery, 1974-77, assoc. prof., 1977-82, prof., 1982—; chmn. dept. surgery Bklyn. Hosp., 1982—; cons. head and neck surgery Bklyn. VA Hosp., 1974—. Author: Principles of Surgery Oncology; contbr. articles in med. to profl. jours., chpts. to med. books. Recipient research essay prize N.Y. Colon and Rectal Surg. Soc., 1973; grantee Am. Cancer Soc., 1978. Mem. Assn. Academic. Surgeons, Am. Soc. Clin. Oncology, Am. Assn. Cancer Edn., Soc. Head and Neck Surgeons, ACS, N.Y. Surg. Soc., Bklyn. Surg. Soc., N.Y. Cancer Soc., SOc. Surg. Oncology, N.Y. Head and Neck Soc., N.Y. Soc. Colon and Rectal Surgeons, Phi Kappa Phi. Roman Catholic. Home: 50 Olive St Forest Hills NY 11375 Office: Dept Surgery 121 Dekalb Ave Brooklyn NY 11201

ALFONSO, ROBERT JOHN, university administrator; b. N.Y.C., Dec. 17, 1928; s. Robert Richard and Bertha Rose (Schmitt) A.; m. Martha Sue Ralston, June 9, 1956; children: Allison Denise, Robert John, Andrea Diane (dec.). B.A., Roberts Wesleyan Coll., 1952; postgrad., N.Y. U., 1952-53; Ph.D., Mich. State U., 1962. High sch. English tchr. Syracuse, N.Y., 1956-58, Billings, Mont., 1958-59; asst. to dean Coll. Edn., Mich. State U., 1959-60; asst. prof. edn. Queens Coll., N.Y.C., 1962-64; assoc. exec. sec. Assn. for Supervision and Curriculum Devel., 1964-67; assoc. prof. curriculum and supervision Coll. Edn., U. Ala., 1967-68; asst. dean instrn. and grad. studies, prof. Coll. Edn., Kent State U. (Ohio), 1968-71; dean Coll. Edn. and Grad. Sch. Edn., also prof., 1971-80, assoc. v.p., dean faculties, 1980-82; v.p. acad. affairs East Tenn. State U., 1984—; vis. prof. U. Ga., 1982-83. Author: Instructional Supervision: A Behavior System, 1975, 2d edit., 1981; Asst. editor: Mich. Jour. Secondary Edn, 1959-62. Bd. dirs. Nat. Interagy. Council on Smoking and Health, 1964-67; Inter-Profl. Research Commn. on Pupil Personnel Services, 1965-68. Served to 1st lt. USMCR, 1953-56. Recipient Alumnus of Year award Roberts Wesleyan Coll., 1967. Mem. Assn. for Supervision and Curriculum Devel. (dir.), Am. Assn. Sch. Adminstrs., Nat. Council Tchrs. English (dir. 1965-68), Ohio Assn. for Supervision and Curriculum Devel. (pres.), Am. Ednl. Research Assn., Ohio Congress Sch. Adminstr. Orgns. (v.p.), Phi Delta Kappa, Kappa Delta Pi. Methodist. Home: 918 Maple St Johnson City TN 37601 Office: Dossett Hall East Tenn State U Johnson City TN 37614

ALFORD, BOBBY RAY, physician, educator, university administrator; b. Dallas, May 30, 1932; s. Bryant J. and Edith M. (Garrett) A.; m. Othelia Jerry Dorn, Aug. 28, 1953; children: Bradley Keith, Raye Lynn, Alan Scott. A.S., Tyler Jr. Coll., 1951; postgrad., U. Tex., 1951-52; M.D., Baylor U., 1956. Diplomate: Am. Bd. Otolaryngology (dir.). Intern Jefferson Davis Hosp., Houston, 1956-57; resident Baylor U. Coll. Medicine Affiliated Hosps. Program, 1957-60; mem. faculty Baylor U. Coll. Medicine, 1962—, prof. otolaryngology, chmn. dept., 1967—, v.p. and dean acad. affairs, 1980—; Mem. rev. panel surgeon gen. on neurol. and sensory disease USPHS, 1965-68; cons. Nat. Inst. Neurol. Disease and Stroke, 1970-74; cons. to surgeon gen. U.S. Army, 1963-73; mem. Nat. Adv. Neurol. and Communicative Disorders and Stroke Council, NIH, 1977-80. Author: Neurological Aspects of Auditory and Vestibular Disorders, 1964; Chief editor: A.M.A. Archives of Otolaryngology, 1970-79. Recipient Herman Johnson award Baylor U. Coll. Medicine, 1956; spl. NIH fellow Johns Hopkins Hosp., 1961-62. Fellow A.C.S. (bd. govs. 1977—); mem. Am. Laryngol. Assn., Soc. Univ. Otolaryngologists (sec. 1965-69), Am. Otol. Soc., Assn. Acad. Dept. Otolaryngology, Am. Laryngol., Rhinol. and Otol. Soc., Am. Soc. Head and Neck Surgery, Am. Acad. Otolaryngology Head and Neck Surgery (councillor 1977-79), Head and Neck Surgery (pres. 1981), Am. Council Otolaryngology (pres. 1981), Am. Bronchoesophagological Assn., Soc. Head and Neck Surgeons, Acoustical Soc. Am., Collegium Oto-Rhino-Laryngologicum Amicitae Sacrum, Alpha Omega Alpha. Clubs: Texas Corinthian Yacht (gov. 1978—), Doctor's (Houston) (bd. govs. 1967-70). Office: 1200 Moursund Ave Houston TX 77030

ALFORD, JACK LELAND, mechanical engineer, educator; b. Long Beach, Calif., Nov. 19, 1920; s. Leon Otto and Ethelind (Humphrey) A.; m. Edith Elizabeth Humann, Mar. 8, 1944; children: Christopher John, Margaret Ann. Student, U.S. Naval Acad., 1937-39; B.S., Calif. Inst. Tech., 1942, M.S., 1946, Ph.D., 1950. Registered profl. engr., Calif. With Turbodyne Corp., Hawthorne, Calif., 1948-50; postdoctoral fellow Calif. Inst. Tech., 1950-52; research engr. Jet Propulsion Lab., 1957-59; head engring. div. U.S. Naval Ordnance Test Sta., 1952-55; asst. to tech. dir. Technicolor Corp., 1955-57; prof. Harvey Mudd Coll., Claremont, Calif., 1959-65, James Howard Kindelberger prof. engring., 1965—, chmn. dept. engring., 1967-72, 73-79. Served to lt. USNR, 1942-46. Mem. Am. Soc. M.E., Earthquake Engring. Research Inst., Am. Soc. Engring. Edn., Am. Assn. U. Profs., Sigma Xi, Tau Beta Pi. Office: Harvey Mudd Coll Claremont CA 91711

ALFORD, JOHN MORRIS, former naval officer, foundation executive; b. Galva, Ill., Apr. 13, 1915; s. John Merlin and Shirley (Foote) A.; m. Mary Anne Carlsen, Aug. 30, 1948; children: Douglas Blakeshaw, John Morris III, Stephanie Anne, Glenna Maria. Grad., Marion (Ala.) Mil. Inst., 1932; B.S., U.S. Naval Acad., 1936, Armed Forces Staff Coll., 1952, Nat. War Coll., 1960. Commd. ensign USN, 1936, advanced through grades to rear adm., 1962; sea duty in combat ships Pacific Ocean area, 1936-45, Atlantic and Mediterranean, 1949-51, 54-57, 66-67, Pacific and Far East, 1948-49, 60-64, staff duty, Washington, 1946-47, 52-54, 57-59, 64-66, 67-69, ret., 1969; exec. dir. Navy Marine Coast Guard Residence Found., Inc., 1971—. Decorated Legion of Merit, Bronze Star; Korean Order of Merit. Mem. Navy League U.S., Naval Acad. Alumni Assn., Ret. Officers Assn., Mil. Order World Wars. Home: 3525 Trinity Dr Alexandria VA 22304 Office: US Naval Obs Washington DC 20390

ALFORD, JOHN WILLIAM, banker; b. Balt., Oct. 21, 1912; s. James Perry and Lydia (Turner) A.; m. Mary Elizabeth Anderson, Jan. 3, 1951; children: Barbara Lynne Alford Cantlin, Ronald Bradford. A.B., DePauw U., 1935. With Park Nat. Bank, Newark, Ohio, 1935—, v.p., 1946-56, pres., 1956-60, chmn. bd., 1979—, dir., 1952—; dir. Contour Forming Inc., ALLTEL Ohio, Inc., Stocker & Sitler Oil Co., H. W. Martin & Son Co., W.E. Shrider Co. Mem. Licking County Hosp. Commn., 1962—; gen. chmn. citizens com. for Licking County Meml. Hosp., 1962; mem. adv. bd. Salvation Army, 1946—; pres., trustee Licking County Indsl. Growth Corp.; chmn. Thomas J. Evans Found.; trustee Dawes Arboretum, Denison U., Licking County Found. Public Giving; trustee, treas. Meth. Theol. Sch. in Ohio. Served to lt. comdr. USNR, 1942-46. Mem. Ohio Bankers Assn. (pres. 1966-67), Am. Bankers Assn. (exec. council 1967-70, nat. bank div. exec. com. 1967-70), Newark C. of C. (pres. 1955-56), Ohio C. of C. (dir., vice chmn.), Am. Legion, VFW. Methodist. Clubs: Elks, Rotary, Columbus, Moundbuilders Country. Home: 671 Carriage Ct Newark OH 43055 Office: 50 N 3d St Newark OH 43055

ALFORD, LIONEL DEVON, manufacturing company executive; b. Winnsboro, La., Mar. 1, 1925; s. Columbus F. and Jennie A. (Lee) A.; m. Sallie Julia Bryan, Feb. 2, 1951; children: Lionel Devon, Scott Franklin. B.S. in M.E, La. Tech. U., 1951; postgrad. (Sloan fellow), Stanford U., 1966. Test pilot Boeing Co., Seattle, 1955-59, mgr. various missile test ops., 1959-65, v.p. missiles and space div., 1969-77, sr. v.p., Seattle and Wichita, Kans., 1984—; pres. Boeing Mil. Airplane Co., Seattle and Wichita, Kans., 1977—, Kans. Foodbank Warehouse, Inc.; dir. Fourth Fin. Co., Wichita. Kans. vol. state chmn. U.S. Savs. Bonds, 1980—; bd. dirs. St. Francis Regional Med. Ctr., Wichita. Served with USAF, 1943-46, 51-54. Decorated D.F.C., Air medal with 3 oak leaf clusters. Mem. Soc. Mfg. Engrs., Am. Def. Preparedness Assn., Air Force Assn., Stanford U. Alumni Assn. Republican. Baptist. Home: 14223 N Point Dr Wichita KS 67230 Office: 3801 S Oliver St Wichita KS 67210

ALFORD, NEILL HERBERT, JR., legal educator; b. Greenville, S.C., July 13, 1919; s. Neill Herbert and Elizabeth (Robertson) A.; m. Elizabeth Talbot Smith, June 26, 1943; children: Neill Herbert III, Margaret Dudley, Eli Thomas Stackhouse. B.A., The Citadel-Mil. Coll. S.C., 1940; LL.B., U. Va., 1947; J.S.D., Yale U., 1966. Bar: Va. 1954. Mem. faculty law U. Va. Law Sch., Charlottesville, 1947-61, 62-74, Doherty Found. prof., 1966-74, spl. cons. to pres. univ., legal adviser to rector and bd. dirs., 1972-74; Joseph Henry Lumpkin prof., dean Law Sch. U. Ga., Athens, 1974-76; Percy Brown Jr. prof. law U. Va., 1976—; state reporter Supreme Ct. Va., 1977-84; prof. chair internat. law Naval War Coll., 1961-62, cons., 1962—; Spl. counsel Va. Code Commn., 1954—; dir. Va. Bankers Assn. Trust Sch., 1958-61; summer tchr. George Washington U., U. N.C.; chmn. bd. dirs. U. Va. Press., 1970-74. Author: Cases and Materials on Decedents Estates and Trusts, 5th edit, 1977, Modern Economic Warfare: Law and the Naval Participant, 1967; Contbr. articles to profl. jours. Comdr. civil affairs group U.S. Army Res., 1947-66. Served to lt. col. AUS, 1941-46; ETO. Decorated Bronze Star, Combat Inf. badge.; Sterling fellow Yale, 1950-51; Ford fellow U. Wis., 1958. Mem. Selden Soc., Am. Soc. Legal History, Am. Judicature Soc., Am. Soc. Internat. Law, Am. Law Inst., Am. Coll. Probate Counsel, Va. State Bar, Va., Am. bar assns., Order of Coif, Phi Alpha Delta, Omicron Delta Kappa. Club: Colonnade (Charlottesville). Home: 1868 Field Rd Charlottesville VA 22901 Office: Law Sch U Va Charlottesville VA 22901

ALFORD, ROBERT ROSS, sociologist; b. Stockton, Calif., Apr. 18, 1928; s. Ellsworth and Grace (Ross) A.; m. Gloria Kramer, June 18, 1949; children—Heidi, Jonathan, Elissa. A.B., U. Calif., Berkeley, 1950, M.A., 1952, Ph.D., 1961. Lectr. sociology U. Calif., Berkeley, 1959-61; mem. faculty U. Wis., 1961-74, prof. sociology, 1966-74; asso. dir. Survey Research Lab., 1961-63; vis. prof. govt. U. Essex, Eng., 1966-67; vis. fellow Netherlands Inst. Advanced Study, 1981-82; vis. prof. sociology Columbia U., 1970-71, 80-81; prof. sociology U. Calif., Santa Cruz, 1974—, chmn. bd. studies in sociology, 1974-76; dir. Interdisciplinary Grad. Program in Sociology, 1976-79. Author: Party and Society, 1963, Bureaucracy and Participation: Political Cultures in Four Wisconsin Cities, 1969, Health Care Politics, 1975; editor: Stress and Contradiction in Advanced Capitalist Societies, 1975. Mem. Am. Sociol. Assn., Am. Polit. Sci. Assn. (Woodrow Wilson Found. award 1976). Home: 435 Meder St Santa Cruz CA 95060

ALFORD, WILLIAM PARKER, educator; b. London, Ont., Can., Mar. 22, 1927; s. William Alexander and Ruby (Parker) A.; m. Jeannette Wadland, June 15, 1949; children—David, Mary Joan, Stephen. B.Sc., U. Western Ont., 1949; Ph.D., Princeton, 1954. Instr. Princeton (N.J.) U., 1953-55; mem. faculty U. Rochester, N.Y., 1955-73; prof., chmn. dept. physics U. Western Ontario, 1973—; Vis. prof. Inst. Nuclear Research, Amsterdam, The Netherlands, 1961-62, U. Munich, Germany, 1970-71, U. Colo., 1978-79. Fellow Am. Phys. Soc.; mem. Am. Assn. Physics Tchrs. Office: Dept Physics U Western Ontario London ON Canada

ALFRED, STEPHEN JAY, lawyer; b. N.Y.C., Aug. 15, 1934; s. George J. A. and Janet (Brenner) Miller; m. Norma Richman, June 24, 1956 (div. 1980); children: Deborah Susan, Lynda Beth, Bruce David, Julianna Richman; m. Lynne Belofsky Durchslag, Jan. 10, 1981. A.B., Princeton U., 1956; J.D., Harvard U., 1959. Bar: Ohio 1959, Fla. 1978. Assoc. Squire, Sanders & Dempsey, Cleve., 1959-69, ptnr., 1969—. Contbr. articles to profl. jours. Councilman City of Shaker Heights, Ohio, 1972-79, mayor, Ohio, 1984—; trustee Citizens League of Cleve., 1976-83, Beech Brook Children's Home, Orange, Ohio, 1968—; pres. Beech Brook Children's Home, Orange, Ohio, 1971-72, treas., Orange, Ohio, 1979-81; pres. Lomond Assn., Shaker Heights, 1965-67. Mem. ABA, Bar Assn. Greater Cleve., Cleve. Tax Inst. (gen. chmn. 1981), Harvard Law Sch. Assn. of Cleve. (pres. 1982). Democrat. Jewish. Home: 20856 S Woodland Rd Shaker Heights OH 44122 Office: Squire Sanders & Dempsey 1800 Huntington Bldg Cleveland OH 44115

ALFRED, WILLIAM, author, educator; b. N.Y.C., Aug. 16, 1922; s. Thomas Allfrey and Mary (Bunyan) A. B.A., Bklyn. Coll., 1948; M.A., Harvard U., 1949, Ph.D., 1954. Mem. faculty Harvard U., 1954—, prof. English, 1963—. Author: The Annunciation Rosary, 1948; verse plays Agamemnon, 1954, Hogan's Goat, 1956, Cry For Us All, 1970, To Your Heart's Desire, 1978, Nothing Doing, 1978; Contbr. poems, articles to profl. jours.; co-editor: Of Reformation, The Prose Works of John Milton, 1954; asso. editor: American Poet, 1942-44. Served with AUS, 1943-46. Recipient Lit. Assos. award Bklyn. Coll., 1953; Creative Arts Theatre grantee Brandeis U., 1960; Amy Lowell Travelling Poetry scholar, 1956; Nat. Inst. Arts and Letters grantee. Mem. Mediaeval Acad. Am., Modern Lang. Assn., Dramatists Guild. Home: 31 Athens St Cambridge MA 02138

ALFVEN, HANNES OLOF GOSTA, physicist, educator; b. May 30, 1908. Ph.D., U. Uppsala, Sweden, 1934. Prof. theory of electricity Royal Inst. Tech., Stockholm, 1940-45, prof. electronics, 1945-63, prof. plasma physics, 1963-73; prof. applied physics and info. sci. U. Calif., San Diego, 1967—; past mem. Swedish Sci. Adv. Council, Swedish Atomic Energy Commn.; past bd. govs. Swedish Def. Research Inst., Swedish Atomic Energy Co.; past sci. adv. Swedish Govt.; past pres. Pugwash Confs. Sci. and World Affairs; mem. panel comets and astroids NASA. Author: Cosmical Electrodynamics, 1950, On the Origin of the Solar System, 1954, Cosmical Electrodynamics: Fundamental Principles, 1963, Worlds-Antiworlds, 1966, The Tale of the Big Computer, 1968, Atom, Man and the Universe, 1969, Living on the Third Planet, 1972, Evolution of the Solar System, 1976, Cosmic Plasma, 1981. Recipient Nobel prize for physics, 1970; Lomonsov Gold medal USSR Acad. Scis., 1971; Franklin medal, 1971. Mem. Swedish Acad. Scis., Akademia NAUK (USSR), U.S. Acad. Scis. (fgn. asso.), Royal Soc. (fgn. mem.), numerous others. Office: Dept Electrical Engineering and Computer Science U Calif La Jolla CA 92093 *

ALGER, CHADWICK FAIRFAX, educator, polit. scientist; b. Chambersburg, Pa., Oct. 9, 1924; s. Herbert and Thelma (Drawbaugh) A.; m. Elinor Reynolds, Aug. 28, 1948; children—Mark, Scott, Laura, Craig. B.A., Ursinus Coll., 1949; M.A., Johns Hopkins, 1950; Ph.D., Princeton, 1958; LL.D., Ursinus Coll., 1979. Internat. relations specialist Dept. Navy, 1950-54; instr. Swarthmore Coll., 1957; faculty Northwestern U., Evanston, Ill., 1958-71, prof. polit. sci., 1966-71, dir. internat. relations program, 1967-71; Mershon prof. polit. sci. and pub. policy, dir. transnat. intellectual cooperation program Ohio State U., 1971—; vis. prof. UN affairs N.Y.U., 1962-63. Co-author: Simulation in International Relations, 1963, You and Your Community in the World, 1978; Contbr. articles profl. jours. Served with USNR, 1943-46. Recipient Disting. Scholar award Internat. Soc. for Ednl., Cultural and Sci. Interchanges, 1980. Mem. Am. Polit. Sci. Assn. (council 1970-72), Internat. Polit. Sci. Assn., AAAS, Internat. Studies Assn. (pres. 1978-79), Internat. Peace Research Assn. (council 1971-77), Midwest Conf. Polit. Scis. (recipient prize 1966), Consortium on Peace Research, Edn. and Devel. (exec. com. 1971-77, chmn. 1976-77), Union Internat. Assns. Home: 2674 Westmont Blvd Columbus OH 43221

ALHADEFF, DAVID ALBERT, economics educator; b. Seattle, Mar. 22, 1923; s. Albert David and Pearl (Taranto) A.; m. Charlotte Pechman, Aug. 1, 1948. B.A., U. Wash., 1944; M.A., Harvard U., 1948, Ph.D., 1950. Faculty U. Calif. at Berkeley, 1949—, prof. bus. adminstrn., 1959—, asso. dean, 1980-82. Author: Monopoly and Competition in Banking, 1954, Competition and Controls in Banking, 1968, Microeconomics and Human Behavior, 1982; Contbr. articles to profl. jours., chpts. to books. Served with AUS, 1943-46. Mem. Am., Western econ. assns., Am. Finance Assn. Home: 2101 Shoreline Dr Apt 456 Alameda CA 94501 Office: U Calif Barrows Hall Berkeley CA 94720

ALHADEFF, MORRIS JEROME, organization executive; b. Seattle, Nov. 14, 1914; s. Solomon David and Esther (Almeleh) A.; m. Joan Gottstein, Apr. 2, 1942; children: Michael David, Kenneth. B.A., U. Wash., 1938. News reporter radio sta. KJR, Seattle, 1938; night news editor radio sta. KVI, Tacoma, Wash., 1940-41; program dir., news analyst radio sta. KOL, Seattle, 1942-47; mem. staff Wash. Jockey Club, Renton, 1947—, pres., chief exec. officer, 1971—; pres. Broadacres, Inc., Seattle, 1971—, Miken Corp., 1971—; owner M.J. Alhadeff Co., Seattle, 1945—. Instituted 4-H Club Horsemen's award, 1943—; Chmn. Seattle Arts Commn., 1974-75, Mayor Seattle Task Force Com. for U.S. Bicentennial, 1973, Seattle-King County Am. Revolution Bicentennial Commn., 1975-76, Art in Pub. Places Com., 1975—; chmn. regional orgn. drive Boy Scouts Am., 1962; pres. Patrons N.W. Civic, Cultural and Charitable Orgns., 1970, Contemporary Arts Council of Seattle Art Mus., 1971; mem. Mayor Seattle Task Force Conv. and Bus. Facility, 1975—, Seattle Center Adv. Commn., 1971—, Seattle Found., 1970—; Bd. dirs. Found. Preservation Gov.'s Mansion, 1974-75, NCCJ, 1962-74, Greater Seattle, 1968, Bumbershoot Arts Festival, 1973—; bd. dirs., mem. exec. com., v.p. Seattle Art Mus.; bd. dirs., mem. exec. com. Fifth Ave. Theatre Assn.; trustee Seattle Repertory Theatre, 1968-74; bd. dirs. Evergreen Safety Council, 1984—; founder Joseph Gottstein Meml. Cancer Research Lab., U. Wash.; mem. med. vis. com. U. Wash., 1972; co-chmn. Seattle Parks Centennial Commn., 1984; exec. com. Fifth Ave. Theatre Assn., 1980-81. Served with USCGR, 1944-45. Recipient Distinguished Service award Wash. Horse Breeders, 1974; Round Table award Jockey Club, 1974; 1st Pub. Service award in arts Mayor Seattle, 1975. Mem. Thoroughbred Racing Assn. U.S. (dir., v.p., pres. 1983-84), Puget Sound Sportswriters and Sportscasters (sec.), Turf Publicists Am. (v.p. 1968), Seattle Advt. Club (hon. life), Internat. Footprinter Assn. Clubs: Variety (dir. 1968-72), 101, Rainier, Glendale Golf and Country. Home: 6006 Lake Shore Dr S Seattle WA 98118 Office: PO Box 60 Renton WA 98055

AL-HAFEEZ, HUMZA (LEONARD 12X WEIR), police officer; b. N.Y.C., Feb. 28, 1931; s. Asa Mose and Rose Mae (Danielson) Weir; m. Clarissa Ramona Mitchell, Mar. 1, 1980; children: Rasul, Roland, Habib, Wardi, John, Larry, Don, Mariama. Student, Food Trades Vocat. Sch., 1947-48. Patrolman N.Y.C. Police Dept., from 1959; now owner, dir. Al-Hafeez Security and Investigations Service, Bklyn.; founder Nat. Soc. Afro-Am. Policemen Inc.; also past pres.; cons. community relations to chief insp. N.Y.C. Police Dept., to; U.S. Dept. Justice; investigator of corruption among N.Y.C. police officers Knapp Commn.; undercover narcotic officer, investigator Manhattan office Dist. Atty.; investigator Office of 1st Dep. Policy Commr.; undercover investigator U.S. Dept. Justice.; insp. N.Y. State Athletic Commn.; Lectr. Princeton U., Mich. State U., N.Y. State U., Pace Coll., Bklyn. Coll., U. Chgo., NYU, Satellite Acad., N.Y.C., Kinlock Mission for Blind, City N.Y. Police Acad., Nassau Community Coll.; others. Appeared on radio and TV.; Editor-in-chief: Your Muhammad Speaks newspaper. Mem. pastoral bd. Interfaith Hosp. Recipient Father of Yr. award Kinlock Freedom Found. for the Blind, 1973; Community Service award United Council of Chs., 1975. Mem. Internat. Platform Assn. Mem. Nation of Islam; minister Muhammad's Temple of Islam, Bklyn. Home: 361 Clinton Ave Brooklyn NY 11238 Office: 549 Nostrand Ave Brooklyn NY 11216

ALI, MEHDI RAZA, food and beverage company executive; b. Lahore, Pakistan, Nov. 22, 1944; came to U.S., 1954, naturalized, 1980; m. Raelene, Sept. 19, 1966; children: Mehdi, Hadi. B.A., Yale U., 1965, M.A., 1967. Vice pres. Morgan Guaranty Trust Co., 1968-75; asst. treas. Gen. Motors Corp., N.Y.C., 1976-79, v.p., 1980; v.p., treas. Pepsi Co., Inc., Purchase, N.Y., 1981—. Home: 181 Lounsbury Rd Ridgefield CT 06877 Office: Anderson Hill Rd Purchase NY 10577

ALI, MIR KURSHEED, mathematician; b. Hyderabad, India, Apr. 16, 1926; came to U.S., 1961, naturalized, 1974; s. Mir Warris and Haleema (Begum) A.; m. Mohammadi Begum, Jan. 13, 1952; 2 children. B.Sc., Osmania U., Hyderabad, 1947, M.A., 1949; M.S., Mont. State U., 1964; Ph.D., Wash. State U., 1968. Lectr. math. City Coll. Hyderabad, 1949-52; lectr. math. Sci. Coll., Saifabad, India, 1952-58, head dept., 1958-61; part time faculty Mont. State U., 1961-64; instr. Wash. State U., 1964-66, part time faculty, 1966-68; mem. faculty Calif. State U., Fresno, 1968—, prof. math., 1975—; vis. prof. Abadan (Iran) Inst. Tech., 1976-77. Author articles. NSF fellow, 1965; Edwin W. Rice fellow, 1966. Mem. Am. Math. Soc., Math. Assn. Am., AAUP, Soc. Muslim Scientists U.S. and Can., World Affairs Council. Office: Dept Math Calif State U Fresno CA 93740

ALI, MUHAMMAD (CASSIUS MARCELLUS CLAY), professional boxer; b. Louisville, Jan. 17, 1942; s. Marcellus and Odessa (Grady) Clay; m. Sonji (div. 1966); m. Kalilah Tolona (Belinda Boyd), Apr. 18, 1967 (div. 1977); 3 daus., 1 son; m. Veronica Porshe, June 19, 1977; 1 dau. Ed. pub. schs., Louisville. Appeared in: movie The Greatest, 1977; TV movie Freedom Road; Author: The Greatest: My Own Story, 1975. Mem. World Community Islam. Light heavyweight champion AAU, 1959, 60; light heavyweight champion Golden Gloves, 1959, heavyweight champion, 1960; light heavy weight champion Olympic Games, 1960, world heavyweight champion, 1964-67, 74-78, 78-79; lost to heavyweight champion Larry Holmes, 1980. Address: PO Box 76972 Los Angeles CA 90076 *

ALIBER, ROBERT Z., economist; b. Keene, N.H., Sept. 19, 1930; s. Norman H. and Sophie (Becker) A.; m. Deborah Baltzly, Sept. 9, 1955; children: Jennifer, Rachel, Michael. B.A., Williams Coll., 1952, Cambridge U., 1954, M.A., 1957; Ph.D., Yale U., 1962. Staff economist Commn. Money and Credit, N.Y.C., 1959-61, Com. on Econ. Devel., Washington, 1961-64; sr. econ. advisor AID, Dept. State, Washington, 1964-65; assoc. prof., then prof. internat. econs. and fin. Grad. Sch.Bus., U. Chgo., 1965—. Author: The International Money Game, 1973, 76, 79, 83, Exchange Risk and Corporate International Finance, 1978, Your Money and Your Life; Editor: National Monetary Policies and the International Financial System,

1974, The Political Economy of Monetary Reform, 1976. Served with U.S. Army, 1952-54. Fulbright fellow, 1952-54. Mem. Am. Econs. Assn., Acad. Internat. Bus., Canadian Econs. Assn., Assn. Pub. Policy Analysis and Mgmt. Clubs: Quadrangle, Nat. Economists. Home: 5638 S Dorchester Ave Chicago IL 60637 Office: 1101 E 58th St Chicago IL 60637

ALIMANESTIANU, CALIN, hotel consultant; b. Bucharest, Roumania, Dec. 29, 1925; came to U.S., 1953, naturalized, 1961; s. Virgil and Nineta (Leon) A.; m. Betty Lou Nicholas, Aug. 1, 1959; 1 dau., Simone. Ed. in, Rome. Mgmt. trainee Woodner Hotel, Washington, 1955, Bismarck Hotel, Chgo., 1957; asst. to gen. mgr. Oxford House, Chgo., 1958-60; gen. mgr. Holiday Inn, Newburgh, N.Y., Plainview, L.I., N.Y., 1960-67, v.p. operation, gen. mgr., N.Y.C., 1967-71; mng. dir. Dering Harbor Inn, Shelter Island, N.Y.; hotel cons., 1973—; pres. Creative Hotel Cons. Internat., St. Petersburg Beach, Fla., 1977—. Mem. GOP Heritage Groups (nationalties div.), Julio Maniu Am. Roumanian Relief Found. Mem. Royal Automobile Club Roumania. Mem. Eastern Orthodox Ch. Home and office: 8080 29th Ave N Saint Petersburg FL 33710

ALINDER, JAMES GILBERT, photographer, museum executive, author; b. Glendale, Calif., Mar. 31, 1941; s. Gilbert Leonard and Alice (Gustafson) A.; m. Mary Kathlyn Street, Dec. 17, 1965; children: Jasmine, Jesse, Zachary. B.A., Macalester Coll., 1962; M.F.A., U. N.Mex., 1968. Dir. photography program dept. art U. Nebr., Lincoln, 1968-77; exec. dir. Friends of Photography, Carmel, Calif., 1977—; lectr., cons. in field. Author: Wright Morris: Structures and Artifacts, 1975, Crying for a Vision, 1976, Twelve Midwestern Photographers, 1977, Ansel Adams: 50 Years of Portraits, 1978, Robert Cumming, Photographs, 1978, Collecting Light: The Photographs of Ruth Bernhard, 1979, Ansel Adams: Photographs of the American West, 1980, The Contact Print, 1982, Picture America, 1982; contbr. articles on art photography to profl. jours.; editor: Self-Portrayal: The Photographer's Image, 1978, Carleton Watkins: Photographs of Oregon and the Columbia River, 1979, 9 Critics, 9 Photographs, 1980, Roy DeCarava, Photographs, 1981, Wright Morris, Photographs and Words, 1982; jours. Exposure, 1973-77, Untitled, 1977—; one-man shows, Sheldon Art Mus., Lincoln, Nebr., 1969, 73, Focus Gallery, San Francisco, 1970, Halsted's 831 gallery, Birmingham, Mich., 1971, Once Gallery, N.Y.C., 1974, U. Colo., Boulder, 1976, Camerawork Gallery, San Francisco, 1979, Spiva Art Mus., Joplin, 1980, Weston Gallery, Carmel, 1981, 83, others, group shows include, George Eastman House, Rochester, N.Y., 1969, 71, 72, M.I.T., 1968-70, U. Calif., Davis, 1972, Hudson River Mus., N.Y., 1973, Nelson gallery, Kansas City, 1974, Pratt Inst., N.Y.C., 1975, U. Colo., 1977, Northwestern U., 1978, Santa Barbara Mus. Art, 1979, Spiritus Gallery, Newport Beach, Calif., 1981, 291 Gallery, Kansas City, numerous others; represented in permanent collections, Mus. Modern Art, N.Y.C., Victoria and Albert Mus., London, Bibliotheque Nationale, Paris, George Eastman House, Rochester, N.Y., Art Inst. Chgo., Center for Creative Photography, Tucson, others. Nat. Endowment for Arts photographer's fellow, 1973, 80; Woods Found. fellow, 1974. Mem. Soc. Photog. Edn. (sec. 1973-75, vice-chmn. 1975-77, chmn. bd. 1977-79), Am. Assn. Museums. Office: PO Box 500 Carmel CA 93921

ALIO, IVAN STAMENITOV, physician, medical consultant; b. Sofia, Bulgaria, May 26, 1921; came to U.S., 1954, naturalized, 1958; s. Peter and Elizabeth (Alio) Stamenitov; m. Geraldine Riley, July 1, 1955; children: Elizabeth, John, Richard, Jamila. D.M., Sofia Gymnasium, 1940; M.D., U. Tubingen, Germany, 1945; M.P.H., Johns Hopkins U., 1955; D.P.H. in Epidemiology, Columbia U., 1968; hon. prof., Sch. Chinese Medicine, Seoul, 1958. Intern Alexander Hosp., Sofia, 1946-47; practice medicine, Bulgaria and Italy, 1947-49; med. officer jungle despensary Bruzual de Apure, Venezuela, 1949-50; dir. floating health ctr. along Orinoco River, Venezuela, 1950-53; phys. malariologist 10th Internat. Course Metaxenic Diseases, Maracay, Venezuela, 1953-54; chief preventive medicine, Ft. Chaffee, Ark., 1955-57; resident in family practice Ireland Army Hosp., Ft. Knox., 1957-58; preventive medicine adviser to surgeon gen. Korean Army, 1958-60; phys. epidemiologist Dhahran Health Ctr., Saudi Arabia, 1960-69; cons. WHO, 1970; tech. specialist Peace Corps, Washington, 1970-73, dir. profl. activities, 1973-81; cons. on internat. health and tropical medicine. Served to maj. AUS, 1955-60. Recipient Physician Recognition award AMA, 1969. Fellow Am. Pub. Health Assn., Royal Soc. Tropical Medicine and Hygiene; mem. Am. Soc. Tropical Medicine and Hygiene, Assn. Mil. Surgeons U.S., Res. Officers Assn., 38th Parallel Med. Soc., Gulf Med. Soc., Tri-Dist. Med. Assn., Lebanon Med. Assn., Am. Assn. Fgn. Med. Grads., Soc. Epidemiol. Research, Med. Soc. D.C., Interagy. Com. Nutrition Edn., Epidemiol. Working Group, Smithsonian Assocs., Internat. Health Soc., Nat. Council for Internat. Health. Home: 5021 Sudley Rd West River MD 20778

ALIOTO, ROBERT FRANKLYN, supt. schs.; b. San Francisco, Nov. 22, 1933; s. Michael P. and Evelyn (Blohm) A.; m. Dominica Ann Deuel, June 28, 1980; children—Deborah Ann, Robert Franklyn, David R., Diane A. A.A., Hartnell Coll., 1953; B.E., San Jose State Coll., 1958, M.A., 1961; Ed.D., Harvard, 1968. Tchr. elem. and jr. high schs., Greenfield, Calif., 1956-60; prin. Carneros Elem. Sch., Napa, Calif., 1960-62; supt. Shurtleff Elementary Sch. Dist., Napa, 1962-65; adminstrv. asst. Center for Research and Devel. on Ednl. Differences, Harvard, 1965-66; dir. Inst. Tng. Selected Tchrs. Liaison Role, 1966-67; supt. schs. Pearl River (N.Y.) Sch. Dist., 1966-71, Yonkers (N.Y.) City Sch. Dist., 1971-75, San Francisco Unified Sch. Dist., 1975—. Author: (with J.A. Jungherr) Operational PPBS for Education, 1971. Home: 24 Dellbrook Ave San Francisco CA Office: 135 Van Ness Ave Room 209 San Francisco CA 94102

ALJIAN, JAMES DONOVAN, investment company executive; b. Oakland, Calif., Nov. 5, 1932; s. George W. and Marguerite (Donovan) A.; m. Marjorie L. Townsend, Oct. 17, 1959; children: Mark Donovan, Mary Anne, Reed Townsend. B.S., U. Calif., Berkeley, 1955; M.B.A., Golden Gate U., 1965. Office mgr. Uniroyal Co., San Francisco, 1957-60; audit supr. Ernst & Ernst, San Francisco, 1960-65; sec.-treas. Tracy Investment Co., Las Vegas, 1965-73, Internat. Leisure Corp., 1967-70; sr. v.p. fin. MGM, Culver City, Calif., 1973-79; pres. Tracinda Corp., Las Vegas, 1979-82; sr. v.p. fin. planning MGM/UA Entertainment Co., Culver City, Calif., 1982—; dir. MGM Grand Hotels, Inc., MGM/UA Entertainment Co., Southwest Leasing Corp. Served with AUS, 1955-57. Mem. Am. Inst. C.P.A.s, Calif. Soc. C.P.A.s. Office: 10202 W Washington Blvd Culver City CA 90230

ALKER, HAYWARD ROSE, JR., educator, political science educator; b. N.Y.C., Oct. 3, 1937; s. Hayward Rose and Dorothy (Fitzsimmons) A.; m. Judith Ann Tickner, June 3, 1961; children: Joan Christina, Heather Jane, Gwendolyn Ann. B.S., MIT, 1959; M.S., Yale U., 1960, Ph.D., 1963. Instr. to assoc. prof. polit. sci. Yale U., 1963-68; vis. prof. U. Mich., 1968, others; prof. polit. sci. MIT, 1968—; Chmn. Math. Social Scis. Bd., 1970-71. Author: Mathematics and Politics, 1965, (with others) World Handbook of Political and Social Indicators, 1966, (with Russett) World Politics in the General Assembly, 1966, (with Bloomfield and Choucri) Analyzing Global Interdependence, 1974, (with Hurwitz) Resolving Prisoner's Dilemmas, 1981; Bd. editors: Jour. Interdisciplinary History, 1969-71, (with Hurwitz) Internat. Orgn, 1970-76, Quality and Quantity, 1974—, Internat. Studies Quar, 1980—, Internat. Interactions, 1981—. Congl. intern Office of Chester Bowles, 1960. Fellow Center for Advanced Studies in Behavioral Scis., Stanford, Calif., 1967-68. Mem. Am. Polit. Sci. Assn., Internat. Polit. Sci. Assn., Internat. Studies Assn., Peace Sci. Soc. Democrat. Home: 288 Mill St Newtonville MA 02160 Office: E53-407 Mass Inst Tech Cambridge MA 02139

ALKON, PAUL KENT, English educator. A.B., Harvard U., 1957; Ph.D. in English Lit., U. Chgo., 1962. Instr., asst. prof. English lit. U. Calif.-Berkeley, 1962-70; assoc. prof. U. Md., 1970-71; assoc. prof. English U. Minn., Mpls., 1971-73, prof., 1973-80; Leo S. Bing prof. English U. So. Calif., Los Angeles, 1980—; vis. prof. English Ben Gurion U. of the Negev, Israel, 1977-78. Author: Samuel Johnson and Moral Discipline, 1967, Defoe and Fictional Time, 1979. Mem. MLA, Am. Soc. 18th Century Studies. Office: Dept English U So Calif Los Angeles CA 90007 *

ALLABY, STANLEY REYNOLDS, clergyman; b. Providence, Dec. 28, 1931; s. Edwin T. and Hope (Swift) A.; m. Marion Arlene Johnson, Dec. 18, 1954; children—Norman R., Darlene R., Kimberly A., Stephen R. A.B., Gordon Coll., 1953; M.Div., Gordon Conwell Sem., 1956; D.D., Barrington (R.I.) Coll., 1977; D.Min., Westminster Theol. Sem., 1978. Ordained to ministry, 1956; pastor Black Rock Conglist. Ch., Fairfield, Conn., 1956—; dir. Sudan Interior Mission, N.J., 1970—; vice chmn. Billy Graham New Haven Crusade, 1982; Ockenga lectr. Gordon-Conway Sem., 1983. Bd. dirs. United Neighbors for Self Devel., Bridgeport Bd. dirs. United Neighbors for Self Devel., Conn., 1963-64, Christian Freedom Found., 1960-70; trustee Gordon Coll., Wenham, Mass., 1965-69, 77-81, Gordon Div. Sch., Wenham, Mass., 1965-69. Recipient George Washington honor medal Freedoms Found., 1968, 69; Alumnus-of-Year award Gordon Coll., 1976. Mem. Gordon Coll. Alumni Assn. (past pres.), Nat. Assn. Evangelicals (dir. 1974—, exec. com. 1980-82, nat. conv. coordinator 1981-82), Greater Bridgeport Fellowship Evangelicals (chmn. resolutions com. 1982-83), Bridgeport Pastors Assn. (past pres.), Greater Bridgeport Fellowship Evangelicals (past pres.). Home: 1371 Bronson Rd Fairfield CT 06430 Office: 3685 Black Rock Turnpike Fairfield CT 06430

ALLAIN, EMERY EDGAR, paper co. exec.; b. Northbridge, Mass., Oct. 22, 1922; s. Emery and Florida (Pelletier) A.; m. Florance Chabot, Feb. 10, 1945; children—Amy Louise, John Emery. Student, Bentley Coll., 1939-41, Northeastern U., 1941-43. C.P.A., Mass., Me. With Arthur Andersen & Co. (C.P.A.s), Boston and N.Y.C., 1944-49; controller Royal Lace Paper Works, 1949-51, treas., 1951-54; with Great No. Paper Co., 1954—, controller, 1962-68, v.p. finance, 1968—, Gt. No. Nekoosa Corp., 1970—. Mem. Am. Inst. C.P.A.s, Financial Execs. Inst., Nat. Assn. Accountants. Home: 108 Valley Rd Greenwich CT 06807 Office: 75 Prospect St Stamford CT 06901

ALLAIN, WILLIAM A., governor Mississippi; b. 1928. Grad., U. Notre Dame; LL.B., U. Miss. Bar: Miss. 1950. Former asst. atty. gen. State of Miss., atty. gen., 1980-84; gov. Miss., 1984—. Office: Office of Gov PO Box 139 Jackson MS 39205 *

ALLAM, MARK WHITTIER, veterinarian, former university administrator; b. Fernwood, Pa., Aug. 17, 1908; s. Clyde Macfarl and Helen (Hubbard) A.; m. Lila Josephine Griswold, Apr. 15, 1933; children: Shelley Lee, Maryjane Whittier. V.M.D., U. Pa., 1932. Gen. practice vet. medicine, 1932-45; instr. vet. surgery Sch. Vet. Medicine, U. Pa., 1943-45, asst. prof., 1945-48, assoc. prof., 1948-51, prof., 1951-77, prof. emeritus, 1977—, chmn. dept. surgery, 1951-55; research Harrison Dept. Surg. Research, Sch. Medicine, 1947-51, dean of faculty, 1952-73, asst. v.p. for health affairs, 1973-77; cons. Pan Am. San. Bur., WHO; mem. med. adv. bd. FDA, 1965-69, mem. vet. med. adv. bd., 1967-70; pres. Pa. Health Council, 1969-72; mem. expert panel on vet. edn. FAD-WHO, 1966—; Pres. bd. edn. Media Borough Sch. Dist., 1941-60; pres. Media Civic Forum, 1964-67, Media Historic Preservations, 1977-80. Contbr.: (edited by Hoskins and Lacroix), revised edit.) General Surgery, 1953; Author articles in field. Fellow Coll. Physicians Phila.; mem. Vet. Medicine Alumni Assn. (pres. 1943), Am. Vet. Med. Assn. (v.p. 1956, exec. bd. 1958-63), Pa. Keystone Vet. Med. Assn., Royal Coll. Vet. Surgeons (U.K.) (hon. assoc.), N.Y. Acad. Scis., Sigma Xi, Phi Zeta (nat. pres. 1948). Republican. Presbyterian. Home: 211 E 5th St Media PA 19063 Office: 3451 Walnut St Philadelphia PA 19174

ALLAN, BARRY DAVID, govt. ofcl.; b. Steubenville, Ohio, Jan. 20, 1935; s. John Young and Frances Lucy (Halbrunner) A.; m. Inge Elisabeth Bergeler, Aug. 5, 1961; children—Barbara Diane, Stephen Barry. B.S., Ariz. State U., 1956; M.S., U. Ala., 1964, Ph.D., 1968. Chemist White Sands Missile Range, N.M., 1956; aero fuels research chemist Army Missile Command, Redstone Arsenal, Ala., 1958-62, research chemist-phys., 1962-68, research chemist, 1968—; prof. J.C. Calhoun Coll., Decatur, Ala., 1969-73, Athens (Ala.) Coll., 1970-73, U. Ala., Huntsville, 1974-76; cons., 1965—; reviewer Nat. Sci. Found., 1973—. Publs. in field. Active Huntsville Civic Assn., 1961—. Served to capt. AUS, 1956-58. Recipient Army Research And Devel. Achievement award, 1962, Navy commendation, 1968, Army commendation, 1971, 72. Mem. Am. Chem. Soc. (treas. 1969-73, pres. 1974-76), Combustion Inst., Pasteur Soc., Assn. U.S. Army, N.Y. Acad. Scis., Joint Army, Navy, NASA, Air Force Propellant Characterization Group on Fluids and Materials, Sigma Xi, Gamma Sigma Epsilon, Theta Chi. Patents. Home: 7803 Michael Circle Huntsville AL 35802 Office: US Army Missile Command AMSMI-RK Redstone Arsenal AL 35809

ALLAN, HARRY THAIN, university dean; b. Saugus, Mass., Aug. 12, 1928; s. William Thain and Florence Louise (Horswell) A.; m. T. Jane Haught, July 4, 1952; children: Linda J., William H. B.A., Washington and Jefferson Coll., 1953; B.S., MIT, 1953; J.D., U. Chgo., 1956; postgrad., Carnegie Inst. Tech., 1962-63. Well logging engr. Hycalog Co., Sheveport, La., 1952-53; indsl. engr. R.R. Donnelley & Sons Co., Chgo., 1953-55; instr. Ill. Inst. Tech., 1955-56; from instr. to assoc. prof. Oreg. State U., 1956-65; from assoc. prof. to prof. U. Mass., Amherst, 1965-70, dean Sch. Bus. Adminstrn., 1978—; dean Sch. Mgmt., Syracuse U., 1970-76; provost Northeastern U., 1976-78; dir. Hartford Mut. Funds, HVA Mut. Funds. Author: (with H. Richard Hartzler) An Introduction to Law: a Functional Approach, 1969; mng. editor: U. Chgo. Law Rev., 1955-56; managerial law editor: Am. Bus. Law Jour., 1965-70; contbr. articles to profl. jours. Alternate county chmn. Benton County (Oreg.) Dem. Central Com., 1964-65; town moderator, Amherst, Mass., 1969-70. Served with AUS, 1946-47. Mem. Am., Oreg. bar assns., Am. Bus. Law Assn., Law and Society Assn., Am. Legal Studies Assn., Unitarian-Universalist Assn. Office: Sch Mgmt U Mass Amherst MA 01003

ALLAN, HUGH DAVID, electric company executive; b. Toronto, Feb. 25, 1925; s. Arthur Alexander and Gladys (Gurneys) A.; m. Susan Mary Barclay, May 17, 1947; children: Hugh Michael, David Gurney, Barbara Susan. B.A.Sc., U. Toronto, 1946. Design and application engr. Inglis Ltd., Toronto, 1947-48, sales engr.-sales mgr., 1949-55; asst. to gen. mgr. Worthington Pump Inc., 1956, gen. sales mgr., 1957-60, v.p., gen. mgr., 1960-65, chmn., pres., and gen. mgr., 1965-76, group v.p., 1976-78; pres. Emerson Electric Can. Ltd., Markham, Ont., Can., 1980—; dir. A.B. Chance Can. Ltd., Toronto. Thermo-Disc Can. Ltd., Skill Can. Ltd. Mem. Assn. Profl. Engrs. Ont Club: Rosedale Golf Badminton and Racquet. Home: 418 Russell Hill Rd Toronto Ont. Can. M5P 2SE Office: Emerson Electric Can Ltd PO Box 150 Markham Ont. Canada L3P 3J6

ALLAN, HUGH JAMES PEARSON, bishop; b. Winnipeg, Man., Can., Aug. 7, 1928; s. Hugh Blomfield and Agnes Dorothy (Pearson) A.; m. Beverley Edith Baker, Sept. 10, 1955; children—Douglas, Mary, Barbara, Jennifer. L.Th., St. John's Coll., Winnipeg, 1956, D.D. (hon.), 1974; B.A., U. Man., 1957. Ordained priest Anglican Ch., 1955; asst. St. Aidan's Ch., Winnipeg, 1954, All Saints Ch., 1955; incumbent Peguis Indian Res., Man., 1956-59; rector St. Mark's Ch., Winnipeg, 1960-68, St. Stephen's Ch., Swift Current, Sask., 1968-70, St. Paul's Cathedral, Regina, Sask.; dean Diocese of Qu'Appelle, Regina, 1970-74; bishop Diocese of Keewatin, Kenora, Ont., Can., 1974—. Office: Box 118 Kenora ON P9N 3X1 Canada

ALLAN, RUPERT MORTIMER, JR., public relations executive; b. St. Louis, Oct. 25, 1912; s. Rupert Mortimer and Edna Bates (Weil) A. B.A., Washington U., St. Louis, 1933; postgrad., U. Toulouse, France, 1934-35; M.A., Oxford (Eng.) U., 1937. Master Taylor Sch. Boys, Clayton, Mo., 1938-41; book reviewer St. Louis Post-Dispatch, 1940-41; writer Sta. KSD, St. Louis, 1941; polit. affairs officer Dept. State, 1945-46; asst. dir. public relations Universal-Internat. Studios, Universal City, Calif., 1946-47; asst. continental mgr. Motion Picture Assn. Am., Paris, 1947-49; West Coast corr. Flair mag., 1949; a West Coast editor Look mag., 1950-55; v.p. Arthur P. Jacobs Co. (public relations), Beverly Hills, Calif., 1955-60; partner ICPR (and predecessors, public relations), Los Angeles and Beverly Hills, 1960-77; exec. v.p. Stone/Hallinan Assos. Inc., Public Relations, 1978—; consul of Monaco in, Los Angeles, 1976—. Served as lt. comdr. USNR, 1942-45. Democrat. Episcopalian. Home: 1455 Seabright Pl Beverly Hills CA 90210 Office: Stone/Hallinan Assos Inc 7449 Melrose Ave Los Angeles CA 90046

ALLAN, STANLEY NANCE, architect; b. Phila., July 26, 1921; s. Henry and Nancy (Winkler) A.; m. Mary Willis Sledge, Sept. 9, 1950; children: Christopher, Mollie, Sarah, Stanley. B.A., U. N.C.-Chapel Hill, 1948; M.Arch., Harvard U., 1953. Registered architect, Ill., Va., D.C. Designer Skidmore Owings & Merrill, Portland, Oreg., 1952-63, Chgo. and Colorado Springs, 1952-63; exec. Harry Weese & Assocs., Chgo., Washington, 1964—. Served to lt. (j.g.) USNR, 1943-46. Fellow AIA; mem. Lambda Alpha. Democrat. Clubs: Cosmos (Washington); Arts (Chgo.). Home: 999 N Lakeshore Dr Chicago IL 60611 Office: Harry Weese & Assocs Ltd 10 W Hubbard St Chicago IL 60610

ALLAN, T.S., data processing executive; b. Philipsburg, Que., Can., Nov. 7, 1927; m. Katharine Allan; children: Ross, Scott, Christie. B.Marine-Mech. Engring., Royal Can. Naval Coll., 1946; student, Royal Naval Engring. Coll., 1946-50, Aero. Engr., 1951. Registered profl. engr., Que. Commd. Can. Navy, 1944, advanced through grades to rear admiral; chief engrig. and maintenance Dept. Nat. Def. Can. Armed Forces, 1976-78, ret., 1978; pres. Computer Devices Co., Ottawa, Ont., Can., 1978-82, Control Data Can. Ltd., Mississauga, Que., Can., 1982—, dir., Mississauga, Que., 1978—. Mem. Royal Mil. Inst., Air Industries Assn. Can. (dept. chmn.). Club: Ottawa Golf. Home: 4 Ancroft Pl Toronto ON Canada M4W 1M4 Office: Control Data Can Ltd 1855 Minnesota Ct Missisauga ON Canada L5N 1K7

ALLAN, VIRGINIA RACHEL, business executive, educator; b. Wyandotte, Mich., Oct. 21, 1916; d. Clare Floyd and Leta (Benedict) A. Student, Olivet Coll., 1935-36, LL.D., 1974; A.B., U. Mich., 1939, M.A. (fellow), 1945; L.H.D., Central Mich. U., 1976; D.P.A., Eastern Mich. U., 1981. With Detroit Bd. Edn., 1939-55; pres., co-owner Cahalan Drug Stores, Wyandotte, Mich., 1955-72; dep. asst. sec. state for pub. affairs, Washington, 1972-77; spl. asst. to dean Grad. Sch. Arts and Scis., George Washington U., 1977-83; pres. Cahalan Corp., 1971-82; Pub. mem. fgn. service officer selection bd. State Dept., 1971, 80; mem selection bd. USIA, 1975-83; prin. observer U.S. UN Seminar on Participation of Women in Econ. Life, Gabon, Africa, 1971; del. UN Seminar on Women, Moscow, 1970; chmn. Pres. Nixon's Task Force Women's Rights and Responsibilities, 1969; founding mem. Nat. Women's Polit. Caucus, 1971; alt. rep. World Conf., Internat. Women's Year, Mexico City, 1975-82; del. at large Nat. Women's Conf., 1977; alt. rep. World Conf. UN Decade for Women, Copenhagen, 1980; bd. dirs. Population Reference Bur., 1977-80; trustee WEAL's Marquerite Rawaet's Legal Det. Fund, 1977—; bd. dirs. Equity Policy Center, 1979—; regent Eastern Mich. U., Ypsilanti, 1964-74; adv. bd. Girl Scouts U.S.A. Recipient Outstanding Achievement award U. Mich., 1964, Athena award Intercollegiate Assn. Women Students, 1971, Diamond award City Wyandotte, 1963; named one of Top Ten Working Women in Met. Detroit, 1963. Mem. Nat. Fedn. Bus. and Profl. Women's Clubs (nat. pres. 1963-64), Citizens Council Edn. (co-chmn. 1982—), Mortar Bd., Phi Beta Kappa, Phi Kappa Phi, Delta Kappa Gamma. Home: 2512 Riverside Pkwy Sarasota FL 33581 Office: George Washington U Washington DC 20052

ALLAN, WALTER SCOTT, communications cons., former ins. co. exec.; b. Saugus, Mass., May 30, 1913; s. Walter S. and Lena (Boynton) A.; m. Leah Clapp, Aug. 21, 1937; children—Donald, Walter S. B.A., Clark U., 1935. With claims dept., later med. and rehab. services div. Liberty Mut. Ins. Co., 1935-59, asst. v.p., mgr. med. services, 1959-64, asst. v.p. pub. relations, 1964-75; now communications cons. Author: Rehabilitation-A Community Challenge, 1958. Pres. Am. Hearing Soc., 1963; bd. dirs., exec. com., chmn. rehab. policy com. Nat. Rehab. Assn., pres., 1966; bd. dirs., exec. com. Nat. Health Council; trustee, 1st v.p. Easter Seal Soc. Mass., pres., 1972-73; mem. Nat. Citizens Adv. Com. on Vocational Rehab.; chmn. Mass. Vocational Rehab. Planning Commn.; mem. Adv. Com. on Health Protection and Disease Protection to Sec. Dept. Health, Edn. and Welfare, Presdl. Task Force on Problems Physically Handicapped. Served to lt. (s.g.) USNR, 1943-46. Recipient President's award Nat. Rehab. Assn., 1960, Goodwill award Goodwill Industries Am., 1961. Mem. Pub. Relations Soc. Am. (accredited), N.A.M. (pub. affairs com.), Phi Beta Kappa. Address: 11 Truman Ln West Yarmouth MA 02673 *The significant guidepost in my life has been a faith in the power of people—to reason, to decide, to effect constructive change. Coupled with this has been a determination to achieve a balanced approach to human events, large or small, based on a strong sense of historical perspective.*

ALLAN, WILLIAM ALEXANDER, newspaper editor; b. Turtle Creek, Pa., May 4, 1924; s. Alexander Malcolm and Isabel (Young) A.; m. Rita McEvoy, Mar. 17, 1951; children—William Alexander, Jeffrey, Marianne. Student, U. Va., 1943; B.S. in Physics and Journalism, U. Pitts., 1949. With McKeesport (Pa.) Daily News, 1947-51; with Pitts. Press, 1951—, bus. and financial editor, 1963-70, features editor, 1970-80, roving editor, 1980—. Served with USAAF, 1943-45; ETO. Decorated Air medal; Croix de Guerre, France; recipient Golden Quill award bus. writing Pitts. chpt. Sigma Delta Chi and Pitts. Club: Press Club. Home: 26 McKelvey Ave Pittsburgh PA 15218 Office: Pittsburgh Press Pittsburgh PA 15230

ALLANSMITH, MATHEA REUTER, ophthalmologist; b. Santa Barbara, Calif., May 31, 1930; s. Harry and Mary (Benthall) Reuter; children: Lynn, Lauren, Kathryn, Carolyn, Andrew, Jennifer. M.D.,

U. Calif.-San Francisco, 1955. Diplomate: Am. Bd. Pediatrics, Am. Bd. Ophthalmology. Intern San Francisco Hosp., 1955-56; resident in ophthalmology Stanford Hosp., San Francisco, 1957, resident in pediatrics, 1958-59, U. Calif. Hosp., San Francisco, 1957-58, fellow in pediatric allergy, 1959-60; postdoctoral fellow in immunology dept. med. microbiology Stanford U., 1960-63, resident in ophthalmology, 1969-72, research asso. depts. med. microbiology, surgery and ophthalmology, 1963-67, acting asst. prof. surgery and ophthalmology, 1967-68, asst. prof., 1968-74; head Stanford Eye Bank, 1970-75; asst. prof. ophthalmology Harvard Med. Sch., 1975-77, asso. prof., 1977—; sr. scientist Eye Research Inst., Retina Found., 1975—. Mem. editorial bd.: Am. Jour. Ophthalmology, 1973—, Ophthalmology, 1979—. Fellow Am. Acad. Allergy; mem. Am. Assn. Immunology, Assn. Research in Vision and Ophthalmology, New Eng. Ophthalmol. Soc., Phi Beta Kappa, Sigma Xi. Research in immunology of the eye, diseases of the external eye. Office: 20 Staniford St Boston MA 02114

ALLARD, ANDRE MICHEL, advertising executive; b. Montreal, Que., Can., Apr. 19, 1925; s. Louis Joseph and Aline (Laurendeau) A.; m. Marguerite Janette, Apr. 22, 1965; children: Marie-Suzanne, Christian Janelle. Grad., Concordia U., 1948. Asst. advt. mgr. T. Eaton Co., Montreal, 1950-52; editor Guide Mont-Royal, Rosemount Jour., Montreal, 1955-57; pres. Allard-LeSiege, Montreal, 1958—; founder, pres. Ad Agy. Council Que., Montreal, 1973-75; pres. Mut. Advt. Agy. Network, 1979-80; dir. Inst. Can. Advt., Toronto, 1975-78, 81-83; communication cons. Liberal party Que. province and Montreal, 1959-65. Clubs: St. James/house com.; St. Denis/house com. (Montreal). Home: 20285 Lakeshore Rd Baie d'Urfe PQ Canada H9X 1P9 Office: Allard-LeSiege Inc 555 Dorchester W Montreal PQ Canada H2Z 1B1

ALLARD, CLAUDE HENRY, rubber company executive; b. Lowell, Mass., Jan. 5, 1921; s. Joseph J. and Cora (Pratt) A.; m. Clare Wildgoose, Mar. 11, 1977; children—Charles D., Joseph, James, Philip, Julia, Edward, Jacqueline. B.S. in Chemistry, Lowell Technol. Inst., 1947. With U.S. Rubber Co., 1947-66, asst. gen. mgr. textile div., 1963-64, v.p., gen. mgr., 1964-66; v.p. Uniroyal Inc., 1967—, pres. Uniroyal Internat. div., 1967-70, pres. Uniroyal Tire div., 1970—, corporate group v.p. Uniroyal Tire div., 1972—, pres., chief exec. officer Uniroyal Ltd., Uniroyal Tire div., Toronto, Ont., Can., 1974-77, chmn., pres., chief exec. officer, 1977-82, Corp. v.p. automative, worldwide, Troy, Mich., 1982—. Served with AUS, 1942-44. Mem. Rubber Assn. Can., Bus. Council Nat. Issues, Ont. Bus. Adv. Council. Home: 852 W Glengarry Circle Birmingham MI 48010 Office: Uniroyal Inc 3290 W Big Beaver Rd Suite 200 Troy MI 48084

ALLARD, DAVID HENRY, judge; b. Snohomish, Wash., Jan. 10, 1929; s. Clayton Frederick and Ruth Elizabeth (Winston) A.; m. Elizabeth Ellen Burrill, Nov. 26, 1960; children: John M., Clayton Frederick II. A.B., Whitman Coll., 1951; LL.B., Duke U., 1956. Bar: Wash. 1957, U.S. Supreme Ct. 1965. Mem. staff ICC, Washington, 1958-67, adminstrv. law judge, 1967-72, 73-80, chief adminstrv. law judge, 1980—; adminstrv. law judge FTC, 1972-73; Law reporter Presdl. Task Force on Career Advancement, 1967. Served with AUS, 1951-53. Mem. ABA (Achievement award young lawyers sect. 1965), Fed. Bar Assn. (editor-in-chief jour. 1972, pres. 1974, chmn. edn. bd. 1976—), Fed. Adminstrv. Law Judges Conf., Delta Tau Delta. Presbyterian. Home: 7514 Honesty Way Bethesda MD 20817 Office: Room 6139 ICC Washington DC 20423

ALLARD, JAMES E., oil company executive; b. Rockville, Conn., Dec. 10, 1942; s. Napoleon G. and Dorothea A. (Barbero) A.; m. Vicky Sanford, Oct. 3, 1964; children: Valerie, Marjorie, Jessica. B.S. in bus. adminstrn., U. Conn., 1964; grad. exec. devel. program, Cornell U., 1976. Mgr. fin. AIOC, London, 1977-79; div. controller, then treas. Standard Oil Co. of Ind., Chgo., 1980-81, controller, 1981—. Mem. acctg. adv. bd. and bus. adv. council U. Ill.; mem. vis. adv. com. DePaul U. Office: 200 E Randolph Dr Chicago IL 60601

ALLARD, JEAN, lawyer; b. Trenton, Mo., Dec. 16, 1924; d. Ben J. and Marion (Watson) McGuire; 1 son, John Preston. A.B., Culver-Stockton Coll., 1945, LL.D. (hon.), 1977; A.M., Washington U., St. Louis, 1947; J.D., U. Chgo., 1953; LL.D. (hon.), Elmhurst Coll., 1979. Bar: Ill. 1953, Ohio 1959. Dept. counselor, psychology dept. U. Chgo., 1948-51, research asso. Law Sch., 1953-58, asst. dean, 1956-58; asso. firm Fuller, Harrington, Seney & Henry, Toledo, 1958-59, Lord, Bissell & Brook, Chgo., 1959-62; sec., gen. counsel Maremont Corp., Chgo., 1962-72; v.p. for bus. and finance U. Chgo., 1972-75; partner firm Sonnenschein Carlin Nath & Rosenthal, Chgo., 1976—; dir. Commonwealth Edison Co., La Salle Nat. Bank, Marshall Field & Co., 1976-82, AM Internat., Inc., Maremont Corp. Trustee Culver-Stockton Coll., 1976—; bd. dirs. Chgo. Sch. Fin. Authority, 1980—; mem. Chgo. 1992 World's Fair Corp. Mem. Am., Ill., Chgo. bar assns., Am. Law Inst., Am. Soc. Corp. Secs., Chgo. Assn. Commerce and Industry. (dir.). Clubs: Economic, Commercial, Law., Chicago. Home: 5844 Stony Island Ave Chicago IL 60637 Office: 8000 Sears Tower Chicago IL 60606

ALLARD, ROBERT WAYNE, geneticist, educator; b. Los Angeles, Sept. 3, 1919; s. Glenn A. and Alma A. (Roose) A.; m. Ann Catherine Wilson, June 16, 1944; children: Susan, Thomas, Jane, Gillian, Stacie. B.S., U. Calif. at Davis, 1941; Ph.D., U. Wis., 1946. From asst. to asso. prof. U. Calif. at Davis, 1946—, prof. genetics, 1955—. Author books; contbr. articles to profl. jours. Served to lt. USNR. Recipient Crop Sci. award Am. Soc. Agronomy, 1964, DeKalb Disting. Career award Crop Sci. Soc. Am., 1983; Guggenheim fellow, 1954, 60; Fulbright fellow, 1955. Mem. Nat. Acad. Scis., Am. Soc. Naturalists (pres. 1974-75), Genetics Soc. Am. (pres. 1983-84), Phi Beta Kappa, Sigma Xi, Alpha Gamma Rho, Alpha Zeta. Democrat. Unitarian. Home: 2515 Bombadie Ln Davis CA 95616

ALLARD, SERGE BRUNO, librarian; b. Sherbrooke, Que., Can., June 3, 1931; s. Omer and Colette (Bruneau) A. B.A., U. Ottawa, 1953, B.Ph., 1954, L.Ph., 1955, L.Th., 1960, B.Edn., 1961, B.L.S., 1964. Tchr. Coll. de Rouyn, Que., 1961-64, chief librarian, 1964—, U. Quebec, 1970—. Mem. Am., Can. library assns., Assn. pour l'Avancement Scis. et Tecniques Documentation. Home: 235 Pinder West St Rouyn PQ J9X 2Y5 Canada Office: PO Box 8000 Rouyn PQ J9X 5M5 Canada

ALLARD, WILLIAM KENNETH, mathematician; b. Lowell, Mass., Oct. 29, 1941; s. Frederic Pratt and Jeannette Edna (Perrault) A.; m. Priscilla Elaine May, Aug. 10, 1968; children: Felicia, Christopher. Sc.B., Villanova U., 1963; Ph.D. in Math, Brown U., 1968. Asst. prof. math. Princeton U., 1971-75; prof. math. Duke U., Durham, N.C., 1975—. Mng. editor: Duke Math. Jour. Alfred P. Sloan fellow, 1970-72. Mem. Am. Math. Soc. Home: 200 Monticello Ave Durham NC 27707 Office: Duke Univ Dept Math Durham NC 27706

ALLBRITTON, JOE LEWIS, business executive; b. D'Lo, Miss., Dec. 29, 1924; s. Lewis A. and Ada (Carpenter) A.; m. Barbara Jean Balfanz, Feb. 23, 1967; 1 son, Robert Lewis. LL.B., Baylor U., 1949, LL.D. (hon.), 1964, J.D., 1969; L.H.D., Calif. Bapt. Coll., 1973. Bar: Tex. 1949. Dir. Perpetual Corp., Los Angeles, 1958—, pres., 1965-76, 78-81, chmn. bd., 1973—; chmn. bd. Pierce Nat. Life Ins. Co., Los Angeles, 1958-72, 75—, dir., 1958—; chmn. bd. Univ. Bancshares, Inc., Houston, 1975—, Allbritton Communications Co., 1976—, WJLA,Inc., 1976—, Houston Fin. Services, Ltd., London, 1977—, Riggs Nat. Corp., Washington, 1981—; dir. Riggs Nat. Bank, Washington, 1981—, chmn., 1983—; Bd. dirs. Inst. Internat. Edn., N.Y.C.; mem. Greater Washington Bd. Trade, 1983—. Trustee Fed. City Council, Washington, 1975—; chpt. mem. Protestant Episcopal Ch. Found. of D.C., Washington, 1976—. Served with USN, 1943-46. Mem. State Bar Tex., Assn. Res. City Bankers. Office: 5615 Kirby Dr Suite 310 Houston TX 77005 also Washington DC

ALLCOCK, HARRY MELVIN, JR., information company executive; b. Balt., Nov. 3, 1932; s. Harry Melvin and Sadie Gladus (Leake) A.; m. Ann Beatrice Orlosky, Sept. 23, 1954 (dec. 1967); children: Stephanie, Jeffrey, Christine, Shannon; m. Marilyn Jeane Bowen, July 28, 1968. B.A. in Bus. Adminstrn, George Washington U., 1956. Br. mgr. Ency. Brit., Silver Spring, Md., 1956-61; v.p. IFI—Plenum Data Co., Alexandria, Va., 1961—. Served with U.S. Army, 1953-55. Mem. Am. Chem. Soc. Roman Catholic. Roman Catholic. Clubs: University (Washington); Lakewood Country (Rockville, Md.) (pres. 1980-81). Home: 12007 Whippoorwill Ln Rockville ND 20852 Office: IFI-Plenum Data Co 302 Swann Ave Alexandria VA 22301

ALLDREDGE, ERNEST GEORGE, quality assurance executive; b. Ft. Worth, Apr. 23, 1938; s. Ernest George and Sarah Lou (Malicoat) A.; m. Linda J. Mobley, Sept. 14, 1963; children: Kelly, Denise. Engring. draftman, Ft. Worth Tech. High Sch., 1955; B.M.E., U. Tex.-Arlington, 1959. Inspection engr. Magnaflux Corp., Houston, 1959-63, lab. mgr., 1963-68, nat. gen. mgr., Chgo., 1968-73; pres. testing services Peabody Testing Internat., Chgo., 1973-79, group pres., pres., 1979-83; exec. v.p. GEO Internat., Stamford, Conn., 1980—. Mem. Am. Soc. for Non-Destructive Testing, ASTM, Am. Welding Soc., Am. Metal Assn. Republican. Baptist. Office: 7300 W Lawrence St Chicago IL 60656

ALLDREDGE, LEROY ROMNEY, geophysicist; b. Mesa, Ariz., Feb. 6, 1917; s. Leo and Ida (Romney) A.; m. Larita Williams, Dec. 27, 1940; children—Carol, David Leroy, Joseph Leo, Gary Dean, Mark Evans, Janice, Luann. B.S., U. Ariz., 1939, M.S., 1940; M.Sc. in Engring, Harvard, 1953; Ph.D., U. Md., 1955. Instr. physics U. Ariz., 1940-41; fed. radio insp. FCC, Los Angeles, also Washington, 1941-44; radio engr. dept. terrestrial magnetism Carnegie Inst. of Washington, 1944-45; chief electricity and magnetism div. Naval Ordnance Lab., White Oak, Md., 1945-55; analyst operations research office Johns Hopkins, 1955-59; research geophysicist Coast and Geodetic Survey, Dept. Commerce, Washington, 1959-66; acting dir. Inst. Earth Scis., Environmental Sci. Services Adminstrn., Boulder, Colo., 1966; dir. Earth Scis. Labs., 1967-69, Earth Sci. Lab. Nat. Oceanographic and Atmospheric Adminstrn., 1969-73; research geophysicist U.S. Geol. Survey, 1973—; gen. sec., dir. central bur. Internat. Assn. Geomagnetism and Aeronomy, 1963-75. Asso. editor: Jour. Geophys. Research, 1966-69. Mem. Am. Geophys. Union (sect. on geomagnetism and aeronomy 1950-56, v.p. sect. 1956-59, pres. sect. 1959-61, chmn. Eastern meeting com. 1962-66), Sigma Xi, Phi Kappa Phi. Mem. Ch. of Jesus Christ of Latter-day Saints. Home: 4475 Chippewa Dr Boulder CO 80303 Office: USGS Br Global Seismology and Geomagnetism Denver Fed Center Mail Stop 964 Denver CO 80225 *Science and engineering are very precise. For a man to properly help with the orderly development in any area of science he must treat his data and report them with strict honesty. The same principle is even more valuable in ordinary daily contacts with his friends and acquaintances. A performance that includes half truths or deceit in any form will very likely lead to unhappiness.*

ALLEE, JOHN GAGE, English educator; b. Helena, Mont., Feb. 28, 1918; s. John and Pearla (Townshend) A.; m. Harriet Dow, Apr. 17, 1943; children: John Gage, Stephen Dole. B.A., George Washington U., 1939, M.A., 1940; Ph.D., Johns Hopins U., 1955. Jr. instr. Johns Hopkins U., Balt., 1945-49; asst. prof. English George Washington U., Washington, 1949-56, assoc. prof., 1956-62, prof., 1962—, asst. dean div. univ. students, 1953-58, assoc. dean univ. students, 1958-62, dean univ. students, 1962-79; lectr. Fgn. Service Inst., Smithsonian Instn., Washington, 19756. Served with U.S. Army, 1941-45. Fulbright grantee, Iceland, 1961, 69-70. Mem. Soc. Advancement Scandinavian Study, Mediaeval Acad. Am., Linguistic Soc. Am., Icelandic Archaeol. Soc., Am. Name Soc., New Chaucer Soc., Phi Beta Kappa. Home: 3726 Ingomar St NW Washington DC 20015 Office: Dept English George Washington Univ Washington DC 20052

ALLEMAN, JOAN, editor; b. Hanover, Pa., Oct. 1, 1931; d. Richard B. and Katharine (Eckert) A.; m. Robert Rubin, July 30, 1955 (div. Jan. 1983); children: Thomas, Andrew; m. Arthur T. Birsh, May 1983. B.A., Coll. William and Mary, 1953. Asst. to feature editor, career editor Mademoiselle Mag., N.Y.C., 1954-61; free-lance mag. writer, N.Y.C., 1961-64; editor-in-chief Playbill, N.Y.C., 1964—; Vice pres. Film Modules; affiliated Drama Forum; mem. nominating com. Tony award, 1975, 76, 76-77, 79-80, mem. eligibility com., 1977-78, 81-82, 82-83. Mem. Phi Beta Kappa. Club: Corinthian Yacht. Home: 7 1/2 Leroy St New York NY 10012 Office: care Playbill 151 E 50th St New York NY 10022 *I believe that in a lifetime only two or three things are truly important. This conviction has enabled me to live and work with realistic priorities and a minimum of anxiety.*

ALLEMAN, RAYMOND HENRY, conglomerate executive; b. Yonkers, N.Y., Sept. 18, 1934; s. William A. and Anna L. (White) A.; m. Evelyn M. McEnery, 1954; children: Mark, Brian, Bruce, Gregg, Paul, Blair, Lynn, Janet. B.B.A., Manhattan Coll., 1956. C.P.A., N.Y. Audit mgr. Arthur Andersen & Co., N.Y.C. and Newark, 1956-65; controller Oneida Paper Products/Deerfield Glassine Co., Clifton, N.J., 1965-67; v.p., dep. comptroller ITT World Hdqrs., N.Y.C., 1967—; v.p., dir. ITT Industries, Internat. Standard Electric Corp., ITT Holdings, Inc. Mem. Am. Inst. C.P.A.s, Nat. Assn. Accts., Machinery and Allied Products Inst. (Fin. Council II). Roman Catholic. Office: ITT World Hdqrs 320 Park Ave New York NY 10022 *

ALLEN, ALFRED KEYS, construction company executive; b. Birmingham, Ala., Feb. 18, 1914; s. Charles Morehead and Nannie (Thompson) A.; m. Barbara Moose, Sept. 15, 1938 (dec.); children: Charles Morehead II, Louise Condon, Alfred Keys, Barbara Marie. B.S., Auburn U., 1935; postgrad., Birmingham Law Sch., 1939. Vice pres. Dunn Constrn. Co., Birmingham, 1945-57, Utah Constrn. Co., San Francisco, 1957-59, Blount Bros., Montgomery, Ala., 1959-62; pres. South Engring. & Constrn. Co., Montgomery, 1954—; v.p., dir. Perini Corp., San Francisco, 1963-69, exec. v.p., dir., Miami, Fla., 1969-70; pres., dir. OKC Dredging, Inc., Dallas, 1970-80; sr. v.p., dir. OKC Corp., Dallas, 1970-80; exec. Lone Star Industries, Inc., Greenwich, Conn., 1980-83. Served to lt. col. C.E. U.S. Army, 1940-45; CBI. Decorated Legion of Merit; Order of Cloud and Banner, China). Mem. Moles, Beavers. Clubs: Bent Tree Country, Lancers, Elks. Office: 16144 Chalfont Circle Dallas TX 75248

ALLEN, ANNA FOSTER, librarian; b. West Pittston, Pa., Feb. 20, 1901; d. Henry J. and Mary H. (Ainey) Foster; m. C. Spencer Allen, Sept. 1, 1927. Ph.B., Muhlenberg Coll., 1927; B.L.S., Drexel Inst. Tech., 1931. Asst. reference librarian Bryn Mawr Coll., 1931-36; circulation librarian Temple U., 1936-66; librarian Lehigh County Hist. Soc., Allentown, Pa., 1967—, sec., 1968-71. Author: Leopold Paul Unger Allentown Artist. Vol. Allentown Hosp., 1967—; pres. Muhlenberg Coll. Aux., 1971-75, 80—, fin. sec., 1975-80; mem. coordinating council Allentown Girls Club, 1972-73, Vols. of Am. Day Care Center; mem. Lehigh Valley Com. on Historic Areas; sec. West Park Civic Assn., 1975—. Recipient Four Chaplains Legion of Honor award. Mem. Middle Atlantic Regional Archivist Conf. Lutheran. Clubs: Woman's, Athenaeum (pres. 1972-73), Athenaeum (treas. 1975-81), Gamma Delphian (Allentown)). Home: 1553 Turner St Allentown PA 18102 Office: Old Court House 5th and Hamilton Sts Allentown PA 18101

ALLEN, BELLE, management consulting firm executive; b. Chgo.; d. Isaac and Clara (Friedman) A. Student, U. Chgo. Cons., then v.p., treas., dir. William Karp Cons. Co., Inc., Chgo., 1961-79, chmn., pres., treas., 1979—; v.p., sec., dir. Mgmt. Performance Systems, Inc., 1976-77; v.p., treas., dir. Cultural Arts Surveys, Inc., Chgo., 1965-80; cons., dir. Belle Allen Communications, Chgo., 1961—; cons. Am. Diversified Research Corp., Chgo., 1967-70, Ill. Commn. on Tech. Progress, 1965-67, The City Club of Chgo., 1962-65; mem. bd. govs. consumer adv. council Fed. Res. System, 1979—; mem. Ill. Gov.'s Grievance Panel for State Employees, 1979—; mem. adv. governing bd. Ill. Coalition on Employment of Women, 1980—; spl. program advisor The Pres.'s Project Partnership, 1980—. Editor, contbr.: Operations Research and the Management of Mental Health Administration, 1968; contbr. and editor articles, papers to bus., profl. jours., other publs.; editor, columnist: The Bulletin, 1981—. Founding mem. women's bd. United Cerebral Palsy Assn., Chgo., 1954, bd. dirs., Chgo., 1954-58; mem. Welfare Pub. Relations Forum, 1960-61; dir., chmn. personnel placement com. Indsl. Relations Research Assn., 1960-61; bd. dirs., mem. exec. com., chmn. pub. relations com. Regional Ballet Ensemble, Chgo., 1961-63; bd. dirs. Soc. Chgo. Strings, 1963-64; mem. Community Relation Com., alternate Labor Relations Com. Ill. C. of C., 1961-74; mem. merit employment com. Chgo. Assn. Commerce and Industry, 1961-63, mem. pub. relations com., 1961-63; mem. nat. conf. program Nat. Assn. Inter-group Relations Ofcls., 1959; chmn. inter-city relations com. Publicity Club of Chgo., 1960-61; chmn. "A Retrospective View of An Historical Decade 160-70"/The Fashion Group, 1970; mem. campaign staff Adlai F. Stevenson II, 1952-56, John F. Kennedy, 1960; pres. conf. staff Eleanor Roosevelt, 1960; pres. Democratic Fedn. Ill., 1958-61; mem. Ind. Dem. Coalition, 1968-69; dir. Citizens for Polit. Change, 1969; campaign mgr. City Council Chgo. aldermanic election, 42d ward, 1969. Recipient Outstanding Service award United Cerebral Palsy Assn., Chgo., 1954, Communications Program, The White House, 1961; mem. Welfare Pub. Relations Forum, 1960-61; recipient Disting Service award Am. Bicentennial Research Inst, Library of Human Resources, 1973. Mem. Affirmative Action Assn. (bd. dirs. 1981—, chmn. membership and program coms. 1981—, pres. 1984—), Fashion Group (bd. dirs. 1981-83), Indsl. Relations Research Assn., AAAS, NOW, Sarah Siddons Soc., Soc. Personnel Adminstrs., Women's Equity Action League (Chgo.), Publicity Club of Chgo. Club: Chgo. Press (chmn. women's activities 1969-71). Address: 111 E Chestnut St Chicago IL 60611

ALLEN, BETTY (MRS. RITTEN EDWARD LEE, III), mezzo-soprano; b. Campbell, Ohio; d. James Corr and Dora Catherine (Mitchell) A.; m. Ritten Edward Lee, III, Oct. 17, 1953; children: Anthony Edward, Juliana Catherine. Student, Wilberforce U., 1944-46; certificate, Hartford Sch. Music, 1953; pupil voice, Sarah Peck More, Paul Ulanowsky, Carolina Segrera Holden; L.H.D., Wittenberg U., 1971; D.Mus., Union Coll., 1981. Faculty Phila. Mus. Acad., 1979, Manhattan Sch. Music, 1971, N.C. Sch. Arts, 1978—; exec. dir. Harlem Sch. Arts, 1979; vis. faculty Sibelius Akademie, Helsinki, Finland, 1976; mem. adv. bd. music panel Amherst Coll.; mem. music panel N.C. State Council of the Arts, Dept. State Office Cultural Presentations, Nat. Endowment Arts.; Bd. dirs. Karl Weigl Found., Diller-Quaile Sch. Music, U.S. Com. for UNICEF, Carnegie Hall, Harlem Boys Choir, Chuck Davis Dance Theater; mem. adv. bd. Bloomingdale House of Music, John F. Kennedy Center Opera Co., Rockefeller Found.; bd. vis. artists Boston U. Appeared as soloist: Leonard Bernstein's Jeremiah Symphony, 1951, Virgil Thomson's Four Saints in Three Acts, 1952, N.Y.C. Light Opera Co., 1954; recitalist, also soloist with major symphonies on tours including, ANTA-State Dept. tours., Europe, N. Africa, Caribbean, Can., U.S., S. Am., Far East, 1954-, S. Am. tour, 1968, Bellas Artes Opera, Mexico City, 1970, recital debut, Town Hall, N.Y.C., 1958, ofcl. debuts, London, Berlin, 1958, formal opera debut, Teatro Colon, Buenos Aires, Argentina, 1964; U.S. opera debut San Francisco Opera, 1966; N.Y.C. opera debut, 1973, Mini-Met. debut, 1973; Broadway debut in Treemonisha, 1975; opened new civic theaters in, San Jose, Calif. and Regina, Sask., Can., concert hall, Lyndon Baines Johnson Library, Austin, Tex., 1971; artist-in-residence, Phila. Opera Co.; appeared with, Caramoor Music Festival, summer 1971, Cin. May Festival, 1972, Santa Fe Opera, 1972, 75, Canadian Opera Co., Winnipeg, Man., 1972, 77, Washington Opera Co., 1971, Tanglewood Festival, 1974, Kansas City, Houston and Santa Fe operas, 1975, Saratoga Festival, Casals Festival, 1968, 69, 76, Helsinki Festival, 1976, numerous radio and TV performances, U.S., Can., Mex., Eng., Germany, Scandinavia; rec. artist, London, Vox, Capitol, Odeon-Pathe, Decca, Deutsche Grammophon, RCA Victor records; represented U.S. in Cultural Olympics, Mexico City. Recipient Marian Anderson award, 1953-54, Nat. Music League Mgmt. award, 1953; named Best Singer of Season Critics' Circle, Argentina and Chile, 1959, Critics' Circle, Uruguay, 1961; Martha Baird Rockefeller Aid to Music grantee, 1953, 58; John Hay Whitney fellow, 1953-54; Ford Found. concert soloist grantee, 1963-64. Mem. NAACP, Urban League, Hartford Mus. Club, Am. Guild Mus. Artists, Actors Equity, AFTRA, Silvermine Guild Artists, Jeunesses Musicales, Gioventu Musicale, Student Sangverein Trondheim, Unitarian-Universalist Women's Fedn., Nat. Negro Musicians Assn. (life), Concert Artists Guild, Met. Opera Guild, Amherst Glee Club (hon. life), Union Coll. Glee Club (hon. life), Met. Mus. Art, Mus. Modern Art, Am. Mus. Natural History, Sigma Alpha Iota (hon.). Unitarian-Universalist. Club: Cosmopolitan. Office: Harlem School of the Arts 645 St. Nicholas Ave New York NY 10030 *To be able to combine childhood fantasies of self-expression, to travel and roam the world, to meet again and make new friends, to serve the demanding, yet fulfilling art of music - these are some of the wonderful joys of being a singer. I have been free to be me.*

ALLEN, CHARLES EUGENE, educator; b. Burley, Idaho, Jan. 25, 1939; s. Charles William and Elsie Permelia (Fowler) A.; m. Connie Jeanette Block, June 19, 1966; children—Kerry Janelle, Tamara Sue. B.S., U. Idaho, 1961; M.S., U. Wis., 1963, Ph.D., 1966. Research asst. U. Wis., Madison, 1961-65; NSF fellow Commonwealth Sci. and Indsl. Research Orgn., Div. Food Research, Sydney, Australia, 1966-67; mem. faculty depts. animal sci. and food sci. and nutrition U. Minn., St. Paul, 1967—, prof., 1972—; vis. prof. animal sci. Pa. State U., 1978. Contbr. articles profl. jours. Pres. Falcon Heights P.T.A., 1973-74. Mem. Am. Soc. Animal Sci., Nat. Inst. Food Technologists, Am. Meat Sci. Assn., Am. Inst. Nutrition, Minn. Inst. Food Technologists, Sigma Xi. Lutheran. Office: 1354 Eckles Ave Saint Paul MN 55108

ALLEN, CHARLES JOSEPH, II, advertising agency executive; b. Providence, June 8, 1917; s. John Alfred and Emily (Smith) A.; m. Fay Eleanore Manne, Nov. 19, 1941; children: Linda Fay (Mrs. Marc D. Constant), June Lee (Mrs. Michael L. Traviolia). A.B. with honors, U. Pitts., 1939. Corporate sales service mgr. Kroger Co., Cin., 1945-52; v.p. Gardner Advt., Inc., St. Louis, 1952-56, McCann-Erickson, Inc., Chgo., 1956-58; chmn. bd., chief exec. officer Allen, Anderson, Niefeld & Paley, Inc., Chgo., 1958-69; pres. Charles J. Allen & Assos., Woodridge, Ill., 1970—; v.p., dir. Grabin-Shaw Advt., Milw., 1960-73;

pres., dir. A A Gift Shopper Plan, Elmhurst, 1970—; dir. EFS Service Corp., Elmhurst, Sales Force Cos. Chgo., Elmhurst Fed. Savs. & Loan, A/C/T Enterprises, Chgo., Press Syndicate Service, Pitts.; cons. in field, 1960—. Contbr. articles to profl. jours.; Speaker in field. Pres. bd. dirs. Village IV Orgn., Woodridge, Ill., 1978—. Mem. Assn. Food Execs. (pres. 1967—), Chgo. Assn. Commerce and Industry, Elmhurst C. of C. (dir., past pres.), U. Pitts. Alumni Assn., Am. Marketing Assn. (past dir.), Indsl. Advt. Club. Clubs: Chicago Press, Executives, Itasca (Ill.) Country. Home: 2668 Foxglove St Woodridge IL 60517 Office: 8280 Janes Ave Suite 104 Woodridge IL 60517

ALLEN, CHARLES KELLER, assn. exec., cattleman; b. Independence, Va., Dec. 15, 1942; s. Lavada Charles and Gladys Kyle (Poole) A.; m. Berna Jo Menge, Apr. 29, 1976; children—Rachael Suzanne, Kristin Kellie, Clint Keller. B.S., Va. Poly. Inst. and State U., 1968; M.S., Mich. State U., Ph.D., 1972. Mgr. Beef Cattle Research Center, Mich. State U., East Lansing, 1970-72; dir. edn. and research Am. Polled Hereford Assn., Kansas City, Mo., 1972-78; chief adminstrv. officer Am. Angus Assn. and subs. Angus Prodns., Inc., St. Joseph, Mo., 1978-81; pres. Profl. Cattle Adv. Service, Savannah, Mo., 1981—; gov. Agr. Hall Fame, 1981; bd. govs., bd. dirs. Am. Royal, 1979-80; ofcl. Am. Royal Inter-Collegiate Judging Contest, 1975-77. Contbr. articles to profl. jours. Served with USAF, 1962-65. Recipient Industry award Va. Poly. Inst. and State U. Block and Bridle Club, 1980. Mem. Nat. Cattleman's Assn. (research com. 1975-76), Beef Improvement Fedn. (dir. 1975-77), U.S. Beef Breeds Council (sec., v.p. 1978-81), World Angus Forum (sec. 1979-81), Nat. Soc. Livestock Record Assn. (dir. 1979-80), Am. Soc. Animal Sci. (program com. 1979-81, chmn. 1981), Am. Soc. Assn. Execs., Am. Angus Assn., Am. Polled Hereford Assn., Am. Simmental Assn., Mo. Cattleman's Assn., St. Joseph C. of C. (livestock and econ. devel. coms. 1979-80), Kansas City C. of C. (livestock com. 1974-76). Republican. Methodist. Home and Office: Route 3 Box 177 Savannah MO 64485

ALLEN, CHARLES MENGEL, judge; b. Louisville, Nov. 22, 1916; s. Arthur Dwight and Jane (Mengel) A.; m. Betty Anne Cardwell, June 25, 1949; children: Charles Dwight, Angela M. B.A., Yale U., 1941; LL.B., U. Louisville, 1943. Bar: Ky. 1944. Practiced in Louisville, 1947-55; asst. U.S. atty. for Western Dist. Ky., 1955-59; mem. firm Booth & Walker, Louisville, 1959-61; circuit judge 4th Chancery div. Jefferson County, 1961-71; dist. judge U.S. Dist. Ct., Louisville, 1971—, now chief judge. Pres. Ky. Ry. Mus.; bd. dirs. Louisville Art Center; mem. Ky. Humane Soc., local chpt., Nat. Ry. Hist. Soc. Mem. Am., Fed., Ky., Louisville bar assns. Office: Room 252 US Courthouse Louisville KY 40202 *

ALLEN, CHARLES RICHARD, financial exec.; b. Cleve., Mar. 10, 1926; s. Charles Ross and Jennie (Harmon) A.; m. Marion Elizabeth Taylor, Aug. 17, 1946; children—Kathleen Allen Templin, Jeanne Allen Duffy, Kenneth. Student, Occidental Coll., 1942-43; B.S., UCLA, 1945. Acctg. supr. N.Am. Aviation, Inc., Los Angeles, 1946-55; div. controller TRW, Inc., Los Angeles, 1955-61, dir. finance, 1961-64, asso. controller, Cleve., 1964-66, controller, 1966-67, v.p., 1967-77, exec. v.p., 1977—, chief financial officer, 1967—, also dir.; adv. New Court Partners, N.Y.C. Trustee John Carroll U. Served with USNR, 1943-46. Mem. Financial Execs. Inst., Am. Finance Assn., Greater Cleve. Growth Assn., Inst. of Dirs. (London). Clubs: Shaker Heights Country, Union, Pepper Pike (Cleve.); Wall Street (N.Y.C.). Home: 17503 Shelburne Rd Cleveland Heights OH 44118 Office: TRW Inc 23555 Euclid Ave Cleveland OH 44117

ALLEN, CHARLES ROBERT, physician, educator; b. Bowling Green, Ky., June 26, 1911; s. Samuel H. and Eva (Lawrence) A.; m. Lucille Fitzhugh, June 27, 1934; children—Charles Robert, Richard F., Elizabeth (Mrs. McEldowney). B.S., Western Ky. State Tchrs. Coll., 1932, M.A., 1933; Ph.D., U. Wis., 1941, M.D., 1946. Diplomate: Am. Bd. Anesthesiology. Lab. instr. Western Ky. State Tchrs. Coll., 1933-34; grad. asst. Ohio State U., 1934; sci. tchr. Bowling Green Pub. Schs., 1934-35, Louisville Pub. Schs., 1935-38; research asst. U. Wis., 1938-40, instr. physiology, 1940-42; asst. prof. anesthesiology U. Tex. Med. Br., Galveston, 1942-46, asso. prof., 1946-53, prof., 1953—, chmn. dept. anesthesiology, 1953-77, intern, Galveston, 1946-47; practice medicine, specializing in anesthesiology, Galveston, 1946—; med. cons. U.S. Army, Brooke Army Med. Center, Ft. Sam Houston, Tex., 1945-70, Oak Ridge Inst. Nuclear Studies, 1949-54, Wilford Hall USAF Hosp., Lackland AFB, Tex., 1953-67, USPHS Hosp., Galveston, 1953-77; chief of staff U. Tex. Med. Br. Hosps., 1966-67; mem. respiratory and anesthetic drugs adv. com. FDA, Washington, 1966-70. Contbr. articles to profl. jours. Mem. adv. bd. Galveston Citizens Comprehensive Planning, 1964-66; Bd. dirs. William Temple Found. Fellow Am. Coll. Anesthesiologists (past bd. govs., chmn. oral exams.); mem. Am. Soc. Anesthesiologists (past com. chmn.), Tex. Soc. Anesthesiologists (past pres.), So. Soc. Anesthesiologists (past pres.), AMA, Tex., So. med. assns., Galveston County Med. Soc. (mem. exec. com., past chmn. bd. censors), Am. Physiol. Soc., Acad. Anesthesiology, Tex. Gulf Coast Anesthesia Soc., Internat. Anesthesia Research Soc., Soc. Acad. Anesthesia Chairmen (pres. 1973-74), Assn. U. Anesthetists (past mem. adminstrv. council), AAUP, Sigma Xi. Home: 20 Cedar Lawn S Galveston TX 77550 Office: 800 Mechanic St Galveston TX 77550

ALLEN, CHARLES WILLIAM, engineering educator; b. Newbury, Eng., July 24, 1932; s. Isaac William and Emily (Butler) A.; m. Rita Joyce Pembroke, Dec. 28, 1957; children: Malcolm Charles, Verity Simone. B.S., U. London, 1957; M.S., Case Inst. Tech., 1962; Ph.D., U. Calif., Davis, 1966. Design engr. Lear Siegler, Cleve., 1957-62; group leader Aerojet Gen., Sacramento, 1962-63; asso. engring. U. Calif., Davis, 1965-66; asso. prof. Calif. State U., Chico, 1966-71, prof. engring., 1971—, head mech. engring., 1976-79, 82—; vis. fellow U. Leicester, Eng., 1974. Contbr. articles to profl. jours. Fellow NASA, 1967, 68, 69. Mem. ASME, Am. Soc. Engring. Edn., Sigma Xi. Home: 1691 Filbert Ave Chico CA 95926 Office: Mech Engring Dept Calif State U Chico CA 95926

ALLEN, CHARLES WILLIAM, lawyer; b. Portland, Maine, Nov. 14, 1912; s. Neal W. and Margaret (Stevens) A.; m. Genevieve Lahee, Sept. 5, 1936; children—Thomas H., Ruth W., William N. A.B., Bowdoin Coll., 1934; J.D., U. Mich., 1937. Bar: N.Y. bar 1938, Maine bar 1946. Practiced in, N.Y.C., 1937-41, Portland, 1946—; assoc. firm Sullivan & Cromwell, 1937-41; ptnr. Pierce, Atwood, Scribner, Allen, Smith & Lancaster, 1946—; Trustee Portland Savs. Bank, 1959-80. Mem. Portland City Council, 1964-70, chmn., 1966; Treas., trustee Bowdoin Coll., 1959-67, bd. overseers, 1967-76; treas. Hebron Acad., 1954-59, trustee, 1953-65; trustee Colby, Bates, Bowdoin Ednl. Telecasting Corp., 1961-74, Portland Pub. Library, 1971—; pres. Portland Pub. Library, 1980-82; mem. com. visitors U. Mich. Law Sch., 1967-68; bd. dirs. Maine Civil Liberties Union, 1973-76, treas., 1974-76; mem. exec. com. Portland SANE, 1970—, chmn., 1971-75. Served to lt. comdr. USNR, 1942-46. Mem. Am., Maine, Cumberland County bar assns., Order of Coif. Home: 41 Rackleff St Portland ME 04103 Office: 1 Monument Sq Portland ME 04111

ALLEN, CLARENCE RODERIC, geologist, educator; b. Palo Alto, Cal., Feb. 15, 1925; s. Hollis Partridge and Delight (Wright) A. B.A., Reed Coll., 1949; M.S., Cal. Inst Tech., 1951, Ph.D., 1954. Asst. prof. geology U. Minn., 1954-55; mem. faculty Cal. Inst. Tech., 1955—, prof. geology and geophysics, 1964—; interim dir. Seismological Lab., 1965-67, acting chmn. division of geological scis., 1967-68; Chmn. cons. bd. earthquake analysis Cal. Dept. Water Resources, 1965-74; chmn. geol. hazards adv. com. for program Cal. Resources Agy., 1965-66; mem. earth scis. adv. panel NSF, 1965-68, chmn., 1967-68, mem. adv. com. environmental scis., 1970-72; mem. U.S. Geol. Survey adv. panel to Nat. Center Earthquake Research, 1966-75, Cal. Mining and Geology Bd., 1969-75, chmn., 1975; mem. task force on earthquake hazard reduction Office Sci. and Tech., 1970-71. Served to 1st lt. USAAF, 1943-46. Recipient G.K. Gilbert award seismic geology Carnegie Instn., 1960. Fellow Am. Geophys. Union, Geol. Soc. Am. (counselor 1968-70, pres. 1973-74), Am. Acad. Arts Scis.; mem. Am. Assn. Petroleum Geologists, Nat. Acad. Scis., Earthquake Engring. Research Inst., Seismological Soc. Am. (dir. 1970—, pres. 1975-76), Assn. Engring. Geologists, Nat. Acad. Engring., Soc. Exploration Geophysicists, Phi Beta Kappa. Home: 700 S Lake Ave Apt 322 Pasadena CA 91106

ALLEN, CLIVE VICTOR, communications company executive, lawyer; b. Montreal, Que., Can., June 11, 1935; s. John Arthur and Norah (Barnett) A.; m. Barbara Mary Kantor, Feb. 22, 1964; children—Drew, Blair. B.A., McGill U., 1956, B.C.L., 1959. Bar: Called to bar. Mem. firm Hackett, Mulvena,& Drummond & Fiske, 1960-63, Fiske, Emery, Allen & Lauzon, 1964-66; v.p., sec. Allied Chem. Can. Ltd., 1966-74; sr. v.p., gen. counsel No. Telecom Ltd., 1974—. Mem. Can., Internat. bar assns., Am. Soc. Corporate Secs., Assn. Can. Gen. Counsel, Can. Tax Found. Clubs: Montreal Badminton & Squash; St. James's (Montreal); Granite (Toronto). Home: 18A Deer Park Crescent Toronto ON M4V 2C2 Canada Office: 33 City Center Dr Mississauga ON L5B 2N2 Canada

ALLEN, COURTNEY KEITH, profl. hockey team exec.; b. Saskatoon, Sask., Can., Aug. 21, 1923; came to U.S., 1941; s. Courtney Bliss and Gertrude Marguerite (Armitage) A.; m. Joyce Adele Webster, Apr. 21, 1948; children: Bradford Keith, Traci Jo, Blake Patrick. Hockey player with Buffalo Bisons, Springfield Indians, Detroit Redwings, Edmonton Flyers, Regina Capitals, Brandon Regals, Seattle Americans, 1942-57, gen. mgr., coach, also Seattle Totems, 1956-66; coach, then asst. gen. mgr. Phila. Flyers Profl. Hockey Club, 1967-68, exec. v.p., gen. mgr., 1968—. Served with Canadian Navy, 1943-45. Club: Overbrook Country (Radnor, Pa.). Team winner Stanley Cup, 1973-74, 74-75. Office: care Phila Flyers Pattison Pl Philadelphia PA 19148 *

ALLEN, DARRYL FRANK, glass company executive; b. Detroit, Sept. 7, 1943; s. Hairston Ulyssess and Frances (Akers) A.; m. Sharon Mae Baines, Aug. 27, 1966; children: Richard Baines, James Bretten, Michael Jeffery. B.A., Mich. State U., 1965; M.B.A., U. Mich., 1966. Mgr. Arthur Andersen & Co., Detroit, 1965-72; corporate controller Aeroquip Corp., Jackson, Mich., 1972-76, v.p. finance, 1976-78, v.p. fin. and adminstrn., 1978-79; v.p. fin. services Libbey-Owens-Ford Co., 1980—, chief fin. officer, 1981-83, group v.p., 1983—. Mem. Am. Inst. C.P.A.s, Mich. Assn. C.P.A.s, Financial Execs. Inst. Home: 5565 Sturbridge Toledo OH 43623 Office: 811 Madison Ave Toledo OH 43624

ALLEN, DAVID DONALD, ins. co. exec.; b. Scranton, Pa., Feb. 17, 1931; s. Robert William and Muriel Joan (Malia) A.; m. Eleanor M. Corwin, May 17, 1952; children—Lisa and Laura (twins), Joan. B.A., Harpur Coll., 1956. With IBM Corp., 1956-69, Eastern region mgr. systems, N.Y.C., 1965-67, data processing div. mgr. comml. analysis, White Plains, N.Y., 1967-69; v.p. operations Computer Tech. East, N.Y.C., 1969-70; v.p. mgmt. information systems CBS, N.Y.C., 1970-76; v.p. Lincoln Nat. Life Ins. Co., 1976-79, sr. v.p., 1979—. Served with AUS, 1950-53. Home: 12204 Covington Rd Ft Wayne IN 46804 Office: 1300 S Clinton St PO Box 1110 Ft Wayne IN 46801

ALLEN, DAVID T., physician, commissioner of health; b. Crawfordsville, Ind., Apr. 29, 1940; s. Joseph Percival and Harriet (Taylor) A.; m. Carol Ann Ruppel, Jan. 27, 1968; children: Tim, Heather. B.A., DePauw U., 1961; M.D., Case Western Reserve U., 1966; M.P.H., U. Mich., 1971. Intern in pediatrics Palo Alto-Stanford Hosp., Palo Alto, Calif., 1966-67; with USPHS, 1967-70; acting epidemiologist W. Va. Dept. Health, 1967-68; cons. family planning Ga. Dept. Pub. Health, 1968-69, tech. assistance officer family planning evaluation activity, 1969-70; dir. family and maternal health Tenn. Dept. Pub. Health, 1970-71, dir. family health services, 1971-72, dir. local health adminstrn., 1972-75; health officer Williamson County, Tenn., 1973-80; asst. commnr. pub. health, dir. bur. regional and local health Tenn. Dept. Pub. Health, 1975-77, dep. commnr. med. services, 1977-79, dir. community health services adminstrn., 1979-80; commnr. Ky. Dept. Health Services, Frankfort, KY., 1980—; mem. faculty dept. preventive medicine and community health Vanderbilt U. Sch. Medicine, 1980, Meharry Med. Coll., 1975; spl. reporter on health WSM-TV News, 1979; cons. AID-Kenya Ministry of Health, 1976; cons. in field. Contbr. articles to profl. jours. Mem. Tenn. Med. Assn., Nashville Acad. Medicine, Am. Pub. Health Assn., Ky. Med. Assn., Woodford County Med. Soc. Home: 31 Heritage St Versailles KY 40383 Office: Ky Dept Health 275 E Main St Frankfort KY 40621

ALLEN, DIOGENES, clergyman, educator; b. Lexington, Ky., Oct. 17, 1932; m. Jane Mary Billing, Sept. 8, 1958; children: Mary, George, John, Timothy. B.A. with high distinction, U. Ky., 1954; postgrad., Princeton U., 1954-55; B.A. with honors, Oxford U., 1957, M.A., 1961; B.D., Yale U., 1959, Ph.D., 1965. Ordained to ministry United Presbyterian Ch., 1959. Minister Windham Presbyn. Ch., N.H., 1958-61; asst. prof. York U., Toronto, Ont., Can., 1964-66, assoc. prof. philosophy, 1966-67; assoc. prof. Princeton Theol. Sem., N.J., 1967-74; prof. Princeton Theol. Sem., N.J., 1974—, Stuart prof. philosophy, 1981—; trustee Blair Acad., Harvey Sch. Author: The Reasonableness of Faith, 1968, Finding Our Father, 1974, Between Two Worlds, 1978, Traces of God, 1981, Three Outsider: Pascal, Kierkegaard and S. Weil, 1983, Mechanical Explanations and Their Relation to the Ultimate Origin of the Universe According to Leibniz, 1983; editor: Theodicy (Leibniz), 1966; mem. editorial bd.: Theology Today. Rhodes scholar, 1955-57, 63-64; Rockefeller fellow, 1962-64. Home: 29 Alexander St Princeton NJ 08540 Office: 21 Dickinson St Princeton NJ 08540 *In my life I have found that there are many people who are glad to encourage and help another person in the pursuit of worthwhile tasks.*

ALLEN, DON LEE, dentistry educator, college dean; b. Burlington, N.C., Mar. 13, 1934; s. William Arthur and Gena (Davis) A.; m. Winifred Rouse, Aug. 2, 1958; children: Don Lee, Michael Denmark, Susan Winifred. Student, Elon Coll., 1952-55; D.D.S., U. N.C., 1959; M.S. in Periodontics, U. Mich., 1964. Instr. U. N.C. Sch. Dentistry, Chapel Hill, 1959-62, asst. prof., 1962-65, asso. prof., 1965-69, prof., asso. dean, 1969-70, U. Fla. Coll. Dentistry, Gainesville, 1970-73, dean, 1973-82, U. Tex. Dental Br. at Houston, 1982—; staff Shands Teaching Hosp., 1970-82; mem. nat. adv. council health profl. edn. Dept. Health and Human Services, 1978-82; mem. Commn. Dental Edn. and Practice Fedn. Dentaire Internationale, 1981—; cons. USPHS, Council Dental Edn., VA Hosp., Gainesville and Houston. Author: (with G. Hunter, W. McFall) Periodontics for the Dental Hygienist, 1968, 2d edit., 1974, 3d edit., 1980; contbg. editor: Gould Med. Dictionary. Active Y-Indian Guides, Chapel Hill, 1968-70, Gainesville, 1973-75; elder Presbyterian Ch., 1972-75, 78-82. Recipient teaching award U. N.C. Class of 1966. Fellow Am. Coll. Dentists (chmn. Fla. sect. 1980-81), Internat. Coll. Dentists (pres. 1981-82); mem. Am. Acad. Periodontology, ADA (commn. on dental accreditation 1978—), Am. Assn. Dental Schs. (pres. 1982-83), Internat. Assn. Dental Research, So. Conf. Dental Deans and Examiners (pres. 1983-84), So. Acad. Periodontology, Omicron Kappa Upsilon. Address: Univ of Texas Health Sciences Center School of Dentistry Houston TX 77025

ALLEN, DONALD CLINTON, lawyer; b. Spokane, Wash., Nov. 5, 1931; s. Donald Eldon and Alice Adillah (Diediker) A.; m. Carolyn J. Gray; children: Joan C., Susan P., Patsy A., Michael E. Student, Princeton, 1950-53; LL.B., U. Md., 1959. Bar: Md. bar 1959. Asso. firm Rollins, Smalkin, Weston & Andrew, Balt., 1959-64; partner firm Allen, Thieblot & Hughes, Balt., 1964-69, Allen, Thieblot & Alexander, 1969—; Instr. Mt. Vernon (Md.) Sch. Law div. Eastern Coll. Commerce, Law, 1967-68; instr. Essex (Md.) Community Coll., 1967-69; asst. Md. Dept. Legis. Reference, 1963-64; reporter Md. Legis. Council Com. to Revise Health Laws, 1963-65, Gov. Md. Commn. to Revise Mental Health Laws, 1966-69; mem. inquiry com. Atty. Grievance Commn. of Md., 1978-81, mem. rev. bd., 1981-84. Pres. Randallstown (Md.) P.T.A., 1964-65. Served with AUS, 1953-55. Mem. Am., Md. bar assns., Bar Assn. Balt. City (chmn. com. unins. motorists 1965), Assn. Def. Trial Counsel Met. Balt. (pres. 1976-77), Md. Assn. Def. Trial Counsel (pres. 1977-79), Randallstown Jaycees (dir. 1960-62), Sky Valley Assn. (chmn. adv. bd. 1974-77), Delta Theta Phi. Club: Optimist. Office: 444 World Trade Center Baltimore MD 21202

ALLEN, DUANE DAVID, singer, mem. vocal group; b. Taylortown, Tex., Apr. 29, 1943; s. Fred and Loretta (Bell) A.; m. Norah Lee Stuart, Sept. 22, 1969; children—Jamie Dionne, Duane David II (Dee). B.S. in Music, E. Tex. U., 1965; H.L.D. (hon.) in Christian Music, Victory Bible Inst., Lewistown, Ohio, 1975. Disc jockey Sta. KPLT, Paris, Tex., 1963-65; co-owner, pres. Silverline, Goldline Music Pub. Cos.; owner, pres. Superior Sound Studios. Partner, lead singer, Oak Ridge Boys, 1966—; composer: gospel songs He Did It All For Me, Here's a Song for the Man, How Much Further Can We Go, I Will Follow the Sun; Co-author: The History of Gospel Music, 1971. Recipient Grammy awards, 1970, 74, 76, 77; 12 Dove awards Gospel Music Assn.; named Vocal Group of Yr. Country Music Assn., 1978. Mem. Country Music Assn., Gospel Music Assn., AFTRA, Nat. Acad. Rec. Arts and Scis., Acad. Country Music. *

ALLEN, DURWARD LEON, biologist, educator; b. Uniondale, Ind., Oct. 11, 1910; s. Harley J. and Jennie M. (LaTurner) A.; m. Dorothy Ellen Helling, Sept. 23, 1935; children: Stephen R., Harley W., Susan E. A.B., U. Mich., 1932; Ph.D., Mich. State Coll., 1937; L.H.D. (hon.), No. Mich. U., 1971. Game research biologist Mich. Dept. Conservation, 1935-46; wildlife research biologist U.S. Fish and Wildlife Service, Laurel, Md., 1946-50, asst. chief br. wildlife research, Washington, 1951-54; prof. wildlife ecology Purdue U., Lafayette, Ind., 1954—; Mem. Adv. Bd. on Nat. Parks, Monuments and Historic Sites, U.S. Dept. Interior, 1966-72, chmn., 1971-72; Chmn. Nat. Sci. Adv. Com. on Fish and Wildlife and Parks, U.S. Dept. Interior, 1975-76. Author: Michigan Fox Squirrel Management, 1943, Pheasants Afield, 1953, Our Wildlife Legacy, 1954, The Life of Prairies and Plains, 1967, Wolves of Minong, 1979; Editor: Pheasants in North America, 1956. Recipient medal of honor Anglers' Club of N.Y., 1956. Fellow AAAS; mem. Wildlife Soc. (hon. life mem., pres. 1956-57, Annual Tech. Publ. award 1946, Annual Conservation Edn. award 1955, Leopold Meml. medal 1968), Am. Soc. Mammalogists, Ecol. Soc. Am., Washington Biologists' Field Club, Am. Inst. Biol. Scis., Am. Forestry Assn. (bd. dirs.), Wilderness Soc., Outdoors Writers Assn. Am. (Jade of Chiefs award 1968), Nature Conservancy, Conservation Found., Nat. Parks and Conservation Assn., Sierra Club, Ind. Acad. Sci., Nat. Audubon Soc. (bd. dirs.), Seminarium Botanicum, Sigma Xi, Phi Sigma, Xi Sigma Pi. Clubs: Boone and Crockett, Cosmos (Washington); Explorers (N.Y.C.). Home: 1010 Windwood Lane West Lafayette IN 47906 *Humanity emerged from the natural order and must continue to survive as a part of it. I believe that professionals in any way concerned with the earth relationships of man have a prior obligation to serve generations of the future equally with those of the present.*

ALLEN, DWIGHT WILLIAM, education educator; b. Stockton, Calif., Aug. 1, 1931; s. John William and Valera (Fisher) A.; m. Carole Jeanine Swall, Apr. 12, 1953; children: Douglas Bruce, Dwight Dennis, Dana Lee, Carla Jeanne and Cheryl Elaine (twins). A.B. with distinction, Stanford U., 1953, M.A. in Edn., 1957, Ed.D., 1959. Instr. Athens (Greece) Coll., 1953-54; secondary sch. tchr., 1957-59; faculty Stanford, 1958-67; assoc. prof. edn. Stanford U., 1965-67; dean U. Mass. Sch. Edn., Amherst, 1968-74, prof., 1976-78; Univ. prof. urban edn. Old Dominion U., Norfolk, Va., 1978-80, Univ. prof. arts and letters, 1981—; prof. edn. Norfolk State U., 1978—; chief tech. adviser UNESCO, Nat. Tchr. Tng. Coll., Lesotho, 1974-76; cons. Calif. Commn. Pub. Edn., 1966-67; pres. Jr. Statesmen Found., 1964-66; chmn. planning coordination com., chief cons. ednl. professions devel. act. U.S. Office Edn., 1967; cons. AID, Dept. State, 1976-78, Internat. Monetary Fund, 1981—. Author: (with Robert N. Bush) A New Design for High School Education: Assuming a Flexible Schedule, 1964, (with Don Bushnell) The Computer in American Education, 1967, (with others) Technical Skills of Teaching for Elementary and Secondary Education, 1968, (with Kevin Ryan) Microteaching, 1969, (with Eli Seifman) The Teacher's Handbook, 1971, (with Jeffrey C. Hecht) Controversies in Education, 1972; Editor: (with Robert Madgic) Great Issues Series, The Scholastic Press, 1967—; Contbr. numerous articles to profl. jours., chpts. in books. Served with AUS, 1954-56. Am. Edn. Research Assn., AAAS, NEA, Phi Delta Kappa. Mem. Nat. Spiritual Assembly of Baha'is of U.S., 1966-74, 80—. Office: Sch Arts and Letters Old Dominion U Norfolk VA 23508

ALLEN, EDWARD LAWRENCE, govt. ofcl., economist; b. Stony Point, N.Y., Feb. 28, 1913; s. Ernest John and Clara Adelaine (Termansen) A.; m. Doris Anne Hoffman, Mar. 16, 1963; children—Edward Lawrence, Anne Beatrice. B.S., Columbia, 1935; M.A., Am. U., 1946, Ph.D., 1948. Various statis. and research positions with financial firms, N.Y.C., 1935-41; statis. analyst WPB, 1942-43; dep. for research, target analysis USAF, 1946-51; project leader, weapons systems evaluation group OSD, 1951-53; chief econ. research CIA, 1953-71; dep. asst. sec. Dept. Commerce, 1971-73, econ. cons., 1974—; adj. prof. econs. Am. U., 1949—. Author: Economics of American Manufacturing, 1952, Soviet Progress vs. American Enterprise, 1958, Can the United States Maintain its World Leadership, 1960, Energy and Economic Growth, 1979, also articles. Served as officer USNR, 1943-46. Mem. Am. Econ. Assn. Home: 6028 Woodley Rd McLean VA 22101

ALLEN, ELBERT ENRICO, dentist; b. Shreveport, La., Sept. 19, 1921; s. William and Mathilde (Durr) A.; m. Carolyn Sims, Nov. 11, 1963. B.S., Wiley Coll., 1942; D.D.S., Meharry Med. Coll., 1945. Practice dentistry, Shreveport, 1945—. Chmn. finance com. Pioneer div. Boy Scouts Am., 1954-62; bd. dirs. Norwela council, 1949—; vice chmn. The Shreveport Story, 1969; mem. La. State Fair, 1972-74; div. planning and services for aging Caddo-Bossier Council of Local Govt., 1970-74, Northwest La. Area-wide Health Planning Council, Inc., 1973-74; Mem. Caddo Parish Sch. Bd., 1970-72; mem. exec. com. Shreveport City Charter Com., 1970; Bd. dirs. Mt. Moriah Day Care Center and Nursery, Shreveport Mental Health Center, Am. Cancer Soc., Shreveport chpt. A.R.C., Shreveport Assn. for Blind, David H.

Raines Assn., Family Counseling and Children Services, United Fund, Rutherford House, Kappa Towers, Kappa Alpha Psi Found., 1982-84; pres., bd. dirs. Community Council of Caddo and Bossier Parishes; bd. dirs., past 1st v.p. N.W. Coordinating Council; trustee Wiley Coll.; chmn. mgmt. com. George Washington Carver YMCA; mem. Better Bus. Bur., Shreveport, 1980-81; mem. adv. bd. Salvation Army, Shreveport, 1981; mem. exec. com. Community Council-Caddo Parish and Bossier Parish, 1979-81. Served with AUS, 1943-44; as capt. USAF, 1951-53. Recipient Liberty Bell award Shreveport Bar Assn., 1970. Mem. Am. Dental Assn., Nat. Dental Assn. (past editor jour.), Pelican State Dental Assn. (past pres.), 4th Dist. Dental Assn., La. Dental Assn., N. La. Dental Soc. (past sec.), Chgo. Dental Soc. (asso.), Acad. Gen. Dentistry (past parliamentarian), Acad. Pierre Fauchard (Pierre Fauchard award), Fedn. Dentaire Internat., Royal Soc. for Promotion Health (London, Eng.), Shreveport C. of C., Meharry Med. Coll. Alumni Assn., Am. Inst. Parliamentarians, Nat. Rehab. Assn., Am. Legion (past post comdr., past chmn. for Boys State, vice chmn. Americanism council 1980-81, historian), Shreveport Negro C. of C., Kappa Alpha Psi (grand polemarch). Methodist. Club: Am. Woodman (supreme comdr.). Home: 2119 Carver Pl Shreveport LA 71103 Office: 1004 Sprague St Shreveport LA 71101

ALLEN, ERNEST MASON, library director; b. Terrell, Tex., Dec. 1, 1904; s. Louis L. and Ada (Turner) A.; m. Virginia Williamson, June 7, 1928; children: Anton M., E. Raworth, James W. Ph.B. magna cum laude, Emory U., 1926, M.A., 1939, D.Sc. (hon.), 1956; LL.D., Clemson U., 1968. Instr. French, Jr. Coll. Augusta (Ga.), 1926-41; sec., treas. Augusta Bus. Coll., 1930-41; project mgr. NYA, Ga., 1941-43; sr. pub. health rep. div. veneral diseases USPHS, 1943-45, operations officer, 1945-46; asst. chief div. research grants NIH, 1946-51, chief div. research grants, 1951-60; asso. dir. NIH, 1960-63; grants policy officer USPHS, 1963-68, dir. Office of Extramural Programs, 1968-69; dep. asst. sec. for grant adminstrn. policy HEW, 1969-73; asso. dir. Nat. Library of Medicine, 1973—; chmn. gov. bd. BioSciences Info. Exchange, 1952-55; mem. adv. com. U.S. sci. exhibit Century 21 Expn.; mem. 1963 Nat. Health Forum Com.; cons. Pres.'s Commn. on Health Needs of Nation, mem. com. on acad. sci. and engring., 1968-70; mem. adv. council AAAS, 1973—. Recipient Yorktown medal Govt. France, 1932; Disting. Service award HEW, 1971. Mem. Phi Beta Kappa, Phi Sigma Iota, Phi Theta Kappa. Home: 8507 Hazelwood Dr Bethesda MD 20814

ALLEN, EUGENE MURRAY, chemist; b. Newark, Nov. 7, 1916; s. Mitchell and Celia (Schnitter) Kaplan; m. Beatrice Hyman, Jan. 23, 1937; children: Marlene, Julian Lewis. A.B., Columbia, 1938; M.S., Stevens Inst. Tech., 1944; Ph.D., Rutgers U., 1952. Research chemist Utility Color Co., Newark, 1938-39, United Color & Pigment Co., 1939-41, E.R. Squibb & Sons, Bklyn., 1941-42; chemist Picatinny Arsenal, Dover, N.J., 1942-45; research chemist Am. Cyanamid Co., Bound Brook, N.J., 1945-63, research asso., 1963-66, research fellow, 1966-67, cons., 1967-72; prof. chemistry Lehigh U., 1967—, dir. Color Sci. lab., 1968—, Consortium for Color Tech., 1973—; cons. IBM Corp., Celanese Can., Pantone, Inc.; Mem. U.S. nat. com., cons. colorimetry com. Internat. Commn. Illumination. Asso. editor: Color Engineering, 1964-71, Jour. Color and Appearance, 1971; Contbr. articles to sci. jours. Recipient Sr. Research award Am. Cyanamid Co., 1958, Armin J. Bruning award Fedn Socs. for Coatings Tech., 1982. Fellow Optical Soc. Am.; mem. Am. Chem. Soc., Am. Assn. Textile Chemists and Colorists (chmn. color tech. com. 1965), Inter-Soc. Color Council (chmn. fluorescence subcom. 1952-67, dir. 1974-76, Godlove award 1983), Sigma Xi. Home: 2100 Main St Bethlehem PA 18017 *Artists and scientists are driven by the same creative impulse, and are engaged in the same pursuit-that of creating new entitites out of disparate elements. Just as a good painting has the inner logic of a scientific demonstration, so does a well executed and reported scientific investigation have the beauty of a Mozart symphony. That is why every good scientific work bears the unmistakable imprint of the man who made it, and could only have been effected at that time, in that place, and by that person.*

ALLEN, FRANCES ELIZABETH, computer scientist; b. Peru, N.Y., Aug. 4, 1932; d. John Abram and Ruth Genevieve (Downs) A.; m. Jacob T. Schwartz, July 22, 1972. B.S., State U. N.Y., Albany, 1954; M.A., U. Mich., 1957. Research computer scientist IBM Research Lab., Yorktown Heights, N.Y., 1957—; adj. asso. prof. N.Y. U., 1970-72; mem. computer sci. adv. bd. NSF, 1972-75, cons., 1975—; lectr. Chinese Acad. Scis., 1973, 77; IEEE disting. visitor, 1973-74; cons. prof. Stanford U., 1977-78. Mem. Assn. Computing Machinery (nat. lectr. 1972-73), Programming Systems and Langs. (Paper award 1976). Home: Finney Farm Croton-on-Hudson NY 10520 Office: IBM Corp PO Box 218 Yorktown Heights NY 10598

ALLEN, FRANCIS ALFRED, legal educator; b. Kansas City, Kan., Oct. 25, 1919; s. Oliver Boyd and Justa Lee (Wingo) A.; m. June Florence Murphy, Feb. 16, 1947; children: Neil Walsh, Susan Lee. A.B., Cornell Coll., 1941, J.D. (hon.), 1958; LL.B. magna cum laude, Northwestern U., 1946; LL.D., U. Victoria, 1980. Bar: Ill. 1950, Mich. 1968. Legal sec. Chief Justice Fred M. Vinson, 1946-48; asst. prof. law Northwestern U., 1948-50, asso. prof., 1950-53; prof. law Harvard, 1953-56, U. Chgo., 1956-62, U. Mich., 1962-63; Univ. prof. also prof. law U. Chgo., 1963-66; dean law U. Mich., Ann Arbor, 1966-71, prof., 1966-72, Edson R. Sunderland prof., 1972—; faculty Salzburg Seminar in Am. studies, summers 1963, 73; Holmes lectr. Harvard, 1972-73; Storrs lectr. Yale, 1979; Spl. cons. ESA, 1951; pres. Assn. Am. Law Schs., 1976. Author: The Borderland of Criminal Justice, 1964, The Crimes of Politics, 1974, Law, Intellect and Education, 1979, The Decline of the Rehabilitative Ideal, 1981; editor-in-chief: Ill. Law Rev., 1942-43; Editor: Standards of American Legislation (Freund), 1965; Contbr. articles on legal subjects to jours. Chmn. citizens adv. com. Ill. Sex Offenders Commn., 1952-53; drafting chmn. Ill. Criminal Code, 1961; mem. citizens adv. com. Family Ct. of Cook County, 1962. Served as sgt. USAAF, 1942-45. Recipient Arthur von Briesen medal Nat. Legal Aid and Defender Assn., 1963, Guggenheim fellow, 1971-72, 78. Mem. Am. Acad. Arts and Scis., Am. Bar Assn., Am. Law Inst. (mem. council 1969-74), Ill. Acad. Criminology (pres. 1961-62), Phi Beta Kappa, Order of Coif. Methodist. Home: 11 Eastbury Ct Ann Arbor MI 48105

ALLEN, FRANK CARROLL, banker; b. Hazlehurst, Miss., Nov. 10, 1913; s. Walter Scott and May (Ellis) A.; m. Clara Marnee Alford, June 23, 1937; children: Marnee Louise, Susan Carroll, Elizabeth Jane. A.A. with high honors, Copiah-Lincoln Jr. Coll., Wesson, Miss., 1933; student, Am. Inst. Banking, 1935, 36, 37, 47, 49. Bookkeeper, teller Georgetown Bank, Miss., 1933-34, cashier, dir., 1937-41; bookkeeper Deposit Guaranty Bank & Trust Co., Jackson, Miss., 1934-37; bank examiner, Miss., 1942-46; cashier, dir. Brookhaven Bank & Trust Co., Miss., 1947-49; pres., dir. Lawrence County Bank, Monticello, Miss., 1949-65; pres. Monticello Bank br. Deposit Guaranty Nat. Bank, 1966-78; chmn. adv. bd. Monticello/Newhebron Bank brs., 1966—; adv. bd. Deposit Guaranty Nat. Bank of Jackson, 1966—, Deposit Guaranty Corp.; chmn. bd. Ins. & Realty Underwriters, 1971-75, dir., 1961-76; Bd. dirs. Miss. Econ. Council, 1950-53; commr. Monticello Planning Bd., 1964-74; commr. banking and consumer fin. State of Miss., 1980; bd. dirs. S.W. Miss. Devel. Assn., 1960-72; Chmn. scholarship bd. Monticello Mfg. Co., 1960-72. Mem. exec. bd. Andrew Jackson council Boy Scouts Am., 1975—. Served to 1st lt. AUS, 1942-46. Mem. Am. Bankers Assn. (chmn. Miss. dist. 7 on U.S. Savs. Bonds 1952—), Miss. Bankers Assn. (chmn bank mgmt. com. 1948-49, group v.p. 1948-49), Monticello C. of C. (pres. 1951-53, 60-61, dir. 1951-81), Newcomen Soc. N. Am. Baptist (deacon 1953—, Sunday sch. supt. 1958-60). Club: Lion (pres. Monticello 1954-55). Home: PO Box 368 Monticello MS 39654 Office: PO Box 458 Monticello MS 39654

ALLEN, FRED CARY, ret. army officer; b. Vine Grove, Ky., Apr. 29, 1917; s. Fred P. and Alice (Peterson) A.; m. Eunice Bond, Jan. 25, 1958; children—Joyce Gail (Mrs. David Schimberg), David Frederick, Richard Forsythe, Joan Meissner. B.S., Western Ky. U., 1940. Commd. 2d lt. U.S. Army, 1940, advanced through grades to brig. gen., 1967; inf. and transp. assignments, U.S., Far East, Korea, Alaska, 1940-58; comdg. officer Transp. Bn., 1st Inf. Div., Ft. Riley, Kan., 1958-60; student Indsl. Coll. Armed Forces, Washington, 1960-61; comdg. officer Army Support Command, Alaska, 1962-63; chief of staff U.S. Army, Alaska, 1964-65; dir. army transp. Dept. of Army, Pentagon, 1966-67; dir. logistics (J-4) U.S. Strike Command, MacDill AFB, Fla., 1967-69; dir. prodn. ships, weapons and electronics system Office Sec. of Def., 1969-72; owner, developer land devel. co. Decorated D.S.M., Legion of Merit with 3 oak leaf clusters, Bronze Star, Army Commendation medal. Mem. Nat. Def. Transp. Assn. (hon. nat. pres., v.p. for Alaska 1963-69), Assn. U.S. Army. Club: Rotarian. Home: 8410 Porter Lane Alexandria VA 22308 *Self confidence is the greatest thing to have going for you. There's little hope without it. Avoid cockiness yet cultivate self esteem and the right amount of egotism. Be a team member and partner but don't forsake your own ideas and principles. Get involved, even take charge, yet be prepared to see it through. Be resolute yet recognize the need and way to change direction.*

ALLEN, FRED HAROLD, JR., physician, educator; b. Holyoke, Mass., Feb. 23, 1912; s. Fred Harold and Harriet (Ives) A.; m. Frances Williams Brown, July 16, 1938; children: Philip Brown, Mark Harold, Barbara Allen Brewster, Dwight Bickford. A.B., Amherst Coll., 1934; M.D., Harvard, 1938. Intern Children's Hosp., Boston, 1938-42; practice pediatrics, Holyoke, Mass., 1946-47, asso. dir. Blood Grouping Lab., Boston, 1947-63; sr. investigator N.Y. Blood Center, 1963—; clin. asso. prof. pediatrics Cornell U. Med. Coll., 1963—. Author: (with L. K. Diamond) Erythroblastosis Fetalis, 1958; also articles.; Chief editor for N. and S. Am.: Vox Sanguinis, 1963-76; Assoc. editor: Transfusion. Served to maj., M.C. AUS, 1942-46. Recipient Karl Landsteiner Meml. award Am. Assn. Blood Banks, 1963; Joseph P. Kennedy Internat. award research mental retardation, 1966; Philip Levine award Am. Soc. Clin. Pathology, 1976; Buffalo award State U. N.Y. at Buffalo, 1976; Schweitzer Research award Greater N.Y. Acad. Prosthodontics, 1978. Discovered cause and prevention of brain damage in erythroblastosis fetalis, 1950. Home: 3 Merestone Terr Bronxville NY 10708 Office: 310 E 67th St New York NY 10021

ALLEN, GARLAND EDWARD, biology educator, science historian; b. Louisville, Feb. 13, 1936; s. Garland Edward and Virginia (Blandford) A.; children: Tania Leigh, Carin Tove. A.B., U. Louisville, 1957; A.M.T., Harvard U., 1958, 1963, Ph.D., 1966. Programmer, announcer WFPL-WFPK, Louisville, 1956-58; tchr. Mt. Hermon (Mass.) Sch., 1958-61; Allston-Burr sr. tutor, instr. history of sci. Harvard, 1965-67; asst. prof. biology Washington U., St. Louis, 1967-72, asso. prof., 1972-80, prof., 1980—; cons. Ednl. Research Corp., Cleve., 1967—; Commr. Commn. Undergrad. Edn. in Biol. Scis., 1967-70; mem. NSF Panel for Social Scis., 1968-71; Sigma Xi Nat. lectr., 1973-74, bicentennial lectr., 1974-77. Author: (with J.J.W. Baker) Matter, Energy and Life, 1965, 70, 75, 80, The Study of Biology, 2d edit, 1971, 3d edit., 1976, 4th edit., 1982, The Process of Biology, 1970, Hypothesis, Prediction and Implication, 1969, Life Sciences in the Twentieth Century, 1975, 78, T.H. Morgan, The Man and His Science, 1978; Editorial bd.: San José Studies, Jour. History of Biology, Folia Medeliana. Fellow Charles Warren Ctr. for Studies in Am. History, Harvard U., 1981-82. Mem. AAAS (council, sect. L exec. com.), Am. Assn. History of Sci., History Sci. Soc., Sigma Xi. Home: 1812 Lafayette Ave St Louis MO 63104 Office: Biology Dept Washington U St Louis MO 63130

ALLEN, GAY WILSON, educator; b. Lake Junaluska, N.C., Aug. 23, 1903; s. Robert Henry and Ethel (Garren) A.; m. Evie Allison, July 15, 1929. A.B., Duke U., 1926, M.A., 1928; Ph.D., U. Wis., 1934; D.Lit., Duke, 1975, U. Wis.-Madison, 1983. Instr. in English Lake Erie Coll., Painesville, O., 1929-31, Shurtleff Coll., Alton, Ill., 1934-35, State Univ., Bowling Green, O., 1935-46; prof. English N.Y.U., 1946-69; tchr. summer schs. Harvard, Duke, U. Tex., U. Hawaii; vis. prof. Harvard U., 1969-70, Emory U., 1979. Author: American Prosody, 1935, Literary Criticism: Pope to Croce, (with H. H. Clark), 1941, Walt Whitman Handbook, 1946, Masters of American Literature, (with H. A. Pochmann), 1949, The Solitary Singer. A Critical Biography of Walt Whitman, 1955, Walt Whitman Abroad, 1955, Walt Whitman's Poems, (with C.T. Davis), 1955, Walt Whitman: Evergreen Profile Book, 1959, Walt Whitman as Man, Poet and Legend, 1961, American Poetry, (with Walter Rideout and James K. Robinson), 1965, William James, A Biography, 1967, The World of Herman Melville, 1971; Editor: A William James Reader, 1971, Studies in Leaves of Grass, 1972, The New Walt Whitman Handbook, 1975, Waldo Emerson, A Biography, 1981; Gen. editor: (with Sculley Bradley) Collected Writings of Walt Whitman, 1961—; Contbr. articles and reviews to nat., internat. jours. Fellow Rockefeller Found., 1944-45; Guggenheim fellow, 1952-53, 59-60. Mem. Internat. Assn. Univ. Profs. English, MLA (Lowell prize 1982), Phi Beta Kappa. Club: P.E.N. Home: 454 Grove St Oradell NJ 07649 *Writing biography is a one-way transaction in friendship.*

ALLEN, GEORGE, professional football coach; b. Detroit, Apr. 29, 1922; s. Earl R. and Loretta (Hannigan) A.; m. Etty L. Lumbroso, May 26, 1951; children: George, Gregory, Bruce, Jennifer. B.A., M.A., U. Mich.; postgrad., U. So. Calif. Formerly football coach Morningside Coll., Sioux City, Iowa, Whittier (Calif.) Coll.; coach defense Chicago Bears; head coach Los Angeles Rams, 1978; head coach, v.p., gen. mgr. Washington Redskins (Nat. Football Conf.), 1971-77; football commentator and analyst CBS Sports, 1979-82; coach and gen. mgr. Chgo. Blitz, 1982-83; coach Ariz. Wranglers, Phoenix, 1983—. Address: care Ariz Wranglers 515 N 48th St Phoenix AZ 85008 *

ALLEN, GEORGE HOWARD, publishing executive; b. Boston, June 1, 1914; s. Albert Hacker and Myrtie A. (Lawton) A.; m. Virginia Russell, Sept. 7, 1940; children: Russell Lawton, Douglas Winslow (dec.). B.S., U. Mass., 1936, LL.D., 1967; M.B.A., Harvard U., 1938. Asst. to pres. Nat. Theatre Supply Co., N.Y.C., 1938-40; research mgr. Sta. WOR, 1941, asst. dir. promotion and research, 1942-43; radio cons. U.S. Treasury Dept., 1943-45; gen. mgr., sec. bd. Coop. Analysis of Broadcasting, N.Y.C., 1944-46; N.E. sales mgr. N.Y. Herald Tribune, 1946, promotion mgr., 1947-50; chmn. 20th Nat. Bus. Conf., Harvard, 1950; dir. sales promotion McCall's mag., 1950-57, asst. pub., gen. mgr., 1957-60; pub. Better Living mag., 1956; v.p. Mass Markets Publs., Inc., 1953-54, pres., 1954-55, dir., 1953-55; spl. asst. to pres. Meredith Pub. Co., N.Y.C., 1960-61, v.p., 1961-66, dir., 1965-66, gen. mgr. mag. pub. div., Des Moines, 1962-66; pub. Better Homes and Gardens, Successful Farming mags., 1964-66; chmn. bd. Nat. Plan Service, Chgo., 1965-66; pub., v.p. Fawcett Publs., Inc., N.Y.C., 1966-72, exec. v.p., dir., 1972-77; sr. v.p. mags. CBS Publs., 1977—, spl. interest group pub. (Audio, Road & Track, World Tennis, Am. Photographer, Cycle World), 1982—; pub. Woman's Day, 1966-80, Audio, Road & Track, World Tennis, Am. Photographers, Cycle World, 1982—; Mem. panel Pres.'s White House Conf. on Food and Nutrition, 1969; Bd. dirs. Internat. Exchange Program, Ann Arbor, chmn., 1978-79; bd. dirs. Advt. Council, 1969—; chmn. Intercorp. Communications Group; mem. council judges Advt. Hall of Fame, 1982. Author: Individual Initiative in Business; Contbr. articles profl. mags. Mem. Chancellor's Council U. Mass, 1982, mem. bus. adv. Council Sch. Mgmt., 1983. Recipient leadership award Am. Legion, 1932; Young Advt. Man of Year, 1956; Achievement Award Wash. Ad Club, 1956; Silver Anvil award Am. Pub. Relations Assn., 1957; Bell Ringer award Salt Lake City Ad Club, 1957; Pub. Relations News award, 1957; Mgmt. Man of Year, 1965; named Pub. of Year; also recipient Henry Johnson Fisher award of mag. industry, 1980. Mem. Am. Mktg. Assn. (pres. N.Y. 1946), NAM (dir. 1965-66), Mag. Pubs. Assn. (dir., sec. 1974-75, chmn. 1977, chmn. Kelly awards com. 1980—), Advt. Fedn. Am. (dir. 1965-67), U.S. C. of C. (edn. com. 1964-66), Advt. Research Found. (dir. 1965, sec.-treas. 1971, vice chmn. 1972, chmn. 1974-75), U. Mass. Alumni Assn. (v.p.), Harvard Bus. Sch. Assn. (pres. 1967), Pubs. Information Bur. (dir. 1966, vice chmn. 1974), Harvard Alumni Assn. (dir. 1958-59), Sales Promotion Execs. Assn. (mem. nat. bd. 1958), Pub. Relations Soc. Am., Newcomen Soc., Lambda Chi Alpha, Adelphia. Congregationalist. Clubs: Harvard, Canadian, Economic, Dutch Treat, Sky (N.Y.C.); International (Chgo.). Home: 14 Long Hill Rd Guilford CT 06437 Office: CBS Publs 1515 Broadway New York NY 10036 *Togetherness is still the glue that structures our society.*

ALLEN, GINA, author; b. Trenton, Nebr.; d. R.V. and Osa (Hanel) Hunkins; 1 dau., Ginita Allen Wall. B.A., Northwestern U., 1940. Exec. sec. Youth Commn. 3d Jud. Dist., N.Mex., 1955-60; mem. bd. Golden Gate chpt. NOW, 1970—; pres. Humanist Assn. San Francisco, 1976—; sec. Am. Humanist Assn., 1973-77, sr. humanist counselor, 1972—, chmn. women's caucus, 1977—, v.p., 1979-83. Author: Prairie Children, 1941, On the Oregon Trail, 1942, Rustics for Keeps, 1948, (with R.V. Hunkins) Tepee Days, 1941, Trapper Days, 1942, Sod-House Days, 1945, The Forbidden Man, 1961 (Anisfield-Wolf award 1962), Gold!, 1964, Gold Is, 1969, Intimacy, 1971; also short stories, articles in popular mags. Chairwoman N.Mex. Democratic Central Com., 1956-59. Recipient Pioneer award Am. Humanist Assn., 1983. Unitarian. Mailing Address: 2424 Castro St San Francisco CA 94131

ALLEN, GORDON ERWIN, apparel company executive; b. Whitinsville, Mass., Feb. 4, 1926; s. George R. and Margaret (Gibson) A.; m. Sally Sprague, Sept. 15, 1951; children: Janet, Judith, Betsy. B.A., Brown U., 1950. Various postitions in sales and merchandising Arrow Co., 1950-68; v.p. mktg. Alatex, Inc., 1969-70, pres., 1971-75; exec. v.p. Cluett, Peabody & Co., Inc., N.Y.C., 1975-78, pres., 1979—; dir. City Fed. Savs. & Loan Assn.; mem. adv. bd. Mfrs. Hanover Trust Co. Served with USAAF, 19744-46. Mem. Am. Apparel Mfrs. Assn. (chmn.). Republican. Presbyterian. Home: 335 Woodland Ave Westfield NJ 07090 Office: 510 Fifth Ave New York NY 10036

ALLEN, HARLAND HILL, economist; b. Loyalton, S.D., Dec. 9, 1887; s. Albert Barnes and Harriet Mabel (Hill) A.; m. Florence Brooks, May 28, 1927 (dec. Dec. 1964); children—Franklin (dec.), Rolaine Kay Allen Groves; m. Alma Louise Petersen, Aug. 8, 1965. Student, Dakota Wesleyan U., LL.D. (hon.), 1958; A.B., Colo. Tchrs. Coll., 1916, A.M., 1917; postgrad., U. Chgo., 1920-21, Columbia U., 1924, univs. Paris, London, Berlin, Leipzig, summers 1926, 29. Editor, pub. Roscoe (S.D.) Reveille, 1911-12; supt. pub. schs., Kersey, Colo., 1915-16; prof. econs. North Tex. State Tchrs. Coll., Denton, 1917-19; fellow, teaching asst. U. Chgo., 1919-21; instr. econs. U. Ill., 1921-22; prof. econs., dean Sch. Commerce, Okla. Agrl. and Mech Coll., 1923-24; economist Halsey, Stuart & Co., Chgo., 1927-29, Foreman State Nat. Bank, 1929-31; pres. Growth Research, Inc. (successors to Harland Allen Assos., investment mgrs.), 1931-61, chmn. bd., 1961-68; founder, chief exec. Growth Industry Shares, Inc., 1946-64; dean Roosevelt Coll. Sch. Commerce, Chgo., 1947-49, exec. com., chmn. bd., 1959-63; charter mem. bd. La Salle Fund, Chgo.; fin. and indsl. research, S.Am., 1972; vis. lectr. Dakota Wesleyan U., 1973. Lectr., writer.; Author: Whither Interest Rates, 1939, The Businessman's Stake in American-Soviet Friendship, 1943, Investing for Growth-Why and How, 1957, How the Science Revolution is Changing the Social Order, 1964; series World Economic Perspectives for the 1970's, 1970-71, Portentous Credit Inflation, 1979; syndicated newspaper column Your Money Problems, 1924-29, Harland Allen Economic Letter, 1932-44; contbr.: articles to Business and Society; others. Bd. dirs. Dakota Wesleyan U., Mitchell, S.D., Edward A. Filene Good Will Fund; chmn. Chgo. chpt. Com. to Defend Am., 1941. Recipient Man of Year citation Dakota Weslyan U., 1961. Mem. Am. Econs. Assn., Am. Statis. Assn. (past pres. Chgo.). Unitarian. Clubs: City (dir.), Mid-Am., Investment Analysts (pres. 1932-33). Home: 3940 E Timrod Ave Apt 225 Tucson AZ 85711 *The highest priority in my life is, and will always be, to add whatever I can to people's understanding of their problems, opportunities, and aspirations—as individuals and as citizens of the wide world. The hope for Peace and Progress seems to me to hinge entirely on such understanding.*

ALLEN, HAROLD BYRON, educator; b. Grand Rapids, Mich., Oct. 6, 1902; s. Arthur Kingsbury and Edith (Welch) A.; m. Elizabeth Mitchell, June 19, 1934; children: Marjorie Lyle (Mrs. Alexander G. Russell), Susan Kingsbury (Mrs. David Stevenson). B.A., Kalamazoo Coll., 1924; M.A., U. Mich., 1928, Ph.D., 1941. From asst. prof. to prof. rhetoric, also asst. to pres. Shurtleff Coll., Alton, Ill., 1925- 34; asst. editor Early Modern English Dictionary, 1934-39, Middle English Dictionary, 1939-40; asst. prof. English San Diego State Coll., 1940-43; mem. faculty U. Minn., 1944—, prof. English, 1958-68, prof. English and linguistics, 1968-71, prof. emeritus, 1971—, lectr. in linguistics, 1976-77; vis. summer prof. Mills Coll., 1943, U. So. Cal., 1961, U. Victoria, Can., 1973, 74, 75, Moorhead State U., 1976, Chadron State Coll., 1978; Fulbright lectr. U. Cairo, Egypt, 1954-55; Smith-Mundt vis. prof. linguistics UAR Ministry of Edn., Cairo, 1958-59; Fulbright-Hayes lectr. Kossuth Lajos U., Debrecen, Hungary, 1972; dir., editor Linguistic Atlas of Upper Midwest, 1947—; linguistic cons. Economy Co., 1967—, Ency. of the States, 1980; adv. bd. Doubleday dictionaries, 1975—; mem. nat. adv. council Teaching English as Fgn. Lang., 1962-65, 69—, chmn., 1974-77; English lang. cons. U. Tehran, Iran, 1971, 73; Chmn. lang. arts adv. com. Minn. Bd. Edn., 1962-67. Author: An Introduction to English Sound Structure, 1960, TENES-A Survey of the Teaching of English to Non-English Speakers in the U.S, 1966, Linguistic Atlas of the Upper Midwest, Vol. 1, 1973, Vol. 2, 1975, Vol. 3, 1976, Pathways to English, 1984; also articles.; Editor, compiler in field. Recipient Disting. Alumnus award Kalamazoo Coll., 1980; Am. Council Learned Soc. fellow, summers, 1938-40; fellow Fund Advancement Edn., 1951-52. Mem. ACLU, AAUP, Nat. Council Tchrs. English (pres. 1961, dir. commn. English lang. 1964-68, chmn. Conf. Coll. Composition and Communication 1952, Distinguished service award 1969, David Russell award for research 1973), Tchrs. English to Speakers of Other Langs. (pres. 1966-67, Distinguished service citation 1970), Linguistic Soc. Am., Am. Dialect Soc. (mem. exec. council 1963-68, pres. 1971, 72), Am. Name Soc. (bd. mgrs. 1961-63), Canadian Linguistic Assn., Internat. Assn. U. Profs. English, Speech Communication Assn., Minn. Group Linguistics (chmn. 1948, 64-67, 74), Phi Delta Kappa, Phi Kappa Phi,

Pi Kappa Delta, Sigma Tau Delta, Theta Alpha Phi. Home: 8100 Highwood Dr Bloomington MN 55438

ALLEN, HAROLD G., life ins. co. exec.; b. Mecosta County, Mich., Oct. 9, 1911; s. William and Verna R. (Phelps) A.; m. Jean D. Crawford, Aug. 1, 1937; children—Margaret D., Nancy R. B.A., U. Mich., 1933, M.A., 1934. With Bankers Life Co., Des Moines, 1934—, actuary, 1956-63, 2d v.p., 1956-59, v.p., 1959-66, sr. v.p., 1966-68, pres., 1968-73, chmn., chief exec. officer, 1973-76, ret., also dir. Served to 1st lt. USMCR, 1943-46. Fellow Soc. Actuaries; mem. Am. Acad. Actuaries, Des Moines C. of C. (pres., dir.). Club: Des Moines. Home: 4333 Greenwood Dr Des Moines IA 50312

ALLEN, HARRY CLAY, JR., chemist, educator; b. Saugus, Mass., Nov. 26, 1920; s. Harry Clay and Sarah Elizabeth (Thorburn) A.; m. Carolyn A. Bliss, Feb. 1, 1948; children—Carol B., Paul T. B.S., Northeastern U., 1948; Sc.M., Brown U., 1949; Ph.D., U. Wash., 1951. Research fellow Harvard, 1951-53; asst. prof. Mich. State U., 1953-54; chemist Nat. Bur. Standards, 1954-61, chief analytical and inorganic chemistry div., 1961-63, chief inorganic materials div., 1963-65; dep. dir. Inst. for Materials Research, 1965-66; asst. dir. minerals research Bur. Mines, 1966-69; prof. chemistry Clark U., 1969—, chmn. dept., 1969-78, dean Grad. Sch., 1978-81, coordinator research, 1978-83, acting provost, 1980-81, asso. provost, 1981-83; research assoc. U. Cambridge, Eng., 1959-60; vis. research prof. U. Wash., 1958; vis. prof. U. N.C., Chapel Hill, 1978; Postdoctoral fellow AEC, 1951-53. Author: (with P. C. Cross) Molecular Vib-rotors, 1963. Served with AUS, 1942-46. Recipient Samuel Wesley Stratton award Nat. Bur. Standards, 1965. Fellow Am. Phys. Soc., Am. Inst. Chemists; mem. Am. Chem. Soc., Sigma Xi, Phi Lambda Upsilon. Club: Cosmos (Washington). Home: 21 Rittenhouse Rd Worcester MA 01602

ALLEN, HENRY FREEMAN, ophthalmologist, educator; b. Boston, Nov. 23, 1916; s. Freeman and Ethel (Gibson) A.; m. Emily L. Tuckerman, June 7, 1941; children: Emily T., Rosamond W., Freeman. A.B. magna cum laude, Harvard, 1939, M.D., 1943; Sc. D. hon., Colby Coll., 1976. Intern Mass. Gen. Hosp., Boston, 1944; resident Mass. Eye and Ear Infirmary, Boston, 1947-49; practice ophthalmology, Boston, 1949; chief ophthalmology Mass. Eye & Ear Infirmary, 1968-73, cons. chief ophthalmology, 1973—; cons. Mass. Gen. Hosp., Children's Hosp. Med. Center; clin. prof., head dept. Harvard Med. Sch., 1968-74, Henry Willard Williams clin. prof., 1970—. Pres. Channing Home, Boston, 1951-57; Trustee Episcopal Theol. Sch., Cambridge, 1960-74, Perkins Sch. for Blind, Watertown. Served to capt., M.C. AUS, 1944-45; ETO. Mem. Am. Assn. Ophthalmology (pres. 1971-72), Am. Acad. Ophthalmology, A.M.A. (chief editor Archives Ophthalmology, chmn. sect. ophthalmology 1966—, Lucien Howe medal 1967), New Eng. Ophthal. Soc., Phi Beta Kappa. Episcopalian. Office: 200 Beacon St Boston MA 02116

ALLEN, HERBERT, steel company executive; b. Ratcliff, Tex., May 2, 1907; s. Jasper and Leona (Matthews) A.; m. Helen Daniels, Aug. 28, 1937; children: David Daniels (dec.), Anne (Mrs. Jonathan Taft Symonds), Michael Herbert. B.S. in Mech. Engring., Rice U., 1929. Registered profl. engr., Tex. Engaged in research, 1929-31; with Cameron Iron Works, Inc. (and predecessor), Houston, 1931—, v.p. engring. and mfg., 1942-50, v.p., gen. mgr., 1950-66, pres., 1966-73, chmn. bd., 1973-77, also dir.; dir. Tex. Commerce Bank. Bd. govs. Rice U., Houston, 1949-64, trustee, 1964-76, chmn., 1972-76. Named Inventor of Year Houston Patent Attys. Assn., 1977; recipient Gold medal for distinguished service Assn. Rice Alumni, 1975. Hon. mem. ASME (Petroleum Div. award 1977); mem. Nat. Acad. Engring., Am. Inst. Mining, Metall. and Petroleum Engrs., Am. Petroleum Inst., Tex. Soc. Profl. Engrs. (named Engr. of Year 1961), Houston C. of C. (bd. dirs. 1952-54, v.p. 1954-55, dir.-at-large 1962), Houston Engring. and Sci. Soc., Tau Beta Pi. Episcopalian. Clubs: River Oaks Country, Petroleum, Ramada, Houston; Bayou, Metropolitan (N.Y.C.). Patentee in field. Home: 3207 Groveland Ln Houston TX 77019 Office: PO Box 1212 Houston TX 77251

ALLEN, HERBERT ELLIS, environmental chemistry educator; b. Sharon, Pa., July 19, 1939; s. Jacob Samuel and Florence (Safier) A.; children: Francine Joy, Julie Michelle. B.S. in chemistry, U. Mich., 1962; M.S., Wayne State U., 1967; Ph.D., U. Mich., 1974. Chemist U.S. Bur. Comml. Fisheries, Ann Arbor, Mich., 1962-70; lectr. U. Mich., Ann Arbor, 1970-74; asst. prof. Ill. Inst. Tech., Chgo., 1974-76, assoc. prof., 1976-80, prof. environ engring., 1980-83; dir. Environ. Studies Inst., Drexel U., Phila., also prof. chemistry, 1983—; vis. prof. Water Research Centre, Madmenham, Eng., 1980-81; cons. WHO; cons U.S. EPA. Editor: Nutrients in Natural Waters, 1972. WHO fellow, 1981. Mem. Am. Chem. Soc. (chmn. div. environ. chemistry 1972-75), Water Pollution Control Fedn., Am. Soc. Limnology and Oceanography, Internat. Assn. Water Pollution Research and Control. Home: 21 E Levering Mill Rd Bala Cynwyd PA 19004 Office: Drexel Univ Environmental Studies Inst Philadelphia PA 19104

ALLEN, HOWARD D., insurance company executive; b. Boston, Apr. 1, 1927; s. Elmer F. and Bessie D. (Dyer) A.; children: April, May, Mark, June, Juliette. B.A., Harvard U., 1950. Asst. actuary Pan Am Life, New Orleans, 1955-57, John Hancock Mutual Life Insurance Co., Boston, 1957-61, assoc. actuary, 1961-66, 2d v.p., 1966-68; v.p. John Hancock Mutual Life Insuranceco., Boston, 1968-78; sr. v.p. John Hancock Mutual Life Insurance Co., Boston, 1978—; chmn. research planning com Life Ins. Mgmt. Assn., Hartford, Conn., 1976-78; chmn. N.Y. subcom. Am. Council of Life Ins., Washington, 1978-80. Chmn. sch. survey com. Westwood, Mass., 1968; chmn. EDP study com. Stoughton, Mass. Served to 1st lt. USAF, 1950-52. Fellow Soc. of Actuaries, Am. Acad. Actuaries. Clubs: Harvard (Boston); Braeburn Country (Newton, Mass.). Home: 685 Oak St Apt 15-203 Brockton MA 02401 Office: John Hancock Mutual Life Ins co PO Box 111 Boston MA 02117

ALLEN, HOWARD PFEIFFER, electric utility executive; b. Upland, Calif., Oct. 7, 1925; s. Howard Clinton and Emma Maud (Pfeiffer) A.; m. Dixie Mae Illa, May 14, 1948; 1 dau., Alisa Cary. B.A. cum laude, Pomona Coll., 1948; J.D., Stanford U., 1951. Bar: Calif. 1952. Asst. dean, asst. prof. law Stanford Law Sch., 1951-54; with So. Calif. Edison Co., 1954—, v.p., 1962-71, sr. v.p., 1971-73, exec. v.p., 1973-80, pres., 1980—, also dir.; dir. Calif. Fed. Savs. & Loan Assn., Calif. Fed. Inc., Pacific Southwest Airlines, PSA Inc., MCA, Inc., ICN Pharms., Inc., Republic Corp., Computer Scis., Inc. Bd. dirs. Los Angeles County Fair Assn., Los Angeles Civic Light Opera, Pacific Coast Elec. Assn., Calif. Council for Environ. and Econ. Balance; trustee Pomona Coll., 1978—, Los Angeles County Mus. Art, NCCJ; vice-chmn. bd. dirs., mem. exec. com. Mayor's Spl. Com. on Olympics; mem. Los Angeles Olympic Organizing Com. Mem. Los Angeles C. of C. (dir., pres. 1978, chmn. 1979), ABA, Los Angeles County Bar Assn., State Bar Calif., Bar Assn. San Francisco., Phi Beta Kappa, Phi Delta Phi. Clubs: California (Los Angeles); Pacific-Union, Bohemian (San Francisco). Office: 2244 Walnut Grove Ave Rosemead CA 91770

ALLEN, IRWIN, motion picture writer, producer, director; b. N.Y.C.; s. Joseph and Eva (Davis) A. Student, CCNY, Columbia U. Radio news commentator KLAC, Hollywood, Calif.; syndicated newspaper columnist, motion picture editor Atlas Features Syndicate, Hollywood; lit. agt. motion pictures; television producer, commentator, Hollywood. Prodn. exec.: Double Dynamite; assoc. producer: Where Danger Lives; co-producer: A Girl in Every Port; producer, dir., screenplay writer: The Sea Around Us; producer: Dangerous Mission, When Time Ran Out; writer, producer, dir.: Animal World; producer, dir., co-writer screenplay: The Story of Mankind; producer, co-writer screenplay: The Big Circus; producer, dir., co-writer: The Lost World, Voyage to the Bottom of the Sea, Five Weeks in a Balloon, City Beneath the Sea; producer, dir.: spl. action sequences The Towering Inferno, The Poseidon Adventure; dir.: The Swarm; producer: Beyond the Poseidon Adventure; creator, producer: TV series Land of The Giants, Lost in Space, The Time Tunnel, Voyage to the Bottom of the Sea, Swiss Family Robinson, Code Red; producer: TV movies Memory of Eva Ryker, Adventures of the Queen, The Time Travellers, Flood, Fire, The Return of Captain Nemo, Hanging by a Thread, Cave-In, The Night the Bridge Fell Down. Recipient Academy award for The Sea Around Us, Internat. Laurel award Motion Picture Exhibitors, Blue Ribbon award for excellent motion picture prodn. Box Office mag. (5 times), Merit award So. Calif. Fedn. Womans Clubs (5 times), David Donatello award for The Towering Inferno; named NATO Producer of Yr., Fox Showman of Yr. Office: Columbia Pictures Burbank CA 91505

ALLEN, IVAN, JR., merchant; b. Atlanta, Mar. 15, 1911; s. Ivan and Irene (Beaumont) A.; m. Louise Richardson, Jan. 1, 1936; children—Ivan III, Inman, Beaumont. Grad., Georgia Inst. Tech., 1933; LL.D., Morris Brown Coll., Clark Coll., Atlanta U., La Grange Coll., Emory U., Davidson Coll. With Ivan Allen Co., Atlanta, 1933—, pres., 1946-57, vice chmn. bd., 1957, chmn. bd., 1969—; dir. Equitable Life Assurance Soc. Scout, scoutmaster, area pres., regional committeeman, mem. nat. exec. bd. Boy Scouts Am.; chmn. Greater Atlanta Community Chest, 1949; Lt. col. Gov.'s Staff, 1936; treas. Ga. State Hosp. Authority, 1936; sec. exec. dept. State Ga., 1945-46; mayor of Atlanta, 1961-69; Trustee Ga. Tech. Found. Served as maj. inf. AUS, World War II. Awarded Silver Beaver, Silver Antelope, Silver Buffalo; Recipient Armin Maier award Atlanta Rotary Club, 1952. Mem. Ga. Tech. Alumni Assn. (pres. 1953-54), Atlanta C. of C. (pres. 1961), Nat. Stationery and Office Equipment Assn. (dist. gov. 1938-40, pres. 1955-56), Sigma Alpha Epsilon. Club: Rotarian. Home: 3700 Northside Dr Atlanta GA 30305 Office: 221 Ivy St Atlanta GA 30303

ALLEN, JACK, emeritus educator; b. Prestonsburg, Ky., June 18, 1914; s. Edward L. and Anna (Mayo) A.; m. Cherry Falls, Aug. 16, 1941; children—David E., Robert L., Edward L. A.B., Eastern Ky. State Coll., 1935; M.A., George Peabody Coll. Tchrs., 1938, Ph.D., 1941. High sch. tchr., Ky., 1935-37; asst. prof. history Eastern Ky. State Coll., 1940-42, 46; asso. prof. history George Peabody Coll., 1946-52, prof., 1952-80, prof. history emeritus, 1980—, head dept., 1954-74, chmn. div. social sci., 1963-74, acting exec. dean academic affairs, 1974-75, dir. programs for ednl. policy specialists, 1974-77; instr. Peabody-in-Athens, Greece, 1968; Asso. dir. for academic programs Nashville U. Center Council, 1969-70; Cons. Nova Sch., Ft. Lauderdale, Fla., 1963-67, Oak Ridge Schs., 1964-66; Social studies cons., Republic of Korea, 1961, 69; cons. Tri-Univ. project U. Wash., 1967-69, Bel air Sch., Mandeville, Jamaica, 1970; Adv. council council Edn. Policies Commn.; adv. bd. Am. Viewpoint, Inc., Am. Edn. Publs., 1970-73; Coordinating Council Tchr. Edn. Alliance for Met., Nashville, 1969-75; author cons. Gt. Am. Achievement program Bicentennial Fund, 1978—. Author elementary and high sch. textbooks, workbooks; author: (with Hershel Gower) Pen and Sword, 1960 (received Merit award Soc. State and Local History), A Charter for Social Studies in Korea, 1961, (with Adelene E. Howland) The United States of America, 1964, The Americas, 1964, The Earth and Our States, 1966, Nations Around the Globe, 1966, Nations of Other Lands, 1966, Documents U.S.A, 1967, (with others) The Problems and Promise of American Democracy, 1964, (with John L. Betts) History; USA, 1967, 71, 76, (with others) Contemporary Issues in American Democracy, 1969, Teachers Manual for Contemporary Issues in American Democracy, 1969, The Social Studies, 1969, American Public School, 1969, USA; History with Documents, 1971, American Society: Inquiry into Civic Issues, 1973, (with others) Design for the Future, 1974, American Society, 1978, Americans, 1979, One Nation Indivisable, 1979, A New Republic Among Nations, 1980, Of, By, and For the People, 1980, Education in the Eighties: Social Studies, 1980, American Society: Civics and Citizenship, 1984; Contbr. articles to profl. jours., yearbooks. Chmn. nat. alumni fund campaign Peabody Coll. of Vanderbilt U., 1983. Served with USNR, 1942-45. Recipient Alumnus of Yr. award Eastern Ky. State Coll., 1960, Centennial award Eastern Ky U., 1974. Mem. Am. Studies Assn., Nat. Council Social Studies (pres. 1958, chmn. publs. com. 1967), Orgn. of Am. Historians, Phi Delta Kappa, Kappa Delta Pi, Pi Gamma Mu, Pi Omega Pi. Clubs: Old Oak., Hillwood. Home: 3705 Hilldale Dr Nashville TN 37215

ALLEN, JAMES ALBERT, librarian; b. Alexandria, La., Nov. 7, 1930; s. James Ogden and Nena (McGrew) A.; m. Gloria Ann Bausewein, Aug. 17, 1963; 1 dau., Janet Ann. B.S. in Bus. Adminstrn, La. State U., 1954, M.S. in L.S, 1962. Tchr. schs. in, La., 1958-61; instr., asst. dir. La. Coll. Library, 1962, asst. prof., asst. dir., 1963-64, chmn. dept. library sci., dir. library, 1964-65; head librarian Little Rock U., 1965-69; dir. library U. Ark., Little Rock, 1969—, asso. prof. library sci., 1971—, chmn. dept., 1969-76; mem. Central Ark. Network Delivery Library and Ednl. Services, 1972-73; mem. bd. AMIGOS Bibliog. Council, 1975-76, 80-83, vice chmn. bd., 1981-82; chmn. Ark. Union Catalog Com., 1976-77, Ark. Union List of Serials Com., 1982-83; cons. in field. Bd. dirs. Walnut Valley Homes Assn., 1974-75, sec., 1974; mem. vestry Christ Episc. Ch., 1978. Mem. Am. Library Assn., Southwestern Library Assn. (chmn. coll. and univ. library div. 1972), Ark. Library Assn. (chmn. coll. and univ. div. 1971, membership v.p. 1973, pres. resources and tech. services div. 1975), Assn. Coll. and Research Libraries, O.C.L.C. Users Council, Pi Tau Pi, Alpha Tau Omega. Home: 39 Walnut Valley Dr Little Rock AR 72211 Office: Univ Ark Library University and 33d Sts Little Rock AR 72204

ALLEN, JAMES HARRILL, physician, educator; b. Chattanooga, Jan. 31, 1906; s. George Henry and Mary (Harrill) A.; m. Ruth Sanford, Aug. 17, 1934; children—Mary Helen, George Sanford, John Robert. A.B., U. Tenn., 1926; M.D., U. Mich., 1930; M.S., U. Ia., 1938. Diplomate: Am. Bd. Ophthalmology (mem. 1951-59). Intern, resident Univ. Hosps., 1930-34; fellow ophthalmology U. Ia., 1934-36, research asst., 1936-37, instr. ophthalmology, 1937-38, asst. prof., 1938-45, asso. prof., 1945-46, prof., 1946-50; prof. ophthalmology Tulane U., 1950-71, chmn. dept., 1952-67; asso. dean med. dir. Tulane Clinics, 1967-71, clin. prof. ophthalmology, 1971-76, emeritus prof., 1976—; 16th Proctor Meml. lectr. U. Cal., 1961; 1st Dwight Townes vis. prof. ophthalmology U. Louisville, 1967; 4th Conrad Berens Meml. lectr., 1971; cons. Nat. Soc. Prevention Blindness, Nat. Council to Combat Blindness, Eye Bank for Sight Restoration, N.Y., USPHS Hosp., Carville, La., New Orleans, New Orleans VA Hosp.; cons. ophthalmology to air surgeon, 1952-58; Dir. So. Eye Bank, Gulf States Eye Surgery Found., 1950-60; bd. dirs. Information Council Americas, 1960—, New Orleans Lighthouse for the Blind, 1962—, pres., 1973—. Editor: Strabismus, A Symposium, 1950, Strabismus Symposium II, 1958, Proc. Assn. Research in Opthalmology, 1948-54; survey of: Opthalmology, 1962-68; cons. editor, 1968—; editor: Mays Diseases of the Eye, 23d edit, 1963, 24th edit., 1968, The Pen, 1977—; collaborating editor: Opthalmologico Ibero Americano, 1952-60; associate: Archives of Ophthalmology, 1950-53; editorial bd.: Investigative Opthalmology, 1961-68, Annals of Ophthalmology, 1968—; cons. editor: Audio Digest, 1963—; Contbr. articles to med. jours. Served from capt. to lt. col. USAAF, 1942-46. Recipient Beverly Meyers Nelson achievement award for meritorious contributions in field of vision, 1958; Egyptian Med. Syndicate medal, 1966; Distinguished Service award Soc. Contemporary Ophthalmology, 1973; Meritorious Service award Contact Lens Assn. Ophthalmologists, 1973; decorated Legion of Honor Order of DeMolay, 1962; Order of Red Cross of Constantine, 1969; knight comdr. Ct. of Honor, 1973; Dr. Felix Formento Meml. award La. Pub. Health Assn., 1975. Mem. N.Y. Acad. Scis., Pan Am. Assn. Ophthalmology (asst. sec. 1953-74), Aerospace Med. Assn., Am. Soc. for Microbiology, Assn. Mil. Surgeons, Soc. Am. Bacteriologists, A.A.A.S., A.M.A. (Gold medal ophthalmology sect. 1976), Assn. Research Ophthalmology (asst. sec. 1938-47, sec.-treas. 1947-54, trustee 1955-60, chmn. 1960), Assn. Am. Physicians and Surgeons, Am. Acad. Ophthalmology and Otolaryngology, La. Ophthalmology Assn. (sec.-treas. 1975—), Am. Assn. Ophthalmology (dir. 1968-76), Orleans Parish med. socs., Pan Am. Ophthal. Found. (pres. 1966-74), Contact Lens Assn. Ophthalmologists (exec. com. 1965-75, v.p. 1970-71, pres. 1972), European Contact Lens Assn. Ophthalmologists, Internat. Contact Lens Assn. Ophthalmologists (exec. com. 1966-76), World Med. Assn., Verhoeff Soc., So. Ophthalmic Pathology Club, Physicians Ednl. Network (chmn. 1977—), Sigma Xi, Theta Kappa Psi; hon. mem. Minn. Acad. Ophthalmology and Otolaryngology, Ft. Worth Eye, Ear, Nose and Throat Soc., Central Ill., Kansas City socs. ophthalmology and otolaryngology, Ark.-La.-Tex. Otolaryng. and Ophthalmological Soc., Dallas So. Clin. Soc., Chilean Ophthalmology Soc., Mont. Acad. Otolaryngology and Ophthalmology, Ophthal. Soc. Valley of Cauca (Colombia), Sociedad Neurologica de Colombia (corr.), Royal Soc. St. George, Royal Order Scotland. Clubs: Mason, Shriner, Elk, Rotarian., Pendennis, Jesters., City. Home: 9104 Quince St New Orleans LA 70118

ALLEN, JAMES LOVIC, JR., humanist, educator; b. Atlanta, Jan. 2, 1929; s. James Lovic and Effie Grace (Schell) A.; m. Barbara Foster, June 13, 1953 (div.); children: Melinda Sue, Algernon Foster. B.A., Tulane U., 1953, M.A., 1954; Ph.D., U. Fla., 1959. Instr. in English U. Tenn., 1954-56; asst. prof. English Stephen F. Austin State U., Nacogdoches, Tex., 1959-60; assoc. prof. English U. So. Miss., Hattiesburg, 1960-63, U. Hawaii, Hilo, 1963-69, prof., 1969—; vis. prof. English Stephen F. Austin State U., 1970-71, U. Tenn., 1976-77. Author: Locked in: Surfing for Life, 1970, Yeats's Epitaph: A Key to Symbolic Unity in His Life and Work, 1982; editor: Yeats Four Decades After: Some Scholarly and Critical Perspectives, 1979; Editorial bd.: 20th Century Lit, Yeats Eliot Rev.; Contbr. articles to profl. publs. Served with USN, 1946-49. So. Fellowship Fund grantee, 1956-58. Mem. AAUP, MLA, Can. Assn. for Irish Studies, Am. Com. Irish Studies, Canadian Assn. Irish Studies, Assn. for Study of Anglo-Irish Lit., Phi Beta Kappa. Democrat. Unitarian. Researcher W.B. Yeats. Home: 2405 Kalanianaole Ave Apt 304 Hilo HI 96720 Office: U Hawaii 1400 Kapiolani St Hilo HI 96720

ALLEN, JAMES R., retired air force officer, business executive; b. Louisville, Nov. 17, 1925; s. James Smoot and Ruth (Rodgers) A.; m. Kathryn Lewis; children: Jeffrey, Kathryn. B.S. in Mil. Engring, U.S. Mil. Acad., 1948; postgrad., Army Command and Gen. Staff Coll., 1959-60, Indsl. Coll. Armed Forces, 1964-65; M.S. in Bus. Adminstrn, George Washington U., 1965. Commd. 2d lt. USAF, 1948, advanced through grades to gen., 1977; comdr. flying tng. classes, Randolph AFB, Tex., Nellis AFB, Nev., 1948-49; with 18th Fighter Group P.I., 1949-51; aide to comdr. Fifth Air Force, Korea, 1951; mem. 71st Fighter Squadron, Greater Pitts. Airport, 1951-53; co. tactical officer U.S. Mil. Acad., West Point, N.Y., 1953-56; flight comdr., squadron ops. officer 53d Fighter Day Squadron, Ramstein Air Base, Germany, 1956-58; with Directorate Plans Hdqrs. U.S. Air Forces in Europe, 1958-59; with directorate Plans Hdqrs. USAF, Pentagon, 1960, asst. dep. dir. plans, 1968-69; dep. dir. plans and policy Directorate of Plans, dep. chief staff plans and operations, 1969-72; comdr. 4th Tactical Fighter Squadron, Eglin AFB, Fla., 1965; dep. comdr. for operations 12th Tactical Fighter Wing, Cam Ranh Bay, Vietnam, 1965-67, 3615th Pilot Tng. Wing, Craig AFB, Ala., 1967-68; comdr. 19th Air Div., Carswell AFB, Tex.; asst. dep. chief staff for ops. SAC, Offutt AFB, Nebr., 1972-73, chief staff, after 1973; supt. USAF Acad., 1974-77; chief staff SHAPE, 1977-79; dep. comdr.-in-chief U.S. European Command, 1979-81; comdr.-in-chief Mil. Airlift Command, 1981-83, ret., 1983; chmn., chief exec. officer Internat. Planning and Analysis Ctr., Inc., 1983—. Decorated D.S.M. with oak leaf cluster, Legion of Merit with two oak leaf clusters, D.F.C. with one oak leaf cluster, Bronze Star, Air medal with eleven oak leaf clusters, Air Force Commendation medal with one oak leaf cluster, Army Commendation medal, comdr. French Ordre Nationale du Mérite, Sudanese Order of the Two Niles. Address: 450 5th St NW Washington DC 20001

ALLEN, JAMES ROSS, psychiatrist; b. Wroexter, Ont., Can., Mar. 16, 1935; s. James John and Mary Mable (Ross) A.; m. Barbara Ann Pearman, Nov. 28, 1968; 1 son, Michael David. B.A., U. Toronto, 1957, M.D., 1961; diploma psychiatry, McGill U., 1967. Diplomate: Am. Bd. Psychiatry and Neurology. Fellow Lab. Community Psychiatry Harvard, 1967-68; asst. prof. U. Okla. Health Scis. Center, Tulsa, 1969-71, assoc. prof., 1971-75, prof., 1975—, head dept. psychiatry and behavioral scis.; chief exec. officer Tulsa Psychiat. Center; cons. Indian Health Service, VA, Muskogee, Okla.; Chmn. Tulsa Alcohol Adv. Commn., 1979; mem. Ken Found. Task Force on Alcoholism. Author: Guide to Psychiatry, 1982; contbr. articles to profl. jours. Fellow Royal Coll. Physicians of Can.; mem. Internat. Transactional Analysis Assn. (trustee), Gestalt Therapy Inst. Dallas, AMA, Am. Psychiat. Assn. (cert. in adminstrn.), Tulsa Psychiat. Inst. Office: 1612 E 12th St Tulsa OK 74120

ALLEN, JAY PRESSON, writer, producer; b. Fort Worth, Mar. 3, 1922; d. Albert Jeffry and Willie (Miller) Presson; m. Lewis Maitland Allen, Mar. 12, 1955; 1 dau., Anna Brooke. Screenplays include Cabaret, Prince of the City; plays include The Prime of Miss Jean Brodie; creator: TV series Family; author screenplay; exec. producer: Deathtrap, Prince of the City; author book, screenplay; exec. producer: Just Tell Me What You Want. Recipient David di Donatello award, 1980. Mem. Writers Guild, Dramatists Guild, Acad. Motion Picture Arts and Scis. Office: 156 W 56th St New York NY 10019

ALLEN, JEREMIAH MERVIN, educational administrator, English educator; b. Boston, Sept. 3, 1919; s. Jeremiah Mervin and Dorothy (Lucas) A.; m. Aldith Kent Sutton, Oct. 5, 1941; children: Jeremiah Mervin, Peter, Barbara, Stanley, Jonathan. A.B., Duke U., 1947; M.A., Tufts U., 1948; Ph.D., U. Colo., 1956. Instr. English U. Colo., Boulder, 1948-55, asst. prof., 1956-60, assoc. prof., 1960-62, prof., 1962-68; prof., assoc. provost U. Mass., Amherst, 1968-70, dean and prof. English, 1970—. Co-author: Writing Clinical Reports, 1953, Curricula in Solid Mechanics, 1961, Honors Program in Engineering, 1964, contbr., articles to profl. jours. Served to lt. comdr. USNR, 1940-45. Mem. Council Coll. of Arts and Scis. (pres. 1974-75), Phi Beta Kappa. Democrat. Home: 160 Lincoln Ave Amherst MA 01002 Office: U Mass Amherst MA 01003

ALLEN, JERRY CLYFF, gallery and collections director; b. St. Anthony, Idaho, Jan. 21, 1941; s. Clifton J. and Vida Valria (Hurst) A.; m. Myrne Freeman, Aug. 9, 1963; children: Jerye, Derryk, Dustyn, Ryial, Alyshia. A.A., Valley Jr. Coll., 1967; B.A., U. Calif.-Northridge,

1970; M.F.A., Brigham Young U., 1975. With Fine Arts Collection/ Brigham Young U., Provo, Utah, 1973—, dir., 1978—. Mem. Am. Mus. Assn., Utah Mus. Assn. Home: 460 S 1079 E Provo UT 84601 Office: Brigham Young Univ Gallery F-303 HFAC Provo UT 84602

ALLEN, JOHN ELIOT, geology educator; b. Seattle, Aug. 12, 1908; s. Eric William and Ida (Sally) (Elliott) A.; m. Margaret Lucy Moss, July 26, 1933; 1 dau., Margaret (Sally) (Mrs. Scott McNall). B.A., U. Oreg., 1931, M.A., 1932; Ph.D., U. Calif. at Berkeley, 1944. Geologist Oreg. Dept. Geology and Mineral Industries, 1938-47; asso. prof. Pa. State Coll., 1947-49; head dept. geology N.Mex. Sch. Mines, 1949-52; sr. geologist N.Mex. Bur. Mines, 1952-56; head dept. geology Portland (Oreg.) State U., 1956-74, prof. emeritus, 1974—; prof. Whitman Coll., 1975; research geologist Nev. Bur. Mines, 1976, N.Mex. Bur. Mines, 1977; faculty U. Calif., Santa Barbara, summers 1952, 61, 65, U. Hawaii, summer 1966. Author: Magnificent Gateway, 1979. Bd. dirs. Oreg. Nature Conservancy, 1980—. Hon. mem. Oreg. Mus. Sci. and Industry.; Recipient Silver Beaver award Boy Scouts Am., 1955; SEATO prof. U. Peshawar., Pakistan, 1963-64. Mem. Geol. Soc. Am., Nat. Assn. Geology Tchrs. (pres. 1967), Am. Inst. Profl. Geologists (pres. Oreg. sect. 1973), Geol. Soc. Ore. Country, Phi Beta Kappa, Sigma Xi, Delta Upsilon. Club: Portland City. Home: 507 1717 SW Park Ave Portland OR 97201 *In teaching, there is no substitute for enthusiasm, which is contagious. In learning, there is no substitute for motivation, which overcomes many difficulties. In a profession, there is no substitute for a firm ethical code, which outlines the limits beyond which self-respect is lost.*

ALLEN, JOHN LEO, utilities exec.; b. Boston, Oct. 7, 1928; s. James Michael and Christine Pauline (McKeon) A.; m. Mary Ann Long, Aug. 23, 1952; children—Helen, Diane, John, Virginia. Student, Bentley Coll., 1950, Northeastern U., 1954; Advanced Mgmt. Program, Harvard U., 1976. Trainee, supr. Boston Gas Co., 1950-65, mgr., 1965-67, exec. asst. to pres., 1967, asst. treas., 1969-71, treas., 1971—, v.p., 1975—, also dir.; asst. to treas. Eastern Gas & Fuel Assos., 1968. Served with AUS, 1946-47. Mem. Am. Gas Assn., New Eng. Gas Assn. (treas), Nat. Assn. Accountants, Fin. Execs. Inst. Club: K.C. Home: 5 Homeward Ln Walpole MA 02081 Office: One Beacon St Boston MA 02108

ALLEN, JOHN LOGAN, geographer; b. Laramie, Wyo., Dec. 27, 1941; s. John Milton and Nancy Elizabeth (Logan) A.; m. Anne Evelyn Gilroy, Aug. 9, 1964; children: Traci Kathleen, Jennifer Lynne. B.A. (Gen. Motors Corp. scholar 1959-63), U. Wyo., 1963, M.A., 1964; Ph.D. (univ. grad. fellow 1964-67), Clark U., Worcester, Mass., 1969, 1970-71. Mem. faculty U. Conn., Storrs, 1967—, prof. geography, 1979—, head dept., 1976—; cons. in field. Author: Passage Through the Garden: Lewis and Clark and the Geographical Lore of the American Northwest, 1975; editor: Environment 82/83, Environment 83/84; contbr. articles to profl. jours., chpts. to books. Pres. Mansfield (Conn.) Middle Sch. Assn., 1979-80; mem. Mansfield Conservation Commn.; vice chmn. Mansfield Zoning Bd. Appeals. Recipient Meritorious Achievement award Lewis and Clark Trail Heritage Found., 1976. Fellow Am. Geog. Assn., Royal Geog. Soc.; mem. Assn. Am. Geographers, Western History Assn., Soc. Historians Early Am. Republic, Soc. History Discovery, AAAS, Phi Beta Kappa, Phi Kappa Phi, Omicron Delta Kappa. Democrat. Congregationalist. Clubs: Elks, Masons. Home: 21 Thomas Dr Storrs CT 06268 Office: U-148 Univ Conn Storrs CT 06268 *As a scientist and educator, I have tried to abide by the principle that learning is necessary for the public good and that academicians should make their skills and knowledge available to society at large. Service to others is as important an educational function as the more frequently recognized components of teaching and research.*

ALLEN, JOHN LOYD, technical consultant; b. Estherville, Iowa, June 13, 1931; s. John C. and Ruth Hines; m. Dorothy G. Hooper, Sept. 4, 1952; children: Jacqueline, Linda, David, Stephen. B.S., Pa. State U., 1958; M.S., M.I.T., 1962; Ph.D., MIT, 1968. Jr. engr. HRB-Singer, 1954-58; staff mem., group leader, assoc. div. head M.I.T. Lincoln Labs., 1958-71; assoc. dir. research U.S. Naval Research Lab., 1971-74; dep. dir. def. research and engring. Dept. Def., 1974-77; v.p. Gen. Research Corp., 1977-78, pres., 1978-81; cons. John L. Allen Assocs. Ltd., Arlington, Va., 1981—; mem. Air Force Studies Bd. NRC, 1982—. Bd. visitors Air U., 1980—. Served with USAF, 1950-54. Fellow IEEE. Home: 1708 Besley Rd Vienna VA 22180 Office: 1901 N Fort Myer Dr Suite 1120 Arlington VA 22209

ALLEN, J(OSEPH) GARROTT, surgeon, educator; b. Elkins, W.Va., June 5, 1912; s. James Edward and Susan H. (Garrott) A.; m. Dorothy O. Travis, July 15, 1940 (div. 1968); children: Barry Worth, Edward Henry, Nannette (Mrs. Antonio Alarcón), Lester Travis, Joseph Garrott; m. Kathryn L. Shipley, Dec. 27, 1968; children: Robert Kelman, Grant Frederick, Susan. Student, Davis and Elkins Coll., 1930-32; A.B., Washington U., St. Louis, 1934; M.D., Harvard, 1938. Diplomate: Am. Bd. Surgery (mem. bd. 1958-64). Intern Billings Hosp., U. Chgo., 1939; asst. resident surgery U. Chgo., 1940-44, instr. surgery, 1943-47, asst. prof., 1947-48, asso. prof., 1948-51, prof., 1951-59; research asso. metall. labs. Manhattan Project, 1944-46; group leader Argonne Nat. Lab., 1946-59; prof. Stanford, 1959-77, active emeritus, 1977—; exec. dept. surgery, 1959-61; Mem. surgery study sect. USPHS, 1955-59. Author: (with others) Surgery-Principles and Practice, 1957, 4th edit., 1970, Shock and Transfusion, Therapy, 1959, The Epidemiology of Hepatitis, 1972, also sci. papers.; Editor: Peptic Ulcer, 1959; co-editor: Family Health Ency, 1970; chief editor: Archives of Surgery, 1960-70; mem. editorial bd.: Lab World, 1978. Trustee Am. Youth Found., 1954-67; Mem. NRC, 1950-54; Mem. standards com. Am. Assn. Blood Banks, 1958. Recipient prize for protamine sulfate/heparin work Chgo. Surg. Soc., 1940; John J. Abel prize for research irradiation injury Am. Assn. Pharmacology and Exptl. Therapeutics, 1948; Ednl. award Am. Assn. Blood Banks, 1954; Gold medal for original research Ill. Med. Soc., 1948, 52; Samuel D. Gross award Pa. Acad. Surgery, 1955; First Merit award Chgo. Tech. Securities Council, 1955; First John Elliott award Am. Assn. Blood Banks, 1956; citation Washington Alumni Assn., 1960. Fellow AAAS; Mem. Soc. Exptl. Biology and Medicine, Am. Physiol. Soc., A.C.S. (chmn. com. blood and allied problems), Internat. Surg. Group (founder), AMA (Gold medal for original research 1948), Am. Surg. Assn., Soc. Clin. Surgery (sec. 1958-60), S.F. Surg. Soc., Soc. Univ. Surgeons, Am. Cancer Soc. (chmn. com. cancer therapy), Western, Pacific Coast surg. assns., Surg. Infection Soc. (founder mem. 1980), Halsted Soc., Alpha Omega Alpha. Introduced protamine sulfate clinically to control anticoagulant heparin, 1937; proved nutritional value of intravenous plasma, 1950; proved high risk of commercial blood after 30 years of study, and stimulated formation of all-volunteer nat. blood program, 1975; labeling of vol. and purchased blood, 1977. Home and office: 583 Salvatierra Stanford CA 94305

ALLEN, JOSEPH HENRY, educator; b. Evanston, Ill., Nov. 9, 1916; s. Joseph Henry and Ann Eugenia (Jansen) A.; m. Eleanor Clark, June 14, 1941; children—David, Elisabeth Allen Adams, Melinda Allen Cary. B.A., Kenyon Coll., 1938; advanced mgmt. program, Stanford Grad. Sch. Bus., 1953. Joined McGraw-Hill Inc., 1938, regional editor and advt. salesman, 1938-42, established S.W. office, Dallas, also mgr., 1948, div. mgr., Los Angeles, 1951-55, v.p., dir. mktg., N.Y.C., 1955-63, v.p. ops., 1963-66; pres. McGraw-Hill Publs. Co., 1966-70; group pres. McGraw-Hill, Inc., 1970-74, dir., 1966-75; sr. v.p. United Techs. Corp., Hartford, Conn., 1974-77; assoc. dean Sch. Bus. Adminstrn., U. Conn., 1977—; dir. Sci. Research Assocs., Inc., Muir, Cornelius, Moore, Inc., Advt. Council, Inc. Served as lt. USNR, 1942-45. Clubs: University (N.Y.C.); Wee Burn Country (Darien, Conn.). Home: 29 Tokeneke Trail Darien CT 06820

ALLEN, JOSEPH PERCIVAL, astronaut; b. Crawfordsville, Ind., June 27, 1937; s. Joseph P. and Harriet (Taylor) A.; m. Bonnie Jo Darling, July 9, 1961. B.A. (Rector scholar 1955-59), DePauw U., 1959, Christian Albrechts U., Kiel, Germany, 1959-60; M.S., Yale U., 1961, Ph.D., 1965. Guest research asso. Brookhaven Nat. Lab., 1962-65; staff physicist Nuclear Structure Lab., Yale U., 1965; research asso. U. Wash., 1966; scientist-astronaut Lyndon B. Johnson Manned Spacecraft Center, NASA, Houston, 1967-75, asst. adminstr. for legis. affairs, Washington, from 1975; now on staff and astronaut Lyndon B. Johnson Space Center., astronaut, crew mem. first operational flight of Space Shuttle Columbia, 1982; Mem. staff Pres.'s Council Internat. Econ. Policy, 1973. Author articles in field. Mem. Am. Phys. Soc., Am. Astronautical Soc., N.Y. Acad. Scis., Am. Astron. Soc., AAAS, Phi Beta Kappa, Sigma Xi, Beta Theta Pi, Phi Eta Sigma. Address: Lyndon B Johnson Space Center NASA Houston TX 77058

ALLEN, KAREN JANE, actress; b. Carrollton, Ill., Oct. 5, 1951; d. Carroll Thompson and Patricia (Howell) A. Student, George Washington U., 1974-76. Mem. Washington Theatre Lab., 1973-77. Appeared in: film The Whidjit-Maker, 1977; films Animal House, 1978, The Wanderers, 1979, A Small Circle of Friends, 1979, Cruising, 1979, East of Eden, 1980, Raiders of the Lost Ark, 1980, Shoot The Moon, 1981, Split Image, 1981; play Two For the Seesaw, (orgn.) Berkshire Theatre Festival, 1981; films Monday After The Miracle, Actors Studio (N.Y.C.), Kennedy Ctr. (Washington), Broadway, 1983 (Theatre World award 1983); play Tennessee Williams: A Celebration, Williamstown Theatre Festival, 1982, Extremities, West Side Arts Theatre, N.Y.C., 1983. Mem. Screen Actors Guild, Actor's Equity Assn. Office: Press Relations Paramount Pictures Corp 1 Gulf & Western Plaza New York NY 10023

ALLEN, KENNETH DALE, insurance executive; b. Carthage, Mo., Apr. 5, 1939; s. Herbert Herman and Viola Elizabeth (Woodley) A.; m. Donna Sue Viator, Aug. 26, 1961; children: Jeffrey Scott, Kristin Michelle, Timothy Brian, Bradley Todd. A.B., Central Mo. State U., 1960; LL.B., George Washington U., 1963. Legis. and research asst. Office Sen. Stuart Symington, Washington, 1960-65; asst. Washington counsel Health Ins. Assn., 1965-72; exec. v.p. Am. Nat. Ins. Co., Galveston, Tex., 1972-78; sr. exec. v.p., gen. counsel, dir. Southwestern Life Ins. Co., Dallas, 1978—. Mem. Am., D.C. bar assns., Assn. Life Ins. Counsel. Democrat. Episcopalian. Office: Southwestern Life Ins Co PO Box 2699 Dallas TX 75221 *

ALLEN, L. CALHOUN, JR., university official; b. Shreveport, La., Feb. 8, 1921; s. L. Calhoun and Lel (Goodwin) A.; m. Mary Lenore Miller, Aug. 20, 1948 (dec. Oct. 1975); children: Frances Olivia, L. Calhoun, III; m. Jacqueline Spell Schober, Jan. 14, 1978. Asso. Allen Constrn. Co., Shreveport, 1954-62; commr. pub. utilities City of Shreveport, 1962-70, mayor, 1970-78; commr. La. Stadium, Expn. Dist., 1972-78; asso. coordinator plans and programs La. State U. Med. Center, Shreveport, 1979—. Elder Presbyn. Ch. Served with USNR, 1943-75; capt. Res. (ret.). Mem. Am. Legion, 40 and 8 (comdr. 1959-60, chef de gare La. 1966-67). Democrat. Home: 4739 Fairfield Ave Shreveport LA 71106 Office: PO Box 33932 Shreveport LA 71130

ALLEN, L. SCOTT, clergyman; b. Meridian, Miss., May 4, 1918; s. Louis and Mable (Fiedler) A. A.B., Clark Coll., 1940; B.D., Gammon Theol. Sem., 1942; M.A., Northwestern U., 1961; LL.D., Bethune-Cookman Coll.; D.C.L., Emory and Henry Coll.; D.D., Wiley Coll., Duke U. Ordained to ministry United Methodist Ch., as deacon, 1939, as elder, 1942; minister George Oliver Meth. Ch., Atlanta, 1938-39, Grace Meth. Ch., Covington, Ga., 1939-41, Eastpoint Meth. Ch., Fairborn, Ga., 1941-42, Asbury Meth. Ch., Savannah, 1942-48, Central Meth. Ch., Atlanta, 1948-56; instr. philosophy and religion Clark Coll., Atlanta, 1956; consecrated bishop, 1967, resident bishop, Holston Area, 1968-76, Charlotte (N.C.) Area, 1976—; mem. Meth. Bd. Higher Edn. and Ministry, 1978—; past pres. Coll. Bishops, Southeastern Jurisdiction, World Div. Bd. Global Ministries; chmn. Gen. Commn. on Archives and History, United Meth. Ch., 1980; past del. numerous ch. confs. Chmn. bd. Gammon Theol. Sem., 1976—, bd. dirs., 1968—. Editor: Central Christian Advocate, New Orleans, 1956-67. Trustee Bennett Coll., Brevard Coll., Greensboro Coll., High Point Coll., Pfeiffer Coll.; v.p. bd. trustees Lake Junaluska Assembly, Southeastern Jurisdiction, 1976—. Mem. NAACP. Office: PO Box 18005 Charlotte NC 28218 *

ALLEN, LAWRENCE A., educator. Prof. library sci. U. Ky.; orgn. devel. cons. Address: University of Kentucky Coll of Library Science Lexington KY 40506

ALLEN, LAYMAN EDWARD, legal educator; b. Turtle Creek, Pa., June 9, 1927; s. Layman Grant and Viola Iris (Williams) A.; m. Christine R. Patmore, Mar. 29, 1950 (dec.); children: Layman G., Patricia R.; m. Emily C. Hall, Oct. 3, 1981; children: Phillip A., Kelly C. Student, Washington and Jefferson Coll., 1945-46; A.B., Princeton U., 1951; M.Pub. Admnstrn., Harvard U., 1952; LL.B., Yale U., 1956. Bar: Conn. 1956. Fellow Center for Advanced Study in Behavioral Scis., 1961-62; sr. fellow Yale Law Sch., 1956-57, lectr., 1957-58, instr., 1958-59, asst. prof., 1959-63, assoc. prof., 1963-66; assoc. prof. law U. Mich. Law Sch., Ann Arbor, 1966-71, prof., 1971—; research scientist Mental Health Research Inst., U. Mich., 1966—; cons. legal drafting Nat. Life Ins. Co., Mich. Blue Cross & Blue Shield (various law firms); quar. electronic data retrieval com. Am. Bar Assn.; ops. research analyst McKinsey & Co.; orgn. and methods analyst Office of Sec. Air Force.; Trustee Center for Study of Responsive Law. Editor-in-chief: Jurimetrics Jour; newspaper corr.; editor: Games & Simulations; Author: WFF 'n Proof: The Game of Modern Logic, 1961, latest rev. edit., 1973, (with Robin B.S. Brooks, Patricia A. James) Automatic Retrieval of Legal Literature: Why and How, 1962, WFF: The Beginner's Game of Modern Logic, 1962, latest rev. edit., 1973, Equations: The Game of Creative Mathematics, 1963, latest rev. edit., 1973, (with Mary E. Caldwell) Reflections of the Communications Sciences and Law: The Jurimetrics Conference, 1965, (with J. Ross and P. Kugel) Queries 'n Theories: The Game of Science and Language, 1970, altest rev. edit., 1973, (with F. Goodman, D. Humphrey and J. Ross) On-Words: The Game of Word Structures, 1971, rev. edit., 1973; contbr. articles to profl. jours. Served with USNR, 1945-46. Mem. AAAS, Assn. Symbolic Logic, Nat. Council Tchrs. Math., Am. Bar Assn. (council sect. sci. and tech.), ACLU. Democrat. Unitarian. Home: 1407 Brooklyn Ave Ann Arbor MI 48104

ALLEN, LEE NORCROSS, university dean; b. Shawmut, Ala., Apr. 16, 1926; s. Leland Norcross and Dorothy (Whitaker) A.; m. Catherine Ann Bryant, Aug. 24, 1963; children—Leland Norcross, Leslie Catherine. B.S., Auburn U., 1948, M.S., 1949; Ph.D., U. Pa., 1955. From instr. to prof. history Eastern Baptist Coll., St. Davids, Pa., 1952-61; prof. history Samford U., Birmingham, Ala., 1961—, grad. dean, 1965—; dean Howard Coll. Arts and Scis., 1975—. Author: (with Mrs. E.S. Bee) History of Ruhama, 1969, The First One Hundred Fifty Years: First Baptist Church of Montgomery, 1979, Born for Missions, 1984; also articles. Served with AUS, 1944-46. Research fellow Auburn U., 1948-49; Harrison fellow U. Pa., 1949-52; recipient Commendation certificate Am. Assn. State and Local History. Mem. Am., So., Ala. hist. assns., Omicron Delta Kappa, Phi Alpha Theta, Kappa Phi Kappa, Pi Gamma Mu. Southern Bapt. Club: Rotarian (pres. Shades Valley club 1969-70). Home: 24 Pine Crest Rd Birmingham AL 35223

ALLEN, LEW, JR., former air force officer, jet propulsion laboratory executive; b. Miami, Fla., Sept. 30, 1925; s. Lew and Zella (Holman) A.; m. Barbara Frink, Aug. 19, 1949; children: Barbara Allen Miller, Lew, Marjorie Allen Dauster, Christie Allen Jameson. B.S., U.S. Mil. Acad., 1946; M.S., U. Ill., 1952, Ph.D., 1954. Commd. 2d lt. USAAF, 1946; advanced through grades to gen. USAF, 1977; physicist AEC, Los Alamos, 1954-57, Air Force Weapons Lab., 1957-61; mem. staff Office Sec. Def., 1961-65; with Air Force Space Program, 1965-72; dir. Nat. Security Agy., Ft. Meade, Md., 1973-77; comdr. Air Force Systems Command, 1977; vice chief staff USAF, 1978, chief staff, 1978-82; ret., 1982; dir. Jet Propulsion Lab., Pasadena, Calif., 1982—. Decorated D.S.M. (5), Legion of Merit with 2 oak leaf clusters, Joint Service Commendation medal. Mem. Am. Phys. Soc., Am. Geophys. Union, Nat. Acad. Engring., Sigma Xi. 1040 S Arroyo Blvd Pasadena CA 91105 Office: Jet Propulsion Lab California Inst Tech 4800 Oak Grove Dr Pasadena CA 91125

ALLEN, LOUIS G., bank holding company executive; b. 1929; (married). B.B.A., U. Mich., 1951, M.B.A., 1956. Fin. analyst Ford Motor Co., 1954-58; with Mfrs. Nat. Bank, Detroit, 1958—, asst. cashier, 1961-63, v.p. mortgage dept., 1965, v.p. adminstrn. mortgage dept., 1966-68, sr. v.p. adminstrn. mortgage dept., 1968-70, exec. v.p., 1970-73, pres., 1973—, also dep. chmn.; dir. Arnold Home Inc., CBDA Inc.; trustee Citizens Mortgage Invest Trust. Served with U.S. Army, 1951-53. Office: Mfrs Bank Tower 100 Renaissance Center Detroit MI 48243 *

ALLEN, LUCILE, educational consultant; b. Paris, Tex., Jan. 27, 1906; d. Charles Newton and Enola (Hendrick) A. A.B., Trinity U., 1927; A.M., So. Meth. U., 1931; Ed.D., Tchrs. Coll., Columbia U., 1945; LL.D., Chatham Coll., 1959; D.Litt., Austin Coll., 1965. Tchr., English and sr. counselor Highland Park High Sch., Dallas, 1930-43; Gen. Edn. Bd. fellow in human devel. U. Chgo., 1943; Grace Dodge fellow Tchrs. Coll., Columbia U., 1943-44; exec. sec. Womans Found., 1944-45; prof. edn. Cornell U., 1945-52, counselor of students, 1945-48, dean of women, 1948-52; dean, prof. Chatham Coll., Pitts., 1952-59; ednl. cons., spl. asst. to pres. Austin Coll., Sherman, Tex., 1959-61; dean women, asso. prof. edn. Stanford, 1961-65; asst. to pres. Fresno State Coll., 1967-70; tchr. English East Texas State Coll., summer 1936, North Texas State Tchrs. Coll., summers 1937-38; lectr. Trinity U., summer 1940; asso. U. Tex. Grad. Curriculum Workshop, summer 1941; lectr. The Hogg Found. for Mental Hygiene and Higher Edn., 1940-43; chmn. Eastern Hazen Conf., 1948; mem. Nat. Commn. on Higher Edn. Author profl. articles and brochures. Trustee Woman's Found., Inc.; bd. dirs. Citizens Council, State of N.Y.; mem. Nat. Commn. on Edn. of Women for Am. Council of Edn., 1953-60, Nat. Adv. Bd. Civil Def., 1953-56. Recipient Distinguished Alumnus award So. Meth. U., 1955. Mem. N.Y. Assn. Deans and Guidance Counselors (pres. 1952), AAUW, Nat. Assn. Deans of Women (sec. 1950, pres. 1953-54), NEA, LWV, Mortar Board, Alpha Chi, Kappa Delta Pi, Pi Lambda Theta. Presbyn. Home: 5483A Paseo del Lago Laguna Hills CA 92653

ALLEN, LYLE WALLACE, lawyer; b. Chillicothe, Ill., June 17, 1924; s. Donald M. and Mary Ellen (McEvoy) A.; m. Helen Kolar, Aug. 16, 1947; children: Mary Elizabeth Watkins, Bryan James. Student, N.C. State Coll., 1943-44; B.S., Northwestern U., 1947; postgrad., Columbia Law Sch., 1947-48; J.D., U. Wis., 1950. Bar: Ill. 1950. Partner firm Heyl Royster Voelker & Allen, Peoria, Ill., 1957—. Served with 87th Inf. Div. U.S. Army, World War II. Decorated Purple Heart. Mem. Am. Bar Assn., Ill. State Bar Assn. (pres. 1972-73), Assn. of Ins. Attys. (pres. 1965-66), Wig and Pen (London). Democrat. Presbyterian. Clubs: Creve Coeur; Country (Peoria); Chgo. Athletic Assn.; Mission Valley Country (Venice, Fla.); Venice Yacht. Office: 600 Jefferson Bank Bldg Peoria IL 61602

ALLEN, MARTIN, computer company executive; b. 1931. With Martin-Marietta Corp., 1952-62, Gen. Precision Equipment Corp., 1962-69; co-founder, pres., chief exec. officer Computervision Corp., Bedford, Mass., 1969—, also dir. Address: Computervision Corp 201 Burlington Rd Bedford MA 01730 *

ALLEN, MARYON PITTMAN, former U.S. Senator, journalist, lectr., interior designer; b. Meridian, Miss., Nov. 30, 1925; d. John D. and Tellie (Chism) Pittman; m. Joshua Sanford Mullins, Jr., Oct. 17, 1946 (div. Jan. 1959); children—Joshua Sanford III, John Pittman, Maryon Foster; m. James Browning Allen, Aug. 7, 1964 (dec. June 1978); 1 stepson, James Browning. Student, U. Ala., 1944-47, Internat. Inst. Interior Design, 1970. Office mgr. for Dr. Alston Callahan, Birmingham, Ala., 1959-60; bus. mgr. psychiat. clinic U. Ala. Med. Center, Birmingham, 1960-61; life underwriter Protective Life Ins. Co., Birmingham, 1961-62; women's editor Sun Newspapers, Birmingham, 1962-64; v.p., partner Pittman family cos., J.D. Pittman Partnership Co., J.D. Pittman Tractor Co., Emerald Valley Corp., Mountain Lake Farms, Inc., Birmingham; mem. U.S. Senate (succeeding late husband James B. Allen), 1978; dir. public relations and advt. C.G. Sloan & Co. Auction House, Washington, 1981—; owner Maryon Allen's Cliff House Antiques. Feature writer: Birmingham News, 1964; writer: syndicated column Reflections of a News Hen, Washington, 1969-78; feature writer, columnist: Maryon Allen's Washington, Washington Post, 1979—. Mem. Ladies of U.S. Senate ARC Unit, Ala. Hist. Commn., Blair House Fine Arts Commn.; charter mem. Birmingham Com. of 100 for Women; trustee Children's Fresh Air Farm, Ind. Presbyn. Ch., Birmingham; Democratic Presdl. elector, Ala., 1968. Recipient 1st place award for best original column Ala. Press Assn., 1962, 63, also various press state and nat. awards for typography, fashion writing, food pages, several awards during Senate service. Clubs: Washington Press, 1925 F Street, 91st Congress, Congressional. Home: 3215 Cliff Rd Birmingham AL 35205 *You have to believe in yourself, your talents and the premise that you were put here to contribute of yourself. . .not always to take.*

ALLEN, MAURICE BARTELLE, JR., architect; b. Lansing, Mich., Mar. 20, 1926; s. Maurice Bartelle and Marguerite Rey (Stahl) A.; m. Nancy Elizabeth Huff, June 29, 1951; children—Robert (dec.), Katherine, David. Student, Western Mich. U., 1944, Notre Dame U., 1944-46; B.Arch., U. Mich., 1950. Registered profl. architect, Mich., Ohio. Draftsman, designer Smith, Hinchman & Grylls (architects), Detroit, 1950-51; designer, asso. Eero Saarinen & Assos., Bloomfield Hills, Mich., 1951-61; v.p. design and planning TMP Assos. (architects, engrs. and planners), Bloomfield Hills, 1961—; design critic Coll. Architecture and Design, U. Mich., 1958—. Prin. archtl. works include Gen. Motors Inst. campus devel. and bldgs, Flint, Mich., Mackinac and Manitou halls, Grand Valley State Coll, O'Dowd Hall, Oakland U, Prototype Regional Correctional Facilities, Mich. Dept. Corrections, Fine Arts Ctr. and Theater, Allied Scis. Bldg., Macomb Community Coll. Active Detroit Area council Boy Scouts Am., 1969—; mem. environmental arts com. Mich. Council for Arts, 1970—; vice chmn. Mich. Gov.'s Spl. Commn. on Architecture, 1971—. Served with USNR, 1944-47. Honor awards Mich. Soc.

Architects, 1970, 71; citation for design high rise structures Am. Iron and Steel Inst., 1971; Recipient Citation of excellence Architecture for Justice Exhbn., 1982. Fellow AIA (honor award Detroit chpt. 1970); Mem. Nat. Council Archtl. Registration Bds., Mich. Soc. Architects, Alpha Tau Omega. Republican. Episcopalian. Clubs: Mason., Detroit Economic. Home: 4325 Derry Rd Bloomfield Hills MI 48013 Office: 1191 W Square Lake Rd Bloomfield Hills MI 48013

ALLEN, MERLE MAESER, JR., lawyer; b. Prescott, Ariz., June 6, 1932; s. Merle Maeser and Centenna (Haymore) A.; m. Carol Beckstrand, Aug. 16, 1954; children: Leslie Ann, Shauna, Denise, Colette, Mark M., Brian T. B.A., Brigham Young U., 1954; J.D., U. Ariz., 1960. Bar: Ariz. 1960. With firm Moore & Romley, Phoenix, 1960-72; partner firm Udall, Shumway, Blackhurst, Allen, Lyons & Davis, Mesa, Ariz., 1973—; Dir. Pioneer Bank Life Ins. Co., 1968-69. Author: Advertising Protection Through Copyright, 1960. Active membership drive Downtown Phoenix YMCA, 1963-73; bd. dirs. Mesa YMCA, 1974-77, Mesa Pub. Safety Found., 1976-82; v.p., membership chmn. Mesa Fine Arts Assn., 1978-79; active Theodore Roosevelt council Boy Scouts Am., 1963-83. Served as pilot USAF, 1954-57. Recipient award for interest in and services to youth of community Boy Scouts Am., 1968. Mem. Am., Ariz., Maricopa County bar assns., State Bar Ariz. (com. on examinations 1982—), Fedn. Ins. Counsel. Mormon (bishop 1977-81). Club: Rotarian (pres. Mesa West 1975-76). Home: 904 N Heritage St Mesa AZ 85201 Office: 30 W First St Mesa AZ 85201

ALLEN, MICHAEL GLYNNE, business exec.; b. London, Eng., July 10, 1938; came to U.S., 1968; s. George and Lucy (Munden) A.; m. Diana Tonge, June 6, 1964 (div. Dec. 1980); children: Sarah, Mark.; m. Kathleen Cashman, May 14, 1983. B.S. in Math, London U., 1959; M.A. in Physics, Cambridge U., 1962. Mgr. ops. research Richard Thomas & Baldwin, Newport, Eng., 1962-65; sr. asso., engagement mgr. McKinsey & Co., London and N.Y.C., 1966-72; mgr. group strategic planning and review Gen. Electric Co., Bridgeport, Conn., 1972-73, staff exec. corporate strategy and systems, 1973-76, v.p., 1976-79; pres. The Michael Allen Co., Rowayton, Conn., 1979—; speaker profl. orgns. Contbr. articles to, AMA, World Future Soc. Bull., Conf. Bd., Planning Rev. Mem. Am. Cybernetics Assn., N.Am. Soc. Corporate Planning, Ops. Research Soc., Planning Execs. Inst., Silvermine Guild Artists (pres., trustee). Office: Center Strategic Management 65 Rowayton Ave Rowayton CT 06820

ALLEN, NANCY SCHUSTER, librarian; b. Buffalo, Jan. 10, 1948; d. Joseph E. and Margaret (Cormack) Schuster; m. Richard R. Allen, Sept. 2, 1967; children: Seth Cormack, Emily Margaret. B.A., U. Rochester, 1971, M.A. in Art History, 1973; M.L.S., Rutgers U., 1973. Asst. librarian Mus. Fine Arts, Boston, 1975-76, librarian, 1976-76; reference librarian Medford Pub. Library, Mass., 1973-75; lectr. Grad. Sch. Library and Info. Scis., Simmons Coll., Boston, 1984; cons. in field. Mem. Art Library Soc. N.Am. (chmn. 1983—), Soc. Am. Archivists. Home: 29 Myrtle St Belmont MA 02178 Office: 465 Huntington Ave Boston MA 02115

ALLEN, NEWTON PERKINS, lawyer; b. Memphis, Jan. 3, 1922; s. James Seddon and Sarah (Perkins) A.; m. Malinda Lobdell Nobles, Oct. 4, 1947; children: John Lobdell, Malinda Nobles, Newton Perkins, Cannon Fairfax. A.B., Princeton, 1943; LL.B., U. Va., 1948. Bar: Tenn. bar 1947. Assoc. Armstrong, Allen, Braden, Goodman, McBride & Prewitt (and predecessor firm), Memphis, 1947—, ptnr., 1950—. Mem. Chickasaw council Boy Scouts Am., 1958-60, exec. bd. mem., 1961-69; Trustee LeBonheur Children's Hosp., Memphis, 1964-72, vice chmn. bd., 1965; mem. alumni council Princeton, 1954-64; pres. bd. trustees St. Mary's Episcopal Sch., 1966-67, v.p., 1972-73; chmn. Greater Memphis Council on Crime and Delinquency, 1976—; co-chmn. Memphis conf. Faith at Work, 1975, bd. dirs., 1976—; bd. dirs. Memphis Orchestral Soc., pres., 1979-81. Mem. Am. Coll. Probate Lawyers, Am., Tenn., Memphis, Shelby County bar assns., Tenn. Def. Lawyers Assn. Republican. Episcopalian sr. warden 1984,. Club: Memphis Lions (pres. 1956). Home: 950 Audubon Dr Memphis TN 38117 Office: One Commerce Sq Memphis TN 38103

ALLEN, NICHOLAS EUGENE, lawyer; b. Atlanta, July 24, 1907; s. Columbus Eugene and Maude Anne (Allen) A.; m. Adelaide Whitford, June 11, 1938; children: Sandra, Susanne. B.S., Princeton U., 1929; LL.B., Harvard U., 1932. Bar: N.J 1933, D.C 1940, Md. 1956. Pvt. practice, N.J., 1933-35, D.C., 1953—, Md., 1957—; atty. Solicitor's Office, U.S. Dept. Labor, 1936-42, 1947; asst. gen. counsel Dept. of Air Force, 1948, asso. gen. counsel, 1949-51; steel industry div. adviser Office Gen. Counsel, NPA, 1951-52; spl. asst. to Sec. Commerce, dep. acting asst. sec. of commerce for internat. affairs, 1952-53; now mem. Herrick, Allen & Glassman; lectr. Am. U. and George Washington U. law schs., 1954-60. Served in Judge Adv. Gen.'s Dept. AUS, 1942-46; parachutist and staff judge advocate of 82d Airborne Div. in; Ardennes, Rhineland and Central European campaigns; staff judge adv. U.S. Hdqtrs.; Berlin Dist.; exec. officer ETO Judge Adv. Div.; brig. gen. USAF Res.; ret.; dep. comdr. 1st (formerly 2d) Air Force Res. Region, 1960-67. Decorated Legion of Merit, Bronze Star Medal, commendation award, U.S.; Belgian and Dutch fourrageres. Mem. Am., Fed. Md., D.C. bar assns., 82d Airborne Div. Assn., Judge Advocates Assn. (nat. pres. 1956-57), Phi Beta Kappa. Conglist. Home: 5313 Blackistone Rd Westmoreland Hills Bethesda MD 20816 Office: 1200 18th St NW Washington DC 20036

ALLEN, PHILLIP RICHARD, actor; b. Pitts., Mar. 26, 1939; s. Michael and Helen (Sarna) A.; m. Joan Snyder, Feb. 17, 1974. Student, Neighborhood Playhouse, N.Y.C., 1960-61. Appeared in: motion pictures Midway, 1975, Spl. Delivery, 1977, Onionfield, 1979, Mommie Dearest, 1981, Star Trek III, 1984; appeared in: television movies Friendly Fire, 1979, A Family Upside Down, 1978, Washington, D.C, 1976, Quincy, 1978, Snafu, 1976, Helter Skelter, 1975, Trapped Beneath the Sea, 1975, Sheila Levine, 1977, Uncommon Love, 1983; appeared on: television shows Hagen, 1979, Husbands and Wives, 1978, Black Sheep Squadron, 1978, Eight Is Enough, 1977, Lou Grant, 1977, Forever Fernwood, 1977, Baretta, 1977, Most Wanted, 1976, Joe Forrester, 1975, Police Story, 1974, Get Christie Love, 1975, Mary Tyler Moore, 1976, Bob Newhart Show, 1976, Kojak, 1977, Streets of San Francisco, 1976, Mary Jane Harper Cried Last Night, 1977, Bad News Bears, 1979—, Benson, 1983; appeared in: Broadway play Sticks and Bones (Tony award, New York Critics award 1972); appeared in Off-Broadway plays: Adaptation/Next, 1968, The Village Wooing, 1965, N.Y.C. Nat. Co. in, That Championship Season, 1974 (nominated Drama Critics award); appeared in Los Angeles theatre in: Are You Now or Have You Ever Been, 1974 (Drama Critics award); appeared in Triangle Theatre in: Cafe Chino, 1965; appeared in Phoenix Repertory Co. in: Harvey; appeared in Los Angeles Pub. Theatre world premiere: Desert Fire, 1983. Mem. Screen Actors Guild, AFTRA, Equity. Address: care Phil Gersh Agy Inc 222 N Canon Dr Beverly Hills CA 90210 *The Theatre is like a gigantic arena. Here you are rolling along nicely with the punches and all of a sudden—bang! You're on the canvas, not once, but many times. Well, you just pick yourself up, dust yourself off and, by God, start all over again. Think ahead, so it won't happen exactly that way again, and persevere. Because no matter how big or how small, success is sweet.*

ALLEN, POLLY REYNOLDS, economist, educator; b. Peoria, Ill., Mar. 9, 1940; d. Robert Bacon and Gertrude E. (Moretz) Reynolds; m. Irvine Lewis Allen, Dec. 1966. B.A., U. Iowa, 1962; Ph.D., Brown U., 1970. Asst. prof. econs. Princeton U., N.J., 1970-76; assoc. prof. U. Conn., Storrs, 1976-82, prof., 1982—. Author: (with Peter B. Kenan) Asset Markets, Exchange Rates and Economic Integration: A Synthesis, 1980. Mem. Am. Econ. Assn. Office: Univ Conn Storrs CT 06268

ALLEN, RALPH DEAN, corporate executive; b. Stanhope, Iowa, July 3, 1941; s. Ralph Carlton and Arvella Ruth (Tade) A.; children: June Ann, Lisa Renee, Jeffrey Carlton. B.S. in Bus. Adminstrn, Drake U., Des Moines, 1964; postgrad., U. Rochester, N.Y. With Eastman Kodak Co., 1964-80, dir. shareowner relations, 1976-80; dir. investor relations ITT Corp., N.Y.C., 1980—, v.p., 1981—; guest lectr. Fordham U. Grad. Sch. Mem. Investor Relations Assn. (pres. 1981-82), Fin. Analysts Fedn. Office: 320 Park Ave New York NY 10022

ALLEN, RALPH GILMORE, dramatist, producer, educator; b. Phila., Jan. 7, 1934; s. Ralph Bergen and Sara Beddoe (Walker) A.; m. Harriet Phyllis Nichols, Aug. 24, 1957. B.A. summa cum laude, Amherst Coll., 1955; D.F.A., Yale U., 1960; D.H.L. (hon.), amherst coll., 1980. Asst. prof. theatre and drama U. Pitts., 1960; assoc. prof. theatre and drama U. Pitts., 1960-68; prof., chmn. dept. drama U. Victoria, B.C., Can., 1968-72; chmn. dept., prof. theatre U. Tenn., Knoxville, 1972-80; prof. drama Queens Coll., N.Y.C., 1983—; dir. Clarence Brown Theatre Co., Knoxville, 1972-77; theatre cons., producer John F. Kennedy Ctr., Washington, 1980—. (With RL Stevens) 9 plays, Washington and N.Y.C.; author: (with John Gassner) Theatre and Drama in the Making, 1965; playwright: (with Joshua Logan) Rip Von Winkle, 1976, The Tax Collector, 1977; dir.: plays including Everyman, 1972-75, The New Majestic Follies, 1977; author: sketches, revue Sugar Babies, 1979; editor Theatre Survey, 1965-69; contbr. numerous articlesto profl. jours. John Golden fellow, 1957-59; Guggenheim fellow, 1965; Charles E. Merrill fellow, 1961; named Artist of Yr. Phi Kappa Phi, 1983; recipient Award for Service to Arts Mayor of Phila., 1983, Award of Merit Am. Theatre Assn., 1983. Fellow Am. Theatre Assn. (v.p. 1972); mem. Am. Soc. Theatre Research (dir., exec. com. 1977-80), Theatre Can. (gov. 1970-71), Nat. Theatre Conf. Club: Players (N.Y.C.). Office: John F Kennedy Ctr Washington DC 20566

ALLEN, REGINALD, collection curator; b. Phila., Mar. 22, 1905; s. Alfred Reginald and Helen Johnson (Warren) A.; m. Helen Howe, May 31, 1946. Grad. cum laude, Phillips Exeter Acad., 1922; B.A., Harvard, 1926. With advt. dept. Victor Talking Machine Co., 1926-30; copywriter N.W. Ayer, 1930-32, J. M. Mathes, 1932-35; bd. dirs. Phila. Orch. Assn., 1933-35, mgr., 1935-39; head story dept. Universal Pictures, 1939-42; Pacific Coast rep. J. Arthur Rank Orgn., Universal City, Calif., 1946-49; asst. mgr., bus. adminstr., sec. to bd. dirs. Met. Opera Co., N.Y.C., 1949-57, asst. to pres., gen. mgr., 1962-69; exec. dir. operations Lincoln Center Performing Arts, 1957-62; exec. v.p. Am. Acad. Rome, 1969-71, acting dir., 1969-70; curator Gilbert & Sullivan Collection, Pierpont Morgan Library, 1971—; Mem. DeSchauensee S. African Expdn. to Kalahari Desert, 1930, Pres.' Adv. com. Nat. Cultural Center, 1958-63; mem. N.Y. State Council Arts, 1961-65, Pres.' Exec. Com. for Shakespeare Anniversary, 1964; Pres. D'Oyly Carte Inc., 1973—. Author: The First Night Gilbert & Sullivan, 1958, rev. edit., 1976, W. S. Gilbert, An Anniversary Survey and Exhibition Checklist, 1963, Sir Arthur Sullivan, Composer and Personage, 1975, Gilbert and Sullivan in America, 1979. Trustee D'Oyly Carte Opera Trust; pres. Am. Friends of D'Oyly Carte & Gilbert & Sullivan, 1981. Served to lt. comdr. USNR, 1942-45. Guggenheim fellow, 1973-74. Life fellow Pierpont Morgan Library.; Mem. Phila. Acad. Natural Scis. Clubs: Century Assn., Grolier. Home: 2512 Q St NW Washington DC 20007 Office: Pierpont Morgan Library 29 E 36th St New York NY 10016

ALLEN, REGINALD EDGAR, philosophy and classics educator; b. Phila., Mar. 13, 1931; s. Amos Samuel and Alice (Bodine) A.; m. Ann Branin Usilton, June 6, 1961; children: Alice, Ruth, Elizabeth, William. A.B. with highest honors, Haverford Coll., 1953; M.A., Yale U., 1955, Ph.D., 1958; B.Phil., St. Andrews U., 1957. Prof. philosophy and classics Northwestern U., Evanston, Ill., 1978—. Author: Studies in Plato's Metaphysics, 1966, Plato's Earlier Theory of Forms, 1970, Socrates and Legal Obligation, 1980, Plato's Pormenides, 1983. Mem. Phi Beta Kappa. Address: PO Box 1776 Evanston IL 60204

ALLEN, REX E., actor, producer; b. Willcox, Ariz., Dec. 31, 1920; s. Horace E. and Faye Louella (Clark) A.; m. Jean Redder, Aug. 25, 1947; children: Rex E., Curtis Lee, Mark Wayne, Bonita Kaye. Grad. high sch. Pres. Quality Five Prodns. Acting debut: Nat. Barn Dance, Chgo., 1944-49; actor motion pictures, Republic Studios, 20th Century Fox, Disney Prodns.; TV appearances Frontier Doctor; also guest appearances; rec. artist, Decca, Mercury Records, 1966-73. Del. Republican Nat. Conv., 1972; Trustee Cowboy Hall Fame, 1969—; bd. dirs. Willcox Hosp., John Edwards Meml. Found. Named Ariz. Man of Year, 1965, Rodeo Man of Year, 1970, Number 1 Box Office Western Star, 1953-54. Lodges: Masons; Shriners. *

ALLEN, REX WHITAKER, architect; b. San Francisco, Dec. 21, 1914; s. Lewis Whitaker and Maude Rex (Allen) A.; m. Elizabeth Johnson, Oct. 11, 1941 (div. 1949); children: Alexandra A. (Mrs. Daniel D. Fleckles), Frances Lambert (Mrs. Andrew Dunn); m. Ruth Batchelor, Apr. 1, 1949 (div. 1971); m. Bettie J. Crossfield, Nov. 6, 1971. A.B., Harvard U., 1936, M.Arch., 1939; student, Columbia U. Arch. Sch., 1936-37. With Research and Planning Assos., N.Y.C., 1939-42, Camloc Fastener Corp., 1942-45, Isadore Rosenfield (architect), 1945-48, Blanchard and Maher (architects), San Francisco, 1949-52; established pvt. practice, San Francisco, 1953; pres. Rex Whitaker Allen & Assos., San Francisco, 1961-71, Archtl. Prodns., Inc., 1971-76; prin. Hugh Stubbins/Rex Allen Partnership, 1968, Rex Allen Partnership, 1971-76; pres. Rex Allen-Drever-Lechowski, Architects, 1976—; Chmn. Mill Valley Adv. Edn. Council, 1956; mem. Calif. Bldg. Safety Bd., 1973—. Author: (with Ilona von Karolyi) Hospital Planning Handbook, 1976; Contbr. articles to profl. jours.; prin. works include French Hosp, San Francisco, Mercy Hosp, Sacramento, Roseville (Calif.) Dist. Hosp, Highland Hosp, Oakland, St. Francis Hosp, San Francisco, Dominican Hosp, Santa Cruz, Alta Bates Hosp, Berkeley, Calif., Boston City Hosp, Out-Patient bldg. Woodland (Calif.) Meml. Hosp, Stanislaus Meml. Hosp, Modesto, Calif., Madera (Calif.) Community Hosp, Sacred Heart Hosp, Eugene, Oreg., St. Joseph Hosp, Mt. Clemens, Mich., Commonwealth Health Center, Saipan. Fellow AIA (v.p. No. Calif. chpt. 1964, bd. dirs. Calif. council 1955-56, 1962-64, nat. pres. 1969-70); hon. fellow Royal Archtl. Inst. Can.; mem. Constrn. Specification Inst. (pres. San Francisco 1961), San Francisco Zool. Soc. (trustee), Assn. Western Hosps. (chmn. arch. sect. 1957-58), Calif. Hosp. Assn., Am. Hosp. Assn., Internat. Hosp. Fedn., Am. Assn. Hosp. Planning (pres. 1971-72), Union Internat. des Architectes Public Health Work Group (dir. 1979-80), La Sociedad de Arquitectos Mexicanos (hon. mem.), Federación Panamericana de Asociaciones de Arquitectos (v.p. 1980-84), San Francisco Planning and Urban Renewal Assn., San Francisco Mus. Art, San Francisco Symphony Found., Sierra Club. Club: Harvard (N.Y.C. and San Francisco). Home: 4718 17th St San Francisco CA 94117 Office: 425 Battery St San Francisco CA 94111 also 1033 Massachusetts Ave Cambridge MA 02138

ALLEN, RICHARD BLOSE, lawyer, editor; b. Aledo, Ill., May 10, 1919; s. James Albert and Claire (Smith) A.; m. Marion Treloar, Aug. 27, 1949; children: Penelope, Jennifer, Leslie Jean. B.S., U. Ill., 1941, J.D., 1947; LL.D., Seton Hall U., 1977. Bar: Ill. bar 1947. Staff editor ABA Jour., 1947-48, 63-66, exec. editor, 1966-70, editor, 1970-83, editor, pub., 1983—; pvt. practice law, Aledo, 1949-57; gen. counsel Ill. State Bar Assn., 1957-63. Served from pvt. to maj. Q.M.C. AUS, 1941-46. Mem. Am. Bar Assn., Ill. Bar Assn. (mem. assembly 1972-74), Chgo. Bar Assn., Selden Soc., Scribes, Sigma Delta Chi, Kappa Tau Alpha, Phi Delta Phi, Alpha Tau Omega. Clubs: Michigan Shores (Wilmette); Law (Chgo.); Cosmos (Washington). Home: 702 Illinois Rd Wilmette IL 60091 Office: 750 N Lake Shore Dr Chicago IL 60611

ALLEN, RICHARD GARRETT, educator, hosp. exec.; b. St. Paul, July 8, 1923; s. John and Margaretta (Taggert) A.; m. Ida Elizabeth Vernon, July 5, 1944; children—Richard Garrett, Barbara Elizabeth, Julie Frances (dec.). B.S. cum laude, Trinity U., 1954; M.H.A., Baylor U., 1957; postgrad., Indsl. Coll. of Armed Forces, 1962, USAF Command and Staff Coll., 1962. Commd. 2d lt. Med. Service Corps U.S. Air Force, 1948, advanced through grades to maj., 1961; served in, U.S., Pacific and, Germany, ret., 1964; asst. adminstr. U. Ala. Hosp. and Clinics; dir. Center for Hosp. Continuing Edn., Sch. for Health Services, U. Ala., Birmingham, 1965-68; dir. edn. New Eng. Hosp. Assembly, Inc., New Eng. Center for Continuing Edn., U. N.H., Durham, 1968-74; dir. Office Health Care Edn., 1970-74; exec. v.p. Edn. and Research Found., San Francisco, 1974-77, Assn. West Hosps., 1974-77; v.p. health affairs M G & M Communications, Foster City, Calif.; pres. Calif. Coll. Podiatric Medicine; chief exec. officer Calif. Podiatry Hosp. and Outpatient Clinic, San Francisco, 1977-81; prof. health care adminstrn. St. Mary's Coll. of Calif., Moraga, 1982—; mem. Nat. Adv. Council on Vocat. Edn., 1969-71; also cons.; cons. Booz, Allen & Hamilton, Washington, Ops. Research, Inc., Silver Spring, Md., Republic of Korea Air Force Med. Services, Seoul, Bio-Dynamics, Inc., Cambridge, Mass., HEALTHSAT—Appalachia Community Services Network, Washington, 1980—. Pub.: Hosp. Forum, San Francisco, 1974-77; Contbr. articles to profl. jours. Decorated Air Force Commendation medal with oak leaf cluster. Fellow Am. Coll. Hosp. Adminstrs.; mem. Am. Soc. for Health Manpower Edn. and Tng., Am. Hosp. Assn., AAUP, Am. Soc. Hosp. Edn. and Tng. (pres. 1972), Am. Assn. Colls. Podiatric Medicine (pres. 1979-81). Episcopalian. Clubs: Masons, LAMBS. Home: 10 Van Tassel Ln Orinda CA 94563 Office: PO Box 784 St Mary's Coll Calif Moraga CA 94575 *Uncertainty is a fact of life; there is no progress free of the risk of change. Sharpen your sense of timing and know when it is time to let go and when to hang on. Trials and defeats are inevitable elements of the committed life; welcome these conflicts for it is your principles that are involved. Appreciate the past, but focus on today's tasks—while realizing that tomorrow will be nothing like you expect it to be. Cultivate a cheerful acceptance of your own mortality, and its attendant limitations and blessings.*

ALLEN, RICHARD STANLEY (DICK ALLEN), educator, author; b. Troy, N.Y., Aug. 8, 1939; s. Richard Sanders and Doris (Bishop) A.; m. Loretta Mary Negridge, Aug. 13, 1960; children: Richard Negridge, Tanya Angell. A.B., Syracuse U., (N.Y.), 1961; M.A., Brown U., 1963. Teaching assoc. Brown U., 1962-64; instr. English Wright State U., Dayton, Ohio, 1964-68; mem. faculty U. Bridgeport, (Conn.), 1968—, prof. English, 1976-79, Charles A. Dana prof. English, 1979—, also dir. creative writing. Author: Anon and Various Time Machine Poems, 1971, Science Fiction: The Future, 1982, Overnight in the Guest House of the Mystic, 1984, Regions with No Proper Names, 1975; poems, articles, revs.; editor, poetry editor: Mad River Rev., 1964-68; co-editor: Detective Fiction: Crime and Compromise, 1974, Looking Ahead: The Vision of Science Fiction, 1975; contbg. editor: Am. Poetry Rev.; book reviewer: Poetry, Am. Book Rev. Recipient Union Arts and Civic League Poetry prize, 1971, Assoc. Depts. English-MLA Disting. Teaching award, 1971, San Jose Poetry prize, 1976; Hart Crane Meml. Poetry fellow, 1966; Robert Frost Poetry fellow, 1972; Mellon research fellow, 1981; Nat. Endowment Arts poetry writing grantee, 1984—. Mem. AAUP, Poets and Writers. Republican. Unitarian. Home: 74 Fern Circle Trumbull CT 06611 Office: Dept English U Bridgeport Bridgeport CT 06601

ALLEN, RICHARD VINCENT, business consultant; b. Collingswood, N.J., Jan. 1, 1936; s. Charles Carroll and Magdalen (Buchman) A.; m. Patricia Ann Mason, Dec. 28,1957; children: Michael, Kristin, Mark, Karen, Kathryn, Kevin, Kimberly. B.A., U. Notre Dame, 1957, M.A., 1958; postgrad., U. Munich, W. Ger., 1958-61; hon. doctorate, Hanover Coll., Korea U. Instr. U. Md. Overseas Div., 1959-61; asst. prof. polit. sci. Ga. Inst. Tech., 1961-62; sr. staff mem. Center for Strategic and Internat. Studies, Georgetown U., 1962-66, Hoover Instn. on War, Revolution and Peace, Stanford U., 1966-69, Nat. Security Council, White House, 1969; dep. asst. to Pres. U.S., White House, 1971-72; pres. Potomac Internat. Corp., Washington, 1972-80; sr. fgn. policy and nat. security adv. to Pres. Ronald Reagan, 1978-80; asst. for nat. security affairs Pres. U.S., White House, 1981-82; pres. Richard V. Allen Co., Washington, 1982—; disting. fellow and chmn. Asian Studies Ctr. Heritage Found., 1982—; sr. counselor for fgn. policy and nat. security Republican Nat. Com., 1982—; sr. fellow Hoover Instn., 1983—; vice chmn. Internat. Democratic Union, 1983—; chmn. German-Am. Tricentennial Found., 1983—. Author: Peace or Peaceful Coexistence?, 1966, (with others) Communism and Democracy: Theory and Action, 1967; editor: (with David M. Abshire) National Security: Political, Military and Economic Strategics in the Decade Ahead, 1963, Yearbook on International Communist Affairs, 1969. Chmn. com. on intelligence Republican Nat. Com., 1977-80; trustee St. Francis Prep. Sch., Spring Grove, Pa. Named Patriot of Yr. SAR, 1981; H.B. Earhart fellow Relm Found., 1958-61; decorated Order of Diplomatic Merit Republic of Korea, 1982, Knight Comdr.'s Cross Fed. Republic of Germany, 1983, Badge and Star of Order of Merit, 1983. Mem. Am. Polit. Sci. Assn., Intercollegiate Studies Inst. (trustee), Com. on Present Danger (dir.). Clubs: Univ., Fed. City, 1925 F St. (Washington). Office: 905 16th St NW Washington DC 20006

ALLEN, ROBERT COX, banker; b. Phila., Mar. 16, 1924; s. Bertram Risley and Mary Catherine (Cox) A.; m. Elizabeth Purvis, Sept. 9, 1950; children: Robert Cox, Deborah Elizabeth, Meredith Anne. A.B., Dartmouth Coll., 1947; M.B.A., U. Pa., 1949. Asst. treas. Corn Exchange Nat. Bank, Phila., 1949-51; exec. v.p. Girard Bank, Phila., 1951-78; exec. v.p., dir. Farmers Bank of State of Del., Wilmington, 1978-80; pres., dir., 1980-82; pres., chief exec. officer, dir. The Hershey Bank (Pa.), 1982. Author: Bank Mergers, 1968, Selecting and Promoting Branch Banking Locations, 1972. Pres. Nat. Cystic Fibrosis Research Found., 1960-65; mem. standing com. Episcopal Diocese of Pa., 1974-78; chmn. exec. com., trustee Med. Coll. Pa., 1975-78. Served with USNR, 1942-44. Mem. Am. Mgmt. Assn., Del. Bankers Assn. Republican. Club: Hershey Country. Home: 16 Springcreek Manor Hershey PA 17033 Office: 9 W Chocolate Ave Hershey PA 17033

ALLEN, ROBERT DAY, educator, biologist; b. Providence, Aug. 28, 1927; s. Richard Day and Mary (Cottrell) A.; m. Margaret Dampman, Dec. 23, 1950 (div. 1970); children—Elizabeth, Wayne; m. Nina Strömgren, Sept. 12, 1971; 1 dau., Barbara. A.B., Brown U., 1949; Ph.D., U. Pa., 1953. Asst. instr. zoology U. Pa., 1950-51; instr. zoology U. Mich., 1954-56; asst. prof., then asso. prof. biology Princeton, 1956-66; prof. biology dept. State U. N.Y. at Albany, 1966-74, chmn., 1966-

72; prof., chmn. dept. biol. scis. Dartmouth Coll., 1975-78, Ira Allen Eastman prof. biology, 1978—; cons. to industry, 1963—, lectr., Eng., Japan, Mexico, USSR, Poland, East and West Germany, France, Sweden, Denmark; vis. prof. Osaka (Japan) U., Japan Soc. for Promotion of Sci., 1974; Trustee Marine Biol. Lab., Woods Hole, Mass., 1966-74, 75-79. Editor: Primitive Motile Systems in Cell Biology, 1964, Cell Motility, 1980—; asso. editor: Jour. Mechanochem. and Cell Motility, 1971-75; editor: Microscopica Acta, 1977—; Contbr. articles to U.S. and fgn. jours. Guggenheim fellow, 1961, 66; recipient Golden Eagle award for non-theatre motion picture Mitosis Council Internat. Non Theatrical Events, 1965; USPHS; predoctoral fellow U. Pa., 1951-53; USPHS; postdoctoral fellow, Sweden and Italy, 1953-54. Fellow AAAS (council 1976-79, com. on fellows 1977—, nominating com. 1978), Royal Micros. Soc.; mem. Soc. Gen. Physiologists (treas. 1963-65, pres. 1973-74), Am. Soc. for for Cell Biology (council 1973-75), Biophys. Soc. Office: Dept Biol Scis Dartmouth Coll Hanover NH 03755

ALLEN, ROBERT DEE, lawyer; b. Tulsa, Oct. 13, 1928; s. Harve and Olive Jean (Brown) A.; m. Mary Latimer Conner, May 18, 1957; children: Scott, Randy, Blake. B.A., U. Okla., 1951, LL.B., 1955, J.D., 1970. Bar: Okla. 1955. Asso. Abernathy & Abernathy, Shawnee, Okla., 1955; law clk. to judge 10th U.S. Ct. Appeals, Denver, 1956; to judge Western Dist. Okla., 1956-57; asst. ins. commr., counsel Okla. Ins. Dept., 1957-63; partner firm Quinlan, Allen & Batchelor, Oklahoma City, 1963-65, DeBois & Allen, 1965-66; counsel AT&T, Washington, 1966-67; gen. atty. Southwestern Bell Telephone Co., Okla., 1967-79; v.p., gen. counsel Ill. Bell Telephone Co., Chgo., 1979-83; sole practice law, Chgo., 1983—; mem. Gov.'s Ad Valorem Tax Structure and Sch. Fin. Commn., 1972; dir. Taxpayers Fedn. Ill., 1980—. Bd. dirs. Oklahoma County Legal Aid Soc., 1973—. Served to sgt. AUS, 1946-48; lt. col. Res. Mem. Am. Judicature Soc., Am. Bar Assn., Fed. Bar Assn. (v.p. Okla. Chpt. 1977—), Okla. Bar Assn., Ill. Bar Assn., Chgo. Bar Assn., Order of Coif, Phi Delta Phi, Sigma Phi Epsilon (dir.). Presbyterian. Home: 8101 Glenwood Ave Oklahoma City OK 73114 *Being genuine and candid are traits which cause others to place confidence in you. Insincere platitudes are sandy foundations upon which mutual trust and respect simply cannot be built. I place honest, tactful, candor at the top of the list of important traits for success in business, love and in life generally.*

ALLEN, ROBERT EUGENE, communications company executive; b. Joplin, Mo., Jan. 25, 1935; s. Walter Clark and Frances (Patton) A.; m. Elizabeth Terese Pfeffer, Aug. 4, 1956; children: Jay Robert, Daniel Scott, Katherine Louise, Ann Elizabeth, Amy Susan. B.A., Wabash Coll., 1957, LL.D. (hon.), 1984; postgrad., Harvard Bus. Sch., 1965. With Ind. Bell Telephone Co. Inc., Indpls., 1957—, traffic student, 1957-61, dist. traffic supr., Bloomington, 1961-62, dist. comml. mgr., 1962-66, div. comml. mgr., Bloomington; and Indpls., 1966-68, asst. to operations v.p., 1968, gen. comml. mgr., 1968-72, v.p., sec., treas., 1972-74; v.p., gen. mgr. Bell Telephone Co. of Pa., Phila., 1974-76; v.p., chief operating officer, dir. Ill. Bell Telephone Co., 1976-78; v.p. AT&T, Basking Ridge, N.J., 1978-81, exec. v.p., chief fin. officer, N.Y.C., 1983-84, exec. v.p. corp. adminstrn. and fin., 1984—; pres. C&P Telephone Cos., Washington, 1981-83, chmn., chief exec. officer, 1983; dir. Cluett Peabody, Inc., Mfrs. Hanover Trust, Elizabeth, N.J., Mfrs. Hanover Corp. Trustee, co-chmn. devel. com. Wabash Coll.; trustee Columbia U. Mem. Nat. Assn. Wabash Men. Presbyterian. Clubs: Short Hills, Baltusrol Golf., Burning Tree, Congressional Country. Home: 60 Stewart Rd Short Hills NJ 07078 Office: A T&T Co. 550 Madison Ave. New York NY 10022

ALLEN, ROBERT FAY, manufacturing company executive; b. Syracuse, N.Y., Oct. 7, 1923; s. Fay O. and Ruth R. (Gorman) A.; m. Vivian R. Rott, May 31, 1951; children: Kathleen, Joan, Barbara, Thomas, Robert. B.S. in Mech. Engring, Princeton U., 1945. With Carrier Corp., 1945—, v.p., gen. mgr. unitary equipment div., 1972-74, pres. Carrier Air Conditioning div., 1974-75, corp. group v.p. air conditioning div., exec. v.p. air conditioning and refrigeration group, 1978—, corp. pres., 1981—; dir. Lincoln Nat. Bank-Central, Elizondo S.A., Le Compresseur Frigorifique S.A. Mem. council Upstate Med. Center, Syracuse, Syracuse U. Sch. Mgmt.; trustee LeMoyne Coll.; bd. dirs. Syracuse Opera Theatre; mem. President's Nat. Alliance for Bus. Mem. N.Y. State Bus. Council (bd. dirs.), Mfrs. Assn. Central N.Y. (bd. dirs.). Clubs: Century (Syracuse); Onondaga (Fayetteville, N.Y.); Princeton (N.Y.C.). Office: Carrier Corp Carrier Pkwy Syracuse NY 13221

ALLEN, ROBERT HUGH, communications corp. exec.; b. Breckenridge, Tex., Jan. 13, 1924; s. Charles Stanley and Mildred Mary (Dow) A.; m. Claire P. O'Keefe, Oct. 22, 1949; children—Christopher, Patricia, Colin. A.B., Bowdoin Coll., 1946; postgrad., Princeton U., 1944, Trinity U., 1945, U. Rochester, 1945-46. With Taylor Instrument Co., 1949-51; regional sales mgr. Am. Optical Corp., 1951-54; sales mgr. N.Am. Philips Corp., 1955-63; v.p., product group mgr. ITT, N.Y.C., 1963—. Active Boy Scouts Am., 1970-72. Served with USNR, 1943-46. Mem. VFW. Republican. Club: Minuteman Yacht. Home: 15 Harding St Westport CT 06880

ALLEN, ROBERT HUTTON, telephone company executive; b. Douglaston, N.Y., Nov. 16, 1921; s. Archibald John and Grace Browne (MCGuire) A.; m. Elise Eaton, Oct. 16, 1954; children: Warren Eaton, Janet, Martha, Grace. B.A., Williams Coll., 1946. With Cin. Bell Inc., 1946—, gen. comml. mgr., 1963-65, asst. to pres., 1965-67, pub. relations dir., 1967-68, dir. adminstrn. and planning, 1968-70, v.p., sec., treas., 1970-82, v.p. fin., sec., dir., 1982—. Trustee Merc. Library, Cin. Symphony Orch. Served with USAAF, 1942-46. Republican. Clubs: University, Cincinnati Country; Williams (N.Y.C.). Home: 2285 Grandin Rd Cincinnati OH 45208 Office: 201 E 4th St Cincinnati OH 45202

ALLEN, ROBERT SCOTT, educator, biochemist; b. Tabiona, Utah, Nov. 13, 1917; s. Robert Ernest and Genevieve (Michie) A.; m. Louise Pierce, Sept. 4, 1940; children: Don Robert, Gary Wayne, Ross Michael. B.S., Brigham Young U., 1939, M.S., 1940; Ph.D., Iowa State Coll., 1949. Research assoc. Iowa State U., Ames, 1947-49, faculty, 1949-67, prof., 1957-67, chmn. dept. biochemistry and biophysics, 1960-63; prof. La. State U., Baton Rouge, 1967—, head dept. biochemistry, 1967-83. Editor: (with others) Physiology of Digestion in the Ruminant, 1965. Recipient Am. Feed Mfrs. award in dairy cattle nutrition, 1955; named Disting. prof. agr. Iowa State U., 1965. Mem. Am. Chem. Soc. (past chmn. Ames sect.), Am. Dairy Sci. Assn., Am. Inst. Nutrition, Sigma Xi, Phi Kappa Phi, Phi Lambda Upsilon, Gamma Sigma Delta. Research, numerous publs. on biochemistry of vitamin A and carotene metabolism, lipid absorption and metabolism, forage preservation and utilization, etiology of bloat in ruminants, marine biochemistry. Home: 256 Court St Baton Rouge LA 70810

ALLEN, ROBERTA L., painter, writer; b. N.Y.C., 1945; d. Sol and Jeanette (Waldner) A. A.A.S., Fashion Inst. Tech., N.Y.C., 1964; student, Instituto de Bellas Artes, Mex., 1970. Lectr. Corcoran Sch. Art, Washington, 1975, Kutztown State Coll., 1979, C.W. Post Coll., 1979. Author: Partially Trapped Lines, the Invisible Line of Limitation, 1975, Pointless Arrows, 1976, Possibilities, 1977, Pointless Acts, 1977, Everything In The World There Is To Know Is Known By Somebody, But Not By the Same Knower, 1981; Solo exhibitions include, Galerie 845, Amsterdam, Netherlands, 1967, John Weber Gallery, N.Y.C., 1974, 75, 77, 79, Inst. for Art and Urban Resources, N.Y.C., 1977, 80, Galerie Maier-Hahn, Dusseldorf, W. Ger., 1977, MTL Galerie, Brussels, 1978, C.W. Post Coll., Glenvale, N.Y., Galerie Walter Storms, Munich, W. Ger., 1981, Kunstforum, Stadt. Galerie in Lenbachhaus, Munich, Galleria Primo Piano, Rome, Italy. MacDowell Colony fellow, 1971, 72; Ossabaw I. Project fellow, 1972; Creative Artists Public Service grantee, 1978-79; Yaddo fellow, 1983. Home and Office: 5 W 16th St New York NY 10011

ALLEN, RONALD ROYCE, educator; b. Horicon, Wis., Dec. 8, 1930; s. Clayton Francis and Hazel Ann (Whipple) A.; m. JoAnne Elizabeth Kuehl, Feb. 2, 1957; children—John Jeffery, David Jennings. B.S., Wis. State Coll., 1952; M.A., U. Wis., 1957, Ph.D., 1960. Mem. faculty Amherst (Mass.) Coll., 1960-63; mem. faculty U. Wis., Madison, 1963—, prof. communication arts, curriculum and instrn., 1970—; prin. investigator Wis. Research and Devel. Center Cognitive Learning, 1964-69; de. White House Conf. on Children, 1971. Author: (with W.A. Linkugel and R.L. Johannsen) Contemporary American Speeches, rev. ed. 1978, (with S. Anderson and Jere Hough) Speech in American Society, 1968, (with Clay Wilmington) Speech Communication in the Secondary School, rev. ed, 1976, (with S. Parish and C. David Mortensen) Communication: Interacting Through Speech, 1974, (with P. Judson Newcombe) New Horizons for Teacher Education in Speech Communication, 1974, (with Kenneth Brown) Developing Communication Competence in Children, 1976, (with Ray E. McKerrow) The Pragmatics of Public Communication, 1977. Served to lt. USNR, 1952-56. Mem. Wis. Speech Assn. (pres. 1968-70), Speech Communication Assn. (pres. 1979). Home: 1809 Peacock Ct Sun Prairie WI 53590 *When retirement arrives and salary checks discontinue, my work will go on because it is important to me. In my judgment, commitment to one's work is a necessary ingredient of a meaningful and happy life.*

ALLEN, SALLY LYMAN, biologist; b. N.Y.C., Aug. 3, 1926; d. Alexander Victor and Dorothy (Rogers) Lyman; 1 dau., Susan L. A.B., Vassar Coll., 1946; Ph.D. (John M. Prather fellow), U. Chgo., 1954. Research asso. dept. zoology U. Mich., Ann Arbor, 1955-73, asso. prof. botany, 1967-71, prof., 1971-75, prof. zoology, 1973-75, prof. biol. scis., 1975—; chmn. dept. cellular and molecular biology, div. biol. scis., 1975-77; vis. prof. genetics Ind. U., 1967; cons. Am. Type Culture Collection, 1975—. Mem. editorial bd.: Jour. of Protozoology, 1974-76; asso. editor: Genetics, 1973—; contbr. articles to profl. jours. Fellow AAAS; mem. Am. Inst. Biol. Sci., Genetics Soc. Am., Soc. Protozoologists, Am. Naturalists Soc. (v.p. 1978), Am. Soc. for Cell Biology (mem. council 1973-75), Phi Beta Kappa, Sigma Xi. Office: Div Biol Scis U Mich Ann Arbor MI 48109

ALLEN, SAMUEL WASHINGTON, poet, educator; b. Columbus, Ohio, Dec. 9, 1917; s. Alexander Joseph and Jewett Elizabeth (Washington) A.; 1 dau., Marie-Christine Catherine. A.B., Fisk U., 1938; J.D., Harvard U., 1941; postgrad., New Sch. Social Research, N.Y.C., 1947-48, Sorbonne, Paris, 1949-50. Bar: N.Y. 1942. Dep. asst. dist. atty. N.Y., N.Y.C., 1946-47; claims atty. U.S. Armed Force Europe, 1951-55; practice law, N.Y.C., 1956-57; asso. prof. law Tex. So. U., 1958-60; atty. U.S. Govt., Washington, 1961-68; Avalon prof. humanities Tuskegee Inst., Ala., 1968-70; vis. prof. Wesleyan U., Middletown, Conn., 1970-71; prof. English, Boston U., 1971-81; vis. prof. third world lit. Duke U., 1972-73, 73-74, Rutgers U., 1981. Author: (as Paul Vesey with epilogue, trans. by Janheinz Jahn) Elfenbeinzahne, 1956, Ivory Tusks and Other Poems, 1968, Paul Vesey's Ledger, 1975; editor: Poems from Africa, 1973; transl.: (Jean Paul Sartre) Orphée Noir, 1951; pub. reading, rec. poetry, Library of Congress, Nov. 1972; Contbr. articles to profl. jours. Bd. dirs. So. Edn. Found., Atlanta, 1969-76. Served with AUS, 1942-46. NEA Creative Writing fellow, 1979-80. Mem. MLA, Coll. Lang. Assn., African Lit. Assn., N.Y. Bar Assn.

ALLEN, STEPHEN VALENTINE PATRICK WILLIAM, television humorist, song writer; b. N.Y.C., Dec. 26, 1921; s. Carroll and Isabelle (Donohue) A.; m. Dorothy Goodman, Aug. 23, 1943; children: Stephen, Brian, David; m. Jayne Meadows, July 31, 1954; 1 son, William Christopher. Student journalism, Drake U., 1941, State Tchrs. Coll., Ariz., 1942. Radio announcer, Sta. KOY, Phoenix, 1942, Stas. KFAC and KMTR, Los Angeles, 1944; comedian, MBS, 1945; disc jockey, CBS, 1948; wrote narration and appeared in movie: Down Memory Lane; also appeared in: own TV show Warning Shot, after 1950; appeared in: Broadway play The Pink Elephant, 1953; creator, host: Tonight Show, NBC, 1954-56; host: TV shows Steve Allen Show, NBC, 1956-59, WBC syndicate, 1961-64, I've Got A Secret, 1964-66, Laughback, 1976-77, Meeting of Minds, 1977-78; Recipient (Grammy award for Gravy Waltz 1964); Writer: more than 3000 songs, including Mary Hartman, Mary Hartman; Author: Fourteen for Tonight, 1955, Bop Fables, 1955, The Funnymen, 1956, Wry on the Rocks, 1956, The Girls on the Tenth Floor, 1958, The Question Man, 1959, Mark It and Strike It; autobiography, 1960, Not All Your Laughter, Not All Your Tears, 1962; Letter to a Conservative, 1965, The Ground is Our Table, 1966, Bigger Than A Breadbox, 1967, A Flash of Swallows, 1969, The Wake, 1972, Princess Snip-Snip, 1973, Curses, 1973, Schmock-Schmock!, 1975, What To Say When It Rains, Meeting of Minds, Vol. I, Chopped Up Chinese, Ripoff, Explaining China, Funny People, The Talk Show Murders, More Funny People, Beloved Son: A Story of the Jesus Cults. Address: 15201 Burbank Blvd Van Nuys CA 91401

ALLEN, THOMAS JOHN, management educator; b. Newark, Aug. 20, 1931; s. Thomas John and Margaret Ann (Conley) A.; m. Joan Marie Gilmartin, Jan. 28, 1961; children: Thomas John, Susan Marie, Mairin. B.S., Upsala Coll., East Orange, N.J., 1954; postgrad., U. Wash., 1957-58; S.M., MIT, 1963, Ph.D., 1966. Design engr. Tung-Sol Electric Co., Bloomfield, N.J., 1956-57; research engr. Boeing Co., Seattle, 1957-64; research assoc. MIT, Cambridge, 1963-66, prof. mgmt., 1966—; cons. to bus., govt agencies. Author: Managing the Flow of Technology, 1977. Chmn. Cath.-Jewish Com., Boston, 1977-79; chmn. bd. Rosary Acad., Watertown, Mass., 1976-79. Served to sgt. USMC, 1954-56. Hon. sr. research fellow U. Manchester, 1970—. Fellow AAAS; mem. IEEE, Am. Psychol. Assn., Irish Am. Cultural Assn., Sigma Xi. Office: Massachusetts Institute of Technology 50 Memorial Dr Cambridge MA 02139

ALLEN, THOMAS OSCAR, petroleum engineering consultant; b. Weimar, Tex., Dec. 8, 1914; s. Dee Hansworth and Anna (Uzzell) A.; m. Ninette Marie Smith, Aug. 23, 1938; children: Thomas E., Jeannie Allen Shaw. B.S. in Elec. Engring, Tex. A&M, 1936; grad., Army Command and Gen. Staff Coll., 1943. With Humble Oil & Refining Co., Houston, 1936-58, supervising petroleum engr., 1949-53, sr. supervising petroleum engr., 1953-58; research mgr. petroleum prodn. research div. Jersey Prodn. Research Co., Standard Oil Co., N.J., Tulsa, 1958-63, sr. engring. asso., 1964; pres. Oil and Gas Cons. Internat., Inc., Tulsa, 1965—; Chmn. nat. petroleum subcom. Smithsonian Hall of Petroleum, Washington, 1961-67. Co-author: Production Operations, Vols. 1-2, 1978. Served to maj. AUS, 1942-46. Mem. AIME (disting. lectr. 1966-67), Am. Petroleum Inst. (chmn. prodn. com. south dist. 1955-56), Soc. Petroleum Engrs. Home: 2661 E 33d Pl Tulsa OK 74105 Office: 4554 S Harvard Tulsa OK 74135

ALLEN, TOBY, resort complex exec.; b. Saffron Walden, Essex, Eng., Apr. 3, 1941; s. John Piers and Modwena Margaret (Sedgwick) A. Student, Friends' Sch., Saffron Walden, 1952-58; B.A. Hotel/ Restaurant Mgmt, Westminster Coll., London, 1961. Mgmt. trainee Claridge's Hotel, London, Eng., 1960; maitre d'hotel Monte-Carlo Palace Hotel, Monte-Carlo, 1961-62; food and beverage mgr. Fred Harvey, Inc., Napa, Calif., 1967-70; gen. mgr. Esso Hotel, Maidenhead, Berkshire, Eng., 1973-74, Pheasant Run, Inc., St. Charles, Ill., 1974-76, Fred Harvey-Amfac, Furnace Creek Inn and Ranch Resort, Death Valley, Calif., 1976-80, Fred Harvey-Amfac/ Grand Canyon, Ariz., 1980—. Pres. Student's Union. Westminster Coll., London, 1960-61. Served with U.S. Army, 1963-65. Recipient Vanencia Award Sherry Shippers Assn., 1961; Trust House award, 1961. Mem. Food and Cookery Assn. Great Britain, Hotel and Catering Inst. Great Britain. Republican. Presbyterian. Club: Grand Canyon Soccer. Home: PO Box 256 104 Kaibab St Grand Canyon AZ 86023 Office: PO Box 699 Grand Canyon AZ 86023

ALLEN, WALLACE WILBUR, journalism educator; b. Norwich, Conn., Sept. 22, 1919; s. Samuel Prescott and Catherine Bell (McEwen) A.; m. Gladys E Wiseman, July 10, 1948; 1 son, Stewart David. A.B. summa cum laude, Brown U., 1941; M.A., U. Wis., 1946; M.S., Columbia U., 1947. Reporter Cape Cod Standard-Times, Hyannis, Mass., 1947-49; city editor Monroe (Mich) Eve. News, 1949-51; mem. staff Mpls. Tribune, 1951-82, mng. editor, 1968-77, assoc. editor, 1977-82; assoc. prof. journalism U. N.D., Grand Forks, 1982—. Author: A Design for News, 1981. Served with USAAF, 1942-45. Mem. Am. Soc. Newspaper Editors, AP Mng. Editors Assn., Phi Beta Kappa. Home: 4128 Ewing Ave S Minneapolis MN 55410 Office: Dept Journalism Univ North Dakota Grand Forks ND 58202

ALLEN, WELLS PRESTON, JR., utilities executive; b. Scranton, Pa., Apr. 6, 1921; s. Wells P. and Marguerite (Allen) A.; m. Jessie Jobson, June 23, 1946; children: James, Carolyn, Barbara. B.E.E., Rensselaer Poly. Inst., 1949. Registered profl. engr., N.Y. Cadet engr. N.Y. State Electric & Gas Corp., Binghamton, 1949-51, jr. engr., 1951-54, engr., 1954-58, chief power supply engr., 1958-63, asst. to pres., 1963-65, v.p., 1965-71, sr. v.p., 1971-73, exec. v.p., 1974-76, pres., 1976-83, chmn., chief exec. officer, 1983—, also dir.; dir. Utilities Mut. Ins. Co.; regional adv. bd. dirs. First City div. Lincoln First Bank, N.A.; dir. Bus. Council of N.Y. State, Inc., Lincoln First Banks Inc., Columbian Mut. Life Ins. Co. Past pres. Broome-Tioga chpt. N.Y. State Assn. for Retarded Children; council Rensselaer Poly. Inst.; mem. SUNY at Binghamton Found., 1973—; bd. dirs. Pathfinder Village. Served with AUS, 1942-45. Mem. IEEE, Am. Legion. Presbyterian. Club: Masons. Office: 4500 Vestal Pkwy E Binghamton NY 13903

ALLEN, WILLIAM CECIL, physician, educator; b. LaBelle, Mo., Sept. 8, 1919; s. William H. and Viola O. (Holt) A.; m. Madge Marie Gehardt, Dec. 25, 1943; children: William Walter, Linda Diane Allen Deardeuff, Robert Lee, Leah Denise. A.B., U. Nebr., 1947, M.D., 1951; M.P.H., Johns Hopkins U., 1960. Diplomate: Am. Bd. Preventive Medicine, Am. Bd. Family Practice. Intern Bishop Clarkson Meml. Hosp., Omaha, 1952; practice medicine specializing in family practice, Glasgow, Mo., 1952-59, specializing in preventive medicine, Columbia, Mo., 1960—; dir. sect. chronic diseases Mo. Div. Health, Jefferson City, 1960-65; asst. med. dir. U. Mo. Med. Center, 1965-75; assoc. coordinator Mo. Regional Med. Program, 1968-73, coordinator health programs, 1969—, clin. asst. prof. community health and med. practice, 1962-65, asst. prof. community health and med. practice, 1965-69, assoc. prof., 1969-75, prof., 1975-76, prof. dept. family and community medicine, 1976—; cons. Mo. Regional Med. Program, 1966-67, Norfolk (Va.) Area Med. Sch. Authority, 1965-66; governing body Area II Health Systems Agy., 1977—, mem. coordinating com., 1977—; founding dir. Mid-Mo. PSRO Corp., 1974-75, dir., 1976—. Contbr. articles to profl. jours. Mem. Gov.'s Adv Council for Comprehensive Health Planning, 1970-73; trustee U. Mo. Med. Sch. Found., 1976—. Served with USMC, 1943-46. Fellow Am. Coll. Preventive Medicine, Am. Acad. Family Physicians (sci. program com. 1972-75, commn. on edn. 1975-80), Royal Soc. Health; mem. Mo. Acad. Family Physicians (dir. 1956-59, 76-82, alt. del. 1982—, v.p. 1983—), Mo. Med. Assn., Howard County Med. Soc. (pres. 1958-59), Boone County Med. Soc. (pres. 1974-75), Am. Diabetes Assn. (pres. 1978, dir. 1974-77), Mo. Diabetes Assn. (pres. 1972-73), Soc. Tchrs. Family Medicine, AMA, Mo. Public Health Assn., Am. Heart Assn. (program com. 1979-82), Am. Heart Assn. of Mo. (sec. 1980-81), Mo. Heart Assn. (sec. 1979—, v.p. 1980—, pres.-elect 1982—). Methodist. Club: Optimists. Office: M304 Medical Center U Mo Columbia MO 65212

ALLEN, WILLIAM DALE, editor; b. Joplin, Mo., Aug. 16, 1938; s. William L. and Freda V. (Jones) A.; m. Barbara Bower, Aug. 26, 1960; children: Kendal Maria, Matthew Paul, Anna Elizabeth. A. in journalism, Joplin Jr. Coll., 1959; B.J., U. Mo.-Columbia., 1961. Reporter Joplin Globe, 1957-59; news editor Newport Ind., Ark., 1961-63; Carolinas editor, nat. editor Charlotte Observer, N.C., 1963-70; Sunday editor, assoc. mng. editor Phila. Inquirer, 1970-80; exec. editor Akron Beacon Jour, Ohio, 1980—. Mem. Associated Press Mng. Editors. Office: Akron Beacon Journal 44 E Exchange St Akron OH 44328

ALLEN, WILLIAM FREDERICK, JR., mechanical engineer; b. North Kingstown, R.I., June 22, 1919; s. William Frederick and Anita Lucy (Freeman) A.; m. Doris Evelyn Pendoley, Sept. 6, 1952; children: William Frederick, Janet Anita, Thomas Joseph, Paul Norman. Sc.B. in Engring., Brown U., 1941; S.M. in Mech. Engring., Harvard U., 1947, postgrad., 1947-48. Registered profl. engr., 20 states and Ont. Asst. in engring. Brown U., 1941-43, instr., 1943-44; teaching fellow in mech. engring. Harvard U., 1948; with Stone & Webster Engring. Corp., Boston, 1948—, engring. mgr., v.p., 1968-71, sr. v.p., 1971, pres., 1972-78, chief exec. officer, 1973—, chmn., 1978-83, dir., 1969—; dir. Blue Cross of Mass., vice chmn., 1983—. Trustee Thayer Acad., Braintree, Mass., 1974—, pres., 1979-81; trustee Northeastern U. Served with USNR, 1944-46. Fellow ASME. Roman Catholic. Office: 245 Summer St Boston MA 02107

ALLEN, WILLIAM HAYES, lawyer; b. Palo Alto, Calif., Oct. 19, 1926; s. Ben Shannon and Victoria Rose (French) A.; m. Joan Webster Emmett, July 16, 1950; children: Edwin Hayes, Neal French, William Kent. Student, Deep Springs Coll., 1942-44; B.A. with gt. distinction, Stanford U., 1948, LL.B., 1956. Bar: D.C. bar 1958. Corr. AP, Fresno, Calif., 1948-49, newsman, Sacramento, 1950-53; law clk. to Chief Justice Earl Warren U.S. Supreme Ct., Washington, 1956-57; asso. firm Covington & Burling, Washington, 1957-64, partner, 1964—; acting prof. law Stanford U. Law Sch., 1979; adj. prof. law Howard U. Sch. Law, 1981—; chmn. jud. rev. com. Adminstrv. Conf. of U.S., 1972-82; sr. conf. fellow Adminstrv. Conf. of U.S., 1982—; mem. steering com. Nat. Prison Project, 1975—. Pres.: Stanford Law Rev., vol. 8, 1955-56; contbr. articles to legal jours. Mem. Fair Housing Bd., Arlington County, Va., 1974-79. Served with U.S. Army, 1945-47. Mem. Am. Law Inst., ABA (mem. council adminstrv. law sect. 1969-72, 79-81, chmn. 1982-83), Bar Assn. D.C., D.C. Bar (chmn. legal ethics com. 1976-78), Order of Coif. Democrat. Mem. United Ch. of Christ. Club: Fed. City. Office: 1201 Pennsylvania Ave NW PO Box 7566 Washington DC 20044

ALLEN, WILLIAM RICHARD, economist; b. Eldorado, Ill., Apr. 3, 1924; s. Oliver Boyd and Justa Lee (Wingo) A.; m. Frances Lorraine Swoboda, Aug. 15, 1948; children: Janet Elizabeth, Sandra Lee. A.B., Cornell Coll., Iowa, 1948; Ph.D., Duke U., 1953. Faculty, Washington

U., St. Louis, 1951-52; faculty UCLA, 1952—, prof., 1963—; vis. prof. Northwestern U., 1952, U. Wis., 1964, U. Mich., 1965, So. Ill. U., 1969, Tex. A&M, 1971-73; cons. Dept. Commerce, 1962; v.p. Found. Research in Econs. and Edn., 1971-73; pres. Internat. Inst. Econ. Research, 1974—; nationally syndicated radio commentator; TV commentator, Los Angeles. Author: (with others) Foreign Trade and Finance, 1959, Essays in Economic Thought, 1960, University Economics, 3d edit., 1972, Exchange and Production, 3d edit., 1983, International Trade Theory, 1965, Midnight Economist, 1981; Adv. bd.: (with others) History of Polit. Economy, 1969-84, Social Sci. Quar, 1975—; contbr. articles to profl. jours. Served with USAAF, 1943-46. Social Sci. Research Council grantee, 1950-51, 62; Ford Found. grantee, 1958-59, 72-74; NSF grantee, 1965-66; Earhart Found. grantee, 1972, 74-75. Mem. Western Econ. Soc. (pres. 1970-71), So. Econ. Assn. (v.p. 1978-79), History of Econs. Soc. (v.p. 1974-75), Phi Beta Kappa. Home: 11809 Allaseba Dr Los Angeles CA 90066

ALLEN, WILLIAM STEPHEN, architect; b. Neptune Twp., N.J., July 15, 1912; s. William Stephen and Margaret (Pape) A.; m. Jane Eileen Eikelman, Feb. 12, 1952. B.Arch., U. Pa., 1935, M.Arch., 1936. Traveling fellow U. Pa., 1936-37; archtl. designer Masten & Hurd, San Francisco, 1937-41; partner Anshen & Allen (architects), San Francisco, 1946—; Mem. San Francisco Art Commn., 1952-56; mem. pub. adv. panel on archtl. services GSA, 1967-69; mem. archtl. adv. com. of joint rules com. Calif. Legislature regarding restoration State Capitol Bldg., Sacramento, 1974-75. Prin. works include Chapel of Holy Cross, Sedona, Ariz., 1956, visitor's center, Dinosaur Nat. Monument, Utah, 1957, Internat. Bldg, San Francisco, 1961, Coll. Chemistry, U. Calif. at Berkeley, 1962, Good Samaritan Gen. Hosp, San Jose, 1965, Bank of Calif. office bldg, San Francisco, 1968, Portland, Oreg., 1970, Lawrence Hall of Sci, U. Calif. at Bekeley, 1969, Nat. Sci. Center, Singapore, 1971; cons. architect: San Mateo-Hayward Bridge, 1962 (ASCE and Am. Inst. Steel Constrn. awards 1968), San Diego-Coronado Bridge, (AISC award), So. Crossing, San Francisco Bay, Dumbarton Bridge, San Francisco, West Seattle (Wash.) Bridge, 1979-80. Served to lt. comdr. USNR, 1942-46. Fellow AIA (pres. No. Calif. chpt. 1956-57, pres. Calif. council 1962, mem. jury of fellows 1967-69); mem. Sigma Xi. Home: 168 Harrison Ave Sausalito CA 94965 Office: 461 Bush St San Francisco CA 94108

ALLEN, WOODY, actor, filmmaker, author; b. N.Y.C., Dec. 1, 1935; s. Martin and Nettie (Cherry) Konigsberg; m. Louise Lasser. Student, N.Y. U., 1953, Coll. City N.Y., 1953. Writer TV comedy for, Sid Caesar, 1957, Art Carney, 1958-59, Herb Shriner, 1953; appeared in numerous nightclubs, TV shows, 1961—; author screenplay; also appeared in: motion picture What's New Pussycat, 1964-65; screenplay, dir., actor: Take the Money and Run, 1969, Bananas, 1971, What's Up Tiger Lily?, 1966, Everything You Always Wanted to Know About Sex But Were Afraid to Ask, 1972, Sleeper, 1973, Love and Death, 1975, The Front, 1976, Manhattan (Brit. Acad. award), 1979 (N.Y. Film Critics award), Stardust Memories, 1980; writer, dir., producer, actor: Annie Hall (N.Y. Film Critics Circle award for Best Dir. and Best Screenplay), 1977 (Nat. Soc. Film Critics Screenwriting award); screenplay, dir.: Interiors, 1978; author: play Don't Drink the Water, 1966; play, screenplay Play It Again, Sam, 1969; film, 1972; Author: Getting Even, 1971, Without Feathers, 1975, Side Effects, 1980; play The Floating Lightbulb, 1981; contbr. numerous pieces to, Playboy, New Yorker, other mags. Recipient Sylvania award, 1957; Spl. award Berlin Film Festival, 1975; nominated for Emmy award as TV writer, 1957. Democrat.

ALLER, ROBERT OLEN, scientist; b. Dayton, Ohio, Mar. 26, 1930; s. Olen A. and Carolyn R. (Lewis) A.; m. Nancy B. Rife, June 5, 1953; children: Cynthia L., Carole B., Robert C. B.S., U.S. Naval Acad., 1953; M.S. in Aero. Engring., U. Mich., 1960; P.M.D., Harvard U., 1968. Commd. 2d lt. U.S. Air Force, 1953, advanced through grades to capt., served, U.S. and Europe, res., 1963; with aerospace div. Philco/ Ford, Houston, 1963-64; with NASA space program, Washington, 1964—, div. tracking and data relay satellite program, 1979—. Served with USN, 1949-53. Recipient 2 NASA Exceptional awards, NASA Outstanding Leadership award. Fellow Am. Astron. Soc.; mem. AIAA, Explorers Club, Sigma Xi. Lutheran. Home: 7714 Glenmore Spring Way Bethesda MD 20817 Office: 600 Independence Ave SW Washington DC 20546

ALLERHAND, ADAM, chemist, educator; b. Krakow, Poland, May 23, 1937; s. Jonah and Amalia (Rotstein) A.; m. Nancy Jo Koehler, Apr. 20, 1978. B.S., State Tech. U., Chile, 1958; Ph.D., Princeton U., 1962. Asst. prof. Johns Hopkins U., 1965-67; asst. prof. Ind. U., Bloomington, 1967-69, asso. prof., 1969-72, prof. chemistry, 1972—, chmn. dept. chemistry, 1978-81. Contbr. articles on nuclear magnetic resonance of large molecules to profl. jours. Alfred P. Sloan Found. research fellow, 1966-68. Mem. Am. Chem. Soc., Am. Soc. Biol. Chemists, AAAS. Office: Dept Chemistry Ind U Bloomington IN 47405

ALLERS, FRANZ, orch. condr.; b. Czechoslovakia, Aug. 6, 1905; came to U.S., 1938; s. Carl and Paula (Kellner) A.; m. Carolyn Shaffer, 1941 (div. 1961); 1 dau., Carol Frances; m. Janne Furch, 1963. Student, Praha Conservatory, Prague, 1920, Berlin Hochschule für Musik, Berlin, 1923-26. First violinist, Berlin Philharmonic Orch., 1924-25; condr., Muncpl. Theatre, Carlsbad, 1926; asst. to gen. dir. of music, Wupperthal, Barmen-Elberfeld, 1926-27; 1st condr., United Municipal Theatres, Wupperthal, 1927-33; asst. at, Bayreuth Festival, summer 1927; asst., Wagner Festival, Paris, 1929; chief of opera and condr. Philharmonic concerts, Municipal Theatre, Aussig-on-Elbe, 1933-38; condr., Ballet Russe and Ballet Russe de Monte Carlo, London, 1938; toured U.S., South America and Can. as condr., Ballet Russe de Monte Carlo, 1939-44; musical dir., 1942-44; condr., Met. Opera House, N.Y.C., 1963-76, N.Y. Philharmonic, 1965, Nuremberg Philharmonic, 1967-76, Radio-TV Hilversum-Holland, 1968-79; gen. music dir., State Opera Comique, Munich; guest condr., Opera Munich and Cologne; musical dir., Music Theatre Lincoln Center, N.Y.C., 1964-66, Nat. Symphony, Washington, 1969, 78, 79, 81, 82, Saratoga Festival, 1969-82, Wolf Trap Festival, 1974, 77-82, Philharmonic Orch., London, 1970, Ravinia Festival, 1969, 70, 71, 74-82, Holland Opera, 1973, 74, 75, 76, others; condr. radio broadcast concerts, Czech Philharmonic and Radio Corp. of Prague orchs.; U.S. Condr.: Day Before Spring, 1945-56, Brigadoon, 1947-49, South Pacific, 1950-51, Paint Your Wagon, 1951-52; film Haensel and Gretel, 1953, Plain and Fancy, 1954-55; musical dir., State Fair Musicals, Dallas, Texas, 1953-56, My Fair Lady, 1956-60 (Antoinette Perry award 1957), tour to, Russia, 1960, Berlin, 1961, Munich, 1962, Vienna, 1963, Geneva, 1968, Brussels, 1969, U.S. tour with, Vienna Tonkuenstler Orch., 1978, 80, Hallmark TV program, 1955-63, also Omnibus, Susskind, Firestone programs, Camelot, 1960-63 (Antoinette Perry award 1961); condr. most maj. symphony orchs. of, U.S., also Berlin Philharmonic Orch., 1957, 59, 67, Hamburg Radio Orch., 1958, 59, 62, 64, 65, 66, Munich Radio Orch., 1962-65, Bavaria TV Munich, 1962-69, Radio Oslo, 1962, Cologne Radio Orch., 1965-82, Oslo Philharmonic Orch., 1965, Vienna Tonkuenstler Orch., 1965—, Vienna Symphony Orch., 1964-68, Opera Geneve, 1968-72, Miami Opera, 1977, 80, 81, 84; Rec. artist, Columbia RCA Victor, Vanguard, Phillips, Electrola., Eurodisk.

ALLERTON, JOHN STEPHEN, association executive; b. N.Y.C., Dec. 22, 1926; s. Moses Alexander and Rebecca (Stephens) A.; m. Juanita Grace Lee, Nov. 9, 1956. B.A. in Indsl. Engring, N.Y. U., 1950; grad. Advanced Mgmt. Program, Harvard Bus. Sch., 1971. With Am. Automobile Assn., Falls Church, Va., 1955—, dir. mktg., 1957-62; gen. mgr. Automobile Club of Wash., Seattle, 1962-65; pres. Ohio Motorists Assn., 1965-78; exec. v.p., gen. mgr. Am. Automobile Assn., 1978—; dir. Citizens Fed. Savs. and Loan Assn., Cleve.; Bd. dirs. Salvation Army, Ohio, 1966-76, Am. Cancer Soc., 1966-70, Crawford Automotive-Aviation Mus., Cleve., 1973-78; Bd. govs. Found. Internat. Meetings. Served with U.S. Navy, 1944-46. Mem. Nat. Assn. Corporate Dirs., Internat. Platform Assn. Presbyterian. Clubs: Harvard (Washington); Union (Cleve.). Office: 8111 Gatehouse Rd Falls Church VA 22047

ALLERTON, MICHAEL JOHN, performing arts administrator; b. Torquay, Devon, Eng., Mar. 5, 1935; children: Julie Kathryn, David Graeme. Chartered acct., Can. With Harrods of London, Morgan's (now Hudson's Bay Co.); acct. Coopers & Lybrand; mng. dir. Vancouver (B.C., Can.) Symphony Soc.; pres. Assn. Can. Orchs.; mem. Can. Music Council.; Mem. Vancouver Bd. Trade. Served to Royal Navy. Recipient award of merit Community Arts Council, 1978. Mem. Tory Party. Anglican. *

ALLERY, KENNETH EDWARD, air force officer; b. Holyoke, Mass., Mar. 3, 1925; s. Alfred Edward and Anne (Millen) A.; m. Constance DuFresne, June 22, 1946; children—Katherine Ann, Kenneth Scott, Bryan Keith, David Edward. B.A., Park Coll., 1965; M.S., George Washington U., 1969; grad., Air Command and Staff Coll., 1961, Nat. War Coll., 1969. Commd. 2d lt. U.S. Army Air Force, 1944; advanced through grades to brig. gen. U.S. Air Force, 1972; insp. with Insp. Gen. Team 17th Air Force; exec. officer, ops. officer 526th Fighter Interceptor Squadron, Ramstein Air Base, Germany, 1961; sr. Air Force adviser Oreg. Air N.G., Portland Internat. Airport, 1965-67; dir. ops. and tng. 1st Air Force, Stewart AFB, N.Y., 1967-68; mem. N.Am. br. Directorate Plans and Programs, Orgn. Joint Chiefs of Staff, 1969-71; asst. dep. chief of staff for plans Aerospace Def. Command, Ent AFB, Colo., 1971-72, N.Am. Air Def. Command/Continental Air Def. Command, 1972-73, asst. dep. chief of staff for ops., 1973-74; also dep. chief of staff for ops. Aerospace Def. Command; command insp. gen. NORAD/CONAD/ADC, 1974-76; ret.; asst. to v.p. Syscon Corp., Colorado Springs, 1976—; Bd. dirs. All Services Fund, Inc., Patrick J. Stevens & Assos., Inc. Decorated D.S.M., D.F.C., Air medal with 4 oak leaf clusters, Meritorious Service medal with oak leaf cluster, Air Force Commendation medal. Home: 6955 Mikado Ln Colorado Springs CO 80919 Office: Syscon Corp 3595 E Fountain Blvd Colorado Springs CO 80910

ALLEY, HAROLD PUGMIRE, weed scientist, educator; b. Coleville, Wyo., Mar. 26, 1924; s. Willis David and Della Young (Pugmire) A.; m. Nadra Jeanne Dayton, June 22, 1946; children: Eva Lynette, Willis David. B.S. in Agronomy, U. Wyo., 1949, M.S., 1955; Ph.D. in Bot. Sci., Colo. State U., 1965. Tchr. vocat. agr., coach La Grange High Sch., Wyo., 1949-55; mem. faculty U. Wyo., Laramie, 1955—, prof. weed sci., 1966—, extension weed scientist, 1960—. Author research papers in field. Served with AUS, 1942-46. Recipient George Humphrey award U. Wyo., 1980. Mem. Weed Sci. Soc. Am. (hon., Outstanding Extension Worker award 1975), AAAS, Western Soc. Weed Sci. Mormon. Lodge: Elks. Home: 1121 Reynold Div Laramie WY 80270 Office: Plant Sci Div Univ Wyo Laramie WY 80271

ALLEY, JAMES WILLIAM, physician, educator; b. Follansbee, W.Va., Mar. 13, 1929; s. John Joseph and Mary Edith (Allison) A.; m. Jean Marie Kinney, Nov. 15, 1958; children: Curtis, John, Mark. A.A., Roberts Wesleyan Coll., 1949; A.B. cum laude, U. Buffalo, 1955; M.D., State U. N.Y., 1959; M.P.H., Harvard U., 1962; D.Sc. (hon.), Marquette U., 1969. Intern Rochester (N.Y.) Gen. Hosp., 1959-60; gen. practice medicine, Lodi, Ohio, 1961; missionary United Methodist Ch., Bolivia, 1964-68, 69-72; internat. resident Johns Hopkins U. Sch. Hygiene, 1968-69; dir. div. public health Ga. Dept. Human Resources, Atlanta, 1972—; asso. prof. dept. internat. health Johns Hopkins U. Sch. Hygiene, 1969-72; prof. community health U. San Simon, Cochabamba, Bolivia, 1967-72; clin. prof. dept. preventive medicine Emory U. Sch. Medicine, 1978—; clin. prof. dept. community medicine Mercer Sch. Medicine, 1983. Assoc. editor: A Companion to the Life Sciences. Mem. Bishop's Cabinet, United Meth. Ch. in Bolivia, 1969-72; mem. Gov. Carter's Council on Family Planning, Atlanta, 1973-75, Gov. Busbee's Council on Developmental Disabilities, 1977—; bd. dirs. Ga. div. Am. Cancer Soc., 1978—; bd. dirs. WHO W.Am. Ctr. Perinatal Care and Health Service Research; mem. med. adv. com. Butler St. YMCA, 1981—. Served with U.S. Army, 1950-52. Named Roberts Wesleyan Coll. Alumnus of Year, 1982; WHO fellow Inst. Nutrition, Guatemala, 1962; recipient Disting. Provider award Ga. Assn. Primary Health Care. Mem. Am., Pub. Health Assn., Ga. Pub. Health Assn. (pres.-elect), Assn. State and Territorial Health Ofcls., Utah Acad. Preventive Medicine (hon.), Phi Beta Kappa. Democrat. Club: Rotary. Home: 5098 Timber Ridge Ct Stone Mountain GA 30087 Office: 47 Trinity Ave SW Atlanta GA 30334 *Peace on earth is the ultimate goal which all humankind should seek. It is only attainable as all people come closer to their own right of self-fulfillment.*

ALLEY, WAYNE EDWARD, legal educator, ret. army officer; b. Portland, Oreg., May 16, 1932; s. Leonard David and Hilda Myrtle (Blum) A.; m. Marie Winkelmann Dommer, Jan. 28, 1978; children: Elizabeth, David, John; stepchildren: Mark Dommer, Eric Dommer. A.B., Stanford U., 1952; J.D., Stanford SU., 1957. Bar: Oreg. Ptnr. William & Alley, Portland, 1957-59; commd. officer JAGC, U.S. Army, advanced through grades to brig. gen., ret., 1981; now dean Coll. Law, dir. Law Ctr. U. Okla.-Norman. Decorated D.S.M.; docrated Legion of Merit; decorated Bronze Star. Mem. ABA, Fed. Bar Assn., Oreg. Bar Assn., Bar Assn. Calif., Phi Beta Kappa, Order of Coif. Home: 1905 Joe Taylor Circle Norman OK 73069 Office: 300 Timberdell Rd Norman OK 73019

ALLEY, WILLIAM J., insurance company executive; b. Vernon, Tex., Dec. 27, 1929; s. W. H. and Opal M. (Cater) A.; m. Deborah Bunn, Dec. 28, 1979; children: Susan Jane, Pamela Jean, Patricia Ann, Sarah Elizabeth, Brayton. A.A., Northeastern A. and M. Coll., 1949; B.B.A., U. Okla., 1951, J.D., 1954. Bar: Okla. 1954; C.L.U. Atty. State Ins. Bd. Okla., 1956-57; asst. v.p. Pioneer Am. Ins. Co., 1957-59, v.p., 1959-60, v.p., agy. dir., 1960-66, dir., 1961, sr. v.p. marketing, 1966; v.p. Franklin Life Ins. Co., Springfield, Ill., 1967-69, sr. v.p., agy. dir., 1969-74, exec. v.p., 1974-75, pres., chief exec. officer, 1976—, chmn. bd., 1977—; pres., dir., chmn. bd. Franklin Fin. Service Corp.; chmn. bd., pres. Franklin United Life Ins. Co.; sr. v.p. strategic planning Am. Brands, Inc., 1983—, also dir.; dir. First Bank, Central Ill. Pub. Service Co.; chmn. bd., dir. Am. Franklin Co. Served to capt. USAF, 1954-56. Mem. Springfield Assn. Life Underwriters, Okla. Bar. Assn., Delta Sigma Pi, Phi Kappa Sigma, Phi Alpha Delta. Clubs: Mason, Shriner, Illini Country, Sangamo, Springfield Racquet; Tavern (Chgo.). Office: Franklin Sq Springfield IL 62713

ALLEYN, JACQUES RICHARD, lawyer; b. Quebec City, Que., Can., Nov. 24, 1926; s. Charles Edouard and Germaine (Des Jardins) A. LL.L., Jesuits Coll., Laval U., 1951. Bar: Que. Advocate Alleyn, Labrecque, Bernier & Alleyn, Que., 1952-53, Labrecque, Bernier & Alleyn, 1953, Noel, Alleyn & Rioux, 1957—; sec. Commn. Revision of Que. Mining Laws, 1956-61; gen. counsel CBC, Ottawa, Ont., 1962—. Mem. Can. Bar Assn., Que. Bar Assn. Home: 34 Walton Ct Ottawa ONCanada K1V 9T1 Office: Canadian Broadcasting Corp 1500 Bronson St Ottawa ONCanada K1G 3J5

ALLFREY, VINCENT GEORGE, educator, biochemist; b. N.Y.C., June 28, 1921; s. Thomas Richard and Margaret Theresa (Ryan) A.; m. Joan Lenore Brice, July 9, 1943; children—Barbara Claire, Kevin Mark. B.A., B.S., Coll. N.Y., 1943; M.S., Columbia, 1948, Ph.D., 1949. Mem. faculty Rockefeller U., 1949—, prof. cell biology, 1963—. Editor: Jour. Gen. Physiology, 1958—, Exptl. Zoology, 1964—, Recent Results in Cancer Research, 1965—, Archives Biochemistry and Biophysics, 1970—, Cancer Research, 1977—. Mem. research adv. com. Am. Cancer Soc., Nat. Cancer Inst. Mem. Am. Soc. Biol. Chemists, Am. Soc. Cell Biology, Phi Beta Kappa, Sigma Xi. Spl. research chemistry cell nucleus, chromosomal proteins, role genetic material in RNA synthesis, nuclear energy metabolism, regulation chromosomal activity, mechanisms of carcinogenesis. Home: 24 Winthrop Ct Tenafly NJ 07670 Office: Rockefeller Univ 1230 York Ave New York NY 10021

ALLGOOD, CLARENCE WILLIAM, U.S. judge; b. Birmingham, Ala., Sept. 12, 1902; s. Robert Veneable and Patricia (Robinson) A.; m. Marie Maxwell, June 27, 1927; 1 son, Clarence William. Student, Howard Coll., 1921-23; B.S., Ala. Poly. Inst., 1926; LL.B., Brimingham Sch. Law, 1941. Bar: Ala. 1941. Referee in bankruptcy U.S. Dist. Ct. No. Ala., 1937-61; U.S. dist. judge No. Dist. Ala., 1961—, now sr. dist. judge.; Dir. Fidelity Mortgage Co. Ala., Fidelity Fed. Savs. and Loan Assn. Author articles; contbr. textbooks. Mem. counsel profl. relations Am. Hosp. Assn., 1950-52; chmn. Ala. Hosp. Trustee Assn., 1951; Chmn. trustees S. Highland Infirmary, Brimingham, 1945-55; trustee Crippled Childrens Hosp. and Clinic, 1941—, pres., 1958; trustee Ala. Soc. Crippled Children and Adults, 1946-48. Mem. Am., Ala., Brimingham bar assns., Pi Kappa Alpha, Sigma Delta Kappa, Blue Key. Clubs: Mason, Shriner, Elk., Civitan (Birmingham). Office: 311 Fed Courthouse Birmingham AL 35203 *

ALLIGOOD, BOB, architectural, engineering and planning company executive; b. Moultrie, Ga., Dec. 5, 1932; s. Coy B. and Gladys Lucile (Thomas) A.; m. Celestew Moore, May 11, 1956; children: Randy, Robyn. B.S. in Indsl. Engring., U. Fla.-Gainesville, 1960. Exec. dir. Fla. Engring. Soc., Orlando, 1960-66; v.p. Watson & Co., Architects and Engrs., Orlando; also v.p. First Data Corp., Orlando, 1966-68; pres., dir. Reynolds, Smith & Hills Architects, Engrs, Planners, Inc., Jacksonville, Fla., 1968—; chmn. bd. dirs. Plantec, Inc., RSH Internat. Inc. Mem. Fla. Ho. of Reps., 1964-67, Fla. Gov.'s Task Force on Phys. Fitness, 1975-76, Fla. Gov.'s Productivity Council, 1981. Served with U.S. Army, 1953-56. Mem. Am. Inst. Indsl. Engrs., Fla. Engring. Soc., ASCE, Nat. Soc. Profl. Engrs., Fla. Council of 100, Fla. C. of C., Jacksonville Area C. of C., Jacksonville Com. of 100, Blue Key. Office: Reynolds Smith and Hills PO Box 4850 Jacksonville FL 32201

ALLIK, MICHAEL, food products company executive; b. N.Y.C., Aug. 28, 1935; s. Michael and Alma (Busch) A.; m. Deborah Dixon, Jan. 2, 1983; children by previous marriage: William Michael, Timothy John. B.S., MIT, 1957; M.B.A., Harvard U., 1961. Vice. pres. Kondu Corp., Erie, Pa., 1961-66; assoc. Booz, Allen & Hamilton, Cleve., 1966-69; gen. mgr. Textile Friction Group H.K. Porter, Pitts., 1969-71; gen. mgr. transformer div. Allis Chalmers, Pitts., 1971-75; exec. v.p. Mead Paper Group, Dayton, Ohio, 1975-78; sr. v.p. strategy and adminstrn. Mead Corp., Dayton, 1978-81; sr. v.p. fin. and adminstrn. Dart & Kraft, Inc., Northbrook, Ill., 1981-83, pres. Splty. Products Group, 1984—. Pres. bd. trustees Victory Theatre, Dayton, 1980-81; bd. dirs. Chgo. Hort. Soc., 1982—. Served to 1st lt. C.E. U.S. Army; 1957-59. Republican. Club: Chgo. Economic. Home: 133 Linden Ave Wilmette IL 60091 Office: Dart & Kraft Inc 2211 Sanders Rd Northbrook IL 60062

ALLIN, JOHN MAURY, bishop; b. Helena, Ark., Apr. 22, 1921; s. Richard and Dora (Harper) A.; m. Frances Ann Kelly, Oct. 18, 1949; children: Martha May, Kelly Ann and John Maury (twins), Frances Elizabeth. B.A., U. of South, 1943, M.Div., 1945, D.D., 1962; M.Ed., Miss. Coll., 1960. Ordained to ministry Episcopal Ch., 1944; vicar St. Peter's Ch., Conway, Ark., 1945-49; curate St. Andrew's Ch., New Orleans, 1950-51; chaplain to Episcopal students and institutions, New Orleans, 1950-52; rector Grace Ch., Monroe, La., 1952-58; rector, pres. All Saints Jr. Coll., Vicksburg, Miss., 1958-61; bishop coadjutor Diocese of Miss., P.E. Ch., Jackson, 1961-66, bishop, from 1966; now presiding bishop Episcopal Ch. in U.S.A., N.Y.C.; Examining chaplain Diocese of La., 1952-61; mem. Joint Commn. on Ecumenical Relations, 1964—; chmn. com. on councils of chs., 1969-72; mem. Anglican-Roman Catholic Consultation, 1967—; mem. exec. council Episcopal Ch., 1970—, mem. steering com. of exec. council, 1970—, chmn. program adv. com. on communications, 1970—, mem. ecumenical standing com., 1970—; v.p. Province IV of Episcopal Ch., 1971-73; mem. Miss. Religious Leadership Conf., 1969-73, chmn., 1972-73. Mem. exec. bd. County Health Improvement Project, 1968-71; Trustee All Saints Episcopal Sch., Vicksburg, 1961—, Episcopal Radio-Television Found., 1963-69; trustee U. of South, 1961—, bd. regents, 1965-71, 79—, chancellor, 1973-79. 815 2d Ave New York NY 10017

ALLING, CHARLES BOOTH, JR., management consultant; b. Montclair, N.J., July 7, 1921; s. Charles and Esther (Kelsey) A.; m. Abigail Parsons McMaster, Aug. 23, 1953; children: Charlotte, Beth, Gaie. B.A., Yale U., 1947. Dir. mgmt. services Frank C. Brown & Co., N.Y.C., 1963-68; ptnr. S.D. Fuller & Co. (Investment Bankers), N.Y.C., 1968-73, William H. Clark & Assocs., 1973-78; sr. v.p., mng. ptnr. Spencer Stuart & Assocs., N.Y.C., 1978—. Served to capt. USAAF, 1943-45. Decorated D.F.C., Air Medal with 5 oak leaf clusters. Clubs: N.Y. Racquet and Tennis (N.Y.C.); Bedford (N.Y.) Golf and Tennis.; Racquet and Tennis (N.Y.C.). Home: 200 E 90th St Apt 26F New York NY 10128 Office: Park Avenue Plaza 55 E 52 New York NY 10055

ALLING, NORMAN LARRABEE, educator; b. Rochester, N.Y., Feb. 8, 1930; s. Harold Lattimore and Merle (Kolb) A.; m. Katharine McPherson Page, Aug. 20, 1957; children—Elizabeth Larrabee, Margaret Tilden. B.A., Bard Coll., 1952; M.A., Columbia, 1954, Ph.D., 1958. Lectr. math. Columbia, 1955-57; asst. prof. math. Purdue U., 1957-62, asso. prof., 1962-65; lectr. math. Mass. Inst. Tech., 1962-64; asso. prof. math. U. Rochester, 1965-70, prof., 1970—; on leave as vis. prof. U. Wurzburg, Germany, 1971. Contbr. articles to profl. jours. Postdoctoral fellow NSF, 1961-62; sr. postdoctoral fellow, 1964-65. Mem. Am. Math. Soc. Research on ordered groups and fields, valuation theory, extensions of meromorphic function fields, Banach algebras of analytic functions, real algebraic curves. Home: 215 Sandringham Rd Rochester NY 14610

ALLINGER, NORMAN LOUIS, educator; b. Alameda, Calif., Apr. 6, 1928; s. Norman Clarke and Florence Helen (Young) A.; m. Janet Waldron, Aug. 14, 1952; children—Alan Louis, Ilene Suzanne, James Augustus. B.S., U. Calif. at Berkeley, 1951; Ph.D., U. Calif. at Los Angeles, 1954. Research fellow U. Calif. at Los Angeles, 1954-55, Harvard, 1955-56; asst. prof. chemistry Wayne State U., 1956-59, asso. prof., 1959-60, prof., 1960-69; prof. chemistry U. Ga., 1969—. Author: Topics in Stereochemistry; Editor: Jour. Comp. Chemistry; contbr. articles to profl. jours. Served with AUS, 1946-48. Alfred P. Sloan fellow, 1959-63. Mem. Am. Chem. Soc., Chem. Soc. London. Office: Dept Chemistry U Ga Athens GA 30602

ALLINSON, A. EDWARD, banker; b. Phila., Dec. 11, 1934; s. William R. and MargueriteCatherine (McCaughan) A.; m. Patricia Marie Dooley, July 11, 1959; children: Courtney Ann, A. Edward III, Bradford Joseph. B.S. in Econs., U. Pa. Wharton Sch. of Fin., Phila., 1957; M.S. in Mgmt., MIT, Sloan Sch., Cambridge, Mass., 1971. Salesman IBM Corp., Phila., 1957-65, mktg. mgr., Wilmington, Del., 1964-67, br. mgr., Boston, 1969-70; exec. v.p. State Street Bank, Boston, 1970-77, Chase Manhattan Bank, N.Y.C., 1977—. Dir. Salvation Army, N.Y.C., DST, Inc., Kansas City, Mo.; trustee Tuskegee Inst., Tuskegee, Ala. Served to capt. USAR, 1957-65. Sloan fellow MIT, 1971. Republican. Roman Catholic. Clubs: Wee Burn Country (Darien, Conn.); Doubles (N.Y.C.). Home: 700 Hollow Tree Ridge Rd Darien CT 06820 Office: Chase Manhattan Bank 1211 of the Americas New York NY 10036

ALLIO, ROBERT JOHN, management consultant executive, school official; b. N.Y.C., Sept. 1, 1931; s. Albert Joseph and Helen (Gerbereux) A.; m. Barbara Maria Littauer, Oct. 3, 1953; children: Mark, Paul, David, Michael,. B.Metal. Engring., Rensselaer Poly. Inst., 1952, Ph.D., 1957; M.S., Ohio State U., 1954. Mgr. advanced materials Gen. Electric Co., Schenectady, 1957-60; sr. staff AEC, Washington, 1962; engring. mgr. atomic power div. Westinghouse Corp., Pitts., 1962-68; dir. corp. planning Babcock & Wilcox, N.Y., 1968-75; v.p. Can. Wire Co., Toronto, Ont., Can., 1975-78; pres. Canstar Communications, Toronto, 1976-78; sr. staff mem. Arthur D. Little Co., Cambridge, Mass., 1978-79; pres. Robert J. Allio & Assocs., Cambridge, 1979—; dean Rensselaer Poly. Inst. Sch. Mgmt., Troy, N.Y., 1981—. Author: Corporate Planning, 1981; editor, pub.: Planning Rev. Jour., 1972—. Mem. N. Am. Soc. for Corp. Planning (pres. 1976-77). Club: Union League (N.Y.C.). Home: 15 Maple Ave Cambridge MA 02139 Office: Robert J Allio & Assocs 1000 Massachusetts Ave Cambridge MA 02138

ALLISON, B.R., conservationist, consultant; b. Rockwell City, Iowa, Nov. 12, 1915; s. Bert Ross and Florence June (Anderson) A.; m. Bernice Dwyer, May. 3, 1936; children: Camille Allison Miller, Gere Lynne Allison Brown, Michael R. Student, George Peabody Coll., 1938-39. With Civilian Conservation Corps, 1934; park supt. Tenn. Dept. Conservation, Nashville, 1940-47, dir. div. state parks, 1947-49; exec. dir. Tenn. Rural Electric Coop. Assn., Nashville, 1949-51; owner, mgr. Highland Rim Nursery-Buck Allison Inc., Nashville, 1951-75; commr. Tenn. Dept. Conservation, Nashville, 1975-79; cons., chmn. bot. com. Tenn. Bot. Gardens, Nashville, 1958-62; park commr. Metro Nashville Bd. Parks, Nashville, 1964-72; pres. Tenn. Nurserymen's Assn., Nashville, 1958; sr. fellow Am. Inst. Park Dirs., 1948. Contbr. articles to jours. in field. Bd. dirs. Nashville Boy's Club, 1971, Nashville Children's Mus., 1971-73; mem. Hist. Commn., Nashville, 1981-83; pres. Tenn. Hist. Soc., Nashville, 1981-83. Served with USN, 1943-45. Recipient Athens award Smithsonian Instn., 1960. Life mem. Tenn. Conservation League; life. mem. Nature Conservancy; life mem. Am. Forestry Assn.; mem. Am. Masters Foxhounds Assn., Am. Legion. Democrat. Roman Catholic. Home: 7732 Indian Springs Dr Nashville TN 37221 Office: Natural Resource Mgmt Route 1 McCrory Ln Kingston Springs TN 37082

ALLISON, DWIGHT LEONARD, JR., investment company executive; b. Boston, Oct. 27, 1929; s. Dwight Leonard and Stella (DeGrasse) A.; m. Lyona G. Strohacker, June 19, 1954; children: Dwight Leonard III, Barbara Lynn, Laurie. A.B., Dartmouth Coll., 1951; M.B.A., Amos Tuck Sch. Bus. Adminstrn., 1952; LL.B., Harvard U., 1956. Bar: Mass. 1956. Practiced in, Boston, 1956-66; assoc. Goodwin, Procter & Hoar, 1956-64, partner, 1965-66; v.p., dir. Gardner Assocs., Inc., Boston, 1966-68; chmn. fin. com. C.H. Sprague & Son Co., 1968-69; chmn. bd. Sprague Assoc., Inc., Boston, 1969-71; gen. ptnr. Sprague & Co., 1971—; pvt. investor, 1973-74; pres., chief exec. officer, dir. Boston Co., 1977-81, chmn. bd., 1981-83, chmn. exec. com., 1974-77; dir. Dennison Mfg. Co., Sea-Land Corp. Pres. Permanent Charity Fund of Boston, 1979—. Served to 1st lt. USAF, 1952-53. Mem. Mass., Boston bar assns. Office: 1 Boston Pl Boston MA 02106

ALLISON, FRED, JR., physician, educator; b. Abingdon, Va., Sept. 8, 1922; s. Fred and Elizabeth Harriet (Kelly) A.; m. Clara Knox, Oct. 14, 1949; children: Rebecca Allison Parsley, Martha Allison Brown, Fred III, Robert Gardiner. B.S., Ala. Poly. Inst., 1944; M.D., Vanderbilt U., 1946. Diplomate: Am. Bd. Internal Medicine. Intern Vanderbilt Hosp., Nashville, 1946-47; resident Peter Bent Brigham Hosp., Boston, 1949-50; practice medicine specializing in internal medicine, 1946—; asst. prof. medicine Washington U., St. Louis, 1955; prof. medicine, head infectious disease dept. U. Miss., Jackson, 1955-68; prof. medicine, head dept. medicine La. State U., New Orleans, 1968—; head La. State U. div. Charity Hosp., 1968—. Served with U.S. Army, 1943-46, 47-49. Home: 7821 Freret St New Orleans LA 70118 Office: 1542 Tulane Ave Sch Medicine La State U New Orleans LA 70112

ALLISON, GERALD LOU, architect; b. Seattle, Oct. 27, 1932; s. Cecil Jay and Ruth (Basilidas) A.; m. Charlotte Ann Nelson, July 30, 1955; children—Ruth Anne, Lynn Charlotte. B.Arch., U. Wash., 1955. Registered architect, Hawaii, Wash., Guam, Fiji. Asso., 1960-62; v.p. Wimberly, Whisenand, Allison, Tong & Goo Architects, Ltd., Honolulu, 1962—; Design critic U. Hawaii dept. architecture, 1970-71; guest lectr. East-West Center, 1970-71; lectr. U. Hawaii Sch. Travel Industry Mgmt.; Pres. Interprofl. Com. on Environmental Design, 1970; mem. Gov.'s Task Force on Natural Environment; 1970 Mayor's Com. to Preserve Natural Beauty, 1971; mem. steering com. Hawaii Community Design Center, 1970-71; co-founder Constrn. Industry Pub. Arts Program, 1970; mem. Pacific Area Travel Assn. Devel. Authority, Hawaii Nani Loa State Fedn. to Preserve Natural Beauty, 1971. Designer, Decker & Christensen, Seattle, 1955-57; architect, Wimberly & Cook, Honolulu, 1957-60; Weekly newspaper columnist, 1970, 71—; Editorial bd.: Hawaii Architect; editorial bd., writer: Symposia mag. Bd. dirs. Waialae Iki Ridge Community Assn., 1975-78; Deacon United Ch. of Christ. Recipient Mahalo award for pub. service Hawaii Wood Products Assn., 1970; Kagoshima Prefecture honor award, 1981; Ibusuki City honor award, 1981; named Businessman of Year Hawaii Bus. and Indsl. mag., 1967. Fellow AIA (Design awards 1960, 62, 64, 68, 71, 73, 75, treas. 1968, v.p. 1969, pres. 1970, jury mem. Honor awards 1971, nat. pub. relations com. 1973, nat. design com. 1978, nat. com. architecture, art and recreation); mem. Royal Inst. Brit. Architects, Am. Arbitration Assn. (mem. panel), Outdoor Circle, Life of Land, Alpha Delta Phi. Club: Outrigger Canoe (Honolulu). Home: 1621 Ihiloa Loop Honolulu HI 96821 Office: 2222 Kalakaua Ave Penthouse Honolulu HI 96815

ALLISON, GRAHAM TILLETT, JR., educator; b. Charlotte, N.C., Mar. 23, 1940; s. Graham Tillett and Virginia (Wright) A.; m. Elisabeth Kovacs Smith, Aug. 23, 1968. A.B., Harvard U., 1962, Ph.D., 1968; B.A., M.A., Hertford Coll., Oxford (Eng.) U., 1964. Asst. prof. John F. Kennedy Sch. Govt., Harvard U., Cambridge, Mass., 1968-70, asso. prof., 1970-72, prof., 1972—, asso. dean, 1975-77, dean, 1977—; fellow Center for Advanced Studies, Stanford, Palo Alto, Calif., 1973-74; asso. Center for Internat. Affairs, Harvard; cons. Rand Corp., U.S. Dept. Def., others.; Mem. numerous Nat. Acad. Sci. panels; mem. Trilateral Commn., Council on Fgn. Relations.; Mem. Fgn. Affairs Task Force Democratic Adv. Com., 1973, Vis. Com. on Fgn. Policy Studies, Brookings Instn. Author: Essence of Decision, 1971, Remaking Foreign Policy: The Organizational Connection, 1976, Sharing International Responsibility Among the Trilateral Countries, 1983; Contbr. articles to profl. jours. Home: 69 Pinehurst Rd Belmont MA 02178 Office: John F Kennedy Sch Govt Harvard U 79 John F Kennedy St Cambridge MA 02138

ALLISON, HENRY BARDEN, II, mechanical engineer; b. Indpls., Sept. 27, 1931; s. Henry Barden and Ella (Montgomery) A.; m. Jean Guthrie, June 3, 1953; children: Deborah Gwenn, Audrey Leigh, Derk Bryan, Mark Major. B.S. in Mech. Engring., U. S.C., 1953; M.S., Ga. Inst. Tech., 1959. Devel. engr. Lockheed-Ga. Co., Marietta, Ga., 1956-61; research engr. Lockheed Missiles & Space Co., Sunnyvale, Calif., 1961; devel. engr. Ryan Aeros. Co., San Diego, 1961-62; with Lockheed-Ga. Co., 1962—, chief engr. research and tech., 1971-79, dir. engring., 1979-83, dir. C-5/C-141 programs, 1983, v.p. C-5/C-141 programs, 1984—; dir. Lockheed-Ga. Employees Fed. Credit Union. Bd. dirs. St. John United Methodist Ch., Atlanta, Community Recreational Facility, Sandy Springs, Ga.; mem. House Dist. Republican Exec. Com. Served as lt. (j.g.) USNR, 1953-56. Mem. ASME, AIAA, Tau Beta Pi. Home: 6185 River Chase Circle Atlanta GA 30328 Office: 86 S Cobb Dr Marietta GA 30063

ALLISON, HENRY EDWARD, philosophy educator; b. N.Y.C., Apr. 25, 1957; s. John Phillip and Renee Catherine (Traurig) A.; m. Norma Ann Moore, Aug. 20, 1959; children: Eric Paul, Renee Catherine. B.A., Yale U., 1959; M.A. in Religion, Columbia U. and Union Theol. Sem., 1961; Ph.D., New Sch. for Social Research, 1964. Asst. prof. SUNY-Potsdam, 1964-65, Pa. State U., State College, 1965-68; assoc. prof. U. Fla., Gainesville, 1968-73; prof. U. Calif.-San Diego, La Jolla, 1973—, chmn. dept. philosophy, 1978-82. Author: Lessing and the Enlightenment, 1967, Benedict de Spinoza, 1975, The Kant-Eberhard Controversy, 1973, Kant's Transcendental Idealism: an Interpretation and Defense, 1983. Nat. Endowment for Humanities fellow, 1970-80. Mem. Am. Philos. Assn., AAUP. Home: 6153 Stetson Pl San Diego CA 92122 Office: Univ Calif San Diego B-002 Revelle College La Jolla CA 92093

ALLISON, JAMES CLAYBROOKE, II, broadcasting executive; b. Mason County, Ky., May 26, 1942; s. James Claybrooke and Frances (Orme) A.; m. Rosa Lee Parr, Aug. 29, 1965; children: Frances Michelle, James Claybrooke, III. A.B. in Radio-TV, U. Ky., 1964. Announcer sta. WVLK, Lexington, 1964-65; news dir. sta. WCMI, Ashland, 1965-68; news reporter sta. WLAP, Lexington, Ky., 1965-68, announcer, copywriter, 1968-69, asst. gen. mgr., dir. ops., 1969-70, gen. mgr., 1970—. Vice pres. Ky. chpt. Leukemia Soc., 1977—, Nat. trustee; bd. dirs. Big Bros./Big Sisters, Lexington, 1979—, Central Ky. Youth Orch. Inc. Dir. Sales and Mktg. Execs. Lexington (dir. 1978—), Ky. Assn. Broadcasters. Democrat. Club: Lions. Home: 3528 Coltneck Ln Lexington KY 40502 *

ALLISON, JAMES RALPH, lawyer; b. Salineville, Ohio, Feb. 14, 1930; s. Samuel O. and Lois M. (Willis) A.; m. Eleanor Kathryn Nealis, May 2, 1959; children: James Bradley, Matthew Samuel, Jonathan Alexander, Ann Elizabeth. B.A. Maryville (Tenn.) Coll, 1952; J.D., U. Chgo., 1955. Bar: Ohio 1955. Practiced in, East Palestine, 1957—; mem. firm Cohen & Allison, 1957-74, Allison & Blasdell, 1974—; city solicitor, East Palestine, 1972-75; chmn. bd. Union Comml. & Savs. Bank, East Palestine. Pres. East Palestine Sch. Dist. Bd. Edn., 1965-71; bd. dirs. Columbiana County Mental Health Assn., Columbiana County Mental Health Clinic, 1975-78; mem. alumni bd. Maryville Coll., 1967-72; councilman City of East Palestine, 1978-81; chmn. Columbiana County Republican Central and Exec. Com., 1980—. Served with CIC, U.S. Army, 1955-57. Mem. ABA, Ohio Bar Assn. (council of dels. 1979—), Columbiana County Bar Assn. (sec.-treas. 1960-78, pres. 1983—). Presbyterian (deacon, elder). Club: Rotary (dist. gov. 1969-70, dist. sec.-treas. 1972—). Home: 569 Sugar Camp Dr East Palestine OH 44413 Office: 25 E Rebecca St East Palestine OH 44413

ALLISON, JAMES RICHARD, JR., dermatologist; b. Columbia, S.C., Nov. 8, 1924; s. James Richard and Susy Millikin (FitzSimons) A.; m. Cornelia Elizabeth McElveen, Sept. 10, 1948; children: James Richard, Ann FitzSimons, Robert McElveen, Elizabeth Huger. A.B., U. N.C., 1947; M.D., Med. U. S.C., 1951. Diplomate: Am. Bd. Dermatology. Intern Jefferson-Hillman Hosp., Birmingham, Ala., 1951-52; resident in dermatology U. Mich., 1952-55; practice medicine specializing in dermatology, Columbia, 1955-65; pres. Columbia Skin Clinic P.A., 1965—; part time dir. div. dermatology, prof. medicine Sch. Medicine U. S.C., 1980—, clin. prof. dermatology; cons. VA, U.S. Army, USPHS; cons., mem. health care adv. bd. S.C. Dept. Mental Health. Contbr. to books, med. jours. Bd. dirs. S.C. Nursing Assn. Served to lt. (j.g.) USNR, 1943-46. Fellow Am. Acad. Dermatology (dir.); mem. Am. Dermatol. Assn., Soc. for Dermatol. Surgery (dir. 1979-82), Southeastern Dermatology Assn. (past pres.), So. Med. Assn. (past pres. sect. dermatology), Assn. Profs. Dermatology. Episcopalian. Lodges: Sertoma; Torch. Home: 1535 Haynesworth Rd Columbia SC 29205 Office: 3321 Medical Park Rd Suite 502 Columbia SC 29203

ALLISON, RICHARD CLARK, lawyer; b. N.Y.C., July 10, 1924; s. Albert Fay and Anice (Clark) A.; m. Anne Elizabeth Johnston, Oct. 28, 1950; children: Anne Sidney, William Scott, Richard Clark. B.A., U. Va., 1944, LL.B., 1948. Bar: N.Y. 1948. Practiced in, N.Y.C., 1948-52, 54-55, 55—; partner firm Reid & Priest, 1961—; with U.S. Govt., 1952-54. Trustee Buckley Country Day Sch. Served to ensign USNR, 1942-46. Mem. Am. Bar Assn. (chmn. com. Latin Am. Law 1964-68, vice chmn. internat. law sect. 1969-76, chmn. 1976-77, chmn. Nat. Inst. on Doing Bus. in Far East 1972, chmn internat. legal exchange program 1981—), Internat. Bar Assn., Société Internationale des Avocats, Inter-Am. Bar Assn., Am. Fgn. Law Assn. (dir.), Am. Arbitration Assn. (nat. panel), Southwestern Legal Found. (adv. bd.), Am. Soc. Internat. Law, Council on Fgn. Relations, Am. Bar Found., Assn. Bar City N.Y., Raven Soc., SAR, St. Andrew's Soc. N.Y., Phi Beta Kappa, Omicron Delta Kappa, Pi Kappa Alpha, Phi Delta Phi. Congregationalist. Clubs: Union League, Manhasset Bay Yacht. Home: 224 Circle Dr Plandome Manor NY 11030 Office: 40 W 57th St New York NY 10019

ALLISON, ROBERT ARTHUR, professional stock car driver; b. Miami, Fla., Dec. 3, 1937; s. Edmond J. and Katherine F. (Patton) A.; m. Judith A. Bjorkman, Feb. 20, 1960; children: David, Bonnie, Clifford, Caralene. Ed. parochial schs., Miami. Stock car racer, 1955—; with Grand Nat. Winston Cup div. Nat. Assn. Stock Car Auto Racing, 1965—; pres. Bobby Allison Racing, Inc. Mem. Hueytown (Ala.) Indsl. Devel. Bd.; Active Boy Scouts Am. Named Driver of Yr. Martini & Rossi, 1972, Nat. Motor Sport Press Assn., Olsenite, 1983; named Most Popular Driver Motor Racing Network poll, 1971, 72, 73, 81, 82, 83, Ala. Pro Athlete of 1978 Ala. Sportswriters Assn.; named to Am. Auto Racing Writers and Broadcasters Assn. All Am. Team, 1978. Mem. Nat. Assn. Stock Car Auto Racing (60 Winston cup wins 1961-82, Most Popular Driver in Winston Cup Grand Nat. Div. 1971, 72, 73, 81, 82). Roman Catholic. Club: Lions (Hueytown). Office: 140 Church St Hueytown AL 35023

ALLISON, RUSSELL STAFFORD, railroad company executive; b. Tichborne, Ont., Can., June 1, 1924; s. William Russell and Gertrude (Stafford) A.; m. Jean Edith McKillop, Mar. 5, 1949; children: Joan, John. P. in Civil Engring., Queen's U., Kingston,Ont, 1946. Cert. engr. With CP Rail, 1945—, supt., Montreal, 1964, gen. mgr. Pacific region, Vancouver, B.C., 1966; v.p. Prairie region CP. Rail, Winnipeg, Man., 1969; v.p. Eastern region CP Rail, Toronto, Ont., 1974, exec. v.p., Montreal, 1981—; pres., dir. CanPac Car Inc., Montreal, 1981—, Sault Ste. Marie Bridge R.R. Co., N.Y.C., 1981—, Toronto, Hamilton & Buffalo, Hamilton, 1981—, Toronto Terminals Railway Co., Toronto, 1981—, Soo Line R.R. Co. Mem. Am. Assn. R.R. Supts., Am. Railway Engring. Assn., Corp. Profl. Engrs. Ont., Engring. Inst. Can. Clubs: Mt. Stephen (dir. 1982), Can. Ry. (Montreal)). Home: 378 Olivier Ave Westmount PQ Canada H3Z 2C9 Office: CP Rail PO Box 6042 Sta A Montreal PQ Canada H3C 3E4

ALLISON, STANLEY FREDERICK, corporate consultant; b. Mpls., Apr. 5, 1917; s. Carl J. and Amelia (Marohn) A.; m. Elizabeth H. Spielman, May 15, 1942; children: Richard B., David R., Thomas R. B.B.A., U. Minn., 1939. With Ohio Boxboard Co., 1945-58, v.p., 1953-58, Packaging Corp. Am., Evanston, Ill., 1958-63, sr. v.p., 1963-66, dir., 1965—, pres., chief exec. officer, 1966-74, chmn. bd., 1974-77; sr. v.p. Tenneco, Inc., 1966-74, exec. v.p., 1974-82; dir. Tenn. River Pulp & Paper Co., 1969-74, chmn. bd., 1970-74; trustee Paperboard Packaging Council, 1969-72, Inst. Paper Chemistry, 1974-77. Served with USNR, 1942-45. Mem. Fiber Box Assn. (dir. 1958-68, pres. 1966), Am. Paper Inst. (dir. 1967-74), Fourdrinier Kraft Bd. Inst. (chmn. bd. 1971-72), Rice U. Shepherd Soc. (governing council). Clubs: Mid-America (Chgo.); Lyford Cay (Nassau, Bahamas); Houston. Home: 23 Willowron Dr Houston TX 77024 Office: 1100 Milam Bldg Suite 4300 Houston TX 77002

ALLISON, WILLIAM WHITTAKER, soft drink company executive; b. Nashville, Sept. 10, 1933; s. Andrew J. and Thelma (Whittaker) A.; 1 dau., Tracey Marie. B.A., DePauw U., Greencastle, Ind., 1954; postgrad., U. Philippines, 1958-60; M.P.A., U. Pitts., 1966. Research asst. Council Econ. and Cultural Affairs, Inc., Quezon City, Philippines, 1959-63; dir. Econ. Opportunity Atlanta, 1969-76; dep. dir. Community Services Adminstrn., Washington, 1977-81; v.p. civic affairs Coca-Cola Co., Atlanta, 1981—. Contbr. articles to profl. jours. Chmn. Martin Luther King Nat. Historic Dist.; mem. Leadership Atlanta, United Way Am., Atlanta. Served with U.S. Army, 1954-56. Recipient Urban Service award Office Econ. Opportunity, 1967, Young Man Yr. in Pub. Service award Atlanta Jr. C. of C., 1968, Outstanding Young Man of Yr. award Outstanding Young People in Atlanta, 1968, Ivan Allen Jr. Human Relations award Morris Brown Coll. Nat. Alumni Assn., 1974. Office: The Coca-Cola Co 310 North Ave Atlanta GA 30313

ALLMAND, LINDA F., librarian; b. Port Arthur, Tex, Jan. 31, 1937; d. Clifton James and Jewel Etoile (Smith) A. B.A., N. Tex. State U., 1960; M.A., U. Denver, 1962. Clerical asst. Gates Meml. Library, 1953-55; library asst. Houston Pub. Library, 1955-58; children's librarian Denver Pub. Library, 1960-63; children's coordinator Anaheim Pub. Library, Calif., 1963-65; br. mgr. Dallas Pub. Library, 1965-71; instr. N. Tex. State U., Denton, 1967—; chief br. services Dallas Pub. Library, 1971-81; dir. Ft. Worth Pub. Library, 1981—; instr. Dallas County Community Coll., 1981; bldg. cons. Jacksonville Pub. Library, Tex., 1976-79, Haltom City Pub. Library, 1983—, Carrollton Pub. Library, 1979-81, Hurst Pub. Library, 1977-78, Dallas Pub. Library, 1974-80. Author: 1981-2000, Ft. Worth Public Library—Facilities and Long Range Planning Study, 1982; contbr. chpts. to books, articles to profl. jours. Bd. dirs. City of Dallas Credit Union, 1973-81; com. chmn. Goals for Dallas, 1967-69; mem. Forum Ft. Worth, 1983; bd. dirs. Sr. Citizen's Centers, Inc., 1982. Pilot Club of Port Arthur scholar, 1954; Library Binding Inst. scholar, 1958; recipient Disting. Alumnus award N Tex. State U., 1983, Leadership Ft. Worth, 1982-83. Mem. ALA, Tex. Library Assn. (pres. 1980-81, chmn. planning com. 1982-84), Tarrant Regional Librarians Assn., Am. Mgmt. Assn., Dallas County Librarians Assn. (pres. 1968-69), Freedom to Read Found. Home: 2409 Stanley St Fort Worth TX 76110 Office: 300 Taylor St Fort Worth TX 76102

ALLMAND, W. WARREN, Canadian govt. ofcl.; b. Montreal, Que., Can., Sept. 19, 1932; s. Harold William and Irene (McMorrow) A.; children: Patrick, Julianne, Robin. Grad., St. Francis Xavier U., Antigonish, N.S., 1954; postgrad., McGill U., Montreal, 1957, U. Paris, 1959. Bar: Called to Que. bar 1958, Ont. bar 1974, Yukon and N.W.T. bar 1976, created queen's counsel 1977. Mem. Parliament, 1965—; solicitor gen. Can., 1972-76; minister Indian and No. affairs, 1976-77; tchr. polit. sci. and comml. law, 1962-65. Mem. Canadian Bar Assn. Liberal. Clubs: Mt. Royal Tennis (Montreal); Ottawa Tennis. Address: 783CB House of Commons Ottawa ON Canada *

ALLMENDINGER, PAUL FLORIN, engineering association executive; b. Moline, Ill., Mar. 2, 1922; s. Andrew Louis A. and Nellie L. (Florin) Inman; m. Sara Jo Breazeale, Aug. 31, 1947; children: James, Glen, John. Student, Augustana Coll., Rock Island., Ill., 1940-41; B.S., U.S. Naval Acad., 1944. Dir. engring. Prestolite Co.-Eltra Corp., Toledo, Ohio, 1961-67; dir. engring. Power Tool div. Rockwell Internat., Pitts., 1967-68, v.p. engring. Power Tool div., 1968-77; v.p. tech. affairs Motor Vehicle Mfrs. Assn., Detroit, 1977-81; dept. exec. dir. ASME, N.Y.C., 1981-82, exec. dir., 1982—. Served to lt (j.g.) USN, 1941-47. Mem. ASME (Centennial award 1980), Soc. Automotive Engrs. (bd. dirs. 1963-66), Am. Soc. Engring. Edn., Soc. Mfg. Engrs., Engrs. Council for Profl. Devel. (bd. dirs. 1973-80, pres. 1976-78), Am. Nat. Statndards Inst. (bd. dirs. 1977-82), Tau Beta Pi. Republican. Presbyterian. Club: Univeristy (Washington). Office: ASME 345 E 47th St New York NY 10017

ALLNER, WALTER HEINZ, designer, painter, art director; b. Dessau, Germany, Jan. 2, 1909; came to U.S., 1949, naturalized, 1957; m. Colette Vasselon, Mar. 8, 1938 (div. June 1951); 1 son, Michel; m. Jane Booth Pope, Apr. 4, 1954; 1 son, Peter. Student, Bauhaus-Dessau, 1927-30. Designer Gesellschafts-und Wirtschafts-Museum, Vienna, Austria, 1929; asst. to typographer Piet Zwart, Wassenaar, Holland, 1930; editorial, painting, and advt. designer, Paris, 1932-49; ptnr. Omnium Graphique, Paris, 1933-36; art dir. Formes, Editions d'Art Graphique et Photographique, Paris, 1933-36; Paris editor Swiss art mag. Graphis, 1945-48; founder, editor Internat. Poster Ann., 1948-52; co-dir. Editions Paralleles, Paris, 1948-51; mem. staff Fortune mag., N.Y.C., 1951-74, art dir., 1962-74; mem. faculty Parsons Sch. Design, N.Y.C., 1974—; vis. critic Ecole Superieure d'Arts Graphiques, Paris, 1979-82; free-lance designer design cons. companies. Designer posters for traffic safety campaign, Outdoor Advt. Assn. Am., 1959-60; exhibits, Salon des Surindependants, Paris, Salon des Réalités Nouvelles, Paris, numerous others, Germany, Austria, U.S., Eng., France, Holland, Switzerland, Latin Am., Japan.; Compiler, editor: A.M. Cassandre, Peintre d'Affiches, 1948; Editor: Posters, 1952; Author numerous articles on poster art. Recipient Bauhaus-Dessau German Acad. Architecture, 1979. Mem. Alliance Graphique Internationale (internat. pres.), Am. Inst. Graphic Arts, Art Dirs. Club. Home: 110 Riverside Dr New York NY 10024 Castle Rd Truro MA 02666

ALLNUTT, ROBERT FREDERICK, lawyer, organization executive; b. Richmond, Va., June 15, 1935; s. Robert Carhart and Evelyn

Rosalie (Brooks) A.; m. Jan Latven, July 14, 1938; children: Robert David, Thomas Frederick. B.S. in Indsl. Engring, Va. Poly. Inst., 1957; J.D. with distinction, George Washington U., 1960, LL.M., 1962. Bar: D.C. 1960, Va. 1960. Patent examiner U.S. Patent Office, 1957-60; with NASA, 1960-70, 78-83, asst. adminstr. legis. affairs, 1967-70, assoc. dep. adminstr., 1978-81, assoc. adminstr. external relations, dep. gen. counsel, 1981-83; legal counsel, corp. sec. U.S. Com. Energy Awareness, 1983—; assoc. gen. counsel Commn. Govt. Procurement, 1970-73; staff dir. com. aero. and space scis. U.S. Senate, 1973-75; dep. asst. adminstr. ERDA, 1975-78; lectr. law Am. U. Law Sch., 1964. Recipient Superior Performance award U.S. Patent Office, 1959, Apollo Achievement award NASA, 1969, Meritorious Service medal ERDA, 1976, Exceptional Service medal NASA, 1981, Disting. Service medal, 1983; named Meritorious Fed. Exec. with Presdl. Rank Office of Pres., 1981. Mem. Am. Bar Assn., Fed. Bar Assn., Govt. Patent Lawyers Assn. (v.p. 1967), Order of Coif. Home: 5400 Edgemoor Ln Bethesda MD 20814 Office: US Com Energy Awareness 1735 I St NW Washington DC 20006 *The greatest privilege of my life has been the opportunity for public service: an opportunity that came to me, as it does in our system, not as a familial right or political favor, but because I was willing to start at a junior level and work.*

ALLOWAY, JAMES ALEXANDER, management consultant; b. Erie, Pa.; s. Rawle Allison and and May Ann (Mulligan) A.; m. Tam Thi Nguyen, Feb. 16, 1983; children: James Alexander, Lynn Marie, Ruth Ann. B.A., Grove City (Pa.) Coll., 1951; M. Govt. Adminstrn., Wharton Sch. U. Pa., 1955. Adminstrv. asst., Teaneck, N.J., 1954-55, chief fiscal officer, Fair Lawn, N.J., 1955-58, bus. adminstr., Edison, N.J., 1958-61, Elizabeth, N.J., 1961-64, Woodbridge, N.J., 1964-67; dir. div. local fin. N.J. Dept. Community Affairs, 1967-74; pres. N.J. Civil Service Commn., 1970-74; city mgr., Dayton, Ohio, 1974-79, San Jose, Calif., 1979-80; dir. instl. devel. Royal Commn. Jubailand Yanbu (Saudi Arabia), 1980-82; mgmt. cons. Pub. Adminstrn. Service, 1983—; mem. Pres.'s Adv. Council Intergovtl. Personnel Policy; past pres. N.J. Mcpl. Mgmt. Assn. Served with USMCR, 1951-53. Fels fellow, 1953. Mem. Internat. City Mgmt. Assn., Ohio City Mgrs. Assn. Presbyterian. Office: PO Box 2427 Addis Ababa Ethiopia *

ALLOWAY, LAWRENCE, writer, educator; b. Wimbledon, London, Eng., Sept. 17, 1926; came to U.S., 1961; s. Francis Lawrence and Nora (Hatton) A.; m. Sylvia Sleigh, June 28, 1954. Asst. lectr. Nat. Gallery, London, 1948-54; lectr. Tate Gallery, London, 1952-55; Brit. corr. Art News mag., N.Y.C., 1954-57; dep. dir. Inst. Contemporary Arts, London, 1957-60; instr. art history Bennington (Vt.) Coll., 1961-62; curator Guggenheim Mus., N.Y.C., 1962-66; chmn. div. of fine arts Sch. Visual Arts, N.Y.C., 1967-68; prof. State U. at Stony Brook, N.Y., 1968-81; Mem. com. London County Council Open Air Exhbn., 1960; juror Carnegie Inst. Internat., 1961. Contbg. editor: Art Internat. mag, Zurich, Switzerland, 1957-65; writer, mem. artist-in-residence program, So. Ill. U. at Carbondale, 1966-67; art editor: The Nation, 1968-81; contbg. editor: Artforum, 1972-76; co-editor: Art Criticism, 1979-80; Author: Nine Abstract Artists, 1954, Ettore Colla, 1960, The Metalization of a Dream, 1963, The Venice Biennale, 1895-1968, 1969, Violent America: The Movies, 1946-64, 1970, American Pop Art, 1974, Topics in American Art since 1945, 1975. Fgn. leader grantee Dept. State, 1958; recipient 2d Fgn. Critics prize 30th Venice Biennale, 1961, Frank Jewitt Mather award art for criticism, 1972. Mem. Assn. Internat. Art (hon. joint-sec. Brit. sect. 1957-60). Home: 330 W 20th St New York NY 10011

ALLPORT, PETER WARD, assn. exec.; b. Vienna, Austria, July 28, 1920; s. Fayette Ward and Mildred Dorcas (Burt) A.; m. Margaret Hahr Nichols, Jan. 5, 1946; 1 son, George Nichols. B.A., Brown U., 1941. With Erwin, Wasey & Co. (advt.), N.Y.C., 1944-46; with Assn. Nat. Advertisers, N.Y.C., 1946—, v.p., sec., 1958-60, exec. v.p., 1960, pres., 1960—; Mem. adv. com. distbn. council Dept. Commerce, also U.S. council Internat. C. of C.; bd. dirs. Advt. Council, Advt. Research Found. Contbr. to: Handbook of Advertising Management, 1970. Mem. Alpha Delta Phi. Clubs: Union League (N.Y.C.); Am. Yacht (Rye, N.Y.). Home: 2 Crown Circle Bronxville NY 10708 Office: 155 E 44th St New York NY 10017

ALLRED, ALBERT LOUIS, educator; b. Mount Airy, N.C., Sept. 19, 1931; s. Caleb Haynes and Bessie (Brown) A.; m. Nancy Jean Willis, Aug. 30, 1958; children—Kevin Scott, Gregg Warren, Sarah Elaine. B.S. in Chemistry, U. N.C., 1953; A.M., Harvard, 1955, Ph.D., 1956. Chemist E.I. du Pont de Nemours Co., Wilmington, Del., 1952, 55, Mallinckrodt Chem. Works, St. Louis, 1954, Argonne Nat. Lab., 1958, 76; mem. faculty Northwestern U., 1956—, prof., 1969—; asso. dean Coll. Arts and Scis., 1970-74, chmn. dept. chemistry, 1980—. Alfred P. Sloan fellow, 1963-65; postdoctoral fellow U. Rome, Italy, 1967; hon. research asso. Univ. Coll., London (Eng.), 1965. Mem. Am. Chem. Soc., Chem. Soc.(London), Am. Assn. U. Profs. (pres. Northwestern U. 1968-69), Phi Beta Kappa, Phi Lambda Upsilon, Sigma Xi, Alpha Chi Sigma. Home: 820 Milburn St Evanston IL 60201

ALLRED, EVAN LEIGH, scientist, educator; b. Deseret, Utah, May 22, 1929; s. Leigh Richmond and Louise (Cowley) A.; m. Barbara Klea Hawkins, Apr. 21, 1955; children—Kevin Michael, Richard Paul, Steven Leigh and Craig Lynn (twins). B.S., Brigham Young U., 1951, M.S., 1956; Ph.D., UCLA, 1959. Research chemist Phillips Petroleum Co., Bartlesville, Okla., 1951-54; instr. chemistry U. Wash., 1960-61; sr. research chemist Rohm & Haas Co., Phila., 1961-63; asst. prof. chemistry U. Utah, 1963-67, asso. prof., 1967-70, prof., 1970—. David P. Gardner faculty fellow, 1976; NSF postdoctoral fellow, 1959-60. Mem. Am. Chem. Soc., Sigma Xi, Phi Kappa Phi. Mem. Ch. of Jesus Christ of Latter Day Saints. Research physical and organic chemistry; organic reaction mechanisms; synthesis of molecules of theoretical interest. Home: 4195 S 2700 E Salt Lake City UT 84124

ALLRED, JOHN CALDWELL, physicist; b. Breckenridge, Tex., Apr. 24, 1926; s. Oran Henderson and Katherine (Miller) A.; m. Mary Elizabeth Bode, June 4, 1950; children: Susan Elizabeth, Katherine Anne, John Renne. B.A., Tex. Christian U., 1944; M.A., U. Tex., 1948, Ph.D., 1950. Staff mem. Los Alamos Sci. Lab., 1948-55, mem. vis. staff, 1975—; research scientist Convair Co., 1955-56; mem. faculty U. Houston, 1956-79, prof. physics, 1961-79, v.p., dean faculties, 1962-68. Fellow Am. Phys. Soc.; mem. Am. Nuclear Soc. (charter), Acoustical Soc. Am., Sigma Xi, Alpha Chi, Sigma Pi Sigma. Office: Los Alamos Nat Lab MS 850 Los Alamos NM 87545

ALLSHOUSE, MERLE FREDERICK, college president; b. Pitts., Apr. 26, 1935; s. Merle Lawrence and Helen (Frederick) A.; m. Myrna Mansfield, Apr. 1, 1956; children: Frederick Scott, Kimberly Dawn. B.A. (Rector fellow), DePauw U., 1957; M.A. (Rockefeller Theol. fellow), Yale, 1959; Ph.D. (Rockefeller fellow 1959-61, Kent fellow 1961), Yale, 1965. Instr. philosophy Dickinson Coll., 1963-65, asst. prof., 1965-68, asso. dean of coll., asso. prof. philosophy, 1968-70; dean of coll., prof. philosophy Bloomfield (N.J.) Coll., 1970-71, pres., 1971—; Mem. N.J. Student Assistance Bd. Bd. dirs. N.J. Coll. Fund, Inc.; trustee Montclair Kimberley Acad.; pres. Presbyn. Coll. Union. HEW fellow, 1979-80. Mem. Metaphys. Soc. Am., Am. Philos. Assn., Am. Acad. Religion, Assn. Ind. Colls. and Univs. in N.J. (dir., chmn. bd.), Nat. Assn. Ind. Colls. and Univs. (chmn. secretariat 1983-84). Office: Bloomfield Coll Bloomfield NJ 07003

ALLSOPP, THOMAS, ins. exec.; b. Newark, May 17, 1918; s. Thomas and Amy A. (Hart) A.; m. Margaret Jean Johnson, Sept. 28, 1940; children—Carol (Mrs. Frederick F. Rhines), Barbara (Mrs. John Conathan), Susan. A.B., Princeton, 1939. With Prudential Ins. Co. Am., 1939—, successively sr. methods analyst, asst. personnel dir., gen. mgr. home office, dir. adminstrn. Canadian head office, exec. gen. mgr. South- Central home office, 1939-55, 2d v.p., 1955-62, sr. v.p. Northeastern home office, Boston, 1962-74, sr. v.p. pub. affairs home office, Newark, 1974-76; cons. Am. Council Life Ins., 1976-80; dir. Zurich-Am. Ins. Cos., 1976—; cons. IGA, Inc., 1977—. Author: (with Harry J. Volk) Life Insurance Company Organization, 1955. Mem. nat. adv. bd. Boy Scouts Am. Mem. Am. Coll. Life Underwriters. Clubs: Oyster Harbors (Cape Cod, Mass); Princeton of N.Y. Home: 39 Hornbeam Ln Centerville MA 02632

ALLTOP, JAMES HOWARD, ins. co. exec.; b. cb. Glenville, W.Va., Nov. 28, 1905; s. Evan and Ida and (Miller) A.; m. Lillian O'Bannon, June 11, 1930 (dec. July 7, 1978); children—James H., William O'Bannon; m. Helen Gragg Perlin, Dec. 1, 1979. A.B., Ind. U., 1929. With Eli Lilly Co., 1929-31, Am. United Life Ins. Co., Indpls., 1931—, personnel dir., 1932-52, sec., 1952-61, sr. v.p., dir., 1961—; lectr. Butler U., 1936-52. Gen. chmn. Community Chest, Indpls., 1953-54. Mem. Ind. U. Alumni Assn. (past pres.), Beta Theta Pi. Home: 1720 E 80th St Indianapolis IN 46240 Office: Am United Life Ins Co Box 368 Indianapolis IN 46204

ALLUMS, KENNETH LAMAR, electric utility company executive; b. Dora, Ala., Aug. 31, 1931; s. Ira L. and Ruth (Washburn) A.; m. Peggie Jean HensOn, Dec. 26, 1952; children: Kenneth L., Richard Keith, Michael Wayne. B.S. in Elec. Engring., Auburn U., 1953. Registered profl. engr. Ala. Engr. Gen. Electric Co., Schenectady, 1953-55, Ala. Power Co., Birmingham, 1957-65, dist. mgr., 1965-66, div. mgr., 1966-77, mgr. power delivery, 1977-78, sr. v.p., 1978—. Bd. dirs. Tuscaloosa chpt. ARC, 1967-68. Served to capt. DU.S. Army, 1955-57. Mem. Birmingham C. of C. Republican. Am. Baptist. Lodge: Kiwanis (pres. 1969-70). Home: Route 1 Box 774 Dora AL 35062 Office: Alabama Power Co 600 N 18th St Birmingham AL 35291

ALLWORTH, EDWARD ALFRED, Middle Eastern studies educator; b. Columbia, S.C., Dec. 1, 1920; s. Edward Christopher and Ethel Elaine (Walker) A.; m. Janet Ferne Lovett; 1 son, Clark Edward. B.S., Oreg. State U., 1948; A.M., U. Chgo., 1953; Ph.D., Columbia U., 1959. Instr. Russian and humanities Reed Coll., Portland, 1957-58; program asst. Internat. Tng. and Research div. The Ford Found., 1958-59; asst. to dir. emigrant relations Am. Com., Munich, Germany, 1960-61; asst. prof. Turco-Soviet studies, dept. Middle East lang. and culture Columbia U., 1961-64, assoc. prof., 1965-69, prof., 1970—; chmn. Seminar on Soviet Nationality Problems, 1968—; dir. Program on Soviet Nationality Problems, 1970—; del., bd. dirs., officer Am. Research Inst. in Turkey, Inc., 1968—; founder Central Asian Circle, 1974; dir. Central Asia Ctr., 1983—; cons. in field. Author: Uzbek Literary Politics, 1964, Central Asian Publishing and The Rise of Nationalism, 1965, Nationalities of the Soviet East, 1971, Soviet Asia: Bibliographies, 1975, (with Nishan Parlakian) Shirvanzade's Evil Spirit, 1980, The End of Ethnic Integration in Southern Central Asia, 1982; Editor, co-author: Central Asia: A Century of Russian Rule, 1967, Soviet Nationality Problems, 1971, The Nationality Question in Soviet Central Asia, 1973, Nationality group Survival in Multiethnic States, 1977, Ethnic Russia in the USSR—The Dilemma of Dominance, 1980; gen. editor: Central Asia Book Series, 1983—; Translator: (by Ibrahim Sinasi) The Wedding of a Poet, 1981; also Central Asian, Russian and Turkish prose and poetry. Served with U.S. Army, 1942-47. Ford Found. fellow, 1955-57; Social Sci. Research Council fellow, 1967-68; Am. Philos. Soc. fellow, 1975-76; Middle East Inst. fellow, 1976; guest scholar Kennan Inst. Advanced Russian Studies, The Wilson Ctr., Washington, 1982. Office: 618 Kent Hall Columbia U 116th St and Broadway New York NY 10027 *Twenty years of trying to provide evidence of the importance to the United States and the world of the great Central Asia region (larger than the USA or PR China) has had an insignificant impact on the academic or public mind in comparison with the effect of the 1979 invasion of Afghanistan by the Russians. These ironies usefully remind us of the true dimension of our efforts in human history. To be the composer of one wonderful small poem probably has more lasting value than a multitude of less creative endeavors at making things happen. But I keep trying to prove the opposite.*

ALLY, CARL JOSEPH, advertising executive; b. Detroit, Mar. 31, 1924; s. Carl and Mary (Miglio) A.; m. Patricia M. Nusco, Jan. 15, 1952; children: Christopher Jonathan, Patricia Ann, Matthew Carl. B.A., U. Mich., 1949, postgrad., 1953; cert., Sch. Fgn. Service, Georgetown U., 1952. Advt. exec. Gen. Electric Co., Schenectady, 1948-51; mgr. N.Y.C. office Campbell-Ewald Co., 1955-60; v.p. Papert, Koening, Lois, Inc., N.Y.C., 1960-62; founder, chmn. bd., chief exec. officer Carl Ally Inc., N.Y.C., 1962-76; chmn. bd. Ally & Gargano, Inc., N.Y.C., 1979—; lectr. New Sch. Social Research, 1964—. Served to capt. USAAF, 1942-45; Served to capt. USAF, 1950-52. Decorated D.F.C., Air medal with three oak leaf clusters. Mem. Sigma Nu. Clubs: Wings (N.Y.C.); University. Office: Ally & Aargano 805 3d Ave New York NY 10022 *

ALLYN, ARTHUR CECIL, museum director, lepidopterist; b. Chgo., Dec. 24, 1913; s. Arthur Cecil and Nelle (Musick) A.; m. Dorothy DeWitt, Mar. 21, 1938 (dec.); children: Dorothy Ann (Mrs. Christopher J. Lavick, Jr.), David D., William N. (adopted); m. Dorothy Dunklau, Apr. 22, 1972. Student, Dartmouth Coll., 1931-35, Beloit Coll., 1935; D.Sc. (hon.), U. Fla., 1981. Chmn. bd. A.C. Allyn & Co., Chgo., 1969—; pres., dir. Chgo. White Sox, 1961-70; now mng. dir. Allyn Mus. Entomology of Fla. State Mus.; pres. Sarasota Jungle Garden, 1970—; dir. Allyn Precision Tools (PTY) LTD, Mono Container (PTY) Ltd. Fellow Royal Entomol. Soc.; mem. Lepidopterists Soc., Sigma Chi. Presbyn. Club: University (Sarasota). Home: 888 Blvd of the Arts Sarasota FL 33577

ALLYN, HENRY GREGORY, JR., retired railroad executive; b. Phila., Dec. 4, 1920; s. Henry Gregory and Frances H. (Steen) A.; m. Elizabeth Kendrick Burrows, Sept. 20, 1947; children: Henry Gregory III, Florence Elizabeth, John Steen. Grad., Lawrenceville Sch., 1939; B.A., Princeton, 1943. With Pa. R.R., 1947-68; asst. v.p. freight sales Penn Central Co., N.Y.C., 1968-69; pres., dir. P. & L.E. R.R., Pitts., 1969-70, pres. chief exec. officer, 1970-82; dir. Wheeling-Pitts. Steel Corp.; Duquesne Light Co., Pitts. Bd. dirs. Allegheny Trails council Boy Scouts Am.; trustee Allegheny Gen. Hosp., Pitts. Served with Hosp. Corps USNR, 1943-46; PTO. Republican. Clubs: Duquesne, Harvard-Yale-Princeton (Pitts.); Allegheny Country (Sewickley); Princeton (N.Y.C.); Capitol Hill (Washington).

ALM, JOHN LEVERNE, retail foods executive; b. Denver, Mar. 16, 1920; s. Lenus and Ellen (Nilson) A.; m. Kathryn E. Stenmark, Dec. 5, 1942; children: Linda Kay, Kenton L. B.S., Iowa State U., 1942. Supt. Almhurst Dairy, Denver, 1946-47; mgr. Lucerne Milk Co., Denver, 1947-52; mgr. milk and ice cream plant Safeway Stores Inc., Los Angeles, 1952-61, dist. mgr. deli ops., Oakland, Calif., 1961-68, ops. mgr. milk plants, 1966-71, cheese and butter dept. mgr., 1971-82, v.p.-div. mgr. dairy div., 1982—. Mem. United Dairy Industry (dir. 1982), Nat. Dairy Council (dir. 1982), Calif. Dairy Council (dir. 1984), Am. Dairy Assn. (dir. 1982), Dairy Research Inc. (dir. 1982). Presbyterian. Home: 155 Hall Dr Orinda CA 94563 Office: Safeway Stores Inc Dairy Div Oakland CA 94660

ALM, RICHARD SANFORD, educator; b. Mpls., Aug. 26, 1921; s. Leonard Hilder and Grace Hannah (Leask) A.; m. Julia Nygaard, July 24, 1948; children: Robert Anthony, Steven Scott. B.S., U. Minn., 1942, M.A., 1948, Ph.D., 1954. Instr. U. Minn. High Sch., 1946-48; tchr. Lincoln High Sch., Seattle, 1949-51; mem. faculty U. Hawaii, 1951—, prof. edn., 1962—, chmn. dept. curriculum and instrn., 1968-71, 83—, chmn. grad. studies secondary edn., 1968-75, chmn. grad. studies curriculum and instrn., 1975—; mem. faculties U. Colo., summers 1949-52, 58, U. Wis., summer 1962, U. Calif., Berkeley, summer 1964, Tchrs. Coll., Columbia U., summer 1965; cons. ALA (sch. systems.). Editor: English Jour, 1964-73, Ednl. Perspectives, 1961-64, (with G. Carlsen) Social Understanding Through Literature, 1954, Books for You, 1964, (with Carlsen, Tovatt) Themes and Writers Series, 4 vols, 1967; asso. editor: Internat. Reading Assn. Dictionary of Reading and Related Terms, 1981; contbr. articles to profl. jours., chpts. to books. Served with AUS, 1942-46. Recipient citation secondary sect. Nat. Council Tchrs. English, 1972, Distinguished Service award, 1974; various grants and fellowships. Mem. Internat. Reading Assn. (state coordinator Hawaii 1980-83), Nat. Conf. Research in English, Hawaii Council Tchrs. English (pres. 1955-57, exec. sec. 1958-68), Ka Hui Heluhelu Council (pres. 1978-79), Phi Delta Kappa. Home: 3863 Lurline Dr Honolulu HI 96816 *What are the characteristics of a good teacher? The essential quality is caring about people. He must be knowledgeable, kind, patient, fair, articulate. He experiences a renewal of joy at the successes of his students.*

ALMASI, GEORGE STANLEY, electrical engineer; b. Budapest, Hungary, Oct. 8, 1938; came to U.S., 1948; s. Joseph Charles and Janina (Stollowa) A.; m. Carol Ann Freiberg, Aug. 28, 1965; 1 son, George Michael. B.S.E.E., Syracuse U., 1961; M.S.E.E., MIT, 1962, Ph.D. in E.E., 1966. Research staff mem. IBM Research Ctr., Yorktown Heights, N.Y., 1966—, group mgr., 1973-80, sr. mgr., 1980—. Patentee magnetic bubble sensor, 1972, contiguous disk devices, 1979. Coach Katonah Little League Mets, 1975-76; mem. St. Mary's Planning Com., 1979; pres. Katunah Village Improvement Soc., 1978-79; chmn. Katomah Neighborhood PA Com., 1981-82. Fellow IEEE. Republican. Roman Catholic. Office: IBM TJ Watson Research Center PO Box 218 Yorktown Heights NY 10598 *

ALMEIDA, LAURINDO, guitarist, composer; b. Brazil, Sept. 2, 1917; came to U.S., 1947, naturalized, 1961; s. Benjamin and Placedina (Araujo) A.; m. Maria M. Ferreira, May 20, 1944 (dec. Aug. 1970); m. Deltra Eamon, Aug. 3, 1971. Student, Escola Nacional de Muscica do Rio de Janeiro. Owner, operator Brazilliance Music Pub. Co., 1952—. Featured soloist, Stan Kenton Orch., 1947-50; guitarist motion picture prodns., 1949—; composer musical scores for TV; also motion pictures Maracaibo, 1956, Goodbye My Lady, 1957; rec. artist, Capitol, World Pacific, Decca, Orion and Concord records. Recipient cert. of appreciation Am. String Tchrs. Assn. Mem. ASCAP, AFTRA, Am. Songwriters Assn., Composers Guild Am., Nat. Acad. Rec. Arts and Scis. (bd. govs. classical music, 5 Grammy awards, 14 nominations), Acad. Motion Picture Writers and Producers, Am. Guitar Soc. (Vadah Olcott-Bickford Meml. award). Address: 4104 Witzel Dr Sherman Oaks CA 91423

ALMEN, LOUIS THEODORE, college president; b. Seattle, Dec. 20, 1925; s. Carl William and Agnes Louise (Hedeen) A.; m. Ardis Elaine Swanson, June 24, 1949; children: Peter, Mary, Ruth. B.A., Gustavus Adolphus Coll., 1946, D.D. (hon.), 1976; B.D., Augustana Theol. Sem., 1950; M.Th., Princeton Theol. Sem., 1955; postgrad., Union Theol. Sem., N.Y.C., 1960; Ph.D., State U. Iowa, h1963; L.H.D. (hon.), Lenoir Rhyne Coll., 1979. Ordained to ministry Lutheran Ch. Am.; pastor St. Bartholomew Luth. Ch., Elizabeth, N.J., 1950-53; instr. Upsala Coll., 1950-53; prof. Augustana Coll., Rock Island, Ill., 1953-67; chief exec. bd. coll. edn. Luth. Ch. Am., N.Y.C., 1967-73, exec. dir. div. profl. leadership, Phila., 1973-77; pres. Thiel Coll., Greenville, Pa., 1977—; bd. govs. Nat. Council Chs. of Christ, 1974-78; bd. dirs. Council Ind. Colls., Washington; pres. Luth. Ednl. Conf. N.Am., 1981-82; bd. dirs. div. mission in N.Am. Luth. Ch. Am.; adv. First Seneca Bank, Greenville and Oil City, Pa.; mem. exec. com. Ind. Colls. and Univs., Harrisburg,, Pa.; cons. in field. Editor: Drug Abuse and Use, 1979. Honors scholar Danforth Found., Luth. Ch. Am., Princeton Theol. Sem., State U. Iowa. Mem. Am. Assn. Higher Edn., Am. Acad. Religion, Am. Acad. Polit. and Social Sci., AAUP, Religious Edn. Assn. Club: Iroquois (Conneaut Lake, Pa.). Home: 40 Eagle St Greenville PA 16125 Office: Thiel Coll Greenville PA 16125

ALMEN, LOWELL GORDON, editor; b. Grafton, N.D., Sept. 25, 1941; s. Paul Orville and Helen Eunice (Johnson) A.; m. Sally Arlyn Clark, Aug. 14, 1965; children: Paul Simon, Cassandra Gabrielle. B.A., Concordia Coll., Moorhead, Minn., 1963; M.Div., Luther Theol. Sem., St. Paul, 1967; Litt.D., Capitol U., 1981. Ordained to ministry Lutheran Ch., 1967; pastor St. Peter's Luth. Ch., Dresser, Wis., 1967-69; asso. campus pastor, dir. communications Concordia Coll., Moorhead, Minn., 1969-74; mng. editor Luth. Standard ofcl. publ. Am. Luth. Ch., Mpls., 1974-78, editor, 1979—. Editor: World Religions and Christian Mission, 1967, Our Neighbor's Faith, 1968. Recipient Disting. Alumnus award Concordia Coll., 1982; Bush Found. grantee, 1972. Mem. Asso. Ch. Press, Evangel. Press Assn. Club: Minn. Press. Office: Luth Standard 426 S 5th St Box 1209 Minneapolis MN 55440

ALMENDROS, NESTOR, cinematographer; b. Barcelona, Spain, Oct. 30, 1930; s. Hermino and Maria (Cuyas) A. Ph.D., Havana (Cuba) U., 1955; student cinematoraphy and film editing, CCNY, 1956, Centro Sperimentale di Cinematografia, Rome, 1957. Tchr. Spanish Vassar Coll., 1957-59. Dir. documentary films for, ICAIC, Cuba, 1959-61; films photographed include La Collectioneuse, 1966, The Wild Child, 1969 (Best Photography award U.S. Assn. Film Critics), Claire's Knee, 1970, The Story of Adele H, 1975, The Marquise of O, 1975, Madame Rosa, 1977, The Last Metro, 1980 (Best Photography award French Acad. Motion Picture Arts and Techniques), Days of Heaven, 1979 (Best Photography award Am. Acad. Motion Picture Arts and Scis., U.S. Assn. Film Critics), Kramer vs Kramer, 1980, The Blue Lagoon, 1980, The Last Metro, 1981, Sophie's Choice, 1982; Author: A Man with a Camera, 1980, Improper Conduct, 1984. Decorated chevalier Order Arts and Letters, France, 1976. Mem. Am. Soc. Cinematographers.

ALMERS, WOLFHARD, physiology and biophysics educator; b. Helmstedt, W.Ger., May 29, 1943; came to U.S., 1966; s. Eberhard and Ute (Plathner) A.; m. Hilary M. Turnbull, May 17, 1967; children: Mattias, Lucy. Student, Free U. Berlin, 1963-66, Duke U., 1966-69; Ph.D., U. Rochester, 1971. Tutor Churchill Coll., Cambridge U., Eng., 1972-73; research scientist Cambridge U., 1971-74; asst. prof. physiology biophysics U. Wash., Seattle, 1974-78, assoc. proff., 1978-82, prof., 1982—. Contbr. articles to sci. jours.; mem. editorial bd.: Jour. Physiology, 1981—, Am. Jour. Physiology, 1981—. Muscular Dystrophy Assn. postdoctoral fellow, 1971-74; NIH grantee, 1974—; Muscular Dystrophy Assn. grantee, 1981—. Mem. AAAS, Soc. for Neurosci, Biophys. Soc., Physiol. Soc. Gt. Brit. (assoc.). Home: 825 35th Ave Seattle WA 98122 Office: Dept Physiology and Biophysics SJ-40 Seattle WA 98195

ALMGREN, FREDERICK JUSTIN, JR., mathematician; b. Birmingham, Ala., July 3, 1933; s. Frederick Justin and Sarah Cone (Wright) A.; m. Jean Ellen Taylor, Oct. 6, 1973; children—Robert Frederick, Ann Stewart, Karen Taylor. B.S. in Engring, Princeton U., 1955; Ph.D. in Math, Brown U., 1962. Instr. math. Princeton (N.J.) U., 1962-63, asst. prof., 1965-68, asso. prof., 1968-72, prof., 1972—; scholar Inst. Advanced Study, Princeton, 1963-65, 69, 74-75, 78, 81-82; exchange visitor Steklov Math. Inst., Leningrad, USSR, 1970. Author: Plateau's Problem, 1966; contbr. numerous articles in field to math. jours. Served with USN, 1955-58. Alfred P. Sloan fellow, 1968-70; Guggenheim Meml. fellow, 1974-75; NSF grantee, 1962—. Mem. Am. Math. Soc., Math. Assn. Am., Soc. Indsl. and Applied Math., AAAS. Home: 83 Riverside Dr Princeton NJ 08540 Office: Dept Math Fine Hall Princeton U Princeton NJ 08544

ALMGREN, HERBERT PHILIP, banker; b. Fairfield, Ala., Oct. 22, 1916; s. O. Philip and Lillie (Becker) A.; m. Jean R. Cleaveland, June 10, 1939; children—Caroline C. (Mrs. Douglass N. Ellis Jr.), Nancy B. (Mrs. Robert A. Killam). B.S. magna cum laude, Springfield Coll., 1938; postgrad., Columbia. Tchr. Rectory Sch., Pomfret, Conn., 1938-40; with Monarch Life Ins. Co. (and predecessor), 1940-63, v.p., 1958-63; with Shawmut First Bank & Trust Co. Hampden County, 1963—, sr. v.p., 1964-65, pres., 1965-68, pres., chief exec. officer, 1968-79, chmn., chief exec. officer, 1979-81, ret., 1981, also dir.; dir. Westmass Area Devel. Corp., Am. Pad & Paper Co., Holyoke, Mass., Am Pad Plus, Daniel O'Connell's. Past chmn. bd. Baystate Med. Center; corporator Springfield Boys Club, Springfield Jr. Achievement. Served to lt. (j.g.) USNR, 1943-46. Mem. Mass. Bankers Assn. (former pres.), Greater Springfield C. of C. (dir., past pres.). Clubs: Rotary; Colony (Springfield); Longmeadow Country. Office: 127 State St Springfield MA 01103

ALMIRALL, LLOYD VINCENT, lawyer; b. Bklyn., Nov. 9, 1907; s. Juan A. and Emma (Kuntz) A.; m. Catherine Lewerth, Sept. 17, 1937; children—Danne, Jan Almirall Olmer, Paul L., Irene (Mrs. Wayne Hobin). A.B., Hamilton Coll., Clinton, N.Y., 1929; LL.B., Harvard, 1932. Bar: N.Y. bar 1932. Since practiced in, N.Y.C.; partner firm Breed, Abbott & Morgan, 1946-76, ret. Trustee Lenox Sch., N.Y.C., 1946-59, pres., 1951-56; trustee Harvey Sch., Katonah; N.Y., 1948-76, Hamilton Coll., 1958-64. Mem. Mr. Haight Jr.'s Litchfield County Hounds (M.F.H.), Chi Psi. Clubs: Players, Harvard (N.Y.C.). Home: 4 Walnut Hill Rd PO Box 483 Ridgefield CT 06877

ALMODOVÁR, ISMAEL, university president; b. San Germán, P.R., Apr. 14, 1932; s. Juan B. and Celia (García) A.; m. Magdaline Sosnoski, Jan. 6, 1964; children: John, Liza, Andrew, Paul, Diana, Evelyn. B.Sc. magna cum laude, U. P.R., 1952; M.S. in Chemistry, Carnegie Inst. Tech., Pitts., 1958; Ph.D., Carnegie Mellon U., 1960; postdoctoral, Brookhaven Nat. Lab., Upton, N.Y., 1962; postgrad., Grad. Sch. Law, U. P.R., 1974. Instr. U. P.R., Mayaguez, 1952-53, 55-60, asst. prof., 1960-62, asso. prof., 1962-67, prof. chemistry, 1967—; dir. nuclear sci. and tech. div. Puar Nuclear Center, U. P.R., Mayaguez, 1960-62, dir. neutron diffraction program, 1963-65, dir. grad. studies, 1965-66, chmn. dept. chemistry, Rio Piedras, 1966-70; dean Coll. Natural Scis., 1970-74; dir. Center Energy and Environ. Research, 1976-77, pres., San Juan, 1977—; health scientist adminstr. div. research resources NIH, Bethesda, Md., 1974-75; cons. sci. programs P.R. Dept. Edn., 1967-70; instl. rep. Oak Ridge Associated Univs., 1970-72, 75; mem. P.R. State Bd. Examiners Practice of Chemistry, 1969-77, pres., 1976-77; mem. adv. com. marine affairs Nat. Assn. State Univs. and Land-Grant Colls., 1980-81; v.p. Assn. Caribbean Univs. and Research Insts., 1980—; peer evaluator NIH and NSF, Middle States Assn.; mem. Nat. Commn. Higher Edn. Issues, Am. Council on Edn., 1981; cons. Mem. adv. com. State Conservation Trust Fund, 1973-75; mem. tech. adv. com. Environ. Quality Bd. P.R., 1976-82; mem. Gov.'s Adv. Council on Energy, 1977-82 (on Edn.), 1978—, 1978—; bd. regents Nat. Library Medicine, NIH, 1978-82; trustee UNICA Found. Contbr. numerous articles to sci. jours. Served to 1st lt. U.S. Army, 1952-54; Korea. Mem. Am. Chem. Soc. (chpt. chmn. 1970—), Am. Inst. Chemists, Chemists Assn. P.R. (pres. 1968), Acad. Arts and Scis. P.R., P.R. Sci. Tchrs. Assn., Sigma Xi (chmn. chpt. 1962), Phi Kappa Phi. Office: GPO Box 4984-G San Juan PR 00936 *Where can man stand alone in this universe and be successful? Nowhere.*

ALMON, RENEAU PEARSON, state justice; b. Moulton, Ala., July 8, 1937; s. Nathaniel Lee and Mary (Johnson) A.; m. Deborah Pearson, June 27, 1974; children by previous marriage—Jonathan, Jason, Nathaniel; 1 stepson-Tommy Preer. B.S., U. Ala., 1959; LL.B., Cumberland Sch. Law Samford U., 1964. Bar: Ala. bar 1964. Judge 36th Jud. Circuit Ala., 1965-69, Ala. Ct. Criminal Appeals, 1969-75; justice Ala. Supreme Ct., Montgomery, 1975—. Mem. Am., Ala. bar assns., Am. Judicature Soc. Office: Judicial Bldg 445 Dexter Ave Montgomery AL 36130

ALMOND, CARL HERMAN, physician, educator; b. Latour, Mo., Apr. 1, 1926; s. Hugh Herman and Sylvia (Morrison) A.; m. Nancy Ginn, June 18, 1964; children: Carrie, Callie, Carl, Christopher. B.S., Washington U., St. Louis, 1949, M.D., 1953. Diplomate: Am. Bd. Surgery, Am. Bd. Thoracic Surgery. Rotating intern Los Angeles County Gen. Hosp., 1953-54; resident surgery U. Mich., Ann Arbor, 1954-56, jr. clin. instr. surgery, 1956-57, sr. clin. instr., 1957-58; fellow surg. pathology Barnes Hosp.-Washington U., St. Louis, 1956; sr. surg. resident in urology Baylor U. Affiliated Hosps., 1958-59; resident thoracic surgery U. So. Calif., Los Angeles, 1959, fellow thoracic surgery, 1962-63; staff surgeon Univ. Hosp., Columbia, Mo., 1959-78, dir. thoracic and cardiovascular surgery, 1968-77, VA Hosp., Columbia; fellow Brompton Hosp., London, Eng., 1961; asst. prof. surgery U. Mo. Sch. Medicine, Columbia, 1959-64, asso. prof., 1964-69, prof., chief thoracic and cardiovascular surgery, from 1969; now prof. and chmn. dept. surgery Sch. Medicine, U. S.C., Columbia, dir. gen. surgery residency program, 1979—; vis. prof. U. Geneva, Switzerland, 1972-73; Mem. med. adv. panel FAA, 1970-75; mem. U.S. Commn. on UNESCO, 1983. Contbr. articles to profl. jours. Served with USNR, 1944-52. Fellow A.C.S.; mem. AMA, Boone County Med. Soc., Columbia Med. Soc., S.C. Med. Assn., S.C. Thoracic Soc., Am. Assn. Med. Colls., Frederick H. Coller Surg. Soc., St. Louis Surg. Soc., Am. Coll. Cardiology, Am., S.C. heart assns., Am. Soc. Artificial Internal Organs, Soc. Med. Cons. to Armed Forces, Am. Coll. Chest Physicians, So. Thoracic Surg. Assn., Central Surg. Soc., Am. Assn. Thoracic Surgery, So. Surg. Assn., S.C. Surg. Soc., Chest Club, Soc. Surg. Chairmen, Marion S. DeWeese Surg. Soc., Southeastern Surg. Soc., Internat. Cardiovascular Soc., Soc. Thoracic Surgeons, Sigma Xi, Nu Sigma Nu, Sigma Chi. Home: 10 Sunturf Circle Columbia SC 29204 Office: U South Carolina School Medicine Dept Surgery Columbia SC 29208

ALMOND, GABRIEL ABRAHAM, political science educator; b. Rock Island, Ill., Jan. 12, 1911; s. David Moses and Lisa (Elson) A.; m. Maria Dorothea Kaufmann, Apr. 29, 1937; children: Richard J., Peter O., Susan J. Ph.B., U. Chgo., 1932, Ph.D., 1938. Fellow Social Sci. Research Council, 1935-36, 46; instr. polit. sci. Bklyn. Coll., 1939-42; with OWI, Washington, 1942-44, War Dept., ETO, 1945; research asso. Yale U. Inst. Internat. Studies, 1947-49, asso. prof. polit. sci., 1949-51, prof. polit. sci., 1959-63; asso. prof. internat. affairs Princeton, 1951-54, prof., 1954-57, prof. politics, 1957-59; prof. polit. sci. Stanford, 1963—, exec. head dept. polit. sci., 1964-68; Cons. Air U., 1948, Dept. State, 1950, Office Naval Research, 1951, Rand Corp., 1954-55, Sci. Adv. Bd. USAF, 1960-61; vis. prof. U. Tokyo, Japan, 1962; Overseas fellow Churchill Coll. U. Cambridge, 1972-73. Author: The American People and Foreign Policy, 1950, The Appeals of Communism, 1954, The Politics of the Developing Areas, 1960; author: (with Sidney Verba) The Civic Culture, 1963, (with G. Bingham Powell) Comparative Politics, 1966, Political Development, 1970, (with others) Crisis, Choice and Change, 1973, Comparative Politics Today, 1974, 80, 84, (with G. Bingham Powell) Comparative Politics; System, Process, Policy, 1978, (with Sidney Verba and others) The Civic Culture Revisited, 1980, (with others) Progress and its Discontents, 1982; Editor, author: The Struggle for Democracy in Germany, 1949. Recipient Travel and Study award Ford Found., 1962-63; fellow Center for Advanced Study in the Behavioral Scis., 1956-57; sr. fellow Nat. Endowment for Humanities, 1972-73. Fellow Am. Acad. Arts and Scis.; mem. Nat. Acad. Scis., Am. Philos. Soc., Social Sci. Research Council (bd. dirs., chmn. com. comparative politics), Am. Polit. Sci. Assn. (pres. 1965-66, James Madison award 1981), Am. Assn. Pub. Opinion Research, Acad. Polit. Sci. Home: 4135 Old Trace Rd Palo Alto CA 94306 Office: Stanford Univ Stanford CA 94305

ALMOND, JAMES LINDSAY, JR., judge; b. Charlottesville, Va., June 15, 1898; s. James Lindsay and Eddie Nicholas (Burgess) A.; m. Josephine Katherine Minter, Aug. 15, 1925. LL.B., U. Va., 1923; LL.D., Coll. William and Mary, 1959, Roanoke Coll., 1982, Christopher Newport Coll., 1982. Bar: Va. 1921. Practiced in, Roanoke, 1923-32; prin. Zoar High Sch., 1921-22; asst. pros. atty., Roanoke, 1930-33; Judge Hustings Ct., Roanoke, 1933-45; mem. 79th Congress, 2d session (fill vacancy); elected 80th Congress; mem. post office and civil service com.; atty. gen. Va., 1948-57; gov. State of Va., 1958-62; apptd. interim judge U.S. Ct. Customs and Patent Appeals, Washington, 1962-63, asso. judge, 1963-73, sr. judge, 1973-82, U.S. Ct. Appeals for Fed. Circuit, Washington, 1982—. Served with U.S. Army, World War I. Recipient DAR medal of honor Nat. Soc. DAR, 1983. Mem. Am. Bar Assn. (hon.), Va. Bar Assn., Richmond Bar Assn., United Comml. Travelers, Raven Soc., Delta Theta Phi, Alpha Kappa Psi, Omicron Delta Kappa. Democrat. Lutheran (tchr. men's bible class). Clubs: Mason (33 deg.), Shriner).

ALMOND, LINCOLN CARTER, U.S. attorney; b. Pawtucket, R.I., June 16, 1936; s. Thomas Clifton and Elsie (Carter) A.; m. Marilyn Ann Johnson, Oct. 11, 1958; children: Lincoln Douglas, Amy Elizabeth. B.S., U. R.I., 1958; U.S. Dist. Ct. R.I., 1962. Bar: R.I. 1962, U.S. Dist. Ct. R.I. 1962, U.S. Ct. Appeals (1st cir.) 1969. Sole practice, Providence, 1961-62; adminstr. Town of Lincoln, R.I., 1963-69; U.S. atty. Dist. R.I., Providence, 1969-78, 81—; sole practice, Providence, 1978-81. Chmn. 2d Pawtucket Area Indsl. Found.; moderator Saylesvile Fire Dist.; candiate R.I. Ho. Reps., 1968; candidate Gov., 1978. Mem. R.I. Bar Assn. (bd. govs. 1978-82). Republican. Episcopalian. Home: 12 Hillside Ave Lincoln RI 02865

ALMOND, PAUL, film director, producer; b. Montreal, Que., Can., Apr. 26, 1931; s. Eric and Irene Clarice (Gray) A.; m. Joan Elkins, Sept. 11, 1976; 1 son, Matthew James. Student, McGill U., Montreal, 1948-49; B.A., Balliol Coll., Oxford, 1952, M.A., 1954. TV producer-dir. CBC, Toronto, also in Los Angeles, N.Y.C., London, 1954-67; pres. Quest Films, Montreal, 1967—. Writer, producer, dir.: feature films Isabel, 1968, Act of the Heart, 1970 (Best Can. Dir.), Journey, 1972; dir.: Ups and Downs, 1982; Subject of book: (Janet Edsforth) Paul Almond, The Flame Within, 1973. Recipient Spl. diploma of merit, Prague, 1963; Genie as best Can. TV drama dir., 1980. Mem. Dirs. Guild Am., Dirs. Guild Can., Can. Assn. Motion Picture Producers. Anglican. 54 Malibu Colony Dr Malibu CA 90265

ALMY, THOMAS PATTISON, educator, physician; b. N.Y.C., Jan. 10, 1915; s. Don Robinson and Marie (Pattison) A.; m. Katharine Whitin Swift, Nov. 12, 1943; children: Susan, Anne, Christine. A.B., Cornell U., 1935, M.D., 1939; M.A. (hon.), Dartmouth Coll., 1970. Intern N.Y. Hosp., 1939-40; resident medicine, 1940-43; from asst. prof. to prof. medicine Cornell U. Med. Coll., 1946-68; Nathan Smith prof. medicine, chmn. dept. Dartmouth Med. Sch., 1968-73, Third Century prof., 1973—; disting. physician VA, 1982—; cons NIH, NRC, Am. Cancer Soc. Author articles in clin. physiology gastrointestinal disease. Recipient award of distinction Cornell U. Med. Coll. Alumni Assn., 1967. Master A.C.P. (bd. regents 1968-73); mem. Assn. Am. Physicians, Am. Soc. Clin. Investigation, Am. Gastroenterol. Assn. (pres. 1964, Julius Friedenwald medal 1976). Home: Stevens Rd Etna NH 03750 Office: VA Med Center White River Junction VT 05001

ALNES, ELLIS STEPHEN, journalist, researcher; b. Thief River Falls, Minn., Dec. 1, 1926; s. Lloyd T. and Shirley (Anderson) A.; m. Margaret Elizabeth Grinols, Dec. 17, 1948; children: Susan, Karen, Judith, Lee. B.A., U. Minn., 1949. U.P.I. reporter, Bismarck, N.D., 1949-54; reporter, bus. editor, Sunday editor Pioneer Press & Dispatch, St. Paul, 1954-67; exec. dir. Upper Midwest Council, 1979-82; pub., editor Minn. Jour., 1983—. Editorial writer, Mpls. Star, 1967-71; asso. editorial page editor, 1971-75; editorial page editor, 1975-79. Served with USNR, 1944-46. Office: 908 Park Ave Mahtomedi MN 55115

ALONSO, WILLIAM, population studies educator, demographer; b. Buenos Aires, Argentina, Jan. 29, 1933; married, 1959; 2 children. B.A., Harvard U., 1954, M.C.P., 1956; Ph.D., U. Pa., 1960. Asst. prof., assoc. prof. regional planning Harvard U., 1959-67, R. Saltonstall prof. population policy, dir. ctr. population studies, 1976—; mem. Inst. Urban and Regional Devel., U. Calif.-Berkeley, 1967-76, prof. regional planning, 1966-76; mem. Joint Ctr. for Urban Studies, M.I.T. and Harvard U., 1959-67; UN expert, prof. urban and regional planning, dir. dept. Bandung Inst. Tech., Indonesia, 1960-61; vis. prof. Central U. Venezuela, 1962; vis. lectr. Yale U., 1966; mem. Inter-Univ. Com. on Urban Econs., 1969—; cons. Urban Inst. and Rand corp., 1969—, IBRD, Ford Found., 1970—; mem. Nat. Acad. Sci. Adv. Com. on Dept. HUD, 1972—; adviser, lectr. Inst. Phys. Planning, Cuba, 1972. U.S. Dept. Com. on Econ. Devel. Adminstrn. grantee Inst. Urban and Regional Devel., U. Calif.-Berkeley, 1967—; grantee NSF, 1970—. Mem. Regional Sci. Assn. (v.p. 1969). Office: Ctr for Population Studies Harvard U Cambridge MA 02138 *

ALONZO, MARTIN VINCENT, mining company executive; b. N.Y.C., Apr. 8, 1931; s. Mariano and Mary (Traina) A.; m. Sabina Gallucci, June 7, 1952; children: Martin Vincent, Marlene, Sabrina. B.B.A. in Acctg. cum laude, Baruch Coll., City U. N.Y., 1952, M.B.A. in Fin. and Investments, 1971. C.P.A., N.Y. Accountant Eisner and Lubin (C.P.A.s), N.Y.C., 1952-57; treas., controller Credit-Am. Corp., N.Y.C., 1957-60; asst. v.p. indsl. time sales, financing and leasing A.J. Armstrong Co., Inc., N.Y.C., 1960-65; treas., sec. So. Nitrogen Co., Savannah, Ga., 1965-67; with AMAX Inc., Greenwich, Conn., 1967—, controller, 1970, v.p., 1973-78, sr. v.p. controls and adminstrn., 1978-80, pres. Indsl. Minerals div., 1981-82, exec. v.p. splty. and light metals ops., 1982—; dir. Alumax Inc. Bd. dirs. Greenwich Health Assn. Mem. Nat. Assn. Accountants (chmn. mgmt. acctg. practices com. 1976-79), Extractive Industries Luncheon Group (chmn. 1978-79), Fin. Acctg. Standards Bd., Am. Mining Congress (chmn. acctg. com. 1980—, mem. pension com.), Am. Inst. C.P.A.s, Fin. Execs. Inst., AIME, Phosphate Rock Export Assn. (dir.), Price Inst. for Entreprenurial Studies (dir.), Nat. Assn. Mfrs., U.S. C. of C., U.S. Council of Internat. C. of C., Japan Soc., Beta Alpha Psi, Beta Gamma Sigma. Republican. Roman Catholic. Office: AMAX Center Greenwich CT 06830

ALPEN, EDWARD LEWIS, biophysicist, educator; b. San Francisco, May 14, 1922; s. Edward Lawrence and Margaret Lilly (Shipley) A.; m. Wynella June Dosh, Jan. 6, 1945; children: Angela Marie, Jeannette Elise. B.S., U. Calif., Berkeley, 1946, Ph.D., 1950. Br. chief, then dir. biol. and med. scis. Naval Radiol. Def. Lab., San Francisco, 1952-68; mgr. environ. and life scis. Battelle Meml. Inst., Richland, Wash., 1968-69, asso. dir., then dir. Pacific N.W. div., 1969-75; dir. Donner Lab., U. Calif., Berkeley; also asso. dir. Lawrence Berkeley Lab., 1975—; prof. biophysics U. Calif., Berkeley, 1975—, prof. radiology, San Francisco, 1976—; mem. Nat. Council Radiol. Protection, 1969—; Mem. Gov. Wash. Council Econ. Devel., 1973-75; bd. dirs. Wash. Bd. Trade, 1973-76. Author papers, abstracts in field. Served to capt. USNR, 1942-46, 50-51. Recipient Navy Sci. medal, 1962, Disting. Service medal Dept. Def., 1963, Sustaining Members medal Assn. Mil. Surgeons, 1971; fellow Guggenheim Found., 1960-61; sr. fellow NSF, 1958-59. Fellow Calif. Acad. Scis.; mem. Bioelectomagnetics Soc. (pres. 1979-80), Am. Physiol. Soc., Radiation Research Soc., Soc. Exptl. Biology and Medicine, Biophys. Soc., Am. Philatelic Soc., Sigma Xi. Episcopalian. Home: 1182 Miller Ave Berkeley CA 94708 Office: 466 Donner U Calif Berkeley CA 94720

ALPER, ALBERT, consulting civil engineer; b. St. Louis, Oct. 12, 1912; s. Nathan W. and Anna (Schoenfeld) A.; m. Sylvia Lasky, Nov. 26, 1937; children—Cynthia Merle Raymond, Patricia Ann (Mrs. Norman Gold), Marc Howard. B.S.C.E., Mo. Sch. Mines and Metallurgy, 1936. Various engring. positions, 1936-46; structural engr. J. Gordon Turnbull, Inc. (Engrs.-Architects), St. Louis, 1946-49; design engr. Metz & Eason (Structural Engrs.), St. Louis, 1949-51; cons. structural engr., Creve Coeur, Mo., 1951-70; pres., chmn. bd. Alper Assos., Inc., 1970—. Structural engring. projects include St. Louis Planetarium. Fellow ASCE; mem. Am. Concrete Inst., ASTM, Nat. Soc. Profl. Engrs., Cons. Engrs. Council Mo. (dir. 1967-69, pres. 1981-82), Internat. Assn. Bridge and Structural Engrs. Home: 578 Sarah Ln Creve Coeur MO 63141 Office: 1023 Executive Pkwy Dr Saint Louis MO 63141

ALPER, ALLEN MYRON, precision materials company executive; b. N.Y.C., Oct. 23, 1932; s. Joseph and Pauline (Frohlich) A.; m. Barbara Marshall, Dec. 20, 1959; children: Allen Myron, Andrew Marshall. B.S., Bklyn. Coll., 1954; Ph.D. (Univ. fellow, Dyckman Inst. scholar, Univ. Pres's. scholar), Columbia U., 1957. Sr. mineralogist Corning Glass Works, N.Y., 1957-59, research mineralogist, 1959-62, mgr. ceramic research, sr. research asso., 1962-69; with GTE Sylvania Inc. div. Sylvania Inc., Towanda, Pa., 1969—, chief engr., 1971-72, dir. research and engring., 1972-78, mgr. ops., from 1978; now pres. GTE Walmet, Royal Oak, Mich.; mem. Pa. Gov's Adv. Panel on Materials, 1971—; chmn. adv. com. Materials Research Lab., Pa. State U.; mem. adhoc adv. com. Phase Equilibria Data Center, 1983. Editor: Phase Diagrams: Materials Science and Technology, 1970, High Temperature Oxides, 1970-71; editorial bd.: High Temperature Sci. jour, 1969—, High Temperature Chemistry, 1973—, Materials Handbook, 1974—; editor: Materials Sci. and Tech. Series, 1972—; contbr. articles to profl. jours. Mem. exec. bd. Gen. Sullivan council Boy Scouts Am. Recipient Bklyn. Coll. award Disting. Achievement, 1983; N.Mex. Bur. Mines. grantee, 1954-57; also fellow. Fellow Am. Ceramic Soc., Geol. Soc. Am., Am. Inst. Chemists; mem. Brit. Ceramic Soc., Am. Soc. Metals, Am. Chem. Soc., Sigma Xi. Presbyterian. Club: Towanda Country. Patentee in field. Home: 880 Great Oaks Blvd Rochester MI 48063 Office: GTE Walmet Royal Oak MI 48068

ALPER, HOWARD, chemistry educator; b. Montreal, Que, Can., Oct. 17, 1941; s. Max and Frema (Weinstein) A.; m. Anne Elizabeth, June 4, 1966; children: Ruth, Lara. B.Sc. in Chemistry with honors, Sir George Williams U., Can., 1963; Ph.D., McGill U., 1967. NATO postdoctoral fellow, 1967-68; asst. prof. SUNY-Binghamton, 1968-71, assoc. prof., 1971-74; assoc. prof. chemistry U. Ottawa, Ont., Can., 1975-77, prof., 1978—, chmn. dept., 1982—. Contbr. 155 articles to sci. jours. Recipient E.W.R. Steacie award Natural Scis. and Engring. Research Council Can., 1980. Mem. Am. Chem. Soc., Chem. Inst. Can. (inorganic chemistry award 1980), Chem. Soc. (London). Patentee in field (5). Office: 365 Nicholas St Ottawa ON Canada KIN 9B4

ALPER, JEROME MILTON, lawyer; b. N.Y.C., Aug. 26, 1914; s. David Samuel and Ethel (Gordon) A.; m. Janet Adrian Levy, Jan. 4, 1948 (dec.); children: Jonathan Louis, Alan Irwin, Andrew Michael; m. Muriel C. Pearl, Jan. 17, 1981. B.A., U. Chattanooga, 1934; J.D., U. Chgo., 1937. Bar: Tenn., Ill., D.C. Practiced in, Chattanooga, 1938; atty. SEC, 1939-50; with firm Alper, Schoene Horkan & Mann, Washington, 1950—; counsel Joint Transp. Commn. for Negotiation of Washington Met. Area Transit Regulation Compact and Washington Met. Area Transit Authority Compact, 1959-66; Counsel Gov.'s Steering Com. on Mass Transp. for Balt. Met. Area, 1967-69. Contbr. articles to profl. jours. Pres. Montgomery County Art Center, Inc.; chmn. bus. com. Folger Shakespeare Library, 1975-76; Trustee Urban Am., Inc., 1964-67, Am. Planning and Civic Assn., 1960-64. Served to lt. comdr. USNR, 1941-45; ETO; PTO. Mem. Am., D.C., Tenn., Fed. Power bar assns., Bar Assn. of D.C., Am. Judicature Soc. Jewish religion (dir. temple 1954-58). Clubs: Nat. Lawyers, Nat. Democratic (Washington). Office: 818 18th St Washington DC 20006

ALPER, JONATHAN L., theatre executive; b. Washington, Sept. 14, 1950; s. Jerome M. and Janet (Levy) A. B.A.l, Amherst Coll., 1971; cert., Webber-Douglas Acad., London, 1974. Lit. mgr., dir. Folger Theatre Group, Washington, 1975-78; lit. mgr. Manhattan Theatre Club, N.Y.C., 1980—; dramaturg Sundance Playwriting Conf., Sundance, Utah, 1982—. Dir.: plays Safe House, 1978, Hamlet, 1978, Teeth N'Smiles, 1977, Alls Well That Ends Well, 1976. Mem. Phi Beta Kappa. Home: 785 W End Ave Apt 10A New York NY 10020 Office: Manhattan Theatre Club 321 E 73d St New York NY 10021

ALPER, MERLIN LIONEL, financial executive; b. Bklyn., May 25, 1932; s. James B. and Rose (Mellis) A.; m. Elaine R. Honig, Dec. 21, 1957; children: Jerome Eric, Alyssa Ellen. B.B.A., Adelphi U., 1955. C.P.A., N.Y. With Arthur Andersen & Co., N.Y.C., 1955-68, comml. audit mgr., 1963-68; dir. fin. controls ITT, N.Y.C., 1968-73, asst. comptroller, 1973, corporate v.p., 1979; ITT Europe, Inc., 1978-84; corporate v.p., comptroller ITT Telecommunications Corp., 1984—. Served with Chem. Corps AUS, 1956-58. Named to Adelphi U. Alumni Acad. of Distinction, 1984. Mem. Am. Inst. C.P.A.'s, N.Y. State Soc. C.P.A.'s, Nat. Assn. Accts. (dir. N.Y. chpt. 1965-66), Fin. Execs. Inst. Office: 320 Park Ave New York NY 10022

ALPER, THELMA GORFINKLE, psychologist, educator; b. Chelsea, Mass., July 24, 1908; d. David and Mollie (Herman) Gorfinkle; m. Abraham T. Alper, Apr. 1, 1932. A.B., Wellesley Coll., 1929, A.M., 1933; Ph.D., Radcliffe Coll., 1943. Diplomate: Am. Bd. Examiners Profl. Psychology. Departmental asst. Wellesley Coll., 1929-42, asso. prof., 1952, prof., 1954-73, Helen J. Sanborn prof. psychology, 1969-73, prof. emeritus, 1973—, chmn. dept. psychology, 1963-67; instr. Harvard, 1943-46, lectr., 1946-48; tutor Radcliffe Coll., 1942-43; asso. prof. Clark U., 1948-52; psychologist Judge Baker Guidance Center, 1959-79, emeritus, 1979—; also hon. dir. Wellesley Human Relations Service; pvt. practice individual adult psychotherapy. Former dir.

Internat. Inst. in, Spain. Contbr. articles profl. publs. Trustee Rosenfeld Found. Fellow Am. Psychol. Assn., Mass. Psychol. Assn. (pres. 1952-54, career contbn. award 1975), New Eng. Psychol. Assn. (pres. 1970-71); mem. Phi Beta Kappa, Sigma Xi. Home: 55 Harvard Ave Brookline MA 02146

ALPERN, MATHEW, physiological optics educator; b. Akron, Ohio, Sept. 22, 1920; s. Aaron Harry and Goldie (Ray) A.; m. Rebecca Ann Elsner, Aug. 17, 1951; children: Bowen Lewis, Goldie Ann, Barbara Rachel, Aaron Harry. Student, U. Akron, 1937-38, 42; O.D., No. Ill. Coll. Optometry, 1941; B.M.E., U. Fla., 1946; Ph.D., Ohio State U., 1950. Asst. prof. optometry Pacific U., 1951-55; instr. ophthalmology U. Mich., 1955-56; asst. prof. physiol. optics Med. Sch.; also asst. prof. psychology Coll. Lit., Scis. and Arts, 1956-58, assoc. prof. physiol. optics, also assoc. prof. psychology, 1958-63, prof. physiol. optics dept. ophthalmology and physiology, also prof. psychology, 1963—; NIH spl. fellow, physiol. lab. U. Cambridge, Eng., 1961-62; vis. scientist study sect. NIH, Bethesda, Md., 1970-74; vis. prof. psychobiology Fla. State U., 1968-69; Anna Berliner lectr. Pacific U., 1978, Japanese Soc. Ophthalmic Optics, Kagoshima, Japan, 1980; vis. scientist physics div. NRC Can., 1983-84; mem. Am. Com. on Optics and Visual Physiology, 1969—; mem. sci. adv. bd. Nat. Retinitis Piementosa Found., 1972—. Author: (with others) Sensory Processes, 1966; Contbr. articles to profl. jours.; assoc. editor: Jour. of Optical Soc. Am., 1982-83. Fellow Optical Soc. Am. (Edgar D. Tillyer medal 1984); mem. Am. Physiol. Soc., Am. Psychol. Assn., Soc. Exptl. Psychologists, Assn. Research in Vision and Ophthalmology (Friedenwald award 1974, trustee 1979-83, v.p. 1983), Biophys. Soc. Jewish. Home: 3545 Woodland Rd Ann Arbor MI 48104

ALPEROVITZ, GAR, author; b. Racine, Wis., May 5, 1936; s. Julius and Emily (Bensman) A.; m. Sharon Sosnick, Aug. 29, 1976; children by previous marriage: Kari Fai, David Joseph. B.S. in History, U. Wis., 1958; M.A. in Econs, U. Cal. at Berkeley, 1960; Ph.D. in Polit. Economy, U. Cambridge, Eng., 1964. Congl. asst., 1961-62; mem. U.S. Senate staff, 1964-65; spl. asst. Dept. State, 1965-66; fellow King's Coll., Cambridge (Eng.) U., 1964-68, Inst. Politics Harvard, 1965-68, Brookings Instn., 1966, Inst. Policy Studies, 1968-69; co-dir. Cambridge (Mass.) Inst., 1968-71; co-dir. exploratory project econ. alternatives, 1973—; co-dir. Nat. Center Econ. Alternatives, 1978—; guest prof. Notre Dame U., 1982-83. Author: Atomic Diplomacy: Hiroshima and Potsdam, 1965, Cold War Essays, 1970, Strategy and Program, 1973, Rebounding America, 1984; also articles. Home: 2317 Ashmead Pl NW Washington DC 20009 Office: 2000 P St NW Suite 300 Washington DC 20036

ALPERS, DAVID HERSHEL, physician, educator; b. Phila., May 9, 1935; s. Bernard Jacob and Lillian (Sher) A.; m. Melanie Goldman, Aug. 12, 1977; children: Ann, Ruth, Barbara. B.A., Harvard U., 1956, M.D., 1960. Intern Mass. Gen. Hosp., Boston, 1960-61, resident in internal medicine, 1961-62; instr. medicine Harvard U., 1965-67, asso. in medicine, 1967-68, asst. prof., 1968-69; asst. prof. medicine Washington U., St. Louis, 1969-72, asso. prof., 1972-73, prof., 1973—, dir. GI div., 1969—. Asso. editor: Jour. Clin. Investigation, 1977-82; contbr. articles and revs. to profl. jours., chpts. to books. Served with USPHS, 1962-64. Mem. Am. Soc. Clin. Investigation, Am. Assn. Physicians, Am. Gastroent. Assn., Am. Soc. Biol. Chemists, Am. Fedn. Clin. Research. Office: 660 S Euclid St Saint Louis MO 63110

ALPERT, DANIEL, physicist, educator; b. Hartford, Conn., Apr. 10, 1917; s. Elias and Dora (Prechepa) A.; m. Natalie L. Boyle, Jan. 12, 1942; children—Amy Vincell, Laura Jane. B.S., Trinity Coll., Hartford, 1937, D.Sc. (hon.), 1957; Ph.D., Stanford, 1942. Research physicist Westinghouse Research Lab., Pitts., 1942-50, mgr. physics dept., 1950-55, asso. dir., 1955-57; prof. physics U. Ill. at Urbana, 1957—; dir. Coordinated Sci. Lab., 1959-65; dean Grad. Coll., 1965-72; dir. Center for Advanced Study; assoc. dir. Computer-Based Edn. Research Lab., 1972—. Author articles on ultrahigh vacuum tech., surface physics, computer based edn., sci., tech. and society. Mem. Wilkins Twp. Sch. Bd., 1946-56, Allegheny County Sch. Bd., 1956-57, Def. Sci. Bd., 1963-72; Trustee Trinity Coll., Inst. Def. Analyses. Recipient Newcomb Cleveland award AAAS, 1954; Gaede-Langmuir award Am. Vacuum Soc., 1980. Mem. Am. Phys. Soc., AAAS, Phi Beta Kappa, Sigma Xi. Home: 402 W Pennsylvania Ave Urbana IL 61801

ALPERT, DAVID JONATHAN, orchestra administrator; b. Boston, June 19, 1957; s. Victor and Dorothy Lillian (Rosenberg) A.; m. Quincy Cotton, June 27, 1982. B.A., NYU, 1979; M.B.A., Springfield, Mass., 1981. Fellow Am. Symphony Orch. League, Washington, 1981-82; devel. dir. Buffalo Philharm., 1982-83, orch. mgr., 1983—. Fellow Nat. Endowment for Arts, 1980. Mem. Am. Symphony Orch. League. Democrat. Jewish. Office: Buffalo Philharmonic Orch 71 Symphony Circle PO Box 905 Buffalo NY 14222

ALPERT, HERB, record company executive, musician; b. Los Angeles, Mar. 31, 1935; s. Louis and Tillie (Goldberg) A.; m. Sharon Mae Lubin, Aug. 5, 1956 (div.); children: Dore, Eden; m. Lani Hall; 1 dau., Aria. Student, U. So. Calif. Co-owner, pres. A & M Record Co., 1962—. Leader, trumpeter, arranger mus. group, Tijuana Brass, 1962—; Numerous recs. including Fandango, Magic Man, Rise, Beat of the Brass, Lonely Bull, Solid Brass, South of the Border, What Now My Love, Whipped Cream. Served with AUS, 1955-57. Named one of Top Artists on Campus (album sales), 1968. Address: care A and M Records 1416 N LaBrea Ave Hollywood CA 90028 *

ALPERT, HOLLIS, writer; b. Herkimer, N.Y., Sept. 24, 1916; s. Abram and Myra (Carroll);; s. Abram and Myra (Alpert). Student, New Sch. Social Research, 1946-47. Book reviewer Sat. Rev., N.Y. Times, others, 1947-59; film critic Sat. Review, after 1950, Woman's Day, 1953-60; asso. fiction editor New Yorker, 1950-56; contbg. editor Woman's Day, 1956-69; mng. editor (World Mag.), after 1972, film editor, lively arts editor, after 1973; editor Am. Film, 1975—; Algur Meadows Disting. vis. prof. So. Meth. U., 1982; Past dir. Edward MacDowell Assn. Author: The Summer Lovers, 1958, Some Other Time, 1960, The Dreams and the Dreamers, 1962, For Immediate Release, 1963, The Barrymores, 1964, The Claimant, 1968, The People Eaters, 1971, Smash, 1973, (under name Robert Carroll) A Disappearance, 1974; Editor: The Actors Life-Journals, Charlton Heston, 1978; Contbr.: numerous short stories to mags. including Harper's Bazaar. Served to 1st lt. AUS, 1942-46. Recipient Critic's award Screen Dirs.' Guild Am., 1957. Mem. Nat. Soc. Film Critics (chmn. 1972-73). Address: Box 142 Shelter Island NY 11964

ALPERT, JOSEPH STEPHEN, physician, educator; b. New Haven, Feb. 1, 1942; s. Zelly Charles and Beatrice Ann (Kopsofsky) A.; m. Helle Mathiasen, Aug. 6, 1965; children: Eva Elisabeth, Niels David. B.A. magna cum laude, Yale U., 1963; M.D. cum laude, Harvard U., 1969. Diplomate: Am. Bd. Internal Medicine (cardiovascular disease). Successively intern, resident in internal medicine, fellow in cardiovascular disease Peter Bent Brigham Hosp.-Harvard U. Med. Sch., Boston, 1969-74, dir. Samuel A. Levine cardiac unit, asst. prof. medicine, 1976-78; prof., dir. div. cardiovascular medicine U. Mass. Med. Sch., Worcester, 1978—; cons. W. Roxbury VA Hosp., Boston; sec., treas. med. staff U. Mass. Med. Center, 1979-81, pres. med. staff, 1981-82. Author: The Heart Attack Handbook, 1978, Cardiovascular Physiopathology, 1984; co-author: Manual of Coronary Care, 1977, 80, Manual of Cardiovascular Diagnosis and Therapy, 1980, Valvular Heart Disease, 1981; assoc. editor: Jour. History of Medicine and Allied Scis, 1977-80; editorial cons., Little, Brown & Co.; mem. editorial bd., Jour. Am. Coll. Cardiology, 1983—; contbr. numerous articles med. jours. Served to lt. comdr. USNR, 1974-76. Decorated Commendation medal, 1976; recipient Gold medal U. Copenhagen, 1968, Edward Rhodes Stitt award San Diego Naval Hosp., 1976, George W. Thorn award Peter Bent Brigham Hosp., 1977; Fulbright scholar, Copenhagen, 1963-64; USPHS-Mass. Heart Assn. fellow, 1971-72; NIH spl. research fellow, 1972-73. Fellow A.C.P., Am. Coll. Cardiology, Am. Coll. Chest Physicians (gov. for Mass. 1983-86); mem. Am. Heart Assn. (fellow council clin. cardiology), AAAS, Am. Assn. History Medicine, Am. Fedn. Clin. Research, Aesculapian Club, Phi Beta Kappa, Sigma Xi, Alpha Omega Alpha. Home: 55 Nathan Rd Newton Center MA 02159 Office: 55 Lake Ave N Worcester MA 01605 *I have lived my life following 3 rules: (1) maintain enthusiasm for living and learning; (2) love family and friends; and (3) work hard.*

ALPERT, NORMAN, chemical company executive; b. Phila., May 5, 1921; s. Barnet and Celia A.; m. Adeline Edna Gushman, Apr. 9, 1948; children: Rosalind Alice, Barbara Naomi. A.B. in Chemistry, Temple U., 1942, M.A., 1947; Ph.D. (AEC research fellow 1948-49), Purdue U., 1949. Devel. engr. Publicker Industries, Phila., 1942-45; group head Texaco, Inc., Beacon, N.Y., 1949-59; div. mgr. Exxon Inc., Linden, N.J., 1959-79; v.p., dir. research Hooker Chem. Co., Grand Island, N.Y., 1979-82; v.p. spl. environ. projects Occidental Chem. Corp., Niagara Falls, N.Y., 1982-84, v.p. corp. environ. affairs, 1984—. Author. Mgr. Career Explorer Post local Boy Scouts Am., 1981. Mem. Am. Chem. Soc., Soc. Automotive Engrs., Niagara Frontier Assn. Research and Devel. Dirs. Patentee in field. Home: 4060 Lower River Rd Youngstown NY 14174 Office: Occidental Chem Corp Niagara Falls NY 14302

ALPERT, NORMAN JOSEPH, merchandising executive; b. Cleve., Mar. 12, 1931; s. Hyman and Jessie (Abramson) A.; m. Shirley Marcia Forman, Dec. 25, 1956; children: Gary, Andrea. Student, Phoenix Coll., 1952-54; B.A., Ariz. State U., 1956. Store mgr. Fed. Mart, San Diego, 1970-71, dir. catalog, 1971-74, furniture and traffic appliance buyer, 1974-76, v.p. gen. merchandising, 1976-78, sr. v.p., 1978-81; ptnr. retail chain, San Diego, 1981—; bd. dirs. Fed. Mart Credit Union, 1979—. Served with Signal Corps, U.S. Army, 1950-52. Democrat. Jewish. Clubs: Masons, Shriners, Legion of Honor, Elks. Home: 4365 Mount Abernathy St San Diego CA 92117 Office: 7961 Clairemont Mesa Blvd San Diego CA 92111

ALPERT, SEYMOUR, physician; b. N.Y.C., Apr. 20, 1918; s. Louis and Ida (Freedman) A.; m. Cecile Bernadine Cohen, Sept. 7, 1941. A.B., Columbia U., 1939; M.D., SUNY, Downstate Med. Center, 1943; LL.D. (hon.), George Washington U., 1984. Diplomate: Am. Bd. Anesthesiology. Intern Beth Israel Hosp., N.Y.C., 1943-44; resident in anesthesiology Gallinger Mcpl. Hosp., Washington, 1946-47; mem. faculty dept. anesthesiology George Washington U. Sch. Medicine and Hosp., Washington, 1948—, prof., 1961-83, prof. emeritus, 1983—; v.p. for devel. George Washington U., 1969-83; cons. in anesthesiology Walter Reed Army Hosp., Washington, 1948-83, VA Hosp., 1948-70, D.C. Gen. Hosp., 1948-69, Mead Dental Hosp., 1949-69; dir. Jefferson Fed. Savs. and Loan Assn., 1979-82; adv. bd. Washington Fed. Savs. & Loan, 1982—. Contbr. articles to med. jours. Bd. govs. Hewbrew U., Jerusalem, 1968—; bd. govs. State of Israel Bonds, 1964—, nat. chmn. med. div., 1969—; bd. dirs. Israel Investors Corp., 1965-82, exec. com., 1974-82; bd. dirs. Am. Friends of Hebrew U., 1966—, chmn. med. div., 1969—, v.p., 1969—; bd. dirs. Council Jewish Fedn. and Welfare Funds, 1966-73; examining physician Met. Police Boys Clubs, 1952-76; pres. United Jewish Appeal, 1966-67, exec. com., 1955—; bd. dirs. United Givers Fund, 1972-74; exec. com. Jewish Community Council, 1958-75; bd. mgrs. Adas Israel Congregation, 1963—; bd. dirs. Kaufmann Camp for Boys and Girls, 1964-78, Jewish Community Found., 1966—; v.p. Jewish Community Found., 1968-69; vice chmn. United Jewish Endowment Fund, 1984—. Served to capt. AUS, 1944-46. Recipient Man of Yr. award State of Israel Bonds, 1964; Freedom award, 1970; Disting. Service award Phi Delta Epsilon, 1971, 73; Torch of Learning award Am. Friends of Hebrew U., 1975; Med. award United Jewish Appeal, 1980. Fellow Am. Coll. Anesthesiology; mem. Am. Soc. Anesthesiologists (dir. 1963-66, trustee Wood Library Mus. Anesthesiology 1968-74, v.p. 1970-74), Md.-D.C. Soc. Anesthesiologists (pres. 1968-69), AMA, Med. Soc. D.C. (mem. numerous coms.), Jacobi Med. Soc., Pan Am. Med. Soc. (pres. 1967), Assn. Am. Med. Colls. (co-dir. nat. med. library study 1965-66), Assn. Univ. Anesthetists, Internat. Anesthesia Research Soc., Phi Delta Epsilon (nat. pres. 1961-62, exec. com. 1961—, exec. sec. 1963-72, v.p. bd. trustees 1972-73, pres. bd. trustees 1973-74). Home: 2801 New Mexico Ave NW Washington DC 20007

ALPERT, WARREN, corporate executive; b. Boston, Dec. 2, 1920; s. Goodman and Tena (Horowitz) A. B.S. Boston U, 1942; M.B.A., Harvard U., 1947. Mgmt. trainee Standard Oil Co. of Calif., 1947-48; financial specialist The Calif. Oil Co., 1948-52; pres. Warren Petroleum Co., 1952-54; now chmn. bd.; founder, pres., chmn. bd. Warren Equities, Inc., from 1954; pres., chmn. Ritz Tower Hotel; chmn. bd. Kenyon Oil Co., Inc., Mid-Valley Petroleum Corp., Puritan Oil Co., Inc., Drake Petroleum Co., Inc.; Mem. of U.S. Com. for UN, 1958; exec. com. Small Bus. Adminstrn., 1958; asst. sec. of state U.S. AID, 1962; Former trustee, mem. exec. com. Boston U.; trustee Emerson Coll.; former v.p. Petroleum Marketing Edn. Found.; bd. dirs. Assos. of Harvard Bus. Sch.; mem. com. for resource and devel. Harvard Med. Sch. Served with Signal Intelligence AUS, 1943-45. Andrew Wellington Cordier fellow Sch. Internat. Affairs, Columbia U. Mem. Am. Petroleum Industry 25 Year Club, Young Presidents Orgn (past dir.), Am. Petroleum Inst. (dir. mktg. div.). Clubs: Harvard Business School (exec. com., dir., bd. govs., pres. 1960-61), Harvard (N.Y.C.); Harvard (Boston); Friars, Atrium. Home: 465 Park Ave New York NY 10022 Office: Warren Equities Inc 10 E 53d St New York NY 10022

ALPHER, RALPH ASHER, physicist; b. Washington, Feb. 3, 1921; s. Samuel and Rose (Maleson) A.; m. Louise Ellen Simons, Jan. 28, 1942; children: Harriet Alpher Lebetkin, Victor. B.S. George Washington U, 1943; M.S., 1945; Ph.D., 1948. Physicist Bur. Ordnance and Naval Ordnance Lab., U.S. Navy, Washington, 1940-44, Applied Physics Lab., Johns Hopkins U., Silver Spring, Md., 1944-55, Gen. Electric Research and Devel. Center, Schenectady, 1955—; adj. prof. Rensselaer Poly. Inst., 1958-63. Contbr. articles to books and profl. jours. in fields astrophysics, cosmology, physics of fluids. Bd. dirs. Mohawk-Hudson Council for Ednl. TV, 1974-80, 82—, chmn., 1978-80; bd. dirs. Dudley Obs., Union U., Albany, N.Y., 1968-72, 80—. Recipient Magellanic Premium Am. Philos. Soc., 1975; Georges Vanderlinden prize Belgian Royal Acad. Scis., Letters and Fine Arts, 1975; John Price Wetherill medal Franklin Inst., 1980. Fellow Am. Phys. Soc. (councillor-at-large 1979-82, exec. com. 1980-81), AAAS; mem. Fedn. Am. Scientists, Sigma Xi. Club: Internat. Torch. Home: 2159 Orchard Park Dr Schenectady NY 12309 Office: General Electric Research and Devel Center PO Box 8 Schenectady NY 12301

ALPS, GLEN EARL, educator, printmaker; b. Loveland, Colo., June 20, 1914. B.A., U. No. Colo.; M.F.A., U. Wash.; postgrad., U. Iowa. Prof. art U. Wash. Author: works included in numerous art and print books. The Collagraph; Work represented in permanent collections, Mus. Modern Art, N.Y.C., Phila. Art Mus., Chgo. Art Inst., Los Angeles County Art Mus., Library of Congress, others; sculpture includes panels, Seattle Public Library, 1960, fountains, Seattle Mcpl. Bldg., 1961, First Christian Ch, Greeley, Colo., 1962, others; numerous exhbns. prints. Tamarind fellow; Ford Found. fellow; recipient Wash. Gov.'s award. Mem. NW Printmakers (pres. 1951-53, 62-64). Address: 6523 40th Ave NE Seattle WA 98115

ALSAKER, ELWOOD CECIL, meat packing co. exec.; b. Rosholt, S.D., Oct. 31, 1924; s. Conrad Peter and Edla Victoria (Wass) A.; m. Virginia Cumming, Sept., 1947. B.B.A., U. Minn., 1948. With George A. Hormel & Co., Austin, Minn., 1948—, now sr. v.p., treas.; dir. First Bank of Austin, Minn.; Dir. Hormel Found. Dir. Austin YMCA. Served with U.S. Army, 1944-46. Republican. Lutheran. Club: Austin Country (dir.). Home: 800 1st Dr NW Austin MN 55912 Office: PO Box 800 Austin MN 55912

ALSBERG, DIETRICH ANSELM, electrical engineer; b. Kassel, Germany, June 5, 1917; came to U.S., 1939, naturalized, 1943; s. Adolf and Elisabeth (Hofmann) A.; m. Glenna Rose Le Baron, Nov. 6, 1942; children: Peter Allyn, Ronald Ashley, Terry Wayne, David James. B.S. in E.E, Tech. U., Stuttgart, 1938; postgrad., Case Sch. Applied Sci., Cleve., 1939-40. Engr. Wright Tool and Forge Co., Barberton, Ohio, 1940-41, Bridgwater Machine Co., Akron, 1941-43; with Bell Labs., Holmdel, N.J., 1945-82, head various depts., 1965-82, head microwave transmission dept., 1977-80, transmission studies dept., 1980-82; cons., 1982—. Contbr. articles to profl. jours. Mem. Berkeley Heights (N.J.) Bd. Edn., 1955-58; chmn. Environ. Commn., Berkeley Heights, 1971-76. Served with U.S. Army, 1943-45. Fellow IEEE. Methodist. Patentee in field of communications, electromagnetic waves, missile and space guidance. Home: 123 Pine St Lincroft NJ 07738

ALSCHULER, SAM, lawyer; b. Aurora, Ill., June 16, 1913; s. Benjamin P. and Lillian (Reinheimer) A.; m. Winifred King, Feb. 8, 1939; children: Albert W., Therese A. (Mrs. Richard N. Hale). A.B., U. Wis., 1933; J.D., U. Chgo., 1935. Bar: Ill. 1935, U.S. Supreme Ct. 1953. Practiced in, Aurora, 1935—; partner Alschuler, Putnam, McWethy, Funkey & Grometer, P.C., 1935—. Mem. Aurora Planning Commn., 1954-79; chmn. United Fund, 1966; vice chmn., dir. Kane County Council for Econ. Opportunity, 1966-69; Corp. counsel City of Aurora, 1961-65; Pres., trustee Aurora chpt. Ill. Assn. Crippled, 1948-63, 75—, bd. dirs., 1948-63, pres., 1952; v.p., bd. dirs. United Community Services Aurora, 1959-68; governing mem., bd. dirs. Aurora Hosp. Assn., 1940—. Served with AUS, 1944-45. Mem. Am., Ill., Kane County bar assns., Am. Judicature Soc., Greater Aurora C. of C. (past pres., dir.), Sigma Delta Chi, Zeta Beta Tau. Democrat. Clubs: Elk, Moose, Rotarian., Union League. Home: 119 S Buell Ave Aurora IL 60506 Office: 32 Water St Mall Aurora IL 60507 *Living and practising law in a small city have provided the means of meeting, serving and working with many people, both professionally and otherwise. I like to think that over the years I have helped those people at least somewhat, and that thought has given me considerable satisfaction. Although such a life limits the opportunities for fame and fortune, it has made for closer ties, I feel, with family, friends, clients and people generally than would have been possible in a metropolis. I have never regretted my decision, after law school, to come home.*

ALSDORF, JAMES WILLIAM, manufacturing executive; b. Chgo., Aug. 16, 1913; s. Anthony James and Camilie (Lederer) A.; m. Barbara Brach, Aug. 17, 1935 (div. Jan 2, 1950); children: Gregg, Lynne, Jeffery, James; m. Marilynn Markham, 1952. Student, Wharton Sch. Finance and Commerce, U. Pa., 1932-34. Chmn., dir. Alsdorf Internat. Ltd., Chgo.; Pres, and dir. A.J. Alsdorf Corp. (exporters and internat. mchts.); chmn. emeritus Cory Food Services, Inc. (mfrs.), Chgo.; also past officer, dir. subsidiaries and divs. Fresh'nd-Aire Co., Nicro Steel Products Co., Autopoint Co., Chgo.; dir., chmn. exec. com., v.p., sec. Grindmaster of Ky., Inc.; past. pres., treas., dir. Cory Sales Corp., Chgo., Cory Coffee Service Plan, Inc., Cory Coffee Service Plan, Toronto, Ont., Can.; pres., dir. Cory AG, Zurich, Switzerland,; Cory Kaffee Serviceplan, Zurich; past treas., dir. Cory Corp. (Can.) Ltd., Toronto, Ont.; dir. Cory Still Internat. Ltd., London, Unarco Industries, Inc., Hyatt Internat. Corp., Chgo.; past dir. NK Cory AB, Stockholm, Sweden,; Cory Coffee Service A/S, Oslo, Norway, OY Cory Coffee Service AB, Helsinki, Finland; past chmn. bd., dir. Flavor-Seal Corp., Chgo.; past pres., dir. Mitchell Mfg. Co. (and subsidiaries), Chgo. Mem. nat. com. U. Art Mus., U. Calif., Berkeley; mem. exec. com. of adv. council Snite Mus. Art, U. Notre Dame; mem. citizens bd. U. Chgo.; mem. collectors com. Nat. Gallery Art, Washington; asso. Rehab. Inst. Chgo.; mem. Mid-Am. com. Internat. Bus. and Govt. Cooperation, Inc.; mem. univ. library council Northwestern U. Library, Evanston, Ill.; past mem. of Gov. Ill.'s Com. Trade Expansion.; Pres., dir. Alsdorf Found., Chgo.; past bd. dirs. World Wildlife Fund, Washington; mem. 1001 club; trustee Menninger Found. of Topeka; past chmn., life trustee, life gov., disting. benefactor, chmn. nominating com., vice chmn. exec. com. Art Inst. Chgo.; bd. dirs., v.p. Sarah Siddons Soc., Chgo.; life trustee benefactor Indpls. Mus. Art; opus mem. Ravinia Festival Assn.; subscribing mem. Am. Craftsmen's Council, N.Y.C.; vis. com. div. humanities U. Chgo.; mem. adv. bd. Martin D'Arcy Gallery Art, Loyola U., Chgo.; mem. Far Eastern Studies com. U. Chgo., also Pres.'s Fund com.; past governing mem. Orchestral Assn.; life mem. Field Mus. Natural History, Chgo.; mem. internat. council Mus. Modern Art, N.Y.C.; v.p., vice chmn., contbg. mem., trustee com. Am. Assn. Museums, Washington; bd. govs Dumbarton Oaks, Washington; vice chmn. fine arts adv. com. Fed. Res. Bd.; mem. Renaissance Soc., U. Chgo.; founding mem. Old Masters Soc., Chgo.; sponsor Friends of Park, Chgo.; mem. Sustaining Fellows, mem. Textile Soc. Art Inst. Chgo.; trust asso. Chgo. Community Trust. Named to Wisdom Hall of Fame; recipient Wisdom Award of Honor, 1979, Centennial award Art Inst. Chgo., 1979; Bicentennial Arts Award medal King Gustav Adolph of Sweden. Mem. Chgo. Hort. Soc., Oriental Ceramics Soc., Am. Assn. Mus., Archaeol Inst. Am., Nat. Geog. Soc., Newcomen Soc. N.Am., Nat. Housewares Mfrs. Assn. Chgo. (pres. 1949-51, dir., mem. exec. com.), Gen. Alumni Bd. U. Pa., Northwestern U. Assos., Friends of Art of Northwestern U. (patron Block Gallery), Ordre des Compagnons du Beaujolais, Antiquarian Soc. (life), Chgo. Council Fine Arts (bus. adv. com.), Contemporary Art Circle Chgo. (founding mem.), Newberry Library Assn., Chgo. Hist. Soc. (life, gov.), Friends Asia House Gallery, Asia Soc., Chinese Art Soc. Am., Oriental Inst. of U. Chgo. (assoc., mem. adv. council), Friends Chgo. Public Library (mem. centennial com.), The Orientals, Archives Am. Art, Smithsonian Instn. (sustaining), Chgo. Public Sch. Art Soc., Nat. Trust Hist. Preservation, Wedgewood Soc. Chgo. (dir.), Soc. Contemporary Art (sponsor), Chgo. Council Fgn. Relations (mem. Chgo. com.), Friends of Neuberger Mus. (Purchase, N.Y.), Friends of Am. Mus. in Britain (N.Y.C.), Met. Mus. Art (nat. asso.), Historic Pullman Found. (sustaining), David and Alfred Smart Gallery of U. Chgo. (supporting), Chgo. Open Lands Project (governing), Sigma Chi (award 1975). Clubs: Executives (past dir.), Chicago, The Arts (dir., mem. exhbns. com., chmn. nominating com.), University of Pa. (past dir.), Tavern (past gov.), Casino, President's of Loyola U. (Chgo.); Sunset Ridge Country (Northbrook, Ill.); Post and Paddock (Arlington Heights, Ill.) (dir., exec. com.). Office: 4300 W Peterson Ave Chicago IL 60646

ALSOBROOK, HENRY BERNIS, JR., lawyer; b. New Orleans, Nov. 9, 1930; s. Henry Bernis and Ethel (Smith) A.; m. Eugenie Loie Wilson, June 6, 1956; children—Eugenie Wilson, John Gleason, Emily

Woodward. B.A., Tulane U., 1952, J.D., 1957. Bar: La. bar 1957. Since practiced in, New Orleans; sr. partner firm Adams & Reese; mem. faculty Tulane U. Law Sch.; bd. dirs. Def. Research Inst., 1978-81, chmn. med.-legal com., 1967-72; lectr. in field. Author articles in field.; Mem. editorial bds. legal jours. Bd. dirs. New Orleans Philharm. Symphony Soc.; elder St. Charles Ave. Presbyn. Ch., New Orleans. Served with USNR, 1953. Fellow Am. Bar Found., Am. Coll. Trial Lawyers; mem. ABA (past chmn. standing com. commerce), La. Bar Assn. (pres. 1982-83), New Orleans Bar Assn., Internat. Assn. Ins. Counsel (exec. com. 1982-85), Fedn. Ins. Counsel, New Orleans Assn. Def. Counsel, La. Assn. Def. Counsel (gov. 1965), La. Law Inst. (council 1963-64), Soc. Med. Assn. Counsel (charter), Soc. Hosp. Attys. (charter), AMA (hon.). Clubs: New Orleans Country, La., Avoca Duck, Lakeshore. Office: 4500 One Shell Sq New Orleans LA 70139

ALSOP, DONALD DOUGLAS, judge; b. Duluth, Minn., Aug. 28, 1927; s. Robert Alvin and Mathilda (Aaseng) A.; m. Jean Lois Tweeten, Aug. 16, 1952; children—David, Marcia, Robert. B.S., U. Minn., 1950, LL.B., 1952. Bar: Minn. 1952. Practiced in, New Ulm, 1952-75; mem. firm Gislason, Alsop, Dosland & Hunter, 1954-75; judge U.S. Dist. Ct. for dist. Minn., 1975—; Mem. Jud. Conf. Com. to Implement Criminal Justice Act, 1979—. Chmn. Brown County (Minn.) Republican Com., 1960-64, 2d Congl. Dist. Rep. Com., 1968-72, Brown County chpt. ARC, 1968-74. Served with AUS, 1945-46. Mem. Am., Minn. bar assns.; mem. 8th Circuit Dist. Judges Assn. (pres. 1982—); Mem. New Ulm C. of C. (pres. 1974-75), Order of Coif. Office: US Dist Ct 760 Federal Bldg 316 N Robert St Saint Paul MN 55101

ALSOP, JOSEPH WRIGHT, newspaperman, author; b. Avon, Conn., Oct. 11, 1910; s. Wright and Corinne Douglas (Robinson) A.; m. Mrs. Susan Mary Jay Patten, Feb. 16, 1961 (div. 1978). Grad., Groton Sch., 1928; A.B., Harvard U., 1932. Mem. staff N.Y. Herald Tribune, N.Y.C., 1932-35, Washington, 1936-37; Mellon lectr. Nat. Gallery Art, 1978. (With Robert E. Kintner); author of: syndicated column on politics The Capital Parade, for N.Am. Newspaper Alliance, 1937-40; Author: (with Turner Catledge) The 168 Days, 1938, (with Robert E. Kintner) Men Around the President, 1938, American White Paper, 1940, (with Stewart Alsop) We Accuse, 1955, The Reporter's Trade, 1958, From the Silent Earth, 1964, (with brother, Stewart J. O. Alsop) From the Silent Earth; column Matter of Fact, syndicated through N.Y. Herald Tribune Syndicate, 1945-58; sole author, through, Washington Post, then Los Angeles Times Syndicate, 1958-74; Contbr. to: other mags. New Yorker. Commd. lt. U.S. Navy, 1940; sent to India from Navy; joined Am. Vol. Air Group as aide to Gen. Chennault; captured by Japanese at; Hong Kong; and held prisoner until, June 1942; then was exchanged and returned to; U.S.; became chief of Lend Lease Mission to China at, Dec. 1942; Chusking; capt. 14th Air Force and mem. staff of Gen. Chennault, 1943-45. Decorated Legion of Merit, Chinese Cloud Banner. Clubs: Links (N.Y.C.); Turf (London). Address: 2720 Dumbarton Ave NW Washington DC 20007 *

ALSPACH, PHILIP HALLIDAY, mfg. co. exec.; b. Buffalo, Apr. 19, 1923; s. Walter L. and Jean E. (Halliday) A.; m. Jean Edwards, Dec. 20, 1947; children—Philip Clough, Bruce Edwards, David Christopher. B.Engring. in Mech. Engring, Tulane U., 1944. Registered profl. engr., Mass., Wis., La. With Gen. Electric Co., 1945-64, mgr. indsl. electronics div. planning, 1961-64; v.p., gen. mgr. constrn. machinery div. Allis Chalmers Mfg. Co., Milw., 1964-68; exec. v.p., dir., mem. exec. com. Jeffrey Galion, Inc., 1968-69; v.p. I.T.E. Imperial Corp., Springhouse, Pa., 1969-75; pres. E.W. Bliss div. Gulf & Western Mfg. Co., Southfield, Mich., 1975-79; group v.p. Katy Industries, Inc., Elgin, Ill., 1979—; dir. Winnebago Industries, Inc. Author papers in field. Mem. Soc. Automotive Engrs. (sr.), IEEE, Soc. Mfg. Engrs., Inst. Dirs. (U.K.), Am. Mgmt. Assn. Clubs: Canadian, Met. (N.Y.C.). Home: PO Box 493 Elgin IL 60120 Office: 853 Dundee Ave Elgin IL 60120

ALSPAUGH, ROBERT ODO, industrial management consultant; b. Cuyahoga Falls, O., Jan. 30, 1912; s. Odo Albert and Leah (Case) A.; m. Jane Bradner, Dec. 6, 1941; 1 dau., Janet Bradner. Student, U. Akron, 1931-32; B.S. in Bus. Adminstrn., Case-Western Res. U., 1934. Asst. comml. research dir. Forest City Pub. Co., Cleve., 1934-37; mgmt. cons., 1938-41; civilian asst. Office Chief Ordnance, U.S. Army, Washington, 1941-42; chmn. Alspaugh & Co. (mgmt. cons.), Cleve., 1946—; Hon. dep. Cuyahoga County (Ohio) auditor, 1965-66; dir. financial study cost reduction St. Vincent Charity Hosp., 1961-62; financial adviser Decatur and Macon County Hosp. Study, 1956. Author: (with others) Combat and Motor Transport Vehicle Spare Part Policies and Operations of U.S. Army, 1945. Served to maj. AUS, 1942-46. Decorated Legion of Merit. Mem. Cleve. Inst. Arts, Western Res. Hist. Soc., Mus. Natural History, Art Mus., Mus. Arts Assn., Newcomen Soc. N.Am., Met. Mus. Art N.Y.C., Cleve., French, Brit. chambers commerce. Episcopalian. Clubs: Racquet and Tennis, India House, River and Doubles (N.Y.C.); American, Anabels (London, Eng.); Country, Union, Mid-Day (Cleve.). Home: 2952 Fairmount Blvd Cleveland Heights OH 44118 also 160 E 65th St New York NY 10021 Office: 1500 Huntington Cleveland OH 44115 also 111 Broadway New York NY

ALSTADT, DONALD MARTIN, business executive; b. Erie, Pa., July 29, 1921; s. Rheinhold L. and Jean M. A.; m. Lynn Perry, Dec. 26, 1966; 1 dau., Karen. B.S., U. Pitts., 1947; Sc.D. (hon.), Thiel Coll., 1980. With Lord Corp., Erie, 1961—, v.p., gen. mgr., 1964-66, exec. v.p., 1966-68, pres., 1968—; cons. Carborundum Co., Transistor Products Co. of Boston, 1952-56; dir. Keithley Instruments Inc.; cons. Lincoln Project, 1952-53, NSF, 1980—. Contbr. articles to profl. jours. Chmn. bd. overseers Franklin Pierce Law Ctr., 1981—; mem. adv. bd. Ctr. for Advanced Engring. Study, MIT, 1981—; mem. Pa. Sci. and Engring. Found., 1980—; Bd. advisors Case Western Res. Sch. Mgmt., Cleve., 1970—; bd. visitors U. Pitts. Grad. Sch. Bus., 1972—; trustee Poly. Inst. N.Y., Bklyn., 1973—, Kolff Found., Cleve., 1974—, Hamot Med. Center, Erie, Pa., 1973-78, Rose Poly. Inst., 1976-79; mem. adv. bd. Mellon Inst. Research; met. chmn. Nat. Alliance of Businessmen, 1969; mem. president's council Tulane U., 1976—; mem. vis. com. Sch. Engring., M.I.T., 1980—, Sch. Engring., Duke U., 1980—; bd. overseers Franklin Pierce Law Center, 1980—; mem. policy com. Pa. Bus. Council, 1979—. Recipient Medal of Merit Edinboro State Coll., 1979, Univ. medal Pa. State U., 1981. Fellow Am. Inst. Chemists; mem. Am. Phys. Soc., Am. Chem. Soc., Faraday Soc. of Eng., Electrochem. Soc., Chemists Club N.Y., N.Y. Acad. Scis., Inst. Mgmt. Sci., Am. Security Council. Republican. Presbyterian. Office: 2000 W Grandview Blvd Erie PA 16514

ALSTON, ALEX ARMSTRONG, JR., lawyer; b. Cleveland, Miss., July 22, 1936; s. Alex Armstrong and Elizabeth (Davidson) A.; m. Sarah Jane Givens, June 28, 1959; children: Alex Armstrong, Alice Carolyn, Sheldon Givens. B.A., Millsaps Coll., 1958; LL.B., U. Miss., 1964. Bar: Miss. 1964. Assoc. and partner firm Wells, Thomas & Wells, Jackson, Miss., 1964-68; partner firm Thomas, Price, Alston, Jones & Davis, Jackson, 1968—. Editor-in-chief: Miss. Law Jour, 1963-64. Asst. scoutmaster, scoutmaster troop 302 Andrew Jackson Council Boy Scouts Am., 1965—. Served to capt. USMC, 1958-61. Recipient Silver Beaver award Boy Scouts Am., 1981. Mem. Miss. State Bar Assn., Am. Bar Assn. (sects. on ins., negligence and compensation, antitrust, litigation), Hinds County Bar Assn., Defense Research Inst., Am. Law Inst., Am. Coll. Trial Lawyers, Phi Delta Phi, Omicron Delta Kappa. Presbyterian. Home: 1304 Poplar Jackson MS 39202 Office: PO Drawer 1532 Jackson MS 39205

ALSTON, PHILIP HENRY, JR., ambassador, lawyer; b. Atlanta, Apr. 19, 1911; s. Philip Henry and May (Lewis) A.; m. Elkin Goddard, June 27, 1939; children: Elkin Goddard (Mrs. James E. Cushman), John Goddard. A.B., U. Ga., 1932; LL.B., Emory U., 1934; student, Harvard Law Sch., 1935. Bar: Ga. 1934. Since practiced in, Atlanta; with firm Alston & Bird; ambassador to, Australia and, Nauru, 1977-81; Past mem. Atlanta advisory bd. Citizens and So. Nat. Bank; dir. Triton, Inc. Former trustee Charles Loridans Found., Vasser Woolley Found.; past bd. regents Univ. System Ga. Served to lt. USNR, World War II. Mem. U. Ga. Alumni Soc. (pres. 1963-64), Sigma Alpha Epsilon. Episcopalian (past sr. warden). Home: Sea Island GA 31561 also 145 15th St NE Unit 411 Atlanta GA 30361 Office: 35 Broad St Atlanta GA 30335

ALSTON, WILLIAM PAYNE, philosophy educator; b. Shreveport, La., Nov. 29, 1921; s. William Payne and Eunice (Schoolfield) A.; m. Mary Frances Collins, Aug. 15, 1943 (div.); 1 dau., Frances Ellen; m. Valerie Tibbetts Barnes, July 3, 1963. B.M., Centenary Coll., 1942; Ph.D., U. Chgo., 1951. Instr. philosophy U. Mich., 1949-52, asst. prof., then asso. prof., 1952-61, prof., 1961-71, acting chmn. dept., 1961-64; prof. philosophy Rutgers U., 1971-76, U. Ill., Champaign, 1976-80, chmn. dept., 1977-80; prof. philosophy Syracuse (N.Y.) U., 1980—; vis. asst. prof. UCLA, 1952-53; vis. lectr. Harvard U., 1955-56. Author: Religious Belief and Philosophical Thought, 1963, (with G. Nakhnikian) Readings in twentieth Century Philosophy, 1963, Philosophy of Language, 1964, (with R.B. Brandt) The Problems of Philosophy; Introductory Readings, 1967, 3d edit., 1978; also numerous articles in field, chpts. in books; editor: Philos. Research Archives, 1974-77, Faith and Philosophy, 1982—. Served with AUS, 1942-46. Mem. Philos. Assn. (pres. Western div. 1978-79). Home: 120 Windsor Pl Syracuse NY 13210 Office: Dept Philosophy Syracuse U Syracuse NY 13210

ALSUP, RICHARD CLAYBOURNE, lawyer, natural gas corp. exec.; b. Hobbs, N.Mex., Apr. 29, 1940. B.A., U. Tx., El Paso, 1962; LL.B., U. Houston, 1968. Bar: Tex. bar 1968. Pvt. practice law, Houston, 1968-69; sr. v.p., gen. counsel Houston Natural Gas Corp., 1969—. Mem. Am. Bar Assn., Tex. Bar Assn., Houston Bar Assn., Am. Soc. Internat Law. Office: PO Box 1188 Houston TX 77001

ALTABE, JOAN AUGUSTA BERG, artist; b. N.Y.C., Apr. 27, 1935; d. Harold and Evelyn (Cooperman) Berg; m. David F. Altabe, Sept. 28, 1958; children—Richard Jonathan, Madeline Nissa. Studied with, Robert Motherwell; B.A., Hunter Coll., 1956, postgrad., 1956-57. Prodn. mgr. Am. Hairdresser trade mag., 1956-57; fine art tchr. secondary schs., N.Y.C., 1957-72; art dir. Aim mag., 1979-80; Vol. art tchr. N.Y. Lighthouse For Blind, 1950-53; Bicentennial exhibit dir. Long Beach Mus. Art, 1975-76. Artist-muralist, 1972—, prin. work includes 6 stained glass window murals, N.Y. Synagogue, 1973, heraldic design, Smithsonian Instn. Bicentennial Travelling Exhibit, 1976-78; represented in permanent collection, Santa Barbara Mus.; cartoon strip Richie, Bradentons Island Herald; book reviewer syndicated cartoon, Leonardo, Pergamon Press, Gt. Brit., 1980—; author, illustrator: cartoon Novella Fantasy; contbr. articles, illustrations to profl. jours. Mem. Nat. Soc. Mural Painters (treas., bd. dirs., dir. finance). Home: 343 Ben Franklin Dr Sarasota FL 33577 *To transcend my life through painting, or teaching or publishing, with loyalty to my individual spirit and dedication to communication.*

ALTENBERND, A(UGUST) LYNN, educator; b. Cleve., Feb. 3, 1918; s. Adolf Carl and Lucy M. (Cheyney) A.; m. Mary Blazekovich, Apr. 19, 1941; children: Toni (Mrs. Andrew J. Gold), Mark, Nicholas. B.S. in Edn, Ohio State U., 1939, M.A., 1949, Ph.D. in English, 1954. Relief visitor, Cleve., 1939-42; tchr. English John Bryan High Sch., Yellow Springs, O., 1942-44; supply clk. Wright-Patterson AFB, 1944, asst. buyer spl. aircraft Procurement div., 1946-48; instr. Ohio State U., 1949-54; mem. faculty U. Ill. at Urbana, 1954—, prof. English, 1965—, head dept., 1966-71, asso. dean Grad. Coll., 1980-83; cons. English Macmillan Pub. Co., 1963-76. Editor: (with Leslie L. Lewis) Introduction to Literature: Stories, Poems, Plays, 3 vols., 2d edit, 1969, Poems, 3d edit, 1975, Stories, 3d edit, 1980, Handbooks for the Study of Fiction, Poetry, Drama, 3 vols, 1966, Exploring Literature: Fiction, Poetry, Drama and Criticism, 1970, Anthology: An Introduction to Literature, 1977. Served to 2d lt. AUS, 1944-46. Mem. MLA, Nat. Council Tchrs. English, AAUP. Home: 308 E Colorado Ave Urbana IL 61801

ALTER, DAVID EMMET, JR., author, artist, publisher, consultant; b. Mussoorie, U.P., India, July 14, 1921; s. David Emmet and Mary Martha (Payne) A. (parents U.S. citizens); m. Sarah G. McGinnis, July 25, 1981; children by previous marriage: Dismore J., David Emmet III. B.A., Coll. Wooster, 1943; M.A., Mills Coll., 1950. Fgn. service officer AID, 1954-75; alt. U.S. rep. to OAS, 1969-75; author, artist, pub. The Wanderers Almanac, ann., 1969—; treas. Artmakers, Inc., 1981—. Served with AUS, 1943-46, 50-54. Recipient meritorious honor award AID, 1959. Home and office: 181 Magnolia Ave St Augustine FL 32084

ALTER, EDWARD T., state treasurer; b. Glen Ridge, N.J., July 26, 1941; s. E. Irving and Norma (Fisher) A.; m. Patricia R. Olsen, 1975; children: Christina Lyn, Ashly Ann, Darci Lee. B.A., U. Utah., 1966, M.B.A., 1967. C.P.A., Calif., Utah. Sr. acct. Touche Ross & Co., Los Angeles, 1967-72; asst. treas. U. Utah, Salt Lake City, 1972-80; treas. State of Utah, Salt Lake City, 1981—. Bd. dirs. Utah Housing Fin. Agy., Utah State Retirement Bd.; mem. Utah State Republican Central Com., 1981—. Served to sgt. USAR, 1958-66. Mem. Am. Inst. C.P.A.s, Delta Sigma Pi, Delta Phi Kappa. Club: Utah Bond (pres. 1981-82). Office: 215 State Capitol Salt Lake City UT 84114

ALTER, ELEANOR BREITEL, lawyer; b. N.Y.C., Nov. 10, 1938; d. Charles David and Jeanne (Hollander) Breitel; children: Richard B. Zabel, David B. Zabel. B.A. with honors, U. Mich., 1960; postgrad., Harvard U., 1960-61; LL.B., Columbia U., 1964. Bar: N.Y. 1965. Atty., office of gen. counsel, ins. dept. State of N.Y., 1964-66; asso. firm Miller & Carlson, N.Y.C., 1966-68, Marshall, Bratter, Greene, Allison & Tucker, 1968-74, mem. firm, 1974-82, Roseman Colin Freund Lewis & Cohen, 1982—; adj. prof. law NYU Sch Law, 1983—; lectr. in field. Contbr. articles to profl. jours. Mem. Am. Law Inst., Am. Bar Assn., N.Y. State Bar Assn., Assn. Bar City N.Y. (library com. 1978-80, com. on matrimonial law 1977-81, judiciary com. 1981—), N.Y. County Lawyers Assn. (chmn. com. on matrimonial law 1980-82), Am. Acad. Matrimonial Lawyers. Office: 575 Madison New York NY 10022

ALTER, HARVEY, chemist, association executive; b. N.Y.C., Sept. 4, 1932; s. Louis B. and Elsie (Wiener) A.; m. Cora Wolff, Feb. 10, 1957; children: Juli E., Lisa C. B.S., Queens Coll., CUNY, 1952; M.S., U. Cin., 1954, Ph.D. (Applied Sci. fellow), 1957. Physicist Bakelite Co. Union Carbide Corp., Bound Brook, N.J., 1957-59; sr. research chemist Harris Research Lab., Inc. Gillete Co., Washington, 1959-63; research supr. Harris Research Labs., Inc. Gillette Co., Washington, 1963-64, group leader, 1964-65; assoc. dir. research Toni Co div. Gillette Co., Chgo., 1965-66, tech. dir. research, 1966-68; mgr. spl. projects Gillette Research Inst., Rockville, Md., 1968-69, mgr. Harris Research Labs. div., 1969-72, v.p., 1971-72; dir. research programs Nat. Ctr. for Resource Recovery, Inc., Washington, 1972-79; mgr. resources and environ. quality dept. U.S. C. of C., Washington, 1979—; lectr. CCNY, 1958-59, Am. U., Washington, 1974-78, adj. prof. Coll. Pub. Affairs, 1978—. Author: (with J.J. Dunn, Jr.) Solid Waste Conversion to Energy: Current U.S. and European Practice, 1980, Materials Recovery from Wastes Unit Operations and Results, 1983; editor: Resources and Conversation jour., 1974—; mem. editorial bd.: Jour. Adhesion, 1971-73, Polymer-Plastics Tech. and Engring., 1970-75; contbr. articles to profl. jours.; patentee in field. Mem. Civic Ctr. Commn. Rockville, Md., 1970-71, Human Rights Commn. Rockville, 1971-79; chmn. Human Rights Commn., Rockville, 1976-78; mem. Bicentennial Commn. Rockville, 1975-76, Select Caucus (Town Meeting) Northbrook, Ill., 1968; bd. dirs. New Mark Commns Homes Assn., Inc., 1969, 70. Fellow ASTM (Merit award 1980), Washington Acad.-Scis.; mem. Am. Chem. Soc. (pres. Washington sect. 1972), AAAS, Alumni Assn. Queens Coll. (pres. Nat. Capital cpt. 1961, 62), Sigma Xi, Phi Lambda Upsilon. Club: Cosmos (Washington). Office: US C of C 1615 H St NW Washington DC 20062

ALTER, JEAN VICTOR, educator; b. Warsaw, Poland, Oct. 7, 1925; came to U.S., 1951; s. Victor and Melanie (Lorein) A.; m. Michelle Caroly, Aug. 3, 1977; 1 dau. by previous marriage, Nora. M.A., U. Brussels, Belgium, 1948; doctorate, U. Paris, 1951; Ph.D., U. Chgo., 1956. Instr., then asst. prof. Howard U., 1952-58; asst. then asso. prof. U. Md., 1958-67; prof., chmn. dept. Romance langs. Case Western Res. U., 1967-69; prof. French U. Pa., 1970—; lectr., writer in field. Author: Les origines de la satire antibourgeoise en France, 1966, La vision du monde d'Alain Robbe-Grillet, 1966, L'Esprit antibourgeois sous l'ancien regime, 1970, Itineraire d'un Poete, 1980. Recipient Fulbright award, 1951; Smith-Mundt grantee, 1951. Mem. Modern Lang. Assn., Am. Assn. Tchrs. French, Am. Assn. U. Profs., Acad. Lit. Studies. Office: Dept Romance Languages Univ Pa Philadelphia PA 19104 *Work at what you like to do; do well whatever you do; be always lucidly yourself, but do not take yourself too seriously.*

ALTER, JONATHAN HAMMERMAN, journalist; b. Chgo., Oct. 6, 1957; s. James M. and Joanne (Hammerman) A. A.B. cum laude, Harvard U., 1979. Speechwriter The White House, 1978; free lance writer, Washington, 1979-80; lobbyist Save the Dunes Council, Washington, 1979-80; editor The Washington Monthly, 1981-82; assoc. editor Newsweek, N.Y.C., 1983—; cons. Office Pub. Affairs, FAA, 1980. Author: (with Michael Calabrese and Ronald Browstein) Selecting A President, 1980; editor: (with Charles Peters) Inside the System. Vol. V, 1984. Address: 444 Madison Ave New York NY 10022

ALTER, ROBERT B., foreign language educator, critic; b. N.Y.C., Apr. 2, 1935; s. Harry and Tillie (Zimmmerman) A.; m. Judith Berkenbilt, June 4, 1961 (div. 1973); children: Miriam, Dan; m. Carol Cosman, June 17, 1973; children: Gabriel, Micha. B.A., Columbia U., 1957; M.A., Harvard U., 1958, Ph.D., 1962. Instr., then asst. prof. English Columbia U., 1962-66; mem. faculty U. Calif. at Berkeley, 1967—, prof. Hebrew and comparative lit., 1969—, chmn. dept. comparative lit., 1970-72; columnist Commentary mag., 1965-73, contbg. editor, 1973—. Author: Rogue's Progress: Studies in the Picaresque Novel, 1964, Fielding and the Nature of the Novel, 1968, After the Tradition, 1969, Partial Magic: The Novel as a Self-Conscious Genre, 1975, Defenses of the Imagination, 1977, A Lion for Love, 1979, The Art of Biblical Narrative, 1981; Contbg. editor: Tri Quarterly mag, 1975—. Recipient English Inst. Essay prize, 1965, Nat. Jewish Book award for Jewish thought, 1982; Guggenheim fellow, 1966-67, 78-79; NEH sr. fellow, 1972-73; Inst. for Advanced Studies fellow, Jerusalem, 1982-83. Mem. Am. Comparative Lit. Assn. Jewish. Home: 1475 LeRoy Ave Berkeley CA 94708

ALTERMAN, IRWIN MICHAEL, lawyer; b. Vineland, N.J., Mar. 4, 1941; s. Joseph and Rose A.; m. Susan Simon, Aug. 6, 1972; 1 son, Owen. A.B., Princeton U., 1962; LL.B., Columbia U., 1965. Bar: N.Y. bar 1966, Mich. bar 1967. Law clk. Judge Theodore Levin, U.S. Dist. Ct., Eastern Dist. Mich., 1965-67; asso. firm Kaye, Scholer, Fierman, Hays & Handler, N.Y.C., 1967-70, Hyman, Gurwin, Nachman, Friedman & Winkelman, Southfield, Mich., 1970-74, partner, 1974—; lectr. Inst. Continuing Legal Edn., Ann Arbor, Mich. Founding editor: Mich. Antitrust, 1975—; editor: Mich. Antitrust Digest; contbr. articles to profl. jours. Mem. nat. young leadership cabinet United Jewish Appeal, 1978-79, mem. nat. exec. com., 1980; v.p. Adat Shalom Synagogue, Farmington Hills, Mich. Mem. Am. Law Inst., Am. Bar Assn., Assn. Bar City N.Y., State Bar Mich. (chmn. com. on plain English, past chmn. antitrust sect.), Detroit Bar Assn. Club: Princeton (past pres. Mich.). Office: 17117 W Nine Mile Rd Suite 1600 Southfield MI 48075

ALTERMAN, ISIDORE, investment company executive. Chmn., treas. Alterman Investment Fund, Inc., Atlanta. Office: Alterman Investment Fund Inc 1218 Pces Ferry Rd Atlanta GA 30327§

ALTHEIMER, ALAN J., lawyer; b. St. Louis, Sept. 2, 1903. A.B., Columbia U., 1923, J.D., 1925. Bar: Ill. 1926. Since practiced in, Chgo.; mem. firm Altheimer & Gray.; Dir. Conveyor Systems, Inc., Edward Gray Corp., Franklin Picture Co., Inland Constrn. Co., Americana Hotels Corp. V.p., bd. dirs. Albert Pick Jr. Fund; bd. dirs., past pres. Jewish Council on Urban Affairs. Recipient Profl. Merit award Columbia U. Law Sch. Alumni Assn.; Frank L. Weil award Nat. Jewish Welfare Bd. Mem. Am., Ill., Chgo. bar assns., Zeta Beta Tau. Clubs: Standard, Northmoor. Office: 333 W Wacker Dr Chicago IL 60606

ALTHOUSE, ERNEST E., utility executive; b. Strausstown, Pa., Sept. 24, 1904; s. Adam Joseph and Minnie (Burkey) A.; m. Elizabeth Righter Plank, May 29, 1935. E.E., Lehigh U., 1926. Registered profl. engr., N.Y., Pa. With Central Hudson Gas & Electric Corp., Poughkeepsie, N.Y., 1928—, pres., 1968-75, vice chmn., 1975—, also dir. Mem. IEEE, Soc. Gas Lighting. Club: Mason. Home: 1 Alden Rd Poughkeepsie NY 12603 Office: 284 South Ave Poughkeepsie NY 12602

ALTIS, HAROLD DAVID, aircraft manufacturing company executive, mechanical engineer; b. Cabool, Mo., July 9, 1928; s. Ezra Patrick and Elsie May (East) A.; m. Thelma Zeline Amick, Sept. 3, 1950; children: Deborah Gail Altis Gibson, David Eric, Rex Nathaniel. B.S.M.E., U. Mo., 1951; postgrad., Sch. Law, 1950-51. With McDonnell Aircraft Co., St. Louis, 1951-78, dir. advanced engring. div., 1971-77, v.p. engring. tech. div., 1977-78, exec. v.p., 1982—; corp. v.p. engring. and research McDonnell Douglas Corp., St. Louis, 1978—; instr. Univ. Coll., Washington U., St. Louis, 1953-55; mem. engring. adv. council U. Mo., 1978—; mem. U.S. Air Force Sci. Adv. Bd., 1980—. Recipient Mo. Honor award U. Mo., 1979. Mem. Aerospace Industries Assn. (aerospace tech. council), AIAA, ASME, Air Force Assn., Navy League U.S. Baptist. Office: PO Box 516 Saint Louis MO 63166

ALTIZER, THOMAS JONATHAN JACKSON, educator, theologian; b. Cambridge, Mass., Sept. 28, 1927; s. Jackson Duncan and Frances (Greetham) A.; m. children—John Jackson, Katherine

Blake. Student, St. John's Colls., 1944-45; A.B., U. Chgo., 1948, A.M., 1951, Ph.D., 1955. Asst. prof. religion Wabash Coll., 1954-56; asst. prof., then asso. prof. religion Emory U., 1956-68; prof. English State U. N.Y. at Stony Brook, 1968—. Author: Oriental Mysticism and Biblical Eschatology, 1961, Mircea Eliade and the Dialectic of the Sacred, 1963, The Gospel of Christian Atheism, 1966, The New Apocalypse, 1967, Descent into Hell, 1970, The Self-Embodiment of God, 1977, Total Presence, 1980. Served with AUS, 1945-46. Home: 210 Chestnut St Port Jefferson NY 11777 Office: Religious Studies State U NY Stony Brook NY 11794

ALTMAN, EDWARD IRA, finance educator, consultant, editor; b. N.Y.C., June 5, 1941; s. Sidney and Florence (Brown) A.; m. Elaine Karalus, June 24, 1967; 1 son, Gregory. B.A. in Econs., CCNY, 1963; M.B.A., UCLA, 1965, Ph.D. in Fin., 1967. Prof. fin. NYU, 1967—, chmn. M.B.A. program, 1977—; vis. prof. Hautes Etudes Commerciales, Jouy en Joses, Frances, 1971-73, Catholic U., Rio de Janeiro, 1977, U. Paris, 1976, Australian Grad. Sch. Mgmt., Sydney, 1981; cons. Zeta Services, Inc., Mountainside, N.J., Arthur Anderson & Co., Chgo. Author: Corporate Bankruptcy in America, 1971, Corporate Financial Distress, 1983; editor Financial Handbook, 5th edit., 1981, Jai Press, Greenwich, Conn., 1978—, John Wiley & Sons, N.Y.C., 1982—; developer fin. models. Mem. Fin. Mgmt. Assn. (bd. dirs. 1982—), European Fin. Assn. (mem. exec. com. 1978-80). Home: 100 Bleecker St New York NY 10012 Office: NYU 100 Trinity Pl New York NY 10006

ALTMAN, ELLEN, librarian, educator; b. Pitts., Jan. 1, 1936; d. William and Catherine (Wall) Conley. A.B., Duquesne U., 1957; M.L.S., Rutgers, 1965, Ph.D., 1971. Instr., asst research prof. Rutgers U., 1965-67, 70-72; asst. prof. U. Ky., 1972-73, U. Toronto, 1974-76; assoc. prof. Ind. U., 1976-79; dir., prof. Grad. Library Sch., U. Ariz., Tucson, 1979—; cons. various research orgns., state libraries. Active Exec. Women's Council So. Ariz., 1980—. Author: Performance Measures in Pub. Libraries, 1973, A Data Gathering and Instructional Manual for Performance Measures in Public Libraries, 1976, Local Public Library Administration, 1980. Fulbright-Hayes sr. lectr., 1978. Mem. ALA, AAUP, Am. Mgmt. Assn. Office: 1515 E 1st St Tucson AZ 85721

ALTMAN, IRWIN, university official; b. N.Y.C., July 16, 1930; s. Louis L. and Ethel (Schonberg) A.; m. Gloria Seckler, Jan. 2, 1953; children: David Gary, William Michael. B.A., N.Y.U., 1951; M.A., U. Md., 1954, Ph.D., 1957. Asst. prof. Am. U., Washington, 1957-58, sr. research scientist, asso. prof., 1960-62, adj. prof., 1962-69; research scientist human scis. research, Arlington, Va., 1958-60; research psychologist Naval Med. Research Inst., Bethesda, Md., 1962-69; adj. prof. U. Md., 1968-69; prof., chmn. psychology dept. U. Utah, Salt Lake City, 1969-76, prof., 1976-79, dean Coll. Social and Behavioral Scis., 1979-83, v.p. for acad. affairs, 1983—. Author: (with J.E. McGrath) Small Groups, 1966, (with D.A. Taylor) Social Penetration, 1973, Environment and Social Behavior, 1975, (with J. Wohlwill) Human Behavior and Environment: Vol. I, 1976, Vol. II, 1977, Vol. III, 1978, Vol. IV, 1980, Vol. V, 1981, Vol. VI, 1983, (with M. Chrmers) Culture and Environment, 1980; Mem. editorial bd.: Small Groups, 1970-79, Man-Environment Systems, 1969-73, Jour. Applied Social Psychology, 1973, Sociometry, 1973-76, Environment and Behavior, 1975, (with M. Chemras) Jour. Personality and Social Psychology, 1974-83, Contemporary Psychology, 1975, Environ. Psychology and Nonverbal Behavior, Psychology, 1976, Am. Jour. Community Psychology, 1978, Population and Environment, 1979, Jour. Environ. Psychology, 1982; Contbr. articles to profl. jours. Served to 1st lt. Adj. Gen. Corps. AUS, 1954-56. Mem. Am. Psychol. Assn. (pres. div. population and environment), AAAS, Soc. Exptl. Social Psychology, Soc. Psychol. Study Social Issues, Soc. Personality and Social Psychology (pres.). Home: 2827 Commonwealth Ave Salt Lake City UT 84109

ALTMAN, LAURENCE, publisher; b. N.Y.C., Aug. 25, 1933; s. Abraham and Mirabelle (Grant) A.; m. Karen E. Ringnalda, June 10, 1974; children: Phoebe, Hayley, Chelsea, Ben. B.A., Cornell U.; M.S., Ph.D., Lehigh U., 1959. Instr. physics Lehigh U., 1957-61; sr. engr. Sperry Rand Corp., Syosset, N.Y., 1961-65; editor McGraw-Hill, N.Y.C., 1967-78; v.p. Hayden Pub. Co., Hasbrouck Heights, N.J., 1978—; lectr. computer scis. Recipient Jesse H. Neal editorial achievement award, 1977. Mem. IEEE, Am. Bus. Press. Patentee remote measurement techniques. Address: 10 Mulholland Dr Hasbrouck Heights NJ 07604

ALTMAN, LAWRENCE KIMBALL, physician, journalist; b. Quincy, Mass., June 19, 1937; s. William S. and Esther (Kimball) A. A.B. cum laude, Harvard U., 1958; M.D., Tufts U., 1962. Diplomate: Am. Vet. Epidemiology Soc. Intern Mt. Zion Hosp., San Francisco, 1962-63; USPHS epidemic intelligence service officer Centers for Disease Control, Atlanta, 1963-66; med. resident, fellow U. Wash. Hosp., Seattle, 1966-69; med. corr., columnist The Doctors World N.Y. Times, 1969—; assoc. prof. medicine NYU, 1970—; vis. physician Serafimer Hosp., Karolinska Inst., Stockholm, Sweden, 1973; vis. scientist U. Wash., 1971. Author: Science of The Times, 1981; contbr. chpts. to books, articles to profl. jours.; Ency. Brittanica, 1979—, Grolier Ency., 1972—. Recipient Howard W. Blakeslee award Am. Heart Assn., 1982, 83, Claude Bernard award Nat. Soc. Med. Research, 1971, 74, Walter C. Alvarez award Am. Med. Writers Assn., 1980, Journalism award Am. Acad. Pediatrics, 1982, Pub. Service award Nat. Kidney Found. Fellow ACP, Am. Coll. Epidemiology, N.Y. Acad. Medicine; mem. Inst. Medicine/Nat. Acad. Scis., Am. Soc. Tropical Medicine and Hygiene, Soc. for Epidemiol. Research. Clubs: Century (N.Y.C.); Harvard (N.Y.C. and Boston). Home: 140 West End Ave New York NY 10023 Office: New York Times 229 W 43d St New York NY 10036

ALTMAN, MILTON HUBERT, lawyer; b. Mpls., July 18, 1917; s. Harry Edmund and Lee (Cohen) A.; m. Helen Horwitz, May 21, 1942; children—Neil, Robert, James. B.S., U. Minn., 1938, LL.B., 1947. Bar: Minn. bar 1947. Ptnr. firm Altman, Weiss & Bearmon, St. Paul, 1947—; Mem. Minn. Gov.'s adv. com. on Constl. Revision, 1950, on Gift and Inheritance Tax Regulations, 1961-65; chmn. atty. gen.'s adv. com. on Consumer Protection, 1961-65; mem. U.S. Dist. Ct. Nominating Commn., 1979—; spl. atty. Minn. Bd. Med. Examiners, 1963-75, U. Minn., 1963-75; dir. SPH Hotel Co.; Mem. nat. emergency com. Nat. Council on Crime and Delinquency, 1967-69; mem. Minn.-Wis. small bus. advisory council SBA, 1968-70; mem., v.p. Citizens' Council on Delinquency and Crime, 1968-76; bd. dirs. Correctional Service Minn., 1968-76; mem. Lawyers Com. for Civil Rights Under Law, 1965—; Chmn. Minn. Lawyers for Johnson and Humphrey, 1968. Author: Estate Planning, 1966. Bd. dirs. St. Paul Jewish Fund and Council, 1966-69, Minn. Soc. Crippled Children and Adults. Mem. ABA, Minn. Bar Assn. (chmn tax sect. 1960-62), Ramsey County Bar Assn. (exec. council 1968-71), Am. Arbitration Assn. (nat. panel arbitrators), Fgn. Policy Assn. (nat. council 1969), U. Minn. Law Sch. Alumni Assn. (dir. 1967-70), UN Assn. (nat. legacies com. 1967), Am. Law Inst. Clubs: Minn. (dir. 1975-78), St. Paul Athletic.). Home: 2353 Youngman Ave Apt 406 Saint Paul MN 55116 Office: Altman Weiss & Bearmon 711 Degree of Honor Bldg Saint Paul MN 55101

ALTMAN, PETER ALEXANDER, editor, ednl. adminstr.; b. Washington, June 3, 1943; s. Oscar Louis and Alberta Petrie (Smith) A. B.A., U. Calif. at Berkeley, 1963; M.A., U. Pa., 1964; postgrad., Harvard, 1968, 73, Georgetown U., 1964, Columbia, 1965, U. Minn., 1966, U. Urbino, Italy, 1969, Goethe Inst. Passau, W. Ger., 1977. Mem. faculty dept. English U. Minn., 1965-76; lit. mgr. Guthrie Theater, Mpls., 1971; asst. for arts to v.p. Boston U., 1978, exec. officer for arts, 1978—; mem. faculty Sch. Theatre, 1978—, co-dir., 1979-81; asso. dean Sch. for Arts, 1981—; lectr. critics workshops for St. Paul Arts and Scis. Council, Walker Art Center, Mpls., U. Minn., St. Cloud State Coll.; host KSJN-FM series of concert interval broadcasts, 1971-72. Writer, asst. editor: Books, N.Y.C., 1965; drama and music critic, Mpls. Star, 1966-71; books and arts editor, chief critic, 1971-75; theatre critic, WBUR-FM, 1978-81; asso. producer, Hartman Theatre Co., 1981—; Contbr. articles to profl. publs. Served with AUS, 1964. Recipient Mpls. Page One award for criticism, 1968, Am. Polit. Sci. Assn. prize for urban affairs writing, 1968; Bush fellow, 1972. Home: 16 Chauncy St Cambridge MA 02138 Office: 141 Bay State Rd Boston MA 02215

ALTMAN, ROBERT B., film director, writer, producer; b. Kansas City, Mo., Feb. 20, 1925; m. Kathryn Altman; children: Robert, Matthew; children by previous marriage: Michael, Stephen, Christine. Student, U. Mo., 3 years. Owner Lion's Gate Films. Writer, producer, dir. for: TV, including Kraft Theater; writer, producer, dir.: TV pilot The Long Hot Summer; co-producer: film The James Dean Story, 1957; dir.: films The Delinquents, 1957, Countdown, 1968, That Cold Day in the Park, 1969, M*A*S*H, 1970, Popeye, 1980, Come Back to the 5 & Dime, Jimmy Dean, Jimmy Dean, 1982, Streamers, 1983; producer: The Late Show, 1977, Welcome to L.A., 1977, Rich Kids, 1979, Remember My Name, 1979; producer and dir.: A Wedding, 1978, Quintet, 1979, A Perfect Couple, 1979; producer, dir., screenwriter: Three Women, 1977, Health, 1979; dir. and screenwriter: Brewster McCloud, 1970, McCabe and Mrs. Miller, 1971, Images, 1972, The Long Goodbye, 1973, Thieves Like Us, 1974, California Split, 1974, Nashville, 1975, Buffalo Bill and the Indians, 1976; dir.: Broadway play Come Back to the 5 & Dime, Jimmy Dean, Jimmy Dean, 1982. Served with AUS, 1943-47. Recipient Grand prize for M*A*S*H Cannes Film Festival, 1970; M*A*S*H named Best Film Nat. Soc. Film Critics, 1970. Mem. Dirs. Guild Am. Office: Landscape Films 12115 Magnolia Blvd Suite 123 North Hollywood CA 91607 *

ALTMAN, ROBERT HARRY, lawyer; b. Elmira, N.Y., Nov. 8, 1944; s. Harry and Madeline Maria (Limoncelli) A.; m. Susan C. Hecht, Aug. 18, 1968; children: Scott Robert, Jeremy Lawrence, Lee Rachel. B.A., U. Buffalo, 1966; J.D., U. Toledo, 1969. Bar: N.Y. 1970. Assoc. firm Silberfeld, Danziger & Bangser, N.Y.C., 1970-76; gen. counsel, sec. Fay's Drug Co., Inc., Liverpool, N.Y., 1976-80; partner firm Danziger, Bangser, Klipstein, Goldsmith & Greenwald, N.Y.C.; dir. Arrowhead Tool Builders, Inc. Mem. Am. Bar Assn., N.Y. State Bar Assn., Onondaga County Bar Assn., Nat. Assn. Chain Drug Stores. Office: 230 Park Ave New York NY 10017

ALTMAN, ROGER CHARLES, corporate executive, former government official; b. Boston, Apr. 2, 1945; s. Sidney Stanley and Geraldine (Madden) A. B.A., Georgetown U., 1967; M.B.A., U. Chgo., 1969. Asso. Lehman Bros. Kuhn Loeb, Inc., 1969-74, partner gen. banking, 1974-77, mng. dir., 1981—; asst. sec. domestic fin. Dept. of Treasury, Washington, 1977-81; Mem. Select Com. on N.Y. State Pub. Authorities, 1974, Council Fgn. Relations. Clubs: West Side Tennis, El Morocco, Williams (N.Y.C.). Office: Lehman Bros Kuhn Loeb Inc One William St New York NY 10004 *

ALTMAN, STEVEN, university official; b. Jacksonville, Fla., Oct. 24, 1945; s. Harold and Estelle (Avchin) A.; m. Judy Ellen Ovadenko, Feb. 8, 1969. B.A., UCLA, 1967; M.B.A., U. So. Calif., 1969, D.B.A., 1975. Asst. dean Sch. Bus. U. So. Calif., Los Angeles, 1969-72; asst. prof. div. mgmt. Fla. Internat. U., Miami, 1972-76, chmn. div. mgmt., 1972-77, assoc. prof. div. mgmt., 1976-84, prof. div. mgmt., 1984—, asst. v.p. acad. affairs, 1977-78, assoc. v.p. acad. affairs, 1978-80; v.p. acad. affairs Fla. Internat U., 1981—; univ. provost Fla. Internat. U., 1982—; spl. master Fla. Pub. Employees Relations Commn., 1976—; dir. Internat. Ctr. of Fla., Miami, 1982—; cons. in field. Author: Organizational Behavior, 1979, 84, Reading in Organizational Behavior, 1979, Profit Basics, 1977; editor: Organization Development: Progress and Perspectives, 1982. Mem. adv. bd. Assn. for Retarded Citizens, Miami, 1978—; vice chmn. Internat. Health Com., 1984—; exec. com. Metro-Miami Action Plan, 1983—. Served with USAR, 1968-74. Recipient Gold medal for econs. edn. Freedom Found., 1971, Excellence in Teaching award Sch. Bus. Adminstrn., U. So. Calif., 1972; named Outstanding Faculty Mem. Coll. Bus. Adminstrn. Fla. Internat. U., 1975. Mem. Acad. of Mgmt., Am. Soc. Pub. Adminstrn., Inst. for Mgmt. Sci., Am. Inst. Decision Scis., Internat. Personnel Mgmt. Assn., Soc. Profls. in Dispute Resolution, Am. Arbitration Assn. (arbitrator 1977—), Nat. Univ. Extension Assn., Indsl. Relations Research Assn., Am. Assn. Higher Edn., Am. Assn. State Colls. and Univs., South Miami-Kendall Area C. of C. (dir. 1982—, pres. 1983-84), Beta Gamma Sigma. Home: 13911 SW 109th St Miami FL 33186 Office: Florida Internat Univ Tamiami Trail Miami FL 33199

ALTMAN, STUART HAROLD, economist; b. N.Y.C., Aug. 8, 1937; s. Sidney and Florence A.; m. Diane Kleinberg, June 7, 1959; children: Beth, Renee, Heather. B.B.A., CCNY; M.A. in Econs; Ph.D., UCLA. Asso. prof. econs. Brown U., 1966-71; dep. asst. sec. health and planning HEW, 1971-76; dep. dir. for health (Cost of Living Council), 1973-74; dean Florence Heller Grad. Sch., Brandeis U., Waltham, Mass., 1976—; chmn. bd. Univ. Health Policy Consortium; cons. Office Tech. Assessment; mem. Inst. Medicine, Nat. Acad. Scis., 1978—. Author, editor govt. publs., reports. Mem. exec. bd. Beth Israel Hosp., Brookline, Mass., 1979—. Mem. Am. Public Health Assn. Office: Florence Heller Grad Sch Brandeis Univ Waltham MA 02254

ALTMANN, STUART ALLEN, biology educator; b. St. Louis, June 9, 1930; s. Maurice Walter and Deborah (Friedman) A.; m. Jeanne Glaser, June 19, 1959; children: Michael, Rachel. B.A. in Zoology, UCLA, 1953, M.A., 1954; Ph.D. in Biology, Harvard U., 1960. Teaching asst in zoology UCLA, 1953-54; biol. research asst. in med. zoology Walter Reed Inst. Research, 1954-56; teaching fellow in biology Harvard U., 1959, 60; biologist in neuroanatomy NIH, 1956-58, 60; NIH predoctoral fellow in biology Harvard U., 1958-60; asst. prof. zoology U. Alta., Edmonton, Can., 1960-65, assoc. prof., 1965; sociobiologist Yerkes Regional Primate Research Ctr., Atlanta, 1965-70; hon. research assoc. Haile Sellaissie I U., Ethiopia, 1971; prof. biology and com. on evolutionary biology U. Chgo., 1970—, prof. anatomy, 1970-80; mem. primate conservation com. Nat. Acad. Scis.-NRC, 1970-72; mem. exptl. psychology sci. adv. panel NIMH, 1969-73; sci. adviser Yerkes Regional Primate Research Ctr., 1970-75; grantreviewer NSF, NIH, NIMH, Spencer Found., Nat. Geog. Soc., Smithsonian Instn., others. Contbr. articles to profl. jours.; mem. editorial bd.: Behavioral Ecology and Sociobiology, 1976-79, Am. Naturalist, 1977-79, Animal Behavior, 1978-79; mem. bd. editorial commentators: The Behavioral and Brain scis., 1977—; manuscript reviewer various profl. jours. Grantee NIMH, 1959, 62-63, 70-71, 71-72, 72-79, U. Alta., 1960, NSF, 1963-64, 64-71. Fellow Animal Behavior Soc. (pres. 1977, exec. com. 1975-78); mem. Current Anthropology (assoc.). Home: 1507 E 56th Chicago IL 60637 Office: Allee Lab Animal Behavior U Chgo 940 E 57th St Chicago IL 60637

ALTNER, PETER CHRISTIAN, orthopedic surgeon, med. educator; b. Starnberg, Germany, Apr. 19, 1932; came to U.S., 1961, naturalized, 1970; s. Bruno Robert and Gisela (Brüch) A.; m. Louise Ruth Bonney, Feb. 7, 1958; children—Linda Louise, Peter Eric, Karen Christine. M.D., U. Kiel, Germany, 1957. Intern Muhlenberg Hosp., Plainfield, N.J., 1958-59; resident orthopedics U. Chgo., 1962-64; asst. prof. U. Ill., Chgo., 1967-71; asso. prof., chief div. orthopedic surgery Chgo. Med. Sch. and Mt. Sinai Hosp. Med. Center, Chgo., 1971-73; prof. surgery U. Health Scis., Chgo. Med. Sch.; also dir. amputee clinic Cook County Hosp., Chgo., 1967—. Chmn. Village of Northbrook (Ill.) Youth Commn. Recipient Raymond B. Allen instructorship U. Ill., 1968; Outstanding New Citizenship award Met. Chgo. Citizenship Council, 1970. Mem. Am. Acad. Orthopedic Surgeons, Ill., Chgo. orthopedic socs., A.C.S., AMA, Ill., Chgo. med. socs., Assn. Orthopedic Chairmen. Home: 290 Lee Rd Northbrook IL 60062 Office: N Chgo VA Hosp North Chicago IL 60064 *Success is a result of faith, acceptance of people as they are and believing in their basic goodness. The key is confidence in one's ability to change what is not beneficial to mankind.*

ALTOBELLI, JOSEPH SALVATORE, professional baseball manager; b. Detroit, May 26, 1932; s. Michael and Antoinette (Gigliaroi) A.; m. Patsy R. Wooten, May 3, 1952; children: Mike, Mark, Jody, Jackie, Jerry, Joe. Student, Detroit Pub. Schs. Profl. baseball player Daytona Beach, Fla., 1951, Reading, Pa., 1952-53, Indpls., 1954, 56, 58, Cleve., 1955, 57, Toronto, 1959, Montreal, 1960, Omaha, 1961, Minn., 1962, Rochester, N.Y., 1963-65, mgr., Bluefield, W. Va., 1966-67, Stockton, Calif., 1968, Dallas-Ft. Worth, 1969-70, Rochester, 1971-76, Columbus, Ohio, 1980, San Francisco Giants, National League, 1977-79, Balt. Orioles, Am. League, 1983—. Office: care Baltimore Orioles Memorial Stadium Baltimore MD 21218 *

ALTON, BRUCE TAYLOR, college president; b. Cleve., Apr. 11, 1939; s. Ralph Taylor and Marian Bannon (Black) A.; m. Christie Lichliter, Aug. 25, 1962; 1 son, James. B.A., Ohio Wesleyan U., 1961; M.A., Mich. State U., 1962; Ph.D., Ohio State U., 1971. Asst. dean men Ohio Wesleyan U., Delaware, 1965-69; dean students Rocky Mountain Coll., Billings, Mont., 1971-74, acting pres., 1974-75, pres., 1975—, asst. prof. psychology, 1971-80, assoc. prof., 1980—; dir. Norwest Bank, Billings, 1980—; mem. advisory bd. Kampgrounds Am., Inc. Bd. dirs. Billings United Way, 1973-79; trustee, vice chmn. Billings Deaconess Hosp., 1976-82; chmn. bd. Western Ind. Coll. Found., 1983-84; mem. ch. bd. for homeland ministries. United Christ Ch., treas. council higher edn. Served with USAF, 1962-65. Mem. Mont. Ind. Coll. Assn. (founding pres. 1975-78), Phi Delta Kappa, Theta Alpha Phi., Pi Kappa Delta, Delta Tau Delta. Congregationalist (chmn. bd. trustees 1975-78). Lodge: Rotary (dir., past pres.). Home: 3010 Rugby Dr Billings MT 59102

ALTON, ELAINE VIVIAN, mathematics educator; b. Watertown, N.Y., Aug. 30, 1925; s. Keith Earle and Gladys Louise (Freeman) A. A.B., SUNY-Albany, 1946; M.Ed., St. Lawrence U., 1951; M.A., U. Mich., 1958; Ph.D., Mich. State U., 1965. Tchr. math. Fultonville High Sch., N.Y., 1946-48; assoc. prof. math. Ferris State Coll., Big Rapids, Mich., 1948-62; asst. instr. math Mich. State U., East Lansing, Mich., 1962-64; prof. math. edn. Ind.-Purdue U., Indpls., 1964—. Author: Vol. SI-the Metric System, 1977, filmstrip-cassette course, Trigonometry, 1980; contbr. articles in field to profl. jours. NSF grantee, 1970-73. Mem. Nat. Council Tchrs. Math., Assn. Tchr. Educators, Math. Assn. Am., Am. Math. Assn. Two Year Colls., Ind. Council Tchrs. Math. Club: Pilot (Indpls.). Home: 4215 Dahlia Ct Indianapolis IN 46220 Office: Ind U-Purdue U 1125 E 38th St PO Box 647 Indianapolis IN 46223

ALTSCHAEFFL, ADOLPH GEORGE, civil engr.; b. Passaic, N.J., July 20, 1930; s. Ludwig and Crescenz (Liebl) A.; m. Martha Anne Filiatreau, Aug. 6, 1966. B.S.C.E., Purdue U., 1952, M.S.C.E., 1955, Ph.D., 1960. Instr. in civil engring. Purdue U., West Lafayette, Ind., 1952-60, asst. prof. civil engring., 1960-64, asso. prof., 1964-74, prof., 1974—; with Waterways Expt. Sta., C.E., Vicksburg, Miss., 1955, U.S. Geol. Survey, Indpls., 1956; cons. civil engring. with various architect and contractor firms. Contbr. articles to profl. jours. Served with USAR, 1950-61. Mem. Am. Soc. Engring. Edn., ASCE, Nat. Soc. Profl. Engrs., Am. Ry. Engring. Assn., ASTM. Office: Civil Engring Bldg Purdue U West Lafayette IN 47907

ALTSCHUL, AARON MAYER, educator; b. Chgo., Mar. 13, 1914; s. Philip and Sophie (Fox) A.; m. Ruth Braude, Oct. 24, 1937; children—Sandra Betty Altschul Norman, Judy Altschul Bonderman. B.S., U. Chgo., 1934, Ph.D., 1937; D.Sc. (hon.), Tulane U., 1968. Research assoc. dept. chemistry spectroscopic biol. investigations unit U. Chgo., 1937-41; scientist, adminstr. U.S. Dept. Agr. Lab., New Orleans, 1941-58; chief research chemist Seed Protein Pioneering Research lab., 1958-67, spl. asst. to sec. of agr. for nutrition improvement, Washington, 1967-71; prof. dept. community and family medicine Georgetown U., 1971—, dir. div. nutrition, 1975—, dir. diet mgmt. program, 1976—; Underwood-Prescott lectr., 1976; former cons. to Israeli govt.; former cons. UN agencies. Author: Proteins, Their Chemistry and Politics, 1965; Editor: Processed Plant Protein Foodstuffs, 1958, New Protein Foods, Vol. 1, 1974, Vol. 2, 1976, (with H.L. Wilcke) New Protein Foods, Vol. 3, 1978, Vol. 4, 1981, Amino Acid Fortification of Protein Foods, 1971; Contbr. articles in field to profl. jours. Pres. Temple Micah, Washington, 1977-78. Recipient Golden Peanut award, 1964; Distinguished Service award U.S. Dept. Agr., 1970; Rockefeller Public Service award, 1970. Mem. Am. Chem. Soc. (Charles F. Spencer award 1966), Am. Soc. Biol. Chemists, Inst. Food Technologists (Internat. award 1971), Am. Inst. Nutrition, Am. Soc. for Clin. Nutrition, Am. Coll. Nutrition (affiliate fellow), Phi Beta Kappa, Sigma Xi, Phi Tau Sigma. Club: Cosmos. Office: Department of Community and Family Medicine Georgetown University School of Medicine Washington DC 20007

ALTSCHUL, ALFRED SAMUEL, transportation company executive; b. Chgo., Oct. 16, 1939; s. Herman and Lillian (Ginsburg) A.; m. Lynn Silverman, Sept. 8, 1968; children: Howard, Steven, Mark. B.S., U. Wis., 1961; M.B.A., U. Chgo., 1963. C.P.A., Ill. With G.A.T.X. Corp., Chgo., 1964-81, asst. treas., 1967-70, treas., 1970-81; v.p. fin. Midway Airlines, Chgo., 1981—. Lectr. fin. mgmt. Active Talent Assistance Program. Served with AUS, 1963-69. Mem. Financial Mgrs. Assn. (pres.), Alpha Epsilon Pi. Jewish religion. Club: Standard (Chgo.). Home: 8824 N Lowell Skokie IL 60076 Office: 5700 S Ciaro Chicago IL 60638

ALTSCHUL, ARTHUR GOODHART, investment banker; b. N.Y.C., Apr. 6, 1920; s. Frank and Helen (Goodhart) A.; m. Diana Landreth Childs, June 28, 1980; children from previous marriages: Stephen Frank, Charles, Arthur Goodhart, Emily Helen, Serena von Reis; 1 stepdau., Ariel Landreth Childs. Grad., Deerfield Acad., 1939; A.B., Yale, 1943. Partner Goldman, Sachs & Co., N.Y.C., 1959-76, ltd. partner, 1977—; chmn. bd. Gen. Am. Investors Co., Inc.; dir. Solar Kinetics, Inc., Wicat Systems, Inc., Boswell Energy Corp., Sunbelt Energy Corp.; mem. distbn. com. N.Y. Community Trust. Trustee Am. Assembly; former chmn. bd. trustees Barnard Coll.; mem. governing bd. Yale U. Art Gallery.; nat. bd. Smithsonian Assocs.; trustees council Nat. Gallery Art. Served to 1st lt. USMCR, 1943-45. Mem. Council Fgn. Relations. Clubs: Century Assn., Down Town Assn., Yale (N.Y.C.); Stanwich, Century Country, Madison Square

Garden, Turf and Field, Bond. Home: 993 Fifth Ave New York NY 10028 Office: 85 Broad St New York NY 10004

ALTSCHUL, MICHAEL, history educator; b. N.Y.C., Sept. 29, 1936; s. Harry and Ethel (Brahinsky) A.; children: Jennifer, Emily. B.A., NYU, 1957; Ph.D., Johns Hopkins U., 1962. Asst. prof. U. Mich., Ann Arbor, 1962-67; assoc. prof. Case Western Res. U., Cleve., 1967-77, prof. history, 1977—; vis. prof. Cleve. State U., 1972, 82; cons. Ednl. Testing Service, Princeton, N.J., 1982. Author: Baronial Family: Clares, 1965, Anglo-Norman England, 1969. Fulbright fellow (London), 1960-61; Am. Council Learned Socs. fellow, 1976; recipient Outstanding Teaching award Case Western Res. U., 1975. Fellow Royal Hist. Soc.; mem. Medieval Acad. Am. (adv. bd. 1979-82), Conf. Brit. Studies, Hasking Soc. Anglo-Norman Studies, Midwest Medieval Conf., Phi Beta Kappa. Office: Case Western Res U Dept History Cleveland OH 44106

ALTSCHULE, MARK DAVID, physician; b. N.Y.C., July 16, 1906; s. Benedict and Clara (Feldman) A.; m. Julia Diamant, July 6, 1934. B.S., Coll. City N.Y., 1927; M.D., Harvard, 1933. Diplomate: Am. Bd. Internal Med. House officer pathology Peter Bent Brigham Hosp., Boston, 1932; house officer medicine Beth Israel Hosp., Boston, 1932-34, resident med. research, 1934-35, vis. physician, 1946—; dir. internal medicine and research clin. physiology McLean Hosp., Belmont, Mass., 1947-68, cons., clin. physiologist, 1968—; asso. Thorndike Lab., Boston City Hosp., 1955-66; asst. clin. prof. medicine Harvard Med. Sch., 1952-70, asso. clin. prof. medicine, 1970-72, vis. prof., 1972-78; editor-in-chief Lippincott's Med. Sci., 1959-68, Med. Counterpoint, 1969-73. Author: Physiology in Diseases of the Heart and Lungs, rev. edit., 1954, Japanese edit., 1956, Bodily Physiology and Mental and Emotional Disorders, 1953, Acute Pulmonary Edema, 1954, The Pineal Gland: A Review of the Physiologic Literature, 1954, Essays in the History of Psychiatry, 1957, Roots of Modern Psychiatry, 2d edit., 1965, (with A. Osol and R. Pratt) The United States Dispensatory Physicians' Pharmacology, 1967. Hon. curator prints, photographs Francis A. Countway Library of Medicine, Harvard, 1969—. Mem. Assn. Am. Physicians, Soc. Exptl. Biology and Medicine, N.Y. Acad. Scis., Am., New Eng. heart assns., Am. Coll. Clin. Pharmacology and Chemotherapy, Am. Soc. Clin. Investigation, Internat. Cardiology Found., History Sci. Soc., Medieval Acad. Am., Mass. Med. Soc., Alpha Omega Alpha. Home: 23 Warwick Rd Brookline MA 02146 Office: Harvard Med Sch Boston MA 02115 *Doing good for the sake of doing good alone is the most destructive force in human society. It must be avoided.*

ALTSHUL, HAROLD MILTON, drug co. exec.; b. N.Y.C., June 19, 1909; s. Victor I. and Fannie (Kosven) A.; m. Anne Majette Grant, Feb. 13, 1959; children—Victor Anthony, Lindsey Grant. Student, Cornell U., 1928-29. With Ketchum & Co., Inc., N.Y.C., 1930—, sales mgr., 1933, operations mgr., 1934, pres., 1935—, chmn. bd., chief exec. officer, 1978—, dir., 1935—. Fellow Aspen Inst. for Humanistic Studies; mem. Nat. Wholesale Druggists Assn. (v.p. 1938, mem. bd. control 1957-59), Am. Arbitration Assn. (mem. nat. panel 1946-59), Drug, Chem. and Allied Trades Assn. (exec. com. 1942-50, chmn. 1946, adv. council 1947-50), N.Y. Bd. Trade (dir. 1943-51, v.p. 1948-50), Young Presidents Orgn. (dir. 1951-55, chmn. exec. com. 1951-52, v.p. 1952-53), Chief Execs. Forum (dir. 1958—, pres. 1962). Clubs: City Athletic (N.Y.C.); East Hampton (N.Y.); Yacht (gov. 1965—, commodore 1967-68), N.Y. Yacht, Wadawanuck Yacht. Home: 176 Water St PO Box 168 Stonington CT 06378 Office: 16 E 40th St New York NY 10016

ALTSHULER, ALAN ANTHONY, political scientist; b. Bklyn., Mar. 9, 1936; s. Leonard M. and Janet A. (Sonnenstrahl) A.; m. Julie C. Maller, June 15, 1958; children: Jennifer, David. B.A., Cornell U., 1957; M.A., U. Chgo., 1959, Ph.D., 1961. Instr. Swarthmore Coll., 1960-61; Smith-Mundt vis. asst. prof. Makerere (Uganda) Coll., 1961-62; asst. prof. Cornell U., 1962-66; asso. prof. MIT, 1966-69, prof. polit. sci. and urban studies and planning, 1969-71, 1975-83, chmn. dept. polit. sci., 1977-82; dean Grad. Sch. Pub. Adminstrn. NYU, 1983—; sec. transp. and constrn. Commonwealth Mass., 1971-75; chmn. Gov. Mass. Task Force Transp., 1969-70; dir. Boston Transp. Planning Rev. (part-time), 1970-71. Author: The City Planning Process: A Political Analysis, 1965, Community Control: The Black Demand for Participation in Large American Cities, 1970, The Urban Transportation System: Politics and Policy Innovation, 1979; also articles.; Editor: Current Issues in Transportation Policy, 1979; Co-editor: The Politics of the Federal Bureaucracy, 1977. Mem. Nat. Acad. Pub. Adminstrn., Am. Polit. Sci. Assn. Jewish. Home: 29 Washington Sq W New York NY 10011 Office: new york univ office of the dean washington square New York NY 10003

ALTSHULER, KENNETH Z., psychiatrist; b. Paterson, N.J., Apr. 11, 1929; s. Jacob and Altie (Freedman) A.; m. Gloria Seigel, June 14, 1952; children: Steven, Lori, Dara. B.A., Cornell U., 1948; M.D., U. Buffalo, 1952; D.Sc. (hon.), Gallaudet Coll., 1972. Intern Kings County Hosp., Bklyn., 1952-53; resident N.Y. State Psychiat. Inst., N.Y.C., 1955-58; asst. in psychiatry Columbia U., 1958-59, instr., 1959-63, research assoc., 1963-67, asst. clin. prof., 1967-71, assoc. clin. prof., 1971-75, prof., 1975-77; tng. analyst Psychoanalytic Clinic for Tng and Research, 1969-77; project dir. Essential Aspects of Deafness, 1972-76, Trauma and Sleep Physiology, 1975-77; prof. psychiatry Southwestern Med. Sch., Dallas, 1977, chmn. dept. psychiatry, 1977—, Stanton Sharp prof. psychiatry, 1983—; tng. analyst New Orleans Psychoanalytic Inst., 1979—; chief deafness unit Rockland State Hosp., Orangeburg, N.Y., 1966-77; cons. to NIH. Co-editor: Family and Mental Health Problems in a Deaf Population, 1963, Comprehensive Mental Health Services for the Deaf, 1966, Psychiatry and the Deaf, 1968, Expanded Mental Health Care for the Deaf, 1970; others.; Contbr. articles to profl. jours. Served with USNR, 1953-55. Recipient Wilson award in genetics and preventive medicine, 1961. Fellow Am. Psychiat. Assn. (cert. of achievement bd. hosp. psychiatry), Am. Coll. Psychiatrists, Am. Coll. Psychoanalysts; mem. AAAS, AMA, Am. Psychoanalytic Assn., Am. Soc. Human Genetics, Assn. for Psychoanalytic Medicine (recipient Merit award 1965), Tex. Med. Soc., Dallas County Med. Soc., Am. Psychopathol. Assn., Assn. Dirs. Med. Student Edn. in Psychiatry (founder, v.p. 1976-77).

ALTSHULER, NATHAN, educator, anthropologist; b. Detroit, Oct. 31, 1925; s. Aaron and Sylvia (Spitzer) A.; m. Meredith Treene, Apr. 14, 1959; children—Anthea, Linnea, Alyssa. B.A., U. Mich., 1951; postgrad., U. Ariz., 1951-52; Ph.D., Harvard, 1959. Research asst. Am. Mus. Natural History, 1947-49; research asst., teaching fellow Harvard, 1952-56; instr. Boston U., 1956-57; research asso. Joint Com. Mental Illness and Health, 1958-59; postdoctoral Nat. Inst. Mental Health fellow Harvard, 1959-60; asst. prof. to prof., chmn. dept. anthropology Coll. William and Mary, 1960—. Cofounder, editor: Studies in Third World Societies. Served wih inf. AUS, 1944-46. Recipient alumni research award Coll. William and Mary, 1963, faculty award Phi Beta Kappa, 1963, Student Assn., 1967. Fellow Am. Anthropol. Assn., Explorers Club; mem. AAAS, Phi Beta Kappa, Phi Delta Kappa. Research on Cree and Eskimo at Hudson Bay, health programs various African nations and Guyana. Home: 202 Tyler Brooks Dr Williamsburg VA 23185

ALTSTETTER, CARL JOSEPH, metallurgist, educator; b. Lima, Ohio, Oct. 26, 1930; s. Oscar G. and Clara H. A.; m. Nadja Burton Holmes, Aug. 21, 1954; children: Gregory, Mark. Met.E., U. Cin., 1953; M.S., Ill. Inst. Tech., 1954; Sc.D., Mass. Inst. Tech., 1958. With Standard Oil of Ohio, summer 1949, Bendix-Westinghouse Automotive Air Brake Co., 1949-53, Sun Oil Co., summer 1953, Battelle Meml. Inst., summer 1954; research asst. M.I.T., 1954-58; asst. prof. U. Ill., Urbana, 1958-63, asso. prof., 1963-69, prof. phys. metallurgy, 1969—; vis. scientist Max Planck Inst., Stuttgart and Garching, Germany, Nat. Bur. Standards, Washington, 1983; vis. prof. U. Calif., Berkeley, 1980; Bd. dirs. Champaign-Urbana Symphony Orch. Contbr. sci. articles to profl. lit. Recipient Disting. Alumnus award U. Cin., 1978; NATO sr. sci. fellow, 1977. Mem. Am. Soc. Metals, AIME, AAUP. Office: 302 Metallurgy Bldg U Ill Urbana IL 61801

ALTURA, BURTON MYRON, physiologist, educator; b. N.Y.C., Apr. 9, 1936; s. Barney and Frances (Dorfman) A.; m. Bella Tabak, Dec. 27, 1961; 1 dau., Rachel Allison. B.A., Hofstra U., 1957; M.S., N.Y. U., 1961, Ph.D. (USPHS fellow), 1964. Teaching fellow in biology N.Y. U., N.Y.C., 1960-61; instr. exptl. anesthesiology Sch. Medicine, 1964-65, asst. prof., 1965-66; asst. prof. physiology and anesthesiology Albert Einstein Coll. Medicine, N.Y.C., 1967-70, assoc. prof., 1970-74, vis. prof., 1974-76; prof. physiology SUNY Downstate Med. Center, Bklyn., 1974—; research fellow Bronx Mcpl. Hosp. Center, 1967-76; mem. spl. study sect. on toxicology Nat. Inst. Environ. Health Scis., 1977-78; mem. Alcohol Biomed. Research Rev. Com., Nat. Inst. Alcohol Abuse and Alcoholism, 1978—; adj. prof. biology Queens Coll., CUNY, 1983—; cons. NSF, Nat. Heart, Lung and Blood Inst., CUNY, Miles Inst., Upjohn Co., Bayer AG, Ciba-Geigy, Zyma SA.; organizer, condr. symposia. Author: Microcirculation, 3 vols., 1977-80, Vascular Endothelium and Basement Membranes, 1980, Pathophysiology of the Reticuloendothelial System, 1981, Ionic Regulation of the Microcirculation, 1982; editor-in-chief: Physiology and Pathophysiology Series, 1976—, Microcirculation, 1980—, Magnesium: Exptl. and Clin. Research, 1981—; mem. editorial bd.: Jour. Circulatory Shock, 1973—, Advances in Microcirculation, 1976—, Jour. Cardiovascular Pharmacology, 1977—, Prostaglandins and Medicine, 1978—, Substance and Alcohol Actions/Misuse, 1979—, Alcoholism: Clin. and Exptl. Research, 1982—; assoc. editor: Jour. of Artery, 1974—; asso. editor: Microvascular Research, 1978—, Agents and Actions, 1981—; contbr. over 450 articles to profl. jours. Recipient Research Career Devel. award USPHS, 1968-72; travel awards NIH, 1968, Am. Soc. Pharm. and Exptl. Therapeutics, 1969; NIH grantee, 1968—; NIMH grantee, 1974-78; Nat. Inst. Drug Abuse grantee, 1979—. Fellow Am. Heart Assn. (mem. council on stroke 1973—, council basic sci. 1969—, council on thrombosis 1971—, council on circulation 1978—, council on high blood pressure 1978—, cardiovascular A study sect. 1978-81), Am. Coll. Nutrition; mem. Microcirculatory Soc. (past mem. exec. council, mem. nominating com. 1973-74); fellow Am. Physiol. Soc. (mem. circulation group 1971—, public info. com. 1980—); mem. Soc. Exptl. Biology and Medicine (editorial bd. 1976—), AAUP, Am. Public Health Assn., Am. Chem. Soc. (div. medicinal chemistry), Am. Soc. Pharm. and Exptl. Therapeutics, Endocrine Soc., Harvey Soc., Am. Coll. Toxicology, Research Soc. on Alcoholism, Am. Thoracic Soc., Soc. for Neurosci., Shock Soc. (founding), Am. Fedn. Clin. Research, AAAS, European Conf. Microcirculation, Internat. Anesthesia Research Soc., Internat. Soc. Thrombosis and Haemostasis, Internat. Soc. Biomed. Research on Alcoholism (founding mem.), Internat. Soc. Biorheology, Soc. Environ. Geochemistry and Health, Soc. Neurosci., Reticuloendothelial Soc., Gerontol. Soc., Internat. Platform Assn., Am. Inst. Biol. Sci., Assn. Gnotobiotics, Am. Microscopical Soc., Am. Soc. Zoologists, Am. Soc. Cell Biology, Am. Soc. Bone and Mineral Research, N.Y. Acad. Scis., Am. Public Health Assn., N.Y. Heart Assn., Sigma Xi. Office: 450 Clarkson Ave Brooklyn NY 11203

ALTUS, WILLIAM DAVID, psychologist; b. Burlington, Kans., May 28, 1908; s. Samuel Abraham and Cora Jane (Burch) A.; m. Mary Agnes Atkinson, Dec. 14, 1929 (div. 1948); m. Grace Merriman Thompson, Dec. 24, 1951; children: Martha, Elizabeth, Deborah. A.B., B.S., Kans. State Tchrs. Coll., 1930, M.S., 1932; Ph.D., N.Y. U., 1941. Instr. Santa Barbara Coll., 1941-44; asst. prof. U. Calif. at Santa Barbara, 1944-47, asso. prof., 1947-54, prof., 1954-75, prof. emeritus, 1975—; chmn. dept. psychology, 1950-55, faculty research lectr., 1961—. Contbr. articles to profl. jours. Served from 2d lt. to capt. AUS, 1942-46. Fellow Am. Psychol. Assn., AAAS; mem. Sierra Club. Clubs: Univ. Calif. Faculty, Channel City. Home: 767 Las Palmas Dr Santa Barbara CA 93110

ALUTTO, JOSEPH ANTHONY, educator; b. Bronx, N.Y., June 3, 1941; s. Anthony and Concetta (Del Prete) A.; m. Rosemary Kerr, May 15, 1942; children: Patricia, Christine, Kerrie. B.B.A., Manhattan Coll., Riverdaly, N.Y., 1962; M.A., U. Ill., 1965; Ph.D., Cornell U., 1968. Asst. prof. orgnl. behavior SUNY-Buffalo, 1966-72, assoc. prof., 1972-75, prof., 1975—, dean Sch. Mgmt., 1976—; vis. prof. Carnegie-Mellon U., Pitts., 1974-75; arbitrator Fed. Mediation and Concilliation Service, 1971—; dir. Niagara Cutter, Inc., Tonawanda, N.Y., 1975—, Health Care Plan, Inc., Buffalo, 1978—. Author: (with others) Theory Testing in Organizational Behavior: The Varient Approach, 1983; contbr. articles to profl. jours. Bd. dirs. United Way, Buffalo, 1982—; pres. Amherst Central Sch. Bd., 1982—. Mem. Am. Arbitration Assn., Buffalo Area C. of C. (dir. 1982—), Am. Psychol. Assn., Acad. Mgmt. (pres. Eastern Div. 1980-81), Am. Sociol. Assn., AAAS. Club: Buffalo. Home: 655 Lebrun Rd Buffalo NY 14226 Office: Sch Mgmt SUNY 103 Crosby Hall Buffalo NY 14214

ALVA, LUIGI, lyric tenor; b. Lima, Peru, Apr. 10, 1927; s. Augusto Alva Oliva and Virginia (Talledo); m. Anna M. Zanetti, May 11, 1957; children: Juan Luis, Pedro Miguel. Ed., Peruvian Naval Acad., 1948, Singing Sch., La Scala, Milan, Italy, 1954. Artistic dir. Fundacion pro Arte Lirico, Lima. Appeared: various roles in Zarzuela, 1950; participant contest: The Great Caruso, 1951; played role of: Alfredo in La Traviata, Arequipa, Peru, 1952; also in, New Theatre, Milan, 1954; mem.: Little Scala, Milan, 1955-56, La Scala, 1956; appearances: Vienna Staatsoper, 1957, Covent Garden, London, 1960, Colon of Buenos Aires, 1962, Dallas Opera, 1960, Chgo. Lyric Opera, 1961, also festivals in, Aix, Holland, Edinburgh, Glyndebourne, Salzburg, others; performer, Met. Opera House, N.Y.C., Deutsche Oper, Berlin, Germany, 1966—; recording artist for, Columbia, H.M.V., Decca and Ricordi records. Decorated Order of Merit; comdr. Order del Peru, Order del Sol, Peru; others. Address: via Moscova 46 3 Milan Italy *

ALVARADO, FERNANDO L., electrical engineering educator, consultant; b. Lima, Peru. B.E.E., Nat. U., Lima, 1966, P.E., 1967; M.S., Clarkson Coll., Potsdam, N.Y., 1969; Ph.D., U. Mich., 1972. Asst. prof. U. Toledo, 1972-75; asst. prof. elec. engring. U. Wis., Madison, 1975-77, assoc. prof., 1977-82, prof., 1982—. Office: U Wis 1425 Johnson Dr Madison WI 53706 *

ALVAREZ, EVERETT, JR., government official, lawyer, former naval officer; b. Salinas, Calif., Dec. 23, 1937; s. Everett and Soledad (Rivera) A.; m. Thomasine Ilyas, Oct. 27, 1973; children: Marc, Bryan. B.S.E.E., Santa Clara U., 1960, Ph.D. hon., 1982; M.S., Naval Postgrad. Sch., 1976; J.D., George Washington U., 1983. Commd. officer U.S. Navy, 1960, advanced through grades to comdr., 1974; prisoner of war, North Vietnam, 1964-73, ret., 1980; dep. dir. Peace Corps, Washington, 1981-82; dep. adminstr. VA, Washington, 1982—. Bd. dirs. Everett Alvarez Scholarship Found., Santa Clara U., 1973—. Decorated Legion of Merit (2), Bronze Star (2), Silver Star, D.F.C. Republican. Orthodox Catholic. Office: Vets Adminstrn 810 Vermont Ave NW Washington DC 20420

ALVAREZ, LUIS W., physicist; b. San Francisco, June 13, 1911; s. Walter C. and Harriet S. (Smyth) A.; m. Geraldine Smithwick, 1936; children: Walter, Jean; m. Janet L. Landis, 1958; children: Donald and Helen. B.S., U. Chgo., 1932, M.S., 1934, Ph.D., 1936, Sc.D., 1967; Sc.D., Carnegie-Mellon U., 1968, Kenyon Coll., 1969, Notre Dame U., 1976, Ain Shams U., Cairo, 1979, Pa. Coll. Optometry, 1982. Research asso., instr., asst. prof., asso. prof. U. Calif., 1936-45, prof. physics, 1945-78, prof. emeritus, 1978—; asso. dir. Lawrence Radiation Lab., 1954-59, 75-78; radar research and devel. Mass. Inst. Tech., 1940-43, Los Alamos, 1944-45; dir. Hewlett Packard Co. Recipient Collier Trophy, 1946; Medal for Merit, 1948; John Scott medal, 1953; Einstein medal, 1961; Nat. Medal of Sci., 1964; Michelson award, 1965; Nobel prize in physics, 1968; Wright prize, 1981; named Calif. Scientist of Year, 1960; named to Nat. Inventors Hall of Fame, 1978. Fellow Am. Phys. Soc. (pres. 1969); mem. Nat. Acad. Scis., Nat. Acad. Engring., Am. Philos. Soc., Am. Acad. Arts and Scis., Phi Beta Kappa, Sigma Xi; asso. mem. Institut D'Egypte.

ALVAREZ, PAUL HUBERT, public relations consultant; b. Glen Ridge, N.J., Jan. 16, 1942; s. Hubert Peter and Emilie (Stock) A.; 1 dau., Amy Elizabeth. B.A., Muskingham Coll. Account supr. Ketchum Pub. Relations, Pitts., 1972-74, v.p., 1974-77, sr. v.p., 1977-79, exec. v.p., Pitts., 1979-82, chmn., chief exec. officer, 1982—; sec.-treas. Counselor's Acad., N.Y.C., 1983-84; bd. advisors Sch. Journalism, U. Fla., Gainesville, 1981—; co-chmn. Am. Educators in Journalism Study on Grad. Edn. in Pub. Relations, Brimingham, Ala., 1982—. Author, editor: What Happens in Public Relations, 1980. Mem. exec. com., bd. dirs. Civic Light Opera Assn., Pitts., 1979-83; bd. dirs. Arthritis Found. Western Pa., Pitts., 1981-82. Served with USNG. Mem. Pub. Relations Soc. Am. Democrat. Presbyterian. Club: Siwandy Country (Bronxville, N.Y.). Home: 175 Riverside Dr New York NY 10024 Office: Ketchum Pub Relations 1133 Ave of Americas New York NY 10036

ALVAREZ, ROBERT SMYTH, editor, publisher; b. San Francisco, June 7, 1912; s. Walter Clement and Harriet (Smyth) A.; m. Janet Crosby, Nov. 4, 1935; children—David Crosby, Robert Smyth, Nancy (Mrs. Eric Wallace). A.B., U. Chgo., 1934, Ph.D., 1939; B.S. in L.S, U. Ill., 1935. Dir. Brockton (Mass.) Public Library, 1941-43, Nashville Public Library, 1946-59, Berkeley (Calif.) Public Library, 1959-61, South San Francisco Public Library, 1966-80; Editor, pub. Adminstrs. Digest, 1965—, Bus. Info., 1969—, Supt.'s Digest, 1977—; tchr. public library adminstrn. George Peabody Coll., Nashville, 1946-59; library cons., surveyor. Author: Qualifications of Public Library Directors in North Central States, 1943; Contbr. articles to profl. jours. Chmn. Boy Scouts Am., North San Mateo County, 1973. Named Boss of Year Nashville Secs. Assn., 1958, Citizen of Year, South San Francisco, 1976. Mem. Phi Gamma Delta. Episcopalian. Clubs: Rotarian (pres. South San Francisco 1979-80), Sequoia (organizer), Glendale (Nashville) (organizer); Reliez Valley Country (Pleasant Hills, Calif.) (organizer); Calif. Golf (South San Francisco)). Home: 432 Dorado Way South San Francisco CA 94080 Office: PO Box 993 South San Francisco CA 94080

ALVAREZ TENA, VICTORINO, clergyman; b. Puruándiro, Mex., Mar. 10, 1920; s. Joaquín Alvarez Parra Tena Álvarez and Concepción (Tena) Álvarez. Ed., Colegio Morelos de Puruandiro, Seminary Morelia, Seminario de Montezuma. Ordained priest Roman Cath. Ch.; bishop, Celaya, Mex. Home: Altamirano 404 en Celya GTO Mexico Office: Manuel Doblado 110 En Celaya GTO Mexico

ALVARINO DE LEIRA, ANGELES (ANGELES ALVARINO), biologist, oceanographer; b. El Ferrol, Spain, Oct. 3, 1916; came to U.S., 1958, naturalized, 1966; d. Antonio Alvarino-Grimaldos Carmen and Gonzalez (Diaz-Saavedra); m. Eugenio Leira-Manso, Mar. 16, 1940; 1 dau., Angeles. B.S. and Letters summa cum laude, U. Santiago de Compostela (Spain), 1933; M. Natural Scis., U. Madrid, 1941, cert. Doctorate, 1951, D.Sc. summa cum laude, 1967. Cert. Biologist-Oceanographer, Spanish Inst. Oceanography, 1952. Prof. biology Coll. El Ferrol, Spain, 1941-48; fishery research biologist dept. Sea Fisheries Spain, 1948-52; histologist Superior Council Sci. Research, 1948-52; biologist, oceanographer Spanish Inst. Oceanography, 1950-57; biologist Scripps Inst. Oceanography, U. Calif.-LaJolla, 1958-69; fishery research biologist Nat. Marine Fisheries Service Southwest Fisheries Ctr., NOAA, U.S. Dept. Commerce, La Jolla, 1970—; assoc. prof. U. Nat. Autonomous Mexico, U. San Diego, 1982—; research assoc. San Diego State U.; vis. prof. Poly. Tech. Mexico, U. Parara (Brazil). Contbr. articles to profl. jours., chpts. to sci. books; discoverer new soecies of animals. Brit. Council fellow, 1953-54; Fulbright fellow, 1956-57; NSF grantee, 1961-69; U.S. Office Navy grantee, 1958-69; Calif. Coop. Oceanic Fishery Investigation grantee, 1958-69; UNESCO grantee, 1979. Fellow Am. Inst. Fishery Research Biologists, San Diego Soc. Natural History; mem. Assn. Natural History Soc., Western Naturalists Soc., Calif. Acad. Scis., Biol. Soc. Washington, Hispano-Am. Assn. Researchers on Marine Scis., Marine Biol. Assn. U.K., Sigma Xi. Home: 7535 Cabrillo Ave La Jolla CA 92037 Office: PO Box 271 La Jolla CA 92038

ALVARY, LORENZO, bass singer; b. Hungary, Feb. 20, 1909; came to U.S., 1938, naturalized, 1944; s. William and Elizabeth (Kras) A.; m. Hallie Carr Fox, 1959. B.L., U. Geneva, Switzerland, 1930; LL.M., U. Budapest, Hungary, 1932. Gen. mgr., artistic dir. Opera Guild Greater, Miami, 1972-73; producer Scarlatti Spectacle, Venice, Brussels, Paris, 1961, 62. Made debut, Royal Opera House, Budapest, 1934; toured in concerts and operas throughout world, Vienna State Opera, 1977-78, Met. Opera Co., N.Y.C., 1942—; soloist, N.Y. Philharmonic Symphony, (under Bruno Walter and Arturo Toscanini, Leonard Bernstein, others), 1942—; has appeared in, Rio de Janiero, Sao Paulo, Brazil, Mexico City, Montevideo, Uruguay, Teatro Colon—Buenos Aires, 1956, Opera Paris, 1957, San Francisco Opera, 1940—, Stuttgart, Berlin, Naples, Venice, Brussels, Genoa, 1956—, Salzburg Festival, 1974-75; host weekly program: Opera Topics, sta, WKCR, 1964—; Judge internat. vocal contests, Busseto, Enna, Cento; Vercelli (all Italy), Geneva, Barcelona, Rio de Janeiro, Paris, Pretoria, Munich, Toulouse, Met. Opera Auditions. Calvinist. *Work, discipline and competitive spirit.*

ALVERSON, HOYT SUTLIFF, anthropology educator; b. Washington, June 7, 1942; s. Elwyn Sutliff and Myrtle (Hall) A.; m. Marianne Melchior, June 6, 1964; children: Keith, Brian. B.A., George Washington U., 1964, M.Phil., Yale U., 1967, Ph.D., 1968. Reading room attendant Library of Congress, Washington, 1960-64; instr. So. Conn. State Coll., New Haven, 1965; asst. prof. Dartmouth Coll., Hanover, N.H., 1968-74, assoc. prof., chmn., 1974-80, prof., chmn., Hanover, 1980—; cons. U.S. Peace Corps, Botswana, 1974, AID, Washington, 1975, 81, Can. Internat. Devel. Aid., Botswana, 1978; project humanist N.H. Council on Humanities, Concord, 1983. Author: Mind in the Heart of Darkness, 1978 (Herskovits U. Chgo. Folklore prize 1979); contbr. articles to profl. jours. Presdoctoral fellow NIH, 1965-67; research grantee NSF, 1971, NIMH, 1974-75;

recipient summer stipend NEH, 1981. Home: Freeman Rd Hanover NH 03755 Office: Dartmouth Coll Hanover NH 03755

ALVERSON, WILLIAM H., lawyer; b. Rockford, Ill., July 23, 1933. A.B., Princeton U., 1955; LL.B., U. Wis., 1960. Bar: Wis. bar 1960. Mem. firm Godfrey & Kahn. Pres. Milw. Profl. Sports and Services, 1972-76; chmn. Houston Rockets basketball team, 1977-79; chmn. bd. govs. Nat. Basketball Assn., 1975-76. Mem. Milw., Am. bar assns., State Bar Wis., Phi Delta Phi. Office: 780 N Water St Milwaukee WI 53202

ALVINE, ROBERT, rubber manufacturing company executive; b. Newark, Aug. 25, 1938; s. James C. and Marie A.; m. Diane C. Marzulli, May 6, 1961; children: Robert James, Laurie Anne. B.S., Rutgers U., 1960; postgrad., Harvard Bus. Sch., 1972. With Celanese Corp., 1960-77; bus. mgr. Celanese Plastics Co., Newark, 1969-72; mktg. mgr. Celanese Piping Systems, Hilliard, Ohio, 1972-75; v.p. comml. Celanese Polymer Spltys. Co., Louisville, 1975-77; dir. strategy planning and bus. devel. Uniroyal, Naugatuck, Conn., 1977, v.p. corp. planning and devel., Middlebury, Conn., 1978-79; v.p., gen. mgr. Uniroyal Tire Co. and; pres. Uniroyal Merchandising Co., 1979-80, Uniroyal Devel. Co., 1980—; group v.p. Engineered Products, Worldwide, 1983—. Served with AUS, 1962-68. Named Ky. Col., 1976. Mem. Am. Inst. Mgmt., Nat. Planning Inst., Comml. Devel. Assn., N. Am. Planning Soc., Nat. Assn. Corp. Growth, Rubber Mfrs. Assn., Newcomen Soc. Am., Soc. Plastics Industry, Soc. Plastics Engrs., Mfg. Chemists Assn., Nat. Paint and Coatings Assn., Pres.'s Assn. Mem. Ch. of Christ. Home: 55 N Racebrook Rd Woodbridge CT 06525 Office: Uniroyal World Hdqrs Middlebury CT 06749

ALVORD, JOEL BARNES, bank executive; b. Manchester, Conn., Nov. 29, 1938; s. Martin Earl and Elizabeth (Barnes) A.; m. Anne Stilson, June 23, 1962; children: Sarah, Seth. A.B., Dartmouth Coll., 1960, M.B.A., 1961. With Hartford Nat. Corp., Conn., 1963—, exec. v.p. investments and exec. v.p., 1976-78, pres., 1978—, also dir.; dir. Hartford Steam Boiler Inspection and Ins. Co., N.Am. Reins. Corp., Swiss Re Advs., Inc., Swiss Reins. Co. (N.Am.), Inc., Moore McCormack Resources. Bd. dirs. Inst. of Living, Hartford; trustee Loomis-Chaffee Sch., Windsor, Conn., Wadsworth Atheneum. Served with Ordnance Corps U.S. Army, 1961-62. Mem. Res. City Bankers Assn. Congregationalist.

ALVORD, WILLIAM HOWARD, accountant; b. Syracuse, N.Y., Sept. 17, 1925; s. D. Eaton and Maryon (McNamara) A.; m. Shirley Ann Knott, Mar. 31, 1951; children: Nancy Lynn, Sharon Elizabeth (Mrs. Jeffrey Skerry). B.S., Syracuse U., 1949; M.S., Grad. Sch. Bus., Columbia U., 1953. C.P.A., N.Y. Auditor Hurdman & Cranstoun (C.P.A.s), N.Y.C., 1949-52; with Carrier Corp., Syracuse, 1953-72, v.p. fin., 1968-72; v.p., chief fin. officer, mem. exec. com., dir. USM Corp., Boston, 1972-76; sr. v.p. fin. Investors Diversified Services, Inc., Mpls., 1976-83; pvt. practice acctg., Mpls., 1983—; trustee Suffolk Franklin Savs. Bank, Boston, 1973-76; Chmn. corp. adv. council Syracuse U., 1969-78. Served with AUS, 1943-46. Mem. Fin. Execs. Inst., Am. Inst. C.P.A.'s. Presbyterian. Clubs: N.Y. Athletic, Mpls., Mpls. Athletic. Home: 4634 Edgebrook Pl Edina MN 55424 Office: 2407 IDS Ctr Minneapolis MN 55402

AL YASIRI, KAHTAN ABBASS, coll. dean; b. Hindia, Iraq, Jan. 20, 1939; came to U.S., 1958; s. Abbass and Fakria Al Y.; m. Ann M. Johnson, June 8, 1961; children—Jeanan, Shawn, Seanan, Javon. B.Sc., U. Nebr., 1962; M.S., 1963; Ph.D., Ia. State U., 1965. Research asst. U. Nebr., Lincoln, 1961-63; inst. Ames (Iowa) pub. schs., 1963-65; instr. Iowa State U., Ames, 1964-65; asso. prof., head dept. bus. and econs. U. Wis. at Platteville, 1965-66; prof. econs. dean Coll. Bus. and Econs., 1966-76; dean Coll. Bus., Industry and Communications, 1976—. Author: Economic Work and Program Study, 1966, Growth and Progress in Business, 1966, The Foundations of Economic Analysis, Key Ideas and Statements in Economics, 1976, Glossary of Important Economic Terms and Concepts, 1976. Mem. Am., Midwest, Western econ. assns., Agr. Econ. Assn., Am. Soc. Personnel Adminstrs., Omicron Delta Epsilon, Phi Kappa Phi. Home: 6756 N Elm St Platteville WI 53818

ALYEA, ETHAN DAVIDSON, lawyer; b. Clifton, N.J., Feb. 2, 1896; s. Joseph Pascal Strong and Sarah May (Dinsmore) A.; m. Dorothy Collins, Aug. 2, 1924; children—Jane D., Ethan Davidson. A.B., Princeton U., 1916, M.A., 1917; LL.B., Harvard U., 1922. Bar: N.Y. bar 1923. Since practiced in, N.Y.C.; mem. firm Dewey, Ballantine, Bushby, Palmer & Wood.; Pres. Montclair (N.J.) Council Social Agys., 1948-50; Bd. dirs. Grand Central Art Galleries, Inc., 1961-69. Pres., dir. Cintas Found.; trustee Montclair Community Chest, 1954-57; pres. Montclair Adult Sch., 1946-48, trustee, 1946—; trustee Montclair Library, 1947-57; v.p., trustee Montclair Art Mus., 1953-67. Served as sgt. U.S. Army, 1918-19. Mem. ABA, N.Y. Bar Assn., Assn. Bar City N.Y., N.Y. County Lawyers Assn., Phi Beta Kappa. Club: Downtown Assn. (N.Y.C.). Home: 77 Highland Ave Montclair NJ 07042 Office: 140 Broadway New York NY 10005

ALYEA, ETHAN DAVIDSON, JR., educator; b. Orange, N.J., Mar. 7, 1931; s. Ethan Davidson and Dorothy (Collins) A.; m. Sandra Dement, June 17, 1957; children—Caroline Dinsmore, Peter Gerritse, Clark Vreeland, Garret Merselis. A.B., Princeton, 1953; Ph.D., Calif. Inst. Tech., 1962. Mem. faculty dept. physics Ind. U., Bloomington, 1962—, asso. prof., 1967-71, prof., 1971—. Recipient Distinguished Teaching award Standard Oil (Ind.) Found., 1970. Mem. Am. Phys. Soc., Am. Assn. Physics Tchrs. Home: 2217 Georgetown Rd Bloomington IN 47401

ALZADO, LYLE MARTIN, professional football player; b. Bklyn., Apr. 3, 1949. B.A., Yankton (S.D.) Coll., 1971. Profl. football player Denver Broncos, 1971-79, Cleve. Browns, 1979-82, Los Angeles Raiders, 1982—; fought Muhammed Ali in exhbn. match, Denver, 1979. Host radio sports talk show, Sta. KWBZ, Denver, 1976-77. Colo. hon. head coach Spl. Olympic Program for Retarded; vol. staff Children's Hosp.; co-chmn. Bike-a-thon for Cystic Fibrosis, Read-a-thon; hon. chmn. Walk for Mankind; hon. nat. sports com. Muscular Dystrophy, Arapahoe County chmn.; bd. dirs. Am. Cancer Soc.; mem. Fight for Life St. Anthony's Hosp.; active juvenile delinquent program and Police Athletic League of Denver Police Dept.; active civic orgn. fund raising. Recipient Earl Hartman Meml. award as outstanding defensive lineman on Denver Broncos, 1975; Byron Whizzer White Humanitarian award Nat. Football League, 1977; Friend of Youth award Optimists Internat., 1978; named Man of Year Denver Jaycees, 1976, Nat. Football League, 1977; AFC Defensive Player of Yr., 1977; All-Pro Defensive Lineman, 1977. Office: care Los Angeles Raiders 332 Center St El Segundo CA 90245 *I have felt that to be successful and happy, one must believe in these three things: God, oneself, and friends.* *

AMACHER, RICHARD EARL, literature educator; b. Ridgway, Pa., Dec. 13, 1917; s. Albert and Emma (Luchs) A.; m. Cordelia Anne Ward, Aug. 26, 1953; 1 dau., Alice Marie. A.B., Ohio U., 1939; postgrad., U. Chgo., 1939-42; Ph.D., U. Pitts., 1947. Instr. English Yale U., New Haven, 1944-45; instr. Rutgers U., New Brunswick, N.J., 1945-47, asst. prof., 1947-53, lectr., 1953-54; chmn. English dept. Henderson State Tchrs. Coll., Arkadelphia, Ark., 1954-57; asso. prof. English Auburn (Ala.) U., 1957-65, prof., 1965-78, Hargis prof. Am. Lit., 1978—; Fulbright prof., Wurzburg, W. Ger., 1961-62, Konstanz, W. Ger., 1969-70. Author: Franklin's Wit and Folly, 1953, Practical Criticism, 1956, Benjamin Franklin, 1962, Edward Albee, 1969, (with Margaret Rule) Edward Albee at Home and Abroad, 1973, (with Victor Lange) New Perspectives in German Literary Criticism, 1979, American Political Writers, 1788-1800, 1979; editor: (with G. Polhemus) J.G. Baldwin's The Flush Times of California, 1966. Chmn. Auburn Chamber Music Soc., 1980—; elder Presbyterian Ch. Am. Council Learned Socs. grantee, 1972. Mem. MLA, S. Atlantic MLA, AAUP, Am. Studies Assn. (pres. southeastern sec. 1977-79), Société Historique d'Auteuil et de Passy, Nat. Soc. Lit. and Arts. Democrat. Club: Auburn Univ. Faculty. Home: 515 Auburn Dr Auburn AL 36830 Office: English Dept Auburn Univ Auburn AL 36830

AMADEO, JOSE H., physician, educator; b. N.Y.C., July 16, 1928; s. H. R. and Carmen (Nigaglioni) A.; m. Patricia Carron; children—Jose F. Javier, Luis Robert, Carmen Patricia; children (by previous marriage)—Mary Martha, Jose H., John Michael, Jennifer. B.Sc., Ursinus Coll., 1948; M.D., Jefferson Med. Coll., 1952. Diplomate: Am. Bd. Surgery, Am. Bd. Thoracic Surgery, Nat. Bd. Med. Examiners. Intern Jefferson Med. Coll. Hosp., Phila., 1952-53, resident surgery, 1953-57, Am. Cancer Soc. fellow, 1956-57; instr. surgery Jefferson Med. Coll., 1959-61; chief surg. service San Juan (P.R.) VA Hosp., 1961—; prof., co-chmn. dept. surgery U. P.R. Sch. Medicine, San Juan, 1961—. Contbr. articles to med. and surg. publs. Mem. Phila. Dist. Health and Welfare Council, 1960-61. Served to capt. M.C. USAF, 1957-59; now col. P.R. Army N.G. Fellow A.C.S. (gov.), Internat. Soc. Surgery; mem AMA, Pan Am Med. Assn., Soc. Thoracic Surgery, Assn. Mil. Surgeons, U.S., Am. Fedn. Clin. Research, Soc. for Surgery of Alimentary Tract, Southeastern Surg. Congress, Res. Officers Assn., Alpha Omega Alpha, Alpha Kappa Kappa. Republican. Roman Catholic. Home: PO Box 10837 Caparra Heights PR 00922 Office: VA Hospital San Juan PR 00936

AMADO, RALPH DAVID, educator; b. Los Angeles, Nov. 23, 1932; s. Richard Joseph and Suzanne (Nahoum) A.; m. Carol Stein, May 28, 1961; children—Richard Lewis, David Philip. B.A., Stanford, 1954; Ph.D. (Rhodes scholar), Oxford U., 1957. Research asso. U. Pa., 1957-59, asst. prof., 1959-62, asso. prof., 1962-65, prof. physics, 1965—; Cons. Arms Control and Disarmament Agy., 1962-65, Los Alamos Sci. Lab., 1965—. Fellow Am. Phys. Soc.; mem. A.A.A.S. Home: 509 Latmer Rd Merion PA 19066

AMADOR, LUIS VALENTINE, surgeon; b. 1920. M.D., Northwestern U., 1944. Diplomate: Am. Bd. Neurosurgeons. Intern U. Ill., 1944-45, resident in neurology and neurosurgery, 1945-46, 48-50, Rockefeller Found., 1951-52; Guggenheim fellow, 1954; neurosurgeon Children's Meml. Hosp., Northwestern Meml. Hosps. (Wesley and Passavant Pavillions); clin. prof. neurol. surgery U. Ill., Chgo., 1966-78; prof. clin. neurol. surgery Northwestern U., 1978—; Bd. dirs. Spastic Paralysis Research Found. Contbr. articles to books and profl. jours. Served to capt. M.C. AUS., 1946-48. Fellow A.C.S., Royal Soc. Medicine; mem. AMA, Congress Neurol. Surgeons, Am. Assn. Neurol. Surgeons, Central Neurosurg. Soc. (pres.), Internat. Soc. Pediatric Neurosurgery, Interurban Neurol. Soc. (dir.), Am. Soc. Stereotaxic Neurosurgery, AAAS, Sigma Xi. Office: 707 N Fairbanks Ct Chicago IL 60611

AMAN, GEORGE MATTHIAS, III, lawyer; b. Wayne, Pa., Mar. 2, 1930; s. George Matthias and Emily (Kalbach) A.; m. Ellen McMillan, June 20, 1959; children: James E., Catherine E., Peter T. A.B., Princeton U., 1952; LL.B., Harvard U., 1957. Bar: Pa. 1958. Assoc. Townsend Elliot & Munson, Phila., 1960-65; ptnr. Morgan Lewis & Bockius, Phila., 1965—. Commr. Radnor Twp., Pa., 1976-80, planning commr., Pa., 1981—; pres. bd. trustees Wayne Presbyn. Ch., Pa., 1981-84. Served to 1st lt. U.S. Army, 1952-54. Mem. ABA, Pa. Mcpl. Authorities Assn., Phila. Regional Mcpls. Fin. Officers Assn. (dir. 1983—), Am. Law Inst. Republican. Clubs: Merion Cricket (Haverford, Pa.); Princeton (Phila.) (dir 1977-79). Home: 425 Darby Paoli Rd Wayne PA 19087 Office: Morgan Lewis & Bockius One Logan Sq Philadelphia PA 19103

AMAN, MOHAMMED MOHAMMED, university dean, library science and information educator; b. Cairo, Jan. 3, 1940; U.S., 1963, naturalized, 1975; s. Mohammed Aman and Fathia Ali (al-Maghrabi) Mohammed; m. Mary Jo Parker, Sept. 15, 1972; 1 son, David. B.A., Cairo U., 1961; M.S., Columbia U., 1965; Ph.D., U. Pitts., 1968. Librarian Egyptian Nat. Library, 1961-63, Duquesne U., Pitts., 1966-68; asst. prof. library sci. Pratt Inst., N.Y.C., 1968-69; asst. prof., then assoc. prof. St. John's U., Jamaica, N.Y., 1969-73, prof., dir. div. library and info. sci., 1973-76; prof. library sci., dean Palmer Grad. Library Sch., C.W. Post Center, L.I. U., 1976-79; prof., dean Sch. Library and Info. Sci., U. Wis., Milw., 1979—; cons. for UNESCO, AID and; UNIDO. Author: Librarianship and the Third World, 1976, Cataloging and Classifications of Non-Western Library Material: Issues, Trends and Practices, 1979, Arab Serials and Periodicals: A Subject Bibliography, 1979, On line Access to Databases (Arabic). Fellow Middle East Studies Assn.; mem. ALA (chmn. internat. relations roundtable 1976-77, chmn. internat. relations com. 1984-85), Am. Soc. Info. Sci., Am.-Arab Affairs Council, Spl. Libraries Assn., Egyptian-Am. Scholars Assn., Assn. for Library and Info. Sci. Edn. (chmn. internat. relations com. 1983-84), Wis. Library Assn. (chmn. library careers com. 1981-1982). Democrat. Islam. Office: Sch Library and Info Sci Univ Wis Milwaukee WI 53201

AMAN, REINHOLD ALBERT, philologist, publisher; b. Fuerstenzell, Bavaria, Apr. 8, 1936; came to U.S., 1959, naturalized, 1963; s. Ludwig and Anna Margarete (Waindinger) A.; m. Shirley Ann Beischel, Apr. 9, 1960; 1 dau., Susan. Student, Chem. Engring. Inst., Augsburg, Germany, 1953-54; B.S. with high honors, U. Wis., 1965; Ph.D., U. Tex., 1968. Chem. engr., Munich and Frankfurt, Ger., 1954-57; petroleum chemist Shell Oil Co., Montreal, Que., Can., 1957-59; chem. analyst A. O. Smith Corp., Milw., 1959-62; prof. German U. Wis., Milw., 1968-74; editor, pub. Maledicta Jour., Maledicta Press Publs., Waukesha, Wis., 1976—; pres. Maledicta Press, Waukesha, 1976—; dir. Internat. Maledicta Archives, Waukesha, 1975—. Author: Der Kampf in Wolframs Parzival, 1968, Bayrisch-oesterreichisches Schimpfwoerterbuch, 1973, 81; gen. editor: Mammoth Cod (Mark Twain), 1976, Dictionary of International Slurs (A. Roback), 1979, Graffiti (A. Read), 1977; editor: Maledicta: The Internat. Jour. Verbal Aggression, 1977—; contbr. articles to profl. jours. Recipient scholarships U. Wis., 1963-65, French-German award, 1965; U. Wis. research grantee, 1973, 74; NDEA Title IV fellow, 1965-68. Mem. Internat. Maledicta Soc. (pres.). Home and Office: 331 S Greenfield Ave Waukesha WI 53186

AMANDES, RICHARD BRUCE, lawyer; b. Berkeley, Calif., Mar. 29, 1927; s. F. Frederic and Nellie (McHoul) A.; m. Carolyn Jordan, Jan. 1, 1983; children: Christopher Bruce, Robin Michelle. A.B., U. Calif. at Berkeley, 1950; J.D., Hastings Coll. Law, 1953; LL.M., NYU, 1956. Bar: Calif. 1954. Pvt. practice law, San Francisco, 1954; instr. U. Wash. Sch. Law, 1954-55, vis. asst. prof., 1956-57, asst. prof., asst. dean, 1958-60, asso. prof., asst. dean, 1960-64; asst. prof. U. Wyo. Sch. Law, 1957-58; asso. dean, Robert W. Harrison prof. law Hastings Coll. of Law, U. Calif., 1964-66; dean, prof. law Tex. Tech U., Lubbock, 1966-77; vis. asst. prof. So. Meth. U. Sch. Law, summer 1957; vis. prof. Gonzaga U. Sch. Law, fall 1974, Southwestern U. Sch. Law, spring 1975, U. San Diego Sch. Law, 1977-78; Disting. prof. law U. LaVerne Coll. Law, 1978-81, asso. dean, 1980-81; vis. prof. law Vanderbilt U., Nashville, 1981-82, U. Santa Clara (Calif.), 1982-83; gen. counsel Planning Cons., Inc., Lubbock, 1983—; adminstr. Continuing Legal Edn., State of Wash., 1959-64; participant Summer Workshop for Internat. Legal Studies, U. Calif., Berkeley, 1958; Chmn. Conf. Western Law Schs., Seattle, 1959, Lubbock, 1971, San Diego, 1978; mem. exec. com. Law Sch. Admission Test Council, 1962-64; chmn. Bar Exam. Revision Com. Tex., 1969-77; sec.-treas. Tex. Tech. Law Sch. Found., 1966-77; commr. on Uniform State Laws, Tex., 1972-74; ednl. dir. Uniform Land Transactions Act and Uniform Simplification of Land Transfers Act, 1979—; hearing referee Calif. State Bar Ct., 1979—; participant Law and Econs. Workshop, Law and Econs. Inst., summer 1980; cons. law sch. accreditation, 1974—. Contbr. articles to profl. publs. Served with AUS, 1945-47. Teaching fellow N.Y. U. Sch. Law, 1955-56. Mem. ABA (chmn. com. on significant real property decisions 1965-66), Wash. Bar Assn., State Bar Calif., State Bar Tex., Assn. Am. Law Schs. (council on new and expanding law schs.), Edward S. Thurston Honor Soc., Order of Coif, Phi Alpha Delta, Lambda Alpha Epsilon, Phi Kappa Phi (pres. Tex. Tech U. chpt. 1976-77). Office: PO Box 6870 Lubbock TX 79493

AMANN, PETER HENRY, history educator; b. Vienna, Austria, May 31, 1927; came to U.S., 1941, naturalized, 1950; s. Paul and Dora (Iranyi) A.; m. Enne Niemi, June 19, 1947; children: Paula, Sandra, David. B.A., Oberlin Coll., 1947; M.A., U. Chgo., 1953, Ph. D., 1958. Instr. history Bowdoin Coll., Brunswick, Me., 1956-59; asst., then assoc. prof. Oakland U., Rochester, Mich., 1959-65; assoc. prof. State U. N.Y. at Binghamton, 1965-68; prof. history U. Mich., Dearborn, 1968—, William E. Stirton disting. prof. history, 1978—. Author: Revolution and Mass Democracy: The Paris Club Movement in 1848, 1975; Editorial bd.: French Hist. Studies, 1972-75; Contbr. articles to profl. jours.; current research areas Am. fascism during 1930's, French peasant history. Guggenheim fellow, 1963-64; sr. research Fulbright fellow, Paris, 1963-64; Nat. Endowment for the Humanities fellow, Toulouse; France, 1982. Mem. Am. Hist. Assn., French Hist. Soc. Home: 2472 Grant Ann Arbor MI 48104 Office: 4901 Evergreen Rd Dearborn MI 48128

AMARA, LUCINE, opera and concert singer; b. Hartford, Conn., Mar. 1, 1927; d. George and Adrine (Kazanjian) Armaganian;, Jan. 7, 1961 (div. June 1964). Student, Music Acad. of West, 1947, U. So. Calif., 1949-50. Appeared at Hollywood Bowl, 1948; soloist, San Francisco Symphony, 1949-50; with, Met. Opera, N.Y.C., 1950—; appeared on, Met. Opera: In Performance, 1982, 83, 84; recorded Pagliacci, 1951, 60; singer with, New Orleans, Hartford, Pitts., Central City operas, 1952-54; appeared, Glyndebourne Opera, 1954, 55, 57, 58, Edinburgh Festival, 1954; singer, Aida, Terme Di Caracalla, Rome, 1954, also Stockholm Opera, N.Y. Philharmonic, St. Louis Civic Light Opera, 1955-56; has appeared in: leading or title roles in several operas including Tosca, Aids, Amelia in Un Ballo in Maschera, others; appeared with, St. Petersburg (Fla.) Opera; opera and concert tour, Russia, 1965, Manila, 1968, Paris, Mex., 1966, Hong Kong and China, 1983; rec. artist, Columbia, RCA, Victor, Angel records, Met. Opera Record Club. Recipient 1st prize Atwater-Kent Radio Auditions, 1948. Mem. Sigma Alpha Iota. Home: 260 West End Ave New York NY 10023 Office: Metropolitan Opera New York NY 10023 *My life has been filled with new experiences. I have been most fortunate to have achieved a career that has introduced me to so many wonderful people. Some have become close friends; others, because of time and distance, have become warm acquaintances. I am humbly grateful for all God's blessings.*

AMARAL, JESUS EDUARDO, architect; b. Humacao, P.R., Oct. 13, 1927; s. Jesus and Ana Maria (Carmona) A.; m. Maria Luisa Bibiloni, Apr. 11, 1953; children—Ana Maria, Maria Luisa, Maria Teresa, Eduardo Jose. B.C.E., Cornell U., 1948, B.Arch., 1951. Lic. architect, P.R., Pa. Civil engr. P.R. Housing Authority, 1948; constrn. insp. Caribe Hilton Project, San Juan, P.R., 1949; archtl. designer Office Rene Ramirez, San Juan, 1953; practice architecture, San Juan, 1954-55; architect urban renewal br. San Juan Mcpl. Housing Authority, 1955; partner Amaral y Morales-Arquitectos, San Juan, 1956-69; prin. J.E. Amaral, Arquitecto y Asocs., San Juan, 1970—; in charge orgn. Sch. Architecture, U. P.R., 1965-69; dir. Sch. Architecture, 1966-69; mem. alumni secondary schs. com. Cornell U., 1966—; mem. adv. council Coll. Architecture, Art and Planning, 1977—, vis. prof. archtl. design, 1977; dir. Roig Comml. Bank, Humacao, Johnson Wax of P.R.; adv. to spl. com. on natural resources Chamber of Reps. of P.R., 1967-68; counselor to Mayor San Juan on Model City Program, 1969. Archtl. works include, Hotel Delicias, Fajardo, P.R., 1964 (Progressive Architecture Design Awards citation 1961), Catholic Ch., Yabucoa, P.R., 1968, Coll. Campus of U., P.R., Humacao (P.R. chpt. AIA Honor Awards Program citation of merit 1977 and), Coll. Campus of U., P.R., Humacao (Honor Design award 1978), Coll. Campus of Bayamon Regional Coll., U. P.R., 1971—, Prototype Schs. for Govt. P.R., 1976 (P.R. chpt. AIA Honors Awards Program spl. mention 1976); interior designer, Velasco Store at Plaza Las Americas Shopping Center, Hato Rey, P.R., 1968 (Urbe Design award). Served with USAF, 1951-53. Recipient 2d prize San Juan Mcpl. Baseball Stadium Competition, 1959. Fellow AIA (pres. P.R. chpt. 1978); mem. Colegio de Arquitectos de P.R., Colegio de Ingenieros de P.R., Nat. Council Archtl. Registration Bds. (cert.), Instituto de Arquitetos do Brasil (hon.). Roman Catholic. Clubs: Penn-Cornell of P.R.; Rio Mar Country (Rio Grande, P.R.). Office: PO Box 896 Hato Rey PR 00919

AMAREL, SAUL, educator, computer scientist; b. Thessaloniki, Greece, Feb. 16, 1928; came to U.S., 1957, naturalized, 1962; s. Albert and Sol (Pelossof) Amario; m. Marianne Kroh, Dec. 20, 1953; children: Dan, David. B.Sc., Israel Inst. Tech., Haifa, 1948, Ingenieur EE, 1949; M.S., Columbia, 1953, D.Eng. Sci, 1955. Sci. dep. Israel Ministry Def., Israel, 1948-52, project leader control and computer systems, 1955-57; research engr. Electronic Research Lab., Columbia, 1953-55; head computer theory research RCA Labs., Princeton, N.J., 1957-69; prof., chmn. computer sci. dept. Rutgers U., New Brunswick, N.J., 1969—; dir. Lab. Computer Sci. Research, 1977—, Rutgers Research Resource in Computers in Medicine, 1971—; vis. prof. computer sci. Carnegie Mellon U., 1966; vis. scholar Stanford U., 1979; vis. research fellow SRI Internat., spring 1983; Mem. chem./biol. info. handling rev. com. NIH, 1971-75; mem. info. scis. adv. com. N.J. Dept. Higher Edn., 1973—; mem. exec. and adv. coms. SUMEX-AIM, 1974—; trustee Internat. Joint Confs. Artificial Intelligence, 1981—; bd. dirs. N.J. Ednl. Computer Network, 1975-80. Mem. editorial bd.: Artificial Intelligence, Internat. Jour., 1969—, Jour. Computer Langs., 1974—; contbr. articles to sci. jours. Trustee Ramapo Coll., N.J., 1969-73. Mem. IEEE (sr.), Soc. Indsl. and Applied Math., Assn. Computing Machinery, AAAS, Sigma Xi. Home: 25 White Pine Ln Princeton NJ 08540 Office: Rutgers U New Brunswick NJ 08903

AMATO, VINCENT VITO, bus. exec.; b. Bklyn., Oct. 14, 1929; s. Anthony and Josephine (Maniscalco) A.; m. Marie Dioguardi, Apr. 24, 1955; children—Stephanie, Janine, Anthony, Christopher. B.B.A., CCNY, 1951, M.B.A., 1958. Liaison to div. controller Allied Chem. Corp., N.Y.C., 1951-59; acctg. systems rep. Olivetti-Underwood, N.Y.C., 1959-61; v.p. planning, controller, acquisitions exec. Ingredient Tech. Corp., N.Y.C., 1961-72, v.p. planning, treas., 1972-73, pres. splty. products, 1973-80; pres., mktg. and mgmt. cons. Market Makers Inc., 1980—; adj. asst. prof. N.Y. U.; also Am. Mgmt. Assn.

seminars. Pres. Lakeridges Civic Assn. Mem. Fin. Execs. Inst., Assn. for Corp. Growth, Am. Mgmt. Assn. (tech. adviser). Home: 7 Alder Ct Matawan NJ 07747 Office: 900 Route 9 Woodbridge NJ 07095

AMAYA, MARIO ANTHONY, art administrator, editor, writer; b. N.Y.C., Oct. 6, 1933; s. Mario A. and Maria Sophia (Garofalo) A. B.A. in Art and English Lit, Bklyn. Coll.; postgrad., London (Eng.) U. Editor, author, art critic, exhbn. organizer, 1956-69; art adviser, founding asso. editor Royal Opera House mag., 1962-68; founding editor Art and Artists Mag., London, 1965-68; chief curator Art Gallery of Toronto, Ont., Can., 1969-72; dir. N.Y. Cultural Center, Farleigh Dickinson U., 1972-76, adj. prof., 1972-76; Am. editor Connoisseur mag., 1976-79; dir. Chrysler Mus., Norfolk, Va., 1976-79; pres. Fine Arts Collection Services, Inc., art cons., 1979; head of devel. NAD, 1980—; vis. prof. N.Y. State U. at Buffalo, 1971-72; lectr. abroad USIS. Organizer opening exhbn., Inst. Contemporary Arts, London, 1968; guest dir., Queens Mus., Flushing Meadow, 1976; organizer exhbns.: The Obsessive Image, London, 1968, Sacred and Profane in Symbolist Art, Toronto, 1969, (with Pierre Rosenberg) French 17th and 18th Century Master Drawings, Toronto, 1973, Blacks: USA: Now, 1973, Women Choose Women, 1973, (with Robert Isaacson) Bouguereau, 1975, Man Ray, N.Y.C., London, Rome, 1974-75, Art Deco, Can., 1974; Author: Pop as Art, 1965, Art Nouveau, 1966, Tiffany Glass, 1967; numerous exhbn. catalogues; Am. editor: Connoisseur, 1977-79; contbg. editor: Archtl. Digest. Home: 229 E 79th St New York NY 10021 Home: 37 Redcliffe Sq London SW 10 England

AMBACH, DWIGHT RUSSELL, foreign service officer; b. Highland Park, Ill., Jan. 9, 1931; s. Russell William and Ethel (Repass) A.; m. Betsy Hunter, Aug. 27, 1955; children: Hunter Mackay, Nancy Cole, James Gordon. A.B., Brown U., 1952; M.A., Fletcher Sch., 1953; postgrad., MIT, 1963-64. Dep. dir. Office Regional Econ. Policy, Bur. Inter-Am. Affairs Dept. State, Washington, 1971-74; exec. asst. to chmn. Export-Import Bank, Washington, 1974-76; counselor for econ. and comml. affairs Am. Embassy, Vienna, Austria, 1976-80; dean Sch. Area Studies Fgn. Service Inst., Washington, 1980—. Mem. Chevy Chase Town Council. Recipient Superior Honor award Dept. State, 1973. Mem. Am. Fgn. Service Assn., Am. Econ. Assn., Phi Beta Kappa. Office: 1400 Key Blvd Arlington VA 22209

AMBACH, GORDON MAC KAY, state education official, university official; b. Providence, Nov. 10, 1934; s. Russell W. and Ethel (Repass) A.; m. Lucy DeWitt Emory, Mar. 9, 1963; children: Kenneth Emory, Alison Repass, Douglas Mac Kay. B.A., Yale U., 1956; M.A., Harvard U. Grad. Sch. Edn., 1957, cert. advanced study, 1966. Tchr. social studies 7th and 8th grades East Williston Sch. Dist., L.I., N.Y., 1958-61; asst. program planning officer U.S. Office Edn., Washington, 1961-62, asst. legis. specialist, 1962-63, exec. sec., 1963-64; adminstrv. asst. to mem. Boston Sch. Com., 1964-65; staff seminar mgr., mem. staff Harvard U. Grad. Sch. Edn., 1966-67; spl. asst. to commr. for long range planning N.Y. State Edn. Dept., Albany, 1967-69, asst. commr. for long range planning, 1969-70, exec. dep. commr., 1970-77; commr. edn. and pres. U. State N.Y., 1977—; mem. Nat. Commn. on Libraries and Info. Service; mem. local and univ. coms. for Yale and Harvard univs.; Bd. dirs. Lincoln Center Inst., N.Y. State Sci. and Tech. Found., Saratoga Performing Arts Center; co-chmn. Albany United Way, 1979-80. Served with USAR, 1957-63. Mem. Edn. Commn. States, Council Chief State Sch. Offices (pres.-elect), Acad. Polit. Scis., Am. Assn. Sch. Adminstrs., Phi Delta Kappa. Office: State Edn Dept Albany NY 12234

AMBASZ, EMILIO, architect, industrial designer, graphic designer; b. Resistencia, Chaco, Argentina, June 13, 1943. M.F.A., Sch. Architecture, Princeton U., 1966. Curator design Mus. Modern Art, N.Y.C., 1970-76; pres. Emilio Ambasz & Assocs., N.Y.C., 1981—, Emilio Ambasz Design Group Ltd., 1981—; chief design cons. Cummins Engine Co., Inc., Columbus, Ind., 1981—; coordinator Com. Architecture and Design Mus. Modern Art. Archtl. works include, Grand Rapids Art Mus., 1976, Mus. Am. Folk Art, N.Y.C., 1980, San Antonio Bot. Garden Conservatory, 1983, interior design includes, Banque Bruxelles Lambert, Milan, Italy, 1979, Banque Bruxelles Lambert, 1983; insdl. design works include Vertebra Seating System; indsl. design works Dorsal Seating System; indsl. design works include Logetec Spotlight Range, Oseris Lighting System. Recipient Progressive Architective award, 1976. Home: 295 Central Park West 14 D New York NY 10024 Office: Emilio Ambasz & Assocs 207 E 32d St New York NY 10016

AMBEAULT, GEORGE JOHN WALLACE, newspaper executive; b. Sault Ste. Marie, Ont., Can., Nov. 30, 1946; s. Wallace William and Margaret Mary (Parson) A.; m. Irene Michelle Mytka, Apr. 22, 1972; children: Marcia Michelle, Jason Mathew, Jonathan George. B.A., U. Windsor, Ont., 1969, M.B.A., 1971. Mgr. case soap fin. analysis Procter & Gamble Can., Toronto, 1975-76, mgr. plant acctg., 1976-77, mgr. case food and toilet foods fin. dept., 1977-79; mgr. fin. planning The Glove and Mail, Toronto, 1979-80, mgr. fin. and adminstrn., 1980-82, mgr. systems and adminstrn., 1982—. Treas. Provincial Assn., Mississauga, Ont., 1979; dir. Fed. Riding Assn., Mississauga, 1980-83. Mem. Inst. Newspaper Controllers and Fin. Officers, Phi Kappa Theta. Roman Catholic. Club: Logic (Toronto) (dir. 1983—). Home: 1700 Wembury Rd Mississauga ON Canada L5J 4G3 Office: The Globe and Mail 444 Front St W Toronto ON Canada M5V 2S9

AMBER, EUGENE LEWIS, insurance company executive; b. Buffalo, Mar. 8, 1923; s. Harrison L. and Emma M. (Cobb) A.; m. Katherine M. Midgette, Nov. 17, 1945; children—Lisa K. Amber Sampson, Deborah Amber Heffernan, John L., Gilbert H. Student, Cornell U., 1940-42, B.A., 1948. Underwriter, spl. agt. Hartford Accident & Indemnity Co., 1948-53; with Berkshire Life Ins. Co., Pittsfield, Mass., 1953—, 1st v.p. investment, 1962-63, sr. v.p. investments, 1963—; pres., dir. Berkshire Mgmt. and Research Co., Pittsfield, 1968—; dir. Mass. Bus. Devel. Corp., Boston, Bank of Boston, N.A., of Berkshire County, The Fla. Cos. Pres., Coolidge Hill Found., 1956—; treas. Boys' Club Pittsfield, 1963—. Bd. dirs. Berkshire Rehab. Center. Served to capt. USMCR, 1942-46. Decorated Air medal. Club: Country (Pittsfield). Home: 152 Main St Dalton MA 01226 Office: 700 South St Pittsfield MA 01201

AMBERG, JOHN RAYMOND, radiology educator; b. Mpls., June 5, 1926; s. Raymond Michael and Margaret (McHugh) A.; m. Lorraine Arnoldt, Oct. 22, 1949; children: John, Janet, James, Joseph, Jill, Joan, Jeffrey, Jay, Jerry, Judd. Student, DePauw U., 1944-45; B.S., U. Minn., 1947; M.B., 1949; M.D., 1950. Intern Clinics U. Chgo., 1949-50; resident Western Res. U., Cleve., 1952-53, U. Minn., Mpls., 1953-55; assoc. prof. dept. radiology Sch. Medicine, Marquette U., Milw., 1957-62, prof., chmn. dept., 1962-65; prof. radiology U. Calif. at San Francisco, 1965-72; prof., chmn. dept. radiology Vanderbilt U., Nashville, 1972-74; prof. U. Calif. at San Diego, 1974—. Served with AUS, 1949-52. Am. Cancer Soc. fellow, 1952-54. Mem. AMA, Am. Coll. Radiology, Radiologic Soc. N. Am., Am. Gastroenterological Assn., Assn. Am. Med. Colls. Home: 6821 Avenida Andorra La Jolla CA 92037

AMBLER, ERNEST, government official; b. Bradford, Eng., Nov. 20, 1923; came to U.S., 1953, naturalized, 1958; s. William and Sarah Alice (Binns) A.; m. Alice Virginia Seiler, Nov. 19, 1955; children: Christopher William, Jonathan Ernest. B.A., New Coll., Oxford U., 1945, M.A., 1949, Ph.D., 1953. With Armstrong Siddeley Motors, Ltd., Coventry, Eng., 1944-48; Nuffield Research fellow Oxford U., 1953; with Nat. Bur. Standards, Commerce Dept., 1953—, div. chief inorganic materials div., Washington, 1965-68; dir. Inst. for Basic Standards, Washington, 1968-73; dep. dir. Nat. Bur. Standards, Washington, 1973, acting dir., 1975-78, dir. bur., 1978—; Liaison rep. to div. phys. scis. Nat. Acad. Sci.-NRC, 1968-69; Sponsor's del. Nat. Conf. Standards Lab., 1968; U.S. rep. Internat. Com. on Weights and Measures, 1972—. D.C. mem. bd. govs. Israel/U.S. Binat. Indsl. Research and Devel. Found.; mem. Md. High Tech. Roundtable. Recipient Arthur S. Flemming award Washington Jr. C. of C., 1961; John Simon Guggenheim Meml. Found. fellow, 1963; recipient William A. Wildmack award in metrology, 1976, Pres.'s award for Distinguished Fed. Civilian Service, 1977. Mem. Am. Phys. Soc. (editor Rev. Modern Physics 1966-69), Washington Acad. Scis., AAAS. Patentee low temperature refrigeration apparatus. Home: 6920 Blaisdell Rd Bethesda MD 20817 Office: Nat Bur Standards Washington DC 20234

AMBLER, GEORGE POWELL, insurance company executive; b. Milw., Dec. 14, 1926; s. Harold George and Sarah (Goodsen) A.; m. Dorothy S. Collins, Jan. 10, 1948; children: Carolyn. B.A., Drake U., 1947; postgrad., Rÿksuniversiteit te gent, 1948. With Prudential Insurance Co. Am., Chgo., 1948—, v.p., 1949-58; sr. v.p. Prudential Insurance Co.Am., 1958-78; exec. v.p. Mid-Am. ops. Prudential Insurance Co. Am., 1978—; dir. Am. Cyananrid Corp., Eagle Picher Industries, Inc., Central Bancorp., Ohio Nat. Life Ins. Co. Bd. dirs. Chgo. area chpt. ARC; trustee U. Ill.; commr. Kane County Park Dist. Mem. Am. Insurance Assn., Life Office Mgmt. Assn. (past pres.). Clubs: Glenview Country; Cliff dwellers, Tavern (Chgo.). Office: Werik Bldg 24 N Wabash Ave Suite 823 Chicago IL 60602

AMBLER, JOHN DOSS, petroleum company executive; b. Buena Vista, Va., July 24, 1934; s. Robert Cary and Ella A.; m. Annette Virginia Chase, Mar. 25, 1959; children—John Chase, Cynthia. B.S., Va. Poly. Inst., 1956. Dist. sales mgr. Texaco, Inc., Harrisburg, Pa., 1965-67, asst. div. mgr., Norfolk, Va., 1967-68, staff asst. to gen. mktg. mgr., N.Y.C., 1968-72, asst. to gen. mgr. petroleum products dept., Europe, N.Y.C., 1972; gen. mgr. Texaco Olie Maatschappij B.V., Rotterdam, Netherlands, 1972-75; mng. dir. Texaco Oil A.B., Stockholm, 1975-77, asst. to pres., Harrison, N.Y., 1977-80, v.p., asst. to pres., 1980, v.p., asst. to chmn. bd., 1980—; pres. Texaco Europe, 1981—; chmn. bd., chief exec. officer Texaco Ltd., London, Eng; dir. Texaco Trinidad, Inc., Caltex Petroleum Corp. Served with U.S. Army, 1957-58. Methodist. Club: Silver Springs Country (Ridgefield, Conn.). Address: 1 Knightsbridge Green London England SW1

AMBROSE, JAMES RICHARD, government official; b. Brewer, Me., Aug. 16, 1922; s. James and Helen A.; m. Diane Ruth Johnson, Nov. 11, 1981; children by previous marriage: James, David, Gregory, Jeffery. Degree in engring., U. Me., 1943; postgrad., Georgetown U., Cath. U., U. Md. Staff Naval Research Lab., Washington, to 1955; with Lockheed Corp., 1955; prin. firm Systems Research Corp. (later Ford Aerospace and Communication Corp.), to 1979; now undersec. army. Mem. Am. Phys. Soc. Office: Dept Army Pentagon Washington DC 20301

AMBROSE, JOHN WILLIAM, JR., educator; b. Worcester, Mass., Jan. 23, 1931; s. John W. and Vivian (Lavallee) A.; m. Frances McKillop, 1961; children: John William, Matthew R. Peter J. A.B., Brown U., 1952, A.M., 1959, Ph.D., 1962. Tchr. Latin Roxbury Latin Sch. (Mass.), 1956-61; instr. Latin and Greek Phillips Acad., Andover, Mass., 1961-64; chmn. dept. classics Taft Sch., Watertown, Conn., 1964-66; asst. prof. to assoc. prof. Bowdoin Coll., Brunswick, Maine, 1966-76, prof. classics, 1976—, chmn. dept. classics, 1971—, Merrill prof. Greek classics, 1977—; teaching asst. Brown U., 1959-60. Author: Horace on Foreign Policy, 1973; co-author: (with others) Greek Attitudes, 1974, Preparatory Latin, 2d edit., 1977, A Commentary to Euripides Hecuba, 1981. Mem. Am. Philos. Assn., Classical Assn. New Eng., Archaeol. Inst. Am. Office: Dept Classics Bowdoin Boll Brunswick ME 04011 *

AMBROSE, MYLES JOSEPH, lawyer; b. N.Y.C., July 21, 1926; s. Arthur P. and Anna (Campbell) A.; m. Elaine Miller, June 26, 1948 (dec. Sept. 1975); children: Myles Joseph, Kathleen Anne Ley, Kevin Arthur, Elise Mary, Nora Jeanne Ambrose Baker, Christopher Miller; m. Joan Fitzpatrick, June 24, 1978. Grad., New Hampton Sch., N.H., 1944; B.B.A., Manhattan Coll., 1948, LL.D. (hon.), 1972; J.D., N.Y. Law Sch., 1952. Bar: N.Y. 1952, U.S. Supreme Ct. 1969, D.C. 1973, U.S. Ct. Customs and Patent Appeals 1970, U.S. Ct. Internat. Trade 1970, D.C. Ct. Appeals 1973. Personnel mgr. Devenco, Inc., 1948-49, 51-54; adminstrv. asst. U.S. atty. So. dist., N.Y., 1954-57; instr. econs. and indsl. relations Manhattan Coll., 1955-57; asst. to sec. U.S. Treasury, 1957-60; exec. dir. Waterfront Commn. of N.Y. Harbor, 1960-63; pvt. practice law, N.Y.C., 1963-69; chief counsel N.Y. State Joint Legislative Com. for Study Alcoholic Beverage Control Law, 1963-65; U.S. commr. customs, Washington, 1969-72, spl. cons. to Pres., spl. asst. atty. gen., 1972-73; mem. firm Spear & Hill, 1973-75, Ambrose and Casselman, P.C., 1975-79; now mem. firm O'Connor & Hannan, Washington.; U.S. observer 13th session UN Commn. on Narcotics, Geneva, Switzerland, 1958; chmn. U.S. delegation 27th Gen. Assembly, Internat. Criminal Police Orgn., London, 1958, 28th Extraordinary Gen. Assembly, Paris, 1959; U.S. observer 29th Gen. Assembly, Washington, 1960; mem. U.S. delegation, Mexico City, 1969, Brussels, 1970, Ottawa, 1971, Frankfurt, 1972; chmn. U.S.-Mexico Conf. on Narcotics, Washington, 1960, mem. confs., Washington and; Mexico City, 1969, 70, 71, 72; chmn. U.S.-Canadian-Mexican Conf. on Customs Procedures, San Clemente, Calif., 1970; chmn. U.S. del. Customs Cooperation Council, Brussels, 1970; chmn., Vienna, 1971, U.S.-European Customs Conf. Narcotics, Paris and; Vienna, 1971; hon. consul Principality of Monaco, Washington, 1973—. Bd. dirs. Daytop Village.; vice chmn. Reagan-Bush Inaugural Com. Recipient Presdl. Mgmt. Improvement certificate Pres. Nixon, 1970, Sec. Treasury Exceptional Service award, 1970; decorated knight comdr. Order Merit Italian Republic; recipient Distinguished Alumnus award N.Y. Law Sch., 1973, Alumni award for pub. service Manhattan Coll., 1972. Mem. Am. Bar Assn. (past chmn. standing com. on custom law), Assn. Bar City N.Y., Friendly Sons of St. Patrick, Alpha Sigma Beta, Phi Alpha Delta (hon.). Republican. Roman Catholic. Clubs: Sleepy Hollow Country; Metropolitan (N.Y.C.); University, Army-Navy (Washington). Home: 2614 31st St NW Washington DC 20008 Office: O'Connor & Hannan 1919 Penn Ave NW Suite 800 Washington DC 20006

AMBROSE, SAMUEL SHERIDAN, JR., urologist; b. Jacksonville, N.C., Oct. 2, 1923; s. Samuel Sheridan and Beatrice (Collins) A.; m. Betty Stuart Stansbury, Oct. 7, 1950; children: Charles Stuart, Ann Collins, Samuel Bruce. A.B. in Chemistry, Duke U., 1943, M.D., 1947. Diplomate: Am. Bd. Urology, Nat. Bd. Med. Examiners. Intern in surgery, then asst. resident in urology Duke U. Hosp., 1947-50, resident in urology, 1953; instr. physiology Duke U. Med. Sch., 1947, instr. urology, 1953; mem. faculty Emory U. Med. Sch., 1954—, prof. urology, 1972—; mem. staff Emory U. Hosp., 1972—, chief urology, 1972—; pvt. practice medicine specializing in urology, Atlanta, 1954-71; mem. staff Piedmont Hosp., 1954-72, chief urology, 1960; mem. staff St. Joseph's Infirmary, 1954—, Grady Meml. Hosp., 1954—, Henrietta Egleston Hosp. for Children, 1956—. Contbr. numerous articles to med. jours. Served as officer M.C. USNR, 1950-52. Mem. AMA, Am. Urol. Assn. (pres. Southeastern sect. 1974-75, chmn. nat. sci. exhibits com. 1974—, exec. com. 1983), Soc. Pediatric Urology (pres. 1971-72), Am. Assn. Clin. Urologists, Am. Acad. Pediatrics, Am. Assn. Genito-Urinary Surgeons, A.C.S., Soc. Internat. D'Urologie, Pan-Pacific Surg. Assn., Med. Assn. Ga., Ga. Urol. Assn. (pres. 1967), So. Med. Soc. (chmn. urology sect. 1970-71), Fulton County Med. Soc., Atlanta Clin. Soc. (v.p. 1964). Presbyterian. Clubs: Piedmont Driving, Cherokee Town and Country (pres. 1968-69), University Yacht (commodore 1973); Homosassa Fishing (Atlanta)). Home: 1014 Nawench Dr NW Atlanta GA 30327 Office: 1365 Clifton Rd NE Atlanta GA 30322

AMBROSE, TOMMY W., chemical engineer, executive; b. Jerome, Idaho, Oct. 14, 1926; s. Fines M. and Avice (Barnes) A.; m. Shirley Ann Ball, June 23, 1951; children: Leslie Ann, Julie Lynn, Pamela Lee. B.S., U. Idaho, 1950, M.S., 1951, Ph.D. hon., 1981, Oreg. State U., 1957. Registered engr., Wash., Ohio. Engr. Gen. Electric Co., Richland, Wash., 1951-54, 57-60, supr. reactor fuels, 1960-63, mgr. process and reactor devel., 1963-65, mgr. research and engring., 1965, Douglas United Nuclear Co., Richland, Wash., 1965-69; asst. dir. Battelle Seattle Research Center, 1969-70, exec. dir., 1971-74; dir. Battelle Pacific N.W. Labs., Richland, Wash., 1975-79; corp. dir. multicomponent ops. Battelle Meml. Inst., Columbus, Ohio, 1979—, v.p., 1976—; mem. adv. com. Coll. Engring. U., Idaho, Moscow, 1974—; mem. vis. com. Coll. Engring., U. Wash., 1974-83; mem. govs. adv. council for dept. of commerce and economic Devel., 1975-79; Wash. State council on Postsecondary Edn., 1977-79; chmn. bd. trustees Columbia Basin Coll., 1967-69; bd. dirs. N.W. Coll. and U. Assn. for Science, 1976-79; v.p., trustee, mem. exec. com. Pacific Sci. Center Found. Trustee, mem. exec. com. Columbus Symphony Orch., 1982; trustee Jefferson Acad., 1984—. Served with USNR, 1944-46. Mem. Am. Inst. Chem. Engrs., Am. Nuclear Soc.; mem. Ohio Acad. Sci. (indsl. acad. com. 1983—); Mem. Sigma Xi, Pi Lambda Upsilon. Methodist. Home: 530 Plymouth St Worthington OH 43085 Office: 505 King Ave Columbus OH 43201

AMBROZIC, ALOYSIUS MATTHEW, bishop; b. Gabrje, Slovenia, Yugoslavia, Jan. 27, 1930; s. Aloysius and Helen (Pecar) A. Student, St. Augustine Sem., 1955; S.T.L., Universitá San Tomaso, Rome, 1958, Sacrae Scripturae Licentiatus, Biblicum, Rome, 1960; Th.D., U. Wurzburg, 1970. Ordained priest Roman Catholic Ch., 1955, ordained aux. bishop of, Toronto, 1976—; parish work Port Colborne, Ont., Can., 1955-56; faculty St. Augustines Sem., Scarborough, Ont., Can., 1956-76, dean studies, 1971-76; prof. N.T. exegesis Toronto Sch. Theology, 1970-76. Author: The Hidden Kingdom: A Redaction-Critical Study of the References to the Kingdom of God in Mark's Gospel, 1972, Remarks on the Canadian Catechism, 1974. Office: 291 Cosburn Ave Toronto ON Canada M4J 2M4 *

AMBRUS, CLARA MARIE, physician; b. Rome, Dec. 28, 1924; U.S., 1949, naturalized, 1955; d. Anthony and Charlotte (Schneider) Bayer; m. Julian Lawrence Ambrus, Feb. 17, 1945; children—Madeline Ambrus Lillie, Peter, Julian, Linda, Steven, Katherine, Charles. Student, U. Budapest (Hungary), 1943-47; M.D., U. Zurich, Switzerland, 1949; postgrad., U. Paris, 1949; Ph.D., Jefferson Med. Coll., 1955. Diplomate: Am. Bd. Clin. Chemists. Research asst. Inst. Histology, Embryology and Biology U. Budapest, 1943-45; demonstrator in pharmacology U. Budapest Med. Sch., 1946-47; asst. dept. pharmacology U. Zurich Med. Sch., 1947-49; asst. dept. therapeutic chemistry and virology Inst. Pasteur, Paris, 1949; asst. prof. pharmacology Phila. Coll. Pharmacy and Sci., 1950-52, asso. prof., 1952-55; research asso. Roswell Park Meml. Inst., Buffalo, 1955-58, sr. cancer research scientist, 1958-64, asso. scientist, 1964-69, prin. cancer research scientist, 1969—; prof. pharmacology State U. N.Y.; Buffalo Med. and Grad. Schs., 1955—, asso. prof. pediatrics, 1955-76, prof. pediatrics, 1976—. Contbr. articles to med. and sci. jours. Trustee Nichols Sch., Buffalo. Named Outstanding Woman of Western N.Y. Community Adv. Council, SUNY, Buffalo, 1980. Fellow A.C.P., Am. Coll. Clin. Pharmacology, Internat. Soc. Hematology; mem. Am. Soc. Pharmacology and Exptl. Therapeutics, Am. Soc. Cancer Research, Soc. Exptl. Biology, Medicine, AMA, Am. Fedn. Clin. Research, Am. Physiol. Soc., Am. Soc. Hematology, Buffalo Acad. Medicine, AAUW, Am. Med. Women's Assn., Sigma Xi, Rho Chi. Clubs: Women's Faculty of U. Buffalo, Clarksburg Country, Saturn, Garrett. Home: 143 Windsor Ave Buffalo NY 14209 also West Hill Farm Boston NY 14025 Office: 666 Elm St Buffalo NY 14263

AMBRUS, JULIAN L., physician, medical educator; b. Budapest, Hungary, Nov. 29, 1924; came to U.S., 1949, naturalized, 1955; s. Alexander and Elizabeth A.; m. Clara M. Bayer, Feb. 18, 1945; children—Madeline (Mrs. David Lillie), Peter, Julian, Linda, Steven, Katherine, Charles. Student, U. Budapest, 1942-47; M.D., U. Zurich, 1949; postgrad., Sorbonne, 1949-50; Ph.D. in Med. Sci, Jefferson Med. Coll., 1954. Diplomate: Am. Bd. Clin. Chemistry. Research asst., instr. histology U. Budapest, 1943-45, demonstrator pharmacology, 1946-47; asst. pharmacology U. Zurich, 1947-49; asst. dept. therapeutic chemistry, virology and tropical medicine Inst. Pasteur, Paris, 1949; asst. prof., asso. prof., prof. Phila. Coll. Pharmacology and Sci., 1950-55; prin. cancer research scientist Roswell Park Meml. Inst. and Hosp., 1955-65, asst. to the dir., 1961-65; dir. Springville Labs., 1965-75, dir. cancer research head dept. pathophysiology, 1975—; asst. prof. pharmacology U. Buffalo Med. Sch., 1955-61, asso. prof. pharmacology, 1961-65, prof., 1965-72; chmn. Roswell Park div. exec. com. Grad. Sch., 1955-65; prof. biochem. pharmacology State U. N.Y. at Buffalo, 1964—, asso. in internal medicine, 1961-64, asst. prof. internal medicine, 1964-66, asso. prof. internal medicine, 1966-71, prof., 1971—; prof., chmn. dept. exptl. pathology Grad. Sch., 1972—; dir. Instnl. Cancer Tng. Program USPHS, 1956-65; Mem. com. Thrombolytic agts. USPHS-NIH, 1960-66; cons. A.M.A. Council Drugs, Adv. Com. on; Blood Coagulation Components, Protein Found., Cambridge, Mass.; Bur. Drugs FDA, WHO, Geneva.; Commr. Lake Erie chpt. U.S. Pony Clubs, mem. intercollegiate com. Contbr. articles profl. jours.; Editor-in-chief: Revs. of Hematology; editorial bd.: Research Communications in Chem. Pathology and Pharmacology. Trustee Calasanctius Prep. Sch. for Acad. Gifted, Elmwood-Franklin Sch., Buffalo Chamber Music Soc., Internat. Inst. Buffalo; bd. regents Am. Coll. Law and Sci. Recipient first prize med. student paper Hungarian Med. Sch., 1947, 1st prize surgery U. Budapest, 1947; Nelson lectureship and medal U. Calif., Davis, 1972. Fellow ACP, Am. Coll. Nuclear Physicians, Am. Coll. Angiology, Royal Soc. Medicine, Am. Coll. Pharmacology and Chemotherapy, Council on Clin. Cardiology, Am. Heart Assn., Internat. Coll. Angiology, Am. Geriatrics Soc., N.Y. Acad. Sci., A.A.A.S., Internat. Soc. Hematology; mem. Am. Soc. Hematology, Am. Soc. Pathologists, Am. Soc. Nuclear Medicine, Am. Soc. Pharmacology and Exptl. Therapeutics, Am. Soc. Physiology, Am. Assn. Cancer Research, Am. Soc. Clin. Oncology, Fedn. Clin. Research, Soc. Exptl. Biology and Medicine, Assn. Am. Med. Colls., Cath. Physicians Guild, Sigma Xi, Rho Chi, Physiol. Soc. Phila., Radiation Research Soc., Buffalo Zool. Soc. (chmn. Sci. Council 1965-66), Buffalo Acad. Medicine (pres. 1976-77). Home: 143 Windsor Ave Buffalo NY 14209 also West Hill Farm Emmerling Rd Boston NY 14025 Office: 666 Elm St Buffalo NY 14263

AMBUEL, JOHN PHILIP, med. educator; b. Broadus, Mont., Mar. 23, 1918; s. Henry J. and Bertha (Preus) A.; m. Marion Storck;

children—Jack, Bruce, David. A.B., Luther Coll., Decorah, Ia., 1941; M.D., U. Chgo., 1946. Diplomate: Am. Bd. Pediatrics, Am. Acad. Pediatrics. Intern Doctor's Hosp., Seattle, 1946-47; resident Children's Hosp., Detroit, 1949-51; fellow hematology U. Chgo., 1951-53; med. dir. outpatient dept. Children's Hosp., Columbus, Ohio, 1953-74; mem. faculty Ohio State U., Columbus, 1953-74; sch. physician Univ. Sch., 1953-58, prof. pediatric medicine, 1965-74, prof. preventive medicine, 1968-74; med. dir. ambulatory services Children's Meml. Hosp., Chgo., 1974-78, prof. dept. pediatrics, Northwestern U. Med. Sch., 1974-78, prof. dept. community and preventive medicine, 1974-78; prof. dept. family practice and pediatrics, Med. Coll., Wis., Milw., 1978—; Project dir. children and youth project, Columbus and Franklin County, Children's Hosp., 1966-74. Served to lt. (j.g.) USNR, 1947-49. Mem. Ambulatory Pediatric Assn., Am. Acad. Pediatrics, Am. Pediatric Soc., Am. Pub. Health Assn., Am. Assn. Maternal and Child Health, Mid-West Soc. Pediatric Research. Home: 2490 Anita Dr Brookfield WI 53005

AMDAHL, BYRDELLE JOHN, biomedical engineering and manufacturing company executive; b. Ossian, Iowa, June 5, 1934; s. John G. and Mae (Vikse) A.; m. Agnes Nestegard, June 17, 1955 (div. May 1981); children: Gary, Mark. Student, Luther Coll., Decorah, Iowa, 1952-54; B.B.A., U. Minn., 1958, postgrad., 1971. C.P.A., Minn. Auditor Dept. Agr., Mpls., 1958; auditor Ernst & Ernst, Mpls., 1958-64; exec. Cornelius Co., Mpls., 1964-74, treas., controller, 1968-69, v.p. fin., 1969-72, v.p. finance and adminstrn., 1972-73, exec. v.p., 1973-74, dir., 1971-74; exec. v.p. fin. and adminstrn., chief fin. officer Medtronic Inc., Mpls., 1974-77, exec. v.p. diversified ops., 1977-81; pres., chief exec. officer Bionexus, Inc., 1981—. Bd. dirs. Lutheran Youth Encounter, 1968-75. Served with AUS, 1954-56. Mem. Alpha Kappa Psi. Republican. Clubs: Minneapolis, Capital City, Rotary Internat. Office: 5257 North Blvd Raleigh NC 27604 *Success seems to be less expressed in the objectives we achieve and more in the way we process life.*

AMDAHL, DOUGLAS KENNETH, justice Minnesota Supreme Court; b. Mabel, Minn., Jan. 23, 1919. B.B.A., U. Minn., 1945; J.D. summa cum laude, William Mitchell Coll. Law, 1951. Bar: Minn. 1951, Fed. Dist. Ct. 1952. Ptnr. Amdahl & Scott, Mpls., 1951-55; asst. county atty., Hennepin County, Minn., 1955-61; judge Mcpl. Ct., Mpls., 1961-62, Dist. Ct. 4th Dist., Minn., 1962-80, chief judge, 1973-75; assoc. justice Minn. Supreme Ct., 1980-81, chief justice, 1981—; asst. registrar, then registrar Mpls. Coll. Law, 1948-55; prof. law William Mitchell Coll. Law, 1951-65; moot ct. instr. U. Minn.; faculty mem. and advisor Nat. Coll. State Judiciary; mem. Nat. Bd. Trial Advocacy. Mem. ABA, Minn., Hennepin County bar assns., Internat. Acad. Trial Judges, State Dist. Ct. Judges Assn. (pres. 1976-77). Office: 230 State Capitol Saint Paul MN 55155

AMDAHL, GENE MYRON, computer company executive; b. Flandreau, S.D., Nov. 16, 1922; s. Anton E. and Inga (Brendsel) A.; m. Marian Quissell, June 23, 1946; children: Carlton Gene, Beth Delaine, Andrea Leigh. B.S.E.E., S.D. State U., 1948, D.Eng. (hon.), 1974; Ph.D., U. Wis., 1952, D.Sc. (hon.), 1979, Luther Coll., 1980, Augustana Coll., 1984. Project mgr. IBM Corp., Poughkeepsie, N.Y., 1952-55; group head Ramo-Wooldridge Corp., Los Angeles, 1956; mgr. systems design Aeronutronics, Los Angeles, 1956-60; mgr. systems design advanced data processing systems IBM Corp., N.Y.C., Los Gatos, Calif., Menlo Park, Calif., 1960-70; founder, chmn. Amdahl Corp., 1970-80, Trilogy Ltd., 1980—. Served with USN, 1942-44. Recipient Disting. Alumnus award S.D. State U., 1973, Data Processing Man of Yr. award Data Processing Mgmt. Assn., 1976, Disting. Service citation U. Wis., 1976, Michelson-Morley award Case-Western Res. U., 1977, Harry Goode Meml. award for outstanding contbns. to design and manufacture of large, high-performance computers Am. Fedn. Info. Processing Socs., 1983; IBM fellow, 1965; IEEE fellow, 1969. Fellow Brit. Computer Soc.; mem. Nat. Acad. Engring., IEEE (W.W. McDowell award 1976), Quadrato della Radio, Pontecchio Marcon. Lutheran. Club: La Rinconada Country (Saratoga, Calif.). Patentee in field. Home: 165 Patricia Dr Atherton CA 94025 Office: Trilogy Systems 10500 Ridgeview Ct Cupertino CA 95014

AMELING, ELLY, soprano; b. Rotterdam, Netherlands, Feb. 8, 1938; d. Dirk and Aleida (Zikking) A.; m. Arnold W. Belder, Nov. 6, 1964. Student, Conservatory of Music, The Hague, Netherlands, 1954-58. Debut, Victoria Hall, Geneva, Switzerlands; numerous solo recitals, also with orchs. throughout world, rec. artist, Philips, CBS, Decca London, EMI Angel, RCA, Odeon, Harmonia Mundi, Peters Internat. and, Vanguard records. Decorated Order Oranje Nassau, Netherlands; recipient preis der Deutschen Schallplattenkritic; Grand prix du Disque. Office: care Sheldon Soffer Mgmt 130 W 56th St New York NY 10019 *

AMELIO, GILBERT FRANK, semiconductor company executive; b. N.Y.C., Mar. 1, 1943; s. Anthony and Elizabeth (DeAngelis) A.; m. Miriam LeDora Rupert, Apr. 1, 1963; children: Anthony Todd, Tracy Elizabeth, Andrew Ryan. B.S. in Physics, Ga. Inst. Tech., 1965, M.S., 1967, Ph.D., 1968. Tech. dir., co-founder Info. Sci., Atlanta, 1962-65; mem. tech. staff Bell Telephone Labs., Murray Hill, N.J., 1968-71; div. v.p., gen. mgr. Fairchild, Mountain View, Calif., 1971-83; pres. semiconductor products div. Rockwell Internat., Newport Beach, Calif., 1983—; dir. Ga. Inst. Tech. Nat. Adv. Bd., Atlanta, 1981—, Ga. Inst. Tech. Research Inst., 1982—; dir., chmn. Recticon, Pottstown, Pa., 1983—. Patentee in field. Fellow IEEE (chmn. subcom. 1974-81); mem. Semiconductor Industry Assn. (dir. 1983—). Republican. Roman Catholic. Home: 38 Rockingham Dr Newport Beach CA 92660 Office: Semiconductor Products Div Rockwell Internat 4311 Jamboree Rd Newport Beach CA 92660

AMEMIYA, TAKESHI, economist; b. Tokyo, Mar. 29, 1935; s. Kenji and Shizuko A.; m. Yoshiko Miyaki, May 5, 1969; children: Naoko, Kentaro. B.A., Internat. Christian U., 1958; M.A. in Econs., Am. U., 1961; Ph.D., Johns Hopkins U., 1964. Mem. faculty Stanford U., (Calif.), 1964-66, 68—, prof. econs., 1974—; lectr. Inst. Econ. Research, Hitotsubashi U., Tokyo, 1966-68; cons. Author articles; editorial profl. jours. Ford Found. fellow, 1963; Guggenheim fellow, 1975; NSF grantee. Fellow Econometric Soc., Am. Statis. Assn.; mem. Phi Beta Kappa. Home: 923 Casanueva Pl Stanford CA 94305 Office: Stanford Univ Econs Dept Stanford CA 94305

AMEN, IRVING, artist; b. N.Y.C., July 25, 1918; s. Benjamin and Bessie (Glusack) A.; m. Dora Beck, May 21, 1941. Student, Pratt Inst., N.Y.C., 1933-35, Art Students League, N.Y.C., 1946-48, Academie de la Grande Chaumiere, Paris, France, 1949-50. Tchr. Pratt Inst., 1957, 58, U. Notre Dame, 1962. One man shows, N.Y.C., San Francisco, Denver, Washington, Louisville, Detroit, Albuquerque, Cleve., Phila., Memphis, Salt Lake City, numerous other cities in, U.S., also in, Jerusalem, Israel, rep. permanent collections, Met. Mus. Art, Mus. Modern Art, Library of Congress, Smithsonian Instn., Bibliotheque Nationale, Paris, Bibliotheque Royale, Brussels, Belgium, Bezalel Nat. Mus., Jerusalem, Victoria and Albert Mus., London, Eng., Albertina Mus., Vienna, Austria, Stadtische Mus., Wilberfeld, Germany, N.Y. Pub. Library, Phila. Mus. Art, Boston Mus. Fine Art, Balt. Mus. Art, Cambridge (Mass.) Pub. Library, Cin. Mus. Art, de Cordova and Dana Mus., Lincoln, Mass., numerous others; designer peace medal to commemorate end of Vietnam War, illus., Gilgamesh for Ltd. Edits. Club; designer stained glass windows depicting 12 Tribes of, Israel, Agudas Achim Synagogue, Columbus, Ohio. Served with USAAF, 1942-45. Mem. Artists Equity (dir.), Soc. Am. Graphic Artists (dir.), Internat. Inst. Arts and Letters, Internat. Soc. Wood Engravers, Am. Color Print Soc., Audubon Artists, Boston Printmakers, L'Accademia Fiorentina delle arti del disegno Florence (hon.). Address: 90 SW 12th Terr Boca Raton FL 33432

AMENDOLA, ANTHONY JOSEPH, brewing company executive; b. N.Y.C., May 18, 1926; s. Charles and Elizabeth (Pizzuto) A.; m. Margaret McGee, June 6, 1947; children: Victoria, Joan, Lorraine. A.B., Columbia U., 1946. Sales rep. Birmingham News, Ala., 1947-49; rep. Anheuser-Busch, Inc., N.Y.C., 1950-53; advt. sales Esquire, Inc., N.Y.C., 1953-55, Western Advt. mgr., Chgo., 1955-56; regional account exec. D'Arcy Advt. Co., N.Y.C., 1956-60, dir. regional mktg. service, St. Louis, 1960-65, v.p. nat. mktg. services, account supr., 1965-70, sr. v.p. dir., account supr., mng. dir. St. Louis office, then pres.; now exec. v.p. Loseph Schlitz Brewing Co., Milw. Served to ensign USNR, 1943-45. Mem. Advt. Club Greater St. Louis. Clubs: Media, Friars (N.Y.C.); St. Louis Ad, Sunset County (St. Louis). Lodge: K.C. Office: Joseph Schlitz Brewing Co 235 W Galena St Milwaukee WI 53201

AMENT, RICHARD, anesthesiologist, educator; b. N.Y.C., Jan. 27, 1919; m. Esther Abrams, Apr. 18, 1943; children—Sara Lauren Baron, David S., Robert H., Victor C. M.D., U. Buffalo, 1942. Diplomate: Nat. Bd. Med. Examiners, Am. Bd. Anesthesiology (sr. examiner, mem. nominating com. 1973-75, 78-83). Intern Buffalo Gen. Hosp., 1942-43, asst. in anesthesiology, 1949-54, asst. attending anesthesiologist, 1954-62, asso. attending, 1962-63, attending, 1963—; fellow in physiology U. Rochester, 1946-47; resident anesthesiology Bellevue Hosp., N.Y.C., 1947-49, Boston Childrens Hosp., 1949; clin. instr. anesthesiology U. Buffalo, 1949, asst. clin. prof., 1956; asso. clin. prof. anesthesiology State U. N.Y. at Buffalo, 1960-71, clin. prof., 1971—, dir. anesthesia edn., 1978—; faculty council Sch. Medicine, 1972-74; vis. prof. U. Md., 1975, U. Tex., Dallas, 1976, N.Y. U., 1977, U. Colo., 1977, U. Wash., 1977, U. Tex., San Antonio, 1977. Contbr. articles to med. jours. Trustee Temple Beth Zion, 1960-66, 68-75, pres., 1971-73; mem. nat. med. staff Nat. Jamboree, Boy Scouts Am., Colorado Springs, 1961, Boy Scouts Am., Valley Forge, 1964; mem. exec. bd. Greater Niagara Frontier council, 1960-70, chmn. health and safety com. Buffalo Area council, 1961-68, mem. exec. bd., 1959-70, rep. Nat. council, 1965-70; pres. Jewish Center Greater Buffalo, Inc., 1970-72, 74-75, chmn. nominating com., 1977; bd. govs. Jewish Fedn. Greater Buffalo, 1964-69, 71-73, 77-79, chmn. social planning com., 1968-69. Served to capt., M.C. USAAF, 1943-46. Silver Beaver award, 1965. Fellow Am. Coll. Anesthesiologists (gov. 1973-75); mem. Am. Soc. Anesthesiologists (pres. 1977, chmn. govt. affairs com. 1980—), N.Y. State Soc. Anesthesiologists, pres. 1967), World Fedn. Socs. of Anesthesiologists (sec. U.S. del. 1976—, chmn. fin. com. 1980—), N.Y. State Med. Soc. (com. on forensic medicine 1965-67), Erie County Med. Soc. (chmn. anesthesia study com. 1953-62), AMA (vice chmn. anesthesia sect. 1978—, rep. to Intersplty. Adv. Bd. 1978-80, rep. to Council Med. Splty. Socs. 1978—, bd. dirs. 1980—, treas. 1980—). Home: 22 Lake Ledge Dr Williamsville NY 14221 Office: Buffalo Anesthesia Assos PO Box 488 Buffalo NY 14205

AMENTA, PETER SEBASTIAN, researcher, anatomist; b. Cromwell, Conn., Mar. 26, 1927; s. Peter and Mary (DeMauro) A.; m. Rose Phyllis Russo, June 20, 1953; children: Mary Vincenza, Rosemarie. Student, Conn. Wesleyan U., 1947-49; B.S., Fairfield U., 1952; M.S., Marquette U., 1954; Ph.D., U. Chgo., 1958. Undergrad. asst. Fairfield U., 1949-52; grad. asst. Marquette U., 1952-54, U. Chgo., 1955-58; instr., ind. investigator Marine Biol. Lab., Woods Hole, Mass., summer 1956; instr. anatomy Hahnemann Med. Coll., 1958-60, asst. prof. anatomy, 1960-63, asso. prof., 1963-71, prof., 1971—, acting chmn. dept., 1973-75, chmn. dept., 1975—; head microscopic anatomy, 1968-75, treas., exec. faculty, 1970-73, dir. div. electron microscopy, 1970-75; vis. prof. cytology Rome U., 1966, 76, Estacao Agronomica National, Oeiras, Portugal, 1970, Edinburg (Scotland) U., 1972; instr. Trenton Diocese High Sch. Religion, 1967-72; lectr. N.J. Right to Life Com., 1969-73, Am. Cancer Soc., 1969—; Continuing Edn. Program, Roxborough Hosp., Phila., 1970; pres. Humanity Gifts Registry, U. Pa., 1976-81. Author: Histology and Embryology Review, 1977, 2d edit., 1983, Review of Medical History, 1977, Histology, 3d edit., 1983. Twp. chmn. Burlington County Juvenile Conf. Com., 1967-70; mem. Trenton Diocesan Pastoral Council, 1968-73, vice-chmn., 1970-72; dir. St. Joan of Arc Choir; mem. S. Jersey String Band. Served with AUS, 1946-47. Named Man of Year, Fairfield U., 1962; Distinguished Alumnus, Am. Jesuit U., 1967. Fellow AAAS; mem. Am. Assn. Anatomists, Assn. Anatomy Chairmen, Albertus Magnus Guild of Catholic Scientists, AMA, N.Y. Acad. Scis., Am. Inst. Biol. Scis., Tissue Culture Assn., Am. Soc. Photogiology, Internat. Congress Photogiology, Am. Soc. Zoologists, Hahnemann Alumni Assn. (hon.), Sigma Xi, Phi Sigma. Office: Dept Anatomy #408 Hahnemann U Broad and Vine Philadelphia PA 19102

AMERINE, MAYNARD ANDREW, educator, enologist; b. San Jose, Calif., Oct. 30, 1911; s. Roy Reagan and Tennie (Davis) A. B.S., U. Calif., Berkeley, 1932, Ph.D. in Plant Physiology, 1936. Mem. faculty U. Calif. at Davis, 1935—, prof. enology, enologist Exptl. Sta., 1952-74, emeritus Exptl. Sta., 1974—, chmn. dept. viticulture and enology, 1957-62; cons. Wine Inst., 1974—. Author: (with M. A. Joslyn) Table Wines: The Technology of Their Production in California, 1951, 2d edit., 1970, (with Louise Wheeler) A Check-List of Books and Pamphlets on Grapes and Wines and Related Subjects, 1951, A Short Check-List of Books and Pamphlets in English on Grapes, Wine and Related Subjects, 1949-1959, 1959, (with others) The Technology of Wine Making, 4th edit., 1980, (with G. L. Marsh) Wine Making at Home, 1962, (with M.A. Joslyn) Dessert, Appetizer and Related Flavored Wines: The Technology of Their Production, 1964, (with V.L. Singleton) Wine: An Introduction for Americans, 1965, 2d edit., 1977, (with Rose M. Pangborn and E. B. Roessler) Principles of Sensory Evaluation of Food, 1965, A Check List on Grapes and Wines, 1960-68, (with supplement for) A Check List on Grapes and Wines, 1949-59, 1969, (with G.F. Stewart) Introduction to Food Science and Technology, 1973, 2d edit., 1982, (with C.S. Ough) Wine and Must Analyses, 1974, 80, (with E.B. Roessler) Wines: Their Sensory Evaluation, 1976, 2d edit., 1983; Editor and contbr.: Wine Production Technology in the U.S, 1981. Served to maj. AUS, 1942-46. Decorated chevalier de Merite Agricole, France, 1947, officier Ordre National du Merite, (France), 1976; recipient diplôme d'honneur Office Internat. du Vin, 1952, 65; 2d prize Oberly award A.L.A., 1953; Guggenheim fellow, 1954-55; Merit award Am. Soc. Enologists, 1967; Am. Wine Soc., 1976; Man of Year award Les Amis du Vin, 1976. Mem. Am. Soc. Enologists (pres. 1958-59), AAAS, Am. Chem. Soc., Inst. Food Technologists. Republican. Baptist. Club: Bohemian (San Francisco). Home: PO Box 208 St Helena CA 94574

AMERMAN, DAVID PETER, publishing executive; b. Syracuse, N.Y., Nov.l 30, 1926; s. Peter and Adele Louise (Dodge) A.; m. Lois Marjorie Behnke, May 24, 1951; children: Peter Duguid, Scott Charles, Arthur Caldwell. B.A., Hamilton Coll., 1951. With Atlantic Refining co., Syracuse, 1951-53, Prentice-Hall, Inc., Englewood Cliffs, N.Y., 1953-77, pres. Coll. div., 1977-81, group v.p., 1981—; mem. bd. publs. Luth. Ch. Am., 1970-80, pres. bd. publs., 1976-80. Trustee Wyckoff Pub. Library, N.J., 1962-75, treas., N.J., 1965-68, pres., N.J., 1969-72; mem. Fedn. Libraries, No. Bergen County, N.J., 1970-76, pres., 1972-73. Served with USN, 1944-46. Mem. Assn. Am. Publs. (dir. 1978-80), N.J. Library Assn., ALA, Nat. Assn. Coll. Stores, Holland Soc. Republican. Lutheran. Home: 390 Annette Ct Wyckoff NJ 07841 Office: Prentice Hall Inc Englewood Cliffs NJ 07362

AMES, ALFRED CAMPBELL, journalist, educator; b. Spokane, Wash., July 21, 1916; s. William Porter and Anna (Campbell) A.; m. Eleanor Alice Holliday, Feb. 4, 1951. A.B., U. Kans., 1936; A.M., U. Ill., 1937, Ph.D., 1943. Asst. English U. Ill., 1937-43, instr., 1943-44; instr. English Ill. Inst. Tech., 1944-46, asst. prof., 1946-51; asso. editor book sect. Chgo. Tribune, 1951-56, editorial writer, 1956-81; lectr. bus. English Northwestern U., 1945-64, lectr. journalism, 1964-81; adj. prof. English Brevard (N.C.) Coll., 1981-83. Mem. Modern Lang. Assn., Phi Beta Kappa. Methodist. Home: Sherwood Forest 9 Warbler Way Brevard NC 28712 Office: Brevard Coll Brevard NC 28712

AMES, BARBARA FRANCES, advertising agency executive; b. Bklyn., Jan. 26, 1936; d. George and Selma C. (Ruderman) Levine; m. Jonathan Ames, Oct. 14, 1956 (div. 1964). Student, Hunter Coll., 1953-55. Computer liaison Young & Rubicam, N.Y.C., 1958-66; spot broadcast coordinator Ted Bates, N.Y.C., 1966; office mgr. Advt. Info. Services, N.Y.C., 1966-67, media supr., planning, 1969-73, sr. v.p., mgr. communication service, 1974—. Office: Young & Rubicam Inc 285 Madison Ave New York NY 10017

AMES, BRUCE CHARLES, machinery company executive; b. Elgin, Ill., June 27, 1925; s. Daniel Franklin and Ruth Maude (Wright) A.; m. Joyce Grace Eichhorn, Sept. 9, 1950; children: Paula, Richard, Cynthia. Ph.B., Ill. Wesleyan U., 1950; M.B.A., Harvard U., 1954. Service engr. Ill. Bell Telephone Co., 1950-52; gen. comml. mgr. Gen. Telephone Co. N.Y., 1954-56; dir. mktg. Cin. Telephone Co., 1956-57; dir. McKinsey & Co., 1957-71; pres. Reliance Electric Co., Cleve., 1971-80, Acme-Cleve. Corp., 1981-83, chief exec. officer, 1981—, chmn., 1983—; dir. Diamond Shamrock Corp., Warner-Lambert Co., Hanna Mining Co., Cleve. Center for Econ. Edn. Author articles. Served with U.S. Army, 1943-46. Office: Acme-Cleveland Corp 30195 Chagrin Blvd Cleveland OH 44124 *

AMES, BRUCE N(ATHAN), biochemist, geneticist; b. N.Y.C., Dec. 16, 1928; s. Maurice U. and Dorothy (Andres) A.; m. Giovanna Ferro-Luzzi, Aug. 26, 1960; children: Sofia, Matteo. B.A., Cornell U., 1950; Ph.D., Calif. Inst. Tech., 1953. Chief sect. microbial genetics NIH, Bethesda, Md., 1953-68; prof. biochemistry U. Calif., Berkeley, 1968—. Mem. Nat. Cancer Adv. Bd. Recipient Eli Lilly award Am. Chem. Soc., 1964, Flemming award, 1966; Rosenstiel award, 1976; FASEB award, 1976; Environ. Mutagen Soc. award, 1977; Felix Wankel award, 1978; John Scott medal, 1979; New Brunswick award, 1980; Corson medal, 1980; Mott prize, 1983; Gardner award, 1983. Mem. Am. Soc. Biol. Chemists, Am. Soc. Microbiology, Environ. Mutagen Soc., Genetics Soc., Am. Assn. Cancer Research, Soc. of Toxicology, Am. Chem. Soc., Am. Acad. Arts and Scis., Nat. Acad. Scis. Research, publs. on bacterial molecular biology, histidine biosynthesis and its control; RNA and regulation; mutagenesis; detection of environmental mutagens and carcinogens, genetic toxicology, oxygen radicals and disease. Home: 1324 Spruce St Berkeley CA 94709

AMES, CLINTON G., JR., manufacturing company executive; b. Norfolk, Va., 1922; married. B.S., Va. Poly Inst., 1946. With Calvert Distilling Co., 1946-47; plant project engr. Eli Lilly & Co., 1948-51; staff engr. Merck & Co., 1951-54; mgr. tech. services Scott Paper Co., 1954-63; v.p. engring. Rice Barton Corp., 1963-68; asst. to gen. mgr. Continental Can Co., 1968; gen. mgr. ops. and engring. Inland Container Corp., Indpls., 1968-70, v.p. container bd. div., 1970-71, sr. v.p. ops., 1971-72, exec. v.p. ops., 1972-77, pres., 1977—, chief exec. officer, 1979—, dir.; v.p. Time Inc. Served with 1st lt. USAAF, 1942-45. Office: Inland Container Corp 151 N Delaware St Indianapolis IN 46204 *

AMES, DONALD PAUL, phys. chemist; b. Brandon, Man., Can., Sept. 13, 1922; s. Paul Main and Della Johanna (Hebel) A.; m. Doris Elizabeth Ubbelohde, Dec. 30, 1949; children—Elizabeth Carol, Barbara Louise. B.S., U. Wis., 1944, Ph.D. in Phys. Chemistry, 1949; LL.D. (hon.), U. Mo., St. Louis, 1978. Staff chemist Los Alamos Sci. Lab., 1950-52; asst. prof. phys. chemistry U. Ky., Lexington, 1952-54; staff chemist duPont Co., Aiken, S.C., 1954-56; sr. chemist, scientist Monsanto Co., St. Louis, 1956-61; scientist, then sr. scientist research div. McDonnell Aircraft Co., St. Louis, 1961-68; dep. dir. research, then dir. research McDonnell Douglas Research Labs., St. Louis, 1968-71, dir. labs., 1971-76, staff v.p., 1976—; mem. physics research evaluation group, directorate physics Air Force Office Sci. Research; adv. com. corp. assos. Am. Inst. Physics. Contbr. numerous profl. publns. Served with U.S. Army, 1944-46. Wis. Alumni research fellow, 1946-48; predoctoral fellow AEC, 1948-49; postdoctoral fellow, 1949. Mem. Am. Chem. Soc., Am. Phys. Soc., Phi Beta Kappa, Sigma Xi, Phi Lambda Upsilon, Phi Kappa Phi, Phi Eta Sigma, Alpha Chi, Sigma, Gamma Alpha. Office: McDonnell Douglas Research Labs PO Box 516 St Louis MO 63166

AMES, FISHER, lawyer; b. Oklahoma City, July 6, 1905; s. Charles Bismark and Elizabeth P. (Allen) A.; m. Jewell Turner, Nov. 5, 1934; children—Judith (Mrs. James P. Rhoads), Sarah (Mrs. Bruce B. Lenz). A.B., Harvard Coll., 1926; LL.B., U. Okla., 1930. Bar: Okla. bar 1930. Since practiced in Oklahoma City; of counsel firm Ames, Daugherty, Black, Ashabranner & Rogers, 1950—. Served to comdr. USNR, 1941-45. Home: 821 NW 38th St Oklahoma City OK 73118 Office: 6440 Avondale Oklahoma City OK 73116

AMES, FRANK ANTHONY, percussionist; b. Wheeling, W.Va., Oct. 12, 1942; s. Louis Higgins and Camille (O'Brien) A.; m. Susan Whalley, June 14, 1966 (div.); 1 dau., Kristin Suzanne; m. Annette Beck, 1980. Student, Linsley Mil. Inst., 1960-64; Mus.B., Eastman Sch. Music, 1964; M.F.A., Carnegie Mellon U., 1964. Teaching fellow Carnegie Mellon U., 1960-64; founder, exec. dir. 20th Century Consort, Millennium Ensemble, Martha's Vineyard Music Festival.; founder, pres. Potomac Prodns., Inc.; percussionist Pitts. Symphony, 1964-66, Balt. Symphony, 1966-68; prin. percussionist Nat. Symphony Orch., Washington, 1968—. Office: 1235 Potomac St NW Washington DC 20007

AMES, GEORGE JOSEPH, investment banker; b. N.Y.C., May 14, 1917; s. George Stanley and Catherine (Diercks) A.; m. Marion Patterson, July 19, 1941; children: Ruth Ames Solie, Joan (Mrs. Asa J. Berkowitz), Margery, Dorothy. A.B., Columbia U., 1937; J.D., Fordham Sch. Law, 1942. Bar: N.Y. 1942. With firm Lazard Freres & Co., N.Y.C., 1937-42, 46, gen. partner, 1957—; Chmn. bd. dirs. Louis August Jonas Found. Bd. dirs. Citizens Housing and Planning Council.; trustee Hartley House. Served to lt. USNR, 1942-46. Mem. ABA, Assn. Bar City N.Y. Clubs: Westchester Country, Am. Yacht (Rye, N.Y.). Home: Seville Ave Rye NY 10580 Office: 1 Rockefeller Plaza New York NY 10020

AMES, JAMES BARR, lawyer; b. Wayland, Mass., Apr. 10, 1911; s. Richard and Dorothy (Abbott) A.; m. Mary Ogden Adams, June 14, 1941 (dec. 1967); children: Elizabeth Bigelow (dec.), Richard, Charles Cabell; m. Suzannah Ayer Parker, Oct. 10, 1969. A.B., Harvard U., 1932, J.D. cum laude, 1936. Bar: Mass. 1936. Assoc. Ropes & Gray,

Boston, 1936-41, ptnr., 1947-83, of counsel, 1983—; dir. Fiduciary Trust Co., Boston; trustee Cambridge Savs. Bank. Author: Boston: A City Upon a Hill, 1980; co-author: How to Live and Die with Massachusetts Probate, 1982. Pres. Hosp. Planning for Greater Boston Inc., 1965-71, Mt. Auburn Hosp., Cambridge, 1953-59, Boston Athanaeum, 1961-81, Mass. Hist. Soc., 1975-78; treas. Mus. Fine Arts, 1977-83; chmn. Animal Rescue League Boston, 1958-70, Greater Boston Charitable Trust, 1970-73; trustee Buckingham Sch., Cambridge, 1959-62. Served to col. USAF, 1942-45. Decorated Legion of Merit, Bronze Star with oak leaf cluster. Fellow Am. Bar Found., Am. Coll. Probate Counsel (past state chmn.); mem. Am. Law Inst., ABA, Boston Bar Assn. (past chmn. probate com.), Cambridge Bar Assn. (past pres.), Am. Bar Found., Am. Humane Soc. (hon.), Phi Beta Kappa (chpt. pres.). Unitarian. Clubs: Somerset, Tavern, Cohasset Yacht. Home: 8 Dunstable Rd Cambridge MA 02138 Office: 225 Franklin St Boston MA 02110

AMES, JOHN DAWES, banker; b. May 7, 1904; s. K.L. and A.S. A.; m. Charlotte Schoonmaker, Nov. 9, 1928; children: John D., William S., Knowlton; m. Constance Hasler, Oct. 1, 1949. Grad., Princeton, 1928. Pres. Chgo. Jour. Commerce, 1929-50; exec. dir. Midwest div. Dow Jones & Co., Inc.; pubs. Wall Street Jour., 1951—; partner Bacon, Whipple & Co. Served as lt. col. AUS, World War II. Decorated Bronze Star. Episcopalian. Home: 600 N Washington Rd Lake Forest IL 60045 Office: 135 S LaSalle St Chicago IL 60603

AMES, JOHN LEWIS, lawyer, advertising executive; b. Norfolk, Va., July 15, 1912; s. Harry Lee and Catherine I. (Betty) A.; m. Margaret Kilbon, Apr. 8, 1939; children: Margaret Lee, John Lewis. A.B., Randolph-Macon Coll., 1933; LL.B., U. Richmond, Va., 1937; postgrad., N.Y. U. Law Sch., 1939-40. Bar: Va. bar 1936, N.Y. bar 1940. Mem. tax div. Home Life Ins. Co., N.Y.C., 1937-38; trial atty. Tanner, Sillocks & Friend, N.Y.C., 1938-41; house counsel Ruthrauff & Ryan, Inc., N.Y.C., 1941-42, house counsel and asst. to pres., 1945-48, sec., counsel, 1948-50, v.p., sec., 1950-55, v.p., sec., treas., 1955-57; also dir.; v.p., sec. Erwin, Wassey, Ruthrauff & Ryan, Inc., 1957-59; asst. dir. bus. affairs CBS TV Network, Inc., N.Y.C., 1959-62; v.p., sec., treas. Kudner Agy., Inc., 1962-65; also dir.; sr. v.p. adminstrn. and finance West, Weir & Bartel, Inc., N.Y.C., 1966, exec. v.p., dir., until 1968; v.p., sec. Lennen & Newell, Inc., 1968-73; v.p. bus. and legal affairs Dancer-Fitzgerald-Sample, Inc., 1973-83, legal cons., 1983—; dir. Carroll Products, Inc.; spl. agt. FBI, Washington and; N.Y.C., 1942-45; Spl. dep. atty. gen. N.Y. State, 1946-48; Mem. Nassau County N.Y. Crime Commn., 1973—; Trustee Randolph-Macon Coll., 1955—; Mem. Massapequa Bd. Edn., 1952-79, pres., 1957-78; past pres. Nassau-Suffolk Sch. Bds. Assn.; Past chmn. trustees Am. Assn. Advt. Agencies Group Ins. Mem. N.Y. County Lawyers Assn., Am. Arbitration Assn. (mem. nat. panel), Soc. Former Spl. Agts. F.B.I. (past nat. sec.), Alumni Soc. Randolph-Macon Coll. (past pres.), Phi Kappa Sigma, Omicron Delta Kappa, Tau Kappa Alpha. Methodist. Club: Indian Creek Yacht and Country (Kilmarnock, Va.). Home: 129 Rumson Rd Harbour Green Massapequa NY 11758 Office: 405 Lexington Ave New York NY 10017

AMES, LINCOLN, investment co. exec.; b. Glen Ridge, N.J., Aug. 8, 1932; s. Wyllys P. and Anna (Lincoln) A.; m. Aubin Wells Zabriskie, Nov. 26, 1960; children: Hyla Lincoln, Mark Zabriskie, David Wyllys. B.S., Yale U., 1954; M.B.A., Harvard U., 1960. Sr. v.p., dir. Blyth & Co., Inc., N.Y.C., 1960-72; exec. v.p., nat. dir. investment banking dir. Dean Witter Reynolds Inc., N.Y.C., 1972—; also mem. exec. com. Dean Witter Reynolds Overseas Ltd. Served with USNR, 1954-58. Mem. N.Y. Soc. Security Analysts, N.Y. Bond Club. Presbyterian. Republican. Clubs: City Midday, Montclair Golf, The Brook, Hartwood. Office: Dean Witter Reynolds Inc 130 Liberty St New York NY 10006

AMES, LOUISE BATES, child psychologist; b. Portland, Maine, Oct. 29, 1908; d. Samuel Lewis and Annie Earle (Leach) Bates; m. Smith Whittier Ames, May 22, 1930 (div. 1937); 1 dau., Joan Ames Ames Chase. A.B., U. Maine, 1930, M.A., 1933, Sc.D., 1957; Ph.D., Yale U., 1936; D.Sc., Wheaton Coll., 1967. Cert. psychologist, Conn. Research sec., personal asst. to Dr. Gesell Yale Clinc Child Devel., Yale Med. Sch., 1933-36, instr., 1940-44, asst. prof., 1944-50; curator Yale Films of Child Devel., 1944-50; co-founder Gesell Inst. Child Devel., dir. research, sec.-treas., 1950—, asso. dir., chief psychologist, 1968, co-dir., 1971-77, acting dir., 1978, pres., 1978—. Author: daily syndicated newspaper column Parents Ask; weekly TV broadcast on child behavior, WBZ, Boston, 1952-55; Author 2 dozen books, including: (with Arnold Gesell and others) The Gesell Institute's Child from One to Six; editorial bd.: Jour. Learning Disabilities, Jour. Genetic Psychology. Mem. Conn. Psychol. Soc., Am. Psychol. Assn., Soc. Research Child Devel., Internat. Council Psychologists (dir. 1945-47), Soc. Projective Techniques (pres. 1970), Sigma Xi. Home: 283 Edwards St New Haven CT 06511 Office: 310 Prospect St New Haven CT 06511 *Both by nature and upbringing, I am highly sympathetic to the Puritan ethic. I not only am extremely single minded and goal oriented, but I pretty much live to work. By good fortune, the work I do is of the greatest pleasure and interest to me, and I have been extremely fortunate in my associates.*

AMES, MILTON BENJAMIN, JR., retired aerospace researcher; b. Norfolk, Va., Sept. 21, 1913; s. Milton B. and Mabel (Roberts) A.; m. Martha Nuland, Jan. 22, 1944 (dec. 1979); children: Carol Diane, Linda Anne, Milton Stephen; m. Alice Warren, Nov. 19, 1979. Student, William and Mary Coll., Va. Poly. Inst., 1931-32, Ga. Inst. Tech., 1933-34; B.S. in Aero. Engring, Guggenheim Sch. Aeros., Ga. Inst. Tech., 1936. Aero. research engr. Langley Meml. Aero. Lab., Langley Field, Va., 1936-41; instr. aeros. Norfolk div. Va. Poly. Inst., 1940-41; engring. asst. to G.W. Lewis; dir. NACA, Washington, 1941-43; engring. asst. to chief mil. research NACA hdqrs., 1943-46, chief aerodynamics div., 1946-58; asst. dir. aero. and space research NASA, 1959-60, dep. dir. advanced research, 1960-61; dir. space vehicles Office Advanced Research and Tech., 1961-70, sr. research asso., 1970-72; spl. asst. to asst. adminstr. for DOD and Interagy. Affairs, 1972; dir. NASA hdqrs. projects Fire, Pegasus and Lifting Body flight research program; chmn. panel on reusable launch vehicle tech. (space shuttle) NASA-Dept. Def., 1965-66; cons. to NASA hdqrs.; also spl. tech. asst. to U.S. Nat. Dels. to AGARD, NATO, 1972-74; partner Ames Bros., Norfolk.; Mem. fluid dynamics panel, adv. group aero. research and devel. NATO. Author research publs., tech. summaries. Recipient NASA awards for projects Fire, Pegasus, Apollo, X-15, Lifting Bodies and Space Shuttle; named Distinguished Alumnus Old Dominion U., 1966. Fellow Inst. Aeros. and Astronautics (chmn. Washington sect. 1948-49); mem. AAAS, Nat. Aeros. Assn. (policy com. of contest and record bd. 1958-72), Theta Chi. Clubs: University (Washington); Belle Haven Country (Alexandria, Va.). Home: 1605 River Farm Dr River Bend Estates Alexandria VA 22308

AMES, OAKES, college president; b. Boston, Oct. 9, 1931; s. Amyas and Evelyn Ingeborg (Perkins) A.; m. Louise Voorhees Kimball, June 25, 1960; children: Geoffrey A., Michael P., Stephen K., Letitia V. A.B., Harvard U., 1953; Ph.D., Johns Hopkins U., 1957. Instr., then asst. prof. physics Princeton U., 1958-66; asso. prof., then prof. SUNY-Stony Brook, 1966-74; asst. to pres. SUNY, 1966-68, chmn. dept. physics, 1970-74; pres. Conn. Coll., New London, 1974—. Trustee Eugene O'Neill Meml. Theatre Center, Lawrence and Meml. Hosps., Mystic Seaport. Mem. Am. Assn. Physics Tchrs., Am. Phys. Soc., AAAS. Clubs: Harvard, Century Assn. (N.Y.C.).

AMES, RALPH WOLFLEY, univ. dean; b. Etna, Wyo., June 27, 1920; s. John Coburn and Emma (Wolfley) A. B.S., U. Wyo., 1940, M.S., 1941; Ph.D., U. Ill., 1950. Asst. prof. botany U. Mass., 1950-51; asso. plant pathologist Ill. Natural Hist. Survey, 1951-52; asso. prof. Utah State Agrl. Coll., 1952-54, prof., head dept. botany, 1954-58; plant pathologist Los Angeles Arboretum, 1958-60; mem. faculty Calif. State Poly. U., Pomona, 1960—, now prof. botany, head dept., dean Sch. Sci. Served to capt. M.C. AUS, 1942-46. Mem. Am. Phytopath. Soc., Bot. Soc. Am., Mycol. Soc. Am., Internat. Shade Tree Conf. Office: 3801 W Temple Ave Pomona CA 91768

AMES, ROBERT ARTHUR, research scientist; b. Fresno, Calif., Dec. 5, 1925; s. Harry G. and Martha A. (Davison) A.; m. Delila, Nov. 24, 1955; children: Douglas, Matthew, Duncan, Dee. B.Sc., U. Calif.-Berkeley, 1942, M.Sc., 1950; Sc.D., U. Utah, 1956, Inst. Sci. Research, Salt Lake City, 1964. Research and devel. engr. ARAMCO, 1948-50; research engr. Filtroc Corp., Salt Lake City, 1950-52, ANPEX Corp., Red Wood City, Calif., 1952-54; dir. research Inst. Sci. Research, Salt Lake City, 1963—; dir. Ele-Metals Corp., Salt Lake City, Eden Glo Corp. Author: Subjective Science, 1980; contbr. articles to profl. jours. Bd. dirs., pres. Utah Opera Soc., 1976-77. Served with U.S. Army, 1942-46; ETO; PTO. Mem. ASTM, Am. Chem. Soc., Am. Electroplating Soc., Am. Nuclear Soc., AAAS, Am. Inst. Chem. Engrs. Office: 3585 Via Terra Salt Lake City UT 84115

AMES, ROBERT SAN, retired manufacturing company executive; b. N.Y.C., Jan. 23, 1919; s. Leonard and Felicia (San) A.; m. Margaret Grossman, Oct. 14, 1945; children: Linda (Mrs. K.J. Cassady), David, Elizabeth. B.A., Columbia U., 1940, B.S. in Mech. Engring., 1941, M.S., 1942, Mass. Inst. Tech., 1954. With Goodyear Aircraft Corp., Akron, Ohio, 1942-60; v.p. Aeroprojects, Inc., West Chester, Pa., 1960-62; mgr. planning RCA Def. Elec. Products, Camden, N.J., 1962-64; v.p. mfg. Bell Aerospace Co., Buffalo, 1964-68; group v.p. Textron, Inc., Providence, 1968-71, sr. v.p. ops., 1971-79, mem. adminstrv. and investment coms., exec. v.p.-aerospace, 1979-84; Pres., dir. Am. Research and Devel. Corp., Boston, 1972-73; dir. Sippican Ocean Systems (Marion), Mass., Criton Corp., Precision Castparts, Pneumo Corp., Esterline Corp. Bd. dirs. Providence Athenaeum, 1972-75; bd. dirs. Lincoln Sch. Mem. Nat. Security Indsl. Assn. (chmn. bd. dirs. 1982), Aerospace Industries Assn. (chmn. bd. govs. 1983). Home: 626 Angell St Providence RI 02906 Office: RI Hosp Trust Nat Bank Bldg Rm 1103 15 Westminster St Providence RI 02903

AMES, VAN METER, educator; b. De Soto, Iowa, July 9, 1898; s. Edward Scribner and Mabel (Van Meter) A.; m. Betty Breneman, June 12, 1930; children—Sanford Scribner, Christine (Mrs. Judson E. Cornish), Damaris. Ph.B., U. Chgo., 1919, Ph.D., 1924. Faculty U. Cin., 1925, head dept. philosophy, 1959—, Obed J. Wilson prof. ethics, 1960-66, Obed J. Wilson prof. ethics emeritus, 1966—; fellow Grad. Sch., 1957—; Vis. prof. Cornell U., summer 1931, U. Tex., 1934-35, U. Hawaii, 1947-48; Faculté des Lettres U. Aix-Marseille, France, spring 1949, Columbia, summer 1957; Mem. 2d East-West Philosophers Conf., U. Hawaii, summer 1959. Author: Aesthetics of the Novel, 1928, Introduction to Beauty, 1931; poetry Out of Iowa, 1936, Proust and Santayana, 1937, Andre Gide, 1947, (with Betty B. Ames) Japan and Zen, 1961, Zen and American Thought, 1962; Editor: Beyond Theology: The Autobiography of Edward Scribner Ames, 1959, The Prayers and Meditations of E.S. Ames, 1970. Rockefeller grantee, France, 1948; Fulbright research prof. philosophy Komazawa U., Tokyo, Japan, 1958-59; Humanist fellow, 1976. Mem. Am. Philos. Assn. (pres. Western div. 1959-60), Am. Soc. Aesthetics (pres. 1961-62), Am. Humanist Assn. Home: 448 Warren Ave Cincinnati OH 45220 *It is basic to examine the values of life. Socrates said that the unexamined life is not worth living. The question of the Good, the True, and the Beautiful must be understood as curiosity and wonder about the most persistent, often unanswerable questions.*

AMES, WILLIAM FRANCIS, mathematician; b. Brandon, Man., Can., Dec. 8, 1926; s. Paul Main and Della Johanna (Hebel) A.; m. Theresa Danielson, May 29, 1951; children: Karen Anne, Susan Lynn, Pamela Margaret. M.S., U. Wis., 1950. Instr. U. Wis., Racine, 1953-55; sr. engr. DuPont Co., Wilmington, Del., 1955-59; prof. U. Del., Newark, 1959-67, U. Iowa, Iowa City, 1967-75, Ga. Inst. Tech., Atlanta, 1975—, Regents prof., 1981—; research prof. U. Ga., Athens, 1977-79; cons. in field. Author: Nonlinear Partial Differential Equations in Engineering, Vol. I, 1965, Vol. II, 1972, Nonlinear Ordinary Differential Equations in Transport Processes, 1968, Numerical Methods for Partial Differential Equations, 1970, 77; Editor 3 books.; Contbr. articles to profl. jours. Served with USNR, 1944-46, 51-52. NSF faculty fellow, 1963-64; grantee, 1964-67, 76-79; NBS grantee, 1967-71; USPHS grantee, 1961-63; EPA grantee, 1978-81; U.S. Army grantee, 1968-75, 81—; NATO sr. fellow, 1972-73; Humboldt sr. scientist, 1974-75. Mem. Soc. Indsl. and Applied Maths. (mem. council), Math. Assn. Am., Soc. Natural Philosophy. Home: 125 Tamarisk Dr Atlanta GA 30342 Office: Sch Math Ga Inst Tech Atlanta GA 30332

AMICK, ROBERT O'NEIL, retail company executive; b. Columbia, S.C., Feb. 12, 1933; s. Robert Walter A. and Emma Dell (Courtney) Walker; m. Barbara Moore, Nov. 27, 1960. B.S., U. So. Miss., 1959. Cert. internal. auditor. Asst. mgr. auditing J.C. Penney Co., Inc., N.Y.C., 1959-65, audit mgr., 1968-73, asst. controller, 1976-81, v.p., controller, 1982—; controller Treasury Stores, N.Y.C., 1965-68, Thrift Drug Co., Pitts., 1973-76. Treas. Penney PAC, N.Y.C., 1982. Served to lt. U.S. Army, 1953-57. Mem. Fin. Execs. Inst. (dir., N.Y.C.), Nat. Assn. Accts. (v.p. 1973-74), Inst. Internal Auditors. Methodist. Home: Route 1 Box 91 Smithfield NC 27577 Office: JC Penny Co Inc 1301 Ave of the Americas New York NY 10019

AMIDON, ELLSWORTH LYMAN, ret. physician, educator; b. West Barnet, Vt., Apr. 3, 1906; s. Freeman Ellsworth and Mary Ward (Walker) A.; m. Mae Agnes Elizibeth Liddle, June 29, 1932; children—Roger Lyman, Cynthia Jean. Student, Goddard Sem., 1922-23; B.S., Tufts Coll., 1927; M.D., U. Vt., 1932, D.Sc. (hon.), 1974; M.S., U. Pa. Grad. Sch., 1936. Diplomate: Am. Bd. Internal Medicine. Intern Mary Fletcher Hosp., Burlington, Vt., 1932- 33, med. dir., 1934; instr. pathology U. Vt. Med. Coll., 1933-35, instr. pathology and internal medicine, 1936-37, asst. prof. internal medicine, 1937-40, asso. prof., 1940-45, chmn. dept., 1945-64, prof., 1945—; Med. chmn. fund-raising Chittenden unit Vt. Heart Assn.; Surgeon USPHS Res. Mem. editorial bd.: Book of Health, 1953; Contbr. articles profl. jours. Recipient Distinguished Service award Vt. Med. Soc., 1965, recipient U. Vt. Alumni, 1973. Master A.C.P. (regent 1957—, 1st v.p. 1963); fellow Am. Coll. Cardiology; mem. Am. Heart Assn. (dir. 1958-63), Vt. Heart Assn. (liaison to Am. Heart Assn., pres. 1956-57), Am. Diabetic Assn., Am. Fedn. Clin. Research, Vt., Montreal med. socs. Home: 144 Deforest Rd Burlington VT 05401 Office: Mary Fletcher Unit Burlington VT 05401

AMIDON, ROGER LYMAN, health administration educator; b. Burlington, Vt., Apr. 8, 1938; s. Ellsworth L. and Mae (Liddle) A.; m. JoAnn Reiland, Aug. 1, 1968. B.A., U. Vt., 1960; M.A., U. Iowa, 1965, Ph.D. (USPHS trainee), 1968. Asst. prof. hosp. and health adminstrn. U. Iowa, 1968-73, asso. prof., 1973-77; prof., chmn. dept. health adminstrn. U. Okla., 1977-81, U. S.C., 1981—; exec. sec. Nat. Center Health Services Research, 1975-76; dir. Am. Indian Grad. Program in Health Adminstrn., U. Okla., 1977-81. Contbr. articles to profl. jours. Served with M.S.C. U.S. Army, 1961-62. Mem. AAAS, AAUP, Am. Hosp. Assn., Am. Public Health Assn., Inst. Soc., Ethics and the Life Scis. Home: 6423 Gill Creek Rd Columbia SC 29206 Office: Dept of Health Administration School Public Health South Carolina Columbia SC 29208

AMINO, LEO, sculptor, designer; b. Japan, June 26, 1911; came to U.S., 1929; s. Ichiju and Yufu A.; m. Julie Blumberger, 1947; 1 dau., Eriko. Student, N.Y.U., Am. Artists Sch. Tchr. sculpture Black Mountain (N.C.) Coll., 1946, 50; formerly tchr. sculpture Cooper Union, N.Y.C. One man shows include, Montross Gallery, 1940, Artists' Gallery, 1940-43, Clay Club Gallery, 1941, Bonestell Gallery, 1945, Sculptors Gallery, 1946-49, Sculpture Center, 1951, 52, 54, 57, 71, 73, Art Alliance, Phila., 1951, East Hampton Gallery, 1969, 70; represented in, Mus. of Modern Art, Massillon Mus., Addison Gallery, Am. Art, U. Neb., Grand Rapids Mus., Olsen Found., New Haven, Tex. State Coll., Women, Des Moines Art Center, Whitney Mus. Am. Art, Provincetown, Mass., pub. and pvt. collections. Studio: 58 Watts St New York City NY 10013

AMIOKA, SHIRO, educator; b. Honolulu, Oct. 26, 1922; s. Tsurumatsu and Reye (Yoshimura) A.; m. Toshiko Watanabe, July 25, 1956. Ed.B., U. Hawaii, 1949, Ed.M., 1952; Ph.D., U. Ill., 1959; postgrad., U. Minn., 1951-52, U. Tokyo, Japan, 1962-63, 69-70; Ph.D., Ashiya U., Japan, 1978. Instr. edn. U. Ill., Urbana, 1954-55, 58-59; instr. edn. U. Hawaii, Honolulu, 1955-57, asst. prof., 1957-63, assoc. prof., 1963-66, prof., 1966—, chmn. dept. ednl. founds., 1981—, also asst. dean summer session, 1960-65, assoc. dean summer session, 1965-71, chancellor for community colls., 1975-77; supt. edn. Hawaii State Dept. Edn., Honolulu, 1971-74. Served with AUS, 1943-47. Mem. Philosophy of Edn. Soc., John Dewey Soc., Hawaiian Acad. Sci., AAUP, Assn. for Asian Studies, History Edn. Soc., Soc. Profs. Edn., Nat. Soc. for Study Edn., John Dewey Soc. of Japan, Phi Kappa Phi, Phi Delta Kappa, Kappa Delta Pi. Home: 308-B Kuliouou Rd Honolulu HI 96821 Office: Coll Edn U Hawaii 1776 University Ave Honolulu HI 96822

AMIRIKIAN, ARSHAM, engineering company executive; b. Armenia, May 17, 1899; U.S., 1919, naturalized, 1927; s. Paravon and Pearl (Delbarian) A.; m. Philomena Elizabeth Boardman, Aug. 8, 1925; children: Richard Armen, Joyce Eleanor (Mrs. Robert A. Harrison). B.S., Ecole superieure des Ponts et Chaussees, Constantinople, 1919; C.E., Cornell U., 1923; D.Tech.Sc., Technische Hochschule, Vienna, 1960. Steel fabricator draftsman and designer 1923-28; various engring. positions to chief engring. cons. Naval Facilities Engring. Command, U.S. Navy Dept., Washington, 1928-71; pres. Amirikian Engring. Co., 1971—; cons. engr. shore and floating structures, harbor and docking facilities; adj. prof. engring. George Washington U., 1965-66. Author: Analysis of Rigid Frames, 1942; Contbr. articles tech. periodicals. Recipient Fuertes Grad. gold medal Cornell U., 1943, Lincoln gold medal Am. Welding Soc., 1949, A.E. Lindau award Am. Concrete Inst., 1958, Distinguished Service award Dept. of Navy, 1966, Def. Dept., 1969, Civilian Career Achievement award Dept. Navy, 1971, Goethals medal Soc. Am. Mil. Engrs., 1971. Fellow Am. Concrete Inst., Soc. Am. Mil. Engrs.; mem. Nat. Acad. Engring., ASCE (hon., E.E. Howard award 1978), Am. Welding Soc. (hon.), Soc. Naval Architects and Marine Engrs., Internat. Inst. Welding (hon.), Sigma Xi. Inventor of Ammi lift dock and transfer system, biserrated rib framing, split-beam prestressing, thin-shell hollow-rib and cellular precast concrete framing systems. Home: 6526 Western Ave Chevy Chase MD 20815 Office: 35 Wisconsin Circle Chevy Chase MD 20815

AMIS, EDWARD STEPHEN, chemistry educator; b. Himyar, Ky., Nov. 9, 1905; s. Jack and Artie (Southard) A.; m. Annie Velma Birdwhistle, Sept. 2, 1934; children: Edward Stephen, Velma Dianne. B.S., U. Ky., 1930, M.S., 1933; Ph.D., Columbia U., 1939. Mem. faculty La. State U., 1939-45, asso. prof., 1943-45; staff Carbide & Carbon Chems. Corp., Oak Ridge, 1945-47; prof. chemistry U. Ark., Fayetteville, 1947—; Mem. bd. alumni Union Coll., Barbourville, Ky., 1979—. Author: Kinetics of Chemical Change in Solution, 1949, A Book of Verse and Prose, 1965, Solvent Effects on Reaction Rates and Mechanisms, 1966, Russian edit., 1968, (with James F. Hinton) Solvent Effects on Chemical Phenomena, 1973, Saga of Racehorse and Other Items, 1969, A Novice in Europe and Other Writings, 1971, Beautiful But Dangerous and Other Poetry, 1977; numerous articles. Recipient Distinguished Research award U. Ark., 1967. Fellow N.Y. Acad. Scis.; mem. Am. Chem. Soc. (So. Chemist award 1959, S.W. award 1960, Tour Speaker plaque 1975), Am. Inst. Chemists (La., Ark., Miss. sect. honor scroll 1975), Ark. Acad. Scis., Sigma Xi, Alpha Chi Sigma, Pi Mu Epsilon, Phi Lambda Upsilon, Sigma Pi Sigma. Research on electromotive chemistry, conductance and transference of electrolytes in solution, kinetics and mechanism of chem. reactions in pure and mixed solvents, solvation of ions in pure and mixed solvents using conductance, transference and nuclear magnetic resonance procedures, theories of ion-diplolar molecule reactions, temperature coefficients of reaction rates, electron exchange reactions. Home: 1655 Woolsey Ave Fayetteville AR 72701

AMIS, KINGSLEY, novelist; b. Apr. 16, 1922; s. William Robert and Rosa A.; m. Hilary Ann Bardwell (div. 1965); m. Elizabeth Jane Howard, 1965; 3 children. Ed., City of London Sch., St. John's, Oxford. Lectr. English U. Coll., Swansea, 1949-61; vis. fellow creative writing Princeton, 1958-59; fellow in English Peterhouse, Cambridge U., Eng., 1961-63. Author: verse A Frame of Mind, 1953, Lucky Jim, 1954; filmed, 1957, That Uncertain Feeling, 1955; filmed as Only Two Can Play, 1961; verse A Case of Samples, 1956, I Like it Here, 1958, Take a Girl Like You, 1960; non-fiction New Maps of Hell, 1960, My Enemy's Enemy, 1962, One Fat Englishman, 1963, The James Bond Dossier, 1965, (with Robert Conquest) The Egyptologists, 1965, The Anti-Death League, 1966, A Look Round the Estate; verse, 1967, I Want It Now, 1968, The Green Man, 1969; non-fiction What Became of Jane Austen, 1970, Girl, 20, 1971, On Drink, 1972, The Riverside Villas Murder, 1973, Ending Up, 1974, Rudyard Kipling and his World, 1975, The Alteration, 1976, Jake's Thing, 1978, Russian Hide-and-Seek, 1980; collected Short Stories, 1980; editor: The New Oxford Book of Light Verse, 1978, The Faber Popular Reciter, 1978, The Golden Age of Science Fiction, 1981; contbr. to publs. Served with Army, 1942-45. Office: Jonathan Clowes & Co 19 Jeffrey's Pl London England NW1

AMISANO, JOSEPH, architect; b. N.Y.C., June 10, 1917; s. Ernest and Mary (Farrais) A.; m. Dorotht Baxter, June 10, 1946; children: Paul, Tina, Lisa; m. 2d Rosellen Goodrich, July 12, 1958. B.Arch., Pratt Inst., 1941. Registered architect, 14 states including Ga. Designer Walter Sanders, N.Y.C., 1940-41, Harrison & Fouihoux, 1941-42, Harrison & Abramovitz, 1942-44; structural engr. Pan Am. Airport, N.Y.C., 1944-45; designer Ketchum, Gina & Sharp, N.Y.C., 1946-49; pres. Toombs, Amisano & Wells, Atlanta, 1955—; guest lectr. Washington U., St. Louis, 1963. Mem. placement com. Regional Office Dept. Edn., Washington, 1961; mem. local com. Nat. Assn. Real Estate Execs., Miami, 1979; bd. dirs. Atlanta Art Inst., Atlanta, 1981. Recipient various awards AIA, 1946-83. Fellow AIA; mem. NAD, Am. Acad. Rome (Prix de Rome 1952), Internat. Council Shopping

Centers, Am. Inst. Planners. Democrat. Roman Catholic. Club: Commerce (Atlanta). Home: 1028 Newench Dr NW Atlanta GA 30327 Office: Toombs Amisano & Wells Inc 401 W Peachtree St NE Suite 1570 Atlanta GA 30308

AMISH, KEITH WARREN, utility executive; b. Rochester, N.Y., Feb. 13, 1923; s. Elmer J. and Florence E. (Zimmerman) A.; m. Josephine B. Merman, June 1, 1946; children: Paul, Richard, James, Barbara, Patricia. B.S. in Elec. Engring, Lehigh U., Bethlehem, Pa., 1947; M.B.A., U. Rochester, N.Y., 1971. Registered profl. engr., N.Y. With Rochester Gas and Electric Corp., 1947—, sr. v.p., then exec. v.p., 1971-80, pres., chief operating officer, 1980—, also dir.; dir., past pres. Empire State Electric Energy Research Corp.; dir. Mfrs. Hanover, N.A., Central Region; corp. rep. N.E. Power Coordinating Council; alt. mem. exec. com. N.Y. State Power Pool. Mem. exec. bd. Otetiana council Boy Scouts Am.; mem. exec. adv. bd. Roberts Wesleyan Coll., Rochester. Served with AUS, 1943-46. Mem. IEEE, Nat. Soc. Profl. Engrs., Edison Electric Inst., Am. Gas Assn., Am. Mgmt. Assn., Rochester Engring. Soc., Rochester Area C. of C. (trustee), Tau Beta Pi, Eta Kappa Nu, Pi Mu Epsilon.. Clubs: University (Rochester); Chemists (N.Y.C.). Home: 1454 Webster-Fairport Rd Penfield NY 14526 Office: 89 East Ave Rochester NY 14649

AMITAY, NOACH, radio communicatio electrical engineer; b. Tel Aviv, Israel, Apr. 30, 1930; came to U.S., 1956; s. Haim and Bilhah (Pesker) A.; m. Joan Pilchard, Apr. 10, 1960; children: Elisa, Tamar, Rena, Sarah. B.S. cum laude, Technion, Israel, 1953; M.S., Carnegie Inst. Tech., 1957, Ph.D., 1960. Engr. Signal Corps, Israeli Army, 1954-56; research engr. Carnegie Inst. Tech., Pitts., 1956-59, asst. prof., 1960-62; cons. Magnetics, Inc., Butler, Pa., 1957-60; mem. tech. staff AT&T Bell Labs., Holmdel, N.J., 1962—; cons. Westinghouse Electric Corp., Pitts., 1960-62. Con-arthor: Theory and Analysis of Phased Array Antennas, 1972; contbr. articles to profl. jours.; Patentee in field. Fellow IEEE; mem. Internat. Sci. Radio Union. Jewish. Home: 57 Wilshire Dr Tinton Falls NJ 07724 Office: AT&T Bell Labs 4G-616 Crawford Corner Rd Holmdel NJ 07733

AMLEN, SEYMOUR, TV program executive; b. N.Y.C., Apr. 28, 1928; s. Herman and Ray (Silverman) A.; m. Elinor Schlossberg, June 29, 1958; children—David Jonathan, Jennifer Jean. B.A., U. Mo., 1949; M.A., Ohio State U., 1950. Supr. audience measurements ABC-TV, N.Y.C., 1955-58, mgr. program research, 1958-64, asso. research dir., 1964-73; v.p. ABC-TV research, 1973-75, ABC-TV Program Planning, after 1975; now v.p. ABC Entertainment. Democrat. Jewish. Office: 1330 6th Ave New York NY 10019 *When I was a young man there were older people who took an interest in me and encouraged me as my career advanced. I have tried ever since to do the same for young people who seek my help in entering or climbing the ladder in the broadcasting business. I strongly believe that no one can or should have to do it alone.*

AMLING, FREDERICK, educator; b. Cleve., Dec. 23, 1926; s. Gustav and Elsie (Fisher) A.; m. Gwendolyn Stewart, Feb. 17, 1951; children: Jeffrey, Scott, Terrance. B.A., Baldwin Wallace Coll., 1948; M.B.A., Miami U., Oxford U., 1949; Ph.D., U. Pa., 1957. Instr. U. Maine, 1948-50, U. Pa., 1950- 52, U. Conn., 1952-55; prof. finance and investment chmn. dept. Miami U., Oxford, 1955-66; prof. finance U. R.I., Kingston, 1966-69; dean Coll. Bus. Adminstrn., 1966-69; now prof. bus. finance Grad. Sch. Bus. and Fin. George Washington U.; pres. Frederick Amling & Assocs., investment advisors; cons. finance and investment, 1959—; cons. Riggs Nat. Bank, Am. Psychiat. Assn.; Dir. Keystone Internat. Fund, Boston. Author: Investments: An Introduction to Analysis and Management, rev. edit., 1984, Plaid on Investments, 1983, Dow Jones Irwin Guide to Personal Financial Planning and Personal Financial Management, 1982; Contbr. articles on finance to profl. jours., newspapers. Chmn. local Cancer Crusade, 1964; trustee Georgetown Presbyn. Ch., 1977-79. Served with USNR, World War II. Recipient Alumni Merit award Baldwin Wallace Coll., 1973, Alumni award George Washington U., 1982, George Washington U. Bus. Sch., 1982. Mem. Washington Soc. Financial Analysts (treas.), Financial Mgmt. Assn., Am. Finance Assn. (membership chmn.), Eastern Finance Assn. (v.p. 1979), Smithsonian Assos., Beta Gamma Sigma, Delta Sigma Pi, Lambda Chi Alpha. Presbyn. (elder 1962- 66). Clubs: University (Miami U., Oxford) (pres. 1964); Turks Head (Providence); George Washington Univ., Cosmos, Congl. Country. Home: 7312 Masters Dr Potomac MD 20854 also 17 New Salt Rd Ocean Park ME 04063 Office: Hall of Govt and Business George Washington U 21st St and G St Washington DC 20006 *To work for family and society with God's help.*

AMMAR, RAYMOND GEORGE, physicist, educator; b. Kingston, Jamaica, July 15, 1932; came to U.S., 1961, naturalized, 1965; s. Elias George and Nellie (Khaleel) A.; m. Carroll Ikerd, June 17, 1961; children—Elizabeth, Robert, David. A.B., Harvard U., 1953; PhD., U. Chgo., 1959. Research asso. Enrico Fermi Inst., U. Chgo., 1959-60; asst. prof. physics Northwestern U., Evanston, Ill., 1960-64, asso. prof., 1964-69; prof. physics U. Kans., Lawrence, 1969—; cons. Argonne (Ill.) Nat. Lab., 1965-69, vis. scientist, 1971-72; project dir. NSF grant for research in high energy physics, 1962—. Contbr. articles to sci. jours. Fellow Am. Phys. Soc.; mem. AAUP. Home: 1651 Hillcrest Rd Lawrence KS 66044 Office: Dept Physics U Kans Lawrence KS 66045

AMMARELL, JOHN SAMUEL, security services executive; b. nr. Reading, Pa., Mar. 21, 1920; s. John Samuel and Marie (Rothermel) A.; m. Florence Rebecca Althouse, June 27, 1942; children—John David, Robert Lynn. A.B., Muhlenberg Coll., 1941; postgrad., George Washington U., 1942-43. Spl. agt., asst. chief liaison FBI, Washington, 1942-54; asso. Gt. Am. Tchrs. Agy., Allentown, Pa., 1955-56; mgr. personnel, dir. security Air Products & Chems., Inc., Trexlertown, Pa., 1956-58; chmn. exec. com., dir., exec. v.p. Wackenhut Corp., Coral Gables, Fla., 1958-83, chmn. exec. com., dir., 1983—; pres. Newberry Coll., S.C., 1984—; exec. v.p. Wackenhut Services, Inc., 1960-81, dir., 1960—, Wackenhut Internat. Inc., Stellar Systems.; Bd. dirs. Asso. Industries Fla., 1966—, sec., 1968-69; treas., 1969-70, v.p., 1970-73, pres., 1973-74, chmn., 1974-75; bd. dirs. Greater Miami Citizens Crime Commn., 1975—, pres., 1979-80; Trustee Newberry Coll., 1970-73, 74—. Recipient Alumni Achievement award Muhlenberg Coll., 1971; named Community Leader Am., 1970-78. Mem. Soc. Former Spl. Agts. FBI (pres. Pan Am. chpt. 1967-68), Com. Nat. Security Cos. (chmn. 1975-77), Am. Soc. Indsl. Security (chmn. pvt. security services council 1976-79), Lambda Chi Alpha, Omicron Delta Kappa, Phi Alpha Theta. Lutheran. Clubs: Elk., Country of Coral Gables. Office: 3280 Ponce de Leon Blvd Coral Gables FL 33134 Office: Newberry Coll Newberry SC 29108

AMMEN, JAMES, textile company executive; b. 1939. Bachelor, Columbia U., Master. With Burlington Industries, Inc., Greensboro, N.C., 1962—; mgr. sales promotion Pacific Mills div., Burlington Industries, Inc., 1962-75, pres., 1975-78; corp. group v.p. Burlington Industries, Inc., 1978-80, exec. v.p., Greensboro, N.C., 1980—; mem. mgmt. policy com. Greensboro, Greensboro, N.C. Office: Burlington Industries Inc 3330 W Friendly Ave Greensboro NC 27420 *

AMMERMAN, ROBERT RAY, philosopher, educator; b. Buffalo, Sept. 5, 1927; s. John Raymond and Frances Mura (Pettit) A.; 1 son, Robert Thompson. A.B. with highest honors, Swarthmore Coll., 1952; M.A., Brown U., 1954, Ph.D., 1956. Mem. faculty dept. philosophy U. Wis., Madison, 1956—, prof., 1967—; vis. researcher U. London, 1965. Author: (with M.G. Singer) Introductory Readings in Philosophy, 1962, Classics of Analytic Philosophy, 1965. Served with U.S. Army, 1945-48. Mem. Phi Beta Kappa. Home: 1415 Hwy B Cambridge WI 53523 Office: Dept Philosophy U Wis Madison WI 53706

AMMIDON, HOYT, banker; b. Balt., June 30, 1909; s. Daniel Clark and Estelle H. (Hoyt) A.; m. Elizabeth Macl. K. Callaway, May 19, 1933; children: Hoyt, Lee Thorne. Student, Loomis Sch., Windsor, Conn., 1923-25, 1926-28, Le Rosey Sch., Rolle, Switzerland, 1925-26; B.A., Yale U., 1932; LL.D., Hofstra U., 1968. With Central Hanover Bank (now Mfrs. Hanover Trust Co.), 1932—, asst. sec., 1937-43, v.p., 1950-52, trustee, 1957; chief exec. officer Vincent Astor, 1952-58; pres. U.S. Trust Co., N.Y.C., 1958-62, chmn., 1962-74; chmn. bd. U.S. Internat. Adv. Co., 1966-74; dir., exec. com., chmn. audit com. Perkin-Elmer Corp., 1967-79; dir., mem. exec. com. Bullock Fund, Ltd., Carriers & Gen. Corp., Dividend Shares, Inc., High Income Shares, Inc., Monthly Income Shares, Inc., Nation-Wide Securities Co., Inc., Aggressive Growth Shares, Bullock Fund, Bullock Tax-Free, Pacific Gen. Devel. Co.; chmn. bd. WestAm. Properties, S.A.; mem. N.Y. Banking Bd., 1963-67; commr. Port N.Y. Authority, 1969-72, vice chmn., 1970-72, chmn. operations com., 1970-72; mem. adv. bd. Quadrex Securities Corp., Metroscape Systems, Inc.,, 1984. Hon. chmn., founding mem. Am. Friends Can. Com., Inc.; mem. nat. businessmen's com. A Better Chance, 1969-73; Mem. devel. bd. Yale U.; mem. adv. bd. YMCA, Huntington Twp., N.Y.; former bd. dirs. Meml. Hosp.; mem. com. N.Y. Clearing House Assn.; bd. dirs. emeritus Lincoln Center Performing Arts; bd. dirs. Fed. Hall Meml. Assocs., N.Y.C., 1959-74, N.Y.C. Nat. Shrines Assocs., 1969-74, N.Y. div. Am. Cancer Soc., 1969-73; bd. govs. Hundred Year Assn. of N.Y., 1963-71; trustee, pres. emeritus bd. Loomis Sch.; trustee emeritus Cooper Union Advancement Sci. and Art; trustee, founding mem. Bus. Com. for the Arts, Inc.; life fellow Met. Mus. Art; fellow Pierpont Morgan Library, 1962-74; pres. bd. dirs. adv. council Am. Ditchley Found.; adv. com. Marine Hist. Assn.; mem. council Fedn. Protestant Welfare Agys., Inc.; bd. govs. N.Y. Coll. Osteo. Medicine. Served as lt. USCGR, 1942-45. Decorated grand ofcl. Order Crown of Italy; Fundacion Internacional Eloy Alfaro, Panama; officer Am. Soc. Most Venerable Order of Hosp. of St. John of Jerusalem; hon. comdr. Order Brit. Empire; recipient Medal of Merit St. Nicholas Soc. City N.Y., 1969; Gold medal St. Paul's Cathedral, London; Distinguished Service award Loomis-Chaffee Sch. Mem. Soc. Colonial Wars, Soc. Mayflower Descs., Am. Inst. Banking (adv. council N.Y. chpt. 1959-74), Grad. Club Assn. New Haven, Assn. Internat. Anciens Roseens, Pilgrims, U.S. Srs. Golf Assn. (former dir.), Chi Psi. Clubs: Economic (N.Y.C.); Cove Neck Tennis Courts, Cruising of America, Elihu (Yale) (grad. pres. 1958-60), River, Links, Piping Rock, St. Nicholas Hockey, Mory's Assn.; Royal and Ancient Golf of St. Andrews (Scotland). Office: 45 Wall St New York NY 10005

AMMON, HARRY, history educator; b. Waterbury, Conn., Sept. 4, 1917; s. Grover and Lena Mary (Pyne) A. B.S., GeorgeTown U., 1939, M.A., 1940; Ph.D., U. Va., 1948. Editor Md. Hist. Mag., Balt., 1948-50; asst. prof. So. Ill. U., Carbondale, 1950-57, assoc. prof., 1957-66, prof. history, 1966—; Fulbright lectr. U. Vienna, Austria, 1954-55; vis. prof. U. Va., Charlottesville, 1968-69. Author: James Monroe: The Quest for National Identity, 1971, The Genet Mission, 1973. Mem. Phi Beta Kappa. Home: 318 W Oak St Carbondale Il 69201 Office: History Dept So Ill U Carbondale Il 62901

AMMON, JAMES E., retailing exec.; b. Carmi, Ill., May 17, 1935; s. Otis Elwell and Katherine Bernice (Lairmer) A.; m. Patricia Carol Kucera, Aug. 30, 1958; children—Lynn Allison, Scott Anderson. B.B.A., Tulane U., 1959. C.P.A., La. Sr. accountant Haskins & Sells, New Orleans, 1959-63; sr. accountant Middle South Services, Inc., New Orleans, 1963-67, asst. sec., asst. treas., 1968, treas., 1968-78, v.p., 1975-78; treas. Middle South Utilities, Inc., New Orleans, 1970-78, v.p., 1977-78; sr. v.p. fin. D.H. Holmes Co. Ltd., New Orleans, 1978—. Served with USMC, 1954-56. Mem. Fin. Exec. Inst., Am. Inst. C.P.A.s, Nat. Retail Mchts. Assn., New Orleans C. of C. Democrat. Clubs: Metairie (La.) Country, Internat. House. Home: 462 Homestead Ave Metairie LA 70005 Office: 819 Canal St New Orleans LA 70112

AMMONS, ARCHIE RANDOLPH, poet; b. Whiteville, N.C., Feb. 18, 1926; s. Willie M. and Lucy Della (McKee) A.; m. Phyllis Plumbo, Nov. 26, 1949; 1 son, John Randolph. B.S., Wake Forest Coll., 1949; student, U. Calif.-Berkeley, 1951-52; Litt.D., Wake Forest U., 1972, U. N.C.-Chapel Hill, 1973. Prin., Hatteras (N.C.) Elem. Sch., 1949-50; exec. v.p. Freidrich & Dimmock, Inc. (biol. glassware mfr.), Millville, N.J., 1952- 61; asst. prof. English, Cornell U., 1964-68, asso. prof., 1968-71, prof., 1971—, Goldwin Smith prof. poetry, 1973—. Author: Ommateum, 1955, Expressions of Sea Level, 1964, Corsons Inlet, 1965, Tape for the Turn of the Year, 1965, Northfield Poems, 1966, Selected Poems, 1968, Uplands, 1970, Briefings, 1971, Collected Poems, 1951-1971, 1972, Sphere: The Form of a Motion, 1974, Diversifications, 1975, The Selected Poems: Nineteen Fifty One-Nineteen Seventy Seven, 1977, The Snow Poems, 1977, Selected Longer Poems, 1980, A Coast of Trees, 1981, Worldly Hopes, 1982, Lake Effect Country, 1983; poetry editor: Nation, 1963. Served with USNR, 1944-46. Recipient Bollingen prize in poetry, 1973-74; Guggenheim fellow, 1966; traveling fellow Am. Acad. Arts and Letters, 1967; recipient Levinson prize Poetry mag., 1970; Nat. Book award for poetry, 1973; Nat. Book Critics Circle award, 1982. Fellow Am. Acad. Arts and Scis. Address: 606 Hanshaw Rd Ithaca NY 14850

AMMONS, EDSEL ALBERT, bishop; b. Chgo., Feb. 17, 1924; s. Albert Clifton and Lila Kay (Sherrod) A.; m. June Billingsley, Aug. 18, 1951; children—Marilyn, Edsel, Carol, Kenneth, Carlton, Lila. B.A., Roosevelt U., 1948; B.D., Garrett Theol. Sem., 1956; D.Min., Chgo. Theol. Sem., 1975; D.D. (hon.), Westmar Coll., 1975. Social case worker Dept. Welfare Cook County, Chgo., 1951-56; ordained to ministry Meth. Ch., 1949; pastor Whitfield Meth. Ch., Chgo., 1957-60, Ingleside-Whitfield Meth. Ch., 1960-63; dist. dir. urban work Rockford dist. No. Ill. Conf. United Meth. Ch., 1963-66; council staff ann. conf. No. Ill. Conf., 1966-68; urban ch. cons., prof. ch. and soc., dir. basic degree studies Garrett Evang. Theol. Sem., Evanston, Ill., 1968-76; bishop United Meth. Ch., Mich. area, 1976—; exec. dir. Ednl. and Cultural Inst. Black Clergy, Chgo., 1972-73. Vice pres. Chatham-Avalon Community Council, Chgo., 1958-61; pres. W. Avalon Community Council, Chgo., 1959-60. Served with U.S. Army, 1943-46. Mem. Alpha Phi Alpha. Office: 155 W Congress St Suite 200 Detroit MI 48226 *

AMMONS, ROBERT BRUCE, pub., psychologist; b. Denver, Feb. 27, 1920; s. Bruce and Margaret Ann (Gates) A.; m. Carol Hamrick, Aug. 29, 1949; children: Carl, Bruce, Douglas, Elizabeth, Richard, Stephanie, Glenyss. B.A., San Diego State U., 1939; M.A., U. Iowa, 1941, Ph.D., 1946. Instr. Syracuse U., 1946; asst. prof. U. Denver, 1946-48, Tulane U., 1948-49, U. Louisville, 1949-55; asso. prof. U. N.D., 1956-57; prof. psychology U. Mont., Missoula, 1957—; Chmn. Solar div. Am. Assn. Variable Star Observers, 1980—. Also co-editor, pub.: Psychol. Reports, 1955—, Perceptual and Motor Skills, 1949—; Contbr. over 200 articles to profl. jours. Fellow Am. Psychol. Assn.; mem. Rocky Mountain, Midwest, Mont., Brit. psychol. Assns., Psychonomic Soc., Am. Statis. Assn., Am. Coll. Sports Medicine, Cheiron Soc., Sigma Xi. Home: 411 Keith Ave Missoula MT 59801 Office: Univ Montana Missoula MT 59812

AMON, ARTHUR HOWARD, JR., retailing executive; b. N.Y.C., Oct. 1, 1927; s. Arthur Howard and Constance (Kreuter) A.; m. Barbara Joan Brown, Oct. 29, 1948; children: Arthur, Scott, Patricia. Student, NYU, 1946-48, U. Va., 1948-49; LL.B., N.Y. Law Sch., 1951. Bar: N.Y. Assoc. Abberley Kooiman Marcellino & Clay, N.Y.C., 1951-56; house counsel Modern Transfer Co., Allentown, Pa., 1956-60; with real estate dept. J.C. Penney Co., 1960—, western real estate mgr., San Francisco, Buena Park, Calif., 1965-78, mgr. real estate ops., N.Y.C., 1978-79, v.p., dir. real estate, 1979—. Served with USN; 1945-46. Mem. Real Estate Bd. N.Y., Internat. Council Shopping Ctrs. (trustee), Urban Land Inst. Office: 1301 Ave of Americas New York NY 10019

AMON, WILLIAM FREDERICK, JR., genetic engring. co. exec.; b. Chelsea, Mass., Jan. 11, 1922; s. William Frederick and Esther H. (Rautenberg) A.; m. Barbara Marie Erlandson, Aug. 2, 1944; children—William Frederick III, Janet B., Carol J., Robert J. B.S. Ch.E., Northeastern U., 1943. Vice pres. new bus. ventures Borden Chem., N.Y.C., 1968-72; pres., chief exec. officer Electrospin Inc., Columbus, Ohio, 1972-76; v.p. Story Chem. Co., Muskegon, Mich., 1975-76, Cetus Corp., Berkeley, Calif., 1976—. Mem. Comml. Devel. Assn., Am. Chem. Soc., Soc. Indsl. Microbiology. Lutheran. Club: Chemists (N.Y.). Holder numerous patents. Home: 831 Matadera Circle Danville CA 94526 Office: 600 Bancroft Way Berkeley CA 94710

AMORY, CLEVELAND, writer; b. Nahant, Mass., Sept. 2, 1917; s. Robert and Leonore (Cobb) A. A.B., Harvard U., 1939; L.H.D., New Eng. Coll., Mercy Coll. Newspaper reporter Nashua (N.H.) Telegraph, Ariz. Daily Star, Tucson; then mng. editor Prescott (Ariz.) Evening Courier; asso. editor Saturday Evening Post, 1939-41; free lance writer, 1943—; editor Celebrity Register, 1959, 63. Author: The Proper Bostonians, 1947, Home Town, 1950, The Last Resorts, 1952, Who Killed Society?, 1960, Vanity Fair (anthology), 1960, Mankind? Our Incredible War on Wildlife, 1974, Animail, 1976; novel The Trouble With Nowadays, 1979; radio syndicated Curmudgeon at Large; TV commentator; syndicated newspaper column Animail. Founder, pres. The Fund for Animals. Clubs: Harvard, N.Y. Athletic, Dutch Treat (N.Y.C.). Office: 200 W 57th St New York NY 10019

AMORY, ROBERT, JR., lawyer; b. Boston, Mar. 2, 1915; s. Robert and Leonore (Cobb) A.; m. Mary Armstrong, June 17, 1938; children: Robert III, Daniel. A.B., Harvard, 1936, LL.B., 1938. Bar: N.Y. 1939, N.H. and Mass. 1946, D.C. 1965. Practiced in, N.Y.C., 1938-40; prof. law and accounting Harvard Law Sch., 1946-52; dep. dir. CIA, 1952-62; chief internat. div. Bur. Budget, 1962-65; mem. NSC Planning Bd., 1953-61; mem. firm Corcoran, Foley, Youngman & Rowe, Washington, 1965-72; sec., gen. counsel Nat. Gallery Art, Washington, 1973-80; U.S. del. Bermuda Conf., 1953, Bangkok, 1955; Trustee Arena Stage; bd. overseers Harvard U., 1963-69; mem. adv. council Sch. Advanced Internat. Studies, Johns Hopkins U.; mem. Cambridge Sch. Com., 1949-51; treas. Washington Cathedral Found., 1969-77. Author: Surf and Sand, 1947, Materials on Accounting, 1949. Entered Army as pvt., 1941; commanded amphibian engr. battalion and regiment; New Guinea and Philippine campaigns; discharged as col., 1946; lt. col. Armor Mass. N.G., 1946-51. Mem. Am. Law Inst. (life), Harvard Alumni Assn. (pres. 1961-62, dir. 1959-63, 75-77), Harvard Law Sch. Alumni Assn. pres. 1974-76). Clubs: Metropolitan, Cosmos (Washington); Chevy Chase, Cruising of America. Home: 4833 Dexter Terr Washington DC 20007

AMORY, THOMAS CARHART, management consultant; b. N.Y.C., Oct. 29, 1933; s. George Sullivan and Marion Renee (Carhart) A.; m. Carolyn Marie Pesnell, May 10, 1969; children: Renee Elizabeth, Caroline Carhart, Gillian Brookman. A.B., Harvard U., 1956. Comml. mgr. N.Y. Telephone Co., N.Y.C., 1957-60; sales mgr. Royce Chem. Co., East Rutherford, N.J., 1960-62; asst. to chmn. Seatrain Lines, Inc., Edgewater, N.J., 1963-65; mgmt. cons. Booz Allen & Hamilton, N.Y.C., 1966-67; ptnr. William H. Clark Assocs., Inc., N.Y.C., 1967-75, pres., 1975-79, chmn., 1979—. Trustee Mus. City, N.Y., 1971—. Mem. Assn. Exec. Recruiting Cons., Inc., Swiss Soc., Brit.-Am. C. of C. Republican. Episcopalian. Clubs: Union League, Brook, River, Tuxedo, Nantucket Yacht. Home: 435 E 52nd St New York NY 10022 Office: 330 Madison Ave New York NY 10017

AMOS, JAMES LYSLE, photographer; b. Kalamazoo, Jan. 25, 1929; s. George Elsworth and Lois Hazel (Noffsinger) A.; m. Martha Imogene Holbrook, Sept. 1975. Student, U. Idaho, 1947-49; Asso. Applied Sci., Rochester Inst. Tech., 1951. Trainee Eastman Kodak Co. (various locations), 1951-53, salesman, Des Moines, 1956, tech. sales rep., Balt., 1957-67. Free lance photographer, 1967-69; photographer, Nat. Geog. Soc., Washington, 1969—; prin. photographer books on Hawaii and America's Inland Waterway. Served with AUS, 1953-55. Mem. Nat. Press Photographers Assn. (named Mag. Photographer of Year 1969, 70), White House News Photographers Assn. Home: PO Box 118 Centreville MD 21617 Office: 17th and M Sts NW Washington DC 20036

AMOS, JOHN BEVERLY, insurance company executive; b. Enterprise, Ala., June 5, 1924; s. John Shelby and Mary Helen (Mullins) A.; m. Elena Diaz-Verson, Sept. 23, 1945; children: John Shelby, II, Maria Teresa. Ed., U. Miami, Fla., 1947, LL.D., 1979; J.D., U. Fla., 1949. Bar: Fla. 1949. Pvt. practice, Ft. Walton Beach, Fla., 1949-55, founder, 1955, Am. Family Life Assurance Co., Columbus, Ga., 1955; former pres., now chmn. bd., chief exec. officer, 1955; former pres., now chmn. bd., chief exec. officer Am. Family Corp. Past pres. Goodwill Industries, Columbus; past chmn. 3d Dist. Ga. Democratic Com.; trustee Morris Brown Coll., Atlanta; mem. nat. com. Nat. Mus. Jewish History, Phila.; vice chmn. Nat. Bipartisan Polit. Action Com. Mem. Nat. Assn. Life Cos. (v.p.), Fla. Bar Assn. Episcopalian. Clubs: Metropolitan (N.Y.C.); Big Eddy, Harmony (Columbus). Office: PO Box 1459 Columbus GA 31999 *

AMOS, JOHN ELLIS, lawyer; b. Charleston, W.Va., July 16, 1905; s. John Ellison and Louise Hampton (Delaney) A.; m. Edith Johnston, Oct. 5, 1935; children: John Delaney, Mary Amos Kolstad. Student, Augusta Mil. Acad.; LL.B., W.Va. U., 1929. Bar: W.Va. 1929. Since practiced in, Charleston.; Dir. Vulcan Materials Co., Birmingham, Ala.; Mem. W.Va. Ho. Dels. from Kanawha County, 1935-47, speaker, 1943-45, 47; mem. W.Va., Senate, 1947-56; Mem. Dem. Nat. Com. from W.Va., 1959-68; Pres. W.Va. Bd. Regents, 1969, sec., 1970. Mem. Am. Trucking Assn. (pres. 1965, chmn. bd. 1966, v.p. at large). Home: 291 Llwyd's Ln Vero Beach FL 32963 Office: PO Box 28 Charleston WV 25321

AMOS, MARVIN CYRIL, airline executive; b. Seymour, Ind., July 29, 1924; s. David Lawrence and Mary Eva (Hill) A.; m. Anne Addison, June 11, 1949; children: Patrick Marvin, Joanne Lee, Mark Addison, Judy Mitchell, Steven Lawrence. B.A., Hanover (Ind.) Coll., 1949. Edn. specialist RCA, Indpls., 1956-57; mgr. edn. and profl. placement, mgr. profl. placement and devel. Hotpoint div. Gen. Electric Co., Chgo., 1957-62; asst. to pres., dir. indsl. relations Wright Aero div. Curtiss-Wright Corp., Woodbridge, N.J., 1962-64; dir. planning and research, dir. personnel, v.p. personnel Eastern Air Lines, Inc., Miami,

1965-76, v.p. personnel and corporate adminstrn., 1976-78, sr. v.p. personnel and corporate adminstrn., 1978—; Trustee Hanover (Ind.) Coll., 1971—, chmn. bldgs. and grounds com., 1973—; bd. dirs. Sanibel Moorings Assn., 1975—. Served with U.S. Army, 1943-46, 51-53. Named Alumnus of Yr. Hanover Coll., 1976. Mem. Greater Miami C. of C. Republican. Roman Catholic. Home: 7745 SW 138th Terr Miami FL 33158 Office: Eastern Air Lines Inc Miami Internat Airport Miami FL 33148

AMOS, PAUL SHELBY, insurance corporation executive; b. Enterprise, Ala., Apr. 23, 1926; s. John Shelby and Mary Ellen (Mullins) A.; m. Mary Jean Roberts, Oct. 24, 1948; 1 son, Daniel P. Student, pub. schs. Co-founder, v.p. Am. Family Life Assurance Co., Columbus, Ga., 1956-64, state mgr. Ala., 1964-74, 1st v.p., dir. mktg., 1974-78, pres., 1978-83; vice chmn. Am Family Life Assurance Co., Columbus, Ga., 1983—; pres. Am. Family Corp., 1981-83, vice chmn., 1983—; owner Ben Franklin Stores, Milton, Fla., 1946-66; ptnr., v.p. Service Oil Co., Milton, 1958-66; pres., chmn. First Fed. Savs. & Loan, Milton, 1957-74. Served with USCGR, 1944-46; PTO. Mem. Columbus C. of C. (dir. 1981—). Democrat. Methodist. Club: Country of Columbus. Lodge: Lions (pres. Milton 1955). Home: 939 Overlook Ave Columbus GA 31906 Office: Am Family Ctr 1932 Wynnton Rd Columbus GA 31999

AMOSS, W. JAMES, JR., shipping company executive; b. 1924; married. B.B.A., Tulane U. With Lykes Bros. Steamship Co. Inc., New Orleans, 1947—, v.p. traffic, 1967-70, exec. v.p., 1970-73, pres., 1973—, chief exec. officer, dir., 1981—; dir. Hibernia Nat. Bank. Served with USN, 1940-46, 50-52. Office: Lykes Bros Steamship Co Inc 300 Poydras St Lykes Ctr PO Box 53068 New Orleans LA 70153 *

AMPER, ALAN, metals company executive; b. Brownsville, Pa., Sept. 20, 1923; s. Robert and Lillian (Ehrenpreis) A.; m. Jacqueline Friedman Levy, Mar. 18, 1976; children by previous marriage: Neil, Martha Coopersmith, Leslie; stepchildren: Madelyn Levy, Janice Levy, Sharon Levy. Student, U. Va., 1941-43. With Southwest Steel Corp., Pitts., 1946-61, v.p., 1948-61; founder, 1961; chief exec. officer, chmn. bd. Steelmet, Inc., Pitts. Bd. dirs. Montefiore Hosp., United Jewish Fedn., McKeesport Symphony Soc., Pitts. Symphony. Served with AUS, 1943-46. Mem. Inst. Scrap Iron and Steel, Nat. Assn. Recycling Industries, Pi Lambda Phi. Clubs: Ocean Reef (Key Largo, Fla.); Westmoreland Country (Export, Pa.); Concordia (Pitts.). Home: Gateway Towers Pittsburgh PA 15222 Office: PO Box 369 McKeesport PA 15134

AMRAM, DAVID WERNER, III, composer, conductor, musician; b. Phila., Nov. 17, 1930; s. Philip and Emilie (Weyl) A.; m. Loralee Ecobelli, Jan. 7, 1979; children: Alana, Adira, Adam. Student, Oberlin Conservatory Music, 1948-49, Manhattan Sch. Music, 1955-56; B.A. in European History, George Washington U., 1952; LL.D., Moravian Coll., Bethlehem, Pa., 1979; student composition with, Vitorio Giannini; student horn with, Gunther Schuller, N.Y.C., 1956. Composer incidental music for prodns., N.Y. Shakespeare Festival, 1956-67, Broadway plays, 1958—, films, 1957—, (collaboration with Jack Kerouac and Allen Ginsberg) also TV; first composer-in-residence, N.Y. Philharmonic Orch., 1966-67; condr., Bklyn. Philharmonic Youth Series; guest condr., soloist, Phila. Orch., Toronto Symphony, Houston Symphony, Rochester Symphony, Kansas City Symphony, Montreal, Winnipeg, Milw. symphony orchs.; appearances folk and jazz festivals, combining symphony, jazz and folk music with audience participation.; Compositions for orch. include Ode to Lord Buckley for saxaphone and orch., Violin Concerto; numerous others; operas include The Final Ingredient, 12th Night; Recording artist for, Elektra/Musician, Flying Fish Records.; Author: operas include Adventures and Musical Times of David Amram, 1968; Subject of: one-hour Nat. Ednl. TV documentary The World of David Amram, 1969, David Amram and Friends, 1979; for PBS Soundstage; Collection of papers at, Mugar Library of Boston U. Served with AUS, 1952-54. Recipient Obie award for compositions for Phoenix Theater and N.Y. Shakespeare Festival, 1959. Home: 461 6th Ave New York NY 10011 *'Music is a mountain, and all stones in that mountain are part of the whole." Dimitri Mitropolous, to whom I dedicated my book, "Vibrations", felt this way. As a composer—conductor—musician, I try in my conduct with other musicians and the audience, to include everyone, by not putting myself or anyone else above the music. By including audience participation, and by playing folk and jazz festivals and workshops, as well as conducting symphony concerts! There are no more walls in music*

AMRAM, PHILIP WERNER, lawyer; b. Phila., Mar. 14, 1900; s. David Werner and Beulah (Brylawski) A.; m. Emilie S. Weyl, Dec. 18, 1924; children—Mariana B., David Werner, III.; m. Helen M. Costello, June 5, 1982. A.B., U. Pa., 1920; B.S.A., Pa. State Coll., 1922; LL.B. cum laude, U. Pa., 1927. Bar: Pa. 1927, D.C. 1945. Practiced as mem. law firm of Wolf, Block, Schorr & Solis-Cohen, Phila., 1927-42; mem. Amram, Hahn & Sundlun (and successor firms), Washington; tchr. Pa. practice and practice ct. U. Pa. Law Sch., 1929-42; in charge aviation activities, as chief internat. air transport div. Bd. Econ. Warfare, Washington, 1942; chief rep. S. Pacific area, 1943, spl. asst. to Atty. Gen. U.S. in charge litigation against, Standard Oil Co., N.J., 1943-45; also spl. adviser to Alien Property Custodian.; Mem. civil procedural rules com. Supreme Ct. Pa., 1938—, chmn., 1958-82; chmn. adv. com. to U.S. Commn. on Internat. Rules of Jud. Procedure, 1959-66; mem. adv. rules com. U.S. Dist. Court, Eastern Dist. Pa., Circuit Ct. of Appeals, 1939-42; mem. State Dept. Adv. Com. on Internat. Pvt. Law, 1964-76, vice chmn., 1971-76; Ofcl. U.S. observer Hague Conf. Internat. Pvt. Law, 1956, 60, mem. ofcl. delegation, 1964, 68, 72, 76, chmn. delegation, 1972. Author: Amram's Pennsylvania Common Pleas Practice, 7th edit, 1970, New Federal Rules in Pennsylvania, 1938, Goodrich-Amram Pennsylvania Procedural Rules Service, 1940-80; Editor-in-chief: U. Pa. Law Rev, 1926-27; contbr. law revs. Assoc. trustee law sch. U. Pa., 1959-76; Pres. United Community Services of Washington, 1956-6, La Fondation de l'Ecole Française Internationale de Washington, 1966-76. Served as 2d lt. inf. U.S. Army, World War I. Decorated officier French Legion of Honor, comdr. Ordre des Palmes Academiques. Mem. Am. Law Inst., Mil. Order Fgn. Wars, Am., Fed., Internat., state and local bar assns., Order of Coif, Phi Kappa Phi. Club: Cosmos. Home: 4000 Cathedral Ave NW Apt 413B Washington DC 20016 Loveladies NJ 08008 Office: 1155 15th St NW Washington DC 20005 *I believe that God placed man on the earth to develop himself to the maximum limit of his capability. Any man or woman who does not devote his or her life to this aim is defrauding not only himself or herself, but also his or her maker.*

AMREIN, YOST URSUS LUCIUS, zoologist, educator; b. Arosa, Switzerland, Jan. 3, 1918; came to U.S., 1938, naturalized, 1942; s. Otto Friederich and Anna Elisabeth (Beerli) A.; m. Margaret Cuthbertson Brown, Dec. 28, 1948; 1 son, Lucius George. B.A., U. Calif. at Los Angeles, 1947, M.A., 1948; Ph.D., 1951. Asst. ranch supr. Teesdale Ranch, nr. Ndola, No. Rhodesia, 1937-38; from instr. to asso. prof. zoology Pomona (Calif.) Coll., 1951-59, prof. zoology, chmn. dept., 1959-68, Willard G. Halstead prof., 1961-81, emeritus, 1981—; Research fellow Swiss Tropical Inst., Basel, 1964-65. Contbr. articles to profl. jours. Served with AUS, 1942-45; CBI. Decorated Bronze Star with one cluster.; Pub. Health fellow Nat. Inst. Med. Research, London, Eng., 1957-58; research grantee, 1959-74; recipient Outstanding Grad. Achievement award Phi Sigma, U. Calif. at Los Angeles, 1951. Fellow Royal Soc. Tropical Medicine and Hygiene, A.A.A.S.; mem. Western Soc. Naturalists (pres. 1969), So. Calif. Soc. Parasitologists, Sigma Xi, Phi Sigma. Home: 456 Harrison Ave Claremont CA 91711

AMSEL, ABRAM, experimental pyschologist; b. Montreal, Que., Can., Dec. 4, 1922; came to U.S., 1946, naturalized, 1957; s. Aaron Harry and Annie (Levitt) A.; m. Tess Steinbach, June 11, 1947; children: Steven David, Andrew Jay, Geoffrey Neal. B.A., Queen's U., Kingston, Ont., 1944; M.A., McGill U., Montreal, 1946; Ph.D., U. Iowa, 1948. Mem. faculty Tulane U., 1948-60, U. Toronto, 1960-69; vis. prof. U. Calif., Berkeley, 1962; mem. faculty U. Tex., Austin, 1969—, prof. exptl. psychology, 1969—, Ashbel Smith prof., 1981—; vis. prof. U. Pa., 1974-75, U. Oxford, Eng., fall 1979. Editor: Psychonomic Science, 1970-72, Animal Learning and Behavior, 1972-76; mem. editorial bd.: Internat. Jour. Psychophysiology, 1982—; contbr. articles to profl. jours., monographs and chpts. to books. NSF sr. postdoctoral fellow Univ. Coll., London, 1966-67; research grantee NSF, 1956-78, NRC, Can., 1962-69, NIMH, 1978—. Mem. Internat. Brain Research Orgn., Internat. Soc. Devel. Psychobiology, Soc. Exptl. Psychologists (chmn. 1976, Warren medal 1980), AAUP (chpt. pres. 1958-59), Psychonomic Soc. (chmn. gov. bd. 1978), Internat. Soc. Psychophysiology (hon.), Midwestern Psychol. Assn., So. Psychol. Assn., So. Soc. Philosophy and Psychology, Sigma Xi (chpt. pres. 1957-58). Home: 4707 Crestway Dr Austin TX 78731 Office: Dept Psychology Univ Tex Austin TX 78712

AMSLER, JAMES THOMAS, college president; b. Boston, Dec. 13, 1921; s. Gustavus Adolphus and Anna Marie (Egan) A.; m. Frances Vallely, May 13, 1944; children: Jane, Mary, Patricia, James. B.S.E., Fithburg (S.C.) U., 1943; Ed.M., Harvard U., 1950; Ed.D., Boston U., 1955. Tchr., 1946-49; lab. sch. supr. Salem (Mass.) State Coll., 1949-55, faculty, 1955-61, dean of admissions, 1961-68, pres., 1979—; asso. dir. Mass. State Coll., 1968-70; pres. North Adams (Mass.) State Coll., 1970-79; dir. First Agrl. Bank, Century N. Shore Bank. Trustee North Adams Regional Hosp.; corporator Salem Hosp. Served to capt. USN. Mem. Epsilon Pi Tau, Phi Delta Kappa, Salem C. of C. (pres.). Club: Rotary. Office: 352 Lafayette St Salem MA 01970

AMSPOKER, JAMES MACK, gas company executive; b. East Liberty, Ohio, July 28, 1926; s. Charley Mack and Blanche (Richardson) A.; m. Anne M. Guido, Dec. 2, 1955; children: Charley M., Stephanie. B.M.E., Ohio State U., 1948. With Columbia Engring. Corp., Columbus, Ohio, 1948-50, Columbia Gas System Service Corp., N.Y.C., 1950-53; gen. engr. Ohio Fuel Gas Co., Columbus, 1953-63; supervisory engr. Columbia Gas of Ohio, Columbus, 1963-67, chief engr., 1967, v.p., 1967-70, sr. v.p., dir., 1970-73, Columbia Gas Transmission Corp., Charleston, W.Va., 1973—. Served with USNR, 1944-46. Mem. Am. Gas Assn., Ohio State U. Com. for Tomorrow, Ohio Order of Engrs. Clubs: Mason., Berry Hills Country, Charleston Tennis. Home: 1 Pinetop Pl Charleston WV 25314 Office: PO Box 1273 Charleston WV 25325

AMSTER, HARVEY JEROME, educator, physicist; b. Cleve., Sept. 30, 1928; s. Sidney Nelson and Hilda (Klein) A.; m. Kathy S. Kyohn; 1 dau., Heidi J. B.S. in Physics, Calif. Inst. Tech., 1950; Ph.D., Mass. Inst. Tech., 1954. Sr. scientist Bettis Atomic Power Lab., Westinghouse Electric Corp., 1954-57, fellow scientist, 1957-60, adv. scientist, 1960-61; mem. faculty U. Calif., Berkeley, 1961-77, prof. nuclear engring., 1965-77; physicist Lawrence Radiation Lab., Livermore, Calif., 1961; sr. physicist Northrop Space Labs., Hawthorne, Cal., 1963; vis. prof. U. Wis., 1963, Western Res. U., 1965, Queen Mary Coll. U. London, Eng., 1971; staff Inst. Def. Analyses, Arlington, Va., 1969; cons. to industry, 1962—; vis. scientist applied physics div. Argonne (Ill.) Nat. Lab., 1975; individual practice, 1977. Author articles, models of atomic nucleus, neutron cross sections, spatially dependent neutron slowing down distbns., theory of statis. errors in Monte Carlo calculations and environ. consequences of nuclear tech. Mem. Am. Phys. Soc., Am. Nuclear Soc., A.A.A.S. Home: 2 Admiral Dr Apt 473 Emeryville CA 94608 *If you want to do good scientific work, don't go where engineers have positions of importance.*

AMSTER, LINDA EVELYN, newspaper executive, consultant; b. N.Y.C., May 21, 1938; d. Abraham and Belle Shirley (Levine) Meyerson; m. Robert L. Amster, Feb. 18, 1961 (dec. Feb. 1974). B.A., U. Mich., 1960; M.L.S., Columbia U., 1968. Tchr. English Stamford High Sch., Conn., 1961-63; research librarian The Detroit News, 1965-67, The N.Y. Times, N.Y.C., 1967-69, supr. news research, 1969-74, news research mgr., 1974—; bd. dirs. Council for Career Planning, N.Y.C., 1982—. Contbr. articles in field to bokos, N.Y. Times and other publs. Mem. Spl. libraries Assn. Home: 336 Central Park W New York NY 10025 Office: The NY Times 229 W 43d St New York NY 10036

AMSTERDAM, ANTHONY GUY, legal educator; b. Phila., Sept. 12, 1935; s. Gustave G. and Valla (Abel) A.; m. Lois P. Sheinfeld, Aug. 29, 1968. A.B., Haverford Coll., 1957; LL.B., U. Pa., 1960. Bar: D.C. bar 1960. Law clk. to U.S. Supreme Ct. Justice Felix Frankfurter, 1960-61; asst. U.S. atty., 1961-62; prof. law U. Pa. Law Sch., 1962-69, Stanford Law Sch., 1969-81, Montgomery prof. clin. legal edn., 1980-81; prof. law, dir. clin. programs and trial advocacy N.Y. U. Law Sch., 1981—; cons. litigating atty. numerous civil rights groups; cons. govt. commns. Mem. Commn. to Study Disturbances at Columbia, 1968; Trustee Center Law and Social Policy, Am. Civil Liberties Union No. Calif., Lawyers Constl. Defense Com., So. Poverty Law Center. Author: The Defensive Transfer of Civil Rights Litigation From State to Federal Courts, 1964, (with B. Segal and M. Miller) Trial Manual for the Defense of Criminal Cases, 3d edit, 1974; also numerous articles.; Editor-in-chief: U. Pa. Law Rev, 1959-60. Named Outstanding Young Man of Year Phila. and Pa. Jaycees, 1967; recipient First Disting. Service award U. Pa. Law Sch., 1968, Haverford award Haverford Coll., 1970; Arthur V. Briesen award Nat. Legal Aid and Defender Assn., 1972, 76; named Lawyer of Year Calif. Trial Lawyers Assn., 1973; 1st Earl Warren Civil Liberties award No. Calif. chpt. ACLU, 1973; Citizen of Merit award Sun Reporter, 1974; Walter J. Gores award Stanford U., 1977; William O. Douglas award Pub. Counsel, 1977; 2d Am. award Calif. Attys. Criminal Justice, 1978; award for enhancement human dignity Durfee Found., 1982. Fellow Am. Acad. Arts and Scis. Home: 29 Washington Sq W New York NY 10011 Office: New York Univ Law Sch New York NY 10012

AMSTUTZ, HAROLD EMERSON, veterinarian, educator; b. Barrs Mill, Ohio, June 21, 1919; s. Nelson David and Viola Emma (Schnitzer) A.; m. Mabelle Josephine Bower, June 26, 1949; children: Suzanne Marie, Cynthia Lou, Patricia Lynn, David Bruce. B.S. in Agr, Ohio State U., 1942, D.V.M., 1945. Diplomate: Am. Coll. Vet. Internal Medicine (pres. 1972-73, chmn. bd. regents 1973-74). Pvt. practice vet. medicine, Orrville, Ohio, 1946-47; instr. vet. medicine Ohio State U., 1947-52, asst. prof., 1952-54, asso. prof., 1954-56, prof., 1957-61; prof., head dept. vet. medicine Purdue U., Lafayette, Ind., 1956-61, head dept. vet. clinics, 1961-75, prof. large animal clinics, 1975—. Editor: Bovine Medicine and Surgery Book, 1979; contbg. editor: Modern Veterinary Practice, 1979; contbr. chpts. to books on diseases of large domestic animals. Pres. World Assn. for Buiatrics, 1972—. Served with U.S. Army, 1945-46. Recipient Borden award for outstanding research in diseases of dairy cattle, 1978; named Disting. Alumnus Ohio State U. Coll. Vet. Medicine, 1974. Mem. Am. Vet. Med. Assn., Am. Assn. Vet. Clinicians (pres. 1972), Am. Assn. Bovine Practitioners (exec. sec. 1971—), Sigma Xi, Phi Zeta (Gamma award), Gamma Sigma Delta. Republican. Lutheran. Office: Purdue U West Lafayette IN 47907

AMUNDSON, DUANE MELVIN, gas company executive; b. Niagara, Wis., Apr. 3, 1925; s. Melvin Oscar and Thalia (McSweeny) A.; m. Marian Force, Nov. 21, 1948; children: Melvin, Robert, Jeffrey, Kimberly. B.S. in Civil Engring., Purdue U., 1950. With Ind. Gas Co., Inc., Indpls., 1950—, v.p. ops. engring., 1963-74, sr. v.p. ops. engring., 1974-77, exec. v.p., 1977-80, pres. and chief exec. officer, 1980—; also dir.; pres., chief exec. officer IGC Energy, Inc., Ohio River Pipeline Corp., 1980—. Served with USNR, 1943-46, 51-52. Mem. Nat., Ind. socs. profl. engrs., Am., Ind. gas assns. Clubs: Masons, Lions, Elks. Home: 19720 Allisonville Ave Noblesville IN 46060 Office: 1630 N Meridian St Indianapolis IN 46202

AMUNDSON, JOHN MELVIN, JR., architect; b. Sunnyside, Wash., Mar. 4, 1926; s. John Melvin and Atta Faye (Swanay) A.; m. Janet Louise Barnard, June 19, 1947; children—Kathleen Faye, David William, Kristin Marie. Student, Wash. State U., 1946-48; B.Arch. with honors, U. Oreg., 1951; diploma Civic Design, U. Liverpool, 1952. Draftsman, architect, designer, Portland, Oreg., 1952-55; planning cons. Bur. of Municipal Research and Services, U. Ore., 1955-57; co-founder Lutes and Amundson, Architects and Community Planners, 1957-72; founder, pres. Amundson Assos., Architects and Planners, Springfield, Oreg., 1972—; asso. prof. U. Oreg., summers, 1974, 76. Mem. Oreg. State Council on Aging, 1961-65; mem. bd. appeals City of Springfield, 1962-72; mem. Mayor's Sign Com., City of Eugene, Oreg., 1963-66; bd. govs. Friends of Mus. U. Oreg., 1965-68; moderator 1st Congregational Ch., 1968-69. Served with USNR, 1944-46. Fulbright scholar, 1951-52; named Eugene Jr. First Citizen, 1961; Recipient Dean Gustafson award Nat. Council Architectural Registration Bds., 1976, Outstanding Vol. for Service to Lane County award, 1983. Fellow AIA, Western Conf. Archtl. Registration Bds., Nat. Archtl. Accrediting Bd. (pres. 1973-74), Council of Ednl. Facilities Planners, Eugene Area C. of C. (pres. 1981), Airplane Owners and Pilots Assn. Democrat. Clubs: Eugene Yacht, Eugene Downtown Lions, Elks. Home: 938 E 22d Ave Eugene OR 97405 Office: 200 S Mill St Springfield OR 97477

AMUNDSON, NEAL RUSSELL, chemical engineer; b. St. Paul, Jan. 10, 1916; s. Oscar and Hazel (Cottrell) A.; m. Shirley Dimond, Sept. 25, 1941; children: Gregg Russell, Beth Eva, Erik Neal. B.Chem. Engring., U. Minn., 1937, M.S., 1941, Ph.D. in Math, 1945. Postdoctoral fellow applied math. Brown U., 1944-45; asst. prof. math. U. Minn., 1945-47, asso. prof. chem. engring., 1947-51, prof., head dept., 1951-74, Regents' prof. chem. engring., 1967-77; Cullen prof. chem. engring. U. Houston, 1977—. Editor: Internat. Series on Phys. and Chem. Engring. Sci; Contbr. Research papers profl. jours. Fulbright scholar, Guggenheim fellow Cambridge (Eng.) U., 1954-55; Guggenheim fellow, 1975, 76; NATO Sr. fellow, 1975. Mem. Am. Chem. Soc. (recipient indsl. and engring. chemistry award 1960), Am. Inst. Chem. Engring. (William H. Walker award 1962, Warren K. Lewis award 1971, R.H. Wilhelm award 1973), Nat. Acad. Engring., Am. Soc. Engring. Edn. (Vincent Bendix award 1970), Sigma Xi, Tau Beta Pi, Phi Lambda Upsilon, Alpha Chi Sigma. Home: 5327 Cherokee St Houston TX 77005

AMUSSEN, THEODORE SMITH, publisher; b. Salt Lake City, Aug. 15, 1915; s. Theodore S. and Lorna Addison (Russell) A.; m. Anne Nelson Cutler, Oct. 14, 1939 (dec. Nov. 1958); children: Deborah, Daniel, David, Timothy Dwyer; m. Moira Martin, Dec. 23, 1971 (div. 1978); 1 son, James. Student, Brooks Sch., North Andover, Mass., 1930-35, Sorbonne, Paris, 1935-36, Harvard U., 1936-37. Asst. editor Rinehart & Co., Inc. (formerly Farrar & Rinehart Inc.), N.Y.C., 1938-45, assoc. editor, 1945-47, v.p., gen. mgr. trade dept., editor-in-chief gen. book dept., 1953-60; exec. editor Reynal, Hitchcock & Co., Inc., 1947; editor Harcourt, Brace & Co., Inc.; also Reynal & Hitchcock when merged, 1948; editor-in-chief Henry Holt & Co., Inc., 1950-53; v.p. Peters Co., Inc., 1961-65; editor spl. publs. div. Nat. Geog. Soc., 1966-68; chief div. books Nat. Park Service, 1968-70; editor-in-chief Nat. Gallery of Art, 1970-81; dir. Rinehart & Co., Inc., Fred Feldkamp Prodns., Inc. Served as pub. relations specialist USNR, 1945-46. Mem. P.E.N., Am. Assn. Mus. Clubs: Harvard (Washington); Overseas Press, Publishers Lunch, Coffee House. Home and Office:: 2400 41st St NW Apt 104 Washington DC 20007

AMYX, DARRELL ARLYNN, educator; b. Exeter, Calif., Apr. 2, 1911; s. Buford Elmore and Maude (Kirkman) A.; m. Eleanor Wilkinson, July 6, 1936; 1 dau., Ellen Anne. A.B. in Classics, Stanford, 1930; M.A. in Latin, U. Calif. at Berkeley, 1932; Ph.D. in Latin and Classical Archaeology, U. Calif. at Berkeley, 1937. Instr. in Latin U. Chgo., 1937-39; successively asst., research asso., instr. classics U. Calif. at Berkeley, 1939-42; with U.S. Office of Censorship, San Francisco, 1942-45; mem. faculty U. Calif. at Berkeley, 1946-78, emeritus, 1978—; chmn. dept. art, 1966-71; asst. dean Coll. Letters and Scis., 1964-65, curator classical art univ. art museum, 1965—; curator ancient Mediterranean art R.H. Lowie Mus. Anthropology, 1958—, humanities research prof., 1969; vis. prof. fine arts Ind. U., 1979. Asso. editor: Calif. Studies in Classical Antiquity, vols. 1-5, 1968-72; Author: An Amphora with a Price Inscription, 1941, Corinthian Vases at San Simeon, 1943, (with W.K. Pritchett) The Attic Stelai, 1958, (with others) Cypriote Antiquities in San Francisco Bay Area Collections, 1974, Echoes from Olympus, 1974, (with Patricis Lawrence) Corinth VII: 2, Archaic Corinthian Pottery and the Anaploga Well, 1975; also articles. Recipient Berkeley citation, 1978; Fellow Am. Sch. Classical Studies, Athens, Greece, 1935-36; Guggenheim fellow, 1957-59, 73-74; Fulbright sr. research grantee to Greece, 1957-58; grantee Am. Council Learned Socs., 1941, 62, 71, 80; fellow, 1965-66; grantee Am. Philos. Soc., 1956, 76. Mem. Archaeol. Inst. Am., Am. Philol. Assn., Phi Beta Kappa; corr. mem. Deutsches Archäologisches Institut, Istituto di Studi Etruschi ed Italici. Home: 671 Oberlin Ave Kensington CA 94708 Office: Dept History of Art U California Berkeley CA 94720

ANAGNOSTOPOULOS, CONSTANTINE EMMANUEL, company executive; b. Athens, Greece, Nov. 1, 1922; came to U.S., 1946; s. Emmanuel Constantine A. and Helen (Michaelides) Kefalas; m. Maria Tsagarakis, July 10, 1949; 1 son, Paul Constantine. Sc.B. in Chemistry, Brown U., 1949, M.S., Harvard U., 1950, Ph.D., 1952; postgrad. in bus. adminstrn., Columbia U., 1964. Dir. research and devel. organic div. Monsanto Co., St. Louis, 1962-67, bus. dir., 1967-71, gen. mgr. New Enterprise div., 1971-75, gen. mgr. rubber chem. div., 1975-80; v.p. mng. dir. Monsanto Europe-Africa, Brussels, 1980-82; corp. v.p. corp. devel. Monsanto Co., St. Louis, 1982—; chmn. bd. Monsanto Europe S.A., Brussels, 1980-82; dir. Polyolefin Industries Ltd., Bombay, India, Advent Eurofund Ltd., Eng. Patentee in organic and polymer chemistry, 1953-67; contbr. articles to profl. jours. Bd. dirs. Am. C. of C., Brussels, 1981-82; mem. European Govt. Bus. Council, Strasbourgh, France, 1981-82; pres. United Fund Belgium, 1982; mem. presdl. com. prizes for innovation, Washington, 1972, U.S.-USSR Trade and Econ. Council, Washington, 1980-82. Served to capt. Brit. Army, 1944-46. Recipient chemistry prize Brown U., 1949, teaching award Harvard U., 1950, 51, 52. Mem. Nat. Inventors Council, Research Soc. Am., Nat. Acad. Engring. (patent com.), Indsl. Research Inst., Comml. Devel. Assn., Am. Chem. Soc. Republican. Episcopalian. Club: Bellerive Country (St. Louis). Home: 13003

Starbuck Rd Saint Louis MO 63141 Office: Monsanto Co 800 N Lindbergh Saint Louis MO 63167

ANARGYROS, SPERO, sculptor; b. N.Y.C., Jan. 23, 1915; s. Drosos Speros and Martha Gustafson (Carlson) A. Scholarship student, Art Students League, 1934-35, Master Inst. United Arts, 1935-36; travel study, Europe, North Africa, Mexico, Central Am. With Overseas Project 19, N.E. Africa, 1942-44. Exhibited in group shows, N.A.D., 1938-40, 53-56, 59, 77, 78, Archtl. League N.Y., Pa. Acad. Fine Arts, 1940, Calif. State Fair, 1952, 53, DeYoung Mus., San Francisco, 1953-62, Erickson Gallery, Palo Alto, 1972, Rosicrusian Egyptian Mus., San Jose, Calif., Nat. Sculpture Soc. Ann., 1975, 77, 78 (award 1978), one man shows, Houston Gallery, 1968, Corpus Christi Gallery; works include: Redwood basrelief, Pacific Mut. Life Ins. Bldg., San Francisco, 1955; bronze bas-relief, Main Office Bldg., First Western Bank, San Francisco, 1957; seal of City and County of San Francisco, Hall of Justice Bldg., 1960, Hawaii Statehood Medallion, 1962, Russell Varian Portrait Plaque on Physics Lab., Stanford U., 1962, Lawrence Mario Giannini, Bank of Am. Medallion, 1962, Gold Gate Bridge Medallion, 1962; bronze base relief, Crocker Citizens Nat. Bank, San Mateo, 1967; Alaska Centennial coin, 1967, San Diego Coronado Bay Bridge Medallion, 1969; marble portrait Benjamin Franklin, facade of Franklin Savs. Bldg., San Francisco, 1964; Am. Negro Commemorative Coin, 1969; life size lion sculptures for, Chinatown br. of Hong Kong Bank, San Francisco, 1967; heroic monument Pedro Martinez K.C.S.S., Guam, 1972; Yellowstone Park Centennial Commemorative Coin, Nat. Commemorative Soc., 1972; portrait bust William Bechtle, San Francisco, 1973, Clarence Berry, U. Alaska, 1973; Risen Christ figure, Guam, 1974; medallion, Calif. Hist. Soc., 1974; over life size bronze Pedro C. Lujan, 1974; meml. bust Jack Robinson, Guam; Jockey of Year trophy, Bay Meadows Race Track, Calif., 1974, 25th Anniversary medallion, Sta. KGO-TV, Calif., 1974; master model Twin Bicentennial Commemorative Medallion, San Francisco and U.S.A., 1976; restored: bronze bas-relief plaques for the Eagle Alaska monument to N.W. Passage of 1905, 1976; works include 4 heroic groups for restoration project, State Capitol Bldg., Sacramento, 1982; numerous portrait busts and heads, medals including Mr. and Mrs. Garcia Lourdes, Mrs. Edward Goldie, Mrs. William W. Meir, Edwin Herring, Sen. Ernest Gruening of Alaska; restored all sculpture on, Palace of Fine Arts, San Francisco, 1965-66. Recipient Best Sculpture award Acad. Artists Assn., 1959, John Spring Founders award Nat. Sculpture Soc., 1975. Fellow Internat. Inst. Arts and Letters, Nat. Sculpture Soc. (Council Am. Artist Socs. prize 1978); life mem. Art Students League, N.Y. Club: Bohemian (San Francisco). Address: 541A Tunnel Ave Brisbane CA 94005

ANASTASI, ANNE (MRS. JOHN PORTER FOLEY, JR), educator; b. N.Y.C., Dec. 19, 1908; d. Anthony and Theresa (Gaudiosi) A.; m. John Porter Foley, Jr., July 26, 1933. A.B., Barnard Coll., 1928; Ph.D., Columbia, 1930; Litt.D. (hon.), U. Windsor (Can.), 1967, Sc.D., Cedar Crest Coll., 1971, La Salle Coll., 1979, Fordham U., 1979, Paed.D., Villanova U., 1971. Instr. psychology Barnard Coll., N.Y.C., 1930-39; asst. prof., chmn. dept. Queens Coll., N.Y.C., 1939-46; asso. prof. Fordham U., N.Y.C., 1947-51, prof., 1951-79, prof. emeritus, 1979—, chmn. dept. psychology, 1968-74; Mem. NRC, 1952-55; Pres. Am. Psychol. Found., 1965-67. Author: Differential Psychology, 1937, rev. edit., 1949, 58, Psychological Testing, 1954, rev. edit. 1961, 68, 76, Fields of Applied Psychology, 1964, 2d edit., 1979; also articles in field.; Editor: Individual Differences, 1965, Testing Problems in Perspective, 1966; Contributions to Differential Psychology, 1982. Recipient award for disting. service to measurement Ednl. Testing Service, 1977, award disting. contbns. to research Am. Ednl. Research Assn., 1983. Mem. Am. Psychol. Assn. (rec. sec. 1952-55, pres. div. gen. psychology 1956-57, bd. dirs. 1956-59, 68-70, pres. div. evaluation and measurement 1965-66, pres. 1971-72, Disting. Sci. award 1981), Eastern Psychol. Assn. (pres. 1946-47, dir. 1948-50), Psychonomic Soc., Psychometric Soc., Phi Beta Kappa, Sigma Xi.

ANASTASIO, JAMES, ins. co. exec.; b. N.Y.C., Sept. 28, 1930; s. Alphonse and Clara (Santangini) A.; m. Lucy Di Staulo, Feb. 14, 1953; children—Michael, Janis. Student, Pace Coll., 1959. With Union Reinsurance Co., N.Y.C., 1955-62; with Am. Re-Ins. Co., N.Y.C., 1962—; now v.p., treas.; dir. Am. Excess Ins. Co.; faculty Coll. of Ins., 1977. Served with USN, 1951-55. Mem. Soc. Ins. Accountants (exec. com.), Ins. Accounting and Statis. Assn. Club: K.C. (past grand knight). Home: 39 Nottingham Rd Manalapan NJ 07726 Office: One Liberty Plaza New York NY 10006

ANASTOS, GEORGE, emeritus zoology educator; b. Akron, Ohio, Jan. 9, 1920; s. Peter and Kaliroy (Kakarakis) A.; m. Angelica Pappas, Sept. 8, 1946; children: Phyllis Catherine, Barbara Ann. B.S. with distinction, U. Akron, 1942; M.A., Harvard U., 1947, Ph.D., 1949. Teaching fellow biology Harvard, 1947-49; asst. prof. zoology Miami U., Oxford, Ohio, 1949-51; mem. faculty U. Md., 1951-82, prof. zoology, 1958-82, prof. emeritus, 1982—, head dept., 1961-68; exec. sec. Inst. Acarology, 1953-58, asst. dir., 1958-61; lectr. Inst. Acarology, Ohio State U., 1962-68; Spl. cons. USPHS, 1954; cons. Dept. Def., 1955-65, NSF, 1961-68; prin. investigator grants and contracts NIH and; Dept. Army, 1953; sci. adviser WHO, Geneva, Switzerland, 1968-75; dir. WHO Regional Reference Center, 1970-75; sec. gen. XV Internat. Congress Entomology, 1975-76. Author: The Scutate Ticks of Indonesia, 1950, The Ticks of the USSR, 1957, Index Catalogue to Russian, Central and Eastern European and Chinese Literature in Medical Entomology, vols. 1-12, 1963-67, Ixodid Ticks of Central Africa, vols. 1-4, 1966-67; Editor: Jour. Econ. Entomology, 1970-82. Served to lt. USNR, 1942-46. Guggenheim fellow, 1958. Mem. Washington Acad. Sci., Am. Soc. Parasitologists, Helminthological Soc. Washington, Soc. Systematic Zoology, Entomol. Soc. Am., Sigma Xi (pres. Md. chpt. 1962), Phi Sigma Kappa, Alpha Sigma Omicron (pres. Akron U. 1941-42). Home: 3021 Crest Ave Cheverly MD 20785 *I believe that it is the responsibility of each educator to receive high the "torch of knowledge" and to pass it on to the next generation even higher than he received it.*

ANASTOS, MILTON VASIL, educator; b. N.Y.C., July 10, 1909; s. Vlassios and Stella Hope (Spartali) A.;, Sept. 7, 1935 (div. 1938); 1 son, Milton Vasil; m. Rosemary Park, July 31, 1965. A.B. magna cum laude (First Boylston prize 1929, Latin oration 1931), Harvard U., 1930, S.T.B. summa cum laude, 1935, Ph.D., 1940, student Law Sch., 1932-33. Asst. history Harvard U., 1935-37, 40-41, asst. English, 1939-41; Jr. fellow Dumbarton Oaks Research Library and Collection, 1941-43, fellow, 1944-46, asst. prof. Byzantine theology, 1946-51, asso. prof., 1951-59, prof., 1959-64; librarian Div. Sch., 1936-39; vis. asso. prof. church history, 1956-59, vis. prof., 1959-64; sec. Harvard Theol. Rev., 1937-39; prof. Byzantine Greek UCLA, 1964-67, prof.Byzantine Greek and history, 1967—; instr. Bibl. history Wellesley Coll., 1937; lectr. U. Munich, U. Thessalonike, Conn. Coll. Women, U. Wash., U. Calif.-Berkeley and Los Angeles, Manhattanville Coll.; orator Medieval Acad. Am., 1982—. Author: Pletho's Calendar and Liturgy, Dumbarton Oaks Papers, 1948, Byzantine Influence on the Latin Culture of the Twelfth Century, 1961, Nestorius Was Orthodox, 1963, Studies in Byzantine Intellectual History, 1978; co-editor: Vigiliae Christianae, 1966—, Viator, 1969—. Vice chmn. Harvard Found. Advanced Study and Research, Washington, 1951-52; mem. U.S. Commn. Preservation Monuments, 1942-43; research analyst OSS, 1943-45; bd. scholars Harvard U. Dumbarton Oaks Research Library and Collection, 1952—, dep. chmn., 1973-75, hon. asso., 1975—. Grantee Am. Council Learned Socs., 1948; Fulbright sr. research fellow, 1954-55; Guggenheim fellow, 1954-55, 66-67. Fellow Acad. Athens, Am. Acad. Arts and Scis., Mediaeval Acad. Am., Am., Royal numis. socs., Soc. Macedonian Studies (corr.), Soc. Byzantine Studies (Athens); mem. Am. Hist. Assn., Internat. Com. für den Nachdruck griechischer Handschriftenkataloge, Am. Philos. Soc., Phi Beta Kappa (pres. UCLA 1967-68). Democrat. Mem. Greek Orthodox Ch. Home: 10501 Wilshire Blvd Apt 2101 Los Angeles CA 90024

ANBAR, MICHAEL, biophysics educator; b. Danzig, Danzig, June 27, 1927; came to U.S., 1967, naturalized, 1973; s. Joshua and Chava A.; m. Ada Komet, Aug. 11, 1953; children: Ran D., Ariel D. M.Sc., Hebrew U., Jerusalem, 1950, Ph.D., 1953. Instr. chemistry U. Chgo., 1953-55; sr. scientist Weizmann Inst. Sci., 1955-60; prof. Frienberg Grad. Sch., Rehovoth, Israel, 1960-67; sr. research asso. Ames Research Center, 1967-68; dir. phys. sci. SRI Internat., Menlo Park, Calif., 1968-72, dir. mass spectrometry, 1972-77; prof. biophysical sci., chmn. dept. Sch. Medicine, SUNY, Buffalo, 1977—, exec. dir. Health Instrument and Device Inst., 1983—. Author: The Hydrated Electron, 1970, The Machine of the Bedside—Strategies for Using Technology in Patient Care, 1984; author: Clinical Biophysics, 1984; Contbr. articles to profl. jours. Served with Israeli Air Force, 1947-49. Grantee in field. Mem. Assn. Am. Med. Colls., N.Y. Acad. Sci., Am. Chem. Soc., Biophys. Soc., Am. Inst. Ultrasound in Medicine, Am. Assn. Clin. Chemistry, Internat. Assn. Dental Research, Radiation Research Soc., Am. Assn. Dental Research, Am. Assn. Mass Spectrometry, Assn. Advancement of Med. Instrumentation, AAAS. Office: State Univ New York 118 Cary Hall Buffalo NY 14214 *Any scientist should first try to understand Nature and then to utilize knowledge for the betterment of the quality of life. Even a single modest contribution to medicine can help many thousands, making it a worthwhile cause for any scientist. My research and teaching focus, therefore, is on the application of the physical sciences to medicine.*

ANCELL, NATHAN S., diversified company executive; b. N.Y.C., 1908. A.B., Columbia Coll., 1929; LL.B., Columbia U., 1931. Vice pres. Interco Inc., also dir., chmn. bd. subs. Ethan Allen Inc. Office: Ethan Allen Inc Ethan Allen Dr Danbury CT 06810 *

ANCES, I. G(EORGE), medical educator; b. Balt., July 3, 1935; s. Harry and Fanny A.; m. Marlene Roth, Oct. 23, 1966; 1 son, Beau Mark. B.S., U. Md., 1956, M.D., 1959. Diplomate: Am. Bd. Obstetrics and Gynecology. Intern Ohio State U. Hosp., 1959-60; resident in obstetrics and gynecology Univ. Hosp., Balt., 1960-61, 63-65; mem. faculty U. Md. Med. Sch., Balt., 1966—, prof. obstetrics and gynecology, 1975—, dir. labs. obstetrics and gynecol. research and clin. labs., 1967—, dir. div. adolescent obstetrics and gynecology and family planning, 1981—. Contbr. chpts. to books, articles to profl. jours. Capt. sustaining fund drive Balt. Symphony Orch.; med. adv. com. Fire Dept. Balt. City. Served with USAF, 1961-63. Fellow Am. Coll. Obstetrics and Gynecology; mem. Endocrine Soc., Soc. Gynecol. Investigation, Soc. Study Reprodn. (charter), Internat. Soc. Research in Biology Reprodn. (charter), Md. Obstetrics and Gynecol. Soc. (sec. 1978-81, dir. 1979—), Med. and Chirurgical Soc. Md., Soc. Adolescent Medicine, Douglas Obstet. and Gynecol. Soc., English Speaking Union, Md. Conservation Council, Sigma Xi. Clubs: Maryland, Towson Golf and Country. Home: 22 Charlcote Pl Baltimore MD 21218 Office: Dept Obstetrics and Gynecology Univ Md Hosp Baltimore MD 21218

ANCKER, CLINTON JAMES, JR., educator; b. Cedar Falls, Iowa, June 21, 1919; s. Clinton James and Fern (Lalan) A.; m. Margaret Wright Rees, Apr. 11, 1947; children—Clinton James III, Evan Randolph, Megan Lalan, Scott Rees. B.S. in Mech. Engring, Purdue U., 1940; M.S., U. Calif. at Berkeley, 1949, Mech. Engr., 1950; Ph.D., Stanford, 1955. Jr. engr. Detroit Edison Co., 1941, 46; instr. Purdue U., 1946-47; asst. prof. U. Calif. at Berkeley, 1947-55; operations analyst Operations Research Office, Chevy Chase, Md., 1955-56; sr. engr. Booz-Allen Applied Research, Inc., Chgo., 1956-58; mgr. Analco Services Co., Chgo., 1958-59; head math. and operations research program System Devel. Corp., Santa Monica, Calif., 1959-67; dir. Nat. Hwy. Safety Inst., Dept. Transp., 1967-68; prof., chmn. dept. indsl. and systems engring. U. So. Calif., 1968—. Author papers in field. Served to capt. AUS, 1941-46. Mem. ASME, Operations Research Soc. Am. (nat. council 1970-73), Soc. Cincinnati, Am. Inst. Indsl. Engrs., Mil. Operations Research Soc. (exec. com. 1964-65), Sigma Xi, Tau Beta Pi, Pi Tau Sigma, Alpha Pi Mu, Omega Rho (nat. pres. 1976-78). Home: 23908 Malibu Knolls Rd Malibu CA 90265 Office: Dept Indsl and Systems Engring Univ So Calif Los Angeles CA 90007

ANCKER-JOHNSON, BETSY, physicist, automotive company executive; b. St. Louis, Apr. 29, 1927; d. Clinton James and Fern (Lalan) Ancker; m. Harold Hunt Johnson, Mar. 15, 1958; children: Ruth P. Johnson, David H. Johnson, Paul A. Johnson, Martha H. Johnson. B.A. in Physics with high honors (Pendleton scholar), Wellesley Coll., 1949; Ph.D. magna cum laude, U. Tuebingen, Germany, 1953; D.Sc. (hon.), Poly. Inst. N.Y., 1979, LL.D., Bates Coll., 1980. Instr., jr. research physist U. Calif., 1953-54; physicist Sylvania Microwave Physics Lab., 1956-58; mem. tech. staff RCA Labs., 1958-61; research specialist Boeing Co., 1961-70, exec., 1970-73; asst. sec. commerce for sci. and tech., 1973-77; dir. phys. research Argonne Nat. Lab., Ill., 1977-79; v.p. environ. activities staff Gen. Motors Tech. Center, Warren, Mich., 1979—; affiliate prof. elec. engring. U. Wash., 1964-73; dir. Gen. Mills; mem. Energy Research Adv. Bd. Dept. Energy. Author. Mem. staff Inter-Varsity Christian Fellowship, 1954-56; Trustee Wellesley Coll., 1972-77. AAUW fellow, 1950-51; Horton Hollowell fellow, 1951-52; NSF grantee, 1967-72. Fellow Am. Phys. Soc. (councillor-at-large 1973-76), IEEE; mem. Nat. Acad. Engring., Phi Beta Kappa, Sigma Xi. Patentee in field. Office: Environmental Activities Staff GM Technical Center Warren MI 48090

ANCONA, BARRY, publisher; b. N.Y.C., Apr. 23, 1948; s. Victor and Ruth (Bronner) A. B.A., Grinnell Coll., 1968. Editor Cedar Valley Daily Times, Vinton, Iowa, 1968-69, Orange (N.J.) Transcript, 1971-72; pub. Videography mag., N.Y.C., Biomed. Communications (mag.), Media Horizons. Pres. N.Y. alumni com. Grinnell Coll.; Bd. dirs., pres. West 16th St. Block Assn., N.Y.C., 1974-77. Served as corr. and chief bur. pub. info. office AUS, 1969-71; Vietnam. Mem. Deadline Club, Photog. Adminstrs. Inc., Sigma Delta Chi. Home: 49 W 16th St New York NY 10011 Office: 475 Park Ave S New York NY 10016

ANCONA, GEORGE EPHRAIM, photographer, film producer, author; b. N.Y.C., Dec. 4, 1929; s. Ephraim Jose and Emma Graziana (Diaz) A.; m. Helga Von Sydow, July 20, 1968; children: Lisa, Gina, Tomas, Isabel, Marina, Pablo. Student, Academia de San Carlos, Mexico, 1949, Art Students League, 1950, Cooper Union Sch. Design, 1950. Art dir. Esquire Inc., N.Y.C., 1951-53, Seventeen mag., 1953-54, Grey Advt. Agy., 1954-58, Daniel & Charles Advt. Agy., 1958-60; free lance photographer, film producer, N.Y.C., 1960—; lectr. graphic design, photography Rockland Community Coll., 1973—, Parsons Sch. Design, 1974—, Sch. Visual Arts, 1978—. Author: Handtalk, 1974, Monsters on Wheels, 1974, What Do You Do?, 1976, I Feel, 1977, Growing Older, 1978, It's a Baby!, 1979, Dancing Is, 1981, Bananas, from Manolo to Margie, Team work, Monster Movers; designer, photographer numerous other books. Address: Crickettown Rd Stony Point NY 10980 *Curiosity is the biggest element in my work. Watching people and making contact through my photographs have given me a sense of myself. My work keeps me in touch with the world around me. Whether a person bakes, builds, sings or drives, people reach one another in their own way. Mine is taking pictures. Reaching out to others... I think that's what living is all about.*

ANDELSON, ROBERT VERNON, educator, social philosopher; b. Los Angeles, Feb. 19, 1931; s. Abraham and Ada (Andersen) A.; m. Bonny von Orange Johnson, June 7, 1964. A.A., Los Angeles City Coll., 1950; A.B. equivalent, U. Chgo., 1952; A.M., U. So. Calif., 1954, Ph.D., 1960. Exec. dir. Henry George Sch. Social Sci., San Diego Extension, Calif., 1959-62; instr. philosophy and religion Northland Coll., Wis., 1962-63; asst. prof. govt. and philosophy Northwestern State U., La., 1963-65; mem. faculty Auburn U., Ala., 1965—, prof. philosophy, 1973—, mem. grad. faculty, 1969—; inaugural lectr. philosophy lecture series U. Ala. at Birmingham, 1975; mem. acad. staff Ludwig von Mises Inst., 1983—; ordained to ministry Congregational Ch., 1959. Author: Imputed Rights: An Essay in Christian Social Theory, 1971; editor, co-author: Critics of Henry George, 1979; mem. editorial bd.: Am. Jour. Econs. and Sociology, 1969—, The Personalist, 1975-80; contbr. articles to scholarly jours. Asst. sgt. at arms Republican Nat. Conv., 1952; mem. Lee County Rep. Exec. Com., 1967-79; trustee Henry George Found. Am., 1971-75, mem. adv. commn., 1975—. Recipient research awards Found. Social Research, 1959, Relm Found., 1967, 2 George Washington Honor medals Freedoms Found., 1970, 72. Mem. So. Soc. Philosophy and Psychology, Ala. Philos. Soc. (pres. 1968-69, 78-79), AAUP. (pres. Auburn chpt. 1975-76). Home: 534 Cary Dr Auburn AL 36830

ANDERBERG, EDWARD CLARENCE, banker; b. N.Y.C., Nov. 28, 1918; s. Eberhard I. and Selma (Bogren) A.; m. Carol Kirkwood, Oct. 12, 1951; children—Thomas, Robert, Karen, Stephen. B.S., NYU, 1951, M.B.A., 1966. With Green Point Savs. Bank, Bklyn., 1935—, asst. sec., 1954-60, asst. v.p., 1960-66, v.p., 1966-67, exec. v.p., 1967-82, pres., 1982—. Bd. mgrs. Greenpoint br. YMCA, 1970—, chmn. world service com., 1967—. Served with AUS, 1942-46. Home: 15 Shady Ln Laurel Hollow NY 11791 Office: 807 Manhattan Ave Brooklyn NY 11222

ANDEREGG, KAREN KLOK, magazine editor; b. Council Bluffs, Iowa, Dec. 19, 1940; d. George J. and Hazel E. (Durham) Klok; m. George F. Anderegg, Jr., Aug. 27, 1970. B.A., Stanford U., 1963. Copywriter Vogue mag., N.Y.C., 1963-72; copy editor Mademoiselle mag., N.Y.C., 1972-77, mng. editor, 1977-80; asso. editor Vogue Mag., N.Y.C., 1980—. Mem. Am. Soc. Mag. Editors. Office: 350 Madison Ave New York NY 10017

ANDERER, JOSEPH HENRY, textile company executive; b. Phila., Oct. 12, 1924; s. Joseph L. and Catherine (Fleck) A.; m. E. T'Lene Brinson, Apr. 4, 1948; children: Joseph D., Mark H., Nancy T. B.M.E., Ga. Inst. Tech., 1947, B.I.E., 1948. Chem. engr. Atlantic Richfield Corp., 1947-55; fiber research mgr., textile devel. lab. mgr. Am. Viscose Corp., 1955-62; with Celanese Corp., 1962-69, exec. v.p. textile mktg., 1967-68; pres. cosmetic and fragrance div., also dir. Revlon, N.Y.C., 1969-71; pres., chief operating officer dir. M. Lowenstein, 1972-77; chmn. bd., chief exec. officer Warren Corp., Stafford Springs, Conn., Grendel Corp., Greenwood, S.C.; trustee Lincoln Savs. Bank, N.Y.C.; dir. Fairtex Mills, N.Y.C., 1977-82, U.S. Shoe Corp., Cin.; Chmn. nat. adv. bd. Ga. Inst. Tech., 1976-82; trustee N.Y. Ocean Sci. Lab., Montauk. Served to lt. USMCR, 1943-45. Mem. Wool Mfg. Council (exec. com.); Mem. Tau Beta Pi, Pi Tau Sigma. Methodist. Clubs: N.Y. Yacht, Stamford Yacht (dir., comdr.). Patentee fiber technology. Office: 1290 Ave of Americas Suite 1359 New York NY 10017

ANDERHALTER, OLIVER FRANK, educator; b. Trenton, Ill., Feb. 14, 1922; s. Oliver Valentine and Catherine (Vollet) A.; m. Elizabeth Fritz, Apr. 30, 1945; childrenSharon, Stephen, Dennis. B.Ed., Eastern Ill. State Tchrs. Coll., 1943, Ped.D. (hon.), 1956; A.M., St. Louis U., 1947, Ph.D., 1949. Mem. faculty St. Louis U., 1947—, prof. edn., 1957—; dir. Bur. Instl. Research, 1949-65, 1949-65, Univ. Computer Center, 1961-69, chmn. research methodology dept., 1968-76; v.p. Scholastic Testing Service, Chgo., 1951—; Chmn. finance com. Greater St. Louis Campfire Girls Orgn., 1958-59. Author, editor standardized tests. Served as pilot USNR, 1943-46. Mem. Am. Ednl. Research Assn., Nat. Council Measurement, Am. Statis. Assn., N.E.A. Home: 12756 Whispering Hills Creve Coeur MO 63104 Office: 62 Weldon Pkwy St Louis MO 63043

ANDERLE, DONALD FRANK, librarian; b. Chgo., Feb. 18, 1936; s. Frank Jerome and Mildred Dorothy (Pinnow) A.; m. Sylvia Ann Ramos, May 31, 1969; children: Laura Elena, Julian Edward. B.F.A., State U. Iowa, 1957; M.L.S., Columbia U., 1969. First asst. art and arch. dir. N.Y. Pub. Library, N.Y.C., 1969-72, chief art and architecture dir., 1972-80, chief art prints, and photographs, 1980, assoc. dir. for spl. collections, 1980—. Home: Maple Ave Peekskill NY 10566 Office: New York Pub Library 5th Ave and 42d St New York NY 10018

ANDERS, EDWARD, educator, chemist; b. Libau, Latvia, June 21, 1926; came to U.S., 1949, naturalized, 1955; s. Adolph and Erica (Leventals) Alperovitch; m. Joan Elizabeth Fleming, Nov. 12, 1955; children: George Charles, Nanci Elizabeth. Student, U. Munich, Germany, 1949; A.M., Columbia U., 1951, Ph.D., 1954. Instr. U. Ill., 1954-55; mem. faculty U. Chgo., 1955—, prof. chemistry, 1962-73, Horace B. Horton prof. chemistry, 1973—; vis. prof. Calif. Inst. Tech., 1960, U. Berne, Switzerland, 1963-64, 70, 78, 80, 83; research asso. Field Mus. Natural History, Chgo., 1968—; resident research asso. NASA, 1961; cons., 1961-69, mem. lunar sample analysis planning team, 1967-69. Asso. editor: Geochimica et Cosmochimica Acta, 1966-73, Icarus, 1970—, The Moon and the Planets, 1974—; contbr. articles to profl. jours. Recipient Univ. medal for excellence Columbia U., 1966; J. Lawrence Smith medal Nat. Acad. Scis., 1971; Quantrell award for excellence in undergrad. teaching U. Chgo., 1973; NASA medal for exceptional sci. achievement, 1973; Guggenheim fellow, 1973-74. Fellow AAAS (Newcomb Cleveland prize 1959), Meteoritical Soc. (v.p. 1968-72, Leonard medal 1974), Am. Acad. Arts and Sci., Am. Geophys. Union; asso. Royal Astron. Soc.; mem. Nat. Acad. Sci., Am. Astron. Soc. (chmn. div. planetary scis. 1971-72), Internat. Astron. Union (pres. com. on moon 1976-79), Am. Chem. Soc., Geochem. Soc. Spl. research origin, age, composition of meteorites and lunar rocks, origin moon and planets. Office: Enrico Fermi Inst Univ Chgo 5630 S Ellis Ave Chicago IL 60637

ANDERSEN, DONALD EDWARD, chemical company executive; b. New Haven, June 3, 1923; s. Edward L. and Jane (Nesbit) A. B.S., Brown U., 1948, Ph.D., 1952; M.S., Stanford U., 1950. With E.I. duPont de Nemours, Inc., Wilmington, Del., 1952—; works mgr. Beaumont Works, 1966-70, lab. dir., mgr. research and devel., 1970-81, mgr. facilities planning exptl. sta., 1981—; cons. Mgmt. Resources. Served with USAAF, 1943-46. Recipient Potter prize for Ph.D. thesis of outstanding merit Brown U., 1952. Fellow AAAS; mem. Am. Chem. Soc. Home: 1608 N Rodney St Wilmington DE 19806 Office: Wilmington DE 19899:

ANDERSEN, ELMER L., manufacturing executive, governor of Minnesota; b. Chgo., June 17, 1909; s. Arne and Jennie (Johnson) A.;

m. Eleanor Johnson, 1932; children: Anthony L., Julian L., Emily E. B.B.A., U. Minn., 1931; LL.D. (hon.), Macalester College, St. Paul, 1965; L.H.D., Carleton Coll., 1972. With H.B. Fuller Co. (mfrs. indsl. adhesives), 1934—, sales mgr., 1937-41, pres., 1941-61, 63-71, chmn., 1961-63, 71—, chief exec. officer, 1971-74, chmn. bd., 1974—; dir. Davis Consol. Industries, Sydney, Australia, Prenor Group Ltd., Montreal, Que., 1972-76, Geo. A. Hormel & Co., Austin, 1971-75, First Trust Co., St. Paul, 1969-74; mem. Minn. Senate, 1949-58; gov. of Minn., 1961-63; pub. Princeton (Minn.) Union Eagle, 1976—, Sun Newspapers, 1978—. Campaign chmn. St. Paul Community Chest, 1959—; exec. com. Boy Scouts Am.; mem. Nat. Parks Centennial Commn., 1971, Gov.'s Voyageurs Nat. Park Adv. Commn., Select Com. on Minn. Jud. System; chmn. Minn. Constl. Study Commn.; Bd. dirs., pres. Child Welfare League Am., 1965-67; past pres. St. Paul Gallery and Sch. of Art; past trustee Augsburg Coll., Mpls.; pres. Charles A. Lindbergh Meml. Fund, 1978—; regent U. Minn., 1967-75; chmn. bd., 1971-75; chmn. Bush Found., St. Paul; bd. dirs. Council on Founds., N.Y.C; chmn. U. Minn. Found.; mem. exec. council Minn. Hist. Soc. Decorated Order of Lion, Finland; recipient Outstanding Achievement award U. Minn., 1959; award of merit Izaak Walton League; Silver Beaver award; Silver Antelope award Boy Scouts Am.; Conservation award Mpls. C. of C.; Taconite award Minn. chpt. Am. Inst. Mining Engrs., 1976; Nat. Phi Kappa Phi award U. Minn., 1977; Minn. Bus. Hall Fame award, 1977; Greatest Living St. Paulite award St. Paul C. of C., 1980; award Adhesive and Sealant Council, 1980; others. Fellow Morgan Library (N.Y.C); Mem. Adhesive Mfrs. Assn. Am. (past pres.), Voyageurs Nat. Park Assn. (past pres.), Minn. Hist. Soc. (exec. com., pres. 1966-70), Am. Antiquarian Soc. Republican. Lutheran. Clubs: Rotarian (past pres. St. Paul, past dist. gov.), Grolier (N.Y.C.); St. Paul Gavel (past pres.). Office: 800 Rosedale Towers Roseville MN

ANDERSEN, HANS CHRISTIAN, educator; b. Bklyn., Sept. 25, 1941; m. June Jenny, Jne 17, 1967; 1 son, Hans Christian. S.B., MIT, 1962, Ph.D., 1966. Jr. fellow Soc. Fellows Harvard U., Cambridge, 1965-68; asst. prof. chemistry Stanford U., Calif., 1968-74, prof., Calif., 1980—; vis. prof. chemistry Columbia U., N.Y.C., 1981-82. Mem. editorial com.: Ann. Rev. of Phys. Chemistry, 1983—. Recipient Gores Award for Excellence in Teaching Stanford U., 1973; Sloan fellow, 1972-74; Guggenheim fellow, 1976-77. Mem. Am. Phys. Soc., Am. Chem. Soc. Adress: Dept Chemistry Stanford U Stanford CA 94305

ANDERSEN, HAROLD WAYNE, newspaper publisher; b. Omaha, July 30, 1923; s. Andrew B. and Grace (Russell) A.; m. Marian Louise Battey, Apr. 19, 1952; children: David, Nancy. B.S. in Edn., U. Nebr., Omaha, 1945, L.H.D. (hon.), 1975; L.H.D. (hon.) Dana Coll., 1983. Reporter Lincoln (Nebr.) Star, 1945-46; with Omaha World-Herald, 1946—, pres., 1966—; dir. AP, Raleigh (N.C.) News & Observer, Newspaper Advt. Bur.; chmn. World Press Freedom Com.; past chmn. Fed. Res. Bank, Kansas City (Mo.). Bd. dirs. United Arts/Omaha; trustee U. Nebr. Found.; trustee, past pres. Jr. Achievement Omaha. Recipient Disting. Journalist award U. Nebr. chpt. Kappa Tau Alpha, 1972, Americanism citation Henry Monsky lodge B'nai B'rith, 1972, Nebr. Builder award U. Nebr., Lincoln, 1976. Mem. Am. Newspapers Pubs. Assn. (past chmn., dir.), Internat. Fedn. Newspapers Pubs. (past pres.), Nebr. Press Assn. (Master Editor-Pub. award 1979), Council Fgn. Relations, Omaha C. of C. (dir.), Phi Beta Kappa, Phi Gamma Delta. Republican. Presbyterian. Home: 6545 Prairie Ave Omaha NE 68132 Office: Omaha World-Herald World-Herald Sq Omaha NE 68102

ANDERSEN, IB STEEN, ballet dancer; b. Copenhagen, Dec. 14, 1954; s. Ingolf Henry and Anna Marie (Hansen) A. Student, Royal Danish Ballet Sch., 1962-73. Dancer, Royal Danish Ballet, 1973—; prin. dancer, 1975—, N.Y.C. Ballet, 1980—.

ANDERSEN, KENNETH BENJAMIN, association executive; b. Jamestown, N.Y., Apr. 6, 1905; s. Benjamin Gaylord and Esther Lydia (Nelson) A.; m. Mildred Mary Cederquist, June 1, 1935; children: Richard Tyler, Mary Gaylord, Kendal Elizabeth. B.S., Dartmouth, 1927; grad. student, N.Y.U., 1930-31. Budget supr., mgr. sales estimating dept. Dahlstrom Metallic Door Co., Jamestown, N.Y., 1927-30, 33-34; sec. Am. Management Assn., N.Y.C., 1930-33, asst. to pres., 1939-41; asst. sec. Rubber Mfrs. Assn., 1934; adminstrv. asst. Office of Sec. Dept. Commerce, Washington, 1935-39; adminstrv. sec. Nat. Elec. Mfrs. Assn., N.Y.C., 1941-46; asst. to pres. Sci. Apparatus Makers Assn., 1947-48, exec. v.p., 1948-67; pres. Assn. Mem. Services, Inc., Chgo., 1967—. Assoc. editor: Handbook of Business Administration, 1931; contbg. author: Association Management, 1958. Mem. Winnetka Planning Commn., 1966-71; chmn. Winnetka Caucus Com., 1964-65, 70—; mem. St. James Cathedral Com., Chgo.; Pres. bd. mgrs. Nat. Inst., Mich. State U., 1956-57; regent Inst. Orgn. Mgmt. Mem. Trade Assn. Execs. Forum Chgo. (pres. 1954-55), Am. Soc. Assn. Execs. (pres. 1958), Nat. Indsl. Council (chmn. 1950), Phi Beta Kappa, Zeta Psi. Episcopalian (vestryman). Club: The Tower (Chgo.). Home: 607 Oak St Winnetka IL 60093 Office: 230 N Michigan Ave Chicago IL 60601

ANDERSEN, KENNETH ELDON, speech communication educator; b. Harlan, Iowa, Dec. 28, 1933; s. Edward and Anna Christina (Christiansen) A.; m. Mary Ann Klaaren, Aug. 20, 1964; 1 son, Erik LaMont. B.A., U. No. Iowa, 1954, M.A., 1955; Ph.D. (Merchant scholar, Knapp fellow), U. Wis., 1961. Instr. U. Colo., Boulder, 1955-56; instr. U. Mich., Ann Arbor, 1961-63, asst. prof., 1963-67, asso. prof., 1967-70, U. Ill., Urbana, 1970-73, prof. speech communication, 1973—, asso. head dept., 1971-78, asso. dean, 1981—, chmn. senate council, 1981—84, vis. prof., Chgo., 1966, U. So. Calif., Los Angeles, 1968. Author textbooks; editor: Jour. Am. Forensic Assn, 1968-71; editorial bd., 1964-68; editor: Speaker and Gavel, 1975-78; contbr. articles profl. jours. Served with AUS, 1956-58. Mem. Speech Communication Assn. (fin. bd. 1974-76, adminstrv. com. 1974-76, 80-84, 2d v.p. 1980-81, 1st v.p. 1981-82, pres. 1982-83), Rhetoric Soc., AAUP (chpt. pres.), Central States Speech Assn. (Outstanding Young Tchrs. Speech award 1962, exec. sec., conv. mgr. 1969-72, editorial bd. 1967-70, pres. 1974-75), Am. Forensic Assn., Ill. Speech and Theatre Assn., Commn. on Am. Parliamentary Procedure, Am. Assn. Pub. Opinion Research, Internat. Communication Assn., Delta Sigma Rho-Tau Kappa Alpha (Service award 1979, Disting. Alumni award 1983). Home: 2002 Galen Dr Champaign IL 61821 Office: Dept Speech Communication 244 Lincoln Hall U Ill Urbana IL 61801

ANDERSEN, KENNETH KAAE, educator; b. Perth Amboy, N.J., May 13, 1934; s. Anton Carl and Kristine (Kaae) A.; m. Barbara Estelle Fowler, July 20, 1957; children—David Kaae, Peter Carl, Joyce Karen. B.S., Rutgers U., 1955; Ph.D., U. Minn., 1959; student, Pa. State U., 1959-60. Prof. chemistry U. N.H., 1960—; vis. prof. Tech. U. Denmark, Lyngby, Denmark, 1971, U. East Anglia, Norwich, Eng., 1966-67, Colo. State U., Ft. Collins, 1979. NSF fellow, 1966-67; Fulbright lectr., 1971. Mem. Am. Chem. Soc. Research organic sulfur chemistry. Home: 16 Garden Lane Durham NH 03824

ANDERSEN, LAIRD BRYCE, educator, univ. dean; b. Madison, S.D., Sept. 16, 1928; s. Andrew Christopher and Alyce (Farrington) A.; m. Joan Roberta Westwood, Nov. 23, 1961; children—Christopher Frederick, Elizabeth Virginia. B.S., U. Minn., 1950, M.S., 1951, M.A., 1961; Ph.D., U. Ill., 1954. Registered profl. engr., Mass., N.J. Asst. prof. Lehigh U., 1954-59; asso. prof. Rice U., 1959-60, U. Nebr., 1961-63; prof., asso. dean engring. N.J. Inst. Tech., 1963-66, dean engring., 1966-75, dean acad. affairs, 1972-74, v.p. acad. affairs, 1974-75, prof. chem. engring., 1975-80; dean Coll. Engring., Southeastern Mass. U., North Dartmouth, 1980—. Co-author: Principles of Unit Operations, 1960, 2d edit., 1980, Introduction to Chemical Engineering, 1960. Mem. Am. Soc. Engring. Edn. (chmn. chem. engring. div. 1967), Am. Inst. Chem. Engrs., Sigma Xi, Phi Lambda Upsilon, Tau Beta Pi, Alpha Chi Sigma, Triangle. Home: 28 Holly Ln Mattapoisett MA 02739 Office: Southeastern Mass U North Dartmouth MA 02747

ANDERSEN, NIELS HJORTH, chemist; b. Copenhagen, Oct. 9, 1943; U.S., 1950, naturalized, 1959; s. Orla and Inger Tryde (Larsen) A.; m. Sidnee Helen Lee, May 18, 1963; children—Marin Christine, Beth Arkady. B.A. cum laude, U. Minn., 1962; Ph.D. in Organic Chemistry, Northwestern U., 1967. Research fellow Harvard U., Boston, 1967-68; asst. prof. chemistry U. Wash., 1968-72, asso. prof., 1972-76, prof., 1976—; prin. scientist ALZA Corp., Palo Alto, Calif., 1970, cons., 1971-75. Recipient Dreyfus Found. Tchr.-Scholar award, 1974-79, Career Devel. award NIH, 1975-80; Sloan Found. research fellow, 1972-74; USPHS grantee, 1971—. Mem. Am. Chem. Soc., Chem. Soc. (London), AAAS, Phytochem. Soc., Fedn. Am. Scientists, N.Y. Acad. Scis. Democrat. Research, numerous publs. on natural products chemistry, synthesis, molecular pharmacology, and prostaglandins. Home: 19538 67th Ave NE Seattle WA 98155 Office: U Wash Dept Chemistry BG-10 Seattle WA 98195 *In seeking a solution, a way to an objective, your questions, in order of priority, should be: How?, Why Not?, and rarely, Why? Never make verifiable assumptions.*

ANDERSEN, ROBERT ALLEN, government official; b. Denver, Aug. 27, 1936; s. Emmet Christian and Margaret Irene (Maupin) A.; m. Jane Eng., May 13, 1967. A.B. in Polit Sci., U. S.C., 1958, M.A., 1961; postgrad., U. Colo Law Sch., 1958-59; Ph.D. in Internat. Relations, Am. U., 1973. Area coordinator for econ. devel. Area Redevel. Adminstrn., Commerce Dept., 1962-64; acting dir. urban projects div., program officer, chief Project Adminstrn. VISTA (OEO), Washington, 1964-66; implementation programming, planning and budgeting system Office Program Planning and Evaluation, Office Edn., 1966-67; staff asst. to dep. postmaster gen. Postal Service, 1967-72, sr. planning officer, 1972-74; dir. evaluation Immigration and Naturalization Service, Washington, 1974—. Vice pres. bd. dirs. D.C. Assn. Retarded Citizens. Mem. Am. Soc. Pub. Adminstrn., Sigma Phi Epsilon. Episcopalian. Home: 5701 Nebraska Ave NW Washington DC 20015 Office: Immigration and Naturalization Service 425 I St NW Washington DC 20001

ANDERSEN, RONALD MAX, health services educator, researcher; b. Omaha, Fed. 15, 1939; s. Max Adolph and Evangeline Dorothy (Wobbe) A.; m. Diane Borella, June 19, 1965; 1 dau., Rachel. B.S., U. Santa Clara, 1960; M.S., Purdue U., 1962, Ph.D., 1968. Research assoc. Purdue U., West Lafayette, Ind., 1962-63; assoc. study dir. Nat. Opinion Research Ctr., Chgo., 1963-66; research assoc. U. Chgo., 1963-77, assoc. prof. then prof. Grad. Sch. Bus., 1974-83, dir. Program in Hosp. Adminstrn. and Ctr. for Health Adminstrn. Studies, 1980—; mem. Panel on Health Services Research, Nat. Acad. Scis., Washington, 1980-83; dir. Health Adminstrn. Press, Ann Arbor, Mich., 1980-83, Social Service Rev., Chgo., 1982-83; coms. Nat. Ctr. for Health Services Research, Rockville, Md., 1970-83. Author, A Decade of Health Services, 1967, Two Decades of Health Service, 1976, Total Survey Error, 1979, Health Services in the U.S., 1980. Active Art Inst., Chgo., Field Mus., Chgo., Smithsonian Mus., Washington. NIH fellow, 1960-62; grantee Robert Wood Johnson Found., 1983, Kaiser Family Found., 1983, Nat. Ctr. for Health Services Research, 1982. Mem. Am. Sociol. Assn. (chmn. med. sociology sect. 1980-81), Nat. Acad. Scis., Nat. Inst. Medicine, Assn. for Health Services Research (dir. 1981-83), Am. Pub. Health Assn., Assoc. Univ. Program in Health Adminstrn. Roman Catholic. Home: 17737 Howe Ave Homewood IL 60430 Office: U Chicago 1101 E 58th St Chicago IL 60637

ANDERSON, ALAN T., business exec.; b. 1927. Pres. Apgar Food Products Co., 1973-79, Patrick Cudahy Inc.; pres., chief operating officer Bluebird Inc., Phila., 1979— *

ANDERSON, ALBERT ESTEN, publisher; b. Mpls., Aug. 29, 1921; s. Albert and Viola (Gullickson) A.; m. Delores Wennblom, July 17, 1954; children—Barbara, David. B.A., St. Olaf Coll., 1944; postgrad., Luther Theol. Sem., 1945, U. Minn., 1946; Litt.D., Wartburg Coll., 1975. Mktg. mgr. Augsburg Pub. House, Mpls., 1947-68, asst. gen. mgr., 1963-70, chief exec. officer, 1970—; dir. Fourth Northwestern Nat. Bank, Mpls., 1967—. Bd. dirs. Lutheran Student Found. Minn., 1960-68, Fairview-Southdale Hosp., 1977-80; regent Augsburg Coll., 1964-70, St. Olaf Coll., 1974—. Served with USMCR, 1943; Served with USNAC, 1944. Recipient Distinguished Alumnus award St. Olaf Coll., 1970. Mem. Protestant Ch.-Owned Pubs.' Assn. (dir. 1963—). Republican. Lutheran. Home: 4809 Hibiscus Ave Minneapolis MN 55435 Office: 426 S 5th St Minneapolis MN 55415

ANDERSON, ALEXANDRA C., writer, editor; b. Boston, May 14, 1942; d. Henry and Marion Ruth (Thompson) Fuller; children: Lafcadio, Genevieve, Oscar. B.A., Sarah Lawrence Coll., 1961. Art editor: Village Voice, N.Y.C., 1974-77; features asso.: Vogue Mag, 1977-78; sr. editor: Portfolio Mag, N.Y.C., 1979-83; editor-in-chief: Arts and Antiques Mag., N.Y.C., 1983—; author: Anderson and Archer's SoHo: The Essential Guide to Art and Life in Lower Manhattan, 1979; free-lance writer. Trustee Skowhegan Sch. Painting and Sculpture; bd. dirs. N.Y. State Small Press Assn., Franklin Furnace. Recipient Art Critics' award NEA, 1978; Japan Found. travel grantee, 1976. Office: 271 Madison Ave New York NY 10016

ANDERSON, ALLAN CROSBY, hospital executive; b. Jamestown, N.Y., Sept. 18, 1932; s. Emmons E. and Gertrude (Sweet) A.; m. Pauline Culver, June 24, 1956; children: Todd Culver, Emily Ann. B.S., Syracuse U., 1954; M.H.A., U. Minn., 1956. Asst. adminstr. Highland Hosp., Rochester, N.Y., 1959-62, adminstr., 1965-68; asst. dir. Presbyn. Hosp., Phila., 1962-65; exec. dir. Strong Meml. Hosp., U. Rochester, 1968-79; pres. Lenox Hill Hosp., N.Y.C., 1979—; asst. prof. health services U. Rochester Sch. Medicine and Dentistry.; Mem. exec. com. Sub-Regional Adminstrs. Group, Adminstrs. Conf., Sub-Regional Exec. Conf.; chmn. bd. dirs. Rochester Regional Hosp. Assn.; also vice chmn. hosp. planning group; chmn. pub. relations com., bd. dirs. Rochester Hosp. Service Corp. Mem. blood program com. Rochester-Monroe County chpt. A.R.C.; mem. med. adv. com. Planned Parenthood of Rochester and Monroe County.; Bd. dirs. Rochester Presbyn. Home, 1967-70, Home Care Assn. Rochester and Monroe County, Health Council Monroe County. Served to 1st lt., Med. Service Corps USAF, 1957-59. Mem. Am. Coll. Hosp. Adminstrs., Assn. Am. Med. Colls. (assembly), Hosp. Assn. N.Y. State (dir., regional orgns. com., govt. relations com. 1966—, trustee 1980), Greater N.Y. Hosp. Assn. (gov. 1980—, treas. 1982, sec. 1983, chmn. fiscal policy com. 1982-83, chmn. ambulatory care comm. 1980), Am. Hosp. Assn. (regional adv. bd. 1983—, alt. del. ho. of dels. 1983—), League Vol. Hosps. (pres.-elect 1983—). Presbyn. (ruling elder). Home: 75 East End Ave New York NY 10028 Office: 100 E 77th St New York NY 10021

ANDERSON, ANDREW HERBERT, army officer; b. Bklyn., Sept. 8, 1928; s. Hjalmar and Anna (Rantanen) Andreason; m. Ellen Lee Miller, Sept. 1, 1956; children—James Andrew, Glenn Robert, Steven Michael. B.S. in History, Park Coll., 1963; M.S. in Personnel Adminstrn, George Washington U., 1968. Commd. in N.G., 1951; entered active duty as 1st lt. U.S. Army, 1954, advanced through grades to maj. gen., 1981—; troop comdr., Ft. Benning, Ga., 1958-60, in Korea, 1964, mem. army staff, Washington, 1965-67, bn. comdr., Vietnam, 1968, Ger., 1970-71; comdr. Support Command, 1st Armored Div., Ger., 1973-74, chief of staff, 1975-76; dep. comdr. Tank-Automotive Materiel Readiness Command, Warren, Mich., 1977-79; comdr. U.S. Army Tank Automotive Research/Devel. Command, Warren, 1979-80; dep. insp. gen., Washington, 1980-81; dep. comdr. VII Corps, Ger., 1981—. Decorated Silver Star, Legion of Merit with oak leaf cluster, D.F.C., Bronze Star with 3 oak leaf clusters, Air medals with V device, Army Commendation medal with 3 oak leaf clusters, Purple Heart. Mem. Assn. U.S. Army, Armor Assn., Am. Def. Preparedness Assn., VFW. Republican. Clubs: Order Purple Heart, Masons (32 deg.), Shriners.). Office: HQ VII Corps APO NY 09107

ANDERSON, ANSEL COCHRAN, physics educator; b. Warren, Pa., Sept. 17, 1933; s. Andrew Conrad and Elpha (Cochran) A.; m. Janet Arlene Belles, June 11, 1955; children: Gail Marie, Alan Belles. B.S., Allegheny Coll., 1955; M.A., Wesleyan U., 1957; Ph.D., U. Ill., 1961. Research asso. U. Ill., 1961-62, research asst. prof., 1962-64, asst. prof., 1964-66, asso. prof., 1966-69, prof. physics, 1969—. Contbr. numerous articles to profl. jours. Guggenheim Found. fellow, 1966-67; NSF fellow, 1958-60; Hays-Fulbright grantee, 1966-67. Fellow Am. Phys. Soc. Office: Physics Dept U Ill 1110 W Green St Urbana IL 61801

ANDERSON, ARNOLD HERBERT, life insurance company executive; b. Chgo., Oct. 3, 1915; s. Hilding A. and Alma (Johnson) A.; m. Christine Mitchell, Jan. 11, 1947; children—Robert N. Power (step-son), Betsy E. A.B., Western Mich. U., 1937; M.A., U. Mich., 1941. Instr. math., Dundee, Mich., 1938-40; with Life & Casualty Ins. Co., Nashville, 1946—, chief actuary, 1955-66, exec. v.p. adminstrn., 1966—, exec. v.p., 1977-79, also mem. exec. com., dir.; ret., 1979; vice chmn. bd. Life Ins. Co. Okla., 1978; dir. Life Ins. Investors Fund, Mid-Tenn. Auto Club. Bd. dirs. Nashville Jr. Achievement, 1969. Served to lt. (s.g.) USNR, 1941-46. Mem. Southeastern Actuaries Club, Nashville Actuarial Club (pres. 1966-67), Am. Mgmt. Assn., Am. Acad. Actuaries, Am. Legion (post comdr. 1948-49). Home: 6217 Ramsgate Ct Brentwood TN 37027

ANDERSON, ARNOLD SEVEREN, pediatrician; b. Mpls., Jan. 11, 1918; s. Arnold Severen and Myrtle (Sholl) A.; m. Ruth Rusk Dalton, Aug. 31, 1940; children: Renner, Jeffrey, Kimball, Lucinda, Susanna, Whitney, Tyler (dec.), Colin, Amy, Martha. B.A., S. Olaf Coll., 1939; M.D., U. Minn., 1944; M.S. in Pediatrics, Mayo Found., Rochester, Minn., 1950. Diplomate: Am. Bd. Pediatrics. Intern San Diego County Hosp., 1944, resident, 1944-45; a founder, pediatrician St. Louis Park (Minn.) Med. Center, 1950-69, pres., 1960-66, bd. dirs., 1960-69; a founder, mem. staff, trustee Children's Health Center and Hosp., Mpls., 1967—; pres. Children's Health Center, 1972-77, dir. patient care, 1978-83, sr. pediatric cons., 1984—; mem. nutrition edn. tng. com. Minn. Dept. Edn.; clin. prof. pediatrics U. Minn.; mem. Minn. Gov.'s Council on Nutrition; cons. Met. Council on Pediatric Emergency Med. Care. Contbr. articles to profl. publs. Mem. Com. on Scouting for Handicapped, Viking council Boy Scouts Am. Served with M.C. U.S. Army, 1945-47. Recipient Dr. Francis E. Harrington award Mpls. Jaycees, 1975, Disting. Alumnus award St. Olaf Coll., 1979, Harold S. Diehl award for outstanding contbns. to practice of medicine, 1984. Mem. Am. Acad. Pediatrics (chmn. sect. community pediatrics 1984), Ambulatory Pediatric Assn., AMA, Northwestern Pediatric Soc., Minn. Med. Assn., Hennepin County Med. Soc. (Charles Bolles Bolles-Rogers 1978 award), Mpls. Met. Pediatric Soc. Quaker. Office: Mpls Children's Med Center 2525 Chicago Ave Minneapolis MN 55404

ANDERSON, ARNOLD STUART, lawyer, retail company executive; b. N.Y.C., June 4, 1934; s. David and Mary (Bilgoray) A.; m. Barbara Sapkowitz, Oct. 1, 1955; children: David Jay, Randi Lee. B.A., CCNY, 1956; J.D., Columbia U., 1959. Bar: N.Y. 1959, U.S. Supreme Ct. 1971. Gen. atty., office gen. counsel FAA, Washington, 1960-61; assoc. Fly, Shuebruck, Blume & Gaguine, N.Y.C., 1962-63; asst. counsel N.Y. Moreland Commn. on Alcoholic Beverage Control Law, N.Y.C., 1963-64; assoc. Winthrop, Stimson, Putnam & Roberts, N.Y.C., 1964-79; v.p., gen. counsel F.W. Woolworth Co., N.Y.C., 1979-80, sr. v.p., gen. counsel, 1980-82, exec. v.p. adminstrn., gen. counsel, 1982—; asst. counsel investigation into jud. conduct Supreme Ct. Appellate Div. 2d Dept., 1970. Author: (with R.S. Taft) N.Y. Practice Series, Personal Taxation, Vol. I, 1975; contbr. articles to profl. jours. Mem. Am. Bar Assn., Fed. Bar Assn., N.Y. Bar Assn., N.Y.C. Bar Assn. Office: World Wide Exec Office Woolworth Bldg 233 Broadway New York NY 10279

ANDERSON, ARTHUR ALLAN, lawyer; b. Grand Rapids, Mich., Apr. 16, 1939; s. Alvin Alexander and Mildred Jane (Grice) A. A.B., Brown U., 1962, Sc.B. in Chemistry, 1962; LL.B., Yale U., 1965. Bar: N.Y. 1966. Assoc. Fish & Neave, N.Y.C., 1965-69; founder, pres. Source Securities Corp., 1970-72; gen. counsel Teleprompter Corp., N.Y.C., 1973-74; ptnr. Anderson & Rubin and predecessors, N.Y.C., 1975-82, Choate, Moore, Hahn & McGarry, 1982—; dir. Am. Transcommunications Inc., Dalton Communications Inc. Mem. N.Y. State Bar Assn., ABA, Bar Assn. City N.Y. (sec. com. on copyright and lit. property). Club: Maltby Valley Falls. Home: 136 W 24th St New York NY 10011 Office: 420 Lexington Ave New York NY 10170

ANDERSON, ARTHUR G., JR., educator; b. Sioux City, Iowa, July 1, 1918; s. Arthur G. and Lois (Mueller) A.; m. Sue Rinker, Sept. 16, 1944; children—Lynn, Joyce, Beth. A.B., U. Ill., 1940; M.Sc., U. Mich., 1942, Ph.D., 1944. Chemist Manhattan Project, Tenn. Eastman Corp., Oak Ridge, 1944-45; mem. faculty U. Wash., Seattle, 1946—, asso. prof. chemistry, 1952-57, prof., 1957—, asso. chmn., 1979—; Research fellow U. Ill., 1946; NSF fellow Heidelberg U., 1960-61; Vis. prof. Australian Nat. U., Canberra, 1966. Contbr. articles to profl. jours. Recipient Petroleum Research Fund Internat. award, 1966. Fellow N.Y. Acad. Scis., Am. Inst. Chemists, Chem. Soc. London; mem. Sigma Xi, Phi Beta Kappa, Phi Kappa Phi, Phi Lambda Upsilon. Research in synthesis and properties of nonbenzenoid aromatic, heterocyclic compounds. Home: 7035 53d Ave NE Seattle WA 98115

ANDERSON, ARTHUR GEORGE, computer company executive; b. Evanston, Ill., Nov. 22, 1926; s. Arthur G. and Margaret (Bree) A.; m. Eliza Chavez Heninger, 1975; children: Joseph S., Robin R., Jennifer M. B.S., U. San Francisco, 1947-49; M.S., Northwestern U., 1951; Ph.D., N.Y. U., 1958. With IBM Corp., 1951—, head numerous engring. and managerial positions, 1951-65, staff dir. corporate tech. com., Armonk, N.Y., 1965-67, dir. research, Yorktown, N.Y., 1967-69, v.p., dir. research, Yorktown, 1969-70, dir. tech. assessment, 1971-72; pres. Gen. Products div., San Jose, Calif., 1972-79, 81—; v.p., group exec. DP products group, White Plains, N.Y., 1979-81; vis. fellow Center for Study of Democratic Instns., 1970-71. Served with USNR, 1944-46. Recipient Invention award IBM. Fellow Am. Phys. Soc., IEEE; mem. AAAS, Am. Soc. for Quality Control, Nat. Acad.

Engring. Patentee in field of spin echo storage techniques and digital circuitry. Home: Box 8747 Incline Village NV 89450 Office: Bldg 0282 5600 Cottle Rd San Jose CA 95193

ANDERSON, ARTHUR N., utility company executive; b. N.Y.C., Jan. 18, 1912; s. Nels and Mathilda (Sandlund) A.; m. Marion A. Olson, Aug. 8, 1937; children: Marian Elaine, Nils A. B.S. in Mech. Engring, N.Y.U., 1933. With Consol. Edison Co. of N.Y., Inc., 1933-50, 54-73, various engring. and supervisory positions, gas and electric prodn. depts., engring. and constrn. depts., v.p. constrn., 1961-73; sec., treas. Asso. Edison Illuminating Cos., N.Y.C., 1973—; power engr. indsl. devel. atomic energy AEC, 1950-52; with Atomic Power Devel. Assos., Detroit, 1952-54. Mem. ASME, Soc. Gas Lighting N.Y.C. Club: Engineers (N.Y.C.). Home: 7 Elm Sea Ln Plandome Manor NY 11030 Office: 51 E 42d St New York NY 10017

ANDERSON, ARTHUR SALZNER, advertising agency executive; b. Bosie, Idaho, Jan. 17, 1923; s. Howard Ballantyne and Mildred Ina (Salzner) A.; m. Janice Virginia Jacobsen, June 21, 1948; children: Roger Bruce, Gregory Bryan, Julie Janice, Lane Jacobsen, Margaret Virginia, Heidi Gail, Steven Jacobsen. B.A., U. Utah, 1947. Sales promotion asst. Internat. Harvester Co., 1947-48, zone mgr., 1948-51; sr. v.p., dir., chmn. exec. com. David W. Evans, Inc., Salt Lake City, 1977—; chmn. bd. Panoram Prodns., 1977-82; pres. Deseret Book Co., 1975-80, dir., 1975—. Author: By Example, 1961. Vice-pres. Salt Lake Area United Fund, 1977-80; mem. governing bd. Primary Children's Med. Center, 1977—, vice chmn., 1981—; bd. dirs. Osmond Found., 1982—. Served with AUS, 1943-46. Mem. Utah Advt. Fedn. (pres. 1967-68), Sales and Mktg. Execs. Utah (pres. 1965-66). Mormon. Home: 2242 Kensington Ave Salt Lake City UT 84108 Office: 110 Social Hall Ave Salt Lake City UT 84111:

ANDERSON, AUSTIN GOTHARD, university adminstrator, lawyer; b. Calumet, Minn., June 30, 1931; s. Hugo Gothard and Turna Marie (Johnson) A.; m. Catherine Antoinette Spellacy, Jan. 2. 1954; children: Todd, Susan, Timothy, Linda, Mark. B.A., U. Minn., 1954, J.D., 1958. Bar: Minn. 1958, Ill. 1962, Mich. 1974. Mem. Spellacy, Spellacy, Lano & Anderson, Marble, Minn, 1958-62; dir. Ill. Inst. Continuing Legal Edn., Springfield, 1962-64; dir. dept. continuing legal edn. U. Minn., Mnpls., 1964-70, assoc. dean gen. extension div., Mpls., 1968-70; mem. Dorsey, Marquart, Windhorst, West & Halladay, Mpls., 1970-73; assoc. dir. Nat. Ctr. State Cts., St. Paul, 1973-74; dir. Inst. Continuing Legal Edn. U. Mich., Ann Arbor, 1973—; adj. faculty U. Minn., 1974, Wayne State U., 1974-75, William Mitchell Coll. Law, 1973-74; project dir. Select Com. on Judiciary State of Minn., 1974-76. Co-editor, contbg, author: Lawyer's Handbook, 1975. Chmn. City of Bloomington Park and Recreation Adv. Commn., Minn., 1970-72; pres. bd. King Sch. Parent-Tchr. Orgn., 1977-78; mem. adv. com. Ferris State Coll.; mem. Ann Arbor Citizens Recreation Adv. Com., 1983-84, Ann Arbor Parks Adv. Com., 1983-84; sec. Ann Arbor Amateur Hockey Assn., 1983-84. Served with U.S. Navy, 1950-51. Mem. Assn. Legal Adminstrs. (pres. 1969-70), ABA (chmn. sect. econ. of law practice 1981-82), Mich. Bar Assn., Ill. Bar Assn., Minn. Bar Assn., Washtenaw County Bar Assn., Am. Mgmt. Assn., Assn. Continuing Legal Edn. Adminstrs. Home: 3617 Larchmont Dr Ann Arbor MI 48109 Office: U Mich 432 Hutchins Hall Ann Arbor MI 48109

ANDERSON, B(ENARD) HAROLD, educator; b. Greeley, Colo., Mar. 21, 1935; s. Benard Joel and Ethel Frances (Robinson) A.; m. Joyce Yvonne Lira, June 10, 1961; children—Tod Allen, Brett Benard. B.S., Colo. State U., 1957, M.Ed., 1963; Ph.D., Ohio State U., 1966. Instr. vocat. agr., Cortez, Colo., 1958-63; research asso. Nat. Center Vocat. Edn., Columbus, Ohio, 1964-65; asst. state supr. Colo. State Bd. Vocat. Edn., 1965-66; asso. prof. Colo. State U., Fort Collins, 1966-73, prof., head dept., 1973—; cons. Mont. State Dept. Edn., 1970, Utah State Dept. Edn., 1972. Author: Planning and Conducting Cooperative Work Experience Programs, 1965, Learning Through Experience in Agricultural Industry, 1978; Editor: Agr. Edn. Round-up, 1963-64, 66-69, Am. Assn. Tchr. Educators in Agr. Newsletter, 1971-72. Chmn. Public Sch. Parents Adv. Com., 1971-73; chmn. legis. com. public sch. Parent Tchr. Orgn., 1971-73; chmn. Am. Inst. Coop. Summer Inst. Young Farmers, 1971. Recipient Charles Shepardson award for teaching Colo. State U., 1972. Mem. Am. Assn. Tchr. Educators in Agr. (pres. 1972-73), Nat. Soc. Study Edn., Am. Vocat. Assn., Colo. Vocat. Assn., Nat. Vocat. Agr. Tchrs., Colo. Vocat. Agr. Tchrs., U. Council Vocat. Edn. (pres. 1978-79), Colo. Assn. Vocat. Adminstrs., Nat. Council Local Adminstrs., Colo. Schoolmasters Club, Alpha Zeta, Alpha Tau Alpha, Phi Kappa Phi, Gamma Sigma Delta, Phi Delta Kappa, Alpha Delta Epsilon, Omicron Tau Theta, Iota Lambda Sigma. Home: 3316 Canadian Pkwy Fort Collins CO 80524

ANDERSON, BETTE B., business exec., former govt. ofcl. Grad. degree, Stonier Grad. Sch. Banking, Rutgers U., 1975. Former v.p. Citizens & So. Nat. Bank, Savannah, Ga.; undersec. Dept. Treasury, Washington, 1977-81; dir. ITT, N.Y.C., 1981—. Office: ITT 320 Park Ave New York NY 10022 *

ANDERSON, BRADLEY JAY, cartoonist; b. Jamestown, N.Y., May 14, 1924; s. Perle J. and Jennie (Solomonson) A.; m. Barbara Marie Jones, Sept. 8, 1945; children: Christine Dorothy (Mrs. Ruben Castaneda, Jr.), Craig Bradley, Paul Richard, Mark Stephen. B.F.A., Syracuse U., 1951. Art dir. audio visual dept. Syracuse U., 1950-51; free-lance mag. cartoonist, 1950—; art dir. Ball & Grier (pub. relations), Utica, N.Y., 1952-53. Syndicated cartoonist: Marmaduke, 1954—, Grandpa's Boy, 1954—, exhbns. include, San Deigo Fair Fine Arts and Cartoons, 1966, Punch mag. exhbn., 1954, Selected Cartoons of 14 Sat. Eve. Post Cartoonists, 1958, Americana Overseas exhbn., 1957, Burchfield Center, State U. Coll. at Buffalo, 1976, San Francisco Mus. Fine Arts, 1978; represented in permanent collections, Albert T. Reid Coll., William Allen White Found., Syracuse U. Manuscripts Library.; Author: Marmaduke, 1955, More Marmaduke, 1958, 1973, Marmaduke, 1966, Marmaduke Rides Again, 1968, Marmaduke... Again?, 1976, Down Marmaduke!, 1978, Marmaduke Digs In, 1978, The Marmaduke Treasury, 1978, Marmaduke on the Loose, 1980, Marmaduke Super Dog, 1983, Meet Marmaduke, 1983, Marmaduke Mystery Puzzles, 1983, Marmaduke Large and Lovable, 1983. Served with USNR, 1943-46. Mem. Newspaper Comics Council, Nat. Cartoonists Soc., Sigma Delta Chi. Club: Mason. Home: 422 Santa Marina Ct Escondido CA 92025

ANDERSON, BRUCE CARL, architect, architecture educator; b. Montreal, Que., Can., Jan. 8, 1941; s. Ralph Fritjof and Doris Amy (Smith) A.; m. Bissera Anderson Doneff, June 26, 1971; children: Diana, Christina. B.Arch., McGill U., 1964; M.Arch. in Urban Design, Harvard U., 1966. Asst. prof. McGill U., Montreal, Que., 1966-69, assoc. prof., 1969-81, prof. architecture, 1981—; vis. prof. U. Pa., Phila., 1968, Carleton U., Ottawa, Ont., Can., 1972, U. Houston, 1970; architect Anderson/Cove Architects, Montreal, 1980-82; vis. prof. Bruce Anderson Architect, Montreal, 1982—. Recipient Bronze medal Royal Archtl. Inst. Can., 1964, Lt. Govs. Gold medal McGill U., 1964; Hugh McLennan Travelling scholar, 1964; Pilkington scholar, 1964; Dunlop Travelling scholar, 1964; Frank Knox fellow Harvard U., 1965. Mem. Royal Archtl. Inst. Can., Order of Architects Que. Club: McGill Faculty (Montreal) (pres. 1976-77). Home: 403 Cote Saint Antoine Rd Westmount PQ Canada H3Y 2J8 Office: McGill Univ Sch of Architecture 3480 University St Montreal PQ Canada H3A 2A7

ANDERSON, BRUCE MURRAY, educator; b. Detroit, July 14, 1929; s. Harold Bruce and Elizabeth (Miller) A.; m. Constance Burchard Derr, June 29, 1950; children—David Bruce, Marcia Anne, Nancy Louise. B.S., Ursinus Coll., 1953; M.S., Purdue U., 1954; Ph.D., Johns Hopkins, 1958. Postdoctoral fellow Brandeis U., 1958-60; asst. prof. biochemistry U. Louisville, 1960-63; asso. prof. biochemistry U. Tenn., 1963-67, prof., 1967-70; prof., head dept. biochemistry and nutrition Va. Poly. Inst. State U., 1970—. Served with USAAF, 1946-49. Mem. Am. Chem. Soc., Am. Soc. Biol. Chemists, Sigma Xi, Phi Lambda Upsilon. Research and publs. on enzymology and pyridine nucleotide chemistry. Home: 1013 Highland Circle SE Blacksburg VA 24060

ANDERSON, BUIST MURFEE, lawyer; b. Marion, Ala., Nov. 17, 1904; s. Edward Buist and Mary Agnes (Murfee) A.; m. Dorothy Mary Crawford, Feb. 27, 1932; children: Mary Jeanne Anderson Jones, David Crawford, Dudley Buist. B.S., U. Va., 1924; LL.B., Yale U., 1929. Bar: Ala. 1928, Conn. 1930, U.S. Supreme Ct. 1937. Statistician, U.S. Dept. Agr., 1924-27; atty. Conn. Gen. Life Ins. Co., 1929-39, counsel, 1939-69, v.p., 1949-69; with firm Murtha, Cullina, Richter & Pinney, Hartford, 1969-82; dir. Colonial Life & Accident Ins. Co. Editor: Vance on Insurance, 3d edit., 1951, Legal Notes, Transactions (Soc. Actuaries), 1941-64. Mem. Am. Arbitration Assn., ABA, Assn. Life Ins. Counsel (pres. 1959-60), Am. Life Conv. (chmn. legal sect. 1948). Baptist. Home: Gale Rd Bloomfield CT 06002 Office: 101 Pearl St Hartford CT 06103

ANDERSON, CARL DAVID, scientist; b. N.Y.C., Sept. 3, 1905; s. Carl David and Emma Adolfina (Ajaxson) A.; m. Lorraine Elvira Bergman; children—Marshall David, David Andrew. B.S., Calif. Inst. of Tech., 1927, Ph.D. magna cum laude, 1930; hon. Sc.D., Colgate U., 1937, Gustavus Adolphus Coll., 1963; LL.D. (hon.), Temple U., 1948. Coffin research fellow Calif. Inst. Tech., 1927-28, teaching fellow in physics, 1928-30, research fellow in physica, 1930-33, asst. prof. physics, 1933-37, asso. prof., 1937-39, prof., 1939-76, prof. emeritus, 1976—, chmn. div. physics, math. and astronomy, 1962-70. Awarded gold medal Am. Inst. of City of N.Y., 1935; Nobel prize in physics, 1936; Elliott Cresson medal of the Franklin Inst., 1937; John Ericsson medal Am. Soc. Swedish Engrs., 1960. Mem. Am. Phys. Soc., Am. Philos. Soc., Nat. Acad. Scis., Sigma Xi, Tau Beta Pi. Research on X-Ray photoelectrons, 1927-30; research on gamma rays and cosmic-rays since 1930. Discoverer of positron, 1932, 1st meson, 1937. Address: Dept Physics California Institute of Technology Pasadena CA 91109 *

ANDERSON, CAROLYN JENNINGS, columnist; b. Franklin, Tenn., Apr. 8, 1913; d. Robert Harmon and Carrie (Estes) Jennings; m. Thomas Jefferson Anderson, Dec. 24, 1936; 1 dau., Carol Anderson Porter. Student, Woman's Coll. Ala., 1931-33; B.A., Vanderbilt U., 1935. Asso. woman's editor Farm & Ranch, Nashville, 1962-72; syndicated columnist American Way Features, Pigeon Forge, Tenn., 1967—; treas. So. Farm Publs. Author: Collector's Items, 1965. Mem. Davidson County (Tenn.) Republican Exec. Com., 1965; asst. to chmn. American Party, 1972-78; local chmn. Stop ERA, Pigeon Forge, 1978. Elected Miss Woman's Coll. Ala., 1932, Miss Vanderbilt, 1934. Mem. Delta Delta Delta. Mem. Jupiter Bible Fellowship. Clubs: Belle Meade Country (Nashville); Little Rock Country, D.A.R. (mem. nat. resolutions com.), D.A.R. (early 1960's), Colonial Dames Am.). Norton Creek Gatlinburg TN 37738 *The old false values such as wealth and popularity fade in importance in the light of the eternal verities set forth in the Word of God. No longer is it a question of try-try-try—but, rather—submit-submit-submit—to Jesus Christ.*

ANDERSON, CHARLES ARNER, physician; b. Cortland, Ohio, June 13, 1907; s. James Cossatt and Halle Lenore (Clark) A.; m. Mary Pond Hughes, July 9, 1949; children—Charles Arner, David James, Grayson Carroll, Warren Rice. Student, Miami U., 1927, Cleve. Coll., 1928, Ohio Wesleyan U., 1929-31; M.B., Ch.B., U. Edinburgh, 1937, L.R.C.P., 1938, D.N.B., 1939. Postgrad. tng. urology Genesee Hosp., U. Rochester, St. Francis Hosp., Peoria, Ill., Watts Hosp., U. N.C., 1937-42; asso. urology St. Louis U., 1946-47; pvt. practice urology, Warren, Ohio, 1947—; chief urol. service St. Joseph Riverside Hosp., Warren, 1948-62, asso. staff, 1962—, Trumbull Meml. Hosp., Warren, 1962-64, staff urologist, 1964—, chief urological service, 1973-76; pres., treas. Warndeer Land Co., Inc., 1962-76, Denusurg Corp., 1967—. President Patriotic Edn., Inc., 1968-69, chmn., 1970—; Mem. Ohio Republican Cent. Com. Served as capt., M.C. AUS, 1942-46; chief urol. and surg. service 29th Evacuation Hosp. Recipient Minute Man award Nat. Soc. S.A.R.; named Ky. col., Miss. col. Mem. Am. Urol. Assn., Trumbull County Hist. Soc. (v.p. 1964-68, pres. 1969-78), AMA, Ohio, Trumbull County med. socs., Am. Soc. Clin. Hypnosis, S.A.R. (nat. pres. 1962-63), Order Ky. Cols., Order Miss. Cols., Symposiarchs (nat. pres. 1968-69), Kappa Sigma (dist. grand master 1964-67, 73—, nat. alumni commr. 1967-70). Clubs: Mason (Shriner, Jester), Buckeye, Trumbull Country. Office: 546 Washington N E Warren OH 44483

ANDERSON, CHARLES ARNOLD, educator; b. Platte, S.D., Jan. 13, 1907; s. Edward Thomas and Edith (Orvis) A.; m. Mary Jean Bowman, July 18, 1942; 1 son, Lloyd Barr. B.A., U. Minn., 1927, M.A., 1928, Ph.D., 1932; Ph.D. (hon.), U. Stockholm, 1978. Faculty U. Minn., 1929, Harvard U., 1930-35, 43, Iowa State U., 1936-43, U. Ky., 1945-58; various U.S. govt. assignments, 1944-45; faculty U. Calif. at Berkeley, 1948-49; vis. prof. U. Lund, Sweden, 1954-55; Fulbright scholar Uppsala (Sweden) U., 1955-56; prof. U. Chgo., 1958—, also dir., 1958-73; cons. UNESCO, Ford Found., World Bank, OECD; vis. prof. U. Stockholm, 1974, U. London, 1975. Author: Social Selection in Education and Economic Development, 1983; editor: Am. Jour. Sociology, 1967-73; Joint editor: Edn., Economy and Soc, 1961, Edn. and Econ. Growth, 1965; Contbr. articles profl. jours. Mem. Comparative Edn. Soc. (pres.), Swedish Royal Acad. Sci., Phi Beta Kappa, Sigma Xi. Home: 5650 Dorchester Ave Chicago IL 60637

ANDERSON, CHARLES ARTHUR, former research institute administrator; b. Columbus, Ohio, Nov. 14, 1917; s. Arthur E. and Huldah (Peterson) A.; m. Elizabeth Rushforth, Oct. 27, 1942; children: Peter C., Stephen E., Julia E. A.B., U. Calif. at Berkeley, 1938; M.B.A., Grad. Sch. Bus. Adminstrn., Harvard U., 1940; L.H.D., Colby Coll., 1975. Asst. prof. Grad. Sch. Bus. Adminstrn., Harvard U., Boston, 1945-48; v.p. Magna Power Tool Corp., Menlo Park, Calif., 1948-58; prof., asso. dean Stanford Grad. Sch. Bus., 1959-61; v.p. Kern County Land Co., San Francisco, 1961-64; pres. Walker Mfg. Co., Racine, Wis., 1964-66, J.I. Case Co., Racine, 1966-68; pres., chief exec. officer SRI Internat., Menlo Park, 1968-79, also dir.; dir. Eaton Corp., NCR Corp., Owens-Corning Fiberglas Corp., Boise Cascade Corp., Saga Corp.; Mem. adv. council Bus. Sch., Stanford, 1966-72, 74-79; Mem. Menlo Park Planning Commn., 1955-60; mem. industry adv. council Dept. Def., 1971-73. Mem. Menlo Park City Council, 1961-62; mem. Gov.'s Commn. on Reorgn. Wis. State Govt., 1965-67; bd. dirs. Childrens Hosp. at Stanford, 1979—, Internat. House, U. Calif., Berkeley, 1979-82. Served to lt. comdr. USNR, 1941-45. Recipient Exceptional Service award USAF, 1965. Presbyn. Clubs: Palo Alto; Pacific-Union (San Francisco); Menlo Country. Home: 2434 Sharon Oaks Dr Menlo Park CA 94025 Office: Suite 120 Bldg 1 3000 Sand Hill Rd Menlo Park CA 94025

ANDERSON, CHARLES BURROUGHS, bookseller; b. Washington, Iowa, Mar. 4, 1905; s. Marion T. and Lucy (Burroughs) A.; m. Herta Lindke, Sept. 16, 1938 (div.); m. Frances L. Wallace, May 28, 1946. Ph.B., U. Chgo., 1926; M.A., Columbia, 1929; student, U. Paris, France, 1931; diplomiert, U. Berlin, Germany, 1932. Faculty Edgewood Sch., 1926-28; instr. English Columbia, 1929-31; faculty Horace Mann Sch., 1934-45; supr. Coll. Entrance Exam. Bd., 1933-39; chmn. bd. Anderson's Book Shop, Inc., Larchmont, N.Y., 1946—; lectr. Grad. Inst. Book Publishing, N.Y.U., 1959-62; Bd. dirs. Am. Booksellers Assn., 1954-62, 64-74, pres., 1958-60. chmn. bd. dirs., 1960-62; bd. judges Carey-Thomas Book award, 1958; bd. dirs. Library Club Am., 1959; steering com. Nat. Library Week, 1958-61; Bd. dirs. Nat. Com. for Florence Agreement, 1960-68; Am. del. Internat. Community Booksellers, Wiesbaden, Germany, 1962; rep. R.R. Bowker Co. to Internat. Book Fair, Frankfurt, 1965-70. Editor-in-chief ABA Publs., 1972-75; Author: Guide to Good Pronunciation; Co-translator: World History of Dance (Sachs), 1938; Editor: Bookselling in America and the World; Contbr. articles to profl. publs. Mem. English Grad. Union (Columbia), Alpha Delta Phi. Clubs: Lions (pres. 1951); Columbia University, Princeton (N.Y.C.); Larchmont Shore; Halifax (Daytona Beach, Fla.). Home: 554 Riverside Dr Ormond Beach FL 32074 Office: 96 Chatsworth Ave Larchmont NY 10538

ANDERSON, CHARLES E., forest products company executive; b. Coos Bay, Oreg., 1929; (married). B.A., Whitman Coll., 1950; M.B.A., Harvard U., 1956. With ITT Rayonier Inc., 1956—, personnel mgr. Jesup div., 1957, asst. mgr. indsl. reins. S.E., 1958-63, gen. mgr. indsl. reins., N.Y.C., 1963-67, v.p. adminstrn., 1967, sr. v.p., 1970, pres., chief operating officer, 1970-73, pres., chief exec. officer, 1973-76, chmn. bd., pres., chief exec. officer, 1976-78, chmn. bd., chief exec. officer, from 1978, now chmn. bd., also dir. Served with USAF, 1950-54.

ANDERSON, CHARLES FREDERICK, banker; b. Binghamton, N.Y., Feb. 6, 1933; s. Oscar Frederick and Olive Lucy (Greene) A.; m. Ruth Ann Camp, June 19, 1954; children: Matthew Frederick, Kathryn Frances. B.S. in Bus. Mgmt, Ariz. State U., 1958. With Valley Nat. Bank, Phoenix, 1956-63, asst. mgr. data processing, 1959-63; gen. mgr., then pres. Bank Computer Center Conn., Hartford, 1963-66; mgr., bank cons. Peat, Marwick & Mitchell & Co. (C.P.A.s), Chgo., 1966-69; v.p., mgr. data processing First Interstate Bank Washington, N.A., Seattle, 1969-71, v.p., mgr. banks ops. and data processing, 1971-73, sr. v.p. adminstrn., 1973-75; sr. v.p. ops. and mktg. First Interstate Bancorp., Los Angeles, 1975-78; chief exec. officer N.W. Mgmt. Services, Inc., 1978-81; sr. v.p. Southeast Bank, Miami, Fla., 1981—; vice chmn. bd. First Interstate Services, 1975-78; dir. Southeast Services Co., Plus System Inc.; Mem. Wash. Data Processing Commn., 1973-74. Pres. Oakbrook P.T.A., Lakewood, Wash., 1970-71; mem. exec. bd. South Fla. Council Boy Scouts Am.; Trustee Steilacoom Community Coll., 1969-71; bd. dirs. Evergreen Safety Council, Seattle; mem. Bainbridge Island Juvenile Conf. Com., 1980-81. Recipient Order of Arrow Boy Scouts Am., 1975—. Mem. Am. Bankers Assn. (lectr.), Soc. Mgmt. Info. Systems (charter), Nat. Electronic Funds Transfer Assn. (bd. dirs. 1978-82), Delta Sigma Phi. Republican. Episcopalian. Clubs: Bankers (Miami); Riviera Country. Home: 4821 Campo Sano Ct Coral Gables FL 33146 Office: 100 S Biscayne Blvd Miami FL 33131

ANDERSON, CHARLES ROBERTS, educator; b. Macon, Ga., Oct. 17, 1902; s. Robert Lanier and Gertrude (Roberts) A.; m. Eugenia Blount, June 1, 1935; m. Mary Pringle, May 3, 1963. A.B., U. Ga., 1924, A.M., 1928; Ph.D., Columbia U., 1939. Instr., English U. Ga., 1927-30; instr. English Duke U., 1930-35; asst. prof., 1935-39, assoc. prof., 1939-41; assoc. prof. Am. lit. Johns Hopkins U., Balt., 1941-45, prof., 1946-69, chmn. dept., 1950-56, Caroline Donovan prof. Am. lit., 1957-69, prof. emeritus, 1969—; Lamar Found. lectr. Wesleyan Coll., 1957; vis. prof., summers George Washington U., 1938, Johns Hopkins U., 1940, U. Calif., 1946, Columbia U., 1947-48, U. So. Calif., 1950, U. Hawaii, 1956; guest prof. U. Heidelberg, 1949; vis. lectr. Nagano Seminar, Japan, summer 1954; auspices U.S. Dept. State, Am. specialist lectr., Singapore, Manila, Taiwan and Japan, 1965-66, Korea, Bangkok, Katmandu, Bucharest, 1969; lectr. USIA, Yugoslavia, 1974, Taiwan, Japan, Singapore, Kuala Lumpur, Bangkok, Burma, India, Pakistan, Iran, Egypt, Greece, Austria, 1976-77, Hong Kong, Bangkok, Burma, Pakistan, Aghanistan, 1978, Japan, Hong Kong, Kuala Lumpur, Singapore, Java, Bangkok, India, 1979, Hong Kong, Dacca, Bangkok, India, Saudi Arabia, India, 1980, Lyon, Paris, 1981, Portugal, 1982, Germany, Czechoslovakia, Portugal, Italy, 1983. Mng. editor: Am. Lit, 1932-33; Author: Melville in the South Seas, 1939, Emily Dickinson's Poetry, Stairway of Surprise (Christian Gauss award Phi Beta Kappa 1960), The Magic Circle of Walden, 1968, Person, Place and Thing in Henry James's Novels, 1978 (Christian Gauss award Phi Beta Kappa); Editor: Journal of a Cruise in the Frigate United States with notes on Melville, 1937, Sidney Lanier: Poems and Letters, 1970, Thoreau's World: Miniatures from his Journal, 1971, Thoreau's Vision: The Major Essays, 1973, The Bostonians (Henry James), 1983; Gen. editor: Centennial Edition of Sidney Lanier (10 vols.), 1945, American Literary Masters, 2 vols, 1965; Assoc. editor: Modern Lang. Notes, 1942—; Contbr. articles to profl. jours.; Mem. adv. bd.: Jour. Am. Lit, 1955-58; editorial bd., 1959-62. Rosenwald fellow, 1938-39; Fulbright fellow U. Rome, 1942-43, U. Torino, Italy, 1959-60, Kyoto U., Doshisha U., 1969; fellow Huntington Library, summer 1952; Guggenheim fellow, 1965-66. Fellow Soc. Am. Studies; mem. MLA (chmn. Am. lit. group 1957), AAUP, Soc. Am. Historians, Melville Soc. Am. (pres. 1946), Internat. Assn. Univ. Profs. English, Phi Beta Kappa, Phi Delta Theta, Sigma Upsilon. Home: 4 Legare St Charleston SC 29401 and Church Cottage Linton Cambridgeshire UK *My purpose as a professor, scholar, and author has been to (1) open the eyes of undergraduates to the magical world of literature, (2) inspire post-graduate students to undertake original research, (3) further international understanding by presenting American literature to many countries of Europe and Asia in my lectures and books.*

ANDERSON, CHESTER GRANT, educator; b. River Falls, Wis., Dec. 8, 1923; s. C.A. Chester and Inga Amelia (Grant) A.; m. Carole Nygard, Apr. 23, 1945; children—Stephen, Mark, Jonathan. Student, St. Olaf Coll., 1941-43; M.A., U. Chgo., 1948; Ph.D., Columbia U., 1962. Asst. prof. English Creighton U., Omaha, 1948-50, asst. prof., 1954-57, Fordham U., N.Y.C., 1951-52; dir. State Soc. Services, Am. Inst. C.P.A.'s, 1952-54; asso. prof. Western Conn. State U., 1957-63; asst. prof. Columbia U., 1963-68; prof. English U. Minn., Mpls., 1963—; Fulbright prof. Helsinki (Finland) U., 1963-64. Author: James Joyce and His World, 1967, Critical Edit. of James Joyce's A Portrait of the Artist, 1968, Growing Up in Minnesota, 1976. Served to ensign AC, USNR, 1943-45. Mem. MLA, MLA Helsinki, James Joyce Found. 400 Groveland Ave Minneapolis MN 55403 Office: Dept English 207 Lind Hall U Minn 207 Church St SE Minneapolis MN 55455

ANDERSON, CORTLAND EDWIN, JR., educational administrator; b. Laurelton, N.Y., Oct. 10, 1935; s. Cortland Edwin and Helen (O'Krinsky) A.; m. Fidella Purdin, Feb. 2, 1958; children: Laura, Sharon, Mary. A.B. in English, Fla. So. Coll., Lakeland, 1958. City editor, mng. editor St. Petersburg (Fla.) Times, 1959-66; editor, v.p. Suffolk (N.Y.) Sun, 1966-69; asst. v.p. public relations N.Y. Telephone Co., 1970-76; exec. v.p. Corp. for Public Broadcasting, Washington, 1977-79; v.p. Washington Post Co., Washington, 1979-81; dir. E.W. Scripps Sch. Journalism, Ohio U., Athens, 1981—. Mem. editorial adv. bd.: Sci. 83 Mag; adv. bd.: Children's Express, N.Y.C. Mem. energy com. Atlantic Council; mem. adv. bd. Third Sector Project,

Washington. Episcopalian. Office: Sch Journalism Ohio U Athens OH 45701

ANDERSON, CURTISS MARTIN, editor, writer; b. Mpls., July 16, 1928; s. Otto and Hilda Marie (Holman) A.; m. Anne Sonopol, Dec. 12, 1953. B.A., U. Minn., 1951. With Meredith Pub. Co., Des Moines, 1951-60; editor Vacation Ideas book, also Home Building Ideas book for Better Homes & Gardens mag., 1951-52, asso. editor, sr. writer mag., 1956-57, spl. features editor mag., 1957-60; asso. editor, staff writer Ladies Home Jour., Phila., 1960, mng. editor, 1961-62, editor-in-chief, 1962-64; contract writer McCall's mag., 1964; editor Venture-The Traveler's World, N.Y.C., 1964-71, v.p., 1967-71; editor Hallmark Cards, Inc., Kansas City, Mo., 1971-72; editor, pub. dir. Diversion Mag., 1972-75; mng. editor Look mag., 1978-79; editor mag. devel. Hearst Corp., 1979—. Author: Collections from the American Past, 1975, (with J.C. Hall) When You Care Enough, 1979. Served with USN, 1946-48. Recipient award for best article on architecture in non-profl. mag. AIA, 1955; named one of ten outstanding young men of year S. Jr. C. of C., 1963. Mem. Am. Soc. Mag. Editors, Sigma Delta Chi. Clubs: Metropolitan, Washington Press. Home: 150 E 69th St New York NY 10021

ANDERSON, CYNTHIA LEE, ballet dancer; b. Pasadena, Calif., Sept. 23, 1956; d. Robert Warren and Shirley (Bennetts) A. Student public schs. Dancer, Joffrey II Ballet Co., N.Y.C., 1974-76, Joffrey Ballet Co., N.Y.C., 1976—. Mem. Am. Guild of Musical Artists. Address: 130 W 56th St New York NY 10019

ANDERSON, DANIEL OGREN, mfg. co. exec.; b. Jamestown, N.Y., Mar. 11, 1928; s. Paul Nathanial and Cecille (Ogren) A.; m. Mary Joan Olson, Mar. 31, 1951; 1 dau., Catherine Louise Anderson Carr. A.B., Princeton U., 1951. With Gen. Electric Co., 1951-70, mgr. fin. planning and adminstrn. ops. advanced systems div., 1969-70; controller N. Am. ops. Honeywell Info. Systems, Waltham, Mass., 1970-74, v.p. fin. and adminstrn., 1974-75; v.p., chief fin. officer Itek Corp., Lexington, Mass., 1975-77, exec. v.p. indsl. and bus. products group, 1978—; pres. Graphic Systems and Communications Industries, 1981—. Mem. Fin. Execs. Inst. Clubs: Princeton (N.Y.C.); Cap and Gown, Weston Golf. Office: 10 Maguire Rd Lexington MA 02173

ANDERSON, DAREL BURTON, paper company executive; b. North Branch, Minn., Dec. 6, 1927; s. Axel and Verna (Johnson) A.; m. Lois Maxine Olson, June 12, 1948; children: Gregory, Gayle, Gretchen. With Leslie Paper Co., Fargo, N.D., 1950-64, sales mgr., Mpls., 1965-76, exec. v.p., 1982—, pres., 1982—. Republican. Lutheran. Club: Mpls. Athletic. Home: 15000 Cherry Ln Minnetonka MN 55343 Office: Leslie Paper Co PO Box 1351 Shelard Tower Minneapolis MN 55440

ANDERSON, DARRYL KENT, investment executive; b. Lake Charles, La., Apr. 18, 1941; s. Byrum Lavelle and Doris Marie (Goodman) A.; m. Linda Clarke, Aug. 29, 1969; children: Whitney Paige, Huntley Clarke, Clarke Kent. B.A., Rice U., 1962; M.B.A., U. Va., 1964. Pres. Rivercrest Investment Corp., Houston, 1966-70; v.p. Underwood Neuhaus & Co., Houston, 1970-78; sr. v.p. Allied Bancshares, Inc., Houston, 1978-81, exec. v.p., 1981—; dir. Allied Beltway Bank-Farmers State Bank, Austin Broadcasting Co.-Central Tex. Broadcasting Co. Pres. Rivercrest Civic Assn., Houston; bd. dirs. Houston Inst. Cancer Research. Served with U.S. Air N.G., 1964-70. Named Outstanding Mil. Grad. Citizens Com. Army and Air Force, San Antonio, 1964. Presbyterian. Clubs: Houston, Lakeside Country, Athletic, Garden of the Gods, Coronado. Office: Allied Bancshares Inc 7th Floor 1000 Louisiana Houston TX 77002

ANDERSON, DARYL, actor; b. Seattle, July 1, 1951; stepson Patrick and Shirley Joan (Gerard) Gallagher. B.F.A., U. Wash., Seattle, 1975. Actor, Seattle Repertory Theatre, 1975-76, Los Angeles Actors Theatre, 1976-77; actor: TV series Lou Grant, 1977-82. Recipient Vet.'s Employment award Dept. Labor, 1979. Mem. Screen Actors Guild (nat. dir. 1980—), Nat. Acad. TV Arts and Scis. Democrat. Address: care Screen Actors Guild 7750 Sunset Blvd Hollywood CA 90046

ANDERSON, DAVID, ambassador; b. Scotland, Jan. 3, 1937; emigrated to U.S., 1952; s. Alexander Peggie and Janet Barclay (Brown) A.; m. Doris helen Heitmann, Nov. 15, 1979; children: Natalie, Scott, Nina. B.A., Union Coll., 1958; M.A., Fletcher Sch. Law and Diplomacy, 1959. Commd. fgn. service officer Dept. State, 1959, intelligence research officer, Washington, 1959-62, polit. officer, Yugoslavia, 1962-65, Mali, 1965-67, Berlin, 1967-70, Brussels, 1970-71, Bonn, W. Ger., 1971-75, dep. exec. sec., dir. Central European affairs, Washington, 1975-77, dep. exec. sec., 1977-78; U.S. Minister, Berlin, 1978-81, ambassador to Yugoslavia, Belgrade, 1981—. Mem. Phi Beta Kappa. Address: American Embassy Kneza Milosa 50 Belgrade Yugoslavia

ANDERSON, DAVID DANIEL, educator; b. Lorain, Ohio, June 8, 1924; s. David and Nora Marie (Foster) A.; m. Patricia Ann Rittenhour, Feb. 1, 1953. B.S., Bowling Green State U., 1951, M.A., 1952; Ph.D., Mich. State U., 1960. From instr. to prof. dept. Am. thought and lang. Mich. State U., East Lansing, 1957—; lectr. Am. Mus., Bath, Eng., 1980; editor U. Coll. Quar., 1971-80; Fulbright prof. U. Karachi, Pakistan, 1963-64, Am. del. to, Internat. Fedn. Modern Langs., and Lit., 1969-78, Internat. Congress Orientalists, 1971-79. Author: Sherwood Anderson, 1968 (Book Manuscript award 1961), Louis Bromfield, 1964, Critical Studies in American Literature, 1964, Sherwood Anderson's Winesburg, Ohio, 1967, Brand Whitlock, 1968, Abraham Lincoln, 1970, Suggestions for the Instructor, 1971, Robert Ingersoll, 1972, Woodrow Wilson, 1978, Ignatius Donnelly, 1980, William Jennings Bryan, 1981; editor: The Black Experience, 1969, The Literary Works of Abraham Lincoln, 1970, Sunshine and Smoke: American Writers and the American Environment, 1971, (with others) The Dark and Tangled Path, 1971, MidAmerica I, 1974, II, 1975, III, 1976, IV, 1977, V, 1978, VI, 1979, VII, 1980, VIII, 1981, IX, 1982, X., Sherwood Anderson: Dimentions of his Literary Art, 1976, Sherwood Anderson: The Writer at His Craft, 1979, Critical Essays on Sherwood Anderson, 1981, Michigan: A State Anthology, 1983. Served with USN, 1942-45; Served with AUS, 1952-53. Decorated Silver Star, Purple Heart; recipient Disting. Alumnus award Bowling Green State U., 1976; Disting. Faculty award Mich. State U., 1974. Mem. AAUP, Popular Culture Assn., Modern Lang Assn., Soc. Study Midwestern Lit. (founder, exec. sec., Disting. Service award 1982), Assn. Gen. and Liberal Edn. Am. Assn. Advancement Humanities. Club: University. Home: 6555 Lansdown Dr Dimondale MI 48821 Office: Dept Am Thought and Lang Mich State U East Lansing MI 48824

ANDERSON, DAVID E., telephone company executive; b. Sioux City, Iowa, 1926. B.E.E., Iowa State U., 1948. In various positions Gen. Telephone Co. Wis., 1948-67; chief engr. Gen. Telephone Co. Ohio, 1967-68; pres. Gen. Telephone Co. Ill., 1968-78; v.p. network engring. and constrn. Gen. Telephone Co. Calif., 1977-79, pres., chief exec. officer, dir., 1979—. Bd. dirs. United Way, Los Angeles; trustee Santa Monica Hosp. Med. Ctr., Calif. Served with USN, 1944-46. Mem. Nat. Soc. Profl. Engrs., Los Angeles Area C. of C. (bd. dirs.). Office: Gen Telephone Co Calif 100 Wilshire Blvd Santa Monica CA 90401 *

ANDERSON, DAVID GILROY, forestry educator, college official; b. Skaneateles, N.Y., Aug. 3, 1930; s. Edwin G. and Laura L. (Wickham) A.; m. Judith B. Valentine, Dec. 2, 1978; children: Linda, David Andrew, Timothy; stepchildren: Timothy Wadsworth, Duane Wadsworth. A.A.S., N.Y. State Ranger Sch., 1950; b.S., N.Y. State Coll. Forestry, 1953; M.S., U. Utah, 1958; M.P.A., Syracuse U., 1977, postgrad., 1979. Instr. N.Y. State Ranger Sch., Wanakena, 1959-62, asst. prof., 1963-65; asst. dean, assoc. prof. forestry SUNY-Syracuse, 1965-70; prof., univ. v.p. N.Y. State Ranger Sch., 1970—; dir. Univ. Hill Corp. Bd. dirs., v.p. N.Y. State Coll. Forestry Found., Inc., 1978-81. Served with USNR, 1953-59. Am. Council Edn. fellow, 1970-71. Mem. Am. Forestry Assn., AAAS, Soc. Am. Foresters, N.Y. Forest Owners Assn., Nat. Audubon Soc., Nature Conservancy, Am. Soc. for Pub. Adminstrn., Am. Legion, Syracuse U. Alumni Assn., U. Utah Alumni Assn., Sigma Xi. Republican. Presbyterian. Club: Clayton Yacht. Home: 3928 Derby Dr Syracuse NY 13215 Office: SUNY Coll Environ Sci and Forestry Sycracuse NY 13210

ANDERSON, DAVID POOLE, journalist; b. Troy, N.Y., May 6, 1929; s. Robert P. and Josephine (David) A.; m. Maureen Ann Young, Oct. 24, 1953; children: Stephen, Mark, Mary Jo, Jean Marie. B.A., Holy Cross Coll., 1951. Sports writer Bklyn. Eagle, 1951-55, New York Jour.-Am., 1955-66, New York Times, 1966—. Author: Countdown to Super Bowl, 1969, (with Ray Robinson) Sugar Ray, 1970, (with Larry Csonka and Jim Kiick) Always On The Run, 1973, Pancho Gonzalez, 1974, (with Frank Robinson) Frank: The First Year, 1976, Sports of Our Times, 1979, The Yankees, 1979, (with John Madden) Hey, Wait a Minute, I Wrote a Book, 1984; editor: The Red Smith Reader, 1981. Recipient Best Sports Stories award (mag.), 1965; Best Sports Stories award (features), 1972; Page One award for sports features, 1972; Nat. Fleischer award for boxing writing, 1974; Pulitzer Prize for commentary, 1981. Home: 8 Inness Rd Tenafly NJ 07670 Office: 229 W 43d St New York NY 10036

ANDERSON, DAVID PREWITT, university dean; b. Twin Falls, Idaho, Sept. 14, 1934; s. Robert Kyle and Margaret Elizabeth (Prewitt) A.; m. Janice Gale Schmied, Dec. 21, 1962; children: Kathryn Lynn, Christopher Kyle. Student, U. Idaho, 1952-54; B.S., Wash. State U., 1959, D.V.M., 1961; M.S., U. Wis., 1964, Ph.D., 1965. Diplomate: Am. Coll. Vet. Microbiologists. NIH trainee U. Wis., 1961-64, asst. prof. vet. sci., asst. dir. biotron, 1965-69; prof. med. microbiology, dir. Poultry Disease Research Center, U. Ga., 1969-71, asso. dean research and grad. affairs, 1971-73, prof., 1974—, dean, 1975—; mem. com. animal health Nat. Acad. Sci., 1977-80, Animal Health Sci. Research Advisory Bd. U.S. Dept. Agr., 1978—; chmn. commn. on vet. medicine Nat. Assn. State Univs. and Land Grant Colls., 1982-83. Editor: Avian Diseases. Mem. AVMA, Am. Assn. Avian Pathologists, Poultry Sci. Assn. Home: 190 Harris St Winterville GA 30683

ANDERSON, DAVID TURPEAU, government official, judge; b. Cin., Aug. 9, 1942; s. Randall Hudson and Florida (Turpeau) A.; m. Marta Camille, Dec. 29, 1962 (div. 1970); children: David Malcolm, Daniel Michel. B.S., U. Cin., 1963; J.D., George Washington U., 1972. Staff aide U.S. Senator Robert Taft, Jr., Washington, 1967-69; asst. congl. relations U.S. HUD, Washington, 1970; asst. for legislation Am. Hosp. Assn., Washington, 1971-73; assoc. Stanley, Durham & Johnson, Phila., 1973-74; asst. city solicitor Office City Solicitor, Phila., 1974-81; chmn. Bd. Contract Appeals, HUD, Washington, 1981—. Mem. ABA, Fed. Bar Assn., Nat. Bar Assn., Phila. Bar Assn., Nat. Conf. Bd. Contract Appeals Mems., Nat. Lawyers Club. Club: Nat. Press. Home: PO Box 23859 Washington DC 20024 Office: Bd Contract Appeals HUD Room 2158 451 7th St SW Washington DC 20410

ANDERSON, DENNIS ALBIN, bishop; b. Glenwood, Minn., July 8, 1937; s. Albin G. and Florence Elizabeth (Larson) A.; m. Barbara Ann Forse, Dec. 30, 1960; children: Kristin, Charles. B.A., Gustavus Adolphus Coll., 1959; M.Div., Luth. Sch. Theology, Chgo., 1963; D.Div. hon., Gustavus Adolphus Coll., 1978; D.H.L. HON., Midland Luth. Coll., Fremont, Nebr., 1980. Ordained to minstry Lutheran Ch. Am., 1963. Mission developer Luth. Ch. in Am., Austin, Tex., 1963-64; pastor Holy Cross Luth. Ch., Austin, 1964-66, Luth. Ch. Good Shepherd, Prospect Heights, Ill., 1966-71, St. Paul Luth. Ch., Grand Island, Nebr., 1973-78; bishop Nebr. synod Luth. Ch. in Am., Omaha, 1978—, mem. exec. council, 1976-84. Author: Searching for Faith, 1975, Baptism and . . ., 1976, Jesus My Brother in Suffering, 1977. Office: Nebr Synod Lutheran Ch in Am 124 S 24th St Amana NE 68144

ANDERSON, DON LYNN, educator, geophysicist; b. Frederick, Md., Mar. 5, 1933; s. Richard Andrew and Minola (Phares) A.; m. Nancy Lois Ruth, Sept. 15, 1956; children: Lynn Ellen, Lee Weston. B.S., Rensselaer Poly. Inst., 1955; M.S., Calif. Inst. Tech., 1959, Ph.D., 1962. With Chevron Oil Co., Mont., Wyo., Calif., 1955-56; with Air Force Cambridge Research Center, Boston, 1956-58, Arctic Inst. N.Am., 1958; mem. faculty Calif. Inst. Tech., Pasadena, 1962—, asso. prof. geophysics, 1964-68, prof., 1968—, dir. seismol. lab., 1967—; Prin. investigator King Mars Seismic Expt.; mem. various coms. NASA, Nat. Acad. Scis.; chmn. seismology com. Nat. Acad. Sci., 1975, mem. Acad., 1982—. Asso. editor: Jour. Geophys. Research, 1965-67, Tectonophysics, 1974-77; editor: Physics of the Earth and Planetary Interiors. Recipient Exceptional Sci. Achievement award NASA, 1977; Sloan Found. fellow, 1965-67. Fellow Am. Geophys. Union (James B. Macelwane award, 1966, pres. tectonophysics sect. 1971-72, chmn. Macelwane award com. 1975), Geol. Soc. Am. (asso. editor bull. 1971—); mem. Am. Acad. Arts and Scis., AAAS, Royal Astron. Soc., Seismol. Soc. Am., Sigma Xi. Home: 669 E Alameda St Altadena CA 91001 Office: 1201 E California Blvd Pasadena CA 91109

ANDERSON, DONALD BERNARD, oil co. exec.; b. Chgo., Apr. 6, 1919; s. Hugo August and Hilda (Nelson) A.; m. Patricia Gaylord, 1945 (dec. 1978); m. Sarah Midgette, 1980. B.S. in Mech. Engring, Purdue U., 1942. Vice pres. Hondo Oil & Gas Co. (formerly Malco Refineries, Inc.), Roswell, N.Mex., 1946-63; pres. Anderson Oil Co., Roswell, 1963—, Cotter Corp., 1966-70, chmn. bd., 1966-74; founder, pres. Anderson Drilling Co., Denver, 1974-77, chmn. bd., 1977—. Curator fine arts, mem. acquisitions com. Roswell Mus. and Art Center, 1949-56, trustee, 1956—, pres. bd., 1957—; bd. dirs. Sch. Am. Research, Santa Fe, Jargon Soc., Penland, N.C.; regent Eastern N.Mex. U., 1966-72; commr. Smithsonian Instn., Nat. Mus. Am. Art, 1980—. Served to lt. USNR, 1942-46. Address: PO Box 1 Roswell NM 88201

ANDERSON, DONALD EDWARD, research and development executive; b. Delavan, Minn., Sept. 16, 1931; s. Levi Edward and Sarah (Hillman) A.; m. Cynthia Jane Luedtke, June 16, 1954; children: Scott Mark, Gwen Marie, Bruce Alan, Gail Diane. B.S., U. Minn., 1952, M.S., 1954, Ph.D. in Elec. Engring, 1958. Research asst. U. Minn., 1952-54, research fellow, 1954-58, mem. faculty, 1958-68, prof. elec. engring., 1967-68; with Sheldahl, Inc., Northfield, Minn., 1967-77, v.p., dir. corp. research and devel., 1968-77; dir., chief exec. officer Mid-Am. Solar Energy Complex, Mpls., 1976-81; pres., chief exec. officer Suntec Systems, Inc., St. Paul, 1982-83; pres. Inno Ventors, Inc., Northfield, Minn., 1981—; cons. in field, 1958—. Mem. IEEE, Am. Phys. Soc., Soc. Information Display, Internat. Solar Energy Soc., Sigma Xi, Tau Beta Pi, Eta Kappa Nu, Kappa Eta Kappa. Research electron emission, superconductivity, phys. electronics, solar thermal energy. Patentee electromagnetic energy storage, direct energy conversion, display devices, optical films, solar collectors, acoustics; teaching elec. circuit theory field theory, energy conversion, electronics. Home: 1109 E Woodley Northfield MN 55057

ANDERSON, DONALD GEORGE, educator; b. Burlington, Iowa, Oct. 11, 1930; s. George H. and Esther (McCaleb) A.; m. Beulah Esther Fargo, June 6, 1959; children—David A., Susan R. A.A., Burlington Jr. Coll., 1950; B.S., U. Iowa, 1956; M.A., 1957, Ph.D., 1962. Instr. U.S.D., 1957-59; instr. mktg. U. Iowa, 1959-61; asst. prof. mktg. U. N.D., 1961-62, prof., 1963—, chmn. dept. mktg., 1963-75, 78—; asst. prof. mktg. U. South Fla., 1962-63; vis. prof. bus. adminstrn. Moorhead State Coll., 1972. Contbg. editor: Small Bus. Mgmt, 1973. Chmn. New Indsl. Devel. Subcom. N.D. Economic Devel. Commn., 1967. Served with USN, 1951-54. Mem. Am., So. mktg. assns., So., Midwest econ. assns., Small Bus. Inst. Dirs. Assn., VFW, Beta Gamma Sigma, Order Artus, Delta Sigma Pi. Home: 2910 Clover Dr Grand Forks ND 58201

ANDERSON, DONALD GORDON MARCUS, educator; b. Sarnia, Ont., Can., Jan. 4, 1937; s. Gordon Lincoln and Jean Merritt (McNaughton) A. B.S., U. Western Ont., 1959; A.M., Harvard, 1960, Ph.D., 1963. Lectr., research fellow Harvard, 1963-65, asst. prof. applied math., 1965-69, Gordon McKay prof. applied math., 1969—. Mem. AAAS, Soc. for Indsl. and Applied Math. Office: Aiken Computation Laboratory Harvard University Cambridge MA 02138

ANDERSON, DONALD KEITH, chem. engr.; b. Iron Mountain, Mich., July 15, 1931; s. Milton Eugene and Edna Olive (Van Court) A.; m. Gina Dale Garrett, July 12, 1957; children—Shannon Elizabeth, Amanda Juliet. B.S., U. Ill., 1956; M.S., U. Wash., 1958, Ph.D., 1960. Asst. prof. chem. engring. Mich. State U., 1960-64, asso. prof., 1964-69, prof. chem. engring. and physiology, 1970—, chmn. dept. chem engring., 1977—; cons. to industry. Contbr. numerous articles to profl. jours. Recipient Disting. Faculty award Mich State U., 1973. Mem. Am. Inst. Chem. Engrs., Am. Chem. Soc., Am. Soc. Engring. Edn., Sigma Xi, Tau Beta Pi, Sigma Tau, Phi Lambda Upsilon, Omega Chi Epsilon. Club: Lions. Office: Dept Chem Engring Mich State U East Lansing MI 48824

ANDERSON, DONALD KENNEDY, JR., educator; b. Evanston, Ill., Mar. 18, 1922; s. Donald Kennedy and Kathryn Marie (Shields) A.; m. Kathleen Elizabeth Hughes, Sept. 11, 1949; children: David J., Lawrence W. A.B., Yale U., 1943; M.A., Northwestern U., 1947; Ph.D., Duke U., 1957. Instr. Geneva Coll., Beaver Falls, Pa., 1947-49; from instr. to asst. prof. Rose Poly. Inst., Terre Haute, Ind., 1952-58; asst. prof., assoc. prof. Butler U., Indpls., 1958-65; assoc. prof. U. Mo., Columbia, 1965-67, prof. dept. English, 1967—, assoc. dean Grad. Sch., 1970-74. Author: John Ford, 1972; editor: John Ford's Perkin Warbeck, 1965, John Ford's The Broken Heart, 1968. Served to lt. (j.g.) USNR, 1943-46. Folger fellow, 1965; U. Mo. Summer Research fellow, 1966, 68, 76, 79. Mem. MLA (midwest regional del. 1972-75), AAUP (sec.-treas. 1962-63). Democrat. Methodist. Home: 1309 Ridge Rd Columbia MO 65201 Office: Dept English U Mo Columbia MO 65211

ANDERSON, DONALD MILTON, diplomat; b. Sioux City, Iowa; s. Milton Ernest and Hazel Fern (Cunningham) A.; m. Blanche McGehee Snowden, July 2, 1954; children: Susan Snowden, Jeanne Katherine Anderson Hulit. B.A., La. State U., 1954. With Fgn. Service U.S. Dept. State, 1958—, vice consul, Hong Kong, 1962-65; staff Office Asian Communist Affairs, Dept. State, 1966-70; 2d sec. Am. Embassy, New Delhi, 1970-72, Paris, 1972-73; polit. counselor U.S. Liaison Office, Beijing, China, 1973-75; chief China reporting sect. U.S. Consulate Gen., Hong Kong, 1975-77; dep. U.S. rep. Office Micronesian Status Negotiations, Washington, 1977-78; dep. dir. Office People's Republic of China Affairs, Washington, 1978-80; dir. Office Chinese Affairs, 1983—; consul gen. U.S. Consulate Gen., Shanghai, China, 1980-83. Served to 1st lt. U.S. Army, 1955-57. Recipient Meritorious Honor award Dept. State, 1981; named La. State U. Hall of Distinction, 1982, Significant Sig Sigma Chi, 1983. Mem. Am. Fgn. Service Assn. Episcopalian. Home: 3050 Harrison St NW Washington DC 20015 Office: Dept State Washington DC 20520

ANDERSON, DONALD MORGAN, entomologist; b. Washington, Dec. 27, 1930; s. John Kenneth and Alice Cornelia (Morgan) A. B.A., Miami U., Oxford, Ohio, 1953; Ph.D., Cornell U.l, 1958. Grad. teaching asst. Cornell U., 1954-57; asst. prof. sci. SUNY-Buffalo, 1959-60, research fellow, 1960; research entomologist Dept. Agrl., Washington, 1960—; research assoc. Buffalo Mus. Sci., 1972—, Smithsonian Instn., 1978—. Contbr. articles to profl. jours. Sigma Xi grantee, 1959. Mem. Entomol. Soc. Washington (corr sec. 1963-65, pres.-elect 1984), Entomol. Soc. Am., Soc. Systematic Zoology, Coleopterists Co., Am. Inst. Biol. Scis., St. Andrews Soc. Washington, Clan Anderson Soc. (editor 1979—), Sigma Xi, Phi Kappa Phi. Home: 3701 Connecticut Ave NW Washington DC 20008 Office: Systematic Entomology Lab Dept Agr Nat Mus Natural History Washington DC 20560

ANDERSON, DONALD SUTHERLAND, business executive; b. Winnipeg, Man., Can., Sept. 21, 1913; s. James Wilson and Madeleine Caroline Mary (Chivers) A.; m. Margaret Richmond Stoddart, Aug. 16, 1941; children: Ian S., Jocelyn (Mrs. Roger A. Green), R. James. Grad. high sch. With Royal Bank of Can., Winnipeg, 1930—, various positions br. offices and supr.'s dept., 1930-41, mem. Canadian credits staff, Montreal, Que., 1941-45, asst. mgr. Winnipeg br., 1947-49, mgr. 3d St. br., Calgary, Alta., 1949-51, mgr. Calgary br., 1951-52, mgr. Toronto (Ont.) br., 1952-57, asst. gen. mgr. head office, 1957-58, asst. gen. mgr., Toronto, 1958-61, gen. mgr., Ont., 1961-64, v.p., dir., 1964-70, sr. v.p., dir., Toronto, 1970-71, dir., 1971—; chmn., chief exec. officer Metro Centre Devels. Ltd., 1971-75; chmn. Can. Realties Ltd., 1975—; dir. Slough Estates (Can.) Ltd., Denison Mines Ltd., Crum & Forster Can. Ltd., Herald Ins. Co., Continental Group Can. Ltd., Wheeling-Pitts. Steel Corp., Pitts., Algonquin Merc. Corp., Hardee Farms Internat., Inglis Ltd.; Mem., past pres. Bd. Trade Met. Toronto. Trustee Toronto Gen. Hosp.; nat. adv. bd. Boys Clubs Can. Served with Royal Canadian Army, 1942-45. Clubs: York, Toronto, Rosedale Golf (Toronto); Ranchmen's (Calgary); Manitoba (Winnipeg); The Goodwood; Lost Tree (Fla.); Ristigouche Salmon; Matapedia Royal and Ancient Golf of St. Andrews (Scotland). Home: 42 Arjay Crescent Willowdale ON Canada M2L 1C7

ANDERSON, DONNA KAY, musicologist; b. Underwood, N.D., Feb. 16, 1935; d. Freedolph E. and Olga (Mayer) A. Ph.D., Ind. U., 1966. Instr. piano MacPhail Sch. Music, 1956-59, Summit Sch., 1959-61; asst. prof. music history SUNY, Cortland, 1967-70, asso. prof., 1970-78, prof., 1978—, faculty research fellow, 1967-69. Author: Charles T. Griffes: An Annotated Bibliography-Discography, 1977, The Works of Charles T. Griffes: A Descriptive Catalogue, 1983; editor: Three Preludes for Piano, 1967, Four Impressions, 1970, Legend for Piano, 1972, De Profundis, 1978; editor, translator: Four German Songs, 1970. Summer grantee, 1972. Mem. Am. Musicol. Soc., Coll. Music Soc., Sonneck Soc., Music Library Assn., Mu Phi Epsilon, Pi Kappa Lambda, Delta Kappa Gamma. Office: 262 Music Dept SUNY Cortland NY 13045

ANDERSON, DOUGLAS MCDOUGALL, consultant; b. Jamestown, R.I., Dec. 1, 1918; s. James William and Miriam Ellen

(Hawkins) A.; m. Charlotte Hall, Dec. 29, 1945 (div. 1978); children: Deborah, Douglas, Jr., Carol, Craig. B.A., Harvard, 1941, M.B.A., 1948. Sr. asso. Bruce Payne & Assos., Westport, Conn., 1948-53; dir. mfg. ITT-Kellogg, Chgo., 1954-60; sr. v.p. Arthur D. Little, Cambridge, Mass., 1960—. Served with USNR, 1942-45. Home: 21 River Ln Duxbury MA 02332 Office: Arthur D Little Inc Acorn Park Cambridge MA 02140

ANDERSON, DUWAYNE MARLO, earth and polar scientist, university administrator; b. Lehi, Utah, Sept. 9, 1927; s. Duwayne LeRoy and Fern Francell (Fagan) A.; m. June B. Hodgin, Apr. 2, 1980; children by previous marriage: Lynna Nadine, Christopher Kent, Lesleigh Leigh. B.S., Brigham Young U., 1954; Ph.D. (Purdue Research Found. fellow), Purdue U., 1958. Prof. soil physics U. Ariz., Tucson, 1958-63; research scientist, chief earth scis. br. (Cold Regions Research and Engring. Lab.), Hanover, N.H., 1963-76; chief scientist, div. polar programs NSF, Washington, 1976-78, mem. Viking sci. team, 1969-76; dean faculty natural scis. and math. SUNY, Buffalo, 1978-84; univ. assoc. provost for research Tex. A&M U., College Station, 1984—; Pegrum lectr. SUNY, 1980; cons. NASA, 1964—, NSF, 1979—; sr. U.S. rep., Antarctica, 1976, 77, vis. prof., lectr. numerous univs. Editor: (with O.B. Andersland) Geotechnical Engineering for Cold Regions, 1978; Cons. editor: Soil Sci, 1965—, (with O.B. Andersland) Cold Regions Sci. and Tech, 1978-82; Contbr. numerous sci. and tech. articles to profl. jours. Bd. dirs. Ford K. Sayre Meml. Ski Council, Hanover, 1969-71; bd. dirs. Grafton County Fish and Game Assn., 1965—, pres., 1968-70; bd. dirs. Hanover Conservation Council, 1970-76, v.p., 1970-73; bd. dirs. Buffalo Mus. Sci., 1980-84, v.p., 1982-84. Served in USAF, 1946-49. Recipient Sci. Achievement award Cold Regions Research and Engring. Lab., 1968; Sec. of Army Research fellow, 1966. Fellow Am. Soc. Agronomy; mem. Internat. Glaciological Soc., Am. Polar Soc., Am. Geophys. Union, AAAS, Soil Sci. Soc. Am., Niagara Frontier Assn. Research and Devel. Dirs. (pres. 1983-84), Sigma Xi, Sigma Gamma Epsilon. Republican. Home: 8720 Bent Tree Dr College Station TX 77841 Office: Office of Provost Tex A&M U College Station TX 77843

ANDERSON, E. KARL, lawyer; b. Huntington, W. Va., Mar. 30, 1931; s. Earle Karl and Helen Emerie (Johnson) A.; m. Mary Elizabeth Williams, Nov. 13, 1953; children—Sharon Elizabeth, Charles Wesley. B.B.A., So. Methodist U., 1953, LL.B., 1960. Bar: Tex. bar 1960. Field supr. Travelers Ins. Co., Dallas, 1956-57; claim mgr. Allstate Ins. Co., Dallas, 1958-62; practiced in, Dallas, 1963—; partner firm Lastelick, Anderson and Hilliard, 1968—. Served with USAF, 1954-56. Mem. Am. Bar Assn., Dallas Assn. Trial Lawyers (dir. 1964-65, 74-75), Tex. Trial Lawyers Assn., Assn. Trial Lawyers Am., Delta Theta Phi, Sigma Iota Epsilon, Sigma Alpha Epsilon. Presbyn. Club: Dallas Country. Home: 4549 Belclaire Dallas TX 75205 Office: 1st Tex Bank Bldg Dallas TX 75229

ANDERSON, EDITH HELEN, nursing school administrator; b. N.J., June 3, 1927. B.S., Manhattanville Coll., 1951; M.A., N.Y. U., 1958, Ph.D., 1963. Staff nurse Halloran VA Hosp., S.I., N.Y., 1948-49; camp nurse Ten Mile River camp Boy Scouts Am., N.Y., 1949; pub. health nurse Vis. Nurse Assn., Elizabeth, N.J., 1950-54, Community Service Soc., N.Y.C., 1954-56; instr. practical nursing program Elizabeth (N.J.) Bd. Edn., 1956-58; teaching fellow grad. program in parent-child nursing N.Y. U., 1958-60, asst. prof., dir. grad. program in parent-child nursing, 1960-64; acting chief nursing sect. Children's Bur., Social and Rehab. Service, HEW, Washington, 1967-68; nursing edn. cons. Nursing Sect. Children's Bur., Welfare Adminstrn., 1964-69; dean Sch. Nursing, Coll. Health Scis. and Social Welfare, U. Hawaii, Honolulu, 1969-76; dean coll. nursing U. Del., Newark, 1976—; Cons. P.R. Dept. Health, U. P.R., 1963, V.I. Dept. Health, 1964, Inst. Tech. Interchange East-West Center, U. Hawaii; tchr./trainer field tng. program Provincial Health Dept., Republic of China, Taiwan, 1969, tchr./trainer Tb control, Ryukya Islands, Inst. Tech. Interchange, East-West Center, Lyndon B. Johnson Tropical Med. Center, Am. Samoa, 1970, 71; mem. med. adv. bd. VA Hosp., Elsmere, Del., 1977—; mem. Del. State Coordinating Health Council, 1978-84. Author: Commitment to Child Health, 1967, (with others) Maternity Care in the United States: Gains and Gaps, 1966, Current Concepts in Clinical Nursing, Vol. I, 1967, Vol. II, 1969, Vol. III, 1971, Vol. IV, 1973. Fellow Am. Acad. Nursing; mem. Am. Nurses Assn., Hawaii Nurses Assn. (editor mag. 1973-75, chmn. publicity com. 1973-75), Nat. League Nursing (chmn. maternal child nursing sect. So. region 1965, chairperson bd. rev. of accreditation 1980-81), Hawaii League Nursing (1st v.p. 1973), Mid-Atlantic Regional Nursing Assn. (1st governing bd. 1981, v.p. 1982-83), Pi Lambda Theta, Sigma Theta Tau. Home: 1403 Shallcross Ave Hamilton House Apt 502 Wilmington DE 19806 *

ANDERSON, EDWIN JOHN, profl. football exec.; b. Rockford, Ill., Aug. 3, 1902; s. John A. and Emma (Wallin) A.; m. Isabelle B. Bort, Mar. 31, 1928; children—Suzanne Jane (Mrs. Harold J. Stenglein, Jr.) (dec.), Marynell (Mrs. Richard G. Williams). A.B., Beloit (Wis.) Coll., 1927. Advt. mgr. ABC Washing Machine Co., Peoria, Ill., 1927; with Goebel Brewing Co., Detroit, 1938—, pres., 1941-58, Goebel Brewing Co. of Cal., Oakland; dir., mem. adv. bd. Kemper Co.; pres., gen. mgr. dir. Detroit Lions Football Co., 1949-62, exec. v.p., 1962-73, sr. v.p., 1973—. Former mem. bd. dirs. Detroit Community Fund, United Found., Detroit Bd. Commerce, Met. Bldg. Com. of Detroit; past pres. Children's Hosp. of Mich., Birmingham Community House. Episcopalian. Clubs: Detroit Athletic, Bloomfield Hills Country, Detroit (Detroit); Seven Lakes Country, Racquet (Palm Springs, Calif.). Home: 2945 N Woodward Ave Apt 62 Bloomfield Hills MI 48013 Office: Detroit Lions Inc Pontiac MI 48057

ANDERSON, EILEEN RUTH, mayor; b. Bell, Calif., Oct. 18, 1928; d. Elmer E. and Ellen S. (Martini) Pulling; m. Clifford F. Anderson, Oct. 10, 1950; children: Mark Alexander, Patricia Maulani Anderson Dauterman, Lorita Ellen Anderson Naipo. Student, UCLA, 1946-47; B.A., U. Hawaii, 1950, postgrad., 1972-73. Personnel technician Dept. Personnel Services State of Hawaii, 1956-61, mgmt. analyst Dept. Budget and Fin., 1961-64, tech. cons. Pub. Employees Compensation Appeals Bd., 1964-54, legis. analyst Office of Legis. Auditor, 1966-70, program evaluation analyst Dept. Budget and Fin., 1970-72, acting chief Program Evaluation Br., 1972-73, chief Budget Planning and Mgmt. div. Dept. Budget and Fin., 1974, dir. fin. Dept. Budget and Fin., 1974-80; personnel mgmt. services technican Dept. Civil Service City and County of Honolulu, 1965-66; legis. analyst Office of Council Services State of Hawaii, 1973-74, mayor, 1981—. Den mother Aloha council Boy Scouts Am., 1961-62; sec. Kaneohe Little League, 1962-63; asst. leader Aloha council Girl Scouts U.S.A., 1963-64; mem. altar guild Calvary Episcopal Ch., 1970-73; mem. budget and allocations com. Aloha United Way, 1978-79; mem. adv. council Liliuokalani Trust, 1979-80; active Honolulu Symphony, ARC, Hawaii Muscular Dystrophy Assn., Citizens Against Noise, Kaneohe Community Sr. Citizen Council, Hawaii Mental Health Assn., others. Named Woman of Yr. for 1980 Hawaii Bus. Mag., 1981. Mem. U.S. Conf. Mayors, Nat. Acad Pub. Adminstrn., Bus. and Profl. Women's Assn., Honolulu com. on Fgn. Relations, Women in Acad. Adminstrn. Program, Ala Moana Jaycees, Hawaiian Businessmen's Assn., Kaimuki Businessmen and Profl. Assn. Democrat. Clubs: Oahu Country, Waialae Country, Plaza, Honolulu, Hawaii Yacht, Kaneohe Yacht. Office: City and County of Honolulu 530 S King St Honolulu HI 96813

ANDERSON, ELLIS B., drug company executive; b. Michigan City, Ind., Aug. 30, 1926; s. A.B. and Esther (Nicholson) A.; m. Adrienne Scotchbrook, Aug. 6, 1955; children: Rebecca J., Katherine V. A.B. cum laude, Ind. U., 1949, J.D., 1952; grad., Advanced Mgmt. Program, Harvard U., 1970. Bar: Ind. bar 1952. Partner firm Butt, Bowers & Anderson, Evansville, Ind., 1952-60; with Baxter Labs. Inc., Morton Grove, Ill., 1961-65; sr. v.p., gen. counsel, dir., mem. exec. com. Hoffmann-La Roche Inc., Nutley, N.J., from 1965. Served with AUS, World War II. Mem. Phi Beta Kappa. Club: Nassau. Home: 52 Elm Rd Princeton NJ 08540 Office: 340 Kingsland St Nutley NJ 07110

ANDERSON, ELMER EBERT, physics educator; b. Ottawa, Ill., June 28, 1922; s. Oscar Elmer and Ruth (Ebert) A.; m. Amelia Gabriel, Oct. 30, 1943; children: Kenneth, Mark, Scott, Ruth, Carl; m. Diane Cayey, July 22, 1976; children: Sven, Kurt. A.B., Occidental Coll., 1950; M.S., U. Ill., 1956; Ph.D., U. Md., 1964. Instr. Deep Springs Coll., 1952-53, dean, 1953-55; teaching asst. U. Ill., 1955-57; research physicist Electromagnetics div. U.S. Naval Ordnance Lab., White Oak, Md., 1957-62, div. chief, 1962-65; asso. prof. physics Clarkson Coll. Tech., 1965-68, prof., 1968-77, chmn. dept., 1966-74, dean Arts and Scis., 1974-76; prof. physics, dean sci. and humanities Ind. U.-Purdue U., Fort Wayne, Ind., 1977-79; v.p. acad. affairs U. Ala., Huntsville, 1979—, prof. physics, 1979—. Author: Modern Physics and Quantum Mechanics, 1971, Introduction to Modern Physics, 1981; contbr. articles to profl. jours. Served with USN, 1940-46, 50-52; comdr. Res. ret. Fulbright-Hayes lectr., Turkey, 1972-73. Fellow Am. Phys. Soc., Am. Assn. Physics Tchrs; mem. Sigma Xi, Phi Kappa Phi, Sigma Pi Sigma. Home: 3220 Monarch Dr SW Huntsville AL 35801

ANDERSON, ERIC WILLIAM, food service company executive; b. Woburn, Mass., Aug. 15, 1923; s. Eric and Valborg A.; m. Freda M. Shaw, Sept. 17, 1948; children: Deborah Jean, Karen Ellen, Patricia Lynn, Lesa Mary. B.S. in Bus. Adminstrn, Boston U., 1948; LL.B., Suffolk U., 1953. Bar: Mass. bar 1953. Staff accountant Flaherty Bliss & Co., Boston, 1948-50; office mgr. Alfred J. Thibeault, Inc., Arlington, Mass., 1950-52; staff accountant Gordon E. Brennan & Co., Arlington, 1952-53; controller Emerson & Cuming, Inc., Canton, Mass., 1953-65; v.p., treas. Friendly Ice Cream Corp., Wilbraham, Mass., 1965—; dir. Park West Bank & Trust Co. Corporator Bay State Med. Center, 1972-78; bd. dirs. Springfield (Mass.) YMCA, 1978—, Springfield Orch. Assn., 1982—; bd. govs. Nat. Assn. Securities Dealers, 1976-78. Served with AUS, World War II. Decorated Bronze Star medal, Purple Heart. Mem. Fin. Execs. Inst. Club: Masons. Home: 226 Monson Rd Wilbraham MA 01095 Office: 1855 Boston Rd Wilbraham MA 01095

ANDERSON, ERNEST LEROY, lumber co. exec.; b. Logan, Utah, Aug. 11, 1910; s. Anthon Edward and Nora (Egbert) A.; m. Grace Rasmussen, Sept. 8, 1936; children—Robert Monte, Kristen Anderson Bennett, Ross Carl. B.S., Utah State U., 1937. With Anderson Lumber Co., 1929—, pres., chief exec. officer, Ogden, Utah, 1963-79, chmn. bd., 1979—; mgr. Pioneer Wholesale Supply Co., 1960-61, chmn. bd., 1979—; pres. Bonneville Lumber Co.; adv. bd. No. div. First Security Bank Utah; mem. nat. adv. council, mem. bus. partners program Utah State U., Logan. Pres. Logan C. of C., 1954; chmn. Logan City Planning Commn., 1957. Mem. Nat. Lumber Dealers Assn. (dir. 1974-75), Intermountain Lumber Dealers Assn. (dir. 1951-54), Mountain States Lumber Dealers Assn. (pres. 1967), Odgen C. of C. (treas. 1966), Old Main Soc. (past pres.; mem. president's club), Sigma Chi (life), Alpha Kappa Psi. Republican. Mormon. Clubs: Rotary (past pres. Logan), Ogden Golfand Country; Ambassador Athletic (Salt Lake City). Home: 4130 Skyline Dr Ogden UT 84403 Office: First Security Bank Bldg Ogden UT 84403

ANDERSON, ERNEST WASHINGTON, mfg. co. exec.; b. Corydon, Ind., Feb. 22, 1922; s. Roscoe Irvin and Orpah (Dick) A.; m. Jeanne Elizabeth Schoonover, July 12, 1944; children—Thomas, Carol, Steven, Jane. B.S., Ind. U., 1943. With Gen. Motors Corp., Detroit, 1948-52; with Fed.-Mogul Corp., Detroit, 1952—. Also v.p., sec. Advisory bd. Providence Hosp.; bd. dirs. Citizens Research Council Mich. Served to capt. AUS, 1943-48. Mem. Tax Execs. Inst. (nat. v.p., treas., dir., chpt. pres.), NAM, U.S. C. of C., Fin. Execs. Inst., Am. Soc. Corp. Secs., Mich. C. of C., Southfield C. of C. Clubs: Detroit Athletic, Economic, Orchard Lake Country. Home: 434 Whippers-in Ct Bloomfield Hills MI 48013 Office: PO Box 1966 Detroit MI 48235

ANDERSON, EUGENE I., auto parts co. exec.; b. Crothersville, Ind., Oct. 5, 1917; s. Irving and Grace (Rawlings) A.; m. Rosemary Tulley, Oct. 9, 1941; children—David E., John F., Carol, Judy J. B.S. in Indsl. Engring, Purdue U., 1939. Indsl. engr. Goodyear Tire & Rubber Co., Akron, O., 1939-43, P.R. Mallory Co., Indpls., 1946-47; indsl. engr., plant mgr., works mgr., gen. mgr., exec. v.p., pres., now chmn., dir. Arvin Industries; dir. Irwin Union Bank & Trust Co., Columbus, Ind. Gas. Co., Indpls. Served with USNR, 1943-46. Home: 4011 Shoshonee Dr Columbus IN 47203 Office: 1531 E 13th St Columbus IN 47201

ANDERSON, EUGENE NEWTON, educator; b. Tehuacana, Tex., July 24, 1900; s. Jesse and Luda Lee (Newton) A.; m. Pauline Relyea, June 25, 1932; 1 son, Eugene Newton. A.B., U. Colo., 1921; Ph.D., U. Chgo., 1928; postgrad., U. Berlin, 1924-25. Instr. U. Chgo., 1925-32, asst. prof. European history, 1932-36; prof. European history Am. U., Washington, 1936-41; coordinator info., 1941-42; with Office Strategic Services, 1942-45; asst. chief div. cultural cooperation Dept. State, Washington, 1945, assoc. chief German-Austrian activities div., occupied areas, 1946-47; expert on humanities in German and Austrian univs. War Dept. and Am. Council Learned Socs., summer 1949; prof. European history U. Nebr., 1947-55, UCLA, 1955-68, emeritus prof., 1968—; vis. prof. U. Calif.-Santa Barbara, 1968-70; faculty Peshawar U., West Pakistan, summer 1961. Author: The First Moroccan Crisis: 1904-06, 1930, Nationalism and the Cultural Crisis in Prussia: 1806-15, 1939, The Humanities in the German and Austrian Universities, 1950, Process versus Power, 1952, The Prussian Elections of 1862 and 1863, 1954, The Social and Political Conflict in Prussia, 1858-64, 1954; Modern Europe in World Perspective, 1958; European Issues in the 20th Century, 1958; co-author: Political Institutions and Social Change in Continental Europe in the 19th Century, 1968; co-editor: Medieval and Historiographical Essays in Honor of J.W. Thompson, 1940; co-author: Europe in the 19th Century: A Documentary Analysis, 2 vols., 1961; co-editor, co-translator: Eckart Kehr, Battleship Building and Party Politics in Germany, 1894-1901, 1975; bd. editors: Jour. Modern History, 1952-55. Served with U.S. Army, 1918. Social Sci. Research fellow, 1930-31, 37. Mem. AAUP, Am. Hist. Assn. (chmn. program com. 1939), Phi. Beta Kappa, Phi Delta Theta. Presbyterian. Home: 552 Pintura Dr Santa Barbara CA 93111 Office: Dept Asian Studies U Calif Riverside Riverside CA 92521

ANDERSON, EUGENE ROBERT, lawyer; b. Portland, Oreg., Oct. 24, 1927; s. Andrew E. and Ruth Beatrice (White) A.; m. Hildegard M. Bleibtreu, Nov. 26, 1955; children—Matthew, Martin. B.S., UCLA, 1949; attended, Oreg. State Coll., 1945; J.D., Harvard U., 1952; LL.M., N.Y. U., 1960. Bar: N.Y. bar 1953, Mass., So. and Eastern dists. N.Y., Second Circuit, D.C. Circuit, U.S. Ct. Claims, U.S. Supreme Ct. bars 1953. Asso. firm Chadbourne, Parke, Whiteside & Wolff, N.Y.C., 1953-61, partner, 1965-69; asst. U.S. atty. So. Dist. N.Y., Foley Square, 1961-65, chief civil div., 1963-65; ptnr. firm Anderson Russell Kill & Olick (P.C.), N.Y.C., 1969—; asst. dist. atty. N.Y. County, 1977; dir. Keene Corp., N.Y.C., Am. Brands, Inc., White Cap Inc., Lester, Pa.; Spl. hearing officer U.S. Dept. Justice, 1965-68; arbitrator Am. Arbitration Assn., 1965—, Small Claims Ct., 1970-76; mem. com. on trial practice and technique Second Circuit, 1967-73. Mem. St. George's Ch., vestryman, 1966-68. Served with AUS, 1946. Mem. Assn. Bar City N.Y., Fed., Am. bar assns., Police Athletic League (dir., gen. counsel). Home: 64 Round Hill Rd Scarsdale NY 10583 Office: 666 3d Ave New York NY 10017

ANDERSON, FLETCHER NEAL, chemical executive; b. Kansas City, Mo., Nov. 5, 1930; s. Chester Gustav and Astrid Cecilia (Crone) A.; m. Marilyn Lucille Henke; children: Karl C., Keith F., Susan L. B.S. in Chem. Engring., U. Mo., Columbia, 1951; M.S., Washington U., St. Louis, 1956; grad. exec. program, Stanford U., 1972. Registered profl. engr., Mo., Pa. With Mallinckrodt, Inc., St. Louis, 1951-81, group v.p. food, drug and cosmetic chems. div., 1974-76, group v.p. chem. group, 1976-78, sr. v.p. chem. group, 1978-81, also dir.; pres., dir. Chomerics, Inc., Woburn, Mass. Adv. com. Engring. Sch., U. Mo., Columbia, 1978—; Mem. Florissant (Mo.) Charter Commn., 1961-63. Recipient Disting. Service to Engring. award U. Mo., Columbia, 1978. Mem. Am. Inst. Chem. Engrs. Lutheran. Club: Brae Burn Country.

ANDERSON, FLOYD EDWARD, author, newspaperman; b. Superior, Wis., July 15, 1906; s. John Elmer and Paula (Hagen) A.; m. Joy Eder, Oct. 29, 1932; children—Joan (Mrs. J. Anderson Holleman), Peter, Thomas, Martin, Joseph, Mary Teresa (Mrs. J. Fred Carey), Stephen. Editorial asst. Am. mag., N.Y.C., 1932-36; engaged in pvt. bus., 1936-45; sales mgr. Am. Press, N.Y.C., 1945-48; mng. editor Catholic Light, Scranton, Pa., 1948-51, Advocate, Newark, 1951-61, Register system of papers, Denver, 1961-62, Central Calif. Register, Fresno, 1962-63; dir. NC News Service (U.S. Catholic Conf.), Washington, 1963-69; v.p. Internat. Fedn. Cath. Press Agys., 1968-69; editor The New World, Chgo., 1969-76; mem. adv. bd. Arlington (Va.) Cath. Herald, 1976—, dir., 1977—. Author: The Bishop's Boy, 1957, Father of the American Navy, 1959, Father Baker, 1960, Gold Rush Bishop, 1962, The Birth Control Encyclical, 1969; Co-author: 1683-1982: The Anders Gustaf Andersson Family; Editor: Council Daybook, Vatican II, sessions 1 and 2, 1965, session 3, 1965, session 4, 1966. Bd. dirs. Pederson Family Assn., 1977-79, 81—. Recipient award Cath. War Vets, N.J., 1956; decorated knight of St. Gregory, 1959. Mem. Cath. Press Assn. (bd. dirs. 1954-63, sec. 1954-59, v.p. 1959-61, pres. 1961-63, St. Francis de Sales award 1963), Internat. Fedn. Dirs. Cath. Publs. (v.p. 1967-69), Internat. Cath. Fedn. Newspapers and Pubs. (v.p. 1971-76). Home: 8016 Bethelen Woods Ln Springfield VA 22153

ANDERSON, FRED WOODROW WILSON, educator; b. Lisco, Nebr., June 14, 1918; s. George Washington and Etta (Smith) A.; m. Mary Louella Lindsay, Aug. 29, 1942; children—Barbara Elaine, Lorraine Sue. B.S., Nebr. State Coll., Chadron, 1940; M.A., U. Nebr., 1949, Ed.D., 1959. Tchr., coach Cairo (Nebr.) pub. schs., 1940-41; prin., tchr. Alma (Nebr.) pub. schs., 1941, Walton (Nebr.) consol. schs., 1946; supt. schs., Cairo, 1946-51, Cambridge, Nebr., 1951-60; dean, prin. Jefferson County (Colo.) schs., 1960-62; prof. edn. So. State Coll., Springfield, S.D., 1962-64, dir. student personnel, 1963-64; vis. instr. Black Hills State Coll., Spearfish, S.D., summers 1959-62, prof. edn., chmn. div. edn. and psychology, 1964—; Mem. S.D. Commn. Tchr. Edn. and Profl. Standards, 1964-67, S.D. Com. Evaluation Tchr. Edn. Programs, 1966-67. Served with USMCR, 1942-46. Mem. Nat. Edn. Assn., Nebr. Edn. Assn. (treas. dist. V 1958), Furnas County Edn. Assn. (sec. 1953, pres. 1959), Am. Legion (past post comdr.), Black Hills State Coll. Edn. Assn. (pres. 1967-68). Methodist (chmn. ofcl. bd. 1967-68). Clubs: Rotarian (pres. Cambridge 1953), Mason, Shriner. Home: 1311 W Jackson St Spearfish SD 57783

ANDERSON, FREDERICK RANDOLPH, JR., lawyer, legal educator; b. Rutherfordton, N.C., June 28, 1941; s. Frederick Randolph and Ophelia (Meeler) A.; m. Ann Clyde Hart, May 31, 1980. B.A. with highest honors (Morehead Scholar, Nat. Merit Scholar), U. N.C., 1963, Oxford (Eng.) U., 1965; J.D., Harvard U., 1968. Bar: D.C. 1969. Teaching fellow Harvard U., Cambridge, Mass., 1966-68; staff assoc. Nat. Acad. Engring., Washington, 1969-70; editor-in-chief Environ. Law Reporter, Washington, 1970-73; exec. dir. Environ. Law Inst., Washington, 1973-78, pres., 1978-80, bd. dirs., 1980—; prof. law U. Utah Coll. Law, Salt Lake City, 1980—; adj. prof. law George Washington U. Nat. Law Center, 1970-74; vis. prof. law Duke U. Law Sch., Spring 1977, U. Utah Sch. Law, summer 1979; mem. panel on high-level radioactive waste disposal Nat. Acad. Scis., 1979—, mem. congressional study of common law relief for hazardous waste injuries, 1980-82. Author: NEPA in the Courts, 1973, Environmental Improvement Through Economic Incentives, 1978, Environmental Law and Policy, 1984; contbg. author: Federal Environmental Law, 1974, Occupational and Environmental Health, 1982. Bd. dirs. W.Va. Highlands Conservancy, 1970-73; Ford Found.-U.S. Office Edn. fellow, 1968-69. Mem. ABA (standing com. on environ. law 1973—), Am. Bar Assn. (chmn. 1980—), Internat. Soc. Environ. Law, Adminstrv. Conf. of U.S., Am. Law Inst. Club: Univ. (Washington). Office: Coll Law U Utah Salt Lake City UT 84112

ANDERSON, GEORGE FREDERICK, educator, former association executive; b. Buffalo, Sept. 15, 1914; s. Gustaf Edmund and Harriett Manelva (Paulding) A.; m. Julia Jane Ackley, Nov. 26, 1942; children: Lois A. Ezell, Cheri A. Goodson. B.S., SUNY, Cortland, 1940; M.S., Syracuse U., 1947, Ed.D., 1950. Tchr. phys. edn., coach, vice prin. Gorham (N.Y.) Central Sch., 1940-43; instr. Syracuse U., 1947-48, dual prof. liberal arts and edn., 1948-51; asso. exec. sec. Am. Alliance Health, Phys. Edn., Recreation and Dance, Washington, 1951-74, exec. v.p., 1974-80, dir., 1974-80; ret., 1980; dir. Center for Ednl. Assns., 1974-80. Contbr. articles to profl. jours. Served with USNR, 1943-46. Mem. NEA (life), Am. Alliance Health, Phys. Edn., Recreation and Dance (life), Am. Soc. Assn. Execs., Soc. State Dirs. of Health, Phys. Edn. and Recreation. Republican. Lutheran. Home: 10408 Gatewood Terr Silver Spring MD 20903 *Good fortune, sound judgement, and hard work are the basic ingredients of financial success, but only when they are combined with honesty and integrity do they produce the personal success one needs to cope with today's stress.*

ANDERSON, GEORGE HARDING, broadcasting company executive; b. Buffalo, Mar. 6, 1931; s. Gordon and Adeline (Harding) A.; m. Sandra Bradley, Aug. 24, 1957 (div. 1972); 1 son, Geoffrey Bradley; m. Barbara Rich Tisdole, Jan. 18, 1974. B.A., Harvard, 1954. With First Nat. Bank Boston, 1955-58, Randolph Assos., Wellesley, Mass., 1959-61; pres. Precision Products Co. Inc., Waltham, Mass., 1961-64; sales mgr. WBZ-TV, Boston, 1964-66; office mgr. Blair Radio, Boston, 1966-67; sales mgr. WHDH-TV, Boston, 1967-68; exec. v.p., dir. Guy Gannett Broadcasting Services, Sta. WGAN-AM-FM-TV, Portland, Maine, Sta. WHYN-AM-FM-TV, Springfield, Mass., Sta. WINZ-AM-FM, Miami, Fla., 1968-78; pres. Sta. KENS-TV, San Antonio, 1980—; pres., chief operating officer Harte-Hanks TV Group, 1981—; corp. v.p. Harte-Hanks Communications, 1981—; dir. WTLV, Jacksonville, Fla., 1978—, Maine Nat. Bank, Southworth Machine Co. Pres. Maine Audubon Soc., 1971, Portland Soc. Natural History, 1971; maj. Portland United Fund Drive, 1971, advance gifts chmn., 1972; co-chmn. fund drive Edward Waters Coll., 1979; Bd. dirs. Maine Cancer Soc., Jacksonville United Way, 1979—, San Antonio Red Cross, 1981—; vice chmn. San Antonio Red Cross, 1983—; Bd. dirs. S.W. Tex. Blood Bank. Served with USAF, 1951-53.

Mem. New Eng. Broadcasters (bd. dirs.), Jacksonville C. of C. (bd. dirs. 1979—). Clubs: Harvard (Boston); Harvard Varsity, Owl (Cambridge, Mass.); University. Home: 725 College Blvd San Antonio TX 78209 Office: Sta KENS PO Box 5 San Antonio TX 78299

ANDERSON, GEORGE LEE (SPARKY ANDERSON), profl. baseball team mgr.; b. Bridgewater, S.D., Feb. 22, 1934. Profl. baseball player Phila. Phillies, 1959; mgr. Cin. Reds, 1970-78, Detroit Tigers, 1979—. Named Nat. League Mgr. of Year, 1972. Winner Nat. League championship, 1970, 72, 75, 76; mgr. Nat. League All Star Team, 1971, 73, 76, 77. Office: care Detroit Tigers Tiger Stadium Detroit MI 48216 *

ANDERSON, GEORGE MCCULLOUGH, III, financial consulting company executive; b. Balt., Oct. 16, 1935; s. George McCullough and Sophie (Miller) A.; m. Phoebe N. Matthews, June 14, 1980; children: Kristina, Susan, George. B.A., Yale U., 1958; M.B.A., U. Pa., 1960. Asst. v.p. Mellon Nat. Bank & Trust Co., Pitts., 1960-68; v.p. corp. services Equitable Trust Co., Balt., 1968-78; v.p., sec. Equitable Bancorp., Balt., 1972-78; pres. 1st Nat. Bank of Georgetown, Del., 1978-81, P&G Anderson, Inc. (cons. to fin. instns.), Phila., 1981—. Presbyterian. Clubs: Maryland, L'Hirondelle. Home: PO Box 78 Bethel DE 19931 Office: P&G Anderson Inc 8611 Germantown Ave Box 27564 Philadelphia PA 19118

ANDERSON, GEORGE ROSS, JR., fed. judge; b. Anderson, S.C., Jan. 29, 1929; s. George Ross and Eva Mae (Pooler) A.; m. Dorothy M. Downie, Dec. 2, 1951; 1 son, G. Ross. B.Comml. Sci., Southeastern U., 1949; postgrad., George Washington U., 1949-51; LL.B., U. S.C., 1954. Bar: S.C. bar 1954. Mem. identification div. FBI, Washington, 1945-47; clk. to U.S. Senator Olin D. Johnston, Washington, 1947-51, Columbia, S.C., 1953-54; individual practice law, Anderson, S.C., 1954-79; U.S. dist. judge Dist. of S.C., Greenville, 1980—. Asst. editor: U. S.C. Law Rev, 1953-54. Bd. dirs. Salvation Army, 1968, YMCA, 1968-79, Anderson Youth Assn., 1978-80. Served with USAF, 1951-52. Fellow Internat. Acad. Trial Lawyers (dir. 1979-81), Internat. Soc. Barristers; mem. S.C. Bar Assn. (dir. 1977-80, past circuit v.p.), Am. Bar Assn., Assn. Trial Lawyers Am. (bd. govs. 1969-71), S.C. Trial Lawyers Assn. (v.p. 1970-71, pres. 1971-72), Ga. Trial Lawyers Assn., Am. Assn. Forensic Scientists. Democrat. Baptist. Office: US Courthouse and Fed Bldg 315 S McDuffie St Anderson SC 29621

ANDERSON, GERALD EDWIN, utilities executive; b. Boston, Apr. 9, 1931; s. Clarence Gustav and Lela Pauline (Kelley) A.; m. Mary Elizabeth Iverson, May 21, 1955; children: Todd K., Timothy J., Kristin E. A.A., Worthington (Minn.) Jr. Coll., 1950; B.B.A., U. Minn., 1952. C.P.A., Minn. Staff accountant, audit mgr. Arthur Andersen & Co., Mpls., 1953-65; asst. comptroller Commonwealth Energy System (formerly New Eng. Gas & Electric Assn.), Cambridge, Mass., 1966, system comptroller, 1967-71, v.p., comptroller, 1971-72, treas. parent co., financial v.p. system, 1972-74, pres., 1974—, chief exec. officer, 1975—; trustee parent co.; also dir. operating subsidiaries Commonwealth Energy System; dir. Algonquin Gas Transmission Co., Bay Bank Harvard Trust Co., Liberty Mut. Ins. Co., Edison Electric Inst., New Eng. Council, Inc. Mem. town finance com., Carlisle, Mass., 1968-73, chmn., 1972-73. Served to 1st lt. USAF, 1952-53. Mem. Am. Inst. C.P.A., Mass., Minn. socs. C.P.A., Financial Execs. Inst., Beta Alpha Psi, Beta Gamma Sigma. Lutheran. Club: Algonquin. Home: Hornbeam Ln Centerville MA 02632 Office: 675 Massachusetts Ave Cambridge MA 02139

ANDERSON, GERALD LESLIE, steel industry financial executive; b. Washington, May 24, 1940; s. Paul Hash and Edith (Hathaway) A.; m. Margaret Marie Curley, June 8, 1974; children: Paul Charles, Laura Marie. B.S. in Indsl. Mgmt, Carnegie Mellon U., 1961, M.S. in Indsl. Adminstrn, 1962. Econ. analyst Sun Oil Co., Phila., 1962-66; asst. treas. Selas Corp. Am., Dresher, Pa., 1966-74; treas. Midrex Corp., Charlotte, N.C., 1974-76; v.p., treas. Korf Industries, Inc., Charlotte, 1976—. Mem. Fin. Execs. Inst., Tax Execs. Inst., Am. Mgmt. Assn., Delta Tau Delta. Republican. Presbyterian. Home: 3625 Pickwick Ln Charlotte NC 28211 Office: 1 NCNB Plaza Charlotte NC 28280

ANDERSON, GLENN ELWOOD, investment banker; b. Asheville, N.C., July 24, 1914; s. James Garrett and Lottie Lee (Alexander) A.; m. Grace Elizabeth Curtis, Oct. 10, 1936; children: Glenn Elwood, Charlotte A. Straney. A.B., Duke U., 1934. With Kirchofer & Arnold, Inc. (and successor firm); Carolina Securities Corp., Raleigh, N.C., 1934—, beginning as sec., successively v.p., dir., asst. to pres. and dir., exec. v.p. and dir., 1934-55, pres., dir., 1955-81, chmn., chief exec. officer, dir., 1981—; dir. Investors Mgmt. Corp., Raleigh, N.C.; Natural Gas Corp., Fayetteville, N.C., NCNG Exploration Corp., Cape Fear Energy Corp., Golden Corral Corp., Raleigh; dir. Securities Investor Protection Corp., 1971-78. Past v.p. United Fund of Raleigh and Wake County.; Trustee Rex Hosp., Raleigh. Mem. Nat. Assn. Securities Dealers (bd. govs. 1958-60, chmn. bus. conduct com. 1959, chmn. bd. 1960), Investment Bankers Assn. Am. (chmn. southeastern group 1962, bd. govs. 1967-69), Securities Dealers Carolinas (organizer, 1st pres.), Sigma Phi Epsilon. Methodist. Clubs: Raleigh-Durham Bond (past pres.); Capital City (past gov.), Sphinx (pres. 1965), Carolina Country (Raleigh)). Home: 121 Pasquotank Dr Raleigh NC 27609 Office: Carolina Securities Corp: P O Box 1071 Raleigh NC 27602

ANDERSON, GLENN MALCOLM, congressman; b. Los Angeles; m. Lee Dutton; children: Melinda (Mrs. Ming Tang), Evan, Glenn Michael. B.A., UCLA. Mayor, Hawthorne, Calif., 1940-43; mem. Calif. Assembly from South Bay Area, Los Angeles, 1943-51; lt. gov., Calif., 1958-67; mem. 91st-98th congresses from 32d Dist. Calif.; mem. pub. works and transp. com., Mcht. Marine and fisheries com.; chmn. State Lands Commn., 1959-67; past mem. Commn. Califs., Calif. Council Urban Growth; past chmn. Calif. Interstate Cooperation Commn. Hon. life mem. PTA.; Regent U. Calif., 1959-67. Served with AUS, World War II. Mem. Secondary Sch. Adminstrs. Assn., Am. Legion, DAV, Amvets, Native Sons Golden West, Redmen, Hawthorne C. of C. Democrat. Clubs: Elks, Kiwanis. Office: 2329 Rayburn House Office Bldg Washington DC 20515 *

ANDERSON, GORDON CALDWELL, metal service center exec.; b. Sherbrook, Que., Can., Aug. 22, 1920; s. James and Euphemia (Pettigrew) A.; m. Marjorie Jane Welty, Feb. 2, 1944; children—Karen V., James D., Christine E., Thomas G., William R., David J. B.S., Northwestern U., Evanston, Ill., 1942. Regional mgr. Kaiser Aluminum & Chem. Sales, Inc., Oakland, Calif., 1946-52; chmn., dir. Fullerton Metals Co., Northbrook, Ill., 1952—. Trustee Fullerton Metals Found.; Vice pres. fund raising Northfield Community Fund; chmn. steel industry Scout-O-Ree Luncheon for Chgo. Boy Scouts Am., 1978. Served as 1st lt. U.S. Army, 1943-46. Mem. Nat. Assn. Alumnium Distbrs. (past pres.), Copper and Brass Servicenter Assn. (past pres.), Steel Service Inst. (chmn. exec. com.). Club: Sunset Ridge Country (past pres.). Home: 280 Maple Row Northbrook IL 60062 Office: 3000 Shermer Rd Northbrook IL 60062

ANDERSON, GORDON MACKENZIE, petroleum service contractors executive; b. Los Angeles, Mar. 25, 1932; s. Kenneth C.M. and Edith (King) A.; m. Elizabeth Ann Pugh, Mar. 21, 1959; children: Michael James, Greg Mark, Jeffrey Stevens. A.A., Glendale Coll., 1951; B.S., U. So. Calif., 1954; grad., Officers Candidate Sch., Newport, R.I., 1955; student, various Navy Schs. including CIC Sch. Mgr. Santa Fe Drilling Co., Chile, 1960-63, Libya, 1963-67, mgr. contracts adminstrn., Calif., 1967-70, pres., Orange, Calif., 1970—; sr. v.p., dir. Santa Fe Internat. Corp. Mem. adv. bd. U. So. Calif. Sch. Engring.; bd. dirs. St. Jude Hosp., Fullerton, Calif. Served to lt. (j.g.) USN, 1955-58. Mem. Young Pres.'s Orgn. (chmn. 1978-79), Internat. Assn. Oilwell Drilling Contractors (chmn. 1978-79). Office: PO Box 4000 Alhambra CA 91802

ANDERSON, GRACE MERLE, educator; b. London, Eng., Oct. 31; d. Ernest William and Nettie May (Harwood) A. B.A., McMaster U., 1961; M.A., 1964; Ph.D., U. Toronto, Ont., Can., 1971. Chemist Wolsey, Leicester, Eng., 1944-47; head chemist Wolsey of Can., Quebec City, Que., Can., 1947-50; chemist L. B. Holliday, Montreal, Que., 1950-53; mem. tech. staff Can. Baptist Overseas Mission, Costa Rica and Bolivia, 1954-60; asst. prof. sociology Acadia U., N.S., 1963-67; asso. prof. sociology and anthropology Wilfrid Laurier U., Waterloo, Ont., 1970-77, prof., 1977—; adj. prof. U. Waterloo, 1974—. Author: Town Lake Road: Urban Fringe Poverty in Nova Scotia, 1967, A Selected Bibliography on Portuguese Immigration, 1970, Networks of Contact: The Portuguese and Toronto, 1974, A Future to Inherit: Portuguese Communities in Canada, 1976, Non-Milk Cookbook, 1976, 2d edit., 1977, Spanish-Speaking Immigrants in Selected Canadian Cities, 1977. Fellow Am. Anthropol. Assn.; mem. Am. Sociol. Assn., Can. Assn. Sociology and Anthropology, Internat. Sociol. Assn., Can. Ethnic Studies Assn. Baptist. Office: 75 University Ave Waterloo ON N2L 3C5 Canada *Christian faith is the pivot of my life—it has prevented me from becoming easily discouraged.*

ANDERSON, GRANT THRALLS, lawyer; b. Portland, Oreg., Apr. 5, 1910; s. James Clifford and Nettie Avis (Thralls) A.; m. Mildred Lucille Shields, June 19, 1937 (dec. July 1961); children: Sharon Shields (Mrs. John R. Greiner), Franklin Vance (killed in action in Vietnam); m. Maryesther Agnew, July 1, 1967. B.A., U. Oreg., 1933, J.D., 1936. Bar: Oreg. 1936. Since practiced in Portland; assoc. firm Miller, Nash, Wiener, Hager & Carlsen and predecessors, 1936-48; partner Miller, Nash, Yerke, Wiener & Hagen (and predecessors), 1948-80, of counsel, 1980—; instr. Northwestern Coll. Law, 1944-48. Mem. Am., Multnomah County bar assns., Am. Judicature Soc., Oreg. State Bar, Lang Syne Soc., Phi Delta Phi. Republican. Clubs: Mason (32 deg.), Waverley Country, Multnomah Athletic (Portland); Portland Yacht; Thunderbird Country (Rancho Mirage, Calif.); Rotary. Home: 6326 SE Reed College Pl Portland OR 97202 Office: 111 SW 5th Ave Portland OR 97204

ANDERSON, GUY IRVING, artist; b. Edmonds, Wash., Nov. 20, 1906; s. Irving Lodell and Edna Marie (Bolduc) A. One-man shows, Seattle Art Mus., 1936, 45, 77, Smolin Gallery, N.Y.C., 1962, Francine Seders Gallery, Seattle, 1971, 73, 75, 77, 80, Henry Art Gallery, Seattle, 1977, group shows include, U. Oreg., 1968, Am. Fedn. Arts Drawing Soc. Nat. Exhbn., 1970, Smithsonin Instn., Washington and other museums, 1974, Portopia, 81, Portopia, Kobe, Japan, 1981, Henry Gallery, U. Wash., Nat. Mus. Art, Osaka, Japan, 1982; represented in permanent collections, Met. Mus. Art, N.Y.C., Smithsonian Instn., Seattle Art Mus., Bklyn. Mus., Wichita Art Mus., Munson-William Proctor Inst., Utica, N.Y., Santa Barbara Mus., Henry Gallery, U. Wash., others, commd. murals include, Opera House, Seattle, 1st Nat. Bank, Seattle. Tiffany Found. scholar, 1926; Guggenheim Found. fellow, 1975-76. Address: Box 217 La Conner WA 98257

ANDERSON, HAROLD ALBERT, engring. and bldg. exec.; b. Beverly, Mass., Jan. 19, 1908; s. John Albert and Ann (Westerberg) A.; m. Grace Whittaker, Apr. 24, 1936; children—Harold Albert, Richard A. C.E., Tufts Coll., 1928. Registered profl. engr., numerous states. With Austin Co., Cleve., 1928-73, exec. v.p., gen. mgr., 1958-63, pres., 1963-73, also chief exec. officer, 1969-73, ret., 1973. Mem. ASCE, Nat. Soc. Profl. Engrs. Clubs: Cleve. Skating (Cleve.); Bay Head (N.J.) Yacht. Home: 2731 Chesterton Rd Shaker Heights OH 44122 Office: 3650 Mayfield Rd Cleveland OH 44121

ANDERSON, HARRY, artist, illustrator; b. Chgo., IL, Aug. 11, 1906; s. Joseph Reynold and Clara Emily (Stahl) A.; m. Ruth E. Young, Nov. 12, 1938; children: Jared Huebel, Tim, Kristen Anderson Geddis. Student, U. Ill., 1925-26; B.F.A., Syracuse U., 1931; D.F.A. hon., Andrew U., 1977. Artist-illustrator Steven-Gross Studio, Chgo., 1935-41, Sunblom and Anderson, 1941-46; freelance artist-illustrator, Hyattsville, Md., 1946-51, Ridgefield, Conn., 1951—. Mem. Am. Watercolor Soc., Am. Acad. Design (assoc.).

ANDERSON, HARRY FREDERICK, JR., architect; b. Chgo., Feb. 4, 1927; s. Harry Frederick and Sarah Matilda (Anderson) A.; m. Frances Annette Zeilstra, Jan. 27, 1951 (div. Jan. 1979); children—Scott H., Mark S., Robert R., Grant Alan; m. Elizabeth Jane Elden, Jan. 17, 1979 (dec. Apr. 1982); m. Joanell Vivian Mangan, Mar. 22, 1983. B.Arch., Ill. Inst. Tech., 1953. Chief draftsman Stade & Cooley, Chgo., 1953-55; partner firm Stade, Dolan & Anderson, Chgo., 1955-65; project architect Perkins & Will Partnership, Chgo., 1965-67, partner, v.p., 1967—, sr. v.p., 1973-74, exec. v.p., 1974-75, pres., chief exec. officer, 1975—, chmn. bd., 1982—; bd. dirs. Chgo. Bldg. Congress. Prin. works include Rockford (Ill.) Coll. Library, 1967, Sci. Bldg, 1968, Arts Complex, 1970, Women's Dormitory, 1969, Silver Cross Hosp, Joliet, Ill., 1971, Westlake Hosp, Melrose Park, Ill., 1970, Am. Soc. Clin. Pathologists bldg., Chgo., 1971, Ingalls Hosp, 1974, St. Mary of Nazareth Hosp, 1975, Childrens Meml. Hosp., Chgo., 1980, U. Chgo. Hosp, 1980. Chmn. adv. council Booth Meml. Hosp., Chgo., 1969—; adv. bd. Chgo. Salvation Army, 1969—. Served with USN, 1944-47. Fellow AIA; Mem. Internat. Hosp. Fedn., Am. Pub. Health Assn. Clubs: Chicago, Univ. (Chgo.); Park Ridge Country. Home: 2650 N Lakeview Ave Apt 310 Chicago IL 60614 Office: 2 N LaSalle St Chicago IL 60602

ANDERSON, HERBERT E., clergyman; b. Madrid, Iowa, Mar. 1, 1916; s. Oscar Albim and Ellen (Peterson) A.; m. Alice Elizabeth Johnson, Sept. 28, 1942; children: Mark, Karen, Stephen, Timothy, James, Peter. B.A., Wheaton (Ill.) Coll., 1941; B.D., Princeton Theol. Sem., 1947; D.D. (hon.), Western Baptist Theol. Sem., Portland, Oreg., 1962. Ordained to ministry Bapt. Ch., 1948; dir. Salem (Oreg.) Youth Center, 1947-48; pastor in, Gladstone, Oreg., 1948-52, The Dalles, Oreg., 1952-58, Lebanon, Oreg., 1958-62; gen. dir. Conservative Bapt. Fgn. Mission Soc., Wheaton, Ill., 1967-71; pastor Hinson Meml. Bapt. Ch., Portland, Oreg., 1963-67, 71-73, First Bapt. Ch., Corvallis, Oreg., 1973-78, Monmouth, Oreg., 1978-82; pres., chmn. dept. Bible and philosophy Judson Bapt. Coll., The Dalles, 1980—; Mem. bd. Conservative Bapt. Assn. Am., 1958-63, pres., 1963-67; moderator Conservative Bapt. Assn. Oreg., 1961-62. Bd. dirs. Western Bapt. Theol. Sem., Judson Bapt. Coll., Portland. Home: 4850 Alsip Rd Monmouth OR 97361

ANDERSON, HERSCHEL VINCENT, librarian; b. Charlotte, N.C., Mar. 14, 1932; s. Paul Kemper and Lillian (Johnson) A. B.A., Duke U., 1954; M.S., Columbia U., 1959. Library asst. Bklyn. Public Library, 1954-59; asst. bookmobile librarian King County Public Library, Seattle, 1959-62; asst. librarian Longview (Wash.) Public Library, 1962-63; librarian N.C. Mus. Art, Raleigh, 1963-64; audio-visual cons. N.C. State Library, Raleigh, 1964-68; dir. Sandhill Regional Library, Rockingham, N.C., 1968-70; asso. state librarian Tenn. State Library and Archives, Nashville, 1970-72; unit dir. Colo. State Library, Denver, 1972-73; state librarian S.D. State Library, Pierre, 1973-80; dir. Mesa (Ariz.) Public Library, 1980—; dir. Bibliographical Center for Research, Denver, 1974-80, v.p., 1977; v.p; Western Council State Libraries, 1978, mem., 1975-80, v.p., 1978, pres., 1979; mem. Ariz. State Library Adv. Council, 1981-84, pres., 1982-83. Served with AUS, 1955-57. Mem. ALA, S.D. Library Assn. (Librarian of Yr. 1977, hon. life 1980), Mountain Plains Library Assn. (pres. 1974, dir. 1974-77), Ariz. Library Assn., Chief Officers of State Library Agys. (dir. 1974-76), Phi Kappa Psi. Episcopalian. Clubs: Mesa Kiwanis (dir. 1981—, v.p. 1983. Home: Mesa AZ Office: Mesa Public Library Mesa AZ 85201 Mailing address: 1850 S Westwood Unit 42 Mesa AZ 85202

ANDERSON, HOWARD CLEVENGER, lawyer; b. Gloucester, N.J., Dec. 3, 1910; s. Howard C. and Bertha M. (Ducey) A. A.B., Princeton U., 1931; LL.B., Harvard U., 1934. Bar: N.Y. 1934, D.C. 1958. Asso. firm Root, Clark, Buckner & Ballantine, N.Y.C., 1934-46; atty. Western Electric Co., Inc., N.Y.C., 1946-56, gen. solicitor, 1956-58; v.p., gen. counsel Chesapeake & Potomac Telephone cos. of Washington, Va., Md. and W.Va., 1958-75; partner firm Debevoise & Liberman, Washington, 1976-77; counsel firm Dewey, Ballantine, Bushby, Palmer & Wood, Washington and N.Y.C., 1977—. Mem. Am. Bar Assn., Bar Assn. of D.C., Bar Assn. City N.Y., Phi Beta Kappa. Clubs: Metropolitan, Chevy Chase (Washington); Princeton (N.Y.C.). Home: 5302 Elliott Rd Washington DC 20016 Office: 1775 Pennsylvania Ave NW Washington DC 20006

ANDERSON, IAIN MAIR, automobile mfg. co. exec.; b. Calcutta, India, May 11, 1931; came to U.S., 1963; s. Ian Hoyle and Elizabeth (Wilson) A.; m. Joan Gordon Sutherland, Oct. 30, 1954; children—Ian Gordon, Kenneth Sutherland, Joan Elizabeth. Chartered accountant, Glasgow (Scotland) U., 1953. Chartered accountant, 1948-53; asst. treas. Boynton Acceptance Co., Toronto, Can., 1954-55; financial, mfg. and purchasing positions with Ford Motor Co. Cn., 1955-63; with Am. Motors Co., 1963-78, ops. control dir., 1965-66, controller, 1966—, v.p. finance, 1967-75, group v.p. fin. and govt. affairs, 1975-77, exec. v.p., 1977; exec. v.p. fin. and adminstrn., treas. Volkswagen of Am., 1978—. Office: 888 W Big Beaver Rd Troy MI 48084

ANDERSON, IAN, musician; b. Blackpool, Eng., Aug. 10, 1947. Ed., Blackpool Coll. Art. Mem. John Evan Band, 1966-67; leader Jethro Tull group, 1967—. Records include Storm Watch; producer: album Now We Are Six for Steeleye Span. Address: care Premier Talent Agy 3 E 54th St New York NY 10022 *

ANDERSON, IRVING CHARLES, business consultant; b. Morton, N.Y., Aug. 25, 1916; s. Charles and Bessie (Altpeter) A.; m. Lucille Stothard, Aug. 21, 1941; children: Stephen Stothard, Debra Lee. B.S. in Chem. Engring., Syracuse U., 1937; grad., Northwestern U. Inst. Mgmt., 1956. Refinery engr. affiliate of Standard Oil Co. (N.J.), Aruba, Netherlands Antilles, head control group, 1937-42; with Esso Research & Engring. Co., 1942-47, Creole Petroleum Corp., 1947-61, mgr. export sales, 1958-60, v.p., 1960-61; v.p. cargo sales dept. Esso Internat., Inc., 1961-66, v.p. dir., 1966-69, sr. v.p., dir., mem. exec. com., 1969-70; fuel oil coordinator Exxon Corp., N.J., 1970-72; mem. faculty U. Ga. Sch. Bus. Adminstrn., 1973-74; bus. cons., 1974—; pres. Manatee Energy Co., 1978-80, dir., 1978—. Mem. Am. Petroleum Inst., Pi Kappa Alpha, Alpha Chi Sigma. Methodist. Clubs: Rotary, Countryside Country, Cypress Run Golf, Touchdown, N.Y. Athletic, Eastern Sportsman's. Home: 3206 Masters Dr Clearwater FL 33519

ANDERSON, IVAN DELOS, impressionist painter; b. Yankton, S.D., Feb. 13, 1915; s. Albert and Elizabeth (Cooper) A.; m. Bette Stanley, Feb. 19, 1944; 1 son, Greg. B.A., Yankton Coll., 1937; diploma cosmetology, Poly. Coll., Los Angeles, 1939. Designer Ivan of Hollywood, Calif., 1938-40, House of Westmore, Hollywood, 1946-47; v.p. Nutri-Tonic Corp., Hollywood, 1948-59. Author; illustrator: Creative Hairshaping and Hairstyling, 1947 (Best Litho Textbook of Yr. award Am. Lithography Soc. 1948), Hairstyling, 1948; one-man exhbns. include, Falco Gallery, Sherman Oaks, Calif., 1967, Cagle Galleries, Lubbock, Tex., 1974, Norton Simon's Hunt-Wesson Gallery, Fullerton, Calif., Huney Gallery, San Diego, 1975, The Gallery, Catalina Island, Calif., Expressions Gallery, Newport Beach, Calif., 1976, Moulton Playhouse, Laguna Beach, Calif., 1977, group exhbns. include, Festival of Arts, Laguna Beach, (1973-74), Chaffey Coll., Cucamonga, Calif., (1974), Art-A-Fair Festival, Laguna Beach, 1975, 76, 77, Laguna Beach Mus., 1974, 75, 76; represented in permanent collections, Mus. Modern Art, N.Y.C., Los Angeles Mus., Buffalo Bill Hist. Mus. Cody, Wyo., Roy Rogers Mus., Victorville, Calif., Library of Congress, Los Angeles Children's Hosp., also numerous pvt. collections including, Ronald Reagan, John Wayne, Mary Pickford; posters commd. include Hopalong Cassidy, 1976, Catalina Island Casino, 1977, Laguna Beach, 1977; paintings commd. for Anderson's Children of World Serigraph series, 1975-76; paintings commd. Beachcomber and Beachgirl, 1983. Served with AUS, 1941-46. Recipient Gold trophy Grand Nat., 1940; Best Portrait of Yr. award Wilshire Ebel Club, 1967; Best of Show Catalina Art Festival, 1967; Grand Prize United Meth. Ch., Los Angeles, 1969; Wrigley award P.K. Wrigley, 1968; 1st prize Catalina Art Festival, 1976. Mem. Art-a-Fair. Address: 1060 Flamingo Rd Laguna Beach CA 92651 *To most people, specialization means spending your life at one endeavor. After four successful careers, I've learned that boredom starts to set in as goals are reached. When there is little left to learn, I change careers, and I can truthfully say every working day of my life has been and is fun. At 66, I have as much zest for life as I did when I was 22*

ANDERSON, J. BLAINE, judge; b. Trenton, Utah, Jan. 19, 1922; s. Leslie Howard and Theo Ellen (Stocking) A.; m. Grace Little, Nov. 14, 1944; children—J. Eric, J. Blaine, Leslie Ann, Dirk Brian. Student, U. Idaho, 1940-41, U. Wash., 1945-46; LL.B., U. Idaho, 1949; J.D. (hon.), Lewis and Clark Coll., 1978. Bar: Idaho bar 1949. Practiced in, Blackfoot, 1949-71; partner firm Furchner and Anderson (and predecessor law firms), 1955-71; U.S. dist. judge Dist. Idaho, Boise, 1971-76; U.S. circuit judge U.S. Ct. Appeals, 9th Circuit, 1976—. Chmn. Idaho Air Pollution Commn., 1959-60. Served with USCG, 1942-45. Fellow Am. Coll. Trial Lawyers; mem. Am. Bar Assn. (mem. ho. of dels. 1959-60, 64-71, gov. 1971-74, mem. council gen. practice sect. 1962-66, 70-71, mem. adv. bd. editors Jour. 1969-71), Idaho State Bar (bd. commrs. 1958-61, pres. 1960-61, chmn. unauthorized practice of law com. 1955-58), S.E. Idaho Dist. Bar (pres. 1957-58), Am. Judicature Soc. (dir. 1961-66), Am. Coll. Probate Counsel. Office: US Court Bldg 550 Fort St Boise ID 83724

ANDERSON, J. JOSEPH, banker; b. Cortland, N.Y., Apr. 12, 1938; s. Edward J. and Agnes E. A.; m. May B. Marovich; children: Daniel F., George P., Mark E. B.B.A., U. Notre Dame, 1960; M.B.A., U. Chgo., 1968. Bar: C.P.A., Ill. Gen. acct. UARCO Bus. Forms, Inc., 1960-63; with Continental Ill. Nat. Bank and Trust Co., 1963—, 2d v.p., 1968, operating rep. methods research, 1969, v.p., 1970; auditor Continental Bank and parent co., 1972, v.p., 1974, sr. v.p., 1975, head multinat. banking services, 1976, head controller's and systems, 1980, controller, 1980, exec. v.p., 1981—; past mem. faculty Loyola U., Chgo.; mem. acctg. adv. bd. U. Ill.-Chgo. Bd. dirs. A.R.C., Cath. Charities Chgo.; bd. advisers Dartmouth Inst., Dartmouth Coll.; bd. dirs. Ill. Benedictine Coll; trustee Morehouse Coll., Atlanta. Served with U.S. Army, 1961-62. Mem. Ill. Soc. C.P.A.s. Clubs: Bankers,

Economic. Address: Continental Ill Corp 231 S LaSalle St Chicago IL 60693

ANDERSON, JACK NORTHMAN, newspaper columnist; b. Long Beach, Calif., Oct. 19, 1922; s. Orlando N. and Agnes (Mortensen) A.; m. Olivia Farley, Aug. 10, 1949; children: Cheri, Lance F., Laurie, Tina, Kevin N., Randy N., Tanya, Rodney V., Bryan W. Student, U. Utah, 1940-41, Georgetown U., 1947-48, George Washington U., 1948. Reporter, Salt Lake Tribune, 1939-41; war corr. Deseret News, 1945; reporter Washington Merry-go-Round, 1947—, partner, from 1965, owner, from 1969; Washington editor Parade mag., 1954-68, bur. chief, from 1968; Missionary in So. states for Church Jesus Christ of Latter Day Saints, 1941-44. Author: (with Ronald May) McCarthy the Man, the Senator, The Ism, 1952, (with Fred Blumenthal) The Kefauver Story, 1956, (with Drew Pearson) U.S.A. Second Class Power?, 1958, Washington Expose, 1966, Case Against Congress, 1968, (with Carl Kalvelage) American Government-Like It Is, 1972, (with George Clifford) The Anderson Papers, 1973, (with James Boyd) Confessions of a Muckraker, 1979, (with Bill Pronzini) The Cambodia File, 1981, (with John Kidner) Alice in Blunderland, 1983, (with James Boyd) Fiasco, 1983. Sec., trustee Chinese Refugee Relief, from 1962. Served with U.S. Mcht. Marine, 1944-45; with AUS, 1946-47. Recipient Pulitzer Prize for Nat. Reporting, 1972. Mem. White House Corr. Assn. Club: National Press (Washington). Office: care United Feature Syndicate 200 Park Ave New York NY 10166 *

ANDERSON, JACK OLAND, college administrator; b. Mich., Aug. 5, 1921; s. Seymour and Laura (Fox) A. Student, Ferris State Coll., 1940-41; B.S., Central Mich. U., 1948; M.A., U. Mich., 1950; Ed.D., Mich. State U., 1962. Tchr. pub. schs. Mich., 1949-59; asst. instr. Mich. State U., 1959-62; dir. edn. Lansing (Mich.) Bus. Inst., 1963-65; exec. dir. Lockyear Bus. Coll., 1965-66; acad. dean Detroit Coll., 1966-69; pres. Bristol (Tenn.) Coll., 1969-83, chmn. bd. dirs., 1983—; past chmn., mem. Sullivan County Vocat. Adv. Com.; vice chmn. region IV proprietary sch. coordinatin council U.S. Dept. Edn. Mem. Tenn. Pub. Service Council; past mem. bd. adminstrn. First Baptist Ch., Bristol. Served to capt. U.S. Army, 1942-46. Mem. Tenn. Bus. Coll. Assn. (past pres., dir.), Southeastern Bus. Coll. Assn. (past pres., dir.), Nat. Rehab. Assn., Bristol C. of C. (past dir., chmn. congl. action 1979, chmn. exon. impact subcom. of coal commn.). Club: Elks. Address: PO Box 757 Bristol TN 37621 *It has been a fact of my life that the more I do for others, the more abundant my life becomes. Problems are not obstacles; they are opportunities; to solve problems is to grow.*

ANDERSON, JACK ROY, health care executive; b. Mansfield, Ohio, Feb. 14, 1925; s. Roy L. and Katherine (Munson) A.; m. Rose-Marie J. Garcia, June 24, 1950; children: Gail Ellen, Neil Robert, Barbara Ann. B.S., Miami U., 1947; M.S., Columbia U., 1949.; Acctg. mgr. Time, Inc., N.Y.C., 1950-59; asst. to controller W.R. Grace & Co., N.Y.C, 1959-62; v.p., treas. Hartford Publs., Inc., N.Y.C., 1962-65; controller McCall Corp., N.Y.C., 1965-68; v.p. Reliance Group, Inc., N.Y.C., 1968-70; pres., dir. Hosp. Affiliates Internat., Inc., Nashville, 1970-76, chmn. bd. dir., 1977—; dir. Hillhaven Corp., Tacoma; vis. lectr. Vanderbilt U., Duke U.; adj. faculty Vanderbilt Owen Grad. Sch. Mgmt., 1978-79. Author: The Road to Recovery, 1976. Vice pres. Greenwich Council Parent-Tchr. Assn., Conn., 1961-62; vis. com. Vanderbilt Owen Grad. Sch. Mgmt., 1973-77; bd. dirs. Tulane Med. Ctr. Hosp. and Clinic, New Orleans, Hillhaven corp., Tacoma, Hosp. Underwriting Group Ltd., Bermuda; trustee, mem. com. quality health care River Oaks Found., Nat Com Quality Health Care; mem. bus. adv. council Miami U., 1975-78, chmn., 1978. Served to lt. j.g. USNR, 1943-46. Mem. Columbia Bus. Assocs., Fin. Execs. Inst. (chmn. health care subcom. of employee benefits com.), Sigma Chi, Beta Alpha Psi, Beta Gamma Sigma. Clubs: Board Room (N.Y.C.); Stanwich (Greenwich, Conn.); Pres's (Oxford, Ohio); University (Nashville). Home: 110 Lynwood Terr Nashville TN 37205 Office: 4525 Harding Rd Nashville TN 37205

ANDERSON, JAMES ARTHUR, mining company executive; b. Aurelia, Iowa, Mar. 25, 1935; s. Vernon L. and Agnes (Weiland) A.; m. Ann Charlene Sutherland, Sept. 9, 1956. B.S. in Geol. Engring., U. Utah, 1957; M.S. in Mining Geology, Harvard U., 1960; Ph.D. in Econ. Geology, Harvard U., 1965; M.B.A., Stanford U., 1978. Staff geologist, sr. exploration geologist, exec. exploration geologist Kennecott Copper Corp., Salt Lake City, 1960-68; v.p. U.S. metal exploration, U.S. exploration mgr. Occidental Minerals Corp., Denver, 1968-75; exec. v.p. exploration and bus. devel., dir. v.p. and gen. mgr. exploration Homestake Mining Co., San Francisco, 1975—; chmn. policy research com. Calif. State Mining and Geology Bd., Sacramento, 1978—, also vice-chmn. bd. Contbg. author: Advances in Geology of the Porphyry Copper Deposits, Southwest NA, 1982; contbr. articles in tech. jour. Mem. Soc. Mining Engrs., AIME, Geol. Soc. Am., World Affairs Council Calif., Mining and Metall. Soc. Am., Colo. Mining Assn. Republican. Methodist. Clubs: Commonwealth Calif. (San Francisco); Banker San Francisco. Office: Homestake Mining Co 650 California St 9th Floor San Francisco CA 94108

ANDERSON, JAMES FREDERICK, clergyman; b. Elizabeth, N.J., Aug. 23, 1927; s. Fred and Hazel Minerva (Brown) A.; m. Bette Dillensnyder, Sept. 8, 1951; children—Judith (Mrs. Wayne Westbury), James Frederick, Mark, Rebecca. B.A., Princeton, 1949; B.D., Princeton Theol. Sem., 1952; D.D., Alma Coll., 1974. Ordained to ministry Presbyn. Ch., 1952; chaplain Hun Sch. for Boys, Princeton, 1953; instr. religion Lafayette Coll., Easton, Pa., 1954-55; pastor Presbyn. chs., Catasauqua, Pa., 1956-61, Narberth, Pa., 1961-66, Second Presbyn. Ch., Richmond, Va., 1966-72, Kirk in the Hills, Bloomfield Hills, Mich., 1972—; Trustee Alma (Mich.) Coll., Princeton Theol. Sem., William Beaumont Hosp., Royal Oak, Mich. Served with USNR, 1945-46. Home: 1420 W Long Lake Rd Bloomfield Hills MI 48013 Office: 1340 W Long Lake Rd Bloomfield Hills MI 48013

ANDERSON, JAMES GEORGE, sociologist, educator; b. Balt., July 24, 1936; s. Clair Sherrill and Kathryn Ann (Plovanich) A.; children: Robin Marie, James Brian, Melissa Lee, Derek Clair. B.Engring. Scis. in Chem. Engring, Johns Hopkins U., 1957, M.S.E. in Ops. Research and Indsl. Engring, 1959, M.A.T., 1960, Ph.D. in Edn. and Sociology, 1964. Adminstrv. asst. to dean Eve. Coll., Johns Hopkins U., 1964-65, dir. div. engring., 1965-66; research prof. ednl. adminstrn. N.Mex. State U., 1966-70; mem. faculty Purdue U., 1970—, prof. sociology, 1974—; asst. dean for analytical studies Sch. Humanities, Social Sci. and Edn., 1975-78; cons. in field. Author: Bureaucracy in Education, 1968, also articles, chpts. in books. Served as officer C.E. USA, 1960-61. USPHS grantee. Mem. Am. Sociol. Assn., Am. Public Health Assn., Am. Acad. Polit. and Social Scis., Am. Ednl. Research Assn. (treas. spl. interest group 1969-71), AAUP, Am. Assn. Eve. Colls. Home: 615 Meridian St West Lafayette IN 47906 Office: Dept Sociology and Anthropology Purdue U West Lafayette IN 47907

ANDERSON, JAMES GILBERT, chemistry educator. Philip S. Weld prof. atmospheric chemistry Harvard U., Cambridge, Mass. Office: Harvard U Ctr for Earth and Planetary Physics Cambridge MA 02138§

ANDERSON, JAMES HENRY, dean; b. Odum, Ga., Jan. 11, 1926; s. James Tillman and Mamie (Aspinwall) A.; m. Dorothy Allen, Dec. 29, 1951; children: Alicia Carol, Laurie Beth, James Hampton, Sue Ellen, John Allen. B.S., U. Ga., 1949; M.S., N.C. State U., 1955; Ph.D., Iowa State U., 1957. Bar: Registered profl. engr., Miss. Prof., head agrl. engring. dept U. Tenn., Knoxville, 1960-61; prof., head agrl. engring. dept. Miss. State U., Starkville, 1961-68; dean resident instrn. Coll. Agr., 1967-68; dir. Miss. Agrl. and Forestry Exptl. Sta., Starkville, 1969-77; dean Coll. Agrl. and Natural Resources, Mich. State U., Lansing, 1977—. Contbr. articles to various publs. Mem. exec. com S. Bapt. Conv., 1973-77. Served with U.S. Army, 1944-46. Fellow Am. Soc. Agrl. Engrs. Baptist. Club: Rotary. Office: Michigan State U 104 Agriculture Hall East Lansing MI 48824 *

ANDERSON, JAMES KEITH, magazine editor; b. Grand Junction, Colo., June 27, 1924; s. Arnold Plumer and Helen Catherine (Enright) A.; m. Doris Mae Johnson, Aug. 5, 1952; children: Catherine E., Charles E., William H. II. A.B., U. Mich., 1949. Reporter Jefferson City (Mo.) News and Tribune, 1949, Tampa (Fla.) Daily Times, 1949-51; editor Detroit Labor News, 1951-53; reporter Detroit News, 1953-68; editor VFW mag., Kansas City, Mo., 1968—. Contbr.: articles to Omaha World-Herald. Adv. bd. Hospitalized Vets. Writing Project, 1973—; Bd. dirs. Internat. Inst. Met. Detroit, 1963-68, Shepherd's Center, 1979-81. Served with inf. AUS, 1943-45. Decorated Bronze Star, Purple Heart, Combat Inf. badge; Gold Cross of Merit Polish Govt. in Exile; Royal Yugoslav Commemorative War Cross; Latvian Pro Merito; numerous awards for ethnic coverage. Mem. VFW, S.R., DAV, Ancient and Honorable Artillery Co. of Mass., Sons and Daus. 1st Settlers Newbury, Mass., Sigma Delta Chi, Sigma Tau Gamma. Episcopalian (vestry). Clubs: Detroit Press, Kansas City Press. Home: 621 W 63d St Kansas City MO 64113 Office: 406 W 34th St Kansas City MO 64111

ANDERSON, JAMES WILLIAM, III, performing artist, composer; b. Columbia, S.C., Nov. 1, 1937; s. James William and Elizabeth (Smith) A.; m. Rebecca Joyce Stegall, Oct. 2, 1970; children: Terri Lee, Jennifer Lane, James William IV. A.B., U. Ga., 1959. Disc jockey radio sta. WGAU, Athens, Ga., Sta. WJJC, Commerce, Ga., 1956-59; sportswriter DeKalb New Era; corr. Atlanta Jour. Became rec. artist for Decca Records after Ray Price recorded his song City Lights; since has written: numerous songs, including I Get the Fever, 1966, For Loving You, 1967, Happy State of Life, 1968, But You Know I Love You, 1969, Quits, 1971, The Corner of My Life, 1973; rec. artist: recs. include Mama Sang a Song, 1962; albums include Nashville Mirrors; world-wide concert appearances; appeared on: syndicated TV series the Bill Anerson Show; syndicated TV show Road to Nashville; with, Grand Ole Opry, Nashville, 1961—; host: Backstage at the Grand Ole Opry, 1980; TV show Fandango, 1983—; exec. producer: You Can Be a Star, 1983—; performer, lectr. and composer country music touring the U.S., Can., Europe syndicated TV show, 1974—. Hon. state chmn. Tenn. Christmas Seal Drive, Nashville, 1971, Tenn. Assn. Retarded Children and Adults, 1974. Recipient Country Music Songwriter of Year award Billboard Mag., 1963, 64, 65, 73, 74; Country Music Male Artist of Year award Billboard, Cashbox, Music Reporter, Music Vendor mags., 1963. Mem. Country Music Assn. (dir. 1961-62, 74-75), Assn. Country Entertainers (dir. 1974-75), Nashville Songwriters Assn. (dir. 1974-75), Phi Kappa Phi, Kappa Sigma. Methodist. Office: 4223 Lebanon Rd Suite 201 Hermitage TN 37076

ANDERSON, JERRY MAYNARD, university administrator; b. Deronda, Wis., Sept. 16, 1933; s. Jens B. and Mamie P. (Hanson) A.; m. Betty Lou Schultz, Feb. 7, 1959; children: Gregory J., Timothy B. B.S., Wis. State U. at River Falls, 1958; M.S., No. Ill. U., 1959; Ph.D., Mich. State U., 1964. Instr. speech U. Maine, 1959-61; asst. prof. speech, dir. forensics Mich. State U., 1961-68; prof., chmn. dept. speech and dramatic arts Central Mich. U., Mt. Pleasant, 1968-72, vice provost, 1972-73; v.p. acad. affairs Western Wash. U., 1973-75; vice chancellor, prof. speech U. Wis., Oshkosh, 1975-79; pres., prof. speech Ball State U., Muncie, Ind., 1979-81; sr. cons. Am. Assn. State Colls. and Univs., Washington, 1981-82; research adminstr. U. Wis., Stout, Menomonie, 1982—. Author: (with Paul J. Dovre) Readings in Argumentation, 1968; also articles. Served with USN, 1952-54. Recipient 1st Sr. Disting. Professionalism award Central Mich. U., 1971; Research fellow Harry S Truman Found., 1965; fellow Am. Council on Edn. Acad. Adminstrn. Internship Program, 1971—; Recipient Disting. Alumnus award Delta Sigma Rho-Tau Kappa Alpha, 1980; Sagamore of Wabash Public Service award Gov. of Ind., 1980. Mem. Central States Speech Assn. (pres. 1973, Outstanding Young Tchr. award 1966), Mich. Speech Assn. (pres. 1967-68), Am. Forensic Assn. (pres. 1972-74), Midwest Forensic Assn. (pres. 1969-72), Speech Communication Assn. (mem. legis. council 1967, legis. assembly 1975). Club: Rotary. Office: Route 2 Box 79B Amery WI 54001

ANDERSON, JOHN BAYARD, former congressman, lawyer; b. Rockford, Ill., Feb. 15, 1922; s. E. Albin and Mabel Edna (Ring) A.; m. Keke Machakos, Jan. 4, 1953; children: Eleanora, John Bayard, Diane, Karen, Susan Kimberly. A.B., U. Ill., 1942, J.D., 1946; LL.M., Harvard U., 1949; hon. doctorates, U. Ill., Wheaton Coll., Shimer Coll., Biola Coll., Geneva Coll., North Park Coll. and Theol. Sem., Houghton Coll., Trinity Coll. Bar: Ill. 1946. Practice law Rockford, 1946-52; with U.S. Fgn. Service, 1952-55; assigned, West Berlin, 1952-55; mem. 87th-95th Congresses from 16th Dist. Ill., mem. rules com.; chmn. Ho. Republican Conf., 1969-79; polit. commentator WLS-TV, Chgo., from 1981; ind. candidate for Pres. U.S., 1980. Author: Between Two Worlds: A Congressman's Choice, 1970, Vision and Betrayal in America, 1976; editor: Congress and Conscience, 1970. Trustee Trinity Coll., Deerfield, Ill.; bd. dirs. Youth for Christ Internat. Served with F.A., AUS, World War II. Named Outstanding Layman of Year, Nat. Assn. Evangelicals, 1964. Mem. Phi Beta Kappa. Mem. Evang. Free Ch. (past trustee). *

ANDERSON, JOHN CRAWFORD, rail corporation executive; b. Oxbow, Sask., Can., Sept. 27, 1921; s. John Robert and Barbara Ethel (Crawford) A.; m. Doris Kathleen Maloney, May 8, 1948; children: Brenda, Patricia, Nancy, John, Laura. Student, United Coll., Winnipeg, 1938-39. With Canadian Pacific Ltd., 1939—, clk., Winnipeg, Man., Can., 1939-57, supr., 1957-62, labor relations officer, Montreal, Que., Can., 1962-66, asst.to v.p. personnel, 1966-68, v.p. indsl. relations, 1968-81, v.p. personnel, 1981—; gov. Que. Blue Cross, Montreal, 1969—; dir. Que Mut. Life Assurance Co., Montreal, 1975—, mem. exec. com., 1981—. Served with RCAF, 1943-45. Home: 66 White Pine Dr Beaconsfield PQ Canada H9W 5E3 Office: Canadian Pacific Ltd 910 Peel St PO Box 6042 Station A Montreal PQ Canada H3C 3E4

ANDERSON, JOHN DAVID, architect; b. New Haven, Dec. 24, 1926; s. William Edward and Norma Vere (Carson) A.; m. Florence A. Van Dyke, Aug. 26, 1950; children—Robert Stewart, David Carson. A.B. cum laude, Harvard U., 1949, M.Arch., 1952. Draftsman John K. Monroe (Architect), Denver, 1952-54; draftsman, designer, asso. Wheeler & Lewis (Architects), Denver, 1954-60; prin. John D. Anderson, Denver, 1960-64; partner Anderson, Barker Rinker (Architects), Denver, 1965-69, A-B-R Partnership (Architects), 1970-75; prin., pres. Anderson Architects, P.C., Denver, 1975—; vis. lectr. U. Colo., U. N.Mex., U. Nebr., U. Cape Town, Colo. State U., Plymouth Polytech., Eng.; Chmn. Denver Bldg. Dept. Bd. Appeals, 1974-75; chmn. Colo. Gov.'s Task Force on Removal of Archtl. Barriers, 1972-74; vice chmn. Colo. Bd. Non-Residential Energy Conservation Standards, 1978—. Prin. works include, Community Coll. Denver, North campus, Westminster, 1977, Yale and Jewell elem. schs., Aurora (award winning solar heated structures). Served with USNR, 1944-46. Fellow AIA (pres. Colo. chpt. 1967); mem. Colo. Soc. Architects (pres. 1971), Internat. Solar Energy Soc., Council Ednl. Facility Planners (internat. chmn. energy com. 1980). Republican. Congregationalist. Home: 30262 Rainbow Hills Rd Golden CO 80401 Office: 1522 Blake St Denver CO 80202

ANDERSON, JOHN DAVID, agri-business executive; b. Toledo, May 17, 1922; s. Harold and Margaret (Meilink) A.; m. Mary K. Wenzel, Sept. 4, 1948; children: John David, Michael, Jeffrey, Kathleen, Elizabeth, Mark, Susan, Jane, William, Amy, Sarah. Student, Mich. State U., 1942; D.C.S. (hon.), U. Toledo, 1974, LL.D., Tri-State U., 1979. Gen. mgr. The Andersons, Maumee, Ohio, 1947-79, sr. partner, 1979—; mem. U.S. Feed Grains Council, 1970-78. Trustee Greater Toledo Corp., U. Toledo Corp., U. Toledo, Toledo Mus. Art, United Way; bd. dirs. Fed. Res. Bank of Cleve., 1981—; bd. regents St. John's Jesuit High Sch., 1965—; exec. com. Lucas County Republican Party, 1978—; pres. bd. trustees Toledo YMCA, 1964-78, Toledo Bd. Trade, 1956-71, Toledo Community Chest, 1948—; chmn. St. Charles-St. Luke's Hosp. Fund Dr., Toledo United Appeal Fund dr.; trustee, chmn. Mary Manse Coll., 1973-74. Served with USAAF, 1943-45. Mem. Ohio C. of C. (dir.), Toledo C. of C. (pres. 1967-68). Roman Catholic. Clubs: Pres. Ohio State U., Pres. Bowling Green State U., Toledo, Toledo Country, Rotary (pres. 1972-73). Home: 1833 S Holland Sylvania Rd Maumee OH 43537 Office: PO Box 119 Maumee OH 43537

ANDERSON, JOHN DAVID, JR., aerospace engineer; b. Lancaster, Pa., Oct. 1, 1937; s. John David and Esther Pearl (Stoneback) A.; m. Sarah Allen West, Sept. 11, 1960; children: Katherine Josephine, Elizabeth Esther. B.Aero. Engring. with honors (Gen. Motors scholar, J. Hillis Meml. scholar), U. Fla., 1959; Ph.D. in Aero. Engring., Ohio State U. Chief hypersonics group Naval Ordnance Lab., White Oak, Md., 1966-73; prof., chmn. dept. aerospace engring. U. Md., College Park, 1973—. Author: Gasdynamic Lasers: An Introduction, 1976, Introduction to Flight: Its Engineering and History, 1978; author: Modern Compressible Flow: with Historical Perspective, 1982, Fundamentals of Aerodynamics, 1984; contbr. articles to profl. jours. Served with USAF, 1959-62. Named disting. scholar/tchr. U. Md., 1981-82; NSF fellow, NASA fellow Ohio State U., 1966; Recipient Meritorious Civilian Service award Naval Ordnance Lab., 1972. Fellow Washington Acad. Scis. (Engring. Sci. award 1975), AIAA (asso. fellow, mem. council Nat. Capital sect.); mem. Am. Soc. Engring. Edn., Am. Phys. Soc., Sigma Xi, Tau Beta Pi, Sigma Tau, Phi Kappa Phi, Phi Eta Sigma. Roman Catholic. Office: Dept Aerospace Engring U Md College Park MD 20742 *A prescription for success in professional life involves a proper balance of hard work, long hours, awareness and clear thinking, with a goal-oriented philosophy and outright love of one's profession. In addition, one must have the desire, abilities and opportunities to accomplish his goals.*

ANDERSON, JOHN EDWARD, mechanical engineering educator; b. Chgo., May 15, 1927; s. Claus Oscar and Ruth Melvina (Engstrom) A.; m. Cynthia Louise Howard, May 24, 1975; children: Candice, James, Stanley. B.M.E., Iowa State U., 1949; M.S. in M.E., U. Minn., 1955; Ph.D., MIT, 1962. Registered profl. engr., Minn. Aero. research scientist Nat. Adv. Com. for Aeros., Langley Field, Va., 1949-51; devel. engr. Honeywell, Inc., Mpls., 1951-53, research engr., 1953-55, prin. research engr., 1955-58, research project engr., 1954-58, sr. staff engr., 1958-62, mgr. space systems, 1963; mem. faculty U. Minn., Mpls., 1963—, prof. mech. engring., 1971—; cons. Colo. Regional Transp. Dist., 1974-75, Raytheon Co., 1975-76, Mannesmann Demag, 1978-79, Arthr D. Little, Inc., 1981, Indpls. Transit Commn., 1979-81. Author: Transit Systems Theory; editor: Personal Rapid Transit. Served with U.S. Navy, 1945-46. Convair fellow. Nat. Acad. Sci., 1967-68. Mem. AAAS, AIAA, Am. Inst. Indsl. Engrs., Fedn. Am. Scientists, Union Concerned Scientists, Mensa, World Federalists Assn., Sci., Tech. and Soc. Assn., Sierra Club. Unitarian. Home: 1920 S 1st St 2003 Minneapolis MN 55454 Office: 111 Church St SE Minneapolis MN 55455

ANDERSON, JOHN EDWARD, lawyer; b. Mpls., Sept. 12, 1917; s. William Charles and Myrtle (Grosvenor) A.; m. Margaret Stewart, Sept. 14, 1942 (dec.); children: Margaret Susan, Judith Grosvenor, John Edward, Deborah Lee (dec.), William Stewart; m. Marion Redding, Mar. 3, 1967. B.S. cum laude, UCLA, 1940; M.B.A. with distinction (Baker scholar), Harvard U., 1942; J.D. cum laude, Loyola U., 1950. Bar: Calif. 1950; C.P.A., Calif. Accountant Arthur Andersen & Co. (C.P.A.'s), Los Angeles, 1945-48; since practiced in, Los Angeles, Santa Ana and, Newport Beach; ptnr. Kindel & Anderson, 1953—; dir. Diamond Perforated Metals, Summit Health, Ltd., Emett & Chandler Cos. Inc., Applied Magnetics Corp., Sloan Tech. Corp., Topa Equities, Ltd., Topa Mgmt. Co., Indsl. Tools, Inc., Angeles Corp., Bourns, Inc., Eldon Industries Inc. Trustee Claremont McKenna Coll.; trustee St. John's Hosp. and Health Center Found.; bd. dirs. YMCA Met., Los Angeles. Served to lt. USNR, 1942-45. Mem. ABA, State Bar Calif., Am. Inst. Accountants, Calif. Soc. C.P.A.s, Phi Delta Phi, Beta Gamma Sigma, Beta Theta Pi. Presbyterian (elder). Clubs: Los Angeles Country, Calif., Regency (Los Angeles); Eldorado Country (Palm Desert, Calif.); Outrigger Canoe (Honolulu). Home: 10445 Bellagio Rd Los Angeles CA 90077 Office: 555 S Flower St 26th Floor Los Angeles CA 90071 4000 MacArthur Blvd Newport Beach CA 92660

ANDERSON, JOHN FIRTH, church administrator, librarian; b. Saginaw, Mich., Oct. 5, 1928; s. Harlan Firth and Irene Martha (Bowser) A.; m. Patricia Ann Goble, June 18, 1950; children: Douglas Firth, Elizabeth Ann. B.A., Mich. State U., 1949; M.S. in L.S, U. Ill., 1950. Young people's librarian Enoch Pratt Free Library, Balt., 1950-52; with Balt. County Pub. Library, 1952-58, supr. adult work, 1955-56, asst. county librarian, 1956-58; dir. Knoxville (Tenn.) Pub. Library System, 1958-62, Tucson Pub. Library, 1962-68, 73-82; exec. presbyter, stated clk. Presbytery of Santa Barbara (Calif.), 1982—; city librarian San Francisco Pub. library, 1968-73; cons. on library bldgs., devel. and mgmt. Contbr. articles to profl. publs. Bd. dirs. Amigos Bibliographic Council, 1977-81, vice-chmn., 1977-79, sec., 1980-81; mem. Ariz. Library Adv. Council, 1975-81; charter mem. Freedom to Read Found.; Bd. dirs. Ariz. Theatre Co., 1978-82, Tucson Pub. Library. Recipient Disting. Citizen award U. Ariz., 1981. Mem. ALA (mem. at large council 1961-65, 66-70, bd. dirs. pub. library assn. 1961-65, bd. dirs. library administrn. div. 1964-65, chmn. library orgn. and mgmt. sect. 1964-65, pres. library administrn. div. 1968-69), Calif. Library Assn. (mem. council 1970-71), Southwestern Library Assn. (pres. 1976-78), Ariz. Library Assn. (pres. pub. libraries div. 1964-65, pres. 1967-68, Librarian of Year 1968, Rosenzweig award 1981), Ariz. Assn. County Librarians (pres. 1979-80), Ariz. China Council (pres. 1979-80), Beta Phi Mu. Presbyn. (elder). Lodges: Kiwanis (pres. Tucson 1968, 75-76); Rotary. Office: Presbytery of Santa Barbara 6067 Shirrell Way Goleta CA 93117

ANDERSON, JOHN FRANKLIN, JR., clergyman; b. Dallas, May 27, 1920; s. John Franklin A.; m. Nancy Lee Love, 1943; children: William Earl, Paul Burris, Rebecca. B.A., Austin Coll., 1941; D.D., B.D., Union Presbyn. Theol. Sem., 1944; Th.M., Austin Presbyn. Sem., 1953. Ordained to ministry Presbyn. Ch. Pastor 1st Presbyn. Ch., Tyler, Tex., 1946-51, assoc. pastor, Tyler, Dallas, 1951-52, pastor,

1952-58, Orlando, Fla., 1958-65; mem. exec. sec. Bd. Nat Ministries, Atlanta, 1965-73; pastor 1st Presbyn. Ch., Dallas, 1973—; moderator 122d Gen. Assembley Presbyn. Ch. U.S., Columbus, Ga., 1982. Trustee Austin Coll., Sherman, Tex.; pres. Greater Dallas Community of Chs., Dallas, 1982, Presbyn. Village Retirement Ctr., Dallas, 1982—. Served with USNR, 1944-46.

ANDERSON, JOHN GASTON, electrical engineer; b. Dante, Va., Aug. 21, 1922; s. Harvey Ellis and Lenora (Ingram) A.; m. Elizabeth Amelia Weller, Sept. 18, 1948; 1 son, David John. B.S. with honors in Elec. Engring., Va. Poly. Inst., 1943. Registered profl. engr., Mass. With Gen. Electric Co., 1946—, mgr. AC transmission studies, Schenectady, 1972-74, mgr. high voltage lab., Pittsfield, Mass., 1974-80, cons. engr. transmission systems, Schenectady, 1980—; cons., lectr. on high voltage and power transmission; mem. U.S. USSR Tech. Exchange for High Voltage Transmission. Co-author books in field; contbr. articles to profl. publs.; editor: GE Transmission Mag., 1972-74. Active Boy Scouts Am., 1960-79. Served to capt. USAAF, 1943-45. Recipient Nat. prizes for papers Am. Inst. Elec. Engrs., 1957. Fellow IEEE; mem. Nat. Acad. Engring., Power Engring. Soc. (chmn. nat. public affairs subcom. 1979, chmn. tech. ops. dept. 1982—), Nat. Eagle Scout Assn., Tau Beta Pi, Eta Kappa Nu, Phi Kappa Phi. Patentee in field. Office: Gen Electric Co 1 River Rd Schenectady NY 12345

ANDERSON, JOHN HAROLD, advertising executive; b. Brantford, Ont., Can., Apr. 30, 1943; s. Harold N. and Greta (Marion) A.; m. Janet Theresa Ward, July 10, 1970; children: Melinda N., Bronwyn K. Grad. with honors in bus. adminstrn., U. Western Ont., 1967. With MacLaren Advt. Ltd., Toronto, Ont., 1967-72, Imperial Oil Ltd., Toronto, 1972-81; pres., chief exec. officer Foote, Cone & Belding, Toronto, 1981—. Bd. dirs. Fedn. Against Child Abuse, Toronto, 1983, Can. Advt. Found. Office: 496 Queen St E Toronto ON Canada M5A 4G8

ANDERSON, JOHN JOSEPH BAXTER, nutritionist, educator; b. Cleve., June 12, 1934; s. Francis Morrow and Phyllis Suzette (Wallbridge) A.; m. Elizabeth Elsemore, Aug. 17, 1957; children: Edward E., John P., Timothy W. B.A. in History, Williams Coll., 1956; M.A. in Edn, Harvard U., 1958, Boston U., 1962; Ph.D. in Phys. Biology, Cornell U., 1966. Instr. Bradford (Mass.) Jr. Coll., 1959-62; asst. prof. physiology U. Ill., 1966-71; assoc. prof. U.N.C. at Chapel Hill, 1971-76, prof., 1977—; cons. USPHS. Co-author: Human Ecology, 1975; editor: Parturient Hypocalcemia, 1971, Applied Nutrition for Health Professions, 1977. FDA grantee, 1979. Mem. AAAS, Am. Physiol. Soc., Am. Public Health Assn., N.C. Public Health Fund, Am. Inst. Nutrition., Brit. Soc. Nutrition, Am. Coll. Nutrition. Home: 15 Rogerson Dr Chapel Hill NC 27514 Office: 315 Pittsboro St Chapel Hill NC 27514

ANDERSON, JOHN LEONARD, chemical engineering educator; b. Wilmington, Del., Sept. 29, 1945; s. Leonard Theodore and Leona (Kause) A.; m. Patricia Siemen, June 8, 1968; children: Brian Christopher, Lauren Kathleen. B.Ch.E., U. Del., 1967; M.S., U. Ill., 1969, Ph.D., 1971. Asst. prof. chem. engring. Cornell U., Ithaca, N.Y., 1971-76; assoc. prof. chem. engring. Carnegie-Mellon U., Pitts., 1976-79, prof., 1979—, head dept. com. engring., 1983—; dir. biomed. engring. Carnegie-Mellon U., Pitts., 1980—. Contbr. articles to profl. jours. Served to 2d lt. U.S. Army, 1972. NIH predoctoral fellow, 1969-71; NIH grantee, 1981—; John Simon Guggenheim Meml. Found. fellow, 1982-83; MIT vis. prof., 1982-83; vis. scholar Irish Am. Tech. Exchange Programme, Dept. Chem. Engring., U. Coll. Dublin, 1983. Mem. Am. Inst. Chem. Engrs. (symposium chmn. 1974—), Am. Chem. Soc. (symposium chmn. 1974—), AAAS, Tau Beta Pi, Alpha Tau Omega. Office: Carnegie-Mellon U Dept Chem Engring 5000 Forbes Ave Pittsburgh PA 15213

ANDERSON, JOHN MELVIN, physicist; b. Kansas City, Mo., Oct. 9, 1924; s. Melvin C. and Myrtle E. (Wooley) A.; m. Lois Emma Koester, June 16, 1950; children—Charles M., James M., Ruth C., Julie C. B.S. in Elec. Engring, U. Ill., 1947, M.S., 1948, Ph.D., 1955. Research asst. radio direction finding U. Ill., 1947-51, research asso. gaseous electronics, 1951-55; physicist plasma research Gen. Electric Co., Schenectady, 1955—; adj. prof. elec. engring. Rensselaer Poly. Inst., Troy, N.Y., 1964-71. Author. Served with AUS, 1943-46. Fellow IEEE (sect. chmn. 1967-68), Am. Phys. Soc.; mem. Sigma Xi, Tau Beta Pi, Eta Kappa Nu. Patentee in field. Home: 17 Cedar Ln Scotia NY 12302 Office: PO Box 8 Gen Electric Research and Devel Center Schenectady NY 12301

ANDERSON, JOHN MUELLER, emeritus philosophy educator; b. Cedar Rapids, Iowa, July 29, 1914; s. Arthur G. and Lois A. (Mueller) A.; m. Mary A. Gale, 1936; m. Barbara C. Lax., 1970. B.A., U. Ill., 1935, M.A. 1936; Ph.D., U. Calif. at Berkeley, 1939. Credit mgr. retail store Sears, Roebuck & Co., New Albany, Ind., 1939-41; research engr. Elgin Nat. Watch Co., Ill., 1941-42; chief spl. project Mpls.-Honeywell Co., 1942-43, asst. to chief engr., 1943-45; lectr. math. U. Minn., 1945-46; mem. faculty Pa. State U., 1946-80, prof. philosophy, 1951-68, Evan Pugh research prof. philosophy, 1968-80, emeritus, 1980—; head dept., 1948-49, 52-55, 58-67, acting asst. dean for research, 1964, summer 1965; founder, 1st dir. Inst. Arts and Humanistic Studies, 1966-68; liberal arts editor Pa. State Studies; vis. lectr. U. Ill., summer 1965; guest prof. U. Otago, New Zealand, 1955, Free U. Berlin, Germany, 1961-62, U. Calif., Santa Cruz, 1979; cons. ops. research, computer design. Author: (with Anderson and Mandeville) Industrial Management, 1942, Calhoun Basic Documents, 1952, The Individual and the New World, 1955, (with H.W. Johnstone, Jr.) Natural Deduction, 1962, The Realm of Art, 1967, The Truth of Freedom, 1977; also articles; founding editor: Man and World, 1966—; editor: Dialogue Press, 1971—; translator: (with E.H. Freund) Heidegger: Discourse on Thinking, 1966. Mem. Am. Philos Assn., Western Pa. Philos. Assn., AAUP, Assn. Am. Studies, Assn. Symbolic Logic, Soc. Phenomenology and Existential Philosophy (exec. com. 1965-68), Am. Soc. for Aesthetics, Am. Math. Soc., Phi Beta Kappa, Sigma Xi, Pi Gamma Mu, Alpha Tau Omega. Patentee computers. Home: RD 1 Box 290-A Port Matilda PA 16870 Office: 246 Sparks Bldg University Park PA 16802

ANDERSON, JOHN MURRAY, consultant, former university president; b. Toronto, Ont., Can., Sept. 3, 1926; s. Murray Alexander and Eleanor Montgomery (Valentine) A.; m. Eileen Anne McFaul, Nov. 3, 1951; children: Nancy, Susan, Peter, Katherine. B.Sc.F., U. Toronto, 1951, Ph.D., 1958; LL.D., St. Thomas U., 1974, Dalhousie U., 1979; D.Ped., U. Maine, Orono, 1976. Asst. prof. U. N.B., Can., 1958-63; asso. prof. Carleton U., 1963-67; dir. Fisheries Research Bd. Can. Biol. Sta., St. Andrews, N.B., 1967-72; dir. gen. Canadian Research and Devel., Fisheries and Marine Service, Dept. Environment, Ottawa, Ont., 1972-73; pres. U. N.B., 1973-79, J.M. Anderson Consultants Inc., 1980—; dir. Atlantic Salmon Research Inst., 1984—; pres., chmn. bd. dirs. Huntsman Marine Lab., St. Andrews, N.B., 1973-77; Bd. govs. Rothesay (N.B.) Collegiate Sch., 1976—, Kenya Tech. Tchrs. Coll., Nairobi, 1977-79; chmn. Assn. Atlantic Univs., 1978-79; v.p. Biol. Council Can., 1977-79. Contbr. numerous articles on fish physiology to profl. jours. Bd. dirs. Internat. Atlantic Salmon Found., 1979—, J.R. Bradfield Edn. Fund, Noranda, 1979—; pres., chmn. bd. trustees Sunbury Shores Arts and Nature Center, Inc., 1982—; bd. dirs. Aquaculture Assn. N.B., 1981—. Served with Royal Can. Navy, 1945. Mem. Inst. Can. Bankers (gov. 1974-79), Canadian Soc. Zoologists (pres. 1973-74), Agr. Ass. Can. (pres. 1984—), Assn. Univs. and Colls. Can. (dir. 1975-79), Sigma Chi. Unitarian. Clubs: Union (St. John, N.B.); Fredericton Garrison. Office: Atlantic Salmon Research Inst Saint Andrews NB NB Canada E0G 2X0

ANDERSON, JOHN RICHARD, educator; b. Fargo, N.D., May 5, 1931; s. John Raymond and Mary Ann (Beaulieu) A.; m. Shereen V. Erickson, Mar. 26, 1955; children: Scott F., Lisa K., Steven F. B.S., Utah State U., 1958; M.S., U. Wis., 1958, Ph.D., 1960. Asst. prof. entomology U. Calif., Berkeley, 1961-66, asso. prof., 1967-70, prof., 1970—; chmn. div. parasitology Coll. Natural Resources, 1970-71, assoc. dean research, 1979—; Trustee, past chmn. Alameda County (Calif.) Mosquito Abatement Dist., 1961-73, 79—. Editoral bd.: Jour. Med. Entomology, 1968-72, Jour. Econ. Entomology, 1977-81, Thomas Say Found, 1968-72. Served with USN, 1950-54. Research grantee. Mem. AAAS, Entomol. Soc., Am., Can., Pacific Coast entomol. socs., Am., Calif. mosquito control assns., Calif. Acad. Sci., N.Y. Acad. Sci., No. Calif. Parasitologists, Oakland Mus. Assn. Home: 2881 Shasta Rd Berkeley CA 94708 Office: U Calif Berkeley CA 94720

ANDERSON, JOHN ROBERT, university administrator; b. Stromsburg, Nebr., Aug. 1, 1928; s. Norris Merton and Violet Charlotte (Stromberg) A.; m. Bertha Margery Nore, Aug. 27, 1950; children: Eric Jon, Mary Lynn. Student, Midland Coll., 1945-46; A.A., Luther Jr. Coll., 1949; B.S. (Regents scholar), U. Nebr., Lincoln, 1951; M.A. in Math, U. Nebr., Lincoln, 1954; Ph.D., Purdue U., 1970. Tchr. math., coach Bloomfield (Nebr.) High Sch., 1951-52; control systems analyst, Allison div. Gen. Motors Corp., Indpls., 1954-60; prof. math. Depauw U., Greencastle, Ind., 1960, asst. dean, dir. grad. studies, 1973-76, dir. grad. studies, 1976—, resident dir. W. European studies program, W. Ger., France, 1975, resident dir. Mediterrenean Studies program, 1982; dir. NSF Coop. Coll. Sch., Sci. Inst., 1969-70; instr. NSF summer inst., 1972; instr. Challenge sci. and math. program U.S. Students in Europe, 1976, 77, 78, 80, 82; bd. dirs. Law Focused Edn., Indpls., 1975—, Ind. Regional Math. Consortium, 1977—. Bd. dirs. Bd. No. 8657 Lutheran Brotherhood; officer Peace Evangel. Luth. Ch., 1960—. Served with U.S. Army, 1946-48. Danforth Tchr. fellow, 1963-64; NSF sci. faculty fellow, 1964-65; Lilly Found. edn. grantee, summers 1961-63. Mem. Math. Assn. Am., Nat. Council Tchrs. Math., North Central Assn. (commr. 1974-78), Sigma Xi, Pi Mu Epsilon, Kappa Delta Pi, Beta Sigma Psi. Clubs: Rotary Internat. (sec. 1976-77, v.p. 1977-78), Rotary Internat. (pres. 1978-79). Home: 1560 Bloomington St Greencastle IN 46135 *In working with people always keep in mind: "If I were in their place, is this the way I would like to be treated by someone in my position?"*

ANDERSON, JOHN ROBERT, psychology and computer science educator; b. Vancouver, B.C., Can., Aug. 27, 1947; came to U.S., 1968, naturalized, permanent resident 1974; s. John Leonard and Adeline (Langraff) A.; m. Lynne Marie Reder, Mar. 29, 1973; 1 son, John Frank. B.A., U.B.C., 1968; Ph.D., Stanford U., 1972. Asst. prof. psychology Yale U., New Haven, 1972-73, prof., 1976-78; jr. fellow U. Mich., Ann Arbor, 1973-76; prof. psychology and computer sci. Carnegie Mellon U., Pitts., 1978—. Author: Language, Memory and Though, 1976, Cognitive Psychology and Its Implications, 1980, Cognitive Skills and Their Acquisitions, 1981, the Architecture of Cognition, 1983, Human Associative Memory, 1973. Mem. Am. Psychol. Assn., Am. Assn. Artificial Intelligence, Psychonomics Soc., Cognitive Sci. Soc. Office: Carnegie Mellon U Pittsburgh PA 15213 *My professional life has been devoted to understanding the concept of intelligence rather than to following and specific scientific or pro-fessional methodology. I have done research on human cognition, worker on creating artificial intelligence in computers, and have most recently been working on using artificial intelligence to improve human itelli-gence. I have been fortunate to be part of a generation of scientists that have made revolutionary progress on these issues*

ANDERSON, JOHN WEIR, editor; b. Phila., Sept. 29, 1928; s. Henry Ince and Marian (Carter) A.; m. Madelyn Anne Streeter, Apr. 28, 1956; children—Hilary Elissa, Adam Weir. A.B., Williams Coll., 1950. Reporter York (Pa.) Dispatch, 1953-55, Reading (Pa.) Times, 1955-56; reporter Washington Post, 1957-61, editorial writer, 1961-67, city editor, 1968-69, fgn. editor, 1970-71, editorial writer, 1971—. Author: Eisenhower, Brownell and the Congress, 1964. Served with AUS, 1946-48. Home: 514 Prince St Alexandria VA 22314 Office: 1150 15th St NW Washington DC 20071

ANDERSON, JOSEPH JAMES, state librarian; b. Dubuque, Iowa, June 28, 1932; s. George James and Agnes Irene (Melroy) A. B.A., St. Mary's U., San Antonio, 1953. Library asst. Bolt Hall Sch. of Law Library U. Calif., Berkeley, 1960-61; tech. librarian Lockheed Missiles & Space Co., Van Nuys, Calif., 1961-64; mgr. tech. processing Ampex Corp., Redwood City, Calif., 1964-67; dir. reference services Nev. State Library, Carson City, 1967-70, state librarian, 1970—; chmn. western states adv. council edn., 1974-76; state coordinator Nev. State Hist. Records Adv. Bd., 1977—; mem. Western State Com. on Higher Edn., 1970-77. Lt. comdr. USNR, 1954-66. Mem. ALA, Mountain Plains Library Assn. (pres. 1980), Spl. Libraries Assn., Nev. Library Assn., Calif. Library Assn., Western Council State Libraries (past pres., treas. 1978—). Republican. Roman Catholic. Home: PO box 1693 Carson City NV 89702

ANDERSON, JOSEPH NORMAN, food company executive, former college president; b. Mpls., May 12, 1926; s. Joseph E. and Helen (Larson) A.; m. Ruth E. Anderson, Sept. 6, 1952; children: Peter, Timothy, Paul, Matthew, Robin, Kathryn, Charles. B.B.A. with distinction, U. Minn., 1947. With Sears, Roebuck & Co., 1947-49, Gamble-Skogmo, Inc., 1950-64; v.p. finance, dir. Nat. Bellas Hess, Inc., 1964-67, pres., chief exec. officer, dir., 1967-69, chmn. bd., pres., chief exec. officer, 1969-75; pres. Jamestown (N.D.) Coll., 1975-83, Dakota Bake-n-Serv, Inc., 1983—; Pres. Merchants Research Council, 1961-62. Served with AUS, 1953-55. Mem. Phi Beta Kappa, Beta Gamma Sigma. Republican. Presbyn.

ANDERSON, JUDITH HELENA, English educator; b. Worcester, Mass., Apr. 21, 1940; d. Oscar William and Beatrice Marguerite (Beaudry) A.; m. E. Talbot Donaldson, May 18, 1971. A.B. magna cum laude, Radcliffe Coll., 1961; M.A., Yale U., 1962, Ph.D., 1965. Instr. Cornell U., Ithaca, N.Y., 1964-65, asst. prof., 1965-72; vis. lectr. Yale U., New Haven, 1973; vis. asst. prof. U. Mich., Ann Arbor, 1973-74; assoc. prof. Ind. U., Bloomington, 1974-79, prof. English, 1979—. Author: The Growth of a Personal Voice, 1976, Biographical Truth, 1984; editorial bd.: Spenser Ency., 1979—, Duquesne Studies in Lang. and Lit., 1976—. Woodrow Wilson fellow 1961-62, 63-64; NEH summer fellow and sr. research fellow, 1979, 81-82; Huntington Library research grantee, 1978. Mem. Spenser Soc. (pres. 1980), MLA (exec. com. Renaissance div. 1973-78), Renaissance Soc. Am., Milton Soc., AAUP, Phi Beta Kappa. Home: 2525 E 8th St Bloomington IN 47401 Office: Dept English Ind U Bloomington IN 47405

ANDERSON, KARL HERBERT, ins. co. exec.; b. Los Angeles, June 14, 1929. A.A., Pasadena City Coll., 1949; student, U. Calif., Los Angeles, 1949-51; B.A., Los Angeles State Coll., 1954. With Occidental Life Ins. Co. of Calif., Los Angeles, 1953—, 2d v.p., div. head group underwriting div., 1968-69, v.p., 1969-71, exec. v.p., 1971-79, sr. v.p. industry and provider relations, 1979—; Mem. Dist. Atty.'s Adv. Council. Fellow Life Office Mgmt. Inst.; mem. Health Ins. Assn. Am. Club: Transamerica Toastmasters. Office: 1150 S Olive St Los Angeles CA 90015

ANDERSON, KEITH, lawyer, banker; b. Phoenix, June 21, 1917; s. Carl Andreson and Helen (Fairchild) A.; m. Grace R. VanDenburg, 1941 (div. 1957); m. Catherine Huber, 1960; children: Fletcher F., Warren, Nicholas H. A.B., Dartmouth Coll., 1939; LL.B., Harvard U., 1942. Bar: N.Y. 1942, Ariz. 1946, Colo. 1950. Assoc. firm Carter, Ledyard & Milburn, N.Y.C., 1946-50; counsel Gen. Securities Co., Denver, 1950-54; ptnr. Holme, Roberts & Owen, Denver, 1954-70; v.p. Eagle County Devel. Co., Denver, 1970-71; pres. Mountain Banks, Ltd., Denver, 1972-74; ptnr. Banker & Hostetler, 1980—; chmn. Republic Nat. Bank of Englewood; dir. Mt. Banks Ltd., 1st Nat. Bank of Pueblo, Exchange Nat. Bank, Colorado Springs; chmn. bd., pres. Mine & Smelter Corp., First Charter Bank of Denver. Mem. Denver Planning Bd., 1960-63; pres. Graland Sch., Denver, 1963, Denver Mental Health Assn., 1962; treas. Rocky Mountain Planned Parenthood, Denver, 1980-81. Served with inf. U.S. Army, 1943-45. Mem. ABA, Denver Bar Assn., Colo. Bar Assn. Democrat. Clubs: University (Denver); Arapahoe Tennis. Office: Baker & Hostetler 303 E 17th Ave Denver CO 80203

ANDERSON, KENNETH ALLAN, professional football player; b. Batavia, Ill., Feb. 15, 1949; m. Bonnie Anderson; children: Matt, Megan, Elizabeth. B.S., Augustana Coll., 1971; J.D., No. Ky. U., 1981. Quarterback Cin. Bengals, 1971—. Player NFL Pro Bowl, 1975, 81, 82, NFL Championship Game, 1982; named NFL Player of Yr. Sporting News, 1981, Most Valuable Player in NFL Profl. Football Writers, 1981, A.P., 1981. Address: care Cincinnati Bengals 200 Riverfront Staduim Cincinnati OH 45202 *

ANDERSON, KENNETH EUGENE, educator; b. Mpls., Mar. 2, 1910; s. Peter Wilhelm and Alma Annette (Ekstrum) A.; m. Dorothy Woodruff Smith, Aug. 1, 1934; children: Peter Alden, Philip Norman. B.S., U. Minn., 1932, M.A., 1934, Ph.D., 1949. Tchr., adminstr. pub. schs., Minn., 1934-44; instr. U. Minn. High Sch., 1944-46, dir., 1946-47; prin. Campus High Sch., Iowa State Tchrs. Coll., 1947-48; asst. prof. ed. U. Kans., 1948-50, asso. prof. edn., dir. bur. edn. research service, 1950-52, prof. edn., 1952—, dean sch. edn., 1952-69; exec. dir. Kans. Master Planning Commn. on Post High Sch. Edn., 1970-73. Author: Anderson-Fisk Chemistry Test, 1966, (with Collister, Ladd) The Educational Achievement of Indian Children, 1953, (with others) The Indian Child Goes to School, 1957, (with H.A. Smith) Topics In Statistics for Students in Education, 1959; Exec. editor: Bull. Edn. and Kan. Studies in Education, 1953-68; Contbr. profl. publs. Recipient Outstanding Achievement award U. Minn., 1965; Master Tchr. award Kans. State Tchrs. Coll., Emporia, 1971; Fullbright-Hays scholar, Colombia, S.Am., summer 1974. Fellow AAAS (v.p. Sect. Q 1961-62); mem. Nat. Assn. Research Sci. Teaching (pres. 1954-55), North Central Assn. Colls. and Secondary Schs. (dir., exec. com. 1961-65), Nat. Soc. Study Edn., Am. Statis. Assn., Am. Ednl. Research Assn. (pres. 1959), Fulbright Alumni Assn., Sigma Xi. Home: 2312 Princeton Pl Lawrence KS 66044

ANDERSON, KENNETH G., corporation executive; b. N.Y.C., Jan. 14, 1924; m. Elayne M. Tranchina, Feb. 14, 1953; children: Kenneth G., Kristine E., Kathleen L., Kimberly A. B.S., Rennselaer Poly. Inst., 1950; M.B.A., Columbia U., 1953. Mgr. compensation Sylvania Electric Co., N.Y.C., 1959-62; mgr. compensation and benefits Celanese Corp., N.Y.C., 1962-64, asst. dir. personnel, dir. personnel, 1964-68, dir. personnel and orgn., 1968-73, v.p. personnel and orgn., 1973-79, v.p. employee affairs, 1979—. Chmn. Town Planning Bd., River Vale, N.J., 1963-78. Served to maj. USAF, 1940-45; ETO. Home: 567 Bernita Dr River Vale NJ 07675 Office: Celanese Corp 1211 Avenue of the Americas New York NY 10036

ANDERSON, KINSEY A., physicist, educator; b. Preston, Minn., Sept. 18, 1926; s. Malvin R. and Allene (Michener) A.; m. Lilica Athena Vassiliades, May 29, 1954; children—Danae, Sindri. B.A., Carleton Coll., 1949; Ph.D., U. Minn., 1955. Research assoc., faculty U. Iowa, Iowa City, 1955-59; Guggenheim fellow Royal Inst. Tech., Stockholm, Sweden, 1959-60; faculty U. Calif. at Berkeley, 1960—, prof. physics, 1966—; dir. Space Sci. Lab., 1970-79; Cons. NSF, NASA. Contbr. numerous articles to profl. jours. Mem. Nat. Acad. Scis., Am. Geophys. Union, Am. Phys. Soc., Am. Astron. Soc., Internat. Astron. Union, Phi Beta Kappa, Sigma Xi. Research in space plasma physics, magnetospheric particles, magnetic and electric fields using balloon, rocket and satellite instruments. Home: 8321 Buckingham Dr El Cerrito CA 94530 Office: Space Sci Lab U Calif Berkeley CA 94720

ANDERSON, LAURENS, biochemistry educator, scientist; b. Belle Fourche, S.D., May 19, 1920; s. Adolph and Mary E. (Slaughter) A.; m. Doris Elaine Young, Sept. 15, 1945; children: Eric Edward, Karl Arnold, Kristine Elaine. B.S., U. Wyo., 1942; M.S., U. Wis., 1947, Ph.D., 1950. Tchr., Campbell County, Wyo., 1936-38; asst. prof. biochemistry U. Wis.-Madison, 1951-56, assoc. prof., 1956-61, prof., 1961—, Steenbock prof. biomolecular structure dept. biochemistry, 1981—. Mem. editorial bd.: Advances in Carbohydrate Chemistry and Biochemistry, 1972, Carbohydrate Research, 1976—; contbr. sci. paper on organic chemistry and biochemistry of sugars and related substances. Mem. Council on Higher Edn., Wis. Conf. of United Ch. of Christ, 1966-73. Served to 1st lt. USAF, 1942-45; Italy. NRC fellow, (Zurich, Switzerland), 1950-51; NIH sr. postdoctoral fellow, 1971-72. Mem. Am. Chem. Soc. (Claude S. Hudson award in carbohydrate chemistry 1984), Am. Soc. Biol. Chemists, Sigma Xi. Mem. United Ch. of Christ. Home: 5639 Lake Mendota Dr Madison WI 53705 Office: Dept Biochemistry U Wis 420 Henry Mall Madison WI 53706

ANDERSON, LAURIE, performance artist; b. Wayne, Ill., 1947; d. Arthur T. and Mary Louise (Rowland) A. B.A. magna cum laude in Art History, Barnard Coll., 1969; M.F.A. in Sculpture, Columbia U., 1972. Composer and performer of multi-media exhbns. consisting of music, photography, film, drawings, animation and accompanying text, also sculptor, writer and violinist; art history instr. CCNY, 1973-75; freelance critic Art News; freelance Art Forum. Freelance critic: Art News, Art Forum; works include Story Show, 1972, Automotive, 1972, O-Range, 1973, Duets on Ice, 1973, Songs and Stories for the Insomniac, 1975, Refried Beans for Instants, 1976, For Instants Part 5, The Kitchen, N.Y.C., 1977, Handphone Table, Mus. Modern Art, N.Y.C., 1978, Americans on the Move, The Kitchen, 1979, United States 1-IV, Bklyn. Acad. Music, 1983; other compositions include Like a Stream-3, Born, Never Asked, It's cold Outside; recordings include O Superman, 1981, Big Science, 1982, Let X-X, Artforum Flexi-disc, 1982; contbr.: to album anthology You're the Guy I Want to Share My Money With, 1982; Mister Heartbreak album, 1984. ZBS Media artist-in residence, 1975; N.Y. State Council on Arts grantee, 1975, 77; Nat. Endowment for Arts grantee, 1977, 79; Guggenheim fellow, 1983. Mem. Phi Beta Kappa. Home: 530 Canal St New York NY 10013 Office: care Gail Turner 530 Canal St New York NY 10013 *

ANDERSON, LAVERNE ERIC, lawyer; b. Rockford, Ill., Feb. 24, 1922; s. Eric J. and Alma M. (Johnson) A.; m. Lucille Hardy, Feb. 14, 1954. LL.B., U. Ill., 1944, J.D., 1946. Bar: Ill. bar 1947. Admitted to practice U.S. Treasury Dept., Fed. Ct.; individual practice law,

Rockford, 1947—, city atty., 1947-53, corp. counsel, 1953-57. Mem. Am., Ill., Winnebago County bar assns., Broadway Bus. Assn., Phi Eta Sigma, Phi Beta Kappa, Phi Kappa Phi. Lutheran. Clubs: Masons, Shriners (rep. Imperial Council, dir., El Hajj Caravanserai No. 4, potentate Tebala Shrine Temple 1977). Office: 724 Broadway Rockford IL 61108

ANDERSON, LAWRENCE BERNHART, architect, educator; b. Geneva, Minn., May 7, 1906; s. Andrew S. and Lena (Christianson) A.; m. Rosina duPont, July 30, 1936; children: Judith, Karen, Lawrence. B.S., U. Min., 1926, 1927; M.Arch., Mass. Inst. Tech., 1930; student, Ecole des Beaux-Arts, Paris, 1930-33. Practice architecture, 1936—; partner H.L. Beckwith, Cambridge, 1938-54, Anderson, Beckwith and Haible, Boston, 1954-73; mem. faculty M.I.T., 1933-76, prof., 1945-71, charge dept. architecture, 1946-67; dean Sch. Architecture and Planning, 1965-71, prof. emeritus, sr. lectr., 1971-76; vis. prof. Universidad Católica, Santiago, Chile, 1975, U. Utah, 1977, U. Ariz., 1980, U. Calif., Berkeley, 1981; T. Jefferson prof. U. Va., 1976. Academician NAD. Fellow Am. Acad. Arts and Sci., AIA; mem. Assn. Collegiate Schs. Architecture (pres. 1953-55). Address: 44 Beaver Pond Rd PO Box 64 Lincoln Center MA 01773

ANDERSON, LAWRENCE KEITH, elec. engr.; b. Toronto, Ont., Can., Oct. 2, 1935; came to U.S., 1957; s. Wallace Ray and Irene Margaret (Linn) A.; m. Katherine Florence Drechsler, Sept. 21, 1963; children—Susan Barbara, Robert Keith. B. in Engring. Physics, McGill U., 1957; Ph.D. in E.E, Stanford U., 1962. With Bell Labs., 1961—, dir. electronic components and Subsystems lab., Allentown, Pa., 1981—. Fellow IEEE (pres. Electron Devices Soc. 1976-77, dir. 1979-80). Home: 3574 Stafore Dr W Bethlehem PA 18017 Office: 555 Union Blvd Allentown PA 18103

ANDERSON, LAWRENCE LESLIE, JR., manufacturing company executive, executive recruitment company executive; b. Mataredonda, Veracruz, Mexico, Apr. 5, 1930; s. Lawrence Leslie and Barbara Graham (Ryan) A. (parents Am. citizens); m. Stella Lee Edwards, Aug. 26, 1958; children: Lawrence Leslie, John Edwards, Elizabeth Hope, Stella Lee, Tobias Belford. A.B., Princeton U., 1952; M.A., Columbia U., 1956, Yale U., 1957; M.B.A., NYU, 1966. Salesman Procter & Gamble, 1954-55; internat. account rep. J. Walter Thompson, Columbia, 1957-61; product devel. mgr. Gen. Foods, White Plains, N.Y., 1961-63; product mgr. CPC, N.Y.C., 1963-68; with Imasco Ltd., Montreal, Que., Can., 1968-72, pres., chief exec. officer Growers Wine and S & W Fine Foods subs., Victoria, B.C., Can., San Francisco, 1969-72, Anderson Indsl. Products; pres., chief ops. officer Frank Foods Co., Cin., 1972-74, Reed Candy Co., Chgo., 1977-80; owner Lawrence Anderson & Assocs., Meriden, Conn., 1981—. Served with USMCR, 1952-54. Mem. Young Pres. Orgn., Am. Mgmt. Assn. (pres.'s Council 1971-72). Republican. Episcopalian. Office: 885 Wells Rd Wethersfield CT 06109

ANDERSON, LEE STRATTON, newspaper editor; b. Trenton, Ky., Dec. 15, 1925; s. Herbert Love and Corinne (Kirkpatrick) A.; m. Elizabeth McDonald, June 10, 1950; children—Corinne Elizabeth (Mrs. Jeffrey P. Adams), Mary Stewart. A.B., U. Chattanooga, 1948. Reporter Chattanooga News-Free Press, 1942-48, asso. editor, 1948-58, editor, 1958—; pres. Anderson-Meyers Enterprises, Inc.; operator Confederama; pres. Hamilton Enterprises Inc. Author: Battles of Chickamauga and Chattanooga 1863. Pres. Chattanooga Conv. and Visitor's Bur., 1958; chmn. Chattanooga chpt. ARC, 1968-70, United Fund Campaign, 1979. Served with USAAF, World War II; maj. Army Res. Recipient numerous Freedoms Found. awards for editorials and lectrs. Mem. Sigma Chi. Presbyn. (elder). Club: Rotarian (pres. Chattanooga 1964-65). Home: 220 N Crest Rd Chattanooga TN 37404 Office: 400 11th St Chattanooga TN 37401

ANDERSON, LEMOYNE W., librarian; b. Wheaton, Minn., Aug. 16, 1923; s. Walter E. and Ruth (Lundquist) A.; m. Hollis Annetta Pearson, June 2, 1950; children—Kristine Marie, Victoria Annetta. Student, Gustavus Adolphus Coll., 1942, 46; A.B., U. Minn., 1948, B.S. in L.S, 1948; M.S., U. Ill., 1951, Ph.D., 1970. Serials librarian Iowa State U., 1948-50; counselor librarian U. Ill., Chgo., 1951-55, reference librarian, asst. prof. library sci., 1955-57; dir. libraries, prof. library sci. Colo. State U., 1957—; Chmn. Research Libraries Group, Inc., 1980-81. Pres. U.S. Book Exchange, 1979. Served to sgt. AUS, 1942-45. Decorated Bronze Star medal, Purple Heart. Mem. Am. Library Assn., Mountain-Plains Library Assn., Colo. Library Assn. (pres. 1972-73), Assn. Coll. and Research Libraries (pres. 1979-80), Assn. Research Libraries (pres. 1978-79), AAUP, Am-Scandinavian Found., AAAS, Sigma Xi, Phi Kappa Phi, Alpha Tau Omega. Lutheran. Club: Lion. Home: 3606 Woodridge Rd Fort Collins CO 80524

ANDERSON, LENNART, artist; b. Detroit, Aug. 22, 1928. B.F.A., Art Inst. Chgo., 1950; M.F.A., Cranbrook Acad. Art Mich., 1952. Instr. Chatham Coll., Pitts., 1961-62, Pratt Inst., N.Y.C., 1962-69, Skowhegan Sch., 1965, 67, Art Students League, N.Y., Yale U., 1967, Finch Coll., N.Y.C., Bklyn. Coll. Exhbns., Carnegie Inst. Mus. Art, 1964, 67, Vassar Coll., 1968, Corcoran Gallery, Washington, 1964, 65; represented in permanent collections, Whitney Mus. Am. Art, Bklyn. Mus., Hirschorn Mus., Washington, Mus. Fine Arts, Boston, Cleve. Mus. Tiffan Found. grantee, 1957, 61; recipient Prix de Rome, 1958-60; Raymond A. Speiser Meml. prize Pa. Acad. Fine Arts, 1966; Nat. Council on Arts prize, 1966. NAD (academician 1983). Office: Dept of Art Brooklyn College Bedford Ave and Ave H Brooklyn NY 11210 *

ANDERSON, LEO E., lawyer; b. Gettysburg, S.D., Feb. 20, 1902; s. Laurits Martin and Leonora (Ellis) A.; m. Hollis Norris, Nov. 1, 1931 (dec. 1959); children: Denise, David H.; m. Pauline Murray, Feb. 12, 1961. Student, U. Redlands, 1921-22; B.S., B.A., U. So. Calif., 1924, LL.B., 1927. Bar: Calif. bar. With firm Meserve, Mumper & Hughes, Los Angeles, 1927—, partner, 1938—; Dir. Lennox Industries. Chmn. Los Angeles County Republican Central Com., 1936-40, Calif. Rep. Central Com., 1946-48; Pres., dir. Forest Lawn Meml. Parks; chmn. bd. govs. Shriners Hosps. for Crippled Children Los Angeles Unit, 1973-74; trustee U. Redlands (Calif.), 1968-72, Los Angeles Philanthropic Found., 1968—; pres. Orange Grove Terr. Owners Assn., 1976—. Clubs: Mason (grandmaster Calif. and Hawaii 1958), Shriner (potentate temple 1968). Home: 1215 S Orange Grove Blvd Pasadena CA 91105 Office: 333 S Hope St 35th Floor Los Angeles CA 90071

ANDERSON, LEONARD GUSTAVE, business executive; b. Danville, Ill., Jan. 16, 1919; s. Andrew John and Hedvig (Engstrom) A.; m. Perrin Louise Johnston, Aug. 25, 1946. B.S., U. So. Miss., 1947; LL.B., Emory U., 1949. Bar: Ga. 1949. Lawyer Atlantic Coast Line R.R. Co., 1950-67, Seaboard Coast Line R.R. Co., 1967-68, v.p., treas., dir., 1968-80; v.p., treas. Seaboard Coast Line Industries, Inc., 1969-80, CSX Corp., Richmond, 1980—; dir. L. & N. R.R., 1972-80; mem. finance com. Norfolk & Portsmouth Belt Line R.R. Co. Served to capt. AUS, 1942-46; maj. Res.; ret. Mem. Am. Bar Assn., State Bar Ga., Phi Delta Phi. Methodist. Club: Commonwealth (Richmond, Va.). Home: 300 W Franklin St Richmond VA 23220 Office: 1500 Fed Res Blvd Richmond VA 23213

ANDERSON, LYLE ARTHUR, mfg. co. exec.; b. Jewell, Kans., Dec. 29, 1931; s. Arvid Herman and Clara Vera (Herman) A.; m. Harriet Virginia Robson, June 12, 1953; children—Brian, Karen, Eric. B.S., U. Kans., 1953; M.S., Butler U., 1961. C.P.A., Mo., Kans. Mgmt. trainee, internal auditor RCA, Camden, N.J. and Indpls., 1955-59; auditor Ernst & Ernst (C.P.A.'s), Kansas City, Mo., 1959-63; v.p. fin. and adminstrn., treas., dir. Affiliated Hosp. Products, Inc., St. Louis, 1963-71; sr. v.p. Kitchens of Sara Lee div. Consol. Foods Corp., Deerfield, Ill., 1971-74, exec. v.p. fin., dir. parent co., Chgo., 1974-76; pres., chief exec. officer Autotrol Corp., Crystal Lake, Ill., 1976—; chmn. bd. Valley Electromagnetics Corp., Spring Valley, Ill. Bd. dirs. Meml. Hosp. of McHenry County. Served with AUS, 1953-55. Mem. Ill. Mfrs. Assn. (bd. dirs.), Am. Inst. C.P.A.'s, Omicron Delta Kappa. Republican. Methodist. Home: 9804 Partridge Ln Crystal Lake IL 60014 Office: 365 E Prairie St Crystal Lake IL 60014

ANDERSON, LYNN (RENE ANDERSON), singer; b. Grand Forks, N.D., Sept. 26, 1947; d. Casey and Liz Anderson; m. Glenn Sutton; 1 dau., Lisa. Began singing and recording, 1966; appearances on: Lawrence Welk Show, from 1967—, Porter Waggoner Show, 1967, Gran Old Opry, 1967, Bill Anderson Show, 1967, 68; recorded songs include Sweet Talkin Man, I Never Promised You a Rose Garden, You're My Man, Top of the World, What a Man My Man Is. Address: care International Creative Management 40 W 57th St New York NY 10019 *

ANDERSON, MARIAN, contralto; b. Phila., Feb. 27, 1902; d. John Berkeley and Anna A.; m. Orpheus H. Fisher, July 24, 1943. Ed. Phila. pub. schs.; mus edn., pvt. study in Phila., N.Y. and abroad, Spelman Coll., 1979,. As child sang in Union Bapt. Ch. choir, Phila.; U.S. del. 13th Gen. Assembly, UN, 1958; ret., 1965. Began singing career, 1924; Debut in Un Ballo in Maschera, Met. Opera, 1955; has made many concert tours of the, U.S. and, Europe; one of the leading contraltos in world; appearances in all famous concert halls, stadia; Author: My Lord, What a Morning, 1966. Recipient Bok Award, 1940; Am. Freedom medal, 1963; Congl. gold medal, 1978; awarded Finnish decoration "probenignitate humana, 1940; decorations from Sweden, Philippines, Haiti, Liberia, France, numerous states and cities in U.S.; Yokus Lo medal (Japan); named Woman of the Decade Ladies Home Jour., 1980; won 1st prize in competition with 300 others at N.Y. Lewisohn Stadium, 1925. Mem. Alpha Kappa Alpha. A fund raised through a church concert enabled her to take singing lessons under an Italian instr. Office: care ICM Artists Ltd 40 W 57th St New York NY 10019 *

ANDERSON, MARION CORNELIUS, medical educator; b. Concordia, Kans., Oct. 9, 1926; s. Cornelius Oscar and Mildred Marian (Watson) A.; m. Sonia Blue Bennett, Jan. 30, 1949; children: Dudley Scott, James Christopher, Julia, Laura Gail. Student, U. Kans., 1946-49; B.S., Northwestern U., 1950, M.D., 1953, M.S., 1960. Diplomate: Am. Bd. Surgery. Intern Passavant Meml. Hosp., Chgo., 1953-54, resident in surgery, 1954-55, Kanavel fellow in surgery, 1956-57; resident in surgery VA Research Hosp., Chgo., 1955-56; assoc. in surgery Cook County Hosp., Chgo., 1957-59; clin. asst. dept. surgery Northwestern U. Med. Sch., 1958, instr., 1958-59, assoc., 1960-62, asst. prof., 1962-64, asso. prof., 1964-68; prof., chmn. dept. surgery Med. Coll. Ohio, Toledo, 1969-72, pres., 1972-77; vice chmn. dept. surgery Med. U. S.C., 1977, chmn. dept. surgery, 1978; cons. Stedmans Med. Dictionary, 1970. Editorial bd.: Am. Jour. Surgery, Am. Surgery; Contbr. articles to profl. jours. Served with USNR, 1944-46. ACS. Kemper research scholar, 1960. Mem. AAAS, Am. Assn. Med. Writers, Am. Assn. for Surgery of Trauma, A.C.S. (gov. 1984—), Am. Gastroent. Assn., AMA., Am., Central, Western surg. assns., Cleve., Midwest, Pan-Pacific, Toledo (pres. 1970-71) surg. socs., So. Surg. Assn., Assn. Am. Med. Colls., Detroit Gastroent. Soc., Internat. Soc. Surgery, Nat. Soc. Med. Research, N.Y. Acad. Sci., Northwestern U. Med. Sch. Alumni Assn. (pres. 1965-66, Service award 1968), Pancreas Club (sec. 1968-69), Soc. Clin. Surgery, Soc. for Surgery Alimentary Tract (v.p. 1983), Soc. Surg. Chairmen, Southeastern Surg. Congress, Soc. Univ. Surgeons, Surg. Biology Club III, S.C. Med. Assn., Charleston County Med. Soc., Sigma Xi, Alpha Omega Alpha, Phi Chi. Club: Charleston Country. Home: 1580 Fairway Dr Charleston SC 29412

ANDERSON, MARQUARD JOHN, mfg. exec.; b. Clairton, Pa., Apr. 15, 1920; s. Carl J. and Anna C. (Carlson) A.; m. Catherine Markey, June 2, 1945; children—Carl, John, Ruth C. B.S., U. Pitts., 1942. With Aro Corporation, Bryan, Ohio, 1945—, successively asst. sales mgr., asst. to v.p., v.p., 1945-56, pres., 1956—; also dir.; dir. Citizens Nat. Bank, Bryan, Union Pump Co., Battle Creek, Mich., Libby Owens Ford, Toledo, Ohio, Ammco Tools Inc., Chgo. Served as capt. USAAF, 1942-45. Clubs: Mason, Shriner. Home: Center Ridge Rd Bryan OH 43506 Office: Aro Corp: 1 Aro Center Bryan OH 43506

ANDERSON, MARTIN CARL, economist; b. Lowell, Mass., Aug. 5, 1936; s. Ralph and Evelyn (Anderson) A.; m. Annelise Graebner, Sept. 25, 1965. A.B. summa cum laude, Dartmouth, 1957; M.S. in Engring. and Bus. Adminstrn, Thayer Sch. Engring. and Amos Tuck Sch. Bus. Adminstrn.; Ph.D. in Indsl. Mgmt, Mass. Inst. Tech., 1962. Asst. to dean, instr. engring. Thayer Sch. Engring., Hanover, N.H., 1959; research fellow Joint Center for Urban Studies, Mass. Inst. Tech. and Harvard, 1961-62; asst. prof. finance Grad. Sch. Bus., Columbia, N.Y.C., 1962-65, asso. prof. bus., 1965-68; spl. asst. to Pres. of U.S., 1969-70, spl. cons. for systems analysis, 1970-71; sr. fellow Hoover Inst. on War, Revolution and Peace, Stanford U., 1971-81; asst. to Pres. of U.S. for policy devel., Washington, 1981—; pub. interest dir. Fed. Home Loan Bank of San Francisco, 1972-79; Mem. Commn. on Critical Choices for Ams., 1973-75, Def. Manpower Commn., 1975-76, Com. on the Present Danger, 1977—. Author: The Federal Bulldozer: A Critical Analysis of Urban Renewal, 1949-62, 1964, Conscription: A Select and Annotated Bibliography, 1976, Welfare: The Political Economy of Welfare Reform in the U.S, 1978. Dir. research Nixon presdl. campaign, 1968; issues adviser Reagan presdl. campaign, 1976, 80. Served as 2d lt. AUS, 1958-59. Mem. Am. Econ. Assn., Am. Finance Assn., U.S. C. of C. (council on trends and perspectives 1974-76), Phi Beta Kappa. Office: The White House 1600 Pennsylvania Ave Washington DC 20050

ANDERSON, MARY JANE, information brokerage and consulting firm executive; b. Des Moines, Jan. 23, 1935; d. William Kenneth and Margaret Louise (Snider) McPherson; m. Charles Robert Anderson, Oct. 21, 1965; 1 dau., Mary Margaret. B.A. in Edn, U. Fla., 1957; M.A.L.S., Fla. State U., 1963. Elem. sch. librarian Dade County Schs., Miami, Fla., 1957-61; children's/young adult librarian Santa Fe Regional Library, Gainesville, Fla., 1961-63; br. librarian Jacksonville (Fla.) Public Library, 1963-64, chief of children's services, 1964-66, head of circulation, 1966-67; public library cons. Fla. State Library, Tallahassee, 1967-70; dir. tech. processing St. Mary's Coll. of Md., St. Mary's City, 1970-72; coordinator children's services Baltimore County Public Library, Towson, Md., 1972-73; exec. dir. young adult services div. ALA, Chgo., 1973-75, exec. dir. assn. for library service to children, 1973-82; pres. Answers Unltd., Inc., 1982—; instr. and cons. in field. Bd. dirs. Child Devel. Assos. Consortium, 1975-83, Coalition for Children and Youth, 1978-80; mem. exec. com. U.S. sect. Internat. Bd. on Books for Young People, 1973-82; mem. adv. bd. Reading Rainbow, TV series, 1981—. Editor: Top of the News, 1971-73, Fla. State Library Newsletter, 1967-70; contbr. articles to profl. jours. Mem. ALA, Beta Phi Mu. Episcopalian. Office: 1618 Elder Ln Northfield IL 60093

ANDERSON, MILTON HENRY, psychiatrist, hospital administrator; b. Omaha, July 31, 1919; s. Milton Henry and Emma Fay (Anderson) A.; m. Margaret Cushing, July 24, 1943 (dec. 1960); children: Gregory Cushing, Milton Henry III, Herbert Clark, Eric Austin; m. J. Sue Roberts, Sept. 12, 1966. Student, Northwestern U., 1937-38; A.B., Omaha U., 1941; M.D., U. Nebr., 1943. Bar: Diplomate Am. Bd. Psychiatry and Neurology. Intern Long Island Coll. Medicine, 1943-44; resident Lenox Hill Hosp., N.Y.C., 1944- 45; clin. dir. Hastings (Nebr.) State Hosp., 1948-51; med. supt. Osawatomie (Kans.) State Hosp., 1951-53, Evansville State Hosp., 1953-69; dir. psychiatry Welborn Meml. Hosp., 1969-82; Cons. Deaconess, St. Mary's hosps., regional VA hosps., states Ill. and Ind.; bd. dirs. Evansville Child Guidance Clinic, 1953-62, Vanderburgh County Mental Health Clinic, 1964-72. Active local health fund drives. Served to capt., M.C. AUS, 1945-47. Bishop Clarkson resident physician, 1947-48; fellow Bennett Found., 1947-48. Fellow Am. Psychiat. Assn. (life), Am. Orthopsychiat. Assn., AAAS, Am. Geriatric Soc.; mem. Central Neuropsychiat. Assn., Am. Med. Electroencephalographic Soc., Western Electroencephalographic Soc., Am. Epilepsy Soc., Am. Group Psychotherapy Assn., Assn. Research Nervous and Mental Diseases, Sigma Chi, Phi Rho Sigma. Clubs: Mason (Shriner), Indpls. Athletic, Evansville Country, Rotary (pres. 1968-69). Address: 3700 Bellemeade Ave Suite 109 Evansville IN 47715

ANDERSON, MYLES NORMAN, mining and refining metals company executive; b. Flin Flon, Man., Can., Jan. 22, 1931; m. Tania Lorette Babienko; children: Kristopher, Paul, Kathryn. B.Sc., U. Man. Chmn., chief exec. officer Cominco Ltd., Vancouver, B.C., Can.; dir. Toronto-Dominion Bank, Gulf Can. Ltd., Fording Coal Ltd., Aberfoyle Ltd., Cominco Australian Pty. Ltd., Cominco Binani Zinc Ltd., Vestgron Mines Ltd. Mem. Mining Assn. Can., Can. Inst. Mining and Metallurgy, Am. Inst. Metall. Engrs., B.C. Profl. Engrs., Mo. Profl. Engrs., Alta. Profl. Engrs., Coal Assn. Can. Clubs: Vancouver, Shaughnessy Golf and Country. Office: Cominco Ltd 200 Granville Sq Vancouver BC V6C 2R2 Canada

ANDERSON, NEIL MARTIN, insurance company executive; b. Boone, Iowa, May 2, 1937; s. Wilbert Martin and Leona Jeannette (Larson) A.; m. Barbara Gordon Nall, June 11, 1960; children—Keith Gordon, Sally Wadsworth. B.A. with distinction, U. Iowa. Actuarial asst. Nat. Life & Accident Ins. Co., Nashville, 1959-62, asst. actuary, 1962-65, 2d v.p., asso. actuary to v.p. and chief actuary individual ins. div., 1965-75, sr. v.p., chief actuary, 1975-79; sr. v.p. NLT Corp., Nashville, 1979-80, exec. v.p., 1980—, chief actuary, 1983—, also dir.; dir. Nat. Life & Accident Ins. Co., Gt. So. Life Ins. Co., Guardsman Life Ins. Co. Fellow Soc. Actuaries; mem. Am. Acad. Actuaries, Southeastern Actuaries Club (past pres.). Lutheran. Home: 1242 Jefferson Davis Ct Brentwood TN 37027 Office: Am Gen Center Nashville TN 37250

ANDERSON, NILS, JR., business executive; b. Plainfield, N.J., Jan. 28, 1914; s. Nils and Marguerite (Stephens) A.; m. Jean Derby Ferris, July 30, 1938; children: Nils III (dec.), Derby Ferris, Stephens Massie, Ward Reynolds. B.A., Williams Coll., 1937; student, Colo. Sch. Mines, George Washington U. Law Sch. With Koppers Co., summers 1933-37, Bakelite Corp., 1937-41; dir. Deveboise-Anderson Co., Inc., 1937—, pres., 1950-58, chmn. bd., 1965—; v.p. Casein Co. Am. (subsequently chem. div. Borden Co.), 1945-50; also dir. Am., S.Am. cos.; with WPB, 1941-45, chief adhesives unit, 1942, chief plastics br., 1944-45; also govt. presiding officer adhesives, plastics industry adv. coms., chem. div. adviser to Dept. Agr.; combined Raw Materials Bd., Stock Pile and Shipping Br. during World War II; mem. U.S. Trade Mission to Rumania and Poland, 1965. Author tech. articles on adhesives and plastics. Trustee, U.S. Naval War Coll. Found. Mem. ASME, Am. Coke and Coal Chems. Inst., Am. Iron and Steel Inst., Soc. Colonial Wars, Soc. War 1812, Pilgrims Soc., Alpha Delta Phi. Clubs: Links, University (N.Y.C.); Country (Fairfield); Travellers (Paris); Duquesne (Pitts.); Rolling Rock (Pa.); Pequot Yacht (Southport). Home: 935 Harbor Rd Southport CT 06490

ANDERSON, ODIN WALDEMAR, sociologist, educator; b. Mpls., July 5, 1914; s. Edwin and Anna (Ormbreck) A.; m. Helen Hay, June 24, 1939; children: Kristin Alice, Thor Edwin. B.A., U. Wis., 1937, M.A., 1938; B.A. in L.S., U. Mich., 1940, Ph.D., 1948; Ph.D. (hon.), U. Uppsala, Sweden, 1977. Instr., U. Mich. Sch. Pub. Health, 1944-49; asso. prof. dept. clin. preventive medicine, med. faculty U. Western Ont., London, 1949-52; research dir. Health Info. Found., N.Y.C., 1952-62, Health Info. Found., U. Chgo., 1962-64, Center Health Adminstrn. Studies, 1964-66, asso. dir., 1966-72, dir., 1972-80, asso. prof. sociology, dept. sociology and Grad. Sch. Bus., 1962-64, prof., 1964-80, prof. emeritus, 1980—; prof. sociology U. Wis., Madison, 1980—; Mem. research com. Nat. Tb Assn., 1959- 64; mem. U.S. Nat. Com. Vital and Health Stats., 1959-63. Author: (with Jacob J. Feldman) Family Medical Care and Voluntary Health Insurance, 1956, (with others) Family Medical Care and Health Insurance, 1963, (with Ronald Andersen) A Decade of Health Services: Social Survey Trends in Use and Expenditures, 1968, The Uneasy Equilibrium: Private and Public Financing of Health Services in the U.S., 1875-1965, 1968, Health Care: Can There Be Equity? The United States, Sweden, and England, 1972. Fellow Am. Sociol. Assn. (past chmn. sect. med. sociology, Disting. Med. Sociologist sect. med. sociology 1980), Am. Pub. Health Assn., Am. Coll. Hosp. Adminstrs. (hon.), AAAS; mem. Inst. Medicine of Nat. Acad. Sci. Home: 2105 Kendall Ave Madison WI 53705

ANDERSON, ORSON LAMAR, educator; b. Price, Utah, Dec. 3, 1924; s. Orson Bryner and Elda Mae (Edwards) A.; m. Berneice Hoggatt; children—Bonnie, Sherri. B.S., U. Utah, 1948, Ph.D., 1951. Physicist Bell Telephone Labs., Murray Hill, N.J., 1951-60; mgr. materials research Am. Standard Research Labs., New Brunswick, N.J., 1960-63; adj. prof. Lamont Geol. Obs., Columbia U., 1963-66, prof. geology, 1966-71; prof. geophysics U. Calif., Los Angeles, 1971—; dir. Inst. Geophysics and Planetary Physics, 1978—. Research on mineral physics, planetary physics, energy and environ. studies. Office: Institute of Geophysics University of California Los Angeles CA 90024

ANDERSON, O(RVIL) ROGER, biology educator, researcher, marine biology; b. East St. Louis, Ill., Aug. 4, 1937; s. Orvil Noel and Marie Elizabeth (Diekemper) A. B.A., Washington U., St. Louis, 1959, M.A., 1961, Ph.D., 1964. Ordained to ministry, Reorganized Ch. of Jesus Christ of Latter Day Saints, 1962. Asst. prof. sci. Columbia U. Tchrs. Coll., N.Y.C., 1964-67, assoc. prof., 1968-70, prof., 1971—; research assoc. Lamont-Doherty Obs., Palisades, N.Y., 1965-70, sr. research scientist, 1971—; minister Reorganized Ch. of Jesus Christ of Latter Day Saints, N.Y.C., 1964—. Author: Quantitative Analysis of Stucture in Teaching, 1971, Teaching Modern Ideas of Biology, 1972, The Experience of Science, 1976, Radiolaria, 1983; editor: Jour. of Research in Sci. Teaching, 1970-75; contbr. articles to profl. jours. NSF grantee, 1972—. Fellow AAAS; mem. Soc. Protozoologists, Am. Soc. Limnology and Oceanography, Nat. Assn. for Research in Sci. Teaching (pres. 1976-77), Sigma Xi. Home: 501 W 120th St New York NY 10027 Office: Columbia U Tchrs Coll 525 W 120th St New York NY 10027

ANDERSON, OWEN RAYMOND, scientific and educational organization executive; b. Chestertown, Md., Aug. 27, 1919; s. Owen Raymond and Ida Frances (Jenkins) A.; m. Ida Lois Pritts, June 8, 1946; children: Penny Pritts, Jeri Alyce. B.A., Washington Coll., 1940. Tchr. Garrett County Bd. Edn., Kitzmiller, Md., 1940-41, 1946; with Nat. Geog. Soc., Washington, 1946—, div. supr., 1950, adminstrv. asst., 1952-61, asst. sec., 1961-66, asso. sec., 1966-76, v.p., sec., 1976-80, exec. v.p., 1980—, trustee, 1981—, vice chmn. bd., 1984—. Served to capt. U.S. Army, 1941-46, 50-52; ETO, Korea. Decorated Bronze Star, Purple Heart, Combat Infantry badge; recipient Alumni Citation award Washington Coll., 1981. Mem. Am. Legion, Lambda Chi Alpha. Methodist. Club: Alfalfa. Home: 3213 Pickwick Ln Chevy Chase MD 20815 Office: 17th and M Sts NW Washington DC 20036

ANDERSON, PAUL EDWARD, cement company executive; b. Pottsville, Pa., Aug. 19, 1921; s. Thomas and Virginia (Nolan) A.; m. Florence Joan White, Oct. 16, 1948; children: Paul Edward, Barbara Jane. Grad., Peirce Sch. Bus. Adminstrn., Phila., 1948. With Lehigh Portland Cement Co., Allentown, Pa., 1948—, credit mgr., 1957-64, treas., 1958-67, v.p. corp. devel., 1967-70, mgr. real estate, 1970-72, treas., 1971—, v.p., 1979—, dir., 1983—. Roman Catholic. Clubs: Livingston, Lehigh Country (Allentown, Pa.). Home: 3756 Turner St Allentown PA 18104 Office: 718 Hamilton St Allentown PA 18101

ANDERSON, PAUL F., bishop; b. Boston, Apr. 20, 1917; s. Philip Leo and Mary Elizabeth (Doyle) A. B.A., St. John's Sem., Brighton, Mass., 1943. Ordained priest Roman Cath. Ch., 1943; pastor Sioux Falls (S.D.) Cath. Diocese, 1946-68; coadjutor bishop of, Duluth, 1968-69, bishop, 1969—. Office: 215 W 4th St Duluth MN 55806 *

ANDERSON, PAUL GENE, national space administration official; b. Grandy, Minn., Aug. 10, 1943; s. Oliver Eugene and Elvera Deborah (Burke) A.; m. Loretta Lorraine West, July 13, 1963; children: Wendy, Kathleen. B.A., U. Minn., 1965, postgrad., 1965-66. With NASA, 1966—, dir. program analysis div. Office Space Scis. and Applications, Washington, 1980-82; comptroller NASA Lewis Research Ctr., Cleve., 1982—. Home: 29460 Lake Rd Bay Village OH 44140 Office: Comptroller Code 3000 Lewis Research Ctr Cleveland OH

ANDERSON, PAUL IRVING, electronics company executive; b. Portland, Oreg., Mar. 23, 1935; s. William F. and Ruth M. A.; m. Lorraine A. Franz, Nov. 21, 1959; children: Todd, Susan, Cheryl, Cynthia. B.S., Oreg. State U., 1956. Various positions in mktg., sales and engring. mgmt. 3M Co., St. Paul and Boston, 1956-74, product dir., Brussels, Belgium, 1974-77, group bus. planning mgr., St. Paul, 1977-79; sr. v.p., gen. mgr. Rayovac Corp., Madison, Wis., 1979-82; pres. Anderson Cons. Co., Madison, 1982-83; div. v.p. RCA Corp., Indpls., 1983—. Mem. Am. Mgmt. Assn., Tau Beta Pi, Pi Tau Sigma, Sigma Tau. Republican. Presbyterian. Clubs: Columbia (Indpls.); Madison; Nakoma Golf (Madison). Home: 13061 Andover Dr Carmel IN 46032

ANDERSON, PAUL MAURICE, electrical engring. educator, researcher, consultant; b. Des Moines, Jan. 22, 1926; s. Neil W. and Buena Vista (Thompson) A.; m. Virginia Ann Worswick, July 8, 1950; children: William, Mark, James, Thomas. B.S.E.E., Iowa State U., 1949, M.S.E.E., 1958, Ph.D. in Elec. Engring., 1961. Registered profl. engr., Ariz., Calif., Iowa; registered control systems engr., Calif. Elec. engr. Iowa Pub. Service Co., Sioux City, 1949-55; prof. elec. engring. Iowa State U., Ames, 1955-75; program mgr. Electric Power Research Inst., Palo Alto, Calif., 1975-78; cons. Power Math Assocs. Inc., Palo Alto and Tempe, 1978—; prof. elec. engring. Ariz. State U., Tempe, 1980—. Author: Analysis of Faulted Power Systems, 1973, (with others) Power Control and Stability, 1977; editor: Ency. Sci. and Tech., 1979; contbr. articles to profl. jours. NSF faculty fellow, 1960-61; recipient Faculty citation Iowa State U. Alumni Assn., 1973, Profl. Achievement citation Iowa State U., 1981. Fellow IEEE (pres. Iowa sect. 1959-60), Conf. Internat. des Grands Reseaux Electriques, Sigma Xi, Phi Kappa Phi, Eta Kappa Nu, Pi Mu Epsilon. Republican. Lodge: Masons. Home: 1236 E Malibu Dr Tempe AZ 85282 Office: Arizona State U Dept Elec and Computer Engring Tempe AZ 85287

ANDERSON, PHILIP SIDNEY, lawyer; b. Little Rock, May 9, 1935; s. Philip Sidney and Frances (Walt) A.; m. Rosemary Gill Wright, Sept. 26, 1959; children: Sidney Walt, Philip Wright, Catherine Gill. B.A., U. Ark., 1959, LL.B., 1959. Bar: Ark. 1960. Since practiced in, Little Rock; partner firm Wright, Lindsey & Jennings.; Lectr. Ark. Law Sch., 1963-65; mem. Ark. Supreme Ct. Com. on Jury Instrns., 1962—, U.S. Circuit Judge Nominating Panel for 8th Circuit, 1978-79. Co-author: Arkansas Model Jury Instructions, 1965, 74. Pres. Friends of Little Rock Pub. Library, 1968-69, Little Rock Unlimited Progress, Inc., 1973-74, Greater Little Rock Chamber Found., 1980—; trustee George W. Donaghey Found., pres., 1979-81; trustee Central Ark. Library System; sponsor Little Rock Chamber Music Soc. Served to 2d lt. AUS, 1959-60. Recipient Spl. award Ark. Bar Assn., 1966. Fellow Ark. Bar Found. (chmn. 1973-74); mem. Am. Law Inst. (council), Am. Judicature Soc., ABA (state del. 1979—, council legal edn. sect.), Ark. Bar Assn., Pulaski County Bar Assn., Greater Little Rock C. of C. (bd. dirs.), Blue Key, Kappa Sigma. Episcopalian. Home: 4716 Crestwood St Little Rock AR 72207 Office: 2200 Worthen Bank Bldg Little Rock AR 72201

ANDERSON, PHILIP WARREN, physicist; b. Indpls., Dec. 13, 1923; s. Harry W. and Elsie (Osborne) A.; m. Joyce Gothwaite, July 31, 1947; 1 dau., Susan Osborne. B.S., Harvard U., 1943, M.A., 1947, Ph.D., 1949; D.Sc. (hon.), U. Ill., 1979. Mem. staff Naval Research Lab., 1943-45; mem. tech. staff Bell Telephone Labs., Murray Hill, N.J., 1949—, chmn. theoretical physics dept., 1959-60, asst. dir. phys. research lab., 1974-76, cons. dir., 1976—; Fulbright lectr. U. Tokyo, 1953-54; Loeb lectr. Harvard U., 1964; prof. theoretical physics Cambridge (Eng.) U., 1967-75; prof. physics Princeton U., 1975—; Overseas fellow Churchill Coll., Cambridge U., 1961-62; fellow Jesus Coll., 1969-75, hon. fellow, 1978—. Author: Concepts in Solids, 1963, Basic Notions of Condensed Matter Physics, 1984. Recipient Oliver E. Buckley prize Am. Physical Soc., 1964; Dannie Heinemann prize Göttingen (Ger.) Acad. Scis., 1975; Nobel prize in physics, 1977; Guthrie medal Inst. of Physics, 1978; Nat. Medal Sci., 1982. Fellow Am. Phys. Soc., Am. Acad. Arts and Scis., AAAS; mem. Nat. Acad. Scis., Royal Soc. (fgn.), Phys. Soc. Japan, European Phys. Soc. Research in quantum theory, especially theoretical physics of solids, spectral line broadening, magnetism, superconductivity. Address: Bell Telephone Labs Murray Hill NJ 07974

ANDERSON, POUL WILLIAM, science fiction author; b. Pa., 1926. Degree physics, U. Minn., 1948. Works include: Brain Wave, 1954, Planet of No Return, 1956, War of the Wing-Men, 1958, Earthman Go Home!, 1960, Mayday Orbit, 1961, After Doomsday, 1962, Let the Spaceman Beware, 1963, Orbit Unlimited, 1963, Is There Life on Other Worlds, 1963, Time and Stars, 1964, Agent of the Terran Empire, 1965, The Trouble Twisters, 1966, The Horn of Time, 1968, Infinite Voyage: Man's Future in Space, 1969, Tau Zero, 1970, Brain Wave, 1970, Circus of Hells, 1970, Guardians of Time, 1970, Seven Conquests, 1970, Tales of the Flying Mountains, 1970, Operation Chaos, 1971, Byworlder, 1971, The Broken Sword, 1971, Hrolf Kraki's Saga, 1973, Virgin Planet, 1973, The Rebel World, 1973, People of the Wind, 1973, Fire Time, 1974, The Many Worlds of Poul Anderson, 1974, The Book of Poul Anderson, 1975, Mirkheim, 1977, The Avatar, 1978, The Merman's Children, 1979, Orion Shall Rise, 1983; numerous others. Recipient Hugo award, Nebula award. Issue of Mag. Fantasy and Sci. dedicated to him, 1972. Office: care Scott Meredith Lit Agy 845 3d Ave New York NY 10022

ANDERSON, QUENTIN, English educator, critic; b. Minnewaukan, N.D., July 21, 1912; s. Maxwell and Margaret E. (Haskett) A.; m. Margaret Pickett, May 27, 1933 (div. Aug. 1946); 1 dau., Martha Haskett; m. Thelma Ehrlich, Dec. 13, 1947; children: Abraham Bruce, Maxwell Lincoln. Student, Dartmouth, 1931-32; A.B., Columbia, 1937, Ph.D., 1953; M.A., Harvard, 1945. Mem. faculty Columbia, N.Y.C., 1939—, prof. English, 1961—, Julian Levi prof. humanities, 1978-81, prof. emeritus, 1981—, spl. lectr., 1981-82; vis. prof. U. Sussex, Eng., 1966-67; Paley lectr. Hebrew U. of Jerusalem, 1982. Editor: Henry James, Selected Short Stories, 1950, The American Henry James, 1957, (Hawthorne) Twice Told Tales, 1960, (with Joseph A. Mazzeo) The Proper Study, 1962, The Imperial Self, 1971, (with others) Art, Politics and Will: Essays in Honor of Lionel Trilling, 1977. Fulbright grantee, France, 1962-63; Nat. Endowment for Humanities sr. fellow, 1973—; Nat. Humanities Center fellow, 1979-80; N.Y. Inst. for Humanities fellow, 1981-84. Mem. Acad. Lit. Studies, Modern Lang. Assn., P.E.N. Home: 29 Claremont Ave New York NY 10027

ANDERSON, RALPH ALEXANDER, JR., architect; b. Houston, Jan. 1, 1923; s. Ralph Alexander and Ruby (Ellison) A. B.A. in Arch, Rice Inst., 1943, B.S., 1947. With firm Wilson, Morris & Crain, Houston, 1947-52, partner, 1952-62; partner firm Wilson, Morris, Crain & Anderson, Houston, 1962-72, Wilson/Crain/Anderson/Reynolds, 1972-78, Crain/Anderson Inc., 1978—. Prin. works include Spl. Events Centers, U. Tex., Austin, 1977, U. Tex., El Paso, Kelsey-Seybold Clinic, Houston, 1963, WISH-TV, Indpls., 1966, Western Nat. Bank, Houston, 1967, Houston Post Bldg, 1969. Pres. Contemporary Art Mus. Houston, 1957, Houston Bot. Soc., 1967-68; chmn. Billboards, Ltd., action group, 1967-71. Served with inf. AUS, 1943-45; ETO. Fellow A.I.A. (pres. Houston 1966); mem. Phi Beta Kappa. Home: 1638 Banks St Houston TX 77006 Office: 4828 W Loop S South Houston TX 77081

ANDERSON, RAYMOND CHARLES, family physician, educator; b. Burns, Wyo., Mar. 24, 1933; s. Edward Charles and Grace Lucille (Johnson) A.; children: Lisa, Eric, Kristen, Kurt. B.S., U. Wyo., 1958; M.D., U. Rochester, 1962. Diplomate: Am. Bd. Family Practice. Intern Henry Ford Hosp., Detroit, 1962-63; resident in family practice Community Hosp., Santa Rosa, Calif., 1963-65; practice medicine specializing in family medicine, Santa Rosa, Calif., 1965-72; dir., asst. clin. prof. family practice residency program Community Hosp., Santa Rosa, 1972-74; assoc. prof., chmn. dept. family medicine U. Calif., Irvine, 1974-79, assoc. prof., 1979—; med. dir. Chem. Dependency Treatment Unit Meml. Hosp., Long Beach, Calif., 1982—; cons. Bur. Health Profession, HHS, USPHS, 1977—; chair diversion com. impaired physicians Calif. State Bd. Med. Quality Assurance, 1980. Editorial bd.: Jour. Family Practice Recertification, 1979—; contbr. chpts. in family medicine texts. Pres. Coast Opera Assos., Orange County, 1979—. Served with USNR, 1951-55. Mem. AMA, Calif. Med. Assn., Orange County Med. Assn., Am. Acad. Family Physicians, Am. Med. Soc. Alcoholism, Soc. Tchrs. of Family Medicine. Office: Memorial Hosp Box 1428 2801 Atlantic Ave Long Beach CA 90801-1428

ANDERSON, RAYMOND QUINTUS, diversified company executive; b. Jamestown, N.Y., Nov. 27, 1930; s. Paul N. and Cecille (Ogren) A.; m. Sondra Rumsey, June 5, 1954; children: Heidi, Kristin, Gerrit, Mitchell, Tracy, Brooks. Grad., Phillip Acad., Andover, Mass., 1949; B.S. in Engring., Princeton U., 1953; postgrad., Grad. Sch. Indsl. Mgmt., Mass. Inst. Tech. With Dahlstrom Corp., Jamestown, 1957-76, exec. v.p., 1965, pres., 1968-76; founder, pres. Aarque Steel Corp., 1976-78, Aarque Mgmt. Corp., Jamestown, 1978—; founder, chmn. Aarque Cos., 1980—; chmn. Aarque Office Systems, Inc., Aarque Holdings Ltd., Cold Metal Products Co., Inc., Aarque Steel Group; dir. Lincoln 1st Bank, N.A., Meridian Industries, Inc.; chmn. Van Huffel Tube Corp., Kardex Systems, Inc. Chmn. Jamestown United Fund drive, 1964, 74. Served with USNR, 1954-57. Mem. Mfrs. Assn. Jamestown Area (pres. 1967-68), Empire State C. of C. (pres. 1974-76), Tau Beta Pi. Republican. Episcopalian. Clubs: Moon Brook Country (Jamestown); Sportsmen's (Chautaqua, N.Y.); Union League Metropolitan (N.Y.C.). Patentee in field. Home: 65 E Terrace Ave Lakewood NY 14750 Office: Aarque Mgmt Corp 111 W 2d St Jamestown NY 14701

ANDERSON, REX HERBERT, insurance executive; b. Rockford, Ill., Jan. 18, 1920; s. Herbert E. and Ethel V. (Helin) A.; m. Martha Jean Baker, Sept. 11, 1943; 1 son, Rex Herbert. A.B., Beloit Coll., 1941. Group field rep. Wash. Nat. Ins. Co., 1951-52, advt. and sales promotion, 1946-50; supr. Great West Life Assurance Co., 1950-52, br. office supr., St. Louis, 1952-53; dir. accident and sickness sales N.Y. Life Ins. Co., 1953-55, dir. sales promotion, 1955-56, asst. v.p. charge sales devel., 1956-57; v.p. mktg. Life Ins. Co. N.Am., Phila., 1957-62, charge individual sales and agy. ops., 1962-64, exec. officer charge individual life and health lines, life reins. dept., 1964-72, sr. v.p., 1970-79, in charge internat. life ins. ops., 1972-79; chmn. bd. Hawkeye Nat. Life Ins. Co., Des Moines, 1982—; vice chmn. bd., dir. Interam. Life, Athens, Greece, 1971-79, dir., 1982—, Inter Trust Ins. Co., Athens, INA Security Corp., GAN Anglo-Am. Ins. Co., N.Y.C.; Am. rep. Groupe des Assurances Nationales, Paris, 1979—. Trustee Phila. Coll. Art, 1966-75. Served with USAAF, 1942-46. Mem. Life Ins. Agy. Mgmt. Assn., Tau Kappa Epsilon, Delta Sigma Rho. Republican. Presbyterian. Home: 1210 Pine Wood Rd Villanova PA 19085 Office: PO Box 431 Villanova PA 19085

ANDERSON, RICHARD EDMUND, business executive; b. Ferndale, Mich., Dec. 23, 1938; s. Richard H. and Carolyn Jeanne (Figg) A.; m. Kay M. Clarke, Sept. 9, 1961; children: Pam, Mark, Linda. B.A., Mich. State U., 1962; postgrad. in advanced mgmt., Harvard U., 1979. Adminstrv. asst. City of Fort Lauderdale, Fla., 1964-67, dep. city mgr., 1967-75, city mgr., 1975-80; v.p. Fla. Innovation Group, Tampa, Fla., 1980-81; pres. Integrated Systems Assocs., Inc., Ft. Lauderdale, 1981—; chief exec. officer Power Control, Inc., Ft. Lauderdale, 1982—; instr. pub. adminstrn. Broward Community Coll. Contbr. articles to profl. jours. Mem. Internat. City Mgmt. Assn., Am. Soc. Pub. Adminstrn. Home: 4209 Country Club Dr Fort Lauderdale FL 33308 Office: PO Box 1274 Fort Lauderdale FL 33302

ANDERSON, RICHARD L(OREE), mathematician educator; b. North Liberty, Ind., Apr. 20, 1915; s. George W. and Mabel (Schrader) A.; m. Mary E. Turner, Jan. 31, 1946; children: Kathryn Hart, William Bayard. A.B., DePauw U., 1936; M.S., Iowa State Coll., 1938, Ph.D., 1941. Mem. faculty dept. stats. N.C. State U., Raleigh, 1941-66, asso. prof., 1945-50, prof., 1951-66; research mathematician Princeton U., 1944-45; prof. stats. Purdue U., Lafayette, Ind., 1950-51; research prof. stats. U. Ga., Athens, 1966-67; prof. dept. stats. U. Ky., Lexington, 1967-80, chmn. dept., 1967-79, asst. to dean Coll. Agr., 1980—; mem. econ. research adv. com. U.S. Dept. Agr., 1965-68; cons. various def., govt. instns., 1955-67, also Internat. Math. and Stats. Libraries, 1970—; vis. prof. U. Umea, Sweden, 1977, Indian Statis. Inst., 1977. Mng. editor: Statis. Theory and Method Abstracts, 1958-67; Author: (with T.A. Bancroft) Statistical Theory in Research, 1952; editorial bd.: Communications in Stats., 1972—; contbr. articles to profl. jours. Ford Found. grantee London Sch. Econs., 1958, sci. computer center U. Cairo, 1969; NSF vis. lectr., 1964-65. Fellow Am. Statis. Assn. (mem. census adv. com. 1972-77, chmn. com. 1977, dir. 1976-78, chmn. com. on stats. and environ. 1979—, pres. 1983), Inst. Math. Statistics (mem. council 1955-57, 62-64), AAAS (chmn. Sect. U 1979); mem. Biometric Soc. (pres. Eastern N. Am. region 1966), Internat. Statis. Inst., Phi Beta Kappa, Sigma Xi, Phi Kappa Phi, Gamma Sigma Delta. Home: 3349 Braemer Dr Lexington KY 40502

ANDERSON, RICHARD LOUIS, electrical engineer; b. Mpls., Feb. 4, 1927; s. Ben Walter and Anna Elizabeth (Zitcowicz) A.; m. Claire Louise Petersen, Sept. 15, 1951; children: Gretchen, Betty Lise, Karl. B.S., U. Minn., 1950, M.S., 1952; Ph.D., Syracuse (N.Y.) U., 1960; D.Sc. (hon.), U. Sao Paulo, Brazil, 1969. Research asst. U. Minn., 1950-52; research engr. IBM Corp., Poughkeepsie, N.Y., 1952-60; from. instr. to prof. elec. and computing engring. Syracuse U., 1954-79; prof. elec. engring. U. Vt., Burlington, 1979—, dir. materials sci. program, 1981—; Fulbright-Hayes prof. U. Madrid, 1960-61, U. Sao Paulo, 1967-69; cons. to govt. and industry.; cons. UN Devel. Program, 1980—. Author. Served with USNR, 1944-47. Recipient 1st Brazilian prize microelectronics, 1980; fellow Ford Found., 1967-69; grantee NSF, 1974-80, 80—, N.Y. State Sci. and Tech. Found., 1974-75, 77-78, Dept. Energy, 1979—. Fellow IEEE; mem. Internat. Solar Soc., Am. Phys. Soc., AAUP, Electrochem. Soc., Brazilian Phys. Soc., Sigma Xi. Patentee in field. Home: Hills Point Rd Charlotte VT 05445 Office: Elec Engring Dept U Vt Burlington VT 05405

ANDERSON, RICHARD NORMAN, actor; b. Long Branch, N.J., Aug. 8, 1926; s. Henry and Olga (Lurie) A.; children: Ashley, Brooke Dominique, Deva Justine. Pres. Richard Anderson Film Corp., 1977—. Film actor, 1950—; prin. films include Long Hot Summer, Paths of Glory, Compulsion, Tora, Tora, Tora, Scaramouche, The Magnificent Yankee, Seven Days in May, Wackiest Ship in the Army, Doctors Wives, Seconds; numerous TV appearances Fall Guy; numerous TV appearances include Whiz Kids, Fantasy Island, Love Boat, Condominium, The Immigrants, Big Valley, Gunsmoke, The Rifleman, Playhouse 90, The Eighty Yard Run; played: regular role in Bus Stop, 1960, Perry Mason, 1961, Dan August, 1969, Six Million Dollar Man, 1972-77, Bionic Woman, 1974-77, Cover-Up, 1984—; appeared on Broadway in: The Highest Tree; appeared in summer stock, Lobero Theatre, Santa Barbara, Calif., Laguna Beach Playhouse (Calif.). Served with AUS, 1944-46. Mem. Acad. Motion Picture Arts and Scis., Screen Actors Guild. Office: care William Morris Agy 1350 Ave of Americas New York NY 10019

ANDERSON, RICHARD PAUL, agr. co. exec.; b. Toledo, Apr. 10, 1929; s. Harold and Margaret Mary (Meilink) A.; m. Frances Mildred Heilman, Nov. 28, 1953; children—Christopher, Daniel, James, Martha, Jennifer, Timothy. B.S magna cum laude, Mich. Stte U., 1953. With The Andersons, Maumee, Ohio, 1946—, gen. partner, 1951—, gen. mgr., 1980—; dir. Toledo Edison Co. Pres. Toledo Area council Boy Scouts Am., 1966-69; gen. chmn. Crusade of Mercy, Toledo, 1972; bd. dirs. Childrens Services, St. Luke's Hosp.; chmn. support council Ohio Agrl. Research and Devel. Center. Served with AUS, 1954-56. Named Toledo Area Citizen of Yr. Toledo Bd. Realtors, 1974, Outstanding Lay Leader N.W. Ohio chpt. Nat. Assn. Social Workers, 1971. Republican. Roman Catholic. Club: Rotary (Toledo.) (pres. 1976-77). Home: 1833 S Holland Sylvania Rd Maumee OH 43537 Office: PO Box 119 Maumee OH 43537

ANDERSON, RICHARD WILLIAM, psychiatrist, educator; b. Brainerd, Minn., Sept. 11, 1919; s. John Peter and Christine (Erichsen) A.; m. Bette Ann Simonson, July 31, 1943; children: Peter, John, Erik. Student, Carleton Coll., 1936-38; B.S., U. Minn., 1941, M.B., M.D., 1943. Diplomate: Am. Bd. Psychiatry and Neurology. Intern U.S. Marine Hosp., Seattle, 1943; grad. tng. Mass. Mental Health Center, 1946-47, part-time 1949-50; resident psychiatrist Baldpate, Inc., Georgetown, Mass., 1947-50; dep. commr. mental health, Minn., 1950-51, pvt. practice, St. Paul, 1951-53; mem. faculty U. Minn. Med. Sch., 1953-75, prof. psychiatry, 1961-75; chief psychiatry service Mpls. Gen. Hosp., 1953-57, dir. adult psychiatry clinic, 1958-70, chief clin. services, dept. psychiatry, 1970-75; psychiatrist Scripps Clinic, La Jolla, Calif., 1975—. Contbr. articles to profl. jours. Served with AUS, 1943-46. Commonwealth Fund fellow, Ipswich, Eng., 1963-64. Fellow Am. Psychiat. Assn. (life). Home: 6363 Via Maria La Jolla CA 92037

ANDERSON, ROBBIN COLYER, former college dean; b. DeRidder, La., June 8, 1914; s. Ward and Elizabeth (Richardson) A.; m. Margaret Foster Ball, July 20, 1946; children: Charles Ward, Robbin Bruce, Richard Ball. B.S. in Chem. Engring, La. State U., 1934, M.S. in Chemistry, 1936; Ph.D. in Phys. Chemistry, U. Wis., 1939. Mem. faculty U. Tex., 1939-67, asso. dean Grad. Sch., 1966-67; head insts. sect. div. sci. personnel and edn. NSF, 1960-61; dean Coll. Arts and Sci., U. Ark., 1967-79, dean emeritus, 1981—, prof. chemistry, 1967-81; cons. in field, 1942—. Contbr. articles to profl. jours. Mem. Ark. Sci. and Tech. Council (chmn. 1971-73), Am. Chem. Soc., Ark. Deans Assn. (pres. 1976-77), Tex. Acad. Sci. (pres. 1966-67), Chem. Soc., Council Coll. Arts and Scis. (dir. 1977-78), Ark. Acad. Sci. (pres. 1982-83), AAAS, Fayetteville C. of C., Nat. Assn. State U. and Land-Grant Colls. (commn. on arts and scis.), Sigma Xi, Phi Kappa Phi, Omicron Delta Kappa, Lambda Chi Alpha. Club: Rotarian. Home: 1599 Halsell Rd Fayetteville AR 72701

ANDERSON, ROBERT, ambassador; b. Mass., Jan. 6, 1922; m. Elena Fenoaltea; children: Cynthia, Christina, Mark. B.A., Yale, 1944. Joined Fgn. Service, Dept. State, 1946; vice consul, Shanghai, 1946-47, polit. officer, Nanking, 1947-49, prin. officer, Chiengmai, 1950-51, polit. officer, Bangkok, 1951-53, New Delhi, 1953-55; internat. relations officer Dept. State, 1955-57, staff asst. to asst. sec. pub. affairs, 1957-59; polit. officer, Bordeaux, 1959-61, asst. comml. attache, Paris, 1961-62, spl. asst. to ambassador, 1962-63, spl. asst. to under sec. state, 1963-65; dep. dir. Office West European Affairs, 1965-66; country dir. for France-Benelux, Bur. European Affairs, 1966-68; counsellor polit. affairs, Paris, 1968-72, ambassador E. and P. to Dahomey, Cotonou, 1972-74, spl. asst. to sec. state for press relations and Dept. Spokesman, Washington, 1974-76, ambassador E. and P. to Morocco, 1976-78; spl. asst. for internat. affairs to supreme allied comdr., Atlantic and to U.S. Comdr.-in-Chief, Atlantic, Norfolk, Va., 1978-82; ambassador E. and P. to Dominican Republic, 1982—. Mem. corp. bd. Tangier Am. Sch.; pres. Tangier Am. Legation Mus. Soc. Served to 1st lt. AUS, 1943-46. Recipient Commendable Service award Dept. State, 1959. Mem. Council on Fgn. Relations, Internat. Inst. for Strategic Studies (London). Clubs: Chevy Chase, Met. (Washington); Polo (Paris). Address: 35-36 Am Embassy APO Miami FL 34041

ANDERSON, ROBERT, manufacturing company executive; b. Columbus, Nebr., Nov. 2, 1920; s. Robert and Lillian (Devlin) A.; m. Constance Dahlun Severy, Oct. 2, 1942 (div.); children: Robert, Kathleen D.; m. Diane Clark Lowe, Nov. 2, 1973. B.S. in Mech. Engring, Colo. State U., 1943, LL.D., 1966; M. Automotive Engring., Chrysler Inst. Engring., 1948. With Chrysler Corp., 1946-68, v.p. corp., gen. mgr. Chrysler-Plymouth div., 1965-67; with Rockwell International Corp., 1968—, pres. comml. products group, 1968-69, v.p. corp., 1968-69, exec. v.p., 1969-70, pres., chief operating officer, 1970-74, pres., 1974-79, chief exec. officer, 1974—, chmn., 1979—, dir., 1968—; dir. Security Pacific Corp. and subs. Security Pacific Nat.

Bank, Los Angeles, Celanese Corp., Owens-Ill., Inc., Hosp. Corp. Am. Trustee Calif. Inst. Tech., Carnegie-Mellon U., Pitts.; bd. dirs. Nat. Council for U.S.-China Trade, Exec. Council Fgn. Diplomats; chmn. bus.-higher edn. forum Am. Council on Edn.; chmn. Western Hwy. Inst., 1983-84. Served to capt. F.A. AUS, 1943-46. Named Exec. of Yr. Nat. Mgmt. Assn., 1980. Mem. Soc. Automotive Engrs., Phi Kappa Phi, Tau Beta Pi, Sigma Nu. Clubs: Rolling Rock, Laurel Valley Golf (Ligonier, Pa.); Fox Chapel (Pa.) Golf, Eldorado (Calif.) Country, Desert Horizons (Calif.), Country; Duquesne (Pitts.); Los Angeles Country. Office: Rockwell International Corp 6O0 Grant St Pittsburgh PA 15219

ANDERSON, ROBERT BERNARD, chemical engineering educator; b. Moline, Ill., Aug. 31, 1915; s. Gustav Adel and Hilda (Benson) A.; m. Jane Elizabeth Udden, July 3, 1942; children: Robert Udden, Susan Jane. A.B., Augustana Coll., 1938; M.S., State U. Iowa, 1940, Ph.D., 1942. Grad. asst., instr. chemistry dept. State U. Iowa, 1938-42; NDRC project dept. chem. engring. Johns Hopkins, 1942-44; phys. chemist U.S. Bur. Mines, Pitts., 1944-64; Petroleum Research Fund fellow, 1965; prof. chem. engring. McMaster U., Hamilton, Ont., Can., 1965—; Spinks lectr. U. Sask., 1982; Mem. NRC grants awards com., 1967-70; Mem. adv. bd. Petroleum Research Fund, 1958-61. Author: (with others) The Fischer-Tropsch and Related Syntheses, 1951; Editor: Experimental Methods in Catalytic Research, vol. I, 1968; co-editor, vol. II, vol. III, 1976; Contbr. to: Emmett's Catalysis, vol. IV, 1956; Contbr. many articles to jours. Recipient Pitts. award, 1960, Outstanding Alumni award Augustana Coll., 1961, Distinguished Service award U.S. Dept. Interior, 1966, Catalysis award Pitts. Catalysis Soc., 1983. Fellow Chem. Inst. Can. (chmn. div. catalysis 1971, Catalysis award 1979), Royal Soc. Can.; mem. Am. Chem. Soc. (Ipatieff prize 1953, chmn. Pitts. sect. 1959), Catalysis Soc., Sigma Xi. Home: 149 Colleen Crescent Ancaster ON Canada Office: Chem Engring Dept McMaster U Hamilton ON Canada

ANDERSON, ROBERT BERNERD, lawyer, former secretary of the Treasury; b. Burleson, Tex., June 4, 1910; s. Robert Lee and Elizabeth (Haskew) A.; m. Ollie Mae Anderson, Apr. 10, 1953; children: James Richard, Gerald Lee. Student, Weatherford Coll., Tex., 1927; LL.B., U. Tex., 1932; LL.D., McMurry Coll., Tex., 1950, Tex. Christian U., 1951; Litt.D., Mid.-Western U., Tex., 1951. Bar: Tex. 1932. Sole practice law, Fort Worth, 1932—; mem. Tex. Ho. of Reps., 1932; asst. atty. gen. Tex., 1932-33; prof. law U. Tex., Austin, 1933-34; tax commr. State of Tex., 1934-37, racing commr., 1934-37, mem. State Tax Bd., 1934-37; chmn., exec. dir. Tex. Unemployment Commn., 1936-37; sec. Dept. Navy, 1953-54; dept. sec. Dept. Def., 1954-55; pres. Ventures Ltd., N.Y.C. and Toronto, 1955-57; sec. Dept. Treasury, 1957-61; ptnr. Loeb, Rhoades & Co., N.Y.C., 1961-73; ptnr. Anderson & Pendleton, Washington, 1980—; ptnr. Anderson, Liu & Choo, Chgo., 1982—; chmn. Robert B. Anderson Co. Ltd., 1971—, Am. Gas & Chem. Co. Ltd.; dir. Pantry Pride Inc., Servamatic Solar Systems Inc., Intercontinental Trailsea Corp. Chmn. bd. overseers Eisenhower Coll.; mem. nat. exec. bd. Boy Scout Am., Bus Council. Decorated cross of Order of Boyaca, Colombia, Most Exalted Order of White Elephant, Thailand, medal of Freedom, 1955, Grand Cross Ct. of Honour, 1959; recipient Tex. award, 1954, Navy Disitng. Pub. Service award, 1955, Army Exceptional Service award, 1955, Air Force Civilian Service award, 1955; named Texan of Yr., 1955. Mem. Nat. Geog. Soc. (life), Washington Nat. Cathedral Navy League Am., ABA, Assn. Bar City N.Y., The Chancellors, Phi Delta Phi. Clubs: Links, Metropolitan, University (N.Y.C.); Greenwich Country; Round Hill (Greenwich, Conn.); Metropolitan (Washington). Lodges: Order of DeMolay; Masons. Home: Khakum Wood Rd Greenwich CT 06830 Office: 535 Fifth Ave Suite 1004 New York NY 10017

ANDERSON, ROBERT CLETUS, educator; b. Birmingham, Ala., July 18, 1921; s. Allie Cletus and Dana (Hilliard) A.; m. Evalee R. Pilgrim, 1977; children by previous marriage: Margaret Campbell, William Robert. B.S., Auburn U., 1942; M.A., U. N.C., 1947; Ph.D., N.Y. U., 1950. Research asst. Inst. Research in Social Sci., U. N.C., 1946-47; asst. to dean Sch. Edn., N.Y. U., 1948-50; dean Grad. Sch., Memphis State U., 1950-53; exec. assoc. So. Regional Edn. Bd., 1953-55, assoc. dir., 1955-57, dir., 1957-61; exec. v.p. Auburn U., 1961-65; v.p. research U. Ga., Athens, 1965—, prof. sociology, 1965—; pres. U. Ga. Research Found., 1978—; dir. So. Regional Project on Ednl. TV, So. Regional Edn. Bd., 1952, So. Regional Conf. on Edn. Beyond the High Sch., 1957; mem. Surgeon Gen.'s cons. group on Med. Edn., 1958-59, W.K. Kellogg Found. Ednl. Adv. Com., 1960-64, Joint Council on Ednl. Telecommunications, 1961-70, v.p., 1965-67; mem. council for research policy and adminstrn. Nat. Assn. State Univs. and Land-Grant Colls., 1965—, chmn., 1965-67; Chmn. exec. com. Skidaway Inst. Oceanography, 1968-69; mem. exec. com. Nat. Conf. Advancement Research, 1981—, Nat. Council Univ. Research Administrs., 1982—; dir. Nat. Conf. Future Univ. Research, 1982—. Served from 2d lt. to capt. AUS, 1942-46; ETO. Decorated Purple Heart. Mem. AAAS, N.Y. Acad. Scis., Am. Council on Edn. (council on fed. relations 1963-67), Am. Assn. Higher Edn., Nat. Council Univ. Research Adminstrs., Phi Kappa Phi, Alpha Tau Omega, Alpha Kappa Delta, Kappa Delta Pi, Omicron Delta Kappa, Phi Delta Kappa, Phi Eta Sigma, Pi Gamma Mu. Home: 110 Holmes Ct Athens GA 30606

ANDERSON, ROBERT DALE, business executive; b. McPherson, Kans., July 25, 1930; s. Ralph E. A.; m. Sara Jane Todd, June 8, 1952; children: David T., Cynthia J. Anderson Grittman. B.S. in Milling Adminstrn., Kans. State U., 1952. Asst. plant mgr. Internat. Multi-Foods, Kansas City, Mo., 1954-57, div. by-product mgr., 1957-59, gen. mgr. by-product sales, Mpls., 1959-62; by-product merchandiser I.S. Joseph Co. Inc., Mpls., 1962-74, sr. v.p. mktg., 1974-80, pres. and chief operating officer, 1980—; dir. Nat. Sun Industries, Enderlin, N.D., I.S. Joseph Co., Inc., Mpls., I.S. Joseph Barge Co., I.S. Joseph Netherlands B.V., Rotterdam. Served to 1st lt. USAF, 1952-54. Republican. Presbyterian. Lodge: Rotary. Office: IS Joseph Co Inc 777 Grain Exchange Minneapolis MN 55415

ANDERSON, ROBERT E., manufacturing company executive; b. N.Y.C., 1929; (married). B.A., Brown U., 1959. With N.Y. Telephone Co., 1954-56; asso. brand promotion mgr. Procter & Gamble Co., 1956-62; v.p., mgmt. supr. William Esty Co., 1962-63; exec. v.p., dir. Lever Bros. Co., 1963-78, R.J. Reynolds Tobacco Co., 1978-79; pres., chief operating officer Mattel Inc., 1979—, also dir. Office: 5150 Rosecrans Ave Hawthorne CA 90250 *

ANDERSON, ROBERT FERDINAND, mining company executive; b. Hibbing, Minn., Apr. 26, 1921; s. A.G. and Anna (Tanquist) A.; m. Marjorie Mahon, Mar. 9, 1944; children: Judith A., Christopher R., Mark M. B. Engring., Mich. Tech. U., 1946. With Hanna Mining Co., 1947—, pres., chief exec. officer, 1978—; chmn. pres., chief exec. officer, 1982—; also dir. Hanna Mining Co.; chmn., dir. Iron Ore Co. Can.; dir. Que. N. Shore and Labrador Ry. Co., Midland SouthWest Corp., Norcen Energy Resources Ltd., St. John D'el Rey Mining Co. Ltd., WellTech, Inc., Society Corp., Society Nat. Bank. Served with USAAF, 1943-46. Mem. AIME, Am. Iron and Steel Inst. (dir.), Am. Iron Ore Assn. (dir.), Am. Mining Congress (dir.). Clubs: Cleveland Athletic, Union, Pepper Pike, Westwood Country (Cleve.); Mt. Royal (Montreal, Que., Can.); Laurel Valley Golf, Rolling Rock (Ligonier, Pa.); Duquesne (Pitts.). Home: 3585 Eldorado Dr Rocky River OH 44116 Office: Hanna Mining Co 100 Erieview Plaza 36th Floor Cleveland OH 44114

ANDERSON, ROBERT GREGG, realty and development company executive; b. St. Joseph, Mo., Oct. 3, 1928; s. Clarence William and Marie Louise (Newman) A.; 1 son, Robert Gregg. Student, U. Okla., 1948-49, U. Tulsa, 1950. Pres. Gregg Anderson Realty, San Diego, 1959-63; v.p. Trousdale Constrn. Co., Los Angeles, 1963-67, cons., 1967—; pres. Amfac Properties div.; v.p. Amfac, Inc., Honolulu, 1967-69, sr. v.p., 1969-74; pres., chmn. bd. Accent Enterprises, Inc., Amfac Communities, Inc., Amfac Silverado Corp., Neilson Way Corp., 745 Fort St. Corp., Central Oahu Land Corp., Los Angeles Environmental Structures, Inc.; chmn. bd. West Maui Properties, Inc.; v.p. Silverado Country Club & Resort, Inc., 1969-74; pres. Gregg Anderson Realty & Devel., Inc., 1974—, Villa Pacific Bldg. Co., 1980—. Served with USNR, 1950-54. Clubs: Kaanapali Country (Maui); Silverado Country (Napa, Calif.). Office: 15233 Ventura Blvd Suite 212 Sherman Oaks CA 91403

ANDERSON, ROBERT HENRY, educator; b. Milw., July 28, 1918; s. Robert Dean and Eleanor (Weil) A.; m. Mary Jane Hopkins, July 19, 1941 (div. Jan. 1979); children: Dean Robert, Lynn Mary (Mrs. William D. Grant), Scott William, Carol Jane; m. Karolyn J. Snyder, Jan. 24, 1979. B.A., U. Wis., 1939, M.A., 1942; Ph.D., U. Chgo., 1949; A.M. (hon.), Harvard, 1959. Tchr., Oconomowoc, Wis., 1940-43; research asst. ednl. field service U. Chgo., 1946-47; prin. Roosevelt Sch., River Forest, Ill., 1947-49; supt. schs. dist. 163, Park Forest, Ill., 1949-54; mem. faculty Grad. Sch. Edn., Harvard, 1954-73, prof. edn., 1962-73; prof., dean Coll. of Edn. Tex. Tech. U., Lubbock, 1973-83, prof. and dean emeritus, 1983—; pres. Pedamorphosis, Inc., Lubbock, 1977—; lectr., cons. sch. orgn., adminstrn., architecture. Author: Teaching in a World of Change, 1966, Education in Anticipation of Tomorrow, 1973, Opting for Openness, 1973; Co-author: The Nongraded Elementary School, rev. edit, 1963, Clinical Supervision, 2d edit, 1980; co-editor: As the Twig is Bent, 1971; sr. editor: Current Trends in Education (pub. in Japanese), 1971; editor: Tex. Tech. Jour. Edn, 1973—; contbr. chpts. books. Served with USNR, 1943-46. Mem. Nat. Soc. Study Edn., NEA, Am. Ednl. Research Assn., Assn. Supervision and Curriculum Devel., Phi Delta Kappa. Episcopalian. Home: 13604 Waterfall Way Tampa FL 33624 Office: PO Box 4560 Lubbock TX 79409

ANDERSON, ROBERT HYMAN, retired retail company executive; b. Chgo., Oct. 31, 1919; s. Benedict and Grace (Hyman) A.; m. Sylvia Josephine Pelikan, Aug. 26, 1940; children: Sylvia (Mrs. Bruce McConnell), Elizabeth (Mrs. Charles Vinicky). Student, U. Wis.-Madison, 1937; grad., Advanced Mgmt. Program, Harvard, 1966. Vice pres. retail merchandising Sears Roebuck & Co., Chgo., 1939-74; pres., chief operating officer W. T. Grant Co., N.Y.C., 1975-76; exec. v.p. retail group W.R. Grace & Co., N.Y.C., 1978-82. Vice chmn. N.Y. council Boy Scouts Am., 1975-83, mem. exec. bd., 1971-75. Served with USNR, 1944-46. Recipient Good Scout award Boy Scouts Am., 1972. Republican. Club: Harvard. Home: 383 Long Hill Dr Short Hills NJ 07078

ANDERSON, ROBERT MARSHALL, bishop; b. S.I., N.Y., Dec. 18, 1933; s. Arthur Harold and Hazel Schneider A.; m. Mary Artemis Evans, Aug. 24, 1960; children: Martha, Elizabeth, Catherine, Thomas. B.A., Colgate U., 1955; S.T.B., Berkeley Div. Sch., 1961; D.D. (hon.), Seabury Western Sem., 1978, Berkeley Divinity Sch., Yale U., 1977. Ordained priest Episcopal Ch.; curate St. John's Ch., Stamford, Conn., 1961-63, vicar, 1963-67; priest in charge, Middle Haddan, Conn., 1963-67, rector, 1967-68; asso. rector St. John's Ch., Stamford, 1968-72; dean St. Mark's Cathedral, Salt Lake City, 1972-78; bishop Episcopal Diocese of Minn., Mpls., 1978—. Served with U.S. Army.; Danforth fellow, 1959-60. Mem. Berkeley Alumni (pres. 1972-76). Democrat. Clubs: Mpls., Minikahda. Office: 309 Clifton Ave Minneapolis MN 55403 *

ANDERSON, ROBERT MORRIS, JR., electrical engineer; b. Crookston, Minn., Feb. 15, 1939; s. Robert Morris and Eleanor Elaine (Huotte) A.; m. Janice Ilene Pendell, Sept. 3, 1960; children—Erik Martin, Kristi Lynn. B.E.E., U. Mich., 1961, M.E.E., 1963, M.S. in Physics, 1965, Ph.D. in Elec. Engring, 1967. Asst. research engr. U. Mich., Ann Arbor, 1964-67; research engr. Conductron Corp., Ann Arbor, summer 1967; asst. prof. elec. engring. Purdue U., West Lafayette, Ind., 1967-71, asso. prof., 1971-79, prof., 1979, engring. coordinator for continuing edn., 1973-79, Ball Bros. prof., 1976-79; mgr. engring. edn. and tng., corp. cons. services Gen. Electric Co., Bridgeport, Conn., 1979-82, mgr. tech. edn. ops., corp. engring. and mfg., 1982—. Author: multi-media learning package Fundamentals of Vacuum Technology, 1973, (with others) Divided Loyalties, 1980; contbr. articles to profl. jours. Named Best Tchr. Elec. Engring. Purdue U., 1974; recipient Dow Outstanding Young Faculty award, 1974. Mem Am. Soc. Engring. Edn. (certificate of merit 1977), AAAS, Am. Vacuum Soc., Am. Soc. Tng. and Devel., IEEE. Lutheran. Home: 128 Hurd Rd Trumbull CT 06611 Office: Bldg 29EE Gen Electric 1285 Boston Ave Bridgeport CT 06602

ANDERSON, ROBERT ORVILLE, industrialist; b. Chgo., Apr. 13, 1917; s. Hugo A. and Hilda (Nelson) A.; m. Barbara Phelps, Aug. 25, 1939; children—Katherine, Julia, Maria, Robert Bruce, Barbara Burton, William Phelps, Beverley. B.A., U. Chgo., 1939. With Am. Mineral Spirits Co., Chgo., 1939-41; pres. Malco Refineries, Inc. (now Hondo Oil and Gas Co.), Roswell, N.Mex., 1941-63; chmn. bd. Atlantic Richfield Co., Los Angeles; owner Diamond A Cattle Co., Roswell.; Mem. Com. Econ. Devel., Nat. Petroleum Council, Washington. Chmn. Aspen Inst. for Humanistic Studies; chmn. Lovelace Found.; trustee Calif. Inst. Tech., U. Chgo. Mem. Am. Petroleum Inst. (dir.). Clubs: Century (N.Y.C.); California (Los Angeles); Metropolitan (Washington); Chicago; Pacific-Union (San Francisco). Home: PO Box 1000 Roswell NM 88201 Office: 515 S Flower St Los Angeles CA 90071

ANDERSON, ROBERT T., state lieutenant governor; b. Marshalltown, Iowa, Mar. 8, 1945; s. Robert T. and Ida (Halvorson) A.; m. Elsie Ulland, 1967; 1 son, Robert Elias. B.A., U. Iowa, 1967, M.A., 1971. Mem. Iowa Ho. of Reps., Des Moines, 1974-82, majority whip 67th Gen. Assembly, asst. minority leader 68th and 69th assemblies; lt. gov. State of Iowa, Des Moines, 1983—. Mem. United Teaching Profession, Izaak Walton League. Democrat. Methodist. Office: Office of Lt Gov State Capitol Des Moines IA 50319 *

ANDERSON, ROBERT THEODORE, music educator, organist; b. Chgo., Oct. 5, 1934; s. Albert Theodore and Lillian Gertrude (Chalbeck) A. B.Sacred Music, Ill. Wesleyan U., 1955; M.Sacred Music, Union Theol. Sem., N.Y.C., 1957, D.Sacred Music, 1961. Mem. faculty So. Methodist U., 1960—, Univ. disting. prof. organ, 1972—, Meadows Found. disting. teaching prof., 1981-82; organ cons., lectr., tchr. master classes. Concert organist; Author articles; composer anthems. Fulbright grantee, 1957-59; named Distinguished Alumnus Ill. Wesleyan U., 1972. Mem. Am. Guild Organists (council), Internat. Bach Soc., Blue Key, Pi Kappa Lambda, Phi Mu Alpha, Phi Beta Phi. Methodist. Home: 6810 Stichter Ave Dallas TX 75230 Office: Div Music Sch Arts So Methodist Univ Dallas TX 75275

ANDERSON, ROBERT WOODRUFF, playwright, novelist, screenwriter; b. N.Y.C., Apr. 28, 1917; s. James Hewston and Myra Esther (Grigg) A.; m. Phyllis Stohl, June 24, 1940 (dec. 1956); m. Teresa Wright, Dec. 11, 1959 (div. 1978). A.B. magna cum laude, Harvard U., 1939, M.A., 1940. Tchr. playwriting Am. Theatre Wing, 1946-50; mem. Playwrights Co., 1953-60; faculty Salzburg Seminar in Am. Studies, 1968, Iowa Writers Workshop, 1976; Bd. govs. Am. Playwrights Theatre; past chmn. bd. overseers' com. to visit the performing arts Harvard U. Playwright: Love Revisited; produced: Westport Country Playhouse, 1951, All Summer Long, Arena Stage, Washington, 1953, Arena Stage, N.Y.C., 1954, Tea and Sympathy, N.Y.C., 1953; writer in residence, U. N.C.; 969; author: screenplays Tea and Sympathy, 1956, Until They Sail, 1957, The Nun's Story, 1959, The Sand Pebbles, 1966; plays Silent Night, Lonely Night, 1959, The Days Between, 1965, You Know I Can't Hear You When the Water's Running, 1967, I Never Sang for My Father; play, 1968, screenplay, 1970 (Writers Guild Am. award for best screenplay); play Solitaire/Double Solitaire, 1971; novel After, 1973, Getting Up and Going Home, 1978. Served as lt. USNR, 1942-46. Recipient 1st prize for Come Marching Home Army-Navy Playwriting Contest for servicemen overseas, 1945; named to Theater Hall of Fame, 1981. Mem. Dramatists Guild (past pres.), New Dramatists Com. (past pres.), Authors League (v.p., council). Clubs: Coffee House, Century Assn., Harvard (N.Y.C.). Office: care Audrey Wood-ICM 40 W 57th St New York NY 10019 *

ANDERSON, ROGER E., banker; b. 1921. B.A., Northwestern U., 1942. With Continental Ill. Nat. Bank and Trust Co., Chgo., 1946—, exec. v.p., 1968-73, chmn. bd., 1973—; chmn. bd. Continental Ill. Corp., 1973—, also dir.; dir. Amsted Industries, S.C. Johnson & Son, Inc., Eastman Kodak Co. Served with USNR, 1942-46. Address: Continental Bank 231 S LaSalle St Chicago IL 60697

ANDERSON, ROLPH ELY, marketing educator; b. Buchanan, Mich., Aug. 27, 1936; s. Eugene Jefferson and Susanna (James) A. B.A., Mich. State U., 1958, M.B.A., 1964; Ph.D., U. Fla., 1971. Mgr. new product devel. Quaker Oats Co., Chgo., 1964-67; prof., chmn. dept. bus. mgmt. Old Dominion U., Norfolk, Va., 1971-75; prof., chmn. dept. mktg. Drexel U., Phila., 1975—. Co-author: Multivariate Data Analysis, 1979, Sales Management, 1982, Applications in Multivariate Data Analysis, 1983; contbr. articles to profl. publs. Served to capt. USNR (Ret.). Mem. S.E. Am. Inst. Decision Scis. (pres. 1977-78), Am. Inst. Decision Scis. (mem. nat. council 1977-78), Internat. Mktg. Assn. (conf. co-chmn. 1978), Sales and Mktg. Execs. Internat., So. Mktg. Assn., Naval Res. Assn., N.E. Am. Inst. Decision Scis., Res. Officers Assn., Beta Gamma Sigma. Methodist. Office: Coll Bus and Adminstrn Drexel Univ Philadelphia PA 19104

ANDERSON, RON J., hospital administrator, physician; b. Chickasha, Okla., Sept. 6, 1946; s. Ted J. and Ruby (Harston) Anderson B.; m. Sue Ann Blakely, Apr. 12, 1975; children: Sarah Elizabeth, Daniel Jerrod, John Charles. B.S. in Pharmacy, Southwest U. Okla., 1969; M.D., U. Okla., 1973. Diplomate: Am. Bd. Internal Medicine. Intern U. Tex. Southwestern Med. Sch., Parkland Meml. Hosp., VA Hosp., Dallas, 1973-74, resident and chief resident in internal medicine, 1974-76; asst. prof. internal medicine U. Tex. Health Sci. Ctr., Dallas, 1976-81, asst. dean clin. affairs, 1979-82, assoc. prof. internal medicine, 1981—; med. dir. ambulatory-emergency services Dallas County Hosp. Dist., 1979-82, acting. med. dir., 1981-82, chief exec. officer, 1982; mem. task force on teaching hosps. Tex. Hosp. Assn., 1982—, task force on indigent health care, 1983—; cons. on high blood pressure Am. Heart Assn., 1981-83; advisor Tex. Assn. Physician Assts.; chmn. Neighborhood Clinic Cooperating Com., Dallas, 1980-82; dir. Children's Oncology Services Tex., Dallas, 1982—, Dallas Council on Alcoholism, 1982—, Addison, Carrollton, Copell, Farmers Branch chpt. Am. Heart Assn., 1978-80; mem. Tex. Gov.'s Task Force on Indigent Health Care, 1983—, Tex. Health and Human Services Coordinating Council, 1983—; chmn. Tex. Bd. Health, 1983—, Tex. Assn. Pub. Hosps., 1983—. Contbr. articles to profl. jours. Preceptor Dallas Ind. Sch. Dist. Talented and Gifted Program, 1977; mem. Dallas Commrs. Ct. Task Force on Mental Patients, 1979. Fellow ACP; mem. AMA, Tex. Med. Assn., Dallas County Med. Soc., Am. Soc. Internal Medicine, Soc. Research and Edn., Primary Care Internal Medicine. Democrat. Baptist. Home: 1022 Windridge St Duncanville TX 75116 Office: Dallas County Hosp Dist 5201 Harry Hines Blvd Dallas TX 75235

ANDERSON, RONALD DELAINE, educator; b. Poplar, Wis., Aug. 25, 1937; s. Leslie A. and Linnea A. (Bergsten) A.; m. Sandra Jean Wendt, June 1, 1963; children—Debra Jean, Timothy James, Nathan David. B.S., U. Wis., 1959, Ph.D., 1964. Asst. prof. edn. Kans. State U., Manhattan, 1964-65; mem. faculty U. Colo., Boulder, 1965—, prof. edn., 1971—, assoc. dean edn., 1972-78, dir. lab. for research in sci. and math. edn., 1980—; pres. Profl. Services Inst., 1978—. Co-author: Developing Children's Thinking Through Science, 1970; contbr. articles to profl. jours. Fellow AAAS; mem. Nat. Assn. Research Sci. Teaching (pres. 1975-76), Assn. Edn. Tchrs. in Sci. (pres. 1972-73), Nat. Sci. Tchrs. Assn., Phi Delta Kappa. Home: 875 Bluebird Ln Lafayette CO 80026 Office: Sch Edn Univ Colo Boulder CO 80309

ANDERSON, RONALD DESMOND, business and economics columnist; b. Yorkton, Sask., Cn., Dec. 25, 1922; s. Carl Emmanuel and Edla victoria (Pearson) A.; m. Georgina Mary Carpenado, Jan. 30, 1946; children: Gary, Russell, Nathan, Shelly. B.A., U. Sask., 1951; B.J., Carleton U., 1952. Reporter Calgary Herald, Alta., Can., 1952-57; columnist Globe and Mail, Toronto, Ont., Can., 1971—. Served with Canadian Army, 1942-44. Recipient Univ. Medal in Journalism Carleton U., 1952. Office: 444 Front St W Toronto ON Canada M5V 2S9

ANDERSON, RONALD R., corporate executive. Chmn., pres., chief exec. officer GF Corp., Youngstown, Ohio. Office: GF Corp 229 E Dennick Ave Youngstown OH 44505§

ANDERSON, ROY ARNOLD, aerospace company executive; b. Ripon, Calif., Dec. 15, 1920; s. Carl Gustav and Esther (Johnson) A.; m. Betty Leona Boehme, June 10, 1948; children: Ross David, Karyn Dale, Debra Elayne, James Patrick. A.B., Stanford U., 1947, M.B.A., 1949. C.P.A., Calif. With Westinghouse Electric Corp., 1952-56; mgr. accounting and finance, then dir. mgmt. controls Lockheed Missiles & Space Co., 1956-65; dir. finance Lockheed-Ga. Co., 1965-68; asst. treas. Lockheed Corp., 1968-69, v.p., controller, 1969-71, sr. v.p. finance, 1971-75, Vice chmn. bd., chief financial and adminstrv. officer, 1975-77, chmn. bd., chief exec. officer, 1977—; dir. Avantek, Santa Clara, Calif., SRI Internat., Menlo Park, Calif., 1st Interstate Bank Calif., 1st Interstate Bancorp., Los Angeles, So. Calif. Edison Co. Trustee Occidental Coll. Served with USNR, 1942-46, 50-52. Mem. Phi Beta Kappa. Office: 2555 N Hollywood Way Burbank CA 91503

ANDERSON, SHIRLEY FLORENCE LORD, cosmetics magazine executive; b. London, Aug. 28; U.S., 1971; d. Francis J. and Mabel Florence (Williamson) Stringer; m. David Anderson, Aug. 3, 1974; children: Mark, Richard. Grad., S.W. Essex Coll., London, 1948. Fiction editor Woman's Own, 1950-53; features editor Good Taste mag, 1953-56; features, fiction editor Woman and Beauty, 1956-59; fashion editor Star Evening newspaper, 1959-60; women's editor

London Evening Standard, 1960-63, London Evening News, 1963-68; beauty editor Harper's Bazar, London, 1963-71, Harper's Bazaar, N.Y.C., 1971-73; beauty, health editor Vogue mag. Condé Nast Publs, N.Y.C., 1973-75; v.p. corp. relations Helena Rubinstein, N.Y.C., 1975-80. Dir. spl. projects, beauty and fitness, 1980—; Syndicated Field columnist on beauty, health. City commr. Craigavon City, No. Ireland, 1963-68. Home: 210 Central Park S New York NY 10019 Office: 350 Madison Ave New York NY 10017

ANDERSON, SPARKY *See* **ANDERSON, GEORGE LEE**

ANDERSON, STANFORD OWEN, architect, archtl. historian; b. Redwood Falls, Minn., Nov 13, 1934; s. Carl Alfred and Dora Helena (Paulson) A. B.A., U. Minn., 1957; M.A. in Architecture, U. Calif., Berkeley, 1958, postgrad., 1958-59; Ph.D., Columbia U., 1968. Tchr. Archtl. Assn., London, 1962-63, 74-78; co-dir. research project Inst. for Architecture and Urban Studies, N.Y.C., 1970-72, fellow, 1971-81; asst. prof. history and architecture MIT, 1963-69, assoc. prof., 1969-72, prof., 1972—; co-dir. archtl. transl. project Am. Acad. Arts and Scis., 1977-80; mem. adv. council Mcpl. Art Soc., City N.Y., 1972-78; mem. Boston Landmarks Commn., 1980—. Editor: Planning for Diversity and Choice, 1969, On Streets, 1978. Fulbright scholar, 1961-62; John Simon Guggenheim fellow, 1969-70; Graham Found. fellow, 1971; Am. Council Learned Socs. fellow, 1977-78. Mem. Assn. Collegiate Schs. Architecture, Brit. Soc. for Philosophy of Sci., Coll. Art Assn., Nat. Trust Hist. Preservation, Soc. Archtl. Historians (dir. 1969-72, 76,77). Home: 63 Commercial Wharf Boston MA 02110 Office: Dept Architecture 77 Massachusetts Ave Cambridge MA 02139

ANDERSON, STANLEY JOSEPH, naval officer; b. Mpls., Nov. 5, 1927; s. Joseph Ferdin and Alma Victoria (Anderson) A.; m. Lora Zarubin, Jan. 24, 1953; 1 son, Stanley Joseph. B.S., U.S. Naval Acad., 1951. Served as enlisted man U.S. Navy, 1946-47, commd. ensign, 1951, advanced through grades to rear adm., 1975; served on U.S.S. St. Paul, 1951-54; student Submarine Sch., New London, Conn., 1954—; served on diesel submarine, 1955-56, nuclear power trainee, New London and, Arco, Idaho, 1956, served aboard five nuclear submarines, 1957-70; comdr. U.S.S. Haddock, 1965-70; sr. mem. Nuclear Power Exam. Bd., Atlantic Fleet, 1971-72; comdr. Submarine Squadron 4, Charleston, S.C., 1973-74; chief of staff to comdr. Submarine Force U.S. Atlantic Fleet, 1974-75; comdr. Submarine Group 6, Charleston, 1975-77; naval insp. gen. Navy Dept., Washington, 1977-80; comdr. naval logistics command, dep. chief staff U.S. Pacific Fleet; also comdr. Naval Base, Pearl Harbor, Hawaii, 1980-83; asst. dep. chief naval ops. logistics, Washington, 1983—. Decorated Legion of Merit with 3 gold stars, Meritorious Service medal with gold star, Navy Commendation medal. Mem. U.S. Naval Inst., U.S. Naval Acad. Alumni Assn., Officer's Christian Fellowship. (pres.). Office: Navy Dept Washington DC 20350

ANDERSON, STANLEY ROBERT, college president; b. Rudyard, Mich., Mar. 11, 1920; s. John Leslie and Henrietta (Farrish) A.; m. Dorothy Anne Austin, Aug. 27, 1946; children: Anne (Mrs. Robert Rahrig), William, Carol (Mrs. Kimball Bishop). B.S., Mich. State U., 1946, M.S., 1949; Ph.D., Iowa State U., 1954. Field rep. Mich. Crop Improvement Assn., 1946-49; instr. Charlevoix (Mich.) pub. schs., 1949-50; instr. agronomy Iowa State U., 1950-54; mem. faculty Ohio State U., 1954-67, prof. agronomy, 1963-67; dean, prof. agr. Tex. A. and I. U., Kingsville, 1967-75; pres. Abraham Baldwin Agrl. Coll., Tifton, Ga., 1975—. Contbr. articles to profl. jours. Pres. Make and Keep Kingsville Beautiful, Inc., 1968; pres. Coastal Bend Agribus. Council, 1972-73; active local Boy Scouts Am. Served to 1st lt. USAAF, 1943-45. Decorated D.F.C., Air medal with 3 clusters; Named Prof. of Year Ohio State U., 1958—, Distinguished Adviser, 1967; recipient Merit Tchr. award Ohio State U., 1967; named State Farmer Ohio, 1958, State Farmer Ga., 1980. Fellow Am. Soc. Agronomy (bd. dirs. 1956-58, chmn. seed prodn. and tech. div. 1955-56, chmn. resident teaching div. 1957-58, chmn. physiology and metabolism div. 1965-66); mem. Crop Sci. Soc. (bd. dirs. 1955-57,67, tech. editor jour. 1966-69), Am. Assn. U. Agrl. Adminstrs. (chmn. 1974-75), Gamma Sigma Delta, Alpha Zeta, Phi Delta Kappa, Farmhouse Frat. Methodist. Clubs: Spring Hill Country, Rotary. Home: President's Home ABAC Sta Tifton GA 31793 *Work is the key to success and is to be enjoyed.*

ANDERSON, STEFAN STOLEN, banker; b. Madison, Wis., Apr. 1934; s. Theodore M. and Siri (Stolen) A.; m. Joan Timmermann, Sept. 19, 1959; children—Sharon Jill, Theodore Peter. A.B. magna cum laude, Harvard, 1956; M.B.A., U. Chgo., 1960. With Am. Nat. Bank & Trust Co. of Chgo., 1960-74, v.p., 1966-68, group v.p., 1968, exec. v.p., 1969-74; exec. v.p., dir. Mchts. Nat. Bank, Muncie, Ind., 1974-79, pres., 1979—; pres., dir. First Mchts Corp., 1983—. Vice pres. Nat. Youth Adv. Council for White House Conf. on Children and Youth, 1950; Bd. dirs. Crossroads council Boy Scouts Am., Jr. Achievement, Muncie Symphony Orch., Goodwill Industries, Delaware County United Way; trustee Roosevelt U., 1970-74. Served with USNR, 1956-58. Mem. Independent Bankers Assn. Ind. (dir.), Phi Beta Kappa, Beta Gamma Sigma. Clubs: Delaware Country, Rotary, Muncie (Muncie). Home: 2705 W Twickingham Dr Muncie IN 47304 Office: 200 E Jackson St Muncie IN 47305

ANDERSON, STUART LEROY, clergyman, coll. chancellor; b. Elmore, Ohio, Jan. 24, 1912; s. George Alfred and Grace Pearl (Longfellow) A.; m. Raezella Tom Klepper, Sept. 25, 1935; children—Philip, Catherine. A.B., Albion Coll., 1933, D.D. honoris causa, 1945; B.D., Chicago Theol. Sem., 1936; M.A., U. Chgo., 1936; Litt.D., Pacific U., 1960. Ordained to ministry Congl. Ch., 1936; minister First Ch., Argo, Ill., 1935-36, Glendale, Calif., 1938- 43, Long Beach, 1943-50, minister youth, Los Angeles, 1936-37; pres., prof. homiletics Pacific Sch. Religion, Berkeley, Calif., 1950-71, chancellor, 1971-77, pres. emeritus, 1977—; Moderator Los Angeles Assn. Congl.-Christian Chs., 1943-44, Congl. Conf. So. Calif. and S.W., 1949-50, Northern Calif. Congl. Conf., 1952-53; mem. Congl. Commn. on Theol. Edn., 1956—; mem. nat. com. war victims and reconstrn. Congl. Christian Chs.; mem. Prudential com. Am. Bd. Commrs. for Fgn. Missions, 1943-46, v.p., 1946-53; mem. U.S. Conf. for World Council Chs., 1961—; asst. moderator for Gen. Synod United Ch. Christ, 1961-63; protestant observer Second Vatican Council, 1965; mem. theol. commn. United Ch. of Christ, 1971—; Bd. dirs. Rockefeller Bros. Theol. Fellowship Program, 1958-64. Author: A Faith to Live By, 1959. Mem. Tau Kappa Epsilon, Alpha Phi Gamma, Delta Sigma Rho. Clubs: Rotary, U. Calif. Faculty (Berkeley); Commonwealth (San Francisco). Home: 344 Quincy Ave Long Beach CA 90814

ANDERSON, SUSAN LOU, lawyer; b. Washington, July 14, 1947; d. Howard Lester and Katherine (Anderson) Hershock. A.B., Eastern Coll., 1969; J.D., Villanova U., 1972. Bar: Pa. Staff atty., asso. counsel Fidelcor Inc., Phila., 1973-75, asst. v.p., asst. sec., asst. counsel, 1975-76, dep. head legal dept., v.p., asst. sec., asst. counsel, 1976-78, acting head personnel, 1975-76; partner firm Littleton and Anderson, Phila., 1978-82, Law Offices of Susan L. Anderson, 1982—; lectr. Temple U.; sec.-treas. Pa. Bd. Law Examiners. Trustee Marriage Council Phila., 1977; bd. dirs. Girl Scouts Phila., 1982—. Recipient cert. leadership Phila. YWCA, 1976. Mem. Am. Bar Assn., Pa. Bar Assn., Phila. Bar Assn. Home: 3644 Darby Rd Bryn Mawr PA 19010 Office: 225 Christ Church Walkway Philadelphia PA 19106

ANDERSON, THEODORE WILBUR, statistics educator; b. Mpls., June 5, 1918; s. Theodore Wilbur and Evelynn (Johnson) A.; m. Dorothy Fisher, July 8, 1950; children: Robert Lewis, Janet Lynn, Jeanne Elizabeth. B.S. with highest distinction, Northwestern U., 1939; M.A., Princeton U., 1942, Ph.D., 1945. Asst. dept. math. Northwestern U., 1939-40; instr. math. Princeton U., 1941-43, research assoc., 1943-45, Cowles Commn., U. Chgo., 1945-46; staff Columbia U., 1946-67, successively instr. math. stats., asst. prof., assoc. prof., 1946-56, prof., 1956-67, chmn. math. stats. dept., 1956-60, 64-65, acting chmn., 1950-51, 63; prof. stats. and econs. Stanford U., 1967—; dir. project Office Naval Research, 1968—; prin. investigator NSF project, 1969—, Army Research Office project, 1982—; vis. prof. math. U. Moscow, 1968; vis. prof. stats. U. Paris, 1968; acad. visitor math. Imperial Coll. Sci. and Tech., U. London, 1967-68, London Sch. Econs. and Polit. Sci., 1974-75; research visitor Tokyo Inst. Tech., 1977; cons. RAND Corp.; mem. com. on basic research adv. Office Ordnance Research, Nat. Acad. Scis.-NRC, 1955-58; mem. panel on applied math. adv. Nat. Bur. Standards, 1964-65; chmn. com. on stats. NRC, 1961-63; mem. com. on support research in math. scis. Nat Acad. Scis., 1965-68; mem. com. Pres.'s Statis. Socs., 1962-64; sci. dir. NATO Advanced Study Inst. on Discriminant Analysis and Its Applications, 1972; mem. panel reviewers Nat. Acad. Sci. Author: An Introduction to Multivariate Statistical Analysis, 1958, The Statistical Analysis of Time Series, 1971, (with Somesh Das Gupta and George P.H. Styan) A Bibliography of Multivariate Statistical Analysis, 1972, (with Stanley Sclove) Introductory Statistical Analysis, 1974, An Introduction to the Statistical Analysis of Data, 1978; editor: Annals of Math. Statistics, 1950-52; editorial bd.: Psychometika, 1954-72; assoc. editor: Jour. Time Series Analysis, 1980—. Guggenheim fellow, 1947-48; fellow Center for Advanced Study in Behavioral Scis., 1957-58; vis. scholar, 1972-73, 80; Sherman Fairchild disting. scholar Calif. Inst. Tech., 1980. Fellow Am. Statis. Assn. (v.p. 1971-73), Econometric Soc., Royal. Statis. Soc., AAAS, Inst. Math. Stats. (pres. 1963), Am. Acad. Arts and Scis.; mem. Am. Math. Soc., Indian, Internat. statis. insts., Conf. Bd. Math. Scis. (exec. com.), Psychometric Soc. (council dirs.), Nat. Acad. Scis., Bernouilli Soc. for Math. Stats. and Probability, Phi Beta Kappa. Home: 746 Santa Ynez St Stanford CA 94305 Office: Dept Statistics Sequoia Hall Stanford U Stanford CA 94305

ANDERSON, THOMAS DUNAWAY, lawyer; b. Oklahoma City, Mar. 9, 1912; s. Frank Ervin and Burdine (Clayton) A.; m. Helen Sharp, Feb. 21, 1938; children: Helen Shaw, Lucille Clayton Streeter, John Sharp. Student, Rice Inst., 1930-31; LL.B., Washington and Lee U., 1934; LL.D. (hon.), Lambuth Coll., 1967. Bar: Va. 1933, Tex. 1934. Assoc. firm Andrews, Kurth, Campbell & Bradley, 1934-41, 46-47; sr. v.p., trust officer Tex. Commerce Bank and predecessors, 1947-65; partner firm Anderson, Brown, Orn & Jones, 1965-80, of counsel, 1980—; dir. GOE Resources Co., Columbia Sci. Industries. Trustee emeritus Washington and Lee U.; Trustee emeritus Lambuth Coll.; pres. Kelsey Seybold Found., Protestant Episcopal Ch. Council, Diocese of Tex., Washington-on-the-Brazos State Park Assn.; past pres. Mus. Fine Arts of Houston, Houston Grand Opera; bd. visitors Univ. Cancer Found.; bd. dirs. Bayou Bend Gardens Endowment, Bayou Bend Adv. Com., Retina Research Found., San Jacinto Mus., Harris County Hist. Commn. Mem. Am., Houston bar assns., State Bar Tex., Philos. Soc. Tex., Phi Delta Phi. Episcopalian. Clubs: Bayou, Tejas, Eagle Lake Rod and Gun, Houston Country, River Oaks Garden (hon.). Home: 3925 Del Monte Houston TX 77019 Office: 900 Texas Commerce Tower Houston TX 77002

ANDERSON, THOMAS HAROLD, agribusiness company executive; b. Toledo, Jan. 21, 1924; s. Harold and Margaret (Meilink) A.; m. Mary Pat Adamshick, Sept. 13, 1952; children: Mary, Andrew, Margaret, Anthony, Matthew, Janet, Ellen, Edward, Frederick, Alex, Katherine, Thomas, Angel. Grad. magna cum laude, Mich. State U., 1965. Gen. Partner The Andersons, 1947—, asst. gen. mgr., 1979—. Trustee Toledo-Lucas County Public Library, 1970, pres., 1970-72; trustee Toledo Zool. Soc., Med. Coll. Ohio, Toledo, Toledo Community Chest, United Way; gen. chmn. United Way, 1977. Served with USAAF. Roman Catholic. Clubs: Maumee Rotary (past pres.), Ottawa Skeet.). Home: 1833 S Holland Sylvania Rd Maumee OH 43537 Office: PO Box 119 Maumee OH 43547

ANDERSON, THOMAS J., publisher, rancher, public speaker, syndicated columnist; b. Nashville, Nov. 7, 1910; s. William J. and Nancy Lucas (Joseph) A.; m. Carolyn Montague Jennings, Dec. 24, 1936; 1 dau., Carolyn (Mrs. Sam M. Porter, Jr.). B.A., Vanderbilt U., 1934; LL.B. (hon.), Bob Jones U., 1967. Securities salesman Gray-Shillinglaw & Co., Nashville, 1934-36; salesman Nunn-Schwab Securities Co., 1936-39; mgr. unlisted securities dept. J.C. Bradford Co., 1939-43; So. sales mgr. So. Agriculturist, Nashville, 1943-47; owner, pub. (So. Farm Publs.), 1947-71, Farm and Ranch mag., 1953-63, The American Way Features (nat. newspaper syndicate), Straight Talk (weekly newsletter Anderson Enterprises); radio commentator, world traveler, also cattle and timber ranch. Author: Straight Talk, 1967, Silence Is Not Golden It's Yellow, 1973. Vice presdl. candidate Am. Party, 1972, nat. chmn., 1972-78, presdl. candidate, 1976; mem. council John Birch Soc., 1959-76; nat. chmn. We-the-People, 1966-72. Served to lt. U.S. Navy, 1943-46. Recipient Liberty awards Congress of Freedom, 1964—, Pub. Address award Freedoms Found. Valley Forge, 1959, 60; named Man of Yr. God and Country Rally, 1966. Mem. Am. Agrl. Editors Assn. (pres. 1954), Phi Delta Theta (province pres. 1936-39). So. Methodist. Clubs: Jupiter Inlet Beach, Jupiter Ocean and Racquet (Fla.). 128 Lighthouse Dr Jupiter Inlet Colony Jupiter FL 33458

ANDERSON, THOMAS KEMP, JR., editor; b. Christoval, Tex., Jan. 19, 1926; s. Thomas Kemp and Ruth Mary (Starbuck) A.; m. Wanda Dale Hill, May 11, 1951; children—Robert, Sharon, Deena, Brent, Bryan. B.S., McMurry Coll., 1948; M.S., Okla. State U., 1949. Copy editor Corpus Christi (Tex.) Caller, 1953-55, Dallas Times Herald, 1955-56; bur. chief McGraw-Hill World News, Dallas, 1957-59, Los Angeles, 1959-64; mng. editor news Electronics Mag., N.Y.C., 1964-67; editor in chief, 1970-79; dir. editorial tng. McGraw-Hill Pub. Co., N.Y.C., 1967-70, v.p. bus. systems devel., 1979—; Chmn. engring. student mag. advisers' com. Am. Soc. Engring. Edn., 1973-74; Mem. editorial com. Am. Bus. Press, 1973-75. Served with USNR, 1944-46. Recipient Jesse H. Neal Editorial Achievement award Am. Bus. Press, 1978. Methodist. Home: 385 Hopper Ave Ridgewood NJ 07450 Office: 1221 Ave of Americas New York NY 10020

ANDERSON, THOMAS P., constrn. co. exec.; b. Ithaca, N.Y., July 20, 1916; s. Clarence E. and Frances A. A.; m. Louise Howard, July 3, 1954; children—Beth, Jeffrey, Peggy, Linda, Eric. B.S. in Acctg, Syracuse U. C.P.A., N.Y., Ohio. Engaged in acctg. and auditing, prior to 1951; with Morrison-Knudsen Co., Inc. (and affiliates), 1951—; treas. H.K. Ferguson Co., Cleve. Served with USAAF, 1942-46. Mem. Ohio Soc. C.P.A.s, N.Y. State Soc. C.P.A.s. Methodist. Home: 4261 Martin Dr North Olmsted OH 44070 Office: HK Ferguson Co 1 Erieview Plaza Cleveland OH 44114

ANDERSON, THOMAS PATRICK, mechanical engineer, educator; b. Chgo., Oct. 22, 1934; s. Clarence Kenneth and Anne (Moran) A.; m. Elizabeth Ann Toof, July 9, 1960; children—Patricia, James. B.S. in Mech. Engring, Northwestern U., 1956, M.S., 1958, Ph.D., 1961. Registered profl. engr., Ill., Iowa. Engr. Askania Regulator Co., Chgo., 1953-55; research engr. Cook Research Labs., Skokie, Ill., summer, 1956, ARO Inc., Tullahoma, Tenn., summers 1958, 59; asst. prof., then asso. prof. Northwestern U., 1960-66; prof. mech. engring. U. Iowa, 1966-75, chmn. dept., 1966-70; program mgr. Office Systems Integration and Analysis, NSF, 1974-75, program mgr. div. intergovtl. sci. and pub. tech., 1975-78, acting dir. indsl. program, 1976-78; dean Sch. Sci. and Engring., So. Ill. U., Edwardsville, 1978-82, prof. Sch. Engring., 1982—; cons., asso. dep. dir. interdeptl. energy study Office Sci. and Tech., 1963-65. Contbr. numerous articles to profl. jours. Named One of Ten Outstanding Young Men Chgo. Jr. Assn. Commerce and Industry, 1964. Fellow Iowa Acad. Sci.; mem. AAAS, AAUP, Am. Geophys. Union, Am. Inst. Aero. and Astronautics, Am. Phys. Soc., Am. Soc. Engring. Edn., ASME, N.Y. Acad. Scis., Sigma Xi. Home: 1527 Lewis Rd Edwardsville IL 62025

ANDERSON, THOMAS RALPH, financial services company executive; b. Aurora, Ill., Feb. 12, 1938; s. Ralph A. and Jeannette C. (Malmer) A.; m. Carol Tremaine, Oct. 6, 1962; children: Brian, Rodney, Nicole. B.S., U. Ill., 1961. C.P.A., Ill. Auditor Arthur Young & Co., Chgo., 1961-66; comptroller Kemper Fin. Services, Inc., Chgo., 1966-71, v.p., comptroller, 1971-75, exec. v.p., 1975-77, pres., chief exec. officer, dir., 1977-83, chmn., chief exec. officer, dir., 1983—; chmn., treas. Kemper Investors Life Ins. Co., Chgo., 1976-78, chmn., chief exec. officer, treas., 1978-79, chmn., chief exec. officer, 1979—, mgr. (dir.) separate accounts, 1983—; sr. v.p., dir. Kemper Corp., 1983—, Lumbermens Mut. Casualty Co., 1983—, Am. Motorists Ins. Co., 1983—, Am. Mfrs. Mut. Ins. Co., 1983—; chmn., dir. kemper/Cymrot, Inc., 1983—; v.p., dir. Tech. Fund, Inc., Kemper Growth Fund, Inc., Kemper Summit Fund, Inc., Kemper Total Return Fund, Inc., Kemper Income & Capital Preservation Fund, Inc., Kemper Money Market Fund, Inc., Kemper Municipal Bond Fund, Inc., Kemper Option Income Fund, Inc., Kemper U.S. Govt. Securities Fund, Inc., Kemper High Yield Fund, Inc., Cash Equivalent Fund, Inc., Kemper Internat. Fund, Inc., Kemper Govt. Money Market Fund, Inc., Tax-Exempt Money Market Fund, Inc., Kemper Calif. Tax-Free Income Fund, Inc.; dir. Fin. Guaranty Ins. Co., Bateman Eichler Hill Richards, Inc., Blunt, Ellis & Loewi, Inc., Prescott, Ball & Turben, Inc. Trustee, chmn. fin. com. Ill. chpt. Leukemia Soc. Am., 1980—; trustee James S. Kemper Found., 1983—. Mem. Am. Inst. C.P.A.s, Ill. Soc. C.P.A.s, Am. Inst. Corp. Controllers, Alpha Tau Omega. Congregationalist. Clubs: Economics, LaGrange Country (LaGrange, Ill.); University, Attic, Whitehall (Chgo.). Lodge: Masons. Home: 209 S Blackstone Ave LaGrange IL 60525 Office: 120 S LaSalle St Chicago IL 60603

ANDERSON, THURMAN EUGENE, army officer; b. Glennville, Ga., June 2, 1932; s. John Thurman and Myrtice (Girardeau) A.; m. Gloria Mae Jones, Aug. 26, 1951; children: Michael Eugene, Marvin Paul. B.S., North Gal. Coll., 1953; M.B.A., Syracuse U., 1968; grad., U.S. Army War Coll., 1973, U.S. Army Command and Gen. Staff Coll., 1967. Commd. 2d lt. U.S. Army, 1953, advanced through grades to maj. gen, 1981; comptroller U.S. Army Forces Command, Atlanta, 1978-80; comdg. gen. 2d Armored Div., Garlstedt, W.Ger., 1980-82, 3d Armored Div., Grankfurt, W.Ger., 1982—; mem. U.S. Army Gen. Officer Selection Bd., Washington, 1982. Decorated Legion of Merit (2), Bronze Star, Meritorious Service medal, Honor Cross medal in Gold, Germany. Mem. Am. Soc. Mil. Comptrollers, Assn. U.S. Army. Baptist. Home: Box 253 Reidsville GA 30453 Office: US Army Headquarters 3d Armored Div APO New York NY 09039

ANDERSON, TIMOTHY CHRISTOPHER, association executive; b. Hinsdale, Ill., Dec. 27, 1950; s. Paul Eugene and Mary Agnes (Donnell) A. B.A. in Polit. Sci. with honors, Boston Coll., (1973.). Research asst. Congressman O'Neill's Office, Washington, 1973; ednl. cons. E.F. Shelly Co., Washington, 1973-74; asso. dir. Boston Zool. Soc., 1974-76, exec. dir., adminstr. Boston's two zoos, 1976-81; New Eng. regional v.p. Nat. Alliance Bus., Boston, 1981—; cons. NEH, 1977-78; v.p. Boston Harbor Assocs. Mem. Blue Hill Ave. Commn., 1977-80; program com. Boston Cultural Edn. Collaborative, 1976-80; polit. cons., Western Mass., Sen. Kennedy, 1974; field coordinator for, Western Mass., Jimmy Carter's Primary Election Campaign, 1975-76; bd. dirs. Franklin Park Coalition, 1974-81; mem. council, treas. Madison Park Community Sch., 1979-83; trustee, v.p. Mass. Cultural Alliance; v.p. Artists Found.; mem. Baptist Assos., Boston Coll.; mem. advocacy steering com. Mass. Council on Arts and Humanities, 1979-81; incorporator Boston Zool. Soc., 1982. Office: Nat Alliance Bus 190 High St Boston MA 02110

ANDERSON, TOTTON JAMES, political science educator; b. Beirut, May 26, 1909; s. Samuel M. and Agatha (Totton) A.; m. Frances Elizabeth Moore, Aug. 17, 1934. A.B., U. Calif. at Berkeley, 1930, M.A., 1931; Ph.D., U. So. Calif., 1946. Registrar, dean Ventura (Calif.) Coll., 1935-42, 46-47; mem. faculty U. So. Calif., 1947—, prof. polit. sci., 1958—, disting. emeritus prof., 1983—, chmn. dept. polit. sci., 1957-60, 64-66, asso. dean div. social scis. Coll. Letters, Arts and Scis., 1966-69, cons. prof. Sch. Bus., 1975—; vis. prof. U. Hawaii, summer 1958; Disting. vis. prof. U. San Diego, 1978-79; polit. cons., 1960—; exec. com. Calif. Constl. Revision Commn., 1964-73; chmn. exec. com. Calif. Legis. Intern Program, 1957-71; mem. Mayor Los Angeles Community Redevel. Adv. Com., 1966-68; asso. dir. Nat. Center Edn. in Politics, 1954-55; regional dir. Citizenship Clearing House, 1959-63; Trustee Coro Found., 1959-72. Co-author: Introduction to Political Science, 4th edit., 1983, Western Politics, 1958, Bibilography on Western Politics, 1958, Politics in the American West, 1969, Political Dynamiting, 1970; contbg. author: Cooperation and Conflict: Readings in American Federalism, 1969; contbr. articles to profl. jours. Served to lt. col. USAAF, 1943-45; ret. col. Res. Decorated Bronze Star. Mem. Am. Polit. Sci. Assn., Western Polit. Sci. Assn. (pres. 1952-53), Am. Acad. Polit. and Social Scis., Phi Beta Kappa (pres. Alpha Alumni Assn. in So. Calif. 1964-66). Home: 3234-C San Amadeo Laguna Hills CA 92653

ANDERSON, VICTOR CHARLES, applied physics educator; b. Shanghai, China, Mar. 31, 1922; s. Elam Johnathan and Colina (Michael) A.; m. Anne Dowden, May 9, 1943; children: Victor C., Judith. B.A., U. Redlands, 1943; Ph.D., UCLA, 1953. Research technician U. Calif. Radiation Lab., Berkeley, 1943-46; research asst. Scripps Instn. Oceanography, La Jolla, 1947-53; postdoctoral fellow Harvard U. Acoustics Research Lab., 1954-55; research physicist Scripps Instn. Oceanography, U. Calif., 1955—, prof. applied physics, 1969—; chmn. dept. elec. engring. and computer sci. Scripps Instn. Oceanograpy, U. Calif., 1981—; dep. dir. marine Phys. Lab. Scripps Instn. Oceangraphy, U. Calif., 1969—. Patentee digital multibeam steering, delay line time compressor. Recipient Disting. Civilian Service award Office of Naval Research, 1976. Fellow Acoustical Soc. Am.; mem. IEEE, Sigma Pi Sigma. Presbyterian. Home: 2325 Poinsettia Dr San Diego CA 92106 Office: EECS Dept U Calif-San Diego La Jolla CA 92093

ANDERSON, VICTOR ELVING, educator, geneticist; b. Stromsburg, Nebr., Sept. 6, 1921; s. Edwin L. and Olga (Elving) A.; m. Carol Esther Rexion, Aug. 31, 1946; children: Catherine, Carl, Christine, Martha. A.A., Bethel Jr. Coll., 1941; student, Bethel Theol. Sem., 1941-43; B.A., U. Minn., 1945, M.S., 1949, Ph.D., 1953. Faculty dept. biology Bethel Coll., 1946-60; asst. dir. Dight Inst. for Human Genetics, U. Minn., 1954-78, acting dir., 1978—, asso. prof. zoology and genetics, 1961-66, prof. genetics and cell biology, 1966—; Cons. Nat. Inst.

Neurol. Disease and Blindness, 1961-68; mem. developmental behavioral scis. study sect. NIH, 1972-75, chmn., 1974-75; Bd. regents Bethel Coll. and Sem., 1969-74, 82—; bd. dirs. Inst. for Advanced Christian Studies, 1971-76, 77-81, 82—. Author: (with H.O. Goodman and S.C. Reed) Variables Related to Human Breast Cancer, 1958, (with S.C. Reed, C. Hartley, V.P. Phillips, N.A. Johnson) The Psychoses: Family Studies, 1973; (with W.A. Hauser, J.K. Penry, C.F. Sing) also articles. Genetic Basis of the Epilepsies; contbr. articles to profl. jours. Named Alumnus of Year Bethel Coll. and Sem., 1965. Mem. AAAS (pres. Acad. Conf. 1967), Am. Soc. Human Genetics (dir. 1967-70), Minn. Acad. Sci. (pres. 1964-65), Am. Sci. Affiliation (pres. 1963-65), Behavior Genetics Assn. (sec. 1972-74, pres. 1979-80), Genetics Soc. Am., Phi Beta Kappa, Sigma Xi (exec. bd. 1972—, pres. 1982-83). Research on genetics in human behavior, mental retardation, epilepsy, and diabetes. Home: 1775 N Fairview Ave Saint Paul MN 55113 Office: Dight Inst Human Genetics U Minn Minneapolis MN 55455

ANDERSON, WALLACE ERVIN, physicist, educator, univ. ofcl.; b. Scranton, S.C., Oct. 28, 1913; s. Miles Hannibal and Laura (Wallace) A.; m. Rheta M. Frierson, Sept. 12, 1939; children—Sarah Graham, Mary Wallace. B.S., The Citadel, 1934, D.Sc. (hon.), 1981; M.S., U. Ky., 1936; Ph.D. (Rackham fellow 1947), U. Mich., 1949. Mem. faculty The Citadel, 1936-42, 46-79, prof. physics, head dept., 1953—, acad. dean, 1966—, v.p. for acad. affairs, 1970-79, interim pres., 1978-79, dean emeritus, 1979; spl. tutor Med. Coll. S.C. Teaching Hosp., Charleston, 1959-67; research asso. Duke, 1949, 50. Served to lt. col. AUS, 1942-46; col. Res. Decorated Legion of Merit. Mem. Am. Phys. Soc., Am. Assn. Physics Tchrs., Sigma Xi, Sigma Pi Sigma, Phi Kappa Phi. Episcopalian. Clubs: Country of Charleston, Rotary. Home: 11 Country Club Dr Charleston SC 29412

ANDERSON, WALLACE LUDWIG, educator; b. Hartford, Conn., Sept. 9, 1917; s. Ludwig and Greta (Askerbloom) A.; m. Mary Elizabeth Belden, Mar. 10, 1943; children: Hale, Whit. B.A., Trinity Coll., Conn., 1939, M.A., 1945; Ph.D., U. Chgo., 1948. Tchr. pub. schs., Conn., 1939-42; asst. prof. English U. No. Iowa, Cedar Falls, 1948-54, asso. prof., 1954-58, prof., 1958-72, asst. dean instr., 1959-63, assoc. dean instrn., 1963-65, dean undergraduate studies, 1965-72; prof. English Bridgewater (Mass.) State Coll., 1972-82, prof. emeritus, 1983—, acad. dean, 1972-78, v.p. acad. affairs, 1978-83; Mem. intercultural edn. com. Edn. and World Affairs. Author: (with N.C. Stageberg) Poetry as Experience, 1952, Introductory Readings on Language, 1962, Edwin Arlington Robinson: A Critical Introduction, 1967; Contbr.: articles profl. jours. Edwin Arlington Robinson: A Critical Introduction. Served with USAAF, 1942-45. Fulbright award The Netherlands, 1957-58; Guggenheim fellow, 1967-68. Mem. MLA. Home: 185 Lakeside Dr Bridgewater MA 02324

ANDERSON, WALTER DIXON, trade assn. exec.; b. Elizabeth, N.J., July 22, 1932; s. Charles Michael and Hazel Mildred (Fieldstad) A. B.A., Emory U., 1954; M.A., U. Ga., 1958. State rep. Nat. Found. March of Dimes, Jacksonville, Fla., 1958-61; exec. sec. Fla. Turf-Grass Assn., Jacksonville, 1961-69; exec. dir. Irrigation Assn., Silver Spring, Md., 1969-80, exec. v.p., 1980—. Served with U.S. Army, 1954-56. Mem. Am. Soc. Assn. Execs., Washington Soc. Assn. Execs., Soil Conservation Soc. Am., Sigma Delta Chi. Republican. Methodist. Home: 6700 Heatherford Ct Rockville MD 20855 Office: 13975 Connecticut Ave Silver Spring MD 20906

ANDERSON, WALTER HERMAN, editor; b. Mt. Vernon, N.Y., Aug. 31, 1944; s. William Henry and Ethel Magdalena (Crolly) A.; m. Loretta Gritz, Sept. 9, 1967; children: Eric Christian, Melinda Christe. A.A., Westchester Community Coll., 1970; B.S. summa cum laude, Mercy Coll., 1972. Reporter Reporter Dispatch, White Plains, N.Y., 1967-68, night city editor, 1968-69, editor, gen. mgr., 1975-77; police reporter Westchester Rockland Newspapers, White Plains, N.Y., 1969-70, help editor for action line, 1970-71, investigative reporter, 1971-72; editor, gen. mgr. Standard Star, New Rochelle, N.Y., 1974-75; sr. editor Parade mag., N.Y.C., 1977-78, mng. editor, 1978-80, editor, 1980—; guest lectr. Columbia U., NYU, U. Mass.; adj. prof. psychology, sociology Westchester Community Coll., 1972—. Chmn. bd. trustees Mercy Coll., Dobbs Ferry, N.Y., 1980—; bd. dirs. St. Vincent's Hosp., 1975-80; mem. Nat. Com. for Lit. Arts. Served with USMC, 1961-66. Recipient Frank Tripp Meml. award Gannett Group, 1971, Valedictory award Westchester Community Coll., 1970, others. Mem. Soc. Silurians, Sigma Delta Chi, Psi Chi. Club: Overseas Press. Office: 750 3d Ave New York NY 10017 *I hope a single driving desire remains with me always—that is, to encourage talented people. To share, even in the least of ways, in the growth of a creative talent is the highest goal of an editor, if his career is to matter at all.*

ANDERSON, WARREN M., diversified company executive; b. Bklyn., Nov. 29, 1921; s. John M. and Ida M. (Peterson) A.; m. Lillian K. Christensen, Feb. 22, 1947. A.B., Colgate U., 1942; LL.B., Western Res. U., 1956. Chem. sales rep. Union Carbide Co., N.Y.C., 1945, v.p. sales and mktg., Olefins div., 1962, pres. Process Chems. div., 1967-69, v.p., 1969-73, exec. v.p., 1973-77, pres., 1977-82, chmn., chief exec. officer, 1982—, also dir. Served with USNR, 1943-45. Mem. Am. Chem. Soc., Soc. Chem. Industry, ABA. Office: Union Carbide Corp Old Ridgebury Rd Danbury CT 06817

ANDERSON, WARREN MATTICE, state senator; b. Bainbridge, N.Y., Oct. 16, 1915; s. Floyd E. and Edna (Mattice) A.; m. Eleanor C. Sanford, June 28, 1941; children: Warren David, Lawrence, Richard, Thomas. B.A., Colgate U., 1937; J.D., Albany Law Sch., 1940, LL.D. (hon.), 1979, Hartwick Coll., 1976, Coll. of New Rochelle, 1979, Fordham U., 1980, Union Coll., 1981, Colgate U., 1982. Bar: N.Y. bar 1940. Since practiced in, Binghamton, asst. atty., Broome County, N.Y., 1940-42; assoc. firm Hinman, Howard & Kattell, 1949-52, partner, 1952—; mem. N.Y. State Senate, 1953—, chmn. fin. com., 1966-72, pres. pro tem, majority leader, 1973—; Del. Republican Nat. Conf., 1972, 76, 80, mem. platform com., 1976; regional mem.-at-large governing bd. Council State Govts.; also mem.-at-large governing bd.; trustee Colgate U., 1964-70, Cornell U., 1973—. Served with AUS, 1943-44; to lt. JAGC AUS, 1944-45. Recipient Alumni award Colgate U., 1972. Fellow Am. Bar Found., N.Y. State Bar Found.; mem. Am., N.Y. State, Broome County bar assns. Presbyterian. Clubs: Binghamton; Ft. Orange (Albany, N.Y.). Home: 34 Lathrop Ave Binghamton NY 13905 Office: 724 Security Mut Bldg Binghamton NY 13901

ANDERSON, WENDELL WILLIAM, JR., metal and plastic products maufacturing company executive; b. Pitts., 1925. Student, Yale U., 1945. Chmn., chief exec. officer Bundy Corp., Detroit; dir. Detroit Edison Co., Ex-Cell-O Corp., Mfrs. Nat. Bank, Detroit. Office: Bundy Corp 333 W Fort St Detroit MI 48226 *

ANDERSON, WILLIAM (ALBION), JR., oil and gas holding company executive; b. Paris, Ark., July 12, 1939; s. William A. and Maude (Rogers) A.; m. Patricia P. Puterbaugh, July 5, 1968; stepchildren—Charles L. Kuehn, Cynthia P. Kuehn. B.S.B.A., U. Ark., 1961; M.B.A., Harvard U., 1963. With Blyth Eastman Dillon & Co., Inc., 1963-75, exec. asst. to chief exec. officer, dir. planning, N.Y.C., 1973-74, sr. v.p., 1974-75; sr. v.p., chief fin. officer ENSTAR Corp., Houston, 1975—; dir. Republic Bank Houston. Mem. Fin. Execs. Inst. Clubs: River Oaks Country, University, Petroleum (Houston). Office: PO Box 6554 Houston TX 77005

ANDERSON, WILLIAM BANKS, JR., ophthalmology educator; b. Durham, N.C., June 14, 1931; s. William Banks and Mildred Ursula (Everett) A.; m. Nancy Eldridge Walker, Sept. 17, 1960; children: Mary Banks, Mark Eldridge, Elizabeth Perry. A.B., Princeton U., 1952; M.D., Harvard U., 1956. Diplomate: Am. Bd. Ophthalmology. Intern Duke U. Med. Ctr., Durham, N.C., 1956-57, resident, 1959-62, asst. prof. ophthalmology, 1962-67, assoc. prof. ophthalmology, 1967-76, prof. ophthalmology, 1976—; mem. profl. adv. com. N.C. Div. Services to the Blind, Raleigh, 1972—. Chmn. bd. trustees Durham Acad., 1975-77. Served to capt. M.C. U.S. Army, 1957-59. Fellow ACS; mem. Am. Ophthalmol. Soc., Am. Acad. Ophthalmology (bd. councillors). Episcopalian. Home: 2401 Cranford Rd Durham NC 27706 Office: Duke U Eye Center Erwin Rd Durham NC 27710

ANDERSON, WILLIAM BRECKENRIDGE, lawyer; b. St. Louis, July 28, 1927; s. Albert Lyon and Gladys Winifred (King) A.; m. Mary Lou McCullough, June 7, 1952; children—William Breckenridge, Nancy. Student, Ill. Wesleyan U.; J.D., U. Mo., Columbia, 1952. Bar: Mo. bar 1952. Partner firm Anderson, Gilbert, Wolfort, Allen & Bierman, St. Louis, 1956-68; prof. law U. Mo. Law Sch., Kansas City, 1968—, asso. dean, 1977—; dir. Mo. Bar Research, Inc. Served with USAF, 1952-56. Recipient Lon O. Hocker Meml. Trial Lawyer award Mo. Bar Found., 1961. Mem. Am. Bar Assn., Mo. Bar Assn., Kansas City Bar Assn., St. Andrews Soc. Home: 901 W Santa Fe Trail Kansas City MO 64145 Office: 5100 Rockhill Rd Kansas City MO 64110

ANDERSON, WILLIAM EDWARD, broadcasting co. exec.; b. Wilmington, Del., June 5, 1942; s. William Marion and Glenda (Allen) A.; m. Margaret Elizabeth Baynard, July 23, 1960; children—William Edward, Karen Elizabeth, Sheryl Evette. Announcer Sta. WSNJ, Bridgeton, N.J., 1962-65; security supr. Del. State Hosp., New Castle, 1965-71; juvenile group leader Ferris Sch. for Boys, Wilmington, 1971-72; program dir. Sta. WSTW-FM, Wilmington, 1972—; Communication cons. Del. div. Am. Cancer Soc.; publicity chmn. United Negro Coll. Fund, Del. campaign, 1974-80. Mem. citizens adv. council Colonial Sch. Bd. Recipient Disting. Service award United Negro Coll. Fund, 1978. Democrat. Methodist. Home: 122 Halcyon Dr New Castle DE 19720 Office: 2727 Shipley Rd Wilmington DE 19899

ANDERSON, WILLIAM EDWARD, editorial consultant; b. Mpls., July 1, 1922; s. Oscar Emmanuel and Lillian Ann (Clark) A. Certificate, State U. Iowa, 1942; A.B., Columbia, 1949, postgrad., 1950-51. Prodn. mgr. Palmer Publs. (mag. pub.), N.Y.C., 1951-55; mng. editor Chem. Engring. Progress publ. Am. Inst. Chem. Engring., N.Y.C., 1955-58, Electro-Tech. publ. C-M Tech. Publs., 1958-62, Stereo Rev. mag. Ziff-Davis Pub. Co., N.Y.C., 1963-64, editor, 1965-78, editor-in-chief, 1979-82; editorial cons., 1982—. Served with USAAF, 1942-46. A.M. Proudfit fellow. Mem. Music Critics Assn., Nat. Acad. Rec. Arts, Scis., Am. Soc. Mag. Editors, Phi Beta Kappa. Home: East Quogue NY 11942

ANDERSON, WILLIAM ERNEST, lawyer; b. Chgo., July 31, 1895; s. Andrew and Mary (Lofqvist) A.; m. Marjorie Allen, June 18, 1927; children: Laurel Joyce, Lois Winifred; m. Beatriz Hernandez del Valle. LL.B., Webster Coll., 1920; LL.M., Loyola U., Chgo., 1926. Bar: Ill. 1920. Since practiced in, Chgo.; specializing in patents, unfair competition, trade-marks and copyrights; counsel to firm Fitch, Even, Tabin & Flannery (and predecessor firm), Chgo., 1931—; U.S. claims commr. for, Morocco, Algeria, Tunisia, 1943-45. Author: Spanish Adjectives and Adverbs, 1941. Served to lt. col. AUS, 1942-46. Mem. Inter-Am., Am., Ill., Chgo. bar assns., Am., Chgo. patent law assns. Club: Union League (Chicago). Home: 7212 Oak Ave River Forest IL 60305 Office: 135 S LaSalle St Chicago IL 60603

ANDERSON, WILLIAM HENRY, physician, educator; b. Phila., Nov. 10, 1940; s. William Henry Schoen and Elizabeth Winifred (Laverty) A.; m. Catherine Sacchetti, Oct. 7, 1967; 1 dau., Jennifer Ann Gist. B.S., MIT, 1962; M.A., U. Pa., 1967; M.D., Thomas Jefferson U., 1967; M.P.H., Harvard U., 1977. Diplomate: Am. Bd. Psychiatry and Neurology. Intern. Pa. Hosp., Phila., 1967-68; resident in psychiatry Mass. Gen. Hosp., Boston, 1968-71, assoc. psychiatrist dept. psychiatry, 1976—, dir. postgrad. edn., 1976-81; instr. psychiatry Harvard U., Boston, 1973-75, asst. prof., 1975-81, asst. clin. prof., 1981-82, lectr., 1982—; chief psychiatry St. Elizabeths Hosp., Boston, 1981—; asst. attending psychiatrist Mclean Hosp., Belmont, Mass. Contbg. editor: The New Physician, 1977-79. Served to lt. comdr., M.C. USNR, 1971-73. Fellow Am. Psychiat. Assn.; mem. AAAS, Am. Acad. Clin. Psychiatrists, Internat. Soc. Polit. Psychology, Com. on Fgn. Relations (Boston com.), Med. Assn. P.R. (hon.), Mass. Med. Soc., Am. Coll. Emergency Physicians, Am. Pub. Health Assn., Boston Athenaeum, Handel and Hayden Soc., Sigma Xi. Club: Harvard (Boston). Office: Mass Gen Hosp Boston MA 02114 Office: St Elizabeth Hosp Boston MA 02135

ANDERSON, WILLIAM HOPPLE, lawyer; b. Cin., Feb. 28, 1926; s. Robert Waters and Anna (Hopple) A.; (m), Feb. 3, 1951; children—Susan Hopple, Nancy, Barbara, William Hopple, Francie. Student, Carleton Coll., 1946; LL.B., U. Cin., 1952. Bar: Ohio bar 1952, U.S. Supreme Ct 1964. Mem. firm Becker, Loeb, & Becker, Cin., 1952-54; asst. pros. atty., Hamilton County, Ohio, 1953-57; partner firm Graydon, Head & Ritchey, Cin., 1957—; judge Wyoming (Ohio) Mcpl. Ct., 1960-67; mem. Ohio Ho. of Reps., 1967-69. Served with USMC, 1944-46. Mem. Ohio Bar Assn., Cin. Bar Assn. Republican. Presbyterian. Home: 297 Mount Pleasant Ave Wyoming OH 45215 Office: 511 Walnut St Cincinnati OH 45202

ANDERSON, WILLIAM LON, veterinarian; b. Royse City, Tex., Jan. 1, 1931; s. William Lyman and Lucile (McCoulskey) A.; m. Mary Lou Humphreys, July 17, 1970; children—Andra Flournoy, William Chilton; stepchildren—Linda Humphreys, Cindi Humphreys. D.V.M., Tex. A. and M. U., 1953. Practice veterinary medicine, Rockwall, Tex., 1955-58, Addison, Tex., 1958—; partner Dallas Veterinary Assos., Addison, 1958-80; owner Dallas Vet. Med. Center, 1980—; mem. Tex. Animal Health Commn., 1971-75; dir. Prestonwood Nat. Bank.; Trustee Dallas Health and Sci. Museum. Served with USAF, 1953-55. Recipient Disting. Alumnus award Coll. Vet. Medicine, Tex. A&M U. Mem. AVMA (pres. 1977-78), Tex. Veterinary Med. Assn. (pres. 1970), Dallas County Veterinary Med. Assn. (pres. 1968), Am. Animal Hosp. Assn., Am. Assn. Equine Practitioners, U.S. Animal Health Assn., Dallas Execs. Assn. Episcopalian. Clubs: Kiwanis, Hi Noon (Dallas); Masons, Shriners, Dallas Assembly. Home: 6615 Regal Bluff Dallas TX 75240 Office: 15000 Beltway Dr Addison TX 75001

ANDERSON, WILLIAM ROBERT, corporate executive; b. Bakerville, Tenn., June 17, 1921; s. David Hensly and Mary (McKelvey) A.; m. Yvonne Etzel, June 10, 1943 (div. Apr. 1979); children: Michael David, William Robert; m. Patricia Walters, Dec. 26, 1980; 1 dau., Jane Hensley. Grad., Columbia Mil. Acad., 1939; B.S. in Elec. Engring, U.S. Naval Acad., 1942; D.Sc., Defiance Coll., 1958. Commd. ensign U.S. Navy, 1942, advanced through grades to capt., 1960; assigned submarines (Tarpon, Narwhal, Trutta, Pacific combat patrols), World War II, postwar service submarines, Sarda, comdr. attack submarine, Pearl Harbor, 1953-55, head tactical dept., 1955-56; staff naval reactors br. AEC, Washington, 1956-57; comdr. U.S.S. Nautilus, 1957-59; ret., 1962; cons. to Pres. J.F. Kennedy, until 1963; mem. 89th-92d Congresses from 6th Tenn. Dist. Author: Nautilus 90 North, 1959, First Under the North Pole, 1959, The Useful Atom, 1966; Contbr. articles to nat. mags. and profl. publs. Decorated Bronze Star, Legion of Merit; recipient Stephen Decatur prize Navy League U.S., Distinguished Service award, N.Y.C., Christopher Columbus Internat. Communications award, Genoa, Italy; Elisha Kent Kane medalist Geog. Soc. Phila., 1959; Patron's medal Royal Geog. Soc., 1959; Leadership award Freedoms Found., 1960. Mem. Am. Legion, Amvets. Club: Explorers (N.Y.C.). Home: Arlington VA Office: 444 N Capitol St NW Washington DC 20001

ANDERSON, WILLIAM SCOVIL, classics educator; b. Brookline, Mass., Sept. 16, 1927; s. Edgar Weston and Katrina (Brewster) A.; m. Lorna Candee Bassette, June 12, 1954 (div. Dec. 1977); children: Judith, Blythe, Heather, Meredith, Keith; m. Deirdre Burt, May 28, 1983. B.A., Yale U., 1950, Ph.D., 1954; A.B., Cambridge U., (Eng.), 1952, M.A., 1955. Prix de Rome fellow Am. Acad. in Rome, 1954-55; instr. classics Yale U., 1955-59; resident in Rome, Morse fellow, 1959-60; mem. faculty U. Calif.-Berkeley, 1960—, prof. Latin and comparative lit., 1966—, prof. charge Intercollegiate Ctr. Classical Studies, 1967-68; chmn. classics U. Calif-Berkeley, 1970-73. Author: The Art of the Aeneid, 1969, Ovid, Metamorphoses, Critical Text, 1977; mem. editorial bd.: Classical Jour., Vergilius; mem.: Satire newsletter; contbr. articles to profl. jours. Served with AUS, 1946-48; Korea. NDH sr. fellow, 1973-74. Mem. Am. Philol. Assn. (pres. 1977), Danforth Assocs., Soc. Religion. Episcopalian. Office: Dept Classics Univ Calif Berkeley CA 94720

ANDERSON, WILLIAM, JR., college president. Pres. Mary Washington Coll., Fredericksburg, Va. Office: Office of Pres Mary Washington Coll Fredericksburg VA 22401§

ANDERSON-IMBERT, ENRIQUE, educator, author; b. Cordoba, Argentina, Feb. 12, 1910; came to U.S., 1947, naturalized, 1953; s. Jose Enrique and Honorina (Imbert) Anderson; m. Margarita Di Clerico, Mar. 30, 1935; children: Carlos Eduardo, Anabel. M.A., Universidad Nacional de Buenos Aires, 1940, Ph.D., 1946. Prof. lit. Universidad Nacional de Cuyo, Argentina, 1940, Universidad Nacional de Tucuman, 1941-46; lectr. Spanish lit. Smith Coll., Northampton, Mass., 1944; prof. Spanish lit. Mich. U., 1947-65; Victor S. Thomas prof. hispanic lit. Harvard, 1965—. Author: El arte de la prosa en Juan Montalvo, 1948, Historia de la literatura hispanoamericana, 1954, Que es la prosa, 1958, El grimorio, 1961, Vigilia Fuga, 1963, El gato de Cheshire, 1965, Genio y figura de Sarmiento, 1967, La originalidad de Ruben Dario, 1968, La Sandia y otros cuentos, 1969, Una aventura de Sarmiento en Chicago, 1969, La locura juega al ajedrez, 1971, La flecha en el aire, 1972, Los domingos del profesor, 1972, Estudios sobre letras hispanicas, 1974, La botella de Klein, 1975, El realismo magico, 1976, Los primeros cuentos del mundo, 1977, Victoria, 1977, Teoria y tècnica del cuento, 1979, La critica literaria y sus mètodos, 1979, Dos mujeres y un Julián, 1982. Mem. Am. Acad. Arts and Scis., Academia Argentina de Letras. Home: 20 Elizabeth Rd Belmont MA 02178 Office: 94 Widener Library Harvard Cambridge MA 02138

ANDES, CHARLES LOVETT, coin co. exec.; b. Phila., Sept. 23, 1930; s. Charles Lovett and Gladys (Stead) A.; m. Dorothea Roberta Abbott, Aug. 25, 1961; children: Elizabeth, Susan, Karen, Page. Student, Swarthmore Coll., 1948-50; B.A., Syracuse U., 1952. Pres. Adtech Industries, Phila., 1954-68; exec. v.p., dir. The Franklin Mint Corp., Franklin Center, Pa., 1969-73, pres., 1972-73, chmn. bd., 1973—; dir. Franklin Inst. Fidelcor, Inc., Phila., Fidelity Bank. Bd. dirs. Greater Phila. Partnership, Epilepsy Found. Am., Honor Am. Com., UN Assn. of U.S., Phila. Orch. Assn. Presbyterian. Clubs: Phila. Country, Union League, Merion Cricket (Phila.); La Mirador (Vevey, Switzerland). Office: Franklin Mint Corp Franklin Center PA 19091 *

ANDES, JOHN WILBUR, medical association executive; b. Knoxville, Tenn., July 18, 1928; s. John Wilbur and Irene (Garrett) A.; m. Patricia Jane Guy, Nov. 20, 1954; children: Alan Patrick, Jane Alison. A.B., Princeton U., 1948. Claims mgr. Blue Cross-Blue Shield of Fla., Jacksonville, 1948-50, 52-57, profl. relations dir., 1955-57; asst. exec. sec. Am. Soc. Anesthesiologists, Park Ridge, Ill., 1957-58, exec. sec., 1958—. Served with U.S. Navy, 1950-52. Mem. Am. Assn. Med. Soc. Execs., Profl. Conv. Mgmt. Assn., Park Ridge C. of C., Am. Soc. Assn. Execs., Chgo. Soc. Assn. Execs. Club: Princeton (Chgo.). Home: 1810 Walnut St Park Ridge IL 60068 Office: Am Soc Anesthesiologists 515 Busse Hwy Park Ridge IL 60068

ANDO, ALBERT K., economist, educator; b. Tokyo, Japan, Nov. 15, 1929; came to U.S., 1950, naturalized, 1963; s. T. and H.M. A.; m. Faith G. Halfter, June 23, 1967; children—Matthew, Clifford, Alison. B.S., Seattle U., 1951; M.A., St. Louis U., 1953; M.S., Carnegie Inst. Tech., 1956, Ph.D., 1959. Asst. prof. econs. M.I.T., Cambridge, 1957-62, asso. prof., 1962-64; prof. econs. and fin. U. Pa., Phila., 1966—; Chmn. subcom. on monetary research Social Sci. Research Council, 1970-81. Author: (with H.A. Simon and F.M. Fisher) Essays on Social Science Models, 1963, (with E. Cary Brown and Ann F. Freidlaender) Studies in Stabilization Policies, 1968, International Aspects of Stabilization Policies, 1975; contbr.: articles to profl. jours. International Aspects of Stabilization Policies. Guggenheim fellow, 1971-72; recipient Sr. Am. Scientist award A. Van Humboldt Found., 1977; NSF grantee, 1959—. Fellow Econometric Soc.; mem. Am. Econs. Assn. Home: 205 Dove Ln Haverford PA 19041 Office: Dept Econs Univ Pa Philadelphia PA 19104

ANDOLSEK, CHARLES MERRICK, liquor company executive; b. Hackensack, N.J., Mar. 18, 1947; s. Charles F. and Winifred M. A. B.S., U. Va., 1969; M.B.A., Columbia U., 1971. Officers asst. Chem. Bank, N.Y.C., 1971-73; fin. analyst Bristol Myers Co., 1973-74; fin. analyst, then asst. treas. Joseph E. Seagram & Sons, Inc., N.Y.C., 1974-79, v.p., treas., 1979—. Office: 800 3d Ave New York NY 10022

ANDRADE, EDNA, artist, emeritus art educator; b. Portsmouth, Va.; d. Thomas Judson and Ruth (Porter) Wright; m. C. Preston Andrade, Jr., July 12, 1941 (div. 1960). B.F.A., Pa. Acad. Fine Arts/U. Pa., 1937. Supr. art elem. schs., Norfolk, Va., 1938-39; instr. drawing and painting Newcomb Art Sch., Tulane U., 1939-41; lectr. U. N.Mex., 1971; prof. Phila. Coll. Art, 1959-72, 73-82, prof. emeritus, 1982—; prof. art Temple U., 1972-73. Artist, designer, OSS, 1942-44; free-lance designer, Washington, 1944-46; free-lance painter, designer, muralist, Phila. and, N.Y.C., 1946—; artist-in-residence, Hartford Sch. Art and Tamarind Inst., 1971, U. Sask., Can., 1977, U. Zulia, Maracaibo, Venezuela, 1980, Ariz. State U., Tempe, 1981, Fabric Workshop, Phila., 1984; vis. artist, Skidmore Coll., 1973, 74, one-woman shows, E. Hampton Gallery, N.Y.C., Peale Galleries Pa. Acad., Rutgers U., U. Hartford, Marian Locks Gallery, Phila., group shows include, AAAL, In This Acad., Pa. Acad. Fine Arts, Phila., William Penn Meml. Mus., Harrisburg, Phila. Coll. Art, Three Centuries Am. Art, Phila. Mus. Art, Bklyn. Mus., Ft. Worth Art Center, Des Moines Art Center, Philbrook Art Center, Tulsa, others; represented in permanent collections, Phila. Mus. Art, Pa. Acad. Fine Arts, Print Club, Balt. Mus. Art, Addison Gallery Am. Art, McNay Art Inst., San Antonio, Montclair (N.J.) Art Mus., Nat. Collection Fine Arts, Library of Congress, USIA, Albright-Knox Art Gallery, Buffalo, Colonial Penn Group, First Pa. Banking & Trust Co., Phila., Tamarind Collection, U. N.Mex. Mus., Yale Art

Gallery, Atlantic Richfield, Phila., Am. Telephone & Telegraph Co., Day & Zimmerman, Phila. Recipient 1st and 2d Cresson European traveling scholarships, 1936, 37, prizes Pa. Acad., 1964, 68, Eyre medal Phila. Water Color Club, 1968, Childe Hassam Meml. purchases AAAL, 1967, 68, Merit award Pa., 71, Hazlett Meml. award for excellence in arts, 1980, Hunt award for visual arts Phila. Women's Way, 1984. Mem. Fellowship of Pa. Acad. Fine Arts, Coll. Art Assn., Women's Caucus for Art (Honor award 1983), Print Club.

ANDRAS, OSCAR SIDNEY, oil company executive; b. Bogalusa, La., July 23, 1935; s. Oscar Severin and Rosalyn (Rogers) A.; m. Mary Louise Sisk, June 3, 1957; children: Louis James, David Sisk. B.S., La. State U., 1957. With Gulf Oil Corp., Port Arthur, Tex., 1957-59, Dow Chem. Co., Baton Rouge, 1959-67, Dow Chem Co., Houston, 1967-74, Dow Chem. Co., Midland, Mich., 1974-77, Houston, 1977-80, Enterprise Cos. Inc., 1980—; dir. Oasis Pipeline Co., Houston, 1974-80. Mem. Tex. Gov.'s Energy Council, Auston, 1975-77; pres. F.U.N. Football, Houston, 1972; bd.dirs. Meyerland Little League, Houston, 1970. Served to 2d lt. U.S. Army, 1958. Republican. Roman Catholic. Office: Enterprise Cos Inc 2727 W Loop N Houston TX 77052

ANDRAS, ROBERT KNIGHT, mining company executive; b. Lachine, Que., Can., Feb. 20, 1921; s. John Donald and Angela Eva (Knight) A.; m. Frances Hunt, Oct. 20, 1945; children: Robert Hunt, Angela Knight. Grad., Wesley Coll., Winnipeg, 1938; D. Pub. Service, Northland Coll., Ashland, Wis., 1970; LL.D., Lakehead U., 1978. Exec. Ford Motor Co., 1946-55; pres. 4 automotive equipment and leasing firms, Thunder Bay, Ont., Can., 1955-68; Liberal mem. Fed. Parliament, 1965—; apptd. mem. Queen's Privy Council for Can., cabinet minister without portfolio with responsibility for Indian policy, 1968, minister responsible for housing, 1969, minister of state for urban affairs, from 1971, minister consumer and corporate affairs and registrar gen. Can., 1972, minister manpower and immigration, 1972; pres. Treasury Bd., 1976, Bd. Econ. Devel. Ministers, 1978; sr. v.p., dir. Teck Corp., Vancouver, B.C.; dir. Lornex Mining Corp.; Nat. co-chmn. Liberal campaign, 1972; bd. dirs. Vancouver Bd. Trade. Served to maj. Canadian Army, 1942-46. Decorated Voluntary medal, France and Germany medal, Def. medal, War medal, 39-45; recipient Centennial medal, Jubilee medal. Mem. Elec. Vehicle Assn. Can. (dir.), Inter-Parliamentary Union, NATO, Commonwealth parliamentary assns., Alta. Indian Assn. (hon. pres. 1969). Clubs: Vancouver, Shaughnessy Golf and Country, Canadian (Vancouver); Le Cercle Universitaire (Ottawa). Office: 1199 W Hastings Vancouver BC V6E 2K5 Canada

ANDRASICK, JAMES STEPHEN, agribusiness company executive; b. Passaic, N.J., Mar. 27, 1944; s. Stephen Adam and Emily (Spolnik) A.; m. Kathleen Hancock Dudden, Mar. 5, 1966; children: Christopher J., Gregory O. B.S., U.S. Coast Guard Acad., 1965; M.S., MIT, 1971. Systems analyst Jamesbury Corp., 1970; mem. corp. fin. and product devel. staffs Ford Motor Co., 1971-74; mgr. corp. devel. IU Internat. Corp., Phila., 1974-78; v.p. planning, controller C. Brewer & Co., Ltd., Honolulu, 1978-81, sr. v.p. fin., chief fin. officer, 1981-83, exec. v.p. fin. and adminstrn., 1983—; dir. Bay & River Nav. Co., San Francisco, 1981—. Chmn. comml. div. Aloha United Way, Honolulu, 1981. Served to lt. USCG, 1965-69; Vietnam. Mem. Fin. Execs. Inst. Episcopalian. Club: Plaza (Honolulu). Home: 609 Ahakea St Honolulu HI 96816 Office: C Brewer & Co Ltd 827 Fort St Honolulu HI 96813

ANDRASSY, TIMOTHY FRANCIS, trade assn. exec.; b. Cleve., Feb. 13, 1948; s. Robert Steven and Matilda A.; m. Grace Elizabeth Wills, Jan. 3, 1970; children—Timothy Francis, Courtney, Alyson. B.S., John Carroll U., Cleve., 1970. Asso. producer, prodn. asst. Sta. WKBF-TV, Cleve., 1968-69; asst. dir. public relations Thistledown Racing Club, N. Randall, Ohio, 1969-70, dir. promotions, 1976-77; asst. to pres. Gaffney Advt., Mentor, Ohio, 1970-71; stadium mgr., dir. broadcast ops. Cleve. Indians Profl. (Baseball Club), 1971-74; mgr. communications Am. Soc. Metals, Metals Park, Ohio, 1974-76; exec. dir. Assn. Steel Distbrs., Cleve., 1977-81; v.p. Steel Service Center Inst., Cleve., 1981—. Dir. community relations Geauga County Bi-Centennial Organizing Com., 1975-76. Mem. Am. Soc. Assn. Execs., Meeting Planners Internat., Greater Cleve. Growth Assn., Greater Cleve. Soc. Assn. Execs., Downtown Euclid Assn. Home: 496 Babbitt Rd Euclid OH 44123 Office: 1600 Terminal Tower Bldg Cleveland OH 44113

ANDRE, CARL, sculptor; b. Quincy, Mass., Sept. 16, 1935; s. George Hans and Margaret (Johnson). Represented in public collections, Tate Gallery, London, Mus. Modern Art, N.Y.C., Aldrich Mus., Ridgefield, Conn., Pasadena (Calif.) Mus. Art, Rose Art Mus., Brandeis U., Columbus (Ohio) Gallery Fine Arts, Walker Art Center, Mpls., Milw. Art Center, La Jolla (Calif.) Mus. Contemporary Art, Dayton (Ohio) Art Inst., Albright Knox Art Gallery, N.Y.C., Monchengladbach Mus., Germany, Wallraf-Richartz Mus., Cologne, Haus Lange Mus., Krefeld, Germany, Staatsgalerie, Stuttgart, Germany, Kunstmus. Basel, Switzerland, Hessisches Landesmus., Darmstadt, Germany, Stedelijk Mus., Amsterdam, Van Abbe Mus., Eindhoven, Netherlands, Art Soc. Ghent, Belgium, Chgo. Art Inst., Los Angeles County Mus. Art, Musée Nat. d'Art Moderne, Paris, Carnegie Inst Mus. Art, Pitts., Musèo de Art Moderno, Bogota, Colombia, Seattle Art Mus., High Mus. Art, Atlanta, Ohio State U. Gallery Fine Art, Bayerischen Staatsgemäldesammlungen, Munich, Kröller-Müller Mus., Otterlo, Netherlands, Detroit Inst. Arts, Guggenheim Mus., N.Y.C., City of Hartford, Conn., Mus. Boymans-van Beuningen, Rotterdam, Netherlands. Address: PO Box 1001 Cooper Sta New York NY 10003 Office: care Paula Cooper 155 Wooster St New York NY 10012

ANDRÉ, OSCAR JULES, lawyer; b. Charleroi, Belgium, May 15, 1900; came to U.S., 1908, naturalized, 1914; s. Oscar Jean and Aline (Bastin) A.; m. Ruby E. Cox, June 14, 1932; children—Nancy André Baker, Elise, David J. A.B. magna cum laude, Salem Coll., 1925, LL.D., 1977; LL.B., U. Va., 1929. Bar: W.Va. bar 1929, Va. bar 1978, U.S. Supreme Ct. bar 1973. Mem. firm Steptoe & Johnson, Clarksburg, 1929—, partner, 1934—, sr. partner, 1950-76; counsel firm Larrick, White, André & Rabun, Winchester, Va., 1978—; Vice pres., dir. Osborn Machinery Co., Inc., Clarksburg Theatre Co. Pres. Clarksburg Community Concert Assn., 1950-78; past pres., bd. dirs. W.Va., Harrison County Tb and health assns.; bd. dirs. Salem Coll., 1930-51, Union Protestant Hosp., United Hosp. Center, Clarksburg; adv. bd. Clarksburg YWCA. Fellow Am. Coll. Trial Lawyers; mem. W. Va. State Bar (bd. govs. 1957-60, v.p. 1960-62, pres. 1962-63), Va. State Bar, Am. Bar Assn., W. Va. Bar Assn., Harrison County Bar Assn. (past pres.), Winchester-Frederick County Bar Assn., Fed. Jud. Conf. 4th Circuit, Order of Coif, Phi Beta Kappa. Republican. Presbyterian. Home: 112 N Washington St Apt 1 Winchester VA 22601 Office: PO Box 3337 29 N Braddock St Winchester VA 22601

ANDRE, PAUL DEAN, magazine editor; b. Mechanicsville, Iowa, Sept. 5, 1928; s. Marvin Leonard and Beryl Madge (Anderson) A.; m. Frances Valeria Tjaden, Dec. 27, 1952; 1 dau., Carol Lea. B.S., Iowa State U., 1952. Farmer, 1955; asso. farm editor Cedar Rapids (Iowa) Gazette, 1956-61; asst. extension editor Iowa State U., 1961-62; editor Better Farming Methods, Mt. Morris, Ill., 1962-64, BEEF, St. Paul, 1964—. Served with USAF, 1952-54; Korea. Recipient 35 awards for photography and writing, including; Top Choice award Colo. Cattle Feeders Assn., 1980. Mem. Am. Agrl. Editors Assn. (1st place award for writing prodn. category 1975), Newspaper Farm Editors Am. (asso.), Livestock Publs. Council (dir.), Ret. Officers Assn. Republican. Lutheran. Club: Ft. Snelling Officers. Home: 109 N Heritage Circle Burnsville MN 55337 Office: 1999 Shepard Rd Saint Paul MN 55116

ANDREANO, RALPH LOUIS, economist, educator; b. Waterbury, Conn., Apr. 11, 1929; s. John and Loretta (Creasia) A.; m. Carol Jean Wessbecher, Sept. 5, 1955; children: Maria Carol, Nicholas George. A.B., Drury Coll., 1952; M.A., Washington U., St. Louis, 1955, U. Oslo, Norway, 1952-53; Ph.D., Northwestern U., 1961. Instr. econs. Northwestern U., 1959-60; asst. prof. econs. Earlham Coll., 1961, asso. prof., chmn. dept., 1962-65; asst. prof. bus. adminstrn. Harvard Bus. Sch., 1961-62; Brookings Nat. Research prof., 1964-65; asso. prof. econs., dir. undergrad. program econs. U. Wis., 1965-67, prof., 1967—, dir. Health Econs. Research Center, 1969—, chmn. dept. econs., 1980-83; Ofcl. del. Am. Econ. Assn. to Am. Council Learned Socs., 1964-70; adminstr. Div. Health State of Wis., 1976-78; economist WHO, Geneva, 1973-74. Author: (with H.F. Williamson and others) A History of American Petroleum Industry, 2 vols., 1959, 63, No Joy in Mudville: The Dilemma of Major League Baseball, 1965, Student Economists Handbook, 1967, (with B.A. Weisbrod and others) Disease and Economic Development, 1973, (with B.A. Weisbrod) American Health Policy, 1973; Editor, author: New Views on American Economic Development, 1965; Editor: Economic Impact of the Civil War, 1963, rev., 1967, The New Economic History: Papers on Methodology, 1971, (with J. Siegfried) Economics of Crime, 1981; Editor, founder: Explorations in Entrepreneurial History, 2d series, 1963-71; editor: Jour. Econ. History, 1974-75; sr. editor (econs.): Social Sci. and Medicine, 1983—; contbr. articles to profl. jours. Ford Faculty Research fellow, 1968-69. Mem. Inst. Medicine of Nat. Acad. Scis. Home: 1815 Vilas Ave Madison WI 53711

ANDREAS, DWAYNE ORVILLE, corporation executive; b. Worthington, Minn., Mar. 4, 1918; s. Reuben P. and Lydia (Stoltz) A.; m. Bertha Benedict, 1938 (div.); 1 dau., Sandra Ann Andreas McMurtie; m. Dorothy Inez Snyder, Dec. 21, 1947; children: Terry Lynn Bevis, Herbert Burns, Michael D. Student, Wheaton (Ill.) Coll., 1935-36; hon. degree, Barry U. Vice pres., dir. Honeymead Products Co., Cedar Rapids, Iowa, 1936-46, chmn. bd., chief exec. officer, Mankato, Minn., 1952-72; v.p. Cargill, Inc., Mpls., 1946-52; exec. v.p. Farmers Union Grain Terminal Assn., St. Paul, 1960-66; chmn. bd., chief exec. officer Archer-Daniels-Midland Co., Decatur, Ill., 1970—, also mem. exec. com., dir.; pres. Seaview Hotel Corp., 1958—; dir. Nat. City Bank Mpls., Phibro Salomon, Inc., Lone Star Industries, Inc., Greenwich, Conn.; Mem. Pres.'s Gen. Adv. Commn. on Fgn. Assistance Programs, 1965-68, Pres.'s Adv. Council on Mgmt. Improvement, 1969-73; chmn. Pres.'s Task Force on Internat. Pvt. Enterprise. Pres. Andreas Found.; trustee U.S. Naval Acad. Found., Freedom from Hunger Found.; nat. dir. Boys' Club Am. Mem. Fgn. Policy Assn. N.Y. (dir.). Clubs: Union League (Chgo.); Indian Creek Country (Miami Beach, Fla.); Mpls., Minikahda (Mpls.); Blind Brook Country (Purchase, N.Y.); Links, Friars (N.Y.). Office: Archer Daniels Midland Co PO Box 1470 Decatur IL 62525

ANDREAS, LOWELL WILLARD, manufacturing executive; b. Lisbon, Iowa, Feb. 24, 1922; s. Reuben P. and Lydia (Stoltz) A.; m. Nadine B. Hamilton, May 30, 1943; children: Pamela Jane Andreas Lee, David Lowell. Student, Wheaton (Ill.) Coll., 1939-41, U. Iowa, 1941-42. With Honeymead Products Co., Mankato, Minn., 1947-67, pres., 1952-67; treas., dir., mem. exec. com. Nat. City Bancorp, Mpls., 1960—, chmn. bd., 1983—; exec. v.p. Archer Daniels Midland Co., Mpls., 1967-68, pres., Decatur, Ill., 1968-72, chmn. mgmt. com., 1972—, now chmn. fin. com., also dir., mem. exec. com.; dir., mem. exec. com. Nat. City Bank Mpls.; dir. Kayot, Inc., Nat. City Bancorp, Mpls., Mankato Citizens Telephone Co., Advt. Unltd., Inc. Bd. dirs., exec. v.p. Andreas Found. Served with AUS, 1942-46. Mem. Phi Delta Theta. Presbyterian. Clubs: Union League (Chgo.); Mpls. Home: 10 Trail Dr Mankato MN 56001 Office: ADM Box 728 3d and Harper Sts Mankato MN 56001

ANDREAS, MICHAEL DWAYNE, agricultural business executive; b. Coral Gables, Fla., Dec. 30, 1948; s. Dwayne Orville and Inez (Snyder) A.; m. Sally Ann Whitley, Sept. 26, 1981; children: Eric Michael, Regan Inez, Melissa Ann. B.A., Northwestern U., 1970. Grain trader Archer Daniels Midland, Decatur, Ill., 1970-79, exec., Decatur, 1979—; dir. Toepfer Internat., Hamburg, W.Ger., 1983—. Mem. Chgo. Bd. Trade (dir.), Decatur C. of C. (dir. 1980). Episcopalian. Clubs: Decatur Country; Indian Creek (Miami, Fla.). Home: 83 N Country Club Dr Decatur IL 62521 Office: Archer Daniels Midland PO Box 1470 Decatur IL 62525

ANDREASEN, GEORGE FREDRICK, dentist; b. Fremont, Nebr., Feb. 16, 1934; s. George T. and Laura Mae (Hynek) A.; m. Nancy Coover, June 13, 1959; children—Susan, Robin. B.S. (Regents scholar), U. Nebr., 1959; D.D.S., 1959; M.S. (NIH fellow), 1963. Research fellow Worcester Coll., Oxford, Eng., 1960-61; asst. prof. orthodontics U. Iowa Coll. Dentistry, Iowa City, 1963-67, asso. prof., acting head dept. orthodontics, 1967, asso. prof., head dept., 1968, prof., head dept. orthodontics, 1968—; practice dentistry, Iowa City, 1963—; cons. to various dental corps. on dental materials. Contbr. articles to profl. jours. U. Nebr. alumnus master, 1974. Fellow Am. Coll. Dentists, Royal Soc. Health (Eng.); mem. Am. Assn. Orthodontists (chmn. sci. com. 1971-72, nat. com. on research 1976-79), Iowa Orthodontic Soc. (pres. 1972-73), Am., Iowa dental assns., Univ. Dist. Dental Assn., Iowa Alumni Assn. (life), U. Iowa Med. Center (life), Am. Oxonion, Phalanx Blue Print Key, Sigma Xi, Pi Tau Sigma, Omicron Kappa Upsilon, Delta Tau Delta, Xi Psi Phi. Club: Athletic (Iowa City). Patentee in field. Home: 1104 Penkridge St Iowa City IA 52240 Office: Room 5221 DSB U Iowa Iowa City IA 52240

ANDREASON, JOHN CHRISTIAN, lawyer; b. Marysville, Calif., Nov. 18, 1924; s. John Christian and Sadie Louisa (Duus) A. B.A., J.D., Stanford U., 1958. Bar: Calif. 1958. With Aerojet-Gen. Corp., La Jolla, Calif., 1958—, v.p., gen. counsel, 1980—. Mem. ABA, Nat. Contract Mgmt. Assn. Republican. Lodge: Masons. Office: Aerojet General Corp 10300 N Torrey Pines Rd La Jolla CA 92037

ANDREASSEN, PAUL, business executive; b. Stubbekobing, Denmark, Feb. 18, 1928; s. Walther and Edith (Thulin) A.; m. Elsa Mogelbjerg Pedersen, Dec. 23, 1949; children: Lasse, Lise, Peter. Grad. in Machine Constrn. Enging., Kobenhavns Maskinteknijum, Copenhagen, 1951. Dir. Det Danske Rengorings Selskab, Copenhagen, 1962, mng. dir., 1962-72; pres., mng. dir. Internat. Service System, Charlottenlund, Denmark, 1972—; chmn. Prudential Bldg. Maintenance Inc., N.Y.C.; dir. Privatbanken A-S, Cph., Rockwool Internat. A-S, Cph., Politiken A-S. Bd. dirs. Egmont H. Petersen Found.; chmn. Assn. for Aid to Mothers and Their Children, Copenhagen. Mem. Pres. Assn. Office: Prudential Bldg Maintenance Corp 1430 Broadway New York NY 10018

ANDREJEVIC, MILET, painter; b. Petrovgrad, Yugoslavia, Sept. 25, 1925; came to U.S., 1958, naturalized, 1961; s. Dimitrije and Jelena (Dragicevic) A.; m. Helen Bardeen, Apr. 30, 1955; 1 son, Mark. B.F.A., Belgrade Acad. Fine Arts, 1944, M.F.A., 1950. Instr. N.Y. U., 1965-66, Bklyn. Coll., 1974-76; asst. prof. Pratt Inst., 1981—. One man shows, Green Gallery, N.Y.C., 1961, 63, Goldowsky Gallery, N.Y.C., 1970, 71, 72, 76, R. Schoelkopf Gallery, N.Y.C., 1981, group shows include, Whitney Mus. Anns., N.Y.C., 1963, 64, 65, Mus. Modern Art, N.Y.C., 1977, Hirsch & Adler Gallery, N.Y.C., 1980, Phila. Acad., 1981, Am. Acad. and Inst. Arts and Letters, 1984; represented in permanent collections, Whitney Mus., Hirschorn Mus., Washington, Met. Mus., N.Y.C., U. Tex., Austin, U. Va., Charlottesville, R.I. Sch. Design, Allentown Mus., U. N.C.; mem., The Green Gallery, N.Y.C., 1961-64, Bellamy Goldowsky Gallery, N.Y.C., 1970-79, Robert Schoelkopf Gallery, N.Y.C., 1979—. Nat. Endowment for Arts grantee, 1976; Ingram Merrill Found, grantee, 1980. Mem. Nat. Acad. Design. Home: 35 W 82d St New York NY 10024 Office: 133 W 72d St New York NY 10023

ANDREOLI, KATHLEEN GAINOR, nurse, educator; b. Albany, N.Y., Sept. 22, 1935; d. John Edward and Edmunda Elizabeth (Ringlemann) Gainor; m. Thomas Eugene Andreoli, Sept. 17, 1960; children: Paula Kathleen, Thomas Anthony, Karen Marie. B.S.N., Georgetown U., 1957; M.S.N., Vanderbilt U., 1959; D.S.N., U. Ala., Birmingham, 1979. Staff nurse Albany Hosp. Med. Center, 1957; instr. St Thomas Hosp. Sch. Nursing, Nashville, 1958-59, Georgetown U. Sch., Nursing, 1959-60, Duke U. Sch. Nursing, 1960-61, Bon Secours Hosp. Sch. Nursing, Balt., 1962-64; ednl. coordinator, physician asst. program, instr. coronary care unit nursing inservice edn. Duke U. Med. Center, Durham, N.C., 1965-70; ednl. dir. physician asst. program dept. medicine U. Ala. Med. Center, Birmingham, 1970-75, clin. assoc. prof. cardiovascular nursing Sch. Nursing, 1970-77, asst. prof. nursing dept. medicine, 1971, assoc. prof., 1972—, assoc. prof. nursing Sch. Pub. and Allied Health, 1973—; assoc. dir. Family Nurse Practitioner Program, 1976, assoc. prof. community health nursing Grad. Program, 1977-79, assoc. prof. dept. pub. health, 1978-79; prof. nursing, spl. asst. to pres. for ednl. affairs U. Tex. Health Sci. Center, Houston, 1979—; acting dean Sch. Allied Health Scis.; exec. dir. acad. services, prof. nursing, cons. in field. Author, editor: (with others) Comprehensive Cardiac Care, 1983; editor: Heart and Lung, Jour. of Total Care, 1971; contbr. articles to profl. jours. Recipient Founder's award N.C. Heart Assn., 1970. Fellow Am. Acad. Nursing; mem. Inst. Medicine, Am. Nurses Assn., Nat. League Nursing, Am. Assn. Critical Care Nurses, Ala. Heart Assn., Council Family Nurse Practitioners and Clinicians, Am. Heart Assn. Council Cardiovascular Nursing, Sigma Theta Tau, Alpha Eta, Phi Kappa Phi. Roman Catholic. Office: Office of Pres U Tex Health Scis Center PO Box 20036 Houston TX 77225

ANDREOLI, THOMAS EUGENE, physician; b. Bronx, N.Y., Jan. 9, 1935; s. Eugene and Lydia (Bertoldi) A.; m. Kathleen Gainor, Sept. 17, 1960; children—Paula Kathleen, Thomas Anthony, Karen Marie. B.A. cum laude, St. Vincent Coll., 1956; M.D. magna cum laude, Georgetown U., 1960. Diplomate: Am. Bd. Internal Medicine and subsplty. in nephrology. Intern, resident in medicine Duke U., Durham, N.C., 1960-61, 64-65, asso. prof. medicine and asst. prof. physiology, 1965-70; prof. medicine and physiology, dir. nephrology research and tng. center U. Ala. Sch. Medicine, Birmingham, 1970-78; prof., chmn. dept. internal medicine U. Tex. Med. Sch., Houston, 1979—; chief medicine Hermann Hosp., Houston, 1979—; mem. physiology study sect. NIH, 1974-78; chmn. adv. com. for Nat. Biotechnology Resource in Electron Probe Microanalysis, Harvard U., 1977—; coordinating com. on evaluation research needs in nephrology and urology Nat. Inst. Arthritis, Metabolism and Digestive Diseases, 1974-78; bd. trustees End-Stage Renal Disease Network 18, HEW, 1976-78; co-chmn. Gordon Research Conf.-Biol. Interaction and Transport, 1971, chmn., 1973. Author: Disturbances in Body Fluid Osmolality, 1977, Physiology of Membrane Disorders, 1978, Membrane Physiology, 1980; Editor: Am./Jour. Physiology: Renal, Fluid and Electrolyte Physiology, 1976—; asso. editor: Annual Rev. Physiology, 1977—, Am. Jour. Medicine, 1979—; mem. editorial bd.: Jour. Clin. Investigation, 1976-81, Mineral and Electrolyte Metabolism, 1977-80, Tex. Health Letter, 1980—, Seminars in Nephrology, 1980—, Kidney Internat, 1981—, Physiol. Revs, 1982—. Served with USPHS, 1961-64. Fellow A.C.P.; mem. Assn. Am. Physicians, Assn. Profs. Medicine, Central Soc. Clin. Research, Am. Fedn. Clin. Research, Am. Soc. Clin. Investigation, Am. Soc. Nephrology, Internat. Soc. Nephrology, Am. Heart Assn., So. Soc. Clin. Investigation, Biophysical Soc., Am. Physiol. Soc., Red Cell Club, So. Salt and Water Club. Office: Dept Internal Medicine U Tex Med Sch at Houston PO Box 20708 Houston TX 77025

ANDRES, FREDERICK WILLIAM, lawyer; b. Alexandria, Egypt, Sept. 21, 1906; s. Frederick Henry Augustus and Laura Edith (Beazell) A.; m. Katherine Pratt Weeks, Sept. 9, 1931; children: Katherine Weeks Andres Moore, Anita Andres Rogerson, William McKenzie. A.B., Dartmouth Coll., 1929, A.M. (hon.), 1963, LL.D., 1979; LL.B., Harvard U., 1932; LL.D. (hon.), Colby Coll., 1977. Bar: Mass. bar 1932. Since practiced in, Boston; mem. firm Sherburne, Powers & Needham, 1940-83, of counsel, 1983—; dir. George B.H. Macomber Co.; clk., dir. London Harness Co., Hamilton Constrn. Corp., Investors Bank & Trust Co.; dir. Health Systems, Inc.; trustee Boston Broadcasters Liquidating Trust. Author: (with others) The College on the Hill-A Dartmouth Chronicle, 1964. Regional chmn. Dartmouth Capital Fund campaign, 1958-61; sec.-chmn. Dartmouth class 1929, 1929-63; trustee Dartmouth Coll., 1963-77, chmn. bd. trustees, 1972-77; pres. Dartmouth Alumni Assn., Boston, 1950; chmn. Dartmouth Athletic Council, 1956-61; regional chmn. United Negro Coll. Fund, 1960; mem. Brookline (Mass.) Town Meeting, 1947-53, Brookline Personnel Bd., 1957-66; bd. dirs. Brookline Citizens Com., 1948-57; trustee Phillips Exeter Acad., 1962-72, 77-81, pres. bd., 1965-72; trustee Champlain Coll., 1966-70, Bennington Coll., 1956-63, Beaver Country Day Sch., Chestnut Hill, Mass., 1947-64; pres. Beaver Country Day Sch., 1949-64; trustee Elizabeth Carleton House, Boston, 1954-72, pres., 1957-66; mem. corp. New Eng. Deaconess Hosp., 1963—; bd. dirs. Grenville Clark Fund at Dartmouth Coll., Inc., 1973—. Recipient Alumni award Dartmouth Coll., 1963, Disting. Friend Edn. award Counsel Advancement and Support Edn., 1982. Mem. Am. Bar Assn., Boston Bar Assn. (council 1966-68), Mass. Bar Assn., Dartmouth Alumni Assn. Boston (pres. 1950), Phi Gamma Delta, Casque and Gauntlet Sr. Soc., Gen. Alumni Assn. Phillips Exeter Acad. (pres. 1962-63), Nisi Prius Club. Republican. Episcopalian (vestry 1957-60). Clubs: The Country (Brookline); Harvard, Union (Boston). Home: 106 Laurel Rd Chestnut Hill Brookline MA 02167 Office: 1 Beacon St Boston MA 02108

ANDRES, RONALD PAUL, chem. engr., educator; b. Chgo., Jan. 9, 1938; s. Harold William and Amanda Ann (Breuhaus) A.; m. Jean Mills Elwood, July 15, 1961; children—Douglas, Jennifer, Mark. B.S., Northwestern U., 1959; Ph.D., Princeton U., 1962. Asst. prof. Princeton U., 1962-68, asso. prof., 1968-76, prof. chem. enging., 1976-81, Purdue U., West Lafayette, Ind., 1981—, head, 1981—. Mem. Am. Chem. Soc., Am. Inst. Chem. Engrs., AAAS, Sigma Xi, Tau Beta Pi, Pi Mu Epsilon, Phi Lambda Upsilon, Phi Eta Sigma. Office: Sch Chem Enging Purdue U West Lafayette IN 47907

ANDRES, WILLIAM ALFRED, retail chain executive; b. Fayette, Iowa, Aug. 9, 1926; s. Alfred G. and Eva Levetta (Eide) A.; m. Betty Ruth Follett, June 4, 1947; children: Robert A., Charles W., Richard W. B.A., Upper Iowa U., 1948, D.B.A. (hon.), 1977; M.A., U. Pitts., 1949. With Dayton Co. (later became Dayton Hudson Corp.), Mpls., 1958—, exec. v.p. retail ops., 1971-74, pres., 1974-77, chief exec. officer, 1976—, chmn. bd., 1977—, chmn. exec. com., 1983—; dir. First Bank System, Inc., Internat. Multifoods, St. Paul Cos., Exxon Corp. Bd. dirs.

United Way of Mpls. Area, 1975—, Fairview Community Hosps., Catalyst. Served to 2d lt., inf. U.S. Army, 1944-46. Mem. Am. Retail Fedn. (dir.). Club: Minneapolis. Office: 777 Nicollet Mall Minneapolis MN 55402

ANDRESS, JAMES GILLIS, health care company executive; b. Hamlin, Tex., Jan. 5, 1939; s. James Auvice and Ruth (Gillis) A.; m. Carolyn Given Holt, Aug. 3, 1963; children: Carolyn, Andrew, Sarah. B.S., U.S. Mil. Acad., 1962; M.B.A., U. Pa., 1969. Cons. Booz, Allen & Hamilton, Chgo., 1969-74; dir. corp. planning Abbott Labs., North Chgo., Il., 1974; pres. Abbott Can., 1974-78; v.p. Abbott Labs., Pacific and Far East, 1978-81, v.p. corp. planning, 1981-83, pres. home care, 1983—. Bd. dirs. Lake Forest Sch. Mgmt., 1980. Served to capt. U.S. Army, 1962-68. Decorated Bronze Star. Office: Abbott Labs Abbott Park North Chicago IL 60064

ANDRESS, SAMUEL COE, lawyer; b. Hayesville, Ohio, June 27, 1906; s. Upton Samuel and Millicent Alma (Coe) A. A.B., Wittenberg U., 1925; LL.B., U. Cin., 1928. Bar: Ohio 1928. Since practiced in, Akron; sr. partner firm Roetzel & Andress. Trustee Akron Beacon Jour. Charity Fund, Akron Community Trusts. Served to lt. USNR, 1942-45. Mem. Am., Ohio, Akron bar assns., 6th Circuit Jud. Conf., Akron C. of C. (past pres.), Order of Coif, Lambda Chi Alpha, Delta Sigma Rho, Phi Alpha Delta. Episcopalian. Clubs: Rotary, City, University, Sharon, Portage Country (Akron). Home: 161 E Fairlawn Blvd Akron OH 44313 Office: 1 Cascade Plaza Akron OH 44308

ANDRESS, VERN RANDOLPH, psychologist, marriage and family therapist, college dean; b. Boulder, Colo., Mar. 29, 1935; s. Victor William and Frances Willette (Boyer) A.; m. Monika Pia Heep, Oct. 22, 1960; children: Vivian Monica, Kimberley Dawn. A.A., Southwestern Coll., Chula Vista, Calif., 1967; B.A., San Diego State Coll., 1969; M.S., San Diego State U., 1971; Ph.D., U.S. Internat. U., 1976. Pres. Beauty Boutique, Inc., San Diego, 1961-67; counselor San Diego Acad., 1969-70; dir. adminstrn. of justice Loma Linda U., Riverside, Calif., 1970-80, asst. prof. psychology, 1972-76, assoc. prof., 1976-79, prof., 1979—, chmn. dept. psychology, 1977-80, dean Coll. Arts and Sci., 1980—; psychologist Riverside County Coroner's Office, 1976—; cons. psychology to law enforcement and industry, 1970—. Contbr. numerous articles to profl. jours., popular publs.; editor: Jour. Adventist Behavioral Scientists, 1974-79. Mem. Grand Terrace Planning Commn., Calif., 1978—. Served with U.S. Army, 1954-56; France. Named Disting. Researcher Inland Counties Psychol. Assn., 1980; recipient Disting. Service award Calif. Sex Crimes Investigators, 1983. Mem. Am. Assn. Suicidology, Am. Psychol. Assn., Calif. State Psychol. Assn., Calif. Assn. Marriage and Family Therapists, Am. Orchid Soc., John Steinbeck Soc., Sigma Xi. Adventist. Office: Loma Linda U 4700 Pierce St Riverside CA 92515 *One should optimize the choice options available to him by careful, deliberate planning with and eye set early on those goals he wants to attain and a full awareness of the price he is willing to pay. The process of education should be designed to enrich the quality of his life and the lives of those who share his world.*

ANDRETTI, MARIO GABRIEL, race car driver; b. Montona, Trieste, Italy, Feb. 28, 1940; came to U.S., 1955, naturalized, 1959; s. Louis Alvise and Rina (Giovanelli) A.; m. DeeAnn Beverly Hoch, Nov. 25, 1961; children: Michael Mario, Jeffrey Louis, Barbra Dee. Foreman Retter Line, Inc., Easton, Pa., 1959-61; with Delwick Co., Easton, 1961; foreman Motovator, Springfield, N.J., 1961-64; profl. race car driver Dean Van Lines, Long Beach, Calif., 1964-68, STP Corp., Des Plaines, Ill., 1969-71, Vel's Parnelli Jones, Torrance, Calif., 1972-76, John Player Team Lotus, Norwich, Eng., 1976-80, Penske Racing, Reading, Pa., 1976-80, Patrick Racing, 1981, Alfa Romeo, 1981—, Newman, Haas Racing, 1983; pres. Andretti Racing Enterprises, Nazareth, 1968—; Mem. Pres.'s Conf. Phys. Fitness and Sports, 1970—. Mem. Automobile Hall of Fame, Sebring, Fla.; recipient Athlete of Year award ABC, 1969, Phila. Sports Writers, 1979; nat. champion U.S. Auto Club, 1965, 66, 69. Mem. Jr. C. of C. Nazareth, United Airlines Million Mile Club, TWA Amabassador Club, 100 Mile an Hour Club, U.S. Auto Club, Fedn. Internationale de L'automobile. Roman Catholic. Winner Indpls. 500, 1969, 81; world champion race car driver, 1978. Address: 53 Victory Ln Nazareth PA 18064

ANDREW, CHARLES CURTIS, hotel corp. exec.; b. Belfry, Mont., Dec. 4, 1928; s. Chester Arthur and Bertha Columby (Thomas) A.; m. Jacqueline M. McElhiney, Mar. 2, 1951; children—Curtis C., Jack T., Mark S., Paul C. B.S. in Psychology, U. Wash., 1956, postgrad., 1956-58. Tchr., counsellor Highline Sch. Dist. 401, Seattle, 1956-61; gen. mgr. Seattle Hyatt House, 1961-70; operation v.p. Hyatt Central Offices, Hyatt Hotel Corp., Burlingame, Calif., 1970-73, regional v.p., Kissimmee, Fla., 1973—. Served with USNR, 1945-48, 50-52. Mem. C. of C., Tourist Devel. Council, Am. Soc. Travel Agts., Nat. Restaurant Assn., Am. Hotel-Motel Assn., Hotel Sales Mgrs. Assn., Central Fla. Hotel-Motel Assn. (pres., founder), Skal. Clubs: Masons, Shriners, Rotary, Toastmasters. Office: Hyatt Orlando I-4 and US 192E Kissimmee FL 32741

ANDREW, GWEN, univ. dean; b. Plattville, Wis., June 18, 1922; d. Harry Roscoe and Lulu Mae (Howery) A. B.A., U. Wis., 1944, M.A., 1945; Ph.D., Mich. State U., 1961. Chief psychometrician U. Wis., Madison, 1946-49; research psychologist to dir. research Mich. Dept. Mental Health, Lansing, 1950-66; prof., dir. Sch. Social Work, Mich. State U., East Lansing, 1967-75, dean Coll. Social Sci., 1975—. Contbr. articles on mental health and orgn. theory to profl. jours. Mem. Am. Sociol. Assn., Am. Psychol. Assn., AAAS, Phi Beta Kappa, Phi Kappa Phi, Alpha Kappa Delta, Psi Chi. Home: 1936 Vassar Dr Lansing MI 48912 Office: Coll Social Sci Mich State U East Lansing MI 48823

ANDREW, LLOYD B., JR., chemical company executive; b. Joliet, Ill., Nov. 30, 1923; s. Lloyd Brummond and Elizabeth (Frick) A.; m. Frances Burdett, Dec. 31, 1948; children: Joyce, Cindy, Lloyd B. III. Student, Ill. Inst. Tech., 1944-46; B.S.M.E. with distinction, Purdue U., 1948; M.S.M.E., La. State U., 1956. Process engr. Phillips Petroleum, Oklahoma City, 1948-50, Borger, Tex., 1950-51; with Ethyl Corp., 1951—, gen. mgr. VisQueen div., Baton Rouge, 1963-68, dir. fin. relations parent co., Richmond, Va., 1968-74, v.p. fin. relations, 1974-81, v.p., treas., 1981-83, sr. v.p., treas., 1983—. Served with USAAC, 1942-44; ETO. Decorated D.F.C., Air medal with 4 oak leaf clusters. Mem. Nat. Investor Relations Inst. Republican. Methodist. Clubs: Wall St. (N.Y.C.); Downtown (Richmond); Kiwanis. Home: 103 Roslyn Hills Dr Richmond VA 23229 Office: PO Box 2189 Richmond VA 23217

ANDREW, R. D., plastics and resins company executive. Pres. Celanese Plastics & Specialties Co., Louisville. Office: Celanese Plastics & Specialties Co 1 Riverfront Plaza Louisville KY 40201§

ANDREWS, ALFRED WINCHESTER, manufacturing executive; b. Bklyn., Sept. 20, 1919; s. Alfred W. and Nancy Copeland (Goodyear) A.; m. Grace Marie Flynn, Jan. 9, 1943; children: Patricia Andrews O'Connor, John F. B.Eng., Yale U., 1941. Supr. engring. Monsanto Co., Springfield, Mass., 1941-51, mgr., dir. engring., 1951-63, bus. dir., Texas City, Tex., 1963-66, gen. mgr. plastics, St. Louis, 1966-75, v.p., dir. engring., 1975—; dir. Fisher Controls Internat., St. Louis, 1979-82. Fellow Am. Inst. Chem. Engrs.; mem. Nat. Soc. Profl. Engrs. (Outstanding Engr. in Industryaward 1982), Mo. Soc. Profl. Engrs. (Outstanding Engr. in Industryaward 1981). Republican. Home: 243 Ladue Oaks Dr Saint Louis MO 63141 Office: Monsanto Co 800 N Lindbergh Blvd Saint Louis MO 63167

ANDREWS, ARCHIE MOULTON, government official; b. Greenwich, Conn., July 29, 1919; s. Archie M. and Eleanor (Underwood) A.; m. Margaret Jane Jones, Mar. 3, 1944 (dec. Sept. 1977); children: Archie Moulton III, Peter Underwood, Duncan Trumbull; m. Nike Smith Middleton, Oct. 3, 1978. A.B., Princeton U., 1941. Exec. trainee W.R. Grace & Co., 1941-42; econ. analyst State Dept., 1942-43; U.S. rep. blacklist com. Ministry Econ. Warfare, Am. embassy, London, 1943-45; with Dictograph Products, Inc., Danbury, Conn., 1946-63, pres., 1962-63; also dir.; pres. Acousticon-Dictograph Co. Ltd., Can., 1963, dir., 1958-63, Gen. Acoustics Ltd., Eng., 1950-63; dep. dir. Bur. Internat. Commerce, Dept. Commerce, 1964-69; dir. U.S. trade mission to N. Africa, 1966; comml. counsellor Am. embassy, London, 1970-75; dir. bus. services Office Internat. Affairs, HUD, Washington, 1976-77; dir. exporters service Office Export Adminstrn., Dept. Commerce, Washington, 1978—. Mem. SAR. Clubs: Princeton (Washington and N.Y.C.); Pilgrims. Home: 307 Yoakum Pkwy Alexandria VA 22304 Office: US Dept Commerce Washington DC

ANDREWS, BENNY, artist; b. Madison, Ga., Nov. 13, 1930; s. George Clevel and Viola (Perryman) A.; m. Mary Ellen Jones Smith, Apr. 3, 1957; children: Christopher, Thomas Michael, Julia Rachael. Student, Ft. Valley State Coll., 1948-50, U. Chgo., 1956-58; B.F.A., Chgo. Art Inst., 1958. Instr. art New Sch. Social Research, N.Y.C., 1967-70, Queens Coll., 1968—; vis. artist Calif. State Coll. at Hayward, 1969; vis. art critic Yale, 1974. Author: Between the Lines, 1978; illustrator: Applachee Red (Raymond Andrews), 1978, Rosebell Lee Wildcat Tennessee (Raymond Andrews), 1980; contbr. articles on black art, culture to profl. jours.; Asso. editor (art): Encore mag; one man shows, Kessler Gallery, Provincetown, Mass., 1960-70, Forum Gallery, N.Y.C., 1962-64-66, Henri Gallery, Alexandria, Va., 1963-64, Studio Mus., N.Y.C., 1970, ACA Gallery, N.Y.C., 1972, U. Md., Aronson-Midtown Gallery, Atlanta, 1973, Lerner-Heller Gallery, N.Y.C., 1979, 80, 81, Gallery of Sarasota, 1979; exhibited in group shows at, Detroit Inst., 1959, Phila. Acad. Art, 1960, Bklyn. Mus., 1963, Butler Inst. Am. Art, 1967, Mus. Modern Art, N.Y.C., 1968-71, High Mus., Atlanta, 1971, Wadsworth Atheneum, 1979, Art Inst. Chgo., Los Angeles County Mus. Art, 1982; represented in permanent collections, Mus. Modern Art, N.Y.C., High Mus., Atlanta, African Mus., Washington, Norfolk Mus., Va., Butler Inst. Am. Art, Youngstown, Ohio, Chrysler Mus., Provincetown, Mass., La Jolla (Calif.) Mus., NYU, N.Y.C., Detroit Inst. Art, U. Kans. Art Mus., Lawrence, U. Wyo. Art Gallery, Laramie, Joslyn Mus. Art, Omaha, Bklyn. Mus., Joseph H. Hirschhorn Mus., Ohara Mus., Japan, Edwin A. Ulrich Mus., Wichita, Kans. Co-chmn. Black Emergency Cultural Coalition, 1969—; bd. dirs. Children's Art Carnival. Served with USAAF, 1950-54. John Hay Whitney fellow, 1965-67; Dorne Professionship U. Bridgeport, Conn., 1970; N.Y. Council Arts grantee, 1971; MacDowell Colony fellow, 1973-74; Nat. Endowment for Arts; grantee, 1974. Office: care Lerner-Heller Gallery 956 Madison Ave New York NY 10021 *My whole existence as a person and as an artist rests on how I relate to my principles. It is very important for me to keep those principles high, and in so doing, I hope to inspire others to do the same.* *

ANDREWS, CHARLES EDWARD, university administrator, physician, educator; b. Stratford, Okla., Jan. 22, 1925; m. Theresa Markley, Nov. 1982; children: Evelyn, Mary Ellen, Jeffrey. Student, NYU, 1943-45; M.D., Boston U., 1949. Diplomate: Am. Bd. Internal Medicine. Intern U. Kans. Med. Center, 1949-50, resident, 1953-55, VA Hosp., Wichita, 1950-51; instr. U. Minn., 1955-56, U. Kans. Med. Center, 1955-56, assoc. in medicine, 1956-57, asst. prof. medicine, 1957-60, assoc. prof., 1960-61, W.Va. U. Med. Center, 1961-63, prof., 1963-83, acting dir. med. center, 1967-68, provost for health scis., 1968-77, v.p. health scis., 1978-81; gen. practice medicine, Omaha, 1983—; chancellor, v.p., prof. medicine U. Nebr. Med. Center, Omaha, 1983—; mem. staff U. Nebr. Hosp. and Clinic, 1983—; lectr. medicine U. Kansas City Sch. Dentistry, 1958-61; mem. W.Va. Regional Med. Program Adv. Group, 1966-76, W.Va. Comprehensive Health Planning Adv. Council, 1968-76; cons. Nat. Inst. Occupational Safety and Health, 1968-78; mem. adv. council Ctr. for Communicable Disease Control, 1969-73; dir. W.Va. Health Systems Agt., 1976-79; acting dir. W.Va. State Dept. Health, 1977; mem. Statewide Health Coordinating Council, 1978—, Mine Health Research Adv. Com., 1979-84. Bd. dirs. Am. Lung Assn., 1972—. Served to capt. USAAF, 1943-46, 53-57. Mem. ACP, Am. Fedn. for Clin. Research, Am. Thoracic Soc., Am. Coll. Chest Pysicians, So. Soc. for Clin. Investigation, Central Soc. for Clin. Research. Home: 11313 Canyon Rd Omaha NE 68112 Office: U Nebr Med Center 42d and Dewey Ave Omaha NE 68105

ANDREWS, CLARENCE ADELBERT, historian, educator, writer, publisher; b. Waterloo, Iowa, Oct. 24, 1912; s. Harry Leon and June Jennie (Jones) A.; m. Ollie Mae Easley, June 12, 1937; children: Linda Andrews Thompson, Terry Andrews Lasansky, Steven Randall. B.A., U. Iowa, 1954, M.A., 1960, Ph.D., 1963. Mem. War Price and Rationing Bd., Sheldon, Iowa, 1941-42; exec. sec. Sheldon C. of C., 1941-42; owner House of Andrews, Sheldon, 1942-49; asst. prof. Colo. State U., Ft. Collins, 1960-61; from instr. to asso. prof. English and journalism U. Iowa, 1961-69; vis. prof. journalism, 1976-82; prof. lang. and lit. Mich. Tech. U., Houghton, 1971-75; also dir. tech. and sci. communications; adj. prof. Am. thought and lang. Mich. State U., E. Lansing, 1975—; pub. Midwest Heritage Pub. Co., 1979—; vis. prof. Naval Ordnance Test Sta., China Lake, Calif., 1959; cons. Measurement Research Center, 1960; Mem. Mich. Council Humanities, 1974-76. Author: Technical and Scientific Writing, 1964, Writing, 1972, A Literary History of Iowa, 1972, Technical and Business Writing, 1974, Growing Up In Iowa, 1978, A Bibliography of Chicago Literature, 1978, The American Dream in the Heartland, 1982, Chicago in Story, 1983; Editor: Personnel Adminstr, 1960-61, Christmas in Iowa, 1979, Growing Up in the Middle West, 1981. Bd. dirs. N.W. Iowa Def. Bonds Sales, 1942. Served with USAAF, 1944-46. Recipient Mid-Am. Award, 1982; Grantee NDEA, 1968, NSF, 1964, 66, Ednl. Profl. Devel. Act, 1969, Mich. Tech. U., 1973. Mem. Soc. Study Midwest Lit., Am. Bus. Communicators, Western Lit. Assn., Phi Beta Kappa, Kappa Tau Alpha. Address: 108 Pearl St Iowa City IA 52240

ANDREWS, DAVID STANLEY, banker; b. Youngstown, Ohio, Dec. 17, 1947; s. James Beatty and Ada Blanche A.; m. Julia Lynn Dulin, June 23, 1973. B.S. in Bus. Adminstrn., Ohio State U., 1969; M.B.A., U. Mich., 1970. C.P.A., Fla., Mich. Mgr. Coopers and Lybrand (C.P.A.s), Ft. Lauderdale, Fla., 1974-80; v.p. fin., treas. Gulfstream Banks, Inc., Boca Raton, Fla., 1980-82; sr. v.p., controller NCNB Nat. Bank Fla., 1983—; instr. Wayne State U., Detroit, 1976-77. Served with USAF, 1971-74. Mem. Am. Inst. C.P.A.s, Fla. Soc. C.P.A.s. Republican. Episcopalian.

ANDREWS, FRANK MEREDITH, social science educator; b. N.Y.C., Apr. 2, 1935; s. Frank Emerson and Edith Lilian (Severance) A.; m. Ann Katharine Skilling, July 6, 1962; children: Kenneth Skilling, Steven Severance. B.A., Dartmouth Coll., 1957; postgrad. (Rotary Found. Internat. fellow), U. Sydney, Australia, 1958, New Sch. for Social Research, 1959; Ph.D. (Rackham fellow), U. Mich., 1962. Asst. study dir. Inst. for Social Research U. Mich., Ann Arbor, 1959-61, study dir., 1962-67, sr. study dir., 1968-70, program dir., 1971—, research sci., 1973—, lectr. psychology, 1963-66, asst. prof., 1967-70, asso. prof., 1971-75, prof., 1976—, prof. population planning, 1979—; cons. to Pan-Am. Health Orgn., UNESCO, AID, UN Research Inst. for Social Devel., Korea Devel. Inst., Can. Council, Philippine Inst. for Devel. Studies, Chinese Acad. Scis., various corps. and univs. Author: (with D.C. Pelz) Scientists in Organizations, 1966, Japanese edit., 1971, Russian edit., 1973, rev. English edit., 1976, (with others) Justifying Violence, 1972, (with S.B. Withay) Social Indicators of Well-Being, 1976, A Study of Company Sponsored Foundations, 1959, (with others) Multiple Classification Analysis, 1967, 2d edit., 1973, (with R.C. Messenger) Multivariate Nominal Scale Analysis, 1973, (with others) A Guide for Selecting Statistical Techniques for Analyzing Social Science Data, 1974, 2d edit., 1981, Hebrew edit., 1976, French edit., 1977; Editor: Scientific Productivity, 1979; co-editor: Quality of Life: Comparative Studies, 1980; Contbr. chpts. to books, articles to profl. jours. Pres. Whitmore Lake E. Shore Assn., 1970-71, 73—; bd. dirs. Whitmore Lake Homeowners Assn., 1972—, Whitmore Lake Health Clinic, 1981—. Grantee NSF, NIMH, NASA, UNESCO. Mem. Am. Statis. Assn., Am. Psychol. Assn., Am., Internat. sociol. assns., Soc. for Social Studies of Sci., Soc. for Internat. Devel., Population Assn. Am., Phi Beta Kappa, Sigma Xi. Home: 11720 E Shore Dr Whitmore Lake MI 48189 Office: Institute for Social Research U Michigan Ann Arbor MI 48109

ANDREWS, FRED CHARLES, educator; b. Aylesbury, Sask., Can., July 13, 1924; s. Henry Marmaduke and Margaret (Van de Bogart) A.; m. Joyce Davenny, Apr. 5, 1944; children—Linda (Mrs. Pierre Dunn), David W., Gail E. B.S. in Math, U. Wash., 1946, M.S. in Math. Statistics, 1948; Ph.D., U. Calif., Berkeley, 1953. Research asso. Applied Math. and Statistics Lab., Stanford, 1952-54; asst. prof. math., asso. statistician U. Nebr., 1954-57; asso. prof. math. U. Oreg., 1957-66, dir., 1960-69, prof. math., 1966—, head dept. math., 1973-80; Vis. statistician Math Centrum, Amsterdam, The Netherlands, 1963-64. Contbr. articles to profl. jours. Pres. Met.-Civic Club, Eugene-Springfield, 1967-68; Trustee Oreg. Grad. Center, 1967-77. Served to lt. (j.g.) USNR, 1943-46. Fulbright-Hays sr. lectr. U. Tampere, Finland, 1969-70, Univ. Coll., Cork, Ireland, 1976-77. Mem. Inst. Math. Statistics, Am. Statis. Assn., Biometric Soc., AAAS, AAUP, Sigma Xi. Office: Dept Math U Oreg Eugene OR 97403

ANDREWS, FREDERICK NEWCOMB, university dean; b. Boston, Feb. 5, 1914; s. Frederick Huntoon and Gertrude (Macomber) A.; m. Gertrude Evelyn Martin, Sept. 3, 1938; children: Frederick Martin, Donna Elaine. B.S., U. Mass., 1935, M.S., 1936, D.Sc., 1962; Ph.D., U. Mo., 1939; D.Agr. (hon.), Purdue U., 1983. Instr. animal husbandry U. Mass., 1936; coop. agt. U. Mo.-U.S. Dept. Agr., 1936-40; asst. prof. animal sci. Purdue U., 1940-45, assoc. prof., 1945-49, prof., 1949—, asst. to dean, 1949-54, dir., 1960—, head dept. animal scis., 1962, dean Grad. Sch., v.p. research, 1963—; v.p., bd. dirs. Purdue Research Found., 1964—; chmn. bd. dirs. Indpls. Ctr. Advanced Research, 1981; Spl. cons. Latin Am. programs in agrl. sci. Rockefeller Found., 1956, 61, bd. cons. agrl. programs, 1962—; v.p. Indpls. Center for Advanced Research, 1973—; mem. Ford Found. ednl. mission to, Mexico, 1962, Fulbright award com.; research grant reviewer NSF-NIH; mem. numerous coms. nutrition and animal physiology Nat. Acad. Scis., mem. agr. bd., 1972—; mem. Internat. Conf. on Use Isotopes in Animal Biology and Med. Scis., Mexico City, 1961; mem. council on fed. regulations Assn. Am. Univs., 1968—; mem. selection com. Showalter Trust, 1983. Author: Breeding Better Livestock, 1953, Breeding and Improving of Farm Animals, rev. edit, 1967, Swine Production, rev. edit, 1962; Editorial bd.: Jour. Animal Sci. Selection com. Tyler Ecology award, 1971—. Recipient research award Sigma Xi, 1949, Morrison research award Am. Soc. Animal Sci., 1961. Fellow A.A.A.S.; mem. Am. Soc. Zoologists, Am. Soc. Animal Sci., N.Y. Acad. Scis., Am. Dairy Sci. Assn., Poultry Sci. Assn., Ind. Vet. Med. Assn. (hon.), Am. Assn. Anatomists, Assn. Grad. Schs., Council Grad. Schs., Phi Beta Kappa, Sigma Xi, Phi Kappa Phi, Gamma Sigma Delta. Home: 691 Sugar Hill Dr West Lafayette IN 47906 Office: Purdue Research Found Purdue U Lafayette IN 49707

ANDREWS, GLENN, former congressman, farmer; b. Anniston, Ala., Jan. 15, 1909; s. Roger Lee and Beryl Elizabeth (Jones) A.; m. Ethel Standish Jackson, Jan. 1937; children—Ethel Houston (Mrs. George Kilby), Arthur Glenn, Frank Scott. Student, Mercersburg Acad., 1926-27; A.B., Princeton, 1931. With IBM, Nat. City Bank, N.Y.C., 1931-37; salesman, dist. mgr. subsidiary Eastman Kodak Co., New Orleans, 1937-47; advt. exec., pres. Andrews Advt., Inc., Anniston, 1947—; mem. 89th Congress 4th Dist., Ala.; farmer, Anniston, Ala., 1960—; pres. Glendale Realty Co., Inc., Anniston.; Mem. James Madison Commn., 1964—; standing trustee in bankruptcy ct., Anniston.; Chmn. Republican Party, Calhoun County, 1952—; candidate sec. state, 1956; candidate Ala. Ho. of Reps., 1958; regional coordinator Rep. Com., 1960-64, dist. chmn., del. state conv., 1962, del. nat. conv., 1964, 72; Rep. chmn. 4th Congl. Ala. Dist. Mem. com. sponsors MacArthur Meml. Com., Former Mems. Congress, Assn. Ex-Mems. Squadron A. Episcopalian. Clubs: Rotarian, Mason (32, K.T.), Anniston Country; Nassau (Princeton, N.J.). Home: 1205 Champaign St Anniston AL 36201 Office: Andrews Advt Inc PO Box 1589 Anniston AL 36201

ANDREWS, GORDON CLARK, lawyer; b. Boston, Mar. 25, 1941; s. Loring Beal and Flora Spencer (Hinckley) A.; m. Deborah M. Devere, July 9, 1966; children: Christine Leigh, Cynthia Lyn, Carey Loring. B.A., Dartmouth Coll., 1963; J.D., N.Y. U., 1969. Bar: N.Y. State bar 1970, Conn. bar 1971. Asso. firm Morgan Lewis & Bockius (and predecessor), N.Y.C., 1969-72; asst. sec. Howmet Corp., Greenwich, Conn., 1973-75; sec., asst. gen. counsel Beker Industries Corp., Greenwich, 1976—, v.p., 1978-81; gen. counsel M&T Chems., Inc., Woodbridge, N.J., 1982—. Served to lt. USNR, 1963-69. Recipient Am. Law award, 1969. Mem. Am., N.Y. State, Conn. bar assns., Am. Soc. Corporate Secs., Westchester-Fairfield Corporate Counsel Assn. Republican. Club: Greenwich Country. Home: 46 Club Rd Riverside CT 06878 Office: One Woodbridge Ctr Woodbridge NJ 07095

ANDREWS, HENRY NATHANIEL, JR., scientist, educator; b. Melrose, Mass., June 15, 1910; s. Henry Nathaniel and Florence Clara (Hollings) A.; m. Elisabeth Claude Ham, Jan. 12, 1939; children—Hollings T., Henry III, Nancy R. B.S., M.I.T., 1934; M.S., Washington U., St. Louis, 1937, Ph. D., 1939; student, Cambridge (Eng.) U., 1937-38. Mem. staff Washington U., 1939-64; prof. Bot. Garden, St. Louis, 1941-64, asst. to dir., 1944-47; part time employee U.S. Geol. Survey; chmn. botany dept. U. Conn., Storrs, 1965-67, head systematic and environ. biol. sect., 1967-70, prof. emeritus, 1975—. NSF postdoctoral fellow Swedish Mus. Natural History, Stockholm, 1964-65; Fulbright teaching fellow Poona Univ., India, 1960-61; vis. prof. Aarhus (Denmark) U., 1976. Mem. Bot. Soc. Am. (Merit award 1966), Nat. Acad. Scis., Paleontol. Soc., Torrey Bot. Club, Phi Beta Kappa, Sigma Xi. Research work deals primarily with fossil plants of central coal fields, Devonian age Fossils, Arctic paleobotany. Home: RFD 1 Box 146 Laconia NH 03246

ANDREWS, IKE FRANKLIN, congressman; b. Bonlee, N.C., Sept. 2, 1925; s. Archie F. and Ina (Dunlap) A.; m. Pat Goodwin, 1977;

children by previous marriage: Alice, Nina Patricia. B.S., U. N.C., 1950, LL.B., 1952. Bar: N.C. 1952. Partner firm Andrews & Stone, Siler City, 1966-72; mem. 93d-98th congresses from, N.C.; Mem. N.C. Senate, 1959-61; mem. N.C. Ho. of Reps., 1961-67, 69, 71, majority leader, speaker pro-tem, 1971; Bd. govs. U. N.C., 1959-71, chancellor selection com., 1971. Served with F.A. AUS, 1943-45. Decorated Bronze Star, Purple Heart. Mem. Siler City C. of C., Am. Legion. Club: Rotarian. Office: 2201 Rayburn House Office Bldg Washington DC 20515 *

ANDREWS, J. DAVID, lawyer; b. Decatur, Ill., July 5, 1933; s. Jesse D. and Louise Glenna (Mason) A.; m. Helen Virginia Migely, July 12, 1958; children: Virginia, Robert, Michael, Betsy. B.A. magna cum laude, U. Ill., 1955, J.D., 1960. Bar: Wash. 1961. Partner firm Perkins, Coie, Stone, Olsen & Williams, Seattle, 1960—; Bd. dirs. Cornish Inst., Seattle, 1977—; dirs. Am. Bar Endowment; bd. visitors Law Sch., U. Puget Sound., 1976—; trustee AEF Pension Fund, 1975-79; bd. govs. Am. Bar, 1975-79. Dir.: Am. Bar Jour, 1975-79; Contbr. articles to profl. jours. Served to capt. USAF, 1955-57. Fellow Am. Bar Found. (former treas.), Am. Coll. Trial Lawyers; mem. Am. Bar Assn. (ho. of dels. 1967-69, 75—, asst. treas. 1972-74, treas. 1975-79, bd. govs. 1975-79), Wash. Bar Assn. (chmn. pub. relations com. 1971-73), Seattle-King County Bar Assn., Am. Judicature Soc., Phi Beta Kappa, Phi Kappa Phi, Phi Eta Sigma. Home: 10320 Bedford Ct NW Seattle WA 98177 Office: 1900 Washington Bldg Seattle WA 98101

ANDREWS, JAMES CRANDALL, librarian; b. Phila., Apr. 18, 1921; s. James Clarence and Kathleen Bardshar (Crandall) A.; m. Katherine Hamrick, Mar. 27, 1943; children: James H., Robert C., Kenneth B. B.S. in Physics, U. N.C., 1946, U. Ill., 1947, M.S., 1949. Radar research U.S. Naval Research Lab., Washington, 1942-46; acquisiton dept. U. Ill.-Urbana, 1947-48; head librarian K-25 plant Carbide & Carbon Chem. Corp., Oak Ridge, 1948-50; head tech. info. service E.I. duPont de Nemours & Co., Savannah River Lab., Aiken, S.C., 1951-58; dir. library Argonne Nat. Lab., Ill., 1959-70; univ. librarian U. Tex.-Dallas, 1970-72; dir. libraries Rensselaer Poly. Inst., Troy, N.Y., 1972—; Ford Found. library cons. C. Am., 1965, 68, 72. Contbr. articles to profl. jours. Active Boy Scouts Am., 1959-71. Recipient Silver Beaver award Boy Scouts Am., 1968. Mem. Am. Philatelic Soc. Club: Appalachian Mountain

ANDREWS, JAMES EDGAR, church official, clergyman; b. Whittenburg, Tex., Dec. 29, 1928; s. Bryan McEvrie and Rose Ellen (Simpson) A.; m. Sarah Elizabeth Crouch, Sept. 16, 1962; children: Charis Megan, Bryan Hugh. B.A., Austin Coll., 1952, M.A., 1953, D.D., 1974; B.D., Austin Presbyn. Theol. Sem., 1956. Ordained to ministry Presbyterian Ch. U.S., 1956; asst. minister St. Andrews Presbyn. Ch., Houston, 1956-58; sec. for info. World Alliance of Ref. Chs., Geneva, Switzerland, 1958-60; dir. info. Princeton (N.J.) Theol. Sem., 1960-68, asst. to pres., 1963-71; asst. to stated clk. Presbyn. Ch. U.S., 1971-73, stated clk., 1973-83, interim co-stated clk., 1983-84; Mem. governing bd. Nat. Council Chs., 1973—; sec. Caribbean and N. Am. Area Council World Alliance Ref. Chs., 1977—. Mem. Common Council of Borough of Princeton, 1968-70. Home: 2668 E McKinnon Dr Decatur GA 30030 Office: Presbyn Ch in US 341 Ponce de Leon Ave NE Atlanta GA 30308

ANDREWS, JOHN CHARLES, lawyer; b. Duncan, Okla., Oct. 24, 1926; s. John Charles and Eva L. (Loos) A.; m. Patricia Coffey, Nov. 22, 1952; children: John Charles, Patricia Kathleen, Michael Joseph, Margaret Ann, Daniel Coffey, Timothy Jerome. Student, Oklahoma City U., 1944; J.D., Okla. U., 1949. Bar: Okla. 1949. Asst. ins. commr. State of Okla., 1949-50; mem. firm Andrews Davis Legg Bixler Milsten & Murrah, Inc. (and predecessors), Oklahoma City, 1967—; dir. Founders Bank & Trust Co., Balliet's Inc. Trustee Central Cemetery Co. of Ill. Served with AUS, 1944-46. Mem. Am., Okla. bar assns., Phi Delta Phi. Roman Catholic. Clubs: Whitehall, Beacon. Home: 1709 Wilshire Blvd Oklahoma City OK 73116 Office: 500 W Main St Oklahoma City OK 73102

ANDREWS, JOHN FRANK, educator; b. Cave City, Ark., July 10, 1930; s. Frank Ferd and Ruth Lanell (Puckett) A.; m. Margery Ann Hall, June 21, 1952; children: John Patrick, Carol Ann, Laurie Lanell. B.S. in Civil Engring, U. Ark., 1951, M.S., 1953; Ph.D., U. Calif. at Berkeley, 1964. Registered profl. engr., Ark., S.C., Tex.; diplomate Am. Acad. Environ. Engrs. Instr. civil engring. U. Ark., 1953-55, asst. prof., 1955-59, asso. prof., 1959-60; project engr. U. Calif. at Berkeley, 1962-63; asso. prof., asso. dir. water resources engring. program Clemson U., 1963-66, prof., dir. environmental systems engring., 1966-68, prof., dept head, 1968-74; prof. civil and environmental engring. U. Houston, 1975-81; prof. environ. sci. and engring. Rice U., 1981—; Cons. water pollution control Engring.-Sci., Inc., Los Angeles, Phila., Chgo., Mpls., Union Carbide, U.S. Army, Bacardi Distilleries, Pan Am. Health Orgn., Greeley & Hansen Engrs., Shell Devel. Co., Weyerhauser Co., also others. Research, publs. in field. NSF grantee. Fellow Royal Soc. Health; mem. ASCE, Am. Inst. Chem. Engrs., Am. Water Works Assn., Water Polution Control Fedn. (Harrison Prescott Eddy award 1975), Am. Soc. Microbiology, Am. Chem. Soc., AAAS, Internat. Assn. Water Pollution Research (U.S. editor Water Research, vice chmn. Vienna conf. 1971, 75, 79, program chmn. London conf. 1973, Stockholm conf. 1977), Am. Soc. Engring. Edn., Assn. Environ. Engring. Profs. (dir. 1967-70, chmn. workshops 1968-70, chmn. nat. conf. 1977), Instrument Soc. Am., N.Y. Acad. Scis., Internat. Water Supply Assn., Sigma Xi, Tau Beta Pi, Phi Kappa Phi. Methodist. Office: Dept Environ Sci and Engring Rice U Box 1892 Houston TX 77251

ANDREWS, JOHN FRANK, educational administrator, editor; b. Carlsbad, N.Mex., Nov. 2, 1942; s. Frank Randolph and Mary Lucille (Wimberly) A.; m. Vicky Roberta Anderson, Aug. 20, 1966 (div. 1983); children: Eric John, Lisa Gail. A.B., Princeton U., 1965; M.A.T., Harvard U., 1966; Ph.D., Vanderbilt U., 1971. Instr. English U. Tenn.-Nashville, 1969-70; asst. prof. English, dir. grad. studies in English Fla. State U., Tallahassee, 1970-74; dir. acad. programs Folger Shakespeare Library, Washington, 1974—, chmn. Folger Inst. Renaissance and 18th Century Studies, 1974—; exec. editor Folger Books, 1974—; cons. Time-Life TV, WNET/Thirteen Corp. for Pub. Broadcasting, Pub. Broadcasting Service, Exxon Corp.; chmn. Nat. Adv. Panel for the Shakespeare Plays, 1979—; mem. adv. bds. Inst. Humanistic Studies SUNY-Albany, Newberry Library Center Renaissance Studies, Adult Learning Listening Network, others; cons. Shakespeare: The Globe and the World, touring exhbn., 1978-81, Doubleday, 1982-83, Nat. Pub. Radio, 1978-81. Asst. editor: Shakespeare Studies, 1972-74; editor: Shakespeare Quarterly, 1974—; editor-in-chief, contbr.: William Shakespeare: His World, His Work, His Influence, 1985; contbr. numerous articles to scholarly jours.; panelist Fellowships, NEH, 1981-82. Recipient Research awards Folger Shakespeare Library, Fla. State U.; adminstr. program grants NEH, Andrew W. Mellon Found., Exxon Found., Met. Life, Surdna Found., others. Mem. AAUP (sec. chpt. 1972-74), Modern Lang. Assn., South Atlantic Modern Lang. Assn., Renaissance Soc. Am. (mem. council 1975—), Southeastern Renaissance Conf. Internat. Shakespeare Conf., Shakespeare Assn. Am. (trustee 1979-82). Home: 2032 Belmont Rd NW 605 Washington DC 20009 Office: Folger Shakespeare Library 201 E Capitol St SE Washington DC 20003

ANDREWS, JOHN HOBART MCLEAN, educator; b. Kamloops, B.C., Can., May 15, 1926; s. John Ernest and Cynthia Maria (Robinson) A.; m. Doris Deborah Payne, Aug. 28, 1948; children: William John, Donald Wilfrid, Jeffrey Peter, Lorraine Doris. B.A. with honours in Physics, U. B.C., 1947, M.A. in Edn, 1954; Ph.D. in Ednl. Adminstrn, U. Chgo., 1957. Tchr., prin. B.C. schs., 1950-55; prof. edn. U. Alta., 1957-65; prof., chmn. ednl. adminstrn., asst. dir. Ont. Inst. for Studies in Edn., 1965-73; dean of edn. U. B.C., Vancouver, 1973-79, prof. ednl. adminstrn., 1979—. Author articles in fields of leadership, orgn. theory, and tchr. edn. Home: 4923 College Highroad Vancouver BC Canada Office: Faculty of Edn Vancouver BC Canada V6T 1Z5

ANDREWS, JOHN STEWART, college official; b. Salem, Ohio, Oct. 28, 1919; s. William W. and Lora (Ressler) A.; m. Marie Louise Adams, Mar. 22, 1944; children: William Douglas, Jeffrey Lynn, Kathleen Margaret, Richard Dale, John Michael (dec.). Student, U. Dayton, 1939-40, U. Queensland, Australia, 1945-46; grad., Advanced Mgmt. Program, Harvard, 1965, Inst. Ednl. Mgmt., 1973; B.A., Goddard Coll., 1974; M.A. (hon.), Goddard Coll., 1975. Exec. v.p. Rike-Kumler Co., Dayton, Ohio, 1965-69; exec. v.p. Shillitos, Cin., 1969, pres., 1970-72; dir. mgmt. Goddard Coll., Plainfield, Vt., 1972-74, acting pres. and chief exec. officer, 1974-75; regional dir. for North Africa, Near East, Orient and Pacific, Peace Corps, Washington, 1976-78; dean of adminstrn. St. Mary's Coll. (Md.), 1979-80; v.p., adminstrn. St. Mary's Coll., 1980—. Served to lt. USAAF, 1940-45. Presbyn. (elder 1961—). Clubs: Harvard of Vt., Chesapeake Country, Washington; Harvard Bus. (Washington). Address: Box 415 Bayside Dr Saint Leonard MD 20685

ANDREWS, JOHN THOMAS, quaternary geologist; b. Millom, Cumberland, Eng., Nov. 8, 1937; came to U.S., 1968, naturalized, 1976; s. George and Dorothy (Black) A.; m. Martha Lee Tuthill, Dec. 16, 1961; children—Melissa Margaret, Thomas George. B.A., U. Nottingham, 1959, Ph.D., 1965, D.Sc., 1978; M.Sc., McGill U., 1961. Research scientist Govt. Can., Ottawa, 1961-67; prof. geol. scis. Inst. Arctic and Alpine Research, U. Colo., Boulder, 1968—. Author: Glacial Isosasty, 1974, Glacial Systems, 1975. Fellow Geol. Soc. Am. (Kirk Bryan medal 1973), Arctic Inst. N.Am.; mem. Internat. Glaciol. Soc., Am. Geophys. Union, Canadian Geol. Assn., Colo. Sci. Soc. (Past President's award 1969). Home: 1407 Kennedy Ct Boulder CO 80303 Office: Inst Arctic and Alpine Research Univ Colo Boulder CO 80309

ANDREWS, JULIE, actress, singer; b. Walton-on-Thames, Eng., Oct. 1, 1935; d. Edward C. and Barbara Wells; m. Tony Walton, May 10, 1959 (div.); 1 dau., Emma; m. Blake Edwards, 1969. Studied with pvt. tutors; studied voice with Mme. Stiles-Allen. Debut as singer, Hippodrome, London, 1947; appeared in: pantomime Cinderella, London, 1953; appeared: Broadway prodn. The Boy Friend, N.Y.C., 1954, My Fair Lady, 1956-60 (N.Y. Drama Critics award 1956), Camelot, 1960-62; films include Mary Poppins, 1964 (Acad. award for best actress 1964), The Americanization of Emily, 1964, Torn Curtain, 1966, The Sound of Music, 1966, Hawaii, 1966, Thoroughly Modern Millie, 1967, Star!, 1968, Darling Lili, 1970, The Tamarind Seed, 1973, 10, 1979, Little Miss Marker, 1980, S.O.B, 1981, Victor/Victoria, 1982, The Man Who Loved Women, 1983; TV debut in High Tor, 1956; star: TV series The Julie Andrews Hour, 1972-73; also spls.; Author: (as Julie Edwards): Mandy, 1971, The Last of the Really Great Whangdoodles, 1974. Recipient Golden Globe award Hollywood Fgn. Press Assn., 1964, 65; named World Film Favorite (female), 1967. Office: care Creative Artists Agy 1888 Century Park E Suite 1400 Los Angeles CA 90067 *

ANDREWS, KENNETH RICHMOND, business administration educator; b. New London, Conn., May 24, 1916; s. William John and Myrtle (Richmond) A.; m. Edith May Platt, Apr. 29, 1945 (div. 1969); children: Kenneth Richmond, Carolyn; m. Carolyn Erskine Hall, Feb. 14, 1970. A.B., Wesleyan U., 1936, M.A., 1937; Ph.D., U. Ill., 1948; M.A. (hon.), Harvard U., 1957. Tchr. English U. Ill., 1937-41; instr. bus. adminstrn. Harvard Grad. Sch. Bus. Adminstrn., 1946-47, asst. prof., 1947-52, asso. prof., 1952-57, prof., 1957-65, Donald K. David prof. bus. adminstrn., 1965—, faculty chmn. Advanced Mgmt. Program, 1967-70, master Leverett House, 1971-81, chmn. gen. mgmt. faculty, 1981-83; cons. on mgmt. devel. and policy problems; dir. Duriron, Inc., Price Bros., Inc., Reed & Barton, Temple Barker & Stone, Inc., Harvard U. Press, Xerox Corp.; Am. Productivity Ctr. Author: Nook Farm, 1950, (with others) Problems of General Management, 1962, Business Policy Text and Cases, 1965, rev. edit., 1969, 73, 77, 79, The Effectiveness of University Executive Development Programs, 1966, The Concept of Corporate Strategy, 1971, rev. edit., 1980; editor: The Case Method of Teaching Human Relations and Administration, 1953; chmn. editorial bd.: Harvard Bus. Rev, 1972-79; editor-in-chief, 1979—. Trustee Wesleyan U., 1955-72, Nat. Ctr. for Econ. Edn. of Children. Served from pvt. F.A. to maj. USAAF, 1941-46. Mem. Phi Beta Kappa. Office: Soldiers Field Boston MA 02163

ANDREWS, LARRY KENNETH, university administrator, English educator; b. Columbia, Mo., Oct. 10, 1940; s. Adam and Betty Dysart (Carruth) A.; m. Kim Maree Crawley, June 10, 1963; children: Wyn, Sally. B.S., U. Mo., 1963, M.Ed., 1967, Ph.D., 1969; postgrad., Iliff Sch. Theology, 1980. Asst. prof. English U. Nebr.-Lincoln, from 1969, now prof., also grad. dean, 1974-77, asst. vice-chancellor, 1977-81, asst. to chancellor, 1981-83; asst. exec. v.p., provost U. Nebr. System, 1983—; cons. univs., pub. schs., 1969—; trustee Nebr. Wesleyan U., Lincoln, 1982—. Author: (with others) Language for a Future, 1969; contbr. chpts., articles to profl. publs., 1969—. Mem. bd. higher edn. Nebr. Methodist Conf., 1980—; bd. dirs. United Way, Lincoln, 1981-84. Named Outstanding Prof. Mortar Bd., Columbia, Mo., 1969, U. Nebr.-Lincoln, 1971. Mem. Nat. Council Tchrs. English (dir. 1972-75), Internat. Reading Assn., Am. Assn. Higher Edn., Nebr. Council Tchrs. English (exec. sec. 1972-76), Phi Delta Kappa. Democrat. Club: Torach (Lincoln). Lodge: Rotary. Office: U Nebr 3835 Holdrege St Lincoln NE 68588 *

ANDREWS, LAVONE D., architect; b. Beaumont, Tex., Sept. 18, 1912; d. Charles and Lavone (Lowman) Dickensheets; m. Mark Edwin Andrews, July 23, 1948; 1 son, Mark Edwin III. Student, Miss Hamlin's Sch., San Francisco, Marlborough Sch., Los Angeles; A.B., Rice Inst., 1933; B.S. in architecture, Rice Inst., 1934. Licensed architect, Tex. and D.C. Assoc. with outstanding architects in Southwest, 1934-37, opened own office, Houston, 1937-41; architect firm Anderson, Clayton & Co. (cotton firm), 1941-51; v.p. Ancon Oil & Gas, Inc. Also pvt. work, museum in, Washington, Naval Hist. Found. & Health Center, schs. for, City of Houston. Trustee Mus. Fine Arts in Houston; mem. YWCA World Service Council. Selected as 3d of the 10 outstanding women architects in Am. Archtl. Record, 1947. Fellow AIA; mem. Royal Inst. Architects Ireland, Pallas Athene Lit. Soc. of Rice Inst. Episcopalian. Clubs: River, Colony (N.Y.C.); Houston, Houston Country, Garden of Houston, Bayou, Garden of Am. Home: 3711 San Felipe Houston TX 77027 Knappague Castle County Clare Ireland also (summer) Sea Wynde Fisher's Island NY 06390 Office: 1000 Bank of Southwest Bldg Houston TX 77002

ANDREWS, MARK, U.S. Senator; b. Fargo, N.D., May 19, 1926; s. Mark and Lillian (Hoyler) A.; m. Mary Willming, June 28, 1949; children: Mark, Sarah Jane, Karen Louise. B.S., N.D. State U., 1949, LL.D., 1978. Farmer, Mapleton, N.D., 1949—; mem. 88th-92d Congresses from 1st Dist. N.D., 93d to 96th Congresses at large, mem. appropriations com.; ofcl. del. FAO Conf., Rome, 1975; now mem. U.S. Senate from N.D., mem. appropriations, budget and agr. coms., chmn. select com. Indian affairs. Past mem. Republican Nat. Com. for N.D.; bd. dirs. Cass County chpt. ARC. Named Hon. Am. Farmer Future Farmers Am., 1976. Mem. Rep. Nat. Farm Council, N.D. Young Reps. (past chmn.), Nat. Reclamation Assn. (chmn. land limitations com.), Farm Bur., Am. Legion, N.D. Stockmen's Assn., N.D. Crop Improvement Assn. (past pres.), Greater N.D. Assn., Northwest Farm Mgrs., N.D. Water Users Assn., Sigma Chi. Episcopalian. Home: Mapleton ND 58059 Office: Hart Senate Office Bldg Room 724 Washington DC 20510

ANDREWS, MARK EDWIN, lawyer, industrialist; b. Houston, Oct. 17, 1903; s. Jesse and Celeste (Bujac) A.; m. Marguerite McLellan (dec. 1946); m. Lavone Dickensheets, July 23, 1948; children—Marguerite McLellan, Mark Edwin. A.B., Princeton U., 1927; LL.B., So. Tex. Coll. Law, 1934; postgrad., U. Colo., 1931-34. Pres. Andrews, Loop & Co., 1928-34, Ryan & Andrews, 1936-42, Westmoreland Mfg. Co., 1936-42, M.E. Andrews, Ltd., 1951—, Ancon Oil & Gas, Inc., 1951—; adv. dir. Bank of Southwest; faculty So. Tex. Coll. Law, 1934-42. Author: Law vs. Equity in The Merchant of Venice, 1965, Buying a Navy, 1946, Wildcatters Handbook, 1952; contbr. articles to legal publs. Chmn. Bayou Bend Mus. Adv. Com.; trustee, ex-officio mem. exec. com. Mus. Fine Arts, Houston. Served USNR, 1942-46; advancing lt. to capt., serving in Office Procurement and Material, Exec. Office of Sec. Navy Dept.; chief of procurement USN, 1945-46; asst. sec. of navy, 1947-49. Decorated Legion of Merit, 1946. Mem. Houston Com. on Fgn. Relations (Carnegie Found.), English Speaking Union (v.p. Houston chpt.), Japan-Am. Soc. Houston (pres.). Republican. Episcopalian. Clubs: Houston Country, Bayou, Allegro, Houston (Houston); Links, River (N.Y.C.); Tiger Inn, Right Wing (Princeton, N.J.); Fishers Island (N.Y.) Country); Shannon Golf (Ireland); Kildare St. (Dublin, Ireland). Home: 3711 San Felipe Houston TX 77027 also Sea Wynde Fishers Island NY Knappogue Castle County Clare Ireland Office: 1000 Bank of Southwest Bldg Houston TX 77002

ANDREWS, MARVIN ARNOLD, city official; b. Kewanee, Ill., Jan. 21, 1929; s. Arthur Wilber and Ethel Belle (Kleinfall) A.; m. Barbara Lorraine Ball, July 15, 1978; children: William L., Barbara L. B.S. in Econs. and Fin, U. Ill., 1955; M.P.A., Syracuse U., 1956; urban execs. course, M.I.T., 1969. Adminstrv. asst. to city mgr., Elgin, Ill., 1956-58, asst. to city mgr., Phoenix, 1958-66, dep. city mgr., 1966-69, asst. city mgr., 1967-76, city mgr., 1976—; mem. steering com. Urban Consortium, 1973-76; mem. Gov.'s Groundwater Users Adv. Com., Gov.'s Merit System Rev. Commn., 1980. Chmn. govt. div. Phoenix United Way, 1978, bd. dirs., 1979. Served with U.S. Army, 1948-51; Korea. Mem. Ariz. City Mgmt. Assn. (pres. 1971), Am. Soc. Public Adminstrn. (dir. Ariz. 1979, Ariz. Superior Service award 1979), Internat. City Mgmt. Assn., Am. Mgmt. Assn., Pres.' Assn. Club: Rotary. Office: 251 W Washington St Phoenix AZ 85003

ANDREWS, MASON COOKE, obstetrician-gynecologist, educator; b. Norfolk, Va., Apr. 20, 1919; s. Charles James and Jean (Cooke) A.; m. Sabine Goodman, Sept. 24, 1949; children: Jean, Mason. B.A., Princeton U., 1940; M.D., Johns Hopkins U., 1943. Diplomate: Am. Bd. Ob-Gyn. Intern ob-gyn Johns Hopkins U., Balt., 1944, resident ob-gyn, 1946-50; pvt. practice ob-gyn, Norfolk, Va., 1950-70; lectr. Johns Hopkins U. Sch. Medicine, Balt., 1971-72; prof., chmn. dept. ob-gyn Eastern Va. Med. Sch., Norfolk, 1974—; dir. First Va. Bank of Tidewater, Chesapeake and Potomac Telephone Co., Waverly Press; chmn. Eastern Va. Med. Authority, 1964-70. Contbr. (numerous articles to sci. jours.). Mem. Norfolk Planning Commn., 1963-65; chmn. Southeastern Va. Planning Dist. Com., 1981-82; vice mayor, Norfolk, 1978-82, Norfolk councilman. Recipient First Citizen citation Norfolk Cosmopolitan Club, 1967, Norfolk Citation for Outstanding Service, 1964. Fellow Am. Gynecol. and Obstet. Soc. (v.p. 1982-83); mem. South Atlantic Assn., Va. Obstet. and Gynecol. Soc. (pres. 1975), Norfolk Acad. Medicine (pres. 1961). Presbyterian. Clubs: Harbor, Norfolk Yacht and Country. Home: 1011 N Shore Rd Norfolk VA 23505 Office: Eastern Virginia Med Sch Dept Ob-Gyn 603 Medical Tower Norfolk VA

ANDREWS, MICHAEL ALLEN, congressman, lawyer; b. Houston, Feb. 7, 1944; s. Frank H. and Jonnie (Allen) A.; m. Elizabeth Ann Bowman, July 10, 1971; children: Carolien Bowman, Emily Allen. B.A., U. Tex., Austin, 1967; J.D., So. Meth. U., 1970. Bar: Tex. 1970, U.S. Supreme Ct. 1971, U.S. Dist. Ct. for so. dist. Tex. 1972, U.S. Ct. Appeals for 5th circuit 1981. Law clk. U.S Dist. Ct., Houston, 1972-76; asst. dist. atty. Harris County Dist. Atty.'s Office, Houston, 1972-76; ptnr. firm. Baker, Brown, Sharman & Wise, Houston, 1976-82; mem. 98th Congress from 25th dist. Tex., 1983—; v.p. Freshman Democtatic Caucus, Washington, 1983—, mem. com. on party effectiveness, 1983—. Mem. ABA, Houston Bar Assn., State Bar Tex., House Women's Caucus, House Arts Caucus, House Space Caucus. Democrat. Methodist. Office: US House of Reps 1039 Longworth Bldg Washington DC 20515

ANDREWS, OLIVER, JR., educator; b. Montclair, N.J., May 26, 1917; s. Oliver and Rosamund (Capen) A.; m. Ann Roberta Wright, Sept. 4, 1953; children: Oliver, Elizabeth W., Rosamund C., Michael C., Anthony W., Anne A., Geoffrey C. B.S. cum laude, Harvard U., 1939; diplome, Institut de Phonetique, Paris, 1948; M.A., Middlebury Coll., 1947; Ph.D., McGill U., 1956. Tchr. Gov. Dummer Acad., Byfield, Mass., 1939-43; asst. prof. Bates Coll., 1948-52, Purdue U., 1956-58, asso. prof., 1958-60; prof., head dept. modern langs. St. Lawrence U., 1960-66, founder, dir. jr. year in, France, 1964; prof., head dept. Romance and classical langs. U. Conn., Storrs, 1966-77, founder, jr. year in; France, 1967, coordinator, 1967—, dir., 1978-79; Exec. dir. Charles I. Travelli Fund, Boston, 1960—; cons. HEW, 1962-67; Bd. dirs. Council on Internat. Ednl. Exchange, 1973-78, 81—. Contbr. articles to lang. jours. Served with AUS, 1943-45. Decorated Bronze Star with oak leaf cluster U.S.; chevalier Ordre des Palmes Académiques; commandeur Société Vinicole de Médoc. Mem. AAUP, Modern Lang. Assn. Am. (cons. 1964-68, chmn. com. N.E. Conf. 1968, dir. Conf. 1969-72), Am. Assn. Tchrs. French. Club: Harvard (N.Y.C.). Home: Dog Ln Storrs CT 06268

ANDREWS, RICHARD VINCENT, physiologist, graduate school dean; b. Arapahoe, Nebr., Jan. 9, 1932; s. Wilber Vincent and Fern (Clawson) A.; m. Elizabeth Williams, June 1, 1954; children: Thomas, William, Robert, Catherine, James, John. B.S., Creighton U., 1958, M.S., 1959; Ph.D., U. Iowa, 1963. Instr. biology Creighton U., Omaha, 1958-60, asst. prof., 1963-65, assoc. prof., 1965-68, prof. physiology, 1968—, asst. med. dean, 1972-75, dean grad. studies, 1975—; instr. physiology U. Iowa, 1960-63; cons. VA, Omaha Pub. Power; plenary speaker USSR Symposium on Environment, 1970. Contbr. articles to profl. jours. Served with M.C. U.S. Army, 1951-54. NSF fellow, 1962-63; NSF-NIH-ONR-AINA grantee, 1963-75. Mem. Am. Physiol. Soc., Am. Ecol. Soc., Am. Mammal Soc., Endocrine Soc., Nebr. Acad. Sci., Soc. Exptl. Biology and Medicine, Explorers Club, Sigma Xi. Office: 2500 California St Omaha NE 68178

ANDREWS, TIGE (TIGER ANDREWS), actor; b. Bklyn., Mar. 19, 1920; s. George Elias Damian and Selma (Shaleesh) A.; m. Norma Nadine Thornton, Dec. 28, 1950; children: Barbara, Gina, John,

Steven, Juli, Anthony. Student, Am. Acad. Dramatic Arts, N.Y.C. Appeared in: Broadway plays Hidden Horizon; appeared off-Broadway: Three Penny Opera; appeared: in films Last Tycoon; appeared on: TV series Sgt. Bilko; as Gander: Mod Squad; Oil painter; sculptor. Served to lt. inf. U.S. Army, World War II; MTO. Mem. Screen Actors Guild, Writers Guild West, AFTRA. Democrat. Greek Orthodox. Office: Talent Mgmt Internat Wilshire Blvd Los Angeles CA

ANDREWS, WAYNE, author, art history educator; b. Kenilworth, Ill., Sept. 5, 1913; s. Emory Cobb and Helen (Armstrong) A.; m. Elizabeth A. Hodges, June 12, 1948; 1 dau., Elizabeth Waties. A.B., Harvard U., 1936; Ph.D., Columbia U., 1956. Curator manuscripts N.Y. Hist. Soc., 1948-56; editor Charles Scribner's Sons, 1956-63; Archives of Am. Art prof. Wayne State U., 1964-84; Phi Beta Kappa vis. lectr., 1975-76. Author: The Vanderbilt Legend, 1941, Battle for Chicago, 1946, Architecture, Ambition and Americans, 1955, rev. edit., 1978, Architecture in America, 1960, rev. edit., 1977, Germaine: A Portrait of Madame de Staël, 1963, Architecture in Michigan, 1967, rev. edit., 1982, Architecture in Chicago and Mid-America, 1968, Architecture in New York, 1969, Siegfried's Curse: The German Journey from Nietzsche to Hesse, 1972, Architecture in New England, 1973, American Gothic, 1975, Pride of the South-A Social History of Southern Architecture, 1979, Voltaire, 1981; pseudonym Montagu O'Reilly: Who Has Been Tampering With These Pianos, 1948; editor: Concise Dictionary of American History, 1962, Best Short Stories of Edith Wharton, 1957. Co-trustee Joseph and Robert Cornell Meml. Found., 1982. Mem. Société Chateaubriand (Paris). Home: 521 Neff Rd Grosse Pointe MI 48230

ANDREWS, WILLIAM COOKE, physician; b. Norfolk, Va., June 7, 1924; s. Charles James and Jean Curry (Cooke) A.; m. Elizabeth Wight Kyle, Nov. 10, 1951; children—Elizabeth Randolph, William Cooke, Susan Carrington. A.A., Princeton U., 1946; M.D., Johns Hopkins U., 1947. Diplomate: Am. Bd. Obstetrics and Gynecology. Intern N.Y. Hosp., 1947, resident in obstetrics and gynecology, 1948-50, 52-53; practice medicine specializing in obstetrics and gynecology, Norfolk, Va., 1953—; asst. in obstetrics and gynecology Cornell U. Med. Sch., 1948-50, 52-53; mem. attending staff Med. Center Hosp.; mem. vis. staff DePaul Hosp.; prof. obstetrics and gynecology Eastern Va. Med. Sch., Norfolk, 1975—, pres. faculty senate, 1976-77. Contbr. articles in field to profl. jours. Chmn. Bicentennial Commn., City of Norfolk, 1969-71; commr. Community Facilities Commn., 1971-73, chmn., 1973—; bd. dirs. Va. League for Planned Parenthood, 1966-68; pres. Norfolk chpt. Planned Parenthood, 1966-68. Served with M.C. USN, 1950-52. Named Hon. Officer of the Most Excellent Order of the Brit. Empire Queen Elizabeth II, 1967. Fellow Am. Coll. Obstetricians and Gynecologists, Am. Assn. Obstetricians and Gynecologists; mem. Am. Fertility Soc. (dir. 1970-73, pres. 1977), Med. Soc. Va., Norfolk Acad. Medicine, Va., Tidewater obstet. and gynecol. socs., Continental Gynecol. Soc., So. Med. Assn., AMA, South Atlantic Assn. Obstetricians and Gynecologists, Norfolk C. of C. (chmn. armed forces com. 1966-68, v.p. 1968-69, pres. 1970), Internat. Fedn. Fertility Socs. (asst. treas. 1974—), Navy League U.S. (pres. Hampton Roads council 1968-70, nat. dir. 1970-74), English Speaking Union U.S. (pres. Norfolk-Portsmouth br. 1964-66), Planned Parenthood Fedn. Am. (cons. nat. med. com. 1975—). Presbyterian. Club: Norfolk Yacht and Country (commodore 1966). Home: 929 Graydon Ave Norfolk VA 23507 Office: 903 Medical Tower Norfolk VA 23507

ANDREWS, WILLIAM FREDERICK, manufacturing executive; b. Easton, Pa., Oct. 7, 1931; s. William Frederick and Lydia Nielson (Cross) A.; m. Carol Beaman, Feb. 8, 1962; children: William Frederick III, Whitney, Carter, Clayton, Sloane. B.S., U. Md., 1953; M.B.A., Seton Hall U., 1961. Product mgr. Scovill Mfg. Co., Waterbury, Conn., 1965-68, v.p., gen. mgr., Raleigh, N.C., 1968-73, group v.p., Nashville, 1973-79, pres., Waterbury, 1979-81, chmn., 1981—; chmn., pres., chief exec. officer Scovill Inc.; dir. Sybron Corp., MCM Corp., So. New Eng. Telephone Co., Bank of Boston. Bd. dirs. St. Margarets-Meterhan Sch., Westover Sch., ARC, Litchfield Jr. Republic, YMCA, Mattatuck Mus., Am. Indian Archeol. Inst., Waterbury Hosp. Served with USAF, 1953-56. Recipient Silver Beaver award Boy Scouts Am., 1979. Mem. Machinery Allied Products Inst. (dir., exec. com.), Nat. Fluid Power Assn. (past pres.), Internat. C. of C. (trustee), Waterbury C. of C. (chmn.), NAM (dir.). Republican. Episcopalian. Clubs: Bellemeade Country (Nashville); Waterbury, Waterbury Country, Litchfield Country. Office: Scovill Sq Waterbury CT 06720

ANDREWS, WILLIAM GEORGE, political science educator; b. Windsor, Colo., Aug. 5, 1930; s. Nathan Edwin and Ellen (Samson) A.; (div.)children: Donna Ellen, William George, Jennifer Louise, Edwin Bartilon; m. Monika Wickert; children—Christopher Scott, Thomas Nathan. B.A., Colo. State U., 1952; C.E.P., U. Bordeaux, France, 1955; Ph.D., Cornell U., 1959. Instr., asst. prof. Dartmouth Coll., 1958-61; asst. prof., asso. prof. govt. Tufts U., 1961-67; research asso. Inst. Polit. Studies, U. Paris; also prof. Am. Coll. in Paris and Inst. Am. Studies, Paris, 1962-63; prof. polit. sci. State U. N.Y. at Brockport, 1967—, chmn. dept., 1967-71, dean social scis., 1970-76, dean liberal studies, 1976-79, faculty exchange scholar, 1976—; dir. social scis. program in Paris, 1983-85; propr. Challenger Press, 1944-45, 69—. Author or editor: American National Political Institutions, 1962, French Politics and Algeria, 1962, European Political Institutions, 2d edit, 1966, Soviet Institutions and Policies, 1966, European Politics I, 1966, Politics and Civil Liberties in Europe, 1967, Constitutions and Constitutionalism, 3d edit, 1968, European Politics II, 1969, Politics of International Crises, 1969, Coordinate Magistrates, 1969, The Politics of Coups d'etat, 1969, The Fifth Republic at Twenty, 1981, Internat. Handbook of Polit. Sci, 1982, Presidential Government in Gaullist France, 1982; also numerous articles; gen. editor: series New Perspectives in Political Science, 1960—. Served to 1st lt. USAF, 1952-54. Fulbright fellow, 1954-55, 62-63; Nat. Endowment for Humanities sr. fellow, 1973-74, summer 1983. Mem. Conf. Group French Politics and Soc. (exec. sec. 1977-78, exec. com. 1978—), Am. Polit. Sci. Assn., N.Y. Polit. Sci. Assn. (exec. com. 1968-69), Internat. Polit. Sci. Assn. Republican. Lutheran. Home: 46 College St Brockport NY 14420

ANDREWS, WILLIAM L., professional football player; b. Thomasville, Ga., Dec. 25, 1955; m. Lydia Andrews; 1 son, Andy. Attended, Auburn U. Running back Atlanta Falcons, NFL, 1979—. Player in NFL Pro Bowl, 1980-82; mem. UPI All Rookie Team, 1979. Office: Atlanta Falcons 185 and Suwanee Rd Suwanee GA 30174 *

ANDREWS, WILLIAM STUART, lawyer; b. Phoenix, Aug. 20, 1927; s. Lloyd J. and Francie (Webb) A.; children—Lloyd James III, William Stuart, Chester D., Teresa Lee, Julie Ann, Elizabeth Francie. Student, Phoenix Coll., 1945-48; LL.B., J.D., U. Ariz., 1952. Bar: Ariz. bar 1952. Since practiced in, Phoenix; mem. firm Andrews, Marenda & Moseley (and predecessor firms), 1958—; dep. Maricopa County atty., 1952-57, asst. atty. gen., Ariz., 1959. Chmn. Maricopa County Bd. Suprs., 1966. Served with USNR, 1946-48. Mem. Am. Bar Assn., Ariz. Bar Assn. (past bd. govs.), Maricopa County Bar Assn. (past dir.), Sigma Alpha Epsilon, Phi Delta Phi. Democrat. Office: 1432 N 7th St Phoenix AZ 85006

ANDRIAN, GUSTAVE WILLIAM, foreign language and literature educator; b. Hartford, Conn., Sept. 17, 1918; s. William and Alexandra (Perakos) A.; m. Margaret Ann Penfield, Aug. 18, 1951; children: Robert, Barbara, William. B.A., Trinity Coll., Hartford, 1940; Ph.D, Johns Hopkins U., 1946. Instr. Army Specialized Tng. Program, U. Md., 1943-44; asst. prof. Spanish and French U. Md.-College Park, 1945-46; asst. prof. Spanish Trinity Coll., Hartford, 1946-53, assoc. prof., 1953-62, prof., 1962—; editorial cons. The Macmillan Co., N.Y.C., 1968-75. Author and editor: Fondo y Forma, 1970; editor: Modern Spanish Prose and Poetry, 1964, Modern Spanish Prose and Poetry, 2d edit., 1969, Modern Spanish Prose and Poetry, 3d edit., 1977. Mem. MLA, Am. Assn. Tchrs. Spanish and Portuguese, AAUP. Home: 94 Midwell Rd Wethersfield CT 06109 Office: Trinity College 300 Summit St Hartford Ct 06106

ANDRINGA, CALVIN BRUCE, investment banker; b. Omro, Wis., Mar. 2, 1941; s. Cornelius and Bessie Irene (McKenzie) A.; m. Patricia Ann Perkins, July 7, 1968; children—Deborah Rene, Gordon Michael, Katherine Beth. B.B.A., U. Wis., 1963, J.D., 1966. Tax accountant Arthur Andersen & Co.; treas. Wausau Paper Mills Co., Wis., 1968-70; v.p., treas. Marriott Corp., Washington, 1970-74; v.p. exec. planning Amtrak, Washington, 1975-76; sr. v.p. fin. and adminstrn. United Nuclear Corp., Falls Church, Va., 1977-79; pres. Andringa & Co., Washington, 1979—; dir. Services Nat. Bank. Served to capt. U.S. Army, 1966-68. Decorated Army Commendation medal. Mem. Am., Wis. bar assns. Home: 9122 Kittery Ln Bethesda MD 20817 Office: 1220 19th St NW Suite 300 Washington DC 20036

ANDRIOLE, STEPHEN JOHN, info. systems exec.; b. Phila., Oct. 22, 1949; s. Frank Richard and Grace Marie A.; m. Denise Marie De Felice, Aug. 7, 1971. B.A. magna cum laude, LaSalle Coll., 1971; M.A., U. Md., 1973, Ph.D., 1974. NDEA research fellow U. Md., 1971-74, instr., 1974, asst. prof., 1975; research analyst Decisions and Designs, Inc., McLean, Va., 1975-76, project dir., 1975-76; program mgr. Def. Advanced Research Projects Agy., Dept. Def., Arlington, Va., 1977-78; dir. Cybernetics Tech. Office, 1977-79; pres. Internat. Info. Systems, Inc., 1979—; participant profl. panels and seminars; professorial lectr. applied nat. security analysis Sch. Advanced Internat. Studies, 1977-78. Contbr. articles to profl. publs.; reviewer: Internat. Studies Quar, 1974—; editorial bd., 1975—. Mem. Am. Polit. Sci. Assn., Internat. Studies Assn., Internat. Polit. Sci. Assn., Alpha Epsilon, Pi Sigma Alpha, Phi Kappa. Roman Catholic. *Tenacity is the real secret of "success" in a world where success has become increasingly hard to define and where persistence, then, becomes almost paramount.*

ANDROS, DEE G., univ. athletic adminstr.; m. Luella Thomas, Jan., 1949; 1 dau., Jeanna. M.A., U. Okla., 1952. Asst. coach Okla. State U., 1950-53; line coach Tex. Tech U., 1954-55, U. Nebr., 1956, U. Calif., Berkeley, 1957, 58, 59, Ill. State U., 1960-61; head coach Idaho State U., 1962, 63, 64, Oreg. State U., Corvallis, 1965-75, athletic dir., 1975—. Served with USMC, 1942-46. Mem. Nat. Football Assn. (trustee), Nat. Athletic Dirs. Assn. Clubs: Masons, Shriners, Elks, Moose. Asst. coach Tex. Tech. U. Sun Bowl game, 1955, Rose Bowl game Calif. State U., 1959. Home: 715 Elizabeth Dr Corvallis OR 97330 Office: Dept Athletics Oregon State U Corvallis OR 97331 *

ANDRUS, CECIL D., former secretary interior; b. Hood River, Oreg., Aug. 25, 1931; s. Hal Stephen and Dorothy (Johnson) A.; m. Carol Mae May, Aug. 27, 1949; children—Tana Lee, Tracy Sue, Kelly Kay. Student, Oreg. State U., 1948-49. State gen. mgr. Paul Revere Life Ins. Co., 1969-70; gov. State of Idaho, 1971-77; sec. of interior, 1977-81; dir. Bekar Industries Corp., 1981—, Gold Fields Am. Corp., 1982-84, Environ. Testing and Certification Corp., 1981-84; Mem. Idaho Senate, 1961-66, 69-70; Mem. exec. com. Nat. Gov.'s Conf., 1971-72, chmn., 1976, Fedn. Rocky Mountain States, 1971-72. Served with USNR, 1951-55. Mem. V.F.W., Idaho Taxpayers Assn. (dir. 1964-66). Democrat. Address: 1280 Candleridge Dr Boise ID 83712

ANDRUS, GERALD LOUIS, utilities holding co. cons.; b. Crowley, La., Nov. 15, 1904; s. Charles D. and Rosa C. (Ramoin) A.; m. Lucile G. Isacks, Apr. 22, 1930; 1 dau., Marion. B.B.A., Tulane U., 1928. C.P.A., La. With New Orleans Pub. Service, Inc., 1928-62, comptroller, 1947-52, v.p., 1952-59, pres., 1959-62, dir., 1959-75; pres. Middle South Utilities, Inc., N.Y.C., 1962-70, chmn. bd., chief exec. officer, 1970-72, chmn. bd., 1972-74, dir., 1960-74, cons. to mgmt., 1974—; pres., dir. Middle South Services, Inc., New Orleans, 1963-70, chmn. bd., chief exec. officer, 1970-72; dir. New Orleans br. Fed. Res. Bank of Atlanta, 1959-61, chmn., 1960; Mem. Bd. City Trusts, 1954-62. Chmn. finance United Fund Drive, 1954; Adv. mem. bd. adminstrs. Tulane U., past vice chmn. bd. adminstrs., chmn. presdl. search com., 1974-75. Clubs: New Orleans Country (pres. 1959-60), Boston (pres. 1967-68), Stratford (New Orleans); Racquet and Tennis, Links (N.Y.C.). King of New Orleans Mardi Gras, 1960. Home: 1309 Nashville Ave New Orleans LA 70115 Office: 225 Baronne St Suite 1704 New Orleans LA 70112

ANDUJAR, JOHN J., physician; b. Chgo., Jan. 26, 1912; s. M.A. and Lily (Kurzenknabe) A.; m. Elizabeth Richards, Aug. 16, 1935; children: Betty Jo, Linda Lee. B.S., Pa. State U., 1930; M.D., Temple U., 1934; postgrad., Union U., 1935-36, Cornell U., 1942. Diplomate: Nat. Bd. Med. Examiners, Am. Bd. Pathology (past pres.). Intern Harrisburg (Pa.) Gen. Hosp., 1934-35; Meml. Hosp., N.Y.C., 1942-43, Bender Hygienic Lab., Albany, N.Y., 1935-36; assoc. prof. U. Ark., 1937-38; practice medicine, Ft. Worth, 1938—; prof. med. technology Tex. Christian U., 1938-50; dir. Ft. Worth Med. Labs., Ft. Worth Dept. Health Labs., Tex. Dept. Health Regional Labs.; cons. pathologist USPHS, John Peter Smith hosps., Carswell AFB Sta. Hosp.; Past pres. Tarrant County Crime Commn., Am. Pathology Found.; past pres. World Pathology Found. Fellow Am. Soc. Clin. Pathologists (past pres.), ACP, Coll. Am. Pathologists (founder); mem. AAAS, AMA, Am. Assn. Blood Banks (founder), Am. Assn. Phys. and Surg., Am. Cancer Soc., Soc. Am. Bacteriologists, Pan-Am. Med. Assn., Tex. Acad. Internal Medicine, Assn. Mil. Surgeons U.S., Internat. Acad. Pathology, Am. Pub. Health Assn., Tex. Acad. Sci., Tex. Hosp. Assn., Tex. Pub. Health Assn., Tex. Soc. Pathologists (past pres.), Tarrant County Med. Soc. (past pres.), Internat. Council Soc. Pathology, Royal Soc. Health, World Assn. Soc. Pathology (pres. 1969-72), Tarrant County Mental Health Soc., Phi Beta Pi. Presbyterian. Clubs: Fort Worth Boat, Peninsula Country, Torch. Address: PO Box 1118 Fort Worth TX 76101

ANFINSEN, CHRISTIAN BOEHMER, biochemist; b. Monessen, Pa., Mar. 26, 1916; s. Christian Boehmer and Sophie (Rasmussen) A.; m. Florence Bernice Kenenger, Nov. 29, 1941; children: Carol Bernice, Margot Sophie, Christian Boehmer; m. Libby Shulman Ely, 1979. B.A., Swarthmore Coll., 1937, D.Sc., 1965; M.S., U. Pa., 1939, D.Sc., 1967; Ph.D., Harvard U., 1943; D.Sc. (hon.), Georgetown U., 1967, Swarthmore Coll., 1965, N.Y. Med. Coll., 1969, Gustav Adolphus U., 1975, Brandeis U., 1977, Providence Coll., 1978, M.D., U. Naples, 1981. Am.-Scandinavian Found. fellow Carlsberg Lab., Copenhagen, 1939; sr. cancer research fellow Nobel Inst., Stockholm, 1947; Markle scholar, 1948—; asst. prof. biol. chemistry Harvard U. Med. Sch.; prof. biochemistry Harvard Med. Sch., 1962-63; Guggenheim fellow Weizmann Inst., Rehovot, Israel, 1958; chief lab. cellular physiology and metabolism Nat. Heart Inst., Bethesda, Md., 1950-62; chief lab. chem. biology Nat. Inst. Arthritis and Metabolic Diseases, Bethesda, 1963-82; mem. faculty dept. biology Johns Hopkins U., Balt., 1982—; Bd. govs. Weizmann Inst. Sci., Rehovot, Israel. Author: The Molecular Basis of Evolution, 1959; Contbr. to sci. publs. Recipient Rockefeller Public Service award, 1954-55; Nobel prize in chemistry, 1972; Myrtle Wreath Hadassah, 1977. Mem. Am. Soc. Biol. Chemists (pres. 1971-72), Am. Acad. Arts and Scis., Am. Philos. Soc., Nat. Acad. Scis., Washington Acad. Scis., Fedn. Am. Scientists (treas. 1958-59, vice chmn. 1959-60, 73-76), Pontifical Acad. Sci. Home: 1740 Vineyard Trail Epping Forest Annapolis MD Office: Dept Biology Johns Hopkins U. 34th and Charles St Baltimore MD 21218

ANGEL, GROVER LAMARR, emeritus education educator; b. Mars Hill, N.C., July 2, 1909; s. Samuel W. and Sue (Gardner) A.; m. Mary Nell English, Dec. 27, 1937; 1 dau., Carolyn Sue (dec.). A.B., High Point Coll., 1929; M.A., George Washington U., 1946, Ed. D., 1952; spl. student, U. N.C., summer 1930, Northwestern U., summer 1950. Tchr. English, sci. Denton (N.C.) High Sch., 1929-31; tchr. English. Spring Creek (N.C.) High Sch., 1931-35; tchr. sci. Beech Glen (N.C.) High Sch., 1935-37; head English dept. Marshall (N.C.) High Sch., 1937-39; prin. Hot Springs (N.C.) High Sch., 1939-42; corr. Asheville (N.C.) Citizen-Times, 1931-42; spl. investigator Dun & Bradstreet, Inc., Washington, 1942-44, mgr., 1944-46; cons. Office of Naval Research, Navy Dept., 1946; employment adviser sci. personnel div. Navy Dept. and Naval Research Lab., 1946-47; research assoc. Am. Council on Edn., 1947-50; asst. to dean Coll. Gen. Studies, George Washington U., 1950-51, asst. dir. off-campus div., 1951-53, dir., 1954-56, asst. dean, 1956-57, dean, 1957-66, lectr. edn. Sch. Edn., 1950-55, professorial lectr. edn., 1955-57, asso. prof. edn., 1957-59, prof., 1959-74, prof. emeritus, 1974—; Lectr. edn. Am. Council Edn., Internat. House, 1954-55; Mem. Naval Labs. Adv. Com. on Sci. Personnel, 1946-50; pres. Washington chpt. Nat. Cystic Fibrosis Research Found., 1959-61, 65-67, pres. region IV, 1960-62, nat. trustee, 1962-79, hon. trustee, 1979-82, nat. v.p., 1971-75, chmn. nat. bd. trustees, 1973-77, hon. trustee N.C. chpt., 1962—; mem. steering com. Tng. Officers Conf., Washington, 1960-62; U.S. del. World Congress U. Adult Edn., Denmark, 1965, Anglo-Am. Adult Edn. Conf., Oxford, Eng., 1965; mem. Spl. Adult Edn. Survey Team, Yugoslavia, 1965, UNESCO study team, Paris, 1965; U.S. del. Higher Edn. Convocation, Libya, 1974. Author: Poetry in Contemporary American Poets, 1937-38, Teacher Application Forms, 1946, The Management of Internal School Finance, 1952. Pres. Greater Ivy Communities Citizens Assn., Madison County, N.C., 1975-79, Madison County Arts Council, 1975-77; mem. Madison County Recreation Commn., 1975—, chmn., 1978—; chmn. Madison County Library Bd., 1975—; secondary rep. Madison County, Land-of-Sky Regional B, Council of Govts., 1977-78; mem. Western N.C. Tomorrow Com., 1980—; bd. visitors High Point Coll., 1983—. Recipient Alumnus of Yr. award High Point Coll., 1957; Alumni Service award George Washington U., 1975; awards Phi Delta Kappa, 1954, Wisdom Soc., 1970, Naval Grad. Dental Sch., 1974, Nat. Naval Med. Center, 1974, D.C. chpt. Cystic Fibrosis, 1974, Higher Edn. Assn. of George Washington U., 1973, 74, Adult Edn. Assn., Washington, 1974, Western N.C. Community Devel. Assn., 1975, 78; named Man of Year Greater Ivy and Madison County, N.C., 1975, 78; Man of Yr. award Western N.C. Community Devel. Assn., 1978; nat. service award Cystic Fibrosis Found., 1979; N.C. Gov's Sr. Citizen award for volunteerism, 1981. Mem. AAAS, Am. Edn. Research Assn., Nat. Vocational Guidance Assn., Am. Assn. Higher Edn., Am. Assn. Profs. Higher Edn., Assn. U. Evening Colls. (pres. region 5 1963), Nat. U. Extension Assn., Adult Edn. Assn. U.S.A., Soc. Advancement Mgmt., Soc. Personnel Adminstrn., NEA, N.C. Edn. Assn., AAUP, Fed. Schoolmen's Club, Jr. Order of United Am. Mechanics, Phi Delta Kappa (chpt. pres. 1953-54, area coordinator dist. VI 1955-58, faculty sponsor George Washington U. 1955-75, faculty sponsor emeritus 1975—), Alpha Sigma Lambda (faculty sponsor George Washington U. 1965), Epsilon Eta Phi. Democrat. Methodist (adminstrv. bd. Mars Hill Ch. 1977-81, chmn. 1979-81, layreader 1981—). Clubs: Mason (32 deg., Shriner), Lion.). Home: California Creek Rd Route 3 Mars Hill NC 28754 also 3602 34th Avenue Dr W Cortez Villas Bradenton FL 33505

ANGEL, JAMES ROGER PRIOR, astronomer; b. St. Helens, Eng., Feb. 7, 1941; came to U.S., 1967; s. James Lee and Joan (Prior) A.; m. Ellinor M. Goonan, Aug. 21, 1965; children—Jennifer, James. B.A., Oxford (Eng.) U., 1963, D.Phil., 1967; M.S., Calif. Inst. Tech., 1966. From research asso. to asso. prof. physics Columbia U., 1967-74; vis. asso. prof. astronomy U. Tex., Austin, 1974; mem. faculty U. Ariz., Tucson, 1974—, prof. astronomy, 1975—. Sloan fellow, 1970-74. Mem. Am. Astron. Soc. (Pierce prize 1976). Research on white dwarf stars, quasars, astron. instruments. Office: Steward Obs Univ Ariz Tucson AZ 85721

ANGEL, RIFKA, painter; b. Kalvaria, Sept. 16, 1899; U.S., 1913, naturalized, 1927; d. Raphael and Esther Blume (Estherson) A.; m. Milton Warren Douthat, June, 1929; 1 dau., Blossom Margaret Douthat. Student, Art Students League, 1926-27. One-man shows include, Knoedler Gallery, Chgo., 1929, 30, Carl Fisher Gallery, N.Y.C., 1936, Findlay Gallery, N.Y.C., 1937, 38, ACA Gallery, N.Y.C., 1947, Van Diemen-Lillienfeld Galleries, 1954, De Aenille Gallery, N.Y.C., 1959, Park Ave. Gallery, 1963, group shows include, Art Inst. Chgo., 1933, Whitney Mus. Am. Art, 1934, Mus. Modern Art, 1933, Bklyn. Mus., 1936; represented in permanent collections, Art Inst. Chgo., Honolulu Acad. Fine Arts, William Rockhill Nelson Art Gallery, Kansas City, Mo., Mary Atkins Mus. Fine Arts, Kansas City, Mo., Brandeis U.; Works in encaustic medium. Recipient award Chgo. Art Inst., 1934, Am. Fedn. Art, 1948, City Mus., St. Louis, 1943. Fellow Internat. Inst. Arts and Letters; mem. Artist Equity Assn. N.Y. *My approach to painting is spontaneous, emotional. I feel that there is in my work an art of balance plus a bit of laughter—pure and unreserved.*

ANGELAKOS, DIOGENES JAMES, electrical engineering educator; b. Chgo., July 3, 1919; s. James and Georgia A.; m. Helen Hatzilambrou, Dec. 29, 1946 (dec.); children: Erica, Demetri (dec.). B.S., U. Notre Dame, 1942; M.S., Harvard U., 1946, Ph.D., 1950. Engr., Westinghouse Electric Co., 1942-43; instr. U. Notre Dame, 1943-46; teaching fellow Cruft Labs., Harvard U., 1947-49, research asst. at univ., 1949-50; asst. prof. U. Notre Dame, 1950-51; mem. elec. engrng. and computer scis. dept. U. Calif.-Berkeley, 1951—, prof., 1960—, dir. Electronics Research Lab., 1964—, vice chmn. dept., 1964—; liaison scientist Office Naval Research, Am. embassy, London, 1961-62. Author: (with T.E. Everhart) Microwave Communications, 1968; also numerous articles. Guggenheim fellow, 1957-58; recipient Axion award Hellenic Am. Profl. Soc. Calif. Fellow IEEE; mem. Sigma Xi, Eta Kappa Nu, Tau Beta Pi. Home: 978 Euclid Ave Berkeley CA 94708

ANGELAKOS, EVANGELOS THEODOROU, physician, physiologist, pharmacologist, educator; b. Tripolis, Greece, July 15, 1929; came to U.S., 1948, naturalized, 1966; s. Theodore A. and Aglaia (Tsiverioti) A.; m. Eleanor Pell, Aug. 28, 1954; 1 son, Theodore. Student, Athens (Greece) U., 1947-48, Cornell U., 1950-51; M.A., Boston U., 1953, Ph.D., 1956; M.D., Harvard, 1959. Mem. faculty Boston U. Sch. Medicine, 1955-68, prof. physiology, 1963-68; prof., chmn. dept. physiology and biophysics Hahnemann U. Sch. Medicine, Phila., 1968-82, interim dean, 1982—; chmn. adv. com. biomed. research inst. Center for Research and Advanced Studies, U. Maine, Portland, 1971—; research assoc. biomath. MIT, 1959-60; vis. scientist Karolinska Inst., Stockholm, 1962-63; cons. U.S. Army Labs. Environ. Medicine, Natick, Mass., 1964—, NASA Electronics Research Center, Cambridge, Mass., 1966-68; Trustee, sec. bd. Hahnemann Med. Coll.

and Hosp., Phila., 1977-81. Contbr. articles to sci. jours. and textbooks. Med. Found. Research fellow, 1959-60; USPHS Research and Career Devel. grantee, 1960-68. Home: 602 Washington Sq Philadelphia PA 19106 Office: Hahnemann U Office of Dean MS 440 Philadelphia PA 19102

ANGELL, CHARLES AUSTEN, physical chemist; b. Canberra, Australia, Dec. 14, 1933; came to U.S., 1964; s. Herbert Raleigh and Kate Rosalind A.; m. Iris Violeta Burgos, June 22, 1958; children: Charles Austen, Sonia Yris, Sandra Jenine. B.Sc. in Chemistry, Melbourne U., 1954, M.Sc., 1956; Ph.D., D.I.C., Imperial Coll. Sci., U. London, 1961. Lectr. U. Melbourne, 1962-64; research asso. Argonne (Ill.) Nat. Lab., 1964-66; mem. faculty Purdue U., 1966, prof. chemistry, 1971—; chmn. (Gordon Research Conf.), 1977, 80. Co-author: Glass: Structure by Spectroscopy, 1976; Editorial adv. bd.: Jour. Phys. Chemistry, 1974-82. Recipient Sigma Xi Faculty Research award Purdue U., 1977. Mem. Am. Chem. Soc., Am. Ceramic Soc., AAAS, AAUP. Office: Dept Chemistry Purdue U West Lafayette IN 47907

ANGELL, JAMES BROWNE, engineering educator; b. S.I., N.Y., Dec. 25, 1924; s. Robert Corson and Jessie (Browne) A.; m. Elizabeth Isabelle Rice, July 22, 1950; children—Charles Lawrence, Carolyn Corson. S.B., S.M., MIT, 1946, Sc.D. in Elec. Engring, 1952. Research asst. MIT, 1946-51; mgr. solid-state circuit research, research div. Philco Corp., Phila., 1951-60; mem. faculty Stanford U., 1960—, prof. elec. engring., 1962—, dir., 1964-71, assoc. dept. chmn., 1970—; cons. to industry and govt., 1960—; Mem. electronics adv. group for comdg. gen. U.S. Army Electronics Command, 1964-74; mem. U.S. Army Sci. Adv. Panel, 1968-74; Carillonneur Stanford, 1960—. Author sect. book. Area chmn. town incorporation com. Portola Valley, Calif., 1963-64; Bd. dirs. Portola Valley Assn., 1964-67. Fellow IEEE (chmn. internat solid state circuits conf. 1964); mem. Am. Guild Organists, Guild Carillonneurs in N. Am. (dir. 1969-75, rec. sec. 1970-75), Am. Assn. U. Profs. Home: 30 Shoshone Pl Portola Valley CA 94025 Office: Dept Electrical Engring Stanford CA 94305

ANGELL, RICHARD BRADSHAW, philosophy educator; b. Scarsdale, N.Y., Oct. 14, 1918; s. Stephen LeRoy and Alice (Angel) A.; m. Imogene Lucille Baker, June 4, 1949; children: John Baker, Paul McLean, James Bigelow, David Bradshaw, Kathryn Elizabeth. B.A., Swarthmore Coll., 1940; M. Govt. Adminstrn., U. Pa., 1948; M.A. in Philosophy, Harvard U., 1948, Ph.D., 1954. Acting asst. prof. Fla. State U., 1949-51; asst. prof. Ohio Wesleyan U., 1954-58, asso. prof., 1958-63, prof., 1963-68; chmn. philosophy dept. Wayne State U., 1968-73, 76-78, prof., 1968—. Author: Reasoning and Logic. Chmn. bd. trustees Friends Sch., Detroit, 1978-80, 81-82. Served to capt. Med. Adminstrv. Corps AUS, 1942-45. Mem. AAUP, Am. Philos. Assn., ACLU., Mem. Soc. of Friends. Office: Dept Philosophy Wayne State U 791 Mackenzie Hall Detroit MI 48202

ANGELL, ROGER, writer, editor; b. N.Y.C., Sept. 19, 1920; s. Ernest and Katharine Shepley (Sergeant) A.; m. Evelyn Ames Baker, Oct. 1942 (div. 1963); children—Caroline S., Alice; m. Carol Rogge, Oct. 1963; 1 son, John Henry. Grad., Pomfret Sch., 1938; A.B., Harvard, 1942. Editor, writer: Mag. X, Curtis Pub. Co., 1946-47; sr. editor: Holiday mag, 1947-56; fiction editor, gen. contbr.: New Yorker mag, N.Y.C., 1956—; Author: The Stone Arbor, 1961, A Day in the Life of Roger Angell, 1971, The Summer Game, 1972, Five Seasons, 1977, Late Innings, 1982. Past com. mem. New York Civil Liberties Union. Served with USAAF, 1942-46; PTO. Recipient George Polk award for commentary, 1981. Mem. Authors Guild (nat. council, v.p.), Authors League (nat. council), P.E.N. Clubs: Century Assn., Coffee House. Home: 1261 Madison Ave New York NY 10028 Office: 25 W 43d St New York NY 10036

ANGELO, FRANK, newspaperman; b. Detroit, Sept. 6, 1914; s. Nicolo and Ida (Dugini) A.; m. Elizabeth Paton Stoll, Feb. 25, 1950; children—Frank, Andrew. B.A., Wayne State U., 1934, D.H.L. (hon.), 1978. From copy boy to copy reader sports dept. Detroit News, 1934-41; sports writer, copy reader, feature editor Detroit Free Press, 1941-52, asst. to exec. editor, 1952-55, mng. editor, 1955-71, asso. exec. editor, 1971-81; ret., 1981. Mem. AP Mng. Editors (past nat. exec. bd.), Mich. AP Assn. (pres. 1967), Mich. Press Assn. (pres. 1969), Mackenzie Honor Soc., Sigma Delta Chi (pres. Detroit 1956-57, nat. pres. 1969-70).

ANGELOU, MAYA, author; b. St. Louis, Apr. 4, 1928; d. Bailey and Vivian (Baxter) Johnson; 1 son, Guy Johnson. Author: I Know Why the Caged Bird Sings, 1970, Just Give Me A Cool Drink of Water 'Fore I Die, 1971, Georgia, Georgia, 1972, Gather Together in My Name, 1974, Oh Pray My Wings Are Gonna Fit Me Well, 1975, Singin' and Swingin' and Gettin' Merry Like Christmas, 1976, And Still I Rise, 1976; appeared on: TV in The Richard Pryor Special?; in ltd. series Roots. Named Woman of Yr. in Communications, 1976. Office: care Dave Le Camera Lordly and Dame Inc 51 Church St Boston MA 02116

ANGER, KENNETH, film maker, author; b. Santa Monica, Calif., 1932. Producer, dir.: films Escape Episode, 1946, Fireworks, 1947, Puce Moment, 1949, Eaux d'Artifice, 1953, Inauguration of the Pleasure Dome, 1954, Thelema Abbey, 1955, Scorpio Rising, 1962-64, Kustom Kar Kommandos, 1965, Invocation of My Demon Brother (Lucifer Rising), 1969, Rabbit's Moon, 1971; others; author: Hollywood Babylon, 1959. Ford Found. fellow, 1964. Address: care American Fedn Arts Film Program 41 E 65th St New York NY 10021 *

ANGEVINE, GEORGE BRAUD, steel co. exec.; b. Newark, June 26, 1918; s. Lewis James and Eugenia Marie (Braud) A.; m. Margaret Muse Collin, Apr. 3, 1976; children by previous marriage—Paula Angevine Craig, Sheryl, Katherine A. Leith, Barbara. B.A., Rutgers U., 1940; LL.B., U. Pitts., 1948. Bar: Pa. bar 1948. Mgr. labor relations West Penn Power Co., Pitts., 1948-56; partner firm Thorp, Reed & Armstrong, Pitts., 1956-63; v.p., gen. counsel, sec. Nat. Steel Corp., Pitts., 1963—, now vice chmn. Bd. dirs. Allegheny Trails council Boy Scouts Am., Pitts; trustee Chatham Coll., Pitts. Served with USAAF, 1942-46. Decorated D.F.C., Air medal. Mem. Am. Iron and Steel Inst., Am., Pa., Mich., Allegheny County bar assns., Pa. Soc. Presbyterian (deacon). Clubs: Duquesne (Pitts.); Allegheny Country (Sewickley, Pa.); Edgeworth (Pa.); Rolling Rock (Ligonier, Pa.); Bath and Tennis (Palm Beach, Fla.). Home: 625 Pine Rd Sewickley PA 15143 Office: 2800 Grant Bldg Pittsburgh PA 15219

ANGLE, JOHN CHARLES, life insurance company executive; b. N.Y.C., Aug. 22, 1923; s. Everett Edward and Catharine Elizabeth (Dodge) A.; m. Catherine Anne Sellers, Oct. 4, 1945; children: Margaret Susan, James Sellers. S.B., U. Chgo., 1944. With Union Nat. Life Ins. Co., Lincoln, Nebr., 1948-51; v.p., actuary Woodmen Accident and Life Co., Lincoln, 1953-73, dir., 1969-73; sr. v.p., chief actuary Guardian Life Ins. Co. Am., N.Y.C., 1973-77, exec. v.p., 1977-80, pres., 1980—, also dir.; dir. Guardian Ins. & Annuity Co., Guardian Park Ave. Fund, Guardian Cash Fund, Guardian Investor Services Corp. Contbr. chpts. to books; cons. editor: Life and Health Insurance Handbook, 2d edit, 1964. Pres. Lincoln Community Chest, 1965, Lincoln Community Council, 1966-68; bd. dirs. Lincoln Gen. Hosp., 1970-73. Served to 1st lt. USAAF, 1943-46; to capt. USAF, 1951-52. Fellow Soc. Actuaries (dir. publs. 1975-79); mem. Am. Acad. Actuaries (dir. 1977-79), Internat. Actuarial Assn. (sec. and nat. corr. U.S. sect.). Office: 201 Park Ave S New York NY 10003

ANGLE, JOHN EDWIN, lawyer; b. Springfield, Ill., June 19, 1931; s. Paul McClelland and Vesta (Magee) A.; m. Shona Lederman, Aug. 15, 1959; children: Brad, Jennifer, Susan. B.A., Brown U., 1953; J.D., Northwestern U., 1956. Bar: Ill. 1956. Assoc. Davis, Boyden, Jones & Baer, Chgo., 1957-59; ptnr. Kirkland & Ellis, Chgo., 1961—. Bd. dirs. Legal Aid Bur., Chgo., 1979—; mem. Caucus Nominating com. Village of Glencoe, Ill., 1979-80, mem. Bd. Zoning Appeals, Ill., 1981. Served with U.S. Army, 1957-58, 60. Mem. ABA, Ill. State Bar Assn. Club: Tavern (Chgo.). Home: 1664 N Orchard St Chicago IL 60614 Office: Kirkland & Ellis 200 E Randolph Dr Chicago IL 60601

ANGLEMIRE, KENNETH NORTON, retired publishing company executive, writer, environmentalist; b. Chgo.; s. Fred Rutherford and Isabel (Alguire) A.; m. Anne Hayes. (dec.). Student, Northwestern U.; B.S., U. Ill., Urbana; LL.B., J.D., Chgo.-Kent Coll. Law, Ill. Inst. Tech. Bar: Ill. bar. Pvt. practice of law, to 1936; atty. Chgo. Title and Trust Co., 1936-42; chief acct., office mgr. Graphic Arts Displays, Inc., Chgo., 1942-50; comptroller Marshall Industries, Chgo., 1950-53, Marquis-Who's Who, Inc., 1953-59, v.p., 1958-59, exec. v.p., chief ops. officer, 1959-69, chmn. bd., pub., 1969-70; pres., dir. A.N. Marquis Co., Inc., Chgo., 1964-69; Mem. Ill. State Scholarship Commn., 1966-69; charter mem. Bus. Adv. Council, Chgo. Urban League; hon. mem. staff N.Mex. Atty. Gen., 1971-74; mem. Adult Edn. Council Greater Chgo., bd. dirs., 1968-70. Writer articles on music, natural history and conservation, mountain adventure. Mem. Ill. Audubon Soc. (v.p. fin., dir. 1961-65), Greater North Michigan Ave. Assn. (dir. 1966-70), Dickens Fellowship, Santa Fe Opera Guild, Internat. Alban-Berg Soc., Sangre de Cristo Audubon Soc. N.Mex. (founder, pres. 1972-73, dir. 1972-75), Friends of Santa Fe Public Library, Historic Santa Fe Found., Wilderness Study Com. N.Mex., Santa Fe Concert Assn., ACLU, Bus. Execs. Move for Peace in Viet Nam, Pi Kappa Alpha, Delta Theta Phi, Sierra Club (founder, chmn. Great Lakes chpt. 1959-61, 64-66, exec. com. 1959-69). Club: N.Mex. Mountain. *To be compassionate to all living things; to strive for the rich adventure of experience this good earth offers; and to contribute to protection of its precious environment, to peace, equality, and tolerance.*

ANGLIM, PHILIP, actor; b. San Francisco, Feb. 11, 1953. B.A., Yale U. Actor: (debut) Rosencrantz and Guildenstern, Yale Theatre, 1970, Southbury Playhouse, 1972, Cin. Playhouse in the Park, 1975-76, American Place, 1976, Berkshire Theatre, Stockbridge, Mass., 1977; N.Y. appearance Snow White, You're Gonna Be Alright, Jamie Boy, The Judgement, The Elephant Man; film All American Boy, 1970; TV appearance The Adams Chronicles, 1970, Tomorrow's Families, 1970. Recipient Drama Desk award for role in Elephant Man, Obie award for role in Elephant Man, Outer Circle Citic's award for role in Elephant Man, Theater World award for role in Elephant Man. Address: care William Morris Agy 1350 Ave of the Americas New York NY 10019 *

ANGOINE, HOWARD FRANCIS, editor; b. N.Y.C., Aug. 3, 1940; s. Charles Francis Angione and Genevieve Rita (McCarthy) A.; m. Maryann Allgaier, June 24, 1971; children: Charles Francis, Mary Christine, Kathleen Elizabeth. B.A. in History, Holy Cross Coll., 1962; M.A. in Internat. Relations, Clark U., 1966. Reporter, sci. writer Worcester Telegram, Mass., 1961-65; writer, day editor, sci. writer AP, Boston, 1965-69, editor, shift supr. Gen. Desk, N.Y.C., 1969-77; tech. editor N.Y. Times, 1977—; tchr. history St. John's Prep., Shrewsburg, Mass., 1964-65. Editor: AP Stylebook, 1977. Sec. Class of 1962 Holy Cross Coll., 1966-80. Mem. Holy Cross Alumni Assn. (dir), Harris Users Group (pres. 1980—). Roman Catholic. Home: 80-47 192d St Jamaica NY 11423 Office: NY Times 229 W 43d St New York NY 10036

ANGRESS, RUTH KLUGER, German educator, editor; b. Vienna, Austria, Oct. 30, 1931; came to U.S., 1947, naturalized, 1952; d. Viktor and Alma (Gredinger) Kluger Hirschel; m. Werner T. Angress, Mar. 1952 (div. 1962); children: Percy, Dan. B.A., Hunter Coll., N.Y.C., 1950; M.A., U. Calif.-Berkeley, 1952, Ph.D., 1967. Asst. prof. German lang. and lit. Case Western Res. U., 1966-70; assoc. prof. U. Kans., Lawrence, 1970-73, U. Va., Charlottesville, 1973-75, prof., 1975-76, U. Calif.-Irvine, 1976-80, Princeton U., 1980—; editor German Quar., 1976—. Author: The Early German Epigram; A Study in Baroque Poetry, 1971; contbr. articles to profl. jours. Am. Council Learned Socs. fellow, 1978. Mem. MLA (exec. council 1978-82), Am. Assn. Tchrs. German (exec. council 1976-81), Lessing Soc. (pres. 1977-79). Democrat. Jewish. Home: 177 Nassau St Princeton NJ 08540 Office: Dept German Princeton U Princeton NJ 08544

ANGRISANI, ALBERT, government official; b. Newark, Aug. 26, 1949; s. Frank and Lillian (Spagnola) A.; m. Caroline Purnell, June 24, 1972; 1 dau., Catherine Frances. B.A., Washington and Lee U., 1971; M.B.A., Fairleigh Dickinson U., 1974. Investment asst. Chase Manhattan Bank, N.Y.C., 1972-74, officer, 1974-77, asst. v.p., 1977-78, v.p., 1978-79; campaign dir. N.J. Reagan-Bush Com., 1979-80; asst. sec. of labor Dept. Labor, Washington, 1981—; dir. Nat. Consumer Coop. Bank, Washington.; Councilman Borough of Bernardsville, N.J., 1977-79, council pres., 1979-80; dir. Somerset County (N.J.) Governing Ofcl. Assn., 1978-80. Republican. Club: Kiwanis. Office: 200 Constitution Ave NW Washington DC 20210 *

ANGULO, MANUEL RAFAEL, lawyer; b. N.Y.C., Sept. 5, 1917; s. Charles and Ysabel (Piedra) A.; m. Carolyn Louise Bonin, Nov. 6, 1937; children: Charles B., M. Ralph; m. Diana Hutchins Rockwell, June 12, 1970. B.A., Yale U., 1939; LL.B., Harvard U., 1942; postgrad., Columbia U., 1952. Bar: N.Y. bar 1947. Practice in, N.Y.C., 1942-48, 61—; asso. Davis, Polk, Wardwell, Sunderland & Kiendl, 1942-48; attaché, econ. analyst Am. embassy, Santo Domingo, 1943-44; attaché embassy, Lisbon, Portugal, 1944-46; with OSS, London, 1944; gen. solicitor Creole Petroleum Corp., Caracas, Venezuela, 1948-54; partner Escritorio J.M. Travieso Paul, Caracas, 1954-61, Curtis, Mallet-Prevost, Colt & Mosle, N.Y.C., 1961—; lectr. Law Sch. U. Va., 1963-71. Contbr. profl. jours. Mem. council Boy Scouts Am., Venezuela, 1955-59; pres. N. Am. Assn. Venezuela, 1957-59. Mem. Am., Internat., Inter Am., N.Y. State, N.Y.C. bar assns., N.Y. County Lawyers Assn., Am. Fgn. Law Assn., Pan Am. Soc. U.S., Sigma Xi. Clubs: Yale, Union League, Broad Street, Metropolitan Opera (N.Y.C.); Metropolitan (Washington); Farmington Country (Charlottesville, Va.); Merion Cricket (Haverford, Pa.); Gulph Mills Golf (King of Prussia, Pa.). Home: 340 E 64th St New York NY 10021 Office: 101 Park Ave New York NY 10178

ANGUS, JOHN COTTON, chemical engineering educator; b. Grand Haven, Mich., Feb. 22, 1934; s. Francis Clark and Margaret (Cotton) A.; m. Caroline Helen Gezon, June 25, 1960; children—Lorraine Margaret, Charles Thomas. B.S. in Chem. Engring, U. Mich., 1956, M.S., 1958, Ph.D. in Engring, 1960. Registered profl. engr., Ohio, Mich. Research engr. Minn. Mining & Mfg. Co., St. Paul, 1960-63; prof. Case Inst. Tech., Cleve., 1963-67, prof. chem. engring., 1967—, chmn. dept., 1974-80; vis. lectr. U. Edinburgh, Scotland, 1972-73; vis. prof. Northwestern U., 1980-81. Vice pres. ARC, Inc.; trustee Ohio Coal Research Lab.; chmn. bd. trustees Ohio Scottish Games. NSF fellow, 1956-57; NATO sr. fellow, 1972-73. Mem. Am. Inst. Chem. Engrs., Am. Chem. Soc., Electrochem. Soc., Sigma Xi, Tau Beta Pi, Phi Lambda Upsilon. Research in fields of crystal growth, laser applications, coal gasification, sulfur removal processes, electrochemical devices, thermodynamics. Home: 2716 Colchester Rd Cleveland OH 44106 Office: Dept Chem Engring Case Western Res U Cleveland OH 44106

ANGUS, MICHAEL RICHARDSON, consumer goods company executive; b. Ashford, Kent, Eng., May 5, 1930; s. William Richardson and Doris Margaret (Breach) A.; m. Eileen Isabel May Elliott, Aug. 4, 1952; children—Barbara Jane Angus Johnson, Simon Richardson, Nicholas William. B.Sc. with honors, U. Bristol, 1951. With Unilever PLC, 1954—; mktg. dir. Thibaud Gibbs, Paris, 1962-65, mng. dir. research bur., 1965-67; sales dir. Lever Bros. U.K., 1967-70, coordinator toilet preparations, 1970-76, coordinator chems., 1976-77, head orgn. div., 1977-79, regional dir. N. Am., 1979—, dir., 1970—; now chmn. bd., chief exec. officer Lever Bros. Co., N.Y.C. and; Unilever U.S., Inc.; dir. Unilever N.V. Gov., Ashridge Mgmt. Coll. Served as officer RAF, 1951-54. Mem. Brit. Inst. Mgmt. (companion). Clubs: University, Economic, Knickerbocker (N.Y.C.). Office: Lever Bros Co 390 Park Ave New York NY 10022

ANISKOVICH, PAUL PETER, JR., insurance company executive; b. New Haven, June 18, 1936; s. Paul Peter and Helen Adele (Postemsky) A.; m. Carol Lacey, Apr. 27, 1957; children: Michael, Nancy, Gary, Peter. Student, Fairfield U., 1956-57, Quinnipiac Coll., 1957-58. C.L.U. Sales mgr. Met. Life Ins. Co., New Haven, 1958-63; regional mgr. Puritan Life Ins. Co., Providence, 1963-67; 2d v.p. Life Ins. Mktg. & Research Assoc., Hartford, Conn., 1968-73; 2d v.p. mktg. Acacia Mut. Life Ins. Co., Washington, 1973-76; pres., dir. Patriot Gen. Life Ins. Co., Concord, Mass., 1976-78; dir. Middlesex Ins. Co., Concord, 1976-78; spl. asst. to pres. State Mut. Life Assurance Co., Worcester, Mass., 1978-80; sr. v.p., chief mktg. officer Union Central Life Ins. Co., Cin., 1980—. Served with USMCR, 1954-56. Mem. Am. Soc. C.L.U.s, Nat. Assn. Life Underwriters. Republican. Roman Catholic. Club: Hyde Park Country (Cin.). Home: 1033 Rookwood Dr Cincinnati OH 45208 Office: Union Central Life Ins Co PO Box 179 Mill and Waycross Rds Cincinnati OH 45201

ANIXTER, ALAN B., electrical manufacturing company executive; b. Chgo., Il, July 25, 1920; s. Juliu B. and Zelda (Rogoff) A.; m. Gail Annenberg, Nov. 6, 1943; children: James, Scott. B.S. in Econs., U. Pa., 1941, M.B.A., 1943. With Webster-Chgo. Corp., 1941-43; ptnr. Telmor Engring. Co., Chgo., Il, 1943-46; v.p. sales R.I. Insulated Wire Co., Cranston, 1946-52; ptnr. Mfrs. Agy., Chgo., Il, 1953-57; pres. Anixter Bros., Inc., Skokie, Ill., 1957—; dir. Cregier Elec. Mfrs. Co., Mark Products, Royal Elec. Co., Turmac, Ltd. Clubs: Standard (Chgo.); Northmoor Country (Highland Park, Ill.). Home: 1111 Turicum Lake Forest Il 60045 Office: Anixter Bros Inc 4711 Golf Rd Skokie IL 60076

ANJARD, RONALD PAUL, SR., materials and processing specialist, author, educator, consultant; b. Chgo., July 31, 1935; s. Auguste L. and Florence M. (Byrne) A.; m. Marie B. Sampler; children: Ronald P., Michael P., Michele M., John R. B.S., Carnegie Mellon U., 1957; M.S., Purdue U., 1968; Asso. Sci., Ind. U., 1973; B.A., T.A. Edison Coll., 1979; postgrad., Butler U., 1962-63, Ind. U. Law Sch., Ivy Tech., 1975, La. State U., 1978, U. Calif., 1978; P.D.E., U. Wis., 1978; B.S. in Bus, SUNY, 1979; Ph.D. in Edn, Columbia Pacific U., 1980, Columbia Pacific U., 1981. Engr. U.S. Steel Corp., Braddock, Pa., 1956-57; metall. engr. Crucible Steel Co., Pitts., 1957-58; process engr. Raytheon Mfg. Co., Newton, Mass., 1958-59; sr. engr. Delco Electronics div. GM, Kokomo, Ind., 1959-81, quality control mgr. Avx. Materials Div., San Diego, 1981-82, div. quality mgr., Johnson Matthey Electronic Materials div., 1982-83, v.p. tech., 1982—; pres. Anjaro Tech. Cons., 1982—, Anjaro Solder Paste Tech., 1983; importer Anjard Imports, 1970—; instr. Ball State U., 1970-71, 75-76, Kokomo Apprentice Program, 1971-81, Ind. Vocat. Tech. Coll., 1978-81, Ala. A&M U., 1983, Chapman Coll., 1983—. Free-lance writer, 1973—; Editor: Solid State Technology. Pres. Greater Kokomo Assn. Chs., 1972-75; chmn. Diocesan Pastoral Council, Diocese Layfayette, Ind., 1977-78, diocesan ecumenical officer, 1972-78, diocesan impact coordinator, 1972—; mem. Ind. Council Chs., 1971—, Howard County (Ind.) Council, 1981; trustee Clayton Twp., 1970-75; dir. 5th dist. Ind. Twp. Trustees Assn.; chmn. Ind. State U. Young Republicans; mem. Ind. State Com. for Med. Assistance, Ind. Citizens Adv. Council on Alcoholism, Ind. Citizens Council on Addictions, Meshingomesia council Boy Scouts Am., Mayor's Human Rights Com.; chmn. Clay Twp. Bicentennial Com., 1974-76; mem. exec. com. Kokomo Bicentennial Com., 1974-76; govt. agys. chmn. Howard County Bicentennial Com., 1974-76; capt. capital fund drive Sangralea Valley Boys Home Campaign, 1968; active Ind. Council of Chs.; del. Rep. State Conv., 1970, 74, 78, 80, dep. registration officer, 1970, 72, 74, 76, 80; mem. Rep. Nat. Com., 1970-75; resolutions chmn. Young Reps. Conv., 1969; state minority chmn., dir. Howard County Young Reps.; regional dir. Leadership Tng. Sch.; chmn. 5th Dist. Young Reps.; bd. dirs. Drug Abuse Council, Howard County; bd. dirs., membership chmn. Mental Health Assn., Howard County, numerous other civic activities. Served to capt., Ordnance Corps U.S. Army, 1957-66. Recipient Ind. Mental Health citations, 1969, 70, Howard County Mental Health citations, 1969, 70, Nat. Young Rep. Hard Charger award, 1970, Gen. Motors Community Service award, 1970, Jaycee Distinguished Service award, 1970, Distinguished Service award Ind. Young Reps., 1971, Layman of Year award K.C., 1971, Ind. Mental Health award, 1971-72, Heart Fund award, 1973, Ind. Gov.'s Vol. Action commendation, 1975, 78, award Greater Kokomo Council of Chs., 1975; named Outstanding Ind. Young Rep., 1970; fellow Harry S. Truman Library, 1974—. Mem. Internat. Soc. for Hybrid Microelectronics (Midwest regional dir., charter state pres., treas., v.p., publicity chmn., program chmn. 1970—, mem., San Diege chpt. officer 1981); Mem. Semicondr. Materials Soc., Am. Soc. Quality Control (editor non-periodic publs., electronics div.), Am. Soc. Metals, Am. Bar Assn., Internat Electronics Packaging Soc. (San Diego chpt officer, liaison coordinator 1983—), ASTM (chmn. subcoms. 1963-68), Am. Inst. Mining and Metall. Engrs., Am. Ceramics Soc. (San Diego chpt. officer, liaison officer 1981—), Kokomo Engring. Soc., Internat. Platform Assn.; mem. Internat. Brich Collector's Assn. (pres. 1983—); Mem. Am. Indian Assn., Ind. Chess Assn., Nat. Hist. Soc., Ind. Hist. Soc., Howard County Hist. Soc. (bd. dirs.), Tippecanoe County Hist. Assn., Found. Ill. Archeology, Epigraphic Soc., Nat., Fla., Clearwater Audubon socs., N.Am. Acad. Ecumenists, Soc. Investigation of Unexplained, Ancient Astronaut Soc.; mem. Internat. Assn. for the investigation of ancient civizations (dir. 1980—); Mem. Internat. UFO Registry, Kokomo Fine Arts Assn., Nat. Wilderness Soc., Whitewater Valley R.R. Assn., Kokomo Mgmt. Club (auditor 1970), Am. Hort. Soc., Nat. Greentown Glass Assn., San Diego Hist. Soc., San Diego Zool. Soc., Sigma Xi, also numerous others. Clubs: Kokomo Photo Guild, Ind. Chess, Donora Sportsman, Sycamore Racquet, Kokomo Rose Soc., Kokomo Astronomy, Kokomo Poetry, Kokomo Swim. Home: 10942 Montego Dr San Diego CA 92124 *It is important that we consider the real reason for our existence and then direct our spirit, our mind, our energies, our talents accordingly. The summation of all things is not God; it is Man's limited perception of God.*

ANKA, PAUL, singer, composer; b. Ottawa, Ont., Can., July 30, 1941; came to U.S., 1959; s. Andrew and Camilia (Tannis) A.; m. Anne de Zogheb, Feb. 16, 1963; 5 children. Ed. pub. schs., Ottawa. Propr.

Spanka Music Corp., 1958—, Flanka Music Corp., 1958—, Camy Prodns., Inc., 1961-66. Appeared maj. cities, S.Am., Caribbean, Europe, U.S., 1956—; motion pictures include: (author title song) The Longest Day, 1961, Girl's Town, Look in Any Window; TV appearances include Ed Sullivan Show, Danny Thomas, Perry Como, Johnny Carson, Dean Martin, Hollywood Palace, Open Mind, Atlantic City U.S.A, Happy Birthday, America, 1976, Sinatra—The First Forty Years; appeared syndicated variety show, 1973; replacement in: Broadway musical What Makes Sammy Run?, 1954; appeared at, Copacabana, N.Y.C., Sands Hotel, Ceasar's Palace, Hilton Hotel, all Las Vegas, Caribe Hilton Hotel, San Juan, P.R., Paladium, London, Olympia, Paris, Uris, N.Y.C., Waldorf Astoria, N.Y.C.; participated: San Remo Music Festival, 1964; recs. include My Way, 1968, (You're) Having My Baby, 1974, One Man Woman/One Woman Man, 1974, I Don't Like To Sleep Alone, 1975, (I Believe) There's Nothing Stronger Than Our Love, 1975, Times of Your Life, 1975, Anytime (I'll Be There), 1976, Happier, 1976, My Best Friend's Wife, 1977, Everybody Ought To Be in Love, 1977, Both Sides of Love, Headlines; wrote: (with Bert Bacharach) score for film Together?, 1979; Composer: Diana, 1957, Crazy Love, Lonely Boy, 1959, Put Your Head on My Shoulder, 1959, Time to Cry, 1959, The Longest Day, 1962, Ogni Volta, 1964, Do I Love You, 1971, Tonight Show theme music; others; also compositions for other artists, including My Way for, Frank Sinatra and, She's A Lady for, Tom Jones. Club: Friars (N.Y.C.). Holder 15 gold records for million dollar world-wide sellers. Office: care Press Relations RCA Records 1133 Ave of Americas New York NY 10036 *

ANKER, SUZANNE CAROL, artist; b. N.Y.C., Aug. 6, 1946; 1 dau., Jocelyn. B.A., Bklyn. Coll.; M.F.A., U. Colo. Asst. prof. art Washington U. Sch. Fine Arts, St. Louis, 1976-79. Exhbns. include, St. Louis Art Mus., Denver Art Mus., Bradford Mus., Eng., 1976, Central Mus., Tokyo, 1977, Alvar Aalto Mus., Finland, Williams Coll. Mus. Art, 1978, Walker Art Center, Mpls., 1979, Richard Gray Gallery, Chgo., Pace Gallery, N.Y.C., Galleria Milano, Italy, 1980, Albright-Knox Gallery, Buffalo, Getler Pall Gallery, N.Y.C., Galleria Arte Verso, Italy, 1981, Nat. Mus. Modern Art, Japan, 1982, Hong Kong Mus. Art, Nat. Mus., Republic of Singapore, Terminal Art Show, N.Y.C., 1983, Bonnier Gallery, N.Y.C., Sunderland Arts Ctr., Eng., Kettle's Yard, Eng., Southampton Gallery, Eng., Nat. Collection Fine Arts, Smithsonian Inst.; represented in permanent collections, St. Louis Art Mus., Denver Art Mus., Williams Coll. Mus. Art. Address: 101 Wooster St New York NY 10012

ANLYAN, WILLIAM GEORGE, surgeon, university administrator; b. Alexandria, Egypt, Oct. 14, 1925; s. Arm and Emmeraude (Nazar) A.; children by previous marriage: William George, John Peter, Louise Barbra, Laura. B.S. magna cum laude, Yale, 1945, M.D., 1949; D.Sc. (hon.), Rush Med. Coll., 1973. Diplomate: Am. Bd. Surgery, Am. Bd. Thoracic Surgery. Intern, resident, instr., assoc. in surgery Duke Hosp., Durham, N.C., 1949-53, asst. prof. surgery, 1958-61, prof. surgery, 1961—; assoc. dean Sch. Medicine Duke, 1963, dean, 1964-69, v.p. health affairs, 1969—; dir. G.D. Searle & Co.; Chmn. Durham VA V.P.'s Com.; surg. cons. Durham VA Hosp.; Markle scholar med. sci., 1953-58; Chmn. regents Nat. Library Medicine, 1971-72; trustee N.C. Sch. Sci. and Math., 1978—. Editorial bd.: Pharos, 1968—. Recipient award for disting. achievement Modern Medicine, 1974; Gov.'s award for disting. meritorious service, 1978. Fellow A.C.S.; mem. AMA (adv. com. med. sci. 1972—), Soc. Univ. Surgeons, Soc. Vascular Surgery, Internat. Cardiovascular Soc., Soc. Clin. Surgery, Am. Heart Assn., Soc. Med. Adminstrs. (pres. 1983-85), Inst. Medicine of Nat. Acad. Sci., Council Deans (chmn. 1968-69), Coordinating Council Med. Edn. (chmn. 1973-74), So. Med. Assn., Surg. Biology Club II, Am., So. surg. assns., Halsted Soc., Allen O. Whipple Surg. Soc., Assn. Am. Med. Colls. (chmn. 1970-71, Abraham Flexner award 1980), Assn. Acad. Health Centers (pres. 1975), Phi Beta Kappa, Sigma Xi, Alpha Omega Alpha. Club: Rotarian. Home: 1516 Pinecrest Rd Durham NC 27705

ANNABLE, WELDON GRANT, manufacturing company executive; b. Evanston, Ill., Jan. 28, 1937; s. Weldon Grant and Julia (Howell) A.; m. Eleanor Jane Scott, June 26, 1960; children: David Ross, Susan Elizabeth. B.S., Purdue U., 1959; M.B.A., Harvard, 1965. Marketing cons. Booz, Allen & Hamilton, Inc., N.Y.C., 1964; mgr. spl. financial projects, controller Columbus (Ind.) ops., dir. product financial analysis Cummins Engine Co., Inc., 1965-68; div. controller Irwin Mgmt. Co., Columbus, 1968-69; v.p., controller Gen. Signal Corp., N.Y.C., 1969-71; exec. v.p. Whittaker Community Devel. Corp., 1971-73; pres. Edwards Co., Inc., Norwalk, Conn., 1973-76; dir. planning (packaging), dir. planning and control, mng. dir. bus. systems mgmt. Am. Can Co., Greenwich, Conn., 1976-82; asst. dir. SCM Corp., Stamford, Conn., 1982—; dir. G.A. Kleissler Co., Edison, N.J. Trustee United Presbyn. Found. Served to lt. C.E.C. USNR, 1959-63. Named Outstanding Young Am., 1970. Home: 104 Chestnut Hill Ln Stamford CT 06903 Office: 117 Prospect St Stamford CT 06901

ANNAN, DOUGLAS BRUCE, aerospace executive; b. Hamilton, Ont., Can., May 5, 1917; s. Oliver Stuart and Margaret Jane (Low) A.; m., Mar. 16, 1945; children: David, Richard. B.S. in Engring., Queen's U., Kingston, Ont., 1940. Profl. engr., Ont. Gen. mgr. spl. products div. de Havilland Aircraft Can., Ltd., Downsview, 1959-62, v.p. spl. products div., 1964-65, v.p. ops., 1965-78, sr. v.p., 1978—; pres. Sprague-TCC Can. Ltd., Toronto, 1962-64. Nat. chmn. Queen's U. Alumni Capital Programs, Kingston, 1970-75; trustee Queen's U., exec. audit, fund council com., 1972—. Served to group capt. RCAF, 1940-45. Recipient commendation King George VI, 1942, 43; decorated D.F.C., Air Force Cross; hon. a.d.c. Gov. Gen. Can., 1950-55. Mem. Assn. Profl. Engrs. Ont., Engring. Inst. Can., Can. Export Assn. (dir. Ottawa 1980—). Presbyterian. Clubs: Oakville; Faculty (Kingston). Lodge: Masons. Home: 153 Claxton Drr Oakville Blvd Downsview ON Canada M3K 1Y5 Office: de Havilland Aircraft Can Ltd Garratt Blvd Downsview ON Canada M3K 1Y5

ANNEAR, PAUL RICHARD, emeritus educator; b. Cedar Rapids, Iowa, Jan. 19, 1915; s. Richard Floyd and Hortense Beatrice (Camp) A.; m. Elizabeth Jane Barkley, Sept. 2, 1939; children—Sandra Sue (Mrs. Robert McMillan Thompson), Marcia Louise (Mrs. Kenneth Eugene Beery), Craig Barkley. B.A. in Astronomy, Drake U., 1936; M.S., Case Inst. Tech., 1938; Ph.D., U. Mich., 1949. Instr. physics, astronomy Hunter Coll., 1940-41; prof. dept. math. and astronomy Baldwin-Wallace Coll., Berea, Ohio, 1941-80, prof. emeritus, 1980—; head dept., 1942-71; Data reduction analyst RCA Missile Test Project, Patrick AFB, Fla., summers 1957, 58, NASA Lewis Research Center, Cleve., 1959, Goodyear Aerospace Corp., Akron, Ohio, 1966. Councilman, Berea, 1956-60. Mem. Cleve. Astron. Soc., Am. Contract Bridge League, Phi Beta Kappa. Club: Oakwood Tennis (Strongsville, Ohio). Home: 66 Barberry Dr Berea OH 44017

ANNEKEN, WILLIAM BERNARD, manufacturing company executive; b. Erlanger, Ky., June 9, 1933; s. William Herman and Ann Catherine (Domaschko) A.; m. Carol Marie Menke, Aug.21, 1954; children: William G., Steven M., James G., Cynthia M., Lisa M. B.S. in Bus. Adminstrn. magna cum laude, Xavier U., 1960, M.B.A., 1964. With Palm Beach Inc., Cin., 1963—, treas., 1972-75, exec. v.p. fin., 1975—, also dir. Served with AUS, 1953-55. Mem. Xavier U. Alumni Assn. (past pres.), Fin. Execs. Inst., Am. Mgmt. Assn., Nat. Assn. Credit Men. Republican. Roman Catholic. Clubs: N.Y. Athletic, U. Cin. Office: 400 Pike St Cincinnati OH 45202

ANNENBERG, WALTER H., publishing company executive, former ambassador; b. Milw., 1908; m. Veronica Dunkelman (div.); 1 dau., Wallis; m. Leonore Cohn. Ed., The Peddie Sch., Wharton Sch., U. Pa.,; D.Journalism, Mt. Sinai Med. Coll., Temple U.; L.H.D., Widener Coll.; LL.D., La Salle Coll., U. Pa., Dropsie Coll., U. So. Calif., 1977; L.H.D., Albert Einstein Coll. Medicine, Elizabethtown Coll., Coll. Podiatric Medicine, Phila., 1977, U. Notre Dame. Pres. Triangle Publs., Inc., Phila., Seventeen Mag., TV Guide, Daily Racing Form; former U.S. ambassador to, Great Britain and No. Ireland.; Pres. M.L. Annenberg Found., Annenberg Fund; founder, pres. Annenberg Sch. Communications, Grad. Sch. U. Pa., U. S.C. Trustee Dermatology Found., Met. Mus. Art, United Fund Phila. Area, U. Pa., Nat. Trust for Historic Preservation; trustee-at-large Found. for Ind. Colls., Inc.; bd. dirs., trustee emeritus Eisenhower Med. Center, Rancho Mirage, Calif.; bd. govs. Acad. Food Mktg. of St. Joseph's Coll.; trustee emeritus Peddie Sch.; adv. bd. lay trustees Villanova U.; mem. Nat. Neiman Fund Com., Navy nat. com. Army-Navy Mus. Former comdr. USNR. Decorated officer French Legion of Honor; comdr. Order of the Lion Finland, Order of Crown of Italy, comdr. Order of Merit, Italy; knight comdr. Order Brit. Empire; recipient Russell H. Conwell award Temple U.; Gold medal award Freedoms Found.; Pa. Meritorious Service medal; Man of Year award Del. Valley Council, 1964; gold medal award Phila. Club of Printing House Craftsmen; Samuel S. Fels medal award, 1968; Ralph Lowell award Corp. Pub. Broadcasting, 1983. Fellow Pa. Acad. Fine Arts; mem. Navy League, Newcomen Soc., Alliance Francaise de Phila., Am. Soc. Newspaper Editors, Internat. Press Inst., Inter Am. Press Assn., Friars Sr. Soc., Cum Laude Soc., English-Speaking Union, Am. Swedish Hist. Found., Am. Newspaper Pubs. Assn., Explorers Club, Phi Sigma Delta, Sigma Delta Chi. Clubs: Rittenhouse, Racquet, Poor Richard, Faculty U. Pa. (Phila.); Tamarisk Country (Palm Springs); Lyford Cay (Nassau, Bahamas); Overseas Press (N.Y.C.); Nat. Press (Washington); Century Country (White Plains, N.Y.); White's (London); Swinley Forest (Ascot, Eng.); California (Los Angeles); Pilgrims; Castle Pines (Denver). Donor Walter H. Annenberg Library and The Masters' House to the Peddie Sch., Hightstown, N.J.

ANNESE, DOMENICO, landscape architect; b. N.Y.C., June 9, 1919; s. Fedele and Antonia (Angelini) A.; m. Serafina Villanova, July 16, 1944; children: Donald F., Loretta S. Student, SUNY Coll. Environ. Sci. and Forestry, 1942; B.S. in Landscape Architecture, Syracuse U., 1942. Registered landscape architect, N.Y., Pa., Conn., Mass., Ohio, Tenn. Landscape architect Clarence C. Combs, N.Y.C., 1946-50, asso., 1955-56; asst. chief landscape architect Nat. Capital Parks, Washington, 1950-55; asso. Clarke and Rapuano, Inc., N.Y.C., 1956-72, v.p., 1972—; vice chmn. N.Y. State Bd. Landscape Architects, 1961-67, chmn., 1967-71; mem. Pleasantville (N.Y.) Parks and Recreation Bd., 1974-83; adj. prof. urban landscape architecture Coll. City N.Y., 1975-76; vis. prof.-lectr. in landscape architecture Sch. Planning and Architecture, New Delhi, India, 1977; pres. Landscape Architecture Found. Served with Coast Arty., F.A. U.S. Army, 1941-46; ETO. Fellow Am. Soc. Landscape Architects; mem. Council Landscape Archtl. Registration Bds. (pres.). Lutheran. Home: 315 Bedford Rd Pleasantville NY 10570 Office: 215 Lexington Ave New York NY 10016

ANN-MARGRET (ANN-MARGRET OLSSON), actress, performer; b. Stockholm, Sweden, Apr. 28, 1941; came to U.S., naturalized, 1949; d. Gustav Olsson; m. Roger Smith, 1967. Student, Northwestern U. Performer radio shows, band tours; appeared with: George Burns, Las Vegas, 1961; headliner numerous appearances, Las Vegas, 1961—; actress: numerous films including Pocketful of Miracles, 1961, State Fair, 1961, Bye Bye Byrdie, 1962, Viva Las Vegas, 1963, The Pleasure Seekers, 1964, Kitten With a Whip, 1964, Bus Riley's Back in Town, 1964, Once A Thief, 1965, Stagecoach, 1966, The Swinger, 1966, Murderers' Row, 1967, The Tiger and the Pussycat, 1967, C.C. & Company, 1971, Carnal Knowledge, 1971, Train Robbers, 1972, Outside Man, 1972, Tommy, 1975, Joseph Andrews, 1976, The Last Remake of Beau Geste, 1977, Magic, 1978, The Cheap Detective, 1978, The Villain, 1979, Middle-Age Crazy, 1980, The Return of the Soldier, 1982, I Ought To Be in Pictures, 1982, Lookin' To Get Out, 1978; several TV spls., 1975-76; TV film A Streetcar Named Desire, 1984; Author: Exercises for the Tired Business Man. Address: care Press Relations Twentieth Century Fox Film Corp Box 900 Beverly Hills CA 90213 *

ANNO, JAMES NELSON, scientist; b. Niles, Ohio, Feb. 6, 1934; s. James Nelson and Opal Mae (Gentry) A.; m. Janet Winkel, June 12, 1955; children—James David, Sara Jennifer, Jefferson Nelson. B.S., Ohio State U., 1955, M.S., 1961, Ph.D., 1965. Technician Battelle Meml. Inst., Columbus, Ohio, 1953-55, supr. research reactor, 1955-60, asst. chief applied nuclear physics div., 1960-65, chief lubrication mechanics div., 1967-70; asso. prof. nuclear engring. U. Cin., 1970-73, prof., 1973—; pres. Research Dynamics, Inc., 1977—. Author: Encyclopedia of Draw Poker, 1973, (with J.A. Walowit) Modern Development in Lubrication Mechanics, 1975, Wave Mechanics for Engineers, 1976, Mechanics of Liquid Jets, 1977; contbr. articles to profl. jours. Recipient Civic award Columbus Jr. C. of C., 1961; honored by Saturday Evening Post, 1961. Mem. Am. Phys. Soc., Am. Nuclear Soc., Sigma Xi, Phi Beta Kappa, Sigma Pi Sigma. Club: Masons. Home: 5882 Ropes Dr Cincinnati OH 45244 Office: U Cin 509 Old Chemistry Bldg Cincinnati OH 45221

ANNUNZIO, FRANK, congressman; b. Chgo., Jan. 12, 1915; m. Angeline Alesia, Dec. 28, 1935; children: Jacqueline (Mrs. Frank Lato), Linda (Mrs. William O'Donnell), Susan (Mrs. Kevin Tynan). B.S., M.Ed., DePaul U. Asst. supr. Nat. Defense Training Program Austin Evening Sch., Chgo.; legislative, ednl. dir. United Steelworkers of Am., Chgo.; mem. 89th-98th congresses from Ill. 11th Dist.; chmn. consumer affairs and coinage subcom. of banking, fin. and urban affairs com., chmn. accounts subcom. of House adminstrn. com.; Dir. Ill. Dept. Labor; chmn. War Ration Bd. 40-20; mem. adv. com. on Unemployment Compensation; mem. adv. com. to Ill. Indsl. Commn. on Health and Safety; mem. adv. bd. Cook County (Ill.) Health and Survey; gen. chmn. Villa Scalabrini Devel. Fund; v.p., lay adv. bd. Villa Scalabrini Italian Old People's Home. Mem. Catholic Youth Orgn., K.C. (4 deg.). Office: Rayburn Bldg Washington DC 20515

ANNUS, JOHN AUGUSTUS, artist; b. Riga, Latvia, Oct. 25, 1935; emigrated to U.S., 1949; s. Augustus and Irma (Gustavs) A.; m. Edite Zeile, Oct. 18, 1981; 1 dau., Aurelia 1 dau., by previous marriage, Fabiola. B.F.A., Pratt Inst., 1958; postgrad., Art Students League, 1958-59, Nat. Acad. Design, 1958-59, Academia de Belli Arti, Rome, 1962-64. One-man shows, American Academy in Rome, 1960, Arte al Berge, Palermo, 1963, Architectural League, N.Y., 1965, Vendo Nubes, Phila., 1965, 70, 76, Galleria del Vantaggio, Rome, 1962, 71, 73, 74, Galerie Clasing, W. Ger., 1982, group shows, Spectrum 5, N.Y.C., 1972, 73, Skidmore Coll., N.Y.C., 1975, U. Pa., 1976, Nat. Acad. Design, 1958, 59, 64, 67, 68, 75, 80; represented permanent collections, Balt. Mus., 1975, Collection of the Italian Govt., 1962, Henry Ranger Fund, Nat. Acad. Design, 1975, Am. Acad. in Rome, 1982, Nat. Acad. Design Permanent Collection, 1982. Recipient Gold medal for oil painting "Labyrinth", 1962, Wallace Truman prize for oil painting "Agrigento", 1967, Ranger Pruchase prize for "By the Sea", 1965, Reflection, 1965, award of Excellence for "By the Sea", 1982; Nat. Acad. Design grantee Nat. Acad. Design, 1958-59; Albert Hallgarten traveling grantee, 1958-59; Prix de Rome Am. Acad. in Rome, 1959-60; Italian Govt. grantee, 1962—. Mem. Nat. Acad. Design, Soc. Fellows, Am. Acad. Rome, Nat. Soc. Mural Painters, others. Lutheran.

ANRIG, GREGORY RICHARD, educational testing company executive; b. Englewood, N.J., Nov. 18, 1931; (M. Charlotte Schlott), June 29, 1957; children: Greg, Susan, Christopher. A.B., Western Mich. U., 1953; M.A. in Teaching, Harvard U., 1956, Ed.D., 1963; D.H.L. (hon.), Northeastern U., 1978, D.L., Amherst Coll., 1978, D.Public Service, Simmons Coll., 1979, D.L., Williams Coll., 1982, D.H.L., Syracuse U., 1982. Tchr. history, asst. to prin. East View Jr. High Sch., White Plains, N.Y., 1956-60; prin. Battle Hill Elementary-Jr. High Sch., White Plains, 1960-64; supt. Mt. Greylock Regional Sch. Dist., Williamstown, Mass., 1964-67; dir. div. equal ednl. opportunities U.S. Office Edn., 1967-69; exec. asst. to U.S. commr. edn., 1969-70; dir. Inst. Learning and Teaching, U. Mass., Boston, 1970-73; commr. edn. Commonwealth of Mass., 1973-81; pres. Ednl. Testing Service, 1981—. Author numerous papers, reports. Served to 1st lt. AUS, 1953-55; Korea. Recipient Distinguished Service award White Plains C. of C., 1963; Superior Service award HEW, 1970; Friend of Edn. award Mass. Tchrs. Assn., 1978; Outstanding Educator award Mass. Jr. High/Middle Sch. Prins. Assn., 1980. Mem. Nat. Acad. Edn. Address: Ednl Testing Services Rosedale Rd Princeton NJ 08541

ANSARY, CYRUS A., lawyer, publisher, investor; b. Shoraz, Oram, Nov. 20, 1933; s. Adbul and Jamali (Mostmand) A.; m. Janet C. Hodges, Aug. 1, 1970; children: Douglas, Pary Ann, Jeffrey C., Bradley C. B.S., Am. U., 1955; LL.B., Columbia U., 1948. Bar: Md. 1959, D.C. 1960, Va. 1961. Practiced law, Washington, 1959-72; sr. ptnr. firm Ansary, Kirkpatrick and Rosse, 1964-72; chmn. bd. Industry Reports, Inc., Washington, 1960-72; organizer, 1st chmn. bd., pres. Woodland Nat. Bank, Alexandria, Va., 1963-67; lectr. Sch. Bus. Adminstrn., Am. U., 1967-71; chmn. bd. Fin. Dynamics Corp., Washington, 1967-72, Campbell Music Co., 1968-72, John L. Lindstrom and Assocs., Inc., 1962—, Freid, Krupp GmbH, Essen, W.Ger., 1974-79, Metalurgica Campo Limpo Ltda., Sao Paulo, Brazil, 1976-79; pres. IK Investment A.G., Zurich, Switzerland, 1974-79, Investment Services Internat. Co., Washington, 1973-83, Lambert Publs., Inc., 1978—; dir. Deutsche Babcock and Wilson, A.G., Oberhausen, W.Ger., 1975-79, 1st Am. Bank Md., Silver Springs, Washington Mut. Investors Fund, Potomac Asset Mgmt. Co., Washington, Accumetric, Inc., Elizabethtown, Ky. Trustee Am. U., 1968—, chmn. bd., 1982—; trustee Wolf Trap Found., Vienna, Va., 1978-81, Krupp Found., Esen, 1977-79, Washington Opera Soc., 1982—; pres. Ansary Found., Washington, 1983—. Served with USMCR, 1959-63. Mem. Washington Soc. Investment Analysts, Nat. Assn. Execs. Clubs: Nat. Press, Metropolitan (Washington); Congl. Country (Bethesda). Lodge: Rotary. Home: 1030 15th St NW Washington DC 20005

ANSBACHER, CHARLES ALEXANDER, conductor, musician; b. Providence, Oct. 5, 1942; s. Heinz L. and Rowena (Ripin) A.; m. 1 son, Henry Lloyd. B.A., Brown U., 1965; M.Music, U. Cin., 1968, D.M.A., 1979. Nat. adv. bd. Avery Fisher awards music, 1974—; mem. Colo. State Festival Council for Centennial-Bicentennial Commn., 1974-76; chmn. White House Fellows Regional Selection Com. Asst. condr., Kingsport (Tenn.) Symphony Orch., 1965-66; condr., mus. dir., Middletown (Ohio) Symphony Orch., 1967-70, Colorado Springs Symphony Orch., 1970—; music dir., Rockefeller Found., Apprentice Musicians Program, Cin. Playhouse in Park, 1967; guest condr., Cin. Symphony Orch., Denver Symphony Orch., Frysk Orkest in Leeuwarden, Holland; guest conductor, Indpls. Symphony, Omaha Symphony, Ft. Worth Symphony, San Diego Symphony, Seoul Philharm.; condr., music dir., Young Artists Orch. Denver, 1980-84. White House fellow, 1976-77. Mem. Urban League Pike's Peak Region (treas.), Pike's Peak Musicians Assn. (v.p. 1974-76), Condrs. Guild of Am. Symphony Orch. League (chmn. 1979-81), Am. Symphony Orch. League (dir. 1979-81), Colo. Council Arts and Humanities (1978-84), Music Educators Nat. Conf., World Affairs Council Colorado Springs (pres. 1980-84). Clubs: Rotary., El Paso. Home: 1431 N Tejon St Colorado Springs CO 80907 Office: Box 1692 Colorado Springs CO 80901

ANSCHUETZ, NORBERT LEE, international consultant; b. Leavenworth, Kans., May 16, 1915; s. Otto William and Irma (Hilpert) A.; m. Roberta Cook, Mar. 13, 1943; children—Carol Anschuetz Bosley, Ellen Anschuetz Lewis, Susan, Nancy Anschuetz Stahl. A.B., U. Kans., 1936; LL.B., Harvard, 1939; grad., Nat. War Coll., 1957, State Dept. Sr. Seminar, 1967. Bar: Mo. bar 1939. Practice in, Kansas City, Mo., 1939-41; with Dept. State, 1946-68, fgn. service officer, 1951-68; assigned successively to, Washington ahd, Athens, Greece, counselor in, Bangkok, 1954-56, minister-counselor, Cairo, 1958-62, Paris, 1962-64, Athens, 1964-67; rep. for Middle East and Africa First Nat. City Bank N.Y., Beirut, 1968-70; fgn. affairs rep. Citibank, N.Y.C., 1971-74, v.p. internat. relations, 1976-80; dir. Citicorp. Internat. Devel. Orgn., London, 1974-76; now internat. cons. Served to lt. col. AUS, 1941-46. Hon. citizen Athens, 1967. Mem. Council Fgn. Relations, Internat. Inst. Strategic Studies., Royal Inst. Internat. Affairs. Clubs: Bucks (London); Knickerbocker (N.Y.C.); Metropolitan (Washington). Home and office: 4918 Tilden St NW Washington DC 20016

ANSEL, HOWARD CARL, pharmacist, university dean; b. Cleve., Oct. 18, 1933; s. Alex Sandor and Celia A.; m. Suzanne Marie Klein, Aug. 14, 1960; children: Lori Sue, Michael Louis, Jeffrey Stephen. B.S., U. Toledo, 1955; M.S., U. Fla., 1957, Ph.D., 1959. Lic. pharmacist, Ohio, Ga., Fla. Asst. prof. pharmacy U. Toledo, 1959-62; asst. prof. pharmacy U. Ga., Athens, 1962-65, asso. prof., 1965-69, prof., 1969—; head dept. pharmacy, 1968-77; dean Coll. Pharmacy, 1977—; mem. adv. panel; OTC Antacids, FDA, 1972-73. Author: Introduction to Pharmaceutical Dosage Forms, 1981; co-author: Pharmaceutical Calculations, 7th edit, 1980. Fellow Am. Found. Pharm. Edn.; mem. Am. Pharm. Assn., Ga. Pharm. Assn., Acad. Pharm. Scis., Am. Assn. Colls. Pharmacy, Sigma Xi, Rho Chi, Phi Kappa Phi. Club: Rotary Internat. Home: 145 Mansfield Ct Athens GA 30606 Office: Coll Pharmacy U Ga Athens GA 30602

ANSELL, EDWARD ORIN, lawyer, university executive; b. Superior, Wis., Mar. 29, 1926; s. H. S. and Mollie (Rudnitzky) A.; m. Hanne B. Baer, Dec. 23, 1956; children: Deborah, William. B.S. in Elec. Engring, U. Wis., 1948; J.D., George Washington U., 1955. Bar: D.C. 1955, Calif. 1960. Electronic engr. FCC, Buffalo and Washington, 1948-55; patent atty. RCA, Princeton, N.J., 1955-57; gen. mgr. AeroChem. Research Labs., Princeton, 1957-58; patent atty. Aerojet-Gen. Corp., La Jolla, Calif., 1958-63, corp. patent counsel, 1963-82, asst. sec., 1970-79, sec., 1979-82; dir. patents and licensing Calif. Inst. Tech., 1982—; adj. prof. U. La Verne (Calif.) Coll. Law, 1972-78; Spl. adv., task force chmn. U.S. Commn. Govt. Procurement, 1971. Contbr. articles profl. publns. Recipient Alumni Service award George Washington U., 1979. Mem. Am. Bar Assn., Fed. Bar Assn., Am. Patent Law Assn., Assn. Corp. Patent Counsel, Assn. Coll. and Univ. Attys., Los Angeles Patent Law Assn., Licensing Execs. Soc., Soc. Univ. Patent Adminstrs., Patent, Trademark and Copyright Jour. (1971-76). Office: 1201 E California Blvd Pasadena CA 91125

ANSELL, GEORGE STEPHEN, metallurgist, educator; b. Akron, Ohio, Apr. 1, 1934; s. Frederick Jesse and Fanny (Soletsky) A.; m. Marjorie Boris, Dec. 18, 1960; children: Frederick Stuart, Laura Ruth,

Benjamin Jesse. B.Met.E., Rensselaer Poly. Inst., 1954; M.Met.E., 1955; Ph.D., 1960. Registered profl. engr., N.Y. State. Phys. metallurgist U.S. Naval Research Lab., Washington, 1957-58; faculty Rensselaer Poly. Inst., Troy, N.Y., 1960—, Robert W. Hunt prof. metall. engring., 1965—, chmn. materials div., 1969-74, dean engring., 1974—; Cons. to pvt. cos. Recipient Curtis W. McGraw award Am. Soc. for Engring. Edn., 1971. Fellow Am. Soc. for Metals (Alfred H. Geisler award Eastern N.Y. chpt. 1964, Bradley Stoughton award 1968), Metall. Soc.; mem. Am. Inst. Mining, Metall. and Petroleum Engrs. (Hardy Gold medal 1961, chmn. Inst. Metals div. 1974), Nat. Soc. Profl. Engrs., Sci. Research Soc. Am., Sigma Xi, Tau Beta Pi, Phi Lambda Upsilon. Research, publs. on theoretical and exptl. analysis of relationships between defect structure and properties of crystaline solids. Home: 6 Colonial Green Loudonville NY 12211 Office: Sch of Engring Rensselaer Poly Inst Troy NY 12181

ANSELME, JEAN-PIERRE LOUIS MARIE, chemist; b. Port-au-Prince, Haiti, Sept. 22, 1936; came to U.S., 1955, naturalized, 1960; s. Pierre F. and Jeanne (Kieffer) A.; m. Marie-Celine Carrie, Dec. 31, 1960; children—Fabiene, Veronika, Vanessa. B.A., St. Martial Coll., Haiti, 1955; B.S., Fordham U., 1959; Ph.D., Poly. Inst., Bklyn., 1963. Research asso. Poly. Inst. Bklyn., 1963, 65, sr. instr., 1965; NSF fellow Institut fur Organische Chemie, Munich, 1964; asst. prof. chemistry U. Mass. at Boston, 1965-68, asso. prof., 1968-70, prof., 1970—; pres. Organic Preparations and Procedures, Inc., Newton, Mass.; vis. prof. Research Inst. Indsl. Sci., Kyushu U., Fukuoka, Japan, 1972, U. Miami, Coral Gables, Fla., 1979. Author: (with others) Organic Compounds with Nitrogen-Nitrogen Bonds, 1966, N-Nitrosamines, 1979; founder, editor: Organic Preparations and Procedures, 1969-70, Organic Preparations and Procedures Internat, 1971—; contbr. articles to profl. jours. Recipient Seymour Shapiro award as outstanding grad. student organic chemistry Poly. Inst. Bklyn., 1963; Sloan fellow, 1969-71. Fellow Japan Soc. for Promotion Sci.; mem. Am. Chem. Soc., Chem. Soc. London, Sigma Xi, Phi Lambda Upsilon. Office: U Mass at Boston Dept Chemistry Harbor Campus Boston MA 02125

ANSELMO, ANTHONY G., retail stores executive; b. Michel, B.C., Can., Mar. 14, 1918. With Can. Safety Ltd., Calgary, Alta., pres., 1971—, mng. dir. Can. ops., 1978—, chief exec. officer, 1980—, chmn. bd., 1981—. V.p. Kainai Chieftainshop; exec. bd. dirs. Can. Council Christians and Jews, western region; bd. dirs. Jr. Achievement, Calgary; assoc. dir. Calgary Exhbn. and Stampede; mem. adv. bd. Stampedar Football Club; pres. McMahon Stadium Soc. Served to lt. RAF, 1940-45. Decorated Can. medal. Office: Can Safeway Ltd 535 10th Ave SW PO Box 864 Sta M Calgary AB Canada T2P 2T6 *

ANSHEN, MELVIN, educator; b. Boston, July 2, 1912; s. Zalkend and Fanny (Kogan) A.; m. Gertrude Lakson, Sept. 14, 1936. A.B., Harvard, 1933, M.B.A., 1935, D.C.S., 1940. Prof. Ind. U., 1937-51, Grad. Sch. Indsl. Adminstrn., Carnegie Inst. Tech., Pitts., 1951-62; prof. bus. Grad. Sch. Bus., Columbia, 1962—, Garrett prof. pub. policy and bus. responsibility, 1972—; dir. research coordination staff WPB, 1942-46; acting dep. adminstr. program and requirements Def. Prodn. Adminstrn., 1951; vis. lectr. bus. sch. Harvard, 1947; vis. prof. Stanford, 1950. Author: Wartime Production Controls, 1949, Modern Marketing, 1939, An Introduction to Business, 1942, Private Enterprise and Public Policy, 1953, Managing the Socially Responsible Corporation, 1974, Corporate Strategies for Social Performance, 1979. Mem. Am. Econ. Assn. Home: 205 West End Ave New York NY 10023

ANSON, RICHARD WILLIAM, army officer; b. Newburyport, Mass., Feb. 18, 1927; s. Paul E. and Dorothy A. (Wilmot) Wetzel; m. Mary L. Copeland, Apr. 12, 1958; 1 dau., Sandra D. B.S. in Econs., U. Calif., Berkeley, 1952; M.S. in Indsl. Engring, Ohio State U., 1962; grad., Army War Coll., 1969. Commd. 2d lt. U.S. Army, 1952, Advanced through grades to maj. gen., 1979; service in, Korea, Vietnam, Panama; dep. dir. force devel. and strategic plans and policy J-5, Orgn. Joint Chiefs Staff, Washington, 1976-77; comdr. 1933d Inf. Brigade, C.Z.; also comdr. U.S. Security Assistance Agy., Latin Am., 1977-79; dep. insp. gen. Dept. of Army, Washington, 1979-80; chief Army Force Modernization Office, Office Chief Staff, 1980—. Pres. C.Z. council Boy Scouts Am., 1977-79. Decorated Def. Superior Service medal, Legion of Merit, D.F.C., Bronze Star with V, Air medal, Army Commendation medal, Combat Inf. badge, Meritorious Service medal. Mem. Soc. 1st Inf. Div., Assn. U.S. Army. Democrat. Episcopalian. Home: 7404 Park Terrace Dr Alexandria VA 22307 Office: Room 301 Hdqrs LANDSOUTHEAST Izmir Turkey PO Box 6004 APO New York NY 09224

ANSPACH, ERNST, economist; b. Glogau, Germany, Feb. 4, 1913; came to U.S., 1936, naturalized, 1943; s. Hermann and Margarete (Gurassa) A.; m. Ruth Pietsch, Dec. 20, 1950; children: Paul David, Margaret Louise. Js.D., U. Freiburg, Berlin, Munich, Breslau, 1935; M.Sc., New Sch. Social Research, N.Y.C., 1943. With German jud. service, 1934-36; fin. analyst Loeb, Rhoades & Co., N.Y.C., 1936-43; reorgn. of adminstrn. Justice in, Bavaria and Hesse, 1946-49; gen. counsel and polit. adviser Dept. State, U.S. Land Commr. for Hesse, 1949-52; economist, gen. partner Loeb, Rhoades & Co., Investment Bankers, N.Y.C., 1952-77; chief economist, 1st v.p. Loeb Rhoades, Hornblower & Co., N.Y.C., 1978-79, cons., 1980—; tchr. adult edn. program Henry St. Settlement, N.Y.C., 1939-43; lectr. Univs. Munich, Marburg, Frankfurt, 1948-52; lectr. fields econs., polit. sci., theology and primitive art, 1955—. Contbr. articles to sci. jours.; collection African Tribal Art; exhibited, Mus. Primitive Art, N.Y.C., 1967-68. Trustee Bleuler Psychotherapy Center, 1953—, chmn. bd., 1956-65; trustee Nightingale-Bamford Sch., 1971-77; chmn. bd. trustees Madison Ave. Presbyterian Ch., 1975—; mem. vis. com. dept. primitive art Met. Mus. Art, N.Y.C. Served to capt. AUS, 1943-46. Recipient Army commendation ribbon. Mem. Nat. Assn. Bus. Economists, Conf. Bus. Economists. Club: Wall St. Home: 118 W 79th St New York NY 10024

ANSPACH, HERBERT KEPHART, appliance company executive; b. Ada, Ohio, Sept. 3, 1926; s. Eldred W. and Della (Kephart) A.; m. Elizabeth McKenzie, June 5, 1952; 1 dau., Heather. B.S. in Mech. Engring., U. Wis., 1947; J.D., U. Mich., 1952. Bar: Mich. 1953, Ohio 1953. Devel. engr. Goodyear Tire & Rubber Co., St. Mary's, Ohio, 1947-49; labor relations rep. Kaiser Motors, Willow Run, Mich., 1953, supr. indsl. relations, Shadyside, Ohio, 1953-54; patent examiner U.S. Dept. Commerce, Washington, 1954, patent atty., 1955-56, dir. patent sect., 1956-60, asst. sec., asst. gen. counsel, 1961-67, v.p. personnel, 1967-74; chmn. bd., chief exec. officer Inglis Ltd., Toronto, Ont., Can., 1975-77; pres., chief operating officer Whirlpool Corp., Benton Harbor, Mich., 1977-83; cons., 1983—. Served to ensign USNR, 1944-46. Clubs: Metropolitan, Union League (Chgo); Toronto; Point O' Woods (Benton Harbor).

ANSTATT, PETER JAN, marketing services company executive; b. Haworth, N.J., Feb. 9, 1942; s. Herman E. and Margaret (Dunham) A.; m. Jean Ann Sorchiotti, Aug. 13, 1966; children: Chirstopher Ryan, Holley Elizabeth. B.S. in Printing Mgmt., Carnegie Mellon U., 1963; grad. program for mgmt. devel., Harvard U. Bus. Sch., 1977. Estimator Einson Freeman Inc., N.Y.C., 1963, project mgr., 1965-66, account exec., Fairlawn, N.J., 1966-71, gen. mgr., Fairlawn, 1971-76, pres., chief exec. officer, 1977-78, chmn., chief exec. officer, Paramus, N.J., 1978—; v.p. ops. EAC Industires, Paramus, 1978. Mem. alumni bd. govs. Blair Acad., 1974-77; bd. dirs. Ridgewood YMCA, 1981—. Served with C.E. U.S. Army, 1963-65; Korea. Mem. Point of Purchase Advt. Inst. (chmn. trade ethics com. 1973-78, chmn. ann. exhibit com. 1979, dir. 1973-81, vice chmn. bd. 1979, chmn. 1980, speaker ann. industry seminar 1977-80), Beta Theta Pi (pres. 1962-63). Republican. Methodist. Home: 365 Annette Ct Wyckoff NJ 07481 Office: Einson Freeman Inc 299 Route 17 Paramus NJ 07652 *Undying belief in God, country and the free enterprise system. Adherence to the principles of respect, fairness, achievement through teamwork and happiness—with one's self, with what one does, and with interpersonal relationships.*

ANTHES, JACOB, elec. engr.; b. Germany, Oct. 11, 1920; came to U.S., 1924, naturalized, 1933; s. Phillip and Dorothea (Kuehn) A.; m. Johanna Charlotte Petzsche, Jan. 29, 1967; children—John, Richard, Susan, Thomas, James. Student, Marquette U., 1946-47. Inspector U.S. Govt. Civil Service, 1941-42; engr. Centralab div. Globe Union, Inc., Milw., 1946-49; owner-chief engr. Am. Research Lab., Ft. Atkinson, Wis., 1949-64; research dir. Electrocopy Corp., Phila., 1965-67; new product devel. engr. LaBelle Industries, Oconomowoc, Wis., 1967—; owner, new product designer Electro-Photo Products Co., Glidden, Wis. Served with Ordnance Dept. AUS, 1942-46; PTO. Republican. Lutheran. Patentee in field. Home: Lutz Rd Route 1 Glidden WI 54527 *To contribute to society all that my capabilities permit. To accept from society no more than my reasonable fair share.*

ANTHONY, BERYL F., JR., congressman; b. El Dorado, Ark., Feb. 21, 1938; s. Beryl F. and Oma Lee (Roark) A.; m. Sheila Foster, Aug. 4, 1962; children: Alison Roark, Lauren Foster. B.A., U. Ark., 1961, J.D., 1963. Bar: Ark. 1963. Asst. atty. gen., Ark., 1964-65, dep. pros. atty., Union County, Ark., 1966-70; pros. atty. 13th Jud. Dist., 1971-76; legal counsel Anthony Forest Products Co., 1977; individual practice law, 1977; mem. 96th-98 Congresses from 4th Ark. Dist.; dir., legal counsel Union Fidelity Savs. and Loan Assn. of El Dorado, 1977. Mem. Ark. Pros. Attys. Assn. (pres. 1975), Ark. Forestry Assn. (sec., dir. 1977), Union County Bar Assn., Ark. Bar Assn., Am. Bar Assn. Democrat. Episcopalian. Office: 1117 Longworth Office Bldg Washington DC 20515 *

ANTHONY, DONALD CHARLES, librarian; b. N.Y.C., Mar. 29, 1926; s. Charles and Margaret Evelyn (Gleason) A.; m. Mary Miserez, Apr. 18, 1957; children—Stephen, Sheila, Irene. B.A., U. Wis., 1951, M.A., 1954; postgrad., U. Geneva, Switzerland, 1952-53. Library asst. Enoch Pratt Free Library, Balt., 1954-55; librarian Eleutherian Mills-Hagley Found., Wilmington, Del., 1955-59; dir. Fargo (N.D.) Pub. Library, 1959-61; asso. librarian N.Y. State Library, Albany, 1961-66; asst. dir. Columbia Libraries, 1966-69, acting dir., 1969, asso. dir., 1970-74; dir. Syracuse U. Libraries, 1974—; cons. N.Y. State Edn. Dept., 1967—. Producer; host: TV Museum, KXGO-TV, Fargo, 1960; Contbr. articles to profl. jours. Trustee N.Y. Met. Reference and Research Library Agy., 1969-74; chmn. bd. dirs. Five Asso. U. Libraries, Syracuse, 1975-76, 77-79; trustee Bd. Edn., Dobbs Ferry, N.Y., 1971-74, v.p., 1973-74. Served with USNR, 1944-46. Fellow Council on Library Resources (1970); Mem. ALA, Soc. Am. Archivists. Home: 104 Westminster Ave Syracuse NY 13210 Office: Bird Library Syracuse U Syracuse NY 13210

ANTHONY, EARL RODERICK, professional bowler; b. Tacoma, Apr. 27, 1938; s. Earl Roderick and Laura Ellen (Davis) A.; married; children: Jeri Ann, Michael, Tracy. Student pub. schs., Tacoma. Profl. bowler, 1970-84. Author: Winning Bowling, 1977, Championship Bowling, 1983. Served with USAF, 1955-59. Named Bowler of Year Sporting News-Profl. Bowlers Assn., 1974-76, 81-83, Bowling Writers Assn., 1974, 75, 76, 81, 82, 83; recipient George Young Meml. award, 1973-75, 80, 83; AMF Grand Prix Bowling, 1976; named to Profl. Bowlers Assn. Hall of Fame, 1981, Male Bowler of Decade, 1971-80 Bowlers' Jour.; winner Seattle Open, 1970, 73, Mercury Cougar Open, 1971, Japan Star Lanes Open, 1972, Am. Airlines Open, 1972, Portland Open, 1972, Bowling Assn. Nat. tournament, 1973, 81, 82, 83, Firestone Tournament Champions, 1974, 78; Brunswick Profl. Bowling Assn. Nat. Championship, 1974, 75; Home Box Office Open, 1974; Canada Dry Open, 1974; Winston-Salem Invitational, 1974; L.I. Open, 1975, 79, 80, 81; Greater Los Angeles Open, 1975; Quad Cities Open, 1975; Jackson Open, 1975; Buzz Fazio Open, 1975, 76; Midas Open, 1976; AMF Dick Weber 5 Star Open, 1976; Fresno (Calif.) Open, 1974, 76; So. Calif. Open, 1976; Waukegan (Ill.) Open, 1975, 76, 77; Miller Lite Classic, 1977; AMF Magicscore Open, 1978, 81; ABC Masters Championship, 1977, 84; Rolaids Open, 1981; ARC Alameda Open, 1982; Miller High Life Classic, 1982; True Value Open, 1983. Mem. Profl. Bowlers Assn. Mem. All Am. Team, 1972-83; winner 41 Profl. Bowlers Assn. titles.

ANTHONY, EDWARD LOVELL, II, investments executive; b. Boston, Sept. 24, 1921; s. DeForest and Dorothy (Dodge) A.; m. Constance Foss, Oct. 2, 1954; children: Edward Lovell, Victoria Noble, Richard Geoffrey David. A.B., Harvard U., 1943, M.B.A., 1952; postgrad., Boston U., 1943. Asst. to pres. Daltry Opera Co., Middletown, Conn., 1938-40; asst. to headmaster Manter Hall Sch., Cambridge and Wianno, Mass., 1941; assoc. editor Pub. Affairs Press, Washington, 1945-46; asst. chief photog. intelligence tng. U.S. Navy, 1946-50; dir. publs SBA, 1952-62; editor Harvard Bus. Sch. Bull., Boston, 1962-80, Exec. Letter, 1964-70; prin. E.L. Anthony & Co., Cambridge, 1980—; treas., dir. Lomel Corp., 1979—. Editor: Management Aids for Small Business Annual, 5 vols., 1955-59, Equity Capital for Small Business, 1960. Vice chmn. Community Fund, Washington, 1960; trustee, pres. Dr. Franklin Perkins Sch., Lancaster, Mass.; trustee, treas. Pine Manor Coll., Chestnut Hill, Mass. Served with U.S. Army, 1942-45. Mem. Internat. Council for Small Bus., Council Advancement and Support Edn., English Speaking Union, Friends of Boston Symphony Orch., Nat. Assn. Retarded Citizens, Internat. Council Small Bus., Harvard Bus. Sch. Assn. Boston, Navy League U.S. (Boston council; life), USO Council New England (life), Nat. Free Lance Photog. Assn., Order of Lafayette. Episcopalian (vestryman, warden). Clubs: Country (Brookline, Mass.); Univ. (Washington); Harvard (Boston); (N.Y.C.); Hundred of Mass. Home: 68 Woodcliff Rd Wellesley Hills MA 02181 Office: E L Anthony & Co 50 Church St Cambridge MA 02138 *In my observation, the fortunes of an enterprise are linked to its people. Continuing success stems largely from cooperative efforts by people of competence, vision, probity, constancy to purpose, and a friendly welcoming attitude toward change. Lack of those qualities portends decline. No part of an organization exists solely to itself; the condition of every part affects the whole.*

ANTHONY, EDWARD MASON, linguistics educator; b. Cleve., Sept. 1, 1922; s. Edward Mason and Elsie (Haas) A.; m. Ann Louise Terbrueggen, Sept. 18, 1946; children: Lynn Diane Anthony Higgins, Janice Louise, Edward Mason. A.B., U. Mich., 1944, M.A., 1946, Ph.D., 1954. From instr. English to prof. linguistics U. Mich., 1945-64; prof. U. Pitts., 1964—, chmn. dept. gen. linguistics, 1964-74; dir. Lang. Acquisition Inst., 1970, dir. lang. orientation programs, 1974—, dir. Asian Studies program, 1977-82; vis. lectr., Afghanistan, 1951, Thailand, 1955-57, Mexico, 1964-65, Poland, 1977; dir. S.E. Asian English Project, Thailand, Laos, Vietnam, 1958-61, Rockefeller Found. Thai Project, 1967-72; vis. prof. Regional English Lang. Centre, Singapore, 1974-75, Peking Inst. Fgn. Lang., 1979-80; cons. in field; mem. Nat. Adv. Council Teaching English as a Fgn. Lang.; resource person Detroit Bd. Edn., 1964, Pitts. Bd. Edn., 1965; mem. adv. screening com. in linguistics Council for Internat. Exchange of Scholars, 1976. Author: Reading Thai Syllables, 1962, (with others) Foundations of Thai, 2 vols, 1968, Towards a Theory of Lexical Meaning, 1975; book rev. editor: Lan. Learning, 1948; editor, 1949. Smith- Mundt grantee, 1951; recipient Fulbright award, 1955-57; NDEA lang. Research grantee, 1965-67; State Dept. grantee, 1964, 65, 77. Mem. Linguistic Soc., Am. Assn. Applied Linguists, Assn. Asian Studies, Siam Soc. (life), Assn. Tchrs. English to Speakers of Other Langs. (pres. 1967), Nat. Council Tchrs. English. Democrat. Presbyterian. Home: 4118 Northampton Dr Allison Park PA 15101 Office: Dept Gen Linguistic U Pitts Pittsburgh PA 15260

ANTHONY, GUY MAULDIN, retail co. exec.; b. Cleveland, Okla., Apr. 26, 1915; s. Charles Ross and Lutie Lillian (Mauldin) A.; m. Christine Elizabeth Holland, Mar. 27, 1945; children—Charles Ross III, Guy Mauldin Jr., Robert Holland, Roy Jay, Jack Holland, Tom Albert. B.S., Wharton Sch., U. Pa., 1936. With C.R. Anthony Stores, Oklahoma City, 1936—, v.p., dir. personnel, 1942-72, pres., 1972-80, pres. emeritus, 1980—; dir. Liberty Nat. Bank, Oklahoma City, Mid Continent Casualty Co., Tulsa. Bd. dirs. Northside YMCA, Oklahoma City, Cassady Sch., Oklahoma City, Last Frontier council Boy Scouts Am.; Okla. state chmn. Employer Support for N.G. and Res. Served to capt. USAAF, World War II. Decorated Bronze Star with oak leaf cluster. Mem. Oklahoma City C. of C. (corp. dir.). Methodist. Club: Oklahoma City Rotary (pres.). Home: 6707 NW Grand Blvd Oklahoma City OK 73116 Office: PO Box 25725 Oklahoma City OK 73125

ANTHONY, HARRY ANTONIADES, city planner, educator; b. Skyros, Greece, July 28, 1922; came to U.S., 1951, naturalized, 1954; s. Anthony G. and Maria G. (Ftoulis) Antoniades; m. Anne C. Skoufis, Sept. 23, 1950; children: Mary Anne Anthony Smith, Kathryn Harriet. B.Arch., Nat. Tech. U., Athens, Greece, 1945; student, Ecole Nat. Supérieure des Beaux Arts, Paris, France, 1945-46; M.City Planning, U. Paris, 1947; Docteur d'Université, Sorbonne, Paris, 1949; Ph.D. in Arch. and Urban Planning, Columbia, 1955. Architect-planner with Constantinos A. Doxiadis, Athens, 1943-45, LeCorbusier, Paris, 1946-47, ECA, 1949-51; city planner with Maurice E.H. Rotival, N.Y.C., 1951-52; chief planner Brown & Blauvelt, N.Y.C., 1952-54; city planner Skidmore, Owings & Merrill, N.Y.C., 1954-56; prin. planning cons. Brown Engrs. Internat., N.Y.C., 1956-60; prin. Brown & Anthony City Planners, Inc., N.Y.C., 1960-69; v.p. Doxiadis Assocs., Inc., Washington, 1971-72; Mem. faculty Columbia, 1953-72, prof. urban planning, 1963-72, dir. grad. div. urban planning Grad. Sch. Architecture and Planning, 1962-65; prof. urban planning Calif. State Poly. U., Pomona, 1972-83, prof. emeritus, 1983—, chmn. dept., 1972-76; vis. prof. urban design Tulane U., 1967-68; vis. lectr. U. Calif. at Berkeley, Stanford U., Dartmouth, San Diego State U., CUNY, U. Okla., Ohio U., Auburn U., Salk Inst. Biol. Studies, U.S. Internat. U.; vis. prof. urban studies and planning U. Calif., San Diego, 1980-82; scholar-in-residence U. B.C., Vancouver, 1978; planning, zoning, urban renewal and urban design cons. to several cities, U.S. and abroad; also cons. to UN, Am. Med. Bldg. Guild, corps. and pvt. firms, to govts. and univs.; planning commr., Leonia, N.J., 1958-64. Author, co-author, contbr.: Four Great Makers of Modern Architecture: Gropius, Le Corbusier, Mies Van Der Rohe, Wright, Dictionary of American History, The Challenge of Squatter Settlements—With Special Reference to the Cities of Latin America, La Défense à Paris et le Quartier d'Affaires de Vancouver: Une Comparaison Urbaine, New Orleans Air Rights Study, Woodstock Growth Plan and Land Use Controls, others; several master plans, city and regional planning reports, urban design plans and programs, environ. impact reports, zoning ordinances, educational videocassettes on urban planning subjects.; Contbr. articles to profl. jours., mags., newspapers. Recipient Premier Grand Prix Internat. Exhbn. Housing and City Planning, Paris, 1947; William Kinne Fellows travelling fellow in planning, N.Am., 1956; research award Urban Center of Columbia U., 1969; named Outstanding Prof. Calif. State Poly. U., 1975. Mem. AIA (Arnold W. Brunner scholar 1958), Am. Inst. Cert. Planners, Am. Planning Assn. Home: 7665 Caminito Avola La Jolla CA 92037 Office: Dept Urban Planning Sch Environmental Design Calif State Poly Univ Pomona CA 91768

ANTHONY, JOSEPH, theatrical director; b. Milw., May 24, 1912; s. Leonard Deuster and Sophie (Herts) A.; m. Perry Wilson, Aug. 3, 1942; children: Peter Dean, Ellen Roe. Student, U. Wis., 1929-31, Pasadena (Cal.) Playhouse, 1931-35, Daykarhanova Sch. Stage, N.Y.C., 1935-37. Lectr. Am. Theatre Wing, Daykarhanova Sch. Stage; tchr. Vassar Coll., 1966, N.Y. U., 1968-69, Hunter Coll., 1967-70, State U. N.Y. at Purchase, 1972-76. Appeared in amateur theatres, Milw., 1930, Pasadena Playhouse, 1931-35; 1st profl. appearance: (with Helen Gahagan in) Mary Queen of Scots, Los Angeles; also appeared in: Lady in the Dark, 1939; other appearances include: Professor Mamlock, 1936, Truckline Cafe, 1946, Peer Gynt, 1947, Skipper Next to God, 1948, Anastasia, 1954-55, Country Girl, 1951, Camino Real, 1953, Flight into Egypt, 1952; motion picture appearances include: Joe Smith, American; also appeared in TV dramatic prodns.; dancing partner with Agnes de Mille, 1940-41; dir.: theatrical prodns. Bullfight, 1954, The Lark, 1955, The Rainmaker, 1954, Clearing the Woods, 1957, Marriage-go-Round, 1958, Winesburg, Ohio, 1959, The Best Man, 1960, The Most Happy Fella, 1956, Mary, Mary, 1961, Under the Yum-Yum Tree, 1960, Romulus, 1962, 110 in the Shade, 1963, The Last Analysis, 1964, Slow Dance on the Killing Ground, 1964, Rhinoceros, 1961, Mrs. Dally Has a Lover, 1965, The Playroom, 1965, Weekend, 1967, Jimmy, 1969, Finishing Touches, 1973; motion pictures The Rainmaker, 1956, The Matchmaker, 1959, Career, 1959, All in a Night's Work, 1961, The Captive City, 1962, Tomorrow, 1971; also TV prodns., Am. Shakespeare Festival, 1965, 66, Guthrie Theatre, 1969, Ahmondson Theatre, Los Angeles, 1968, The Three Sisters, Juilliard Sch., 1979. Served with AUS, 1942-46. Mem. AFTRA (bd. 1950), Actor's Equity (council 1951-56), Screen Dirs. Guild (bd. 1961), Soc. Stage Dirs. and Choreographers (pres. 1963-65), Am. Actors Co. (founding mem.). Address: S Pamet Rd Truro MA 02666

ANTHONY, RAY TAYLOR, department store executive; b. Cleveland, Okla., June 16, 1913; s. Charles Ross and Lutie Lillian (Mauldin) A.; m. Claudia Chesnut Bettis, Feb. 1, 1940; children: Claudia Raye, Carol Gaye, Linda June, Lutie C., Ray Bettis. B.S. in Bus. Adminstrn, U. Okla., 1934. Salesman C.R. Anthony Co., Oklahoma City, 1934-38, mdse. mgr. shoes, 1938-44, traffic mgr., 1945-52, dir., 1949—, office mgr., treas., 1952-55, v.p., treas., 1955-72, chmn. bd., 1972—; dir. Citizens Nat. Bank & Trust Co., 1976—; Pres. Community Council Central Okla., 1975-77; pres. Better Bus. Bur., 1977-79. Chmn. Areawide Health Planning Orgn., 1969-72; bd. dirs. Oklahoma City YMCA, pres., 1982-83; bd. dirs. Okla. State Fair Bd., Oklahoma City Appeals Rev. Bd.; pres. United Way, 1983; trustee Okla. Zool. Soc. Served with USAAF, 1944-45. Decorated Air Medal, D.F.C. Mem. Fin. Execs. Inst., Oklahoma City C. of C. (v.p.). Democrat. Mem. Disciples of Christ. Clubs: Oklahoma City Golf and Country, Quail Creek Country, Petroleum, Econ., Whitehall, Lions (pres. 1950-51). Home: 6901 Avondale Dr Oklahoma City OK 73116 Office: 701 N Broadway Oklahoma City OK 73102:

ANTHONY, RICHARD ELAND, banker; b. Troy, Ala., May 6, 1946; s. Eiland Eland, Jr. and Jane (Henderson) A.; m. Virginia Fleming, Aug. 5, 1967; children: Richard Eland, Virginia Lee. B.S. in Fin, U. Ala., 1968; M.B.A., U. Va., 1971; diploma, Sch. Banking South, La. State U., 1976. With First Nat. Bank Birmingham, Ala., 1971—, sr.

v.p., mgr. comml. loan dept., 1977-79, exec. v.p., head corporate banking div., 1979—; dir. Engel Mortgage Co., Inc., Assoc. Industries Ala. Bd. dirs. Birmingham YMCA, 1979-80, Diabetes Trust Fund, Birmingham, 1980, Ala. Golf Assn., 1978-80; chmn. bd. dirs. Lakeshore Hosp., Birmingham, 1978-80; vice chmn., bd. dirs. Discovery Place, Birmingham, 1980. Served with USAR, 1968-74. Named Ala. Young Banker of Year Ala. Bankers Assn., 1980. Mem. Am. Inst. Banking, Robert Morris Assocs., Newcomer Soc., U. Ala. Alumni Assn. (exec. com. Jefferson County chpt. 1980), Kappa Alpha. Methodist. Clubs: Shoal Creek, Birmingham Country, Birmingham Kiwanis (dir. 1980), Jefferson, Birmingham Monday Morning Quarterback. Home: 2 Montrose Circle Birmingham AL 35213 Office: PO Box 11007 Birmingham AL 35288

ANTHONY, ROBERT ARMSTRONG, chmn. Adminstrv. Conf. U.S.; b. Washington, Dec. 28, 1931; s. Emile Peter and Martha (Graham (Armstrong) A.; m. Ruth Grace Barrons, Feb. 7, 1959 (div.); 1 son, Graham Barrons. B.A., Yale U., 1953, Oxford U., 1955; J.D., Stanford U., 1957. Bar: Calif. bar 1957, N.Y. Bar 1971, D.C. bar 1972. Asso. firm Pillsburg, Madison & Sutro, San Francisco, 1957-62, Kelso, Cotton & Ernst, 1962-64; asso. prof. law Cornell U. Law Sch., 1964-68, prof., 1968-75, dir. interat. legal studies, 1964-74; chief counsel, later dir. Office Fgn. Direct Investments, Dept. Commerce, 1972-74; lectr. Acad. Am. and Internat. Law, Dallas, 1967-72; cons. Adminstrv. Conf. U.S., Washington, 1968-71, chmn., 1974—. Mem. Sausalito (Calif.) City Planning Commn., 1962-64; bd. dirs. Marin Shakespeare Festival, 1961-64. Mem. Am. Bar Assn., Washington Bar Assn., Calif. Bar Assn., San Francisco Bar Assn., Assn. Am. Rhodes Scholars, Am. Soc. Internat. Law. *

ANTHONY, ROBERT NEWTON, emeritus management educator; b. Orange, Mass., Sept. 6, 1916; s. Charles H. and Grace (Newton) A.; m. Gretchen Lynch, Aug. 28, 1943; children: Robert N., Victoria Stewart; m. Katherine Worley, Aug. 4, 1973. A.B., Colby Coll., 1938, M.A. (hon.), 1959, L.H.D., 1963; M.B.A., Harvard U., 1940, D.C.S., 1952. Faculty Bus. Sch., Harvard U., 1940-42, 46-67, 68-82, Ross Graham Walker prof. mgmt. control, Leatherbee lectr., 1967-82; Ross Graham Walker prof. emeritus, 1982—; pres. Mgmt. Analysis Center, Inc., 1955-63; asst. sec., controller Dept. Def., 1965-68; prof. Mgmt. Devel. Inst., Switzerland, 1957-58; with Stanford Exec. Devel. Program, 1962; mem. advisory bd. IMEDE, Switzerland, 1961-65, 68-77; spl. asst. to chmn. Price Commn., 1971-73; mem. educators cons. com. Gen. Accounting Office, 1973—; dir., chmn. audit com. Carborundum Co., 1971-77, Warnaco, Inc., 1972—; Trustee Colby Coll., 1959-74, 75—, chmn., 1978-83. Author: Cases, Problems and Questions in Practical Controllership, 1949, Management Controls in Industrial Research Organization, 1952, (with Dearborn and Kneznek) Spending for Industrial Research, 1951-52, Shoe Machinery: Buy or Lease?, 1955, (with Reece) Accounting, Text and Cases, 1956, 6th edit., 1979, 7th edit., 1983, Office Equipment, Buy or Rent?, 1957, Problems in Accounting, 1960; (with Reece) 6th edit. as Accounting Principles Workbook, 1983; (with Masson and Hunt) Cases in Financial Management, 1960, Essentials of Accounting, 1964, 2d edit., 1976, Accounting Principles, 1965, 5th edit., 1983, Planning and Control Systems: A Framework for Analysis, 1965, Management Control Systems, 4th edit. (with Dearden), 1980, (with Hekimian) Operations Cost Control, 1967, Plaid in Management Accounting, 2d edit, 1973, (with Welsch) Fundamentals of Financial Accounting, 1974, 3d edit., 1981, Fundamentals of Management Accounting, 1974, 3d edit., 1981, Management Control in Nonprofit Organizations, 1975, 2d edit., 1980, Accounting for the Cost of Interest, 1976, Financial Accounting in Nonbusiness Organizations, 1978, Tell it Like it Was, 1983; Editor: Automatic Data Processing 1956; cons. editor: Richard D. Irwin, Inc; Mem. bd.: Harvard Bus. Rev, 1947-59; Contbr. articles to profl. jours. Town auditor Town of Waterville Valley, N.H., 1976—; mem. audit com. City of N.Y., 1979—. Served from ensign to lt. comdr. USNR, 1941-46. Recipient Distinguished Leadership award Fed. Govt. Accountants Assn., Distinguished Pub. Service medal Dept. Def. Fellow Acad. Mgmt.; mem. Am. Acctg. Assn. (v.p. 1959, pres. 1973-74), Fin. Execs. Inst., Nat. Assn. Accountants (chmn. cost concepts subcom.), Assn. Govt. Accountants, Am. Soc. Mil. Comptrollers, Phi Beta Kappa, Pi Gamma Mu. Club: Cosmos. Home: PO Box 4 Waterville Valley NH 03223

ANTHONY, STEPHEN HOPKINS, real estate company executive; b. Boston, Aug. 3, 1937; s. Julian Danford and Eleanor Caroline (Hopkins) A.; m. Barbara Hilda Mead, June 11, 1960; children—Susan Hamblen, Emily Hopkins. A.B., Hamilton Coll., Clinton, N.Y., 1959; M.B.A., Harvard U., 1961. Exec. v.p. Copley Real Estate Advisors, Boston, 1982—; v.p. New Eng. Mut. Life Ins. Co., 1972—. Pres., dir. Greater Boston Community Devel., Inc.; Trustee Newton-Wellesley Hosp., Mass. Samaritan Corp.; corporator Morgan Meml. Goodwill Industries. Mem. Mortgage Bankers Assn., Mass., Greater Boston Real Estate Bd. Congregationalist. Club: Wellesley. Home: 19 Bay State Rd Wellesley MA 02181 Office: 535 Boylston St Boston MA 02117

ANTHONY, WILLIAM GRAHAM, artist; b. Ft. Monmouth, N.J., Sept. 25, 1934; s. Emile Peter and Martha Graham (Armstrong) A.; m. Norma Neuman, Jan. 16, 1983. B.A. in European History, Yale U., 1958; student, San Francisco Art Inst., 1959. Author: A New Approach to Figure Drawing, 1965, Bible Stories, 1978; Exhibited in one-man shows at, Legion of Honor, San Francisco, 1962, Kavaletten Gallery, Uppsala, Sweden, 1975, Razor Gallery, N.Y.C., 1978, others, exhibited in group shows at, San Francisco Mus. Modern Art, exhibited irn group shows at, Art Inst. Chgo., Whitney Mus. Am. Art, N.Y.C., Allan Stone Gallery, N.Y.C., St. Paul Art Center, Bolles Gallery, San Francisco, works represented in collections at, Art Inst. Chgo., Bklyn. Mus., Cleve. Mus. Art, Corcoran Gallery Art, Washington, Detroit Inst. Arts, Mus. Fine Arts, Houston, Seattle Art Mus., Whitney Mus. Am. Art, N.Y.C., Centre National d'Art Contemporain, Paris, Wallraf-Richartz-Museum, Cologne, Germany, others. Served with U.S. Army, 1953-55. Republican. Home and Studio: 463 West St Apt H-216 New York NY 10014 *My idea in art has been to show something of our unconscious by using the common mistakes which beginners in art make when attempting to draw or paint the human figure. These mistakes (heads too large, arms and legs too small, etc.) can be satirized in a way which I hope reveals something of the world view of the eleven-year-old that remains in all of us.*

ANTIN, DAVID, poet, critic; b. Bklyn., Feb. 1, 1932; s. Max and Mollie (Kitzes) A.; m. Eleanor Fineman, Dec. 16, 1960; 1 son, Blaise Cendrars. B.A., Coll. City N.Y., 1955; M.A. (Herbert Lehman fellow), N.Y. U., 1966. Prof. visual art U. Calif.-San Diego, 1968—; contbg. editor Alcheringa, 1972-80; editorial com. U. Calif. Press, 1972-76; contbg. editor New Wilderness, 1979—. Author: Definitions, 1967, Autobiography, 1967, Code of Flag Behavior, 1968, Meditations, 1971, Talking, 1972, Talking at the Boundaries, 1976, Who's Listening Out There, 1980, Tuning, 1984. Recipient Creative Arts award U. Calif., 1972; Guggenheim fellow, 1976-77; Nat. Endowment Humanities fellow, 1983-84. Home: PO Box 1147 Del Mar CA 92014 Office: Visual Art Dept Univ Calif La Jolla CA 92037

ANTIN, ELEANOR, artist; b. N.Y.C., Feb. 27, 1935; d. Sol and Jeanette (Efron) Fineman; m. David Antin, Sept. 1960; 1 son, Blaise Cendrars. B.A., CCNY, 1958; student, Tamara Daykarhanova Sch. for Stage, N.Y.C., 1954-56. Prof. visual arts U. Calif., San Diego. Producer videotapes Little Match Girl Ballet, 1975, Adventures of a Nurse, 1976; artist: The Nurse and the Hijackers, 1977, The Angel of Mercy, 1980; One-woman shows include, Mus. Modern Art, N.Y.C., 1973, Whitney Mus. Film and Video Program, N.Y.C., 1978, Long Beach (Calif.) Mus. Art, 1979, Ronald Feldman Gallery, N.Y.C., 1977, 79, 80, 83, group shows include, São Paulo Biennial, Brazil, 1975, Phila. Mus. Fine Arts, 1978, Hirschhorn Mus., Washington, 1979, Santa Barbara (Calif.) Mus. Art, represented in permanent collections, Long Beach (Calif.) Mus. Art, Wadsworth Atheneum, Hartford, Conn., artist performer at, Venice Bienale, 1976, Mus. Contemporary Art, Chgo., 1978, Mus. Contemporary Art, Houston, 1978, 80; author: book Being Antinova, 1983. Nat. Endowment for Arts grantee, 1979. Office: Visual Arts Dept U Calif at San Diego La Jolla CA 92093

ANTLE, CHARLES EDWARD, educator; b. East View, Ky., Nov. 11, 1930; s. Bayard Pierpoint and Mary Elizabeth (Blaydes) A.; m. Elna Thomas Hall, Nov. 25, 1953; children—James, Rebecca, Susan Hall, Mark Edward. A.A., Lindsey Wilson Coll., 1950; B.S., Eastern Ky. State U., 1954, M.A., 1955; postgrad., U. Ky., 1954-55; Ph.D. (NDEA fellow), Okla. State U., 1962. Sr. aerophysics engr. Gen. Dynamics Corp., Fort Worth, 1955-57; mem. faculty U. Mo., Rolla, 1957-60, 62-68, prof. math., 1966-68; asso. prof. statistics Pa. State U., University Park, 1968-70, prof., 1970—. Contbr. articles to profl. jours. Served with AUS, 1951-53. Decorated Bronze Star medal. Mem. Am. Statis. Assn., Royal Statis. Soc., Inst. Math. Statistics. Home: 2302 W Branch Rd State College PA 16801 Office: Dept Statistics Pa State U University Park PA 16802

ANTMAN, STUART SHELDON, mathematician, educator; b. Bklyn., June 2, 1939; s. Mitchell and Gertrude (Siegel) A.; m. Wilma Gail Richlin, Mar. 24, 1968; children: Rachel Alexandra, Melissa Dora. B.S., Rensselaer Poly. Inst., 1961; M.S., U. Minn., 1963, Ph.D., 1965. Lectr. U. Minn., summer 1965; vis. mem. Courant Inst., N.Y. U., 1965-67, asst. prof. math. and aeros., 1967-69, assoc. prof. math., 1969-72; sr. vis. fellow U. Oxford, 1969-70, Heriot-Watt U., Edinburgh, summers 1972, 77; prof. math. U. Md., College Park, 1972—; prin. investigator NSF grants, 1972—; mem. Applied Math. Summer Inst., Dartmouth Coll., 1973; prof. Ecole D'Ete D'Analyse Numerique, Breau, France, 1974; vis. prof. U. Paris-Sud, Orsay, 1975, Brown U., Providence, 1978-79, Ecole Polytechnique, Palaiseau, France, 1979, Math. Scis. Research Inst., Berkeley, Calif., 1983, Univ. P. and M. Curie, Paris, 1983; mem. U.S. Nat. Com. on Theoretical and Applied Mechanics, 1980—. Author: The Theory of Rods, 1972; Co-editor: Bifurcation Theory and Nonlinear Eigenvalue Problems, 1969, Springer Tracts in Natural Philosophy, 1972-80; mem. editorial bd.: Archive for Rational Mechanics and Analysis, 1972—, Acta Applicandae Mathematicae, 1982—. John S. Guggenheim Meml. Found. fellow, 1978-79. Mem. Am. Math. Soc., Soc. for Indsl. and Applied Math., Soc. for Natural Philosophy (sec. 1974-76), Math. Assn. Am., Pi Mu Epsilon. Home: 10012 Branch View Ct Silver Spring MD 20903 Office: Dept Math U Md College Park MD 20742

ANTON, DAVID MICHAEL, hospital consultant; b. Bklyn., Jan. 27, 1911; s. Sol and Grace A.; m. Audrey Keller, Oct. 16, 1941. Chief hosp. operations VA br. office, Columbus, Ohio, 1946-47; asst. dir. VA Med. Ctr., Dearborn, Mich., 1947-53, Bklyn., 1953-54, asst. dir. med. ctr., N.Y.C., 1954-57, med. ctr. dir., Castle Point, N.Y., 1957-58; area dir. adminstrv. services VA Area Med. Office, Boston, 1958-63; dir. bldg. mgmt. service VA Central Office, Washington, 1963-66; dir. VA Med. Ctr., West Haven, Conn., 1966-70, hosp. dir., St. Louis, 1970—; asso. chief med. dir. VA, Washington, ret., 1974; hosp. cons., 1974—; Bd. dirs. Lakeview Ctr., Pensacola, Fla. Served to maj. Med. Service Corps AUS; Served to maj. Med. Service Corps USAAF, 1942-46; ETO. Recipient citations Am. Legion, U.S. Customs Port N.Y., 1957, Am. Legion dept. N.Y., 1957, dept. Conn., 1970, AMVETS Spl. Meritorious Commendation Nat., 1967, United Spanish War Vets dept. Conn., 1968, Vets. World War I dept. Conn., 1968, 70, D.A.V. dept. Conn., 1970; Nat. D.A.V. citation for distinguished Service, 1972; others; Adminstrs. Exceptional Service award and Chief Med.; Dirs. certificate for outstanding performance, VA, 1971; Distinguished Service award; Gold medal VA, 1974. Fellow Royal Soc. Health (Eng.); mem. Am. Coll. Hosp. Adminstrs. (life), Assn. Mil. Surgeons U.S. (life), Fed. Hosp. Inst. Alumni Assn., Am. Hosp. Assn. (life), Am. Legion. Club: Mason. Address: 615 Bayshore Dr Apt 207 Pensacola FL 32507

ANTON, DONALD CHRIST, lawyer; b. St. Louis, Mar. 26, 1931; s. Christ J. and Ann L. (Thiel) A.; m. Aurora Ida Viglino, June 13, 1959; children: Donald K., Linda Ann. Student, S.W. Mo. State U., 1949-50, Kans. State U., 1950-51; B.S. in Bus. Adminstrn, Washington U., St. Louis, 1953, J.D., 1956. Bar: Mo. bar 1955, U.S. Fed. Ct. bar 1955, U.S. Supreme Ct. bar 1955, U.S. Tax Ct. bar 1955. Gen. acct. Union Electric Co., St. Louis, 1952-53; practiced in, St. Louis, Hillsboro, Mo., Jefferson City, Mo., also, Washington; mem. firm Evans and Dixon, St. Louis, 1954-55; atty. St. Louis Dist. Engrs., 1957-58; mem. firm Forgey and Sindel, St. Louis, 1958-59; probate and trust officer Merc. Trust Co., St. Louis, 1959-60; mem. firm Hall, Reaban, Seigel & Scheele, St. Louis, 1960-63; partner firm Anton, Raleigh & Wynne, St. Louis, 1969—; Pres. Holiday Ins. Agy., St. Louis, 1960-63, Dory Realtors, 1959-69; sec. Pine Ford Land Co., St. Louis, 1962—; co-propr. Henny Penny Chicken Restaurant, St. Louis, 1966-69; pres. Diversified Cons., Inc., St. Louis, 1969—; counsel SBA, St. Louis and Washington, 1962-65; spl. asst. to Atty. Gen. of Mo., 1967; asst. pros. atty. for Jefferson County, Mo., 1968; counsel for Mo. Senate 75th Gen. Assembly, Legis. Session, 1969; legal counsel Moline, Wellston, Pattonville-Bridgeton Terrace Fire Protection Dists., St. Louis County.; Mem. Econ. Adv. Council, State of Mo., 1968-72; del. Dem. Nat. Conv., 1964, 76, 80, Mo. State Conv., 1968, 72, 76, 80; chmn. Dem. Com., St. Louis County (Mo.), 1972—; Dem. committeeman, Concord Twp., St. Louis County, 1968—. Served to 1st lt. AUS, 1955-58. Mem. ABA (banking and bus. law coms. 1961—, taxation com. 1968—, uniform comml. code com. 1965-70), Fed. Bar Assn. (sec. 1965-66), Mo. Bar Assn. (bus. orgns. com. 1964—), Am. Judicature Soc., St. Louis Council World Affairs, Soc. Disting. Ams., Am. Turners, DAV, Delta Sigma Pi, Phi Delta Phi, Sigma Nu. Roman Cahtolic. Clubs: Kiwanis, Lions, Optimists. Home: 130 Sappington Ave Acres Dr Saint Louis MO 63126 Office: Anton Raleigh & Wynne 50 Crestwood Exec Center Saint Louis MO 63126 *It is my firm belief that by application of the American Work Ethic, perseverance and constant attention to detail, success can be achieved in any endeavor. Further, if these principles are applied through a meticulously organized program which is properly administered, superior results and success will be achieved as the natural logical result.*

ANTON, FRANK ROBERT, economics educator, author; b. Leix., Ireland, July 22, 1920; s. Norman James and Teresa Beatrice (Baker) A. B.S., London Sch. Econs., 1950; M.A., UCLA, 1956; Ph.D., U. London, 1962. Prof. econs. U. Calgary, Alta., Can., 1956—; OECD vis. prof. Middle East Tech. U., Ankara, Turkey, 1964; Chmn. numerous arbitration and conciliation bds. Govt. of Alta. Author: Role of Government on Settlement of Industrial Disputes in Canada, 1962, (with M.K. Inman) Economics in a Canadian Setting, 1965, Wages and Productivity: The New Equation, 1969, Worker Participation: Prescription for Industrial Change, 1980, The Canadian Coal Industry: Challenge in the Years Ahead, 1981. Served with RAF, 1940-46. Can. Council fellow, 1963-64, 71—. Mem. Am., Canadian econ. assns., Am., Canadian indsl. relations research assns. Club: United Services Inst. (Calgary). Home: Box 1 Site 9 SS3 Calgary AB Canada

ANTON, FREDERICK WILLIAM, insurance company executive, lawyer; b. Phila., Mar. 4, 1934; s. Frederick W. and Hilda C. (Winter) A.; m. Elizabeth Daniels, Nov. 27, 1965; children: Sarah, Frederick. B.S., Villanova U., 1955, LL.B., 1958. Bar: Pa. 1959. Practice law Ralph S. Croskey, Phila., 1959-62; trial counsel Pa. Mfrs. Assn. Ins. co., Phila., 1962-72, pres., 1972—; dir. Continental Bank, Phila., 1979—. Bd. dirs. Phila. Partnership, 1981, Walnut St. Theater, Phila., 1983; mem. Pa. State Planning Bd., 1980. Mem. Pa. Mfrs. Assn. (pres. 1975—), Ins. Fedn. Pa. (chmn. 1974-75). Republican. Clubs: Union League (Phila.); Aronimink Golf (Newton Square, Pa.). Home: 303 Orchard Way Saint Davids PA 19087 Office: Pa Mfrs Assn Ins Co 925 Chestnut St Philadelphia PA 19107

ANTON, GEORGE LOUIS, aluminum company executive; b. Savannah, Ga., Nov. 2, 1923; s. Louis George and Pauline (Constantine) A.; m. Sophia Andrianopoulou, Sept. 9, 1951; children: Louis George, Charles John. B.S. in Indsl. Engring., Ga. Inst. Tech., 1949, M.S., 1952. Cert. prof. engr., Calif. Supr. insl. engring. Ethyl Corp., Baton Rouge, 1952-59; dir. indsl. engring. U.S. Borax & Chem. Corp., Los Angeles, 1959-62, dir. prodn. planning, 1963-65, dir. mfg., 1965-70; asst. to pres. Oxford Paper subs. Ethyl Corp., Richmond, Va., 1970-74; v.p. ops. Capitol Products Corp. subs. Ethyl Corp., Harrisburg, Pa., 1974-79, exec. v.p., gen. mgr., 1979—. Spl. editor, Jour. Indsl. Engring., 1954-59. Pres. bd. dirs. United Cerebral Palsy Ctr., 1981-83; cub master Cub Scouts Am., Arcadia, Calif., 1961-65; pres. Civic Assn., Richmond, 1972; mem. Gov. Reagan's Com. Efficiency and Cost Control, 1967. Served with U.S. Army, 1943-46. Decorated Bronze Star, Croix de Guerre (unit). Mem. Am. Inst. Indsl. Engrs. (dir. mgmt. div. 1982-83, chpt. pres. Los Angeles and Baton Rouge), Am. Mgmt. Assn. Greek Orthodox. Club: West Shore Country (Camp Hill, Pa.). Home: 1715 Mountainview Rd Harrisburg PA 17110 Office: PO Box 3070 Harrisburg PA 17105

ANTON, JOHN PETER, philosophy educator; b. Canton, Ohio, Nov. 2, 1920; s. Peter C. and Christine (Giannopoulos) A.; m. Helen Vezos, Nov. 26, 1955; children: James, Christopher, Peter. B.S., Columbia U., 1949, M.A., 1950, Ph.D., 1954. Instr. Pace Coll., 1953-54; vis. lectr. U. N.Mex., 1954-55; asst. prof. U. Nebr., 1955-58; asso. prof. Ohio Wesleyan U., 1958-62; prof. State U. N.Y., Buffalo, 1962-67; asso. dean Grad. Sch., prof., 1967-69; Fuller E. Callaway prof. Emory U., 1969-81, chmn. dept. philosophy, 1969-76; Woods vis. prof. Mills Coll., 1981; prof., provost New Coll. U. South Fla., 1982-83, prof. philosophy, 1983—. Author: Aristotle's Theory of Contrariety, 1957, Science, Philosophy and Educational Tasks, 1966, Naturalism and Historical Understanding, 1967, Philosophical Essays, 1969, Essays in Ancient Greek Philosophy, 1971, Science and the Sciences in Plato, 1980, Critical Humanism as a Philosophy of Culture, 1981; Co-editor jour.: Diotima; editorial cons.: Jour. History of Philosophy, 1968—, The Humanist, 1967—; editorial bd.: Ancient Philosophy, 1979, Idealistic Studies, 1981, Philos. Inquiry, 1981. Served with AUS, 1946-47. Mem. Modern Greek Studies Assn. (v.p. 1969—), Soc. Macedonian Studies (hon.), Am. Philos. Assn., Am. Philol. Assn., Soc. Ancient Greek Philosophy (sec.-treas. 1973-81, pres. 1981-83), Ga. Philos. Soc. (v.p. 1972, pres. 1973), Am. Soc. Aesthetics (trustee 1973-76, 81-84), Internat. Soc. for Neoplatonic Studies (chmn. exec. com.), Soc. for History Philosophy (mem. exec. com.), Acad. Athens (corr.), Phi Beta Kappa (hon.), Eta Sigma Phi (hon.), Phi Sigma Tau (hon.). Office: U South Fla Tampa FL 35520

ANTON, NICHOLAS GUY, consulting physicist, engr.; b. Trieste, Austria, Dec. 14, 1906; came to U.S., 1926, naturalized, 1943; s. Joseph and Ann (Mandle) A.; m. Bernice Irene Skripsky, June 19, 1932; children—Joan Carol Anton Pearlman, Linda Elaine Anton Kincaid, Nancy Helen Anton Bobrow. Grad., Tech. Inst. Leonardo da Vinci, 1926; student, Columbia U., 1926-28. Various engring. positions Duovac Radio Tube Corp., Bklyn., 1928-31; pres., chmn. bd. Electronic Labs., Inc., Bklyn., 1931-32; founder, gen partner in charge mfg., factory engring. Amperex Electronics Products, 1932-48; pres., dir. research, devel., engring. Anton Electronic Labs., Bklyn., 1948-61; chmn. bd. Anton Imco Corp., 1959-61; founder, pres., dir. research, devel. EON Corp., Bklyn., 1961-78; cons., lectr., N.Y.C., 1978-79; pres., chmn. Dosimeter Corp., 1963-75; lectr. L.I. U., 1969-78; indsl. tech. cons. AEC for UN Internat. Conf. on Peaceful Uses of Atomic Energy, Geneva, 1955; Mem. Pres.'s Conf. on Indsl. Safety, 1967—, Albert Gallatin Assos.-N.Y. U., 1951-54; Centennary com. Poly. Inst. Bklyn., 1963-64, U.S. Nat. UN Day Com., 1972-74, 76. Contbr. numerous articles, papers to profl. lit. Recipient cert. of appreciation Office of Pres. Fellow IEEE, Am. Phys. Soc., N.Y. Acad. Scis., N.Y. Acad. Medicine (asso.), AAAS, Am. Philos. Soc.; mem. ASME, Am. Math. Soc., Am. Soc. for Nondestructive Testing, Electronic Industries Assn. (past chmn. various coms.), Am. Standard Assn. Jewish. Clubs: Unity, Engineers. Patentee in field. Home: 2501 Antigua Terr A3 Coconut Creek FL 33066 *Life can be beautiful, interesting and successful if you train yourself assiduously and are ready to grasp opportunities wherever you find them. Dedicate yourself to the task at hand; study, analyze, design, develop; never copy, never follow. Lead! Keep researching, probing, innovating. Be true to yourself; be realistic, be decisive and firm; be considerate to and honest with your associates.*

ANTON, SUSAN, actress; m. Jack Stein. Appeared in film Goldengirl, 1979; appeared in film Spring Fever, 1982; appeared in television series Mel and Susan Together, 1978, Cliffhangers, 1979, Presenting Susan Anton, 1979; appearances on television spls. and commercials, nightclub performer and recording artist. Named Miss California, 1969. Office: care JNS Enterprises 15910 Ventura Blvd Suite 1602 Encino CA 91436

ANTON, THOMAS JULIUS, political science, public policy educator, consultant; b. Worcester, Mass., Sept. 28, 1934; s. Julius and Irene (Dupsha) A.; m. Barbara Jane Lindblom, June 22, 1957; children: Lynn Allison, Leslie Carol, Thomas Rolf. A.B., Clark U., 1956; M.A., Princeton U., 1959; Ph.D., Prnceton U., 1961. Lectr. U. Pa., Phila, 1960-61; asst. prof. U. Ill., Urbana, 1961-63, assoc. prof., Urbana, Chgo., 1964-67; assoc. prof., prof. U. Mich., Ann Arbor, 1967-83; prof. polit. sci., A.A. Taubman prof. Am. instns. Brown U., Providence, 1983—; vis. prof. U. Stockholm., 1968,71, U. Srockholm, 1968, 71; cons. State of Ill., Springfield, Chgo., 1963-70, State of Mich., Lansing, 1972-83, HEW, Washington, 1976-80, Nat. Acad. Sci., 1976-80, Brookings Instn., 1970—; panel mem. Nat. Acad. Scis., Washington, 1981-82; dir. Ph.D. program in urban planning, Ann Arbor, Mich., 1977-80; mem. Swedish Fulbright Commn., Stockholm, 1971. Author: The Politics of State Expenditure in Illinois, 1966, Governing Greater Stockholm, 1975, Moving Money, 1980, Administered Politics, 1980; editor: Policy Scis., Amsterdam, 1977-80. J.F. Kennedy fellow Gov. of Sweden, 1977; NSF grantee, 1980. Mem. Am Polit. Sci. Assn., Assn. Pub. Policy and Mgmt., Midwest Polit. Sci. Assn, Phi Beta Kappa. Democrat. Clubs: Princeton (N.Y.C.); Cosmos (Washington). Home: 276 Sumac Ln Ann Arbor MI 48105 Office: U Mich Inst Pub Policy Studies Ann Arbor MI 48104

ANTONAKOS, STEPHEN, sculptor; b. So., Greece, Nov. 1, 1926; came to U.S., 1930. Ed., Bklyn. Community Coll., Bklyn. Mus. Art Sch. Lectr. Yale, New Haven, 1968; Sculptor, working primarily in neon, vis. artist, artist-in-residence, Madison, 1971, 1972. One-man shows, U. Maine, 1958, Avant-Garde Gallery, N.Y., Miami Mus. Modern Art, 1964, Schramm Gallery, Ft. Lauderdale, Byron Gallery, N.Y.C., Fischbach Gallery, N.Y.C., 1967, 68, 69, 72, John Weber Gallery, N.Y.C., 1974, 75, 76, 77, Ft. Worth Art Mus., 1974-75, Albright-Knox Art Gallery, Buffalo, 1975, Wright State U., Dayton, Ohio, Galleria Marilena Bonomo, Bari, Italy, Galerie 26, Paris, Galleriaforma, Genoa, Italy, Galerie December, Dusseldorf, Germany, 1976, Art & Project, Amsterdam, Galerie Bonnier, Geneva, Nancy Lurie Gallery, Chgo., Galerie Aronowitsch, Stockholm, 1977, Galerie Tanit, Munich, 1978, 80, Lowe Art Mus., Miami, Fla., 1980, Nassau County Mus. Fine Art, Roslyn, N.Y., 1982, Maison de Culture de Nevers (France), 1983, Le Coindu Miroir, Dijon, France, Bonnier Gallery, N.Y.C., exhibited in group shows, Miami Mus. Modern Art, 1958, Martha Jackson Gallery, N.Y., 1960, Allan Stone Gallery, 1961, 62, 64, Byron Gallery, 1963, 64, PVI Gallery, N.Y., 1964, 65, Whitney Mus. Am. Art, 1966 (2), 68, 69, 70, Newark Coll. Engring., 1968, U. N.C., R.I. Sch. Design, 1969, U. Calif. at Los Angeles Art Gallery, U. Nebr., Lincoln, 1970, Documenta 6, Kassel, W.Ger., 1977, Galerie Nancy Gillespie/Elisabeth de Laage, Paris, 1979, numerous others, represented in permanent collections, Fed. Bldg., Dayton, Ohio, Hampshire Coll., Amherst, Mass., U. Mass., Amherst, Atlanta Internat. Airport, Whitney Mus. Am. Art, Mus. Modern Art, N.Y.C., Larry Aldrich Mus., Ridgefield, Conn., Wadsworth Atheneum, Hartford, Conn., Phoenix Art Mus., Weatherspoon Art Gallery, U. N.C., Greensboro, Newark Mus., Milw. Art Center, Guggenheim Mus., La Jolla Mus. Contemporary Art, Seattle Arts Commn., Finch Coll. Mus., N.Y., Miami Mus. Modern Art., Lawrence St. Ventures, Denver, Balt. Mass Transit Adminstrn., Lowertown Redevel. Corp., St. Paul, Niagara Frontier Transp. Authority, Buffalo. Recipient award Nat. Endowment for Arts, 1973, N.Y. Creative Artists Pub. Service Program. Address: 435 W Broadway New York NY 10012

ANTONELL, WALTER JOHN, publishing executive; b. Bklyn., Dec. 23, 1934; s. Vincent Nick and Irene (Virga) A.; m. Natalie Sue Turner, Dec. 10, 1955 (div. 1982); children: Berkeley, Bradley, Deborah; m. Janice Ann Kiernan, Dec. 29, 1982. B.A. in Econs., Gettysburg Coll., 1955; M.B.A., Fairleigh Dickinson U., 1962. Mgr. Olivetti Corp., Hartfold, Conn., 1961-68, dir., N.Y.C., 1968-72; corp. dir. Xerox Corp., Stamford, Conn., 1972-78; v.p. Citibank, N.Y.C., 1979-81, Bantam Books, Inc., 1981—. Patentee on computer enlcosure, 1976. Mem. Am. Mgmt. Assn., Nat. Council Phys. Distbn. Mgmt., Am. Prodn. and Inventory Control, Data Processing Mgmt. Assn. Republican. Roman Catholic. Home: RD3 Stillhouse Rd Freehold NJ 07728 Office: Bantam Books Inc 666 Fifth Ave New York NY 10103

ANTONIO, JUAN, dancer, choreographer, educator; b. Mexico City, May 4, 1945; U.S., 1966; s. Juan and Ofelia (Rodea) A. Dancer, instr. Ballet Nacional, Mexico, 1965, Ballet Folkorico, 1966; co-founder, prin. dancer, assoc. dir. Falco Dance Co., N.Y.C., 1967—, choreographer, 1971—; instr. performer with Joffrey Ballet, N.Y.C.; instr., performer with N.Y.C. Opera, Washington Opera Soc.; guest artist Netherlands Dans Theatre, Jose Limon Dance Co.; guest artist, asst. choreographer Broadway prodn. Indians and Dude; instr. groups, theatres, U.S., Europe; artistic cons., dir. Toronto Dance Ctr., Ont., Can., 1983—. Creator: Imago, B-Mine, I Remember, First Base, Coasting, Memorias for Ballet Nacional de Espana. NEA grantee, 1977; Creative Arts Pub. Services grantee, 1975. Mem. Screen Actor's Guild, Actor's Equity. Home: 484 W 43d St 39-0 New York NY 10036 Office: Louis Falco Dance Co 131 W 24th St New York NY 10011 *I love life, live performances and people in love with life.*

ANTONIO, LOU, actor, director; b. Oklahoma City; s. James Demetrios and Lucille (Wright) A. B.A., U. Okla., 1957. Actor, 1968—; off-Broadway appearances include The Buffalo Skinner (Theatre World award 1969, 70); films include Splendor in the Grass, 1960, American, America, 1963, Hawaii, 1966, Cool Hand Luke, 1967, The Phynx, 1970; TV series include Dog and Cat, 1977, The Snoop Sisters, 1974, Makin' It, 1979; also appearances in movies for TV and episodes of series; movies directed for TV include Someone I Touched, 1975, Lanigan's Rabbi, 1976, The Girl in the Empty Grave, 1977, Something for Joey, 1977 (Humanitas award), The Critical List, 1978, A Real American Hero, 1978, Silent Victory: The Kitty O'Neil Story, 1979, Breaking Up Is Hard To Do, 1979, The Contender, 1981, We're Fighting Back, 1981, The Star Maker, 1981; author: screenplay Mission: Batangas, 1969. Mem. Screen Actors Guild, Actors Equity Assn., AFTRA, Dirs. Guild Am., Writers Guild Am. Address: care Artists Agy 10000 Santa Monica Blvd Suite 305 Los Angeles CA 90067 *

ANTONIOU, THEODORE, composer, condr.; b. Athens, Greece, Feb. 10, 1938; came to U.S., 1969, naturalized, 1972; s. Vassilios and Maria (Veligradi) A. Diploma in violin, Nat. Conservatory of Greece, Athens, 1956, 1958, Ministry Edn. of Greece, 1957, Hellenic Conservatory, Athens, 1961, Hochschule for Musik, Munich, W. Ger., 1964, Siemens Studio for Electronic Music, Munich, 1965. Mem. faculty Nat. Conservatory, Athens, 1956-61; composer in residence, vis. prof. composition, orchestration and drama Stanford U., 1968-69, 69-70, 76; composer in residence U. Utah, 1970, 71-72; prof. composition, dir. New Music Group, Phila. Mus. Acad. (now Phila. Coll. Performing Arts), 1970-79; prof. composition Boston U., 1979—; founder, dir. Stanford New Music Ensemble, ALEA II, 1969, ALFA III Boston's Performing Ensemble, 1979—. Condr., Phila. Mus. Acad. Symphony Orch., 1970-71, 75-76; dir., Politis Prize in Composition, 1979—; numerous compositions, including Concertino for Piano, 1962 (hon. 1st prize Athens Tech. Inst. 1962), Violinkonsert, 1965 (1st prize City Stuttgart, Germany 1966), Mikographies for big Orch, 1964 (1st prize in composition Arts Ministry of Greece 1967), Cassandra, ballet, 1969 k7(Premio Ondas, Barcelona Radi-TV 1970), Stichomythia II, 1977, (22d Concours Internat. de Guitare, Radio France 1978) Stichomythia II; numerous commns., including Koussevtisky Music Found. Commn., 1972; artistic dir., Athens Centre for Creative Arts, 1973-75, composer, condr., dir. contemporary activities, Berkshire Music Center, Tanglewood, 1974—; founder, dir., Hellenic Group Contemporary Music, Athens, 1967—; Contbr. articles to profl. jours. Recipient 1st prize for composition Hellenic Conservatory, 1961, Richard Strauss prize City of Munich, 1964; Kassimatis Found. fellow, 1961-63; Deutsche Akademische Austauschdienst fellow, 1963-65; State Dept. Program for Leaders and Specialist fellow, 1966; Nat. Endowment for Arts fellow, 1975, 77; John Simon Guggenheim Meml. Found. grantee, 1979. Mem. Internat. Soc. Contemporary Music (co-founder, v.p. Greek chpt. 1965-72), Internat. Soc. Heinrich Schutz (co-founder, v.p. Greek chpt. 1966). Office: 855 Commonwealth Ave Boston MA 02215

ANTONOFF, GARY L., realtor; b. Waukon, Iowa, Sept. 29, 1936; s. Ben H. and Florence L. (Rosenberg) A.; m. Carol Pesmen, July 5, 1958; children: Douglas Scott, Wendy Susan. B.S., Colo. U., 1954. Mgr. G.E.M. Dept. Store, St. Louis, 1958-61; pres. Antonoff & Co., realtors, Denver, 1961—; chmn. bd. Denver Nuggets Basketball, Inc., 1977; dir. Colo. Nat. Bank, Denver.; Bd. dirs. Rose Meml. Hosp., Anti-Defamation League, Nat. Jewish Hosp.; bd. dirs. Allied Jewish Fedn., campaign chmn., 1979, pres., 1980, chmn. Endowment Fund, 1981-82; co-chmn. Council on Internat. Jewish Affairs. Mem. Nat. Assn. Realtors, Internat. Council Shopping Centers. Home: 3300 S Columbine Circle Englewood CO 80110 Office: 1720 S Bellaire St Denver CO 80222

ANTONOWSKY, MARVIN, motion picture company executive; b. N.Y.C., Jan. 31, 1929; s. Harry and Dora (Green) A. B.B.A. in Acctg., CCNY, 1949, M.B.A. in Mktg., 1952. Vice pres. research ABC-TV, N.Y.C., 1969-73; v.p. programming NBC-TV, N.Y.C., 1973-76; sr. v.p., liasion with ABC-TV MCA Universal-TV, Universal City, Calif., 1976-79; sr. v.p., asst. to pres. Columbia Pictures, Burbank, Calif., 1979-80, exec. v.p. mktg., 1980-81, pres. mktg. and research, 1981-83; pres. mktg. MCA Universal Pictures, Universal City, Calif., 1982—. Home: 3116 Strand Manhattan Beach CA 90266

ANTONSEN, ELMER HAROLD, educator; b. Glens Falls, N.Y., Nov. 17, 1929; s. Haakon and Astrid Caroline Emilie (Sommer) A.; m. Hannelore Gertrude Adam, Mar. 24, 1956; children: Ingrid Carol, Christopher Walter. B.A., Union Coll., Schenectady, N.Y., 1951; postgrad., U. Vienna, 1951-52, U. Goettingen, 1956; M.A., U. Ill., 1957, Ph.D., 1961. Instr. German, Northwestern U., Evanston, Ill., 1959-61; asst. prof. U. Iowa, Iowa City, 1961-64, asso. prof., 1964-67, U. Ill., Urbana, 1967-70, prof. Germanic langs. and linguistics, 1970—, head dept., 1973-82; assoc. Ctr. for Advanced Studies, 1983-84; vis. prof. U. N.C., Chapel Hill, 1972-73. Author: A Concise Grammar of the Older Runic Inscriptions, 1975; Contbr. articles to profl. jours. Served with AUS, 1953-56. Fulbright scholar, 1951-52. Mem. Linguistic Soc. Am., Modern Lang. Assn., Soc. Advancement of Scandinavian Study, Institut für deutsche Sprache (corr. mem.), Selskab for nordisk filologi, Rogaland Arkeologisk Selskap, Phi Beta Kappa. Home: 2210 Plymouth Dr Champaign IL 61820 Office: 3072 FLB Univ Ill Urbana IL 61801

ANTOSIEWICZ, HENRY ALBERT, mathematics educator; b. Wollersdorf, Austria, May 14, 1925; came to U.S., 1947, naturalized, 1953; s. Adalbert and Margarethe (Kollaritsch) A.; m. Rose Thomasian, Aug. 30, 1958 (div. Mar. 1967); m. Sally Baker, Aug. 13, 1970 (div. May 1977); m. Peri Winkler, Mar. 27, 1981; 1 son, Cedric Henry. Ph.D., U. Vienna, 1947. Asso. editor math. revs. Am. Math. Soc., Providence, 1957-58; prof. math. U. So. Calif., Los Angeles, 1958—, chmn. dept., 1968-77; pres. Analytical Securities Mgmt., 1978—; cons. TRW Systems, Redondo Beach, Calif., 1960-68, also various fin. instns.; Trustee Math. Scis. Research Inst., Berkeley, Calif., 1981—. Contbr. articles to profl. jours. Mem. Am. Math. Soc. Home: 8541 Charl Ln Los Angeles CA 90046 Office: Dept Math MC-1113 U So Calif Los Angeles CA 90089

ANTREASIAN, GARO ZAREH, painter, lithographer, art educator; b. Indpls., Feb. 16, 1922; s. Zareh Minas and Takouhie (Daniell) A.; m. Jeanne Glascock, May 2, 1947; children: David Garo, Thomas Berj. B.F.A., Herron Sch. Art, 1948; D.F.A. (hon.), Ind. U.-Purdue U. at Indpls., 1972. Instr. Herron Sch. Art, 1948-64; prof. art U. N.Mex., 1964—, chmn. dept. art, 1981-84; tech. dir. Tamarind Inst., 1970-72; vis. lectr., artist numerous univs.; Bd. dirs. Albuquerque Mus., 1980—. Prin. author: The Tamarind Book of Lithography: Art and Techniques, 1970; One-man shows include, Malvina Miller Gallery, San Francisco, 1971, Marjorie Kauffman Gallery, Houston, 1975-79, 84, U. Colo., Boulder, 1972, Calif. Coll. Arts & Crafts, Oakland, 1973, Miami U., Oxford, Ohio, Kans. State U., Atlanta Coll. Art, 1974, U. Ga., Athens, Alice Simsar Gallery, Ann Arbor, 1977-79, Elaine Horwich Gallery, Santa Fe, Mus. of N.Mex., Santa Fe, 1979, exhibited group shows, Phila. Print Club, 1960-63, Ind. Artists, 1947-63, White House, 1966, Nat. Lithographic Exhbn. Fla. State U., 1965, Library Congress, 1961-66, Bklyn. Mus., 1958-68, 76, U.S. Pavilion Venice Biennale, 1970, Internat. Biennial, Bradford, Eng., 1972-74, Internat. Biennial, Tokyo, 1972, City Mus. Hong Kong, represented in permanent collections, Bklyn. Mus., Guggenheim Mus., N.Y.C., Cin. Mus., Mus. Modern Art, N.Y.C., Library of Congress, Met. Mus., N.Y.C., also, Met. Mus., Boston, Met. Mus., Seattle, Met. Mus., Phila., Met. Mus., San Diego, Dallas art museums, Los Angeles County Mus., murals, Ind. U., Butler U., Ind. State Office Bldg. Served with USCGR, World War II; PTO. Recipient Distinguished Alumni award Herron Sch. Art, 1972; Grantee Nat. Endowment Arts, 1983. Mem. World Print Council (dir. 1980—), Nat. Print Council Am. (co-pres. 1980-82), Coll. Art Assn. Am. (dir. 1977-80). Address: 4909 Paseo Del Rey NW Albuquerque NM 87120

ANTTILA, RAIMO AULIS, historical linguist; b. Lieto, Finland, Apr. 21, 1935; came to U.S., 1962; s. Lauri Nikolai and Tyyne Raakel A.; m. Seija S. H. Gerdt, July 25, 1959; children: Selene, Matti. Candidate of Humanities, U. Turku, 1959, 1961; Ph.D., Yale U., 1966. Acting asst. prof. UCLA, 1965-66, asst. prof., 1966-71, assoc. prof., 1971-74, prof. dept. linguistics, 1974—; prof. U. Helsinki, Finland, 1971-76; instr. Linguistic Inst., Linguistic Soc. Am., summers 1966, 74, 83; Collitz prof. Indo-European linguistics Linguistics Soc. Am., U. Am., 1974. Author: Proto-Indo European Schwebeablaut, 1969, An Introduction to Historical and Comparative Linguistics, 1972, Analogy, 1977; mem. editorial bd.: Jour. Indo-European Studies, 1972—, Virittaga, 1973—; mem. editorial: Historiographia Linguistica, 1973—; mem. editorial bd.: Folia Linguistica Historica, 1978—; author: Forum Linguisticum, 1978—, Cahiers de L'Institut de Linguistique-Louvain, 1979—, Diachronica, 1983—, NOWELE, 1983. Lutheran. Home: 1022 Cedar St Santa Monica CA 90405 Office: UCLA 405 Hilgard Ave Los Angeles CA 90024

ANTUPIT, SAMUEL NATHANIEL, art dir.; b. West Hartford, Conn., Feb. 14, 1932; s. Louis and Sylvia (Feinberg) A.; m. Rosalie Jane Littman, Dec. 30, 1956; children—Lisa Ruth, Jennifer Carol, Stephen Michael, Peter Louis. Grad., Loomis Sch., 1950; B.A. in English, Yale, 1954; B.F.A. in Graphic Design, Yale, 1956. Asst. art dir. Harper's Bazaar mag., 1958-61, Show mag., 1961-63; asst. corp. art dir. Conde Nast Publs., 1963, Pushpin Studios, 1963-64; art. dir. Art in Am., 1963-64, N.Y. Rev. Books, 1963—, Esquire mag., 1964-68, 77; pres. Hess and/or Antupit, designer, publs., and cons., 1968-70; lectr. pub. procedures course Harvard-Radcliffe Coll., 1965-80; propr. Cycling Frog Press, Pound Ridge, N.Y., 1961—, Antupit & Others Inc., 1971—, Subsistence Press, 1971—; exec. art dir. Book of the Month Club, 1977-81; dir. art and design, mem. pub. com. Harry N. Abrams, Inc., N.Y.C., 1981—; Trustee Hiram Halle Meml. Library. (Emmy award Nat. Acad. TV Arts and Scis. 1974); Author: (with Terry Clifford) Cures, 1980. Served with AUS, 1956-58. Recipient Design awards Art Dirs. Club, N.Y.C., 1960—, Type Dirs. Club, N.Y.C., 1961—, Soc. Illustrators, 1961—, Art Dirs. Club, Boston, Alliance Graphique Internationale. Mem. Nat. Acad. Rec. Arts and Scis., Am. Inst. Graphic Arts (bd. dirs. 1968—, v.p. 1970-72, Design awards 1965—), Yale U. Arts Assn. (exec. com. 1972-76). Office: 110 E 59th St New York NY 10022

ANUSZKIEWICZ, RICHARD JOSEPH, artist; b. Erie, Pa., May 23, 1930; s. Adam Jacob and Victoria (Jankowski) A.; m. Sarah Feeney, Nov. 26, 1960; children: Adam John, Stephanie. B.F.A., Cleve. Inst. Art, 1953; M.F.A., Yale U., 1955; B.S. in Edn., Kent State U., 1956. One-man shows at, Butler Art Inst., Youngstown, Ohio, 1955, The Contempories, N.Y.C., 1960, 61, 63, Sidney Janis Gallery, N.Y.C., 1965-67, Dartmouth Coll., 1967, Cleve. Mus. Art, Kent State U., 1968, Andrew Crispo Gallery, N.Y.C., 1975, 77, La Jolla (Calif.) Mus. Contemporary Art, 1976, Univ. Art Mus., Berkeley, Calif., 1977, Columbus (Ohio) Gallery of Fine Arts, exhibited in group shows at, Mus. Modern Art, 1960-61, 63, 65, U. Ill., 1961, NYU, Pa. Acad. Design, 1962, Whitney Mus. Am. Art, 1962, 63-64, 70, 71, Inst. Contemporary Arts, Boston, 1962, Columbus (Ohio) Gallery Fine Arts, City Art Mus., St. Louis, Munson-Williams-Proctor Inst., Utica, N.Y., Tweed Gallery U. Minn., Silvermine (Conn.) Guild Artists, 1962, 63, Atheneum Sch., Helsinki, Finland, 1962, Mus. Modern Art, Sarasota, Fla., J.B. Speed Art Mus., Louisville, Meml. Art Gallery, Rochester, N.Y., Allentown (Pa.) Art Mus., 1963, Krannert (Ill.) Art Mus., De Cordova Mus., Lincoln, Mass., Washington Gallery Modern Art, U. Mich. Mus. Art, 1964, Sidney Janis Gallery, N.Y.C., 1964, 65, Art Inst., Chgo., 1964, 71, Tate Gallery, London, 1964, Far Gallery, Carnegie Inst., Pitts., Carnegie Inst., Pitts., Corcoran Gallery Art, Washington, 1965, Art Fair Cologne, Germany, 1967, Larry Aldrich Mus., Ridgefield, Conn., 1968, 71, Hopkins Center Art Galleries Dartmouth Coll., Hanover, N.H., 1969, Denver Art Mus., Va. Mus. Fine Arts, Richmond, 1970, Ind. State U., Terre Haute, Masur Modern Art, Monroe, La., Birmingham (Ala.) Mus., 1971, others, represented in permanent collections, Mus. Modern Art, Whitney Mus. Am. Art, Cleve. Mus. Art, Corcoran Gallery Art, Allentown Art Mus., Albright-Knox Art Gallery, Butler Art Inst., Akron (Ohio) Art Inst., Yale Art Gallery, Chgo. Art Inst., Larry Aldrich Mus., Ridgefield, Conn., Fogg Art Mus. of Harvard U., Hirshhorn Mus. and Sculpture Garden, artist-in-residence, Dartmouth Coll., 1967, U. Wis., 1968, Cornell U., Kent State U.; Contbr. articles to profl. jours. Office: care Crispo Gallery 41 E 57th St New York NY 10022 *

ANVARIPOUR, M.A., lawyer; b. Tehran, Iran, Jan. 23, 1935; came to U.S., 1957; s. Ahmed and Monir (Georgi) A.; m. Patricia Matson Lynch (div. 1971); 1 dau., Sandra M.; m. Guilda Eshtehardi, Mar. 31, 1978 (div. 1984); 1 son, Cyrus Ramsey. LL.B., U. Tehran, 1956; B.S., U. San Francisco, 1959; student, U. Calif. Hastings Coll. Law, San Francisco; J.D., Ill. Inst. Tech.-Chgo. Kent Coll. Law, 1973. Bar: Ill. 1973, Fed. cts. Asst. field dir. Am. Friends of Middle East, Inc., Iran, 1962-64, field dir., 1964-66; asst. dean students, dean internat. students and faculty affairs Ill. Inst. Tech., Chgo., 1966-81; practiced in, Chgo., 1973—; ednl. and legal adviser Consulate Gen. Iran, Chgo., 1973-79; aux. lawyer NAACP, Chgo., 1973-74; lectr. immigration and law seminar Ill. Inst. Tech.-Chgo.-Kent Coll. Law Sch., 1974. Mem. Am., Iran-Am. (sec.-gen. 1964-66), Chgo. Bar Assn. (chmn. immigration com. 1982-83), Iran Am. Alumni Assn. (sec. 1964-66), Nat. Assn. Fgn. Student Affairs (Ill. chmn. 1968-69), U. Tehran, U. San Francisco, Idaho State U. (hon.), Ill. Inst. Tech., Chgo.-Kent Coll. Law alumni assns., Nat. Assn. Immigration and Nationality Lawyers (sec.-treas. 1976-78, v.p. 1978-80, pres. 1980-81), Phi Delta Phi. Club: Armour Faculty (pres. 1977-78). Home: 990 N Lake Shore Dr Chicago IL 60611 Office: 20 N Clark St Chicago IL 60602 *My biases have made my life extremely rewarding. I have several. I have a strong bias against intolerance. I have a deep-seated bias against hate and bigotry, a bias against war, a bias for peace, and a bias which guides me to have faith in the basic goodness of my fellow human beings.*

APEL, JOHN RALPH, physicist; b. Absecon, N.J., June 14, 1930; s. Ezio A. and Grace A. (Rose) Baltera; m. Martha Eleise Davis, Sept. 8, 1956; children: Denise Alison, Jacqueline Jeanne. B.S., U. Md., 1957, M.S., 1961; Ph.D. (William S. Parsons fellow), Johns Hopkins, 1970. With Applied Physics Lab., Johns Hopkins U., Laurel, Md., 1957-70, 82—; sr. physicist Applied Physics Lab., Johns Hopkins, 1961-70, asst. group supr., 1966-70; asst. dir. Applied Physics Lab., John Hopkins U., 1982—; dir. Ocean Remote Sensing Lab., Atlantic Oceanographic and Meteorol. Labs., Miami, Fla., 1970-75, Pacific Marine Environ. Lab., NOAA, Seattle, 1976-81; Adj. prof. physics U. Miami, 1970-76; affiliate prof. atmospheric scis. and oceanography U. Wash., 1976-81; cons. NASA, Dept. Def., 1971—, UNESCO, Intergovtl. Oceanographic Commn., 1975—; chmn. ocean dynamics adv. sub com. NASA, 1973-76; mem. Internat. Union of Radio Scis., Commn. F, 1974—, Inter-Union Commn. Radio Meteorology, 1975-82; Sr. fellow Joint Inst. for Study of Atmosphere and Ocean, 1977-81; chmn. Sea Use Council Sci. and Tech. Bd., 1977-81; sr. fellow Joint Inst. for Marine and Atmospheric Research, 1978-81; chmn. aerospace and remote sensing Internat. Council for Exploration of Sea, 1979—; trustee Pacific Sci. Center, 1977-81; mem. Sci. Commn. Ocean Research, 1980—. Contbg. author: Ballistic Missile and Space Technology, Vol. 4, 1961, Advances in Geophysics, Vol. 9, 1962, Advances in Astronautical Sciences, Vol. 30, 1974, Remote Sensing: Energy-Related Studies, 1975, Annual Review of Earth and Planetary Sciences, vol. 8, 1980; guest co-editor: Boundary Layer Meteorology, 1977; Contbr. articles to profl. jours. Served with USNR, 1951-52. Recipient Disting. Authorship award Nat. Oceanic and Atmospheric Adminstrn., 1976; Gold medal for meritorious service Dept. Commerce, 1974. Mem. Am. Phys. Soc., Am. Meteorol. Soc., N.Y. Acad. Scis., AAAS, Am. Geophys. Union, Sigma Xi, Sigma Pi Sigma, Phi Eta Sigma, Phi Delta Theta. Clubs: Cosmos (Washington); Explorers (N.Y.C.). Home: 14605 Carrolton Rd Rockville MD 20853 Office: Applied Physics Lab Johns Hopkins Rd Laurel MD 20707

APFEL, ROBERT EDMUND, engineering educator; b. N.Y.C., Mar. 16, 1943; s. Mark and Anita A.; m. Nancy Howe, July 13, 1968; children: Darren Alexander, Alison Anita. B.A., Tufts U., 1964; M.A., Harvard U., 1967, Ph.D., 1970. Postdoctoral research fellow Harvard U., 1970-71; asst. prof. mech. engring. Yale U., 1971-75, assoc. prof., 1975-81, prof., chmn. dept., 1981—; prin., cons. Robert E. Apfel, Ph.D., New Haven, 1972—. Recipient A.B. Wood Medal and Prize Inst. Physics, 1971. Fellow Acoustical Soc. Am. (Biennial 1976); mem. Am. Phys. Soc., Am. Assn. Physics Tchrs., ASME. Unitarian. Office: Yale U PO Box 2159 New Haven CT 06520

APONE, CARL ANTHONY, journalist; b. Brownsville, Pa., July 9, 1923; s. Peter P. and Carmela (Puglia) A.; m. Kathleen King, Jan. 23, 1965; 1 dau., Elizabeth. B.A. cum laude, U. Notre Dame, 1949; M.A., Boston U., 1950. Asst. prof. journalism and Am. lit. St. Mary's Coll. for Women, Notre Dame, Ind., 1950-53; staff writer UP, Detroit, 1953; city editor Brownsville Telegraph, 1953-57; staff writer Pitts. Sun- Telegraph, 1958-60; music editor Pitts. Press, 1960—; mem. faculty journalism Duquesne U., 1967-72; free-lance writer, 1950—; Mem. panel com. St. Vincent DePaul Soc., 1963—. Served with inf. AUS, 1943-46. Recipient Golden Quill Journalism awards; Pa. Newspaper Pubs. Assn. awards. Mem. Third Order St. Francis. Home: 2016 Worcester Dr Pittsburgh PA 15243 Office: Pitts Press Blvd of Allies Pittsburgh PA 15230

APONTE MARTINEZ, LUIS CARDINAL, archbishop; b. Lajas, P.R., Aug. 4, 1922; s. Santiago E. Aponte and Rosa Martinez. Student, San Ildefonso Sem., San Juan, P.R., 1944, St. John's Sem., Boston, 1950; LL.D. (hon.), Fordham U., 1965. Ordained priest Roman Cath. Ch., 1950; asst. in Patillas, P.R.; pastor in, Maricao, P.R., Sta. Isabel, P.R., 1953-55; sec. to bishop of Ponce, P.R., 1955-57; pastor in Aibonito, P.R., 1957-60; aux. bishop of Ponce, 1960-63, bishop, 1963-64; archbishop of, San Juan, 1964—, elevated to cardinal, 1973; Chancellor Cath. U. P.R., Ponce, 1963—; pres. Puerto Rican Episcopal Conf. Served as chaplain P.R. N.G., 1957-60. Club: Lion. Address: PO Box S-1967 San Juan PR 00903 *

APOSTLE, HIPPOCRATES GEORGE, mathematics educator; b. Tyrnavos, Greece, Jan. 1, 1910; came to U.S., naturalized, 1922; s. George C. and Aspasia (Tzartzanos) A.; m. Margaret Wylie, 1968. B.A., Columbia, 1933, M.A., 1935; postgrad., U. Chgo., 1935-39; Licence en Philosophie, Laval U., Can., 1941; Ph.D. in Philosophy, Harvard, 1943. Asst. prof. math. and physics W. Va. Wesleyan U., 1942-43; asst. prof. math. U. Rochester, 1943-45; asst. prof. math. and philosophy Amherst Coll., 1945-47; asst. prof. philosophy U. Chgo., 1947-48; prof. math. Grinnell Coll., 1948—, Steele prof., 1961—.

Author: Aristotle's Philosophy of Mathematics, 1952, College Algebra, 1954, A Survey of Basic Mathematics, 1960, Aristotle's Metaphysics, 1967, Aristotle's Physics, 1969, Aristotle's Ethics, 1975, Aristotle's Categories and Propositions, 1980, Aristotle's Posterior Analytics, 1981, Aristotle's On the Soul, 1982, Aristotle Selected Works, 1983. Home: 817 East St Grinnell IA 50112

APPEL, ALFRED, lawyer; b. N.Y.C., May 8, 1906; s. Samuel and Sadie (Niedermann) A.; m. Beatrice C. Hoffman, Sept. 3, 1931; children—Alfred, Elizabeth (Mrs. Paul Schaffer), John S. A.B., Cornell U., 1926, J.D., 1928. Bar: N.Y. 1928. Practiced in N.Y.C., 1928—; asso. Proskauer Rose Goetz & Mendelsohn and (predecessor firms), 1928-40, partner, 1940—, now sr. partner; dir. McGregor Doniger, Inc., 1954-79, B. Manischewitz Co., 1954-70; Mem. Bd. Edn. Union Free Sch. Dist. 7, Great Neck, N.Y., 1954-60; mem. Cornell Law Sch. Adv. Council, 1967—, univ. council, 1979—; bd. dirs. The Hoffman-Appel Found., Inc., Charles H. Oestreich Found.; former trustee Soc. of Hillside Hosp.; nat. chmn. Cornell Law Sch. Fund. Editor, bus. mgr.: Cornell Law Rev, 1927-28. Mem. Assn. Bar City N.Y., Internat. Bar Assn., N.Y. County Lawyers Assn., Am., N.Y. State bar assns., Order of Coif, Sigma Alpha Mu, Phi Kappa Phi. Clubs: Harmonie, Cornell (N.Y.C.). Home: 200 E 57th St New York NY 10022 Office: 300 Park Ave New York NY 10022

APPEL, ALFRED, JR., educator, writer, scholar; b. N.Y.C., Jan. 31, 1934; s. Alfred and Beatrice (Hoffman) A.; m. Nina Schick, Sept. 1, 1957; children: Karen Appel Oshman, Richard James. Student, Cornell U., 1952-54; B.A., Columbia U., 1959, M.A., 1960, Ph.D. in English, 1963. Lectr. English Columbia U., 1961-62, perceptor in English, 1962-63; asst. prof. Stanford U., 1963-68, Northwestern U., Evanston, Ill., 1968-69, assoc. prof., 1969-74, prof., 1974—. Author: A Season of Dreams, 1965, Nabokov's Dark Cinema, 1974, Signs of Life, 1983; author and editor: The Annotated Lolita, 1970; editor: John DeForest's Witching Times, 1967, (with Charles Newman) Nabokov: Criticism, Reminiscences, Translations, Tributs, 1970, (with Simon Kazlinsky) The Bitter Air of Exile: Russian Writers in the West 1922-72, 1977; contbg. author: Nabokov: The Man and his Work, 1967, The Single Voice, 1969, A Book of Things About Vladimir Nabokov, 1974, Vladimir Nabokov: A Tribute, 1979, Nabokov's Fifth Arc, 1982. Served with U.S. Army, 1955-57. Guggenheim fellow, 1972; Rockefeller fellow, 1976; recipient Best Creative Essay award Arts Council Ill., 1974. Home: 717 Greenleaf Ave Wilmette IL 60091 Office: Dept English Northwestern U Evanston IL 60201

APPEL, BARRY, securities dealer; b. Bklyn., Mar. 27, 1931; s. George and Rose (Kaufman) A.; m. Joan Diane Lebowitz, Aug. 7, 1960 (div. Feb. 1980); children: James Philip, Alix Liza; m. Barbara Spencer Cole, Feb. 22, 1984. B.A., Bklyn. Coll., 1952; M.B.A., CCNY, 1954. Pub. acct. firm Mayers, Architect & Brown, N.Y.C., 1956-59; pres. Philips, Appel & Walden, Inc., N.Y.C., 1959-71; individual mem. Am. Stock Exchange, N.Y.C., 1971-72, 74—, specialist, 1972-74, also floor ofcl., 1966-73, exchange ofcl., 1975—, bd. govs., 1976-82; bd. govs. Am. Commodities Exchange, 1977-80; bd. dirs. Am. Gold Coin Exchange, 1982—; dir. Securities Industry Automation Corp.; partner firm Greene & Greene, 1972-74. Served with AUS, 1954-56. Mem. Beta Gamma Sigma. Home: 7002 Boulevard East Guttenberg NJ 07093 Office: 175 W 73d St New York NY 10023

APPEL, JOHN J., educator; b. Weimar, Germany, Aug. 11, 1921; s. Jacob and Susanna (Ortweiler) A.; m. Selma Dubin, 1956; 1 son, Michael Jeffrey. B.A., U. Miami, 1948, M.A., 1951; Ph.D. (Harrison fellow), U. Pa., 1960. Instr. U. Miami, Essex Community Coll., Balt.; dir. adult edn. Jewish Community Center, Balt.; asst. prof. Mich. State U., East Lansing, 1961-71, prof., 1971—; vis. scholar ethnic studies Smithsonian Instn., Washington, 1969-70; vis. prof. History Mus. Grad. Program, Cooperstown, N.Y.; asso. prof. James Madison Coll., Mich. State U., East Lansing, 1969-71; cons. Ford Found., Nat. Park Service, various pub. firms. Author: The New Immigration, 1971, The Distorted Image, 1973, Immigrant Historical Societies in the USA, 1980. Served with U.S. Army, 1942-45. Mem. AAUP, Am. Hist. Assn., Soc. Am. Historians, Am. Jewish Hist. Soc., Immigration History Soc. Jewish. Home: 219 Oakland Dr East Lansing MI 48823 Office: Michigan State U East Lansing MI 48824

APPEL, NORMAN, ophthalmologist, educator; b. N.Y.C., Dec. 4, 1945; s. Robert M. and Anne K. (Kleiner) A.; m. Rena Lee Moskovits, Sept. 2, 1973. B.A., U. Louisville, 1966, M.D., 1970; postgrad., Harvard U., 1974. Diplomate: Am. Bd. Ophthalmology. Intern Maimonides Med. Ctr., Bklyn., 1970-71; resident in ophthalmology Strong Meml. Hosp. of U. Rochester, N.Y., 1973-76; fellow The Edward S. Harkness Eye Inst., Columbia-Presbyn. Med. Ctr., N.Y.C., 1976; practice medicine specializing in orbit, lacrimal and oculoplastic surgery and oncology, N.Y.C., 1977—; sr. clin. asst. ophthalmologist Mt. Sinai Hosp., 1977—; asst. attending ophthalmologist Beth Israel Med. Ctr., 1977—; assoc. attending ophthalmologist St. Clare's Hosp., 1977—; asst. attending surgeon ophthalmology N.Y. Infirmary Beekman Downtown Hosp., 1977—; attending ophthalmologist Bronx VA Hosp.; asst. attending ophthalmologist Montefiore Hosp. and Med. Ctr., 1979—, Cabrini Med. Ctr., 1982—, Westchester County Med. Ctr., 1983—; founder, dir. Orbit Clinic Mt. Sinai Hosp., 1977-78, Orbit and Oculoplastic Surgery Clinic Beth Israel Med. Ctr., 1977-79, St. Clare's Hosp., 1977—, Bronx Va Hosp., 1977—, North Central Bronx Hosp., 1980—, Orbit Clinic N.Y. Infirmary Beekman Downtown Hosp., 1977—; physician in charge orbit, lacrimal and oculoplastic surgery service Brookdale Hosp. Med. Ctr., 1982—; founder, dir. Orbit, Lacrimal and Oculoplastic Surgery Clinic, 1982—; cons. Interfaith Med. Ctr.; faculty Mt. Sinai Sch. Medicine, Albert Einstein Coll. Medicine; cons. in field. Served with USAF, 1971-73; Vietnam. N.Y. State Regents scholar, 1963. Fellow ACS, Am. Acad. Ophthalmology and Otolaryngology; mem. N.Y. State Med. Soc., N.Y. County Med. Soc., Bklyn. Ophthalmol. Soc., Phi Delta Epsilon. Office: 1021 Park Ave New York NY 10028

APPEL, STEPHEN BERNARD, department store chain executive; b. N.Y.C., May 28, 1935; s. Joseph and Frances (Soss) A.; m. Martha Patterson Smith, Nov. 26, 1967; children: Susan Dudley, Henry Gamble. A.B., U. Chgo., 1954, M.B.A., 1959. In merchandising and control positions Macy's N.Y., N.Y.C., 1959-65; expense controller Alexanders Dept. Store, N.Y.C., 1965-66; research dir. Federated Dept. Stores, Inc., Cin., 1966-73, dir. plans and analysis, 1974-77; v.p. research and planning Abraham & Straus Dept. Store, N.Y.C., 1977-79; v.p. research May Dept. Stores Co. Inc., St. Louis, 1979—; speaker Nat. Retail Mchts. Assn., Internat. Council Shopping Ctrs. Mem. Y. Chgo. Nat. Alumni Bd., 1969-72. Served with U.S. Army, 1954-56; Korea. Mem. Planning Execs. Inst., Am. Mgmt. Assn., Retail Research Soc., Delta Upsilon. Office: May Dept Stores Co Inc 611 Olive St Saint Louis MO 63101

APPEL, WALLACE HENRY, industrial designer; b. Boston, Sept. 10, 1925; s. Wallace Henry and Isabella (Simpson) A.; m. Marjorie Jeanne Triebold, Nov. 22, 1948; children: Linda, Donna, Sandra. B.F.A., R.I. Sch. Design, 1950. Staff designer Westinghouse Electric, Mansfield, Ohio, 1950-55, mgr. indsl. design, 1955-75, White-Westinghouse, Mansfield, 1975-80; v.p. design Advanced Food Systems, Columbus, Ohio, 1980-82; v.p. design and planning WCI Internat., Grand Rapids, Mich., 1982—. Contbg. author: World of Manufacturing, 1968; patentee in field. Served with USN, 1943-46. Fellow Indsl. Designers Soc. Am. (dir. 1975-80). Home: 5138 Stauffer SE Grand Rapids MI 49508 Office: WCI Internat 4248 Kalamazoo SE Grand Rapids MI 49508

APPEL, WILLIAM FRANK, pharmacist; b. Mpls., Oct. 8, 1924; s. William Ignatius and Elna Antonia (Mulzahn) A.; m. Louise D. Altman, Sept. 24, 1949; children—Nancy, Peggy, James, Elizabeth. B.S. in Pharmacy, U. Minn., 1949; D.Sc. (hon.), Phila. Coll. Pharmacy and Sci., 1978. Intern in pharmacy Northwestern Hosp., Mpls.; pres., pharmacist, mgr. Appel Pharmacy, Inc., Mpls., 1949—; pres. Pharm. Cons. Services, P.A., St. Paul, 1960—, Shenandoah Pharmacy, Inc., Mpls., Pharmco, Inc., Bloomington, Minn., Riverside Pharmacy Corp., Mpls.; mem. Minn. Bd. Pharmacy, 1960-65, pres., 1965; preceptor internship requirement program; chmn. Minn. Gov.'s Commn. on Drug Abuse, 1971-73; mem. Mpls. Health Dept. Task Force on Pub. Health Approaches to Chem. Dependency; clin. instr. U. Minn. Coll. Pharmacy, 1970—; cons. HEW; long term care facilities; rep. Nat. Pharmacy/Industry Com. on Nat. Health Ins.; mem. revision com. U.S. Pharmacopeial Conv., 1980—. Served with USN, 1942-46. Recipient Good Neighbor award Sta. WCCO, Mpls., 1973. Mem. Twin City Met. Drug Assn., Minn. Pharm. Assn. (v.p., Harold R. Popp award 1974, mem. continuing edn. faculty 1970—), Am. Pharm. Assn. (pres. N.W. br., nat. pres. 1976-77, Daniel B. Smith award 1970, treas. 1979—) pharm. assns), Minn. Gerontol. Soc., U. Minn. Coll. Pharmacy Alumni Assn. (v.p., Distinguished Pharmacist award 1971). Home: 7204 Trillium Ln Minneapolis MN 55435 Office: 3952 Lyndale Ave S Minneapolis MN 55409

APPELBAUM, JOEL ALAN, physicist, educator; b. Bklyn., Dec. 30, 1941; s. Emanuel and Sylvia A.; m. Muriel Rothenberg, Sept. 1, 1963; 1 son, Robert. B.S. in Physics, CCNY, 1963, M.S., U. Chgo., 1964, Ph.D. in Physics (NASA fellow), 1966. Mem. tech. staff Bell Labs., Murray Hill, N.J., 1967-68, dept. theoretical physics, 1969-78, supr. econ. analysis group, 1978-80, head demand econ. dept., 1980-82, head bus. planning dept., 1982—; asst. prof. physics U. Calif., Berkeley, 1968-69; vis. lectr. Ecole Polytechnique Federale de Lausanne, 1980, Free U. West Berlin, 1973; Inst. Theoretical Physics U. Colo., 1970. Fellow Am. Phys. Soc. (Davisson Germer prize 1979), AAAS; mem. Phi Beta Kappa. Research, publs. in solid state physics and econs. Home: 100 W Dudley Ave Westfield NJ 07090 Office: Crawford Corner Holmdel NJ 07733

APPELBAUM, JOSEPH, food co. exec.; b. N.Y.C., July 31, 1926; s. Max and Anna (Bader) A.; m. children—Robert, Jeffrey. B.Chem. Engring., Coll. City N.Y., 1947; M.S., Bucknell U., 1948; grad. Advanced Mgmt. Program, Harvard, 1967. Asst. dir. corporate engring. Gen. Mills Corp., 1967-69; pres. Slim Jim, Inc., Phila., 1969-70, Blue Bird Food Products, 1970, Doxsee Food Corp., Balt., 1970—. Served with AUS; World War II. Mem. Am. Chem. Soc., Am. Inst. Chem. Engrs. Home: 9 Pomona S Pikesville MD 21208 Office: 8223 Pulaski Hwy Baltimore MD 21237

APPELMAN, EVAN HUGH, chemist; b. Chgo., June 6, 1935; s. Harry Louis and Mollie Sarah (Hirsch) A.; m. Mary Frances Goold, Sept. 2, 1960; children—Harold Stewart, Hilary Louise. A.B., U. Chgo., 1953, M.S., 1955; Ph.D., U. Calif. at Berkeley, 1960. With Argonne (Ill.) Nat. Lab., 1960—, chemist, 1963-76, sr. chemist, 1976—. Contbr. articles to profl. jours. Guggenheim fellow, 1973-74; Recipient award for service at Argonne Nat. Lab., U. Chgo., 1975; E.O. Lawrence award ERDA, 1976. Mem. AAAS, Am. Chem. Soc., Fedn. Am. Scientists, Phi Beta Kappa, Sigma Xi. Jewish. Office: Argonne National Laboratory 9700 S Cass Ave Bldg 200 Argonne IL 60439:

APPELMAN, WILLIAM HENRY, advertising executive; b. N.Y.C., Mar. 10, 1939; s. Herman and Edna (Adler) A. B.A., Bklyn. Coll., 1959. Copywriter Doyle, Dane, Bernbach, N.Y.C., 1966-73; sr. v.p., group creative dir. Young & Rubicam, N.Y.C., 1974—. Advisor Greenwich Village Trust for Hist. Preservation, N.Y.C., 1982. Recipient Clio awards, 1980, 81, Hollywood and Radio TV Soc. awards, 1979, 80. Mem. Am. Orchid Soc. Republican. Jewish. Office: Young & Rubicam 285 Madison Ave New York NY 10017

APPELQUIST, THOMAS WILLIAM, physicist, educator; b. Emmetsburg, Iowa, Nov. 1, 1941; s. Leroy Applequist and Madeline (McCullum) A.; m. Marion E. Locascio, Aug. 28, 1965; children: Daniel, Karen. B.S., Ill. Benedictine Coll., 1963; Ph.D., Cornell U., 1968; M.S., Yale U., 1976. Research assoc. Stanford Linear Accelerator Ctr., Stanford U., Palo Alto, Calif., 1968-70; asst. prof. Harvard U., Cambridge, Mass., 1970-74; assoc. prof. Yale U., New Haven, 1975-76, prof. physics, 1976—, chmn. physics dept., 1983—; cons. U.S. Dept. Energy, Washington, 1983. Mem. editorial bd.: Phys. Rev., Upton, L.I., N.Y., 1978-81, 84—. Sloane fellow Sloan Found., N.Y.C., 1976-80. Fellow Am. Phys. Soc. (mem. exec. com. 1978-80), AAAS. Home: 400 Livingston St New Haven CT 06511 Office: Dept Physics Yale U New Haven CT 06520

APPELSON, WALLACE BERTRAND, college president; b. Bklyn., June 9, 1930. B.S., NYU, 1951, M.A., 1952; Ed.D., Columbia U., 1959. Chief X-ray technician Samaritan Hosp., Bklyn., 1951-52; tchr. art White Plains Pub. Schs., N.Y., 1954-57; research asst. Inst. Adminstrv. Research (Columbia U.), 1957-58; asst. prof. ednl. adminstrn. Rutgers U., 1958-60; coordinator terminal program N.J. State Dept. Higher Edn., 1960-65; dean acad. affairs Bucks County Community Coll., Newton, Pa., 1965-70; pres. Atlantic Community Coll., Mays Landing, N.J., 1970-73; dean faculty LaGuardia Community Coll., CUNY, 1973-76; pres. Truman Coll., Chgo., 1976—. Editor: Associated Public Schools System Yearbook, 1958, Toward Higher Education Newsletter, N.J. Div. Higher Edn., 1960-65; contbr. articles to profl. jours. Pres. bd. dirs. North Bus. and Indsl. Council Chgo.; bd. dirs. Ravenswood Hosp. Med. Ctr., Chgo., Uptown Chgo. Commn., Dist. Two Edn. Council, Chgo., Orchard Mental Health Ctr., Skokie, Ill. Served with U.S. Army, 1952-54. Mem. Am. Assn. Sch. Adminstrs., Am. Assn. Higher Edn., Am. Assn. Community and Jr. Colls., Phi Delta Kappa, Kappa Delta Pi, Uptown C. of C. (bd. dirs.). Office: 1145 W Wilson Ave Chicago IL 60640

APPENZELLAR, SALLY LOUISE, librarian; b. N.Y.C., Mar. 21, 1948; d. Donald Cameron and Sally (Sanders) A. B.A., Conn. Coll., 1970; M.L.S., U. Md., 1972; M.A., George Washington U., 1977. Reference and computer services librarian U.S. Fed. Trade Commn., Washington, 1972-76; chief law library U.S. Gen. Acctg. Office, 1976-78, tech. info. specialist, 1978-79; chief readers services U.S. Dept. Justice, 1979-81, dir.library staff, 1981—; chmn. Automated Legal Research Interagy. Planning Com., Washington, 1981—; chmn. exec. adv. council Fed. Library and Info. Network, 1982—; lectr. Legal Edn. Inst., 1982—. Contbr. articles to profl. jours.; panelist: procs. Archival Automation, 1981, Evolution in CALR Systems, 1981. Recipient Atty. Gen.'s Spl. Commendation award U.S. Dept. Justice, 1981. Mem. Am. Assn. Law Libraries, Law Libraries Soc. Washington, Beta Phi Mu. Roman Catholic. Home: 535 2d St SE Washington DC 20003 Office: US Dept Justice 10th and Pennsylvania Ave NW Washington DC 20530

APPERSON, JACK ALFONSO, army officer; b. Fredericksburg, Va., Dec. 21, 1934; s. Claude Heywood and Mary Louise (Farmer) A.; m. Alexandra Maynard, Aug. 31, 1957; children: Melissa Heywood, Amy Alexandra, Robert Randall (dec.), Eric Edward. B.S., 1957; M.S. in Nuclear Physics, U. Ala., 1962; A.A. hon., Texarkana Community Coll., 1979. Commd. 2d lt. U.S. Army, 1957, advanced through grades to brig. gen., platoon leader, Ft. Bragg, N.C., 1957-58, Ft. Knox, Ky., 1958-59; comdg. officer 546th Ordnance Co. U.S. Army-Europe, 1963-64, material officer 66th Maintenance Bn., 1964-65, exec. officer bn., 1965-66; asst. prof., instr. dept. ordnance U.S. Mil. Acad., 1967-69; bn. comdr. and material officer 801st Maintenance Bn., Vietnam, 1969-70; assignment officer ordnance br. Office of Personnel Ops., Dept. Army, Washington, 1970-71, chief co. grade assignments, 1971-72; bn. comdr. 1st Inf. Div., Ft. Riley, Kans., 1973-74; assigned to Office of Staff for Logistics, Dept. Army, Washington, 1974-75; chief war res. office Office Chief of Staff for Logistics, Dept. Army, Washington, 1975-76; exec. officer Office Asst. Sec. for Installations and Logistics, Washington, 1976-77; comdr. Red River Army Depot, Texarkana, Tex., 1977-79; dep. comdg. gen. U.S. Army Missile Material Readiness Command, Redstone Arsenal, Ala., 1979-81; comdg. gen. U.S. Army Depot System Command, Chambersburg, Pa., 1981—. Bd. dirs. Redstone Fed. Credit Union; vestryman Sharon Chapel Episcopal Ch., Alexandria, Va., 1975-77. Decorated Legion of Merit, Bronze Star (2), Meritorious Service medal, others. Mem. Assn. Grads. U.S. Mil. Acad., Assn. U.S. Army, Am. Def. Preparedness Assn., Alumni Assn. U.S. Army War Coll., Sigma Pi Sigma. Republican. Lodge: Rotary. Home: Box 90 Letterkenney Army Depot Chambersburg PA 17201 Office: Comdr US Army Depot System Command Chambersburg PA 17201

APPL, FREDRIC CARL, educator; b. Mt. Hope, Kans., Nov. 17, 1932; s. Frederick Carl and Vida Jane (Gates) A.; m. Esther Natalie Simpson, June 13, 1954; children—Sandra Lee, Charlotte Joann, Cynthia Lucille. B.S. in Mech. Engring, Carnegie Mellon U., 1954, M.S., 1956, Ph.D., 1958. Research asst. Carnegie Inst. Tech., 1954-57, instr.-asst. prof., 1957-58; cons. Mine Safety Appliances Co., Pitts., 1957-58; research engr. Jersey Prodn. Research Co., Tulsa, 1958-60; asso. prof. engring. Kans. State U., Manhattan, 1960-64, prof., 1964-65, Jennings prof., 1967—; cons. Christensen Diamond Products Co., Salt Lake City, 1965-67. Reviewer: Applied Mechanics Revs, 1968—; Contbr. articles to profl. jours. NSF grantee, 1961-63, 63-65; coop. research Technische U. Hannover, West Germany, 1974. Mem. ASME, Soc. Petroleum Engrs., Sigma Xi, Tau Beta Pi, Pi Tau Sigma, Phi Kappa Phi, Pi Mu Epsilon. Patentee in field. Home: 1916 Indiana Ln Manhattan KS 66502

APPLE, B. NIXON, lawyer; b. Toronto, Ont., Can., 1924. Ed., U. Toronto, Osgoode Hall Law Sch. Partner firm Salter, Apple, Cousland & Kerbel, Toronto; Queen's counsel. Home: Rural Route 3 Uxbridge ON L0C 1K0 Canada Office: 10 King St E Toronto ON Canada

APPLE, RAYMOND WALTER, JR., journalist; b. Akron, Ohio, Nov. 20, 1934; s. Raymond Walter and Julia (Albrecht) A.; m. Betsy Pinckney Brown, July 14, 1982; stepchildren: Catherine St. George Brown, John Preston Brown. Student, Princeton U., 1952-56; A.B., Columbia U., 1961. Reporter Wall St. Jour., 1956-57, 59-61; writer, corr. NBC News, 1961-63; mem. staff N.Y. Times, 1963—, Albany bur. chief, 1964-65, Vietnam corr., 1965-66, Vietnam bur. chief, 1966-68, Africa bur. chief, 1969, nat. polit. corr., 1970-76, London bur. chief, 1977-80, 81—, Moscow bur. chief, 1980-81. Contbr. to nat. mags., books. Served with AUS, 1957-59. Recipient Krout prize history Columbia, 1961; award Acad. TV Arts and Scis., 1963; George Polk Meml. award, 1967; Overseas Press Club award, 1967. Mem. Am. Newspaper Guild. Clubs: Century (N.Y.C.); Garrick (London). Office: NY Times 76 Shoe Ln London EC4 England

APPLEBAUM, EDWARD LEON, otolaryngologist, editor, educator; b. Detroit, Jan. 14, 1940; s. M. Lawrence and Frieda (Millman) A.; m. Marilyn Novetsky, June 21, 1966; children: Daniel Ira, Rachel Anne. A.B., Wayne State U., 1961, M.D., 1964. Diplomate: Am. Bd. Otolaryngology. Intern Univ. Hosp., Ann Arbor, Mich., 1964-65; resident Mass. Eye and Ear Infirmary Harvard Med. Sch., Boston, 1966-69; practice medicine specializing in otolaryngology, Chgo., 1972—; assoc. prof. Northwestern U. Med. Sch., 1972-79; prof., head dept. otolaryngology, head and neck surgery Coll. Medicine, U. Ill., 1979—; mem. staffs U. Ill. Hosp., Westside VA Med. Ctr., Children's Meml. Hosp. Author: Tracheal Intubation, 1976; editor: Am. Jour. Otolaryngology, 1982. Served as maj. U.S. Army, 1969-71. Recipient Anna Albert Keller Research award Wayne State U. Coll. Medicine, 1964, William Beaumont Soc. Orig. Research award, 1964. Fellow ACS, Am. Soc. for Head and Neck Surgery, Am. Acad. Facial Plastic and Reconstructive Surgery, Am. Acad. Otolaryngology, Head and Neck Surgery, Am. Laryngol. Rhinol. and Otol. Soc. Office: Ill Coll Medicine Dept Otolaryngology-Head and Neck Surgery 1855 W Taylor St Chicago IL 60612

APPLEBAUM, LOUIS, composer, conductor; b. Toronto, Ont., Can., Apr. 3, 1918; s. Morris Abraham and Fanny (Freiberg) A.; m. Janet Hershoff, July 19, 1940; 1 son, David Hersh. Student, Toronto Conservatory Music, 1938-40; LL.D. (hon.), York U., 1979. Music dir. Nat. Film Bd. Can., Ottawa, Ont., 1941-46; music cons. CBC, Toronto, 1960-61, Nat. Arts Centre, Ottawa, 1963-67; exec. dir. Ont. Arts Council, Toronto, 1971-80; chmn. Fed. Cultural Policy Rev. Com., 1980-82; lectr. York U., Toronto, 1974. Music dir., Stratford (Ont.) Festival, 1953-60; composer condr. for films, TV, theatre., 400 scores for film, theatre, TV, ballets, symphonic, chamber, solo music.; contbr. articles to jours. Recipient award Composers, Authors and Pubs. Assn. Can., 1938, Can. film awards, 1968, Can. Centennial medal, 1967; Wilderness award, 1973; officer Order of Can., 1977; Anik award, 1976; Jubilee medal, 1977; nominee Acad. Award.; hon. fellow Ont. Coll. Art, 1981. Mem. Can. Music Council, Can. League Composers, Composers, Authors and Pubs. Assn. Can., Can. Conf. Arts, Assembly Arts Adminstrs., Royal Soc. Arts. Clubs: Arts and Letters (Toronto); Cercle Universitaire (Ottawa). Office: 151 365 Laurier Ave W Ottawa ON K1A OC8 Canada *

APPLEBAUM, SAMUEL, musician, music educator, consultant; b. Passaic, N.J., Jan. 15, 1904; s. Michael and Fanny (Levine) A.; m. Sada Rothman, Aug. 14, 1927 (dec. 1976); children: Michael Tree, Lois Applebaum Leibow. Diploma, Juilliard Sch. Music, 1927; D.Mus. (hon.), Gettysburg (Pa.) Coll., 1974, Southwestern Coll., Winfield, Kans., 1976. Tchr. violin Manhattan Sch. Music, 1956—, Fairleigh Dickinson U., Madison, N.J., 1968—, Kean Coll., Union, N.J., 1973-75; cons. in field, 1945—; cons. applied music dept. Seton Hall U., N.J., 1983—. Composer 400 works for strings and orch., 1936—; author textbooks on string performance, also lecture films. Mem. Nat. Fedn. Music Clubs (nat. good will ambassador 1960, citation 1965), Nat. String Tchrs. Assn. (award 1967), Am. String Tchrs. Assn. (citation 1965), N.J. Fedn. Music Clubs (program chmn. 1956-60), N.J. Music Educators Assn. (pres. 1960-64), Asso. Musicians Greater N.Y., N.Y. Musicians Club, Nat. Sch. Orch. Assn., Bohemians. Jewish. Club: B'nai B'rith. Address: 23 North Terr Maplewood NJ 07040 *In my textbooks and study books, the aim is to inspire teachers to teach creatively; to inspire their pupils to think creatively and to motivate their pupils to develop a strong desire to learn.*

APPLEBAUM, SID, food chain store executive. Pres. Applebaum Super Markets Inc., St. Paul. Office: Applebaum Super Markets Inc PO Box 43509 St. Paul MN 55164

APPLEBAUM, STUART S., publishing company public relations executive; b. N.Y.C., Sept. 19, 1949; s. Jack A. and Anne (Miller) A. B.A., Queens Coll., 1971. Publicity assoc. Alfred A. Knopf, Inc., N.Y.C., 1971-73; publicist MGM Pictures, N.Y.C., 1973, Bantam Books, Inc., 1974-75, publicity mgr., 1976-79, publicity dir., 1979—, v.p., 1982—. Mem. Publishers Publicity Assn. (bd. dirs. N.Y.C. chpt. 1979-84). Office: Bantam Books 666 Fifth Ave New York NY 10103

APPLEBEE, WILLIAM ROBERT, newspaper executive; b. Iowa City, Iowa, Aug. 22, 1936; s. Kenneth O. and Sadie E. A.; m. Katherine R. Payne, Sept. 9, 1956; children: William K., Julie A., Jennifer L., Jessica E. Grad., Iowa Wesleyan Coll., 1959. Gen. mgr. Grand Forks (N.D.) Herald Daily Newspaper, 1966-73; pres., pub. Niles (Mich.) Daily Star, 1973-77; gen. mgr. Bradenton (Fla.) Herald, 1977-79, Pasadena (Calif.) Star-News, 1979-81, pub., 1981—. Mem. Inland Daily Press Assn., Am. Newspaper Pubs. Assn., Calif. Press Assn., C. of C. Republican. Club: Athletic (Pasadena). Office: 525 E Colorado St Pasadena CA 91169

APPLEBERRY, JAMES BRUCE, university president; b. Waverly, Mo., Feb. 22, 1938; s. James Earnest and Bertha Viola (Lane) A.; m. Patricia Ann Trent, June 5, 1960; children: John Mark, Timothy David. B.S. in Edn, Central Mo. State Coll., 1960, M.S., 1963, Ed.S., 1967; postgrad., U. Kans., 1967; Ed.D., Okla. State U., 1969. Tchr. Knob Noster Pub. Sch., 1960-62; prin. Knob Noster Elementary Sch., 1962-63, Knob Noster Jr. High Sch., 1963-64; minister edn. Wornall Rd. Baptist Ch., Kansas City, Mo., 1964-65; grad. fellow Central Mo. State Coll., 1965-66, asst. dir. field service, 1966-67; grad. asst. Okla. State U., 1967-68, asst. prof. ednl. adminstrn., 1967-71, assoc. prof., 1971-73, prof., head dept. adminstrn. and higher edn., 1973-75; Am. Council on Edn. fellow Acad. Adminstrn. Internship Program U. Kans., Lawrence, 1973-74, dir. planning, prof. adminstrn., founds. and higher edn., 1975-76, asst. to chancellor, prof., 1976-77; pres. Pittsburg (Kans.) State U., 1977-83, No. Mich. U., Marquette, 1983—; plenary rep. Univ. Council for Ednl. Adminstrn., 1968-72; mem. exec. com., 1973-76; ednl. adminstrn. rep. Council on Tchr. Edn., 1968-75; dir. 1st State Bank Pittsburg; abstracter ednl. adminstrn. abstracts Univ. Council for Ednl. Adminstrn., Columbus, Ohio, 1969-75; asst. state liaison rep. to Am. Assn. Colls. for Tchr. Edn., 1971; coordinator Interested Profs. Ednl. Adminstrn.; cons. N.Central Okla. Assn. Sch. Adminstrs.; mem. adv. council Nat. Council Edn. Stats., 1980-83; Kans. rep. to Am. Assn. State Colls. and Univs., 1980-81. Contbr. articles to ednl. jours. Trustee Marquette Gen. Hosp. Mem. Am. Assn. for Higher Edn., Am. Ednl. Research Assn., NEA, Nat. Conf. Profs. Ednl. Adminstrn., Mace and Torch, Phi Delta Kappa, Phi Kappa Phi, Kappa Delta Pi, Phi Sigma Phi, Kappa Mu Epsilon., Alpha Kappa Psi. Club: Rotary. Home: 1240 Center St Marquette MI 49855 Office: Northern Michigan Univ Office of the President Marquette MI 49855

APPLEBY, JOYCE OLDHAM, historian; b. Omaha, Apr. 9, 1929; d. Junius G. and Edith (Cash) Oldham; children: Ann Lansburg Bloxham, Mark Lansburgh, Frank Bell Appleby. B.A., Stanford U., 1950; M.A., U. Calif., Santa Barbara, 1959; Ph.D., Claremont Grad. Sch., 1966. With Mademoiselle mag., 1950-52; asst. prof. history San Diego State U., 1967-70, asso. prof., 1970-73; prof. history, asso. dean Coll. Arts and Letters, 1973-75, prof., 1976-81; vis. asso. prof. U. Calif., Irvine, 1975-76; vis. prof. UCLA, 1978-79, prof. history, 1981—; vis. fellow St. Catherine's Coll., Oxford U., 1983; Bd. fellows Claremont Grad. Sch. and U. Center, 1970-73. Author: Economic Thought and Ideology in Seventeenth-Century England, 1978, Capitalism and a New Social Order, 1983; contbr. articles to profl. jours.; bd. editors: Democracy, 1980—, William and Mary Quar., 1980-83, 18th Century Studies, 1982—, Ency. Am. Polit. History. Mem. Calif. Dem. Council, 1964-66; mem. Escondido Human Rights Coordinating Council, 1968-70; Fellow commoner Churchill Coll. Cambridge U., 1977-78. Mem. Am. Hist. Assn. (council), Orgn. Am. Historians, Inst. Early Am. History and Culture (council chmn.). Home: 615 Westholme Ave Los Angeles CA 90024 Office: Dept History UCLA Los Angeles CA 90024

APPLEGATE, DOUGLAS, congressman; b. Steubenville, Ohio, Mar. 27, 1928; s. Earl Douglas and Mary Margaret (Longacre) A.; m. Betty Jean Engstrom, Aug. 25, 1950; children: Kirk Douglas, David Allen. Student pub. schs., Steubenville. Real estate salesman and broker, Steubenville, 1950—; mem. Ohio Ho. of Reps. from 33d Dist., 1961-68, Ohio Senate, 1969-76; mem. 95th-98th Congresses from 18th Dist. Ohio. Del.-at-large Democratic Nat. Conv., 1964; past pres. Jefferson County Young Dems. Named One of 10 Outstanding Young Men U.S. C. of C.; Outstanding Ohio Legislator DAV, 1975. Mem. Young Dems., Farm Bur., Pine Valley, Mingo Sportsmen, Sons of Italy, Polish-Am. Citizens, League Women Voters. Presbyterian. Clubs: Elks, Eagles, Polish Athletic (Steubenville). Home: Route 3 Berkeley Pl Steubenville OH 43952 Office: 2464 Rayburn House Office Bldg Washington DC 20515 *

APPLEGATE, EDWARD TIMOTHY, hotel company executive; b. Dayton, Ohio, Nov. 28, 1934; s. Harold Darst and Mary Gertrude (Harbison) A.; m. Patricia Margaret Kusko, July 11, 1959; children: Elizabeth Ann, Mary Catherine. B.S. in Bus. Adminstrn. cum laude, Ohio State U., 1959, J.D., 1961. Bar: N.Y. 1961. Asso. atty. Hale Russell & Stentzel, N.Y.C., 1961-63; asst. mgr. legal services Comml. Airplane div. The Boeing Co., Renton, Wash., 1963-68; v.p. marketing and contracts Hokanson div. Lear-Siegler, Inc., Santa Ana, Calif., 1968-69; v.p., corporate counsel Internat. Leisure Corp., Las Vegas, Nev., 1969-72; sr. v.p., gen. counsel Hilton Hotels, Beverly Hills, Calif., 1972—. Served with USN, 1952-55. Mem. Am. Bar Assn., Am. Soc. Corporate Secs., Am. Hotel and Motel Assn., Town Hall of Calif. Republican. Office: 9990 Santa Monica Blvd Beverly Hills CA 90212

APPLEMAN, JEAN, lawyer, author; b. Urbana, Ill., Oct. 4, 1939; d. John Alan and Jean Isabelle (Gerber) A. Student, U. Wis., 1956, 62, Georgetown U., 1956-58, Laval U., Quebec, 1957, 59, Catholic U., Washington, 1958; A.B. magna cum laude, U. Ill., 1960, J.D., 1963; postgrad., U. Perugia, Italy, 1960. Bar: Ill. bar 1963, D.C. bar 1963, U.S. Cts. of Appeal 1963, Fifth and Seventh circuits 1963. Atty. R.R. Retirement Bd., Chgo., 1963-64; practiced in, Chgo., 1964—; Adminstrv. dir. Internat. Soc. Barristers, 1965-73; asst. prof. law Loyola U., Chgo., 1970-73; law clk. to Judge Albert E. Hallett Chgo. 2d Dist. Appellate Ct., 1975-76; to Judge Romiti Chgo. 1st Dist. Appellate Ct., 1976—; fin. columnist Better Investing. Author: Insurance Law and Practice, 38 vols, 1965—, Persuasion in Brief Writing, 1968, (with Jerome Mirza) Illinois Tort Law and Practice, 1974, The Midas Touch, Dynamics of Market Investment, 1975, How To Inflate Your Income and Assets During the Reagan Years, 1981; co-author: Problems in Law, 1975; Contbr. articles to World Book Ency., also profl. jours. Recipient U. Ill. Scholarship Key, 1960. Mem. Am., Internat., Ill., Chgo. bar assns., Order Coif, Phi Kappa Phi. Democrat. Roman Catholic. Home and office: 1530 N Dearborn Pkwy Chicago IL 60610 *

APPLEMAN, MARJORIE, playwright, educator; b. Ft. Wayne, Ind.; d. Theodore E. and Martha C. (Rathert) Haberkorn; m. Philip Appleman. B.A., Northwestern U.; M.A., Ind. U.; degre superieur, Sorbonne, U. Paris. Lectr. in English Columbia U., N.Y.C., 1977-80; asst. prof. English (playwriting) NYU, 1976—; mem. membership com. PEN Am. Ctr., N.Y.C., 1980—; mem. playwrights unit Circle Repertory Co., N.Y.C., 1978—. Author: plays The Bedroom, 1978, Thirty-Nine Seconds and Counting, 1983, Seduction Duet, 1981, Foxtrot by the Bay, 1982. Hartfound Found. fellow; finalist Gt. Am. Play Contest Actors Theatre Louisville, 1978, Eugene O'Neill award Nat. Playwrights Conf., 1979; recipient Double Image Short Play award Samuel French, Inc., 1981, 12th Ann. Playwriting award Jacksonville U., 1982. Mem. Dramatists Guild, Authors League Am., Acad. Am. Poets. Home: 411 E 10th St 21A New York NY 10009 Office: Dept English NYU New York NY 10003

APPLEMAN, PHILIP, English educator, writer, poet; b. Feb. 8, 1926; m. Marjorie Haberkorn. B.S. in English, 1950, Ph.D., Northwestern U., 1955, A.M., U. Mich., 1951; postgrad., U. Lyon, (France), 1951-52. Teaching asst. Northwestern U., Evanston, Ill., 1953-55; instr. English Ind. U., Bloomington, 1955-58, asst. prof., 1958-62, assoc. prof., 1962-67, prof., 1967-82, disting. prof., 1982—; dir., instr. in world lit. and philosophy Internat. Sch. Am., 1960-61, 62-63; vis. prof. lit. SUNY-Purchase, 1973; vis. prof. English Columbia U., 1974; panelist NEH, Washington, 1968, applications judge, 1978, 80; mem. adv. panel Ind. Arts Commn., 1971; cons. NEH-sponsored Project on Ethics and Values in Health Care Columbia U. Coll. Physicians and Surgeons, 1979-81; lectr. in field, poetry reader. Author: The Silent Explosion, 1965, (2d edit.) The Silent Explosion, 1966, (Portuguese transl.) The Silent Explosion, 1973; (poetry) Kites on a Windy Day, 1967 (Ind. Authors' Day citation 1968), Summer Love and Surf, 1968 (Friends of Lit. Soc. Robert F. Ferguson Meml. award 1969, Soc. Midland Authors Midland Poetry award 1969), Open Doorways, 1976; novel In the Twelfth Year of the War, 1970, Shame the Devil, 1981; editor: books The Origin of Species, 1975; book An Essay on the Principle of Population, 1976, (2d edit.) Darwin, 1979; contbr. numerous articles, chpts. revs. to various publs. Co-founder Bloomington Civil Liberties Union; faculty adviser Ind. U. Civil Liberties Union, Bloomington. Served with AC U.S. Army, 1944-45; served with U.S. Mcht. Marine, 1946, 48-49. Recipient citation for In the Twelfth Year of the War, Ind. Author's Day, 1971; Fulbright scholar, France, 1951-52; Huntington Hartford Found. fellow, 1964; Nat. Endowment for Arts fellow, 1975. Mem. AAUP (pres. Ind. U. chpt. 1968-69, mem. nat. council 1969-72), MLA (sec. English sect. II 1965, chmn. English sect. II 1966, chmn. sect. exec. com. 1972), Nat. Council Tchrs. English, PEN, Poetry Soc. Am. (Christopher Morley Meml. award 1970, Alice Fay di Castagnola award 1975, awards judge 1970, 71, 74, 76, 79, mem. governing bd. 1981-83), Acad. Am. Poets, Authors Guild, Phi Beta Kappa. Office: Dept English Ind U Bloomington IN 47405

APPLETON, ARTHUR IVAR, electric products manufacturing company executive; b. Chgo., Oct. 14, 1915; s. Albert Ivar and Lillian (Wihk) A.; m. Martha O'Driscoll, July 20, 1947; children: Thomas Albert, Arthur Ivar; by previous marriage: James Kenneth, John Stephen, Linda Charlotte, William Paul. B.A., Dartmouth, 1936. With Appleton Electric Co., 1936—, pres., chmn. bd., 1947-83, now chmn. bd.; dir., v.p. Gulfstream Park Racing Assn.; propr. Appleton Oil Co. Served with USNR, 1943-45. Decorated Letter of Commendation. Mem. Phi Delta Theta. Presbyn. (pres. bd. trustees 1958-59). Clubs: Bob O'Link Golf; Exmoor Country (Highland Park, Ill.); Surf (Surfside) (Fla.); Indian Creek (Miami Beach, Fla.). Home: 22 Indian Creek Dr Indian Creek Village Miami Beach FL 33154 Office: 1701 W Wellington Ave Chicago IL 60657

APPLETON, JOSEPH HAYNE, civil engr., educator; b. Collinsville, Ala., Aug. 5, 1927; s. Shelton and Helen (Gower) A.; m. Patricia Ann Zimmerman, May 8, 1954; children—Joseph F., Sandra K., Jeffrey T., Tricia A., Kevin L., Kathryn L. B.C.E., Auburn U., 1947; M.S., U. Ill., 1949, Ph.D., 1959. Research asst. U. Ill., Urbana, 1947-49, research asso., 1951-54; structural engr. U.S. Bur. Pub. Rds., Washington, 1949-50; instr. N.C. State U., 1950-51; structural engr. Ala. Cement Tile Co., Birmingham, 1954-59; prof. engring. U. Ala., Birmingham, 1959—, asso. prof. dentistry, 1960—, asso. prof. physiology and biophysics, 1966—; dean Sch. Engring., 1971-78; cons. structural analysis and design, 1959—. Contbr. numerous articles to profl. jours. Mem. ASCE, Am. Soc. Engring. Edn., Am. Concrete Inst., Nat. Soc. Profl. Engrs., AAUP, Newcomen Soc., Sigma Xi, Tau Beta Pi, Phi Kappa Phi, Chi Epsilon. Methodist. Club: Exchange of Birmingham (pres. 1981-82). Home: 4237 Antietam Dr Birmingham AL 35213

APPLEY, LAWRENCE A., business executive; b. Nyack, N.Y., Apr. 22, 1904; s. Rev. Joseph Earl and Jessie (Moore) A.; m. Ruth G. Wilson, Sept. 1, 1927 (dec. Mar. 1977); children: Ruth Ann, Judith (Mrs. William Schatz); m. Katherine F. Coffey, Dec. 1979. A.B., Ohio Wesleyan U., 1927, LL.D., 1946; LL.D., Bethany Coll., 1951, St. Lawrence U., 1951, Colgate U., 1955; Litt.D., Bryant Coll., 1970; L.H.D., Lakeland Coll., 1979. Instr. Colgate U., 1927-30; personnel mgr. Buffalo div. Mobil Oil Co., Inc., 1930-34, ednl. dir., N.Y.C., 1934-41; v.p. Vick Chem. Co., N.Y.C., 1941-46, dir., 1945-47; v.p., dir. Montgomery Ward & Co., Chgo., 1946-48; pres. Am. Mgmt. Assn., 1948-68, chmn., 1968-74, chmn. emeritus, 1974—; adj. prof. Fla. Atlantic U., 1980—; chmn., chief exec. officer A&S Mgmt. Corp., 1979—; dir. Nat. Can Corp., Kohler Co., Oneida, Ltd.; expert cons. to Sec. of War on civilian personnel, 1941-42; exec. dir., dep. chmn. War Manpower Commn., Washington, 1943-44; mem. personnel policy com. Hoover Commn., 1948; personnel adv. com. AEC, 1948-52. Author: TV series Management in Action. Pres. Truman's Adv. Com. on Mgmt., 1949-52, U.S. Commn. on Intergovtl. Relations, 1953-54; mem. U.S. Bus. Ethics Adv. Council, 1961-63; pres. Glen Ridge (N.J.) Bn. Forum, 1945-46, Bd. of Edn., 1940-46; former trustee Colgate U., Am. U., Cazenovia Coll., Ohio Wesleyan U., Northfield Mt. Herman Sch. Recipient War Dept. citation for meritorious civilian service, 1944; Presdl. citation Medal for Merit, 1946; Skipper Allen award Nat. Assn. Training Directors, 1958; Human Relations award, 1952; Taylor Key Soc. Advancement Mgmt., 1961; Henry Laurence Gantt medal, 1963; Applause award Sales Execs. Club N.Y., 1966; Horatio Alger award, 1971. Fellow Internat. Acad. Mgmt.; mem. Am. Mgmt. Assn. (v.p. charge personnel div. 1942-44, dir., mem. exec. com. 1944-47), producer mgr. skill tng. program, ASME (chmn. exec. com. mgmt. 1945), Soc. Advancement Mgmt., Phi Beta Kappa Assos., Omicron Delta Kappa, Chi Phi, Delta Sigma Rho, Sigma Iota Epsilon. Methodist. Home: 1536 SE 15th Ct Deerfield Beach FL 33441 *The basic difference between the human and the dumb animal is that the human animal was given judgment—the ability to differentiate between right and wrong. . . . I have great faith in the inherent goodness and value of human beings. I cannot believe that the Supreme Being who created the human body, the human mind, and the human soul did so to fail.*

APPLEY, MORTIMER HERBERT, psychologist, university president; b. N.Y.C., Nov. 21, 1921; s. Benjamin and Minnie Albert; m. Dee Gordon, June 5, 1942 (div. Oct. 1969); children: Richard Gordon, John Benton; m. Mariann B. Hundahl, Jan. 10, 1971; stepchildren: Scott, Eric, Heidi Hundahl. B.S., CCNY, 1942; M.A., U. Denver, 1946; Ph.D., U. Mich., 1950; D.Sc. (hon.), York U., 1975, D.H.L., Northeastern U., 1983, Litt.D., Am. Internat. Coll., 1984, LL.D., Clark U., 1984. Instr. U. Denver, 1945-47; instr. U. Mich., 1947-49; asst. prof. Wesleyan U., Middletown, Conn., 1949-52; prof., chmn. psychology Conn. Coll., New London, 1952-60, So. Ill. U., Carbondale, 1960-62, York U., Toronto, Ont., Can., 1962-67, dean faculty grad. studies, 1965-68; prof., chmn. psychology U. Mass., Amherst, 1967-69; dean Grad. Sch., 1969-74, asso. provost, 1973-74; pres. Clark U., Worcester, Mass., 1974—; cons. NSF, NIMH, NRC of Can., Can. Council, VA. Author: (with C.N. Cofer) Motivation: Theory and Research, 1964, (with R. Trumbull) Psychological Stress, 1967, (with J. Rickwood) Psychology in Canada, 1967; Editor: Adaption Level Theory: A Symposium, 1971, Motivation and Emotion, 1976—; assoc. editor: Psychol. Abstracts, 1961-62; editor, contbr. to: Psychoanalysis and Psychology; contbg. author: Internat. Ency. Neurology, Psychology, Psychoanalysis and Psychiatry, Ency. Brit.; Contbr. articles to profl. jours. Served with USAAF, 1942-45. NSF Sci. Faculty fellow, 1959-60; Fulbright fellow, Germany, 1973-74. Fellow Am. (past chmn. edn. and tng. bd.), Canadian psychol. assns.); mem. Conn. Psychol. Assn. (past pres.), New Eng. Psychol Assn. (past pres.), Sigma Xi, Psi Chi, Phi Sigma. Democrat. Unitarian (chmn. bd. mgrs. congregation). Clubs: Worcester, Worcester Econ. (pres. 1980-81); University (N.Y.C.).

APPLEYARD, EDWARD CLAIR, geologist; b. Strathroy, Ont., Can., June 22, 1934; s. Harold Frederick and Muriel A.; m. Elizabeth Ann Curtis, July 28, 1962; children—Gregory David Jarvis, Mary Louise Desborough. B.Sc., U. Western Ont., 1956; M.Sc., Queen's U., 1960; Ph.D., Cambridge U., 1963. Asst. Lectr. Bedford Coll., U. London, 1962-65; asst. prof. U. Waterloo, Ont., Can., 1965-68, asso. prof., 1968—; exec. dir. Can. Geosci. Council, 1972-80. Mem. Geol. Assn. Can., Mineral. Assn. Can., Geol. Soc. Norway. Office: Dept Earth Scis Univ of Waterloo Waterloo ON N2L 3G1 Canada

APPLEYARD, MILTON HERBERT, hospital administration; b. Johnstown, Pa., Apr. 30, 1929; s. Milton A. and Leona (Cook) A.; children: Lorraine Marie, Karl Wallace, Milton John. B.S., U. Pa., 1956, postgrad., 1959-60; M.S., Columbia U., 1964. Asst. dir. Presbyn.-U. Pa. Med. Center, Phila., 1957-66; exec. dir. United Hosp., Inc., Beaver Falls, Pa., 1966-70, Harrisburg (Pa.) Hosp., 1970-77, pres., 1977—; pres., chief exec. officer Harrisburg Hosp. Health Found., 1983—; dir. Dauphin County Mental Health/Mental Retardation Program, 1970-72, chmn. bd., 1973; mem. Commonwealth of Pa. Comprehensive Health Planning Adv. Council, 1970-73; pres. Council on Alcoholism, Beaver County, 1968-69; vice chmn. Regional Med. Program, Beaver County, 1969-70; chmn. adminstrs. conf. Hosp. Council Western Pa., 1969. Adviser Med. Explorer post 29 Boy Scouts Am.; Bd. dirs. Harrisburg YMCA, 1972, Beaver County Joint Hosp. Planning Assn., 1968-70. Served with USMC, 1948-52. Fellow Am. Coll. Hosp. Adminstrs. (regent Dist. II 1981-84); mem. Am. Hosp. Assn., Hosp. Assn. Pa. (dir. 1969-72, pres. elect 1973, chmn. bd. 1974). Rotarian. Office: Harrisburg Hospital S Front St Harrisburg PA 17101

APRISON, MORRIS HERMAN, biochemist, neurobiologist, educator; b. Milw., Oct. 6, 1923; s. Henry and Ethel (Mollin) A.; m. Shirley Reder, Aug. 21, 1949; children—Barry, Robert. B.S. in Chemistry, U. Wis., 1945, tchrs. certificate, 1947, M.S. in Physics, 1949, Ph.D. in Biochemistry, 1952. Grad. teaching asst. in physics U. Wis., Madison, 1947-49; grad. research asst. in pathology Sch. Medicine, 1950-51, grad. research asst. in biochemistry, 1951-52; tech. asst. in physics Inst. Paper Chemistry, Appleton, Wis., 1949-50; biochemist, prin. investigator, head biophysics sect. Galesburg (Ill.) State Research Hosp., 1952-56; prin. research investigator in biochemistry Inst. Psychiat. Research; asst. prof. depts. biochemistry and psychiatry Ind. U. Med. Sch., Indpls., 1956-60, asso. prof., 1960-64, prof. biochemistry, 1964-78, distinguished prof. psychiatry and biochemistry, 1978, distinguished prof. neurobiology and biochemistry, 1978—, chief neurobiology sect., 1969-74; mem. exec. com. dept. psychiatry, exec. adminstr. Inst. Psychiat. Research, 1973-74, dir. inst., 1974-78, chief sect. applied and theoretical neurobiology, 1978—; co-chmn. session on neurotransmitters 23d Internat. Physiol. Congress, 1965; chmn. session neurochemistry and neuropharmacology 25th Congress, 1971; ad hoc mem. study sect. psychopharmacology NIMH, 1967-71, mem. neuropsychology study sect., 1970-74; vis. prof. 4th ASPET Workshop, Vanderbilt U., 1972; guest scholar Grad. Sch., Kans. State U., 1973. Adv. editor: Neurosci. Research, 1968-73, Jour. Biol. Psychiatry, 1968-83, Neuropharmacology, 1969—, Jour. Neurochemistry, 1972-75, Pharmacology, Biochemistry and Behavior, 1973—, Jour. Comparative and General Pharmacology, 1974-75, Jour. Gen. Pharmacology, 1975—, Jour. Developmental Psychobiology, 1974-77; regional editor: Life Scis, 1970-73; co-editor: Advances in Neurochemistry, 1973—; mem. editorial bd.: Jour. Neurochemistry, 1975-79; dep. chief editor, 1980-83; mem. editorial bd.: Neurochem. Research, 1975-82; co-editor 6 books; contbr. articles to profl. jours., chpts. to books. Mem. Ind. regional adv. bd. Anti-Defamation League, 1973-76; bd. overseers St. Meinrad Sem., 1974-77. Served with USNR, 1944-46. Mem. Am. Physiol. Soc., Biophys. Soc., Soc. Biol. Psychiatry (program com. 1974-75, co-chmn. 1975-76, gold medal 1975), Internat. Brain Research Orgn., Internat. Soc. Neurochemistry (co-chmn. 1 session 1st internat. meeting Strasbourg, France 1967, 4th meeting Tokyo 1973, 7th meeting Jerusalem 1979, council 1973-75, sec. 1975-79, chmn. 1979-81, publicity com. 1975-83, nominating com. 1983—), Am. Soc. Neurochemistry (co-chmn. 1 session 1970, 71, council 1971-73, 75-79, chmn. sci. program com. 1972, mem. 1973), Soc. for Neurosci. (pres. Indpls. chpt. 1970-71), Sigma Xi. Home: 5810 N Dearborn St Indianapolis IN 46220 Office: Inst Psychiat Research Ind Univ Sch Medicine Indianapolis IN 46223

APRUZZI, GENE, stock broker; b. Trani, Bari, Italy, Feb. 16, 1934; came to U.S., 1956, naturalized, 1959; s. Francesco and Giulia (Tritto) A.; m. Ida G. Italiano, May 12, 1956; 1 dau., Claire J. Chartered acct., Sch. Econs., Bari, 1952; student, Università di Bari, 1952-56, NYU, 1956-58. Accountant Am. Hull Ins. Syndicate, N.Y.C., 1956-58; Acct., F.I. duPont & Co., N.Y.C., 1958-59; asst. ops. mgr. Cyrus J. Lawrence & Sons, N.Y.C., 1959-61, ops. mgr., 1961-67, gen. partner charge ops. and adminstrn., mem. exec. com., 1968-73; sr. v.p., chief financial and ops. officer Cyrus J. Lawrence, Inc., 1973-76, exec. v.p., chief fin. and ops. officer, 1976—; also dir., mem. exec. com.; v.p., treas., dir. C.J. Lawrence & Co., Inc., 1973—; pres., dir. Cyrus J. Lawrence Capital Holdings Inc., 1977—; pres., chief exec. officer, trustee The 59 Wall Street Fund; dir. Devlin Allen Communications, Lawrence-Williams Broadcasting Corp., Deulin Allen Communications, LWB Atlanta, LWB Allentown; Mem. Am. stock exchange, Pacific Stock Exchange, Midwest Stock Exchange; mem. Phila. Stock Exchange; dir. Wall St. Tax Assn., 1970-72. Bd. govs. Strathmore Village Civic Assn., 1970-73; chmn. bd. Cathedral Sch. St. Mary, Garden City, 1977. Mem. Securities Industry Assn. Clubs: Downtown Athletic (N.Y.C.); Plandome (N.Y.) Country, World Trade Center. Home: 74 Dover Rd Manhasset NY 11030 Office: 115 Broadway New York NY 10006

APSTEIN, MAURICE, electrical engineer; b. Bridgeport, Conn., May 5, 1910; s. David and Mary A.; m. Martha Keck, June 21, 1936; children—Carl Stephen, Michael Donald. B.S. in Elec. Engring, City U. N.Y., 1932; M.E.A., George Washington U., 1959; Ph.D., Am. U., 1963. Engr. Morlen Electric Co., 1932-40; tchr. radio communications, N.Y.C., 1940-45; chief engr. Cardwell Mfg. Co., 1945-49; electronic scientist Nat. Bur. Standards, Washington, 1949-53; asso. tech. dir. Harry Diamond Labs., U.S. Army, Washington, 1953-75; research prof. Sch. Engring. and Applied Sci., George Washington U., Washington, 1975—. Recipient Exceptional Service Gold medal U.S. Dept. Commerce, 1952; Exceptional Civilian Service award U.S. Army, 1972. Fellow IEEE, Washington Acad. Sci.; mem. AAAS, Nat. Acad. Engring. Club: Cosmos (Washington). Patentee in fields of electronics, instrumentation, mil. tech. Home: 4611 Maple Ave Bethesda MD 20814 Office: Sch of Engring George Washington U Washington DC 20052

APT, CHARLES, artist; b. N.Y.C., Dec. 10, 1933; s. Gustav Lee and Tami (Vera Salzman) A.; m. Ursula Edith Betz, July 24, 1959; children—Gregory, Sam. B.F.A., Pratt Inst., 1956. Exhibited in group shows at, Mus. Fine Art, Springfield, Mass., 1966, Expn. Intercontinentale, Monaco, France, 1966, 68, NAD, 1965, 68, 77, 78, 79, 80, 81, 83, Am. Watercolor Soc., 1965, 66, 68, 69, Allied Artists Am., 1964, 65, 67, 69, 70, 72, Nat. Mus. Racing, Saratoga, N.Y., 1967, Atlantic City Race Track, Nat. Arts Club, one-man shows, Ground Floor Art Gallery, N.Y.C., 1967, 68, 69, Aqueduct Race Track Art Gallery, N.Y.C., 1967, Grand Central Art Galleries, 1969, Far Gallery, N.Y.C., 1972, 78, Talisman Gallery, Bartlesville, Okla., 1976, Gallery 52, South Orange, N.J., 1976, 77, two-man show, Palm Beach (Fla.) Galleries, 1973. Served with AUS, 1956-58. Recipient Gold medal Am. Vets. Soc. Artists, 1965; Best in Show award Saratoga Mus. Racing Ann., 1967; 2d Benjamin Altman award for figure painting NAD, 1968; Le Prix Prince Souverain, Monaco, 1968; hon. mention Allied Artists Am., 1970; Bronze medal Annual Open Watercolor Exhbn. Nat. Arts Club, 1971; Sutherland prize Annual Open Oil Exhbn., 1972; Ject-key prize Salmagundi Club, 1972. Mem. Artists Fellowship, Allied Artists Am., NAD (academician), Artists Equity Assn. N.Y. Home: Route 45 Warren CT 06754 Studio: 27 W 67th St New York NY 10023

APT, LEONARD, physician; b. Phila., June 28, 1922; s. Morris and Rebecca A. A.B., U. Pa., 1942; M.D., Jefferson Med. Coll., 1945. Diplomate: Am. Bd. Pediatrics, Am. Bd. Ophthalmology and Otolaryngology. Intern Jefferson Med. Coll. Hosp., Phila., 1945-46; pediatric resident and research fellow in hematology Children's Hosp., Detroit, 1946-49, pediatric resident, Cin., 1949-50, Children's Med. Center, Boston, 1950-52, chief med. resident, 1952-53, asst. physician, 1953-55; teaching fellow in pediatrics Harvard U. Med. Sch., Boston, 1950-52, instr. pediatrics, 1953-55; sr. physician radioisotope unit Boston VA Hosp., 1953-55; ophthalmology resident Wills Eye Hosp., Phila., 1955-57, fellow in pediatric ophthalmology research, 1959-61; fellow pediatric ophthalmology NIH, 1958-59; practice medicine specializing in pediatric ophthalmology, Los Angeles, 1961—; attending surgeon Jules Stein Eye Inst., UCLA, dir. pediatric ophthalmology, 1966—; asso. prof. ophthalmology UCLA Sch. Medicine, 1968-72, prof., 1972—; cons. pediatric ophthalmology Cedars-Sinai Med. Center, Los Angeles, St. John's Hosp., Santa Monica, Calif., Bur. Maternal and Child Health, Dept. Public Health, Calif., Dept. Health, Los Angeles. Contbr. numerous articles on pediatric ophthalmology to med. jours.; contbr. chpts. in field to med. books; editor: Diagnostic Procedures in Pediatric Ophthalmology, 1963. Served to 1st. lt. M.C. U.S. Army, 1943-46. Mem. Am. Acad. Ophthalmology, Am. Acad. Pediatrics, Am. Ophthal. Soc., Assn. for Research in Ophthalmology, Soc. Pediatric Research, Am. Assn. of Pediatric Ophthalmology and Strabismus, Pacific Coast Oto-Ophthal. Soc., AMA, Am. Med. Writers Assn. Office: Jules Stein Eye Inst UCLA School of Medicine Los Angeles CA 90024

APTHEKER, HERBERT, historian, lecturer; b. Bklyn., July 31, 1915; s. Benjamin and Rebecca (Komar) A.; m. Fay Aptheker, Sept. 4, 1942; 1 dau., Bettina. B.S., Columbia U., 1936, A.M., 1937, Ph.D., 1943; Ph.D. (hon.), Martin Luther U., Halle, Germany, 1966. Editor Masses and Mainstream, 1948-52, Polit. Affairs, 1952-63; dir. Am. Inst. Marxist Studies, N.Y.C., 1964—; prof. Hostos Community Coll., City U. N.Y., 1971-77; lectr. throughout, U.S. and Europe, 1946—; vis. lectr. dept. history Bryn Mawr Coll., 1969-71; vis. lectr. U. Mass., 1971-72, Yale U., 1976, U. Calif. at Berkeley Law Sch., 1978—, U. Santa Clara, 1982-83; vis. prof. Afro-Am. studies U. Calif., Berkeley, 1984. Author: To Be Free: Studies in American Negro History, 1948, World of C. Wright Mills, 1960, Soul of the Republic, 1964, Negro Slave Revolts in the United States, 1939, Negro in the Civil War, 1938, Nat Turner's Slave Rebellion, 1966, Mission to Hanoi, 1966, Labor Movement in the South During Slavery, 1954, The Truth about Hungary, 1957, The Nature of Democracy, Freedom and Revolution, 1967, History of the American People, 2 vols, 1959, 60, Essays in the History of the American Negro, rev. edit, 1964, Era of McCarthyism, 1955, Dare We Be Free?, 1960, American Foreign Policy and the Cold War, 1962, American Negro Slave Revolts, 1943; rev. edit., 1963, American Civil War, 1961, Urgency of Marxist-Christian Dialogue, 1970, Afro-American History: the Modern Era, 1971, Annotated Bibliography of the Published Writings of W.E.B. DuBois, 1973, Early Years of the Republic, 1783-1793, 1976, The Unfolding Drama: Studies in U.S. History, 1979; Editor: Disarmament and American Economy, 1960, One Continual Cry, 1965, Marxism and Democracy, 1964, And Why Not Every Man?, 1961, Marxism and Alienation, 1965, Documentary History of the Negro People in the United States, Vols. 1-3, 1951-74, Marxism and Christianity, 1967, Autobiography of W.E.B. DuBois, 1968, The Correspondence of W.E.B. DuBois, Vol. 1, 1973, Vol. II, 1976, Vol. III, 1978, The Published Writings of W.E.B. DuBois, 40 vols, 1973—, Education for Black People (DuBois), 1973, Prayers for Dark Folk (DuBois), 1980. Ind. Peace candidate for U.S. Congress, 1966; candidate Communist party for U.S. Senate, 1976. Served to maj. F.A. AUS, 1942-46; ETO. Guggenheim fellow, 1946-47; grantee Social Sci. Research Council, 1961, Rabinowitz Found., 1965, Am. Council Learned Studies, 1974. Mem. Am. Hist. Assn., Assn. Study Negro Life (History award 1939, 69). Office: 480 N 1st St San Jose CA 95112

AQUILINO, DANIEL, banker; b. Needham, Mass., Feb. 4, 1924; s. Michael Aquilino and Anna (Bruno) A.; m. Theresa H. Barberio, Nov. 9, 1946; children: Donna Lee (Mrs. Herbert F. Fraser), Daniel C., Michael D. B.S. magna cum laude, Northeastern U., 1949; grad., Stonier Grad. Sch. Banking, Rutgers U., 1962. With Fed. Res. Bank Boston, 1949—, exec. v.p., 1970—. Served with AUS, 1943-45. Home: 3 Bakers Hill Rd Weston MA 02193 Office: 600 Atlantic Ave Boston MA 02106

ARABIE, PHIPPS, psychology educator; b. Mar. 13, 1948; s. Wade Joseph and Betty Jo (Thomason) A. A.B., Harvard U., 1970; Ph.D., Stanford U., 1974. Asst. prof. psychology U. Minn., Mpls., 1974-77, assoc. prof., 1977-80; prof. psychology and sociology U. Ill., Champaign-Urbana, 1970—; cons. Bell Telephone Labs, Murray Hill, N.J., 1975—. Editor: Jour. Classification, 1983—; contbr. articles to profl. jours. Grantee NSF, Office Naval Research; Beckman Assoc. U. Ill., 1983-84. Fellow Am. Psychol. Assn.; mem. Am. Statis. Assn., Psychometric Soc., Soc. Math. Psychology, Am. Sociol. Assn., N.Am. Classification Soc., AAAS. Office: U Ill Dept Psychology 603 E Daniel Champaign IL 61820

ARAGALL, GIACOMO, opera singer; b. Barcelona, Spain, June 6, 1939; s. Ramon and Paula (Garriga) A.; m. Luisa Sabiron; children: Jaime, Daniel, Juan. Ed., Barcelona Conservatory. Preliminary debut at, Teatro Liceo Barcelona; profl. debut, Teatro la Fenice, Venice, Italy, 1963; appearances Rome Opera, singing tenor roles, La Scala (Milan), Covent Garden, London, Munich (W. Ger.) Staatsoper, Weiner Staatsoper, Vienna, Met. Opera, N.Y.C., Budapest (Hungary) Opera, Paris Opera; Hamburg (W. Ger.) Opera, Phila. Lyric Opera, San Francisco Opera.; rec. artist. Served with Spanish Army. Recipient medal Los Reyes Catolicos, Parma Premio Verdi award, Turin Premio D'Oro award. Roman Catholic. Office: care Robert Lombardo Assocs 61 W 62d St New York NY 10023 *

ARAGON, JOHN ANTHONY, univ. pres.; b. Albuquerque, May 3, 1930; s. John D. and Marcia S. (Garcia) A.; m. Martha Jean Maurice, Mar. 1, 1952; children—John, Judith Alison, Marcia Alicia, Joel Timothy. B.A., N.Mex. Highlands U., 1952; M.A., U. N.Mex., 1959, Ed.D., 1966. Tchr. pub. schs., Espanola, N.Mex., 1952-54, Los Alamos, 1954-56; dir. profl. services N.Mex. Tchrs. Assn., 1956-59; exec. dir. N.Mex. Sch. Bds. Assn., 1959-65; prof. ednl. adminstr. U. N.Mex., 1965-75; pres. N.Mex. Highlands U., Las Vegas, 1975—; chief cultural cons. Bicultural Childrens TV; cons. HEW, AID, Yale U., Ford Found., Mountain Bell Telephone Co., U. Tex., U. Calif. at Los Angeles, Stanford U. Mus. rec. poetry Que Es Poesia, 1975. Recipient NEA Nat. award on cultural understanding and improvement teaching, 1972. Mem. Phi Delta Kappa. Office: NMex Highlands U Las Vegas NM 87701

ARAGONÉS, SERGIO, cartoonist; b. Castellon, Spain, Sept. 6, 1937; came to U.S., 1962; s. Pascual and Isabel (Domenech) A.; m. Lilio Chomette, Sept. 14, 1962. Student, U. Mex. Sch. Architecture, 1960. Freelance cartoonist, 1954—; cartoonist: Mad mag, 1962—; frequent TV appearances, speaker in field; illustrator drawings for TV prodns. Shirley MacLaine Spl, Cher Show, Jim Stafford Show; spls. for Real Kids, Laugh-In, Speak Up America; illustrator: 14 books including Mothers are Funnier than Children (Betty Rollin), 1964, Sam, the Ceiling Needs Painting, 1964, Up Your Lexicon, 1966, Henry the Smiling Dog (Henry Blankfort), 1966, The Seven Secrets of Sales Success (Edward J. Hegarty), 1966; author/illustrator: Viva Mad, 1968, Mad About Mad, 1970, Mad-ly Yours, 1972, In Mad We Trust, 1974, Mad as the Devil, 1975, Incurably Mad, 1977, Sergio Aragones on Parade, 1979, Shootin' Mad, 1979, Mad Marginals, 1980; illustrator 14 books including Mad as a Hatter, 1981. Mem. Nat. Cartoonists Soc. (Reubens award), Screen Actors Guild, AFTRA, Writers Guild Am., Cartoonists Guild, Comic Art Profl. Soc. (v.p. 1980-81). Office: Mad Mag 485 Madison Ave New York NY 10022

ARAKAWA, KASUMI, physician, educator; b. Toyohashi, Japan, Feb. 19, 1926; came to U.S., 1954, naturalized, 1963; s. Masumi and Fayuko (Hattori) A.; m. Juen Hope Takahara, Aug. 27, 1956; children—Jane Riet, Kenneth Luke, Amy Kathryn. M.D., Tokyo Med. Coll., 1953. Diplomate: Am. Bd. Anesthesiology. Intern Iowa Meth. Hosp., Des Moines, 1954-56; resident U. Kans. Med. Center, Kansas City, 1956-58; practice medicine specializing in anesthesiology, Kansas City, 1958—; instr. anesthesiology U. Kans. Med Center, Kansas City, 1961-64, asst. prof., 1964-71, asso. prof., 1971-77, prof., 1977—, chmn. dept. anesthesiology, 1977—; clin. asso. prof. U. Mo.-Kans. City Sch. Dentistry, 1973—; dir. Kansas City Health Care, Inc. Fulbright scholar, 1954. Recipient Outstanding Faculty award Student AMA, 1970. Fellow Am. Coll. Anesthesiology; mem. Asso. Univ. Anesthesiologists (sec.-treas. 1969—), Acad. Anesthesiology, Japan-Am. Soc. Midwest (v.p. 1965, 71). Home: 7917 El Monte St Shawnee Mission KS 66208 Office: U Med Center 39 Rainbow St Kansas City KS 66103

ARAMANY, MOHAMED ABDELAL, prosthodontist, educator; b. Cairo, Egypt, Mar. 24, 1935; m. Janet Jacqueline Young, July 31, 1964; children: Jacqueline, Elizabeth, Andrew, Richard. P.N.S., Cairo U., 1954, D.D.S., 1958; M.S., U. Pitts., 1963, D.M.D., 1973. Am. Bd. Prosthodontics; cert. N.E. Regional Dental Bd.; lic. dentist, Pa. Intern Univ. Hosp., Egypt, 1958-59, instr. Sch. Dentistry, 1959-60, asst. prof. Sch. Dentistry, 1964-68; resident in prosthodontics U. Pitts. Sch. Dental Medicine and Hosps., 1961-63; teaching fellow Sch. Dental Medicine, U. Pitts., 1961-63, asst. prof., 1968-71, assoc. prof., 1971-75, prof., 1975—; resident in maxillofacial prosthetics Tex. U. Dental Br., M.D. Anderson Hosp. and Tumor Inst., Houston, 1969-70; dir. Regional Ctr. for Maxillofacial Rehab., Eye and Ear Hosp., Pitts., 1973—; dir. dept. maxillofacial prosthodontics and gen. practice dentistry West Penn Hosp., Pitts.; cons. maxillofacial prosthodontics VA Hosp., Pitts., Mercy Hosp. Fellow Internat. Coll. Dentists; mem. Am. Cleft Palate Assn., Internat. Assn. Dental Research, Am. Prosthodontic Soc., ADA, Pa. Dental Assn., Odontol. Soc. Western Pa., Am. Acad. Maxillofacial Prosthetics, Internat. Assn. for Study of Dento Facial Abnormalities, Am. Coll. Prosthodontics, Am. Assn. Dental Schs. Office: Sch Medicine Univ Pitts 5 Ave Bigelow Blvd Pittsburgh PA 15260

ARAMONY, WILLIAM, community service organization executive; b. Jewett City, Conn., July 27, 1927; s. Russell and Nazley (Farrah) A.; m. Bebe Ann Nojeim, Apr. 29, 1951; children: William S., Susan Jean, Robert David. Student, Clark U., 1946-49; M.A. in Social Work, Boston Coll., 1951. Exec. dir. United Community Services, Columbia, S.C., 1958-61; exec. dir. St. Joseph County, Ind., 1961-64; exec. v.p. United Fund of Dade County, Miami, Fla., 1964-70; pres. United Way Am., Alexandria, Va., 1970—, United Way Internat.; Vice pres. Internat. Standing Conf. on Philanthropy, London; sec.-gen. Internat. Council United Fund Raising; trustee Clark U., Worcester, Mass., Independent Sector, Washington. Served as 1st lt. Med. Service Corps U.S. Army, 1951-53. Recipient Man of Action award Greater Miami C. of C., 1970; Disting. Citizen award Nat. Health and Welfare Mut. Ins. Council, 1981. Home: 7410 Gatewood Ct Alexandria VA 22307 Office: 701 N Fairfax St Alexandria VA 22314

ARAMS, FRANK ROBERT, electronics company executive; b. Danzig, Germany, Oct. 18, 1925; came to U.S., 1939, naturalized, 1945; s. Richard and Alice (Frank) A.; m. Edith Knoll, July 24, 1952; children: Mark, Ronald. B.E.E., U. Mich., 1947; M.S. in Applied Physics, Harvard U., 1948, Stevens Inst. Tech., 1953; Ph.D. in Electrophysics, Poly. Inst. N.Y., 1961. Sr. staff mem. RCA Microwave div., Harrison, N.J., 1948-56; cons. AIL div. Eaton Corp., Melville, N.Y., 1956-65; head electrophysics and infrared dept. Cutler Hammer Corp., 1965-71; v.p. LNR Communications, Inc., Hauppauge, N.Y., 1971—. Author: Infrared-to-Millimater Wave Detectors, 1972; contbr. articles to profl. jours. Served with AUS, 1942-44. Fellow IEEE; mem. Optical Soc. Am. Home: 37 Schoolhouse Ln Lake Success NY 11020 Office: 180 Marcus Blvd Hauppauge NY 11788

ARANDA, JACOB VELASCO, neonatologist; b. Philippines, Dec. 29, 1942; emigrated to Can., 1969, naturalized, 1976; s. Anacleto T. and Gorgonia S. (Velasco) A.; m. Betty I. Sasyniuk, Dec. 28, 1974; children—Kenneth Frederic, Christopher James. M.D., Manila Central U., 1965; Ph.D. in Pharmacology, McGill U., 1975. Diplomate: Am. Bd. Pediatrics (perinatal and neonatal medicine). Intern U.S. Naval Hosp., Subic Bay, 1964-65, Washington Hosp. Center-George Washington U., 1965-66; resident in pediatrics SUNY Upstate Med. Center, Syracuse, 1966-68; fellow neonatology Case Western Res. U. Med. Sch.-Cleve. Met. Gen. Hosp., 1968-69; research fellow neonatology McGill U.-Montreal, Children's Hosp., 1969-71; attending neonatologist Montreal Children's, Royal Victoria, Jewish Gen., Montreal Gen. hosps.; cons. pediatrician St. Mary's Hosp.; acting dir. neonatal research Montreal Children's Hosp., 1974-79, dir. developmental pharmacology and perinatal research, 1979—; asst. prof. pediatrics, pharmacology and therapeutics McGill U. Med. Sch., 1974-77, asso. prof., 1977—; Med. Research Council Can. fellow, 1971-74; Queen Elizabeth II scientist, 1975. Editor-in-chief: Developmental Pharmacology and Therapeutics; contbr. articles to med. jours. Fellow Am. Coll. Clin. Pharmacology, Am. Acad. Pediatrics; mem. Am. Fedn. Clin. Research, Am. Thoracic Soc., Fedn. Med. Specialists Que., Canadian Pediatric Soc., Canadian Assn. Research in Toxicology, Canadian Thoracic Soc., Canadian Pharmacol. Soc., N.Y. Acad. Scis., Soc. Pediatric Research, Canadian Soc. Clin. Investigation. Methodist. Club: Canadian. Home: 3800 Grey Ave Montreal PQ H4R 3N7 Canada Office: 2300 Tupper Ave Montreal PQ H3H 1P3 Canada

ARANDA, THOMAS, JR., ambassador; b. Nogales, Ariz., Apr. 9, 1934; (married); 2 children. B.S., U. Ariz., 1956; J.D., 1967. Mem. firm Hiser and Aranda, Phoenix, 1968-69; mem. firm DePrima and Aranda, Phoenix, 1969-70, DePrima, Aranda and DeLeon, 1970-76; spl. asst. to Pres. Ford, White House, Washington, 1976-77; individual practice law, Phoenix, 1977-79; mem. firm Aranda and Fisher, 1979-81; ambassador to Uruguay, Montevideo, 1981—. Served to lt. col. USAF, 1955-60. Office: Am Embassy Calle Lauro Muller 1776 Montevideo Uruguay *

ARANDA DÍAZ MUÑÓZ, PEDRO, bishop; b. Leon, Mex., Apr. 29, 1933. Ordained priest Roman Catholic Ch., 1956; named bishop of Tulancingo, 1975. Address: Obispado Apartado 14 Tulancingo Mexico

ARANGO, JORGE SANIN, architect; b. Bogota, Colombia, Nov. 29, 1916; s. Fernando Arango and Maria Sanin A.; m. Elizabeth Leighton, 1944; 1 son, Pedro; m. Judith Brooks Wolpert, Dec. 14, 1951; children: Richard, Virginia; m. Penelope Corey, Aug. 18, 1976. Student, Universidad Catolica de Chile Sch. Architecture, 1935-42, Harvard Grad. Sch. Design, 1942-43. Head archtl. firm Arango & Murtra, Bogota, 1946-59; prof. architecture and urban design Nat. U., Bogota, 1945-47; vis. prof. Sch. Architecture U. Calif., Berkeley, 1956, 58; Pub. bldgs. dir., Colombia, 1948-49; pres. Colombian Soc. Architects, 1946-51, Colegio Engrs. and Architects of Colombia, 1955. Co-author basic plan for devel. Bogota, 1948; Author: (with C. Martinez) Architecture in Colombia, 1951, The Urbanization of the Earth, 1970. Recipient Excellence in Design awards Miami and Fla. chpts. AIA, 1967. Mem. AIA. Invited to U.S. by State Dept. and Mus. Modern Art, N.Y.C. Home: 3920 Wood Ave Miami FL 33133

ARANOW, HENRY, JR., emeritus medical educator; b. N.Y.C., May 5, 1913; s. Harry and Dora (Bittman) A.; m. Doris Elaine Jones, Apr. 26, 1941; children—Peter Jones, Philip Thompson, Michael Henry, Robert Bittman. Grad., Horace Mann Sch. Boys, 1930; A.B. magna cum laude, Harvard U., 1934; M.D., Columbia U., 1938, Med.Sci.D., 1944. Intern Presbyn. Hosp., N.Y.C., 1938-40, resident, 1942-44, mem. staff, adminstrn., 1944—, acting dir. med. service, 1970-71, 75-76, attending physician, 1969—; mem. faculty Columbia Coll. Physicians and Surgeons, N.Y.C., asso. prof. clin. medicine, 1960-67, prof., 1967—, Samuel W. Lambert prof. medicine, 1976-78, Lambert prof. emeritus, 1978—, acting chmn. dept. medicine, 1970-71, 75-76; sr. adj. assoc. Inst. Society, Ethics and Life Scis., 1981—; Harlow Brooks fellow N.Y. Acad. Medicine, Johns Hopkins Hosp., Balt., 1941-42; dir., mem. exec. com., hon. counselor Group Health, Inc.; Trustee Mary Imogene Bassett Hosp., Cooperstown, N.Y., 1977—, chmn. bd. trustees, pres., 1982—; bd. visitors Helen Hayes Rehab. and Research Hosp., N.Y., 1978—. Contbr. articles to profl. jours.; asso. editor: Man and Medicine; mem. editorial bd.: The Pharos, 1979—. Benjamin Franklin fellow Royal Soc. Arts, London, Eng., 1970. Mem. N.Y. Acad. Medicine, Endocrine Soc., Am. Thyroid Assn., Harvey Soc., Phi Beta Kappa, Alpha Omega Alpha. Club: Century Assn. (N.Y.C.). Home: 665 N Broadway Hastings-on-Hudson NY 10706 Office: 630 W 168th St New York NY 10032

ARANT, EUGENE WESLEY, lawyer; b. North Powder, Oreg., Dec. 21, 1920; s. Ernest Elbert and Wanda (Haller) A.; m. Juanita Clark Flowers, Mar. 15, 1953; children: Thomas W., Kenneth E., Richard W. B.S. in Elec. Engring, Oreg. State U., 1943; J.D., U. So. Calif., 1949. Bar: Calif. 1950. Mem. engring. faculty U. So. Calif., 1947-51; practiced in, Los Angeles, 1950-51; patent atty. Hughes Aircraft Co., Culver City, Calif., 1953-56; pvt. practice, Los Angeles, 1957—. Author articles. Mem. La Mirada (Calif.) City Council, 1958-60; trustee Beverly Hills Presbyn. Ch., 1976-78. Served with AUS, 1943-46, 51-53. Mem. Am. Bar Assn., Los Angeles County Bar Assn., Wilshire Bar Assn. (sec. 1979-80), State Bar Calif., Los Angeles Patent Law Assn. (chmn. legis. com. 1981-82), Ala. State Bar. Democrat. Lodge: Wilshire Rotary of Los Angeles (dir. 1981-83). Patentee med. devices. Home: 2444 Jupiter Dr Los Angeles CA 90046 Office: 3435 Wilshire Blvd Los Angeles CA 90010

ARANT, WILLIAM DOUGLAS, lawyer; b. Waverly, Ala., May 19, 1897; s. William Jackson and Emma (Baker) A.; m. Letitia Tyler McNeel, Dec. 31, 1929 (dec. July 14, 1977); children: Adele Goodwyn (Mrs. Richard J. Stockham, Jr.), Letitia Christian, Frances Fairlie (Mrs. David R. Maginnes). B.S., M.S., U. Va., 1920; LL.B. magna cum laude, Yale U., 1923; LL.D. (hon.), U. Ala., 1978, Birmingham-So. Coll., 1978, D.C.L., Southwestern at Memphis, 1984. Bar: Ala. 1923. Instr. polit. sci. U. Va., summers 1920-22; with Tillman, Bradley & Baldwin, Birmingham, Ala., mem. successor firms, 1927—; now Bradley, Arant, Rose & White; spl. asst. to atty. gen. U.S. and chief counsel for Petroleum Adminstrv. Bd. (N.R.A.), Washington, 1933-34; chmn. Regional Labor Bd., 6th Dist., N.R.A., 1934-35; public mem. 4th Regional Labor Bd., Atlanta, 1942-44; mem. nat. com. study Anti-Trust Laws, 1953-54. Editor in chief: Yale Law Jour, 1922-23. Mem. Bd. Appeal, Dist. 2 Ala. SSS, 1940-45; pres. Birmingham Civic Symphony Assn., 1936-38, Birmingham Civic Opera Assn., 1957-60; mem. distbn. com. Greater Birmingham Found.; trustee Brooke Hill Sch., 1940-73, Eye Found.; bd. dirs. Norton Center Birmingham-So. Coll., 1972—. Enlisted as pvt. U.S. Army, June 1918; later assigned Field Arty. C.O.T.S.; Camp Taylor, Ky.; 2d lt., 1919. Fellow Am. Bar Found.; mem. Am. Bar Assn. (com. on bill of rights 1938-45, chmn. 1941-43), Ala. State Bar Assn. (pres. 1936-37, bd. commrs. 1931-40), Birmingham Bar Assn., Am. Law Inst., Assn. Bar City N.Y., Beta Theta Pi, Phi Delta Phi, Phi Beta Kappa, Order of Coif. Episcopalian. Clubs: Redstone, Mountain Brook Country. Home: 2815 Argyle Rd Birmingham AL 35213 Office: Park Place Tower 2001 Park Pl Birmingham AL 35203

ARANT, WILLIAMS EDWARD, JR., banker; b. Kingstree, S.C., Oct. 29, 1935; s. Williams Edward and Evelyn Lanham (Coskrey) A.; m. Barbara Unger, June 17, 1961; children: Jenifer Layne, Williams Edward. B.A., Duke U., 1959; postgrad., Stonier Sch. Bank, Rutgers U., 1968. Sr. v.p. Wachovia Corp., Winston-Salem, N.Y.C., 1970-73, pres., Winston-Salem, 1973-78; exec. v.p. Hibernia Nat. Bank, New Orleans, 1978-80; pres., chief adminstrv. officerr, dir. Park Nat. Bank, Knoxville, Tenn., 1980—. Chmn. United Way Major 1st div., 1981; trustee Webb Sch. Knoxville; active U. Tenn. Chancellor's Assocs. Mem. Am. Bankers Assn., Knoxville C. of C. (v.p. econ. devel. 1980—). Lodge: Rotary. Office: Park Nat Bank 505 S Gay St Knoxville TN 37901

ARANYOS, ALEXANDER SANDOR, international operations executive; b. Zilina, Czechoslovakia; s. Ludwig and Ethel (Wilhelm) A.; m. Gertrude Reisman, Aug. 22, 1937; children: Alexander Paul, Vivian Jane. Degree Comml. Engring. cum laude, Grad. Sch. Commerce U. Prague, 1931. Adminstrv. asst. to pres. and export mgr. Coburg Mining & Foundry Co., Bratislava, Czechoslovakia, 1940-41; mgr. import div. Gen. Motors Distbrs., Republic of Panama, 1940-41; mgr. Latin Am. div. Van Raalte Co., N.Y.C., 1945-53; with Fruehauf Corp., Detroit, 1953—, v.p. internat. ops., 1956—, dir., 1973—; pres., dir. Fruehauf Internat. Ltd., 1957, chmn., dir., 1976-82, hon. chmn., 1982—; mem. adminstrv. council Viaturas PNV-Freuhauf S.A., Sao Paulo, Brazil; dir. Fruehauf Trailers (Australasia) Pty. Ltd., Fruehauf Finance Corp. (Pty.) Ltd., Melbourne, Australia, Fruehauf France,

S.A., RIS-ORANGIS, France, Fruehauf de Mexico, S.A., Coacalco, Nippon Fruehauf Co., Ltd., Tokyo, Henred-Fruehauf Trailers (Pty.) Ltd., Johannesburg, S. Africa, Fruehauf S.A., Madrid, Spain, Industrias Colombo Andina Inca, S.A., Bogota, Colombia; asso. dir., Clyde Industries Ltd., Sydney, Australia. Mem. regional export expansion council U.S. Dept. Commerce, 1970-73. Decorated French Legion of Honor. Mem. Research Inst. Am., AIM, Detroit Bd. Commerce, Internat. Execs. Assn. N.Y., World Trade Club Detroit, Am. Australian Assn. N.Y., C. of C. U.S. (internat. com.). Clubs: Rotary, Rockefeller Center Luncheon (N.Y.C.); Detroit Athletic. Home: 2 Bridle Ln Sands Point NY 11050 10020 and 10900 Harper Ave Detroit MI 48232

ARASKOG, RAND VINCENT, business executive; b. Fergus Falls, Minn., Oct. 30, 1931; s. Randolph Victor and Hilfred Mathilda A.; m. Jessie Marie Gustafson, July 29, 1956. B.S.M.E., U.S. Mil. Acad., 1953; postgrad., Harvard U., 1953-54. Spl. asst. to dir. Dept. Def., Washington, 1954-59; dir. mktg. aero. div. Honeywell, Inc., Mpls., 1960-66; v.p. ITT; group exec. ITT Aerospace, Electronics, Components and Energy Group, Nutley, N.J., 1971-76; pres., chief exec. ITT Corp., N.Y.C., 1979—, chmn. bd., chmn. exec. and policy coms., 1980—; dir. ITT Corp., Hartford Ins., Dayton-Hudson Corp.; chmn. Nat. Security Telecommunications Adv. Com., 1983—. Served with U.S. Army, 1954-56. Mem. Aerospace Industries Assn. (bd. govs.), Air Force Assn. (mem. exec. council). Episcopalian. Office: ITT World Hdqrs 320 Park Ave New York NY 10022 *

ARASTEH, ABDAL-REZA, psychologist, psychotherapist, educator, author; b. Shiraz, Iran, Sept. 27, 1927; came to U.S., 1951, naturalized, 1976; s. Mirza Khalil A. and Sarah Bigum Sadat Mirzai; m. Josephine Durkatz, July 14, 1957; children: Dariush K., Roya Louise. B.A., U. Tehran, 1948, M.A. in Psychology and Philosophy, 1951; Ph.D., La. State U., 1953; postgrad., U. Chgo., 1953-54. Assoc. prof. U. Tehran and Inst. for Pub. Adminstrn., 1954-57; lectr. dept. near Eastern studies Princeton U., N.J., 1958-60; collaborator with Erich Fromm, 1960-62; mem. faculty dept. psychiatry and social behavior George Washington U., 1962-69; vis. prof. social and analytical psychology U. Tehran, 1969-71, advisor to mgmt. and social devel., 1969-71; vis. prof. Princeton U., 1971-72; internat. lectr. and advisor in devel. and tng. various univs., U.S., Can., Asia, Iran, India, Japan, 1972—; mem. adj. faculty Grad Sch. Dept. Agr., 1962-75; advisor Indian Inst. Tech., 1972-78, UN Inst. for Research and Devel., 1971-72, NIH, 1968-69, Med. Women's Internat. Assn., 1975; dir. Inst. for Perspective Tng. and Devel., Bethesda, Md., 1973—; vis. prof. Jung Inst., Zurich, Switzerland, 1982. Author: Faces of Persian Youth, 1970, (Spanish edit.) Rumi the Persian, The Sufi, 1974, Man and Society in Iran, 1969, Education and Social Awakening in Iran, 1960, Teaching Through Research, 1968, Toward Final Personality Integration, 1975, Creativity and Human Development, 1976, Growth to Selfhood, 1980, (in Persian) The Process of Human Growth, 1956, Development of Western Psychology, 1970, Rebirth of Youth in the Age of Cultural Change, 1961, Role of Science and Technology in Human Society, 1969; contbr. numerous articles on Persian culture nad psycho-cultural analyses and human devel. to profl. jours. Recipient UNESCO, 1972; Fulbright scholar, 1951. Fellow Am. Psychol. Assn., Royal Soc. Medicine, Internat. Ctr. for Integrative Studies; mem. Congress for Asian Psychology (founding mem.), Inst. Advanced Islamic Studies (hon.), Am. Mgmt. Assn., Internat. Congress Psychotherapy, Soc. for Interdevel, World Union and Consortium for Rural Tech. Address: 7705 Custer Rd Bethesda MD 20814

ARBEENY, HENRY, investment company executive; b. N.Y.C., June 9, 1930; s. Samuel S. and Martha (Strenk) A.; m. Marlene Arbeeny; children: Marc H., Karen L., Loren E. Student public schs. Bond broker Drake and Co., N.Y.C., 1960-62; exec. v.p., dir. Paine Webber & Co., N.Y.C., 1962-75; dir. Reynolds Securities Co., N.Y.C., 1975-78; sr. v.p., dir. Dean Witter Reynolds Inc., N.Y.C., 1978—. Served as pilot USAF, 1950-59. Office: 130 Liberty St New York NY 10006

ARBIB, MICHAEL ANTHONY, cybernetician, computer scientist, neuroscientist, educator; b. Eastbourne, U.K., May 28, 1940; came to U.S., 1961; s. John R. and Helen (Arbib) A.; m. Prue Hassell, Dec. 29, 1965; children: Phillipa Jane, Benjamin Giles. B.Sc., U. Sydney, 1960; Ph.D. in Math, MIT, 1963. Vis. lectr. U. New South Wales (Australia), 1962, 65, 68, Mont. State U., summers 1963, 65, Imperial Coll. London, 1968; vis. prof. U. Western Australia, Perth, 1974, Technion, Israel, 1975, Washington U., St. Louis, 1976, U. Edinburgh, 1976-77, Gifford lectr. in natural theology, 1983; lectr. tours, U.S., Europe, USSR, 1963-64, Japan, 1972, U. Calif., Irvine, 1980; mem. faculty Stanford U., 1965-70, assoc. prof. elec. engring., 1969-70; adj. prof. psychology, prof. computer and info. sci. U. Mass. at Amherst, 1970—, chmn. computer and info. sci., 1970-75; dir. Center for Systems Neurosci., 1974—, co-dir. cognitive sci., 1980-82. Author: Brains, Machines and Mathematics, 1964, Theories of Abstract Automata, 1969, The Metaphorical Brain, 1972, Computers and the Cybernetic Society, 1977, (with others) Topics in Mathematical System Theory, 1969, System Theory, 1974, Discrete Mathematics, 1974, Conceptual Models of Neural Organization, 1974, Arrows, Structures and Functors, 1975, Design of Well-Structured and Correct Programs, 1978, A Basis for Theoretical Computer Science, 1981, A Programming Approach to Compatability, 1982; editor: Algebraic Theory of Machines, Languages and Semigroups, 1968, Neural Models of Language Processes, 1982; editorial bd.: Competition and Cooperation in Neural Nets, 1982, Adaptive Control of Ill-Defined Systems, 1983; Contbr. articles to profl. jours. Mem. Am. Math. Soc., Assn. Computing Machinery, IEEE, AAAS, Soc. Neurosci. Home: 164 Aubinwood Rd Amherst MA 01002

ARBITER, NATHANIEL, Metallurgical engineer; b. Yonkers, N.Y., Jan. 2, 1911; s. David and Ida Cora (Rockman) A.; m. Carolyn Stella Metz, Mar. 1, 1961; children: Jane F. Arbiter Latane, Jerome L., Laurie N., Elizabeth R., Dorothy, Corinna. A.B., Columbia U., 1932, postgrad., 1932-36. Research asso. Columbia U., N.Y.C., 1937-43; research metallurgist Battelle Meml. Inst., Columbus, Ohio, 1943-44, Phelps Dodge Corp., 1944-51; prof. mineral engring. Krumb Sch. Mines Columbia U., 1951-69, prof. emeritus, 1977—; dir. research, group cons. metallurgist Anaconda Co., Tucson, 1969-77; adj. prof. U. Ariz., Tucson, 1977—; vis. prof. U. Calif., Berkeley, 1977; spl. lectr. Columbia U., 1977-81; cons. various mining and engring. cos., UN, World Bank. Contbr. numerous articles to sci. jours. Recipient R.H. Richards award AIME, 1961, Mineral Industry Edn. award, 1971; A.M. Gaudin award, 1980; A.F. Taggart award, 1981; Krumb lectr., 1982. Mem. Nat. Acad. Engring., Am. Inst. Mining, Metall. and Petroleum Engrs. (hon.), Soc. Mining Engrs. (disting. mem.). Patentee in field. Home: X9 Ranch Vail AZ 85641 *No goal in science or in life is impossible. We may not reach it ourselves, but others surely will. To agree that a task is beyond us forecloses further effort. Better to have failed than not to have tried.*

ARBIZU, RAY LAWRENCE, tenor, educator; b. Phoenix, Aug. 10, 1929; s. Ray Cahill and Margarita (Trujillo) A.; m. Annie Marion Albrecht, Jan. 27, 1953; children—Ray Lawrence, Kathleen DeEtte, Marcus Adrian, Ann Amelia, Linda Fe, Blaine Thomas, Beth Eileen, David Lloyd, Heidi Renee. B.A., Ariz. State U., 1952, M.A., 1954; postgrad., U. So. Calif., 1956-60. Mem. faculty No. Ariz. U., Flagstaff, 1968-70; prof. music Brigham Young U., Provo, Utah, 1970—. Leading tenor, Bonn (W. Ger.) Opera Co., 1962-65, Essen Opera Co., 1965-67; on tour with, Am. Nat. Opera Co., 1967-68; performances with, Aachen, Essen, Cologne, Hannover, Karlsruhe (Germany), Boston, Tucson, Nev. opera cos., Chgo. Grant Park Series, St. Louis Summer Festival, Utah Symphony Orch., Utah Opera Co., Salt Lake City Opera Co. Chmn. Republican Com., Orem, Utah, 1973-76; bd. dirs. Community Concert Series, Flagstaff, 1968-70. Served with U.S. Army, 1952-54. Fulbright scholar, Vienna, 1960. Mem. Nat. Opera Assn., Music Educators Nat. Conf., Am. Guild Music Artists, Nat. Assn. Tchrs. of Singing. Home: 661 W 700 St N Orem UT 84057 Office: Dept Music Brigham Young U Provo UT 84601

ARBOGAST, ZOLLIE O., JR., lawyer; b. Kansas, Ill., June 6, 1929; s. Zollie O. and Helen (Ryan) A.; m. Mary Anita Stewart, June 2, 1951; children—Daniel Steven, Alane Annette. Student, Eastern Ill. State U., 1947-49; J.D., Chgo.-Kent Coll. Law, 1952. Bar: Ill. bar 1952. Practiced in, Marshall, 1952-63, Casey, 1967—; county judge Clark County, Ill., 1958-64; asso. judge 5th Jud. Circuit Ill., 1964-67; partner firm Partlow & Arbogast, 1967-75; individual practice law, Casey, 1976-80, 81—; partner firm Arbogast & Arbogast, 1980-81. Mem. Am., Ill., Clark County bar assns., Phi Alpha Delta. Republican. Mem. Christian Ch. Club: Mason. Home: 801 E Alabama St Casey IL 62420 Office: 110 E Main St Casey IL 62420

ARBOUR, ALGER, professional hockey coach; b. Sudury, Ont., Can., Nov. 1, 1932. Defenseman Detroit Red Wings, chgo. Black Hawks, Montreal Canadiens, St. Louis Blues of Nat. Hockey League, 1953-71; coach St. Louis Blues, 1970, 71-72, asst. gen. mgr., 1971; coach N.Y. Islanders, Uniondale, 1973—. Mem. (3 Stanley Cup championships teams, including), Detroit Red Wings, 1954, Chgo. Black Hawks, 1961, Toronto Maple Leafs, 1964; coach Stanley Cup chmapionship teams, 1980-83. Office: NY Islanders Uniondale NY 11553 *

ARBOUR, HAROLD CYRIL, planetarium dir.; b. Baton Rouge, Apr. 10, 1939; s. Cyril Thomas and Murnie Lee (Knight) A.; m. Doris L. Watkins, May 14, 1966; children—Stephen David, Virginia Leigh. B.S. in Astrophysics, La. State U., Baton Rouge, 1967. Asst. dir. La. Arts and Scis. Center Planetarium, Baton Rouge, 1967-72, dir., 1972—. Served with AUS, 1962-65. Decorated Commendation medal. Mem. Internat. Planetarium Soc. Home: 10958 Worthington Ave Baton Rouge LA 70815 Office: 502 North Blvd Baton Rouge LA 70802

ARBUCKLE, ERNEST COMINGS, banker; b. Lee, N.H., Sept. 5, 1912; s. Frank Albert and Ernestine C. (Weeden) A.; m. Katherine Norris Hall, Dec. 10, 1942; children—Ernest C., Joan, Katherine, Susan. A.B., Stanford U., 1933, M.B.A., 1936; Dr. h.c., U. Centroamericana, 1970; LL.D., Golden Gate U., 1973. Personnel specialist Standard Oil of Calif., 1937-41, orgn. analyst, 1945-46; dir. procurement, asst. to pres. Golden State Co., Ltd., 1946-50; exec. v.p. Pacific Coast div. W.R. Grace & Co., 1950-58; dean Grad. Sch. Bus., Stanford U., 1958-68, now dean emeritus; chmn. bd. Stanford Research Inst., 1966-70, dir., 1966—; chmn. Wells Fargo Bank, San Francisco, 1968-77; now dir. emeritus; chmn. Saga Corp., Menlo Park, Calif., 1978—, chmn. exec. com., 1982; dir. Owens-Ill., Inc., Hewlett-Packard Co., Utah Internat. Inc., A. Johnson & Co., Inc.; mem. adv. com. Export-Import Bank U.S., 1972-75; Mem. Commn. on White House Fellows, 1964-68; mem. Adv. Com. on Pvt. Enterprise in Fgn. Aid, 1964-65, Pres.'s Commn. on Internat. Trade and Investment Policy, 1970-71; mem. industry adv. council Dept. Def., 1969-72; mem. Trilateral Commn., 1973-77. Bd. dirs. Bay Area Council, Inc., chmn., 1976-77; chmn. Community Found. Santa Clara County, 1982—; trustee Stanford U., 1968-76, Packard Found., 1970—, Calif. Acad. Scis., 1979—. Served as lt. comdr. USNR, 1941-45. Decorated Silver Star; recipient Freedoms Found. award, 1950; Adminstrv. Excellence award Stanford Bus. Sch. Assn., 1968; Bus. Leadership award U. Mich. Grad. Sch. Bus. Adminstrn., 1969; Disting. Achievement medal Stanford Athletic Bd., 1971; Bus. Statesman award Harvard Bus. Sch. Alumni Assn., 1975. Republican. Clubs: Pacific Union, Bohemian. Home: 12 Arastradero Rd Menlo Park CA 94025 Office: One Saga Ln Menlo Park CA 94025

ARCARA, RICHARD JOSEPH, lawyer, County district attorney; b. Buffalo, June 6, 1940; s. Philip and Angela (Arcara); m. Gwendolyn White, July 1, 1976. B.A. in History, St. Bonaventure U., 1962; J.D., Villanova U., 1965. Bar: N.Y. bar 1966. Law clk. Legal Aid Bur., Buffalo, 1965; asso. firm Lipsitz, Green, Fahringer, Roll, Schuller & James, Buffalo, 1968-69; asst. U.S. atty. Western Dist. N.Y., 1969-73, 1st asst. U.S. atty., 1973-74, U.S. atty., after 1975; Erie County dist. atty., 1982—. Mem. Buffalo Fed. Exec. Bd.; Hon. chmn. United Cerebral Palsy, 1978. Served to capt., Mil. Police U.S. Army, 1966-68. Mem. Erie County Bar Assn., N.Y. State Bar Assn., Am. Bar Assn. Republican. Roman Catholic. Clubs: Buffalo Yacht, Buffalo Athletic. Office: 25 Delaware Ave Buffalo NY 14202 *

ARCARI, MARIO MARCO, banker; b. Florence, Italy; came to U.S., 1974; s. Giuseppe and Luisa (Lanini) A.; 1 dau., Silvia. Law degree, U. Florence, 1954. V.p. Banca Commerciale Italiana, London, 1970-74, sr. v.p., N.Y.C., 1974-81, regional mgr., Milan, 1981-82; pres., chief adminstrv. officer Long Island Trust Co., Garden City, N.Y., 1982, pres., chief exec. officer, 1983—; chmn. Sociedad Mexicana para la Industria y el Comercio; dir. BCI of Can. Ltd., Toronto, BCI Realty Ltd.

ARCARO, EDDIE (GEORGE EDWARD), sports broadcasting journalist, former jockey; b. Cin., Feb. 19, 1916; s. Pasquale and Josephine (Giancola) A.; m. Ruth Arcaro, 1937; children—Carolyn, Bobbie. Profl. jockey, 1931-62; now commentator horse racing ABC. One of 2 jockeys to ride five Kentucky Derby winners; rider of six Preakness Stakes winners, six Belmont Stakes winners, including Whirlaway, 1941, Triple Crown winner Citation, 1948. Address: ABC Sports 1330 Ave of Americas New York NY 10019

ARCE, A. ANTHONY, psychiatrist; b. San Juan, P.R., June 13, 1923; s. Angel and Juana (Baez) A.; m. Malvene Balkind, Oct. 7, 1971; children—Alan I. Scheer, Judith Ann Scheer, Michael Anthony Arce. B.S., Washington and Jefferson Coll., 1942; M.D., Temple U., 1946. Diplomate: Am. Bd. Psychiatry and Neurology; certified in adminstrv. psychiatry. Intern Mercy Hosp., Bay City, Mich. and; Frankford Hosp., Phila., 1946-47; dir. Aguadilla (P.R.) Dist. Hosp., 1947-48; chief health officer, Utuado, P.R., 1950-51; physician U.S. Mil. Acad., West Point, N.Y., 1951-52; med. officer Pa. R.R., 1952-53; practice medicine, Yonkers, N.Y., 1953-59; resident psychiatrist Payne Whitney Clinic, N.Y.C., 1959-62; asso. dir. psychiatry Grasslands Hosp., Valhalla, N.Y., 1962-67; dir. psychiatry Lincoln Hall Sch., Lincolndale, N.Y., 1967-68; dir. Bur. Aftercare Services N.Y. State Dept. Mental Hygiene, 1968-71; dir. Manhattan Psychiat. Center, Ward's Island, N.Y., 1971-76, Hahnemann Community Mental Health and Mental Retardation Center, Phila., 1976—; pvt. practice medicine specializing in psychiatry, 1962—; prof. psychiatry, dep. chmn. dept. mental health services Hahnemann Med. Coll., 1976—. Mem. president's council N.Y. U. Sch. Social Work, 1963-66; bd. dirs. P.R. Family Inst., N.Y.C., 1970-72. Served with AUS, 1943-46, 48-50. Mem. World Psychiat. Assn., Am. Psychiat. Assn. (chmn. task force continuing care), Phila. Psychiat. Soc., Pan Am. Med. Assn., Assn. Mental Health Adminstrs. Home: 7805 Chandler Rd Laverock PA 19118 Office: 314 N Broad St Philadelphia PA 19102

ARCE, PHILLIP WILLIAM, hotel/casino executive; b. N.Y.C., June 25, 1937; s. Joseph F. and Margaret (Degnan) A.; m. Dorothy Fiss, June 25, 1966; children: Joseph, William, Serena. Student, U. Notre Dame, 1955-56; A.A., San Diego Jr. Coll., 1958; postgrad., San Diego State U., 1958-60, San Diego U., 1960-62; student, LaSalle Law Sch., 1963-65. Various positions Del Webb Corp., Las Vegas and Reno, Nev., Oahu, Hawaii, 1963-75; exec. Caesars Palace, Las Vegas, 1975-78; pres. Frontier Hotel, Las Vegas, 1978—; tchr. hotel div. U. Nev., Las Vegas, 1966-67, 1976-77. Mem. exec. com. Boulder Dam Area council Boy Scouts Am., 1976—; vice chmn. United Way So. Nev., 1968—; pres. Easter Seals Nev., 1974-76; bd. dirs. Air Force Acad. Found., 1982—. Served with USMC, 1962. Recipient numerous awards including Appreciation awards Easter Seals, 1972, 73, United Way, 1975, Silver Beaver award Boy Scouts Am., 1984. Mem. Am. Hotel and Motel Assn. (bd. dirs. 1979-82), Nev. Hotel and Motel Assn. (pres. 1980, Hotelier of Yr. award 1981), Las Vegas C. of C. (dir. 1979—, pres. 1984). Republican. Roman Catholic. Home: 4243 Ridgecrest Dr Las Vegas NV 89121 Office: Frontier Hotel 3120 Las Vegas Blvd South Las Vegas NV 89109

ARCENEAUX, GEORGE, JR., federal judge; b. New Orleans, May 17, 1928; s. George and Louise (Austin) A. B.A., La. State U., 1949; J.D., Am. U., 1957. Bar: La. 1959. Partner Duval, Arceneaux, Lewis and Funderburk, Houma, La., 1960-79; spl. counsel La. Mineral Bd., Baton Rouge, 1960-62; city atty. City of Houma, 1970-71; judge U.S. Dist. Ct. Eastern Dist. La., New Orleans, 1979—. Mem. Houma-Terrebonne Regional Planning Commn., 1963-65, chmn., 1963-71; mem. La. Ho. of Dels., 1973-74. Mem. Fed. Terrebonne Parish Bar Assn. (pres. 1964-65). Office: US Courthouse Chambers C-405 New Orleans LA 70130

ARCENEAUX, WILLIAM, historian, educator, state ofcl.; b. Lafayette, La., Aug. 19, 1941; s. Teddy and Regina (Begnaud) A.; m. Patricia Boozman; children—Ted, Angelle, Leah, Scott. B.A., U. Southwestern La., 1962; M.A., La. State U., 1965, Ph.D., 1969. Instr. La. State U., 1966-67; asst. prof. Northwestern State U., Natchitoches, La., 1967-69; asso. prof., chmn. dept. history So. U., New Orleans, 1969-72; exec. dir. La. Coordinating Council for Higher Edn., Baton Rouge, 1972-75; commr. higher edn. La., Baton Rouge, 1975—; mem. Edn. Commn. States. Author: Acadian General-Alfred Mouton and the Civil War, 1972, 2d edit., 1981, AGB Reports, 1977; Editor: Postsecondary Education in Transition: Planning for Change in Louisiana, 1975. Bd. dirs. Student Loan Mktg. Assn.; mem. adv. bd. Odyssey House of La. Named one of 100 Young Leaders of Academy Change mag., 1978; recipient Jefferson Davis medal UDC. Mem. State Higher Edn. Exec. Officers Assn., Am. Hist. Assn., Fgn. Relations Assn. New Orleans, La. Hist. Assn., Omicron Delta Kappa, Phi Alpha Theta. Democrat. Roman Catholic. Club: Rotary (Baton Rouge). Office: 161 Riverside Mall Baton Rouge LA 70801

ARCHAMBAULT, BENNETT, corp. exec.; b. Oakland, Calif.; s. Albert Joseph and May (Smales) A.; m. Margaret Henrietta Morgan; children—Suzanne Morgan, Michele Lorraine, Steven Bennett. Student, Ga. Inst. Tech.; S.B., Mass. Inst. Tech. Vice pres., gen. mgr. M.W. Kellogg Co., N.Y.C., 1946-54; pres. Stewart-Warner Corp., Chgo., 1954—, chmn. bd., 1959—; pres., dir. Thor Power Tool Co.; exec. com., dir. Kemper Corp., Lumbermens Mut. Casualty Co., Am. Motorists Ins. Co., Am. Mfrs. Mut. Ins. Co., Lawter Chems., Inc.; head London Mission for OSRD, 1942-45. Mem. Mayor's Com. Econ. And Cultural Devel. Chgo.; bd. govs. United Republican Fund Ill.; former chmn. for Ill. Rep. Nat. Fin. Com.; trustee, mem. exec. com. Ill. Inst. Tech.; trustee Ill. Inst. Tech. Research Inst.; trustee, mem. exec. com., nominating com. Mus. Sci. and Industry; mem. com. on devel., past mem. corp. Mass. Inst. Tech.; adv. council Grad. Sch. Mgmt. Northwestern U.; trustee Better Govt. Assn.; bd. dirs. Protestant Found. Greater Chgo. Decorated Medal Merit, U.S.; His Majesty's Medal for Service in Cause of Freedom, Brit.). Mem. Employers Assn. Greater Chgo. (dir.), Newcomen Soc. N.Am., Research Soc. Am., C. of C. U.S., Ill. Mfrs. Assn. (adv. bd.), NAM. Republican. Clubs: Racquet, Saddle and Cycle, Commercial, MIT of Chgo., Executives, Chicago, Economic (Chgo.); Glen View, Westmoreland. Home: 3240 Lake Shore Dr Chicago IL 60657 Office: 1826 Diversey Pkwy Chicago IL 60614

ARCHAMBAULT, GEORGE FRANCIS, editor, pharmaceutical consultant; b. Springfield, Mass., Apr. 29, 1909; s. George Charles and Catherine V. (Mayette) A.; m. Lillian Herbert, Sept. 3, 1934; children: Joan Anne Archambault Rubis, Lillian Kathleen Archambault Matan, Patricia Gay Archambault Kachik, Frances Helen Archambault Parks, George Francis, William Herbert. Ph.G., Mass. Coll. Pharmacy, 1931, Ph.C., 1933, Pharm.D. (hon.), 1960; J.D., Northeastern U., 1941; D.Sc. (hon.), Phila. Coll. Pharmacy, 1951, LL.D., Temple U., 1961. Bar: Mass. 1942, U.S. Supreme Ct. 1976, D.C. 1980; Registered pharmacist in Mass., 1932. Mem. faculty Mass. Coll. Pharmacy, 1933-45, lectr. pharmacy and bus. adminstrn., 1933-47; practiced in, Belmont, Mass. and Washington, 1945-47; dir. profl. relations in New Eng. states Liggett Drug Co., 1945-47; commd. pharmacist officer USPHS, 1947-67, pharmacist dir., 1952; chief pharmacy br., div. hosps. Bur. Med. Services, 1947-65; also pharmacy liasion officer Office Surgeon Gen. USPHS, 1960-67, medicare pharmacy planning cons. div. med. care adminstrn., 1965-67; dean, prof. pharmacy adminstrn. Coll. Pharmacy, U. Fla., Gainesville, 1967; editor Hosp. Formulary Jour., 1967-79; Washington editor Drug Intelligence and Clin. Pharmacy Jour., 1979—; cons. on pharmacy and instnl. and other drug distbn. systems, 1967—; cons. United Mine Workers Am. Health and Retirement Fund, 1971-76, Am. Soc. Cons. Pharmacists, 1972—, Hill-Burton program USPHS, 1969-79; mem. revision com. U.S. Pharmacopeia, 1950-60, trustee, 1960-75, USPHS del., mem.-at-large, 1975, cons. to exec. dir., 1976—, mem. subcoms. on external and internal preparations; hon. mem., 1980—; mem. faculty Inst. Hosp. Law of Am. Hosp. Assn., 1954-69; mem. joint com. Am. Soc. Hosp. Pharmacists and Am. Hosp. Assn., 1955-68; pharm. cons. Catholic Hosp. Assn., 1950—; pharmacy cons. profl. exam. service Am. Pub. Health Assn., 1949-59; adv. pub. health service pharmacy and prescription trend, div. prices and cost of living Bur. Labor Statistics, 1955-67; mem. nat. adv. com. Law-Medicine Research Inst., Boston U., 1960-65; lectr. law hosp. pharmacy and drugs including investigational drugs; Samuel Melendy Meml. lectr. U. Minn. Coll. Pharmacy, 1962. Author numerous articles, chpts. in books. Recipient Harvey A. Whitney Hosp. Pharmacy award Am. Soc. Hosp. Pharmacists, 1956; Andrew Craigie award Assn. Mil. Surgeons, 1962; certificate of appreciation Cath. Hosp. Assn., 1956, Kappa Psi Pharm. Frat, 1962, U.S. Naval Sch. Hosp. Adminstrn., 1964; Disting. Service medal USPHS, 1965; Remington medal Am. Pharm. Assn., 1969; Disting. Alumni award Mass. Coll. Pharmacy, 1976, Northeastern U. Sch. Law, 1980; named Man of Year Am. Druggist, 1966; George Archambault ann. award established in his honor by Am. Soc. Cons. Pharmacists, 1972; Pres.'s award Am. Soc. Pharmacy Law, 1982. Life mem. Am. Pharm. Assn. (chmn. council 1959-60, com. publs. 1958-59, pres. Washington chpt. 1950, nat. pres. 1962-63); fellow AAAS (v.p. 1958, mem. council 1959—), Am. Pub. Health Assn., Am. Soc. Hosp. Pharmacists (hon. charter, pres. 1954-55); mem. Commd. Officers Assn. USPHS (chmn. exec. com. 1961-62), Mass. Soc. Hosp. Pharmacists (founder, hon.), La. Socs. Hosp. Pharmacists (hon.), Nat. Health Lawyers Assn., Am. Soc. Law and Medicine, Am. Soc. Hosp. Attys., Am. Med. Writers Assn., Fed. Bar Assn., D.C. Bar Assn., Nat.

Press Club, Am. Soc. Pharmacy Law, Nat. Assn. Uniformed Services, Ret. Officers Assn., Kappa Psi, Rho Chi.

ARCHAMBAULT, LOUIS, sculptor; b. Montreal, Que., Can., Apr. 4, 1915; s. Anthime Sergius and Annie (Michaud) A.; m. Mariette Provost, June 7, 1941; children: Aubert, Eloi, Patrice. Student, Coll. Jean-de-Brebeuf, Montreal; B.A., U. Montreal, 1936; Diploma, Ecole des Beaux Arts, Montreal, 1939. Mem. faculty Musée des Beaux-Arts, Montreal, Ecole des Beaux-Arts, U. B.C. (Can.), Vancouver, U. Que., Montreal, Concordia U. Works exhibited, Internat. Sculpture Exhbn., Festival of Gt. Britain, London, 1951, 10th Triennale, Milan, Italy, 1954, 28th Biennial, Venice, 1956, 11th Triennale, Milan, 1957, Brussels Universal and Internat. Exhbn., 1958, Pitts. Internat., Internat. Exhbn. Contemporary Sculpture, Expo '67, Montreal, 11th Biennial, Middelheim, 1971; several one-man shows in, Can., France, Eng.; represented in permanent collections, Nat. Gallery, Ottawa, Musée du Que., Quebec City, Musée d art contemporain, Montreal, Museo Internazionale della Ceramica, Faenza, Italy, Can. Imperial Bank of Commerce, Montreal, Art Gallery Ont., Toronto, Sun Life Bldg., Toronto, Upland Air Terminal, Ottawa, Place des Arts, Montreal, Malton Airport, Toronto, Scarborough Coll., Toronto, Macdonald Block, Queen's Park, Toronto, Fed. Food and Drug Bldg., Longueuil, Que., Can. Council Art Bank, Ottawa, Winnipeg Art Gallery, Justice Ct. Bldg., Quebec City, also others; commd. free-standing sculpture and mural wall for Can. Pavillion, Brussels Exhbn., 1958, sculptures for Can. Pavilion, Expo '67, Montreal, also others. Decorated officer Order Can., 1968; recipient Arts medal Royal Archtl. Inst. of Can., 1958; Recipient Diplome d'honneur Can. Conf. Arts, 1982; Canadian Govt. fellow for travel in, France, 1953-54; Can. Council grantee, 1959, 62, 69. Academician Royal Canadian Acad. Arts. Address: 278 Sanford Ave St Lambert PQ Canada J4P 2X6

ARCHAMBAULT, REGINALD DONAT, educator; b. West Warwick, R.I., Dec. 20, 1928; s. Reginald Donat and Doris (Sarvis) A.; m. Claire Marie Antonelli, May 30, 1951; children: Katharine, Carmel, Reginald, Sarah. A.B., Brown U., 1952; M.A.T., Wesleyan U., 1954; Ed.D., Harvard U., 1959. Instr., asst. prof. Wesleyan U., Middletown, Conn., 1955-62; assoc. prof. Grinnell Coll., Iowa, 1962-65, chmn. edn., 1962-65; assoc. prof., then prof. dept. edn. Brown U., Providence, 1965—, chmn. edn., 1967—, dir. M.A. in Teaching, 1967—; vis. prof. Harvard U., 1959, 67. Editor: John Dewey on Education, 1965, Dewey's Lectures, 1899, 1967, Philosophical Analysis and Education, 1965. Served with U.S. Army, 1946-48. Ford. Found. fellow, 1962. Mem. Phi Delta Kappa. Roman Catholic. Home: 289 Wayland Ave Providence RI 02906 Office: Brown U Box 1938 Providence RI 02912

ARCHER, BILL, congressman; b. Houston, Mar. 22, 1928; (m); 5 children. Student, Rice U., 1945-46; B.B.A., LL.B. with honors, U. Tex. Bar: Tex. bar. Pres. Uncle Johnny Mills, Inc., 1953-61; rancher, bus. exec.; partner firm Harris, Archer Parks & Graul, Houston, 1968-71; mem. 92d-98th Congresses from 7th Dist. Tex.; mem. Banking and Currency Com., 1971-72, Ways and Means Com., from 1973; Ad Hoc Com. on Energy, from 1977. Mem. Hunters Creek Village (Tex.) City Council, 1955-62, also mayor pro tem.; mem. Tex. Ho. of Reps., 1966-70, Republican Task Force on Energy and Resources, 1971-72. Served with USAF, 1951-53. Mem. Tex., Houston bar assns., Phi Delta Phi, Sigma Alpha Epsilon (Houston Man of Year 1968). Roman Catholic. Club: Rep. Chowder and Marching. Office: 1135 Longworth House Office Bldg Washington DC 20515 *

ARCHER, EDMUND MINOR, artist; b. Richmond, Va., Sept. 28, 1904; s. William Wharton and Rosalie (Pleasants) A. Student, Nora Houston and Adele Clark Studio, Richmond, 1911-18; grad., St. Christopher's Sch., Richmond, 1921; student, U. Va., 1921-22, Art Students League N.Y., 1923-25; ind. study in, including Academie Colarossi, Paris, 1925-26. Asst. and asso. curator Whitney Mus. Am. Art, N.Y.C., 1930-40; instr. drawing, painting composition Corcoran Sch. Art; also faculty George Washington U., 1944-68, emeritus, 1968—; Mem. bd. control Art Students League N.Y., 1924-25. One-man shows, various U.S. cities; works exhibited prin. museums and nat. exhbns., N.Y. and Chgo. world fairs, 1930—, N.A.D., 1956, Corcoran Gallery of Art, Washington, 1959, paintings in collections, Boston Museum Fine Arts, Corcoran Gallery Art, Fisk U., Naval Acad. Mus., Va. Mus. Fine Arts, Whitney Mus. Am. Art, Valentine Mus., Va. Commonwealth U., U. Va., portraits represented in collections of, univs. Va., Princeton, Richmond, Mich., Va. State Capitol, Med. Coll. Va.; executed mural, Hopewell (Va.) Post Office. Served with 603d Engrs. AUS, World War II. Recipient Corcoran bronze medal, 3d William A. Clark prize Corcoran Gallery Art, 1930, Purchase award Va. Mus. Fine Arts, 1941; painting prize; also popular prize Norfolk Mus. Arts and Scis., 1950. Fellow Internat. Inst. Arts and Letters, Switzerland (1961). Address: 13 S Foushee St Richmond VA 23220

ARCHER, GLENN LEROY, JR., lawyer, government official; b. Densmore, Kans., Mar. 21, 1929; s. Glenn LeRoy and Ruth Agnes (Ford) A.; m. Vera Poe Wiseman, Dec. 29, 1956; children: Susan Elaine, Sharon Jane, Glenn LeRoy, Thomas Wiseman. B.A., Yale U., 1951; J.D. with honors, George Washington U., 1954. Bar: D.C. 1954. Ptnr. Hamel Park McCabe & Saunders, Washington, 1956-81; asst. atty. gen. U.S. Dept. Justice, Washington, 1981—. Served to 1st lt. USAF, 1954-56. Mem. ABA (sec. taxation sect. 1975-77), Fed. Bar Assn., Bar Assn. D.C. Republican. Methodist. Club: Metropolitan (Washington). Home: 6227 Lakeview Dr Falls Church VA 22041 Office: Tax Division Dept Justice 10th St and Constituiton Ave NW Washington DC 20530

ARCHER, JAMES ELSON, educator; b. Hedley, Tex., Dec. 1, 1922; s. James M. and Mary Minerva (Bolles) A.; m. Reta Faye Turner, Nov. 8, 1942; 1 son, James Elson. B.S., Tex. Tech. U., 1947; Ph.D., Mass. Inst. Tech., 1950. Instr. Mass. Inst. Tech., 1950-52, Sloan fellow in indsl. mgmt., 1963-64; researcher Pitts. Plate Glass Co., Pitts., 1952-53, asst. dir., 1953-54, asso. dir., 1954-56, dir. research, 1956-62; mng. partner Archer Assos., Dallas, 1962-64; corporate dir. mgmt. systems Tex. Instruments, Dallas, 1964-68; prof. Tex. Tech U., Lubbock, 1968—. Served with USAAF, 1943-46. Home: 6208 Lynnhaven Dr Lubbock TX 79413 Office: PO Box 4200 Lubbock TX 79409 *

ARCHER, JOHN DALE, physician, editor medical journal; b. Brady, Tex., Mar. 10, 1923; s. John Andrew and Mattie Rae (Willis) A.; m. Dora Alice Bullard, June 10, 1952; children: Linda Dale, Diana Lee. B.A., U. Tex., 1950, M.D., 1952, postgrad. Sch. Law, 1954-57. Intern Brackenridge Hosp., Austin, Tex., 1952-53; research asso. dept. pharmacology and toxicology U. Tex. Med. Br., Galveston, 1951-52, instr., 1952-53, asst. prof., 1953-55; team physician dept. intercollegiate athletics U. Tex., Austin, 1955-57; staff physician Student Health Center, 1955-57; asst. med. dir. State Dept. Pub. Welfare, Austin, 1957-58; med. officer div. new drugs FDA, HEW, Washington, 1958-61, dep. dir., 1961-62, acting dir., 1962; staff physician med. service VA Center, Temple, Tex., 1962-64; asst. dir. dept. of drugs, div. of science activities AMA, Chgo., 1964-67, dir. drug evaluation sect., 1967-72, asst. dir. dept. of drugs, 1972; sr. editor Jour. of A.M.A., Chgo., 1972—. Author: The Archer Method of Winning at 21, 1973, also other trade books; Contbr. articles to med. jours. Served with USMC, 1941-45. Mem. AMA, Drug Info. Assn. (pres. 1972-73), Am. Med. Writers Assn., Research Soc. Am., Am. Acad. Clin. Toxicology, Am. Soc. for Clin. Pharmacology and Therapeutics, Phi Beta Kappa, Phi Eta Sigma. Club: Elks. Instrumental in prevention of U.S. sale of thalidomide. Home: 375 Wilshire St Park Forest IL 60466 Office: 535 N Dearborn St Chicago IL 60610

ARCHER, KENNETH DAVIDSON, lawyer, utility executive; b. Chgo., Feb. 15, 1940; s. Martin A. and Madeline D. (Davidson) A.; m. Barbara Elizabeth Clark, Aug. 22, 1970; children: Matthew Clark, Anthony Miles. B.S. with honors, U. Ill., 1961; J.D. cum laude, Harvard U., 1965. Bar: N.Y. State bar 1966, Ill. bar 1976. Asso. firm Shearman & Sterling, N.Y.C., 1965-70; assoc. counsel GAF Corp., N.Y.C., 1970-73; asst. counsel Cerro Corp., Chgo., 1973-75, gen. counsel, sec., v.p., 1975-76; v.p. law and adminstrn., sec. Orange and Rockland Utilities, Inc., Pearl River, N.Y., 1976-80, sr. v.p. law and adminstrn., sec., 1980—. Bd. dirs. Chgo. Lyric Opera Guild, 1975-76; trustee Pascack Valley Hosp., Westwood, N.J., 1979—, pres. bd. trustees, 1981-83; mem. exec. bd. Bergen County Council Bay Scouts Am., 1983—. Mem. Am. Bar Assn., N.Y. State Bar Assn. (utilities law com.), Assn. Bar City N.Y., Edison Electric Inst. (legal com.), Am. Soc. Corporate Secs. Clubs: Harvard, University (N.Y.C.); Hackensack Golf (Oradell, N.J.); Union League (Chgo.). Home: 175 Werimus Rd Hillsdale NJ 07642 Office: One Blue Hill Plaza Pearl River NY 10965

ARCHER, LORAN DUANE, government official; b. San Bernardino, Calif., Nov. 26, 1929; s. Loran Edward and Irma Elsie (Chance) A.; m. Cecilia Maria Gajan, June 9, 1956; children: John, Stephen, Michael, James, Patricia, Anne. B.S., UCLA, 1952; postgrad., San Francisco State U., 1956-58. Rehab. adminstr. Dept. Rehab., State of Calif., Sacramento, 1956-65, alcoholism program adminstr., 1967-70, dir. Office of Alcoholism, 1970-77; alcoholism clinic dir. Sacramento County Alcoholism Program, 1965-67; dep. dir. Nat. Inst. on Alcohol Abuse and Alcoholism, USPHS, Rockville, Md., 1977—; mem. Nat. Adv. Council, Rockville, 1976; cons. on alcoholism Calif. State Bd. Pub. Health, 1967-69, Calif. Med. Assn., San Francisco, 1969-71. Served to 1st lt. Med. Service Corps USAF, 1952-56. Recipient Spl. Recognition award Health and Welfare, State of Calif., 1976, Senate and Assembly Joint Resolution Commendation Calif. Legislature, 1977, Adminstrs. award for Meritorious Achievement Alcohol, Drug Abuse, and Mental Health Adminstrn., HHS, 1979. Mem. Council State and Territorial Alcoholism Authorities (nat. award for outstanding service 1978), Nat. Assn. State Alcohol and Drug Abuse Dirs. (nat. award for outstanding service 1978-79). Democrat. Roman Catholic. Home: 13828 Dowlais Dr Rockville MD 20853 Office: Nat Inst Alcohol Abuse and Alcoholism Room 16-105 5600 Fishers Ln Rockville MD 20857

ARCHER, RICHARD ALLEN, insurance broker; b. Los Angeles, June 24, 1927; s. Allen T. and Violet M. (McIlwaith) A.; m. Jean Bailey, Oct. 20, 1951; children—Kathy Archer Hampar, Pamela Archer Trinen, John Andrew. B.S. in Bus. Adminstrn, U. So. Calif., 1949; C.P.C.U., 1956. Pres. Allen T. Archer & Co. (ins. brokers), Los Angeles, 1959-72; (co. merged with Frank B. Hall & Co., Inc., 1972); with Frank B. Hall & Co., Inc., 1972-79, pres., then chmn. bd. chief exec. officer parent corp., 1974-77, gen. mgr. Western div., 1978-79; chmn. bd., chief exec. officer subsidiary Frank B. Hall & Co., Los Angeles, 1972-73; vice chmn. bd. Pinehurst Corp., Los Angeles, 1979—, also dir.; dir. Hydril Co., Imperial Corp. Am.; trustee Coll. Inst., N.Y.C., 1975-77. Trustee Seaver Inst., 1972—; chmn. trustees Loyola Marymount U., 1978—; pres. Republican Assn. So. Calif., 1971. Served to ensign USNR, World War II. Mem. Nat. Assn. Ins. Brokers (pres. 1964-66), Nat. Assn. Surety Bond Producers (pres. 1968-69), Nat. Assn. Casualty and Surety Agts. (past dir.), Am. Soc. C.P.C.U.'s (Man of Year award Pacific chpt. 1965), Ins. Brokers Soc. So. Calif. (pres. 1963), Young Pres. Orgn. (pres. Los Angeles chpt. 1974-75), Chief Execs. Orgn. (v.p.). Clubs: California, Los Angeles Country, Santa Monica Beach. Office: 1800 Ave Stars Los Angeles CA 90067

ARCHER, RICHARD JOSEPH, lawyer; b. Virginia, Minn., Mar. 24, 1922; s. William John and Margaret Leanore (Duff) A.; m. Kristina M. Hanson, Jan. 29, 1977; children: Alison P., Cynthia J. A.B., U. Mich., 1947, J.D., 1948. Bar: Calif. 1949, U.S. Supreme Ct. 1962, Hawaii 1982. Partner firm Morrison and Foerster, San Francisco, 1954-71, Sullivan, Jones and Archer, 1971-81, Archer Rosenak & Hanson, 1981—. Served with USN, 1942-45. Decorated Bronze Star. Mem. Am. Law Inst., Am. Coll. Trial Lawyers, Am. Bar Assn., ACLU, Am. Soc. Internat. Law. Republican. Clubs: Stock Exchange, Bankers (San Francisco). Home: 3110 Bohemian Hwy Occidental CA 95465 Office: 130 Sutter St San Francisco CA 94104

ARCHER, RONALD DEAN, chemist, educator; b. Rochelle, Ill., July 22, 1932; s. Don Adam and Irma Cecil (Olson) A.; m. Joyce Hilder Carlson, Jan. 31, 1954; children: Paul Dean, Lynn Sue, Sharon Jean, Julie Anne. B.S., Ill. State U., 1953, M.S., 1954; Ph.D., U. Ill., 1959. Tchr. Larson Jr. High Sch., Elgin, Ill., 1954; asst. prof. U. Calif., Riverside, 1959-63, Tulane U., New Orleans, 1963-65, assoc. prof., 1965-66, U. Mass., Amherst, 1966-70, prof. chemistry, 1970—, head chemistry dept., 1977-83; vis. prof. Tech. U. Denmark, 1972; research scientist Naval Research Lab., Washington, spring 1980; cons., 1960-63, 64-70, 72—. Contbr. chem. articles to research jours. Served with U.S. Army, 1954-56. Grantee USAF, Research Corp., NSF, Am. Chem. Soc., NIH, Army Research Office, Office Naval Research. Fellow AAAS; mem. Am. Chem. Soc. (chmn. Conn. Valley sect. 1979), Am. Crystallographic Assn., Royal Soc. Chemistry, Internat. Union Pure and Applied Chemistry, New Eng. Assn. Chemistry Tchrs., Sigma Xi, Phi Lambda Upsilon. Republican. Lutheran. Home: 19 Lantern Ln Amherst MA 01002 Office: Grad Research Tower A U Mass Amherst MA 01003 *Nothing surpasses the joy in the eyes of a student who has just synthesized a new chemical compound, especially if it has unique properties or may benefit the human endeavor.*

ARCHER, SARA KATHERINE, nursing educator; b. Goldsboro, N.C., July 17, 1918; d. Charles Robert and Millie (S.) Layton; children by previous marriage—Benjamin J. Archer, Charles Robert Layton III, Zelda Lourdes Archer, Stephen J. Layton. R.N., Washington Sanatarium and Hosp., 1940; B.S., U. Miami (Fla.), 1962; M.S., Boston U., 1965, Ed.D., 1970. Staff nurse Dade County (Fla.) Dept. Public Health, 1959-61; coordinator Health Maintenance for the Aged, Miami, 1962-64; asst. prof., coordinator gerontology program Boston U., Sch. of Nursing, 1966-68; assoc. prof. grad. program med.-surg. nursing Vanderbilt U. Sch. Nursing, Nashville, Tenn., 1969-71, assoc. dean, 1970-72, dean, 1972-82, prof., 1972—; geriatrical cons. VA Hosp., Mountain Home, Tenn., Murfreesboro, Tenn., Birmingham, Ala., 1974—. Contbr. articles on nursing edn. to profl. jours. Recipient Outstanding Service award U. Miami, 1972, Gov.'s Outstanding Tennessean award, 1978. Fellow Am. Acad. Nursing; mem. Am. Nurses Assn., Tenn. Nurses Assn., Nat. League Nursing, Tenn. League Nursing, Am. Assn. Colls. Nursing, Am. Public Health Assn., Gerontol. Soc., Sigma Theta Tau.

ARCHER, STEPHEN HUNT, economist, educator; b. Fargo, N.D., Nov. 30, 1928; s. Clifford Paul and Myrtle Mona (Blair) A.; m. Carol Rosa Mohr, Dec. 29, 1951 (div. Feb. 1971); children—Stephen Paul, Timothy William, David Conrad; m. Lana Jo Urban, Sept. 23, 1972. B.A., U. Minn., 1949, M.S., 1953, Ph.D., 1958; postdoctoral student (Ford Found. grantee), U. Calif. at Los Angeles, 1959-60. Mgr. J.M. Dain Co., Mpls., 1950, account exec., 1952-53; instr. econs. U. Minn., Mpls., 1954-56; asst. prof. fin. U. Wash., Seattle, 1956-60, asso. prof., 1960-65, prof., 1965-73, chmn. dept. fin., bus. econs. and quantitative methods, 1966-70; dean Grad. Sch. Adminstrn. Willamette U., Salem, Oreg., 1973-76, prof., 1976-79, Guy F. Atkinson prof., 1979—; Fulbright sr. lectr. Bocconi U., Milan, Italy, 1982; v.p. Hinton, Jones & Co., Inc. (investment brokers), Seattle, 1969-70; cons. Wash. Bankers Assn., 1971-72, Weyerhaeuser Co., 1971, Bus.-Econs. Adv. & Research Inc., 1969-77. Author: Introduction to Mathematics for Business Analysis, 1960, Business Finance: Theory and Mgmt, 1966, revised edit., 1972, The Theory of Business Finance, 1967, 2d revised edit., 1983, Portfolio Analysis, 1971, revised edit., 1979, Introduction to Financial Management, 1979, revised edit., 1983; editor: Jour. Fin. and Quantitative Analysis, 1966-70, Economic Perspectives, Economica Aziendale, Jour. Fin. Edn. Served with USNR, 1950-52. Mem. Fin. Mgmt. Assn. (pres. 1973-74), Western Fin. Assn., Acad. Internat. Bus., Am. Inst. Decision Scis. (treas. 1975-77), Phi Beta Kappa. Home: 4587 Orchard Heights Rd NW Salem OR 97304

ARCHER, STEPHEN MURPHY, educator; b. Winfield, Kans., May 14, 1934; s. William A. and Cecilia (Kumbera) A.; m. Paula Karalyn Agrelius, Aug. 3, 1959; 1 son, Steven Michael. B.A., B.S., Emporia State U., 1957, M.S., 1958; Ph.D., U. Ill., 1964. Prof. theatre Kearney State U., Nebr., 1964-66, So. Ill. U.-Edwardsville, 1966-71, U. Mo., Columbia, 1971—. Author: How Theatre Happens, 1978, 83, American Actors and Actresses, 1983; (script) TKO, 1971. Recipient Gold Medallion for Excellence Amoco, 1982. Mem. Am. Theatre Assn., Am. Soc. Theatre Research, Soc. Theatre Research. Club: Players. Home: 715 Spring Valley Rd Columbia MO 65201 Office: 129 Fine Arts U Mo Columbia MO 65211

ARCHER, SYDNEY, educator; b. N.Y.C., Jan. 23, 1917; s. Samuel and Eva (Cohen) A.; m. Therese Neiman, Jan. 26, 1946; children: Eve, David, Daniel. B.A., U. Wis., 1937; Ph.D., Pa. State U., 1940. Chemist, dir. chemistry div. Sterling-Winthrop Research Inst., Rensselaer, N.Y., 1943-68, assoc. dir., v.p., 1968-73; research prof. medicinal chemistry Rensselaer Poly. Inst., Troy, N.Y., 1973—, dean sch. sci., 1980—; cons. WHO, Geneva, 1975—; mem. exec. com. Com. on Problems of Drug Dependence, 1980—. Bd. editors: Medicinal Chemistry Rev., 1981—. Fellow AAAS; mem. Am. Chem. Soc. (Medicinal Chemistry award 1968), Chem. Soc. (London) (1968), Am. Soc. for Pharmacology and Exptl. Therapeutics, Sigma Xi. Home: 52 Wisconsin Ave Delmar NY 12054 Office: Rensselaer Poly Inst Sch of Sci Troy NY 12181

ARCHER, VIOLET BALESTRERI, educator, composer, pianist; b. Montreal, Que., Can., Apr. 24, 1913; d. Cesar B. and Beatrice (Azzi) A. Licentiate in piano, McGill U., 1934, B.Mus., 1936, D.Mus. (hon.), 1971; Asso., Royal Canadian Coll. Organists, 1939; B.Mus., Yale, 1948, M.Mus., 1949. Instr. music McGill U., 1945-47; (concert season), Eng., 1950; resident composer N. Tex. State Coll., Denton, 1950-53; asst. prof. music U. Okla., Norman, 1953-61; asso. prof. U. Alta., Edmonton, Can., 1962-70, prof. music, 1970-78, prof. emeritus, 1978—; also chmn. div. music theory and composition; vis. prof. music Cornell U., Ithaca, N.Y., summer 1952; mem. theory com. Can. Assn. U. Schs. Music; voting mem. council Can. Music Centre, Toronto; artistic adviser N.Y. Music Soc.; mem. bd. Can. Music Competition, Montreal. Composer: works including Sonatina for Organ; opera Sganarelle; sonatas for oboe and piano, clarinet and piano, alto saxophone and piano; anthems for mixed chorus and organ Psalmody; for orch., chorus and baritone voice, sonata no. 2 for piano; song cycles Divertimento for Saxophone Quartet; compositions performed extensively in Can., U.S., Europe, also many commd. works. Recipient citation Yale Sch. Music Alumni Assn., 1968; Merit award Govt. Alta., 1970; Creative and Performance award City of Edmonton, 1972; Queen's Jubilee Silver medal, 1977; Cert of Recognition for contbns. to musical heritage of Alta., 1980; Fellow MacDowell Colony, 1956; Can. Council sr. fellow, 1958-59. Mem. Can. Music Council (exec. bd.), Am., Can. music centres, PRO Can., Am. Fedn. Musicians, Can. League Composers, Can. Assn. Univ. Profs., Alta. Registered Music Tchrs. Assn., Canadian Fedn. Music Tchrs., Internat. Folk Music Council, Canadian Folk Music Soc., Canadian Music Educators Assn., Music Educators Nat. Conf., Alta., Composers Assn. (a founder, 1st v.p.), Am. Women Composers (asso.), Latitude 53 Soc. Artists (dir.), Accademia Tiberina of Rome (hon. life acad. mem.), Frau und Musik, Internationaler Arbeitskreis, Assn. Can. Women Composers, Sigma Alpha Iota, Pi Kappa Lambda. Home: 10805 85 Ave Edmonton AB T6E 2L2 Canada

ARCHER, WILLIAM REYNOLDS, JR., congressman; b. Houston, Mar. 22, 1928; s. William Reynolds and Eleanor M. (Miller) A.; m. Sharon Sawyer; children: William Reynolds III, Richard M., Sharon, Elizabeth, Barbara. B.B.A., U. Tex., Austin, LL.B. with honors. Bar: Tex. Pvt. practice law; pres. Uncle Johnny Mills, Inc.; dir. Heights State Bank, Houston; councilman, mayor pro-tem Village of Hunters Creek, 1955-62; mem. Tex. Ho. of Reps., 1966-70, 98th Congress from 7th Dist. Tex. Bd. dirs. Houston Soc. Prevention Cruelty to Animals; past chmn. Republican Study Com. Task Force on Regulatory Reform. Served with USAF; Korea. Recipient numerous service and honor awards. Named Most Respected Congressman from Tex., Tex. Bus. mag. Address: 1135 Longworth House Office Bldg Washington DC 20515

ARCHIBALD, ADAMS GORDON, utility executive; b. Truro, N.S., Can., Jan. 7, 1911; s. Harry Adams and Willana A.; m. Marion D. Muggah, Sept. 14, 1938; 3 sons, 1 dau. B.Comm., Dalhousie U., Can. Salesman Maritime Telegraph & Telephone Co., Ltd., Halifax, N.S., 1934-35, chief clk., Sydney, N.S., 1935-39, local mgr., Amherst, N.S., 1939-40, gen. comml. supr., Halifax, 1940-43, gen. comml. mgr., 1943-56, gen. plant mgr., 1956-58, gen. mgr., 1958-59, v.p., gen. mgr., 1959-63, pres, 1963-78, chmn., pres., 1968-75, chmn. bd., chief exec. officer, 1975-76, chmn. bd., from 1976, ICG Scotia Gas Ltd., Halifax, 1979—; dir. Eastern Tel. and Tel. Co., Comml. Life Assurance Co., Halifax Ins. Co., Toronto-Dominion Bank, Stanfield's Ltd., Island Telephone Co. Ltd. Past pres., mem. council Halifax Bd. Trade; past pres. Canadian C. of C. Clubs: Saraguay, Halifax. Office: ICG Scotia Gas Ltd PO Box 907 Halifax NS Canada B3J 2V9 *

ARCHIBALD, DOUGLAS NELSON, college dean, educator; b. N.Y.C., Apr. 20, 1933; s. H. Douglas and Dorothy (Olsen) A.; m. Marie Palms Thurber, May 13, 1961; children: Nathan, Jennifer, Michael, Timothy, Galen. B.A., Dartmouth Coll., 1955; M.A., U. Mich., 1959, Ph.D., 1966. Asst. prof. English Cornell U., Ithaca, N.Y., 1964-73, asst. dean, 1969-73; prof. English Colby Coll., Waterville, Maine, 1973-82, v.p., dean faculty, 1982—. Author: J.B. Yeats, 1974, Yeats, 1983; contbr. articles to profl. jours. Served to lt. USAF, 1956-59. Woodrow Wilson fellow, 1958-59; Horace Rackham fellow, 1962-64; Soc. Humanities Jr. fellow, 1968. Home: Weeks Rd RFD 1 Pittsfield ME 04967 Office: Colby Coll Mayflower Hill Waterville ME 04901

ARCHIBALD, NATHANIEL "NATE", professional basketball player; b. N.Y.C., Apr. 18, 1948. Ed., U. Tex. at El Paso, Ariz. Western Coll. Guard Cin. Royals basketball team, 1970-72, Kansas City Kings, Kansas City, Mo., 1973-76; mem. N.Y. Nets Basketball Team, Carl Place, N.Y., 1976-77, Buffalo Braves Basketball Team, 1977-78, Boston Celtics Basketball Team, 1978-83, Milw. Bucks, 1983—. Office: care Milw Bucks 901 N 4th St Milwaukee WI 53203 *

ARCHIBALD, REGINALD MAC GREGOR, physician, chemist, educator; b. Syracuse, N.Y., Mar. 2, 1910; s. Eben Henry and Minnie (Archibald) A.; m. Evelyn Stroh, June 12, 1948; children—Ruth, Lawrence. B.A., U. B.C., 1930, M.A., 1932; Ph.D., U. Toronto, 1934, M.D., 1939. Tchr., research asst. U. B.C., 1930-32; teaching and research asst. U. Toronto, 1932-33, fellow pathol. chemistry, 1933-35; intern Hosp. for Sick Children, Toronto, 1937, surgery, 1938, medicine, 1939; intern Toronto Gen. Hosp., 1939-40; fellow div. med. scis. NRC, 1940-42; asst. resident physician Rockefeller Hosp., 1941-46; asso. Rockefeller U., 1946, mem., 1948—, prof., 1955-80, prof. emeritus, 1980—; sr. physician Rockefeller Hosp., 1955-80; prof. biochemistry, sch. hygiene and pub. health Johns Hopkins, j1946-48. Mem. editorial bd.: Jour. Biol. Chemistry, 1948-58, Jour. Clin. Endocrinology and Metabolism, 1952-60, Child Development, 1954-56; adv. bd.: Analytical Chemistry, 1957-60. Fellow A.A.A.S.; mem. Am. Chem. Soc., Am. Soc. Biol. Chemists, Harvey Soc., Am. Fedn. Clin. Research, Coll. Phys. and Surg. Ont., Med. and Chirurg. Faculty Md., Endocrine Soc., Soc. Exptl. Biology and Medicine, Soc. Research in Child Devel., Brit. Biochem. Soc., Lawson Wilkins Soc. Pediatric Endocrinology, Soc. Adolescent Medicine, Nat. Acad. Clin. Biochemistry, Sigma Xi. Club: Explorers. Med. research in pediatric endocrinology and biochemistry, devel. clin. lab. methods, study of influence of hormones on enzymes. Home: 266 Ancon Ave Pelham NY 10803 Office: Hospital of Rockefeller U 1230 York Ave New York NY 10021

ARCHIBECK, PHILIP JAMES, public service company executive; b. Albuquerque, Dec. 6, 1941; s. Conrad William and Mary (Geurs) A.; m. Ruth Ann Elsbrock, Feb. 26, 1964; children: Michael, Patricia, Christine. B.S., Regis Coll. With Public Service Co. N. Mex., Albuquerque, 1966—, office mgr., 1967-70, budget dir., 1970-74, treas., 1974—; dir. Am. Bank Commerce. Bd. dirs. Salvation Army, Heart Assos. Served to capt. USMC, 1964-66. Republican. Roman Catholic. Home: 5921 Camino Placido Albuquerque NM 87109 Office: Public Service Co Alvarado Sq Albuquerque NM 87158

ARCHIE, JAMES LEE, artist; b. Orlander, N.C., June 14, 1924; s. Eddie and Elizabeth (Mitchell) A.; m. Marjorie Ann Booth, June 7, 1959; children: Victoria Esther, Olivia Rebecca, Daniel James, Enoch Lee. Ed. Cath. schs. Dir. Tucker Galleries, N.Y.C.; mgr. Wilfred G. Gooden Contracting, Inc., N.Y.C.; art instr. elem. schs. Exhbtd. group shows, Harlem Hosp., 1968, Studio Museum, N.Y.C., 1969, Mary Rogers Coll., Afro-American Art Festival, Tucker Galleries, N.Y.C., Freedom Bank, N.Y.C., 1969, Africa I'Leto Galleries, N.Y.C., 1970, Youth Devel. Agy. Exhbt., Countee Cullen Library, N.Y.C., 9th Ann. Outdoor Afro-Am. Art Festival, N.Y.C., 1972; participant, Westchester Panorama, White Plains, N.Y., 1971, 1st Black Arts Exhbn., Albany, N.Y., 1972; guest artist Sunday Gallery traveling art exhibit, Westchester County, 1971-72; dir., Creative Community Workshop, N.Y.C.; decorator, Broadway producer David Merrick, also actress Leslie Uggams; designer, Apollo Theater, Harlem, N.Y., dressing rooms; Works include: Destitute Meets Tranquility, 1969, Cry of Hunger at Midnight, Strength of Black Beauty, 1969. Vol. art therapist for adults in disadvantaged areas, vol. cons. to tchrs. to improve their understanding of problems facing slum-bred youngsters; vol. cons. with prisoners N.Y.C. prisons; vol. community cons. Museum Arts Projects in slum areas.; vol. tchr. furniture design and mfr. Genesis Campbell Christian Jr. Acad., Bronx, N.Y. Mem. Museum Art N.Y.C., Internat. Platform Assn., Federated Cultural Commn. Mem. Seventh-day Adventist Ch. Address: 61-15 98th St Rego Park Queens NY 11374 *I regard my skill in art as a God-given talent which I have used to reflect and to portray the needs, desires and capabilities of the less fortunate in our society.*

ARCILESI, VINCENT JASPER, artist; b. St. Louis, May 5, 1932; s. Vincent P. and Lucia (Burnett) A.; m. Nan Chapin, May 6, 1967; children: Piero Dante, Francesca Vincenza. B.F.A. in Info. Design, U. Okla., 1953, Sch. Art Inst. Chgo., 1956, M.F.A., 1961. Lectr. in art Chgo. City Coll., southeast br., 1962-64; asso. prof. art Southwest Coll., 1964-72; adj. asso. prof. art Finch Coll., N.Y.C., 1972-73; adj. asst. prof. art Fashion Inst. Tech., N.Y.C., 1974—; vis. critic Grad. Sch. Painting, U. Pa., Phila., 1977. One-man shows of paintings include, Noho Gallery, N.Y.C., 1981, Fairweather-Hardin Gallery, Chgo., 1964, Main Street Galleries, Chgo., 1968, Alverno Coll. Gallery, Milw., 1969, Ill. Art Council Gallery, Chgo., 1970, SUNY, Stony Brook, 1975, Westbroadway Gallery, N.Y.C., 1973, 74, 75, 77, Capricorn Galleries, Bethesda, Md., 1978; numerous group shows include, Corcoran Gallery Art, Washington, 1976, Wadsworth Atheneum, Hartford, Conn., 1976, Fogg Art Mus., Boston, Inst. Contemporary Art, Boston, No. Ariz. U. Art Gallery, Flagstaff, 1978, Mpls. Inst. Arts, 1977, Mulw. Art Center, Fort Worth Art Mus., San Francisco Mus. Modern Art, High Mus. Art, Atlanta, 1978, Bklyn Mus., N.A.M.E. Gallery, Chgo., Internat. Fair Contemporary Art, Bologna, Italy, 47 Bond Street Gallery, N.Y.C., NAD, N.Y.C., 1980, 82, Krannert Art Mus., U. Ill., Urbana, 1980, Landmark Gallery, N.Y.C., 1975, 78, 80, Allan Frumkin Gallery, N.Y.C., 1980, 82, Joanna Dean Gallery, N.Y.C., 1982, Am. Acad. and Inst. Arts and Letters, N.Y.C., 1981, Bilbao Internat. Exhbn. Ctr. (Spain), 1982; represented in permanent collections, Art Inst. Chgo., Joseph H. Hirshhorn Collection, Fashion Inst. Tech., N.Y.C., Mus. of Contemporary Art, Chgo., Southwest Coll., Chgo., Lake Shore Nat. Bank, Chgo., Ill. State Mus., Springfield, Kemper Ins. Co., Long Grove, Ill., Daicel Chem. Industries, Japan, also pvt. collections. Served with U.S. Army, 1953-54. U.S. Dept. Interior grantee, 1974; Nat. Endowment Arts grantee, 1982; CAPS fellow, 1981-82. Mem. Orgn. of Ind. Artists, Alliance of Figurative Artists (mem. program com. 1972-74). Address: 116 Duane St New York NY 10007

ARCINIEGA, TOMAS ABEL, college president; b. El Paso, Tex., Aug. 5, 1937; s. Tomas Hilario and Judith G. (Zozaya) A.; m. M. Concha Ochotorena, Aug. 10, 1957; children: Wendy, Lisa, Judy, Laura. B.S., N. Mex. State U., 1960; M.A., U. N. Mex., 1966, Ph.D., 1970. Asst. dean Grad. Sch. U. Tex.-El Paso, 1972-73; co-dir. Southwestern Schs. Study, U. Tex.-El Paso, 1970-73; dean Coll. Edn. San Diego State U., 1973-80; v.p. acad. affairs. Calif. State U., Fresno, 1980-83; pres. Calif. State Coll., Bakersfield, 1983—; prof. ednl. adminstrn. and supervision U. N. Mex., U. Tex.-El Paso, San Diego State U., Calif. State U., Fresno, Calif. State Coll., Bakersfield; cons. in edn. to state and fed. agys., instrns.; dep. chief party U. N. Mex. AID Project, Colombia, 1969-70. Author: Public Education's Response to the Mexican-American, 1971, Preparing Teachers of Mexican Americans: A Sociocultural and Political Issue, 1977; co-author: Chicanos and Native Americans: The Territorial Minorities, 1973; guest editor: Calif. Jour. Tchr. Edn., 1981. Trustee Carnegie Corp. N.Y., N.Y.C.; bd. dirs. Math., Engring., Sci. Achievement, Berekeley, Calif.; mem. steering com. Nat. Urban Coalition, Washington. Served to lt. inf. U.S. Army, 1961-63. Recipient Legis. commendation for higher edn. Calif. Legislature, 1975-78; recipeint Meritorious Service award Am. Assn. Colls. Tchr. Edn., 1978, recipient League United Latin Am. Citizens, 1983; named to Top 100 Acad. Leaders in Higher Edn. Change Mag., 1978. Mem. Am. Ednl. Research Assn. (editorial com. 1979-82), Assn. Mexican Am. Educators (various commendations), Am. Assn. Higher Edn. (instl. rep.), Am. Council on Edn. (instl. rep.). Democrat. Roman Catholic. Home: 300 Coffee Rd Bakersfield CA 93309 Office: Calif State Coll-Bakersfield 9001 Stockdale Hwy Bakersfield CA 93311 *Insuring the right of every American youngster to a first-rate public education has been a driving interest in my life. I consider my self extremely fortunate in having had numerous opportunities to become involved in meaningful efforts to insure that basic right in our country.*

ARCOMANO, JOSEPH PETER, radiologist; b. Bklyn., June 7, 1924; s. Frank and Mary G. (Mugavero) A.; m. Ellen I. Gustafson, June 4, 1949; children—Peter, Lisa, Paul. B.S., U. Chgo., 1946, M.D., 1949. Diplomate: Am. Bd. Radiology. Intern Greenpoint Hosp., 1949; resident in radiology L.I. Coll. Hosp., 1952-55; practice medicine specializing in radiology, Bklyn., 1955-60, Huntington, N.Y., 1960—; mem. staff Northport VA Hosp., Nassau County Med. Center, Mercy Hosp., St. Charles Hosp., Mather Meml. Hosp., Sagamore Children's Hosp.; asso.prof. radiology Sch. Medicine, N.Y. U., 1967-70; prof. radiology Med. Sch., State U. N.Y., Stony Brook, 1977—; dir. radiology North Shore Med. Group, 1970—; dir. sch. radiologic tech. Northport VA Hosp.; mem. X-Ray Technician Bd. of Examiners, N.Y. State, 1964-69. Contbr. articles to radiol. jours. Served with U.S. Army, 1942-45; with M.C., 1950-52; Korea. Recipient Dir.'s Outstanding Service award Northport VA Hosp., 1972, 77. Fellow Am. Coll. Radiology; mem. AMA (Physicians Recognition award 1969, 72, 77), Radiol. Soc. N. Am., Am. Roetngen Ray Soc., Soc. Nuclear Medicine, Am. Soc. Compensation Medicine, 38th Parallel Med. Soc. Korea. Roman Catholic. Home: 1 Richard Ln Huntington NY 11743 Office: 325 Park Ave Huntington NY 11743

ARD, HAROLD JACOB, library adminstr.; b. Herrick, Ill., Aug. 26, 1940; s. Jacob S. and Hazel E. (Taylor) A.; m. Erma Chapman, Jan. 30, 1960 (div. June 1974); children—Teri Ann, Mark Alan. B.S. in Edn, Ill. State U., 1962, M.S. in Psychology, 1964; M.L.S., Rosary Coll., River Forest, Ill., 1968. Tchr., materials cons. Decatur (Ill.) Pub. Schs., 1962-64; head librarian Barrington (Ill.) Pub. Library, 1964-68; exec. librarian Arlington Heights (Ill.) Meml. Library, 1968-72; library system dir. Jackson (Miss.) Met. Library System, 1972-77; asso. dir. Rowland Med. Library, U. Miss. Med. Center, Jackson, 1978—; cons., lectr. in field. Mem. ALA, Miss., Southeastern library assns., Med. Library Assn., Beta Phi Mu. Methodist. Club: Rotary. Home: 3932 N State St Jackson MS 39206 Office: U Miss Med Center 2500 N State St Jackson MS 39216

ARDEN, BRUCE WESLEY, computer science and electrical engineering educator; b. Mpls., May 29, 1927; s. Wesley and Clare Montgomery (Newton) A.; m. Patricia Ann Joy, Aug. 25, 1951; children: Wayne Wesley, Michelle Joy. Student, U. Del., 1944; B.S. in Elec. Engring, Purdue U., 1949; postgrad., U. Chgo., 1949; M.A., U. Mich., 1955, Ph.D., 1965. Detail engr. Allison div. Gen. Motors Corp., Indpls., 1950-51; asst. prof. dept. computing and communication scis. U. Mich., Ann Arbor, 1965-67, assoc. prof., 1967-70, prof., 1970-73, chmn. dept., 1971-73, from research asst. to asso. dir. Computing Facilities, 1951-73; prof., chmn. dept. elec. engring. and computer sci. Princeton, 1973—, Arthur Le Grand Doty prof. engring., 1981—; vis. prof. U. Grenoble, France, 1971-72; guest prof. Siemons Research, Munich, Germany, 1983, also cons.; cons. to Gen. Motors Corp., Ford Corp., Westinghouse Co., RCA, Xerox Data Systems, IBM.; Mem. sci. council Inst. for Computer Applications in Sci. and Engring., 1973-79; chmn. com. on anti-ballistic missile data processing Nat. Acad. Sci., 1966-71; mem. panel Inst. Computer Sci. and Tech., 198—; mem. acad. adv. council Wang Inst., 1978—. Author: An Introduction to Digital Computing, 1963, (with K. Astil) Numerical Algorithms: Their Origins and Applications, 1970; editor: What Can Be Automated?, 1980. Served with USNR, 1944-46, 49-50. Mem. IEEE (sr.), AAAS, Assn. for Computing Machinery, Univs. Space Research Assn. (bd. dirs. 1982—), Sigma Xi, Tau Beta Pi, Eta Kappa Nu. Home: 148 Springdale Rd Princeton NJ 08540

ARDEN, EUGENE, univ. ofcl.; b. N.Y.C., June 25, 1923; s. Harry and Gussie (Shevach) A.; m. Sandra E. Rose, July 11, 1948; children—Stacey, Jonathan. B.A., N.Y.U., 1943; M.A., Columbia, 1947; Ph.D., Ohio State U., 1953. Mem. faculties Ohio State U., Queen's Coll., also Hofstra U., 1947-56; from asst. prof. to prof., chmn. dept. English and humanities div. C.W. Post Coll., Greenvale, N.Y., 1956-62, dean, 1962-64; dean grad. faculties L.I. U., 1964-70, dean Conolly Coll., 1970-71, exec. dean Bklyn. Center, 1971; vice chancellor, dean acad. affairs U. Mich., Dearborn, 1972—. Contbr. articles to profl. jours., mags. Bd. dirs. Mid-Island YM and YWHA, 1962-64; mem. nat. exec. com. Hillel Founds.; asso. chmn. civil liberties com. Jewish Community Council, Met. Detroit. Served with AUS, 1943-46; ETO. Mem. AAUP., B'nai B'rith (pres. Central Nassau lodge 1966-68). Home: 27416 Aberdeen Southfield MI 48076

ARDEN, EVE (EUNICE GUEDENS), actress; b. Mill Valley, Calif., Apr. 30, 1912; d. Charles Peter and Lucille (Frank) Quedens; m. Edward G. Bergen (div. 1948); adopted children: Liza, Constance; m. Brooks West, Aug. 24, 1951; 1 son, Douglas Brooks; 1 adopted son, Duncan Paris. Student pub. schs. Actress: N.Y. shows Shubert Ziegfield Follies, 1933, Very Warm for May, Two for the Show, Let's Face It, 1941; motion pictures include Stage Door, 1938; Cover Girl, 1944, The Doughgirls, 1944, Mildred Pierce, 1945, Goodbye My Fancy, 1951, We're Not Married, 1952, Anatomy of a Murder, 1959, Dark at the Top of the Stairs, 1960, Sergeant Deadhead, 1965, Grease, 1978, Under the Rainbow, 1981, Grease II, 1982; TV movie Alice in Wonderland, 1983; began in: radio series Our Miss Brooks, 1948; TV series, 1952; television series The Eve Arden Show, 1957-58, Mothers-in-Law, 1967; star: nat. company Butterflies Are Free, Chgo. and Los Angeles, 1970; appeared on: stage in Auntie Mame, 1958. Recipient Emmy award, 1953, Sarrah Siddons award as Actress of Yr. in Hello Dolly, Chgo., 1967-68. Office: care Glenn Rose 9665 Wilshire Blvd Beverly Hills CA 90210

ARDEN, GEORGE JUSTIN, insurance company executive; b. N.Y.C., July 4, 1923; s. James Ezra and Beatrice (Seltzer) A.; m. Patricia Martin, June 30, 1964; children—James, George Justin, Andrea. B.A., Lafayette Coll., 1944. Pres. Great Century Life Ins. Co., Scottsdale, Ariz.; pres., chmn. bd. Arden Group of Cos., N.Y.C., Physicians Planning Service Corp.; chmn. bd. Appa-Gt. Century Money Market Fund, N.Y.C., Appa-Gt. Century Art and Antiquities Fund; dir. Energy Exchange Corp.; Mem. U.S. Senatorial Bus. Adv. Bd. Bd. dirs. Manhattan Ind. League for Blind, Arthritis Found., Lafayette Coll. Served with AUS, 1941-42. Mem. Key Biscayne (Fla.) C. of C., Marquis Soc., Nat. Assn. Residents and Interns (dir., trustee), Am. Profl. Practice Assn., The Attys. Group, Am. Bus. Assn., Am. Farmers Assn., Murray Hill Assn. Clubs: Sky, El Morroco, Commodore of Barbados, N.Y. Turf & Field, Jockey, Key Biscayne Beach, Thorobred Racing Assn. Office: 292 Madison Ave New York NY 10017

ARDEN, SHERRY WARETNICK, publisher; b. N.Y.C., Oct. 18, 1930; d. Abraham and Rose (Bellak) Waretnick; m. Hal Marc Arden (div. 1974); children: Doren, Cathy; m. George Ballak, Oct. 20, 1979. Student, Columbia U. Publicity dir. Coward-McCann, N.Y.C., 1965-67; producer Allan Foskko Assoc., ABC-TV, N.Y.C., 1967-68; sr. v.p., pub. William Morrow & Co., N.Y.C., 1968—. Mem. Assn. Am. Pubs. (dir.). Clubs: Pubs. Lunch.

ARDERY, PHILIP PENDLETON, lawyer; b. Lexington, Ky., Mar. 6, 1914; s. William Breckenridge and Julia (Spencer) A.; m. Anne Stuyvesant Tweedy, Dec. 6, 1941; children: Peter Brooks (dec.), Philip Pendleton, Joseph Lord Tweedy, Julia Spencer. A.B., U. Ky., 1935; J.D., Harvard U., 1938; M.B.A., U. Louisville, 1957. Bar: Ky. 1938. Practice law, Frankfort, 1938-40, 45-50, Louisville, 1952—; partner Brown, Todd & Heyburn, 1972—; sec. Ky. Aero. Commn., 1946-48; commr. Jefferson County, 1958-61. Author: Bomber Pilot: A Memoir of World War II, 1978; also articles. Pres. Ky. Heart Assn., 1955, chmn. bd., 1956; chmn. bd. Am. Heart Assn., 1966-69; pres. Louisville Community Concert Assn.; bd. dirs. Louisville Inst. Phys. Medicine and Rehab., pres., 1977-80; trustee U. of South, 1977-80; bd. dirs. Louisville Hospice, 1979—, St. Francis High Sch., Louisville, 1979-83. Served to col. USAAF, 1940-45; Served to col. USAF, 1950-52; now maj. gen. USAF-Res.; ret. Decorated Silver Star, D.F.C. (2), Air medal (4); Croix de Guerre with palm (France). Mem. Am., Ky., Louisville bar assns., Phi Beta Kappa. Democrat. Episcopalian. Club: Pendennis (Louisville). Home: 448 Swing Ln Louisville KY 40207 Office: 1600 Citizens Plaza Louisville KY 40202

ARDITTI, FRED D., economist, educator; b. N.Y.C., Jan. 30, 1939; s. David A. and Marie (Ben Nathan) A.; m. Margaret Monroe, Jan. 1981; children: Elizabeth, Anne Sarah. B.S. in Elec. Engring, M.I.T., 1960, M.S. in Indsl. Mgmt, 1962, Ph.D. in Econs, 1966. Economist Rand Corp., Santa Monica, Calif., 1965-67; lectr., asst. prof. fin. U. Calif., Berkeley, 1967-71; from asso. prof. to prof. fin. U. Fla., Gainesville, 1971-77, Walter J. Matherly chair fin. and econs., 1974-80, chmn. dept. econs., 1977-80; v.p. research, chief economist Chgo. Merc. Exchange, 1980—; v.s. prof. Hebrew U., 1973, U. Toronto, 1976-77. Contbr. articles to profl. jours., chpts. to books. NSF fellow; Ford Found. research grantee; NDEA fellow; other fellowships. Mem. Am. Econs. Assn., Am. Fin. Assn. Jewish. Office: GNP Fin Inc 222 S Riverside Plaza Suite 846 Chicago IL 60606

ARDLEIGH, JOSEPH D., research institute executive; b. Scranton, Pa., May 24, 1914; s. Hugh Granville and Pauline (Danvers) A.; m. Susan Bell; children: Paul, Carl, Hugh, Teri. Ed., N.Y.U. Devel. mgr., operating mgr. and personnel mgr. Hoover Co., North Canton, O., 1933-37; established Sales Methods, Inc., N.Y.C., 1937-39; membership dir. Research Inst. of Am., 1939—, v.p., 1944-53, exec. v.p., 1953-67, pres., 1967-79, pres., chief exec. offier, 1979; mng. partner Ardleigh Assos., 1979—; past pres. Nat. Law Press; dir. Emery Air Freight Corp. Author books and articles on marketing and human relations. Trustee Manhattan Coll. Mem. Nat. Soc. Sales Tng. Execs. (hon. life), Nat. Sales Execs., C. of C., Sales Execs. Club N.Y. (past pres.). Clubs: Greenwich Country (gov.), Board Room; Union League (N.Y.C.) (pres.). Home: 100 Rowayton Woods Rowayton CT 06854 Office: Rowayton CT 06854

ARDOIN, JOHN LOUIS, newspaperman; b. Alexandria, La., Jan. 8, 1935; s. Louis and Ruth (Herren) A. Mus.B., U. Tex., 1955; Mus.M., U. Okla., 1956; postgrad., Mich. State U., 1958-59. Asst. editor Mus. Am. mag., 1959-63, asso. editor, 1963-64, editor, 1964; mng. editor Philharmonic Hall program; mem. music staff Saturday Rev., 1965-66; music editor, amusements critic Dallas Morning News, 1966—; N.Y. music critic London Times, 1964-66, Opera mag., 1965-66; Guest lectr. Ind. U., 1971-72, Eastman Sch. Music, 1973, Am. Inst. Mus. Studies, 1973; music cons. WNET-13, N.Y.C. Co-author: Callas, The Tenors; author: The Callas Legacy; author film documentaries on Maria Callas, Beyreuth Festival, Spoleta U.S.A. Festival. Mem. N.Y. Music Critics Circle (1960-64). Home: 4318 Abbott Ave Dallas TX 75205 Office: Communications Center Dallas TX 75222

ARDOYNO, DOLORES (DORR), opera company administrator; b. Mobile, Ala., Sept. 23; d. William John and Kathryn Cecelia (Hickey) A.; m. Donald Dorr, Apr. 29, 1971. Student, Webster Coll., 1939-41, Springhill Coll., 1944, St. Louis U., 1944-45, Loyola U., Los Angeles, 1951-52. Asst. prodn. coordinator western div. ABC-TV, Hollywood, Calif., 1950-54; head radio/TV Whitlock, Swigart & Evans Advt. Co., New Orleans, 1956-59; mgr. New Orleans Summer Pops, 1960-66; owner, dir. PR Service, New Orleans, 1960-68; dir. public relations New Orleans Opera, 1968-71; gen. mgr. Opera/South, Jackson, Miss., 1971-80, Baton Rouge Opera, 1981—. Democrat. Roman Catholic. Office: 427 Laurel St Baton Rouge LA 70801

AREEDA, PHILLIP, lawyer, educator; b. Detroit, Jan. 28, 1930; s. Elias Herbert and Selma (Cope) A. A.B., Harvard U., 1951, LL.B., 1954; Harvard travelling fellow, 1954-55. Bar: Mich. 1954. Mem. White House staff, asst. spl. counsel to Pres. U.S., 1956-61; mem. faculty Harvard Law Sch., 1961, prof. law, 1963—, Langdell prof., 1981—; counsel to Pres. U.S., 1974-75; exec. dir. U.S. Cabinet Task Force on Oil Import Control, 1969. Author: Antitrust Analysis, 1967, 3d edit., 1981, Antitrust Law, 1982; co-Author: Antitrust Law, 5 vols., 1978, 80. Served to 1st lt. USAF, 1955-57. Mem. Am. Law Inst., Am. Acad. Arts and Scis. Office: Langdell Hall Cambridge MA 02138

AREEN, GORDON E., finance company executive; b. Chgo., Feb. 10, 1918; s. Eric G. and Tillie S. (Nyberg) A.; m. Pauline J. Payberg, June 28, 1942; children: Judith Carol, Patricia Ann, Richard Gordon. Grad., Sch. Commerce, Northwestern U., 1940. C.P.A., Ill. Accountant Arthur Andersen & Co. (C.P.A.s), 1945, Allstate Ins. Co., Chgo., 1946-47; asst. comptroller to exec. v.p. Assos. Investment Co., South Bend, Ind., 1947-64; pres., dir., chief exec. officer Chrysler Fin. Corp., 1964-80, chmn. bd., chief exec. officer, dir., 1980-81; v.p. Chrysler Corp., 1974-81; pres., dir. Chrysler Ins. Co., 1964-81; pres., chief exec. officer, dir. Internat. Harvester Credit Corp., Chgo., 1981-84, chmn. bd., chief exec. officer, dir., 1984—; v.p. Internat. Harvester Co., Chgo., 1981—. Trustee Alma (Mich.) Coll., chmn. bd., 1981—; trustee Inst. Advanced Pastoral Studies, Kirk in Hills Presbyterian Ch.; past pres. Jr. Achievement S.E. Mich.; v.p., dir. Detroit Swedish Council, Inc. Served to maj. U.S. Army, 1940-45. Mem. Am. Inst. C.P.A.s, Alpha Kappa Psi. Republican. Clubs: Masons, Shriners, Mid Am., Meadow, Oakland Hills Country. Home: 3932 Maple Hill E West Bloomfield MI 48033

AREEN, JUDITH CAROL, legal educator; b. Chgo., Aug. 2, 1944; d. Gordon Eric and Pauline Jeanette (Payberg) A.; m. Richard M. Cooper, Feb. 17, 1979; 1 son, Benjamin Eric. A.B., Cornell U., 1966; J.D., Yale U., 1969. Bar: Mass. 1971, D.C. 1972. Program planner for higher edn. Mayor's Office City of N.Y., 1969-70; dir. edn. voucher study Center for Study Pub. Policy, Cambridge, Mass., 1970-72; mem. faculty Georgetown U. Law Center, Washington, 1971—, asso. prof., 1972-76, prof. law, 1976—; gen. counsel, dir. Fed. Legal Representation Study of Pres.'s Reorgn. Project Office of Mgmt. and Budget, Washington, 1977-80; prof. community and family medicine U. Mich., 1982; sr. research fellow Kennedy Inst., Georgetown U. Author: Youth Service Agencies, 1977, Cases and Materials on Family Law, 1978. Mem. Def. Adv. Com. Women in Services; dep. counsel credentials com. Democratic Nat. Conv., 1976. Mem. Am., D.C. bar assns., D.C. bar (gov.), Women's Legal Def. Fund. Office: 600 New Jersey Ave NW Washington DC 20001

AREL, BULENT, composer.; b. Istanbul, Turkey, Apr. 23, 1919; came to U.S., naturalized, 1973. Grad., Ankara State Conservatory, 1947. Tchr., Ankara, Turkey, 1945-51; music dir. Radio Ankara, 1951-59, 63-65; formerly research asst. (Rockefeller Found. grantee) Columbia-Princeton Electronic Music Center; mem. faculty Yale U., 1961-62, 65-70; founder, dir. Yale U. Electronic Music Studio, 1965; prof. music, dir. Electronic Music Studios, SUNY, Stony Brook, 1971—; vis. prof. Columbia U. Has engaged in teaching composition of symphonies, ballets, chamber and theatre music, electronic music; composer:

instrumental works, electronic music including Electronic Music No. 1, 1960; Mimiana I, II, III, 1968, 69, 73; film score Out of Into, 1972, also others; recs. for Stereo Electronic Music No. 1, CRI, Columbia, Finnadar, Opus One. Recipient Nat. Endowment for Arts awards (2); N.Y. State research grantee. Office: Electronic Music Studio SUNY Stony Brook NY 11794 *

ARELLANO, IGNACIO, advertising executive; b. Mexico City, Nov. 3, 1928; s. Emilio A. and Guadalupe (Orozco) de Arellano; m. Maria Elenade la Garza, Oct. 19, 1956; children: Ignacio, Ma Elena, Jose Antonio, Mauricio, Roberto. Student, Colegio Cristobal Colon, Mexico City, 1935-44. Brand mgr. Orgn. Procter and Gamble, Mexico City, 1950-60; advt., mktg. mgr. Gen. Foods, Mexico City, 1960, The Sydney Ross Co., 1961-64, Anderson Clayton, 1965-69; gen. mgr. Arellano Ted Bates, Mexico City, 1970—. Mem. Internat. Advt. Assn. (pres. 1974), Mexican Assn. Advt. Agys. (pres. 1976). Clubs: Club de Industriales (Mexico City); Cuernavaca Raquet (Cuernavaca) (Mexico). Home: Brisa 356 Mexico City DF Mexico Office: Arellano Ted Bates Publicidad Goldsmith 225 Mexico DF Mexico 11560

ARENA, JAY M., pediatrician, educator; b. Clarksburg, W.Va., Mar. 3, 1909; s. Anthony M. and Rose (Sandy) A.; m. Pauline Elizabeth Monteith, July 10, 1931; children—Rosanne (Mrs. Oscar Green), Jay Morris Jr., Carolyn Jean (Mrs. Harry C. Wood), Mary Margaret (Mrs. Robert Beeching), Katherine (Mrs. Arthur Prosser), Pauline (Mrs. William Myers), Regina (Mrs. Needham Smith). B.A., W.Va. U., 1930; M.D., Duke U., 1932. Intern Strong Meml. Hosp., Rochester, N.Y., 1932, Johns Hopkins Hosp., 1932-33; asst. resident Duke Hosp., 1933-34, resident, 1934-35; instr. pediatrics Vanderbilt U., 1936; asst. prof. pediatrics Duke Hosp., 1936-50, asso. prof., 1951-56, prof., 1956—, prof. community health scis., 1970—; dir. Poison Control Center, 1953—; editorial bds. Council Family Health, Clin. Pediatrics, Nutrition Today, Pediatric News, Highlights; mem. adv. bd. Pediatrics Annals.; Chmn. Z 66 standards com. Nat. Standards Inst., 1969—; mem. com. U.S. Consumer Products Safety Commn., 1976-78; pres. Am. Assn. Poison Controls Centers, 1968-70. Author: The Compleat Pediatrician, 1969, (with James W. Hardin) Human Poisoning from Native and Cultivated Plants, 1969, 2d edit., 1973, Poisoning: Toxicology-Symptoms-Treatments, 3d 4th edit, 1979, Dangers to Children and Youth, 1971, (with Miriam Bachar) Child Safety is No Accident, 1978, (with Barbara Echols) The Common Sense Guide to Good Eating, 1978, Davison of Duke: His Reminiscences, 1980, also numerous articles on poisoning and varied pediatric subjects. Mem. Am. Acad. Pediatrics (exec. bd. 1965-71, pres. 1971-72), Am. Pediatric Soc., Phi Beta Kappa, Sigma Xi, Alpha Omega Alpha. Home: 1403 Woodburn Rd Durham NC 27705 *Although children may be victims of fate, they should never be the victims of our neglect.*

ARENA, JOHN I., publisher, reading specialist; b. Alameda, Calif., Sept. 12, 1929; s. Anthony and Nina Helen (Culotta) A.; m. Anna Maria Arena, Oct. 31, 1964; 1 son, James Anthony. A.B., San Francisco State Coll., 1951, M.A., 1959; postgrad., U. San Francisco, 1951-52, U. Calif., Berkeley, 1959-62. Tchr. Ashland Sch., San Lorenzo, Calif., 1954-56, Sunset Sch. for Physically Handicapped Children, San Lorenzo, 1956-59; prin. Marindale Sch., San Rafael, Calif., 1959-61; home tchr. Oakland Pub. Schs., 1961-62; instr., program dir. Dewitt Reading Clinic, San Rafael, Calif., 1961-68; editor, publisher Academic Therapy Publs., Inc., San Rafael, Calif., 1965—; exec. dir. Arena Sch. and Learning Center, remedial center and school, San Rafael, 1970-77; lectr. in Edn., Reading Dominican Coll. of San Rafael, 1972—; cons. in field to various sch. dists. Editor: Jour. Spl. Edn, 1968—, Bull. of Orton Soc, 1968-74, many others. Recipient award Calif. Assn. Neurologically Handicapped Children, 1971, pres.'s award, 1977; award Assn. Children with Learning Disabilities, 1970; also Pioneer-Profl. award, 1979. Mem. Optometric Extension Program Found., Inc. (hon.). Home: 50 Corte Morada Greenbrae CA 94904 Office: 20 Commercial Blvd Novato CA 94947

ARENAL, JULIE (MRS. BARRY PRIMUS), choreographer. Tchr. Herbert Berghof Studio; asst. on tng. program Lincoln Center Repertory Theatre. Dancer with cos. of, Anna Sokolow, Sophie Maslow, John Butler, Jack Cole, Lose Limon; choreographer: Marat/Sade for, Theatre Co. of Boston, Harvard U. Loeb Theatre, Municipal Theatre, Atlanta, Hair, on Broadway (Most Original Choreographer of Year award Sat. Rev. 1968), also London; dir., choreographer: Hair, Stockholm (Best Dir.-Choreographer of Year award 1969); choreographer: Indians on Broadway; choreographer, dir.: Isabel's a Jezebel; choreographer: Fiesta for Ballet Hispanico, 1972, 20008 1/2, Boccaccio, 1975, A Private Circus, 1975, Free to Be You and Me, 1976, The Referee, 1976, El Arbito, 1978; choreographer for, San Francisco Ballet, Nat. Ballet de Cuba; film King of the Gypsies; dir., choreographer: Funny Girl, Tokyo, 1979-80; choreographer: Four Friends, 1980. Nat. Endowment for Arts grantee for A Puerto Rican Soap Opera, Ballet Hispanico, 1973. Home: 205 E 10th St New York NY 10003

ARENBERG, JULIUS THEODORE, JR., acctg. co. exec.; b. Chgo., May 29, 1923; s. Julius Theodore and Ellen A. (Foran) A.; m. Jean E. Young, June 19, 1948; children—Robert, Thomas, Mary, James, Michael, Douglas. B.S. in Acctg, U. Ill., 1947. C.P.A., Ill. With Arthur Andersen & Co. (C.P.A.'s), Chgo., 1947—, partner, 1962—, head fin. services div., 1975—; chmn. C.P.A. adv. com. Nat. Assn. Ins. Commrs., 1974-75; mem. faculty Bank Adminstrn. Inst. Sch., U. Wis., 1966-69, Nat. Installment Credit Sch., U. Chgo., 1965-70. Mem. Lombard (Ill.) Elementary Bd. Edn., 1960-66, pres., 1962-66. Served with USNR, 1943-46. Mem. Am. Inst. C.P.A.'s (chmn. com. ins. acctg. and auditing 1966-73), Ill. Soc. C.P.A.'s. Roman Catholic. Clubs: Attic (Chgo.); St. Charles Country, Bay Hill, Metropolitan. Office: 33 W Monroe St Chicago IL 60603

AREND, FEROLD GENE, retail exec.; b. Fairbury, Nebr., July 18, 1925; s. Henry Fredrick and Alice Gurtrude (Pearson) A.; m. Melba Jane Courmier, June 19, 1951; children—Deborah Jean, William Curtis, Thomas Scott, Michael Charles. Student public schs. Fairbury. With Hested Variety Stores, 1946-59; dist. mgr. to mdse. coordinator and inventory controller Central div. J.J. Newberry Co., Omaha, 1960-66; with Wal-Mart Stores, Inc., Bentonville, Ark., 1966—, exec. v.p., 1968-74, pres., 1974-78, vice chmn., 1978—; also dir. Served with USN, 1943-45; PTO. Republican. Roman Catholic. Office: Wal Mart Stores Inc 702 SW 8th St Bentonville AR 72712

AREND, THOMAS EDWARD, advertising agency executive; b. Fremont, Ohio, Jan. 27, 1928; s. Chester E. and Betty Louise (Schmidt) A.; m. Judith Ann Carr, Dec. 9, 1961; children: Katherine, Thomas. B.S., Northwestern U., 1951. TV producer NBC-TV, Cleve., 1951-53, Chgo., 1954-59; TV mgr. FCB Advt., Chgo., 1959-64, v.p. TV, San Francisco, 1964-70, v.p. creative services, Chgo., 1970-75, sr. v.p. corp. ops., 1975—; dir. FCB Found., Chgo., 1981—. Bd. dirs. Lake Bluff (Ill.), Open Lands Assn., 1983—. Served with U.S. Army, 1946-48. Roman Catholic. Clubs: Bath and Tennis (Lake Bluff) (v.p. 1974-76); Internat. (Chgo.)). Office: Foote Cone Belding Communications Inc 401 N Michigan Ave Chicago IL 60611

ARENDALL, CHARLES BAKER, JR., lawyer; b. Portsmouth, Va., Feb. 13, 1915; s. Charles B. and Kate (Peacock) A.; m. Nan Eager Boone, Oct. 26, 1944; children—Nan Boone McGinley, Lawrence Barclay Manley, Kathryn Baker Cox, Elizabeth Charles Tilney. A.B., U. Richmond, 1935; LL.B. cum laude, Harvard, 1938. Bar: Ala. bar 1938. Asso. firm Smith & Johnston, Mobile, 1938-41; mem. firm Hand, Arendall, Bedsole, Greaves & Johnston (and predecessor), Mobile, 1941—; Adv. bd. Cumberland Law Sch., Samford U. Trustee Mobile Coll. Fellow Am. Coll. Trial Lawyers; mem. Internat., Am., Ala., Inter-Am., Mobile bar assns., Am. Judicature Soc., Assn. Bar City N.Y., Internat. Assn. Ins. Counsel, Am. Law Inst., Assn. Railroad Trial Counsel, Omicron Delta Kappa, Pi Delta Epsilon, Alpha Psi Omega, Kappa Sigma. Baptist. Clubs: Athelstan, Lakewood, Country. Home: Point Clear AL 36564 Office: First Nat Bank Bldg Mobile AL 36601

ARENS, JAMES F., anesthesiologist, educator; b. Hamel, Minn., Apr. 20, 1934; s. Frederick and Aurelia (Boldwc) A.; m. Mary Helen, Feb. 9, 1960; children: Patricia, James F. M.D., Creighton U., Omaha, 1959. Cert. Am. Bd. Anesthesiology. Commd. officer U.S. Air Force; advanced through grades to capt. U.S Air Force; ret. U.S. Air Force, 1966; dir. anesthesia Ochsner Clinic, New Orleans, 1967-72; prof., chmn. anesthesiology U. Miss. Med. Ctr., Jackson, 1972-77; prof., chmn. U. Tex. Med. Br., Galveston, 1977—, dir. surg. operating and acute care support services, 1977—, med. dir. respiratory therapy dept., 1980-81, exec. dir. operating room, 1977—; chmn., sec. Joint Com. on Critical Care Medicine, 1982—. Mem. Am. Coll. Anesthesiology, Am. Bd. Med. Specialities, Soc. Acad. Anesthesia Chmn. (pres. 1979), Am. Soc. Anesthesiologists. Roman Catholic. Home: 22 S Shore Dr Galveston TX 77550 Office: U Tex Med Br 8th St and Market St Galveston TX 77550

ARENSBERG, CONRAD MAYNADIER, anthropologist, sociologist; b. Pitts., Sept. 12, 1910; s. Charles F. C. and Emily Wright (Maynadier) A.; m. Vivian Garrison, July 14, 1974; children—Emily Maynadier, Margaret Farrell. A.B., Harvard U., 1931, Ph.D., 1934. Cornelius Wright. Jr. fellow Harvard U., 1934-37; with indsl. relations sect. Mass. Inst. Tech., 1937-40; chmn., organizer dept. sociology and anthropology Bklyn. Coll., 1940-42; chmn. sociology Barnard Coll., 1946-50; cons. research in Ruhr, Socialforschungstelle, Dortmund, Germany, 1950-51; research dir. UNESCO Inst. Social Scis., Cologne, 1952; prof. anthropology Columbia U., 1953—; co-dir. (with Alan Lomax) Cantometrics-Choreometrics Project, 1969-79. Author: Irish Countryman, 1936, Family and Community in Ireland, 1940, Measuring Human Relations, (with Eliot D. Chapple), 1942; editor: Human Orgn, 1946-52, Am. Anthropol. Assn. Manual for Point 4 Workers, 1953, Indsl. Relations Research Assn. Summary Human Relations Research, 1955, (with Karl Polanyi) Trade and Markets in the Early Empires, 1957, (with Solon T. Kimball) Culture and Community, 1965, (with Arthur Niehoff) Introducing Social Change, 1964. Served from capt. to maj. AUS, 1943-45. Mem. Soc. Applied Anthropology (founder), Am. Anthrop. Assn. (pres. 1979-80). Episcopalian. Clubs: Century (N.Y.C.); St. Botolph (Boston). Home: 460 Riverside Dr New York NY 10027 Office: Schermerhorn Hall Columbia U New York NY 10027

ARENSON, KAREN WATTEL, journalist; b. Long Beach, N.Y., Jan. 3, 1949; d. Harold Louis and Sara (Gordon) Wattel; m. Gregory Keith Arenson, Sept. 4, 1970. S.B., MIT, 1970; M.Pub. Policy, Harvard U., 1972. Assoc. dir. Nat. Affiliations of Concerned Bus. Students, Chgo., 1972-73; corr. Bus. Week Mag., 1973-79, editor, 1977-78; reporter N.Y. Times, N.Y.C., 1978—; mem. vis. com. dept. econs. (MIT), ednl. counselor. Author: The New York Times Guide to Making the New Tax Law Work for You, 1981. Recipient Matrix award Women in Communications, 1982, Journalism award Washington Monthly, 1981. Home: 125 W 76th St New York NY 10023 Office: 229 W 43d St New York NY 10036

ARENT, ALBERT EZRA, lawyer; b. Rochester, N.Y., Aug. 25, 1911; s. Hyman J. and Sarah (Weller) A.; m. Frances Feldman, Nov. 23, 1939; children: Stephen Weller, Margery Arent Grovet. A.B., Cornell U., 1932, LL.B., 1935. Bar: N.Y. bar 1935, D.C. bar 1945. Research asst. N.Y. State Law Revision Commn., 1934; atty. U.S. Bur. Internal Revenue, 1935-39; spl. asst. to Atty. Gen. U.S., 1939-44; chief trial atty. Alien Property Unit, U.S. Dept. Justice, 1942-44; pvt. law practice specializing in taxation; partner firm Arent, Fox, Kintner, Plotkin and Kahn and (predecessor firms), Washington, 1944—; lectr. taxation Am. U., 1948-52; prof. taxation Georgetown Law Sch., 1951-73; also lectr. tax subjects before Practising Law Inst., N.Y. U., U. Chgo. tax insts., Am., Fed., various local and state bar assns.; prosecuted leading fgn. agt. registration act cases, World War II.; chmn. adv. council Cornell Law Sch., 1979-82. Contbr. articles to legal publs. Vice pres. Jewish Community Council of Greater Washington, 1953-57, pres., 1957-61; chmn. Commn. on Social Action of Reform Judaism, 1973-77; chmn. Cornell Law Sch. Fund, 1975-77; mem. council Cornell U.; mem. steering com. Nat. Urban Coalition, 1970-77, mem. exec. com., 1970-72; mem. governing bd. and exec. com. Common Cause, 1970-72; bd. dirs. Overseas Edn. Fund of LWV, 1961-79; vice chmn. Nat Jewish Community Relations Adv. Council, 1967-70, chmn., 1970-73; vice chmn. Conf. Pres.'s Major Jewish Orgns., 1970-73; trustee Cornell U., 1978-83, trustee emeritus, 1983—; 1st v.p. Washington Hebrew Congregation, 1978-80; v.p. United Jewish Appeal Fedn. Greater Washington, 1979-81. Recipient Stephen S. Wise medallion award Nat. Capital chpt. Am. Jewish Congress, 1965, Vicennial medal Georgetown U., 1971, Humanitarianism award B'nai B'rith, 1975, Disting. Alumnus award Cornell U. Law Sch., 1982, award for outstanding service Overseas Edn. Fund, 1983. Mem. Am. Law Inst., Am. Judicature Soc., Am., Fed., D.C. bar assns., Telluride Assn., Phi Beta Kappa, Phi Kappa Phi. Home: 2510 Virginia Ave NW Washington DC 20037 Office: Federal Bar Bldg Washington DC 20006

ARENTS, CHESTER ABBO, engineer, educator; b. Leonardville, Kans., Apr. 19, 1910; s. Abbo Edward and Hazel Amanda (Johnson) A.; m. Edna Louisa Van Vleet, Feb. 18, 1935. B.S., Oreg. State U., 1932, M.S., 1946; M.E., 953; D.Sc., Marshall U., 1968. Registered profl. engr., Oreg., W.Va. Test engr. (automotive) City of Portland, Oreg., 1936-41; asso. elec. engr. Bonneville Power Adm., 1941-43; asst. prof. mech. engring. Oreg. State Coll., 1943-46; asso. prof. mech. engring. in charge machine design and heat power engring. Mont. State Coll., 1946-47; asso. prof. mech. engring. and asst. dept. dir. Ill. Inst. Tech., Chgo., 1947-49, asst. dean engring., 1949-51, coordinator research and prof. mech. engring. in charge sponsored research program, 1951-55; dean Coll. Engring. W.Va. U., 1955-75, dean emeritus, 1975—, tech. cons., engring. analyst, 1975—; also dir. of engring. Expt. Sta. Cons. div. air pollution NIH; past sec. Nat. Conf. Indsl. Hydraulics; mem. Bldg. Research Adv. Bd.; mem. bd. rev. Marine Engring. Lab., U.S. Navy; mem. Pub. Land Corp. W.Va.; past pres. W.Va. Registration Bd. Profl. Engrs.; Past dir. N.E. zone Nat. Council State Bd. Engring. Examiners; pres. Nat. Council Engring. Examiners, 1970-71. Author manuals on insulation. Mem. W.Va. Soc. Profl. Engrs., ASME, Am. Soc. Engring. Edn., Nat. (dir.), W.Va. socs. profl. engrs.), Morgantown C. of C. (pres. 1962), Morgantown Community Assn. (trustee), Sigma Xi, Pi Tau Sigma, Tau Beta Pi, Eta Kappa Nu, Alpha Pi Mu. Mem. Pentecostal Ch. Home: 1244 Oxford Pl Morgantown WV 26505

ARENZ, ROBERT JAMES, engineering educator, administrator; b. Primghar, Iowa, Aug. 20, 1924; s. George and Gladys (Moore) A. B.S., Oreg. State U., 1945; M.S., St. Louis U., 1957; Ph.D., Calif. Inst. Tech., 1964; S.T.M., Santa Clara U., 1966. Registered profl. engr., Calif.; ordained priest S.J., Roman Catholic Ch. Aerodynamicist Douglas Aircraft Co., Santa Monica, Calif., 1945-50; research fellow Calif. Inst. Tech., Pasadena, 1963-66; prof. mech. engring. Loyola Marymount U., Los Angeles, 1967-78; dean faculty, prof. Parks Coll., St. Louis, 1978-80; dean arts and sci. Gonzaga U., Spokane, Wash., 1980—; cons. Lockheed Missiles & Space Co., Sunnyvale, Calif., 1964-66; vis. research scientist Ernst-Mach-Institut, Freiburg, Germany, 1966-67; cons. sr. scientist Jet Propulsion Lab., Pasadena, Calif., 1969-78. Critical reviewer Applied Mechanics Reviews, 1965-75; paper referee: Exptl. Mechanics Jour. Polymer Sci., 1969-78; contbr. articles to profl. jours. Chmn. Citizens Airport Adv. Com., Los Angeles, 1973-74. Recipient Summer Symposium award NSF, Va. Poly. Inst., 1970. Fellow AIAA (assoc.); mem. ASME, Soc. Exptl. Stress Analysis, Am. Soc. Engring. Edn., Am. Acad. Mechanics, Sigma Xi, Tau Beta Pi, Pi Tau Sigma. Home and Office: Gonzaga U Spokane WA 99258

AREY, LESLIE BRAINERD, anatomist, educator; b. Camden, Maine, Feb. 15, 1891; s. Arthur Brainerd and Mary Josephine (Page) A.; (m), 1913-15; m. Mary E. Holt, 1926. A.B., Colby Coll., Waterville, Maine, 1912, D.Sc., 1937; Ph.D., Harvard, 1915; LL.D., Chgo. Med. Sch., 1934; L.H.D., Ill. Coll. Podiatric Medicine, 1983. Asst. in zoology Harvard, 1912-13, teaching fellow, 1913; asst. in zoology Radcliffe, 1913-14, instr. anatomy, 1915-17, assoc. prof., 1917-19, prof. microscopic anatomy, 1919-24; Robert L. Rea prof. anatomy, chmn. dept. anatomy Northwestern U. Med. Sch., 1924-56, emeritus prof. anatomy, 1956—; mem. staff Wesley Meml. Hosp., Passavant Hosp., Children's Meml. Hosp; spl. cons. NIH.; Sometime investigator U.S. Bureau Fisheries; sometime chmn. Com. Basic Scis., White House Conf. on Child Health and Protection; sometime guest lectr. Chgo. Jr. Colls; vis. prof. U. P.R., 1963, 64; Chmn. Internat. Com. on Embryological Terminology, 1962—; pres. Internat. Anatomical Nomenclature Com., 1975-80; Sec.-treas. Interfraternity Confs., 1938-42, pres., 1944-47; mem. exec. com. Profl. Interfraternity Conference, 1942-44. Author: Tratado de Endocrinologia Clinica, 1951, Word Book Encyclopedia, 1949, Morris Human Anatomy, 1966, Developmental Anatomy, 1974, Human Histology, 1974, Medical Dictionary, 1974, Anatomia Desarrollo, 1958, Histologia Humana, 1958, Centennial History of Northwestern University Medical School, 1959, Northwestern University Medical School, 1979, istologia umana, 1976; Assoc. editor: Excerpta Medica; editor: Northwestern U. Med. Sch. Mag, 1963-74; Writer papers and monographs on anatomy and physiology; contbr. to 13 books and 6 encys. Recipient Alumni medal Northwestern U., 1959, Service award, 1973, Hamilton Interstate Teaching award, 1973; Coll. award Am. Coll. Obstetrics and Gynecology, 1975; William H. Byford Northwestern award, 1980; Disting. Alumnus award Colby Coll., 1980; named to City of Chgo. Hall of Fame, 1967. Fellow Chgo. Acad. Sci. (pres. 1956-73, pres. emeritus 1973—, trustee 1973—); mem. Am. Soc. Zoologists (sec. 1928, treas. 1925-30), Am. Assn. Anatomists (exec. com. 1930-34, v.p. 1942-46, pres. 1952-54, Henry Gray award 1974), Phi Beta Kappa, Sigma Xi, Delta Upsilon, Phi Beta Pi (praetor 1932-34, 40-47, supreme archon 1934-41, trustee and supreme councillor 1934-73, supreme editor 1942, moderator 1951—), Alpha Omega Alpha (hon.), Pi Kappa Epsilon, Pi Delta. Republican. Clubs: Mason (K.T., 32 deg.), Shriner, University, Chaos. Address: 3440 Lake Shore Dr Chicago IL 60657

ARGENTO, DOMINICK, composer; b. York, Pa., Oct. 27, 1927; s. Michael and Nicolina (Amato) A.; m. Carolyn Bailey, Sept. 6, 1954. B.Mus., Peabody Conservatory, 1951; Fulbright fellow, Conservatorio Cherubini, Florence, 1951-52; Ph.D., Eastman Sch. Music, 1957. Prof. music U. Minn., Mpls., 1958—; Co-founder Center Opera, Mpls., Hilltop Opera, Balt. Composer numerous operas, song cycles, choral and orchestral works. Served with AUS, 1945-47. Guggenheim grantee, 1957-58, 64-65; Recipient Pulitzer prize, 1975. Mem. A.S.C.A.P., Am. Acad. and Inst. Arts and Letters. Office: Dept Music U Minn Minneapolis MN 55455 *

ARGIRION, MICHAEL, editor; b. Chgo., May 2, 1940; s. Gus and Angela A.; m. Sherrie Berlant, Feb. 10; children: Carrie, Glen. Student, DePaul U., 1958-59, Northwestern U., 1959-60, U. Chgo., 1961-62. Copy editor Chgo.'s Am., 1959-68, wire editor, 1969; news editor Chgo. Today, 1970-71, Sunday and features editor, 1971-74; asst. Sunday editor Chgo. Tribune, 1974-75, features editor, 1975-79, asst. mng. editor features, 1979-81, asst. mng. editor news editing, 1981-82, exec. news editor, 1982—. Editor: History of Your World, 1969. Served with U.S. Army, 1962. Mem. AP Mng. Editors, Newspaper Comics Council (mem. exec. com., chmn. bd.). Clubs: Chgo. Press, Buffalo Grove Golf, Skyline, Tam Racquet. Office: Chgo Tribune 435 N Michigan Ave Chicago IL 60611

ARGON, ALI SUPHI, mechanical engineering educator; b. Istanbul, Turkey, Dec. 19, 1930; came to U.S., 1948, naturalized, 1980; s. Mehmet Ali Suphi and Seniha Margaret (Grosche) A.; m. Xenia Mary Lacher, Sept. 6, 1953; children—Alice Leyla, Arif Kermit. B.S., Purdue U., 1952; S.M., MIT, 1953, Sc.D., 1956. Project engr. High Voltage Engring. Corp., Burlington, Mass., 1956-58; lectr. Middle East Tech. U., Ankara, Turkey, 1959; mem. faculty MIT, 1960—, prof. mech. engring., 1968—, Quentin Berg prof. mech. engring., 1982; vis. prof. polymer physics U. Leeds, 1972; cons. indsl. and govt. labs. Author: (with F.A. McClintock) Mechanical Behavior of Materials, 1966, (with U.F. Kocks and M.F. Ashby) Thermodynamics and Kinetics of Slip, 1975; Editor: Physics of Strength and Plasticity, 1969, Constitutive Equations in Plasticity, 1975; Contbr. articles to profl. jours. Recipient Charles Russ Richards Meml. award ASME, 1976. Home: 16 Plymouth Ave Belmont MA 02178 Office: Room 1-306 Mass Inst Tech Cambridge MA 02139 *Always strive for perfection, but never take yourself seriously.*

ARGOW, KEITH ANGEVIN, forester, association executive; b. New Haven, Sept. 3, 1936; s. Walter Webster and Claire (Angevin) A.; m. Mary Lou Morgan, Apr. 12, 1969; children: Brittina, Kristen, Kenton. B.A. in Econs, Colo. Coll., 1958; B.S. in Forest Mgmt; M.Forestry, U. Mich., 1961; Ph.D. in Forestry and Polit. Sci, N.C. State U., 1970. With U.S. Forest Service, 1961-74; adminstr. Mt. Rogers Nat. Recreation Area, Marion, Va., 1970-74; assoc. prof. forestry, sect. leader forest recreation and park mgmt. Va. Poly. Inst. and State U., Blacksburg, 1974-78; exec. dir. Trout Unlimited, Washington, 1978-81; pres. Am. Resources Group, Vienna, Va., 1981—; Washington rep. Nat. Woodland Owners Assn.; editor Conservation News Digest; exec. com. Natural Resurces Council Am.; bd. dirs. Am. Forestry Assn.; past trustee Fontana Conservation Roundup; past chmn. for Va., Nature Conservancy. Author 46 articles in field. Div. dir. Nat. Ski Patrol System, 1972-77. Served to capt., inf. AUS, 1958-59. Recipient award merit U.S. Forest Service, 1965, Silver Star Adminstrv. award Nat. Ski Patrol System, 1977. Mem. Soc. Am. Foresters, Am. Soc. Assn. Execs., Phi Beta Kappa, Xi Sigma Pi. Unitarian. Club: Rotary. Home: 2614 Lakevale Dr Vienna VA 22180 Office: Am Resources Group Suite 210 Bank of Vienna Bldg Vienna VA 22180

ARGUE, HAZEN R., Canadian government official; b. Moose Jaw, Sask., 1921; s. Howard B and Legia (Scharf) A.; m. Jean Ignatescu, 1945; 4 children. B.S. in Agr. with distinction, U. Sask., 1944. Mem. Can. Ho. of Commons. for Assiniboia, 1945-63; parliamentary leader, then nat. leader Coop. Commonwealth Fedn., 1958-62; mem. Can. Senate, 1963—, chmn. com. agr., 1972-80; mem. privy cabinet, minister of state for Can. Wheat Bd., 1980—; also minister for Two-Price Wheat Act and Western Grain Stblzn. Act; chmn. Grains Group.

Mem. numerous internat. dels.; engaged in farming, Kayville, Sask. Office: Minister State for Wheat Bd Parliament Bldg Ottawa ON K1A 0AS Canada *

ARGUE, JOHN CLIFFORD, lawyer; b. Glendale, Calif., Jan. 25, 1932; s. J. Clifford and Catherine Emily (Clements) A.; m. Leah Elizabeth Moore, June 29, 1963; children: Elizabeth Anne, John Michael. A.B. in Commerce and Finance, Occidental Coll., 1953; LL.B., U. So. Calif., 1956. Bar: Calif. 1957. Since practiced in, Los Angeles; mem. firm Argue & Argue, 1958-59, Flint & MacKay, 1960-72, Argue, Freston, Pearson, Harbison & Myers, 1972—; dir. LAACO, Inc., Trust Services Am., Inc., 1st Bus. Bank, Los Angeles. Pres. So. Calif. Com. Olympic Games, 1972—; founding-chmn. Los Angeles Olympic Organizing Com., 1978-79, now vice chmn.; trustee Pomona Coll.; chmn. Greater Los Angeles affiliate Am. Heart Assn.; trustee Verdugo Hills Hosp., chmn., 1979; bd. govs. Alumni Occidental Coll., 1962-64; bd. dirs. U. So. Calif. Assocs., Town Hall; chmn. PGA Championship, 1983. Served with U.S. Army, 1956-58. Mem. Los Angeles, Calif., Am. bar assns., Legion Lex (dir. 1974), So. Calif. Golf Assn. (pres. 1979), Calif. Golf Assn. (v.p. 1979), Phi Delta Phi, Alpha Tau Omega. Clubs: Chancery, Calif. (pres.), Los Angeles Athletic, Riviera Country, Flint Canyon Tennis, Oakmont Country (pres. 1972), Rotary (Los Angeles)). Home: 1314 Descanso Dr La Canada LA 91011 Office: 626 Wilshire Blvd Suite 1000 Los Angeles CA 90017

ARGYRES, PETROS NICHOLAOS, educator; b. Lefkas, Greece, Mar. 9, 1927; came to U.S., 1947, naturalized, 1956; s. Nicholaos Constantinos and Georgia (Aretha) A.; m. Nita M. Dressler, Aug. 2, 1958; children: Peter N., Philip C., Anneta Z. A.B. with highest honors, U. Calif., Berkeley, 1950, M.A., 1952, Ph.D. (fellow), 1954. Research physicist Westinghouse Research Lab., Pitts., 1954-58, Lincoln Lab., M.I.T., 1958-67; vis. asso. prof. physics M.I.T., 1965-67; mem. faculty Northeastern U., Boston, 1967—, prof. physics, 1967—; vis. prof. Ecole Normale Superieure, U. Paris, France, 1969-70, Tech. U. of Greece, Athens, 1982-83. Contbr. articles to books and profl. jours. IBM fellow, 1952-53. Fellow Am. Phys. Soc.; mem. AAAS, Acad. of Athens (corr.), Sigma Xi, Phi Beta Kappa. Home: 39 Meriam St Lexington MA 02173

ARGYRIS, CHRIS, educator; b. Newark, July 16, 1923; s. Stephen and Sophia (Papasthathis) A.; m. Renee Brocoum, July 23, 1950; children: Dianne Ellen, James Phillip. A.B., Clark U., 1947; M.A., U. Kans., 1949; Ph.D., Cornell U., 1951; M.A. (hon.), Yale U., 1960, Harvard U., 1971, LL.D., McGill U., 1977; D.Psychology and Pedagogy, U. Louvain, 1978; D.Econs., Stockholm Sch. Econs., 1979. Asst. prof. Yale U., 1951-55, asso. prof., 1956-60, prof., 1960-65, Beach prof. adminstrv. sci., 1965-71; James Bryant Conant prof. edn. and orgnl. behavior Harvard U. Grad. Schs. Edn. and Bus., 1971—; cons. in field. Author 21 books including: Intervention Theory and Method, 1970; Author: 21 books including Management and Organizational Development, 1971, The Applicability of Organizational Sociology, 1972, Organization and Innovation, 1965, Integrating the Individual and the Organization, 1965, Interpersonal Competence and Organizational Effectiveness, 1964, Behind the Front Page, 1974, (with Donald Schon) Theory in Practice, 1974, Organizational Learning, 1978, Increasing Leadership Effectiveness, 1976; Inner Contradictions of Rigorous Research, 1980, Reasoning, Learning, Action, 1982; also articles. Trustee Clark U., Mass., Nat. Tng. Labs. Served with Signal Corps, AUS, 1941-45. Ford disting. vis. prof., 1967-68; Sloan prof. U. London, 1970—; vis. scholar Cambridge U., Eng., 1970—. Mem. Phi Beta Kappa, Sigma Xi, Phi Kappa Phi. Home: 58 Sylvan Ln Weston MA 02193 Office: Grad Sch Edn Harvard U Cambridge MA 02138

ARGYROS, GEORGE L., development company executive, professional sports team owner; b. Detroit; m. Judie Argyros. Student, Mich. State U.; B.S. in Bus. and Econs., Chapman Coll., 1959. Pres. Arnel Devel. Co.; chmn. bd. Arnel Mgmt.; chmn., dir. Air Cal, 1981—; dir. comml. financing services Newport bancorp and Coast Thrift and Loan Co.; prin. owner Seattle Mariners Baseball Team, 1981—; mem. Baseball's Revenue sharing Com., Restructuring Com., Commr. Selection Com.; bd. dirs. Am. League. Chmn. Western Wash.'s United Cerebral Palsy Telethon; chmn. fundraising Nat. Multiple Sclerosis Soc., Puget Sound chpt.; active NCCJ, Boy Scouts Am., World Affairs Council, Young Pres.'s Orgn.; chmn. bd. trustees Chapman Coll. Office: Seattle Mariners Baseball Club PO Box 4100 Seattle WA 98104 *

ARIAS, IRWIN MONROE, physician, educator; b. N.Y.C., Sept. 4, 1926; s. Henry Robert and Sylvia (Hirsh) A.; children: Jonathan, Linda, Wendy, Nancy. B.S., Harvard U., 1947; M.S., Columbia U., 1948; M.D. cum laude, State U., N.Y. Med. Center, 1952. Diplomate: Am. Bd. Internal Medicine. Intern Fourth Med. Service (Harvard) Boston City Hosp., 1952-54, asst. resident, 1954-55; USPHS fellow gastroenterology/liver disease Second and Fourth Med. Service, 1955-56; fellow hematology Boston VA Hosp., 1954-55; research fellow N.Y. Heart Assn., Albert Einstein Coll. Medicine, Bronx, N.Y., 1956-57, sr. research fellow, 1956-58, asst. prof., 1960-64, asso. prof., 1964-69; asst. vis. physician Bronx Mcpl. Hosp. Center, 1956-64, asso. attending physician, 1964-67, attending physician, 1969—; prin. investigator USPHS GI tng. program; dir. program and chief div. gastroenterology-liver disease Albert Einstein Coll. Medicine, Bronx, 1967—, prof. medicine, 1969—, vice chmn. dept. medicine, 1973—; dir. Liver Research Center, 1973—, asso. chmn. academic devel., dept. medicine, 1980—; cons. Rockefeller Found., 1958-60, Pan Am. Union, 1959-63. Editor: (with others) Glutathione: Metabolism and Function, 1976, the Liver: Biology and Pathobiology, 1980, the Liver; Contbr. numerous articles to sci. publs. Mem. overseas med. adv. bd. Tel Aviv U. Sch. Medicine, 1963-69; mem. nat. adv. bd. La Leche League, 1970—; trustee Mount Desert Island Biol. Lab., 1969-71; mem. adv. bd. Children's Med. Research Center, Cin., 1976-81. Recipient numerous awards including Disting. Achievement awards Am. Gastroenterologic Assn., 1970, Am. Coll. Gastroenterologists, 1971, Can. Gastroenterologic Assn., 1972; B.B. Vincent Lyons award Am. Gastroenterologic Assn., 1965; San Diego-Spl. fellow. E.B. Scripps Inst. for Comparative Biology, 1967; Disting. Commendation medal medicine U. Recife, Brazil, 1972. Mem. AAAS, Am. Soc. Clin. Investigation (v.p.), Am. Assn. Study Liver Disease, Am. Fedn. Clin. Research, Am. Gastroenterol. Assn., The Harvey Soc., Am. Physiol. Soc., Internat. Assn. Clin. Investigation, Internat. Assn. Study of Liver, Assn. Am. Physicians, Alpha Omega Alpha. Office: 1300 Morris Park Ave Bronx NY 10461

ARIAS, JULIO JAVIER, foreign service officer; b. Nogales, Ariz., Feb. 19, 1921; s. Julio and Maria Luisa (Lopez) A. Student, U. Ariz., UCLA; B.A. with highest honors, U. Calif.-Berkeley, 1949. Rate clk. So. Pacific R.R., Ariz., 1934-42; commd. fgn. service officer Dept. State, 1950, served with, Philippines, Italy, Japan, Spain, 1950-74, dep. asst. sec. for visa services, Washington, 1974-78, prin. officer Am. Consulate Gen., Guadalajara, Mexico, 1981—. Served to master sgt. U.S. Mil. Ry. Service, 1942-45; Algeria, Europe. Recipient Meritorious Honor award Am. Embassy, Madrid, 1970, Honor with silver platter Orgn. Cuban Refugees, Madrid, 1970, Citation Assn. Immigration and Nationality Lawyers, San Francisco, 1976, Superior Honor award Dept. State, Washington, 1978, citations, awards, honors, plaques numerous orgns. Mem. Am. Soc. Jalisco (hon. pres. 1981—), Am. Legion, Phi Beta Kappa. Clubs: Country, Club de Guadalajara, Cinegetico de Guadalajara. Office: Am consulate Gen Progresso 175 Guadalajara Jalisco Mexico 44100

ARIAS, MORTIMER, theology educator, bishop emeritus; b. Durazno, Uruguay, Jan. 7, 1924; emigrated to U.S., 1980; m. Esther Leguizamon, Jan. 3, 1948; children: Eunice Esther, Ruben Daniel. B.Th., Union Theol. Sem., Buenos Aires, 1946, M.Th., 1957; B.Pre-Medicine, Montevideo U., 1948; D.Min., Perkins Sch. Theology, Dallas, 1977. Ordained to ministry Methodist Ch., 1947; Deacon, Elder, and Bishop orders; exec. pastor Meth. Ch., Uruguay, 1947-56, 58-61, pastor, dist. supt., Bolivia, 1962-67, nat. exec. sec., 1668-69; bishop Evang. Meth. Ch., Bolivia, 1969-76; vis. prof. Perkins Sch. Theology, Boston U., 1976-78, Sch. Theology, Claremont, Calif., 1981—; exec. sec. Latin Am. Meth. Council, 1978-80; sec. of mission Latin Am. Council of Chs., 1979-80; mem. Com. on World Mission World Council Chs., Geneva, 1973-83, Intenat. Assn. Missiology (Amsterdam), Holland, 1980—. Author: Salvation is Liberation(Spanish and Portuguese), 1973, Your Kingdom Come (Spanish), 1980, Announcing the Reign of God (English), 1983; co-author: The Cry of My People (English and Spanish), 1980. Active Assembly of Human Rights, Bolivia, 1975—, Justice and Peace Commn., Bolivia, 1970-75, Meth. Fedn. for Social Action, U.S., 1981—, Central Am. Task Force, U.S., 1981—. Mem. Assn. Profs. of Mission U.S., Acad. of Evangelism U.S. Home: Casilla 3532 Cochabamba Bolivia Office: Sch Theology at Claremont 1325 N College Ave Claremont CA 91711

ARIS, RUTHERFORD, applied mathematician, educator; b. Bournemouth, Eng., Sept. 15, 1929; came to U.S., 1955, naturalized, 1962; s. Algernon Pollock and Janet (Elford) A.; m. Claire Mercedes Holman, Jan. 1, 1958. B.Sc. (spl.) with 1st class honours in Math, London (Eng.) U., 1948, Ph.D., 1960, D.Sc., 1964; student, Edinburgh (Scotland) U., 1948-50. Tech. officer Billingham div. I.C.I. Ltd., 1950-55; research fellow U. Minn., 1955-56; lectr. tech. math. Edinburgh U., 1956-58; mem. faculty U. Minn., 1958—, prof. chem. engring., 1963—, Regents' prof., 1978—; O.A. Hougen vis. prof. U. Wis., 1979; Sherman Fairchild Disting. Scholar Calif. Inst. Tech., 1980-81; cons. to industry, lectr., 1961—. Author: Optimal Design of Chemical Reactors, 1961, Vectors, Tensors and the Basic Equations of Fluid Mechanics, 1962, Discrete Dynamic Programming, 1964, Introduction to the Analysis of Chemical Reactors, 1965, Elementary Chemical Reactor Analysis, 1969, (with N.R. Amundson) First-Order Partial Differential Equations with Applications, 1973, (with W. Strieder) Variational Methods Applied to Problems of Diffusion and Reaction, 1973, The Mathematical Theory of Diffusion and Reaction in Permeable Catalysts, 1975, Mathematical Modelling Techniques, 1978, Chemical Engineering in the University Context, 1982, Springs of Scientific Creativity, 1982; co-editor: An Index of Scripts for E.A. Lowe's Codices Latini Antiquiores, 1982. Sr. research fellow NSF, 1964-65; Guggenheim fellow, 1971-72; Recipient E. Harris Harbison award for distinguished teaching, 1969; Alpha Chi Sigma award Am. Inst. Chem. Engrs., 1969; Chem. Engring. lectr. award Am. Soc. Engring. Edn., 1973. Fellow Inst. Math. and Applications; mem. Nat. Acad. Engring., Soc. Nat. Philosophy, Soc. for Math. Biology, Soc. Indsl. and Applied Math., Am. Chem. Soc., Am. Inst. Chem. Engrs. (R.H. Wilhelm award 1975), Mediaeval Acad. Am., Soc. Scribes and Illuminators, Soc. Textual Scholarship, Internat. Soc. Math. Modeling. Lutheran. Office: Dept of Chemical Engineering Univ of Minnesota Minneapolis MN 55455

ARISON, TED, cruise lines company executive, bank executive, real estate developer; b. Tel Aviv, Feb, 24, 1924; U.S., 1952; s. Meir and Vera (Avrutin) Arisohn; m. Mina Wassermam, Apr. 1948 (div.); children: Mickey Michael, Sharon Arison Sueiras; m. Marilyn B. Hersh Lin, Aug. 1968; 1 son, Michael A. Student, Am. U. Beirut, 1940-42. Mgr. M.Dizengoff & Co., Tel Aviv, 1946-48, 49-51; owner, chmn., pres. Tran-Air Co., N.Y.C., 1952-66, Arison Shipping Co., Miami, Fla., 1966-71, Hamilton Holding Co., 1979—, Carnival Cruise Lines, 1972—; trustee Nat. Found. Advancement in Arts, Miami, Fla., 1981—. Founder Soc. Univ. Founders U. Miami, Fla., 1981—. Albert Einstein Coll. Medicine, N.Y.C., 1983—, mt. Sinai Med Ctr., Miami Beach, Fla., 1983, Tel Aviv U., 1983; mem. Mayor's Ad Hoc Econ. Devel. Council, Miami Beach, Fla., 1983—, Republican Eagles, Washington, 1983—. Served to col. Israeli Army, 1948-49. Recipient Disting. Achievement award Albert Einstein Coll. Medicine, 1983. Republican. Jewish. Office: Carnival Cruise Lines Inc New World Tower Suite 2302 100 N Biscayne Blvd Miami FL 33132

ARISS, HERBERT JOSHUA, artist; b. Guelph, Ont., Can., Sept. 29, 1918; s. William Minno and Wilhemina Helen (Zinger) A.; m. Margot Joan Phillips, July 5, 1950; children—Joshua Herbert, Jeffrey Earl. Student, Ont. Coll. Edn., 1947. Artist, designer Vibra-Lite Co., 1940-42; art tchr. H.B. Beal Secondary Sch., London, Ont., 1947-63, head art dept., 1964-77; lectr. U. Western Ont., Doon Sch. Fine Arts, 1954-64. Executed murals, Huron and Erie Bldg., Chatham, Ont., 1958, John Labatt Head Office, 1959, Macdonald Block, Ont. Govt., 1966. Pres. Western Art League, 1956-58. Served with Canadian Army, 1942-46. Can. Council fellow for creative painting, 1960-61. Mem. Royal Can. Acad. Art, Can. Soc. Painters in Water Colour (Honour award 1964), Ont. Soc. Artists. Anglican. Home and studio: 770 Leroy Crescent London ON N5Y 4G7 Canada

ARIYOSHI, GEORGE RYOICHI, governor Hawaii; b. Honolulu, Mar. 12, 1926; s. Ryozo and Mitsue (Yoshikawa) A.; m. Jean Miya Hayashi, Feb. 5, 1955; children: Lynn Miye, Todd Ryozo, Donn Ryoji. Student, U. Hawaii, 1944-45, 47; B.A., Mich. State U., 1949, LL.D. (hon.), 1979; J.D., U. Mich., 1952; LL.D. (hon.), U. Philippines, 1975, U. Guam, 1975, H.H.D., U. Visayas, Philippines, 1977. Bar: Hawaii 1953. Practiced in, Honolulu, 1953-70; Mem. T.H. Ho. of Reps., 1954-58, T.H. Senate, 1958, Hawaii State Senate, 1959-70; chmn. Senate Ways and Means Com., 1963-64, Senate majority leader, 1965-66, majority floor leader of State Senate, 1969-70; lt. gov., Hawaii, 1970-73, acting gov., 1973-74, gov., 1974—; chmn. Western Govs. Conf., 1977-78; dir. Hawaiian Ins. & Guaranty, Ltd., 1966-70, First Hawaiian Bank, 1962-70, Honolulu Gas Co., Ltd. (Pacific Resources, Inc.), 1964-70. Chmn. small bus. div. Community Chest, 1963; fund raiser pub. employees div. Aloha United Fund, 1971-72; exec. bd. Aloha council Boy Scouts Am., 1970-72; chmn. Citizenship Day Com., 1971; pres. Pacific Basin Devel. Council, 1980-81; bd. mgrs. YMCA, 1955-57. Served with M.I. Service AUS, 1945-46. Recipient Distinguished Alumni awards U. Hawaii, 1975, Mich. State U., 1975. Mem. Am. Bar Assn. (ho. dels. 1969—), Hawaii Bar Assn. (pres. 1969), Hawaii Bar Found. (charter mem., pres. 1969—). Democrat. Club: Military Intelligence Service Vets (pres. 1968-69). Office: State Capitol Honolulu HI 96813

ARKFELD, LEO, archbishop; b. Butte, Nebr., Feb. 4, 1912; s. George and Theresa (Siemer) A. Ed., Divine Word Sem., Techny, Ill. Ordained priest Roman Catholic Ch., 1943; missionary to, New Guinea, 1945, bishop of Wewak, 1948-76; archbishop of Madang, adminstr. Diocese of Wewak, 1976-80. Address: Box 750 Madang Papua New Guinea

ARKIN, ALAN WOLF, actor; b. N.Y.C., Mar. 26, 1934; s. David I. and Beatrice (Wortis) A.; m. Barbara Dana, June 16, 1964; 1 son, Anthony; children by previous marriage: Adam, Matthew. Student, Los Angeles City Coll., 1951-53, Bennington Coll., 1954-55. Broadway appearances include From The Second City, 1961, Enter Laughing, 1963, Luv, 1964; motion picture appearances include The Russians are Coming, The Russians Are Coming, 1966 (Golden Globe award as best actor in musical or comedy 1967), Woman Times Seven, 1967, Wait Until Dark, 1967, Inspector Clouseau, 1968, The Heart is a Lonely Hunter, 1968, Popi, 1969, Catch-22, 1970, Last of the Red Hot Lovers, 1972, Seven Per Cent Solution, 1976, The In Laws, 1979, Chu Chu and the Philly Flash, 1981, Improper Channels, 1981, The Last Unicorn, 1982; TV appearances include To America, 1976, The Defection of Simas Kudirka, 1978, Capt. Kangaroo, The Love Song of Barney Kempinski; mem. theatre group, Second City Chicago and Off-Broadway, 1961; rec. of children's music The Babysitters, 1958, Songs and Fun with The Babysitters, 1960, The Family Album, 1965, The Babysitters Menagerie, 1968; short motion pictures include That's Me, 1963, The Last Mohican, 1965; dir.: movie short People Soup; motion picture Little Murders, 1971; Broadway play The Sunshine Boys, 1972; TV drama Twigs, 1975; author: (juvenile) Tony's Hard Work Day, 1972, The Lemming Condition, 1979; (adult-jour.) Halfway Through the Door, 1979. Address: care Robinson, Luttrell & Assos 141 El Camino Real #110 Beverly Hills CA 90212 *

ARKOFF, SAMUEL Z., motion picture executive, producer; b. Ft. Dodge, Iowa, June 12, 1918; m. Hilda Rusoff. Ed., U. Colo., U. Iowa; J.D., Loyola U., Los Angeles, 1948. Bar: Calif. Co-founder Am. Releasing, 1954, Am. Internat. Pictures, 1955; pres., chmn. bd. Am. Internat. Pictures, Inc., until 1979; pres., chmn. Samuel Z. Arkoff Co., Los Angeles, 1980—; pres. Arkoff Internat. Pictures, 1981—. Producer or co-producer: more than 250 films, including The House of Usher, 1960, The Pit and the Pendulum, 1961, Beach Party, 1963, The Wild Angels, 1966, The Trip, 1967, Wild in the Streets, 1968, Wuthering Heights, 1971, Dillinger, 1973, Heavy Traffic, 1973, Cooley High, 1975, Futureworld, 1976, A Matter of Time, 1976, Empire of the Ants, 1977, The Island of Dr. Moreau, 1977, The People That Time Forgot, 1977, Our Winning Season, 1978, Love at First Bite, 1979, Something Short of Paradise, 1979, Meteor, 1979, Amityville Horror, 1979, How to Beat the High Cost of Living, 1980, Dressed to Kill, 1980, The Earthling, 1981, Underground Aces, 1981. Trustee Loyola-Marymount U., Los Angeles, 1979—. Served as cryptographer USAAF, World War II. Named with partner James H. Nicholson as Producers of Year Allied States Assn. Motion Picture Theatre Owners, 1963; Master Showman of Decade Theatre Owners Am., 1964; Producers of Year Show-A-Rama VIII; Motion Picture Pioneer of Yr. (with Nicholson) Found. Motion Picture Pioneers, Inc., 1971; decorated commendatore of Order of Merit, Italy, 1970; named Internat. Ambassador, v.p. Variety Clubs Internat., 1973. Office: 9200 Sunset Blvd PH3 Los Angeles CA 90069 *

ARKOWITZ, MARTIN ARTHUR, mathematics educator; b. Bklyn., Apr. 17, 1935; s. William and Ruth (Levine) A.; m. Eleanor Silver, Aug. 25, 1957; children: David, Robert, Steven. B.A., Columbia Coll., N.Y.C., 1956, M.A., 1957; Ph.D., Cornell U., 1960. Postdoctoral assoc. Johns Hopkins U., 1960-61; instr. math. Princeton U., 1961-64; asst. prof. Dartmouth Coll., Hanover, N.H., 1964-67, assoc. prof., 1967-71, prof., 1971—, chmn. dept. math. and computer sci., 1981—; vis. prof. Aarhus U., Denmark, 1972-73, U. Ariz., Tucson, 1979-80; vis. scholar Oxford U., Eng., 1967-68; mem. adv. com. Dartmouth-Andover Math. Inst., Andover, Mass., 1981—. Author: (with C.R. Curjel) Groups of Homotopy Classes, 1964, Localization and H-spaces, 1974. Mem. Am. Math. Soc., Math. Assn. Am. Home: 10 Brockway Rd Hanover NH 03755 Office: Dartmouth Coll Hanover NH 03755

ARKUS, LEON ANTHONY, art consultant, former museum director; b. Passaic, N.J., May 6, 1915; s. Mayer and Elizabeth (Hoffman) A.; m. Jane L. Callomon, Dec. 19, 1971. Ed., Townsend Harris Prep., Coll. City N.Y. Asst. to dir. Masterpieces of Art Exhbn., N.Y. World's Fair, 1939-40; cons. fgn. relief orgns. Art Aid Corp., N.Y.C., 1941; personnel mgr. Foley Bros., Inc.; also Spencer, White & Prentice, Inc., Ahwaz, Iran, 1942-43; mgr. Douglas Curry Assos., Inc., N.Y.C., 1946-47; spl. asst. to pres. Am. Fedn. Arts, 1948; v.p., dir. Raymond & Raymond, Inc., N.Y.C., 1949-54; asst. dir. Mus. Art, Carnegie Inst., 1954-62, asso. dir., 1962-68, dir., 1968-80, dir. emeritus, 1980—; now cons.; Bd. govs. Pitts. Plan for Art, 1958-83. Author: Three Self-Taught Pennsylvania Artists: Edward Hicks, John Kane, Horace Pippin, 1966, Carl-Henning Pedersen, 1968, Art of Black Africa, 1969, Pittsburgh International Exhibition of Contemporary Art, 1970, John Kane Painter, A Catalogue Raisonne, 1971, Fresh Air School: Sam Francis, Joan Mitchell, Walasse Ting, 1972, Art in Residence, 1973, Twelve Years of Collecting, 1974, Celebration, 1974, Pittsburgh Corporations Collect, 1975, Pittsburgh International Series: Pierre Alechinsky, 1977, Eduardo Chillida/Willem De Kooning, 1979. Vice pres. Pitts. New Music Ensemble; bd. dirs. Three Rivers Art Festival, Allegheny County Courthouse Gallery/Forum, Pub. Art Rev. Com. of Allegheny County; exec. com. Asger Jorn Found., Denmark.; mem. Com. on Arts for Light Rail System, Port Authority of Allegheny County. Served to capt. AUS, 1943-45. Decorated Bronze Star; knight's cross Order of Dannebrog, Denmark; recipient Honor award AIA. Hon. mem. Am. Soc. Interior Designers, Asso. Artists Pitts.; mem. Am. Assn. Museums., Assn. Profl. Art Advisors (bd. dirs.). Club: Century Assn. Office: 303 S Craig St Pittsburgh PA 15213

ARLEDGE, CHARLES STONE, manufacturing executive; b. Bonham, Tex., Oct. 20, 1935; s. John F. and Mary Madeline (Jones) A.; m. Barbara Jeanne Ruff, June 18, 1966; children: John Harrison, Mary Katherine. B.S., Stanford U., 1957, M.S. (Standard Oil Co. Calif. scholar 1958), 1958, M.B.A., 1966. Engr. Shell Oil Co., Los Angeles, 1958-64; with Signal Cos., La Jolla, Calif., 1966—, v.p., 1970-79, group v.p., 1979—, dir., 1974-83; dir. Ampex Co., Rancho Santa Fe Nat. Bank, UOP Inc. Trustee Orme Sch., Mayer, Ariz., 1977—; bd. dirs. San Diego Symphony, 1981—. Republican. Presbyterian. Clubs: California; Men's Garden (Los Angeles) (dir. 1976-80). Home: PO Box 957 Rancho Santa Fe CA 92067 Office: 11255 N Torrey Pines Rd La Jolla CA 92037

ARLEDGE, ROONE, TV exec.; b. Forest Hills, N.Y., July 8, 1931; s. Roone and Gertrude (Stritmater) A.; m. Joan Heise, Dec. 27, 1953 (div. 1971); children—Elizabeth Ann, Susan Lee, Patricia Lu, Roone Pinckney. B.B.A., Columbia Coll., 1952. With Dumont TV, 1952-53; producer-dir. children's and pub. affairs programming NBC, 1955-60; producer network sports ABC-TV, 1960-61, v.p. charge sports, 1963-68; now pres. ABC Sports, Inc., ABC News; exec. producer all ABC sports programs, including 1964, 1968, 1972 Olympic games; created the Wide World of Sports program, 1961; producer entertainment spls. including Frank Sinatra, The Main Event at Madison Sq. Garden. (Recipient Emmy award 1958, 66, 67, 68, 69, 70, 71, 72, 73, 74, TV Guide award 1964, Cannes Film Festival Grand prize 1965, 66). Mem. Pres.'s Council on Phys. Fitness, also chmn. sports com. Served with AUS, 1953-54. George Foster Peabody awards internat. understanding (3); Nat. Headlines spl. citation, 1968; Saturday Rev. award; Distinguished Service award N.Y. chpt. Broadcast Pioneers, 1968; Kennedy Family award, 1972; award N.Y. chpt. Nat. Football Found. and; Hall of Fame, 1972; named Man of Yr. Nat. Assn. TV Program Execs., Phila. Advt. and Sales Club, Football News, Ohio State U., Gallagher Report. Office: 1330 Ave of Americas New York NY 10019 *

ARLEN, MICHAEL J., writer; b. London, Eng., Dec. 9. 1930; s. Michael and Atlanta (Mercati) A.; m. Ann Warner, 1957 (div. 1971); children—Jennifer, Caroline, Elizabeth, Sally; m. Alice Albright Hoge,

1972; stepchildren—Alicia, James Patrick, Robert Hoge. Grad., St. Paul's Sch., Concord, N.H., 1948, Harvard, 1952. Reporter Life mag., 1952-56; contbr., TV critic The New Yorker mag., 1957—; juror Columbia U.-Dupont awards for broadcast journalism, 1969-72, 78-80; faculty Bread Loaf Writers Conf., 1980. Author: Living-Room War, 1969, Exiles, 1970, An American Verdict, 1973, Passage to Ararat, 1975, The View from Highway 1, 1976, Thirty Seconds, 1980, The Camera Age, 1981. Recipient award for television criticism Screen Dirs. Guild, 1968; Nat. Book award for contemporary affairs, 1976; Le Prix Brémond, 1976. Office: care The New Yorker 25 W 43d St New York NY 10036

ARLETT, ALLAN, fund raising executive; b. Aldershot, Eng., Apr. 21, 1941; emigrated to Can., 1943; s. Allan J. and Dorothy (Jameson) A.; m. Lynn Marshall Hoppe, Oct. 8, 1977; children: Karin, Neil. B.S., U. London, 1967. Asst. dir. U. Toronto, 1964-67; asst. devel. officer Carleton U., Ottawa, Ont., 1967-68; dir. ann. fund Clarkson Coll. Tech., Potsdam, N.J., 1968-71; dir. alumni relations and devel. Queens Coll., CUNY, 1975-77; v.p. Gordon L. Goldie Ltd., Toronto, 1977-80; exec. dir. Candian Centre for Philanthropy, Toronto, 1980—. Editor: Canadian Directory to Foundations and Granting Agencies. Bd. dirs. Trillium Found., Ont., 1982—. U.S. Steel Found. grantee, 1971; recipient maj. award alumni programming Am. Alumni Council, 1974. Club: Whitby Yacht. Home: 154 Neville Park Blvd Toronto ON Canada M4E 3P8 Office: 185 Bay St Suite 504 Toronto ON Canada M5J 1K6

ARLOW, ARNOLD JACK, advertising executive; b. Bklyn., Sept. 29, 1933; s. Louis and Sylvia (Spitzberg) A.; m. Phyllis Banschick, Apr. 20, 1958; children: Susan, Noah. B.F.A., 1978. Certificate in Art, Cooper Union, 1954. Art dir. N.Y. Times, 1958-61, Altman Stoller Advt., N.Y.C., 1961-65, Daniel & Charles Advt., 1965, McCaffrey McCall Advt., 1965-66; partner, creative dir. Martin Landey, Arlow Advt., N.Y.C., 1966-80; exec. v.p., creative dir. Geers Gross Advt., 1980-83; cons. communications industry, 1983—; tchr. design Wagner Coll., Staten Island, 1964-69. Trustee Cooper Union. Served with USAF Res., 1961-66. Fulbright-Hays grantee, Paris, 1954-55. Mem. N.Y. Art Dirs Club, N.Y. Copy Club, Am. Inst. Graphic Arts. Democrat. Jewish. Home: 3 N Clover Dr Great Neck NY 11021

ARLOW, JACOB A., psychiatrist; b. N.Y.C., Sept. 3, 1912; s. Adolph A. and Ida (Feldman) A.; m. Alice Diamond, Oct. 31, 1936; children—Michael Saul, Allan Joseph, Seth Martin, Jonathan Bruce. B.S., N.Y. U., 1932, M.D., 1936. Diplomate: Am. Bd. Neurology and Psychiatry. Rotating intern Harlem Hosp., N.Y.C., 1936-38; resident neuropsychiatrist USPHS Hosp., Ellis Island, N.Y., 1938-39; resident psychiatrist Kings County Hosp., Bklyn., 1939, asst. psychiatrist mental hygiene clinic, 1941; asst. resident neurologist Montefiore Hosp., Bronx, N.Y., 1940-41, asst. neurologist, 1942-44; resident psychiatrist N.Y. State Psychiat. Inst. and Hosp., N.Y.C., 1940-41; cons. psychiatrist Pride of Judea Children's Home, Bklyn., 1940-45; pvt. practice parttime, N.Y.C., 1941, full time, 1942; grad. psychiatrist Profl. Sch. N.Y. Psychoanalytic Inst., N.Y.C., 1948, lectr. psychosomatic medicine, 1948-50; instr. psychoanalysis and religion Sch. Applied Pschoanalysis of inst., 1951-52; instr. neurology Columbia Coll. Phys. and Surg., 1942-44, instr. psychiatry psychosomatic service of psychoanalytic clinic for tng. and research, 1947-51, John B. Turner vis. prof. psychiatry, 1967-68; research asso, instr. psychiatry Presbyn. Hosp.-Columbia Med. Center, 1944-51; clin. asst. prof. psychoanalytic medicine State U. N.Y. Coll. Medicine at N.Y.C., 1952-55, clin. asso. prof., 1955-62, clin. prof., 1962-79, N.Y. U., 1979—; faculty N.Y. Psychoanalytic Inst., 1956—; vis. prof. psychiatry La. State U. Sch. Medicine, 1969-70, Yeshiva U.-Albert Einstein Coll. Medicine, 1971-72, Mt. Sinai Sch. Medicine, N.Y.C., 1972-73. Author: Legacy of Sigmund Freud, 1956, (with Charles Brenner) Psychoanalytic Concepts and the Structural Theory, 1964; Editor: Selected Writings of Bertram D. Lewin; editor-in-chief: Psychoanalytic Quar, 1970-79; mem. editorial bd.: Psyche. Vice pres. Great Neck (L.I.) Coop. Sch.; trustee, sec. N.Y. Psychoanalytic Inst., 1956-59. Recipient Heinz Hartman award, 1980; Lenox Hill Disting. Clinicians award, 1980. Mem. AMA, Am. Psychoanalytic Assn. (pres. 1960-61), Internat. Soc. Study of Time, Am. Psychoanalytic Assn. (chmn. COPE 1962-66, bd. editors jour. 1958-60, chmn. bd. profl. standards 1967-70), Am. Psychiat. Assn., Psychosomatic Soc., N.Y. Psychoanalytic Inst. (pres. 1966-68), Internat. Psycho-Analytic Assn. (treas., v.p.). Home: 94 Wildwood Rd Great Neck NY 11024 Office: 120 E 36th St New York NY 10016

ARMACOST, MICHAEL HAYDEN, diplomat; b. Cleve., Apr. 15, 1937; s. George H. and Verda Gay (Hayden) A.; m. Roberta June Bray, Mar. 8, 1959; children—Scott, Timothy, Christopher. B.A., Carleton Coll., 1958; postgrad., Friedrich Wilhelms Universität, 1959; M.A., Columbia U., 1961, Ph.D., 1965. Asso. prof. govt. Pomona Coll., 1962-70, Wig Disting. prof., 1966; spl. asst. to ambassador Am. embassy, Tokyo, 1972-74; mem. policy planning staff Dept. State, Washington, 1974-77; sr. staff mem. NSC, 1977-78; dep. asst. sec. def., internat. security affairs Dept. Def., Washington, 1978-79; prin. dep. asst. sec. East Asian and Pacific affairs Dept. State, 1980-81; ambassador to Philippines, 1982—. Author: The Politics of Weapons Innovation, 1969, The Foreign Relations of the United States, 1969. Recipient Superior Honor award Dept. State, 1976; Disting. Civilian Service award Dept. Def., 1980; White House fellow, 1969-70. Mem. Council on Fgn. Relations. Methodist. Home: 18 Jacaranda Rd Forbes Park Makati Metro Manila Philippines Office: Am Embassy APO San Francisco CA 96528 *

ARMACOST, PETER HAYDEN, college president; b. N.Y.C., July 12, 1935; s. George Henry and Verda Gay (Hayden) A.; m. Suzanne Lee Sadosky, June 22, 1957; children: Martha Hayden, David Keys, Sarah Jane, Rebecca Ann. B.A., Denison U., 1957; Ph.D., U. Minn., 1963. Dean students, chmn. dept. psychology Augsburg Coll., Mpls., 1959-65; program dir. Assn. Am. Colls., Washington, 1965-67; pres., prof. psychology Ottawa U., (Kans.), 1967-77; pres. Eckerd Coll., St. Petersburg, Fla., 1977—. Author materials in field. Chmn. Kansas City (Mo.) Regional Council Higher Edn., 1972-74; pres. Am. Bapt. Chs., U.S., 1974-75. Recipient Disting. Alumnus citation Denison U.; Woodrow Wilson fellow; Danforth fellow. Mem. Assn. Am. Colls. (dir.), Am. Council Edn., Nat. Assn. Student Personnel Adminstrs. (dir. div. research, publs. and conf. chmn., Disting. Service award), Assoc. Ind. Colls. Kans. (pres. 1970-72), Young Pres. Orgn., Am. Assn. Higher Edn., Soc. Values in Higher Edn., Nat. Assn. Ind. Coll. and U. Pres., Suncoast C. of C. (v.p. govt. relations 1981—), Blue Key, Phi Beta Kappa, Omicron Delta Kappa, Pi Gamma Mu, Psi Chi. Republican. Clubs: Kansas City, St. Petersbury Yacht, Rotary, Suncoasters. Home: 6320 Bahama Shores Dr S St Petersburg FL 33705 Office: PO Box 12560 St Petersburg FL 33733

ARMACOST, SAMUEL HENRY, bank executive; b. NewportNews, Va., Mar. 29, 1939; s. George Henry and Verda Gae (Hayden) A.; m. MAry Jane Levan, June 16, 1962; children: Susan Lovell, Mary Elizabeth. B.A., Denison U., 1961; M.B.A., Stanford U., 1964. With BAnk of Am. NT & SA, 1961—; v.p. mgr. London br. Bank of Am. NT & SA, 1972-74, sr. v.p., mgr. San Francisco, 1975-77, exec. v.p. Europe, Middle East and Africa div., London, 1977-79, exec. v.p., cashier, San Francisco, 1979-81; pres., chief exec. officer Bank of Am. and Bank Am. Corp., 1981—; chmn. Bank Am. Internat. Ltd., London, Banco Comercial para America, Madrid; dir. Banco Intercontinental Espanol, Madrid, Bank Am. Internat. S.A., Luxembourg, Bank Am. N.Y., Fin. Group Kuwait, Banca d'America d'Italia, Milan, Societe Financiere puor le Pays d'Outre Mer, Geneva. Mem. Bankers Assn. for Fgn. Trade (dir.). Republican. Presbyterian. Clubs: Overseas Bankers (London); Olympic, Burlingame Country (San Francisco). Office: Bank Am Corp Bank of Am Ctr San Francisco CA 94104 *

ARMALY, MANSOUR F(ARID), ophthalmologist; b. Shefa Amer, Palestine, Feb. 25, 1927; came to U.S., 1955, naturalized, 1965; s. Fareed M. and Fadwa M. (Bahouth) A.; m. Aida Makdis, July 2, 1950; children: Raya, Fareed. B.A., Am. U., Beirut, 1947, M.D., 1952; M.Sc., U. Iowa, 1957. Diplomate: Am. Bd. Ophthalmology. Intern Am. U. Hosps., Beirut, Resident, 1952-55; research fellow U. Iowa, 1955-57, instr., 1957-58, asst. prof. ophthalmology, 1958-60, asso. prof., 1960-66, prof., 1966-70; prof., chmn. dept. ophthalmology George Washington U. Med. Center, 1970—; cons. in field; Univ. prof. U. Paraguay. Contbr. articles to profl. publs.; mem. editorial bd.: Investigative Ophthalmology, 1969-73, Ophthalmology Digest, 1971—; asso. editor: Archives Ophthalmology, 1970. Decorated knight Order of Cedars, Lebanon; recipient Alumni Gold Medal Am. U. Beirut; NIH grantee, 1957-69, 58-75, 58-63, 63-73, 68-73; Nat. Eye Inst. grantee, 1972, 73-76, 74-76. Fellow ACS, Internat. Coll. Surgeons; mem. AMA (Knapp award 1968, Hektoen Silver medal 1969, Merit award 1976), Am. Acad. Ophthalmology and Otolaryngology, Assn. for Research in Vision and Ophthalmology (Fight for Sight award 1966), Am. Ophthalmol. Soc., Internat. Glaucoma Com., Internat. Glaucoma Congress (Ann. Achievement award 1979), French Ophthalmologic Soc., Introcular Lens Implant Soc., Internat. Eye Found. Office: 2150 Pennsylvania Ave NW Washington DC 20037

ARMAN, ARMAND PIERRE, sculptor; b. Nice, France, Nov. 17, 1928; came to U.S., 1961, naturalized, 1972; m. Corice Canton-Arman, July 13, 1971; 1 dau., Yasmine Valentine; m. Eliane Radigue, 1953 (div. 1968); children: Yves, Francoise Olry, Anne Person. Student, 1946-49; M.A. in Art History, Ecole du Louvre, Paris, 1949-51. Exhibited one-man shows, Walker Art Ctr., Mpls., 1964, Musees des Arts Decoratifs, Paris, 1969, La Jolla Mus. Contemporary Art, Calif., 1974, Albright-Knox Gallery, Buffalo, 1975, Kunstmuseum, Hannover, W.Ger., 1981, Hessisches Landesmuseum, Darmstadt, W.Ger., 1982, Tel Aviv Mus., Israel, Tubingen Kunstmuseum, W.Ger., 1983, group shows include, Mus. Modern Art, N.Y.C., 1961, Kaiser Wilhelm Mus., Krefeld, W.Ger., 1963, Tate Gallery, London, 1964, Janis Gallery, N.Y.C., Nat. Mus. Modern Art, Tokyo, 1969, Kunsthaus, Zurich, 1979, Westfalishes Landesmuseum, Munster, W.Ger., 1980, Stedelijk Mus., Amsterdam, Netherlands, 1982; represented in permanent collections, Albright-Knox Gallery, Buffalo, Guggenheim Mus., N.Y.C., Met. Mus. Art, N.Y.C., Musee des Arts Decoratifs, Louvre, Paris, Kaiser Wilhelm Mus., Krefeld, Israel Mus., Jerusalem, Hirshhorn Mus. and Sculpture Garden, Washington, Nat. Gallery, Canberra, Australia, La. Mus. Modern Art.

ARMANI, GIORGIO, fashion designer; b. Emilia Romagna, Italy, 1936. Studied medicine, Italy. Asst. menswear buyer, fashion coordinator La Rinascente, Milan; then worked 8 yrs. as designer Cerutti Co., Milan; freelance designer, opening own business, Milan, 1975; head Giorgio Armani Corp., N.Y.C. and; Georgio Armani boutiques. Recipient Neiman Marcus award, 1979; named Most Influential Designer Outside Am. Council of Fashion Designer of Am., 1983. Office: Giorgio Armani Corp 650 Fifth Ave New York NY 10019 *

ARMBRECHT, WILLIAM H., lawyer, business executive; b. Mobile, Ala., Nov. 1, 1908; s. William H. and Anna Bell (Paterson) A.; m. Katherine Little, Oct. 8, 1927; children: William H. III, Katherine, Anna Bell, Conrad Paterson, Clara. LL.B., U. Ala., 1932. Bar: Ala. 1932. Since practiced in, Mobile; partner Armbrecht, Jackson, DeMouy, Crowe, Holmes & Reeves; dir. emeritus 1st Nat. Bank of Mobile. Mem. Mobile Indsl. Devel. Bd.; bd. regents Spring Hill Coll. Mem. Am. Bar Assn., Ala. Bar Assn., Mobile Bar Assn. (pres. 1954), C. of C., Phi Delta Phi, Alpha Tau Omega. Episcopalian (trustee). Clubs: Kiwanian., Lakewood Country (Point Clear, Ala.); Country, Athelstan, Propeller, Bienville, Internat. Trade (Mobile); Down Town (N.Y.C.). Home: 112 Pinebrook W Spring Hill AL 36608 Office: Mchts Bank Bldg Mobile AL 36602

ARMBRECHT, WILLIAM HENRY, III, lawyer; b. Mobile, Ala., Jan. 13, 1929; s. William Henry and Katherine (Little) A.; m. Dorothy Jean Taylor, Sept. 1, 1951; children—Katherine Handley, William Taylor, Alexander Paterson. B.S., U. Ala., 1950, J.D., 1952. Bar: Ala. bar 1952. Asso. firm Inge, Twitty, Armbrecht & Jackson, Mobile, 1952-56; partner firm Armbrecht, Jackson, McConnell & DeMouy, Mobile, 1956-65, Armbrecht, Jackson & DeMouy, 1965-75, Armbrecht, Jackson, DeMouy, Crowe, Holmes & Reeves, 1976—. Served to 1st lt. AUS, 1952-54. Mem. Am. Bar Assn., Ala. Bar Assn. (chmn. grievance com. 1973-74, chmn. sect. corp. banking and bus. law 1976-78), Mobile C. of C., Southeastern Corp. Law Inst. (mem. planning com.), Phi Delta Phi, Delta Kappa Epsilon. Episcopalian. Clubs: Mobile Country, Athelstan, Internat. Trade (Mobile). Home: 600 Fairfax Rd East Mobile AL 36608 Office: 1101 Merchants Nat Bank Bldg PO Box 290 Mobile AL 36601

ARMBRUSTER, KERNEL LANTIN, ins. co. exec.; b. Haines City, Fla., Sept. 24, 1925; s. Francis H. and Maude M. (Griffin) A.; m. LaVerne M. Ahtipus, June 9, 1950; 1 dau., Jenny L. B.A. in Bus. Adminstrn, Washington U., St. Louis, 1949; J.D., St. Louis U., 1954. Bar: Mo. bar 1954, Ohio bar 1956. With St. Paul Fire & Marine Ins. Co., 1949—, adjuster, St. Louis, 1949-54, claim mgr., Cin., 1954-64, gen. counsel home office, St. Paul, 1964—. Served with USNR, 1943-45.

ARMEL, LARRY DANIEL, insurance company executive; b. Iola, Kans., Feb. 12, 1942. B.A., Kans. U., 1965, J.D., 1968. Bar: Kans. 1968. Assoc. Stinson, Mag & Fizzell, 1968-72; sr. v.p., gen. counsel, sec. Security Benefit Life Ins. Co., Topeka, 1972—; dir. Security Equity Fund, Security Ultra Fund. Active fund raising YMCA, Topeka United Fund, YWCA, Stormont-Vail Hosp. Fellow Life Office Mgmt. Assn.; mem. ABA, Nat. Assn. Security Dealers (registered prin.), Kans. Bar Assn., Topeka Bar Assn. Home: 3200 W 33d Ct Topeka KS 66614 Office: Security Benefit Life Bldg 700 Harrison St Topeka KS 66636

ARMENTANO, ANTHONY JOHN, state supreme court justice; b. Hartford, Conn., June 12, 1916; s. Joseph and Rosina (DiDonato) A.; m. Mary Fraticelli, Feb. 6, 1943; children: Frank J., James A. B.S., Boston U., 1938, J.D., 1941. Bar: Conn. bar 1941. Mem. Conn. Senate, 1957-63, pres. pro tempore, 1959-61; lt. gov. State of Conn., 1961-63; judge of Ct.of Common Pleas, 1963-65; judge Superior Ct., 1965-81; asso. justice Conn. Supreme Ct., Hartford, 1981—. Served to capt. U.S. Army, 1942-46. Mem. Am. Bar Assn., Conn. Bar Assn., Hartford County Bar Assn. Democrat. Roman Catholic. Office: Drawer N Station A Hartford CT 06106 *

ARMENTROUT, STEVEN ALEXANDER, physician; b. Morgantown, W.Va., Aug. 22, 1933; s. Walter W. and Dorothy (Gasch) A.; m. Barbara Jean Lamson, July 18, 1977; children—Marc, Susan, Sandra, Nancy, Julie, Chris, Victor. A.B., U. Chgo., 1953, M.D., 1959. Intern U. Hosp., Cleve., 1959-60; resident in medicine, fellow Am. Cancer Soc. Western Res. U. Hosp., 1960-63; project dir. USPHS, 1963-65; asst. prof. Case Western Res. U. Med. Sch., 1965-71; mem. faculty U. Calif. Med. Sch., Irvine, 1971—, prof. medicine, chief div. hematology-oncology, 1978—, also dir. program in oncology. Mem. Am. Assn. Cancer Research, AAUP, A.C.P., Am. Cancer Soc. (chmn. bd. 1973), AMA, Am. Soc. Clin. Oncology, Am. Soc. Hematology, Orange County Med. Assn., Am. Soc. Internal Medicine, Calif. Med. Assn. Research in multiple sclerosis. Office: 101 City Dr S Orange CA 92668

ARMERDING, HUDSON TAYLOR, retired college president; b. Albuquerque, June 21, 1918; s. Carl and Eva May (Taylor) A.; m. Miriam Lucille Bailey, Dec. 26, 1944; children—Carreen, Taylor, Paul, Miriam, Jonathan. A.B., Wheaton (Ill.) Coll., 1941; A.M., Clark U., 1942; Ph.D., U. Chgo., 1948; postgrad., Harvard, 1949-50; D.D., Gordon-Conwell Theol. Sem., 1972; LL.D., Houghton Coll., 1973, John Brown U., 1982; S.T.D., Greenville Coll., 1976; Litt.D., Asbury Coll., 1977. Instr. social sci. Wheaton Coll, 1946-48; successively prof. history, dean, also acting pres. Gordon (Mass.) Coll., 1948-49, 50-61; ordained to ministry Baptist Ch., 1951; minister in, Manchester, N.H., 1949-50, Brockton, Mass., 1951-54; prof. history Wheaton Coll., 1961-82, provost, 1963-65, pres., 1965-82. Author: Christianity and the World of Thought, 1968, Leadership, 1978, A Word to the Wise, 1980. Bd. dirs. North Conway (N.H.) Inst., 1959-67; chmn. trustees Columbia Bible Coll., 1974-83. Served with USNR, 1942-46; comdr. Res. ret. Mem. Nat. Assn. Evangelicals (past pres.), World Evang. Fellowship (past pres.), Officers Christian Fellowship, U.S. Naval Inst., Am. Legion, Pi Gamma Mu, Pi Kappa Delta. Address: Care Wheaton Coll Wheaton IL 60187

ARMISTEAD, MOSS WILLIAM, III, ret. newspaper exec.; b. Suffolk, Va., Sept. 7, 1915; s. Moss William, Jr. and Mary Judith (Smith) A.; m. Mary Ragan Bridges, Dec. 30, 1939; 1 dau., Elfleda Bridges (Mrs. Peter Huff Ring). Student, Randolph-Macon Coll., 1933-36; LL.D., Washington and Lee U., 1967. Reporter Covington Virginian, 1936; reporter, state editor utility editor, legislative corr. Roanoke (Va.) Times, 1936-42; exec. sec. to Gov. of Va. and Sec. of Commonwealth, 1946-47; asst. to pub. Times & World-News, Roanoke, 1947-51, asso. pub., 1951, v.p., pub., 1954; pres., dir. Times-World Corp.; also pub. Roanoke Times and World-News, 1954-73, chmn. bd., 1955-69; exec. v.p., dir. Landmark Communications, Inc., 1973-74, pres., dir., 1974-78, chmn. exec. com., 1978—. Pres. Roanoke Valley Devel. Corp., 1957-59; Mem. State Bd. Welfare and Instns., 1947-51; Pres. Roanoke Community Fund, 1952, Central YMCA, 1957-58; pres. Community Hosp., Roanoke Valley, 1960-73; mem. Va. Port Authority, 1958-70. Served from pvt. to 1st lt., inf. AUS, 1942-46; capt. Va. N.G., 1947-50. Decorated Purple Heart. Mem. U.S. Chamber Commerce, Va. Chamber Commerce (v.p.), Roanoke Chamber Commerce (pres. 1953), Am. Newspaper Pubs. Assn. (dir. 1965-74), So. Newspaper Pubs. Assn. (pres. 1975-76), Phi Kappa Sigma, Sigma Delta Chi, Alpha Kappa Psi. Club: Shenandoah (Roanoke). Home: Route 3 Moneta VA 24121

ARMISTEAD, WILLIS WILLIAM, university administrator; b. Detroit, Oct. 28, 1916; s. Eber Merrill and Josephine Brunell (Kindred) A.; m. Martha Sidney Clark, Sept. 17, 1938 (dec. 1964); children: Willis William, Jack Murray, Sidney Merrill; m. Mary Wallace Nelson, 1967. D.V.M., Tex. A. and M. Coll., 1938; M.Sc., Ohio State U., 1950; Ph.D., U. Minn., 1955.. Pvt. practice veterinary medicine, 1938-40; instr. Sch. Veterinary Medicine, Tex. A. and M. Coll, 1940-42, asst. prof. to prof., 1946-53; dean Sch. Veterinary Medicine, 1953-57, Coll. Veterinary Medicine, Mich. State U., East Lansing, 1957-74, Coll. Veterinary Medicine, U. Tenn., Knoxville, 1974-79; v.p. agr. U. Tenn. System, 1979—; collaborator animal diseases and parasite research div. Dept. Agr., 1954-65; cons., adviser commn. veterinary edn. of South So. Regional Edn. Bd., 1953-56; mem. gov.'s sci. adv. bd., 1958-60; nat. cons. to Air Force Surgeon Gen., 1960-62; mem. adv. council Inst. Lab. Animal Resources, NRC, 1962-66; pres. Assn. Am. Veterinary Med. Colls., 1964-65, 73-74; veterinary med. resident investigators selection com. U.S. VA, 1967-70; veterinary medicine rev. com. Bur. Health Professions Edn. and Manpower Tng., HEW, 1967-71; mem. Nat. Bd. Veterinary Med. Examiners, 1970-74; mem. adv. panel for veterinary medicine Inst. Medicine, Nat. Acad. Scis., 1972-74; mem. bd. agr. and renewable resources NRC, 1976-77; 1st Allam lectr. Am. Coll. Veterinary Surgeons, 1972. Contbg. author: Canine Surgery, rev. edit, 1957, Canine Medicine, rev. edit, 1959; editor: The N.Am. Veterinarian, 1950-56, Jour. Veterinary Med. Edn, 1974-80; asso. editor: Jour. Am. Animal Hosp. Assn, 1964-70; contbr. tech. articles to profl. jours. Bd. dirs. Tenn. Farm Bur. Fedn., 1979—. Served from 1st lt. to maj. Veterinary Corps AUS, 1942-46. Recipient Meritorious Service award Selective Service System, 1972; hon. alumnus Mich. State U., 1972, Disting. Alumnus award Coll. Vet. Medicine, Tex. A. and M. U., 1980. Mem. AAAS, U.S. Animal Health Assn., Am. Veterinary Med. Assn. (pres. 1957-58, award 1977), Tex Veterinary Med. Assn. (pres. 1947-48), Mich. Veterinary Med. Assn. (trustee Edn. and Sci. Trust 1970-74), Tenn. Veterinary Med. Assn., Inst. Medicine of Nat. Acad. Scis., N.Y. Acad. Scis., Sigma Xi, Phi Kappa Phi, Alpha Zeta, Phi Zeta, Omega Tau Sigma (nat. Gamma Award Ohio State U. 1962). Episcopalian. Club: Rotary. Home: 1101 Cherokee Blvd Knoxville TN 37919 Office: Box 1071 Knoxville TN 37901

ARMITAGE, RICHARD, former university official; b. Ravenna, Ohio, Apr. 15, 1918; s. Harry and Inez (Hughes) A.; m. Janet Plummer, Mar. 28, 1942 (div. 1978); children: Bruce, Suzanne, Barry, Daniel, Douglas, John; m. Mary Beth Snyder, July 29, 1978. A.B., Oberlin Coll., 1939; M.A., Ohio State U., 1940, Ph.D. (Univ. scholar 1940-41), 1945; postdoctoral student, U. Tex., 1951-52. Faculty Ohio State U., Columbus, 1941-70, 71—, prof. Romance langs., 1966-70, 71-78, asst. dean Coll. Arts and Scis., 1954-55, asst. dean Grad. Sch., 1956-60, assoc. dean, 1960-63, dean, 1963-70, univ. ombudsman, 1971-73, v.p. student services, 1973-78; provost, dean faculties U. Mo., Kansas City, 1970-71; vice chancellor student affairs U. Calif., San Diego, 1978-81; dir. student acad. services UCLA, 1981-82; mgmt. cons., 1982—; vis. prof. Kenyon Coll., fall 1947; cons. Minn. State Coll. Bd., 1968, Inst. Internat. Ed., 1967—; mem. Grad. Record Exam. Bd., 1973-78, chmn., 1976-77; Chmn. region VIII Woodrow Wilson Fellowship Found., 1961-65; bd. dirs. Ohio State U. Research Found.; chmn. editorial bd. Ohio State U. Press. Author: (with W. Meiden) Beginning Spanish Fundamentals of Spanish Grammar; also articles, revs. Trustee Children's Hosp., 1967-70; mem. adv. com. on grad. programs Ohio Bd. Regents, 1965-70. Ford Fellow, 1951-52. Mem. Am. Assn. Tchrs. Spanish and Portuguese, Nat. Assn. Student Personnel Adminstrs. Address: 2308 Alva Ave El Cerrito CA 94530

ARMITAGE, RICHARD LEE, federal government official; b. Boston, Apr. 26, 1945; s. Leo Holmes and Ruth H. A.; m. Laura Alice Samford, Apr. 15, 1968; children: Beth, Lee, Jenny, Paul. B.S., U.S. Naval Acad. Naval ops. coordinator Def. Attache Office, Saigon, Vietnam, 1973-75; cons. Dept. Def., Washington, 1975-76, Iran, 1975-76; ptnr. Agt.-Export, Bangkok, 1976-78, Washington, 1976-78; adminstrv. asst. to U.S. Senator Robert Dole, Washington, 1978-79, self-employed cons., Fairfax, Va., 1979-80; fgn. policy advisor Reagan for Pres. campaign, Washington, 1980; trans. advisor U.S. Govt., Washington, 1980-81; asst. sec. def. East Asia Dept. Def., Washington,

1981-83, asst. sec. def. internat. security affairs, 1983—. Served to lt. USN, 1967-73; Vietnam. Mem. Assn. Asian Studies. Republican. Roman Catholic. Office: Office Sec Defense Pentagon Washington DC 10301

ARMITAGE, WILLIAM BARCLAY, drug store chain executive; b. Portland, Oreg., Mar. 13, 1908; s. William J. and Bertha C. (Rice) A.; m. Erma L. McManus, Sept. 11, 1930; 1 son, Barclay M. Ph.G., Oreg. State Sch. Pharmacy, 1930. Sales rep. McKesson & Robbins Inc., Portland, 1934-42; partner, founder Payless Drug Stores N.W., Portland, 1942—; now sec., dir.; dir. Pacific Progressive Shippers, 1968-72. Mem. Oreg. State Pharm. Assn., Vet. Druggists Assn., Kappa Sigma. Clubs: Elk, Mason., Internat., Multnomah Athletic (Portland). Office: 9275 Peyton Ln Wilsonville OR 97070 *

ARMOR, JAMES BURTON, retail drug company executive; b. Pauls Valley, Okla., Sept. 14, 1926; s. James Dennis and Maida Bland (Beckham) A.; m. Mary Ann Stump, Sept. 4, 1948; children: James Burton, Nancy Diane, John Andrew, Jeffrey David. Student, La. Tech. U., 1944-45, Duke U., 1945-46; B.S. in Mktg, Okla. U., 1948. With J.C. Penney Co., 1948—, store mgr., 1960-62, merchandising coordinator Hdqrs., N.Y.C., 1962-64, mdse. mgr., 1964-70; dir. store ops. Thrift Drug Co. (div. J.C. Penney), Pitts., 1971-73, v.p., 1974-75, exec. v.p., 1975-80, pres., 1980—. Mem. North Caldwell (N.J.) Sch. Bd., 1968-69, North Caldwell Planning and Zoning Bd., 1969-70; assoc. program mem. U. Pitts. Grad. Sch., 1980—, exec. com., 1984—. Served with USN, 1944-46. Mem. Bus. Assn. Regional Indsl. Devel. Corp. (pres. 1978-80), Nat. Assn. Chain Drug Stores (dir. 1980—, exec. com. 1982—), Phi Delta Theta. Republican. Presbyn. Office: 615 Alpha Dr Pittsburgh PA 15238

ARMOUR, DAVID EDWARD PONTON, association executive; b. Toronto, Ont., Can., Sept. 6, 1921; s. Ponton Edward Burton and Grace Marie (Magann) A.; m. Kathleen Marie Bridge-Williams, May 24, 1945 (div. Nov. 1974); children: Richard, Robin, Moira, Sheila, Anne; m. 2d Eve Denise Arnoldi, Oct. 8, 1974. Student, Trinity Coll., Port Hop, Ont.; grad., Royal Mil. Coll., Kingston, Ont. Gen. mgr. Hammermill Paper, Erie, Pa.; with woodlands ops. Howard Smith, Montreal, Que., Can., 1946-58; mgmt. cons. Currie, Copper & Lybrands, Toronto, 1958-65; corp. dir. Salada Foods Ltd., Toronto, 1965-67; v.p., gen. mgr. Crush Internat., Toronto, 1967-75; pres. Elec. and Electronic Mfrs. Assn. Can., Toronto, 1976—; chmn. exec. council Can. Soft Drink Assn., Toronto, 1969-74; bd. dirs. Fedn. Aggregate Studies, Toronto, 1981-83. Aide-de-camp Lt.-Gov. Ont., 1959-63; pres. Uxbridge Ratepayers Assn., Ont., 1970-74. Served to maj. Can. Army, 1942-46; ETO. Decorated Can. decoration Dept. Nat. Def., Ottawa. Progressive-Conservative. Clubs: Toronto North York Hunt (Aurora, Ont.); Royal Can. Mil. Inst. (Toronto). Office: Elec and Electronics Mfrs Assn Can One Yonge St Suite 1608 Toronto ON Canada M5E 1R1

ARMOUR, LAURANCE HEARNE, JR., banker; b. Chgo., May 20, 1923; s. Laurance Hearne and Frances Lacy (Withers) A.; m. Margot Caroline Boyd, Apr. 7, 1954; children—Laurance Hearne, Steven Shelby, Margot Brooks. Grad., Hotchkiss Sch., 1941; A.A., Princeton, 1945; student, Northwestern U., 1947-48. With LaSalle Nat. Bank, Chgo., 1948—, dir., 1951—, vice chmn., 1953-63, chmn. exec. com., 1964-73. Bd. dirs. Espiscopal Charities, Chgo.; trustee Northwestern Meml. Hosp., Goodwill Industries, Chgo.; nat. bd. govs. Inst. Living, Hartford, Conn. Served from pvt. to 1st lt. AUS, 1943-46. Home: 930 Rosemary Rd Lake Forest IL 60045 Office: 135 S LaSalle St Chicago IL 60603 *My generation inherited great opportunities. If I can make some contribution, however small, toward assuring that the next generation may have similar opportunities, then my life will have been worth living.*

ARMOUR, RICHARD (WILLARD ARMOUR), educator, author; b. San Pedro, Calif., July 15, 1906; s. Harry Willard and Sue (Wheelock) A.; m. Kathleen Fauntleroy Stevens, Dec. 25, 1932; children—Geoffrey Stevens, Karin Elizabeth. A.B., Pomona Coll., 1927, Litt.D., 1972; A.M., Harvard, 1928, Ph.D., 1933; Litt.D., Coll. of Ozarks, 1944; L.H.D., Whittier Coll., 1968, So. Calif. Coll. Optometry, 1972; LL.D., Coll. Idaho, 1969, Claremont Men's Coll., 1974. Instr. in English U. Tex., 1928-29, Northwestern U., 1930-31; Dexter Scholar (research fellow) from Harvard at John Forster Library, Victoria and Albert Museum, London, 1931; prof. English, head div. of modern langs. Coll. of the Ozarks, 1932-33; Am. lectr. U. Freiburg, Germany, 1933-34; asst. prof., asso. prof. and prof. English Wells Coll., 1934-45; prof. English Scripps Coll. and Claremont Grad. Sch., 1945-63; dean of faculty Scripps Coll., 1961-63, Balch lectr. in English lit., 1963-66, dean and prof. emeritus, 1966—; Chancellor's lectr. Calif. State U. and Colls., 1964—; writer-in-residence U. Redlands, 1974; vis. prof. Whittier Coll., 1975; served as Am. specialist abroad for U.S. State Dept., 1964, 66, 67, 68, 70; Fund Advancement Edn.; faculty fellow, 1953-54; Carnegie vis. prof. English U. Hawaii, 1957; leader of European tours, summers, 1926-31. Author: (with Raymond F. Howes) of numerous books, including Coleridge the Talker, 1940, Yours for the Asking, 1942, Golf Bawls, 1946, Writing Light Verse, 1947, For Partly Proud Parents, 1950, It All Started with Columbus, 1953, Light Armour, 1954, It All Started with Europa, 1955, It All Started with Eve, 1956, Twisted Tales from Shakespeare, 1957, Nights with Armour, 1958, It All Started with Marx, 1958, Drug Store Days, 1959, The Classics Reclassified, 1960, Golf Is a Four-Letter Word, 1962, Armour's Almanac, 1962, The Medical Muse, or What to Do Until the Patient Comes, 1963, Through Darkest Adolescence, 1963, Our Presidents, 1964, The Year Santa Went Modern, 1964, American Lit Relit, 1964, An Armoury of Light Verse, 1964, The Adventures of Egbert the Easter Egg, 1965, Going Around in Academic Circles, 1965, Animals on the Ceiling, 1966, Punctured Poems, 1966, It All Started with Hippocrates, 1966, It All Started with Stones and Clubs, 1967, A Dozen Dinosaurs, 1967, Odd Old Mammals, 1968, My Life with Women, 1968, English Lit Relit, 1969, On Your Marks: A Package of Punctuation, 1969, A Diabolical Dictionary of Education, 1969, All Sizes and Shapes of Monkeys and Apes, 1970, A Short History of Sex, 1970, Who's in Holes?, 1971, Writing Light Verse and Prose Humor, 1971, All in Sport, 1972, Out of My Mind, 1972, The Strange Dreams of Rover Jones, 1973, It All Started with Freshman English, 1973, Going Like Sixty: A Lighthearted Look at the Later Years, 1974, Sea Full of Whales, 1974, The Academic Bestiary, 1974, The Spouse in the House, 1975, The Happy Bookers: A History of Librarians and Their World, 1976, It All Would Have Startled Columbus, 1976, It All Started with Nudes: An Artful History of Art, 1977, Strange Monsters of the Sea, 1979, Insects All Around Us, 1981; dept. editor: Quote: The Weekly Digest; mem. editorial bd.: The Writer; writer: syndicated feature in Family Weekly; Contbr. articles and poems to nat. mags. Trustee Claremont Men's Coll. Served as 2d lt. inf. Res. Corps U.S. Army, 1927-37; active duty in Antiaircraft Arty., 1942-46; lt. col., detailed to War Dept. Gen. Staff (mem.), 1944-46; col. U.S. Army Res. Decorated Legion of Merit with oak leaf cluster. Mem. Modern Lang. Assn. Am., Am. Assn. Univ. Profs., Calif. Writers Guild, P.E.N., Phi Beta Kappa. Conglist. Home: 894 W Harrison Ave Claremont CA 91711 *I owe much to that sixth sense, the sense of humor, as important for our enjoyment of life and our survival as any of the five physical senses. Like a muscle, with use it develops and with lack of use it wastes away. It is especially important that we use it on ourselves.*

ARMOUR, T. STANTON, financial consultant; b. Chgo., Jan. 3, 1924; s. Lester and Mary Leola (Stanton) A.; m. Jean Ann Reddy, July 3, 1948; children: Audrey Lester, Thomas Stanton. Grad., St. Mark's Sch., Southboro, Mass., 1942; B.A., Yale, 1949. With Marathon Corp., Menasha, Wis., 1949-56, regional sales mgr., 1955-56; with Mitchell, Hutchins, Inc. (investments), Chgo., 1957—, pres., 1967-69, chmn. operating com., 1970-73, chmn. bd., 1973-77, sr. mng. dir., 1977-78; also dir.; sr. v.p., dir. Paine, Webber, Jackson & Curtis Inc., 1977-78, Paine Webber Mitchell Hutchins Inc., Chgo., 1979-80; dir. Paine Webber Inc., N.Y.C. Chmn. Northwestern Meml. Found., Chgo.; trustee Shedd Aquarium, Chgo.; vice chmn. adv. bd. Chgo. Salvation Army. Served with USNR, 1943-46. Mem. Northwestern U. Assn., Comml. Club Chgo., Ruffled Grouse Soc. (exec. v.p.). Clubs: Attic, Casino (Chgo.); Onwentsia, Shore Acres, Winter (Lake Forest). Home: 1144 Hawkweed Ln Lake Forest IL 60045 Office: 55 W Monroe St Suite 3800 Chicago IL 60603

ARMS, BREWSTER LEE, business executive; b. Pasadena, Calif., Dec. 18, 1925; s. Louis Lee and Mae Warne (Marsh) A.; m. Shirley Smallwood, Mar. 17, 1962; children: Emily Diane, Stephen Brewster, Andrew Marsh. B.A., Stanford U., 1948, J.D., 1951. Bar: Calif. 1952. Atty., corp. sec. Bankline Oil Co., 1952-59; atty. The Signal Companies, Inc. (formerly Signal Oil and Gas Co.), Los Angeles, 1959-63, corp. sec., 1963-72, sr. v.p., gen. counsel, 1970—. Served with inf. AUS, 1944-45. Mem. Am., Calif., San Diego County bar assns., Am. Soc. Corp. Secs. (dir.). Club: Rotarian. Office: 11255 N Torrey Pines Rd La Jolla CA 92037

ARMSTRONG, ANNE LEGENDRE (MRS. TOBIN ARMSTRONG), corporate director, educator; b. New Orleans, Dec. 27, 1927; d. Armant and Olive (Martindale) Legendre; m. Tobin Armstrong, Apr. 12, 1950; children: John Barclay, Katharine A., Sarita S., Tobin and James L. (twins). Grad., Vassar Coll., 1949. Trustee Kenedy County (Tex.) Sch. Bd., 1968-74; mem. Rep. Nat. Com. from Tex., 1968-73, co-chmn., 1971-73; del. Rep. Nat. Conv., 1964, 68, 72; counsellor to Pres., U.S., 1973-74; U.S. ambassador to, Gt. Britain and, No. Ireland, 1976-77; dir. Gen. Motors Corp., Halliburton Co., Gen. Foods Corp., First City Bancorp. Tex. Inc., Boise Cascade Corp.; chmn. adv. bd., vice-chmn. exec. bd. Center for Strategic and Internat. Studies, Georgetown U., 1977—, professorial lectr. in diplomacy, 1977—; chmn. Pres.'s Fgn. Intelligence Adv. Bd., 1981—; Bd. dirs. Atlantic Council, 1977-82; trustee So. Meth. U., 1977—, Guggenheim Found., 1980—; mem. vis. com. Kennedy Sch. Govt., Harvard U., 1978-82; mem. pres.'s council Tulane U., 1977-80; bd. regents Smithsonian Instn., 1978—; bd. overseers Hoover Instn., 1978—; mem. Congl. Awards Bd., 1980-81. Co-chmn. Reagan-Bush Campaign, 1980. Recipient Rep. Woman of Yr. award, 1979, Texan of Yr. award, 1981. Mem. English-Speaking Union (chmn. 1978-80), Council Fgn. Relations, Phi Beta Kappa. Clubs: Econ., N.Y.; F St. (Washington).

ARMSTRONG, ARTHUR JAMES, bishop; b. Marion, Ind., Sept. 17, 1924; s. Arthur J. and Frances (Green) A.; m. Phyllis Jeanne Shaeffer, Feb. 26, 1942; children: James, Teresa, John, Rebecca (Mrs. Ed Putens), Leslye (Mrs. David Hope). A.B. Fla. So. Coll, 1948; B.D., Candler Sch. Theology, Emory U., 1952; D.D., Fla. So. U., 1960, DePauw U., 1965; L.H.D., Ill. Wesleyan U., 1970, Dakota Wesleyan U., 1970, Westmar Coll., 1971, Ind. Central U., 1982, Emory U. Ordained to ministry Meth. Ch., 1948; minister in, Fla., 1945-58; sr. minister Broadway Meth. Ch., Indpls., 1958-68; bishop United Meth. Ch., Dakotas area, 1968-80, Ind. area, Indpls., 1980—; instr. Christian Theol. Sem., Indpls., 1961-68; del. 4th Gen. Assembly World Council Chs., 1968, 6th Gen. Assembly World Council Chs., 1983, Nat. Council Chs., 1970, pres., 1982-84; pres. bd. ch. and society United Meth. Ch., 1972-76, chmn. com. for peace and self-devel. of peoples, 1972-76, pres. commn. on religion and race, 1976—. Author: The Journey That Men Make, 1969, The Urgent Now, 1970, Mission: Middle America, 1971, The Pastor and the Public Servant, 1972, United Methodist Primer, 1973, 77, Wilderness Voices, 1974, The Nation Yet To Be, 1975, Telling Truth: The Foolishness of Preaching in a Real World, 1977, The Miracle of Easter, 1980, From the Underside, 1981, Preaching on Peace, 1982; contbg. author: The Pulpit Speaks on Race, 1966, War Crimes and the American Conscience, 1970, Rethinking Evangelism, 1971, What's a Nice Church Like You Doing in a Place Like This?, 1972. Vice-chmn. Hoosiers for Peace, 1968; mem. Ind. State Platform Com. Democratic Party, 1968, Nat. Coalition for a Responsible Congress, 1970; trustee, exec. com. Christian Century Found.; trustee Ewha U., Seoul, Korea, DePauw U., U. Evansville, Ind. Central U., United Theol. Sem., Dayton, Ohio. Served with USNR, 1942. Recipient distinguished service award Indpls. Jr. C. of C., 1959. Office: 1100 W 42d St Indianapolis IN 46208

ARMSTRONG, BENJAMIN LEIGHTON, association executive; b. Newark, Oct. 18, 1923; s. Benjamin L. and Margaret D. (Denison) A.; m. Ruth Freed, Apr. 11, 1946; children: Robert, Bonnie, Debbie. B.S., NYU, 1948, M.A., 1950, Ph.D., 1968; M.Div., Union Theol. Sem., N.Y.C., 1955. Ordained to ministry United Presbyn. Ch., U.S.A., 1949; pastor Central Presbyn. Ch., Paterson, N.J., 1950-54; dir. radio Trans World Radio, 1958-67; exec. dir. Nat. Religious Broadcasters, Morristown, N.J., 1967—; chmn. communications commn. World Evang. Fellowship, 1974-81. Author: The Electric Church, 1979; editor: Ann. Directory Religious Broadcasting, 1984-85. Recipient Founders Day award NYU, 1968, Faith and Freedom award Religious Heritage of Am., 1982. Mem. Nat. Assn. Evangelicals, Kappa Delta Pi. Office: I 80 and New Maple Ave Pine Brook NJ 07058

ARMSTRONG, C. MICHAEL, computer business executive; b. Detroit, Oct. 18, 1938; s. Charles H. and Zora Jean (Brooks) A.; m. Anne Gossett, June 17, 1961; children: Linda, Julie, Kristy. B.S. in Bus. Econs, Miami U., Oxford, Ohio, 1961; grad., Dartmouth Inst., 1976. With IBM Corp., 1961—; mktg. div. dir. systems mgmt. IBM, White Plains, N.Y., 1975-76, v.p. market ops. East, 1976-78, pres. data processing div., 1978-80, v.p., asst. group exec. plans and controls, data processing product group, 1980-83; v.p., group exec. IBM Corp., 1983. Mem. bus. adv. council Miami U., Columbia U.; bd. dirs. A Better Chance, Darien, Conn., pres., Darien, Conn., 1983; bd. dirs. Darien YMCA; active United Way Tri-State.; mem. Council on Fgn. Relations. Mem. Council Fgn. Relations. Home: 699 Hollow Tree Ridge Rd Darien CT 06820

ARMSTRONG, CARL HINES, former state official; b. DeKoven, Ky., May 1, 1926; s. Oral M. and Ethel M. (Wilson) A.; m. Ferrell Mann, May 16, 1947; children: Carla, Gayle, Dawn. Student, U. Evansville, Ind., 1945-47, Internat. Corr. Schs., 1947, Am. Inst. Banking, 1948-49, Butler U., 1959-61, Ind. U. Sch. Art, 1961-62, Christian Theol. Sem., 1977—. Bus. mgr. Dairy Service, Evansville, 1946-48; owner, operator Cardell Models, Evansville, 1959-69; bus. mgr. Children's Mus., Indpls., 1959-66; mus. specialist Ind. State Mus., Indpls., 1967-70, dir., 1970-82; dir. div. historic preservation Ind. Dept. Natural Resources, 1970-82; adminstr. Yellowwood Terr., 1982—; com. mem. for feasibility study Central Exhibits Lab., U.S. Nat. Mus., Washington. Com. mem. Ind./Ky. Conf., United Ch. of Christ, 1971-72; lay minister United Ch. of Christ, 1975—. Served with AUS, 1944. Mem. Am. Assn. Museums, Assn. Ind. Museums, Ind. State Mus. Soc. (exec. sec.), Midwest Museums Conf., Assn. for Preservation Tech., Assn. Sci. Mus. Dirs., Hoosier Homestead Commn., Ind. Am. Revolution Bicentennial Commn. Republican. Clubs: Masons, Order Eastern Star. Designer, Ind. State Mus. Master Plan and Complex, Gus Grisson Meml., Mitchell, Ind. Home: 1009 Meadowview Dr New Albany IN 47150 *God's gift to me was the breath of life. My pledge to life is my best effort in all that I am called to do.*

ARMSTRONG, CHARLES HARRY, veterinarian, educator; b. Mt. Vernon, Ohio, Mar. 10, 1925; s. Charles Edward and Nettie Edith (Potter) A.; m. Caroline Jayne Schraeder, Sept. 5, 1945; children: Bruce Edward, Brian Lee. D.V.M., Ohio State U., 1951; M.S., Purdue U., 1963, Ph.D., 1966. Pvt. practice veterinary medicine, Chgo., Evanston and Skokie, Ill., 1951-61; instr. veterinary microbiology Purdue U., West Lafayette, Ind., 1961-66, asst. prof., 1966-68, asso. prof., 1968-73, prof., 1973—; dir. microbiology sect. Animal Disease Diagnostic Lab. Contbr. sci. articles to profl. jours. Pres. Lafayette Bd. Health, 1971-72. Served with USMC, 1942-46. Named Tchr. of Year Sch. Veterinary Medicine, Purdue U., 1967; NIH postdoctoral fellow, 1964-66. Mem. Am. Veterinary Med. Assn., Am. Assn. Veterinary Lab. Diagnosticians (chmn. mycoplasmosis com.), Am. Soc. for Microbiology, Internat. Orgn. Mycoplasmology (chmn. internat. membership com.), Conf. Research Workers in Animal Diseases, Sigma Xi, Phi Zeta. Home: 2400 Maumee Pl Lafayette IN 47905 Office: ADDL Purdue U West Lafayette IN 47907

ARMSTRONG, CLYDE WILSON, lawyer; b. New Kensington, Pa., Apr. 22, 1926; s. Clyde Allman and Ethlyn Wilson (Logan) A.; m. Jean Marvin Forncrook, June 12, 1948; children: Cathy Mitchell, Melissa Anne, Christopher Lee. A.B., Princeton U., 1948; LL.B., U. Pa., 1951. Bar: Pa. 1951, U.S. Dist. Ct. 1951. Mem. firm Thorp, Reed & Armstrong, Pitts., 1951—, ptnr., 1957—; dir. Shannopin Mining Co., Delray Connecting R.R. Co. Vice-pres. Community Chest of Allegheny County, 1971-73; v.p. United Way of Allegheny County, 1974-75; bd. dirs. Community Services of Pa., 1973-79, v.p., 1977-78. Served with USNR, 1944-46. Mem. Am. Law Inst., Am. Coll. Trial Lawyers, ABA, Pa. Bar Assn., Allegheny County Bar Assn., Am. Bar Found. Clubs: Duquesne, Longue Vue Country. Home: 5621 Northumberland St Pittsburgh PA 15217 Office: One Riverfront Center Pittsburgh PA 15222

ARMSTRONG, DICKWIN DILL, c. of c. exec.; b. Muncie, Ind., Aug. 18, 1934; s. Colby Cooler and Elizabeth A. (Houck) A.; m. Janice A. Flora, June 2, 1957; children—Brent D., Stacey J. B.S. in Gen. Bus, Ind. U., 1956. Chief exec. officer Madison (Ind.) C. of C., 1959-61, Frankfort (Ind.) C. of C., 1961-63, Marion (Ind.) C. of C., 1963-66, Lakeland (Fla.) C. of C., 1966-80, Portland (Oreg.) C. of C., 1980—; bd. dirs. Nat. Alliance Bus., Oreg. Joint Council Econ. Edn. Served to capt. AUS, 1957-59. Mem. Am. C. of C. Execs. (past dir.), U.S. C. of C. (faculty center continuing edn.), Oreg. Chamber Execs. (dir., com. chmn.), Sigma Alpha Epsilon. Republican. Methodist. Clubs: Rotary, Masons. Home: 5722 SW Windsor Ct Portland OR 97221 Office: 824 SW 5th Ave Portland OR 97024

ARMSTRONG, DON L(EIGH), chemist, educator; b. Alhambra, Calif., June 7, 1916; s. Roy C. and Frankie L. A.; m. B. Caroline Hayes, May 24, 1940; children: Alan L., Carol L. A.B., UCLA, 1937; M.S., U. So. Calif., 1938, Ph.D., 1942, M.S., 1945. Research asso. U. So. Calif., Los Angeles, 1941-46; mgr. chem. div. Aerojet Gen. Corp., Azusa, Calif., 1946-65; pres. Tech. Assistance Group, Covina, Calif., 1964-79; prof. chemistry Whittier (Calif.) Coll., 1965-81, disting. service prof., 1981—, chmn. dept. chemistry, 1966-79; Mem. spl. adv. com. to sec. Def., 1958-59. Contbr. chpts. to books. Mem. Am. Chem. Soc., Marine Tech. Soc., AAUP, Sigma Xi. Clubs: Santa Barbara Yacht, Masons. Patentee in field. Office: Whittier Coll Whittier CA 90608

ARMSTRONG, DONALD, physician; b. Montclair, N.J., Mar. 25, 1931; s. James John and Lillian (Ragan) A.; m. Elizabeth Freeman Sweet, July 17, 1954; children: Rebecca, Alison, Priscilla, Bradford. A.B., Lehigh U., Bethlehem, Pa., 1953; M.D., Columbia U., 1957. Diplomate: Am. Bd. Internal Medicine, Bd. Med. Microbiology. Intern Cornell div. Bellevue Hosp., N.Y.C., 1957-58; resident U. Colo. Hosps., 1958-59; resident, then chief resident Meml. Cancer Center, 1959-61; Sloan-Kettering fellow-Nat. Cancer Inst. trainee, 1959-61; research asso. Lab. Infectious Diseases, NIH, 1961-63; Nat. Cancer Inst. spl. fellow virology lab. Children's Hosp. Phila., 1963-65; mem. staff Meml. Hosp., N.Y.C., 1965—, attending physician, 1971—, co-dir. microbiology lab., 1965-69, dir., 1969—; asst. vis. physician James Ewing Hosp., N.Y.C., 1965-68, Cornell div. Bellevue Hosp., 1968; mem. staff N.Y. Hosp., 1970—, attending physician, 1976—; asso. Sloan-Kettering Inst., 1965-76, mem., 1977—; chief infectious disease service Meml. Sloan-Kettering Cancer Center, 1970—; mem. faculty Cornell U. Med. Sch., 1965—, prof. medicine, 1976—; med. dir. Chinatown Health Clinic, N.Y.C., 1971-79, bd. dirs., 1979—. Author articles papers in field, chpts. in books; editor: Infectious Diseases: Diagnosis and Treatment; mem. editorial bd. profl. jours. Vol. physician Khao-I-Dang Refugee Camp, Thailand, 1980; mem. com. for scholarly exchange with People's Republic of China, Nat. Acad. Scis., 1981. Served with USPHS, 1961-63. Spl. fellow NIH, 1963-65; grantee Commonwealth Fund, 1977-78. Fellow ACP, Am. Acad. Microbiology, N.Y. Acad. Medicine, Acad. Medicine N.J.; mem. Infectious Disease Soc. Am., Am. Soc. Microbiology, Am. Fedn. Clin. Research, Tissue Culture Assn., Harvey Soc., Am. Thoracic Soc., Linnaean Soc., N.Y. Clin. Soc., Med. Soc. County N.Y., Royal Soc. Medicine, Charaka Club. Home: 440 Riverside Dr New York NY 10027 Office: 1275 York Ave New York NY 10021

ARMSTRONG, DONALD EUGENE, economist, educational administrator; b. Nanton, Alta., Can., May 10, 1925; s. Samuel Thomas and Laura (Brydges) A.; m. Muriel Gladys Buchanan, May 14, 1947; children—Susan Deryl, Patricia Joanne, Terrence Bruce. B.A., U. Alta., Edmonton, 1950, B.Com., 1951; Ph.D., McGill U., 1954. Lectr. in econs. McGill U., 1954-55, asst. prof., 1955-60, prof. mgmt., 1960—, assoc. dean Faculty of Mgmt., 1983—, dir. Sch. Commerce, 1960-65, founder, dir. Grad. Sch. Bus., 1963-66; founder, pres. Fin. Research Inst., 1968-70; dir. FRI, Ventures, Manecon; mem. Conseil D'Orientation Economique du Que., 1964-68. Author: (with John Lindeman) Policies and Practices of United States subsidiaries in Canada, 1961, Education and Achievement, 1970, Competition Versus Monopoly, 1982; contbr. articles to profl. jours. Served to lt. Inf. Corps., Can. Army, 1943-45. Recipient Gold medal in econs. U. Alta., 1950; Bronfman fellow, 1950-51; U. Manchester fellow, 1951-52; Imperial Oil fellow, 1952-53. Mem. Can. Econ. Assn., Am. Econ. Assn., Royal Econ. Soc., others. Home: 3 Westland Dr Montreal PQ H4X 1M1 Canada Office: 1001 Sherbrooke St W Montreal PQ H3A 1G5 Canada

ARMSTRONG, GEORGE RICHARD, manufacturing company executive; b. Sterling, Ill., Oct. 6, 1918; s. Otha Allen and Eva Marie (Rigg) A.; m. Doris Allen, June 7, 1942; children: Ross Alan, Rita Ann Fitch. Student, Bradley U.; B.S. in Mech. Engring., U. Iowa, 1946. With Caterpillar Tractor Co., 1937—, asst. dir. mfg. gen. offices, 1963-64, dir. mfg., 1964-66, plant mgr., Aurora, Ill., 1966-69, gen. mgr. mfg. and facilities planning gen. offices, 1969-70, v.p., 1970-77, exec. v.p., Peoria, Ill., 1977—, also dir., Aurora, Ill.; dir. Provident Savs. and Loan Assn., Peoria, Computer Aided Mfg. Internat., Inc. Trustee Eureka Coll. Served with AUS, 1944-46. Decorated Purple Heart. Mem. Soc. Automotive Engrs., Soc. Mfg. Engrs. Republican. Presbyterian. Clubs: Country (Peoria); Union League (Chgo.). Home:

124 E Coventry Ln Peoria IL 60614 Office: Caterpillar Tractor Co 100 NE Adams Peoria IL 61629

ARMSTRONG, GERALD STUART, diversified co. exec.; b. N.Y.C., May 6, 1943; s. George William and Eleanor (Bovenizer) A.; m. Kristina M. Becker., Dec. 10, 1977; 1 son, Jeffrey Stuart. A.B. in English, Dartmouth Coll., 1965; M.B.A. in Fin. with distinction, N.Y. U., 1976. With Chase Manhattan Bank, N.A., N.Y.C., 1969-80, v.p., div. exec. corp. banking dept., 1975-79, sr. v.p. corp. banking dept., 1980; exec. v.p., chief operating officer Filmways, Inc., Los Angeles, 1980—, also dir. Served to lt. USN, 1965-69. Clubs: Creek (Locust Valley, N.Y.); Yale, Sky (N.Y.C.). Office: 2049 Century Park E Los Angeles CA 90067

ARMSTRONG, GRANT, lawyer; b. Raymond, Wash., Sept. 30, 1907; s. Oren G. and Clara (Knutson) A.; m. Elbertine Adams, Jan. 25, 1933 (dec. Jan. 1979). LL.B., U. Wash., 1929. Bar: Wash. bar 1930. Practiced in, Chehalis, 1930—; mem. firm Armstrong, Vander Stoep & Remund (and predecessor firms), 1946—; Bd. regents U. Wash., 1950-57; bd. visitors Law Sch., U. Puget Sound. Served to lt. comdr. USNR, 1943-46. Fellow Am. Coll. Trial Lawyers, Am. Bar Found., Am. Coll. Probate Counsel; mem. Am. Bar Assn. (state del. 1965-74, gov. 1975-77), Wash. Bar Assn. (gov. 1958-61, pres. 1964-65), Sigma Nu, Phi Delta Phi, Order of Coif (hon.). Republican. Episcopalian. Clubs: Rotarian., Seattle Golf, Tacoma. Home: 215NE Glen Rd Chehalis WA 98532 Office: 345 NW Pacific Ave Chehalis WA 98532

ARMSTRONG, GREGORY TIMON, religion educator, clergyman; b. Evanston, Ill, Dec. 23, 1933; s. John Robert and Clara Joanna (Carlson) A.; m. Edna Louise Stagg, May 11, 1957; children: Edna Louise, Elizabeth Stagg. B.A. with honors, Wesleyan U., 1955; B.D. with highest honors, McCormick Theol. Sem., 1958; Th.D. magna cum laude, U. Heidelberg, 1961. Ordained to ministry United Presbyterian Ch., 1961; instr. ch. history McCormick Theol. Sem., Chgo., 1961-62; asst. prof. ch. history Vanderbilt U. Div. Sch., Nashville, 1962-68; assoc. prof. religion Sweet Briar Coll., Va, after 1968, then prof., chmn. dept. currently Charles A. Dana prof. religion, dir. inter-disciplinary studies; research fellow U. Goettingen, W. Ger., 1974-75; vis. prof. hist. studies Union Theol. Sem., Richmond, 1983—. Author: Die Genesis in der Alten Kirche, 1962; contbr.: articles and book revs. on ch. history and art to scholary jours. Mem. Nashville United Givers Fund, 1966-68; pres. local PTA, Amherst, Va., 1971-72; mem. Wesleyan U. Alumni Fund, 1971-74. Rotary Internat. fellow, 1958-59; Rockefeller doctoral fellow, 1959-61; Nettie F. McCormick fellow, 1959-61; Presbyn. Grad. fellow, 1960-61; Am. Council Learned Soc. Study fellow, 1965-66; NEH grantee, 1971; Fulbright Hays sr. research fellow, 1974-75; Sweet Briar faculty fellow, 1981-82; Vanderbilt U. Research Council grantee, 1966-68; Am. Philos. Soc. grantee, 1981. Mem. Am. Hist. Assn., Am. Soc. Ch. History (membership chmn. 1972-74), Am. Catholic Hist. Assn., Am. Acad. Religion, Archaeol. Inst. Am., AAUP (pres. chpt. 1976), Phi Beta Kappa (chpt. pres. 1976-78). Address: PO Box AY Sweet Briar VA 24595

ARMSTRONG, HENRY CONNER, Canadian government official; b. Winnipeg, Man., Can., June 16, 1925; s. William Arthur Laird and Archena May (Conner) A.; m. Barbara Fay Jackson, May 20, 1950; children: Barbara E., Nancy M., Scott J. B.Sc. in Metall. Engring, Queen's U., Kingston, Ont., 1949; M.B.A. (Kresge fellow), U. Toronto, 1954; diploma in indsl. adminstrn. (Alcan fellow), Centre D'Etudes Industrielles, Geneva, Switzerland, 1958. Various sales and marketing positions Aluminum Co. of Can., Ltd., 1954-64; commodity officer Dept. Trade and Commerce, Ottawa, Ont., 1964-66; comml. counsellor Canadian Embassy, Washington, 1966-74; chief research and planning div., resource industries and constrn. br. Dept. Industry, Trade and Commerce, Ottawa, Ont., Can., 1974-75; dir. minerals and metals div. Dept. Energy, Mines and Resources, Ottawa, Ont., 1975-81, exec. dir. internat. minerals, 1981-82, mgr. spl. projects, 1982-83; counselor for metals, minerals and energy Can. High Commn., Canberra, Australia, 1983—. Served with RCAF and Royal Navy Fleet Air Arm, 1944-45. Mem. Assn. Profl. Engrs. Ont., Canadian Inst. Mining and Metallurgy, Am. Soc. Metals. Mem. United Ch. of Can. Home: 26 Garsca St Campbell ACT 2601Australia Office: Can High Commn Commonwealth Ave Canberra ACT 2600Australia

ARMSTRONG, HERBERT STOKER, ret. univ. dean; b. Toronto, Ont., Can., Nov. 23, 1915; s. George Reidy and Ethel (Stoker) A.; m. Kathleen Halbert, Sept. 6, 1941; children—Catherine, Margaret. B.A., U. Toronto, 1938, M.A., 1939; Ph.D., U. Chgo., 1942; D.Sc., McMaster U., 1967; D.U.C., U. Calgary, 1972. Mem. faculty McMaster U., 1941-62, prof. geology, 1948-62, dean arts and scis., 1950-62; dean sci. U. Alta., 1962-63, v.p. acad., 1963-64; pres. U. Alta. at Calgary, 1964-66; pres., vice chancellor U. Calgary, 1966-68; prof. geology U. Guelph, Ont., 1968-82, dean grad. studies, 1968-80; from asst. to field geologist Ont. Dept. Mines, summers 1937-46, 52, 55, 56. Contbr. articles to profl. jours. Mem. bd. mgmt. Art Gallery Hamilton, 1949-62, pres., 1957-59; mem. council Hamilton Assn., 1946-53, pres., 1951-52; chmn. camp com. Hamilton YMCA, 1958-61, bd. dirs., 1961-62; bd. dirs. Hamilton Philharmonic Orch., 1959-62, Edmonton Symphony Soc., 1963-64, Calgary Philharmonic, 1965-68. Fellow Royal Soc. Can., Royal Canadian Geog. Soc., Geol. Assn. Can. (charter); mem. Canadian Inst. Mining and Metallurgy, Can. Soc. Petroleum Geologists, Geol. Soc. Finland, Geochem. Soc., Heraldry Soc. Can. (dir. 1974-78). Mem. United Ch. Can. Club: Mason. Home: 75 Glasgow St N Guelph ON N1H 4W1 Canada

ARMSTRONG, HERBERT W., evangelist; b. Des Moines, July 31, 1892; (married); children: Richard David (dec.), Garner Ted, Beverly Gott, Dorothy Mattson. Ordained to ministry, 1931; founder Worldwide Ch. of God, 1933, now chmn.; founder, chmn. Ambassador Found.; broadcaster Radio Ch. of God (now World Tomorrow), 1934—. Author: The Autobiography of Herbert W. Armstrong, 1967, The United States and British Commonwealth in Prophecy, 1967, Incredible Human Potential, 1978, The Missing Dimension in Sex, 1964, 71, 81, The Wonderful World Tomorrow, 1979; Editor: The Plain Truth, 1934—, The Good News, Youth, 83. Chmn. bd. Ambassador Coll. Address: Worldwide Ch of God 300 W Green St Pasadena CA 91129

ARMSTRONG, JAMES SINCLAIR, lawyer, banker; b. N.Y.C., Oct. 15, 1915; s. Sinclair Howard and Katharine Martin (LeBoutillier) A.; m. Charlotte Peirce Horwood Faircloth, Nov. 22, 1978. Grad., Milton (Mass.) Acad., 1934; A.B. cum laude, Harvard, 1938, J.D., 1941; postgrad., Northwestern U., 1942-44, 46-48. Bar: Ill. bar 1941, N.Y. bar 1959. Asso. firm Isham, Lincoln & Beale, Chgo., 1941-45, 46-49, mem., 1950-53, SEC, Washington, 1953-57, chmn. commn., 1955-57; asst. sec. navy for financial mgmt., also comptroller Dept. Navy, Washington, 1957-59; exec. v.p. U.S. Trust Co. of N.Y., 1959-80; mem. firm Whitman & Ransom, N.Y.C., 1980—; dir. Rexham Corp., Royal Life Ins. Co. N.Y.; sec. S. Eleuthera Properties (Bahamas). Trustee, chmn. Samuel Rubin Found.; bd. dirs. Internat. Ctr. in N.Y.; trustee, sec. The Gunnery Sch., Washington, Conn.; bd. dirs., pres. St. Mark's Historic Landmark Fund, N.Y.C., Nat. Inst. Social Scis., N.Y.C.; bd. dirs., chmn. Com. to Oppose Sale of St. Bartholomew's Ch., N.Y.C.; chmn., bd. dirs. Fund for Peace, N.Y.C.; bd. dirs. Internat. Ctr. in N.Y. Served as lt. (j.g.) USNR, 1945-46. Decorated Knight Order Orange-Nassau Netherlands. Mem. Am. Bar Assn., Am. Law Inst. (life), Practicing Law Inst., Assn. Bar City of N.Y., Legal Club Chgo., Co. of Adventurers (Mass.) (sec.), Navy League U.S. (life), Hort. Soc. N.Y. (dir., treas.), N.Y. Hist. Soc. (life), N.Y. Soc. Library (life), Pilgrims U.S., Am. Soc. Venerable Order St. John of Jerusalem, English-Speaking Union U.S. (dir., v.p.), St. Andrews Soc. State N.Y. (life, standing com.), Huguenot Soc. Am. (life; chancellor), St. Nicholas Soc. City N.Y. (life, bd. dirs.), Soc. Colonial Wars of N.Y. (life), Kappa Beta Phi. Clubs: Church, Century, Down Town, Harvard, N.Y. Yacht, Thursday Evening, Union (N.Y.C.); Chevy Chase (Md.); Washington (Conn.); Washington Garden; Edgartown (Mass.); Reading Room; Yacht Metropolitan (Washington). Home: 501 E 79th St Apt 3C New York NY 10021 Office: 522 Fifth Ave New York NY 10036

ARMSTRONG, JANE BOTSFORD, sculptor; b. Buffalo; d. Samuel Booth and Edith (Pursel) Botsford; m. Robert Thexton Armstrong, July 3, 1960. Student, Middlebury Coll., 1939-40, Pratt Inst., 1940-41, Art Students' League, 1962-64. One-man shows, Frank Rehn Gallery, N.Y.C., 1971, 73, 75, 77, Columbus (Ohio) Gallery Fine Arts, 1972, Columbia (S.C.) Mus. Art, 1975, New Britain (Conn.) Mus. Am. Art, 1972, Johnson Gallery, Middlebury Coll., 1973, Mary Duke Biddle Gallery for Blind N.C. Mus. Art, 1974, J.B. Speed Art Mus., Louisville, 1975, Buffalo State U., Marjorie Parr Gallery, London, 1976, Ark. Art Center, 1977, Dallas Mus. Fine Art, 1978, Wichita (Kans.) Art Mus., 1978, 82, Wadsworth Atheneum, 1979, Harmon Gallery, 1979, 81, Washington County (Md.) Mus. Fine Arts, Hagerstown, 1979, Chautauqua (N.Y.) Nat. Exhbn. Am. Art, 1980, Southeastern Center Contemporary Art, Winston-Salem, N.C., Rollins Coll., Winter Park, Fla., 1981, The Sculpture Center, N.Y.C.; One-man shows, Sid Deutsch Gallery, N.Y.C., 1983, Boca Raton Center Arts (Fla.), 1983; exhibited in, USIA group exhbn., Europe, 1975-76, Artists of Am., Denver, 1981, 82, 83; represented in numerous acad., indsl., pub. and pvt. collections. Recipient Pauline Law prize Allied Artists Am., 1969, 70, Gold medal, 1976, Ralph Fabri medal honor, 1978, Chaim Gross Found. award, 1980; cert. merit NAD, 1973; Council Am. Artists' Socs. prize Nat. Sculpture Soc., 1973; Porton award, 1981. Fellow Nat. Sculpture Soc. (Bronze medal 1976); Mem. Nat. Arts Club (gold medal for sculpture 1968, 69, 71, best in show 1973, Edith W. Macguire award 1975, Plaque Honor 1977, Alexander Saltzman award 1983), Audubon Artists (medal of honor 1972), Sculptors Guild, Allied Artists Am., Nat. Assn. Women Artists (Charles N. Whinston Meml. prize 1973, Anonymous Mem. award. 1975, 77, Mrs. C. D. Murphy Meml. prize 1979, Elizabeth S. Blake prize 1980), Knickerbocker Artists (Knickerbocker award 1982, Elliot Liskin award 1979), Catharine Willard Wolfe Art Club (Liskin award 1981, Anna Hyatt Huntington award 1982). Home: 2909 S Ocean Blvd Highland Beach FL 33431 Home: Orchard Hill PO Box 38 Saluda NC 28773

ARMSTRONG, JOHN ALEXANDER, political science educator; b. St. Augustine, Fla., May 4, 1922; s. John Alexander and Maria (Hernandez) A.; m. Annette Taylor, June 14, 1952; children: Janet Ann, Carol Louise, Kathryn Marie. Ph.B., U. Chgo., 1948, M.A., 1949; student, U. Frankfurt, Germany, 1949-50; Ph.D., Columbia U., 1953. Research analyst War Documentation Project, Alexandria, Va., 1951, 53-54; asst. prof. internat. relations U. Denver, 1952; vis. asst. prof. internat. relations Columbia U., 1957; mem. faculty U. Wis., Madison, 1954—, prof. polit. sci., 1960—, Philippe de Commynes prof. polit. sci., 1978—, exec. sec. Russian area studies program, 1959-63, 64-65, acting dir. Western European area studies program, 1966-67; mem. adv. panel European affairs State Dept., 1966-69, cons. bur. intelligence and research, 1972-81; mem. bd. dirs. Conf. on European Problems, 1972—. Author: Ukrainian Nationalism, 2d edit, 1963, The Soviet Bureaucratic Elite, 2d edit, 1966, The Politics of Totalitarianism, 1961, Ideology, Politics and Government in the Soviet Union, 4th edit, 1978, The European Administrative Elite, 1973, Nations Before Nationalism, 1982; editor: Soviet Partisans in World War II, 1964. Served with AUS, 1942-46; ETO. Guggenheim fellow, 1967-68, 75-76. Mem. Am. Assn. Advancement Slavic Studies (pres. 1965-67), Council Fgn. Relations, Academic Com. on Soviet Jewry, Ukrainian Polit. Sci. Assn. U.S., Am. Hist. Assn., Am., Midwest polit. sci. assns., Internat. Polit. Sci. Assn. (council 1979-82), Kennan Inst. Advanced Russian Studies (acad. council 1981—), Phi Beta Kappa. Home: 2118 Chamberlain St Madison WI 53705

ARMSTRONG, JOHN ARCHIBALD, oil company executive; b. Dauphin, Man., Can., Mar. 24, 1917; s. Herbert H. and Louise I. (McDonald) A.; m. June Keith, Oct. 7, 1943; children: David Duncan, Douglas Keith, Willard Drew. B.Sc. in Geology, U. Man., 1937, Queen's U., 1942. With Imperial Oil Ltd., 1940—; successively gen. mgr. producing dept., exec. v.p., pres., chief exec. officer, chmn. Standard Oil Co., N.J., now ret.; dir. Export Devel. Corp., Royal Bank of Can.; mem. Brit. N.Am. Commn. Trustee Fraser Inst. Mem. Conf. Bd. Office: 1235 Bay St Suite 601 Toronto ON M5R 3K4 Canada *

ARMSTRONG, JOHN CHACE, industrial engineer; b. Rochester, N.Y., Nov. 25, 1918; s. George Simpson and Dorothy (Miller) A.; m. Helga Evensen, Dec. 28, 1950 (dec.); children: Karin A. Newhouse, Christine Armstrong Furney, Elizabeth Anne Lamb; m. Mary Helen Hurlimann, Mar. 4, 1977; m. stepchildren: Mary Ann, Lily and Susan A. Hurlimann., Mar. 4, 1977. B.A., Williams Coll., 1940; B.S. in Chem. Engring., NYU, 1942. Research chemist, indsl. engr. E.I. duPont de Nemours & Co., Niagara Falls, N.Y., 1942-46; cons. indsl. engr. Geo. S. Armstrong & Co., Inc., N.Y.C., 1946—, pres., 1961—, also dir. Pres. Alumni Fedn., NYU, 1973-76, alumni trustee, 1977-81; chmn. Albert Gallatin Assocs., 1977-79. Mem. Am. Chem. Soc., Am. Inst. Chem. Engrs., N.Y. Soc. Security Analysts, Zeta Psi. Congregationalist. Clubs: Williams (N.Y.C.); Riverside Yacht; Round Hill (Greenwich, Conn.). Home: 8 Grahampton Ln Greenwich CT 06830 Office: 2 Park Ave New York NY 10016

ARMSTRONG, JOHN DALE, lawyer; b. Petersburg, Va., Dec. 7, 1918; s. William Davis and Ethel Kathryn (Walter) A.; m. Geneva Pratt, Aug. 3, 1951; children: Dale Armstrong James, William Taylor. B.S. in Bus. Adminstrn, U. Fla., 1941; LL.B., U. Va., 1948; LL.M. in Taxation, N.Y. U., 1951. Bar: N.Y. 1949, Fla. 1950. Assoc. firm Cadwalader, Wickersham & Taft, N.Y.C., 1948-49, Shutts & Bowen, Miami, 1949-50; trial atty. Office Regional Counsel IRS, Phila., 1951-56; assoc. firm Mershon, Sawyer, Johnston, Dunwody & Cole, Miami, 1956-60, ptnr., 1960—; Mem. South Fla. Coordinating Council, 1979; pres. Estate Planning Council of Greater Miami, 1970-71; chmn. planning and program com. U. Miami Ann. Tax Conf., 1960-79. Treas., bd. dirs. Sch. Vol. Program; chmn. bd. mgrs. S.W. YMCA, 1970-71, now bd. dirs.; bd. dirs. Miami Civic Music Assn., Lighthouse for the Blind, Dade Heritage Trust. Served to col., Transp. Corps AUS, 1941-46. Decorated Bronze Star. Fellow Am. Coll. Tax Counsel; Mem. Am. Law Inst., ABA (past chmn. regional liaison com., sect. taxation), Fed. Bar Assn., N.Y. Bar, Fla. Bar (chmn. tax sect. 1962-63), Mil. Order World Wars (comdr. Miami chpt.), Res. Officers Assn. (life), Miami C. of C. (trustee). Democrat. Christian Scientist. Clubs: Miami, Riviera Country., Two Hundred of Greater Miami. Office: 1600 Southeast First Nat Bank Bldg Miami FL 33131

ARMSTRONG, JOHN KENASTON, insurance and financial services company executive; b. Springfield, Mass., Sept. 2, 1929; s. Ralph A. and Avice E. (Bliss) A.; m. Katherine Kipp, Dec. 17, 1955; children: Leigh, Stephen Kipp. B.A., Wesleyan U., Middletown, Conn., 1950; M.B.A., Harvard U., 1956. Budget and credit mgr. W.R. Grace & Co., N.Y.C., 1956-58; asst. controller Ford Motor Co., Dearborn, Mich., 1958-63, mktg. dir., 1963-68; fin. v.p. Keene Corp., N.Y.C., 1968-77; exec. v.p., chief fin. officer INA Corp., Phila., 1977—; dir. Franklin Fed. Savs. & Loan Assn., N.Y.C., United Chem. Corp., INA Comml. Fin., Inc., Phila., Investors Life Ins. Co., Phila. Investment Group, Wilmington, Del., Ins. Co. N.Am., Phila., INA Reins Co., Life Ins. Co. N.Am., INA Internat. Corp, INA Capital Advisers, INA Life Ins. Co., Los Angeles, Sealed Air Corp., Fairlawn, N.J., Hosp. Affiliates Internat., Inc., Nashville. Trustee Thomas Jefferson U., 1977—; bd. dirs. Phila. Conv. and Vistors Bur. Served with Signal Corps U.S. Army, 1951-53. Mem. Phi Beta Kappa. Republican. Clubs: Harvard Bus. Sch. of N.Y. (v.p. 1976-77), Wesleyan of Phila. (pres. 1977). Home: 854 Mount Pleasant Rd Bryn Mawr PA 19010 Office: INA Corp 1600 Arch St Philadelphia PA 19101

ARMSTRONG, JOSEPH GRAVITT, publishing company executive; b. Fort Worth, Aug. 23, 1943; adopted s. Doyle C. A. and Gravitt. B.A., Trinity U., 1965; J.D., U. Tex., 1968. Bar: Tex. 1968. Assoc. Wertheim & Co., Inc. (investment bankers), N.Y.C., 1968-72; asst. to pub. Family Weekly Mag., N.Y.C., 1972-73; with Straight Arrow Pubs., N.Y.C., 1973-77; advt. dir. Rolling Stone mag., 1973-74, pres., pub., 1975-77; pres. N.Y. Mag. Corp.; editor-in-chief and pub. N.Y. Mag. and New West Mag., 1977-80; pres., pub., founder The Movies, 1981—. Mem. ABA. Home: 10 Mitchell Pl New York NY 10017 The Movies 310 Madison Ave New York NY 10017

ARMSTRONG, KARAN, soprano; b. Havre, Mont., Dec. 14, 1941. B.A., Concordia Coll., Moorhead, Minn. European debut as: Salome, Strasbourg; also appeared as: Salome at, Munich (W. Ger.) Festival, 1976; with, Stuttgart Opera, 1977, Frankfurt Opera; Am. debut as Musetta: (La Boheme), San Francisco Spring Opera, 1966; Venice Opera debut as Marie in: Wozzeck, 1979; other appearances with, Zurich (Switzerland) Opera, Berlin Opera, N.Y.C. Opera, also Hamburg, Frankfurt, Oslo, Hawaii, Strasbourg, Munich, Balt., Houston, San Antonio, Seattle, Santa Fe, Memphis, opera cos.; and with, Ravinia Festival, Chgo., Hollywood Bowl, Los Angeles, Boston Pops Orch.; former mem., Roger Wagner Chorale; N.Y. recital debut at, Town Hall, 1976; film version of Falstaff, 1980; TV appearances include: Evening at Pops. Winner San Francisco Opera audition, 1965; Met. Opera audition, 1966. Address: care Columbia Artists Mgmt 165 W 57 St New York NY 10019

ARMSTRONG, LLOYD, JR., physicist, educator; b. Austin, Tex., May 19, 1940; s. Lloyd and Beatrice (Jackson) A.; m. Judith Glantz, July 9, 1965; 1 son, Wade Matthew. B.S. in Physics, M.I.T., 1962, Ph.D., U. Calif., Berkeley, 1966. Postdoctoral physicist Lawrence Berkeley (Calif.) Lab., 1965-66, cons., 1976; sr. physicist Westinghouse Research Labs., Pitts., 1967-68, cons., 1968-70; research asso. Johns Hopkins U., 1968-69, asst. prof. physics, 1969-73, asso. prof., 1973-77, prof., 1977—; maitre de recherche associe Centre National de la Recherche Scientifique, Orsay, France, 1972-73; vis. fellow Joint Inst. for Lab. Astrophysics, Boulder, Colo., 1978-79; program officer NSF, 1981-83. Author: Theory of Hyperfine Structure of Free Atoms, 1971; contbr. articles to profl. jours. NSF grantee, 1972—; Dept. Energy grantee, 1975—. Mem. Am. Phys. Soc. Office: Physics Dept Johns Hopkins U Baltimore MD 21218

ARMSTRONG, MINNIE OLIVER, supermarket chain executive; b. Boise, Idaho, Sept. 3, 1927; d. Joseph and Minnie Belle (Houde) Oliver; m. Charles L. Armstrong, July 30, 1955. Grad., high sch. Stenographer C.C. Anderson Co., Boise, 1945; with Ada County Assitance Dept., Idaho, 1945-48, Albertson's Inc., Boise, 1948—, sec., 1969—; asst. sec. Skaggs-Albertson's Properties, Inc., 1971-75, sec., 1975-82; sec., dir. Albertson's Realty Inc., 1960—, Monte Mart, Inc., 1975-82. Bd. dirs., sec. J.A. and Kathryn Albertson Found.; trustee Joseph Buell Scott Trust. Mem. Am. Soc. Corp. Secs. Seventh-day Adventist. Office: Abertson's Inc 250 Parkcenter Blvd Boise ID 83726

ARMSTRONG, NEIL A., computer systems company executive, former astronaut; b. Wapakoneta, Ohio, Aug. 5, 1930; s. Stephen A.; m. Janet Shearon; children: Eric, Mark. B.S. In Aero. Engring, Purdue U., 1955; M.S. in Aero. Engring, U. So. Calif. With Lewis Flight Propulsion Lab., NACA, 1955; then aero. research pilot for NACA (later NASA, High Speed Flight Sta.), Edwards, Calif.; astronaut Manned Spacecraft Center, NASA, Houston, 1962-70; command pilot Gemini 8, Mar. 1966; comdr. Apollo II; dep. asso. adminstr. for aeros. Office Advanced Research and Tech., Hdqrs. NASA, Washington, 1970-71; prof. aerospace engring. U. Cin., 1971-79; chmn. bd. Cardwell Internat., Ltd., Lebanon, Ohio, 1980-82; chmn. CTA, Inc., 1982—; dir. Gates Learjet Corp., Cin. Gas & Electric Co., Eaton Corp., Taft Broadcasting Co., Cin. Milacron, UAL, Inc. Chmn. bd. trustees Cin. Mus. Natural History. Served as naval aviator USN, 1949-52; Korea. Recipient numerous awards, including Octave Chanute award Inst. Aero. Scis., 1962, Presdl. Medal for Freedom, 1969, Exceptional Service medal NASA, Hubbard Gold medal Nat. Geog. Soc., 1970, Kitty Hawk Meml. award, 1969, Pere Marquette medal, 1969, Arthur S. Fleming award, 1970, Congl. Space Medal of Honor, Explorers Club medal. Fellow AIAA (hon., Astronautics award 1966), Internat. Astronautical Fedn. (hon.), Soc. Exptl. Test Pilots; mem. Nat. Acad. Engring. 1st man to walk on moon, 1969. Office: 31 N Broadway Lebanon OH 45036

ARMSTRONG, NEILL, football coach; b. Tishomingo, Okla., Mar. 9, 1926; (married); 3 children. Student, Okla. A and M U. Player Phila. Eagles, Nat. Football League, 1947-51, Winnipeg Blue Bombers, Can. Football League, 1951-54; asst. coach Okla. State U., 1955-61; asst. def. coach Houston Oilers, Nat. Football League, 1962-63; head coach Edmonton Eskimos, Can. Football League, 1964-69; defensive coach Minnesota Vikings, Nat. Football League, 1970-78; head coach Chgo. Bears, Nat. Football League, 1978-81; with research and devel. dept. Dallas Cowboys, Nat. Football League, 1981—. Office: Dallas Cowboys 6116 N Central Expressway Dallas TX 75206

ARMSTRONG, OLIVER WENDELL, oil company executive; b. Mound Valley, Kans., July 13, 1919; s. Charles Eugene and Elva (Williams) A.; m. Betty Jane Nichols, June 24, 1945; 1 dau., Julia Anne. Student, Kans. State U., 1937-40; B.S., Pittsburg State U., 1941. With Phillips Petroleum Co., 1944—, div. credit mgr., Chgo., 1951-55, regional credit mgr., Bartlesville, Okla., 1955-59, adminstrv. asst., 1959-60, asst. treas., 1960-65, sec., treas., 1965-71, v.p. and treas., 1971-78, v.p. treasury, 1978—; dir. 1st Nat. Bank Bartlesville, Transatlantic Reins. Co., Okla. Bus. Devel. Corp., Trenwick Ltd.; Bd. advisers Sch. Bus. and Econs. Pittsburg State U. Mem. Am. Petroleum Inst., Fin. Execs. Inst. Republican. Presbyterian. Clubs: Elk, Mason, Shriner, Jester, Rotarian. Home: 2000 Skyline Dr Bartlesville OK 74003 Office: Phillips Bldg Bartlesville OK 74004

ARMSTRONG, RICHARD ALFORD, editor; b. D'Lo, Miss., Aug. 29, 1929; s. Thomas Richard and Mildred (Alford) A.; m. Nancy Trimble Ray, Oct. 1, 1957; 1 dau., Lucy Isabelle. Student, U. Ala., 1946-47; B.J., U. Mo., 1950; M.A. in English, Columbia U., 1955. Reporter Gadsden (Ala.) Times, 1950-54; contbg. editor Time Mag., 1956-61, Saturday Evening Post, 1962-69; mng. editor USA-1 mag., 1961-62; with Fortune mag., N.Y.C., 1969—, asso. editor, bd. editors, 1971-75, asst. mng. editor, 1975-77, exec. editor, 1977—. Served to 1st lt. U.S. Army, 1951-52; Korea. Decorated Bronze Star. Presbyterian. Home: 521 Wynnewood Rd Pelham Manor NY 10803 Office: Fortune Mag Time & Life Bldg Rockefeller Center New York NY 10020

ARMSTRONG, RICHARD BURKE, television dir.; b. Bklyn., May 12, 1924; s. John Andrew and Christine (Dougherty) A.; m. Carolyn Millett Jones, Oct. 2, 1954; children—Robert James, Jennifer Marlowe, Christina Louise. Student, U. Scranton, 1942-43; B.A., Catholic U. Am., 1950, postgrad., 1952. Stage mgr. Sta WMAL-TV, Washington, 1953-54, dir., 1954-62, ABC-TV News Bur., Washington, 1962—. Actor, Players Inc., Washington, 1952-53. Served with U.S. Army, 1943-46. Office: 1717 De Sales St Washington DC 20036

ARMSTRONG, RICHARD QUINE, beverage company executive; b. Boston, June 27, 1935; s. Oren Arthur and Katherine Isobel (Quine) A.; m. Pamela Bartholomew, Oct. 7, 1961; children: Matthew, Roderick. B.A. cum laude, Bowdoin Coll., 1957. Vice pres., account supr. Rockwell, Quinn & Wall, advt., N.Y.C., 1966-68; v.p., account dir. Ted Bates Advt., N.Y.C., 1968-72; v.p., dir. ops. Dobbs-Life Savers Internat., N.Y.C., 1972-76; pres., chief exec. officer Can. Dry Corp., N.Y.C., 1976-82; pres., chief operating officer Dr. Pepper Co., Dallas, 1982—. Fund raiser ARC, Bowdoin Coll., Brunswick Sch., Greenwich, Conn. Served to 1st lt. AUS, 1957-59. Episcopalian. Clubs: Union League (N.Y.C.); Milbrook (Greenwich). Office: Dr Pepper Co 5523 E Mockingbird Ln Dallas TX 75265 *

ARMSTRONG, ROBERT ARNOLD, petroleum company executive; b. Chgo., Feb. 17, 1928; s. Arnold Gustave and Lillian (Laver) A.; m. Jane Victoria Colestock, May 13, 1951 (dec. 1964); children: Michael, Richard, Patricia, Casey; m. Margaret Soden, Nov. 17, 1973; children: Gregory, Jennifer. Student, Mo. Sch. Mines, 1946-48; B.S., Stanford U., 1951; postgrad., Colo. Sch. Mines, 1956-58; M.S., U. So. Calif., 1961, 1961-64. Petroleum engr. S.Am.; with Standard Oil Co. of Calif., 1951-58; research engr. Chevron Research Labs., La Habra, Calif., 1958-61; sr. evaluation engr. Union Oil Co., Los Angeles, 1961-6?; v.p. Lee Keeling & Assos., Los Angeles, 1963-65; dir., pres. Armstrong Petroleum Corp., Newport Beach, Calif., 1965—; dir. Richards Armstrong Drilling Co., Armstrong Petroleum, Calif. Ind. Oil Producers; vis. prof. engring. U. So. Calif., Los Angeles, 1960-65. Mem. adv. bd. Stanford Mineral Sci. Sch. Assos., Stanford Bus. Sch.; bd. dirs. Sta. KUSI-TV, San Diego; trustee U.S. Internat. U.; advisor Mission of the Californias. Mem. AAAS, Ind. Oilman's Assn., Calif. Conservation Commn., Am. Inst. Mining Engrs. (pres. jr. group, petroleum br. 1960-61), Am. Petroleum Inst., Western Oil and Gas Assn.; mem. Orange County Petroleum Assn. Patentee subsea prodn. systems. Home: 81 Emerald Bay Laguna Beach CA 92651 Office: 2244 Coast Hwy Newport Beach CA 92663

ARMSTRONG, ROBERT BRADLEY, mfg. co. exec.; b. Mpls., Dec. 25, 1929; s. Harry George and Mary Evelyn (Sutherl) A.; m. Lucille Dolores Miller, Mar. 12, 1960; children—Mary Gregg, Brad Lee. B.Mech. Engring., Gen. Motors Inst., 1959. With Gen. Motors Corp., Detroit and Flint, Mich., 1958-69; v.p., gen. mgr. Simplicity Engring. Co., Durand, Mich., 1969-71; exec. v.p. Cardinal of Adrian, Dryden, Mich., 1971-72; sr. v.p. Champion Home Builders Co., Dryden, 1972-75; founder, pres. Bending Spltys., Inc. (spl. machinery), Madison Heights, Mich., 1976—. Bd. dirs. Blue Shield of Mich. Served with USAF, 1950-54. Recipient 10 Year key for outstanding job performance Gen. Motors Inst., 1958. Club: Lion. Home: 2624 Hounds Chase Troy MI 48098 Office: 580 Ajax Dr Madison Heights MI 48071 *If the events in one's life are not daring and exciting, then you have no life, simply an existence.*

ARMSTRONG, ROBERT DOUGLAS, former mining company executive; b. Ottawa, Ont., Can., Apr. 25, 1916; s. William Allan and Jennie (Betty) A.; m. Dorothea Christine Fairleigh, Dec. 29, 1943; children: Robert Michael, Reginald Brock, Barbara Elizabeth, Robert Douglas. B. Commerce, Queen's U., 1937. Chartered acct., 1941. With Price Waterhouse & Co., C.P.A.'s, Toronto, 1937-41, Imperial Oil Ltd., 1941-50, A.V. Roe Can., 1951-53; comptroller Can. Nat. Rys., Montreal, 1953-56, v.p., 1956-59; with Chrysler Corp., 1959-62; pres. Chrysler Leasing Corp., 1962-64, Can. Found. Co., Ltd., Toronto, 1966-74, chmn., chief exec. officer, 1975-83. Served with Can. Army, World War II. Home: 30 Glenorchy Rd Don Mills ONCanada

ARMSTRONG, ROBERT PLANT, editor, educator; b. Wheeling, W.Va., May 19, 1919; s. Clarence Warren and Dorothy Johanna (Green) A. B.A., U. Ariz., 1944; M.A., U. Iowa, 1946; Ph.D., Northwestern U., 1957. Traveler Houghton Mifflin & Co., 1945-46; instr. English Mont. State U., Missoula, 1946-50; field editor Harper and Bros., 1956-58; editor Alfred A. Knopf, N.Y.C., 1958-59; dir. publs. U. Ariz. Press, 1959-60; dir. Northwestern U. Press, 1960-73, prof. Coll. Arts and Scis., 1967-73; prof. anthropology U. Tex. at Dallas, 1974—; vis. prof. art history State U. N.Y., Buffalo, summer 1970; vis. curator African art Buffalo Mus. Sci., summer 1970; vis. prof. U. Ibadan, Nigeria, 1972-73; also vis. dir. Univ. Press. Columnist: Book Forum, 1975—; Author: The Affecting Presence: An Essay in Humanistic Anthropology, 1971, Forms and Processes in Africa, 1970, Wellspring: On the Myth and the Source of Culture, 1975, The Powers of Presence: Myth, Consciousness, and Affecting Presence, 1981; chmn. editorial bd.: Book Forum; mem. editorial bd.: Arts Inquiry; cons. editor: Studies in Visual Communications; contbr. numerous articles to profl. jours. Served with USNR, 1940-43. Fellow African Studies Assn., Am. Anthrop. Assn. Office: Sch Arts and Humanities U Tex at Dallas Richardson TX 75080

ARMSTRONG, ROBIN LOUIS, university dean, physics educator; b. Galt, Ont., Can., May 14, 1935; s. Robert Dockstader and Beatrice Jenny (Grill) S.; m. Karen Elisabeth Feilberg Hansen, July 8, 1960; children: Keir Grill, Christopher Drew. B.A., U. Toronto, 1958, M.A., 1959; Ph.D., 1961; Ph.D. Rutherford Meml. fellow, Oxford (Eng.) U., 1961-62; FRSC, 1979. Mem. faculty U. Toronto, 1962—, prof. physics, 1971—, chmn. dept., 1974-82, dean Faculty of Arts and Sci., 1982—. Co-author: Mechanics, Waves and Thermal Physics, 1970, Electromagnetic Interaction, 1973; contbr. articles to profl. jours. Mem. Canadian Assn. Physicists (Herzberg medal 1973), Am. Assn. Physicists, Internat. Soc. Magnetic Resonance. Home: 540 Huron St Toronto ON M5R 2R7 Canada Office: Faculty of Arts and Science Univ Toronto 100 St George St Toronto ON M5S 1A1 Canada

ARMSTRONG, RODNEY, librarian; b. Atlanta, Mar. 5, 1923; s. Harold Rodney and Mary Blair (Armstrong) A.; m. Katherine Price Cortesi, June 14, 1969; children: Louise Spencer, Robert Knowlton. B.A., Williams Coll., 1948; M.S., Columbia U., 1950. Librarian Phillips Exeter Acad., N.H., 1950-73; dir., librarian Boston Athenaeum, 1973—; bd. dirs. New Eng. Deposit Library, 1973; hon. sec. Hakluyt Soc., 1973—; sec., trustee Donations for Edn. in Liberia, 1973—; mem. corp., trustee Fruitlands Mus., Harvard, Mass.; cons. in field. Served with USNR, 1943-45. Decorated Purple Heart; Benjamin Franklin fellow Royal Soc. Arts, 1974. Fellow Am. Acad. Arts and Scis., Soc. Antiquaries; mem. ALA (life), N.H. Library Assn. (past officer, dir.), Am. Antiquarian soc., Colonial Soc. Mass., Mass. Hist. Soc., Manuscript Soc. (dir., past pres.), New Eng. Historic Geneal. Soc. (pres. 1977-82). Episcopalian. Clubs: Century Assn., Grolier (N.Y.C.); Odd Volumes (Boston) (pres. 1979—). Home: 101 Chestnut St Boston MA 02108 Office: 10 1/2 Beacon St Boston MA 02108

ARMSTRONG, RONALD WILLIAM, metallurgical engineering educator; b. Balt., May 4, 1934; s. John Paul and Elizabeth (Novotny) A.; m. Mary Ann Manarczyk, Feb. 15, 1958; children: Lisa Joan, Lori Bess. B.Engring. Sci., Johns Hopkins U., 1955; Ph.D., Carnegie Mellon U., 1958; M.A. (hon.), Brown U., 1966. Metallurgist Westinghouse Electric Corp., Pitts., 1959-64; assoc. prof. engring. Brown U., Providence, 1965-68; prof. materials U. Md., College Park, 1968—; cons. Oak Ridge Nat. Lab., 1967-70, Lawrence Livermore (Calif.) Lab., 1968-72, Inst. Def. Analysis, McLean, Va., 1969-75, Naval Surface Weapons Center, White Oak, Md., 1979—; program mgr. sci. edn. directorate NSF, 1976-77, rotator div. sci. edn. resources improvement, 1976-77; vis. prof. metall. engring. U. Strathclyde, Scotland, 1982-85; vis. fellow Clare Coll., U. Cambridge, 1984. Contbr. to profl. jours. Recipient Robert Lansing Hardy Gold medal Am. Inst. Mining and Metall. Engrs., 1964; research fellow Leeds (Eng.) U., 1958-59, U. Melbourne (Australia), 1964; research grantee Def. Dept., 1963-73, 81—, NSF, 1973-75, Dept. Energy, 1978-83; sr. Fulbright-Hays fellow, Lower Hutt, N.Z., 1974; NSF research participant United Technologies Research Center, Conn., 1975; NATO lectr. award, Eng., 1979; U.S.-France Coop. Sci. Program participant, Paris, 1980; sci. liaison officer European sci. office Office of Naval Research, London, 1982-84. Mem. AAAS, AIME, ASME, Am. Soc. Metals, N.Y. Acad. Scis., Sigma Xi, Phi Kappa Phi, Alpha Sigma Mu, Pi Tau Sigma. Home: 1514 Rosewick Ave Baltimore MD 21237 Office: Dept Mech Engineering Univ Md College Park MD 20740

ARMSTRONG, THEODORE MORELOCK, corporate executive; b. St. Louis, July 22, 1939; s. Theodore Roosevelt and Vassar Fambrough (Morelock) A.; m. Carol Mercer Robert, Sept. 7, 1963; children: Evelyn Anne, Robert Theodore. B.A., Yale U., 1961; LL.B., Duke U., 1964. Bar: Mo. bar 1964. With Mississippi River Transmission Corp. and affiliated cos., St. Louis, 1964—; corporate sec. Mo. Pacific Corp., 1971-75, River Cement Co., 1968-75; asst. v.p. Mississippi River Transmission Corp., 1974-75, v.p. gas supply, 1975-79, exec. v.p., 1979-83, pres., chief exec. officer, 1983—, dir., 1982—, United Mo. Bank of St. Louis. Mem. ABA, Mo. Bar, Met. St. Louis Bar Assn., So. Gas Assn. (dir. 1984—), Phi Alpha Delta. Republican. Presbyterian. Clubs: Bellerive, St. Louis, Yale (St. Louis); Yale (N.Y.C.). Home: 43 Countryside Ln St Louis MO 63131 Office: 9900 Clayton Rd St Louis MO 63124

ARMSTRONG, THOMAS NEWTON, III, museum dir.; b. Portsmouth, Va., July 30, 1932; s. Thomas Newton, Jr. and Mary Saunders (Tabb) A.; m. Virginia Whitney Brewster, May 18, 1963; children—Thomas Newton IV, Whitney, Eliot, Amory. Student, Cornell U., 1950-54, Art Students League, summer 1953, Inst. Fine Arts, N.Y. U., 1965-67. Personnel coordinator, asst. to chmn. bd. Stone & Webster, Inc., N.Y.C., 1957-65; curator, asso. dir. Colonial Williamsburg-Abby Aldrich Rockefeller Folk Art Collection, Williamsburg, Va., 1967-71; dir. Pa. Acad. Fine Arts, Phila., 1971-73; asso. dir. Whitney Mus. Am. Art, N.Y.C., 1973-74, dir., 1974—. Office: 765 Madison Ave New York NY 10021 *

ARMSTRONG, W. J., bank executive. Pres., chief exec. officer Northwestern Nat. Bank Mpls. Office: Northwestern Nat Bank Mpls 7th and Marquette Ave Minneapolis MN 55480§

ARMSTRONG, WALTER PRESTON, JR., lawyer; b. Memphis, Oct. 4, 1916; s. Walter Preston and Irma Lewis (Waddell) A.; m. Alice Kavanaugh McKee, Nov. 3, 1949; children: Alice Kavanaugh, Walter Preston III. Grad., Choate Sch., Wallingford, Conn., 1934; A.B., Harvard U., 1938, J.D., 1941; D.C.L. (hon.), Southwestern at Memphis, 1961. Bar: Tenn. 1940. Practiced in, Memphis, 1941—; assoc. firm Armstrong, Allen, Braden, Goodman, McBride & Prewitt (and predecessor firms), 1941-48, partner, 1948—; Commr. for Promotion of Uniformity of Legislation in U.S. for Tenn., 1947-67. Author law rev. articles. Pres. bd. edn. Memphis City Schs., 1956-61; mem. Tenn. Higher Edn. Commn., 1967-84, chmn., 1974-75; mem. Tenn. Hist. Commn., 1969-80; hon. French consul, 1978—. Served from pvt. to maj. AUS, 1941-46. Fellow Am. Bar Found. (sec. 1960-62), Tenn. Bar Found. (chmn. 1983-84), Am. Coll. Trial Lawyers; mem. Am. Bar Assn. (ho. of dels. 1952-75), Tenn. Bar Assn. (pres. 1972-73), Memphis and Shelby County Bar Assn., Inter-Am. Bar Assn., Internat. Bar Assn., Fed. Bar Assn., Assn. Bar City N.Y., Am. Law Inst., Am. Judicature Soc., Nat. Conf. Commrs. on Uniform State Laws (pres. 1961-63), Harvard Law School Assn. (sec. 1957-58), Order of Coif, Scribes (pres. 1960-61), Phi Delta Phi, Omicron Delta Kappa. Home: 1530 Carr Ave Memphis TN 38104 Office: 1900 One Commerce Sq Memphis TN 38103 *Faith in God, love of family, devotion to duty, and respect for my fellow man.*

ARMSTRONG, WALTER WILLIAM, investment copany executive; b. Bklyn., Oct. 25, 1928; s. Harry Howard and Isabella Clementine (Campbell) A.; m. Joan Winifred Coulter, June 25, 1955; children: Margaret Ann, Catherine Ann, James Gerard, Walter William, Thomas Paul, Michael Andrew. B.B.A., Pace U., 1957, M.B.A., 1963. Asst. sec. Dreyfus Corp., N.Y.C., 1955-64; asst. mgr. First Jersey Nat. Bank, Jersey City, 1964-66; v.p. adminstrn. Nat. Securities & Research Corp., N.Y.C., 1966-69; mgmt. cons. Coopers & Lybrand, N.Y.C., 1969-75; dir. internal audit Blyth Eastman Dillon Capital Markets, Inc., N.Y.C., 1976-79; v.p., treas. Calvin Bullock, Ltd., N.Y.C., 1979—; treas. Bullock Fund, Ltd., N.Y.C., 1979—, Bullock Tax-Free Shares, Inc., 1979—, Can. Fund. Inc., 1979—, Dividend Shares, Inc., 1979—, High Income Shares, Inc., 1979—, Money Shares, Inc., 1979—, Monthly Income Shares, Inc., 1979—, Nation-Wide Securities Co., Inc., 1979—, Agressive Growth Shares, Inc., 1982—. Served with AUS, 1951-53. Mem. Nat. Investment Co. Service Assn. (exec. com. 1968-72, chmn. exec. com. 1973-74). Roman Catholic. Home: 450 Derby Rd Baldwin NY 11510 Office: Calvin Bullock Ltd 1 Wall St New York NY 10005

ARMSTRONG, WARREN BRUCE, university president, history educator; b. Tidioute, Pa., Oct. 16, 1933; s. Mead C. and Mary (Griffin) A.; m. Elizabeth Ann Fowler, Aug. 7, 1954 (div. 1973); children: Linda Susan, Heidi Jo; m. Joan Elizabeth Gregory, Apr. 19, 1974; children: Susan Elizabeth, Pamela Anne. Th.B., Bapt. Coll. Pa., 1956; A.M., U. Mich., 1958, Ph.D., 1964. Instr. history Olivet Coll., 1961-63, asst. prof., 1963-65, chmn. dept., 1964-65; asst. prof. U. Wis.-Whitewater, 1965-66, asso. prof., 1966-69, prof., 1969-70, asst. dean Coll. Arts and Scis., 1966-69, asso. dean, 1969-70; dean St. Cloud (Minn.) State U., 1970-75, prof. history, 1970-75; pres. Eastern N.Mex. U., Portales, 1975-83, Wichita State U. (Kans.), 1983—, prof. history, .1983—. Author: (with Dae Hong Chang) The Prison: Voices from the Inside, 1972; Contbr. articles to profl. jours. Councilman, Whitewater, 1968-70. Mem. AAUP, Orgn. Am. Historians, Am. Conf. Acad. Deans., Am. Assn. Higher Edn., Phi Kappa Phi. Democrat. Home: 1820 N Hillside Wichita KS 67214 Office: wichita state univ office of the president 1845 fairmont Wichita KS 67208

ARMSTRONG, WILLIAM HOWARD, educator, author; b. Lexington, Va., Sept. 14, 1914; s. Howard G. and Ida (Morris) A.; m. Martha Stonestreet Williams, Aug. 24, 1942; children: Christopher, David, Mary. A.B., Hampden-Sydney Coll., 1936; postgrad., U. Va., 1937-38. Tchr. history Kent (Conn.) Sch., 1945—. Author: Through Troubled Waters, 1956, Study is Hard Work, 1957, Peoples of the Ancient World, 1959, 87 Ways to Help Your Child in School, 1961, Sounder, 1969 (Newbery award), Barefoot in the Grass (Life of Grandma Moses), 1970, Sour Land, 1971, Hadassah: Esther the Orphan Queen, 1972, The Maclead Place, 1972, The Mills of God, 1973, The Education of Abraham Lincoln, 1974, Study Tips: How To Improve Your Study Habits and Improve Your Grades, 1976, Joanna's Miracle, 1977, The Tale of Tawny and Dingo, 1979, Study Tips: New and Revised Edition, 1983, Studying Tactics, 1983. Recipient Nat. Sch. Bell award for distinguished service in interpretation of edn., 1963; Mark Twain award for Sounder, 1972. Home: Kimadee Hill Kent CT 06757

ARMSTRONG, WILLIAM L., Senator; b. Fremont, Nebr., 1937; s. William L. and Dorothy (Steen) A.; m. Ellen M. Eaton, July 15, 1962; children: Anne Elizabeth, William. Pres., Sta. KOSI AM-FM, Aurora, Colo., 1959—; mem. 93d-95th Congresses from 5th Dist., Colo., U.S. Senate from, 1979—; dir. Peoples Bank & Trust Co., 1968-73, Peoples Bank of Arapahoe County, 1970-73, Intermountain Network, 1969-73; Mem. Colo. Senate, 1965-72, majority leader, 1969-72; mem. Colo. Ho. of Reps., 1963-64. Bd. govs., exec. com. Metro Denver Urban Coalition, 1969-72; bd. dirs. Denver Organizing Com. for the XII Winter Olympic Games, 1971-72, Adams County-Aurora unit Am. Cancer Soc., 1972. Recipient Disting. Service award Aurora Jr. C. of C., 1970; named one of three Outstanding Young Men in Colo. State Jaycees, 1970. Mem. AP Broadcasters Assn. (dir. 1971-72, v.p. 1972). Office: Senate Office Bldg Washington DC 20510

ARMSWORTHY, FRANK JOSEPH, retail executive; b. Balt., Aug. 15, 1927; s. Frank M. and Eva C. (Cooney) A.; m. Joan Marie Colamaria, June 15, 1963; children: Frank, Richard, Scott. B.S., U. Md., 1951. Intelligence officer CIA, 1951-56; with Sears, Roebuck & Co., 1956-63, personnel and employee relations rep. for New Eng., 1958-63; personnel dir. Noxaema Chem. Co., 1964-66, Horn & Hardart Baking Co., 1966-68; from personnel dir. to v.p. ops. Filene's, Boston, 1968-78; pres. Goldsmiths' Dept. Store, Memphis, 1978-80; vice chmn. Saks Fifth Ave., N.Y.C., 1980—; dir. Asso. Mdsg. Corp., 1978-80, chmn. personnel com., 1973-75. Bd. dirs. United Way Greater Memphis, 1978-80; chmn. mcht. council N.Y.U. Retail Inst.; Bd. dirs. Visitors and Conv. Bur., Memphis, 1978-80, Liberty Bowl Festival Assn., 1978-80, Greater Memphis State Inc., 1979-80, Memphis chpt. ARC, 1978, Met. N.Y. council Boy Scouts Am.; mem. Gov. Mass. Task Force Child Care, 1974-75, Nat. Football Found. and Hall of Fame, 1979—; mem. president's round table Le Moyne-Owen Coll., Memphis, 1979-80. Served with AUS, 1945-46. Mem. Nat. Retail Mchts. Assn., Met. N.Y. Retails Mchts. Assn. (v.p.), N.Y. State Retail Council (chmn.), Fifth Ave. Assn. Home: 150 E 69th St Apt 16E New York NY 10021 Office: 17 E 49th St New York NY 10022

ARNABOLDI, LEO PETER, JR., lawyer; b. Paterson, N.J., Dec. 28, 1924; s. Leo Peter and Stella (Bannes) A.; m. Sheila Gallagher, Dec. 27, 1958; children: Leo, Clinton, Lilla. A.B. summa cum laude in Econs., Amherst Coll., 1947; J.D., Yale U., 1950. Bar: N.Y. 1951. Assoc. Willkie Farr & Gallagher, N.Y.C., 1950-52, Olwine, Connelly, Chase, O'Donnell & Weyher, 1952-59; ptnr. Olwine, Connelly, Chase, O'Donnelly & Weyher, N.Y.C., 1960—; sr. ptnr. Olwine, Connelly, Chase, O'Donnell & Weyher, N.Y.C., 1969—; chmn. exec. com. Lionel Corp., N.Y.C., 1968—; dir., mem. exec. com. Seabrook Foods, Inc., 1967-73. Editor: Yale Law Jour., 1949-50. Served to lt. USAF, 1944-46. Mem. Phi Beta Kappa, Beta Theta Pi. Clubs: Greenwich Country, Stanwich (Greenwich, Conn.); Raquet and Tennis (N.Y.C.). Home: 26 Cedar Wood Dr. Greenwich CT 06832 Office: Lionel Corp 9 W 57th St New York NY 10019

ARNALL, ELLIS GIBBS, lawyer, former governor of Georgia; b. Newnan, Ga., Mar. 20, 1907; s. Joe Gibbs and Bessie Lena (Ellis) A.; m. Mildred DeLaney Slemons, Apr. 6, 1935 (dec. June 29, 1980); children: Alvan Slemons, Alice Slemons Arnall Harty; m. Ruby Hamilton McCord, July 15, 1981. Student, Mercer U., 1924; A.B., U. of South, 1928, D.C.L., 1947; LL.B., U. Ga., 1931; LL.D., Atlanta Law Sch., 1942, Piedmont Coll., 1943, Bryant Coll., 1948. Bar: Ga. 1931. Mem. Ga. Ho. of Reps., speaker pro tem, 1933-37; atty. gen., Ga., 1939-43, gov., 1943-47; pres. Columbus Nat. Life Ins. Co. (formerly Dixie Life Ins. Co.), Newnan, 1946-60, Soc. Ind. Motion Picture Producers, Beverly Hills, Calif., 1948-60, Ind. Film Producers Export Corp., Beverly Hills, 1953-60; sr. partner law firm Arnall, Golden & Gregory, Atlanta; chmn. bd. Coastal States Life Ins. Co., Atlanta, 1956—, Atlanta Americana Motor Hotel Corp.; vice chmn., dir. Sun Life Group, Inc.; dir. First Nat. Bank in Newnan, Alterman Foods Inc., Midland Capital Corp., The Rushton Co., Simmons Plating Works, U.S. Office Price Stblzn., Feb.-Sept. 1952; mem. Nat. Commn. for UNESCO, 1947-51, 63—; mem. U.S. del. Fifth Conf. UNESCO, Paris, 1949; mem. U.S. del. Anglo-Am. Film Conf., London, 1950, 53-56. Author: The Shore Dimly Seen, 1946, What the People Want, 1947. Mem. Franklin D. Roosevelt Warm Springs Meml. Commn., 1970—; trustee U. South, 1946-50, Mercer U., 1960-70. Named to Transp. Hall of Fame, 1977. Fellow Internat. Inst. Arts and Scis.; mem. Am. Judicature Soc., Nat. Assn. Life Ins. Co. (chmn. bd. 1955—), Am., Fed., Ga. bar assns., Soc. Motion Picture Arts and Scis., Phi Beta Kappa, Phi Delta Phi, Kappa Alpha. Democrat. Club: Atlanta Lawyers. Office: 55 Park Pl Atlanta GA 30335

ARNASON, HJORVARDUR HARVARD, art historian; b. Winnipeg, Man., Can., Apr. 24, 1909; came to U.S., 1927, naturalized, 1940; s. Sveinbjorn and Maria (Bjarnadottir) A.; m. Elizabeth Hickcox Yard, July 25, 1936; children: Eleanor Atwood, Jon Yard. Student, U. Man., 1925-27; B.S., Northwestern U., 1931, A.M., 1937; M.F.A., Princeton U., 1939. Instr., Northwestern U., 1936-38; research asst. and lectr. Frick Collection, N.Y.C., 1938-42; lectr. Hunter Coll, 1939-42; field rep. OWI, Iceland, 1942-44, asst. dep. dir. for Europe, hdqrs. Washington, 1944-45; chief program planning and evaluation unit Office of Internat. Info. and Cultural Affairs, Dept. State, Washington, 1945-46; vis. asso. prof. art U. Chgo., 1947; prof., chmn. dept. art U. Minn., 1947-61; dir. Walker Art Center, Mpls., 1951-61; v.p. for art adminstrn. Solomon R. Guggenheim Found., N.Y.C., 1961-69; former cons. Guggenheim Mus.; Fulbright fellow, France, 1955-56; Carnegie vis. prof. U. Hawaii, 1959; sr. research fellow NEH, 1971-72; U.S. rep. Prep. Commn. on UNESCO, London and Paris, 1946. Author: Modern Sculpture, 1962, Conrad Marca-Relli, 1962, Sculpture by Houdon, 1964, Alexander Calder, 1966, History of Modern Art, 1968, 2d, 1977, Jacques Lipchitz: Fifty Years of Sketches in Bronze, 1969, (with Ugo Mulas) Alexander Calder, 1969, (with Jacques Lipchitz) Jacques Lipchitz: My Life in Sculpture, 1972, The Sculptures of Houdon, 1975, Jean-Antoine Houdon, French edit., 1976, (with Barbaralla Diamonstein) Robert Motherwell: New & Revised, 1982, Robert Motherwell, 1977; also monographs, catalogues, articles on medieval, 18th century and modern art. Trustee Adolph Gottlieb Found.; mem. exec. bd., chmn. adv. com. Internat. Found. for Art Research. Decorated chevalier de l'Ordre des Arts et des Lettres (France); knight Order St. Olav (Norway), Order of Falcon (Iceland). Mem. Coll. Art Assn., Am. Assn. Mus., AAUP, Am. Soc. 18th Century Studies, Société Française d'Étude du 18ème Siècle. Clubs: Century, Princeton (N.Y.C.). *

ARNAUD, CLAUDE DONALD, JR., educator; b. Hackensack, N.J., Dec. 4, 1929; s. Claude Donald and Alice Marie (Minnet) A.; children: Claude Michael, Ellen Marie. B.A., Columbia Coll., 1951; M.D., N.Y. Med. Coll., 1955. Intern St. Luke's Hosp., N.Y.C.; also resident; resident, endocrine fellow Milwaukee County Hosp.; fellow U. Wis.; instr. biochemistry U. Pa., 1965-66; cons. dept. endocrine research Mayo Clinic, Rochester, Minn., 1967-77, head mineral research unit, 1972-74, head endocrine research unit, mineral research lab., 1974-77, asso. prof. medicine Grad. Sch. Medicine, 1970-74, prof., 1974-77; prof. medicine and physiology U. Calif., San Francisco, 1977—; chief endocrine unit San Francisco VA Med. Center, 1977—. Contbr. numerous articles to profl. jours. Served with M.C. U.S. Navy, 1957-59. NIH grantee, 1968—. Mem. Am. Fedn. Clin. Research, Am. Soc. Biol. Chemists, Am. Soc. Clin. Investigation, Am. Physiol. Soc., Assn. Am. Physicians, Endocrine Soc., Western Assn. Physicians, AAAS., Am. Soc. Bone Mineral Research.

ARNAUD, DANIEL LEONARD, educator, business executive; b. N.Y.C., May 29, 1935; s. Leonard Ellison and Martha Lindemuth A.; m. Carol Ann Tosi, Mar. 21, 1967; children: Martha Beasley, Frances Ellison, Maxwell Charles Leonard. Grad., Groton Sch., 1953; A.B., Carleton Coll., 1957; M.A., U. S.D., 1960; Ph.D., Stanford, 1968. Tchr. Latin Groton Sch., Mass., 1957-58; acting instr. classics Stanford, 1960-63; instr. classics Lawrence U., Appleton, Wis., 1964-68, asst. prof., 1968-72, Danforth faculty asso., 1970-71, chmn. dept. classics, 1967-68, 70-72, dir. freshman program, 1971-72, on leave, 1968-70, 72-74; asst. dir. Salzburg Seminar in Am. Studies, Austria, 1968-69, asso. dir., 1969-70, v.p., 1977-80; exec. dir. Thomas J. Watson Found., Providence, 1972-77; dir. planning and group devel. EG&G Environ. Group, Waltham, Mass., 1980-81; mng. dir. Earth Watch, 1981-82; head alumni affairs and devel. Groton Sch., (Mass.), 1982—; Mem. adv. council Sch. for Field Studies, 1981—; mem. alumni standing com. Groton Sch., 1981—. Mem. Archeol. Inst. Am., Am. Philol. Assn., Providence Art Club. Home and Office: Groton Sch Groton MA 01450

ARNAZ, LUCIE DESIREE, actress; b. July 17, 1951; d. Desi and Lucille Ball; m. Laurence Luckenbill; 1 son, Simon. Appeared on: television series Here's Lucy; television appearances include: The Sixth Sense, Marcus Welby, M.D., Timex Presents Words and Music, Ed Sullivan's Clown Around, Lucie at Walt Disney World, Kraft Music Hall, Death Scream, The Black Dahlia, The Mating Game; stage appearances include leading roles in: nat. touring co. of Seesaw; West Coast premiere Vanities; N.Y. prodn. Annie Get Your Gun, 1978; Broadway prodn. They're Playing Our Song; other appearances include, Mack and Mabel, Cabaret, Once Upon a Mattress; television appearances include: Good Bye Charlie; other appearances include: L'il Abner, Bye Bye Birdie; appeared in: motion picture The Jazz Singer, 1980; host: radio interview show Tune in with Lucie, So. Calif. Easter Seals Telethon. Recipient Los Angeles Drama Critics' award. *

ARNDT, ROGER EDWARD ANTHONY, hydraulic engr.; b. N.Y.C., May 25, 1935; s. Ernest Otto Paul and Olive (Walters) A.; m. Sofia Smyk, June 16, 1962 (div.); children—Larysa Tamara, Tanya Sofia. B.C.E., CCNY, 1960; S.M., M.I.T., 1962, Ph.D., 1967. Chemist Consol. Testing Labs., New Hyde Park, N.Y., 1956-57; jr. civilengr. N.Y.C. Dept. Public Works, 1960; research engr. Allegheny Ballistics Lab., Cumberland, Md., 1962-63; sr. research engr. Lockheed Calif. Corp., Burbank, 1963-64; asso. prof. aerospace engring. Pa. State U., 1967-77; prof. hydromechanics, dir. St. Anthony Falls Hydraulic Labs., U. Minn., Mpls., 1977—; mem. Com. for Mpls. Hydropower Mus., 1980—; 1st Theodor Ranov disting. lectr. SUNY, Buffalo, 1979; cons. in field. Author articles in field, chpts. in books.; Editor: Flow Studies in Air and Water Pollution, 1971, Fluid Mechanics Research in Water Resources Engineering, 1981; asso. editor: Jour. Fluids Engring, 1977-79. Recipient George Taylor Teaching award U. Minn., 1978, Lorenz G. Straub award, 1968; NASA fellow, 1965-67. Mem. Internat. Assn. Hydraulic Research, AIAA (Outstanding Faculty Adv. award 1971, 72, 73, 74), Acoustical Soc. Am., ASCE, Am. Soc. Engring. Edn., ASME, ASTM, Am. Water Resources Assn., N.Y. Acad. Scis., Sigma Xi. Club: Twin City Cloud 7. Home: 1820 N Ham Lake Dr Anoka MN 55303 Office: U Minn St Anthony Falls Hydraulic Lab Mississippi River at 3d Ave SE Minneapolis MN 55414

ARNDT, WALTER WERNER, Russian language educator, poet; b. Constantinople, Turkey, May 4, 1916; came to U.S., 1949, naturalized, 1955; s. Fritz Georg and Julia (Heimann) A.; m. Sophie Miriam Bach, Jan. 6, 1945; children: Robert Michael, Joachim David, Prudence Joy, Corinne Constance. Dipl.Econ.Pol.Sc., Oriel Coll., Oxford (Eng.) U., 1936; cand. mag., Sch. Bus. Adminstrn., Warsaw (Poland) U., 1939; B.S. summa cum laude in Mech. Engring., Robert Coll., Istanbul, 1943; Ph.D., U. N.C., 1956; M.A. (hon.), Dartmouth, 1967. Asst. dir., Turkey office; Internat. Rescue and Relief Com., 1942-49, Intergovtl. Com. Refugees, 1945-47, UN Internat. Refugee Orgn., 1947-49; instr. Robert Coll., Istanbul, 1945-48; corr. The Economist, 1946-48; instr., then asst. prof. classical and modern langs. Guilford Coll., 1950-56; asst. prof., then asso. prof. Slavic and linguistics U. N.C., 1957-66, chmn. dept. linguistics, Slavic and Oriental langs., 1965-66; prof. Russian Dartmouth, 1966—, chmn. dept. Russian lang. and lit., 1967-70; Fulbright prof. U. Münster, Germany, 1961-62; guest prof. Polish U. Colo., summer 1965. Author: Alexander Pushkin: Eugene Onegin, 1963, 2d edit., revised and expanded, 1981, Wilhelm Busch, Clement Dove, The Thwarted Poet, 1967, (with L. Levine) Grundzüge moderner Sprachbeschreibung, 1969, Pushkin Threefold, 1972, Alexander Pushkin: Ruslan and Liudmila, 1974, J.W. von Goethe, Faust: A Tragedy (verse translation), 1976, Anna Akhmatova, Selected Poems (verse translation), 1976, The Genius of Wilhelm Busch: Comedy of Frustration, 1981. Served with OSS, 1943-45; OWI. Ford fellow U. Mich., 1952, Harvard, 1956-57; research grantee Am. Philos. Soc., 1967, Rockefeller Found., 1975, Guggenheim Found., 1977-78, NEH, 1978-79; Kennan fellow Wilson Ctr., Smithsonian Instn., NEH, 1981-82; fellow Va. Ctr. for Creative Arts, 1983; co-recipient Bollingen prize for translation poetry, 1963. Mem. Linguistic Soc. Am., Am. Assn. Advancement Slavic Studies, South Atlantic Modern Lang. Assn. (chmn. Slavic sect. 1959-60, sec. 1962-63, chmn. 1963-64), Am. Assn. Tchrs. Slavic and E. European Langs. (v.p. 1964—), South Conf. Slavic Studies (v.p. 1964-65, pres. 1965-66), Phi Beta Kappa (hon.). Home: 38 Maple St Hanover NH 03755

ARNER, CHARLES EDWARD, banker; b. St. Paul, June 16, 1922; s. George Henry and Alice Alvina (Schroeder) A.; m. Barbara E. Mannheimer, Jan. 22, 1948; children: Cort, Stephanie. Asst. cashier First Bank St. Paul, 1958-60, asst. v.p., 1960-62, v.p., 1962-67, s.r. v.p., 1968-80, chmn., chief exec. officer, 1980-83, vice chmn., 1983-84; pres. First Computer Corp., 1967-68. Trustee Sci. Mus. of Minn., St. Paul, 1981—; bd. dirs., treas. St. Paul Progress Corp., 1982—. Episcopalian. Clubs: Mineapolis, Minnesota; North Oaks Golf (Minn.); Tucson Nat. Golf. Home: 5 West Shore Rd Saint Paul MN 55110 Office: 332 Minnesota St Saint Paul MN 55101

ARNESEN, KENNETH GEORGE, banker, lawyer; b. Chgo., Nov. 24, 1928; s. George T. and Alva E. (Baier) A.; m. Lois Fisher, Sept. 28, 1957; children: Nancy Eileen, David Eric, Robert Kirk. B.S.C., State U. Iowa, 1951; LL.B., U. Ill., 1954. Bar: Ill. 1955. Atty., asso. gen. counsel, then sr. v.p., gen. counsel, cashier First Nat. Bank Chgo., 1956—, sr. v.p., gen. counsel, 1980—. Served with AUS, 1954-56. Clubs: Law, Legal (Chgo.). Office: 1 First Nat Plaza Chicago IL 60670

ARNESON, GEORGE STEPHEN, manufacturing company executive; b. St. Paul, Apr. 3, 1925; s. Oscar and Louvia Irene (Clare) A.; m. Maria Fernanda Suarez; children: George Stephen Fernando, Deborah Clare Fernanda, Diane Elizabeth Fernanda, Frederick Oscar Fernando. B.E.E., U. Minn., 1949; B.S. in Marine Transp, U.S. Mcht. Marine Acad., 1945. Certified mgmt. cons.; sr. mem. Am. Soc. Appraisers. Sales engr. Hubbard & Co., Chgo., 1949-54; cons. Booz, Allen & Hamilton, Chgo., 1954-57; mgr. mktg. cons. services, dir. mktg., plant mgr. Borg-Warner Corp., Chgo., 1957-60; asst. gen. mgr., then v.p., gen. mgr. Delta-Star Electric div. H.K. Porter Co., Inc., Pitts., 1960-63, v.p., gen. mgr. elec. divs., 1963-65; v.p. mktg. Wheeling Steel Corp., 1965-66; pres., chief exec. officer Vendo Co., Kansas City, Mo., 1966-72, also dir., chmn. exec. com.; pres., chmn. Dun-Lap Mfg. Co., Newton, Iowa, 1973-77; pres. Arneson & Co., Kansas City, Mo., 1974—; dir. TelCon Assocs., Shawnee Mission, Kans., Richard Muther & Assocs., Kansas City. Chmn. adv. bd. Kans. Dept. Corrections; trustee Park Coll., Parkville, Mo. Served to lt. (j.g.) USNR, 1943-46. Recipient Outstanding Achievement award U.S. Mcht. Marine Acad.; Past Dir. award Automatic Merchandising Assn. Mem. Am. Soc. Appraisers, Phi Gamma Delta (life), Alpha Phi Omega (life). Republican. Presbyterian. Clubs: Masons, K.T., Shriners. Home: 12715 High Dr Leawood KS 66209

ARNESON, ROBERT CARSTON, sculptor, educator; b. Benicia, Calif., Sept. 4, 1930. B.A. in Edn, Calif. Coll. Arts and Crafts, 1954; M.F.A. Mills Coll, 1958; student ceramics with, Antonio Prieto. Instr. design Mills Coll., 1960-62; prof. art U. Calif.-Davis, 1962—. One man shows, various galleries, U.S. and London, retrospective exhbn., Mus. Contemporary Art, Chgo., also San Francisco Mus. Art, 1974; exhibited in group shows, U. Calif. Art Mus., Berkeley, 1967, Johnson Wax Collection, touring U.S. and Europe, 1968-73, Whitney Mus. Am. Art, N.Y.C., 1969, 81-82, Mus. Contemporary Crafts, N.Y.C., 1971, Mus. Modern Art, Kyoto, also Tokyo, Japan, 1971-72, Crocker Art Mus., Sacramento, 1981, San Francisco Mus. Modern Art, 1982; represented in permanent collections, San Francisco Mus. Modern Art, Oakland (Calif.) Art Mus., Santa Barbara (Calif.) Mus. Art, U. Calif. Art Mus., Berkeley, Nat. Mus. Modern Art, Kyoto, Utah Mus. Fine Arts, Salt Lake City, Stedlijk Mus., Amsterdam, Holland. Office: Art Dept U Calif Davis CA 95616 *

ARNESS, JAMES, actor; b. Mpls., May 26, 1923; s. Rolf C. and Ruth (Duesler) A.; m. Virginia Chapman, Feb. 12, 1948; children: Craig, Jenny Lee, Rolf. Student, Beloit Coll., 1942. Motion pictures include Gun the Man Down; actor live and filmed TV shows, 1954—; star: series CBS-TV Gunsmoke, 1955-75; TV series How the West Was Won, from 1977, McClain's Law, NBC; TV movie The Macahans, 1976. Served as pvt. AUS, World War II. Mem. Beta Theta Pi. Home: Pacific Palisades CA 90272 *

ARNEST, BERNARD PATRICK, artist; b. Denver, Feb. 19, 1917; s. Bernard Patrick and Marie Josephine (Kaelin) A.; m. Barbara Irene Maurin, June 5, 1948; children: Paul, Lisa, Mark. Student, Colorado Springs Fine Arts Center, 1936-39. Instr. Mpls. Sch. Art, 1947-49; asst. prof., assoc. prof. art U. Minn., Mpls., 1949-57; prof. art Colo. Coll., Colorado Springs, 1957-82, chmn. dept., 1957-71, 79-82; initiator advanced placement in art Coll. Entrance Exam Bd., 1966-72, co-chmn. examining com., 1966-72; cons. Coll. Art Programs, Ford Found., 1965. One-man shows, San Francisco Mus. Art, Mpls. Inst. Art, Walker Art Center, U. Minn. Galleries, Denver Art Mus., Colorado Springs Fine Arts Center, Kraushaar Galleries, N.Y.C., group shows, Whitney Annual, Pitts. Internat., Corcoran Biennial, Am. Acad., Mpls. Art Inst., Walker Art Center, Denver Art Mus., Colorado Springs Fine Arts Center. Served to 1st lt. U.S. Army, 1941-45; ETO. Guggenheim fellow, 1940; U.S. State Dept. grantee, 1960. Mem. Coll. Art Assn., AAUP, Artists Equity (head Mpls. chpt. 1948-50). Home: 1502 Wood Ave Colorado Springs CO 80907

ARNETT, EDWARD MCCOLLIN, chemistry educator, researcher; b. Phila., Sept. 25, 1922; s. John Hancock A. and Katherine (Williams) McCollin; m. Mary Hall Founders, Aug. 18, 1951 (div.); children: Eric, Brain; m. Sylvia Gettmann, Dec. 10, 1970; stepchildren: Elden, Byron, Colin. B.S., U. Pa., 1943, M.S., 1946, Ph.D., 1949. Research dir. Max Levy Co., Phila., 1949-53; assoc. prof. chemistry Western Md. Coll., Westminster, 1953-55; research fellow Harvard U., 1955-57; prof. U. Pitts., 1955-80; Reynolds prof. Duke U., Durham, N.C., 1980—. Contbr. numerous articles to profl. jours. Guggenheim fellow, 1968-69. Mem. Am. Chem. Soc. (Pitts. award 1976, James Flack Norris award 1976), Nat. Acad. Scis. Quaker. Home: 2529 Perkins Rd Durham NC 27706 Office: Dept Chemistry Duke U Gross Chem Lab Durham NC 27706

ARNETT, FOSTER DEAVER, lawyer; b. Knoxville, Tenn., Nov. 28, 1920; s. Foster Greenwood and Edna (Deaver) A.; m. Jean Medlin, Mar. 3, 1951; children: Melissa Lee, Foster Deaver. B.A., U. Tenn., 1946; LL.B., U. Va., 1948. Bar: Va. and Tenn. 1948. Practice law, Knoxville, 1948—; partner Arnett, Draper & Hagood (and predecessors), 1954—. Pres., Knox Children's Found., 1959-61, 75-76, U. Tenn. Hearing and Speech Center, 1963-65, Knoxville Teen Ctr., 1969-71; v.p. Ft. Loudon Assn., 1972-75; bd. dirs. Knoxville News-Sentinel Charities, 1979—; del. Republican Nat. Conv., 1964. Served to 1st lt. AUS, 1942-46; lt. comdr. USAR; ret. Decorated Silver Star, Purple Heart. Fellow Am. Coll. Trial Lawyers (fed. rules and adj. state coms.), Internat. Acad. Trial Lawyers (chmn. profl. malpractice com.), Internat. Soc. Barristers, Am. Bar Found.; mem. Southeastern Legal Found. (legal adv. bd.), Nat. Conf. Commrs. Uniform State Laws, ABA, Tenn. Bar Assn. (pres. 1968-69), Tenn. Bar Found. (charter), Knoxville Bar Assn. (pres. 1959-60), Internat. Assn. Ins. Counsel (sec.-treas.), S.E. Def. Counsel Assn. (v.p. 1966), Am. Trial Lawyers Assn., Am. Acad. Hosp. Attys. of Am. Hosp. Assn. (charter), U. Tenn. Nat. Alumni Assn. (pres. 1961-62, chmn. nat. ann. giving program 1961-63), Scribes, Scabbard and Blade, Phi Gamma Delta, Phi Delta Phi, Omicron Delta Kappa. Clubs: Civitan, Cherokee Country, LeConte, U. Tenn. Faculty, Men's Cotillion (dir. 1960-61, 63-64, 66-68), Men's Cotillion (trustee 1962—), Appalachian (pres. 1974-76). Home: 4636 Alta Vista Way SW Knoxville TN 37919 Office: 2300 Plaza Tower Knoxville TN 37929

ARNETT, G. RAY, govt. ofcl.; b. Quantico, Va., June 14, 1924; (married); 4 children. Ed., UCLA, U. So. Calif. Formerly dir. Nat. Wildlife Fedn.; head Calif. Dept. Fish and Game; now asst. sec. fish, wildlife and parks Dept. Interior, Washington. Chmn. bd. dirs. Wildlife Legis. Fund Am., Wildlife Conservation Fund Am. Served with USMC, 1942-46, 50-52. Address: Dept Interior Office Asst Sec Fish Wildlife and Parks 18th and C Sts NW Washington DC 20240 *

ARNETT, HAROLD EDWARD, educator; b. Hegeler, Ill., Jan. 20, 1931; s. Dumous Clay and Amie (Netherton) A.; m. Betty Joanne Carter, Aug. 31, 1952; children—John Brockman, Carl Edward, Melia Louise. B.S., U. Ill., 1955, M.S., 1957, Ph.D., 1963. C.P.A., Ill. Instr. accountancy U. Ill., 1955-60; tax accountant firm Filbey, Andrews & Filbey, Champaign, Ill., 1957-59; student counselor, faculty adviser Office of Dean, Coll. Commerce and Bus. Adminstrn., U. Ill., 1955-57; research asso. Research div. Am. Inst. C.P.A.'s, N.Y.C., 1960-62; asst. prof., U. Mich., 1962-66, asso. prof., 1966-69, prof., 1969—, head dept. accounting, 1969-72; cons. various bus. orgns. Contbr. articles to accounting jours., also monographs. Vice-pres. Wines Sch. PTO, 1965-66, pres., 1966-67; mem. subcom. City of Detroit Commn. on Community Relations, 1971—; cubmaster Portage Trails council Boy Scouts Am., 1963-66, treas., 1967-68; mem. Municipal Finance Com., Ann Arbor, 1971-72; trustee Walsh Coll., 1975-79. Served with USNR, 1948-52. Mem. Am. Inst. C.P.A.'s, Am. Accounting Assn., Financial Execs. Inst., Mich. Assn. C.P.A.'s, Nat. Assn. Accountants (dir. Ann Arbor chpt. 1963-71, sec. 1967-68, 2d v.p. 1968-69, pres. 1969-70, nat. dir. 1974-76, 81-84, internat. v.p. 1981-82, exec. com. 1981-82), Ann Arbor C. of C. (tax com. 1969-70), U. Ill. Scholarship Key, Beta Alpha Psi, Beta Gamma Sigma, Chi Gamma Iota, Phi Eta Sigma, Sigma Iota Epsilon. Republican. Presbyn. Club: Mason. Home: 2113 Delaware Dr Ann Arbor MI 48103

ARNETT, JUDSON WOODROW, journalist; b. Russell, Ky., Nov. 11, 1911; s. Thomas Frank and Claudia (Dillon) A.; m. Fern Haver, Dec. 22, 1934 (dec. 1983). Owner, editor 3 weeklies, Ohio, Ill., Fla.,, 1945-56; bur. mgr. St. Petersburg Times, Bradenton, Fla., 1956-57; assoc. editor Savannah Morning News, Ga., 1957-58, editor, 1958-59; columnist Detroit Free Press, 1959—, editorial bd., 1970-76. Mem. bd. control Lake Superior State Coll., Sault Ste. Marie, Mich., 1978—; chmn. Livingston County United Way campaign, 1982. Served with USN, 1942-45. Recipient Mich. Disting. Citizen award Lake Superior State Coll., 1976. Mem. Soc. Profl. Journalists (pres. Detroit chpt. 1966-68). Home: 5360 Golf Club Rd Howell MI 48843 Office: Detroit Free Press 321 W Lafayette Blvd Detroit MI 48231

ARNETT, ROSS HAROLD, JR., entomologist, editor, publisher; b. Medina, N.Y., Apr. 13, 1919; s. Ross Harold and Hazel Dell (Oderkirk) A.; m. Mary Catherine Ennis, Feb. 16, 1942; children: Ross Harold, Michael J., Mary Anne, Barbara E., Frances X. C., Joseph A., Bernadette T., Matthew C. B.S., Cornell U., 1942, M.S., 1946, Ph.D., 1948. Instr. Cornell U., 1945-48; entomologist U.S. Nat. Mus., Washington, 1948-54; asso. prof. St. John Fisher Coll., Rochester, N.Y., 1954-58; prof. biology Cath. U. Am., Washington, 1958-66, head dept. biology, 1962-66, dir., 1961-66; prof. entomology Purdue U., Lafayette, Ind., 1966-70; Henry L. Beadel fellow Tall Timbers Research Sta., Tallahassee, 1970-73; prof. biology Siena Coll., Loudonville, N.Y., 1973-79; dir. Oxycopis Pond Research Sta., Kinderhook, N.Y., 1980-82; prof. entomology U. Fla., 1983—; pres. World Digests, Inc., 1973-74; v.p. Am. Entomol. Inst., Ann Arbor, Mich.; exec. dir. Biol. Research Inst. Am., 1973-80. Author: Beetles of the United States, 1962, (with D.C. Braungart) Introduction to Plant Science, 1962, 2d edit., 1965, 3d edit, (with G.F. Bazinet, Jr.), 1970, 4th edit., 1977, Entomological Information Storage and Retrieval, 1970, (with R.E. Blackwelder) Checklist of the Beetles of Canada, U.S., Mexico, Central America and the West Indies, 1977, The Naturalists' Directory and Almanac, 43d edit, 1978, (with N.M. Downie) How to Know the Beetles, 1980, (with R.L. Jacques, Jr.) Simon & Schuster's Guide to the Insects, 1980, Checklist of the Beetles of North and Central America and West Indies, 10 Vols., 1983; also numerous articles. Fellow Royal Entomol. Soc. London; mem. Entomol. Soc. Am., Bot. Soc. Internat., Am. Soc. Plant Taxonomists, Am. Ornithol. Soc., Am. Entomol. Soc., AAAS, Am. Inst. Biol. Sci., Soc. Systematic Zool., Sigma Xi, Phi Kappa Phi. Clubs: Cosmos, Explorers. Standardized classification beetles U.S. and families beetles world; research on speciation as it affects evolutionary process. Home: 2406 NW 47th Terr Gainesville FL 32606

ARNETT, WARREN GRANT, interior designer; b. Charleston, W.Va., Aug. 16, 1923; s. Bernice Buell and Verla Dessie (Ash) A.; (div.)1 dau., Linda Arnett McCulloch. Student, Carnegie Mellon Inst., 1941-42, Parsons Sch. Design, N.Y.C., 1959, N.Y. Sch. Interior Design, 1959-60. Studio mgr. NBC, N.Y.C., 1949-57; interior designer Myrick's Furniture, Inc., Orlando, Fla., 1957-59, W. and J. Sloane's, Manhasset, N.Y., 1959-60, Myrick's Interiors, Orlando, 1960-67; pres. Warren G. Arnett, Inc., Orlando, 1967—; sec., bd. dirs. Nat. Council Interior Design Qualifications, 1973-75, dir., 1979-81; mem. barrier free design com. President's Com. Employment Handicapped, 1971-72; rep. Fed. Design Assembly, 1972, 74; trustee Found. Interior Design Edn. Research, 1973—; lectr. in field, judge competitions. Free-lance actor radio, stage and TV, 1935—. Pres. Central Fla. Civic Theatre, Orlando, 1967-69, bd. dirs., 1963—, chmn. bldg. com., 1968-73; founding mem., bd. dirs. Council Arts and Scis. Central Fla., 1967-71; bd. dirs. Participation Enriches Arts and Scis. Orgn. (PESO), 1968—, sec., 1969-70, v.p., 1980-81, pres., 1981-82; mem. beautification com. Orlando C. of C., 1974-75; bd. dirs. Loch Haven Park, Orlando, 1977—. Served with U.S. Army, 1943-46. Decorated Bronze Star. Fellow Am. Soc. Interior Designers (life mem., Gold T Square award 1973, pres. 1971-73, chmn. bd. 1973-75, dir. 1965-68, 69-75, Presdl. citation 1975, 80, dir. 1976-81); hon. mem. Interior Design Educators Council. Home: 1500 Gay Rd Winter Park FL 32789 Office: 745 N Thornton Ave Orlando FL 32803:

ARNEZ, NANCY LEVI, educational leadership educator; b. Balt., July 6, 1928; d. Milton Emerson and Ida Barbour (Rusk) Levi. A.B., Morgan State Coll., 1949; M.A., Columbia U., 1954, Ed.D., 1958. Chr. English Druid Jr. High Sch., Balt., 1949-52; tchr. English Houston Jr. High Sch., Balt., 1952-57; asst. to admissions officer Tchrs. Coll., Columbia U., N.Y.C., 1957-58, grad. asst., 1957; head dept. English Cherry Hill Jr. High Sch., Balt., 1958-62; assoc. prof., dir. student teaching Morgan State Coll., Balt., 1962-66; prof., dir. Ctr. for Inner City Studies, Northeastern Ill. U., Chgo., 1966-74; prof., assoc. acting dean Sch. Edn. Howard U., Washington, 1974-80, prof., chmn. dept. ednl. leadership, 1980—. Author: Partners in Urban Education: Teaching the Inner City Child, 1973, The Struggle for Equality of Educational Opportunity, 1975, Administrative Issues in the Implementation of the Response to Educational Needs Project, 1979, The Besieged School Superintendent, 1981, School Based Administrator Training, 1982; mem. editorial bd.: Phi Delta Kappan, 1975-80, Jour. Negro Edn., 1975—, Black Child Jour., 1980—; contbr. articles to profl. jours. State treas., mem. exec. com. Md. State council UN Children's Fund, 1965; founder Operation Champ, Balt, 1965; mem. adv. bd. Better Boys Found., Chgo., 1966-74, Mus. African-Am. History, Chgo., 1969; state chmn. Right to Read, Washington, 1973-80; treas. Com. to Elect Douglass Moore to City Council, Washington, 1982. African Am. Inst. grantee, 1974; Spencer Found. grantee, 1976, 77. Mem. Am. Assn. Sch. Adminstrs. (editorial bd. 1982). Presbyterian. Home: 3122 Cherry Rd NE Washington DC 20018 Office: 2400 6th St NW Washington DC 20059

ARNHEIM, RUDOLF, psychologist, educator; b. Berlin, July 15, 1904; U.S., 1940, naturalized, 1946; s. Georg and Betty (Gutherz) A.; m. Mary Elizabeth Frame, Apr. 11, 1953; 1 dau., Margaret. Ph.D., U. Berlin, 1928; D.F.A. (hon.), R.I. Sch. Design, 1976, Litt.D., Bates Coll., 1981. Asso. editor publs. Internat. Inst. Ednl. Films, Rome, 1933-38; lectr., vis. prof. Grad. Faculty, New Sch. Social Research, N.Y.C., 1943-68; mem. faculty Sarah Lawrence Coll., 1943-68; prof. psychology of art Carpenter Center for Visual Arts, Harvard U., 1968-74, emeritus, 1974—; vis. prof. U. Mich., Ann Arbor, 1974—. Author: Art and Visual Perception, 1954-74, Film as Art, 1957, Picasso's Guernica, 1962, Toward a Psychology of Art, 1966, Visual Thinking, 1969, Entropy and Art, 1971, Radio, 1971, The Dynamics of Architectural Form, 1977, The Power of the Center, 1982. Recipient Disting. Service award Nat. Art Edn. Assn., 1976; Guggenheim fellow, 1941-42; Fulbright lectr. Ochanomizu U., Tokyo, 1959-60; resident Am. Acad., Rome, 1978. Fellow Am. Psychol. Assn. (pres. div. psychology and arts 1957-58, 65-66, 70-71), Am. Acad. Arts and Scis.; mem. Am. Soc. Aesthetics (pres. 1959-60, 79-80), Coll. Art Assn. Home: 1133 S 7th St Ann Arbor MI 48103

ARNHOFF, FRANKLYN NATHANIEL, psychologist, sociologist, educator; b. N.Y.C., Nov. 6, 1926; s. Abraham A. and Florence Wilner (Arnhoff); m. Lorraine Silver, Dec. 28, 1952; children: Stuart Brett, Gwen Alison. B.S., L.I. U., 1948; M.A., NYU, 1949; Ph.D., Northwestern U., 1953. Clin. psychology intern Elgin State Hosp.,

(Ill.), 1950, NRC fellow, 1950-51; USPHS fellow Northwestern U., Evanston, Ill., 1951-53, research assoc., instr. evening div., 1953-54; instr. med. psychology, chief psychologist adult out-patient services U. Nebr. Coll. Medicine, Omaha, 1954-56; research clin. psychologist VA Hosp., Salisbury, N.C., 1956-57; asst. prof. SUNY Upstate Med. Ctr., Syracuse, 1957-60; assoc. research scientst N.Y. Dept. Mental Hygiene, 1957-60; assoc. prof. psychology U. Miami, (Fla.), 1960-62, research assoc. prof. psychiatry Coll. Medicine, 1960-63; grants assoc. NIH, 1963-64; chief manpower and analytic studies br., div. manpower and tng. programs NIMH, 1964-70; John Edward Fowler prof. psychology U. Va., Charlottesville, 1970—, Univ. prof., 1975—, prof. psychiatry, biomed. engring., anesthesiology, professorial lectr. sociology and anthropology, co-dir. pain studies clinic, head behavioral sci. Coll. Medicine, 1970-75; cons., lectr. in field. Author: Manpower for Mental Health, 1969, Social Consequences of Policy Toward Mental Illness, 1975; The Sociology of Health, 1979, articles, reports. Served with USNR, 1944-46. Fellow Inst. Social Gerontology, U. Mich., 1958. Fellow AAAS, Am. Psychol. Assn.; mem. Am. Sociol. Assn., So. Sociol. Soc., Eastern Psychol. Assn., Am. Acad. Polit. and Social Sci. Jewish. Home: 756 Broomley Rd Charlottesville VA 22901 Office: Cabell Hall U Va Charlottesville VA 22903

ARNING, JOHN FREDRICK, lawyer; b. Lansing, Mich., MaY 4, 1925; s. Clarence W. and Leatha Mae (Stoner) A.; m. Mary Kiver, Apr. 6, 1947; children: Valerie P., John Frederick, William A. LL.B. magna cum laude, Harvard U., 1949. Bar: N.Y. 1949. Assoc. firm Sullivan & Cromwell, N.Y.C., 1949-57, ptnr., 1957—. Mem. ABA, Assn. Bar City N.Y., Union Internationale des Avocats. Home: 201 E 28th St New York NY 10016 Office: Sullivan & Cromwell 125 Broad St New York NY 10004

ARNING, LEE DONCOURT, insurance company executive; b. Palenville, N.Y., Aug. 12, 1923; s. Herman G. and Grace Todd (Doncourt) A.; m. Sarah Louise Deacon, June 12, 1947; children: Charles, Cynthia, Lee Doncourt. B.S. in Bus. Adminstrn, Rutgers U., 1951. With Dun & Bradstreet, Inc., 1947-55; with N.Y. Stock Exchange, 1955-72, sr. v.p., 1971-72; exec. v.p., treas. Tucker, Anthony & R.L. Day, Inc., 1972-76; pres., dir. USLIFE Corp., N.Y.C., 1976-81, vice chmn., dir., 1981—; vice chmn., dir. USLIFE Income Fund, Inc., 1977—; trustee Montclair Savs. Bank, N.J., 1972-76, 80—; bd. dirs. Chgo. Bd. Options Exchange, 1973-75. Chmn. Montclair chpt. ARC, 1975-77; pres. Eagle Rock council Boy Scouts Am., 1956; trustee Montclair Art Mus., 1977—, Mountainside Hosp., Montclair, N.J., 1982; warden, vestryman St. James Episcopal Ch., Montclair, 1963-74; mem. Montclair Bd. Edn., 1966-71, v.p., 1971. Served with AUS, 1942-46. Office: 125 Maiden Ln New York NY 10038:

ARNOFF, E. LEONARD, management scientist and consultant; b. Cleve., Oct. 15, 1922; s. David and and Lena (Mentz) A.; m. Ann Edith Kolisch, Aug. 21, 1948; children: Janice Lee (dec.), Susan Renee. B.S., Western Res. U., 1943; M.S, Case Inst. Tech., 1948; Ph.D., Calif. Inst. Tech., 1951. Mathematician, hydrodynamicist Naval Ordnance Test Station, Pasadena, Calif., 1950-51; mathematician, aero. research scientist NACA, Cleve., 1951-52; prof. ops. research Case Inst. Tech., Cleve., 1952-61; cons. Japanese Govt., U.S. Dept. State, summer 1959; prin., nat. dir. planning and ops. services Ernst & Whinney (C.P.A.s), Cleve., 1960—; instr. Case Inst. Tech., 1946-48; teaching fellow, Inst. scholar Calif. Inst. Tech., 1948-51. Author: Introduction to Operations Research, 17th printing, 1957, (Co-author) also articles.; textbooks.; Editor: Mgmt. Sci, 1955-70. Co-pres. Cleveland Heights PTA, 1964-65; vis. com. Case Western Res. U., 1980—; bd. dirs. Panorama Services and Products. Served with inf. AUS, 1943-46. Decorated Bronze Star, Purple Heart with 2 oak leaf clusters. Fellow Ops. Research Soc. Am., AAAS; mem. Inst. Mgmt. Scis. (internat pres. 1968-69), N.Am. Soc. Corporate Planning, Inst. Mgmt. Cons., Math. Assn. Am., Greater Cleve. Growth Assn., U.S. Figure Skating Assn., Sigma Xi, Omicron Delta Kappa, Beta Alpha Psi., Omega Pho. Clubs: Plaza Figure Skating (pres. 1971-73), Cleve. Skating, Clevelander, Mid-Day, Masons (Cleve.) (master 1961-62). Home: 17150 S Woodland Rd Shaker Heights OH 44120 Office: 2000 National City Center Cleveland OH 44114

ARNOLD, ARMIN HERBERT, German educator; b. Zug, Switzerland, Sept. 1, 1931; s. Franz and Ida (Baumgartner) A. Student, U. Zurich, 1953-54, Queen Mary Coll., U. London, 1954-55; Dr. ès Lettres, U. Fribourg, 1956. Asst. prof. U. Alta., Edmonton, 1959-61; mem. faculty McGill U., Montreal, Que., 1961—, prof. German, 1968—. Author: books on D.H. Lawrence, 1958, 63, 72, Heinrich Heine, 1959, James Joyce, 1963, G.B. Shaw, 1965, Friedrich Durrenmatt, 1969, Expressionism, 1966, 72, Crime Novel, 1978. Mem. Royal Soc. Can. Office: Dept German McGill U 1001 Sherbrooke W Montreal PQ Canada H3A 1G5

ARNOLD, CHARLES BURLE, JR., medical researcher; b. Seattle, Aug. 13, 1934; s. Charles Burle and Ruth Helene (Hadley) A.; m. Sarah J. Slagle, Dec. 16, 1972; children: Geoffrey, Christopher, Jonathan. B.S. cum laude, U. Puget Sound, 1956; M.D., C.M., McGill U., 1960; M.P.H., U. N.C., 1965. Diplomate: Am. Bd. Preventive Medicine. Intern U. Wash. Hosp., Seattle, 1960-61, resident, 1961; physician Peace Corps, La Paz, Bolivia and; Washington, 1961-64; asst. prof. health adminstrn., asso. Carolina Population Center, U. N.C., Chapel Hill, 1965-69; asst. prof. Albert Einstein Coll. Medicine, Bronx, N.Y., 1969-72; prof. public adminstrn. and clin. asso. prof. preventive medicine N.Y. U., N.Y.C., 1972—; lectr. community health Mt. Sinai Med. Sch., N.Y.C.; dir. Mahoney Inst. Health Maintenance, Am. Health Found., 1975-83, v.p. research, 1978-83, cons., 1983—. Assoc. editor: Preventive Medicine Jour, 1975-83; sr. assoc. editor, 1983—; editor: Advances in Disease Prevention, 1981-82; contbr. articles to profl. jours. Milbank Faculty fellow, 1967-74; OEO grantee, 1968-74; Population Council grantee, 1971-75; Health Research Council N.Y.C. grantee, 1972-75; Nat. Cancer Inst. grantee, 1975—; Nat. Heart, Lung and Blood Inst. grantee, 1977—; HEW Office Health Promotion grantee, 1978-80. Fellow Am. Coll. Preventive Medicine (pres. 1977-78); mem. Pan Am. Community Health Assn. (sec. 1971—). Research in fertility, heart disease and cancer, health care services. Home: 25 Forest Ln Scarsdale NY 10583 Office: Am Health Found 320 E 43d St New York NY 10017

ARNOLD, DANNY, writer, director, producer; b. N.Y.C., Jan. 23, 1925; s. Abraham and Esther (Colker) Rothman; m. Donna Cooke, Feb. 16, 1961; children: David, Dannel. Student pub. schs., N.Y.C. Motion picture film editor, 1944-46, actor, 1947-51, writer, 1951—, writer screenplays and TV shows, until 1961; pres. Four D Prodns., Inc., 1958—. Producer, writer, dir.: TV series The Real McCoys, 1961-62, Bewitched, 1963-64, Wackiest Ship in the Army, 1964-65, That Girl, 1967-69, My World and Welcome to It, 1969-70, Barney Miller, 1973-82 (Emmy award as producer 1982), Fish, 1975—. Served with USMC, 1942-44. Recipient Emmy award Acad. TV Arts and Scis., 1970. Mem. Writers Guild Am. West, Screen Actors Guild, Dirs. Guild Am., AFTRA. Club: Brentwood Country. Office: care ABC 1438 N Gower Hollywood CA 90028 *

ARNOLD, DAVID CLEMENT, electronics co. exec.; b. Farson, Iowa, Sept. 28, 1919; s. David Edwin and Hazel (Brown) A.; m. Ann Robel, Mar. 20, 1941; children—Nancy, Susan, John David, Robert Edwin. B.S. in Elec. Engring, Iowa State U., 1942. Engr. Gen. Electric Co., 1942-45, Gilfillan Bros., Los Angeles, 1945-48; chief engr., then dir. research and devel. Collins Radio Co., 1948-59; v.p. Alpha Radio, Richardson, Tex., 1959-61; operations mgr. RCA, Burlington, Mass., 1961-65; v.p., gen. mgr. Hoffman Electronics Corp., El Monte, Calif., 1965, exec. v.p., dir., 1965-66, pres., 1966-70, Conductron Corp., 1970-71; corporate v.p. McDonnell Douglas Corp., 1971—; pres. McDonnell Douglas Electronics Co., 1971—. Mem. IEEE, Electronics Industries Assn. (bd. govs., v.p.), Am. Astronautical Soc., Am. Ordnance Assn. Home: RFD 1 Box 72 Portage Des Sioux MO 63373 Office: 2600 N 3d St Saint Charles MO 63301

ARNOLD, DIANNE EKBERG, banker; b. Kenmare, N.D., Oct. 14, 1944; d. Gustave S. and Helen M. (Nelson) Ekberg; m. Robert A. Arnold, Dec. 19, 1964; children: Dawn, Jeffrey. B.S. in Stats. and Econs., U. Minn., 1966. Ops. analyst First Bank St. Paul, 1966-74, comml. banking officer, 1974-77, asst. v.p., 1977-78, v.p., div. head, 1978-80, sr. v.p., 1980-82, exec. v.p., 1982—; dir. AHW Corp. Trustee Bapt. Hosp. Fund, Inc., 1982-83, Mpls. Soc. Fine Arts, 1982—; exec. devel. center steering com. U. Minn.; exec. bd. Indianhead Council Boy Scouts Am.; adv. com. St. Paul C. of C. Mem. Robert Morris Assocs., Am. Bankers Assn., Minn. Women's Econ. Roundtable (exec. v.p., dir.). Clubs: Minn. of St. Paul (sec.-treas., dir.), St. Paul Athletic). Office: First Bank of Saint Paul 332 Minnesota St Saint Paul MN 55101

ARNOLD, EDDY, singer; b. Henderson, Tenn., May 15, 1918; m. Sally, Nov. 28, 1941; children—Dick, Jo Ann (Mrs. Pollard). Owner Eddy Arnold's Tenn. Fried Chicken, Inc., 1968—. Appeared on, WSM Radio, Nashville, (with Pee Wee King's western band Golden West Cowboys), 1940-43; co-host Grand Ole Opry radio program, 1943-48; guest appearances on: numerous radio shows, including Western Theatre, RCA Victor Show, We the People, Spike Jones Show, Luncheon at Sardi's, Paul Whiteman Show, Breakfast Club; own radio show Checkerboard Square, 1947-55; made: first television appearnce on Milton Berle Show, 1949; appeared in: motion pictures Feudin Rhythm, 1949, Hoedown, 1950; N.Y.C. debut at, Carnegie Hall, 1966; debut at, Coconut Grove nightclub, Los Angeles, 1967, television appearances include shows hosted by, Ed Sullivan, Perry Como, Danny Kaye, Dinah Shore, Danny Thomas, Mike Douglas, Jackie Gleason, Johnny Carson, Les Crane, Dean Martin and, Red Skelton; featured on: TV spls. Profile from the Land, 1968, Kraft Music Hall Spls, 1967, 68, 69, 70, 71; appeared with symphony orchs. of, Hartford, Memphis, Nashville, 1967-68; recordings include Mommy, Please Stay Home With Me, 1945, That's How Much I Love You, Bouquet of Roses, Anytime, I'll Hold You In My Heart, Don't Rob Another Man's Castle, What's He Doing in My World?, Make the World Go Away, The Last Word in Lonesome is Me, Misty Blue, Turn the World Around, Here Comes Heaven; Author: It's a Long Way from Chester County, 1969. Hon. chmn. Tenn. Young Democrats. Named to Country Music Hall of Fame, 1966; Entertainer of Year, 1967. Address: care Gerard W Purcell Assos 133 Fifth Ave New York NY 10003

ARNOLD, EVERETT JOHN, life ins. co. exec.; b. Wisconsin Rapids, Wis., Dec. 4, 1932; s. John George and Margaret Elizabeth (Schroder) A.; m. Bernadeen Evelyn Yonko, June 25, 1955; children—Karoline Kay, Richard Bert. B.B.A. in Accounting, U. Wis., 1958. C.P.A., Wis. Asst. state auditor Wis. Dept. Audit, 1958-61; with Nat. Guardian Life Ins. Co., Madison, Wis., 1961—, v.p., dir. adminstrn., 1969-73, exec. v.p., dir. adminstrn., 1973-74, exec. v.p., treas., 1974—. Mem. budget com., loaned exec. Madison United Way; adv. bd. Madison YWCA; mem. peer rev. com. Wis. Chiropractors Assn. Served with AUS, 1953-54; Korea. Mem. Wis. Soc. C.P.A.s, Life Office Mgmt. Assn. (asso.), Madison C. of C., Beta Alpha Psi. Clubs: Kiwanis, Maple Bluff Country. Home: 4900 Kirkwood Dr Waunakee WI 53597 Office: 2 E Gilman St Madison WI 53703

ARNOLD, G. DEWEY, JR., accountant; b. Montgomery, Ala., Jan. 30, 1925; s. G. Dewey and Janie Esther (Terry) A.; m. Dorothy Louise Wenger, Dec. 4, 1954; children: Susan O., G. Dewey III. B.A. in Econs, U. of South, 1949; postgrad. in acct., U. Tenn. C.P.A., Pa., D.C., Md. With Aladdin Industries, Inc., Nashville, 1949-50; with Price Waterhouse (C.P.A.s), 1950—; ptnr. Price Waterhouse & Co. (C.P.A.s), 1961—, ptn charge Washington office, 1965-76, mem. policy com., 1975-80, regional mng. ptnr., 1976—; instr. acctg. Robert Morris Sch. Acctg., 1952-53; lectr., course dir. mgmt. acctg. Inst. Mexicano de Administracion de Negocias, A.C., 1958-64; bd. dirs. Washington Bd. Trade, 1973-75; mem. audit adv. com. Sec. Navy, 1972-75. Bd. dirs. Jr. C. of C., 1954-55; trustee Fed. City Council, 1966—; bd. dirs. Greater Washington Ednl. TV Assn., Inc., 1970-82, Minority Contractors Center, 1972-74, Redskins Found., 1973—, D.C. Mcpl. Research Bur., 1974-76, Wolf Trap Found., 1975—; chmn. bd. trustees Landon Sch., 1974-79; vice chmn. D.C. BiCentennial Commn., 1971-75. Served with USNR, 1943-45. Mem. Am. Inst. C.P.A.s; mem. D.C. Inst. C.P.A.s; Mem. Nat. Assn. Accts.; mem. Md. Inst. C.P.A.s; Mem. Am. Arbitration Assn. Episcopalian. Clubs: Chevy Chase, Burning Tree, Pine Valley Golf, Metropolitan (Washington); Rolling Rock. Home: 3 Chalfont Ct Bethesda MD 20816 Office: 1801 K St NW Washington DC 20006

ARNOLD, GARY HOWARD, film critic; b. Princeton, Ind., Aug. 22, 1942; s. Charles Howard and Ferris (Smith) A.; m. Sue Datz, Dec. 29, 1967; children—Pauline, Jane, Esther. Student, N.Y.U., 1959-60, U. Calif. at Berkeley, 1960-63. Film critic Diplomat mag., 1966; film critic, reporter Ind. Film Jour., 1968-69; film critic Washington Post, 1969—. Home: 5133 N 1st St Arlington VA 22203 Office: 1150 15th St NW Washington DC 20005

ARNOLD, HARRY BARTLEY, lawyer; b. Columbus, Ohio, Aug. 27, 1912; s. Harry Bartley and Grace (Russell) A.; m. Mary Jane Hubbard, July 8, 1936 (dec.); children—Thomas Bartley, Susan Hubbard Arnold Baumgartner (dec.), Nancianne Arnold Below, Katherine Arnold Wade; m. Barbara Miller Boothby, July 28, 1972. A.B. summa cum laude, Princeton U., 1933; LL.B., Yale U., 1936. Bar: Ohio bar 1936. Since practiced in, Columbus; of counsel firm Porter & Wright; dir. Midland Mut. Life Ins. Co., Columbus, 1951-83, asst. counsel, 1956-62, asso. counsel, 1962-69, v.p., gen. counsel, 1969-79, gen. counsel emeritus, 1979—. Chmn. screening com. Columbus United Appeal, 1965; chmn. budget and admissions com. United Community Council Columbus, 1958-59, trustee, 1958-65, pres., 1961-63; mem. Nat. Budget and Consultation Com. Nat. Health and Welfare Agys., 1958-61; trustee Children's Hosp., Columbus, 1959-76, Columbus Acad., 1938-62; pres. Columbus Acad., 1948-55; trustee Columbus Symphony Orch., 1964-67; mem. grad. bd. Yale Law Sch., 1957-59; trustee Columbus YMCA, 1937-63, exec. com., 1948-56, 1st v.p., 1956. Served to lt. USNR, 1942-46; PTO. Recipient George Meany Community Service award Franklin County (Ohio) AFL-CIO, 1962. Fellow Am. Coll. Trial Lawyers; mem. Am., Ohio, Columbus bar assns., Assn. Life Ins. Counsel, Am. Judicature Soc. Republican. Clubs: Columbus Country, Rocky Fork Hunt and Country (Columbus); Castalia (Ohio) Trout; Naples Yacht, Hole-in-the-Wall Golf (Naples, Fla.); Princeton of Central Ohio (pres. 1959-62). Home: 9351 Harlem Rd Westerville OH 43081 Office: Huntington Trust Bldg Columbus OH 43215

ARNOLD, HARRY LOREN, JR., dermatologist, editor, author; b. Owosso, Mich., Aug. 7, 1912; s. Harry L. and Meda (Sheldon) A.; m. Blanche G. Wetherald, 1934 (div. 1941); m. Jeanne M. Prevost, July 11, 1942; children: Sara Joan, Charles R., Harry Loren III, John P., Susan M.; m. Jeanne S. Herman, Dec. 16, 1983. A.B. cum laude, U. Mich., 1932, M.D., 1935; M.S., 1939. Diplomate: Am. Bd. Dermatology (mem. bd. 1966-76, pres. 1972-73). Intern U. Mich. Hosp., 1935-36, resident, 1936-37, instr. dermatology, 1937-39; chief dermatology Straub Clinic, Honolulu, 1939-69; clin. prof. dermatology U. Hawaii.; Pres. Straub Med. Research Inst., 1961-63; Frederick G. Novy, Jr. vis. scholar in dermatology U. Calif. Med. Sch., Davis, 1975; cons. emeritus Tripler Army Med. Center, 1980. Author: Modern Concepts of Leprosy, 1953, Raibyo Gentaiteki Gainen, 1956, (with P. Fasal) Leprosy, 1973, (with A. Domonkos and R.B. Odom) Andrews' Diseases of the Skin, 7th edit, 1981; also numerous articles, editorials, columns, and chpts. in textbooks.; Editor: Hawaii Med. Jour, 1941—, Straub Clinic Procs, 1941-77; editor emeritus, 1978—, The Schoch Letter, 1975—, Soc. Trans., Internat. Jour. Dermatology, 1978—; corr. editor: Internat. Jour. of Leprosy, 1950—; editorial bd.: Cutis, 1965—, Group Practice, 1966-74, Jour. Internat. Med. Research, 1972—, Archives Dermatology, 1973-83, Jour. AMA, 1973-74. Named Practitioner of Yr. Dermatol. Found., 1983. Fellow A.C.P., AAAS, Royal Soc. Medicine; mem. Hawaii Med. Assn. (past pres.), Honolulu County Med. Assn. (past pres.), Hawaiian Acad. Sci. (past pres.), Am. Acad. Dermatology (hon.; pres. 1975-76), Internat. Soc. Tropical Dermatology (past v.p.), Internat. Leprosy Assn., Hawaii Dermatol. Soc., Pacific Dermatol. Soc. (hon. mem., pres. 1968), AMA (past del., sect. chmn., del. sect. dermatology), Am. Dermatol. Assn. (bd. dirs. 1969-70, pres. 1971), Phila. Coll. Physicians (corr.), Sociedad Argentina de Leprología (corr.), Sociedad Cubana de Dermatología y Sifilografía (corr.), Asociacion Argentina de Dermatología (corr.), Sociedad Venezolana de Dermatología, Venereología y Leprología (corr.), Sociedad Mexicana de Dermatología (hon.), Sociedad Brasileira de Dermatologia (hon.), S. African Dermatol. Assn. (hon.), N.Y. Dermatol. Assn. (hon.), Swedish Dermatol. Soc. (corr.), Honolulu chpt. Internat. Wine and Food Soc. (pres. 1977), Social Sci. Assn. Honolulu (pres. 1984), Sigma Xi, Kappa Beta Phi, Alpha Omega Alpha, Nu Sigma Nu, Phi Kappa Psi, Zeta Psi. Home: 250 Laurel St Apt 301 San Francisco CA 94118 Office: Queens Physicians Office Bldg 1380 Lusitana St 412 Honolulu HI 96813 *I have for most of my life tried to act toward others as I'd like them to act toward me; to accept responsibilities when asked, and to do my best with them; to be tolerant, moderate, and punctual.*

ARNOLD, HASKELL N., JR., state official; b. Savannah, Ga., July 20, 1945; s. Haskell N. Arnold, Sr. and Rosalyn J. Griffin; m. Linda Hebron Grayson, July 30, 1966; children: Shaun, Tia. B.S. in Acctg, Hampton Inst., 1966; M.B.A., Harvard U., 1971; postgrad. in public utility mgmt, Ga. Inst. Tech., 1976. C.P.A., Md. Staff auditor Arthur Andersen & Co., Washington, 1971-72; controller H.G. Parks, Inc., Balt., 1972-74; mgr. corp. budget adminstrn. Potomac Electric Power Co., Washington, 1974-76; v.p. fin. Public Broadcasting Service, Washington, 1977-80; commr. Md. Public Service Commn., Balt., 1980—. Coach Columbia (Md.) Youth Basketball League, 1978-80; mem. black exec. exchange program Nat. Urban League.; active Boy Scouts Am., United Way of Central Md. Served with U.S. Army, 1967-69. Mem. Am. Inst. C.P.A.s, D.C. Inst. C.P.A.s, Kappa Alpha Psi., Beta Gamma Sigma. Democrat. Presbyterian. Club: Harvard Bus. Sch. (Balt.). Office: 231 E Baltimore St Suite 1500 Baltimore MD 21202 *

ARNOLD, HENRI, cartoonist; b. Bethlehem, Pa., Oct. 15, 1918; s. Samuel Max and Dora (Schnur) A.; m. Harriet Chefetz, Feb. 14, 1980; children by previous marriage—Nora Sally, Ned Michael. Student, Cooper Union, 1946. Editorial/sports cartoonist Bridgeport (Conn.) Sun. Herald, 1941; author weekly humor page Chgo. Tribune, 1955-65; art dir. Chgo. Tribune-N.Y. News Syndicate, Inc., N.Y.C., 1957-77; lectr. in field. Creator: This Man's Army, N.Y. Sun. News, 1954-64; writer/cartoonist for: Ching Chow, 1977—; co-producer: Jumble, That Scrambled Word Game, 1960—; Illustrator: (Tommy Armour) The ABC's of Golf, 1967, 22 vols. of Jumble, That Scrambled Word Game, 1962—. Served with USAAF, 1942-45. Mem. Nat. Cartoonists Soc., Artists and Writers Guild. Club: Tamarack Country. Office: Tribune Co Syndicate Inc 220 E 42d St New York NY 10017

ARNOLD, HERBERT ANTON, educator; b. Buchau, June 23, 1935; U.S., naturalized, 1963; s. Josef and Maria (Rothberger) A.; m. Annemarie Stuck, Feb. 11, 1961; children: Bettina, Corinna Maria, Christiane Vivian. Abitur, Oberrealschule Kaufbeuren, 1956; Staatsexamen, Julius-Maximilians U., Wurzburg, Germany, 1962, Dr. phil., 1966; M.A., Wesleyan U., 1980. Teaching asst. Liverpool (Eng.) Collegiate, 1959-60; referendar Siebold Realgymnasium, Wurzburg, 1962-63; instr. Wesleyan U., Middletown, Conn., 1963-66, asst. prof., 1966-72, 1972-80, prof. dept. German lang. and lit., 1980—, dir. Wesleyan Program in Germany., 1967-69, 73, 81, 82, chmn. dept. German, 1982—. Author: N. Chamberlain's Appeasement Policy, 1966. Trustee Am. Field Service, N.Y.C., 1970-73, 81-83, chmn. bd. dirs, N.Y.C., 1979-81. Mem. Am. Assn. Tchrs. German (pres. 1975-76), MLA, Western Assn. German Studies, Am. Hist. Assn. Home: 1 Edwards Rd Portland CT 06480 Office: Wesleyan U Middletown CT 06457

ARNOLD, JAMES RICHARD, chemist, educator; b. New Brunswick, N.J., May 5, 1923; s. Abraham Samuel and Julia (Jacobs) A.; m. Louise Clark, Oct. 11, 1952; children: Robert C., Theodore J., Kenneth C. A.B., Princeton U., 1943, M.A., 1945, Ph.D., 1946. Postdoctoral fellow Inst. Nuclear Studies, U. Chgo., 1946-47, mem. faculty, 1948-55; NRC fellow Harvard U., 1947-48; mem. faculty chemistry Princeton U., 1955-58; asso. prof. chemistry U. Calif., San Diego, 1958-60, prof., 1960—, Harold C. Urey prof., 1983—, chmn. dept. chemistry, 1960-63; asso. Manhattan Project, 1943-46; dir. Calif. Space Inst., 1980—; mem. various bds. NASA, 1959—; mem. space sci. bd. Nat. Acad. Sci., 1970-74, mem. com. on sci. and public policy, 1973-77. Mem. editorial bd.: Ann. Rev. Nuclear Chemistry, 1972; asso. editor: Revs. Geophysics and Space Physics, 1972-75, Moon, 1972—; contbr. articles to profl. jours. Pres. Torrey Pines Elem. Sch. PTA, 1964-65; pres. La Jolla Democratic Club, 1965-66; mem. nat. council World Federalists-U.S.A., 1970-72. Recipient E.O. Lawrence medal AEC, 1968; Leonard medal Meteoritical Soc., 1976; asteroid 2143 named Jimarnold in his honor, 1980; Guggenheim fellow, India, 1972-73. Mem. Nat. Acad. Sci., Am. Acad. Arts and Scis., Am. Chem. Soc., AAAS, Fedn. Am. Scientists, World Federalist Assn., Internat. Acad. Astronautics (corr.).

ARNOLD, JAMES ROMER, mgmt. cons.; b. Chgo., May 8, 1933; s. William Joseph and Beatrice (Romer) A.; m. June Lenore Clissold, Aug. 18, 1956; children—Kathryn Anne, Douglas Joseph, Robert Clissold. B.S., Denison U., Granville, Ohio, 1955; M.B.A., Northwestern U., 1957. Asst. to exec. v.p. McGraw-Edison Co., Elgin, Ill., 1960-65; officer No. Trust Co., Chgo., 1965-67; pres. Kearney Exec. Search div.; also officer, mem. mgmt. com. parent co. A.T. Kearnney, Inc., Chgo., 1967—; mem. dean's adv. com. U. Ill. Sch. Bus., 1976—. Served to 1st lt. AUS, 1957-60. Mem. Assn. Exec. Recruiting Cons. (exec. v.p., dir. 1980-81). Republican. Mem. Glenview Community Ch. Clubs: Tower (Chgo.); Westmoreland Country. Office: 222 S Riverside Plaza Chicago IL 60606

ARNOLD, KENNETH LLOYD, publisher, playwright; b. Washington, Mar. 29, 1944; s. Lloyd Cecil and Violet Henrietta (Workman) A.; m. Susan Thomson Viguers, Apr. 26, 1975; children: Nicholas Viguers, Ruth Viguers. B.A., Lynchburg Coll., 1966; M.A.,

Johns Hopkins U., 1967. Asst. adv. mgr. John Hopkins U. Press, Balt., 1967-70, social sci. editor, 1970-74; editor in chief Temple U. Press, Phila., 1974-82; dir. Rutgers U. Press, New Brunswick, N.J., 1982—. Author: plays Pope Joan, 1976, The House of Bedlam, 1978, She Also Dances, 1980, Wanting Marie, 1982. Woodrow Wilson fellow, 1966; Eugene O'Neill Nat. Playwright Eugene O'Neill Theatre Center, Waterford, Conn., 1979. Mem. Dramatist's Guild. Democrat. Episcopalian. Home: 6363 Germantown Ave Philadelphia PA 19144 Office: Rutgers U Press 30 College Ave New Brunswick NJ 08103

ARNOLD, MARGARET LONG (MRS. DEXTER OTIS ARNOLD), association executive; b. Lusk, Wyo., Aug. 15, 1914; d. S. Burman and Margaret M (Hoch) Long; m. Dexter Otis Arnold, June 27, 1939. A.B., Syracuse U., 1934; LL.D. (hon.), New Eng. Coll., 1951. Dir. speech and dramatics Syracuse Schs., 1935-39; pres. N.H. Fedn. Women's Clubs, 1950-52; chmn. UN specialized agys. Gen. Fedn. Women's Clubs, 1952-54, communications dept., 1954-56, rec. sec., 1956—, 1st v.p., 1960, pres., 1962-64, hon. pres., 1964—; asst. exec. dir. Nat. Ret. Tchrs. Assn./Am. Assn. Ret. Persons, 1974, now exec. asst. for women's activities; also daily radio commentator. Chmn. N.H. Council Problems of Aging; mem. nat. adv. com. White House Conf. on Aging; vice chmn. Nat. Conf. on Citizenship; chmn. Def. Adv. Com. on Women in the Services; N.Y. State chmn. Continuing Edn. Council; mem. N.Y. Council Women, N.Y. Council on Aging, Fed. Council on Aging, U.S. Interdeptl. Adv. Council on Status of Women, Citizens Council Status of Women, N.Y. State Council Continuing Edn.; v.p. Washington Forum; dir. Nat. Women's Party, Council World Affairs; dir., v.p. CARE, N.H. Social Welfare Council, Old Ft. No. 4, N.Y. World's Fair; bd. govs. Arthritis and Rheumatism Found.; bd. visitors Am. Freedom Center, Freedoms Found. at Valley Forge; trustee Am. Freedom from Hunger Found., Inc.; chmn. bd. Outstanding Young Women Am.; bd. dirs. Girls' Clubs Am., USO, Mid Hudson Patterns for Progress; alumni council rep. Syracuse Univ. Named N.H. Distinguished Citizen; recipient Pettee medal U. N.H.; Arents medal U. Syracuse; Nat. Recognition award Freedoms Found.; Alumni award 4-H, 1966. Mem. Ch. Women's Assn., Concord Hosp. Assn. (v.p. 1952-53), Nat. Press Club, Am. Newspaper Women's Club, LWV, AAUW, Nat. Laymens League (dir.), Delta Gamma (past nat. officer). Presbyterian. Home: Apt 1406 Watergate West 2700 Virginia Ave Washington DC 20037

ARNOLD, MARTIN, journalist; b. N.Y.C., May 14, 1929; s. A.M. and Evelyn (Goodman) A.; m. Irmgard Alexy, May 25, 1952; children: Mark William, Christopher Curt. B.A., Adelphi Coll., 1951. With Newsday, 1952-54, N.Y. Herald Tribune, 1954-59; reporter N.Y. Times, 1959-76, asst. met. editor, 1976-77; asst. editor Mag., 1977-83, dep. editor, 1983—. Friend of Robert F. Kennedy Meml. Found. Served with AUS, 1946-48. Recipient George Polk award for polit. reporting, 1968; Page One award for feature writing N.Y. Newspaper Guild, 1970; Press award Am. Bar Assn., 1974. Mem. Acad. Polit. Sci. Soaring Soc. Am. Office: 229 W 43d St New York NY 10036

ARNOLD, MELVIN CHESTER, paper products manufacturing company executive; b. Toledo, Mar. 8, 1923; s. Chester E. and Esther (Lauffer) A.; m. Margaret Scott, Apr. 23, 1976; children: Douglas McDonald, David Lauffer, Barbara Jean, Melvin Chester, Mark Emerick, Wendy Lauretta, Francis John, Julie Ann. B.S., Ohio State U., 1944; LL.B., U. Toledo, 1948. Bar: Ohio 1949, Nebr. 1953. Legal counsel Toledo Scale Corp., 1946-52; sec., dir. Omaha Retinning Corp., 1955-59; sec., treas., dir. Omaha Foods Inc., 1957-59; legal consel Omar, Inc., Omaha, 1953-59; sec., assoc. counsel Eaton Corp., Cleve., 1959-67, v.p., gen. counsel, 1967-73, exec. v.p. law and corp. relations, Cleve., 1973—; dir. St. John del Rey Mining Co p.l.c., (Brazil). Bd. dirs. Bus. Council for Internat. Understanding, Cleve. State U. Devel. Found.; chmn. bd. trustees Cleve. State U.; bd. dirs. Greater Cleve. Growth Assn.; mem. Internat. Mgmt. and Devel. Inst.; former chmn. Met. Cleve. JOBS Council; bd. dirs. U.S. Yugoslav Econ. Council; chmn. Pvt. Industry Council Cleve.; co-chmn. Greater Cleve. Roundtable. Mem. Am., Ohio, Cleve. bar assns., NAM (dir.), Ohio Mfrs. Assn. (trustee), Alpha Tau Omega. Clubs: Mayfield Country (trustee), Pepper Pike, Union, Cleveland Playhouse, Clevelander (trustee), Mid-Day (Cleve.); Wilderness Country (Naples, Fla.). Home: 10401 Lake Shore Blvd Bratenahl OH 44108 Office: 100 Erieview Plaza Cleveland OH 44114

ARNOLD, MORRIS FAIRCHILD, bishop; b. Mpls., Jan. 5, 1915; s. LeRoy and Kate (Fairchild) A.; children: Jaqueline Fairchild (Mrs. Arnold Crocker), William Morris; m. Harriet Borda Schmidgall, 1978. B.A. magna cum laude, Williams Coll., 1936; M.Div. cum laude, Episcopal Theol. Sch., 1940; D.D., Kenyon Coll., 1961, Williams Coll., 1972. Ordained priest Episcopal Ch., 1940; priest-in-charge St. John's Ch., Saugus, Mass., 1940-43; chaplain U.S. Army, 1943-45; rector Grace Ch., Medford, Mass., 1945-50; Episcopal students chaplain Tufts Coll., Boston, 1945-50; rector Christ Ch., Cin., 1950-72; consecrated suffragan bishop, 1972; suffragan bishop Episcopal Diocese of Mass., 1972—. Del. to Anglican Congress from So. Ohio, 1954; dep. to 7 Gen. Convs. of Episcopal Ch., 1958-70; co-founder U.S. Ch. and City Conf., 1959, pres., 1964-66; mem. Joint Commn. on Edn. for Holy Orders, 1961-68; program and budget com. of Episcopal Ch., 1961-70, 77-80; pres. Council of Chs. of Greater Cin., 1961-63; treas. Cin. Met. Area Religious Coalition, 1968-72; v.p. Episcopal City Mission, Boston, 1972—; Trustee ARC, 1957-63, Family Service, 1962-71, Better Housing League, 1951-72; mem. Cathedral Deans Assn., 1955-72; mem. steering com. Urban Bishop's Coalition, 1977—. Mem. Soc. for the Relief of Aged or Disabled Clergymen (v.p. 1972—), Alumni Assn. Episcopal Theol. Sch. (pres. 1969-72), Phi Beta Kappa, Delta Phi. Home: 445 Pleasant St Belmont MA 02178

ARNOLD, PAUL BEAVER, artist, educator; b. T'aiyuanfu, Shansi, China, Nov. 24, 1918; s. Roger David and Eleanor (Tracy) A.; m. Sarah Ann Clagett, May 29, 1942; children: Margaret C., Tacie L., Juduth L., Kemper D. A.B., Oberlin Coll., 1940, M.A., 1941; M.F.A. (Ford Found. fellow), U. Minn., 1955. Instr. fine arts Oberlin (Ohio) Coll., 1941-42, instr. to prof., 1946—, Young-Hunter prof. art, 1982—, acting chmn. dept. fine arts, 1967-68, chmn., 1970-72, 73-79; dir. NDEA East Asian Lang. and Area Center, 1967-68; project dir. Peace Corps Tng. Program, summer 1964-65; dir. Taiwan Summer Chinese Lang. Program, 1969; preceptor U. Minn., 1951; vis. prof. architecture dept. Tunghai U., Taichung, Taiwan, 1973; vis. prof. Sarah Lawrence Coll., Lacoste, France, 1979, 80. Exhibited in one man shows at Allen Art Mus., Oberlin, 1946, 62, Ohio U., Athens, 1953, Cleve. Inst. Art, 1955, Ohio State U., 1956, 63, Bates Coll., Lewiston, Maine, 1957, Lafayette (Ind.) Art Assn., 1959, Purdue U., U. Mont., Bluffton (Ohio) Coll., 1960, Ashland (Ohio) Coll., 1963, Jewish Center, Columbus, Ohio, 1964, Jersey City State Coll., 1966, 78, Mt. Herman (Mass.) Sch., 1967, Northfield (Mass.) Sch., May Co., Cleveland Heights, Ohio, Lorain County Community Coll., Elyria, Ohio, 1968, 74, Miami U., Oxford, Ohio, 1968, Laurel Sch., Cleve., 1969, Summer Gallery, Wattsburg, Pa., Hiram (Ohio) Coll., 1970, U. Kans., Northwestern Mich. Coll., Traverse City, 1974, 78, Design Corner Gallery, Cleve., 1974, Heidelberg Coll., Tiffin, Ohio, 1975, Traverse City Arts Center, 1978, Barton Center, Cleve., 1981, Chautauqua (N.Y.) Art Center, numerous group shows at galleries, museums and schs., 1942—; represented in permanent collections at, Seattle Art Mus., Library of Congress, Dayton Art Inst., Butler Art Inst., Brooks Meml. Collection, Memphis, Univ. Gallery, U. Minn., Allen Art Mus., Canton (Ohio) Art Inst., Cleve. Mus. Art, Wadsworth Atheneum, Hartford, Conn., Balt. Mus., DePauw U. Mus., U. Kans. Mus.; executed murals Adminstrn. Bldg., Gilford Instrument Labs., Oberlin, 1971, Student Union, Oberlin Coll., 1973; co-author: Zoning Ordinance, Oberlin, 1959; Author: Pheasant, 1956, White Peacock, 1957, (with others) The Humanities at Oberlin, 1957; Illustrator: General Chemistry, 1955, Laboratory Experiments, 1955, also articles. Mem. Oberlin Zoning Bd. Appeals, 1955-57; chmn. Oberlin Planning Commn., 1960-61, 63-65; mem. Oberlin City Council, 1968-69; bd. dirs. Karamu Found.; chmn. bd. trustees Oberlin Shansi Meml. Assn., 1974-76. Served with AUS, 1942-46. Recipient Oberlin Coll. Research Status award, 1965-66, also numerous art prizes; Gt. Lakes Colls. Assn. Non-Western Studies grantee, 1965-66. Mem. Nat. Assn. Schs. of Art and Design (dir. 1970-80, 82—, pres. 1975-78), Mid-Am. Coll. Art Assn. (exec. bd. 1963-66), Coll. Art Assn. (dir. 1979—, sec. 1982-84, v.p. 1984—). Republican. Mem. United Ch. of Christ. Office: Dept Art Oberlin Coll Oberlin OH 44074

ARNOLD, PHILIP MILLS, retired oil company executive; b. Springfield, Mo., Feb. 9, 1911; s. Anthony L. and Mary Genevieve (Hodnett) A. B.S., Washington U., 1932, Chem. E., 1941, Sc.D. hon., 1983. Chem. engr. research div. Philips Petroleum Co., 1937-45, asst. mgr. chem. engring. div., 1946-48, asst. mgr. chem. dept., 1948-50, mgr. research and devel. dept., 1950-64, v.p. research and devel., 1964-76; Exec. com. div. chemistry and chem. tech. NRC, 1961-65; mem. U.S. nat. com. Internat. Union Pure and Applied Chemistry, 1961-75, chmn., 1964-68, mem. bur., 1969-75; dir. Coordinating Research Council, 1964, pres., 1969-71, Indsl. Research Inst., 1964-65, bd. dirs., 1958-61; mem. Com. on Scholarly Communication with People's Republic of China. Mem. World Petroleum Congresses (permanent council 1965-71), AAAS, Dirs. Indsl. Research, Nat. Acad. Engring., Sigma Chi, Tau Beta Pi, Alpha Chi Sigma. Republican. Home: Box 1457 Bartlesville OK 74005

ARNOLD, RALPH MOFFETT, artist; b. Chgo., Dec. 5, 1928; s. Roy Ralph and Bertha Ethel (Harris) A. B.A., Roosevelt U., 1955; M.F.A., Art Inst. Chgo., 1977. Asst. prof. art Rockford (Ill.) Coll., 1969-70; asst. prof. art Barat Coll., Lake Forest, Ill., also acting chmn. art dept., 1970-72; asst. prof. art Loyola U., Chgo., 1972—, also chmn. dept. fine arts. One man shows, Benjamin Gallery, Chgo., 1966-68, Gilman Galleries, 1969-71, Van Stratten Galleries, Chgo., 1971, Ill. Arts Council, Chgo., 1970, Chgo. State Coll., 1982, Loyola U., Chgo., 1983; exhibited in group shows, Mus. Contemporary Art, Chgo., 1969, Mus. Art, Utica, N.Y., 1970, Whitney Mus. Am. Art, 1971, Fisk U., 1972, Ill. State Mus., 1971; represented in permanent collections, Whitney Mus., N.Y.C., Rockford (Ill.) Coll., Fisk U., Johnson Publs., First Nat. Bank of Chgo., Tuesday Found. Mem. community youth project Ill. Arts Council, 1970. Served with AUS, 1951-53; Korea. Home: 1858 N Sedgwick St Chicago IL 60614

ARNOLD, RICHARD KEITH, educator, forester; b. Long Beach, Calif., Nov. 17, 1913; s. Park and Mayme F. (Swan) A.; m. Helen Louise DuBose, Feb. 7, 1942 (dec. 1970); children: Bruce Gaillard, Richard Park, Jay Ross; m. Lilliam C. DeAngelis, Oct. 24, 1970. A.A., Glendale Jr. Coll., 1935; B.S., U. Calif.-Berkeley, 1937; M.F., Yale U., 1938; Ph.D., U. Mich., 1950. Asso. in forestry U. Calif.-Berkeley, 1939-41, asst. prof. forestry, 1946-51, 53-55; forester Forest Service U.S. Dept. Agr., Berkeley, 1951-53, chief of fire research, 1955-57; dir. Pacific S.W. Forest Expt. Sta., 1957-63; dir. div. Forest Protection Research, Forest Service U.S. Dept. Agr., Washington, 1963-66, dep. chief research, 1969-73; dean Sch. Natural Resources, U. Mich., Ann Arbor, 1966-69; asso. dean Lyndon B. Johnson Sch. Pub. Affairs, U. Tex., Austin, 1974-76, asst. v.p.-research, 1976-79, dir. div. natural resources and environ., 1974-76; Cons. CD and fire research State of Calif., 1949-54; U.S. mem. FAO Com. on Forestry Edn., 1968-69; mem. adv. com. Yale U. Sch. Forestry, 1969—; chmn. fire working group N.Am. Forestry Commn., 1965-66. Mem. Mich. Gov.'s Commn. on Urban Affairs, 1968. Served to lt. USNR, 1942-46. Fellow Soc. Am. Foresters (pres. 1975-77); mem. Internat. Union Forestry Research Orgns., Internat. Union Socs. Foresters, AAAS, Am. Forestry Assn., Sigma Xi, Phi Beta Kappa. Club: Kiwanis. Home: 23 Santana Way Hot Springs Village AR 71909

ARNOLD, RICHARD SHEPPARD, judge; b. Texarkana, Tex., Mar. 26, 1936; s. Richard Lewis and Janet (Sheppard) A.; children: Janet Sheppard, Lydia Palmer; m. Kay Kelley, Oct. 27, 1979. B.A. summa cum laude, Yale U., 1957; J.D. magna cum laude, Harvard U., 1960. Bar: D.C. 1961, Ark. 1960. Practiced in Washington, 1961-64, Texarkana, 1964-74; law clk. to Justice Brennan, Supreme Ct. U.S., 1960-61; asso. Covington & Burling, 1961-64; partner Arnold & Arnold, 1964-74; legis. sec. Gov. of Ark., 1973-74, staff coordinator, 1974; legis. asst. Senator Bumpers of Ark., Washington, 1975-78; judge U.S. Dist. Ct. Eastern and Western Dists. Ark., 1978-80, U.S. Ct. Appeals 8th Circuit, Little Rock, 1980—; part-time instr. U. Va. Law Sch., 1962-64; mem. Ark. Constl. Revision Study Commn., 1967-68. Case editor: Harvard Law Rev., 1959-60; contbr. articles to profl. jours. Gen. chmn. Texarkana United Way Crusade, 1969-70; pres. Texarkana Community Chest, 1970-71; mem. overseers com. Harvard Law Sch., 1973-79; candidate for Congress 4th Dist. Ark., 1966, 72; del. Democratic Nat. Conv., 1968, Ark. Constl. Conv., 1969-70; chmn. rules com. Ark. Dem. Com., 1968-74, mem. exec. com., 1972-74; mem. Com. on Legis. Orgn., 1971-72; trustee U. Ark., 1973-74. Mem. Am. Law Inst., Cum Laude Soc., Phi Beta Kappa. Episcopalian. Home: 3901 Cedar Hill Rd No 5 Little Rock AR Office: US Court of Appeals PO Box 429 Little Rock AR 72203

ARNOLD, RICHARD THOMAS, educator; b. Indpls., June 18, 1913; s. Robert Henry and Sarah Anne (Jones) A.; m. Doris Marie Madsen, Sept. 1, 1939; children—Mary Lyn, Robert Henry. B.E., So. Ill. State Tchrs. Coll., 1934; M.S., U. Ill., 1935, Ph.D., 1937; D.Sc. (hon.), Northwestern U., 1979. Research fellow U. Ill., 1936-37; became mem. faculty U. of Minn., 1937, prof. chemistry, 1946, head dept. chemistry, 1953-55; program adminstr., basic research in phys. sci. Alfred P. Sloan Found., N.Y.C., 1955-60; dir. research Mead Johnson & Co., 1960, v.p. in charge research, 1961-62, v.p., chmn. sci. adv. bd., 1968—; pres. Mead Johnson Research Center, 1962—, Organic Syntheses, 1970—; prof., chmn. dept. chemistry So. Ill. U., 1969—; sci. adviser to U.S. High Commr., Germany, 1952-53. Recipient award in pure chem. Am. Chem. Soc., 1949; Guggenheim fellow, 1948. Mem. Am. Chem. Soc., A.A.A.S., Phi Beta Kappa, Sigma Xi, Alpha Chi Sigma. Home: 5 Heritage Rd Carbondale IL 62901

ARNOLD, ROBERT MORRIS, banker; b. Seattle, June 6, 1928; s. Lawrence Moss and Grace Elizabeth (Heffernan) A.; children: Grace Allen, Lauren McLellan. B.A. in Fin. and Bus. Adminstrn, Yale U., 1951; grad., Pacific Coast Sch. Banking, 1963. With Seattle-First Nat. Bank, 1951, 55—, v.p., 1965-73, mgr. nat. accounts dept., 1969-73, dir., 1969—, sr. v.p., mgr. corp. bus. devel., 1973—; dir. Societe Candy Co. Bd. dirs. Centrum Found., Fred C. Hutchinson Cancer Research Center; mem. joint founder Contemporary Art Council of Seattle Art Mus.; trustees Poncho; bd. dirs. exec. com., fin. com. Seattle Art Mus. Served as officer USNR, 1951-55. Mem. Am. Inst. Banking, Mcpl. League Seattle, Yale Assn. Western Wash., Newcomen Soc. (treas. Pacific N.W. com.). Republican. Clubs: Seattle Golf, Seattle Tennis, Seattle Yacht, Harbor (a founder), Rainier; University (Seattle and San Francisco); Bohemian (San Francisco). Home: 1535 Parkside Dr E Seattle WA 98112 Office: 1004 4th Ave Seattle WA 91804

ARNOLD, ROBERT MOSES, public relations consultant, business editor; b. Wilkinsburg, Pa., Dec. 15, 1948; s. Robert Hickman and Helen Elizabeth (Moses) A. B.S. in Journalism, W.Va. U., 1970; M.A., New Sch. for Social Research, 1976. Editor front page Morgantown (W.Va.) Dominion-News, 1968-70; sr. editor, account exec. Alexander Co. (pub. relations), N.Y.C., 1970-78; pres. Riverside Services (editorial and communications cons.), N.Y.C., 1978—; sr. editor Mktg. Times; dir. fin. relations Churchill Group, N.Y.C.; cons. pub. relations Sales and Mktg. Execs. Internat., The Maleck Group, Lincoln Logs, Ltd., Lifeboat Assos. Author: booklet The Greening of West Virginia; film documentaries Protecting Your Healthy Home; Contbr. to: Investment Dealers Digest. Mem. Pub. Relations Soc. Am., Publicity Club N.Y., Sigma Delta Chi. Presbyn. (pres. bd. trustees, ruling elder). Home: 617 W 113th St New York NY 10025 Office: 239 E 32d St New York NY 10016

ARNOLD, STANLEY RICHARD, lawyer; b. Los Angeles, Apr. 20, 1932; s. Aaron Leon and Lucille May (Singer) A.; m. Jennie Ann Sabow, June 16, 1962; children: Abby Sue, James Andrew, Kathryn Rose, Julianna Marie. Student, UCLA, 1949-52; A.B., Stanford U., 1953, J.D., 1955; LL.M., McGill U., 1956. Bar: Calif. 1956. Practiced in, Los Angeles, 1959—; trial atty. Dryden, Harrington, Horgan & Swartz, 1959-61; mem. firm Stapleton, Weinberg & Isen, 1961-63; partner firm Goldman, Goldman & Arnold, Los Angeles, 1967-75, Arnold & Fink, Encino, Calif., 1976-79; prin. Stanley R. Arnold (P.C., Encino), 1979—; mem. bus. law arbitration panel Los Angeles Superior Ct. Mem. exec. com. Los Angeles County Com. to Re-Elect Pres., 1972—; Los Angeles chmn. Spl. Com. to Re-Elect Pres., 1972. Served to capt. USAF, 1956-59. Mem. Comml. Law League Am., State Bar Calif., San Fernando Valley Bar Assn., Am., Los Angeles bus. trial lawyers assns., Assn. Trial Lawyers Am., Internat. Bar Assn., Am. Arbitration Assn. (arbitrator), B'nai B'rith (past pres.). Office: 15910 Ventura Blvd Suite 1606 Encino CA 91436 also One Century Plaza 2029 Century Park E 6th Floor Los Angeles CA 90067

ARNOLD, TERRELL E. S., foreign service officer; b. Bluefield, W.Va., Dec. 14, 1925; s. Carl Eugene and Mary Elizabeth (Craven) A.; m. Yvonne Iris Wright, Nov. 25, 1951. A.B., Stanford U., 1953; M.A., San Jose (Calif.) State Coll., 1958. Tchr. English and pub. speaking Fremont High Sch., Oakland, Calif., 1954-56; joined U.S. Fgn. Service, 1957; analyst Bur. Intelligence and Research, State Dept., 1958-59; econ. officer embassy, Cairo, 1960-61, consulate gen., Calcutta, 1962-64; economist Bur. Econ. Affairs, State Dept., 1965-67, chief food for freedom div., 1967-69; dep. chief mission embassy, Colombo, Ceylon, 1969-70; assigned Nat. War Coll., 1970-71; counselor for econ.-comml. affairs Am. embassy, Manila, Philippines, 1971-76; sr. fgn. service insp., Washington, 1976-78, consul gen., Sao Paulo, Brazil, from 1978, assigned to Nat. War Coll.; now dep. dir. Office for Combating Terrorism, Dept. State, Washington. Served with USNR, 1943-46, 51-52. Recipient Meritorious Service award State Dept., 1966. Mem. Am. Fgn. Service Assn. Episcopalian. Office: Office for Combating Terrorism M/CT Room 2238 Dept State Washington DC 20520

ARNOLD, THOMAS CLINGMAN, investment counselor; b. Asheville, N.C., Sept. 6, 1943; s. Richard Marion and Virginia (Penland) A.; m. Genevieve Preston Hunter, June 8, 1965; children: Susan Copland, Thomas Hunter. A.B., U. N.C., 1965; M.B.A., U. Pa., 1967. Mem. sales and mktg. staff Am. Enka Co., N.C., 1965-69, v.p., gen. mgr., 1975-82; asst. treas. Akzona (Am. Enka), Asheville, 1969-72; fin. dir. Armak Co., Chgo., 1972-74; v.p., treas. Akzona, Inc., Asheville, 1982-83; investment counselor G. Waring Boys Co., Asheville, 1983—. Trustee U. N.C.-Asheville, 1981—; mem. alumni council Asheville Sch., 1981—. Mem. Am. Mgmt. Assn. Presbyterian. Clubs: University (N.Y.C.); Biltmore Forest Country (Asheville). Home: 406 Vanderbilt Rd Asheville NC 28803 Office: G Waring Boys Co Box 15167 Asheville NC 28813

ARNOLD, TOM, lawyer; b. Houston, Nov. 20, 1923; s. Thomas Jewel and Georgia (Buck) A.; m. Grace Gordon, Dec. 8, 1956; children: Vivian, Gordon Thomas. B.S.E.E., U. Tex., 1944, LL.B., 1949. Bar: Tex., D.C. bars 1949. Practice in, Houston, 1951—; atty. U.S. Dept. Justice, 1949-51; asso., partner Hutcheson, Taliaferro & Hutcheson, 1951-56; partner Arnold & Roylance, 1957-66, Arnold, Roylance, Kruger & Durkee, 1966-69, Arnold, White & Durkee, 1969—; occasional lectr. patent, trade mark and copyright law U. Tex., U. Houston, S. Tex. Coll. Law; chmn. Nat. Council Patent Law Assns., 1968-69; mem. adv. com. Tex. Legis. Council, 1966-67; mem. patent adv. com. U.S. Dept. Commerce, 1968-71; mem. adv. com. Pres.'s Domestic Policy Rev. on Indsl. Innovation, 1978-79; mem. Tex. Bd. Legal Specialization, 1976-77; mem. adv. com. on internat. intellectual property Dept. State, 1978-79; mem. chancellor's council U. Tex., 1976—. Co-author: Patentee Trial Advocacy; asst. editor: Tex. Law Rev, 1948-49; contbr. articles to profl. jours.; frequent lectr. at continuing legal edn. insts. Served to lt. (j.g.) USNR, 1943-46. Recipient Jefferson medal for outstanding contbn. to patent law and practice, 1974. Fellow Am. Bar Found., Tex. Legal Found.; mem. ABA (chmn. patent, trademark, copyright sect. 1964-65), Tex. Bar Assn. (chmn. patent, trademark, copyright sect. 1955-56), Houston Bar Assn. (pres. 1977-78), Am. Patent Law Assn. (pres. 1977-78), Houston Patent Law Assn., Gulf Coast Legal Found. (dir. 1976-79), U. Tex. Ex-students Assn. (exec. council 1970-73), Tex. Conf. Bar Pres.'s, Tex. Execs. of Houston (pres. 1969-70), Licensing Execs. Soc. (pres. 1979-80), Order of Coif, Phi Gamma Delta, Phi Eta Sigma. Republican. Methodist. Home: 6014 Deerwood St Houston TX 77057 Office: Suite 4000 One Bering Park 750 Bering Dr Houston TX 77057

ARNOLD, WALTER MARTIN, educator; b. Steelton, Pa., June 14, 1906; s. Philip and Ella (Sullenberger) A.; m. Evelyn Reeser, June 5, 1931; children: Jean Elizabeth (Mrs. Francis A. Rudolph, Jr.), Philip Elbert, Marilyn Ethel (Mrs. James A. Miller). B.S., Pa. State U., 1929, M.Ed., 1935; Ed.D., Okla. State U., 1957. Instr. Lancaster (Pa.) Boys High Sch., 1929-37; supt. Stevens Trade Sch., Lancaster, 1937-41; spl. rep. trade and indsl. edn. U.S. Office Edn., 1941-43; dir. vocat. edn. Allentown (Pa.) city schs., 1943-45; personnel mgr. Mack Mfg. Corp., 1945-49; assoc. H.W. Beyer Assos., pension cons., Allentown, 1949-50; supr. trade and indsl. edn., Okla., 1950-54, dir., exec. officer vocat. edn., Kans., 1954-59; dir. area vocat. edn. br., div. vocational and tech. edn. U.S. Office Edn., 1959-61, asst. commnr. vocat. and tech. edn., 1961-67; cons. vocat. and tech edn., also dir. of Pa. Study of Vocational Edn., 1967-69; pres. Am. Vocat. Research Corp., 1969-71; Walter M. Arnold Assocs., Inc. Am. Vocational Research Corp., Arlington, Va., 1971-75; adj. prof. Fla. Internat. U., 1976-78. Pres. Kans. Adult Edn. Assn., 1958-59; mem. Gov. Kans. Com. Mental Retardation, 1958, Gov. Kans. Inter-Deptl. Com. Aging, 1956-59, Kans. Adv. Council Edn., 1954-59; chmn. planning com. Four State Conf., 1957; tng. dir. Kans. Survival Plan Project, 1956-59; mem. north area Broward County Sch. Dist. Adv. Exec. Bd. and Com., 1979—; chmn. adv. com. Atlantic Area Vocat. Tech. Center, 1976—; mem. Curriculum task force Supts. Commn. on Public Edn., chmn. task force on vocat. edn., 1980-81; council mem. Coconut Grove City Council (Fla.), 1983—. Mem. Am. Soc. Engring. Edn., Am. Tech. Edn. Assn., Council Local Admistrs. Vocat. Edn. and Practical Arts, Am. Vocat. Assn., NEA, Pa. State U. Alumni Assn., Okla. State U. Alumni Assn., Nat. Assn. State Directors Vocational Edn., Alpha Chi Rho, Kappa Phi Kappa, Kappa Delta Pi, Phi Delta Kappa, Iota Lambda Sigma. Home and office: 1201 Bahama Bend H-1 Coconut Creek FL 33066 *Throughout my life, I have applied a principle of reinvesting part* *of my income continuously in my education, training and experience. The returns have been phenomenal.*

ARNOLD, WILLARD MAX, printing and publishing company executive; b. Williamport, Pa., Sept. 5, 1918; s. Charles Elliott and Blanch Ann (Hughes) A.; m. Dorothy N. Bradford, Feb. 1, 1944; 1 son, Robert Bradford. B.S. in Econs., Pa State U., 1941. With IBM, 1941-42, 46-47, Snapout Forms Co., 1948-51, Arnold Graphic Industries, Inc., Akron, 1952—, now chmn.; chmn. Graphic Mgmt. Cons., Akron, Colorcraft Corp., Loftins Bus. Forms Co. Bd. dirs. Salvation Army, Cleve., 1960-71, local council Boy Scouts Am., Cleve., 1962-67. Served to capt. USMC, 1942-46. Mem. Am. Mgmt. Assn., Nat. Bus. Forms Assn., Am. Horse Council, Bluecoats, Inc. Clubs: Country (Cleve.); Manalapan Yacht (Manalapan, Fla.); Delray Beach (Fla.). Lodge: Masons. Home: 13404 W State Rd 40 Ocala FL 32670 Office: 1600 E Turkeyfoot Lake Rd Uniontown OH 44685

ARNOLD, WILLIAM HOWARD, energy company executive; b. Jefferson Barracks, Mo., May 13, 1931; s. William Howard and Elizabeth Welsh (Mullen) A.; m. Josephine Inman Routheau, June 13, 1952; children: William, Frances, Edward, David, Thomas. A.B., Cornell U., 1951; A.M., Princeton U., 1953, Ph.D., 1955. Instr., research assoc. Princeton U., 1955; sr. engr., mgr. reactor physics Westinghouse Atomic Power Div., Pitts., 1955-61; dir. nuclear fuel mgmt. NUS Corp., Washington, 1961-62; various mgmt. positions to gen. mgr. PWR Systems, Pitts., 1962-79; pres. Westinghouse Nuclear Internat., Pitts., 1979-80, gen. mgr. Advanced Reactor div., 1981—, gen. mgr. Advanced Energy Systems div., 1983—; tchr. nuclear tech. U. Pitts., 1957, U. Ala., 1963. Contbr. articles to profl. jours. Fellow Am. Nuclear Soc., AAAS; mem. Nat. Acad. Engring., Am. Phys. Soc., Sigma Xi. Clubs: Longue Vue Country, Chevy Chase. Office: Box 158 Madison PA 15663

ARNOLD, WILLIAM PERRY, retail department stores executive; b. Omaha, Mar. 21, 1925; s. John Chappel and Rachel Harriet (Heiss) A.; m. Barbara Lee Powell, Feb. 16, 1949; children: Stephen P., Alice Lee. B.S., U. Mo., 1947. With L.S. Ayres, Indpls., 1947-58; pres., gen. mdse. mgr. subsidiary John Bressmer Co., Springfield, Ill., 1958-64; v.p. mdse. and publicity, dir., mem. exec. com. L.S. Ayres & Co., 1964-68; exec. v.p., then pres., chmn. bd. J.W. Robinson Co., Los Angeles, 1968-74; vice chmn., exec. officer merchandising Asso. Dry Goods Co., N.Y.C., 1974-76, pres., exec. officer merchandising, 1976-79, pres., chief exec. officer, 1979-81, chmn., chief exec. officer, 1981-84, chmn. exec. com., 1984—, also dir.; dir. Asso. Dry Goods (U.K.) Ltd., Central Hudson Gas and Electric Corp., Poughkeepsie, Black & Decker Mfg. Co.; trustee, exec. com. Am. Savs. Bank, N.Y.C. Mem. adv. bd. Salvation Army, N.Y.C.; trustee Nat. Jewish Hosp. and Research Center, Denver. Clubs: N.Y. Athletic, Union League, Turf and Field (N.Y.C.). Home: 18 Steeple Chase Rd Greenwich CT 06830 Office: 417 Fifth Ave New York NY 10016

ARNOLD, WILLIAM STRANG, lawyer; b. Yonkers, N.Y., Feb. 5, 1921; s. L.J. and Hazel (Strang) A.; m. Mary Ellen Gittinger, Sept. 17, 1943; children—Patricia (Mrs. Henry King), Richard L. A.B., U. Ark., 1942, J.D., 1947; LL.M., Columbia, 1948. Bar: Ark, bar 1947. Practice in, Crossett and Hamburg, 1948—; sr. partner Arnold, Hamilton & Streetman.; Dir. Ashley Life Ins. Co., MonArk Boat Co., First Nat. Bank of Crossett, Ashley County Abstract Co. Mem. Ark. Commn. on Uniform State Laws; mem. adv. bd. DeSota Area council Boy Scouts Am., 1970; Mem. Crossett Health Found. Served with USAAF, 1942-45. Mem. ABA, Ark. Bar Assn. (past pres.), Am. Coll. Probate Counsel, Am. Coll. Trial Lawyers, Am. Judicature Soc. Address: PO Drawer A Crossett AR 71635

ARNON, DANIEL I(SRAEL), biochemist, educator; b. Poland, Nov. 14, 1910; s. Leon and Rachel (Chodes) A.; m. Lucile Jane Soule, Feb. 24, 1940; children: Anne Arnon Hodge, Ruth Arnon Hanham, Stephen, Nancy, Dennis. B.S., U. Calif., 1932; Ph.D., 1936; Ph.D. hon. doctorate, U. Bordeaux, France, 1975. Instr. U. Calif. at Berkeley, 1936-41, asst. prof., assoc. prof., 1941-50, prof. plant physiology, 1950-60, prof. cell physiology, 1960—, research biochemist, 1978—; founding chmn. dept. cell physiology, 1961-78; biochemist Calif. Agrl. Expt. Sta., 1958-78; Guggenheim fellow, Cambridge U., Eng., 1947-48; lectr. Belgian Am. Found., U. Liège, Belgium, 1948; Fulbright research scholar Max-Planck Inst., Berlin-Dahlem, Germany, i955-56. Author sci. articles. Served from lt. to maj. AUS, 1943-46. Recipient Gold medal U. Pisa, 1958; Charles F. Kettering award photosynthesis research; Nat. medal of Sci.; Guggenheim fellow, 1962-63. Fellow Am. Acad. Arts and Scis., AAAS (recipient Newcomb Cleveland prize 1940); mem. Nat. Acad. Scis., Royal Swedish Acad. Scis., Acad. d'Agriculture de France, Deutsche Akademie der Naturforscher Leopoldina, Am. Chem. Soc., Am. Soc. Biol. Chemists, Biochem. Soc. (London), Am. Soc. Photobiology, Am. Soc. Plant Physiologists (pres. 1952-53, Stephen Hales prize, Charles Reid Barnes life membership award), Scandinavian Soc. Plant Physiologists, Spanish Biochem. Soc. (hon.). Home: 28 Norwood Ave Berkeley CA 94707

ARNOT, DAVID SHELDON, steel co. exec.; b. San Francisco, May 8, 1930; s. Philip Howard and Ruth (Sheldon) A.; m. Ann Neville Crary, Dec. 15, 1951; children—Thomas C., Todd S., James P. B.A., U. Calif., Berkeley, 1953; postgrad., Stanford U., (1977). With Bethlehem Steel Corp., Pa., 1956—, v.p. sales, 1977-78, sr. v.p., comml., 1978-80, exec. v.p., 1980—, also dir. Chmn. Northampton County (Pa.) chpt. Am. Cancer Soc., 1976-78. Served with Ordnance Corps, m2U.S. Army, 1953-56. Mem. Am. Iron and Steel Inst., Farm and Indsl. Equipment Inst. Aux. Clubs: Saucon Valley Country, Bethlehem; Sky (N.Y.). Office: Bethlehem Steel Corp 701 E 3d St Bethlehem PA 18016

ARNOTT, HOWARD JOSEPH, educator; b. Los Angeles, Mar. 9, 1928; s. Andrew Hugh and Evelyn Leonore (Donelly) A.; m. Wanda Jean Cross, Jan. 28, 1950; children—John Joseph, Catherine Jean, Susan Leonore, Virginia Anne. A.B., U. So. Calif., 1952, M.S., 1953; Ph.D., U. Calif. at Berkeley, 1958. Asst. prof. biology Northwestern U., Evanston, Ill., 1958-64; asso. prof. dept. botany U. Tex., Austin, 1965-68, prof., 1968-72, acting chmn. dept., 1970-71; prof., chmn. dept. biology U. So. Fla., Tampa, 1972-74; prof., dean Coll. Sci. U. Tex., Arlington, 1974—; vis. mem. dept. biology Tex. A. and M. U., 1971-75; cons. Ency. Brit. Films, NASA. Advisory editor: Protoplasma; Contbr. articles, abstracts to sci. jours., chpts. to books. Served with USN, 1946-48. NSF grantee, 1963-65; NIH postdoctoral fellow U. Tex., 1964-65. Mem. Bot. Soc. Am., Am. Soc. Cell Biology, Soc. Invertebrate Pathology, Am. Microscopical Soc., AAAS, Sigma Xi, Phi Sigma. Home: 1723 Prestonwood Dr Arlington TX 76012

ARNOTT, STRUTHER, univ. ofcl., molecular biologist; b. Larkhall, Scotland, Sept. 25, 1934. B.Sc., Glasgow (Scotland) U., 1956, Ph.D., 1960, D.Sc., 1978. Scientist biophysics unit Med. Research Council Kings Coll., London, 1960-70; prof. biology Purdue U., West Lafayette, Ind., 1970—, chmn. dept. biol. scis., 1975-80, v.p. research, dep. provost, dean grad. sch., 1980—. Contbr. numerous articles on molecular structures of nucleic acids, fibrous proteins and polysaccharides to profl. jours. Fellow Royal Soc. Chemistry. Home: 421 Robinson St West Lafayette IN 47906 Office: Grad Sch Purdue U West Lafayette IN 47907

ARNOVITZ, BENTON MAYER, editor; b. Butler, Pa., July 21, 1942; s. Paul and Miriam (Shapiro) A. A.B., Cornell U., 1964; M.A., N.Y. U., 1969; grad., U.S. Army Command and Gen. Staff Coll., 1982. Editor Macmillan Pub. Co., N.Y.C., 1966-73; sr. trade editor Chilton Book Co., Radnor, Pa., 1973-76; exec. editor Stein and Day Pubs., Briarcliff Manor, N.Y., 1976—. Served to capt. AUS, 1964-66, 70; lt. col. USAR. Mem. Alpha Phi Delta. Home: 19 Putnam Rd Continental Village RD 3 Peekskill NY 10566 Office: Scarborough House Briarcliff Manor NY 10510

ARNOW, LESLIE EARLE, scientist; b. Micanopy, Fla., June 22, 1909; s. Joseph Leslie and Mable Annie (Thrasher) A.; m. Jennie Martin, July 17, 1933 (dec. Sept. 1976); 1 son, Peter Leslie. Ph.G. and B.S., U. Fla., 1930; Ph.D., U. Minn., 1934, M.B. and M.D., 1940. Grad. asst. in physiol. chemistry and biophysics U. Minn., 1931-34, instr. physiol. chemistry, 1934-40, asst. prof., 1940-42; dir. biochem. research, med.-research div. Sharp and Dohme div. Merck & Co., Inc., 1942-44, dir. research, 1944-53, v.p., dir. research, 1953-56; v.p. Merck Sharp & Dohme Research Labs. div. Merck & Co., Inc.; exec. dir. Merck Inst. for Therapeutic Research, 1956-58; pres. Warner-Lambert Research Inst., 1958-65, sr. scientific cons., 1965-74; v.p. Warner-Lambert Pharm. Co., 1958-65. Author, Introduction to Physiological and Pathological Chemistry, 1976, Introduction to Laboratory Chemistry, 1976, Introduction to Organic and Biological Chemistry, (with H.C. Reitz), 1949, Health In A Bottle, 1970, Food Power, 1972, also articles in tech. publs. Past pres. bd. trustees Morris County Easter Seal Soc. Recipient Centennial award U. Fla., 1953, Outstanding Achievement award U. Minn., 1955. Fellow AAAS, N.Y. Acad. Sci.; mem. Morris County Med. Soc., AMA, Med. Soc. N.J., Research Dirs. Assn., Am. Chem. Soc., Am. Soc. Biol. Chemists, Am. Soc. for Clin. Pharmacology and Therapeutics, Soc. Exptl. Biology and Medicine, Phi Beta Kappa, Sigma Xi, Alpha Omega Alpha, Phi Beta Pi, Gamma Sigma Epsilon, Rho Chi, Phi Sigma, Alpha Epsilon Delta, Gamma Alpha, Sigma Chi. Club: Morris County Golf. Home: 14 Fairfield Dr Convent Station NJ 07961 *I have tried to conduct myself so that my associates, both business and social, would respect me as a competent scientist, a fair and efficient adminstrator, and a valued friend. I hope—and believe—that some of the activities in which I have been involved have contributed, however briefly in a historical sense, to the happiness and physical well-being of many of my fellow men and women.*

ARNOW, WINSTON EUGENE, federal judge; b. Micanopy, Fla., Mar. 13, 1911; s. J. Leslie and Mable (Thrasher) A.; m. Frances Day Cease, Jan. 11, 1941; 1 dau., Ann. B.S. in Bus. Adminstrn, U. Fla., 1932. Bar: Fla. bar 1933. J.D., 1933; research clk. Supreme Ct. of Fla., 1934; gen. practice Gainsville, Fla., 1935-42; mem. firm Clayton, Arnow, Duncan, Johnston, Clayton & Quincey, Gainesville, 1946-67; judge U.S. Dist. Ct., No. Dist. Fla., Pensacola, 1968—, chief judge, 1969-81, sr. judge, 1981—. Contbr. articles profl. jours. Chmn. steering com. Fla. Civil Practice before trial. Served to maj. AUS, 1942-46. Recipient Distinguished Alumni award U. Fla., 1972. Fellow Am. Coll. Probate Counsel; mem. Am. Bar Assn., Fla. Bar, Am. Law Inst., Soc. Bar 1st Jud. Circuit, Am. Judicature Soc., Order of Coif (hon.), Scabbard and Blade, Fla. Blue Key, Sigma Phi Epsilon, Phi Delta Phi, Tau Kappa Alpha, Phi Delta Epsilon. Clubs: Pensacola Rotary, Exec., Mustin Beach Officers. Office: PO Box 12347 Pensacola FL 32581

ARNS, ROBERT GEORGE, univ. adminstr., physics educator; b. Buffalo, July 24, 1933; m. Carol T. Sulecki, June 15, 1957; children: Susan, Thomas, Paul. B.S., Canisius Coll., 1955; M.S., U. Mich., 1956, Ph.D., 1960. Asst. prof. physics SUNY-Buffalo, 1960-63, asso. prof., 1963-64, Ohio State U., Columbus, 1964-69, prof., 1969-77, vice chmn. dept., 1970-75, vice provost univ., 1971-73, asso. provost univ., 1975-77; prof. physics, v.p. for acad. affairs U. Vt., Burlington, 1977—. Contbr. articles to profl. jours. Mem. Am. Phys. Soc., Am. Assn. Physics Tchrs., Sigma Xi, Phi Beta Kappa. Home: RD 2 Box 2440 Martindale Rd Shelburne VT 05482

ARNSTEIN, WALTER LEONARD, history educator; b. Stuttgart, Germany, May 14, 1930; came to U.S., 1939, naturalized, 1944; s. Richard and Charlotte (Heymann) A.; m. Charlotte Culver Sutphen, June 8, 1952; children: Sylvia, Peter. B.S.S., CCNY, 1951; M.A., Columbia U., 1954; Ph.D., Northwestern U., 1961; postgrad., U. London, Eng., 1956-57. Asst. prof. history Roosevelt U., Chgo., 1957-62, assoc. prof., 1962-66, prof., acting dean grad. div., 1966-67; prof. history U. Ill., 1968—, chmn. dept., 1974-78; assoc. U. Ill. Center for Advanced Study, 1972-73; vis. assoc. prof. history Northwestern U., 1963-64, spring 1966; vis. fellow Clare Hall, Cambridge U., 1982. Author: The Bradlaugh Case: A Study in Late Victorian Opinion and Politics, 1965, Britain Yesterday and Today, 1966, 71, 76, 83, Protestant Versus Catholic in Mid-Victorian England, 1982; co-author: The Age of Aristocracy (William B. Willcox), 3d edit, 1976, 4th edit., 1982; editor: The Past Speaks: Sources and Problems in British History since 1688, 1981; bd. editors: The Historian, 1976—, Am. Hist. Rev., 1982—; Mem. bd. advisers: Victorian Studies, 1966-75; Contbr. articles profl. jours. Vice chmn. Ill. Humanities Council, 1983-84. Served with AUS, 1951-53; Korea. Fulbright scholar, 1956-57; Fellow Am. Council Learned Socs., 1967-68. Fellow Royal Hist. Soc.; mem. Am. Hist. Assn., Brit. Hist. Assn, Conf. Brit. Studies (exec. com. 1971-76), Midwest Conf. on Brit. Studies (pres. 1980-82), Midwest Victorian Studies Assn. (pres. 1977-80), Phi Beta Kappa, Phi Alpha Theta. Home: 804 W Green St Champaign IL 61820 Office: Dept History 309 Gregory Hall U Ill Urbana IL 61801

ARON, WILLIAM, government official, biologist; b. Bklyn., June 26, 1930. B.S. in Biology, Bklyn. Coll., 1952; M.S., U. Wash., 1957, Ph.D. in Fisheries-Oceanography, 1960. Biologist, Wash. State Dept. Fisheries, Seattle, 1952-53; research asst. prof. oceanography U. Wash., Seattle, 1956-61; head group biol. oceanography Gen. Motors Def. Research Lab., Santa Barbara, Calif., 1961-67; dep. head office oceanography and limnology Smithsonian Instn., Washington, 1967-69, dir. oceanography and limnology program, 1969-71; dir. office ecology and environ. conservation NOAA, Commerce Dept., Rockville, Md., 1971-78; dir. Office Marine Mammals and Endangered Species, Nat. Marine Fisheries Service, 1978-80, N.W. and Alaska Fisheries Center, Seattle, 1980—; prof. U. Wash., Seattle, 1980—; mem. com. on oceanography Nat. Acad. Sci.-NRC; chief scientist Project Neptune, Office Naval Research; U.S. commr. Internat. Whaling Commn. Mem. Am. Soc. Limnology, Oceanography, AAAS. Research in zoogeography of pelagic fish and plankton, instrumentation for sampling, role of Suez Canal and other canals as pathway for dispersion. Home: 11809 NE 30th Pl Bellevue WA 98005 Office: 2725 Montlake Blvd E Seattle WA 98112

ARONOW, WILBERT SOLOMON, physician, educator; b. N.Y.C., Oct. 30, 1931; s. Simon and Bella (Safrin) A.; m. Ina Gloria Brody, Sept. 20, 1958; children—Michael Steven, Janice Susan. B.S., Queens Coll., 1953; M.D., Harvard U., 1957. Diplomate: Am. Bd. Internal Medicine. Intern Michael Reese Hosp. and Med. Center, Chgo., 1957-58; resident, 1958-61; practice medicine specializing in internal medicine and cardiology; cardiologist, chief Noninvasive Cardiovascular Lab., Long Beach (Calif.) VA Hosp., 1964-72, chief cardiovascular diseases, 1973-82, asst. chief medicine for research, 1975-80; asso. prof. medicine U. Calif., Irvine, 1972-75, prof. medicine, 1975-82, prof. community and environ. medicine, 1975-82, prof. pharmacology and therapeutics, 1976-82, vice chief cardiovascular div., chief cardiovascular research, 1974-82; prof. medicine, chief cardiovascular research Creighton U., Omaha, 1982—; vis. prof. U. Tex. Southwestern Med. Sch., Dallas, 1976, U. Man., 1979, U. Toronto, 1979, Tex. Tech U. Sch. Medicine, Lubbock, 1983, U. Medicine and Dentistry of N.J.-Rutgers Med. Sch., 1983; cons. cardiology Orange County Med. Center, 1968-82; staff cardiology service St. Joseph Hosp., Omaha, 1982—; cons. FDA, 1970-77, mem. ad hoc sci. advisory coms., 1970-72, mem. cardiovascular and renal advisory com., 1973-76; cons. U. Calif. Project Clear Air, 1970, Calif. Air Resources Bd., 1973, 78, 80, EPA, 1973, 78, 79, 80, 81, 82, 83, dept. drugs AMA, 1974, 78, 81, NIH, 1976, 80, W. Ger. Dept. Health, 1978, U.S. Dept. Justice Law Enforcement Assistance Adminstrn., 1978, Nat. Heart, Lung and Blood Inst., 1979, FTC, 1980, 81, Dept. Health and Environ. Scis., State of Mont., 1980, Nat. Ctr. Health Stats., 1981; cons. and chmn. spl. rev. com. Nat. Cancer Inst., 1980; cons. and mem. subcom. on smoking Am. Heart Assn., 1980-83. Mem. editorial bd.: Jour. Pharmacology and Exptl. Therapeutics, 1977—; guest field editor, 1981; Editorial bd.: Am. Jour. Cardiology, 1980-82, Jour. Circulation, 1980-83, E R Reports, 1981—, Physician's Drug Alert, 1982—, Jour. Cardiovascular and Pulmonary Technique, 1983—; contbr. to research publs. Served to capt., M.C. AUS, 1961-63. Fellow A.C.P., Am. Coll. Cardiology, Am. Coll. Chest Physicians (vice-chmn. coronary disease sect. 1978-79, gov. So. Calif. 1977-83, chmn. coronary disease sect. 1979-81, vice chmn. gov.'s council, mem. exec. council 1979-81, chmn. forum on cardiovascular disease 1980-81, sec. council on govs. 1981-82), Council Clin. Cardiology of Am. Heart Assn.; mem. Am. Soc. Clin. Pharmacology and Therapeutics (chmn. cardiovascular and pulmonary diseases sect. 1973-74, 1975-77), Am. Fedn. Clin. Research, Assn. VA Cardiologists (pres. 1975-77), Long Beach Heart Assn. (dir. 1972-75), Orange County Heart Assn. (dir. 1979-81), Phi Beta Kappa. Jewish. Home: 9961 Essex Rd Omaha NB 68114 Office: Creighton Univ Sch Medicine 601 N 30th St Omaha NB 68131 *Concern for the public health as well as for individual patient care has been the motivating force behind my medical research, teaching, and patient care. Performing work in a very careful, scientific fashion, being honest, being helpful and supportive to others, working very hard and efficiently, and being true to my principles of conduct has contributed to my success.*

ARONSON, DAVID, artist, art educator; b. Shilova, Lithuania, Oct. 28, 1923; came to U.S., 1929, naturalized, 1931; s. Peisach Leib and Gertrude (Shapiro) A.; m. Georgianna B. Nyman, June 10, 1956; children: Judith, Benjamin, Abigail. Certificate, Boston Mus. Sch., 1946. Instr. painting Boston Mus. Sch., 1943-54; prof. art Boston U., 1962—, chmn. div., 1954-62. Contbr. articles to profl. jours.; one man shows include, Niveau Gallery, N.Y.C., 1945, 56, Mus. Modern Art, N.Y.C., 1945, Boris Mirski Gallery, Boston, 1951, 59, 64, 69, Downtown Gallery, N.Y.C., 1953, Nordness Gallery, N.Y.C., 1960, 63, 69, Rex Evans Gallery, Los Angeles, 1961, Long Beach (Calif.) Mus., Westhampton (N.Y.) Gallery, J. Thomas Gallery, Provincetown, Mass., 1964, N.Y. World's Fair, 1964-65, Smithsonian Instn., 1965, Zora Gallery, Los Angeles, Hunter Gallery, Chattanooga, Kovler Gallery, Chgo., 1966, Bernard Danenberg Galleries, N.Y.C., 1969, 72, Pucker-Safrai Gallery, Boston, 1976, 78, Louis Newman Galleries, Los Angeles, 1977, Louis Newman Galleries, Beverly Hills, Calif., 1981, 84, Sadye Bronfman Art Ctr., Montreal, Que., Can., 1982, retrospective exhbns. include, Rose Mus., Brandeis U., Waltham, Mass., 1978, Jewish Mus., N.Y.C., 1979, Mus. Am. Jewish History, Phila., So. Middlesex U., South Dartmouth, Mass., 1983; represented in permanent collections, Art Inst. Chgo., Va. Mus. Fine Arts, Richmond, Bryn Mawr Coll., Brandeis U., Tupperware Mus., Orlando, Fla., Decordova Mus., Lincoln, Mass., Mus. Modern Art, Atlanta U., Atlanta Art Assn., U. Nebr., Krannert Art Mus. of U. Ill., Whitney Mus. Am. Art, Colby Coll., U. N.H., Portland Mus. Art, Corcoran Gallery Art, Washington, Munson Williams Proctor Art Inst., Ithaca, N.Y., Boston Mus. Fine Arts, Smithsonian Instn., Washington, Milw. Art Inst., Pa. Acad. Fine Arts, Johnson Found., Racine, Wis., Worcester (Mass.) Art Mus., Brockton (Mass.) Mus. Art, Longy Sch. Music, Cambridge, Mass., Boston U., Joseph Hirschhorn Collection, Hebrew Tchrs. Coll., Brookline, Mass., Pa. State U. Mus. Art, U. Judaism, Los Angeles, numerous others, sculpture commns., Container Corp. Am., 1963, 65, Reform Jewish Appeal, 1980, Combined Jewish Appeal, 1981, Temple Beth Elohim, Wellesley, Mass., 1982, Bradeis U. Library, Waltham, Mass., 1983. Recipient 1st Judges prize Inst. Modern Art, Boston, 1944, 1st Popular prize, 1944; Choice Friends of Art Art Inst. Chgo., 1946; Purchase prize Va. Mus. Fine Arts, 1946; Travelling fellow Boston Mus. Sch., 1946; Grand prize Boston Arts Festival, 1952, 54; 2d prize, 1953; 1st prize Tupperware Art Fund, 1954; grantee in art; Nat. Inst. Arts and Letters, 1958; Purchase prize, 1961, 62, 63; purchase prize Pa. Acad. Fine Arts; other purchase prizes; Samuel F.B. Morse Gold medal NAD, 1973; Isaac N. Maynard prize, 1975; Joseph S. Isidor gold medal NAD, 1976; Guggenheim fellow, 1960; Academician NAD (Adolph and Clara Obrig prize, 1968). Home: 137 Brimstone Ln Sudbury MA 01776 also Fairview PEI Canada Office: 855 Commonwealth Ave Boston MA 02215

ARONSON, DAVID, rabbi; b. Vitebsk, Russia, Aug. 1, 1894; came to U.S., 1906, naturalized, 1918; s. Jekuthiel Zalman and Yetta (Kudritzin) A.; m. Bertha Friedman, May 1, 1927; children—Raphael, Hillel. A.B., N.Y. U., 1916; A.M., Columbia, 1917; Rabbi, Jewish Theol. Sem. of Am., 1919, D.H.L. (honoris causa), 1946; D.D., U. Judaism, 1969. Served with Jewish Welfare Bd.; camp rabbi Camp Upton, L.I., 1917-19; rabbi, Salt Lake City, 1920-22, Duluth, Minn., 1922-24, Beth El Synagogue, Mpls., 1924-59; since emeritus; prof. rabbinics grad. sch. U. Judaism, Los Angeles, 1959—; vis. lectr. Jewish Theol. Sem.; Mem. Gov.'s Human Relations Commn., 1943-59, Mayor's Council on Human Relations, Citizen's Charter Commn.; rep. Am. Jewish Conf., 1943; pres. Rabbinical Assembly, 1948-50; bd. dirs., bd. overseers Jewish Theol. Sem. and others. Author: The Jewish Way of Life; Asso. editor of the: Am. Jewish World, 1930-59; Contbr. articles relating to Jewish affairs to profl. jours. Recipient Outstanding Service award Mpls. Jewish Fedn., 1959, Distinguished Service award City of Mpls., 1959; Prime Minister's award State of Israel, 1976; Mordecai M. Kaplan medal of honor U. Judaism, 1981. Home: 8555 Saturn St Los Angeles CA 90035 Office: 15600 Mulholland Dr Los Angeles CA 90077 *There can be no perfect world without perfect people; I am one of the people. What I do with my life is, therefore, a factor in the character of the world.*

ARONSON, DAVID, chemical and mechanical engineer; b. Bklyn., Sept. 24, 1912; s. Oscar and Amy (Maas) A.; m. Hannah Unger, Feb. 11, 1945; children: Deborah, Judi. B.S., Cooper Union Sch. Engring., 1936; B.S. Ch.E., Poly. Inst. Bklyn., 1944. Chem. engr. Sanderson & Porter, Pine Bluff, Ark., 1942-43, Kellex Corp., N.Y.C., 1943-45, Elliott Co., Jeannette, Pa., 1945-51; staff engr. Worthington Corp., Harrison, N.J., 1951-54; partner Deutsch & Loonam, N.Y.C., 1954-55; cons., dir. research and devel. Worthington Corp., Harrison, N.J., 1955-70; cons. engr. David Aronson Assocs., Upper Montclair, N.J., 1970—, dir. research and devel. Contbr. articles to profl. jours. Chmn. community relations com. Congregation Shomrei Emunah, 1971—. Fellow ASME (mem. exec. com. tech. and soc. div. 1970—); mem. Am. Inst. Chem. Engrs., AAAS, Sigma Xi, Tau Beta Pi. Patentee in field. Address: 9 Riverview W Dr W Upper Montclair NJ 07043

ARONSON, EDGAR DAVID, brokerage company executive; b. N.Y.C., June 17, 1934; s. Aaron Solomon and Ida Claire (Minevitch) A.; m. Nancy Carol Pforzheimer, Dec. 23, 1956; children: Edgar David, Alison C., Edith S., Peter Borrah. A.B., Harvard U., 1956,

M.B.A., 1962. Successively trainee, asst. cashier, v.p. 1st Nat. Bank of Chgo., 1962-67; v.p. Republic Nat. Bank of N.Y., 1968; trainee Salomon Bros., N.Y.C., 1968-69, ltd. partner, 1970, v.p., 1971-72, gen. partner, 1972-79; mng. dir. Salomon Bros. Internat. Ltd., London, 1971-76; chmn. bd. Dillon, Read Internat., 1979-81; pres. EDACO, Inc., 1981—; dir. Merrie-Go-Round, Inc., Dallas, APL N.V., Curacao, Indogas Ltd., Hong Kong, Burnwood Corp., N.Y.C., Calif. Energy Co., Santa Rosa. Author: (with others) New Old World, 1962, Response to Change, 1963. Corporator Lesley Coll., Cambridge, Mass. Served to 1st lt. USMCR, 1956-60. Mem. Marine Corps Res. Officers Assn., 1st Marine Div. Assn., The Cruising Assn. (U.K.), Mensa. Clubs: N.Y. Yacht, Harvard of N.Y.C. Home: 115 E 79th St New York NY 10021 Office: 46 William St New York NY 10005

ARONSON, HOWARD ISAAC, linguist, educator; b. Chgo., Mar. 5, 1936; s. Abe and Jean A. B.A., U. Ill., 1956; M.A., Ind. U., 1958, Ph.D., 1961. Asst. prof. Slavic langs. and lit. U. Wis., Madison, 1961-62; asst. prof. Slavic linguistics U. Chgo., 1962-65, asso. prof. depts. slavic langs. and lit. and linguistics, 1965-73, prof., 1973—, chmn. dept. linguistics, 1972-80, chmn. dept. Slavic langs. and lits., 1983—. Mem. Linguistics Soc. Am., Am. Assn. Tchrs. Slavic and East European Langs. Jewish. Home: 415 Aldine Apt 7B Chicago IL 60657 Office: Dept Slavic Langs and Lits Univ of Chicago Chicago IL 60637

ARONSON, JAY RICHARD, economics educator, researcher, academic administrator; b. N.Y.C., Aug. 26, 1937; s. Lester and Rose (Hacken) A.; m. Judith Libby Klein, Sept. 13, 1959; children: Sarah, Miriam, Anne. A.B., Clark U., 1959, Ph.D., 1964; M.A., Stanford U., 1961. Asst. prof. econs. Worcester Poly. Inst. (Mass.), 1961-65, Lehigh U., Bethlehem, Pa., 1965-68, assoc. prof., 1968-72, prof., 1972—; dir. Fairchild-Martindale Ctr. for Study Pvt. Enterprise, Lehigh U., Bethlehem, 1980—; vis. lectr. Clark U., 1964-65, 66; grant referee NSF, Social Sci. Research Council, London; vis. scholar U. York (Eng.), 1973; cons. Internat. City Mgmt. Assn. Author: books including (with J. Maxwell) Financing Stte and Local Governments, 1977, Public Finance; editor: (with E. Schwartz) management policies in Local Government Finance, 1975; contbr. articles to profl. publs. Recipient Lindback award Lehigh U., 1968, Stabler award Lindback award, 1974; Rockefeller fellow, 1959-61; named hon. fellow Clark U., 1962; grantee Ford Found., 1971-72, 76-77, HEW, 1978-79, Scaife Found., 1982; Fulbright research scholar, 1978. Mem. Am. Econ. Assn., Nat. Tax Assn., Am. Fin. Assn., Roya Econ. Soc. Democrat. Jewish. Home: 1804 Jennings St Bethlehem PA 18017 Office: LeHigh U Bethlehem PA

ARONSON, LOUIS VINCENT, II, mfg. exec.; b. Newark, Jan. 18, 1923; s. Alexander H. and Leona L. (Lazarus) A.; m. Joan Barbara Fisch, Nov. 2, 1945; children—James Richard, Robert A., Kathryn Ann, Diane Barbara. B.S., U.S. Naval Acad., 1945. Methods engr. Ronson Corp., 1947-48, supr. prodn. control, 1948-50, v.p. charge material procurement, 1950-52, v.p. charge ops., 1952, dir., 1952—, pres., 1953—. Bd. dirs. NCCJ. Served as ensign USN, 1945-47. Mem. Am. Naval Acad. Athletic Assn., Am. Ordnance Assn. Club: 24 Karat. Home: PO Box 548 Far Hills NJ 07931 Office: 1 Ronson Rd Bridgewater NJ 08807

ARONSON, MICHAEL ANDREW, editor, publishing co. exec.; b. Bklyn., Apr. 27, 1939; s. Jesse Besthoff and Marcia (Sacks) A. B.A., Johns Hopkins, 1960. Asst. dir. Ind. U. Press, Bloomington, 1966-69; London editor U. Chgo. Press, 1970, sci. editor, 1971-73; editor-in-chief Johns Hopkins U. Press, Balt., 1973-78; gen. editor Harvard U. Press, Cambridge, Mass., 1978—. Jewish. Office: Harvard U Press 79 Garden St Cambridge MA 02138

ARONSON, SIDNEY HERBERT, sociology educator; b. Boston, Aug. 11, 1924; s. Max and Lena (Shuffel) A.; m. Selma Bornstein, Dec. 25, 1949; children: Nancy, Mark. A.B., Harvard U., 1949, A.M., 1958; A.M., Tufts U., 1949; Ph.D., Columbia U., 1961. Assoc. prof., chmn. dept. sociology NYU, N.Y.C., 1967-72; prof. sociology Bklyn. Coll. and Grad. Ctr.-CUNY, 1972—. Author: Status and Kinship in the Higher Civil Service, 1964, Life in Society, 1965; assoc. editor: Social Problems, 1953-58; adv. editor: Sociol. Inquiry, 1982—. Bd. dirs. New Rochelle (N.Y.) Mental Health Assn., 1963-64; mem. exec. com. Westchester County Anti-Defemation League, 1972—. Served with inf. U.S. Army, 1943-45. Decorated Bronze Star; postdoctoral fellow Harvard U., 1961-62; NIMH fellow Cornell U., 1956-57; Fulbright prof., Israel and India, 1978-79. Mem. Am. Sociol. Assn. (pres. 1979-80), Eastern Sociol Soc., Soc. Study Social Problems. Democrat. Jewish. Club: Harvard of Westchester. Home: 47 Ellsworth St Larchmont NY 10538 Office: Bklyn Coll Brooklyn NY 11210

ARONSON, STANLEY MAYNARD, educator, physician; b. N.Y.C., May 28, 1922; s. Eliuh and Lena (Hassner) A.; m. Betty Ellis, June 3, 1947; children: Susan, Lisa, Sarah. B.S., CCNY, 1943; M.D., N.Y. U., 1947; M.A., Brown U., 1971; M.P.H., Harvard U. Sch. Public Health, 1981. Diplomate: Am. Bd. Pathology., Am. Bd. Neuropathology. Residency tng. Bellevue Hosp.; Residence tng. Meml. Center for Cancer, Mt. Sinai Hosp., all N.Y.C., 1947-53; faculty Columbia Coll. Physicians and Surgeons, 1951-54; prof. pathology, asst. dean SUNY, Bklyn., 1954-70; prof. med. sci., dean medicine Brown U., 1970-81, Univ. prof. med. sci., 1981—; dir. labs. Kings County Hosp. Center, Bklyn., 1965-70; pathologist-in-chief Miriam Hosp., Providence, 1970-75; vis. prof. community medicine Dartmouth Coll. Med. Sch., 1982—; lectr. Yale Sch. Medicine, 1964-65; lectr. pathology Tufts U. Sch. Medicine, 1978—; cons. physician neuropathology Jewish Chronic Disease Hosp., Bklyn., 1951—, NIH, 1962—; cons. physician R.I. Hosp., Roger Williams Hosp., Meml. Hosp., Providence VA Hosp., Butler Hosp., Providence, Luth. Med. Center, N.Y.C. Author: (with B.W. Volk) Cerebral Sphingolipidoses, 1962, Inborn Disorders of Sphingolipid Metabolism, 1966, Sphingolipids, Sphingolipidoses and Allied Disorders, 1972, (with A. Sahs and E Hartman) Guidelines for Stroke Care, 1976; also numerous articles; mem. editorial bd.: Jour. Submicroscopic Cytology, R.I. Med. Jour., Jour. Neuropathology and Exptl. Neurology. Mem. Nat. Adv. Commn. on Multiple Sclerosis, 1973-74; commr. U.S. Commn. Control of Huntington's Disease, 1976—; mem. NIH Perinatal Research Commn., Joint Commn. on Stroke Facilities; chmn. Legis. Commn. Dementia Related to Aging; mem. med. adv. bd. Nat. Multiple Sclerosis Soc., Dysautonomia Found., Nat. Tay-Sachs Assn., Nat. Fund for Med. Edn., Hospice R.I., Interfaith Health Care Ministries. Served with U.S. Army, 1942-46. Mem. AMA, Am. Neurol. Assn., Am. Assn. Neuropathology (pres. 1971-72), N.Y. Acad. Medicine, Am. Acad. Neurology, Am. Assn. Pathologists and Bacteriologists, Internat. Soc. Neuropathology, Assn. Am. Med. Colls., N.Y. Neurol. Soc. Research on genetics epidemiology, pathology and diagnostic features of cerebral degenerative diseases, population dynamics, pathology and epidemiology of cerebral vascular disease and stroke. Home: 26 Elm St Rehoboth MA 02769 Office: Office Med Affairs Brown U Providence RI 02912

ARONSTEIN, MARTIN JOSEPH, lawyer, educator; b. N.Y.C., Jan. 25, 1925; s. William and Mollie (Mintz) A.; m. Sally K. Rosenau, Sept. 18, 1948; children: Katherine Aronstein Porter, David M., James K. B.E., Yale U., 1944; M.B.A., Harvard U., 1948; LL.B., U. Pa., 1965. Bar: Pa. bar 1965. Bus. exec., Phila., 1948-65; asso. firm Obermayer, Rebmann, Maxwell & Hippel, Phila., 1965-67, partner, 1968-69; asso. prof. law U. Pa., 1969-72, prof., 1972-78; counsel firm Ballard, Spahr, Andrews & Ingersoll, Phila., 1978-80, partner, 1980-81; prof. law U. Pa., 1981—. Contbr. articles to law revs.; mem.: Permanent Editorial Bd. Uniform Comml. Code, 1978—, Counsel, 1980—. Served with USN, 1943-46. Mem. Am. Law Inst., Am. Bar Assn. (reporter com. on stock certs. 1973-77, chmn. subcom. on investment securities 1982—), Pa. Bar Assn., Phila. Bar Assn., Order of Coif, Sigma Xi, Tau Beta Pi. Home: 1820 Rittenhouse Sq Philadelphia PA 19103 Office: 3400 Chestnut St Philadelphia PA 19104

ARPE, JOHN EDWIN, transp. systems and solid waste systems mfg. co. exec.; b. Milw., June 10, 1916; s. Walter C. and Amanda (Bruck) A.; m. Germaine M. Brever, Aug. 10, 1940; children—James F., John E., Christine Mary, Janet Emily. Student, U. Wis., 1938-42, Marquette U., 1943-46; Advanced Mgmt. Program, Harvard U., 1966. Various depts. including gen. accounting, govt. accounting, contract adminstrn., mfg. Heil Co., Milw., 1934-61, v.p. in charge mfg., 1961, v.p. adminstrn. and fin., 1962-68, dir., 1964—, treas., v.p., 1968, exec. v.p., treas., 1968-77, pres., 1977—; mem. exec. com., dir. W.A. Krueger Co., Scottsdale, Ariz.; dir. Valuation Research Corp., Milw. Bd. dirs. Luth. Hosp. Milw. Club: Univ. (Milw.). Home: 12520 Stephen Pl Elm Grove WI 53122 Office: 3000 W Montana St Milwaukee WI 53201

ARPEL, ADRIEN, cosmetic co. exec.; b. N.J., July 15, 1941; d. Samuel and Ada (Stark) Joachim; m. Ronald Monroe Newman, Oct. 30, 1960; 1 dau., Lauren Nicole. Student, Pace Coll., 1960-62. Pres. Adrienne Cosmetics, Englewood, N.J., 1959-60, Lisa Lauren Cosmetics, N.Y.C., 1962-65, Adrien Arpel, Inc., 1965—; dir. Seligman and Latz, Inc., 1975-77. Author: Adrien Arepl 21 Day Make Over Shape Over, 1978, Adrien Arpel How to Look 10 Years Younger, 1980. Bd. dirs. Cradle Adoption Agy., Chgo., Kings Point (N.Y.) Civic Assn., Children's Aid Soc., N.Y.C. Mem. Cosmetic Career Women. Office: 666 Fifth Ave New York NY 10103

ARPINO, GERALD PETER, choreographer; b. Staten Island, N.Y., Jan. 14, 1928; s. Luigi and Anna (Santana) A. Student, Wagner Coll.; studied ballet under, Mary Ann Wells; studied modern dance under, May O'Donnell and Gertrude Shurr. Dancer Ballet Russe, 1951-52, Joffrey Ballet, to 1962; with faculty Joffrey Ballet Sch. N.Y.C., from 1953, now co-dir.; choreographer, assoc. dir. The Joffrey Ballet. (Formerly called Undine) choreographer ballets including Incubus, all 1962, Viva Vivaldi!, 1965, Olympics, Nightwings, both 1966, Cello Concerto, Arcs and Angels, Elegy, all 1967, Secret Places, The Clowns, Fanfarita, A Light Fantastic, 1968, Animus, The Poppet, 1969, Confetti, Solarwind, Trinity, all 1970, Reflections, Valentine, Kettentanz, all 1971, Chabriesque, Sacred Grove on Mount Talmalpais, both 1972, Jackpot, 1973, The Relativity of Icarus, 1974, Drums, Dreams on Banjos, 1975, Orpheus Times Light 2, 1976, Touch Me, 1977, Choura, L'Air d 'Esprit, Suite Saint-Saens, all 1978, Epode, 1979, Celebration, 1980. Served with USCG, 1945-48. Recipient award Dance Mag., 1974. Address: City Center Joffrey Ballet 130 W 56th St New York NY 10019

ARPS, LESLIE HANSEN, lawyer; b. Leipzig, Germany, July 14, 1907; s. George F. and Alice (Black) A; m. Ruth Collicott, Oct. 26, 1959. A.B., Stanford, 1928; LL.B., Harvard, 1931. Bar: N.Y. bar 1932. Asso. Root, Clark, Buckner & Ballantine, N.Y.C., 1931-42, 46-48; mem. firm Skadden, Arps, Slate, Meagher & Flom, N.Y.C., 1948—; spl. asst. atty. gen. State of N.Y.; asst. chief counsel N.Y. State Crime Commn., 1951-52; asso. gen. counsel to N.Y. State Moreland Commn. to Investigate State Agys. in relation to Pari-Mutuel Harness Racing, 1953-54; cons. N.Y. State Moreland Commn. on Alcoholic Beverage Control law, 1963-64. Chmn. bd. trustees Gateway Sch. N.Y., 1965-67; trustee The Gunnery, Inc., 1978—. Served to lt. col. USAAF, 1942-45. Mem. Am. Bar Assn., N.Y. State Bar Assn., N.Y.C. Bar Assn. (chmn. exec. com. 1973-74), N.Y. County Lawyers Assn., Am. Bar Found., Am. Judicature Soc., Fed. Bar Council, Merc. Library Assn. (dir.), Am. Arbitration Assn. (dir.), Phi Beta Kappa. Clubs: Union League, Sky, Harvard (N.Y.C.). Home: 530 Park Ave New York NY 10021 Office: 919 3d Ave New York NY 10022

ARQUILLA, ROBERT, general contractor; b. Chgo., Nov. 13, 1926; s. George, Sr. and Emelia (Pechacek) A.; m. Thelma Fay Fresen, June 4, 1948; children: Scott, Roberta Ann, Keith, Bruce. B.S. in Bus. Adminstrn, Northwestern U., 1950. With Burnside Constrn. Co., Glenwood, Ill., 1950—, sr. v.p., 1976—, dir., 1957—; chmn. bd. Heritage-Glenwood Bank. Bd. dirs. Glenwood Sch. for Boys; mem. Fed. Savs. and Loan Adv. Council, 1975-76. Served with USNR, 1944-46. Mem. Nat. Assn. Home Builders (pres. 1977), Lambda Alpha. Club: Olympia Fields Country. Home: 2333 Golfview Ln Flossmoor IL 60422 Office: 18400 S Halsted St Glenwood IL 60425

ARRAJ, ALFRED ALBERT, U.S. district judge; b. Kansas City, Mo., Sept. 1, 1906; s. Elias and Mary (Dervis) A.; m. Madge L. Connors, Nov. 12, 1929; 1 dau., Sally Marie. J.D., U. Colo., 1928, LL.D., 1977. Bar: Colo. 1928. Gen. practice law, Denver, Springfield, Colo., 1928-36; county atty. Beca County, Colo., 1936-42, 46-48, dep. dist. atty., 1946-48; dist. judge 15th Jud. Dist. Colo., 1949-57; U.S. judge Dist. of Colo., 1957-59, chief judge, from 1959, now sr. judge. Bd. dirs. Fed. Jud. Center. Served from 1st lt. to maj. USAAF, 1942-46; CBI. Recipient Norlin Recognition award for distinguished achievement U. Colo., 1968, William Lee Knous award U. Colo. Sch. Law, 1970. Mem. Am. Judicature Soc., Am. Bar Assn., Colo. Bar Assn., S.E. Colo. Bar Assn. (pres. 1940), Fed. Bar Assn., Denver Bar Assn., Order of Coif, Jud. Conf. U.S., Phi Delta Phi. Episcopalian. Club: University. Home: 200 Ivy St Denver CO 80220 Office: U S Courthouse Denver CO 80294

ARRAU, CLAUDIO, concert pianist; b. Chillan, Chile, Feb. 6, 1903; (married); children: Carmen, Mario, Christopher. Endowed as child prodigy by Chilean Govt. to study at, Stern Conservatory, Berlin, with Martin Krause, 1912-18. Made debut, Berlin, 1915; London debut, 1920; toured, Germany, Europe, S.Am., 1st U.S. tour, 1923-24; returned permanently, 1941; toured, USSR, 1929, 30, 68, Australia, 1947, 57, 62, 68, 70, 74, S. Africa, 1949, 52, 56, Japan, 1965, 68, 72, 79, Israel, 1950, 52, 58, 60, 64, 67, 71, 72; presented 32 Beethoven piano sonatas in, N.Y., 1953, 62; toured world many times.; Recorded: major piano works of Debussy, Beethoven, Brahms, Chopin, Liszt, Schumann, Schubert. Recipient Liszt prize, 1913, 14; Ibach prize, 1917; Grand Internat. prize at, Geneva, 1927; decorated chevalier Order Arts and Letters, France; Deutsches Verdienst Kreuz, Ger.; streets named in his honor in, Santiago and Chillan. Home: New York NY also VT Office: care Internat Creative Mgmt Artists 40 W 57th St New York NY 10019

ARREDONDO, ELISEO LUIS, advertising agency executive; b. Mexico City, Dec. 11, 1947; s. Eliseo and Angelina (Garcia) A.; m. Lourdes Arredondo Reynaud, Mar. 11, 1983; m. Dulce Sanchez, Feb. 17, 1973 (div. 1980); children: Paulina, Adriana. B.B.A., Universidad Iberoamericana, 1971. Brand mgr. BIMBO, 1969-72; account exec. Nielsen Co., Mex., 1972-76, NCK, Mexico, 1976-78; mgmt. supr. McCann Erickson, Mex., 1978-80; gen. mgr. SSC & B Lintas, Mexico City, 1980—. Recipient Exceptional Leadership in Account Service award McCann Erickson, 1979. Home: 256 Cofre de Perote 401 Mexico City Lomas de Chapultepec Mexico 11000 Office: Quadrant Dante 36-11 Mexico City Anzures Mexico 11590

ARRIGONI, LOUIS, cooperative food distributor; b. S. Cle Elum, Wash., Aug. 4, 1916; s. Joseph and Esther (Paganelli) A.; m. Evelyn I. Pierson, Apr. 26, 1944; children: Nancy, Evelyn, James. B.S., U. Wash., 1938, M.S., 1940, Ph.D., 1945. Asst. prof. chemistry U. Wash., Seattle, 1943-49; with Consol. Dairy Products Co., Seattle, 1949-67, v.p., 1962-67, dir., 1962—, pres., 1971—; pres. Assoc. Grocers Inc., Seattle, 1967-71, also dir., chmn. exec. com.; dir. Rainier Internat. Bank, Dairy Export Co., Inc., Rainier Nat. Bank. Mem. Am. Pharm. Assn., Sigma Xi. Clubs: Wash. Athletic, Rainier (Seattle). Lodge: Elks. Home: 4845 NE 85th St Seattle WA 98115 Office: Consolidated Dairy Products Co 635 Elliott Ave Seattle WA 98119

ARRINGTON, CHARLES HAMMOND, JR., research director; b. Rocky Mount, N.C., Dec. 23, 1920; s. Charles Hammond and Annie (Barrett) A.; m. Elsie Jane Woodlief, Aug. 20, 1941; children: Charles Hammond, Roger W. B.S., Duke U., 1941; Ph.D., Calif. Inst. Tech., 1949. Research chemist E.I. DuPont De Nemours & Co. Inc., Wilmington, Del., 1949-52, research supr., 1952-57, assoc. research dir., 1957-67, dir. research, 1967-74, asst. gen. dir. research and devel., 1974-78, gen. dir. research and devel., 1978—. Served to lt. USNR, 1943-46. Mem. Am. Chem. Soc., Am. Phys. Soc., AAAS, Soc. Photog. Scientists and Engrs. Indsl. Research Inst., Sigma Xi. Democrat. Am. Baptist. Clubs: Wilmington Country, DuPont Country. Home: 711 Greenwood Rd Wilmington DE 19807 Office: 10th and Market Sts Wilmington DE 19898

ARRINGTON, LEONARD JAMES, history educator; b. Twin Falls, Idaho, July 2, 1917; s. Noah Wesley and Edna Grace (Corn) A.; m. Grace Fort, Apr. 24, 1943; children: James Wesley, Carl Wayne, Susan Grace. B.A. in Econs, U. Idaho, 1939, L.H.D. (hon.), 1977; Ph.D. in Econ. History, U. N.C., 1952; H.H.D. (hon.), Utah State U., 1982. Prof. econs. Utah State U., 1946-72; summer prof. Brigham Young U., Provo, Utah, 1956, 58, 66; Lemuel H. Redd prof. Western history, dir. Charles Redd Center for Western Studies, 1972-80; dir. Joseph Fielding Smith Inst. for Ch. History, 1980—; ch. historian Ch. of Jesus Christ of Latter-day Saints, 1972-80, dir. history div., 1978-80; Fulbright prof. Am. econs. U. Genoa, Italy, 1958-59; vis. prof. history UCLA, 1966-67. Author: Great Basin Kingdom: An Economic History of the Latter-day Saints, 1830-1900, 1958, The Changing Economic Structure of the Mountain West, 1850-1950, 1963, Beet Sugar in the West: A History of the Utah-Idaho Sugar Company, 1891-1966, 1966, Charles C. Rich, Mormon General, Western Frontiersman, 1974, David Eccles, Pioneer Western Industrialist, 1975, Building the City of God: Community and Cooperation Among the Mormons, 1976, From Quaker to Latter-day Saint: Bishop Edwin D. Woolley, 1976, The Mormon Experience: A History of the Latter-day Saints, 1979; Editor: Western Hist. Quar., 1969-72; bd. editors: Pacific Hist. Rev, 1959-62; adv. editor: Dialogue: A Jour. of Mormon Thought, 1966-69. Served with AUS, 1943-46. Recipient Charles Redd Humanities award Utah Acad. Scis., Arts and Letters, 1966, David O. McKay Humanities award Brigham Young U., 1969; Huntington Library fellow, 1956-57. Mem. Mormon History Assn. (pres. 1965-66), Western History Assn. (pres. 1968-69), Am. Hist. Assn. (pres. Pacific Coast br. 1981-82), Agrl. History Soc. (pres. 1969-70), Sons Utah Pioneers, SAR, Am. Legion. Club: Rotary. Home: 2236 South 2200 E Salt Lake City UT 84109 Office: 301 Knight Mangum Bldg Brigham Young U Provo UT 84602 *A religious historian must be tenacious in preserving his bi-linguality; he must attempt to speak with authority and excellence in addressing his professional colleagues in the language of scholarship and, in the language of faith, seek to provide his fellow communicants another experience, another soul, new understandings of life.*

ARRINGTON, RICHARD, mayor; b. Livingston, Ala., Oct. 19, 1934. A.B., Miles Coll., 1955; M.S., U. Detroit, 1957; Ph.D. in Zoology, U. Okla., 1966. Asst. prof. Miles Coll., 1957-63, prof., from 1966, counselor, 1962-63, dir. Summer Sch., acting dean, 1966-67, dean, 1967-70; exec. dir. Ala. Center for Higher Edn., 1970-79; mayor City of Birmingham, Ala., 1979—. Mem. Birmingham City Council, 1971-75. Office: Office of Mayor 710 20th St N Birmingham AL 35203 *

ARROL, JOHN, corporate executive; b. Scotland, Aug. 6, 1923; U.S., 1924, naturalized, 1934; s. William and Isabella (Gordon) A.; m. Jane Trice, June 18, 1949; children: Robert, Nancy, David, William. B.S. in Bus. Adminstrn, Xavier U., 1953; M.A., Vanderbilt U., 1964. Cost supr. Ford Motor Co., 1950-57; planning supr. Curtiss Wright Corp., 1957-58; with Avco Corp., 1958-64, asst. controller, 1962-64; corp. controller Globe-Union, Inc., Milw., 1964-70, v.p., controller, 1970-72, chief fin. officer, 1972-73; sr. v.p. finance Rucker Co., Oakland, Calif., 1973-77, NL Industries-Petroleum Services, Oakland, 1977-78; v.p., chief fin. officer, dir. Gardner-Denver Co., Dallas, 1978-79; v.p. fin. and adminstrn. Systron Donner Corp., Concord, Calif., 1980—; pres. Data Automation Scis., 1967-73; chmn. bd. San Jose Capital Corp., 1976—, Hughes Electronic Devices Corp., Grass Valley, Calif., 1981—; dir. Roconex Corp., Los Gatos, Calif., Pantle Mining Corp., Grass Valley, Paragon Tech. Co., Pleasant Hill, Calif., Lightgate Inc., Berkeley, Calif.; instr. cost accounting U. Tenn., 1960-62; instr. bus. adminstrn. Ind. U., 1964; mem. adv. bd. Fin. Ctr. Bank, San Francisco, 1983—. Bd. dirs. Dallas Civic Opera, Milw. chpt. ARC.; mem. adv. council Sch. Bus., San Francisco State U., 1981—; mem. adv. bd. Mt. Diablo chpt. Boy Scouts Am., Walnut Creek, Calif., 1983—. Mem. Nat. Assn. Accountants, Fin. Execs. Inst. Clubs: Rotary; Round Hill Country (Alamo, Calif.). Home: 2427 Alamo Glen Dr Danville CA 94526 Office: 2750 Systron Dr Concord CA 94518

ARROW, KENNETH JOSEPH, economist, educator; b. N.Y.C., Aug. 23, 1921; s. Harry I. and Lillian (Greenberg) A.; m. Selma Schweitzer, Aug. 31, 1947; children: David Michael, Andrew. B.S. in Social Sci., CCNY, 1940; M.A., Columbia U., 1941, Ph.D., 1951, D.Sc., 1973; LL.D. (hon.), U. Chgo., 1967, City U. N.Y., 1972, Hebrew U. Jerusalem, 1975, U. Pa., 1976, D.Social and Econ. Scis., U. Vienna, Austria, 1971, D.Social Scis., Yale, 1974, Doctor, Université René Descartes, Paris, 1974; Dr.Pol., U. Helsinki, 1976; M.A. (hon.), Harvard U., 1968. Research asso. Cowles Commn. for Research in Econs., 1947-49; asst. prof. econs. U. Chgo., 1948-49; acting asst. prof. econs. and statistics Stanford, 1949-50, asso. prof., 1950-53, prof. econs., statistics and ops. research, 1953-68; prof. econs. Harvard, 1968-74, James Bryant Conant univ. prof., 1974-79; exec. head dept. econs. Stanford U., 1954-56, acting exec. head dept., 1962-63, Joan Kenney prof. econs. and prof. ops. research, 1979—; economist Council Econ. Advisers, U.S. Govt., 1962; cons. RAND Corp. Author: Social Choice and Individual Values, 1951, Essays in the Theory of Risk Bearing, 1971, The Limits of Organization, 1974, Collected Papers, Vols. I and II, 1983; Co-author: Mathematical Studies in Inventory and Production, 1958, Studies in Linear and Nonlinear Programming, 1958, Time Series Analysis of Inter-industry Demands, 1959, Public Investment, The Rate of Return and Optimal Fiscal Policy, 1971, General Competitive Analysis, 1971, Studies in Resource Allocation Processes, 1977. Served as capt. AUS, 1942-46. Social Sci. Research fellow, 1952; fellow Center for Advanced Study in the Behavioral Scis., 1956-57, Churchill Coll., Cambridge, Eng., 1963-64, 70, 73; Guggenheim fellow, 1972-73; Recipient John Bates Clark medal Am. Econ. Assn., 1957; Alfred Nobel Meml. prize in econ. scis., 1972. Fellow Am. Acad. Arts and Scis. (v.p. 1979-81), Econometric Soc. (v.p. 1955, pres. 1956), Am. Statis. Assn., Inst. Math. Statistics, Am. Econ. Assn. (mem. exec. com. 1967-69, pres. 1973), AAAS (chmn. sect K 1983), Internat. Soc. for Inventory Research (pres. 1983-84);

mem. Nat. Acad. Scis., Am. Philos. Soc., Inst. Mgmt. Scis. (pres. 1963, chmn. council 1964), Finnish Acad. Scis. (fgn. hon.), Brit. Acad. (corr.), Western Econ. Assn. (pres. 1980-81). Office: Dept Econs Stanford U Stanford CA 94305

ARROWSMITH, WILLIAM AYRES, educator, writer; b. Orange, N.J., Apr. 13, 1924; s. Walter Weed and Dorothy (Ayres) A.; m. Jean Reiser, Jan. 10, 1945 (div. 1980); children: Nancy, Beth. B.A., Princeton U., 1947, Ph.D., 1954; B.A. (Rhodes scholar), Oxford (Eng.) U., 1951, M.A., 1958; LL.D. hon., Loyola U., 1968, L.H.D., St. Michael's Coll., Burlington, Vt., 1968, D.Litt., Westminster Coll., Fulton, Mo., 1969, Dartmouth Coll., 1970, Dickinson Coll., 1971, Lebanon Valley Coll., 1973, D.L.H., U. Detroit, 1973, Grand Valley State Colls., 1973. Instr. classics Princeton U., 1951-53; instr. classics and humanities Wesleyan U., Middletown, Conn., 1953-54; asst. prof. classics and humanities U. Calif., Riverside, 1954-56; mem. faculty U. Tex., Austin, 1958-70, prof. classics, 1959-70, chmn. dept., 1964-66, Univ. prof. arts and letters, 1965-70; vis. prof. humanities M.I.T., 1971; prof. classics, Univ. prof. Boston U., 1971-76; vis. Henry McCormick prof. dramatic lit. Sch. Drama, Yale U., 1976-77; prof. writing seminars and classics Johns Hopkins U., 1977-81; Ednl. cons. Ford Found., 1970-71; cons. Leadership Tng. Inst., Office of Edn., 1970-71; vis. prof. M.I.T., spring 1971; fellow Center Advanced Studies, Wesleyan U., 1967, Battelle Meml. Inst., Seattle, 1968; founding editor Chimera, 1942-44, Hudson Rev., 1948-60, Arion, Jour. Classical Culture, 1962—; adv. editor Tulane Drama Rev., 1960-67; adv. bd. Mosaic, 1967—; mem. exec. com. Nat. Translation Center, 1965-70; mem. faculty, mem. bd. Nat. Humanities Faculty, 1972-74; mem. Acad. Lit. Studies, 1975, Internat. Council on Future of the Univ. Translator: (Petronius) The Satyricon, 1959, (Euripides) The Bacchae, Cyclops, Heracles, Orestes and Hecuba, 1960, (Aristophanes) The Birds, 1961, Clouds, 1962, (with R. Shattuck) The Craft and Context of Translation, 1962, (with D. S. Carne-Ross) (Cesare Pavese) Dialogues with Leucò, 1965, (Cesare Pavese) Hard Labor, 1976; Editor: Image of Italy, 1961, Five Modern Italian Novels, 1964; gen. editor: The Greek Tragedy in New Translation (33 vols.), 1973—, Alcestis (Euripides), 1975; Contbr. numerous articles to profl. jours. Served with AUS, 1943-46. Woodrow Wilson fellow, 1947-48; Guggenheim fellow, 1957-58; Prix de Rome sr. research fellow Am. Acad. Rome, 1956-57; Phi Beta Kappa vis. scholar, 1964-65; Rockefeller fellow in humanities, 1980-81; recipient Longview award criticism, 1960; Bromberg award excellence in teaching U. Tex., 1959; Morris L. Ernst award excellence in teaching, 1962; Piper prof. for disting. teaching, 1966; Harbison award for disting. teaching, 1971; award for lit. Am. Acad. and Nat. Inst. Arts and Letters, 1978. Mem. P.E.N., Assn. Am. Rhodes Scholars, Phi Beta Kappa. Democrat. Club: Cosmos. Office: Emory Univ Dept of Classics Atlanta GA 30322

ARROYO, MARTINA, soprano; b. N.Y.C. Pupil, Marinka Gurevich Mo Martin Rich, Joseph Turnau, Rose Landver; student, Kathryn Long Course Met. Opera. Debut, Carnegie Hall, 1958; leading soprano, Met. Opera, N.Y.C.; in roles including: Tosca; performed opening night Met. season, 1970-71, 71-72, 73-74; performed at, La Scala, Milan, Munich Staatsoper, Berlin Deutsche Oper, Rome Opera, Vienna State Opera, Covent Garden, Teatro Colon, Buenos Aires, Teatro Colon, San Francisco, Teatro Colon, Chgo., and all maj. opera houses; soloist, N.Y., Vienna, Berlin, Royal (London), Paris philharmonics, San Francisco, Pitts., Phila., Chgo., Cleve. symphonies, Concertgebouw, other maj. orchs.; frequent performer, Saratoga, Ravinia, Tanglewood festivals and festivals Vienna, Berlin, Edinburgh, Helsinki; oratorios include Judas Maccabaeus; others., Recs. for, Columbia, London, Angel, DGG, Philips, EMI, RCA. Former mem. Nat. Endowment of Arts, Washington; trustee Carnegie Hall, N.Y.C. Named Outstanding Alumna Hunter Coll., N.Y.C. Address: care Thea Dispeker 59 E 54th St New York NY 10022

ARSEM, ALVAN DONALD, educator; b. Schenectady, July 3, 1923; s. William Collins and Helen Theresa (Moran) A.; m. Katharine L. Brooks, June 30, 1945; children: Nancy, Marilyn, Harold, Beverly. B.S. in Elec. Engring, M.I.T., 1945; postgrad., Syracuse U., 1950-52; M.B.A., Northwestern U., 1978. Devel. engr. RCA, Camden, N.J., 1945-48; mgr. advanced product devel. Gen. Electric Electronics Lab., Syracuse, N.Y., 1948-55; mgr. engring. Stewart-Warner Electronics, Chgo., 1955-58; mgr. engring. and research Wurlitzer Co., North Tonawanda, N.Y., 1958-60, v.p. engring. and research, 1960-68, exec. v.p., 1968-74, chmn. bd., chief exec. officer, 1974-78, now chmn. bd.; asso. prof. Sch. Mgmt., dir. corp. relations, dir. internat. exec. program SUNY, Buffalo, 1978—. Served with AUS, 1942-43. Mem. IEEE (sr.), N.Y. Acad. Sci., U.S. Naval Inst., Acoustical Soc. Am., Sci. Research Soc. Am., Inst. Mgmt. Scis. Clubs: Economic, Chgo. Yacht, Union League (Chgo.); Olcott (N.Y.) Yacht; Royal Canadian Yacht (Toronto, Ont.). Home: 25 Northledge Dr Snyder NY 14226 Office: Sch Mgmt Crosby Hall SUNY Buffalo NY 14214

ART, ROBERT JEFFREY, political scientist, educator; b. Canton, Ohio, Aug. 24, 1942; s. Herbert and Dorothy (Levine) A.; m. Suzanne Straus, June 4, 1968; children: David, Robyn. A.B., Columbia Coll., 1964; Ph.D., Harvard U., 1967. Asst. prof. Brandeis U., Waltham, Mass., 1967-72, assoc. prof., 1973-77, Christian A. Herter prof. internat. relations, 1977—, dean Grad. Sch. Arts and Scis., 1977-83. Author: The TFX Decision: McNarmara and the Military, 1968. Guggenheim fellow, 1975-76. Mem. Council Fgn. Relations (internat. affairs fellow 1971-72), Internat. Inst. Strategic Studies. Home: S Great Rd Lincoln MA 01773 Offic: Dept Politics Brandeis U South St Waltham MA 02254

ARTER, ROBERT, army officer; b. Massillon, Ohio, Sept. 7, 1929; s. Robert Alfred and Mary Bernice (Lemley) A.; m. Lois Caroline Sayles, Sept. 23, 1950; children: Caroline, Robert John. B.S. in Personnel Mgmt, Ohio U., Athens, 1950; M.S. in Public Adminstrn, Shippensburg (Pa.) State Coll., 1972. Commd. U.S. Army, 1950, advanced through grades to maj. gen.; service in, Vietnam; dep. comdr. U.S. Army Command and Gen. Staff Coll., Ft. Leavenworth, Kans., 1977-79; comdr. U.S. Army Mil. Dist. Washington, 1979-81, U.S. Army Milpercen, 1981-83, U.S. Army Readiness and Mobilization Region VIII, Hdqrs. Fitzsimons Army Med. Ctr., Aurora, Colo., 1983—. Decorated Silver Star, Legion of Merit with 1 oak leaf cluster, D.F.C., Bronze Star, Air medal with 19 oak leaf clusters and V device, Joint Service Commendation medal with oak leaf cluster, Purple Heart, Combat Inf. badge (2), Parachutist badge. Methodist. Home: Quarters 3 Fort Lesley J McNair Washington DC 20319 Office: Quarters 14-1 Fitzsimons Army Med Ctr Aurora CO 80045

ARTHOS, JOHN, English language educator; b. Wilmington, Del., July 18, 1908; s. James and Norma (Bennett) Exarchoulakos; m. Martha Rose Ennen, May 10, 1952; children: Lydie, John, James, Maria, Martha. A.B., Dartmouth Coll., 1930; A.M., Harvard U., 1933, Ph.D., 1937. Mem. faculty English dept. U. Mich., Ann Arbor, 1938-42, 45—, assoc. prof., 1949-54, prof., 1954—, Henry Russell Lectr., 1970, Hereward T. Price univ. prof. English, 1972—; faculty U. Wash., Seattle, 1963, Tex. A&M U., 1980; research prof. U. Florence, 1949-50, U. Rome, 1970-71; vis. lectr. Ala. Shakespeare Festival, Jacksonville State U., 1977-78; cons. Nat. Humanities faculty. Author: Minturno to The Apennines, 1946, Language of Natural Description in Eighteenth Century Poetry, 1949, On a Mask Presented at Ludlow-Castle, 1954, On the Poetry of Spenser and the Form of Romances, 1956, Dante, Michelangelo and Milton, 1963, The Art of Shakespeare, 1964, Milton and the Italian Cities, 1968, Shakespeare: The Early Writings, 1972, Shakespeare's Use of Dream and Vision, 1976, The Status of the Humanities, 1980, An Invitation to India, 1983; Editor: Love's Labor's Lost, 1965, Life of Adam (G. B. Loredano), 1968, Selected Poetry of John Dryden, 1970. Am. del. U. Delhi and Aurobindo Centre, 1980. Served with AUS, 1942-45. Decorated Bronze Star; Guggenheim fellow, 1956-57; Am. Council Learned Socs. fellow, 1963-64. Mem. Modern Lang. Assn. Am., Milton Soc., Dante Soc., Renaissance Soc. Club: U. Mich. Research (pres. 1977). Home: 2026 Hill St Ann Arbor MI 48104

ARTHUR, ANDREW RAYMOND, manufacturing company executive, consultant; b. Chgo., July 18, 1936; s. Hurshel and Margaret (Schurr) A.; m. Ruth Ann Wolf; children: Thomas, William, Daniel, Philip, Catherine, Patricia, Michael. B.S., U. Notre Dame, 1958; J.D., N.Y.U., 1962. Patent atty Western Electric Co., N.Y.U., 1958-63; sr. v.p. and adminstrn. Bell & Howell Co., Chgo, 1963-82, cons., Chgo., 1982-83; sr. v.p. AM Internat., Chgo., 1983—. Mem. Winnetka Caucus, Ill., 1981-83; vice chmn. Chgo. Community Ventures Inc. Mem. State Bar Calif., ABA. Roman Catholic. Office: AM Internat Prudential Plaza 130 E Randolph St Chgo Il 60601

ARTHUR, BEATRICE, actress; b. N.Y.C., May 13, 1926; d. Philip and Rebecca Frankel; m. Gene Saks, May 28, 1950; 2 sons. Student, Blackstone Coll., also Franklin Inst. Sci. and Art; student acting with, Erwin Piscator, Dramatic Workshop, New Sch. Social Research. Theatrical appearances include: Lysistrata, 1947, Dog Beneath the Skin, 1947, Gas, 1947, Yerma, 1947, No Exit, 1948, The Taming of the Shrew, 1948, Six Characters in Search of An Author, 1948, The Owl and the Pussycat, 1948, Le Boungeois Gentil Homme, 1949, Yes Is for a Very Young Man, 1949, Creditors, 1949, Heartbreak House, 1949, Three Penny Opera, 1954, 55, Shoestring Revue, 1955, Seventh Heaven, 1955, The Ziegfield Follies, 1956, What's The Rush?, summer 1956, Mistress of the Inn, 1957, Nature's Way, 1957, Ulysses in Nightown, 1958, Chic, 1959, Gay Divorcee, 1960, A Matter of Position, 1962, Mame, 1966 (Tony award best supporting mus. actress), Fiddler on the Roof, 1964; stock appearances with Fiddler on the Roof, Circle Theatre, Atlantic City, summer 1951, State Fair Music Hall, Dallas, 1953, Music Circus, Lambertville, N.J.; resident commedienne, Tamiment (Pa.) Theatre; numerous TV and nightclub appearances, 1948—; motion picture appearances That Kind of Woman, 1959; Lovers and Other Strangers, 1970, Mame, 1974, History of the World Part I, 1981; TV appearances include All in the Family, 1971; leading role: TV series Maude, 1972-78; The Beatrice Arthur Spl; TV series 30 Years of TV Comedy's Greatest Hits. Mem. Artists Equity Assn., Screen Actors Guild, AFTRA. Office: care Tanden Prodns 1901 Ave of Stars Los Angeles CA 90067 *

ARTHUR, BETTIE, psychologist, educator; b. Detroit, Oct. 5, 1924; d. John Gordon and Elizabeth (Gillies) A. B.S., Wayne State U., 1947, M.A., 1949; M.S., U. Mich.-Ann Arbor, 1953, Ph.D., 1958, M.P.H., 1971. Lic. psychologist, Mich. Staff psychologist U. Mich., Ann Arbor, 1958-60, instr. psychology, 1960-63; asst. prof. U. Mich, Ann Arbor, 1963-65; assoc. prof. U. Mich., Ann Arbor, 1965-73, prof., 1973—; cons. Mercywood Sanitarium, Ann Arbor, 1965—, Ann Arbor VA Hosp. Mem. Am. Psychol. Assn. Office: Children's Psychiatric Hosp U Mich Med Ctr Ann Arbor MI 48109

ARTHUR, CHARTHEL, ballerina; b. Los Angeles, Oct. 8, 1946; d. Charles Joseph and Thelma Kathryn (Simonson) A.; m. Robert Marc Estner, Apr. 1, 1971; 1 son, Daniel Adam. Student pub. schs., Pasadena, Calif. Mem. Joffrey Ballet, N.Y.C., 1965-78; tchr. classical ballet Am. Ballet Center, N.J. Ballet Co. and Sch., Joffrey Workshop. Danced: leading roles in Feast of Ashes, Petrouchka, The Green Table, Cakewalk; performed at, White House, 1965, 1968. Mem. Am. Guild Mus. Artists. Home: 25 Minnehaha Blvd Oakland NJ 07436

ARTHUR, GEORGE ROLAND, electronics engineer; b. Phila., Feb. 22, 1925; s. George Gardner and Laura (Mager) A.; m. Madeline Wilma Alby, Feb. 23, 1946 (div. Oct. 1982); children: George Roland, Stephen, Lesley, Randy, Gail.; m. Linda M. Smith, Dec. 28, 1982. Student, Webb Inst., 1944-45; B.Eng., Yale U., 1948, M.Eng., 1949, Ph.D., 1952. Instr. elec. engring. Yale, 1949-52; sect. head missile guidance Sperry Gyroscope, 1952-56; mgr. airborne missile electronics RCA, Camden, N.J., 1956-59; mgr. adv. manned systems engring. Gen. Electric Co., Phila., 1959-63; dep. dir. aerospace ITT Labs., Nutley, N.J., 1963-66; tech. dir. ITT U.S. Def. Group, 1966-67; v.p. ITT-Europe, 1967-78; product group mgr. def., space, marine ITT World Hdqrs., 1979-80; v.p. bus. devel. Fairchild Space/Elec., Germantown, Md., 1980-83; mktg. cons., South Yarmouth, Mass., 1983—. Served with USNR, 1943-46. Fellow Brit. Interplanetary Soc., AAAS, Am. Astron. Soc. (pres. 1959, 60); sr. mem. IEEE, AIAA; mem. Sigma Xi, Tau Beta Pi. Home: 108 Main St South Yarmouth MA 02664

ARTHUR, JAMES CARLTON, advertising executive; b. Galax, Va., Oct. 3, 1933; s. Lanier L. and Elizabeth (Hurt) A.; m. Holly Ann Peck, Apr. 6, 1959; children: Allison Lee, Forrest Carlton. B.S., U. Wis.-Madison, 1960. Assoc. creative dir. Foote, Cone & Belding Advt., Chgo., 1960-69; pres. Arthur & Wheeler, Inc., Chgo., 1969-74; mng. ptnr. Tatham, Laird & Kudner Advt., Chgo., 1974-77; pres. Clinton E. Frank Advt., Chgo., 1977—. Mem. Chgo. Advt. Club. Republican. Congregationalist. Office: 120 S Riverside Plaza Chicago IL 60606

ARTHUR, JAMES GREIG, mathematics educator; b. Hamilton, Ont., Can., May 18, 1944; s. John Greig and Katherine Mary Patricia (Scott) A.; m. Dorothy Pendleton Helm, June 10, 1972; children: James Pendleton, David Greig. B.Sc., U. Toronto, 1966, M.Sc., 1967; Ph.D., Yale U., 1970. Instr. Princeton U., 1970-72; asst. prof. Yale U., 1972-76; prof. Duke U., 1976-79, U. Toronto, 1979—. Contbr. articles to profl. jours. Sloan fellow, 1975-77. Fellow Royal Socl. Can.; mem. Can., Am. math. socs. Address: 23 Woodlawn Ave W Toronto ON Canada M4V 1G6

ARTHUR, JOHN MORRISON, utility executive; b. Pitts., Aug. 17, 1922; s. Hugh Morrison and Ann Matilda (Crowe) A.; m. Sylvia Ann Martin, June 19, 1948; children: William Robert, John Martin, Andrew Scott. B.S. in Elec. Engring, U. Pitts., 1944, M.S., 1947. With Duquesne Light Co., Pitts., 1944—, asst. to chmn. bd. and pres., 1966-67, pres., 1967-68, chmn. bd., chief exec. officer, 1968-83, chmn. bd., pres., 1983—, also dir.; dir. Joy Mfg. Co., Mellon Bank N.A., Mellon Nat. Corp., Mine Safety Appliances Co. Vice pres. Allegheny Conf. on Community Devel.; chmn. Regional Indsl. Devel. Corp. S.W. Pa., Penn's Southwest Assn.; Bd. dirs. Edison Electric Inst., Pa. Economy League; trustee U. Pitts., Robert Morris Coll. Served with AUS, 1942-43. Mem. IEEE, Greater Pitts. C. of C., Profl. Engrs. Soc., Engrs. Soc. Western Pa. Clubs: Duquesne (Pitts); Montour Heights Country (Coraopolis, Pa.); Rolling Rock (Ligonier, Pa.). Office: Duquesne Light Co One Oxford Ctr 301 Grant St Pittsburgh PA 15279

ARTHUR, MACON MICHAUX, lawyer; b. Goldsboro, N.C., Mar. 1, 1922; s. Joseph Dogan and Sarah Borden (Michaux) A.; m. Marianne de Roubaix, Sept. 16, 1950; children: Patrick, Danielle, Elizabeth. B.A., U. Va., 1947, LL.B., 1948. Bar: D.C. 1949, Md. 1959, Ill. 1961. Assoc. Adair, Ulmer, Murchison, Kent & Ashby, Washington, 1948-58, ptnr., 1958-61, Mayer, Brown & Platt, Chgo. and Paris, 1961—. Trustee Eastern Mineral Law Found., Morgantown W.Va., 1983—. Served to capt. U.S. Army, 1942-46; ETO, PTO; served to maj. USAR, 1946-66. Mem. ABA, Chgo. Bar Assn. Clubs: University, Metropolitan (Chgo.). Home: 800 Walden Rd Winnetka IL 60093 Office: Mayer, Brown & Platt 231 S LaSalle Chicago IL 60604

ARTHUR, MAX, nursing home adminstr.; b. Maynard, Iowa, Dec. 25, 1921; s. William Leonard and Marie (Meyer) A.; m. Anita Delores Blake, Nov. 4, 1944; children—Bradley Kent, Gregory Len, David Alan. Student, Upper Iowa Coll., 1940-42, Albright Coll., 1943-44. Lic. nursing home adminstr., Wis. Sales rep. Ohio Equipment Co., Madison, Wis., 1951-57; adminstr. Grundy County Hosp., Grundy Center, Iowa, 1957-60, Summit Hosp., Oconomowoc, Wis., 1960-62; hosp. and phys. relations Asso. Hosp. Services, Milw., 1963-65; adminstr. Waukesha (Wis.) County Instns., 1965-73, Four Winds Manor Nursing Home, Verona, Wis., 1973—; pres. Four Winds Manor, Inc., 1973—. Served with USAAF, 1942-44. Mem. Am. Coll. Nursing Home Adminstrs., Wis. Assn. Nursing Homes (dir.). Lutheran. Address: 302 Lincoln St Verona WI 53593

ARTHUR, RANSOM JAMES, psychiatrist, educator; b. N.Y.C., Dec. 5, 1925; s. Ransom James and Barbara Remick A.; m. Frances Nickolls, Dec. 18, 1954; children: Jane, Shelley. A.B. with honors, U. Calif., Berkeley, 1947; M.D. cum laude, Harvard U., 1951. Intern Mass. Gen. Hosp., Boston, 1951-52; teaching fellow Harvard Med. Sch., 1951-54; resident in pediatrics Children's Med. Center, Boston, 1952-54; resident in psychiatry Queens Hosp., Honolulu, 1954-55; commd. lt U.S. Navy, 1958, advanced through grades to capt., 1968; resident U.S. Naval Hosp., Bethesda, Md., 1957-60; comdg. officer U.S. Naval Med. Neuropsychiat. Res. Unit, San Diego, 1963-74, ret., 1974; prof. psychiatry, assoc. dean Sch. Medicine (Sch. Medicine); dir. Neuropsychiat. Inst. Hosp. and Clinics, UCLA, 1974-79; dean Sch. Medicine, U. Oreg., Portland, 1979-83; prof. UCLA, 1983—; chief of staff Brentwood VA Hosp., Los Angeles, 1983—; cons. Founder Masters' Swimming, 1970, nat. chmn., 1970-72, nat. chmn. goals and objectives, 1972—. Author: An Introduction to Social Psychiatry, 1971; contbr. articles to profl. jours.; mem. editorial bd.: Mil. Medicine, 1972—, Am. Jour. Psychiatry, 1975-79. Served with USMCR, 1943-46. Decorated Legion of Merit (2). Mem. Am. Coll. Psychiatrists, Am. Psychiat. Assn., Royal Soc. Medicine, AMA (Physicians Recognition award), Assn. Am. Med. Colls., Assn. Mil. Surgeons, Phi Beta Kappa, Sigma Xi. Home: 2666 SW Buckingham Ave Portland OR 97201

ARTHUR, ROBERT MILTON, cons., biol. engr.; b. Fond du Lac, Wis., Mar. 21, 1924; s. Simon Albert and Irma Minnie (Spielberg) A.; m. Sally K. McMillan, Mar. 13, 1965; 1 son, Robert McMillan. B.A., Ripon Coll., 1949; B.S., Northwestern U., 1953; M.S., Harvard, 1956; Ph.D., State U. Ia., 1963. Asst. engr. City of Fond du Lac, 1949-52; asst. engr. Chgo. Pump Co., Chgo., 1953-56; prof., chmn. dept. biol. engring. Rose-Hulman Inst. Tech., Terre Haute, Ind., 1956-72; pres. Arthur & Assos. (Cons. Engrs.), Fond du Lac, 1957-77, Arthur Tech., Inc., 1965—, Biotech. Research Center, 1971—. Editor: 3d, 4th, 5th Bioengring. Symposia Rose-Hulman Inst. Served with AUS, 1943-46; ETO. Mem. Water Pollution Control Fedn. (chmn. instrumentation com. 1970-78), Am. Soc. Engring. Edn. (biomed. com. 1964-66, 71-73), Instrument Soc. Am. (Kermit Fischer Environ. award 1981), ASTM, Tau Beta Pi. Tech. Patentee in field; developer biol. engring. dept. Rose-Hulman Inst. Tech., 1967. Home: 2496 Winnebago Dr Fond du Lac WI 54935

ARTHUR, THOMAS DONNELLY, securities company executive; b. Greenville, N.C., Apr. 24, 1944; s. Robert Bruce and Marie (Donnelly) A.; m. Bretta Barrs, June 24, 1967; children: Marie Treadway, Anne Stuart. A.B. in Econs., U. N.C., 1966; M.B.A., East Carolina U., 1971. Vice pres. Pierce, Wulburn, Murphy Corp., 1971-74; v.p. fin. Eli Witt Co., Tampa, Fla., 1974-77; exec. v.p., sec.-treas. Eli Securities Co., Tampa, Fla., 1977—; pres. Havatampa Inc., Tampa, Fla., 1978—. Served to 1st lt. U.S. Army, 1966-69. Decorated Silver Star, Bronze Star, Air medal, Army Commendation medal, Cross of Gallantry Vietnam. Office: Eli Securities Co 500 S Falkenburg Rd Tampa FL 33601

ARTHUR, WALLACE, univ. adminstr.; b. N.Y.C., Nov. 22, 1932; s. Adolph and Helen (Beckerman) Heimlich; m. Lois Shiller, Jan. 17, 1960; children—David A., Edward S., Stephen D. B.Eng.Sci., N.Y. U., 1957, B.E.E., Ph.D., 1962. Research asso. N.Y. U., 1957-61; lectr. Rutgers U., Newark, 1961-62; mem. faculty dept. physics Fairleigh Dickinson U., Teaneck, N.J., 1962-73, prof., chmn. dept., dean Coll. Sci. and Engring., 1973—; cons. in field. Author: Mechanics, 1969. Served with U.S. Army, 1952-54. Mem. AAUP (pres. chpt. 1964-65), Sigma Xi (pres. chpt. 1967-68, 71-73). Home: 22 Raymond Harrington Park NJ 07640 Office: 1000 River Rd Teaneck NJ 07666

ARTHUR, WILLIAM BOLLING, assn. exec.; b. Louisville, Sept. 6, 1914; s. Stanley H. and Margaret (Carter) A.; m. Frances Lee Young, Aug. 19, 1939; children—William Bolling, Richard Houghton. A.B., U. Ky., 1937, LL.D., 1967. Asst. state editor Louisville Courier-Jour., 1939-41; asst. mng. editor Look mag., 1949-54, mng. editor, 1954-66, editor, 1966-71; v.p. Cowles Mag. & Broadcasting Inc., 1962-70; v.p., dir. Cowles Communications, Inc., 1970-71; v.p. Hill and Knowlton, Inc., 1971-73; exec. dir. Nat. News Council, N.Y.C., 1973—; Chief press br. Bur. Pub. Relations, War Dept., 1944-46. Trustee Berea Coll., Ky. Decorated Legion Merit.; Recipient Freedoms Found. award, 1948; named to Ky. Journalism Hall of Fame, 1981. Mem. Am. Soc. Mag. Editors (chmn. 1969-71), Sigma Delta Chi (nat. pres. 1968-69). Presbyn. Home: 715 Bleker Ave Mamaroneck NY 10543 Office: One Lincoln Plaza New York NY 10023

ARTHURS, ALBERTA BEAN, foundation executive; b. Framingham, Mass., Dec. 20, 1932; d. Maurice and Eleanor Irene (Levenson) Bean; m. Edward Arthurs, Dec. 20, 1960; children: Lee Michael, Daniel Jacob, Madeleine Hope. B.A., Wellesley Coll., 1954; Ph.D., Bryn Mawr Coll., 1972. Editor Liberty Mut. Ins. Co. Mag., Boston, 1954-56; dir. admissions Eliot-Pearson Sch.-Tufts U., Medford, Mass., 1957-59, instr. English, 1958-62; instr., lectr. Rutgers U., New Brunswick, N.J., 1964-72, asst. prof., 1972-73; dean Radcliffe Coll., Cambridge, Mass., 1973-75, Harvard U., Cambridge, 1975-77; pres., prof. English Chatham Coll., Pitts., 1977-82; dir. arts and humanities Rockefeller Found., N.Y.C., 1982—; dir. Culbro Corp., Salzburg Seminar in Am. Studies. Bd. dirs. Harbridge House, 1980-82, Presbyn.-Univ. Hosp., Pitts, 1979-82, Pitts. Symphony Soc., 1980-82; trustee Hotchkiss Sch., 1975-83, Pine Manor Coll., 1976-81, Ellis Sch., 1977-82. Clubs: Duquesne (Pitts.); Harvard (N.Y.C.); Signet Soc. (Cambridge). Office: Rockeller Found 1133 Ave of Americas New York NY 10036

ARTHURS, HARRY WILLIAM, legal educator; b. Toronto, Ont., Can., May 9, 1935; s. Leon and Ellen (Dworkin) A.; m. Penny Milnes, June 22, 1974. B.A., U. Toronto, 1955, LL.B., 1958; LL.M., Harvard, 1959. Prof. Osgoode Hall Law Sch., York U., Downsview, Ont., 1961—, dean, 1972-77; arbitrator, mediator; chief adjudicator Pub. Service of Can., 1967-68. Contbr. various articles on labor law, legal history, adminstrv. law and legal edn. to profl. jours. Vice pres. Can. Civil Liberties Assn., 1964-67, pres., 1976-77; mem. U.A.W. Pub. Rev. Bd., 1967-77; vice chmn. Ont. Ednl. Relations Commn., 1976-77; chmn. S.S.H.R.C. Study on Legal Research and Edn. in Can., 1980-83;

bencher Law Soc. Upper Can., 1979-83; mem. Econ. Council Can., 1978-81. Fellow Royal Soc. Can. Home: 11 Hillcrest Pk Toronto ON Canada Office: Osgoode Hall Law Sch York U 4700 Keele St Downsview ON Canada

ARTINIAN, ARTINE, scholar French literature; b. Pazardjick, Bulgaria, Dec. 8, 1907; came to U.S., 1920, naturalized, 1930; s. Peter and Akaby (Berberian) A.; m. Margaret Willard Woodbridge, June 27, 1936; children—Margaret, Robert Willard, Ellen (Mrs. David Artinian Strickland.). A.B., Bowdoin Coll., 1931; diploma, U. Paris, 1932; A.M., Harvard U., 1933; Ph.D., Columbia U., 1941; Litt.D. (hon.), Bowdoin Coll., 1966; postgrad., U. Grenoble, France, 1931, U. Poitiers, France, 1932. Asst. French Bowdoin Coll., 1930-31; ednl. worker dept. correction organizing inmate sch. Welfare Island Penitentiary, N.Y.C., 1934-35; prof. French John Marshall Coll. Law, N.J., 1935-36; chmn. French dept. Bard Coll., Annandale, N.Y., 1935-64, chmn. div. langs., lits., 1939-40, 44-45, 56-57, 58-59, 60-64, prof. emeritus French, 1964—, head instr. French, 1943-44; prof.-in-charge Sweet Briar (Va.) Jr. Year in France, 1953-55; acting dir. U.S. house Cité Universitaire, Paris, summers 1955, 56, 58; mem. com. examiners (French sect.) Coll. Entrance Exam. Bd., 1962-64; Trustee Am. Students Center, Paris, 1954-65; guest of French govt., summer 1946. Compiler extensive Guy de Maupassant collection, also French lit. manuscripts now at, U. Tex., Austin; exhibited collection drawings and paintings of French writers, U.S. tour sponsored by French govt., 1968-70; Century and a Half of French Illustrators, Cornell U., Brandeis U., Harvard U., 1968, Cornell U., Brandeis U., Harvard U., Tex., 1972, Auckland (N.Z.) Mus., 1977, The French Visage, A Century and a Half of French Portraits, Bowdoin Coll. Mus. Art, Hopkins Art Center, Dartmouth Coll., others, 1969, Music in Art at, Henry Morrison Flagler Mus., Palm Beach, Fla., Brandeis U., Wellesley Coll., 1971, Cornell U., 1972; also exhibited other collections numerous other univs. U.S. including, Columbia, Harvard, French Inst. N.Y.C., Vassar, U. Va.; Author: Maupassant Criticism in France, 1880-1940, With an Inquiry into His Present Fame and a Bibliography, 1941, 69; Editor: La Correspondance inédite de Guy de Maupassant, 1951, Pour et Contre Maupassant, 1955, Complete Short Stories of Guy de Maupassant, 1955, La Queue de la Poire de la Boule de Monseigneur (Flaubert 1st edit.), 1958, Là-Haut (Huysmans 1st edit.), 1963, From Victor Hugo to Jean Cocteau, 1965; Contbr. to profl. jours., books. Decorated officier d'Academie, France, 1948; Am. Council Learned Socs. fellow, 1943-44; Fulbright research scholar, France, 1949-50; Am. Philos. Soc. research grantee, Paris, 1960. Mem. Société des Amis de Guy de Maupassant (v.p. 1950-65), MLA (sec. 19th Century French sect. 1947, chmn. 1948), Am. Assn. Tchrs. French, AAUP (pres. Bard Coll. chpt. 1951-52), Société Littéraire des Amis d'Emile Zola (U.S. rep. bd. dirs. 1954-65), Theta Delta Chi, Pi Delta Epsilon. Home: 100 Worth Ave Palm Beach FL 33480

ARTIS, JAY WILLIAM, sociologist, educator; b. Augusta, Wis., Nov. 20, 1925; s. Jay Ralph and Elsie Hazel (Mierow) A.; m. Virginia Cooper, June 15, 1947; children: Deborah Lee, Ronald Jay. B.A., Hamline U., 1949; M.A., Pa. State U., 1950; Ph.D., U. Wis., 1955. Asst. prof. Vanderbilt U., 1953-56; faculty Mich. State U., East Lansing, 1956—, prof. sociology, 1963—, acting dean Coll Social Sci., 1972, chmn. dept. sociology, 1973-83; vis. prof. Makerere U., Kampala, Uganda, 1970-72. Served with U.S. Army, 1943-46. Mem. Am. Sociol. Assn., African Studies Assn. Home: 6230 Cobblers Dr East Lansing MI 48823 Office: Dept Sociology Berkey Hall Michigan State U East Lansing MI 48824

ARTNER, ALAN GUSTAV, journalist; b. Chgo., May 14, 1947; s. Gustav and Katherine Rose (Lucas) A. B.A., Northwestern U., 1968, M.A., 1969. Apprentice music critic Chgo. Tribune, 1972-73, art critic, 1973—. Rockefeller Found. grantee, 1971-72. Office: Chgo Tribune 435 N Michigan Ave Chicago IL 60611

ARTSCHWAGER, RICHARD, artist; b. Washington, Dec. 26, 1924; s. Ernst and Eugenia (Brodsky) A.; m. Catherine Kord, Sept. 16, 1972; 1 dau. by previous marriage, Eva. A.B., Cornell U., 1948; pupil of, Amedee Ozenfant, N.Y.C., 1949-50. One-man shows include, Leo Castelli Gallery, N.Y.C., 1965, 67, 72, 73, 75, 76, 78, 79, Konrad Fischer, Dusseldorf, Germany, 1968, Illeana Sonnabend, Paris, Geneva, Stockholm, 1975, Kunstverein, Hamburg, Germany, 1979, Albright-Knox Art Gallery, Buffalo, Inst. Contemporary Art, U. Pa., Phila., La Jolla (Calif.) Mus. Contemporary Art, 1980, Mus. Contemporary Art, Houston, numerous gallery and mus. group shows, 1963—; represented in permanent collections, Milw. Art Center, Mus. Modern Art, Whitney Mus., The Rockhill-Nelson Mus., Kansas City, Mo., Detroit Art Center, Stroer Mus., Darmstadt, Germany, Aachen (Germany) Mus., Wadsworth Athenaeum, Conn., Rotterdam (Netherlands) Mus., Basel (Switzerland) Mus., La Jolla (Calif.) Mus., also pvt. collections. Originated mode in which art work, surroundings, participant/viewer form single context. Address: Box 99 Charlotteville NY 12036

ARTUSIO, JOSEPH FRANCIS, JR., anesthesiologist; b. Jersey City, Nov. 26, 1917; s. Joseph and Jennie (Cuneo) A.; m. Mary Louise Ellis, Oct. 8, 1945; children: Marianne, Suzanne (Mrs. Neil McIntyre), Evelyn, Joseph Francis, Mark, Douglas. B.S., St. Peters Coll., 1939; M.D., Cornell U., 1943. Diplomate: Am. Bd. Anesthesiology. Intern Bellevue Hosp., N.Y.C., 1943-44; resident anesthesiology N.Y. Hosp., 1946-47, asst. attending anesthesiologist, 1947-48, attending anesthesiologist in charge, 1948-57, anesthesiologist-in-chief, 1957—; instr. surgery Cornell U. Med. Coll., 1947-48, asst. prof. surgery, 1948-52, assoc. prof., 1952-57, prof. anesthesiology in surgery, 1957-67, prof. anesthesiology, chmn. dept., 1967—. Mem. bd. edn. Pelham (N.Y.) Pub. Schs., 1961-69, pres., 1968-69; trustee, sec. Anesthesia Found., 1974-78. Served with M.C. AUS, 1944-46. Fellow Am. Coll. Anesthesiologists; mem. AMA, Acad. Anesthesiology, Am. Soc. Anesthesiologists, Am. Soc. Pharmacology and Exptl. Therapeutics, Assn. Univ. Anesthetists, Soc. Academic Anesthesia (chmn. placement com. 1970-81), Soc. Exptl. Biology and Medicine (unitarian com. 1956), Med. Soc. State N.Y., N.Y. Acad. Medicine (chmn., sec. anesthesiology and resuscitation 1970), N.Y. State Soc. Anesthesiologists (gen. chmn. postgrad. assembly 1968-70), Med. Soc. County N.Y. Home: 238 Corlies Ave Pelham NY 10803 Office: Dept Anesthesiology Cornell U Med Coll New York NY 10021

ARTZ, FREDERICK BINKERD, historian; b. Dayton, Ohio, Oct. 19, 1894; s. J. Elam and May (Binkerd) A. A.B. summa cum laude, Oberlin Coll., 1916, D.Litt., 1966; student, U. Toulouse, 1919, U. Paris, 1922-23; Ph.D., Harvard, 1924; D.Litt., Carthage Coll., 1970. Instr. history Antioch Coll., 1916-17, Harvard, 1923-24; prof. history Oberlin Coll., 1924—; vis. prof. Harvard, 1930-31; lectr. Harvard Summer Sch., 1931, 34. Author: France Under the Bourbon Restoration, 1931, Reaction and Revolution, 1814-32; W.L. Langer series of Rise of Modern Europe The Intellectual History of Europe from St. Augustine to Marx-a Guide, 1951, The Mind of the Middle Ages, 200-1500 A.D., an Historical Survey, 1954, 3d rev. edit., 1980, From the Renaissance to Romanticism A.D. 1300-1830, 1962; also Japanese transl. Memoirs, 1964, The Enlightenment in France, 1968; Contbr. to: Ency. of Soc. Sciences; Mem. bd. editors: Jour. Modern History, 1932-35. Served with A.E.F., 1917-19; France. Fellow Social Sci. Research Council, 1928-29. Mem. Am. Hist. Assn., AAUP, Royal Hist. Soc., Société d'Histore Moderne, Phi Beta Kappa. Home: 157 N Professor St Oberlin OH 44074

ARTZ, KENNETH BUCKLEY, financial exec.; b. Reading, Pa., July 14, 1928; s. Clarence Bright and Naomi (Floyd) A.; m. Ann Louise Wildermuth, June 2, 1956. B.S. in Econs, Albright Coll., Reading, 1957. C.P.A., Pa., D.C. Sr. accountant Price Waterhouse & Co., Phila., 1957-63; asst. to controller Curtis Pub. Co., Phila., 1963-66, treas., 1966-69, v.p., treas., 1969-71; v.p. finance and adminstrn. Ballantine Books, Inc. (subsidiary Internat. Textbook Corp.), N.Y.C., 1971-73; treas. Madison Group, Inc., N.Y.C., 1973-75; v.p. finance Phila. mag., 1975—. Served with AUS, 1951-53. Mem. Am. Inst. C.P.A.s. Home: Hopkinson House Philadelphia PA 19106 Office: Phila Mag 1500 Walnut St Philadelphia PA 19102

ARTZT, EDWIN LEWIS, consumer products co. exec.; b. N.Y.C., Apr. 15, 1930; s. William and Ida A.; m. Ruth Nadine Martin, May 12, 1950; children—Wendy Anne, Karen Susan, William M., Laura Grace, Elizabeth Louise. B.J., U. Oreg., 1951. Account exec. Glasser Gailey Advt. Agy., Los Angeles, 1952-53; with Procter & Gamble Co., Cin., 1953—, brand mgr. advt. dept., 1956-58, asso. brand promotion mgr., 1958-60, brand promotion mgr., 1960, 62-65, copy mgr., 1960-62, advt. mgr. paper products div., 1965-68, mgr. products food div., 1968-69, v.p., 1969, v.p., acting mgr. coffee div., 1970, v.p., group exec., 1970-75, dir., 1972-75, 80—, group v.p., Europe, Belgium, 1975-80, exec. v.p. internat., 1980—. Past chmn. residential div. United Appeal; past chmn. Public Library Capital Funds campaign; past dist. chmn. Capital Fund Raising dr. Boy Scouts Am., past leadership tng. chmn.; past chmn. advt. com. Sch. Tax Levy, County Govt. Issue; past trustee Kansas City Philharmonic, Nutrition Found., Boys' Clubs Greater Cin.; past bd. dirs. Kansas City Lyric Theater; past bd. govs. Kansas City Art Inst. Mem. Am. C. of C. Belgium (v.p.), Conf. Bd. Europe (adv. council), Internat. C. of C. (exec. com. U.S. council), Nat. Fgn. Trade Council. Clubs: Queen City, Cin. Country, Comml. (Cin.). Home: 9005 Cunningham Rd Cincinnati OH 45243

ARUM, ROBERT, lawyer, sports events promotor; b. N.Y.C., Dec. 8, 1931; s. Samuel and Celia (Baumgarten) A.; m. Barbara Mandelbaum, July 2, 1960 (div. 1977); children: John, Richard, Elizabeth; m. Sybil Ann Hamada, Dec. 18, 1977. B.A., N.Y. U., 1953; J.D. cum laude, Harvard, 1956. Bar: N.Y. 1956. Atty. firm Root, Barrett, Cohen, Knapp & Smith, N.Y.C., 1956-61; asst. U.S. atty., chief tax sect. U.S. Atty.'s Office, So. Dist. N.Y., 1961-64; partner firm Phillips, Nizer, Benjamin, Krim & Ballon, N.Y.C., 1964-72, Arum & Katz, 1972-79; chmn. Top Rank, Inc.; pres. Bob Arum Enterprises, Inc.; Promoter Ali-Frazier Super Fight II, 1974, Evel Knievel Snake River Canyon Jump, 1974, Ali-Norton World Heavyweight Championship, 1976, Monzon-Valdez World Middleweight Championship, 1976, 77, Ali-Shavers Heavyweight Championship, 1977, Ali-Spinks Championship, 1978, Tate-Coetzee Championship, 1979, Leonard-Duran Championship, 1980, Tate-Weaver Championship, 1980, Arguello-Pryor Championship, 1983, Moore-Duran Championship, 1983, Hagler-Duran Championship, 1983. Mem. Am. Bar Assn., Assn. Bar City N.Y. Club: Friars. Home: 250 E 63d St New York NY 10021

ARUMI, FRANCISCO, architecture educator, consultant; b. Valparaiso, Chile, Feb. 4, 1940; came to U.S., 1957; s. Francisco and Piedad (Noe) Arumi S.; m. Betys E. Battle, Dec. 22, 1963 (div. Apr. 1981); children: Ana Marie, Francisco Alexander. B.S., U. N.C., 1962, M.S., 1964; Ph.D., U. Tex., 1970. Asst. prof. Calif. Poly Inst., San Luis Obispo, 1964-65; vis. prof. U. Costa Rica, San Jose, 1965-66; physics specialist NSF, San Jose, 1966-67; research assoc. U. Tex., Austin, 1967-72, now prof. architecture; cons. in field. Author: Fisica de Plasmas, 1972; contbr. articles to profl. publs.; author: computer program DEROB. Grantee NSF, 1972-75, Dept. Energy, 1978-83. Mem. Am. Phys. Soc., ASHRAE. Roman Catholic. Office: Sch Architecture U Tex Austin TX 78731 *

ARUNDEL, ARTHUR WINDSOR, publishing company executive; b. Washington, Jan. 12, 1928; s. Russell Moore and Marjorie (Sale) A.; m. Margaret Crenshaw McElroy, May 18, 1957; children: Sarah Harwood, Paul Windsor, Marjorie Sale, John Howard, Thomas Brooke. B.A., Harvard U., 1951. Corr. CBS Washington Bur., 1955-56, UPI, Washington, 1957-59; spl. asst. to sec. U.S. Dept. Commerce, Washington, 1959-60; founder, chief exec. officer Arundel Communications, Washington, 1960—; chmn. bd. Pepcom Industries, Washington, 1957-80; dir. Nat. Savs. & Trust Co., Washington. Contbr. numerous articles to profl. jours. Bd. dirs. Kennedy Sch. Govt., Harvard U., African Wildlife Leadership Found., Nairobi, Kenya and Washington, Washington Journalism Center, Nat. Press Found., Suburban Newspapers Am. Served with USMC, 1951-55. Democrat. Episcopalian. Clubs: Nat. Press, Met. (Washington); Racquet & Tennis (N.Y.C.). Office: 1707 L St NW 500 Washington DC 20036

ARVESON, RAYMOND GERHARD, supt. schs.; b. Jamestown, N.D., May 11, 1921; s. Gerhard B. and Josephine B. (Akre) A.; m. Adelaide M. Severson, June 21, 1942; children—Raymond, Susan, John. B.A., Mayville State Coll., 1942; M.A., U. Minn., 1948; Ed.D., U. Calif., Berkeley, 1962. High sch. prin., Alamo, N.D., 1942-43, high sch. prin., supt. schs., Langdon, N.D., 1943-45, supt. schs., Leeds, N.D., 1945-57, high sch. counselor, asst. prin., prin., Hayward, Calif., 1957-63, asst. supt., 1963-68, supt. pub. schs., 1968-76; supt. Mpls. Public Schs., 1976-80, East Baton Parish Schs., Baton Rouge, 1980—; prof. Calif. State U., Hayward, 1962-63; cons. numerous Calif. sch. dists. Contbr. articles to ednl. jours. Mem. standing com. on research and analysis Am. Lutheran Ch., 1973-80; bd. dirs. United Way, Far West Regional Lab. for Ednl. Research and Devel.; bd. regents Golden Valley Luth. Coll.; mem. exec. bd. San Francisco, Istrouma and Viking councils Boy Scouts Am.; trustee Fairview Hosp. Recipient Silver Beaver award Boy Scouts Am., 1963, Man of Year award Boys Clubs Am., 1976. Mem. NEA (life), Calif. Tchrs. Assn. (life), N.D. Edn. Assn. (life), Hayward C. of C. (life), Baton Rouge C. of C., Am. Assn. Sch. Adminstrs. (joint com. Nat. Sch. Bds. Assn.), Calif. Assn. Sch. Adminstrs., La. Assn. Sch. Execs., La. Assn. Sch. Supts., Assn. Supervision and Curriculum Devel. (nat. bd., Calif. pres.), Nat. Soc. for Study Edn., Scholia, Phi Delta Kappa. Club: Rotary. Home: 3017 Belle Cherie Dr Baton Rouge LA 70808 Office: 1050 S Foster Dr Baton Rouge LA 70806

ARVESON, WILLIAM BARNES, mathematics educator; b. Oakland, Calif., Nov. 22, 1934; s. Ronald Magnus and Audrey Mary (Hichens) A. B.S. in Math, Calif. Inst. Tech., 1960; M.A., UCLA, 1963, Ph.D., 1964. Benjamin Pierce instr. Harvard U., 1965-68; lectr. dept. math. U. Calif., Berkeley, 1968-69, assoc. prof., 1969-74, prof., 1974—, Miller research prof., 1985-86. Author: An Invitation to C*-algebras, 1976, assoc. editor: Duke Math. Jour, 1975—, Jour. of Operator Theory, 1977—; contbr. articles to math. jours. Served with U.S. Navy, 1952-55. John Simon Guggenheim fellow, 1976-77. Mem. Am. Math. Soc. Office: Dept Math U Calif Berkeley CA 94700

ARZBAECHER, ROBERT C(HARLES), research institute executive, electrical engineer, researcher; b. Chgo., Oct. 28, 1931; s. Hugo L. and Caroline G. A.; m. Joan Collins, June 16, 1956; children: Carolyn, Robert, Mary Beth, Jean, Thomas. B.S., Fournier Inst., 1953; M.S., U. Ill., 1958; Ph.D., 1960. Asst. prof. elec. engring. Christian Bros. Coll., Memphis, 1960-63, assoc. prof., 1963-67; assoc. prof. elec. engring. U. Ill.-Chgo., 1967-70, prof., 1970-76; chmn. dept. elec. engring. U. Iowa, Iowa City, 1976-81; dir. Pritzker Inst. Med. Engring., Ill. Inst. Tech., Chgo., 1981—; v.p. U. Iowa Research Found., 1978-81; pres. Arzco Inc., Chgo., 1980—. Contbr. articles to profl. jours.; inventor Arzco pill electrode. Trustee Ill. Cancer Council, Chgo., 1981—. Mem. IEEE (sr.). Home: 5757 N Sheridan Rd Chicago IL 60660 Office: Ill Inst Tech IIT Ctr Chicago IL 60616

ARZOUMANIDIS, GREGORY G., chemist; b. Thessaloniki, Greece, Aug. 16, 1936; came to U.S., 1964, naturalized, 1976; s. Gerasimos and Sophia A.; m. Anastasia Anastasopoulos, Jan. 2, 1966; children: Sophia, Alexis. B.S. in Chemistry, U. Thessaloniki, 1959, M.S., 1959; Ph.D. in Inorganic Chemistry, U. Stuttgart, (Germany), 1964; M.B.A., U. Conn., 1979. Research assoc. MIT, 1964-66; research chemist Monsanto, Everett, Mass., 1966-69; sr. research chemist Am. Cyanamid Co., Stamford, Conn., 1969-72, Stauffer Chem. Co., Dobbs Ferry, N.Y., 1972-79, Amoco Chems. Corp., Naperville, Ill., 1979—. Inventor comml. catalysts for polypropylene plastics, new processes; patentee (U.S. and fgn.); contbr. articles to profl. jours. Served to 2d lt. Greek Army, 1959-61. Recipient acad. award Govt. of W.Ger., 1963. Mem. Am. Chem. Soc., Sigma Xi. Greek Orthodox. Home: 7 S 610 Carriage Way Naperville IL 60540 Office: PO Box 400 Naperville IL 60566

ARZUBE, JUAN ALFREDO, bishop; b. Guayaquil, Ecuador, June 1, 1918; came to U.S., 1944, naturalized, 1961; s. Juan Bautista and Maria (Jaramillo) A. B.S. in Civil Engring, Rensselaer Poly. Inst., 1942; B.A., St. John's Sem., 1954. Ordained priest Roman Catholic Ch., 1954; asso. pastor St. Agnes Ch., Los Angeles, Resurrection Ch., Ascension Ch., Our Lady of Guadalupe Ch., El Monte, Calif.; aux. bishop of, Los Angeles, 1971—. Episcopal vicar for Spanish speaking, 1973—; mem. nat. bishops coms. Ad Hoc Com. for Spanish Speaking; chmn. Com. for Latin Am. Recipient Humanitarian award Mexican Am. Opportunity Found., 1978, John Anson Ford award Los Angeles County Commn. Human Relations, 1979. Home: 5223 Hastings St Los Angeles CA 90022 Office: 1531 W 9th St Los Angeles CA 90015

ASAKAWA, TOKAKO, dancer, choreographer; b. Toyko, Feb. 23, 1939; U.S., 1962; d. Kamenosuke and Chiaki A.; m. David Hatch Walker, Dec. 20, 1970. Student, Tokyo schs. Dancer Martha Graham Dance Co., N.Y.C., 1962-76, 81—, Alvin Ailey, 1968-69, Pearl Lang, 1967, Lar Lubovitch, 1971; guest performer Japanese Govt., 1974; co-founder Asakawalker Dance Co. Performer, Bell Telephone Hours, Los Angeles, 1970; performed as Eliza: The King and I; choreographer: Fantasy II, Eclipse, Ambrosia, Daybreak, Reflections of Roman. Named Legendary Woman of Am. St. Vincent's Hosp., Birmingham, Ala., 1975; recipient Tokyo Shibun dance award, 1950-62. Mem. Am. Guild Musical Artists. Toured Japan with USIS, 1975. Home and Office: 77 Greene St New York NY 10012

ASANTE, MOLEFI KETE, communications educator; b. Valdosta, Ga., Aug. 14, 1942; s. Arthur Lee and Lillie Bell (Wilkson) Smith; m. Kariamui Welsh, Jan. 8, 1982; children: Kasina Eka, Dauki, Molefi Khumalo. B.A., Okla. Christian U., 1964; M.A., Pepperdine U., 1965; Ph.D., UCLA, 1968; L.H.D., U. New Haven, 1976. Prof. dept. communications UCLA, 1969-73; Fulbright prof., Zimbabwe, 1981-82; chmn. dept. communication SUNY-Buffalo, 1973-79, prof., 1973—. Author: Afrocentricity, Handbook of Inter-Cultural Communication, Transracial Communication, Rhetoric of Black Revolution, Contemporary Public Communication; contbr. articles to profl. jours. Fulbright-Hayes fellow, 1981-82. Mem. Internat. Communications Assn. (v.p. 1977-80), African Heritage Studies Assn., Soc. Intercultural Edn., Tng. and Research. Democrat. Home: 59 Ashland Ave Buffalo NY 14222 Office: Dept CommunicationSUNY Baldy Hall Buffalo Ny 14260

ASBELL, BERNARD, author; b. Bklyn., May 8, 1923; s. Samuel and Minnie (Zevin) A.; m. Mildred Sacarny, Jan. 2, 1944; children: Paul, Lawrence, Jonathan, Jody; m. Marjorie Baldwin Farrell, June 11, 1971. Student, U. Conn., 1943-44; L.H.D., U. New Haven, 1978. Reporter Richmond (Va.) Times-Dispatch, 1945-47; engaged in pub. relations, Chgo., 1947-55; mng. editor Chgo. mag., 1955-56; tchr. non-fiction writing U. Chgo., 1956-60, Bread Loaf Writers Conf., Middlebury (Vt.) Coll., 1960, 61, U. Bridgeport, 1961-63; vis. lectr. Yale U., 1979-80, Pa. State U., 1984-85; dir. New Eng. Writers Center, 1979—; writer in residence Clark U., 1982; cons. Ednl. Facilities Labs., 1963, U. Ill., 1964, Ford Found., 1965, 1968-69; cons. to sec. HEW, 1965-68, IBM Corp., Carnegie Corp. N.Y.; asso. fellow Trumbull Coll., Yale U., 1981—. Free lance author, 1956—; Author: When F.D.R. Died, 1961, The New Improved American, 1965, What Lawyers Really Do, 1970, Careers in Urban Affairs, 1970, The F.D.R. Memoirs, 1973; pseudonym Nicholas Max: President McGovern's First Term, 1973, (with Clair F. Vough) Productivity, 1975, The Senate Nobody Knows, 1978, (with David Hartman) White Coat, White Cane, 1978; editor: Mother & Daughter: The Letters of Eleanor and Anna Roosevelt, 1982; contbr. to nat. mags. Justice of peace, Wilton, Conn., 1966-67; chmn. Wilton Democratic party, 1964-66. Served with AUS, 1943-45. Recipient Sch. Bell award NEA, 1965; Edn. Writers Assn. 1st prize mag. coverage, 1965; spl. citation, 1966. Mem. Am. Soc. Journalists and Authors (pres. 1963, exec. council 1964-66), P.E.N., Authors Guild, Nat. Press Club, Mensa. Club: Coffee House. Address: 265 College St New Haven CT 06510

ASBILL, MAC, JR., lawyer; b. Atlanta, Mar. 15, 1922; s. Mac and Jennie (Sutherl) A.; m. Jane Winchester, Jan. 29, 1943; children: Richard M., Henry W., William S., Anne W. B.A., Princeton U., 1942; LL.B. magna cum laude, Harvard U., 1948. Bar: D.C. 1948, Ga. 1957. Clk. to assoc. justice U.S. Supreme Ct., 1948-49; assoc. firm Sutherland, Asbill & Brennan (and predecessors), Washington, 1949-53, partner, 1953—; atty. office dept. counsel Dept. U.S. Army, 1950-51; mem. Commr. of Internal Revenue's Adv. Group, 1975. Contbr. articles to profl. jours. Mem. Fed. City Council, 1973—, mem. exec. com., 1975—; pres. D.C. Mcpl. Research Bur., 1977-79; vice-chmn. Greater Washington Research Center, 1979-82, trustee, 1982—. Fellow ABA (chmn. sect. taxation 1971-72, ho. of dels. 1978—); mem. D.C. Bar Assn., Am. Law Inst. Home: 9717 Corral Dr Potomac MD 20854 Office: 1666 K St NW Washington DC 20006

ASBURY, ARTHUR KNIGHT, neurologist, educator; b. Cin., Nov. 22, 1928; s. Eslie and Mary (Knight) A.; m. Carolyn Holstein, May 17, 1980; children by previous marriage: Dana, Patricia Knight, William Francis. Grad., Phillips Acad., Andover, Mass., 1946; student, Stanford, 1947-48; B.S., U. Ky., 1951; M.D., U. Cin., 1958; M.A. (hon.), U. Pa., 1974. Intern in medicine Mass. Gen. Hosp., Boston, 1958-59, resident, 1959-63, fellow, 1963-65, staff neurologist, 1965-69; chief neurology San Francisco VA Hosp., 1969-74; prof. dept. neurology U. Pa., Phila., 1974—, chmn. dept. neurology, 1974-82; teaching fellow Harvard Med. Sch., 1958-65, instr., 1965-68, assoc., 1968-69; assoc. prof. neurology U. Calif. at San Francisco, 1969-73, prof., vice-chmn., 1969-74. Sr. editor: Internat. Med. Rev. Series-Neurology, Butterworth & Co., London, 1980—; Asso. editor: Archives of Neurology, 1975-76; Assoc. editor: Annals of Neurology, 1976-81; mem. editorial bd.: Muscle and Nerve, 1977—, Neurology, 1981—, Jour. Neuropathology and Exptl. Neurology, 1981-83; contbr. chpts. to med. textbooks, articles to med. jours. Vice-pres., bd. dirs. Forest Retreat Farms Inc., Carlisle, Ky., 1970—. Served with AUS, 1951-53. USPHS grantee, 1967—; Muscular Dystrophy Assn. grantee, 1974—. Fellow Am. Acad. Neurology (v.p. 1977-79); mem. Am. Neurol. Assn. (councillor 1976-81, pres. 1982-83), Am. Assn. Neuropathologists (v.p. 1983-84), Soc. Neurosci., Assn. Univ. Profs.

Neurology (pres. 1980-82). Episcopalian (vestryman). Home: 2409 Naudain St Philadelphia PA 19146 Office: Dept Neurology Hospital Univ Pa Philadelphia PA 19104

ASBURY, LARRY WAYNE, real estate management company executive; b. Mexico City, Mo., Aug. 13, 1947; s. Donald Earl and Mary Juanita (Brower) A.; m. Debbie G. Widmer, Sept. 8, 1973. B.A. in Bus. Adminstrn., Southwest Mo. State U.-Springfield, 1973, postgrad., 1973-74. Regional field rep. Vernon & James Smith Co., Dallas, 1973-76; v.p., regional mgr. Nat. Corp. Housing Partnerships, Nashville, 1976-79, v.p., Washington, 1979-81, sr. v.p., 1981—; v.p. subs. Nat. Corp. for Housing Partnerships Property Mgmt., Inc., Washington, 1979-81, sr. v.p., 1981-83, exec. v.p., 1983—. Chmn. campaign United Way, Washington, 1981. Served with U.S. Army, 1967-70. Mem. Nat. Assn. Home Builders, Inst. Real Estate Mgmt., Nat. Leased Housing Assn. (speaker 1982). Republican. Methodist. Home: 10407 Rodney Rd Silver Springs MD 20903 Office: Nat Corp Housing Partnerships 1133 15th St NW Washington DC 20005

ASBURY, WILLIAM FITTS, editor; b. Tacoma, Wash., Apr. 19, 1924; s. Joseph Lester and Isabel (Fitts) A.; m. Janet Ward, May 20, 1955; children—Jefferson, Sarah, April, David, Alexandra. B.A. in Journalism, U. Wash., 1949. Corr. far east Christian Herald mag., 1950-52; asst. internat. dir. China Children's Fund, Hong Kong, 1952-54; rep. East Pakistan The Asia Found., Dacca, 1955-58, dir. S. Asia countries, 1958-59; editor, pub., owner The Weekly Trinity Jour., Trinity County, Calif., 1959-61; news editor Oroville (Calif.) Mercury Register, 1961-63; bus. editor Redding (Calif.) Record-Searchlight, 1963-66; mng. editor Bremerton (Wash.) Sun, 1966-69; pub. adviser U. Wash. Daily, 1969-71; exec. Seattle Times; assigned to nat. desk, then transferred as editor, v.p. to Walla Walla Union-Bull., 1971-75; editor Seattle Post-Intelligencer, 1975-81; regional dir. Cordovan Bus. Jours., Houston, 1981—. Adv. bd. Salvation Army. Served with USN, 1943-46. Mem. Allied Daily Newspapers, Asso. Press Mng. Editor's Assn., Am. Soc. Newspaper Editors, Forest Protection Assn., Sigma Nu, Sigma Delta Chi. Democrat. Methodist. Clubs: Washington Athletic, Inquiry, Family Sports. Home: 9011 NE 34th Bellevue WA 98004 Office: Cordovan Bus Jours 5314 Bingle Rd Houston TX 77092

ASCH, MOSES, record company executive. Owner, founder, head Folkways Records, N.Y.C., 1948—. Office: Folkways Records 43 W 61st St New York NY 10023

ASCHAFFENBURG, WALTER EUGENE, composer, music educator; b. Essen, Germany, May 20, 1927; came to U.S., 1938, naturalized, 1944; s. William Arthur and Margarete (Herz) A.; m. Nancy Dandridge Cooper, Aug. 14, 1951; children: Ruth Margareta, Katherine Elizabeth. Diploma, Hartford Sch. Music, 1945; B.A., Oberlin Coll., 1951; M.A., Eastman Sch. Music, 1952. Prof. composition and music theory, chmn. composition dept. Oberlin (Ohio) Coll. Conservatory Music, 1952—, also former chmn. dept. music theory. Composer: Ozymandias-Symphonic Reflections for Orch, 1952, Cello Sonata, 1953, Sonata for Solo Violin, 1954, Piano Sonatina, 1954, String Quartet, 1955, Bartleby-opera, 1962, Elegy for Strings, 1961, Three Dances for Orch, 1966, Three Shakespeare Sonnets, 1967, Quintet for Winds, 1967, Proem for Brass and Percussion, 1969, Duo for Violin and Cello, 1971, Conversations-Six Pieces for Piano, 1973, Libertatem Appellant for Tenor, Baritone and Orch, 1976, Carrousel—24 Pieces for Piano, 1980, Concertino for Violin, Ten Winds and Contrabass, 1982, Laughing Time for Mixed Chorus, 1983. Served with AUS, 1945-47. Recipient award Fromm Music Found., 1953; Nat. Inst. Arts and Letters award, 1966; Cleve. arts prize, 1980; Guggenheim fellow, 1955-56, 73-74. Mem. ACLU, AAUP (past chpt. pres.), Am. Soc. U. Composers, Am. Music Center, Soc. for Music Theory, ASCAP. Home: 49 Shipherd Circle Oberlin OH 44074

ASCHAUER, CHARLES JOSEPH, JR., health products company executive; b. Decatur, Ill., July 23, 1928; s. Charles Joseph and Beulah Diehl (Kniple) A.; m. Elizabeth Claire Meagher, Apr. 28, 1962; children: Karen Claire, Thomas Arthur, Susan Jean, Karl Andrew. B.B.A., Northwestern U., 1950; certificate internat. bus. adminstr., Centre d'Etudes Industrielles, Geneva, Switzerland, 1951. Prin. McKinsey & Co., Chgo., 1955-62; v.p. mktg. Mead Johnson Labs. div. Mead Johnson & Co., Evansville, Ind., 1962-67; v.p., pres. automotive group Maremont Corp., Chgo., 1967-70; v.p., group exec. Whittaker Corp., Los Angeles, 1970-71; v.p., pres. hosp. products div. Abbott Labs., North Chicago, Ill., 1971-76, v.p., group exec., 1976-79, exec. v.p., dir., 1979—; dir. Benefit Trust Life Ins. Co., Chgo., Stearns Chem. Corp., Madison, Wis., Marine Corp., Milw. Served to lt. Supply Corps USNR, 1951-55. Mem. Chgo. Pres.'s Orgn., Proprietary Assn., Sigma Nu. Clubs: University, Economics (Chgo.); Sunset Ridge Country (Northbrook, Ill.). Office: Abbott Park North Chicago IL 60064

ASCHENBRENNER, KARL, educator, philosopher; b. Bison, Kans., Nov. 20, 1911; s. John and Elisabeth Nathalia (Schnell) A.; m. Margaret Marie Kerr, Jan. 19, 1937; children: Lisbeth, Peter, John. A.B., Reed Coll., 1934; M.A., U. Calif.-Berkeley, 1938, Ph.D., 1940. Instr. philosophy Reed Coll., 1940-42; mem. faculty U. Calif.-Berkeley, 1946—, prof. philosophy, 1959—, chmn. philosophy, 1960-63, chmn. dept. design, 1964-65; vis. lectr. Amerika Inst., U. Munich, 1950. Co-editor, translator: (Baumgarten) Reflections on Poetry, 1954, Aesthetic Theories, 1965; author: The Concepts of Value, 1971; Author: The Concepts of Criticism, 1974, Analysis of Appraisive Characterization, 1983, Companion to Kant's Critique of Pure Reason, 1983; also articles, reviews in field. Del. Internat. Congress Aesthetics, 1956, 60, 64, 72, 76, 80. Served to lt. USNR, 1943-46. Guggenheim fellow, Vienna and London, 1956-57; Fulbright research fellow U. Munich, 1963-64; sr. fellow Nat. Endowment for Humanities, 1972; exchange scholar Inst. Cultural Relations, Budapest, Hungary, 1974-75, 77. Mem. Am. Soc. Aesthetics, Brit. Soc. Aesthetics, Phi Beta Kappa. Club: University Faculty (Berkeley). Home: 1616 La Vereda Rd Berkeley CA 94709

ASCHHEIM, JOSEPH, economist, educator; b. Hannover, Germany, May 28, 1930; came to U.S., 1947, naturalized, 1952; s. Max and Sarah (Pfeffer) A.; married. A.B. with highest honors, U. Calif. at Berkeley, 1951; A.M. (Charles H. Smith scholar), Harvard U., 1953; Ph.D. (John E. Thayer scholar), Harvard U., 1954. Mem. faculty Johns Hopkins U., 1956-63; mem. faculty George Washington U., Washington, 1963—, prof. econs., 1964—; at various times cons. to U.S. govt. and internat. orgns.; dir. research, econ. adviser to gov. Central Bank Kenya, 1971-72; vis. lectr. various European and Asian univs. Author books and numerous articles in profl. jours.; editorial bd.: So. Econ. Jour, 1960-62, Atlantic Econ. Jour, 1973—. Served with AUS, 1954-56. Ford Found. Faculty Research fellow. Mem. Am. Econs. Assn., Atlantic Econs. Assn. (v.p. 1973-76), Royal Econ. Soc., Phi Beta Kappa. Jewish. Office: Dept Econs George Washington U Washington DC 20052

ASH, MARY KAY WAGNER, cosmetics company executive; b. Hot Wells, Tex.; d. Edward Alexander and Lula Vember (Hastings) Wagner; m. Melville Jerome Ash, Jan. 6, 1966 (dec.); children: Marylyn Rogers, Ben Rogers, Richard Rogers. Student, U. Houston, 1942-43. Mgr. Stanley Home Products, Houston, 1939-52; nat. tng. dir. World Gift Co., Dallas, 1952-63; founder, chmn. May Kay Cosmetics, Inc., Dallas, 1963—; speaker to various orgns. Vol. Dallas County Community Action Com.; mem. chancellor's council U. Tex. Mem. Bus. and Profl. Women's Club. Office: Mary Kay Cosmetics Inc 8787 Stemmons Freeway Dallas TX 75247 *Our company philosophy of God first, family second, career third has contributed immeasurably to our company's success. I feel I simply verbalized what most women feel their priorities should be.*

ASH, PHILIP, psychologist; b. N.Y.C., Feb. 2, 1917; s. Samuel Kieval and Estella (Feldstein) A.; m. Ruth Clyde, Sept. 16, 1945 (div. Dec. 1972); children—Peter, Sharon; m. Judith Nelson Cates, June 6, 1973; 1 son, Nelson E. B.S. in Psychology, City U. N.Y., 1938; M.A. in Personnel Adminstrn, Am. U., 1949; Ph.D. in Psychology, Pa. State U., 1949. Diplomate: Indsl. Psychlogy Am. Bd. Profl. Psychology. Analyst to unit chief occupational research Dept. Labor, 1940-47; research fellow Pa. State U., 1947-49, asso. prof., 1949-52; asst. to v.p. indsl. relatons Inland Steel, 1952-68; prof. psychology U. Ill., Chgo., 1968-80, prof. emeritus, 1980—; dir. research John E. Reid Assos., Chgo., 1969—; dir. Ash, Blackstone & Cates, Blacksburg, Va. Author: Guide for Selection and Placement of Employees, 2d edit, 1977, also articles.; Editor: Forensic Psychology and Disability Evaluation, 1972. Mem. public adv. com. Chgo. Commn. Human Relations, 1957-80; retirement com. Chgo. Commn. Sr. Citizens, 1960-80; chmn. Ill. Psychologist Examining Com., 1963-72. Fellow Am. Psychol. Assn. (pres. div. indsl. psychology 1968-69), AAAS; mem. Ill. Psychol. Assn. (pres. 1963-64), Chgo. Psychol. Assn., Midwest Psychol. Assn., Am. Personnel and Guidance Assn., Am. Psychology-Law Soc., Indsl. Relations Research Assn., Internat. Assn. Applied Psychology, Internat. Gerontol. Assn., Phi Beta Kappa, Sigma Xi, Psi Chi. Home and Office: 817 Hutcheson Dr Blacksburg VA 24060

ASH, ROY LAWRENCE, business executive; b. Los Angeles, Oct. 20, 1918; s. Charles K. and Fay E. (Dickinson) A.; m. Lila M. Hornbek., Nov. 13, 1943; children—Loretta (Mrs. Truman T. Ackerson), James, Marilyn Ash Hodge, Robert, Charles. M.B.A., Harvard, 1947. With Bank of Am., 1936-42, 47-49; chief fin. officer Hughes Aircraft Co., 1949-53; co-founder Litton Industries, Inc., Beverly Hills, Calif., 1953-72, dir., 1953-72, pres., 1961-72; asst. to Pres. U.S.; dir. Office Mgmt. and Budget, Washington, 1973-75; chmn. bd., chief exec. officer AM Internat., 1976-81; dir. Global Marine, Inc., 1965-72, 75-81, BankAmerica Corp., Bank of Am. NT & SA, Consol. Foods Corp., Trus-Joist Corp.; Chmn. Pres.'s Adv. Council on Exec. Orgn., 1969-71; co-chmn. Japan-Calif. Assn., 1965-72, 80-81; vice chmn. Los Angeles Olympic Organizing Com. Trustee Calif. Inst. Tech., 1967-72, Com. for Econ. Devel., 1970-72, 75—, Urban Inst., 1971-72; dir. Los Angeles World Affairs Council, 1968-72, 78—, pres., 1970-72; chmn. adv. council on gen. govt. Rep. Nat. Com., 1977-80. Mem. C. of C. U.S. (dir. 1979—), Conf. Bd. Clubs: Bel Air Country, Harvard (Los Angeles). Office: 1900 Ave of Stars Los Angeles CA 90067

ASHBERY, JOHN LAWRENCE, author; b. Rochester, N.Y., July 28, 1927; s. Chester Frederick and Helen (Lawrence) A. Grad., Deerfield Acad., 1945; B.A., Harvard U., 1949; M.A., Columbia U., 1951; postgrad., NYU, 1957-58; D.Litt. hon., Southampton Coll. of L.I.U., 1979. Copywriter Oxford U. Press, N.Y.C., 1951-54, McGraw Hill Book Co., 1954-55; art critic European edit. N.Y. Herald Tribune, Paris, 1960-65; Paris corr. Art News, 1964-65, exec. editor, N.Y.C., 1966-72; prof. English Bklyn. Coll., 1974—, Disting. prof., 1980—; editor quar. rev. Art and Lit., Paris, 1963-66; art critic Art Internat., Lugano, Switzerland, 1961-64; editor Locus Solus, Lans-en-Vercors, France, 1960-62; poetry editor Partisan Rev., 1976-80; art critic New York Mag., 1978-80, Newsweek, 1980—. Author: poems Turandot and Other Poems, 1953, Some Trees, 1956, 70, 78, The Poems, 1960, The Tennis Court Oath, 1962, Rivers and Mountains, 1966, 77, Selected Poems, 1967, Three Madrigals, 1968, Sunrise in Suburbia, 1968, Fragment, 1969, The Double Dream of Spring, 1970, 76, The New Spirit, 1970, Three Poems, 1972, 77, The Vermont Notebook, 1975, Self-Portrait in a Convex Mirror, 1975, 76, 77, Houseboat Days, 1977, As We Know, 1979, Shadow Train, 1981, 82; plays The Heroes, 1952, The Compromise, 1956, The Philosopher, 1963; (with James Schuyler) novel A Nest of Ninnies, 1969, 76; works represented in numerous anthologies; also author numerous articles art criticism, translations.; Contbr. verse to lit. periodicals.; verse set to music. Recipient Yale Series of Younger Poets prize, 1956; Harriet Monroe Poetry award Poetry Mag., 1963, 75; Union League Civic and Arts Found. prize, 1966; Nat. Inst. Arts and Letters award, 1969; Shelley award Poetry Soc. Am., 1973; guest of honor Poetry Day Modern Poetry Assn., 1973; Frank O'Hara prize Modern Poetry Assn., 1974; Pulitzer prize, 1976; Nat. Book award, 1976; Nat. Book Critics Circle award Harvard U., 1976; poetry award English-Speaking Union, 1980; Mayor's award, N.Y.C., 1983; Charles Flint Kellogg award Bard Coll., 1983; named Phi Beta Kappa Poet Harvard U., 1979; Fulbright scholar, Montpellier, France, 1955-56, Paris, France, 1956-57; Poets' Found. grantee, 1960, 64; Ingram Merrill Found. grantee, 1962, 72; Guggenheim fellow, 1967, 73; Rockefeller Found. grantee, 1979-80. Fellow Acad. Am. Poets, Mem. Am. Acad. and Inst. Arts and Letters. Spl. research life and work Raymond Roussel. Address: care Georges Borchardt Inc 136 E 57th St New York NY 10022

ASHBROOK, JAMES BARBOUR, theology educator; b. Adrian, Mich., Nov. 1, 1925; s. Milan Forest and Elizabeth (Barbour) A.; m. Patricia Jane Cober, Aug. 14, 1948; children: Peter, Susan, Martha, Karen. A.B. with honors, Denison U., 1947, LL.D., 1976; B.D., Colgate Rochester Div. Sch., 1950; M.A., Ohio State U., 1962, Ph.D., 1964; postdoctoral fellow, U. Rochester, 1971-73; postgrad., Union Theol. Sem., 1954-55. Diplomate: Am. Assn. Pastoral Counselors, Am. Bd. Profl. Psychology (subsplty. clin. psychology). Ordained to ministry Am. Bapt. Ch., 1950; asst. chaplain U. Rochester, 1948-50; pastor South Congl. Ch., Rochester, N.Y., 1950-54, First Baptist Ch., Granville, Ohio, 1955-60; asso. prof. pastoral theology Colgate Rochester Div. Sch., 1960-65, prof., 1965-69, prof. psychology and theology, 1969-81; prof. religion and personality Garrett-Evang. Sem., 1981—; adv. mem. Grad. Faculty Northwestern U., 1982—; vis. lectr. Denison U., 1958-60; vis. asso. prof. Ohio State U., 1966; vis. prof. Princeton Theol. Sem., 1970-71. Author: Become Community, 1971, In Human Presence-Hope, 1971, Humanitas, 1973, The Old Me and A New i, 1974, Responding to Human Pain, 1975; co-author: Christianity for Pious Skeptics, 1977; Contbr.: chpts. to Religion and Medicine, 1967, Psychological Testing for Ministerial Selection, 1970, Explorations in Ministry, 1971. Bd. mgrs. ministers and missionaries benefit bd. Am. Bapt. Chs., 1962-71, 72-80. Faculty fellow Am. Assn. Theol. Schs., 1963-64, 71-72; recipient W.C. and J.V. Stone Found. grants, 1969-72; Alumni citation Denison U., 1972. Mem. Am. Psychol. Assn., Am. Assn. Pastoral Counselors, Soc. Sci. Study Religion, Phi Beta Kappa. Home: 1205 Wesley Ave Evanston IL 60202 Office: 2121 Sheridan Rd Evanston IL 60201

ASHBURN, ANDERSON, editor; b. Winston-Salem, N.C., Aug. 24, 1919; s. Arthur Lee and Nonnie Mae (Boyles) A.; m. Sue Shermer, Aug. 4, 1941; children: Kit (Mrs. Robert Champlin), Terri, Edward Lee. B.S.E., U. Mich., 1940. Editor Mich. Technic, Ann Arbor, 1939-40; assoc. editor Tool Engr., Detroit, 1940-41; asst. editor Am. Machinist (McGraw-Hill Publs. Co.), N.Y.C., 1942, asso. editor, 1946-54, mng. editor, 1955-64, chief editor, 1965—, Product Engring., N.Y.C., 1970-71; mem. mfg. studies bd. NRC. Pres. Asbury Terr. Housing Devel. Fund.; Mem. adv. council Tools for Freedom Program Pan Am. Devel. Found.; trustee Am. Precision Mus., Meth. Ch. of Tarrytown. Served to capt. AUS, 1942-46, 51-52. Recipient Jesse H. Neal Editorial Achievement awards, 1966, 68, 71, 76, 78, Nat. Mag. award Columbia Grad. Sch. Journalism, 1969, Crain award Am. Bus. Press. Mem. Soc. Automotive Engrs. (past v.p., chmn. mfg. activity), ASME, Am. Soc. Mag. Editors (chmn. 1973-75), Numerical Control Soc., Kappa Sigma, Tau Beta Pi. Clubs: Nyack (N.Y.) Boat; Dutch Treat (N.Y.C.). Home: 45 Highland Ave Tarrytown NY 10591 Office: 1221 Ave of Americas New York NY 10020

ASHBY, DONALD WAYNE, JR., accountant; b. Camden, N.J., Feb. 17, 1926; s. Donald Wayne and Dorothy (Childers) A.; m. Jo Rutan, July 13, 1977; children—Pamela Anne, Donald Wayne III. B.S., Ohio State U., 1949. C.P.A., N.Y., Ohio. Partner Deloitte Haskins & Sells (C.P.A.'s), 1961—, partner in charge, 1961—. Served with USNR, 1944-46; with USAF, 1950-51. Mem. Am. Inst. C.P.A.'s, Ohio Soc. C.P.A.'s (pres. Columbus chpt. 1969), Ohio State U. Alumni Assn. (pres. 1981), Phi Gamma Delta. Episcopalian. Clubs: Scioto Country (treas. 1972-74), Columbus Athletic (pres. 1968), Execs. (pres. 1971), Columbus (pres. 1980-81), The Golf (Columbus)). Home: 4906 Riverside Dr Columbus OH 43220 Office: 155 E Broad St Columbus OH 43215

ASHBY, HAL, film director; b. Ogden, Utah, 1936. Ed., Utah State U. Film editor, asso. producer, dir., 1970—. Films directed include The Landlord, 1970, Harold and Maude, 1971, The Last Detail, 1973, Shampoo, 1974, Bound for Glory, 1976, Coming Home, 1978, Being There, 1979, Lookin' To Get Out, 1982, Let's Spend the Night Together, 1983. Office: care Dir's Guild Am 7950 Sunset Blvd Hollywood CA 90046 *

ASHBY, HUGH C(LINTON), transportation company executive; b. Slaughters, Ky., Oct. 23, 1934; s. Clint and Ruth Helen (Orton) A.; m. Alma Joyce Atwood, Dec. 23, 1960; children: Forrest W., Sarah C. B.S., Murray State U., 1960. Tchr. Pub. Schs. Paducah, Ky., 1960-62; budget analyst Ky. Dept. Fin., Frankfort, 1962-64; dir. div. of rates Ky. Dept. Motor Transp., Frankfort, 1964-68; dir. rates and budgets Am. Transit Corp., St. Louis, 1968-71, v.p. adminstrn., 1971-76, exec. v.p., 1976—. Served with USAF, 1954-58. Home: 2039 Barnhill Ct Saint Louis MO 63141 Office: American Transit Corp 120 S Central Saint Louis MO 63105

ASHBY, JOHN FORSYTHE, bishop; b. Tulsa, Mar. 26, 1929; s. Thomas Albert and Margaret (Mote) A.; m. Mary Carver, Aug. 12, 1954; children: Anne Carver Ashby Jones, Elizabeth Ashby McBride. B.A., Okla. State U., 1952; M.Div., Episcopal Theol. Sem. Southwest, Austin, Tex., 1955, D.D. hon., 1981; M.A., Cambridge U., Eng., 1967. Ordained to minstry Episcopal Ch., 1955. Vicar St. John's Episcopal Ch., Burant, Okla., 1955-59; rector St. Luke's Episcopal Ch., Ada, Okla., 1959-81; bishop Episcopal Diocese of Western Kans., Salina, 1981—. Served to lt. col. USAR, 1960-81. Home: 512 Sunset Dr Salina KS 67401 Office: Episcopal Diocese of Western Kans PO Box 1383 Salina KS 67402

ASHBY, ROBERT SAMUEL, lawyer; b. Crawfordsville, Ind., July 9, 1916; s. William Wallace and Nellie (Graybill) A.; m. Susan Gatch, June 4, 1949; children: Jean G., Willis G. A.B. with highest honors, Ind. U., 1938; LL.B. magna cum laude, Harvard, 1941. Bar: Ind. 1941, N.Y. 1942. Asso. firm Carter, Ledyard & Milburn, N.Y.C., 1941-42; partner firm Barnes & Thornburg, Indpls., 1946—; dir. Fed. Home Life Ins. Co. Ind., Home Ins. Co. Ind., Ind. Nat. Corp., Altamil Corp., Danner's, Inc. Editor: Harvard Law Rev, 1941; Contbr. articles to tax and legal jours. Trustee Indpls. Mus. Art, 1960—. Served to lt. comdr. USNR, 1942-46. Mem. Am., Ind., Indpls. bar assns., Assn. Bar City N.Y., Bar Assn. 7th Fed. Circuit, Phi Beta Kappa, Sigma Nu. Clubs: Indianapolis Dramatic, Contemporary, University. Home: 7248 Pennsylvania St Indianapolis IN 46240 Office: 1313 Merchants Bank Bldg Indianapolis IN 46204

ASHCROFT, JOHN, state official; b. Chgo.; married; children—Martha, Jay, Andrew. Grad. cum laude, Yale U., 1964; J.D., U. Chgo., 1967. Bar: Mo., U.S. Supreme Ct. Asso. prof. S.W. Mo. State U., Springfield, 5 yrs; practice law, Springfield, Mo., until 1973; state auditor State of Mo., 1973-75, asst. atty. gen., 1975-77, atty. gen., 1977—. Gospel singer: records include In the Spirit of Life and Liberty; Author: (with wife) College Law for Business, 7th, 8th, 9th edits., It's the Law, 1979. Mem. Am. Bar Assn. (ho. of dels.), Mo. Bar Assn., Cole County Bar Assn., Nat. Assn. Attys. Gen. (past pres., chmn. budget com., mem. exec. com.). Republican. Mem. Assembly of God Ch. Office: Office Atty Gen PO Box 899 Jefferson City MO 65102

ASHE, A.J., retired rubber company executive; b. Kenton, Tenn., Nov. 20, 1924; s. Walter Dee and Audelle (Keathley) A.; m. Robbie Jean Nixon, Sept. 5, 1946; children: John Allen, Robert Edwin, David Nixon. B.S., U. Tenn., 1948; M.S., Cornell U., 1949, Ph.D., 1951. Mktg. specialist U.S. Dept. Agr., Cornell U., Ithaca, N.Y., 1951-52; commodity analyst Armour & Co., Chgo., 1952-57; sales and econ. forecaster Butler Mfg. Co., Kansas City, 1957-60; mgr. econ. research, dir. bus. research, asso. dir. corp. planning, dir. bus. research and planning B.F. Goodrich Co., Akron, Ohio, 1960-70, v.p. econs. and planning, 1970-72, v.p. planning and devel., 1972-76, sr. v.p., 1976-83; cons. dir. BancOhio Nat. Bank, 1972—. Mem. bus. research adv. council to Commr. of Labor Statistics, 1965-68; mem. balance of payments adv. tech. com. to Sec. Commerce, 1965-68; adviser UN Conf. on Trade and Devel., 1969, 76; econ. adv. bd. to Sec. Commerce, 1968-70, 1975-76; mem. tech. cons. to Bus. Council, 1965-70, 1972-77, 79-83; adviser Pres.'s Council on Wage and Price Stability, 1978-80, U.S. Dept. State Internat. Commodity Agreement on Natural Rubber, 1977-79; Mem. planning and priorities com. United Community Council, Akron, 1963-64; mem. citizens panel Econ. Growth of Akron Area, 1962; mem. discussion group indsl. economists Harvard Bus. Sch., 1965-80; mem. com. on ch. and econ. life Nat. Council Chs., 1967-69; mem. Akron Human Relations Commn., 1970-73; fin. adv. com. Mayor of Akron, 1976-77; mem. Akron Action Com., 1978—, Akron Econ. Council, 1978—; bd. dirs. Akron U., 1967-70, Eastern Coll., 1980—, Eastern Bapt. Theol. Sem., 1980—; trustee Akron Gen. Med. Center, 1972—, United Way of Summit County, 1975-82, Stan Hywet Hall Found., 1970. Served with USNR, 1943-45. Mem. Am. Mgmt. Assn., Conf. Bus. Economists (chmn. 1972-73), Nat. Soc. Corp. Planning, Rubber Mfrs. Assn. (econ. and statis. coms. 1960-76), Nat. Assn. Bus. Economists, U.S. C. of C. (mem. banking, monetary and fiscal affairs com. 1971—), Internat. Rubber Study Group (adviser U.S. Dept. State 1969, mem. com. of experts on rubber 1972-73), Internat. Rd. Fedn. (dir. 1977-79), UN Assn. of U.S.A. (dir. 1979-82), Phi Kappa Phi, Alpha Zeta. Republican. Baptist. Home: 2319 Chatham Rd Akron OH 44313 Office: BF Goodrich Co 500 S Main St Akron OH 44318 *What success I have enjoyed is attributed to the merits of the American enterprise system which rewards those who are willing to acquire the proper training, take initiative, exert self-confidence and discipline, work hard, be a team player, maintain integrity, and place their trust in God.*

ASHE, ARTHUR, tennis player; b. Richmond, Va., 1943. Grad., UCLA, 1966. Mem. U.S. Davis Cup Team, capt., 1981; pres. Players Enterprises, Inc., Washington. Served with AUS. Winner two U.S. Inter-collegiate championships during coll.; winner U.S. Men's Hard Court Championship, 1963, U.S. Men's Clay Ct., 1967, U.S. Amateur title, 1968, U.S. Open championship, 1968, Australian open Winner, 1970, French Open Doubles, 1972, Wimbledon Singles, 1975, World

Championship Tennis Singles, 1975, Australian Open Doubles, 1977. Address: 360 E 72d St Apt C-1801 New York NY 10021

ASHE, ARTHUR JAMES, III, chemistry educator; b. N.Y.C., Aug. 5, 1940; s. Arthur James and Helen Louise (Hawelka) A.; m. Penelope Guerard Vaughan, Aug. 25, 1962; children: Arthur J., Christopher V. B.A., Yale U., 1962, M.S., 1965, Ph.D., 1966; postgrad., Cambridge U., 1962-63. Asst. prof. chemistry U. Mich., Ann Arbor, 1966-71, asso. prof., 1971-76, prof., 1976—, chmn. dept., 1983—; vis. scientist Phys. Chemistry Inst., U. Basle, Switzerland, 1974. Alfred P. Sloan fellow, 1972-76. Mem. Am. Chem. Soc., Chem. Soc. (London). Home: 2001 Shadford Rd Ann Arbor MI 48104 Office: Dept Chemistry U Mich Ann Arbor MI 48109

ASHE, DAVID I(RVING), lawyer; b. Bklyn., Nov. 13, 1910; s. Morris and Bessie (Newman) A.;, 1934 (div. 1959); children: Judith Ashe Handelman, Deborah Lucy Ashe Warheit; m. Amelia H. Wexler, Dec. 26, 1962; stepchildren: Richard Wexler, Susan Wexler Lahn. B.S.S. magna cum laude, CCNY, 1929; J.D., Columbia U., 1932. Bar: N.Y. 1933. Since practiced in N.Y.C.; specializing in law of labor relations and representing internat. and local labor unions; mem. firm Ashe & Rifkin, 1940—; instr. labor law and labor problems Trade Union Inst. of Rand Sch. Social Sci., 1936-45, dir., 1940-44; mem. bd. dirs. New Leader (pub.), 1944-50; labor law cons. ACLU. Author: Yellow Dog Contracts, Legal and Social Aspects, 1931, The Taft-Hartley Law: How It Affects Unions and Workers, 1947, The Labor-Management Reporting and Disclosure Act of 1959, An Analysis, 1959; adv. editor: Parents mag., 1948-50; contbr. to labor ednl. publs. Mem. state adv. com. for study of vocat. edn. in N.Y. City Schs., 1949-52, mem. com. (N.Y. City Bd. Edn.) to study impact of increased birth rate on N.Y. City Schs., 1948-49; mem. N.Y. Gov.'s Task Force Aid to Edn., 1974-75; adv. bd. Center Advanced Study in Edn., 1975—; mem. adv. bd. Nat. Center for Study of Collective Bargaining in Higher Edn., 1972—; mem. adminstrv., nat. exec. coms. Jewish Labor Com., 1965—, chmn. N.Y. div., 1966—; mem. exec. com. Nat. Jewish Community Relations Adv. Council, 1965—, Jewish Community Relations Council of N.Y., 1977—; v.p. Jewish Community Relations Council of N.Y., 1980—; mem. adv. com. Robert F. Wagner Labor Archives; mem. edn. com. United Negro Coll. Fund, 1960-62; mem. com. on legis. Citizens Union, N.Y.C., 1960-64; pres. Musicians Service Corp.; mem. Bd. Higher Edn. N.Y.C., 1966-73; bd. dirs. Research Found. CUNY, v.p., 1975-77, pres., 1977-81; bd. dirs. Italian-Am. Inst. to Promote Higher Edn., 1977-80; bd. dirs., chmn. nat. com. Fund for Open Society, 1977—; exec. com. City U. Faculty Welfare Trustees, 1967—. Mem. Am. Arbitration Assn. (nat. panel arbitrators), Workers Def. League (nat. com. 1956-58), Nat. Planning Assn. (nat. council), Workmen's Circle (gen. counsel), Alumni Assn. Columbia Sch. Law, Bar Assn. N.Y.C. (labor and social security legis. com. 1951-54, 67-70, com. on post admission legal edn. 1971-74), Alumni Assn. City Coll., United Parents Assns. N.Y.C. (counsel, past pres., chmn. exec. council and legis. com. and v.p.), Pub. Edn. Assn. (legis. and sch. adminstrn. com. 1950-62), N.Y. County Lawyers Assn. (com. labor relations 1976—), Phi Beta Kappa. Home: 1020 Park Ave New York NY 10028 Office: 225 Broadway New York NY 10007

ASHEIM, LESTER EUGENE, librarian, educator; b. Spokane, Jan. 22, 1914; s. Sol and Bertha (Bergman) A. A.B., U. Wash., 1936, B.A. in Librarianship, 1937, M.A., 1941; Ph.D., U. Chgo., 1949. Jr. reference asst. Library U. Wash., 1937-41; librarian U.S. Fed. Penitentiary, McNeill Island, Wash., 1941-42; regional librarian Fed. Pub. Housing Authority, 1946; vis. lectr., library sch. U. Ill., summer 1949; asst. prof. U. Chgo. Grad. Library Sch., 1948-52, dean students, 1951-52, dean, asso. prof., 1952-62, prof., 1971-74; editor Library Quar., 1972-74; dir. Internat. Relations Office, ALA, 1962-66, dir. office for library edn., 1966-71; William Rand Kenan Jr. prof. library sci. U. N.C. at Chapel Hill, 1975—; Fulbright lectr. U. Brasilia, 1979. Author: (with Bernard Berelson) The Library's Public, 1949, Librarianship in the Developing Countries, 1966; editor: A Forum on the Public Library Inquiry, 1950, The Core of Education for Librarianship, 1954, The Future of the Book, 1955, Humanities and the Library, 1957, New Directions in Public Library Development, 1957, Persistent Issues in American Librarianship, 1961, (with Sara Fenwick) Differentiating the Media, 1975, (with D. Philip Baker and Virginia Mathews) Reading and Successful Living, 1983. Served with Signal Intelligence AUS, 1942-45. Recipient Distinguished Alumnus award U. Wash. Sch. Librarianship, 1966; Intellectual Freedom award Ill. Library Assn., 1966; Scarecrow Press award for library lit., 1968; Beta Phi Mu award, 1973; Joseph W. Lippincott award, 1976; presented with Festschrift, As Much to Learn as to Teach: Essays in Honor of Lester Asheim, 1979. Mem. ALA, AAUP, Phi Beta Kappa, Zeta Beta Tau. Home: 21 Banbury Ln Chapel Hill NC 27514

ASHENFELTER, DAVID LOUIS, newspaper reporter; b. Toledo, Oct. 20, 1948; s. Duaine Louis and Betty Jean (Porter) A.; m. Barbara Ann Dinwieddie, Feb. 22, 1974. B.S. in Edn., Ind. U., 1971. Reporter Kokomo Morning Times, Ind., 1966-67, Bloomington Daily Herald-Telephone, 1968-69, Bloomington Courier-Tribune, 1970-71, Detroit News, 1971-83, Detroit Free Press, 1983—. Recipient Pulitzer prize for meritorious pub. service Columbia U., 1982, Disting. Service award for gen. newspaper reporting Sigma Delta Chi, 1981, AP, 1981, UPI, 1981, pub. service medallion Detroit Press Club, 1981. Mem. Sigma Delta Chi, Sigma Xi. Office: Detroit Free Press 321 W Lafayette Blvd Detroit MI 48231

ASHENHURST, ROBERT CARL, mining company executive; b. Uxbridge Twp., Ont., Can., Apr. 5, 1918; s. John and May (Davis) A.; m. Rita M. Thrasher, July 23, 1943; children: Mary Jane, John Robert, Carol Ann, James Thomas. Student, Gregg Coll., 1937, U. Toronto, 1965-67. Chartered acct. Sec., treas. Milliken Lake Uranium Mines, 1956-58, Stanleigh Uranium Mines, 1958-60; treas., dir., v.p. fin. and corp. devel. Mattagami Lake Mines Ltd., Toronto, Ont., 1960-78; v.p., sec. Noranda Mines Ltd., Toronto, 1967—; pres. Heath Steele Mines Ltd., Toronto, 1979—; treas., dir. Mattabi Mines Ltd., Toronto, 1970—. Mem. Can. Inst. Mining and Metallurgy. Clubs: Engineers (Toronto); Toronto Golf. Home: 1681 Bramsey Dr Mississauga ON Canada L5S 2H9 Office: PO Box 45 Commerce Ct W: Toronto ON Canada M5L 1B6

ASHENHURST, ROBERT LOVETT, educator; b. Paris, France, Aug. 9, 1929; (parents Am. citizens); m. Julia Brewster Brown, June 18, 1949 (div. Feb. 1964); children: Julia Brewster, John Cobden, David Russell, Martha Lovett. A.B., Harvard U., 1950, S.M., 1954, Ph.D., 1956. Research assoc. Harvard U., 1950-56, instr., 1956-57; asst. prof. U. Chgo., 1957-60, assoc. prof., 1960-65, prof., 1965—, marshal of univ., 1968—; dir. Inst. for Computer Research, 1969-78, chmn. com. on info. scis., 1969-74, asso. dir., 1965-69. Mem. Woodlawn Hosp. Corp., Chgo., 1965-79; treas. Hyde Park-Kenwood Community Conf., 1969-71, Gilbert and Sullivan Opera Co., 1974—, Hyde Park-Kenwood Community Health Center, 1976-78. Mem. Assn. for Computing Machinery (editor-in-chief Communications of the ACM 1973-83, council mem.-at-large 1976—), Soc. Indsl. and Applied Math., IEEE, Inst. Mgmt. Scis., AAAS, N.Y. Acad. Sci., Phi Beta Kappa, Sigma Xi. Clubs: Tavern, Quadrangle (Chgo.). Home: 5545 S University Ave Chicago IL 60637 Office: 1101 E 58th St Chicago IL 60637

ASHER, AARON, editor; b. Memel, Lithuania, Aug. 26, 1929; s. Samuel and Henny (Meyer) A.; m. Linda Wofsey, Oct. 11, 1956; children—Rachel, Abigail. B.A. with honors, U. Chgo., 1949, M.A., 1952. Mem. editorial staff Alfred A. Knopf, Inc., N.Y.C., 1956-58; exec. editor Meridian Books, Inc., N.Y.C., 1958-64; sr. editor Viking Press, Inc., N.Y.C., 1964-69; dir. gen. book dept. Holt, Rinehart and Winston, Inc., N.Y.C., 1969-74; editor-in-chief Macmillan Pub. Co., Inc., N.Y.C., 1974; editor-in-chief, v.p. Farrar, Straus and Giroux, Inc., N.Y.C., 1975-81; exec. editor Harper & Row, N.Y.C., 1981—; instr. pub. N.Y. U., 1968-69. Served with AUS, 1953-55. Office: 10 E 53d St New York NY 10022

ASHER, FREDERICK, mail order company executive; b. Chgo., Mar. 6, 1915; s. Louis Eller and Alice (Wormser) A.; m. Frances Reitler, June 30, 1938; children—Frederick Matheson, Alice, Deborah Helene. B.A. cum laude, Dartmouth, 1937; student, Coll. Agr. U. Wis., 1938. Gen. mgr. Louis G. Cowan, Chgo., 1938-41; advt. mgr. Consol. Book Publ. Co., Chgo., 1945-50; pres. Frederick Asher, Inc. (advt.), Chgo., 1950-55, John Plain & Co. (mail order), 1955-66, pres., chief exec. officer, 1966-72, Bellwether Devel. Corp., Highland Park, Ill., 1972—; pres., chief exec. Earth Products Corp., Highland Park, 1982—; dir. Glencoe Nat. Bank, Ill., 1958-73, chmn. bd., 1974—. Mem. Chgo. exec. com. Anti-Defamation League, 1952-56; mem. budget reviewing com. Community Chest Chgo., 1957-59; Trustee Highland Park Hosp., 1950-72, bd. mgr., 1970-72; bd. dirs. Highland Park Community Chest, 1951-68, pres., chmn., 1955-57; bd. dirs. Immigrants' Service League, 1951-68, pres., 1955-56; bd. dirs. Highland Park Civic Assn., 1952-56, Scholarship and Guidance Assn., 1953-55; adminstrv. bd. Travelers Aid Soc. Chgo.; trustee Lake Forest (Ill.) Acad., 1968-73, 83—. Served with AUS, 1944-45. Mem. Mail Order Assn. Am. (dir. 1958-69), Dartmouth Club Chgo. (dir. 1965-67), Nat. Planning Assn. (mem. nat. council 1967-69). Clubs: Mid-America (Chgo.); Lake Shore Country (Glencoe, Ill.); Ojai (Calif.) Valley Country. Home: 405 Moraine Rd Highland Park IL 60035 Office: 1866 Sheridan Rd Highland Park IL 60035

ASHER, LILA OLIVER, artist; b. Phila., Nov. 15, 1921; d. Benjamin O. and Mollie (Finkelstein) Oliver; m. Sydney S. Asher, Jr., May 5, 1946 (dec.); children—Bonnie Asher-Doar, Warren Oliver; m. Kenneth P. Crawford, Apr. 26, 1980. Certificate, Phila. Coll. Art, (Bd. Edn. scholar), 1943; student, Frank B. A. Linton, Phila. Sketch Club. Faculty Wilson Tchrs. Coll., Washington, 1953-54; instr. art dept. Howard U., 1947-51, lectr., 1961-64, asst. prof., 1964-66, asso. prof., 1966-71, prof., 1971—. Artist in sculpture, graphics, watercolor, oil including murals one-woman shows, Barnett-Aden Gallery, 1951, William C. Blood Gallery, 1955, Arts Club, Washington, 1957, Collectors Gallery, 1959, Garrett Park Pub. Library, Md., 1960, Art Shop, Silver Spring, Md., 1961, Potters' House, Washington, 1963, Burr Galleries, N.Y.C., Gallery 222, El Paso, Tex., 1965, Thomson Gallery, N.Y.C., 1968, B'nai B'rith Nat. Hdqrs. Gallery, 1969, U. Va., Charlottesville, 1970, Green-Field Gallery, El Paso, 1972, Franz Bader Gallery, retrospective, Washington, 1972, Northwestern Mich. Coll., 1972, Am. Club, Tokyo, 1973, Govt. Coll. Arts and Crafts, Madras, India, 1974, Fisk U., Nashville, Tenn., USIS, Karachi, Lahore, Islamabad, Pakistan, 1975, Am. Cultural Center, Bombay, India, Am. Cultural Center, Madras, Am. U. Center, Calcutta, India, USIS, Ankara and Adana, Turkey, 1976, Via Gambaro Gallery, Washington, 1977, Howard U., Washington, 1978, Gallery Kormendy, Alexandria, Va., Northeastern U., Boston, 1980; exhibited in group shows, World's Fair, N.Y.C., 1965, Pa. Acad. Fine Arts, Smithsonian Instn., Washington, 1950, 54-58, 60-63, Library of Congress, 1954, Corcoran Gallery Art, Washington, 1949, 51, 52, 55, 57-59, Howard U., 1952, 61-63, 65, 67, 70, 72, 73, 74, 75, 76, 77, 78, George Washington U., 1968, Pan-Am. Union, Woodmere Gallery, 1949-50, Phila. Print Club, Washington Printmakers Soc., Balt. Mus. Art, 1959, Hood Coll., U. Va., Maine, Riverside Mus., N.Y.C., Rochester, (N.Y.) Meml. Art Gallery, 1954, Franz Bader Gallery, Washington, 1955, 71, Graphic Arts Soc., N.Y.C., Va. Intermont Coll., Nat. Collection Fine Arts, Washington Watercolor Assn., Arts Club Washington, Soc. Washington Artists Ann., 1971, 72, Soc. Washington Printmakers, Dimock Gallery, George Washington U., numerous others, retrospective shows, Franz Bader Gallery, Washington, 1972, Fisk U., Nashville, 1974, Howard U., Washington, 1978; represented in permanent collections, Nat. Mus. Am. Art, Howard U., Georgetown U., Corcoran Gallery, U. Va., U. Tex., Sweetbriar (Va.) Coll., Superior Ct. D.C., B'nai B'rith Washington, City of Wolfsburg, Germany, Down East Gallery, Washington, U.S. Mediation and Conciliation Service, Bur. Nat. Affairs, Center for Research in Edn. Disadvantaged, Jerusalem, Am. Embassy, Tel Aviv, Montgomery County (Md.) Contemporary Print Collection, also pvt. collections; guest artist, U. Tex., print program, 1972. Recipient prize for print Corcoran Gallery Art 10th Area Exhbn., 1956; U. Va. award, 1963, 70; guest artist City of Wolfsburg, 1968, 71, 75, 80; honoree Nat. Mus. Am. Art, 1981. Mem. Soc. Washington Artists (past pres.), Soc. Washington Printmakers (past treas. and rec. sec.), Washington Water Color Club, Artist's Equity (past treas.). Address: 4100 Thornapple St Chevy Chase MD 20015

ASHER, M(ARTIN) RICHARD, lawyer; b. N.Y.C., Mar. 1, 1932; s. George Joseph and Rose (Rosenblatt) A.; m. Sheila Delores Seigal, June 27, 1954; children: Jeffrey David, Jonathan Andrew, Janet Maxine. B.A., Tufts U., 1953; J.D., Cornell U., 1956. Bar: N.Y. State 1956. Asso. firm Raphael, Searles, Levin & Vischi & Paul G. Marshall, Esq., N.Y.C., 1958-61; mem. firm Asher, Beldock & Kushnik, N.Y.C., 1961-66; with CBS Records, 1966-83; mng. dir. CBS Records U.K., London, 1972-75; pres. CBS Records Internat., N.Y.C., 1975-79; dep. pres., chief operating officer CBS Records Group, N.Y.C., 1979-83 also pres. CBS Records Div.; ptnr. Aarow, Edelstein, Gross & Asher N.Y.C., 1983—. Dist. leader Democratic Party, Dobbs Ferry, N.Y., 1958-60. Served to lt. USMCR, 1956-58. Honored by Anti-Defamation League, B'nai B'rith Mus. and Performing Luncheon, 1977; honored as maj. contbr. to advancement human rights and furtherance of interreligious understanding Anti-Defamation League Appeal, 1979; named one of Tomorrow's Top 200 Execs. Billboard, 1976. Mem. Internat. Fedn. Phonograph Industries (v.p., dir.), Records Assn. Am., Am. Bar Assn., Country Music Assn. Office: Arrow Edelstein Gross & Asher 919 3d Ave New York NY 10022

ASHFORD, DOUGLAS ELLIOTT, comparative politics educator; b. Lockport, N.Y., Aug. 28, 1928; s. Howard John and Doris (Saunders) A.; m. Margaret Anderson, May 25, 1955 (div. 1970); children: Elizabeth, Douglas, David, Michael; m. 2d Karen V. Knudson, June 8, 1974; 1 son, Matthew. B.A., Brown U., 1950; M.A., Oxford U., (Eng.), 1952; Ph.D., Princeton U., 1961. Asst. prof. comparative politics Ind. U., Bloomington, 1961-63; assoc. prof. Johns Hopkins U., Balt., 1963-64, Cornell U., Ithaca, N.Y., 1964-68, prof., 1968-82; Andrew W. Mellon prof. comparative politics U. Pitts., 1982—; cons. NSF, Washington, 1968—, NEH, 1972—; mem. steering com. Council for European Studies, N.Y.C., 1974-78. Author: Financing Cities n the Welfare State, 1980, Policy and Politics in Britain: Limits of Consensus, 1981, British Dogmatism and French Pragmatism, 1982, Policy and Politics in France: Living with Uncertainty, 1982. Served to 1st lt. USAF, 1952-55. Rhodes scholar, 1950; fellow Netherlands Inst. Advanced Study, 1977; Simon fellow U. Manchester, Eng., 1980; fellow Guggenheim Found., 1982. Mem. mem. Am. Polit. Sci. Assn., Am. Oxonian Soc., Policy Studies Assn., Brit. Studies Group (mem. exec. com. 1979-82). Democrat. Presbyterian. Office: Dept Polit Sci 4R15 Forbes Quard U Pitts Pittsburgh PA 15260

ASHFORD, JAMES KNOX, auto parts company executive; b. Starkville, Miss., Jan. 20, 1937; s. Charles Rabb and Nannie (Smith) A.; m. Jacqueline Martin, July 23, 1961; children: Diane Marie, James Knox, Catherine Nan. B.S. in Accounting, Miss. State U., 1958; grad., Advanced Mgmt. Program, Harvard U., 1976. Mgr. budgets Kern County Land Co., San Francisco, 1965-67; corporate controller Walker Mfg. Co., Racine, Wis., 1967-71, v.p. fin., 1971-73, exec. v.p., 1973-77; exec. v.p. fin. and adminstrn. Tenneco Automotive, Deerfield, Ill., 1977; pres. Monroe Auto Equipment Co. Mich. subs. Tenneco Automotive, 1978-81; v.p. corp. planning and devel. Tenneco Inc., Houston, 1981-82; pres., chief exec. officer Tenneco Automotive div. Tenneco Inc., 1982—; bd. dirs. Automotive Info. Council, 1982—. Served with USNR, 1954-62. Mem. Motor and Equipment Mfrs. Assn. (bd. dirs. 1982—). Republican. Presbyterian. Office: 2275 Half Day Rd Bannockburn IL 60015

ASHFORD, NICKOLAS, singer, songwriter; b. Willow Run, Mich., 1943; m. Valerie Simpson; 1 dau., Nicole. Songwriter-producer with, Valerie Simpson; with, Scepter Records, then, Motown Records; rec. artist (with Valerie Simpson), 1973—; (with Simpson) include) songs co-written You're All I Need to Get By, Let's Get Stoned, Ain't No Mountain High Enough, Ain't Nothing Like the Real Thing; albums Musical Affair, Is It Still Good to Ya, Stay Free. Address: care William Morris Agy 1350 Ave of Americas New York NY 10019 *

ASHIN, MARK, English language educator; b. N.Y.C., Mar. 1, 1917; s. Max and Zina (Rudin) A.; m. Alice Elaine Froyd, Jan. 9, 1949; 1 son, Paul. B.A., U. Chgo., 1937, M.A., 1938, Ph.D., 1950. Instr. Mich. State Coll., East Lansing, 1938-41; instr. U. Chgo., 1947-51, asst. prof., 1951-57, assoc. prof., 1957-67, prof. English, 1967—; vis. prof. Rochester U., 1961, N.Y. U., 1964; Dir. NDEA Special Inst. for Advanced Study in English, 1968; dir. Spl. Summer Session Disadvantaged Students, U-Chgo., 1970. Served to 2d lt. OSS AUS, 1943-46. Recipient Quantrell Distinguished Teaching award U. Chgo., 1954. Home: 5541 Dorchester Ave Chicago IL 60637

ASHJIAN, MESROB, clergyman; b. Beirut, Lebanon, Jan. 3, 1941; s. Nerces and Martha (Kassabian) A. Student, Armenian Theol. Sem., Antelias, Lebanon, 1957-61, Ecumenical Inst., Bossey, Switzerland, 1962-63; B.A., Princeton Theol. Sem., 1964, postgrad., 1970-74. Ordained priest Armenian Apostolic Ch., 1961; mem. faculty Armenian Theol. Sem., Antelias, Lebanon, 1961-62, 64, 65, 66-70, vice dean, 1964-65, dean, 1966-70; instr. Karen Jeppe Coll., Aleppo, Syria, 1965-66; preacher St. Gregory Ch., Aleppo, Syria, 1965-66; prelate Diocese of Armenians in Iran and India, Isfahan, Iran, 1974-77; consecrated bishop, 1977, consecrated archbishop, 1984; prelate Armenian Apostolic Ch. of Am., Eastern States and Can., N.Y.C., 1978—. Editor: Hask monthly, 1966-70, Deghegadou, 1976-77, The Holy Week in the Armenian Church Tradition, 1978, Unpublished Papers and Works of Mesrob Taliatine, 1979. Decorated grand protector, Order Hospitallers St. George of Carinthea. Mem. World Council Chs. Club: Princeton (N.Y.C.). Office: 138 E 39th St New York NY 10016

ASHKENAZL, ELY EZRA, electronics co. exec.; b. Mexico City, Sept. 13, 1922; U.S., 1936; s. Ezra and Sofia (Hakim) A.; m. Grace Franco, June 18, 1950; children—Ezra, Isaac, Ronald, Shefie, David, Allegra. Diploma, Am. Acad. Accounting, 1942. Partner E.S.&E. Ashkenazi, Charlotte, N.C., 1939-53, Nanasi Co., West New York, N.J., 1953-68; pres. Soundesign Corp., Jersey City, 1961—. Bd. govs. Jewish Community Center, Ocean Twp., N.J., Hillel Sch., Wanamassa, N.J. Served with USAAF, 1943-45. Home: 77 Monmouth Dr Deal NJ 07723 Office: 34 Exchange Pl Jersey City NJ 07203

ASHKENAZY, VLADIMIR DAVIDOVICH, concert pianist; b. Gorky, USSR, July 6, 1937; s. David and Evstolia (Plotnova) A.; m. Thorunn Johannsdottir, Feb. 25, 1961; children—Vladimir Stefan, Nadia Liza, Dimitri Thor, Sonia Edda, Alexandra Inga. Ed., Central Music Sch., Moscow, also Moscow Conservatory; studied with, Sumbatyan, Lev Oborin. London debut, London Symphony Orch. under George Hurst; later solo recital, Festival Hall, 1963, recordings, concerts throughout world. Recipient 2d prize Internat. Chopin Competition, Warsaw, 1955, Gold medal Queen Elizabeth Internat. Piano Competition, Brussels, 1956; with John Ogdon winner Tchaikovsky Piano Competition, Moscow, 1962. Home: Sonnenhof 4 6004 Luzern Switzerland

ASHLER, PHILIP FREDERIC, consultant; b. N.Y.C., Oct. 15, 1914; s. Philip and Charlotte (Barth) A.; m. Jane Porter, Mar. 4, 1942 (dec. 1968); children: Philip Frederic, Robert Porter, Richard Harrison; m. Elise Barrett Duvall, June 21, 1969; stepchildren: Richard Edward, Jeffries Harding. B.B.A. cum laude, St. Johns Coll., 1935; M.B.A., Harvard U., 1937; grad., Indsl. Coll. Armed Forces, 1956; Sc.D., Fla. Inst. Tech., 1969; LL.D., U. W. Fla., 1969. Enlisted USMCR, 1932; commd. ensign USN, 1938, advanced through grades to rear adm., 1959; served in, Normandy, So. France, Iwo Jima, Korea; dir. Office Small Bus. Dept. Def., Washington, 1948-51; mem. joint staff Joint Chiefs Staff, 1957-59; ret., 1959; dir. devel. Pensacola Jr. Coll., 1960-68; vice chancellor adminstrn. State Univ. System Fla., 1968-70, exec. vice chancellor, 1970-75; treas., ins. commr., fire marshal State of Fla., 1975-76, sec. of commerce, 1977-79; pres. Philip F. Ashler & Assos., Tallahassee, 1979—; chmn. bd. Cambridge Community Care, Inc., Tallahassee, 1981—, Mfrs. Internat. Trade Corp., Tampa, Fla.; dir. Fidelity Guaranty Life Ins. Co., Balt., U.S. Fidelity & Guaranty Co., Lewis State Bank, Tallahassee; Mem. Fla. Edn. Council, 1967-68; commr. from Fla. Edn. Commn. States, 1967-68; mem. U.S. Dept. Commerce Dist. Export Council, 1978—; mem. legis. adv. council So. Regional Edn. Bd., 1966-68; mem. Fla. Bd. Ind. Colls. and Univs., 1971-75, mem. adv. council for mil. edn., 1980—; chmn. Fla. Civil Def. Adv. Council, 1966-69; mem. Fla. Council Internat. Devel., 1973-79, vice chmn., 1979-80, chmn., 1980—; mem. Select Council on Post High Sch. Edn., 1967-68; chmn. Fla. Med. Liability Ins. Commn., 1975-76, Fla. Task Force on Auto and Workers Compensation, 1975-76; mem. Yugoslavia Adv. Council, 1976—, InterAm. Congress on Psychology, Bogota, Colombia, 1974, NATO Advanced Sci. Inst., W.Ger., 1973; guest lectr. U. Belgrade, Yugoslavia, 1973; adviser econ. devel. to gov. Fla., 1977-78; mission leader Japan/S.E. U.S. Assn., Tokyo, 1977; mem. U.S. Council Internat. C. of C., 1979—; trustee Fla. Council on Econ. Edn., 1979-81; mem. services policy adv. com. Office of U.S. Trade Rep., Exec. Office of Pres., Washington, 1980—. Mem. Fla. Ho. Reps., 1963-68; Chmn. bd. dirs. Fla. Heart Assn., 1969-71; bd. dirs., treas. Internat. Cardiology Found.; bd. dirs. Tallahassee Meml. Hosp., Easter Seal Soc., 1963-68; bd. dirs., exec. com. Am. Heart Assn., 1971-77, Internat. Cardiology Fedn., Geneva, Switzerland, 1975-77; founding chmn. Tallahassee Symphony Orch., 1981-82. Decorated Bronze Star with Combat V, Korean Presdl. citation; recipient Internat. Distinguished Service award Kiwanis Internat., 1965; Distinguished Service award Am. Heart Assn., 1965, 71; Distinguished Achievement award, 1975; Legislative award St. Petersburg Times, 1967. Mem. Fla. Med. Malpractice Joint Underwriting Assn. (chmn. bd. govs. 1975-76), Nat. Assn. Ins. Commrs. (vice chmn. exec. com. 1976), U.S. S.E./Japan Assn. (chmn. 1981-83), Kappa Delta, Fla. Council 100. Democrat. Episcopalian (licensed lay reader). Clubs: Masons (32 deg.), Shriners, Rotary,

Capital City Tiger Bay (Tallahassee) (chmn. bd. dirs.); Curzon House (London); Fla. Econs. (dir.). Home: 2115 E Randolph Circle Tallahassee FL 32312 also 11 Riad Sultan Kasbah Tangier Morocco Office: Cambridge Group Internat 425 E Call St Suite 72 Tallahassee FL 32301

ASHLEY, ELIZABETH, actress; b. Ocala, Fla., Aug. 30, 1941; d. Arthur Kingman and Lucille (Ayer) Cole; m. George Peppard (div.); 1 son, Christian Moore; m. James Michael McCarthy. Student ballet with, Tatiana Semenova, La. State U., 1957-58; grad., Neighborhood Playhouse, N.Y.C., 1961. Apptd. Pres.'s council 1st Nat. Council on the Arts, 1965-69; dir. Am. Film Inst., 1968-72. Appeared on Broadway in: The Highest Tree, 1961, Take Her, She's Mine, 1962, Barefoot in the Park, 1963; appeared: movies The Carpet Baggers, 1963, Ship of Fools, 1964, The Third Day, 1965, Marriage of a Young Stockbroker, 1971, Paperback Hero, 1974, Golden Needles, 1974, Rancho Deluxe, 1975, 92 in the Shade, 1976, The Great Scout and Cathouse Thursday, 1976, Coma, 1978, Windows, 1980; TV movies include Second Chance, 1972, The Heist, 1972, Your Money or Your Wife, 1972; stage appearances include The Enchanted, Washington, 1973, The Skin of Our Teeth, Washington, 1975, Broadway, Cat on a Hot Tin Roof, Stratford, Conn. and Broadway, 1974, approximately 200 TV films.; Author: Postcards from the Road, 1978. Recipient Antoinette Perry award, 1962. Mem. Actors Equity, Screen Actors Guild, AFTRA. *

ASHLEY, FLETCHER, architect; b. Orange, N.J., May 28, 1926; s. Raymond Eliot and Hilda Fletcher (Brazer) A.; m. Joan Shepard, June 10, 1948; children: Hilda B. (Mrs. Stanley L. Rideout), Karen S. (Mrs. S. Leon Hughes, Jr.), Gail H. Ashley-Rollman, Alison F. (Mrs. John W. Sheetz IV). A.B. cum laude in Archtl. Sci., Harvard U., 1950, M.Arch., 1953. Asso. Hugh Stubbins (architect), Cambridge, Mass., 1954-59; self-employed architect, Lexington, Mass., 1954-64; partner firm Ashley & Myer, Cambridge, 1961-64; prin., dir., treas. Ashley, Myer & Assos., Inc., Cambridge, 1964-69, Ashley/Myer/Smith Inc., 1969-72; prin., dir., v.p., treas. Arrowstreet Inc., Cambridge, 1972-77; trustee, v.p., treas. Environ. Design Group, Inc., Cambridge, 1975-77; individual practice architecture, Lexington, Mass., 1977—. Trustee, corporator Cambridge Savs. Bank, 1969—; treas. Orchard Tennis Cts., Lexington. Served with USNR, 1944-46. Recipient Progressive Architecture design award, 1958; Homes for Better Living award, 1962; 1st prize Internat. Archtl. Design competition New Boston Archtl. Center, 1964; Nat. award merit, 1970; HUD nat. award, 1970; Archtl. Record award for excellence, 1971. Clubs: Belmont Hill (Mass.); Cliff Country (Ogunquit); Coral Beach and Tennis (Bermuda). Home: 6 Moon Hill Rd Lexington MA 02173 Office: 6 Moon Hill Lexington MA 02173

ASHLEY, GEORGE EDWARD, lawyer; b. Bloomfield, Mo., Nov. 28, 1919; s. John Lucas and Emma (Weber) A.; m. Elizabeth Cottingham, July 11, 1942; children: George Lucas, Ruth Ashley Lewing, Anne Elizabeth, Ernest Cottingham. A.B., U. Mo., Columbia, 1947, LL.B., 1948. Bar: Mo. 1948, Tex. 1954, N.Y. 1956. Gen. atty. AT&T, 1962-73, asso. gen. counsel, 1981—; v.p., gen. counsel N.Y. Telephone Co., N.Y.C., 1973-81. Dir. United Energy Resources, Inc., United Gas Pipe Line Co. Served with inf. AUS, 1942-45. Decorated Purple Heart; recipient Silver Beaver award Boy Scouts Am., 1974. Fellow Am. Bar Found.; mem. ABA, N.Y. State, FCC bar assns., Assn. Bar City N.Y., Am. Law Inst., Phi Beta Kappa, Order of Coif. Clubs: Larchmont Yacht, Century Assn., Pinnacle (N.Y.C.); Masons. Home: 66 Vine Rd Larchmont NY 10538: Office: 195 Broadway New York NY 10007

ASHLEY, HOLT, aero. scientist, educator; b. San Francisco, Jan. 10, 1923; s. Harold Harrison and Anne (Oates) A.; m. Frances M. Day, Feb. 1, 1947. Student, Calif. Inst. Tech., 1940-43; B.S., U. Chgo., 1944; S.M., Mass. Inst. Tech., 1948, Sc.D., 1951. Faculty Mass. Inst. Tech., 1946-67, prof. aero., 1960-67; prof. aeros. and astronautics Stanford U., 1967-; spl. research aeroelasticity, aerodynamics; cons. govt. agys., research orgns., indsl. corps.; dir. office of exploratory research and problem assessment and div. advanced tech. applications NSF, 1972-74; mem. sci. adv. bd. USAF, 1958-80; research adv. com. structural dynamics NASA, 1952-60, research adv. com. on aircraft structures, 1962-70, chmn. research adv. com. on materials and structures, 1974-77; mem. Kanpur Indo-American program Indian Inst. Tech., 1964-65; AIAA Wright Bros. lectr., 1981. Co-author: Aeroelasticity, 1955, Principles of Aeroelasticity, 1962, Aerodynamics of Wings and Bodies, 1969, Engineering Analysis of Flight Vehicles, 1974. Mem. Greater Boston coordinating council Boy Scouts Am., also mem.-at-large and adviser air explorer squadron. Recipient Goodwin medal M.I.T., 1952; Exceptional Civilian Service award U.S. Air Force, 1972, 80; Public Service award NASA, 1981; named one of 10 outstanding young men of year Boston Jr. C. of C., 1956. Fellow Am. Acad. Arts and Scis.; hon. fellow AIAA (asso. editor jour., v.p. tech. 1971, pres. 1973, Structures, Structural Dynamics and Materials award 1969); mem. Am. Meterol. Soc. (profl., recipient 50th Anniversary medal 1971), AAAS, Nat. Acad. Engring. (aeros. and space engring. bd. 1977—), Phi Beta Kappa, Sigma Xi, Tau Beta Pi. Address: 475 Woodside Dr Woodside CA 94062

ASHLEY, JAMES WHEELER, lawyer; b. Chgo., Sept. 23, 1923; s. Frederick and Elizabeth (Wheeler) A.; m. Courtney Collidge, Dec. 27, 1947 (div. 1975); children: James W., Cooper S., Courtney, Christopher R., John M.; m. Joan Allbright, Sept. 25, 1975. Student, Fordham U., 1941-43; J.D., Northwestern U., 1948. Bar: Ill. 1948. Asst. sec. Continental Ill. Nat. Bank, Chgo., 1948-57; assoc. McDemott, Will & Emery, Chgo., 1957-59, ptnr., 1959—; dir. Madison-Kipp Corp., Chgo. Tube & Iron Co., Globe Corp. Contbr. articles to legal jours. Bd. dirs. Chgo. YMCA, 1964—, chmn., 1974-75, mem. nat. bd. dirs., 1975—; bd. dirs. Bus. and Profl. People Pub. Interest, Chgo., 1973—, pres., Chgo., 1982—; trustee Village of Hinsdale, 1969-72. Served to capt. USAAF, 1943-45; PTO. Mem. ABA, Ill. Bar Assn., Chgo. Council Lawyers, Chgo. Bar Assn. Clubs: Monroe of Chgo. (pres., dir.); Plaza. Home: 1815 N Howe St Chicago IL 60614 Office: McDermont Will & Emery 111 W Monroe St Chicago IL 60603

ASHLEY, MERRILL, ballerina; b. St. Paul; m. Kibbe Fitzpatrick. Student, N.Y.C. Ballet Sch. Joined N.Y.C. Ballet, 1967, prin. dancer, 1977—. Prin. roles in: Balanchine's Ballo della Regina and Ballade, Jerome Robbins' Four Chamber Works. Address: care New York City Ballet Lincoln Center Plaza New York NY 10023 *

ASHLEY, ROBERT PAUL, JR., English literature educator; b. Balt., Apr. 15, 1915; s. Robert Paul and Ethel (Rice) A.; m. Virginia Woods, June 24, 1939; children—Virginia Ashley Hager, Dianne Ashley Per-Lee, Cynthia, Robert Paul, Jacquelyn. A.B., Bowdoin Coll., 1936; M.A., Harvard U., 1937, Ph.D., 1949. Tennis coach and instr. English Portland (Maine) Jr. Coll., 1938-39; instr. English Colby Jr. Coll., 1939- 43; tng. instr. Boston Q.M. Depot, 1944; teaching fellow English Harvard U., 1946-48, coach tennis, 1946; asst. prof. English, asst. dean, coach tennis Washington and Jefferson Coll., 1948-51; asst. prof. English U.S. Mil. Acad., 1951-55; prof. English Ripon Coll., 1955—, dean of coll., 1955-74, tennis coach, 1955-64, acting pres., 1966, v.p., 1968-74, chmn. English dept., 1977-80; vis. prof. U.S. Naval Acad. 2d Sem., 1968-69; dir. news and records Midwest Athletic Conf., 1956-61, v.p., 1957-58, pres., 1958-59, 80-81, commr., 1960-66, acting commr., 1977-78; examiner, cons. North Central Assn., 1963-79; mem. Commn. on Colls. and Univs., 1968-72, Wis. Commn. Higher Ednl. Aids, 1964-67, chmn., 1965-66, Nat. Summer Conf. Acad. Deans, 1968. Author: Wilkie Collins, Understanding the Novel; author: juveniles The Stolen Train, Rebel Raiders; Elizabeth Fiction, The Short Stories of Wilkie Collins, Civil War Poetry; co-author: The Bible as Literature; editor: anthologies Faulkner at West Point; contbr. articles to profl. jours. Served as lt. (j.g.) USNR, 1944-46; maj. U.S. Army Res., 1951-55; now col. (ret.). Mem. Modern Lang. Assn. Am., Midwest Modern Lang. Assn., Dickens Soc., Thomas Hardy Soc., Wilkie Collins Soc., Phi Beta Kappa, Zeta Psi. Home: 504 Watson St Ripon WI 54971

ASHMAN, ALLAN, lawyer; b. Boston, July 3, 1940; s. Joseph and Sylvia (Shatz) A.; m. Sandra Rachel Silverton, July 4, 1965; children: Laura Beth, Jonathan Ben. B.A. cum laude, Brown U., 1962; J.D., Columbia U., 1965. Bar: N.C. 1966, U.S. Supreme Ct. 1970. Asst. prof. public law and govt., asst. dir. Inst. Govt., U. N.C. at Chapel Hill, 1965-68; dir. research and spl. projects Nat. Legal Aid and Defender Assn., Chgo., 1968-71; dir. research Am. Judicature Soc., Chgo., 1971-77, asst. exec. dir., 1977-80; exec. dir. Nat. Conf. Bar Examiners, Chgo., 1980—; adj. prof. Ill. Inst. Tech.; lectr. Chgo.-Kent Coll. Law. Author: The New Private Practice: A Study of Piper & Marbury's Neighborhood Law Office, 1972, (with James J. Alfini) The Key to Judicial Merit Selection: The Nominating Process, 1974, (with John P. Ryan) America's Trial Judges, 1980; Research editor: Columbia Jour. Law and Social Problems, 1964-65; Contbr. articles to law jours. Mem. Am. Law Inst., ABA, N.C. Bar Assn., Chgo. Bar Assn. Home: 748 Chilton Ln Wilmette IL 60091 Office: 333 N Michigan Ave Chicago IL 60601

ASHMEAD, LAWRENCE PEEL, editor; b. Rochester, N.Y., July 4, 1932; s. Lawrence Henry and Lillian Jessie (Peel) A. B.A., U. Rochester, 1954, M.S., 1958. Editor, editorial dir. Doubleday & Co., N.Y.C., 1960-75, Simon & Schuster, 1975-77; exec. editor J.B. Lippincott, N.Y.C., 1975-79, Harper & Row, 1979—. Clubs: Yale; Dutch Treat (N.Y.C.); Franklin Inn (Phila.). Home: 2 Sutton Pl S New York NY 10022 Office: Harper & Row Publishers Inc Trade Div 10 E 53d St New York NY 10022

ASHMORE, HARRY SCOTT, editor, found. executive; b. Greenville, S.C., July 27, 1916; s. William Green and Nancy Elizabeth (Scott) A.; m. Barbara Edith Laier, June 2, 1940; 1 dau., Anne Rogers. B.S., Clemson Coll., 1937; Nieman fellow journalism, Harvard, 1941-42; LL.D., Oberlin Coll., 1958, Grinnell Coll., 1963, U. Ark., 1972. Reporter-columnist Greenville (S.C.) Piedmont, 1937-39; polit. writer Greenville News and Charlotte (N.C.) News, 1939-41; asso. editor Charlotte News, 1945-47, editor, 1947; editor editorial page Ark. Gazette, Little Rock, 1947, exec. editor, 1948-59, on leave to serve as asst. Stevenson for presdl. campaign, 1955-56; cons. Center for Study Democratic Instns., Fund for Republic, 1959-60; editor in chief Ency. Brit., 1960-63; editor Brit. Perspectives, 1964-68; sr. fellow Center for Study Dem. Instns., 1959-75; exec. v.p., 1967-69, pres., 1969-74; sr. fellow in communications Duke, 1973-74; Howard R. Marsh vis. prof. U. Mich., 1975. Author: The Negro and the Schools, 1954, An Epitaph for Dixie, 1957, The Other Side of Jordan, 1960, The Man in the Middle, 1966, (with William C. Baggs) Mission to Hanoi, 1968, Fear in the Air, 1973, Arkansas: A Bicentennial History, 1977, Hearts and Minds: The Anatomy of Racism from Roosevelt to Reagan, 1982; editor: The William O. Douglas Inquiry, 1978. Mem. bd. Nat. Com. for an Effective Congress, 1966—; vice chmn. adv. council Am. Civil Liberties Union, 1970—; Bd. dirs. Fund for Republic, 1954-79. Served from 2d lt. to lt. col. 95th Inf. Div. AUS, 1942-45; mem. War Dept. Gen. Staff, 1945. Decorated citation for spl. duty as chief staff Task Force Faith, Ruhr Pocket, 1945; Bronze Star with two oak leaf clusters; recipient Sidney Hillman award, 1957; Pulitzer Prize, editorial writing, 1958; Freedom House award, 1958; Lillian Smith award, 1982. Home: 1373 E Valley Rd Santa Barbara CA 93108

ASHMORE, HENRY LUDLOW, education association administrator; b. Tallahassee, July 4, 1920; s. John Henry and Nursie (Whaley) A.; m. Clarice Langston, Aug. 16, 1946; children: Randan Ludlow, Jerri. B.A. with honors, U. Fla., 1942, Ed.M., 1948, Ed.D. (grad. fellow 1947-50), 1950. Prin. St. Marks (Fla.) Sch., 1946-47; dir. student teaching Ga. Tchrs. Coll., 1950-53; pres. Pensacola Jr. Coll., 1954-64, Armstrong State Coll., Savannah, Ga., 1964-82; assoc. exec. dir. Commn. on Colls., So. Assn. Colls. and Schs., 1982—. Bd. dirs. Candler Hosp., Savannah; mem. exec. com. S.E. Ga. Health Systems, Inc. Served to 1st lt. AUS, 1942-46. Mem. Kappa Delta Pi, Phi Delta Kappa, Phi Kappa Phi, Phi Theta Kappa. Democrat. Baptist (chmn. bd. deacons). Club: Rotary. Home: 1416 N Camden Circle Savannah GA 31406

ASHTON, DAVID JOHN, business and finance educator; b. Somerville, Mass., June 29, 1921; s. Albert Carter and E. Edna (Spry) A.; m. Grace Christine Higgins, June 21, 1943; children: Leslie Jean (Mrs. John Koles), Jeffrey Carter, John Mark. B.S., Tufts Coll., 1942; M.B.A., Boston U., 1950; M.A., Fletcher Sch. Law and Diplomacy, 1952, Ph.D., 1959. Instr., asst. prof. Coll. Bus. Adminstrn. Boston U., 1947-59, assoc. prof., 1959-61, prof., 1961—; editor Boston U. Bus. Review, 1958-59; chmn. Internat. Bus. Curriculum, 1958-64; chmn. dept. Internat. Bus., 1964-68, 74-79, internat. curriculum coordinator, 1968—, chmn. dept. fin. and econs., 1979-82; acting chmn. acctg., 1983-85; mng. dir. Boston U., Brussels, Belgium, 1972-74, 77-78; vis. lectr. U. Libre de Bruxelles, 1972-74, Luxembourg Econ. Inst., 1982; econ. cons. U.S. Naval War Coll., 1963-64, vis. lectr., 1964-65; v.p., dir., mem. exec. com. Internat. Bus. Center of New Eng., Inc., 1975—; econ. and fin. cons. U.S. Dept. Commerce, U.S. Dept. Treasury, Fed. Res. Bank of Boston, Ednl. Testing Service, Internat. Exec. Service Corps, New Eng. Econ. Research Found., New Eng. Regional Commn., Saudi Iron and Steel Corp. Author: New England Manfacturers and European Investments, 1963, The International Component in England's Economic Base, 1968, New England's Exports of Manufactures, 1975, Business Services and New England's Export Base, 1978, also numerous articles in field.; Editorial bd.: The International Executive. Mem. Arlington (Mass.) Bd. Pub. Edn., 1955-58, chmn. bd., 1957-58; mem. Planning Bd., Arlington, 1959-62, Tufts Alumni Council, 1959—; mem. exec. com. Tufts Alumni Council, 1959-62; mem. exec. bd. Fletcher Sch. Alumni Assn., 1958-65; mem. Mass. Gov.'s Adv. Council on Internat. Trade, 1964, Winchester (Mass.) Town Meeting, 1964-70, 76—; vice chmn. Town Govt. Study Commn., 1968-70; mem. Town Mgr. Selection Com., 1975; Bd. dirs. Found. for Advancement of Edn. in Internat. Bus., 1962—, Income Fund Boston. Served to lt. USNR, 1942-45. Decorated chevalier Order of Leopold II, Belgium; recipient George L. Plimpton Alumni award Tilton Sch., 1976. Mem. Am. Econ. Assn., Nat. Planning Assn., Am. Acad. Polit. and Social Sci., Acad. Internat. Bus., Am. Arbitration Assn., Delta Tau Delta, Beta Gamma Sigma, Alpha Kappa Psi. Club: Harvard (Boston). Home: 22 Myrtle St Winchester MA 01890 Office: 704 Commonwealth Ave Boston MA 02215

ASHTON, DORE, author, educator; b. Newark; d. Ralph N. and Sylvia (Ashton) Shapiro; m. Adja Yunkers, July 8, 1952; children—Alexandra Louise, Marina Svietlana. B.A., U. Wis., 1949; M.A., Harvard, 1950; Ph.D. honoris causa, Moore Coll., 1975, Hamline U., 1982. Asso. editor Art Digest, 1951-54; asso. critic N.Y. Times, 1955-60; lectr. Pratt Inst., 1962-63; head humanities dept. (Sch. Visual Arts), 1965-68; prof. Cooper Union, 1968—; art critic, lectr., dir. exhbns. Bd. dirs. Found. for Edn. in Arts; adv. bd. John Simon Guggenheim Found.; chmn. Freedom to Write Com. of P.E.N. Author: Abstract Art Before Columbus, 1957, Poets and the Past, 1959, Philip Guston, 1960, The Unknown Shore, 1962, Rauschenberg's Dante, 1964, Modern American Sculpture, 1968, Richard Lindner, 1969, A Reading of Modern Art, 1970, Pol Bury, 1971; cultural guide New York,, 1972; Picasso on Art, 1972, The New York School: A Cultural Reckoning, 1973, A Joseph Cornell Album, 1974, Yes, But, A Critical Biography of Philip Guston, 1976, A Fable of Modern Art, 1980, American Art Since 1945, 1982, About Rothko, 1983; co-author: Rosa Bonheur, A Life and Legend, 1981; co-editor: Redon, Moreau, Bresdin, 1961; N.Y. contbg. editor: Studio Internat, 1961-74, Opus Internat, 1968-74, XXième Siècle, 1955-70, Arts, 1974—; Contbr. to: Vision and Value series (Gyorgy Kepes), 1966, The New Art Anthology (Gregory Battcock), 1966. Adv. bd. Ctr. Advanced Study in Visual Arts, Nat. Gallery, Swann Found. Recipient Mather award for art criticism Coll. Art Assn., 1963; Guggenheim fellow, 1964; Graham fellow, 1963; Ford Found. fellow, 1960; Nat. Endowment for Humanities grantee, 1980. Mem. Internat. Assn. Art Critics, Coll. Art Assn., Phi Beta Kappa. Home: 217 E 11th St New York NY 10003

ASHTON, GEOFFREY CYRIL, educator, geneticist; b. Croydon, Eng., July 5, 1925; s. Cyril Hanniss and Ethel (Pate) A.; m. Kathleen J. Stanley, Feb. 25, 1951; children—Carolyn Joy, Kathryn Alison, Melinda Jane, Jonathan Geoffrey. B.Sc., Liverpool U., 1943, Ph.D., 1958, D.Sc, 1967. Research asst. U. Toronto, Ont., Can., 1948-50; sect. leader Glaxo Labs., Eng., 1951-56; sr. sci. officer Farm Livestock Research Centre, Eng., 1956-58; prin. research officer Commonwealth Sci. and Indsl. Research Orgn., Australia, 1958-64; prof. genetics U. Hawaii, 1964—, chmn. dept., 1965-72, 79—, asst. vice chancellor, 1972-74, vice chancellor, 1974-78; mem. blood group scientists panel FAO, 1963—, chmn. subcom. on protein polymorphism nomenclature, 1963—. Mem. Genetics Soc. Am., Am. Soc. for Human Genetics, Am. Soc. Naturalists, Behavioral Genetics Assn., Sigma Xi, Phi Delta Kappa. Home: 5414 Kirkwood Pl Honolulu HI 96821

ASHTON, GWYNNE, ballet school director, choreographer; b. Sydney, Australia; d. William Thomas Evans and Irene (Reuter) Pike; m. John Lansbury Botha, Sept. 3, 1959; 1 dau., Natalia Irene Botha. Ed., Sydney, Australia. Mem. faculty Nat. Acad. Arts, Champaign, Ill., 1972-76, dir., 1976, Nat. Ballet Ill., Champaign, 1976. Dancer, Kirsova Ballet, Australia, 1942; Royal Acad. Dance scholar, Sadlers Wells Ballet Sch., London, 1945; dancer, Sadlers Wells Opera Ballet, 1947, Continental Ballet Co., 1949; dancer, choreographer, dir., Pretoria Ballet Theater, Johannesburg, 1952; ballet mistress, Royal Winnipeg Ballet, 1965-68; assoc. dir., 1968; ballet mistress, Pitts. Ballet Theater, 1978-81; asst. dir., Pitts. Ballet Theater, 1981—; dir., Pitts. Ballet Theatre Sch., 1983—; also master classes. Nat. Endowment Arts fellow, 1979. Fellow Imperial Soc. Tchrs. Dancing Checchetti; assoc. Royal Acad. Dancing. Home: 147 Lilmont Dr Swissvale PA 15218 Office: 244 Blvd of the Allies Pittsburgh PA 15222

ASHTON, HARRIS JOHN, business executive; b. Elizabeth, N.J., June 21, 1932; s. Earle S. and Dorothy (Black) A.; m. Angela Murphy, Oct. 20, 1962; children: Kelly Elizabeth, Victoria Catherine. B.A., Yale U., 1954; LL.B., Columbia U., 1959. Bar: N.Y. 1960. Assoc. Breed, Abbott & Morgan, 1959-62, Lovejoy, Wasson, Lundgren & Huppuch, 1962-64; partner Lovejoy, Wasson, Lundgren & Ashton, 1964-75, of counsel, 1975-81; pres., chief adminstrv. officer Gen. Host Corp., 1967-69, chmn., pres., chief exec. officer, 1970—; chmn. Cudahy Co., 1980—; dir. Royal Bank and Trust Co., Franklin Custodian Funds, Inc. Bd. dirs. Madison Square Boys' Club; trustee Greenwich Acad., 1977-81, Miss Porter's Sch., 1981—; bd. visitors Columbia U. Sch. Law, 1982—. Served to lt. AUS, 1955-57. Mem. Am., N.Y. State bar assns., Bar Assn. City N.Y. Clubs: Yale, Sky (N.Y.C.); Blind Brook, Stanwich., Lyford Cay. Home: 191 Clapboard Ridge Rd Greenwich CT 06830 Office: 22 Gate House Rd Stamford CT 06902

ASHTON, SISTER MARY MADONNA, state health commissioner; b. St. Paul; d. Avon B. and Ruth (Fehring) A. B.A., St. Catherine's Coll., St. Paul, 1944; M.S., St. Louis U., 1946; M.H.A., U. Minn., 1958. Mem. Congregation of Sisters St. Joseph of Carondelet; dir. med. social service dept. St. Joseph's Hosp., St. Paul, 1949-56; dir. outpatient dept. St. Mary's Hosp., Mpls., 1958-59, asst. adminstr., 1959-62, adminstr., 1962-68, exec. v.p., 1968-72, pres., 1972-82; commr. health State of Minn., 1983—; dir. Nat. City Bank, Mpls.; preceptor, mem. faculty U. Minn. Program in Hosp. Adminstrn.; Bush summer fellow Harvard Sch. Bus., 1976. Trustee Minn. Blue Cross Assn. Recipient Sabra Hamilton award Program in Hosp. Adminstrn. U. Minn., 1958; Minn. Health Citizen of Yr. award, 1977. Fellow Am. Coll. Hosp. Adminstrs.; sec. Nat. Catholic Health Assn. Home: 5101 W 70th St Minneapolis MN 55435 Office: 717 SE Delaware St Minneapolis MN 55440

ASHTON, PETER SHAW, botanist, educator; b. Boscombe, Eng., June 27, 1934; came to U.S., 1978; s. Dudley Shaw and Edna Marjory (Knott) A.; m. Helen Mary Spence, June 14, 1958; children—Peter Mark, Mellard John, Rachel Mary. B.A., Cambridge U., 1953-56, M.A., 1960, Ph.D., 1962. Forest botanist Forest Dept., Brunei, 1956-62, forest botanist, Sarawak, 1962-65; sr. lectr. Aberdeen (Scotland) U., 1966-72, 1972-78; dir. Arnold Arboretum Harvard U., Cambridge, Mass., 1978—, prof. botany, 1978—. Author books on Borneo trees. Fellow Am. Acad. Arts and Scis., Royal Soc. Edinburgh; Mem. Bot. Soc. Am., Brit. Ecol. Soc., Assn. Tropical Biology, Linnean Soc. London, Internat. Soc. Tropical Ecology, New Eng. Botanical Club. Office: 22 Divinity Ave Cambridge MA 02138

ASHTON, RICH JAMES, librarian; b. Middletown, Ohio, Sept. 18, 1945; s. Ralph James and Lydia Marie (Thornbery) A.; m. Marcia K. Zuroweste, Dec. 23, 1968; children: Jonathan Paul, David Andrew. A.B., Harvard U., 1967; M.A., Northwestern U., 1969, Ph.D., 1973; M.A., U. Chgo., 1976. Instr., asst. prof. history Northwestern U., Evanston, Ill., 1972-74; curator local and family history Newberry Library, Chgo., 1974-77; asst. dir. Allen County Pub. Library, Ft. Wayne, Ind., 1977-80, dir., 1980—; mem. Ind. Coop Library Services Authority, 1980—, Ft. Wayne Cable TV Adv. Council, 1982—; cons. Nat. Endowment Humanities, Nat. Ctr. Edn. Stats., Northwestern U. Office Estate Planning. Author: The Life of Henry Ruiter, 1742-1819, 1974, The Genealogy Beginner's Manual: A New Edition, 1977. Bd. dirs. Community Coordinated Child Care, Evanston, 1972-74, Three Rivers Montessori Sch., Ft. Wayne, 1977-80; bd. dirs., sec., v.p., pres. Allen County-Ft. Wayne Hist. Soc., 1977—. Conscientious objector. Recipient Nat. Merit scholar, 1963-67; NDEA fellow, 1967-69; Woodrow Wilson fellow, 1971-72. Mem. ALA, Ind. Library Assn., Fedn. Geneal. Soc. Clubs: Fortnightly, Quest. Lodge: Kiwanis. Home: 4617 Calumet Ave Fort Wayne IN 46806 Office: 900 Webster St PO Box 2270 Fort Wayne IN 46801

ASHTON, SAMUEL COLLIER, research institute executive; b. Hohenwald, Tenn., Sept. 26, 1922; s. Arch Will and Lulu Earle (Collier) A.; m. Rita Jane Anderson, Oct. 18, 1947; 1 son, Craig Collier. B.S.E.E., U.S. Naval Acad., 1945. Head cryogenic lab. The Tex. Co., Long Beach, Calif., 1947-48; asst. dir. phys. sic. div. Stanford Research Inst., Menlo Park, Calif., 1948-59; corp. v.p. Research Triangle Inst., Research Triangle Park, N.C., 1959—. Co-patentee continuous ion exchange sugar beet refining. Served to engisn USN, 1945-47; PTO. Mem. Am. Def. Preparedness Assn. (chmn. Carolinas chpt. 1965). Republican. Episcopalian. Club: Hope Valley Country (Durham, N.C.). Home: 3104 Buckingham Rd Durham NC 27707

ASHTON, WENDELL JEREMY, publisher; b. Salt Lake City, Oct. 31, 1912; s. Marvin Owen and Rae (Jeremy) A.; m. Marian Reynolds, Apr. 24, 1940 (dec. Mar. 1963); children: Wendy Jane (Mrs. Neil Christiansen), Susan, Ellen (Mrs. J. Robert Van Orman), Marged, Owen, Kay; m. Belva Barlow, June 26, 1964; 1 dau., Allyson Louise. B.S. magna cum laude, U. Utah, 1933; LL.D., Westminster Coll., 1980. Reporter Salt Lake City Telegram, 1931-34; asso. editor Millennial Star, London, Eng., 1935-36; salesman for bldg. materials co., 1936-42; gen. sec. Sunday Schs., Ch. of Jesus Christ of Latter Day Saints, 1942-46; mng. editor Deseret News, Salt Lake City, 1947-48; v.p. Gillham Advt., Inc., Salt Lake City, 1951-72; mng. dir. pub. communications Ch. of Jesus Christ of Latter Day Saints, 1972-77; pub. Deseret News Pub. Co., Salt Lake City, 1978—; partner Oneida Investment Co., 1952—; chmn. bd. Salt Lake br. Fed. Res. Bank San Francisco, 1979—. Author: (with Ab Jenkins) Salt of the Earth, 1939, Theirs is the Kingdom, 1945, Voice in the West, 1950, It's Your Life to Enjoy, 1955, In Your Own Image, 1959, Bigger Than Yourself, 1965, To Thine Own Self, 1972. Pres., chief exec. officer Utah Symphony, 1966—; pres. Sons Utah Pioneers, 1946-47; chmn. Utah Cancer Crusade, 1964; v.p. Great Salt Lake council Boy Scouts Am., 1957-60; vice chmn. Utah Bicentennial Commn. for Am.'s Ind., 1972—; state adv. com. Citizens for Better Utah, 1968—; mem. Utah Travel Commn., 1975—; bd. govs. DS Hosp., 1975—, Stevens Henager Coll., 1957-72, Deseret Utah Art Found., 1974—; adv. bd. dept. journalism U. Utah, 1967—; mem. nat. adv. bd. Brigham Young U. Coll. Bus., 1972—; exec. com. Utahns Against Pornography, 1976—; bd. dirs. Newspaper Agy. Corp. Recipient Distinguished Alumni award U. Utah, 1968, Service to Journalism award, 1967; Silver medal Am. Advt. Fedn., 1967; Silver Beaver award Boy Scouts Am., 1957; Meritorious Service award Dept. Communications Brigham Young U., 1975; Disting. Service award U. Utah Coll. Bus., 1979; Disting. Service to Edn. award Phi Delta Kappa, 1983. Mem. Salt Lake Area C. of C. (bd. govs. 1976-79, 1st v.p., pres. 1978-79), Sigma Nu (Utah Hall of Fame 1976). Republican. Mem. Ch. of Jesus Christ of Latter Day Saints (stake pres. 1960-62; regional rep. of 12, 1967-73). Home: 4229 Park Terrace Dr Salt Lake City UT 84117 Office: 30 E 1st S Salt Lake City UT 84110

ASHWORTH, JOHN LAWRENCE, lawyer; b. Huntington, W.Va., Apr. 15, 1934; s. W.L.J. and Johnnie (Summers) A.; m. Rosemary L. Baxter, Aug. 10, 1957; children: Julie, Amy, Molly. B.A., Ohio Wesleyan U., 1956; J.D., U. Mich., 1959. Bar: Ky. 1962, Ohio 1960, U.S. Supreme Ct. 1976. Practice in, Ashland, 1960-64, Marion, 1964—; staff atty. Ashland Oil & Refining Co., 1960-64. Comment editor: Pages Ohio Revised Code, 1978—. Chmn. Nat. Found. March of Dimes, 1970; chmn. profl. div. Marion County United Appeal, 1970, chmn. employee div., 1971; pres. United Way Marion County, 1972, drive chmn., 1973; mem. Marion City Bd. Edn., 1972—, v.p., 1977-78, 82, pres., 1978-79, 83; Bd. dirs. Marion County United Community Services, 1970-72; bd. govs. Community Meml. Hosp., 1972-76; trustee Mary Elizabeth Smith Found., 1972-76. Recipient award of merit Ohio Legal Center Inst., 1964. Mem. Am. Bar Assn., Ohio Bar Assn. (past com. chmn.), Ky. Bar Assn., Marion County Bar Assn. (pres. 1973). Baptist. Club: Rotary (pres. Marion 1972-73). Home: 725 King Ave Marion OH 43302 Office: 255 Executive Dr Marion OH 43302

ASHWORTH, KENNETH HAYDEN, educational administrator; b. Abilene, Tex., Feb. 24, 1932; s. Harold Laverne and Mae Beatrice (Grote) A.; children: Rodney Brian, Karen Grace. B.A., U. Tex., 1958, Ph.D., 1969; M. Pub. Adminstrn., Syracuse U., 1959. Asst. commr. coordinating bd. Tex. Coll. and Univ. System, Austin, 1965-69, commr. higher edn., 1976—; vice chancellor for acad. affairs U. Tex. System, Austin, 1969-73; exec. v.p. U. Tex. at San Antonio, 1973-76. Author: Scholars and Statesmen, 1972, American Higher Education in Decline, 1979. Served with USN, 1951-55. Mem. Philos. Soc. Tex., Sembradores de Amistad, Phi Beta Kappa, Phi Delta Kappa, Phi Kappa Phi, Pi Sigma Alpha. Democrat. Unitarian. Club: Town and Gown. Home: 6631 Valleyside Rd Austin TX 78731 Office: PO Box 12788 Austin TX 78711

ASHWORTH, MAYNARD RICHARD, newspaper publisher; b. Holden, Mo., July 21, 1894; s. Henry Brinkley and Eunice Mary (West) A.; m. Annie Laurie Page, Jan. 26, 1926; children—Maynard Richard, Peggy. Ed., State Tchrs. Coll., Warrensburg, Mo., 1912-15, U. Chgo., summer 1916, U. Minn., summer 1917. Tchr., Guthrie, Okla., 1915-16, Mpls., 1917, dept. store work, Pitts., 1919-24, real estate, Pitts., Los Angeles, Miami, 1924-26, in newspaper work, 1927—; with Ledger-Enquirer, Columbus, Ga., 1927-28, Durham (N.C.) Sun, 1929; gen. mgr. Wilmington (N.C.) Star-News, 1929-30, Long Beach (Calif.) Sun, 1930-31; newspaper broker, Los Angeles, 1932; with San Pedro News Pilot, 1932-34; gen. mgr. Ledger-Enquirer, Columbus, 1934-73; pub. Columbus Ledger and Columbus Enquirer, 1936-73; pres. R.W. Page Corp., 1961-73, pres. emeritus, 1973—; dir. Columbus Bank & Trust Co. Served to 2d lt. U.S. Army, 1917-19; commd. 1st lt. inf. Res. Corps, 1919; capt., 1924; served in World War II, Aug. 1941-Oct. 1944; capt. to lt. col. inf., 17 months; Africa and Italy. Mem. Phi Kappa Phi. Democrat (ind.). Methodist. Clubs: Masons (32 deg.), Shriners; Rotary (dist. gov. 165th dist. 1939-40), Country, Big Eddy (Columbus); Officers (Fort Benning, Ga.). Home: 821 Peachtree Dr Columbus GA 31906 Office: Columbus Bank & Trust Co Bldg Columbus GA 31901 *A goal early in life, burning ambition to achieve, preparation by education and practical experience, then relentless drive, work, and love of this work, and behind it all, an incentive; loved ones first, and equally strong, desire to serve mankind in a worthwhile manner, to do something for this opportunity of life—to help my fellow man.*

ASIMAKOPULOS, ATHANASIOS, economics educator; b. Montreal, May 28, 1930; s. Antonios and Paraskevi (Sepentzie) A.; m. Marika Salamis, Aug. 18, 1961; children: Anna, Julia. B.A., McGill U., 1951, M.A., 1953; Ph.D., U. Cambridge, 1959. Asst. prof. Royal Mil. Coll., Kingston, Ont., Can., 1957-59; asst. prof. econs. McGill U., Montreal, 1959-63, assoc. prof., 1963-66, prof., 1966—, chmn. dept. econs., 1974-78; mem. research staff Royal Commn. on Govt. Orgns., 1961, Royal Commn. on Banking and Fin., 1962. Author: The Reliability of Selected Price Indexes as Measures of Price Trends, 1964, An Introduction to Economic Theory: Microeconomics, 1978, The Nature of Public Pension Plans: Intergenerational Equity, Funding and Saving, 1980; mng. editor: Can. Jour. Econs., 1968-72. Fellow Royal Soc. Can.; mem. Am. Econ. Assn., Royal Econ. Soc., Can. Econ. Assn. Home: 3230 The Boulevard Westmount PQ Canada H3Y 1S3 Office: 855 Sherbrooke St W Montreal PQ Canada H3A 2T7

ASIMOV, ISAAC, author, biochemist; b. Petrovichi, Russia, Jan. 2, 1920; came to U.S., 1923, naturalized, 1928; s. Judah and Anna Rachel (Berman) A.; m. Gertrude Blugerman, 1942; children: David, Robyn Joan; m. Janet Jeppson, 1973. B.S., Columbia U., 1939, M.A., 1941, Ph.D., 1948. With Boston U. Sch. Medicine, 1949—, asso. prof. biochemistry, 1955-79, prof., 1979—. Author: Pebble in the Sky, 1950, I, Robot, 1950, The Stars, Like the Dust, 1951, Foundation, 1951, Foundation and Empire, 1952, Currents of Space, 1952, Second Foundation, 1953, Caves of Steel, 1954, End of Eternity, 1955, Races and People, 1955, The Naked Sun, 1957; textbook Biochemistry and Human Metabolism, rev. edit, 1957; World of Carbon, 1958, World of Nitrogen, 1958, Nine Tomorrows, 1959, The Words of Science, 1959, Realm of Numbers, 1959, The Living River, 1960, Kingdom of the Sun, 1960, Realm of Measure, 1960, Wellsprings of Life, 1960, Words from Myths, 1961, Realm of Algebra, 1961, Life and Energy, 1962, Words in Genesis, 1962, Fact and Fancy, 1962, Words on the Map, 1962, Search for the Elements, 1962, Words from the Exodus, 1963, The Human Body, 1963, The Genetic Code, 1963, Intelligent Man's Guide to Science, 1960, View from a Height, 1963, Kite that Won the Revolution, 1963, Human Brain, 1964, A Short History of Biology, 1964, Quick and Easy Math, 1964, Adding a Dimension, 1964, A Short History of Chemistry, 1965, The Greeks, 1965, Of Time and Space and Other Things, 1965, The New Intelligent Man's Guide to Science, 1965, An Easy Introduction to the Slide Rule, 1965, Fantastic Voyage, 1966, The Noble Gases, 1966, The Neutrino, 1966, The Roman Republic, 1967, Understanding Physics, 1966, Is Anyone There?, 1967, To the Ends of the Universe, 1967, Mars, 1967, Egyptians, 1967, Asimov's Mysteries, 1968, Science, Numbers and I, 1968, Stars, 1968, Galaxies, 1968, A Whiff of Death, 1968, Near East, 1968, Asimov's Guide to the Bible, vol. 1, 1968, vol. 2, 1969, The Dark Ages, 1968, Words from History, 1968, Photosynthesis, 1969, The Shaping of England, 1969, Twentieth Century Discovery, 1969, Nightfall and Other Stories, 1969, Opus 100, 1969, ABC's of Space, 1969, Great Ideas of Science, 1969, Solar System and Back, 1970, Asimov's Guide to Shakespeare (2 vols.), 1970, Constantinople, 1970, ABC's of the Ocean, 1970, Light, 1970, The Stars in Their Courses, 1971, Where Do We Go from Here?, 1971, What Makes the Sun Shine?, 1971, The Sensuous Dirty Old Man, 1971, The Best New Thing, 1971, Isaac Asimov's Treasury of Humor, 1971, The Hugo Winners, Vol. 2, 1971, The Land of Canaan, 1971, ABC's of the Earth, 1971, The Left Hand of the Electron, 1972, The Gods Themselves, 1972, Asimov's Guide to Science, 1972, More Words of Science, 1972, ABC's of Ecology, 1972, The Early Asimov, 1972, The Shaping of France, 1972, The Story of Ruth, 1972, Asimov's Annotated Don Juan, 1972, The Shaping of North America, 1973, Today and Tomorrow and, 1973, Jupiter, the Largest Planet, 1973, Please Explain, 1973, How Did We Find Out About Numbers, 1973, How Did We Find Out About Dinosaurs, 1973, The Tragedy of the Moon, 1973, Asimov on Astronomy, 1974, The Birth of the United States, 1974, Before the Golden Age, 1974, Our World in Space, 1974, How Did We Find Out About Germs, 1974, Asimov's Annotated Paradise Lost, 1974, Tales of the Black Widowers, 1974, Earth: Our Crowded Spaceship, 1974, Asimov on Chemistry, 1974, How Did We Find Out About Vitamins, 1974, Of Matters Great and Small, 1975, The Solar System, 1975, Our Federal Union, 1975, How Did We Find Out about Comets, 1975, Science Past—Science Future, 1975, Buy Jupiter and Other Stories, 1975, Eyes on the Universe, 1975, Lecherous Limericks, 1975, Heavenly Host, 1975, The Ends of the Earth, 1975, How Did We Find Out About Energy, 1975, Asimov on Physics, 1976, Murder at the ABA, 1976, How Did We Find Out About Atoms, 1976, The Planet That Wasn't, 1976, The Bicentennial Man and Other Stories, 1976, More Lecherous Limericks, 1976, More Tales of the Black Widowers, 1976, Alpha Centauri, The Nearest Star, 1976, How Did We Find Out About Nuclear Power, 1976, Familiar Poems Annotated, 1977, The Collapsing Universe, 1977, Asimov on Numbers, 1977, How Did We Find Out About Outer Space, 1977, Still More Lecherous Limericks, 1977, Hugo Winners, Vol. II, 1977, The Beginning and the End, 1977, Mars, The Red Planet, 1977, The Golden Door, 1977, The Key Word and Other Mysteries, 1977, Asimov's Sherlockian Limericks, 1977, One Hundred Great Science Fiction Short Short Stories, 1978, Quasar, Quasar, Burning Bright, 1978, How Did We Find Out About Earthquakes, 1978, Animals of the Bible, 1978, Life and Time, 1978, Limericks: Too Gross, 1978, How Did We Find Out About Black Holes, 1978, Saturn and Beyond, 1979, In Memory Yet Green, 1979, Opus 200, 1979, Extraterrestrial Civilizations, 1979, How Did We Find Out About Our Human Roots?, 1979, The Road to Infinity, 1979, A Choice of Catastrophes, 1979, Isaac Asimov's Book of Facts, 1979, The Science Fictional Solar System, 1979, The Thirteen Crimes of Science Fiction, 1979, How Did We Find Out About Antarctica?, 1979, Casebook of the Black Widowers, 1980, How Did We Find Out About Oil?, 1980, In Joy Still Felt, 1980, Microcosmic Tales, 1980, Who Dun It?, 1980, Seven Deadly Sins of Science Fiction, 1980, The Annotated Gulliver's Travels, 1980, How Did We Find Out About Coal, 1980, In the Beginning, 1981, Asimov on Science Fiction, 1981, Venus: Near Neighbor of the Sun, 1981, How Did We Find Out About Solar Power, 1981, How Did We Find Out About Volcanoes, 1981, Views of the Universe, 1981, The Sun Shines Bright, 1981, Change, 1981, A Glossary of Limericks, 1982, How Did We Find Out About Life in the Deep Sea, 1982, The Complete Robot, 1982, Laughing Space, 1982, Exploring the Earth and the Cosmos, 1982, How Did We Find Out About the Beginning of Life, 1982, Foundations Edge, 1982, How Did We Find Out About the Universe, 1982, Counting the Eons, 1983, The Winds of Change and other Stories, 1983, The Roving Mind, 1983, The Measure of the Universe, 1983, The Union Club Mysteries, 1983, Norby, the Mixed-Up Robot, 1983, How Did We Find Out About Genes, 1983, The Robots of Dawn, 1983, others. Recipient James T. Grady award Am. Chem. Soc., 1965, AAAS-Westinghouse sci. writing award, 1967. Address: 10 W 66th St Apt 33A New York NY 10023 *I have been avid to learn and avid to teach. When I was seven years old, I taught my five year old sister to read. I have been fortunate to be born with a restless and efficient brain, with a capacity for clear thought and an ability to put that thought into words. Placing it all at the service of my avidity, I have published 237 books as of now and am well-thought of in consequence. As you see, none of this is to my credit. I am the beneficiary of a lucky break in the genetic-sweepstakes.*

ASIMOW, MICHAEL R., lawyer, educator; b. Los Angeles, July 22, 1939; s. William E. and Frieda (Miller) A.; children: Daniel Bryan, Paul David. B.S., UCLA, 1961; LL.B., U. Calif., Berkeley, 1964. Bar: Calif. bar 1965. Asso. firm Irell & Manella, Los Angeles, 1964-66; acting prof. law UCLA, 1967-71, prof., 1971—; cons. Adminstrv. Conf. U.S. Sec., UCLA Faculty Assn.; bd. dirs. Tax Analysts and Advs., Washington. Author: Advice to the Public from Federal Administrative Agencies, 1973. Home: 1626 Malcolm Ave Los Angeles CA 90024 Office: Sch Law U Calif Los Angeles CA 90024 *

ASKANAS-ENGEL, VALERIE, neurologist, educator, researcher; b. Poland, May 28,1937; came to U.S., 1969, naturalized, 1975; d. Marian and Leontyne Askanas; m. W. King Engel; 1 dau., Eve Monique. M.D., Warsaw Med. Sch., Poland, 1960, Ph.D., 1967. Rotating intern Univ. Hosp. Warsaw Med. Sch., 1960-61, resident in neurology, 1961-64, fellow in neuromuscular diseases, 1964-65; asst. prof. neurology Warsaw Med. Sch., 1965-69; assoc. mem. Inst. Muscle Diseases, N.Y.C., 1969-73; asst. prof. NYU Med. Sch., 1973-77; sr. investigator NIH, Bethesda, Md., 1977-81; prof. neurology and pathology U. So. Calif., Los Angeles, 1981—; co-dir. Neuromuscular Ctr. at Hosp. Good Samaritan, 1981—, Muscular Dystrophy Assn. Clinic, 1981—. Contbr. numerous articles, chpts., abstracts to med. publs. Recipient Premio Associazione Stampa Medica Italiana Di Giurnal ItalianaIsmo Medico, 1980; grantee NIH, 1974-77, 83—, Muscular Dystrophy Assn., 1969-77, 81—. Mem. Am. Acad. Neurology, Soc. for Neurosci., Am. Soc. Cell Biology, Am. Assn. Neuropathology, Histochem. Soc., Los Angeles County Med. Assn. Home: 527 S Arden Blvd Los Angeles CA 90020 Office: Hosp Good Samaritan U So Calif Neuromuscular Ctr 637 S Lucas Ave Los Angeles CA 90017

ASKEW, REUBIN O'DONOVAN, lawyer; b. Muskogee, Okla., Sept. 11, 1928; s. Leo Goldberg and Alberta (O'Donovan) A.; m. Donna Lou Harper, Aug. 11, 1956; children: Angela Askew Cook, Kevin O'Donovan. B.S., Fla. State U., 1951; LL.B., U. Fla., 1956. Bar: Fla. 1956. Practiced in, Pensacola, 1956-70; gov. State of Fla., 1971-79; apptd. Pres.'s spl. rep. for trade negotiations, Washington, 1979-81, practice law, Miami, Fla., 1981—; chmn. Presdl. Adv. Bd. on Ambassadorial Appointments, 1977-79, Select Commn. on Immigration and Refugee Policy, 1979; asst. solicitor Escambia County, 1956-58; mem. Fla. Ho. of Reps., 1958-62, Fla. Senate, 1962-70; vice chmn. So. Govs. Conf., 1973-74, chmn., 1974-75, Nat. Govs. Conf., 1977, 78, Nat. Democratic Govs. Conf., 1976-77, So. Growth Policies Bd., 1977; keynote speaker Nat. Dem. Conv., 1972. Mem. Fla. Exec. Com. Tb and Health Assn., 1960-65, Children's Home Soc., 1965—; chmn. Edn. Commn. of States, 1973-74; co-chmn. Citizens Com. on Immigration Reform. Served with AUS, 1946-47; to capt. USAF, 1951-53. Recipient John F. Kennedy Profiles in Courage award B'nai B'rith, 1971, award for conservation work Nat. Wildlife Fedn., 1972, Outstanding Conservationist of Year award Fla. Audubon Soc., 1972, Herbert H. Lehman Ethics award, 1973, John F. Kennedy award Nat. Council Jewish Women, 1973, William Booth award Salvation Army, 1973, Theodore Roosevelt award Internat. Platform Assn., 1975, Herbert Harley award Am. Judicature Soc., 1975, Human Relations award NCCJ, 1976, Leadership Honor award Am. Inst. Planners, 1978, medal Fla. Bar Found., 1979, others. Mem. Fla., Am. bar assns., Am. Judicature Soc. (dir. 1979—), Am. Legion., Order of Coif. Democrat. Presbyn. (elder 1960—). Clubs: Masons (33°), Rotarian. Office: 1401 Brickell Ave PH-1 Miami FL 33131

ASKEY, RICHARD ALLEN, mathematician; b. St. Louis, June 4, 1933; s. Philip Edwin and Bessie May (Yates) A.; m. Ellizabeth Ann Hill, June 14, 1958; children: James, Suzanne. B.A., Washington U., St. Louis, 1955; M.A., Harvard U., 1956; Ph.D., Princeton U., 1961. Instr. in math. Washington U., 1958-61, U. Chgo., 1961-63; asst. prof. math. U. Wis., Madison, 1963-65, asso. prof., 1965-68, prof., 1968—. Author: Orthogonal Polynomials and Special Functions, 1975; editor: Theory and Application of Special Functions, 1975, Collected Papers of Gabor Szego, 1982. Guggenheim fellow, 1969-70. Mem. Am. Math. Soc., Math. Assn. Am., Soc. Indsl. and Applied Math. Home: 2105 Regent St Madison WI 53705 Office: Van Vleck Hall U Wis Madison WI 53706

ASKIN, LEON, director, actor, producer, writer; b. Vienna, Austria, Sept. 18, 1907; came to U.S., 1940, naturalized, 1943; s. Samuel and Malvine (Susman) Aschkenasy; m. Annelies Ehrlich, Apr. 12, 1955; 1 stepdau., Irene Hartzell. Grad., New Sch. for Dramatic Arts, (later called Reinhardt-Seminar), Vienna, 1927; postgrad., Columbia U., summer 1951. Artistic dir. Washington Civic Theatre, 1940-42; tchr. modern play analysis Am. Theater Wing, 1946-47; directing Dramatic Workshop, N.Y.C., 1947-48; founder Actors Equity Community Theater, 1948; chmn. various coms. Actors Equity Library Theatre, 1947-52; hon. life dir. Equity Library Theatre. Actor, Dumont Playhouse, Dusseldorf, Germany, 1927; cabaret dir., writer, actor, Paris, 1933-35; dir. First Legion, Linz, Austria, 1935; artistic dir. lit. and polit. cabaret, ABC, Vienna, 1935-38; writer: motion pictures including Rappel Immediat, Paris, 1938-40; artistic dir.: Troilus and Cressida (Most Outstanding Prodn. 1941), The Applecart (Shaw), American Way; Broadway actor and dir., 1946-52; staged: Faust for, Goethe Festival, 1948-49; dir., played Shylock in: Merchant of Venice, 1952; motion picture appearances include The Robe, 1953, One, Two, Three, 1962, Guns for San Sebastian, 1967, Do Not Disturb, 1966, Hammersmith is Out, Going Ape, 1980, Horror Star, 1981, Airplane II, 1982; starred as Gen. Burkhalter in: TV series Hogan's Heroes, 1966-71; starred as Martin Luther and Karl Marx: Meeting of Minds TV series; dir.: West Coast plays St. Joan (Bernard Shaw), 1954, Julius Caesar (Shakespeare), 1960, The Egg (Felicien Marceau), 1975, Fever in the Brain (Marvin Aron), 1980; played Othello (in German), Hamburg and Berlin, 1957 (acclaimed as greatest German Othello of 20th Century); Contbr.: articles to Los Angeles Times; essays to U. Hamburg Arbeitastelle fur Exilliteratur. Served with U.S. Army, 1942-46; editor-in-chief The Orientation Digest Air Tech. Service Command (15 citations). Recipient Medal of honor City of Vienna, 1983. Mem. Actors Equity (dir. West Coast adv. com. 1952-55), Screen Actors Guild (dir. 1973), AFTRA; mem. Am. Film Inst.; Mem. Acad. Motion Picture Arts and Scis., Acad. TV Arts and Scis., ANTA (nat. bd.), Am. Nat. Theatre and Acad. West (chmn. bd. 1976-78, pres. 1979-82, pres. emeritus 1983—, organized, presented Nat. Artist award to Fred Astaire, Henry Fonda, Bob Hope, Jimmy Stewart, and Roger Stevens, initiated ANTA West/Hearst Discovery Theatre, Calif. Mus. Sci. and Industry). Home: 625 N Rexford Dr Beverly Hills CA 90210 Office: Am Nat Theatre and Acad West 9777 Wilshire Blvd Suite 900 Beverly Hills CA 90213 *I probably would have been far more successful if I had believed less in people, but I doubt that I should have been happier.*

ASKIN, WALTER MILLER, artist, educator; b. Pasadena, Calif., Sept. 12, 1929; s. Paul Henry and Dorothy Margaret (Miller) A.; m. Doris Mae Anderson, Sept. 16, 1950; 1 dau., Nancy Carol Oudegeest. B.A., U. Calif at Berkeley, 1951, M.A., 1952; postgrad., Ruskin Sch. Drawing and Fine Art, Oxford. Asst. curator edn. Legion of Honor Mus., San Francisco, 1953-54; prof. art Calif. State U., Los Angeles, 1956—; vis. artist Pasadena Art Mus., 1962-63, U. N.Mex., 1972, Calif. State U., Long Beach, 1974-75, Cranbrook Acad. Art, Michigan, 1978, Ariz. State U., Tempe, 1979, Art Center Athens Sch. Fine Arts, Mykonos, Greece, 1973, Kelpra Studio, London, 1969, 73; chief reader Advanced Placement Program Ednl. Testing Service, 1982—; chmn. visual arts panel Art Recognition and Talent Search Nat. Found. Advancement in Arts-Commn. on Presdl. Scholars. Numerous exhbns. including one-man shows, Kunstlerhaus, Vienna, Austria, 1981, Santa Barbara Mus. Art, 1966, Hellenic-Am. Union, Athens, Greece, 1973, Hank Baum Gallery, San Francisco, 1970, 74, 76, Ericson Gallery, N.Y.C., 1978, Abraxas Gallery, Calif., 1979,80,81. Trustee Pasadena Art Mus., 1963-68; bd. dirs. Los Angeles Inst. Contemporary Art, 1978-81; Bd. govs. Baxter Art Gallery, Calif. Inst. Tech., 1980—. Recipient Outstanding Prof. award Calif. State U., 1973, Artists award Pasadena Arts Council, 1970, also over 50 awards in competitive exhns. art. Mem. Coll. Art Assn. Am. Home: 846 Bank St South Pasadena CA 91030 Office: 26 W Dayton St Pasadena CA 91105 *As an artist I'm always after the impossible: works embodying a total conceptual enclosure. I try to break through the fog of habit, to see freshly, to cook up an upsetting, unassimilable, corruptive, subversive and indigestible visual stew that combines seriousness and laughter, sobriety and gaity, holiness and vulgarity, commitment and detachment, earnestness and disinterestedness, activity and idleness, work and play, concern and unconcern, reality and fantasy, stability and transformation.*

ASKINS, WALLACE BOYD, manufacturing company executive; b. Chgo., June 2, 1930; s. Wallace Fay and Evelyn Mae (Baker) A.; m. Trieste M. Olivieri, May 20, 1954; 1 son, Justin Wallace. B.A., Lake Forest (Ill.) Coll., 1952; J.D. with honors, John Marshall Law Sch., Chgo., 1961. Bar: Ill. 1961; C.P.A., Ill. Sr. accountant Ernst & Whinney (C.P.A.s), Chgo., 1952-55; controller, house counsel Nat. Lock Co., Rockford, Ill., 1955-65; asst. corp. controller Xerox Corp., Stamford, Conn., 1965-77; exec. v.p., chief fin. officer White Motor Corp., Cleve., 1977-81, chmn. bd., chief exec. officer, 1981-84; v.p., chief fin. officer ARMCO Corp., Middletown, Ohio, 1984—; also dir. White Motor Corp.; dir. Corporate Property Services, Enre Investment Co., Surety Title Agy., Inc. Mem. Am. Bar Assn., Am. Inst. C.P.A.s,

Fin. Execs. Inst., Tax Execs. Inst., Ill. Soc. C.P.A.s, N.Y. Soc. C.P.A.s, Conn. Soc. C.P.A.s, Ill. Bar Assn. Republican. Presbyterian. Club: Shrine. Home: 1155 Country Club Dr Bloomfield Hills MI 48013 Office: ARMCO Middletown OH

ASKWITH, HERBERT, publishing company executive, public relations counselor; b. Boston, May 6, 1889; s. Barry and Gertrude (Aron) A.; m. Margaret A. Long, June 30, 1910; children: Bertram, Edna Abbey, Jean, Marjorie Louise. A.B. magna cum laude, Harvard U., 1907. Asst. English, comparative lit. Harvard U., 1907; mem. editorial staff Good Health Pub. Co., Battle Creek, Mich., 1908-12; publ. mgr. The Independent, N.Y.C., 1916-21; editor, pub. World Rev., 1922-26; v.p. Horace Liveright, Inc. (book pubs.), 1927-29; pub. relations counselor, N.Y.C., 1935—; cons. to pres. New Haven R.R., 1954-56. Author: A Common-Sense Guide to Children's Reading; editor: (with Arnold Herrick) This Way to Unity; author mag. and newspaper articles.; lectr.; frequent radio-TV guest speaker. Mem. N.Y. Gov.'s Panel Commuting Problems, 1959; initiator plan r.r. terminal and shopping center, New Rochelle, N.Y.; chmn. Westchester Commuters Group; mem. Larchmont Park Commn.; promotion Garden of a Million Tulips, N.Y. World's Fair, 1939. Twice recipient Bowdoin Lit. prize Harvard U.; endowed ann. Herbert Askwith Symposium on Higher Edn. Harvard U. Mem. Phi Beta Kappa. Clubs: Harvard (Westchester); Publicity (N.Y.C.) (v.p.). Home: 57 N Chatsworth Ave Larchmont NY 10538

ASLANIDES, PETER CONSTANTINE, lawyer; b. Jersey City, May 20, 1940; s. Louis P. and Denise E. (Vosiandes) A. B.A., Columbia U., 1962; LL.B., Georgetown U., 1965; LL.M. in Taxation, NYU, 1970. Bar: N.J. 1965, N.Y. 1981, D.C. 1965. Partner McCarter & English, Newark, 1969—; adj. prof. Georgetown U. Law Sch., 1980-82; dir. J.L. Prescott Co. Author papers in field. Trustee Christ Hosp., Jersey City., Garden State Ballet. Served as capt. USAF, 1966-69. Mem. Am. Bar Assn., Am. Coll. Probate Counsel, Am. Coll. Tax Counsel, Am. Law Inst., N.J. Bar Assn., Essex County Bar Assn., Internat. Fiscal Assn., N.Y. Hellenic-Am. C. of C. Clubs: Essex (Newark); Princeton (N.Y.C.); Baltrusol Golf (Springfield). Home: One Fifth Ave New York NY 10003 Office: 550 Broad St Newark NJ 07102 Office: One World Trade Ctr New York NY 10048

ASLING, CLARENCE WILLET, anatomist, educator; b. Duluth, Minn., June 17, 1913; s. Clarence D. and S. Elizabeth (Woolverton) A.; m. Irene Savostin, 1970; children: Joseph H., Carol J. Asling Clewell. B.A. in Chemistry, U. Kans., 1934, M.A. in Anatomy, 1937, M.D., 1939; Ph.D. in Anatomy, U. Calif., Berkeley, 1947. Intern Collis P. and Howard Huntington Meml. Hosp., Pasadena, Calif., 1939-40; instr. Vanderbilt U., 1940-41, U. Kans., 1941-44, U. Calif., San Francisco, 1945-47, asst. prof. anatomy, 1947-51, assoc. prof., 1951-57, prof. anatomy, 1957-80, prof. emeritus, 1980—; acting chmn., 1967-68, state curator for anatomy for No. Calif., 1966-76; vis. prof. U. Geneva, 1962. Contbr. articles to profl. jours. Fulbright fellow, 1953-54; Guggenheim fellow, 1962-63; Recipient medal U. Liege, 1954. Mem. AAUP, Am. Assn. Anatomists, Soc. Exptl. Biology and Medicine, Teratology Soc., Anat. Soc. Gt. Britain and Ireland, Congenital Anomalies Research Soc. Japan, Consejo Nacional de Professores de Ciencias Morfológicas (hon.), Sigma Xi, Phi Beta Pi. Office: 1334 Med Scis Bldg Sch of Medicine 513 Parnassus Ave San Francisco CA 94143

ASMUS, JOHN FREDRICH, physicist; b. Pasadena, Calif., Jan. 30, 1937; s. William F. and Eleanor E. (Kocher) A.; m. Barbara Ann Flaherty, Feb. 23, 1963; children—Joanne M., Rosemary H. B.S. in E.E, Calif. Inst. Tech., 1958, M.S., 1959, Ph.D. in E.E. and Physics, 1965. Head optical systems dept. Aero Geo Astro Corp., Alexandria, Va., 1960-64; head laser dept. Gulf Gen. Atomic, San Diego, Calif., 1964-69; research staff Inst. Def. Analyses, Arlington, Va., 1969-71; v.p. Sci. Applications, Inc., Albuquerque, 1971-73; lectr. U. Calif., Davis, 1974, research physicist, co-founder art and sci. center, San Diego, 1973—; cons.; mem. adv. group on electron devices Smithsonian Assos. Contbr. sci. articles to profl. jours. Schlumberger fellow, 1959-60; Tektronix fellow, 1960-61. Mem. Internat. Inst. Conservation of Historic and Artistic Works, IEEE, Am. Inst. Conservation, Nat. Trust Historic Preservation, Venice Soc., Bay Area Art Conservation Guild, Sigma Xi, Tau Beta Pi. Patentee metallic vapor laser, embedded pinch laser; introduced laser, ultrasonic and computer image enhancement techniques to art conservation. Home: 8239 Sugarman Dr LaJolla CA 92037 Office: IGPP A 025 University California San Diego LaJolla CA 92093

ASNER, EDWARD, actor; b. Kansas City, Mo., Nov. 15, 1929; s. Morris David and Lizzie (Seliger) A.; m. Nancy Lou Sykes, Mar. 23, 1959; children: Matthew and Liza (twins), Kathryn. Student, U. Chgo., 1947-49. Debut at, Playwrights Theatre, Chgo., 1953; appeared on TV, in Off-Broadway and Broadway shows, N.Y.C., 1955-61; appeared in numerous motion pictures and TV shows, Los Angeles, 1961—; appeared on: Mary Tyler Moore Show, CBS-TV, 7 years, Lou Grant Show, CBS-TV, 1977-82, This Side of Eden; narrator: TV film Narco; appeared in: motion pictures Fort Apache, The Bronx, 1981, Daniel, 1983. Served with Signal Corps U.S. Army, 1951-53. Recipient 4 Golden Gobe Awards, 6 Emmy Awards. Mem. Screen Actors Guild (pres. 1981—). Office: care Jack Fields & Assos 9255 Sunset Blvd Suite 1105 Los Angeles CA 90069 *

ASP, RAYMOND J., meat packing company executive; b. 1928; m. B.A., Carleton Coll., 1950. With George A. Hormel & Co., Inc., Austin, Minn., 1950—, prodn. foreman, 1954-59, products merchandiser, 1959-61, div. mgr., 1961-69, v.p. grocery products div., 1965-69, group v.p. prepared foods, 1969-79, exec. v.p. prepared foods, 1970—, dir. Served with U.S. Army, 1950-52. Office: George A Hormel & Co Inc 501 16th Ave NE Austin MN 55912 *

ASP, WILLIAM GEORGE, librarian; b. Hutchinson, Minn., July 4, 1943; s. George William and Blanche Irene (Mattson) A. B.A., U. Minn., 1966, M.A., 1970; postgrad., U. Iowa, 1972-75. Dir. East Central Regional Library, Cambridge, Minn., 1967-70; asst. prof. Sch. Library Sci., U. Iowa, 1970-75; dir. Minn. Office Pub. Libraries and Interlibrary Coop., St. Paul, 1975—; cons. in field. Mem. Nat. Council for Quality Continuing Edn. for Info., Library and Media Personnel.; Bd. dirs. Bakken Library Electricity and Life, Mpls.; vice chmn. White House Conf. on Library and Info. Services Task Force, 1980—. Mem. Am., Minn. library assns., Chief Officers State Library Agencies (chmn. 1979-80), Minn. Ednl. Media Orgn., Minn. Assn. Continuing and Adult Edn., Am. Field Service. Home: 1315 Edgecumbe Rd St Paul MN 55116 Office: 301 Hanover Bldg 480 Cedar St St Paul MN 55101

ASPEN, MARVIN EDWARD, U.S. dist. judge; b. Chgo., July 11, 1934; s. George Abraham and Helen (Adelson) A.; m. Susan Alona Tubbs, Dec. 18, 1966; children—Jennifer Marion, Jessica Maile, Andrew Joseph. B.S. in Law, Northwestern U., 1956, J.D., 1958. Bar: Ill. bar 1958. Individual practice, Chgo., 1958-59; draftsman joint com. to draft new Ill. criminal code Chgo. Bar Assn.-Ill. Bar Assn., 1959-60; asst. state's atty., Cook County, Ill., 1960-63; asst. corp. counsel City of Chgo., 1963-71; individual practice, 1971; judge Circuit Ct. Cook County, 1971-79; U.S. dist. judge No. Dist. Ill., Eastern div., Chgo., 1979—; mem. part-time faculty Northwestern U. Law Sch.; chmn. adv. bd. Inst. Criminal Justice, John Marshall Sch. Law; mem. Ill. Law Enforcement Commn., Gov. Ill. Adv. Commn. Criminal Justice, Cook County Bd. Corrections; chmn. coms. Commn. Ill. Supreme Ct. Appointments; mem. faculty Nat. Inst. Trial Advocacy, Nat. Jud. Coll.; past chmn. coms. Ill. Jud. Conf. Programs. Co-author: Criminal Law for the Layman-A Citizen's Guide, 2d edit, 1977, Criminal Evidence for the Police, 1972; Contbr. articles legal publns. Served with USAF, 1958-59. Mem. Am. Bar Assn., Am. Judicature Soc., Ill. Bar Assn. (past chmn. coms.), Chgo. Bar Assn. (bd. mgrs. 1978-79), Decalogue Soc. Lawyers (past chmn. coms.), John Howard Assn. (dir.). Jewish. Office: 219 S Dearborn St Chicago IL 60604

ASPER, ISRAEL HAROLD, corporation executive; b. Minnedosa, Man., Can., Aug. 11, 1932; s. Leon and Cecilia (Zevit) A.; m. Ruth Miriam Bernstein, May 27, 1956; children: David, Gail, Leonard. B.A., U. Man., Winnipeg, 1953, LL.B., 1964. Assoc. Drache, Meltzer & Co., Winnipeg, Man., 1957-59; sr. ptnr. Asper, & Co., Winnipeg, 1959-70, Buchwald, Asper, Henteleff, 1970-77; chmn., chief exec. officer CanWest Capital Corp., Winnipeg, 1977—; chmn. bd. Global Communications, Ltd., Toronto, 1974—, CanWest Broadcasting, Ltd., Winnipeg, 1977—; dir. Western Approaches, Ltd., Vancouver, Air Can., Montreal. Author: The Benson Iceberg, 1970; syndicated newspaper column Taxation, 1966-77. Recipient Alumni award U. Man., 1979. Mem. Can. Bar Assn., Can. Tax Found., Man. Bar Assn., Man. Law Soc., Man. Assn. Rights and Liberties. Jewish. Clubs: Canadian, UniCity Racquet (Winnipeg). Lodge: B'nai B'rith. Home: 1063 Wellington Crescent Winnipeg MB Canada R2N 0A1 Office: CanWest Capital Corp 1900-155 Carlton St Winnipeg MB Canada R3C 3H8

ASPER, MERLE WILLIS, JR., mfg. co. exec.; b. Buena Park, Calif., Oct. 27, 1929; s. Merle Willis and Ruby Josephine (Jackson) A.; m. Nancy Jeanne Hampton, Apr. 8, 1961; children—Merle Willis III, Jeanne Elizabeth. A.B., Stanford, 1953; LL.B., Boston Coll., 1958. Bar: Calif. bar 1958. Gen. counsel, v.p. legal relations, sec. Purex Industries, Inc., Lakewood, Calif., 1971—. Home: 942 River Ln Santa Ana CA 92706 Office: 5101 Clark Ave Lakewood CA 90712

ASPIN, LES, congressman; b. Milw., July 21, 1938; s. Leslie and Marie (Orth) A. B.A. summa cum laude, Yale U., 1960; M.A., Oxford (Eng.) U., 1962; Ph.D., MIT, 1965. Mem. staff Sen. William Proxmire, 1960, campaign dir., 1964; staff asst. to Walter Heller; chmn. Pres. Kennedy's Council Econ. Advisers, 1963; mem. 92d-98th congresses from 1st Wis. Dist., chmn. subcom. mil. personnel and compensation. Served to capt. AUS, 1966-68. Mem. Jr. C. of C., Am. Legion, Phi Beta Kappa. Episcopalian. Office: 442 Cannon Office Bldg Washington DC 20515

ASPLIN, EDWARD WILLIAM, packaging co. exec.; b. Mpls., June 25, 1922; s. John E. and Alma (Carlbom) A.; m. Eleanor Young Rodgers, Oct. 20, 1951; children—Sarah L., William R., Lynn E. B.B.A., U. Minn., 1943; postgrad., U. Mich., 1947-48, Wayne State, 1949-50, Rutgers U. Sch. Banking, 1957-59. Cost accountant Nat. Bank Detroit, 1947-50; asst. v.p. adminstrn. Northwest Bancorp., Mpls., 1950-59; v.p. mktg. Northwestern Nat. Bank, Mpls., 1959-67; chmn., chief adminstrv. officer Bemis Co., Inc., Mpls., 1967—, also dir.; dir. Cin. Milacron Inc., DeLuxe Check Printers, Inc. Adviser Opportunity Workshop, Inc.; bd. dirs. YMCA. Served with USNR, 1943-46. Mem. NAM. Clubs: Minikahda, Minneapolis; University (N.Y.C.). Office: 800 Northstar Center Minneapolis MN 55402

ASPLUNDH, BARR ELDER, utility line clearance executive; b. Abington, Pa., Sept. 10, 1927; s. Griffith and Myrtle (Elder) A.; m. Jeanne Leedecker, Sept. 22, 1979; 1 dau., Alex Asplundh Walter. B.S. in Agrl. Econs, Pa. State U., 1952. With Asplundh Co., Willow Grove, Pa., 1945—, supr. ops., then pres., 1968—; chmn. bd. Asplundh Tree Expert Co., 1982—; dir. First Pa. Bank, Phila., Gigliotti Corp. Bd. dirs. Abington (Pa.) Hosp., Phila. Zoo, Wills Eye Hosp., Phila. Served with AUS, World War II. Mem. Internat. Game Fishing Assn., Soaring Soc. Am., N.J. Shade Tree Commn. (hon.), Sigma Chi. Republican. Mem. Swedenborgian Ch. Clubs: Seaview Country, Ocean Reef, Huntingdon Valley Country (dir.), Ocean City Marlin and Tuna (dir.), Bryn Athyn Civic and Social (dir.). Home: 2625 Alnwick Rd Bryn Athyn PA 19009 Office: Asplundh Co Blair Mill Rd Willow Grove PA 19090

ASPLUNDH, LESTER, tree care company executive; b. Bryn Athyn, Pa., 1901. Grad., Swarthmore Coll., 1923. Chmn. bd. Asplundh Tree Expert Co., Inc., Willow Grove, Pa., also dir.; chmn. Utilities Line Constrn. Co. Office: Tree Expert Co Blair Mill Rd Willow Grove PA 19070

ASPREY, WINIFRED ALICE, emeritus mathematics educator; b. Sioux City, Iowa, Apr. 8, 1917; d. Peter and Gladys (Brown) A. A.B., Vassar Coll., 1938; M.S., State U. Iowa, 1943, Ph.D., 1945. Student tchr. Brearley Sch., N.Y.C., 1938-40; tchr. Girls Latin Sch., Chgo., 1940-42; asst. instr. math. State U. Iowa, 1942-45; faculty math. Vassar Coll., Poughkeepsie, N.Y., 1945—, prof., chmn. dept., 1958-62, now Elizabeth Stillman Williams prof. math. and dir. Computer Center emeritus; vis. assoc. math. Ednl. Testing Service, summer 1959; dir. an acad. year inst. in math. under N.Y. State Edn. Dept., 1962-63, computer inst. high sch. tchrs., 1964, 66, 67; vis. prof. on exchange program IBM, Poughkeepsie, 1969-70; cons., mem. vis. staff, computer div. U. Calif. Los Alamos Sci. Lab., 1972—; vis. disting. prof. computer sci. Bethany Coll. (W.Va.), 1983; vis. prof. math. and computer sci. St. Louis U. in Madrid, 1983—. Vassar Coll. fellow, 1950-51, 79-80; NSF grantee summer inst., Eugene, Oreg., 1954, U. Calif. at Los Angeles, 1962; IBM post-doctoral indsl. research fellow, 1957-58; NSF faculty fellow, 1964-65. Fellow AAAS, Iowa Acad. Sci.; mem. Am. Math. Soc., Math. Assn. Am. (com. on undergrad. program in math. 1980—), Soc. Indsl. and Applied Math., AAUP, Iowa Acad. Scis., Am. Statis. Assn., Assn. Computing Machinery (nat. lectr. 1970-71), Nat. Council Tchrs. Math., Phi Beta Kappa, Sigma Xi. Address: Box 87 Vassar Coll Poughkeepsie NY 12601

ASQUITH, PHILIP ERNEST, financial executive; b. Stockport, Eng., Sept. 24, 1940; came to U.S., 1964; s. Ernest and Gladys (Hibert) A.; m. Lynn Lorna Poole, June 1, 1963; children: Jonathan, Christina, Nicole. B.Sc., Birmingham U., Eng., 1962; M.B.A., Harvard U., 1966. Chem. engr. British Petroleum Co. Ltd., London, 1962-64; fin. analyst Standard Oil Co. (Ind.), N.Y.C., 1966-68; gen. ptnr. Bear, Stearns & Co., N.Y.C., 1981—; dir. Revere Copper & Brass, Inc., N.Y.C. Office: 55 Water St New York NY 10041

ASSAEL, HENRY, marketing educator; b. Sofia, Bulgaria, Sept. 12, 1935; s. Stanley Isaac and Anna (Behar) A.; m. Alyce Friedman, Aug. 19, 1961; children: Shaun Eric, Brenda Erica. B.A. cum laude, Harvard U., 1957; M.B.A., U. Pa., 1959; Ph.D., Columbia, 1965. Asst. prof. mktg. Sch. Bus., St. John's U., Jamaica, N.Y., 1962-65, Hofstra U., Hempstead, N.Y., 1965-66; prof. mktg. Grad. Sch. Bus. Adminstrn., N.Y. U., 1966—, chmn. mktg. dept., 1979—; cons. AT&T, N.Y. Stock Exchange, Nestle Co., Inc., GTE, CBS, Am. Can Co. Author: Educational Preparations for Positions in Advertising Management, 1966, The Politics of Distributive Trade Associations: A Study in Conflict Resolution, 1967, Consumer Behavior and Marketing Action, 1981; also numerous articles; editor: A Century of Marketing, 33 vols, 1978, Early Development and Conceptualization of the Field of Marketing, 1978. Mem. Am. Mktg. Assn., Assn. Consumer Research. Office: 100 Trinity Pl New York NY 10006

ASSELIN, MARTIAL, Canadian govt. ofcl.; b. La Malbaie, Que., Can., Feb. 3, 1924; s. Ferdin and Eugenie (Tremblay) A.; m. Pierrette Bouchard, Feb. 14, 1953 (dec. Jan. 1969); 1 son, Jean-Louis; m. Ginette D'Auteuill, Sept. 17, 1976. Ed., Laval U., Quebec. Bar: Called to Que. bar 1951. Dir. Barreau du Saquenay, 1955; mayor City of La Malbaie, 1957-63; mem. Ho. of Commons, 1958-63, 65-72; privy councillor, from 1963; mem. Can. Senate, from 1972; partner firm Asselin, Lapointe and Simard, La Malbaie, 1969-79; minister of state in charge Can. Internat. Devel. Agy. and Francophonie, 1979—; del. numerous nat. and internat. meetings; dir. Prévoyants du Can., 1973-79. Mem. Progressive Conservative Party. Roman Catholic. Address: Blvd des Falaises Point-au-Pic Charlevois PQ Canada

ASSOUSA, GEORGE ELIAS, physicist, foundation executive; b. Jerusalem, Mar. 15, 1936; emigrated to U.S., 1953, naturalized, 1965; s. Elias Theodore and Virginia George (Saboura) A.; divorced; children: Mark Andrew, Virginia Noel. B.A., Earlham Coll., 1957; postgrad. (Rockefeller Bros. fellow), Union Theol. Sem., 1957-58; M.A., Columbia U., 1960; Ph.D. (Nuclear Sci. fellow, Grad. fellow), Fla. State U., 1968. Mem. faculty Earlham Coll., Richmond, Ind., 1960-63; research asst., instr. nuclear physics Fla. State U., Tallahassee, 1963-68; fellow Carnegie Instn. of Washington, 1968-70, research prof., mem. sci. staff, 1970-80, sr. fellow, 1980—; sci. and ednl. affairs v.p. Ideas, Inc., Washington, 1974-75; cons. Princeton U. Obs., 1971-72; cons. on Mid-East sci. Nat. Acad. Scis., 1975; advisor sci. and tech. policy to Crown Prince Hassan of Jordan, 1976-78; cons. N.J. Marine Scis. Consortium, 1980—; Presdl. fellow, fellow program in sci., tech. and humanism Aspen Inst. for Humanistic Studies, 1978—. Contbr.: articles in field to Phys. Rev. Co-founder, pres. Found. for Arab-Israeli Reconciliation, Washington, 1974-77, co-chmn. bd., 1977—; founder, dir. Salzburg Internat. Affairs Seminar, 1979—; dir.-gen. Trust for Internat. Devel. and Edn., London, 1980—; pres. Partnership for Internat. Devel., Inc., Washington, 1981—. Mem. Internat. Astron. Union, Am. Astron. Soc., AAUP, Am. Phys. Soc., Arab Phys. Soc. (U.S. rep.), Lebanese Assn. for Advancement Sci., Council Fgn. Relations, Sigma Xi. Club: Cosmos (Washington). Co-discoverer supernova induced star formation, 1977; specialist Middle East affairs. Office: Partnership for Internat Devel Inc 108 Park St London England W1Y 3RB

ASTAIRE, FRED, actor, dancer; b. Omaha, May 10, 1899; s. Frederic and Ann (Geilus) Austerlitz; m. Phyllis Baker, July 12, 1933 (dec. died 1954); children: Fred, Ava, Peter Potter (step-son); m. Robyn Smith, June 1980. Ed. pub. schs. Co-starred with sister as team of: Fred and Adele (Mrs. Kingman Douglass) Astaire, 1916-32; appeared in: Funny Face, Over the Top, Passing Show of 1918, Apple Blossoms, Lady Be Good, The Bandwagon; following sister's marriage to Lord Charles Cavendish, starred alone in musical comedies later motion pictures; films include Gay Divorcee, Roberta, Follow the Fleet, Swingtime, Top Hat, Shall We Dance?, Damsel in Distress, Carefree, The Story of Vernon and Irene Castle, Broadway Melody of 1940, Second Chorus, You'll Never Get Rich, Holiday Inn, You Were Never Lovelier, The Sky's the Limit, The Ziegfield Follies, Yolanda and the Thief, Blue Skies, Easter Parade, Barkleys of Broadway, Three Little Words, Let's Dance, Royal Wedding, The Belle of New York, The Bandwagon, Daddy Longlegs, Silk Stockings, Funny Face, On the Beach, The Pleasure of His Company, Notorius Lady, Finnian's Rainbow, 1967, Midas Run, 1968, That's Entertainment, 1974, The Towering Inferno, 1974 (Acad. award nominee), That's Entertainment, Part Two, 1976, Ghost Story, 1981; star: musical comedies later motion pictures, including Fred Astaire Show, 1968; appeared on TV in: It Takes A Thief; starred in TV specials; host, occasional star: Alcoa Premier; appeared in TV in: Santa Claus Is Coming to Town, 1970, The Easter Bunny Is Coming to Town, 1977, A Family Upside Down, 1978 (Recipient 9 Emmy awards, Acad. award for raising standards all musicals 1949, Lifetime Achievement award Am. Film Inst. 1981); Author: Steps In Time, 1959. Episcopalian. Clubs: Racquet and Tennis, Lambs, The Brook (N.Y.C.). Address: care Internat Creative Mgmt 8899 Beverly Blvd Los Angeles CA 90048 *

ASTENGO, GEORGE, government management executive; b. Los Angeles, Aug. 6, 1940; s. Henry Astengo Catherine Contreras and Rodriquez (Astengo); m. Minerva Maria Garcia, Feb. 1, 1964; children: Monique Therese, David Alfred. B.A., Calif. State U.-Los Angeles, 1964; A.A., Los Angeles City Coll., 1961; cert., UCLA, 1972. Mgr. personnel adminstrn. ITT, Los Angeles, 1970-75; corp. mgr. personnel adminstrn. Am. Corp., Monterey Park, Calif., 1975-79; v.p. employee relations and adminstrv. services Benefical Standard Corp., Los Angeles, 1979-81; presdl. personnel assoc. dir. The White House, Washington, 1981; dep. asst. sec. U.S. Treasury Dept., Washington, 1981—; instr. Loyola Marymount U., Los Angeles, 1978-80; con. Mchts. & Mfrs., Los Angeles, 1978-79. Mem. Maryo's Com. for Hiring the Handicapped, Glendale, Calif., 1973, Nat. Alliance of Businessmen, Los Angeles, 1974; mem. sch. site council Verdugo Woodlands Elem. Sch., Glendale, 1980. Mem. Am. Soc. Personnel Admistrn., Calif. State C. of C., Los Angeles Area C. of C. Republican. Roman Catholic. Home: 2707 Hermosita Dr Glendale CA 91208

ASTILL, KENNETH NORMAN, university dean; b. Westerly, R.I., July 16, 1923; s. John Henry and Mabel Nellie (Robotham) A.; m. Hazel Patricia Lamb, Apr. 10, 1948; children: Kenneth John, Robert Michael. B.S., U. R.I., 1944; M.A.E., Chrysler Inst. Engring., 1946; M.S., Harvard U., 1953; Ph.D., MIT, 1961. Lab engr. Chrysler Corp., Detroit, 1944-47; prof. mech. engring. Tufts U., Medford, Mass., 1947-80, assoc. dean engring., 1980—; cons. Sylvania Electric Co., Natick Labs., Kaye Instruments, C.S. Draper Labs.; vis. fellow U. Sussex, 1968, 83; vis. prof. U. Leeds, 1976, U. Sussex, 1983. Author: (with B. Arden) Numerical Algorithms, 1970, Elementary Experiments in Mechanical Engineering, 1971, (with others) Laboratory Demonstrations in Heat Transfer and Fluid Mechanics, 1968. Recipient Ralph R. Teeter award Soc. Automotive Engrs., 1981; NSF fellow, 1968. Mem. ASME (chmn. Boston sect. 1981-82), AAUP, Am. Soc. Engring. Edn., Engring. Soc. New Eng. (dir. 1982-83), Sigma Xi, Tau Beta Pi. Home: 72 Yale St Winchester MA 01890 Office: Anderson Hall Tufts Univ Medford MA 02155

ASTIN, ALEXANDER WILLIAM, educator; b. Washington, May 30; s. Allen Varley and Margaret L. (Mackenzie) A.; m. Helen Stavridou, Feb. 11, 1956; children: John Alexander, Paul Allen. A.B., Gettysburg (Pa.) Coll., 1953, Litt.D. (hon.), 1981; M.A., U. Md., 1956, Ph.D., 1958. Dep. chief psychology service USPHS Hosp., Lexington, Ky., 1957-59; dep. chief psychology research unit VA Hosp., Balt., 1959-60; research asso., dir. research Nat. Merit Scholar Corp., Evanston, Ill., 1960-64; dir. research Am. Council Edn., Washington, 1965-73; prof. higher edn. UCLA, 1973—; pres. Higher Edn. Research Inst., Los Angeles, 1973-83. Author: The College Environment, 1968, The Educational and Vocational Development of College Students, 1969, The Invisible Colleges, 1971, The Power of Protest, 1975, Preventing Students from Dropping Out, 1975, Four Critical Years, 1977, Maximizing Leadership Effectiveness, 1980, Minorities in American Higher Education, 1982; others. Trustee St. Xavier Coll., Chgo., Marjorie Webster Jr. Coll., Washington., Gettysburg Coll., 1983—. Recipient Disting. Research award Am. Personnel and Guidance Assn., 1965, Nat. Assn. Student Personnel Adminstrs., 1976; Outstanding Service award Am. Coll. Personnel Assn., 1978; Lindquist award for outstanding research on college students Am. Ednl. Research Assn., 1983; fellow Center Advanced Study Behavioral Sci.

Fellow Am. Psychol. Assn., AAAS; mem. Am. Assn. Higher Edn. (dir.). Home: 2681 Cordelia Rd Los Angeles CA 90049 Office: 924 Westwood Blvd Suite 835 Los Angeles CA 90024

ASTIN, JOHN ALLEN, actor, director, writer; b. Balt., Mar. 30, 1930; s. Allen Varley and Margaret Linnie (Mackenzie) A.; m. Anna Marie (Patty) Duke, Aug. 5, 1972; children: David, Allen, Thomas, Sean, Mackenzie. Student, Washington and Jefferson Coll., 1948-50; B.A., Johns Hopkins U., 1952; postgrad., U. Minn., 1952-53. Appeared on and off Broadway in: Laughton's prodn. of Major Barbara; Ulysses in Nighttown, The Threepenny Opera; others, 1954-60; appeared in: motion pictures West Side Story, 1961, That Touch of Mink, 1962, The Wheeler Dealers, 1963, Move Over Darling, 1963, Candy, 1968, Prelude, 1968, Viva Max, 1969, Get to Know Your Rabbit, 1972, Every Little Crook and Nanny, 1972, The Brothers O'Toole, 1973, Freaky Friday, 1976; TV appearances include I'm Dickens, He's Fenster, 1962-63; The Addams Family, 1964-66; TV appearances include: Evil Roy Slade (world premiere), 1972, Only with Married Men, 1974, The Dream Makers, 1975, Phillip and Barbara, 1976; dir. numerous TV shows including: McMillan and Wife, Night Gallery; dir.: pilot films for Rosetti and Ryan; numerous TV shows, including Mr. Merlin, Just Our Luck; actor, dir.: TV show Operation Petticoat, 1977; motion picture dir., writer: Prelude, 1968 (Acad. award nominee); motion picture writer: (with Coslough Johnson) All Boxed Up, 1972, Cummins and Kinneys, 1973. Mem. Actors Equity Assn., Screen Actors Guild, AFTRA, Dirs. Guild Am., Writers Guild Am. West. (dir. 1981—). Office: Box 49698 Los Angeles CA 90049 *It's important to understand that the world is, for the most part, a collective madhouse, and that practically everyone, however "normal" his facade, is faking sanity. One must try to recognize these aberrations, for they can be the enemy of love.*

ASTIN, PATTY DUKE (ANNA MARIE DUKE), actress; b. N.Y.C., Dec. 14, 1946; d. John P. and Frances (McMahon) Duke; m. John Astin, 1973. Grad., Quintano's School for Young Profls. TV appearances include Armstrong Circle Theatre, 1955, The Prince and the Pauper, 1957, Wuthering Heights, 1958, U.S. Steel Hour, Meet Me in St. Louis, 1959, Swiss Family Robinson, 1958, The Power and the Glory, 1961; appearances include Patty Duke Show, 1963–1964; TV appearances include Before and After, 1979, Women in White, The Baby Sitter, The Women's Room; numerous others; TV appearances include All's Fair, 1981-82; numerous others; theatrical appearances include The Miracle Worker, 1959-61, Isle of Children, 1962; motion picture appearance in The Miracle Worker, 1962 (Acad. award as best supporting actress 1963), Valley of the Dolls, 1967, Me, Natalie, 1969 (Golden Globe award as best actress 1970), My Sweet Charlie, 1970, You'll Like My Mother, 1972, The Swan, 1978, Billie, 1965; appeared in: TV film George Washington, 1984. Nat. youth chmn. Muscular Dystrophy Assns. Am. Recipient Emmy Award, 1979. Address: care Creative Artists Agy 1888 Century Park E Los Angeles CA 90067

ASTMAN, JOSEPH GUSTAV, educator; b. Willimantic, Conn., Nov. 8, 1916; s. Joseph and Helen (Mueller) A.; m. Dorothy Rennie, Dec. 31, 1941; children: Joseph Gustav, William Rennie, Dorthe Rennie, Selda. B.A., Trinity Coll., Hartford, Conn., 1938; M.A., Yale U., 1942, Ph.D., 1948; grantee, Am. Council Learned Socs., U. Mich., summer 1956. Tchr. German, Trinity Coll., 1941-42, 46-48; tchr. English and German, Avon (Conn.) Old Farms Sch., 1942-43; tchr. German, St. Joseph Coll., West Hartford, Conn., 1947-48; mem. faculty Hofstra U., Hempstead, N.Y., 1948—, prof. German, chmn. dept. fgn. langs. and lit., 1954-66, dean Coll. Liberal Arts and Scis., 1966-72, on leave, 1972-73, prof. comparative lit. and langs., 1973—, dir. univ. center for cultural and intercultural study, 1975—, dir. Cultural Ctr., 1982—; dir. NDEA Summer Lang. Inst., 1960-63; asso. Yale Library, 1955—; dir. testing MLA, N.Y.C., 1964-65; mem. Woodrow Wilson fellowship selection com., 1966-70, Middle-States Evaluation Teams. Contbr. articles to profl. publs. Bd. dirs. Friends Nassau County Mus., now treas.; bd. fellows Trinity Coll., Hartford, 1964-71. Served with AUS, 1944-46; ETO. Recipient Dean's award for excellence Hofstra U., 1977; NEH grantee U. Calif.-Berkeley, summer 1981, 1983; Alumni medal Trinity Coll., 1983, Hon. Alumnus, Hofstra U., 1983. Mem. AAUP (pres. Hofstra chpt. 1951-52), MLA, Assn. Tchrs. Slavic E. European Langs. (v.p. N.Y. State 1951-55), Nat. Assn. Standard Med. Vocabulary, Am. Legion (past post vice comdr.), Early Trades and Crafts Soc., Maynard Hill Hist. Soc. (charter), Am. Soc. 18th Century Studies, Sigma Kappa Alpha, Sigma Delta Pi. Home: 2 Border Ln Levittown NY 11756 Office: Hofstra U Hempstead Turnpike Hempstead NY 11550

ASTON, JAMES WILLIAM, banker; b. Farmersville, Tex., Oct. 6, 1911; s. Joe A. and Jimmie Gertrude (Jackson) A.; m. Sarah Camilla Orth, June 29, 1935; 1 son, James William. B.C.E., A. and M. U., U. Tex., 1933. Registered profl. engr. Asst. city mgr., Dallas, 1935-39, city mgr., 1939-41, Bryan, Tex., 1939; v.p. Republic Nat. Bank of Dallas, 1945-55, exec. v.p., 1955-57, pres., 1957-61, pres., chief exec. officer, 1961-65; chmn., chief exec. officer, 1965-74, dir., 1957-77, chmn. dirs. exec. com., 1977—; dir. Republic Bank Corp., Dallas, Indsl. Properties Corp. Mem. Tex. Gov.'s Energy Adv. Council, Greater Dallas Planning Council; pres. Southwestern Med. Found.; trustee S.W. Legal Found.; bd. dirs. Hoblitzelle Found. Served from lt. to col. USAAF, 1941-45; air orgn. planning, hdqrs. A.A.F.; asst. chief, later chief staff ATC. Decorated D.S.M., Legion of Merit. Mem. Trinity Improvement Assn. (v.p.), Am. Bankers Assn. (exec. council 1965-68), Tex. Bankers Assn. (past pres.), Internat. C. of C. (trustee U.S. council), Tau Beta Phi. Mem. Christian Ch. Clubs: Dallas, Dallas Country (Dallas); Las Colinas Country. Home: 5000 Royal Ln Dallas TX 75229 Office: Republic Bank Corp PO Box 222105 Dallas TX 75222

ASTOR, MRS. VINCENT, foundation executive, civic worker; b. Portsmouth, N.H.; d. John Henry and Mabel (Howard) Russell; m. Vincent Astor. LL.D., Columbia U., 1971, Brown U., 1980; H.H.D. (hon.), Fordham U., 1980. Feature editor House and Garden, N.Y.C.; pres., trustee Vincent Astor Found., N.Y.C.; v.p., trustee Astor Home for Children; bd. overseers Cornell U.; trustee Marconi Internat. Fellowship, Sleepy Hollow Restorations; trustee, chmn. Far Eastern art; com. mem. Met. Mus. Art, N.Y.C.; trustee and hon. chmn., mem. devel. com., mem. exec. com. N.Y. Public Library, N.Y.C.; trustee, mem. conservation com., mem. exec. com., hon. chmn. women's com. N.Y. Zool. Soc.; trustee, mem. exec. com., mem. council of fellows Pierpont Morgan Library; trustee, mem. exec. com. Rockefeller U., Sta.-WNET-TV/Channel 13; mem. N.Y. State Park Commn., 1967-69, Mrs. Lyndon Johnson's Beautification Com., Washington. Author: Footprints, Patchwork Child, The Bluebird Is At Home. Decorated dame Venerable Order of St. John of Jerusalem; recipient Anniversary medal N.Y. Public Library Astor, Lenox and Tilden Founds., 1961, award Sisters of Good Shepherd and Children of Madona Hts. Sch. for Girls, 1963, Client Award cert. N.Y. State Assn. Architects, 1964, Honor award HUD, 1966, cert. appreciation City N.Y., 1967, Michael Friedsam medal Archtl. League N.Y., 1968, award Brotherhood-In-Action, Inc., 1968, Outstanding Contbn. award Am. Soc. Landscape Architects, 1968, Spirit of Achievement award Albert Einstein Coll. Medicine, Yeshiva U., 1969, Good Samaritan award P. Ballentine & Sons, 1969, Prospect Block Civic Assn., 1969; Albert Gallatin medal N.Y. U., 1972; spl. citation AIA, 1973; Medal of Merit award Lotos Club, 1973; Pres.'s medal Mcpl. Art Soc., 1976; Gold Medal award N.Y. Zool. Soc., 1978; Elizabeth Seton Humanitarian award N.Y. Foundling Hosp., 1978; Little Apple award Met. Mus. Art, Morgan Library, N.Y. Public Library, N.Y. Zool. Soc., Rockefeller U., South St. Seaport and Sta. WNET-TV/Channel 13, 1978; Albert S. Bard Merit award in urban landscape architecture City Club N.Y., 1967; Forsythia award Bklyn. Bot. Garden, 1981; Woman of Conscience Award Appeal Conscience Found., 1981; Gold medal Nat. Inst. Social Scis., 1981; Bishop's cross; numerous others. Mem. Pilgrims of U.S., Mcpl. Art Soc., Navy League, Nat. Park Found. (asso.), Asia Soc., China Soc., Japan Soc. Clubs: Colony, Grolier, Sleepy Hollow, N.Y. Yacht, Coffee House. Office: Astor (The Vincent) Found 405 Park Ave New York NY 10022

ASTRIN, MARVIN H., broadcasting co. exec.; b. Chgo., Feb. 10, 1925; s. Abe and Lena (Mandel) A.; m. Angie Brown. Student, DePaul U., 1945-48, Roosevelt U., 1948-49, Northwestern U., 1949-50. Account exec. Batten, Barton, Durstine & Osborn, 1945-53, Weiss & Geller Advt., 1953-54, Tatham-Laird Advt., 1954-57; v.p. radio sales WGN Continental Broadcasting Co., Chgo., 1957-81; v.p., gen. mgr. WGN Radio, 1970-73, exec. v.p., gen. mgr., 1974; pres. WGN Continental Sales Co., 1974-78; pres., chief exec. officer WAIT 820 Radio, 1978-79; mgr. Chgo. Office Bernard Howard, 1980; with CBS, Chgo., 1981—. Served with AUS, 1943-45. Mem. Broadcaster Advt. Club (pres. 1977-78), Radio Advt. Bur. (dir.), B'nai B'rith. Home: 6415 N Kilbourn Ave Lincolnwood IL 60646

ASTUTO, PHILIP LOUIS, educator; b. N.Y.C., Jan. 5, 1923; s. Salvatore and Anna (Insalaco) A.; m. Natella M. Digia, July 4, 1953; children—Philip, Anne Marie. B.A., St. John's U., 1943; M.A., Columbia, 1947, Ph.D., 1956. Mem. faculty St. John's U., 1947—, prof. Spanish, 1958—, dir. Latin Am. studies, 1957-60, chmn. dept. modern fgn. langs., 1961-65; Participant Prof.-Student Summer Seminar, sponsored State Dept., 1950; OAS research fellow, Quito, Bogota, 1973-74. Contbr. articles to profl. jours. Served to 1st lt., inf. AUS, 1943-46; ETO. Mem. Am. Assn. Tchrs. Spanish and Portuguese, Am. Hist. Assn., Assn. Latin Am. Studies Modern Lang. Assn., Nat. Acad. History of Ecuador (fgn. corr.). Home: 11 Steuben Dr Jericho NY 11753 Office: St John's U Jamaica NY 11432

ASUNCION, JACOBO ROSALES, JR., surgeon, educator; b. Legaspy City, Philippines, June 12, 1932; emigrated to Can., 1961, naturalized, 1971; s. Jacobo Ramirez and Trinidad (Rosales) A.; m. Erlinda Yniesta Obellos, Feb. 9, 1963; children: Michael Anthony, Paul Daniel. A.A., U. Philippines, 1949; M.D., C.M., U. Santo Tomas, Philippines, 1956; diploma in anatomy (fellow), Queen's U., Kingston, Ont., Can., 1964. Diplomate: Am. Bd. Urology. Intern Homer G. Phillips Hosp., St. Louis, 1956-57, resident in surgery, 1957-58; resident in urology Washington U., St. Louis, 1958-60, chief resident in urology, 1960-61; sr. surg. resident Winnipeg Gen. Hosp., Can., 1962-63, chief resident in pediatric surgery, 1963; teaching fellow in anatomy Queen's U., 1963-64; lectr. in anatomy Dalhousie U., Halifax, N.S., 1964-66, prof. anatomy, 1966, 1966—, 1966—; curator Richard L. de C.H. Saunders Med. Mus., 1967—, mem. med. and dental curriculum coms., 1974—; instr. pub. speaking, human relations and leadership tng. Mgmt. Devel. Center, Warren Adams & Assos., Halifax, 1970—. Author course outline series in anatomy, 1967—. Founder, pres., chmn. bd. Filipino Assn., N.S., 1968-69, 73-74, chmn. standing com. on constn. and by-laws, 1969—, chmn. nominating com., 1976-77; pres. Jollimore PTA; project dir. The Filipino Music Revival, 1975-76; band mgr. Filipino Band of Filipino Assn. N.S., 1975-76; social dir. Fiesta Filipino Exec. Council, 1977-78. Recipient Distinguished Service award United Council Filipino Assns. in Can., 1973, Most Outstanding Filipino in Can. award, 1974, Filipino of Year award Filipino Assn. N.S., 1975; Canadian Govt. grantee, 1975. Mem. Canadian, Am. assns. anatomists, Dalhousie Research Assn., Canadian Med. Assn., Dalhousie Faculty Assn., St. Thomas Aquinas, N.S. ednl. assns., Canadian Fedn. Biol. Socs., Dalhousie Speakers Bur., N.S. Physicians for Life, Canadian Assn. Univ. Tchrs., Dalhousie U., Santo Tomas U. alumni assns., N.W. Arm Planning Assn., Filipino Assn. N.S. Inc. (advisor, bd. dirs. 1978-80, presdl. advisor 1980—), United Council Filipino Assns. in Can. (awards selection com. 1982-83), Phi Xenian Med. Soc., Tau Mu Sigma Phi, Phi Chi. Roman Catholic. Clubs: K.C. (certificate of recognition 1975, chmn. award selection com. 1974-75), K.C. (pro life com. 1974-75). Home: 46 Inverness Halifax NS B3P 1X7 Canada Office: Sir Charles Tupper Medical Bldg Faculty of Medicine Dalhousie University Halifax NS B3H 4H7 Canada *Our life is what our thoughts make it. What we do, compared with what we can do, is like comparing the waves on top of the ocean with the ocean's mighty depths.*

ATAL, BISHNU SAROOP, electrical engineer; b. Kanpur, India, May 10, 1933; came to U.S., 1961; s. Jagannath Prasad and Lashmi Devi (Lakshmi) A.; m. Kamla, July 3, 1959; children: Alka, Namita. B.S with honors, U. Lucknow, 1952; degree, Indian Inst. Sci., Bangalore, Mysore, India, 1955; Ph.D. in E.E., Poly Inst. Bklyn., 1968. Sr. research asst. Indian Inst. Sci., Bangalore, Mysore, 1955-56, lectr., 1957-60; sr. research fellow Central Electronic Engr. Research Inst., Pilani, Rajasthan, India, 1960; mem. tech. staff, supr. Bell Telephone Labs., Murray Hill, N.J., 1961—. Contbr. articles to various publs. Recipient Tech. Achievement award, 1976, Sr. award, 1980. Fellow Acoustical Soc. Am., IEEE. Office: AT&T Bell Labs 600 Mountain Ave Murray Hill NJ 07974 *

ATCHESON, JAMES EDWARD, architect; b. Terrell, Tex., Jan 26, 1906; s. Frank and Bessie (Barton) A.; m. Armista Lucille Heggen, June 20, 1936; children: Michael Edward, Daniel Benn, Timothy Jon, Anne Louise. B.Arch., Tex. Tech. Coll., 1936. Draftsman Eickenroht & Cocke (architects), San Antonio; also part-time instr. Tex. Tech. Coll., 1928-34; designer O.R. Walker (architect), Lubbock, Tex., 1935-40; asso. archtl. engr. C.E. U.S. Army, Albuquerque and Pyote, Tex., 1942-44; partner Walker & Atcheson (architects), Lubbock, 1941-46; prin. James Atcheson (architects), Lubbock, 1947-48; partner Atcheson & Atkinson (architects), Lubbock, 1949-55, Atcheson Cartwright & Assocs. architects and engrs., and predecessor firms 1956-83, Atcheson & Assocs., architects, 1984—. Prin. works include Lubbock Country Club, 1960, Citizens Nat. Bank, Lubbock, 1963, First Christian Ch., Lubbock, 1964, Bell System Telephone Bldg., Lubbock (merit award for architectural excellence 1967), Am. State Bank, Lubbock, 1969, Lubbock, 1969, Courthouse and Fed. office bldg, Lubbock, 1971, Lubbock, 1971. Mem. AIA (pres. Panhandle chpt. 1945, Lubbock chpt. 1963), Tex. Soc. Architects (v.p. 1960), Constn. Specifications Inst. (pres. Lubbock chpt. 1966), Phi Delta Theta. Lutheran (pres. 1966-67). Clubs: Kiwanian (pres. 1973), Lubbock Country.). Home: 3203 26th St Lubbock TX 79410 Office: 3330 70th St Lubbock TX 79413

ATCHISON, RICHARD CALVIN, food company executive; b. Altadena, Calif., Aug. 4, 1932; s. Floyd and Clara (Warwick) A.; m. Mildred Platt, Jan. 14, 1957; children—Tracey, Hayley. B.S., UCLA, 1958. Salesman, product mgr. Lever Bros., N.Y.C., 1958-61; product mgr., group product mgr., then regional sales mgr. Purex Corp., 1961-65; with Van Camp Sea Food Co. div. Ralston Purina Co., San Diego, 1966—, pres., 1965-81, Mitsubishi Foods (U.S.A.) Inc., 1981—. Served with USAF, 1952-56. Office: 2010 Jimmy Durante Blvd Suite 220 Delmar CA 92014

ATCHISON, WILLIAM FRANKLIN, computer scientist, educator; b. Smithfield, Ky., Apr. 7, 1918; s. William Duncan and Mary Lou (Beatty) A.; m. Lois Ethel Bruinkool, June 7, 1947; children—Allen Franklin, Glen Ray, Mary Beth, David Duncan. A.B., Georgetown Coll., 1938; M.A., U. Ky., 1940; Ph.D., U. Ill., 1943; postgrad., Harvard, 1950-51. Physics lab. asst. Georgetown Coll., 1936-38; teaching asst. math. U. Ky., 1939-40; teaching asst., instr. math. U. Ill., 1940-44, instr., asst. prof. math., 1946-55; research asso. prof. math. Ga. Inst. Tech., 1955-63, research prof. math., 1963-66, head programming and coding group, 1956-57, chief, 1957-66, acting dir Sch. Info. Sci., 1963-64; prof. computer sci. U. Md., College Park, 1966—, dir., 1966-73, acting chmn. dept. computer sci., 1973-74; sr. computer scientist Nat. Inst. Edn., Washington, 1974-75; Mem. curriculum com. on computer sci., mem. edn. com. Am. Fedn. Info. Processing Socs.; mem. edn. bd. Assn. Computing Machinery, chmn., 1967-80; mem. working group on computer sci. edn. at secondary sch. level Internat. Fedn. Info. Processing, chmn. working group advanced curriculum; chmn. Interuniv. Communications Council, 1973-74. Contbr. articles profl. jours. Home: 10711 Gatewood Ave Silver Spring MD 20903 Office: Dept Computer Sci U Md College Park MD 20742

ATCHLEY, BILL LEE, university president; b. Cape Girardeau, Mo., Feb. 16, 1932; s. William Cecil and Mary (Bicket) A.; m. Pat Limbaugh, Aug. 1954; 3 children. B.S. in Civil Engring, U. Mo., Rolla, 1957, M.S., 1959; Ph.D., Tex. A. and M. U., 1965. Registered profl. engr., Mo., W.Va., S.C. From asst. prof. to prof. engring. mechanics U. Mo., Rolla, 1957-75; prof., dean Coll. Engring., W.Va. U., Morgantown, 1975-79; pres. Clemson (S.C.) U., 1979; cons. Systems Cons. Inc., Savannah River Lab.; chmn. Gov. W.Va. Commn. Energy, Economy and Environment, 1975; sci. and tech. adviser to Senate and Ho. of Dels. W.Va., 1976; mem. W.Va. Bd. Registration Profl. Engrs.; sci. and tech. adviser to Gov. Mo., 1972-75, to; Gov. W.Va., 1975-79; W.Va. gov.'s rep. to U.S. Govs. Commn. on Energy, 1979; energy advisor to Gov. S.C., 1980; mem. Gov.'s Council on Alcohol Fuels; mem. fed. fossil energy adv. com. Dept. Energy. Author papers in field. Bd. dirs. Southeast Energy Research Inst., S.C. Energy Forum, S.C. Research Authority, S.C. Sea Grant Consortium; mem. sports com. USIA. Served with AUS, 1952-54. Recipient alumni merit award Southeast Mo. State U.; Ford Found. fellow; recipient Distinguished Service award Rolla Bicentennial Com., 1975. Mem. Nat. Govs. Conf., Am. Soc. Engring. Edn., ASCE, Nat. Soc. Profl. Engrs., Newcomen Soc. N.Am., Future Farmers Am. (hon.), Sigma Nu, Phi Kappa Phi (hon.), Beta Sigma Gamma (hon.). Methodist. Office: Office of Pres Clemson U PO Box 992 Clemson SC 29631

ATCHLEY, DANA WINSLOW, JR., electronics manufacturing company executive; b. N.Y.C., Oct. 27, 1917; s. Dana Winslow and Mary Cornelia (Phister) A.; m. Barbara Welch, Aug. 26, 1939 (div. 1953); children: Dana Winslow III, Mary Babcock, Elizabeth Ross, Sarah Ross; m. Barbara Standish Payne, May 1, 1954; children: Marion Woodward, Abigail Adams (dec.), Cornelia Phister, Katherine Saltonstall. Grad., Loomis Sch., 1935; B.S., Harvard U., 1940. Engr. Hygrade-Sylvania, Inc., 1940-41; govt. sales mgr. electronics div. Sylvania Electric Products, 1945-47; sales mgr. Tracerlab, Inc., 1947-50, dir. engring., 1950-51; tech. coordinator United Paramount Theatres, Inc., 1951-52; pres., dir. Microwave Assos., Inc., Burlington, Mass., 1952-69; chmn., chief exec. officer, dir. Microwave Assocs., Inc., 1969-75, chmn., dir., 1969-78, chmn. exec. com., 1975-77, vice-chmn., Burlington, 1981-83; vice chmn., dir. M/A-COM Inc., 1978-81, chmn. emeritus, 1983—. Bd. dirs. Anorexia Nervosa Aid Soc. Mass. Inc. Served to lt. comdr. USNR, 1941-45. Fellow Radio Club Am.; Mem. IEEE (life), Am. Radio Relay League. Clubs: Appalachian Mountain, St. Botolph (Boston); Marblehead Frostbite Sailing, Edgartown Yacht (trustee 1980-83). Home: Granville Rd Lincoln MA 01773 Office: M/A COM Inc Burlington MA 01803

ATCHLEY, ROBERT CLAUDE, gerontologist; b. San Antonio, Sept. 18, 1939; s. Ray Clayton and Roberta Ova (Maddox) A.; children—Christopher, Melissa. A.B., Miami U., Oxford, Ohio, 1961; M.A., Am. U., 1965, Ph.D., 1968. Mem. faculty George Washington U., 1965-66; asst. prof. sociology Miami U.; also research asso. Scripps Found., Oxford, 1966-74, dir. found., 1974—. Author: Understanding American Society, 1971, The Social Forces in Later Life, 3d edit., 1980, The Sociology of Retirement, 1976, Families in Later Life, 1979, Social Problems of the Aged, 1978, also articles. Served to capt. USMCR, 1961-65. NIMH fellow, 1965. Mem. Geront. Soc. Am. (editor-in-chief spl. publns. 1980—), Am. Psychol. Assn., Am. Sociol. Assn., Western Geront. Soc. Home: 5991 Contreras Rd Oxford OH 45056 Office: 354 Hoyt Library Miami Univ Oxford OH 45056

ATHA, STUART KIMBALL, JR., banker; b. Newark, May 28, 1925; s. Stuart Kimball and Katharine Grosvenor (Dixon) A.; m. Eleanor Hendry, July 6, 1946; children—Stuart Kimball III, Susan Hendry, Peter William. B.A., Princeton, 1950. With Hanover Bank, N.Y.C., 1950-62, asst. sec., 1955-56, asst. treas., 1956-62; asst. sec. Chem. Bank, Co., N.Y.C., 1962, asst. v.p., 1962-65, v.p., 1965-71, regional v.p., 1971-72, sr. v.p., 1972—. Served to 1st lt. USAAF, 1943-46. Clubs: Bd. Room (N.Y.C.); Cannon (Princeton). Home: Russet Rd Valley Cottage NY 10989 Office: 277 Park Ave New York NY 10172

ATHANASSOULAS, SOTIRIOS, clergyman; b. Epirus, Greece, Feb. 19, 1936; s. George and Anastasia A. B.D., U. Athens, 1961; M.A., U. Montreal Scis. Religieuses, 1971. Ordained priest Greek Orthodox Ch., 1962; priest St. George Ch., Edmonton, Alta., Can., 1962-65, St. George Cathedral, Montreal, Que., Can., 1965-73; elevated to bishop, 1973, Greek Orthodox bishop of, Toronto, Ont., Can., 1973—; head Greek Orthodox Ch. of Can., 1979—; mem. archdiocese council Greek Orthodox Archdiocese, 1968—, pres. diocesan council, 1974, mem. holy synod, 1977—, mem. archdiocese council, 1968, pres. diocesan council, 1974—; mem. exec. com. Can. Council Chs., 1974—; hon. pres. Thalassemia Found., 1975—; mem. Presbyters Council, 1970-73. Vice pres. Christian Pavilion, Expo 67; mem. governing council U. Toronto, 1975-78. Recipient Centennial medal of Can., 1967. Office: Greek Orthodox Diocese of Toronto 27 Teddington Park Ave Toronto ON M4N 2C4 Canada *

ATHANS, MICHAEL, electrical engineering educator; b. Drama, Greece, May 3, 1937; came to U.S., 1954, naturalized, 1962; s. Joannis M. and Chrissi C. (Konstantinou) Athanassiades. S.B., U. Calif., Berkeley, 1958, S.M., 1959, Ph.D., 1961. Staff mem. Lincoln Lab., Lexington, Mass., 1961-64; asst. prof. Mass. Inst. Tech., Cambridge, 1964, assoc. prof., 1966-73, prof., 1973—; dir. Electronic Systems Lab., 1974-78, Lab. for Info. and Decision Systems, 1978-81, ALPHATECH Inc., Burlington, Mass.; cons. systems and control engring. Author: (with P.L. Falb) Optimal Control, 1966, (with others) Systems, Networks and Computation: Basic Concepts, 1972, Systems, Networks and Computation: Multivariable Methods, 1974; Contbr.: numerous articles to profl. jours. Systems, Networks and Computation: Multivariable Methods. Recipient Donald P. Eckman award, 1964, Frederic Terman award, 1969, AACC Edn. award, 1981. Fellow IEEE (pres. control systems soc. 1972-74), AAAS; mem. Phi Beta Kappa, Sigma Xi. Home: 40 Kendel Common Weston MA 02193 Office: Room 35 406 Massachusetts Institute Technology Cambridge MA 02139

ATHEARN, JAMES LOMEN, insurance educator; b. Kremlin, Mont., Oct. 2, 1916; s. Fred D. and Clarinda E. (Lomen) A.; m. Helen L. Bowery, Nov. 21, 1940; children: Sydney Jane, Teri Lei. B.A., U. Mont., 1947, M.A., 1949; Ph.D., Ohio State U., 1953. C.L.U.;

C.P.C.U. Instr. econs. Coll. Commerce, Ohio State U., 1949-53, asst. prof., 1953-57; prof. Coll. Bus. Adminstrn., U. Fla., Gainesville, 1957-64; dean Sch. Bus., U. Mont., 1964-67; W. Frank Hipp prof. ins. U. S.C., Columbia, 1967-82; bd. govs. Internat. Ins. Seminars. Author: General Insurance Agency Management, 1965, Risk and Insurance, 1977, It Pays to Shop for Life Insurance, 1977; co-author: Questions and Answers on Insurance, 1960. Postdoctoral fellow S.S. Huebner Found., 1956-57. Mem. Am. Risk and Ins. Assn. (past pres.), Am. Soc. C.L.U.'s, Am. Soc. C.P.C.U.'s, So. Risk and Ins. Assn., Western Risk and Ins. Assn. Home: PO Box 123 West Glacier MT 59936

ATHERTON, ALEXANDER SIMPSON, newspaper exec.; b. Honolulu, Mar. 29, 1913; s. Frank Cooke and Eleanore Alice (Simpson) A.; m. LeBurta Marie Gates, Oct. 8, 1941; children—Burta Lee, Frank Cooke II, Marjory Gates. Grad., Tabor Acad., Marion, Mass., 1931; B.A., Dartmouth, 1936. With Hawaiian Trust Co., Honolulu, 1954-66, asst. v.p., 1958-66; pres. Honolulu Star-Bull., 1963—; pres. Guam Publs.; dir. Hawaiian Trust Co., Castle & Cooke, Inc.; Pres. Mid-Pacific Inst., 1955—. Past campaign chmn. Honolulu Community Chest.; Trustee Hawaii Loa Coll., Atherton Family Found.; bd. dirs. Africare, Inc., Honolulu Zoo, Bishop Mus. Mem. Navy League U.S., Royal Philatelic Soc. London, Theta Delta Chi. Republican. Mem. United Ch. Christ. Clubs: Pacific, Adventurers, Waialae Country (Honolulu); Collectors (N.Y.C.). Home: 2150 Puualii Pl Honolulu HI 96822

ATHERTON, ALFRED LEROY, JR., foreign service officer; b. Pitts., Nov. 22, 1921; s. Alfred Leroy and Joan (Reed) A.; m. Betty Wylie Kittredge, May 26, 1946; children: Lynne Kittredge, Michael Anton, Reed Wylie. B.S., Harvard U., 1944, M.A., 1947; LL.D. (hon.), Muskingum Coll., 1984; spl. student econs., U. Calif. at Berkeley, 1961-62. Joined U.S. Fgn. Service, 1947, accorded rank of career ambassader, 1981; vice consul, Stuttgart, Germany, 1947-50, Bonn, Germany, 1950-52, 2d sec., Damascus, Syria, 1953-56, consul, Aleppo, Syria, 1957-58; internat. relations officer Bur. Near Eastern and South Asian Affairs, State Dept., 1959-61; consul, Calcutta, India, 1962-65; dep. dir. Office Near Eastern Affairs, State Dept., 1965-66; country dir. Arab States North, State Dept., 1966-67, country dir. Israel and Arab Israel affairs, 1967-69; dep. asst. sec. Bur. Near East and South Asian Affairs, State Dept., 1970-74; asst. sec. Bur. Near East and South Asian Affairs, 1974-78, ambassador-at-large, 1978-79; ambassador to, Egypt, 1979-83; dir. gen. Fgn. Service, State Dept., 1983—. Served to 1st lt. F.A. AUS, 1943-45; ETO. Decorated Air medal, Silver Star; recipient Career Service award Nat. Civil Service League, 1975; President's award for disting. fed. civilian service, 1980; Presdl. Disting. Service award, 1983. Mem. Fgn. Service Assn, Council on Fgn. Relations. Unitarian. Home: 4301 Massachusetts Ave NW Apt 5003 Washington DC 20016 Office: state department foreign service 2201 c street nw Washington DC 20520

ATHERTON, CHARLES HENRY, federal commission administrator; b. Kingston, Pa., June 24, 1932; s. Thomas Henry and Mary A.; m. Mary Bringhurst Davis, Dec. 15, 1967; children: Sarah Scott, Thomas Henry, Charles Henry. B.A. summa cum laude, Princeton U., 1954, M.F.A., 1957. Practice architecture, Washington, 1957; asst. sec. Fine Arts Commn., 1960-64, sec., adminstrv. officer, 1964—. Trustee Nat. Child Research Center, 1975-79; bd. govs. Columbia Hist. Soc. Served to lt. j.g. USNR, 1957-67. Mem. AIA (pres. Washington chpt. 1983). Clubs: Potomac Boat (Washington); Princeton. Home: 3127 Newark St NW Washington DC 20008 Office: 708 Jackson Pl Washington DC 20006

ATHERTON, JAMES DALE, publisher; b. Browder, Ky., Aug. 20, 1935; s. Homer and Hettie Flora (Tucker) A.; m. Donna Marie Zajicek, Sept. 29, 1956; children: Lisa Marie, James Anthony, Lora Dianne. Student, Cuyahoga Community Coll., Mich. State U. With Penton Press, 1958-64, Steel Mag., 1964-70, Industry Week Mag., 1970-74; sales mgr. New Equipment Digest, Cleve., 1974-75, pub., 1975—, also v.p.; chmn. standards and practices com. Media Comparability Council. Chmn. div. IV United Way. Served with U.S. Army, 1955-58. Mem. Nat. Fluid Power Assn., Indsl. Marketers of Cleve. (dir.), Bus. Profl. Advt. Assn., Sales and Mktg. Execs., Material Handling Inst., T.F. Club of Cleve. (pres. 1973), Cleve. Advt. Club, Scribes Internationale. Republican. Roman Catholic. Clubs: Lakewood Country, Mid-Day, Communicators. Office: 1111 Chester Penton Plaza Cleveland OH 44114

ATHERTON, JAMES KENNETH WARD, photographer; b. Washington, Dec. 16, 1927; s. Fairfax Malcolm, Sr. and Mildred (Herrcher) A.; m. Patricia Ann Hall, Oct. 18, 1949; children: Michael, Robin, Jamie, Steven. Ed. pub. schs., Nat. Sch. Photography. Telephoto operator Acme Newspictures, 1949-50; photographer U.P.I., Washington, 1950-70; picture editor Washington Post, 1970-73, staff photographer, 1973—; owner Atherton's Used Book Shop, Kensington, Md., 1973—; mem. standing com. Senate Press Photographer's Gallery. Served with USN, 1946-47. Recipient 2d prize feature class World Photo Exhbn., Hague, Netherlands, 1966, Bill Pryor Meml. award Washington-Balt. Newspaper Guild, 1962, 63, 64, 66, 69; award for newsfeature picture Nat. Headlines Club, 1969; 1st prize gen. news category, Pictures of Year competition Nat. Press Photographers Assn., 1964; 1st prize annual photo contest White House Press Photographers Assn., 1952, 57, 61, 62, 63, 64; 1st prize presdl. class, 1970; grand award, White House contest, 1961; Ernest E. Grass Meml. award Kent State U., 1957. Mem. Nat. Press Photographers Assn., White House News Photographers Assn. Home: 2913 Stanton Ave Silver Spring MD 20910 Office: 1150 15th St N W Washington DC 20005

ATHERTON, JAMES PEYTON, JR., tenor; b. Montgomery, Ala., Apr. 27, 1943; s. James Peyton and Anna Avery (Thomas) A. B.Music, Peabody Conservatory Music, Balt., 1965, M.Music, 1966. Debuts include, Met. Opera, N.Y.C., 1977, Gyndebourne Festival, 1979, Holland Festival, 1976; mem., Santa Fe Opera, 1973-78, Met. Opera, 1977—; appeared also with, San Francisco Opera, Houston Grand Opera, Miami Opera, Dallas Opera, Canadian Opera. Recipient Nat. Opera Inst. award, 1972. Office: care Columbia Artists 165 W 57th St New York NY 10019 *

ATHERTON, SELWYN L., banker; b. Nashua, N.H., Dec. 11, 1929; s. Ives and Doris (White) A.; m. Margery S. Bugbee, May 10, 1952; children: Alynn W., Lois C., Lee P., Mark R. B.A., Dartmouth Coll., 1951; A.M.P., Harvard U., 1978. Asst. treas. Mfrs. Trust Co., N.Y.C., 1951-57; v.p. 1st Nat. Bank, Auburn, Maine, 1957-61; pres. 1st Agrl. Bank, Pittsfield, Mass., 1961-82; pres., chief operating officer Multibank Fin. Corp., Quincy, Mass., 1982—; chmn. bd. South Shore Bank, Quincy, 1982—; dir. Butternut Basin, Inc., Great Barrington, Mass., Multibank Fin. Corp., South Shore Bank. Mem. Robert Morris Assocs. Home: 75 Simon Hill Rd Norwell MA 02061 Office: Multibank Financial Corp 1400 Hancock St Quincy MA 02169

ATHEY, ROBERT MARSH, hospital administrator; b. Salisbury, N.C., Jan. 3, 1937; s. Gilbert David and Kathleen (Calder) A.; m. Dianne Fleming, Oct. 3, 1981; children: Robert Mark, David Gregg, Thomas Earl; stepchildren: Kellie Dianne, Beverly Lynn. A.B., Catawba Coll., 1959; M.S., U. Ala., Birmingham, 1973. Acct. pvt. firms, Salisbury and Cleveland, N.C., 1959-62; fiscal positions with VA hosps., N.C., S.C., Va., 1962-71; health care adminstr., asst. hosp. dir. trainee VA Hosp., Birmingham, 1971-73, asst. hosp. dir., Lake City, Fla., 1973-75; hosp. adminstrn. specialist, staff asst., spl. asst. VA Central Office, Washington, 1975-76; assoc. med. ctr. dir. VA Med. Ctr., Augusta, Ga., 1976—; mem. Augusta Area Hosp. Council, 1980—, pres., 1983-84; dir. Shepard Community Blood Ctr., Augusta, 1977-81. Asst. pack master Cub Scouts, Boy Scouts Am., 1967-70. Recipient Superior Performance award VA, 1964, 65, Dir.'s commendation VA, 1966, 67, commendation Med. Dist. Dir., 1983. Mem. Ga. Hosp. Assn., Assn. Mil Surgeons, Am. Coll. Hosp. Adminstrs., Am. Hist. Soc. (founding mem.). Lutheran. Home: 29 W Va Med Ctr Augusta GA 30910 Office: Va Med Ctr 2460 Wrightsboro Rd Augusta Ga 30910

ATHOW, KIRK LELAND, plant pathologist; b. Tacoma, Wash., Jan. 22, 1920; s. Leland J. and Ethel M. (Johnson) A.; m. Evelyn M. Klapstein; children: Morris, Debra, Diana, Gary. B.S., Wash. State U., 1946; M.S., Purdue U., 1948, Ph.D., 1951; Honoris Causa, Fed. U. Vicosa, Brazil, 1976. Asst. prof. plant pathology Purdue U., 1949-54, asso. prof., 1954-64, prof., 1964—; technician Purdue-USAID Brazil Project, 1965-68, cons., 1970-73. Contbr. articles in soybean research to profl. jours. Served with U.S. Army, 1942-45. Mem. Am. Phytopath. Soc., Ind. Acad. Sci., Am. Soybean Assn., Pi Kappa Alpha. Methodist. Home: 2104 Crestview Ct Lafayette IN 47905 Office: Dept Plant Pathology Purdue U West Lafayette IN 47907

ATIK, ABRAHAM, found. exec.; b. Jerusalem, June 23, 1936; s. Joseph and Briendl A.; m. Harriet Windwehr, Sept. 1, 1958; children—David Charles, Shira Miriam. B.A., Yeshiva Coll., 1958; M.A., N.Y. U., 1962. Asst. dir. Jewish Welfare Fedn., New Orleans, 1964-66; mgmt. cons. Nelson Assos., N.Y.C., 1967-70; sr. mgmt. analyst Office of the Mayor, N.Y.C., 1970-73; asso. dir. Nat. Found. Jewish Culture, N.Y.C., 1973-80, exec. dir., 1980—. Mem. Conf. Jewish Communal Service. Jewish. Home: 3950 Blackstone Ave Riverdale NY 10471 Office: 122 E 42d St New York NY 10168

ATIYEH, VICTOR GEORGE, governor of Oregon; b. Portland, Oreg., Feb. 20, 1923; s. George and Linda (Asley) A.; m. Dolores Hewitt, July 4, 1944. Student, U. Oreg., 1941-43. With Atiyeh Bros., Inc., Portland, until 1979; resigned as pres.; gov. State of Oreg., Salem, 1979—; mem. Oreg. Ho. of Reps., 1959-65, Oreg. Senate, 1965-78, minority leader, 1971-78; past chmn. Western Govs. Conf. Past pres. Columbia-Pacific council Boy Scouts Am.; past mem. Nat. Explorer Bd.; mem. United Fund, St. Vincent Med. Found., Tuality Community Hosp. Found.; dir.-at-large U. Oreg. Devel. Fund; del. Republican Nat. Conv., 1968, 72, 76, mem. nat. platform com., 1968, 72. Served with USCGR, 1944-45. Recipient Silver Beaver and Silver Antelope awards Boy Scouts Am. Mem. Rep. Govs. Assn. (chmn.). Episcopalian. Office: Office of Gov State Capitol Salem OR 97310

ATKESON, TIMOTHY BREED, lawyer; b. Phila., Apr. 18, 1927; s. Clarence Lee Conner and Mary Paulding (Breed) A.; m. Paula Granger, Aug. 18, 1956; children: Timothy, Christopher, Andrew, Nicholas, Mark, Benjamin, Erica, Jonathan. B.A., Haverford Coll., 1947; Rhodes scholar, Oxford U., 1947-49, M.A., 1954; J.D., Yale U., 1952. Bar: D.C. 1962. Asso., partner firm Steptoe & Johnson, Washington, 1962-67, 1975—; gen. counsel Asian Devel. Bank, 1967-69, Pres.'s Council on Environ. Quality, 1970-73, Office Tech. Assessment, U.S. Congress, 1974; vis. prof. environ. law Dartmouth Coll., 1974; lectr. environ. law Catholic U. Law Sch., 1972; adj. prof. environ. law Georgetown U. Law Sch., 1980—. Bd. dirs. Sidwell Friends Sch., 1970-79, chmn., 1977-79, Am. Farm Sch. in Greece, 1981—. Served with USMC Res., 1945. Mem. Am. Law Inst., Am. Soc. Internat. Law, Environ. Law Inst. (dir. 1974—), Am. Bar Assn., D.C. Bar Assn. Episcopalian. Clubs: Metropolitan, Cosmos. Home: 3141 Highland Pl NW Washington DC 20008 Office: 1250 Connecticut Ave NW Washington DC 20036

ATKEY, RONALD GEORGE, lawyer; b. St. John, N.B., Can., Feb. 15, 1942; s. Osborne Lorne George and Mary Agnes (Hills) A.; m. Marie Catherine Rounding, Oct. 8, 1976; children: Jennifer, Matthew, Erin, Jonathan. B.A., U. Western Ont., Can., 1962, LL.B., 1965; LL.M., Yale U., 1966. Bar: apptd. Queen's counsel, Ont. 1979. Counsel Ont. Law Reform Commn., Toronto, 1969-71; prof. law U. Western Ont., 1967-71, Osgoode Hall Law Sch., York U., Toronto, 1971-72; mem. Can. Parliament for St. Paul's, 1972-74, 79-80; ptnr. firm Osler, Hoskin & Harcourt, barristers and solicitors, Toronto, 1974-79, 80—; minister of employment and immigration Can. Dept. Employment and Immigration, Ottawa, Ont., 1979-80; prof. law U. Toronto, 1974-77, 80—. Author: (with J. N. Lyon) Canadian Constitutional Law in a Modern Perspective, 1970. Recipient Gold medal in law U. Western Ont., 1965. Mem. Law Soc. Upper Can., Can. Bar Assn., Can. Civil Liberties Assn. (dir.), Internat. Freedom of Journalism Inst (chmn.). Progressive Conservative. Clubs: Albany, Empire. Office: Suite 6600 First Canadian Pl Toronto ON Canada

ATKIN, J. MYRON, College dean; b. Bklyn., Apr. 6, 1927; s. Charles Z. and Esther (Jaffe) A.; m. Ann Spiegel, Dec. 25, 1947; children—David, Ruth, Jonathan. B.S., City Coll. N.Y., 1947; M.A., N.Y. U., 1948, Ph.D., 1956. High sch. sci. tchr., N.Y.C., 1948-50; elementary sch. sci. tchr. Great Neck (N.Y.) pub. schs., 1950-55; prof. sci. edn. Coll. Edn., U. Ill. at Urbana, 1955-79, asso. dean, 1966-70, dean, 1970-79; prof., dean Sch. Edn., Stanford U., 1979—; Cons. OECD, Paris, Nat. Inst. Edn.; mem. edn. adv. bd. NSF, 1973-76; mem. Ill. Tchr. Certification Bd., 1973-76; Sir John Adams lectr. U. London Inst. Edn., 1980. Author children's sci. textbooks. Served with USNR, 1945-46. Fellow AAAS (v.p. sect. Q 1973-74); mem. Council Elementary Sci. Internat. (pres. 1969-70), Am. Ednl. Research Assn. (exec. bd. 1972-75, chmn. govt. and profl. liaison com.). Office: Sch Edn Stanford U Stanford CA 94305

ATKIN, JAMES BLAKESLEY, lawyer; b. Orange, N.J., Sept. 23, 1930; s. I.C. Raymond and Alice W. (Flanagan) A.; m. Margarita Lean, Jan. 29, 1957 (div. 1972); children: Deirdre Winifred, James Raymond, Blakesley; m. Eva Auchincloss, Aug. 1, 1972 (div. 1976). B.A., U. Va., 1953, LL.B., 1958. Bar: Calif. 1959, D.C. 1981. Assoc. Pillsbury, Madison & Sutro, San Francisco, 1958-66, ptnr., 1967-81, Washington, 1981—; dep. dir. transition team Dept. Energy, Washington, 1980-81; project dir. com. on indsl. orgn. Am. Petroleum Inst., Washington, 1976-80. Trustee Women's Sports Found., San Francisco, 1978—, Reed Union Sch. Dist., Belvedere-Tiburon, Calif., 1966-68; bd. dirs. Washington Performing Arts Soc., 1982—, Celebrate Women!, Washington, 1982—. Recipient Disting. Service medal Dept. Energy, 1981. Mem. Natural Gas Supply Assn. (chmn legal subcom. 1973-75, chmn. legal subcom. 1981-83). Republican. Episcopalian. Clubs: Bohemian (San Francisco); Union (N.Y.C.). Home: 1150 25th St NW Washington DC 20037 Office: Pillsbury Madison & Sutro 1050 17th St NW Washington DC 20036

ATKIN, KENWARD LOUIS, university official; b. Houghton, Mich., Mar. 12, 1919; s. Charles W. and Ella W. (Young) A.; m. Jane Follis, Dec. 16, 1945; children: Charles, Thomas, Penelope, David. A.B., U. Mich., 1942, M.B.A., 1952; Ph.D., Mich. State U., 1961. Partner, mgr. C.W. Atkin & Son, Soo, Mich., 1946-51; mktg. specialist Ford Motor Co., Detroit, 1952; merchandising mgr. Ex-Cell-O Corp., Detroit, 1953-56; instr. to prof., chmn. dept. advt. Mich. State U., East Lansing, 1956-75; prof., chmn. dept. communications Calif. State U. at Fullerton, 1975-83; dir. Ctr. for Communication Arts So. Meth. U., Dallas, 1983—; cons. State of Mich., Gen. Motors Co., Foote, Cone & Belding Advt. Agy. Author: Communications and Consumer Behavior, 1961; Contbr. articles to profl. jours. Served to maj. AUS, 1942-46; with Mich. N.G., 1946-50. Fellow Am. Assn. Advt. Agys. (educator coordinator), Econ. Found.; mem. Am. Mktg. Assn., Assn. for Edn. in Journalism (chmn. advt. div.), Am. Acad. Advt. (pres. 1974—), Am. Soc. Journalism Sch. Adminstrs. (exec. dir., pres. 1982—), Kappa Tau Alpha. Home: 7314 Centenary Dallas TX 75225

ATKIN, MICHAEL PRENTISS, advertising executive; b. N.Y.C., Sept. 19, 1932; s. Charles Bekcinton and Ellen Parker (Love) A.; m. Vivi Thomas, Feb. 24, 1979; children: Nicole Ellen, Geoffrey Charles, Jillian Claire. B.A., Williams Coll., 1965. Media researcher, planner J. Walter Thompson, N.Y.C., 1971-73; assoc. dir., media research dir. William Esty Co., N.Y.C., 1973-76; v.p., media research dir. McCaffrey & McCall, N.Y.C., 1976-78; sr. v.p. media info., systems Needham Harper & Steers, U.S.A., Inc., N.Y.C., 1978—. Served to capt. USAF, 1966-70. Episcopalian. Home: 71 Round Lake Rd Ridgefield CT 06877 Office: Needham Harper & Steers USA Inc 909 3d Ave New York NY 10022

ATKINS, C(ARL) CLYDE, judge; b. Washington, Nov. 23, 1914; s. C. C. and Marguerite (Criste) A.; m. Esther Castillo, Jan 18, 1937; children: Julie A. Landrigan, Carla A. Schulte (dec.), Carl Clyde. Student, U. Miami, Fla., 1931-32; LL.B., U. Fla., 1936, J.D., 1967; LL.D., Barry Coll., Miami Shores, 1966, Biscayne Coll., Miami, 1970. Bar: Fla. bar 1936. Practice in, Stuart, 1936-41, Miami, 1941-66; partner firm Walton, Lantaff, Schroeder, Atkins, Carson & Wahl (and predecessors), 1941-66; U.S. dist. judge So. dist. Fla., 1966—, chief judge, 1977-82, sr. judge, 1983—; founder-trustee Lawyers Title Guaranty Fund, 1948—, treas., 1963-66. Contbr. articles to profl. jours. Pres. St. Augustine Diocesan Union Holy Name Societies, 1950-51, Miami Archdiocesan Council Cath. Men, 1959-70. Recipient Outstanding Cath. award Nat. Conf. Christians and Jews, 1959. Jud. fellow Am. Coll. Trial Lawyers; mem. ABA (ho. of dels. 1960-66, 79-80), Dade County Bar Assn. (pres. 1953-54), Fla. Bar (bd. govs. 1954-59, pres. 1960-61), Nat. Conf. Fed. Trial Judges (chmn. exec. com. 1975-77, del. Jud. Adminstrn. Council 1979-82), Tau Kappa Alpha, Phi Kappa Tau, Phi Alpha Delta. Clubs: Kiwanis (past dir. Miami), Miami, Coral Gables Country. Office: PO Box 013009 Miami FL 33101

ATKINS, CHESTER B., record co. exec., guitarist, publisher; b. Luttrell, Tenn., June 20, 1924; s. James A. and Ida (Sharp) A.; m. Leona Johnson, June 3, 1946; 1 dau., Merle (Mrs. Will Russell). Student pub. schs., Hamilton, Ga. Cons. Gretsch Guitar Co., Bklyn.; div. v.p. country music RCA Records; chmn. bd. Famous Am. Musicians and Educators, Inc.; dir. Aurora Pub. Co.; Bd. dirs. Nashville Symphony. Performer with, Johnny & Jack; performer with, Grand Ole Opry, Nashville, The Old Dominion Barn Dance, Richmond, Va., Radio Ozark, Springfield, Mo.; (Recipient Grammy award 1967). Named Instrumentalist of Year Country Music Assn., 1969; Most Outstanding Guitarist Guitar Player mag., 1970; Instrumentalist of Year Playboy, 1969; recipient Humanitarian Service award Nat. Conf. Christians and Jews, 1970. Mem. Nashville C. of C. (bd. govs.), AFTRA, Nat. Acad. Rec. Arts and Scis., Am. Fedn. Musicians, Country Music Assn.

ATKINS, DALE MORRELL, physician; b. Somerset, Colo., Jan. 20, 1922; s. James Perry and Lura May (Morrell) A.; m. Loretta Ilene Davidson, June 20, 1943; children—Loretta, Linda, Peter, John. B.A., U. Colo., 1943, M.D., 1945, M.S., 1953. Intern Mass. Meml. Hosp., 1945-46; resident medicine Colo. U. Sch. Medicine, 1948-50, resident urology, 1950-53; pvt. practice genitourinary surgery, Denver, 1953—; clin. asst. prof. surgery U. Colo. Sch. Medicine, 1955—; Mem. bd. regents U. Colo., 1963-74. Served to capt., M.C. AUS, 1946-48. Mem. Phi Beta Kappa. Republican. Methodist. Club: Rotarian. Home: 3982 S Chase Way Denver CO 80235 Office: 2005 Franklin St Denver CO 80205

ATKINS, GORDON LEE, architect; b. Calgary, Alta., Can., Mar. 5, 1937; s. Grant Lee and Dorothy (Atkins) Kearl; m. Constance Joan Lecoq, Mar. 21, 1956; children—Lisa Dawn, Laura Celine, Drew Gordon, Ryan Blake, Murray Kyle, Seth Myer. B.Arch., U. Wash., 1960. Design architect R.R. Campbell & Assos., Seattle, 1958-60, Green, Blankenstein, Russell & Assos., Winnipeg, Man., Can., 1960-61; free lance designer, 1961; partner Alton, McCaul, Bowers, 1961-62; pvt. practive architecture, Calgary, 1962—; pres., prin. Gordon Atkins & Assos., Architects, Ltd., 1977—; sessional instr. Mt. Royal Coll., So. Alta. Inst. Tech.; lectr. U. Calgary; academician Royal Can. Acad. Art.; Mem. Mid-Can. Devel. Corridor Conf. Author: Plywood World, 1970; contbr. articles to profl. jours.; works include Calgary Centennial Planetarium (2d place design award 1964), Leavitt residence, (City of Calgary Urban Design award), Indian Friendship Center, (City of Calgary Urban Design award), Shouldice Change Pavilion, Calgary, (Can. Architect design award 1980), also residences, schs., works displayed, Nat. Gallery, 1967, 69. Recipient Massey medal, 1967, award of excellence Can. Architects Yearbook, 1968; numerous archtl. awards. Mem. Royal Archtl. Inst. Can., Alta. Assn. Architects (pres. Calgary chpt. 1964, Practice Profile award 1981). Mormon. Home: 1008 Durham Ave SW Calgary AB T2T 0E9 Canada Office: 1909 17th Ave Sw Calgary AB T2T 0E9 Canada

ATKINS, JAMES FREDERICK, helicopter company executive; b. Buffalo, Dec. 4, 1918; s. Frederick James and Kathryn Elizabeth (Corbett) A.; m. Elizabeth Marie Shields, June 12, 1948; children: James Frederick, Mary Beth, Kathryn Ann, Susan Gail. Student, U. Denver, 1943-44; B.B.A., Canisius Coll., Buffalo, 1950. Acct., Bell Aircraft Corp., Buffalo, 1940-52; with Bell Helicopter Co., Ft. Worth, 1952-72, treas., asst. sec., 1956-57, sec.-treas., 1957-60, exec. v.p., 1960-72; pres. Bell Helicopter Textron Co., Ft. Worth, 1972-83, chmn. bd., 1983—; dir. First Nat. Bank of Ft. Worth. Active Ft. Worth Progress, Inc.; bd. dirs. So. Meth. U. Found. for Sci. and Engrng., Tex. Christian U. Research Found., Arts Council of Ft. Worth. Served with USAAF, 1942-46. Mem. Newcomen Soc., Am. Helicopter Soc. (past pres.), Helicopter Assn. Am., Assn. U.S. Army, Army Aviation Assn. Am., Air Force Assn., Navy League, Aerospace Industries Assn., Nat. Aviation Assn., Nat. Security Indsl. Assn., Ft. Worth C. of C. (dir.). Roman Catholic. Clubs: River Crest Country, Shady Oaks Country (Ft. Worth). Office: PO Box 482 Fort Worth TX 76101 *

ATKINS, STUART (PRATT), educator; b. Balt., Mar. 8, 1914; s. (George) Robert and Huldah M. (Pratt) A.; m. Lillian E. Reed, June 7, 1946; 1 son, Stuart Reed. A.B. summa cum laude, Yale U., 1935, Ph.D., 1938; A.M. (hon.), Harvard U., 1948. Instr. Dartmouth Coll., 1938-41, Harvard U., 1941-43, Princeton U., 1946; asst. prof. German Harvard U., 1946-48, asso. prof., 1948-56, prof., 1956-65, chmn. dept. Germanic langs. and lits., 1952-57, 60-65; prof. German U. Calif., 1965—, faculty research lectr., 1973; Guggenheim fellow, 1955, 68; vis. prof. U. Goettingen, Germany, 1962; guest prof. Ripon Coll., 1964; Jasper-Jacob-Stahl lectr. Bowdoin Coll., 1972. Author: The Testament of Werther, 1949, Goethe's Faust: A Literary Analysis, 1958, The Age of Goethe, 1969; editor, author revision: Bayard Taylor's Faust, trans, 1962, Goethe's Faust, Part I, bilingual edit, 1963, Heine: Werke, Bd. I, 1973, Bd. II, 1977, Goethe: Torquato Tasso, 1977; also articles.; Editor: German Quar, 1952-57; Contbr.: articles to profl. jours. Served with USAAF, 1943-46. Decorated Bronze Star, Croix de Guerre;

recipient gold medal Goethe Institut, 1968. Mem. Am. Acad. Arts and Scis., Goethe Soc. N.Am., Heinrich Heine-Gesellschaft, Modern Lang Assn. Am. (pres. 1972), Modern Humanities Research Assn., Am. Assn. Tchrs. German (exec. council 1966-68, hon. mem.), Philol. Assn. Pacific Coast, Goethe-Gesellschaft, Phi Beta Kappa. Home: 752 Woodland Dr Santa Barbara CA 93108

ATKINS, VICTOR KENNICOTT, JR., investment banker; b. Seattle, Feb. 8, 1945; s. Victor Kennicott and Elizabeth (Tanner) A. A.B., Harvard U., 1967, M.B.A., 1972. Assoc. Blyth Eastman Dillon & Co., N.Y.C., 1972-75, v.p., 1976-78, 1st v.p., 1978-79, E.F. Hutton & Co., 1979-81, sr. v.p., 1981—. Clubs: The Brook (N.Y.C.); Southampton; Nat. Golf Links (Southampton, N.Y.); Pacific Union (San Francisco). Home: Boheson Rd Box 310 Southampton NY 11968 Office: EF Hutton Group Inc One Battery Park Plaza New York NY 10004

ATKINSON, ANDERSON WATKINS, ret. air force officer; b. Fordyce, Ark., Dec. 31, 1923; s. Henry Harrison and Grace (Elliot) A.; m. Shirley Marie Seaman, June 6, 1946; children—Randall Lee, John Delong. Student, Syracuse U., 1941-42; B.S., U.S. Mil. Acad., 1946; M.S.E. (Aero.), U. Mich., 1956; postgrad., Indsl. Coll. Armed Forces, 1966-67. Commd. officer U.S. Air Force, 1946, advanced through grades to maj. gen.; fighter pilot, Mich., 1946-49, Alaska, 1949-51, N.Y., 1951-56; weapons officer Lincoln Lab. M.I.T., Cambridge, 1956-60; sta. hdqrs. U.S. Air Force, Pentagon, Washington, 1960-64, hdqrs. Europe, 1964-66; dep. comdr. ops. 15th Fighter Wing, Fla., 1967-68; with 366th Fighter Wing, Danang, Vietnam, 1968-69; wing comdr., Tex., 1969-71, vice comdr. tng. center, 1971-73; dep. dir. current ops. Joint Chiefs of Staff, 1973-78; chief def. attache system Def. Intelligence Agy., Washington, 1978-80; ret., 1980. Decorated D.S.M., Legion of Merit with 2 oak leaf clusters, D.F.C., Bronze Star, Vietnamese medal of Honor, others. Mem. Air Force Assn., Daedalisn. Republican. Methodist. Clubs: Rocky Bayou Country, Kiwanis. Office: 203 John Sims Pkwy Niceville FL 32578 *

ATKINSON, ARTHUR JOHN, physician; b. Chgo., Dec. 4, 1900; s. William James and Bertha (Behn) A.; m. Inez Hill, Apr. 27, 1929; children—Inez, Arthur John. B.S. and M.S., U. Chgo., 1921; M.D., Rush Med. Coll., 1924. Asso. in pharmacology and physiology U. Chgo., 1920-24; intern Presbyn. Hosp., 1924-25; med. residency Cook County, 1926-27; asso. in medicine Rush Med. Coll., 1925-31; asst. physician Presbyn. Hosp., 1926-30; mem. faculty Northwestern U., 1931—; now prof. medicine; attending physician Northwestern Meml. Hosp., 1931—; specializing in internal medicine, 1926—. Mem. Am. Gastroenterol. Assn., AMA, Central Soc. for Clin. Research, Inst. of Medicine of Chgo., Chgo. Soc. Internal Medicine, Am. Coll. Gastroenterology, Chgo. Med. Soc. Clubs: Mid-America, Chicago Yacht (Chgo.). Home: 54 E Division St Chicago IL 60610 Office: Prudential Bldg Prudential Plaza Chicago IL 60601

ATKINSON, ARTHUR SHERIDAN, fin. and mgmt. cons.; b. Sacramento, Dec. 5, 1918; s. Arthur Garratt and Fay (Mosher) A.; m. Didi Crutcher, Dec. 12, 1968; children—Marsha Fay, Sheridan Earle. B.S. with highest honors, U. Calif., Berkeley, 1939; postgrad., Sch. Bus., Stanford U., 1942-43. Investment advisor to regents U. Calif., 1946-51; asso. McKinsey & Co., 1951-53; investment counsel Scudder Stevens & Clark, San Francisco, 1953-55; chmn. bd. Atkinson & Assos., fin. mgmt. consultants, N.Y.C. and San Francisco, 1955—; chmn. bd., pres. Botany Industries, N.Y.C., 1974—; chmn. bd., chmn. Crown Internat. Group, N.Y.C., San Francisco, 1974—; chmn. bd. Crown Fin. Inc., Dallas, 1974—; chmn. bd., chief exec. officer Spl. Earth Equipment Corp., Emoryville, Calif., 1976-79; pres. The Myers Co., Orlando, Fla., 1973-74; chmn. bd. Devel. and Tech. Assistance Internat., Inc., Palo Alto, Calif., 1960-64; spl. fin. adviser to atty. gen. State of Calif., 1976—; chmn. Joan Hansent & Co. (internat. licensing cons.), N.Y.C., 1977—; mng. dir. World Vision, Inc., Pasadena, Calif., 1958-59; treas. W.R. Grace & Co., Calif. and W.Va., 1953; v.p. Fry Consultants, 1964-67; pres. Fry Fin., Inc., 1964-67; fin. cons. to pres. and chmn. Transam. Corp., 1963-64; dir. various cos.; lectr., author in field. Served with U.S. Army, 1944. Mem. Newcomen Soc. N. Am., Nat. Fedn. Fin. Analysts Socs., Assn. for Corp. Growth, Soc. for Advancement Mgmt., Internat. Platform Assn., Inter-Varsity Christian Fellowship (dir.), Brit. Philos. Soc., Univ. Christian Fellowship (chmn.), Chinese Christian Coll. Assn. (trustee), U. Calif. Alumni Assn., Beta Alpha Psi, Beta Gamma Sigma. Presbyterian. Clubs: San Francisco Stock Exchange, U. Calif. Faculty. 220 Montgomery St Penthouse San Francisco CA 94104

ATKINSON, BILL, designer; b. Utica, N.Y., Feb. 22, 1916; s. J. Harry and Elizabeth Anne (Woolfenden) A.; m. Sylvia Small, 1940; children: Lynn, Gail; m. Jeanne Marie Pagnucco, 1969; stepchildren: Robert, Rachael. B. Arch./Landscape Arch., Cornell U., 1940; postgrad., New Sch. Social Research, 1965, Sch. Visual Arts, N.Y.C., 1966. Spl. asst. to Eero Saarinen, Bloomfield Hills, Mich.; research engr. Chrysler Corp., Detroit, 1942-46; pres., designer Bill Atkinson Ltd., N.Y.C., 1974—, Atkinson Internat., Ltd., 1983—; dir. Glen Mfg. Co., Milw.; cons. to bd. trustees R.I. Sch. Design. Set designer, Metro-Goldwyn Meyer, 1938-39; draftsman/designer, Architects Edward Stone, Phillip Goodwin, N.Y.C.; designer, renderer, Architects McKim, Meade & White, N.Y.C.; pvt. practice architecture, design, Bloomfield Hills, 1946-49; fashion designer, 1950-70; designer, V.P. Glen of Michigan, N.Y.C.; photographer: book series Time-Life, N.Y.C., 1971; designer career apparel, Amtrak, N.Y.C., St. Louis, Washington, 1972; originator, designer: Hilton Hotel's Rainbow Concept, N.Y.C., St. Louis, Beverly Hills, Calif., 1973. Co-winner Rome Collaborative in Architecture, 1937; recipient numerous awards including Designer of Yr. award Sports Illustrated, Corduroy Council awards, Made in U.S.A. award for Am. Sportswear, 1965 awards Am. Retailers, Coty award for Am. fashion, 1978, Am. Design award Leather Industries Am., 1979; Flying Colors Fashion award, 1980; winner Silver Medal del Amo Internationale Invitational Competition for Sculpture and Fashion for Yr. 2000. Mem. Council Am. Fashion Designers, Cornell U. Alumni Assn., Sch. Visual Arts Alumni Assn., New Sch. Social Scis. Alumni Assn. Office: 32 W 40th St New York NY 10018

ATKINSON, CARROLL HOLLOWAY, educator; b. Fairbury, Nebr., Oct. 24, 1896; s. Charles Raymond and Florence (Bennie) A.; m. Ruby Baker, Aug. 23, 1921 (dec. 1925); children—Yvonne Dorothy, Carroll Holloway; m. Mary Hansen, 1926 (dec. 1941); m. Carol Mary Gonzales, 1959; children—Ardith Anne, Alicia Arthurita, Arthur Amigo. A.B., Lawrence Coll., 1920; student, U. Grenoble, France, 1919, Pacific U., 1922, U. Oreg., 1922, U. Wash., 1923, U. Calif. Los Angeles, 1926, U. So. Calif.; M.A., U. Tex., 1937, George Peabody Coll. for Tchrs.; Ph.D., 1937-38. Jr. clerk Met. Life Ins. Co., 1915-16; steno. Sheridan (Wyo.) Iron Works, 1917-18; statistician Kimberly-Clark Paper Co., Wis., 1920-21; athletic coach Lawrence Coll., 1915-17, 19-21; prof. and athletic coach Coll. of Idaho, 1921-22; prin. and coach, Forest Grove, Oreg., 1922-23, Thorp, Wash., 1923-24, North Bend, Oreg., 1924-25; salesman Acme Fast Freight Service, 1925-26; tchr. Pasadena Pub. Schs., 1926-30; prin. and coach San Luis Obispo, Calif., 1930-35; ednl. adviser Civilian Conservation Corps, 1935-36; asso. prof. North Tex. State Tchrs. Coll., 1936-37, Edinboro (Pa.) State Tchrs. Coll., 1938-39; asso. prof. and dir. radio Jersey City and Newark (N.J.) State Tchrs. colls., 1939-41; dir. Nelson and McLucas Meml. Libraries, Detroit, 1941-45; pub. relations dept. Key System., Oakland, Calif., 1945-46; columnist Honolulu Star-Bull. (and radio producer), 1946-47, Santa Fe New Mexican, 1951-52; dean of men Southwestern U., 1947-49; dir. tchr. tng. Dakota Wesleyan U., 1949-51; lectr. St. Michaels Coll., Santa Fe, 1951-54, also summer; supervising prin. pub. schools, Pojoaque, N.Mex., 1951-54; tchr. (summers) U. Wash., 1940, U. Wyo., No. Mont. Coll. and Eastern Mont. State Normal Sch., 1941, U. Utah, 1943, N.Mex. Highlands U., 1949; supervising prin. Belen (N.Mex.) pub. schs., 1954-57; tchr. pub. schs., Grants, N.Mex., 1957-60; prof. edn., psychology Tex. Luth. Coll., Sequin, Tex., 1960-61; chmn. psychology dept. Pacific U., 1961-64; vis. prof. history Fla. Meml. Coll., 1964-66; asso. prof. edn. Bethune-Cookman Coll., 1966-72; Extension staff faculty N.Mex. Western Coll., 1954-57; radio producer, 1931—; with Wally Gluck Enterprises. Author 20 books, 1938—, including, Intellectual Tramp, 1955, Story of Education, 1962, 65, The Show Must Go On—Even For Children, 1977. Mem. exec. com. Boy Scouts Am. Served with A.E.F., World War I. Life mem. NEA; mem. AAAS, Tex. Acad. Sci., Texas Psychol. Assn., Am. Assn. Sch. Adminstrs., Soc. Advancement Learning, Am. Legion, Acad. Polit. Sci., United Comml. Travelers, Portland Psychol. Assn., Am. Assn. of Croix de Guerre, VFW, AAUP, Daytona Beach Psychol. Assn., Internat. Platform Assn., Vets. Bus. Men's Club. Methodist. Address: 3021 N Oleander Ave Daytona Beach FL 32018 *To sacrifice the pleasures of today to gain the satisfactions of tomorrow has been a chief motivation in my life.*

ATKINSON, DANIEL EDWARD, educator, biochemist; b. Pawnee City, Nebr., Apr. 8, 1921; s. Max and Amy (Neiswanger) A.; m. Elsie Ann Hemmingson, 1948; children: Kristine Ruth, Owen Rolf, Joyce Elaine, Ellen Lee, David Eric. B.Sc., U. Nebr., 1942, D.Sc., 1975; Ph.D., Iowa State U., 1949. Research fellow Calif. Inst. Tech., 1949-50; asso. scientist Argonne Nat. Lab., 1950-52; mem. faculty UCLA, 1952—, prof. chemistry, 1962-81, 1981—; vis. prof. M.I.T., 1966-67, U. B.C., 1975. Author: Cellular Energy Metabolism and Its Regulation, 1977; asso. editor: Jour. Biol. Chemistry, 1972-77; Contbr. articles to profl. jours. Served with USNR, 1943-46. Guggenheim fellow, 1966-67. Mem. Am. Soc. Biol. Chemists, Am. Chem. Soc. (chmn. div. biol. chemistry 1978), Am. Soc. Microbiology, Am. Soc. Plant Physiologists. Home: 3123 Malcolm Ave Los Angeles CA 90034

ATKINSON, DAVID SKILLMAN, manufacturing company executive; b. Phila., Jan. 30, 1921; s. James Clarence and Margaret (Skillman) A.; m. Mary H. Headley, Jan. 15, 1943; children: Susan, Sara, Ann Gayley. B.S., Yale U., 1942, B.A., 1942. Various positions in mfg. Procter & Gamble, Cin., 1942-56; with Thiokol Chem. Co., Bristol, Pa., 1956-65, Standard Pressed Steel Co., Jenkintown, Pa., 1965-68, Northwest Industries, Chgo., 1968-73; group v.p., dir. Dennison Mfg. Co., Framingham, Mass., 1973—; dir. Laidlaw Corp., Scottsdale, Ariz., Erving Paper Mills., Mass. Served to lt. USNR, 1943-46; ETO. Episcopalian. Club: Yale (Chgo.) (bd. dirs. 1968-73). Office: Dennison Mfg Co 300 Howard St Framingham MA 01701

ATKINSON, FREDERICK GRISWOLD, former dept. store exec.; b. Aspinwall, Pa., Dec. 5, 1904; s. John Frederick and Dee (Griswold) A.; m. Joyce Mallory Hill, May 25, 1934; 1 son, Frederick (dec.). Student, Columbia Coll., 1922-26. With Cities Service Co. N.Y., 1926-34; with Procter & Gamble Co. of Cin., 1935-40, R.H. Macy & Co., Inc., N.Y.C., 1940-70, v.p. for personnel adminstrn., 1948-67, sr. v.p., dir., 1967-70, cons., 1970-72; trustee Seamen's Bank for Savs., N.Y.C., 1955-72; dir., cons. THinc. Career Planning Corp., N.Y.C., 1972-80; Chmn. Am. Retail Fedn. Employee Relations Com., 1951-55; chmn. personnel adv. council Nat. Indsl. Conf. Bd., 1952-53; mem. labor-mgmt. Manpower Policy Com., U.S. Dept. Labor. Pres. bd. trustees St. Paul's Am. Ch., Rome, Italy, St. James Am. Ch., Florence, Italy; pres. bd. of fgn. parishes Nat. Episcopal Ch.; trustee Gen. Theol. Sem., N.Y.C., 1965-75, Roosevelt Hosp., N.Y.C., Aspen Valley Hosp., Aspen Valley Med. Found., Voice Found., N.Y.C.; bd. dirs. U.S. Com. for UNICEF. Served as col. USAF, 1942-45; brig. gen. USAF Res., 1954—; spl. cons. to sec. Air Force, 1950-51. Awarded D.S.M. for mil. service in Air Force personnel adminstrn., World War II. Fellow Internat. Acad. Mgmt. (Geneva); mem. Am. Mgmt. Assn. (dir., v.p. personnel div. 1954-56, hon. life mem.), Delta Upsilon. Clubs: Union, Wings, Pilgrims of U.S. (N.Y.C.); Army and Navy (Washington); Singing Beach (Manchester); (Mass.); Everglades (Palm Beach, Fla.). Home: 160 Chilean Ave Palm Beach FL 33480 also 1 Church Row Manchester MA 01944

ATKINSON, GORDON, chemistry educator; b. Bklyn., Aug. 29, 1930; s. John and Margaret (Barrie) A.; m. Betty Lou Dilmore, Apr. 1, 1976; children: Alan Gordon, Gwyneth, Valerie. B.S. in Chemistry, Lehigh U., 1952; Ph.D. in Phys. Chemistry, Iowa State U., 1956. Instr chemistry U. Mich., Ann Arbor, 1957-61; asst. prof. U. Md., College Park, 1961-64, asso. prof., 1964-67, prof., 1967-71; prof. chemistry U. Okla., Norman, 1971—, chmn. dept. chemistry, 1971-74; dean Grad. Coll., 1974-79, vice provost for research adminstrn., 1974-79; cons. in field.; Fulbright prof. Copenhagen U., 1967-68. Author: Reactions and Reason, 1973; Contbr. articles to profl. jours. Recipient Excellence in Teaching award U. Md., 1963, Regent's award for research U. Okla., 1983. Fellow N.Y. Acad. Sci., Am. Inst. Chemists; mem. Am. Chem. Soc., AAAS, AAUP, Sigma Xi, Phi Beta Kappa, Tau Beta Pi, Phi Kappa Phi, Phi Lambda Upsilon, Kappa Sigma. Democrat. Unitarian-Universalist. Home: 1419 Greenbriar Dr Norman OK 73069: Office: Dept Chemistry Oklahoma 620 Parrington Oval Norman OK 73019

ATKINSON, HUGH CRAIG, univ. library adminstr.; b. Chgo., Nov. 27, 1933; s. Craig and Margaret (Ritchey) A.; m. Mary Nugent, Jan. 12, 1957; children—George, Mary Susan, Ann. Student, St. Benedict's Coll., 1951-53, U. Chgo., 1953-57; M.A., Grad. Library Sch., 1959. Certificate in archival adminstrn. U.S. Nat. Archives, 1958. Asst. in rare books U. Chgo. Library, 1957-58; reader's service librarian Pa. Mil. Coll. Library, 1958-61; with State U. N.Y. at Buffalo, 1961-67, asst. dir., 1964-67; with Ohio State Univs. Libraries, 1967-76, prof. and dir., 1971-76; prof. and univ. librarian U. Ill., Urbana, 1976—; Mem. adv. com. for research in info. scis. Ohio Project for Research in Info. Sci., 1972-73; chmn. com. direct borrowing Ohio Coll. Library Center, 1973-76, trustee, chmn. audit com., 1978—. Author HEW report: Optimum Speed of Library Access as Related to Optimum Size Library Collections, 1970; Contbg. author: Advances in Librarianship, 1974; Editor: (with Joseph Katz, Richard A. Ploch) Twenty-One Letters from Hart Crane to George Bryan, 1968, (with William White gen. editor) Theodore Dreiser: a checklist, 1971; Compiler: The Merrill Checklist of Theodore Dreiser, 1969; Contbg. editor, complier: The Bowker Annual of Library and Book Trade Information, 16th-23d edits, 1971-78; Contbr. articles to profl. jours. Trustee Interuniv. Communications Council, 1976-79. Mem. ALA, Ill. Library Assn., Assn. Research Libraries, Center Research Libraries, U. Chgo. Grad. Library Sch. Alumni Assn. (pres. 1974-75), AAUP. Home: 904 Sunnycrest Dr Urbana IL 61801 Office: U Ill Library Urbana IL 61801

ATKINSON, JOHN WILLIAM, educator, psychologist; b. Jersey City, Dec. 31, 1923; s. Frank Gray and Wilhelmina (Meyer) A.; m. Mary Jane Wanta, Apr. 15, 1944; children: Ann Mina, David John, William Frank. B.A., Wesleyan U., Middletown, Conn., 1947; M.A., U. Mich., 1948, Ph.D., 1950; Dr.Phil. honoris causa, Ruhr U. Bochum, 1980. Asst. prof. Wesleyan U., 1949-50; asst. prof., then prof. psychology U. Mich., Ann Arbor, 1950—; also research assoc. Survey Research Center, 1966-69. Author: (with D.C. McClelland and others) The Achievement Motive, 1953, 76, An Introduction to Motivation, 1964, rev. edit. (with David Birch), 1978, (with David Birch) The Dynamics of Action, 1970, (with J.O. Raynor) Personality, Motivation, and Achievement, 1978, Personality, Motivation and Action: Selected Papers, 1983; Editor, contbg. author: Motives in Fantasy, Action and Society, 1958, (with N.T. Feather) A Theory of Achievement Motivation, 1966, (with J.O. Raynor) Motivation and Achievement, 1974. Served to 2d lt. USAAF, 1943-45. Social Sci. Research Council fellow, 1952-55; Center for Advanced Study in Behavioral Scis. fellow, 1955-56; Guggenheim fellow, 1960-61; USPHS spl. research fellow, 1969-70. Fellow Am. Psychol. Assn. (Disting. Sci. Contbn. award 1979), Am. Acad. Arts and Scis.; mem. Am. Ednl. Research Assn., AAAS, AAUP. Address: Psychology Dept Univ Mich Ann Arbor MI 48109

ATKINSON, RICHARD CHATHAM, educator, experimental psychologist, university chancellor; b. Oak Park, Ill., Mar. 19, 1929; s. Herbert and Margaret (Feuerbach) A.; m. Rita Loyd, Aug. 20, 1952; 1 dau., Lynn Loyd. Ph.B., U. Chgo., 1948; Ph.D., Ind. U., 1955. Lectr. applied math. and stats. Stanford (Calif.) U., 1956-57, assoc. prof., 1961-64, prof., 1964-80; asst. prof. psychology, 1957-61; dep. dir. NSF, 1975-76, acting dir., 1976-77; dir., 1977-80; chancellor U. Calif., San Diego, 1980—; Mem. Pres.'s Com. Nat. Medal Sci. Author: (with Atkinson and Hilgard) Introduction to Psychology, 8th edit, 1983, Computer Assisted Instruction, 1969, An Introduction to Mathematical Learning Theory, 1965, Studies in Mathematical Psychology, 1964, Contemporary Developments in Mathematical Psychology, 1974, Mind and Behavior, 1980. Served with AUS, 1954-56. Guggenheim fellow, 1967; fellow Center for Advanced Study in Behavioral Scis., 1963; recipient Distinguished Research award Social Sci. Research Council, 1962. Fellow Am. Acad. Arts and Scis., Am. Psychol. Assn. (pres. exptl. div. 1974-75, Disting. Sci. Contbn. award 1977, Thorndike award 1980), AAAS (chmn. psychology sect. 1975-76); mem. Soc. Exptl. Psychologists, Nat. Acad. Scis., Am. Philos. Soc., Nat. Acad. Edn., Inst. of Medicine, Psychonomic Soc. (chmn. 1973-74), Western Psychol. Assn. (pres. 1975-76), Psychometric Soc., Sigma Xi. Clubs: Cosmos (Washington); Explorers (N.Y.C.). Home: 9630 La Jolla Farms Rd La Jolla CA 92037 Office: Chancellor's Office U Calif at San Diego La Jolla CA 92093

ATKYNS, (WILLIE) LEE, (JR.), artist, museum director; b. Washington, Sept. 13, 1913; s. Willie Lee and Marion Amelia (Van Horn) A. Retouch artist, negative cutter Bur. Engraving & Printing, Washington, 1936-42; map maker, retouch artist Army Map Service, Dalcavlia, Md., 1942-45; tchr. Lee Atkyns Art Sch., Washington, 1945-47, Lee Atkyns Studio, Puzzletown, Pa., 1946-50, Lee Atkyns Art Mart, Johnstown, Pa., 1948-50, Lee Atkyns Little Bohemia, Indiana, Pa., 1948-49, Lee Atkyns Art Sch., Altoona, Pa., 1948-50, Lee Atkyns Art Studio, Washington, 1950-75; dir. Lee Atkyns Studio Gallery (Puzzletown), Duncansville, Pa., 1975—. Exhibited group shows, Corcoran Art Gallery, Smithsonian Inst., Catholic U. Am., American U.; George Washington U.; exhibited, Balt. Mus., Nat. Acad. Design, Carnegie Inst. Art, Butler Art Inst.; represented by: Hirshon Galleries, State College, Pa. Recipient numerous awards profl. assns. Mem. Artists Equity, Internat. Platform Assn., Soc. Washington Artists, Landscape Club, Arts Club, Water Color Club (past pres.), Puzzletown Artists Guild, Art for the Home Group. Republican. Home: Route 2 Box 120 Duncansville PA 16635

ATLAS, DAVID, research scientist; b. Bklyn., May 25, 1924; s. Isadore and Rose (Jaffee) A.; m. Lucille Rosen, Sept. 26, 1948; children: Joan Linda, Robert Fred. B.Sc., NYU, 1946; M.Sc., MIT, 1951, D.Sc. in Meteorology, 1955. Chief weather radar br. Air Force Cambridge Research Labs., Bedford, Mass., 1948-66; prof. meterology U. Chgo., 1966-72; dir. atmospheric tech. div. Nat. Center for Atmospheric Research, Boulder, Colo., 1972-73, dir. nat. hail research expt., 1974-75; dir. lab. for atmospheric sci. NASA, Goddard Space Flight Center, Greenbelt, Md., 1977—; Chmn. Nat. Acad. Scis. Panel Remote Atmospheric Probing, also mem. com. on atmospheric scis., 1975-82. Served as 1st lt. USAAF, 1943-46. Recipient Loeser award Air Force Cambridge Research Labs., 1957, O'Day award, 1964; Robert M. Losey award AIAA, 1966; NASA Outstanding Leadership medal, 1982; NSF sr. postdoctoral fellow Imperial Coll., London, Eng., 1959-60. Fellow Am. Meteorol. Soc. (councilor 1961-64, 72-74, Meisinger award 1957, asso. editor publs. 1957-74, pres. 1975—, Cleveland Abbé award 1983), Am. Geophys. Union, Am. Astronautical Soc., Royal Meteorol. Soc., AAAS; mem. Internat. Radio Sci. Union (pres. inter-union commn. on radio meteorology 1969-72). Inventor weather radar devices. Home: 7420 Westlake Terr Bethesda MD 20034

ATLAS, JAMES ROBERT, magazine editor; b. Chgo., Mar. 22, 1949; s. Donald and Nora (Glassenberg) A.; m. Anna O'Conor Sloane Fels, Aug. 2, 1975. B.A., Harvard U., 1971; postgrad. (Rhodes scholar), Oxford (Eng.) U., 1971-73. Staff writer Time, N.Y.C., 1977-78; asst. editor N.Y. Times Book Rev., N.Y. Times, 1978-81; asso. editor Atlantic Monthly, 1981—. Author: Delmore Schwartz: The Life of an American Poet, 1977; contbr. articles to various nat. mags. Home: 40 W 77th St New York NY 10024 Office: Atlantic Monthly 8 Arlington St Boston MA 02116

ATLURI, SATYA N(ADHAM), theoretical and applied mechanics educator, consultant; b. Gudivada, Andhra, India, Oct. 7, 1945; came to U.S., 1966; s. Tirupati Rao and Tulasi (Devi) A.; m. Revati Adusumilli, May 17,, 1972; children: Neelima, Niroupa. B.E., Andhra U., Vizag, 1964; M.E., Indian Inst. Sci., Bangalore, India, 1966; Sc.D., MIT, 1969. Research MIT, Cambridge, Mass., 1966-71; asst. prof. U. Wash., Seattle, 1971-74; assoc. prof. civil engring. Ga. Inst. Tech., Atlanta, 1974-77, prof., 1977-79, Regents prof. mechanics, 1979—, dir. Ctr. for Advancement Computational Mechanics, 1980—. Contbr. articles to profl. jours.; author: books, including Computational Methods in the Mechanics of Solids and Structures, 1984; editor: Hybrid and Mixed Finite Element Methods, 1983. Grantee NSF, 1975—, USAF Office Sci. Research, 1973—, Office Naval Research, 1978—, Air Force Rocket Propulsion Lab., 1976-79, NASA, 1980—, NRC, 1978-80. Fellow Am. Acad. Mechanics; mem. AIAA (assoc. editor AIAA Jour. 1983—), ASCE (assoc. editor Jour. Engring. Mechanics 1982—), ASME (chmn. com. computing in applied mechanics 1983—). Home: 2794 Woodland Park Dr NE Atlanta GA 30345 Office: Ctr for Advancement Computational Mechanics Sch Civil Enging Ga Inst Tech Atlanta GA 30332

ATSUMI, TAKAYORI PAUL, musician, educator; b. Tokyo, Jan. 8, 1934; U.S., 1956, naturalized, 1966; s. Kohichi and Fujie (Itoh) A.; m. Sally Bigelow, Dec. 28, 1963; children: Edith Yoriko, Takase Andrew, Nancy Yasuko. B.F.A., Kunitachi Music Coll., 1956; Mus.M., New Eng. Conservatory Music, 1958; postgrad., Cath. U. Am., 1960-61. Prof. cello Ariz. State U., Tempe, 1964—; mem. Salud Casals, N.Y.C., 1970; established Pablo Casals Internat. Cello Library, Ariz. State U., 1972; ann. cello ensemble composition competition Ariz.-Cello Soc.-Am. Soc. Univ. Composers.; founding dir.-condr. Los Celistas, 1975. Cellist, Boston Pops Orch., 1958-64, New Orleans Philharm. Orch., 1958-59, Nat. Symphony Orch., Washington, 1959-64; solo cellist, Flagstaff Summer Festival, 1964—, Phoenix Symphony Orch.; cellist, New Art Quartet, 1965—; solo recitals, Jordan Hall Boston, Boston Mus. Fine Arts, WGBH-TV, Boston, others. Rockefeller Found. fellow, 1957; faculty grantee Ariz. State U., 1973, 74, 76. Mem. Ariz. Music Educators Assn. (v.p. higher edn. sect. 1973—), Ariz. Cello Soc.

(founding pres. 1970), Violincello Soc. N.Y., Phi Mu Alpha, Pi Kappa Lambda. Office: Dept Music Ariz State U Tempe AZ 85287 *

ATTEBERRY, WILLIAM DUANE, diversified manufacturing company executive; b. Decatur, Ill., Mar. 24, 1920; s. William Herman and Lucile (Hunter) A.; m. Doris Jean Walker, Dec. 19, 1946; children: William Thomas, James Norman, Thomas Hunter. B.E., U. So. Calif., 1943. Engr. P.R. Mallory & Co., Indpls., 1946; v.p. Western Lead Products Co., Los Angeles, 1946-51; engr., prodn. mgr. chems. and metals div. Eagle-Picher Co., Cin., 1951-60; pres. chems. and metals div. Eagle-Picher Industries, Inc., Cin., 1960-65, exec. v.p. corp., 1965-67, pres., 1967-78, chmn. bd., 1978—, chief exec. officer, 1968-82, also dir.; dir. Fifth-Third Bank Cin., 1st Nat. Bank Joplin, Mo., Empire Dist. Electric Co., Xtek Inc., Kroger Inc., Vulcan Materials Co. Chmn. bd. dirs. Bethesda Hosp.; bd. dirs. Joplin YMCA; trustee Ohio No. U., Boys Club Cin.; assoc. bd. dirs. Greater Cin. Found. Served to capt. USMCR, 1943-46; PTO. Mem. AIME, Am. Zinc. Inst. (dir., v.p.), Sigma Chi. Republican. Presbyterian (trustee). Clubs: Queen City (Cin.); Cincinnati Country; Tippecanoe Lake Country (Ind.); Hole-in-the-Wall Golf, Naples Yacht (Fla.). Home: 6050 Redbird Hollow Ln Cincinnati OH 45243 Office: Eagle-Picher Industries Inc 580 Walnut St Cincinnati OH 45202

ATTENBOROUGH, SIR RICHARD (SAMUEL ATTENBOROUGH), actor, producer, director; b. Aug. 29, 1923; s. Frederick L. A.; m. Sheila Beryl Grant Sim. Student (Leverhulme scholar, Bancroft medal), Royal Acad. Dramatic Art. Chm. Capital Radio, London; pro-chancellor Sussex U. Theatrical appearances include Ah Wilderness, 1941, Awake and Sing, 1942, The Little Foxes, 1942, Brighton Rock, 1943, The Way Back Home (Home of the Brave), 1949, To Dorothy, a Son, 1950, Sweet Madness, 1952, The Mouse Trap, 1952-54, Double Image, 1956-57, The Rape of the Belt, 1957-58; motion pictures include The Human Factor; co-founder, co-producer: Beaver Films; appeared in: The Angry Silence, 1959; formed: Allied Makers and; appeared in: 1st prodn. The League of Gentlemen; produced: Whistle Down the Wind, 1961, The L-Shaped Room, 1962; dir.: Oh! What a Lovely War, 1968; produced, appeared in: Seance on a Wet Afternoon, 1963; dir.: Young Winston, 1971-72, A Bridge Too Far, 1975, Magic, 1978; producer, dir.: Gandhi, 1980-81. Decorated comdr. Order Brit. Empire, 1967; Knighted, 1976; recipient Best Actor award Brit. Film Acad., 1964; three Golden Globe awards.; Acad. award best dir., 1983. Mem. Brit. Acad. Film and TV Arts (v.p.). Clubs: Garrick, Beefstake, Green Room. Address: c/o Creative Artists Agency Inc 1888 Century Park E Suite 1400 Los Angeles CA 90067

ATTINELLO, JOHN SALVATORE, aeronautical engineer; b. Phillipsburg, N.J., Aug. 2, 1920; (married); 4 children. B.S.M.E. cum laude, Lafayette Coll., Easton, Pa., 1943; student, Cal. Inst. Tech.; M.S. in Aero. Engring, Cath. U. Am., 1950; postgrad., U. Md., 1950-55. Engring. officer overhaul and repair div. Naval Air Sta., Kodiak and Attu, Alaska, 1943-45, spl. project officer service test dept., Patuxent River, Md., 1945-46; aircraft design, research div. Bur. Aeros. Navy Dept., Washington, 1946-48, asst. head supersonic aerodynamics, 1949-52, head supersonic aerodynamics, 1952-56; asst. chief research Fairchild Aircraft div., Hagerstown, Md., 1955-57; asst. to chief engr. tech. Fairchild Aircraft and Missiles div. Fairchild Engine & Airplane Corp., 1957-59, corp. sci. adv. bd., 1958-60, asst. to dir engring., 1959-60; chief Scout Class vehicles NASA, 1961, chief exptl. devel., 1961-62; sr. tech. staff Inst. Def. Analyses, research and engring. support div., 1962—, cons. weapons systems evaluations div., 1962—, projects mgr. sr. tech. staff systems evaluation div., 1966-79, System Planning Corp., 1979-82; head aviation and surface effects dept. Program Planning Office David Taylor Naval Ship Research and Devel. Ctr., 1982—; numerous sci. lectures. Cons. Brit. Ministry Supply and Royal Navy, 1952-53; cons. U. Mich., 1958, AEC, 1962—. Contbr. Articles tech. publs. Active Boy Scouts Am.; sec. Franklin County Authority, Greencastle, Pa., 1957-60; v.p. Pinecrest Citizens Assn., 1962-63; bd. dirs. Pinecrest Community Center, Inc., 1963, pres., 1964. Recipient Meritorious Civilian Service award devel. highlift BLC system jet aircraft U.S. Navy, 1953, citation and award for co-invention recording gun camera for use in Korea, 1954. Asso. fellow Inst. Aerospace Scis. (council 1958-60, 60-62), Royal Aero. Soc.; mem. Nat. Security Industries Assn., Inst. Aero. Scis. (chmn. Hagerstown sect. 1958-59), Tau Beta Pi. Presbyn. (ruling elder). Club: Toastmasters Internat. Patentee in field. Home: 6474 Woodridge Rd Alexandria VA 22312

ATTLES, ALVIN A. (AL ATTLES), professional basketball team executive; b. Newark, Nov. 7, 1936; m. Wilhemina Rice; children: Alvin III, Erica. Grad., N.C. A & T State U., 1960. Player Phila. Warriors, Nat. Basketball Assn., 1960-62, San Francisco Warriors, Nat. Basketball Assn., 1962-71; coach Golden State Warriors, Nat. Basketball Assn., 1971-83, gen. mgr., Oakland, Calif., 1983—. Coach Nat. Basketball Assn. championship teams, 1975. Office: Golden State Warriors Oakland Coliseum Arena Oakland CA 94621 *

ATTNEAVE, CAROLYN ADAMS LEWIS, psychologist, educator; b. El Paso, Tex., July 2, 1920; d. James Irwin and Carrie Florence (Adams) Lewis; m. Fred Attneave III, Oct. 1949 (div. 1956); children: Dorothy Maud Attneave Jackson, Philip Henry. A.A., Yuba Jr. Coll., 1939; B.A., Chico Stte Coll., 1940; M.A., Stanford U., 1947, Ph.D., 1952; postgrad., U. Okla. Med. Sch., 1957, 63-64, U. Chgo., 1949, 58, Yeshiva U., 1968; Sc.D. (hon.), St. Vincent Coll., 1981. Dir student personnel services Tex. Women's U., Denton, 1956-57; asst. prof. psychology and human devel. Tex. Technol. Coll., Lubbock, 1957-61; coordinator Community Guidance Services Region V Okla. Dept. Healthl, Shawnee, 1961-67; sr. psychologist Phila. Child Guidance Clinic, 1967-69; coordinator Mass. Dept. Mental Health Pub. Service Career Program, 1969-71; clin. dir. Family Intervention unit Boston State Hosp., 1971; research assoc. and lectr. dept. behavioral scis. Harvard Sch. Pub. Health, Boston, 1972-75; clin. assoc. prof. dept. psychiatry Tufts Sch. Medicine, Boston, 1969-75; prof. psychology U. Wash., Seattle, 1975—; also dir. Am. Indian Studies, 1975-77; cons. Am. Psychiat. Assn. Task Force on Am. Indian Affairs, 1972—; pvt. practice psychol. counseling, family therapy, 1965—; teaching fellow Boston Family Inst., 1969-75. Author: (with Ross Speck) Family Networks, 1973, transl. Spanish, German, Swedish, Japanese, (with M. Beiser) Service Networks and Patterns of Use: Indian Mental Health, 1975; editor: (with Alan Tulipan) Beyond Clinic Walls, 1974, Bibliography of American Indian Mental Health, 1979-82; contbr. numerous articles to profl. jours. Mem. Nat. Adv. Council on Women's Equity in Edn., 1979—, vice chmn., 1980-81; mem. Del.-Cherokee Tribe of Okla.; del. White House Conf. on Family, 1980; Pres. Shawnee (Okla.) Community Planning Council, 1966-69; mem. bd. registration for psychologists Mass., 1974-75. Served to lt. (s.g.) USCGR, 1942-46. Recipient Research award Okla. Pub. Health Assn., 1967; Disting. Psychologist award Wash. State Psychol. Assn., 1981; NSF vis. professorship for women, 1983-85. Fellow Am. Psychol. Assn., Am. Orthopsychol. Assn.; mem. Soc. Family Therapy and Research, Am. Family Therapy Assn. (dir. 1978—), LWV (dir. 1953-56), Gen. Systems Soc., Soc. Psychol. Study of Social Issues, Soc. Am. Indian Psychologists (pres. 1979-80). Roman Catholic. Home: 5206 Ivanhoe Seattle WA 98105 Office: Dept Psychology NI 15 U Wash Seattle WA 98195 *Integrating oneself amongst American Indian and Mainstream cultures sensitizes one to the culturally determined patterns of behavior in all peoples, including the institutionalized, the blind, the deaf, as well as other ethnic and racial groups. This makes one impatient with narrow dogmatism, but increases awareness of the common range of human needs and the multiplicity of feasible solutions to familiar problems.*

ATTWELL, KIRBY, business executive; b. Houston, June 1, 1935; s. Khleber VanZandt and Lucille (MacAshan) A.; m. Nancy McGrory, Nov. 26, 1965; children: Kirby Andrew, Meredith McAshan. B.A., U. Tex., Austin, 1957; M.B.A., Harvard U., 1960. C.L.U., 1967. Investment analyst T.J. Bettes Co., Houston, 1960-61; v.p., investment analyst Bus. Funds, Inc., Houston, 1961-65; v.p. Lincoln Liberty Life Ins. Co., Houston, 1965-67; v.p., sec., then treas. Lincoln Fin., Inc., Houston, 1967-71, pres., chief exec. officer, 1971-79, Supply Corp., Houston, 1979-83, Attwell Interests, 1983—; chmn. NDX Corp., 1983—; dir. Vallen Corp., Houston. Founder Houstonian Found., 1976; bd. dirs. Tex. Children's Hosp., Houston. Served with USAF, 1957. Mem. Young Pres. Orgn., Nat. Assn. Life Underwriters, Houston C. of C. Episcopalian. Clubs: Houston, River Oaks Country, Harvard Bus. Sch. (Houston). Home: 2410 Locke Ln Houston TX 77019 Office: PO Box 27225 Houston TX 77227

ATTWOOD, JAMES ALBERT, insurance company executive; b. Detroit, June 1, 1927; s. Albert Messenger and Tyyne Marie (Koskela) A.; m. Pauline Veryl Ellwood, June 18, 1955; children: Terry Jo, James Albert, Dorothy Tyyne, Katherine Pauline. B.A., U. Mich., 1950; student, Ohio State U., 1952-53, Salmon Chase Coll. Law, 1952-53. With Equitable Life Assurance Soc. U.S., N.Y.C., 1950-56, 61-83, v.p., 1966-68, sr. v.p., 1969-72, exec. v.p., 1973-77, exec. v.p., chief ins. officer, 1977-79, exec. v.p., chief investment officer, 1980-83, dir., 1973-83; chmn., chief exec. officer, trustee Mut. Life Ins. Co. N.Y., N.Y.C., 1983—; partner Hewitt Assocs., Libertyville, Ill., 1956-61; chmn. MONY Reins.; dir. Monyco, Inc., Sherwin-Williams Co.; bus. exec. in residence Mt. Holyoke Coll., 1976; vis. prof. polit. sci. Hunter Coll., CUNY, 1977-78. Mem. Bronxville (N.Y.) Bd. Edn., 1972-77; v.p. Adoption Service Westchester, 1964-70; deacon, elder Bronxville Ref. Ch., 1973-78, 83—; adv. dir. Internat. Found. Employee Benefit Plans, 1973-77; bd. dirs. Coll. of Ins., 1983—. Served with USNR, 1945-46; with USAF, 1952-53. Fellow Soc. Actuaries (dir. 1979-82, v.p. 1983—); mem. Am. Acad. Actuaries (dir. 1978-81), Internat. Assn. Actuaries, Am. Pension Conf. (steering com. 1970-73), Phi Beta Kappa, Phi Kappa Phi, Phi Eta Sigma. Clubs: Univ. (N.Y.C.); Siwonoy Country (Bronxville). Home: 10 Woodland Ave Bronxville NY 10708 Office: 1740 Broadway New York NY 10019

ATTWOOD, WILLIAM, journalist; b. Paris, July 14, 1919; s. Frederic and Gladys (Hollingsworth) A.; m. Simone Cadgene, June 22, 1950; children—Peter, Janet duPont, Susan. A.B., Princeton U., 1941. Corr. N.Y. Herald Tribune in Paris and; with UN bur., 1946-49; European corr. Colliers mag., 1949-51; European editor Look mag., 1951-54, nat. editor, 1955-57, fgn. editor, 1957-61; U.S. ambassador to Guinea, 1961-63; spl. adviser U.S. del. UN, 1963-64; U.S. ambassador to Kenya, 1964-66; editor-in-chief, v.p. Cowles Communications, Inc., N.Y.C., 1966-70; pres., pub. Newsday, Inc., Garden City, N.Y., 1970-78, chmn. bd., 1978-79; adj. prof. journalism C. W. Post Coll., 1980, Yale U., 1981; Mem. John F. Kennedy (presdl. campaign staff), 1960; Regional alumni trustee Princeton, 1967-71; trustee Kress Found., 1971-80; bd. dirs. Overseas Devel. Council, Am. Com. for East-West Accord; mem. U.S. del. UNESCO Gen. Conf., 1978; exec. com. Internat. Center of Photography U.S. Nat. Commn. for UNESCO, 1980—. Author: The Man Who Could Grow Hair, 1949, Still the Most Exciting Country, 1955, (with George B. Leonard, Jr. and J. Robert Moskin) The Decline of the American Male, 1958, The Reds and the Blacks, 1967, The Fairly Scary Adventure Book, 1969, Making It Through Middle Age: Notes While in Transit, 1982. Mem. New Canaan (Conn.) Town Council. Served to capt. AUS, 1941-45. Recipient Nat. Headliners award, 1955, 57, George Polk Meml. award, 1956, N.Y. Newspaper Guild Page One award, 1960. Mem. Council Fgn. Relations. Democrat. Clubs: Century, Princeton of N.Y.C., Country of New Canaan. Home: 423 Carter St New Canaan CT 06840

ATWATER, FRANKLIN SIMPSON, business adviser; b. New Britain, Conn., Aug. 24, 1916; s. George Franklin and Ida (Simpson) A.; m. Marion Jane Brian, May 9, 1947; children: Mary-Jane, Brian, Sally. B.S., MIT, 1938. Mem. staff MIT, 1938-39; with Fafnir Bearing Co. (div. Textron Inc.), New Britain, 1939-75, prodn. engr., indsl. engring. mgr., asst. gen. works mgr., gen. works mgr., 1956-59, v.p. mfg., 1959-63, v.p. operations, 1963-67, exec. v.p., 1967-69, pres., 1969-75, Charlotte, N.C., 1975-76, chmn., 1976-77; dir. Goss & DeLeeuw Machine Co., Fusion Systems Corp., Galileo Electro-Optics Corp., First Union Nat. Bank, Carolina Pump & Supply Co., Cronus Industries, Inc., LogEtronics Inc. Author: (with L.L. Bethel and others) Industrial Organization and Management, 1945, Essentials of Industrial Management, 1954, Production Control, 1942. Home: 91 Heritage Dr River Hills Plantation Clover SC 29710 Office: 14401 Carowinds Blvd Charlotte NC 28217

ATWATER, HARVEY LEROY, government official; b. Atlanta, Feb. 27, 1951; s. Harvey Dillard and Alma (Page) A.; m. Sally Dunbar, June 24, 1978; 1 dau., Sarah Lee. B.A., Newberry Coll., 1973; M.A. in Journalism, U. S.C., 1977, postgrad., 1980. Pres. Baker & Assocs., Columbia, S.C., 1974-80; spl. asst. to pres. White House, Washington, 1981-82, dep. asst. to pres., 1982—; active polit. campaigns; campaign dir. Sen. Strom Thurmond, 1977-78, Reagan for Pres., S.C., 1980; regional polit. dir. Reagan-Bush campaign, So. States, 1980; cons. congl. campaign Ga. and S.C., 1976-80. Del. Republican Nat. Conv., 1972; nat. dir. Coll. Reps., 1974; del. Rep. Nat. Conv., 1980. Recipient Outstanding Alumni award Newberry Coll., 1981. Mem. Nat. Heritage Found. (bd. regents). Methodist. Home: 500 N St SW 505N Washington DC 20024 Office: 175 Old Executive Office Bldg Washington DC 20500

ATWATER, JAMES DAVID, journalist, university dean; b. Westfield, Mass., Oct. 25, 1928; s. William Henry and Vesta Buffum (Gannett) A.; m. Patricia Anne Levington, Jan. 15, 1955; children: Mary Elizabeth, Stephen Gannett, Christopher Perry, Andrew, Katharine, Jennifer. B.A., Yale U., 1950. Corr., writer Time mag., 1953-62, 73-77, sr. editor, 1978—; sr. journalist-in-residence Duke U., Durham, N.C., spring 1981; contbg. editor Saturday Evening Post, 1963-66, sr. editor, 1966-69; dean Sch. Journalism, U. Mo.-Columbia, 1983—. Author: novel Time Bomb, 1977. Spl. asst. to Pres. U.S., 1969-70; mem. sch. bd. Union Free Sch. Dist. 2, Town Greenburgh, N.Y., 1965-69, 74-76, pres., 1968, 75. Served to 1st lt. USAF, 1950-53. Office: U Mo Sch Journalism Box 838 Columbia MO 65205

ATWATER, JOHN SPENCER, physician; b. Cin., Oct. 12, 1913; s. Carleton William and May (Spencer) A.; m. Laura Virginia Zipplies, July 29, 1939; children—John Spencer, Paul Carleton, Elizabeth Baron. Student, Western Res. U., 1931-32; A.B., Denison U., 1935, Ind. U. Sch. Medicine, 1934-36; M.D., Johns Hopkins, 1939; M.S. in Medicine, U. Minn., 1944. Diplomate: Am. Bd. Internal Medicine, Am. Bd. Gastroenterology. Intern medicine U. Chgo. Clinics, 1939-40, asst. resident medicine, 1940-41; fellow Mayo Found., 1941-44; 1st asst. medicine Mayo Clinic, Rochester, Minn., 1943-44; practice medicine specializing in internal medicine and gastroenterology, Atlanta, 1946—; mem. staffs Ga. Bapt. Hosp., Crawford W. Long Meml. Hosp.; asso. chief medicine Ga. Baptist Hosp., 1948-57, acting chief medicine, 1958-60, chief medicine, 1973-77, pres. staff, 1962, mem. exec. com., 1961-64, chmn. exec. com., 1963, chief gastroent. sect., 1948—; chief dept. medicine Atlanta Hosp., 1968-69, chief medicine, 1969-72, mem. exec. com., 1968-72, chmn. credentials com., 1968-69, mem. utilization rev. com., 1968-69, mem. med. recs. com., 1968, mem. joint conf. com., 1970-72; cons. in gastroenterology Robert T. Jones Meml. Hosp., Canton, Ga., 1962—, Cobb Gen. Hosp., Austell, Ga., 1968-73; instr. in medicine U. Minn., 1943-44, Emory U., 1946-54, asso. in medicine, 1954-65; cons. internal medicine VA, Ga. Dept. Edn., Fgn. Mission Bd. So. Bapt. Conv., U.S. Dept. State, Chmn. Atlanta Grad. Med. Assembly, 1958-59, exhibit chmn., 1960, mem. advisory com., 1961, mem. emergency care service com., 1964-65; mem. Gov.'s Commn. on Aging, 1959-62, chmn. health com., 1959-62; del. White House Conf. on Aging, 1961; chmn. Gov.'s Conf. on Aging, 1960, Ga. Joint Council to Improve Health Care of Aged, 1959—; mem. health advisory com. Ga. Commn. on Aging, 1964—; mem. clin. lab. blood and bank and tissue bank com. Ga. Dept. Pub. Health, 1971—; Partner Caduceus Properties, 1969—; dir. So. Gen. Ins. Co., Stuyvesant Ins. Co., Stuyvesant Life Ins. Co., Jersey Ins. Co. N.Y., 1st Ga. Bank, Peoples Am. Bank Atlanta, GAC Corp. Author numerous articles in field, (with others) sci. exhibits at med. meetings, films, TV demonstrations in field. Bd. dirs. Atlanta Boys Club, med. dir., 1953-65, mem. endowment com., 1970-72; bd. dirs. Atlanta Girls Club, vice-chmn., 1957-58, chmn. bd., 1958-59, 3d v.p., 1960; bd. dirs. Atlanta Ballet, 1978—. Served as lt. M.C. USNR, 1944-46. Recipient Certificate of Appreciation Fulton County Med. Soc., 1960, 63; Aven Citizenship award, 1961; Award of Recognition Atlanta Boys Club, 1966; Keystone Bronze award Boys Clubs Am., 1968, 74; Letter of Appreciation Med. Assn. Ga., 1969; Certificate of Appreciation, 1970. Fellow A.C.P., Am. Geriatrics Soc.; mem. AMA (cons. council med. services 1960—, chmn. reference com. med. edn. 1969, mem. reference com. fin. med. care 1967, mem. reference com. ins. and med. services 1971), Med. Assn. Ga. (chmn. bd. spl. activities 1961—, treas. 1962—, mem. publs. com. jour. 1962—, mem. exec. com. 1962—, mem. fin. com. 1962—, mem. spl. fin., central billing, hdqrs. expansion and bldg. coms., chmn. awards com.), Fulton County Med. Soc. (chmn. com. on aging 1959, 60, 61), 5th Dist. Med. Soc., So. Med. Assn. (past chmn.), Am. Gastroent. Assn., Am. Gastroscopic Soc., Am. Soc. Gastrointestinal Endoscopy, World Congress Gastroenterology, N.Y. Acad. Scis., Am. Heart Assn., Alumni Assn. Mayo Found. Med. Edn. and Research, Mayo Gastrointestinal Alumni Assn., Johns Hopkins Med. and Surg. Soc., U. Chgo. Med. Alumni Assn., Am., Ga. socs. internal medicine, Johns Hopkins Alumni Assn. (past pres. Ga. soc., past nat. v.p.), Atlanta C. of C., SAR, Phoenix Soc., Phi Gamma Delta, Nu Sigma Nu. Baptist. Clubs: Kiwanian (mem. boys and girls work com. 1966-70, fund raising com. 1969-70), Kiwanian (vocat. guidance com. 1969), Kiwanian (operation drug alert com. 1970-71), Commerce, Atlanta City (charter mem.). Home: 2625 Howell Mill Rd NW Atlanta GA 30327 Office: 478 Peachtree St NE Atlanta GA 30308

ATWATER, TANYA MARIA, marine geophysicist, educator; b. Los Angeles, Aug. 27, 1942; d. Eugene and Elizabeth Ruth (Ransom) A.; 1 child, Alyosha Molnar. Student, M.I.T., 1960-63; B.A., U. Calif., Berkeley, 1965; Ph.D., Scripps Inst. Oceanography, 1972. Vis. earthquake researcher U. Chile, 1966; research asso. Stanford U., 1970-71; asst. prof. Scripps Inst. Oceanography, 1972-73; U.S.-USSR Acad. Scis. exchange scientist, 1973; asst. prof. M.I.T., from 1974, asso. prof., until 1980; prof. dept. geoscis. U. Calif., Santa Barbara, 1980—; chmn. ocean margin drilling Ocean Crust Planning Adv. Com.; mem. public adv. com. on law of sea Dept. State, 1979—; Sigma Xi lectr., 1975-76. Contbr. articles to profl. jours. Sloan fellow, 1975-77; recipient Newcomb Cleveland prize AAAS, 1980. Fellow Am. Geophys. Union, Geol. Soc. Am.; mem. AAAS, Assn. Women in Sci. Office: Dept Geoscis U of Calif Santa Barbara CA 93106

ATWATER, VERNE STAFFORD, finance educator, former banker; b. Pitts., Aug. 22, 1920; s. Verne L. and Priscilla (Brodeur) A.; m. Evelyn Lowe, May 29, 1943; children: Lynda, Louise. B.A., Heidelberg Coll., 1942; M.B.A., Harvard U., 1943; Ph.D., NYU, 1961. Dir. placement, asst. prof. bus. adminstrn. Syracuse U., 1946-50; asst. to chmn. bd. N.J. Bank, Paterson, 1950-56; dir. adminstrn. Ford Found., 1956-61; rep. Argentina/Chile, 1961-63; dir. Latin Am. and Caribbean Program, 1963-64, v.p., 1964-68; pres. Westinghouse Learning Corp., N.Y.C., 1968-71; chmn., chief exec. officer Central Savs. Bank, N.Y., 1971-81; prof. fin., dir. Ctr. for Internat. Bus., Lubin Grad. Sch. Bus. Pace U., 1981—; dir. Grolier, Inc.; dir. Instl. Group Info. Corp. Hudson City Savs. Bank N.J.; mem. Nat. Commn. Electronic Fund Transfers, 1975-77; Mem. Pres.'s Task Force Career Devel., 1967-68, N.Y. State Bus. Adv. Council, 1969-73, N.J. Housing Finance Agy., 1966-70; chmn. Ave. of Americas Assn., 1980-81. Chmn. bd. trustees Heidelberg Coll., 1982—; trustee Center for Fin. Studies at Fairfield U., James T. Lee Found., Ridgewood YWCA; chmn. exec. com. Inst. Internat. Edn. Served to lt. USNR, 1943-46. Clubs: Arcola Country (Paramus, N.J.); University (N.Y.C.). Home: 6 Maynard Ct Ridgewood NJ 07450

ATWELL, ROBERT HERRON, assn. exec.; b. Washington, Pa., Jan. 26, 1931; s. R. Boice and Elsie (Herron) A.; m. Constance Woodruff, Sept. 4, 1972; children—Catherine, Cynthia; children by previous marriage—Mary, Robert, John, Nancy, Carl. B.A., Coll. Wooster, 1953; M.A. in Pub. Adminstrn, U. Minn., 1957. Budget examiner U.S. Bur. Budget, Washington, 1957-60; fiscal economist, loan officer U.S. Devel. Loan Fund, Dept. State, 1960; budget examiner, program analyst for higher edn. and med. research programs U.S. Bur. Budget, 1961-62; program planning officer, asst. chief Community Mental Health Centers br. NIMH, HEW, 1962-65; vice chancellor for adminstrn. U. Wis., Madison, 1965-70; pres. Pitzer Coll., Claremont, Calif., 1970-78; v.p. Am. Council Edn., 1978—; Chmn. Council Claremont Coll., 1971-72; pres. Ind. Colls. So. Calif., 1974-75. Served with AUS, 1953-55. Home: 8608 Timber Hill Ln Potomac MD 20854

ATWELL, ROBERT JAMES, emeritus medical educator; b. Gary, Ind., Sept. 1, 1919; s. Oswald B. and Helen N. (Neuding) A.; m. Paula Mozelle Mitchell, Apr. 28, 1945; children: Robert, David M., Paul N. A.B., Duke U., 1941, M.D., 1944. Intern Duke Hosp., 1944-45, resident, 1945-47, Bellevue Hosp., N.Y.C., 1947-48; chief med. service Ohio Tb Hosp., Columbus, 1950-66; mem. faculty Coll. Medicine Ohio State U., 1951-83, prof., 1966-83; acting dean Coll. Medicine, 1972-73; dir., prof. Sch. Allied Med. Professions Ohio State U., 1966-83, prof. emeritus Sch. Allied Med. Professions, 1983—; mem. attending staff U. Hosp., Columbus, 1952—; cons. asst. sec. health affairs HEW, 1971-74, Nat. Library Medicine, 1970-74, AMA, 1969-83, Regional Med. Programs, 1969-72, Bur. Health Manpower Edn., NIH, 1968-70, Nat. Inst. Arthritis and Metabolic Diseases, 1962, VA, 1954—; chmn. med. adv. coms. State Tchrs. Retirement System and Sch. Employees Retirement System, State of Ohio, 1966—. Contbr. articles to profl. jours. Fellow A.C.P.; mem. Assn. Schs. Allied Health Professions (sec.-treas. 1969, pres. 1971), Central Soc. Clin. Research. Home: 2372 West Lane Ave Columbus OH 43221

ATWOOD, ALAN FRANCIS, manufacturing executive; b. Lewiston, Idaho, Aug. 15, 1927; s. Frank Thomas and Helen Delphine (Allen) A.; 1 dau., April. B.S., U. Idaho, 1952; M.B.A., Harvard U., 1954. Acctg. exec. Gen. Motors Corp., 1956-68; v.p., controller White Motor Corp., Cleve., 1968-76; v.p. fin. Joy Mfg. Co., Pitts., 1976—. Served with USNR, 1945-46. Mem. Fin. Execs. Inst. Clubs: Duquesne, Highland Country, Masons. Home: 506 Cherry Ct Pittsburgh PA 15237 Office: 301 Grant St Pittsburgh PA 15219

ATWOOD, ANN MARGARET, author; b. Heber, Calif., Feb. 12, 1913; d. Howard C. and Marie (Jones) A. B.A., U. Redlands, 1934; student, Art Center Sch., Los Angeles, summer 1935. Owner, mgr. Ann Atwood Studio Children's Portraiture, Riverside, Calif., 1937-40, San Marino, Calif., 1940-60, South Laguna, Calif., 1960-67; founder, dir. adult edn. class in poetry writing, Riverside, 1938-40; tchr. poetry Hollywood (Calif.) High Sch., 1943-44. Author, illustrator (or author-photographer): poetry Being Made of Earth, 1940, The Little Circle, 1967; author, illustrator: New Moon Cove, 1969 (awards 1969, 70), The Wild Young Desert, 1970, Haiku: The Mood of Earth, 1971 (award So. Calif. Council on Lit. for Children and Young People), The Kingdom of the Forest, 1972, My Own Rhythm, 1973; author-photographer: filmstrips Sea, Sand and Shore series, 1969, The Making of a Desert, 1970, Life Conquers the Desert, 1970, The Little Circle, 1970 (Silver medal Internat. Film and TV Festival), The Heart of Haiku, 1971, Haiku: A Photographic Interpretation, 1971 (Chris award Columbus Internat. Film Festival), The Gods Were Tall and Green, 1972 (Silver medal Internat. Film and TV Festival N.Y.), Haiku: The Hidden Glimmering, 1973 (Gold medal Atlanta Film Festival), (with Elizabeth B. Hazelton) Sammy, the Crow, 1970, Tahiti is My Island, 1969, Teeka, the Otter, 1971, My Forty Years with Beavers, 1975, For All That Lives, 1975, Day Into Night, 1981; photographer: Sammy, The Crow Who Remembered, 1969; (with Erica Anderson) book For All That Lives, 1975; film strips Inscape: The Realm of Haiku, 1976 (Gold Cindy award Informational Film Producers Assn.), Haiku-Vision (named Best of Yr., Previews), book, 1977 (ALA Notable Book 1978), Fly With the Wind-Flow With the Water, 1979; (with Günther Klinge) book Im Kreis des Jahres, 1982; book Lebe den Tag, 1983. Mem. Sierra Club. Laguna CA 92677

ATWOOD, DONALD JESSE, JR., automotive executive; b. Haverhill, Mass., May 25, 1924; s. Donald Jesse and Doris Albertine (French) A.; m. Curina Harian, Sept. 8, 1946; children: Susan Albertine, Donald Jesse. B.S.E.E., MIT, 1948, M.S.E.E., 1950. With AC Electronics div. Gen. Motors Corp., 1961-70, dir. ops., Milw., 1968-70; mgr. Indpls. ops. Detroit Diesel Allison div. (Gen. Motors Corp.), 1970-73, 1st gen. mgr. Transp. Systems div., 1973-74, gen. mgr. Delco Electronics div., Kokomo, Ind., 1974-78, gen. mgr., Detroit, 1978-80; v.p., group exec. Gen. Motors Corp., 1981—; dir. Charles Stark Draper Lab. Corp. Bd. dirs. Automotive Hall of Fame, Inc., Western Hwy. Inst. Served with AUS, 1943-46. Mem. Am. Helicopter Assn., Soc. Automotive Engrs., Motor Vehicle Mfrs. Assn. (policy com.), Nat. Acad. Engring., AIAA, Air Force Assn., Assn. U.S. Army, Navy League. Home: Franklin MI 48025 Office: 31 Judson St Pontiac MI 48058

ATWOOD, EDWARD CHARLES, JR., univ. dean; b. N.Y.C., Dec. 2, 1922; s. Edward Charles and Bertha Margaret (Moloney) A.; m. June Matilda Ruschmeyer, Mar. 30, 1946; children—Edward Terrell, Jeffrey Terrell. A.B., Princeton U., 1946, M.A., 1950, Ph.D. in Econs, 1959. Teaching fellow U. Buffalo, 1946-47; part-time instr. Princeton U., 1948-50; instr. Denison U., 1950-52; from asst. to asso. prof. Washington and Lee U., 1952-60, dean students, 1961-69, dean Sch. Commerce, 1969—, also prof. econs.; econ. cons. Bankers Trust Co., N.Y.C., 1956; economist Gen. Electric Co., 1960-61; tchr. courses Am. Inst. Banking, Va. Sch. Banking, 1957-59; dir. United Va. Bankshares/Rockbridge, Lexington. Pres. Rockbridge Area Housing Corp., 1974-75; trustee Lawrenceville Fathers Assn. Served with USNR, 1942-46. Mem. Am. Assembly Collegiate Schs. Bus. (initial accreditation com.), Am., So. econ. assns., Am. Bankers Assn (selection com. 1973-74), Beta Gamma Sigma, Omicron Delta Kappa, Omicron Delta Epsilon. Presbyterian. Home: 4 University Pl Lexington VA 24450

ATWOOD, GERALD FRANCIS, pediatric cardiologist, educator; b. Cedar Rapids, Iowa, Feb. 11, 1940; s. Lucian M. and Evelyn (Larchick) A.; m. Susan Dunkley, Mar. 7, 1981; 1 dau., Kathleen; children by previous marriage: Michael, Karen, Mark. B.S., Loyola U., Chgo., 1960; M.D., U. Ill., 1964. Diplomate: Am. Bd. Pediatrics with subsplty. in pediatric cardiology. Intern Presbyterian St. Luke's Hosp., Chgo., 1964-65, resident in pediatrics, 1965-66, chief resident, 1966-67; instr. pediatrics U. Ill., 1965-67; research asso. Nat. Communicable Disease Center, Atlanta, 1967-69; clin. instr. pediatrics Emory U., 1967-69; fellow pediatric cardiology Duke U. Med. Center, 1969-71; research asso. biochemistry, 1970-71; asst. prof. pediatrics and pharmacology Vanderbilt U., 1971-77, asso. dir., 1971-77, dir. pediatric student teaching program, 1972-77; prof. pediatrics U. N.D., 1977—, chmn. dept., 1977-82; practice medicine specializing in pediatric cardiology, Fargo, N.D., 1983—. Contbr. articles to profl. jours. Served with USPHS, 1967-69. Fellow Am. Coll. Cardiology; mem. Am. Heart Assn., So. Soc. Pediatric Research, Southeastern Pediatric Cardiology Soc., Great Plains Perinatal Soc., Am. Acad. Pediatrics. Home: Rural Route 1 Box 407 Fargo ND 58103 Office: Fargo Clinic 737 Broadway Fargo ND 58123

ATWOOD, HAROLD LESLIE, physiology and zoology educator; b. Montreal, Que., Can., Feb. 15, 1937; s. Carl Edmond and Margaret (Killam) A.; m. Lenore Gertrude Mandelson, DEc. 23, 1959; children: David, Robert, Evan. B.A., U. Toronto, 1959; M.A., U. Calif.-Berkeley, 1960; Ph.D., Glasgow U., 1963, Sc.D., 1978. Research assoc. U. Oreg., Eugene, 1962-64; research fellow Calif. Inst. Tech., Pasadena, 1964-65; asst. prof. U. Toronto, 1965-68, assoc. prof., 1968-72, prof. zoology, 1972—, chmn. dept. physiology, 1981—. Guggenheim fellow U. Calif.-San Diego, 1972. Fellow royal Soc. Can.; mem. soc. Neurosci., AAAS, Can. Soc. Zoologists, Am. Physiol. Soc., Can. Physiol. Soc. Office: Dept. Physiology NL U Toronto Med. Sci. Bldg Toronto ON Canada M5S 1A8

ATWOOD, JAMES R., lawyer; b. White Plains, N.Y., Feb. 21, 1944; s. Bernard D. and Joyce Rose A.; m. Wendy Fisler, Aug. 22, 1981; 1 son, Christopher Charles. B.A., Yale U., 1966; J.D., Stanford U., 1969. Bar: Calif. 1969, D.C. 1970. Law clk. to judge U.S. Ct. Appeals, Los Angeles, 1969-70; law clk. to Chief Justice Warren Burger U.S. Supreme Ct., 1970-71; mem. firm Covington & Burling, Washington, 1971-78, partner, 1977-78, 81—; dep. asst. sec. for transp. affairs Dept. State, Washington, 1978-79, dep. legal adviser, 1979-80; acting prof. Stanford Law Sch., 1980. Author: (with Kingman Brewster) Antitrust and American Business Abroad, 2d edit, 1981. Mem. ABA, D.C. Bar Assn., Am. Soc. Internat. Law., Washington Inst. Fgn. Affairs. Club: Met. (Washington). Office: 1201 Pennsylvania Ave NW PO Box 7566 Washington DC 20044

ATWOOD, KENNETH WARD, JR., elec. engr., educator; b. Cedarview, Utah, Dec. 21, 1922; s. Kenneth Ward and Luella (King) A.; m. Ruth Marjorie Johnson, Dec. 7, 1944; children—Mary Lou, Kenneth LeRoy, Judy Ruth. B.S., U. Utah, 1950, M.S., 1954, Ph.D., 1957. Engr. stas. KSL and KSL-TV, Salt Lake City, 1949-55; sr. engr. Gen. Electric Co., Richland, Wash., 1962-63; instr. elec. engring. U. Utah, Salt Lake City, 1956-58, asst. prof., 1958-65, asso. prof., 1965-76, prof., 1976—. Author: Electronic Engineering, 1962, rev., 1966, 73, Semiconductor Devices and Circuits, 1971. Served with USAAC, 1943-46. Mem. IEEE (sr.; Community Service award Utah sect. 1975, 81), Am. Soc. Engring. Edn., Sigma Xi, Tau Beta Pi, Sigma Pi Sigma, Eta Kappa Nu. Mormon. Home: 140 W 8600 S Midvale UT 84047 Office: Merrill Engring Bldg U Utah Salt Lake City UT 84112

ATWOOD, KIMBALL CHASE, geneticist; b. N.Y.C., May 15, 1921; s. Kimball Chase, Jr. and Mary Evelyn (Girdner) A.; m. Barbara Frances Drew, Mar. 31, 1945; children—Barbara Johnston Atwood Fukuda, Jane Evelyn, Kimball Chase IV, Nathaniel Bradbury. A.B., Columbia U., 1942; M.D., N.Y. U.-Bellevue Coll. Medicine, 1946. Intern Bellevue Hosp., N.Y.C., 1946-47; research asso. Columbia U., 1948-51; sr. biologist Oak Ridge Nat. Lab., 1951-58; asso. prof. med. genetics U. Chgo., 1958-61; prof. microbiology U. Ill., Urbana, 1961-69; prof. human genetics and devel. Columbia U., 1969—. Home: 100 Haven Ave New York NY 10032 Office: 701 W 168th St New York NY 10032

ATWOOD, MARGARET ELEANOR, author; b. Ottawa, Ont., Can., Nov. 18, 1939; d. Carl Edmund and Margaret Dorothy (Killam) A. B.A., U. Toronto, 1961; A.M., Radcliffe Coll., 1962; D. Litt. (hon.), Trent U., 1973, Concordia U., 1980, LL.D., Queen's U., 1974. Mem. faculty U. B.C., 1964-65, Sir George Williams U., 1967-68, U. Alta, 1969-70, York U., 1971-72; writer-in-residence U. Toronto, 1972-73. Author: poetry Double Persephone, 1961, The Circle Game, 1967, The Animals in That Country, 1968, The Journals of Susanna Moodie, 1970, Procedures for Underground, 1970, Power Politics, 1973, Poems for Voices, 1970, You Are Happy, 1975, Selected Poems, 1976, (Am. edit., 1978) Selected Poems, Two-Headed Poems, 1978, True Stories, 1981; novel The Edible Woman, 1969, (Am. edit.) The Edible Woman, 1970, Surfacing, 1972, (Am. edit.) Surfacing, 1973, Lady Oracle, 1973, Life Before Man, 1979, Bodily Harm, 1981, Murder in the Dark, 1983; short stories Dancing Girls, 1977, Bluebeard's Egg, 1983; juvenile Up in the Tree, 1978, Anna's Pet, 1980; non-fiction Survival: A Thematic Guide to Canadian Literature, 1972, Second Words: Selected Critical Prose, 1982; contbr. poems, short stories, revs. and articles to scholarly jours. Recipient E.J. Pratt medal, 1961, Pres.'s medal U. Western Ont., 1965, Gov. Gen.'s award, 1966, 1st pl. Centennial Commn. Poetry Competition, 1967, Union Poetry prize, Chicago, 1969, Bess Hoskins prize of Poetry, Chicago, 1974, City of Toronto Bookaward, 1977, Can. Booksellers Assn. award, 1977, award for short fiction Periodical Distbr. Can., 1977, St. Lawrence award for Fiction, 1978, Radcliffe Grad. medal, 1980, Molson award, 1981, Internat. Writers prize Welsh Arts Council, 1982; Guggenheim fellow, 1981; decorated companion Order of Can., 1981. Office: care Oxford Univ Press 70 Wymford Dr Don Mills Ont Canada M3C 1J9

ATWOOD, ROBERT BRUCE, editor, publisher; b. Chgo., Mar. 31, 1907; s. Burton H. and Mary Beach (Stevenson) A.; m. Evangeline Rasmuson, Apr. 2, 1932; children: Marilyn A. Odom, Sara Elaine. A.B., Clark U., 1929; Litt.D. (hon.), Alaska Meth. U., 1967; D.Journalism (hon.), U. Alaska, 1979. Reporter Worcester (Mass.) Telegram, 1926-29, 34-35, Ill. State Jour., Springfield, 1929-34; editor and pub. The Anchorage Times, 1935—. Author pamphlets, articles, editorials pub. in various jours. Chmn. Alaska Statehood Com., 1949-59; hon. Norwegian consul at Anchorage; mem. civilian adv. bd. Alaskan Air Command, 1962—, now chmn. Mem. AP, Am. Newspaper Pubs. Assn., Internat. Press Inst., Pacific N.W. Newspaper Assn., Nat. Municipal League (council), Allied Daily Newspapers, Am. Soc. Newspaper Editors, Am. Polar Soc. (bd. govs.), C. of C. (pres. 1944, 48), Sigma Delta Chi. Republican. Presbyterian. Clubs: Rotary, Explorers, Nat. Press. Home: 2000 Atwood Dr Anchorage AK 99503 Office: 820 4th Ave Anchorage AK 99501 Mailing Address: Box 40 Anchorage AK 99510

AU, TUNG, civil engineer; b. Hong Kong, Sept. 8, 1923; U.S., 1947, naturalized, 1963; s. Tung C. and Fuk K. (Leung) A.; m. Isabel Szeto, June 18, 1955; children—Thomas, Yolande. B.S., St. John's U., 1943; M.S., U. Ill., 1948, Ph.D., 1951; M. Sci. Engring., U. Mich., 1954. Registered profl. engr., Pa., Ill. Structural engr., 1951-55; asst. prof. U. Detroit, 1955-57; asso. prof. Carnegie-Mellon U., 1957-64, prof., 1964—, acting head civil engring. dept., 1971; engring. cons. Sch. dir. Fox Chapel Area Sch. Dist., 1976-79; trustee Lingnan U., 1973—. Author or co-author: Elementary Structural Mechanics, 1963, Introduction to Systems Engineering-Deterministic Models, 1969, Fundamentals of Systems Engineering—Probabilitic Models, 1972, Engineering Economics for Capital Investment Analysis, 1983; Author: maj. reports Ride Shared Vehicle Paratransit (RSVP) System, 1977, Productivity Improvement for Taxi/Paratransit Industry, 1978. Mem. ASCE, Nat. Soc. Profl. Engrs., Am. Soc. Engring. Edn., Am. Assn. Cost Engrs., Ops. Research Soc. Am., Sigma Xi, Phi Kappa Phi, Tau Beta Pi. Home: 5211 Forbes Ave Pittsburgh PA 15217

AUBERGER, KENNETH JAMES, government official; b. Rochester, N.Y., Sept. 23, 1926; s. Joseph and Evelyn (McGinness) A.; m. Patricia Frances Sacco, Apr. 14, 1951. B.B.A., St. Bernardine-Siena Coll., 1950; J.D., Am. U., 1959, M.B.A., 1961. Bar: D.C. bar 1960; C.P.A., Md. Accountant-auditor Carl Thomy & Co., Rochester, 1950-51, GAO, 1952-64; dep. gov., chief examiner Farm Credit Adminstrn., 1965-82, dep. gov., chief of staff, 1982—. Served with USNR, 1945-46, 51-52. Mem. Am., D.C. bar assns., Am. Inst. C.P.A.'s, Md. Soc. C.P.A.'s. Home: 10410 Gary Rd Potomac MD 20854 Office: Farm Credit Adminstrn Washington DC 20578

AUBERJONOIS, RENÉ MURAT, actor; b. N.Y.C., June 1, 1940; s. Fernand and Laura (Murat) A.; m. Judith Helen Mihalyi, Oct. 19, 1963; children: Tessa Louise, Rémy-Luc. B.F.A., Carnegie-Mellon U., 1962. Tchr. acting U. Calif. at Berkeley, San Francisco State U., Julliard Sch. Appeared in: films M.A.S.H, 1970, Brewster McCloud, 1971, McCabe and Mrs. Miller, 1971, Pete N' Tillie, 1972, Images, 1971, The Hindenberg, 1973, King Kong, 1976, Eyes of Laura Mars, 1978, Where the Buffalo Roam, 1980; appeared in repertory theatre, Washington, 1962-65, A.C.T., San Francisco, 1965-68, Mark Twain Forum, Los Angeles, 1980-83, Arena Stage; Broadway plays Coco, 1970 (Tony award), The Good Doctor, 1974 (Tony nominee), Tricks, 1972; star: TV series Benson; other TV appearances. Office: 124 W 79th St New York NY 10024

AUBIN, WILLIAM M., aerospace manufacturing company executive; b. Detroit, Dec. 17, 1929; s. Hector and Alice (Nittinger) A.; m. Joyce N. Gauthier, June 26, 1952; children: Mark, Julie, Denise, Brian, Bruce, Allison, Elaine. B.Aero. Engring., U. Detroit, 1953; M.S. in Math., Adelphi Coll., 1956. With Grumman Aerospace Corp., Bethpage, N.Y., 1953—, staff to gen. mgr. for product devel.; cons. NASA. Mem. West Islip Library Bd., N.Y., 1963-67. Mem. AIAA, Metal Sci. Club. Roman Catholic. Home: 9 Pansmith Ln West Islip NY 11795 Office: Grumman Aerospace Corp Bethpage NY 11714

AUBREY, ROGER FREDERICK, psychology and education educator; b. Waterloo, Iowa, Nov. 1, 1929; s. Earl F. and Ruth M. (Schminke) A.; m. Dixie L. Cook, Mar. 15, 1963; children: Joshua, David, Christopher. A.B., U. Miami, 1954; M.A., U. Chgo., 1964; Ed.D., Boston U., 1975. Tchr. United Twp. High Sch., East Moline, Ill., 1959-62; counselor Sch. Dist. 133, Chgo., 1964-69; psychologist-counselor, dir. guidance U. Chgo. Lab. Schs., 1964-69; dir. guidance and health Brookline (Mass.) Schs., 1969-77; prof. psychology and edn. Vanderbilt U., Nashville, 1977—; cons. in field. Author: The Counselor and Drug Abuse Programs, 1973, Experimenting with Living: Pros and Cons, 1973, Career Development Needs of Thirteen Year Olds, 1978; editor: Practices of Guidance, 1972, Guidance: Strategies and Techniques, 1975; contbr. articles to profl. jours. Served with U.S. Army, 1951. Named Writer of Yr. Am. Sch. Counselor Assn., 1973. Mem. Assn. Counselor Edn. and Supervision (pres. 1973-74), Am. Psychol. Assn., Am. Personnel and Guidance Assn., Am. Ednl. Research Assn., AAAS. Democrat. Unitarian. Home: 6304 Torrington Rd Nashville TN 37205 Office: PO Box 52 Nashville TN 37203

AUBRY, EUGENE EDWARDS, architect; b. Galveston, Tex., Nov. 15, 1935; s. Frank J. and Christine C. (Anderson) A.; m. Elizabeth Hunter, July 12, 1958; children: Camilla Elizabeth, Christian Eugenia, Adrian Helen. B.S., U. Houston, also B.Arch. Partner firm Barnstone and Aubry, 1966-70, Wilson, Morris, Crain & Anderson, Houston, 1970-72; partner S.I. Morris Assocs., Houston, 1972-80, Morris/Aubry Architects, 1980—. Prin. works include: offices of Schlumberger Ltd, N.Y.C., 1967, offices of Paul, Weiss, Goldberg, Rifkind, Wharton and Garrison, N.Y.C., 1968, Inst. Arts and Media Center, Rice U., Houston, P.G. Bell residence, 1970 (1st Honor award Tex. Soc. Architects), U. St. Thomas dormitory (Merit award Tex. Soc. Architects); dormitory, 1971 (Merit award Tex. Soc. Architects); Rothko Chapel, 1970 (Merit award Tex. Soc. Architects), Texaco Hdqrs., Houston, 1976, Houston Central Library, 1976 (Honor award AIA), Mus. Fine Arts Sch., Houston, 1978 (honor award Tex. Soc. Architects), Houston, 1978 (honor award Tex. Soc. Architects), Allied Chem. Bldg, Houston, 1978, Alfred C. Glassell Sch. Art, Houston, 1978, Prudential Ins. Co. S.W. Home Office, Houston, 1978 (honor award Tex. Soc. Architects), Julia Ideson Library Bldg. Restoration, 1978 (honor award Tex. Soc. Architects), First City Tower, Houston, 1981, Inn on Park at Riverway, Houston, 1981, Gulf States Utilities Bldg, Beaumont, Tex., 1981, Mid-Am. Plaza, Oklahoma City, 1981, Tex. Wesleyan Coll. Library, Fort Worth, Tex., 1984. Fellow AIA; Mem. Contemporary Art Assn., Mus. Fine Arts Houston, Mus. Modern Art, N.Y.C., Tex. Soc. Architects. Home: 3043 Reba Houston TX 77019 office: 3355 W Alabama Houston TX 77098

AUBURN, NORMAN PAUL, university president; b. Cin., May 22, 1905; s. Joseph and Huldah A.; m. Kathleen Montgomery, June 28, 1930 (dec. 1974); children: Ames Auburn Latta, Richard, Mark, David Bruce; m. Virginia Kirk, Jan. 4, 1977. A.B., U. Cin., 1927; student, Law Sch., 1927-28, Grad. Sch., 1934-35, LL.D., 1952, Parsons Coll., 1945, U. Liberia, 1959, U. Akron, 1971; D.Sc., U. Tulsa, 1957; Litt.D., Washburn U., 1961; L.H.D., Coll. of Wooster, 1963; D.C.L., Union Coll., 1979. Editor Cin. Constructor, 1928-33; asst. mgr. Asso. Gen. Contractors of Am., 1928-33; publicity mgr. Allied Constrn. Industries, 1930-33; exec. sec. U. Cin. Alumni Assn., 1933-36; editor Cin. Alumnus, 1929-36; asst. dir., asst. prof. Evening Coll., U. Cin., 1936-38; asso. prof. U. Cin., 1938-40, acting dean, 1940-41, dean and prof., 1941-43, dean of univ. adminstrn., clk. bd. dirs., 1943-51, v.p., 1943-51, acting pres., 1949; exec. dir. U. Cin. Research Found., 1943-51; pres. U. Akron, 1951-71, pres. emeritus, cons., 1971—; acting pres. Council Fin. Aid to Edn., N.Y.C., 1957-58, bd. dirs., 1957-71; spl. asst. univ. relations AID, U.S. State Dept., 1965-66, cons., 1966—, Acad. Ednl. Devel., Inc., N.Y.C., 1965-70, sr. v.p., dir. institutional ops., 1971—; acting pres. Poly. Inst., Bklyn., 1973, Stephens Coll., Columbia, Mo., 1974-75, Cedar Crest Coll., Allentown, Pa., 1977-78, Union Coll., Schenectady, N.Y., 1978-79; acting chancellor Union U., Albany, N.Y., 1978-79; sr. v.p., provost Widener U., Chester, Pa., 1979-82; acting pres. Salem Coll., W.Va., 1982-83; spl. asst. to pres. for planning W.Va. U., Morgantown, 1983—; chmn. Univ. Council on Edn. for Pub. Responsibility, 1965-66; dir. Great Lakes Megalopolis Research Project, 1968-74; vice chmn. Am. Council Edn., 1963-64, dir., 1969-72, First Fed. Savs. and Loan Assn., Akron, chmn. bd., 1973—; dir. emeritus 1st Nat. Bank Akron. Contbr. articles to ednl. jours. Bd. dirs. Akron Gen. Hosp.; trustee Greater Akron Musical Assn., 1967—, Lane Theol. Sem., Ohio Coll. Assn.; pres. Ohio Coll. Assn., 1960-61; mem. Air Force ROTC Adv. Panel to Dept. USAF, 1960-64; mem. exec. com. Ohio Research and Devel. Bd., 1962-65; pres. Herman Muehlstein Found., 1965—. Fellow AAAS; mem. Assn. Am. Colls. (vice chmn. commn. coll. adminstrn. 1965-68), Am. Soc. Engring. Edn., Am. Assn. State Colls. and Univs. (chmn. com. on internat. programs 1970-71), Assn. Univ. Evening Colls. (pres. 1944), Assn. Urban Univs. (pres. 1955-56, sec.-treas. 1956-65), Newcomen Soc., Cincinnatus Soc., Summit County Hist. Soc. (trustee 1975—), Queen City Assn., Alpha Kappa Psi, Phi Alpha Delta, Lambda Chi Alpha, Omicron Delta Kappa, Scabbard and Blade. Presbyterian. Clubs: Rotary (pres. Cin. 1950-51, Akron 1958-59); Commonwealth (Cin.); University (Akron, N.Y.C., Columbus, Ohio); City, Portage Country (Akron). Office: Office of Pres Emeritus U Akron Akron OH 44325

AUBUT, MARCEL, sports association official; b. St. Hubert de Riviere-du-Loup, Que., Can., Jan. 5, 1948; s. Rol and Omerine (Prouxl) A.; (married); children: Melanie, Julie, Catherine. LL.M., Laval U., 1971. Bar: Que. 1971. Legal advisor, sec., treas. Que. Nordiques Hockey Club, Charlesbourg, Que., 1976-78, pres., 1978—; sr. asso. firm Beauvais, Truchon and Aubut, Que.; dir. various corps. Bd. dirs., gov. Nat. Office: Quebec Nordiques 2205 Ave du Colisee Quebec PQ Canada G1L 4W7 *

AUCH, WALTER EDWARD, securities company executive; b. Detroit, Apr. 12, 1921; s. Fred J. and Beatrice H. (Higgins) A.; children: Walter Edward, Timothy R., Terrance H. Student, Albion Coll., also U. Detroit, 1939-42. Stockbroker William C. Roney & Co., Detroit, 1946-55; sr. partner Bache & Co., N.Y.C., 1955-64, Paine, Webber, Jackson & Curtis, 1964-70; pres. Nat. Securities & Research Corp., N.Y.C., 1970-72; exec. v.p. duPont, Glore, Forgan, Inc., N.Y.C., 1972-73; pres. duPont Walston, Inc., 1973-74; exec. v.p. Paine, Webber, Jackson & Curtis, N.Y.C., 1974-79; chmn., chief exec. officer Chgo. Bd. Options Exchange, 1979—; dir. Essex Chem., Amarco Resources, Patlex Corp. Trustee Albion Coll. Served with USAAF, 1942-45. Mem. Bond Club N.Y., Bond Club Chgo., N.Y. Stock Exchange Club, Sigma Chi. Clubs: City Midday, Union League (N.Y.C.); Chicago, Attic (Chgo.); Greenwich Country; Milbrook (Greenwich); Landmark (Stamford, Conn.); Stratton Mountain Country. Home: 1040 Lake Shore Dr Chicago IL 60611 also 92 Husted Ln Greenwich CT Office: Chgo Bd Options Exchange LaSalle at Jackson Chicago IL 60604 *When I was a boy, my grandfather advised me to "live every day in such a way that the line behind the hearse gets longer." I've tried hard to follow that advice.*

AUCHINCLOSS, DAVID, publisher; b. N.Y.C., Mar. 16, 1943; s. Douglas and Eleanor (Grant) A.; m. Robin Matilda Gorham, June 12, 1966; children: Conrad McIntire, Hilary Miller; m. Judith Haskell Kress, Aug. 19, 1979. B.A., Trinity Coll., Hartford, Conn., 1965; M.B.A., Columbia U., 1967. With exec. tng. program Newsweek, N.Y.C., 1967, asst. to gen. mgr., 1968, asst. to mng. dir. internat. edit., 1969, asst. advt. mgr.-ops., 1970-72, asst. to pub., 1972-75, v.p., dir. planning and adminstrn., 1975-77, sr. v.p., 1977, pub., 1977-79, exec. v.p., 1979-80, Instl. Investor, Inc., N.Y.C., 1981-82; pres., pub. Atlantic Monthly, N.Y.C., 1982—. Office: The Atlantic Monthly 8 Arlington St Boston MA 02116

AUCHINCLOSS, KENNETH, editor; b. N.Y.C., July 3, 1937; s. Douglas and Eleanor (Grant) A.; m. Eleanor Muir Johnson, June 5, 1971; children: Malcolm Grant, Emily Johnson. A.B., Harvard U., 1959; B.A., M.A. (Henry fellow), Balliol Coll., Oxford (Eng.) U., 1961. Asst. to dep. asst. sec. commerce, Washington, 1962-63, exec. asst. Pres.'s spl. rep. for trade negotiations, 1963-65; asst. to trustees Inst. for Advanced Study, Princeton, N.J., 1965-66; asso. editor Newsweek, N.Y.C., 1966-69, gen. editor, 1969-72, sr. editor, 1972, exec. editor, 1973-75, mng. editor, 1975—. Trustee Groton Sch. Home: 40 E 62d St New York NY 10021 Office: 444 Madison Ave New York NY 10022

AUCHINCLOSS, LOUIS STANTON, author; b. Lawrence, N.Y., Sept. 27, 1917; s. Joseph Howl and Priscilla (Stanton) A.; m. Adele Lawrence, Sept. 1957; children: John, Blake, Andrew. Student, Yale U., 1939; LL.B., U. Va., 1941; Litt.D., N.Y. U., 1974, Pace U., 1979. Bar: N.Y. bar 1941. Asso. firm Sullivan & Cromwell, 1941-51; asso. Hawkins, Delafield & Wood, N.Y.C., 1954-58, partner, 1958—. Author: The Indifferent Children, 1947, The Injustice Collectors, 1950, Sybil, 1952, A Law for the Lion, 1953, The Romantic Egoists, 1954, The Great World and Timothy Colt, 1956, Venus in Sparta, 1958, Pursuit of the Prodigal, 1959, The House of Five Talents, 1960, Reflections of a Jacobite, 1961, Portrait in Brownstone, 1962, Powers of Attorney, 1963, The Rector of Justin, 1964, Pioneers and Caretakers, 1965, The Embezzler, 1966, Tales of Manhattan, 1967, A World of Profit, 1968, Motiveless Malignity, 1969, Second Chance, 1970, Edith Wharton, 1971, I Came As a Thief, Richelieu, 1972, The Partners, A Writer's Capital, 1974, Reading Henry James, 1975, The Winthrop Covenant, 1976, The Dark Lady, 1977, The Country Cousin, 1978, Persons of Consequence, 1979, Life, Law and Letters, 1979, The House of the Prophet, 1980, The Cat and the King, 1981, Watchfires, 1982, Exit Lady Masham, 1983. Trustee Josiah Macy, Jr. Found.; pres. Mus. City of N.Y. Served as lt. USNR, 1941-45. Mem. Am. Coll. Probate Counsel, Nat. Inst. Arts and Letters, Assn. Bar City N.Y. Episcopalian. Clubs: Century Assn., Downtown Assn. Home: 1111 Park Ave New York NY 10028 Office: 67 Wall St New York NY 10005

AUCHTER, THORNE G., govt. ofcl.; b. Jacksonville, Fla., Mar. 6, 1945. B.A., Jacksonville U., 1968. Constrn. supr. Auchter Co., Jacksonville, 1968-75, exec. v.p., 1975-81; legis. coordinator Fla. Senate rules com., 1975; asst. sec. Occupation Safety and Health Adminstrn., Dept. Labor, Washington, 1981—. Office: Dept Labor 200 Constitution Ave Washington DC 20210 *

AUCLAIR, JACQUES LUCIEN, entomologist, educator; b. Montreal, Que., Can., Apr. 2, 1923; s. Alfred and Clothilde (Boucher) A.; m. Suzanne Strub, Apr. 28, 1951; children: Danielle, France,; Monique Marsil; May 31, 1975. B.Sc., U. Montreal, 1942; M.Sc., McGill U., 1945; Ph.D., Cornell U., 1949. Asst. prof. dept. biology U. Montreal, 1949-53, prof., 1967—, chmn. dept. biol. scis., 1967-73; Research entomologist Can. Agr. Dept., St. Jean, Que., 1949-64; research prof. N.Mex. State U., Las Cruces, 1964-67. Contbr. sci. articles to profl. jours. Fellow Entomol. Soc. Can.; mem. Entomol. Soc. Am., Entomol. Soc. Que., Am. Inst. Biol. Scis. Home: 405 Riverside Dr Saint Lambert PQ Canada JAP 1B2 Office: U Montreal Biology Dept Montreal PQ Canada H3C 3J7

AUCOIN, LES, congressman; b. Portland, Oreg., Oct. 21, 1942; s. Francis Edgar and Alice (Atkinson) AuC.; m. Susan Swearingen, June 11, 1963; children: Stacy, Kelly. B.A., Pacific U., 1969. Reporter, editor Redmond (Oreg.) Spokesman, 1964; with Portland Oregonian, 1965-66; dir. pub. info. and publs. Pacific U., 1966-73; adminstr. Skidmore, Owings & Merrill, Portland, 1973-74; mem. 94th-98th Congresses from 1st Oreg. Dist., Com. on Appropriations; chmn. House Task Force on Indsl. Innovation and Productivity., House Dem. Trade Caucus, 1983—; Mem. Oreg. Ho. of Reps., 1971-74, majority leader, 1973-74, chmn., 1973, 1974; mem. State Emergency Bd., 1973-74. Served with inf. U.S. Army, 1961-64. Recipient One of 10 Outstanding Young Men of Am. award U.S. Jaycees, 1977; Brotherhood award B'nai, B'rith, 1978. Office: 2159 Rayburn House Office Bldg Washington DC 20515

AUDET, JEAN-PAUL, educator; b. St. Anselme, Que., Can., July 12, 1918; s. Alphonse and Marie-Anne (Gagne) A.; m. Jeanne-Marie Gingras, July 16, 1975; children: Isabelle, Paul-Emmanuel, Dominique. B.A., Levis Coll. U. Laval, Quebec, Que., 1939; Lector Theologiae, Dominican Faculty Philosphy and Theology, Ottawa, Ont., Can., 1947; D.Theology U. St. Thomas, Rome, 1949; postgrad. in Egyptology, Oxford (Eng.) U., 1950, Ecole Biblique et Archeologique Francaise, Jerusalem, 1952. Prof., Dominican Faculty Philosophy and Theology, Ottawa, 1952-58, Ecole Biblique et Archeologique Francaise de Jerusalem, 1958-68; prof. philosophy U. Montreal, Que., Can., 1969—, chmn. dept. philosophy, 1974-78, chmn. univ. research commn., 1974-78; mem. Can. Council, 1969-77; mem. exec. com., mem. council Can. Assn. U. Tchrs., 1973-76. Author: books, including La Didache, 1958, Mariage et Celibat dans Le Service Pastoral del'Eglise, 1967, (with A. Diessler and H. Schlier) Der Priesterliche Dienst, 1970; contbr. numerous articles, essays, revs. on history, philosophy, Bibl. scholarship to profl. publs. Recipient Molson award Can. Council, 1970; fellow, 1960, 63, 72-74. Mem. Royal Soc. Can., Academie des Scis. Morales et Politiques., Internat. Assn. for Study Prehist. and Ethnol. Religion., Strategic Mgmt. Soc. Home: Rural Route 2 Magog PQ J1X 3W3 Canada Office: U Montreal 2910 Edouard-Montpetit Blvd Montreal PQ Canada

AUDET, LEONARD, theologian; b. Maria, P.Q., Can., Nov. 26, 1932; s. Ernest and Emilie (Loubert) A. D.Th., U. Montreal, (1964); Licence en Ecriture Sainte, Pontificium Institutum Biblicum, Rome, 1964. Prof. Scolasticat de Theologie de Joliette, Que., Can., 1965-67; prof. Bible Faculty of Theology U. Montreal, 1967-77; dean Faculty of Theology, 1977—. Author: Apres Jesus, Autorite et Liberte dans le peuple de Dieu, 1977, A Companion to Paul, 1975, Vivante est ta parole, 1975. Mem. Can. Cath. Soc. of the Bible (adminstrv. council), Can. Soc. Theology, Cath. Assn. Bibl. Study of Can. (treas. 1968-77). Home: 450 rue Querbes Montreal PQ H2V 3W5 Canada Office: Faculte de Théologie U Montreal PQ H3C 3J7 Canada

AUDET, LIONEL, clergyman; b. Ste.-Marie de Beauce, Que., Can., May 22, 1908; s. Louis and Eugenie (Turcotte) A. Ph.L., Grand Seminaire de Que., (1931); D.Th., Angelicum, Rome, 1936. Ordained priest Roman Catholic Ch., 1934; Prof. theology Grand Seminaire de Que., 1936-52, dir. spiritual, 1945-47, superieur, 1950-52; aux. bishop, Que., 1952—. Author: Notre Participation au Sacerdoce du Christ, 1945. Address: Archbishop's House CP 459 Quebec PQ G1R 4R6 Canada *

AUDET, PAUL ANDRE, newspaper executive; b. Quebec, Can., Mar. 14, 1923; s. Sylvio and Rose Aimee (Cloutier) A.; m. Michele Richard, Sept. 13, 1947; children: Francine, Andre, Marc. Newspaper reporter L'Evenement Jour., 1942-44; staff writer The Canadian Press, 1944, asst. mng. editor, 1945-48, sales and sales mgr. printing dept., 1948-54; advt. dir. Le Soleil, Quebec, 1955-74, pres., gen. mgr., 1974—; pres. Le Soleil Limitee, Edimedia, Inc. Named hon. lt. col. Les Voltigeurs de Que. Regt. Mem. Société Française de Quebec, Ordre des Chevaliers de Meduse. Roman Catholic. Clubs: Garrison, Gastrononique Prosper Montagne., Cercle Universitaire. Home: 9 Jardins Merici Apt 1803 Quebec PQ G1S 4N8 Canada Office: 340 St Vallier Suite E Quebec PQ Canada

AUDET, RENE, bishop; b. Montreal, Que., Can., Jan. 18, 1920; s. Louis Napoleon and Marie-Louise (Blais) A. Student, St. Ignace Coll., 1936-41, Brebeuf Coll., 1941-43; B.A., Montreal U., 1943; postgrad., Immaculate Conception Scolasticate, 1943-48; B.Sc. in Sociology, St. Louis U., 1953, M.A., 1955. Ordained priest Roman Catholic Ch., 1948; curate St. Joseph's Ch., Rouyn, Que., 1948-51; chaplain Syndicates, 1948-51, Youville Hosp., Noranda, Que., 1951-52; curate, Kirkland Lake, Ont., 1952-55; diocesan procurator Bishop's House, Timmins, Ont., 1955-63; chaplain St. Mary's Acad., Haileybury, Ont., 1955-63; aux. bishop of, Ottawa, Ont., Can., 1963, consecrated bishop, 1963, vicar gen. of, Ottawa, 1963-68, bishop of, Joliette, Que., 1968—; ecclesiastical asst. World Fedn. Christian Life Communities, 1967—. Mem. Comité Episcopal du Laicat, Comité Episcopal de L'Education Chretienne, Comité Episcopal de la Legislation et de l'Administration Financière, Comité Provincial d'Enseignement Religieux. Clubs: Optimist, K.C. Home: 2 St Charles Borromeo N Joliette PQ J6E 6H6 Canada Office: Bishop's House Joliette PQ J6E 6H6 Canada

AUDET-LAPOINTE, PIERRE, physician, medical foundation executive; b. Montreal, Que., Can., Aug. 26, 1935; s. Lionel and Irene (Lacasse) Audet-L.; m. Lyette Chartrand, Sept. 10, 1960; children: Catherine, Mylene, Valerie, Marika. B.A., Coll. Jean-de-Brebeuf, Montreal, 1960. Diplomate: Am. Bd. Ob-Gyn. Intern. Maisonneuve Hosp., Montreal, 1961-63; resident Notre Dame Hosp., Montreal, 1963-68, Meml. Hosp., N.Y.C., 1963-68; mem. staff Notre-Dame Hosp., Montreal, 1966—; prof. ob-byn U. Montreal, 1977—; pres. Que. Cancer Found. Served to lt. Can. Army Res., 1952-58. Recipient Isaac Blatt award Cardio-Vascular Diseases Found., Montreal, 1959, Parizeau award Assn. des Diplomes, U. Montreal, 1960, McEachren award Can. Cancer Soc., 1967, Allan Blair award, 1968, Union Medicale du Can award, 1968. Fellow Royal Coll. Surgeons Can.; mem. Assn. des Medecins de Langue Francaise du Can., Soc. Obstetriciens and Gynecologues du Can., Assn. Obstetriciens and Gynecologues du Que., Fedn. des Gynecologues and Obstetriciens de Langue Francaise, James Ewin Soc., Gynecologie Laser Soc. Roman Catholic. Home: 167 Pagnuelo Outrmont PQ Canada H2V 3C3 Office: Pavillon Louis-Charles Simard Room 27913 2065 Alexandre-de-Sevres Montreal PQ Canada H2L 4K8

AUER, EDWARD THOMAS, psychiatrist; b. Phila., Jan. 18, 1919; s. William Harper and Anna (Maguire) A.; m. Mary Hedesh, Sept. 23, 1944; children: Robert, Thomas, Kenneth, Mary Ann, Edward. B.A., U. Rochester, 1940; M.D., Temple U., 1943. Intern Abington (Pa.) Meml. Hosp., 1943-44, chief resident, 1947-48; fellow psychiatry U. Pa. Med. Sch., 1948-50, mem. faculty, 1950-62, assoc. prof. psychiatry, 1956-62, clin. prof., 1976—, asst. instr. medicine, 1950-53; practice medicine specializing in psychiatry with Dr. Kenneth Appel & Assos., Phila., 1950-56; with Drs. Edward T. Auer, William T. Donner & Assos., Pa., 1956-62; cons. psychiatry Coatesville VA Hosp., Phila., 1954-56; prof. psychiatry, chmn. dept. neurology and psychiatry St. Louis U. Sch. Medicine, 1962-76, Samuel W. Fordyce prof. psychiatry, 1967-76; chief mental health and behavioral sci. service St. Louis VA Hosp., 1972-76; med. dir. Inst. Pa. Hosp., Phila., 1976-80; mem. Nat. Task Force Homosexuality, 1967-70; vice chmn. Mental Health Planning Com., St. Louis, 1966-69. Cons. editor: Jour. Human Sexuality; contbr. articles to med. jours. Served to capt. M.C. AUS, 1944-47. Fellow Am. Psychiat. Assn. (chmn. council on emerging issues 1972-75, chmn. task force on sex edn. and sex therapy 1976-82), Am. Coll. Psychiatry, Am. Coll. Psychoanalysts (charter, chmn. com. invitations to membership 1973—); mem. AMA, Pa., Phila. med. socs., Group Advancement Psychiatry (dir. 1966-68), Eastern Mo. Psychiat Assn. (pres. 1967-68), So. Psychiat. Assn., AAAS, Sigma Xi, Alpha Omega Alpha. Home: 525 Fox Run Ln Bryn Mawr PA 19010 Office: Phila VA Med Center 39th and Woodland Aves Philadelphia PA 19139

AUER, JAMES MATTHEW, journalist; b. Neenah, Wis., Dec., 2, 1928; s. Matthew George and Charlotte Agnes (Friedland) A.; m. Marilyn Mills, Feb. 1, 1964; 1 son, Charles William. B.A., Lawrence Coll., Appleton, Wis., 1950. With accounting dept. George Banta Co., 1950-51; reporter Twin City News-Record, 1953-56, asst. to editor, 1957-60, news editor, 1960-61; asst. Sunday editor Appleton Post-Crescent, 1960-65, Sunday editor, 1965-72; art critic Milw. Jour., 1972—. Author: The Spirit Is Willing, 1960; plays The City of Light, 1961, Tell It to Angela, 1971. Presiding officer Attic Theatre, Inc., 1959-62; pres. Friends of Bergstrom Art Center, 1967-68; mem. Neenah Municipal Mus. Found., Inc. Recipient Pres.'s award Wis. Heart Assn., 1969. Mem. Am. Assn. Sunday and Feature Editors (pres. 1972-73), State Hist. Soc. Wis. (award of merit 1962), Phi Kappa Tau. Conglist. Home: 1849 N 72d St Wauwatosa WI 53213 Office: 333 W State St Milwaukee WI 53201

AUER, LOUIS, venture capital company executive; b. Milw., July 28, 1926; s. Stuart F. and Ruth Valentine (Bartlett) A.; m. Jean W. Patchett, Mar. 30, 1951; children: Ward Bartlett, Amy Stuart. B.A., Yale U., 1947. Asst. v.p. Chem. Bank N.Y. Trust Co., 1948-59; gen. partner Shields & Co., N.Y.C., 1960-72; sr. v.p. Shields Model Roland Inc., N.Y.C., 1972-77; exec. v.p., dir. Bache Halsey Stuart Shields Inc., N.Y.C., 1977-82; propr. Auer Capital Co., La Quinta, Calif., 1983—; bd. govs. Am. Stock Exchange, 1969-70. Served with U.S. Navy, 1944-46. Episcopalian. Clubs: Yale of N.Y., Shinnecock Hills Golf, Westhampton Country, La Quinta Country. Office: 77599 Ave Madrugada La Quinta CA 92253

AUER, PETER LOUIS, plasma physicist, educator; b. Budapest, Hungary, Jan. 12, 1928; came to U.S., 1937, naturalized, 1942; s. Laszlo and Irma (Morgenstern) A.; m. Rheta E. Siegel, Aug. 27, 1952; children—Deborah, Douglas, Andrea, Matthew. A.B., Cornell U., 1947; Ph.D., Calif. Inst. Tech., 1951. Physicist Gen. Electric Research Lab., Schenectady, 1954-61; head plasma physics Sperry Rand Research Center, Sudbury, Mass., 1961-64; dir. Ballistic Missile Def., Office Sec. Def., Washington, 1964-66; prof. aerospace engring. Cornell U., Ithaca, N.Y., 1966—, dir. lab. plasma studies, 1967-74; cons. Office Sec. Def., Gen. Electric Co., Electric Power Research Inst., AEC, NRC, Nat. Acad. Scis., Dept. of Energy, Inst. for Energy Analysis; vis. scientist Frascati, Italy, 1960-61; vis. prof. Oxford U., 1972-73. Editor: Plasma Physics, 1970; asso. editor: Energy, 1976; Contbr. articles to profl. jours. Guggenheim fellow, 1960-61. Fellow Am. Phys. Soc. Pantentee in field. Home: 220 Devon Rd Ithaca NY 14850

AUERBACH, ARNOLD JACOB (RED AUERBACH), profl. basketball exec.; b. N.Y.C., Sept. 20, 1917; s. Hyman and Marie (Thompson) A.; m. Dorothy Lewis, June 6, 1941; children: Nancy, Randy. B.S. in Phys. Edn, George Washington U., 1940, M.A. in Edn, 1941; hon. degrees, Franklin Pierce Coll., U. Mass., Boston U. Coach Washington Capitols, 1946-49, Tri-Cities Blackhawks, 1949-50; coach Boston Celtics Basketball Team, 1950-66, now pres., gen. mgr.; rep. State Dept. for clinics, demonstrations, exhbns.; dir. basketball sch. Camp Milbrooks, Marshfield, Mass.; sports commentator, lectr.; dir. Seacrest Hotel, North Falmouth, Mass. Author: Fan and Coach, 1953, (with Paul Sann) Red Auerbach: Winning the Hard Way, (with Joe Fitzgerald) Red Auerbach, An Autobiography. Chmn. in, Mass., Easter Seal Soc. Served to lt. USN, 1943-46. Recipient Arch McDonald Achievement award, 1962, Boston's Distinguished Achievement medal, 1965, Sports Achievement award B'nai B'rith; named Nat. Basketball Assn. Coach of Year, 1965; named to Nat. Basketball Hall of Fame, 1968, Naismith Meml. Basketball Hall of Fame, 1968; chosen All-Time NBA Coach. Mem. Nat. Coaches Assn., Omicron Delta Kappa, Colonials (George Washington U.). Club: Touchdown (award) (Washington). Coach 11 Consecutive all star games; winner 10 Eastern div. titles, 9 world titles. Office: Boston Celtics North Sta Boston MA 02114

AUERBACH, CARL ABRAHAM, educator; b. N.Y.C., Oct. 2, 1915; s. Moritz and Rose (Auerbach) A.; m. Laura Kron, Sept. 12, 1940; children—Linda Eugenie, Eric Hart. A.B., L.I. U., 1935; LL.B., Harvard U., 1938. Bar: N.Y. State bar 1938, Wis. bar 1953, Minn. bar 1973, also U.S. Supreme Ct 1946. With firm Ansell, Ansell & Marshall, Washington, 1938; atty. Dept. Labor, 1938-40; asst. gen. counsel OPA, 1940-43, gen. counsel, 1946-47; asso. gen. counsel Office Econ. Stblzn., 1946; prof. law U. Wis. Law Sch., 1947-61, U. Minn. Law Sch., Mpls., 1961—, dean, 1972-79; vis. fellow Hoover Instn. on War, Revolution and Peace, 1979-80, 82; Staff dir. com. internal orgn. and procedure Adminstrv. Conf. U.S., 1961-62; cons. AID, 1963, 66; mem. Commn. Marine Sci., Engring. and Resources, 1966-69, Nat. Hwy. Safety Adv. Com., 1968-71, Adminstrv. Conf. U.S., 1970-74, Minn. Constl. Study Commn., 1971-72. Author: (with others) The Legal Process, 1961, (with Nathanson) The Federal Regulation of Transportation, 1953; also articles. Served with AUS, 1943-46; ETO. Fulbright fellow, 1953-54; fellow Center Advanced Study Behavioral Scis., 1958-59. Mem. Am. Acad. Arts and Scis., Am. Law Inst., Law and Soc. Assn., Am. Bar Assn. Home: 3230 Kyle Ave N Golden Valley MN 55422

AUERBACH, ISAAC LEVIN, computer scientist, publisher, cons.; b. Phila., Oct. 9, 1921; s. Philip and Rose (Levin) A.; 1 son, Philip B. B.S. in Elec. Engring, Drexel U., 1943; M.S. in Applied Physics, Harvard U., 1947. Research engr. Sperry Univac, 1947-48; dir. spl. products div. Burroughs Corp., 1949-57; chmn. bd., pres. Auerbach Corp. for Sci. and Tech., Phila., 1957—; pres. Auerbach Assocs., Inc., 1957-76, Auerbach Cons. (cons.), 1976—; chmn. Auerbach Pubs., Inc., 1960—; pub. Auerbach Computer Tech Reports; treas., dir. The Baupost Group Inc., 1982—; dir. The Software Group Inc., 1983—; U.S. cons. on info. processing and automation UNESCO, 1957-60; chmn. U.S. com. 1st Internat. Conf. Info. Processing, 1959; founder, 1st pres. Internat. Fedn. for Info. Processing, 1960-65, hon. life mem., 1969; mem. Nat. Planning Assn. Editor: The Auerbach Annual-Best Computer Papers, 1971-74, 79-80. Trustee Fedn. Jewish Agys.; internat. bd. govs. Boy's Town Jerusalem; bd. dirs. Jewish Publ. Soc., 1966-73; assoc. trustee, bd. govs. Drexel U. Served as lt. (j.g.) USNR, 1943-46. Recipient Grand medal City of Paris, 1959, alumni citation Drexel U., 1961, Tower of David award State of Israel, 1969. Fellow IEEE (Phila. sect. award 1961), AAAS; distinguished fellow Brit. Computer Soc.; mem. Nat. Acad. Engring. (publs. com. 1983), Franklin Inst., Japan Computer Soc. (hon. fellow), Nat. Acad. Sci. (com. inter sci. and tech. info. programs), Am. Friends Hebrew U., Sigma Xi, Eta Kappa Nu.; Mem. B'nai B'rith. Pioneered devel., design and use computers and digital communications systems; dir. devel. 1st ICBM guidance computer. Home: 900 Centennial Rd Narberth PA 19072 Office: 455 Righters Mill Rd Narberth PA 19072

AUERBACH, JOSEPH, business educator, lawyer; b. Franklin, N.H., Dec. 3, 1916; s. Jacob and Besses Mae (Reamer) A.; m. Judith Evans, Nov. 10, 1941; children: Jonathan L., Hope B. Pym. A.B., Harvard U., 1938, LL.B., 1941. Bar: N.H. 1941, Mass. 1952, U.S. Ct. Appeal (Lst, 2d, 3d, 5th, 7th and D.C. cirs.). Class of 1957 prof. Harvard Bus. Sch., Boston, 1983—; atty. SEC, Washington and Phila., 1941-43, prin. atty., 1946-49; fgn. service staff officer U.S. Dept. State, Dusseldorf, W. Ger., 1950-52; ptn. Sallivan & Worcester, Boston, 1952-82; lectr. Boston U. Law Sch., 1975-76, Harvard Bus. Sch., Boston, 1980-82, prof., 1982-83; dir. The Williams Cos., Tulsa, Nat. Benefit Life Ins. Co., N.Y.C. Mem. editorial bd., Harvard Bus. Rev. Bd. dirs. Friends of Boston U. Libraries; vice-chmn., bd. dirs. Eastern br. Shakespere Globe Ctr. (N.A.), N.Y.C., 1983—; trustee Mass. Eye and Ear Infirmary, Boston, 1981—, Old Colony Charitable Found., Boston, 1976—. Served with AUS, 1943-46. Mem. ABA, Mass. Bar Assn., Boston Bar Assn. Clubs: Federal, Harvard, Sky, Grolier. Home: 23 Lime St Boston MA 02108 Office: Harvard Bus Sch Soldiers Field Boston MA 02163

AUERBACH, MARK, manufacturing company executive; b. N.Y.C., Apr. 27, 1938; s. Milton and Anita A.; m. Loryne Christine Ashley, Mar. 4, 1972; children: Lisa Dori, David Lawrence, Kimberlee Dawn, Michael Benjamin. B.S. in Commerce, Rider Coll., 1961. Acct. Coopers & Lybrand, N.Y.C., 1962-65; chief fin. officer Amicor, Inc., Tulsa, 1965-70, Atlanta, 1972-77, pres., chief exec. officer, Tulsa, 1977—; fin. cons. Masco Assocs., 1970-72. Served with USAF, 1955-59. Mem. Am. Inst. C.P.A.s. Jewish. Office: 468 Getty Ave Clifton NJ 07015

AUERBACH, NORBERT THEO, motion picture company executive, consultant; b. Vienna, Austria, Nov. 4, 1922; s. Josef and Olga A.; m. Margaret Crosby; children: Martin, David, Alexander, Adam. B.A. in Bus. Adminstrn, U. Calif., 1946. Continental mgr. Columbia Pictures Corp., also United Artists Corp., Paris, 1962-66; head sales ops. Seven Arts Corp., Paris, from 1967; continental mgr. Warner Bros. Corp., Paris, until 1972; v.p. CBS Cinema Center, 1972-73; ind. cons., 1973-77; sr. v.p. internat., then pres., chief exec. officer United Artists Corp., N.Y.C., 1977-82; co-pres. United Internat. Pictures, 1982; founder Elektra, Inc., Los Angeles, 1983—; cons. Samuel Goldwyn Co., 1983—. Office: Samuel Goldwyn Pictures Inc 1041 N Formosa Ave Los Angeles CA 90046 *

AUERBACH, RED *See* **AUERBACH, ARNOLD JACOB**

AUERBACH, SEYMOUR, architect; b. N.Y.C., May 28, 1929; s. Nathan and Jennie (Norman) A.; m. Alyce Kelly, Oct. 21, 1963 (div. 1977); children: Kalin Marie, Alison Kelly. B.Arch., Yale U., 1951. Asso. firm Satterlee & Smith (Architects), Washington, 1955-59; partner Cooper & Auerbach (Architects), Washington, 1960-69, Walton, Madden, Cooper & Auerbach (Architects), 1970-71; prin. Offices Seymour Auerbach (Architect), Washington, 1971—; pres. Kamak Devel. Co.; prof. architecture Cath. U. Am. Prin. works include Nat. Visitor Center, Washington, campus plan and dormitories,, Georgetown U.; campus plan and dormitories Olam Tikvah Synagogue, Fairfax, Va.; also resort community, Rehoboth Beach, Del., patentee in field. Bd. mgrs. Chevy Chase Village, Md., 1973-77, vice chmn. bd., 1976-77. Served with C.E. U.S. Army, 1951-54. William Wirt Winchester fellow, 1951; award excellence in architecture Met. Washington Bd. Trade, 1964. Fellow AIA (1st award architecture Potomac Valley chpt. 1963); mem. Soc. Archtl. Historians, Guild Religious Architecture, AAUP. Republican. Jewish. Clubs: Cosmos, Yale (Washington). Home: 115 Hesketh St Chevy Chase MD 20815 Office: PO Box 4146 Chevy Chase MD 20815 *I consider it to be of the highest calling to be involved in the improvement of man's physical environment: not only his shelter, but also his public environment and the implements he uses. In this context I have held architecture to be an Applied, rather than a Fine, Art. I consider it to be a higher calling to be a designer than to be an architect and I find the greatest of personal pleasure in solving individual problems of design for man, by myself, without regard to "style", and without regard to political or other irrelevant considerations.*

AUERBACH, STANLEY IRVING, ecologist; b. Chgo., May 1921; s. Abraham and Carrie (Friedman) A; m. Dawn Patricia Davey, June 12, 1954; children: Andrew J., Anne E., Jonathan B., Alison M. B.S., U. Ill., 1946, M.S., 1947; Ph.D., Northwestern U., 1949. Instr., then asst. prof. Roosevelt U., Chgo., 1950-54; asso. scientist, then scientist health physics div. Oak Ridge Nat. Lab., 1954-59, sr. scientist, sect. leader, 1959-70, dir. ecol. sci. div., 1970-72, dir. environ. scis. div., 1972—; adj. prof. ecology U. Tenn., 1976—; adj. research prof. radiation ecology U. Ga., 1963—; mem. U.S. exec. com. Internat. Biol. Program, co-chmn. program coordinating com., dir. deciduous forest biome project,

1969-74; mem. Nat. Acad. Sci. Adv. Commn. on Research to Sec. Agr., 1969-70, NAE Power Plant Siting Program Commn., 1970-71; chmn. archtl. rev. com. Oak Ridge Nat. Lab., 1971—; mem. aquatic biology com. ORSANCO; mem. ecol. adv. bd. Bur. Reclamation; mem. Nat. Acad. Sci.-NAE Bd. on Energy Studies, 1974-77, chmn. com. on energy and the environment, 1974-77; mem. C.E. bd. environ. cons. Tenn.-Tombigbee Waterway, 1976—; mem. ad hoc com. on transuranic burial ERDA (Dept. Energy), 1976-78; mem. Pres.'s Adv. Com. on Environ. Health and Ecol. Effects of Nat. Energy Plan, 1977-78, Resources for the Future Research Adv. Com., 1978—; mem. commn. natural resources NRC, 1979—; mem. adv. council Water Resources Research Center, U. Tenn., 1980—; Mem. Tenn. Citizens Wilderness Planning, bd. dirs., 1968; trustee Inst. Ecology, 1972-75. Ecology editor: Environment Internat, 1979—; adv. bd.: Environ. and Exptl. Botany, 1967—; bd. editors: Radiation Research, 1975-77. Served to 2d lt. AUS, 1942-44. Fellow AAAS; mem. Am. Inst. Biol. Scis. (bd. govs.), Soc. Zoology (chmn. ecology div.), Am. Soc. Agronomy, Brit. Ecol. Soc., Health Physics Soc., Entomol. Soc. Am., Soc. Systematic Biology, Ecol. Soc. Am. (chmn. com. radioecology 1963-65, sec. 1964-69, chmn. fin. com. 1969, pres. 1971-72), Sigma Xi (pres. Oak Ridge br. 1972-73, chmn. admissions 1980—), Alpha Epsilon Pi. Spl. research ecology centipedes, radioecology and radioactive waste disposal, environ. behavior of radionuclides, ecosystem analysis. Home: 24 Wildwood Dr Oak Ridge TN 37830 Office: PO Box X Oak Ridge TN 37831

AUERBACH, STUART CHARLES, journalist; b. N.Y.C., Oct. 28, 1935; s. Jack and Betty (Segnes) A.; m. Carol A. Honsa, Apr. 6, 1979. B.A., Williams Coll., 1957. Reporter Berkshire Eagle, Pittsfield, Mass., 1957-60, Miami (Fla.) Herald, 1960-66; reporter, then sci.-med. corr. Washington Post, 1960-76, Middle East corr., 1976-77, legal corr., columnist, 1977-79, South Asia corr., 1979-83, econ. corr., 1983. Recipient Pub. Service award Nat. Kidney Found., 1973; certificate commendation Am. Acad. Family Physicians, 1976. Mem. Nat. Assn. Sci. Writers (Sci.-in-Society award 1976). Clubs: Washington Press, Fed. City (Washington); Overseas Press (N.Y.C.); Delhi Gymkhana. Home: 4624 Asbury Pl NW Washington DC 20016 Office: 1150 15th St NW Washington DC 20071

AUERBACH, WILLIAM, lawyer; b. N.Y.C., Aug. 14, 1914; s. Max and Jennie (Geller) A.; m. Tess Kasper, Apr. 15, 1946; children: Sue Ellen, Alan Jeffrey, Melissa Jo. B.S.S., City Coll. N.Y., 1936; J.D., Harvard, 1939. Bar: N.Y. 1940; Certificate Far Eastern Specialization, AUS Specialized Tng. Program, 1944. Practiced in, N.Y.C., 1939-42, 47—; asso. firms Hirson & Bertini, 1939-41, Morris A. Edelman, 1941-43; partner firm Cohen & Auerbach, 1949-51, Auerbach, Labes & Woicik, 1967—; sr. atty. Office Price Adminstrn., Washington, 1946. Served as cryptanalyst and intelligence analyst OSS AUS, 1943-46. Mem. Assn. Bar City N.Y. Jewish. Home: 61 Paine Ave New Rochelle NY 10804 Office: 605 3d Ave New York NY 10016

AUERBACK, ALFRED, psychiatrist; b. Toronto, Can., Sept. 20, 1915; came to U.S., 1939, naturalized, 1944; s. Murray M. and Lena (Breslin) A.; m. Molly Loy Friedman, June 21, 1942; children— Norman L., Sandra J., Diana K. Auerback Gleave. M.D., U. Toronto, 1938. Intern Toronto Gen. Hosp., 1938-39; resident French Hosp., San Francisco, 1939-40; resident in neurology and psychiatry U. Calif. Hosp., San Francisco, 1940-42; practice medicine specializing in psychiatry, San Francisco, 1943—; staff psychiatrist Sheppard Pratt Hosp., Towson, Md., 1942-43; staff U. Calif., San Francisco, 1943—, asst. clin. prof., 1953, asso. clin. prof., 1962, clin. prof., 1970—; cons. San Francisco Gen. Hosp., 1953—; mem. Mental Health Adv. Bd. of San Francisco, 1962-77, chmn., 1967-70; bd. dirs. San Francisco Mental Health Assn., 1981—; cons. Nat. Adv. Council on Alcohol Abuse and Alcoholism, Washington, 1971-76, Calif. Alcoholic Rehab. Commn., 1955-57; mem. Citywide Alcoholism Adv. Bd., San Francisco, 1972-74; chmn., 1972-73, 1st Pacific Congress of Psychiatry, Melbourne, Australia, 1975; chmn. psychiat. congresses, Tokyo, Jerusalem, 1963, Mexico City, Lima, Rio de Janeiro, Sao Paulo, 1964, Edinburgh, 1965. Editor: Schizophrenia, An Integrated Approach, 1959. Recipient Royer award U. Calif., 1966. Fellow Am. Psychiat. Assn. (life, v.p. 1966), San Francisco Med. Soc. (bd. dirs. 1955), Am., Royal, Royal Australian, New Zealand colls. psychiatrists; mem. No. Calif. Psychiat. Soc. (pres. 1956), Am. Assn. Social Psychiatry (councillor 1980—), Pi Lambda Phi, Phi Delta Epsilon. Club: Masons. Home: 1000 North Point St San Francisco CA 94109 Office: 450 Sutter St San Francisco CA 94108

AUFFENBERG, WALTER, curator, educator; b. Detroit, Feb. 6, 1928; s. Walter and Ida (Lange) A.; m. Elinor Ann Wright, July 1, 1947; children: Walter (dec.), Kurt, Garth, Troy. B.S., Stetson U.; M.S., U. Fla., Ph.D. Asst. prof. U. Fla., Gainesville, 1956-59, prof. dept. zoology, 1963—; asst. dir. Biol. Scis. Curriculum Study, Boulder, Colo., 1959-63; chmn. natural scis. Fla. State Mus., Gainesville, 1963-73, curator herpetology, 1963—; AID cons. Bombay (India) U., 1963; NSF cons. Madurai (India) U., 1967; cons., Israel, Uruguay, Argentina, 1965. Author: Behavioral Ecology of the Komodo Moniter, 1981 (Best Book of the Wildlife Soc. 1983); contbr. articles to profl. jours. Served with USN, 1943-45. Fellow AAAS; mem. Am. Soc. Naturalists, Am. Soc. Zoologists, Am. Inst. Biol. Scis., Am. Soc. Ichthyology and Herpetology. Republican. Office: Fla State Mus U Fla Museum Rd Gainesville FL 32611

AUFSES, ARTHUR H(AROLD), JR., surgeon, medical educator; b. N.Y.C., Feb. 8, 1926; s. Arthur Harold and Beatrice (Hauser) A.; m. Harriet Whitman, Dec. 28, 1947; children: Arthur Harold III, Carolyn Aufses Blashek. Student, Columbia U., 1942-43, Union Coll., 1943-44; M.D., Columbus U., 1948. Diplomate: Am. Bd. Surgery. Intern Presbyn. Hosp., N.Y.C., 1948-49, resident in surgery, 1950-51, 53-54, Mt. Sinai Hosp., N.Y.C., 1954-56; practice medicine specializing in surgery, N.Y.C., 1956—; prof., chmn. dept. surgery Mt. Sinai Med. Ctr., N.Y.C., 1974—; chmn. dept. surgery L.I. Jewish Med. Ctr., 1971-74; prof. surgery SUNY-Stony Brook, 1971-74; surgeon-in-chief Mt. Sinai Hosp., N.Y.C., 1974—; nat. sci. adv. council Nat. Found. Ileitis and Colitis, 1965—. Contbr. articles to med. jours. Bd. dirs. 92d St. YMHA, 1974—. Served to 1st lt. U.S. Army, 1951-53. Recipient Jacobi medallion, Mt. Sinai Med. Ctr., 1979, Gold Headed Cane award, Mt. Sinai Med. Ctr., 1982. Fellow ACS, Am. Surg. Assn., Am. Coll. Gastroenterology (trustee), N.Y. Acad. Medicine; mem. Soc. Surg. Oncology, Am. Gastroent. Assn., N.Y. Surg. Soc. (pres. 1979-80), Soc. Surgery Alimentary Tract, Brazilian Coll. Surgeons, Chilean Congress Surgeons, Portuguese Soc. Gastroenterology. Jewish. Home: 1185 Park Ave New York NY 10028 Office: Mount Sinai Medical Center 1 gustave L Levy Pl New York NY 10029

AUGELLO, WILLIAM JOSEPH, lawyer; b. Bklyn., Apr. 5, 1926; s. William J. and Catherine (Ehalt) A.; m. Elizabeth Deasy, July 1, 1950; children: Thomas, Charles, Patricia, William, Peggy Ann, James. LL.B., Fordham U., 1950; B.A., Dartmouth Coll., 1946. Bar: N.Y. 1951. Individual practice law, N.Y.C., 1953-71; mem. firm Augello, Deegan & Pezold, Huntington, N.Y., 1971-78; sr. mem. firm Augello, Pezold & Hirschmann, Huntington, 1978—; treas., dir. Transp. Arbitration Bd., Inc., 1978-81; chmn. accreditation com. Certified Claims Profl. Accreditation Council, Inc., Washington, 1981—; exec. dir., gen. counsel Shippers Nat. Freight Claim Council, Inc., Huntington, 1974—. Author: Freight Claims in Plain English, 1979, 82; author, lectr.: Course I - The Beginning of Freight Claims - The Bill of Lading Contract, 1979, Course II - Documenting Claims, 1980, Course III - Liability Rules and Shipping/Receiving Practices Affecting Loss, Damage and Delay, 1981, Course IV - Changes in Carrier Liability: Court Decisions, Statutes and Regulations, 1983. Served with USN, 1944-46. Named Nat. Transp. Man of Yr. Delta Nu Alpha, 1980-81. Mem. Maritime Lawyers Assn., Motor Carrier Lawyers Assn., Suffolk County Bar Assn., Assn. Interstate Commerce Commn. Practitioners, Delta Nu Alpha. Republican. Roman Catholic. Club: Indian Hills Country. Home: 76 Norwood Ave Northport NY 11768 Office: 120 Main St Huntington NY 11743 *Few things in life are more gratifying than helping others reach their full potential or just providing them with a means to advance up the corporate ladder with their heads higher than before.*

AUGENSTEIN, BRUNO W., research executive; b. Germany, Mar. 16, 1923; came to U.S., 1927, naturalized, 1935; s. Wilhelm C. and Emma (Mina) A.; m. Kathleen Greenlaw, May 30, 1950; children—Karen, Eric, Christopher. Sc.B. in Physics and Math, Brown U., 1943; M.S. in Aero, Calif. Inst. Tech., 1945. Supr. N.Am. Aviation Co., 1946-48; asst. prof. Purdue U., 1948-49; sr. scientist Rand Corp., 1949-58; chief scientist satellite programs; dir. planning Lockheed Missiles & Space Co., 1958-61; spl. asst. Office Sec. Def., 1961-65; now cons.; research adviser Inst. Def. Analyses, 1965-67; v.p. research Rand Corp., Santa Monica, Calif., 1967-71, chief scientist, 1971-72, resident cons., 1972—, sr. scientist, 1976—; cons. Nat. Acad. Sci., Bur. Budget, 1965—, Nat. Bur. Standards, 1971—, Xerad, Inc., 1972—, Dept. Navy, NSF, NASA, 1973—, OSTP, 1978—, Dept. Def., 1978—, Hi Tech Investment Mgmt., Inc., 1983; v.p. research, dir. Spectravision, Inc.; Bd. Regents Nat. Library of Medicine, HEW. Recipient Distinguished Pub. Service award Dept. Def., 1965. Mem. Am. Inst. Physics, AIAA, AAAS, IEEE, Am. Nuclear Soc., Philosophy of Sci. Assn. Club: Cosmos (Washington). Home: 1144 Tellem Dr Pacific Palisades CA 90272 Office: 1700 Main St Santa Monica CA 90406

AUGÉR, ARLEEN JOYCE, soprano; b. Los Angeles, Sept. 13, 1939; d. Everett N. and Doris (Moody) A. B.A., Calif. State U., Long Beach, 1963. Music tchr., in Los Angeles, Denver, Chgo., 1963-67; prof. Music U., Frankfurt, Germany, 1977. Coloratura and lyric soprano, Vienna State Opera, 1967-74; free lance artist, 1974—; master course of voice tng. and interpretation, Internat. Summer Acad. Mozarteum, Salzburg, Austria, 1974-77; debut at, Teatro alla Scala, Milan, Italy in, Ravel's opera L'enfant et les sortileges, 1975, Met. Opera, N.Y.C. in, Beethoven's opera Fidelio, 1978. 1st prize winner I. Viktor-Fuchs-Competition, Los Angeles, 1967; Recipient numerous record prizes. Home: 77 Oeder Weg Frankfurt/Main 1 West Germany D-6000 Office: c/o Hamlen/Landau Mgmt Inc 140 W 79th St Suite 2A New York NY 10024

AUGER, JACQUES GERALD, corporation executive; b. Montreal, Que., Can., Aug. 31, 1941; s. Gerard and Georgette A.; m. Claudette Roussel, June 13, 1964; children: Pascal, Stephane, Francois. B.B.A., U. Montreal, 1968; postgrad., Hates Etudes Commerciales, Montreal, 1969. Dir. Ministry of Transport, Ottawa, Ont., Can., 1976-77; exec. dir. Nat. Harbours Bd., Ottawa, 1977-80, v.p., 1980-83; pres. Ports Canada, Ottawa, 1983—; dir., chmn. bd. Ridley Terminals Inc., Vancouver, B.C., Can., 1981—. Roman Catholic. Clubs: Rideau, Cercle Universitaire (Ottawa). Home: 520 McConnel Rd Aylmer PQ Canada J9J 1G6 Office: Ports Canada Tower A Place de Ville 320 Queen St Ottawa ON Canada K1A 0N6

AUGHENBAUGH, NOLAN BLAINE, geological engineer, university dean; b. Akron, Ohio, July 29, 1928; s. Russell Lowell and Virginia Elena (Squires) A.; m. Barbara Alinora Hill, Feb. 17, 1959; children: Debra Jean, Lowell Doric, Amy Elena. B.S. in Civil Engring, Purdue U., 1955, Ph.D., 1963; M.S. in Geology, U. Mich., 1959. Registered profl. engr., Mo. Geologist, glaciologist, engr. IGY, Antarctica, 1956-59; instr. Purdue U., 1959-63; asst. prof. Sch. Civil Engring., 1963-66; prof. geol. engring. U. Mo., Rolla., 1966-70, chmn. dept. mining, petroleum and geol. engring., 1970-80; dean. Sch. Mineral Industry U. Alaska, 1983—; cons. engr., Rolla., 1960—. Served with USMCR, 1946-48, 50-51. Mem. AIME, Ill. Mining Inst., Internat. Soc. Rock Mechanics, Nat. Assn. Geology Tchrs., Arctic Inst. N.Am., Am. Underground Space Assn., Assn. Engring. Geologists, Rocky Mountain Coal Mining Inst., Sigma Xi, Sigma Gamma Epsilon. Home: PO Box 479 Rolla MO 65401

AUGSBURGER, MYRON SHENK, educator, minister Mennonite Ch.; b. Elida, Ohio, Aug. 20, 1928; s. Clarence A. and Estella (Shenk) A.; m. Esther Kniss, Nov. 28, 1950; children—John Myron, Michael David, Marcia Louise. A.B., Eastern Mennonite Coll., 1955, Th.B., 1958; B.D., Goshen Coll. Bibl. Sem., 1959; Th.M., Union Theol. Sem., 1961, Th.D., 1964; LL.D., Houghton Coll. and Alderson-Broaddus, 1972. Ordained to ministry Mennonite Ch., 1951; pastor chs., Sarasota, Fla., 1951-53; pastor students Eastern Mennonite Coll., Harrisonburg, Va., 1953-55, asst. prof. theology, 1962-65, pres., prof. theology, 1965-80; adj. prof. theology Eastern Mennonite Sem., Harrisburg, Va., also Asso. Mennonite Sems., Elkhart, Ind.; dir., pastor Washington Community Fellowship, 1981—; moderator Gen. Assembly Mennonite Ch., 1983—; Bd. dirs. Presbyn. Ministers' Fund, Phila.; Mem. Christian Leadership Found., Landsville, Pa., Outreach Ministries, York, Pa.; adv. bd. Christian Coll. Calition. Author: Called to Maturity, 1963, Quench Not the Spirit, 1964, Plus Living, 1965, Invitation to Discipleship, 1966, Principles of Biblical Interpretation, 1966, Pilgrim Aflame, 1967, Faith for A Secular World, 1968, the Broken Chalice, 1971, The Expanded Life, 1972, Walking in the Resurrection, 1976, Faithful Unto Death, 1978, Practicing the Presence of the Spirit 1981, Communicators Commentary, Matthew, 1981, Evangelism as Discipling, 1982. Home: 229 9th St NE Washington DC 20002 Office: 9th and Maryland Ave NE Washington DC 20013

AUGUST, ROBERT OLIN, journalist; b. Ashtabula, Ohio, Oct. 6, 1921; s. Frank and Lillian (Olin) A.; m. Marilynn Eccles, Sept. 23, 1943; 1 dau., Allson. B.A., Coll. Wooster, 1943. With Cleve. Press, 1946-82, staff sports dept., 1950—, covered profl. football, 1953-58, exec. sports editor, 1957-58, sports editor, 1958-64, sports columnist, 1964-67, sports columnist, sports editor, 1967-79, gen. columnist, asst. to editor, 1979-81, assoc. editor, 1981-82; sports editor Lake County News-Herald, 1982—; sports columnist 4 Horvitz newspapers, 1982—; nationally syndicated columnist Wiser Side of 60 United Press Syndicate, 1982—. Served from ensign to lt. (j.g.) USNR, 1943-46. Recipient Cleve. Newspaper Guild awards, 1958, 61, 81. Mem. Sigma Delta Chi. Home: 912 Trevitt Circle North Euclid OH 44143 Office: Cleve Press Plaza Cleveland OH 44114

AUGUSTINE, NORMAN RALPH, industrial executive; b. Denver, July 27, 1935; s. Ralph Harvey and Freda Irene (Immenga) A.; m. Margareta Engman, Jan. 20, 1962; children: Gregory Eugen, René Irene. B.S.E. magna cum laude, Princeton U., 1957, M.S., 1959; postgrad., Columbia U., UCLA, U. So. Calif. Research asst. Princeton U., 1957-58; program mgr., chief engr. Douglas Aircraft Co., Inc., Santa Monica, Calif., 1958-65; asst. dir. def. research and engring. U.S. Govt., Office of Sec. Def., Washington, 1965-70; v.p. advanced systems Missiles and Space Co., LTV Aerospace Corp., Dallas, 1970-73; asst. sec. army The Pentagon, Washington, 1973-75, undersec. army, 1975-77; v.p. ops. Martin Marietta Aerospace Corp., Bethesda, Md., 1977-82; pres. Martin Marietta Denver Aerospace Co., 1982—; dir. Internat. Laser Systems, Inc., Orlando, Fla., Colo. Nat. Bank; mem. corp. bd. C.S. Draper Lab.; cons. Office of Sec. Def., 1971—, Exec. Office of Pres., 1971-73, Dept. Army, 1971-73, Dept. Air Force, 1978—, Dept. Navy, 1979—; mem. USAF Sci. Adv. Bd.; chmn. Def. Sci. Bd.; adv. bd. Soc. Logistics Engrs.; mem. NATO Group Experts on Air Def., 1966-70, NASA Research and Tech. Adv. Council, 1973-75; chmn. adv. bd. dept. aeromech. engring. Princeton U., 1975-83; chmn. bd. visitors procurement and acquisition program Am. U., 1977-82; bd. advisors Center for Advancement of Procurement, Fla. State U. Author: Augustine's Laws; Mem. adv. bd.: Jour. of Def. Research, 1970—; asso. editor: Def. System Mgmt. Rev, 1977-82; editorial bd.: Astronautics & Aeros; contbr. articles to profl. jours. Fund raiser YMCA, Arlington, Tex., 1971-72; chmn. nat. program evaluation com. Boy Scouts Am., 1974-79; mem. Immanuel Presbyterian Ch., McLean, Va. Recipient Meritorious Service medal Dept. of Def., 1970; Distinguished Service medal Dept. Army, 1975; Distinguished Civilian Service medal Dept. Def., 1975; Bronze Palm, 1977. Fellow Am. Astron. Soc.; fellow AIAA (v.p. pub. policy 1978-82, dir. 1978—, pres. 1983—); mem. Am. Helicopter Soc. (dir. 1974-75), Assn. U.S. Army (pres. 1980—), Phi Beta Kappa, Sigma Xi, Tau Beta Pi. Home: 2102 Green Oaks Ln Littleton CO 80121 Office: PO Box 179 Denver CO 80201

AUGUSTYN, FRANK JOSEPH, dancer; b. Hamilton, Ont., Can., Jan. 27, 1953; s. Walter and Elizabeth (Schmider) A. Student, Nat. Ballet Sch., 1965-70; LL.D. (hon.), York U., 1977, McMaster U., 1979. Mem., Corps de Ballet, Nat. Ballet Co. of Can., Toronto, 1970-71; soloist, 1971-72; prin., 1972—; co-founder, Ballet Revue; prin. dancer, Berlin Opera Ballet, 1980-81; has performed in, Can., U.S., London Festival Ballet, Germany, London Festival Ballet, France, London Festival Ballet, Holland, London Festival Ballet, Monaco, London Festival Ballet, Belgium, London Festival Ballet, USSR, London Festival Ballet, Italy, London Festival Ballet, Swtizerland, London Festival Ballet, Cuba; TV appearances include Giselle, CBC, 1975, La Fille Mal Gardé, CBC, 1979, Pleasure of Your Company, Magic Show; Author: Kain-Augustyn, 1977. Winner best couple award 2d Internat. Ballet Competition, Moscow, 1973; decorated Order of Can. Office: 157 King St E Toronto ON M5C 1C9 Canada *

AULD, DAVID VINSON, civil engineer; b. Washington, Dec. 18, 1907; s. Robert Edgar and Elizabeth (Vinson) A.; m. Saranell Wilson, Nov. 21, 1931; 1 son, David. B.C.E., Princeton U., 1929. Registered profl. engr., D.C., Md.; Diplomate Am. Acad. Environ. Engrs. With Govt. D.C., 1929-64, supt., chief engr. water div., 1946-53, dir. dept. san. engring., 1953-64; pvt. practice engring., 1965-77; mem. Interstate Commn. Potomac River Basin, 1953-64, chmn., 1959-61, Washington Sanitation Conf., 1947-48. Chmn. Talbot County Historic Dist. Commn., 1975-81. Flotilla comdr. USCG Aux., 1967. Recipient Merit citation for outstanding career pub. service Nat. Civil Service League, 1957, Career Service award, 1962. Fellow ASCE; mem. Water Pollution Control Fedn. (life), Am. Water Works Assn. (life, dir. 1954-57, George Warren Fuller award 1962), Am. Pub. Works Assn. (Pub. Works Man of Year award 1961), Washington Soc. Engrs. (dir. 1959-60, award 1962), Princeton Engring. Assn., Hist. Soc. Talbot County (pres. 1971-74, 79-80). Episcopalian. Clubs: Cosmos, City Tavern (Washington); Chesapeake Bay Yacht (gov. 1973-75). Home: Doncaster Box 418 Route 5 Easton MD 21601

AULD, FRANK, psychologist, educator; b. Denver, Aug. 9, 1923; s. Benjamin Franklin and Marion Leland (Evans) A.; m. Elinor James, June 29, 1946; children—Mary, Robert, Margaret. A.B., Drew U., 1946; M.A., Yale U., 1948, Ph.D., 1950. Diplomate: certified psychologist, Mich., Conn., Ont. Instr. psychology Yale U., New Haven, 1950-52, asst. prof., 1952-59; asso. prof. Wayne State U., Detroit, 1959-61, prof., 1961-67, dir. clin. psychology tng. program, 1960-66; prof. U. Detroit, 1967-70, dir. clin. psychol. clinic, 1967-69; prof. U. Windsor, Ont., Can., 1970—; cons. in field. Author: Steps in Psychotherapy, 1953, Scoring Human Motives, 1959; contbr. articles to profl. jours. Chmn. Dearborn (Mich.) Community Council, 1962; mem. adv. com. on coll. work Episcopal Diocese Mich., 1962-71. Recipient Alumni Achievement award Drew U., 1965. Fellow Am. Psychol. Assn. (evaluation com. 1961-66); mem. Can. Assn. U. Tchrs., Can., Mich. psychol. assns., Ont. Psychol. Assn. (edn. and tng. bd. 1976—), Conn. State Psychol. Soc. (pres. 1958), Soc. Psychotherapy Research, Econ. Club Detroit, Sigma Xi. Home: 1340 Pierce St Birmingham MI 48009 Office: Dept Psychology U Windsor Windsor ON N9B 3P4 Canada

AULD, ISABEL GEORGE, university official; b. Winnipeg, Man., Can., Sept. 21, 1917; d. Charles George and Maggie (Davidson) Hutcheson; m. W. Murray Auld, Sept. 21, 1942; children: Nancy Birt, Hedley, Catherine. B.A., U. Sask., 1938, M.A., 1940, LL.D., 1979. Cytogenetic researcher Canadian Dept. Agr., 1941-42; mem. nat. exec. Consumers Assn. Can., 1963-67; mem. bd. Middlechurch Home Winnipeg, Family Bur. Winnipeg, 1968-76; bd. govs. U. Man., 1968-73, 77—, chancellor, 1977—; Bd. dirs. Klinic, Inc., Winnipeg, 1976-80, Social Planning Council Winnipeg, 1975—, Can. World Youth, Montreal, 1979—, Winnipeg Health Scis. Centre, 1980—, Mount Carmel Clinic, 1977-79. Recipient Centennial medal, 1967; Queen Elizabeth Silver Jubilee medal, 1977; Woman of Year award YWCA, 1978. Clubs: Women's Canadian, Univ. Women's. Office: U Man 204 Adminstrn Bldg Winnipeg MB R3T 2N2 Canada

AULT, CHARLES ROLLIN, lawyer; b. Cleve., Aug. 2, 1923; s. Charles Maurice and LoRena Minnie (Wiswell) A.; m. Janice Mary McLeod, Apr. 9, 1949; children: Charles R., Marcia A., Jonathan M. Student, Brown U., 1941-43; A.B. in Polit. Sci., Case Western Res. U., 1948, J.D., 1951. Bar: Ohio 1951. Assoc. Falsgraf, Reidy, Shoup & Ault, Cleve., 1951-58, ptnr., 1959-71, Baker & Holstetler, 1971—; dir., officer various privately held corps.; mem. corp. bd. Dyke Coll., 1979—; vis. com. Case Western Res. U., Cleve., 1976-78. Contbr. articles to profl. jours. Pres. Citizens League of Cleve., 1972; v.p., life trustee YMCA, Cleve., 1971—; pres., dir. Eastern Cleve. Rotary, 1968; v.p., trustee Forest Hill Ch. Housing Corp., Cleve., 1971-73. Served to capt. U.S. Army, 1941-45, 51-53. Recipient Soc. Benchers Case Western Res. U., 1981; John Hay fellow, 1941-42. Fellow ABA; mem. Ohio Bar Assn., Bar Assn. Greater Cleve. Republican. Presbyterian. Clubs: Cleve. Skating, Cheshire Cheese, Waldon Country. Home: 624-7 Fairington Oval Aurora IL 44202 Office: 3200 National City Ctr Cleveland OH 44114 *Z Honor your heritage whatever it may be, for it became yours without asking and can't be changed. Strive to enhance the heritage of those yet unborn, whatever your limitation. Perserve and even most limitations can be overcome. Appreciate your material successes with humility, for they can be taken from you, but treasure courage, integrity, honesty, humar, love, diligence, dependability, and a good name, for no one can steal them. . . only you can give them away.*

AULT, JAMES MASE, clergyman; b. Sayre, Pa., Aug. 24, 1918; s. Tracey Everett and Bessie (Mase) A.; m. Dorothy Mae Barnhart, Dec. 22, 1943; children: James Mase, Kathryn Louise, Elizabeth Ann, Christopher John (dec.). A.B. magna cum laude, Colgate U., 1949, B.D., Union Theol. Sem., N.Y.C., 1952, S.T.M., 1964; postgrad., St. Andrews U., Scotland, 1966; D.D., Am. U., Washington, 1968; LL.D., Albright Coll., 1973, Ohio Wesleyan U., 1973. Tool engr. Ingersoll-Rand Co., 1936-42; ordained to ministry Methodist Ch., 1951; pastor Meth. Ch., Preston, N.Y., 1946-49, Carlton Hill Meth. Ch., East Rutherford, N.J., 1951-53, Meth. Ch., Leonia, N.J., 1953-58, First Meth. Ch., Pittsfield, Mass., 1958-61; dean students, asso. prof.

practical theology Union Theol. Sem., N.Y.C., 1961-64, prof. practical theology, dir. field edn., 1964-68; dean, prof. pastoral theology Theol. Sch., Drew U., Madison, N.J., 1968-72; bishop Phila. area United Meth. Ch., 1972-80, bishop Pitts. area, 1980—, sec. council of bishops, 1980—; Mem. governing bd. Nat. Council Chs. of Christ in U.S.A.; mem. central com. World Council of Chs., 1981—; mem. exec. com. World Meth. Council, 1981—. Author: Responsible Adults for Tomorrow's World, 1962. Served to 1st lt. AUS, 1942-46. Faculty fellow Am. Assn. Theol. Schs. (1965-66); Mem. AAUP, Acad. Polit. and Social Sci., Phi Beta Kappa. Home: 1230 Greystone Dr Upper Saint Clair PA 15241 Office: 223 4th Ave Pittsburgh PA 15222

AULT, SAMUEL GORDON KEYES, foods corporation executive; b. Winchester, Ont., Can., Feb. 2, 1916; s. Jack Wellesley and Eliza Jane (Keyes) A.; m. Betty Margaret, June 20, 1942; children: Jane Ault Campbell, Stephen, Patricia Ault Olsen. B.S.A., U. Toronto. Pres. Dundas Cheese Co. Ltd., Beurrerie Lafrenieree Ltee., Laiterie Dalliare Ltee., Dominion Dry Milk; v.p. Ogilvie Mills; now chmn. Ault Foods Ltd., Winchester, Ont., Can.; pres. Nat. Dairy Council, Ont. Dairy Council.; Adv. bd. Can. Dairy Commn. Chmn. N. Dundas Sch. Bd.; v.p. St. Lawrence Parks Commn.; pres. Conservative Assn. Dundas. Served to capt. Army of Can., 1941-45. Mentioned in dispatches. Clubs: Laurentian, Ottawa Hunt, Morrisburg Golf, Masons (Winchester). Office: 490 Gordon Winchester ON K0C 2K0 Canada

AUMONT, JEAN-PIERRE, actor, author; b. Paris, Jan. 5, 1911; m. Maria Montez, July 13, 1943 (dec. Sept. 1951); 1 dau., Maria-Christina; m. Marisa Pavan, Mar. 27, 1956; children—Jean-Claude, Patrick. Author: plays L'Ile Heureuse, 1951, Un Beau Dimanche, 1952, Ange le Bienheureux, 1956, Farfada, 1957, Lucy Crown, 1958; autobiography Sun and Shadow, 1978; Motion pictures include Assignment in Brittany, 1943, The Cross of Lorraine, 1943, Heartbeat, 1945, Sheherazade, 1946, Atlantis, 1947, Lilli, 1952, Charge of Lancers, 1954, Hilda Crane, 1956, The Seventh Sin, 1957, John Paul Jones, 1958, The Enemy General, 1959, The Blonde From Buenos Aires, 1960, The Devil at 4 O'Clock, 1960, The Horse Without A Head, 1962, Gigi, 1967, Blind Man's Bluff, 1967, Castle Keep, 1968, Day for Night, 1973, Mahogany, 1976, Blackout, 1978, Cat and Mouse, 1978, Two Solitudes, 1979, Something Short of Paradise, 1979; theatrical appearances include My Name is Aquilon, 1949, Heavenly Twins, 1955, Design for Living, 1948, A Second String, 1960, As You Like It, 1953, Julius Caesar, 1956, Tovarich, 1963, Incident at Vichy, 1965, The Tempest, 1967, South Pacific, 1967, Hostile Witness, 1967, There's A Girl in My Soup, 1969, Camino Real, 1970, Murderous Angels, 1971, Jacques Brel Is Alive and Well and Living in Paris, 1972, Perfect Pitch, 1974, Janus, 1975, Des Journees Entieres dans les Arbres, 1976, La guerre de Troie h'aura pas lieu, 1977, Heartbreak House, 1978, Sound of Music, 1979; TV appearances Beggerman Thief, Arms and the Man, No Time for Comedy, A Month in the Country, Hold Back the Dawn, The Imposter, The Memory of Eve Ryker, The Patty Duke Show, The Name of the Game, Crime and Punishment, The Tempest, Intermezzo, Love Boat, The French Atlantic Affair. Served with French Army, 1939-45. Decorated chevalier Legion of Honour, Croix de Guerre. Address: care Charter Mgmt 9000 Sunset Blvd Los Angeles CA 90069

AUNGST, CLARENCE WILLIAM, cancer institute administrator; b. Chgo., Oct. 8, 1926; s. Arthur St. Clair and Anna Veronica (McHugh) A.; m. Catherine Marie Deinzer, Aug. 31, 1957; children: William, Frank, Edward, Catherine, Caroline, Clair. B.A., SUNY Buffalo, 1952; M.D., SUNY-Syracuse, 1956. Diplomate: Am. Bd. Internal Medicine. Intern Buffalo Gen. Hosp., 1956-57; resident Buffalo Gen. Hosp., 1957-59, Roswell Park Meml. Inst., Buffalo, 1959-60, sr. cancer research internist, 1960-65, assoc. cancer research internist, 1965-67, cancer research internist II, 1967-71, assoc. chief cancer research internist, 1972-74, assoc. inst. dir. clin. affairs, 1974—; cons. Buffalo Gen. Hosp., 1966—; asst. research prof. exptl. pathology SUNY-Buffalo, 1972—, research assoc. prof. medicine, 1973—; research prof. Roswell Park div. Niagra U. (N.Y.), 1978—. Pres. Am. Cancer Soc., N.Y. State div., 1982-83. Served with U.S. Army, 1945-47. Fellow ACP; mem. Am. Assn. Cancer Research, Gastrointestinal Tumor Study Group, Eastern Coop. Oncology Group. Democrat. Roman Catholic. Home: 95 Oakland Pl Buffalo NY 14222 Office: Roswell Park Meml Inst 666 Elm St Buffalo NY 14263

AURAND, CHARLES HENRY, JR., university dean, music educator; b. Battle Creek, Mich., Sept. 6, 1932; s. Charles Henry and Elisabeth Dirk (Hosekstra) A.; m. Donna Mae Erb, June 19, 1954; children: Janice, Cheryl, Sandra, Charles, William. B.M., Mich. State U., 1954, M.M., 1958; Ph.D., U. Mich., 1971. Asst. prof. music Hiram Coll., Ohio, 1958-60; dean, prof. music Dana Sch. Music Youngstown State U., 1960-73; dean., prof. music Coll. Creative Arts, No. Ariz. U., Flagstaff, 1973—; chmn. Ariz. Alliance for Arts Edn., 1974-77; solo clarinetist Flagstaff Symphony; solo, chamber music and orch. musician, 1973—; fine arts cons. Miami U. of Ohio, 1982. Author: Selected Solos, Methods, 1963. Elder Presbyterian Ch., 1965; chmn. Boy Scouts Am., Coconino dist., 1974-78; bd. dirs. Ariz. Com. Arts for the Handicapped, 1982—, Flagstaff Symphony Orch., 1973—, Flagstaff Festival of Arts, 1973—. Served to 1st lt. USAF, 1955-57. Recipient award of merit Boy Scouts Am., 1977. Mem. Am. Assn. Higher Edn., Ariz. Humanities Assn., Music Educators Nat. Conf., State Adminstrs. of Music Schs. (chmn. 1971-73). Republican. Presbyterian. Lodge: Kiwanis. Home: 3251 S Little Dr Flagstaff AZ 86001 Office: College of Creative Arts No Ariz U Flagstaff AZ 86011

AURBACH, GERALD DONALD, research institute administrator; b. Cleve., Mar. 24, 1927; s. Philip S. and Lenora (Weinberg) A.; m. Hannah Leah Rose, Oct. 16, 1960; children: Elissa G., Pamela K. B.A., U. Va., 1950, M.D., 1954. Intern New Eng. Ctr. Hosp., Boston, 1954-55, resident in medicine, 1955-56, USPHS fellow, 1956-59; commd. officer USPHS, 1959—, med. dir., 1966—; research assoc. Nat. Inst. Arthritis, Metabolism and Digestive Diseases, NIH, HEW, Bethesda, Md., 1959-61, sr. investigator, 1961-64, chief sect. on mineral metabolism, 1965-73, chief metabolic diseases dir., 1973—; mem. endocrinology study sect. div. research grants NIH, 1968-70; mem. program organizing com. 3d Internat. Congress Endocrinology, sec.-treas. 4th Congress; Gordon Wilson lectr. Am. Clin. and Climatol. Assn., 1973. Assoc. editor: Endocrinology, 1968-72; vol. editor: Handbook of Physiology; editor-in-chief: Vitamins and Hormones, 1982—; contbr. articles on clin. and basic endocrine research to profl. jours. Recipient John Horsley Meml. prize U. Va., 1960, Andrew Lichtwitz prize French Nat. Inst. for Med. Research, 1968, Disting. Service award USPHS, 1969, Gairdner Internat. award, 1983. Mem. Am. Soc. Clin. Investigation (editorial com. 1971—), AAAS, AMA, Am. Fedn. Clin. Research, Am. Assn. Physicians, Endocrine Soc. (v.p. 1978-79, council 1983—), Am. Soc. Biol. Chemists, Internat. Soc. Endocrinology (exec. com.), Laurentian Hormone Conf. (v.p.), Am. Soc. Bone and Mineral Research (William F. Neuman award 1981), Internat. Conf. on Calcium Regulating Hormones, Inc. (bd. dirs.), Peripatic Club. Home: 10909 Cripple Gate Rd Potomac MD 20854 Office: Nat Inst Arthritis Metabolism and Digestive Diseases Bethesda MD 20205

AURBACH, HERBERT ALEXANDER, sociology educator; b. Cleve., Aug. 6, 1924; s. Nate and Sara (Munitz) A.; m. Rebecca Rachel Blumenfeld, Nov. 2, 1952; children—Jacquelyn Aurbach Scheidlinger, Seth Adam. B.S., Western Res. U., 1948; Ph.D., U. Ky., 1960. Asst. rural sociologist Miss. State Coll., 1954-55; asst. prof. sociology and research asso. N.C. State Coll., Raleigh, 1955-57; research dir. Pitts. Commn. Human Relations, 1957-61; research asso., asst. prof. U. Pitts., 1961-66; assoc. prof. edn. and sociology Pa. State U., 1966-70; prof. SUNY Coll. at Buffalo, 1970—; chmn. dept. sociology SUNY, 1970-74; assoc. dir. Nat. Study Am. Indian Edn., 1968-69. Author: (with Estelle Fuchs) The Status of American Indian Education, 1970; Assoc. editor: Social Problems, 1966-74; Contbr. profl. jours. Bd. dirs. Citizens Commn. Criminal Justice, Buffalo and Erie County, 1972-74, Anti-Defamation League of B'nai B'rith, Buffalo, 1971-75; co-chmn. Self-Study Task Force Bur. Jewish Edn., Greater Buffalo, 1979-80. Served with USAAF, 1942-45. Decorated Air medal with 4 clusters.; So. Fellowship Fund fellow, 1956-57. Mem. Am. Sociol. Soc., Soc. Study Social Problems (sec. 1965-69, treas. 1966-74, exec. officer 1975—). Home: 23 Millbrook Ct Amherst NY 14221 Office: Dept Sociology SUNY Coll at Buffalo Buffalo NY 14222

AURELI, GILES, educator; b. Phila., Jan. 8, 1926; s. Gaetano and Julienne (Bellenger) A.; m. Eileen Johns, Sept. 13, 1951. B.Arch., Pratt Inst., Bklyn., 1950, M.Arch., 1958. Archtl. designer numerous firms, N.Y.C. and Chgo., 1950-65; partner Aureli-Jeffe Design, White Plains, N.Y., 1965-67; project dir. Katz, Waisman, Weber, N.Y.C., 1968—, chmn. interior and indsl. design depts., 1976—; prof. indsl. design Pratt Inst., 1958—. Author: Steel in Home Building, 1964, Reducing Costs of Public Housing, 1966. Served with U.S. Army, 1943-46. Recipient Unesco Design award, 1962. Mem. Indsl. Designers Soc. Am. Office: Pratt Studios Bldg Pratt Inst 200 Willoughby Ave Brooklyn NY 11205

AURIN, ROBERT JAMES, advertising agency executive; b. St. Louis, Feb. 13, 1943; s. George Henry and Elizabeth Anastasia (Krauska) A.; m. Mary L. Martin, Mar. 1981. B.J., U. Mo., 1965. Copywriter Leo Burnett Co., Chgo., 1971-72, Young & Rubicam, Inc., 1972-73; from copywriter to v.p., creative dir. Foote, Cone & Belding, Inc., Chgo., 1973-79; exec. v.p., dir. creative services Grey-North Inc., Chgo., 1979-82; pres. Robert Aurin Assocs., Chgo., 1982—. Served to lt. USN, 1965-70; Vietnam. Mem. Chgo. Council Fgn. Relations., Art Inst. Chgo. Roman Catholic. Office: 415 Aldine St Chicago IL 60657

AURNER, ROBERT RAY, corporate executive, author; b. Adel, Iowa, Aug. 20, 1898; s. Clarence Ray and Nellie (Slayton) A.; m. Kathryn Dayton, June 16, 1921; 1 son, Robert Ray II. B.A. summa cum laude, U. Iowa, 1919, M.A., 1920, Ph.D., 1922. Dir. customer relations, new bus. The State Bank, Madison, Wis., 1925-28; research dir. Walker Co., 1925-30; established Aurner and Assos., cons. mgmt., bus. adminstrn., market distbn. and human relations, pres., exec. dir., 1938—; v.p., dir. Pacific Futures, Inc., 1962—; dir., chmn. bus adv. com. VNA Corp., 1959-62; fin. cons., dir. Carmel Savs. & Loan Assn., Calif., 1960-71; lectr. NBC Station WTMJ, 1929-30; state commr. Wis. Library Certification Bd., 1931-38; pres. Am. Bus. Communication Assn., 1939-40; mem. faculty, adminstrv. staff U. Wis., 1925-48, ranking research prof. bus. adminstrn., chmn. adminstrn. and mgmt. div., 1930-48; vis. prof. bus. mgmt. U. Pitts., 1934, 36, 39; adminstrv. cons. Internat. Cellucotton Products Co., Chgo., 1947-52; cons., dir. Communications Div., Fox River Paper Corp., Appleton, Wis., 1947-60; v.p., gen. cons., dir. Scott, Inc., Milw. and; Carmel, 1949—; cons. U.S. Naval Postgrad. Sch., Mgmt. Sch. Div., Dept. Navy, Dept. Def., 1957—, Jahn & Ollier Corp., Morris, Schenker, Roth, Inc., First Nat. Bank, Chgo., Library Research Service, New Haven, Nat. Assn. Real Estate Bds., N.Y.C., Allis-Chalmers Corp., Milw.; ltd. partner Salinas-Peninsula Investment Co., 1963-72; cons. Wis. Div. Vital Statistics, 1930-48; Dean Coll. of Commerce, Biarritz Am. U., France, U.S. Army Univ. Center No. 2, ETO, 1945-46; attached U.S. Army, USFET, I. and E. Div., Field Grade, rank of col., 1945-46; spl. lectr. Netherlands Sch. Econs., Rotterdam, 1945; U.S. State Dept. rep. Dutch-Am. Conf., The Hague, Holland, 1945; mem. nat. adv. com. Conf. Am. Small Business Orgns., 1947—; Dir. SAE Corp., Evanston, Ill., 1943-53, pres., chmn. bd., 1951-53; mem. nat. adv. counsel Atlantic Union, Inc., 1949—. Author: books, publs. relating to top mgmt. and exec. decision making, latest being Specialized Field Approach, 1963, Language Control for Business, 1965, Success Factors in Executive Development, 1967; Effective English for Colleges, 6th edit, 1980, Effective English for Business Communication, 8th edit, 1982, Effective Communication in Business with Management Emphasis, 7th edit, 1980; Contbg. editor: Am. Ency. Social Scis; Co-author, contbg. editor, American Business Practice (4 vols.). Trustee Levere Meml. Found., Chgo., 1943-53, pres., chmn. bd., 1951-53; chmn. bd., pres., chief exec. officer Carmel Found., Calif., dir., past chmn. fin. com., past chmn. meml. policy com. mem. internal trusteeship com., exec. com., 1954—; mem. bd. investment mgmt. Hazeltine Fund Calif., 1963-83; adv. gov., bd. dirs. Monterey Fund Edn., 1965—; dir., chmn. com. endowments York Sch., 1966-69; bd. dirs. Wis. div. AAA, 1936-47. Recipient Disting. Service award with gold medal Sigma Alpha Epsilon, 1967; Championship Gold Medal award N.O.L. Big Ten Univ. Competition, 1919. Fellow Am. Bus. Communication Assn. (hon.); mem. Am. Mktg. Assn., Nat. Assn. Mktg. (v.p. 1931), Smithsonian Instn. Nat. Assos., Wis. Acad. Scis., Arts and Letters, State Hist. Soc. Iowa, Phi Beta Kappa, Delta Sigma Rho, Alpha Kappa Psi (vice chmn. com. profl. programs, exec. group 1955—), Sigma Alpha Epsilon (supreme council 1943-53, nat. pres. 1951-53). Clubs: Continental (Chgo.); Highlands, Decemvir, Convivium (Monterey Peninsula); Statesman's (Los Angeles); The Group (Pebble Beach, Calif.). Home: San Antonio and Inspiration Aves Carmel Point PO Box 3434 Carmel-by-the Sea CA 93921 Office: PO Box 3434 Carmel CA 93921 *Hold forever in trust the advantages you have enjoyed; and to the peak of your powers, let it be your mandated obligation to pass these advantages on to all who come within your sphere of influence.*

AUSBY, ELLSWORTH AUGUSTUS, artist, educator; b. Portsmouth, Va., Apr. 5, 1942; s. Raymond Robert and Helen Mae (Hodges) A.; m. Lorraine Eskeles, June 15, 1966 (dec.); children: Amber R., Andra F., Dawn M.; m. Jamillyh Mae Jennings, May 1, 1972; 1 child, Kalif S. B.F.A., Sch. Visual Arts, N.Y.C.; postgrad., Pratt Inst., N.Y.C. Instr. painting The Sch. Visual Arts, 1976—; resident artist Cultural Council Found., N.Y.C., 1980-82. Author: Some American History, 1971; designer cover and inside drawings: Black Review Number 2, 1972; designer cover: Tuesdays and Every Other Thursday Off, A Domestic Rap, 1972. CETA grantee, 1978; N.Y. State Council Arts fellow, 1980. Democrat. Islamic. Home: 342 Flushing Ave Brooklyn NY 11205 Office: PO Box 15 Brooklyn NY 11211

AUSFAHL, WILLIAM FRIEND, household products company executive; b. San Francisco, Apr. 20, 1940; s. Robert Hugh and Doris Jane (Friend) A.; m. Trudy Lynn Wierman, June 23, 1962; children: Thomas, Andrew, Matthew. A.B. in Econs., U. Calif., Berkeley, 1961; M.B.A., Stanford U., 1963. Asst. to dean Stanford U. Grad. Sch. Bus., 1963-64; with Cutter Labs., Inc., 1964-82, treas., dir. fin., Emeryville, Calif., 1973-77, v.p. fin., mem. ops. com., 1977-82; sr. v.p. fin., mem. ops. com. Miles Labs., Elkhart, Ind., 1979-82; group v.p., chief fin. officer Clorox Co., Oakland, Calif., 1982—. Active local YMCA Indian Guides, Cub Scouts, home owners assn., youth sports. Mem. Fin. Execs. Inst. Republican. Club: Moraga Country. Office: 1221 Broadway Oakland CA 94612

AUSMAN, ROBERT K., surgeon, research executive; b. Milw., Jan. 31, 1933; s. Donald Charles and Mildred (Shafrin) A.; m. Alice Holmes, May 21, 1969. Ed., Kenyon Coll., 1953; M.D., Marquette U., 1957. Damon Runyon cancer fellow U. Minn., 1958-61; dir. Health Research Inc. Roswell Park Meml. Inst., 1961-69; dep. dir. Fla. Regional Med. Assn., 1969-70; v.p. clin. research Baxter Travenol Labs., 1970-82, pres. advanced devel. group, 1982—; clin. prof. surgery Med. Coll. Wis., 1972—. Named Outstanding Young Man in N.Y. Buffalo Evening News, 1966, Citizen of Year, 1967. Mem. Am. Soc. Clin. Oncology, Am. Assn. Cancer Research. Club: Masons. Home: Box 3538 RFD Long Grove IL 60047 Office: One Baxter Pkwy Deerfield IL 60015

AUSNEHMER, FRED CHARLES, manufacturing company executive; b. Youngstown, Ohio, Sept. 22, 1940; s. Earl George and Gelorma Ann (Tito) A.; m. Grace Ellen Reubendale, June 29, 1963; children: Lynne Ellen, Douglas Earl, Jeffrey Joseph. B.A. in Econs, Colgate U., 1962. With Gen. Electric Co. (various locations), 1962-78; v.p. fin. Mueller Co., Decatur, Ill., 1979, now v.p. ops. Bd. dirs. United Way, Decatur. Lutheran. Clubs: Decatur, South Side Country. Home: 2664 Forrest Green Dr Decatur IL 62521 Office: 500 W Eldorado St Decatur IL 62525

AUST, JOE BRADLEY, surgeon, educator; b. Buffalo, Sept. 8, 1926; s. Joe Bradley and Edith (Derby) A.; m. Constance Ann MacMullin, June 18, 1949; children—Jay Bradley, Bonnie Jean, Barbara Ann, Linda Lee, Mary Louise, Tracey Roberta. M.D., U. Buffalo, 1949; M.S. in Physiology, U. Minn., 1957; Ph.D. in Surgery, U. Minn., 1958. Diplomate: Am. Bd. Surgery, Am. Bd. Thoracic Surgery. Intern U. Minn. Hosps., 1949-50, resident, 1950-58; scholar Am. Cancer Soc. U. Minn., 1957-62, mem. faculty, 1957-66, prof. surgery, 1964-66; prof. surgery, chmn. dept. U. Tex. Med. Sch. at San Antonio, 1966—; cons. Minn. State Prison, 1958-62, Anoka State Hosp., 1962-65, Brooke Army Med. Hosp., 1967—, Wilford Hall USAF Hosp., 1967—, Audie Murphy Meml. VA Hosp., 1973—; nat. cons. to surgeon gen. USAF, Washington, 1975-78. Served with M.C. USNR, 1950-52. Fellow A.C.S.; mem. Am., Western, So., Central surg. assns., Soc. Univ. Surgeons, Soc. Head and Neck Surgeons, Am. Assn. Cancer Research, Am. Soc. Exptl. Pathologists, San Antonio, Allen O. Whipple, Tex. surg. socs., Am. Assn. for Cancer Edn., Halsted Soc., Soc. Clin. Oncology, Transplantation Soc., Soc. Exptl. Biology and Medicine, Sigma Xi, Alpha Omega Alpha, Phi Chi. Spl. research cancer immunity, regional cancer chemotherapy, shock, homotransplantation. Home: 902 Serenade Dr San Antonio TX 78213

AUSTAD, MARK EVANS, ambassador; b. Ogden, Utah, Apr. 1, 1917; s. Jacob and Signe (Anderson) A.; m. Lola Brown, Aug. 20, 1941; children: Nancy Roth, Penny Davis, Wendy Durfee. Student, Weber State Coll., D.Humanities hon., 1973. Broadcast personality CBS, WTOP, Washington, 1950-60, U.P. Metromedia, Inc., Washington and N.Y.C., 1960-73; U.S. rep. Gen. Assembly, UN, N.Y.C., 1973; ambassador to Finland, Helsinki, 1974-77, now ambassador to Norway, Oslo; lectr. Nat. Geog. Soc., Washington, 1960—. Producer: full length travel film Visit with Albert Schweitzer, Soviet Union, Machu Piccu to Sao Paulo, U.S. Nat. Parks, others. Chmn. Washington Cherry Blossom Festival, 1964-65, Inaugural balls, 1968, 72. Decorated Order of White Rose, Finland; named Outstanding Citizen State of Wash. Clubs: Burning Tree, Paradise Valley, Bald Peak, Broadcast Pioneers. Lodge: Rotary. Address: Am Embassy 6641 N Tatum Oslo Norway

AUSTELL, EDWARD CALLAWAY, banker; b. Spartanburg, S.C., Aug. 9, 1937; s. Edward and Frances Roberta (Glenn) A.; m. Louise Arnold Zimmerman, May 14, 1966; children: Frances Barrett, Elizabeth Callaway. A.B., Davidson Coll., 1959; M.B.A., U.N.C., 1960; postgrad., Nat. Trust Sch. Northwestern U., 1968. Vice pres. trust dept. First Nat. Bank S.C., 1964-71; sr. v.p. trust dept. Ga. R.R. Bank & Trust Co., Augusta, 1971—; dir. Ga.-Carolina Warehouse & Compress, Inc., Augusta; Instr. Am. Inst. Banking; past pres. Augusta Estate Planning Council. Trustee Augusta Symphony League, Augusta Opera Assn.; bd. dirs., exec. com. Met. YMCA; past pres. Richland County Hist. Soc.; trustee Historic Augusta; mem. exec. com. Univ. Health Care Found.; past pres. YM-YWCA Property Holding Co.; trustee So. Trust Sch., Birmingham, Ala.; treas., trustee Gertrude Herbert Inst. Art. Served with AUS, 1960-62. Mem. Atlanta Soc. Financial Analysts, Ga. Bankers Assn. (past pres.), Beta Theta Pi. Elder Presbyterian Ch. Clubs: Pinnacle, Augusta Country (Augusta); Tarantella (Columbia, S.C.). Home: 481 staffordshire drive winston-salem nc 27104 Office: p o box 3099 winston-salem nc 27102

AUSTELL, ROBERT RHETT, JR., executive search consultant; b. Middletown, N.Y., May 7, 1925; s. Robert Rhett and Mary Van Etten (Stivers) A.; m. Madeleine Pohlmann, Sept. 27, 1947; children—Elizabeth, Robert Rhett III, Sarah. B.A., Williams Coll., 1948; M.B.A., Harvard U., 1950. With Time, Inc., 1950-76, v.p., 1965-69; gen. mgr. Time Mag., 1960-64; pub. Time-Life Books, 1964-69, group v.p., 1969-75; pres. Am. Heritage Pub. Co., Inc., 1976-78; partner Ward Howell Internat., Inc., 1978—. Trustee Hotchkiss Sch., 1967-80; trustee N.Y. Pub. Library, 1973-82, vice chmn., 1977-79. Served with inf. AUS, World War 11. Mem. Williams Coll. Soc. Alumni (pres.), Phi Beta Kappa. Clubs: Century Assn., Williams, Harvard (N.Y.C.); Sleepy Hollow (Scarborough, N.Y.). Home: 47 Quinn Rd Briarcliff Manor NY 10510 Office: 99 Park Ave New York NY 10016

AUSTEN, K(ARL) FRANK, physician; b. Akron, Ohio, Mar. 14, 1928; s. Karl and Bertle (Jehle) A.; m. Joycelyn Chapman, Apr. 11, 1959; children: Leslie Marie, Karla Ann, Timothy Frank, Jonathan Arthur. A.B., Amherst Coll., 1950; M.D., Harvard U., 1954. Intern in medicine Mass. Gen. Hosp., 1954-55, asst. resident, 1955-56, sr. resident, 1958-59, chief resident, 1961, asst. in medicine, 1962-63, asst. physician, 1963-66, chief pulmonary unit, 1964-66, also cons. in medicine; practice medicine, specializing in internal medicine, allergy and immunology, Boston, 1962—; USPHS postdoctoral research fellow Nat. Inst. Med. Research, Mill Hill, London, 1959-61; asst. in medicine Harvard Med. Sch., 1960-1961, instr., 1961-62, asso. in medicine, 1962-64, asst. prof., 1965-66, asso. prof., 1966-68, prof., 1969-72, Theodore B. Bayles prof., 1972—; physician-in-chief Robert B. Brigham Hosp., 1966—; physician Peter Bent Brigham Hosp., 1966—; chmn. dept. rheumatology and immunology Brigham and Women's Hosp., 1980—; mem. fellowship subcom. Arthritis Found., 1968-71, chmn., 1971; mem. council Infectious Disease Soc. Am., 1969-71; mem. arthritis tng. grants com. Nat. Inst. Arthritis and Metabolic Diseases, NIH, 1970-73; mem. directing group, task force on immunology and disease Nat. Inst. Allergy and Infectious Diseases, 1972-73; bd. dirs. Arthritis Found., 1972—, mem. manpower study com., 1972-73, chmn. research com., 1972—, Med. Found., Inc., 1972—; mem. Am. Bd. Allergy and Immunology, 1973-78, Nat. Commn. on Arthritis and Related Musculoskeletal Diseases, 1975-76, Allergy and Immunology Research Commn., 1975—, chmn., 1976-79. Mem. editorial bd.: Arthritis and Rheumatism, 1968—, Proc. of Transplantation Soc, 1968—, Jour. Infectious Diseases, Jour. Exptl. Medicine, 1971—, Immunol. Communications, 1972—, Clin. Immunology and Immunopathology, 1972—, Proc. of Nat. Acad. Scis, 1978—, Clin. and Exptl. Immunology, 1978—, Immunopharmacology, 1979—, Receptors and Recognition, 1980—, Rheumatology Internat, 1980—, Clin. Immunology Revs, 1981—; contbr. articles to profl. jours. Trustee Amherst Coll., 1981—. Served to capt., M.C. U.S. Army, 1956-58. Mem. Nat. Acad. Scis. (chmn. sect. on med. microbiology and immunology 1983—), Am. Soc. Pharm. and Exptl. Therapeutics, Am.

Soc. Exptl. Pathology, Am. Assn. Immunologists (pres. 1977-78), Brit. Soc. Immunology, Am. Soc. Clin. Investigation, Am. Rheumatism Assn., A.C.P., Transplantation Soc., Am. Acad. Arts and Scis., Assn. Am. Physicians (recorder 1978—), Am. Acad. Allergy (exec. com. 1970-72, sec. 1977-80, pres. 1981), Interurban Clin. Club, Fedn. Am. Soc. Exptl. Biology (dir. 1977—). Home: 34 Bradford Rd Wellesley Hills MA 02181 Office: Brigham and Women's Hosp 75 Francis St Boston MA 02115 also 250 Longwood Ave Boston MA 02115

AUSTEN, W(ILLIAM) GERALD, surgeon, educator; b. Akron, Ohio, Jan. 20, 1930; s. Karl A. and Bertl (Jehle) A.; m. Patricia Ramsdell, Jan. 28, 1961; children: Karl Ramsdell, William Gerald, Jr., Christopher Marshall, Elizabeth Patricia. B.S., MIT, 1951; M.D., Harvard U., 1955. Intern, then resident surgery Mass. Gen. Hosp., Boston, 1955-60, chief of surgery, 1969—; Edward D. Churchill prof. surgery Harvard Med. Sch., 1974—; mem. surgery tng. com. NIH, 1965-68, mem. surgery study sect., 1968-72; mem. heart and lung program project com. Nat. Heart and Lung Inst., Bethesda, Md., 1973-76. Contbr. articles to med. jours. Mem. corp. MIT, 1972—. Served as surgeon USPHS, 1961-62. Markle scholar, 1963-68. Fellow Am. Acad. Arts and Scis.; mem. Soc. Univ. Surgeons (sec. 1967-70, pres. 1972-73), Inst. Medicine of Nat. Acad. Scis., Am. Surg. Assn. (sec. 1979—), Am. Heart Assn. (pres. 1977-78), Mass. Heart Assn. (pres. 1972-74), New Eng. Cardiovascular Soc. (pres. 1972-73). Home: 163 Wellesley St Weston MA 02193 Office: Mass Gen Hosp Boston MA 02114

AUSTERLITZ, ROBERT PAUL, educator; b. Bucharest, Rumania, Dec. 13, 1923; came to U.S., 1938, naturalized, 1946; s. Otto and Rose (Zellenka) A.; m. Sylvi Nevanlinna, Mar. 21, 1953 (dec. Jan. 28, 1981); children—Monica, Paul. A.B., New Sch. Social Research, 1950; M.A., Columbia U., 1950, Ph.D., 1955; student, Japan, 1953-54, 56-58. Mem. faculty Columbia U., N.Y.C., 1958—, prof. linguistics and Uralic studies, 1965—, chmn. dept. linguistics, 1965-68; vis. faculty mem. Linguistic Inst., U. Wash., Seattle, summers 1962-63; vis. asso. prof. Yale U., 1964-65; vis. prof. U. Calif. at Berkeley, 1969, U. Cologne, Ger., 1977, U. Hawaii, 1979; cons. map lang. families Eurasia Smithsonian Instn., 1967. Author: Ob-Ugric Metrics, 1958; Co-editor: Jour. Word, 1960-65, Readings in Linguisitics II, 1966; editor: The Scope of American Linguistics, 1975. Served with AUS, 1943-45. Decorated knight 1st class Order Lion Finland; sr. fellow Nat. Endowment for Humanities, 1971-72. Mem. Linguistic Soc. Am. (life), Soc. Finno-Ougrienne (corr.), Kalevala-Soc. (corr.), Am. Oriental Soc. (pres. 1981-82), Linguistic Soc. Paris. Address: 404 Philosophy Hall Columbia Univ New York NY 10027

AUSTERN, HERMAN THOMAS, lawyer; b. N.Y.C., Sept. 19, 1905; s. Lester and Gertrude (Phillips) A.; m. Esther Kramer, Oct. 16, 1934; children—Helen Theresa (Mrs. Earl M. Colson), David Thomas. B.S., N.Y. U., 1926; LL.B. magna cum laude (Langdell fellow), Harvard U., 1929. Bar: N.Y. bar 1931. Legal sec. to U.S. Circuit Judge Julian W. Mack, 1929, Justice Louis D. Brandeis, 1930; lectr. bus. law N.Y. U., 1947-48, adj. prof. law, 1957—; lectr. Harvard Law Sch., 1968; practiced in, Washington, 1931—; partner firm Covington & Burling, 1936—; chief counsel Nat. Canners Assn., 1942—; dir. Ludlow Corp., Boston, 1947-78; mem. Patent Adv. Panel AEC, 1949-56; adv. council Food and Drug Law Inst., 1949—; mem. adv. bd. Regulatory Toxicology and Pharmacology. Chmn. editorial adv. bd.: Food Drug Cosmetic Law Jour; mem. adv. bd.: Jour. of Reprints for Antitrust Law and Econs; Contbr. articles to profl. jours. Mem. ABA (council antitrust sect. 1959-62, chmn. 1963-64, adv. bd. antitrust and trade regulation report 1970—, chmn. com. food standards, banking, comml. law sect.), N.Y. State Bar Assn. (chmn. FTC com., antitrust law sect.), D.C. Bar Assn., AAAS, Phi Beta Kappa, Alpha Lambda Phi, Delta Kappa Delta. Clubs: Metropolitan, Cosmos, Harvard. Home: 4200 Massachusetts Ave NW Washington DC 20016 Office: 1201 Pennsylvania Ave Washington DC 20044

AUSTILL, ALLEN, university dean; b. Newton, Mass., June 22, 1927; s. William E. and Anna (Pifer) A.; m. Joan Mildred Sellery, June 4, 1950; children: Randolph Allen, Christopher Scott, Lara Anne. B.A., U. Chgo., 1948, M.A., 1951. Research asso. Council State Govts., Chgo., 1951-52; mem. faculty, dir. admissions and placement St. Johns Coll., 1953-55; dir. student housing U. Chgo., 1955-57; tchr., dean students SUNY-Stony Brook, 1957-61; cons. Ford Found., Middle East, Amman, Jordan, 1962; mem. faculty, asso. dean New Sch. Social Research, 1962-64, dean, 1964-79, v.p. acad. affairs and exec. dean, 1979-82, dean, 1982—; cons. title I Higher Edn. Act, State N.Y.; mem. council academic fellows Shimer Coll., 1971—; mem. N.Y. Regents Adv. Task Force for Adult Edn., 1972—, chmn., 1976-77. Author: (with others) Higher Education in the Forty-Eight States, 1952; Summary of State Legislation and Elections, 1953. Pres. Friends of Cresskill Library, 1969-71; mem. vis. com. continuing edn. Harvard U., 1977-83. Served with AUS, 1945-46. Home: 1 Lambs Ln Cresskill NJ 07626 Office: 66 W 12th St New York NY 10011

AUSTIN, ALBERT ADOLPHUS, manufacturing company executive; b. Boston, Sept. 29, 1924; s. John J. A.; m. Elizabeth Bovee Driscoll, June 7, 1952; children: Albert A., Greg, Stacy, Ted, Ken. B.S., Yale U., 1948; M.B.A., Harvard U., 1951. With Container Corp. Am., Chgo., 1952—, sr. v.p. corporate devel., 1977—, also dir., 1977—. Served with USN, 1943-46. Clubs: Owentsia, Midday. Home: 830 Lane Lorraine Lake Forest IL 60045 Office: Container Corp Am 1 First Nat Plaza Chicago IL 60603

AUSTIN, ARTHUR DONALD, II, lawyer, educator; b. Staunton, Va., Dec. 2, 1932; s. George Milnes and Mae (Eichner) A.; m. Irene Clara Wittenberg, June 12, 1960; 1 son, Brian Carl. B.S. in Commerce, U. Va., 1958; J.D., Tulane U., 1963. Bar: Va. bar 1964, D.C. bar 1970. Asst. prof. Coll. of William and Mary, Williamsburg, Va., 1963-64, Bowling Green (Ohio) State U., 1964-66; asst. prof. law Cleve. State U., 1966-68; prof. law Case Western Res. U., Cleve., 1968-70, 72-78, Edgar A. Hahn prof. jurisprudence, 1978—; atty. Dept. Justice, Washington, 1970-71. Author: Antitrust: Law, Economics, Policy, 1976; Contbr. articles to law revs. Served with U.S. Army, 1952-54. Decorated Bronze Star medal with V, Purple Heart. Home: 1174 Stony Hill Rd Hinckley OH 44233 Office: 11075 East Blvd Cleveland OH 44106

AUSTIN, DALE, petroleum products company executive. Pres. Golden Eagle Refining Co., Los Angeles. Office: Golden Eagle Refining Co. 707 Wilshire Blvd Los Angeles CA 90017

AUSTIN, DANIEL ANTHONY, JR., lawyer, consultant; b. Hartford, Conn., Mar. 5, 1928; s. Daniel A. and Mary (Ganley) A. B.A. in Govt, Yale U., 1948; J.D., Harvard U., 1952. Bar: Conn. 1952, U.S. Supreme 1958, D.C. 1957. Trial atty. FTC, Washington, 1957-59; asso. firm Baker, McKenzie & Hightower, Washington, 1959-60; asst. gen. atty., patent officer Rheem Mfg. Co., N.Y.C., 1960-62; asst. sec., asst. gen. counsel Pitney-Bowes, Inc., Stamford, Conn., 1962-70; v.p., sec., gen. counsel Cooper Labs., Inc., Parsippany, N.J., 1970-76; asso. gen. counsel, asst. sec. Am. Home Products Corp., N.Y.C., 1976-77; practice law, Greenwich, Conn., 1977—; pres. Case Corp. Services, Inc., 1979-80; partner Robinson, Robinson & Cole, 1980—; adj. prof. corp. law Pace U.; panelist Am. Mgmt. Assn., 1978-80; Adv. council Sch. Law Pace U., White Plains, N.Y., Manhattanville Coll. Paralegal Program, 1976-77. Author, lectr. corporate directorship, law mgmt. Served to lt. (j.g.) USNR, 1953-56. Recipient Meritorious Service award FTC, 1958. Mem. Am., Conn., Greenwich bar assns., Yale Alumni Assn. (regional chmn. 1968-70), Westchester-Fairfield Corporate Counsel Assn. (founding mem. exec. com. 1973-74, chmn. law dept. mgmt. com. 1975-79), Assn. Corporate Counsel N.J. (co-founder 1975), Harvard Law Sch. Assn. (chmn. Fairfield County 1978—, mem. council 1981—), Inst. Corp. Counsel (chmn. 1978-80). Clubs: Union League, Yale (N.Y.C.); Harvard of Fairfield County (dir. 1981—); Army-Navy (Washington); Bedford (N.Y.) Golf and Tennis. Home and office: Mayfair Ln Greenwich CT 06830

AUSTIN, DARREL, artist; b. Raymond, Wash., June 25, 1907; s. Albert and Ella (Caruthers) A.; m. Margot Helser, Feb. 24, 1933; 1 son, Darrel. Ed. pub. schs.; studied art at, Oregon and Notre Dame univs. and with Emile Jacques. Began painting, 1925; painted murals for, Med. Coll. U. Oreg., 1934; one-man shows, Perls Gallery, N.Y.C., 12 times 1940-64, Mus. Modern Art, N.Y.C., A.C.A. Gallery, N.Y.C., 1970, Harmon Gallery, Naples, Fla., 1973, 79, Perls Gallery, N.Y.C., 1979, Harmon Gallery, Sarasota, Fla., 1983, Harmon-Meek Gallery, Naples, Fla., one-man retrospective show, McNay Inst., San Antonio, 1982, Perls Gallery, N.Y.C., group shows, Whitney Mus., N.Y.C., Carnegie Inst., Pitts., Art. Inst., Chgo., Inst. Modern Art, Boston, City Art Mus., St. Louis, Springfield, Mass., Mus. Fine Arts, Soc. Four Arts, Palm Beach, Fla.; spl. exhbn. Contemporary Painting in the U.S. at, Met. Mus., N.Y.C.; later on tour of Latin Am. countries; represented in permanent collections, Met. Mus., N.Y.C., Mus. Modern Art, Mus. Fine Arts, Boston, Detroit Inst. Art, Albright Art Gallery, Buffalo, Smith Coll. Mus. Art, Phillips Meml. Gallery, Washington, Nelson Gallery Art, Kansas City, Mo., Rochester Meml. Art Gallery, Clearwater (Fla.) Mus., Pa. Acad. Art, Phila., Permanent Collection (Walter Lippincott award), Montclair (N.J.) Mus. Art, IBM Collection, Portland (Oreg.) Mus. Art, U. Nebr., Sarah Lawrence Coll., Norton Gallery Art, Omaha Mus. Art, Ency. Brit., U. Del., Los Angeles County Mus. Art, Ga. Mus. Fine Arts, Morse Gallery Art. Address: Saw Mill Hill Rd New Fairfield CT 06812

AUSTIN, DAVID H., trucking company executive; b. Toronto, Ont., Can., 1935. B.A., Ryerson Poly. Inst., Toronto, Ont., Can., 1957; chartered acct., Queen's U., Kingston, Ont., Can., 1962. Exec. v.p. Direct Trans system Ltd. and predecessor cos., 1962-79; pres., dir. Interstate Motor Freight System, Grand Rapids, Mich., 1979—; dir. Direct Trans. System Ltd. Office: Interstate Motor Freight System Grand Rapids MI 49501 *

AUSTIN, DONALD STAFFORD, engring./surveying co. exec.; b. Honolulu, Dec. 2, 1922; s. Herbert Ashford Robertson and Beatrice Margaret (Hancock) A.; m. Ruth Woolley, Aug. 20, 1947; children—Donald Stafford, Margaret, Herbert, Allan. Student, Stanford U., 1941-43; B.S. in Civil Engring, U. Hawaii, 1951. Jr. engr. Hawaiian Airlines, Ltd., Honolulu, 1944-47; asst. civil engr. H.A.R. Austin & Assos., Ltd., Honolulu, 1951-57, v.p., treas., 1957-59; pres. Austin, Smith & Assos., Inc., Honolulu, 1959-75; pres., chmn. bd. Austin, Tsutsumi & Assos., Inc., Honolulu, 1975—; instr. dept. engring. U. Hawaii, 1952. Fellow Am. Cons. Engrs. Council, ASCE (Commendation award 1962-66, nat. dir. 1976-79, nat. v.p. 1979-80); mem. Am. Concrete Inst., Am. Water Resources Assn., Am. Water Works Assn., Cons. Engrs. Council Hawaii (nat. dir. 1976-77), Engring. Assn. Hawaii, Hawaii Water Pollution Control Fedn., Nat. Soc. Profl. Engrs., Soc. Am. Mil. Engrs., Water Pollution Control Fedn., C. of C. in Honolulu. Mormon. Club: Pacific (Honolulu). Home: 1353 Kainui Dr Kailua HI 96734 Office: 745 Fort Street Mall Suite 900 Honolulu HI 96813

AUSTIN, GABRIEL CHRISTOPHER, publisher; b. N.Y.C., Sept. 3, 1935; s. Robert and Gabrielle (Connolly) A.; m. Florence Heilbrun, Oct. 16, 1967; 1 dau., Louise. B.A., St. John's U., Jamaica, N.Y., 1956; M.S. in L.S, Pratt Inst., 1957. Reference librarian N.Y. Pub. Library, 1952-62; librarian Grolier Club, N.Y.C., 1963-69; asst. v.p. Sotheby Parke Bernet, N.Y.C., 1969-75; pres. Wittenborn Art Books, Inc., N.Y.C., 1975—. Author: Iter Italicum, 1962, Library of Jean Grolier, 1970. Fellow Pierpont Morgan Library, since 1963. Mem. Grolier Club, Bibliog. Soc. Am., Internat. Assn. Bibliophiles. Democrat. Roman Cath. Club: Century Assn. (N.Y.C.). Home: 1009 Park Ave New York NY 10028 Office: 1018 Madison Ave New York NY 10021

AUSTIN, HARRY GUIDEN, engineering and construction company executive; b. Belton, Tex., Dec. 10, 1917; s. Harry Guiden and Emma Lena (Brown) A.; m. Elizabeth Ann Heard, Aug. 31, 1940; children—Lucy Ann, Elizabeth Austin Page, Catherine Marshall.; m. Catherine Austin Wyatt. B.S. in Elec. Engring, Tex. A&M Coll., 1938; M.B.A., Harvard U., 1940; H.H.D., Wiley Coll. Registered profl. engr., Tex. With Pan Am. Airways, Miami, Fla., 1940-41; elec. engr. Brown Shipbldg. Co., Houston, 1941-45; with Brown & Root, Inc., Houston, 1945—, v.p., 1960-65, sr. v.p., 1965-68, sr. group v.p., 1968-70, exec. v.p. engring. and constrn., 1970-78; also dir.; pres. Hael, Inc., Houston, 1978—; mem. Tex. A. and M. Geosci. Council; dir. Harris County Bankshares, Harris County Bank N.W., Atlas Travel, Inc., Houston. Mem. adv. bd. Houston Salvation Army, past chmn. bd.; bd. dirs. Retina Research Found.; trustee Wiley Coll., Marshall, Tex. Mem. Nat. Soc. Profl. Engrs., IEEE, Houston Engring. and Sci. Soc. (past pres.), Houston Com. Fgn. Relations, Harris County Heritage Soc., Mus. Nat. Sci., Mus. Fine Arts. Methodist. Clubs: Petroleum, Houston Country, Ramada (Houston). Home: 267 Pine Hollow Ln Houston TX 77056 Office: 2900 Wesleyan St Ste 400 Houston TX 77027

AUSTIN, JACOB, Canadian government official; b. Calgary, Alta., Can., Mar. 2, 1932; s. Morris and Clara Edith (Chetner) A.; m. Natalie Veiner Freeman, Apr. 2, 1978; children: Edith Clare, Sharon Jill, Barbara Joan. B.A., LL.B., U. B.S.; LL.M., Harvard U.; postgrad., U. Calif., Berkeley. Bar: B.C. 1958, Yukon 1966. Prin. sec. to prime minister, 1974-75, dep. minister energy, mines and resources, 1970-74; mem. Seante, 1975-81; minister of state, 1981-82, minister of state for social devel., 1982—. Liberal. Jewish. Clubs: Univ. (Vancouver, B.X.); Rideau, Le Cercle Universitaire d'Ottawa; Met. (N.Y.C.). Home: 1461 Connaught Dr Vancouver BC V6H 2H5 Canada Office: Rm 283-S The Senate Ottawa ON Canada K1A 0A4 *

AUSTIN, JAMES HENRY, neurologist; b. Cleve., Jan. 4, 1925; s. Paul Weber and Bertha Emily (Holtkamp) A.; m. Judith St. Clair, Feb. 7, 1948; children—Scott Whiting, Lynn St. Clair, James Winslow. B.A. magna cum laude, Brown U., 1961; M.D. cum laude, Harvard U., 1948. Intern Boston City Hosp., 1948-49, asst. resident neurol. unit, 1949-50; neurol. resident Neurol. Inst. N.Y., 1953-55; practice medicine specializing in neurology, Portland, Oreg., 1955-67, Denver, 1967—; asso. in neurology U. Oreg. Med. Sch., 1955-56, prof. neurology, 1966-67; prof., head div. neurology U. Colo. Med. Center, 1967—, chmn. dept. neurology, 1974. Author: Chase, Chance and Creativity: The Lucky Art of Novelty, 1978. Served with USNR, 1942-45, 50-52. Recipient Am. Assn. Neuropathologists prize, 1959; Kenny Research fellow, 1959-63; Saul Korey Meml. lectr., 1967; Alan Gregg fellow, 1974. Mem. United World Federalists, Sigma Xi, Delta Upsilon. Unitarian. Home: 128 S Fairfax St Denver CO 80222

AUSTIN, JAMES WILLIAM, hotel executive; b. Fountain Run, Ky., Nov. 5, 1905; s. James William and Leighton (Barr) A.; m. Esther Amick, Nov. 11, 1934. A.B., Colo. Coll., 1929; LL.D., New Eng. Coll., 1966. Investment banker, 1931-41; v.p., dir. Capital Airlines, 1948-58; pres., dir. NE Airlines, Inc., 1958-64, chmn., 1966-68, dir., 1958-72. Served as col. USAAF, 1942-46. Mem. Beta Theta Pi. Clubs: Metropolitan (Washington); Sky, Wings (N.Y.C.). Home: 220 MacFarlane Dr Delray Beach FL 33444 Office: 250 Park Ave New York City NY 10017

AUSTIN, JAMES WILLIS, naval officer; b. Fort Worth, Jan. 4, 1932; s. Robert Edward and Jessie Lou (Kersey) A.; m. Elizabeth Marshall, July 2, 1955; children—Deborah Ann, James Willis, Susan Louise. B.S., U.S. Naval Acad., 1954; B.S.A.E., U.S. Naval Postgrad. Sch., 1962; M.S. in Aero. and Astronautical Engring, 1963. Commd. ensign U.S. Navy, 1954, advanced through grades to rear adm., 1980; fighter pilot various squadrons, comdg. Fighter Squadron Fourteen; later exec. officer USS Enterprise; then comdr.; now assigned comdr. Fleet Air, Western Pacific, NAF ATSUGI, Japan. Decorated D.F.C., Legion of Merit, Air medal. Mem. U.S. Naval Inst., U.S. Naval Acad. Alumni Assn., Sigma Xi. Methodist. Address: Comdr Fleet Air West PAC Box 3 FPO Seattle WA 98767 *Always attempt to do more than what is required by supervisors.*

AUSTIN, JOHN HOGG, JR., utilities executive; b. Bryn Mawr, Pa., Apr. 16, 1928; s. John Hogg and Helen Elizabeth (Miner) A.; m. Joan Dorothy Bickel, Oct. 14, 1950; children: Nancy, Thomas, Patricia, Katherine. B.S., Yale U., 1950. With Phila. Electric Co., 1950—, comptroller, 1967-71, v.p. finance and accounting, 1971-78, exec. v.p., dir., 1978-82, pres., dir., 1982—, chief operating officer, 1980—; dir. Central Penn Nat. Bank, Meridian Bancorp, Inc., Selas Corp. Am., Phila. Suburban Water Co., Phila. Suburban Corp. Trustee United Way, So. Home Services; bd. dirs. YMCA of Met. Phila., Pa. Economy League. Mem. IEEE, Edison Electric Inst., Pa. Electric Assn. (exec. com.), Fin. Execs. Inst., Franklin Inst. Episcopalian. Clubs: Union League, Yale (Phila.). Home: 330 Bair Rd Berwyn PA 19312 Office: 2301 Market St Philadelphia PA 19101

AUSTIN, JOHN PAUL, retired beverage company executive; b. La Grange, Ga., Feb. 14, 1915; s. Samuel Yates and Maude (Jernigan) A.; m. Jeane Weed, July 12, 1950; children: John Paul, Samuel Weed. A.B., Harvard U., 1937, LL.B., 1940. Bar: N.Y. bar 1940. Practiced in, N.Y.C., 1940-41, 45-49; mem. legal dept. Coca-Cola Co., 1949-50, exec. v.p., 1961-62, pres., dir., 1962-83, chief exec. officer, 1966-81, chmn. bd., 1970-81; exec. v.p. Coca-Cola Export Corp., 1958-59, pres., dir., 1959—. Served as lt. comdr. USNR, 1942-45. Clubs: Racquet and Tennis, Links (N.Y.C.); Blind Brook Golf (Purchase, N.Y.); Capital City, Peachtree Golf (Atlanta). Office: 25 Park Pl NE Suite 1110 Atlanta GA 30303

AUSTIN, KENNETH RALPH, insurance executive; b. Keosauqua, Iowa, Mar. 15, 1920; s. James Clayton and Nancy M. (Landreth) A.; m. LaVerne Eleanor Turin, May 9, 1942; children: Marilyn Ruth, Alan Karl. B.C.S., Drake U., 1941; M.S., U. Iowa, 1942. With Equitable Life Ins. Co. Iowa, Des Moines, 1947—, asst. sec., 1953-59, supt. policy issue, 1959-60, agy. v.p., 1960-64, v.p., controller, 1964-66, exec. v.p., 1966-69, pres., 1969—, chief exec. officer, 1970-83, chmn., 1981—. Bd. dirs. Drake U.; past bd. dirs. Simpson Coll., Marycrest Coll., South Iowa Methodist Homes, Am. Assn. Homes for Aging; bd. govs. Iowa Coll. Found. Served to comdr. USNR, 1942-45. Fellow Life Mgmt. Inst.; mem. Life Office Mgmt. Assn. (past dir.), Am. Council Life Ins. (past dir.). Home: 111 30th St Des Moines IA 50312 Office: PO Box 1635 Des Moines IA 50306

AUSTIN, PATRICIA, advertising agency executive; b. Fort Worth. B.A., So. Meth. U. Art dir., account exec. Read-Poland Agency, Fort Worth, 1955-63; account exec. Bloom Agency, Dallas, 1963-66, account supr., v.p., 1968-73, mgmt. supr., v.p., 1973-76; pres. The Collateral Group, Inc., Dallas, 1976—, Pub. Relations Advisors, Inc., 1977—, Bloom Advt. Too, Inc., Dallas, 1978—; sales promotion and advt. dir. Sakowitz Dept. Store, 1966-68. Office: 7701 Stemmons Dallas TX 75247

AUSTIN, PHILIP EDWARD, university president; b. Fargo, N.D., 1942; s. William and Angelyn A.; m. Susan Gates. B.S., N.D. State U., 1964, M.S., 1966; M.A., Mich. State U., 1968, Ph.D., 1969. Economist U.S. Office of Mgmt. and Budget, Washington, 1971-74; dep. asst. sec. HEW, Washington, 1974-77, acting asst. sec., 1977; prof. econs. George Washington U., Washington, 1977-78; provost, v.p. for acad. affairs Bernard Baruch Coll., N.Y.C., 1978-84; pres. Colo. State U., Fort Collins, 1984—. Served with U.S. Army, 1969-71. Decorated Bronze Star. Mem. Am. Econ. Assn., Am. Assn. Higher Edn., Beta Gamma Sigma. Home: 860 United Nations Plaza New York NY 10017 Office: Office of the Pres Colo State U Fort Collins CO 80523

AUSTIN, RICHARD HENRY, state ofcl.; b. Ala., May 6, 1913; s. Richard H. and Lelia (Hill) A.; m. Ida B. Dawson, Aug. 19, 1939; 1 dau., Hazel. B.S., Detroit Inst. Tech., 1937; LL.D. (hon.), Detroit Coll. Bus., 1971. Pvt. practice accounting, Detroit, 1941-71, auditor, Wayne County, Mich., 1967-70, sec. of state Mich., Lansing, 1971—; del. Mich. Constl. Conv., 1961-62. Bd. dirs. Harper-Grace Hosp., Detroit, Mercy Coll., Detroit, Met. Detroit United Found., Detroit YMCA, Detroit council Boy Scouts Am. Mem. Am. Inst. C.P.A.s, Mich. Assn. C.P.A.s (Distinguished Achievement award 1972). Democrat. Home: 3374 Oakman Blvd Detroit MI 48238 Office: Office of Sec of State State Capitol Lansing MI 48913

AUSTIN, RICHARD WILLIAM, lawyer; b. Harvey, Ill., Jan. 23, 1931; s. Richard Beven and Louise (Crew) A.; m. Susan Stewart, Apr. 9, 1955; children: Mark R., Bryan W., Douglas B., Thomas S. B.A., Denison U., 1952; J.D., Northwestern U., 1955. Bar: Ill. 1955. Assoc. Winston & Strawn, Chgo., 1957-65, ptnr., 1965—; officer, dir. Ill. Inst. Continuing Legal Edn., 1980—; chmn. adv. com. Chgo. Vol. Legal Services Found., 1982—, U.S. Dist. Ct. admissions com., 1982—; mem. com. to study caseflow mgmt. Circuit Ct. of Cook County, Ill., 1979-81. Chmn. Chgo. South Suburban Mass Transit Dist., 1967-71; village atty., Homewood, Ill., 1960-66; chmn. Citizens for a New Ill. Constn., 1968-70. Served with U.S. Army, 1955-57. Fellow Am. Bar Found.; mem. Chgo. Bar Assn (pres. 1979-80, award of appreciation young lawyers sect. 1980), ABA (membership com. chmn. Ill. 1983—), Nat. Conf. Bar Presidents (exec. council 1981—), Chgo. Bar Found. (pres. 1982—), Omicron Delta Kappa. Episcopalian. Clubs: Legal; Law (Chgo.); Olympia Fields Country (Ill.). Office: Winston & Strawn One First National Plaza Chicago IL 60603

AUSTIN, ROBERT CLARKE, naval officer; b. Cleve., Sept. 5, 1931; s. Clarke Albert and Margaret Jane (Richardson) A.; m. Joyce Ann Bisese, Apr. 22, 1957; children—Susan Lynn, James Holden, Robert Clarke, Cecelia Ann. B.S., U.S. Naval Acad., 1954; M.S. in Physics, Naval Postgrad. Sch., 1963. Enlisted U.S. Navy, 1948, commd. ensign, 1954, advanced through grades to rear adm., 1980; comdg. officer USS Finback, 1968-72; comdr. Submarine Devel. Group Two, 1974-76; comdg. officer Naval Submarine Sch., 1976-78; chief of staff submarine force U.S. Atlantic Fleet, 1979-80; dep. dir. for internat. negotiations for Plans and Policy Directorate, Joint Chiefs of Staff, Pentagon, Washington, 1981-82; chief naval tech. tng., 1982—. Decorated Def. Superior Service Medal, Legion of Merit with 2 gold stars, Meritorious Service medal, others. Mem. Sigma Xi. Episcopalian. Office: CNTECHTRA NAS Memphis Millington TN 38054

AUSTIN, ROBERT EUGENE, JR., lawyer; b. Jacksonville, Fla., Oct. 10, 1937; s. Robert Eugene and Leta Fitch A.; m. Jayne Talley, Dec. 28, 1964; children: Robert Eugene, George Harry Talley. B.A., Davidson Coll., 1959; J.D., U. Fla., 1964. Bar: Fla. 1965, D.C. 1983, U.S. Supreme Ct. 1970. Legal asst. Fla. Ho. Reps., 1965; assoc. firm Jones & Sims, Pensacola, Fla., 1965-66; ptnr. firm Warren, Warren & Austin, Leesburg, Fla., 1966-68, McLin, Burnsed, Austin & Cyrus, Leesburg, 1968-77, Austin & Burleigh, 1977-81; sole practice Law Offices of Robert E. Austin, Jr., Leesburg, 1981—; asst. state atty., 1972; mem. Jud. Nominating Commn. and Grievance Com. 5th Dist. Fla.; gov. Fla. Bar, 1983—. Chmn. Lake Dist. Boy Scouts Am.; asst. dean Leesburg Deanery, Diocese of Central Fla.; trustee Fla. House, Washington., U. Fla. Law Center, 1983—. Served to capt. U.S. Army, 1959-62. Mem. Acad. Fla. Trial Lawyers, Am. Arbitration Assn., ABA, Am. Judicature Soc., Am. Law Inst., Assn. Trial Lawyers Am., Nat. Inst. Trial Advocacy, Def. Research Inst., Fed. Bar Assn., Lake County Bar Assn., Roscoe Pound Am. Trial Found., Kappa Alpha, Phi Delta Phi. Democrat. Episcopalian. Clubs: Timuquana Country (Jacksonville, Fla.); University (Orlando, Fla.). Home: 6300 N Silver Lake Dr Leesburg FL 32748 Office: 1000 W Main St Leesburg FL 32748

AUSTIN, RODNEY ELMER, diversified mfg. co. exec.; b. Mardela Springs, Md., Oct. 3, 1926; s. Nathaniel Oakl and Margaret Gertrude (Adkins) A.; m. Dorothy Jacobson, June 18, 1949; children—Nancy Austin Macfarlane, Richard Edward, Susan Pierce, Elizabeth Anne. A.B., Western Md. Coll., 1948; postgrad., George Washington U. Job analyst C.E., Dept. Army, Washington, 1949-53; compensation specialist R.J. Reynolds Tobacco Co., Winston-Salem, N.C., 1953-70; with R.J. Reynolds Industries Inc., Winston-Salem, 1970—, v.p., 1974—; dir. AJR Archer, RJR Foods, Winston-Salem Savs. & Loan Assn. Pres. Winston-Salem Health Care Plan, 1976, Winston-Salem Dental Care Plan, 1978; trustee Western Md. Coll.; adv. bd. Planned Parenthood Greater Winston-Salem. Served with USN, 1945-46. Mem. Am. Mgmt. Assn., Winston-Salem C. of C. Episcopalian. Club: Winston-Salem Rotary. Home: 140 Plymouth Ave Winston-Salem NC 27104 Office: World Hdqrs RJ Reynolds Industries Reynolds Blvd Winston-Salem NC 27102

AUSTIN, RONALD, producer, director, writer; b. Hollywood, Calif., Apr. 9, 1934; s. Charles J. and Mildred (Wood) Munns; m. Ruth Lois Barnett, Aug. 16, 1952; children: Teresa Mildred, Beth Charlene. A.A., Los Angeles City Coll., 1952; B.A. in Theatre Arts, UCLA, 1956. Producer, dir.: TV series and pilots films including Charlie's Angels; writer: TV films including Death Squad; feature films The Happening, 1967; The Midas Run, 1969, Harry in Your Pocket, 1973. Mem. Writers Guild Am. (dir. 1977—, Morgan Cox award for Life Service 1981), Producers Guild Am., Dirs. Guild Am. Office: 13455 Ventura Blvd #209 Sherman Oaks CA 91423

AUSTIN, SPENCER PETER, clergyman; b. Lone Wolf, Okla., Dec. 15, 1909; s. Otis Frank and Bertha Ethel (Sinclair) A.; m. Margaret Ellen Wolfinger, Dec. 15, 1932 (dec. Apr. 1968); children—Roy Frank, Jack Spencer, Margaret Anna; m. Kathleen B. Bailey, Dec. 30, 1969 (dec. June 1981); m. Kathleen B. Havens, Dec. 28, 1982. A.B., Phillips U., 1931, M.A., 1932, B.D., 1933, D.D., 1957; student, Boston U. Sch. Theology, 1943-45. Ordained to ministry Christian Ch. (Disciples of Christ), 1931; pastor in Cedardale and Tangier, Okla., 1929-33, Sayre, Okla., 1933-36, Mangum, Okla., 1937, Duncan, Okla., 1937-43, Everett, Mass., 1943-45; nat. dir. evangelism United Christian Missionary Soc., 1945-50, exec. resources dept., 1950-56; exec. Unified Promotion Christian Chs., 1957-74, chmn. com. relief appeals, 1957-63, adminstrv. sec. com. fraternal aid to Brit. chs., 1954-70; chmn. Week of Compassion com., 1963-76; pres. Christian Ch. Found., 1961-69; Trustee Nat. Christian Missionary Conv., 1957-69; exec. com. Council Christian Unity, 1957-82; mem. grad. sem. council Phillips U., 1962-70; denomination rep. Nat. Council Chs., 1950-72; also mem. exec. com. dept. stewardship and chmn. benevolence promotion com.; mem. exec. com. Ch. World Service, chmn., 1966-70; interim com. Council Agencies Christian Chs., 1952-68; pres. Ch. Finance Council, 1974-76; dir. spl. resources Christian Theol. Sem., 1976-82. Author: Evangelism, 1947. Mem. Disciples of Christ Hist. Soc. (life). Clubs: Rotarian, Kiwanian (pres. Sayre 1936), Odd Fellow.). Home: 287 S Downey Ave Indianapolis IN 46219 Office: 222 S Downey Ave Indianapolis IN 46219 *Most of our own advantages were a gift from others beyond what we deserve. Simple justice demands that we provide similar opportunities for other human beings.*

AUSTIN, TOM NOELL, tobacco company executive; b. Greeneville, Tenn., May 11, 1916; s. Clyde Bernard and Felice (Noell) A.; m. Emily Donaldson, Nov. 19, 1938; children: Tom Noell, Merrily (Mrs. Charles L. Teasley, Jr.), Jay Donaldson, Richard Lyon. Student, UCLA, 1936; B.A., U. Tenn., 1937. Shipping clk. Douglas Tobacco Co., 1937; with Austin Co., Greeneville, 1940—, v.p., 1944-48, pres., 1948-70, chmn. bd., 1970—; dir. Carolina and Northwestern Ry., Tennessee Valley Bancorp., First Nat. Bank, Greeneville; v.p. Unaka Co., Greeneville, Austin Carolina Co., Kinston, N.C., Mullins Leaf Tobacco Co., S.C.; mem. Ky. and Tenn. Dist. Export Council. Trustee Tusculum Coll.; mem. devel. council U. Tenn. Mem. Young Pres.'s Orgn., Chief Execs. Forum, Phi Gamma Delta, Omicron Delta Kappa. Clubs: Elks, Exchange (Greeneville). Home: RFD 7 Greeneville TN 37743 Office: Austin Co Hall and Willis St Greeneville TN 37743

AUSTIN, TRACY ANN, professional tennis player; b. Rolling Hills, Calif., Dec. 12, 1962; d. George and Jeanne A. Student public schs. Amateur tennis player, 1970-78, profl., 1978—; mem. U.S. Fedn. Cup Team, 1978-80, U.S. Wightman Cup Team, 1978, 79, 81. Named AP Female Athlete of year, 1979, 82, Player of the Yr. Women's Tennis Assn., 1980, Women's Sports Found. Profl. Sportswoman of Year, 1980; recipient Ann. Victor award, 1980, 81. Life mem. U.S. Tennis Assn.; mem. Women's Tennis Assn. Champion Gunze Invitational, Japan, 1978, 82, Porsch Classic, Stuttgart, W. Ger., 1978, 79, 80, 81, Emeron Cup, Tokyo, 1979, Avon of Washington, 1979, Wells Fargo Tennis Open, San Diego, 1979, 80, 81, 82, Family Circle Cup, Hilton Head, S.C., 1979, 80, Italian Open, 1979, U.S. Open, 1979, 81, Avon Championships, 1980, Clairol Crown, La Costa, Calif., 1980, BMW Challenge, Eastbourne, Eng., 1980, 81, Can. Open, 1981; champion mixed doubles with brother, Wimbledon, Eng., 1980, Wimbledon Jr. champion, 1978. Office: 888 17th St NW Suite 1200 Washington DC 20006

AUSTIN, WALTER JAMES, civil engineering educator; b. St. Louis, Feb. 6, 1920; s. Walter James and Florence (Knappmeier) A.; m. Helen Evelyn Green, June 18, 1949; children: James Randall, Elaine Kathryn. B.S. in C.E, Rice U., 1941; M.S., U. Ill., 1946, Ph.D., 1949. Structural designer Chgo. Bridge & Iron Co., 1942-46; mem. faculty U. Ill. at Urbana, 1947-60, asso. prof. civil engring., 1952-60; prof. civil engring. Rice U., 1960—, chmn. dept. civil engring., 1963-64, 77-82; cons. structural analysis and design, plates and shells. Author tech. papers. Fellow ASCE (Moisseiff award 1958); mem. Structural Stability Research Council (life), Sigma Xi, Tau Beta Pi. Home: 5211 Rutherglenn Dr Houston TX 77096

AUSTIN, WILLIAM BENNETT, JR., banker; b. Upper Darby, Pa., Feb. 10, 1932; s. William Bennett and Inez Katheryn (Brock) A.; m. Donna Frederick; children: W. Bennett III, Abigail, Amy. A.B. in Econs., Princeton U., 1954; postgrad. in bus. adminstrn., NYU, (1956-59). With Bankers Trust Co., N.Y.C., 1954-74; sr. v.p. South Shore Bank, Quincy, Mass., 1975, exec. v.p., 1975-77, pres., chief operating officer, 1977-82, pres., chief exec. officer, 1982—, dir., 1977—; chmn., dir. Multibank Leasing, Inc., Quincy, 1978—, pres., 1976-78; chmn., dir. Multibank Internat., Quincy, 1978—; dir. Multibank Service Corp., Auburn, Mass., 1980—, Quincy Mut. Fire Ins. Co. Mem. Progress Downtown Quincy, Inc., 1979—, bd. dirs., mem. exec. com., 1982—; mem. nominating com. United Way of Mass. Bay, Inc., 1979, orgn. mem., 1980—; mem. Quincy Devel. and Fin. Corp., 1979—; trustee Thayer Acad., Braintree, Mass., King Family Fund. Served to 1st lt. U.S. Army, 1954-56. Mem. Mass. Bankers Assn. (dir. 1980-82), Better Bus. Bur. Eastern Mass. (dir.), South Shore, C. of C. (dir.). Clubs: Marshfield Country, Neighborhood. Office: South Shore Bank 1400 Hancock Quincy MA 02169

AUSTIN, WILLIAM LAMONT, supt. schs.; b. Detroit, June 18, 1915; s. William Lamont and Dorcas Sahar (Allen) A.; m. Virginia Martha Holm, June 6, 1942; children—Anne, Frank. A.B., Mich. State U., 1937, M.A., 1946, Ph.D., 1970; LL.D. (hon.), Adrian (Mich.) Coll., 1966. Classroom tchr., Charlotte, Mich., 1938-42; with Bendix Aviation Co., also Naval Bur. Ordnance, 1942-46; mem. faculty N.Y.C. Coll., Columbia and Hunter Coll., 1946-48; supt. sch., Wyoming, Mich., 1948-52, Adrian, 1952-65, Muskegon, Mich., 1965—; pres. Am. Assn. Sch. Adminstrs., 1973; Dir. Mich. Consol. Gas Co. Contbr. articles to ednl. jours. Bd. dirs. Muskegon County Community Found.; pres., bd. dirs. Lenawee Youth Center; pres. Huron Valley Child Care Center, 1961. Mem. Mich. Assn. Sch. Adminstrs. (pres. 1963). Club: Rotarian (past local pres.). Home: 3276 Boltwood Dr Muskegon MI 49441 Office: 349 Webster Ave Muskegon MI 49440

AUSTIN, WILLIAM NEWSOME, appliance industry executive; b. Raleigh, N.C., June 22, 1930; s. Robert Smith and Bettie Louise (Yelverton) A.; m. Joanne Louesa Murphy, Sept. 21, 1963; 1 son, William Newsome. B.S., Wake Forest Coll., 1952; M.B.A., Harvard U., 1956. Research asst. Harvard U. Bus. Sch., 1956-57; research assoc. Inst. pour les Etudes de Direction de l'Enterprise, Lausanne, Switzerland, 1957-58; with Magic Chef, Inc., 1959-81, dir. indsl. relations, Cleve., 1966-69, v.p. adminstrn., 1969, v.p., 1978—, pres., Los Angeles, 1969-80, Columbus, Ohio, 1976-80, also dir. parent co.; pres., Cleveland, Tenn., 1980-81; pres., chief exec. officer Raypak, Inc., Westlake Village, Calif., 1983—. Served with U.S. Army, 1952-54. Mem. Chief Execs. Orgn., Gas Appliance Mfrs. Assn. (dir. 1972-81, chmn. 1976-77), Phi Beta Kappa. Clubs: Calif., Palos Verdes Tennis, Palm Desert Tennis. Address: Raypak Inc 31111 Agoura Rd West Lake Village CA 91361

AUSTIN, WILLIAM WEAVER, musicologist; b. Lawton, Okla., Jan. 18, 1920; s. William McKinley and Leone Elizabeth (Weaver) A.; m. Elizabeth Jane Hallstrom, June 20, 1942; children: Ann Elizabeth, Margery Jane. A.B., Harvard U., 1939, A.M., 1940, Ph.D., 1951. Asst. prof. music U. Va., 1946-47; mem. faculty Cornell U., Ithaca, N.Y., 1947—, chmn. music dept., 1958-63, prof., 1960-69, Goldwin Smith prof. musicology, 1969—; vis. asso. prof. Princeton U., 1957-58. Author: Music in the Twentieth Century, 1966, Susanna, Jeanie, and the Old Folks: Songs of Stephen C. Foster, 1975; editor: New Looks at Italian Opera, 1968, Debussy, Prélude à "L'Apres-midi d'un faune", 1970; translator: Carl Dahlhaus, Esthetics of Music, 1981; contbr. articles to music publs. Served from ensign to lt. USNR, 1942-46. Guggenheim fellow, 1961-62. Mem. Am. Musicol. Soc., Soc. Ethnomusicology, Music Library Assn., Music Educators Nat. Conf., AAUP, Coll. Music Soc. (pres. 1960-62), Internat. Musicol. Soc., Am. Acad. Arts and Scis., Gesellschaft für Musikforschung. Home: 205 White Park Rd Ithaca NY 14850 *Greed for learning protects me from sloth, rage, envy, scorn, and even lust and pride. Does my greed need tempering? Can I learn to be more prudent in indulging it? Can I learn to act more bravely in applying some of my learning? Can I learn to make some of it serve justice?*

AUSTRIAN, NEIL R., advertising agency executive; b. N.Y.C., Feb. 21, 1940; s. Joseph H. and Jessie Davis A.; m. Nancy Hewitt, Sept. 8, 1962; children: Neil, John, Jennifer, Jessie Davis. B.C.E., Swarthmore Coll., 1961; M.B.A. (Baker scholar), Harvard U., 1968. Vice-pres. Laird Inc., N.Y.C., 1968-70; founder, pres. Dryden & Co., N.Y.C., investment banker, 1970-74; pres., chief exec. officer Doyle Dane Bernbach Internat. Inc., N.Y.C., 1974-84; chmn., chief exec. officer Showtime Movie Channel, N.Y.C., 1984—; dir. Telecredit Inc., Los Angeles., Refac Techs. Bd. dirs. Young Life Lower East Side, 1968-72; bd. mgrs. Swarthmore Coll. Served to lt. USNR, 1963-66. Mem. ASCE, Nat. Venture Capital Assn., Harvard Bus. Sch. Club, Delta Upsilon. Office: Showtime Movie Channel 1633 Broadway New York NY 10019 *

AUSTRIAN, ROBERT, physician; b. Balt., Apr. 12, 1916; s. Charles Robert and Florence (Hochschild) A.; m. Babette Friedmann, Dec. 29, 1963; stepchildren: Jill Bernstein, Toni Bernstein. A.B., Johns Hopkins U., 1937, M.D., 1941; D.Sc. honoris causa, Hahnemann Med. Coll., 1980, Phila. Coll. Pharmacy and Sci., 1981. Diplomate: Am. Bd. Internal Medicine. House officer Johns Hopkins Hosp., 1941-50, asst. dir. med. out-patient dept., 1951-52; assoc. prof. medicine, then prof. medicine SUNY Coll. Medicine, 1952-62; John Herr Musser prof., chmn. dept. research medicine U. Pa. Sch. Medicine, 1962—; attending physician Hosp. U. Pa.; Tyndale vis. lectr. and prof. Coll. Medicine U. Utah, 1964; spl. research on infectious diseases, bacterial genetics; mem. Meningococcal Infractions Commn., 1964-72, Commn. on Acute Respiratory Disease, 1965-72, Commn. Streptococcal and Staphylococcal Diseases, 1970-72, Armed Forces Epidemiol. Bd.; cons. surg. gen. U.S. Army Research and Devel. Command, 1966-69; mem. subcom. streptococcus and pneumococcus Internat. Com. Bacteriol. Nomenclature; mem. allergy and immunology study sect. Nat. Inst. Allergy and Infectious Diseases, 1965-69, mem. bd. sci. counselors, 1967-70, chmn., 1969-70. Mem. editorial bd.: Jour. Bacteriology, 1964-69, Am. Rev. Respiratory Diseases, 1963-66, Bacteriol. Rev, 1967-71, Jour. Infectious Diseases, 1969-74, Antimicrobial Agents and Chemotherapy, 1972—, Infection and Immunity, 1973-81, Revs. of Infectious Diseases, 1979—. Trustee Johns Hopkins U., 1963-69. Served to capt. M.C. AUS, 1943-45. Recipient U.S. Typhus Commn. medal, 1947; Albert Lasker Clin. Med. Research award, 1978; Phila. award, 1979; Willard O. Thompson award Am. Geriatric Soc., 1981, others. Fellow ACP (master, James D. Bruce Meml. award 1979), N.Y. Acad. Scis., Am. Acad. Microbiology, AAAS (chmn. sect. on med. scis. 1975); mem. Assn. Am. Physicians, Am. Soc. Clin. Investigation, Am. Clin. and Climatol. Assn. (pres. 1984), Am. Soc. Microbiology (v.p. N.Y. br. 1961-62), Nat. Acad. Scis., Soc. Exptl. Biology and Medicine, Harvey Soc., Am. Fedn. Clin. Research, Balt. Med. Soc., Am. Assn. Immunologists, N.Y. Acad. Medicine (sec. sect. microbiology 1961-62), Phila. County Med. Soc. (Strittmatter award 1979), Coll. Physicians Phila. (award of Meritorious Service 1980), Interurban Clin. Club (pres. 1970), Infectious Disease Soc. Am. (pres. 1971, Maxwell Finland lecture award 1974), Johns Hopkins Soc. Scholars, Phi Beta Kappa, Sigma Xi, Alpha Omega Alpha, Omicron Delta Kappa. Club: 14 W. Hamilton Street (Balt.). Address: Dept Research Medicine U Pa Sch Medicine Philadelphia PA 19104

AUTEN, DAVID CHARLES, lawyer; b. Phila., Apr. 4, 1938; s. Charles Raymond and Emily Lillian (Dickel) A.; m. Suzanne Crozier Plowman, Feb. 1, 1969; children: Anne Crozier, Meredith Smedley. B.A., U. Pa., 1960, J.D., 1963. Bar: Pa. 1963. Ptnr. firm Reed Smith Shaw & McClay (and predecessor), Phila., 1963—. Author articles in field. Vice pres. Northeast Community Mental Health Center, 1971-72; vice chmn. alumni ann. giving U. Pa., 1975-77, 81-82, chmn. alumni ann. giving, 1982—, trustee, 1977-80; pres. Gen. Alumni Soc., 1977-80; chmn. Benjamin Franklin Assos., 1975-77, 81-82; pres. Soc. of Coll., 1975-77; v.p. Assn. Republicans for Educated Action, 1971-79; bd. mgrs. Kearsley Home, 1974—, Presbyn.-U. Pa. Med. Center, 1980—, Phila. City Inst., 1981—, St. Peter's Sch., 1975—; pres. St. Peter's Sch., 1978-79. Mem. ABA, Pa. Bar Assn., Phila. Bar Assn. (vice chmn. young lawyers sect. 1971-72), Juristic Soc. (pres.), Interfrat. Alumni Council U. Pa. (pres. 1970-74), Phi Beta Kappa, Theta Xi (pres. 1974-76). Episcopalian (vestryman). Clubs: Rittenhouse (pres.), Union League, Fourth St. Home: 120 Delancey St Philadelphia PA 19106 Office: 1600 Ave of the Arts Bldg Broad and Chestnut Sts Philadelphia PA 19107

AUTEN, JOHN HAROLD, govt. ofcl.; b. Ames, Iowa, June 29, 1922; s. John T. and Dorothy (Davis) A.; m. Ethel Anne Pye, Jan. 20, 1951; children—Susan Irene, John Aaron, Joanne Marie. B.Sc., Ohio State U., 1947; Ph.D., Mass. Inst. Tech., 1954. Instr. Ohio State U., 1952; from instr. to prof. econs. Rice U., 1952-64; with Office Fin. Analysis, Treasury Dept., 1963—, dir., 1966—. Contbr. articles to profl. jours. Served with USAAF, 1943-46. Mem. Am. Econs. Assn., Am. Finance Assn. Home: 2713 Arlington Blvd Arlington VA 22201 Office: Treasury Dept 15th and Pennsylvania Ave NW Washington DC 20220

AUTERA, MICHAEL EDWARD, chemical company executive; b. Passaic, N.J., June 16, 1938; s. Michael and Laura (Vandervliet) A.; m. Martha Bolton Tilt, Jan. 31, 1959; children—Michael Edward, Katherine T., Stephen G. B.S., Lehigh U., 1960; M.B.A., Rutgers U., 1962. C.P.A., N.Y. Indsl. engr. Eastman Kodak Co., Rochester, N.Y., 1960-61; sr. accountant Haskins & Sells, C.P.A.s, N.Y.C., 1962-66; sr. v.p. finance Bristol-Myers Co., N.Y.C., 1966—. Mem. Am. Inst. C.P.A.s, N.Y. State Soc. C.P.A.s, Fin. Execs. Inst., Beta Gamma Sigma. Presbyterian. Home: 844 Wickam Way Ridgewood NJ 07450 Office: 345 Park Ave New York NY 10022

AUTH, TONY, artist; b. Akron, Ohio, May 7, 1942; s. William Anthony and Julia Kathleen (Donnally) A. B.A., U. Calif. at Los Angeles, 1965. Chief med. illustrator Rancho Los Amigos Hosp., Downey, Calif., 1964-70. Editorial cartoonist, Phila. Inquirer, 1971—; anthology of drawings Behind the Lines, 1978. Recipient awards Overseas Press Club, 1975, 76, Sigma Delta Chi, 1976; Pulitzer prize, 1976. Home: 1137 Rodman St Philadelphia PA 19147 Office: 400 N Broad St Philadelphia PA 19101

AUTHEMENT, RAY, college president; b. Chauvin, La., Nov. 19, 1929; s. Elias Lawrence and Elphia (Duplantis) A.; m. Barbara B. Braud, June 1, 1950; children: Kathleen Elizabeth, Julie Ann. B.S., U. Southwestern La., 1950; M.S., La. State U., 1952; Ph.D., 1956. Instr. La. State U., Baton Rouge, 1952-56; asso. prof. McNeese State Coll., Lake Charles, La., 1956-57, U. Southwestern La., 1957-59, prof. math., from, 1959, acad. v.p., 1966-73, pres., 1973—; vis. prof. U. N.C., Chapel Hill, 1962-63. Mem. Downtown Devel. Com. Lafayette, 1972—; mem. La. Bicentennial Commn., 1973, Lafayette Bicentennial Commn., 1973, Econ. Devel. Com., Lafayette, 1973, Sch. Bd. Fatima Parish, Lafayette, 1963-65; bd. dirs. United Way, Lafayette, 1973, U. Southwestern La. Found., 1967; trustee Lafayette Gen. Hosp., 1981—; mem. bd. advisers John Gray Inst., 1982—, St. Joseph Sem., 1967; mem. Commn. Colleges So. Assn. Colls., 1981-83. Mem. Math. Assn. Am., AAAS, Lafayette C. of C. (dir. 1983—), Blue Key, Phi Kappa Phi, Kappa Mu Epsilon, Sigma Pi Sigma, Phi Kappa Theta. Roman Catholic. Club: Rotary. Home: PO Drawer 1008 USL Station Lafayette LA 70504 Office: U Southwestern La Office of Pres Lafayette LA 70504

AUTIAN, JOHN, researcher; b. Phila., Aug. 20, 1924; s. Zaker and Minnie (Castian) A.; m. Ginny Darlene Langford, Nov. 19, 1962; 1 son, Zaker John. B.S., Coll. Pharmacy, Temple U., 1950; M.S., U. Md., 1952, Ph.D., 1954. Asst. prof. Coll. Pharmacy, Temple U., 1954-56, Coll. Pharmacy, U. Md., 1956-57, U. Mich., 1957-60; assoc. prof. U. Tex., 1960-65, prof., dir. drug-plastic research and toxicology lab., 1965-67; prof. pharmaceutics, prof. dentistry, also dir. Material Sci. Toxicology Lab., U. Tenn. Med. Center, 1967—; chmn. dept. molecular biology Coll. Pharmacy, U. Tenn., 1974, dean Coll. Pharmacy, 1975—; cons. Clin. Center, NIH, 1960—; spl. research plastics for med. and para-med. applications. Author numerous articles in field; contbr. to textbooks. Served with AUS, 1943-46. Recipient Distinguished Alumni award Temple U., 1964; citation for research U. Md. Sch. Medicine, 1964; award for pub. service contbns. U. Tenn. Alumni, 1973. Mem. AAAS (v.p. 1962), Am. Pharm. Assn. Home: 5841 Park 4 Memphis TN 38119 Office: Coll Pharmacy U Tenn Center Health Scis Memphis TN 38103

AUTRY, CAROLYN, artist, art history educator; b. Dubuque, Iowa, Dec. 12, 1940; d. William Tilden and Vela (Laseman) A.; m. Peter Elloian, May 27, 1966; 1 dau., Cybele Justine. B.A., U. Iowa, 1963, M.F.A., 1965. Instr. art, art history Baldwin-Wallace Coll., Berea, Ohio, 1965-66; instr. art history Toledo Mus. Art-U. Toledo, 1966—. Exhbns. include, San Francisco Mus. Art, 1973, Oakland Mus., 1975, Santa Barbara Mus., U. Mo., Ljubljana Internat. Biennial, 1975, 81, Internationale Grafik Biennale, Frechen, W. Ger., 1976, Internationale Grafik Biennale, Biella, Italy, Internationale Grafik Biennale, Genoa, Italy, Internationale Grafik Biennale, Leverkusen, W. Ger., 1977, Phila. Mus. Art, 1980, Visual Arts Center, Anchorage, Alaska, U. Louisville, 1981, U. Dallas, 1981, numerous others, Grunwald Ctr. Graphic Arts, UCLA, 1981, Ohio State U., 1982, Belle Arts & Graphic Inc., Nyack, N.Y., Mus. Arts and Scis., Macon, Ga., 1983, U. Tenn., Knoxville, Pratt Graphics Ctr., N.Y.C., Calif. State Coll., San Bernardino; represented in permanent collections, Library of Congress, Phila. Mus. Art, Worcester Art Mus., Mount Holyoke Coll., U. Colo., Bradley U., Calif. State U., San Diego, Ga. State U., U. S.D., U. N.D., U. Louisville, St. Lawrence U., U. Dallas, Hunterdon Art Ctr., Clinton, N.J., Fitchburg Mus., (Mass.), Duxbury Art Complex, (Mass.). Ford Found. grantee, 1961-63; Yale-Norfolk Summer Sch. Art and Music scholar, 1962; Ohio Arts Council grantee, 1979; recipient Louis Black award Boston Printmakers, 1971, Ture Bengtz Meml. prize Boston Printmakers, 1981, Pennell award Library of Congress, 1971, 75, Phila. Print Club awards, 1972, 75, 79, Wesleyan Coll. Internat. award of merit, 1980, numerous others. Mem. The Boston Printmakers, Los Angeles Printmakers Soc., Soc. Am. Graphic Artists, Phila. Print Club, Calif. Soc. Printmakers, Coll. Art Assn. Am., Phi Beta Kappa. Address: 3348 Indian Rd Toledo OH 43606

AUTRY, ORVON GENE, singer, actor, radio entertainer, broadcasting exec.; b. Tioga, Tex., Sept. 29, 1907; s. Delbert and Elnora (Ozment) A.; m. Ina Mae Spivey, Apr. 1, 1932; m. Jacqueline Ellam, 1981. Grad., Tioga (Tex.) High Sch., 1925. Began as r.r. telegraph operator, Sapulpa, Okla., 1925; chmn. bd. Calif. Angels; pres. Flying A Prodns.; owner Sta. KTLA-TV, Phoenix, KTLA-TV, Hollywood, radio stas. KMPC, KSFO, San Francisco, KVI-AM & FM, Seattle, KEX and KQFM, Portland, Oreg., WCAR and WTWR-FM, WCXI-Am, Detroit. Made first phonograph record of cowboy songs, 1929; radio artist, Sta. WLS, Chgo., 1930-34; motion picture actor since 1934, including: In Old Santa Fe; starred in 88 musical Western feature pictures, 95 half-hour TV pictures; Has written over:

250 songs including That Silver-Haired Daddy of Mine, 1931, You're the Only Star in My Blue Heaven, 1938, Dust, 1938, Tears On My Pillow, 1941, Be Honest With Me, 1941, Tweedle O'Twill, 1942, Here Comes Santa Claus, 1948. Served with USAAF, 1942-45. Mem. Internat. Footprinters. Clubs: Masons (32 deg.), Shriners, Elks. Address: care Golden West Broadcasters 5858 W Sunset Blvd Hollywood CA 90028 *

AUWERS, STANLEY JOHN, motor carrier exec.; b. Grand Rapids, Mich., Mar. 22, 1923; s. Joseph T. and Cornelia (Moelhoek) A.; m. Elizabeth Kruis, Apr. 6, 1946; children—Ellen (Mrs. William Northway), Stanley John, Thomas. Student, Calvin Coll., 1940-41; B.B.A., U. Mich., 1943. C.P.A., Mich. With Ernst & Ernst, Detroit, 1943-51; controller Interstate Motor Freight System, Grand Rapids, Mich., 1951-61, v.p., controller, 1961-65, v.p. finance, 1965-69, exec. v.p., 1969-72; also dir.; pres. Transam. Freight Lines, Detroit, 1973—; Chmn. cost com. Mich. Trucking Adv. Bd. to Mich. Pub. Service Commn., 1958-63; mem. citizens com. to study Mich. tax structure advisory Mich. Ho. Reps., 1958. Mem. Am. Motor Carriers Central Freight Assn. (gov. regular common carrier conf.), Mich. Motor Carriers Central Freight Assn. (v.p., gov.), Tax Execs. Inst., Am. Inst. C.P.A.s, Trucking Employers. Presbyn. Home: 7478 Cascade Rd SE Grand Rapids MI 49508 Office: 2843 E Paris Ave Grand Rapids MI 49506

AVALLE-ARCE, JUAN BAUTISTA, language educator; b. Buenos Aires, Argentina, May 13, 1927; came to U.S., 1948; s. Juan B. and Maria Avalle-A.; m. Constance Marginot, Aug. 20, 1953 (dec. 1969); children: Juan Bautista, Maria Martina, Alejandro Alcantara; m. Diane Janet Pamp, Aug. 30, 1969; children: Maria la Real Alejandra, Fadrique Martín Manuel. A.B., Harvard U., 1951, M.A., 1952, Ph.D., 1955. Tutor, Harvard U., 1953-55; asst. prof., then asso. prof. Spanish, Ohio State U., 1955-62; prof. Spanish, Smith Coll., 1962-66, Sophia Smith prof. Hispanic studies, 1966-69; William Rand Kenan, Jr. prof. Spanish, U. N.C., from 1969; now prof. Spanish U. Calif.-Santa Barbara; lectr., 1961-—; vis. scholar Univ. Center in Ga., 1972, Univ. Center Va., 1976; vis. prof. U. Salamanca, 1982; Ph.D. program evaluator N.Y. State Bd. Regents; cons. Council Grad. Schs. in U.S. Author: Conocimiento y vida en Cervantes, 1959, La novela pastoril española, 1959, 2d enlarged edit., 1974, La Galatea de Cervantes, 2 vols., 1961, Gonzalo Fernandez de Oviedo, 1962, El Inca Garcilaso en sus Comentarios, 1961, Deslindes cervantinos, 1961, Three Exemplary Novels, 1964, Bernal Frances y su Romance, 1966, El Persiles de Cervantes, 1969, Los entremeses de Cervantes, 1969, Don Juan Valera y Morsamor, 1970, El cronista Pedro de Escavias Una vida del Siglo XV, 1972, Suma cervantina, 1973, Narradores hispoamericanos de hoy, 1973, Las Memorias de Gonzalo Fernández de Oviedo, 2 vols., 1974, El Peregrino en su patria de Lope de Vega, 1973, Nuevos deslindes cervantinos, 1974, Temas hispánicos medievales, 1975, Don Quijote como forma de vida, 1976, Dintorno de una época dorada, 1978, Cervantes, Don Quixote, annotated critical edit., 2 vols., 1978, 2d rev. edit., 1983, Cervantes, Novelas ejemplares, annotated edit., 3 vols., 1982. Trustee Teutonic Order of the Levant Trust, Marquês de la Lealtad. Recipient Bonsoms medal, Spain, 1961; Guggenheim fellow, 1961; grantee Am. Council Learned Socs., 1965, 68, NEH, 1968, 1978-80, Am. Philos. Soc., 1961, 67; recipient Susan Anthony Potter Lit. prize, 1951; Centro Gallego Lit. prize, 1947. Sr. fellow Southeastern Inst. Medieval and Renaissance Studies; hon. fellow Soc. Spanish and Spanish Am. Studies; fellow Colegio Mayor Arzobispo D. Alonso de Fonseca of U. Salamanca; mem. Am. Acad. Research Historians Medieval Spain, Academia Argentina de Letras, Anglo Am. Basque Studies Soc., Cervantes Soc. Am. (pres. 1979—), Soc. de Bibliofilos Espanoles, Modern Humanities Research Assn., South Atlantic Modern Lang. Assn., Assn. Internac. de Hispanistas, Modern Lang. Assn., Renaissance Soc. Am. (nat. del. to exec. council 1971), Real Sociedad Vascongada de Amigos del País, Centro de Estudios Jacobeos, Inst. d'Etudes Medievales, Inst. de Lit. Iberoamericana, Hispanic Soc. Am., Acad. Lit. Studies (charter), Mediaeval Acad. Am., Anglo Am. Basque Studies Soc., Instituto Internacional de Literatura Iberoamericana, Sovereign Mil. Teutonic Order of the Levant (bailiff, knight grand cross, Grand Prior, Grand Priory in U.S.). Clubs: Triangle Hunt (Durham) (gentleman Whipper-in); U. N.C. Polo, Combined Training Events Assn. Home: Etxeberria 4640 Oak View Rd Santa Ynez CA 93460

AVALLON, JOHN CLEMENT, manufacturing company executive; b. Revere, Mass., 1924; s. Anthony and Rose A.; m. Jean, Oct. 19, 1949; children: John, Judy, James, Joanne. B.S., M.I.T. Formerly with Sylvania Electric Co.; now pres. elec. products GTE Co., Danvers, Mass. Served to capt. AUS; ETO; Served to capt. AUS; CBI; Served to capt. AUS; Korea. Mem. Electrochem. Soc. Roman Catholic. Office: 100 Hutchinson Dr Danvers MA 01923

AVALLONE, MICHAEL ANGELO, author; b. N.Y.C., Oct. 27, 1924; s. Michael Angelo and Marie Antoinette (Antonelli) A.; m. Frances Weinstein, May 27, 1960; children: Stephen Michael, Susan, David Prill. Author: Five Minute Mysteries, 1978, The Judas Judge, 1979, Slaughter in September, 1979, Kill Them Silently, 1980, Coffin Corner, U.S.A, 1981, Death in Yellow, 1981, The Hoodoo Horror, 1981, The Cannonball Run, 1981, Charlie Chan and the Curse of the Dragon Queen, 1981, Beneath the Planet of the Apes, Tales of the Frightened, Man from U.N.C.L.E, Hawaii Five-O, Mannix, Felony Squad, The Doctors, The Partridge Family, Craghold House, The Girl From U.N.C.L.E; series Ed Noon Pvt. Detective; There is Something About a Dame, 1963, Lust Is No Lady, 1964, The Fat Death, 1966, Assassins Don't Die in Bed, 1968, The Horrible Man, 1968, The Flower-Covered Corpse, 1969, Death Dives Deep, 1971, Little Miss Murder, 1971, Shoot It Again, Sam, 1972, The Girl in the Cockpit, 1972, London, Bloody London, 1972, The X-rated Corpse, 1973, The Big Stiffs, 1977, Dark on Monday, 1978, A Woman Called Golda, 1982, Friday the 13th Part II, 1982, Go Die in Afghanistan, 1982, Gotham Gore, 1982, The Man from White Hat, 1982, The Gunfighters, 1982, Red Roses Forever, 1983; numerous others. Served with AUS, 1943-46. Mem. Mystery Writers Am. (dir. 1955—, mem. awards com. 1961-71), Authors League. Democrat. Address: 80 Hilltop Blvd East Brunswick NJ 08816 *A professional writer should be able to write anything—from the Bible to a garden seed catalogue and everything there is that lies in between. . . Writing is the last frontier of individualism in the world—the one art a man can do alone that basically resists collaboration.*

AVANT, GRADY, JR., lawyer; b. New Orleans, Mar. 1, 1932; s. Grady and Sarah (Rutherford) A.; m. Katherine Willis Yancey, Feb. 23, 1963; children: Grady M., Mary Willis Yancey. B.A. magna cum laude, Princeton U., 1954; J.D., Harvard U., 1960. Bar: N.Y. 1961, Ala. 1962, Mich. 1972. Assoc. Bradley, Arant, Rose & White, Birmingham, Ala., 1961-63; assoc., ptnr. Long, Preston, Kinnaird & Avant, Detroit, 1972—. Contbr. articles to legal jours. Served to lt. USMC, 1954-57. Mem. Am. Law Inst.; mem. ABA (antitrust sect., corp., fin. and bus. law sect., fed. regulation of securities com.), State Bar of Mich. (council sect. of antitrust law 1978—, chmn. sect. 1983—), Detroit Com. on Fgn. Relations (rapporteur 1979—, exec. com. 1979—). Episcopalian. Clubs: Grosse Pointe, Detroit Athletic; Mountain Brook (Ala.); Knickerbocker (N.Y.C.); Met. (Washington); Princeton of Mich. (pres. 1976-77). Home: 406 Lincoln Rd Grosse Pointe MI 48230 Office: 4300 Penobscot Bldg Detroit MI 48226

AVE, JOHN ROBERT, tobacco company executive; b. Lafayette, Ind., May 27, 1932; s. John and Zola Marie (Evans) A.; m. Aurora Gasparelli, Sept. 20, 1968; children: Christopher Evan, Dana Kathryn, Jonathan Eric. B.A., DePauw U., 1954; postgrad., Harvard U. Bus. Sch., 1956. With Lorillard Co., N.Y.C., 1973—, v.p. advt. and brand mgmt., 1973-77, sr. v.p. mktg., 1977-79, exec. v.p. mktg., 1979-84, pres., 1984—. Served with USAF, 1956-60. Mem. Phi Beta Kappa. Methodist. Home: 1050 Park Ave New York NY 10128 Office: 666 5th Ave New York NY 10103

AVEDISIAN, ARMEN G., corporation executive, investor; b. Chgo., Oct. 28, 1926; s. Karekin Der and Kardovil (Ignatius) A.; m. Dorothy D. Donian, Nov. 22, 1952; children: Guy A., Vann A., Donna A. B.S., U. Ill., 1949. Civil engr. Standard Paving Co., Chgo., 1949; constrn. supt. Gallagher Asphalt Corp., Thornton, Ill., 1950-55; v.p., dir. Am. Asphalt Paving Co., Chgo., 1956-64; chmn. bd., pres. Lincoln Stone Quarry, Inc., Joliet, Ill., 1964—, Avedisian Industries, Inc., Hillside, Ill., 1964—; chmn. bd. Delta Constrn. Corp., Joliet, 1968—, Swenson, Inc., 1970—, Midstate Stone Corp., Gillespie, Ill., 1970—; chmn. bd., chief exec. officer Hillside Stone Corp., 1969—, Avedisian Co., 1978—; chmn. bd., chief exec. officer Geneva Capital Corp., Lake Geneva, Wis.; chmn. bd. Citizens Nat. Bank, Geneva. Mem. pres.'s com., bd. dirs. Lyric Opera, Chgo., 1968—; mem. classical art acquisitions com. Art Inst. Chgo., 1961—; trustee Avery Coonley Sch., Chgo. Symphony Orch., 1978—; trustee, chmn. European tour com. Chgo. Symphony Orch.; trustee Glenwood (Ill.) Sch. for Boys, Max McGraw Wildlife Found.; mem. exec. bd. Boy Scouts Am., 1978—; mem. Statue of Liberty / Ellis Island Centennial Commn., 1982; v.p. Geneva Lake Water Safety Patrol; mem. gen. com. Société des Bains de Mer de Monte Carlo World Backgammon Championship. Served with AUS, 1944-45. Recipient Disting. Eagle Scout award, 1983. Mem. Nat. Limestone Inst. (chmn. bd. 1971—), Midwest Crushed Limestone Inst. (pres. 1966-67), Nat. Crushed Stone Inst. (bd. govs. 1972—), Ill. Rd. Builders Assn. (dir., treas. 1963), Am., Western socs. civil engrs., Ill. Assn. Aggregate Producers (dir., pres. 1968), Sigma Nu. Clubs: Chgo., Casino, Racquet (Chgo.); Butler Nat. Golf (Oak Brook, Ill.) (gov. 1978—); Casade Campo Golf (Dominican Republic); Dunham Woods Riding (Wayne, Ill.); Lake Geneva Country, Palm Beach (Fla.) Polo and Country. Patentee impermeable ecol. shale barrier in U.S., Can., U.K., W. Ger., France. Office: Citizens Nat Bank Box 432 401 Broad St Lake Geneva WI 53147

AVEDISIAN, EDWARD, painter; b. Lowell, Mass., 1936. Student, Boston Museum Sch. Art. Artist-in-residence U. Kans., 1969; instr. Sch. Visual Arts, N.Y.C., 1969-70. One-man exhbns. include, Boyston Print Center Gallery, Cambridge, Mass., 1957, Hansa Gallery, 1958, Tibor de Nagy Gallery, 1959, 60, Robert Elkon Gallery, N.Y.C., 1962-75, Galerie Zigler, Zürich, 1964, Nicholas Wilder Gallery, Los Angeles, 1966, 68, 69, Kasmin Gallery, London, 1966, 67, Bucknell U. Art Gallery, 1970, Walter Moos Gallery, 1971, Jack Glenn Gallery, Corona del Mar, Calif., Janie C. Lee Gallery, Houston, 1974, Carriage House, Buffalo, 1975, 78, Fishback Gallery, 1979, group exhbns. include, Tibor de Nagy Gallery, Hansa Gallery, Boston Mus. Art, Mus. Modern Art, Washington, Whitney Mus. Art, Dayton (Ohio) Art Internat., Kasmin Gallery, Mus. Modern Art, N.Y.C., Jewish Mus., N.Y.C., Larry Aldrich Mus., San Francisco Mus. Art, Paintings From Expo '67, Boston Inst. Contemporary Art, Berkshire Mus., 1980; represented in permanent collections, Guggenheim Mus., Whitney Mus. Art, Mus. Modern Art, Los Angeles Mus. Art, Pasadena (Calif.) Mus. Art, Larry Aldrich Mus., Wadsworth Atheneum, Chrysler Mus. Art, others. Address: care 26 Warren Hudson NY 12534 *

AVEDON, RICHARD, photographer; b. N.Y.C., May 15, 1923; s. Jack and Anne (Polonsky) A.; m. Dorcas Nowell, 1944; m. Evelyn Franklin, Jan. 29, 1951; 1 son, John. Student, Columbia U. Staff photographer Jr. Bazaar, 1945-47, Harper's Bazaar, 1945-65; photographer French fashions, 1947—; staff photographer Theatre Arts, 1952, Vogue mag., 1966—. Author: (comments by Truman Capote) Observations, 1959, (text by James Baldwin) Nothing Personal, 1964, (intro. by Harold Rosenberg) Portraits, 1976, (essay by Harold Brodkey) Avedon Photographs, 1947-1977, 1978; author: spl. bicentennial edit. Rolling Stone mag. The Family, 1976; editor: Diary of a Century (photographs by Jacques Henri Lartigue), 1970, (with Doon Arbus) Alice in Wonderland: The Forming of a Company, The Making of a Play, 1973; photographs in permanent collections, Smithsonian Instn., Met. Mus. Art, N.Y.C., Mus. Modern Art, N.Y.C., one-man retrospective exhbn., Smithsonian Instn., Washington, 1962, Washington, Mpls. Inst. Arts, summer 1970, Univ. Art Mus., Berkeley, Calif., 1980, one-man show, Mus. Modern Art, 1974, Marlborough Gallery, 1975, Met. Mus. Art, N.Y.C., 1978, group shows include, Mus. Modern Art, 1955, Met. Mus. Art, 1959, 60, 63, 67, Musée Réattu, Arles, France, 1965, N.Y. World's Fair, 1965-66, Fogg Art Mus., Cambridge, Mass., 1967, Rhodes Nat. Gallery, Salisbury, Rhodesia, 1968, Mus. Modern Art, N.Y.C., 1964, 65, 69, Expo '70, Osaka, Japan, 1970, Whitney Mus. Am. Art, 1974. Recipient highest achievement medal awards Art Dirs. Show, 1950—; voted one of world's ten greatest photographers Popular Photography, 1958; citation of dedication to fashion photography Pratt Inst., 1976; Nat. Mag. award Visual Excellence, 1976; Pres.'s fellow R.I. Sch. Design, 1978; Chancellor's citation U. Calif., Berkeley, 1980; named to Hall of Fame Art Dirs. Club, 1982. Photographed civil rights movement in South, 1963; anti-war movement across U.S., 1969; Vietnam, 1971. Address: 407 E 75th St New York NY 10021

AVELLA, WILLIAM R., land development and utilities company executive; b. 1936; married. B.A., CCNY, 1961, M.B.A., 1965. With Black-Clawson Co., 1957-61, IBM Corp., 1961-69; v.p. Levitt & Sons Inc., 1969-73, Larwin Group Inc., 1973-74; with Dell Labs Inc., 1977-78; sr. v.p. Gen. Devel. Corp., Miami, Fla., 1974-78, pres., chief exec. officer, 1978-80, chmn. bd., 1980—, dir.; pres., chief exec. officer Servomation Corp. Office: Gen Devel Corp 111 S Bayshore Dr Miami FL 33131 *

AVENI, ANTHONY FRANCIS, astronomy and anthropology educator, researcher; b. New Haven, May 5, 1938; s. Anthony Mark and Frances (Cremonie) A.; m. Lorraine Reiner, Sept. 5, 1959; children: Patricia, Anthony Francis. A.B., Boston U., 1960; Ph.D., Ariz. U., 1965. Instr. astronomy Colgate U., Hamilton, N.Y., 1963-65, asst. prof., 1965-68, assoc. prof., 1968-75, prof. astronomy, 1976-81, prof. astronomy and anthropology, 1981-82, C.A. Dana prof. astronomy and anthropology, 1982—; vis. prof. U. South Fla., Tampa, 1973-74. Author: Skywatchers of Ancient Mexico, 1980. Named Nat. Prof. of Yr. Council Advancement and Support of Edn., 1982; grantee NSF, Nat. Geog. Soc., Wenner Gren Found., Osco Found., 1973—. Fellow AAAS; mem. Am. Astron. Soc., N.Y. Acad. Scis. Home: RD 2 Box 68 Hamilton NY 13346 Office: Dept Physics-Astronomy and Dept Sociology and Anthropology Colgate U Hamilton NY 13346

AVERCH, HARVEY ALLAN, economist; b. Denver, Dec. 18, 1935; s. Louis and Gussie (Weiner) A.; m. Barbara Ann Duvall, July 5, 1962; children: Elizabeth, Caroline. AB. summa cum laude (Univ. scholar), U.Colo., 1957; Ph.D. (Univ. fellow, Ford Found. fellow), U. N.C., 1962. Sr. staff economist Rand Corp., Santa Monica, Calif., 1961-71; dir. Div. Social Systems and Human Resources, Research Applications Directorate, NSF, Washington, 1971-74, dep. asst. dir. for analysis and planning, 1974-75, acting asst. dir. for sci. edn., 1975-76, asst. dir. for sci. edn., 1976-77, asst. dir. sci., technol. and internat. affairs, 1977—; mem. faculty UCLA, 1963-64, Calif. Inst. Tech., 1967, Rand Grad. Inst., 1970-71; vis. prof. policy scis. and econs. U. Md.-Baltimore County, 1982—. Author: Asymmetry and Arms Control: Some Basic Considerations, 1963, (with M. Lavin) Simulation of Decision-Making in Crisis: Three Manual Gaming Experiments, 1964, (with F. Denton and J. Koehler) A. Crisis of Ambiguity: Political and Economic Development in the Philippines, 1970, The Matrix of Policy in the Philippines, 1971, (with others) How Effective is Schooling? A Critical Review and Synthesis of Research Findings, 1972, How Effective is Schooling? A Critical Review of Research, 1974; contbr. articles to profl. jours. Chmn. U.S./Israel Binat. Sci. Found., 1979. Recipient Meritorious Service award NSF, 1973, Disting. Service award, 1977. Mem. Phi Beta Kappa. Office: NSF 1800 G St NW Washington DC 20550

AVERHILL, JAMES REED, psychology educator; b. San Francisco, Nov. 29, 1935; s. Dupree Reed and Rosalie (Diamond) Averill; m. Judith Wittenberger, June 9, 1962; children: Annalaura, Andrea. B.A., San Jose U., 1959; Ph.D., UCLA, 1966. Psychologist U. Calif.-Berkeley, 1966-71; mem. faculty U. Mass., Amherst, 1971—, prof. psychology, 1976—. Served with U.S. Army, 1954-57. Fulbright fellow, W. Germany, 1959-60. Mem. Am. Psychol. Assn. Office: Dept Psychology U Mass Amherst MA 01003

AVERILL, BARRY WILLIAM, public health educator, health care administrator; b. Bklyn., May 14, 1938; s. William Patrick and Gertrude Ellen (Crowley) A.; m. Betsy Ross Lord, Oct. 15, 1962; children: Barbara, Timothy, Christopher. B.S., U. Ky., 1966. Asst. dir. univ. health services U. Ky., 1964-66, asst. dean Coll. Medicine, 1966-68; asst. dir. univ. health services U. Mass., Amherst, 1968-72, dir. univ. health services, 1972—, instr. dept. pub. health, 1982—; incorporator, dir. Valley Health Plan, Inc., 1976—, Accreditation Assn. for Ambulatory Health Care, Inc., Skokie, Ill., 1979—, treas., 1983—. Contbr. articles to profl. jours. Mem. Western Mass. Health Planning Council, 1970-74; trustee Marshall Field Meml. Library, Conway, Mass. Served in U.S. Army, 1961-63. Mem. Am. Coll. Health Assn. (pres. and treas. 1974—), Am. Pub. Health Assn., Group Health Assn. Am. Roman Catholic. Club: Rotary. Home: Reeds Bridge Rd Conway MA 01341 Office: Univ Health Services U Mass Amherst MA 01003

AVERILL, LLOYD JAMES, JR., religion educator; b. Warrenville, Ill., Apr. 5, 1923; s. Lloyd James and Dorothy Mae (Rogers) A.; m. Shirley Mae Karr, Feb. 9, 1944 (div. June 1968); children: Shelley Ann, Leslie Jean, Scott Alan; m. Carol Anne White, July 13, 1968. Student, Beloit Coll., 1942-43; B.A. with honors, U. Wis., 1947; M.Div., Colgate Rochester Div. Sch., 1950, Th.M., 1966; M.A. in Sociology, U. Rochester, 1952; sr. mem., Fitzwilliam Coll., Cambridge U., 1965-66; asso. mem., Westminster Coll., Cambridge, 1965-66; L.H.D., Lewis and Clark Coll., 1962, Coll. of Idaho, 1975; LL.D., Carroll Coll., 1967, William Jewell Coll., 1967; Litt.D., Augustana (Ill.) Coll., 1968; D.D., Tusculum Coll., 1968. Ordained to ministry Baptist Ch., 1949; asso. dir. field work, instr. practical theology Colgate Rochester Div. Sch., 1951-54; dean chapel Kalamazoo Coll., 1954-67, asst. prof. religion, then asso. prof., 1954-62, prof., 1962-67, asst. to pres., 1957-63, v.p. coll., 1963-67; pres. Council Protestant Colls. and Univs., 1967-68; vis. disting. prof. Ottawa U., mem. faculty, 1968-70; v.p., dean of faculty Davis and Elkins Coll., Elkins, W.Va., 1970-72; pres. Kansas City Regional Council for Higher Edn., 1972-79; v.p. acad. affairs, prof. religious studies Barat Coll., 1979-80; cons. coll. curriculum and adminstrn., 1980—; adj. prof. religion Graceland Coll., 1972—; frequent speaker, lectr.; adj. prof. San Francisco Theol. Sem., 1965-71, Central Bapt. Theol. Sem., 1979; cons. asso. Assn. Am. Colls., 1967-68; cons. commn. on fed. relations Am. Council on Edn., 1967-68; mem. adv. bd. Johnson Assos., Inc.; mem. adv. council on campus ministry programs Danforth Found. Author: A Strategy for the Protestant College, 1966, American Theology in the Liberal Tradition, 1967, Between Faith and Unfaith, 1968, The Problem of Being Human, 1974, The Human Shape of Liberal Learning: Proposals for a Humanistic Curriculum, 1981, Learning to Be Human: A Vision for the Liberal Arts, 1983; also articles, book revs.; editor: Leadership in Colleges and Universities: Assessment and Search, 1977; co-editor: Colleges and Commitments, 1971; cons. editor: Jour. Higher Edn., 1974-77. Served with USAAF, 1943-46. Recipient Campus Ministry grant Danforth Found., 1958-59; grad. fellow Colgate Rochester Div. Sch., 1950. Fellow Soc. Values in Higher Edn.; mem. Am. Acad. Religion, Am. Assn. Higher Edn. Democrat. Address: 533 N Clarendon Kalamazoo MI 49007

AVERILL, RICHARD WOOD, professional society administrator; b. Tarrytown, N.Y., Dec. 26, 1933; s. Lawrence Herman and Margaret Mae (Wood) A. B.S., U. Md., 1955; J.D. cum laude, Am. U., 1958; D.H.L., So. Coll. Optometry, 1972, So. Calif. Coll. Optometry, 1973. Asso. rep. Nat. Retail Mchts. Assn., 1959-61; legis. counsel C. of C. U.S., 1961-68; with Am. Optometric Assn., St. Louis, 1968—, exec. dir., 1977—. Recipient Gold Medal award Beta Sigma Kappa, 1979. Mem. ABA, Am. Soc. Assn. Execs. (dir.), Internat. Assn. Optometric Execs. (past pres.), C. of C. U.S. (com. of 100), Delta Theta Phi, Sigma Nu. Clubs: Congressional Country, Masons. Office: 243 N Lindbergh Saint Louis MO 63141

AVERY, DAVID ROGER, pedodontics educator; b. Kokomo, Ind., Apr. 20, 1940; s. Walter Kenneth and Friedi Rachel (Farmer) A.; m. Myra Jean Avery, Sept. 2, 1961; children: Lisa, Jean, Scott David. B.S., Purdue U., 1963; D.D.S., Ind. U., 1966, M.S.D., 1971. Diplomate: Am. Bd. Pedodontics. Undergrad. research asst. Ind. U. Sch. Dentistry, Indpls., 1962-66, grad. teaching asst. pedodontics, 1968-70, asst. prof. pedodontics, 1970-73, assoc. prof., 1973-79, prof., 1979—, chmn. dept. pedodontics, dir. postdoctroal pedodontics program, 1976—; cons. Am. Bd. Pedodontics, Chgo., 1982—, U.S. Army Gen. Practice Residency Program, Fort Knox, Ky., 1978—, ADA Commn. on Accreditation, 1983-84. Co-author and assoc. editor: Dentistry for the Child and Adolescent, 1978, (3d edit.). Served to lt. (s.g.) USNR, 1966-68. Fellow United Cerebral Palsy Research and Ednl. Found., 1980. Felloq Am. Acad. Pedodontics; mem. Am. Soc. Dentistry for Children, fedn. Dentaire Internat., Omicron Kfappa Upsilon (Theta Theta chpt.). Club: Bass Anglers Sportsmen Soc. Office: Sch Dentistry Ind U 1121 W Michigan St Indianapolis IN 46202

AVERY, DONALD HILLS, metallurgist, educator; b. Hartford, Conn., May 7, 1937; s. Charles Raymond and Loma Elinor (Mullhoil) A.; children: Jon Weymouth, Nathaniel Caleb, Jessica van Voast. Student, Loomis Inst., 1951-55; B.S., M.I.T., 1959, Sc.D., 1962; M.A., Brown U., 1969. Pres. Strathmore Research Co., Cambridge, Mass., 1961-69; dir. research Armor Flite Group, Rangely, Maine, 1973—; dir. A.P.C. Engrs., East Providence, R.I.; asst. prof. M.I.T., 1962-66, Brown U., 1966-69, asso. prof., 1969-74, prof. engring., 1974—; vis. scholar, prof. U. Capetown, 1974. Contbr. articles to profl. jours. NSF fellow, 1959-62; Ford fellow, 1965; research scholar, Tanzania, 1976, 79, Malawi, 1982, 83. Mem. AIME (Metall. Soc.), Am. Soc. Metals (past chmn. R.I., Howe medal 1965), Soc. Plastics Engrs., Hist. Metall. Soc., AAAS, AAUP, History Sci. Soc., Soc. History Tech. Clubs: Explorers Club., Hope, 2000, Barrington Yacht, Kasungu Farmers. Patentee in field. Home: 45 Jennys Ln Barrington RI 02806 Office: Div Engring Brown U Providence RI 02912

AVERY, FREDERICK FIFIELD, food company executive; b. Peoria, Ill., Oct. 8, 1930; s. N. Kirk and Elisabeth (Fifield) A.; m. Joan Oldberg, Sept. 7, 1956; children: Cynthia Allison, Richard Kirk, Karen Lynn. B.A. in Econs., Williams Coll., 1952; M.B.A. in Mktg., U. Wis., 1953. Asst. buyer, then group mgr. Marshall Field & Co., Chgo., 1953-57; brand mgr. Procter & Gamble Co., Cin., 1957-65; mktg. mgr. Folger Coffee Co., Kansas City, Mo., 1965-69; pres., chief operating officer, dir. ENRG Internat. Co., Mpls., 1969-70; v.p., gen. mgr. corp. bottling plants, then exec. v.p. ops. and adminstrn. Dr. Pepper Co., Dallas, 1970-75, exec. v.p. sales and mktg., 1975-80; exec. v.p., chief operating officer Anderson Clayton Foods, Dallas, 1980-82, pres., chief exec. officer, 1982—; dir. Acton Corp., Mass., Tex. Commerce Bank, Anderson Clayton Co.; adj. prof. Cox Sch. Bus., So. Methodist U. Councilman, Leawood, Kans., 1969. Mem. Aerobics Activity Center, Dallas, 1971—; devel. council Trinity Christian Acad., Dallas, 1972-76; exec. v.p., parade chmn. Cotton Bowl Council.; pres. Cotton Bowl Council, 1982-83, chmn., 1983-84. Mem. Sales and Mktg. Execs. Dallas (past pres., dir., Ray Bill award 1976), Mustang Club, Beta Theta Pi. Presbyterian. Clubs: Bent Tree Country, Lancers. Home: 4407 Melissa Ln Dallas TX 75229 Office: PO Box 226165 Dallas TX 75266

AVERY, JAMES KNUCKEY, dental educator; b. Holly, Colo., Aug. 6, 1921; s. Willard Smith and Bertha (Knuckey) A.; m. Dorothy Jane Thuerk, Aug. 26, 1950; children—Nancy Jane, David Lloyd, Robert Hugh. B.A., U. Rochester, 1948, Ph.D., 1952; D.D.S., U. Kansas City, 1945. Instr. anatomy U. Rochester Dental Sch., 1952-54; mem. faculty U. Mich. Med. and Dental Sch., 1954—; prof. oral biology Sch. Dentistry, 1963—, prof. anatomy, 1970—, chmn. dept. oral biology, 1977—; dir. Dental Research Inst., 1975—; mem. dental tng. com. NIH, 1964-68; research cons. VA, Ann Arbor, 1964—. Editorial bd.: Jour. Dental Research, 1968-72. Served to lt. (j.g.) USNR, 1945-47. Recipient award Acad. Dental Medicine. Fellow Am. Coll. Dentists, AAAS (chmn. dentistry sect. 1976); mem. ADA (cons. sci. session 1960-70), Internat. Assn. Dental Research (pres. 1974-75), Am. Assn. Anatomists, Electron Microscopic Soc. Am., Teratology Soc., Sigma Xi (hon.), Omicron Kappa Upsilon o3(hon.). Home: 2465 Adare St Ann Arbor MI 48104

AVERY, JAMES STEPHEN, oil company executive; b. Cranford, N.J., Mar. 24, 1923; s. John Henry and Martha Ann (Jones) A.; m. Joan Avery; children: Sheryl Ann, James Stephen. B.A., Columbia U., 1948, M.A., 1949. Pub. relations rep. Esso Standard Oil Co. (named changed to Exxon Co. U.S.A.), N.Y.C., 1956-63; coordinator community relations Humble Oil and Refining Co. (named changed to Exxon Co. U.S.A.), N.Y.C., 1963-68; mgr. pub. relations Exxon Co., Pelham, N.Y., 1968-71; mgr. pub. affairs Exxon Co. U.S.A., 1971-83, pub. affairs cons., 1983—. Vice-chmn., chmn. adv. com. to Vice Pres.'s Task Force on Youth Motivation, 1966-69; chmn. Union County (N.J.) Coordinating Agy. for Higher Edn., 1968-81; nat. vice-chmn. annual campaigns United Negro Coll. Fund, 1962, 63, 64; trustee N.Y. State Council Econ. Edn., 1974—, N.Y. State Traffic Council, 1974—, Council Mcpl. Performance, 1983—. Served with AUS, 1942-46. Named one of 100 most influential blacks in Am. Ebony Mag., 1973. Mem. Nat. Assn. Market Devel. (pres. 1964-66, chmn. bd. 1967), Omega Psi Phi (Grand Basileus 1970-73). Baptist. Home: Prince's Pine Rd Norwalk CT 06850 Office: 101 Merritt 7 Norwalk CT 06851

AVERY, LUTHER J., lawyer; b. New London, Conn., July 25, 1923; s. Lauriston D. and Dorothy A.; m. Mary Catherine Looney, Aug. 22, 1948; children—Shelley, Matthew, Mark. B.S., U. Calif., Berkeley, 1946, M.B.A., 1947; J.D., Stanford U., 1952. Bar: Calif. bar 1952, U.S. Supreme Ct. bar 1952; C.P.A., Calif. Partner firm Bancroft, Avery & McAlister, San Francisco, 1952—; mem. faculty U. San Francisco Law Sch., 1955-65. Contbr. articles to profl. jours. Served with USNR, 1943-45. Fellow Am. Bar. Found., Am. Coll. Probate Counsel; mem. Am. Law Inst., Am. Bar Assn., San Francisco Bar Assn., State Bar Calif. (cert. tax specialist). Home: 8 16th Ave San Francisco CA 94118 Office: 601 Montgomery St San Francisco CA 94111

AVERY, MARY ELLEN, pediatrician, educator; b. Camden, N.J., May 6, 1927; d. William Clarence and Mary (Miller) A. A.B., Wheaton Coll., Mass., 1948, Sc.D., 1974; M.D., Johns Hopkins U., 1952; Sc.D. (hon.), Trinity Coll., 1976, U. Mich., 1975, Med. Coll. Pa., 1976, Albany Med. Coll., 1977, Med. Coll., Wis., 1978, Radcliffe Coll., 1978, M.A., Harvard U., 1974; L.H.D., Emmanuel Coll., 1979, Northeastern U., 1981, Russell Sage Coll., 1983. Intern Johns Hopkins Hosp., 1953-54, resident, 1954-57; research fellow in pediatrics, Boston, 1957-59, Balt., 1959-69; asso. prof. pediatrics Johns Hopkins U., 1964-69; prof., chmn. dept. pediatrics McGill U. Med. Sch., 1969-74; prof. pediatrics Harvard U., 1974—; physician-in-chief Montreal Children's Hosp., 1969-74, Children's Hosp. Med. Center, Boston, 1974—; mem. council Med. Research Council Can.; mem. study sect. NIH, 1967—. Author: The Lung and Its Disorders in the Newborn Infant, 4th edit, 1981, (with A. Schaffer) Diseases of the Newborn, 1971, 5th edit., 1984; also articles; editorial bd.: Pediatrics, 1965-71, Am. Rev. Respiratory Diseases, 1969—, Am. Jour. Physiology, 1967-73, Jour. Pediatrics, 1974-84, Johns Hopkins Med. Jour, 1978-82, Clin. and Investigative Medicine, 1978—. Trustee Wheaton Coll., Radcliffe Coll., Johns Hopkins U., 1982—. Recipient Mead Johnson award in pediatric research, 1968, Trudeau medal Am. Thoracic Soc., 1984; Markle scholar in med. scis., 1961-66. Fellow Am. Acad. Pediatrics, Am. Acad. Arts and Scis., Royal Coll. Physicians and Surgeons Can.; mem. Am., Canadian pediatric socs., Am. Physiol. Soc., Soc. Pediatric Research (pres. 1972-73), Brit. Paediatric Assn. (hon.), Inst. Medicine, Assn. Med. Sch. Dept. Chairmen, Am. Pediatric Soc., Phi Beta Kappa. Office: 300 Longwood Ave Boston MA 02115

AVERY, NATHAN MARK, oilfield equipment and services company executive; b. Tulsa, May 6, 1934; s. Nathan and Rena (Dean) A.; m. Sally Galbreath, Feb. 5, 1957; children: Mark Galreath, Paige Elizabeth, Jonathan Stuart. Petroleum Engr., Colo. Sch. Mines, 1956. Petroleum engr. Texaco, Harvey, La., 1956-57, Cable Engring., Wichita Falls, Tex., 1958-60, Schultz & Brannan Drilling, Wichita Falls, 1960-61; ind. petroleum engr., Wichita Falls, 1961-64; pres. Power Generation, Inc., Houston, 1964-66, Mattco, Inc., 1967—; pres., chmn. bd., chief exec. officer Galverston-Houston Co., Houston, 1967-82; chmn. bd., chief exec. officer Galveston-Houston Co., Houston, 1982—; chmn. bd. Coco-Cola of Miami, Inc., Coral Gables, Fla., 1983—; dir. First Matagorda Corp., First City Nat. Bank of Houston. Trustee Houston Ballet; bd. dirs. YMCA, Houston, Tex. Hart Inst., 1982-83, Jones Grad. Sch. Bus. Adminstrn., Rice U.;. Served to 2d lt. C.E. U.S. Army, 1957-58. Recipient Disting. Achievement award Colo. Sch. Mines, 1982. Mem. Petroleum Equipment Suppliers Assn. (dir.). Republican. Episcopalian. Home: 3456 Inwood St Houston TX 77019 Office: Galveston-Houston Co 4900 Woodway St Houston TX 77001

AVERY, WILLIAM HENRY, oil company executive, former governor Kans.; b. Wakefield, Kans., Aug. 11, 1911; s. Herman W. and Hattie M. (Coffman) A.; m. Hazel Bowles, June 16, 1940; children: Bill, Barbara Ann, Bradley Eugene, Martha Sue. A.B., U. Kans., 1934. Farmer, stockman, nr. Wakefield, Kans., 1935-55; mem. 84th to 90th Congresses from 2d Kans. Dist.; gov. Kans., 1965-67; with Garvey Enterprises, 1967-68; asst. to pres. Clinton Oil Co., 1969, exec. v.p. adminstrn., 1971—, also mem. exec. com.; pres. Real Petroleum (merged with Clinton Oil Co. 1971), 1969-71; Congl. liaison Dept. Interior, Washington, 1973-77; chmn. bd. Farmers and Mchts. Bank, Wakefield, Kans., 1977-80, now dir.; mem. Kans. Legislature, 1951-55, Legis. Council Kans., 1953-55; dir. bd. edn. Wakefield High Sch. Mem. Kans. Farm Bur., Delta Upsilon. Republican. Methodist. Clubs: Masons, Lions (Wakefield). Home: 5111 Westbard Ave Bethesda MD 20816 Wakefield KS 67487

AVERY, WILLIAM HERBERT, lawyer; b. Jacksonville, Fla., July 16, 1905; s. William Herbert and Annelyle (Graves) A.; m. Eugenie Petrequin, Oct. 6, 1934; children: Nancy (Mrs. H. Paul Pressler), Cameron Scott, Richard Manchester. B.S. magna cum laude, Princeton U., 1927; J.D., Harvard U., 1930. Bar: bar 1930. Practiced in Chgo. with Cutting, Moore & Sidley (and successor firms); now partner Sidley & Austin, 1944—; lectr. Nat. Trust Sch., 1947-64; dir. Carson, Pirie, Scott and Co., Chgo. Title and Trust Co., Equitable Life Assurance Soc. of U.S.; Mem. adv. council Ill. Dept. Public Welfare, 1948-52; pres. Kenilworth Sch. Bd., 1950-53; mem. citizens' bd. U. Chgo., Northwestern U. Assos. Trustee or dir. Civic Fedn.; past v.p. George Williams Coll.; past chmn. Legal Aid Bur. Chgo., Nat. Legal Aid and Defender Assn., Sunday Evening Club, YMCA; past pres. United Charities, Council Legal Edn. for Profl. Responsibility, Presbyn. Home, Evanston, Ravinia Festival Assn. Mem. Ill. Bar Assn., Chgo. Bar Assn., Internat. Bar Assn., Am. Judicature Soc., Am. Law Inst., Chgo. Estate Planning Council, Chgo. Assn. Commerce and Industry (dir.). Presbyterian (elder). Clubs: Commercial (past pres.), Commonwealth (past pres.), Economic (past pres.), Harvard Law (past pres.), Law, Legal, Princeton (past pres.), Tax (past pres.), Mid-Day, University (Chgo.); Indian Hill (Winnetka, Ill.); Old Elm (Lake Forest, Ill.). Home: 99 Indian Hill Rd Winnetka IL 60093 Office: One First Nat Plaza Chicago IL 60603

AVERY, WILLIAM HINCKLEY, physicist; b. Ft. Collins, Colo., July 25, 1912; s. Edgar Delano and Mabel Abbey (Gordon) A.; m. Helen Wallace Palmer, July 18, 1937; children—Christopher, Patricia (Mrs. W. Randolph Bartlett, Jr.). A.B., Pomona Coll., 1933; A.M., Harvard, 1935, Ph.D., 1937. Postdoctoral research asst. infrared spectroscopy Harvard, 1937-39; research chemist Shell Oil Co., St. Louis, Houston, 1939-43; head propulsion div. Allegany Ballistics Lab., Cumberland, Md., 1943-46; cons. in physics and chemistry Arthur D. Little Co., Cambridge, Mass., 1946-47; profl. staff mem. Applied Physics Lab., Johns Hopkins, Laurel, Md., 1947-73, asst. dir. exploratory devel., 1973-78, dir. ocean energy programs, 1978—; mem. various coms. DOD, NASA, NRC, Nat. Acad. Scis.; Nat. Acad. Engring., 1955—; mem. tech. adv. bd. panel on SST environ. research Dept. Commerce, 1971; mem. subcom. AEC, Pres.'s Energy Report, 1973. Contbr. articles to profl. jours. Recipient C.N. Hickman award, 1951, Presdl. certificate of merit, 1948, Naval Ordnance Devel. award, 1945. Fellow Am. Inst. Aeros. and Astronautics (tech. dir. 1968-71); mem. Am. Chem. Soc., Combustion Inst. (dir. 1960-80, Sir Alfred C. Egerton Gold medal 1971), Phi Beta Kappa. Club: Cosmos (Washington). Home: 724 Guilford Ct Silver Spring MD 20901 Office: Johns Hopkins Rd Laurel MD 20707

AVERY, WILLIAM JOSEPH, packaging manufacturing company executive; b. Chgo., June 20, 1940; s. Floyd Joseph and Margaret Mildred (Musard) A.; m. Sharon Bajorek, Sept. 5, 1959; children: Michelle, Martin, Sheryl. Grad. in indsl. mgmt., U. Chgo., 1968. With Crown Cork & Seal Co. Inc., 1959—, v.p. sales, Phila., 1974-79, sr. v.p. mfg. and sales, 1979-80, exec. v.p., 1980-81, pres., 1981—, also dir. Roman Catholic. Address: Crown Cork & Seal Co Inc 9300 Ashton Rd Philadelphia PA 19136

AVERYT, GAYLE OWEN, insurance executive; b. Montgomery, Ala., Oct. 13, 1933; s. Edwin Franklin and Asenath Pratt (Murfee) A.; m. Margaret Rosborough Finlay, July 15, 1963; children: Caroline Elliott, Margaret McQueen, Elinor Finlay. B.S., Davidson Coll., 1955; M.B.A., Harvard U., 1958. Asst. v.p. Colonial Life and Accident Ins. Co., Columbia, S.C., 1958-64, v.p., 1964-68, exec. v.p., 1968-70, chmn. bd. and chief exec. officer, 1970-82, pres. and chmn. bd., 1982—; dir. Citizens and So. Corp., Columbia, 1966—; mem. HIAA Fed. Programs Commn., Washington, 1982—, S.C. Ins. Commn., Columbia, 1976-80; treas. Assn. S.C. Life Ins. Cos., Columbia, 1970-73. Trustee Davidson Coll., N.C.; trustee, treas. U. S.C. Bus. Partnership Found., Columbia; treas. Palmetto Bus. Forum, Columbia; active Republican Senatorial Trust Com., Washington. Served to 2d lt. U.S. Army, 1955-56. Recipient Lyre award Columbia Music Festival Assn., 1972, U. S.C. Ednl. Found. Cum Laude Club award, 1981, Jonathan Maxcy Club award, 1980. Episcopalian. Clubs: Forest Lake, Summit (Columbia). Home: 1717 Greene St Columbia SC 29201 Office: Colonial Life and Accident Ins Co 1200 Colonial Life Blvd W Columbia SC 29210

AVIADO, DOMINGO M., pharmacologist, toxicologist; b. Manila, Aug. 28, 1924; U.S., 1946; s. Domingo Gatus and Severina O. (Mariano) A.; m. Asuncion Palma Guevara, Aug. 15, 1953; children: Maria Cristina Aviado Gentile, Carlos G., Domingo G., Maria Asuncion. Student, U. Philippines, 1940-46; M.D., U. Pa., 1948. From asst. instr. pharmacology to assoc. prof. U. Pa. Med. Sch., 1948-65, prof., 1965-77, acting chmn. dept., 1969-70; sr. dir. biomed. research Allied Chem. Corp., Morristown, N.J., 1977-80; pres. Atmospheric Health Scis., Inc., 1980—; adj. prof. pharmacology Coll. Medicine and Dentistry N.J., Newark, 1977—; vis. lectr. anesthesiology Albert Einstein Med. Center, 1955-77; vis. prof. pharmacology U. of East Med. Center, Philippines, 1959-77; vis. lectr. physiology Women's Med. Coll., Phila., 1961-62, Rutgers U., 1966-67; cons. Council for Drug Research, 1972-73, Poison Control Program of Phila., 1964-70; mem. clean air sci. adv. com. EPA, 1978-80. Author textbook, 7 monographs, 2 med. dictionaries; editorial bd.: Cardiology, 1967-79, Drug Info. Jour, 1974-77, Jour. Cardiovascular Pharmacology, 1978—, Biol. Abstracts, 1984—; adv. editorial bd.: Archives Internationales de Pharmacodynamie et de Therapie, 1965—; editor inhalation sect.: Jour. Pathology and Environ. Toxicology, 1978-80; contbr. articles to profl. jours. Recipient Linnaeus medal, Stockholm, 1961, Purkinje medal, Prague, 1963; Presdl. trophy for most outstanding Filipino, 1975; named Physician of Year Philippine Med. Assn., 1969, numerous other awards; Guggenheim fellow, 1962-63. Mem. Physiol. Soc. Phila. (pres. 1959-60), Am. Soc. Pharmacology and Exptl. Therapeutics (fin. com. 1965-70), Am. Physiol Soc., AAAS, Am. Heart Assn., Internat. Union Pharmacology (treas. 1965-66), Am. Soc. Tropical Medicine and Hygiene, Internat. Leprosy Assn., Am. Coll. Clin. Pharmacology (bd. regents 1978-83), Soc. Toxicology, AMA, Coll. Physicians Phila., Drug Info. Assn., Sigma Xi. Home: 225 Hartshorn Dr Short Hills NJ 07078 Office: 152 Parsonage Hill Rd PO Box 307 Short Hills NJ 07078

AVIAN, BOB, choreographer, producer; b. N.Y.C., Dec. 26, 1937; s. John Hampar and Esther (Keleshian) Avedisian. B.F.A., Boston U., 1959. Dancer, 1959-68; danced in: West Side Story, Broadway, 1960, Funny Girl, Broadway, 1964-65; asso. choreographer, dir., Michael Bennett Prodns., N.Y.C., 1967—; choreographer-producer, 1975—; Broadway prodns. include: Henry, Sweet Henry, 1967, Promises, Promises, 1968, Coco, 1969, Company, 1970, Follies, 1971, Twigs, 1971, Seesaw, 1973, God's Favorite, 1974, A Chorus Line, 1975 (Tony award for best choreography 1976, Los Angeles Drama Critics award for best choreography 1977), Ballroom (Tony award for best choreography 1979, Drama Desk award for choreography 1979); producer: Dreamgirls, 1981. Office: 890 Broadway New York NY 10003

AVIGNONE, FRANK TITUS, III, physics educator; b. N.Y.C., May 9, 1933; s. Frank Titus and Nina Eugenia (Acquini) A.; m. Norma Lloraine Novia, July 17, 1954; children: Michelle, Frank. B.S., Ga. Inst. Tech., 1960, M.S., 1962, Ph.S., 1965. Instr. physics Ga. Inst. Tech., Atlanta, 1963-65, vis. prof., 1976—; asst. prof. physics U. S.C., Columbia, 1965-68, assoc. prof., 1968-73, prof., 1973—, chmn. dept., 1979—; vis. scientist Internat. Centre Theoretical Physics, Trieste, Italy, 1974; chmn. exec. com. U. Isotope Separation, Oak Ridge Nat. Lab., 1975-77; U. S.C. counciller Oak Ridge Assoc. U., 1982—. Contbr. articles to profl. jours. Recipient Russell Research award U. S.C., 1973. Mem. Am. Phys. Soc. Home: 950 Wordsworth Dr Columbia SC 29209 Office: Dept Physics U SC Columbia SC 29209

AVILDSEN, JOHN GUILBERT, film director; b. Ill., Dec. 21, 1935; s. Clarence John and Ivy (Guilbert) A.; children: Anthony Guilbert, Jonathan-Rufus. Student, N.Y. U., 1955. Advt. mgr. Vespa Motor Scooters, 1959. Asst. dir.: Greenwich Village Story, 1961; prodn. mgr.: Mickey One, 1964; 2d unit dir.: Hurry Sundown, 1964; with, Muller, Jordan & Herrick Indsl. Films, 1965-67; dir.: photography Out of It, 1967; films Turn on to Love, 1967, Sweet Dreams, 1968, Guess What We Learned in School Today, 1969, Joe, 1970, Cry Uncle, 1971, Save the Tiger, 1972, Inaugural Ball, 1973, W.W. and the Dixie Dancekings, 1974, Rocky, 1976 (Acad. award for best direction), Slow Dancing in the Big City, 1978, The Formula, 1980, Neighbors, 1981, A Night in Heaven, 1983, The Karate Kio, 1984. Trustee Churchill Sch. Served with U.S. Army, 1959-61. Mem. Dirs. Guild Am., Motion Picture Photographers Union, Motion Picture Editors Union, Writers Guild Am. Home and Office: 45 E 89th St New York NY 10128

AVIRETT, JOHN WILLIAMS, II, lawyer; b. Cumberland, Md., May 13, 1902; s. John Williams and Sarah Donnell (Roemer) A.; m. Barbara Brooke Dennis, July 22, 1947; stepchildren: G.R. Dennis Rawlins, William Murray Rawlins. A.B., U. Va., 1923, M.A., 1924; LL.B., Harvard U., 1927. Bar: Md. bar 1927. Since practiced in, Balt.; partner firm Piper & Marbury, and predecessors, 1933—; led efforts resulting in passage Md. Fireworks Law, 1941, active in passing Balt. law assisting med. research on stray dogs, 1949; First pres. pub. relations council Community Fund Balt., 1936-37; counsel, dir. Jr. Assn. Commerce Balt., 1936-38; trustee Balt. Mus. Art; pres., 1962-68, St. James Sch., Hagerstown, Md., 1962-72; bd. dirs. Md. Soc. Prevention Blindness, 1935—, pres., 1935-41; bd. dirs. Nat. Soc. Prevention Blindness, 1937-68, Balt. Council Social Agys., 1939-42; an organizer, mem. exec. com. Md. Soc. Med. Research, 1950—; bd. mgrs. Uplands Home Ch. Women, Balt., 1953-63, v.p., 1957-63; mem. standing com. Episcopal Diocese Md., 1954-55. Served to capt. USNR, 1943-46. Decorated Legion of Merit. Fellow Md. Bar Found.; mem. Am., Md., Balt. bar assns., Am. Law Inst., Raven Soc., Phi Beta Kappa, Phi Gamma Delta. Clubs: Md., Elkridge, 14 W. Hamilton St., Mchts., Bachelors Cotillon (Balt.). Home: 122 B Melrose E Baltimore MD 21212 Office: 1100 Charles Center S 36 S Charles St Baltimore MD 21201

AVISCHIOUS, RAYMOND, food distbn. co. exec.; b. Chgo., Oct. 23, 1931; m. Arlene Lentner; children—Tom, Gary. B.S. in Mktg, U. Ill., 1953. With Kroger Co., 1953; with Shurfine Central Corp., Northlake, Ill., 1955—, pres., gen. mgr., 1971—, also dir.; dir. Mdse. Nat. Bank, Chgo. Bd. dirs. Aid Assn. Lutherans, Appleton, Wis. Served with AUS, 1953-55. Address: Shurfine Central Corp 2100 N Mannheim Rd Northlake IL 60164

AVISON, DAVID, photographer; b. Harrisonburg, Va., July 13, 1937; s. Charles and Kathryn (Driver) A.;, July 10, 1973. Sc.B., M.I.T., 1959; Ph.D., Brown U., 1966; M.S., Ill. Inst. Tech., 1974. Tchr. photography Columbia Coll., 1970—; owner, operator Avison Photo Products. Exhibited at, Art Inst., Chgo., 1977-83, Grey Art Gallery, N.Y. U., 1977, Dittmar Meml. Gallery, Northwestern U., 1974, 75, 76, 78, Crocker Art Gallery, Sacramento, 1978; represented in permanent collections, Mus. Modern Art, Art Inst. Chgo., Mus. Fine Art, Boston, Internat. Mus. Photography at George Eastman House, Rochester, N.Y., Dallas Mus. Fine Arts, Columbia Coll. Permanent Collection, Chgo., Ball State U. Gallery, Muncie, Ind., No. Ill. U. Sven Parson Gallery, DeKalb; Recipient (award Time-Life Search for Photog. Talent 1974, Phototographers fellow Nat. Endowment for Arts 1977); represented in: permanent collections Ball State U. Gallery, Muncie, Ind., No. Ill. U. Sven Parson Gallery, DeKalb. Mem. Soc. Photog. Edn., Soc. Photog. Scientists and Engrs., Chgo. Artists Coalition, Chgo. Optical Soc. Home: 399 Fullerton Pkwy Chicago IL 60614

AVNER, LOUIS LEONARD, drug company executive; b. California, Pa., Apr. 22, 1915; s. Samuel and Rose (Hoffman) A.; m. Helen L. Huffman, Feb. 22, 1941; children: Constance (Mrs. Bruce Buchanan), Robin. B.A., U. Mich., 1936, postgrad., 1937. Vice pres. Thrift Drug Co., Pitts., 1945-62, exec. v.p., 1962-68, pres., 1968-80; chmn. bd. Apex Resources Inc., 1980—, R&A Devel. Inc., 1980—; dir. Union Nat. Bank Pitts. Bd. dirs. Montefiore Hosp., Am. Friends of Hebrew U. Mem. Beta Gamma Sigma. Home: Hampton Rd Pittsburgh PA 15215

AV PAUL, ANNETTE, ballet dancer; b. Stockholm, Sweden, Feb. 11, 1944; m. Brian Macdonald. Solist then prin. Royal Swedish Ballet, Stockholm; dancer Harkness Ballet, The Ballet Spectacular of Miami, The Royal Winnipeg Ballet, Les Grands Ballets Canadeins, prin., 1973—. Dancer: (repertoire includes) Giselle, Romeo and Juliet, Swan Lake, Double Quartet, Pas de Quatre, Othello, Concerto Barocco, The Four Temperaments, Adieu Robert Schumann, Etapes, Les Valses and Jardin aux Lilas; guest artist: Nat. Film Bd. Can. documentary For The Love of Dance, Film: Gala. Office: Les Grands Ballets Candieus 4869 rue St Denis Montreal PQ Canada M2J 2L7 *

AVRAM, HENRIETTE DAVIDSON, government official; b. N.Y.C., Oct. 7, 1919; d. Joseph and Rhea (Olsho) Davidson; m. Herbert Mois Avram, Aug. 23, 1941; children: Lloyd, Marcie, Jay. Student, Hunter Coll., N.Y.C., George Washington U.; Sc.D. (hon.), So. Ill. U., 1977. Systems analyst, methods analyst, programmer Nat. Security Agy., 1953-59; systems analyst Am. Research Bur., 1959-61, Datatrol Corp., 1961-65; supervisory info. systems specialist Library of Congress, Washington, 1965-67, asst. coordinator info. systems, 1967-70; chief MARC Devel. Office, 1970-76; dir. Network Devel. Office, 1976-80, dir. processing systems, network and automation planning, 1980—, chmn. network adv. com., 1981—; lectr. dept. library sci. Cath. U. Am., 1973—; Chmn. subcom. 2 sectional com. Z39 Am. Nat. Standards Inst., 1966—; chmn. working group on content designators Internat. Fedn. Library Assns., 1972-77; chmn. subcom. 4 working group 1 on character sets Internat. Orgn. for Standardization, 1971—; mem. Com. for Coordination of Nat. Bibliog. Control, 1976-79; mem. steering com. MARC Internat. Network Study, 1975—; chmn. profl. bd. Internat. Fedn. Library Assns. and Instns., 1979—, chmn. info. tech. sect., 1978—, chmn. mgmt. and tech. div., 1979—; chmn. RECON Working Task Force, 1968-73; mem. Internat. Standards Coordinating Com., 1983—, Info. Systems Standards Bd., 1983—; del. to U.S. nat. com. UNESCO/Gen. Info. Program, 1983—; mem. strategies com. Cath. U. Library and Sch. Library and Info. Sci., 1980-81, bd. visitors, 1981—. Bd. editors: Jour. Library Automation, 1970-72; contbr. articles to profl. jours. Recipient Superior Service award Library of Congress, 1968, Margaret Mann citation in cataloging and classification, 1971, Fed. Woman's award, 1974; award for achievement in library and info. tech. ALA-Library Info. Tech. Assn., 1980; co-recipient ACRL Acad./Research Librarian of Year award, 1979. Mem. ALA (dir., past pres. info. sci. and automation div., Melvil Dewey award 1981), Am. Soc. Info. Sci., Assn. Computing Machinery. Home: 1776 Elton Rd Silver Spring MD 20903 Office: Library of Congress Washington DC 20540:

AVRETT, JOHN GLENN, advertising executive; b. Atlanta, Mar. 16, 1929; s. Robert Cary and Annie Berry (Hinton) A.; m. Rosalind Case, Dec. 31, 1972; 1 stepson, Gerald. B.J., U. Ga., 1950. With advt. dept. Rich's Dept. Store, Atlanta, 1950-52; v.p. Foote, Cone & Belding, N.Y.C., 1959-66, Wells, Rich, Greene Inc., 1966-69; sr. v.p. Sullivan, Stauffer, Colwell & Bayles, Inc., N.Y.C., 1968-69; pres. Marchalk Co., N.Y.C., 1969-71; founder, chmn. bd. Avrett, Free & Ginsburg, Inc., N.Y.C., 1971—. Bd. dirs. The Acting Co., N.Y.C. Recipient profl. awards. Mem. N.Y. Advt. Club, N.Y. Copy Club. Methodist. Clubs: Univ. (N.Y.C.); Seawanhaha Corinthian Yacht (Oyster Bay, N.Y.); Piping Rock (Locust Valley, N.Y.); St. Louis Racquet. Home: 155 E 73d St New York NY 10021 also 391 Mill River Rd Oyster Bay NY 11771 Office: 800 3d Ave New York NY 10022

AVRIT, RICHARD CALVIN, naval officer; b. Tilamook, Oreg., Feb. 18, 1932; s. Roy Calvin and Mary Louise (Morgan) A.; m. Alice Jane Tamminga, July 10, 1959; 1 dau., Tamra Jane. B.S. in Engring, U.S. Naval Acad., 1953; M.S. in Engring. Electronics, U.S. Naval Postgrad. Sch., 1960; postgrad., U.S. Naval War Coll., 1971-72. Commd. ensign U.S. Navy, 1953, advanced through grades to rear adm., 1979; served weapons dept. U.S.S. George K. Mackenzie, 1953-54; ops. dept. U.S.S. Willis A. Lee, 1954-57; comdg. officer U.S.S. Sumner County, 1960-63; project officer, staff of comdr. Operational Test and Evaluation Force, Key West, Fla., 1963-66; exec. officer U.S.S. Berkeley, 1966-68; ops. officer, AAW project officer Comdr. Cruiser Destroyer Florilla Nine, 1968-70; comdg. officer U.S.S. Sellers, 1970-71; mil. asst. for surface guns and missiles to asst. dir. Ocean Control Directorate, Def. Research and Engring., Office Sec. of Def., 1972-76; comdg. officer U.S.S. Harry E. Yarnell, 1976-78; chief of staff, comdr. Naval Surface Force U.S. Atlantic Fleet, 1978-79; project mgr. for Saudi Naval Expansion Program, Naval Material Command, Washington, 1979-82; dir. navy logistics plans Office Chief of Naval Ops., Washington, 1982—. Decorated Legion of Merit (2), Bronze Star with Combat V, Meritorious Service Medal (2). Mem. Naval Inst., IEEE. Methodist. Home: 6901 Northfield Dr Annandale VA 22003 Office: Pentagon Room 4B 546 Navy Dept Washington DC 20350

AWEIDA, JESSE ISSA, business executive; b. Rafidya, Palestine, Feb. 19, 1931; came to U.S., 1952, naturalized, 1960; s. Saleh J. and Jameeleh S. (Abbed) A.; m. Maria Klemperer, June 9, 1956; children: Lisa, Robin, Daniel, Neil. B.S. in Mech. Engring., Swarthmore Coll., 1956; M.S., Syracuse (N.Y.) U., 1960. Successively engr., engring. mgr., program mgr. IBM Corp., Poughkeepsie, 1956-66, Boulder, Colo., 1966-69; pres., chmn. bd., chief exec. officer Storage Tech. Corp., Louisville, Colo., 1969-82, chmn., chief exec. officer, 1982—; also dir.; dir. Prime Computer Co. Unitarian. Home: 7184 Spring Ct Boulder CO 80303 Office: 2270 S 88th St Louisville CO 80027 *

AWEIDA, NAIM SALEH, computer company executive; b. Nablus, Palestine, Dec. 9, 1928; U.S., 1969, naturalized, 1974; s. Saleh J. and Jameeleh A. (Abbed) A.; m. Aida N. Salfiti, Dec. 17, 1955; children: Rema, Lena, Ramzi, Andy. Student schs., Haifa, Palestine. Auditor Saba & Co., Haifa, 1946-48; mgr. field ops. Internat. Red Cross Soc., Jordan, 1948-50; project mgr. UN Relief and Works Agy., Jordan, 1950-51; auditor, acct. Arabian Am. Oil Co., Dhahran, Saudi Arabia, 1951-55; with Am. embassy, Amman, Jordan, 1955-67; coordinator Middle East activities Luth. World Relief, Amman, 1967-69; exec. v.p. field ops. div. Storage Tech. Corp., Louisville, Colo., 1969-82, pres., 1982—. Decorated Annahdha medal (Jordan). Home: 7474 Spring Dr Boulder CO 80303 Office: Storage Tech Corp 2270 S 88th St Louisville CO 80027

AWES, GERALD A., chain store executive; b. Colorado Springs, Colo., 1914; married; 3 children. Hon. chmn. Lucky Stores Inc., Dublin, Calif. Mem. Food Market Inst. (past. chmn. bd.). Office: 1630 Newell Ave Walnut Creek CA 94596

AX, EMANUEL, pianist; b. Lvov, Poland. Student of, Mieczyslaw Munz, Juilliard Sch. Music. Appeared as soloist, Chgo., Los Angeles, Phila., Rochester, Seattle, St. Louis and London, Philharmonic orchs.; toured extensively in, C.Am. and S.Am.; performed in joint recital (with violinist Nathan Milstein), extensive tours, Europe, Japan; with maj. orchs.; also recs.; Winner (Arthur Rubinstein Internat. Competition 1974, Avery Fisher prize 1979); recipient (Young Concert Artist's Michaels award 1975). Office: care ICM Artists Ltd 40 W 57th St New York NY 10019 *

AXAM, JOHN ARTHUR, library adminstr.; b. Cin., Feb. 12, 1930; m. Dolores L. Ballard, Sept. 20, 1958. B.S., Cheyney State Coll., 1953; M.S. in L.S, Drexel U., 1958. Head Queen Meml. br. Free Library of Phila., 1960-62, head, 1962-64, head stas. dept., dir., reader devel. program, 1964-78, area adminstr. N. Central and S. Phila., 1978—. Contbr. articles to profl. jours. Chmn. youth services rev. com. United Fund of Phila., 1974-76; opportunity funds and planet Earth coms. Girl Scouts of Phila., 1974-78; trustee, mem. central allocations com. United Way of Southeastern Pa.; lay disciple United Methodist Ch. Recipient Chapel of the Four Chaplins award, 1968. Mem. ALA (council 1970-73), Pa. Library Assn. Home: 1803 Chew Ave Philadelphia PA 19141 Office: Logan Sq St Philadelphia PA 19103

AXEL, JOHN WERNER, office furniture manufacturing executive; b. Muscatine, Iowa, June 10, 1941; s. Chester Walter and Wilma Pauline (Marolf) A.; m. Joan Carol Urenn, June 6, 1964; children—Andrew, Brad. B.S., Iowa State U., 1964; M.Govtl. Adminstrn., U. Pa., 1966. With Hon Industries Inc., Muscatine, 1966—; v.p. adminstrn. Hon Industries, Inc., 1972-78, v.p. fin., 1978—; dir. Mut. Selection Fund., Positech Corp., Ring King Visibles, Inc. Mem. Iowa Republican Central Com., 1975-, state fin. chmn., 1979-81; pres., founder Friends of Musser Public Library, 1976-78. Joseph Wharton scholar, 1964-66; recipient Danforth Found. award, 1955. Mem. Nat. Office Products Assn., Nat. Investor Relations Inst., Fin. Execs. Inst. Republican. Episcopalian. Clubs: Rotary, Elks. Home: 2007 Circle Dr Muscatine IA 52761 Office: 414 E 3d St Muscatine IA 52761

AXEL, RICHARD, pathology and biochemistry educator; b. N.Y.C., July 2, 1946. A.B. magna cum laude, Columbia U., 1967; M.D., Johns Hopkins U., 1970. Intern dept. pathology Columbia U. Coll. Physicians and Surgeons, N.Y.C., 1970-71; fellow Inst. Cancer Research, 1971-72; vis. fellow dept. pathology Columbia U., 1971-72; research assoc. USPHS, NIH, 1972-74; asst. prof. dept. pathology Inst. Cancer Research, Columbia U., 1974-78, prof. depts. pathology and biochemistry, 1978—; mem. molecular biology study sect. NIH, 1981—; Univ. lectr. Columbia U., 1983. Assoc. editor: Cell, 1976—; contbr. articles to profl. jours. Recipient Irma T. Hirschl Career Scientist award, 1976, Young Scientistaward Passano Found., 1979, Alan T. Waterman award, 1982, Eli Lillyaward, 1983. Mem. Nat. Acad. Scis., Am. Acad. Arts and Scis., Phi Beta Kappa. Office: Inst Cancer Research Columbia U 701 W 168th St New York NY 10032

AXELRAD, IRVING IRMAS, lawyer, oil co. exec.; b. Huron, S.D., Dec. 21, 1915; s. Simon and Anna Irmas A.; m. Ethel Ritter Rosenberg, Jan. 1, 1973; Children—Allan, Stephen, Karen, Eve, Joel. A.B., U. Chgo., 1937, J.D. cum laude, 1939. Bar: Ill. bar 1939, Calif. bar 1952. Atty. antitrust div. Dept. Justice, 1939-40; gen. counsel's office mem. SEC, Washington, 1940-41; spl. asst. to atty. gen. tax div. Dept. Justice, 1942-52; sr. partner firm Mitchell, Silberberg & Knupp, Los Angeles, 1952-80; sr. v.p. Occidental Petroleum Corp., Los Angeles, 1980—; lectr. taxation Grad. Sch. Law, U. So. Calif., 1953-54; guest lectr. UCLA, 1956-68, U. Calif., Berkeley, 1958, 65, 68; lectr. U. Chgo. Law Sch. Fed. Tax Conf., 1956, 58, 68; Bd. dirs. Western region United Way, 1980—; mem. adv. bd. Loyola Marymount U. Inst. for Intergroup Relations Tng., 1973-78; mem. exec. bd. Los Angeles chpt. and mem. nat. bd. govs. Am. Jewish Com., 1958—; bd. dirs. Scott Newman Found., 1980—, pres., 1981—. Served to lt. (j.g.) USNR, 1944-46. Mem. Am. Bar Assn., Los Angeles Bar Assn., State Bar of Calif., U. Chgo. Alumni Assn. (pres. So. Calif. chpt. 1964-67), Phi Beta Kappa, Order of Coif. Club: Hillcrest Country (Los Angeles). Office: 10889 Wilshire Blvd Los Angeles CA 90024

AXELRAD, NORMAN DAVID, franchise business executive; b. Chgo., Nov. 13, 1929; s. Samuel and Bessie (Young) A.; m. Sandra Ann Gault, Aug. 26, 1964; 1 son, John E. B.A. in Econs., U. Mich., 1951; J.D., Northwestern U., 1954. Bar: Ill. 1955. Mem. firm Chapman, Anixter & Delaney, Chgo., 1955-60; v.p. McDonald's Corp., Oak Brook, Ill., 1960-81, v.p. pub. affairs; pres. The Franchising Bd., Ltd.; lectr. in legal symposiums. Contbr. articles profl. jours. Bd. dirs. several civic, ednl. and community orgns. Served with U.S. Army, 1954-56. Mem. Am., Ill., Chgo. bar assns. Home: 6727 N Lemai St Lincolnwood IL 60646 Office: 43 E Ohio St Chicago IL 60611

AXELROD, DANIEL ISAAC, geology and botany educator; b. Bklyn., July 16, 1910; s. Morris and Augusta (Gallup) A.; m. Nancy Robinson, June 3, 1939 (div. Sept. 1965); 1 son, James Peter. A.B., U. Calif. at Berkeley, 1933, M.A., 1936, Ph.D., 1938. Asst. prof. UCLA, 1946-48, asso. prof., 1948-52, prof. geology, 1952—, prof. geology and botany, 1962—; prof. botany U. Calif. at Davis, 1968—. Decorated Bronze Star; recipient N.Y. Bot. Garden award Bot. Soc., 1972, Hayden Meml. Geol. award Phila. Acad. Natural Scis., 1979, Fellows medal Calif. Acad. Scis., 1980; Guggenheim fellow, 1952-53; NRC fellow U.S. Nat. Mus., 1939-41. Fellow Am. Acad. Arts and Sci.; Mem. Geol. Soc. Am., AAAS, Paleontol. Soc., Soc. for Study Evolution. Research on evolution of Madro-Tertiary Geoflora; theory of angiosperm evolution; origin and age of desert vegetation; poleward migration of angiosperms in Cretaceous period; evolution of insular floras; determination of altitude of Tertiary floras; topographic history of Snake River Plain and Rio Grande trough; evolution of subalpine Tertiary forests; role of equability in evolution and extinction; role of plate tectonics in biogeography and evolution, role of volcanism in evolution and extinction. Home: 750 Oeste Dr Davis CA 95616

AXELROD, DAVID, public health physician, state health official; b. Gt. Barrington, Mass., Jan. 7, 1935; m. Janet Claire Ross, Aug. 30, 1964; 1 son, Jonathan. A.B magna cum laude, Harvard U., 1956, M.D., 1960. Intern Strong Meml. Hosp., Rochester, N.Y., 1960-61, resident in medicine, 1961-62; research asso. public health service Lab. Biology of Viruses, Nat. Inst. Allergies and Infectious Disease, NIH, Washington, 1962-65, virologist, 1965-68; dir. Infectious Disease Center, Div. Labs. and Research, N.Y. State Dept. Health, Albany, 1968-77, dir. div., 1977-79, commr. of health, 1979—; pres. bd. dirs. Health Research, Inc.; com. mem. NRC Assembly of Life Scis. Served with USPHS, 1962-68. Mem. Assn. State and Territorial Health Ofcls. Home: 98 Terrace Ave Albany NY 12203 Office: Nelson A Rockefeller Empire State Plaza Albany NY 12237

AXELROD, DIANE M., retirement equities fund executive; b. New Haven, Mar. 3, 1943; d. Milton L. and Augusta F. A. B.A. in Psychology, Boston U., 1964; M.A., Columbia U., 1966. Programmer Bank of Am., 1967; systems analyst Topaz Computer Corp., 1968-70; officer computer systems div. Tchrs. Ins. & Annuity Am., N.Y.C., 1971-77, v.p. adminstrn., trading securities and lending, 1977—; bd. dirs. EDP adv. bd. Borough of Manhattan Community Coll., 1978-79. Home: 201 E 66th St Apt 16E New York NY 10021 Office: 730 3d Ave New York NY 10017

AXELROD, GEORGE, playwright; b. N.Y.C., June 9, 1922; s. Herman and Beatrice (Carpenter) A.; m. Gloria Washburn, Feb. 28, 1942 (div. June 1954); children: Peter, Steven; m. Joan Stanton, Oct. 1954; 1 dau., Nina. Radio and TV script writer, 1947—; including sketches for comedians and TV Celebrity Time series, also films; Author: Beggar's Choice, 1947, Blackmailer, 1952, Where Am I Now-When I Need Me, 1971, Small Wonder (revue with Max Wilk), 1948; plays The Seven Year Itch, 1953, Will Success Spoil Rock Hunter?, 1955; films Bus Stop; producer: (with Clinton Wilder) play Visit to a Small Planet, 1957, Goodbye Charlie, 1959; dir.: film Breakfast at Tiffany's, 1959; author: (produced with John Frankenheimer) screenplays The Manchurian Candidate, 1962, and Paris When it Sizzles, 1963, How To Murder Your Wife, 1965; dir. play: Once More, With Feeling, 1958; producer, dir., co-author film: Lord Love a Duck; dir. play: Star Spangled Girl; writer, producer, dir. film: The Secret Life of an American Wife. Mem. Authors League Am., Dramatists Guild. Office: Irving Paul Lazar Agy 211 S Beverly Dr Beverly Hills CA 90212

AXELROD, JULIUS, biochemist, pharmacologist; b. N.Y.C., May 30, 1912; s. Isadore and Molly (Leichtling) A.; m. Sally Taub, Aug. 30, 1938; children: Paul Mark, Alfred Nathan. B.S., Coll. City N.Y., 1933; M.A., N.Y. U., 1941, D.Sc. (hon.), 1971; Ph.D., George Washington U., 1955, LL.D. (hon.), 1971, D.Sc., U. Chgo., 1965, Med. Coll. Wis., 1971; LL.D., Coll. City N.Y., 1972; Dr.h.c., U. Panama, 1972; Sc.D., Med. Coll. Pa., 1974; Dr. honoris causa, U. Paris (Sud), 1982. Chemist Lab. Indsl. Hygiene, 1935-46; research asso. 3d N.Y. U. research div. Goldwater Meml. Hosp., 1946-49; asso. chemist sect. chem. pharmacology Nat. Heart Inst., NIH, 1949-50, chemist, 1950-53, sr. chemist, 1953-55; acting chief sect. pharmacology Lab. Clin. Sci. NIMH, 1955, chief sect. pharmacology, 1955—; Otto Loewi meml. lectr. N.Y. U., 1963; Karl E. Paschkis meml. lectr. Phila. Endocine Soc., 1966; NIH lectr., 1967; Nathanson meml. lectr. U. So. Calif., 1968; James Parkinson lectr. Columbia U., 1971; Wartenberg lectr. Am. Acad. Neurology, 1971; Arnold D. Welch lectr. Yale U., 1971; Harold Carpenter Hodge distinguished lectr. toxicology U. Rochester, 1971; Bennett lectr. Am. Neurol. Assn., 1971; Harvey lectr., 1971; Mayer lectr. Mass. Inst. Tech., 1971; distinguished prof. sci. George Washington U., 1972; Salmon lectr. N.Y. Acad. Medicine, 1972; Eli Lilly lectr., 1972; Mike Hogg lectr. U. Tex., 1972; Fred Schueler lectr. Tulane U., 1972; vis. scholar Herbert Lehman Coll. City U. N.Y., 1973; cons. George Washington U., 1959—; panelist U.S. Bd. Civil Service Examiners, 1958-67; mem. research adv. com. United Cerebral Palsy Assn., 1966-69; mem. psychopharmacology study sect. NIMH, 1970-74; mem. Internat. Brain Research Orgn.; mem. research adv. com. Nat. Found.; vis. com. Brookhaven Nat. Lab., 1972-76; bd. overseers Jackson Lab., 1974. Editorial bd. Jour. Pharmacology and Exptl. Therapeutics, 1956-72, Jour. Medicinal Chemistry, 1962-67, Circulation Research, 1963-71, Currents in Modern Biology, 1966-72; editorial adv. bd.: Communication in Behavioral Biology, 1967-73, Jour. Neurobiology, 1968-77, Jour. Neurochemistry, 1969-77, Jour. Neurovisceral Relation, 1969, Rassegna di Neurologia Vegetativa, 1969—, Internat. Jour. Psychobiology, 1970-75; hon. cons. editor: Life Scis, 1961-69; co-author: The Pineal, 1968; contbr. papers in biochem. actions and metabolism of drugs, hormones, action of pineal gland, enzymes, neurochem. transmission to profl. jours. Recipient Meritorious Research award Assn. Research Nervous and Mental Diseases, 1965; Gairdner award distinguished research, 1967; Nobel prize med. physiology, 1970; Alumni Distinguished Achievement award George Washington U., 1968; Superior Service award HEW, 1968; Distinguished Service award, 1970; Claude Bernard professorship and medal U. Montreal, 1969; Distinguished Service award Modern Medicine mag., 1970; Albert Einstein award Yeshiva U., 1971; medal Rudolf Virchow Med. Soc., 1971; Myrtle Wreath award Hadassah, 1972. Fellow Am. Acad. Arts and Scis., Am. Soc. Neuropsychopharmacology; mem. German Pharmacol. Soc. (corr.), Am. Chem. Soc., Am. Soc. Pharmacology and Exptl. Therapeutics (Torald Sollmann award 1973), Am. Soc. Biol. Chemists, AAAS, Nat. Acad. Scis., Am. Neurol. Assn. (hon.), Royal Soc. London (fgn.), Inst. Medicine (sr.), Sigma Xi, Am. Psychopathol. Assn. (hon.). Home: 10401 Grosvenor Pl Rockville MD 20852 Office: NIH Bethesda MD 20014

AXELSON, CHARLES FREDERIC, food company executive; b. Chgo., Apr. 24, 1917; s. Charles Frederic and Katherine (Strong) A.; m. Dorothy L. Jepson, July 23, 1940; children: Linda Axelson Hoy, Fred, Lori. A.B., M.B.A., U. Chgo., 1937. Staff accountant Lybrand, Ross Bros. & Montgomery, Chgo., 1938-41; with U.S. Gypsum Co., Chgo., 1941-70, asst. controller, 1946-52, controller, 1952-60, controller, asst. treas., 1960-70; v.p. controller Libby, McNeill & Libby, Chgo., 1970-78; v.p., chief fin. officer Lawry's Foods, Inc., Los Angeles, 1978-82; prof. acctg. U. So. Calif., Los Angeles, 1982—; lectr. accounting Northwestern U., 1946-53; dir. Air Conditioning Co. Trustee emeritus Nat. Coll. Edn.; bd. dirs. Crippled Children's Soc. So. Calif. Mem. Am. Inst. C.P.A.'s, Fin. Execs. Inst. (dir. Los Angeles chpt., past pres. Chgo. chpt., past nat. dir., past v.p. Midwestern area), Phi Delta Theta. Presbyterian. Clubs: Execs. (Chgo.); Town Hall (Los Angeles). Home: 292 Palmetto Dr Pasadena CA 91105 Office: Bridge Hall U So Calif Los Angeles CA 90089

AXELSON, JOSEPH ALLEN, professional athletics executive; b. Peoria, Dec. 25, 1927; s. Joseph Victor A. and Florence (Ealen) Massey; m. Malcolm Rae Smith, Oct. 7, 1950; children: David Allen, Mark Stephen, Linda Rae. B.S., Northwestern U., 1949. Sports info. dir. Ga. So. Coll., Statesboro, 1957-60, Nat. Assn. Intercollegiate Athletics, Kansas City, Mo., 1961-62; tournament dir. Bowling Proprs. Assn. Am., Park Ridge, Ill., 1963-64; asst. exec. sec. Nat. Assn. Intercollegiate Athletics, Kansas City, Mo., 1964-68; exec. v.p., gen. mgr. Cin. Royals Profl. Basketball Team, Cin., 1969-72; mgr. Cin. Gardens, 1970-72; pres., gen. mgr. Kansas City Kings Profl. Basketball Team, Kansas City, Mo., 1972-79, 1982—; v.p. ops. NBA, N.Y.C., 1979-82, chmn. competition and rules com., 1975-79. Served to capt. Signal Corps. AUS, 1949-54. Named Nat. Basketball Exec. of Yr. The Sporting News, St. Louis, 1973; recipient Annual Dirs. award Downtown, Inc., Kansas City, Mo., 1979. Mem. Naismith Basketball Hall of Fame (exec. com., 2d v.p. 1983—). Republican. Presbyterian. Lodge: Rotary Kansas City, Mo. Home: 9535 Ash St Apt 111 Overland Park KS 66207 Office: Kansas City Kings 1800 Genessee St Kansas City MO 64102

AXENE, DEAN LANE, electrical manufacturing company executive; b. Kansas City, Mo., Aug. 1, 1923; s. Oscar Frederick and Marlow (Gross) A.; m. Sally Ann Haas, June 7, 1944; children—Eric Christopher, Kristen (Mrs. Ronald R. Wenning). B.S., U.S. Naval Acad., 1944, M.I.T., 1948. Commd. ensign USN, 1944, advanced through grades to rear adm., 1969; electronics officer, engring. officer, nav. officer U.S.S. Tiru, 1948-50; electronics officer of staff comdr. Submarine Squadron 1, 1950-51, Submarine Force, U.S. Pacific Fleet, 1951-52; exec. officer U.S.S. Sea Robin, 1952-53; tng. at Westinghouse Bettis Plant, AEC, Pitts., 1953, Naval Reactor Testing Sta., Arco, Idaho, 1953; commissioning exec. officer U.S.S. Nautilus, 1954-55; comdr. U.S.S. Croaker, 1955-57; dir. nuclear dept. Submarine Sch., New London, 1957-59; instrn. at Naval Reactors br. AEC, Washington, 1959-60; prospective comdg. officer U.S.S. Thresher, Portsmouth (N.H.) Naval Shipyard, 1960-61, comdr., 1961-63; attended Polaris command course Naval Guided Missiles Sch., Dam Neck, Va., 1963; prospective comdg. officer U.S.S. John C. Calhoun, Newport News (Va.) Shipbuilding & Drydock Co., 1963-64, comdr., 1964-66; mem. State Dept. Sr. Seminar in Fgn. Policy, 1966-67; head policy coordination, diplomatic clearance and internat. aviation br. Politico-Mil. Policy div. Office Chief Naval Ops., Navy Dept., Washington, 1967-69; dir. Pan-Am. affairs Naval Missions and Adv. Group div., 1969-70; dep. chief of staff, asst. chief of staff for plans, policy and ops. Staff of NATO's Supreme Allied Comdr. Atlantic, Norfolk, Va., 1970-72; dep. chief naval edn. and tng., Pensacola, Fla., 1972-74, ret., 1974; mgr. contracts and internat. support Westinghouse Electric Corp., Pensacola, 1974—. Past pres. Pensacola Symphony Orch. Decorated Bronze Star with combat V, Legion of Merit, Gt. Star of Mil. Merit, Chile). Mem. U.S. Naval Acad. Found., U.S. Naval Hist. Found., U.S. Naval Inst., Navy League (dir. Pensacola chpt.), Nat. Geog. Soc., Greater Pensacola Area C. of C. (chmn. world trade council). Club: Scenic Hills Country (dir.). Home: 8777 Thunderbird Dr Pensacola FL 32504 Office: Westinghouse Electric Corp PO Box 1313 Pensacola FL 32596 *Personal fulfillment depends on being a contributing member of society.*

AXFORD, ROY ARTHUR, nuclear engineering educator; b. Detroit, Aug. 26, 1928; s. Morgan and Charlotte (Donaldson) A.; m. Anne-Sofie Langfeldt Rasmussen, Apr. 1, 1954; children: Roy Arthur, Elizabeth Carole, Trevor Craig. B.A., Williams Coll., 1952; B.S., Mass. Inst. Tech., 1952, M.S., 1955, Sc.D., 1958. Supr. theoretical physics group Atomics Internat., Canoga Park, Calif., 1958-60; asso. prof. nuclear engring. Tex. A&M, 1960-62, prof., 1962-63; asso. prof. nuclear engring. Northwestern U., 1963-66; asso. prof. U. Ill. at Urbana, 1966-68, prof., 1968—; cons. Los Alamos Sci. Lab., 1963—. Vice-chmn. Mass. Inst. Tech. Alumni Fund Drive, 1970-72, chmn., 1973-75. Recipient cert. of recognition for excellence in undergrad. teaching, U. Ill., 1979, 81. Mem. Am. Nuclear Soc., ASME, AIAA, SAR (sec.-treas. Piankeshaw chpt. 1975-81, v.p. chpt. 1982-83, pres. chpt. 1984—), Sigma Xi., Tau Beta Pi. Home: 2017 S Cottage Grove Urbana IL 61801

AXINN, DONALD EVERETT, real estate investor, developer, acad. adminstr.; b. N.Y.C., July 13, 1929; s. Michael and Ann (Schneider) A. A.B., Middlebury Coll., 1951; M.A., Hofstra U., 1975. Founder, owner Donald E. Axinn Co., Jericho, L.I., N.Y., 1958—; dir. Farrar, Straus & Giroux, Inc., N.Y.C.; asso. dean Hofstra Coll. Liberal Arts and Scis., Hempstead, N.Y., 1971-72; also dir. Inst. Arts. Chmn., commr.; Nassau County Fine Arts Commn., 1970-73; mem. Gov.'s Task Force on Cultural Life and Arts, 1975—; Trustee N.Y. Ocean Scis. Labs., Montauk, N.Y., 1969-71, Waldemar Cancer Research Inst., Woodbury, N.Y., 1966-68; trustee Hofstra U., 1970, 72—, sec., 1973-74, vice chmn., 1974—; bd. dirs. Pro Arte Symphony Orch., 1967-70, N.Y. Quar. Poetry Rev. Found., Inc., 1969—; v.p. bd. dirs. Leukemia Soc.; asso. trustee North Shore-Cornell U. Hosp., 1980-81; trustee N.Y. State Nature and Hist. Preserve Trust, 1978-83, Nassau County Mus., 1980-83; treas. Interfaith Nutrition Network; bd. dirs. Eglevsky Ballet Co., Outward Bound, Inc. Author: Sliding down the Wind, 1978, The Hawk's Dream and Other Poems, 1982; Contbr. poetry to mags. and newspapers. Recipient archtl. design and community enhancement awards L.I. Assn. and Plainview C. of C., 1962-70; NCCJ Brotherhood award, 1977; Humanitarian award Am. Jewish Com., 1978; Hon. award Beta Gamma Sigma, 1978; Tennessee Williams fellow in Poetry, Bread Loaf, 1979; L.I. Disting. Leadership award, 1979; others. Mem. Nat. Pilots Assn., P.E.N., Aircraft Owners and Pilots Assn., Middlebury Coll. Alumni Assn. (v.p., adv. bd. 1978, Delta Upsilon.). Clubs: The Players (N.Y.C.); L.I. Early Fliers (Glen Cove N.Y.); Old (Westbury (N.Y.); Racquet. Designer, developer Long Island Office Park, Engineers Hill Indsl. Parks, 7 locations. Office: 131 Jericho Turnpike Jericho NY 11753 *A wonderful characteristic of this great democracy of ours is the right to fail—which is, of course, the opportunity to succeed. As we pursue some goal, especially a noble one, we learn about the aspects and degrees of success or failure. The aspiration, therefore, becomes a worthwhile endeavor in itself.*

AXINN, GEORGE HAROLD, agricultural economics educator; b. Jamaica, N.Y., Feb. 1, 1926; s. Hyman and Celia (Schneider) A.; m. Nancy Kathryn Wigsten, Feb. 17, 1945; children: Catherine, Paul, Martha, William. B.S., Cornell U., 1947; M.S., U. Wis., 1952, Ph.D., 1958. Editorial asst. Cornell U. Geneva, N.Y., 1947; bull. editor U. Md., College Park, 1949; chmn. dept. rural communication U. Del., Newark, 1950; mem. faculty Mich. State U., East Lansing, 1953—, asso. dir. coop. extension service, 1955-60; coordinator U. Nigeria program, 1961-65, prof. agrl. econs., 1970—, asst. dean internat. studies and programs, 1964—; pres., exec. dir. Midwest Univs. Consortium for Internat. Activities, Inc., 1969-76; FAO rep. to Nepal, 1983—; cons. World Bank, 1973-74, Ford Found., 1968, UNICEF, 1978, FAO, 1974; vis. prof. Cornell U., Ithaca, N.Y., 1958-60, U. Ill., Urbana, 1969-70. Author: Modernizing World Agriculture: A Comparative Study of Agricultural Extension Education Systems, 1972, New Strategies for Rural Development, Rural Life Associates, 1978; contbr. articles to various publs. Served with USNR, 1944-46. W.K. Kellogg Found., fellow, 1956-57. Mem. Rural Sociol. Soc., Am. Agrl. Econs. Assn., Soc. Internat. Devel., Assn. for Advancement Agrl. Scis., Africa, Indian Soc. Extension Edn., Adult Edn. Assn. USA, AAAS, Assn. U.S. Univ. Dirs. Agrl. Programs. Clubs: Lansing Tennis, Michigan State U. Home: 2513 Bentley Ct East Lansing MI 48823 Office: 205 International Center Michigan State U East Lansing MI 48824

AXTHELM, PETE, columnist, author; b. N.Y.C., Aug. 27, 1943; s. Ralph Axthelm and Marjorie Axthelm Scholly; 1 dau., Megan. B.A., Yale U., 1965. Racing writer, columnist, N.Y. Herald Tribune, N.Y.C., 1965-66; staff writer, Sports Illus., 1966-68; sports editor, Newsweek, N.Y.C., 1968-73; columnist, contbg. editor, 1973—; commentator, NBC Sports, N.Y.C., 1979—; author: The Modern Confessional Novel, 1967, (with William F. Talbert) Tennis Observed, 1969, (with O. J. Simpson) O.J.: Education of a Rich Rookie, 1971, The City Game, 1971, The Kid, 1978. Recipient Page One award Newspaper Guild; Nat. Headliners award; Silver Gavel award Am. Bar Assn.; Schick award; Eclipse award. Mem. Nat. Turf Writers Assn., Nat. Pro Football Writers Assn. Office: Newsweek 444 Madison Ave New York NY 10022 *

AXTMANN, ROBERT CLARK, nuclear engineering educator; b. Youngstown, Ohio, Feb. 25, 1925; s. Charles Frank and Marguerite (Conklin) A.; m. Annabell Hoxie, Apr. 9, 1949; children: Connelle Marguerite, Tyrrell Charles, Ellen Virginia. A.B., Oberlin Coll., 1947; Ph.D., Johns Hopkins U., 1950. Instr. Johns Hopkins U., 1949; physicist Aberdeen Proving Ground, 1950; from scientist to sr. research supr. E.I. duPont de Nemours & Co., 1950-59; mem. faculty Princeton U., 1959—, chmn. program nuclear studies in engring., 1960-68; chmn. Council Environ. Studies, 1970-73; vis. fellow Israel AEC, 1964, Comision Nacional de Energia Nuclear, Mexico, 1969, Dept. Sci. and Indsl. Research, N.Z., 1974, 79-80; mem. N.J. Commn. Radiation Protection, 1966-70; adv. com. on geothermal energy Dept. Energy, 1976-78; mem. adv. com. on reactor safeguards U.S. NRC, 1980—. Editor, contbr.: Rescuing Man's Environment: Nine Essays on Environmental Reform, 1972; co-editor: Water and the Environmental Crunch, 1974; contbr. articles to profl. jours. Served with USNR, 1944-46. Mem. Am. Phys. Soc., Am. Inst. Chem. Engrs., Am. Chem. Soc., AAAS. Clubs: Indian John Point (Ont., Can.); Yacht. Home: Burnt Hill Rd Skillman NJ 08558 also Indian John Point Spanish ON Canada

AXTON, HOYT WAYNE, singer, composer; b. Duncan, Okla., Mar. 25, 1938; s. John Thomas and N. Mae (Boren) A.; m. Kathy Roberts, 1963 (div. Oct. 1973); children: Mark Roberts, Michael Stephen, April Laura. Student, Okla. State U., 1957-58. Singer, rec. artist, performer, 1961—, albums recorded on, Horizon, VeeJay, Columbia, Capitol, MCA and A. & M. labels, latest being Hoyt Axton Live; TV performances include Bonanza, 1964, I Dream of Jeannie, 1964, Chryslers Theatre, 1965, Johnny Carson Shows (10), 1976-77, Dinah Shore Show (4), 1975-77, Smothers Bros. Show, 1975, The Hoyt Axton Country Western, Boogie Woogie, Gospel, Rock and Roll Show, 1975, Bionic Woman, 1976, McCloud, 1976, Hee Haw, 1977, Music Hall America, 1977, Midnight Special, 1975-77, Nashville On The Road, 1980-81, Barbara Mandrell Show, 1981, Dukes of Hazard, 1981; numerous others; movie appearances include The Story of a Folk Singer, 1963, Smoky, 1966, Black Stallion, 1980, Junk Man, 1981; composer: numerous recorded songs, including Greenback Dollar, 1962, The Pusher, 1964, Snowblind Friend, 1967, Joy to the World (Jeremiah), 1971, Never Been to Spain, 1972, When the Morning Comes, 1974, Boney Fingers, 1974, Ease Your Pain, 1973, Less Than The Song, 1973, Lion in the Winter, 1974, The No, No, No Song, 1975, Fearless Free Sailin', Less Than The Song, Life Machine, My Griffin Is Gone, Snowblind Friend, Southbound; a musical The Happy Song, 1972, Outlaw Blues; movie sound track, 1977; Record producer, song pub., pres. bd., Jeremiah Records, from 1979, now chmn. bd., Jeremiah Records; performer, Grand Ole Opry, Nashville, 1974, 75, 76, 80, Earnest Tubb Record Shop, Nashville, 1974-75, Ralph Emery Show, Nashville, 1974-76; performed: Jimmy Carter Inaugural Ball; Author, illustrator: Line Drawings, Vols. I-V, 1974-78; author: song books Life Machine, 1973, Southbound, 1975, Less Than the Song, 1977. Spokesman Am. Heart Assn., 1975, UNICEF, 1975-76; organizer fund raising INTERPLAST, for Stanford U. dept. reconstructive surgery, 1975-76; fund raiser Free Clinics, Calif., 1971-74, Redwing Found., 1976, 77; subsidizing founder Bread and Roses Found., Mill Valley, Calif., 1974—; performer at numerous state and fed. prisons, including San Quentin, 1965-75; Active Democratic presidential campaigns Eugene McCarthy, Senator McGovern, Dem. gubernatorial campaigns Gov. Edmond Brown, Calif., Gov. David Borean, Okla. Served with USN, 1958-62. Mem. Country Music Assn., Am. Fedn. Musicians, AFTRA, Screen Actors Guild, Broadcast Music Inc., Okla. Cattlemen's Assn. Mem. Christian Ch. Office: Jeremiah Records Inc PO Box 1077 Hendersonville TN 37075

AXWORTHY, N. LLOYD, Canadian government official; b. North Battleford, Sask., Can., Dec. 21, 1939; s. Norman and Gwen (Thomas) A. B.A., United Coll., (now U. Winnipeg), 1961; M.A. in Polit. Sci. (Woodrow Wilson fellow), Princeton U., 1963; Ph.D. (Woodrow Wilson doctoral fellow), Princeton U., 1972. Prof. polit. sci. U. Winnipeg, Man., Can., 1965-67, 69-79; dir. Inst. of Urban Studies, from 1969; spl. asst. to Hon. John Turner, 1967; apptd. exec. asst. for housing and urban devel. to Hon. P. Hellyer; mem. Legis. Assembly Man., 1973-79; Liberal M.P. for Winnipeg-Fort Garvy, 1979—; apptd. Cabinet Minister Employment and Immigration and Minister Responsible for Status of Women, 1980-83; minister of transport, 1983—.

AYAD, BOULOS AYAD, archaeology educator; b. Egypt, May 3, 1928; U.S., 1967; s. Ayad A.; m. Suzanne E., Feb. 14, 1970; children: Mary, Thereza, Boulos. B.A., U. Cairo, 1952, M.A., 1957, Ph.D. with honors, 1963; M.A., U. Ain Shams, 1953, Higher Inst. Coptic Studies, 1960. Asst. prof. U. Utah, 1967-68, U. Colo., Boulder, 1968-72, assoc. prof., 1972-77, prof. archaeology and ancient langs. of Middle East, 1977—, univ. fellow, 1974-75. Author: Coptic Grammar and Texts, 1971, The Jewish-Aramaean Communities in Ancient Egypt, 1975, The Aramaeans in Egypt, 1975, The Aramaeans in the Ancient Middle East, 1983, The Jewish-Aramaean Civilization and Its Relationship to the Ancient Egyptian Civilization, 1982, The Four Gospels, 1983; translator: Book of Job (from Syriac into Arabic), 1975; contbr. articles to profl jours. Mem. African Studies Assn., Societe d'Archeologie Copte, AAUP, Am. Assn. Tchrs. Arabic, Smithsonian Instn., Soc. Bible Friends. Coptic Orthodox. Home: 1332 Scrub Oak Circle Boulder CO 80303 Office: Dept Anthropology U Colo Boulder CO 80309

AYALA, FRANCISCO JOSE, geneticist, educator; b. Madrid, Mar. 12, 1934; U.S., 1961, naturalized, 1971; s. Francisco and Soledad (Pereda) A.; children—Francisco Jose, Carlos Alberto. B.S., U. Madrid, 1954; M.A., Columbia U., 1963, Ph.D., 1964; D. honoris causa, Universidad de León (Spain), 1982. Research asso. Rockefeller U., 1964-65; asst. prof. Providence Coll., 1965-67, Rockefeller U., 1967-71; asso. prof. to prof. genetics U. Calif., Davis, 1971—; nat. adv. council Nat. Inst. Gen. Med. Scis.; exec. com. EPA. Author: Population and Evolutionary Genetics, 1982, Modern Genetics, 1980, Evolving: the Theory and Processes of Organic Evolution, 1979, Evolution, 1977, Molecular Evolution, 1976, Studies in the Philosophy of Biology, 1974. Recipient medal College de France, 1979. Fellow AAAS; mem. Soc. Study of Evolution (pres. 1979-80), Am. Soc. Naturalists (sec. 1973-76), Genetics Soc. Am., Am. Genetic Assn., Ecology Soc. Am., Nat. Acad. Scis., Am. Acad. Arts and Scis. Home: 747 Plum Ln Davis CA 95611 Office: Dept of Genetics University of California Davis CA 95616

AYALA Y AYALA, RAFAEL, bishop; b. Coatepec de Harinas, Mex., Oct. 25, 1913. Ordained priest Roman Cath. Ch., 1942; elevated to bishop, 1962, named bishop of, Tehuacán, 1962. Address: Apartado Postal 137 Tehuacán Pueblo Mexico

AYARS, ALBERT LEE, former school superintendent; b. Kettle Falls, Wash., Sept. 17, 1917; s. Glen Garrison and Ama Belle (Jennings) A.; m. Frances Louise Schaaf, June 21, 1941; children: Cheron Marie Ayars Holman, Judith Louise Templeman, Albert Lee, Danielle Jo Ayars Alexander, Garrison Hubert, Debora Ann Ayars Dillon, Theodora Ama, Virginia Darlene Dick. B.A., Wash. State U., 1939, B.E., 1940, M.A., 1942, Ed.D., 1956. Tchr. Davenport (Wash.) High Sch., 1940-42; prin. Colville (Wash.) High Sch., 1942-45; supt. Omak (Wash.) Pub. Schs., 1945-49, Sunnyside (Wash.) Pub. Schs., 1949-52; assoc. dir. Joint Council Econ. Edn., N.Y.C., 1952-53; dir. edn. dept. Hill and Knowlton, Inc.; also v.p. John W. Hill Found., N.Y.C., 1953-65; supt. schs., Spokane, 1965-72, Norfolk, Va., 1972-83; vis. prof., lectr. sch. adminstrn., curriculum and pub. relations Wash. State U., Mich. State U., No. Mich. U., Gonzaga U., U. Del., others; cons. in field, mem. adv. coms., speaker and panelist; adv. bd. Seven Colls. Vocat. Workshops, 1962-65, Robert A. Taft Inst. Govt., 1961—, W.E. Upjohn Inst. Employment Research, 1963-70; pres. council nat. orgn. adult edn. Nat. Assn. Industry-Edn. Coop., 1959, hon. life mem., 1965—; chmn. bd. advisers, pres. Assn. Internat. des Etudiants en Sciences Economiques et Commerciales, 1960. Author: Administering the People's Schools, 1957, How to Plan Community Resources Workshops, 1954, 2d edit., 1975, The Teenager and Alcohol, 1970, The Teenager and the Law, 1978, also articles, chpts. in books. Bd. dirs. Horace Mann League, pres., 1981-82; bd. dirs. Four Cities United Communities Fund, Urban League of Tidewater, Tidewater Epilepsy Assn., Norfolk Symphony Assn., Cultural Experiences Unlimited, Norfolk Council PTAs, Tidewater United Community Fund, Norfolk Mental Health and Retardation, Norfolk Health Council, Va., Council Econ. Edn., Joint Council Econ. Edn. Life Supt. emeritus Norfolk Pub. Schs.; Recipient service recognition Council Nat. Orgns. Adult Edn., 1959, first service citation Nat. Workshop Dirs. Conf., 1962, service plaque Whitworth Coll., 1963, Coronat medal St. Edwards U., 1963, first life membership, service plaque Nat. Assn. Industry-Edn. Coop., 1965, Leadership for Learning award Am. Assn. Sch. Adminstrs., 1983; recipient Outstanding Contbn. to Elem. Edn. award Va. Assn. Elem. Sch., Outstanding Service to Econ. Edn. award Va. Council Econ. Edn., 1983; Recipient YMCA Service Plaque, Bahai Human Rights award, citation for contbn. to edn. Va. Grand Lodge of Masons. Life fellow Internat. Inst. Arts and Letters; fellow AAAS; mem. N.Y. Acad. Scis., Am. Acad. Polit. and Social Sci., Internat. Platform Assn., Internat. Assn. Parliamentarians (hon.), Inland Empire Edn. Assn. (pres. 1968-69), Wash. State U. Alumni Assn. (pres. 1949-50, N.Y. area 1954-65), Am. Assn. Sch. Adminstrs. (dir., mem. exec. com. 1969—, v.p. 1973—), Wash. Congress Parents and Tchrs., Va. Congress Parents and Tchrs., Distributive Edn. Clubs Am., Va. chpt. (hon. mem.), Horace Mann League (hon. life mem.), Phi Kappa Phi, Phi Delta Kappa, Kappa Delta Pi. Baptist. Clubs: Norfolk Rotary (pres. 1980-81), Univ., Knife and Fork, Manito Golf and Country (Spokane). Home: 512 Mowbray Arch Norfolk VA 23507 Office: 800 E City Hall Ave Norfolk VA 23510

AYARS, MRS. JAMES *See* **CAUDILL, REBECCA**

AYASO, MANUEL, artist; b. Coruna, Galicia, Spain, Jan. 1, 1934; came to U.S., 1947, naturalized, 1955; s. Jose and Dolores (Dios) A.; m. Lucia Rivas, May 2, 1959; children: Monica, Jose Luciano. Student, Newark Sch. Fine and Indsl. Art, N.J., 1953-56. Exhibited one-man shows, Cober Gallery, N.Y.C., 1961-63,65,66,68, Forum Gallery, 1970,72,74, Ft. Worth Art Ctr., 1964, SUNY-Oswego, 1965, Witt Meml. Mus., San Antonio, 1967, group shows, 22d Biennial Internat. Watercolor Exhbn., Bklyn. Mus., 1963, U. Mex., Mexico City, Exhibit Contemporary Am. Artists, Nat. Inst. Arts and Letters, 1962,63,64,71, Whitney Mus. Am, 1963, Vatican Exhibit Contemporary Am. Spiritual Art, Rome, 1976. Served with U.S. Army, 1956-58. Recipient St. Paul Gallery and Sch. Art Purchase award, 1961, Tiffany Found. Award, 1962; Ford Found. grantee, 1964; recipient Nat. Inst. Arts and Letters Childe Hassam Purchase award, 1971. Mem. Nat. Geog. Soc., Smithsonian Instn., Whitney Mus. Am. Art, N.J. State Mus. Roman Catholic. Address: 12 Vincent Pl Verona NJ 07044

AYBAR, ROMEO, architect; b. Buenos Aires, Argentina, Feb. 8, 1930; came to U.S., 1960, naturalized, 1965; s. Aristobulo Romeo and Maria Sara (Figoli) A.; m. Rose Delia Caceres, Oct. 18, 1954; children: Patricia Monica Aybar Smith, Viviana Sylvia Aybar Pugaczewski, Cynthia Jenny. B.Arch., U. Buenos Aires, 1954. Lic. architect, N.J.; registered planner, N.J.; cert. fall-out shelter analyst. Pvt. practice architecture, Buenos Aires, 1955-60; sr. draftsman Widersum Assocs., N.Y.C., 1960-61; job capt. Mahony Troast, Clifton, N.J., 1961-63; project mgr. R. Cadien Architect, Cliffside Park, N.J., 1963-67; ptnr. Cadien & Aybar, Cliffside Park, N.J., 1968-69; sr. ptrn. The Aybar Partnership-Architect and Planners, Ridgefield, N.J., 1969—; mem. adv. bd. archtl. drafting course The Plaza Sch., Paramus, N.J., 1971—; lectr. Ft. Lee High Sch., Ridgefield High Sch., N.J. Sch. Architecture, N.J. Inst. Tech., others; mem. adj. faculty Montclair State Coll., 1971-74. Mem. Indsl. Safety Council N.J., 1973-78, Ridgefield Zoning Bd. Adjustments, 1969-71; chmn. Ridgefield Zoning Bd. Adjustments, 1972-73; mem. Hudson Riverfront Planning Commn. State of N.J., 1979-81; acting bldg. insp. City of Ridgefield, 1968; 1st lt., pilot N.J. wing CAP, 1978. Recipient Dir.'s award Architects League N.J., 1971, Vegliante Meml. award Architects League N.J., 1973, Outstanding Excellence in Design award N.J. Soc. Architects, 1971, 73. Fellow AIA (N.J. regional dir. 1981-83, 125th Anniversary Presdl. citation 1982); mem. Archtl. League No. N.J. (pres. 1975), N.J. Soc. Architects (dir. 1973, Romeo Aybar Scholarship established 1974, treas. 1974-75, pres. 1979), Aircraft Owners and Pilots Assn., Nat. Pilots Assn. Republican. Clubs: Ridgefield Exchange (pres.) (1972-73); (dir. N.J. dist.) (1973-74). Home: 2150 Center Ave Fort Lee NJ 07024 Office: 605 Broad Ave Ridgefield NJ 07657

AYCOCK, ALICE, artist; b. Harrisburg, Pa., 1946; d. Jesse N. and Alyce F. (Haskins) A. B.A., Douglass Coll.; M.A., Hunter Coll. Tchr. Hunter Coll., N.Y.C., 1972-73, Sch. Visual Arts, 1977—; vis. tchr. sculpture Princeton U., spring 1979. One-woman exhbns. include, N.S. Coll. Art and Design, Halifax (Can.), 1972, 112 Green St. Gallery, N.Y.C., 1974, 77, Project Inc., Cambridge, Mass., 1974, Williams Coll. Mus. Art, Watson Gallery, Wheaton Coll., Norton, Mass., 1976, Studies for a Town, projects room Mus. Modern Art, N.Y.C., 1977-78, Portland (Oreg.) Center Visual Arts, 1978, How to Catch and Manufacture Ghosts; The Machine that Makes the World, John Weber Gallery, N.Y.C., 1978, 79, U. R.I., 1978, Project entitled "The Angels Continue Turning the Wheels of the Universe Despite their Ugly Souls. . .", Salvatore Ala, Milan, Italy, 1978, Projects for PCA 4 at Phila. Coll. Art, 1978, Cranbrook Acad. Art, Bloomfield Hills, Mich., Projects and Proposals at Muhlenberg Coll., Allentown, Pa., Brown U., 1979, Explanation, An, of Spring and the Weight of Air, Contemporary Art Center, Cin., 1979, San Francisco Art Inst., 1979, Protetch-McIntosh Gallery, Washington, U. Mass., Amherst, Inst. Art and Urban Resources, Long Island City, 1980, Artemisia Gallery, Chgo., Ghosts, U. Calif.-Irvine, 1980, Protetch-McIntosh Gallery, Washington, 1980, The Game of Fliers, Washington Public Arts, (D.C.), 1980, The Large Scale Dis/Integration of Micro-Electronic Memories, Battery Park City Landfill, N.Y.C., 1980, Collected Ghost Stories from the Workhouse, U. South Fla., Tampa, 1980, The Savage Sparkler, State U. Plattsburgh, N.Y., 1981, A Theory for Universal Causality (Time/Creation Machines), Lawrence Oliver Gallery, Phila., 1982, The Miraculating Machine in the Garden (Tower of the Winds), Douglass Coll., New Brunswick, N.J., 1982, The Nets of Soloman, Phase II, Mus. Contemporary Art, Chgo., 1983, The Thousand and One Nights in the Mansion of Bliss, Protetch McNeil Gallery, N.Y.C., 1983, The Solar Wind, Roanoke Coll., Salem, Va., 1983, The Thousand and One Nights in the Mansion of Bliss., Wurttembergischer Kunstverein, Stuttgart, W. Ger., 1983; outdoor works include Sun/Glass, Silver Springs, Pa., 1971, Maze, New Kingston, Pa., 1972, Low Bldg. with Dirt Roof, New Kensington, 1973, Walled Trench/Earth Platform/Center Pit, New Kensington, 1974, Williams Coll. Project, 1974, Simple Network of Underground Wells and Tunnels, Far Hills, N.J., 1975, Circular Bldg. with Narrow Ledges for Walking, Silver Springs, 1976, Wooden Shacks on Stilts with Platform, Hartford Art Sch., Conn., 1976, The Beginnings of a Complex, Kassel, W. Ger., 1977, Artpark, Lewiston, N.Y., The Sign on the Door Read the Sign on the Door, U. R.I., 1978, On the Eve of the Indsl. Revolution, Bloomfield Hills, 1978; group exhbns. since 1971 include Documenta 6, Kassel, W. Ger., 1977, Venice Biennial, Italy, 1978, The Angels Continue Turning the Wheels of the Universe: Part II, Stedelijk Mus., Amsterdam, 1978, Whitney Biennial, Whitney Mus. Am. Art., N.Y.C., 1978, 81; including, Whitney Mus. Am. Art, N.Y.C., 1979, 81; group exhbns. since 1971 include, Montreal Mus. Fine Art, Que., Can., 1980, Ft. Worth Art Mus., Machineworks, Inst. Contemporary Art, U. Pa., Phila., 1981, Hoodo (Laura) Vertical and Horizontal Cross Sections of the Ether Wind, Hirshhorn Mus. and Sculpture Garden, Washington, 1981, Past-Present-Future, Wurttembergischer Kunstverein, Stuttgart, Ger., 1982, Nets of Solomon (permanent installations), Fattoria de Celle, Pistoria, Italy, 1982, The Leonardo Swire II, Middelheim, Antwerp, Belgium, 1983, The Hundred Small Rooms, Houston Festival for Arts, Texas, 1984. Grantee CAPS, 1975; fellow Nat. Endowment Arts, 1975, 80. Office: care John Weber Gallery 142 Greene St New York NY 10012

AYCOCK, EZRA KENNETH, state ofcl., educator, physician; b. Pinewood, S.C., Mar. 23, 1927; s. Robert James and Helen Beatrice (Geddings) A.; m. Mary Echo Cook, June 3, 1954; children—Doris Dawson, Ezra Kenneth. B.D., Duke U., 1950; M.D., Med. Coll. S.C., 1954; M.P.H., Harvard U., 1964. Diplomate: Am. Bd. Preventive Medicine, Am. Bd. Pediatrics. Intern Columbia (S.C.) Hosp., 1954-55; resident in pediatrics Children's Hosp., Los Angeles, 1955-56, Med. Coll. Hosp., Charleston, S.C., 1956-57; pvt. practice medicine specializing in pediatrics, Columbia, 1957-63; asst. dir. S.C. Maternal and Child Health div. S.C. Bd. Health, Columbia, 1963-67, state health officer, sec. exec. com., 1967-73; dir. Charleston Co. Health Dept., 1965-67; chmn. S.C. Pollution Control Authority, 1967-70; commr. S.C. Dept. Health and Environ. Control, Columbia, 1973-77; chmn. pub. health services adminstrn. U. S.C., 1977-80; dir. West Ala. Health Dist., 1980—; clin. prof. preventive medicine Med. U. Ala. Contbr. numerous articles to profl. jours. Fellow Am. Coll. Preventive Medicine, Am. Pub. Health Assn. (pres., exec. and governing councils So. Br.); mem. AMA, S.C. Pub. Health Assn., Assn. State and Terr. Health Officers (sec.-treas., pres., chmn. com. relations with affiliates), Ala. Med. Assn., Columbia, S.C. med. socs., Am. Acad. Pediatrics, S.C. Pediatric Assn., S.C. Acad. Gen. Practice, S.C. State Employees Assn., Alpha Omega Alpha. Home: 46 High Forest Tuscaloosa AL 35406 Office: 1101 Jackson Ave Tuscaloosa AL 35406

AYCOCK, WILLIAM BRANTLEY, educator; b. Lucama, N.C., Oct. 26, 1915; s. William P. and Myrtle (Moore) A.; m. Grace Mewborn, Oct. 25, 1941; children—William Preston 11, Nancy W. B.S., N.C. State Coll., 1936; M.A., U. N.C., 1937, J.D., 1948; LL.D., Atlantic Christian Coll., 1959, Wake Forest Coll., 1959, Duke, 1963. Tchr. pub. schs., Greensboro, N.C., 1937-40; adminstr. FSA, 1940-42; prof. law U. N.C., 1948-57, 64-66, chancellor, 1957-64, Kenan prof. law, 1966—. Author: (with Seymour Wurfel) Military Law Under the Uniform Code of Military Justice, 1955. Served from 1st lt. to lt. col., inf. AUS, 1942-45; col. Judge Adv. Gen.'s Corps, Res., 1956. Decorated Silver Star, Legion of Merit, Bronze Star. Mem. Order of Coif, Omicron Delta Kappa, Phi Kappa Tau. Home: 902 Arrowhead Rd Chapel Hill NC 27514

AYDELOTTE, MYRTLE KITCHELL, nursing adminstr., cons.; b. Van Meter, Iowa, May 31, 1917; d. John J. and Larava Josephine (Gutshall) Kitchell; m. William O. Aydelotte, June 22, 1956; children—Marie Elizabeth, Jeannette Farley. B.S., U. Minn., 1939, M.A., 1947, Ph.D., 1955; postgrad., Columbia U. Tchrs. Coll., summer 1948. Head nurse Charles T. Miller Hosp., St. Paul, 1939-41; supr. surg. teaching St. Mary's Hosp. Sch. Nursing, Mpls., 1941-42; instr. U. Minn., 1945-49; dir., dean State U. Iowa Coll. Nursing, 1949-57, prof., 1957-62; asso. chief nurse VA Hosp. Research for Nursing, Iowa City, 1963-64, chief nursing research, 1964-65; prof. U. Iowa Coll. Nursing, 1964-77; exec. dir. Am. Nurses Assn., 1977-81; dir. nursing U. Iowa Hosps. and Clinics, 1968-76; mem. sci. adv. bd. Center for Health

Research, Wayne State U., 1972-76, Inst. Medicine, 1973—; cons. U. Minn., 1970, U. Rochester, 1971, U. Mich., 1970, 73, U. Colo., 1970-71, U. Hawaii, 1972-73, Ariz. State U., 1972, U. Nebr., 1972-73. Contbr. articles to profl. jours.; editorial bd.: Nursing Forum, 1969—, Jour. Nursing Adminstrn, 1971. Mem., v.p. Iowa City Library Bd., 1961-67; mem. Johnson County Bd. Health, 1967-70; mem. adv. com. on family living courses Iowa City Bd. Edn., 1970-72. Served with Army Nurse Corps, 1942-46. Mem. Am. Nurses Assn., Am. Hosp. Assn., Sigma Theta Tau (research com. 1968-72). Home: 201 N 1st Ave Iowa City IA 52240 also 149 Oswegatchie Rd Waterford CT

AYDELOTTE, WILLIAM OSGOOD, historian; b. Bloomington, Ind., Sept. 1, 1910; s. Frank and Marie Jeannette (Osgood) A.; m. Myrtle Elizabeth Kitchell, June 22, 1956; children: Marie Elizabeth, Jeannette Farley. A.B., Harvard U., 1931; Ph.D., U. Cambridge, Eng., 1934. Asst. in chmn.'s office Fed. Home Loan Bank Bd., Washington, 1934-36; mem. faculty Trinity Coll., Hartford, Conn., 1937-43, Smith Coll., Northampton, Mass., 1943-45, Princeton U., 1945-47, U. Iowa, Iowa City, 1947—, prof. history, 1950—, chmn. dept. history, 1947-59, 65-68, Carver prof., 1976-78, emeritus, 1978—; vis. prof. Harvard U., Cambridge, Mass., 1966, U. Leicester, Eng., 1971; fellow Center Advanced Study Behavioral Scis., 1976-77; chmn. Midwest sect. selection com. for Marshall scholarships, 1955-60; mem. selection com. for dissertation fellowships Woodrow Wilson Nat. Fellowship Found., Princeton, 1962-68. Author: Bismarck and British Colonial Policy, 1937, rev. edit., 1970, Quantification in History, 1971; Editor: The Dimensions of Quantitative Research in History, 1972, The History of Parliamentary Behavior, 1977; bd. editors: Am. Hist. Rev, 1976-78; contbr. articles to profl. jours. Decorated hon. officer Order Brit. Empire, 1961. Fellow Royal Hist. Soc.; mem. Am. Hist. Assn., AAUP (com. A and exec. com. 1963-66), Social Sci. Research Council (dir. 1964-70), Nat. Acad. Scis., Iowa Acad. Sci., Social Sci. History Assn. (steering com. 1973—, v.p. 1978-79, pres. 1979-80), Phi Beta Kappa. Clubs: Athenaeum (London); Century (N.Y.C.). Home: 201 N 1st Ave Iowa City IA 52240 also 149 Oswegatchie Rd Waterford CT 06385

AYER, SIR ALFRED JULES, educator, philosopher, author; b. Oct. 29, 1910; s. Jules Louis Cyprien A.; m. Grace Isabel Renee Lees, 1932; children: 1 son, 1 dau.; m. Alberta Constance Chapman (Dee Wells), 1960 (div. 1983); 1 son; m. Vanessa Mary Addison Lawson Salmon. Scholar, Eton Coll., Christ Church Oxford, 1932, M.A., 1936; Dr. hon., U. Brussels, 1962, D.Litt., East Anglia, 1972, DHL, Bard Coll., 1983. Lectr. in philosophy Christ Church, 1932-35, research student, 1935-44; fellow Wadham Coll., Oxford, Eng., 1944-46, hon. fellow, 1957, dean, 1945-46, Grote prof. philosophy of mind and logic, 1946-59, dean arts faculty, 1950-52; Wykeham prof. logic U. Oxford, 1959-78, New Coll., U. Oxford, 1959-78, hon. fellow, 1980; fellow Wolfson Coll., 1978—; hon. fellow U. London, 1979; vis. prof. N.Y.U., 1948-49, CCNY, 1961-62, Surrey U., 1978; Montgomery fellow Dartmouth Coll., 1982-83. Editor: The Humanist Outlook, 1968; author: Metaphysics and Common Sense, 1969, Russell and Moore: The Analytical Heritage, 1971, Probability and Evidence, 1972, Russell, 1972, Bertran Russell as a Philosopher, 1973 (Brit. Acad. lectr.), The Central Questions of Philosophy, 1974, Part of My Life, 1977, Perception and Identity, 1979 (Festschrift reply to critics), Hume, 1980, Philosophy in the Twentieth Century, 1982; contbr. articles to profl. jours.; lectr.: William James, Harvard U., 1970, John Dewey, Columbia U., 1970, Gifford, St. Andrews, 1972-73; author: Language, Truth and Logic, 1936, 1946, The Foundations of Empirical Knowledge, 1940, Thinking and Meaning, 1947 (Inagural lectr.); editor: (with Raymond Winch) British Empirical Philosophers, 1952; author: Philosophical Essays, 1954, The Problem of Knowledge, 1956; editor: Logical Positivism, 1959; author: Privacy, 1960 (Brit. Acad. lectr.), The Concept of a Person and Other Essays, 1963, Man As a Subject for Science, 1964 (Auguste Comte lectr.), The Origins of Pragmatism, 1968. Mem. Central Advisory Council for Edn., 1963-66; pres. ind. Adoption Soc., 1965—. Served in Welsh Guards, 1940-45; served to capt. Welsh Guards, 1943-45; Attache at HM Embassy, Paris 1945. Decorated Chevalier de la Legion d'Honneur, 1977, Order of Cyril and Methodius, 1st class, Bulgaria, 1977. Mem. Humanist Assn., Modern Lang. Assn., Internat. Inst. Philosophy (chmn. Booker Prize Com. 1978), Am. Acad. Arts and Scis. (hon.), Royal Danish Acad. Scis. and Letters (fgn. mem.). Office: 51 York St London England, UK W1H 1PU

AYER, DONALD BELTON, lawyer; b. San Mateo, Calif., Apr. 30, 1949; m. Anne Norton; 1 son, Christopher. B.A. in History with great distinction and honors, Stanford U., 1971, M.A., Harvard U., 1973, J.D. cum laude, 1975. Bar: Calif. 1975, D.C. 1978. Summer assoc. Arent, Fox, Kintner, Plotkin & Kahn, Washington, 1973, Heller, Ehrman, White & McAuliffe, San Francisco, 1974; law clk. to judge U.S. Ct. Appeals D.C. Cir., 1975-76; law clk. to Justice William H. Rehnquist, U.S. Supreme Ct., Washington, 1976-77; asst. U.S. atty. criminal div. No. Dist. Calif., San Francisco, 1977-79, in charge San Jose office, 1978-79; assoc. Gibson Dunn & Crutcher, San Jose, Calif., 1979-81; U.S. atty. Eastern Dist. Calif., Sacramento, 1982—; mem. exec. com. 9th Cir. Jud. Conf. Fed. Cts. Commn. Editor: articles Harvard Law Rev., 1974-75. Pres. Stanford Young Republicans. Mem. ABA, Calif. State Bar Assn., Harvard U. Law Alumni Assn., Stanford U. Alumni Assn. Home: 1308 Normandy Sacramento CA 95822 Office: US Atty's Office 3305 Federal Bldg 650 Capitol Mall Sacramento CA 95814

AYER, MARY JANE, univ. dean; b. Goodman, Wis., May 5, 1930; d. Owen Lee and Alice Nina A. B.S., U. Wis., 1959, M.S., 1964, Ph.D., 1966. Mem. staff Univ. Hosps., Madison, Wis., 1952-57; mem. faculty U. Wis., Madison, 1966, 67—, prof. counseling, 1970—; asso. dean Sch. Edn., 1975—; mem. faculty U. Iowa, 1966-67; adminstr. HEW research grants U. Wis., 1968-74. Editor: (1969-74) Rehab. Counseling Bull; contbr. articles to profl. jours. Mem. Am. Personnel and Guidance Assn., Nat. Assn. Women Deans, Adminstrs. and Counselors, Am. Psychol. Assn. Home: 3050 Shadyside Dr Stoughton WI 53589 Office: 1000 Bascom Mall Madison WI 53704

AYER, WILLIAM ALFRED, chemist; b. Middle Sackville, N.B., Can., July 4, 1932; s. Charles Frederic and Elizabeth Main (Harper) A.; m. Dorothy Kathleen Monteith, May 10, 1954; children: Susan, Stephen, Judith, Andrew, Katherine, Carol. B.Sc., U. N.B., 1953, Ph.D., 1956. Research asso. Harvard U., 1957-58; asst. prof. to asso. prof. chemistry U. Alta, Edmonton, 1958-67, prof., 1967—. Sr. editor: (1976) Can. Jour. Chemistry; contbr. articles to sci. jours. Fellow Chem. Inst. Can. (Merck, Sharpe & Dohme award 1971), Royal Soc. Can.; mem. Am. Chem. Soc., Chem. Soc. London. Home: 8440 117th St Edmonton AB T6G 1R4 Canada Office: Chemistry Dept U Alberta Edmonton AB T6G 2G2 Canada

AYERS, DONALD HOWARD, health management executive; b. Barnesville, Ohio, Apr. 2, 1936; s. John C. and Helen R. A.; m. Waneta J. Murphy, June 1, 1959; children: Teresa Jean, Jeff. B.S. in Edn, Muskingum Coll., 1962; M. Health Care, George Washington U., 1965. Tchr. Schs., Barnesville, 1958-67; assoc. adminstr. Riverside Meth. Hosp., Columbus, Ohio, 1965-72; exec. dir. Grant Hosp., Columbus, 1972—; pres. Health Mgmt. Services, Inc., Associated Mgmt. Cons.; dir. Columbus Auto Club. Served with U.S. Army, 1955-57. Mem. Ohio Hosp. Assn. (past chmn.), Mid Ohio Health Planning Fedn. Methodist. Clubs: Muirfield Country, Brookside Country, Athletic, Masons, Rotary. Office: 300 E Town St Columbus OH 43215

AYERS, DONALD WALTER, tax preparation executive; b. Manhattan, Kans., Dec. 10, 1933; s. David Paul and and Marguerite Elizabeth (Stingley) A.; children: Donald Stephen, Karen Elizabeth. B.A., Kans. State Coll., 1955; postgrad., Kans. State U., 1961. C.P.A., Kans., Mo. Audit mgr. Peat, Marwick, Mitchell & Co. (C.P.A.s), Kansas City, Mo., 1961-73; v.p. fin., treas. H & R Block, Inc., Kansas City, 1973—. Served as officer USAF, 1945-60. Mem. Am. Inst. C.P.A.s, Mo. Soc. C.P.A.s, Fin. Execs. Inst., Nat. Assn. Accts. Republican. Episcopalian. Club: Woodside Racquet (Shawnee Mission, Kans.). Home: 447 E 79th St Kansas City MO 64131 Office: 4410 Main St Kansas City MO 64111

AYERS, GEORGE EDWARD LEWIS, university president; b. Quincy, Ill., Nov. 20, 1938; s. David Lewis and Mary Elizabeth (Wheeler) A.; m. Carolyn Sue Wasson, May 5, 1960; children: Deanne, Danita, Darryl. B.S., Western Ill. U., 1961; M.A., U. No. Colo., 1963, Ed.D., 1965. Prof. Mankato State U., Minn., 1969-71; asst. v.p. acad. affairs Met. State U., St. Paul, 1971-73, v.p. adminstrv. affairs, 1973-74, v.p., dean acad affairs, 1974-78; pres. Massasoit Community Coll., Brockton, Mass., 1978-82, Chgo. State U., 1982—; bd. dirs. Am. Council Edn.; adv. bd. Inst. Mgmt. Lifelong Edn.; chmn. bd. trustees Council Advancement Exptl. Learning. Co-author: Conflict Management: A 1976 Human Relations Training Guide, 1976; ednl. reports; editor: Recruitment and Selection of Support Personnel, 1969. Mem. adv. bd. Brockton Art Ctr.; trustee Milton Acad.; bd. dirs. Minn. Sci. Mus., Spring Hill Conf. Ctr. Recipient Nat. Rehab. Assn. Cordelia Shelving Ellis award, 1969, Western Ill. U. Alumni Achievement award, 1981. Mem. Am. Assn. Higher Edn., Am. Personnel and Guidance Assn., Am. Council Edn., Kappa Delta Phi. Home: 10400 Longwood Dr Chicago IL 60643 Office: Chicago State U 95th at King Dr Chicago IL 60628

AYERS, RICHARD WINSTON, architect; b. Jefferson, Ga., Nov. 23, 1910; s. Jere Sanford and Eva Pierce (McNeill) A.; m. Vaughan Benz, Nov. 14, 1941; children: Richard Allan, Allan Winston, Claire Vaughan. Student, Piedmont Coll., 1926-28; B.F.A., Yale U., 1932, M.F.A., 1934; fellow, Am. Acad. in Rome, 1936-38. Draftsman Frederick A. Godley, Architect, N.Y.C., 1934-36; mem. Buckler & Fenhagen, Architects, Balt., 1938-42; ptnr. Buckler, Fenhagen, Meyer & Ayers, Balt., 1946-55, Meyer & Ayers, 1955-64, Meyer, Ayers & Saint, 1964-70, Saint Steward, Inc., 1970-75, Ayers Saint, 1975—. Mem. Balt. Art Commn., 1955-68; chmn. bldg. com. Balt. Mus. Art, 1955-60; chmn. Mt. Vernon Place Archtl. Adv. Commn., 1958-62; mem. Selection Com. for Fulbright Fellows, 1959-62; bd. archtl. rev. Md., 1947-55, 63—, chmn. bd. archtl. rev., 1963-68; bd. archtl. rev. Baltimore County, 1952-57, 64-67, chmn. archtl. rev., 1952-57; trustee Balt. Bldg. Congress, 1956-58. Served to lt. USNR, 1942-46. Recipient Prix de Rome, 1936; Garland fellow, 1933-34. Fellow AIA (sec. Balt. chpt. 1948-50); mem. NAD (assoc.). Home: 105 Cotswold Rd Baltimore MD 21210 Office: Ayers & Saint 344 N Charles St Baltimore MD 21201

AYERS, THOMAS G., utility executive; b. Detroit, Feb. 16 1915; s. Jule C. and Camilla (Chalmers) A.; m. Mary Andrew, Nov. 25, 1938; children—Catherine Mary Ayers Allen, Thomas G., William Charles, Richard James, John Steven. A.B., U. Mich., 1937; LL.D., Elmhurst Coll., 1966. With Pub. Service Co. No. Ill., 1938-52, mgr. indsl. relations, 1948-52; asst. v.p. Commonwealth Edison Co., Chgo., 1952, v.p., 1953-62, exec. v.p., 1962-64, pres., 1964-73, chmn., pres., chief exec. officer, 1973-80; also dir.; dir. 1st Nat. Bank Chgo., Northwest Industries, Inc., Zenith Radio Corp., Tribune Co., Gen. Dynamics Corp. Chmn. Dearborn Park Corp.; chmn. Met. Crusade of Mercy, 1969, Leadership Council for Met. Open Communities; chmn. bd. trustee Northwestern U., Chgo. Symphony Orch.; mem. Chgo. Econ. Devel. Commn.; chmn., pres. Chgo. World's Fair 1992 Corp. Mem. Chgo. Assn. Commerce and Industry (dir., past pres.). Clubs: Chgo., Mid-Day, Comml., Tavern (Chgo.); Glen Oak Country. Home: 199 Montclair Ave Glen Ellyn IL 60137 Office: PO Box 767 One 1st Nat Plaza Chicago IL 60690

AYKAN, KAMRAN, chemical company executive; b. Istanbul, Turkey, May 19, 1930; s. Mehmet Emin and Fatma (Hikmet) A. Student, U. Hamburg, Germany, 1951-53; M.S., U. Istanbul, 1954. Chemist Bergbau A.G., Koenig Ludwig, Germany, 1956-57; chemist William T. Burnett & Co., Inc., Balt., 1957-58; with E.I. DuPont de Nemours & Co., Inc., 1958-71, staff scientist, 1969-71; mgr. chem. research Engelhard Industries div. Engelhard Minerals and Chems. Corp., Edison, N.J., 1971-72, tech. dir. autoexhaust catalyst group, 1972-74, dir. research and devel., 1974-76, v.p. research and devel., 1976-81, group v.p. research, 1981—; Bd. dirs. Research and Devel. Council N.J. Contbr. articles to profl. jours. Served with Turkish Army, 1954-56. Mem. Am. Crystallographic Assn., Am. Chem. Soc., Indsl. Research Inst., Am. Ceramic Soc., Catalysis Soc. N.Y. Patentee in field. Office: Engelhard Industries Div Engelhard Corp Menlo Park Edison NJ 08817

AYKROYD, DANIEL EDWARD, writer, actor; b. Ottawa, Ont., Can., July 1, 1952; came to U.S., 1975; s. Peter Hugh and Lorraine G. (Gougeon) A.; m. Maureen Lewis, May 10, 1974; children—Mark, Lloyd, Oscar. Mem., Toronto Co. of Second City Theater; star in: CBS TV series Coming Up Rosie; writer, actor: NBC's Saturday Night Live, 1975-79; other TV appearances include All You Need is Cash; appeared in: movies Mr. Mike's Mondo Video, 1979, Neighbors, 1981, Doctor Detroit, 1983, Trading Places, 1983, Twilight Zone, 1983; writer, actor in: movie The Blues Brothers, 1980; performed and records: (with John Belushi as) Blues Brothers; albums include Made in America; v.p., Arc-Ray Productions, Inc. (Recipient Emmy award 1976-77). Mem. Writers Guild Am. West, AFTRA. Office: care Atlantic Records 75 Rockefeller Plaza New York NY 10019 *

AYLESWORTH, THOMAS GIBBONS, author, editor; b. Valparaiso, Ind., Nov. 5, 1927; s. Carrol Wells and Margaret Ruth (Gibbons) A.; m. Virginia Lillian Boelter, Aug. 13, 1949; children: Carol Jean, Thomas Paul. A.B., Ind. U., 1950, M.S., 1953; Ph.D., Ohio State U., 1959. Tchr. Harvard High Sch., Ill., 1951-52, New Albany Jr. High Sch., Ind., 1952-54; head sci. dept. Battle Creek High Sch., Mich., 1955-57; asst. prof. Mich. State U., East Lansing, 1957-61; spl. lectr. Wesleyan U., Middletown, Conn., 1961-64; sr. editor Doubleday & Co., Inc., N.Y.C., 1964-80; pres. Update Pub. Corp., 1976—; editor-in-chief Bison Books Corp., Greenwhich, Conn., 1981—; vis. prof. Ohio State U., Columbus, 1962, Whitewater State U., Wis., 1964. Author: Planning for Effective Science Teaching, 1963, Our Polluted World, 1964, This Vital Air, This Vital Water, 1968, (rev. edit.) This Vital Air, This Vital Water, 1973, It Works Like This, 1968, Teaching for Thinking, 1969, Into the Mammal's World, 1970, Traveling Into Tomorrow, 1970, Servants of the Devil, 1970, Mysteries From the Past, 1971, Werewolves and Other Monsters, 1971; auhtor: Vampires and Other Ghosts, 1972; author: Monsters from the Movies, 1972, The Alchemists, 1973, Astrology and Fortelling the Future, 1973, Who's Out There?, 1975, The World of Microbes, 1975, Cars, Boats, Trains and Planes of Today and Tomorrow, 1975, ESP, 1975, The Search for Life, 1975, Plamistry, 1976, Graphology, 1976, Science Update, 1977, 78, Science at the Ball Game, 1977, The Story of Vampires, 1977, The Store of Werewolves, 1978, Understanding Body Talk, 1978, The Story of Witches, 1979, The Story of Dragons and Other Monsters, 1980, Storm Alert, 1980, Animal Superstitions, 1981, Science Looks at Mythical Monsters, 1982, The Mount St. Helens Disaster, 1983, America This Beautiful Land, 1984, History of Movie Musicals, 1984; New Eng. editor: Am. Biology Tchr., 1962-64; sr. editor: Current Sci., 1961-64. Served with AUS, 1946-47. Mem. N.Y. Acad. Sics., Nat. Sci. Tchrs. Assn., Nat. Assn. Biology Tchrs., Nat. Assn. Research Sci. Teaching, Am. Assn. Sci. Writers, Authors Guild, Phi Delta Kappa. Club: Stamford Yacht (Conn.). Home: 48 Van Rensselaer Ave Stamford CT 06902

AYLLON, CÁNDIDO, educator; b. Bklyn., Oct. 3, 1929; s. Pedro José and Juana (Chevere) A. B.A., Bklyn. Coll., 1951; M.A., U. Wis., 1952, Ph.D., 1956. Instr. Spanish lang. and lit. U. Wash., 1956-57, asst. prof., 1957-63; asst. prof. Spanish lang. and lit. U. Calif. at Riverside, 1963-64, asso. prof., 1964-69, prof., 1969—, dept. chmn. Spanish and Portuguese, 1967—; dir. Edn. Abroad Program, Madrid, Spain, 1979-81; vis. lectr. U. Wis., 1961; dir. U. Wis.-Case Inst. Tech. Spanish program, Monterrey, Mexico, 1962-63; Cons. Peace Corps U. Wash., 1962. Author: La visión pesimista de La Celestina, 1965, (with Paul Smith) Spanish Composition through Literature, 1968; Editorial staff: (1968-72.) Alaluz; Contbr. articles to profl. jours. Recipient Distinguished Teaching award U. Calif. at Riverside, 1972; Fellow Humanities Inst. U. Calif., 1967, 73. Mem. Modern Lang. Assn., Am. Assn. Tchrs. Spanish and Portuguese, Phi Beta Kappa, Sigma Delta Pi, Phi Sigma Iota. Home: 126 Barrett Rd Riverside CA 92507

AYLWARD, RONALD LEE, lawyer; b. St. Louis, May 30, 1930; s. John Thomas and Edna (Ketcherside) A.; m. Margaret Cecilia Hellweg, Aug. 10, 1963; children: Susan Marie, Stephen Ronald, Carolyn Ann. A.B., Washington U., St. Louis, 1952, J.D., 1954; student, U. Va., 1955. Bar: Mo. 1954, Ill. 1961, U.S. Supreme Ct. 1968. Assoc. Henghan, Roberts & Cole, St. Louis, 1958-59; asst. counsel Olin Corp., East Alton, Ill., 1960-64; asst. gen. counsel INTERCO, Inc., St. Louis, 1964-66, asso. gen. counsel, mgr. law dept., 1966-69, asst. sec., 1966-74, gen. counsel, 1969-81, mem. operating bd., 1970—, v.p., 1971-81, mem. exec. com., dir., 1975—, exec. v.p., 1981—; mem. dist. export council U.S. Dept. Commerce, 1974-77; dir., mem. exec. com., trust estates com. Boatmen's Nat. Bank St. Louis, 1982—; dir. Boatmen's Bancshares, Inc. Bd. dirs. St. Louis County chpt. Nat. Found. March of Dimes, 1974—, sec., 1976—, chmn., 1979—; bd. dirs. Cardinal Ritter Inst., 1975—, St. Louis chpt. ARC, 1977-83, Linda Vista Montessori Sch., 1975-77, Better Bus. Bur. Greater St. Louis, 1978—; sec. Better Bus. Bur. Greater St. Louis, 1980—; bd. dirs. YMCA Greater St. Louis, 1981—; trustee St. Louis Council World Affairs, sec., 1978—; chmn. lay bd. DePaul Health Center, 1979—, mem. exec. com. lay bd., 1981—; mem. lay adv. bd. Chaminade Coll. Prep. Sch., 1980—, chmn. bd. trustees, 1981—; mem. lay bd. Acad. of the Visitation, 1981—. Served with AUS, 1955-58. Mem. ABA, Mo. Bar Assn., St. Louis Bar Assn. (chmn. bus. law 1960-72, chmn. corp. law 1964-67, chmn. spl. projects 1964-65, moot ct. coms. 1966-67), Am. Judicature Soc., Am. Footwear Industries Assn. (nat. affairs, vice-chmn. 1970, chmn. 1971-75), Am. Apparel Mfrs. Assn. (dir. 1983—), NAM (taxation com. 1970-78, pub. affairs com. 1973-78, govt. ops./expenditures com. 1973-78), St. Louis C. of C. (legis. and tax com. 1966-74, vice chmn. 1970-71), Asso. Industries Mo. (dir. 1973—, exec. com. 1974—, 2d v.p. 1974-76, pres. 1976-78), Am. Soc. Corp. Secs. (pres. St. Louis regional group 1972-73), Delta Theta Phi (dist. chancellor Mo. 70-77, pres. St. Louis alumni 1963). Clubs: Noonday, Mo. Athletic (dir. 1976-78), Rotary, Bellerive Country (dir. 1981—). Home: 55 Muirfeld Saint Louis MO 63141 Office: 10 Broadway Saint Louis MO 63102 *Having something to achieve is the essence of my career. Continuing to set higher goals throughout life has made it both interesting and rewarding.*

AYLWARD, THOMAS JAMES, JR., communication arts and theatre educator; b. Milw., Nov. 4, 1923; s. Thomas James and Dorothy (Leary) A.; m. Mary L. Lakeman, Jan. 30, 1954; children: Mary Virgina, Thomas James III, Kathleen Grace, Matthew Maxwell, Peter Richard, Anne Marie, Wendy. B.S., U. Wis., Madison, 1947, M.S., 1949, Ph.D., 1960. Tchr. Shorewood (Wis.) High Sch., 1947-48; instr. U. Md., College Park, 1949-59, asst. prof., 1959-62, asso. prof., 1962-68, prof., 1968—, chmn. dept. communication arts and theatre, 1970—; interim dean Coll. Arts and Scis., 1971; cons. to govt. agys.; cons., mem. College Park Cable TV Com., 1976—. Producer, dir. numerous radio and TV programs. Chmn. Md. Dance Theatre Inc., 1971—. Ford Found. fellow in adult edn., 1953-54. Mem. Speech Communication Assn., Eastern Communication Assn., Internat. Communication Assn., Broadcast Edn. Assn., Phi Kappa Phi, Sigman Circle of Omicron Delta Kappa. Republican. Roman Catholic. Home: PO Box 123 Olney MD 20832 Office: U Md College Park MD 20742

AYMAR, GORDON CHRISTIAN, portrait painter; b. East Orange, N.J., July 24, 1893; s. William Howard and Maud (Christian) A.; m. Margaretta Kneass White, Jan. 24, 1920 (dec.); children—Carol Penrhyn Aymar Armstrong, Barbara Aymar Earle, Gordon Christian (dec.). A.B., Yale U., 1914; postgrad., Sch. Mus. Fine Arts, Boston, 1917. Art dir. J. Walter Thompson, N.Y.C., 1920-30; art dir., v.p. Compton Advt. Agy., N.Y.C., 1930-45; cons. designer, portrait work, 1945-59, lectr. in field. Exhibited, Darien Library, Darien Art Festival, Housatonic Art League, New Milford, Conn., Rowayton (Conn.) Art Center, Conn. Classic Arts, Nat. Acad., Christ Ch., Redding, Conn., Bridgeport (Conn.) Mus. Art, Sci. and Industry, Am. Watercolor Soc., Canton (Ohio) Art Inst., Boise (Idaho) Art Inst., Charles and Emma Frye Mus., Seattle, Abilene (Tex.) Fine Arts Mus., Orlando (Fla.) Art Assn., Columbia (S.C.) Mus. Art, Davenport (Iowa) Municipal Art Gallery, Moore Coll. Art, Phila., Arnot Art Gallery, Elmira, N.Y., Baldwin-Wallace Coll., Berea, Ohio, Brooks Meml. Art Gallery, Memphis, Phoenix Art Mus., Century Assn., Yale Club, N.Y.C., Nat. Arts Club, Dayton Art Inst., Montreal (Can.) Mus. Art, Royal Soc. Painters in Water Colour, London, Washington (Conn.) Art Assn., Kent (Conn.) Art Assn., The Gallery, House of Books, Kent, Pomperaug Valley Art League, Southbury, Conn., Gunnery Sch., Washington, Conn., portraits in permanent collections, Am. Cyanamid Co., N.Y., Madison Ave. Presbyn. Ch., N.Y.C., Nat. Council Chs., N.Y.C., Phillips Acad., Andover, Mass., Union Theol. Sem., N.Y.C., Racquet Club, N.Y.C., Little Mgmt. Co., N.Y.C., Bennett Coll., Milford, N.Y., Lazarus Co., Columbus, Ohio, South Kent (Conn.) Sch., Loomis Chaffee Sch., Windsor, Conn., Temple of Justice, Olympia, Wash., Yale U. Art Gallery, New Haven, Neurol. Inst., N.Y.C., Middlebury (Vt.) Coll., Drew U., Madison, N.J., India House, Young & Rubicam, Ogilvy and Mather, N.Y.C., Pratt Inst., Bklyn., Art Dirs. Club, others, photographs in permanent study coll., Mus. Modern Art, N.Y.; art dir., Darien Hist. Soc.; Author: An Introduction to Advertising Illustration, 1930, Bird Flight, 1934, Start 'Em Sailing, 1941, Treasury of Sea Stories, 1944, (with Gordon C. Aymar, Jr.) Second Book on Sailing, 1960, (with Margaretta W. Aymar) Michael Sails the Mud Hen, 1960, Yacht Racing Rules and Tactics, 7th edit, 1973, The Art of Portrait Painting, 1967. Chmn. Park and Recreation Com., rep. town meetings, Darien, Conn., 1952-58. Served as lt. (j.g.) USNR, World War I. Recipient award Nat. Soc. Art Dirs., 1951. Mem. N.Y. Art Dirs. Club (adv. bd., past pres., Hall of Fame 1975), Nat. Soc. Art Dirs. (charter pres., bd.), Am. Watercolor Soc. (dir. 1960-61, 1st v.p. 1961-62), Kent Art Assn. (exec. com., exhbn. com.). Club: Salmagundi (N.Y.C.). Address: RFD 1 Flat Rock Rd South Kent CT 06785 *In my portrait painting I have three objectives: To achieve a physical likeness; to reveal the sitter's spiritual* *characteristics, to produce a work of art per se which will last through the years regardless of the sitter.*

AYMOND, ALPHONSE HENRY, public utilities official, lawyer; b. St. Louis, Sept. 27, 1914; s. Alphonse H. and Anne (Putz) A.; m. Elizabeth Shierson, Sept. 30, 1939; children: Charles H., Robert D., William G. A.B., Northwestern U., 1936; J.D., U. Mich., 1939; D., Olivet Coll., 1970; D. Pub. Service, Western Mich. U., 1974. Bar: Ill. 1939, Mich. 1947. With firm Miller, Gorham, Wescott & Adams, Chgo., 1939-44; with Commonwealth & So. Corp., N.Y.C., 1946-47; atty. Consumers Power Co., Jackson, Mich., 1947-51, gen. atty., 1951-55, v.p., gen. counsel, 1955-57, exec. v.p., dir., 1957-60, chmn. bd., 1960-79, pres., 1972-75, chief exec. officer, 1960-78; of counsel Aymond, Sullivan, Whedon & Thompson, 1979—; dir. Mich. Gas Storage Co., 1960—, C.B. Fin. Corp.; pres. Mich. Gas Storage Co., 1960-78; dir. City Bank & Trust Co., Jackson, NBD Bancorp., Inc., Nat. Bank Detroit, Kellogg Co., K Mart Corp.; trustee Northwestern Mut. Life Ins. Co. Former mem. Jackson Planning Commn.; regional exec. com. Boy Scouts Am.; past chmn. Mich. Found. for Arts; trustee W.K. Kellogg Found., Mich. Colls. Found.; past trustee, pres. Jackson Found. Served to lt. (j.g.) Supply Corps, USNR, 1944-46. Mem. Am. Bar Assn., Edison Electric Inst. (past pres.), Assn. Edison Illuminating Cos. (past pres.), Am. Gas Assn. (past dir.), Nat. Assn. Electric Cos. (past dir.), Order of Coif. Episcopalian (past trustee Diocese Mich.). Clubs: Detroit; Lost Tree (North Palm Beach, Fla.); Jackson Country, Town (Jackson, Mich.). Office: 180 W Michigan Ave Jackson MI 49201 *There are many attributes that are important for any individual to achieve success, but the one essential for it to be meaningful and rewarding is integrity.*

AYO, DONALD JOSEPH, college administrator; b. Bourg, La., Apr. 1, 1934; m. Barbara Brown, 1960; children: Debra, Nancy, Mary. B.S., L.A. State U., 1956; M.S., La. State U., 1958, Ph.D., 1964. Asst. prof. horticulture La. State U., 1958; from instr. to prof. plant sci. Nicholls State U., Thibodaux, La., 1958-67, head dept. agr., 1966-68; dean div. sci. Nicholls Stat U., Thibodaux, La., 1968-69; dean div. life sci. and tech. Nicholls State U., Thibodaux, La., 1969-77, Alcee Fortier Disting. Honor prof. plant sci., 1967—, v.p., 1971-83, provost, 1975-83, pres., 1983—. Asst. editor: Nat. Assn. Coll. Tchrs. Am. Jour., 1963-65. Mem. Am. Soc. Hort. Sci., Am. Soc. Agronomy, Soil Sci. Soc. Am., N.Y. Acad. Sci., Am. Inst. Biol. Scis. Office: Nicholls State Univ Nicholls Univ Sta Thibodaux LA 70301 *

AYOUB, MOHAMED M., industrial engineer, educator; b. Tanta, Egypt, Feb. 17, 1931; s. Mohamed E. and Fatima A. (Salem) A.; m. Beverlie J. Glasscock, Aug. 12, 1959; children: Minda J., Tanya S. B.S.M.E., U. Cairo, 1953; M.S.I.E., State U. Iowa, 1955, Ph.D., 1964. Registered profl. engr., Tex. Sr. indsl. engr., 1958-61; asst. prof. indsl. engring. Tex. Tech. U., Lubbock, 1961-64, asso. prof., 1964-68, prof., 1968-74, Horn prof. indsl. engring. and biomed. engring., dir. Inst. Biotech., 1978—, dir. Inst. Ergonomics Research, 1978—; cons. ergonomics. Author: A Manual on Occupational Ergonomics, 1975; research numerous publs. in field. Recipient Outstanding Service award Tex. Safety Assn. Mem. Am. Inst. Indsl. Engrs. (David Baker Research award), Am. Soc. Engring. Edn., Human Factor Soc. (Paul Fitts award), Am. Indsl. Hygiene Assn., Ergonomics Research Soc., Am. Soc. Biomechanics. Home: 3613 60th Lubbock TX 79413 Office: Dept Indsl Engring Tex Tech U Lubbock TX 79409

AYOUB, SAM, soft drink company executive; b. Tantah, Gharbia, Egypt, Dec. 24, 1918; came to U.S., 1958; s. Youssef and Basima (Malek) A.; m. Louisa Elmasry, May 8, 1948. B.B.A. in Fin., Hofstra U., 1962; postgrad., Harvard Bus. Sch., 1967. Mgr. State Bank Ethiopia, 1945-55, Ethiopia Air Lines, 1955-58; with Coca-Cola Co., 1959—, Coca-Cola Export Corp., N.Y.C., 1959-76; v.p., treas. Coca-Cola Co., Atlanta, 1976-79, sr. v.p. gen. ops., 1979-81, sr. exec. v.p., chief fin. officer, 1981—; dir. Tex. Commerce Bancshares, Houston, Rose Stores Inc., Henderson, N.C.; exec. com. Egypt-U.S. Bus. Council. Bd. dirs. Ga. Dept. Industry and Trade, Piedmont Hosp. Found., Atlanta Humane Soc., Atlanta C. of C., U.S.-China Bus. Council, Japan-Am. Soc., Ga.; trustee Inst. Internat. Edn. Recipient Service award Ga. Bus. and Trade Industry, 1980, Internat. award Ga. Gov.'s, 1981; fellow Atlanta Internat. Bus., 1981. Clubs: World Trade (hon. chmn.); Capital City, Commerce (Atlanta). Home: 30 Willow Glen 5425 Glenridge Dr NE Atlanta GA 30342 Office: Coca-Cola Co 310 North Ave Atlanta GA 30313

AYRES, JAMES MARX, mechanical engineer; b. Pomona, Calif., Nov. 28, 1922; s. James Albert and Martha (Oathout) A.; m. Anita Landa, June 10, 1952; children—Denise, Ron, Gary. B.S. in Mech. Engring, U. Calif., Berkeley, 1944; M.S., Purdue U., 1948. Registered profl. engr., Calif., 5 other states. Chief mech. engr. various engring. firms, 1949-52, then Pereira & Luckman (architects and engrs.), Los Angeles, 1952-56; pvt. practice mech. engring., Los Angeles, 1957-59; pres. Ayres & Hayakawa, Los Angeles, 1959-74, Ayres & Hayakawa Energy Mgmt., 1974-77, Ayres Assocs., 1977—; research fellow radiant heating Purdue U., 1947-48; teaching asst. mech. engring. U. Calif., Berkeley, 1948; guest lectr. U. So. Calif., 1965—, UCLA Sch. Architecture, 1965—; mem. Los Angeles Code Adv. Bd., 1960-72, Calif. Dept. Pub. Health Bldg. Safety Bd., 1973-75, Calif Seismic Safety Commn., 1975-79. Contbr. profl. jours. Chmn. Los Angeles Citizens Com. Music Edn. in Schs., 1964-65; trustee Carthay Circle Assos., 1965-73. Served to lt. (j.g.) USNR, World War II. Recipient Outstanding Engr. Merit award Inst. for Advancement of Engring., 1975. Fellow Earthquake Engring. Research Inst., Am. Soc. Heating, Refrigerating and Air Conditioning Engrs.; mem. Automated Procedures Engring. Cons. (trustee 1967-70, 72, pres. 1971), ASME, Nat. Soc. Profl. Engrs., Cons. Engrs. Council, Cons. Engrs. Assn. Calif., Mech. Engrs. Assn. (pres. 1969), Internat. Solar Energy Soc., Tau Beta Pi. Address: 1180 S Beverly Dr Los Angeles CA 90035

AYRES, JOHN CECIL, pub. health exec.; b. Lawrence, Mass., Apr. 20, 1919; s. John and Dominica (Jarusavicius) Aiauskas; m. Dora Boynton Hoxie, Nov. 6, 1944; children—Janet Claudia, John Boynton, Jeffrey Peabody. B.S., U. Mass., 1941; M.D., Boston U., 1943; M.P.H., Harvard U., 1949. Dir. div. alcoholism Mass. Dept. Pub. Health, 1950-53, epidemiologist div. communicable disease, 1947-48, asst. dir. div., 1949-50; commr. pub. health, Springfield, Mass., 1953—; hosp. dir. Springfield Municipal Hosp., 1958-73, trustee, 1953—; instr. Harvard U., 1949-59; dir. Mass. Blue Shield, 1972-77; Vice pres., chmn. health sect. Springfield Community Council, 1955-57; chmn. Pioneer Valley chpt. Nat. Found., 1968-74. Editor-in-chief: The Hampden Hippocrat, 1966-73. Served with M.C., USNR, 1943-46. Fellow Am. Pub. Health Assn., Am. Coll. Preventive Medicine; mem. AMA, Am. Assn. Pub. Health Physicians, Mass. Med. Soc. (pres. 1974-75), Mass. Pub. Health Assn. (pres. 1955), Mass. Hosp. Assn., Delta Omega. Home: 55 Bridle Path Rd Springfield MA 01118 Office 1414 State St Springfield MA 01109

AYRES, JOHN SAMUEL, chemical engineer; b. Kansas City, Mo., Oct. 12, 1914; s. William I. and Jessie C. (Heinlein) A.; m. Dorothy Rule Fritts, Jan. 19, 1939. B.S., U. Mo., 1935. With Cook Paint & Varnish Co., 1936—, successively chemist, Kansas City, Mo., mgr. research Detroit div., v.p. indsl. sales, Kansas City, 1936-60, pres., 1960-80, vice chmn., cons., 1980—, also dir.; dir. North Kansas City State Bank, Gas Service Co., Asso. Industries Mo. Commr. commerce and indsl. devel., State of Mo.; Bd. govs. Am. Royal Assn.; exec. com. Midwest Research Inst.; treas., exec. com. Kansas City area Boy Scouts Am.; exec. com. Starlight Theatre Assn., pres., 1973-75; trustee U. Kansas City, Midwest Research Inst., Rehab. Inst.; bd. dirs. Clay County Devel. Commn. Recipient engring. honor award U. Mo., 1962, Faculty-Alumni award U. Mo., 1970. Mem. Greater Kansas City C. of C. (past pres.), NAM (past dir.), Nat. (past exec. com., treas.), Kansas City paint and coatings assns., Am. Chem. Soc. (Citizen Chemist award 1968), Detroit Soc. Paint Tech. (past pres.), Nat. Alliance Businessmen (metro chmn. 1975), State of Mo. C. of C. (dir.). Clubs: Kansas City (past pres.), River, Mission Hills Country; Detroit Athletic, Orchard Lake Country (Detroit). Home: 1238 W 63d Terr Kansas City MO 64113 Office: PO Box 389 Kansas City MO 64141

AYRES, LEE SPENCER, real estate developer; b. Belleville, Ill., Nov. 26, 1941; s. William Ransom and Grace Margaret (Player) A.; m. Deanna Mae Reed, Apr. 15, 1967; children: Ashley, Bradley, Wesley. B.A., U. Kans., 1964, M.P.A., 1966. Staff asst. City of Wichita (Kans.), 1965-67; asst. city mgr. Titusville, Fla., 1969, city mgr., 1969-74, Overland Park, Kans., 1974-77, Sunnyvale, Calif., 1977-79; pres., The Centare Corp., Palo Alto, Calif., 1980—. Served as 1st lt. U.S. Army, 1967-69. Decorated Army Commendation medal. Mem. Internat. City Mgmt. Assn., Am. Soc. Public Adminstrn. Home: 866 Groton Ct Sunnyvale CA 94087 Office: 755 Page Mill Rd Suite A241 Palo Alto CA 94304

AYRES, LEW, actor; b. Mpls., Dec. 28, 1908; m. Lola Lane, 1931 (div. 1933); m. Ginger Rogers, 1933 (div. 1939); m. Diana Hall, 1964; 1 son, Justin Bret. Began career as a musician; performed with own orch. and Henry Halstead's Orch.; film debut in The Kiss, 1929; other films include The Sophomore, 1929, Many a Slip, 1930, All Quiet on the Western Front, 1930, Common Clay, 1930, East is West, 1930, Doorway to Hell, 1930, Iron Man, 1931, Up for Murder, 1931, the Spirit of Notre Dame, 1931, Heaven on Earth, 1931, Mississippi, 1931, The Impatient Maiden, 1932, Night World, 1932, Okay America, 1932, State Fair, 1933, Don't Bet on Love, 1933, My Weakness, 1933, Cross Country Cruise, 1934, She Learned About Sailors, 1934, Servants' Entrance, 1934, Let's Be Ritzy, 1934, Lottery Lover, 1935, The Silk Hat Kid, 1935, the Leathernecks have Landed, 1936, Panic on the Air, 1936, Shakedown, 1936, Lady be Careful, 1936, Murder with Pictures, 1936, The Crime Nobody Saw, 1936, Last Train from Madrid, 1937, Hold Em Navy, 1937, Scandal Street, 1938, King of the Newsboys, 1938, Holiday, 1938, Rich Man Poor Girl, 1938, Young Dr. Kildare, 1938; star of: movie series Dr. Kildare, 1938-42, Spring Madness, 1938, Ice Follies, 1939, Broadway Serenade, 1939, These Glamour Girls, 1939, Remember?, 1939, The Golden Fleecing, 1940, Maisie Was a Lady, 1941, Fingers at the Window, 1942, the Dark Mirror, 1946, the Unfaithful, 1947, Johnny Belinda, 1948, the Capture, 1950, New Mexico, 1951, No Escape, 1953, Donovan's Brain, 1954, Advise and Consent, 1961, The Carpetbaggers, 1964, Damien—Omen II, 1978, Battlestar Galactica, 1979; TV pilot Hawaii Five-O, 1968, Marcus Welby M.D, 1968, Earth II, 1971; other TV appearances include: She Waits, 1972, The Man, 1972, The Biscuit Eater, 1972, The Stranger, 1972, The Questor Tapes, 1973, Battle for Planet of the Apes, 1973, Heatwave, 1974, Francis Gary Powers, 1976, End of the World, 1977, Altars of the World, 1976. Recipient Golden Globe award, 1976. Office: care William Morris Agy 151 El Camino Beverly Hills CA 90212 *

AYRES, LYMAN S., merchant; b. Indpls., July 5, 1908; s. Frederic Murray and Alma (Hoegh) A.; m. Isabel Ferguson, Sept. 22, 1934; 1 dau., Elise. Ph.B., Yale U., 1930; LL.D., Franklin (Ind.) Coll., 1962, Butler U., 1974. With L.S. Ayres & Co., Indpls., 1930—, mdse. mgr., 1938-42, v.p., 1940-54, pres., 1954-62, chmn. bd., 1962-73, hon. chmn., 1973—; past dir. Mchts. Nat. Corp., Indpls.; dir. Indpls. Water Co.; dir. emeritus Asso. Dry Goods Corp.; past dir. Ind. Bell Telephone Co. Bd. dirs. Indpls. United Way; trustee emeritus Hanover (Ind.) Coll.; trustee Crown Hill Cemetery, YMCA, Indpls. Served as lt. USNR, 1942-44. Episcopalian. Home: 521 Bent Tree Ln Indianapolis IN 46260 Office: 1 W Washington St Indianapolis IN 46204

AYRES, MARY ANDREWS, advertising agency executive; b. DeSmet, S.D.; d. Frank Malcolm and Anne (Wright) Andrews; m. Charles Thatcher Ayres, July 15, 1946. B.A., U. Minn. Account exec. Sullivan Stauffer Colwell & Bayles, N.Y.C., 1947-50, account supr., 1950-60, v.p., mgmt. supr., 1960-65, sr. v.p., mgmt. supr., 1965-70, exec. v.p., 1, 970-78, mktg. cons., 1978—. Dir. SSC&B, Lintas, Bombay, India.; Active UN, This We Believe, Common Cause.; Bd. dirs. Inwood House, N.Y.C. Named Headliner of Year, Women in Communications, 1974, Advt. Woman of Year, 1972; Nat. Achievement award U. Minn., 1978. Mem. Fashion Group Inc., Women in Communications, Advt. Women N.Y., Alpha Chi Omega. Republican. Presbyterian. Clubs: Wee Burn Country (New Canaan, Conn.); Innisbrook Country (Fla.). Home: 45 Sutton Pl S New York City NY 10022

AYRES, MARY ELLEN, government official; b. Spokane, Wash., June 23, 1924; d. Frank H. and Marion (kellogg) A. Reporter Wenatchee Daily World, Wash., 1948-50, Washington Post, 1951-52; with U.S. Fgn. Service, Dept. State, 1950-51; mem. editorial staff Changing Times, 1952-61; editor Family Guide, Kiplinger Washington Editors, 1952-61, Bur. Labor Stats., Manpower Adminstrn., U.S. Dept. Labor, 1962-67; pub. info. specialist Bur. Indian Affairs, U.S. Dept. Interior, 1967-75; writer-editor Bur. Labor Stats., 1975—; past treas. Govt. Info. Orgn. Mee. publicity com. Nat. Capitol YWCA, 1982-83. Mem. Nat. Assn. Govt. Communicators (treas., dir. 1975-80), Am. News Women's Club, Am. Econ. Assn., Stanford U. Alumnae Assn., Kappa Kappa Gamma. Episcopalian. Club: Nat. Press (Washington). Home: 2400 Virginia Ave NW Apt C802 Washington DC 20037 Office: 441 G St NW Washington DC 20212

AYRES, ROBERT MOSS, JR., university president; b. San Antonio, Sept. 1, 1926; s. Robert Moss and Florence (Collett) A.; m. Patricia Ann Shield, Sept. 10, 1955; children: Robert Atlee, Vera Patricia. Student, Tex. Mil. Inst., 1944; B.A., U. of South, 1949; postgrad., Oxford (Eng.) U., 1949; M.B.A., U. Pa., 1952; D.C.L., U. of South, 1974. With Kidder, Peabody & Co., Phila., N.Y.C., 1950-52; with Dittmar & Co., San Antonio, 1952-53; pres., dir. Russ & Co., Inc., San Antonio, 1953-73; sr. v.p., dir. Rotan Mosle Inc., San Antonio, 1973-77; pres. U. South, Sewanee, Tenn., 1977—, Coll. Athletic Conf.; chmn. So. Coll. and Univ. Union; former allied mem. N.Y. Stock Exchange, Am. Stock Exchange. Past pres. Asso. Alumni U. of South; past pres. bd. dirs. Bexar County chpt. ARC; past pres. bd. trustees Tex. Mil. Inst.; trustee, past chmn. bd. regents U. of South; trustee Brother's Bro. Found.; mem. exec. council Episcopal Ch., 1976-82, also mem. nat. and world mission com.; bd. dirs. Inst. European Studies, Presiding Bishop's Fund World Relief, Alfalit, Internat.; vol. exec. dir. Vol. in Mission, 1976. Served with USN, 1944-46; lt. Res., 1949-60. Mem. San Antonio Soc. Fin. Analysts (past pres.), Securities Industries Assn. (past mem. governing council), Investment Bankers Assn. Am. (past chmn. Tex. group), Nat. Assn. Securities Dealers (past mem. dist. com.), Young Pres. Orgn., Order of Alamo, Tex. Cavaliers, Argyle, Sigma Alpha Epsilon. Episcopalian (mem. exec. bd. diocese W. Tex.; vestryman). Clubs: San Antonio German, San Antonio Country (San Antonio.). Home: Sewanee TN 37375 Office: U of South Sewanee TN 37375

AYRES, ROBERT UNDERWOOD, educator; b. Plainfield, N.J., June 29, 1932; s. John Underwood and Alice Conrow (Hutchinson) A.; m. Leslie Wentz, June 26, 1954; 1 dau., Jennifer Leigh. B.S. in Math, U. Chgo., 1954; M.S. in Physics, U. Md., 1956; Ph.D., U. London, 1958. Research assoc. Hudson Inst., Croton-on-Hudson, N.Y., 1962-67; vis. scholar Resources for Future, 1967-68; v.p., dir. Internat. Research & Tech. Corp., Washington, 1968-76, Delta Research Corp., Arlington, Va., 1976—; chmn. bd. Variflex Corp., Pitts., 1969—; prof. engring. and pub. policy Carnegie-Mellon U., 1979—; cons. in field; mem. tech. and water com. Nat. Acad. Scis., 1971, new transp. systems and tech. com., 1971—, strategic and critical materials com., 1971-72, com. steel research, 1978, com. alts. for reduction chlorofluorocarbon emissions, 1979. Author: Technological Forecasting and Long Range Planning, 1969, (with others) Economics and the Environment, 1971, Alternatives to the Internal Combustion Engine, 1972, Resources, Environment and Economics, 1978, Uncertain Futures, 1979, (with others) Robotics: Applications and Social Implications, 1983; contbr. articles to profl. jours.; assoc. editor: Jour. Transp. Tech. and Planning, 1970-74. Fellow AAAS (council, com.-at-large sect. indsl. sci. 1972-74); mem. Am. Econ. Assn., Soc. Automotive Engrs., World Futures Studies Fedn., Internat. Inst. Forecasters. Home: 703 W Waldheim Rd Pittsburgh PA 15215 Office: Carnegie-Mellon U Pittsburgh PA 15213

AYRES, SAMUEL, III, physician; b. Kansas City, Mo., May 1, 1919; s. Samuel and Helen (Lowry) A.; m. Norma Jean Pritchard, Jan. 1957; 1 son by previous marriage, Richard Lowry. A.B., Stanford, 1940, M.D., 1944. Diplomate: Am. Bd. Dermatology. Intern Los Angeles Gen. Hosp., 1943; resident dermatology and syphilology Cleve. City Hosp., 1944-45; pvt. practice dermatology, dermatologic and cosmetic surgery (now limited to hair transplantation), 1947—; mem. sr. attending staff dermatology Los Angeles County-U. So. Calif. Med. Center, 1947—, chmn., 1962-63; dir. Surg. Skin Planing (dermabrasion) Clinic, 1955—, Hair Transplantation Clinic, 1965—; attending staff Hosp. Good Samaritan, Los Angeles; mem. faculty U. So. Calif. Med. Sch., 1947—, asso. clin. prof. dermatology, 1961—. Co-author textbooks.; Contbr. numerous articles to med. jours. Asso. Council Performing Arts, Los Angeles Music Center. Served to capt. M.C. AUS, 1945-47. Mem. Am., Calif. (chmn. sect. dermatology 1967-68), Los Angeles County (councillor 1956-58) med. assns), Pacific Dermatol. Assn., Los Angeles Dermatol. Soc. (pres. 1963-64), Am. Acad. Dermatology (dir. cutaneous surgery course 1961-65), Am. Dermatol. Assn., Soc. Investigative Dermatology, Hollywood Acad. Medicine, Med. Symposium Soc. Los Angeles (pres. 1965), Los Angeles Acad. Medicine, Far Western Med. Assn., Dermatol. Therapy Assn., N. Am. Clin. Dermatol. Soc., Noah Worcester Dermatol. Soc., Med. Research Assn. Calif., Beverly Hills Acad. Medicine, Am. Acad. Facial Plastic and Reconstructive Surgery, Am. Assn. Cosmetic Surgeons, Am. Soc. for Dermatologic Surgery, Internat. Soc. Dermatol. Surgery, Los Angeles Art Assn., Los Angeles County Mus. Art, Los Angeles County Mus. Natural History, Alpha Kappa Kappa. Office: 405 N Bedford Dr Beverly Hills CA 90210

AYRES, STEPHEN MCCLINTOCK, physician; b. Elizabeth, N.J., Oct. 29, 1929; s. Malcolm B. and Florence M. A.; m. Dolores Kobrick, June 11, 1955; children—Stephen, Elizabeth, Margaret. B.A., Gettysburg Coll., 1951; M.D., Cornell U., 1955. Intern N.Y. Hosp., N.Y.C., 1955, resident, 1958-61; dir. cardio-pulmonary lab. St. Michael's Hosp., Newark, 1961-63, St. Vincent's Hosp. and Med. Center, N.Y.C., 1963-73; physician-in-chief St. Vincent Hosp., Worcester, Mass., 1973-75; prof., chmn. dept. internal medicine St. Louis U. Med. Center, 1975—. Contbr. articles to profl. jours. Served with M.C., USN, 1956-58. Fellow A.C.P., Am. Coll. Cardiology, Am. Coll. Chest Physicians; mem. Soc. Critical Care Medicine (pres. 1979-80), Am. Lung Assn., Assn. Am. Physicians, Am. Soc. Clin. Investigation. Home: 16 Picardy Ln Saint Louis MO 63124 Office: 1325 S Grand Blvd Saint Louis MO 63104

AZAR, HENRY AMIN, pathologist; b. Egypt, Dec. 21, 1927; s. Amin Antonios and Agnes Garabed (Nazaretian) A.; m. Rose Theresa Connell, Apr. 19, 1960; children: Henry Amin, Philip John. B.A., Am. U., Beirut, 1948, M.D., 1952. Diplomate: Am. Bd. Pathology. Intern N.Y.C. Hosp., 1952-53; resident Columbia-Presbyn. Hosp. Med. Center, N.Y.C., 1955-56, N.Y.-Cornell, Med. Center, 1956-57, Mass. Meml. Hosp., Boston, 1957-58; asst. prof. pathology Am. U., Beirut, 1958-60; asst. prof. and asso. prof. pathology Coll. Physicians and Surgeons, Columbia U., 1960-70; dir. surg. pathology, prof. U. Kans., 1970-72; chief lab. service VA Med. Center, Tampa, Fla., 1972-83, chief anatomic pathology, 1983—; prof. U. South Fla., 1972—. Author: Multiple Myeloma and Related Disorders, 1973, Diagnostic Electron Microscopy: The Hemopoietic System, 1979; contbr. articles to profl. jours. Fellow Coll. Am. Pathologists; mem. Am. Assn. Pathologists, Assn. Vet. Assoc Chiefs Lab. Service (pres. 1981-83), Arthur Purdy Stout Soc. (sec. 1983—), Fla. West Coast Assn. Pathologists, Harvey Soc., Am. Soc. Hematology, Internat. Acad. Pathology., Hematopathology Soc. Syrian Orthodox. Home: 97 Adriatic Ave Tampa FL 33606 Office: 13000 N 30th St Tampa FL 33612 *As a pathologist I strive to recognize diseases in terms of aberrations from the normal. The normal is an idealized concept; the patient and his lesion are real and beg for answers that can be only fragmented, sketchy, stylized. There is so much to learn yet about the normal from its countless aberrations, and there is so much to admire in Life.*

AZAR, RAYMOND GEORGE, manufacturing company executive; b. Cleve., Mar. 29, 1924; s. Sam G. and Lydia (Fetlha) A.; m. Eleanor Swezea, Oct. 6, 1945; children: Michelle, Sidneye, Robert. B.S., George Pepperdine Coll., 1949. Chief cost accountant Garrett Corp., Los Angeles, 1953-56, chief accountant, 1956-59, controller, 1959-61, adminstrv. asst. to pres., 1961-63, v.p. contracts-pricing, license agreements, 1963-69, group v.p., 1969-83, exec. v.p., 1983—; dir. Aero Hydrolics, Normalair-Garrett, Ltd., Eng. Served with USAAF, 1942-45; PTO. Decorated Air Medal. Mem. Am. Mgmt. Assn., Nat. Assn. Accountants. Home: 1261 Via Landeta Palos Verdes Estates CA 90274 Office: 9851 Sepulveda Blvd Los Angeles CA 90009

AZARIAN, MARTIN VARTAN, publishing company executive; b. N.Y.C., May 5, 1927; s. Marderos and Altoon (Toutoian) A.; m. Margaret Emery, Aug. 9, 1980; 1 dau., Carol Lydia. B.A., Hunter Coll., 1950; M.S., NYU, 1954; student, Bklyn. Poly. Inst., 1957. Mgr. Claremont Polychem. Corp., Roslyn, N.Y., 1953-54; tech. dir. Borden Chem. Co., Fairlawn, N.J., 1957—; pres. Internat. Universities Press Inc., N.Y.C., 1963—. Served with AUS, 1945-46. Mem. Chemists Club N.Y. (trustee 1972—, chmn. library com. 1972-74), Am. Chem. Soc. Clubs: Turf and Field, N.Y. Athletic. Home: One Fifth Ave New York NY 10003 Office: 315 Fifth Ave New York NY 10016

AZARNOFF, DANIEL LESTER, pharmaceutical company executive; b. Bklyn., Aug. 4, 1926; s. Samuel J. and Kate (Asarnow) A.; m. Joanne Stokes, Dec. 26, 1951; children: Rachel, Richard, Martin. B.S., Rutgers U., 1947, M.S., 1948; M.D., U. Kans., 1955. Asst. instr. anatomy U. Kans. Med. Sch., 1949-50, research fellow, 1950-52, intern, 1955-56, resident, Nat. Heart Inst. research fellow, 1956-58, asst. prof. medicine, 1962-64, assoc. prof., 1964-68, dir. clin. pharmacology study unit, 1964-68, assoc. prof. pharmacology, 1965-68, prof. medicine and pharmacology, 1968, dir. Clin. Pharmacology-Toxicology Center, 1967-78, Disting. prof. Clin. Pharmacology-

Toxicology Center, 1973-78, also prof. medicine, 1965-67, pres. Sigma Xi Club, 1968-69; Nat. Inst. Neurol. Diseases and Blindness spl. trainee Washington U. Sch. Medicine, St. Louis, 1958-60; asst. prof. medicine St. Louis U. Sch. Medicine, 1960-62; vis. scientist Fulbright scholar Karolinska Inst., Stockholm, Sweden, 1968; sr. v.p. worldwide research and devel. G.D. Searle & Co., Chgo., 1978; pres. Searle Research and Devel., Skokie, Ill., 1979—; prof. pathology, clin. prof. pharmacology Northwestern U. Med. Sch., 1978—; professorial lectr. U. Chgo., 1979; dir. Second Workshop on Prins. Drug Evaluation in Man, 1970; chmn. com. on problems of drug safety NRC-Nat. Acad. Sci., 1972-76; cons. numerous govtl. agys. Editor: Dev. of Drug Interactions, 1974-77, Yearbook of Drug Therapy, 1977-79; series editor: Monographs in Clin. Pharmacology, 1977—; mem. editorial and adv. bds. various jours. Served with U.S. Army, 1945-46. Recipient Ginsburg award in phys. diagnosis U. Kans. Med. Center, 1953; Outstanding Intern award, 1956, Ciba award for gerontol. research, 1958, Rectors medal U. Helsinki, 1968; John and Mary R. Markle scholar, 1962; Burroughs Wellcome scholar, 1964; William N. Creasy vis. prof. clin. pharmacology Med. Coll. Va., 1975; Bruce Hall Meml. lectr. St. Vincents Hosp., Sydney, 1976; 7th Sir Henry Hallett Dale lectr. Johns Hopkins U. Med. Sch., 1978. Fellow A.C.P., N.Y. Acad. Scis.; mem. Am. Soc. Clin. Nutrition, Am. Nutrition Instn., Am. Soc. Pharmacology and Exptl. Therapeutics (chmn. clin. pharmacology div. 1969-71, mem. exec. com. 1966-73, 78—, del. 1975-78, bd. publ. trustees), Am. Soc. Clin. Pharmacology and Therapeutics, Am. Fedn. Clin. Research, Brit. Pharmacol. Soc., AMA (vice chmn. council on drugs 1971-72, editorial bd. Jour.), Central Soc. Clin. Research, Royal Soc. for Promotion Health, Inst. Medicine of Nat. Acad. Scis., Soc. Exptl. Biology and Medicine (councillor 1976—), Internat. Union Pharmacologists (sec. clin. pharmacology sect. 1975—, internat. adv. com. Paris Congress 1978), Sigma Xi. Home: 1030 Lake Shore Blvd Evanston IL 60202 Office: 4901 Searle Pkwy Skokie IL 60076

AZAROFF, LEONID VLADIMIROVITCH, physics educator; b. Moscow, June 19, 1926; U.S., 1939, naturalized, 1945; s. Vladimir Ivanovitch and Maria Yulievna (Odlen) A.; m. Carmen Wade, Mar. 9, 1946 (div. July 1968); m. Beth Sulzer, Mar. 4, 1972; children: David, Richard, Lenore. B.S. cum laude, Tufts Coll., 1948; Ph.D., M.I.T., 1954. Research physicist Armour Research Found., Chgo., 1953-54, sr. scientist, 1954-57; asso. prof. metall. engring. Ill. Inst. Tech., 1957-61, prof., 1961-66; prof. physics, dir. Inst. Material Sci., U. Conn., 1966—; guest physicist Brookhaven Nat. Lab., 1961, 62, 64; vis. prof. U. Mass., 1978-79; cons. Owens-Ill., Philips Electronics, Hilger-Watts, Inc.; U.S. del. Internat. Union Crystallography, teaching commn., 1963-69; dir. Conn. Product Devel. Corp., Rogers Corp. Asso., Conn. Devel. Corp., 1977—. Author: 7 books, including X-Ray Diffraction and X-Ray Spectroscopy, 1973; also articles. Served with AUS, 1944-46. Fellow Am. Phys. Soc. (cons. editor), Mineral. Soc. Am.; mem. AAAS (dir.), IEEE (sr.), Am. Soc. Engring. Edn., Conn. Acad. Sci. and Engring. (pres. 1976-82), Am. Crystallographic Assn., Am. Inst. Mining Engrs., Internat. Union Physics, Internat. Union Crystal Growth, Sigma Xi, Phi Kappa Phi, Sigma Pi Sigma. Home: PO Box 103 Storrs CT 06268 *I have always adhered to the principle that anything worth doing at all is worth doing as well as possible. Therefore, I select very carefully the tasks to undertake.*

AZAROW, CHARLES, sugar corporation; b. Jersey City, Dec. 12, 1918; s. Isaac and Ruth (Laurie) A.; m. Dolores Marie Willcockson. Student, Hudson Coll. With B.W. Dyer & Co., N.Y.C., 1937-52; v.p. sugar div. Pepsico, Purchase, N.Y., 1952-68; pres. sweetener div. Sucrest Corp., N.Y.C., 1968-77; pres. Revere Sugar Corp., N.Y.C., 1977-81; pres., chief exec. officer Nat. Sugar Refining, N.Y.C., 1981-82; vice chmn. Holly Sugar Corp., Colorado Springs, Colo., 1982—. Counsilman Demarest, N.J., 1975-77. Served with U.S. Army, 1941-45. Mem. U.S. Beet Sugar Assn., Internat. Sugar Club (past pres.), Sugar Industry Technologists, N.Y. Coffee/Sugar Exchange (on spot com.). Office: Holly Sugar Corp 100 Chase Stone Center Colorado Springs CO 80903

AZCARRAGA MILMO, EMILIO, communication company executive; s. Emilio and Laura (Milmo) Azcarraga. Grad., Culver Mil. Aca., Ind., 1948. Various positions in TV; pres. Televisa S.A.; owner major Mexican TV stas. Office: Televisa SA Edificio Televicentro Avda Chapulteped 18 Mexico City 1 DF Mexico *

AZE, MICHAEL JOHN, arts administrator; b. Littlehampton, Eng., Jan. 2, 1943; emigrated to Can., 1973, naturalized, 1977. B.S. with honors, Univ. Coll. London U., 1964. Mgr. Toronto (Ont., Can.) Symphony, 1973-78; music adminstr. Nat. Arts Centre, Ottawa, Ont., from 1978. Mem. Internat. Soc. Performing Arts Adminstrs., Am. Symphony Orch. League. Office: care Nat Arts Centre PO Box 1534 Station B Ottawa ON K1P 5W1 Canada

AZEN, STANLEY PAUL, biomedical engineering educator, statistician; b. Inpls., Nov. 13, 1938; s. Harry and Shirley (Primack) A.; m. Colleen Anne Gillen, Mar. 7, 1971; 1 son, Matthew. B.A., UCLA, 1960, M.S., 1962, Ph.D., 1969. Mathematician Rand Corp., Santa Monica, Calif., 1962-69; asst. prof. biomed. engring. U. So. Calif., Los Angeles, 1969-72, assoc. prof., 1972-79, prof., 1979—, dir. biometry programs, 1972—. Author: Statistical Analysis: A Computer Oriented Approach, 1972, Statistical Analysis: A Computer Oriented Approach, 2d rev. edit, 1979; editor: Computational Stats. and Data Analysis, 1983—. Mem. Am. Statis. Assn. (sec. 1970-71, pres. 1971-72, chmn. teaching stats. in health scis. 1982-83), Sigma Xi, Pi Mu Epsilon. Office: U So Calif 2025 Zonal PMB B101 Los Angeles CA 90033 *

AZNAVOUR, CHARLES (VARENAGH AZNAVOURIAN), singer, performer; b. May 22, 1924; m. Micheline Rugel, 1945; m. Evelyne Plessis, 1955; m. Ulla Thorssell, Jan. 11, 1967; children: Katia, Patricia, Patrick, Misha. Ed., Ecole centrale de T.S.F., Centre de spectacle, Paris, France. Mem., Jean Daste Co., 1941, (with Pierre Roche in) Les Facheux, also Arlequin, 1944; song recitals in, France, Europe, U.S.; motion picture appearances include La Tete contre les murs, 1959, Les Draguecors, 1959, Tirez sur le pianiste, 1960, le Passage du Rhin, 1960, Un taxi pour Tobrouk, 1964, Le testament d'Orphee, 1964, Horace 62, 1964, Le Diable et les Dix Commandements, 1964, Tempo di Roma, 1964, Cherchez l'idole, 1964, Haute-Infidelite, 1964, la Metamorphose des cloportes, 1965, Paris au mois d'auot, 1966, Le facteur s'en va-t-en Guerre, 1966, Caroline cherie, 1967, l'Amour, The Adventuriers, 1968, Candy, 1969, le Temps des loups, 1970, The Games, 1970, Blockhouse, 1972, Ten Little Indians, 1973, Skyrider, 1975, The Twist, 1976, The Tin Drum, 1979; motion picture music includes Soupe au lait, l'ile du bout du monde, Ces dames preferente le mambo, Le cercle vicieux; music for mus. comedy Monsieur Carnaval, 1965; author: Douchka, 1973; author, composer numerous songs; author: book Aznavour par Aznovour, 1970 (Decorated chevalier Arts et des Lettres, recipient Nashville Best Country Song award for Yesterday When I Was Young 1973, other awards.). Address: 12 rue de Penthievre 75008 Paris France *

AZNEER, J. LEONARD, university president; b. Roumania, May 26, 1921; s. Morris and Ida (Stein) A.; m. Patricia A. Cottrille; children: Jay Barry, Reva Azneer Pearlstein, Ira Brant. B.A., Yeshiva Coll., 1941; grad., Jewish Theol. Sem. Am., 1945, M.H.L., 1949; Ph.D., U. Pitts., 1959; Docteur Osteopathie (hon.), A.T. Still Acad., Lyon, France, 1979. Tchr., English in secondary sch., N.Y.C., 1940-41, ordained rabbi, 1945; asso. prof. edn. Youngstown U., 1951-67; sr. mem. grad. faculty Youngstown State U., 1967-70; pres. Coll. Oseteo. Medicine and Surgery, Des Moines, 1971-81, U. Osteo. Medicine and Health Scis., 1981—; mem. Adv. Com. Osteo. Edn. Author: (with others) Diabetic Acidosis: A Programmed Text, 1964, Resuscitation: A Programmed Text, 1965. Dir. Valley Nat. Bank. Recipient Henry Goode medal award Jewish Theol. Sem., 1945. Mem. Am. Osteo. Assn. (assoc.; vice chmn. task force to study postdoctoral edn.), Am. Assn. Colls. Osteo. Medicine (pres.), Sigma Sigma Phi (hon.). Office: U Osteo Medicine and Health Scis 3200 Grand Ave Des Moines IA 50312 *Only a person born in Europe understands that America is still the only country where a person can hope to grow and achieve in proportion to his ability and efforts. In Romania I might have been a holocaust victim. In the U.S., I have achieved the freedom and the privilege to be a contributor to my society.*

AZOFF, IRVING L., record company executive; b. Chgo., Dec. 12, 1947; s. Louis and Edith A.; m. Shelli Cumsky, Mar. 26, 1978; children: Jennifer, Allison. Agt. Jerry Heller Agy., Los Angeles, ABC Booking Agy.; mgr. Front Line Mgmt., Los Angeles, to 1983; pres. MCA Records Group; v.p. MCA, Inc., Universal City, Calif., 1983—. Named Man of Yr. City of Hope, Los Angeles, 1983. Office: MCA Records 70 Universal City Plaza Universal City CA 91608 *

AZRIN, NATHAN HAROLD, psychologist; b. Boston, Nov. 26, 1930; s. Harry and Esther (Alper) A.; m. Victoria Behar Besalel, Jan. 25, 1953; children—Rachel, Michael, David, Richard. B.A. cum laude, Boston U., 1951, M.A., 1952; Ph.D., Harvard U., 1956. Mem. faculty So. Ill. U., Carbondale, 1958-80, prof. rehab., 1959-80; research dir. Anna (Ill.) Mental Health Center, 1958-80; prof., dir. Nova Psychol. Clinic, Nova U., Ft. Lauderdale, Fla., 1980—. Author: Token Economy, 1968, Toilet Training in Less than a Day, 1974, Toilet Training the Retarded, 1973, Habit Control, 1977; Editor psychol. jours. Served with AUS, 1956-58. Mem. Am. Psychol. Assn. (pres. div. 25 1963, ann. award applications in psychology 1975), Midwestern Psychol. Assn. (pres.), Assn. Advancement Behavior Therapy, Midwestern Analysis of Behavior Assn. Home: 5151 Bayview Dr Fort Lauderdale FL 33308 Office: Nova U 3301 College Ave Fort Lauderdale FL 33314

AZUMA, NORIO, artist, art dealer; b. Kii-Nagashima, Mie-ken, Japan, Nov. 23, 1928; came to U.S., 1959; s. Tobei and Yasu A.; m. Kazuko Kamiya, July 1, 1959; 1 child, Chieko. B.F.A., Kanazawa (Japan) Art Coll., 1952; student, Chouinard Art Inst., Los Angeles, 1955-57, Art Students League, N.Y.C., 1957-59. Dir. art gallery, N.Y.C. Exhibited works in numerous shows. Recipient various art awards. Mem. Assn. Am. Graphic Artists (mem. council), Japanese Artist Assn. N.Y. (mem. council). Developed new medium serigraph on canvas. Home: 276 Riverside Dr New York NY 10025 Office: 142 Greene St New York NY 10012

AZZARA, CANDY, actress; b. Bklyn., May 18, 1947; d. Samuel and Josephine (Bravo) A. Appeared in: films Made for Each Other, 1971, They Might Be Giants, 1971, Hail, 1973, Hearts of the West, 1975, World's Greatest Lover, 1976-77, House Calls, 1976-77, Fatso, 1979, Pendemonium, 1982, Easy Money, 1983; appeared on: TV shows N.Y.P.D, 1970, Those Were the Days, 1971, Kraft Music Hall, 1972, Secret Storm, 1972, Calucci's Dept, 1973, The Girl Who Couldn't Lose, 1974-75, Wives, 1974-75, Kojak, 1974-75, Rhoda, 1974-75, Barney Miller, 1974-75, Fay, 1974-75, Montefusco's, 1974-75, The Cop and the Kid, 1974-75, Love Boat II, 1976-77, Kojak, 1976-77, Baretta, 1976-77, Eddie and Herbert, 1976-77, Barney Miller, 1976-77, The Practice, 1976-77, Rhoda, 1976-77, Soap (five shows), 1978-80, Chips, 1978-80, Trapper John M.D, 1978-80, Barney Miller, 1978-80, Diff'rent Strokes, 1980-82, Love Boat, 1980-82, Dinah Shore, 1980-82; TV movies Divorce Wars, 1980, Million Dollar Infield, 1982; appeared in: Broadway plays Engagement Baby, 1970-72, Lovers and Other Strangers, 1970-72; plays Why I Went Crazy, 1971-72, Only the Shadow Knows, 1971-72, Any Wednesday, Lake Placid Playhouse, 1968, Barefoot in the Park, 1969, Cactus Flower, Bucks County Playhouse, 1973. *I get great fulfillment when I forget self and become one with my character. I have so much to learn.*

AZZATO, LOUIS E., mfg. co. exec.; b. N.Y.C., Oct. 8, 1930; s. John A. and Margaret (Ronca) A.; m. Margaret Jean McCarthy, June 25, 1955; children—Jean Bernadette and Patricia Bernadette (twins), John Kevin, Maureen Ann. B.S. in Chem. Engring. cum laude, CCNY, 1952. With Foster Wheeler Corp., 1952-74; 78—; v.p. Foster Wheeler Italiana, Milan, 1967-74, sr. v.p. parent corp., Livingston, N.J., 1978-80, exec. v.p., 1980-81, pres., chief exec. officer, 1981, also dir.; chmn. bd., chief exec. officer Glitsch, Inc., Dallas, 1974-78; dir. Foster Wheeler Energy Corp., Fidelity Union Bank (other subs. cos.). Bd. dirs. Newark Acad. Roman Catholic. Club: Springbrook Country (Morristown, N.J.). Patentee catalytic cracking. Home: 22 Lord William Penn Dr Morristown NJ 07960

BAAR, EMIL N., lawyer; b. Vienna, Austria, Sept. 9, 1891; s. Jacob and Fannie (Sonnenschein) B.; m. Amelia A. Wasch, June 19, 1919 (dec. 1966); m. Grace Arenson, 1974. A.B., Columbia U., 1913, J.D., 1915; D.H.L. (hon.), Hebrew Union Coll., 1965. Bar: N.Y. State 1915. Mem. firm Baar, Bennett & Fullen, N.Y.C., 1926-74, Palmer, Serles & Baar, 1974-78; counsel Baar, Bennett & Metz, 1978-81, Keenan, Powers & Andrews, N.Y.C., 1981—; justice N.Y. State Supreme Ct., 1951. V.p., dir. JHMCB Nursing Home Co., Inc.; hon. trustee Met. Savs. Bank, Bklyn.; Hon. life chmn. bd. Interfaith Med. Ctr.; trustee Bklyn. Inst. Arts and Scis. (hon. life), United Hosp. Fund N.Y., Jewish Braille Inst. Am. (hon. pres.), Fedn. Jewish Philanthropies; governing com. Bklyn. Mus.; hon. life pres. Union Temple; hon. gov. Hebrew Union Coll.-Jewish Inst. Religion; hon. life v.p., gov. World Union for Progressive Judaism, Ltd. Served with 49th Inf. AUS, World War I. Adopted as hon. chief Algonquin Tribe of Am. Indians of Bklyn., 1951. Mem. Union Am. Hebrew Congregations (hon. life chmn. bd.), Am., N.Y. State, Bklyn. bar assns., Assn. Bar City N.Y., Am. Legion (county comdr. 1925). Clubs: Masons (32 deg.), Elks, Sojourners; Unity (Bklyn.) (dir.); Fresh Meadow Country (pres., chmn. bd. 1936-46). Home: 225 E 57th St New York NY 10022 Office: 4 World Trade Center Suite 1682 New York NY 10048 *Integrity, industry, imagination, impartiality.*

BAAR, JAMES A., public relations executive, author; b. N.Y.C., Feb. 9, 1929; s. A.W. and Marguerite R. B.; m. Beverly Hodge, Sept. 2, 1948; 1 son, Theodore Hall. A.B., Union Coll., Schenectady, 1949. Washington corr. UPI, also other wire service burs. and newspapers, 1949-59; sr. editor Missiles and Rockets mag., 1959-62; mgr. various news bur. ops. Gen. Electric Co., 1962-66; mgr. European mktg. communications ops., 1966-70; pres. Gen. Electric subs. Internat. Mktg. Communications Cons., 1970-72; sr. v.p., dir. public relations Lewis & Gilman, Inc., Phila., 1972-74; exec. v.p. Creamer Dickson Basford, Inc., 1974-78; pres. Creamer Dickson Basford-New Eng., 1978-83; sr. v.p./mgr. N.E. region Hill & Knowlton, Inc., Boston, 1983—. Author: Polaris, 1960, Combat Missileman, 1961, Spacecraft and Missiles of the World, 1962; novel The Great Free Enterprise Gambit, 1980; also numerous articles. Mem. Nat. Investor Relations Inst., Public Relations Soc. Am., Counselors Acad., Internat. Public Relations Assn., Chi Psi, Nat. Press Club, Overseas Press Club. Republican. Episcopalian. Clubs: Hope, Agawam Hunt, Dunes, Mohawk.; Union (Boston). Office: 1 Post Office Sq Boston MA 02109

BABB, ALBERT LESLIE, biomedical engr.; b. Vancouver, C., Can., Nov. 7, 1925; came to U.S., 1948, naturalized, 1954; s. Clarence Stanley and Mildred (Gutteridge) B.; m. Marion A. McDougall; children—Eugene Matthew, Philip Leslie, Christine Louise. B.A.Sc., U. B.C., 1948; M.S., U. Ill., 1949, Ph.D., 1951; student Internat. Sch. Nuclear Sci. and Engring., Argonne Nat. Lab., 1956, 57. Chem. engr. Nat. Research Council Can., 1948; research engr. Rayonier, Inc., 1951-52; faculty U. Wash., Seattle, 1952—, chmn. nuclear engring. group, 1957-65, prof. chem. engring., 1960—, dir. nuclear reactor labs., 1962-72, prof., chmn. dept. nuclear engring., 1965—; del. Japan-U.S. Seminar on Nuclear Engring. Edn., 1974; lectr. hemodialysis engring. USSR Ministry of Health, Moscow, 1976; lectr. biomed. engring. Norwegian Nephrological Soc., Oslo, 1980; lectr. hemodialysis engring. Kuratorium für Hemodialyse, Münster, Germany, 1980, Clinique Iser, Munich, Germany, 1980, Mcpl. Hosp., Hvidovre, Denmark, 1980, State Hosp., Copenhagen, 1980; mem. Assembly Engring., NRC, Com. Transp. Plutonium by Air; cons. med. engring., 1952—. Contbr. chpts. to books, profl. jours. Active local Services to Children's Orthopedic Hosp., N.W. Artificial Kidney Center; trustee Pacific Sci. Center Found., mem. exec. com., 1973-80. Recipient citation Wash. Joint Legis. Com. Nuclear Energy, 1968; named Engr. of Year Wash. State Profl. Engrs. Assn., 1969; Am. Specifying Engr. award for excellence in design artificial kidney systems, 1970; Nat. Kidney Found. Pioneer award., 1982, Sigma Xi award, 1982. Fellow Am. Inst. Chemists; mem. Am. Nuclear Soc. (exec. com. environ. scis. div. 1976—, exec. com. environ. sci. div. 1976, Mem., chmn. div. 1983-84); mem. Am. Chem. Soc., Am. Inst. Chem. Engrs. (named Engr. of Distinction), Engrs. Joint Council, Nat Acad. Engring. (membership com.), Am. Soc. Engring. Edn. (chmn. nuclear engring. div. 1965-66), Am. Nephrology Soc., Am. Soc. Artificial Internal Organs, European Dialysis and Transplantation Assn.; Mem. Inst. Medicine, Nat. Acad. Scis.; mem. Sigma Xi, Tau Beta Pi, Pi Mu Epsilon, Alpha Chi Sigma. Presbyterian. Clubs: Explorers (fellow), U. Wash. Pres.'s). Co-inventor continous central artificial kidney system for low cost treatment in centers, also co-inventor automatic artificial kidney system for overnight unattended hemodialysis of patients in homes, and techniques for early diagnosis of cystic fibrosis in children using a nuclear reactor; formulated dialysis index for prescribing minimum adequate treatment for patients undergoing hemodialysis; co-inventor, dir. design and devel. extracorporeal system for treatment of sickle cell anemia; co-developer computerized wearable insulin pump for diabetics; patentee systems for stblzn. of structures in permafrost, also field of artificial kidney and artificial pancreas. Home: 3237 Lakewood Ave S Seattle WA 98144

BABB, ALVIN CHARLES, beverage company executive; b. Rising City, Nebr., Sept. 25, 1932; s. Lorren William and Merna Janet (Ruth) B.; m. Patricia Ann Schworer, Feb. 14, 1951; children: Mike, Terri, Cae, Al. Student, Kearney State Coll., 1950-51, U. Denver, 1963-64, U. Colo., 1957-60. Warehouse mgr. Adolph Coors Co., Golden, Colo., 1964-71, packaging warehouse v.p., 1971-75, packaging/shipping/utility v.p., 1976-78, sr. v.p. brewery ops., 1978-82, group v.p., 1982-83, group v.p. container ops., exec. v.p., plant mgr., 1983—. Author: Quality in Vertically Integrated Brewery, 1983, Beer Packaging: The Human Element, 1982, Management Commitment of Hearing Conservation, 1976, Scheduling-Packaging to Shipping by Computer, 1970. Eucharistic minister St. Joseph's Ch., Golden, 1976-82, pres. parish council, Golden, 1970; mem. City Charter Commn., Golden, 1960. Named Jaycees Boss of Yr., 1971; recipient Disting. Service Jaycees, 1968. Mem. Master Brewery Assn. Am., Master Brewer Rev. Bd., Golden C. of C. (dir. 1968-71). Republican. Roman Catholic. Club: Lions (pres.) (1976-77). Home: 16106 W 32d Ave Golden CO 80401 Office: Adolf Coors Co 17755 W 32d Ave Golden CO 80401

BABB, ANDREW BIRD, JR., advertising agency executive; b. Winchester, Va., Jan. 11, 1946; s. Andrew B. and Lillian (Oakes) B.; m. Laura A. Longley, Oct. 27, 1970; 1 son, Paul Longley. B.J., U. Mo., 1968, M.A., 1970. Copywriter Leo Burnett Co., Chgo., 1972; v.p. Van Sant Dugdale, Balt. and Washington, 1973-78; sr. v.p., creative dir. Weitzman, Dym & Assocs., Bethesda, Md., 1978-80, Brouilland Communications, Washington, 1980-81, J. Walter Thompson, U.S.A., 1981—. Author: (with Jann Alexander) The No Book, 1983. Bd. trustees Am. Cancer Soc. Washington, 1975—. Recipient Clio awards, 1973-79, Andy award Advt. Club of N.Y.C., 1981, Internat. Broadcasting awards, 1974, 78. Democrat. Roman Catholic. Club: Mo and Ed (Chevy Chase) (pres. 1976-78). Home: 801 Duke St Alexandria VA 22314 Office: 1156 15th St NW Washington DC 20005

BABB, F. FREDLOCK, financial executive; s. Arnold Obed and Sue Wells (Fredlock) B.; m. Janet Marie O'Dor, June 23, 1956; children: James, Karen. B.S., Lehigh U., 1956. Cons. Gen. Electric Co., N.Y.C., 1956-72; treas. Eltra Corp., N.Y.C., 1972-80; with Allegheny Internat. Inc., Pitts., 1980—, v.p., treas., 1980—; dir. Scripto Inc., Allied Fin. Instns. Inc., Corp. Ins. and Reins Co. Ltd. Mem. Nat. Assn. Corp. Treas., Soc. Internat. Treas., Treas. Club (dir.). Clubs: Duquesne, Pitts Field, Seabrook Island, Pinehurst Golf and Country, Laurel Valley. Office: Allegheny Internat Inc 2 Oliver Plaza Pittsburgh PA 15222

BABB, FRANK EDWARD, lawyer; b. Maryville, Mo., Dec. 22, 1932; s. Dale Victor and Esther (Hull) B.; m. Patricia McClaren, June 6, 1953; children: Frank Edward Jr., George. B.S., Northwest Mo. State U., Maryville, 1954; LL.B., Harvard U., 1959. Bar: Ill. 1959, D.C. 1980, Fla. 1980, Va. 1980. Ptnr. McDermott, Will & Emery, Chgo., 1959—; dir. La. Gen. Services, Harvey, 1966—. Served with CIC U.S. Army, 1954-56; C.Z. Mem. ABA, Chgo. Bar Assn., D.C. Bar Assn., Fla. Bar Assn., Va. Bar Assn. Clubs: Chicago, University. Office: McDermott Will & Emery 111 W Monroe St Chicago IL 60603 *My journey from a simple, rural childhood to a complex, professional career was immensely aided by the persons who encouraged, taught and comforted me along the way. I view myself as a link in that human chain extending from a murky beginning to the uncertain future of our species. In turn, I hope to impart some measure of knowledge, insight, dedication and compassion to those travelers behind me. In this endeavor we achieve a measure of immortality.*

BABB, HAROLD, psychology educator; b. Mosheim, Tenn., Sept. 4, 1926; s. Ray Edward and Mary Louise (Brown) B.; m. Marjorie Craig Leask (Sept. 27, 1957); children: Patricia Craig, Barbara Lou, David Edward. B.A., Wayne State U., 1950; M.A., Ohio State U., 1951, Ph.D., 1953. Asst. prof., assoc. prof., chmn. dept. psychology Coe Coll., 1953-58; prof., chmn. dept. psychology Hobart and William Smith Colls., 1958-63; NIH, NIMH exec. sec., grants specialist, 1963-64; prof., chmn. dept. psychology U. Mont., Missoula, 1964-71; prof. psychology SUNY-Binghamton, 1971—, chmn. dept., 1971-74. Contbr. articles on psychology to profl. jours. Served with USNR, 1944-46. NIMH research grantee, 1960-62; NSF research grantee, 1968-69. Mem. Am. Psychol. Assn., Eastern Psychol. Assn., Midwestern Psychol. Assn., Psychonomic Soc., AAAS, AAUP, Sigma Xi. Home: 2309 Hemlock Ln Vestal NY 13850 Office: Dept Psychology SUNY Binghamton NY 13901

BABB, RALPH W., JR., banker; b. Sherman, Tex., Feb. 4, 1949; s. Ralph W. and Billie M. B.; m. Barbara L. Alexander, Aug. 30, 1970; children: Dana P., Derek R. B.S. in Acctg, U. Mo., Columbia, 1971. C.P.A., Mo. Audit mgr. Peat, Marwick, Mitchell & Co., C.P.A.s, St. Louis, 1971-78; sr. v.p., treas. Mercantile Bancorp. Inc., St. Louis, 1978-82, sr. v.p. fin., 1982—; sr. v.p., comptroller Mercantile Trust Co.

N.A., St. Louis, 1978-82, sr. v.p. fin., 1982—. Mem. Am. Inst. C.P.A.s, Fin. Execs. Inst., Mo. Soc. C.P.A.s. Methodist. Address: 1 Mercantile Tower St Louis MO 63166

BABB, WYLIE SHERRILL, college president; b. Greenville, S.C., Aug. 20, 1940; s. J. Wylie and Sally P. B.; m. Linda Witmer, June 30, 1963; children: Corinne, Michelle, David. B.A. in History, Post Coll., 1963; Th.M., Dallas Theol. Sem., 1967; Ph.D. in Ednl. Adminstrn, U. Pitts., 1979. Ordained to ministry Scottsdale, Ariz., 1967; pastor Bible Ch., 1967-71; dean acad. affairs Lancaster (Pa.) Bible Coll., 1971-76; dean faculty Moody Bible Inst., Chgo., 1976-79; pres. Phila. Coll. Bible, 1979—; speaker, cons. in field. Mem. Am. Assn. Higher Edn., Doctoral Assn. Educators, Lower Bucks County C. of C., World Affairs Council, Phi Delta Kappa. Home: 161 Andrew Dr Newtown PA 18940 Office: Phila Coll Bible Langhorne Manor Langhorne PA 19047

BABBITT, BRUCE EDWARD, gov. Ariz.; b. June 27, 1938; m. Hattie; children—Christopher, T.J. B.A. magna cum laude, U. Notre Dame; M.A., U. Newcastle, Eng., 1962; LL.B., Harvard U., 1965. Bar: Ariz. bar. Individual practice law, Phoenix; atty. gen. State of Ariz., Phoenix, 1975-78, gov., 1978—; Chmn. Nuclear Safety Oversight Com., Western Gov.'s Policy Office; mem. Adv. Commn. on Intergovtl. Relations. Trustee Verde Valley Sch., Dougherty Found. Democrat. Office: Office of Gov West Wing State Capitol Phoenix AZ 85007

BABBITT, JOHN GEORGE, rancher; b. Flagstaff, Ariz., May 19, 1908; s. Charles J. and Mary B. (Verkamp) B.; m. Elizabeth Quimby, Sept. 16, 1933; children—Elizabeth A. Babbitt Cordasco (dec.), John George (dec.). B.S., Loyola U., Los Angeles, 1929; postgrad., Babson Sch. Bus., Wellesley, Mass., 1939-31; LL.D. (hon.), U. Ariz., 1965, L.H.D., No. Ariz. U., 1966. Partner Babbitt Manwaring Co., Wellesley, 1932-33; pres., chmn. bd., treas. Babbitt Bros. Trading Co., Flagstaff, 1934—; pres., mgr. Babbitt Ranches, Inc., Flagstaff, 1942—; dir. Valley Nat. Bank, Phoenix, 1956-79, Mountain States Tel. & Tel. Co., 1957-77, 1st Fed. Savs. and Loan Assn., Phoenix, 1955-71. Mem. adv. bd. Los Angeles dist. RFC, 1951-53; Mem. Ariz. Senate, 1945-49, pres., 1949; bd. regents U. Ariz., 1949-65; pres. trustees Flagstaff Community Hosp., 1956-57; mem. Ariz. Gov.'s Tax Study Com., 1963; pres. Mus. No. Ariz., 1971-74, No. Ariz. U. Found., 1968-72. Named Flagstaff Citizen of Yr. Ariz. Daily Sun, 1964; knight of Malta. Mem. Am. Soc. Range Mgmt. (chmn. Ariz. sect. 1952), Ariz. Catle Growers Assn. (pres. 1950-51), Ariz. Livestock Prodn. Credit Assn. (dir. 1943-53). Democrat. Roman Catholic. Clubs: Elks, K.C. Office: 12 E Aspen St Flagstaff AZ 86002

BABBITT, MILTON BYRON, composer; b. Phila., May 10, 1916; s. Albert E. and Sarah (Potamkin) B.; m. Sylvia Miller, Dec. 27, 1939; 1 dau., Betty Ann. A.B., N.Y. U., 1935; M.F.A., Princeton U., 1942; D.Mus., Middlebury Coll., N.Y. U., Swarthmore Coll., New Eng. Conservatory, U. Glasgow. Music faculty Princeton U., 1938—, math. faculty, 1943-45, bicentennial preceptor, 1953-56, William Shubael Conant prof. music, 1966—; faculty Salzburg Seminar in Am. Studies, 1952, Princeton Seminar in Advanced Musical Studies; dir. Columbia-Princeton Electronic Music Center; composition faculty Juilliard Sch.; faculty Internationale Ferienkurse, Darmstadt, 1964. Author: The Function of Set Structure in the Twelve Tone System, 1946, also articles in mus. jours.; Composer: Music for the Mass, 1940, String Trio, 1941, Three Compositions for Piano, 1947, Composition for Four Instruments, 1948, Composition for Twelve Instruments, 1948, Composition for Viola and Piano, 1950, Woodwind Quartet, 1953, String Quartet No. 2, 1954, All Set, 1957, Composition for Synthesizer, 1961, Vision and Prayer, 1961, Ensembles, 1964, Philomel, 1964, Relata I, 1965, Relata II, 1968, String Quartets 3 & 4, 1970-71, Occasional Variations, 1971, Tableaux, 1972, Arie da Capo, 1973, Reflections, 1975, Concerti, 1976, Solo Requiem, 1977, Images, 1979, Paraphrases, 1979, Dual, 1980, Ars Combinatoria, 1981, The Head of the Bed, 1981, String Quartet No. 5, 1982, Melismata, 1982, Canonic Form, 1983. Recipient Joseph A. Bearns prize, 1942, N.Y. Music Critic's citation, 1949, 64; Nat. Inst. Arts and Letters award, 1959; Gold medal Brandeis U., 1970; Pulitzer Prize citation, 1982; George Peabody medal, 1983; John Simon Guggenheim fellow, 1960-61. Mem. Internat. Soc. Contemporary Music (pres. 1951-52, del. 1952 Festival), League of Composers, Nat. Inst. Arts and Letters, Am. Acad. Arts and Scis., Am. Inst. Physics, Phi Beta Kappa. Home: 222 Western Way Princeton NJ 08540

BABBITT, NATALIE MOORE, author, illustrator; b. Dayton, Ohio, July 28, 1932; d. Ralph Zane and Genevieve (Converse) Moore; m. Samuel Fisher Babbitt, June 26, 1954; children—Christopher Converse, Thomas Collier II, Lucy Cullyford. B.A., Smith Coll., Northampton, Mass., 1954. Reviewer N.Y. Times, Washington Post, 1968—; tchr. writing Kirkland Coll., Clinton, N.Y., 1970-78. Author: Tuck Everlasting, 1976, Eyes of the Amaryllis, 1977, others; illustrator: (Valerie Worth) Curlicues, 1980, others. Recipient Newbery medal honor book ALA, 1971, Christopher award Christopher's Orgn., 1976, Internat. Bd. Books for Young People U.S. Honor Book, 1977, Lewis Carroll Shelf award U. Wis., 1978. Mem. P.E.N. Am. Center, Authors Guild, Inc., Authors League Am. Democrat. Club: Cosmopolitan (N.Y.C.). Home: Providence RI

BABBITT, SAMUEL FISHER, university administrator; b. New Haven, Feb. 22, 1929; s. Theodore and Margaret (Fisher) B.; m. Natalie Zane Moore, June 28, 1974; children: Christopher Converse, Thomas Collier, Lucy Cullyford. B.A., Yale U., 1953, M.A., 1957, Ph.D., 1965; LL.D. hon., Hamilton Coll., Clinton, N.Y., 1968. Asst. dean Yale Coll. Grad. Sch., New Haven, 1953-57, 63-66; dean of men Vanderbilt U., Nashville, 1957-62; chief coll. and univ. liaison Office Pub. Affairs, U.S. Peace Corpss, Washington, 1962-63; pres. Kirkland Coll., Clinton, N.Y., 1966-78; v.p. program planning and resources Meml. Sloan-Kettering Cancer Ctr., N.Y.C., 1979-83; v.p. devel. Brown U., Providence, 1982—; mem. N.Y. State Commn. on Civil Rights, 1968-76. Author: The 49th Magician, 1966; producer: (film) The Eyes of the Amaryllis, 1981. Served with inf. U.S. Army, 1948-51; Korea. Decorated Silver Star. Democrat. Episcopalian. Clubs: Yale; Century Assn. (N.Y.C.). Office: Brown U Providence RI 02914

BABBY, ELLEN REISMAN, association executive; b. Montreal, Que., Can., Oct. 21, 1950; came to U.S., 1973; d. Mark Reisman and Rose Gutwillig (Reisman); m. Lon Scott Babby, June 17, 1973; 1 son, Kenneth Robert. Student, McGill U., 1968-70; B.A., Beaver Coll., 1972; M.A., Lehigh U., 1973, Yale U., 1976, M.Phil., 1977, Ph.D., 1980. Tchr. elem. schs. to coll. levels; instr. resident assoc. program Smithsonian Instn., Washington, 1980-82; exec. dir. Assn. for Can. Studies in U.S., Washington, 1982—. Contbr. articles on Quebec lit. to profl. jours. Mem. Assn. for Can. Studies in U.S., MLA, N.E. MLA, Am. Assn. Tchrs. French, Soc. for Internat. Edn., Tng. and Research, N.E. Council for Que. Studies. Jewish. Office: Assn for Can Studies in US 1776 Massachusetts Ave NW Washington DC 20036

BABCOCK, CHARLES LUTHER, educator, classicist; b. Whittier, Calif., May 26, 1924; s. Robert Louis and Margarette (Fuller) B.; m. Mary Ayer Taylor, Aug. 6, 1955; children: Robert Sherburne, Jennie Rownd, Jonathan Taylor. A.B., U. Calif., Berkeley, 1948, M.A., 1949, Ph.D., 1953. Instr. classics Cornell U., 1955-57; asst. prof., asso. prof. classical studies U. Pa., 1957-66, asst. dean to vice dean Coll. Arts and Scis., 1960-64, acting dean, 1964; prof. classics Ohio State U., Columbus, 1966—, chmn. dept., 1966-68, 80—, dean Coll. Humanities, 1968-70; Fulbright scholar in classics, fellow Am. Acad. in Rome, 1953-55, prof.-in-charge Summer Sch., 1966, trustee, 1981—; prof.-in-charge Intercollegiate Center for Classical Studies, Rome, autumn 1974, chmn. mng. com., 1975-82. Contbr. articles to profl. jours. Served to capt., inf. AUS, 1943-47. Decorated Bronze Star with V device. Mem. Am. Philol. Assn. (dir. 1967-71), Vergilian Soc. (pres. 1975-76), Classical Assn. Midwest and South (pres. 1977-78), Classical Soc. of Am. Acad. Rome (past pres.), Phi Beta Kappa, Phi Sigma Kappa. Home: 973 Lynbrook Rd Worthington OH 43085 Office: 230 N Oval Mall Columbus OH 43210

BABCOCK, HORACE WELCOME, astronomer; b. Pasadena, Calif., Sept. 13, 1912; s. Harold Delos and Mary Geddie (Henderson) B.;, 1940 (div. 1958); children: Ann Lucille, Bruce Harold; m. Elizabeth Mae Aubrey, 1958; 1 son, Kenneth L. B.S., Calif. Inst. Tech., 1934; Ph.D., U. Calif., 1938; D.Sc. (hon.), U. Newcastle-upon-Tyne (Eng.), 1965. Asst. Lick Obs., Mt. Hamilton, Calif., 1938-39; instr. Yerkes and McDonald Obs., Williams Bay, Wis., Ft. Davis, Tex., 1939-41; with Radiation Lab., MIT, 1941-42, Rocket Project, Calif. Inst. Tech., 1942-45; staff mem. Mt. Wilson and Palomar Obs., Carnegie Instn. of Washington, Calif. Inst. Tech., Pasadena, 1946—; dir. Mt. Wilson and Palomar Obs., 1964-78. Author sci. and tech. papers in profl. jours. Recipient USN Bur. Ordnance Devel. award, 1946; Draper medal Nat. Acad. Scis., 1957; Eddington medal Royal Astron. Soc., 1958; Gold medal, 1970; Bruce medal Astron. Soc. Pacific, 1969. Mem. Royal Astron. Soc. (asso.), Societé Royale des Sciences de Liege (corr. mem.), Am. Philos. Soc., Am. Acad. Arts and Scis., Nat. Acad. Scis. (councilor 1973-76), Am. Astron. Soc. (councilor 1956-58), Astron. Soc. Pacific, Internat. Astron. Union, Tau Beta Pi. Home: 2189 N Altadena Dr Altadena CA 91001 Office: Mt Wilson and Las Campanas Observatories Carnegie Instn of Washington 813 Santa Barbara St Pasadena CA 91101

BABCOCK, JACK EMERSON, retired army officer, educator; b. Milan, Mich., Apr. 24, 1915; s. Charles Emerson and Thelma (Sweet) B.; m. Judith Mary Gritz, Jan. 8, 1943; children: Jill Irene, Carol Anne, Maria Elena, Jack Emerson, Alice Kay. B.S., U. Wash., 1937; grad., Command and Gen. Staff Coll., 1944, Indsl. Coll. Armed Forces, 1946; M.S., Georgetown U., 1947, Ph.D., 1954, NATO Def. Coll., 1952. Commd. 2d lt. U.S. Army, 1937, advanced through grades to brig. gen., 1965; chief logistics system design div. Def. Supply Agy., 1962-64; comdg. officer U.S. Army Chem. Center and comdt. Chem. Sch., Ft. McClellan, Ala., 1964-65; dir. personnel and tng. Army Material Command, Washington, 1965-66, dir. mgmt. systems and data automation, 1966-68; ret., 1968; spl. asst. to assoc. adminstr. for orgn. and mgmt. NASA, Washington, 1968-69; dir. internat. relations Gen. Dynamics Internat. Corp., Brussels and London, 1969-71; pres., chmn. bd. Astral Mgmtm. Corp., Potomac, Md., 1971-76; assoc. prof. Sch. Bus. Adminstrn. Georgetown U., Washington, 1976—; also dir. summer sch. and continuing edn. summer session at Oxford U.; pres., chmn. bd. Internat. Devel. Assos. Ltd., Washington, 1980—. Author: The Evolution of Industrial Mobilization in the United States, 1954, (with others) The Emergency Management of the National Economy, 1950; Contbr. articles to mags. and newspapers, also profl. jours. Past pres. Fontainebleau PTA. Decorated D.S.M., Legion of Merit with two oak leaf clusters, Army Commendation medal, Brazilian medal of War, John Carroll medal Georgetown U., 1983, others. Mem. Armed Forces Mgmt. Assn. (past pres. nat. chpt.), Am. Ordnance Assn. (past pres. So. post), Georgetown U. Alumni Assn. (v.p. 1979—), Georgetown U. Library Assos. (trustee 1979—), Nat. Sojourners (past pres.), Cercle Royal Gaulois - Artistique et Literaire of Belgium, SHAPE Officers Assn. (Belgium), NATO Def. Coll. Alumni Assn. (Rome), Am. Acad. Polit. and Social Sci., AAAS, AAUP. Lodge: Masons. Home: 1424 Knox Pl Alexandria VA 22304 also Fernrock Bluemont VA Office: IDA Ltd 1555 Connecticut Ave Suite 200 Washington DC 20036

BABCOCK, JOHN BODINE, publishing consultant; b. Schenectady, Feb. 12, 1925; s. Frederick Howard and Gertrude A. (Bodine) B.; m. Mary Scheerer, June 25, 1946; children: John, Linda, Joanne, Frederick. Student, Yale U.; B.S. in Psychology, Columbia U., 1950. Sales promotion mgr. McGraw Hill Pub., N.Y.C., 1950-51; dir. info. services Associated Bus. Publs., N.Y.C., 1951-55, v.p. mem. services, 1955-65; pres. Am. Bus. Press, 1965-70; pub. cons., N.Y.C., 1970—; pres. Indsl. Design Mag., N.Y.C., 1977—; cons. v.p. product devel. Billboard Pub., N.Y.C., 1980—. Trustee Barlow Sch., Amenia, N.Y., 1975-80. Served with USAAF, 1943-46. Decorated Purple Heart. Mem. Advt. Council (bd. dirs. 1965-70), Advt. Fedn. (bd. dirs. 1967-70). Clubs: Yale, Sky (N.Y.C.); Millbrook Country, Mashomack (N.Y.). Home: RD2 Box 79A Stanfordville NY 12581 Office: Billboad 1515 Broadway New York NY 10036

BABCOCK, MICHAEL JOSEPH, retail company executive; b. Fort Riley, Kans., Sept. 10, 1941; s. David Edward and Dorothy Jayne (Viner) B.; m. Abigail Wilkins, Dec. 29, 1974; children: Michael Joseph, Elizabeth Anne, Catherine Nielsen, Rebecca Leigh. B.A. in Indsl. Psychology, U. Tulsa, 1965. Mem. corp. personnel staff 3 M Co., St. Paul, 1965-67; mgr. wage and salary adminstrn. Famous-Barr Co., St. Louis, 1967-68, dir. exec. placement, 1968-70, asso. gen. mgr., Crestwood, Mo., 1970; v.p., personnel dir. Strouss' Co., Youngstown, Ohio, 1970-72, v.p. ops. and personnel, 1972-73, May D & F, Denver, 1973-74; v.p. personnel May Co., Los Angeles, 1974-75, sr. v.p. personnel, 1976-80; sr. v.p. personnel and organizational devel. May Dept. Stores Co., St. Louis, 1976-80; chmn. bd. G. Fox & Co., Hartford, Conn., 1980-82; pres. Filene's, Boston, 1982—. Bd. dirs. mgmt. forum St. Louis YMCA, 1977—; bd. dirs. Hartford Arts Council, Hartford Downtown Council, Hartford Area Boy Scouts Am., United Way of Mass. Bay; corporator Mt. Sinai Hosp., St. Francis Hosp., Renbrook Sch. Mem. Nat. Retail Merchants Assn. (dir. personnel retail div. 1973—), Young Pres.'s Orgn., Kappa Sigma. Republican. Presbyterian. Home: 180 Clyde St Chestnut Hill MA Office: Filene's 426 Washington St Boston MA

BABCOCK, RICHARD FELT, lawyer; b. Evanston, Ill., Nov. 3, 1917; s. William Frank and Gertrude (Felt) B.; m. Elizabeth Vaughn Burlingham, June 12, 1943; children—Rebecca, Richard, Elizabeth, Catherine, David, John. A.B. magna cum laude, Dartmouth, 1940; J.D. cum laude, U. Chgo., 1946, M.B.A., 1950. Bar: Ill. bar. Asso. firm Sidley, Austin, Burgess & Harper, Chgo., 1946-48; partner Overton & Babcock, Chgo., 1948-51, Taylor, Miller, Busch & Wagner, 1951-56, Ross, Hardies, O'Keefe, Babcock & Parsons, 1957—; Lectr. bus. law Northwestern U. Sch. Commerce, 1951-58; lectr. U. Chgo. Grad. Sch. Bus., Chgo., 1953-54; adj. prof. Grad. Sch. Urban Scis., U. Ill.; cons. on land use law Ford Found., 1960-62. Author: The Zoning Game, 1966, Billboards, Glass Houses and the Law, 1976; co-author: Big City Zoning: The Once and Future Frontier; contbr. articles to profl. revs. Dir. Met. Housing and Planning Council, Chgo.; commr. Northeastern Ill. Met. Planning Commn., 1964-72; Asso. dir. Nat. Vols. for Stevenson, 1952; chmn. adv. com. Land Use project Am. Law Inst.; co-chmn. Lawyers Com. for Civil Rights Under Law, 1973-75. Served with Am. Field Service, 1941-43; with Brit. 8th Army, 1942-43; Western Desert; then with N.Z. Divisional Cav. Mem. Am. Inst. Planners, Am. Soc. Planning Ofcls. (pres. 1970-71), Order of Coif, Phi Beta Kappa, Lambda Alpha. Democrat. Club: Mid-Am. (Chgo.). Home: 1314 S Fleming Rd Woodstock IL 60098 Office: One IBM Bldg Chicago IL 60611

BABCOCK, STEPHEN LEE, government official; b. Decatur, Ill., Dec. 19, 1939; s. Milton and Virginia (Derrick) B.; m. Christine Alexandra Keller, Oct. 6, 1979; 1 son, Lee David. B.A., Coll. William and Mary, 1963; J.D., U. Chgo., 1966. Bar: D.C. 1967. Assoc. Reavis, Pogue, Neal & Rose, Washington, 1966-72, Cadwalader, Wickersham & Taft, 1973-75; atty. CAB, Washington, 1975-78; exec. dir. Adminstrv. Conf. U.S., Washington, 1978—; lectr. in field. Bd. dirs. D.C. United Way, Washington, 1979—. Served to capt. USMC, 1958-62. Mem. ABA, Fed. Bar Assn., D.C. Bar Assn. Home: 3615 Idaho Ave NW Washington DC 20016 Office: 2120 L St NW Washington DC 20037

BABIAK, WALTER, conductor. Music dir., condr. Royal Winnipeg Ballet, Man., Can. Office: Royal Winnipeg Ballet 289 Portage Ave Winnipeg MB Canada R3B 2B4§

BABIARZ, JOHN EDWARD, former city official; b. Wilmington, Del., June 6, 1915; s. Stanley and Maryanne (Feret) B.; m. Adele F. Barczuk, June 4, 1939; children: John Edward, Francis. B.A., U. Del., 1937. With Del. Bedding Co., Wilmington, 1939—, treas., mgr., 1941-67; register in chancery, clk. orphans ct., New Castle County, 1948-52; chief clk. Del. Ho. of Reps., 1955-56; mayor of Wilmington, 1961-69; pres. Better Bus. Bur. Del., Inc., 1969-73; sec. Del. Dept. Adminstrv. Services, 1973-77; dir. commerce City of Wilmington, 1977-81. Chmn. Regional Conf. Elected Ofcls., 1963-65; Del. Democratic Nat. Conv., 1956, 60, 64, 68; chmn. bd. Port of Wilmington Maritime Soc.; mem. council Acad. Lifelong Learning, U. Del. Sch. Continuing Edn. Served with AUS, World War II. Mem. V.F.W. (condr. Del 1950-51), Am. Legion, Holy Name Soc., Polish Falcons, Pulaski Legion. Club: Press (Wilmington). Lodges: K.C.; Eagles; Kiwanis. Home: 303 Lea Blvd Wilmington DE 19802

BABIGIAN, HAROUTUN MELKON, psychiatrist; b. Jerusalem, May 3, 1935; s. Melkon A. and Iskouhi (Baklayan) B.; m. Alice Guizirian, Dec. 2, 1961; children—Melkon, Lenna. B.Sc. with distinction, Am. U. Beirut, Lebanon, 1956, M.D., 1960. Diplomate: Am. Bd. Psychiatry. Rotating intern Am. U. Hosp., Beirut, Lebanon, 1959-60; psychiat. resident U. Rochester (N.Y.) Sch. Medicine and Dentistry, Strong Meml. Hosp., 1960-63, instr., fellow psychiatry, 1963-64, sr. instr. psychiatry and preventive medicine and community health, 1964-65, asst. prof., 1965-69, asso. prof., 1969-75, prof. psychiatry, 1975—; asst. psychiatrist Strong Meml. Hosp., 1963-65, asso. psychiatrist, 1965-69, sr. asso. psychiatrist, 1969-75, psychiatrist, 1975-77, acting psychiatrist-in-chief, 1977-79, psychiatrist-in-chief, 1979—; acting dir. div. preventive and social psychiatry, 1966-67, dir., 1967-69, dir. psychiat. emergency services, 1969-72; dir. div. community mental health and preventive psychiatry, dir. U. Rochester Community Mental Health Center, 1972—, dep. chmn. dept. psychiatry, clin. and community services, 1973-79, chmn., 1979—, dir. div. clin. and community programs, 1973—; dir. Cumulative Psychiat. Case Register, Monroe County, N.Y., 1966—; mem. Nat. Bd. Med. Examiners, Psychiatry, 1981—. Contbr. articles in field to profl. jours. Fellow Am. Psychiat. Assn. (pres. Genesee Valley dist. br. 1979-81); mem. Am. Public Health Assn., Am. Assn. Suicidology, Soc. Life History Research in Psychopathology, Psychiat. Research Soc., Am. Psychopath. Assn., Med. Soc. State N.Y., Med. Soc. Monroe County, Inc., Sigma Xi. Home: 3 Burr Oak Dr Pittsford NY 14534 Office: 300 Crittenden Blvd Rochester NY 14642

BABIN, CLAUDE HUNTER, history educator; b. Baton Rouge, Feb. 6, 1924; s. Ventress Victor and Essie (Bond) B.; m. Barbara Ann Murphy, Dec. 29, 1947; 1 son, Claude Hunter. B.A., La. State U., 1945; M.A., U. Wis., 1946; Ph.D., Tulane U., 1954; LL.D., Hendrix Coll., 1965. Instr. history U. Miami, Fla., 1946-49; grad. fellow Tulane U., 1949-54; asst. prof., asso. prof., then prof. history Ark. A. and M. Coll., Monticello, 1954-60, acad. dean, 1960-62, pres., 1962-71; chancellor U. Ark. at Monticello, 1971-77, prof. history, 1977—. Ford fellow, 1951-52. Mem. Am. Hist. Assn., Ark. Hist. Assn., Orgn. Am. Historians, Ark. Farm Bur. Fedn., Kappa Sigma, Phi Alpha Theta, Pi Sigma Alpha. Democrat. Methodist. Home: 135 E Ross Monticello AR 71655

BABIN, PETER JOHN, retailing executive; b. Hartford, Conn., Jan. 11, 1944; s. Henry Andrew B. and Mitilda Barbara (Baron) Bibin; m. Barbara Ellen Mfakinen, July 30, 1972; children: Caroline, Elizabeth, Suzanne. B.A., Wesleyan U., 1965; J.D., U. Conn.-West Hartford, 1968. Bar: Conn. 1968. Staff atty. New Britian Legal Aid Assn., Conn., 1968; agy. staff atty., dist. agy. mgr. Conn. Gen. Life, Hartford, also Los Angeles, Springfield, Mass., 1969-76;; v.p. ins. The May Dept. Stores, 1980—. First v.p., bd. dirs. Greater St. Louis Health Systems Agy., 1982; first v.p., bd. dirs. St. Louis Area Bus. Health Coalition, 1983; bd. dirs. Am. Lung Assn. Eastern Mo., St. Louis, 1983. 2d lt. U.S. Army, 1968-69. Mem. ABA, Risk and Ins. Mgmt. Soc. Roman Catholic. Home: 1726 Butternut Dr Saint Louis MO 63131 Office: 611 Olive St Saint Louis MO 63101

BABLER, WAYNE E., retired telephone company executive; b. Orangeville, Ill., Dec. 8, 1915; s. Oscar E. and Mary (Bender) B.; m. Mary Blome, Dec. 27, 1940; children: Wayne Elroy, Marilyn Anne Evans, Sally Jane Sperry. B.A., Ind. Central Coll., 1936; J.D., U. Mich., 1938; LL.D., Ind. Central Coll., 1966. Bar: Mich. bar 1938, N.Y. bar 1949, Mo. bar 1955, Wis. bar 1963, also U.S. Supreme Ct. bar 1963. Asso. firm Bishop & Bishop, Detroit, 1938-42, partner, 1945-48; atty. AT&T, 1948-55; gen. solicitor Southwestern Bell Telephone Co., St. Louis, 1955-63, v.p., gen. counsel, sec., 1965-80, ret., 1980; v.p., gen. counsel Wis. Telephone Co., Milw., 1963-65. Bd. dirs., chmn. St. Louis Soc. Crippled Children; bd. dirs. St. Louis Symphony Soc. Mem. ABA (chmn. pub. utility sect. 1978-79), Fed. Communications Bar Assn., Wis. Bar Assn., St. Louis Bar Assns., Mo. Bar. Assn. Clubs: Delray Dunes Country, Delray Beach. Home: 11943 Date Palm Dr Boynton Beach FL 33436

BABSON, DAVID LEVEAU, investment counsel; b. Gloucester, Mass., Sept. 16, 1911; s. Elmer W. and Emma G. (Leveau) B.; m. Katherine L. Allen, 1934; children: David Leveau, Susan Babson Young, Katherine L. Babson McAvoy. B.S., Harvard, 1932. Vice pres., dir. Babson's Reports, Inc., 1932-40; founder, ret. pres., cons., dir. David L. Babson & Co., Inc., 1940—; dir. Sierra Pacific Power Co., David L. Babson Investment Fund, Inc. Co-author: Investing for a Successful Future, 1959. Mem. Boston Security Analysts Soc., Investment Counsel Assn. Republican. Conglist. Home: Lyndeborough NH 03082 Office: 1 Boston Pl Boston MA 02108

BABSON, IRVING K., publishing company executive; b. Tel Aviv, Apr. 15, 1936; U.S., 1940; s. Matthew and Miriam B.; children—Stacey B., Mia L. B.B.A., N.Y. City Coll., 1957; postgrad., NATO seminars Harvard Grad. Sch. Bus. Adminstrn., 1965. Exec. v.p. Smokeshop mag., U.S. Tobacco Jour., Convenience Store News, Gaming Bus. mag., BMT Publs., Inc., N.Y.C.; dir. ICC Corp. Served with AUS, 1956-57. Mem. Nat. Assn. Tobacco Distbrs. Club: Friars. Home: 10 East End Ave New York NY 10022 Office: 254 W 31st St New York NY

BABULA, WILLIAM, educator, administrator; b. Stamford, Conn., May 19, 1943; s. Benny F. and Lottie (Zajkowski) B.; m. Karen L. Gemi, June 19, 1965; children: Jared, Joelle. B.A., Rutgers U., 1965; M.A., U. Calif.-Berkeley, 1967, Ph.D., 1969. Asst. prof. English U. Miami, Coral Gables, Fla., 1969-75, assoc. prof., 1975-77, prof., 1977-81, chmn. dept. Eng., 1976-81; dean of arts and humanities Sonoma State U., Robnert Park, Calif., 1981—. Author: Shakespeare and the Tragicomic Archetype, 1975, Shakespeare in Production, 1935-79, 1981; short stories Motorcycle, 1982, The First Edsel, 1983, Ranson, 1983, The Last Jogger in Virginia, 1983; play The Fragging of Lt. Jones (1st prize Gualala Arts Competition 1983); contbr. articles to profl. pub. Recipient Fla. Endowment Humanities grant, 1980-81, Inst. for Study of Aging grant. Mem. Modern Lang. Assn., Shakespeare Assn. Am., Phi Beta Kappa. Office: Sch Arts and Humanities Sonoma State Univ Robnert Pk CA 94928

BACALL, LAUREN (BETTY JOAN PERSKE), actress; b. N.Y.C., Sept. 16, 1924; d. William and Natalie (Bacall) Perske; m. Humphrey Bogart, May 21, 1945 (dec. 1957); children: Stephen, Leslie; m. Jason Robards, July 1961 (div.); 1 son, Sam. Student pub. schs., Am. Acad. Dramatic Art. Actress: Broadway plays Franklin Street, 1942, Goodbye Charlie, 1959; motion picture actress, 1942—; pictures include The Big Sleep, 1944, Confidential Agent, 1945, Dark Passage, 1947, Key Largo, 1948, Young Man With a Horn, 1949, Bright Leaf, 1950, How To Marry a Millionaire, 1953, Woman's World, 1954, The Cobweb, Blood Alley, 1955, Written on the Wind, Designing Woman, The Gift of Love, Flame Over India, 1959, Sex and the Single Girl, 1965, Harper, 1966, Murder on the Orient Express, 1974, The Shootist, 1976, Health, 1980; appeared in: Broadway play Cactus Flower, 1966-67, Applause, 1969-71; also road co., 1971-72, London co., 1972-73 (recipient Tony award for best actress in a musical 1970); Broadway play Woman of the Year, 1981 (recipient Tony award for best actress in a musical 1981); TV spl. The Paris Collections, 1968, Applause, 1973, A Commercial Break (Happy Endings), 1975; Author: Lauren Bacall By Myself, 1978. Recipient Am. Acad. Dramatic Arts award for achievement, 1963. Address: care STE Representation Ltd 1776 Broadway New York NY 10019 *

BACALL, TERESA BICKLE, ballet dancer; b. Escondido, Calif.; d. Alfred Merle and Charlotte Margarette Bickle. With Royal Winnipeg Ballet, 1968-82; now prin. dancer; with Pa. Ballet Co., 1972; prin. dancer Basler Stadt Theatre, Basel, Switzerland, 1973-77, San Diego Ballet, 1977-79. Performances include Our Waltzes and Adagietto, Fall River Legend, Giselle. Mem. Actors Equity. Nichiren Shoshu Buddhist. Home: 24-40 Osborne St Winnipeg MB Canada 289 Portage Ave Winnipeg MB R3B 2B4 Canada

BACCHUS, HABEEB, physician; b. Brit. Guiana, Oct. 15, 1928; came to U.S., 1945, naturalized, 1956; s. Noor and Jumratan (Khan) B.; m. Frances Solarczyk, June 26, 1965; children: Paula Bacchus Robey, Andree Jean Bacchus Scalissi, Jeanne Carol, David Michael, Michael Francis, Julie Shireen. B.S., Howard U., 1947; M.S., George Washington U., 1948, Ph.D., 1950, M.D., 1954. Diplomate: Am. Bd. Internal Medicine, Endocrinology and Metabolism. Research analyst NRC, Washington, 1949-51; research assoc. dept. physiology George Washington U., Washington, 1950-54, asst. research prof. physiology, 1954-59; intern Sibley Meml. Hosp., Washington, 1954-55; resident in medicine Providence Hosp., Washington, 1955-57, tng. officer in medicine, 1957-69; practice medicine specializing in internal medicine, endocrinology and metabolism, Riverside, Calif., 1969—; assoc. chief of medicine Riverside Gen. Hosp., 1969—, assoc. clin. pathologist, 1970-75, chief endocrinology and metabolism, 1984; prof. medicine Loma Linda Sch. Medicine, Calif., 1979—. Author: Essentials of Gynecologic and Obstetric Endocrinology, 1975, Essentials of Metabolic Diseases and Endorinology, 1976, Rational Management of Diabetes, 1977, Endocrine and Metabolic Emergencies, 1977; contbr. numerous articles to med. jours. Served with USPHS, 1957-59. Named Tchr. of Yr. in Medicine Loma Linda U., 1978. Fellow ACP; mem. Am. Physiol. Soc., Endocrine Soc., Am. Fedn. Clin. Research, Calif. Med. Assn. Home: 1444 Ransom Rd Riverside CA 92506 Office: 9851 Magnolia Ave Riverside CA 92503

BACCIGALUPPI, ROGER JOHN, agricultural company executive; b. N.Y.C., Mar. 17, 1934; s. Harry and Ethel (Hutcheon) B.; m. Patricia Marie Wier, Feb. 6, 1960 (div. 1978); children: John, Elisabeth, Andrea, Jason; m. Iris Christine Walfridson, Feb. 3, 1979. B.S., U. Calif., Berkeley, 1956; M.S., Columbia U., 1957. Asst. sales promotion mgr. Maco Mag. Corp., N.Y.C., 1956-57; mdsg. asst. Honig, Cooper & Harrington, San Francisco, 1957-58, 1958-60, asst. dir. merchandising, 1960-61; sales rep. Calif. Almond Growers Exchange, Sacramento, 1961-64, mgr. advt. and sales promotion, 1964-70, v.p. mktg., 1970-73, sr. v.p. mktg., 1973-74, exec. v.p., 1974-75, pres., 1975—; bd. dirs. Almond Bd. Calif.; chmn. Nat. Council Farmer Coops., mem. mktg. and internat. trade conf. group; bd. dirs. Agrl. Council Calif., mem. consumer-producer com., adminstrn. com. Mem. Bus. Sch. Bd. U. Calif., Berkeley. Served with AUS, 1957. Calif. C. of C. (internat. trade task force); Mem. Sacramento C. of C. (dir.). Clubs: Sutter, Del Paso Country, Sierra. Address: PO Box 1768 Sacramento CA 95808

BACCUS, IRA BISHOP, retired electrical engineering educator; b. Plano, Tex., Apr. 25, 1903; s. Henry and Jennie (Bishop) B.; m. Marietta Dickey, Sept. 2, 1925; 1 son, Henry Lee. B.S., Tex. A&M Coll., 1924, E.E., 1939; M.S., U. Tex., 1933. Registered profl. engr., Tex. Draftsman, supr. Tex. Power & Light Co., Dallas, 1924-27; instr. engring. drawing Tex. A. and M. Coll., 1927-28; elec. engr. Central Power & Light Co., San Antonio, 1928-32; instr. elec. subjects San Antonio Jr. Coll., 1934-37; asst. prof. elec. engring. Okla. A. and M Coll., 1937-40; asst., later asso. prof. elec. engring. Mich. State U., 1940-44, prof., head dept. elec. engring., 1947-58, asst. to dean students, 1964-69, prof. emeritus, 1969—; Instr. U.S. Naval Acad., 1944-46; comdg. officer Vol. Res. Research Co., 1951-53; comdr. USNR, ret. Mem. Am. Inst. Elec. Engring. (chmn. Mich. sect. 1951-52), Am. Soc. Engring. Edn., Am. Soc. Profl. Engrs., Mich. Socs. Profl. Engrs. (pres. Grand Valley), SAR, Tau Beta Pi, Sigma Tau, Eta Kappa Nu, Pi Kappa Alpha. Republican. Presbyn. (elder). Clubs: Masons (32 deg.), Shriners, Kiwanis. Home: 7024 Leameadow Dr Dallas TX 75248

BACCUS, ROBERT LEE, manufacturing company executive; b. Dallas, Aug. 3, 1918; s. Robert Lee and Mary Ann (Crady) B.; m. Shirley Dolores Pitts, Nov. 10, 1944; children: Shirley Ann, Robert Lee, Cynthia Lee, Penelope Lynn, Michael Buckner. B.S. in Commerce, So. Methodist U., 1941. Vice-pres. ops. Frigeking div. Cummins Engine Co.; sr. v.p. Textar Corp.; now chmn., chief exec. officer ARA Mfg. Co., Grand Prairie, Tex.; pres. Refri-Auto, San Juan, ARA Auto Accessories, Inc. Office: ARA Mfg Co 606 Fountain Pkwy Grand Prairie TX 75050

BACH, ARTHUR JAMES, investment banker; b. Darien, Conn., Aug. 2, 1929; s. Arthur T. and Ann (James) B.; m. Vona Rae Hopkins, Jan. 15, 1983. B.A., Columbia U., 1952. Accountant Gen. Electric Co., Schenectady, 1956-58; with Dean Witter Reynolds Inc., N.Y.C., 1959—, v.p. mktg., 1975—. Served with AUS, 1952-54. Mem. Nat. Assn. Security Dealers. Congregationalist. Clubs: Bond, Down Town Assn. (N.Y.C.); Apawamis (Rye, N.Y.). Home: 160 E 84th St New York NY 10028 Office: 5 World Trade Center New York NY 10048

BACH, BERT COATES, university administrator; b. Jenkins, Ky., Dec. 14, 1936; s. Bert C. and Rowena W. (Coates) B.; m. Diana Miller, Aug. 25, 1957; children: Bert Coates, Nancy Elizabeth. A.B. in English, Eastern Ky. U., 1958; M.A., George Peabody Coll., 1959; Ph.D. in English, NYU, 1966. Asst. prof. English W.Ga. Coll., Carrollton, 1959-61; instr. dept. English Manhattan Coll., N.Y.C., 1961-64, asst. prof., 1964-66; assoc. prof. English Eastern Ky. U., Richmond, 1966-67, prof. English, 1967-70, chmn. English composition program, 1967-70; prof. English Millikin U., Decatur, Ill., 1970-75, asst. to v.p. acad. affairs, 1974-75, chmn. dept. English, 1970-73; dean Coll. Arts and Scis. U. Tenn.-Chattanooga, 1975-78, exec. dean faculty, 1978-81; vice chancellor acad. affairs State U. and Community Coll. System of Tenn., Nashville, 1981—; manuscript cons. Harper & Row pubs., 1969—. Author: Dickens' Great Expectations: A Guide, 1967, (with Gordon Browning) Fiction for Composition, 1968, Drama For Composition, 1973, (with William A. Sessions and William Walling) The Liberating Forum: A Handbook-Anthology of English and American Poetry, 1972; contbr. essays on lit. criticism to scholarly jours. Del. Democratic Conv., Ky., 1964; bd. dirs. Chattanooga Symphony Orch., 1978—; trustee Richland Community Coll., Decatur, 1971-75. Am. Council on Edn. fellow, 1973-74. Mem. MLA, Nat. Council Tchrs. English, Am. Assn. Higher Edn., Phi Kappa Phi. Episcopalian. Office: State Board of Regents 1161 Murfreesboro Rd Nashville TN 37217

BACH, GEORGE LELAND, economist, emeritus educator; b. Victor, Iowa, Apr. 28, 1915; s. James Everett and Ethel (Sies) B.; m. Ruth Bartoo, Sept. 7, 1939; children: Christopher Leland, Barbara Kathleen, Susan Louise, Timothy Lee. A.B., Grinnell Coll., 1936, LL.D., 1956; Ph.D., U. Chgo., 1940; LL.D., Carnegie Inst. Tech., 1967. Instr. Iowa State Coll., 1939-41; spl. asst. and sr. economist Bd. Govs. Fed. Res. System, 1941-44; prin. economist U.S. Dept. Commerce, 1946; prof., head dept. econs. Carnegie Inst. Tech., 1946-62; dean Grad. Sch. Indsl. Adminstrn., 1949-62, Maurice Falk prof. econs., 1962-66; Ford research prof. Stanford U., 1963-64, Frank Buck prof. econs., 1966-83, prof. econs. emeritus, 1983—; chmn. bd. Pitts. br. Fed. Res. Bank Cleve., 1961-66; cons. Commn. on Orgn. of Exec. Br. Govt., U.S. Treasury and; bd. govs. Fed. Res. System., Ford Found. Author: Federal Reserve Policy Making, 1950, Economics, 1954, 10th edit., 1980, Inflation: A Study in Economics, Ethics, and Politics, 1958, Making Monetary and Fiscal Policy, 1971, The New Inflation, 1973; co-author: Economic Analysis and Public Policy, 1943, 49, Management and Corporations, 1960, Economic Analysis and Policy, 1963, 66, 74, Microeconomics, 1966, 80, Macroeconomics, 1966, 80, Improving the Monetary Aggregates, 1976; Contbr. articles various profl. jours. Vice chmn. trustees Joint Council on Econ. Edn.; bd. dirs. Nat. Bur. Econ. Research. Served with USNR, 1944-46. Recipient AACSB-Dow Jones award for disting. contbn. to mgmt. edn.; Walter Gores award for outstanding teaching.; Faculty Research Fellow, 1958-59. Fellow Am. Acad. Arts and Scis.; mem. Am. Econ. Assn. (exec. com. 1959-62, chmn. com. on econ. edn. 1966-79), Nat. Task Force Econ. Edn. (chmn.), Phi Beta Kappa, Phi Kappa Phi. Home: 661 Cabrillo Ave Stanford CA 94305

BACH, JAN MORRIS, composer, educator; b. Forrest, Ill., Dec. 11, 1937; s. John Nicholas and Anne (Morris) B.; m. Dalia Zakaras; children: Dawn, Eva. Mus.B., U. Ill., 1959, Mus.M., 1961, Mus.D., 1971; postgrad., Yale U., Tanglewood, summer 1961, U. Va., Arlington, 1963-65. Instr. music U. Tampa, Fla., 1965-66; prof. music No. Ill. U., DeKalb, 1966—, Presdl. research prof., Dekalb, 1982-86; composer-in-residence Institut de Hautes Etudes Musicales, Montreux, Switzerland, 1976; editor for brass compositions M.M. Cole, Chgo., 1969-72. Composer: Skizzen, 1967, Woodwork, 1970, Eisteddfod, 1972, Turkish Music, 1968, Four Two-Bit Contraptions, 1971, The System, 1973, Dirge for a Minstrel, 1974, Three Choral Dances, 1975, Laudes, 1975, Three Bagatelles, 1978, Hair Today, 1978, The Happy Prince, 1978, My Wilderness, 1979, Student from Salamanca, 1979, Horn Concerto, 1982. Served with AUS, 1962-65. Recipient BMI Student Composers First prize, 1957, Koussevitsky Composition award, 1961, Harvey Gaul Composition award, 1973, Mannes Opera award, 1973, Pulitzer prize nomination, 1973, 81, 82, 84, SAI Composition award, 1974; Tuba Brotherhood Commn., 1977; Internat. Trumpet Guild commn., 1978; Internat. Brass Congress commn., 1980; Greenwich Philharmonia commn., 1981; Orch. of Ill. commn., 1982; NACWPI commn., 1982; Minot Symphony commn., 1984; Excellence in Teaching award No. Ill. U., 1978; Choral Composition award Brown U., 1978; Nebr. Sinfonia Chamber Orch. contest, 1979; N.Y.C. Opera contest, 1980; Nat. Endowment for Arts grantee, 1975; Ill. Arts Council grantee, 1983. Mem. ASCAP, Coll. Mus. Soc., Broadcast Music Inc., Am. Music Ctr., Phi Eta Sigma, Phi Mu Alpha, Phi Kappa Phi, Pi Kappa Lambda., Omicron Delta Kappa. Office: Dept Music No Ill U DeKalb IL 60115

BACH, MARCUS, author, educator; b. Sauk City, Wis., Dec. 15, 1906; s. Louis P. and Albertina (Buerki) B.; m. Lorena Ernest, Aug. 17, 1932. Student, Wis. Sch. Music, Madison, 1920-22, Mission House Coll. and Sem., Plymouth, Wis., 1924-25; A.M., U. Ia., 1937, Ph.D., 1942; Engaged in research and study, Ky., N.M., Cal., Mexico, 1933-35; Engaged in research and study (Rockefeller fellowship in research and creative writing), 1934-36. Instr. dramatic lit. Carleton Coll., Northfield, Minn., 1937; research among Am. religious and folk groups, 1938-40; asso. dir. and prof. Sch. Religion, U. Iowa, 1942—. To write dramatic spectacles and dramas for centennial observances, including Light of Ages, City of Chgo., 1937, Timothy Alden, Allegheny Coll., Meadville, Pa., 1940, The Path of Faith, Iowa Methodism, 1944; Author: religious and folk plays While Mortals Sleep, 1935, Within These Walls, 1936, Champion of Democracy, 1940, Who is Mrs. Chimpsie?, 1940, Common Ground, 1943, Sunrise By Request, 1944; books They Have Found a Faith, 1946, Report to Protestants, 1948, The Dream Gate, 1949, Faith and My Friends of Faith and Learning, 1951, Strange Altars, 1952, The Will to Believe, 1955, The Circle of Faith, 1956, God and the Soviets, 1958, Major Religions of the World, 1959, Adventures in Faith, 1959, Strange Sects and Curious Cults, 1961, Had You Been Born in Another Faith, 1962, The Unity Way of Life, 1963, Let Life Be Like This, 1964, Spiritual Breakthroughs for our Time, 1965, The Power of Perception, 1966, The Wonderful Magic of Living, 1968, The World of Serendipity, 1970, Strangers at the Door, 1971, What's Right With The World, 1973, The Power of Total Living, 1977, I, Monty, 1978; Contbr. to ency. and nat. mags. Founder, dir. Found. for Spiritual Understanding, Internat., Palos Verdes, Calif. Recipient Charles Sergel Nat. Playwriting award for Happy Merger, 1937, Nicholas Copernicus award, 1943. Mem. Am. Acad. Polit. and Social Sci. Commd. Lectr. on interfaith understanding, contemporary religious movements and Am. religious scene with emphasis on America's little-known religions. Home: 100 Via Alameda Palos Verdes Estates CA 90274

BACH, THOMAS HANDFORD, lawyer; b. Vineland, N.J., Dec. 25, 1928; s. Albert Ludwig and Edith May (Handford) B. A.B., Rutgers U., 1950; LL.B., Harvard U., 1956. Bar: N.Y. State bar 1957. Asso. firm Hawkins, Delafield & Wood, N.Y.C., 1956-61, Reed, Hoyt, Washburn & McCarthy, 1961-62; partner Bach & Condren, N.Y.C., 1963-71, Bach & McAuliffe, 1971-79, Stroock & Stroock & Lavan, 1979—; co-counsel N.Y. State Senate Housing and Urban Devel. Com., 1971; fiscal cons. N.Y.C. Fin. Adminstrn., 1967-70; asst. counsel State Fin. Com., N.Y. State Constl. Conv. of, 1967. Contbr. articles to profl. jours. Mem. N.Y. State Commn. to Study Constl. Tax Limitations, 1974-75. Served with U.S. Army, 1951-53. Mem. Am. Bar Assn., N.Y. State Bar Assn., Assn. of Bar of City of N.Y., N.J. Bar Assn., N.Y. Mcpl. Analysts Group (chmn. 1973-74), Mcpl. Forum of N.Y., Mcpl. Fin. Officers Assn. of U.S. and Can., Mcpl. Fin. Officers Assn. N.J. Episcopalian. Home: 4 E 89th St New York NY 10128 Office: 7 Hanover Sq New York NY 10004

BACHARACH, BURT, pianist, composer; b. Kansas City, Mo., May 12, 1929; s. Bert and Irma (Freeman) B.; m. Paula Stewart; m. Angie Dickinson; 1 dau., Lea Nikki. Student, McGill U., Montreal, 3 years; pupil, Darius Milhaud at New Sch. for Social Research, Henry Cowell at Music Acad. West, Santa Barbara, Calif. Accompanist Vic Damone, 1952; later Polly Bergen, Georgia Gibbs, Joel Gray, Ames Bros., Marlene Dietrich; now composer songs, film scores, stage musicals; frequent collaborator Hal David. Composer: Raindrops Keep Fallin' on My Head (Acad. award 1970), Magic Moments, The Story of My Life, Don't Make Me Over, Walk on By, Trains and Boats and Planes, Close to You, Anyone Who Had a Heart, What the World Needs Now, I'll Never Fall in Love Again, Do You Know the Way to San Jose?, The Look of Love, One Less Bell to Answer, Alfie; scores The April Fools, The Man Who Shot Liberty Valence, Wives and Lovers, Send Me No Flowers, A House is Not a Home, What's New Pussycat?; composer: music for play Promises, Promises, 1969; Recs. for, A&M Records, Kapp Records.; Author: The Bacharach-David Song Book, 1970. Served with AUS, 1950-52. Named (with David) Entertainers of Year Cue mag., 1969. Address: care Internat Creative Mgmt 8899 Beverly Blvd Los Angeles CA 90045 *

BACHARACH, MELVIN LEWIS, venture capitalist; b. Oakland, Calif., May 14, 1924; s. Max and Ellen Mildred (LeValley) B.; m. Vera Patricia Mortimer, Aug. 20, 1950; children: Kimberly Bacharach Arnone, Craig Ronald. B.S. in Bus. Adminstrn, U. Calif., 1948. With Levi Strauss & Co., 1948—, v.p., then exec. v.p., 1973—, pres. U.S. group, 1975—; also dir., mem. exec. com.; pres., chief exec. officer Internat. Bus. Sponsors, Inc., 1979—; dir. ECS Microsystems, Britton-Lee, Inc., Internat. Bus. Sponsors, Inc., I.B.S. I. Capital Corp.; mem. adv. council Sch. Bus. Adminstrn., San Francisco State U. Served as pilot USNR, 1942-46, 51-53. Decorated Air medal. Mem. Western Assn. of Venture Capitalists, Am. Mgmt. Assn., U. Calif. Bus. Adminstrn. Alumni Assn., Soc. Advancement Mgmt., Aircraft Owners and Pilots Assn., Am. Bonanza Soc., Beta Gamma Sigma, Pi Lambda Phi. Clubs: Concordia Argonaut., San Francisco Press. Patentee in apparel field. Office: 765 Bridgeway Blvd Sausalito CA 94965

BACHEM-ALENT, ROSE MARIE, comparatice literature educator, journalist; b. Rhineland, Germany, Jan. 15, 1911; came to U.S., 1950, naturalized, 1955; d. H. F. Baaker and E.C. (Beegen) Baake; m. Peter J. Bachem, July 23, 1947 (div. 1964); children: Yvonne C., Suzanne N.; m. Mury B. Alent, June 12, 1965. Staatsexamen, U. Berlin, 1946; M.A., U. Rochester, 1953, Ph.D., 1957. Asst. prof. SUNY, Geneseo, 1956-58, assoc. prof., 1958-63, prof., 1963-74, disting. teaching prof. comparative lt., 1974—. Author: The Companion to Foreign Language Composition, 1972, Beruhte Franen aus deutschen Landen, 1981; contbr. articles to profl. jours. Recipient Chevalier dans l'ordre des palmes academiques French Govt., 1972, Disting. Teaching Prof. SUNY, 1974, Deutsches Bundesverdienstkrenz erster Klasse German Govt., 1977. Home: 39 2d St Geneseo NY 14459 Office: SUNY Geneseo NY 14454

BACHENHEIMER, KLAUS G., utility company executive; b. Wiesbaden, Germany, July 24, 1926; came to U.S., 1934, naturalized, 1943; s. Wilhelm and Katherina M. (Botticher) B.; m. F. Vernele Johnson, Oct. 11, 1958; children: Kimberly Ann, Lisa Marie. B.B.A. in Higher Accountancy, Woodbury U., 1956. With S.W. Gas Corp., Las Vegas, Nev., 1956—, v.p. controller, 1967-75, sr. v.p., 1975-78, exec. v.p., 1978-80, chief operating officer, exec. v.p., 1980-82, pres., chief operating officer, 1982—, also dir.; dir. Utility Fin. & Mortgage Co., S.W. Gas of Ariz., Carson Water Co., Don Harris & Assos. Bd. dirs. Western States Taxpayers Assn., 1965-68, 77-80, United Way, 1983—; bd. dirs., sec. Salvation Army So. Nev., 1977—; exec. bd. Boulder Dam council Boy Scouts Am., 1982—. Served with USNR, 1943-46, 52-53. Recipient Disting. Service award Salvation Army, 1978. Mem. Pacific Coast Gas Assn., Am. Mgmt. Assn., Nat. Assn. Accountants (chpt. founder and dir. 1971, Disting. Service award 1973). Clubs: Rotary, Hualapai. Office: 5241 Spring Mountain Rd Las Vegas NV 89114

BACHER, VERNON ALFRED, food company executive; b. Port Townsend, Wash., Sept. 24, 1936; s. Vernon Alfred and Sara Vorhees (Modes) B.; m. Glennis Anne Page, Dec. 16, 1962. B.A., Yale U., 1958; M.B.A., Harvard U., 1969. Treas., controller Twin City Foods, Inc., Stanwood, Wash., 1958-67; exec. v.p. United Foods, Inc., Memphis, 1970-78; pres., chief exec. officer John Inglis Frozen Foods Co., Modesto, Calif., 1976-78; v.p. ops. Seabrook Foods Inc., Fresno, Calif., 1978-79, pres. No. div., 1979-83; pres., chief exec. officer Buitoni Foods Corp., South Hackensack, N.J., 1983—. Home: 185 E Palisade Ave B-6 Englewood NJ 07631 Office: Buitoni Foods Corp 450 S Huyler St South Hackensack NJ 07606

BACHERT, RAYMOND PAUL, utility executive; b. Aurora, Ill., Nov. 14, 1924; s. William Carl and Mary Babette (Lindenmeyer) B.; m. Marjorie Elaine Miller, June 24, 1950; children: Linda, Paula, Nancy. B.S. in Acctg., U. Ill., 1950. C.P.A., Ill. With Commonwealth Edison Co., Chgo., 1950—, asst. v.p., 1966-71, treas., 1971-73, sec.-treas., 1973-83, comptroller, 1983—. Bd. dirs. Ill. C. of C. Served with USAF, 1943-46. Home: 222 Hartway Ct Montgomery IL 60538 Office: PO Box 767 Chicago IL 60690

BACHMAN, DAVID CHRISTIAN, orthopedic surgeon; b. Peoria, Ill., Apr. 11, 1934; s. Leland Alvin and Elsie May (Springer) B.; m. Betty June Foster, Sept. 9, 1956; children: Lynne Allison, Laura Ailene. B.A., Goshen Coll., 1958; M.D., Northwestern U., 1962. Intern Cook County Hosp., Chgo., 1962-63; resident in orthopaedic surgery Northwestern U. Med. Sch., 1963-67; practice medicine specializing in orthopaedic surgery, Chgo., 1967-80, practice specializing in ski injuries, 1980—; with Mountain Med. Services, Telluride, Colo., 1982—, Ouray Mountain Rescue Team, Inc., Ouray Med. Ctr., Ouray, Colo.; coroner, Ouray County, Colo.; mem. staffs Northwestern Meml. Hosp., Children's Meml. Hosp., Grant hosp., (all Chgo.), 1967-80; dir. Center for Sports Medicine, Northwestern U. Med. Sch., 1978-80; team physician Chgo. Bulls, Nat. Basketball Assn., 1967-80; asst. prof. dept. orthopedic surgery Northwestern U. Med. Sch., 1967-80; syndicated columnist on sports medicine Dr. Jock. Author: (with Marilyn Preston) Dear Doctor Jock... The Peoples Guide to Sports and Fitness, 1980, (with others) The Diet That Lets You Cheat, 1983. Mem. Ill., Chgo., Colo., Curecanti med. socs., AMA, Am. Coll. Sports Medicine, Am. Acad. Orthopaedic Surgery, Clin. Orthopaedic Soc., Am. Assn. Ry. Surgeons, A.C.S., Am. Orthopaedic Soc. for Sports Medicine, Clin. Orthopedic Soc., Phi Rho Sigma. Presbyterian (elder 1965—). Address: 242 County Rd 12B Ridgway CO 81432

BACHMAN, GEORGE, educator; b. N.Y.C., Jan. 17, 1933; s. Frederick Joseph and Ruth (Benson) B.; m. Joan Caggiano. B.E.E., N.Y. U., 1950, M.S., 1952, Ph.D. in Math, 1956. Asst. prof. math. Rutgers U., New Brunswick, N.J., 1957-60; mem. faculty Bklyn. Poly. Inst., 1960—, asso. prof., 1962-66, prof., 1966—. Author: (with L. Narici and E. Beckenstein) Functional Analysis and Valuation Theory,

1971, (with L. Narici) Functional Analysis, 1966, Elements of Abstract Harmonic Analysis, 1964, Introduction to p-adic Numbers and Valuation Theory, 1964; Contbr.: articles to profl. jours. Introduction to p-adic Numbers and Valuation Theory. Recipient Disting. Teaching award Bklyn. Poly. Inst., 1974, Disting. Research award Sigma Xi, 1982; NSF grantee, 1968—. Mem. Am., Indian math. socs., Math. Assn. Am., Canadian Math. Congress, Societe Mathematique de France. Home: 27 Summit Rd Riverside CT 06878 Office: 333 Jay St Brooklyn NY 11201

BACHMAN, JOHN WALTER, clergyman, church official; b. Youngstown, Ohio, May 30, 1916; s. Walter Herbert and Eda (Fisher) B.; m. Elsie Schiefer, Jan. 20, 1942; children: Charles Walter, John Frederick. A.B., Capital U., Columbus, Ohio, 1937, D.D., 1957; grad., Evang. Luth. Theol. Sem., Columbus, 1940; M.A., Ohio State U., 1946. Ordained to ministry Lutheran Ch., 1941; minister in, Warren, Ohio, 1941-44; instr., then asst. prof. speech and chmn. dept. Capital U., 1944-46; asso. prof. then prof. radio and chmn. dept. Baylor U., 1946-52; asso. prof. then prof. practical theology and dir. Center Communication and Arts, Union Theol. Sem., N.Y.C., 1952-64; pres. Wartburg Coll., Waverly, Iowa, 1964-74; dir. communication and mission support Am. Luth. Ch., 1974-80; vis. lectr. Candler Sch. Theology, Emory U., Christian Theol. Sem., Indpls., Hampton Inst., Pine Hill Div. Hall, Halifax, N.S., Can., Princeton Theol. Sem., Queen's Theol. Coll., Kingston, Ont., Can., Wartburg Theol. Sem., Dubuque, Iowa, Southwestern U., Georgetown, Tex.; hon. research asso. Communication Research Centre, Univ. Coll., U. London, 1959-60; mem. adv. com. on higher edn. Midwestern Conf. on Council State Govts., 1969-70; mem. Iowa Coordinating Council for Post High Sch. Edn., 1970-74; Exec. com. Iowa Coll. Found., Iowa Assn. Pvt. Colls., 1970-74. Author: How to Use Audio-Visual Materials, 1956, The Church in the World of Radio-Television, 1960, Faith That Makes a Difference, 1983; editor: (with E.M. Browne) Better Plays for Today's Churches, 1964; editorial bd.: Quar. Jour. Speech, 1960-62; contbr. to periodicals. Bd. mgrs. communication commn. Nat. Council Chs., 1953—, chmn., 1964-67; adv. bd. Center Mass. Communication, Columbia U., 1957-62, chmn. seminar pub. communication, 1962-63; commn. pub. communication Am. Luth. Ch., 1962-72; chmn. communication task force Luth. World Fedn., 1970-72, chmn. communication com., 1973—; Bd. dirs. Luth. World Relief, 1977—, Luth. Film Assos., 1975—. Mem. Speech Assn. Am. (legis. assembly 1956-60), World Assn. Christian Broadcasting (central com. 1964-67), N. Central Assn. Colls. and Secondary Schs. (com. on research and service 1967-73, com. on liberal arts edn. 1968-73). Home: 8549 Irwin Rd Bloomington MN 55437

BACHMAN, NATHAN DULANEY, IV, investment manager; b. Columbus, Ohio, Sept. 16, 1935; s. Nathan Dulaney III and Kathryn F. (Struble) B.; m. Lynda Mae Aughnay; children: Edward H., Nathan D., Keith F., Shannon Lee. B.A. cum laude, Princeton U., 1957; M.B.A., U. Va., 1961. Chartered fin. analyst Inst. Chartered Analysts, 1967. Investment analyst Fla. Capital Corp., Palm Beach, 1961-64; chief fin. officer and treas. Emery Industries, Inc., Cin., 1964-78; exec. v.p., chief fin. officer Burke Internat. Research Corp., Cin., 1979-80; v.p. First Boston Corp., Chgo., 1980-82, E. F. Hutton, 1983—. Served with USMCR, 1957-58. Mem. Cin. Soc. Fin. Analysts (pres. 1975-76), Fin. Execs. Inst., Nat. Investor Relations Assn., Inst. Chartered Fin. Analysts. Clubs: Terrace Park (Ohio) Swim (pres. 1970-71, treas. 1967-70), Indoor Tennis, Cin. Tennis, Princeton Club Cin. Home: 9510 Cunningham Rd Cincinnati OH 45243 Office: 100 Central Trust Ctr Cincinnati OH 45202

BACHMAN, WALTER CRAWFORD, ship designer, marine cons.; b. Pitts., Dec. 24, 1911; s. Clarence E. and Mary Elizabeth (Crawford) B.; m. Helen Elizabeth Van Cleaf, Mar. 25, 1938; children—Van Cleaf, Elizabeth Crawford Bachman Ramjoué. B.S. in Indsl. Engring, Lehigh U., 1933, M.S., 1935. Tchr. mech. engring. Lehigh U., 1935-36; marine engr. Fed. Shipbldg. and Dry Dock Co., 1936, Gibbs & Cox, Inc., N.Y.C., 1936-70, chief engr., 1958-63, v.p., chief engr., 1963-70; marine cons., Short Hills, N.J., 1970—. Fellow ASME; mem. Nat. Acad. Engring. (mem. marine bd. 1967-75), Soc. Naval Architects and Marine Engrs., Am. Soc. Naval Engrs., N.Y. Acad. Scis. Club: Yacht (Beaulieu-St. Jean). Address: 21 Wayside Short Hills NJ 07078

BACHRACH, BRADFORD K., photographer; b. Worcester, Mass., Nov. 8, 1910; s. Louis Fabian and Dorothy Deland (Keyes) B.; m. Rosamond Esselen, Feb. 19, 1939; children—Susan Prentiss, William Bradford, Dorothy Locke, Laura Keyes. Grad., Phillips Exeter Acad., 1929; A.B., Harvard, 1933. With Bachrach, Inc. (portrait photographers), Watertown, Mass., 1933—, v.p., dir., 1938—, pres., 1955-77. Served to lt. USNR, 1943-45. Mem. Mass. Soc. Mayflower Descs. Unitarian. Clubs: Harvard (N.Y.C.); Wellesley Country. Home: 50 Windsor Rd Wellesley Hills MA 02181

BACHRACH, CHARLES LEWIS, advertising agency executive; b. N.Y.C., Feb. 22, 1946; s. Herbert and Lilla Clare (Blumberg) B.; m. Lois Susan Davis, Sept. 12, 1968; 1 dau., Jennifer Leigh. B.S., Ithaca (N.Y.) Coll., 1968. Assoc. producer MPO Sports Co., N.Y.C., 1968-69; unit mgr. NBC, N.Y.C., 1969; with Ogilvy & Mather, Inc., N.Y.C., 1969—, sr. v.p. broadcast, 1978-83, dir. Network and Programming Dept; sr. v.p. network and programming Western Internat. Media, 1983—; pres. Western Internat. Syndication, 1983—; vis. prof. Ithaca Coll. Sch. Communications; vis. lectr. New Sch. Contbr. articles to profl. publs. Judge Internat. Emmy Awards.; Lobbyist N.Y. State pvt. colls. Recipient Disting. Alumni award Ithaca Coll., 1980. Home: 3121 Dona Marta Dr Studio City CA 91604 Office: 8544 Sunset Blvd Los Angeles CA 90069

BACHRACH, HOWARD L., biochemist; b. Faribault, Minn., May 21, 1920; s. Harry and Elizabeth (Panovitz) B.; m. Shirley F. Lichterman, June 13, 1943; children: Eve E., Harrison J. B.A. in Chemistry, U. Minn., 1942, Ph.D. in Biochemistry, 1949. Research asst. explosives research lab. Nat. Def. Research Com. project Carnegie Inst. Tech., Pitts., 1942-45; research asst. U. Minn., Mpls., 1945-49; biochemist foot-and-mouth disease mission U.S. Dept. Agr., Denmark, 1949-50; research biochemist biochem. and virus lab. U. Calif. at Berkeley, 1950-53; chief scientist, head biochem. and phys. investigation Plum Island Animal Disease Center, Greenport, N.Y., 1953-80, research chemist, advisor to dir., 1981—; sr. exec. U.S. Dept. Agr., 1979; mem. viral and rickettsial grants subcom. Walter Reed Army Inst. Research, 1982—. Recipient Naval Ordnance Devel. award, 1945; Certificate of Merit U.S. Dept. Agr., 1960; Disting. Service award U.S. Dept. Agr., 1982; Presdl. citation, 1965, U.S. Sr. Exec. Service award, 1980; Newcomb Cleveland prize AAAS, 1982; Nat. Award for Agrl. Excellence, 1983; Alexander von Humboldt award, 1983. Fellow N.Y. Acad. Scis.; affiliate Am. Coll. Veterinary Microbiologists; mem. Am. Chem. Soc. (Kenneth A. Smith award 1983), Am. Soc. Microbiology, Soc. Exptl. Biology and Medicine, Nat. Acad. Scis., Am. Soc. Virology, Sigma Xi., Gamma Alpha, Phi Lambda Upsilon. Home: Dayton Rd Southold NY 11971

BACHRACH, IRA NATHANIEL, marketing executive; b. N.Y.C., Apr. 29, 1938; s. Sidney and Ruth (Becker) B.; m. Linda Jean Moulton, Sept. 11, 1982. B.A., CUNY, 1960; postgrad., U. Rochester, 1960-61. Pres. Bachrach Advt. Inc., Sunnyvale, Calif., 1969-76, Bachrach-Ketchum, Inc., San Francisco, 1976-79; pres. Namelab. Inc., San Francisco, 1979—. Served with U.S. Army, 1961-63. Mem. U.S. Trademark Assn., Am. Mktg. Assn. Office: 711 Marina Blvd San Francisco CA 94123

BACHUS, WALTER OTIS, association executive; b. Grand Saline, Tex., Oct. 27, 1926; s. Walter Harry and Gladys Marie (L) B.; m. Helen Singer, Dec. 12, 1946; children: Bruce, Leslie. B.S.C.E., Tex. A&M U., 1950; M.I.E., N.Y. U., 1957; grad., Army War Coll., 1968, Harvard U., 1973. Registered profl. engr., Tex., Washington. Commd. 2d lt. C.E. U.S. Army, 1950, advanced through grades; ret., 1978; exec. dir. Soc. Am. Mil. Engrs., Washington, 1978—. Decorated D.S.M., Legion of Merit, Army Commendation medal, Bronze Star. Mem. ASCE, Am. Inst. Plant Engrs. Christian Scientist. Home: 3808 Great Neck Ct Alexandria VA 22309 Office: 607 Prince St Alexandria VA 22314

BACHYNSKI, MORREL PAUL, physicist; b. Bienfait, Sask., Can., July 19, 1930; s. Nick and Karolina (Bachynski) B.; m. Slava Krkovic, May 1959; children—Caroline Dawn, Jane Diane. B.Eng., U. Sask., 1952, M.Sc., 1953; Ph.D., McGill U., 1955. Mem. sci. staff RCA Ltd., Montreal, Que., 1955-58, dir. microwave physics lab., 1958-65, dir. research, 1965-72, dir. research and devel. labs., 1972-75, v.p. research and devel., 1975-76; pres. MPB Technologies Inc., Ste. Anne de Bellevue, Que., 1976—; Scitec, 1974-75. Author: (with Johnston and Shkarofsky) The Particle Kinetics of Plasmas, 1968; contbr. articles to profl. jours. Recipient David Sarnoff Gold medal, 1963, Prix Scientifique du Quebec, 1973; Can. Enterprise Devel. award, 1977. Fellow IEEE, Am. Phys. Soc., Royal Soc. Can., Can. Aero. and Space Inst.; mem. Canadian Assn. Physicists (pres. 1968). Home: 78 Thurlow Rd Montreal PQ H3X 3G9 Canada Office: MPB Technologies Inc 1725 Trans Can Hwy Dorval PQ H9P 1J1 Canada

BACH-Y-RITA, PAUL, neurophysiologist, rehabilitation medicine specialist; b. N.Y.C., Apr. 24, 1934; s. Pedro and Anne (Hyman) Bach-y-R.; m. Esther Wicab Gutierrez, Apr. 2, 1977; children—Jacqueline Anne, Carol Jean, Laura. M.D., Universidad Nacional Autonoma de Mex., 1959. Diplomate: Am. Bd. Phys. Medicine and Rehab. Pub. health officer, Tilzapotla, Mex., 1958-59; intern Presbyterian Hosp., San Francisco, 1960-61; resident in phys. medicine and rehab. Santa Clara Valley Med. Center, Stanford U., San Jose, Calif., 1977-79; prof. Sch. Med. Sci., U. Pacific, San Francisco, 1967-79; chief rehab. medicine service Martinez (Calif.) VA Hosp., 1979—; prof., vice chmn. dept. phys. medicine and rehab., prof. dept. human physiology U. Calif., Davis, 1979-83; Prof., chmn. dept. U. Wis. Sch. Medicine-Madison, 1983—; assoc. dir. Smith-Kettlewell Inst. Visual Scis., San Francisco, 1967-79; dir. San Francisco Rehab. Engring. Center, 1974-78; vis. prof. U. Pisa, Italy, 1970-71, Universidad Nacional Autonoma de Mex., 1974, Universidad Autonoma Metropolitana, Mex., 1975-76. Author: Brain Mechanisms in Sensory Substitution, 1972; editor 3 books; assoc. editor: Perception, 1974-78; mem. editorial adv. bd.: Internat. Jour. Neurosci, 1977—, Internat. Rehab. Medicine, 1978—, Annales Medicine Physique, 1981—. Bank of Am.-Giannini fellow, 1961-62; USPHS postdoctoral fellow, 1962-63; recipient NIH research career devel. awards, 1963-73; Silver Hektoen medal AMA, 1972; Bronze Hektoen medal, 1977; Franceschetti-Liebrecht prize German Ophthal. Soc., 1974. Mem. AAAS, Internat. Rehab. Medicine Assn., Assn. for Research in Vision and Ophthalmology, Am. Physiol. Soc., Acad. Phys. Medicine and Rehab. Democrat. Patentee in field. Home: 3532 Blackhawk Dr Madison WI 53705 Office: 600 Highland Ave Madison WI 53705

BACIOCCO, ALBERT JOSEPH, JR., naval officer; b. San Francisco, Mar. 4, 1931; s. Albert Joseph and Florence Beatrice (Wiegner) B.; m. Mary Jane Rivera, June 25, 1955; children: David Anthony, Delora Ann, Andrew Joseph, Mary Susan. B.S., U.S. Naval Acad., 1953. Commd. ensign U.S. Navy, 1953; advanced through grades to vice adm.; comdr. U.S.S. Gato, 1965-69; with Submarine Div. 42, 1969-71, Submarine Squadron 4, Charleston, S.C., 1974-76; former mem. chief naval ops. staff, Washington, chief naval research, chief naval devel., dep. chief naval material, Arlington, Va.; dir. research, devel, test and evaluation Dept. Navy, Washington, 1983—. Decorated Legion of Merit (3), Meritorious Service medal, Navy Commendation medal. Mem. U.S. Naval Inst., Am. Def. Preparedness Assn., Am. Soc. Naval Engrs., U.S. Naval Acad. Alumni Assn. Roman Catholic. *

BACK, KURT WOLFGANG, social psychologist, educator; b. Vienna, Austria, Oct. 17, 1919; came to U.S., 1938, naturalized, 1943; s. Paul L. and Thekla E. (Fuchs) B.; m. Mary Louise Vincent, Oct. 18, 1969; 1 son, Allan T. B.A., N.Y. U., 1940; M.A., UCLA, 1941; Ph.D., M.I.T., 1949. Statistician Aberdeen Proving Ground, 1946; asst. study dir. Research Center for Group Dynamics, 1946-49; social sci. analyst Bur. of Census, 1949-51; research assoc. Columbia U., 1951-53, U. P.R., 1953-56, Conservation Found., 1955-58; research assoc. prof. U. N.C., 1956-59; assoc. prof. Duke U., Durham, N.C., 1959-62, prof. sociology and psychiatry, 1962—, James B. Duke prof. sociology, 1976—, chmn. sociology dept., 1976-81. Author: (with Festinger and Schachter) Social Pressures in Informal Groups, 1951, The Family and Population Control, 1959, Slums, Projects and People: Social Psychological Problems of Relocation in Puerto Rico, 1962, Beyond Words: The Story of Sensitivity Training and the Encounter Movement, 1972; editor, contbr.: Social Psychology, 1977, In Search of Community: Encounter Groups and Social Change, 1978, The Life Course: Integrative Theories and Exemplary Populations, 1980. Served with AUS, 1943-46. Recipient Helen L. Deroy award Soc. for Study Social Problems, 1956, Competition for Plans in Television research award, 1961, Burgess award Nat. Council for Family Relations, 1961; NIH spl. research fellow, 1967-68, 73-74. Mem. Am. Sociol. Assn. (council 1974-77), Am. Psychol. Assn., Am. Assn. for Pub. Opinion Research, Population Assn. Am., AAAS (chmn. sect. K 1978-79), Soc. for Exptl. Social Psychology, So. Sociol. Soc., So. Soc. Pub. Opinion Research (pres. 1983-84), Sociol. Research Assn. (pres. 1981-82). Home: 2735 McDowell St Durham NC 27705 Office: Dept Sociology Duke U Durham NC 27706

BACKAR, ANDRE O., finiancial company executive, investment adviser; b. Tunis, Tunisia, Dec. 4, 1921; came to U.S., 1947; children: Zachary, Janet. Baccalaureat, French U. Coll. Stephen Pichon, Bizerte, Tunisia. Lic. stock and commodities broker, N.Y. First v.p. Shearson Hamill, N.Y.C., 1966-70; pres. Shearson-Hamill-Intercontinental, 1966-70; v.p. Evans and Co., N.Y.C., 1970-75; sr. v.p. E.F. Hutton and Co., Inc., Internat. N.V., N.Y.C., 1975-80, E.F. Hutton and Co., Inc., 1980—; adviser UN-Tunisian Mission, N.Y.C., 1955-61; hon. consul. Tunisian Consular Corps, N.Y.C., 1982—. Mem. E.F. Hutton Adv. Council, Founders Club, Chmn.'s Club, Blue Chip Club. Clubs: World Trade Ctr. (founding mem.), Doubles; Le Club (N.Y.C.); Club of Clubs (Cologne, W.Ger.); St. James; Harry's Bar (London). Home: 870 United Nations Plaza New York NY 10017 Office: E F Hutton and Co Inc 1 Battery Park Pl New York NY 10004

BACKAS, JAMES JACOB, foundation administrator; b. Chgo., May 3, 1926; s. John and Ernestine (Harms) B.; m. Margot Wells Schutt, Dec. 1973; 1 dau., Amy Elizabeth. B.A., Mich. State U., 1950; postgrad., U. Mich., 1953-54; M.A., U. Iowa, 1960. Teaching fellow U. Iowa, Iowa City, 1958-59, research fellow, 1959-60; field editor Doubleday & Co., San Francisco, 1961-62, mgr. Coll. div., N.Y.C., 1962-66; mktg. dir. publs. Brookings Instn., Washington, 1966-69; mng. editor Am. Mus. Digest, N.Y.C., 1969; asst. dir. Md. State Arts Council, 1969-72, exec. dir., 1972-76; spl. cons. to chmn. Nat. Endowment for Arts, 1976-78; exec. dir. Am. Arts Alliance, 1978-80; mgmt. cons., Washington, 1980-82; exec. dir. So. Arts Fedn., Atlanta, 1982—; music critic Washington Star, 1966-76; lectr. music history Peabody Conservatory, Balt., 1970-73; mem., co-chmn. music adv. panel Nat. Endowment Arts, 1982—. Contbr. numerous articles on arts administration to profl. and govt. publs. Mem. Balt. Mayor's Cultural Commn.; adv. bd. ESEA Title III, Md., 1972-76; mem. policy com. for cultural affairs Johns Hopkins U., 1974-76; mem. exec. bd. Nat. Assembly State Arts Agys. Mem. Assn. Univ. Presses (chmn. market research com. 1967-69), AAUP, Music Critics Assn., Engring. Soc. Balt., Phi Mu Alpha. Home: 3274 P St NW Washington DC 20007 Office: 1401 Peachtree St Atlanta GA 30309

BACKBERG, BRUCE ALLEN, insurance company executive, lawyer; b. Staples, Minn., Oct. 28, 1948; s. Leroy Chris and Florence Emily (Anvid) B.; m. Lucinda Birch, June 20, 1970; children: Katherine Birch, Benjamin Anthony. B.A. magna cum laude, Concordia Coll., Moorhead, Minn., 1970; J.D. cum laude, U. Minn., 1973. Bar: Minn. 1973. Assoc. counsel St. Paul Cos., Inc., 1978-79, corp. counsel, 1980-81, corp. sec., 1982—. Served to capt. USMCR, 1974-77. Mem. Am. Soc. Corp. Secs., Minn. Bar Assn. Republican. Lutheran. Office: St Paul Cos Inc 385 Washington St Saint Paul MN 55102

BACKE, JOHN DAVID, corp. exec.; b. Akron, Ohio, July 5, 1932; s. John A. and Ella A. (Enyedy) B.; m. Katherine A. Elliott, Oct. 22, 1955; children—Kim, John. B.S. in Bus. Adminstrn, Miami U., Oxford, Ohio, 1954, also LL.D. (hon.); M.B.A., Xavier U., 1961, also LL.D. (hon.). Various managerial positions in engring., fin. and mktg. functions Gen. Electric Co., 1957-66; v.p., dir. mktg. Silver Burdett Co. div. Gen. Learning Corp., 1966-68, pres., 1968-69; exec. v.p. Gen. Learning Corp., Morristown, N.J., 1969, pres., chief exec. officer, 1969-73; pres. CBS Pub. Group, 1973-76; v.p., dir. CBS, Inc., 1973-76, pres., chief exec. officer, mem. fin. com., dir., 1976-80; pres., chief exec. officer Tomorrow Entertainment, Inc.; dir. Bus. Mktg. Corp., N.Y.C. Chmn. employee and pub. relations Gen. Electric Park Commn., Cin., 1960; mem. Phoenix City Planning Bd., 1963-64; trustee Salk Inst., United Fund Morris County, 1971-73; mem. campaign cabinet goals for enrichment program Miami U., 1979-81; mem. N.Y. State Alliance to Save Energy, Bus. Com. for Arts, 1977-80. Served to 1st lt. USAF, 1954-57. Mem. Assn. Am. Pubs. (dir.). Office: Kaufman Astoria Studios 34-31 35th St Astoria NY 11106

BACKER, RUSHTON O., food company executive; b. Los Angeles, Apr. 8, 1926; s. Henry Orlo and Dorothy (Rushton) B.; m. Ruth M. Murray; children: Rushton, Regan, Melanie, Kevin. B.S., U. Calif.-Berkeley. Pres. Mktg. Systems Inc., 1959-65; nat. sales mgr. Barker Equipment Co., 1966-67; pres. Sizzler Family Steak Houses, Los Angeles, 1967-80; vice chmn., chief strategy officer Collins Foods Internat., Los Angeles, 1980—. Served to lt. USN, 1944-46. Home: 1207 E Melody Ln Fullerton CA 92631 Office: Collins Foods Internat Inc 5400 Alla Rd Los Angeles CA 90066

BACKER, WILLIAM MONTAGUE, advertising agency executive; b. N.Y.C., June 9, 1926; s. Bill and Ferdinanda (Legare) B.; m. Ann Allderdice Mudge, June 11, 1983. B.A., Yale U., 1950. Creative dir., vice chmn. McCann-Erickson, N.Y.C., 1954-79; pres. Backer & Spielvogel Inc., N.Y.C., 1979—. Composer: (with others) Teach the World to Sing, 1975. Served with USNR, 1944-46. Mem. ASCAP. Episcopalian. Club: Orange County Hunt (Va.). Office: Backer & Spielvogel Inc 11 W 42d St New York NY 10036

BACKLUND, RALPH THEODORE, editor; b. Hoffman, Minn., Aug. 3, 1918; s. Adolph T. and Grace (Sheppard) B.; m. Caroline Hillman Eckel, May 18, 1956; 1 son, Nicholas Sheppard. A.B. magna cum laude, U. Minn., 1940. Newswriter Sta. WCCO, Mpls., 1946-50; producer news and public affairs Columbia Broadcasting System, 1950-55; exec. producer public affairs programs CBS Radio Network, 1955-58; asso. editor Horizon, N.Y.C., 1958-64, mng. editor, 1964-66; spl. asst. for arts Bur. Ednl. and Cultural Affairs, Dept. State, Washington, 1966-69; bd. editors Smithsonian mag., Washington, 1969-76, exec. editor, 1976—. Served with AUS, 1942-46, 51-52. Recipient Heywood Broun award Am. Newspaper Guild, 1948. Episcopalian. Home: 3827 Massachusetts Ave NW Washington DC 20016 Office: Smithsonian Instn Washington DC 20560

BACKUS, CHARLES EDWARD, engineering educator, researcher; b. Wadestown, W.Va., Sept. 17, 1937; s. Clyde Harvey and Opa Daisy (Strader) B.; m. Judith Ann Clouston, Sept. 1, 1957; children: David, Elizabeth, Amy. B.S. in Mech. Engring., Ohio U., 1959; M.S., U. Ariz.-Tucson, 1961, Ph.D., 1965. Supr., system engr. Westinghouse Astronuclear, Pitts., 1965-68; asst. prof. engring. Ariz. State U., Tempe, 1968-71, assoc. prof., 1971-76, prof., 1976—, asst. dean research, 1979—, dir. Ctr. for Research, 1980—. Contbr. chpts. to books, articles to profl. jours. Mem. Ariz. Solar Energy Commn., Phoenix, 1975—. Fellow IEEE; mem. AAAS, Am. Nuclear Soc., ASME, Am. Soc. Engring. Edn., Mesa C. of C., Sigma Xi, Phi Mu Epsilon, Tau Beta Pi. Methodist. Lodge: Rotary. Office: Ctr for Research Coll Engring and Applied Sci Ariz State U Tempe AZ 85287

BACKUS, DANA CONVERSE, lawyer; b. Bayonne, N.J., Feb. 26, 1907; s. Henry M. and Mary E. (Neilson) B.; m. Louise B. Laidlaw, Sept. 16, 1933 (dec. July 5, 1973); children: Mary (Mrs. Douglas Rankin), Janet (Mrs. E. Blythe Stason, Jr.), Elizabeth (Mrs. Stephen Stuart Girard Jr.), Harriet Meredith (Mrs. Conrad H. Todd), Anne Converse (dec.). A.B., Harvard, 1927, LL.B., 1929. Bar: N.Y. State 1930. Practiced in until partial retirement, N.Y.C., 1930—; mem. firm Windels & Marx, Davies & Ives, now ret. Contbr. numerous articles to profl. jours. Dir., past pres. Citizens Union Research Found., N.Y.C.; former dir. Citizens Union, N.Y., Standard Poors Corp.; Am. del. Assn. UN to World Fedn. UN Assns., 1946-47; mem. secretariat UN Conf., San Francisco, 1945; mem. exec. com. Com. for Def. of Constn. by Preserving Treaty Power, 1952-54. Served from capt. to lt. col. Judge Adv. Gen.'s Dept. AUS, 1943-46; col. Res.; ret.). Mem. Assn. Bar City N.Y. (past chmn. coms. including internat. law com.), Am., N.Y. State bar assns., UN Assn. U.S.A., Pilgrims, Phi Beta Kappa. Democrat. Clubs: Harvard (N.Y.C.); (L.I.) (dir.); Manhasset Bay Yacht, Appalachian Mountain. Home: 180 Middle Neck Rd Sands Point Port Washington NY 11050

BACKUS, JOHN, computer scientist; b. Phila., Dec. 3, 1924; s. Cecil Franklin and Elizabeth (Edsall) B.; m. Una Stannard, 1968; children: Karen, Paula. B.S., Columbia U., 1949, A.M., 1950. Programmer IBM, N.Y.C., 1950-53, mgr. programming research, 1954-59; staff mem. IBM T.J. Watson Research Center, Yorktown Heights, N.Y., 1959-63; IBM fellow IBM Research, Yorktown Heights and San Jose, Calif., 1963—. Editorial bd.: Internat. Jour. Computer and Info. Scis. Served with AUS, 1943-46. Recipient W. Wallace McDowell award IEEE, 1967; Nat. medal of Sci., 1975; Harold Pender award Moore Sch. Elec. Engring., U. Pa., 1983; Achievement award Indsl. Research Inst., Inc., 1983. Mem. Nat. Acad. Engring., Nat. Acad. Scis., Assn. Computing Machinery (Turing award 1977), Am. Math. Soc., European Assn. Theoretical Computer Sci. System designer IBM 704, Fortran programming lang., Backus-Naur Form Lang., function level programming; mem. design group ALGOL 60 lang. Home: 91 St Germain Ave San Francisco CA 94114 Office: IBM Research Lab 5600 Cottle Rd San Jose CA 95193

BACKUS, STANDISH, JR., artist; b. Detroit, Apr. 5, 1910; s. Standish and Lotta (Boyer) B.; m. Barbara Babcock, June 9, 1936; 1 dau., Virginia Boyer (Mrs. Sander Vanocur). Student in art and arch., Princeton U., 1929-33, U. Munich, 1933-34. Instr. U. Calif. extension, 1947-48; chmn. Affiliates of Art, U. Calif., Santa Barbara. Exhibited at, Art Inst. Chgo., Los Angeles County Mus., Salt Lake, Denver art museums, Detroit Art Inst., San Francisco, Santa Barbara museums art, Met. Mus. Art, N.Y.C., DeYoung Gallery, Phillips Gallery, Phila., Corcoran Gallery, Washington, Tate Gallery, London; represented in permanent collections, Santa Barbara Mus. Art, Utah State Coll., San Diego Fine Arts Gallery, Beckman Instruments, Inc., mural, 1955, Pacific War Meml., Corregidor Island, Manila, 1968, Nat. Watercolor Soc., Los Angeles County Mus., U.S. Navy Dept., Washington, also pvt. collections; ofcl. artist, IGY Deepfreeze Expdn., Antarctica, 1955-56. Pres. Citizens Planning Assn.; bd. trustees Santa Barbara Mus. Art, Santa Barbara Mus. Natural History, Santa Barbara Art Inst.; bd. dirs. Calif. Tomorrow, Regional Plan Assn., Santa Barbara Cottage Hosp.; mem. Santa Barbara Found., U. Calif., Santa Barbara Found. Served from ensign to comdr. USNR, 1941-46; as comdr., 1955-56; ofcl. navy combat artist, 1945; PTO. Recipient awards Oakland Art Gallery, 1939, Calif. Watercolor Soc., 1940, Calif. State Fair, 1948, 49. Fellow Internat. Inst. Arts and Letters; mem. Am., Nat. watercolor socs., Santa Barbara, Los Angeles art assns., Am. Fedn. Arts. Address: 2626 Sycamore Canyon Santa Barbara CA 93108 *To perceive ultimate truth through pursuit of excellence.*

BACON, CHARLES LANGSTON, lawyer; b. Marshall, Mo., Oct. 14, 1909; s. Charles B. and Nettie (Fry) B.; m. Helen Elizabeth Selvidge, Dec. 28, 1941; children: Sharon Ruth, Charles Langston. A.B., Missouri Valley Coll., 1930, LL.D., 1962; J.D., Mo. U., 1934. Bar: Mo. bar 1933, Fed. Ct 1934, Supreme Ct 1949, D.C. bar 1975. Partner Judge Robert D. Johnson, 1934; mem. firm James & Bacon, 1941-52; chief counsel Marketing div. Skelly Oil Co., 1952; now partner firm Shook, Hardy & Bacon. Editorial bd.: Mo. Law Rev, 1932-33. Sec. Jackson County Bd. Park Commrs., 1954-56; mem. Mo. Citizens Commn. for Study Pub. Schs., 1951-53; pres. Greater Kansas City Armed Forces Council, 1966-68, Mo. Boys' State, 1950-51; trustee Missouri Valley Coll., 1938—; pres. Liberty Meml. Assn., 1969-82. Served with USNR, 1942-46. Decorated commandeur Croix de Merite Combattant, France, 1962; recipient Legion of Honor Order de Molay, 1963; Meritorious Pub. Service citation U.S. Navy, 1962; Patriot of Year award SR, 1976; Disting. Service award Mo. dept. Am. Legion, 1978. Mem. Mo. Bar (gov.), Mil. Order World Wars, Am. Legion (Mo. comdr. 1950, nat. comdr. 1961-62), Acad. Mo. Squires, Phi Delta Phi, Omicron Delta Kappa, Sigma Nu. Club: Masons. Home: 1263 W 67th Terrace Kansas City MO 64113 Office: 1101 Walnut Ave Kansas City MO 64106

BACON, DAISY SARAH, editor, writer; b. Pa.; d. E. Ellsworth and Jessie M. (Holbrook) B. Ed. by pvt. tutors. Editor Love Story mag., 1928—, Ainslee's Mag., 1934-38, Smart Love Stories, 1937-39, Pocket Love mag., 1937, Detective Story and Romantic Range mags., 1940—; spl. overseas edit. Detective Story mag. for armed forces distbd. by Special Services div. A.S.F. U.S. Army, 1942-June 1946; publisher Gemini Books, 1963—. Compiler of four prize story anthologies annually: Love Story Annual; Author: Love Story Writer, 1953, 2d edit., 1959, Love Story Editor, 1963, The Golden Age at Street & Smith, 1975; Contbr. articles to mags. Spur Awards judge Western Writers Am., 1967-68. Mem. D.A.R. Republican. Episcopalian. Desc. Gov. William Bradford of Plymouth Colony, and Capt. John Holbrook of Weymouth. Home: 7 Hillside Ave Port Washington NY 11050

BACON, DAVID WALTER, university dean, chemical engineering educator; b. Peterborough, Ont., Can., Sept. 12, 1935; s. Arthur and Eleanor (Bothwell) B.; m. Lucille Ann Parks, July 6, 1963; children: Ann Marie, David Eric. B.A.Sc., U. Toronto, Can., 1957; M.S., U. Wis., 1962, Ph.D., 1965. Registered profl. engr., Ont., Can. Computations analyst Canadian Gen. Elect. Co., Peterborough, 1957-60; research group leader Du Pont Can. Inc., Kingston, Ont., 1965-67; assoc. prof. chem. engring. Queen's U., Kingston, Ont., 1968-73, prof., 1973—, dean of applied sci., 1980—; cons. Bell Can., Montreal, Que., 1977-80, BASF Wyandotte Corp., Wyandotte, Mich., 1978—, Andre Marsan and Associes, Montreal, 1981—, Imperial Oil Ltd., Sarnia, Ont., 1981—. Contbr. book chpts., articles to profl. jours. Bd. dirs. Kingston Gen. Hosp., 1983. Recipient Excellence in Teaching award Ont. Confdn. U. Faculty Assns., 1978. Fellow Am. Statis. Assn.; mem. Assn. Profl. Engrs. Province Ont., Nat. Com. Deans Enging. and Applied Sci. (chmn. 1982-83), Statis. Soc. Can., Can. Soc. Chem. Enging. Home: 368 Chelsea Rd Kingston ON Canada K7M 3Z9 Office: Queen's University Faculty of Applied Science Kingston ON Canada K7L 3N6

BACON, DONALD CONRAD, magazine editor; b. Jacksonville, Fla., Jan. 15, 1935; s. Francis Herbert and Myrtis Ann (Gunter) B.; m. Barbara Lee Barnwell, June 22, 1957; children—Elizabeth, Jennifer (dec.). B.S. in Journalism, U. Fla., 1957. Staff writer Wall St. Jour., 1957-61; Congl. fellow, 1961-62; staff writer Washington Star, 1962-63; successively Congl. corr., White House corr., sr. corr. and columnist Newhouse News Service, 1962-75; asso. editor U.S. News & World Report mag., Washington, 1975-79, sr. editor, 1979-81, asst. mng. editor, 1981—. Author: Congress and You, 1969; co-author: The New Millionaires, 1961. Recipient Loeb award U. Conn., 1961; award for excellence in journalism Lincoln U., Jefferson City, Mo., 1977. Mem. Sigma Delta Chi. Clubs: Cosmos, Fed. City (Washington). Home: 3809 East-West Hwy Chevy Chase MD 20815 Office: 2300 N St NW Washington DC 20037

BACON, EDMUND NORWOOD, city planner; b. Phila., May 2, 1910; s. Ellis W. and Helen (Comly) B.; m. Ruth Holmes, Sept. 16, 1938; children: Karin Ellis, Elinor Ruth, Hilda Holmes, Michael Comly, Kira, Kevin Norwood. B.Arch., Cornell U., 1932. Archtl. designer, Shanghai, China, 1934; with W. Pope Barney, architect, Phila., 1935; supr. city planning Inst. Research and Planning, Flint, Mich., 1937-39; mng. dir. Phila. Housing Assn., 1940-43; co-designer Better Phila. Exbn.; also sr. land planner Phila. City Planning Commn., 1946-49, exec. dir., 1949-70, also devel. coordinator, 1968-70; v.p. design devel. Mondev Internat. Ltd., 1972—; prof. adviser in Franklin D. Roosevelt Meml. Competition, 1959; adj. prof. U. Pa., 1950—. Author: Design of Cities, 1967, rev. edit., 1974; prod.: Understanding Cities film series Rome: Impact of an Idea, Paris: Living Space, John Nash and London, The American Urban Experience, The City of the Future, 1983. Mem. Pres.'s Citizen's Adv. Com. Recreation and Natural Beauty, 1966-69; Trustee Am. Acad. in Rome, 1965-76. Recipient Art Alliance Phila. medal achievement, 1961; Man of Year award City Bus. Club Phila., 1962; Brown medal award Franklin Inst., 1962; R.S. Reynolds award for community architecture, 1976; Fairmount Park Art Assn. medal of honor, 1976; Gold medal Royal Instn. Chartered Surveyors, 1974; Ford Found. travel fellow, 1959; Rockefeller fellow, 1963. Fellow AIA (medal 1976), Am. Inst. Planners (Distinguished Service award 1971, Phila. award 1983). Address: 2117 Locust St Philadelphia PA 19103

BACON, ERNST, musician; b. Chgo., May 26, 1898; s. Dr. Charles S. and Maria von (Rosthorn) B.; m. Mary Prentice Lillie, 1927; children—Margaret Frances and Joseph Rosthorn; m. Analee Camp, 1937; children—Paul Ernest Bacon, Arthur Bacon; m. Moselle Camp, 1952; 1 dau., Madeline K.; m. Ellen Wendt, 1972; 1 son, David Ernst. Student, Northwestern U., U. Chgo.; M.A., U. Calif., 1935; studied privately with, Alexander Raab, Glenn D. Gunn, Ernest Bloch, Karl Weigl. Appeared in concerts in, U.S. and, Europe; mem. faculty Eastman Sch., Hamilton Coll., Converse Coll.; founder Bach festival of Carmel, Calif., 1935; supr., condr. Fed. Music Project, San Francisco, 1935-37; dean Sch. of Music, Converse Coll., Spartanburg, S.C., 1938-45; dir. New Spartanburg Festival, 1939-45, Sch. Music, Syracuse U., 1945-47, composer-in-residence, now prof. emeritus. Composer 3 symphonies, 2 piano concertos, 4 orchestral suites; Fables for orch. and narrator By Blue Ontario's Shore Usania; oratorios Requiem Great River; orch., 4 series orchestral songs; music to A Tree on the Plains, The Tempest, And Yours, A. Lincoln (Paul Horgan); opera) (Paul Horgan) Take Your Choice; musical comedy in collagoration, 250 Songs; 2 Quintets (string) Spirits and Places; organ, also works for piano, 2 pianos, ch. music; 250 songs Requiem, Usania; oratorios, 2 ballets.; Author: 100 Fables, Words on Music, Notes on the Piano, The Honor of Music, Advice to Patrons, Imaginary Dialogues. Recipient Bispham Award Ditson and League of Composers Louisville Commns.; Pulitzer fellowship, 1932; Guggenheim fellowship, 1939, 1942; Campion citation; grant-citation Nat. Inst. of Arts and Letters, Am. Soc. Authors, Composers and Publishers. Home: 57 Claremont Ave Orinda CA 94563 *Praise and blame are the artist's climate: indifference a mere vacuum.*

BACON, HELEN HAZARD, classics educator; b. Berkeley, Calif., Mar. 9, 1919; d. Leonard and Martha (Stringham) B. B.A., Bryn Mawr Coll., 1940, Ph.D., 1955; postgrad., U. Calif. at Berkeley, 1940-41, Radcliffe Coll., 1941-42; Litt.D., Middlebury Coll., 1970. With communications div. U.S. Navy Dept., 1942; instr. Greek and freshman English Bryn Mawr Coll., 1946-49; instr. Latin N.C. Women's Coll., Greensboro, 1951-52; from instr. to asso. prof. classics Smith Coll., 1953-61; faculty Barnard Coll., N.Y.C., 1961—, prof. Greek and Latin, 1965—, chmn. dept., 1962-74; faculty Grad. Sch. Arts and Scis. Columbia U., 1975—; Scholar in residence Am. Acad. in Rome, 1968-69; faculty Bread Loaf Sch. English, summers 1966, 68, 73, 75; Blegen disting. vis. research prof. Vassar Coll., fall 1979; vis. prof. Harvard U., spring 1983. Author: Barbarians in Greek Tragedy, 1961; Translator: (with Anthony Hecht) Seven Against Thebes (Aeschylus), 1973; Contbr. to profl. jours. articles, revs. Served to lt. WAVES USNR, 1942-46. Fulbright fellow Am. Sch. Classical Studies, Athens, Greece, 1952-53; Founders fellow AAUW, 1963-64. Mem. Am. Philol. Assn. (dir. 1976-79, 2d v.p. 1983), Archaeol. Inst. Am., Classical assns. Empire State, Atlantic States, N.Y. Classical Club (v.p. 1965-67), ACLU (dir. Hampshire-Hamden chpt. 1959-60), Phi Beta Kappa (hon.). Home: 464 Riverside Dr New York NY 10027

BACON, JAMES EDMUND, banker; b. Mt. Vernon, N.Y., Feb. 27, 1931; s. John Anderson and Charlotte (Robb) B.; m. Edith Morgan Williamson, Oct. 5, 1963; children: Charlotte M., Rachel P., J. Nicholas. A.B., Harvard Coll., 1952, LL.B., 1958. Bar: D.C. 1959, N.Y. 1967. Assoc. Steadman, Collier & Shannon, Washington, 1958-61; atty.-adviser Securities and Exchange Commn., Washington, 1961-63; v.p. Am. Stock Exchange, N.Y.C., 1963-68; sr. v.p., dir. White, Weld and Co., N.Y.C., 1968-78; exec. v.p. U.S. Trust Co. of N.Y., 1978—. Trustee The Day Sch., N.Y.C., 1982—. Served to lt. (j.g.) USN, 1952-55. Mem. N.Y. State Bankers Assn. (dir. 1982—), Downtown-Lower Manhattan Assn. (dir., asst. treas. 1980—). Clubs: Racquet and Tennis (N.Y.C.); Metropolitan (Washington). Home: 169 E 69th St New York NY 10021 Office: US Trust Co of NY 45 Wall St New York NY 10005

BACON, JOHN JOSEPH, utility exec.; b. Cohasset, Mass., May 29, 1928; s. William C. and Mary A. (Nagle) B.; m. Mary A. Parrish, Jan. 16, 1954; children—Janice, Joan, John Joseph, Kathleen. B.S., Boston Coll., 1951; A.A. in Indsl. Engring, Northeastern U., 1961; grad. advanced mgmt. program, Harvard U., 1971. With Boston Gas Co., 1956—, staff engr., 1958-60, mgr. various depts., 1960-69, asst. v.p. customer relations, 1970, v.p. customer relations, 1971-75, sr. v.p., 1975-76, pres., 1976—; sr. v.p., trustee parent co. Eastern Gas & Fuel Assos. Dir. Boston Gas, Mass. Taxpayers Found., Inc., Blue Cross of Mass., Inc. Served to lt. (s.g.) USN, 1952-56. Mem. Inst. Gas Tech. (trustee), New Eng. Gas Assn. (2d v.p.), Am. Gas Assn. (dir.). Office: Boston Gas Co One Beacon St Boston MA 02108 *

BACON, LOUIS ALBERT, consulting civil engineer; b. Champaign, Ill., Apr. 10, 1921; s. Harrison Waxler and Mabel Mae (Watson) B.; m. Clara Elizabeth Manny, Aug. 28, 1943; children: Robert Louis, David Kenneth, William Harrison. B.S. in Civil Engring., U. Ill., 1943. Registered profl. engr., 20 states, D.C. Wing designer Douglas Aircraft Co., El Segundo, Calif., 1943-44; structural designer C.A. Metz Engring. Co., Chgo., 1946-47; chief structural engr. Shaw, Metz & Dolio, architects-engrs., Chgo., 1947-53; chief structural engr., asso. partner Shaw, Metz & Assos., Chgo., 1953-66; pres. P&W Engrs., Inc., cons., Chgo., 1966-74; v.p., head Atlanta div. Stanley Cons., Inc., 1974-76; v.p., dir. engring. div. Heery & Heery, Inc., architects-engrs., Atlanta, 1976—. Mem. planning com., Brookfield, Ill., 1951-54, mem. bd. local improvements, 1954-59, village trustee, 1954-59, mem. environ. protection commn., Glen Ellyn, Ill., 1971-74; pres. Ridgeview Neighborhood Civic Assn., Atlanta, 1980-82; chmn. Fulton County Developers Adv. Com., 1981. Served with USNR, 1944-46. Recipient Outstanding Achievement award Engrs. of Met. Atlanta, 1980. Mem. Nat. Soc. Profl. Engrs. (dir. 1966-69, v.p. 1969-71, pres.-elect 1982-83, pres. 1983-84, div. chmn. profl. engrs. in pvt. practice 1971-72, Chmn.'s award profl. engrs. in pvt. practice 1972, PEPP award 1976), Ill. Soc. Profl. Engrs, pres. 1964-65, Ill. award 1968), Ga. Soc. Profl. Engrs. (Pres.'s award Sandy Springs chpt. 1980, Engr. of Yr. award 1983), ASCE, U. Ill. Civil Engring. Alumni Assn. (pres. 1980-82), Chi Epsilon (hon.). Methodist. Club: Dunwoody (Ga.) Country. Home: 5240 W Kingston Ct NE Atlanta GA 30342 Office: 880 W Peachtree St NW Atlanta GA 30367

BACON, PEGGY, artist, writer; b. Ridgefield, Conn., May 2, 1895; d. Charles Roswell and Elizabeth (Chase) B.; m. Alexander Brook, May 4, 1920 (div.); children: Belinda, Alexander Bacon. Diploma, Kent Place Sch., Summit, N.J., 1913; student, Art Students League, Sch. Fine and Applied Arts, N.Y.C. Began as artist, 1920; tchr. art Fieldston Sch., N.Y.C., 1933-39; former tchr. life drawing, painting and composition Art Students League; tchr. drawing Hunter Coll., Stella Elkins Tyler Coll. Fine Arts, Phila., Corcoran Art Sch., Washington; past tchr. New Sch. Social Research, New Art Center, Kennebunk, Me., summers; tchr. Summer Sch. Music and Art, Stowe, Vt. Work represented in permanent collection, Met. and other museums, retrospective exhbn., Smithsonian Instn., 1975-76; Author and illustrator: Funeralities, 1925, Lion-hearted Kitten, 1927, Mercy and the Mouse, 1928, Ballad of Tangle Street, 1929, The Terrible Nuisance, 1931, Animosities, 1931, Mischief in Mayfield, 1933, Off with Their Heads, 1934, The True Philosopher, 1919, Catcalls, 1935, The Mystery of East Hatchett or Eric the Pink Viking, 1939, Starting from Scratch, 1945, The Good American Witch, 1957; author: novel The Inward Eye, 1952, The Oddity, 1962, The Ghost of Opalina, 1967; author, illustrator: The Magic Touch, 1968; illustrator more than 60 books; contbr. verse, drawings and stories to leading mags. Guggenheim fellow, 1934; grant Nat. Acad. Arts and Letters, 1942. Mem. Nat. Inst. Arts and Letters. Office: care Kravshaar Galleries 724 Fifth Ave New York NY 10019 *

BACON, PHILLIP, educator, geographer, author; b. Cleve., July 10, 1922; s. Hollis Phillip and Emma (Schneider) B.; m. Jane Lowrie, Nov. 21, 1980; children by previous marriage: Laura Jane (Mrs. Robert C. Fraser), Phillip Everett. Cadet, The Citadel, 1940-42; A.B., U. Miami, 1946; M.A., George Peabody Coll. for Tchrs., 1951, Ed.D., 1955. Tchr. social studies Castle Heights Mil. Acad., Lebanon, Tenn., 1946-47, Army and Navy Acad., Carlsbad, Calif., 1948-53; grad. asst. geography George Peabody Coll. for Tchrs. (now Vanderbilt U.), 1953-55; dean Grad. Sch., 1963-64; acting dir. Library Sch., 1964; asst. prof. geography U. Pitts., 1955-57; vis. asst. prof. geography Columbia Tchrs. Coll., 1956-57, asso. prof., 1957-60, prof., 1960-63, 64-66; prof. geography and social studies edn. U. Wash., Seattle, 1966-71, co-dir. tri-univ. project in elementary edn., 1967-71; prof. geography U. Houston, 1971—, chmn. dept., 1973-78; vis. prof. geography U. Colo., 1961, U. Wash., 1965, 79; Jennings lectr., 1963; vis. scholar N.C. Central U., 1966; vis. lectr. geography U. Tex., 1966, NSF vis. scientist, 1970-72; Disting. vis. prof. social studies edn. and geography Seattle Pacific U., 1977, 78, 79; editorial adv. bd. World Book Ency., 1965-84; bd. cons. World Book Atlas, 1965-70; cons. editor Golden Press, 1958-61; ednl. dir. Golden Book Inst. Knowledge, 1960-61; cons. book div. Time, Inc., 1960-69; cons. social sci. project Ednl. Research Council Am., 1962-70; mem. steering com. High Sch. Geography Project, 1965-70; cons. U.S. Office Edn., 1964-71; mem. Wash. Social Studies Adv. Commn., 1968-71; dir. Follett Social Studies Program, 1980-83, Allyn and Bacon social studies program, 1983—; curriculum cons. Author: Australia, Oceania, and the Polar Lands, 1961, North America, 1961, Children's Picture Atlas of the World, 1966, (with Norman Carls and Frank E. Sorenson) Knowing Our Neighbors in the United States, 1966, Knowing Our Neighbors in the United States and Canada, 1966, Regions Around The World, 1970, (with R.R. Boyce) Towns and Cities, 1970, (with others) The United States and Canada, 1970, (with P.V. Greco) The Story of Latin America, 1970, (with others) America: In Space and Time, 1976, Exploring Our World, 1982; Editor: Focus on Geography, Key Concepts and Teaching Strategies, 1970; co-editor: Foundations of World Regional Geography Series, 1970; cons. editor: Life Pictorial Atlas of the World, 1961; adv. bd.: Jour. of Geography, 1967-70, Social Edn, 1975-78; editorial dir.: Field Social Studies Program, 1972-73; co-dir.: Addison-Wesley Elementary Social Studies Program, 1973-80; Contbr. articles to profl. jours., also chpts. to books, yearbooks.; author: (with Donald C. Fairweather) World Regions, 1983, (with James B. Kracht) Our World Today, 1983, (with M. Evelyn Swartz) Our State: California, 1983. Served with USNR, 1942-45. Recipient Teaching Excellence award U. Houston, 1975, 79, 80. Fellow Royal Geog. Soc., Explorers Club; mem. Assn. Am. Geographers (council 1976-79, chmn. publs. com. 1976-78), Nat. Council for Geog. Edn. (life mem., pres. 1966, distinguished service award 1974), N.E.A. (life), Alaska Geog. Soc., Southwestern Social Sci. Assn., Geog. Educators Tex. (founder, co-dir. S.E. Tex. region), Am. Assn. Higher Edn., Nat., Tex., Ind. councils social studies, Vanderbilt U. Alumni Assn. (dir. 1979-83), Peabody Coll. Alumni Assn. (pres. 1981-83), Internat. Platform Assn., Sigma Xi, Sigma Alpha Epsilon, Phi Delta Kappa, Kappa Delta Pi, Kappa Phi Kappa (life), Omicron Delta Kappa, Gamma Theta Upsilon, Pi Gamma Mu. Presbyn. Home: 1302 Spyglass Dr Austin TX 78746 Office: Philip Guthrie Hoffman Hall U Houston Houston TX 77004

BACON, RICHARD FRANKLIN, motor transportation company executive; b. La Harpe, Kans., Jan. 13, 1927; s. Frank E. and Helen M. (Alderman) B.; m. Betty Anne Buchanan, Aug. 10, 1950; children: David, Dan, Randall. B.B.A., So. Methodist U., 1950; grad. transp. mgmt., Stamford U., 1969. Supts. ops. M&D Motor Freight Lines, Inc., Dallas, 1950-57; supt. terminals Merchants Fast Motor Lines, Inc., Abilene, Tex., 1957-62, pres., 1972—; with Merchants, Inc., Abilene, 1962—, dir., 1966—, exec. v.p., 1975-76, pres., 1976—, chief exec. officer, 1977—; dir. W. Tex. Utilities. Pres. Abilene Community Theatre's First Nighters, 1976; bd. dirs. Tex. Research League, 1977-83. Served with USNR, 1944-46. Mem. Am. Trucking Assn. (workshop leader), Tex. Motor Transp. Assn. (dir. common carrier group 1973-75, 77—), Dallas Safety Suprs. (chmn. 1956), Common Carrier Motor Freight Assn. (officer), Abilene C. of C. (past dir.), West C. of C. (exec. com., chmn. nat. affairs com. 1979-81), So. Meth. U. Alumni Assn. (past chpt. pres.), Alpha Tau Omega. Methodist. Clubs: Downtown Rotary (dir.), Abilene Country.). Home: 1460 Tanglewood Road Abilene TX 79605 Office: PO Drawer 3257 Abilene TX 79604

BACON, WALLACE ALGER, educator, author; b. Bad Axe, Mich., Jan. 27, 1914; s. Russell Alger and Mana (Wallace) B. A.B., Albion Coll., 1935, Litt. D., 1967; A.M., U. Mich., 1936, Ph.D., 1940; LL.D., Emerson Coll., 1975. Instr. English U. Mich., 1941-47; chmn. dept. interpretation Northwestern U., Evanston, Ill., 1947-79, asst. prof. English and speech, 1947-50, asso. prof. English and speech, 1950-55, prof. speech, 1955-80, prof. emeritus, 1980—; Fulbright lectr., Philippines, 1961-62, Fulbright-Hays lectr., 1964-65; vis. prof. U. Calif.-Berkeley, U. Wash., Nihon U., Tokyo; mem. adv. bd. Inst. for Readers Theatre, 1974—. Author: verse play Savonarola, 1950 (Bishop Sheil award 1946), William Warner's Syrinx, 1950, (with Robert S. Breen) Literature as Experience, 1959, Literature for Interpretation, 1961, (with N. Crame-Rogers and C. V. Fonacier) Spoken English, 1962, (with C.V. Fonacier) The Art of Oral Interpretation, 1965, The Art of Interpretation, 1966, 3d edit., 1979, Oral Interpretation and the Teaching of Literature in Secondary Schools, 1974; also articles, poetry, monographs.; Asso. editor: Quar. Jour. Speech, 1957-59, 63-65, 75-77, Speech Monographs, 1966-71; adv. editor: Lit. in Performance, 1980-82; assoc. editor, 1983—. Served with AUS, 1942-46. Decorated Legion of Merit; Alfred Lloyd postdoctoral fellow U. Mich., 1940-41; Rockefeller fellow, 1948-49; Ford Found. fellow, 1954-55; recipient Hopwood Major award writing drama U. MIch., 1936; spl. citation U. Philippines, 1965, 70; spl. commendation Ednl. Found. Philippines, 1965. Mem. Speech Communication Assn. (past pres. com. interpretation; chmn. com. publs. 1966, Golden Anniversary Prize Fund award 1965, 74, mem. bicentennial com. 1972-76, chmn. interpretation div. 1973, 2d v.p. 1975, 1st v.p. 1976, pres. 1977), N.Mex. Communications Assn., Western Speech Communication Assn., Communications Assn. of the Pacific (adv. bd. 1980—), Malone Soc., AAUP, Phi Beta Kappa, Delta Sigma Rho, Theta Alpha Phi, Zeta Phi Eta. Home: PO Box 2257 Taos NM 87571 *I believe in the significance of man as a social creature, and in the importance of service. No man has ever found himself except through becoming aware of others. A sense of the otherness of others—in a word, a knowledge of love—is for me the greatest of human virtues.*

BACOT, JOHN CARTER, banker; b. Utica, N.Y., Feb. 7, 1933; s. John Vacher and Edna (Gunn) B.; m. Shirley Schou, Nov. 26, 1960; children: Elizabeth, Susan. A.B., Hamilton Coll., Clinton, N.Y., 1955; LL.B., Cornell U., 1958. Bar: N.Y. 1959. With firm Utica, 1959-60; with Bank of N.Y., N.Y.C., 1960—, pres., 1974—, chief exec. officer, chmn., 1982—, also dir.; dir. Cirfico Holdings Corp., Home Life Ins. Co., Centennial Ins. Co., Bank of N.Y. Internat. Corp., Bank of N.Y. Co., Inc.; trustee Atlantic Mut. Ins. Co. Mem. Econ. Club N.Y., Pilgrims of U.S., Assn. Res. City Bankers. Episcopalian. Club: Montclair Golf. Home: 48 Porter Pl Montclair NJ 07042 Office: 48 Wall St New York NY 10015

BADCOCK, WOGAN STANHOPE, JR., company executive; b. Mulberry, Fla., Feb. 5, 1932; s. Wogan Stanhope and Evelyn Marie (Clark) B.; m. Mary Robison, Aug. 7, 1953; children: Mary Badcock

Stiles, Elizabeth Badcock Daughtrey, Wogan S., Henry C., Ben M. B.S. in Bus. Adminstrn., U. Fla. First v.p. W.S. Badcock Corp., Mulberry, Fla., 1959, bd. dirs., 1959-62, exec. v.p., 1963, pres., 1963—; dir. 1st Nat. Bank, Lakeland, Fla. Founding mem. Pres. Council U. Fla., Gainesville; active Pres. Council Fla. So. Coll., Lakeland; bd. dirs. So. Scholarship Found. Inc., Fla. State U., Tallahassee; active Gulf Ridge council Boy Scouts Am.; trustee YMCA, Lakeland. Served to capt. USAF, 1954-58. Episcopalian. Lodge: Kiwanis. Home: 7 Brook Ln Lakeland FL 33803 Office: WS Badcock Corp PO Box 497 200 Phosphate Blvd NW Mulberry FL 33860

BADDELEY, D. JEFFREY, sci. instrument co. exec.; b. N.Y.C., Apr. 8, 1938; s. P. William and Irene G. (Meek) B.; m. Jean C. Youngs, Aug. 11, 1962; children—Deborah Joan, Jeffrey Curtis. B.S. in Bus. Adminstrn, Northwestern U., 1959, J.D., 1962. Bar: Ohio bar 1962, Ill. bar 1967. Law clk. Russell & Bridewell, Chgo., 1961-62; asso. Squire, Sanders & Dempsey, Cleve., 1962-66; sr. atty. Armour & Co., Chgo., 1966-69; v.p., sec., gen. counsel Sargent-Welch Sci. Co., Skokie, Ill., 1969—, dir., 1979—; chmn., sec. Sargent-Welch Sci. Can., Ltd. Chmn. alumni awards com. Northwestern U., 1973-74; v.p., dir. Northwestern U. Alumni Assn., 1977-79; bd. dirs. Law Sch. Alumni Assn., 1977-82; Mem. local village polit. caucuses, 1970, 74; trustee Village of Lake Bluff, 1977-81; bd. dirs. Family Services. Merritt Found. scholar, 1959-62. Mem. Am., Ill., Chgo. bar assns., Am. Soc. Corporate Secs. Episcopalian (clk. vestry 1970-72). Home: 131 Moffett Rd Lake Bluff IL 60044 Office: 7300 N Linder Ave Skokie IL 60077

BADDOUR, RAYMOND FREDERICK, chemical engineer, educator; b. Laurinburg, N.C., Jan. 11, 1925; s. Frederick Joseph and Fannie (Rizk) B.; m. Anne M. Bridge, Sept. 25, 1954; children: Cynthia Anne, Frederick Raymond, Jean Bridge. B.S., U. Notre Dame, 1945; M.S., Mass. Inst. Tech., 1949; Sc.D., 1951. Asst. dir. Engring Practice Sch., Oak Ridge, 1948-49; asst. prof. Mass. Inst. Tech., 1951-57, asso. prof., 1957-63, prof. chem. engring, 1963—, Lammot du Pont prof. chem. engring., 1973—, also head dept., 1969-76; dir. Environ. Lab., 1970-76; Mem. project separation AEC, 1954; Am. Inst. Chem. Engrs. del. Mendeleev Conf. on Pure and Applied Chemistry, Moscow, 1959; lectr. Max Planck Insts., Germany, 1962; Shell lectr. Cambridge (Eng.) U., 1962; P.C. Reily lectr. Notre Dame U., 1964; mem. sci. adv. com. Gen. Motors Corp., 1971—; co-founder Abcor, Inc., Cambridge, Mass., 1963—; dir. Raychem Corp., 1972-80; founder, chmn. Energy Resources Co., Inc. (ERCO), 1974—; co-founder, chmn. ERCO AG, 1980; dir. Amgen, Inc., 1980—, Lam Research, 1980—; cons. Mobil Chem. Co., N.Y.C., 1963—, U.S. Dept. Commerce, 1960-62, Freeport Minerals Co., N.Y.C., 1976-83, Allied Chem. Co., 1980—. Mem. corp. Boston Museum Sci.; mem. sci. and tech. adv. bd. Field Enterprises, Chgo. (World Book Ency.), 1966-68. United Engrs. and Constructors preceptorship, 1956; NSF post-doctoral fellow, 1967-68; recipient honor award U. Notre Dame Coll. of Engring., 1976. Fellow Am. Inst. Chem. Engrs., Am. Inst. Chemists; mem. Am. Acad. Arts and Scis., Am. Chem. Soc., N.Y. Acad. Scis., AAAS, Sigma Xi. Research publs. and patents in field. Home: 96 Fletcher Rd Belmont MA 02178 Office: 77 Massachusetts Ave Cambridge MA 02139

BADEER, HENRY SARKIS, physician, educator; b. Mersine, Turkey, Jan. 31, 1915; came to U.S., 1965, naturalized, 1971; s. Sarkis and Persape Hagop (Koundakjian) B.; m. Mariam Mihran Kassarjian, July 12, 1948; children: Gilbert H., Daniel H. M.D., Am. U., Beirut, Lebanon, 1938. Gen. practice medicine, Beirut, 1940-51; asst. instr. Am. U. Sch. Medicine, Beirut, 1938-45, adj. prof., 1945-51, asso. prof., 1951-62, prof. physiology, 1962-65, acting chmn. dept., 1951-56, chmn., 1956-65; research fellow Harvard U. Med. Sch., Boston, 1948-49; prof. physiology Creighton U. Med. Sch., Omaha, 1967—, acting chmn. dept., 1971-72; vis. prof. U. Iowa, Iowa City, 1957-58, Downstate Med. Center, Bklyn., 1965-67; mem. med. com. Azounieh Sanatorium, Beirut, 1961-65; mem. research com. Nebr. Heart Assn., 1967-70. Author textbook; Contbr. chpts. to books, articles to profl. jours. Recipient Golden Apple award Students of AMA, 1975; Rockefeller fellow., 1948-49; grantee med. research com. Am. U. Beirut, 1956-65. Mem. AAAS, Internat. Soc. Heart Research, Am. Physiol. Soc., Alpha Omega Alpha. Home: 2808 S 99th Ave Omaha NE 68124 Office: Creighton U Med Sch 2500 Calif St Omaha NE 68178 *My success seems to be related to having set a goal and persevering in achieving it; satisfaction in or enjoyment of the performance of my daily task no matter how mundane; and eagerness to learn from personal experience or the experience of others.*

BADEN, THOMAS ARTHUR, filtration equipment manufacturing company executive; b. Mpls., Nov. 2, 1929; s. Arthur S. and Cathern (Royer) B.; m. Murlen Jane Hall, Oct. 7, 1950; children: Nancy S., Jill E., Tom Arthur, Christopher J. Engring. certificate mech. engring, U. Minn., 1953. Draftsman, designer, chief draftsman, contract mgr., chief engr. Donaldson Co., Mpls., 1949-70, dir. product engring., 1970-73, v.p. product engring., 1973-78, v.p./gen. mgr. fluid power div., 1978—; corp. dir. TTA, Inc., Bloomington, Minn., Muggins Stores, Edina, Minn.; assoc. Exec. Adv. Bd. Mem. fin. and bldg. coms. Nativity of Mary Ch. Mem. ASTM, Am. Inst. Design and Drafting (nat. v.p., dir.), Soc. Automotive Engrs., Soc. Plastics Engrs. Clubs: Loch Lomond Beach (pres.), Powdermill Assn. (bd. dirs.). Patentee in field. Office: 1400 W 94th St Bloomington MN 55431

BADER, ALBERT XAVIER, JR., lawyer; b. Bklyn., Oct. 19, 1932; s. Albert Xavier and Elizabeth Delores (Campion) B.; m. Patricia Anne Keeler, June 27, 1959; children: Albert X. III, Christopher F., Thomas J., Paul L. B.S. magna cum laude, Georgetown U., 1953; LL.B., Columbia U., 1956. Bar: N.Y. 1956, U.S. Supreme Ct. 1965. Assoc. firm Simpson Thacher & Bartlett, N.Y.C., 1956-69, ptnr., 1969—. Bd. dirs. St. Christopher-Jennie Clarkson Child Care Services, Dobbs Ferry, N.Y., 1980—. Served with U.S. Army, 1956-58. Mem. ABA, N.Y. State Bar Assn., Assn. Bar City N.Y., Fed. Bar Council, Gold Key Soc. Club: Larchmont Shore. Home: 30 Masterton Rd Bronxville NY 10708 Office: 1 Battery Park Plaza New York NY 10004

BADER, ALFRED ROBERT, chemist; b. Vienna, Austria, Apr. 28, 1924; came to U.S., 1947, naturalized, 1964; s. Alfred and Elizabeth Maria (Serenyi) B.; m. Isabel Overton, Jan. 26, 1982; children from previous marriage: David, Daniel. B.Sc. in Engring. Chemistry, Queens U., Can., 1945, B.A. in History, 1946, M.Sc. in Organic Chemistry, 1947; M.A., Harvard U., 1948, Ph.D., 1949; D.Sc. (hon.), U. Wis.-Milw., 1980, Purdue U., 1984, U. Wis.-Madison, 1984. Research chemist, group leader charge organic research PPG Co., Milw., 1950-54; chief chemist Aldrich Chem. Co., Milw., 1954-55, pres., 1955-81, chmn., 1981—; pres. Sigma-Aldrich Corp., Milw., 1975-80, chmn. bd., chief exec. officer, 1980-83, chmn. bd., 1983—. Author. Guest curator Milw. Art Center, 1976. Recipient Winthrop-Sears medal Chem. Industry Assn., 1980; named Entrepreneur of Year Research Dirs. Assn., 1980. Fellow Royal Soc. Arts; mem. Am. Chem. Soc. (award Milw. sect. 1971), Chem. Soc. London, Biochem. Soc. London, Coll. Art Assn. Jewish. Clubs: University (Milw.); Chemists (N.Y.C.). Patentee in field. Home: 2961 N Shepard Ave Milwaukee WI 53211 Office: 940 W St Paul Ave Milwaukee WI 53233

BADER, KENNETH LEROY, association executive; b. Carroll, Ohio, May 4, 1934; s. Troy Ora and Clara Louise (Walter) B.; m. Linda Mary Silbaugh, Sept. 17, 1955; children: Bradley, Brent. B.Sc., Ohio State U., 1956, M.Sc., 1957, Ph.D., 1960. Instr. agronomy, 1957-60, asst. prof., 1960-63, asso. prof., 1963-67; asst. dean Coll. Agr., 1964-67, prof., dean of students, 1968-72; vice chancellor, prof. agronomy U. Nebr., Lincoln, 1972-76; chief exec. officer Am. Soybean Assn., St. Louis, 1976—; mem. U.S. President's Export Adminstrn. Commn., 1982—, U.S. Agrl. Trade Policy Com., 1981—. Contbr. articles on agronomy to sci. jours. Mem. Regional Planning Com., Crime Commn., 1972; mem. exec. com. Conv. Bur., 1965-71; bd. dirs. YMCA, 1968-72, chmn., 1969-71. Named St. Louis Agribus. Leader of Yr., 1981; Am. Council on Edn. fellow, 1967-68. Mem. AAAS, Am. Soc. Agronomy, U.S. C. of C. (food and agr. com. 1980—), Sigma Xi, Alpha Zeta. Club: St. Louis Export. Address: American Soybean Assn 777 Craig Rd PO Box 27300 Saint Louis MO 63141

BADER, MICHAEL HALEY, lawyer; b. Tacoma, Aug. 28, 1929; s. Francis William and Gertrude Mary (Haley) B.; m. Joan Marie Berry, Aug. 21, 1954; children: Michael Haley, Brian Raymond, Mary Jennifer, Margaret Patricia, Joan Kerry. LL.B., George Washington U., 1952; M.Liberal Studies, Georgetown U., 1980. Bar: D.C. 1954. Since practiced in, Washington; partner firm Haley, Bader & Potts, 1959—; pres. Sta. WTID, Suffolk, Va., 1980—, Sta. WRCV, Mercersburg, Pa., 1983—; dir. MCI Communications Corp., Washington. Bd. advs. Georgetown Visitation Prep. Sch., Washington. Served to capt. AUS, 1952-54. Mem. Fed. Communications Bar Assn. (exec. com. 1971-74), D.C. Bar Assn. Republican. Roman Catholic. Club: Nat. Communications. Home: 5211 Wehawken Rd Bethesda MD 20816 Office: 2000 M St NW Washington DC 20036

BADER, RICHARD EUGENE, performing arts executive, theatre owner, city planner, real estate developer; s. Benjamin and Beatrice A. B. Grad. in econs., Hobart Coll.; M.C.P.A. in City Planning, Yale U. Jr. planner Candub, Fleissig & Assocs., Newark, 1960-61; asst. planner Raymond & May Assocs. for N.Y.C. Community Renewal Program, 1961-63; dir. sch. planning N.Y.C. Planning Commn., 1963-66; exec. dir. United Parents Assn., N.Y.C., 1966-67; asst. to commr. N.Y.C. Dept. Pub. Works, 1967-68; asst. adminstr. N.Y.C. Parks, Recreation and Cultural Affairs Adminstrn., 1968-72, dep. adminstr., 1972-74; curator for met. N.Y.C., N.Y. State Mus., Albany, 1974-76; cons. N.Y. State Mus., N.Y. State Bicentennial Commn., N.Y. City Cultural Affairs Commn., Westchester County Dept. Parks and Recreation, 1976-77; exec. dir. Am. Shakespeare Theatre, Conn. Ctr. for Performing Arts, Stratford, 1977-81; pres. Wilbur Theatre Operating Corp., Boston, 1981—. Hon. bd. dirs. Am. Concern for Art and Craftsmanship; mem. Com. for Harvard Theatre Collection. Recipient Parks Council award, 1973. Mem. Am. Planning Assn., Am. Assn. Museums, Internat. Council Museums, Friends of Cast Iron Architecture, Spanish Inst. Clubs: st. Botolph; Yale (Boston);; Met. Opera (N.Y.C.). Home: 47 E 64th St New York NY 10021 Office: 246 Tremont St Boston MA 02116

BADER, ROBERT SMITH, zoology educator and researcher; b. Falls City, Nebr., June 18, 1925; s. Ray Jay and Grace (Smith) B.; m. Joan Larson; children: Douglas, Jonathan, Eric, Joel. B.S., Kans. State U., 1949; Ph.D., U. Chgo., 1954. Instr., then asst. prof. biology U. Fla., 1952-56; from asst. prof. to prof. zoology U. Ill., Urbana, 1956-68; prof. biology, dean Coll. Arts and Scis., U. Mo.-St. Louis, 1968-83, research prof., 1983—. Served with USNR, 1943- 45. Mem. Soc. Vertebrate Paleontology, Western History Assn., North Central Assn. Colls. and Univs. Research Kans. history, Prohibition history. Home: 2925 SE 61st St Berryton KS 66409

BADER, WILLIAM BANKS, business executive, former government official; b. Atlantic City, Sept. 8, 1931; s. Edward L. and Celeste Nolan (Burkard) B.; m. Gretta Lange, Dec. 19, 1953; children: Christopher, Katharine, John, Karl. B.A., Pomona Coll., Claremont, Calif., 1953; M.A., Princeton U., 1960, Ph.D., 1964. With Library of Congress, 1954-55, Office Nat. Estimates, 1962-64; lectr. history Princeton U., 1964-65; with Dept. State, 1965-66, U.S. Senate Fgn. Relations Com., 1966-69; program officer, then European rep. Ford Found., 1969-73; program officer Office European and Internat. Affairs, Washington and; N.Y.C., 1973-74; fellow Woodrow Wilson Internat. Center Scholars, 1974-75; dir. fgn. intelligence task force U.S. Senate, 1975-76; asst. dep. under sec. for policy Dept. Def., 1976-78; staff dir. U.S. Senate Fgn. Relations Com., 1978-81; v.p. SRI Internat.-Washington, Arlington, Va., 1981—; adj. prof. Georgetown U. Author: Austria Between East and West: 1945-1955, 1966, The U.S. and the Spread of Nuclear Weapons, 1968; also articles. Served as officer USNR, 1955-58; to capt. USNR, ret. Recipient Meritorious Service medal Dept. State, 1966; Public Service medal Dept. Def., 1979. Mem. Council Fgn. Relations, Internat. Inst. Strategic Studies. Roman Catholic. Club: Cosmos (Washington). Office: SRI Internat 1611 N Kent St Arlington VA 22209

BADERTSCHER, DAVID GLEN, law librarian; b. Morrow, Ohio, Jan. 31, 1935; s. Glen C. and Blanche (Cluff) B.; m. Betty Jo Shafer, June 25, 1965. B.S., Ind. State U., 1957, M.S., 1962; M.S., Rosary Coll., 1967. Tchr. Rockville High Sch., Ind., 1957-59, Medinah Elem. Sch., 1961-63; librarian Elgin Acad., Ill., 1963-64; tchr. Beachwood High Sch., Ohio, 1964-65; librarian Chgo. Pub. Library, 1965-66; circulation, asst. reference librarian U. Chgo. Law Sch., 1966-70; librarian Schiff Hardin Waite Dorschel & Britton, Chgo., 1970-73; exec. librarian Georgetown U. Law Ctr., Washington, 1973-78; dir. library Milbank, Tweed, Hadley & McCloy, N.Y.C, 1978-80; prin. law librarian N.Y. Supreme Ct., N.Y.C., 1980—; cons. Urban Research Corp., Chgo., 1970-73, Herner & Co., 1977—, R.R. Bowker & Co., 1981—; advisor Computer Law Service, 1972-82, EIS, 1978—; adj. prof. Baruch Coll., 1982—. Contbr. articles to profl. jours. Served with AUS, 1959-61. Conv. grantee Am. Assn. Law Libraries, 1970. Mem. Medinah Tchrs. Assn. (pres. 1962-63), Am. Assn. Law Librarians (chmn. com. automation, sci. devel. 1970-72), Chgo. Assn. Law Librarians (pres., conf. chmn. 1970-72), Nat. Micrographics Assn., Am. Soc. Info. Sci. (editor SIG/Law Newsletter 1975-79), ABA (assoc.), Assoc. Info. Mgrs. Home: 46 Colony Ct New Providence NJ 07974 Office: 100 Centre St New York NY 10013

BADGLEY, THEODORE MCBRIDE, psychiatrist, neurologist; b. Salem, Ala., June 27, 1925; s. Roy Joseph and Fannie (Limbaugh) B.; m. Mary Bennett Wells, Dec. 30, 1945; children: Lynne Badgley O'Neil, Jan Badgley Wolkov, Mona Jean Badgley Correy, Jason Wells, James John, Mary Rose. Student, Occidental Coll., 1942-44; M.D., U. So. Calif., 1949. Diplomate: Am. Bd. Psychiatry and Neurology. Intern Letterman Gen. Hosp., San Francisco, 1949-50, resident in psychiatry, 1950-53; commd. capt. M.C. U.S. Army, 1950, advanced through grades to lt. col., 1967; chief mental hygiene cons. service, Ft. Gordon, Ga.; and asso. clin. prof. psychiatry and neurology Med. Coll. Ga., 1954-55; resident in neurology Walter Reed Gen. Hosp., Washington, 1955-57, asst. chief psychiatry service, 1957-59, chief psychiatry service, 1959-62, asst. chief dept. psychiatry and neurology, 1962-63, dir. edn. and tng. psychiatry, 1957-63; chief dept. psychiatry and neurology U.S. Army Gen. Hosp., Landstuhl, Germany, 1963-66; chief psychiatry outpatient dept. Letterman Gen. Hosp., 1966-67; ret., 1967; dir. Kern View Mental Health Center, Bakersfield, Calif., 1967-69; pvt. practice medicine specializing in psychiatry, Bakersfield, 1967—; pres. Sans Doloroso Inst., Bakersfield, 1969—; lectr. community health service orgns., profl. confs., seminars. Contbr. articles to profl. jours. Fellow Am. Psychiat. Assn. Home: 1733 Crestmont Dr Bakersfield CA 93306 Office: 1901 Truxtun Ave Bakersfield CA 93301 *My father is—will always be—30 years older than I.*

BADHAM, JOHN MACDONALD, motion picture dir.; b. Luton, Eng., Aug. 25, 1943; came to U.S., 1945, naturalized, 1950; s. Henry Lee and Mary Iola (Hewitt) B.; m. Bonnie Sue Hughes, Dec. 28, 1967 (div. 1979); 1 dau., Kelly MacDonald. B.A., Yale U., 1963, M.F.A., 1965. Asso. producer Universal Studios, 1969-70; pres. John Badham Films, Inc.; chmn. bd. JMB Films, Inc.; guest lectr. U. Calif., Irvine, U. So. Calif., Loyola Marymount Coll., U. Ala., Amherst Coll. Asso. producer: TV movies Night Gallery, 1969, Neon Ceiling, 1970; asso. producer, dir.: The Senator, 1970 (Emmy award nomination 1971); dir.: numerous episodes of The Bold Ones; others; motion pictures for TV include The Law (Emmy nomination 1974), 1974 (ARD reihe 'das film festival award 1975), Isn't It Shocking, 1973, Reflections of Murder, 1973, The Impatient Heart (Christopher award 1971), The Gun, (So. Calif. Motion Picture Council award 1974), The Godchild, 1974; theatrical motion pictures include The Bingo Long Travelling All Stars and Motor Kings (NAACP image award nomination 1976), Saturday Night Fever, 1977, Dracula, 1979 (Grand prize 9th Internat. Sci. Fiction Festival of Paris, Best Horror Film award and, 1st George Pal Meml. award), both Acad. of Sci. Fiction Fantasy and Horror Films. Served with U.S. Army, 1963-64. Mem. Dirs. Guild Am., Filmex Soc., Acad. Motion Picture Arts and Scis. Home: 7475 Mulholland Dr Los Angeles CA 90046

BADHAM, ROBERT E., congressman; b. Los Angeles, June 9, 1929; s. Byron J. and Bess (Kissinger) B.; m. Anne Carroll; children: Sharon, Robert, William, Phyllis, Jennifer. A.B., Stanford U., 1951. Vice pres., dir. Hoffman Hardware Co., Los Angeles, 1955-69; mem. Calif. Assembly from 71st Dist., 1962-76, 95th-98th Congresses from 40th Calif. Dist. Author articles. Mem. Orange Empire Area council Boy Scouts Am.; del. So. Pacific Dist. conv. Am. Lutheran Ch., 1967, Nat. conv., 1968; alt. del. Republican Nat. Conv., 1964-68; mem. Calif. Rep. Central Com., 1962—, Orange County Rep. Central Com., 1962—. Served to lt. (j.g.) USNR, 1952-54. Mem. Am. Soc. Archtl. Hardware Cons., Orange Coast Assn., Orange County Asso. Chambers Commerce, Am. Legion, Nat. Rifle Assn., Phi Gamma Delta. Office: 2438 Rayburn House Office Bldg Washington DC 20515

BADIAN, ERNST, history educator; b. Vienna, Austria, Aug. 8, 1925; came to U.S., 1968; s. Joseph and Sally (Horinger) B.; m. Nathlie A. Wimsett, 1950; children: Hugh I., Rosemary J. B.A., U. N.Z., 1945, M.A., 1946; B.A., Oxford (Eng.) U., 1950, M.A., 1954, D.Phil., 1956; Lit.D., Victoria U., Wellington, N.Z., 1962. Jr. lectr. classics Victoria U., 1947-48; asst. lectr. classics and ancient history U. Sheffield, Eng., 1952-54; lectr. classics U. Durham, Eng., 1954-65; prof. ancient history U. Leeds, Eng., 1965-69; prof. classics and history State U. N.Y., Buffalo, 1969-71; prof. history Harvard, 1971-82, John Moors Cabot prof. history, 1982—; vis. prof. univs. Colo., Oreg., Wash., S. Africa, Heidelberg, Tel-Aviv, U. Calif., Los Angeles; Sather prof. U. Calif., Berkeley, 1976; vis. mem. Inst. Advanced Study, Princeton, fall 1980. Author: Foreign Clientelae, 264-70 B.C (Conington prize Oxford U. 1958), Studies in Greek and Roman History, 1964, Roman Imperialism in the Late Republic, 1967, Publicans and Sinners, 1972; Editor: Polybius, 1966, Ancient Society and Institutions, 1966, Sir Ronald Syme, Roman Papers, 1979, Am. Jour. Ancient History, 1976—. Fellow Am. Council Learned Socs., 1972-73; Leverhulme fellow, Eng., 1973; John Simon Guggenheim Meml. fellow, 1984. Fellow Brit. Acad., Am. Acad. Arts and Scis.; hon. mem. Soc. Promotion Roman Studies; corr. mem. Austrian Acad. Scis., German Archeol. Inst.; mem. Am. Inst. Archaelogy, Am. Numis. Soc., Am. Philol. Assn., Assn. Ancient Historians, Classical Assn. Can., U.K. Classical Assn., Soc. Promotion Hellenic Studies, Virgil Soc., Assn. Univ. Tchrs. U.K. Office: Robinson Hall Harvard Univ Cambridge MA 02138

BADIE, JOHN WILLIAM, history educator; b. Ft. Smith, Ark., Dec. 18, 1935; s. William Robert and Helen (Montgomery) B.; m. Joan Holt, Aug. 19, 1957; children: Robin, Christopher. B.A. with honors, U. Ark., 1957; M.A., U. Chgo., 1959; Ph.D., Univ. Coll., London, 1962. Asst. prof. Ripon Coll., Wis., 1962-63; asst. prof. history U. Mich., Ann Arbor, 1963-67, assoc. prof., 1967-73, prof., Ann Arbor, 1973—, Richard Hudson prof. history, Ann Arbor, 1981-82, assoc. chmn. dept. history, Ann Arobr, 1970-71; humanities-arts advisor Office Vice Pres. for Research, U. Mich., Ann Arbor, 1974—; assoc. dir. Ctr. for Coordination Ancient Modern Studies, U. Mich., Ann Arbor, 1972-74; dir. Summer Inst. in Ancient History, Ann Arbor, 1977; vis. fellow Clare Hall, Cambridge U., Eng., 1968-69; co-dir. Bononia excavation, Banostor, Yugoslavia, 1970-72; dir. Humayama survey, Jordan, 1982—. Author: The Breviarium of Festus: A critical-Edition with Historical Commentary, 1967, The Conversion of Constantine, 1971, (with others) Western Civilization, 1975; editor: Classical traditions in Early America, 1976. Trustee Ann Arbor Summer Festival, 1979—; chmn. Mich. Council for Humanities, E. Lansing, Mich., 1977-80. Marshall scholar Brit. Marshall Commn. Univ. Coll., Eng., 1960-62; recipient Disting. Service award Mich. Council Humanities, 1980. Mem. Am. Hist. Assn., Assn. Ancient Historians, Soc. Promotion Roman Studies, Archaeol Inst. Am. Democrat. Presbyterian. Office: Dept History U Mich Ann Arbor MI 48109

BADIE, RONALD PETER, banker; b. Elizabeth, N.J., Dec. 13, 1942; s. R. Peter and Madeline E. (Knoop) B.; m. Helen Joan Burkhart; children: Tracey, Tamara, Tara. B.S., Bucknell U., 1964; M.B.A., NYU, 1971. Sr. v.p. Bankers Trust Co., N.Y.C., 1979—; dir. B.T. Australia Ltd., Sidney, Thai Investment Securities Co., Bangkok. Republican. Home: 2046 Oak Knoll Ave San Marino CA 91108 Office: Bankers Trust Co 400 S Hope St Los Angeles CA 90071

BADILLO, HERMAN, lawyer, accountant, former congressman; b. Caguas, P.R., Aug. 21, 1929; s. Francisco and Carmen (Rivera) B.; m. Irma Deutsch, May 7, 1961; children: Loren, Mark, David. B.B.A. magna cum laude, City Coll. N.Y., 1951, LL.D., 1972; J.D. cum laude, Bklyn. Law Sch., 1954. Bar: N.Y. bar 1955; C.P.A., N.Y. State. Asso. firm Ferro, Berdon & Co. (C.P.A.'s), N.Y.C., 1951-55; mem. firm Permut & Badillo, N.Y.C., 1955-61; dep. commr. N.Y.C. Dept. Real Estate, 1962; commr. N.Y.C. Dept. Relocation, 1962-65; pres. Borough of Bronx, 1966-69; mem. firm Stroock and Stroock and Lavan, N.Y.C., 1970, of counsel, 1971-73; mem. 92d-95th congresses from 21st dist. N.Y.; dep. mayor for mgmt. City of N.Y., 1978-79, dep. mayor for policy, 1979; mem. firm Cohn Glickstein Lurie Ostrin Lubell & Lubell, N.Y.C., 1979-81, Fischbein Olivieri Rozenholc & Badillo, 1981—; Adj. prof. Fordham U. Grad. Sch. Urban Edn., 1970-81. Author: A Bill of No Rights: Attica and The American Prison System, 1972. Del. N.Y. State Constl. Conv., 1966; Bd. dirs. Mt. Sinai Hosp., N.Y.C.; chmn. Gov.'s Adv. Commn. on Hispanic Affairs, State of N.Y., 1983—. Mem. Beta Gamma Sigma, Alpha Beta Psi, Sigma Alpha. Democrat. Home: 405 W 259th St Bronx NY 10471 Office: 230 Park Ave Suite 2425 New York NY 10169

BADURA-SKODA, PAUL, pianist; b. Vienna, Austria, Oct. 6, 1927; s. Ludwig and Margarete (Winter) Badura; m. Eva L. Halfar, Sept. 19, 1951; children—Ludwig, Maria Christina, Elisabeth, Michael. Pvt. piano lessons with, Viola Thern, Conservatory of Vienna, 1945-48; summer classes with, Edwin Fischer, Lucern, Switzerland, 1948, 1950, 51, 54. Vis. prof. U. Wis., spring 1964, Stanford, summer 1965; artist in residence U. Wis., 1966-71. Concert debut, Vienna, 1948; concerts with condrs. Furtwangler and Karajan, 1949; pianist, Salzburg Festival, 1950, concert tours, Western Europe, 1950-52, Australia,

1952, U.S. and Can., 1952-53, South and Central Am., U.S., Can., 1953, Western Europe, U.S., 1954-55, U.S., Canada, Australia, New Zealand, 1956, Far East, 1960-61, 63, regular concert tours through all European countries, 1956—, S.Am., 1962, 63, N.Y.C., 1964; Author: (with Dr. E. Badura) Mozart Interpretation, 1957, Interpreting Mozart on the Keyboard, 1962, (with Jörg Demus) Die Klaviersonaten von Ludwig van Beethoven, 1970; cadenzas for several Mozart Concertos, 1962, numerous LP recordings.; Completion of Mozart's Larghetto and Allegro; for two pianos, 1960, of five unfinished Schubert piano sonatas, 1968; Editor several Urtext edits. (Mozart concerti, Schubert piano compositions, Chopin studies, others), 1964—. Recipient 1st award in Austrian competition, Vienna, 1947; 2d award Internat. Bartok Competition, Budapest, 1948; Austrian medal in Gold, 1976. Home: 5811 S Dorchester Ave Chicago IL 60637 Office: care Thea Dispeker Artists Representatives 59 E 54th St New York NY 10022

BAECHLE, JAMES JOSEPH, lawyer, banker; b. Lancaster, Ohio, Nov. 25, 1932; s. Robert John and Helen Pauline (Kennedy) B.; m. Christine Broker Ayres, Sept. 24, 1972; stepson, Charles Ayres. B.S., Ohio State U., 1954; LL.B., Harvard U., 1957. Bar: N.Y. Assoc. firm White & Case, N.Y.C., 1959-67, Paris, 1962-64; v.p., sec., gen. counsel Brown Co., N.Y.C. and Los Angeles, 1967-71; v.p., gen. counsel Bankers Trust N.Y. Corp., N.Y.C., 1971-73, Bankers Trust Co., 1971-73, sr. v.p. and gen. counsel, 1973-79, exec. v.p. and gen. counsel, 1979—. Active Pres.'s Council Ctr. for Internat. Studies, NYU, 1967. Served to capt. USAF, 1957-59. Mem. ABA, N.Y. State Bar Assn., Internat. Bar Assn., Bar Assn. City N.Y. Clubs: Harvard (N.Y.C.); Piping Rock (Locust Valley, N.Y.); Beaver Dam Winter (Locust Valley); Seawanhaka Corinthian Yacht (Oyster Bay, N.Y.); Cove Neck Tennis (Oyster Bay). Home: Horseshoe Rd Mill Neck NY 11765 Office: Bankers Trust Co 280 Park Ave New York NY 10017

BAEDER, DONALD LEE, petroleum company executive; b. Cleve., Aug. 23, 1925; s. Arthur and Augusta Wanda (Mather) B.; m. Barbara Ayres, June 9, 1952; children: Donald Scott, David A., Ellen J., Richard L., James D. B.A. in Chemistry, Baldwin Wallace Coll., 1951; B.S. in Chem. Engring, Carnegie Inst. Tech., 1951. With Exxon Research & Engring. Co., 1951-65, 67-76, gen. mgr. chems. research, Linden, N.J., 1967-68, v.p. corp. and govt. research, 1968-76; mgr. Enjay Chem. Co., N.Y.C., 1965-67; pres. Hooker Chem. Corp., Houston, 1976-80; exec. v.p. sci. and tech. Occidental Petroleum, Los Angeles, 1980—. Contbr. articles to tech. publs. Dist. commr. Boy Scouts Am., 1963-64, councilman, 1967-68, mem. dist. fin. com., 1968; pres. Carnegie-Mellon U. Alumni Council; mem. vis. com. U. Tex.; trustee Baldwin-Wallace Coll., Valparaiso U., Carnegie-Mellon U. Served with AUS, 1943-46. Fellow Am. Chem. Soc.; mem. Am. Inst. Chem. Engrs., Assn. Research Dirs. Clubs: Glen Wild Lake Country, Braeburn Country. Office: PO Box 344 Niagara Falls NY 14302

BAENSCH, ROBERT EDUARD, publisher; b. Leipzig, Ger., Sept. 4, 1934; came to U.S., naturalized, 1948; s. Willy E. and Hilda L. (Stoehr) B.; m. June Otani, Dec. 5, 1965; children: Hiroshi Michael, Miyoko Erika. B.S., Johns Hopkins U., 1957; postgrad., Grad. Sch. Bus., Stanford U., 1980. Mng. editor Grune & Stratton, Inc., N.Y.C., 1958-60; with McGraw-Hill Book Co., 1960-68, editorial dir. internat. dept., 1965-68; v.p., dir. internat. div. Harper & Row Pubs., Inc., 1968-80; pres., chief exec. officer Springer-Verlag N.Y., Inc., 1980-83; v.p. McGraw-Hill Internat. Book Co., 1983—; dir. Springer-Verlag, Heidelberg, W. Ger.; mem. faculty Pub. Center, N.Y. U., 1980—, Stanford U. Pub. Inst., 1980-81, Pub. Inst., U. Denver, 1981—. Author articles in field. Recipient Freedom to Publish award Israeli Pubs. Assn., 1977. Mem. Internat. Pubs. Assn. (exec. com.), Assn. Am. Pubs. (bd. dirs. 1981—, exec. com. profl. and scholarly pubs. div., Internat. Service award 1979), Sci., Tech. and Med. Pubs. Assn. Lutheran. Club: N.Y. Caledonian Curling. Office: 1221 Ave of the Americas New York NY 10020

BAER, BEN KAYSER, cotton merchant; b. Charleston, W. Va., June 26, 1926; s. Frank Adler and Helen (Kayser) B.; m. Eleanor Hirsch, Nov. 5, 1953; children: Julie Ann, Ben, Frank Edward. B.A., Phillips Exeter Acad., 1944; A.B., Princeton U., 1948; LL.B., Yale U., 1950. Ptnr. Campbell, McClintic & Jones, Charleston, 1950-57; chmn. bd. Allenberg Cotton Co., Memphis, 1965—, N.Y. Cotton Exchange, 1983; pres. Am. Cotton Shippers, 1974, So. Cotton Shippers, Memphis, 1970. Served with USNR, 1944-46. Mem. Phi Beta Kappa. Jewish. Home: 5026 Greenway Rd Memphis TN 38117 Office: Allenberg Cotton Co PO Box 154 Memphis TN 38101

BAER, BENJAMIN FRANKLIN, federal official, criminologist; b. Peoria, Ill., Jan. 2, 1918; s. Henry and Emma (Siebenthal) B.; m. Dorothea Frances Heiman, Mar. 20, 1942; children: Marc Bradley, Meredith Jan, Bartley Benjamin F. B.A., San Diego State U., 1941; M.S.W., U. So. Calif., 1947, postgrad., 1964. Camp dir. Probation Dept., Los Angeles, 1942-47; sociologist, supr. classification Dept. Corrections San Quentin, Sacramento, 1947-54; assoc. warden San Quentin, 1954-60; dir. Dept. Corrections State of Iowa, Des Moines, 1960-64, Correctional Decision Info. Project, Sacramento, 1965-67; dep. commr., chmn. youth commn. Minn. Dept. Corrections, St. Paul, 1967-72; hearing examiner U.S. Parole Commn., Washington and Burlingam, Calif., 1972-81, commr., Washington and Burlingam, 1981—, chmn., 1982—; planning commn. Nat. Inst. Crime and Delinquency, Minn., 1969; dir. Nat. Inst. Corrections, 1982—, Adv. Correctional Council, Washington, 1982—; mem. Pres. Kennedy's Juvenile Deliquence Commn., 1961-63; treas., exec. com. Nat. Assn. State Juvenile Delinquency Program, Minn., 1968-71. Author (with Harlan Hill) California Correctional Information System: Preliminary Information System Design, 1967. Bd. dirs. Unitarian Ch., Des Moines, 1961-63. Mem. Am. Correctional Assn. (dir. 1962-65), Assn. Paroling Authorities, Nat. Council Crime and Delinquency (profl. council 1961-71), Nat. Assn. Social Work, Calif. Probation, Parole and Correctional Assn., Phi Sigma Kappa. Republican. Home: 11008 Wickshire Way Rockville MD 20852 Office: U S Parole Commn 5550 Friendship Blvd Chevy Chase MD 20815

BAER, ERIC, science educator; b. Nieder-Weisel, Germany, July 18, 1932; came to U.S., 1947, naturalized, 1952; s. Arthur and Erna (Kraemer) B.; m. Ana Golender, Aug. 5, 1956; children: Lisa, Michelle. M.A., Johns Hopkins, 1953, D.Engrng., 1957. Research engr., polychems. dept. E.I. du Pont de Nemours & Co., Inc., 1957-60; asst. prof. chemistry and chem. engring. U. Ill., 1960-62; assoc. prof. engring. Case Inst. Tech., 1962- 66; prof., head dept. polymer sci. Case Western Res. U., 1966-78; dean Case Inst. Tech., 1978-83, Leonard Case prof. macromolecular sci., 1984—; cons. to industry, 1961—. Author articles in field.; Editor: Engineering Design for Plastics, 1963, Polymer Engineering and Science, 1967—. Recipient Curtis W. McGraw award ASEE, 1968. Mem. Am. Chem. Soc. (Borden award 1981), Am. Phys. Soc., Am. Inst. Chem. Engring., Soc. Plastics Engring. (internat. award 1980), Plastics Inst. Am. (trustee). Home: 2 Mornington Ln Cleveland Heights OH 44106 Office: Case Western Res Univ: Cleveland OH 44106

BAER, HANS HELMUT, chemist, educator; b. Karlsruhe, Germany, July 3, 1926; s. Paul and Elsa (Menges) B.; m. Gertrud H. Mackprang, May 1956; children—Thomas, Nicole. Cand. chem., Karlsruhe Tech. U., 1948; Dipl. Chem., U. Heidelberg, Germany, 1950, Dr. rer. nat., 1952. Research asso. Max Planck Inst. for Med. Research, Heidelberg, 1952-57; vis. asst. prof. dept. biochemistry U. Calif. at Berkeley, 1957-59; vis. scientist NIH, Bethesda, Md., 1959-61; faculty U. Ottawa, Ont., Can., 1961—, prof. chemistry, 1965—, chmn. dept., 1969-75. Contbr. articles to profl. jours. Fellow Chem. Inst. Can.; mem. Am. Chem. Soc. (chmn. div. carbohydrate chemistry 1973-74, Claude S. Hudson award 1975), Gesellschaft Deutscher Chemiker. Home: 54 Rothwell Dr Ottawa ON Canada

BAER, HENRY, lawyer; b. Wissen a/sieg, Germany, Dec. 30, 1930; came to U.S., 1940, naturalized, 1946; s. Ernest and Anneliese (Bernstein) B.; m. Anne Sanders, June 16, 1966; children—Lisa Ann, Henry Douglas. Student, Columbia U., 1950; B.A., So. Meth. U., 1952, LL.B., 1955. Asso. firm Wynne & Wynne, Attys., 1957-63; partner firm McKenzie & Baer, Dallas, 1963—; agt. for Don Meredith (in football and TV.). Served with AUS, 1955-57. Mem. Am., Tex. bar assns., Am. Contract Bridge League (exec. sec. dist.), Phi Beta Kappa. Home: 5512 Royal Crest St Dallas TX 75229 Office: 26th floor LTV Tower Dallas TX 75201

BAER, JOSEPH WINSLOW, lawyer; b. Chgo., Sept. 15, 1917; s. Joseph Louis and Gretchen Winslow (Shattuck) B.; m. Nanette Talbot, June 14, 1952; children—Richard, Elizabeth, Jennifer. A.B., U. Chgo., 1938, J.D., 1940. Bar: Ill. bar 1940, U.S. Dist. Ct. bar 1946. Law clk. Judge Ulysses S. Schwartz, 1945-46; asso. firm Brown, Fox & Blumberg, 1946-47; partner firm Jones Baer & Davis, Chgo., 1947—; also lectr. Instr. John Marshall Law Sch., 1956-61; lectr. in matrimonial law. Author: Merit in No Fault Divorce; Contbr. articles on matrimonial law to profl. jours. Active amateur theater., Republican candidate for municipal ct. judge, Chgo., 1956; mem. com. lawyers action Senator Charles Percy campaigns, Gov. Athletic Supporters Inst. Served to lt. comdr. USNR, 1940-45; PTO. Fellow Am. Acad. Matrimonial Law (founding); mem. Am. Bar Assn., Ill. Bar Assn., Chgo. Bar Assn. (chmn. com. entertainment 1976—), Psi Upsilon, Phi Delta Phi. Episcopalian. Clubs: Adventurers of Chicago, Law of Chicago, Tavern of Chicago. Home: 780 Greenwood St Glencoe IL 60022 Office: 140 S Dearborn St Chicago IL 60603

BAER, JULIUS ARTHUR, II, merchant; b. St. Louis, Apr. 18, 1921; s. Arthur B. and Lucile (Calisch) B.; m. Mary Pauline; children: Julius Arthur, Patricia Anne Robin, Terence Michael. A.B., Duke U., 1943. Asst. field dir. ARC, 1943-46; with Stix, Baer & Fuller Co., dept. store, St. Louis, 1946—; div. mdse. mgr. Stix, Baer & Fuller Co., 1955-57, br. store mgr., 1957-59, v.p. charge total store merchandising and publicity, 1959-61, exec. v.p., 1961-63, pres., chief exec. officer, 1963-76, chmn. bd., 1973-76, hon. chmn. bd., 1976—, also dir., 1963-76; v.p. Asso. Dry Goods; dir. Union Electric Co., Merc. Trust Co., Boston Store, CMC Corp. Bd. dirs., past pres. Downtown St. Louis, Inc.; bd. dirs. St. Louis area council Boy Scouts Am.; bd. dirs. Govtl. Research Inst., Jefferson Nat. Expansion Meml., St. Louis Jewish Hosp., St. Louis Symphony Soc., Herbert Hoover Boys' Club of St. Louis, Inc., United Fund of Greater St. Louis; bd. dirs., past chmn., pres. St. Louis Mcpl. Opera; bd. dirs. Mathew Duckey Boys' Club; chmn. bd. Public Edn. TV Sta. KETC, 1980; chmn. Council on World Affairs; bd. dirs. Dance Concert Soc. St. Louis Theatre Project Co. Recipient Medal of Honor Centre Nationale du Commerce Exterieur, French Govt., 1960; Ordre de L'economie French Govt., 1965; Al Mérito Turistico, Spanish Govt., 1968; Am. Legion citation, 1969. Mem. Am. Retail Fedn. (dir. 1977-83), Nat. Retail Mchts. Assn. (dir. 1974-77), Omicron Delta Kappa, Theta Alpha Phi, Zeta Beta Tau. Office: 515 Olive St Suite 1505 Saint Louis MO 63101

BAER, KENNETH PETER, farmer cooperative executive; b. Deer Creek, Okla., May 20, 1930; s. Samuel Benjamin and Viola Emelia (Peter) B.; m. Mary Ann Blumenstein, May 20, 1950; children: Jeff Wayne, James Lee. Grad. exec. program, Stanford U. Salesman Summerfield Farmers Coop Grain Co., Ill., 1948-52; mgr. grain and farm supplies Bond County Service Co., Greenville, Ill., 1952-53; with Growmark, Inc., 1955—, dir. market devel., then v.p. field services, Bloomington, Ill., 1966-76, group v.p. supply ops., 1976-82, exec. v.p., chief exec. officer, 1982—; chmn. bd. CF Industries, Inc., Long Grove, Ill., 1979—; dir. Nat. Coop. Refinery Assn., McPherson, Kans. Vice pres. bd. Mennonite Hosp., Bloomington. Served with AUS, 1953-55. Home: 2810 E Oakland St Bloomington IL 61701 Office: 1701 Towanda Ave Bloomington IL 61701

BAER, MARK HOMER, librarian; b. Pendleton, Oreg., June 24, 1923; s. George Clinton and Ermal Oleta (Mann) B.; m. Elizabeth Carter, Sept. 20, 1947; children: Christopher, Nicholas. B.A. in History, U. Wash., Seattle, 1950, M.L.S., 1955. Catalog librarian Law Library U. Wash., 1955-56, chemistry br. librarian, 1956-57; librarian engring./tech. div. Oreg. State U., 1957-59; dir. tech. info. services Ampex Corp., Redwood City, Calif., 1959-66; dir. libraries Hewlett-Packard Co., Palo Alto, Calif., 1966—; mem. Calif. Library Services Bd., 1982-84; instr. U. Calif., Berkeley, 1965, lectr., 1966-70. Contbr. articles to profl. jours., chpts. to books. Served with AUS, 1942-45. Recipient Distinguished Alumnus award U. Wash. Sch. Librarianship, 1976. Mem. Spl. Libraries Assn. (pres. 1976-77), IEEE, Internat. Fedn. Library Assns., Assn. Computing Machinery. Republican. Home: 11 Bournemouth Rd St Helena CA 94574 Office: Corp Library 1501 Page Mill Rd Palo Alto CA 94304

BAER, MAX ADELBERT, JR., actor, producer, dir.; b. Oakland, Calif., Dec. 4, 1937; s. Max Adelbert and Mary Ellen (Sullivan) B.; m. Joanna Baer, Aug. 1966 (div. 1970). B.A. in Bus, U. Santa Clara, Calif., 1959. Actor for Warner Bros. Pictures, 1960-61. Actor in: TV series Beverly Hillbillies, 1962-71; author, producer, actor: film Macon County Line, 1974; author, producer, dir., actor: The Wild McCulloch's, 1975; producer, dir.: Ode to Billy Joe, 1976, Hometown U.S.A, 1979. Served with USAF. Recipient Venice Film Festival award for Ode to Billy Joe, 1976. Mem. Dirs. Guild Am., Screen Actors Guild. Roman Catholic. Clubs: Tiffanys (dir.), Pips, Jockey (dir.). *

BAER, MICHAEL ALAN, political scientist, educator; b. Atlanta, Feb. 4, 1943; s. Kurt Arthur and Beulah (Mendelson) B.; m. Charlotte Glazer, Aug. 16, 1964; children: Daniel Noach, Naomi Aviva. B.A., Emory U., 1964; M.A., U. Oreg., 1966, Ph.D., 1968. Research asst. Center Advanced Study Ednl. Adminstrn., U. Oreg., 1964-68; mem. faculty U. Ky., Lexington, 1968—, prof. polit. sci., 1980—, chmn. dept., 1977-81, dean Coll. Arts and Scis., 1981—; polit. analyst WAVE-TV, Louisville. Co-author: Lobbying: Influence and Interaction in American State Legislatures, 1969; editorial bd.: State and Local Govt. Rev, 1977-81; contbr. articles to profl. jours. Bd. dirs. Central Ky. Civil Liberties Union, 1973-77, Congregation Ohavay Zion, Lexington, 1976-78, Bluegrass chpt. NCCJ, 1980-81; bd. dirs. Central Ky. Jewish Assn., 1970-74, 79—, pres., 1973-74; rec. sec. Bluegrass chpt. Ky. Assn. Gifted Edn., 1983—. Leverhulme fellow, 1974-75. Mem. Am. Polit. Sci. Assn., Midwest Polit. Sci. Assn. (exec. council 1980-83), Brit. Politics Group (exec. council 1978-80), So. Polit. Sci. Assn., Ky. Conf. Polit. Sci. Home: 985 Maywick Dr Lexington KY 40504 Office: 1615 Patterson Office Tower Univ Ky Lexington KY 40506

BAER, NORBERT SEBASTIAN, chemist, art conservator, educator; b. Bklyn., June 6, 1938; s. William Frederick and Maria (Berger) B.; m. Janet Lucy Depold, June 20, 1959; children: Diana Maria, Norbert Sebastian. B.Sc., Bklyn. Coll., 1959; M.Sc., U. Wis., 1962; Ph.D., NYU, 1969. Researcher Time Inc., 1963-64; lectr. Queensborough Community Coll., 1967, asst. prof., 1968; instr. Conservation Center, Inst. Fine Arts, NYU, 1969, asst. prof., 1970-75, assoc. prof., 1975-78, prof., 1978—; co-chmn., 1975-83; acting dir. adminstrn. Inst. Fine Arts, 1978-79; mem. exec. com. Adv. Council Hist. Preservation, Internat. Center Com., 1976—, del., 1971—; mem. exec. com. Nat. Conservation Adv. Council, 1972-79, chmn. edn. and tng. com., 1972-79, mem. library and archives com., 1975-79; mem. conservation panel Nat. Endowment for Arts, 1976-77; chmn. ad hoc vis. com. Conservation Analytical Lab., Smithsonian Instn., 1977-78; chmn. exec. bd. Scholarly Catalogue of the Robert Lehman Collection, 1978-79; mem. bd. examiners for paper conservation Am. Inst. Conservation, 1976-79; chmn. U.S. steering com. NATO/CCMS Monuments Preservation Pilot Study, 1978—; chmn. adv. com. on preservation Nat. Archives and Records Service, 1980—; chmn. com. on conservation of historic stone bldgs. and monuments Nat. Materials Adv. Bd., Nat. Acad. Scis., 1980-82; mem. vis. com. dept. objects conservation Met. Mus. Art, 1978—. Editorial adv. and asso. editor: Studies in Conservation, 1971—; asso. editor: Restaurator, 1975—; U.S. exec. editor: Butterworth Series on Conservation in the Arts; mem. editorial bd.: Internat. Jour. Mus. Mgmt. and Curatorship, 1982—; contbr. articles to profl. jours. Guggenheim fellow, 1983-84. Fellow Am. Inst. Chemists, Am. Inst. Conservation, Internat. Inst. Conservation; mem. AAAS, Am. Chem. Soc., Coblentz Soc., Instrument Soc. Am. (sr.), Internat. Metallographic Soc. (sr.), N.Y. Acad. Scis., Sigma Xi. Home: 194 Ascan Ave Forest Hills NY 11375 Office: 14 E 78 St New York NY 10021

BAER, ROBERT JACOB, retired army officer; b. Jamestown, Mo., Aug. 12, 1924; s. John William and Esther Elizabeth (Knipker) B.; m. Ann O'Hara, Dec. 31, 1948; children: John, Thomas, Stephen, Teresa. B.S., U.S. Mil. Acad., 1947; grad., Army War Coll., 1967. Commd. 2d lt. U.S. Army, 1947, advanced through grades to lt. gen., 1977; service in, ETO, Japan, Korea and, Vietnam; staff div. chief Dept. Army, 1969-71; dir. devel. office Chief Research and Devel., 1971-72; project mgr. XM-1 Tank Systems Tank Automotive Command, Warren, Mich., 1972-77; dep. comdr. Army Devel./Readiness Command, Alexandria, Va., 1977-80; ret., 1980; sr. v.p. XMCO, Inc., 1980—. Contbr. to mil. jours. Decorated Silver Star, Legion of Merit with oak leaf cluster, Def. Superior Service medal, D.S.M., Meritorious Service medal, Air medal with 11 oak leaf clusters, Army Commendation medal with oak leaf cluster, Combat Inf. badge. Mem. U.S. Armor Assn., Assn. U.S. Army, Am. Def. Preparedness Assn., Kappa Alpha. Roman Catholic. Home: 6213 Militia Ct Fairfax Station VA 22039

BAER, RUDOLF LEWIS, physician, educator; b. Strasbourg, France, July 22, 1910; came to U.S., 1934, naturalized, 1940; s. Ludwig and Clara (Mainzer) B.; m. Louise Jeanne Grumbach, Nov. 6, 1941; children: John Reckford, Andrew Rudolph. M.D., U. Basel, Switzerland, 1934; postgrad. dermatology, N.Y. Postgrad. Med. Sch., 1937-39; M.D. (hon.), U. Munich, Germany, 1981. Diplomate: Am. Bd. Dermatology (mem. 1964-72, pres. 1967-70). Intern Beth Israel Hosp., N.Y.C., 1934-35; resident dermatology Montefiore Hosp., N.Y.C., 1936-37; faculty Columbia Sch. Medicine, 1939-48; dir. dept. dermatology Univ. Hosp., 1961-81; faculty N.Y.U. Sch. Medicine, 1948—, prof. dermatology, 1961—, chmn. dept. dermatology, 1961-81, George Miller MacKee prof., 1961-81; dir. dept. dermatology Bellevue Hosp. Center, 1961-81; sr. cons. VA Hosp., N.Y.C.; cons. Goldwater Meml. Hosp., N.Y.C., Monmouth Meml. Hosp., Long Branch, N.J., Elizabeth A. Horton Meml. Hosp., Middletown, N.J., Jewish Home and Hosp. for Aged, N.Y.C., Hackensack (N.J.) Hosp.; surgeon gen. U.S. Army, FDA; mem. Internat. Com. Dermatology, 1967-82, pres., 1972-77; mem. com. on revision U.S. Pharmacopeia, 1970-75; mem. commn. cutaneous diseases Armed Forces Epidemiologic Bd., 1967-72; Dohi lectr. Editor: Office Immunology, 1947, Atopic Dermatitis, 1955, Year Book Dermatology, 1955-65; also past mem. numerous editorial bds.; Author over 300 articles. Chmn. bd. Dermatology Found., 1974-77; bd. dirs. Rudolf L. Baer Found. for Skin Diseases, 1975—. Also recipient Dohi medal Japanese Dermatol. Soc., 1965; Von Zumbusch lectr., Munich, 1967; Hellerstrom lectr., Stockholm, 1970; O'Leary lectr. U. Rochester, 1971; Robinson lectr. U. Md., 1972; Barrett Kennedy lectr., 1973; Louis A. Duhring lectr., 1974; Samuel M. Bluefarb lectr., 1975; Frederick J. Novy Jr. vis. scholar, 1978; Morris Samitz lectr., 1979; Ruben Nomland-Robert Carney lectr., 1979; Barrett Kennedy meml. lectr., 1980. Fellow N.Y. Acad. Medicine (chmn. sect. dermatology 1963-64), Am. Acad. Dermatology (pres. 1974-75, Dome lectr. 1976, Gold medal 1978, hon. mem. 1980), Am. Acad. Allergy, Am. Coll. Allergists; mem. AMA (chmn. sect. dermatology 1965-66), Am. Dermatol. Assn. (pres. 1977, hon. mem. 1980), Soc. Investigative Dermatology (pres. 1963-64, Stephen Rothman medal 1973, hon. mem. 1980), Bronx Dermatol. Soc. (pres. 1952), N.Y. Dermatol. Soc. (pres. 1982-83), N.Y. Allergy Soc., N.Y. Acad. Scis., N.Y. County and State Med. Soc., Internat. League Dermatol. Socs. (pres. 1972-77, Alfred Marchionini Gold medal 1977); hon. mem. Argentinian, Austrian, Brit., Brazilian, Danish, Finnish, German, Iranian, Israeli, Japanese, Mexican, Polish, Swedish, Yugoslav, Venezuelan dermatol. socs., Brazilian Nat. Acad. Medicine; corr. mem. Pacific, Cuban, French, Italian dermatol. socs., French Allergy Soc. Home: 1185 Park Ave New York NY 10128 Office: 530 1st Ave New York NY 10016

BAER, WALTER S., III, communications co. exec.; b. Chgo., July 27, 1937; s. Walter S., Jr. and Margaret S. (Mayer) B.; m. Miriam R. Schenker, June 18, 1959; children—David W., Alan B. B.S., Calif. Inst. Tech., 1959; Ph.D. (NSF fellow), U. Wis., 1964. Research physicist Bell Telephone Labs., Murray Hill, N.J., 1964-66; White House fellow, Washington, 1966-67, White House sci. adv. staff, 1967-69; cons. and sr. scientist RAND Corp., Santa Monica, Calif., 1970-81, dir. energy policy program, 1978-81; dir. advanced tech. Times Mirror Co., Los Angeles, 1981—; cons. UN, maj. U.S. corps., 1970—; dir. Aspen (Colo.) Cable TV Workshop, 1972-73; mem. computer sci. and engring. bd. Nat. Acad. Scis., 1969-72; mem. cable TV adv. com. FCC, 1972-73; adv. council Aspen Program on Communications, 1974—. Author: Interactive Television, 1971, Cable Television: A Handbook for Decisionmaking, 1973, also articles; editor: The Electronic Box Office, 1974, wc/ RAND Cable Television Series, 1974; editorial bd.: Telecommunications Policy, 1976—. Trustee, So. Calif. chpt. The Nature Conservancy; mem. adv. com. communications law program UCLA; mem. Los Angeles Energy Mgmt. Adv. Bd., European Community Visitor, 1978—, 1979—. Recipient U. Wis. award for excellence in teaching, 1960; Preceptor award Broadcast Industry Conf., 1974—. Mem. AAAS, Am. Phys. Soc. (Congressional fellows selection com. 1976—), Internat. Inst. Communications, Sigma Xi. Democrat. Home: 560 Latimer Rd Santa Monica CA 90402

BAER, WERNER, economist, educator; b. Offenbach, Ger., Dec. 14, 1931; came to U.S., 1945, naturalized, 1952; s. Richard and Grete (Herz) B. B.A., Queens Coll., N.Y.C., 1953; M.A., Harvard U., 1955, Ph.D., 1958. Instr. Harvard U., 1958-61; asst. prof. Yale U., New Haven, 1961-65; asso. prof. Vanderbilt U., Nashville, 1965-69, prof., 1969-74; prof. econs. U. Ill., Urbana, 1974—; vis. prof. U. São Paulo, Brazil, 1966-68, Vargas Found., 1966-68; Rhodes fellow St. Antony's Coll., Oxford (Eng.) U., 1975. Author: The Brazilian Economy: Growth and Development, 1979, 2d edit., 1983. Decorated Order So. Cross (Brazil). Mem. Am. Econ. Assn., Latin Am. Studies Assn. Home: 103 E Daniel St Apt 6 Champaign IL 61820 Office: U Ill 1407 W Gregory Dr Urbana IL 61801

BAERG, RICHARD HENRY, podiatrist, government executive; b. Los Angeles, Jan. 19, 1937; s. Henry Francis and Ruth Elizabeth (Loven) B.; m. Joan Elaine Williams, 1963 (div. 1981); children: Carol Elizabeth, William Richard, Michael David. A.A., Reedley Coll., 1956; B.S., Calif. Coll. Podiatric Medicine, 1965, D.P.M., 1968, M.Sc., 1970; M.P.H., U. Calif.—, Berkeley, 1971; Sc.D. (hon.), N.Y. Coll. Podiatric Medicine, 1980. Diplomate: Am. Bd. Podiatric Surgery, Am. Bd. Podiatric Orthopedics (exec. sec. 1981—), Am. Bd. Podiatric Pub. Intern Highland Gen. Hosp., Oakland, Calif., 1969; resident in surgery Calif. Podiatry Hosp., San Francisco, 1970; acad. dean N.Y. Coll. Podiatric Medicine, N.Y.C., 1971-74; v.p., dean Calif. Coll. Podiatric Medicine, San Francisco, 1974-76, Los Angeles, 1976-78; pres. Ill. Coll. Podiatric Medicine, Chgo., 1978-79; dir. podiatric service, dept. medicine and surgery VA Central Office, Washington, 1979—; assoc. clin. prof. Stanford U. Med. Sch., 1974-76; clin. prof. Pa. Coll. Podiatric Medicine, 1979—, Inst. for Ednl. Mgmt., Harvard U., 1975; mem. podiatry adv. panel Nat. Acad. Scis.-Inst. Medicine, 1974. Editorial bd.: Jour. Podiatric Medicine and Surgery, Yearbook of Podiatric Medicine and Surgery; Contbr. articles to profl. jours. Served with M.C. U.S. Army and U.S. Navy, 1958-61. Mead-Johnson fellow, 1968-69; Am. Podiatric Assn. fellow, 1969-70, 70-71. Mem. Am. Public Health Assn. (governing council 1977), Am. Coll. Foot Orthopedists, Nat. Bd. Podiatry Examiners (bd. dirs.), Am. Podiatry Assn. (com. on public health 1971—, council on podiatric edn., chmn. profl. edn. com. 1977-78, com. on hosp. 1980—), Assn. Podiatrists in Fed. Service, Am. Assn. Colls. Podiatric Medicine (exec. com. 1973, pres. 1980-81), Acad. Ambulatory Foot Surgery, Assn. Mil. Surgeons U.S., Sigma Pi Epsilon, Pi Delta. Republican. Clubs: Masons, Commonwealth of Calif. Home: 903A S Rolfe St Arlington VA 22204 Office: VA Central Office (129 810 Vermont Ave NW)r Washington DC 20420

BAETJER, ANNA MEDORA, scientist, educator; b. Balt., July 7, 1899; d. J. Frank and Katherine (Cook) B. B.A., Wellesley Coll., 1920; D.Sc., Johns Hopkins U., 1924, D.H.L. (hon.), 1979, D.P.H., Woman's Med. Coll. Pa., 1953, D.Sc., Wheaton Coll., 1966. Mem. faculty Johns Hopkins Sch. Hygiene and Public Health, Balt., 1923—, prof. environ. medicine, 1961-70, prof. emeritus, 1970—; Cons. preventive medicine div. Office Surgeon Gen. U.S. Army, 1943—; mem. commn. environ. health Armed Forces Epidemiol. Bd., 1954-73; mem. com. on biol. effects of atmospheric pollutants NRC, 1970-73; cons. toxicology research div. Koppers Co., 1957-82; mem. Permanent Commn. and Internat. Assn. Occupational Health, 1960—; mem. adv. com. on safety pesticide residues in foods FDA, 1966-70; mem. occupational safety and health study sect. Nat. Inst. Occupational Safety and Health, HEW, 1968-70, 72-74; mem. nat. air quality criteria adv. com. EPA, 1972-76; mem. standards adv. com. on heat stress U.S. Dept. Labor, 1973-74; mem. noise control adv. bd. Balt. Health Dept., 1973-76; mem. com. on public info. in prevention occupational cancer NRC, 1975-77; mem. Armed Forces Epidemiology Bd., 1977-82; temporary adviser WHO, 1978—. Author: Women in Industry-Their Health and Efficiency, 1946; also articles research papers, chpts, in books.; Mem. editorial bd.: Archives Environmental Health, 1960-70, Excerpta Medica, 1976-77. Trustee Indsl. Health Found., 1958—, vice chmn., 1964-68. Recipient Disting. Civilian Services award U.S. Army, 1981, Outstanding Med. Educator award Am. Occupational Medicine Assn., 1983. Mem. Am. Physiol. Soc., Am. Public Health Assn., Am. Indsl. Hygiene Assn. (pres. 1951, Cummings Meml. award 1964), Am. Conf. Govt. Indsl. Hygienists (Herbert Stokinger award 1980), Am. Acad. Occupational Medicine (hon., Robert Kehoe award 1976), Am. Acad. Indsl. Hygiene (bd. 1968-72), Md. Acad. Scis. (trustee 1965-76), Phi Beta Kappa, Sigma Xi. Home: 4900 Roland Ave Baltimore MD 21210 Office: Johns Hopkins Sch Hygiene and Public Health 615 N Woffe St Baltimore MD 21205

BAETZHOLD, HOWARD GEORGE, English educator; b. Buffalo, Jan. 1, 1923; s. Howard Kuster and Harriet Laura (Hofheins) B.; m. Nancy Millard Cheesman, Aug. 5, 1950; children: Howard King, Barbara Millard. Student, Brown U., 1940-43, MIT, 1943-44; A.B. magna cum laude, Brown U., 1944, M.A., 1948; Ph.D., U. Wis., 1953. Asst. dir. Vets. Coll., Brown U., Providence, 1947-48, dir., 1948-49, admissions officer, 1948-50; teaching asst. U. Wis.-Madison, 1950-51; asst. to assoc. dean Coll. Letters and Sci., 1951-53; asst. prof. English Butler U., Indpls., 1953-57, assoc. prof., 1957-67, prof. English, 1967—, head dept., 1981, Rebecca Clifton Reade prof., 1981; vis. prof. U. Del., summer 1963. Author: Mark Twain and John Bull: The British Connection, 1970; contbr. articles to profl. jours. Mem. Indpls. Com. Internat. Visitors, 1965—. Served to 1st lt. A.C. AUS, 1943-46. Faculty fellow Butler U., 1957-58, 69-70; grantee Am. Philos. Soc., 1958, Am. Council Learned Socs., 1967. Mem. AAUP (v.p. state conf. 1955), MLA, Assn. Depts. English, Nat. Council Tchrs. of English, Am. Studies Assn. (nat. council 1974-76), Midwest MLA, Ohio-Ind. Am. Studies Assn. (pres. 1967-68), Ind. Coll. English Assn. (exec. bd. 1983—), Ind. Tchrs. of Writing, Am. Philatelic Soc., Greater Ind. Masters Swimming Assn., Art Assn. Indpls., Butler U. Odd Topics Soc., Delta Upsilon. Home: 6723 Riverview Dr Indianapolis IN 46220

BAEUMER, MAX LORENZ, historian of literature; b. Trier, Germany, May 19, 1917; came to U.S., 1952, naturalized, 1958; s. Lorenz Max and Helene (Dahm) B.; m. Helene Heine, Jan. 25, 1945. Ph.L., Coll. of Trier, 1939; postgrad., U. Frankfurt, Germany, 1947-49; Ph.D., Northwestern U., 1959. Instr. Northwestern U., 1958-59; asst. prof. Bowling Green State U., 1959-61, U. Kans., 1961-63, asso. prof., 1963-64; faculty U. Wis., Madison, 1965—, prof. German lit., 1965—; dir. Northwestern U. Summer Inst., Germany, 1963; Fulbright vis. prof. U. Stuttgart, Germany, 1964-65; evaluator NDEA Insts. in, Germany, 1963; vis. prof. U. Wis. Inst. for Research in Humanities, 1968, permanent mem., 1972; dir. seminar on history and lit. of Reformation NEH, 1980, cons. Author: Das Dionysische i.d. Werken W. Heinses, 1964, Heinse-Studien, 1966; Chief editor: W. Heinse, Collected Works and Letters, 1971—, Toposforschung, 1973; author: W. Heinse, Ardinghello, 1975; Nietzsche and the Dionysian Tradition, 1976, Winckelmann, French Classicism and Jefferson, 1978, Sozialkritische und revolutionäre Literatur der Reformationszeit, 1980; author: Reformation in Braunschweig, 1981, Nietzsche and Luther, 1983, Luther and the Rise of the German Language, 1983, Goethe as a Critic and Reader, 1983. Northwestern U. fellow, 1958; E.M. Watkins scholar, 1963; fellow Am. Philos. Soc., 1965; research fellow U. Wis., 1966, 72, 75, 84; fellow Deutscher Akademischer Austauschdienst, 1975, Herzog August Bibliothek Wolfenbüttel, 1977. Mem. MLA, Goethe Soc. N.Am. (dir.), Am. Assn. Tchrs. German, Internat. Germanist. Verband, Deutsche Schillergesellschaft, Arbeitskreis für Renaissanceforschung, Am. Soc. 18th Century Studies, Deutsche Gesellschaft zur Erforschung des 18. Jahrhunderts (dir.), Internat. Archiv f. Sozialgeschichte d. dt. Literatur. Office: Inst for Research in Humanities U Wis Madison WI 53706

BAEZ, JOAN, folk singer; b. S.I., N.Y., Jan. 9, 1941; d. Albert V. and Joan (Bridge) B.; m. David Victor Harris, Mar. 1968 (div. 1973); 1 son, Gabriel Earl. Appeared in coffeehouses, Gate of Horn, Chgo., 1958, Ballad Room, Club 47, 1958-68, Newport (R.I.) Folk Festival, 1959-69, extended tour to colls. and concert halls, 1960's; appeared, Town Hall and, Carnegie Hall, 1962, 67, 68, U.S. tours, 1970—, concert tours, Japan, 1966, 82, Europe, 1970-73, 80, 83; recording artist for, Vanguard Records, 1960-72, A&M, 1973-76, Portrait Records, 1975-80 (awarded 8 gold albums, 1 gold single.), European record albums, 1981, 83; Author: Joan Baez Songbook, 1964; biography Daybreak, 1968, Coming Out, 1971; (with David Harris) songbook And then I wrote, 1979; extensive TV appearances and speaking tours U.S. and Can. for anti-militarism, 1967-68. Visit to Democratic Republic of Vietnam, 1972; Founder, v.p. Inst. for Study Nonviolence (now Resource Center for Nonviolence, Santa Cruz, Calif.), Palo Alto, Calif., 1965; mem. nat. adv. council Amnesty Internat., 1974—; founder, pres. Humanitas/Internat. Human Rights Com., 1979; condr. fact-finding mission to refugee camps, S.E. Asia, Oct. 1979. Began refusing payment war taxes, 1964; arrested for civil disobedience opposing draft, Oct. and Dec. 1967. Office: care Diamonds and Rust Prodns PO Box 1026 Menlo Park CA 94026 PO Box 818 Menlo Park CA 94026

BAFFES, THOMAS GUS, heart surgeon, lawyer; b. New Orleans, Apr. 3, 1923; s. Gus and Tina (Bores) B.; m. Mary Lou Amann, Feb. 23, 1958; children: Kathleen, Christine, Paul, Andrew. B.S., Tulane U., 1943, M.D., 1945; J.D., DePaul U., 1975. Bar: Ill. 1975, La. 1975. Rotating intern Charity Hosp., New Orleans, 1945-46, residency tng. gen. surgery, 1948-51, residency tng. thoracic surgery, 1951-52; residency pediatric pathology Children's Meml. Hosp., Chgo., 1952, residency pediatric surgery, 1953, fellow cardiovascular research, 1954-56, now mem. staff; staff Swedish Covenant Hosp., head dept. surgery, 1960- 84; prof. surgery Rush Med. Coll.; chmn. dept. surgery Mt. Sinai Med Center; staff Augustana Hosp., Lutheran Gen. Hosp., Ill. Central Hosp., Mt. Sinai Hosp., all Chgo.; mem. law firm Pierce, Daley & Penn, Chgo., 1975—. Author med. articles. Served as capt. M.C., AUS, 1946-48; psychiatry and surgery VA hosps. Recipient Beta Mu award biology; Alpha Chi Sigma award chemistry; Isadore Dyer scholastic award Tulane U., 1945; chosen one of Ten Outstanding Young Men, 1957. Mem. Am. Acad. Pediatrics, AMA, ACS, Am. Coll. Chest Physicians, Chgo. Surg. Soc., Am. Soc. Artificial Organs, Am. Assn. Thoracic Surgery, Soc. Thoracic Surgeons, Western Surg. Soc., Chgo. Med. Soc., Protective Med. Assn. Ill. (pres. 1975—), Phi Beta Kappa, Alpha Omega Alpha. Mem. Hellenic Orthodox Ch. Home: 1701 Woodland Ave Park Ridge IL 60068 Office: 4055 Main St Skokie IL 60076 also 180 N LaSalle St Chicago IL 60601 *I am grateful to have had the priviledge of being a small participating part of the political and social miracle called the United States of America. The statement "It could only happen in America!" was never more true than in my life. I feel a deep sense of dedication to her welfare.*

BAGAN, THOMAS P(AUL), dept. store chain exec.; b. Fargo, N.D., Apr. 8, 1943; s. Paul R. and Arvilla J. B.; m. Carol Ann Lucy, Feb. 12 1966; children—Michelle A., Bradley T. B.A., U. N.D., 1966; grad. Advanced Mgmt. Program, Harvard Bus. Sch., 1978. Divisional mgr. personnel Dayton Hudson Corp., Mpls., 1969-74; corp. v.p. Carter Hawley Hale Stores, Inc., Los Angeles, 1974-79; exec. v.p. Marshall Field & Co., Chgo., 1979—. Clubs: Jonathan (Los Angeles); Carlton (Chgo.). Lake Forest IL Office: 25 E Washington St Chicago IL 60690

BAGBY, FREDERICK LAIR, JR., research institute executive; b. Salt Lake City, Aug. 2, 1920; s. Frederick Lair and Marcia Fanny (Fitts) B.; m. Marilla Eudora Barlow, June 19, 1943; children—Dallas Marilla, Marcia Norinne, Ross Frederick. B.S., U. Utah, 1942. Prodn. design engr. airplane div. Curtiss-Wright Corp., Columbus, Ohio, 1942-46; with Battelle Meml. Inst., Columbus, 1946—, mgr. mech. engring. dept., 1966-70, asst. dir. Columbus labs., 1970-72, asst. to dir. Columbus labs., 1973-74, mgr. def. and space systems programs Columbus labs., 1974-76; dir. Advanced Concepts Lab., 1976-78, sr. program mgr., 1978—. Contbr. articles to profl. jours. Fellow ASME, AIAA (asso.; v.p. sect. affairs); mem. AAAS, Sigma Xi, Tau Beta Pi. Research on advanced land warfare and aerospace systems, smokeless combustion of bituminous coal, high temperature aerospace materials, tech. planning and forecasting, research and devel. econs. Home: 1714 Churchview Ln Columbus OH 43220 Office: 505 King Ave Columbus OH 43201

BAGBY, JOHN R., JR., educator, university institute director; b. Aurora, Mo., Mar. 3, 1919; s. John R. and Grace (Seburn) B.; m. Billie M. Hudson, Oct. 17, 1944; children: Caroline Bagby Whitson, John R. III, Charles Thomas. B.S., U. Ark., 1954, M.S., 1956; Ph.D., Emory U., 1962. Pub. health biologist USPHS, 1946-66; dep. dir. Nat. Communicable Disease Center, 1966-69; dir. Inst. Rural Environ. Health, Colo. State U., 1969—, head dept. microbiology, 1978-83; chmn. interagy. commn. on back contamination NASA, 1966-70; lectr., cons. on planetary protection, 1957—; mem. panel health effects of environ. pollution Pres.'s Sci. Adv. Com., 1965; U.S. del. Orgn. de Coordination et de Coop. pour la Lutte Contre les Grandes Endemies, Bobo Dioulasso, Upper Volta, 1967—; cons. jet propulsion lab. Calif. Inst. Tech., 1974—; cons. NASA-Ames Research Center, 1977—; mem. Colo. Bd. Health, 1983-87. Served with USAAF, 1942-45. Recipient Walter F. Snyder award, 1983. Mem. Am. Soc. Tropical Medicine and Hygiene, Am. Mosquito Control Assn., U.S.-Mex. Border Pub. Health Assn., Colo. Pub. Health Assn., N.Y. Acad. Scis., Am. Inst. Biol. Scis. (planetary quarantine adv. panel 1969-76), Sigma Xi, Gamma Sigma Delta., Phi Sigma. Office: Colo State U Dept Microbiology and Environ Health Fort Collins CO 80523

BAGDIKIAN, BEN HAIG, writer; b. Marash, Turkey, Jan. 30, 1920; came to U.S., 1920, naturalized, 1926; s. Aram Theodore and Daisy (Uvezian) B.; m. Elizabeth Ogasapian, Oct. 2, 1942 (div. 1972); children—Christopher Ben, Frederick Haig; m. Betty L. Medsger, 1973. A.B., Clark U., 1941, D.Litt., 1963; L.H.D., Brown U., 1961. Reporter Springfield (Mass.) Morning Union, 1941-42; asso. editor Periodical House, Inc., N.Y.C., 1946; successively reporter, fgn. corr., chief Washington corr. Providence Jour., 1947-62; contbg. editor Sat. Eve. Post, 1963-67; project dir. study of future U.S. news media Rand Corp., 1967-69; asst. mng. editor for nat. news Washington Post, 1970-71, asst. mng. editor, 1971-72; nat. corr. Columbia Journalism Review, 1972-74; M. Lyle Spencer vis. prof. Syracuse U., 1973; prof. Grad. Sch. Journalism U. Calif., Berkeley. Author: In The Midst of Plenty: The Poor in America, 1964, The Information Machines: Their Impact on Men and the Media, 1971, The Shame of the Prisons, 1972, The Effete Conspiracy, 1972, Caged: Eight Prisoners and their Keepers, 1976, The Media Monopoly, 1983; also pamphlets.; Contbr.: The Kennedy Circle, 1961; Editor: Man's Contracting World in an Expanding Universe, 1959; Bd. editors: Jour. Investigative Reporters and Editors, 1980—. Mem. steering com. Nat. Prison Project., 1974-82; Trustee Clark U., 1964-76; bd. dirs. Nat. Capital Area Civil Liberties Union, 1964-66, Com. to Protect Journalists, 1981—; pres. Lowell Mellett Fund for Free and Responsible Press, 1965-76; acad. adv. bd. Nat. Citizens Com. for Broadcasting., 1978—. Served with USAAF, 1942-45. Recipient George Foster Peabody award, 1951; Sidney Hillman Found. award, 1956; Most Perceptive Critic citation Am. Soc. Journalism Adminstrs., 1978; Ogden Reid Found. fellow, 1956; Guggenheim fellow, 1961-62. Mem. ACLU, Authors League. Home: 25 Stonewall Road Berkeley CA 94705 Office: Evans Hall U Calif Berkeley CA 94720 *The most compelling principles in my life have been, in private life the pervasive need of love and trust in human relations, in public life dignity of the individual combined with devotion to the common good, in intellectual life a distrust of detachment from the human condition, and in journalism honesty and clarity.*

BAGERIS, JOHN, artist, educator; b. Fremont, Ohio, May 11, 1924; s. Evangelos and Gustine (Geros) B. B.F.A., Art Inst. Chgo., 1950, M.F.A., 1952. Instr. art Bklyn. Mus. Art Sch., 1961-65, Sch. Visual Arts, N.Y.C., 1962-71, Art Inst., Boston, 1973—, chmn. dept. fine arts, 1978—. Represented permanent collections, Mus. Modern Art, N.Y.C., Permanent collections, Whitney Mus. Art, N.Y.C., permanent collections, Detroit Inst. Arts, Bklyn. Mus., Wadsworth Atheneum, Hartford, Conn., others. Served with USAAF, 1943-45; ETO. Fulbright fellow, 1953-54.

BAGGE, CARL ELMER, association executive, lawyer; b. Chgo., Jan. 12, 1927; s. Hjalmar and Adele (Elmquist) B.; m. Margaret Evelyn Carlson, June 27, 1953; children: Carol Eileen, Charles Edward, Barbara Ann, Beverly Jean. B.A. summa cum laude, Augustana Coll., 1949; postgrad., Uppsala (Sweden) U., 1947, U. So. Calif., 1956; J.D., Northwestern U., 1952; LL.D. (hon.), Alderson Broaddus Coll., 1980. Bar: Ill. 1951, D.C. 1982. Practiced in, Chgo., 1951-52; atty. A., T. & S.F. Ry., Chgo., 1952-62, asst. gen. atty., 1962-63, spl. asst. exec. dept., 1963-64, gen. atty., 1964-65; commr. FPC, Washington, 1965-70, vice chmn., 1966-67; pres., chief exec. officer, dir. Nat. Coal Assn., Washington, 1971—; dir. Bituminous Coal Research, Inc., 1971—, Coal Exporters Assn., 1975—; Mem. gen. tech. adv. com. to Energy Research and Devel. Adminstrn.; mem. nat. adv. com. Project Independence; mem. nat. coal adv. com. Fed. Energy Adminstrn.; mem. coal adv. com. to sec. Interior; vice chmn. Internat. Coal Research Commn., 1974; bd. dirs. U.S. nat. com. World Energy Conf. Contbr. articles to legal and bus. publs.; contbr. to: The Supreme Court, 1961. Bd. dirs. Nat. Energy Found.; Mem. commn. ch. and econ. life Nat. Council Chs. Christ.; Mem. Deerfield Zoning Bd. Appeals, 1955-58, Deerfield Plan Commn., 1958-62; Bd. dirs. Augustana Coll., Bituminous Coal Research; trustee Luth. Student Found. Met. Chgo. Served to ensign USNR, 1945-46. Mem. Nat. Assn. R.R. and Pub. Utility Commrs. (exec. com.), Am., Ill., Chgo. bar assns., ICC Practitioners Assn., Legal Club Chgo., Econ. Club Chgo., Assn. Western Ry. Counsel, Lexington Group Ry. Historians, Ill. Jr. C. of C., Am. Scandinavian Found., Ill. Hist. Soc., Ry. Systems and Mgmt. Assn., Phi Beta Kappa, Phi Alpha Delta, Pi Kappa Delta. Republican. Lutheran. Clubs: Capitol Hill, Nat. Press, University, Congressional Country (Washington). Home: 10019 Kendale Rd Potomac MD 20854 Office: 1130 17th St NW Washington DC 20036

BAGGETT, LEE, JR., naval officer; b. Oxford, Miss., Jan. 11, 1927; s. Lee and Estelle (Brown) B.; m. Doris Simmons, Sept. 22, 1954. B.S., U.S. Naval Acad., 1950; M.S., U.S. Navy Postgrad. Sch., 1958; postgrad., Naval War Coll., 1961-62. Commd. ensign U.S. Navy, 1950, advanced through grades to vice adm., 1979, engr. officer USS Frank Knox, 1950-51, engr. officer, gunnery officer USS C.J. Badger, 1951-53, condg. officer USS Courlan, 1953-55, exec. officer USS Bridget, 1958-60, comdg. officer USS Firm, 1960-61; test plans officer Def. Atomic Support Agy., 1962-64; staff of comdr. operational test and devel. force U.S. Navy, 1964, comdg. officer USS Decatur, 1966-68, mem. staff, comdr. Carrier Div. 7, 1968-70, dir. guided missile div. Naval Ordnance Systems Command, 1970-72, comdg. officr USS Reeves, 1972-73, chief of staff U.S. 6th Fleet, 1974-75; comdr. anti-submarine warfare systems project Naval Material Command, dir. anti-submarine div. Office Chief of Naval Ops., 1975-77; comdr. Naval Surface Group Middle Pacific, 1977-79; comdr. Naval Surface Force U.S. Pacific Fleet, San Diego, 1979-82; dir. naval warfare Dept. Navy, Washington, 1982—. Dist. chmn. Boy Scouts Am., 1978-79. Decorated D.S.M., Legion of Merit, Bronze Star with gold star. Club: Army-Navy Country (Arlington, Va.). Office: Navy Dept Washington DC 20350

BAGWELL, ROSS KENNEDY, advt. exec.; b. Madisonville, Tenn., Jan. 17, 1932; s. Charles H. and Jeanette (Kennedy) B.; m. Sue Burchfield, Sept. 23, 1951; children—Ross Kennedy Jr., Susan Denise. Student, U. Tenn., 1956; B.A. in Broadcasting, N.Y.U., 1958. Program prodn. and merchandising NBC, N.Y.C., 1957-63; salesman sta. WATE-TV, Knoxville, Tenn., 1963; with Lavidge & Assos., Inc., Knoxville, Chattanooga, Atlanta and; Greensboro, 1963-73, pres., 1970-73, Bagwell Communications, Inc., Knoxville, 1973—, Cinetel Prodns. Inc., 1974—. Contbr. articles to mags. Served with USAF, 1950-53. Recipient award Best TV Nat. Campaign Am. Fedn. Advertisers, 1964, 70. Mem. Alpha Delta Sigma. Republican. Presbyn. Home: 7914 Gleason Rd Apt 1077 Knoxville TN 37919 Office: 320 Troy Circle Knoxville TN 37919

BAHAKEL, CY N., broadcasting executive; b. Birmingham, Ala., Apr. 12, 1921; s. S.A. and Mary B.; m. Beverly B.; 6 children. A.B., U. Ala., 1945, J.D., 1947, LL.D., 1969. Bar: Ala. 1947. Practiced law, Tuscaloosa, 1948; owner Sta. WCCB-TV Bahakel Broadcasting Co., Charlotte, N.C., 1963—. Mem. N.C. Senate, 1972-76, mem. appropriations subcom.; dir. Northwestern Bank of N.C., Inc.; Pres. Democratic Men's Club of Mecklenburg County, N.C., 1970; bd. dirs. Charlotte Salvation Army; Charlotte council Boy Scouts Am., Charlotte Symphony, Charlotte Heart Assn., Charlotte Jr. Achievement; trustee Gardner-Webb Coll., Wingate Coll., United Community Service, Charlotte, Carolina Carrousel and Law Enforcement Assistance Found., Charlotte; mem. N.C. Crime Study Commn., N.C. Savs. and Loan Study Commn. Served with U.S. Army, 1945. Recipient Rotary award Boy Scouts Am., 1967; Humanitarian Service award United Cerebral Palsy, 1969; Founders award N.C. Heart Assn., 1970; ABE Lincoln TV award, 1977; hon. Ky. Col.; Pres.'s award Gardner-Webb Coll., 1976. Mem. Charlotte C. of C. (dir.), N.C. Assn. Broadcasters (dir.), Nat. Assn. UHF Broadcasters (pres.). Home: PO Box 32488 Charlotte NC 28232 Office: Sta WCCB-TV Bahakel Broadcasting Co PO Box 22488 1 Television Pl Charlotte NC 28232

BAHARIAN, ROY ESSAYE, manufacturing company executive; b. Worcester, Mass., Oct. 22, 1922; s. Geragos Bedros and Noonoufar Seranoush (Arzouian) B.; m. Ruth Shirley Fosdick, Nov. 20, 1948; children: Mark, Tod, Lesley. B.S. in Mech. Engring., Worcester Tech. Inst., 1944. Registered profl. engr., N.Y. Asst. chief engr. Riley Stoker Corp., Worcester, 1946-56; sr. project engr. Diamond Internat., N.Y.C., 1956-61, dir. mfg., 1964-72, v.p., 1972-74, group v.p., 1974—; asst. mgr. M.W. Kellogg Co., N.Y.C., 1961-64. Patentee in field. Served to lt. (j.g.) USN, 1942-46; ETO. Recipient Admiral Earle award Worcester Engring. Soc., 1953. Mem. TAPPI, ASME. Congregationalist. Office: Diamond Internat Corp 733 3d Ave New York NY 10017

BAHCALL, JOHN NORRIS, astrophysicist; b. Shreveport, La., Dec. 30, 1934; s. Malcolm and Mildred (Lazarus) B.; m. Neta Assaf, Sept. 21, 1966; children—Ron Assaf, Dan Ophir, Orli Gilat. B.A., U. Calif., 1956; M.Sc., U. Chgo., 1957; Ph.D., Harvard U., 1961. Research asso. Ind. U., 1961-62; theoretical physicist, research asso., asst. prof., then asso. prof. theoretical physics Calif. Inst. Tech., 1962-70; mem. Inst. Advanced Study, Princeton, N.J., 1968-70, prof. natural scis., 1971—; mem. physics advisory panel NSF; mem.-at-large, large space telescope mgmt. and ops. working group NASA; mem. com., div. high energy astrophysics; mem. x-ray astron com. URA. Author: (with Field and Arp) The Redshift Controversy, 1973. Sloan Found. fellow, 1968-71. Fellow Am. Phys. Soc.; mem. Nat. Acad. Scis., Nat. Acad. Arts and Scis., Am. Astron. Soc. (Helen B. Warner prize 1969), Internat. Astron. Union. Jewish. Address: Inst Advanced Study Princeton NJ 08540

BAHIRI, MEDHI M., ballet dancer; b. El Harrach, Algier, Jan. 30, 1956; came to U.S., 1979. Soloist-ballet dancer Basler Stadtheatre, Basel, Switzerland, 1974-76; mem. 20th Century Ballet-Maurice Bejart, Brussels, Belgium, 1976-78; guest artist Nat. Ballet of Mex., Mexico City, 1979; prin. dancer Ballet West, Salt Lake City, 1979-82, Boston

Ballet, 1983; freelance guest artist, N.Y.C. Recipient Gold Medal Prix de Lausanne, Switzerland, 1974, Gold medal Varna Internat. Ballet Competition, Varna, Bulgaria, 1978. Home: 64 W 70th St Apt#C5 New York NY 10023

BAHL, OM PARKASH, biological sciences educator, academic administrator, consultant, researcher, inventor; b. Lyallpur, Punjab, India, Jan. 10, 1927; came to U.S., 1957, naturalized, 1974; s. Daulat R. and Hira D. (Tejkaur) B.; m. Nirmal Nanda, Oct. 8, 1952; children: Vikram, Vinita, Meenakshi. B.Sc. first class, Govt. Coll., Llyallpur, 1942, M.Sc., Punjab U., Chandigarh, 1950; Ph.D., U. Minn., 1962. Lectr. in chemistry Arya Coll., Ludhiana, India, 1950-52, Govt. Coll., Ludhiana, 1952-57; research assoc. U. Minn., Mpls., 1962-63, UCLA, 1963-64; career investigator, Dernham fellow Calif. div. Am. Cancer Soc. U. So. Calif., 1964-65, asst. prof. biochemistry, 1965-66, SUNY-Buffalo, 1966-68, assoc. prof., 1968-71, prof., 1971—, prof., dir. div. cell and molecular biology, 1974-78, prof., chmn. dept. biol. scis., 1976—, mem. patent policy bd., 1982—; cons. in field; mem. Biotech. Adv. Bd., Washington, 1983—, India, 1983—. Contbr. articles to profl. jours.; mem. editorial bd.: Archives Biochemistry and Biophysics, 1979—, Preparative Biochemistry, 1980—; patentee antigen for early pregnancy test and contraceptive vaccine. Recipient medal Pres. U. Liege (Belgium), 1971, Presdl. medal Pres. India, 1973, Med. and Life Sci. award Nat. Council Asian Indian Orgns. in N. Am., 1982; NIH grantee, 1966—; WHO grantee, 1976—. Mem. Am. Chem. Soc. (Schoellkopf award 1978), Am. Soc. Biol. Chemists, Brit. Biochem. Soc., N.Y. Acad. Scis., Endocrine Soc., AAAS, Am. Soc. Cell Biology, Sigma Xi, Gamma Alpha, Phi Lambda Upsilon. Democrat. Hindu. Club: Cosmos (Washington). Office: SUNY-Buffalo 347 Cooke Hall Amherst Campus Buffalo NY 14260

BAHLER, DIANA IPSEN, educator; b. N.Y.C., Dec. 6, 1938; d. Walter F. and Marie M. (Kroger) Ipsen; m. Ernst Behler, Nov. 24, 1967; children: Sophia, Caroline. B.A., U. Wash., 1965, M.A., 1966, Ph.D., 1970. Acting asst. prof. Germanics U. Wash., Seattle, 1969-71, asst. prof. Germanics, 1971-74, assoc. prof. Germanics and comparative lit., 1974-81, prof., 1981—. Author: The Theory of the Novel in Early German Romanticism, 1978; contbr. articles to profl. jours. U. Wash. Grad. Sch. summer stipend for research, 1970; Younger Humanist fellow NEH, 1972-73. Mem. MLA, Am. Assn. Tchrs. German, N.Am. Nietzsche Soc., N.Am. Goethe Soc., Philological Assn. of Pacific Coast, Western Assn. German Studies. Home: 5525 NE Penrith Rd Seattle WA 98105 Office: Dept Germanics U Wash Denny 340 DH30 Seattle WA 98195

BAHLMAN, DUDLEY WARD RHODES, history educator; b. Cin., Mar. 19, 1923; s. William T. and Janet (Rhodes) B.; m. Jean Mitchell, Dec. 29, 1951; children: Dudley R., Anne M. B.A., Yale U., 1946, M.A., 1947, Ph.D., 1951. Instr., asst. prof. Yale U., 1951-59; asst. prof. Williams Coll., Williamstown, Mass., 1959-62, assoc. prof., 1962-67, prof., 1967—, dean of faculty, 1968-75, Class of 1924 prof., 1976—, chmn. dept. history, 1978—. Author: The Moral Revolution of 1688, 1957, The Diary of Sir Edward Hamilton, 1972. Served with Med. Dept. AUS, 1943-46. Morse fellow, 1957-58; Guggenheim fellow, 1965-66. Fellow Royal Hist. Soc.; mem. Am. Hist. Assn. Clubs: Elizabethan., Century. Home: Sabin Dr Williamstown MA 01267

BAHLMAN, WILLIAM THORNE, JR., lawyer; b. Cin., Jan. 9, 1920; s. William Thorne and Janet (Rhodes) B.; m. Nancy W. DeCamp, Mar. 21, 1953; children: Charles R., William Ward, Baker D. B.A., Yale U., 1941, LL.B., 1947. Bar: Ohio 1947. Prin. Paxton & Seasongood, L.P.A., Cin., 1947-67, 73—; ptnr. Paxton & Seasongood, 1954—; prof. law U. Cin. Coll. Law, 1967-73, lectr., 1965-67, 73-77. Served with USAAF, 1942-46. Mem. Am. Law Inst., ABA, Ohio State Bar Assn., Cin. Bar Assn. Office: Paxton and Seasongood 1700 Central Trust Tower Cincinnati OH 45202

BAHM, ARCHIE JOHN, educator; b. Imlay, Mich., Aug. 21, 1907; s. John Samuel and Lena (Kohn) B.; m. Luna Parks Bachelor, Feb. 13, 1930; children—Raymond John, Elaine Lucia (Mrs. C.R. Cundiff). A.B., Albion Coll., 1929; M.A., U. Mich., 1930, Ph.D., 1933. Instr. to asso. prof. Tex. Technol. Coll., 1934-46; asso. prof. philosophy U. Denver, 1946-48; prof. philosophy U. N.Mex., Albuquerque, 1948-73, prof. emeritus, 1973—; Fulbright research scholar U. Rangoon, 1955-56, Banaras Hindu U., 1962-63. Author: Philosophy, An Introduction, 1953, Philosophy of the Buddha, 1958, What Makes Acts Right?, 1958, Tao Teh King by Lao Tzu, 1958, Logic for Beginners, 1960, Types of Intuition, 1961, Yoga: Union with the Ultimate, 1961, The World's Living Religions, 1964, Yoga for Business Executives, 1965, The Heart of Confucius, 1969, Directory of American Philosophers vols. I-IX, 1962-79, Bhagavad Gita, The Wisdom of Krishna, 1970, Polarity, Dialectic and Organicity, 1970, Metaphysics, An Introduction, 1974, Ethics as a Behavioral Science, 1974, Comparative Philosophy, 1977, The Specialist, 1977, The Philosopher's World Model, 1979; Editor: Interdependence, 1977; Contbr. articles to profl. jours. Mem. Am. Philos. Assn., AAAS, Planetary Citizens, World Future Soc., Phi Beta Kappa, Phi Kappa Phi, Phi Sigma Tau. Home: 1915 Las Lomas Rd NE Albuquerque NM 87106

BAHNSEN, JOHN CHARLES, JR., U.S. army officer; b. Albany, Ga., Nov. 8, 1934; s. John Charles and Evelyn (Williams) B.; m. Margaret Ann Miller, Aug. 31, 1974; children: Chris, Brad, Leann, James. B.S., U.S. Mil. Acad., 1956; student, George Washington U., 1968; M.S., Shippensburg State Coll., 1972. Commd. 2d lt. U.S. Army, 1956, advanced through grades to brig. gen.; now chief of staff Combined Field Army ROK/US, Korea. Author: Tank Company Commander's Guide, 1964, Reflections on Command, 1972. Decorated Disting. Service Cross, Silver Star, Legion of Merit, D.F.C., Bronze Star with two oak leaf clusters, Purple Heart, numerous Air medals. Mem. Assn. Grads. U.S. Mil. Acad., Nat. Sojourners, Armor Assn., Legion of Valor, Assn. U.S. Army, VFW, U.S. Army War Coll. Alumni., Blackhorse Assn., Hell on Wheels Assn. Episcopalian. Office: HQ Combined Army Korea APO San Francisco CA 96358

BAHR, EHRHARD, educator; b. Kiel, Germany, Aug. 21, 1932; came to U.S., 1956; s. Klaus and Gisela (Badenhausen) B.; m. Diana Meyers, Nov. 21, 1973; stepchildren: Gary, Timothy, Christopher. Student, U. Heidelberg, Germany, 1952-53, U. Freiburg, Germany, 1953-56; M.S. Ed. (Fulbright scholar), U. Kans., 1956-58; postgrad., U. Cologne, 1959-61; Ph.D., U. Calif., Berkeley, 1968. Asst. prof. German UCLA, 1968-70, asso. prof., 1970-72, prof., 1972—, chmn. dept. Germanic langs., 1981-84. Author: Irony in the Late Works of Goethe, 1972, Georg Lukacs, 1970, Ernst Bloch, 1974; edit. of: Kant, What is Enlightenment, 1974, Nelly Sachs, 1980, Goethe, Wilhelm Meister's Apprenticeship, 1982; co-editor: German Studies Rev; contbr. articles to profl. jours. Recipient Disting. Teaching award UCLA, 1970, Humanities Inst. award, 1972, summer stipend NEH, 1978. Mem. MLA, Am. Soc. 18th Century Studies, Am. Assn. Tchrs. German, Western Soc. 18th Century Studies, Western Assn. German Studies, Philological Assn. Pacific Coast, Lessing Soc., Goethe Soc. N. Am. Office: Germanic Langs UCLA Los Angeles CA 90024

BAHR, GUNTER F., pathologist, educator; b. Altona, Germany, Oct. 25, 1922; s. Karl and Elfriede (Wedekind) B.; m. Lotte Leuenberger; children: Josephine Karina, Nina Ingrid. M.D., U. Wurzburg, Germany, 1952, Karolinska Inst., Stockholm, Sweden, 1957. Asst. Nobel Inst. Cell Research and Genetics, Stockholm, 1950-57, asst. prof., 1957-58, Karolinska Inst., 1957-58, Inst. Pathology, 1957-60; chief biophysics br. Armed Forces Inst. Pathology, 1960-74, chmn. dept. cellular pathology, 1974—; clin. prof. pathology Georgetown U., Washington, 1963—; prof. pathology U. Md., 1978—; lectr. medicine and pathology Johns Hopkins U., Balt., 1972—; vis. prof. pathology, Northwestern U., 1958; research prof., clin. prof. pathology Uniformed Services Univ. Health Scis., Bethesda, Md., 1976—. Editorial bds. sci. jours. Scandinavian rep. UNESCO com. on animal resources, 1955. Recipient award for meritorious civilian service, 1965, award for distinguished civilian service, 1967, Army research team award, 1967; Alexander von Humboldt award, 1978. Hon. fellow Internat. Acad. Reproductive Medicine; mem. Mil. Surgeons U.S. (hon.), Internat. Acad. Cytology (Maurice Goldblatt Cytological award 1966), Electron Microscopy Soc. Am. (dir. 1973-76), Histochem. Soc. (pres. 1975-76), NIH (biomath. and computer study sect. 1973-76), Scandinavian Soc. Electron Microscopy. Research, publs. quantitative electron microscopy, malaria. chromosomes, pattern recognition. Home: 3206 Chestnut St NW Washington DC 20015

BAHR, HOWARD MINER, sociologist, educator; b. Provo, Utah, Feb. 21, 1938; s. A. Francis and Louie Jean (Miner) B.; m. Rosemary Frances Smith, Aug. 28, 1961; children: Bonnie Louise, Howard McKay, Rowena Ruth, Tanya Lavonne, Christopher J., Laura L., Stephen S., Rachel M. B.A. with honors, Brigham Young U., 1962; M.A. in Sociology, U. Tex., 1964, Ph.D., 1965. Research asso. Columbia U., N.Y.C., 1965-68; vis. lectr., summer 1968; lectr. in sociology N.Y. U., 1967-68, Bklyn. Coll., City U. N.Y., 1967; asso. prof. sociology Wash. State U., Pullman, 1968-73, prof., 1972-73, chmn. dept. rural sociology, 1971-73; prof. sociology Brigham Young U., Provo, Utah, 1973—; dir. Family Research Inst., 1977-83; vis. prof. sociology U. Va., 1976-77. Author: Skid Row: An Introduction to Disaffiliation, 1973, Old Men Drunk and Sober, 1974, Women Alone: The Disaffiliation of Urban Females, 1976, Ethnic Americans, 1979, Widows: Adapting to Sudden Bereavement, 1980, Middletown Families, 1982, All Faithful People: Change and Continuity in Middletown's Religion, 1983, Life in Large Families, 1983, Divorce and Remarriage: Problems, Adaptations and Adjustments, 1983; contbr. articles to profl. jours.; asso. editor: Rural Sociology, 1978—, Jour. Marriage and the Family, 1978—. NIMH grantee, 1968-70, 71-73; NSF grantee, 1971-72, 76-80. Mem. Am. Sociol. Assn., Soc. Sci. Study Religion, Rural Sociol. Assn., Nat. Council Family Relations, Southwestern Social Sci. Assn. Mormon. Office: Dept Sociology Brigham Young U Provo UT 84602

BAHR, LAUREN S., publishing company executive; b. New Brunswick, N.J., July 3, 1944; d. Simon A. and Rosalind J. (Cabot) B. Student, U. Grenoble, France, 1964; B.A. (Branstrom scholar), M.A., U. Mich., 1966. Asst. editor New Horizons Pubs., Inc., Chgo., 1967, Scholastic Mags., Inc., N.Y.C., 1968-71; supervising editor Houghton Mifflin Co., Boston, 1971; product devel. editor Appleton-Century-Crofts, N.Y.C., 1972-74; sponsoring editor McGraw-Hill, Inc., N.Y.C., 1974-75; editor Today's Sec. mag., 1975-77; sr. editor Media Systems Corp., N.Y.C., 1978; sr. editor coll. dept. CBS Coll. Pub., N.Y.C., 1978-82, mktg. mgr. fgn. langs., dir. mktg. adminstrn., 1982-83; dir. devel. Coll. div. Harper & Row, N.Y.C., 1983—. Democrat. Jewish. Home: 444 E 82d St New York NY 10028 Office: 383 Madison Ave New York NY 10017

BAHRENBURG, D. CLAEYS, publishing company executive; b. East Orange, N.J., Apr. 26, 1947; s. William Stewart and Janet (Claeys) B.; m. Linda Bartlett, Jan. 3, 1981; 1 dau., Genevieve. Student, Ithaca Coll., 1969-71, NYU, 1971-72. Assoc. mgr. N.E. office N.Y. Times, N.Y.C., 1970-72; assoc. pub. On the Sound mag., N.Y.C., 1972-74; sr. sales rep. Saturday Rev., N.Y.C., 1974-76; assoc. pub. Straight Arrow Pubs., Rolling Stone mag., N.Y.C., 1976-81; v.p., pub. Hearst Publs. House Beautiful, N.Y.C., 1981—. Mem. Orient Hist. Soc., Mag. Pubs. Assn. (com.). Republican. Episcopalian. Clubs: New York Athletic, Orient Yacht. Office: Hearst Corp House Beautiful Mag 1700 Broadway New York NY 10019 *

BAHTI, JAMES HOWE, diplomat; b. Hancock, Mich., July 10, 1923; s. Eino A. and Alice (Howe) B.; m. Anita C., June 12, 1948; children: Thomas, Timothy. B.S., Mich. Tech. U.; M.P.A., U. Mich., Ph.D. Commd. fgn. service officer Dept. State, 2d sec., Cairo, 1961-63, dep. desk officer, Washington, 1964-69, consul, Bombay, India, 1970-72, consul gen., Dhahran, Saudi Arabia, 1972-75, Alexandria, Egypt, 1981—. Author: Arab Boycott of Israel, 1966. Pres. Dhahran Acad. Sch. Bd., 1972-75. Served to cpl. USAAF, 1943-46. Recipient Meritorious Honoraward Dept. State, 1965, Superior Honoraward Dept. State, 1977, 80. Mem. Am. Fgn. Service Assn., Middle East Inst. Office: Am Consulate Gen 110 Horreya Ave Alexandria Egypt

BAIARDI, JOHN CHARLES, sci. lab. dir.; b. Bklyn., Feb. 9, 1918; s. Joseph and Vivian (Oddo) B.; m. Rosalind Castaldi, May 15, 1943; children—Robert, Veronica. B.S., St. Francis Coll., 1940; M.A., Bklyn. Coll., 1943; Ph.D., N.Y. U., 1953. Instr., then asst. prof. biology St. Francis Coll., 1942-48; asso. prof. biology St. Johns U., 1948-54; prof. biology, chmn. dept. L.I. U., 1954-62; asso. dean Grad. Sch., 1960-62, v.p., provost, 1962-67, vice chancellor, 1967-70; pres., dir. N.Y. Ocean Sci. Lab., Montauk, 1970—; Mem. med. adv. bd. Cooley's Anemia Found.; mem. Bi-County Marine Resources Council. Chmn. bd. trustees Affiliated Colls. and Univs., Inc. Named to Bklyn. Hall of Fame for sci. activities, 1964. Fellow N.Y. Acad. Scis.; mem. Harvey Soc., Internat. Oceanographic Found., Sigma Xi, Phi Sigma. Home: Edgemeer Rd Montauk NY 11954 Office: New York Ocean Science Lab Drawer EE Montauk NY 11954

BAIER, EDWARD JOHN, industrial hygiene engineer; b. Pitts., Apr. 1, 1925; s. Edward O. and Lucy M. B.; m. Grace Cecelia McDonald, Jan. 15, 1947; children: Edward Michael, Grace Cecelia. B.S., U. Pitts., 1946, M.P.H. (fellow), 1955. Cert. in comprehensive practice of indsl. hygiene, internat. hazard control mgmt., cert. safety profl. Chief indsl. hygiene sect. Dept. Health State of Pa., 1956-68, dir. div. occupational health, 1968-71, Dept. Environ. Resources, 1971; dir. Bur. Mines and Occupational Health and Safety, 1971-72; dep. dir. Nat. Inst. for Occupational Safety and Health, HEW, Rockville, Md., 1972-78; corp. dir. indsl. hygiene and toxicology Diamond Shamrock Corp., Cleve. and; Dallas, 1978-82; dir. tech. support OSHA, Dept. Labor, 1982—; lectr. in field. Contbr. articles to profl. jours. Chmn. West Shore council Boy Scouts Am., 1970-71; sec. Upper Allen Twp. (Pa.) Sewer Authority, 1970-72. Mem. Am. Conf. Govt. Indsl. Hygienists (chmn. 1968-69), Am. Indsl. Hygiene Assn. (pres. 1975-76, Cummings Meml. award 1982, Edward J. Baier Tech. Achievement award 1984), Am. Acad. Indsl. Hygiene (founder), Indsl. Hygiene Roundtable (steward 1975-76), Nat. Am. Indian Safety Council, N.Y. Acad. Scis., Pa. Soc. Profl. Engrs., Am. Bd. Indsl. Hygiene (dir. 1970-76). Roman Catholic. Office: OSHA Dept Labor DTS 200 Constitution Ave NW Washington DC 20210

BAIL, JOE PAUL, educator; b. Herold, W.Va., May 12, 1925; s. Alva Edward and Prudence (Wood) B.; m. Nelma Louise Rapp, Oct. 20, 1945; 1 son, David Joe. B.S., W.Va. U., 1947, M.S., 1947; Ph.D., Mich State U., 1958. Tchr. agr. Spencer (W. Va.) High Sch., 1947; head dept. agr. Glenville (W. Va.) State Coll., 1948-51; asst. prof., assoc. prof. agrl. edn. W.Va. U., 1951-57; asst. prof., then assoc. prof. Cornell U., Ithaca, N.Y., 1957-67, prof. agrl. edn. div., 1967—, chmn. agrl. edn. div., 1963-71, chmn. dept. edn., 1978; vis. prof. U. Ariz., U. Fla.; Cons. pub. schs., N.Y., Mass., W.Va., Ariz, Fla.; mem. com. Nat. Acad. Scis.; field review officer U.S. Office Edn. Contbg. author: Teacher Education in Agriculture, 1967, 79; contbr. articles to profl. jours. Dist. chmn. Boy Scouts Am., 1972-73; mem. Ch.-Community Action, Inc., 1968—; pres. N.Y. Council on Rural Edn. Served to 1st lt. USAAF, 1943-45; ETO. Decorated Soldier's medal, Air medal with four oak leaf clusters; recipient 30-yr. award in agrl. edn. N.Y. Assn. Tchrs. Agr., 1977; named Hon. Am. Farmer Future Farmers Am., 1978, Paul Harris fellow. Mem. Am. Vocat. Assn. (past nat. com. chmn.), Assn. Higher Edn., N.Y. Assn. Deans of Edn. (mem. council), Alpha Zeta, Kappa Delta Pi, Delta Tau Delta, Alpha Tau Alpha. Democrat. Baptist (trustee). Club: Rotarian (past pres.). Home: 111 Winston Dr Ithaca NY 14850

BAILAR, BENJAMIN FRANKLIN, corporate executive; b. Champaign, Ill., Apr. 21, 1934; s. John C. and Florence (Catherwood) B.; m. Anne Tveit, Aug. 22, 1958; children: Christina, Benjamin Franklin. B.A., U. Colo., 1955; M.B.A., Harvard, 1959; D.P.A. (hon.), Monmouth Coll., 1976. With Continental Oil Co., Houston, 1959-62; with Am. Can Co., N.Y.C., 1962-72, v.p., 1967-72; sr. asst. postmaster gen. U.S. Postal Service, Washington, 1972-74, dep. postmaster gen., 1974-75, postmaster gen., 1975-78; exec. v.p., dir. U.S. Gypsum Co., Chgo., 1978-82; pres., chief exec. officer Scott Pub. Co., N.Y.C., 1983—; dir. Sears Bank & Trust Co., Midland Bancorp., Inc., Dana Corp., Toledo., Nat. Info. Utilities Corp. Asso. mem. Pres.'s Commn. on Employment Handicapped, 1976-78; bd. dirs. Monmouth (Ill.) Coll.; mem. exec. council Washington Irving council Boy Scouts Am., White Plains, N.Y., 1969-72; trustee Adler Planetarium. Served with USNR, 1955-57. Mem. U.S. C. of C. (govt. and regulatory affairs com.), Tau Kappa Epsilon. Clubs: Econ. N.Y.; Econ., Chgo. (Chgo.); Glen View. Home: 410 E Walnut Rd Lake Forest IL 60045 Office: 3 E 57th St New York NY 10022

BAILAR, JOHN CHRISTIAN, JR., chemist, educator, consultant; b. Golden, Colo., May 27, 1904; s. John Christian and Rachel Ella (Work) B.; m. Florence L. Catherwood, Aug. 8, 1931 (dec. Mar. 13, 1975); children: John Christian III, Benjamin Franklin; m. Katharine R. Ross, June 12, 1976. B.A., U. Colo., 1924, M.A., 1925, D.Sc., 1959; Ph.D., U. Mich., 1928; D.Sc., U. Buffalo, 1959, Lehigh U., 1973; L.H.D., Monmouth Coll., 1983. Asst. in chemistry U. Mich., 1926-28; instr. chemistry U. Ill., Urbana, 1928-30, asso., 1930-35, asst. prof., 1935-39, asso. prof., 1939-43, prof., 1943-72, prof. emeritus, 1972—, sec. chem. dept., 1937-51; Vis. prof. chemistry U. Colo., summer 1962, U. Ariz., 1970, U. Wyo., 1970, U. São Paulo, 1972, Kyushu U., Japan, 1974, Wash. State U., 1975, U. Guanajuato, Mexico, 1976, 78, 79, 80, 81, 82, U. W.Fla., 1979; Lectr. in field. Author: (with B S. Hopkins) General Chemistry for Colleges, 1951, 56, Essentials of College Chemistry, 1946, (with Therald Moeller and Jacob Kleinberg) University Chemistry, 1965, (with Therald Moeller, Jacob Kleinberg, Cyrus Guss, Mary Castellion, Clyde Metz) Chemistry, 1978; Editor: The Chemistry of the Coordination Compounds, 1956; editor-in-chief: Vol. IV Inorganic Syntheses; mem. editorial bds. several chem. jours; also contbr. articles and revs. to chem. jours. Bd. dirs. Monmouth Coll., 1958-76. Recipient Sci. Apparatus Makers award in chem. edn., 1961, John R. Kuebler award Alpha Chi Sigma, 1962, Priestley medal Am. Chem. Soc., 1964; Frank Dwyer medal Chem. Soc. New South Wales, 1965; Alfred Werner gold medal Swiss Chem. Soc., 1966; Teaching award Mfg. Chemists Assn., 1968; Am. Chem. Soc. award in inorganic chemistry, sponsored by Mallinckrodt Chem. Works, 1972; Midwest award St. Louis sect. Am. Chem. Soc., 1971; J. Heyrovski medal Czechoslovak Acad. Scis., 1978; Monie Ferst medal Sigma Xi, 1983; 1st recipient John C. Bailar Jr. medal U. Ill.; named Distinguished Alumnus U. Mich., 1967, Ky. Col. Mem. Internat. Union Pure and Applied Chemistry (treas. 1963-71), Am. Chem. Soc. (chmn. div. chem. edn. 1946-47, chmn. div. phys. and inorganic chemistry 1949-50, chmn. div. inorganic chem. 1956-57, pres. 1959, dir. 1958-60), Phi Beta Kappa, Sigma Xi, Phi Lambda Upsilon, Alpha Chi Sigma. Presbyn. Home: 605 E Harding Dr Urbana IL 61801

BAILEY, AMOS PURNELL, clergyman, journalist; b. Grotons, Va., May 2, 1918; s. Louis William and Evelyn (Charnock) B.; m. Ruth Martin Hill, Aug. 22, 1942; children—Eleanor Carol (Mrs. Thomas T. Harriman), Anne Ruth (Mrs. Peter S. Page), Joyce Elizabeth (Mrs. David L. Richardson II), Jeanne Purnell (Mrs. Paul H. Dodge). B.A., Randolph-Macon Coll., 1942, D.D., 1956; B.D., Duke, 1948; Th.M., Union Theol. Sem., 1957. Ordained to ministry United Meth. Ch., 1942; pastor, Emporia, Va., 1938, Richmond, Va., 1938-43, New Kent circuit, 1943-44, Norfolk, 1948-50, Newport News, Va., 1950-54, Centenary Ch., Richmond, 1954-61; supt. Richmond dist. United Meth. Ch., 1961-67; sr. minister Reveille Ch., Richmond, 1967-70; asso. gen. sec., div. chaplains Bd. Higher Edn. and Ministry United Meth. Ch., Washington, 1970-79; v.p. Nat. Meth. Found., 1979—; pres. Nat. Temple Ministries, Inc.; Pres. S.E.J. and S.C.U. Communications, 1968-76; dir. Reeves-Parvin Co.; Vice pres. Va. Conf. Bd. Missions, 1955-61, Meth. Commn. Town and Country Work, 1956-67; mem. Meth. Commn. on Higher Edn., 1960-70, Meth. Interbd. Council, 1960-70; del. Southeastern Jurisdictional Conf., 1964, 68, Gen. Conf., 1964, 66, 68, 70, World Meth. Conf., London, 1966, Denver, 1970, Dublin, 1976; frequent chaplain U.S. Senate, U.S. Ho. of Reps., Va. Gen. Assembly; mem. council, exec. com., pres. communications com. Southeastern Jurisdiction, 1968-76; pres. Joint Communications Com., 1968-76; vice chmn. Ministry to Service Personnel in East Asia, 1972-79; mem. Commn. on Interpretation, Va. Conf. Writer: syndicated column Daily Bread, syndicated radio devotional, 1945-69; condr.: weekly radio counseling program The Night Pastor, 1955-69, Sunshine and Shadows, 1967-70; Contbr. articles to profl. pubs. Mem. exec. com. Va. Conf. Bd. Edn., 1968-72; mem. World Meth. Council.; Mem. Va. Commn. Aging; pres. adv. bd. Richmond Welfare Dept., 1956-68; group chmn. industry div. Richmond United Givers Fund, 1961; mem. Va. Conf. Bd. Ministry, Richmond Pub. Assistance Com., Richmond Council on Alcoholism; chmn. chaplains adv. council VA, Washington; bd. mgrs. Richmond YMCA, 1961-69; Bd. dirs. Va. Meth. Advisers; trustee Randolph-Macon Coll., 1960-82; bd. visitors Duke Div. Sch., 1964-70; trustee So. Sem., 1961-76. Served with Chaplains Corps AUS, 1945-47. Mem. Meth. Hist. Soc., Duke Div. Alumni Assn. (pres.). Club: Kiwanis. Home: 7815 Falstaff Rd McLean VA 22102 Office: 1835 N Nash St Arlington VA 22209 *Life for me is rich and meaningful in a Christian committment which allows a free and unfettered search for truth. Discipline of time and resources, the love of persons in my sphere of activity, a devoted family — all are part of the life I cherish daily.*

BAILEY, ANDREW DEWEY, JR., accountant; b. St. Paul, Feb. 18, 1942; s. Andrew Dewey and Lorraine LaBelle B.; m. Irene Sylvia Femrite, Mar. 22, 1964; children: Andrew Dewey, III, Rachelle Irene. B.S. in Bus, U. Minn., 1964, M.S., 1966; Ph.D., Ohio State U., 1971. C.P.A., Minn. Mem. faculty U. Maine, 1970-72, U. Iowa, 1972-74, Purdue U., 1974-80; prof. acctg., chmn. dept. U. Minn., 1980—. Author articles in field. Mem. Fin. Execs. Inst., Am. Acctg. Assn., Inst. Mgmt. Accountants (cert. mgmt. acct.), Inst. Internal Auditors (cert. internal auditor), Am. Inst. C.P.A.s. Republican. Lutheran. Office: Dept Acctg U Minn Minneapolis MN 55455

BAILEY, CECIL CABANISS, lawyer; b. LaGrange, Ga., Oct. 29, 1901; s. Daniel B. and Maude (Layfield) B.; m. Augusta Mann, Feb. 15, 1923; children: Dorothy Bailey McGehee, Marilyn Evans-Jones, William C. Student, Young Harris Coll., 1922, U. Ga., 1923; LL.B.,

Stetson U., 1927; LL.D. (hon.), Stetson U., 1978. Bar: Fla. 1927. High sch. prin., Byromville, Ga. and Madison, Fla., 1923-24; assoc. Scarlett, Jordan, Futch & Fielding, DeLand, 1927-29; clk. Judge's Ct. Volusia (Fla.) County, 1929-30; assoc. Rogers & Towers, Jacksonville, 1930-37; sr. partner Rogers, Towers, Bailey, Jones & Gay, 1937—; sr. v.p., gen. counsel Gulf Life Ins. Co.; sr. dir. Cain & Bultman, Inc. Bd. overseers Stetson U. Coll. Law, St. Petersburg, Fla.; trustee Charles A. Dana Law Center Found., Hope Haven Hosp.; past pres. and trustee Jacksonville Public Library System; mem. Fla. Game and Fresh Water Fish Commn. Mem. ABA, Fla. Bar Assn., Jacksonville Bar Assn. (pres. 1946), Am. Judicature Soc., Newcomen Soc., Phi Alpha Delta. Methodist. Clubs: Civitan, San Jose Country, Univ., River. Home: 6000 San Jose Blvd Unit 11F Jacksonville FL 32217 Office: 1300 Gulf Life Dr and Gulf Life Tower Jacksonville FL 32207

BAILEY, CECIL DEWITT, engineer; b. Zama, Miss., Oct. 25, 1921; s. James Dewitt and Matha Eugenia (Roberts) B.; m. Myrtis Irene Taylor, Sept. 8, 1942; children: Marilyn, Beverly. B.S., Miss. State U., 1951; M.S., Purdue U., 1954, Ph.D., 1962. Commd. 2d lt. U.S. Air Force, 1944, advanced through grades to lt. col., 1965; pilot, 1944-56, sr. pilot, 1956-60, command pilot, 1960-67, ret., 1967; asst. prof. Air Force Inst. Tech., 1954-58, asso. prof., 1965-67; asso. prof. aero. and astronautical engring. Ohio State U., Columbus, 1967-69, prof., 1970—; dir. USAF-Am. Soc. Engring. Edn. summer faculty research program, Wright-Patterson AFB, Ohio, 1976-78. Contbr. numerous articles to profl. jours. Mem. Am. Inst. Aeros. and Astronautics, Soc. Exptl. Stress Analysis, Am. Soc. Engring. Edn., Am. Acad. Mechanics, Soc. Natural Philosophy, Air Force Assn., Sigma Xi, Sigma Gamma Tau. Club: USAF Officers. Research into a unified theory of mechanics, the general energy equation. Home: 4176 Ashmore Rd Columbus OH 43220

BAILEY, CHARLES LYLE, energy company executive; b. Washington-on-Brazos, Tex., Oct. 15, 1934; s. Robert F. and Opal (Lyle) B.; m. Gayle Marie Fread, Oct. 19, 1957; children—Michele Renee, Craig Lyle, Julie Ann. B.B.A., U. Tex., 1957; grad. Advanced Mgmt. Program, Harvard U., 1975. With Tenneco Inc., 1959-83; asst. sec. Tenneco Oil Co., 1970-71, v.p. parent co., Houston, 1971-83; pres., dir. subs. Eastern Ins. Co. Ltd., Bermuda, 1971-83; pres., chmn. bd. subs. Columbine Casualty Co., Denver, 1977-83; pres., chief exec. officer, dir. mem. exec. com., past chmn. bd. Oil Ins. Ltd., Bermuda., 1983—. Served with U.S. Army, 1957-59. Mem. Nat. Petroleum Refiners Assn., Risk Ins. Mgmt. Soc. (past pres. Houston chpt.). Home: Palm Grove Southshore Rd Devonshire Bermuda 77090 Office: PO Box 1751 Hamilton 5 Bermuda

BAILEY, CHARLES WALDO, II, journalist; b. Boston, Apr. 28, 1929; s. David Washburn and Catherine Ruth (Smith) B.; m. Ann Card Bushnell, Sept. 9, 1950; children: Victoria Britton, Sarah Tilden. Grad., Phillips Exeter Acad., 1946; A.B. magna cum laude, Harvard U., 1950. Reporter, corr. Washington bur. Mpls. Tribune, 1950-54; corr. Washington bur. Des Moines Register, Look mag., 1954-67; chief Washington bur. Mpls. Tribune, 1968-72, editor, 1972-82, Mpls. Star and Tribune, 1982; Washington editor Nat. Pub. Radio, 1984—; Mem. Standing Com. Corr., Washington, 1962-63. Author: (with Fletcher Knebel) No High Ground, 1960, Seven Days in May, 1962, Convention, 1964; Contbr. to: Candidates, 1960, 1959, Exeter Remembered, 1965, The President's Trip to China, 1972. Trustee Carnegie Endowment for Internat. Peace., Washington Journalism Ctr. Mem. Overseas Writers, Council on Fgn. Relations. Clubs: Gridiron, Fed. City, Nat. Press., Harvard of N.Y.C. Home: 3001 Albemarle St NW Washington DC 20008 Office: 2025 M St NW Washington DC 20036

BAILEY, DANA KAVANAGH, radiophysicist, botanist; b. Clarendon Hills, Ill., Nov. 22, 1916; s. Dana Clark and Dorothy (Kavanagh) B. B.S. with highest distinction, U. Ariz., 1937; postgrad., Harvard U., 1940; B.A. (Rhodes scholar), Queen's Coll., Oxford (Eng.) U., 1940, M.A., 1943, D.Sc., 1967. Astronomer expdn. to Peru for Hayden Planetarium, N.Y.C., 1937; physicist Antarctic expdn. U.S. Antarctic Service, 1940-41; project engr. Project RAND Douglas Aircraft Co., Santa Monica, Calif., 1946-48; physicist Nat. Bur. Standards, Washington, 1948-55, physicist, cons., Boulder, Colo., 1959-66; radiophysicist, research botanist Space Environment Lab., Environ. Research Labs., Nat. Oceanic and Atmospheric Adminstrn., Boulder, 1966-76; sci. dir. Page Communications Engrs., Inc., Washington, 1955-59; U.S. Exchange rep. Brit. Antarctic Survey Falkland Islands and Antartica; assoc. Gymnosperms U. Colo. Mus., 1972—; internat. chmn. study group internat. radio consultative com. Internat. Telecommunication Union, Geneva, 1956-78. Contbr. articles to profl. jours. Served to maj., Signal Corps AUS, 1941-46. Decorated Legion of Merit; recipient Arthur S. Flemming govt. award Washington Jr. C. of C., 1951; Silver medal Dept. Commerce, 1952; Gold medal, 1956. Fellow AAAS, Am. Phys. Soc., Am. Geog. Soc., Royal Astron. Soc., Royal Geog. Soc.; mem. Sci. Research Soc. Am. (pres. Boulder br. 1967-68), Am. Geophys. Union, Am. Astron. Soc., Geog. Soc. Lima (hon.), Phi Beta Kappa., Sigma Xi. Clubs: Cosmos (Washington); Explorers (N.Y.C.). Home: 1441 Bluebell Ave Boulder CO 80302 Office: Univ Colo Museum Boulder CO 80309

BAILEY, DAVID ROY SHACKLETON, classics educator; b. Lancaster, Eng., Dec. 10, 1917; came to U.S., 1968; s. John Henry Shackleton and Rosamund Maud (Giles) B. B.A., Gonville and Caius Coll., Cambridge, 1939, M.A., 1943, Litt.D., 1958; Litt.D. (hon.), U. Dublin, 1984. Fellow Gonville and Caius Coll., 1944-55, praelector, 1954-55, dep. bursar, 1964, sr. bursar, 1965-68, Univ. lectr., Tibetan, 1948-68; fellow, dir. studies in classics Jesus Coll., Cambridge, 1955-64; vis. lectr. classics Harvard U., 1963, prof. Greek and Latin, 1975-82, Pope prof. Latin lang. and lit., 1982—; prof. Latin U. Mich., Ann Arbor, 1968-75; vis. Andrew V.V. Raymond prof. classics SUNY, Buffalo, 1973-74; vis. fellow Peterhouse, Cambridge, 1980-81. Author: The Satapancasatka of Matrceta, 1951, Propertiana, 1956, Cicero's Letters, 10 vols, 1965-81, Cicero, 1971, Profile of Horace, 1982, Anthologia Latina I, 1982; others; contbr. articles on Oriental and classical subjects to profl. jours.; Editor: Harvard Studies in Classical Philology, 1978—. Recipient Charles J. Goodwin award of merit, 1978; Nat. Endowment for Humanities fellow, 1980-81. Fellow Brit. Acad., Am. Acad. Arts and Scis.; mem. Am. Philos. Soc. Home: Apt 183 988 Memorial Dr Cambridge MA 02138 Office: Dept Classics 319 Boylston Hall Harvard U Cambridge MA 02138

BAILEY, DUDLEY, educator; b. Lamoni, Iowa, Feb. 7, 1918; s. Vaughn Corless and Lida (Hayer) B.; m. Sue Ogden, Apr. 27, 1945; children—Geoffrey Ogden, Paul Fletcher, Jane Barker. B.A., U. Kansas City, 1942, M.A., 1944; Ph.D., U. Ill., 1954. Instr. U. Nebr., 1943-44, 45-46, Wentworth Mil. Acad., 1944-45, U. Kansas City, 1946-48; grad. asst. U. Ill., 1948-54; mem. faculty U. Neb., 1954—, prof. English, 1963—, chmn. dept., 1962-72; Mem. Nat. Council Accreditation Tchr. Edn., 1966-69. Co-author: Form in Modern English, 1958; Editor: Essays on Rhetoric, 1965, Introductory Language Essays, 1965; editorial adv. bd.: World Book Ency. Dictionary; editorial cons., Oxford Univ. Press. Mem. Coll. Conf. Composition and Communication (chmn. 1968), Nat. Council Tchrs. English (exec. com. 1967-68), Coll. English Assn. (dir. 1963-66), Am. Assn. U. Profs., Modern Lang. Assn., Assn. Depts. English. Democrat. Unitarian. Home: 4231 B St Lincoln NE 68510 Office: Andrews Hall Lincoln NE 68588

BAILEY, EDWARD JOSEPH, diversified industry executive; b. New Haven, June 28, 1932; s. Samuel and Sylvia Jean (Joseph) B.; m. Madelyne Grace Strauss, June 10, 1962; children: Paul Spencer, Mark Daniel. B.S. in Econs, U. Pa., 1954. C.P.A., Conn. With Bailey, Moore & Glazer (pub. accountants), New Haven, 1955-57; mgr. financial analysis Ford Motor Co., Dearborn, Mich., 1957-61; controller sales and distbn. consumer products Philco Ford Corp., Phila., 1962-66; asst. controller Celanese Corp., N.Y.C., 1967-70; v.p., asst. corporate comptroller ITT; also dir. finance, v.p. ITT Europe, Brussels, Belgium, 1970-75; v.p., dep. comptroller ITT, N.Y.C., 1975-80; sr. v.p., chief fin. officer Ingersoll-Rand Co., Woodcliff Lake, N.J., 1980-81; exec. v.p. Esteé Lauder, Inc., N.Y.C., 1981—. Mem. Fin. Execs. Inst. (sec. replacement cost adv. com. 1976), Conf. Bd., N.J. Soc. C.P.A.'s, Zeta Beta Tau, Beta Gamma Sigma, Beta Alpha Psi. Clubs: Fairmount Country., University. Home: 10 Beacon Rd Summit NJ 07901 Office: Esteé Lauder Inc 767 Fifth Ave New York NY 10153

BAILEY, EUGENE CARY, retired consulting engineer; b. Chgo., Apr. 7, 1910; s. Alexander Davidson and Alice (Cary) B.; m. Marie F. Kerker, Apr. 21, 1931 (dec.); m. Janet L. Sampson, Jan. 24, 1938; children: Willard N., Robert E., Alice(dec.). B.S. in Mech. Engring, Purdue U., 1932, M.S., 1933. Registered profl. engr., Ill. With Commonwealth Edison Co., Chgo., 1933-75, system mech. and bldg. engr., 1954-62, adminstrv. engr. for v.p., 1962-75; v.p. bus. devel. John Dolio & Assos. (now Dolio & Metz Ltd), Chgo., 1975-82; cons., resource recovery and nuclear and fossil power engring. Trustee Lyons Twp. High Sch., Dist. 204, 1956-69; trustee Coll. of DuPage, Ill., 1970-77; mem. Ill. Commn. Atomic Energy. Served from 1st lt. to capt. U.S. Army, 1942-45. Fellow ASME (life); mem. Western Soc. Engrs., Am. Welding Soc. (life), Am. Nuclear Soc., Ind. Soc. Profl. Engrs. Republican. United Methodist. Clubs: Antique Auto Am., Rolls-Royce Owners. Home: RR6 Box 252 Columbus IN 47201

BAILEY, EXINE MARGARET ANDERSON, soprano, educator; b. Cottonwood, Minn., Jan. 4, 1922; d. Joseph Leonard and Exine Pearl (Robertson) Anderson; m. Arthur Albert Bailey, May 5, 1956. B.S., U. Minn., 1944; M.A., Columbia U., 1945; profl. diploma, 1951. Instr. Columbia U., 1947-51; faculty U. Oreg., Eugene, 1951—, prof. voice, 1966—; faculty dir., Salzburg, Austria, summer 1968, Europe, summer 1976; vis prof., head vocal instrn. Columbia U., summers 1952, 59. Profl. singer, N.Y.C.; including appearances with NBC, ABC symphonies; solo artist on West Coast; appearing with symphonies, Portland and, Eugene, groups in, Wash., Calif., Mont., Idaho, also in concert.; Contbr. articles, book revs. to various mags. Recipient Young Artist award N.Y.C. Singing Tchrs., 1945, Music Fedn. Club (N.Y.C.) hon. award, 1951; Kathryn Long scholar Met. Opera, 1945. Mem. Nat. Assn. Tchrs. Singing (lt. gov. 1968-72), Oreg. Music Tchrs. Assn (pres. 1974-76), Music Tchrs. Nat. Assn. (nat. voice chmn. high sch. activities 1970-74, nat. chmn. voice 1973-75, 81—, NW chmn. collegiate activities and artists competition 1978—), AAUP, Internat. Platform Assn., Kappa Delta Pi, Sigma Alpha Iota. Home: 17 Westbrook Way Eugene OR 97405 Office: Sch Music U Oreg Eugene OR 97403 *My chief goal in life is to realize my potentials through perfecting my innate talents and capabilities.*

BAILEY, FRANCIS LEE, lawyer; b. Waltham, Mass., June 10, 1933; m. Florence Gott (div. 1961); m. Froma Victoria (div. 1972); 1 son, Scott Frederic; m. Lynda Hart, Aug. 26, 1972 (div. 1980). Student, Harvard U.; LL.B., Boston U. Bar: Mass. 1960. Practice law, Boston and, N.Y.C.; partner firm Bailey & Broder, N.Y.C.; dir. Murray Chris Craft. Author: (with Harvey Aronson) The Defense Never Rests, 1972, Cleared for the Approach, 1977, (with John Greenya) For the Defense, 1976; novel Secrets, 1979; How to Protect Yourself Against Cops In California and Other Strange Places, 1982, To Be a Trial Lawyer, 1983. Mem. Am. Bar Assn. Address: PO Box 679 Marshfield MA 02050

BAILEY, FRED COOLIDGE, engineering consulting company executive; b. Claremont, N.H., Oct. 5, 1925; s. Howard Perry and Helen Gare (Coolidge) B.; m. Mary Beecroft Cunningham, June 26, 1948; children: Susan Bailey Hunter (dec.), Stephen Coolidge, Elizabeth Cunningham. B.S., Mass. Inst. Tech., 1948, M.S., 1949. Registered profl. engr., Mass. Research engr. Caterpillar Tractor Co., Peoria, Ill., 1949-51; asst. tech. dir. com. ship structural design Nat. Acad. Scis., Washington, 1952-55; pres. Teledyne Engring. Services, Waltham, Mass., 1955—. Chmn. Bd. Fire Commrs., Lexington, Mass., 1964-69; mem. Bd. Selectmen, 1969-78; trustee Cary Meml. Library, Lexington, 1971-78, pres., 1972-77; trustee Symmes Hosp., Arlington, Mass., 1969—, mem. exec. com., 1977—, v.p., 1978-80, pres., 1980-81; chmn. Choate-Symmes Health Services, 1981-83. Served with USNR, 1944-46. Fellow Soc. for Exptl. Stress Analysis (pres. 1968-69, recipient Tatnall award 1974); mem. Soc. Naval Architects and Marine Engrs. (recipient Linnard prize 1972), ASME, Am. Welding Soc., Nat. Fire Protection Assn. Home: 48 Coolidge Ave Lexington MA 02173 Office:: 130 2d Ave Waltham MA 02154

BAILEY, GEORGE GILBERT, lawyer; b. Wheeling, W.Va., Dec. 1, 1913; s. George Alfred and Anna Gibson (Rose) B.; m. Lucretia Anne Tucker, Aug. 5, 1944; children—Barbara Anne, Bruce Tucker, John Preston. A.B., W.Va. U., 1935, LL.B., 1937. Bar: W.Va. bar 1937. Since practiced in, Wheeling; partner firm Bailey, Byrum & Vieweg; city solicitor, Wheeling, 1955-72; Pres., dir. Central Union Co. Pres. Oglebay Inst., 1958-60; sec. Sandscrest Found., 1954—. Served with USCGR, 1942-45. Fellow Am. Bar Found.; mem. ABA (ho. of dels. 1964-79, gov. 1974-77), W.Va. Bar Assn. (pres. W.Va. 1962-63), Ohio County Bar Assn. (pres. 1957), State Bar Assn. (pres. 1963-64), Am. Coll. Trial Lawyers, Am. Judicature Soc., Am. Legion, Symposiarchs, Theta Chi, Phi Delta Phi. Democrat. Episcopalian. Home: Dement Rd RD 2 Triadelphia WV 26059 Office: Central Union Bldg Wheeling WV 26003

BAILEY, GLENN WALDEMAR, manufacturing company executive; b. Cleve., May 8, 1925; s. Harry W. and Elizabeth B.; m. Cornelia L. Tarrant, June 12, 1952. B.S., U. Wis., 1946; M.B.A., HarvardU., 1951. Project engr. Thompson Ramo Wooldridge, Cleve., 1946-49; Fin. staff Ford Motor Co., Dearborn, Mich., 1951-54; mgr. fin. analysis Curtiss Wright Corp., 1954-57; asst. to v.p., gen. mgr. Overseas div. Chrysler Corp., Detroit, 1957-60; group gen. mgr. ITT Corp., N.Y.C., 1960-67; chmn. bd., pres. Keene Corp., N.Y.C., 1967-81, Bairnco Corp., 1981—. Served to ensign USNR, 1943-46. Home: Ocean Reef Key Largo FL 33037 Office: 200 Park Ave New York NY 10166

BAILEY, HAROLD STEVENS, JR., ednl. adminstr.; b. Springfield, Mass., Apr. 18, 1922; s. Harold Stevens and Grace Evelyn (Anderson) B.; m. Barbara Ann Dewey, Sept. 8, 1946; children—Cynthia Ann, Lynda Jeanne, Gwen, Pamela, Harold Stevens III. B.S., Mass. Coll. Pharmacy, 1944, M.S., 1948; Ph.D., Purdue U., 1951. Grad. asst. Mass. Coll. Pharmacy, 1946-48; instr. pharmacy Purdue U., 1950-51; faculty S.D. State U., Brookings, 1951—, prof. pharm. chemistry, 1958—, head dept., 1960-61, v.p. acad. affairs, 1961—; dean Grad. Sch., 1965-76; sec. inter-instnl. com. curriculum coordination S.D. Bd. Regents of Edn., 1963-71, mem. acad. adv. council, 1971—, mem. budget adv. council, 1975—, coordinator leadership insts., 1980—; asso. leadership tng. project North Central Assn. Colls. and Secondary Schs., 1961—. Contbr. articles to profl. jours.; Editor pharm. sect.: S.D. Jour. Medicine and Pharmacy, 1953-61. Asso. dist. lay leader S.D. Conf. Methodist Ch., 1960-70; active Boy Scouts Am. Served with AUS, 1944-46. Fellow Am. Found. Pharm. Edn., 1948-50. Fellow AAAS; mem. S.D. Dental Assn. (hon.), S.D. Acad. Sci., S.D. Pharm. Assn., soc. Coll. and Univ. Planning, Sigma Xi, Kappa Psi, Phi Kappa Phi, Rho Chi, Phi Lambda Upsilon. Clubs: Mason, Kiwanian (pres. Brookings 1974-75). Home: 336 Eastern Ave Brooking SD 57006

BAILEY, HARRY AUGUSTINE, JR., educator; b. Ft. Pierce, Fla., Dec. 19, 1932; s. Harry Augustine and Ruth (Finlayson) B.; m. Mary L. Howard, Aug. 4, 1952; children—Harry Augustine III, Larry Berisford. B.A. (Distinguished Mil. Grad.), Fla. A. and M. U., 1954; M.A., U. Kans., 1960, Ph.D., 1964. Asst. dean men Fla. A. and M. U., 1958-59; asst. instr. polit. sci., Western civilization U. Kans., 1960-64, instr. sociology, summer 1964; asst. prof. polit. sci. Temple U., Phila., 1964-68, asso. prof., chmn. dept., 1968-70, prof., chmn. dept., 1970-73, prof., 1973—, dir. M.P.A. program, 1978—; Cons. Phila. Antipoverty Action Com., 1965-67. Contbr. articles to profl. jours.; Editor: Negro Politics in America, 1967, Classics of the American Presidency, 1980; co-editor: Ethnic Group Politics, 1969. Precinct committeeman Democratic party, Lawrence, Kan., 1961-63; Phila. commr. Civil Service, 1981—. Served to 1st lt., arty. AUS, 1954-57. Recipient Christian R. and Mary F. Lindback Found. award for disting. teaching, 1978, Coll. Liberal Arts Alumni Assn. excellence in Teaching award, 1978; both Temple U.). Mem. Am. Soc. Pub. Adminstrn., Center Study Presidency, Ams. for Dem. Action, NAACP, Urban League, Am. Polit. Sci. Assn., AAUP, Pi Sigma Alpha. Episcopalian. Home: 18 Appletree Ct Philadelphia PA 19106

BAILEY, HELEN MCSHANE, historian; b. Gardner, Kans., Oct. 17, 1916; d. Harry Cramer and Maude Ethel (Kramer) McShane; m. James Edwin Bailey, Feb. 23, 1946; children: James Edwin, Barbara Ann Bailey Crawford. B.A., Bethany Nazarene Coll., 1938. Adminstrv. asst. Office Cheif of Staff, U.S. Army, Washington, 1941-48; historian U.S. Army ofcl. history of World War II, U.S. Army, Washington, 1948-58; research asst. George C. Marshall Research Found., Washington, 1958-59; historian Orgn. Joint Chiefs of Staff, Dept. Def., Pentagon, Washington, 1968—. Mem. Am. Hist. Assn., Am. Fgn. Relations. Republican. Lutheran. Home: 9451 Lee Hwy Apt 815 Fairfax VA 22031 Office: Room 1A-714 The Pentagon Washington DC 20301

BAILEY, HENRY JOHN, III, lawyer, educator; b. Pitts., Apr. 4, 1916; s. Henry J. and Lenore Powell Bailey Cahoon; m. Marjorie Jane Ebner, May 30, 1949; children: George W., Christopher G., Barbara W., Timothy P. Student, U.S. Naval Acad., 1934-36; B.A., Pa. State U., 1939; J.D., Yale U., 1947. Bar: N.Y. 1948, Mass. 1963, Oreg. 1974. Ins. investigator Liberty Mut. Ins. Co., N.Y.C., 1941-42; atty. Fed. Res. Bank of N.Y., N.Y.C., 1947-55; asst. v.p. Empire Trust Co., N.Y.C., 1955-56; atty., legal dept. Am. Bankers Assn., N.Y.C., 1956-62; editor Banking Law Jour., Boston, 1962-65; asso. prof. law Willamette U., Salem, Oreg., 1965-69, prof., 1969-81, prof. emeritus, 1981—, adj. prof., 1981—; counsel firm Churchill, Leonard, Brown & Donaldson, Salem, 1981—; vis. prof. U. Akron Sch. Law, 1983-84, Fla. State U. Coll. Law, 1984-85; cons., lectr. to bar and banking groups; lectr. Banking Sch. of South, Baton Rouge, 1972, 73, 75; vis. prof. U. Akron, 1983—. Author: The Law of Bank Checks, 1960, 5th edit., 1979; periodic supplements Modern Uniform Commercial Code Forms, 1963; (with Clarke and Young) Bank Deposits and Collections, 1972, UCC Deskbook: A Short Course in Commercial Paper, 1973, (with Robert D. Hursh) The American Law of Products Liability, 3d edit, 1984, (with William D. Hawkland) The Sum and Substance of Commercial Paper, 1976, 80, Secured Transactions in a Nutshell, 1976, 2d edit., 1981, Oregon Uniform Commercial Code, 2 vols., 1983, 84; Contbr. articles on sales, products liability, comml. paper and secured transactions to legal jours. Served to 1st lt. USAAF, 1942-45; lt. col. Res.; ret. Mem. Am. Bar Assn. (chmn. subcom. on comml. paper 1965-66, 79—), Am. Law Inst., Oreg. State Bar, Lambda Chi Alpha. Republican. Roman Catholic. Office: 530 Center St NE PO Box 804 Salem OR 97308 Office: Fla State U Coll Law Tallahassee FL 32306 *My beliefs are simple: Have faith in God, work hard, and do the job on time.*

BAILEY, HERBERT SMITH, JR., publisher; b. N.Y.C., July 12, 1921; s. Herbert Smith and Viola (Howe) B.; m. Elizabeth M. Brown, June 26, 1943; children: John R., James C., Robin Elizabeth, George W. A.B., Princeton U., 1942; L.H.D., Yale U., 1976. Sci. editor Princeton U. Press, 1946-52, editor, 1952-54, dir., 1954—; dir. Princeton Bank; past mem. adv. com. on tech. publs. AEC; Bowker lectr., 1977. Author: The Art and Science of Book Publishing, 1970; Mem. publs. com.: Am. Scientist; contbr. articles to profl. jours. Past mem. Princeton Twp. Bd. Edn., Princeton Regional Bd. Edn.; chmn. sci. info. council NSF, 1970; vol. leader Boy Scouts Am.; bd. dirs. Nat. Enquiry on Scholarly Publs.; bd. govs. Wesleyan U. Press. Served from ensign to lt. USNR, 1942-45. Mem. Am. Univ. Press Services (dir.), Am. Book Pubs. Council (dir.), Franklin Book Programs (dir.), Assn. Am. Pubs. (dir.), Assn. Am. Univ. Presses (pres.), Newcomen Soc. N.Am., Sigma Xi. Club: Princeton (N.Y.C.). Home: RD 1 Princeton NJ 08540 Office: Princeton U Press 41 William St Princeton NJ 08540

BAILEY, HERMAN TRACY, insurance executive, lawyer; b. Winfield, Iowa, Mar. 25, 1922; s. Dan Wood and Genevieve (Tracy) B.; m. Agnes Kohlhoff, Dec. 24, 1944 (div. Mar. 1973); children—Michael Dan, Tracy Wood.; m. Ruth Carpenter Everett, Jan. 16, 1982. B.S., Iowa State Coll., 1948; J.D., State U. Iowa, 1949. Bar: Iowa bar 1949. Individual practice law, Ottumwa, Iowa, 1949-55; with Bankers Life Co., Des Moines, 1955—, sr. v.p., gen. counsel, 1972—; dir. BLC Ins. Co., Petula Assos., Ltd., Patrician Assos., Inc., BLC Equity Mgmt. Co., BLC Investment Co., BLC Life and Annuity Co., BLC Nat. Ins. Co. Bd. dirs. Iowa Childrens and Family Services., Polk County Legal Aid Soc. Served with USAAF, 1942-46. Mem. Am., Iowa, Polk County bar assns., Assn. Life Ins. Counsel (pres. 1982-83), Order of Coif. Republican. Club: Des Moines. Office: 711 High St Des Moines IA 50307

BAILEY, HUGH COLEMAN, college president; b. Berry, Ala., July 2, 1929; s. Coleman Costello and Susie (Jenkins) B.; m. Ahleida Joan Seever, Nov. 17, 1962; children: Debra Jane, Laura Joan. A.B. with honors, Samford U., 1950; M.A., U. Ala., 1951, Ph.D., 1954. Instr. history and polit. sci. Samford U., 1953-54, asst. prof., 1954-56, assoc. prof., 1956-59, prof., 1959-75, chmn. dept., head div. social scis., 1967-70; dean Howard Coll. Arts and Scis., 1970-75; v.p. for acad. affairs Francis Marion Coll., Florence, S.C., 1975-78; pres. Valdosta (Ga.) State Coll., 1978—; Mem. commn. colls. So. Assn. Colls. and Schs., 1974-75; v.p. Ala. Acad. Sci., 1968-69; pres. Ala. Writers Conclave, 1971-73. Author: John Williams Walker, 1964, Hinton Rowan Helper: Abolitionist-Racist, 1965, Edgar Gardner Murphy: Gentle Progressive, 1968, Liberalism in the New South, Southern Social Reformers and the Progressive Movement, 1969, America: The Framing of a Nation, 2 vols, 1975; Editorial bd.: Social Sci. Vice pres. Homewood City Bd. Edn., 1972-75. Guggenheim fellow, 1963-64; Am. Council Learned Socs. fellow, 1965-66; recipient award merit Am. Assn. State and Local History, 1967. Fellow Royal Soc. Arts; mem. Pi Gamma Mu (nat. trustee-at-large 1969-71, nat. 2d v.p. 1971-78, nat. 1st v.p. 1978—). Episcopalian. Lodge: Kiwanis. Home: 222 Georgia Ave Valdosta GA 31601

BAILEY, IRVING WIDMER, II, insurance holding company executive; b. Cambridge, Mass., June 8, 1941; s. Harwood and Esther (Hill) B.; m. Nancy Lawrence, Sept. 21, 1963; children: Chris,

Michele. Grad., Phillips-Exeter Acad., 1959; student, U. Paris, 1961-62; B.A., U. Colo., 1963; M.B.A., NYU, 1968. Investment officer, asst. v.p. Mut. Life Ins. Co., N.Y.C., 1963-71; v.p. bond investment Phoenix Mut. Life Ins. Co., Hartford, Conn., 1971-76, sr. v.p. investments, 1976-81; exec. v.p., chief investments officer Capital Holding Corp., Louisville, 1981—. Bd. dirs. Internat. Ctr., U. Louisville, 1981—, U. Ky. Vus. Partnership Found., Lexington, 1981—. Mem. N.Y. Soc. Security Analysts, Am. Council Life Ins. sub-com. on fiscal and mentary policy, 1983. Republican. Presbyterian. Clubs: Jefferson (Louisville); Hunting Creek Country (Prospect, Ky.). Home: 6703 Tallwood Ct Louisville KY 40059 Office: Capital Holding Corp PO Box 32830 Louisville KY 40232

BAILEY, JACK BLENDON, computer co. exec.; b. Ft. Worth, Aug. 17, 1925; s. Claude E. and Lalla (Davis) B.; m. Alma Herod. A.B., Okla. State U., 1943, A.M., 1951; LL.B., Columbia, 1948. Bar: Okla. bar 1949. Asso. firm Farmer, Woolsey, Flippo & Bailey, Tulsa, 1949-72, partner, 1951-72; vice-pres., gen. counsel Telex Corp., Tulsa, 1972—. Served with AUS, 1943-45. Mem. Am., Okla. bar assns. Home: 1714 E 30th Pl Tulsa OK 74114 Office: 6422 E 41st St Tulsa OK 74135

BAILEY, JAMES (JIM BAILEY), lawyer, professional football team executive; b. Wilmington, Oreg., Aug. 21, 1946; m. Ann Bailey; children:Sarah, Jenny. Grad., Fla. State U.; J.D., U. Mich. Assoc. Guren, Merritt, Sogg & Cohen, Cleve., 1971-76, ptnr., 1976—; v.p., gen. counsel Cleve. Browns, NFL, 1978—. Office: Cleve Browns Tower B Cleve Stadium Cleveland OH 44114 *

BAILEY, JAMES MARTIN, clergyman, editor; b. Emmetsburg, Iowa, July 28, 1929; s. Allen Ransom and Kathryn (Ausl) B.; m. Betty Jane Wenzel, June 5, 1954; children: Kristine Elizabeth, Susan Ruth. B.A. in Journalism, State U. Iowa, 1951; B.D., Eden Theol. Sem., 1954, D.D., 1966; M.S. in Journalism, Northwestern U., 1956; D.D., Lakeland Coll., Sheboygan, Wis., 1967. Ordained to ministry United Ch. Christ, 1954; mem. staff Nat. Council Chs., 1954-60; bus. mgr. Internat. Jour. Religious Edn., 1954-60, mem. news and information dept., 1974—; mem. exec. com. Communications Commn., 1975—; dir. circulation, advt. and promotion United Ch. Herald, 1960-63, editor, 1963-72, A.D. mag., 1973—. Author: Windbreaks, 1959, Youth in the Town and Country Church, 1959, From Wrecks to Reconciliation, 1969, (with Mrs. Bailey) Worship with Youth, 1962, (with Douglas Gilbert) The Steps of Bonhoeffer, 1969; Contbg. editor: Reformed World, Geneva, Switzerland. Mem. Associated Ch. Press (pres. 1979-81), Interchurch Features (chmn. 1969-73). Home: 45 Watchung Ave Upper Montclair NJ 07043 Office: 475 Riverside Dr New York NY 10027

BAILEY, JOE, professional football team executive. V.p. for adminstrn. Dallas Cowboys, NFL. Office: Care Dallas Cowboys 6116 North Central Expressway Dallas TX 75206

BAILEY, JOEL FURNESS, mechanical engineering educator; b. Pittsfield, Mass., Mar. 7, 1913; s. John Bowen and Clara (Cogswell) B.; m. Arlene Sara Lynn, Mar. 29, 1940 (dec. Sept. 1981); children: Richard John, Betty Jo.; m. Sharon P. White, June 12, 1982; children: Joy Annette and Carol Nanette (twins). B.S., Purdue U., 1935; M.S., Lehigh U., 1939, Ph.D., 1949. Instr. mech. engring. Lehigh U., 1939-42; asst. prof. mech. engring. Oreg. State Coll., 1942-43, Northwestern U., 1943-49; prof. mech. engring. U. Tenn., Knoxville, 1949—, head dept., 1952-73; dir. grad. study program at Arnold Engring. Devel. Center, 1956-57, Alumni Disting. Service prof., 1967—; cons. Union Carbide Nuclear Co., 1951-70. Fellow ASME; mem. Am. Soc. Engring. Edn., ASHRAE, Sigma Xi, Tau Beta Pi, Pi Tau Sigma, Phi Kappa Phi. Presbyterian. Home: Route 1 Scenic Point Louisville TN 37777 Office: U Tenn Knoxville TN 37916

BAILEY, JOHN CHARLES, association executive; b. Osage, Tenn., Feb. 27, 1930; s. Roy Lynn and Dorothy Rachel (Bucknam) B.; m. Shirley Ann Senn, July 30, 1950; 1 dau., Carolyn Kay. Student, U. Iowa, 1950. Mgr. Iowa C. of C., Waverly, 1958-59, gen. mgr., Marshalltown, 1959-61; with U.S. C. of C., 1968-81, regional mgr., Dallas, 1977-81; pres. Greater Mpls. C. of C., 1981—. Mayor, Minnetonka, Minn., 1973-77; chmn. bd. Pub. Affairs Leadership Mgmt., 1976-77. Served with USAF, 1971-73. Mem. Am. C. of C. Execs. (sec.-treas. 1981-82), Assn. Soc. Assn. Execs. Congregationalist. Clubs: Mpls., Wayzata Country. Lodge: Mason. Office: 25 S 1st St Minneapolis MN 55402

BAILEY, JOHN LARRIE, state official; b. Weston, W.Va., Mar. 2, 1934; s. John W. and Carrie Elizabeth (Given) B.; m. Joyce Kennedy, Oct. 15, 1966; children—John Kennedy, David Cleveland, Anne Joyce. A.B., U. S.C., 1955; M.A. in Polit. Sci, W.Va. U., 1966. Tchr. Lost Creek (W.Va.) High Sch., 1960-62; mem. W.Va. Ho. of Dels., 1960-62; stockbroker Parker-Hunter, Inc., Clarksburg, W.Va., 1969-71; pres. Bailey & Assos., Inc., Fairmont, W.Va., 1971-76; treas. State of W.Va., 1976—. Served as officer USN, 1956-59. Recipient Meritorious Service award W.Va. Nat. Guard, 1981. Mem. Naval Res. Assn., Res. Officers Assn. (v.p. for navy, marine corps and coast guard 1967-68), SAR (pres. W.Va. 1982-83), Navy League, Phi Kappa Sigma. Democrat. Baptist. Clubs: Elks, Shriners. Home: 5 Jo Harry Rd Fairmont WV 26554 Office: E-141 State Capitol Bldg Charleston WV 25305

BAILEY, JOHN MARTIN, transportation planner; b. Lakewood, Ohio, Feb. 23, 1928; s. Frank Moherman and Elma (Keener) B.; m. Dorothy Jane Stubbs, Apr. 9, 1960; children: Leslie Jane, Brian John. B.A., Hiram Coll., 1949; M.S., MIT, 1951; Ph.D., U. Va., 1959, postgrad., 1977-78. Aero. research scientist NASA, Cleve., 1951-55; mem. faculty dept. physics Beloit (Wis.) Coll., 1959-76; transp. planner Balt. Regional Planning Council, 1976—; sabbatical research Cambridge U., 1965-66; dir. Overseas Seminar in Quantum Physics, Copenhagen, Denmark, 1970. Author: Liberal Arts Physics, 1974. NSF faculty fellow, 1965-66. Mem. Am. Planning Assn., Transp. Research Bd., Sigma Xi. Presbyterian. Home: 9502 Good Lion Rd Columbia MD 21045 Office: 2225 N Charles St Baltimore MD 21218

BAILEY, JOHN MILTON, educator; b. Memphis, June 3, 1925; s. John Milton and Ruth (Gregory) B.; m. Agnes M. Johnston, July 8, 1949; children—Margaret Ruth (Mrs. Sidney Ray Hill, Jr.), Helen Patricia. B.S., Davidson Coll., 1949; M.S., U. Tenn., 1951; Ph.D., Ga. Inst. Tech., 1959. Instrument engr. E.I. duPont de Nemours & Co., Orange, Tex., 1951-54; asst. prof. Ga. Inst. Tech., 1954-59; program mgr. Martin Marietta Corp., Orlando, Fla., 1959-63, tech. dir., 1963-68; head dept. elec. engring. Miss. State U., Starkville, 1963; Alcoa prof. indsl. engring. U. Tenn., Knoxville, 1968—; dir. Sci. Methods, Inc.; cons. Strategic Air Def., Martin Marietta Corp., Environmental Tech., Inc., Orlando. Author: (with J.E. Alexander) Systems Engineering Mathematics, 1962. Served with USMCR, 1943-46. Decorated Purple Heart; recipient M. A. Ferst Sigma Xi award Ga. Inst. Tech., 1959; Publ. award Martin Marietta Corp., 1964. Mem. I.E.E.E., Sigma Alpha Epsilon. Republican. Episcopalian. Club: Rotarian. Home: 364 Seven Oaks Dr Concord TN 37920

BAILEY, JOHN TURNER, public relations executive; b. Cleve., Dec. 2, 1926; s. Theodore Litchfield and Helen (Moyle) B.; m. Katherine Gerwig, June 21, 1952; children—Theodore Gerwig, Mary Katherine. A.B., Harvard U., 1950; student, Columbia Grad. Sch., 1950-51. Circulation mgr. internat. edits. N.Y. Times, N.Y.C., 1952-58; mgr. profl. relations Lederle Labs., Am. Cyanamid Co., Pearl River, N.Y., 1958-61; partner firm Edward Howard & Co., Cleve., 1961-67, exec. v.p., 1967-72, pres., 1972-77, chmn. bd., 1977—, dir., 1967—. Trustee Chautauqua (N.Y.) Instn., Shaker Lakes Regional Nature Center. Served with USCGR, 1944-46. Mem. Pub. Relations Soc. Am. Clubs: Union, Rowfant, Clevelander, Cleve. Skating, Harvard (Cleve., N.Y.C.); Chautauqua (N.Y.); Yacht (commodore 1970-71). Home: 2666 Wicklow Rd Shaker Heights OH 44120 also 25 N Lake Dr Chautauqua NY 14722 Office: 1021 Euclid Ave Cleveland OH 44115

BAILEY, KENNETH KYLE, educator; b. nr. Coldwater, Miss., Dec. 3, 1923; s. John Parham and Ruby Ross (Allen) B.; m. Mary Lou Crain, Aug. 5, 1961. Student, Northwest Miss. Jr. Coll., 1941-42, 45-46; B.A., Vanderbilt U., 1947, M.A., 1948, Ph.D., 1953. Instr. social sci. Cumberland (Ky.) Coll., 1949-50; instr. social sci. N.M. Mil. Inst., 1952-53, asst. prof., 1953-55; instr. history Ind. U., 1955-56, Tex. Western Coll., 1956-57; asst. prof. North Tex. State Coll., 1957-58, La. State U., 1958-60; asso. prof. history U. Tex. at El Paso, 1960-63, prof., 1963—, chmn. dept., 1968-71. Author: Southern White Protestantism in the Twentieth Century, 2d edit, 1968; bd. editors: Jour. So. History, 1975-79. Served with AUS, 1942-45. Social Sci. Research Council grantee, 1955; Guggenheim Meml. fellow, 1966-67. Mem. Am., So. hist. assns., Am. Soc. Ch. History, Orgn. Am. Historians (mem. Pelzer meml. award com. 1965-69). Presbyterian. Home: 3033 Federal Ave El Paso TX 79930

BAILEY, MERRITT ELTON, JR., publishing company executive; b. Denver, Feb. 24, 1921; s. Merritt Elton and Edwina Louise (Cox) B.; m. Grace Alberta Crabtree, Mar. 30, 1940; 1 dau., Shirley Louise (Mrs. Jonathan Ruhe). B.S., Iowa State U., 1949, M.S., 1951. Asso. editor Iowa State U. Press, Ames, 1949-51, sales mgr., 1951-63, dir., 1963—. Pres. Story County Tb and Health Assn., 1954-56, Meeker Sch. PTA, Ames, 1952-54; chmn. Citizens' Com. for Adequate Schs., Ames, 1958-59; mem. Gov.'s Council on Edn., 1959-60; troop chmn. Tall Corn council Boys Scouts Am., 1952-53; pres. bd. trustees Ames Pub. Library, 1977-83. Served with USAF, 1942-45. Mem. Ames Jaycees (dir. 1950-53), Assn. Am. Univ. Presses (dir. 1971), Actors Inc. (dir. 1964-67), Sigma Delta Chi. Mem. Christian Ch. (dir. 1960-65). Club: Moose. Home: 1716 Maxwell St Ames IA 50010

BAILEY, MITCHELL MONTGOMERY, lawyer; b. May 25, 1921; s. Sol and Mary (Shide) B. B.S., CCNY, 1942; J.D., Columbia U., 1947. Bar: N.Y. 1947. Since practiced in, N.Y.C.; ptnr. Pross, Halpern, Lefevre, Raphael & Alter, 1954-71; counsel Forsythe, McGovern & Pearson, 1972-74; sr. ptnr. Bailey, Marshall, Hoeniger & Freitag, 1975-79, Bailey & Marshall, 1980—; sec. Penn Yan Boats, Inc., Automated Environ. Systems, Inc.; dir. Telcoa Internat. Corp., ETC Laser Corp. Editor: The Jagar, Air Force Res., monthly publ., 1962-69. Sec., counsel Citizens for Eisenhower, 1956, Citizens for Rockefeller, 1962, 66; Pres., bd. dirs. North Valley Stream Assn., N.Y.; sec., counsel, trustee Nat. Pollution Control Found.; trustee Valley Stream Sch. Dist.; counsel, trustee Internat. Amateur Sports Devel. Fund. Served with USAAF, 1942-45; ETO; lt. col. Res.; ret. Recipient N.Y. Judge Adv. award, 1962; Air Force Res. Meritorious Service award, 1964. Mem. N.Y. Bar Assn., N.Y. State Trial Lawyers Assn., Air Force Hist. Found., Bar Assn. City N.Y., Ret. Res. Officers Assn., Air Force Assn. Clubs: El Morroco, Lambs N.Y.C. Office: 415 Madison Ave New York NY 10017

BAILEY, NORMAN STANLEY, baritone; b. Birmingham, Eng., Mar. 23, 1933; s. Stanley Ernest and Agnes Train (Gale) B.; m. Doreen Evelyn Simpson, Dec. 21, 1957; children: Brian, Catherine, Richard. Mus.B., Rhodes U., South Africa; Performer's and Tchr's. Licentiate in Singing; Diploma in Opera, Diploma in Lieder, Diploma in Oratorio, Vienna (Austria) State Acad. Mem. companies Linzer Lanes Theater, Austria, 1960-63, Wuppertaler Buhnen, Wuppertal, W.Ger., 1963-64, Deutsche Oper Am Rhein, Dusseldorf, W.Ger., 1964-67, Sadler's Wells Opera, London, 1967-71. Free lance heroic baritone at leading opera house, including, Covent Garden, La Scala, Bayreuth, Vienna State Opera, Met. Opera; appeared with, Paris Opera, Edinburgh Festival; appeared in: BBC-TV performances of Macbeth; recs. include Der Fliegende Hollander, Meistersinger. Decorated comdr. Order Brit. Empire; prize winner Internat. Song Competition, Vienna, 1960; recipient Sankley Meml. prize, 1977. Bahai. *

BAILEY, ORVILLE TAYLOR, neuropathologist; b. Jewett, N.Y., May 28, 1909; s. Milton O. and Ollie (Persons) B. A.B., Syracuse U., 1928; M.D., Albany Med. Coll., 1932. Rotating intern Albany Hosp., 1932-33; house officer pathology Peter Bent Brigham Hosp., Boston, 1933-34, asso. pathologist, 1940-43; resident pathologist Children's Hosp., Boston, 1934-35; instr. pathology Harvard Med. Sch., 1935-40, asso. in pathology, 1940-46, asst. prof., 1946-51; prof. neuropathology Ind. U. Sch. Medicine, 1951-59; prof. neurology U. Ill. Med. Sch., 1959-70, prof. neurol. surgery, 1970-72; prof. neuropathology in dept. neurosurgery and dept. neurology Abraham Lincoln Sch. Medicine, Chgo., 1972-77, prof. emeritus, 1977—; distinguished prof. pathology Rush Med. Sch., Chgo., 1977—; Cons. Cook County Hosp., 1959—, Children's Meml. Hosp., Chgo., 1963-69. Editor: (with D.E. Smith) The Central Nervous System: Some Experimental Models of Neurologic Disease; Contbr. articles on radiation, vascular disease in childhood, brain tumors to med. jours. Chmn. U.S. delegation, v.p. for U.S. Internat. Congress Neuropathology, 1957-65; Mem. Harvard Soc. Fellows, 1937-40. Corr. mem. Scandinavian Neurosurg. Soc. Clubs: University, Literary (Chgo.). Office: PO Box 2517 Chicago IL 60690

BAILEY, PAMELA GILES, government official; b. Reading, Pa., May 24, 1948; d. John S. and Nancy (Clymer) Giles; m. William W. Bailey, Dec. 13, 1980; children: Suzanne, Robert, Nancy Needham. A.B., Mt. Holyoke Coll., 1970. Research asst. to v.p. of U.S., Washington, 1970-71, to pres. of U.S., 1971-73; staff asst. to pres., dir. research, 1973-74; staff asst. Domestic Council, 1974-75, asst. dir., 1975; mgr. govt. and consumer affairs Am. Hosp. Supply Corp., 1975-79, dir. govt. relations, 1980-81; asst. sec. public affairs Dept. Health and Human Services; dep. dir. White House Office Pub. Affairs, dir. White House Office of Planning, 1984—; asst. sec. public affairs Dept. Health and Human Services. Republican. Office: White House Office of Planning 160 Old Executive Office Bldg Washington DC 20500 *

BAILEY, PEARL (MAE), singer; b. Newport News, Va., Mar. 29, 1918; d. Joseph James B.; m. John Randolph Pinkett, Jr., Aug. 31, 1948 (div. Mar. 1952); m. Louis Bellson, Jr., Nov. 19, 1952. Student pub. schs., Phila. Singer, 1933—; vocalist various popular bands; stage debut: St. Louis Woman, N.Y.C., 1946; role: Broadway musical Hello Dolly, 1967-68, Arms and the Girl, House of Flowers, Bless You All, Duey's Tale, Hurry Up America, and Spit; motion pictures include Variety Girl, Carmen Jones, St. Louis Blues, Porgy and Bess, Isn't It Romantic, Norman, Is That You, That Certain Feeling, All the Fine Young Cannibals, The Landlord, Lost Generation; contract artist, Coral Records, Columbia Records, Decca; night club engagements, N.Y.C., Boston, Hollywood, Las Vegas, Chgo., also London, 1950—; Star: Pearl Bailey Show, ABC-TV, 1970-71; guest artist various TV programs; (Spl. Tony award for Hello, Dolly 1967-68); Author: Raw Pearl, 1969, Pearlie Mae, Talking to Myself, 1971, Pearl's Kitchen, 1973, Duey's Tale, 1975, Hurry Up, America and Spit, 1976. Now spl. rep. U.S. delegation to UN. Recipient Spl. Tony award for Hello, Dolly, 1967-68, Donaldson award, 1956; Recipient Donaldson award, 1956; Entertainer of the Year Cue Magazine, 1967; March of Dimes award, 1968; U.S.O. Woman of the Year, 1969; citation from Mayor John V. Lindsay of N.Y.C. Address: care William Morris Agy Inc 1350 Ave of Americas New York NY 10019 *

BAILEY, PETER GEOFFREY, financial services company executive; b. Winnington, Eng., Oct. 27, 1940; came to U.S., 1970; s. Jack Edward and Freda B.; m. Maureen Sullivan, Dec. 20, 1957; children: Janet, Susan, Alison. Ordinary nat. cert. in mech. engring., Wandsworth Tech. Coll., London, 1958, Higher Nat. Cert., 1961. Jr. design engr. Vickery's Ltd., Eng., 1959-61; chief planning engr. Combined Elec. Mfg., Eng., 1961-63; ptnr. Plan Publs., Eng., 1964-66; nat. sales mgr. Precision Data Card, Eng., 1966-67; mgr. European mktg. Audev, Ltd., subs. Control Data Corp., London, 1967-69; with Bus. Products, Mpls., 1970-79, gen. mgr., 1973-74, v.p., group exec., 1974-79; founding pres. Control Data Bus. Advs., Mpls., 1979-81; sr. v.p. corp. devel. Comml. Credit Co., Balt., 1981-83, sr. v.p. leasing realty services, 1983—; chmn., dir. Custom One Internat., Mpls., 1982—. Home & Office: 300 Saint Paul Pl Baltimore MD 21202

BAILEY, PHILIP SIGMON, chemistry educator; b. Chickasha, Okla., June 9, 1916; s. Thomas Leonard and Alma (Sigmon) B.; m. Marie Shultz, Feb. 2, 1941 (div. 1959); children: Philip Sigmon, Thomas F., Evalee F.; m. Louise Randall Field, Aug. 8, 1959 (dec. 1960); m. Jean Cook Allen, Aug. 3, 1973. B.S., Okla. Bapt. U., 1937; M.S., U. Okla., 1940; Ph.D., U. Va., 1944. Chemist Halliburton Oil Well Cementing Co., Great Bend, Kans., 1940-41; research assoc. U Va., 1944-45; asst. prof. chemistry U. Tex., 1945-49, assoc. prof., 1949-57, prof., 1957—; lectr. in field; cons. ozone chemistry, organic peroxides. Author: Ozonation in Organic Chemistry, Vol. I, 1978, Vol. II, 1982; contbr. articles to books, profl. jours. Mem. Am. Chem. Soc., Sigma Xi, Alpha Chi Sigma, Phi Lambda Upsilon, Alpha Epsilon Delta. Episcopalian (vestryman, lay reader). Club: World of Resorts Country. Patentee in field. Home: PO Box 827 Lago Vista TX 78641 Office: Dept Chemistry Univ Texas Austin TX 78712 *An important concept in my life is that science and a belief in God are compatible. I would like for all who have come in contact with me to see me as a person of high integrity and to have benefitted by the contact.*

BAILEY, RALPH E., oil company executive; b. Pike County, Ind., Mar. 23, 1924; s. Enos M. and Gertie L. (Taylor) B.; children: Douglas G., Cinda C., Rhonda Y., Lisa A. B.S. in Mech. Engring, Purdue U., 1949. With No. Ill. Coal Corp., 1949-50, Sinclair Coal Co., 1950-55; with Peabody Coal Co., 1955-65, v.p. charge mining operations, 1963-64, exec. v.p. operations, 1964-65; v.p. Consolidation Coal Co., Pitts., 1965-68, sr. v.p., 1968-70, exec. v.p., 1970-74, pres., from 1974, chmn., to 1977; also dir.; vice-chmn. Continental Oil Co., 1975-77, pres., 1977—, dep. chmn., 1978, chmn., chief exec. officer, 1979—, also dir.; dir. Consolidation Coal Co.; dir., vice chmn. DuPont Co. Office: Conoco Inc 1007 Market St Wilmington DE 19898 *

BAILEY, REEVE MACLAREN, museum curator; b. Fairmont, W.Va., May 2, 1911; s. Joseph Randall and Elizabeth Weston (Maclaren) B.; m. Marian Alvinette Kregel, Aug. 13, 1939; children—Douglas M., David R., Thomas G., Susan Helen. Student, Toledo U., 1929-30; A.B., U. Mich., 1933, Ph.D., 1938. Instr. zoology Iowa State Coll. (now univ.), 1938-42, asst. prof., 1942-44; asst. prof. zoology U. Mich., 1944-50, asso. prof., 1950-59, prof., 1959-81, prof. emeritus, 1981—; asso. curator Mus. Zoology, 1944-48, curator, 1948—. Contbr. over 100 articles, bulls., revs. to profl. jours. Mem. Am. Soc. Ichthyologists and Herpetologists (editorial bd.; v.p. 1954, pres. 1959), Am. Fisheries Soc. (pres. 1974, hon. mem. 1979—, recipient Award of Excellence 1980), AAAS (council 1968-72), Ecol. Soc. Am., Soc. Study Evolution, Soc. Systematic Zoology, Soc. Limnology and Oceanography, Iowa Acad. Sci., Mich. Acad. Sci., Arts and Letters. Ichthyol. expdns. in U.S., Bermuda, Bolivia, Guatemala, Paraguay, Zambia. Home: 2730 Whitmore Lake Rd Ann Arbor MI 48103 Office: Museum Zoology Univ Mich Ann Arbor MI 48109

BAILEY, RICHARD BRIGGS, investment company executive; b. Weston, Mass., Sept. 14, 1926; s. George William and Alice Gertrude (Cooper) B.; m. Rebecca C. Bradford, June 20, 1950 (div. Dec. 1974); children—Ann, Elizabeth, Richard, Rebecca; m. Anne D. Prescott, Dec. 14, 1974 (div. 1980); m. Anita S. Lawrence, Sept. 12, 1980; 1 dau., Alexandra, B.A., Harvard, 1948, M.A., 1951; postgrad., Grad. Sch. Bus. Adminstrn., 1966. Prodn. engr. C. Brewer & Co., Honolulu, 1951-53; prodn. engr. Raytheon Co., Waltham, Mass., 1953-54; security analyst Keystone Custodian Funds, Boston, 1955-59; industry specialist Mass. Investors Trust, 1959-69; now mng. trustee; mng. partner Mass. Fin. Services, Co., Boston, 1969—, pres., 1978-82; chmn., dir. Mass. Fin. Services Co., 1982—; dir. Transatlantic Capital Corp., Cambridge Trust Co., Lombard Odier Internat. Portfolio Mgmt. Ltd., London., Sun Life Assurance Co. Can. (U.S.); Chmn. Finance Com., Lincoln, Mass., 1966-68. Trustee Plimoth Plantation, Inc., Plymouth, Mass., Phillips Exeter Acad., Exeter, N.H., 1978-82; mem. adv. bd. Coll. Mental Health Center of Boston. Served to 2d lt., Signal Corps AUS, 1944-46. Decorated Letter of Commendation. Mem. Boston Security Analysts Soc. Republican. Episcopalian. Clubs: Knickerbocker, Harvard of N.Y. (N.Y.C.); Somerset (Boston); Eastern Yacht (Marblehead); Coral Beach and Tennis (Bermuda). Home: 63 Atlantic Ave Boston MA 02110 Office: 200 Berkeley St Boston MA 02116

BAILEY, RICHARD CLAYTON, retired museum director, historian, author; b. Muskegon, Mich., Apr. 20, 1911; s. Irving Jacob and Blanche Arvilla (Hosler) B.; m. Dorothy Jean Searles, June 17, 1971; children: Richard Hugh, Joyce Carol. B.A., Fresno (Calif.) State U., 1945. Elem. sch. tchr. Mt. View Sch. Dist., Lamont, Calif., 1946-48; asst. dir., edn. dir. Kern County Mus., Bakersfield, Calif., 1948-55, dir., 1955-81, Pioneer Village, Bakersfield, 1955-81; instr. county history Bakersfield Community Coll., 1970-80; instr. local history and tours Calif. State U., Bakersfield, 1974-81; chmn. Ft. Tejon Restoration Com., 1949-73. Author: Kern County Place Names, 1967, Collector's Choice, 1951, Historic Chronology of Kern County, 1954, Heritage of Kern, 1957, Explorations in Kern, 1959, Bakersfield, Heart of the Golden Empire, 1983. Mem. Calif. Bicentennial Commn., 1969-70, Red Rock Canyon Adv. Com., 1969-73; treas. Kern County Centennial Com., 1966-68; adv. Kern County Heritage Commn., 1976-81; mem. Kern County Hist. Records Commn. Recipient Principal's Service to Children's Edn. award Bakersfield City Sch. Dist., 1959. Mem. Am. Assn. Museums (past pres. Western regional conf.), Calif. Conf. Hist. Socs. (past pres.), Kern County Hist. Soc. (pres. 1948-49, 53-54, lifetime hon. v.p.). Republican. Presbyterian. Clubs: Petroleum Prodn. Pioneers, Death Valley 49ers, Masons. Home: 1101 Lomita Ave Bakersfield CA 93307

BAILEY, ROBERT WILLIAM, insurance company executive; b. N.Y.C., June 16, 1944; s. Robert A. and Eleanore (Mason) B.; m. Charlotte J. Johnson, Nov. 10, 1979; children: Robert William, Brian Charles. A.B., Cornell U., 1966; M.B.A., Adelphi U., 1969. Acctg. analyst Nat. Life Ins. Co., N.Y.C., 1966-69; asst. account exec. Gen. Reins. Corp., Greenwich, Conn., 1970-71, asst. sec., 1972-75, 1972-75, asst. v.p., 1975-80, 2d v.p., 1981—, v.p., 1981—. Mem. Am. Soc. C.P.C.U.s. Republican. Congregationalist. Home: 390 Sound Beach

Ave Old Greenwich CT 06870 Office: Gen Reins Corp 600 Steamboat Rd Greenwich CT 06830

BAILEY, RONALD BERESFORD, polit. scientist, educator; b. Ft. Pierce, Fla., Feb. 5, 1936; s. Harry A. and Ruth G. (Finlayson) B.; m. Vera Polk, Mar. 1, 1967 (div.); 1 son, Ronald. B.S. (State of Fla. scholar), Fla. A. and M. U., 1958; M.A. (Woodrow Wilson fellow), U. Ill., 1960, Ph.D., 1965. Prof., chmn. dept. polit. sci. Atlanta U., 1966-68; asst. prof. dept. polit. sci. St. Louis U., 1968-70; asso. prof. polit. sci. and Black studies Washington U., St. Louis, 1970-71; asst. dean University Coll., U. Fla., Gainesville, 1971-76; prof., chmn. dept. polit. sci. Fla. A. and M. U., Tallahassee, 1976-80; prof. dept. polit. sci. Howard U., Washington, 1980—; co-dir. internat. community agy. student exchange program to U. West Indies, summer, 1980. Contbr. articles on edn. and polit. sci. to profl. jours. Served to capt. U.S. Army, 1964-66. Mem. Am. Polit. Sci. Assn., So. Polit. Sci. Assn., Kappa Delta Pi, Pi Sigma Alpha, Omega Psi Phi. Democrat. Episcopalian. Home: 3200 Weeping Willow Ct Silver Spring MD 20906

BAILEY, SCOTT FIELD, bishop; b. Houston, Oct. 7, 1916; s. William Stuart and Tallulah (Smith) B.; m. Evelyn Williams, Dec. 11, 1943; children—Louise (Mrs. Allen C. Taylor), Nicholas, Scott Field, Sarah (Mrs. Hugh A. Fitzsimons III). B.A., Rice U., 1938; postgrad., U. Tex. Law Sch., 1938-39; M.Div., Va. Theol. Sem., 1942, D.D., 1965; S.T.M., U. of South, 1953, D.D., 1965. Ordained to ministry Episcopal Ch., 1942; pastor in, Waco, Lampasas, San Augustine, Nacogdoches, Austin, Tex., 1942-51, asst. to bishop of, Tex., 1951-64, suffragan bishop of, 1964-75, coadjutor bishop of, West Tex., 1976-77, bishop of, 1977—; Sec. ho. of bishops Episcopal Ch., 1967—; exec. officer Gen. Conv., 1973-77. Served as chaplain USNR, World War II. Fellow Coll. of Preachers; mem. Phi Delta Theta. Home: 2422 Toftrees Dr San Antonio TX 78209 Office: PO Box 6885 San Antonio TX 78209

BAILEY, STURGES WILLIAMS, geologist, educator; b. Waupaca, Wis., Feb. 11, 1919; s. Ralph Williams and Katharine (Simmons) B.; m. Marilyn Lorraine Jones, Feb. 19, 1949; children—David S., Linda M. B.A., U. Wis., 1941, M.A., 1948; Ph.D., Cambridge (Eng.) U., 1955. Faculty U. Wis., Madison, 1951—, prof. geology, 1961—, Roland D. Irving prof. geology, 1976—, chmn. dept. geology and geophysics, 1968-71. Editor: Clays and Clay Minerals, 1964-69, Procs. Internat. Clay Congress, 1972-75; Contbr. articles to profl. jours. Served with USNR, 1942-46. Fulbright scholar, 1949-51. Fellow Mineral Soc. Am. (council 1970-72, v.p. 1972-73, pres. 1973-74); mem. Clay Minerals Soc. (exec. com. 1964-69, v.p. 1970-71, pres. 1971-72, distinguished mem. 1975), Assn. Internationale pour l'Etude des Argiles (editor 1972-75, pres. 1975-78), Phi Beta Kappa. Spl. research X-ray crystallography. Home: 5049 LaCrosse Ln Madison WI 53705

BAILEY, WENDELL, former congressman; b. Willow Springs, Mo., July 31, 1940; s. Robert Haz and Ruby (Dell) B.; m. Jane Ann Bray, Dec. 2, 1963; children: Mike, John, Jill. B.B.A., S.W. Mo. State U., 1962. Salesman Bailey Auto Co., Willow Springs, 1962-66, owner, mgr., 1966—; state rep. Mo. 152d Dist., 1972-80; mem. 97th Congress from 8th Mo. Dist. Councilman, mayor pro tem, City of Willow Springs, 1968-72; candidate for treas. State of Mo., 1984. Chmn. bd. dirs. Willow Care Nursing Home, 1978-80. Mem. Mo. Auto Dealers Assn., Nat. Auto Dealers Assn. Republican. Southern Baptist. Clubs: Willow Springs Lions, Elks. Home: 101 W 4th St Willow Springs MO 65793

BAILEY, WILFORD SHERRILL, science administrator, educator, university president; b. nr. Hartselle, Ala., Mar. 2, 1921; s. Ollis Wilford and Bessie (Widener) B.; m. Cratus Hester, May 30, 1942; children: Wilford Edward, Joe Sherrill, Margaret Ann, Sarah Jane. D.V.M., Auburn U., 1942, M.S., 1946; Sc.D., Johns Hopkins U., 1950. Instr. to head prof. dept. pathology and parasitology Sch. Vet Medicine, Auburn U., 1942-62; asso. dean Grad. Sch. and coordinator research, 1962-66, v.p. for academic affairs, 1966-72; health scientist adminstr. Inst. Allergy and Infectious Diseases, NIH, 1972-74; prof. dept. pathology and parasitology Auburn (Ala.) U., 1974—, asso. dean vet. medicine, 1979-80, interim pres., 1983—; research leader Regional Parasite Research Lab., U.S. Dept. Agr., Auburn, 1980-82; custodian Am. Soc. Parasitologists, 1952-79. Mem. NRC, Council, 1962-68; mem. tng. grant com. Nat. Inst. Allergy and Infectious Diseases, 1964-69; mem. Nat. Adv. Allergy and Infectious Disease Council, 1971-72, 75-78; mem. com. on animal health NRC, Nat. Acad. Sci., 1980—. Research fellow Am. Vet. Med. Assn.; Johns Hopkins Univ. scholar; NSF Sci. Faculty fellow; Rockefeller Found. scholar. Mem. Am. Vet. Med. Assn., Am. Soc. Parasitologists (pres. 1971), Am. Soc. Tropical Medicine and Hygiene (pres. 1977), Sigma Xi, Phi Kappa Phi, Phi Zeta, Omicron Delta Kappa. Mem. Ch. of Christ. Club: Cosmos (Washington). Home: 778 Moore's Mill Rd Auburn AL 36830 Office: Auburn U Auburn AL 36849

BAILEY, WILLIAM HARRISON, artist, educator; b. Council Bluffs, Iowa, Nov. 17, 1930; s. Willard Kendall and Marjorie Esther (Cheyney) B.; m. Sandra Stone, May 28, 1958; children: Ford Hamilton, Alix Brook. Student, U. Kans., 1948-51; B.F.A., Yale U., 1955, M.F.A., 1957. Instr. art Yale U., New Haven, 1957-61, asst. prof., 1961-62, prof., 1969—; dean Sch. Art, 1974-75; asst. prof. Ind. U., 1962-65, asso. prof., 1965-68, prof., 1968-69; now Kingman Brewster prof. Yale U. Exhbns. include, Robert Schoelkopf Gallery, N.Y.C., 1968, 71, 74, 79, Galerie Claude Bernard, Paris, 1978; represented in permanent collection, Mus. Modern Art, Whitney Mus., Hirshorn Mus., St. Louis Art Mus., Nev Galerie Der Stadt Aachen, W. Ger. Pa. Acad., Yale Art Gallery. Served with U.S. Army, 1951-53. Alice Kimball English traveling fellow, 1955; Guggenheim fellow, 1965; Ingram Merrill fellow, 1979. Office: Sch Art Yale Univ New Haven CT 06520

BAILEY, WILLIAM JOHN, educator, chemist; b. East Grand Forks, Minn., Aug. 11, 1921; s. Admiral Ross and Erva (Stewart) B.; m. Mary Caroline Worsham, Aug. 27, 1949; children: Caroline Jane, John Robert, Barbara Ann. Arthur D. B.Chemistry, U. Minn., 1943; Ph.D., U. Ill., 1946. Arthur D. Little postdoctoral fellow MIT, 1946-47; asst. prof. chemistry Wayne State U., Detroit, 1947-49, asso. prof., 1949-51; research prof. organic chemistry U. Md., College Park, 1951—; Chmn. Gordon Research Conf. on Organic Reactions, 1960; mem. NSF postdoctoral selection com., 1963-66; NRC adv. com. elastomers to U.S. Army Natick Labs., 1961-67, chmn. com. macromolecular chemistry, 1967-79; U.S. rep. macromolecular div. Internat. Union Pure and Applied Chemistry, 1967-81; Robert A. Welch lectr., 1971, Rensselaer Poly. Inst. Rauscher Meml. lectr., 1976; Gossett award lectr. N.C. State U., 1983. Mem. editorial bd.: Jour. Organic Chemistry, 1957-63, Macromolecular Synthesis, 1960—, Record Chem. Progress, 1950-70, Jour. Macromolecular Science Chemistry, 1966—, Jour. Polymer Science, 1967—, Macromolecules, 1967-72, Chem. Tech, 1972—, Current Abstracts of Chemistry, 1972—, Index Chemicus, 1972—, Polymer Sci. and Tech, 1972—, Chem. and Engring. News, 1974-76, 79, 81. Recipient Fatty Acid Producers Research award, 1955, U. Minn. Distinguished Alumnus award, 1976. Mem. Chem. Soc. Washington (pres. 1961, Service award 1969), Am. Chem. Soc. (chmn. div. polymer chemistry 1968, chmn. com. on nominations and elections council 1969-72, chmn. Middle Atlantic regional councilors 1970-72, mem. coll. chemistry cons. service 1971-77, dir.-at-large 1973, 77-82, pres. 1975, chmn. bd. 1979, 81, Witco Polymer Chemistry award 1977, chmn. U.S.-Japan Polymer Symposium 1980), AAAS, Am. Inst. Chemists (D.C. Inst. honor scroll 1975), Am. Oil Chemists Soc., Council Sci. Soc. Presidents (exec. bd. 1975-77), Fedn. Material Socs. (trustee 1976-80), Phi Beta Kappa, Sigma Xi (ann. achievement award U. Md. chpt. 1979), Phi Kappa Phi, Phi Lambda Upsilon, Pi Mu Epsilon, Alpha Chi Sigma. Developed several new methods for preparation of polymers; discovered several new polymers; produced a correlation between structure and properties in plastics and rubbers; inventor monomers that expand on polymerization. Home: 6905 Pineway University Park MD 20782 Office: U Md Dept Chemistry College Park MD 20742

BAILEY, WILLIAM O., insurance company executive; b. Syracuse, N.Y., July 1, 1926; s. William E. and Kate (Oliver) B.; m. Carole Watts Parsons, 1979; children: George, Janet, Thomas, Carolyn. A.B. in Econs., Dartmouth Coll., 1947; M.B.A. in Ins., Wharton Sch., U. Pa., 1949. Asst. sec. Nat. Bur. Casualty Underwriters, 1952-54; with Aetna Life & Casualty Co., Hartford, Conn., 1954—, sr. v.p. casualty and surety div., 1968-72, exec. v.p., dir., 1972-76, pres., 1976—. Corporator, mem. ins. com. Hartford Hosp.; trustee Hartford Rehab. Ctr.; bd. corporators Hartford Sem. Found.; bd. dirs. St. Francis Hosp. Served with USNR, World War II. Mem. Oil Ins. Assn. (past pres.), Soc. C.P.C.U. Office: Aetna Life Ins Co 151 Farmington Ave Hartford CT 06115

BAILIN, LIONEL J., phys. inorganic chemist; b. N.Y.C., Oct. 28, 1928; s. Julius Bernard and Mildred (Meyer) B.; m. Gisela Lehn, Dec. 19, 1958; children—Daniel Joseph, Mark Lawrence, Julia Michele, Stephanie. A.B. in Chemistry, N.Y. U., 1949, M.S., Poly. Inst. Bklyn., 1952; Ph.D. in Inorganic Chemistry, Tulane U., 1958. Research and devel. chemist, pigment dept. DuPont Co., Wilmington, Del., 1957-62; research scientist Palo Alto (Calif.) Research Lab., Lockheed Missiles & Space Co., 1962-73, staff scientist, 1974-78, sr. staff scientist inorganic chemistry, 1978—. Contbr. articles to profl. jours. Served with AUS, 1952-54. U.S. Army Ordnance research fellow Tulane U., 1956-57; teaching fellow, 1954-55; EPA grantee, 1975—. Mem. Am. Chem. Soc., Am. Inst. Chemists (chmn. Golden Gate chpt. 1965-66, program chmn. 1964-65), Am. Optical Soc., Sigma Xi. Home: 740 Crane Ave Foster City CA 94404 Office: 3251 Hanover St Palo Alto CA 94304

BAILLIE, CHARLES DOUGLAS, banker; b. Bklyn., Sept. 12, 1918; s. Charles Tupper and Nina (Vincent) B.; m. Helene Elizabeth Kuehn, Feb. 15, 1941 (dec. Apr. 1979); children—Barbara Ann (Mrs. John Roland Obenchain), Charles Douglas, Nancy Helene (Mrs. John Michael King); m. Nancy Lee Anderson, Oct. 22, 1982. B.S. in Bus. Adminstrn. with distinction, Ind. U., 1940; certificate exec. program, UCLA, 1956. Personnel and credit supervision Continental Ill. Nat. Bank, Chgo., 1940-52; v.p. treas., dir. Nat. Discount Corp., South Bend, Ind., 1952-54; with United Calif. Bank, Los Angeles, 1954-75, asst. v.p., 1955-56, v.p., 1956-68, sr. v.p., 1968-70, exec. v.p., 1970-75; v.p. Mfrs. Bank, Los Angeles, 1975-78, sr. v.p., dir., 1978-81, Mitsui Mfrs. Bank, Los Angeles, 1981—. Bd. dirs. Mitsui Mfrs. Bank Found.; bd. dirs. San Marino Community Council, 1968-76, AID-United Givers, 1977-80, United Way Los Angeles County, 1980—; councilman City of San Marino, 1972-76; trustee San Marino Community Ch. Served from ensign to lt. Supply Corps USNR, 1942-46. Mem. Am. Inst. Banking, Los Angeles, San Marino chambers commerce, UCLA Exec. Program Alumni Assn., I Men's Assn., Robert Morris Assos., Town Hall, Delta Sigma Pi, Phi Gamma Delta, Beta Gamma Sigma (dirs. table). Clubs: Rotarian., San Marino City (gov. 1979-80), San Gabriel (Calif.) Country.). Home: 118 W Las Flores Ave Arcadia CA 91006 Office: 135 E 9th St Los Angeles CA 90015

BAILLIE, DAVID SAMUEL, manufacturing company executive; b. Hackensack, N.J., Dec. 14, 1934; s. David and Florence (Kooman) B.; m. Sheila Ann Trubacek, June 6, 1958 (div. 1963); children: Deborah, Brett; m. Linda Birgit Christensen, Apr. 10, 1974; children: Christian, Britt. B.S. in Civil Engring., Lehigh U., 1956, M.S., 1959. Design engr. Texaco, Eagle Point, N.J., 1956; instr. Lehigh U., Bethlehem, Pa., 1958-59; dist. mgr. Caterpillar Overseas S.A., Europe and Africa, 1960-68; product mgr. Caterpillar Tractor Co., Peoria, Ill., 1968-69; mng. dir. Allis-Chalmers Overseas, Rome, 1969-73; sr. v.p. Grove Mfg. Co., Shady Grove, Pa., 1974—; dir. Grove Cranes Ltd., Oxford, Eng., Grove GmbH, W. Ger. Served to 1st lt., C.E. U.S. Army, 1956-58. Mem. Constrn. Industry Mfrs. Assn., Specialized Carriers and Riggin Assn. (chmn. allied industries governing com. 1982-84), Nat. Erectors Assn. Republican. Home: 106 Spring Valley Heights Dr Hagerstown MD 21740 Office: Grove Mfg Co PO Box 21 Shady Grove PA 17256

BAILLIF, ERNEST ALLEN, appliance mfg. co. exec.; b. Pine City, Minn., Dec. 8, 1925; s. Allen E. and Adelaide (St. Martin) B.; m. Phyllis Farquharson, Sept. 12, 1947; children—Linda Jean, Allen Scott, Jeffrey Todd. B.S. in Aero. and Mech. Engring, U. Minn., 1948; M.S. in Mech. Engring, 1950; Ph.D., 1953. Instr. U. Minn., 1947-53; with Whirlpool Corp. (and predecessor), 1953—, dir. engring., 1960-63, gen. mgr. laundry div. engring., St. Joseph, Mich., 1963-67, dir. corporate engring., 1967-68, v.p. corporate engring., Benton Harbor, Mich., 1968-71, v.p. research and engring., 1971—; Past mem. adv. com. St. Joseph Sch.; mem. ind. adv. council Dept. Mech. Engring., U. Minn. Contbr. articles to profl. jours. Trustee Ga. Inst. Tech. Research Inst.; mem. ind. adv. com. Herrick Labs., Purdue U. Bd. Served with AUS, 1944. Mem. IEEE, Am. Soc. Heating, Refrigerating, Air-Conditioning Engrs. Congregationalist. Patentee in field. Home: 4479 Tanglewood Trail Saint Joseph MI 49085 Office: Whirlpool Corp Monte Rd Benton Harbor MI 49022

BAILLIO, O. DALLAS, JR., library ofcl.; b. Shreveport, La., Feb. 16, 1940; s. O. Dallas and Edna Oden (Hartsfield) B.; m. Jimmie Lea Dawson, Mar. 14, 1964; children—Emily Rene, Nancy Amy. B.S., La. Tech. U., 1962; M.S., U. So. Calif., 1970, La. State U., 1971. Library dir. Withers Public Library, Bloomington, Ill., 1972-76, Mobile (Ala.) Public Library, 1977—. Served to capt. USAF, 1963-70. Mem. ALA, Ala. Library Assn. (pres. 1980-81), S.E. Library Assn. Presbyterian. Home: 1569 McIntyre Dr Mobile AL 36618 Office: 701 Government St Mobile AL 36602

BAILY, NATHAN ARIEL, business executive, association official, former government official, educator; b. N.Y.C., July 19, 1920; s. Saul and Eleanor (Mintz) B.; m. Judith Bernstein, June 20, 1946; children: Alan Eric, Lawrence Joel. B.S. in S.S, Coll. City N.Y., 1940; M.A., Columbia, 1941, Ph.D., 1946. Economist OPA; sr. editor-econ. analyst Research Inst. Am.; moderator District Viewpoint (weekly TV program); faculty Advanced Sch. Retail Mgmt. Nat. Sales Execs., Stonier Grad. Sch. Banking at Rutgers U.; hon. faculty mem. U.S. Army Mgmt. Sch.; fellow, charter mem. nat. ednl. adv. bd., instr., hon. dean faculty Washington chpt. Am. Inst. Banking; mem. history and econs. dept. Coll. City N.Y.; instr. Fashion Inst. Tech. and Design, N.Y.C.; faculty Am. U. Sch. Bus. Adminstrn., 1946-73, prof. bus. adminstrn. and finance, 1953—, founding dean, 1955-70; faculty Dept. Agr. Grad. Sch., 1962—; commr. U.S. Postal Rate Commn., Washington, 1970-74, chief economist, 1974-75; pres. Seminars, Speakers, Travel, 1975-82; dir. edn. Inst. Indsl. Launderers, 1975-78; pres. Utility Shareholders Assos., 1976-79; ednl. advisor Inst. Scrap Iron and Steel, 1977-79; sr. staff v.p. edn. Mortgage Bankers Assn. Am., 1979-80; vis. prof. bus./govt. relations George Washington U., 1980-82; Disting. vis. prof. mgmt. Nova U., 1980-81; seminar leader, designer, cons. mgmt., mktg., edn. dir. Washington Mut. Investors Fund, Carl M. Freeman & Assos., AW Industries, Gen. Bus. Services, Pioneer Found., Homer Hoyt Inst.; sec.-treas., pres. Homer Hoyt Inst. Md.; sec. Homer Hoyt Inst. Fla.; editorial adv. bd. Internat. Classics Press; cons., participant tng. programs Brookings Instn., Milk Industry Found., Social Security Adminstrn., Electric Inst. of Washington, Internat. Bank for Reconstrn., IBM, Gen. Electric, Dept. Agr. Grad. Sch., Nat. Tire Dealers and Retreaders Assn. Author: Guide to Establishing a Marketing Program for Institute of Industrial Launderers, 1973, also articles, book revs.; Editor: Marketing Profitably Under the Robinson-Patman Act, 1963, Marketing Handbook for Inst. Indsl. Launderers, 1972, 73; contbg. editor: Modern Security Services. Former mem. D.C. Small Bus. Adv. Council; D.C. adv. council for State Tech. Services Act; mem. Commn. on Ch. Family Financial Planning.; Trustee Council on Opportunities in Selling; bd. dirs. Friends of U.S. Latin America; former chmn. Invest-In-Am. nat. adv. council on econ. edn. Recipient fellowship E.I. duPont de Nemours, Swift & Co., Danforth Found.; Harvard Bus. Sch.; Volker Fund U. N.C. Mem. Am. Soc. Tng. and Devel., A.I.M., Am. Econ. Assn., AAUP, Middle Atlantic Assn. Colls. of Bus. Adminstrn. (pres. 1964-65), Am. Soc. Assn. Execs., Washington Soc. Investment Analysts, Washington Sales Execs. Club (dir. 1962-63), Washington Bd. Trade, Washington Real Estate Bd. (affiliate mem.), Suburban Md. Builders Assn. (hon. mem., econ. cons.), Newcomen Soc. N.Am., Soc. for Religious Orgn. Mgmt. (distinguished service award), U.S. C. of C. (com. anti-trust and trade regulation, dir. 1969-71), Phi Beta Kappa, Omicron Delta Kappa. Home and office: 5516 Greystone St Chevy Chase MD 20815

BAILY, NORMAN ARTHUR, physicist, educator; b. N.Y.C., July 2, 1915; s. Louis D. and Ida (Bolet) B.; m. Rose Levine, Nov. 21, 1940; children: Philip, Barbara. B.S., St. John's U., 1941; M.A., N.Y. U., 1943; Ph.D. in Physics, Columbia U., 1952. Diplomate: Am. Bd. Radiology, Am. Bd. Health Physics. Instr. RCA Inst., N.Y.C., 1943-46; research scientist Radiol. Research Lab., Columbia U., 1946-52; radiation physicist Marine Biol. Lab., Woods Hole, Mass., 1946-52; sci. adv. to comdr. SAC, USAF, 1952-54; chief physicist dept. radiation therapy Roswell Park Meml. Inst., Buffalo, 1954-59; asso. in radiology Sch. Medicine, U. Buffalo, 1954-59; lectr. chemistry Canisius Coll., Buffalo, 1957-59; mgr. space scis. dept. Hughes Research Labs., Malibu, Calif., 1959-67; asso. clin. prof. radiology UCLA, 1959-64, clin. prof. radiology, 1965-65, prof. in residence, 1965-68; cons. U.S. Naval Hosp., Balboa Park, San Diego, 1968—; prof. radiology Emory U., Atlanta, 1967-68, U. Calif., San Diego, 1968—; cons. Rand Corp., 1967-71, VA Hosp., San Diego, 1971—; vis. scientist CERN, 1970; vis. prof. oncology Hebrew U., 1972, Hadassah Hosp.; chmn. radioactive drug research com. Univ. Hosp., U. Calif. Med. Center, San Diego, 1975—; mem. sci. adv. com. Sci. Leasing Inc., San Diego, 1975—; mem. radiation study sect. NIH, 1975-79; Henry Goldberg prof. biomed. engring. Technion Inst., 1980-81; vis. prof. Korea Advanced Inst. Sci. and Tech., 1982. Contbr. numerous articles on radiol. physics and med. physics to profl. jours., chpts. in books; asso. editor: Med. Physics, 1976—. NASA grantee, 1963-79. Fellow Am. Coll. Radiology (chmn. physics com., steering com. on pneumoconiosis); mem. Am. Assn. Physicists in Medicine (sci. council, chmn. gen. med. physics com.), Radiation Research Soc., AAAS, Radiol. Soc. N.Am., Am. Phys. Soc., Soc. Photo-optical Instrumentation Engrs. Home: 8656 Cliffridge Ave LaJolla CA 92037 Office: Radiology M 010 U Calif San Diego LaJolla CA 92093

BAILYN, BERNARD, historian, educator; b. Hartford, Conn., Sept. 10, 1922; s. Charles Manuel and Esther (Schloss) B.; m. Lotte Lazarsfeld, June 18, 1952; children: Charles David, John Frederick. A.B., Williams Coll., 1945, Litt.D., 1969; M.A., Harvard U., 1947, Ph.D., 1953; L.H.D., Lawrence U., 1967, Bard Coll., 1968, Clark U., 1975, Yale U., 1976, Grinnell Coll., 1979, Trinity Coll., 1984; Litt.D., Rutgers U., 1976, Fordham U., 1976. Faculty Harvard U., Cambridge, Mass., 1953—, prof. history, 1961-66, Winthrop prof. history, 1966-81, Adams univ. prof., 1981—, editor-in-chief John Harvard Library, 1962-70, dir. Charles Warren Ctr. for Studies in Am. History, 1983—; Colver lectr. Brown U., 1965; Phelps lectr. NYU, 1969; Trevelyan lectr. Cambridge U., 1971; Becker lectr. Cornell U., 1975; Walker-Ames lectr. U. Wash., 1983; Curti lectr. U. Wis., 1984; mem. Inst. Advanced Study Princeton U., 1980-81. Author: New England Merchants in the 17th Century, 1955, (with Lotte Bailyn) Massachusetts Shipping, 1697-1714, A Statistical Study, 1959, Education in the Forming of American Society, 1960, Pamphlets of the American Revolution, 1750-1776, Vol. 1, 1965, The Ideological Origins of the American Revolution, 1967 (Pulitzer and Bancroft prizes 1968), The Origins of American Politics, 1968, The Ordeal of Thomas Hutchinson, 1974 (Nat. Book award 1975); co-author: The Great Republic, 1977; co-editor: The Intellectual Migration, Europe and America, 1930-1960, 1969, Law in American History, 1972, Perspectives in American History, 1967-77, The Press and The American Revolution, 1980. Served with AUS, 1943-46. Recipient Robert H. Lord award Emmanuel Coll., 1967. Mem. Am. Hist. Assn. (pres. 1981), Am. Acad. Arts and Scis., Nat. Acad. Edn., Am. Philos. Soc., Royal, Mass. hist. socs., Mexican Acad. History and Geography. Home: 170 Clifton St Belmont MA 02178

BAIN, BARBARA (MRS. MARTIN LANDAU), actress; m. Martin Landau; children: Susan, Juliet. B.A. in Sociology, U. Ill. Formerly fashion model, N.Y.C. Appeared in: TV series Space: 1999, Mission Impossible; TV movies Goodnight My Love, 1972, Murder Once Removed, 1971, Savage, 1973, A Summer Without Boys, 1973; other TV appearances include Ben Casey (Recipient 3 Emmy awards.). Address: care Bushell 415 N Crescent Dr Suite 320 Beverly Hills CA 90210

BAIN, CONRAD STAFFORD, actor; b. Lethbridge, Alta., Can., Feb. 4, 1923; came to U.S., 1946, naturalized, 1946; s. Stafford Harrison and Jean Agnes (Young) B.; m. Monica Marjorie Sloan, Sept. 4, 1945; children: Kent Stafford, Mark Alexander, Jennifer Jean. Grad., Am. Acad. Dramatic Art, 1948. Founder Actors Fed. Credit Union, 1962. Broadway appearances include Candide, 1957, Lost in the Stars, 1958, Hot Spot, 1963, Advise and Consent, 1961, Uncle Vanya, 1971; off-Broadway appearances include The Iceman Cometh, 1957, Hogan's Goat, 1966, Scuba Duba, 1967, The Kitchen, 1968, Steambath, 1969; film appearances A Lovely Way to Die, 1967, Who Killed Mary Whats er Name, 1968, Up the Sand Box, 1970, C.H.O.M.P.S, 1979, Child Bride of Short Creek, 1982; co-star: TV series Maude, 1971-78; star: Diff'rent Strokes, 1978—. Served with Canadian Army, World War II. Mem. Actors Equity Assn. (councilor 1962-76), ANTA West (dir. since 1977). Club: Players (N.Y.C.). Office: 1901 Ave of Stars Los Angeles CA 90067 *I have come to realize that each job no matter how small must be an end in itself, and that each day of whatever character must be lived for that day, in all its fullness. Yesterday is gone, regret is a waste, and tomorrow is unknown.*

BAIN, JACK MANSFIELD, educator; b. Gregory, S.D., May 25, 1922; s. Ivan Grant and Lola (Wakeman) B.; m. Charlotte O'Neill, Sept. 28, 1945; children—Claudia, Laura, Grant. B.S. in Edn, U. S.D., 1943, M.A. in Speech, 1947; postgrad., Northwestern U., 1946; Ph.D., U. Mo., 1953. Instr. speech U. S.D., 1947-48, U. Mo., 1948-52; instr. Purdue U., 1952-53, asst. prof., 1953-54; instr. Purdue Inst. Ins., 1952-54; asst. prof. Mich. State U., East Lansing, 1954-61, asso. prof., 1963-

67, prof. communication, 1967-72, prof. communication, racial and ethnic studies, 1973—, chmn. dept. racial and ethnic studies, 1973—, asst. dean coll. communication arts, 1960-61, asst. dean student affairs, 1966-67, dean communication arts, 1967-71, acting dir., 1980-81; acting dean Coll. Urban Devel., 1981; dir. housing, research allocations and tech. assistance U. Nigeria, 1961-63; cons. in field. Co-chmn. Statewide Task Force on Sch. Vandalism and Violence, Lansing, Mich.; Chmn. East Lansing Democratic Com., 1954-55, East Lansing Human Relations Com., 1969. Served with U.S. Army, 1942-46. Decorated Silver Star, Bronze Star, Purple Heart (2). Mem. AAUP, Speech Communication Assn., Internat. Communication Assn., Soc. for Internat. Study, Soc. for Ethnic Studies. Home: 630 Camelot St East Lansing MI 48823 Office: Michigan State U East Lansing MI 48823

BAIN, JAMES ARTHUR, pharmacologist, educator; b. Langdon, N.D., May 22, 1918; s. James Hamilton and Mabel (Aldritt) B.; m. Eleanor Theo Hohaus, Dec. 5, 1947; children: Andrew J., Peter T. A.A., Wayland Jr. Coll., 1938; B.S., U. Wis., 1940, Ph.D., 1944. Research asst. McArdle Meml. Lab., U. Wis., 1940-44, Rockefeller fellow, 1946-47; research asso. U. Ill., 1947-50, asst. prof., then asso. prof., 1952-54; mem. faculty dept. pharmacology Emory U., 1954—, prof., 1954—, chmn. dept., 1957-62, dir. div. basic health scis., 1960-76, exec. asso. dean, 1976—; cons. to govt., nat. agys., industry, 1954—. Contbr. articles profl. jours. Mem. Am. Chem. Soc., Am. Soc. Pharmacology and Exptl. Therapeutics, AAAS. Home: 2275 Tanglewood Rd Decatur GA 30033 Office: Woodruff Med Center Adminstrn Bldg Emory U Atlanta GA 30322

BAIN, ROBERT ADDISON, English literature educator; b. Marshall, Ill., Sept. 20, 1932; s. Ernest A. and Linda Gail (Clark) B.; m. Bonnie Jean Baker, Dec. 27, 1951 (div. 1981); children: Susan E., Robin Anne, Michael A. B.S. with honors, Eastern Ill. U., 1954; A.M., U. Ill., 1959, Ph.D., 1964. Tchr. Lanphier High Sch., Springfield, Ill., 1954-58; reporter Ill. State Jour., Springfield, 1954-58; teaching asst. U. Ill., Urbana, 1958-64; prof. English U. N.C., Chapel Hill, 1964—, dir. freshman English, 1967-70, asst. dean The Gen. Coll., 1979-82; editorial cons. Prentice-Hall, Inc., 1966-78, Scott, Foresman & Co., 1966-79. Author: H.L. Davis, 1974; co-editor, author: The Writer and the Worlds of Words, 1975, Southern Writers: A Biographical Dictionary, 1979; editor: (with George F. Horner) Colonial and Federalist American Writing, 1966; editorial bd.: So. Lit. Jour., 1975—. Den leader Cub Scouts Am., 1970-72. Recipient Tanner award U. N.C., 1976. Mem. N.C.-Va. Coll. English Assn. (pres. 1970-71), Conf. Coll. Composition and Communication (exec. com. 1971-74), Nat. Council Tchrs. English (commn. on composition 1976-79), Southeastern Conf. English in Two-Yr. Coll. (exec. com.), S. Atlantic Modern Lang. Assn. Democrat. Baptist. Home: G9 Ridgewood Apts Carrboro NC 27510 Office: Dept English U NC Chapel Hill NC 27514

BAIN, WILFRED CONWELL, former university dean, music educator, opera theater director; b. Shawville, Que., Can., Jan. 20, 1908; came to U.S., 1918, naturalized, 1940; s. James Alexander and Della Mary (Hawn) B.; m. Mary Freeman, July 1, 1929. A.B., Houghton Coll., 1929; B.Mus., Westminster Choir Coll., 1931; M.A., N.Y.U., 1936, Ed.D., 1938; Mus.D. (hon.), Am. Conservatory, 1951, Temple U., 1962, Westminster Choir Coll., 1965; LL.D., Ind. State U.; Mus. D., Ind. U., 1981, Houghton Coll., 1981. Head music dept. Central Coll., S.C., 1929-30; head voice, choral music Houghton Coll., 1931-38; dean music N. Tex. State U., 1938-47; dean Sch. Music, Ind. U., Bloomington, 1947-73; artistic dir. Opera Theater, 1973—; Chmn. music adv. panel USIA, 1967; music adviser, mem. bd. Coolidge Found.; mem. Nat. Council on Arts and Govt., 1966—; trustee Westminster Choir Coll., 1965—; mem. leadership tng. conf., examiners bd. N. Central Assoc.; mem. com. Central Opera Service; nat. council Met. Opera. V.p. bd. dirs. Palm Beach Opera, (Fla.), 1979—. Recipient gold medal Nat. Soc. Arts and Letters, medal Eugene Ysaye Found. of Belgium, certificate of merit Ind. Higher Edn. Music Adminstrs. Assn. Mem. Nat. Assn. Tchrs. Singing., Nat. Assn. Schs. Music (v.p.), Music Tchrs. Nat. Assn. (pres., sec.), Am. Musical Soc., Music Educators Nat. Conf., Am. Friends of Bayreuth (pres.), Ind. Acad. (charter), Phi Kappa Lambda, Phi Delta Kappa, Pi Sigma Kappa, Kappa Kappa Psi. Club: Rotarian (hon.). Home: 2516 Rechter Dr Bloomington IN 47401 *As a musician, conductor, educator I have as a life objective to develop opera at the educational and professional level through performance, composition, education of all opera personnel.*

BAIN, WILLIAM DONALD, JR., lawyer, chemical company executive; b. Rochelle, Ill., July 1, 1925; s. William Donald and Gretchen (Kittler) B.; m. Pauline Thomas, Jan. 14, 1950; children: Elizabeth Kittler, Anne Alexander, Nancy Hemenway. B.S. in Econs, U. Pa., 1947; LL.B., Washington and Lee U., 1949. Bar: S.C. 1952. Mortgage loan field rep. Travelers Ins. Co., Hartford, Conn., Cleve. and; Orlando, Fla., 1949-51; with Moreland-McKesson Chem. Co., Spartanburg, S.C., 1951—, pres., 1965—, also dir.; pres., dir. Moreland Devel. Co. Inc., 1983—; dir. Affiliated Chem. Group Ltd., Bankers Trust Co., Spartan Radiocasting Corp., Chemtech Industries Inc. Mem. Spartanburg Sch. Bd., 1958-72, chmn., 1963-72; trustee Converse Coll., Washington and Lee U. Served with AC U.S. Army, 1943-45. Mem. S.C. Bar Assn. Republican. Episcopalian. Clubs: Rotary, Piedmont, Spartanburg Country, Spectator., Carolina Country (founder, dir.). Office: PO Box 18288 Spartanburg SC 29304

BAIN, WILLIAM JAMES, architect; b. New Westminster, C., Can., Mar. 27, 1896; s. David and Annie Wilson (Forrester) B.; m. Mildred Worline Clark, May 29, 1924; children— Robert Clark, William James, Jr., Nancy Ann (Mrs. Edward George Lowry III). Student, U. Pa., 1919-21; student in, Europe, 1922. Employed in, Boston, N.Y., Los Angeles, Seattle, 1922-24, practice architecture, 1924—; mem. firm Naramore, Bain, Brady and Johanson, 1943—; Mem. Nat. Pub. Adv. Panel for Archtl. Services, 1968-69; regional adv. bd. SBA. Prin. works include Nat. FDA Bldg, Washington, Washington Bldg., Seattle; assoc. architect: 1st Nat. Bank of Missoula (Mont.), U. Wash. Med. Sch., Seattle, IBM Bldg., Seattle, Seattle 1st Nat. Bank, Seattle Post Intelligencer, Batelle Research Centers, addition to Mayo Clinic, Rochester, Minn., Kingdome, 1979—; also numerous residences in, Wash., Oreg., Idaho, Mont. and B.C. Bd. dirs. Salvation Army.; past mem. Seattle Housing Adv. Bd.; pres. Arthritis Found. Western Wash., 1968; trustee Seattle Urban Renewal. Served with 117th Field Signal Bn., attached to 166th Inf., Rainbow Div. U.S. Army, 1917-18. Fellow AIA (jury of fellows 1950-55, mem. bd. past pres. Wash. chpt., sec. coll. fellows 1966, Seattle pres. 1968); mem. English Speaking Union (mem. bd. 1964-70, 78—), C. of C. (mem. exec. com. 1968-69, dir. 1960-70, treas. 1965, constrn. man of year 1966), Am. Arbitration Assn. Clubs: Rainier (dir.), Rotary, Washington Athletic, Seattle Tennis. Home: 1540 Parkside Dr East Seattle WA 98112 Office: 111 S Jackson St Seattle WA 98104

BAIN, WILLIAM JAMES, JR., architect; b. Seattle, June 26, 1930; s. William James and Mildred Worline (Clark) B.; m. Nancy Sanford Hill, Sept. 21, 1957; children: David Hunter, Stephen Frazer, Mark Sanford, John Worthington. B.Arch., Cornell U., 1953. Partner Naramore, Bain, Brady & Johanson, Seattle; juror, lectr. U. Wash., Seattle, Wash. State U. Prin. works include various research insts., mcpl. bldgs., office complexes, and community plans. Bd. dirs. Downtown Seattle Assn., 1980—, Arboretum Found., 1971-74; bd. dirs. Seattle Symphony Orch., 1974—, pres., 1977-79; mem. affiliate program steering com. Coll. Architecture and Urban Planning, U. Wash., 1969-71. Served to 1st lt., C.E. U.S. Army, 1953-55. Recipient cert. of achievement Port of Whittier, Alaska, 1955. Fellow AIA (pres. Seattle chpt. 1969, chmn. N.W. Regional Student-Profl. Fund 1971, pres. Wash. State council 1974), N.W. Regional Archtl. Found. (pres. 1975); mem. Seattle C. of C. (dir. 1980—), Nat. Assn. Indsl. and Office Parks, Urban Land Inst., Nat. Assn. Corp. Real Estate Execs., Am. Arbitration Assn. (comml. panel 1975—), Lambda Alpha. Episcopalian. Clubs: Rotary, Rainier, Wash. Athletic, Tennis (Seattle). Home: 1631 Rambling Ln Bellevue WA 98004 Office: 111 S Jackson St Seattle WA 98104

BAINBRIDGE, FREDERICK FREEMAN, III, architect; b. Charlottesville, Va., Sept. 15, 1927; s. Frederick Freeman and Cornelia Winston (Burnley) B.; m. Binki Baker, Jan. 6, 1948 (div. Nov. 1972); children—Burnley, Susan Winifred, Meriwether, Robin; m. Anna Bacon, Jan. 1976; 1 son, Nicholas Gordon. B.Arch., U. Va., 1950; M. Indsl. Design, Kansas City Art Inst., 1952. Asst. prof. Sch. Architecture Clemson (S.C.) U., 1952-55; asso. firm Toombs, Amisano & Wells (Architects), Atlanta, 1955-62; prin. firm Martin & Bainbridge, Atlanta, 1962-70, Bainbridge & Assos., 1970—; Southeastern project architect U. Ky. civil defense research project, 1964; vis. critic Ga. Inst. Tech., 1964-67. Chmn. archtl. rev. com. Atlanta Civic Design Commn., 1967—. Served with USNR, 1944-46. Recipient honor awards S. Atlantic Region AIA, 1964, 66, 68, 70; honor award prestressed Concrete Inst., 1967. Mem. AIA. Clubs: Fairington Golf and Tennis, Amelia Island Plantation. Home: 400 Orchard Rd Atlanta GA 30339 Office: 4334 Paces Ferry Rd NW Atlanta GA 30339

BAINBRIDGE, JOHN, writer; b. Monticello, Minn., Mar. 12, 1913; s. William Dean and Bess (Lakin) B.; m. Dorothy Alice Hazlewood, June 2, 1936; children—Jonathon, Janet. B.S., Northwestern U., 1935. Mem. editorial staff The New Yorker, 1938—. Contbr.: numerous Profiles to The New Yorker; and articles to other nat. publs.; Author: Little Wonder, or The Reader's Digest and How It Grew, 1946, The Wonderful World of Toots Shor, 1951, Biography of an Idea, 1952, Garbo, 1955, The Super-Americans, 1961, Like a Homesick Angel, 1964, Another Way of Living, 1968, English Impressions, 1981. Mem. Athors Guild. Club: Coffee House (N.Y.C., N.Y.). Home: Terrace Lodge Stourton nr Warminster Wiltshire England Office: care The New Yorker 25 W 43d St New York NY 10036

BAINBRIDGE, KENNETH TOMPKINS, physicist, educator; b. Cooperstown, N.Y., July 27, 1904; s. William Warin and Mae (Tompkins) B.; m. Margaret Pitkin, Sept. 8, 1931 (dec. 1967); children: Martin Keeler, Joan, Margaret Tompkins; m. Helen Brinkley King, Oct. 11, 1969. S.B., Mass. Inst. Tech., 1926, S.M., 1926; M.A., Princeton, 1927, Ph.D., 1929; M.A. (hon.), Harvard, 1942. Physicist, 1928-29; Nat. Research Council fellow Bartol Research Found., 1929-31, Bartol Research Found. fellow, 1931-33; Guggenheim Meml. Found. fellow at Cavendish Lab., Cambridge, Eng., 1933-34; asst. prof. physics Harvard, 1934-38, asso. prof., 1938-46, prof., 1946—, chmn. dept. physics, 1953-55, George Vasmer Leverett prof. physics, 1961-75, emeritus, 1975—; now design cons. linear direct current motors; tech. cons. Nat. Def. Research Council, 1940-44, M.I.T. Radiation Lab., 1940-43, Los Alamos Lab., 1943-45; dir. Alamogordo Atomic Bomb Test, Feb.-Sept. 1945. Contbr.: tech. articles to Jour. of Franklin Inst. Trustee Asso. Univs., Inc., 1957-59; Mem. 7th Solvay Chemistry Congress, 1947. Awarded Louis Edward Levy medal Franklin Inst., 1933; Presdl. certificate of merit for work on radar, 1948. Mem. Am. Phys. Soc., Nat. Acad. Scis., Am. Acad. Arts and Scis., Alpha Tau Omega, Tau Beta Pi. Holder of patents on photo electric cells, electronic multiplier and electro magnetic pumps. Address: 5 Nobscot Rd Weston MA 02193

BAINER, PHILIP LA VERN, college president; b. Pomona, Kans., Aug. 10, 1931; s. Raymond and Ina Leona (Ward) B.; m. Jane Kristine Huhtala, July 1, 1957 (div.); children: Angela Dawn, Jeffrey Philip. A.B. in Biology, Ottawa U., 1953, M.S., Kans. State Tchrs. Coll., 1957. Tchr. Turner High Sch., Kansas City, Kans., 1957-63; instr. Clatsop Community Coll., 1963-64, chmn. div. liberal arts, 1964-66, dean instrn., 1966-70, pres., 1970—. Pres. Columbia River Maritime Museum, Astoria, Oreg., 1977; treas. Clatsop County Kidney Assn. Served with Signal Corps U.S. Army, 1954-56. Mem. Oreg. Community Coll. Assembly, Oreg. Chief Exec. Officers Council (chmn.), Astoria C. of C. Republican. Mem. Brethern Ch. Clubs: Kiwanis (pres. 1984), Elks.). Home: 186 Kensington Astoria OR 97103 Office: Clatsop Community Coll 16th and Jerome Sts Astoria OR 97103

BAINER, ROY, agricultural engineer, educator; b. nr. Ottawa, Kans., Mar. 7, 1902; s. Harry M. and Clara Ellen (Nitcher) B.; m. Lena Mae Cook, May 29, 1926; 1 dau., La Nelle Marie. B.S., Kans. State Coll., 1926, M.S., 1929; LL.D., U. Calif., 1969; D.Sci., Kans. State U., 1983. Instr. Kans. State Coll., 1926-27, asst. prof., 1927-29; asst. prof., asst. agrl. engr. U. Calif.-Davis, 1929-37, assoc. prof., 1937-45, assoc. agrl. engr., 1937-43, agrl. engr., 1943—, prof. agrl. engring., 1945—, chmn. div., 1947-61, asst. dean engring., 1952-61, assoc. dean, 1961-62, dean, 1962-69, dean emeritus, 1969—; Cons. Brit. Ministry Agr., 1945, U.S. Army, Japan, 1948; asso. dir. mechanization center FAO of UN, Chile, 1958, cons., Peru, 1961, 62, 63-64, 65, 66, 69, Dept. State in Laos, 1966, Kasetsart U., Bangkok, Thailand, 1966; cons. to minister agr., Brazil, 1969, Spain, 1971-72; cons. Arya-Mehr U. Tech., Iran, 1975, Guanajuato U., Mexico, 1977, Malawi, 1978; hon. prof. Agrarian U., Peru, 1964; mem. agr. bd. Nat. Acad. Sci.-NRC, 1957-62; mem. at large NRC; resource person Library Congress, 1972—. Co-author: Principles of Farm Machinery; Contbr. articles to profl. jours. Recipient McCormick Gold Medal for outstanding achievement agrl. engring., Distinguished Service award Am. Soc. Sugar Beet Technologists, 1960, Kans. State U., 1960, U. Mo., 1962. Mem. Am. Soc. Agrl. Engrs. (past pres.), Nat. Acad. Engring., Am. Soc. Engring. Edn. (Vincent Bendix gold medal 1962), Calif. Acad. Sci., Sigma Xi, Phi Mu Alpha, Gamma Sigma Delta, Tau Beta Pi. Republican. Methodist. Clubs: Commonwealth, Faculty, Rotary (past pres. Davis). Patentee in field. Home: 623 Miller Dr Davis CA 95616

BAINS, HARRISON MACKELLAR, JR., food company executive; b. Pasadena, Calif., July 8, 1943; s. Harrison MacKellar and Celeste Adele (Callahan) B.; m. Leslie E. Tawney, Mar. 7, 1970; children: Harrison MacKellar, III, Tawney Elizabeth. B.A., U. Redlands, 1964; M.B.A., U. Calif., Berkeley, 1966. Asst. v.p. Citibank N.A., 1968-72; asst. treas. Richardson-Merrell Inc., 1972-76, Nabisco Inc., East Hanover, N.J., 1976-78, treas., 1978—, v.p., 1980-81; v.p., treas. Nabisco Brands, Inc., Parsippany, N.J., 1981-82, Sr. v.p. fin., 1982-83, Sr. v.p., treas., 1983—. Mem. Fin. Execs. Inst., Food Safety Council (treas. 1980—). Office: Nabisco Brands Plaza Parsippany NJ 07054

BAINS, LEE EDMUNDSON, lawyer, state official; b. Birmingham, Ala., June 18, 1912; s. Herman Lipsey and Myrtle (Edmundson) B.; m. Ruel Eneida Burton, Jan. 1, 1938; children: Sandra Anita (Mrs. Henry Barnard Hardegree), Myrtle Lee, Lee Edmundson. Student, Birmingham So. Coll., 1930-31; B.S., U. Ala., 1934, J.D., 1936. Bar: Ala. 1936, U.S. Supreme Ct 1936, diplomate: Nat. Coll. Advocacy. Practiced in, Bessemer, 1936—, city atty., 1950-58; instr. Birmingham Sch. Law, 1937-41; faculty Nat. War Coll., 1960; atty. for Ala. Power Co., South Central Bell Telephone Co., Phillips Petroleum Co., AmSouth Bank; apptd. by gov. as spl. asst. atty. gen., State of Ala., 1980—. Contbr. article to profl. jour.; Author: Basic Legal Skills, 1976. Pres. Bessemer Bd. Edn., 1955-58, Bessemer YMCA, 1961; Mem. Nat. Naval Res. Policy Bd., 1952-53; advisor Bd. Family Ct., Jefferson County, 1966—; chmn. finance com. Nat. Vets. Day for Birmingham, 1973; Alternate del. Democratic Nat. Conv., 1941; tchr. Men's Bible class First United Meth. Ch., 1966—. Served to rear adm. USNR, 1941-46; ETO, PTO; rear adm. Res. Fellow Am. Coll. Trial Lawyers; mem. Am., Ala. assns. trial lawyers, ABA (vice chmn. environ. law sect. 1979—), Ala. Bar Assn. (chmn. unauthorized practice com. 1977-79), Bessemer Bar Assn. (pres. 1983-84), Birmingham Bar Assn., Res. Officers Assn., Naval Res. Assn., Soc. Colonial Wars (state gov. 1972-73, corr. sec. 1976—), SAR (pres. Ala.), Phi Gamma Delta, Beta Gamma Sigma. Clubs: Kiwanian.; Birmingham Ski, Downtown, The Club (Birmingham). Winner numerous swimming, jogging, skiing and figure skating awards, Presdl. sports award. Home: 621 Melody Ln Bessemer AL 35020 Office: 1813 3d Ave Bessemer AL 35020 *If your goal is happiness, you most likely will accomplish little, and not be happy in your pursuit. If your objective is the pursuit of excellence - doing the very best you can with the task upon which you are working now - then there is a probability of producing good and, perhaps, an excellent work product, and finding happiness as an unsought reward. The pursuit of happiness is a political phrase that represents tolerance and the freedom to pursue individual goals. As a personal objective it will not lead to worthwhile achievement. To the contrary, the pursuit of excellenc will lead to the highest and best accomplishments, and happiness will come as an unsought for reward.*

BAINTON, DONALD J., diversified manufacturing company executive; b. N.Y.C., May 3, 1931; s. William Lewis and Mildred J. (Dunne) B.; m. Aileen M. Demoulins, July 10, 1954; children—Kathryn C., Stephen L., Elizabeth A., William D. B.A., Columbia U., 1952; postgrad., Advanced Mgmt. Program, Rutgers U., 1960. With The Continental Group, Inc., 1954—, gen. mgr. prodn. planning, 1967-68, gen. mgr. mfg., 1968-73; gen. mgr. (Pacific div.), 1973-74, 1974-75; v.p., gen. mgr. ops. U.S. Metal, 1975-76; exec. v.p., gen. mgr. CCC-USA, 1976-78, corp. exec. v.p., pres. diversified ops., 1978-79; pres. Continental Can Co., 1979-81, Continental Packaging, 1981—, exec. v.p., operating officer parent co., 1979—; dir. Continental Group, Inc., Continental Group Can., Ltd., Gen. Pub. Utilities. Bd. dirs. Columbia Coll. Served with USN, 1952-54; Korea. Mem. Nat. Center for Resource Recovery (dir.), Can Mfrs. Inst. (dir.), Columbia U. Alumni Assn. Republican. Roman Catholic. Clubs: Milbrook Country (Greenwich, Conn.); Landmark (Stamford, Conn.); Blind Brook (Purchase, N.Y.); Winged Foot (Mamaroneck, N.Y.); Pinnacle (N.Y.C.). Office: care Continental Group 51 Harbor Plaza Stamford CT 06904

BAINUM, PETER MONTGOMERY, aerospace engineer; b. St. Petersburg, Fla., Feb. 4, 1938; s. Charles Joseph and Mildred Trincher (Salyer) B.; m. Carmen Cecilia Perez; 1 son, David P. B.S. in Aero. Engring, Tex. A&M U., 1959; S.M. in Aeros. and Astronautics, M.I.T., 1960; Ph.D. in Aerospace Engring, Cath. U. Am., 1967. Sr. engr. Martin Co., Orlando, Fla., 1960-62; staff engr. IBM Fed. Systems Div., Bethesda, Md., 1962-65; sr. staff engr., cons. Johns Hopkins U. Applied Physics Lab., 1965-69, 69-72; mem. faculty Howard U., 1969—, prof. aerospace engring., dir. grad. studies, 1973—; v.p. research, cons. WHF & Assos. Inc., Bethesda, Md., 1977—; Summer faculty fellow NASA/Am. Soc. Engring. Edn., 1970-71. Contbr. articles to profl. jours. Recipient Teetor award Soc. Automotive Engrs., 1971, Howard U. award for Outstanding Research, 1981. Fellow Brit. Interplanetary Soc., Am. Astronautical Soc. (exec. v.p.); asso. fellow AIAA; mem. Astrodynamics Tech. Com. Home: 9804 Raleigh Tavern Ct Bethesda MD 20814 Office: Dept Mech Engring Howard U Washington DC 20059 *With a doctoral degree comes significant responsibilities - to search out truth scientifically, to safeguard it, and to apply it to the shaping of both private and public life.*

BAIONE, LUKE, banker; b. N.Y.C., Aug. 23, 1921; s. Dominick and Mary (Marotta) B.; m. Juliet F. Bullard, Aug. 26, 1944; children: Mary, Dominick. B.B.A., Coll. City N.Y., 1942. With Brevoort Savs. Bank (name changed to Met. Savs. Bank after merger with Met. 1970), Bklyn., 1946—, pres., 1969-71, chmn. bd., 1971—, dir., 1967—; dir. Instl. Securities Corp.; mem. Bklyn. adv. bd. Mfrs. Hanover Trust Co.; mem. com. Liaison FDIC, Com. N.Y.C. Govt. Relations, Capitol Structure Study, Corporate Securities Portfolio Mgmt. Mem. Bklyn. adv. com. United Hosp. Fund of N.Y.; bd. dirs. Bklyn. chpt. ARC, St. Francis Coll., Bklyn. Bur. Community Services; mem. bishop's lay com. Diocese of Bklyn. Served with USAAF, 1942-46. Decorated Bronze Star. Mem. Bklyn. C. of C. (dir., chmn. environ. com.), Nat. Council Savs. Instns. (com. fed. fin. and fiscal policy), Savs. Banks Assn. (chmn. dir.). Clubs: Richmond County Country, Brooklyn, Metropolitan. Home: 4 Dalemere Rd Staten Island NY 10304 Office: 211 Montague St Brooklyn NY 11201

BAIR, EDWARD JAY, educator; b. Ft. Collins, Colo., June 30, 1922; s. Jay Albert and Edith Hectos (Pegg) B.; m. Dorothy Helen Bimson, June 29, 1958. B.S., Colo. State U., 1943; Ph.D., Brown U., 1949. Chemist Tenn. Eastman Corp., Oak Ridge, 1953-56; research assoc. U. Wash., 1949-54; mem. faculty Ind. U., 1954—, prof. chemistry, 1965—. Mem. editorial bd.: Jour. Photochemistry. Mem. Am. Chem. Soc., Am. Phys. Soc. Home: 117 N Hillsdale Bloomington IN 47401

BAIR, WILLIAM J., radiation biologist; b. Jackson, Mich., July 14, 1924; s. William J. and Mona J. (Gamble) B.; m. Barbara Joan Sites, Feb. 16, 1952; children: William J., Michael Braden, Andrew Emil. B.A. in chemistry, Ohio Wesleyan U., 1949; Ph.D. in Radiation Biology, U. Rochester, 1954. NRC-AEC fellow U. Rochester, 1949-50, research asso. radiation biology, 1950-54; biol. scientist Hanford Labs. of Gen. Electric Co., Richland, Wash., 1954-56, mgr. inhalation toxicology sect., biology dept., 1956-65, Battelle Meml. Inst., 1965-68; mgr. biology dept. Pacific Northwest Labs., Richland, Wash., 1968-74, dir. life scis. program, 1973-75, mgr. biomed. and environ. research program, 1975-76, mgr. environ. health and safety research program, 1976—; lectr. radiation biology Joint Center Grad. Study, Richland, 1955—; cons. to advisory com. on reactor safeguards Nuclear Regulatory Commn., 1971—; also mem. several coms. on plutonium toxicology. Mem. subcom. inhalation hazards, com. pathologic effects atomic radiation Nat. Acad. Sci., 1957-64; mem. ad hoc com. on hot particles of subcom. biol. effects of ionizing radiation Nat. Acad. Scis.-NRC, 1974-76; chmn. task force on biol. effects of inhaled particles Internat. Commn. on Radiol. Protection, 1970-79, mem. com. 2 on permissible dose for internal radiation, 1973—; chmn. Hanford Symposium Inhaled Radioactive Particles and Gases, 1964; co-chmn. Hanford Symposium Biol. Implications of Transuranium Elements, 1971; chmn. Am. Inst. Biol. Scis.-AEC-Energy Research and Devel. Adminstrn. Transuranium Tech. Group, 1972-75; mem. Nat. Council on Radiation Protection and Measurements, 1974—, bd. dirs., 1976-82, mem. com. on maximum permissible concentrations for occupational and non-occupational exposure, 1970-77, mem. com. basic radiation protection criteria, 1975—, chmn. ad hoc com. on hot particles, 1974, chmn. ad hoc com. internal emitter activities, 1976-77, mem. com. 57 on internal emitter standards, 1977—; U.S. participant and rep. numerous internat. confs., including Japan AEC, Nat. Radiol. Health Inst., Chiba, 1969, South African Assn. Physicists in Medicine and Biology, Pretoria, 1980; mem. rev. com. Argonne Univs. Assn., 1977-80; chmn. Marshall Islands radiol. adv. group Dept. Energy,

1978-81; mem. staff Pres.'s Commn. on Accident at Three Mile Island, 1979-80; mem. regional steering com. on health effects from eruption of Mt. St. Helens, 1980—. Author 100 books, articles, reports, chpts. in books.; lectr. Japan AEC. Recipient E.O. Lawrence Meml. award, 1970; Cert. of Appreciation AEC, 1975. Fellow AAAS; mem. Radiation Research Soc., Health Physics Soc. (dir. 1970-73, pres. 1983), N.Y. Acad. Sci., Soc. Exptl. Biology and Medicine (vice chmn. N.W. sect. 1967-70, 74—), Reticuloendothelial Soc., Soc. Occupational and Environ. Health, Sigma Xi. Club: Kiwanis (dir.). Demonstrated toxicology of plutonium and carcinogenesis of radioactive particles in lung. Home: 102 Somerset St Richland WA 99352 Office: Battelle Pacific NW Labs PO Box 999 Richland WA 99352

BAIRD, ALEXANDER KENNEDY, educator; b. Pasadena, Calif., Nov. 22, 1932; s. A. Kennedy and Phyllis May (Stimpson) B.; m. Kathleen White, Oct. 1, 1965. B.A., Pomona Coll., 1954; M.A., Claremont Grad. Sch., 1957; Ph.D., U. Calif. at Berkeley, 1960. Instr. geology Pomona Coll., Claremont, Calif., 1955-56, 58-60, asst. prof. geology, 1960-64, asso. prof. geology, 1964-70, prof. geology, 1970—. NSF predoctoral fellow, 1957-58; NSF research grantee, 1963-68; NASA Viking scientist, 1972-79; prin. investigator NASA Mars Data Analysis Program, 1979-82; research assoc. NRC Jet Propulsion Lab., 1983. Fellow Geol. Soc. Am.; mem. Nat. Assn. Geology Tchrs., Am. Geophys. Union, Planetary Soc., Phi Beta Kappa, Sigma Xi. Home: 265 W 11th St Claremont CA 91711

BAIRD, CHARLES FITZ, business executive; b. Southampton, N.Y., Sept. 4, 1922; s. George White and Julia (Fitz) B.; m. Norma Adele White, Sept. 13, 1947; children: Susan Fitz, Stephen White, Charles Fitz, Nancy Williams. A.B., Middlebury (Vt.) Coll., 1944; grad., Advanced Mgmt. Program, Harvard, 1960; LL.D. (hon.), Bucknell U., 1976. With Standard Oil Co., N.J., 1948-65, dep. European fin. rep., London, 1955-58, asst. treas., 1958-62; dir. Esso Standard SA Française, 1962-65; asst. sec. of navy (fin. mgmt.), 1966-67, undersec. of navy, 1967-69; v.p. fin. Inco Ltd., 1969-72, sr. v.p., 1972-76, vice-chmn., 1976-77, pres., 1977-80, chmn., chief exec. officer, 1980—, also dir.; dir. Bank of Montreal, ICI Ams. Inc., Aetna Life and Casualty Co.; bd. govs. Olympic Trust of Can.; Mem. President's Commn. Marine Sci., Engring. and Resources, 1967-69, Nat. Adv. Commns. on Ocean and Atmosphere, 1972-74. Trustee Bucknell U., 1969—; chmn. bd. trustees, 1976-82; bd. advisers Naval War Coll., 1970-74; bd. dirs. Tennis Can.; mem. Ont. Bus. Adv. Council. Served as capt. USMC, 1943-46, 51-52. Mem. Bus. Council on Nat. Issues, Brit.-N. Am. Com., Council Fgn. Relations, Can. Inst. Mining and Metallurgy, Canadian-Am. Com., Conf. Bd. Can. (bd. dirs.), Chi Psi. Clubs: Chevy Chase (Md.); India House, Links (N.Y.C.); Short Hills (N.J.); Badmington and Racquet, Toronto, Queen's, Rosedale Golf. Home: 35 Rosedale Rd Toronto ON M4W 2P5 Canada Office: First Canadian Pl Toronto ON M5X 1C4 Canada also 1 New York Plaza New York NY 10004

BAIRD, DONALD, museum director; b. Pitts., May 12, 1926; s. George Mahaffey Patterson and Mary Alma Barton (Johnson) B.; m. Lucille Bailey, Feb. 14, 1948 (dec.); children: Andrew Baird, Laurel Jean. B.S., U. Pitts., 1948; M.S., U. Colo., 1949; Ph.D. (Jeffries Wyman scholar), Harvard U., 1955. Asst. geologist Pa. Topographical and Geol. Survey, 1947-49; curator U. Cin. Mus., 1949-51; asst. curator vertebrate paleontology Mus. Comparative Zoology, Harvard U., 1954-57; mem. staff Mus. Natural History, Princeton U., 1957—, curator, 1967-74, dir., 1974—, also curator vertebrate paleontology; pres. Princeton Jr. Mus., 1968-70; research asso. Am. Mus. Natural History, N.Y.C., 1964—; cons., photographer in field. Author papers in field. Served with AUS, 1944-46. NSF grantee, 1980-81. Mem. Soc. Vertebrate Paleontology (exec. com. 1980—), Paleontol. Soc., Paleontol. Assn., Soc. Study of Evolution, Soc. Hist. Archaeology, Assn. Sci. Mus. Dirs., N.J. Acad. Scis., Nat. Muzzle Loading Rifle Assn., Hist. Soc. Princeton, Old Barracks Assn., Princeton Battlefield Area Preservation Soc. (trustee). Democrat. Quaker. Office: Princeton U Museum Guyot Hall Princeton NJ 08544 *

BAIRD, HENRY WELLES, III, pediatric neurologist; b. Fort Leavenworth, Kans., Oct. 10, 1922; s. Henry Welles and Elizabeth (Tower) B.; m. Eleanora C. Gordon, Apr. 21, 1950; children: Henry Welles IV, Douglas G., Bruce C., Matthew C. B.S., Yale U., 1945, M.D., 1949. Fellow, resident neurology and pediatrics Temple U. Sch. Medicine, Phila., 1950-53, faculty pediatrics, 1953—, asso. prof., 1963-68, prof. pediatrics, 1968—; practice medicine specializing in pediatric neurology, Phila., 1953—; attending pediatrician St. Christopher's Hosp. for Children, Phila., 1966—. Author: The Child with Convulsions, 1972, Neurologic Evaluation of Infants and Children, 1983; Mem. editorial bd.: Devel. Medicine and Child Neurology, 1971—; editor, 1977—; contbr. articles to profl. jours. Served to capt. M.C. AUS, 1950-56. Mem. Soc. Pediatric Research, Am. Acad. Pediatrics, Am. Acad. Cerebral Palsy. Office: 2600 N Lawrence St Philadelphia PA 19133 *I have gotten into more difficulty by believing facts that proved to be incorrect than in any other way.* *

BAIRD, HUGH ADAMSON, engring. co. exec.; b. Renfrew, Scotland; came to U.S., 1923, naturalized, 1942; s. Andrew and Betty (Baird); (m), June 12, 1943; children: Suzanne, Mark. B.S., Calif. Inst. Tech., 1942, M.S., 1946. Mem. staff Office Sci. Research and Devel., Calif. Inst. Tech., 1942-45; with C.F. Braun & Co., Alhambra, Calif., 1946—, v.p., 1971-74, exec. v.p., 1974-79, pres., 1979—. Fellow Am. Inst. Chem. Engrs., IAE. Club: Calif. Office: C F Braun & Co Alhambra CA 91802 *

BAIRD, JAMES ABINGTON, lawyer; b. Kirksville, Mo., Jan. 28, 1926; s. James Abington and Dorothy (LaGest) B.; m. Georgia Jane Suliburk, Mar. 29, 1948; children—James Abington III, Mary J. (Mrs. Ralph Kiebach). B.S., U. Mich., 1949; J.D., U. Toledo, 1957. Bar: Ohio bar 1957. Sales rep. Fruehauf Trailer Co., Chgo., 1949-50; pres. Kaiser-Frazer dealership, Caro, Mich., 1950-51; sales rep. Warren-Teed Products Co., Toledo, 1951-52, Dictaphone Corp., 1952-53; claims adjuster Nationwide Ins. Co., Toledo, 1953-57; since practiced in, Toledo; judge Sylvania Ohio Municipal Ct., 1970-82. Chmn. Sch. Levy campaigns Sylvania Pub. Sch. System, 1968-69, candidate Sch. Bd., 1969. Served with USNR, 1944-46. Mem. Toledo Bar Assn., U. Mich., U. Toledo alumni assns., Phi Delta Theta. Club: Mason. Home: Heather Highland Farm 8505 Scotch Ridge Rd Bowling Green OH 43402

BAIRD, JOHN PIERSON, food company executive, lawyer; b. St. Louis, Nov. 1, 1925; s. John Pierson and Janet (Harrison) B.; m. Virginia Marie Traeger, July 24, 1948; children: John Pierson, William Henry. Student, U. Ill., 1946-49; LL.B., St. Louis U., 1952. Bar: Mo. 1952. Asso. firm Fordyce, Mayne, Hartman, Renard & Stribling, St. Louis, 1952-57, partner firm, 1956-57; dir. labor relations and prodn. personnel Ralston Purina Co., 1957-61, sec., gen. counsel, 1961—, v.p., 1967-79, sr. v.p., 1979—, gen. counsel, 1983—; dir. County Bank of Webster Groves; Mem. adv. bd. Southwestern Legal Found. Internat. and Comparative Law Center, 1967—. Served with inf. AUS, 1943-46; ETO. Mem. Fed., Am., Inter-Am., Mo., St. Louis bar assns., Am. Soc. Corporate Secs., Sigma Phi Epsilon, Phi Delta Phi. Home: 11 Bellerive Country Club Grounds Saint Louis MO 63141 Office: Checkerboard Square Saint Louis MO 63164

BAIRD, JOSEPH ARMSTRONG, JR., art history educator; b. Pitts, Nov. 22, 1922; s. Joseph Armstrong and Lulu Charlotte (Fuller) B. B.A., Oberlin Coll., 1944; M.A., Harvard U., 1947, Ph.D., 1951. Lectr., instr. U. Toronto, Ont., Can., 1949-53; mem. faculty U. Calif., Davis, 1953—, prof. art, 1968—; curator, art cons. Calif. Hist. Soc., San Francisco, 1962-63, 68-71; cataloguer Honeyman Collection Bancroft Library U. Calif., Berkeley, 1964-65; owner North Point Gallery, San Francisco, 1972—; vis. prof. U. So. Calif., 1952, 70, U. Mexico, Mexico City, 1957, U. Oreg., 1963; art cons. mus., civic and hist. orgns.; lectr. cultural instns., including Toronto Art Gallery, Royal Ont. Mus. Art, Nat. Gallery, Washington, Crocker Art Gallery, Sacramento. Author: Time's Wondrous Changes: San Francisco Architecture, 1776-1915, 1962, The Churches of Mexico, 1962, California's Pictoral Lettersheets, 1849-1869, 1967, Historic Lithographs of San Francisco, 1972, The West Remembered, 1973, Wine and the Artist, 1979; catalogues Samuel Marsden Brookes: 1816-1892, 1962, Catalogue of Original Paintings, Drawing and Watercolors in the Robert B. Honeyman, Jr. Collection, 1968, Pre-Impressionism: 1860-1869: A Formative Decade in French Art and Culture, 1969, Art: An Interpretive Bibliography, 1977; editor monographs, exhbn. catalogues; contbr. articles to profl. jours. Recipient award of Merit Calif. Hist. Soc., 1961. Mem. Soc. Archtl. Historians, Phi Beta Kappa. Home: 1830 Mountain View Dr Tiburon CA 94920 Office: Dept Art U Calif Davis CA 95616 Office: 872 North Point St San Francisco CA 94109

BAIRD, JOSEPH ARTHUR, religion educator; b. Boise, Idaho, June 17, 1922; s. Jesse H. and Susanna (Bragstad) B.; m. Mary Harriet Chapman, June 10, 1947; children: Andrew Arthur, Paul Chapman. B.A., Occidental Coll., 1943; B.D., San Francisco Theol. Sem., 1949; Ph.D., U. Edinburgh, 1953; student, U. Basel, Switzerland, 1951, U. Marburg, Germany, 1962. Ordained to ministry Presbyn. Ch., 1949; asst. pastor, San Francisco, 1946-47; Western field rep. Intersem. Movement, 1947-48; music tchr. Marin County (Calif.) schs., 1948-49; pastor, White Sulphur Springs, Mont., 1948-49, asst. pastor, Edinburgh, 1949-51, pastor, Burney, Calif., 1952-54; prof. religion Coll. Wooster, Ohio, 1954—, chmn. dept., 1967-71; adj. prof. San Francisco Theol. Sem., 1964-69; Rep. theol. edn. Am. Acad. Religion, 1956-66; chmn. Lilly Endowment study presem. edn., 1958-64, mem. internat. com. computer Bib. studies, 1968-71; chmn. (Pella Archaeol. Bd.), 1965-67; mem. dept. campus Christian life Synod Ohio, 1966-69. Author: Justice of God in the Teachings of Jesus, 1963, Audience Criticism and the Historical Jesus, 1969, A Critical Concordance to the Synoptic Gospels, 1971, Rediscovering the Power of the Gospel, 1982; also articles.; Editor: Internat. Concordance Library, Iona Press. Pres. Bibl. Research Assos.; Mem. Wooster Symphony Bd., 1960-64. Served to lt. (j.g.) USNR, 1943-46. Mem. Am. Acad. Religion, Soc. Bib. Lit., Studiorum Novi Testamenti Societas, Phi Beta Kappa. Club: Rotarian (chmn. com. internat. service Wooster 196869). Pioneer use computers for content research Greek N.T., devel. audience criticism for N.T. research. Home: 1435 Gasche St Wooster OH 44691 *The guiding raison d'etre of my life is a sense of God's calling to the work I am doing. I find this most adequately expressed in the life and teachings of Jesus Christ, who has been the subject of my research, writing and lecturing through the years.*

BAIRD, KEITH ALEXANDER, newspaper publisher; b. Kitchener, Ont., Can., Aug. 19, 1925; s. James Roy and Myrtle Adelaide (Waldron) B.; m. Constance Mary Hamel, Aug. 5, 1949; 1 dau., Judith Leigh Baird Yormak. B.A., U. Western Ont., 1949. With Kitchener-Waterloo Record Ltd., 1949—, v.p., 1971—, pub., 1955—. Served with Can. Navy, 1942-45. Recipient award Western Ont. Press Assn., 1967, 69, 72, 74. Mem. Can. Daily Newspaper Pubs. Assn. (past dir.), Can. Press (past dir.), Ont. Press Council, Internat. Press Inst., Commonwealth Press Union. Presbyterian. Clubs: Toronto Press; Westmount Golf and Country (Kitchener); Masons. Home: 429 St Leger St Kitchener ON N2H 4M8 Canada Office: 225 Fairway Kitchener ON N2G 4E5 Canada

BAIRD, ROBERT DAHLEN, religious scholar, educator; b. Phila., June 29, 1933; s. Jesse Dahlen and Clara (Sonntag) B.; m. Patty Jo Lutz, Dec. 18, 1954; children—Linda Sue, Stephen Robert, David Bryan, Janna Ann. B.A., Houghton Coll., 1954; B.D., Fuller Theol. Sem., 1957; S.T.M., S. Meth. U., 1959; Ph.D., U. Iowa, 1964. Instr. philosophy and religion U. Omaha, 1962-65; fellow Asian religions Soc. for Religion in Higher Edn., 1965-66; asst. prof. religion U. Iowa, Iowa City, 1966-69, asso. prof., 1969-74, prof., 1974—; faculty fellow Am. Inst. Asian Studies, India, 1972. Author: Category Formation and the History of Religions, 1971, (with W.R. Comstock et al) Religion and Man: An Introduction, 1971, Indian and Far Eastern Religious Traditions, 1972; editor, contbr.: Methodological Issues in Religious Studies, 1975; book rev. editor: Jour. Am. Acad. Religion, 1979—; contbr. articles to profl. jours. Mem. Am. Acad. Religion, Assn. Asian Studies. Democrat. Presbyterian. Home: Route 1 Box 67 Iowa City IA 52240 Office: Sch of Religion Univ Iowa Iowa City IA 52242

BAIRD, ROGER ALLEN, retired corporation executive; b. Canton, Ill., Mar. 14, 1914; s. Frederick R. and Ruth E. (Miller) B.; m. Evelyn F. Rittenhouse, July 29, 1939; children: Jane E., Ann R. A.B., U. Chgo., 1936; J.D., 1938. Bar: Ill. 1939, Wis. 1956. Assoc. later partner Kirkland, Ellis, Hodson, Chaffetz & Masters (and predecessors), Chgo., 1939-56; asst. sec., gen. atty. Kimberly Clark Corp., Neenah, Wis., 1956-59, sec., 1959-75; pres. Kimberly Clark Found., 1975-80. Mem. Wis. Govt. Com. of 25, 1963-65; adv. bd. Wis. Regional Med. Program, 1972-76; trustee Appleton Meml. Hosp., 1961-75, pres., 1966-68, chmn., 1969-75; bd. dirs. Area Health Planning Agy., 1971-80, Wis. Health Policy Council, 1976—; vice chmn. Wis. Health Policy Council, 1980—; bd. dirs. Nat. Council Aging, 1976—, Wis. State Council on Econ. Edn., 1980—. Served with USNR, 1943-46. Mem. Ill. Bar Assn., Phi Gamma Delta. Presbyn. Clubs: Law, Legal (Chgo.); North Shore Golf (Menasha); Neenah Racquet; Crystal Downs Country (Frankfort, Mich.). Home: N-7937 State Park Rd Menasha WI 54952

BAIRD, WILLIAM BRITTON (BIL BAIRD), puppeteer; b. Grand Island, Nebr., Aug. 15, 1904; s. William Hull and Louise (Hetzel) B.; m. Evelyn Schwartz, 1932 (div. 1934); m. Cora Burlar, Jan. 13, 1937 (dec. Dec. 1967); children: Peter Britton, Laura Jenne Baird; m. Patricia Courtleigh, June 1969 (div. 1972); m. Susanna Lloyd, Dec. 1974 (div. 1984); 1 dau., Madeleine. A.B., U. Iowa, 1926. Toured, India, Nepal, Afghanistan for; State Dept., 1962, Russia, 1963; toured, India and Turkey for; U.S. AID, 1970. Began with, Tony Sarg Marionettes, 1928-33; started: Bil Baird's Marionettes at, Chgo. World's Fair, 1934; appeared in: vaudeville, nightclubs, 4 Broadway shows including Ziegfeld Follies, 1943-44, Flahooley, 1951; produced: Ali Baba and the Forty Thieves, 1956; Davy Jones' Locker, 1959, Man in the Moon, 1963, Chrysler Show Go Round, N.Y. World's Fair, 1964-65; Puppet sequence, Baker Street, 1965, govt. films, World War II; films Party Lines, 1946, Telezonia AT&T, 1949, Strange Case Cosmic Rays, 1953; starred in: H.B.O. Spl. Puppet Revue, 1979; produced: TV series for CBS Snarky Parker, 1950-51; Whistling Wizard, 1951-52, Bil Baird Show, 1953; appeared on: Morning Show, 1954; appeared in: Peter and the Wolf, 1958, 59-60, Sorcerer's Apprentice, 1959, Winnie the Pooh, 1960, O'Halloran's Luck, 1961; film The Sound of Music, 1965; opened: (with Cora Baird) Bil Baird Theater, N.Y.C., 1967; presented: People Is, 1967, Winnie the Pooh, 1967-68, Wizard of Oz, 1968-69, Sultan of Tuffet, 1969-70, Ali Baba, 1970-71, Peter and the Wolf, 1971-72, Davy Jones' Locker-Band Wagon revue, 1972-73; produced: Pinocchio, 1973-74, Alice in Wonderland, 1975, Winnie the Pooh, 1975-76, Once Upon A Dragon at Busch Gardens, 1977-78, Histoire du Soldat, films for, Social Security Adminstrn., 1973, over 400 commls.; Author: The Art of the Puppet, 1966, Puppets and Population, 1969. Del. Planned Parenthood Fedn., London, 1972; bd. dirs. World Edn., Presidium Unima. Lt. O.R.C., 1926. Recipient Jennie Heiden award for excellence in profl. children's theater Am. Theater Assn., 1974. Mem. Internat. Puppet Fedn. (dir.), Nat. Acad. TV Arts and Scis. (gov. 1957-61), Sigma Chi, Omicron Delta Kappa. Clubs: Lotos., Salmagundi. Address: 40 Fifth Ave New York NY 10011

BAIRD, WILLIAM CAMERON, former foundry executive; b. Buffalo, Apr. 20, 1907; s. Frank B. and Flora (Cameron) B.; m. Marjorie B. Mitchell, July 19, 1930 (div. 1945); 1 dau., Barbara (Mrs. Joseph Jay Palladino). Grad., Phillips Exeter Acad., 1925; B.A., Williams Coll., 1929; L.H.D., D'Youville Coll., 1979, SUNY-Buffalo, 1984. Treas. Buffalo Pipe & Foundry Corp., 1930-49, pres., 1949-67, chmn. bd., 1967-72, Gruber Supply Corp., 1973—; pres., chief exec. officer Central Foundry Co., 1966-67; dir. Mfrs. & Traders Trust Co., 1937-77, Cathedral Sq., Inc. Chmn. Peace Bridge Authority, 1939-60; Pres. Brent Manor, Inc., 1967-70, Niagara Frontier Housing Devel. Corp., 1968-70, Boys' Clubs of Niagara Frontier, 1956-58; bd. dirs. Boys' Clubs of Buffalo, 1933-83, pres., 1962-63; chmn. council State U. Buffalo, 1970-77; Trustee Community Chest; bd. dirs. Forest Lawn Cemetery, Millard Fillmore Hosp., 1937-83. Served to lt. comdr. USNR. Recipient Bishop's Cross Diocese Western N.Y., 1963; Canisius Coll. Disting. award, 1969; Red Jacket award Buffalo Hist. Soc., 1975; Chancellor's Medal State U. Buffalo, 1978; Disting. Citizen award SUNY; named Man of Year Buffalo Evening News, 1969, Buffalo C. of C., 1977. Mem. Soc. Alumni Williams Coll. (pres. 1955-56), C. of C. (past pres.), Delta Upsilon. Episcopalian (dep. gen. conv. 1937, 40, 49, 52, 61, 67, 69, 70, ch. warden). Clubs: Buffalo, Buffalo Yacht, Buffalo Canoe, Buffalo; Williams (N.Y.C.). Home: 4153 Imperial Dr Orchard Park NY 14127 Office: 1880 Elmwood Ave Buffalo NY 14207

BAIRD, WILLIAM DAVID, historian, educator; b. Oklahoma City, July 8, 1939; s. Everett W. and Faye (Shinn) B.; m. Brenda Jane Tacker, Nov. 24, 1961; children: Angela, Anthony. A.A., George Washington U., 1959; B.A., Central State U., Okla., 1963; M.A., U. Okla., 1965, Ph.D., 1969. Teaching asst. dept. history U. Okla., 1966-68; asst. prof. history U. Ark., Fayetteville, 1968-72, asso. prof., 1972-77, prof., 1977-78; prof., chmn. dept. history Okla. State U., Stillwater, 1978—. Author: Peter Pitchlynn: Chief of the Choctaws, 1972, The Osage People, Indian Tribal Series, 1972, The Choctaw People, Indian Tribal Series, 1974, The Quapaw People, Indian Tribal Series, 1975; contbg. author: Indian-White Relations: A Persistent Paradox, 1976, Medical Education in Arkansas, 1879-1978, 1979, The Quapaw Indians: A History of the Downstream People, 1980; contbr. numerous book revs. and articles on Am. history to scholarly jours.; editor: Dictionary of the Osage Lang. (Francis La Flesche), 1975. Adminstrv. asst. to Congressman, 5th Dist., Okla., 1959-64. Recipient Disting. Former Student award Central State U., 1973; T. Harry Williams award Red River Valley Hist. Rev., 1975. Mem. Orgn. Am. Historians, Western History Assn. (council 1980—), Phi Alpha Theta (Ann. Paper Prize award 1971-73, mem. scholarship com. 1976—, adv. 1970-76). Home: 4902 Country Club Dr Stillwater OK Office: Dept History Okla State Univ Stillwater OK 74074

BAISLEY, ROBERT WILLIAM, music educator; b. New Haven, Apr. 5, 1923; s. Joseph V. and Mary (Bergin) B.; m. Jean Shanley, July 30, 1955; children: Joan Ann, Susan Jean, Elizabeth Veronica. Mus.B., Yale U., 1949; M.A., Columbia U., 1950. Tchr. Cherry Lawn Sch., Darien, Conn., 1950-51; dir. Neighborhood Music Sch., New Haven, 1951-56; asst. prof. piano Sch. Music, Yale U., New Haven, 1956-65; chmn. dept. music Pa. State U., University Park, 1965-79, prof. music, 1965—. Concert pianist in various concerts, recitals, radio and TV. Vol. United Fund, New Haven, 1951-65; rep. to Council of Social Agencies, New Haven, 1951-60; mem. adv. council Salvation Army, New Haven, 1963-65; Bd. dirs. Central Pa. Festival of Arts (pres. 1969-71). Served with AUS, 1941-45. Recipient cert. of merit Yale U., 1979. Mem. Coll. Music Soc., Lechetizsky Assn., Music Educators Nat. Council, Music Tchrs. Nat. Assn., Internat. Soc. for Contemporary Music, Yale U. Sch. Music Alumni Assn. (exec. com. 1977—, pres. 1979—). Lodge: Rotary. Home: 454 Park Ln State College PA 16801 Office: Music Dept Pa State U University Park PA 16802

BAKAL, CARL, writer, public relations executive; b. N.Y.C., Jan. 11, 1918; s. William and Esther (Tutelman) B.; m. Shirley Sesser, 1956; children: Stephanie, Emily, Amy, Wendy. B.S., CCNY, 1939; postgrad., Columbia, 1949. Advt. mgr. Fotoshop, N.Y.C., 1939-41; editor Fotoshop Almanac, 1939-41; asso. editor, contbg. editor U.S. Camera, 1939-43; sales promotion mgr. Universal Camera Corp., 1941-43; editorial chief information control div. Mil. Govt., Germany, 1947-48; promotion writer N.Y. Mirror, 1948-50; asso. editor Coronet mag., N.Y.C., 1950-55; free-lance writer, photo-journalist, 1955-57, 58—; editor Real, See mags., 1957-58; pub. affairs cons. U.S. Dept. Commerce, 1961-62; sr. asso. Howard Chase Assos., N.Y.C., 1962-65; dir. mag. dept. Carl Byoir & Assos., 1966-68; account supr. Anna M. Rosenberg & Assos., 1968-84; sr. v.p. Jack Raymond & Co., Inc., N.Y.C., 1984—; Guest lectr. photo-journalism U. Wis., 1953. Author: Filter Manual, 1953, How To Shoot for Glamour, 1955, The Right To Bear Arms, 1966, No Right To Bear Arms, 1968, Charity U.S.A, 1979; Contbr. articles and photographs to publs. including, McCalls, Redbook, Life, Reader's Digest, Harper's, Saturday Rev., Esquire, Good Housekeeping; contbr. to: Ency. Photography, 1942, Treasury of Tips for Writers, 1965; Photo-journalism columnist for, Writers Digest.; travel editor, Sylvia Porter's Personal Fin. mag., 1984—. Served to 1st lt. AUS, 1942-46, 51-52. Recipient 1st prize Popular Photography $25,000 picture contest, 1956. Mem. Violoncello Soc., P.E.N., Soc. Journalists and Authors (v.p. 1968), Nat. Council for a Responsible Firearm Policy (founder-v.p.). Home: 225 W 86th St New York NY 10024 Office: 488 Madison Ave New York NY 10022

BAKALAR, JOHN STEPHEN, printing and publishing company executive; b. Lynn, Mass., Feb. 10, 1948; s. Leo and Ann Beatrice (Lepie) B.; m. Christine Lake Heilman, Sept. 24, 1972; children—Brooke Heilman, Jessica Heilman, Luke Heilman. B.A., U. Pa., 1970; M.B.A., Stanford U., 1973. Investment mgr. First Chgo. Corp., Chgo., 1973-76; treas. Rand McNally & Co., Skokie, Ill., 1976-78, v.p. fin., treas., 1978—; dir. Transitron Electronic Corp., Woburn, Mass. Vice pres., dir. Broader Urban Involvement and Leadership Devel., Chgo., 1976—. Clubs: Econ. of Chgo.; Northmoor Country (Highland Park, Ill.). Home: 290 Woodland Rd Highland Park IL 60035 Office: 8255 Central Park Skokie IL 60076

BAKALY, CHARLES GEORGE, JR., lawyer; b. Long Beach, Calif., Nov. 15, 1927; s. Charles G. and Doris (Carpenter) B.; m. Patricia Murphey, Oct. 25, 1952; children: Charles G., John W., Thomas B. A.B., Stanford U., 1949; J.D., U. S.C., 1952. Assoc. firm O'Melveny & Myers, Los Angeles, 1956-63, ptnr., 1963—; mem. equal opportunity law com. Def. Research Inst. Author: (with Joel M. Grossman) Modern Law of Employment Contracts: Formation, Operation and Remedies for Breach, 1983; contbr. chpts to books. Trustee, mem. exec. com. Scripps Coll.; trustee Claremont U. Ctr.; bd. advisors Calif. Republican League; bd. dirs. Children's Hosp. of Los Angeles; mem. exec. com. Calif. Republican Com. Served to capt. JAG U.S. Army,

1952-56. Fellow ABA (chmn. sect. labor and employment law 1982); mem. Am. Coll. Trial Lawyers, Los Angeles County Bar Assn. (trustee, chmn. labor law sect. 1976-77), D.C. Bar (governing bd.), Mchts. and Mfrs. Assn. (exec. com., exec. com.), NAM (labor adv. task force), Am. Arbitration Assn., U.S. C. of C. (Labor reations com.), Internat. Soc. Labor Law and Social Legis., Chancery Club, Law Soc. Clubs: Valley Hunt (Pasadena, Calif.); California Athletic (Los Angeles). Office: O'Melveny & Myers 400 S Hope St Los Angeles CA 90071

BAKAY, LOUIS, neurosurgeon; b. Bothsony, Hungary, June 18, 1917; came to U.S., 1948, naturalized, 1954; s. Lajos and Elsa (Riedl) B.; m. Patricia Anna Tighe, June 5, 1954; children—Stephanie Margaret, Nicholas Lajos. M.D., U. Budapest, 1942. Intern Univ. Hosps., Budapest, 1941-42; resident Mass. Gen. Hosp., Boston, 1948-52; practice medicine, specializing in neurosurgery, Boston, 1952-61, Buffalo, 1961—; mem. staff Mass. Gen. Hosp., 1952-61; instr. surgery Harvard U. Med. Sch., Boston, 1948-60; prof., chmn. dept. neurosurgery SUNY at, Buffalo, 1961—. Author: The Blood-Brain Barrier, 1956, Cerebral Edema, 1965, Radioisotope Scanning of Brain Tumors, 1969, The Treatment of Head Injuries in the Thirty Years War (1618-1648), 1971, Head Injuries, 1979; editorial bd.: Acta Neurochirurgica, 1975. Fellow A.C.S.; mem. Soc. Neurol. Surgeons, Am. Assn. Neurol. Surgeons, Congress Neurol. Surgeons. Club: Saturn (Buffalo). Home: 152 Bryant St Buffalo NY 14222 Office: 462 Grider St Buffalo NY 14215

BAKER, ADOLPH, physicist; b. Odessa, Russia, Nov. 15, 1917; came to U.S., 1922, naturalized, 1929; s. Isaac I. and Anna (Kornfield) B.; m. Dora E. Krugman, Nov. 7, 1942; children—Linda J., Daniel R., Ellen J. B.A., Coll. City N.Y., 1938, M.S. in Edn, 1939; B.M.E., Poly. Inst. Bklyn., 1946; M.S. in Math, N.Y. U., 1949; Ph.D. in Physics, Brandeis U., 1964. Stress analyst Republic Aviation Corp., Farmingdale, N.Y., 1946-47; sr. engr. Ranger Aircraft Engines, Farmingdale, 1947-48; staff mem. IBM Corp., N.Y.C., 1948-50; sr. engr. Raytheon Co., Newton, Mass., 1950-54; mgr. computer devel., cons. RCA Corp., Burlington, Mass., 1955-63; prof. physics U. Lowell, Mass., 1963—. Author: Modern Physics and Antiphysics, 1970; contbg. author: Physical Science Today, 1973, Concepts in Physics, 1973; contbr. articles to profl. jours. Served to 1st lt., inf. AUS, 1942-46. Decorated Bronze Star, Purple Heart with oak leaf cluster; sr. Fulbright-Hays scholar USSR, 1974-75. Mem. Am. Phys. Soc., Sigma Xi. Home: 7 Gage Rd Wayland MA 01778 Office: U Lowell Lowell MA 01854

BAKER, ALTON FLETCHER, JR., newspaper editor; b. Cleve., Nov. 15, 1919; s. Alton Fletcher and Mildred (Moody) B.; m. Genevieve Mertzke, 1947 (div. 1975); m. Jeannette Workman Vollstedt, Feb. 14, 1976; children: Sue Baker Diamond, Alton Fletcher, III, Sarah Moody, Robin Louise. A.B., Pomona Coll., 1942. Reporter Eugene (Oreg.) Register-Guard, 1946-50, mng. editor, 1950-54, editor, 1954—, pub., 1961-82, chmn. bd., 1982—; chmn. Oreg. Press Conf., 1973. Chmn. fund drive United Way, Eugene, 1965, pres., 1966-67; bd. dirs., pres. YMCA, Eugene. Served to capt. USAAF, World War II. Mem. Oreg. Newspaper Pubs. Assn. (dir. 1965-70), Am. Soc. Newspaper Editors, Am. Newspaper Pubs. Assn. Republican. Clubs: Eugene Country, De Anza Country. Office: 975 High St PO Box 10188 Eugene OR 97401

BAKER, ALTON WESLEY, educator, corporate administrator; b. Chickasha, Okla., May 28, 1912; s. Charles Wesley and Frances Cornelia (Hennington) B.; m. Mary Elizabeth Dill, June 4, 1938; children: Don Wesley, Viki Joan. B.B.A., U. Tex., 1936; A.M., George Washington U., 1947; Ph.D., Ohio State U., 1952; degree, Cambridge U. Asso. prof. Ohio State U., 1947-54; prof., chmn. dept. mgmt. So. Meth. U., 1954—; prof. Southwestern Legal Found. U. Tex.; prof. Southwestern Grad. Sch. Banking; div. head Fairchild Corp.; chmn. bd. Dill Mfg. Corp.; dir. research Ohio State U. Research Found., U.S. and Orient; Chmn. bd. regional postmaster selection U.S. Post Office Service, 1969—; cons. to postmaster gen., 1968—; cons. to industry in, U.S. and S.Am.; cons. S.W. Legal Found., S.W. Grad. Sch. Banking; prof. Air U.; dir. research intelligence SAC, USAF, Far East. Author: numerous publs. including Supervisor and His Job, 3d ed, 1978, internat. edit., 1979, Management: Small Manufacturing Plants, 1955. Chmn. bd. dirs. So. Meth. U. Retirement System, Inc. Mem. Acad. Mgmt. Clubs: Country, Rotary (Dallas). Home: 6211 W Northwest Hwy Unit 1400 Preston Towers Dallas TX 75225 *Man often finds it hard to have true inner security or fulfillment without possessing an ideal to imitate, a leader or leader-friend to follow. This leader-worshiping instinct places heavy ethical burdens on those of us who would be leaders. Our emotions and our moods, as well as our words and our deeds make those who come in contact with us, many of whom cannot help imitating us, either the beneficiaries or the victims of our presence.*

BAKER, BENJAMIN OSWALD, ret. scientist; b. Portage LaPrairie, Man., Can., Jan. 10, 1917; s. Arthur B. and Emma (Chisem) B.; m. Phyllis Ann Davidson, Nov. 2, 1963; children—Dennis B., Barry I., Jillian Elizabeth. B.Sc., U. Man., 1940. Engr. Canadian Gen. Elec., Peterborough, Ont., Can., 1940-46; supt. design Armament Research and Devel. Establishment, Def. Research Bd., Valcartier, Que., 1946-59; dir. weapons and engring. research Def. Research Bd., Ottawa, 1959-66; dir. project formulation Canadian Forces Hdqrs., Ottawa, 1967-68; chief Canadian Def. Research Staff, Washington, 1968-73; sci. adviser Mobile Command, Canadian Armed Forces, St. Hubert, Que., 1973-77; dep. chief research and devel. Canadian Dept. Nat. Def., Ottawa, 1977-80. Mem. Engring. Inst. Can., Profl. Engrs. Ont., Delta Upsilon. Home: 605 Duff Crescent Ottawa ON K1J 7C6 Canada

BAKER, BERNARD ROBERT, II, lawyer; b. Toledo, Nov. 19, 1915; s. Joseph Lee and Grace (Baker) O'Neil; m. Elinor Shutts, Oct. 16, 1943; children—Bernard Robert III, Lynn Agnes. A.B., Kenyon Coll., 1936; J.D., Harvard, 1941. Bar: Ohio 1946. Practice in, Toledo, 1947—; partner Brown, Baker, Schlageter & Craig (and predecessor firm), 1950—; Pres. B.R. Baker Co., 1946-60; dir. First Nat. Bank Toledo, First Ohio Bankshares; sec., dir. Toledo Blade Co.; Regional vice chmn. U.S. Com. for UN, 1955-62. Past pres. St. Vincent Hosp., Toledo United Appeal; past trustee Med. Coll. Ohio at Toledo, Salvation Army, Toledo; trustee Rutherford B. Hayes Found., Rutherford B. Hayes Presdl. Center, Fremont, Ohio, Goodwill Industries Toledo, Boys Club Toledo, Blue Cross Assn. Toledo, St. Vincent Hosp. Found., Med. Coll. Ohio Found. Served from ensign to lt. comdr. USNR, 1940-45. Recipient Boys Club Bronze Keystone award, 1965; named Toledo Outstanding Man of Year, 1948. Mem. Am., Ohio, Toledo bar assns., Toledo C. of C. (past pres.), Chevalier du Tastevin, Psi Upsilon. Roman Catholic. Clubs: Harvard (N.Y.C.); Ottawa Skeet; Toledo, Belmont Country, Carranor Hunt and Polo (Toledo); Rockwell Trout (Castalia, Ohio). Home: 29831 E River Rd Perrysburg OH 43551 Office: 711 Adams St Toledo OH 43624

BAKER, BURKE, JR., retired diversified industry executive; b. Houston, June 27, 1914; s. Burke and Bennie (Brown) B.; m. Elizabeth High, Apr. 26, 1942; children—Burke III, Robert High, Brandon High. B.A., U. Tex., 1935; M.B.A., Harvard, 1937. Sr. accountant firm Ernst & Ernst (C.P.A.'s), Houston, 1937-41; successive positions to pres., dir. Gulf Atlantic Warehouse Co., 1946-66; v.p. adminstrn., exec. com. Anderson, Clayton & Co., Houston, 1967-74, exec. v.p., 1974-79, dir., 1966—; Mem. exec. com. Houston Com. Fgn. Relations, 1962—, chmn., 1962. Mem. exec. bd. Sam Houston council Boy Scouts Am., dist. chmn., 1960, show chmn., 1969, v.p. adminstrn., 1977, council pres., 1979-80. Served to capt. AUS, 1941-45. Decorated Army Commendation medal. Mem. Am. Cotton Compress and Warehouse Assn. (chmn. exec. com. 1964-66), Houston C. of C. (dir. 1963). Episcopalian (vestryman, sr. warden 1962). Clubs: Rotary (Houston) (dir. 1960, treas. 1977); Forest (treas., bd. govs. 1961), Houston Country, Terpsichore (Houston); Jackson Hole Golf and Tennis (Jackson, Wyo.). Home: 602 Buckingham Dr Houston TX 77024 also 455 Moulton Loop Rd Jackson WY 83001

BAKER, CHARLES DUANE, management consultant; b. Newburyport, Mass., June 21, 1928; s. Charles Duane and Eleanor (Little) B.; m. Alice Elizabeth Ghormley, 1955; children: Charles D., Jonathan G., Alexander K. A.B., Harvard, 1951, M.B.A., 1955. Staff Westinghouse Electric Corp., Elmira, N.Y., 1955-57, supr. purchasing, Jersey City, 1957-61; v.p., treas. United Research, Inc., Cambridge, Mass., 1961-65; v.p., dir. transp. services Harbridge House, Inc., Boston, 1965-69, pres., 1971-74, chmn., 1974—; dep. under sec. U.S. Dept. Transp., Washington, 1969-70, asst. sec. policy and internat. affairs, 1970-71; dir. Millipore Corp., Colony Inc. Author various studies and analyses dealing with mgmt. and with transp. Mem. Mil. Airlift Com., 1974—; mem. Mass. Adv. Com., U.S. Commn. on Civil Rights, 1980—; vis. com. Northeastern U., Harvard U. Served to lt. (j.g.) USNR, 1946-48, 51-53. Recipient Award for Outstanding Achievement U.S. Govt., 1971. Mem. New Eng. Council (vice chmn., dir.), N.D.T.A. (v.p., dir.), Pi Eta. Republican. Congregationalist. Clubs: Essex County, Union; Harvard, Comml., Clover (Boston); E. India (London); Met. (Washington). Home: 2 55 Beacon St Boston MA 02116 also Marmion Way Rockport MA Office: 11 Arlington St Boston MA 02116 1301 Pennsylvania Ave NW Washington DC 20004

BAKER, CHESTER BIRD, agricultural economics educator; b. Mt. Union, Iowa, Aug. 25, 1918; s. Herbert Victor and Florence Heston (Bird) B.; m. Virginia Hall, Sept. 11, 1942; children: Edwin C., Barbara C. (Mrs. John F. Chaney), Thomas H. Student, Iowa Wesleyan Coll., 1934-35; B.S., Iowa State U., 1948; Ph.D., U. Calif. at Berkeley, 1953. Asst. sec.-treas. Mt. Pleasant (Iowa) Prodn. Credit Assn., 1938-40; faculty Mont. State U., Bozeman, 1950-56, prof. agrl. econs., 1955-56; assoc. prof. U. Ill., Urbana, 1957-58, prof. agrl. econs., 1958—; J.S. McLean vis. prof. Ont. Agrl. U., 1961; Cons. Western Agrl. Econs. Research Council, 1961, Midwest Research Inst., 1962, Nat. Assn. Food Chains, 1964-66, Ill. Bankers Assn., 1969, Canadian Task Force on Agr., 1967-69, Dept. Agr., 1963—, Ford Found., 1971, AID, 1973, Govt. of Australia, 1973, Nat. Acad. Scis., 1976; vis. lectr. numerous univs., U.S., Eng., Asia, Australia, Caribbean.; disting. visitor Latrobe U., 1982. Author books and articles. Served with AUS, 1941-46. Travelling fellow Social Sci. Research Council, India, 1958; Fulbright-Hays Sr. Research scholar U. Sydney, Australia, 1966-67, U. Melbourne, Australia, 1980-81; recipient Ernest H. Wakefield award, 1975, Paul A. Funk award, 1976; Research fellow Australian Fed. Reserve Bank, U. Melbourne, 1973-74. Fellow Am. Agrl. Economics Assn. (dir.); mem. Australian Assn. Agrl. Economists, Internat. Assn. Agrl. Economists, Am. Econ. Assn., Gamma Sigma Delta, Alpha Gamma Rho. Presbyterian. Home: 601 E Pennsylvania Ave Urbana IL 61801

BAKER, CLIFTON EARL, engring. and constrn. co. exec.; b. Harrietsville, Ohio, May 11, 1923; s. Lewis Raymond and Freda Edith (Parks) B.; m. Louise Hodgson, Aug. 20, 1947; children: Peggy Lee, Terrie Sue. B.S., Ohio U., Athens, 1943; M.S., Ohio State U., Columbus, 1947. Registered profl. engr., Idaho, Ohio, 42 other states. Jr. structural engr. Goodyear Aircraft Co., Akron, Ohio, 1943-44, Austin Co., Cleve., 1945-46; structural designer Design Service Co., Cleve., 1947; with H.K. Ferguson Co., 1947—, v.p, then pres., Cleve., 1963-79, chmn. bd., 1979—, also dir.; pres. H.K. Ferguson Engring. Co., 1961-79; chmn. bd. Hale & Kullgren Co., 1974-79; group v.p. indsl. ops. Morrison-Knudsen Co., Boise, Idaho, 1979—; dir. Morrison-Knudson Internat. Co., Inc., 1979—, Bendy Engring. Co., 1981—. Bd. visitors Ohio U., 1975—. Served with AUS, 1944-45. Decorated Bronze Star (2). Mem. Am Ordnance Assn., ASTM, ASCE, Beavers, Nat. Soc. Profl. Engrs., Moles, Boise Soc. Profl. Engrs. Clubs: Masons; Union (Cleve.); Hillcrest Country (Boise). Office: PO Box 7808 Boise ID 83729

BAKER, CONSTANCE MARIE, nurse, educator; b. Blossburg, Pa., June 29, 1937; d. John T. and Dorothy V. B. Grad., Pa. Sch. Nursing, 1958; student, Mansfield State Coll., 1960-62; B.S., U. Colo., 1964; M.S., U. Calif., San Francisco, 1967, D.Nursing Sci., 1975. Staff nurse Blossburg (Pa.) State Hosp., 1958-62, St. Joseph's Hosp., Fairbanks, Alaska, 1961-62; public health nurse Alameda County (Calif.) Health Dept., 1965-66; research asst. Sch. Nursing, U. Calif., San Francisco, 1968-69, lectr. grad. program in nursing, 1969-71; asso. prof. U. Okla. Coll. Nursing, Oklahoma City, 1972-78, prof., 1978—, dir. multi-media program, 1975—; cons. VA Hosp. Nursing Service, 1977—; mem. joint task force on practice Okla. Nurses Assn./Okla. Med. Assn., 1979-82; cons. and lectr. on teaching strategies, career devel. and research. Contbr. articles to profl. jours. Recipient Cert. of Appreciation Surgeon Gen., SAC Med. Corps, 1977; Regents' Superior Teaching award U. Okla., 1977. Mem. Am. Nurses Assn., Nat. League Nursing, Am. Assn. Higher Edn., Faculty Devel. and Evaluation Assn., Okla. Public Health Assn., Okla. League Nursing (pres.), Okla. Nurses Assn. (mem. legis. com. 1979-81), Okla. Nurses Coalition for Action in Politics (founder, pres. 1977-78, v.p. 1978-79), Sigma Theta Tau, Phi Delta Gamma. Home: 11609 Leaning Elm Oklahoma City OK 73120 Office: Box 26901 1100 N Stonewall St Oklahoma City OK 73190

BAKER, DAVID HIRAM, nutritional biochemist; b. DeKalb, Ill., Feb. 26, 1939; s. Vernon T. and Lucille M. (Severson) B.; m. Norraine A. Baker; children: Barbara G., Michael D., Susan G. B.S., U. Ill., Champaign-Urbana, 1961, M.S., 1963, Ph.D., 1965. Sr. scientist Eli Lilly & Co., Greenfield, Ind., 1965-67; mem. faculty U. Ill., Champaign-Urbana, 1967—, prof. nutrition, dept. animal sci., 1974—. Author: Sulfur in Nonruminant Nutrition, 1977; editorial bd.: Jour. Animal Sci, 1969-73, Jour. Nutrition, 1975-79, Poultry Sci., 1978-82, Nutrition Revs., 1983—; contbr. numerous articles to sci. jours. Chmn. bd. Champaign-Urbana Teen Challenge Drug Rehab. Program, 1977-80. Recipient Nutrition Research award Am. Feed Mfrs., 1973; Merck award, 1977; Paul A. Funk award, 1977; H. H. Mitchell teaching award, 1979; Broiler Research award, 1983. Mem. Am. Soc. Animal Sci. (Young Scientist award 1971), Poultry Sci. Assn., Am. Inst. Nutrition, Fedn. Am. Socs. Exptl. Biology, Sigma Xi, Phi Kappa Phi, Alpha Zeta, Gamma Sigma Delta. Home: 2313 Brookshire W Champaign IL 61820 Office: U Ill Urbana IL 61801

BAKER, DAVID KENNETH, coll. pres.; b. Glasgow, Scotland, Oct. 2, 1923; came to U.S., 1946, naturalized, 1956; s. David Thomas and Edith (Horner) B.; m. Vivian Christian Perry, Sept. 13, 1947; children—Paul D. (dec.), Richard R. B.Sc., McMaster U., 1946; Ph.D., U. Pa., 1953. Prof. physics Union Coll., Schenectady, 1953-65; mgr. profl. personnel, research and devel. lab. Gen. Electric Co., 1965-67; v.p., dean St. Lawrence U., Canton, N.Y., 1967-76; pres. Harvey Mudd Coll., Claremont, Calif., 1976—; cons. NSF. Author: (with A.T. Goble) Elements of Modern Physics. Mem. Am. Inst. Physics, AAUP, Newcomen Soc. Clubs: Rotary; Calif. (Los Angeles); Univ. (Claremont). Home: 495 E 12th St Claremont CA 91711 Office: Pres's Office Harvey Mudd Coll Claremont CA 91711

BAKER, DAVID MURRAY, retail drug chain executive; b. Scranton, Pa., May 23, 1940; s. Louis and Jean B.; m. Barbara Ann Janow, June 21, 1964; children: Lori Beth, Darryl Lance, Jodi Lyn. B.S. in B.A. cum laude, U. Fla., 1962. C.P.A., Fla. Sr. acct. Peat, Marwick, Mitchell & Co., Tampa, Fla., 1963-67; v.p., dir. control Jack Eckerd Drug Co., Clearwater, Fla., 1964-74; corp. controller Jack Eckerd Corp., Clearwater, 1974-78, treas., 1978-80, v.p., treas., 1980—; dir. Atlantic Bank of Largo, Fla., 1979—. Pres. Congregation Beth Shalom, Clearwater, 1981; bd. dirs. Am. Cancer Soc., Pinellas County, Fla., 1980, chmn. fund-raising com., Pinellas County, Fla. Mem. Am. Inst. C.P.A.s, Fla. Inst. C.P.A.s, Fin. Execs. Inst. (dir. Tampa chpt. 1982), Nat. Assn. Corp. Treas. Office: Jack Eckerd Corp PO Box 4689 Clearwater FL 33518

BAKER, DE WITT CLINTON, III, publishing company executive; b. New Rochelle, N.Y., July 31, 1924; s. De Witt Clinton and Helen Jones (Irby) B.; m. Marybob Willson, Jan. 27, 1951 (dec.); children: Scott Delavan, Todd Hamilton. B.A. cum laude, Dartmouth Coll., 1946, M.B.A. with distinction, 1947. With Simon & Schuster, N.Y.C., 1951, Pocketbooks, Western Pub. Co., to 1969; exec. v.p. adminstrn. and fin. Random House Inc., 1969-74; v.p. Baker & Taylor Co. div. W. R. Grace & Co., N.Y.C., 1974-75, pres., 1975-77; pres. edn. group Esquire Inc., N.Y.C., 1977; exec. v.p. Elsevier-Dutton Pub. Co., N.Y.C., 1978, pres., 1979-80; dir. mgmt. studies R.R. Donnelley & Sons Co., 1980-83; pres. Zipsan Systems, Inc., 1983—. Treas. Westchester County (N.Y.) chpt. Nat. Found. March of Dimes, 1959-70; mem. Mamaronek (N.Y.) Union Free Sch. Bd., 1973-76; treas. Mamaronek Life Center, 1979-80. Served to lt. (j.g.) USNR, 1943-46. Mem. Book Industry Study Group (chmn.). Club: Union League. Home: 320 Central Park W New York NY 10025 Office: 160 Fifth Ave New York NY 10010

BAKER, DEXTER FARRINGTON, air products company executive; b. Worcester, Mass., Apr. 16, 1927; s. Leland Dyer and Edith (Quimby) B.; m. Dorothy Ellen Hess, June 23, 1951; children: Ellen L., Susan A., Leslie A., Carolyn J. B.S., Lehigh U., 1950, M.B.A., 1957. Sales engr. Air Products & Chems., Inc., Allentown, Pa., 1952-56, gen. sales mgr., 1956-57, dir., 1964—, group v.p., 1967-68, exec. v.p., 1968-78, pres., 1978—, chief operating officer, 1978—; mng. dir. Air Products, Ltd., 1957-67, dir., 1964-80, Air Products S.A. (Pty.) Ltd., Catalytic, Inc. Bd. assos. Muhlenberg Coll.; trustee, chmn. vis. com. chem. engring. Lehigh U.; adv. com. Minsi Trails council Boy Scouts Am.; bd. dirs. Pennsylvanians for Effective Govt. Served with USNR, 1945-46; with U.S. Army, 1950-52. Mem. Am. Mgmt. Assn., Am. Inst. Chem. Engrs., Soc. Chem. Industry, Asa Packer Soc. Lehigh U., Theta Chi. Presbyterian (elder). Home: RD 2 Allentown PA 18103 Office: PO Box 538 Allentwon PA 18105

BAKER, DONALD, lawyer; b. Chgo., May 28, 1929; s. Russell and Elizabeth (Wallace) B.; m. Gisela S. Carli, Oct. 6, 1960; children: Caryna, Andrew, Russell. Student, Deep Springs Coll., Calif., 1947-49; J.D.S., U. Chgo., 1954. Bar: Ill. 1955, N.Y. 1964. Ptnr. Baker & McKenzie, Chgo., 1955—; dir. Trimedyne, Inc., Pharmatec, Inc., Grantison Holdings, Inc. Bd. dirs. Mid-Am. Com., Chgo., 1980—, Internat. Bus. Council Mid-Am., 1982-84. Mem. ABA, Ill. Bar Assn., Chgo. Bar Assn. Republican. Club: Michigan Shores (Wilmette, Ill.). Home: 544 Earlston Rd Kenilworth IL 60043 Office: Baker 7 McKenzie 2800 Prudential Plaza Chicago IL 60601

BAKER, DONALD JAMES, geophysicist, educator; b. Long Beach, Calif., Mar. 23, 1937; s. Donald James and Lillian Mae (Pund) B.; m. Emily Lind Delman, Sept. 7, 1968. B.S., Stanford U., 1958; Ph.D., Cornell U., 1962. Postdoctoral fellow Grad. Sch. Oceanography, U. R.I., Kingston, 1962-63; NIH fellow in chem. biodynamics Lawrence Radiation Lab., U. Calif., Berkeley, 1963-64; research fellow, asst. prof., assoc. prof. phys. oceanography Harvard U., 1964-73; research prof. dept. oceanography, sr. oceanographer, applied physics lab. U. Wash., Seattle, 1973-77; sr. fellow Joint Inst. for Study Atmosphere and Ocean, 1977—, prof., chmn. dept. oceanography, 1979—, chmn. dept. oceanography, 1979-81; dean Coll. Ocean and Fishery Scis., 1981-83; group leader deep-sea physics group Pacific Marine Environ. Lab., NOAA, Seattle, 1977-79; co-chmn. exec. com. Internat. So. Ocean Studies (NSF project), 1974—; bd. govs. Joint Oceanographic Instns., Inc., 1979—, pres., 1983—; vice-chmn. joint panel, global weather experiment Nat. Acad. Scis., 1976—, mem. ocean scis. bd., ocean scis. policy bd., 1979—, mem. com. on atmospheric scis., 1978-81, mem. climate research com., 1979—; mem. space and earth sci. adv. com. NASA, 1982—. Co-editor in chief: Dynamics of Atmospheres and Oceans Jour, 1975-79; Contbr. sci. articles to profl. jours. Fellow Explorers Club; mem. Am. Geophys. Union, Am. Meteorol. Soc. (council 1982—), Sigma Xi. Patentee deep-sea pressure gauge. Office: Joint Oceanographic Instns Inc 2100 Pennsylvania Ave NW Washington DC 20037

BAKER, EDWARD MARTIN, engineering and industrial psychologist; b. Bklyn., Mar. 13, 1941; s. Harold H. and Paula B.; m. Shige Jajiki, Dec. 16, 1970; 1 son, Evan Keith. B.A., CCNY, 1962, M.B.A., 1964; Ph.D. (Research fellow), Bowling Green State U., 1972. Human factors research engr. environ. and safety engring. staff Ford Motor Co., Dearborn, Mich., 1972-77, tech. tng. asso., Detroit, 1977-79, orgn. devel. cons., personnel and orgn. staff, 1979-81, statis. asso., ops. support, 1981—. Contbr. articles to profl. jours.; editorial referee: Jour. Quality Tech, 1974-75, 77-81. Mem. Am. Psychol. Assn., Human Factors Soc., Am. Soc. Quality Control (chmn. quality control circle subcom. 1976-77, chmn. quality motivation tech. com. 1977-80, mem. QWL task force 1978-81, Brumbaugh award 1975, Craig award 1976, 79). Home: 35823 Smithfield St Farmington MI 48024 Office: Ford Motor Co Statis Methods Office American Rd Dearborn MI 48121

BAKER, EDWIN CLARENCE, life insurance company executive; b. Fayetteville, Ark., July 16, 1925; s. Bert C. and Rena (Roberts) B.; m. Maralee Bell, June 15, 1973; children: Constance, Patricia, Scott. Grad., Washburn U., Topeka. Second v.p. Pilot Life Ins. Co., 1952-63; pres. Am. Defender Life Ins. Co., Raleigh, N.C., 1963—; chmn. bd. Am. Travel Corp., Raleigh, 1973—. Mem. N.C. Environment Mgmt. Com., 1973—, N.C. Ednl. Authority. Served with U.S. Army, 1943-46, 52-53. Decorated Bronze Star. Mem. Raleigh C. of C. (dir.). Republican. Methodist. Office: 900 Wade St Raleigh NC 27605 *

BAKER, ELBERT HALL, II, newspaper publisher; b. Quincy, Mass., July 18, 1910; s. Frank Smith and Gertrude (Vilas) B.; m. Betye Martin, May 27, 1936; children: Suzanne Baker Bethke, Martine Baker Huesman. Grad., Culver (Ind.) Mil. Acad., 1930; student, Rensselaer Poly. Inst., 1932. With Tribune Pub. Co., Tacoma, 1932—, pub., 1960, pres., 1969-77, chmn., 1977—, also dir. bd. dirs. United Good Neighbor Fund, Pierce County, Wash., Tacoma Community Fund. Served with AUS, 1942-46. Mem. Sigma Delta Chi, Delta Kappa Epsilon. Clubs: Tacoma Country and Golf, Tacoma (Tacoma); Bohemian (San Francisco). Home: 29 Forest Glen Ln SW Tacoma WA 98498 Office: Tribune Pub Co PO Box 11000 Tacoma WA 98411

BAKER, ELGAN LOUIS, psychologist, educator; b. Lexington, Ky., June 8, 1949; s. Elgan L. and Mary Mildred (Mays) B. B.A. with honors and highest distinction in Psychology, DePauw U., 1971, 1971; Ph.D. in Clin. Psychology, U. Tenn., 1976. Staff psychologist Tex. Research Inst. Mental Scis., Houston, 1976-77; adj. asst. prof. dept. psychology U. Houston, 1976-80; asst. clin. prof. dept. psychiatry U.

Tex. Med. Sch., Houston, 1976-80, Baylor Coll. Medicine, 1977-80; chief psychologist psychol. therapies Tex. Research Inst. Mental Scis., Houston, 1977-80, asst. dir. non-med. affairs, 1978-80; cons. and lectr. depts. psychiatry and pediatrics M.D. Anderson Hosp. and Tumor Inst., Tex. Med. Ctr., Houston, 1979-80; cons. div. psychology VA Hosp., San Francisco, 1977-79, Student Counseling Ctr., 1977-79; asst. prof. dept. psychiatry Ind. U. Sch. Medicine, Indpls., 1980-83, assoc. prof., 1983—, dir. tng. in clin. psychology, 1980—; cons. dept. neurology Wishard Hosp., Indpls., 1980—, Midtown Mental Health Ctr., 1980—, VA Hosp. Contbr. articles on clin. psychology to profl. jours. Mem. Soc. Clin. and Exptl. Hypnosis (Sherry K. and Harold B. Crasilneck award 1979), Am. Psychol. Assn. (continuing edn. com. 1978-79), Am. Soc. Clin. Hypnosis, Nat. Register Health Service Providers in Psychology, Psychologists Interested in Study of Psychoanalysis, Tex. Psychol. Assn., Southeastern Psychol. Assn., Phi Beta Kappa, Phi Eta Sigma, Sigma Xi, Omicron Delta Kappa, Lambda Chi Alpha (Hall of Fame 1981). Home: 2921 Horsehill E Indianapolis IN 46224 Office: Dept Psychiatry Ind Univ Sch Medicine 1100 W Michigan Indianapolis IN 46223

BAKER, ELIZABETH CALHOUN, magazine editor; b. Boston; d. John Calhoun and Elizabeth Marshall Evans B. B.A. cum laude, Bryn Mawr Coll.; M.A., Radcliffe Coll. Fulbright scholar Inst. d'Art et d'Archeologie and Ecole du Louvre, Paris; Instr. art history Boston U., Wheaton Coll., Norton, Mass.; assoc. editor Art News, N.Y.C., 1963-65, mng. editor, 1965-73; editor Art in Am. mag., N.Y.C., 1973—; instr. art history Sch. Visual Arts, N.Y.C., 1968-74; freelance art criticism. Nat. Endowment for Arts grantee, 1972. Office: 850 3d Ave New York NY 10022

BAKER, ELMER ELIAS, JR., educator; b. Hagerstown, Md., Apr. 15, 1922; s. Elmer Elias and Lena Rivers (Eichelberger) B.; m. Keora Phyllis Kono, Aug. 17, 1945. Student, Emerson Coll., 1941-43, Litt.D., 1969; B.S. summa cum laude, N.Y.U., 1948, M.A., 1949, Ph.D., 1954. Supr. speech therapy dept. phys. medicine and rehab. Bellevue Hosp., N.Y.C., 1948-50; part-time instr. Pratt Inst., 1949-50; faculty N.Y.U., N.Y.C., 1950—, prof. speech pathology and audiology, 1961—, chmn. dept. English and speech edn., 1960-72, dir. summer sessions, 1962-65, head div. English edn., speech and ednl. theatre, 1965-72, acting vice dean, 1966, 68, 69, asso. dean., 1972-75, vice dean, 1975—, clin. prof., 1961-72; cons. St. Vincent's Hosp., N.Y.C., 1965—, VA Hosp., 1967-68, N.Y. League for Hard of Hearing, 1972-81, also dir. Co-author: Bibliography of Speech and Allied Areas, 1962, Listening and Speaking in the English Classroom, 1971, also chpts. in books.; Contbr. articles to profl. jours. Trustee Emerson Coll., chmn. bd., 1978. Danforth Asso., 1964. Mem. Am. Speech and Hearing Assn. (clin. certificate speech 1955), N.Y. State Speech and Hearing Assn. (pres. 1965), Speech Assn. Am., Kappa Delta Pi, Phi Delta Kappa, Sigma Alpha Eta. Episcopalian. Club: Lotos (N.Y.C.). Home: 330 E 63d St New York NY 10021

BAKER, ERNEST BEASLEY, JR., nursing home administrator; b. Waco, Tex., Mar. 26, 1926; s. Ernest Beasley and Annie Virginia (Nichols) B. B.B.A., U. Tex., 1948. Coll. rep. Ginn & Co., 1956-63; med. rep. Pitman-Moore Co., 1963-66; adminstr. St. Jude's Hosp., Austin, Tex., 1966-76, Austin Geriatric Center, 1970—, Capital Area Radiation and Research Found., Austin, 1976—. Bd. dirs. Capital area div. A.R.C., also pub. relations cons. Midwest div. Served with USNR, 1943-46. Fellow Am. Coll. Health Care Adminstrs. (pres. 1977-78); Mem. Tex. Assn. Homes for Aging, Am. Assn. Homes for Aging, Am. Health Care Assn. Methodist. Home: 3803-A Mia Tia Circle Austin TX 78731 Office: 21 Waller St Austin TX 78702

BAKER, FLOYD WILMER, surgeon, army officer; b. Leavenworth, Kans., May 25, 1927; s. Floyd Winfield and Lolita Clare (Somers) B.; m. Darlene Marie Fulk, Apr. 10, 1949; children: Linda Marie, Diane Louise, Barbara Jayne. B.A., U. Kans., 1950, M.D., 1953; grad., Army Command and Gen. Staff Coll., 1964, Indsl. Coll. Armed Forces, 1967. Diplomate: Am. Bd. Surgery. Commd. 1st lt. U.S. Army, 1953, advanced through grades to maj. gen., 1980; intern Madigan Gen. Hosp., Tacoma, 1953-54; resident in gen. surgery Fitzsimons Army Hosp., Denver, 1955-59; dir. personnel and tng. Office of Surgeon Gen., 1970-71; comdg. gen. Brooke Army Med. Center, Ft. Sam Houston, Tex., 1974-78; Letterman Army Med Center, Presidio of San Francisco, 1978-81; chief surgeon U.S. Army, Europe; comdg. gen. U.S. Army 7th Med. Command,, 1981-83, U.S. Army Health Services Command, Ft. Sam Houston, 1983—. Served with USNR, 1945-46. Decorated Legion of Merit (2), Meritorious Service medal, Army Commendation medal (3), Air medal (2). Fellow Am. Coll. Physician Execs.; Mem. AMA, Am. Mgmt. Assn., Soc. U.S. Army Flight Surgeons. Republican. Baptist. Home: 416 Dickman St Fort Sam Houston TX 78234 Office: HQ USAHSC Fort Sam Houston TX 78234

BAKER, FRANCIS PEARSON, business executive; b. London, Jan. 29, 1929; emigrated to Can., naturalized, 1968; s. Francis Pearson and Eva A. (McDermott) B.; m. Felicity Anne Gilmour, June 1957 (dec.); children: Francis, Catherine. Ed., Royal Mil. Acad., Sandhurst, Eng., 1948. Far East rep. Pinchin Johnson Paints, Singapore, 1955-58; mng. dir. Shalimar Paints Ltd., Calcutta, India, 1958-68; pres. Roxalin Can. Ltd., Toronto, 1968, Internat. Paints (Can.) Ltd., Montreal, Que., 1969—. Active Boy Scouts Can., Montreal. Served to capt. Brit. Army, 1946-55. Clubs: Marine (Toronto); United Services; Oriental (London); St. James; Royal Montreal Golf (Montreal). Home: 11,150 Meighen Rd Apt 901 Montreal PQ Canada H8Y 3J1 Office: Internat Paints (Can) Ltd 6615 Park Ave Montreal PQ Canada H2V 4P6

BAKER, FRANK HAMON, education and research administrator; b. Stroud, Okla., May 2, 1923; s. DeWitt and Maude Emma (Hamon) B.; m. Melonee Gaynelle Gray, May 25, 1946; children: Rilda, Necia, Twila, Dayna. B.S., Okla. State U., 1947, M.S., 1951, Ph.D., 1954. County agt., Delaware County, Okla., 1947-48; grad. asst. Okla. State U., 1951-53; asst. prof. animal sci. Kans. State U., 1953-55; asso. prof. animal nutrition U. Ky., 1955-58; extension livestock specialist Okla. State U., 1958-62; nat. coordinator extension animal sci. U.S. Dept. Agr., Washington, 1962-66; prof., chmn. animal sci. dept. U. Nebr., 1966-74; dean agr., prof. Okla. State U., Stillwater, 1974-79, prof., Internat. Program officer, 1979-81; dir. Internat. Stockmen's Sch. Winrock Internat., Morrilton, Ark., 1981—. Contbr. articles to profl. jours. Served with AUS, 1943-45. Decorated Purple Heart. Fellow AAAS, Am. Soc. Animal Sci. (pres. 1974); mem. Council Agr. Sci. and Tech. (pres. 1979), Nat. Beef Improvement Fedn. (sec. 1968-74), Am. Meat Sci. Assn., Am. Inst. Biol. Sci., Sigma Xi, Gamma Sigma Delta, Epsilon Sigma Phi, Alpha Zeta. Democrat. Methodist. Home: 1806 Berry Pl Conway AR 72032 Office: Winrock Internat Route 3 Morrilton AR 72110 *

BAKER, GEORGE R., investment banker; b. Chgo., Nov. 5, 1929; s. G.R. and Lucy I. B.; m. Maryanne Evans; children: Anne Elizabeth, James Robert. B.A., Coe Coll., 1951; D.C.S. (hon.), 1974. With Continental Ill. Nat. Bank and Trust Co., 1951-83, head gen. banking services dept., 1976-83; spl. ltd. ptnr. Bear Stearns & Co., Chgo., 1983—; dir. Williams Electronics, Inc., Am. Fin. Enterprises, Inc., Midland Co., Reliance Group Holdings, W.W. Grainger Inc. Trustee Children's Meml. Hosp., 1981—; trustee Field Mus. Natural History, Coe Coll., 1977—. Clubs: Sunset Ridge Country, Chicago, Standard, Whitehall. Office: Three First Nat Plaza Suite 2500 Chicago IL 60602

BAKER, HALMER LOREN, engineering and construction company executive; b. Duluth, Minn., Mar. 19, 1924; s. Halmer Ludwig and Alma Birdeen (Anderson) B.; m. Sheila Ann Gallaher, Sept. 26, 1947; 1 son, Timothy Louis. B.S. in Elec. Engring, U. Wis., 1948; M.S. in Indsl. Engring, Stevens Inst. Tech., Hoboken, N.J., 1953. Elec. engr. Westinghouse Electric Corp., 1948-50; with Stone & Webster Service Corp., 1951-67, v.p., 1964-67; pres. Savannah Electric & Power Co., Ga., 1967-71, Stone & Webster, Inc., N.Y.C., 1971-75; sr. v.p. constrn. and ops. power group Brown & Root, Inc., Houston, 1976—. Named Indsl. Man of Year Indsl. Devel. Com., Savannah, 1969. Clubs: Oglethorpe (Savannah); Houston, Riverbend Country (Houston). Home: 12318 Overcup Houston TX 77024 Office: Brown & Root Inc Box 3 Houston TX 77001

BAKER, HAROLD ALBERT, fed. judge; b. Mt. Kisco, N.Y., Oct. 4, 1929; s. John Shirley and Ruth (Sarmiento) B.; m. Dorothy Ida Armstrong, June 24, 1951; children—Emily, Nancy, Peter. A.B., U. Ill., 1951, J.D., 1956. Bar: Ill. bar 1956. Practiced in, Champaign, Ill., 1956-78; partner firm Hatch & Baker, 1960-78; judge U.S. Dist. Ct. for Central Dist. Ill., Danville, 1978—; adj. mem. faculty Coll. Law, U. Ill., 1972-78; sr. counsel Presdl. Commn. on CIA Activities within U.S., 1975. Pres. Champaign Bd. Edn., 1967-76, pres., 1967-76. Served to lt. j.g. USN, 1951-53. Mem. Am. Bar Assn., Ill. Bar Assn. Democrat. Episcopalian. Office: Fed Courthouse Danville IL 61832

BAKER, HARVEY WILLIS, surgeon; b. N.Y.C., Oct. 5, 1918; s. Willis P. and Margaret (Darvas) B.; m. Corene C. Fleming, Nov. 9, 1944; children—Kathleen, William. B.A., Cornell U., 1939; M.D., Columbia U., 1943. Intern, resident in surgery Kings County Hosp., Bklyn., 1943-44, 46-50; fellow in surgery Meml. Sloan Kettering Cancer Center, N.Y.C., 1950-53; clin. prof. surgery U. Oreg.; also chief head and neck surg. service Portland Vets. Hosp., 1953—; attending surgeon Good Samaritan Hosp. and Med. Center; bd. dirs., exec. com. Oreg. Comprehensive Cancer Program. Author: (with R.A. Wise) Surgery of the Head and Neck, a Handbook of Operative Surgery, 1958; contbr. numerous articles to surg. jours. and textbooks. Pres. Oreg. div. Am. Cancer Soc., 1969-71, bd. dirs., 1960—, dir. at large, 1970—. Served to maj. M.C. AUS, 1944-46. Recipient Meritorious Achievement award U. Oreg. Alumni Assn., 1977. Fellow A.C.S. (bd. govs. 1966-72, chmn. commn. on cancer 1975-79); mem. North Pacific Surg. Assn. (pres. 1979), Pacific Coast Surg. Assn., Western Surg. Assn., Soc. Surg. Oncology (pres. 1978), Soc. Head and Neck Surgeons (pres. 1971), Am. Joint Com. for Cancer, Isaac Walton League. Presbyterian. Home: 2000 Jolie Pointe Rd West Linn OR 97068 Office: 2222 NW Lovejoy St Portland OR 97210

BAKER, HASTINGS WYMAN, lawyer and business exec.; b. Stovall, N.C., June 12, 1914; s. Hastings Wyman and Sallie (Younger) B.; m. Beverly Higgins, July 7, 1938; children—Hastings Wyman III, Barry. Student, Harvard, 1932-33, Western Res. U., 1933-34, Wittenberg U., 1934-35, George Washington U., 1935-37, Coll. City N.Y., 1937, Columbia, 1937; LL.B., Fordham U., 1941. Bar: N.Y. State bar 1941. Law clk., asso. atty. Chadbourne, Hunt, Jackel & Brown, N.Y.C., 1939-43; asst. to head legal dept. Mathieson Chem. Co., 1943-44; corp. counsel, asst. sec. Tubize Rayon Corp., 1944-46; with Beaunit Mills, Inc., N.Y.C., 1947—, sec., treas., dir., 1959—, head legal dept., 1947—; various positions to sec.-treas. and head legal dept. Skenandoa Rayon Corp., Nat. Weaving Corp., N.Am. Rayon Corp.; also dir.; mng. dir. Sta. Reps. Assn., Inc., 1964—; pres. Care Centers, Inc.; dir. Tyrex, Inc. (subsidiaries 20th Century Fox Film Corp.). Home: 220 W Norwalk Rd Darien CT 06820 Office: 1820 Winters Tower Dayton OH 45402

BAKER, HENRY JOHN, JR., researcher, educator; b. Little Falls, N.J., Apr. 4, 1935; s. Henry John and Jean (Jungkind) B.; m. Gertrude Howard, Aug. 26, 1959; 1 son, Todd Michael. D.V.M., Auburn U., 1960. Instr. lab. animal medicine Johns Hopkins U., Balt., 1963-65, asst. prof., 1965-68; assoc. prof. comparative medicine U. Ala., Birmingham, 1968-74, dir. exptl. animal resources, 1975—, prof., chmn. dept. comparative medicine, 1974—; cons. AAALAC, Joliet, Ill., 1967—; mem. Aging. Rev. Com., Nat. Inst. Aging., 1979-82, NIH, 1979-82. Editor: Lab. Animal Sci., 1976, Lab. Rat, 1980. Bd. dirs. Birmingham Humane Soc., 1981—. Grantee NIH, ARB, 1975—, NIH, NINCDS, 1973—. Mem. Am. Coll. Lab. Animal Medicine (diplomate, pres. 1975-76), Council on Accreditation AAALAC (chmn. 1976-78), Scientists Ctr. Animal Welfare (trustee), Am. Assn. Lab. Animal Medicine, Am. Vet. Medicine Assn. Office: U Ala University Sta Birmingham AL 35294

BAKER, HENRY S., JR., banker; b. Balt., June 10, 1926; s. Henry S. and Frances (Robinson) B.; m. Marian Stockton Towsend, June 12, 1948; children—Frances, Sandra, Stockton. B.A., Johns Hopkins U., 1950; grad. with honors, Grad. Sch. Banking, Rutgers U., 1957. With Md. Nat. Bank, Balt., 1950—, exec. v.p., 1973—, dir., 1975—; chmn. Redwood Capital Mgmt. Co.; vice chmn. AAA Md., Ins. Agy. Inc.; v.p., dir. Manab Properties; dir. Md. Nat. Corp. Trustee, treas. Garrison Forest Sch., 1962-68, St. Paul's Sch. for Girls, 1968-77; pres. Jr. Achievement Met. Balt., 1971, Florence Crittenden Home, 1964-66; bd. dirs. Keswick, The Home for Incurables, 1965, pres., 1979; chmn. investment com. Episcopal Diocese Md., 1974-80; gen. campaign chmn. United Way Central Md., 1979. Served with USNR, 1944-46. Mem. Assn. Res. City Bankers, Md. Bankers Assn. (pres.), Md. State C. of C. (treas., dir.). Republican. Office: Md Nat Bank PO Box 987 Baltimore MD 21203

BAKER, HERBERT, art dealer; b. Chgo., Aug. 14, 1924; s. Joseph David and Ida (Wilk) B.; m. Gwen Weber, Nov. 24, 1948 (div. 1969); children—Alison M. Frank, David A., Lauren B., Todd R.; m. Nadine Hess Spivack, Apr. 3, 1971. Student, U. Ill., 1940, U. Chgo., 1941-42, Inst. Design, Chgo., 1946. Dir. pub. relations Raymond Loewy Assos., Chgo., 1946-47; v.p. Burton Browne Advt., Chgo., 1947-48; creative coordinator Wetzel Bros., Milw., 1949-50; founder Herbert Baker Advt., Inc., Chgo., 1950; mem. com. primitive art Art Inst., Chgo., 1960-70; authority, dealer African, Oceanic primitive art. Pres. Found. Cancer Research, Chgo., 1960. Served with AUS, 1942-45. Mem. Am. Soc. Appraisers (sr. appraiser). Address: 17800 Tramonto Dr Pacific Palisades CA 90272

BAKER, HERBERT GEORGE, botany educator; b. Brighton, Eng., Feb. 23, 1920; came to U.S., 1957; s. Herbert Reginald and Alice (Bambridge) B.; m. Irene Williams, Apr. 4, 1945; 1 dau., Ruth Elaine. B.S., U. London, 1941, Ph.D., 1945. Research chemist, asst. plant physiologist Hosa Research Labs., Sunbury-on-Thames, Eng., 1940-45; lectr. botany U. Leeds, Eng., 1945-54; research fellow Carnegie Instn., Washington, 1948-49; prof. botany U. Coll. Ghana, 1954-57; faculty U. Calif., Berkeley, 1957—, assoc. prof. botany, 1957-60, prof., 1960—, dir. bot. garden, 1957-69. Author: Plants and Civilization, 1965, 70, 78; Editor: (with G.L. Stebbins) Genetics of Colonizing Species, 1965; series editor: Bot. Monographs, 1971—; Contbr. articles to sci. jours. Fellow AAAS (pres. Pacific div.), Assn. Tropical Biology; mem. Am. Inst. Biol. Sci., Internat. Assn. Botanic Gardens (past v.p.), Internat. Orgn. Plant Biosystematists, Ecol. Soc. Am., Soc. for Study Evolution (past pres.), Bot. Soc. Am. (past pres.), Sigma Xi. Home: 635 Creston Rd Berkeley CA 94708

BAKER, HERSCHEL CLAY, educator; b. Cleburne, Tex., Nov. 8, 1914; s. Tyler Alexander and Mae (Deffebach) B.; m. Barbara Morris, Sept. 6, 1939; children—Ann, William, Pamela. A.B., So. Methodist U., 1935, Mus.B., 1935, LL.D., 1966; A.M., Harvard, 1936, Ph.D., 1939; LL.D., U. Vt., 1967. Instr. English U. Tex., 1939-44, asst. prof. English, 1944-46, Harvard, Cambridge, Mass., 1946-49, asso. prof., 1949-56, prof., 1956—, chmn. dept., 1952-57, Higginson prof. English lit., 1967—. Author: John Philip Kemble, 1942, The Dignity of Man, 1947, The Wars of Truth, 1952, Hyder Edward Rollins: A Bibliography, 1960, William Hazlitt, 1962, The Race of Time, 1966; Editor: The Later Renaissance in England, 1975, (with Hyder Rollins) The Renaissance in England, 1954; contbg. editor: The Complete Signet Classic Shakespeare, 1972, The Riverside Shakespeare, 1974; Contbr. articles to profl. jours. Guggenheim fellow, 1957, 63. Mem. Phi Beta Kappa, Kappa Sigma. Home: 22 Clifton St Belmont MA 02178

BAKER, HOLLIS MACLURE, furniture manufacturing company executive; b. Allegan, Mich., Apr. 27, 1916; s. Hollis Siebe and Ruth (MacClure) B.; m. Betty Jane Brown, Aug. 2, 1947; children: Tomelyn Ann, Susan MacClure. Student, U. Va., 1935-37. With Baker Furniture, Inc., Holland, Mich., 1938-40, 45-73, v.p., treas., 1959-61, pres., 1961-70, chmn. bd., 1970-73; v.p., gen. mgr. Grand Rapids Chair Co., Mich., 1959-61, pres., 1961-70; v.p., dir. Manor House, Inc., N.Y.C., 1958-70; pres. Boyne City R.R. Co., Mich., 400 Bldg. Corp., Palm Beach, Fla.; dir. Mich. Nat. Bank, Lansing, 1968-83, Am. Seating Co., Grand Rapids, 1973-83, Mich. Nat. Bank, 1959-84, Norton Gallery, Palm Beach. Bd. dirs. USCG Acad. Found. Served to lt. (s.g.) USNR, 1941-45. Mem. Nat. Assn. Furniture Mfrs. (dir.), Furniture Mfrs. Assn. Grand Rapids (dir., past pres.), Zeta Psi. Episcopalian. Clubs: Brook, New York Yacht, Leash (N.Y.C.); Chicago, Chicago Yacht; Kent Country, University, Indian, Peninsular (Grand Rapids); Everglades, Bath and Tennis (Palm Beach); Royal Yacht (Greece); Buck's (London); Travellers (Paris). Home: 328 El Vedado Rd Palm Beach FL 33480 Office: 900 McKay Tower Grand Rapids MI 49502 Office: 400 Bldg 400 Royal Palm Way Palm Beach FL 33480

BAKER, HOUSTON ALFRED, JR., English language educator; b. Louisville, Mar. 22, 1943; s. Houston A. and Viola Elizabeth (Smith) B.; m. Charlotte Marie Pierce, Sept. 10, 1966; 1 son, Mark Frederick. B.A., Howard U., 1965; M.A. (John Hay Whitney fellow), UCLA, 1966, Ph.D., 1968. Instr. Howard U., summers 1966; instr. English Yale U., 1968-69, asst. prof., 1969-70; assoc. prof., mem. Center Advanced Studies, U. Va., 1970-73, prof., 1973-74; prof. English U. Pa., Phila., 1974—, dir. Afro-Am. studies, 1974-77; Disting. vis. scholar Cornell U., 1977; Phi Beta Kappa vis. scholar, 1975-76. Author: Long Black Song, 1972, Singers of Daybreak, 1974, A Many-Colored Coat of Dreams, 1974; poems No Matter Where You Travel, You Still Be Black, 1979; The Journey Back: Issues in Black Literature and Criticism, 1980; poems Spirit Run, 1982; editor: Black Literature in America, 1971; poems 20th-Century Interpretations of Native Son, 1972, Reading Black: Essays in the Criticism of African, Caribbean and Black American Literature, 1976; contbr. articles and revs. to profl. jours. Recipient Alfred Longueil Poetry award UCLA, 1966; fellow Center for Advanced Study, Stanford, 1977; Guggenheim fellow, 1978; Nat. Humanities Ctr. fellow, 1982. Mem. MLA, Coll. Lang. Assn., Assn. African and African Am. Folklorists, Am. Studies Assn., Phi Beta Kappa. Home: 613 E Phil-Ellena St Philadelphia PA 19119 Office: Dept English U Pa Philadelphia PA 19104

BAKER, HOWARD HENRY, JR., U.S. senator, lawyer; b. Huntsville, Tenn., Nov. 15, 1925; s. Howard Henry and Dora (Ladd) B.; m. Joy Dirksen, Dec. 22, 1951; children: Darek Dirksen, Cynthia. Grad., McCallie Sch., 1943; student, U. of South, Tulane U.; LL.B., U. Tenn., 1949; LL.D., Tusculum Coll.; D.C.L., Southwestern at Memphis. Formerly sr. partner law firm Baker, Worthington, Barnett & Crossley, Knoxville; U.S. senator from, Tenn., 1966-85, minority leader, 1977-81, majority leader, 1981-85; co-chmn. Senate Select Com. on Presdl. Campaign Activities; mem. Com. on Environment and Pub. Works, Com. on Fgn. Relations, Com. on Rules and Adminstrn., Select Com. on Intelligence.; Presdl. elector, Tenn., 1956; chmn. Tenn. del. Republican Nat. Conv., 1968; Keynote Speaker Rep. Nat. Conv., 1976; Candidate for Pres. U.S., 1980. Served to lt. (j.g.) USNR, 1943-46. Mem. Am. Bar Assn. Office: Dirksen Senate Office Bldg Washington DC 20510

BAKER, J. RICHARD, construction corporation executive; b. Montreal, Que., Can., Feb. 26, 1931; s. William Edward and Audrey G. (McKechnie) B.; m. Lorna Margaret Calderwood, Dec. 28, 1957; children: Susan, Stephen, Jeffrey, Hugh. Student, Victoria Coll.; B.A., U. B.C. Chief estimator Vancouver Pile Driving & Contracting Co. Ltd., N. Vancouver, B.C., Can., 1964-70; chief extimator Dillingham Corp. Can. Ltd., N. Vancouver, 1970-73, mgr. civil and marine div., 1973, v.p. ops., 1973-77, v.p. bus. devel., 1977-80; pres., chief exec. officer Dillingham Constrn. Ltd., 1980—. Vice pres. Vancouver-Coast region Boy Scouts Am., 1980—. Mem. Amalgamated Constrn. Assn. (dir.). Clubs: Royal Vancouver Yacht; Whistler Montain Ski (B.C.). Office: Dillingham Constrn Ltd 20 Brooksband Ave North Vancouver BC Canada V7J 2B8

BAKER, JACK SHERMAN, architect, designer; b. Champaign, Ill., Aug. 8, 1920; s. Clyde Lee and Jane Cecilia (Walker) B. B.A. with honors, U. Ill., 1943, M.S., 1949; cert., N.Y. Beaux Art Inst. od Design, 1943. Mem. faculty U. Ill., Urbana, 1946—, prof. architecture, 1961—; assoc. Atkins, Barrow & Lasswith, Champaign, Ill., 1946-50; pvt. practice architecture, Champaign, Ill., 1946—; aero. designer Boeing Aircraft, Seattle, 1943. Exhibited watercolor paintings; archtl. works published in numerous jours. Served with U.S. Army, 1945-46. Recipient cert. of Appreciation for Dedicated and Disting. Voluntary Service on AIA Com. of Design, 1975, numerous awards in field. Fellow AIA; mem. Nat. Soc. Archtl. Historians, Assn. Collegiate Schs. of Architecture, Nat. Council Architecture and Registration Bds., Nat. Trust Hist. Preservation, Alpha Rho Chi. Clubs: Gargoyle, Scarab; Cliff Dwellers (Chgo.). Home: 7 1/2 Chester St Champaign IL 61820 Office: School of Architecture U Ill Taft Dr Champaign IL 61820

BAKER, JACKSON ARNOLD, container shipping co. exec.; b. Saltville, Va., May 1, 1938; s. Joseph Arnold and Katherine Kimmons (Seale) B.; m. Carolyn Josephine Cantrell, Dec. 27, 1957; children—Allison Kimmons, Elizabeth Arnold. B.S. in Indsl. Mgmt, Ga. Inst. Tech., 1960. Dock foreman Roadway Express, Atlanta, 1960-63; asst. terminal mgr. Waterman of P.R., Mobile, Ala., 1963-65; with SeaLand Service, Inc., Seattle, 1965—, v.p., 1972-75, exec. v.p., 1975—. Office: 100 W Harrison St Suite 505 Seattle WA 98119

BAKER, JAMES ADDISON, III, presidential chief of staff; b. Houston, Apr. 28, 1930; s. James A. and Bonner (Means) B.; m. Susan Garrett, Aug. 6, 1973; 8 children. B.A., Princeton U., 1952; LL.B., U. Tex., 1957. Bar: Tex. 1957. Mem. firm Andrews, Kurth, Campbell & Jones, Houston, 1957-81; undersec. Dept. Commerce, Washington, 1975-76; deputy chmn. del. ops. Pres. Ford Com., Washington, 1976; campaign chmn. George Bush, 1979-80; sr. adviser Reagan-Bush Com., 1980-81; mem. Reagan Transition Team, Washington, 1980-81; chief of staff White House, Washington, 1981—. Trustee Woodrow Wilson Internat. Center for Scholars, Smithsonian Inst., 1977—. Served with USMC, 1952-54. Mem. ABA, State Bar Tex., Houston Bar Assn.; mem. Am. Judicature Soc.; Mem. Phi Delta Phi. Office: White House 1600 Pennsylvania Ave Washington DC 20500

BAKER, JAMES ANDERSON, manufacturing company executive; b. Garland, Tex., Oct. 6, 1927; s. Andy Frank and Ruby (Anderson) B.;

m. Patsy Glynn, Feb. 21, 1950; children: Janet Lea, Carol Ann, Laura Susan. B.S.E.E., So. Meth. U., 1952; grad., Advanced Mgmt. program Harvard Bus. Sch., 1968. With Gen. Electric Co., 1952—, gen. mgr. indsl. control products dept., 1968-72, v.p., dir. mgr. lamp products div., 1973-77, v.p., group exec. lighting bus. group, 1977-79, exec. v.p., sector exec. indsl. products and components sector, Fairfield, Conn., 1979—; dir. Gen. Electric Credit Corp., Can. Gen. Electric Co. Ltd. Vice-pres., bd. dirs. United Way Services, 1978-79; trustee Thomas Alva Edison Found.; active Boy Scouts Am. Served with U.S. Army, 1946-48. Recipient Spurgeon award exploring program Boy Scouts Am., 1975. Mem. Cleve. Growth Assn., Elfun Soc. Republican. Methodist. Office: General Electric Co 3135 Easton Turnpike Fairfield CT 06431

BAKER, JAMES B., architect; b. N.Y.C., Feb. 18, 1933; s. William Edgar and Violet (Twachtman) B.; m. Valery Goldberg, Feb. 10, 1979; children: Mary Morgan, James Edgar, Catriona Griswold, Frederick Alden. A.B., Princeton U., 1954; M.Arch., Yale U., 1960. With firms Blake & Neski, N.Y.C., 1960-62, George Lewis, 1962-63, Kahn & Jacobs, 1963-64; partner firm Baker & Blake, N.Y.C., 1964-72, Baker/Grinnell, 1972-74; cons., 1974-77; dir. Llewelyn Davies Assos., N.Y.C., 1976-78; pres. Tower Devel. Group Inc., Ohio, 1978—, Park-Tower Devel. Co., Ltd., Bermuda, 1978-80; dir. Steers Devel. Group; vis. prof. Sch. Architecture, City U. N.Y. Trustee Darrow Sch. Recipient Design awards HUD, AIA, others. Fellow AIA (dir.); mem. Am. Arbitration Assn. Clubs: Holland Soc., St. Nicholas Soc. Home: 105 E 63d St New York NY 10021 Office: 17 Battery Pl New York NY 10004

BAKER, JAMES E., fgn. service officer; b. Suffolk, Va., Jan. 21, 1935; s. Percy H. and Helen Mae B. B.A., Haverford Coll., 1956; M.A., Fletcher Sch. Law and Diplomacy, 1957; postgrad., U. Calif., 1970-71. Commd. fgn. service officer Dept. State, 1960; minister counselor U.S. Mission to UN, N.Y.C.; prin. officer Office of Dir. Gen. of UN, 1980—; sr. asso. Carnegie Endowment for Internat. Peace, 1978. Served with U.S. Army, 1957-58. Mem. Am. Fgn. Service Assn., Council Fgn. Relations, Am. Polit. Sci. Assn., Am. Studies Assn. Home: 4 E 8th St New York NY 10003 Office: 799 UN Plaza New York NY 10017

BAKER, JAMES EDWARD, investments and management consultant; b. Tuckerman, Ark., Nov. 17, 1925; s. Eugene B. and Alma (Moon) B.; m. Ruth Lacko, Jan. 25, 1958; children: Mary Elizabeth, Donald Eugene, Robert James, Linda Ann. B.S. in Bus. Adminstrn. with honors, U. Ark., 1949, M.B.A., 1950. Exec. trainee Southwestern Bell Telephone Co., St. Louis, 1950-51; staff accountant Montgomery Ward & Co., Chgo., 1951-52; with No. Trust Co., Chgo., 1952-63, 2d v.p., 1961-63; treas. Pet Inc., St. Louis, 1963-68, Brown & Williamson Tobacco Corp., Louisville, 1968-69; v.p., chief fin. officer, dir. Kroger Co., Cin., 1969-79; exec. v.p. adminstrn., dir. Tandy Corp., Ft. Worth, 1979-80; now investments and mgmt. cons. Served with AUS, 1944-46. Mem. Fin. Execs. Inst., Am. Mgmt. Assn. (chmn. fin. council, v.p., dir.). Home: 7686 Coldstream Dr Cincinnati OH 45230

BAKER, JAMES EDWARD, insurance company executive; b. Balt., Feb. 9, 1930; s. Edgar Frank and Thelma May (Howe) B.; m. Bernardine Helen Lesnick, June 7, 1952; 1 son, James Edward. Student, pub. schs. Asst. controller Am. Credit Indemnity Co., N.Y., Balt., 1948-58; with Am. Health & Life Ins. Co., Balt., 1958-71, pres., chief exec. officer, 1966-71, dir., 1964—; sr. v.p. Comml. Credit Services Inc., Balt., 1971-77, dir., 1971—; pres., chief exec. officer Cavalier Ins. Corp., Balt., 1977-80; controller ins. group Comml. Credit Co., Balt., 1980—; dir. Gulf Ins. Co., Dallas, 1980—, Comml. Credit Mortgage Ins. Co., Balt., 1972—. Club: Towson Golf and Country. Lodge: Masons. Home: 2521 Londonderry Rd Timonium MD 21093 Office: Comml Credit Co 300 Saint Paul Pl Baltimore MD 21202

BAKER, JAMES EDWARD SPROUL, lawyer; b. Evanston, Ill., May 23, 1912; s. John Clark and Hester (Sproul) B.; m. Eleanor Lee Dodgson, Oct. 2, 1937 (dec. Sept. 1972); children: John Lee, Edward Graham. A.B., Northwestern U., 1933, J.D., 1936. Bar: Ill. 1936, U.S. Supreme Ct. 1957. Practice in, Chgo., 1936—; assoc. Sidley & Austin, and predecessors, 1936-48, ptnr., 1948-81; of counsel Sidley & Austin (and predecessors), 1981—; lectr. Northwestern U. Law Sch., 1951-52; Nat. chmn. Stanford U. Parents Com., 1970-75; mem. vis. com. Stanford Law Sch., 1976-79, 82—, DePaul U. Sch. Law, 1982—, Northwestern U. Law Sch., 1980—, DePaul U. Law Sch., 1982—. Served to comdr. USNR, 1941-46. Fellow Am. Coll. Trial Lawyers (regent 1974-81, sec. 1977-79, pres. 1979-80); mem. ABA, Bar Assn. 7th Fed. Circuit, Ill. Bar Assn., Chgo. Bar Assn., Soc. Trial Lawyers Ill., Northwestern U. Law Alumni Assn. (past pres.), Order of Coif, Phi Lambda Upsilon, Sigma Nu. Republican. Methodist. Clubs: John Evans (Northwestern U.) (chmn. 1982—); University (Chgo.); John Henry Wigmore (past pres.); Midday, Legal, Law (Chgo.) (pres. 1983—); Westmoreland Country (Wilmette, Ill.)). Home: 1300 N Lake Shore Dr Chicago IL 60610 Office: 1 First Nat Plaza Chicago IL 60603

BAKER, JAMES GILBERT, scientist; b. Louisville, Nov. 11, 1914; s. Jesse Blanton and Hattie May (Stallard) B.; m. Elizabeth Katherine Breitenstein, Jan. 1, 1938; children: Kirby Alan, Dennis Graham, Neal Kenton, Brenda Sue. A.B., U. Louisville, 1935, Sc.D., 1948; A.M. (Townsend Scholar), Harvard, 1936; Ph.D. (mem. Soc. Fellows 1937-41), Harvard, 1942. Lowell lectr., 1940; dir. Optical Research Lab., Harvard, 1941-46, asso. prof., 1946-48; research fellow Harvard Obs., 1942-46, research asso., 1949—, (Lick Obs.), 1949-60; pres. Spica, Inc., 1955-60; cons. optical physics Air Force, 1946-57; cons. Polaroid Corp., 1966—; Chmn. U.S. nat. com. Internat. Commn. Optics, 1956-59, internat. v.p., 1959-62; sci. adv. bd. USAF, 1952-57. Author: (with George Z. Dimitroff) Telescopes and Accessories, 1945. Trustee The Perkin Fund, 1970—. Awarded Adolph Lomb medal for contbns. to optics, 1942, Presdl. Medal of Merit for War Work, 1947; Magellanic Medal for Contbns. to Astron. Optics, 1952; Exceptional Civilian Service Award USAF, 1957; Elliott Cresson medal Franklin Inst., 1962; Frederick Ives medal Optical Soc. Am., 1965; Alan Gordon award SPIE, 1976; Gold medal, 1978. Mem. Nat. Acad. Scis., Nat. Acad. Engring., Am. Philos. Soc., Am. Astron. Soc. (councillor 1956-59), Am. Optical Soc. (pres. 1960), Am. Acad. Arts and Scis. (councillor 1957-59), Explorers Club, Gamma Alpha (pres. Harvard chpt. 1939), Sigma Xi (sec.-treas. Harvard chpt. 1946-48). Home: 14 French Dr Bedford NH 03102 Office: Harvard College Observatory Cambridge MA 02138

BAKER, JAMES KENDRICK, splty. metals mfg. co. exec.; b. Wabash, Ind., Dec. 21, 1931; s. Donald Dale and Edith (Swain) B.; m. Beverly Baker, Apr. 11, 1959; children—Betsy Ann, Dirk Emerson, Hugh Kendrick. A.B., DePauw U., 1953; M.B.A., Harvard, 1958. Regional sales mgr. Arvinyl div. Arvin Industries, Inc., Columbus, Ind., 1958-60, gen. mgr. div., 1960-66, v.p., gen. mgr. div., 1966-68, exec. v.p., dir., 1968-81, pres., dir., 1981—; dir. Norlin Corp., N.Y.C., Columbus Bank & Trust Co., Ind. Nat. Corp., Indpls. Bd. dirs. Associated Colls. Ind., De Pauw U.; pres. Columbus Found. for Youth, 1965, United Way of Bartholomew County, 1979, Vinyl-Metal Laminators Inst. div. Soc. for Plastics Industry, 1963-64; dir. Vinyl-Metal Laminators Inst. div. Soc. for Plastics Industry, 1960—; Vice chmn. Ind. Republican Conv., 1966. Served with AUS, 1953-55. Named Outstanding Boss C. of C., 1965; recipient Disting. Service award Ind. Jr. C. of C., 1966; named One of 5 Outstanding Young Men of Ind., 1966. Mem. Columbus C. of C. (dir.). Clubs: Rotary, DePauw University Alumni (pres. 1974), Harrison Lake Country.). Home: 12044 W State Rd 46 Deer Crossing Columbus IN 47201 Office: Gen Offices Arvin Industries Inc 1531 E 13th St Columbus IN 47201

BAKER, JAMES NETTLETON, railroad association executive; b. Springfield, Mass., Dec. 2, 1930; s. Harris Walton and Genevieve (Nettleton) B.; m. Mary Copeland, Oct. 29, 1936; children: Charles Copeland, Ann Caldwell. B.A. in History, Yale U., 1953. ICC practitioner, 1960. Gen. mgr. pricing Western Pacific R.R., San Francisco, 1978-81; chmn. Western R.R. Traffic Assn., Chgo., 1981—; pres. Western R.R. Assn., Chgo., 1981—; dir. Nat. Freight Traffic Assn., 1982—. Trustee Glencoe Union Ch., Ill., 1981—; mem. nominating caucus Town of Glencoe, 1979-82. Mem. Assn. ICC Practitioners. Club: Skokie Country. Home: 777 Bluff St Glencoe IL 60022 Office: Western Railroad Assn 222 S Riverside Plaza Room 1200 Chicago IL 60606

BAKER, JAMES PORTER, physician, educator; b. Hallsobro, Va., Nov. 21, 1931; s. William Howard and Alice Leigh (Dance) B.; m. Patricia Ormand, Apr. 11, 1975; children: David, Daniel, Steven. B.S., Va. Poly. Inst., 1954; M.D., Med. Coll. Va., 1958. Diplomate: Am. Bd. Internal Medicine. Intern Mass. Meml. Hosp., Boston, 1958-59; resident U.S. Naval Hosp., Chelsea, Mass., 1962-63; asst. resident Med. Coll. Va., Richmond, 1964-65, cardiopulmonary research fellow, 1965-67, instr. Medicine, 1966-67, asst. prof., 1967-70, assoc. prof., 1970-75, advisor Sch. Denistry, 1972-75, med. dir. respiratory ICU, 1967-75, med. co-dir. respiratory therapy and pulmonary labs., Richard, 1967-75; med. dir. respiratory car services Med. Ctr. Hosps., Norfolk, Va., 1975; prof. medicine Eastern Va. Med. Sch., Norfolk, 1975—, chmn. dept. internal medicine, 1978—, interim dean, 1983-84; dir. pulmonary div. med. service programs Eastern Va. Med. Authority, Norfolk; cons. pulmonary diseases U.S. Naval Regional Med. Ctr., Portsmouth, Va., VA Med. Ctr., Hampton, Va.; mem. staff Med. Ctrs. Hosps., Norfolk, DePaul Hosps., Bayside Hosp., Virginia Beach. Editorial bd.: Respiratory Therapy, Va. Med. Monthly; contbr. articles to profl. jours. Served with M.C. USN, 1959-64; served to capt. USNR, 1964—. NIH fellow, 1965-66; A.D. Williams fellow, 1966-67. Fellow Am. Coll. Chest Physicians (sic. program com. 1974-75), ACP (Va. bd. govs. 1983—); mem. Am. Thoracic Soc. (exec. com. 1975-78, TB com. 1975-78), AMA join rev. com. respiratory therapy edn. (1973-78), Am. Lung Assn. (respiratory disease consultation team 1974-78), Am. Assn. Respiratory Therapy (bd. med. advisors, chmn. 1982-83), Alpha Omega Alpha. Lodge: Norfolk Rotary. Home: 213 61st St Virginia Beach VA 23451 Office: 600 Gresham Dr Norfolk VA 23507

BAKER, JANET ABBOTT, mezzo-soprano; b. Aug. 21, 1933; d. Robert Abbott and May (Pollard) B.; m. James Keith Shelley, 1957. Student, Coll. for Girls, York, Eng., Wintringham, Grimsby, Eng.; D.Mus. (hon.), Birmingham U., Leicester, Eng., 1973, London U., 1974, Oxford U., 1975, Hull U., 1975, U. Leeds, 1980, LL.D., U. Aberdeen, 1980. Concert artist; co-dir.: Kings Lynn Festival. Fellow St. Anne's Coll., Oxford (Eng.) U., 1975; Decorated dame Brit. Empire; recipient Daily Mail Kathleen Ferrier award, 1956; Queen's prize Royal Coll. Music, 1959; Shakespeare prize, Hamburg, 1971; Sonning prize, Copenhagen, 1979. Fellow Royal Soc. Arts; mem. Munster Trust. Home: 450 Edgware Rd London W2 England Office: care Shaw Concerts Inc 1995 Broadway New York NY 10023

BAKER, JOE DON, actor; b. Groesbeck, Tex., Feb. 12, 1936; s. Doyle Charles and Edna (McDonald) B.; m. Maria Dolores Rivero-Torres, Dec. 25, 1969 (div. 1980). B.B.A., N.Tex. State Coll., Denton, 1958. Appeared in: New York stage plays Marathon 33, 1963, Blues for Mr. Charlie, 1964; appeared in: TV movies Mongo's Back in Town, 1971, To Kill a Cop, 1978, Power, 1979; star: TV series Eischied, 1979; guest star numerous television series, 1966-72; actor, exec. producer: TV movie Power: An American Saga, 1979; appeared in: motion pictures Cool Hand Luke, 1967, Guns of the Magnificent Seven, 1969, Adam at 6 A.M, 1969, Junior Bonner, 1971, The Wild Rovers, 1971, Welcome Home, Soldier Boys, 1972, Walking Tall, 1972, Charlie Varrick, 1972, The Outfit, 1973, Golden Needles, 1974, Mitchell, 1975, Framed, 1975, Checkered Flag or Crash, 1976, Wishbone Cutter, 1976, The Pack, 1977, Speed Trap, 1977, Wacko, 1981, Joysticks, 1982, The Natural, 1984. Served with AUS, 1958-60. Mem. Actors Studio, N.Y.C. and Los Angeles, Sigma Phi Epsilon. Office: care Artists Agy 10000 Santa Monica Blvd Suite 305 Los Angeles CA 90067

BAKER, JOHN ALEXANDER, JR., foreign service officer; b. Bridgeport, Conn., Oct. 3, 1927; s. John A. and Adelaide (Nichols) B.; m. Sarah K. Bragg, July 2, 1955 (dec. Sept. 1962); m. Katharine P. Gratwick, June 30, 1965; children—John, Kendall, Andrew, Mitchell, Malcolm. B.A., Yale U., 1949; License Scis. Politiques, Geneva (Switzerland) U., 1950. Joined U.S. Fgn. Service, 1950; assigned, Belgrade, 1951-52, Voice of Am., 1954-56, Munich, 1956-57, Moscow, 1957-58, Washington, 1958-60, Rome, 1960-63, U.S. mission to UN, 1963-67; fellow Harvard Center Internat. Affairs, 1967-68; counselor of embassy, dep. chief mission, Prague, 1968-70; dir. East European Affairs, Dept. State, Washington, 1970-74, UN polit. affairs, 1974-75; dep. asst. sec. internat. orgn. affairs, 1975-77; minister to UN Agys. for Food-Agr., Rome, 1977-79; dir. refugee programs Dept. State, 1979-80, dep. asst. sec. for current intelligence, 1980; faculty Nat. War Coll., 1981—. Contbr. articles to profl. publs. Served to 2d lt. AUS, 1946-48. Recipient Meritorious Service award Dept. State, 1960. Home: 3610 Idaho Ave NW Washington DC 20016 Office: Nat War Coll Ft McNair Washington DC 20319

BAKER, JOHN FIRTH, editor; b. Lincoln, Eng., Dec. 21, 1931; came to U.S., 1957; s. Louis Albert and Gladys Muriel (Firth) B.; m. Lila Lichtenstein, Nov. 11, 1958 (div. 1982); m. Barbara Braun, Feb. 27, 1983. M.A., University Coll., Oxford U., 1955. Editorial writer Yorkshire Post, Leeds, Eng., 1955-57, Reuter Ltd., N.Y.C., 1957-62, London, 1962-64, Venture Mag., N.Y.C., 1964-71; sr. editor Readers Digest book div., N.Y.C., 1971-73; mng. editor Publishers Weekly, N.Y.C., 1973-77, editor-in-chief, 1980—; editor-in-Chief Bookviews, N.Y.C., 1977-78; mng. editor Next. Mag., N.Y.C., 1979-80; editor-in-chief Small Press Mag., N.Y.C., 1983—; lectr. New Sch., N.Y. U., Radcliffe Coll., U. Denver. Dir.: Dictionary of Lit. Biography; Contbr. articles to profl. jours. Served with Brit. Army, 1950-52. Home: 7 E 14th St New York NY 10003 Office: 205 E 42d St New York NY 10017

BAKER, JOHN FRANKLIN, industrialist; b. Ironton, Ohio, Oct. 25, 1918; s. Joseph Wilson and Almeda Florence (Corn) B.; m. Edna Jane Dole, Mar. 3, 1938; children: Dole Parker, Sandra Jane. B.S. in Indsl. Engring., Ohio State U., 1944. Ptnr. Worden & Risberg, Phila., 1956-64; pres. J. Franklin Baker & Assocs., Wayne, Pa., 1965—; chmn. bd. Patrick & Wilkins Co.; dir. Harley Chem. Co., Dill Products Co., Duby Corp., Concord Chem. Co., Bernville Mfg. Co., Empress Hosiery Co., Pequea Fishing Tackle Co. Mem. Republican fin. com., Chester County, Pa.; mem. bd. Central Baptist Ch., Wayne, Pa.; pres. Grandview Civic Assn., Ohio, 1955. Recipient Disting. Alumni award Coll. Engring. Ohio State U., 1975, Meritorious Service award Coll. Engring. Ohio State U., 1978, Disting. Service award Grandview Civic Assn., 1956. Mem. Ohio Bd. Registration for Profl. Engrs. and Surveyors, Am. Inst. Indsl. Engrs. (sr.). Clubs: Union League of Phila., Order Eastern Star (past worthy patron), Masons). Home: 686 Wallace Dr Wayne PA 19087

BAKER, JOHN LEE, association executive; b. Chambers, Nebr., July 8, 1928; s. Henry J. and Elizabeth T. Lohaus. Student, U. Nebr., 1946-48; J.D. with honors, Creighton U., Omaha, 1962. Bar: Nebr. 1962, U.S. Supreme Ct. 1962. Civil trial atty. Dept. Justice, 1962-64; senatorial legis. asst., 1964-67; dep. program dir. ops. Grumman Aircraft Corp., 1967-69; congressional liaison Dept. Transp., 1969-70; asst. adminstr. FAA, 1970-73; exec. dir. fed. and public affairs Airline Pilots Assn., 1974-78; pres. Aircraft Owners and Pilots Assn., Washington, 1977—; also pres. assn. Air Safety Found.; publisher assn. Pilot mag.; chmn. Destinations Unlimited (travel agy.), 1977—; cons. in field. Author articles in field. Served as jet pilot USAF, 1948-56. Decorated D.F.C., Air medal with 6 oak leaf clusters; recipient numerous citations. Mem. Aircraft Owners and Pilots Assn., Am. Soc. Assn. Execs., Exptl. Aircraft Assn., Nebr. Bar Assn., Alpha Sigma Nu. Republican. Roman Catholic. Clubs: Nat. Aviation, Wings, Frederick Country, Capitol Hill, Columbia Aviation Country, Washington Country. Address: 421 Aviation Way Frederick MD 21701

BAKER, JOHN RUSSELL, utilities exec.; b. Lexington, Mo., July 21, 1926; s. William Frederick and Flora Anne (Dunford) B.; m. Elizabeth Jane Torrence, June 16, 1948; children—John Russell, Burton T. B.S., U. Mo., 1948, M.B.A., 1962. With Mo. Public Service Co., Kansas City, 1948—, treas., 1966-68, v.p. fin., 1968-71, sr. v.p., 1971-73, exec. v.p., 1973—, also dir.; dir. Charter Bank, Lee's Summit, First Mo. Devel. Fin. Corp.; lectr. fin. U. Mo. Vice-pres. Mid-Continent council Girls Scouts, U.S., 1981; adv. council Sch. Acctg., U. Mo., Columbia. Recipient Outstanding alumnus award Sch. Adminstrn. U. Mo., Kansas City, 1965. Mem. Tax Execs. Inst. (pres. Kansas City 1968), U. Mo. Sch. Adminstrn. Alumni Assn. (pres. 1965), Edison Electric Inst. Republican. Methodist. Clubs: Kansas City, Blue Hills Country. Home: 205 Oxford Ln Lee's Summit MO 64063 Office: 10700 E 350 Hwy Kansas City MO 64138

BAKER, JULIUS, musician; b. Cleve., Sept. 23, 1915; s. Max and Jeannette (Selznick) B.; m. Ruth Thorp, Mar. 28, 1961. Student, Eastman Sch. Music, Rochester, N.Y., 1932-33; diploma, Curtis Inst. Music, Phila., 1937. Faculty Julliard Sch. Music, N.Y.C., 1954—, Curtis Inst. Music, Phila. Mem., Cleve. Orch., 1937-41; 1st flutist, Pitts. Symphony, 1941-43, CBS Symphony, 1943-51, Chgo. Symphony, 1951-53; mem., Bach Aria Group, 1947-65; solo flutist, N.Y. Philharm. Orch., 1965-83; solo appearances, throughout U.S., Europe and Japan; rec. artist for, Decca, Oxford, Vanguard records. Named Dean of Am. Flutists. Home: Enoch Crosby Rd RFD 1 Brewster NY 10509

BAKER, KEITH MICHAEL, educator; b. Swindon, Eng., Aug. 7, 1938; came to U.S., 1964; s. Raymond Eric and Winifred Evelyn (Shepherd) B.; m. Therese Louise Elzas, Oct. 25, 1961; children—Julian, Felix. B.A., Cambridge U., 1960, M.A., 1963; postgrad., Cornell U., 1960-61; Ph.D., Univ. Coll. U. London, 1964. Instr. history and humanities Reed Coll., 1964-65; asst. prof. European history U. Chgo., 1965-71, asso. prof., 1971-76, prof., 1977—, master collegiate div. social scis., 1975-78, asso. dean coll., 1975-78, asso. dean div. social scis., 1975-78; vis. asso. prof. history Yale U., 1974; mem. Inst. Advanced Study, Princeton, N.J., 1979-80. Author: Condorcet: From Natural Philosophy to Social Mathematics, 1975; Editor: Condorcet: Selected Writings, 1977, Jour. Modern History, 1980—. Nat. Endowment for Humanities fellow, 1967-68; Am. Council Learned Soc. Study fellow, 1972-73; Guggenheim fellow, 1979. Mem. Am. Hist. Assn., Am. Soc. 18th Century Studies, Soc. French Hist. Studies. Office: 1126 E 59th St Chicago IL 60637

BAKER, KENDALL LEE, polit. science educator, university dean; b. Clearwater, Fla., Nov. 1, 1942; s. Robert B. and Anne E. B.; m. Tobin Ratliff McGough, Apr. 12, 1981; children: Kraig, Kris, Shannon, Brian. B.A. with high honors, U. Md., 1963; M.A., Georgetown U., 1966, Ph.D. (NDEA fellow), 1969. Instr. dept. polit. sci. U. Wyo., Laramie, 1967-69, asst. prof., 1969-73, assoc. prof., 1973-77, prof., 1977-82, chmn. dept. polit. sci., 1979-82, asst. v.p. acad. affairs, 1976-77; dean Coll. Arts and Scis. Bowling Green State U., (Ohio), 1982—; survey research cons. to various agys. and polit. candidates, 1967—; panel chmn. Rocky Mountain Social Sci. Conv., 1973, Western Social Sci. Conv., 1975; guest participant study trip to, W. Ger., 1977; election observer at invitation of W. German Fed. Govt., 1980. Author: The Wyoming Legislature: Lawmakers, The Public and the Press, 1973, (with R. Dalton and K. Hildebrandt) Germany Transformed: Political Culture and the New Politics, 1981; contbr. articles on polit. sci. to profl. jours. Coach Laramie Soccer Assn., 1978—. Mem. Am. Polit. Sci. Assn. (chmn. panel ann. conv. 1983), Midwest Polit. Sci. Assn., Western Polit. Sci. Assn., Conf. Group on German Politics, Phi Kappa Phi, Omicron Delta Kappa, Pi Sigma Alpha. Home: 31 Indian Creek Dr Rudolph OH 43462 Office: Bowling Green State Univ College of Arts and Sciences Bowling Green OH 43403

BAKER, LAWRENCE COLBY, JR., insurance company executive; b. Carleton, Mich., Oct. 6, 1935; s. Lawrence Colby and Margaret Ellen (Close) B.; m. Ida Wasil, June 26, 1960. B.A., U. Mich., 1957. Underwriter SAFECO, Panorama City, Calif., 1960-61; dist. mgr. Travelers Ins. Co., Los Angeles, 1961-71; chief dep. commr. Calif. Dept. Ins., Los Angeles, 1971-75; pres. Argonaut Ins. Co., Menlo Park, Calif., 1975—, also dir.; dir. Argonaut-Midwest Ins. Co., Argonaut-N.W. Ins. Co., Argonaut-S.W. Ins. Co., Ga. Ins. Co. Bd. dirs. Calif. Workers Compensation Inst., v.p. Served with USN, 1957-60. Mem. Calif. Ins. Guarantee Assn. (chmn.), Nat. Assn. Ind. Insurors (dir.), Ins. Ednl. Assn. (chmn.). Office: 250 Middlefield Rd Menlo Park CA 94025

BAKER, LENOX DIAL, orthopaedist, genealogist; b. DeKalb, Tex., Nov. 10, 1902; s. James D. and Dorothy Hamilton (Lenox) B.; m. Virginia Flowers, Aug. 22, 1933 (dec.); children: Robert Flowers, Lenox Dial; m. Margaret Copeland, Apr. 22, 1967. Student, Pierce Sch. Bus. Adminstrn., Phila., 1920-21, U. Tenn., 1925-29, Sch. Medicine, U. N.C., 1929-30; M.D., Duke, 1934. Diplomate: Am. Bd. Orthopaedic Surgery. Athletic trainer U. Tenn., 1925-29, Duke, 1929-33; ofcl. So. Football Conf., 1933-40; orthopaedic intern Johns Hopkins Hosp., 1933-34, surg. intern, 1934-35, asst. resident orthopaedics, 1935-36, resident orthopaedics, 1936-37; asst., instr. orthopaedic surgery, sch. med. Johns Hopkins, 1935-37; asst. orthopaedics Duke, Durham, N.C., 1937-38, asso., 1938-39, asst. prof., 1940-42, asso. prof., 1942-46, prof., 1947-72, emeritus, 1972—, Pres.'s assoc., 1974—; orthopaedist Duke Hosp., 1937-72, dir. div. phys. therapy, 1943-62; co-op. orthopaedic surgeon crippled children's div. N.C. Bd. Health; also vocational rehab. div. N.C. Dept. Pub. Instrn., 1937-74; orthopaedist Lincoln Hosp., 1937-74, trustee, 1939-74, exec. com., 1941-74, chmn. exec. com., 1951-74; vis. orthopaedist Watts Hosp., 1937—; faculty div. pub. health and soc. work U. NC., 1938-41; med. dir. Lenox Baker Children's Hosp. N.C., Durham, 1949-72; mem. gov.'s cabinet, sec. human resources, State of N.C., 1972; orthopaedic cons. to several hosps., founds., sanitaria, govtl. agys.; active in cerebral palsy work; mem. N.C. Bd. Health, 1956-72, pres., 1963-68, v.p., 1968-72. Author: Treatment of Minor Injuries of Baseball Bone Tumors, 1952, (with others) History of Medicine in North Carolina, 1972; Mem. editorial com.: Jour. Bone and Joints

Surgery, 1960-61; trustee, 1967—; Contbr. articles to profl. publs. Recipient U.S. President's Physician's award, 1958; Citizenship award Triangle chpt. Nat. Football Hall of Fame, 1969; Am. Legion 50th Anniversary Physician of Half-Century award, 1969; Service to Athletics award Atlantic Coast Sportswriters, 1970; Derby Day Dedication award Sigma Chi, 1983; N.C. Gov.'s Baseball award, 1979; named to Duke U. Sports Hall of Fame, 1979, N.C. Sports Hall of Fame, 1983. Mem. AMA (chmn. orthopaedic sect. 1958-59), and other nat., regional, state, local profl. and sci. orgns., including, Am. Acad. Cerebral Palsy (pres. 1954-55), Am. Orthopaedic Assn. (pres. 1963-64), So. Med. Assn. (editorial com. 1960—, past. chmn. orthopaedic sect.), Med. Soc. N.C. (pres. 1959), Tex. Orthopaedic Assn. (hon.), Internat. Cerebral Palsy Soc. (spl. mem.), Guatemala Orthopaedic Assn. (hon.), N.C. Geneal. Soc. (dir. 1974-76, v.p. 1978, pres. 1982-83), Friends of Archives of N.C. (pres. 1980—), Soc. of the Cincinnati, Kappa Sigma, Nu Sigma Nu, Alpha Omega Alpha. Presbyterian. Clubs: Hope Valley Country (Durham, N.C.); Sertoma (hon.). Home: 1 Hastings in the Valley Durham NC 27707 Office: Duke Hosp Box 3706 Durham NC 27710 *Every man you meet is your superior in some fashion. Recognize and appreciate him as such.*

BAKER, LEONARD MORTON, manufacturing company executive; b. Medford, Mass., Oct. 2, 1934; s. Abraham and Sarah B.; m. Ruth Lee Edelstein, June 15, 1958; children: Charles Harold, Andrew Mark, Douglas Jon. B.S. in Chemistry, Harvard U., 1956; Ph.D. in Phys.-Organic Chemistry, Mass. Inst. Tech., 1960. With Union Carbide Corp., 1959—, asso. dir. then dir. research and devel., 1969-77, v.p. research and devel., N.Y.C., 1977-80, v.p., gen. mgr. coatings materials div., 1980-82, v.p. splty. chems. div., 1982-84, corporate dir. tech., 1984—. Exec. bd. Cornell Inst. Biotech.; mem. sci. adv. com. MIT. Mass. Inst. Tech. fellow, 1956-57; NSF fellow, 1957-58; Sun Oil Corp. fellow, 1958-59. Mem. Am. Chem. Soc., Nat. Paint and Coatings Assn., Am. Inst. Chem. Engrs., Indsl. Research Inst., Council Chem. Research, Sigma Xi. Home: 60 Lyons Plains Rd Westport CT 06880 Office: Old Ridgebury Rd Danbury CT 06817

BAKER, LEONARD STANLEY, author; b. Pitts., Jan. 24, 1931; s. Charles and Bess (Schwartz) B.; m. Florence (Liva) Weil, Aug. 1, 1958; children: David, Sara. B.A., U. Pitts., 1952; M.S., Columbia U. Grad. Sch. Journalism, 1955. Reporter St. Louis Globe-Democrat, 1955-56; Washington reporter Newsday, 1956-65; author, editor, lectr., 1965—; vis. prof. U. Louisville, Boston U., George Washington U. Author: The Johnson Eclipse, 1966, Back to Back, 1967, The Guaranteed Society, 1968, Roosevelt and Pearl Harbor, 1970, Brahmin in Revolt, 1972, John Marshall—A Life in Law, 1974, Days of Sorrow and Pain—Leo Baeck and the Berlin Jews, 1978, Brandeis and Frankfurter—A Dual Biography, 1984. Served with U.S. Army, 1952-54. Recipient Pulitzer Prize for Biography, 1979; Gold medal Leo Baeck Inst., 1979. Jewish. Home and Office: 3737 Massachusetts Ave NW Washington DC 20016

BAKER, MALCOLM FREDERIC, protective service and products company executive; b. Worcester, Mass., June 7, 1942; s. Solomon Ruben and Rebecca (Darwin) B.; m. Norma Mae Siegel, Sept. 14, 1969; children: Randal Edward, Eric Howard. A.B., Stanford U., 1964; M.B.A., Columbia U., 1967. With Baker Industries, Inc., Parsippany, N.J., 1967—, exec. v.p., 1974-75, pres., 1975—. Treas. Nat. Soc. Autistic Children. Mem. Stanford U. Alumni Assn. Office: 1633 Littleton Rd Parsippany NJ 07054

BAKER, MARGERY CLAIRE, journalist; b. N.Y.C., May 5, 1948; d. Robert Charles and Elizabeth Madeline (Schiro) B. A.B., Barnard Coll., 1970; M.S., Columbia U., 1971. Asso. producer CBS News, N.Y.C., 1971-73, field producer, Los Angeles, 1973-76, broadcast producer, N.Y.C., 1976-78, v.p. public affairs broadcasts, 1978-82, sr. broadcast producer, 1982—; Office alumni bd. Columbia U. Grad. Sch. Journalism. Mem. Nat. Acad. TV Arts and Scis., Internat. Radio and TV Soc. Club: Quaker Ridge Golf (Scarsdale, N.Y.). Office: 524 W 57th St New York NY 10019

BAKER, MARILYN, TV journalist; b. San Francisco, Sept. 13, 1929; d. Charles Alfred Mansfield; children—Jeffrey, Christopher. Grad. high sch. Reporter Los Angeles Examiner, 1945-49; editor The Spectator, Los Angeles and Beverly Hills, 1949-59; news dir. Cameron Broadcasting, Los Angeles and Palm Springs, 1968-70; TV newswoman KQED-TV, San Francisco, 1970-74; investigative journalist, founder first investigative unit in local TV news sta. KPIX-TV, San Francisco, 1974—. (Emmy for investigative reporting 1974, Emmy awards for feature reporting 1975, 77); Author: Exclusive! The Inside Story of Patty Hearst and the SLA, 1974. Mem. Civic Com. to Restructure the Voters Handbook, 1974—; Bd. dirs. Chinese Youth Affirmative Action, 1974—. Recipient Outstanding Investigative Reporting award U. Calif., 1973, Certificate of Honor for outstanding journalism San Francisco Bd. Suprs., 1973, 76, award for outstanding achievement San Francisco chpt. United Jewish Women's Council, 1973, Distinguished Service medallion San Francisco chpt. Nat. Acad. TV Arts and Scis., 1973; George Foster Peabody nat. award, 1974; Woman of Yr. award San Francisco chpt. Am. Women in Radio and TV, 1974; Columbia-du Pont certificate outstanding journalism, 1975. Mem. Nat. Acad. TV Arts and Scis. (chpt. chmn. journalist com. 1972-75, chpt. gov. 1972—), Daus. Mark Twain. *Freedom of the press is not a "right" of journalists, it is an obligation—and one that cannot be fulfilled by "press conference journalism."*

BAKER, MELVIN C., association executive; b. Sioux City, Iowa, Nov. 9, 1920; s. Robert C. and Louise C. (Moran) B; m. Ann Mead Payne, July 10, 1943; children: Michael, Deborah, Alison, Mark, John, Geoffrey, Courtney. Student, U. S.D., 1939; B.S., Northwestern U., 1946; grad., Advanced Mgmt. Program, Harvard, 1959. Advt. exec. Procter & Gamble Co., 1946-54; with Gen. Foods Corp., 1954-68, v.p., gen. mgr., 1964-67, v.p. mktg., 1968; v.p., dir. Thomas J. Lipton, Inc., 1968-69; v.p., pres. gen. edn. div. (N.Am.) FAS Internat., Inc., N.Y.C., 1969-71; sr. asst. postmaster gen. U.S. Postal Service, Washington, 1971-73; pres. Mktg. Services Inc., Washington, 1973-79; v.p. Am. Advt. Fedn., 1979-81, sr. v.p., 1981—. Served to lt. USNR, 1941-45. Home: 2500 Wisconsin Ave Washington DC

BAKER, MERL, university administrator; b. Cadiz, Ky., July 11, 1924; s. Jesse F. and Argie (Coyle) B.; m. Emily Wilson, Sept. 14, 1946; children: Merl Wilson, Marilyn Ruth. B.S. in Mech. Engring., U. Ky., 1945; M.S., Purdue U., 1948, Ph.D., 1952. Grad. asst. Purdue U., 1946-48; mem. faculty U. Ky., 1948-63, prof. mech. engring., 1955-63; exec. dir. Ky. Research Found., 1953-63; coordinator, dir. U. Ky. coop. programs with AID, 1956-63, exec. dir. research and relations with industry, 1957-63; dean U. Mo. Sch. Mines and Metallurgy, 1963; chancellor U. Mo., Rolla, 1964-73, spl. asst. to pres. statewide system, 1973-77; coordinator energy conservation program Oak Ridge Nat. Lab., 1977-79, energy mgmt. specialist, 1979-82; provost U. Tenn.-Chattanooga, 1982—. Vice pres. Blue Grass council Boy Scouts Am., 1958-62; chmn. adv. bd. U. Ky. YMCA, 1957-58. Decorated Order St. John of Jerusalem-Knights Hospitaller of Malta; Pi Tau Sigma Gold medal award ASME, 1953; Disting. Engring. Alumnus award Purdue U., 1965; Disting. Alumnus Award U. Ky., 1968. Mem. ASME, AIME, ASHRAE (award of merit teaching 1959, chmn. edn. com. 1960-61, Disting. Service award 1971), Am. Soc. Engring. Edn. (pres. S.E. sect. 1956-57, chmn. Internat. edn. com. 1961-63, exec. bd., chmn. engring. coll. research council com. on research adminstrn. 1963-66), Am. Soc. Engring. Mgmt., Nat. Soc. Profl. Engrs., Ky. Acad. Sci., Newcomen Soc. N.Am., Lamp and Cross, Blue Key, Scabbard and Blade, Sigma Xi, Phi Kappa Phi, Phi Eta Sigma, Tau Beta Pi, Pi Tau Sigma, Sigma Pi Sigma, Omicron Delta Kappa, Chi Epsilon. Clubs: Rotary (Lexington, Ky.) (v.p. 1962-63); Cosmos (Washington); Mo. Athletic (St. Louis). Home: 110 Cumberland View Dr Oak Ridge TN 37830 Office: U Tenn Office of Provost Chattanooga TN 37402

BAKER, MICHAEL HARRY, chemical engineer; b. Roanoke, Va., Oct. 25, 1916; s. Samuel A. and Freda (Herman) B.; m. Margaret E. Zanger, 1940 (dec. Sept. 1973); children: Ellen, Martha, Zachary; m. Rosalyn Amdur, Mar. 23, 1975. B.Chem. Engring., Pratt Inst., 1938; postgrad., Va. Poly. Inst., 1939-40, U. Md., 1940-41. Chem. engr. Norfolk (Va.) Waterworks, 1938-39, Seagram, Ltd., Balt., 1940-43, Davison Chem. Corp., 1943-47, Gen. Mills Research Labs., 1947-51; pres. M.H. Baker Co. div. Chem/Serv, Inc., 1952-80, chmn., 1980—; Chmn. Minn. chpt. Am. Technion Soc., 1975-78, nat. dir., 1977—. Co-author: Successful Commercial Chemical Development; Former editor: Minn. Chemist; editor: The Chem. Distbr; former editorial dir.: Minn. Engr; editorial bd.: Identity; Contbr. articles to profl. jours. Chmn. Jewish Vocat. Services com., 1974-78; bd. dirs. Nat. Jewish Council Vocat. Services, 1974—, Jewish Family and Children's Service Minn., 1975-79; founding mem. Mpls. Jewish Community Center; Yiddish tchr. Talmud Torah of Mpls. Fellow AAAS; mem. Minn. Fedn. Engring. Soc. (chmn. 1962-63, dir.), Am. Chem. Soc. (past chmn. Minn., chmn. 17th Gt. Lakes regional meeting 1983), AAAS, Minn. Acad. Scis. (pres. elect 1971, pres. 1972-73, dir.), Am. Inst. Chem. Engr. (past chmn. Twin Cities), Mpls. Engrs. Club (program chmn., dir.), Minn. Indsl. Chemists Forum (past pres.), TAPPI, Inst. Food Technologists (nat. councillor 1964-70, chmn. com. on profl. relations and status), Fedn. Soc. Coatings Tech., Comml. Chem. Devel. Assn. (founding mem., past dir.), Chem. Marketing Research Assn. (founding mem., past dir.), Am. Soc. Oenologists, Nat. Assn. Chem. Distbrs. (exec. com.; editor The Chem. Distbr. 1978-80, editorial bd. 1980—), Am. Soc. Cereal Chemists, Fedn. Am. Scientists, Mfrs. Agts. Nat. Assn., Minn. China Council, Asia Soc. Clubs: Campus (Mpls.); Chemists (N.Y.). Home: 2012 Girard Ave S Minneapolis MN 55405 Office: 207 NE 6th St Minneapolis MN 55413 *It is important to help others realize their capabilities for leadership and to promote their increasing involvement in those activities which will help them grow.*

BAKER, NORMAN HENDERSON, association executive; b. Weston, Ohio, July 24, 1917; s. Roscoe Conklin and Ama Belle (Henderson) B.; m. Jane Marie Wilson, Dec. 8, 1945; children: Janice Marie Cook, Donald William, Barbara Louise Hayes. Ph.B., U. Toledo, 1939; M.A., U. Cin., 1941. Adminstrv. asst., editor Cin. Yearbook, 1939-40; sub-unit chief aircraft scheduling unit WPB, Dayton, Ohio, 1941; adminstrv. analyst Ohio C. of C., Columbus, 1946-48; research dir. Syracuse (N.Y.) Govtl. Research, Inc., 1949-51, N.J. Taxpayers Assn., Trenton, 1952-61; taxation and research dir., then adminstrv. v.p. Ohio C. of C., 1962-73, exec. v.p., 1974-78, life dir., 1979—; former mem. exec. com. Council State C. of C.; bd. dirs. C. of C. Execs. Ohio, Ohio Trade Assn. Execs. Pub. mem. Ohio Adv. Council Vocat. Edn.; bd. dirs. Ohio Council Econ. Edn., Central Ohio Center Econ. Edn. Served to maj. USMCR, 1942-45. Presbyterian. Club: Kiwanis. Home: 2711 Folkstone Rd Columbus OH 43220 *I have tried to live up to the belief that the world would quickly cure its ills if, all at once, everyone started minding his own business, stopped filching from others, and turned in a full day's work.*

BAKER, NORMAN HODGSON, JR., educator; b. Fergus Falls, Minn., Oct. 23, 1931; s. Norman Hodgson and Jeannette (Lieber) B.; m. Doris Blum Nagel, Jan. 16, 1976. B.A., U. Minn., 1952; Ph.D., Cornell U., 1959. Vis. fellow Max-Planck Inst. for Physics and Astrophysics, Munich, Germany, 1959-61; staff scientist Convair Sci. Research Lab., San Diego, 1961; research fellow Goddard Inst. for Space Studies, NASA, N.Y.C., 1961-62; 63-64; mem. Inst. for Advanced Study, Princeton, N.J., 1962-63; vis. lectr. astronomy Yale, New Haven, 1963-64; research asso. physics dept. N.Y. U., 1964-65; asst. prof. dept. astronomy Columbia, N.Y.C., 1965-67, asso. prof., 1967-71, prof., 1971—, chmn. dept., 1972-76. Co-editor: The Astron. Jour, 1967-72, 75-79; editor, 1979—; co-editor: Bull. of Am. Astron. Soc, 1975-79; editor, 1979—. NSF grantee, 1966-79. Mem. Am. Phys. Soc., Am. Astron. Soc., Internat. Astron. Union. Office: Dept Astronomy Columbia U New York NY 10027

BAKER, PAUL, theatre director; b. Hereford, Tex., July 24, 1911; s. William Morgan and Retta (Chapman) B.; m. Sallie Kathryn Cardwell, Dec. 21, 1936; children: Robyn Cardwell, Retta Chapman, Sallie Kathryn. B.A., Trinity U., Waxachie, Tex., 1932, D.F.A. (hon.), 1958; student, U. Wis., 1929; M.F.A., Yale U., 1939; student of Elsie Fogarty,, Central Sch. Speech, London, 1932; studied, observed theatre in Japan. Chief entertainment br. spl. services div. ETO, 1944-45; prof. drama, chmn. dept. Baylor U., 1934-63; dir. Dallas Theatre Center, 1959—; prof. drama, chmn. dept. Trinity U., San Antonio, 1963-77; organized S.W. Summer Theatre, Waco, 1939; mem. Tex. Fine Arts Commn., 1967-68; design cons. Taylor Theater, Trinity U.; mem. Ad Hoc Com. on Profl.-Ednl. Theater Relationships; co-organizer, dir. Arts Magnet High Sch., Booker T. Washington Sch., Dallas Ind. Sch. Dist., 1975—; bd. govs. Am. Playwrights Theater; mng. and artistic dir. Dallas Theater Ctr., 1959-81; prin. Paul Baker Inc., cons., 1981—. Built theatre inside Waco Hall, Baylor U., 1939; designed: Studio I, Baylor U., 1942; dir. exptl. prodn.: Othello, 1953; co-designer: Weston Theatre addition, Baylor Theatre, 1954; dir.: exptl. prodn. A Different Drummer, Baylor U. and CBS-TV, 1955; Hamlet with Burgess Meredith and Charles Laughton, Baylor Theatre, 1956, Journey to Jefferson, Theatre des Nations, Paris, 1964 (recipient Spl. Jury Prize for season); promoted bldg. and founding: Frank Lloyd Theatre, Dallas, 1959; also establishment permanent sch. and repertory co. for Am., Dallas, 1959; author: Integration of Abilities, 1972; chpts. in books. Served to maj. U.S. Army, 1943-45; ETO. Rockefeller Found. fellow, 1937-39, 41, 46, 59; recipient Rodgers and Hammerstein award for outstanding theatrical contbn. in S.W., 1961. Mem. Nat. Theatre Conf. (pres. 1958-62), S.W. Theatre Conf. (pres. 1956), ANTA (dir. 1967-68), Am. Ednl. Theatre Assn., Tex. Inst. Letters. Presbyn. (past elder). Office: Dallas Theater Center 3636 Turtle Creek Dallas TX 75219

BAKER, PAUL, JR., govt. ofcl.; b. Ashland, Ky., Feb. 10, 1921; s. Paul and Edna M. (Holbrook) B.; m. Iantha Dunton, Mar. 14, 1948; children—Paul Mark, Miriam Anne, Jon Clark. B.A., Washington and Lee U., 1942; B.S., U.S. Mil. Acad., 1945; M.S., N.C. State U., 1952; Ph.D. in Physics, U. Denver, 1966. Commd. 2d lt. U.S. Army, 1945; advanced through grades to col. U.S. Air Force, 1966; staff officer directorate requirements Hdqrs. USAF, 1952-56; chief tech. br. (Hartford area office AEC), 1956-61, faculty, 1961-67, prof. physics, head dept., 1964-65, research asso., 1965, dir. research, 1966-67; chief tech. div. Directorate of Space, Hdqrs. USAF, 1967-71; project mgr. Advanced Research Projects Agy., Office Sec. Def., 1971-75; ret., 1975; systems project mgr. Nuclear Regulatory Commn., Washington, 1975—. Contbr. papers on cosmic ray physics. Mem. AAAS, Phi Beta Kappa, Sigma Xi, Beta Theta Pi. Congregationalist. Home: 4404 Random Ct Annandale VA 22003 Office: Nuclear Regulatory Commn Washington DC 20555

BAKER, PAUL RAYMOND, history educator; b. Everett, Wash., Sept. 28, 1927; s. Loren Robbins and Alma Irene (Ball) B.; m. Elizabeth O. Kemp, Feb. 12, 1972; 1 dau., Alice Elizabeth. A.B., Stanford U., 1949; M.A., Columbia U., 1951; Ph.D., Harvard U., 1960. Staff editor Ency. Americana, N.Y.C., 1952-55; instr., asst. prof. Calif. Inst. Tech., Pasadena, 1960-63; lectr. U. Calif.-Riverside, 1963-64, U. Oreg., Eugene, 1964-65; assoc. prof., prof. history and dir. Am. Civilization Program NYU, 1965—; cons. editor Am. history Holt, Rinehart, Winston, N.Y.C., 1969—. Editor: Views of Society and Manners in America, 1963; gen. editor: American Problem Studies series, 40 vols., 1968—; author: The Fortunate Pilgrams, 1964, Richard Morris Hunt, 1980; compiler: The Atomic Bomb, 1968, The Atomic Bomb, rev. edit., 1976; co-author: The American Experience, 5 vols., 1976, 79. Kennedy traveling fellow Harvard U., 1958-59; NEH fellow, 1982. Mem. Am. Hist. Assn., Am. Studies Assn., Soc. Archtl. Historians, Orgn. Am. Historians, Victorian Soc. in Am., N.Y. Hist. Soc., Columbia U. Seminar in Am. Civilization, Phi Beta Kappa (v.p., pres. Beta of N.Y. 1966-70). Club: Century Assn. (N.Y.C.). Home: 90 Hillside Ave Glen Ridge NJ 07028 Office: Dept History NYU 19 University Pl New York NY 10003

BAKER, PEGGY LAURAYNE, dancer, educator, choreographer; b. Edmonton, Alta., Can., Oct. 22, 1952; d. Murray Frank Robert and Rean Laurayne (Elston) Smith; m. Michael James Baker, Sept. 8, 1971. Student, U. Alta., 1970-71, Sch. of the Toronto Dance Theatre, 1971-75, London Contemporary Dance Theatre, 1974, Martha Graham Sch., 1974-77, Herbert Bergof Studio, 1976-77, others. Faculty Sch. of the Toronto Dance Theatre, 1973-78, Lois Smith Sch. of Dance, Toronto, 1977-79, York U., summers 1978, 79; guest tchr. Sch. of the Royal Winnipeg Ballet, 1979, 80. Dancer, Toronto Dance Theatre, 1972-75, The Marchowsky Co., 1975; dancer, Dancemakers, 1974-80; dir., 1977-80; created roles in works by, Carol Anderson, Anna Blewchamp, Nomi Cohen, David Earle, Janice Hladki, Judith Marcuse, Jennifer Mascall, Donald McKayle, Paula Ravitz, Karen Rimmer, Lar Lubovitch, Charles Moulton; dancer, Lar Lubovitch Dance Co., N.Y.C., 1980—; Choreographer: (with composers) collaborations Dream; original score, Kirk Elliott, 1976, Disc, Michael J. Baker, 1979, The Nightingale, Michael J. Baker, 1979. Can. Council grantee, 1974, 75, 76, 80; recipient Ont. Arts Council Choreographic award, 1979. Office: care Arts Arcadia Assos 853 Broadway Suite 1208 New York NY 10003

BAKER, PHILIP DOUGLAS, foundation executive, former investment banker; b. Los Angeles, Mar. 19, 1922; s. J. Douglas and Alice (Brown) B.; m. Cornelia Draves, July 16, 1955; children: Brinton, Todd, Claudia, Samuel Baker. B.S., UCLA, 1947; M.B.A., U. Calif.-Berkeley, 1948. Asso. with Marshall Plan, Germany, 1948-52; with White, Weld & Co., Inc., N.Y.C., 1952-76, partner, 1960-72, sr. v.p., dir., 1972-76; cons. Nat. Exec. Service Corps, 1978; pres. Insts. of Religion and Health, 1978—; chmn. bd. Found. Religion and Health, 1982—; adj. asso. prof. Grad. Sch. Bus. Adminstrn., NYU, 1964-66. Trustee Valley Hosp. Served to capt. USMCR, 1943-46. Decorated Purple Heart. Mem. Investment Bankers Assn. Am. (pres. 1971—), Securities Industry Assn. (vice chmn. bd. 1972), Bond Club N.Y. Home: 293 Green Ridge Rd Franklin Lakes NJ 07417 Office: 3 W 29 St New York NY 10001

BAKER, R. ROBINSON, surgeon; b. Balt., Dec. 30, 1928; s. Henry Scott and Frances (Robinson) B.; m. Jean Harvey, Sept. 12, 1953; children—Susan, Scott, Robert, Jean. A.B., Johns Hopkins U., 1950, M.D., 1954. Diplomate: Am. Bd. Surgery and Bd. Thoracic Surgery. Intern Johns Hopkins U., 1954-55; sr. asst. surgeon Nat. Heart Inst., 1955-57; asst. resident Johns Hopkins Hosp., 1957-58, resident, 1958-61, chief surg. resident, 1961-62, surgeon-in-charge, 1970—, 1976; prof. surgery Johns Hopkins U., 1967—, prof. oncology, 1975—; mem. (Coop. Lung Cancer Detection Group), 1971—. Recipient grants Am. Cancer Soc., 1966-71, John A. Hartford Found., 1968-73, Upjohn Co., 1973, Sterling-Winthrop Research Inst., 1975—. Fellow A.C.S.; mem. Soc. Univ. Surgeons, Am. Assn. Thoracic Surgery, So. Thoracic Surg. Assn., Soc. Head and Neck Surgeons, AMA, Am., So. surg. assns. Club: Elkridge (Balt.). Home: 8717 McDonogh Rd McDonogh MD 21208 Office: 601 N Broadway Baltimore MD 21205

BAKER, REX GAVIN, JR., lawyer, savings and loan executive; b. Beaumont, Tex., Apr. 22, 1920; s. Rex Gavin and Edna (Heflin) B.; m. Jeannette M. Russell, Sept. 6, 1947; children: Jeannette Baker Masraff, Bess Baker Sharman, Ann Baker Wise, Rex Gavin III. B.A., U. Tex., 1941, LL.B., J.D., 1947. Bar: Tex. 1946. Practice law, Houston, 1947—; ptnr. Berry, Richards & Baker, 1947-57, Roberts, Baker, Richards, Elledge & Heard, 1957-62, Baker & Heard, Houston, 1962-75, Baker, Brown, Sharman, Wise & Stephens, 1974-83, Baker, Brown, Sharman, Wise & Parker, 1983—; past chmn. bd. Southwestern Group Fin., Inc.; dir., past chmn. exec. com. United Savs. Assn. Tex.; pres. Fin. Futures Inc.; pres., dir. Blanca Devel. Co.; past dir. Fed. Home Loan Bank Bd., Little Rock, United Savs. Assn. Tex., Kaneb Services, Inc.; dir. Inter-Am. Savs. & Loan Bank, Caracas, Venezuela.; Past mem., sect. chmn. finance commn. State of Tex. Councilman, Bellaire, Tex., 1948-49; mem. Houston Juvenile Delinquency and Crime Commn., 1955-56, Tex. Hi-Y Council, 1957-61. Past bd. dirs. Houston Bapt. U.; bd. dirs. Holly Hall, Houston Housing Devel. Corp., Inst. Religion, Internat. Crusades; past chmn. U. Tex. Devel. Bd.; bd. dirs. U. Tex. Women's Athletics, McDonald Obs.; pres. U. Tex. Found., past chmn. chancellor's council of univ. Served to lt. USNR, 1942-46. Recipient Disting. Alumnus award U. Tex., 1977. Mem. ABA, Interam. Bar Assn., Tex. Bar Assn., Houston Bar Assn., Nat. Savs. and Loan League (past pres., mem. exec. com, dist. chmn.), Tex. Partners of Alliance with Peru (past chmn. bd.), Inter-Am. Savs. and Loan Union (past pres., mem. exec. com.), Internat. Union Bldg. Socs. and Savs. Assns. (v.p., exec. com.), Kappa Sigma. Baptist (deacon). Clubs: River Oaks, Sugar Creek, Houston, Ramada, Univ., Headliners. Home: 2200 Willowick Apt 6E Houston TX 77027 Office: 1200 Smith Suite 3600 Houston TX 77002

BAKER, RICHARD FRELIGH, microbiology educator; b. Westfield, Pa., Feb. 14, 1910; s. Klein Dante and Elsie Mabel (Freligh) B.; m. Sheila G. Calvert, May 21, 1939 (dec. Mar. 1983); 1 dau., Amerlia M. B.S., Pa. State U., 1932, M.S. in Physics, 1933; Ph.D., U. Rochester, 1937. Postdoctoral fellow U. Minn., Mpls., 1937-38; research assoc. Columbia U., N.Y.C., 1938-39, Johns Hopkins U., Balt., 1939-41; physicist RCA, Princeton, N.J., 1941-47; asst. prof. exptl. medicine U. So. Calif. Med. Sch., Los Angeles, 1947-49, assoc. prof., 1949-58, prof. microbiology, 1958—; sr. assoc. Calif. Inst. Tech., Pasadena, 1952-58, sr. research assoc., 1965-79. Research and publs. on electron microscopy and biophysics, 1940—; mem. editorial bd.: Jour. Ultra Structure Research, 1970—. Mem. Electron Microscope Soc. Am. (charter), Los Angeles Acad. Medicine, Sigma Xi, Sigma Pi Sigma. Home: 1822 West Dr San Marino CA 91108 Office: U So Calif Med Sch 2025 Zonal Ave Los Angeles CA 90033

BAKER, RICHARD JOINT, lawyer, insurance executive; b. Barre, Mass., June 4, 1931; s. Merton Orrin and Alice Eleanor (Blanchard) B.; m. Carol Hazel Schotte, Apr. 7, 1956; children: Laurie Ann, Richard Joint, Scott Charles. Student, Oberlin Coll., 1949-52; B.B.A., Clark U., 1954; J.D., Boston U., 1959. Bar: Mass. 1959, U.S. Supreme Ct. 1969. With State Mut. Life Assurance Co. Am., Worcester, Mass., 1959—, 2d v.p., assoc. gen. counsel, 1970-73, v.p., assoc. gen. counsel, sec., 1973-81, v.p. govt. affairs, sec., 1981—; v.p. govt. affairs SMA Life

Assurance Co., 1981—; chmn. State Mut. Life Assurance Employees Polit. Action Com.; treas. State Mut. Life Assurance Fed. Polit. Action Com.; mem. operating com. Mass. Capital Resource Co. Past chmn. West Boylston Bd. Zoning Appeals; mem. West Boylston Fin. Com., 1980-81; bd. dirs. United Way of Central Mass., 1979-81. Served with U.S. Army, 1954-56. Mem. Health Ins. Assn. Am. (fed. affairs contact), Am. Council Life Ins. (mem. task force on polit. activities), ABA (antitrust, torts and ins. practice sects.), Assn. Life Ins. Counsel, Mass. Bus. Roundtable (deps. policy com.), Clark U. Alumni Assn. (past pres.), Life Ins. Assn. Mass. (exec. com., sec.), Worcester Area C. of C. (public affairs com.). Republican. Congregationalist. Clubs: Torch (dir., past pres.), Worcester Econ., Worcester Country, Masons. Home: 8 Townsend Circle West Boylston MA 01583 Office: 440 Lincoln St Worcester MA 01605

BAKER, RICHARD LEE, soup company executive; b. Canton, Ohio, July 22, 1925; s. Clyde F. and Janet (Bailey) B.; m. Virginia Price, Nov. 19, 1949; children: Virginia Lee, Phyllis, Richard L. A.B., Coll. William and Mary, 1946; J.D., U. Pa., 1950. Bar: Pa. 1950. Assoc. law firm, Phila., 1950-51; atty. Pa. R.R. Co., Phila., 1951-63; exec. asst. Allied Chem. Corp., N.Y.C., 1963-65; various positions legal dept. Campbell Soup Co., Camden, N.J., 1965—, sec., sr. corp. counsel, 1980—; dir., officer various Campbell Soup Co. subs. Contbr. articles to profl. publs. Coodinator Mgmt. Improvement Program Gov., N.J., 1982-83. Mem. ABA, Am. Soc. Corp. Secs. Presbyterian. Home: 101 W Walnut Ave Moorestown NJ 08057 Office: Campbell Soup Co Campbell Pl Camden NJ 08101

BAKER, RICHARD MARK, lawyer; b. Gary, Ind., June 21, 1945; Gerald and Eleanor K. B.; m. Linda Ellen Leib, Mar. 7, 1976; 1 son, Gerald Emery. B.S. with distinction in Bus. Adminstrn, Ind. U.; J.D., Stanford U., 1970. Bar: Calif. bar. Asso. firm Butterworth & Waller, 1971-73; asso. counsel, atty. Union Bank, Los Angeles, 1973-78; gen. counsel, sec., sr. v.p. American City Bank, Los Angeles, 1978-83; gen. counsel, sr. v.p. Imperial Bank, Los Angeles, 1983—. Mem. Los Angeles Bar Assn., Am. Bar Assn., Fin. Lawyers Conf., State Bar of Calif. (mem. fin. instns. com.). Home: 3388 Patricia Ave Los Angeles CA 90064 Office: 9920 S La Cienaga Blvd Inglewood CA 90301

BAKER, RICHARD SOUTHWORTH, lawyer; b. Lansing, Mich., Dec. 18, 1929; s. Paul Julius and Florence (Schmid) B.; m. Marina Joy Vidoli, July 24, 1965; children: Garrick Richard, Lydia Joy. Student, DePauw U., 1947-49; A.B. cum laude, Harvard, 1951; J.D., U. Mich., 1954. Bar: Ohio bar 1957. Since practiced in, Toledo; mem. firm Fuller & Henry (and predecessors), 1956—; Chmn. nat. com. region IV Mich. Law Sch. Fund, 1967-69, mem.-at-large, 1970—. Bd. dirs. Asso. Harvard Alumni, 1970-73. Served with AUS, 1954-56. Recipient awards of merit Ohio Legal Center Inst., 1968, 75. Fellow Am. Coll. Trial Lawyers; mem. Am., Ohio, Toledo bar assns., Phi Delta Theta, Phi Delta Phi. Clubs: Toledo, Harvard (pres. 1968-77), Inverness (Toledo)). Home: 2819 Falmouth Rd Toledo OH 43615 Office: 1200 Edison Plaza Toledo OH 43604

BAKER, RICHARD WHEELER, JR., real estate executive; b. Cambridge, Mass., May 13, 1916; s. Richard Wheeler and Doris (Newberry) B.; m. Rachel Irvin Cooper, Dec. 23, 1940; children—Eileen Elizabeth (now Lady Strathnaver), Richard Wheeler III, John Cooper. Grad., Groton Sch., 1934; B.A. summa cum laude, Yale U., 1938, Advanced Mgmt. Program, Harvard, 1957. Tchr. St. Paul's Sch., 1939-41; asst. to personnel dir. Mut. Life Ins. Co. of N.Y., 1946-49, gen. asst., 1949-54; adminstrv. asst. N.Y. Life Ins. Co., 1954-55, exec. asst., 1955-56, asst. v.p., 1956-58, 2d v.p., 1958-61, v.p., 1961-69; sr. v.p. finance, dir. Property Devel. Group, Inc., Ann Arbor, 1969-73; trustee Bklyn. Savs. Bank; chmn. First Pa. Mortgage Trust, 1974-81; exec. trustee Instnl. Investors Trust, 1970-83. Vice chmn. Stony Brook dist. com. Boy Scouts Am., 1959-61; mem. Presdl. Task Force on Low Income Housing, 1969; pres. Princeton chpt. Am. Field Service, 1972-73, treas., 1973—; pres. Princeton Battlefield Area Preservation Soc., 1975—; mem. Yale Div. Sch. Assos., 1980-83, Republican County Com., Princeton Twp., 1953-59; capt. Republican County Com., 1960-62; pres. Princeton Young Rep. Club, 1954-56, Princeton Rep. Club, 1956-59, 73-75; chmn. citizen's adv. com. Princeton Twp. Plan Bd., 1958-60; mem. Princeton Borough Rep. Com., 1974-81; Chmn. bd. trustee's Princeton Country Day Sch., 1958-62; vice chmn. Princeton Day Sch., 1962-63; trustee Princeton Hosp., 1964-72; bd. dirs. Yale Alumni Fund, 1968-73. Served to lt. comdr. USNR, 1941-46; capt. Res. Mem. Life Ins. Assn. Am., Am. Life Conv. (chmn. joint sub-coms. housing and mortgage lending policy of both 1965-68), Mortgage Bankers Assn. (vice chmn. research com. 1964-67), English Speaking Union (dir. Princeton br. 1974-83, pres. 1979-81, exec. dir. 1981-83), Archaeol. Inst. Am. (treas. 1980-83), Hist. Soc. Princeton (dir. 1977-80), Berzelius, Phi Beta Kappa. Episcopalian (vestry 1952-55). Clubs: Elizabethan (New Haven); Pretty Brook (Princeton). Address: 1 Armour Rd Princeton NJ 08540

BAKER, ROBERT ALLEN, JR., psychologist, educator; b. Blackford, Ky., June 27, 1921; s. Robert Allen and Audrey Belle (Thurmond) B.; m. Rose Elizabeth Paalz, Aug. 8, 1953; children: Kathryn, Michael, Robert, Carol, John, Belinda. B.S., U. Ky., 1948, M.S., 1949; Ph.D., Stanford U., 1951. Staff scientist Mass. Inst. Tech., 1951-53; research scientist Human Resources Research Office, Ft. Knox, Ky., 1953-56, sr. staff scientist, 1956-60, group leader, 1960-69; chmn. dept. psychology U. Ky., Lexington, 1969—; cons. Lincoln Lab., MIT, 1951-53; prof. Chico State Coll., 1950, U. Ind. S.E. Campus, 1964-69; cons. Ky. Dept. Mental Health, VA, Ky. Bur. Corrections. Author: Miniature Armor Battlefield, 1960, Tank Commander's Guide, 3 edits, 1958-63, Psychology in the Wry, 1963, Stress Analysis of A Strapless Evening Gown, 1963, Psychology for Man, 1982. Served with USAAF, 1942-45; ETO. Fellow Am. Psychol. Assn.; mem. Midwestern Psychol. Assn., Ky. Psychol. Assn. (pres.), Psychonomic Soc., So. Soc. for Philosophy and Psychology, U.S. Armor Assn., Sigma Xi. Club: Torch. Home: 3495 Castleton Way N Lexington KY 40502

BAKER, ROBERT ANDREW, environmental research scientist; b. Lakewood, Ohio, Sept. 8, 1925; s. Andrew J. and Anna M. B.; m. Peggy Plummer, Mar. 22 1947. B.CH.E., N.C. State U., 1949; M.CH.E., Villanova U., 1955, M.S., 1958; D.Sc., U. Pitts., 1969. Sr. chem. engr. Atlantic Refining Co., Phila., 1949-57; sr. staff engr. Franklin Inst., Phila., 1957-64; sr. fellow Mellon Inst., Pitts., 1964-70; dir. environ. systems group Teledyne-Brown Engring. Co., Huntsville, Ala., 1970-73; regional research hydrologist U.S. Geol. Survey, NSTL Sta., Miss., 1973—; cons. to indsl. firms and govt. agys., 1957—; lectr. Villanova (Pa.) U., 1959-63; guest lectr. seminars various colls. and univs., 1959-81. Participant radio and TV interview and documentary programs, 1957-70; author: Contaminants and Sediments, vols. I and 2, 1980; contbr. articles to profl. jours.; patentee in field; developer methods of sampling and storage of gaseous samples in polymeric films, methods of testing for trace contamination of water. Served with USAAF, 1943-45. Named Engr. of Distinction Engrs. Joint Council, 1970; recipient Max Hecht award, 1968; named Outstanding Chem. Engring. Alumnus Villanova U., 1982. Fellow AAAS, Am. Inst. Chem. Engrs. (mem. exec. com. environ. div. 1975-81), ASTM (vice chmn. com on water 1958-69, Merit award 1967); mem. Am. Chem. Soc. (councillor Disting. service award environ. div. 1978), Internat. Assn. Water Pollution Research and Control (ACS del. USA nat. com.), Miss. Water Pollution Control Assn., Am. Water Works Assn. (mem. research com. on organics 1976-81), Sigma Xi, Phi Eta Sigma, Gamma Sigma Epsilon. Office: US Geol Survey Gulf Coast Hydrosci Cr NSTL Station MS 39529

BAKER, ROBERT CARL, food science educator, consultant; b. Newark, N.Y., Dec. 29, 1921; s. Edward William and Francis Ellen (Houghtaling) B.; m. Jcoba Petronella Munson, Oct. 7, 1944; children: Dale, Hermit, Regina, Maureene, Johanna. B.S., Cornell U., 1943; M.S., Pa. State U., 1949; Ph.D., Purdue U., 1956. Asst. county agt. Orange County 4-H, 1945-46; asst. prof. poultry husbandry Pa. State U., 1946-49; asst. prof. poultry ext. Cornell U., Ithaca, N.Y., 1949-53, assoc. prof., 1953-56, prof. food sci., 1970—, dir. Inst. Food Sci., 1956-70, chmn. dept. poultry sci., 1980—; cons. food cos. Contbr. numerous articles to sci. jours. Pres. Lansing Retirement Authority, Ithaca, N.Y. Methodist. Home: 1106 Auburn Rd Groton NY 13073 Office: Cornell U 200 Rice Hall Ithaca NY

BAKER, ROBERT EDWARD, financial corporation executive, lawyer; b. Albion, Mich., May 6, 1930; s. Robert Charles and Loretto A. (Barrett) B.; m. Mary Anne Mulcahy, Feb. 20, 1965. B.B.A., U. Mich., 1952, LL.B., 1955. Bar: Mich. 1956. Atty. legal dept. Chrysler Corp., Detroit, 1955-64; with Chrysler Fin. Corp., 1964—, dir., Troy, Mich., 1969—, v.p. corp. fin., 1970-80, v.p. fin., gen. counsel, 1980—; dir. Mich. Nat. Bank-N. Metro, Troy, Mich., 1979—, Am. Fin. Services Assn., 1972—, chmn. exec. com., 1983-84, pres. assn., 1978-79. Trustee Comprehensive Health Services of Detroit, 1972—, chmn. bd., 1977—. Served with CIC AUS, 1955-57. Recipient Disting. Service award Am. Fin. Services Assn., 1981. Mem. ABA, State Bar Mich., Detroit Bar Assn., Fin. Execs. Inst. Democrat. Roman Catholic. Club: Orchard Lake Country (Mich.). Home: 4327 Stoneleigh Rd Bloomfield Hills MI 48013 Office: Chrysler Pin Corp 900 Tower Dr Troy MI 48098

BAKER, ROBERT ERNEST, JR., found. exec.; b. Tuscaloosa, Ala., Oct. 17, 1916; s. Robert Ernest and Faye (Whitson) B.; m. Billye Louise Driskell, June 25, 1947; 1 son, Brent Driskell. B.S. in Indsl. Engring, U. Ala., 1939. C.P.A.; registered profl. engr., Tex. Indsl. engring., mgmt. and fin. cons., 1939-62; exec. adminstr., sec. Moody Found., Galveston, Tex., 1962—; dir. Moody Nat. Bank, Galveston, Gal-Tex Hotel Corp. Mem. Houston Soc. Fin. Analysts. Presbyterian. Club: Arty. (Galveston). Home: 6 Adler Circle Galveston TX 77550 Office: Moody National Bank Bldg: Galveston TX 77550

BAKER, ROBERT FRANCIS, pub. co. exec.; b. Lyons, N.Y., Nov. 3, 1935; s. Harold Smith and Zenade Cecil (Gillespie) B.; m. Carol Lee Seaver, Nov. 18, 1961; children—Charles Robert, Elizabeth Marie, Matthew Thomas. B.S., State U. N.Y. at Brockport, 1957; M.S., Bowling Green State U., 1958; Ed.D., U. Cal. at Los Angeles, 1961. Contractors overseas rep. Peace Corps, Nigeria, 1961-64; asso. dir. tng. for Africa, Washington, 1964-66; gen. mgr. ednl. systems div. Litton Industires, N.Y.C., 1966-67; publisher ednl. media Am. Book Co., N.Y.C., 1967-70; v.p. planning and bus. devel. edn. group Xerox Corp., Stamford, Conn., 1970-71; pres., chief exec. officer Ginn & Co., Lexington, Mass., 1971—. Mem. adv. bd. NAACP Legal Def. and Ednl. Fund, Inc., Hammond Mus.; bd. visitors Grad. Sch. Edn. U. Calif., Los Angeles. Mem. Assn. Am. Pubs. Office: Ginn and Co 191 Spring St Lexington MA 02173

BAKER, ROBERT J(OHN), hospital administrator; b. Detroit, Feb. 2, 1944; s. Wesley Ries and Irma Louise (Richards) B.; m. Priscilla Horschak, Sept. 10, 1966; children: Scott, Katherine. B.A., Kalamazoo Coll., 1966; M.B.A., U. Chgo., 1968. Adminstr. Indian Hosp., Sells, Ariz., 1968-70; asst. dir. U. Minn. Hosp., Mpls., 1970-73, assoc. dir., 1973-74, assoc. dir. ops., 1974-77, sr. assoc. dir., 1977; dir. U. Nebr. Hosp. and Clinic, Omaha, 1977—. Chmn. Heartland chpt. ARC, Omaha, 1983; clk. of session Presbyterian Ch. of Cross, Omaha, 1983. Served with USPHS, 1968-70. Recipient Mary H. Bachmeyer award U. Chgo., 1968; Carl A. Erickson fellow, 1966. Mem. Consortium for Study Univ. Hosps. (vice chmn. 1983), Council Teaching Hosps., Omaha-Council Bluffs Hosp. Assn. (pres. 1983). Office: U Nebr Hosp and Clinic 42d and Dewey Ave Omaha NE 68105

BAKER, ROBERT LEON, naval med. officer; b. Oak, Nebr., Feb. 7, 1925; s. Oscar E. and Ada Veru (Davis) B.; m. Rebecca Chandler, Dec. 12, 1956; children—Jay Milton, Rebecca Ann, Betsy Jean, Robert Leon, Bruce Chandler, Brenda Carole. B.S. in Liberal Arts, La. Poly. Inst., 1945, U. Ark., 1949, M.D., 1949; grad. program health systems mgmt., Harvard U. Grad. Sch. Bus., 1972. Diplomate: Am. Bd. Obstetrics and Gynecology. Apprentice seaman U.S. Navy, 1943, commd. lt. j.g., M.C., 1949, advanced through grades to rear adm., 1973; rotating intern Tripler Gen. Hosp., Honolulu, 1949-50; resident in obstetrics and gynecology U.S. Naval Hosp., Oakland, Calif., 1954; assigned U.S. and overseas as obstetrician-gynecologist; chmn. dept. obstetrics and gynecology Naval Hosp., Portsmouth, Va., 1969-72; dir. grad. tng. and chmn. dept. OB-GYN Naval Regional Med. Center, Oakland, 1973-75; comdg. officer Naval Regional Med. Center, Phila., 1975-77, Naval Aerospace and Regional Med. Center, Pensacola, Fla., 1977-79; chief ob-gyn service Baxter Gen. Hosp., Mountain Home, Ark., 1980—; clin. prof. Va. Commonwealth U. Med. Sch., 1971—. Contbr. articles to med. jours. Bd. dirs. Phila. YMCA, 1975-77, Phila. USO, 1976-77. Decorated Legion of Merit, Meritorious Service medal, Navy Commendation medal. Fellow Am. Coll. Obstetricians and Gynecologists (chmn. armed forces dist. Navy sect. 1967-69, vice-chmn. armed forces dist. 1971-74, asst. sec. 1977-79); mem. Assn. Mil. Surgeons U.S. (chpt. pres. 1973-74), AMA, Alpha Omega Alpha, Phi Chi. Mem. Christian Ch. (Disciples of Christ). Club: Union League (Phila.). Home: Box 44 Mountain Home AR 72653 Office: 10 Medical Plaza Mountain Home AR 72653 *Time is critical for top management. It is divided into People time and Paper time. People time, almost invariably, must take precedence at any moment, but paper time still demands and must be accomplished. People time demonstrates concern. This perception by people of concern by management is the essential element of true leadership, and the essence of morale. One who can follow this precept while, at the same time completing paper work, is a top manager. This takes time.*

BAKER, ROBERT MAURICE, manufacturing company executive; b. Odessa, Mo., Feb. 11, 1928; s. William F. and Lillian L. B.; m. Marilyn D. Strode, Feb. 2, 1979; children—Deborah E., James E., Richard M., Ross A., Michelle L. B.S. in Bus. Adminstrn, Central Mo. State Coll., 1951. C.P.A., Mo. Audit mgr. Arthur Andersen & Co., C.P.A.s, St. Louis, 1951-63; treas. Angelica Corp., St. Louis, 1963—. Active local Boy Scouts Am., 1966-72; chmn. com. Sing-Out Florissant Valley, 1971-75. Served with AUS, 1946-47. Mem. Tax Execs. Inst. (officer St. Louis chpt. 1983—). Methodist. Home: 242 Pennington Ln Chesterfield MO 63017 Office: 10176 Corporate Square Dr St Louis MO 63132

BAKER, ROBERT STEVENS, educator, organist; b. Pontiac, Ill., July 7, 1916; s. Stevens R. and Hattie (Thrasher) B.; m. Mary F. Depler, June 24, 1943; children: James S., Martha Faye. B.Mus., Ill. Wesleyan U., 1938, Mus.D., 1960; Sacred Mus.M., Union Theol. Sem., 1940, Sacred Mus.D., 1944; L.H.D., Bradley U., 1964; D.F.I., Westminster Choir Coll., 1966; D. Mus. A., Susquehanna U., 1967; M.A., Yale U., 1973. Dean Sch. Sacred Music, Union Theol. Sem., 1961-72; dir. Yale U. Inst. Music and Worship, 1973-75, prof. organ, 1973—; Bd. dirs. Union Theol. Sem., 1959-61; trustee Westminster Choir Coll., 1968-72; chmn. organ award com. Inst. Internat. Edn., 1957-59, 63, 65, 66, 75. Organist, choirmaster, 1st Presbyn. Ch., Bklyn., 1941-53, Temple Emanu-El, N.Y.C., 1945-61, Fifth Ave. Presbyn. Ch., N.Y.C., 1953-61, St. James Episcopal Ch., N.Y.C., 1972-74, 1st Presbyn. Ch., N.Y.C., 1975—; concert organist, 1945—; recitalist, Westminster Abbey, 900th Anniversary, 1966; organ bldg. cons. Mem. Am. Guild Organists (dean N.Y.C. chpt. 1955-57, nat. councillor 1950-57, 72-75, chmn. nat. conv. 1956, rep., opening recitalist 1st Internat. Congress Organists, London 1957, recitalist nat. convs. 1947, 56), Hymn Soc. Am. (dir. 1961-75), Bohemians, St. Wilfrid Soc., Oratorio Soc. N.Y. (dir.), Coll. Ch. Musicians (dir.). Home: 84 Jesswig Dr Hamden CT 06517 Office: 409 Prospect St New Haven CT 06510

BAKER, ROBERT THOMAS, interior designer; b. Kansas City, Mo., Mar. 23, 1932; s. Robert Blume and Justina (Early) B. B.A. in Art, U. Mo., Columbia, 1954, M.A. in Interior Design, 1962; cert., Parsons Sch. Design, N.Y.C., 1958. Interior designer Edward Keith, Inc., Kansas City, Mo., 1958-60, 63-71, Nereoux Interiors, New Iberia, La., 1960-61, Bloomingdales, N.Y.C., 1962-63, Thomas Price Interiors, Kansas City, Mo., 1971-78; owner Robert Baker Interiors Inc., Kansas City, 1978—; mem. guidance com. Found. Interior Designer Edn. Research, 1972—. Served with USAAF, 1954-57. Award of merit Mo.W./Kans. chpt., 1971. Fellow Am. Soc. Interior Designers (pres. Mo.W./Kans. chpt. 1966-69, 73-74, regional v.p. 1969-71, nat. gov. 1969-74). Republican. Presbyterian. Home: 12801 Cherry St Kansas City MO 64145 Office: 121 E Gregory Kansas City MO 64114

BAKER, ROBERT WILLIAM, educator; b. Brookline, Mass., July 30, 1924; s. Chauncey William and Marion (Power) B.; m. Rita Agnes Knox, Dec. 29, 1951; children—Cheryl Alison, Jeffrey Clark, Susan Knox. A.B., Hobart Coll., 1947; Ph.D., Clark U., 1953. Diplomate: Am. Bd. Profl. Psychology (sub-regional examination coordinator). Staff clin. psychologist VA Hosp., Northampton, Mass., 1953-54; asst. prof. psychology Clark U., Worcester, Mass., 1954-57, asso. prof., 1957-66, prof., 1966—; dir. Psychol. Clinic, 1954-55, 56-65, dean students, 1965-68, asst. provost for student affairs, 1969-70; dir. Psychol. Services Center, 1971—; chmn. univ. faculty, 1972-73. Contbr. articles to profl. jours. Field selection officer Peace Corps, 1964-67; Pres. local chpt. Am. Humanist Assn., 1963-64, Med. Com. for Human Rights, 1965-66; mem. exec. council Worcester Forum Study of Values. Served with USNR, 1943-44. Fellow Am. Psychol. Assn.; mem. ACLU (local exec. com. 1957—, co-chmn. 1971-72, vice chmn. 1974-76), AAUP (com. on acad. freedom and tenure state conf. 1969—, co-chmn. 1972-76, mem. chpt. exec. com., v.p., pres.-elect Mass. conf. 1978-80, pres. Mass. conf. 1980-82). Home: 398 May St Worcester MA 01602

BAKER, ROBERT WOODWARD, airline executive; b. ronxville, N.Y., Sept. 3, 1944; s. Richard Woodward and Dorothy Marilyn (Garett) B.; m. Martha Jane Hauschild, June 11, 1966; children: Richard Woodward, Robert Woodward, William Garrett, Suzanne. B.A., Trinity Coll., 1966; M.B.A., U. Pa., 1968. Dir. ramp services Am. Airlines, Inc., N.Y.C., 1973-76, asst. v.p. mktg. adminstrn., 1976-77; v.p. so. div. Am. airlines, Inc., Dallas, 1977-79; v.p. freight mktg. Am. Airlines, Inc., Dallas-Ft. Worth Airport, 1979-80, v.p. sales and advt., 1980-82, v.p. mktg. auto systems, 1982—. Office: American Airlines Inc MD 5K61 PO Box 619616 Dallas-Fort Worth Airport TX 75261

BAKER, ROLAND JERALD, association executive; b. Pendleton, Oreg., Feb. 27, 1938; s. Roland E. and Thersa Helen (Forest) B.; m. Judy Lynn Murphy, Nov. 24, 1973; children: Kristen L., Kurt F., Brian H. B.A., Western Wash. U., 1961; M.B.A., U. Mich., 1968. Asst. dir. purchasing and stores U. Wash., Seattle, 1970-75; mgr. purchasing and material control Foss Launch & Tug Co., Seattle, 1975-79; mem. faculty Shoreline Community Coll., 1972-79, Edmonds Community Coll., 1974-79, Pacific Luth. U., 1977—; chmn. educators group Nat. Assn. Purchasing Mgmt., N.Y.C., 1976-79, exec. v.p., 1979—. Author: Purchasing Factomatic, 1977, Inventory System Factomatic, 1978, Policies and Procedures for Purchasing and Material Control, 1980. Served with USN, 1961-70; comdr. Res. U.S. Navy postgrad. fellow, 1967. Mem. Purchasing Mgmt. Assn. Wash. (pres. 1978-79), Nat. Minority Supplier Devel. Council (bd. dirs.), Am. Prodn. and Inventory Control Soc., Nat. Assn. Purchasing Mgmt., Nat. Contract Mgmt. Assn., Internat. Fedn. Purchasing and Materials Mgmt., Am. Soc. Assn. Execs. Address: Nat Assn Purchasing Mgmt 11 Park Pl New York NY 10007

BAKER, ROLLIN HAROLD, biologist; b. Cordova, Ill., Nov. 11, 1916; s. Charles Laurence and Minnie Louise (Perkins) B.; m. Mary Elizabeth Waddell, Mar. 21, 1939; children: Elizabeth Alice, Bruce Rollin, Byron Laurence. B.A., U. Tex., 1937; M.S., Tex. A. and M. U., 1938; Ph.D., U. Kans., 1948. Wildife tech. Nat. Park Service, Texas Big Bend, summer 1937; field biologist Tex. Coop. Wildlife Research Unit, College Station, 1938-39; biologist Tex. Game and Fish Commn., 1939-43; asst. curator mammals Mus. Natural History, U. Kans., 1948-55, asst. instr., 1946-48, instr., 1948-49, asst. prof., 1949-54, asso. prof. zoology, 1954-55; acting dir. Mus. Natural History, 1950-51; dir. mus., prof. zoology and fisheries and wildlife Mich. State U., East Lansing, 1955-82, dir., prof. emeritus, 1983—; leader mus. expdns. western states and Mex., for collection and observation animal life, 1949-82; also vis. investigator Rockefeller Inst. Med. Author: Michigan Mammals, 1983; Contbr. articles to profl. jours. Served from ensign to lt. USNR, 1943-46; capt. Res. ret. Fellow AAAS; mem. Am. Soc. Mammalogists (dir. 1956-78), Wildlife Soc., Am. Ornithol. Union, Wilson Ornithol. Union, Soc. Southwestern Naturalists, Soc. Study Evolution, Soc. Systematic Zoology (council 1958-61), Ecol. Soc. Am., Sigma Xi, Alpha Epsilon Delta, Beta Beta Beta, Phi Sigma, Tau Kappa Epsilon, Phi Kappa Phi. Clubs: Explorers, Kiwanis, Mich. Polar-Equator (pres. 1976-78). Home: 302 N Strickland St Eagle Lake TX 77434

BAKER, RONALD DALE, dental educator, surgeon, university adminstrator; b. Pitts., Oct. 20, 1932; s. Dale and Bessie (Lyons) B.; m. Dorothy Sue Casper, Sept. 9, 1967; children: Brian Dale, Bradley Drew. D.D.S. summa cum laude, U. Pitts., 1956; M.A. in Edn., George Washington U., 1974. Diplomate: Am. Bd. Oral and Maxillofacial Surgery. Oral surgeon U.S.S. Sanctuary, Vietnam, 1969-70; dir. oral and maxillofacial surgery residency St. Albans Naval Hosp., N.Y., 1970-71; chmn. oral and maxillofacial surgery dept. Nat. Naval Dental Sch., Bethesda, Md., 1971-74; chmn. oral and maxillofacial surgery dept. Nat. Naval Med. Ctr., Bethesda, Md., 1974-76; prof., chmn. dept. oral and maxillofacial surgery U. N.C. Sch. Dentistry, Chapel Hill, N.C., 1978—; cons. Nat. Naval Med. Ctr., Bethesda, Md., 1977—, Naval Regional Med. Ctr., Camp Lejeune, NC, 1977—, Dorothea Dix Hosp., Raleigh, N.C., 1976—, VA Hosp., Fayetteville, N.C., 1976—. Served to capt. USN, 1956-76. Fellow Am. Coll. Dentistry, Am. Assn. Oral and Maxillofacial Surgeons (del. 1972-74), Internat. Assn. Oral and Maxillofacial Surgeons, Fedn. Dentaire Internat., Pierre Fauchard Acad.; mem. ADA, N.C. Dental Soc., Southeastern Soc. Oral and Maxillofacial Surgeons, Omicron Kappa Upsilon, Phi Eta Sigma, Alpha Omega (scholarship award), Dental Sigma Delta. Home: 622 Wells Ct Chapel Hill NC 27514 Offic: Dept Oral and Maxillofacial Surgery School of Dentistry University of North Carolina Chapel Hill NC 27514

BAKER, RONALD JAMES, educator; b. London, Aug. 24, 1924; s. Herbert James Walter and Ethel (Miller) B.; m. Helen Gillespie Elder, Sept. 3, 1949; children: Ann, Lynn, Ian, Sarah, Katherine; m. Frances

Marilyn Frazer; 1 son, Ralph Edward. B.A., U. B.C., Can., 1951, M.A., 1953; LL.D., U. N.B., Can., 1970, Mt. Allison U., 1977. Lectr. U. B.C., 1951-53, instr., 1953-54, 56-57, asst. prof., 1957-62; resident prof. Prince George, 1960-61, assoc. prof., 1962-64; prof., head dept. English, dir. acad. planning Simon Fraser U., 1964-69; first pres. U. P.E.I., Charlottetown, Can., 1969-78, prof., 1979—; Mem. Acad. Bd. B.C., 1963-69, Joint Bd. Tchr. Edn. B.C., 1964-66; mem. Can. Council, 1971-77, Can. Radio-TV and Telecommunication Commn., 1982—; Bd. govs. N.S. Tech. Coll., Holland Coll., 1969-78. Contbr. articles to profl. jours. Served with RAF, 1943-47. Decorated Centennial medal, 1967; Jubilee medal, 1977; officer Order of Can., 1978. Fellow Royal Soc. Arts; mem. MLA, Assn. Univs. and Colls. Can. (dir. 1972-78), Assn. Atlantic Univs. (pres. 1976-78), Can., Nat. councils tchrs. English, Royal Commonwealth Soc., Can. Soc. for Study Higher Edn. (v.p. 1974, pres. 1975-76), Assn. Can. Univ. Tchrs. English (pres. 1967-68), Can. Linguistic Assn. (exec. 1966-67), Philol. Soc. Address: U PEI Charlottetown PE C1A 4P3 Canada

BAKER, RONALD LEE, folklore educator; b. Indpls., June 30, 1937; s. Delbert Everett and Ellen (Haorison) B.; m. Catherine Anne Neal, Oct. 21, 1960; children: Susannah Hill, Jonathan Kemp. B.S., Ind. State U., Terre Haute, 1960, M.A., 1961; postgrad., U. Ill., 1963-65; Ph.D., Ind U., 1969. Instr. English U. Ill., Urbana, 1963-65; teaching assoc. Ind. U., Ft. Wayne, 1965-66; prof. English Ind State U., Terre Haute, 1966—, chmn. dept., 1966—; vis. lectr. U. Ill., 1972-73; vis. assoc. prof. Ind. U., Bloomington, 1975, vis. prof., 1978. Author: Folklore in the Writings of Rowland E. Robinson, 1973, Hoosier Folk Legends, 1982; (with others) Indiana Place Names, 1975. Mem. Am. Folklore Soc., MLA, Am. Name Soc. (v.p. 198-1-82), Hoosier Folklore Soc. (pres. 1970-79). Democrat. Presbyterian. Home: RD 51 Box 434 Terre Haute IN 47805 Office: Indiana State University Terre Haute IN 47809

BAKER, RUSSELL TREMAINE, JR., lawyer; b. Balt., May 29, 1942; s. Russell Tremaine and Grace (Almond) B.; m. Elizabeth Mason, Sept. 12, 1964; children: Abigail, Richard, Emily. A.B., Williams Coll., 1964; J.D., Harvard U., 1969. Bar: Md. 1970, U.S. Supreme Ct. 1975. Vol. Peace Corps, Ethiopia, 1964-66; law clk. U.S. circuit judge, 1969-70; law clk. to Justice Reed, assigned to Chief Justice Warren Burger, U.S. Supreme Ct., 1970-71; asst. U.S. atty. for Md., 1971-74; assoc. firm Piper & Marbury, Balt., 1974-77, ptnr., 1981—; dep. asst. atty. gen. criminal div. Dept. Justice, Washington, 1977-78; U.S. atty. for Md., Balt., 1978-81. Mem. Md. Bar Assn. Democrat. Home: 10342 Sixpence Circle Columbia MD 21044 Office: 1100 Charles Center South 36 S Charles St Baltimore MD 21201

BAKER, RUSSELL WAYNE, columnist, author; b. Loudoun County, Va., Aug. 14, 1925; s. Benjamin Rex and Lucy Elizabeth (Robinson) B.; m. Miriam Emily Nash, Mar. 11, 1950; children: Kathleen Leland, Allen Nash, Michael Lee. B.A., Johns Hopkins U., 1947, D.Litt.; L.H.D., Hamilton Coll., Franklin Pierce Coll., Princeton U.; LL.D., Union Coll.; D.Litt., Wake Forest U. With Balt. Sun, 1947-54; mem. Washington bur. N.Y. Times, 1954-62; author-columnist editorial page Observer, 1962—. Author: American in Washington, 1961, No Cause for Panic, 1964, All Things Considered, 1965, Our Next President, 1968, Poor Russell's Almanac, 1972, The Upside Down Man, 1977, So This Is Depravity, 1980, (with others) Home Again, Home Again, 1979, Growing Up, 1982, The Rescue of Miss Yaskell and Other Pipe Dreams, 1983. Served with USNR, 1943-45. Recipient Frank Sullivan Meml. award, 1976; George Polk award for commentary, 1979; Pulitzer prize for disting. commentary, 1979; Pulitzer prize for biography, 1983; Elmer Holmes Bobst prize for nonfiction, 1983. Mem. Am. Acad. and Inst. Arts and Letters. Office: 229 W 43d St New York NY 10036

BAKER, SHELDON S., lawyer; b. St. Paul, Dec. 4, 1936; s. Joseph L. and Thelma June (Alford) B.; m. Marilyn Jeanette Netschert, Aug. 16, 1958; children: Curtis Duane, Jon Gregory, Melissa Janel. B.A., Rutgers U., 1958; J.D., Stanford U., 1961. Bar: Calif. 1962; cert. tax specialist Calif. Bar Assn. Practice law, Los Angeles, 1962—; partner firm Halstead, Baker & Olson, 1965—; sec. Joe Baker Bldg. Co., Glendale, Calif., 1959—, also dir. Author: treatise Calif. Inheritance Tax Practice; Contbr. articles to profl. jours. Mem. Glendale Community Coll. Bd. Edn., 1965-81, pres., 1967-68, 71-72, 75-76, 80-81; mem. Glendale Bd. Edn., 1965-81, pres., 1967-68, 72-73, 79-80; mem. adv. council U. So. Calif. Sch. Trustee Acad., 1977; host parent Am. Field Service, 1976-77, 78-79; co-pres. Glendale chpt., 1981-82; mem. exec. bd. Verdugo Hills council Boy Scouts Am., 1965—, pres. council, 1979, scoutmaster, 1972-76; mem. exec. bd. Glendale Area council Girl Scouts Am., 1944-68; pres.-elect Calif. Sch. Bd., 1979, pres., 1980, immediate past pres., 1981; del. assembly Calif. Sch. Bds. Assn., 1969-78, mem. personnel com., 1973-78, chmn. personnel task force, 1978, bd. dirs., 1976-78; bd. dirs. Calif. Community Coll. Trustees Assn., 1979-80; mem. del. assembly Nat. Sch. Bds. Assn., 1979, 80, nominating com., 1981; bd. dirs. Glendale Speech and Hearing Found., 1964-68, Glendale Regional Arts Council, 1974-76, Glendale Coll. Found., 1983, Los Angeles County (Calif.) Sch. Trustees Assn., 1972—; v.p. Los Angeles County (Calif.) Sch. Trustees Assn., 1975-76, pres., 1976-78, exec. bd., 1972-81; bd. dirs. Glendale Edn. Found., 1981. Named one of Five Outstanding Young Men of Calif. Calif. Jr. C. of C., 1964; recipient Silver Beaver award Boy Scouts Am., 1972, Disting. Eagle award, 1980. Mem. Am., Calif., Los Angeles County, Glendale bar assns., Brand Park Property Owners Assn. (chmn. 1971), PTA (hon., life), Order of Coif, Phi Beta Kappa, Delta Upsilon. Clubs: Kiwanian (pres. 1969-70); Verdugo (Glendale) (dir. 1979-82). Office: Suite 1750 615 S Flower St Los Angeles CA 90017 *I try to do the best I can each day to put something back into my community.*

BAKER, SHERIDAN WARNER, JR., educator, author; b. Santa Rosa, Calif., July 10, 1918; s. Sheridan Warner and Juliet (Shaw) B.; m. Helen Elizabeth Barker, Apr. 6. 1946 (div. Aug. 1954); m. Sally Baubie Sandwick, June 17, 1955; children: Elizabeth (Mrs. Karl A. Lagler), Elizabeth, William S. Student, Santa Rosa Jr. Coll., 1935-37; A.B., U. Calif.-Berkeley, 1939, M.A., 1946, Ph.D., 1950. Teaching fellow U. Calif.-Berkeley, 1946-49, lectr., 1949-50, vis. prof., 1970; instr. U. Mich., 1950-57, asst. prof., 1957-61, assoc. prof., 1961-64, prof., 1964—. Author: The Practical Stylist, 1962, The Essayist, 1963, The Complete Stylist, 1966, Ernest Hemingway: An Introduction and Interpretation, 1967, (with I.A. Richards and Jacques Barzun) The Written Word, 1971, (with Northrop Frye and George Perkins) The Practical Imagination, 1980, The Practical Handbook to Literature, 1984; Editor: Mich. Quar. Rev, 1964-71, Henry Fielding's Writings; Contbr.: poems to New Yorker and other mags; also articles on 18th century and modern lit. Bd. judges, ann. Explicator mag. prize, 1965-75; Donor Fund for Ann. Clarence D. Thorpe Dissertation prize, also Louis I. Bredvold Publn. prize U. Mich., 1967. Served to lt. comdr. USNR, 1940-46. Recipient U. Mich. Distinguished Service award, 1960; Fulbright lectr. U. Nagoya, Japan, 1961-62; named in the Top Fifty Living Am. Poets Epoch 15, 1966; Rockefeller Found. fellow, Bellagio, Italy, 1978. Mem. AAUP (pres. Mich. Conf. 1959-60, pres. Mich. chpt. 1972-73), Mich. Acad. Sci., Arts and Letters (pres. 1963-64, editor papers 1954-61), Phi Gamma Delta. Democrat. Episcopalian (vestryman 1966-69, 74-77). Clubs: Flounders (U. Mich.); Racquet. Home: 2866 Provincial Dr Ann Arbor MI 48104

BAKER, STEPHEN, advertising executive; b. Vienna, Austria, Apr.17,1925; s. Oscar and Renee (Lavesky) Bacher; m. Oleda Baker, Oct. 1967; 1 son, Stephen Scott. B.A., William Jewell Coll.; postgrad., N.Y.U., Art Students League. Vice pres. Cunningham & Walsh, 1951-62; pres. Baker & Byrne, 1962-65; pres., dir. Mogul, Baker, Byrne & Weiss, N.Y.C., 1965-69, Baker Hartel, 1969-74; pres. Stephen Baker Assos., 1974—; prof. N.Y.U., 1982, N.Y. Visual Arts, 1982—. Columnist: Ad Age; Author: 19 books. Nominated as Art Dir. of Year, 1961, 63. Mem. N.Y. Art Dirs. Club. Club: Lords Valley Country. Creator "Let Your Fingers Do the Walking" for AT&T. Home: 5 Tudor City Pl New York NY 10017

BAKER, THOMPSON SIMKINS, mining company executive; b. Jacksonville, Fla.., Aug. 25, 1905; s. John Daniel and Julia (Simkins) B.; m. Cynithia L'Engle, Nov. 23, 1931 (dec. Dec., 1967); children: Sarah Church, Edward L'Engle, John Daniel II; m. Sarah Burroughs, Apr. 12, 1970. B.S., Davidson Coll., 1926. With Fla. Rock Industries, Inc.(formerly Shands & Baker, Inc.), Jacksonville, Fla., 1929—; chmn. Fla. Rock Industries, Inc. (formerly Shands & Baker, Inc.), Jacksonville, Fla., 1973—. Home: 3761 Ortega Blvd Jacksonville FL 32210 Office: Florida Rock Industries Inc 155 E 21st St Jacksonville FL 32206

BAKER, TIMOTHY DANFORTH, physician, educator; b. Balt., July 4, 1925; s. Frank and Alice Elizabeth (Chandler) B.; m. Susan Lowell Pardee, June 23, 1951; children: Timothy, David, Susan. B.A., Johns Hopkins U., 1948, M.P.H., 1954; M.D., U. Md., 1952. Health officer, Geneva, N.Y., 1954-56, Syracuse, N.Y., 1958-59; assisting and acting chief health AID, Delhi, 1956-58; assoc. prof. Johns Hopkins U. Sch. Pub. Health, Balt., 1959-67, asst. dean, 1959-77, prof. internat. health and health services adminstrn., 1967—; v.p., dir. Univ. Assocs., 1973-77; vis. prof. epidemiology U. Minn., 1976; dir. Intermed., 1982—; cons. health planning, med. edn., Brazil, India, Indonesia, Taiwan, Saudi Arabia, Kuwait, Md., Calif., D.C. Author: Health Manpower in a Developing Economy, Assessment of Health Status and Needs, International Health Perspectives; contbr. articles to profl. publs. First vice chmn. central com. Republican party, Balt.; del., nominating com. Republican party; bd. dirs., treas. Pan Am. Health Edn. Found. Served with USAF, 1943-45; USPHS, 1956-58. Mem. Am. Pub. Health Assn. (chmn. depidemiology sect., internat. health sect.), Md. Med. Soc. (chmn. health manpower com.), Md. Pub. Health Assn. (pres.), Balt. Med. Soc. (chmn. med. care com.), Omicron Delta Kappa, Delta Omega. Republican. Home: 4705 Keswick Rd Baltimore MD 21210 Office: 615 N Wolfe St Baltimore MD 21205

BAKER, WALLACE RUSSELL, lawyer; b. Chgo., June 11, 1927; s. Russell and Elizabeth (Wallace) B.; m. Miriam Nye Loomis, Apr. 10, 1964; children—Ann Graham, Christopher Loomis, Charles Russell, Jonathan Wallace. A.B., Harvard, 1948, LL.B., 1952; LL.D., U. Brussels, 1961; License en Droit, U. Paris, 1972. Bar: Ill. bar 1952. Partner firm Baker and McKenzie, Chgo., 1953-59, partner in, Brussels, Belgium, 1959-62, resident partner, Paris, France, 1963—; hon. consul of Honduras, Chgo., 1954-56. Author, lectr. in field. Served to 1st lt. AUS, 1944-46. Mem. Am. Bar Assn. Clubs: Mid-Day, University (Chgo.); Lincolns Inn (Cambridge, Mass.); Union Interalliee, Travelers (Paris). Home: 21 rue Monsieur Paris 7 France Office: 94 rue du Faubourg St Honore Paris 8e France

BAKER, WALTER LOUIS, engineering company executive; b. Earlton, N.Y., Aug. 7, 1924; s. Alberti and Louise (Schmidt) B.; m. Janet Katherine Sprague, Sept. 7, 1944 (dec.); children: Walter Kent (dec.), Lawrence Albert, Linda Louise, Louis Milton; m. Marion M. King, July 1, 1976 (dec.); stepchildren: Vinton P. King, John S. King. B.E.E. (N.Y. State scholar, Coll. scholar), Clarkson Coll., 1944; M.S., Pa. State U., 1954. Registered profl. engr., Pa. Tech. supr. Tenn. Eastman Corp., 1944-45; sr. engr. Philco Corp., 1945-49; research asso. Pa. State U., State Coll., from 1949, now prof., sr. mem. grad. faculty, 1965—; pres. Baker Engring. Co., Portsmouth, R.I., 1981—; cons. Spartan Electric Corp., 1960-61, U.S. Marine Corps, 1965, John I. Thompson & Co., 1952-68, HRB-Singer Co., 1958-67, Vitro Corp., 1981, Woods Hole Oceanography Inst., 1981—, Dynamic Systems, Inc., 1980—. Co-author: Acoustic Performance Handbook, 1974; contbr. articles to profl. jours. Recipient U.S. Navy Meritorious Public Service citation. Mem. IEEE (sr., chmn., sec.-treas. Central Pa. sect.), Acoustical Soc. Am., N.Y. Acad. Scis., Sigma Xi. Republican. Methodist. Club: Elks. Address: Baker Engring Co 22 Oliver Hazard Perry Rd Portsmouth RI 02871

BAKER, WARREN J(OSEPH), university president; b. Fitchburg, Mass., Sept. 5, 1938; s. Preston A. and Grace F. (Jarvis) B.; m. Carol Ann Fitzsimons, Apr. 28, 1962; children: Carrie Ann, Kristin Robin, Christopher, Brian. B.S., U. Notre Dame, 1960, M.S., 1962; Ph.D., U. N.Mex., 1966. Research assoc., lectr. E. H. Wang Civil Engring. Research Facility, U. N.Mex., 1962-66; assoc. prof. civil engring. U. Detroit, 1966-71, prof., 1972-79, dean engring., 1973-78, acad. v.p., 1976-79; vis. prof. engring., NSF faculty fellow M.I.T., 1971-72; pres. Calif. Poly. State U., San Luis Obispo, 1979—; judge Internat. Sci. and Engring. Fair, 1974, 75, 77, 80; mem. adv. bd. Jr. Humanities and Sci. Symposium, 1976-78; mem. bd. Internat. Food and Agr. Devel. Contbr. articles to profl. jours. Mem. Detroit Mayor's Mgmt. Adv. Com., 1975-76; bd. dirs. Calif. Council for Environ. and Econ. Balance, 1980—. Fellow Engring. Soc. Detroit; mem. ASCE (chmn. geotech. div. com. on reliability 1976—), Nat. Soc. Profl. Engrs. (pres. Detroit chpt. 1976-77), Am. Soc. Engring. Edn., Am. Assn. State Colls. and Univs. (dir.). Office: Pres's Office Calif Poly State U San Luis Obispo CA 93407

BAKER, WESLEY C., food company executive; b. Leon, Iowa, July 20, 1919; s. Vernon L. and Esther (Norman) B.; m. Joan L. Olson, Aug. 19, 1980; children: (by previous marriage) Ronald C., Sheryl L. B.S., Iowa State U. Tchr. pub. schs.; with Multifoods Corp., Mpls., 1951—, now sr. v.p., gen. mgr.; adviser Future Farmers of Am., 1973-78, Nat. Agr. Council of Am., 1976. Bd. dirs. Meth. Ch., New Ulm, Minn., 1954, Edina, Minn., 1963; lay minister Edina, Minn., Grand Island, Nebr., 1952. Served with USN; 1942-44. Mem. Am. Food Mfrs. Assn. (dir. 1970-82). Republican. Clubs: Mpls., Athletic, Edina Country, Am. Legion, V.F.W. Lodge: Odd Fellows. Office: Internat Multifoods Multifoods Tower Minneapolis MN 55402

BAKER, WILDER DUPUY, JR., advertising agency executive; b. Washington, Dec. 4, 1931; s. Wilder DuPuy and Cora (Barry) B.; m. Dorothy Walker, Apr. 23, 1960; children: Brooke DuPuy, Dana Elizabeth. B.A., Yale U., 1953. Account exec. Phillips Ramsey Co., San Diego, 1954-S7, Benton & Bowles Co., N.Y.C., 1957-60; advt. dir. Stahl-Meyer Co., N.Y.C., 1960-61; account supr. Ogilvy & Mather Co., N.Y.C., 1961-65; successively v.p., exec. v.p., pres. Bresnick Co., Boston, 1965-71; also dir.; sr. v.p., gen. mgr. Wilson Haight Welch Co., Boston, 1971-76; exec. v.p., dir. Warwick Advt., Inc., N.Y.C., 1976-82, pres., 1982—. Mem. fin. com. Nat. Assn. Mental Health, 1973-75; mem. Darien (Conn.) Youth Commn.; bd. dirs. Mental Health Assn., Mass., 1973-75, Asthma and Allergy Found. Am. Mem. Am. Mgmt. Assn., Advt. Club Boston. Clubs: Yale (N.Y.C.); Tokoneke (Darien, Conn.) (gov.). Home: 55 Andrews Dr Darien CT 06920 Office: Warwick Advertising Inc 875 3d Ave New York NY 10022

BAKER, WILLIAM DUNLAP, lawyer; b. St. Louis, June 17, 1932; s. Harold Griffith and Bernice (Kraft) B.; m. Kay Stokes, May 23, 1955; children—Mark William, Kathryne X., Beth Kristie, Frederick Martin. A.B., Colgate U., 1954; J.D., U. Calif. at Berkeley, 1960. Bar: Calif. 1961, Ariz. 1961, U.S. Supreme Ct. 1969. Practice in, Coolidge, 1961, Florence, 1963-63, Phoenix, 1963—; law clk. Stokes & Moring, 1960; spl. investigator Office Pinal County Atty., 1960-61, dep. county atty., 1961- 63; partner McBryde, Vincent, Brumage & Baker, 1961-63; asso. atty. Rawlins, Ellis, Burrus & Kiewit, 1963-65, partner, 1965-81; pres., atty. Ellis & Baker, P.C., 1981—; referee Juvenile Ct. Maricopa County Superior Ct., 1966—. Mem. Gov.'s Adv. Council, Phoenix, 1969-71, Ariz. Environ. Planning Commn., 1974-75; bd. dirs. Agri-Bus. Council, 1978—, sec., 1978-82; Spl. legal counsel Ariz. Com. Republican Party, 1964; legal counsel Ariz. Com. Rep. Party, 1965-69, mem. exec. com., 1972-78; vice-chmn. Maricopa County Rep. Com., 1968-69, chmn., 1969-71; bd. dirs. San Pablo Home for Youth, 1964-72, pres., 1971; bd. dirs. Maricopa County chpt. Nat. Found. March of Dimes, 1966-71, campaign chmn., 1970; trustee St. Luke's Hosp., 1976—, sec., 1978-82, chmn., 1982—; bd. dirs. Luke's Men, 1971-80, pres., 1976-77; bd. dirs. Combined Health Resources, 1982—; bd. dirs., v.p. Ariz. Anglican Cursillo Movement, 1982—; regional v.p. Colgate Alumni Corp., 1977—; vice chancellor Episcopal Diocese of Ariz., 1970—; sr. warden Christ Ch. of Ascension, 1983—. Served to 1st lt. USAF, 1954-57. Mem. Am., Ariz., Calif., Maricopa County bar assns., Ariz. Acad., Sigma Chi, Phi Delta Phi. Club: Ariz. Home: 5309 N 34th St Phoenix AZ 85018 Office: 2300 Valley Bank Center Phoenix AZ 85073

BAKER, WILLIAM FRANKLIN, broadcasting exec.; b. Cleve., Sept. 30, 1942; s. William Franklin and Rita Marie (Huebner) B.; m. Jeannemarie Gelin, June 22, 1968; children—Christiane, Angela. B.A. in Communications and Organizational Behavior, Case Western Res. U., 1965, M.A., 1968, Ph.D., 1972; D.C.S. (hon.), St. John's U., N.Y., 1981. Exec. producer Sta. WEWS-TV, Cleve., 1971-75, asst gen. mgr., 1975-77; v.p., gen. mgr. Sta. WJZ-TV, Balt., 1977-78; pres. Group W. Productions, Hollywood, Calif., 1978-79, Group W-TV, N.Y.C., 1979—. Contbr. articles in field to profl. jours. Bd. dirs. United Way, Balt., 1978; mem. exec. bd. Urban League, Balt., 1978; mem. U.S. Catholic Conf. Communications, TV Info. Bd. Recipient 4 Emmy Awards; 2 Twyla M. Conway Awards. Fellow Explorers Club; mem. Nat. Assn. TV Program Execs., Nat. Assn. Broadcasters, Advt. Research Found. (TV audience measurement council), Internat. Radio-TV Soc., Nat. Acad. TV Arts & Scis. Roman Catholic. Club: N.Y. Yacht. Office: 90 Park Ave New York NY 10016

BAKER, WILLIAM GARRETT, JR., investment banker; b. New Orleans, Dec. 21, 1933; s. William Garrett and Susan Katherine (D'Aubert) B.; m. Nancy Jeffress Rodwell, May 29, 1965; children: Rutland Rodwell, Suzanne Tarry, Ashley Hamilton. B.A., Tulane U., 1955; M.B.A., Harvard U., 1960. Partner, mng. dir. Lehman Bros., N.Y.C., 1960-75; exec. v.p., mng. dir. E.F. Hutton & Co., Inc., Los Angeles, 1975-84; chmn. William G. Baker Co., Los Angeles, 1984—; pres. Pachmayr Gun Works; pres. Darnell Corp., Ltd.; chmn. Calif. Bio Tech.; dir. United Foods, Inc., Cliffwood Energy Co. Bd. visitors Kanuga Conf.; bd. dirs. Hollywood Med. Found. Served to 1st lt. USAF, 1955-58. Episcopalian. Clubs: California, Men's Garden, Tennis (Los Angeles); Church (N.Y.C.); Boston (New Orleans); Bayou, Saddle and Sirloin, Rancheros Visitadores. Home: 324 S Rimpau Blvd Los Angeles CA 90020 Office: One Wilshire Bldg Suite 2900 Los Angeles CA 90017

BAKER, WILLIAM GEORGE, publishing company financial executive; b. Bklyn., July 23, 1935; s. George Francis and Martha Mary (Klostermann) B.; m. Marilyn Rose Emmons, Oct. 10, 1959; children: Steven, Paul. B.B.A., St John's U., Bklyn., 1957; M.B.A., Pace U., 1967. C.P.A., N.Y. Mgr. Arthur Andersen & Co., N.Y.C., 1957-63; asst. treas. Harper & Row Pubs., Inc., N.Y.C., 1963-69, comptroller, 1969-71, v.p., comptroller, 1971—. Served to cpl. USMC, 1958-59. Mem. Am. Inst. C.P.A.s, Fin. Execs. Inst. Club: University (N.Y.C.). Lodge: Masons. Home: 19 Lewis Ln Port Washington NY 11050 Office: Harper & Row Pubs Inc 10 E 53d St New York NY 10022

BAKER, WILLIAM KAUFMAN, geneticist; b. Portland, Ind., Dec. 2, 1919; s. Frank K. and Jennie (Schaeffer) B.; m. Margaret Stewart, Mar. 4, 1944; children—Bruce, Ann, Brian. B.A., Coll. of Wooster, 1941; M.A., U. Tex., 1943, Ph.D. (NRC fellow), 1948. Asst. prof. U. Tenn., 1948-51; sr. biologist Oak Ridge Nat. Lab., 1951-55; asso. prof. U. Chgo., 1955-59, prof. zoology, 1959-77, chmn. dept. biology, 1968-72, U. Utah, 1977-80, prof., 1977—. Co-editor: Am. Naturalist, 1965-70; Author articles on genetics. Served to 1st lt. USAAF, 1943-46. NSF sr. postdoctoral fellow U. Rome, 1963-64; NIH spl. postdoctoral fellow, Madrid, 1972-73. Mem. Am. Soc. Naturalists (sec., v.p. 1976), Genetics Soc. Am. (pres. 1980). Home: 4499 Gilead Way Salt Lake City UT 84117

BAKER, WILLIAM OLIVER, research chemist; b. Chestertown, Md., July 15 1915; s. Harold May and Helen (Stokes) B.; m. Frances Burrill, Nov. 15, 1941; 1 son, Joseph Burrill. B.S., Washington Coll., 1935, Sc.D., 1957; Ph.D., Princeton, 1938; Sc.D., Georgetown U., 1962, U. Pitts., 1963, Seton Hall U., 1965, U. Akron, 1968, U. Mich., 1970, St. Peter's Coll., 1972, Poly. Inst. N.Y., 1973, Trinity Coll., Dublin, Ireland, 1975, Northwestern U., 1976, U. Notre Dame, 1978, Tufts U., 1981, N.J. Coll. Medicine and Dentistry, 1981; D.Eng., Stevens Inst. Tech., 1962, N.J. Inst. Tech., 1978; LL.D., U. Glasgow, 1965, U. Pa., 1974, Kean Coll., N.J., 1976, Lehigh U., 1980, Drew U., 1981; L.H.D., Monmouth Coll., 1973, Clarkson Coll. Tech., 1974. With Bell Telephone Labs., 1939-80, in charge polymer research and devel., 1948-51, asst. dir. chem. and metall. research, 1951-54, dir. research, phys. scis., 1954-55, v.p. research, 1955-73, pres., 1973-79, chmn. bd., 1979-80; dir. Ann. Revs., Inc., Summit and Elizabeth Trust Co.; vis. lectr. Northwestern U., Princeton U., Duke; Schmitt lectr. U. Notre Dame, 1968; Harrelson lectr. N.C. State U., 1971; Herbert Spencer lectr. U. Pa., 1974; Charles M. Schwab Meml. lectr. Am. Iron and Steel Inst., 1976; NIH lectr., 1958, Metall. Soc. Am. Inst. Mining Engrs./Am. Soc. Metals disting. lectr., 1976; Miles Conrad Meml. lectr. Nat. Fedn. Abstracting and Indexing Services, 1977; Wulff lectr. M.I.T., 1979; other lectureships; cons. Office Sci. and Tech., 1977—; Mem. Princeton Grad. Council, 1956-64; bd. visitors Tulane U., 1963—; mem. commn. sociotech. systems NRC, 1974-78, also chmn. adv. bd. on mil. personnel supplies, 1964-78; mem. com. on phys. chemistry of div. chemistry and chem. tech., 1963-70; also steering com. Pres.'s Food and Nutrition Study Commn. Internat. Relations Nat. Acad. Scis.-NRC, 1975; mem. panel on phys. chemistry Office Naval Research, 1948-51; past mem. Pres.'s Sci. Adv. Com., 1957-60; nat. sci. bd. NSF, 1960-66; past chmn. Nat. Sci. Info. Council, 1959-61; mem. sci. adv. bd. Nat. Security Agy., 1959-76, cons., 1976—, Dept. Def., 1958-71, 1963-73,; Panel of Ops. Evaluation Group, USN, 1960-62; mem. N.J. Bd. Higher Edn., 1967—, exec. com., 1970—, vice chmn., 1970-72; mem. liaison com. for sci. and tech. Library of Congress, 1963-73; mem. Pres.'s Fgn. Intelligence Adv. Bd., 1959-77; chmn. Pres.'s Adv. Group Anticipated Advances in Sci. and Tech., 1975-76; vice chmn. Pres.'s Com. Sci. and Tech., 1976-77; bd. regents Nat. Library Medicine, 1969-73; bd. visitors Air Force Systems Command, 1962-73; mem. mgmt. adv. council Oak Ridge Nat. Lab., 1970—; mem. Nat. Commn. on Libraries and Info. Scis., 1971-75, Commn. on Critical Choices for Ams., 1973-75, Nat. Cancer Adv. Bd., 1974-80; mem. panel adv. Inst. Materials Research, Nat. Bur. Standards, 1966-69; mem. Council Trends and Perspectives, U.S. C. of

C., 1966-74; chmn. tech. panels adv. to Nat. Bur. Standards, Nat. Acad. Scis.-NRC, 1969-78; mem. Nat. Council Ednl. Research, 1973-75; mem. energy research and devel. adv. council Energy Policy Office, 1973-75; mem. Project Independence adv. com. Fed. Energy Adminstrn., 1974-75, Gov.'s Com. to Evaluate Capital Needs N.J., 1974-75; mem. governing bd. Nat. Enquiry into Scholarly Communication, 1975-79; adv. council N.J. Regional Med. Library, 1975—, Fed. Emergency Mgmt. Adv. Bd., 1980—, Gas Research Inst. Adv. Bd., 1978—; mem. adv. bd. N.J. Sci./Tech. Center, 1980—; Mem. sci. adv. bd. Robert A. Welch Found., 1968—; vis. com. for chemistry Harvard, 1959-72; mem. council Marconi Fellowships, 1978—; vis. com., div. chemistry and chem. engring. Calif. Inst. Tech., 1969-72; vis. com. on scis. and math. Drew U., 1969—; asso. in univ. seminar on tech. and social change Columbia, 1969—; vis. com., dept. materials sci. and engring. M.I.T., 1973-76; bd. overseers Coll. Engring. and Applied Sci. U. Pa., 1975—; bd. dirs. Council on Library Resources, 1970—, Health Effects Inst., 1980—; Clin. Scholar Program Robert Wood Johnson Found., 1973-76, Third Century Corp., 1973-76. Contbr.: High Polymers, 1945, Symposium on Basic Research, AAAS, 1959, Rheology, Vol. III, 1960, Technology and Social Change, 1964, Science: The Achievement and the Promise, 1968, Ann. Rev. Materials Sci, 1976, various other books.; Mem. editorial adv. bd.: Jour. Info. Sci; past mem. adv. editorial bd.: Chem. and Engring. News; hon. editorial adv. bd.: Carbon; Contbr. numerous articles to tech. jours. Trustee Urban Studies, Inc., 1960-78, Aerospace Corp., 1961-76, Carnegie-Mellon U., 1967—, Princeton, 1964—, Fund N.J., 1974—, Harry Frank Guggenheim Found., 1976—, Gen. Motors Cancer Research Found., 1978—, Charles Babbage Inst., 1978—, Newark Mus., 1979—, Rockefeller U., 1960—; chmn. Rockefeller U., 1980—; trustee Andrew W. Mellon Found., 1965—, chmn., 1975—. Named 1 of 10 top scientists in U.S. industry, 1954; recipient Perkin medal, 1963; Honor scroll Am. Inst. Chemist, 1962; award to execs. ASTM, 1967; Edgar Marburg award, 1967; Indsl. Research Inst. medal, 1970; Frederik Philips award IEEE, 1972; Indsl. Research Man of Year award, 1973; Procter prize Sigma Xi, 1973; James Madison medal Princeton, 1975; Mellon Inst. award, 1975; Soc. Research Adminstrs. award for distinguished contbns., 1976; von Hippel award Materials Research Soc., 1978; Fahrney medal Franklin Inst., 1977; N.J. Sci/Tech. medal, 1980; Harvard fellow, 1937-38; Procter fellow, 1938-39; Jefferson medal N.J. Patent Law Assn., 1981; David Sarnoff prize AFCEA, 1981. Fellow Am. Phys. Soc., Am. Inst. Chemists (Gold medal 1975), Franklin Inst., Am. Acad. Arts and Scis.; mem. Dirs. of Indsl. Research, Am. Chem. Soc. (past mem. com. nat. def., cons., past mem. com. chemistry and pub. affairs, Priestley medal 1966, Parsons award 1976, Willard Gibbs award 1978, Madison Marshall award 1980), Am. Philos. Soc., Nat. Acad. Scis. (council 1969-72, com. sci. and pub. policy 1966-69), Nat. Acad. Engring., Inst. Medicine (council 1973-75), Indsl. Research Inst. (dir. 1960-63), Sigma Xi, Phi Lambda Upsilon, Omicron Delta Kappa. Clubs: Chemists of N.Y. (hon.), Cosmos, Princeton of Northwestern N.J. Holder 13 patents. Office: 600 Mountain Ave Murray Hill NJ 07974 *

BAKER, WILLIAM WALLACE, journalism educator, former newspaperman; b. Kansas City, Mo., July 2, 1921; s. William Reaune and Grace (Wallace) B.; m. Virginia Elizabeth Graham, Dec. 21, 1941 (dec.); 1 son, William Wallace (dec.); m. Betty Krall Thomas, Nov. 16, 1979. A.B., U. Mich., 1947. U. Mich. corr. Detroit Times, 1940-41; with SSS, 1945, Kansas City Star, 1947-77, editorial writer, 1954-63, asso. editor, 1963-67, editor, 1967-77, exec. v.p., 1971-75, pres., 1975-77; lectr. William Allen White Sch. Journalism, U. Kans., 1978, asso. prof., 1978—. Mem. nat. exec. council Episcopal Ch.; trustee William Allen White Found. Served with AUS, World War II; PTO. Decorated Bronze Star. Mem. Am. Soc. Newspaper Editors, Nat. Conf. Editorial Writers, Kansas City Press Club, Sphinx, Phi Beta Kappa, Phi Kappa Phi, Phi Eta Sigma, Sigma Delta Chi. Episcopalian. Club: Lake Quivira. Home: 110 W Terrace Trail Lake Quivira KS 66106 Office: Flint Hall Univ Kans Lawrence KS 66045

BAKER, WINTHROP PATTERSON, JR., broadcasting executive; b. N.Y.C., July 12, 1931; s. Winthrop Patterson and Josie Lou (Kendrick) B.; m. Elizabeth Muriel Allegret, July 30, 1955; children: Winthrop Patterson III, John Adams, Michael Kendrick. Student, Vanderbilt U., 1952; B.S. in Bus. Adminstrn, La. State U., 1953. TV dir. sta. WJMR-TV, New Orleans, 1954-55; producer-dir. sta. WBRZ-TV, Baton Rouge, 1955-56; TV program dir. sta. KLFY-TV, Lafayette, La., 1956-57; program dir. sta. WMBD-TV, Peoria, Ill., 1957-60; asst. program mgr. sta. WBZ-TV, Boston, 1960-61; program mgr. sta. WJZ-TV, Balt., 1962-65, sta. KYW-TV, Phila., 1965-67; asst. gen. mgr. sta. KDKA-TV, Pitts., 1967; gen. mgr. WBZ-TV, Boston, 1968-73, v.p., 1970-73; pres. TV sta. group Westinghouse Broadcasting Co., N.Y.C., 1973-79, corp. v.p., dir., 1974-79; dir. TV Advt. Reps., N.Y.C., 1969-79; pres. P.M. Mag. Inc. (subs. Westinghouse Broadcasting Co.), 1978-79; exec. v.p., dir., gen. mgr. New Eng. TV Co., Boston, 1979-81, 82; pres. Gen. Electric Broadcasting and Cablevision Co., Fairfield, Conn., 1981-82; pres., dir., gen. mgr. Sta. WNEV-TV, Boston, 1982-84; v.p. Westfair Prodns., Ridgefield, Conn., 1984—; pres. Target Video Inc., Wilton, Conn., 1984—. Mem. Boston Youth Activities Commn., Boston, 1970-71; Adv. Com. U.S. Youth Games, 1971; mem. Gov.'s Commn. on Ednl. Reorgn., 1972-73; Bd. dirs., vice-chmn. Boston Community Media Com., 1970-73; bd. dirs. Intercom, Boston, 1970-73, Consumer-care Council, Boston, 1970-71; mem. adv. bd. broadcasting and communications curriculum U. Pa. Wharton Sch. Bus., 1978—, Mercer (N.J.) Community Coll., 1978—. Mem. Am. Advt. Fedn. (dir. 1974—), Nat. Assn. TV Program Execs., New Eng. Broadcast Assn., Mass. Broadcasters Assn. (v.p. dir. 1970-71), Mass. Audubon Soc., De Cordova Museum, Phi Kappa Phi, Mu Sigma Rho, Phi Eta Sigma, Pi Tau Pi, Beta Gamma Sigma.

BAKER-BATSEL, JOHN DAVID, clergyman, librarian; b. Greenville, Ky., Nov. 29, 1933; s. Rufus William and Eunice (Henson) Baker-B.; m. Lyda Katherine Dickerson, May 29, 1953 (div.); children: Lee Ann, Laura Grace, Julia Beth, John David; m. Patricia Ann Baker, June 20, 1980; 1 stepson, Michael Pressey. B.A., Lambuth Coll., 1955; B.D., Vanderbilt U., 1959, M.A., 1962; M.L.S., George Peabody Coll., 1963. Ordained to ministry, 1959; student pastor Memphis Ann. Conf., 1951-60; librarian Lambuth Coll., 1963-64; librarian, prof. Garrett Evang. Theol. Sem., Evanston, Ill., 1964-77; dir. Grad. Theol. Union Library, Berkeley, Calif., 1977—; bd. dirs. Calif. Library Authority for Systems and Services, 1981-82. Editor: Union List of United Methodist Serials 1773-1973, 1974. Mem. Am. Theol. Library Assn. (pres. 1973-74), ALA, Beta Phi Mu. Office: Grad Theol Union Library 2400 Ridge Rd Berkeley CA 94709

BAKES, PHILIP JOHN, JR., lawyer, airline executive; b. Little Rock, Mar. 6, 1946; s. Philip John and Theresa B.; m. Priscilla C. Smith, June 19, 1977; children: Tia, Justin. B.A. magna cum laude, Loyola U., Chgo., 1968; J.D. magna cum laude (Sheldon fellow), Harvard U., 1971. Bar: Ill. 1971, D.C. 1975. Assoc. Devoe, Shadur & Krupp, Chgo., 1972-73; asst. spl. prosecutor Watergate Spl. Prosecution Force, Washington, 1973-74; asst. chief counsel Senate Subcom. on Adminstrv. Practice and Procedures, Washington, 1974-77; spl. counsel Senate Antitrust Subcom., Washington, 1977; gen. counsel CAB, Washington, 1977-79; dep. campaign mgr. Kennedy for Pres., 1979-80; sr. v.p. Tex. Air Corp., Houston, 1980-82, exec. v.p., 1982—; exec. v.p., dir. Continental Airlines, Houston, 1982—; dir. N.Y. Airlines, Inc. N.Y.C., 1980—; mem. adv. com. govtl. relations Am. Enterprise Inst. Mem. D.C. Bar Assn., Ill. Bar Assn. Home: 206 Lakemere Houston TX 77079

BAKES, ROBERT E., state justice; b. 1932. B.A., J.D., U. Idaho. Bar: Idaho 1956. Justice Idaho Supreme Ct. Address: Supreme Court of Idaho Boise ID 83720

BAKKEN, DOUGLAS ADAIR, foundation executive, history consultant; b. Breckenridge, Minn., Mar. 12, 1939; s. John and Marie (Folstad) B.; m. Jacquelyn Ann Nielsen, July 8, 1962; children: Amy Michelle, Wendy Kay. B.S., N.D. State U., 1961; cert. archives adminstrn., Am. U., 1966; M.A., in History, U. Nebr., 1967. Archivist Nebr. State Hist. Soc., Lincoln, 1966-67; assoc. archivist Cornell U., Ithaca, N.Y., 1967-71; archivist adminstr. Anheuser Busch Cos., St. Louis, 1971-77; dir. archives and library Henry Ford Mus., Dearborn, Mich., 1977-83; exec. dir. Ball Bros. Found., Muncie, Ind., 1983—; cons. history, archives, 1978—. Editor-in-chief: The Herald, Edison Inst., 1978-81. Served to 1st lt. Intelligence Corps U.S. Army, 1962-64. Fellow Soc. Am. Archivists; mem. Hist. Soc. Mich. (v.p. 1982-83), Am. Assn. State and Local History, Nat. Automotive History Collection (trustee 1981—), Soc. Automotive Historians (dir. 1981-84). Republican. Lutheran. Home: 4801 Everett Rd Muncie IN 47302 Office: Ball Bros Found 100 S Mulberry St Muncie IN 47305

BAKKEN, JAMES KENDALL, automotive company executive; b. Mt. Horeb., Wis., Apr. 17, 1924; s. Raymond and Marion (Earle) B.; m. Jeanne DeBernard, Jan. 26, 1946; children: Claudia, James Kendall, David, Jennifer, Mary Ellen. B.S. in Mech. Engring., U. Wis., 1945; M.S. in Indsl. Mgmt., MIT, 1963. Gen. mgr. metal stamping Ford Motor Co., Dearborn, Mich., 1970-73, gen. mgr. elec. and electronic div., 1973-77, v.p. worldwide tractor ops., 1977-78, v.p. body and assembly, 1978-80, v.p. ops. staff, 1980—; dir. Robotics Inst. Am., 1983—, Met. Ctr. for High Tech., Detroit, 1983—; mem. adv. bd. Inst. for Quality and Productivity, U. Tenn., Knoxville, 1982—. Bd. dirs. YMCA, Dearborn, 1972; mem. teaching staff Guardian Luth. Ch., Dearborn, 1958-83. Alfred P. Sloan fellow MIT, 1963; recipient Disting. Service citation U. Wis., 1978, Eli Whitney Meml. Soc. Mfg. Engrs., 1981. Mem. Soc. Automotive Engrs. Clubs: Renaissance (Detroit); Fairlane (Dearborn). Office: Ford Motor Co American Rd Dearborn MI 48121

BAKKER, CORNELIS B., psychiatrist, educator; b. Rotterdam, Holland, Jan. 6, 1929; came to U.S., 1953, naturalized, 1963; s. Willem and Poulina J. (Reiff) B.; m. Marianne K. Rabdau, June 11, 1955; children: Paul, James, Gabrielle. M.D. with honors, U. Utrecht, Holland, 1952. Intern Clinics of Rotterdam, 1952-53, Sacred Heart Hosp., Spokane, 1953-54; resident in psychiatry Eastern State Hosp., Medical Lake, Wash., 1954-56, U. Utrecht, 1956-57, U. Mich. Med. Sch., 1957-59; instr., research asso. psychiatry U. Mich., Ann Arbor, 1959-60; instr. psychiatry U. Wash., Seattle, 1960-63, asst. prof., 1963-67, asso. prof., 1967-72, prof. psychiatry, 1972-79, dir. Adult Psychiat. Inpatient Service, 1961-68; dir. Adult Devel. Program, 1968-79; prof., head dept. psychiatry U. Ill. Coll. Medicine, Peoria, 1979—; psychiat. cons. Soc. Sec. Hearings and Appeals, 1963-79, Ketchikan Community Mental Health Center, 1972-77. Contbr. articles to profl. jours.; author: (with M.K. Bakker Rabdau) No Trespassing! - Explorations in Human Territoriality, 1973. Dutch Govt. scholar, 1951-52, 52-53; Fulbright grantee, 1953; Fogarty Sr. fellow U. Leuven, Belgium, 1977-78; recipient Significant Achievement award Am. Psychiatric Assn., 1975. Fellow Am. Psychiatric Assn., Am. Coll. Psychiatrists; mem. Assn. for Advancement of Behavior Therapists, World Psychiat. Assn. Office: Dept Psychiatry U Ill Coll Medicine at Peoria Peoria IL 61656

BAKKER, JAMES ORSEN, clergyman; b. Muskegon, Mich., Jan. 2, 1940; s. Raleigh and Furnia (Irwin) B.; m. Tammy Faye LaValley, Apr. 1, 1961; children—Tammy Sue, Jamie Charles. Student, N.Central Bible Coll., Mpls., 1961. Ordained to ministry Assemblies of God, 1964; evangelist; co-founder Trinity Broadcasting Network, Calif., 1973; founder, host 700 Club (TV show), 1965; pres., founder PTL Club, PTL TV Network, Charlotte, N.C., 1974—; pres. Heritage Sch. of Evangelism and Communication, Charlotte, 1978—; pres., chmn. bd. Heritage Village Ch. and Missionary Fellowship, Inc., Charlotte, 1974—; pres., advisor, tchr., cons. Heritage Sch. Evangelism, Vision Media, Sydney, Australia. Producer, dir.: Jim and Tammy Show, 1965; Author: Move That Mountain, 1976, Big 3 Mountain Movers, 1977, Survival, 1981, How to Lose Weight and Keep It Off, 1979, Devotional Guides, 1979, 80. Charter mem. bd. advisors Boys Town, Pineville, N.C.; active Easter Seal and Cystic Fibrosis telethons, Charlotte, 1976. Recipient Amway award, 1976, Easter Seal award, 1976. Mem. Gospel Music Assn. (Dove award, best gospel TV show 1977), Nat. Religious Broadcasters, Assemblies of God, Nat. UHF Broadcasters Assn., N.C. Assn. Broadcasters, Full Gospel Bus. Men's Fellowship Internat., Charlotte Area Clergy Assn., N.C. C. of C. (Arts and Sci. Council, Charlotte). Office: 7224 Park Rd Charlotte NC 28279

BAKLANOFF, ERIC NICOLAS, educator; b. Graz, Austria, Dec. 9, 1925; came to U.S., 1937, naturalized, 1943; s. Nicolas W. and Lucille (King) B.; m. H. Christina Janes, June 17, 1956 (div. June 1973); children: Nicholas, Tanya; m. Joy Driskell, June 6, 1982. Student, Antioch Coll., 1943-44; A.B., Ohio State U., 1949, M.A., 1950, Ph.D., 1958; postgrad. (Fulbright scholar), U. Chile, 1957, Harvard Grad. Sch. Bus. Adminstrn., 1959, U. Tex., summer 1963. Instr. econs. Ohio State U., 1957-58; asst. prof. La. State U., 1958-61, assoc. prof., 1961-62; prof. econs., dir. Latin Am. Studies Inst., 1965-68; assoc. prof. econs., dir. Grad. Center for Latin Am. Studies, Vanderbilt U., 1962-65; prof. econs., dean for internat. studies and programs U. Ala., 1969-73, Bd. visitors research prof. econs., 1974—; Cons. Am. Council on Edn., USAF Inst., Pres.'s Southeastern Council on Latin Am. Studies, 1963-64; cons. U.S. Dept. Edn., Centro de Estudios y Communicacion Economica. Author: Expropriation of U.S. Investments in Cuba, Mexico and Chile, 1975, The Economic Transformation of Spain and Portugal, 1978, La Transformación Económica de España y Portugal: La economía del Franquismo y de del Salazarismo, 1980; author: Developing Corporate Strategies, Vol. 2, 1982; Contbg. author: Modern Brazil: New Patterns and Development, 1971, Revolutionary Change in Cuba, 1971, Background to Revolution: The Development of Modern Cuba, 1979; Editor, contbg. author: The Shaping of Modern Brazil, 1969, New Perspectives of Brazil, 1966, Mediterranean Europe and the Common Market, 1976; Contbr. articles to profl. jours. Active Boy Scouts Am. Served with USNR, 1944-46; PTO. Grantee U.S. State Dept., Spain, 1974; named Outstanding Scholar U. Ala., 1980-81; Fellow Center Advanced Study Behavioral Scis., 1964-65. Mem. Nat. Honor Soc., Delta Chi, Beta Gamma Sigma, Sigma Delta Pi, Omicron Delta Epsilon. Episcopalian. Office: Box J University AL 35486

BAKNWELL, BOYD B., college president, optometrist. Pres. Ill. Coll. Optometry, Chgo. Office: Ill Coll Optometry 3241 S Michigan Ave Chicago IL 60616

BAKROW, WILLIAM JOHN, college president; b. Parson, Kans., Apr. 22, 1924; s. Leonard A. and Edith (Strasberg) B.; m. Maree Janet Walsh; children: Bruce Wrigley, Caren Edith, Lance Adler. B.A., Brown U., 1948; M.S., Ind. U., 1958, Ed.D., 1960; LL.D. (hon.), St. Mary Coll., Omaha. Reporter Providence Jour., 1948-51; legis. corr. U.P., Albany, N.Y., 1951-56; dir. devel. U. Buffalo, 1956-59, Canisius (N.Y.) Coll., 1961-66; pres. Motorola Exec. Inst., Oracle, Ariz., 1966-73, St. Ambrose Coll., Davenport, Iowa, 1973—; dir. Southeast Nat. Bank Moline, Ill., Sears Mfg. Co., Davenport.; Mem. Scott County Govtl. Study Commn., 1974—. Mem. Illowa Council exec. bd. Boy Scouts Am., 1975—; trustee Palmer Jr. Coll., Davenport, St. Katherine's-St. Mark's Sch., Bettendorf, Iowa. Served with USNR, 1942-46. Office: St Ambrose Coll 518 W Locust St Davenport IA 52803 *

BAKSHI, RALPH, motion picture producer and dir. Student pub. schs., N.Y.C. Associated with CBS Terrytoons, Paramount Pictures; pres. Bakshi Productions, Inc., Hollywood, Calif. Producer, dir.: feature films Fire and Ice. Mem. Writers Guild Am., West, Inc., Dirs. Guild Am., Producers Guild Am., ASCAP. Office: Sun Valley CA

BAKWIN, EDWARD MORRIS, banker; b. N.Y.C., May 13, 1928; s. HArry and Ruth (Morris) B. B.A., Hamilton Coll., 1950; M.B.A., U. Chgo., 1961. With Nat. Stock Yards Nat. Bank, National City, Ill., 1953-55; with Mid-City Nat. Bank Chgo., 1955—, asst. cashier, 1957-60, v.p., 1960-62, pres., 1962-72, chmn. bd., 1967—, Darling-Del. Corp., Chgo., 1972—; dir. St. Louis Nat Stock Yards Co., Okla. Nat. Stock Yards Co. Mem. Chgo. Crime Commn. Adv. bd. U. Chgo., 1967—; citizens bd. George Williams Coll., 1968—; bd. dirs. Duncan-Med. YMCA, 1963-72, Northwestern Meml. Hosp., 1980—, West Central Assn., 1962-67; pres. West Central Assn., 1962-65. Served with AUS, 1951-52. Mem. Am. Bankers Assn., Ill. Bankers Assn. (bd. govs. 1966-69), Explorers Club. Clubs: Adventurers, Metropolitan, Chgo. Yacht, Mid-Am. (Chgo.); N.Y. Yacht (N.Y.C). Home: 175 E Delaware St Chicago IL 60611 Office: Mid-City National Bank of Chicago Chicago IL 60607

BAKWIN, RUTH MORRIS, pediatrician; b. Chgo., June 3, 1898; d. Edward Morris and Helen (Swift) Neilson; m. Harry Bakwin, Feb. 2, 1925; children: Edward Morris, Patricia Anne (Mrs. F.R. Selch), Barbara Swift (Mrs. W.S. Rosenthal), Michael. B.A., Wellesley Coll., 1919; M.D., Cornell U., 1923; M.A., Columbia U., 1929; postgrad. grad. sch., Vienna and Berlin, 1924-25. Diplomate: Am. Bd. Pediatrics. Intern Fifth Ave. Hosp., 1923-24; instr. pediatrics Columbia, 1927-30, N.Y. U., 1930-40, asst. prof. clin. pediatrics, 1940-49, asso. prof. clin. pediatrics, 1949-60, prof. clin. pediatrics, 1961—; asst. pediatrician Bellevue Hosp., 1927-43, asst. vis. physician, 1943-48, asso. vis. physician children's medical service, 1948-55, vis. physician, 1955—, dir. child guidance clinic, pediatric dept., 1931-65; asst. pediatrician Fifth Ave. Hosp., 1925-35; asso. pediatrician N.Y. Infirmary, 1929-31; dir. pediatrics, 1936-54; cons. dir. pediatrics N.Y. Infirmary, 1954, dir. emeritus, 1955—, also trustee, 1962—, co-dir. dept. pediatrics, 1966-67; courtesy staff pediatrics Univ. Hosp. Author: Psychologic Care During Infancy and Childhood, 1942, Clinical Management of Behavior Disorders in Children, 1953, 60, 66, 72, Behavior Disorders in Children; also numerous papers. Mem. com. on child health White House Conf., 1960; mem. Nat. Com. Children and Youth, 1964-67; vol. pediatrician Care-Medico, Honduras, Indonesia. Recipient N.Y. Infirmary award of merit, 1960, Med. Woman of Yr. award N.Y. State Med. Soc., 1971. Mem. Pan Am. Med. Women's Alliance, World Med. Assn., AAAS, Am. Acad. Pediatrics (state chmn. 1965-67), Med. Women's Internat. Assn., AMA, N.Y. Acad. Medicine, Child Study Assn. Am., Soc. Research Child Devel., Am. Med. Women's Assn. (Elizabeth Blackwell award 1950), Women's Med. Soc. N.Y. State, Women's Med. Soc. N.Y.C., Nat. Assn. for Mental Health, Inc. (adv. council on childhood mental illnesses 1962—, dir. 1962-66), Alpha Phi (award 1952). Clubs: Cornell Women's of N.Y., Cosmopolitan, Wellesley. Address: 15 E 69th St New York NY 10021 also 335 Croton Dam Rd Ossining NY 10562

BALABANIAN, DAVID MARK, lawyer; b. Wenatchee, Wash., July 29, 1938; s. Mark Sarkis and Ibraxie (Elmas) B.; m. Christine Madath, June 27, 1962; children: Lisa Marie, Mark Sarkis. A.B., Harvard Coll., 1960; B.Phil., Oxford U., 1962; LL.B., Harvard U., 1965. Bar: Calif. 1966. Partner firm McCutchen, Doyle, Brown & Enersen, San Francisco, 1973—; chmn. Conf. of Dels., Calif. State Bar, 1981-82. Mem. Bar Assn. San Francisco (dir. 1974-76, sec. 1983—), San Francisco Barristers Club (pres. 1972), Practising Law Inst. (trustee 1983—). Home: 641 Spruce St Berkeley CA 94707 Office: 3 Embarcadero Center San Francisco CA 94111

BALADA, LEONARDO, composer, educator; b. Barcelona, Spain, Sept. 22, 1933; s. Jose and Lucia (Ibanez) B.; m. Monica McCormack, July 3, 1962 (div. 1977); 1 son, Dylan; m. Joan Winer, July 28, 1979. Profesorado de Teoria, Conservatory of Barcelona, 1953, Profesorado de Music, 1954; diploma in composition, Juilliard Sch. Music, 1960; postgrad., Mannes Coll. Music, 1961-62. Formerly instr. Institucion Cultural, Barcelona; instr. Walden Sch., N.Y.C., 1962-63; head dept. music UN Internat. Sch., N.Y.C., 1963-70. Composer-in-residence, Aspen (Colo.) Inst., 1970; prof. composition, Carnegie-Mellon U., 1970—; Guest composer, U. Tel Aviv, Israel, 1975; guest condr.; Composer: numerous compositions, including Guernica (premiered New Orleans Philharmonic), 1966, Sinfonia en Negro-Homenaje a Martin Luther King; commd. and premiered, Spanish Radio TV Symphony Orch., 1968; Maria Sabina; oratorio, premiered, Carnegie Hall, 1969; Cumbres; premiered at, Carnegie Hall, 1971; Composer: Sinfonia Concertante for guitar and Orch, 1972; Steel Symphony; premiered, Pitts. Symphony, 1972; Composer: commd. and premiered by Nat. Orch. Spain Auroris, 1973; commd. and premiered by Ponce de Leon; for narrator and orch., 1973, premiered by Jose Ferrer and, New Orleans Philharm. Symphony Orch., 1973, Concerto for Piano, Winds and Percussion, 1974; commd. by, Carnegie-Mellon U. Alumni Assn., premiered at, Carnegie Hall, 1974, Homage to Casals and Homage to Sarasate, 1975, premiered by, Pitts. Symphony, 1976 (City of Barcelona Composition prize 1976), Concertino for Castanets and Orch., 1980; concertina for Castanets and Orch. Sonata for Ten Winds, 1980; composer: chamber works, the most recent being Voces; for mixed chorus a capella, 1971, Tresis; for guitar, flute and cello (commd. by), Composers Theatre Inc., premiered at, May Festival in N.Y.C., 1973, Apuntes for guitar quartet, 1974 (Internat. Composition prize Ciudad de Zaragoza), premiered Zaragoza, 1974; solo compositions, the latest being Analogias, for guitar, 1968; premiered by Narciso Yepes at Besançon Music Festival Elementalis, for organ, 1972; premiered by Pitts. Symphony, 1982 Sardana, 1979; commd. by Nat. Endowment Arts, premiered by N.Y. Philharm., 1982 Quasi un Pasodoble, 1981; premiered at Carnegie Hall, 1982 Concerto for Violin and Orch., 1982; commd. and premiered by Internat. Barcelona Music Festival, 1982 Hangman, Hangman (opera), 1982; grand opera in 2 acts, commd. by San Diego Opera Zapata, 1984; commd. by, D. G. Bellas Artes, Spain, premiered, Week of New Music in Barcelona; also composer several ballets and songs; composer works for many soloists, including, Andrés Segovia, Julian Bream, Nicanor Zabaleta, Alicia de Larrocha, music played by numerous orchs., at numerous festivals in U.S. and abroad, music recorded by, Serenus Records, Louisville Orch. First Edit. Records, Deutsche Grammophon, Desto Records, BASF, over 35 works pub. by, Gen. Music and G. Schirmer. Recipient B. Martinu prize in composition Mannes Coll. Music, 1962, Internat. Composition prize Ciudad de Zaragoza, 1974; Fundacion March fellow. Mem. ASCAP (awards), Am. Music Center, Hispanic Soc. Am. (corr.). Office: care Music Dept Carnegie-Mellon U Pittsburgh PA 15213

BALAGOT, REUBEN CASTILLO, anesthesiologist; b. Manila, July 28, 1920; U.S., 1949, naturalized, 1955; s. Pedro G. and Ambrosia (Castillo) B.; m. Lourdes Ramirez, July 10, 1946; children: Joseph, Edgar, Victoria Balagot Hermann, Ophelia Balagot Julien. B.S., U. Philippines, 1941, M.D., 1944. Diplomate: Am. Bd. Anesthesiology. Intern Philippines Gen. Hosp., Manila, 1943-44; resident U. Ill., Chgo., 1949-50, research fellow, 1951, clin. instr., 1952-54, asst. prof., 1954-56, asso. prof., 1956-60, prof., 1960—, chmn. dept., 1974; chmn. dept. anesthesiology Chgo. Med. Sch., Downey, Ill., 1975—; head div. anesthesiology Grant Hosp., 1956-66, Ill. Masonic Hosp., 1966-67; pres. St. Luke's Hosp., Chgo., 1967-71, Hines (Ill.) VA Hosp, 1971-75; chmn. dept. anesthesiology Cook County Hosp., Chgo., 1981—. Contbr. articles to profl. jours. Served with AUS, 1944-46. Named distinguished physician of yr. Philippine Med. Assn., 1968; Outstanding Filipino Overseas in Med. Research award, 1977. Fellow Am. Fedn. Clin. Research; mem. AMA, A.C.S., AAUP, AAAS, N.Y. Acad. Sci., Ill., Chgo. med. socs., Am. Soc. Anesthesiologists, Ill. Soc. for Med. Research, Am. Writers Research, Am. Assn. Med. Instrumentation, Sigma Xi. Home: 4264 Hazel St Chicago IL 60613 Office: 4332 Oakton St Skokie IL 60076 *A tenacity of purpose and curiosity are important; curiosity implies an open mind. Imagination continuously churns new ideas and fresh approaches. Also important is a desire to transmit knowledge. Integrity, especially to personal principles, and luck to amalgamate the foregoing serve as yeast to make it rise into a coherent whole.*

BALAKIAN, ANNA, scholar, educator, critic-writer; b. Constantinople, Turkey, July 14, 1916; came to U.S., 1926; d. Diran and Kohar (Panosian) B.; m. Stepan Nalbantian, Dec. 15, 1945; children: Suzanne, Haig. B.A., Hunter Coll., 1936; M.A., Columbia U., 1938, Ph.D., 1943; L.H.D. (hon.), New Haven U., 1977. Mem. faculty Syracuse U.; prof. French and comparative lit. N.Y. U., 1955—, chmn. comparative lit. dept., 1978—; vis. prof. City U. N.Y., State U. N.Y., Stony Brook; lectr. in numerous univs., including U. Oxford, Eng., College de France, Paris; producer ednl. radio broadcasts. Author: Literary Origins of Surrealism, 1947 (transl. into Spanish), Surrealism: the Road to the Absolute, 1959 (transl. into Japanese), The Symbolist Movement: a critical appraisal, 1967 (transl. into Spanish), Andre Breton: Magus of Surrealism, 1971 (transl. into Spanish); editor, chief contbr.: The Symbolist Movement in the Literature of European Languages, 1983; reviewer: Saturday Rev, 1960-73; contbr. numerous articles on 19th and 20th century lit. to French, Am. and English scholarly jours. Recipient Distinguished Scholar award Hofstra Faculty, 1975; Guggenheim fellow, 1969-70; Nat. Endowment grantee and cons., 1970-79; Am. Council Learned Socs. grantee; Internat. Research Exchange grantee. Mem. Am. Comparative Lit. Assn. (pres. 1977-80), Internat. Comparative Lit. Assn. (v.p. 1979—), Am. Assn. Tchrs. French (nat. v.p. 1968-71), Modern Lang. Assn., PEN Club, Phi Beta Kappa. Mem. Armenian Apostolic Ch. Home: 16 Linden Ln Old Westbury NY 11568 Office: 19 University Ave New York NY 10003 *I have always competed with myself, trying each year to account for the gift of life and good health. In projecting plans for the future I have never let myself be too busy to enjoy the immediate moment. I have never known boredom. My work has been my pleasure and I have never been able to draw a line between what was work and what was pleasure.*

BALAKIAN, NONA HILDA, editor, book critic; b. Istanbul, Turkey; came to U.S., 1926; d. Diran and Koharig (Panossian) B. B.A., Barnard Coll., 1942; M.S. in Journalism, Columbia U., 1943. Mem. editorial bd. N.Y. Times Book Rev., N.Y.C., 71943—; book reviewer Sunday and daily N.Y. Times, 1943—; cons. in field; mem. book selection com. Books-Across-the-Sea, 1978—; mem. Pulitzer Prize jury (for nonfiction), 1977, for poetry, 1979, 81, Hopwood Award jury (for essays), 1979. Contbr. revs., articles, essays to various lit. mags.; Author: Critical Encounters: Literary Views and Reviews, 1953-1977, 1978; editor: (with Charles Simmons) The Creative Present: Notes on Contemporary American Fiction, 1963; editorial bd.: Ararat Quar., 1970—. Recipient Humanities award Rockefeller Found., 1981. Mem. PEN (exec. bd. 1973-80), Nat. Book Critics Circle (founding; exec. bd. 1974—, sec. 1974-76), Authors Guild. Office: NY Times Book Rev 229W 43d St New York NY 10036 *Though confining me to contemporary writing, literary journalism has rewarded me with a sense of progression and innovation in the arts. It has brought me closer to a recognition of a fluid, changing reality, without, I hope, destroying my sense of history; and it has allowed me to straddle the worlds of the creative and the factual mind. In the fusion of my activities as reviewer, essayist and editor, I have been able to view the literary and publishing communities from a variety of perspectives, relating in some degree to all.*

BALAS, EGON, educator; b. Cluj, Romania, June 7, 1922; came to U.S., 1967, naturalized, 1973; s. Ignat and Boriska B.; m. Edith Lovi, 1948; children: Ann, Vera. D.L., Bolyai U., Cluj, 1949; D.Sc.Ec. summa cum laude, U. Brussels; D.U. in Math., U. Paris. Asso. prof. econs. Inst. Econ. Sci., Bucharest, 1949-58; also research economist Inst. Econ. Research of Romanian Acad., 1956-58; analyst Designing Inst. Forestry and Timber Industry, Bucharest, 1959-61, head math. programming group, 1962-64; head math. programming sector Center Math. Stats. of Romanian Acad., 1964-66; research mathematician Internat. Computation Centre, Rome, 1966; vis. prof. ops. research U. Toronto, 1967, Stanford U., 1967; Ford disting. research prof. Carnegie-Mellon U., 1967-68, prof. indsl. adminstrn. and applied math., 1968—; vis. ops. research analyst Fed. Energy Adminstrn., 1976; cons. NSF grantee, 1972—; mem. council Inst. Mgmt. Scis., 1972-75. Asso. editor: Ops. Research, 1967—, Zeitschrift für Operations Research; adv. editor: Discrete Applied Math.; editorial bd.: Naval Research Logistics Quar., Revue Française d'Automatique et Recherche Operationelle; editorial asso.: European Jour. Operational Research; contbr. articles to profl. jours. Recipient Alexander von Humboldt sr. U.S. scientist award, 1980-81. Research on math. programming, especially integer and nonconvex programming, combinatorial optimization, networks, scheduling, energy models, location theory. Home: 104 Maple Heights Rd Pittsburgh PA 15232

BALASSA, BELA, economist, educator; b. Budapest, Hungary, Apr. 6, 1928; came to U.S., 1957, naturalized, 1962; s. George and Charlotte (Andreics) B.; m. Carol Ann Levy, June 12, 1960; children: Mara, Gabor. Diplomkaufmann, Acad. Fgn. Trade, Budapest, 1948; Dr. iuris rerumque Politicarum, U. Budapest, 1951; Ph.D. in Econs, Yale, 1959. Asst., later asso. prof. Yale, 1959-67; adviser, later cons. econs. dept. IBRD, 1966—; prof. polit. economy Johns Hopkins U., 1967—; vis. prof. U. Calif., Berkeley, 1961-62, Columbia U., 1963-64; econ. adviser to internat. orgns. and fgn. govts., cons. to govt. and industry, 1963—. Author: The Hungarian Experience in Economic Planning, 1959, The Theory of Economic Integration, 1961, Trade Prospects for Developing Countries, 1964, Economic Development and Integration, 1965, Trade Liberalization among Industrial Countries: Objectives and Alternatives, 1967, Studies in Trade Liberalization, 1967, The Structure of Protection in Developing Countries, 1971, European Economic Integration, 1975, Policy Reform in Developing Countries, 1977, Industrial Development in Thailand, 1980, Development Strategies in Semi-Industrial Economies, 1982, The Newly-Industrializing Countries in the World Economy, 1981, Turkey: Industrialization and Trade Strategy, 1982; contbg. editor: Changing Patterns in Foreign Trade and Payments, 1964, 70, 77, Economic Progress, Private Values and Public Policy: Essays in Honor of William Fellner, 1977. Rockefeller fellow, 1957-58; Relm Found. grantee, 1958; Ford Found. dissertation fellow, 1958-59; Social Sci. Research Council grantee, 1963; NSF grantee, 1970-74. Mem. Am. Econ. Assn., Econometric Soc., Royal Econ. Soc., Assn. Comparative Econ. Studies (pres. 1979-80). Home: 2134 Wyoming Ave NW Washington DC 20008 Office: 1818 H St NW Washington DC 20433

BALAZS, ENDRE ALEXANDER, physician, educator; b. Budapest, Hungary, Jan. 10, 1920; naturalized, 1956; s. Endre and Vilma (Bonta) B.; children: Marianne, Andre; m. Janet Logan Denlinger, Oct. 7, 1977. M.D., U. Budapest, 1943, U. Uppsala, 1967. Asso. dir. Retina Found., Boston, 1951-61, pres., 1961-63; research dir. dept. connective tissue research Inst. Biol. and Med. Scis., 1961-69, Boston Biomed. Research Inst., 1971-75; also trustee; Malcolm P. Aldrich prof. ophthalmology, dir. research dept. ophthalmology Coll. Physicians and Surgeons, Columbia U., N.Y.C., 1975—; lectr. dept. ophthalmology Harvard Med. Sch., 1957-76. Co-editor-in-chief: Exptl. Eye Research, 1961—; Editor: The Amino Sugars: The Chemistry and Biology of Compounds Containing Amino Sugars, 1965-69, The Chemistry and Molecular Biology of the Intercellular Matrix, 1970. Recipient Friedenwald award Assn. for Research in Ophthalmology, 1963; Guggenheim fellow, 1968. Fellow Gerontol. Soc.; mem. Am. Soc. Biol. Chemists, Soc. Exptl. Biology and Medicine, Biochemical Soc., Internat. Soc. Eye Research (pres. 1978). Office: 630 W 168th St New York NY 10032

BALBACH, STANLEY BYRON, lawyer; b. Normal, Ill., Dec. 26, 1919; s. Nyle Jacob and Gertrude (Cory) B.; m. Sarah Troutt Witherspoon., May 22, 1944; children: Stanley Byron, Nancy Ann Balbach Fehr, Barbara Balbach Lariviere, Edith. B.S., U. Ill., 1940, LL.B., 1942. Bar: Ill. 1942, Fla. 1980, U.S. Supreme Ct. 1950. Practiced in, Hoopeston, 1945-47, Urbana, 1948—; pres. Nat. Title Assurance Fund, Inc.; nat. chmn. Jr. Bar Conf., 1955. Contbr. articles to profl. publs. Chancellor Central Ill. Conf. United Meth. Ch., 1972-77. Served to capt. USAAF, 1942-45. Mem. ABA (ho. of dels. 1956, 65, chmn. spl. com. lawyers title guaranty funds 1962-70, standing mem. 1982—, mem. council, econs. sect. 1975-77), Ill. Bar Assn., Assn. Trial Lawyers Am., Ill. Trial Lawyers Assn., Am. Coll. Probate Counsel (state chmn. 1975-77), Am. Agrl. Law Assn., Am. Judicature Soc., Am. Coll. Real Estate Lawyers, Phi Delta Phi, Alpha Kappa Lambda. Clubs: Masons, Rotary; Union League (Chgo.). Home: 1009 S Douglas St Urbana IL 61801 Office: Box 217 County Bank Plaza Urbana IL 61801

BALCER, CHARLES LOUIS, coll. pres.; b. McGregor, Iowa, May 23, 1921; s. Ludwig Frank and Iva (Vaughan) B.; m. Martha Elizabeth Belgum, Jan. 6, 1944; children—Mary Elizabeth, Mark Lewis, Beth Louise, Brian Charles. B.S., Winona (Minn.) State Tchrs. Coll., 1942; M.A., State U. Iowa, 1949, Ph.D., 1954. Tchr. Minn. and Iowa high schs., 1942-43, 46-47; instr. State U. Iowa, 1947-50; high sch. prin., Detroit Lakes, Minn., 1950-54; asso. prof. speech St. Cloud (Minn.) State Coll., 1954-56, prof., acad. dean, 1958-64; prof. speech State U. N.Y., Oswego, 1956-57; pres. Augustana Coll., Sioux Falls, S.D., 1965-80, Disting. Service prof., 1980—. Author: (with H. F. Seabury) Teaching Speech. Mem. Nat. Luth. Council., S.D. Edn. and Cultural Affairs Planning Commn., 1974—; Bd. dirs. McKennon Hosp., Sioux Falls, Family Life Service, Sioux Falls Symphony Assn. Served with AUS, 1943-46. Decorated knight 1st class Royal Order St. Olav, Norway). Mem. Speech Communication Assn. Am., Central States Speech Assn. (pres. 1954), NEA, Assn. Higher Edn., Delta Sigma Rho, Kappa Delta Pi, Phi Delta Kappa. Republican. Home: 2501 S Kiwanis Apt 206 Sioux Falls SD 57105 Office: Augustana College Sioux Falls SD 57197 *I have learned that the purpose of this earthly life is not happiness. It is to be useful, to be honorable, to be compassionate. It is to matter—to have it made some difference that you lived at all.*

BALCERZAK, MARION JOHN, mech. engr.; b. Balt., Oct. 28, 1933; s. Marion Frank and Cecilia V. (Mazur) B.; m. Mary Joan Kenny, June 21, 1958; children—Stephanie, Susan, Jennifer, Jeffrey. B.Mech. Engring. magna cum laude, U. Detroit, 1956; M.S. (transp. fellow 1957-60), Northwestern U., 1958, Ph.D., 1961. Research engr. Borg-Warner Corp., 1960-62; with GATX Corp., Chgo., 1962—, dir. research and devel., 1980—; tech. dir., then v.p., gen. mgr. subs. GARD, Inc., 1969-80, pres., 1980—. Served with AUS, 1961. Mem. ASME (Charles T. Main award 1956), Am. Mgmt. Assn., AIAA, ASTM, Am. Def. Preparedness Assn., Cumbustion Inst. Home: 2750 Crabtree Ln Northbrook IL 60062 Office: 7449 N Natchez Ave Niles IL 60648

BALCH, CLYDE WILKINSON, chemical engineer, educator; b. Winterset, Iowa, June 11, 1917; s. Harry C. and Beulah (Wilkinson) B.; m. Mary Jo Mitchell, Apr. 13, 1940; children: Charles M., Thomas S., John R. B.S., U. Md., 1937, M.S., 1938; M.S. in Engring. Sci, U. Toledo, 1958. Phys. chemist U.S. Naval Research Labs., 1938-39; chem. engr. E.I. duPont de Nemours & Co., Inc., 1939-46; v.p. Maumee Chem. Co., 1946-65, dir., 1946-66; prof. chem. engring., chmn. dept. U. Toledo, 1965-68, dean adult and continuing edn., dir. evening sessions, 1967-77; cons., lectr. in field, 1960—. Bd. dirs. Toledo Goodwill Industries, 1967-82. Named Toledo Engr. of Year, 1962; recipient Gold T Alumni award U. Toledo, 1979. Fellow Am. Inst. Chem. Engrs., Tau Beta Pi, Phi Kappa Phi, Sigma Rho Tau, Sigma Alpha Epsilon, Alpha Chi Sigma, Alpha Phi Omega. Home: 540 N Kilkenny Dr Onstead MI 49265 *Direct efforts to specific goals and objectives. Maintain personal and intellectual integrity.*

BALCH, GLENN, author; b. Venus, Tex., Dec. 11, 1902; s. Glenn Olin and Edith (Garrison) B.; m. Faula Mashburn (div. 1935); 1 dau., Betty Lou; m. Elise Kendall, May 15, 1937; children—Lynne Kendall, Mary, Olin. Student, North Tex. State Tchrs. Coll., Denton, 1921-23, U. Tex., 1923-24; A.B., Baylor U., 1924; postgrad., Columbia, 1937. Newspaper reporter Idaho Daily Statesman, Boise, 1925-29; bank clerk, 1923-24, forest ranger, 1925, free-lance mag. writer and publicity, 1929—. Author: Riders of the Rio Grande, 1937, Tiger Roan, 1938, Hide-rack Kidnapped, 1939, Indian Paint, 1942, Wild Horse, 1946, Viking Dog, 1948, Christmas Horse, 1949, Lost Horse, 1950 (Boys' Club Book award 1951), Winter Horse, Squaw Boy, Midnight Colt, Indian Saddle-Up, 1953, Little Hawk and The Free Horses, 1956, The Brave Riders, 1958, White Ruff, Horses, 1959, Horse in Danger, 1960, The Stallion King, 1960, Spotted Horse, 1961, Stallion's Foe, 1962, The Runaways, 1963, Guide to Western Horseback Riding, 1965, The Book of Horses, 1966, Keeping Horse, 1966, The Flaxy Mare, 1967, Horse of Two Colors, 1968, Buck, Wild, 1976; Contbr. to periodicals. Served to lt. col. USAAF, 1941-45; CBI. Recipient George Washington Meml. awards Freedoms Found., 1954, 56, 57. Home: 3890 E Victory Rd Meridian ID 83642

BALCH, JOHN N., food chain executive; b. Evanston, Ill., June 27, 1927; m. Olga C. Goy, Nov. 26, 1952; children: Clifton J., Karen, Kathy. B.S., Northwestern U., 1950. Vice pres., treas. Jewel Co., Inc., Chgo. Mem. Am. Inst. C.P.A.s. Home: 2115 Cental Park Ave Evanston IL 60201 Office: Jewel Cos Inc 5725 N East River Rd Chicago IL 60631

BALCH, SAMUEL EASON, lawyer; b. Madison, Ala., Sept. 5, 1919; s. Joseph Austin and Clara Irene (Vaughn) B.; m. Elizabeth Gordon Brock, Apr. 17, 1943; children: Samuel Eason, Elizabeth Gordon Balch Lanier, Gene Austin Balch Limbaugh, Ann Warwick. B.S. in Commerce and Bus. Adminstrn, U. Ala., 1940; LL.B., U. Va., 1948. Bar: Ala. 1948. Since practiced in, Birmingham; mem. firm Martin, Balch, Bingham & Hawthorne (now Balch, Bingham, Baker, Hawthorne, Williams & Ward), 1953—; dir. Ala. Power Co.; chmn. legal com. Edison Electric Inst. Served with AUS, 1941-46. Fellow Am. Bar Found.; mem. Fed. Energy Bar Assn., Am. Bar Assn., Ala. Bar Assn., Birmingham Bar Assn., Newcomen Soc., Am. Judicature Soc., Farrah Law Soc. (trustee), Kappa Sigma. Episcopalian. Clubs: Mountain Brook (Ala.); Downtown, Relay House (Birmingham); Riverchase Country., Pensacola Country. Home: 4229 Old Leeds Rd Birmingham AL 35213 Office: 600 N 18th St Birmingham AL 35203

BALDACCI, LOUIS CHRISTOPHER, utility company executive; b. Chgo., Aug. 4, 1925; s. Louis C. and Irene (Powell) B.; m. Geraldine Barbara Endre, June 22, 1945; children: Susan Marie Baldacci Flor, James Louis, John William, Mark Christopher. Student, Northwestern U., 1942-44, 46-47, B.S.M.E., 1947; student, Stanford U., 1944-45; M.B.A., Northwestern U., Chgo., 1954. Registered profl. engr., Ill. With Peoples Gas Light & Coke Co., Chgo., 1947—, v.p., 1971-81, exec. v.p., 1981—, dir.; dir. North Shore Gas Co., Peoples Energy Corp. Bd. govs. Met. Housing and Planning Council, Chgo., 1972—; bd. dirs. Greater Chgo. Safety Council, 1974—, TRUST, Inc., Chgo., 1982—. Served to sgt. U.S. Army, 1944-46. Roman Catholic. Club: University (Chgo.). Office: Peoples Gas Light & Coke Co 122 S Michigan Ave Chicago IL 60603

BALDAUF, RICHARD JOHN, biology educator; b. Reading, Pa., May 14, 1920. B.S., Albright Coll., 1949; M.S. in Zoology, Tex. A&M U., 1951, Ph.D., 1956. Mem. faculty Tex. A&M U., 1952-72, prof. wildlife, 1964-72; biologist Tex. A&M Research Found., 1951-56; prof. biology U. Mo., Kansas City, 1972-78; dir. edn. Kansas City Museum, 1972-78; prof. biology U. Ark., Little Rock, 1979—; exec. dir. Mus. Sci. and History, Little Rock, 1978-83; mem. Ark. Plan Environ. Edn., Little Rock Wastewater Adv. Com., Ark. Task Force Acid Rain. Author papers in field. Recipient Faculty Disting. Achievement award in teaching Tex. A&M U., 1963, Outstanding Achievement award, 1971; Disting. Service cert. Earth Awareness Found., 1972; named Outstanding Prof. in Agr. Tex. A&M U., 1963. Fellow Tex. Acad. Sci. (past dir.), AAAS; mem. Am. Nature Study Soc. (past pres.), Am. Soc. Ichthyologists and Herpetologists, Tex. Herpetological Soc. (hon. mem., past pres.), Ark. Herpetological Soc., Am. Soc. Zoologists (past div. chmn.), Sigma Xi. Address: 610 Shamrock Dr Little Rock AR 72205 *My research, teaching and museum experiences have been based on my interest and success in writing, teaching, music, advertising, poetry, photography, and lecturing. It appears that my ability to cross disciplines, plus a sense of humor, has contributed in large part to the quality of life I enjoy. I believe that diversity yields stability in the human life.*

BALDERSTON, WILLIAM, III, banker; b. Madison, Wis., Dec. 10, 1927; s. William and Susan (Ramsay) B.; m. Ruth McKinney; children: William IV, David M., Peter R., Mary M. Grad., Dartmouth Coll., 1950. With Philco Corp., 1951-64; with Lincoln First Banks, Inc. (various locations), 1966—, pres., chmn., Syracuse, N.Y., 1974-78, exec. v.p., mgr. regional banking, Rochester, N.Y., 1978-80, pres., chief operating officer, 1980—, also dir.; Bd. govs. Genesee Hosp. Trustee U. Rochester, Landmark Soc., Western N.Y. Served with USNR, 1945. Mem. Rochester C. of C. (trustee). Clubs: Country of Rochester, Genesee Valley; Hillsboro (Hillsboro Beach, Fla.). Office: 1 Lincoln First Sq Rochester NY 14643

BALDESCHWIELER, JOHN DICKSON, chemist, educator; b. Elizabeth, N.J., Nov. 14, 1933; s. Emile L. and Isobel (Dickson) B.; m. Marcia Ewing, June 20, 1959; children—John Eric, Karen Anne, David Russell. B. Chem. Engring., Cornell U., 1956; Ph.D., U. Calif. at Berkeley, 1959. From instr. to asso. prof. chemistry Harvard U., 1960-65; faculty Stanford (Calif.) U., 1965-71, prof. chemistry, 1967-71; chmn. adv. bd. Synchrotron Radiation Project, 1972-75; vis. scientist Synchrotron Radiation Lab., 1977; dep. dir. Office Sci. and Tech., Exec. Office Pres., Washington, 1971-73; prof. chemistry Calif. Inst. Tech., Pasadena, 1973—, chmn. div. chemistry and chem. engring., 1973-78; OAS vis. lectr. U. Chile, 1969; spl. lectr. in chemistry U. London, Queen Mary Coll., 1970; vis. scientist Bell Labs., 1978; Mem. Pres.'s Sci. Adv. Com., 1969—, vice chmn., 1970-71; mem. Def. Sci. Bd., 1973-80, vice chmn., 1974-76; mem. carcinogenesis adv. panel Nat. Cancer Inst., 1973—; mem. com. planning and instl. affairs NSF, 1973-77; adv. com. Arms Control and Disarmament Agy., 1974-76; mem. Nat. Acad. Sci. Bd. Sci. and Tech. for Internat. Devel., 1974-76, ad hoc com. on fed. sci. policy, 1979, task force on synfuels, 1979; mem. Pres.'s Com. on Nat. Medal, 1974-76, Pres.'s Adv. Group on Sci. and Tech., 1975-76; mem. governing bd. Reza Shah Kabir U., 1975—; mem. Sloan Commn. on Govt. and Higher Edn., 1977-79, U.S.-USSR Joint Commn. on Sci. and Tech. Cooperation, 1977-79; vice chmn. del. on pure and applied chemistry to People's Republic of China, 1978, mem. com. on scholarly communication with, 1978—; mem. research adv. council Ford Motor Co., 1979—; mem. Chem. and Engring. Adv. Bd., 1981—. Mem. editorial adv. bd.: Chem. Physics Letters, 1979—. Served to 1st lt. AUS, 1959-60. Sloan Found. fellow, 1962-64, 64-65; recipient Fresenius award Phi Lambda Upsilon, 1968. Mem. Nat. Acad. Scis., Am. Chem. Soc. (award in pure chemistry 1967), Council on Sci. and Tech. for Devel., Am. Acad. Arts and Scis., Am. Philos. Soc. Home: 619 S Hill Ave Pasadena CA 91106 Office: PO Box 5886 Pasadena CA 91107

BALDESSARI, JOHN ANTHONY, artist; b. National City, Calif., June 17, 1931; s. Anton and Hedvig B.; m. Carol Ann Wixom, June 23, 1962; children—Annamarie, Antonio. B.A., San Diego State U., 1953, M.A., 1957. Asst. prof. U. Calif., San Diego, 1968-70; faculty Calif. Inst. Arts, Santa Monica, 1970—, prof., 1970—. One-man shows include, Sonnabend Gallery, N.Y.C., Van Abbemuseum, Eindhoven, Holland, Mus. Folkwang, Essen W. Ger., Rudiger Schöttle Gallery, Munich, Sumangallery, Genoa, Italy, 1981—, group shows include, Paula Cooper Gallery, N.Y.C., Los Angeles County Mus. Art, Westkunst, Cologne, W. Ger., 5th Internat. Biennale, Vienna, Austria; represented in permanent collections, Mus. Modern Art, N.Y.C., Stedelijk Mus., Amsterdam, Holland, Kunstmuseum, Basel Switzerland, Australian Nat. Gallery. Nat. Endowment for Arts grantee, 1973, 74. Home: 3552 Beethoven St Los Angeles CA 90066 Office: 2001 1/2 Main St Santa Monica CA 90405

BALDIN, LIONEL SILUAN, cons. engr.; b. St. Petersburg, Russia, May 28, 1907; came to U.S., 1919, naturalized, 1939; s. Siluan F. and Augusta J. (Malkoff) B.; m. Jane M. Campbell, June 21, 1934. B.S. in Elec. Engring, Columbia, 1927, M.S., 1928. Registered profl. engr., N.Y., Conn. Engr. N.Y. Telephone Co., 1928-29; indsl. engr. Arthur Andersen & Co., N.Y.C., 1929-30; with Ford, Bacon & Davis, Inc., N.Y.C., 1935-72, mgr. valuation, report and indsl. dept., 1954-63, v.p., 1957-72; also dir.; pres., dir. Norwich & Worcester R.R. Co., 1972-74; cons. engr., 1974—; dir. Ford, Bacon & Davis Constrn. Corp., Monroe, La., Ford, Bacon & Davis, Tex., Inc., Dallas, Ford, Bacon & Davis, Can. Ltd., Calgary, Alta. Mem. Newcomen Soc. N.Am., Sigma Alpha Epsilon, Theta Tau, Epsilon Chi. Home: 27 Cannon St Norwalk CT 06851

BALDINGER, MILTON IRVING, lawyer; b. Olyphant, Pa., June 29, 1911; s. Philip and Anne (Ziegler) B.; m. Geraldine Cohen, Mar. 30, 1944; children—Joan Cassin, Joseph Asher. B.A. with 1st honors, Pa.

State U., 1933; LL.B., U. Pitts., 1936; LL.M., Georgetown U., 1939, S.J.D., 1941. Bar: Pa. bar 1936, D.C. bar 1937, U.S. Supreme Ct. bar 1940. Atty. Fed. Home Loan Bank Bd., Washington, 1937-38; asst. counsel REA, Washington, 1938-40; prof. law Nat. U. (later merged with George Washington U.), 1940-51; individual practice law, Washington, 1940—; chmn. bd. emeritus Columbia 1st Fed. Savs. & Loan Assn., Washington; sec. Col. Sanders Ky. Fried Chicken Ltd., Can.; adviser nat. hdqrs. SSS, 1943; lectr. Judge Adv. Gen. Sch., U.S. Army, 1943-45. Author: The General Welfare Clause, 1939, Constitutionality and Other Phases of Selective Service, 1941, Casea and Materials on Federal Income Taxation, 1947, Tax Chats column Washington Law Reporter, 1961-78; editor in chief: U. Pitts. Law Rev, 1935-36, D.C. Bar Jour, 1959-66. Chmn. Met. Washington chpt. Nat. Found., 1966-70; treas. Baldinger Family Found.; trustee Baldinger Found.; sec. Col. Harland Sanders Charitable Orgn., Can., Col. Harland Sanders Found., Ky. Mem. Am. Law Inst., Am., D.C. bar assns., Am. Judicature Soc., Internat. Soc. Investors in Valuable Assets (pres.), Am. Technion Soc., Order of Coif, Tau Epsilon Rho, Delta Sigma Rho, Phi Kappa Phi, Pi Delta Epsilon, Pi Gamma Mu, Zeta Beta Tau. Clubs: Masons (33 deg.), Shriners, B'nai B'rith, Cosmos, Nat. Press, Woodmont Country. Home: 4536 Linnean Ave NW Washington DC 20008 Office: 608 13th St NW Washington DC 20005 *I was taught by my parents: strive to be better than yourself and not better than your neighbor.*

BALDRIDGE, ROBERT CRARY, biochemist, educator; b. Herington, Kans., Jan. 9, 1921; s. Ben Franklin and Lena (Bradshaw) B.; m. Anne E. Dukelow, July 12, 1943; children: Patricia, Ben M., Herbert C., Thomas H., Robert D. B.S., Kans. State U., 1943; M.S., U. Mich., 1948, Ph.D., 1951. Instr. U. Mich., Ann Arbor, 1951-53; asst. prof., prof. biochemistry Temple U. Med. Sch., Phila., 1953-70, assoc. dean Grad. Sch., 1965-70; prof. biochemistry Thomas Jefferson U., Phila., 1970—, dean Coll. Grad. Studies, 1970-81; cons. Uniformed Services U. Health Scis., 1978-82. Pres. bd. dirs. Abington Twp. Library, 1975-78; mem. Montgomery County Govt. Study Commn., 1974-75; bd. dirs. Ken Crest Corp., care retarded children, 1976-81; mem. com. sci. and arts Franklin Inst.; mem. Mayor's Com. on Sci. and Tech., Phila., 1976-80. Served to capt., inf. AUS, 1943-46; col. USAR, 1948-74. NIH grantee. Mem. Phila. Biochem. Soc., Am. Soc. Biol. Chemists, Soc. Exptl. Biology, Sigma Xi, Phi Kappa Phi, Phi Lambda Upsilon. Democrat. Office: 1020 Locust St Philadelphia PA 19107

BALDRIGE, LETITIA, public relations cons.; b. Miami Beach, Fla.; d. Howard Malcolm and Regina (Connell) B. B.A., Vassar Coll.; postgrad., U. Geneva, Switzerland; D.H.L. (hon.), Creighton U., 1979, Mt. St. Mary's Coll., 1980, Robert Hollensteiner. Personal-social sec. to ambassador Am. Embassy, Paris, France, 1948-51, intelligence officer, 1951-53, asst. to ambassador, Rome, Italy, 1953-56; dir. public relations Tiffany & Co., 1956-61; social sec. to The White House, 1961-63; pres. Letitia Baldrige Enterprises, Chgo., 1964-69; dir. consumer affairs Burlington Industries, 1969-71; pres. Letitia Baldrige Enterprises, Inc., N.Y.C., 1972—; trustee N.Y. Bank for Savs.; dir. Dean Witter Reynolds, Inc., The Outlet Co., Fed. Home Loan Bank N.Y.; Bd. dirs. Woodrow Wilson Found., Inst. Internat. Edn., Women's Forum Inc.; trustee Kenyon Coll., Gambier, Ohio, St. David's Sch., N.Y.C. Author: Roman Candle, 1956, Tiffany Table Settings, 1958, Of Diamonds and Diplomats, 1968, Home, 1972, Juggling, 1976; revised: Amy Vanderbilt's Book of Etiquette, 1978, The Entertainers, 1981; Syndicated columnist: Los Angeles Times; contbr. to popular mags.; also lectr. Mem. Fashion Group, Am. Inst. Interior Designers (public relations asso.). Republican. Office: Letitia Baldrige Enterprises Inc 151 E 80th St New York NY 10021

BALDRIGE, MALCOLM, U.S. sec. commerce; b. Omaha, Oct. 4, 1922; s. Howard Malcolm and Regina (Connell) B.; m. Margaret Trowbridge Murray, Mar. 31, 1951; children—Megan Brewster, Mary Trowbridge. B.A., Yale U., 1944. With Eastern Co. (formerly Eastern Malleable Iron Co.), 1947-62, mng. dir., 1951-57, v.p. co., 1957-60, pres., 1960-62; now dir.; exec. v.p. Scovill Mfg. Co., 1962-63, pres., chief exec. officer, 1963-69, chmn. bd., 1969-81; sec. commerce, Washington, 1981—; Co-chmn. Yale Nat. Bus. Gifts Com.; mem. Conn. Republican Fin. Com. Mem. Woodbury Rep. Town Com.; bd. dirs., past chmn. Waterbury ARC; trustee U.S. council Internat. C. of C. Served to capt., F.A. AUS, 1943-46. Mem. Bus. Council, Council for Fgn. Relations, Rodeo Cowboys Assn. Office: Sec of Commerce Washington DC 20230 *

BALDWIN, ARTHUR DWIGHT, JR., academic administrator, geology educator; b. Boston, Oct. 28, 1938; s. Arthur Dwight and Katharine (Balch) B.; m. Barbara H. Hockman, Aug. 1962; children: Arthur Dwight, Timothy Brooks. B.A., Bowdoin Coll., 1961; M.S., U. Kans.-Lawrence, 1963; Ph.D., Stanford U., 1967. Asst. prof. geology Miami U., Oxford, Ohio, 1966-71, assoc. prof., 1972-79, prof., 1980—, dep. dir. Inst. Environ. Sci., 1976-78, chmn. dept. geology, 1978—. Mem. Geol. Soc. Am., Nat. Water Well Assn., AAAS. Home: 4883 James Rd Oxford OH 45056 Office: Dept Geology Miami U Oxford OH 45056

BALDWIN, BENJAMIN ARMISTEAD, JR., advertising executive; b. Carmel, Calif., Jan. 16, 1943; s. Benjamin A. and Violet (Hill) B.; m. Kenny Lynn Griffith, Aug. 12, 1967 (div. 1979); children: Carter Armistead, Lindsay Hill; m. Martha Ann Hale, Jan. 18, 1980. Student, Washington U., 1961-63; B.J., U. Tex., Austin, 1967. Account exec. Aylin Advt., Beaumont, Tex., 1967-69, v.p., gen. mgr., 1969-70, v.p., dir. client servcices, Houston, 1970-71; v.p., ptnr. Smith, Smith, Baldwin & Carlberg, Inc., Houston, 1971-77, pres., 1977-78; pres., chief exec. officer Rives, Smith, Baldwin, Carlberg Y & R, Houston, 1978—. Bd. dirs. Pro-Houston, 1983—, Light House of Houston, 1979—, Gulf Coast chpt. Nat. Arthritis Found., Houston, 1982—, Houston Symphony, 1983—, Children's Drug Abuse Network, 1983—. Named Man of Yr. Houston Advt. Fedn., 1974; recipient Silver medal Houston Advt. Fedn., 1983. Mem. Houston Advt. Fedn. (pres. 1978-79), Am. Advt. Fedn. (dir. 10th dist. 1978-79), Am. Assn. Advt. Agys. (chmn. Houston council). Republican. Episcopalian. Clubs: Houston Yacht (trustee 1980-81), Houston, Houston Racquet. Home: 2047 MacArthur St Houston TX 77030 Office: Rives Smith Baldwin Carlberg & Y&R 5444 Westheimer Houston TX 77056

BALDWIN, BENJAMIN HARRISON, educator; b. St. Louis, Mar. 1, 1919; s. Benjamin H. and Ella (Conley) B.; m. Jeanne Helen Holliger, June 25, 1955; children—Mark Frederick, Claudia Eloise. B.E., So. Ill. U., 1940; M.S. in Journalism, Northwestern U., 1946. News editor Sta. WGN, Chgo., 1946-48, WOR-MBS, N.Y.C., 1948-56; mem. faculty Medill Sch. Journalism, Northwestern U., 1956—, prof. journalism, chmn. editorial dept., 1965-73; dir. Nat. High Sch. Journalism Inst., 1958-67, Teaching Newspaper Program, 1975-77. Served to 1st lt. AUS, World War 11; PTO. Mem. Assn. Edn. Journalism, Nat. Assn. Sci. Writers, Sigma Delta Chi, Phi Kappa Tau. Lutheran (mem. commn. on ch. papers Luth. Ch. Am. 1967-72, cons. com. Luth. mag. 1972—). Home: 1000 Rolling Pass Glenview IL 60025 Office: Medill Sch Journalism Northwestern U Evanston IL 60201

BALDWIN, CALVIN BENHAM, JR., medical adminstrator; b. Radford, Va., Dec. 22, 1925; s. Calvin Benham and Louise (Delp) B.; m. Elizabeth Buell, Mar. 10, 1951; children: Susan B., Sally C., Ann H. A.B., U. N.C., 1949; postgrad., N.C., 1949-51; M.P.A., Harvard U., 1961. Research asst. Inst. Research Social Scis., Chapel Hill, N.C., 1949-50; methods examiner NIH, Bethesda, Md., 1953-55, budget examiner, 1955-57, adminstrv. officer, 1957-58, adminstrv. officer div. gen. med. sci., 1958-61; exec. officerr DGMS, Bethesda, Md., 1961-62; exec. officer Nat. Inst. Child Health, Bethesda, Md., 1963-70, Nat. Cancer Inst., 1970-80, assoc. dir. adminstrn., 1980—. Mem. Montgomery County Econ. Council, Rockville, Md., 1982-83. Served to cpl. U.S. Army, 1944-46; U.S., Germany, Japan. Recipient W.A. Jump meritorious award HEW, 1960, Superior Service award HEW, 1973. Mem. PHI Beta Kappa. Democrat. Unitarian. Home: 10705 Weymouth St Garrett Park MD 20896 Office: NIH-Administration 9000 Rockville Pike Bethesda MD 20205

BALDWIN, DAVID RAWSON, university administrator; b. New Haven, Nov. 2, 1923; s. Albert A. and Hilda (Rawson) B.; m. Dorothy Elizabeth Sonstrom, June 19, 1948; children: Dwight Rawson, Brian Mark, James Albert. B.S. in Govt., U. Conn., 1947; M.P.A. (Volker fellow 1948-49), Wayne State U., 1949. Research asst. Conn. Pub. Expenditure Council, Hartford, 1948-50; exec. sec. Fayette County br. Pa. Economy League, Uniontown, 1950-51; chief assessor Fayette County, 1952-56; fiscal adviser to Pa. gov.-elect George Leader, 1954; research asso. Pa. Economy League, Pitts., 1956-59; budget sec. State of Pa., 1959-64, exec. asst. to treas., 1964-65; asst. sec. U.S. Dept. Commerce, 1965-69; v.p. bus. and finance Wayne State U., Detroit, 1969-71; asso. v.p. for fin. affairs, asst. treas. Temple U., Phila., 1972—; N.E. regional dir. Nat. Assn. State Budget Officers, 1962-64; cons. HEW, 1964. Served to lt. (j.g.) USNR, 1944-46. Mem. Am. Soc. Pub. Adminstrn., Nat. Assn. Coll. and U. Bus. Officers (chmn. com. on ins. 1970-72), Theta Xi (pres. 1947). Presbyn. (ruling elder). Home: 339 Evergreen Rd Jenkintown PA 19046 Office: Carnell Hall Temple U Philadelphia PA 19122

BALDWIN, DAVID SHEPARD, physician; b. Rochester, N.Y., Sept. 5, 1921; s. Jacob and Anna B.; m. Halee Morris, June 24, 1945; children—Neil, Andrew, Daniel, James. B.A., U. Rochester, 1943, M.D., 1945. Intern Barnes Hosp., St. Louis, 1945-46; resident in medicine Bellevue Hosp., N.Y.C., 1946-48; fellow in medicine and physiology N.Y. U. Sch. Medicine, 1948-50, mem. faculty, 1950—, prof. medicine, co-dir. nephrology div., 1972—; attending physician, physician-in-chief hypertension nephritis clinic Bellevue Hosp.; attending physician N.Y. U. Hosp.; cons. nephrology VA Hosp., N.Y.C.; mem. med. adv. bd. council high blood pressure research Am. Heart Assn.; hon. trustee Nat. Kidney Found. N.Y. Author papers in med. jours., chpts. in books. Served as officer M.C. AUS, 1953-55. Mem. Am. Fedn. Clin. Research, Harvey Soc., Am. Heart Assn., Am. Soc. Nephrology, Am. Soc. Clin. Investigation, Internat. Soc. Nephrology, N.Y. Soc. Nephrology (pres. 1974-75), N.Y. Heart Assn. Home: 333 E 69th St New York NY 10021 Office: 550 1st Ave New York NY 10016 also 20 E 68th St New York NY 10021

BALDWIN, DEWITT C., JR., college president. Pres. Earlham Coll., Richmond, Ind., 1983—. Office: Office of Pres Earlham Coll Richmond IN 47374§

BALDWIN, EVERETT NEWTON, food company executive; b. Syracuse, N.Y., May 30, 1932; s. Stanley Everett and Velma Newton B.; m. Carol Fournier, Dec. 23, 1967; children: Gary Everett, Kristen Gay. A.B., Colgate U., 1954; grad., Advanced Mgmt. Program, Harvard U., 1975. With Procter and Gamble, 1957-62, unit sales mgr. New Eng., 1959-62; with Hunt-Wesson Foods, 1962-66, regional sales mgr. West Coast, 1964-66; with Wm. Underwood Co., 1966-75, exec. v.p., 1973-75; v.p. sales and mktg. Grocery Products div. The Pillsbury Co., 1975-77; with Land O'Lakes Foods, Land O'Lakes Inc., Mpls., 1977-82, group v.p., 1978-82; pres., chief exec. officer, dir. Welch Foods Inc., Concord, Mass., 1982—; dir. AG Foods Inc. Harvard Grad. Sch. fund agt. Advanced Mgmt. Program, 1970. Served to capt. USAF, 1954-57. Mem. Nat. Canners Assn. (past dir.), Grocery Mfrs. Am., Assn. Nat. Advertisers. Home: Shepherd's Meadow Route 1 Monument St Concord MA 01742 Office: Welch Foods Inc 100 Main St Concord MA 01742

BALDWIN, GARY LEE, electronics engineer; b. El Centro, Calif., Oct. 12, 1943; s. Benjamin Harrison and Susan Virginia (Webster) B.; m. Lois D. Johnson, Sept. 4, 1965 (div. 1984); children: Christopher, Bryan. B.S., M.S., Ph.D., U. Calif.-Berkeley. Mem. tech. staff Bell Labs., Holmdel, N.J., 1970-78; head dept. Hewlett-Packard Labs., Palo Alto, Calif., 1978—. Contbr. articles to various publs. Fellow IEEE (editor jour. 1980-83); mem. Sigma Xi, Eta Kappa Nu. Office: Hewlett-Packard Labs 1501 Page Mill Rd Palo Alto CA 94304 *

BALDWIN, GARZA, JR., lawyer, manufacturing company executive; b. Litchfield, Ill., Mar. 10, 1921; s. Garza and Hazel (Satterlee) B.; m. Margaret Jean Skinner, Sept. 7, 1946; children—Deborah Baldwin Lyman, Garza, Mary Beth, Daniel David, Benjamin Willis. Student, Vincennes U., 1938-39; B.S., Ind. U., 1942, J.D. with high distinction, 1948. Bar: Ind. bar 1948, U.S. Supreme Ct. bar 1956, N.C. bar 1959. Practiced in, Sullivan, Ind. and, Indpls., 1948-57, city atty., Sullivan, 1951-55; asso. counsel Olin Corp., Pisgah Forest, N.C., 1957-58, div. counsel, 1958-63, sr. counsel, 1963-69, v.p., counsel fine paper and film group, 1969, v.p. corp. group fine paper and film, 1969-71, pres. group, 1971—, v.p. parent co., 1969—; bd. mgrs. Wachovia Bank & Trust Co., Asheville, N.C.; Mem. Gov.'s Council for Econ. Devel., 1967-68, Gov.'s Efficiency Study Commn., 1973-74, N.C. Council on State Policies and Goals, 1974-78, Gov.'s Bus. Council on Arts and Humanities, 1981—; bd. dirs. N.C. Citizens Assn., 1970—, v.p., 1972-73, pres., 1974-75; bd. dirs. Ednl. Found. Commerce and Industry N.C., 1965-73, U. N.C. at Asheville Found., 1971—, N.C. Engring. Found. Trustee Transylvania Community Hosp., Brevard, N.C., Brevard Coll., 1978—, St. Andrews Presbyn. Coll., Laurinburg, N.C., 1978-81, U. N.C. at Asheville, 1974-77, Meml. Mission Hosp., Asheville.; bd. visitors Sch. Engring. Duke U.; mem. acad. alumni fellows Ind. U. Served to lt. (j.g.) USNR, 1942-45. Mem. Am., Ind., N.C. bar assns., Western Carolina Mfrs. Assn. (pres. 1962-71), N.C. Indsl. Council (pres. 1966-67), Am. Judicature Soc., Order of Coif, Am. Legion, Kappa Sigma, Phi Delta Phi. Republican. Presbyterian. Clubs: Masons (32 deg.), Elks, Asheville Country, Asheville City, Biltmore Forest Country; Capital City (Raleigh, N.C.); Sea Pines Country (Hilton Head Island, S.C.). Home: 18 Beaverdam Knoll Asheville NC 28804 Office: PO Box 200 Pisgah Forest NC 28768

BALDWIN, GEORGE CURRIDEN, physicist, educator; b. Denver, May 5, 1917; s. Harry Lewis and Elizabeth (Watson) B.; m. Winifred M. Gould, Apr. 27, 1952; children—George T., John E., Celia M. B.A., Kalamazoo Coll., 1939; M.A., U. Ill., 1941, Ph.D., 1943. Instr. physics U. Ill., Urbana, 1943-44; research asso. Gen. Electric Co., Schenectady, 1944-55, nuclear engr., Cin., 1955-57; reactor mgr. Argonne (Ill.) Nat. Lab., 1957-58, physicist, Schenectady, 1958-67; adj. prof. nuclear engring. and sci. Rensselaer Poly. Inst., 1964-67, prof., 1967-77, prof. emeritus, 1977—; staff mem. Los Alamos Sci. Lab., 1975—. Author: An Introduction to Nonlinear Optics, 1969; Contbr. articles to profl. jours. Councilman, Niskayuna, N.Y., 1965-69; mem. Zoning Bd., 1969-77. Fellow Am. Phys. Soc.; mem. AAAS, N.Y. Acad. Scis., Phi Beta Kappa, Sigma Xi, Phi Kappa Phi, Gamma Alpha. Office: Los Alamos Sci Lab Los Alamos NM 87544

BALDWIN, GORDON BREWSTER, educator, lawyer; b. Binghamton, N.Y., Sept. 1929; s. Schuyler Forbes and Doris Ambeline (Hawkins) B.; m. Helen Louise Hochgraf, Feb., 1958; children—Schuyler, Mary Page. LL.B., Cornell U., 1953; B.A., Haverford Coll., 1950. Bar: N.Y. bar 1953, Wis. bar 1965. Practiced in, Rochester and, Rome, N.Y., 1953-57; prof. law U. Wis.-Madison, 1957—, asso. dean law, 1968-70; dir. officer edn. U. Wis., 1972—; chmn. internat. law U.S. Naval War Coll., 1963-64; Fulbright prof., Cairo, 1966-67, Tehran, Iran, 1970-71; lectr. State Dept., Cyprus, 1967, 1969, 1971; counselor internat. law U.S. Dept. State, Washington, 1975-76, cons., 1976-77, U.S. Naval War Coll., 1961-65; chmn. screening com. on law Fulbright Program, 1974; mem. constl. law com. Multi-State Bar Exam.; chmn. State Public Def. Bd., 1980-83. Served to capt. AUS, 1953-57. Ford Found. fellow, 1962-63. Mem. Wis. State Bar Assn. (vice chmn. sect. on individual rights 1973-75), Fulbright Alumni Assn. (dir. 1979-82), AAUP (nat. council 1975-78), Order of Coif, Phi Beta Kappa. Club: Rotary (Madison) (pres. 1980). Office: Law Sch Univ Wis Madison WI 53706

BALDWIN, HENRY FURLONG, banker; b. Balt., Jan. 15, 1932; s. Henry du Pont and Margaret (Taylor) B.; (divorced); children: Mary Stevenson, Severn Eyre. A.B., Princeton U., 1954. With Merc.-Safe Deposit & Trust Co., Balt., 1956, v.p., 1963-65, sr. v.p., 1965, exec. v.p., 1965-70, pres., 1970-76, chmn. bd., 1976—; pres., dir. Merc. Bankshares Corp., 1970—; dir. Merc. Safe Deposit & Trust Co., U.S. Fidelity & Guarantee Co., USF&G Corp., Fidelity & Guarantee Life Ins. Co., Flow Gen., Inc., So. Md. Oil, Inc., Ellicott Machine Corp. Trustee Johns Hopkins U., Johns Hopkins Hosp.; bd. govs. and visitors Washington Coll. Served with USMCR, 1954-56. Home: 13801 Mantua Mill Rd Glyndon MD 21071 Office: Mercantile-Safe Deposit & Trust Co Box 1477 Baltimore MD 21203

BALDWIN, HOWARD J., professional hockey team executive; b. 1942; children: Scott, Rebecca, Howard. Student, Boston U. Former bus. mgr. Jersey Devils; ticket mgr., head sales and promotions Phila. Flyers, NHL; founder, mng. gen. ptnr. New Eng. Whalers (now Hartford Whalers), NHL, Conn., 1971—. Served with USMC. Office: Hartford Whalers One Civic Ctr Plaza Hartford CT 06103 *

BALDWIN, JACK NORMAN, microbiologist, educator; b. Nephi, Utah, Dec. 6, 1919; s. Ernest Frank and Eva (Christison) B.; m. Adell Holmgren Cheney, Sept. 6, 1946; children—Marian Adell, Jack Norman, Eva Lee. B.A., U. Utah, 1942, M.A., 1947; Ph.D., Purdue U., 1950. Research asso. Purdue U., 1948-50; asst. prof. Ohio State U., Columbus, 1950-56, 1956-60, prof., 1960-63, U. Ky., Lexington, 1963-67; prof. dept. microbiology U. Ga., Athens, 1967—. Contbr. articles to profl. jours. Served with AUS, 1942-45. Mem. Am. Soc. Microbiology, Soc. Gen. Microbiology, Soc. Exptl. Biology and Medicine, AAAS, Sigma Xi, Phi Lambda Upsilon. Mormon. Home: 185 Pendleton Dr Athens GA 30601 Office: Dept Microbiology U Ga Athens GA 30601:

BALDWIN, JAMES, writer; b. N.Y.C., Aug. 2, 1924; s. David and Berdis Emma (Jones) B. Ed. high sch. Author: Go Tell It on the Mountain, 1953; essays Notes of a Native Son, 1955; Giovanni's Room, 1958, Nobody Knows My Name, 1960, Another Country, 1962, The Fire Next Time, 1963, Blues for Mr. Charlie; play The Amen Corner, 1955, 1964, Going to Meet the Man, 1966, Tell Me How Long the Train's Been Gone, 1968, No Name In the Street, 1972, One Day When I Was Lost, 1973, If Beale Street Could Talk, 1974; Little Man, Little Man, 1975; essays The Devil Finds Work, 1976, Just Above My Head, 1979; contbr. numerous articles to nat. mags. Mem. nat. adv. bd. Congress Racial Equality, Nat. Com. for Sane Nuclear Policy; lectr. civil rights. Saxton fellow, 1945; Rosenwald fellow, 1948; Guggenheim fellow, 1954; Partisan Rev. fellow, 1956; recipient Nat. Inst. Arts and Letters award, 1956; Ford Found. grant-in-aid, 1959, George K. Polk award, 1963. Mem. Actors Studio, Nat. Inst. Arts and Letters. Address: care Edward Acton Inc 17 Grove St New York NY 10014 *

BALDWIN, JIM D., supermarket chain executive. Pres. King Soopers Inc., Denver. Office: 65 Tejon St Denver CO 80223

BALDWIN, JOHN (JOHN PAUL JONES), bassist, keyboard player; b. Sidcup, Kent, Eng., Jan. 3, 1946. Played with various groups from his early teens to, 1966; arranger and session musician various groups including, Donovan and Rolling Stones, 1966-68; bass and keyboard player rock group, Led Zeppelin, 1968—, worldwide concert performances, 1968—; performed in film The Song Remains the Same, 1976; albums include In Through the Out Door. Office: care Swan Song Inc 444 Madison Ave New York NY 10022 *

BALDWIN, JOHN ASHBY, JR., naval officer; b. Balt., Apr. 20, 1933; s. John Ashby and Laura (Hanson) B.; m. Leslie Hall, Dec. 30, 1961; children: Charles Gambrill, Dorothy Sewell. B.S., U.S. Naval Acad., 1955; postgrad., U. Wash., 1962-64. Commd. ensign U.S. Navy, 1955, advanced through grades to rear adm., 1980; comdr. Destroyer Squadron 33, Pearl Harbor, Hawaii, 1975-77; dep. dir. Office of Program Appraisal, Office of Sec. of Navy, Washington, 1977-79; mil. asst. to Dep. Sec. Def., Washington, 1979-81; dir. Systems Analysis Div., Office of Chief of Naval Ops., Washington, 1980-82; comdr. Cruiser-Destroyer Group 3, 1982—. Decorated Def. D.S.M., Bronze Star with combat V, Meritorious Service medal. Mem. U.S. Naval Inst. Episcopalian. Clubs: Nantucket Yacht, Transpacific Yacht, Wharf Rat. Home: Quarters V NASNI San Diego CA 92135 Office: Comdr Cruiser-Destroyer Group 3 care Fleet Post Office San Francisco CA 96601

BALDWIN, JOHN EDWIN, educator; b. Berwyn, Ill., Sept. 10, 1937; s. Francis Miller and Irville (Miller) B.; m. Anne Kruesi Nordlander, Sept. 23, 1961; children—Claire Miller, John Nordlander, Wesley Hale. A.B. summa cum laude, Dartmouth, 1959; Ph.D., Calif. Inst. Tech., 1963. Mem. chemistry faculty U. Ill., 1962-68; prof. chemistry U. Oreg., Eugene, 1968—; dean Coll. Arts and Scis., 1975-80; cons. Stauffer Chem. Co., Office Sci. and Tech., NIH. Author: Experimental Organic Chemistry, 1965, also articles.; Adv. bd.: Organic Reactions. Guggenheim fellow, 1967; Sloan fellow, 1966-68; sr. U.S. scientist award Alexander von Humboldt Found., 1974-75. Home: 2550 Fairmount Blvd Eugene OR 97403

BALDWIN, JOHN WESLEY, history educator; b. Chgo., July 13, 1929; s. Edward N. and H. and Gladys (McDaniel) B.; m. Jenny Jochens, Dec. 24, 1954; children: Peter, Ian, Birgit, Christopher. B.A., Wheaton Coll., 1950; M.A., Pa. State U., 1951; Ph.D., Johns Hopkins, 1956. Instr., then asst. prof. U. Mich., 1956-61; mem. faculty Johns Hopkins, 1961—, prof. history, 1966—. Author: The Medieval Theories of the Just Price, 1959, Masters, Princes and Merchants, 2 vols, 1970, The Scholastic Culture of the Middle Ages, 1971, City on the Seine: Paris under Louis IX, 1226-1270, 1975; Editor: (with Richard Goldthwaite) Universities in Politics: Case Studies from the Late Middle Ages and Early Modern Period, 1972. Guggenheim fellow, 1960-61, 83-84; Howard fellow, 1960-61; Fulbright fellow, 1965-66; grantee Am. Council Learned Socs., 1965-66; sr. fellow Nat. Endowment for Humanities, 1972-73. Fellow Medieval Acad. Am.; mem. Soc. for French Hist. Studies, Royal Danish Acad. Scis. and Letters (fgn.), Am. Hist. Assn., Commn. Internationale de Diplomatique. Home: 4828 Roland Ave Baltimore MD 21210

BALDWIN, JOSEPH LYLE, financial executive; b. Washington, Aug. 26, 1931; s. Joseph Lyle and Claire Anderson (Black) B.; m. Mary Burt Holmes, Dec. 9, 1961; children: Pamela Holmes, Kathryn Anderson, Elizabeth Black. B.A., Duke U., 1953; J.D., U. Va., 1956. Bar: Va. 1956, Ill. 1959. Asso. firm Simpson, Thacher & Bartlett, N.Y.C., 1956; with U.S. Gypsum Co., Chgo., 1958-71; v.p. devel. USG Urban Devel. Corp., 1969-71; v.p., treas. Arcata Corp., Menlo Park, Calif., 1971-82; dir. investor relations and investments Crown Zellerbach, San Francisco, 1982—. Mem. planning com. Hoover Sch., Palo Alto, Calif., 1975-76; vestryman All Saints Episcopal Ch., Palo Alto, 1975-77, sr. warden, 1976. Served with AUS, 1956-58. Mem. Va., Chgo. bar assns., Financial Execs. Inst., Kappa Alpha. Clubs: Foothills (Palo Alto); Bankers (San Francisco); Harvard (N.Y.C.); Carlton (Chgo.). Home: 1211 Cowper St Palo Alto CA 94301 Office: 1 Bush St San Francisco CA 94104

BALDWIN, LIONEL V., university dean; b. Beaumont, Tex., May 30, 1932; s. Eugene B. and Wanda (Wiley) B.; m. Kathleen Flanagan, Sept. 3, 1955; children: Brian, Michael, Diane, Daniel. B.S., U. Notre Dame, 1954; S.M., Mass. Inst. Tech., 1955; Ph.D., Case Inst. Tech., 1959. Research engr. Nat. Adv. Com. Aeros., Ohio, 1957-59; unit head NASA, 1959-61; asso. prof. engring. Colo. State U., 1961-64; acting dean Coll. of Engring., 1964-65, dean, 1966—. Served to capt. USAF, 1955-57. Recipient award for plasma research NASA, 1964. Asso. fellow AIAA; mem. Am. Soc. Engring. Edn. (chmn. engring. deans council), ASME, Am. Inst. Chem. Engrs., Nat. Soc. Profl. Engrs., Sigma Xi, Tau Beta Pi, Sigma Pi Sigma. Patentee apparatus for increasing ion engine beam density. Home: 1900 Sequoia St Fort Collins CO 80525 Office: Colorado State University Fort Collins CO 80523

BALDWIN, PAUL CLAY, business executive; b. Tully, N.Y., May 19, 1914; s. Fred Lynn and Grace Ann (Clay) B.; m. Margaret Mary Fargo, Nov. 2, 1940 (dec. July 1970); children: Barbara F., Paul Clay, Robert F.; m. Doris Walsh, May 20, 1972. B.S., Syracuse U., 1936; M.S., Inst. Chemistry, 1938, Ph.D., 1940; Sc.D., Lawrence U., 1972. With Scott Paper Co., 1940-77, tech. dir., prodn. supr., 1940-46, gen. plant mgr., 1946-51, asst. v.p., 1951-53, v.p., 1953-57, v.p. mfg., engring. and research, 1957-60, exec. v.p. mfg., engring. and research, 1960-62, exec. v.p., 1962-68, vice chmn., dir., 1968-77; vice chmn., trustee, dir. Gilman Paper Co., 1981—; cons. Parsons & Whittemore, Inc., N.Y.; past chmn. bd. Brunswick Pulp & Paper Co.; cons. to paper industry, Devon, Pa.; Chmn. corp. adv. council Syracuse U.; chmn. bd. Research Corp.; dir.-at-large Syracuse Pulp and Paper Found.; former chmn. bd., exec. com. Am. Paper Inst.; chmn. bd. trustees Inst. Paper Chemistry. Recipient Honor award U. Maine Pulp and Paper Found., 1972. Fellow TAPPI; mem. World Affairs Council Phila., Tau Beta Pi, Phi Kappa Psi, Alpha Chi Sigma, Pi Mu Epsilon. Clubs: Aronimink; Union League (Phila.); Radnor Hunt; Anglers (N.Y.). Home: 1300 S Leopard Rd Berwyn PA 19312

BALDWIN, PETER ARTHUR, psychologist, educator, clergyman; b. Andover, Mass., Apr. 7, 1932; s. Alfred Graham and Katherine (Ashworth) B.; m. Carolyn Whitmore, Sept 3, 1955; children: Sarah MacDonald, Robert Henry, Judith Helen. B.A., Middlebury Coll., 1955; S.T.B., Boston U., 1959, Ph.D., 1964; student, New Coll., U. London, 1957-58. Certified psychologist, N.H.; registered psychologist Nat. Register Health Providers in Psychology; accredited chaplain supr. Assn. Clin. Pastoral Edn. Ordained to ministry Unitarian-Universalist Ch., 1959; pastor 2d Ch., Boston, 1955-57, in Dighton, Mass., 1958-62; religious counselor M.I.T., 1959-63; exec. dir. Liberal Religious Youth, Unitarian Universalist Assn., 1963-66; asst. prof. Crane Theol. Sch., Tufts U., 1965-67, Meadville Theol. Sch., U. Chgo., 1967-73; pastor All Souls 1st Universalist Soc., Chgo., 1971-73; assoc. prof. psychology New Eng. Coll., Henniker, N.H., 1973-74; vis. assoc. prof. psychology Colby Coll., New London, N.H., 1974-76; founder N.H. Gestalt Inst., 1973—; assoc. prof. psychology Antioch-New Eng. Grad. Sch., Keene, N.H., 1976—; pvt. practice clin. psychology, 1976—; Dir. Sr. High and Family Insts., Rowe, Mass., 1967-74; Nat. Edn. Conf. lectr. Williston Acad., 1967; Judy lectr., Omaha, 1970. Mem. Am. Psychol. Assn., N.H. Psychol. Assn. (pres. 1980-81), Liberal Religious Youth (life), Liberal Religious Edn. Dirs. Assn., AAUP, Unitarian-Universalists Ministers Assn. Democrat. Home: RD2 Pittsfield NH 03263 Office: 81 Court St Keene NH 03431 Pancake Hill Rd Lower Gilmanton NH 03263

BALDWIN, PHILLIP BENJAMIN, U.S. judge; b. Marshall, Tex., Dec. 23, 1924; s. Jack B. and Lucille (Jones) B.; m. Mertie Bellamy, July 2, 1948; children—Rebecca (Mrs. Bruce C. Clark), Nancy, Jane, Phillip Benjamin. Student, U. Tex., 1942-43; B.A. in Biology, N. Tex. State Tchrs. Coll., 1949, E. Tex. Bapt. Coll., 1949, Baylor U. Law Sch., 1950-51, S. Tex. Sch. Law, 1951-52. Bar: Tex. bar 1952. Asst. dist. atty., Marshall, 1953-54, criminal dist. atty., Harrison County, Tex., 1954-58, practice in, Marshall, 1958-68; U.S. asso. judge Ct. Customs and Patent Appeals, 1968—. Served with USAAF, 1943-46; PTO. Mem. ABA, Tex. Bar Assn., N.E. Tex. Bar Assn., Harrison County Bar Assn. (sec. 1957, pres. 1958-60), Tex. Trial Lawyers Assn., Nat. Assn. Def. Lawyers in Criminal Cases, Am. Legion, VFW, Alpha Tau Omega, Phi Delta Phi. Episcopalian. Club: Elk. Office: US Ct of Customs and Patent Appeals 717 Madison Pl NW Washington DC 20439 *

BALDWIN, RALPH BELKNAP, manufacturing company executive, astronomer; b. Grand Rapids, Mich., June 6, 1912; s. Melvin D. and Julie (Belknap) B.; m. Lois Virginia Johnston, Aug. 3, 1940; children: Melvin Dana II, Pamela, Bruce Belknap. B.S., U. Mich., 1934, M.S., 1935, Ph.D., 1937, LL.D., 1975. Asst. dept. astronomy U. Mich., 1935-36, U. Pa., 1937-38; instr. dept. astronomy Northwestern U., 1938-42; lectr. Adler Planetarium, Chgo., 1940-42; sr. physicist applied physics lab. Johns Hopkins, Silver Spring, Md., 1942-46, cons., East Grand Rapids, Mich., 1946-47; acting supt. schs., East Grand Rapids, 1947; prodn. mgr. Oliver Machinery Co., Grand Rapids, 1947—, dir., 1948—, successively personnel dir., prodn. mgr., sec., 1949-56, v.p., 1956-70, pres., 1970—, chmn. bd., 1981—; Chmn. bd. Internat. Woodworking Machinery and Furniture Supply Fair-U.S.A., 1969-70, 77-78. Author: The Face of the Moon, 1949, The Measure of the Moon, 1963, The Moon—A Fundamental Survey, 1966, The Deadly Fuze: Secret Weapon of World War II, 1980; Contbr. articles to profl. jours. Recipient Presdl. Certificate of Merit, 1947; U.S. Naval Bur. Ordnance award; U.S. Army Chief of Ordnance award; Distinguished Alumnus award U. Mich., 1967; Woodworking and Furniture Digest award Forest Products Research Soc., 1973; J. Lawrence Smith medal Nat. Acad. Scis., 1979. Fellow AAAS, Am. Geophys. Union; mem. Am. Acad. Arts and Scis., Am. Astron. Soc., Royal Astron. Soc. Can. (hon.), Grand Rapids Museum Assn., NAM (dir. 1963-64), Employers Assn. Grand Rapids (pres. 1960-64), Woodworking Machinery Mfrs. Assn. (pres. 1964-68). Clubs: Rotary, Peninsular, University, Kent Country. Home: 6190 S Gatehouse Dr SE Grand Rapids MI 49506 Office: 1025 Clancy Ave NE Grand Rapids MI 49503

BALDWIN, ROBERT EDWARD, economics educator; b. Niagara Falls, N.Y., July 12, 1924; s. Gilbert and Margaret (Ostman) B.; m. Janice Murphy, July 31, 1954; children: Jean, Robert, Richard, Nancy. A.B., U. Buffalo, 1945; Ph.D., Harvard U., 1950. Instr., then asst. prof. econs. Harvard, 1950-57; asso. prof., then prof. econs. UCLA, 1957-64; prof. econs. U. Wis. at Madison, 1964—, F.W. Taussig research prof., 1974—, Hilldale prof., 1982—, chmn. econ. dept., 1975-79; chief economist Office Spl. Trade Rep., Exec. Office of President, 1963-64; vis. prof. Brookings Instn., Washington, 1967-68, U.S. Dept. Labor, 1975-76, World Bank, 1978-79; mem. adv. bd. Inst. Internat. Econs. Author: Economic Development and Export Growth, 1966, Nontariff Distortions of International Trade, 1970, Foreign Trade Regimes and Economic Development: The Philippines, 1975, The Political Economy of Protectionism, 1982, The Inefficiency of Trade Policy, 1982; co-author: Economic Development, 1957, Disease and Economic Development, 1973; Mem. bd. editors: Pakistan Devel. Rev, Rev. of Econs. and Stats., World Economy. Mem. Am. Econ. Assn., Council Fgn. Relations. Home: 125 Nautilus Dr Madison WI 53705

BALDWIN, ROBERT GEORGE, university administrator; b. Vancouver, B.C., Can., Jan. 13, 1927; s. Sidney George and Vera Berkeley (Bailey) B.; m. Barbara Kathleen Chew, Aug. 28, 1948; children: Christopher George, John Robert (dec.), Janet Kathleen Werner. B.A., U. B.C., 1948; M.A., U. Toronto, 1949, Ph.D., 1957. Lectr. English U. Alta., Edmonton, 1951-54, asst. prof., 1954-58, assoc. prof., 1958-63, prof., 1963—, chmn. dept. English, 1967-71, assoc. dean arts, 1971-72, dean arts, 1972-79, v.p. (acad.), 1979—, bd. govs., 1971-74. Can. Council sr. fellow, 1966-67. Mem. Assn. Canadian U. Tchrs. English (v.p. 1970-72), Canadian Assn. Deans Arts and Sci. (pres. 1977-79), Canadian Assn. U. Tchrs., Internat. Assn. U. Profs. English. Home: 6504 124th St Edmonton AB Canada T6H 3V3

BALDWIN, ROBERT HAYES BURNS, business executive; b. East Orange, N.J., July 9, 1920; s. John Frank and Anna (Burns) B.; m. Geraldine Gay Williams, May 28, 1949; children: Janet Kimball, Deborah Gay Baldwin Fall, Robert Hayes Burns, Whitney Hayes, Elizabeth Brooks. A.B., Princeton U., 1942. With Morgan Stanley & Co., N.Y.C., 1946—, gen. ptnr., 1958-65, 67-75, ltd. ptnr., 1965-67; now pres., mng. dir. Morgan Stanley & Co., Inc., N.Y.C.; served as under sec. Dept. Navy, 1965-67; dir. Urban Nat., Inc. Trustee Presbyn. Hosp. City N.Y., Morristown Meml. Hosp., N.J., Geraldine Rockefeller Dodge Found., Seeing Eye, Inc., Orgn. Resources Counselors, Inc. Served to lt. USNR, 1942-46. Mem. Securities Industry Assn. (governing council, vice chmn. bd. dirs.), Council Fgn. Relations, Phi Beta Kappa. Republican. Presbyterian. Clubs: Links (N.Y.C.); Chevy Chase (Md.); Met. (Washington); Morris County Golf (Convent, N.J.); Morristown Field (N.J.); Bridgehampton (N.Y.); Chgo.; Augusta Nat. Golf (Ga.). Home: Village Rd New Vernon NJ 07976 Office: 1251 Ave of Americas New York NY 10020

BALDWIN, ROBERT LESH, educator, biochemist; b. Madison, Wis., Sept. 30, 1927; s. Ira Lawrence and Mary (Lesh) B.; m. Anne Theodora Norris, Aug. 28, 1965; children—David Norris, Eric Lawrence. B.A., U. Wis., 1950; D.Phil. (Rhodes scholar), Oxford (Eng.) U., 1954. Asst. prof., then asso. prof. biochemistry U. Wis., 1955-59; mem. faculty Stanford, 1959—, prof. biochemistry, 1964—; vis. prof. Collège de France, Paris, 1972. Asso. editor: Jour. Molecular Biology, 1964-68, 75-79; mem. editorial bd.: Trends Biochem. Sci, 1977—. Served with AUS, 1946-47. Guggenheim fellow, 1958-59. Mem. Nat. Acad. Scis., Am. Soc. Biol. Chemists, Am. Chem. Soc., Am. Biophysics Soc. (council 1977-81), Am. Acad. Arts and Scis. Home: 1243 Los Trancos Rd Portola Valley CA 94025 Office: Dept Biochemistry Stanford Med Sch Stanford CA 94305

BALDWIN, RUTH WORKMAN, pediatrician; b. Chgo., Nov. 3, 1915; d. John J. and Lucille (Hayes) Workman; m. Gary Martin Baldwin, Sept. 2, 1939; children—John Workman, Gary Martin, Thomas Michael, Robert Hayes. Student, Lewis Inst., 1936-38; B.S., U. Md., 1942, M.D., 1943. Diplomate: Am. Bd. Pediatrics. Intern, asst. resident, then resident in medicine West Balt. Gen. Hosp., 1944-46; asst. resident in pediatrics Univ. Hosp., 1947-49; fellow Children's Hosp. Neurology, Boston, 1949; pvt. practice, Catonsville, Md., 1950-52; asst. prof. pediatrics, dir. seizure unit U. Md. Sch. Medicine, 1950-64, asso. prof. pediatrics, 1964-76, prof., 1976—, asst. electroencephalographer, 1952, also dir.; cons. Rosewood State Tng. Sch., Md. Dept. Health; chmn. med. adv. bd. Md. State Motor Vehicle Adminstrn.; Mem. Md. Council Developmental Disabilities, chmn., 1971-72; mem. adv. bd. Assn. Mentally Handicapped Children in Md., Md. Eastern Shore Epilepsy Assn., Chesapeake Assn. Epilepsy, Assn. Children with Specific Learning Disabilities, others; chmn. Exec. Coalition for Handicapped. Med. adv. bd. numerous civic assns. for handicapped and retarded citizens. Postdoctoral fellow Harvard U. Med. Sch., 1949. Fellow Am. Acad. Pediatrics (chmn. handicapped and mental health com.); mem. Med. and Chirurg. Faculty Md., Am. Acad. Neurology (asso.), Eastern Assn. Electroencephalographers, Am. League Against Epilepsy, Nat. Rehab. Assn., Am. Med. Women's Assn., others. Republican. Presbyterian (elder). Club: Soroptimist (Catonsville). Co-discoverer of aminoaciduria in one of the cerebromacular degenerations. Home: 324 Gun Rd Relay MD 21227 Office: University Hosp Baltimore MD 21201 *Over the years I have been concerned about family life, treating others the way I wish to be treated, concerned for 40 years about the health and welfare of children, especially those who have central nervous system disabilities (the developmental disabilities), and running a home and raising a family to be understanding, kind and productive.*

BALDWIN, WILLIAM HOWARD, lawyer, foundation executive; b. Detroit, Feb. 21, 1916; s. Howard Charles and Ruth E. (Jensen) B.; m. Carol Lees, May 24, 1947; children: Susan, Jeffrey, Julie, Deborah. B.A., Williams Coll., 1938; J.D., U. Mich., 1941; LL.D., Oakland U., 1971, Hobart and William Smith Colls., 1972. Bar: Mich. bar 1941. Partner firm Dykema Gossett, Spencer, Goodnow & Trigg, Detroit, 1970-77, of counsel, 1977—; chmn., trustee Kresge Found., Troy, Mich., 1963—; dir. Standard Fed. Savs. & Loan Assn., Troy, 1962—, K Mart Corp. Served with USAAF, 1942-45. Mem. Am., Mich., Detroit bar assns., Delta Upsilon, Phi Delta Phi. Republican. Episcopalian. Clubs: Bloomfield Hills Country, Detroit Athletic, Detroit. Asst. U.S. prosecutor Nuremberg Trials, 1946. Home: 3517 Bloomfield Club Dr Birmingham MI 48010 Home: PO Box 252 Boca Grande FL 33921 Office: 2401 W Big Beaver Rd Troy MI 48084

BALDWIN, WILLIAM LEE, economics educator; b. N.Y.C., Apr. 12, 1928; s. William Lee and Mildred (Karnes) B.; m. Marcia Diane Hurt, Aug. 18, 1956; children: Douglas Lee, Ellen Parker. B.A., Duke U., 1951; M.A., Princeton U., 1953, Ph.D., 1958. Asst. in instrn., instr. Princeton U., 1952-56, vis. asst. prof., 1961-62; instr., asst. prof., asso. prof., prof. Dartmouth Coll., Hanover, N.H., 1956—, chmn. social scis. div., 1970-72, chmn. econs. dept., 1972-74, 75-78; mem. spl. field staff Rockefeller Found., 1974-75; vis. prof. Thammasat U., Bangkok, Thailand, 1968-70; vis. researcher U. Sains, Malaysia, 1979; cons. FTC, 1980. Author: Antitrust and the Changing Corporation, 1961, The Structure of the Defense Market, 1955-64, 1967, (with S.D. Maxwell) The Role of Foreign Financial Assistance to Thailand in the 1980s, 1975, The World Tin Market: Political Pricing and Economic Competition, 1983; contbr. articles to profl. jours. Served with AUS, 1946-47. Brookings research prof., 1963-64. Mem. Am. Econ. Assn., Indsl. Orgn. Soc. (v.p. 1977-78), AAUP, Phi Beta Kappa, Omicron Delta Kappa. Home: 8 Rayton Rd Hanover NH 03755

BALDYGA, DONALD ARTHUR, banker; b. Bloomfield, N.J., Jan. 13, 1926; s. Joseph and Agnes (Sturm) B.; m. Adline Tarantino, June 25, 1955; 1 son, Donald. B.S. magna cum laude, Seton Hall U., 1950, M.B.A., 1957; J.D., Fordham U., 1957. C.P.A., N.J., Washington. Jr. accountant Peat, Marwick, Mitchell & Co. (C.P.A.'s), N.Y.C., 1950-59, mgr., 1960-61; accounting officer Chase Manhattan Bank, N.Y.C., 1962—, now sr. v.p., gen. auditor; adj. asst. prof. accounting Seton Hall U.; instr. accounting Fairleigh Dickinson U.; Mem. N.J. Econ. Devel. Council, 1968-78. Commr., pres. Passaic County (N.J.) Mental Health Bd., 1963-66; finance chmn. Clifton-Garfield dist. Boy Scouts Am., 1968; dir., treas. Community Action Council, Passaic County, 1964-67; Bd. dirs. Family Mental Health Center, Clifton, N.J. Mem. N.Y. Bar, Am. Inst. C.P.A.s, N.Y. Soc. C.P.A.s. Democrat. Home: 180 Magnolia Woods Ct Apt 8D Deltona FL 32725 Office: 1 New York Plaza New York NY 10015

BALE, ERIC GWYNNE, insurance executive; b. Wales, Jan. 23, 1919; s. Adrian Horatio and Clara May (Jones) B.; m. Beryl Doreen Harley, Mar. 2,1942; children: Leslie Patricia, Shirley Elizabeth. Chartered accountant, 1943. Articling clk. J.H. Bartlett (Chartered Acct.), Exeter, Devon, Eng., 1938-45; sr. auditing clk. Edmunds Casey & Co. (Chartered Accts.), Portsmouth, Hampshire, Eng., 1945-47; partner Griffiths & Griffiths (Chartered Accts.), Vancouver, B.C., 1947-49; dir. B.L. Johnson Walton & Co. Ltd. (Ins. Brokers), Vancouver, B.C., 1949-58; asso. partner Reed Shaw & McNaught, Vancouver, B.C., 1958-68; dir., sec. treas. Reed Stenhouse Cos. Ltd., Toronto, 1968-83, v.p. fin., 1983—. Served with Brit. Army, 1940-45. Fellow Chartered Inst. Secs.; mem. Can. Inst. Chartered Accts., Ins. Inst. Can. Anglican. Clubs: Capilano Golf and Country, Seymour Golf. Home: 3155 Travers Ave West Vancouver BC V7V 1G4 Canada Office: Reed Stenhouse Companies Ltd PO Box 10028 Pacific Centre S Vancouver BC V7Y 1B4 Canada

BALES, JERALD KEITH, insurance company executive; b. Newton, Iowa, July 13, 1926; s. Merl A. and Margaret D. (McVicker) B.; m. Irma Lou Rick, Dec. 28, 1949; children: Rick, Anne, Scott. A.B., Kans. U., 1950, LL.B., 1951. Bar: Mo. Assoc. firm Langworthy, Matz, linde, Kansas City, Mo., 1951-55; trust officer Union Nat. Bank, Kansas City, 1955-60; atty., counsel, assoc. gen. counsel, v.p. and assoc. gen. counsel Bus. Men's Assurance Co. Am., Kansas City, 1960—; exec. v.p. law, sec., 1980—, also dir.; dir. Atlas Mut. Ins. Co., 1983—. Serrved with U.S. Army, 1945-47. Mem. ABA, Mo. Bar Assn., Lawyers' Assn. Kansas City. Club: Mission Hills Country. Home: 5328 Falmouth Shawnee KS Mission 66205 Office: Bus Mens Assurance Co 700 Karnes Blvd Kansas City MO 64108

BALES, RICHARD HENRY HORNER, conductor, composer; b. Alexandria, Va., Feb. 3, 1915; s. Henry Ahijah and Henrietta Wyeth (Horner) B.; m. Mary Elizabeth Starley, Nov. 7, 1942; 1 dau., Mary Starley Alterman. Mus.B., Eastman Sch. Music, U. Rochester, 1936; student, Julliard Grad. Sch., 1938-41; pvt. pupil, Serge Koussevitzky, 1940. Tchr. Mass. State Tchrs. Coll., summer 1941, George Washington U., 1953; lectr. music. Debut as condr. with, Nat. Symphony Orch., 1935; condr., Va.-N.C. Symphony, 1936-38; music dir., Nat. Gallery Art and; condr., Nat. Gallery Orch., Washington, 1943—, Washington Cathedral Choral Soc., 1945-46; music dir., Nat. Symphony Orch., summer 1947; guest condr., orchs. in Phila., N.Y.C., St. Louis, Rochester, San Antonio, N.Mex., Cleve., Nat. Symphony Orch., Am. Little Symphony, Naumburg Orch.; Composer various works, orchestral, film, instrumental, choral selections. Recipient first prize string composition Arts Club Washington, 1940; award Merit Nat. Assn. Composers and Condrs., 1959; Alice M. Ditson award Columbia U., 1960, Acad. of Achievement, Monterey, Cal., 1961; First ann. arts award Washington Times, 1983; Life fellow Internat. Inst. Arts and Letters, 1961. Mem. Nat. Assn. Am. Composers and Condrs. (dir.), Am. Fedn. Musicians, Soc. Cincinnati, Civil War Round Table D.C. (Gold medal 1960, pres. 1960-61), U.S. Navy Band (hon. life), Bruckner Soc. in Am. (hon.), Kindler Found. (pres. 1959-62), S.C.V. (hon. life mem., 1st lt. comdr. 1963-64). Episcopalian. Club: Cosmos. Home: 6022 Pike Branch Dr Alexandria VA 22310 Office: Nat Gallery of Art Washington DC 20565

BALES, ROBERT FREED, social psychologist, educator; b. Ellington, Mo., Mar. 9, 1916; s. Columbus Lee and Ada Lois (Sloan) B.; m. Dorothy Louise Johnson, Sept. 14, 1941. B.A., U. Oreg., 1938, M.S., 1940; M.A., Harvard U., 1943, Ph.D., 1945. Research assoc. sect. on alcohol studies Yale U., 1944-45; instr. sociology Harvard U., Cambridge, Mass., 1945-47; asst. prof. sociology, research assoc. Lab. Social Relations, 1947-51, lectr. sociology, research assoc., 1951-55, assoc. prof., 1955-57, prof. social relations, 1957—, dir., 1960-67, chmn. social psychology program, 1970—; cons. psychology Harvard U. Health Services, 1970—; vis. lectr. sociology and social psychology U. Mich., summer 1949, Columbia, summer 1950; lectr. Salzberg Austria Seminar of Am. Studies, summer 1952, 56; Mem. bd. sci. counsellors NIMH, 1957-60. Author: Interaction Process Analysis: A Method for the Study of Small Groups, 1950, Personality and Interpersonal Behavior, 1970, The Fixation Factor in Alcohol Addiction, 1980, (with Talcott Parsons, Edward A. Shils) Working Papers in the Theory of Action, 1953, (with Talcott Parsons, et al) Family, Socialization, and Interaction Process, 1955; Contbr. to: Group Dynamics, Research and Theory, 1953; Contbr. several other compilations.; Editor: (with A. Paul Hare and Edgar F. Borgatta) Small Groups, Studies in Social Interaction, 1955, (with Stephen P. Cohen and Stephen A. Williamson) SYMLOG, A System for the Multiple Level Observation of Groups, 1979, SYMLOG Case Study Kit, with Instructions for a Group Self Study, 1980. Trustee Ella L. Cabot Trust. Mem. Am. Sociol. Assn., Eastern Sociol. Soc. (pres. 1962-63), Am. Acad. Arts and Scis., Am. Psychol. Assn., Soc. Exptl. Social Psychology, Boston Psychoanalytic Soc. (affiliate). Home: 61 Scotch Pine Rd Weston MA 02193 Office: 1320 William James Hall Harvard U Cambridge MA 02138

BALES, RONALD C., aluminum company executive; b. Toronto, ONT, Canada, 1938. B.A.Sc., U. Toronto, 1959; M.B.A., Harvard U., 1963; postgrad., Centre d'Etudes Industrielles, Geneva, 1972. Fin. analyst Alcan Finances Ltd., Toronto, ON, Canada, 1963-69; gen. mgr. Foil & Flexible Packaging Div., Alcan Canada Products Ltd., Toronto, ON, Canada, 1969-72; v.p. Alcan Canada Products Ltd., Toronto, ON, Canada, 1972-75; v.p., area planning officer Alcan Aluminio Am. Latina, Buenos Aires, Argentina, 1975-78, v.p., tech. officer, Rio de Janeiro, Brazil, 1978-81; v.p. corp. planning Alcan Aluminum Ltd., Montreal, Quebec, Canada, 1981—. Office: Alcan Aluminum Ltd 1188 Sherbrooke St West Montreal Quebec Canada H3A 3G2

BALES, WILLIAM BAXTER, railway executive; b. McAlpine, W.Va., Feb. 5, 1935; s. Woodrow and Thelma (Hite) B.; m. Marga Larson, Jan. 9, 1960; children: Marna, William B., Charles. B.S., Marshall U., 1957; postgrad., T.C. Williams Sch. Law, U. Richmond, 1961-62. With Norfolk & Western Ry. Co., 1962—, gen. mgr. coal traffic, sales and service, 1975-77, dir. internat. coal and ore traffic, N.Y.C., 1977-79, v.p. coal and ore traffic, Roanoke, Va., 1979-82, Norfolk So. Corp., 1982—; dir., exec. v.p. Pocahontas Land Corp., Pocahontas Ky. Corp., Pocahontas Devel. Corp.; pres., dir., chmn. exec. com. Powhatan Oil & Gas Corp.; mem. Va. Dist. Export Council, W.Va. Coal Commn. Served with U.S. Army, 1957-59. Presbyterian. Clubs: Sky (N.Y.C.); Harbor (Norfolk, Va.); Hunting Hills Country (Roanoke). Office: 8 N Jefferson St Roanoke VA 24042

BALESTER, RAYMOND JAMES, psychologist, health administrator; b. Albion, N.Y., Dec. 9, 1917; s. Joseph and Mary (Carlo) B.; m. Vivian Shelton, Oct. 19, 1956; children: Walter Eric,

Carla Maria, Mark Shelton. B.E., SUNY, Brockport, 1942; M.S., U. Pitts., 1947; Ph.D., Vanderbilt U., 1954. Asst. prof. psychology Vanderbilt U., 1955-56; dep. commr. Tenn. Dept. Mental Health, 1957-60; with NIMH, HEW, 1960-69, dep. dir. extramural programs, 1968-69; vice provost social and behavioral scis. Case Western Res. U., 1969-74; supt. Cleve. Psychiat. Inst., 1974—, Fairhill Mental Health Ctr., 1982—; vis. asst. prof. U. Tenn., Nashville, 1957-59, George Peabody Coll., 1957-59, Vanderbilt U., 1957-59. Co-editor: Jour. Spl. Edn, 1965-69. Trustee, past pres. Beechbrook; vis. com. Cleve. State U. Served with AUS, 1942-46. Recipient Career Tchr. award USPHS, 1956; Ann. Family Program award Nashville Radio and TV Council, 1957-60. Mem. Am. Psychol. Assn., Sigma Xi, Psi Chi. Home: 2460 Edgehill Rd Cleveland Heights OH 44106 Office: 1708 Aiken Ave Cleveland OH 44109

BALFOUR, JAMES GRANT, retail co. exec.; b. London, Ont., Can., Aug. 1, 1917; s. Richard Colgan and Ethel Margaret (Grant) B.; m. Margaret Adele Schmalz, Sept. 9, 1944; children—Richard, Ian, Barbara. B.A., U. Western Ont., 1938. Mdse. dir. Zeller's Ltd., Montreal, Que., Can., 1959-64, v.p., 1964-71, dir., 1964—, sr. v.p., 1971-74, pres., chief exec. officer, 1975—, chmn. bd., 1979—. Clubs: London Hunt and Country, London. Home: 1009 Hunt Club Mews London ON N6H 4R7 Canada Office: 5250 Decarie Blvd Montreal PQ H3X 3T9 Canada

BALFOUR, REGINALD JAMES, lawyer; b. Regina, Sask., Can., May 22, 1928; s. Reginald Mcleod and Martha (McElmoyle) B.; m. Beverly Jane Davidson, June 6, 1951; children—John Alan, James Roberts, Reginald William, Beverly Ann. Student, Luther Coll., 1946-48; LL.B., U. Saskatchewan, 1950. Bar: Sask. province bar 1952, appointed Queen's Counsel 1969. Sr. partner firm Balfour, Moss, Milliken, Laschuk, Kyle & Vancise, Regina, 1952—; dir. Royal Trust Corp. Can. M.P. for Regina E., 1972-79. Apptd. to Senate of Can., 1979—. Served to lt. Royal Can. Arty., 1950-54. Mem. Can. Bar Assn., Regina Bar Assn. (pres. 1956-57), Law Soc. Sask., United Services Inst. Progressive Conservative. Home: 175 Lansdowne Rd S Ottawa ON K1M 0N8 Canada Office: 1850 Cornwall St Regina SK Canada also Senate of Canada Ottawa ON Canada

BALFOUR, ST. CLAIR, communications executive; b. Hamilton, Ont., Can., Apr. 30, 1910; s. St. Clair and Ethel May (Southam) B.; m. Helen Gifford Staunton, Jan 21, 1933; children: Elizabeth S., St. Clair. B.A., Trinity Coll., U. Toronto, 1931; LL.D. (hon.), U. Western Ont. With Southam Inc., Toronto, Can., 1931—, mng. dir., 1954-69, pres., 1961-75, chmn., 1975—; bd. govs. Toronto Stock Exchange. Active Can. Exec. Service Overseas; bd. dirs. U. Toronto., Toronto Redevel. Adv. Council. Decorated D.S.C. Mem. Commonwealth Press Union (hon. life), Can. Press (hon. life). Home: 17 Ardwold Gate Toronto ON M5R 2W1 Canada Office: Southam Inc: 150 Bloor St W Toronto ON M5S 2Y8 Canada

BALFOUR, WILLIAM MAYO, physician, educator; b. Pasadena, Calif., Nov. 26, 1914; s. Donald Church and Carrie (Mayo) B.; m. Oane McQuarrie, Jan. 7, 1939; children: James, Barbara, Laurie (Mrs. Dale Tremain), Wendy. B.S., U. Minn., 1936, M.D., 1939; M.S., Mayo Grad. Sch., 1948. Intern, resident Strong Meml. Hosp., Rochester, N.Y., 1939-42; resident Mayo Found., Rochester, Minn., 1942-48; cons. sects. metabolism and endocrinology Mayo Clinic, 1948-57; instr. Mayo Found., 1949-57; USPHS postdoctoral fellow U. Kans., Lawrence, 1957-59, research asso., 1959-62, asso. prof., 1962-66, prof., 1966—, univ. ombudsman, 1977—; dir. Pearson Coll., 1967, vice chancellor student affairs, 1968-76; dir. In-Service Inst. for High Sch. Tchrs. Biol. Scis., 1962-63. Contbr. articles to profl. jours. Served to maj., M.C. AUS, 1942-45. Mem. ACP, Am. Physiol. Soc., Sigma Xi. Unitarian. Home: 1505 University Dr Lawrence KS 66044

BALGOOYEN, HENRY WARREN, economist; b. Hadley, Mich., May 16, 1906; s. Albert and Wilhelmina (Seegmiller) B.; m. Violet M. Linden, Sept. 5, 1930; children: Carol Arden, Warren Prentis, Bruce Willard, Marjorie Ellen. A.B., U. Mich., 1928, M.B.A., 1929. With fgn. dept. Chase Nat. Bank, 1930-36; staff Ebasco Services, Inc., 1936-42, economist, 1944—, asst. comptroller, 1945-46, sec., 1946-56, v.p., 1952, exec. v.p., 1955-57; sec. Am. and Fgn. Power Co., Inc., 1946-51, v.p., sec., 1952-55, exec. v.p., sec., 1955-67, pres., chief exec. officer, 1967, dir., 1962-67; sr. v.p. Ebasco Industries, Inc., N.Y.C., 1968, dir., 1968-69; dir. First Fed. Savs. & Loan Assn., Internat. Mining Corp.; dir., mem. exec. com. Woodway Realty Corp.; Mem. U.S. del. Internat. Trade Orgn. Conf. UN, Havana, 1947-48; mem. U.S. del. Rio de Janeiro Econ. Conf., 1954; v.p. Inter-Am. Council Commerce and Prodn., Montivideo, Uruguay, 1958-60. Bd. dirs. Americas Found., 1967—, pres., 1969-71, chmn. bd., 1972-83; mem. nat. council Inst. Internat. Edn., 1970-82; trustee Am. Enterprise Inst., 1950-71, Am. Inst. Free Labor Devel., 1964-82. Recipient Capt. Robert Dollar Meml. award, 1960; Outstanding Achievement award U. Mich., 1964. Mem. Council for Latin Am. (vice chmn. 1964-68), U.S. Inter-Am. Council (trustee, chmn. bd. 1958-60), Pan Am. Soc. U.S. (pres. 1964-67, hon. pres. 1968—), N.Y.C. C. of C. (exec. com. 1965-68), Argentine-Am. Assn. (v.p. 1950-62), Ecuadorian-Am. Assn. (pres. 1964-65), Bolivarian Soc. U.S. (dir. v.p. 1965-82), Alpha Kappa Psi. Methodist. Home: The Crossways Katonah NY 10536

BALIGA, B. JAYANT, scientist; b. Madras, India, Apr. 28, 1948; came to U.S., 1969; m. Pratima Nayak, Dec. 25, 1975; 1 child, Avinash. B.Tech., Indian Inst. Tech., Madras, 1969; M.S., Rensselaer Poly. Inst., Troy, N.Y., 1971, Ph.D., 1974. Mem. staff Research and Devel. Ctr., Gen. Electric Co., Schenectady, N.Y., 1974-79, tech. coordinator, 1979-81, acting mgr., 1981-82, unit mgr., 1982—; adj. prof. Rensselaer Poly. Inst., 1974—; cons. UN, 1979-80. Patentee insulated gate transistor. Recipient Phillips India medal Indian Inst. Tech., 1969, Spl. medal Indian Inst. Tech., 1969, Allen B. Dumont prize Rensselaer Poly. Inst., 1974, Collidge fellow, 1983. Fellow IEEE; mem. Electrochem. Soc. Home: 3 Clove St Clifton Park NY 12065 Office: Gen Electric Co 1 River Rd Schenectady NY 12065

BALIN, HOWARD, obstetrician and, gynecologist; b. Phila., Jan. 22, 1927; s. Michael and Ester (Rubin) B.; m. Doris Levinson, Sept. 10, 1949; children—Marianne, Susan Roberta, Jane Carol, Robert David. B.A., U. Pa., 1947, M.D., 1951, M.Sc., 1957. Diplomate: Am. Bd. Obstetrics and Gynecology. Intern Grad. Hosp. U. Pa., Phila., 1951-52, resident in gen. surgery, 1952-53, resident in gynecology, 1953-55; resident in obstetrics Phila. Naval Hosp., 1955-56; practice medicine specializing in obstetrics and gynecology, Phila., 1956-77; instr. obstetrics and gynecology U. Pa., 1959-61, asso. in obstetrics and gynecology, 1961-64, asst. prof., 1964-70; asso. in gynecology Grad. Hosp. Phila., 1961-70; asso. obstetrician and gynecologist Pa. Hosp., Phila., 1960-70, chief gynecic research sect., 1960-70; adj. prof. dept. biol. scis. Drexel U., Phila., 1968—; prof. obstetrics and gynecology Hahnemann Med. Coll. and Hosp., Phila., 1970-77, acting chmn., 1973-74, prof., chmn., 1974-77, dir. div. reproductive biology, 1970-77; sr. cons. div. endocrinology and metabolism dept. medicine, 1976-77; prin. med. scientist Franklin Inst. Research Labs., Phila., 1973-76; vis. prof. obstetrics and gynecology U. P.R., 1972-78. Author: (with S. Glasser) Reproductive Biology, 1972, (with A. Hontz and L. A. Lo Sciuto) Handbook of Steroid Contraceptives, 1976, office gynecology, 1977; contbr.: chpts. to med. texts, articles to med. jours. office gynecology. Recipient Fulbright-Hayes Am. specialist award, 1967, 69, 77. Fellow A.C.S., Am. Coll. Obstetrics and Gynecology, Internat. Coll. Surgeons, Phila. Coll. Physicians; mem. AMA (Physicians Recognition award 1980—), Philadelphia County Med. Soc., Phila. Obstet. Soc., Am. Soc. Cytology, Phila. Endocrine Soc., Am. Cancer Soc., Am. Fertility Soc., Am. Soc. Abdominal Surgery, Am. Public Health Assn., Nat. Assn. Ednl. Broadcasters, Am. Soc. Colposcopy, Royal Soc. Medicine, AAUP, S. Weir Mitchell Soc., Phi Beta Kappa, Sigma Xi. Club: Cosmos (Washington). Office: 60 E Township Line Elkins Park PA 19117

BALIN, MARTY (MARTYN JEREL BUCHWALD), musician; b. Cin., Jan. 30, 1942; s. Joseph and Catherine E. Buchwald; 1 dau., Jennifer Ann. Student, San Francisco State U. Pres. Great Pyramid Ltd.; owner Diamondback Music Co. Founder, vocalist, Jefferson Airplane/Starship, 1965-71, 75—; film appearances include Gimme Shelter, 1970—; composer: Volunteers, It's No Secret, Plastic Fantastic Lover, Young Girl Sunday Blues, others; album Balin. Office: care Great Pyramid Ltd 10 Waterville St San Francisco CA 94124

BALINT, JOHN ALEXANDER, physician, academic administrator, educator; b. Budapest, Hungary, Feb. 11, 1925; came to U.S., 1958; s. Michael and Alice (Szekely-Kuvaes) B.; m. Jean M. Gibson, Jan. 15, 1949; children: Peter S., Jane P. B.A., Cambridge U., Eng., 1945, M.B.A.Chir., 1948. Resident hosps., London, 1952-58; fellow in medicine Johns Hopkins U., Balt., 1959-60; asst. prof. medicine Ala. Coll. Medicine, Birmingham, 1960-63; assoc. prof. medicine Albany Med. Coll., N.Y., 1963-68, prof. medicine, head gastroenterology, 1968-81, prof., chmn. dept. medicine, 1981—; cons. VA Med. Ctr., Albany, 1963—. Author: Gastrointestinal Bleeding Diagnosis and Management, 1978; contbr. articles to profl. publs. Served with M.C., RAF, 1950-52. Fellow Royal Coll. Physicians, London, ACP; mem. Am. Gastroent. Assn., Am. Soc. Clin. Investigation, Am. Assn. Study Liver Disease, Am. Physiol. Soc. Office: Dept Medicine Albany Med Col Albany NY 12208

BALIS, MOSES EARL, biochemist, educator; b. Phila., June 19, 1921; s. Harry and Frances (Spector) B.; m. Bernice M. Lamborg, Dec. 30, 1945; children—Frances Andrea, Ellen Joyce. B.A., Temple U., 1943; M.S., U. Pa., 1947, Ph.D., 1949. With Sloan-Kettering Inst., 1949—, head nucleoprotein metabolism sect., 1957—, asso. mem., 1960-65, mem., 1965—, chief div. cell metabolism, 1970—; asso. prof. Med. Coll. Cornell U., 1954-66, prof. biochemistry, 1966—, chmn. biochemistry unit, 1969—; vis. lectr. Adelphi U., 1963-64; cons. chemistry dept. Manhattan Coll., 1981—; mem. study sects. Am. Cancer Soc., NIH.; Mem. planning com. Nat. Cancer Plan; mem. rev. com. Nat. Large Bowel Cancer Program, 1977-81. Editorial bd.: Cancer Research, 1969-73; assoc. editor, 1974-82. Served to lt. (j.g.) USNR, 1944-46. Recipient Research Career award USPHS, 1963. Mem. Am. Chem. Soc. (past sect. chmn.), AAAS, Am. Cancer Soc., Am. Soc. Biol. Chemists, Harvey Soc., Am. Assn. Cancer Research, Sigma Xi. Research, numerous publs. on metabolism of purines in normal and malignant tissues; determined biochem. action of anti-cancer drugs. Home: 450 E 63d St New York NY 10021 Office: 1275 York Ave New York NY 10021

BALK, ALFRED WILLIAM, editor; b. Oskaloosa, Iowa, July 24, 1930; s. Leslie William and Clara Irene (Buell) B.; m. Phyllis Lorraine Munter, June 7, 1952; children: Laraine M., Diane M. Student, Augustana Coll., Rock Island, Ill., 1948-49; B.S., Medill Sch. Journalism, Northwestern U., 1952, M.S., 1953. Reporter Rock Island Argus, 1946-50; newswriter-producer WBBM (CBS), Chgo., 1952-53; reporter Chgo. Sun-Times, 1956; mag. writer, pub. relations J. Walter Thompson Co., Chgo., 1957-58; free lance writer nat. mags., including spl. writer Saturday Evening Post, 1958-66; feature editor Saturday Rev., 1966-68, editor at large, 1968-69; vis. scholar Russell Sage Found., 1968-69; lectr. journalism, editor Columbia Journalism Rev., 1969-73; editor World Press Rev., 1974, editor-pub., 1975—; Cons.-rapporteur Twentieth-Century Fund Task Force on Nat. News Council, 1971-72; cons. Ford Found., Markle Found.; exec. sec. N.Y. Gov.'s Com. on Employment of Minority Groups in News Media, 1968-69. Author: A Free and Responsive Press, The Free List, Property Without Taxes; Co-editor: Our Troubled Press. Mem. Am. Soc. Mag. Editors (exec. council 1977-83), Soc. Journalists, Sigma Delta Chi (Wells Meml. key). Clubs: Overseas Press (gov. 1978-79), Univ.). Office: World Press Rev 230 Park Ave New York NY 10169

BALKE, MARY NOËL, librarian; b. Londonderry, N. Ireland, Dec. 25, 1918; emigrated to Can., 1946; d. William and Jenny (Wilson) Schoales; m. Nicholas Balke, Sept. 2, 1944; children: William Greer, Jennifer Mary. B.A., U. Sheffield, Eng., 1939. Librarian and info. officer Signals Research Devel. Establishment Christchurch, Hants, Eng., 1943-45; freelance writer and broadcaster for newspapers and CBC, Montreal, Toronto, Can., 1946-58; librarian Ottawa (Ont., Can.) Pub. Library, 1959-64; chief librarian Nat. Gallery Can., Ottawa, 1964-79. Recipient Meml. award Canadian Women's Press Club, 1956. Mem. Library Assn. Great Britain (asso.), Canadian Library Assn., Spl. Libraries Assn. Anglican. Home: Box 27 Sea Dog Rural Route 1 Nanoose Bay BC Canada V0R 2R0

BALKE, VICTOR H., bishop; b. Meppen, Ill., Sept. 29, 1931; s. Bernard H. and Elizabeth A. (Knese) B. B.A. in Philosophy, St. Mary of Lake Sem., Mundelein, Ill., 1954, S.T.B. in Theology, 1956, M.A. in Religion, 1957, S.T.L. in Theology, 1958; M.A. in English, St. Louis U., 1964, Ph.D., 1973. Ordained priest Roman Catholic Ch., 1958; asst. pastor, Springfield, Ill., 1958-62; chaplain St. Joseph Home Aged, Springfield, 1962-63; procurator, instr. Diocesan Sem., Springfield, 1963-70, rector, instr., 1970-76; ordained, installed 6th bishop of, Crookston, Minn., 1976—. Clubs: K.C., Lions. Address: Diocese of Crookston 1200 Memorial Dr PO Crookston MN 56716 *

BALL, ARMAND BAER, association executive; b. Dubach, La., Sept. 30, 1930; s. Armand Baer and Lovera (Sanderson) B.; m. Beverly Jane Hodges, Sept. 15, 1957; children—Kathryn Lynn, Robin Armand. B.A., La. Coll., 1951; M.R.E., Southwestern Bapt. Theol. Sem., 1953; M.S., George Williams Coll., 1960. Certified assn. exec. Royal Ambassador dir. Fla. Bapt. Conv., Jacksonville, 1953-57; program dir. Woodlawn Boys' Club, Chgo., 1957-58; camp/youth dir. YMCA, Nashville, 1958-62; exec. dir. YMCA Camps Widjiwagan/duNord, St. Paul YMCA, 1962-74; exec. v.p. Am. Camping Assn., Martinsville, Ind., 1974—. Author: (with Beverly H. Ball) Basic Camp Management, 1979. Trustee Fund for Advancement of Camping; cons. Center for Disease Control, Heritage Conservation and Recreation Service, Project Reach. Mem. Am. Soc. Assn. Execs., Nat. Park and Recreation Assn., Audubon Soc., Canadian Camping Assn., Council on Nat. Coop. in Aquatics. Home: 2812 Fawkes Way Bloomington IN 47401 Office: Bradford Woods Martinsville IN 46151

BALL, DAVID GEORGE, lawyer, mining company executive; b. Gloucester, Eng., Nov. 16, 1936; s. Harold George and Irene Elsie (Hadley) B.; m. Carol Knight Gore, July 28, 1973; children: David George, Christopher Robert, Deborah Margaret, Jonathan Frederick. B.A., Yale, 1960; J.D., Columbia, 1964. Bar: N.Y. State bar 1965. Assoc. firm White & Case, N.Y.C., 1964-69; asst. sec. The Babcock & Wilcox Co., N.Y.C., 1970-74, asst. counsel, 1971-74; asst. sec., asst. counsel AMAX Inc., Greenwich, Conn., 1974, sec., sr. atty., 1974—, v.p. investor relations, sec., 1977-82; sr. v.p., sec. AMAX, Inc., 1982—; dir., officer AMAX Inc. subs.'s.; Mem. N.Y.C. Mayor's Task Force on Tax Policy, 1967. Bd. mgrs. Nat. Audubon Soc. of Greenwich. Mem. Am. Soc. Corp. Secs., Council Fgn. Relations, Am., N.Y. State bar assns., Labor Policy Assn., English Speaking Union. Republican. Episcopalian (vestryman). Clubs: Belle Haven (Greenwich); N.Y. Racquet and Tennis. Home: 508 Round Hill Rd Greenwich CT 06830 Office: AMAX Inc AMAX Center Greenwich CT 06830

BALL, DUARD DANIEL, army officer; b. McAlester, Okla., Oct. 11, 1930; s. Lemuel Framklin and Bertha (Shepherd) B.; m. Marion Dods, May 4, 1957; children: Lisa E., Julia L., Daniel R. B.S., Okla. A&M Coll., 1953; M.B.A., Babson Inst., Wellesley, Mass., 1962. Commd. 2d lt. U.S. Army, 1953, advanced through grades to maj. gen., 1979; service in Korea, Taiwan, Vietnam and Europe; comdg. gen., comdt. U.S. Army Ordnance and Chem. Center and Sch., Aberdeen (Md.) Proving Ground, 1977-79; comdg. gen. White Sands Missile Range, 1979-80; program mgr. XM-1 Tank System, Warren, Mich., 1980-83; comdg. gen. U.S. Army Tank Automotive Command, Warren, Mich., 1983—. Decorated Legion of Merit, Soldier's medal, Bronze Star, Meritorious Service medal with 3 oak leaf clusters, Joint Service Commendation medal, Army Commendation medal with 2 oak leaf clusters. Mem. Assn. U.S. Army, Soc. Missile and Space Pioneers, Am. Def. Preparedness Assn., Soc. Automotive Engrs. Home: 424 George Ave Selfridge Air Nat Guard Base MI 48045 Office: Comdg Gen USATACOM Warren MI 48090

BALL, EDMUND FERDINAND, business executive; b. Muncie, Ind., Jan. 8, 1905; s. Edmund Burke and Bertha (Crosley) B.; m. Isabel Urban, Jan. 11, 1936 (dec. Mar. 1949); children: Frank Edmund, Mrs. Marilyn Bertha Heaton, Frederick Crosley; m. Virginia Beall Stewart, June 28, 1952; children: Robert Burke, Nancy Ball Teed. Student, Asheville (N.C.) Sch., 1920-23, Wabash Coll., 1923-25; Ph.B., Yale, 1928; LL.D. (hon.), Ball State U., DePauw U., Ind. U.; H.H.D., Keuka Coll., Wabash Coll. Asso. Ball Corp., 1928—, asst. sec., 1931, v.p., 1938, dir., exec. v.p., 1945, pres., 1948-63, 68-70, chmn. bd., 1956-69, chmn. exec. com., 1970—; pres. Ball Bros. Found., Minnetrista Corp., Muncie Airport, Inc.; hon. dir. Am. Nat. Bank & Trust Co., Muncie, Mchts. Nat. Bank, Muncie. Hon. Trustee Wabash Coll., Muncie YMCA; hon. trustee Asheville (N.C.) Sch.; bd. dirs., chmn. Ball Meml. Hosp.; hon. bd. dirs. Asso. Colls. Ind.; adv. council Wilmer Inst., Johns Hopkins U.; past mem. council The Citadel, U. Chgo. Sch. Bus., S.W. Research Inst.; former mem. bd. Nat. Assn. Ednl. Broadcasters, Eastern Ind. Ednl. TV Bd.; past bd. dirs. Pub. Broadcasting Service; past mem. Nat. Council on Humanities. Served as maj. USAAF, 1941-45. Mem. Glass Container Mfrs. Inst. (past pres. trustee), Explorers Club, Phi Gamma Delta. Republican. Unversalist. Clubs: Mason (K.T., past nat. treas. K.T., trustee K.T. Eye Found., 33 deg.), Yale (N.Y.C.); Adventurers (Chgo.); Columbia (Indpls.). Home: 1707 Riverside Ave Muncie IN 47303 Office: Suite 520 Mchts Nat Bank Bldg Muncie IN 47305

BALL, ERNEST AUBREY, biologist, educator; b. Mangum, Okla., Dec. 22, 1909; s. John Carlo and Dovie Lee (Thompson) B.; m. Carolyn Maud Lindh, May 25, 1941; children: Jeannette, Michael, Linda. B.S., U. Okla., 1937, M.S., 1938; Ph.D., U. Calif.-Berkeley, 1941. Teaching asst. U. Calif.-Berkeley, 1938-41; research assoc. Carnegie Inst., 1943; instr. biology Harvard U., 1943-46; asst. prof. botany N.C. State U., 1946-47, assoc. prof., 1947-55, prof., 1955-59; prof. biology U. Calif.-Irvine, 1959-80; prof. U. Calif.-Santa Cruz, 1980—; dir. Redwood Inst. NRC fellow, 1941-42; Rockefeller Found. grantee, 1947; NSF grantee, 1957-60; USPHS grantee, 1961-64; AEC grantee, 1966-69; EPA grantee, 1972-73; Simpson Timber grantee, 1975-81. Fellow AAAS; mem. Bot. Soc. Am. Democrat. Office: 149 Applied Science U Calif Santa Cruz CA 95064

BALL, FRANK JERVEY, chemist; b. Charleston, S.C., Jan. 29, 1919; s. John Coming and Annie Arden (Jervey) B.; m. Mary Elizabeth Furtwangler, Feb. 16, 1950; children—Frank Jervey, Stuart Furtwangler, Bruce Devon, Steven Moultrie. B.S., U. of South, 1941; Ph.D., U. Rochester, 1944. Research chemist Westvaco Corp., Charleston Research Center, 1944-46, group leader, 1946-53, dir., 1953-75, asso. corp. research dir., 1975—; dir. Tyrone Research Lab., 1958-60; Pres. Empire State Paper Research Assos., 1970-78. Contbr. articles to profl. jours. Mem. Am. Chem. Soc., TAPPI, Charleston C. of C. (chmn. higher edn. com. 1969-74), Phi Beta Kappa, Sigma Xi, Omicron Delta Kappa. Episcopalian. Clubs: South Carolina Soc., St. Cecilia Soc., Carolina Yacht. Patentee in field. Home: 4 Atlantic St Charleston SC 29401

BALL, GEORGE L., securities company executive; b. Evanston, Ill. B.A., Brown U. Pres. E. F. Hutton Group Inc. and E. F. Hutton & Co., N.Y.C., 1969-82; pres., chief exec. officer Prudential-Bache Securities, N.Y.C., 1983—. Mem. Securities Industry Assn. Office: Prudential-Bache Securities Inc. 100 Gold St. New York NY 10038

BALL, GEORGE WILDMAN, lawyer, investment banker, author; b. Des Moines, Dec. 21, 1909; s. Amos and Edna (Wildman) B.; m. Ruth Murdoch, Sept. 16, 1932; children: John Colin, Douglas Bleakly. B.A., Northwestern U., 1930, J.D., 1933. Bar: Ill. 1934, D.C. 1946. With Gen. Counsel's Office, Dept. Treasury, Washington, 1933-35; practice law, Chgo., 1935-42, Washington, 1946-61; mem. firm Cleary, Gottlieb, Steen & Ball; assoc. gen. counsel Lend-Lease Adminstrn., then Fgn. Econ. Adminstrn., 1942-44; dir. U.S. Strategic Bombing Survey, London, 1944-45; gen. counsel French Supply Council, Washington, 1945-46; undersec. of state for econ. affairs, 1961, undersec. state, 1961-66; of counsel firm Cleary, Gottlieb, Steen & Hamilton (attys.), 1966-68, 69—; chmn. Lehman Bros. Internat., Ltd., 1966-68; U.S. permanent rep. to UN, 1968; sr. ptnr. Lehman Bros., Jan-May 1968, 69-82. Author: The Discipline of Power, 1968, Diplomacy for a Crowded World, 1976, The Past Has Another Pattern, 1982. Decorated officer Legion of Honor, France; grand cross Order of Crown, Belgium; Medal of Freedom, U.S.; grand ufficiale Order of Merit, Italy). Office: 325 E 79th St New York NY 10021

BALL, HOWARD GUY, educator; b. Lancaster, Ohio, Aug. 4, 1930; s. Howard Emitt and Edith Mildred (Clark) B.; (m), May 17, 1980; children: Howard, Brian, Maryla. B.S., Ohio State U., 1952, M.S., 1969, Ph.D., 1972. Edn. specialist Ohio Dept. Edn., Columbus, 1964-71; assoc. prof. N.C. State U., 1971-74; faculty Ala. A & M U., Normal, 1974—; now prof. Ala. A&M U. (Sch. Library Media); chmn. Media Services, Inc.; pres. Higby Inc. Mem. editorial bds.: Reading Horizons, Library Scene, 1979-80, Media and Methods: Early Years, 1984-85; contbr. articles to profl. jours.; authored, directed: Training of Librarians in CATV, 1975. Mem. Ala. Council Human Relations, 1978—, Ala. Democratic Council, 1978—; sec. Orgn. Inner City Govts., 1977—. Recipient NAACP Community award, 1976, Raleigh C. of C. educator's award, 1973. Mem. ALA, Assn. Educators Communication and Tech., Phi Beta Kappa, Phi Delta Kappa, Kappa Alpha Psi. Presbyterian. Club: Masons. Office: Dept Instr/Media Ala A&M U Normal AL 35762

BALL, JOHN A., forest products company executive; b. 1928; married. Grad., Loyola U. With Champion Internat. Corp., Stamford, Conn., 1955—, mktg. mgr. hardwood and plywood, 1960-65, dir. mktg. services, 1965-66, v.p., 1966-67, v.p. br. sales, Staford, Conn., 1967-68; pres. U.S. Plywood, 1968-74; exec. v.p. Champion Internat. Corp., Stamford, Conn., from 1974, exec. v.p. bldg. products div. Served to lt.

(J.G.) USN. Office: Champion Internat Corp One Champion Plaza Stamford CT 06921 *

BALL, JOHN DUDLEY, JR., author; b. Schenectady, July 8, 1911; s. John Dudley and Alena (Wiles) B.; m. Patricia Hamilton, Aug. 22, 1942; 1 son, John David. B.A., Carroll Coll., Waukesha, Wis., 1934, L.H.D., 1978. Mem. editorial staff Fortune mag., 1937-40; asst. curator Hayden Planetarium, N.Y.C., 1940-41; with Columbia Rec. Corp., 1945-47; music editor Bklyn. Eagle, 1946-51; columnist N.Y. World Telegram, 1951-52; dir. pub. relations Inst. Aero. Scis., 1958-61; editor-in-chief DMS, Inc., 1961-62; author, 1963—; chmn. mystery library U. Calif.-San Diego Extension. Author: Records for Pleasure, 1947, Operation Springboard, 1958, Spacemaster I, 1960, Edwards: USAF Flight Test Center, 1962, Judo Boy, 1964 (Jr. Lit. Guild selection), In the Heat of the Night (Edgar award, Critics award, London), 1965 (Acad. award Best Picture of Year 1968), Arctic Showdown, 1966, Rescue Mission, 1966, The Cool Cottontail, 1966 (Mystery Guild selection), Dragon Hotel, 1968, Miss 1000 Spring Blossoms, 1968 (Readers Digest Condensed Book Club selection), Johnny Get Your Gun, 1969, Last Plane Out, 1969, The First Team, 1971, Five Pieces of Jade, 1972 (Detective Book Club selection), The Fourteenth Point, 1973, Mark One-The Dummy, 1974 (Detective Book Club selection), The Winds of Mitamura, 1975, The Eyes of Buddha, 1976, Phase Three Alert, 1977 (Mil. Book Club selection), Police Chief, 1977 (Detective Book Club selection), The Killing in the Market, 1978, The Murder Children, 1979, Then Came Violence, 1980, Trouble for Tallon, 1981, Ananda, 1982; editor: Cop Cade, 1978, The Mystery Story, 1976. Served with Air Transport Command, 1942-45. Mem. Aviation and Space Writers Assn., Mystery Writers Am., Baker St. Irregulars, All Am. Karate Fedn., Japanese-Am. Citizens League, Ox-5 Club, Mensa, CAP. Lutheran. Address: 16401 Otsego St Encino CA 91436

BALL, JOHN FLEMING, advertising and film production executive; b. Evanston, Ill., Apr. 26, 1930; s. Edward Hyde and Kathleen (Fleming) B.; m. Anne Idabelle Firestone, Nov. 9, 1957; children—John Fleming, David Firestone, Sheila Anne. B.A., Princeton, 1952. Asso. producer, program exec. CBS, N.Y.C., 1955-59; with J. Walter Thompson Co., N.Y.C., 1959—, v.p., 1965—, dir. programs, 1965-67, dir. broadcasting, 1967—, pres., dir. Survival Anglia Ltd. div., 1972—; pres. Trident Anglia Inc., 1976—. Trustee Found. Am. Dance. Served with USN, 1952-55. Clubs: Cap and Gown of Princeton U., River, Links (N.Y.C.); Round Hill, Field (Greenwich, Conn.); Nassau (Princeton); Am. (London); Princeton Triangle (chmn. grad. bd.). Home: Deer Park Greenwich CT 06830 also Northport Point MI 49670 Office: 420 Lexington Ave New York NY 10017

BALL, JOHN H(ANSTEIN), lawyer; b. N.Y.C., Dec. 14, 1919; s. Nathan and Hattie (Hanstein) B.; m. Alice Wolf, June 12, 1946; children—Joan, Jean. B.S., N.Y. U., 1941; LL.B., Columbia U., 1944. Bar: N.Y. State bar 1945, So. and Eastern dist. fed. ct. bars 1947. Asso. firm Kaye, Scholer, Flerman, Hays & Handler, N.Y.C., 1944-56, counsel, 1977-81; counsel firm Robinson, Silverman, Pearce, Aronsohn & Berman, N.Y.C., 1981—; partner firm Borden & Ball, N.Y.C., 1956-77. Pres. Central Synagogue, N.Y.C., 1979—. Mem. Am., N.Y. State, N.Y.C., N.Y. County bar assns. Home: 737 Park Ave New York NY 10021 Office: 230 Park Ave New York NY 10169

BALL, JOHN PAUL, publishing company executive; b. N.Y.C., Dec. 15, 1946; s. William Emil and Else (Schmidt) B.; m. Jayne Barbara Irwin, Jan. 30, 1970. Student, N.Y. Sch. Printing, 1964. Prodn. assoc. MacMillan Co., N.Y.C., 1964-65; asst. to pres. Frederick Fell, Inc., N.Y.C., 1965-69; v.p., dir. prodn. William Morrow & Co., Inc., N.Y.C., 1969—. Office: William Morrow & Co Inc 105 Madison Ave New York NY 10016

BALL, JOYCE, librarian; b. N.J., Oct. 31, 1932; d. Frank Geza and Elizabeth Martha (Hopper) Csaposs; m. Robert S. Ball, Sept. 10, 1955; children: Stephanie, Valerie, Steven Robert; m. Stefan B. Moses, Mar. 30, 1980. A.B., Douglass Coll., Rutgers U., 1954; M.A., Ind. U., 1959; M.B.A., Golden Gate U., San Francisco, 1979. Fgn. documents librarian Stanford U., 1955-66; head documents librarian, then head reference div. U. Nev., Reno, 1966-75, head public services, 1975-80; univ. librarian Calif. State U., Sacramento, 1980—; mem. Nev. Gov's Adv. Council on Libraries, 1974-78; mem. panel judges Am. Book Awards, 1980. Editorial bd.: Coll. and Research Libraries, 1975-80; Contbr. articles to profl. jours. Mem. Assn. Coll. and Research Libraries (dir., pres. 1983-84), ALA, Calif. Library Assn., Nev. Library Assn. Democrat. Home: 8181 Folsom Blvd 180 Sacramento CA 95826 Office: 2000 Jed Smith Dr Sacramento CA 95819

BALL, LEWIS EDWIN, II, railcar manufacturing company executive; b. Huntsville, Tex., July 1, 1931; s. William Perry and Mary Ethel (Osborne) B.; m. Marion Buchanan, June 5, 1954. B.B.A., U. Tex., Austin, 1952. C.P.A., Tex.; cert. in mgmt. acctg. Mgr. Ernst & Whinney (C.P.A.s), Houston, 1952-71; v.p., treas., dir. Stewart & Stevenson Services, Inc., Houston, 1971-80; v.p. fin. Intercontinental Consol. Cos., Inc., Houston, 1981-82; v.p. fin., treas. Richmond Tank Car Co., Houston, 1983—. Bd. dirs. Soc. Performing Arts, Retina Research Found.; bd. dirs. Vol. Lawyers and Accts. for Arts, v.p., 1983—; mem. allocations com. Cultural Arts Council Houston; trustee, treas. Houston Museum Natural Sci.; mem. trustees com. exec. com., Mountain Plains Regional rep. Am. Assn. Mus. Mem. Am. Inst. C.P.A.s, Nat. Assn. Accountants, Fin. Execs. Inst., Tex. Soc. C.P.A.s. Methodist. Clubs: Houston Country, Ramada, Garden of Gods, Riverhill, Houstonian. Home: 6122 Valley Forge Dr Houston TX 77057 Office: 1700 W Loop S Suite 1500 Houston TX 77027

BALL, LUCILLE, actress; b. Jamestown, N.Y., Aug. 6, 1911; d. Henry D. and Desiree (Hunt) B.; m. Desi Arnaz, Nov. 30, 1940 (div.); children: Lucie Desiree, Desiderio Alberto IV; m. Gary Morton, Nov. 19, 1961. Ed. high sch., dramatic sch.; studied with, John Murray Anderson. Pres. Desilu Prodns., Inc., 1962-67, Lucille Ball Prodns., 1967—. Motion picture actress, 1934—; pictures include Mame; star: TV shows Here's Lucy; starred on: Broadway in Wildcat; (Recipient Emmy award for best comedienne 1952, 55, 67, 68, Golden Apple award 1973, Ruby award 1974, Entertainer of Yr. award 1975). Presbyterian. Address: care Twentieth Century Fox PO Box 900 Beverly Hills CA 90213 *

BALL, REX MARTIN, architect, urban designer; b. Oklahoma City, June 14, 1934; s. Ralph Martin and Sarah Mae (Kellner) B.; m. Margie E. Crowley, Jan. 1, 1960; children—Julie Kay, Linda Carol, Sharon Louise, Renee Marie. B.Arch., Okla. State U., 1956; M.Arch., M.I.T., 1958. Vice pres., office dir. HTB, Inc., Tulsa, 1962-74, exec. v.p., Oklahoma City, 1974-75, pres., 1975—. Author: Designers Handbook of Building Security - Special Security Systems, 1979; contbr. articles to various jours., mags., newspapers. Pres. Downtown Tulsa Unltd., 1969-71; chmn. Keep Okla. Beautiful Awards, 1966; bd. dirs. West-O-Main Assn., 1966-73; charter mem. Met. Tulsa Transit Authority, 1968-74, chmn., 1972-74; mem. Tulsa Mass Transit Policy Study Com., 1969-72; vice chmn. design of city task force Goals for Tulsa, 1969, bd. dirs., steering, resource coms., 1971; mem. central bus. dist. policy com. Tulsa Met. Area Planning Commn., 1969-71, mem. mass. transp. policy com., 1969-74, mem. intermodal transp. policy com., 1972-74; mem. land use policy com. Indian Nation Council Govts., 1970; organizer Central Area Task Force Steering Com.-Tulsa, 1970, bd. dirs., 1970-74; mem. Frontiers Sci. Found., 1971—, corp. trustee, 1974-79, chmn. ann. spring symposium, 1975; mem. Tulsa Mayor's Adv. Com., 1972-74; mem. mass transit policy com.; contbg. editor to state plan Gov.'s Fuel Allocation Commn., 1972-74; chmn. fed. procurement task force White House Small Bus. Conf. Commn., 1979—; Bd. dirs. Okla. Theater Center, 1979—. Served to capt. C.E. USAR, 1956-58. Recipient Leadership Service Merit award Alpha Rho Chi. Fellow AIA (nat. mem. urban planning and design com. 1972—, pres. Tulsa chpt. 1973-74, corp. mem. Okla. chpt. 1974—); mem. Am. Inst. Cert. Planners, Nat. Housing Conf. (dir. 1965—, legis. com. 1968—), Am. Soc. Planning Ofcls., Internat. Downtown Execs. Assn., Soc. Am. Mil. Engrs. (sustaining), Urban Land Inst., Nat. Trust Hist. Preservation (exec. mem. devel. systems and services council 1978—), Nat. Mcpl. League (regional v.p. 1980, governing council 1977—), Okla. Heritage Assn., M.I.T. Alumni Assn. (pres. Okla. club 1978-79), Oklahoma City C. of C. (dir. 1979-80, v.p. 1980—, chmn. small bus. and edn. div. 1979—, chmn. tchr. of year program, housing com. metro action planners 1977—), Tulsa C. of C. (dir. 1972-74), Okla. State U. Alumni Assn. (pres. Tulsa County 1967-69, chmn. presdl. scholar com. 1970), Blue Key, Sigma Tau. Democrat. Methodist. Clubs: Oklahoma City Golf and Country, Petroleum of Oklahoma City; So. Hills Country (Tulsa). Home: 2917 Charing Cross Rd Oklahoma City OK 73120 Office: HTB Inc 1411 Classen Blvd Oklahoma City OK

BALL, ROBERT M., writer, lecturer, social security, welfare and health policy specialist; b. N.Y.C., Mar. 28, 1914; s. Archey Decatur and Laura Elizabeth (Crump) B.; m. Doris Jacqueline McCord, June 30, 1936; children: Robert Jonathan, Jacqueline Elizabeth. A.B., Wesleyan U., 1935, M.A., 1936. With Bur. Old Age and Survivors Ins., Social Security Bd., 1939-46, asst. dir., 1949-52, acting dir., 1953, dep. dir., 1953-62, commr. of social security, 1962-73; sr. scholar Inst. Medicine, Nat. Acad. Scis., 1973-81; writer, lectr., cons., 1981—; asst. dir. com. on edn. and social security Am. Council on Edn., 1946-49; staff dir. adv. council on social security to U.S. Senate Finance Com., 1947-48; staff dir. pension study Nat. Planning Assn., 1950-52, chmn. adv. council social security, 1965; mem. Nat. Commn. Social Security Reform, 1982. Author: Pensions in the United States, 1952, Social Security Today and Tomorrow, 1978; also articles on social security, welfare, health care and nat. health ins. Recipient Disting. Service award Nat. Civil Service League, 1958; Rockefeller Public Service award, 1961; Arthur J. Altmeyer award, 1968; Clarence A. Kulp award, 1980. Mem. Inst. Medicine, Am. Public Welfare Assn., Nat. Acad. Public Adminstrn., Am. Soc. Public Adminstrn., Nat. Conf. Social Welfare, Nat. Council on Aging, Phi Beta Kappa, Delta Kappa Epsilon. Club: Internat. (Washington). Home: 7217 Park Terr Dr Alexandria VA 22307 Office: 236 Massachusetts Ave NE Suite 405 Washington DC 20002

BALL, VAUGHN CHARLES, educator, lawyer; b. St. Louis, Jan. 3, 1915; s. Charles Joseph and Bird (Vaughn) B.; m. Mary Ellen Miller, Aug. 31, 1940. J.D., Washington U., St. Louis, 1937, A.B., 1947. Bar: Mo. 1937, Ohio 1954. Practice law, St. Louis, 1937-42; atty., office of solicitor U.S. Dept. Labor, 1942-46; asst. prof. Washington U., St. Louis, 1946, Ohio State U., Columbus, 1948, asso. prof., 1949-51, 53, prof., 1954-65; dep. div. counsel Office Price Stblzn., 1951; asst. gen. counsel Office Def. Moblzn., 1951-52, dep. gen. counsel, 1952; Legion Lex prof. U. So. Calif., Los Angeles, 1965-74; Thomas Reade Rootes Cobb prof. law U. Ga., Athens, 1974—; mem. faculty Nat. Jud. Coll., 1966-75, Am. Acad. Jud. Edn., 1974-78. Author: Materials on Trial Practice, 1957, Materials on Selected Evidence Problems, 1966, rev. edit. (with Gilmore), 1973; author: (with others) McCormick, Hornbook on Evidence, rev. edit., 1972, supplement, 1978. Served in USAAF, 1943-46. Mem. Order Coif. Home: 185 Duncan Springs Rd Athens GA 30601 Office: U·Ga Law Sch Athens GA 30602

BALL, WILLIAM, producer, director; b. 1931. A.B., Fordham U.; M.A. (NBC/RCA fellow), Carnegie Inst. Tech.; Ph.D. (hon.), Carnegie-Mellon U., 1979. Founder, gen. dir. Am. Conservatory Theatre, 1965—. (Recipient Tony award 1979), Appearances with, Oreg. Shakespeare Festival, 1950-53, Antioch Shakespeare Festival, 1954, Group 20 Players, 1956, San Diego Shakespeare Festival, 1955, Arena Stage, Washington, 1957-58; in: Broadway and on tour Back to Methuselah, 1958, Six Characters in Search of An Author, 1959, Cosi Fan Tutte, 1959, The Inspector General, 1960, Porgy and Bess, 1961, Midsummer Night's Dream, 1963; with off-Broadway, N.Y.C. Center Opera Co. in, The Misanthrope, The Lady's Not for Burning, The Country Wife, Ivanov, A Month in the Country, 1956-58, Under Milkwood, 1956-61, Six Characters in Search of An Author, 1963; in: The Tempest, Stratford (Conn.) Festival, 1964, Yeoman of the Guard, Stratford, Can.; librettist, dir.: Natalia Petrovna, N.Y.C. Center Opera Co., 1964, Tartuffe for, Lincoln Center Repertory Co., 1965. Fulbright scholar to Eng., 1953-54; Ford Found. Director's grantee, 1959; commn. for Natalia Petrovna, 1964. Address: 450 Geary St San Francisco CA 94102

BALL, WILLIAM BENTLEY, lawyer; b. Rochester, N.Y., Oct. 6, 1916; s. Walter Bentley and May Catherine (Foley) B.; m. Caroline Cook, June 26, 1943; 1 dau., Virginia Mary. A.B., Western Res. U., 1940; J.D., U. Notre Dame, 1948; LL.D. (hon.), Cath. U. Am., 1964, St. Francis Coll., 1965, St. Charles Sem., 1974, Our Lady of Angels Coll., 1979, Gonzaga U., 1984, Kings Coll., 1984. Bar: N.Y. State 1953, Pa. 1958, U.S. Supreme Ct. 1958. Atty. legal dept. W.R. Grace & Co., 1948-53, Pfizer, Inc., 1953-55; prof. law Villanova U., 1955-60; exec. dir., gen. counsel Pa. Cath. Conf., Harrisburg, 1960-68; partner firm Ball & Skelly, Harrisburg, 1968—; mem. appellate ct. rules com. Pa. Supreme Ct., 1973—; bd. advisors St. Thomas More Inst. Legal Research; mem. Fed. Jud. Nominating Com. Pa., 1980-81. Contbr. articles to legal publs.; editor: Zoning for Minimum Lot Area, 1958, Dynamics of the Patent System, 1959. Bd. dirs. Pa. Equal Rights Council, 1964—, Human Life and Natural Family Planning Found., Inc., Washington, 1978—; vice chmn. Nat. Com. for Amish Religious Freedom, 1968—; mem. Camp Hill (Pa.) Borough Authority, 1975-82, Nat. Com. for Year of the Bible. Served with USN, 1940-46; lt. comdr. Res., 1946—; Served with USN, 1940-46; lt. comdr. Res. Decorated knight comdr. Order St. Gregory the Gt.; recipient Signum Fidei award LaSalle Coll., 1965; Merit award Nat. Cath. Edn. Assn., 1967; named Man of Yr. Cathedral Latin Alumni Assn., 1978; Brent award, 1978; Clarence Darrow award, 1982. Mem. Am. Law Inst., Pa. Bar Assn. (chmn. com. on legal edn. and bar admission 1972-77), Fed. Bar Assn. (nat. chmn. com. on constl. law 1970-74), Dauphin County Bar Assn. (chmn. com. on fed. ct. relations 1979—), U.S.S. Quincy Assn., Christian Legal Soc. Republican. Roman Catholic. Club: West Shore Country. Home: 854 Wynnewood Rd Camp Hill PA 17011 Office: 511 N Second St Harrisburg PA 17101

BALL, WILLIAM JOHN, manufacturing company executive; b. Hawley, Pa., Dec. 17, 1926; s. William Henry and Mabel Mary (Lintner) B.; m. Harriet Ann Jones, July 27, 1948; children: Catherine, Carol, Joanne, William J. B.S. in Mech. Engring., Purdue U., 1948. Supr. indsl. engring. Sylvania Electric Co., Altoona, Pa., 1948-56; assoc. Booz, Allen & Hamilton, Cleve., 1956-64; dir. mfg. Black, Sivalls and Bryson, Kansas City, Mo., 1964-66; v.p. mfg. Toledo Scale Co., 1966-69; pres. DeZurik Corp., Sartell, Minn., 1969-75; v.p., group exec. Gen. Signal Corp., Stamford, Conn., 1975—. Bd. dirs. United Way, St. Cloud, 1973-75; mem. pres.'s adv. com. St. John's U., St. Joseph., Minn., 1975-76. Served with USN, 1944-46. Mem. Valve Mfrs. Assn. (dir. 1970-77), Air Pollution Control Assn., Water Pollution Control Fedn. Republican. Unitarian. Office: Gen Signal Corp 2 High Ridge Park Stamford CT 06904

BALL, WILLIAM KENNETH, lawyer; b. DeQueen, Ark., Jan. 15, 1927; s. William P. and Lucille (Jeter) B.; m. Ella Hubbard Scaife, Dec. 28, 1950; children—Lucy Jane, William Ramsay, Charles Scaife. J.D., U. Ark., 1953. Bar: Ark. bar 1953. Law clk. to assoc. justice Ark. Supreme Ct., 1953-54; practice in, Monticello, 1954—; partner firm Williamson Ball & Bird, 1958—; city atty., Monticello, 1961—. Served with AUS, 1945-47, 50-52. Mem. ABA, Ark. Bar Assn., S.E. Ark. Bar Assn. (pres. 1957-58), Kappa Sigma, Delta Theta Phi. Presbyterian. Club: Rotary (pres. 1962-63). Home: 104 Westwood Ln Monticello AR 71655 Office: 106 W Oakland Ave Monticello AR 71655

BALLAM, JOSEPH, physicist, educator; b. Boston, Jan. 2, 1917; s. John Joseph and Sarah (Roosov) B.; m. Ethel Ada Hirsh, Dec. 28, 1938; children—John Joseph, Elysa Denise. B.S. in Physics, U. Mich., 1939; Ph.D., U. Calif. at Berkeley, 1951. Physicist Navy Dept., 1940-45; instr., research asso. Princeton, 1951-56; prof. physics Mich. State U., 1956-60; asso. dir., head research div. Stanford Linear Accelerator Center, 1961—, prof. physics, 1963—; Research collaborator, guest physicist Brookhaven Nat. Lab., 1955; NRC sr. vis. fellow Imperial Coll., London, 1980-81; sr. vis. scientist Ecole Polytechnique Paliseau, Paris, 1981. Author articles on cosmic rays, high energy exptl. physics.; Editor proc. VI: Internat. Conf. High Energy Physics, 1956. Ford Found. fellow, Geneva, 1960-61; Guggenheim fellow, 1971-72. Fellow Am. Phys. Soc. Home: 840 Lathrop Dr Stanford CA 94305

BALLANTINE, IAN, publisher; b. N.Y.C., Feb. 15, 1916; s. Edward James and Stella (Commins) B.; m. Elizabeth Jones, June 22, 1939; 1 son, Richard. A.B., Columbia, 1938; student, London Sch. Econs., 1938-39. Gen. mgr. Penguin Books, Inc., N.Y.C., 1939-45; pres., dir. Bantam Books, Inc., N.Y.C., 1945-52, Ballantine Books, Inc., 1952—; pres. Greenwich Press, Trumbull, Conn.; dir. Peacock Press Ltd.; instr. sociology Columbia. Mem. Phi Beta Kappa. Home: 60 E 9th St New York NY 10003 Office: Bearsville NY 12409

BALLANTINE, MORLEY COWLES (MRS. ARTHUR ATWOOD BALLANTINE), newspaper publisher; b. Des Moines, May 21, 1925; d. John and Elizabeth (Bates) Cowles; m. Arthur Atwood Ballantine, July 26, 1947 (dec. 1975); children—Richard, Elizabeth Ballantine Leavitt, William, Helen Ballantine Healy. A.B., Ft. Lewis Coll., 1975; L.H.D. (hon.), Simpson Coll., Indianola, Iowa, 1980. Pub. Durango (Colo.) Herald, 1952—, editor, pub., 1975-83, editor, chmn. bd., 1983—; dir. 1st Nat. Bank, Durango, 1976—, Des Moines Register & Tribune, 1977—, Cowles Media Co. Mem. Colo. Anti-Discrimination Commn., 1959-61, Colo. Com. on Ednl. Endeavor, 1959-63, Colo. Commn. on Status of Women, 1973-75, Colo. Population Adv. Council, 1972—, Colo. Land Use Commn., 1975-81, Supreme Ct. Nominating Commn., 1984—; pres. S.W. Colo. Mental Health Center, 1964-65; bd. dirs. Colo. Nat. Hist. Preservation Act, 1968-78; trustee Choate/Rosemary Hall, Wallingford, Conn., 1973-81, Simpson Coll., Indianola, Iowa, 1981—, Fountain Valley Sch., Colorado Springs, 1976—; pres. Four Corners Opera Assn., 1983—. Recipient 1st place award for editorial writing Nat. Fedn. Press Women, 1955, Outstanding Alumna award Rosemary Hall, Greenwich, Conn., 1969, Outstanding Journalism award U. Colo. Sch. Journalism, 1967, Distinguished Service award Ft. Lewis Coll., Durango, 1970. Mem. Nat. Soc. Colonial Dames, Colo. Press Assn. (bd. dirs. 1978-79), Colo. AP Assn. (chmn. 1966-67), Denver Women's Forum, Federated Women's Club Durango. Episcopalian. Club: Mill Reef (Antigua, W.I.). Address: care Herald PO Drawer A Durango CO 81301

BALLANTINE, THOMAS AUSTIN, JR., judge; b. Louisville, Sept. 22, 1926; s. Thomas Austin and Anna Marie (Pfeiffer) B.; m. Nancy A. Armstrong, June 10, 1953; children—Thomas A., Nancy Adair, Brigid A., Joseph A. Student, Northwestern U., 1944-46; B.A., U. Ky., 1948; J.D., U. Louisville, 1954. Bar: Ky. bar 1954. Asso. firm McElwain, Dinning, Clarke & Winstead, Louisville, 1954-64; dep. commr. Jefferson Circuit Ct., 1958-62; commr. Jefferson Fiscal Ct., 1962-64; judge Jefferson Circuit Ct., 1964-77, U.S. Dist. Ct., Western Dist. Ky., 1977—; instr. U. Louisville Law Sch., 1969-75. Bd. dirs. Louisville Urban League, 1958-64, chmn., 1963-64; dir. NCCJ, 1960-65, Health and Welfare Council, 1969, Louisville Theatrical Assn., 1970. Mem. Louisville Bar Assn., Ky. State Bar. Democrat. Roman Catholic. Club: Pendennis. Home: 48 Hill Rd Louisville KY 40204 Office: 247 USPO and Courthouse Louisville KY 40202

BALLANTYNE, ARNOLD PAUL, economist; b. Cherokee, Iowa, June 18, 1929; s. Alfred L. and Julia M. (Davenport) B.; m. Wanda Eileen Lowry, Aug. 16, 1929; children—Arnold Craig, Lisa Lyn Ballantyne Martin. B.A. in Econs, U. So. Calif., 1952; M.A., Iowa State U., 1954; Ph.D., Stanford U., 1961. Instr. State U. Iowa, 1953-54; mem. faculty U. Colo., Colorado Springs, 1967—, prof. econs., 1967—, dean, 1970-77, dir., 1978—. Served as officer, pilot USAF, 1954-67. Mem. Am. Econ. Assn., Western Econ. Assn., Western Social Sci. Assn. Methodist. Home: 1438 Acacia Dr Colorado Springs CO 80907 Office: Univ Colo Colorado Springs CO 80907

BALLANTYNE, ROBERT JADWIN, internat. ofcl.; b. Mt. Clemens, Mich., Oct. 16, 1925; s. Lowyd Whitcomb and Oneita (Jadwin) B.; m. Isadora de Andrade Falcao, Jan. 30, 1955 (dec. Mar. 21, 1969); children—Maria, Christopher; m. Lygia Maria Flores da Cunha, Feb. 25, 1972; children—Thomas, Anita. B.A., Yale, 1949. With U.S. Fgn. Service, 1951-69, consular officer, Hong Kong, 1951-53; econ. officer Am. embassy, Jidda, Saudi Arabia, 1953-56, polit. officer, London, 1956-60, Dept. State, 1960-65; assigned to Indsl. Coll. Armed Forces, Washington, 1965-66; dep. dir. U.S. AID Mission to Brazil, 1969-72; dir. Office Tech. Support, Bur. Asia, AID, Washington, 1972-74; dep. dir. Office Brazilian Affairs, Dept. State, 1974-76, Office S.Am. affairs AID, 1976-78; dir. program office U.S. AID Mission to Haiti, 1978-80; sectorial specialist Inter-Am. Devel. Bank, Rio de Janeiro, 1981—. Served with AUS, 1943-45. Unitarian. Club: University (Washington). Address: InterAm Devel Bank Caixa Postal 16209 Z0-01 Rio de Janeiro Brazil

BALLANTYNE, VICTOR ADOLPHUS, JR., former church official; b. Dallas, Oreg., Mar. 31, 1916; s. Victor Adolphus and Edna Naomi (Hall) B.; m. Alta Katherine Warren, July 22, 1941; children: Raymond W., Linda Carol Ballantyne Eastman. A.B., Willamette U., 1937; D.D., Western Evang. Sem., 1974. Ordained to ministry Evang. Ch., 1939; pastor Unionvale-Hopewell (Oreg.) Evang. Ch., 1937-41, Evang. Chs. in, Monmouth, Oreg., 1941-43, Portland, Oreg., 1943-50, Yakima, Wash., 1950-55, Evang. United Brethren Ch., Seattle, 1955-58, Eugene, Oreg., 1958-61, conf. supt., 1961-68, Evang. Ch. of N.Am., Indpls., 1968-71, exec. sec., gen. supt., 1971-83; bd. dirs., past chmn. World Gospel Mission. Trustee Western Evang. Sem. Mem. Wesleyan Theol. Soc. Address: 4730 Auburn Rd NE Apt 72 Salem OR 97301 *Believing in the validity of the call of God, I take the stance of trust in God, and in the Scriptures, as the principle ingredient of my life and work. Such trust implies the necessity of bringing my best thought and discipline to the task, with conscious reliance upon Divine aid to make up the difference between my ability and God's standard for my life and performance.*

BALLARD, CHARLES ALAN, investment banker; b. St. Louis, May 9, 1942; s. Fred William and Fern Ann (Markham) B. B.B.A., So.

Meth. U., 1963. V.p. fin. Systems Capital Corp., Phila., 1967-69; exec. v.p., dir. Vanderbilt Corp., Phila., 1969-71; v.p. Dillon, Read and Co. Inc., N.Y.C., 1972-78, sr. v.p., 1979-80, mng. dir., 1980—, dir., Dillon Read Overseas Corp., Dillon Read Inc.; chmn., dir. Ballard Properties Inc., Haverford, Pa., 1982—. Mem. council Nat. Municipal League, N.Y.C., 1981—; mem. adv. bd. Nat. Entrepreneurship Found., Bloomington, Ind., 1983—, The Energy Bur., N.Y.C., 1981—. Recipient Merit award U. Wis.-La Crosse, 1975, Achievement award Lions Club, Houston, 1963. Mem. N.Y. Stock Exchange (assoc.), Securities Industry Assn. (vice chmn. 1980-81), Pub. Fin. Com. (steering com. 1982). Clubs: Union League (Phila.); The Links (N.Y.C.); Merion Golf (Ardmore, Pa.); Wall St. (N.Y.C.). Home: Turnbridge Rd Haverford PA 19041 Office: Dillon Read and Co Inc Dillon Read Bldg 535 Madison Ave New York NY

BALLARD, CLAUDE MARK, JR., insurance company executive; b. Memphis, Sept. 27, 1929; s. Claude Mark and Elsie May (Miner) B.; m. Mary Theresa Birnbach, July 11, 1953; children: Karen Sue, Mary Melinda, Robin Lisa. With Prudential Ins. Co. Am., 1948—, v.p., regional treas. S.W. ops., Houston, 1967-73, sr. v.p. real estate investment dept., Newark, 1973—; dir. PIC Realty Co., Newark, Am. Bldg. Maintenance Industries; guest lectr. Cornell U., 1974-78, Mich. State U., 1975-80, NYU, 1975-80, Harvard U., 1976-80; chmn. Mortgage Inst., NYU; mem. fin. com. Am. Hotel and Motel Assn. Contbr. articles to profl. jours. Chmn. Econ. Devel. Com., Houston, 1972-73; treas., trustee Urban Land Inst., 1975—, mem. exec. com., 1977-80; pres., trustee Urban Land Research Found., Washington, 1977-79; mem. overseers vis. com. Grad. Sch. Urban Design, Harvard U.; mem. HUD Council on Devel. Choices for 80's. Mem. Am. Inst. Real Estate Appraisers. Home: 68 Island View Way Sea Bright NJ 07760 Office: Prudential Ins Co Am 745 Broad St Newark NJ 07101

BALLARD, EDWARD BROOKS, landscape architect; b. Lexington, Mass., Jan. 25, 1906; s. Walter Clark and Clara Abbie (Bigelow) B.; m. Mina Louise McCormick, Dec. 20, 1947; 1 son, Robert Clark. A.B., Harvard U., 1927, M.L.A., 1933. Asst. to editor Horticulture mag., Boston, 1930; landscape architect, asso. field coordinator Nat. Park Service, 1933-39; exec. sec. Nat. Parks Assn., Washington, 1940-42; spl. rep. Nat. Recreation Assn., 1946-47; asst. dir. Md. Dept. Forest and Parks, Annapolis, 1947-48; supt. Cumberland Falls State Park, Corbin, Ky., 1948-49; prin. landscape architect Pa. Bur. Parks, Harrisburg, 1949-52; landscape architect Office Chief of Engrs., Dept. Army, 1952-58, chief army project site planning, 1958-74; mng. landscape architect Miller, Wihry & Lee, Inc. (landscape architects and engrs.), Washington, 1975-80; cons. mktg. profl. services U.S. Govt., 1982—. Pres. Fairlington Civic Assn., Arlington, Va., 1954-55; pres. Broyhill Crest Citizens Assn., Annandale, Va., 1961-62; sec. Annandale Community Council, 1959-60, chmn., 1963-65. Served to capt. U.S. Army, 1942-46; PTO. Emeritus fellow Am. Soc. Landscape Architects (pres. Potomac chpt. 1961-62, trustee 1964-67, nat. sec.-treas. 1967-71, nat. archivist 1972-76, sec.-treas. Council of Fellows 1976-78); mem. Internat. Fedn. Landscape Architects (com. translation tech. terms 1979—), Harvard Sch. Design Assn., Delta Upsilon. Home: 3913 Longstreet Ct Annandale VA 22003 *To make Planet Earth livable for all people in harmony with Nature is to me the highest, though never completely attainable, goal of human existence. In this brief span of life it is enough reward to provide a better world for our posterity.*

BALLARD, EDWARD GOODWIN, emeritus philosophy educator, author; b. Fairfax, Va., Jan. 3, 1910; s. James W. and Margaret (Lewis) G.; m. Lucy McIver Watson, Nov. 22, 1938; children: Susanne Ballard Dowouis, Lucy Ballard Armentrout, Edward Marshall. B.A., Coll. William and Mary, 1931; diploma, U. Montpelier, France, 1933; M.A., U. Va., 1936, Ph.D., 1946; postgrad., U. Sorbonne, Paris, 1951, Harvard U., 1931-32. Asst. prof. English Va. Mil. Inst., 1939-41; asst. in philosophy U. Va., 1941-42; asst. prof. philosophy Tulane U., 1946-52, assoc. prof., 1952-56, prof., 1956-77, W. R. Irby prof. philosophy, 1977-80, emeritus, 1980—; vis. prof. Yale U., 1963-64, La. State U. at Baton Rouge, 1969, U. Mo., 1981, U. of South, 1981-82; mem. selection com. Woodrow Wilson fellowship, 1966-69; selection panel Nat. Endowment for Humanities, 1970-74; Bd. dirs. Center Advanced Research in Phenomenology, 1979—. Author: Art and Analysis, 1957, Socratic Ignorance, 1965, Philosophy at the Cross Roads, 1971, Man and Technology: Toward the Measurement of a Culture, 1978, Principles of Interpretation, 1983; editorial bd.: So. Jour. Philosophy, 1963-78, Research in Phenomenology, 1969—, Tulane Studies in Philosophy, 1970—; cons. editor: Continental Thought series, U. Ohio Press, 1979—, Current Continental Research, Univ. Press Am., 1980—; contbr. articles to philos. jours. Served to comdr. USNR, 1942-46; Res., to 1970; PTO. Grantee Tulane U., 1959-60, 68-69. Mem. So. Soc. Philosophy and Psychology (pres. 1967), Am. Philos. Assn., AAAS, Am. Metaphys. Soc. Office: Dept Philosophy U of South Sewanee TN 37375

BALLARD, EUGENE HENRY, manufacturing company executive; b. Grand Island, Nebr., Aug. 10. 1934; s. Henry James and Ruth Otelia (Jones) B.; m. Janet Lenore Royer., Dec. 20, 1958; children: Brian Cory, Brent Royer. B.S. in Chemistry, U. Nebr., 1961, J.D., 1961. Bar: Nebr. 1961, Del. 1962, Mass. 1976. Atty. Joseph Bancroft & Son Co., Wilmington, Del., 1961-70, asst. sec., 1967-70, gen. counsel, 1968-70; asst. corp. counsel Standex Internat. Corp., Andover, Mass., 1970-72, sec., corp. counsel, 1972-75; sec., gen. counsel No. Telecom, Inc., Waltham, Mass., 1975-76; sec., clk., gen. counsel Simplex Time Recorder Co., Gardner, Mass., 1976—, v.p., 1982—. Chmn. bd. Christ Ch. Profl. Nursery for Handicapped, 1979—. Mem. Am., Nebr., Mass. bar assns. Episcopalian (vestryman 1965-70, 77-80). Office: Simplex Plaza Gardner MA 01441

BALLARD, FREDERIC LYMAN, lawyer; b. Phila., Sept. 29, 1917; s. Frederic Lyman and Frances (Stoughton) B.; m. Ernesta Drinker, Dec. 22, 1939; children: Frederic Lyman, Sophie, Ernesta, Alice Walker. Grad., St. George's Sch., 1935; A.B., U. Pa., 1939, LL.B., 1942. Bar: Pa. 1942. Since practiced in, Phila.; partner firm Ballard, Spahr, Andrews & Ingersoll.; dir. Peirce-Phelps, Inc., Provident Nat. Bank, Provident Mut. Life Ins. Co. Phila. Mem. Pa. Bd. Pub. Welfare, 1966-70; bd. dirs. Greater Phila. Movement, 1958-72; trustee, mem. exec. com. United Fund Phila., 1959-70; trustee Radcliffe Coll., 1964-72; trustee, chmn. Thomas Jefferson U.; chmn. bd. overseers U. Pa. Law Sch., 1977-79. Served with USNR, 1943-46. Rhodes scholar elect, 1939. Mem. Am., Pa., Phila. bar assns., Phi Beta Kappa, Zeta Psi. Club: Philadelphia. Home: 9120 Crefeld St Philadelphia PA 19118 Office: 30 S 17th St Philadelphia PA 19103

BALLARD, FREDERICK ARMSTRONG, lawyer; b. Penn Yan, N.Y., July 13, 1907; s. Hiram C. and Agnes R. (Armstrong) B.; m. Mary Elizabeth Brackett, Apr. 22, 1933; children—Sally Welles, Mary Elizabeth, Kimberly. A.B., Hamilton Coll., 1928; LL.B., Harvard, 1931. Bar: D.C. bar 1932. Since practiced in, Washington; mem. firm Ballard and Beasley; prof. law Washington Coll. Law, 1935-40; vis. lectr. Aviation law U. Va. Law Sch., 1948; adj. prof. law Georgetown U. Law Sch., Washington, 1959-61; mem. Pres.'s Commn. on Crime in D.C., 1965-66; chmn. disciplinary bd. D.C. Bar (Unified), 1972-75. Served to capt. USNR, 1942-45. Fellow Am. Coll. Trial Lawyers, Am. Bar Found. (Samuel Pool Weaver Constl. Law Essay prize 1962); mem. Am. Bar Assn. (state del. D.C. 1964-72), Bar Assn. D.C. (pres. 1959-60, Lawyer of Year 1973), Am. Law Inst. (council 1966—), Am. Arbitration Assn. (mem. nat. panel), Harvard Law Sch. Assn. D.C. (pres. 1948), Phi Beta Kappa, Chi Psi, Sigma Delta Kappa (hon.). Episcopalian (sr. warden 1956-57). Home: 6060 Woodmont Rd Alexandria VA 22307 Office: 1700 K St NW Washington DC 20006

BALLARD, HAROLD E., professional hockey executive; b. 1903; m. Dorothy (dec.); 3 children. Former mgr. Sea Fleas amateur hockey team, West Toronto (Ont., Can.) Nationals jr. team; mgr., later pres. Jr. Toronto Marlboros; dir. Maple Leaf Gardens; now pres., owner Toronto Maple Leafs. Office: Toronto Maple Leafs Hockey Club 60 Carlton St Toronto ON M5B 1L1 Canada *

BALLARD, JOHN STUART, educator, former mayor; b. Akron, Ohio, Sept. 30 1922; s. Irby S. and Sarah (McCormick) B.; m. Ruth Frances Holden, Oct. 22, 1949; children: Susan, Karen, John H., Mark, Ward. A.B., U. Akron, 1943; LL.B., U. Mich., 1948. Bar: Mich. 1948, Ohio 1949. Spl. agt. FBI, 1949-52; practice law, Akron, 1952-56, 64-65, pros. atty., Summit County, Ohio, 1957-64, mayor of, Akron, 1966-80; adj. asso. prof. dept. urban studies U. Akron, 1980—. Mem. Summit County Republican Exec. Com., 1956—; candidate for U.S. senator from Ohio, 1962. Served with inf. AUS, 1943-46. Recipient Distinguished Service award Akron Jr. C. of C., 1957. Episcopalian. Home: 1685 Hampton Knoll Dr Akron OH 44313 *It is true that in giving we receive.*

BALLARD, JOHN WILLIAM, JR., banker; b. Kingston, Ont., Can., Mar. 8, 1922; came to U.S., 1922; s. John William and Evelyn Mary (Toohill) B.; m. Imogen Dean Billings, Dec. 29, 1947; children—John William III, Paul Billings, Jenny Evelyn. B.S., U. Kans., 1947. With Safety Fed. Savs. and Loan Assn., Kansas City, Mo., 1947—, asst. v.p., 1949-58, treas., 1958-62, pres., 1962—, chmn. bd., 1968—; trustee Kansas City Blue Cross, sec., 1960-61, treas., 1961-71, chmn. bd., 1971—; pres. Safety Ins. Agy., 1962—. Vice pres. Jr. C. of C., 1950, C. of C.; dir. Downtown Inc., 1967—; trustee Savs. and Loan Found., Inc., 1966-70. Served with AUS, 1942-45. Decorated Bronze Star. Mem. Am. Royal Assn. (gov. 1962—), Real Estate Bd. (dir. 1964-65, 71-74), Mo. Savs. and Loan League (pres. 1964-65), Kansas City Savs. and Loan League (pres. 1966-67), Sigma Alpha Epsilon. Episcopalian. Clubs: Mission Hills Country (Shawnee Mission, Kans.); Garden of the Gods (Colorado Springs, Colo.); Rotary (past v.p., dir.), Kansas City.). Home: 9311 Buena Vista Prairie Village KS 66207 Office: 910 Grand Ave Kansas City MO 64106 *In our organization no one works for me, but with me. A man seldom becomes a success without the help of others.*

BALLARD, KAYE, actress; b. Cleve., Nov. 1926; d. Vincent and Lena (Nacarata) Balotta. Broadway appearances include Molly, Pirates of Penzance; TV appearances include Fantasy Island; movies include In Love Again; nightclub appearances include, Plaza Hotel, N.Y.C., Bon Soir, N.Y.C., Palmer House, Chgo. Recipient Italian-Am. award; Dallas State Fair award for Gypsy. Mem. Actors Equity Assn., AFTRA, Screen Actors Guild, Am. Guild Variety Artists. Address: care Richard B Francis 328 S Beverly Dr Beverly Hills CA 90212

BALLARD, LARRY COLEMAN, insurance company executive; b. Des Moines, May 31, 1935; s. Coleman Woodrow and Letitia Rebecca (Reaugh) B.; m. Rosalie Phillips, Dec. 24, 1956; children—Coleman, Tamara. B.S. in Actuarial Scis, Drake U., 1957. Asst. actuary Travelers Ins. Co., Hartford, Conn., 1957-62; v.p. Allstate Ins. Co., Northbrook, Ill., 1962-75; sr. v.p. mktg. CNA Co., Chgo., 1975-77, sr. v.p. central ops., 1977—; dir. Continental Assurance Co., Continental Casualty Co., Nat. Fire Ins. Co., Hartford. Served with U.S. Army, 1958. Fellow Soc. Actuaries. Home: 1100 N Lake Shore Dr Chicago IL 60611 Office: CNA Plaza Chicago IL 60685

BALLARD, LOUIS WAYNE, composer; b. Miami, Okla., July 8, 1931; s. Charles Guthrie and Leona Mae (Quapaw) B.; m. Ruth Sands, Dec. 6, 1965; children by previous marriage: Louis Anthony, Anne Marie, Charles Christopher. B.Mus. and Music Edn., U. Tulsa, 1954; M.Mus., 1962; D.Mus. (hon.), Coll. Santa Fe, 1973. Dir. vocal and instrumental music Nelagoney (Okla.) Public Sch., 1954-56; dir. vocal music Webster High Sch., Tulsa, 1956-58; pvt. music tchr., 1959-62; music dir. Inst. Am. Indian Arts, Santa Fe, 1962-65, dir. performing arts, 1965-69; nat. dir. music edn. curriculum and rev. Bur. Indian Affairs, Washington, 1969-79; lectr., clinician, 1960—; pres. First Am. Indian Films, Inc., 1969—. Composer, Santa Fe, 1979—; ballets The Four Moons; orchl. music Fantasy Aborigine, Nos. I, II, III, IV; chamber music Rhapsody for Four Bassoons; choral cantatas Espiritu de Santiago; band works Nighthawk Keetowa; percussion Cecega Ayuwipi; numerous others.; Author: The American Indian Sings, Book 1, 1970, also articles. Recipient 1st Marion Nevins MacDowell award chamber music, 1969, Nat. Indian Achievement award, 1972, Catlin Peace Pipe award Nat. Indian Lore Assn., 1976, ASCAP award, 1966-76; F.B. Parriott grad. fellow, 1969; grantee Ford Found., 1970, Nat. Endowment Arts, 1967, 69, 76, 79; commd. by Martha B. Rockefeller Found., 1969. Mem. ASCAP, Music Educators Nat. Conf. (chmn. minority concerns com. for N.Mex. 1976), Am. Symphony Orch. League. Office: PO Box 4552 Santa Fe NM 87502

BALLARD, STANLEY SUMNER, physicist; b. Los Angeles, Oct. 1, 1908; s. John Hudson and Myrtle (Stanley) B.; m. Mary Elizabeth Miller, Sept. 13, 1935; children: Mary Susan, John Stanley (dec.); m. Carol Reeves Hanke, Feb. 23, 1974. A.B., Pomona Coll., 1928, D.Sc., 1974; M.A., U. Calif. at Berkeley, 1932, Ph.D., 1934. Asst. physics Dartmouth Coll., 1928-30; teaching fellow physics U. Calif. at Berkeley, 1930-34, research fellow, 1934-35; instr. physics U. Hawaii, 1935-37, asst. prof. physics, 1937-41; research asso. geophysics Hawaii Nat. Park, 1936-41; cons. spectroscopy exptl. sta. Hawaiian Sugar Planters' Assn., 1937-40; collaborator in soil chemistry Hawaii Agrl. Expt. Sta., 1939-41; prof. physics, chmn. dept. Tufts Coll., 1946-54; research physicist U. Calif. Scripps Instn. Oceanography, 1954-58; prof. physics U. Fla., Gainesville, 1958—, Disting. Service prof., 1978—, chmn. dept. physics and astronomy, 1958-71, dir. div. phys. and math. scis., 1968-71; cons. physicist Polaroid Corp., 1946-54, Baird Assos., Inc., 1946-51, Planning Research Corp., 1956-58; cons. Rand Corp., 1952-71, physicist electronics dept., 1953-54; cons. Willow Run Labs., U. Mich., 1957-65; infrared cons. USAF Atlantic Missile Range, 1960-63; cons. astrionics div. Aerojet Gen. Corp., 1961-66; cons. Douglas Advanced Research Labs., 1966-70; prof. physics U. Calif. at Berkeley, summer 1949; U.S. del. Internat. Commn. Optics (Internat. Union Pure and Applied Physics), Delft, Holland, 1948, London, 1950, Madrid, 1953, Boston, 1956, Stockholm, 1959, Munich, 1962, Paris, 1966, Reading, Eng., 1969, Santa Monica, Calif., 1972, Prague, Czechoslovakia, 1975, Madrid, 1978, Graz, Austria, 1981; chmn. U.S. nat. com. Internat. Commn. Optics, 1948-57; mem. Armed Forces NRC vision com., exec. sec., 1956-59; v.p. Internat. Commn. Optics, 1948-56, pres., 1956-59. Co-author: Physics Principles, 1954, Polarized Light, 1964; contbr. to: jours. physics, geophysics, and optics. Ency. Americana, Ency. Brit. Served from lt. to comdr. USNR, 1941-46; officer-in-charge research and devel. optics and infrared instruments Bur. Ordnance, Navy Dept. and radiometry sect. tech. staff Joint Task Force One (atom bomb tests). Decorated Royal Order North Star, Sweden, 1972. Fellow Am. Phys. Soc., AAAS (sec. sect. B physics 1960-67, v.p. 1968), Phys. Soc. London, Optical Soc. Am. (sec. local sects. 1947-53, asso. editor jour. 1950—, v.p. for meetings 1955-59, pres. 1963, disting. service award 1977), Soc. Photo-Instrumentation Engrs.; mem. Am. Inst. Physics (governing bd. 1962-65, 67-73), Japan Soc. Applied Physics (hon.), Fla. Acad. Scis. (medalist 1979), Am. Assn. Physics Tchrs. (pres. 1968-69, distinguished service citation 1975), German Soc. Applied Optics, Phi Beta Kappa, Sigma Xi, Omicron Delta Kappa, Gamma Alpha, Sigma Pi Sigma (nat. pres. 1959-62), Sigma Alpha Epsilon. Presbyterian. Club: Torch. Office: Dept Physics U Fla Gainesville FL 32611

BALLARD, WILLIAM C., JR., health care company executive. Exec. v.p., sec. Humana, Inc., Louisville. Office: Humana Inc PO Box 1438 Louisville KY 40201§

BALLARD, WILLIAM MACHAEL, investment banker; b. Green Bay, Wis., Jan. 12, 1951; s. William Cloyd and Polly Ann (Williams) B.; m. Robbin Minn Kaplan, Apr. 15, 1974 (div. 1982); m. 2d Deborah Minton Butler, Jan. 15, 1983. B.S., Ripon Coll., (Wis.), 1973. Vice pres. Fin. Planning Corp., Madison, Wis., 1973-76; v.p. J.C. Bradford & Co., Nashville, 1976-81, ptnr., 1981—. Mem. Nat. Assn. Securities Dealers, Internat. Assn. Fin. Planners. Republican. Clubs: Hillwood Country, Richland Country (Nashville). Home: 5106 Pheasant Run Trail Brentwood TN 37027 Office: JC Bradford & Co 170 4th Ave N Nashville TN 37219

BALLEM, JOHN BISHOP, lawyer, novelist; b. New Glasgow, N.S., Can., Feb. 2, 1925; s. John Cedric and Flora Winifred (Miller) B.; m. Grace Louise Flavelle, Aug. 31, 1951; children: Flavelle Bishop, Mary Mercedes, John Flavelle. B.A., Dalhousie U., 1946, M.A., 1948, LL.B., 1949; LL.M., Harvard U., 1950. Bar: apptd. Queen's counsel 1966. Asst. prof. law U. B.C., Vancouver, Can., 1950-52; with law dept. Imperial Oil Co., Toronto and Calgary, 1952-56; with Pacific Petroleums, Ltd., Calgary, 1956-62; ptnr. Ballem, McDill & MacInnes, Calgary, Alta., 1962—; pres. Scotia Oils, Ltd., 1965—. Author: textbook Oil and Gas Lease in Canada, 1972; novels The Devil's Lighter, 1973, The Dirty Scenario, 1974, The Judas Conspiracy, 1976, The Moon Pool, 1978, Sacrifice Play, 1981, Alberta Alone, 1981, The Marigot Run, 1984; contbr. articles to profl. jours. Pres. Calgary Zool. Soc., 1966-70. Served with Fleet Air Arm, 1944-45. Mem. Can. Bar Assn. (v.p. Alta. 1966), Alta. Law Soc., N.S. Barristers Assn., Law Soc. Upper Can. Presbyterian. Clubs: Calgary Golf and Country, Calgary Petroleum., Runchmen's, Pinebrook Golf and Country. Office: 3600 Scotia Center Calgary AB Canada T2V 2V6

BALLENGEE, JAMES MCMORROW, diversified operating company executive; b. Charleston, W.Va., Jan. 10, 1923; s. Lanty Ernest and Marie Vivian (McMorrow) B.; m. Jo McIlhattan, June 7, 1947; children: James M., Elizabeth Ann, Sarah Jo. A.B., Morris Harvey Coll., 1946, LL.D. (hon.), 1972; J.D., Washington and Lee U., 1948. Bar: W.Va. bar 1948, Pa. bar 1962. Assoc. firm Mohler, Peters & Snyder, Charleston, W.Va., 1948-53, Dayton, Campbell & Love, Charleston, 1953-57; asso. counsel Sears, Roebuck & Co., Phila., 1957-61; partner firm Morgan, Lewis & Bockius, Phila., 1962; pres., chmn. Phila. Suburban Water Co., Bryn Mawr, Pa., 1962-76, Phila. Suburban Corp., Radnor, Pa., 1968-81, Enterra Corp., 1981—; dir. Berwind Corp., Bell Telephone Co. Pa.; trustee Phila. Savs. Fund Soc., Fidelity Mut. Life Ins. Co. Bd. dirs. Bryn Mawr Hosp.; bd. dirs. Greater Phila. Partnership; past pres. met. bd. Phila. area YMCA; past chmn. Eastern Pa. chpt. Arthritis Found.; trustee Phila. Mus. Art, Arthritis Found.; rector bd. trustees Washington and Lee U. Served with U.S. Army, 1943-46; to 1st lt., 1950-52; Korea. Decorated Bronze Star. Mem. Am., Pa., W.Va. bar assns., Greater Phila. C. of C. (dir.), Order of Coif, Phi Beta Kappa. Democrat. Presbyterian. Clubs: Philadelphia, Merion Golf and Racquet. Home: 711 Williamson Rd Bryn Mawr PA 19010 Office: PO Box 26 Radnor PA 19087

BALLENTINE, J. GREGORY, government economist; b. Buffalo, July 21, 1948; s. Richard Edwin and Maryalice (Callanan) B.; m. Martha Elizabeth Scott, Sepst. 16, 1967; children: Greta K., Dorothy E. Student, Georgetown U., 1966-67; B.S., Springhill Coll., 1970; Ph.D., Rice U., 1974. Asst. prof. Wayne State U., Detroit, 1974-77, assoc. prof., 1977-79, U. Fla., Gainesville, 1979-81, prof., 1981—; dep. asst. sec. U.S. Dept. Treasury, Washington, 1981-83; assoc. dir. Office of Mgmt. and Budget, Washington, 1983—; cons. GAO, Washington, 1979-81; dir. grad program Wayne State U., Detroit, 1977-79. Co-editor: Pub. Fin. Quar., 1981—. Mem. Am. Econ. Assn., Nat. Tax Assn., So. Econ. Assn. Office: Office Mgmt and Budget 17th and Pennsylvania Ave NW Washington DC 20503

BALLER, WARREN ROBERT, ednl. psychologist; b. Trenton, Nebr., June 19, 1900; s. Albert Ernest and Mary Louise (Taylor) B.; m. Dorothy Gwendolyn Jensen, Mar. 15, 1941; children—William Warren, John Timothy, Elizabeth Claire. A.B., York Coll., 1923; M.A., U. Nebr., 1927, Ph.D., 1935; student, Columbia U., 1930, U. Minn., 1932; LL.D., George Williams Coll., 1961. Prin. Callaway (Nebr.) High Sch., 1923-24; supt. schs., Cheney, Nebr., 1925-28; tchr. York Coll., 1928-34, dean, 1933-34; asst. prof. ednl. psychology U. Nebr., 1936-38, asso. prof., 1938-43, prof., 1943-67, also chmn., 1961-67, dir. jr. div., 1948-50; vis. prof. edn. U. Calif. at Los Angeles, 1955-57; prof. ednl. psychology Calif. Western U., 1967-68, U.S. Internat. U., San Diego, 1968—; fellow gen. edn. bd. U. Chgo., 1940-41; vis. prof. George Peabody Coll., summer 1941, Northwestern U., summer 1941, U. Fla., summer 1950, U. Calif., summer 1951, U. Tex., spring 1949; cons. child behavior and devel., Lincoln, 1938—. Author: Psychology of Human Growth and Development, 1961, 2d edit., 1968, Readings in the Psychology of Human Growth and Development, 1962, 2d edit., 1969, Nocturnal Enuresis (Bedwetting) Origins and Treatment, 1975. Mem. Am. Psychol. Assn., Soc. Profs. of Edn. (past pres.), Midwestern, Western psychol. assns., Sigma Xi. Democrat. Presbyterian. Home: 325 Kempton St Spring Valley CA 92077

BALLES, JOHN JOSEPH, banker; b. Freeport, Ill., Jan. 7, 1921; s. Louis J. and Kathleen P. (O'Connor) B.; m. Mira Jane Knupp, June 16, 1944; children: Nancy, Janet. B.S., State U. Iowa, 1942, M.A., 1947; Ph.D., Ohio State U., 1951. Instr., then asst. prof. econs. and bus. adminstrn. Ohio State U., 1947-54; sr. v.p. in charge econ. and corp. planning Fed. Res. Bank Cleve., 1954-59; sr. v.p., chief economist Mellon Nat. Bank & Trust Co., Pitts., 1959-72; pres. Fed. Res. Bank San Francisco, 1972—; dir. N. Am. Rockwell Corp., 1966-72. Author: (with Richard W. Lindholm and John M. Hunter) Principles of Money and Banking, 1954. Bd. dirs. Bay Area Council, San Francisco, 1974—. Served with AUS, 1943-46. Decorated Bronze Star with oak leaf cluster. Mem. Am. Finance Assn. (dir. 1962-63), Am. Bankers Assn. (govt. relations council 1970-72), Nat. Assn. Bus. Economists (council 1964-66), Pa. Bankers Assn. (pres. 1965-66), Am. Econ. Assn. Office: PO Box 7702 San Francisco CA 94120

BALLEW, DAVID WAYNE, mathematics and computer science educator; b. Mangum, Okla., Aug. 20, 1940; s. Troy Chester and Mary Margaret (Means) B.; m. Mary Lou Wilson, June 18, 1960; children: Lawrence, Diana. B.A., U. Okla., 1962, M.A., 1964; Ph.D., U. Ill.-Urbana, 1969. Cert. computer programmer. Research asst. U. Okla.-Norman, 1962-64; research fellow U. Ill.-Urbana, 1964-67; prof. math. sci., computer sci. S.D. Sch. Mines and Tech., Rapid city, 1967—. Author: Fortran 77, Calculus I, Calculus II, Calculus III, 1982; editor: Pi Mu Epsilon Jour., 1977—. Named Outstanding prof. S.D. Sch. Mines and Tech., 1981. Mem. Am. Soc. Engring. Edn., Am. Math. Soc., Math. Assn. Am., Pi Mu Epsilon. Republican. Clubs: Lions, Elks, Toastmasters. Home: Box 544 Rapid City SD 57701 Office: Dept Math Scis 500 E St Joe St Rapid City SD 57701

BALLHAUS, WILLIAM FRANCIS, engineering executive; b. San Francisco, Aug. 15, 1918; s. William Frederick and Eva Rose Callero (O'Connor) B.; m. Edna Dooley, Feb. 13, 1944; children: William Francis, Katherine Louise, Martin Dennis, Mary Susan. B.S., Stanford U., 1940, M.E. (Switzer research fellow, Rosenberg research fellow 1940-42), 1942; Ph.D., Calif. Inst. Tech., 1947. Registered profl. engr. Mem. tech. adv. panel on aeros. Office Sec. Def., 1954-60; mem. NACA, 1954-57; chief engr. Northrop Aircraft, 1953-57, v.p. engring., 1957; v.p., gen. mgr. Nortronics, 1957-61; exec. v.p., dir. Northrop Corp., Beverly Hills, Calif., 1961-64; now dir.; pres. Beckman Instruments, Inc., Fullerton, Calif., 1965-82, chief exec. officer, 1983-84; dir. Amerace Corp., Northrop Corp., Union Oil Co. Calif.; Cons. Office of Critical Tables, Nat. Acad. Scis., 1958-65. Trustee Northrop U., Harvey Mudd Coll.; fellow Claremont U. Center; mem. adv. council Sch. Engring., Stanford U. Fellow AIAA; mem. Nat. Acad. Engring., Assn. U.S. Army (pres. Greater Los Angeles chpt. 1963-65, council of trustees 1965-69). Home: 5672 Mountain View Ave Yorba Linda CA 92686 Office: Ames Research Center NASA Moffett Field CA 94305

BALLIETT, GENE (HOWARD EUGENE BALLIETT), writer, lecturer; b. Dayton, Ohio, Aug. 28, 1931; s. Aaron Henry (Ted) and Ruth Paullin (McDorman) B.; m. Dolores Druley, June 12, 1954; children: Philip Druley, Tedi Jo. B.A. in Journalism, Ohio State U. Formerly reporter Hamilton Jour.-News; asst. news editor Cin. Enquirer, 1956-60; make-up editor Newsday, Garden City, N.Y., 1960-62; sr. editor Med. Econs., Oradell, N.J., 1962-67; cons. med. mgmt., 1967—; editor Physician's Mgmt. mag. Harcourt Brace Jovanovich Co., N.Y.C., 1972-76; dir. div. spl. fin. services City Fed. Savs., Elizabeth, N.J., 1978-80; producer, lectr. Family Finances Tax and Investment Seminar, 1980—. Author: Practice Management, How to Get Started in Private Practice, How to Close a Medical Practice. Served with USAF, 1950-53. Recipient Neal award. Mem. Soc. Med.-Dental Mgmt. Cons. (hon.). Club: Oritani Field (Hackensack, N.J.). Home: 268 W Englewood Ave Teaneck NJ 07666 Office: 555 Cedar Ln Teaneck NJ 07666

BALLIETT, WHITNEY, writer, critic; b. N.Y.C., Apr. 17, 1926; s. Fargo and Dorothy (Lyon) B.; m. Elizabeth Hurley King, 1951; children: Julia, Elizabeth, Will; m. Nancy Kraemer, 1965; children: Whitney, James. B.A. with honors, Cornell U., 1951. Mem. editorial staff New Yorker mag., N.Y.C., 1951—, successively collator, proofreader, reporter, 1951-57, staff writer, 1957—; columnist on jazz recs., concerts, book reviewer, movie and theater reviewer, reporter. Contbr.: poetry to Atlantic Monthly, Saturday Rev.; originated: plan CBS-TV show Sound of Jazz, 1957; Author: The Sound of Suprise, 1959, Dinosaurs in the Morning, 1962, Such Sweet Thunder, 1966, Super-Drummer: A Profile of Buddy Rich, 1968, Ecstasy at the Onion, 1971, Alec Wilder and His Friends, 1974, New York Notes: A Journal of Jazz, 1976, Improvising: Sixteen Jazz Musicians and their Art, 1977, American Singers, 1979, Night Creature: A Journal of Jazz, 1981, Jelly Roll, Jabbo, and Fats: Nineteen Portraits in Jazz, 1983. Served as sgt. USAAF, 1946-47. Office: New Yorker Mag 25 W 43d St New York NY 10036

BALLIN, WILLIAM CHRISTOPHER, shipping and energy company executive; b. Ft. Wayne, Ind., May 3, 1929; s. Christopher Theodore and Katherine (Nolles) B.; m. Dolores Mary Jack, June 18, 1948; children: Stuart, Kirk, Scott, Elizabeth. B.A., U. Toledo, 1949; postgrad., Colo. Coll., Am. U., U. Lausanne, Switzerland. Pub. affairs coordinator Marathon Oil Co., Findlay, Ohio, 1954-61, Washington rep., 1961-63, European mgr. govt. relations, Geneva, 1963-69; v.p. Crosby Kelly Fin. Relations, N.Y.C., 1969-70; exec. v.p. Am. Export Lines, Inc., N.Y.C., 1970-77; U.S. and Mid East adv. Overland Trust Bank, Lugano and Geneva, Switzerland; chmn. Convestor, Geneva; dir. Cortship Internat. B.V., Rotterdam, Netherlands. Bd. dirs. Am. Near East Aid, Middle East Inst. Clubs: Downtown Athletic, Whitehall (N.Y.C.). Home: 200 E 66th St New York NY 10021 Office: 17 Battery Pl New York NY 10004 also 3 Rue Du Mont Blanc Geneva Switzerland

BALLINGER, HARRY RUSSELL, artist; b. Port Townsend, Wash., Sept. 4, 1892; s. James Guy and Lourena (Russell) B.; m. Madeline Waters, Feb. 19, 1922; m. Kay Mollison, Oct. 12, 1951. Student, U. Calif., San Francisco, 1910-11, Art Student's League, 1912-13, Acad. Colorossi, Paris, France, 1927; pupil of, Harvey Dunn, 1915-16. Instr. Grand Central Art Sch., 1930-36, Central Conn. Coll., New Britain, 1945-58, Rockport, Mass., 1952-60, U. Hawaii, 1959, 60. Illustrator nat. mags., 1916-17, 19-35; rep. permanent collections, NAD, New Haven Paint and Clay Club, New Britain Mus. Am. Art, Wadsworth Atheneum, Hartford, Conn., Springfield (Mass.) Art Mus., Central Conn. State Coll., Meriden (Conn.) Arts and Crafts Soc., also mural, Plant High Sch., W. Hartford, Conn., ann. exhbns., Allied Artists, Audubon Artists, Nat. Acad. Design, Am. Watercolor Soc., Salmagundi Club, Napier Co., Meriden, Meriden Savs. Bank, Torrington (Conn.) Savs. Bank, one man shows include, New Britain Mus. Am. Art, 1947, Ward Eggleston Gallery, N.Y.C., 1948, Rockport Art Assn., 1951, 53, 55, 58, 61, 65, 68, 71, 74, Marblehead (Mass.) Art Assn., 1954, Choate Sch., 1959, Guild Boston Artists, 1960, Woodmere Art Gallery, Phila., 1962, Central Conn. Coll., 1965, Cayuga Mus. Art, Auburn, N.Y., 1955, U. Conn., 1966, Wisteria Hurst Mus., Chicopee, Mass., 1977, Ellsworth Gallery, Simsbury, Conn.; Author: Painting Surf and Sea, 1957, Painting Boats and Harbors, 1959, Painting Landscapes, 1965, Painting Sea and Shore, 1973, also articles. Recipient numerous watercolor prizes Salmagundi Club; prizes Meriden Arts and Crafts Soc., 1944, 52, 57, 60, 61, 65, 68, 71, 72, 74, Springfield Acad. Artists Assn., 1952, 53, 55, 62, 64, 65, 70, 72, 74, Hudson Valley Art Assn., 1958, 60, 64, 70, 74, Jordan Marsh Co., Boston, 1953, 56, 60, Am. Artists Profl. League, 1961, Rockport Art Assn., 1953, 55, 60 (2), 63, 65, 68, 74, N. Shore Art Assn., 1963, 64, 70, 73, 76, Audubon Artists Ann. Exhbn., 1968, 71, Acad. Artists, Springfield N. Shore Arts Assn., Rockport Art Assn., Allied Artists Am., 1976; citation contbn. to Am. art, 1980. Asso. NAD.; Mem. Allied Artists, Audubon Artists, Salmagundi Club, New Haven Paint and Clay Club, Conn. Acad., Kent (Conn.) Art Assn., Springfield Acad. Art, N. Shore Art Assn., Rockport Art Assn., Guild Boston Artists, Acad. Artists Springfield (council 1977—). Address: RFD 2 New Hartford CT 06057 *After over sixty years of painting, I feel profoundly grateful that I can still enjoy portraying the land and sea around me. If I can continue to give pleasure to others through my paintings, I will feel amply rewarded for the many years of effort that I have spent in trying to paint the world as I see it.*

BALLINGER, WALTER FRANCIS, surgeon, educator; b. Phila., May 16, 1925; s. Robert I. and Frances (Taylor) B.; m. Ellen Fezandie, June 26, 1953 (div. 1980); children: Walter Francis, Christopher Bardin, David Gordon; m. Mary Randolph Gordon Dickson, Oct. 4, 1980. Student, Cornell U., 1942-44; M.D., U. Pa., 1948. Intern 1st Surg. Div., Bellevue Hosp., N.Y.C., 1948-49, asst. resident surgery, 1949-50, chief resident surgery, 1955-56; asst. resident surgery Columbia-Presbyn. Med. Center, 1953-55; from instr. to assoc. prof. Jefferson Med. Coll., Phila., 1956-63; assoc. prof. surgery Johns Hopkins Sch. Medicine, 1964-67; Bixby prof., head dept. surgery Washington U. Sch. Medicine, St. Louis, 1967-78, prof. surgery, 1978—. Editor: Research Methods in Surgery, 1964, The Management of Trauma, 1968, 74, 79, (with T. Drapanas) Practice of Surgery: Current Review, 1972, 74; co-editor-in-chief: (with G. Zuidema) Surgery, 1971—. Served to capt. U.S. Army, 1950-52. Markle scholar med. sci., 1961-66. Mem. Am. Surg. Assn., Soc. Clin. Surgery, Soc. Univ. Surgeons, A.C.S., James IV Assn., Halsted Soc. Home: 800 Barnes Rd Saint Louis MO 63124 Office: Barnes Hosp Plaza Saint Louis MO 63110

BALLIU, WILLIAM LOUIS, insurance executive; b. Moline, Ill., Dec. 6, 1926; s. Clement and Gladys (Spivey) B.; m. Marie Myrtle Balliu, May 25, 1974; children: William Michael, Christina Marie, Kerry Ellen, Robert Timothy, Thomas Anthony, Denise Marie. B.A., St. Ambrose Coll., Davenport, Iowa, 1950. With Farmland Industries, Inc., Kansas City, Mo., 1952—, v.p. agy., 1968-72, exec. v.p., chief operating officer, 1972-76, pres., chief operating officer, 1976-81, pres., chief exec. officer, 1981—; dir. Iowa Inst. Ins., Farmland Mut. Ins. Co. Served with AUS, 1943-46. Office: Farmland Ins Services 1963 Bell Ave Des Moines IA 50315

BALLMER, RAY WAYNE, minerals company executive; b. Santa Rita, N.Mex., Mar. 6, 1926; s. Gerald Jacob and Martha Clara (Wilhelmsen) B.; m. Doris Jean Greer, July 8, 1945; children: Geraldine Lee, Ray James. B.S. in Mining Engring., 1949; M.S. in Indsl. Mgmt., MIT, 1960. Registered profl. engr., Ariz. Various exec. positions Kennecott Copper Corp., Salt Lake City, 1949-69; dir. ops., gen. mgr. Bougainvill copper Ltd., Panguna, Papua New Guinea, 1969-71; mng. dir. Bougainville copper Ltd., Melbourne, Australia, 1971-75; exec. v.p. Amoco Minerals Co., Denver, 1975-82; pres., chief operating officer Rio Algom Ltd., Toronto, Ont., Can., 1982—; dir. Rio Algom Ltd., Lornex Mining Corp., Ltd., Vancouver, B.C. Recipient Brown medal N.Mex. Inst. Mining and Tech., 1949, Daniel C. Jackling award Soc. Mining Engrs., 1981; Sloan fellow, 1959. Mem. AIME, Mining and Metall. Soc. Am., Australian Inst. Mining and Metallurgy. Club: Lombton Golf and Country (Toronto). Home: 228 Glen Rd Toronto ON Canada M4W 2X3 Office: Rio Algom Ltd 120 Adelaide St W Toronto ON Canada M5H 1W5

BALLOTTI, GENO ARTHUR, found. exec.; b. Walsenberg, Colo., Dec. 28, 1930; s. Ernest James and Beatrice Mary (Pini) B.; m. Geraldine A. McCarty, Nov. 21, 1959; children—Geoffrey, Anne, Kathryn, Susan. B.A., Adams State Coll., 1953; M.A., U. Wyo., 1955; postgrad., Johns Hopkins U., 1958-60. Sr. English tchr. Florence (Colo.) High Sch., 1953-54; instr. Dept. English, U. Wyo., Laramie, 1954-55; spl. agt. Counter-Intelligence Corps, U.S. Army, 1956-57; asso. dir. John Hopkins U. Press, Balt., 1957-61; sec. Assembly on Univ. Goals and Governance, Harvard U., 1969-75; mgmt. bd. overseeing editorial/fin. ops. The Chronicle of Higher Edn., 1975—; pub. Oceanus, Woods Hole (Mass.) Oceanographic Inst., 1974—; advisor Pres. of Stonehill Coll., N. Easton, Mass., 1972—; asso. exec. officer Am. Acad. Arts & Scis., Harvard U., 1961-77. Author: Southwest Indian in Literature, 1955, The Embattled University, 1970; editor: Center Pieces, 1973-74. Asso. dir. Permanent Charity Fund of Boston, 1977-78, dir., 1978—; Pres. Beaver brook Mental Health Assn., McLean Hosp., 1968-73; bd. dirs. Nat. Braille Press, 1961-78; trustee Fernald State Sch., Cambridge Center for Adult Edn.; ednl. cons. Boston Sch. Com., 1968-81, Change Mag., 1964-70; town meeting mem. Town of Belmont, 1968-81. Named Outstanding Alumnus Adams State Coll., 1968; Coe fellow U. Wyo., 1954-55. Roman Catholic. Clubs: Tavern, B & M Tennis, Cotuit Yacht Assn., Moose. Home: 208 Rutledge Rd Belmont MA 02178 Office: 1 Boston Pl Boston MA 02106

BALLOU, MILDRED ORALEE TESDAHL (MRS. PHILIP E. BALLOU), educator; b. Clarion, Iowa; d. Henry and Anna (Larson) Tesdahl; m. Philip E. Ballou, Apr. 27, 1946; 1 son, Stephen Philip. B.S. with honors, Drake U., 1949, M.S. in Edn. with honors, 1955; Ed.D. (Iowa Congress Parents and Tchrs. scholar), U. No. Colo., 1960. Tchr. pub. schs., Winterset, Iowa, 1949; operator Ballou Nursery Sch., Winterset, 1950-52; tchr. sci. Sta. KDPS-TV, Des Moines Pub. Schs., 1952-60; elem. tchr. Drake U. Lab. Sch., summers 1951-54; lectr. Drake U. Community Coll., 'Des Moines, 1955-60; faculty Ball State U., Muncie, 1960—, prof. edn., dept. head, 1970-80, dir. doctoral programs, 1980—; coordinator Airborne TV project Purdue U., 1962; condr. edn. mgmt. workshops Dept. Def. Schs., W.Ger., 1982; sci. edn. workshop dir. U.S. Dependent Schs., La Paz, Bolivia, summer 1969; speaker, 1955—, cons. elem. sci., 1958—; tech. asst. Nat. Right to Read Program, 1972—. Co-author: Science for Discovery series, 1967-68, Science for Human Value series, 1972; Contbr. articles and chpts. to profl. jours. and books. Bd. dirs. Muncie Symphony Women's League.; founder, pres. Muncie Children's Mus., 1979. Recipient Outstanding Alumnus award U. No. Colo., 1982. Mem. Nat. Sci. Tchrs. Assn. (sec. 1960-62), Assn. Childhood Edn. Internat., AAAS, NEA, Assn. Supervision and Curriculum Devel., AAUP, Ind. Psychol. Assn., Ind. Assn. for Edn. Young Children (pres. 1972—), Council Elementary Sci. Internat. (pres. 1968-69), Delta Kappa Gamma, Pi Lambda Theta, Delta Zeta (adviser 1964—), Kappa Delta Pi. Republican. Clubs: Delaware Country (social chmn.), Delaware County Woman's (Muncie); Lake Tippecanoe Country, Univ. Women. Home: 601 Brentwood Ln Muncie IN 47304 Home: 1706 Gulfview Club 58 N Collier Blvd Marco Island FL

BALLOWE, JAMES, university adminstrator, educator; b. Carbondale, Ill., Nov. 28, 1933; s. Frank Charles and Wilma Ruth (Maynard) B.; children: Jeffrey, Mary. B.A., Millikin U., 1954; M.A., U. Ill., 1956, Ph.D., 1963. Tchr. pub. schs. Decatur, Ill., 1954-55; grad. asst. U. Ill., 1955-61; asst. prof. English Millikin U., 1961-63; mem. faculty dept. English Bradley U., Peoria, Ill., 1963—, prof., 1971—, dean Grad. Sch., 1974—, assoc.-elect, 1979—; chmn.-elect. North Central Assn., Commn. Instns. Higher Edn., 1984-85. Author: poetry The Coal Miners, 1979; editor: George Santayana's America, 1967. Recipient Poetry Award Ill. Arts Council, 1975, 78. Mem. Ill. Arts Council (1975-83), Ill. State Mus. Bd. (1977—), Ill. Acts Council (1975-83), Ill. State Mus. Bd. (1977—), Ill. Assn. Grad. Schs. (pres. 1979-80), Midwestern Assn. Grad. Schs. (pres. 1978-79). Office: 1501 Bradley Ave Peoria IL 61625

BALLUFFI, ROBERT WEIERTER, physical metallurgist; b. Bayshore, N.Y., Apr. 18, 1924; s. Frank William and Louise (Weierter) B.; m. Ruth S. Nickse, June 1, 1973; children by previous marriage: Andrew W., Barbara W., Frank C. S.B. in Metallurgy, Mass. Inst. Tech., 1947, Sc.D., 1950. Sr. engr. Sylvania Elec. Co., 1950-54; asst. prof. to prof. U. Ill., 1954-64; prof. to Francis N. Bard prof. metallurgy, dir. dept. Cornell U., Ithaca, N.Y., 1964-78; prof. metallurgy M.I.T., 1978—; cons. Oak Ridge Nat. Lab., Argonne Nat. Lab., Nat. Acad. Sci., AEC, Dept. Energy. Contbr. articles to profl. jours., chpts. in books. Served with AUS, 1943-46. Decorated Bronze Star. Fellow Am. Phys. Soc., AIME; mem. Am. Acad. Scis., Am. Acad. Arts and Scis., Inst. Metals, Sigma Xi. Research in phys. metallurgy, including crystal defects, diffusion, radiation damage. Home: 58 Monmouth St Brookline MA 02146 Office: 13-5078 Mass Inst Tech Cambridge MA 02139

BALMER, THOMAS JAMES, metal products co. exec.; b. Chgo., Sept. 9, 1913; s. Edwin and Katharine (MacHarg) B.; m. Eleanor Eliza Hamant, Oct. 19, 1935 (dec. Nov. 1976). Grad., Choate Sch., 1931; A.B., Harvard, 1935; postgrad., Mass. Inst. Tech., 1942-43, N.Y. U., 1946-48. Mem. pub. relations staff N.Y. Stock Exchange, 1939-57; account exec. Fiscal Info. Service, 1957-61; account supr. Dudley-Anderson-Yutzy, 1961-68; all N.Y.C.; corporate sec., dir. pub. relations MSL Industries, Inc., Beverly Hills, Calif., 1968—; cons. pub. relations Pacific Am. Industries, Calif. Shopping Centers, Inc., Exeter Oil Co., Ltd. Author: Investment Facts about Common Stocks and Cash Dividends, 1947, Do Electronics Companies Need a New Kind of Public Relations?, 1967. Dir. fund raising Dobbs Ferry (N.Y.) Hosp., 1964. Served with AUS, 1942-46. Recipient Oscar award Financial World Nat. Contest, 1970. Mem. Nat. Investor Relations Inst., Am. Soc. Corporate Secs., New Eng. Soc. City N.Y., Sigma Alpha Epsilon. Club: Harvard (N.Y.C.). Home: 833 5th St Santa Monica CA 90403 Office: MSL Industries Inc 212 S Gale Dr Beverly Hills CA 90211

BALOFF, NICHOLAS, educator; b. San Francisco, Aug. 9, 1937; s. Nicholas Boris and Emily (Ersunoff) B.; childern—Steven Nicholas, Katherine Louise. B.S. with highest honors, U. Calif., Berkeley, 1959; S.M., M.I.T., 1960; Ph.D., Stanford U., 1963. Registered profl. engr., Okla., Calif. Asst. prof. bus. admnstrn. U. Chgo., 1963-67; prof. U. Del Valle, Colombia, 1965; asso. prof., div. dir. Stanford (Calif.) U., 1967-72; prof., dean Coll. Bus. Adminstrn., U. Okla., Norman, 1972-76; prof. Sch. Bus. and Pub. Admnstrn., Washington U., St. Louis, 1976—; cons. McKinsey & Co., 1962-66, Ford Found., 1965-67; dir. ANTA Corp., Oklahoma City.; Bd., 1972—. Contbr. articles to profl. jours. Mem. Inst. Mgmt. Scis., AAAS, Inst. Decision Scis., Am. Econ. Assn., Sigma Xi, Beta Gamma Sigma, Tau Beta Pi, Alpha Pi Mu. Address: Washington Univ Box 1133 Saint Louis MO 63130

BALOG, JAMES, investment banker; b. Vintondale, Pa., Sept. 9, 1928; s. Michael and Helen B.; m. Alvina Marie Bartos, Oct. 21, 1950; children: James Dennis, Stephen John, Michael George. B.S., Pa. State U., 1950; M.B.A., Rutgers U., 1958. Prodn. engr. Philco Corp., Lansdale, Pa., 1950; budget dir. Merck & Co., Rahway, N.J., 1951-61; v.p., assoc. fin. staff Electric Bond and Share Co., N.Y.C., 1962-63; v.p., dir. Auerbach Pollak & Richardson, N.Y.C., 1964-69; chmn. William D. Witter, Inc., N.Y.C., 1970-75; with Drexel Burnham Lambert, N.Y.C., 1976—, sr. exec. v.p., 1977—; dir. Collaborative Research Inc., Drexel Burnham Lambert Group, Lambert Brussels Corp., Watchung Hills Travel. Mem. Watchung Bd. Edn., N.J., 1961-65. Mem. N.Y. Soc. Security Analysts, Am. Chem. Soc. Clubs: N.Y. Stock Exchange, Plainfield Country. Lodge: Elks. Home: 106 Wildwood Terr Watchung NJ 07060 Office: 60 Broad St New York NY 10004

BALOUN, JOHN CHARLES, moving company executive; b. Chgo., May 1, 1934; s. John Nicholas and Anne (Giera) B.; m. Lynette Anne Jehs, July 27, 1963; children—John Christopher, Michael Warren. B.C.S., DePaul U., 1956. C.P.A., Ill. Mem. audit staff Arthur Andersen & Co. (C.P.A.s), Chgo., 1956-63; controller, asst. sec. Super Food Services, Inc., Chgo., 1963-67, treas., 1967-68, Dog'N Suds, Inc., Champaign, Ill., 1968-69; dir. planning and control distbn. div. Champion Internat., Inc., Chgo., 1969-74; treas. IGA, Inc., Chgo., 1974-77, v.p., 1977-80; v.p. fin. Allied Van Lines, Inc., Broadview, Ill., 1980—. Served as 2d lt. AUS, 1957. Mem. Ill. Soc. C.P.A.s, Nat. Assn. Corp. Treas. Republican. Home: 610 Western Ave Glen Ellyn IL 60137 Office: 25th Ave and Roosevelt Rd Broadview IL 60153

BALOW, IRVING HENRY, educator; b. Wabasha, Minn., Jan. 19, 1927; s. Laurence Christian and Katherine (Yost) B.; m. Joyce Elizabeth Binner, June 8, 1950 (dec. 1980); children: Mary, Thomas, Michael, Robert, Ann.; m. Alta Sitton, June 27, 1981. B.S., U. Minn., 1951, M.A., 1957, Ph.D., 1959. Elementary sch. tchr., Theilmam, Minn., 1951-53, Wabasha, 1953-54, 56-57; instr. U. Minn., 1957-59; mem. faculty U. Calif. at Riverside, 1959—, prof. edn., 1968—, chmn. dept., 1963-70, asso. dean, 1970-71, acting dean, 1971-72, dean, 1972—; reading cons., 1959—. Contbr. articles to profl. jours. Served with USAAF, 1945-47. Mem. Am. Ednl. Research Assn., Nat. Council Tchrs. English, Nat. Council Measurement Edn., Internat. Reading Assn. Home: 138 Green Oak Dr Riverside CA 92507

BALOWS, ALBERT, microbiologist, educator; b. Denver, Jan. 3, 1921; s. Lazerus and Anna (Kleiner) B.; m. Patricia Ann Barker, Oct. 7, 1956; children: Eve Ellen, Daniel Scott. B.A. in Biology (Lowell scholar), Colo. Coll., 1942; M.S. in Microbiology, Syracuse U., 1948; Ph.D. (Haggin fellow), U. Ky., 1952. Diplomate: Am. Bd. Med. Microbiology. Microbiologist St. Joseph Hosp., Lexington (Ky.) Clinic, 1952-69; dir. bacteriology div. Center Disease Control, USPHS, Atlanta, 1969-81, asst. dir. lab. sci., 1981—; asst. prof. medicine U. Ky. Med. Center, Lexington, 1960-63, assoc. prof. medicine and cell biology, 1963-69; assoc. prof. pathology Emory U. Sch. Medicine, 1970—; prof. biology Ga. State U., Atlanta, 1970—; lectr. Am. Soc. Microbiology Found., 1974-76; cons. clin. microbiology VA Hosp., Good Samaritan Hosp., both Lexington, 1965-69, Med. Service Corps, Dept. Army, 1973-79; mem. expert panel bacterial disease WHO, Geneva. Editor-in-chief: Jour. Clin. Microbiology, 1974-79; editor: Applied Microbiology, 1965-74, Ann. Rev. Microbiology, 1979—, C. C. Thomas med. microbiology series, 1964—, Current Microbiology, 1982—; author, editor over 25 books on microbiology and infectious disease; contbr. articles to profl. jours. Bd. dirs. Lexington chpt. NCCJ, 1960-64. Served with M.C. AUS, 1943-45. Named Lab World Microbiologist of Yr., 1980; recipient Becton-Dickinson award in clin. microbiology, 1981, Silver medallion for outstanding contbns. to clin. microbiology Iatolian Soc. Microbiology, 1983. Fellow Am. Acad. Microbiology (bd. govs. 1973-77, chmn. 1975-76), N.Y. Acad. Scis., AAAS, Am. Pub. Health Assn.; mem. Am. Soc. Microbiology (pres.-elect 1979-80, pres. 1980-81, council, also mem. council policy com. 1974-82), Am. Soc. Clin. Pathology, Soc. Gen. Microbiology, AAUP, Med. Mycol. Soc. Am., Soc. Applied Bacteriology, Infectious Diseases Soc. Am., Acad. Lab. Physicians and Scientists, Am. Veneral Disease Assn., Sci. Writers Guild, Sigma Xi, Blue Key, Omicron Delta Kappa, Tau Kappa Alpha, Zeta Beta Tau. Club: B'nai B'rith. Home: 7640 Ryefield Dr NE Atlanta GA 30338 Office: Center Disease Control 1600 Clifton Rd NE Atlanta GA 30333 *Understanding, good will and peace are achieved by effective communication. Regrettably we fail because we do not listen. I have patterned my life after an ancient Chinese proverb. "First you must learn to listen well; then you will know that you have talked too much."*

BALSAM, ARTUR, pianist; b. Warsaw, Poland, 1906; m. Ruth R. Balsam. Ed., Berlin. Tchr. piano and chamber music Manhattan Sch. Music, N.Y.C., Eastman Sch. Music, Rochester, N.Y. Editor: Mozart Concertos, Oxford U. Press and Schirmer; Debut, 1918, appearances in concerts and recitals throughout, U.S. and Europe, has accompanied, Menuhin, Milstein Francescatti, Morini, many others; former mem., Balsam-Kroll-Heifetz Trio, sonata recitals and recs. with, Szigeti, Oistrach, Rostropowitch, also others; soloist with, NBC, BBC, London Symphony, Royal Philharmonic, London Philharmonia orchs., radio orchs. of, Milan, Warsaw, Berlin, Hamburg, Cardiff, Munich, also others; recorded complete piano works of, Mozart and Haydn, all Beethoven violin sonatas with, Fuchs, all cello sonatas with, Nelsova, all Mozart violin sonatas with, Shumsky. Address: 258 Riverside Dr New York NY 10025

BALSAM, MARTIN HENRY, actor; b. N.Y.C., Nov. 4, 1919; s. Albert and Lillian (Weinstein) B.; m. Pearl L. Somner, Oct. 1952 (div. 1954); m. Joyce Van Patten, Aug. 1959 (div. 1962); 1 dau.; m. Irene Miller, Nov. 1963. Ed., New Sch. Social Research, 1946-48. Profl. acting debut in The Play's the Thing, Locust Valley, N.Y., 1941; N.Y.C. debut in Ghost for Sale, 1941; stage appearances include Lamp at Midnight, N.Y.C., 1947, The Wanhope Building, N.Y.C., High Tor, A Sound of Hunting, Macbeth, N.Y.C., 1948, Sundown Beach, 1948, The Closing Door, 1949, You Know I Can't Hear You When the Water's Running, 1967 (Tony award), Cold Storage (Obie award); appeared in summer stock, 1949—; appearances include The Iceman Cometh; motion pictures include On the Waterfront, 1954, 12 Angry Men, 1957, Marjorie Morningstar, 1957, Al Capone, 1959, Middle of the Night, 1959, Psycho, 1960, All at Home, 1960, Breakfast at Tiffany's, 1961, Ada, 1961, Cape Fear, 1962, The Captive City, 1962, Who's Sleeping in My Bed, 1963, Seven Days in May, 1963, The Carpetbaggers, 1963, 1000 Clowns, 1964 (Acad. award), Bedford Incident, Harlow, After the Fox, 1965, Hombre, 1966, Among the Paths to Eden, 1967, Me, Natalie, Good Guys and Bad Guys, 2001: A Space Odyssey, 1968, Catch 22, Tora Tora Tora, Little Big Man, 1969, The Anderson Tapes, The Commissioner, 1970, The Sentinel, 1977, Silver Bears, 1978, Cuba, 1979, There Goes the Bride, 1980; numerous nightclub, TV appearances; regular on: TV series Archie Bunker's Place, 1979. Served with AUS, 1941-45. Mem. Actors Equity Assn., AFTRA, Screen Actors Guild, Actor's Studio. Office: care Robinson's Assos Inc 132 S Rodeo Dr Beverly Hills CA 90212 *

BALSER, GLENNON CRAVEN, religious executive, clergyman; b. Blakeley, Va., Apr. 8, 1929; s. Brinferd and Elsie Mae (Ramsey) B.; m. Glenna Jean Phillips, Mar. 22, 1952; children: Sandra, Mark, Nancy. B.A., Aurora Coll., 1954, B.Th., 1955; M.Div., Evangelical Theol. Sem., 1957. Ordained to ministry Advent Christian Ch., minister, Columbus, Ohio, 1957-60, Clendenin, W.Va., 1960-64, Lenoir, N.C., 1964-69, Charlotte, N.C., 1969-80, Wilmington, N.C., 1980—; pres. Advent Christian Conf., Ohio, W.Va., N.C., 1958-70, Appalachian Assn., Blowing Rock, N.C., 1974-80; v.p. Advent Christian Gen. Conf., Charlotte, N.C., 1974-80, pres., 1980—; tchr. Caldwell Community Coll., Lenoir, N.C., 1968. Chaplain Fire Dept., Lenoir, 1966; mem. bd. Council Human Relations, Hire the Handicap, Lenoir, 1968; pres. Caldwell County Mental Retardation, Lenoir, 1968. Recipient Leadership Piedmont Advent Christian Conf., 1980, Appalachian Bd. Dirs., 1980, Leadership Advent Christian Gen. Conf., 1980. Lodge: Kiwanis (sec., treas. 1968-69). Home: 801 Pine Forest Rd Wilmington NC 28403 Office: United Advent Christian Ch 5540 S College Rd Wilmington NC 28403

BALSIGER, DAVID WAYNE, author, educator, advertising executive; b. Monroe, Wis., Dec. 14, 1945; s. Leon C. and Dorothy May (Meythaler) B.; m. Robyne Lynn Betzold, July 10, 1982; children: Lisa Atalie, Lori Faith. Student, Pepperdine Coll., Los Angeles, 1964-66, Cypress Jr. Coll., 1966, Chapman Coll. World Campus Afloat, Orange, Calif., 1967-68, Internat. Coll., Copenhagen, 1968; B.A., Nat. U., San Diego, 1977; L.H.D., Lincoln Meml. U., Harrogate, Tenn. Cert. talent agt., Calif.; cert. real estate, Calif.; cert. diamond couselor. Chief photographer, feature writer Anaheim (Calif.) Bull., 1968-69; publisher, editor Money Doctor (consumer mag.), Anaheim, 1969-70; media dir. World Evangelism, San Diego, 1970-72; dir. mktg. Logos Internat. Christian Book Publishers, Plainfield, N.J., 1972-73; pres., dir. Master Media (advt. agy.), Costa Mesa, Calif., 1973-75; pres. Balsiger Lit. Service, Costa Mesa, 1973-78; v.p. communications Donald S. Smith Assos., Anaheim, Calif., 1975-78; asso. producer, dir. creative devel. Sunn Classic Pictures, Los Angeles, Salt Lake City, 1976-78; owner Writeway Profl. Lit. Assos., Santa Ana, Calif., 1978—; pub. Mini Guide Books, Santa Ana, Calif., 1979-80; owner Balsiger Enterprises, Costa Mesa, Calif., 1978—; v.p. Donald S. Smith Assocs., Anaheim, Calif., 1982—; vis. prof. Nat. U., San Diego, 1977-80. Author: The Satan Seller, 1972, The Back Side of Satan, 1973, Noah's Ark: I Touched It, 1974, One More Time, 1974, It's Good to Know, 1975, In Search of Noah's Ark, 1976, The Lincoln Conspiracy, 1977, Beyond Defeat, 1978, On the Other Side, 1978, Mister Abe, 1980, 8 Mini Guide Books; travel series, 1979, Presidential Biblical Scoreboard, 1980; producer, researcher: TV and motion pictures, including Operation Thanks, 1965, The Life and Times of Grizzly Adams, 1976-77, In Search of Noah's Ark, 1976, The Lincoln Conspiracy, 1977, The Bermuda Triangle, 1977. Press agt. John G. Schmitz congl. campaign, 1972, Gordon Bishop supr. campaign, Orange County, 1970; press agt. asst. Ronald Reagan for Gov., statewide, 1966; statewide campaign mgr. James E. Johnson for U.S. Senate, 1974; campaign mgr. Dave Gubler Congl. campaign, 1974; candidate Costa Mesa City Council, 1980; Rep. candidate for Congress from 38th Dist. Calif., 1978; mem. Calif. Republican Assembly, 1975-78; Rep. Assos. Orange County, 1977-79; mem. World Affairs Council Orange County and San Diego, 1969-70; assoc. mem. Calif. Republican Central Com., 1969-70; Bd. dirs. Chapman Coll. World Campus Afloat, 1967, Chrisma Ministries, Orange, Calif., 1969-73; Nat. exec. dir. Ban the Soviets Coalition, 1983-84. Recipient Leadership citation Pepperdine Coll. Alumni Bd., 1965, Vietnam appreciation citation Am. Soldiers in Vietnam, 1966; George Washington Honor medal Freedoms Found., 1978, 79; Religion in Media award, 1979; named writer of month Calif. Writer, 1967; named to Lit. Hall of Fame, 1977. Mem. Nat. Writers Club, U. Calif. Friends Library, Nat. U. Presidents Assos., Christians for Polit. Action. Address: PO Box 10428 Costa Mesa CA 9267 *I believe successful people have a purpose strong enough to make them form the habit of doing things they don't like to do in order to accomplish their purpose. Every single qualification for success is acquited through habit. People form habits and habits form futures.*

BALSLEY, HOWARD LLOYD, educator; b. Chgo., Dec. 3, 1913; s. Elmer Lloyd and Katherine (McGlashing) B.; m. Irol Verneth Whitmore, Aug. 24, 1947. A.B., Ind. U., 1946, M.A., 1947, Ph.D., 1950; postgrad., Johns Hopkins U., 1947-48, U. Chgo., summer 1948. Asst. prof. econs. U. Utah, Salt Lake City, 1949-50; assoc. prof. econs., dir. Sch. Bus., Russell Sage Coll., Troy, N.Y., 1950-52; asso. prof. econs. Washington and Lee U., Lexington, Va., 1952-54; prof. bus. stats., head dept. bus. and econ. research La. Tech. U., Ruston, 1954-65; prof. bus. adminstrn. and stats. Tex. Tech U., Lubbock, 1965-75; head dept. econs. and fin., prof. econs. and stats. U. Ark., Little Rock, 1975-80; adj. prof. econs. and stats. Hardin-Simmons U., Abilene, Tex., 1980—. Author: (with James Gemmell) Principles of Economics, 1953, Readings in Economic Doctrines, vols. 1 and 2, 1961, Introduction to Statistical Method, 1964, Quantitative Research Methods for Business and Economics, 1970, (with Vernon Clover) Business Research, 1974, 3d edit., 1984, Basic Statistics for Business and Economics, 1978. Served with USAAF, 1943-46. Mem. Am. Econ. Assn., So. Econ. Assn., Am. Statis. Assn., S.W. Fedn. Adminstrv. Disciplines, Am. Inst. Decision Scis. Home: 6501 15th Ave W Bradenton FL 33529 *Those who devote their lives to serving others will find themselves richly served.*

BALSLEY, JOHN GERALD, sculptor, educator; b. Cleve., Apr. 15, 1944; s. John Edward and Celia (Hatala) B.; m. Diane Marie Fankell, Dec. 13, 1974; 1 dau., Katharine. B.F.A., Ohio No. U., 1967; M.F.A., No. Ill. U., 1969. Assoc. prof. art Drake U., Des moines, 1969-76, U. Wis.-Milw., 1976—. One man shows, Toledo Mus. Art, 1968, Coll. of Wooster, Ohio, 1967, No. Ill. U., Dekalb, 1969, Fairweather Hardin Gallery, Chgo., 1969, 71, 75, Cedar Rapids Art Ctr., Iowa, 1970, 71, Simpson Coll., Indianola, Iowa, 1971, Grinnell Coll, Iowa, Henri Gallery, Washington, Des Moines Art Ctr., 1972, Morgan Gallery, Kansas City, 1974, 76, 81, Allan Stone Gallery, N.Y.C., 1972, 74, 76, 78, Walter Kelly Gallery, Chgo., 1975, Mpls. Coll. Art and Design, 1975, 76, Nancy Lurie Gallery, Chgo., 1977, 80, Bienville Gallery, New Orleans, 1978, 79, Kohler Art Ctr, Sheboygan, Wis., 1978, Delta Gallery, Houston, Madison Art Ctr, Wis., 1979, U. Del., Frumkin-Struve Gallery, Chgo., 1979-80, New Gallery Contemporary Art, Cleve., 1980, Rahr-West Mus., Manitowoc, Wis., 1982, Dee Dee Phillips Gallery, N.Y.C., 1983, also 2-man shows; group shows Cleve. Mus. Art, 1966, 67, 68, 71, 73, 74, Toledo Mus. Art, 1965, 66, 67, 68, Ind. State U., 1970, U. Ill., 1969, Josly Art Mus., 1970, 72, Nelson Atkins Mus. Art, Kansas City, 1970, Allan Stone Gallery, N.Y.C., 1974, Mus. Art, U. Iowa, Am. Painters and Sculptors, U.S. Pavillion Expo 74, Spokane, Wash., 1975, Indpls. Art Mus., 1976, New Gallery, Cleve., 1977, Des Moines Art Ctr., 1978, U. N.D., 1981, Frumkin-Struve Gallery, Chgo., 1981, 82; represented: permanent collections St. Louis Mus. Art, Nelson Gallery-Atkins Mus., Des Moines Art Ctr., Joslyn Mus. Art, Mus. Art, U. Iowa; contbr. articles on art to profl. jours. NEA grantee, 1972, 80; Tiffancy fellow, 1972. Office: U Wis Kenwood Blvd Milwaukee WI 53211

BALSLEY, PHILIP ELWOOD, entertainer; b. Augusta County, Va., Aug. 8, 1939; s. Henry Elwood and Marjorie Walden (Fielding) B.; m. Wilma Lee Kincaid, July 21, 1962; children—Gregory, Mark, Leah. Grad. high sch. With group Statler Bros., 1961—; treas. Statler Bros. Prodns., 1973—, Am. Cowboy Music Co., 1973—. (Recipient numerous Grammy awards, Country Music Assn. awards.). Bd. dirs. Happy Birthday U.S.A. Presbyn. Home: Route 1 Box 33A Swoope VA 24479 Office: PO Box 2703 Staunton VA 24401

BALTAKE, JOE, journalist; b. Camden, N.J., Sept. 16; s. Joseph John and Rose Clara (Bearint) B.; m. Susan Hale, Apr. 10, 1984. B.A., Rutgers U., 1967. With Phila. Daily News, film critic, 1969—. Contbg. editor: Screen World, 1970—; Author: The Films of Jack Lemmon, 1977; contbr. articles: Films in Rev., 1969—. Home: 124 Kings Hwy W Haddonfield NJ 08033 Office: 400 N Broad St Philadelphia PA 09101 *Life's philosophy: "If you can't get it perfect, what's the point?"*

BALTAY, CHARLES, physics educator; b. Budapest, Hungary, Apr. 15, 1937; came to U.S., 1950, naturalized, 1955; s. John A. and Ilona T. (Herczeg) B.; m. Virginia B. Rohan, Oct. 7, 1961; children: Peter, Michael, Thomas, Matthew, Annemarie Susan. B.S., Union Coll., Schenectady, 1958; M.S., Yale U., 1959, Ph.D., 1963. Research asso. Yale U., 1963-64; mem. faculty Columbia U., 1964—, prof. physics, 1972—; dir. Nevis Labs., 1979—. Editor: Neutrino Interactions, 1972; co-editor: Meson Spectroscopy, 1968, Experimental Meson Spectroscopy, 1970. Sloane fellow, 1966-70. Fellow Am. Phys. Soc.; mem. Sigma Xi. Roman Catholic. Home: 21 Hardscrabble Hill Chappaqua NY 10514 Office: Physics Dept Columbia U New York NY 10027

BALTHROP, CARMEN ARLENE, opera singer; b. Washington, May 14, 1948; d. John William and Clementine Estelle B. Mus.B., U. Md., 1970; Mus.M., Catholic U., 1971. Tchr. music St. Patricks Acad., Washington.; Testified, singer before Senate and House Coms. for Nat. Endowment for Arts, 1977. Mem., Wolf Trap Co.; appeared with, Balt. Lyric Opera, Dallas Civic Opera, San Francisco Opera, Opera Soc. of Washington, Boston Symphony, Detroit Symphony, Houston Grand Opera, Cin. Music Festival, San Antonio Symphony, Carnegie Hall Debut, RAI Rome, Balt. Symphony, Aspen Music Festival, San Francisco Symphony, St. Louis Symphony, Los Angeles Philharmonic, Detroit Opera, Met. Opera, 1972—; recorded: Treemonisha for, DGG. Recipient Arts and Letters Scholarship award, Carling Brewing Co. Competition award, plaque Mayor of D.C.; winner Met. Opera Nat. Councils 1975 Auditions; Nat. Opera Inst. grantee. Mem. Met. Opera, Sigma Alpha Iota. Office: care Met Opera Assn Lincoln Center New York NY 10022 *Ideas first make themselves known to us through dreams—so Dream* *

BALTIMORE, DAVID, microbiologist, educator; b. N.Y.C., Mar. 7, 1938; s. Richard I. and Gertrude (Lipschitz) B.; m. Alice S. Huang, Oct. 5, 1968; 1 dau., Teak. B.A. with high honors in Chemistry, Swarthmore Coll., 1960; postgrad., Mass. Inst. Tech., 1960-61; Ph.D., Rockefeller U., 1964. Research assoc. Salk Inst. Biol. Studies, LaJolla, Calif., 1965-68; assoc. prof. microbiology Mass. Inst. Tech., Cambridge, 1968-71, prof. biology, 1972—, Am. Cancer Soc. prof. microbiology, 1973—, dir. Whitehead Inst. Biomed. Research, 1982—. Editorial bd.: Jour. Virology. Recipient Gustav Stern award in virology, 1971; Warren Triennial prize Mass. Gen. Hosp., 1971; Eli Lilly and Co. award in microbiology and immunology, 1971; U.S. Steel Found. award in molecular biology, 1974; Gairdner Found. ann. award, 1974; Nobel prize in physiology or medicine, 1975. Fellow AAAS; mem. Nat. Acad. Scis., Am. Acad. Arts and Scis., Pontifical Acad. Scis. Home: 28 Donnell St Cambridge MA 02138 Office: Mass Inst Tech Cambridge MA 02139

BALTZ, LEWIS, photographer; b. Newport Beach, Calif., Sept. 12, 1945; s. Charles Lewis and Lola Berenice (Anderson) B.; m. Mary Ann Rayner, Dec. 28, 1974; 1 dau., Monica Diane. B.F.A., San Francisco Art Inst., 1969; M.F.A., Claremont Grad. Sch., 1971. Mem. individual grants panel Nat. Endowment Arts, 1977; mem. vis. com. George Eastman House, 1978-80. One-man shows, Leo Castelli Gallery, N.Y.C., 1971, 73, 75, 78, 81, 83, Corcoran Gallery Art, Washington, 1974-76, George Eastman House, 1972, Balt. Mus. Art, 1976, Mus. Fine Arts, Houston, La Jolla Mus. Contemporary Art, Otis Art Inst., Los Angeles, 1981, San Francisco Mus. Modern Art, over 125 group exhbns.; represented in permanent collections 56 mus. in U.S., Europe, Australia, Can., U.S.; Photog. monographs include New Industrial Parks, Near Irvine, Calif., 1975, Md., 1976, Nev., 1978, Park City, 1981. Guggenheim fellow, 1976; U.S.-U.K. exchange fellow, 1979. Home: 70 Glen Dr Sausalito CA 94965 Office: PO Box 42 Sausalito CA 94966

BALTZAN, MARCEL ALTER, physician; b. Saskatoon, Sask., Can., Oct. 31, 1929; s. David Mortimer and Rose Cristall B.; m. Betty Lou Ray, Aug. 2, 1958; children: Marcel Alter, Frances B., Elizabeth Virginia. B.Sc., McGill U., 1953, M.D., C.M., 1953. Physician Baltzan Assoc. Med. Clinic, Saskatoon, 1959—; prof., chmn. dept. medicine U. Sask., 1974-79. Contbr. articles to med. jours. Fellow Royal Coll. Physicians and Surgeons of Can., ACP; mem. Can. Med. Assn. (pres. 1982-83). Club: Saskatoon. Office: Baltzan Associate Medical Clinic 366 3d Ave S Suite 200 Saskatoon SK Canada S7K 1M5 *

BALTZELL, E(DWARD) DIGBY, sociologist; b. Phila., Nov. 14, 1915; s. Edward Digby and Caroline Adelaide (Duhring) B.; m. Jane Piper, Feb. 21, 1943; children—Eve, Jan Carles. B.S., U. Pa., 1939; Ph.D. in Sociology, Columbia U., 1952. Prof. sociology U. Pa., Phila., 1947—. Author: Philadelphia Gentlemen: The Making of a National Upper Class, 1958, Protestant Establishment, 1964, Puritan Boston and Quaker Philadelphia: Two Protestant Ethics and the Spirit of Class Authority and Leadership, 1979. Served with USNR, 1942-45. Decorated Air medal; Danforth fellow Soc. for Religion in Higher Edn. Princeton Theol. Sem., 1967-68; Charles Warren research fellow Harvard U., 1972-73; Hardy Chair lectr. Hartwick Coll., 1975; Guggenheim fellow, 1978-79. Mem. Am. Sociol. Assn., Am. Studies Assn., Eastern Sociol. Soc., Pa. Hist. Soc. Democrat. Episcopalian. Home: 1724 Delancey St Philadelphia PA 19103 Office: Dept Sociology 113 McNeil Bldg 3718 Locust Walk Philadelphia PA 19104

BALUKAS, JEAN, professional pocket billiard player; b. Bklyn., June 28, 1959; d. Albert Michael and Josephine (Greene) B. Student public schs., N.Y.C. Worldwide personal and TV exhbns., 1965—; participant billiard tournament U.S. Open, 1968 placed 6th out of 16. Mem. Billiard Congress Am., Women's Profl. Billiard Alliance, Profl. Pool Players Assn. Republican. Baptist. U.S. Open Champion, 1972, 73, 74, 75, 76, 77, 83; Women's World Champion, 1975; 77, 78, 79, 80, 82, 83; placed 2d ABC-TV Superstars, 1976, 77; beat Willie Mosconi in CBS TV Challenge of Sexes, 1975; competed in Men's World Championship, 1978 (33d), 1979 (27th), 1980 (23th). Office: care Billiard Congress 14 S Linn St Iowa City IA 52240

BALYO, JOHN GABRIEL, clergyman, educator; b. Greenville, S.C., Jan. 18, 1920; s. John Gabor and Etta (Groce) B.; m. Betty Louise Lindstrand, Oct. 14, 1945; 1 son, John Michael. Student, Atlanta Law Sch., 1937-40; LL.B., Valparaiso U., 1945, Goshen Coll., 1945-46; A.B., Grace Theol. Sem., 1944; B.D. magna cum laude, Grace Theol. Sem., 1946; D.D., Grand Rapids Theol. Sem., 1960. Ordained to ministry Bible Baptist Ch., 1950; pastor in, Three Oaks, Mich., 1942-45, Elkhart, Ind., 1945-46, Kokomo, Ind., 1946-53, Cedar Hill Bapt. Ch., Cleve., 1953-72; prof. Bible and practical theology Grand Rapids (Mich.) Bapt. Theol. Sem., 1972-80; chmn. council of ten Sunshine State Fellowship of Regular Bapt. Chs., Fla., 1980-81; pastor Sun Coast Bapt. Ch., New Port Richey, Fla., 1980-81; prof. theology and Bible Bapt. Bible Coll. and Sch. Theology, Clarks Summit, Pa., 1981—; mem. gen. council Bapt. Mid-Mission, 1954—, adminstrv. com., 1962-73, trustee, 1963-75, chmn. bd. trustees, 1968-75, chmn. council, 1966-68; mem. council 14 Gen. Assn. Regular Bapt. Chs., 1955-59, 60-64, sec. council, 1957-58, chmn. publs. com., 1956-60, 63-66, chmn. council 14, 1966-68, mem. finance com., 1968-69, publs. com., 1968-69, chmn. program com., 1968-69, chmn. edn. com., 1960-62, vice chmn. council, 1962-64, chmn., 1970-72, chmn. publs. com., 1972-73, chmn. council of 18, 1973-74, vice chmn. council of 18, 1977-79, chmn., 1979-81; exec. bd. dirs. Grand Rapids Bapt. Bible Coll. and Sem., 1961-72, chmn. curriculum com., 1963-66; missionary survey trips to, Europe and Africa, 1957-58, Ecuador, 1962, Peru, 1969, Brazil, 1975; Bd. dirs. Hebrew Christian Soc., 1956-64. Author: Sunday sch. material for Regular Bapt. Press; also booklet Creation and Evolution. Address: 1017 Sleepy Hollow Rd Clarks Summit PA 18411

BALZEKAS, STANLEY, JR., museum dir.; b. Chgo., Oct. 8, 1924; s. Stanley and Emily B.; (widower); children—Stanley, III, Robert, Carole Rene. B.S., DePaul U., Chgo., 1950, M.A., 1951. Pres. Balzekas Mus. Lithuanian Culture, Chgo., 1966—, Balzekas Motor Sales, 1952—; advisor Chgo. Council Fine Arts. Editor: Lithuanian Mus. Rev, 1969—. Sec. bd. dirs., chmn. programs and exhibits Chgo. Public Library; commr. Human Relations Commn. Chgo. Served with AUS, 1942-45. Decorated Bronze Star. Mem. Ethnic Cultural Preservation Council (pres. 1977—), Elder Artisans Chgo. (dir.), Nat. Am. Vets. Press Assn. (v.p. 1976—). Clubs: Press, Literary, City (Chgo.) (ethnic chmn.). Office: 4030 Archer Ave Chicago IL 60632

BALZHISER, RICHARD EARL, research and development company executive; b. Wheaton, Ill., May 27, 1932; s. Frank E. and Esther K. (Merrill Warner) B.; m. Christine Karnuth, 1951; children: Gary, Robert, Patricia, Cheryl. B.S. in Chem. Engring., U. Mich., 1955, M.S. in Nuclear Engring., 1956, Ph.D. in Chem. Engring., 1961. Mem. faculty U. Mich., Ann Arbor, 1961-67; White House fellow, spl. asst. to sec. Dept. Def., Washington, 1967-68; chmn. dept. chem. engring. U. Mich., 1970-71; assoc. dir. energy, environ. and natural resources White House Office of Sci. and Tech., Washington, 1971-73; dir. fossil fuel and advanced systems Electric Power Research Inst., Palo Alto, Calif., 1973-79, v.p. research and devel., 1979—; chmn. U.S. Energy R&D Exchange with USSR, 1973-74; mem. adv. bd. Gas Research Inst., Chgo., 1979—, EPCOT Ctr., Orlando, Fla., 1977-80. Editorial bd.: Sci. mag., 1977—; co-author: Chemical Engineering Thermodynamics, 1972, Engineering Thermodynamics, 1977. Mem. Ann Arbor City Council, 1965-67, mayor pro tem, 1967. Charles M. Schwab Meml. lectr. Am. Iron And Steel Inst., 1983. Mem. Am. Inst. Chem. Engrs., AAAS, ASME, Sigma Chi. Republican. Lutheran. Club: Cosmos (Washington). Home: 560 Sand Hill Rd Palo Alto CA 94025 Office: 3412 Hillview Ave Palo Alto CA 94304

BAM, FOSTER, lawyer; b. Bridgeport, Conn., Jan. 11, 1927; s. Frederick and Alma (Foster) B.; children: Sylvia Carol, Sheila Catherine, Eric Foster. Grad., Loomis Sch., 1944; A.B., LL.B., Yale, 1950. Bar: N.Y. 1954, Conn. Mem. faculty accounting Yale, 1952-53; with firm Spence & Hotchkiss, N.Y.C., 1954-55; asst. U.S. dist. atty. So. Dist. N.Y., 1955-58; partner firm Feldman, Kramer, Bam Nessen, N.Y.C., 1958-67; now partner Cummings & Lockwood.; dir. Interstate Bakeries Corp.; Dir. Cities Service Co., Aviation Group, Evergreen Fund, Evergreen Total Return Fund; hon. dir. State Nat. Bank, Greenwich, Conn. Trustee Phoenix Sci. Center. Recipient Johny Foyle Meml. award, 1969. Mem. ABA, Conn. Bar Assn., Greenwich Bar Assn., Oceanic Soc. (chmn. bd. trustees), N.Y. County Lawyers Assn., N.Y. State Dist. Attys. Assn., Exptl. Aircraft Assn., Phi Beta Kappa. Home: 51 Londonderry Dr Greenwich CT 06830 Office: 2 Greenwich Plaza Greenwich CT 06830

BAMBAS, KARL JOHN, chemical company executive; b. Buffalo, Aug. 8, 1933; s. Julius John and Martha Rebecca (Ochsner) B.; m. Inga-Britt Lenore Johnson, 1957 (div. 1977); 1 son, Karl John III; m. Kathleen Gorga, 1978. B.S., Syracuse U., 1955, M.S. (W.R. Grace fellow), 1957; M.B.A., Harvard, 1960. Financial analyst Union Carbide Corp., N.Y.C., 1965-70; mgr. planning and analysis, specialty chems. div. Allied Chem. Corp., Morristown, N.J., 1970-71, asst. controller, 1971-72, controller, 1972-74, asst. to pres., 1974-76; v.p. fin. and adminstrn. Allied Gen. Nuclear Services, Barnwell, S.C., 1976—; instr. bus. policy W.Va. State U., 1962. Contbr. articles on nuclear materials mgmt. to profl. jours. Active Cub Scouts, Boy Scouts Am. Served as 1st lt. USAF. Mem. Fin. Execs. Inst., Inst. Nuclear Materials Mgmt., Alpha Chi Sigma, Sigma Nu. Home: 219 Northwood Dr Aiken SC 29801 Office: Box 847 Barnwell SC 29812

BAMBERG, ROBERT DOUGLAS, educator; b. Buenos Aires, Argentina, Feb. 6, 1928; came to U.S., 1938, naturalized, 1946; s. David Tobias and Hilda (Seagle) B.; m. Jane Hindle, Sept. 3, 1952; children: Winifred, Katharine, Elizabeth; m. Barbara Berndtson Cole, Nov. 22, 1975. B.A., Cornell U., 1951, M.A., 1958, Ph.D., 1961. Instr. English Cornell U., 1959-61; mem. faculty U. Pa., 1961-70, assoc. prof., 1968-70, undergrad. chmn., 1965-70; Charles Dana prof., chmn. English dept. Bates Coll., Lewiston, Maine, 1970-72, prof., dean faculty, 1972-74; prof., chmn. English dept. Kent (Ohio) State U., 1975—. Author: Writers for Tomorrow II, 1954; Editor: The Confession of Jereboam O. Beauchamp, 1965; Norton critical edit. The Portrait of a Lady (Henry James), 1975. Served with USAAF, 1946-47. Home: 1258 Greenwood Ave Kent OH 44240 Office: Dept English Kent State U Kent OH 44242

BAMBERGER, EDWARD CLINTON, JR., lawyer, educator; b. Balt., July 2, 1926; s. Edward Clinton and Anna (Russo) B.; m. Katharine Elizabeth Kelehar, Feb. 16, 1952; children—Edward Clinton III, Christine Ann. B.S., Loyola Coll., Balt., 1949; J.D., Georgetown U., 1951, U. Pa. Law Sch., 1981. Bar: Md. bar 1951, D.C. bar 1975, Mass. bar 1979. Law clk. to judge Ct. Appeals Md., 1951-52; asso. firm Piper & Marbury, Balt., 1952-60, mem. firm, 1960-69; prof., dean Catholic U. Law Sch., 1969-75; exec. v.p. Legal Services Corp., Washington, 1975-79; atty. Legal Services Inst., Boston, 1979—; mem. faculty Harvard Law Sch., 1979—, Northeastern U. Sch. Law, 1979—;

asst. atty. gen. Md., 1958-59; vis. prof. Stanford Law Sch., 1974-75, U. New South Wales, Australia, 1977; dir. legal services program OEO, 1965-66; mem. commn. legal edn. Supreme Jud. Ct. Mass. Contbr. articles to profl. publs. Del. Md. Constl. Conv., 1967; Bd. dirs. Micronesian Legal Services Program, 1970-75, Citizens Communications Center, 1970-75, Am. Indian Lawyer Tng. Program, 1970-75; bd. dirs., exec. com. Lawyers' Com. for Civil Rights Under Law, 1970-75; mem. Boston steering com., 1980—. Served with USAAF, 1945. Mem. Nat. Legal Aid and Defender Assn. (pres. 1971-73, v.p. 1974-75), Soc. Am. Law Tchrs. (bd. govs. 1973-77), ABA (chmn. council legal edn. and admissions to bar 1975-76, ho. of dels. 1971-73, 78-81), Mass. Bar Assn., Boston Bar Assn., D.C. Bar Assn. Democrat. Roman Catholic. Office: Legal Services Inst 3529 Washington St Jamaica Plain Boston MA 02130

BAMBERGER, FRITZ, coll. adminstr.; b. Frankfurt-am-Main, Germany, Jan. 7, 1902; came to U.S., 1939, naturalized, 1944; s. Max and Amalie (Wolf) B.; m. Kate Schwabe, Mar. 21, 1933 (dec.); children: Michael Albert, Gay; m. Maria E. Nussbaum, Sept. 29, 1963. Ph.D., U. Berlin, 1923; D.H.L. hon., Hebrew Union Coll., 1982. Research prof. Acad. for Jewish Research, Berlin, 1926-33; prof. philosophy Coll. Jewish Studies, Berlin, 1933-34; Bd. Edn. for Jews, Berlin, 1934-38; also pres. Jewish Tchrs. Coll. of Prussia; mem. Bd. Jewish Edn., Chgo.; mem. faculty Coll. Jewish Studies, 1939-44; dir. research Coronet and Esquire mags., 1942-48; editorial dir. Coronet, 1948-52, editor, 1952-56; exec. dir. Esquire and Coronet, 1956-61; cons. Esquire, 1962-71; prof. intellectual history, asst. to pres. Hebrew Union Coll., N.Y.C., 1962—, emeritus prof., 1979—; Mem. exec. com. scholars Inst. Advanced Studies in Religion and Humanities; v.p. Leo Baeck Inst. Author: Entstehung des Wertproblems, 1924, Moses Mendelssohn, 1929, Das System des Maimonides, 1935, Das neunte Schuljahr, 1937, Zunz's Conception of History, 1941, Leo Baeck-The Man and the Idea, 1958, The Philosophy of Julius Guttmann, 1960, Hebrew edit., 1976, Books Are the Best Things, 1962; Editor or compiler: Lehren des Judentums, 1928-30, Moses Mendelssohn's Gesammelte Schriften, 1929-32, rev. edit., 1971-81, Denkmal der Freundschaft, 1929, Das Buch Zunz, 1932, Herder's Blaetter der Vorzeit, 1936; Contbr. articles to various publs. Mem. governing body World Union for Progressive Judaism; bd. dirs. Selfhelp Community Services, United Help. Home: 415 E 52d St New York NY 10022 Office: One W 4th St New York NY 10012

BAMBERGER, GERALD FRANCIS, plastics resins co. exec.; b. Hannover, Germany, Sept. 20, 1920; came to U.S., 1938, naturalized, 1943; m. Ursula Friede, Mar. 27, 1946; children—Gale, Richard, Annette, Peter. Comml. diploma, Ecole Superieure de Commerce, Neuchatel, Switzerland, 1938. Pres. A. Bamberger Corp., Bklyn., 1938-54, Interplastics Corp., N.Y.C., 1955-62; prodn. mgr. plastics div. Cities Service Corp., Hicksville, N.Y., 1963-67; pres. Bamberger Polymers, Inc., New Hyde Park, N.Y., 1967—. Served with M.I. AUS, 1943-46. Decorated Bronze Star. Mem. Soc. Plastics Industry, Soc. Plastics Engrs. Office: 3003 New Hyde Park Rd New Hyde Park NY 11042

BAMFORD, THOMAS TRUMAN, bus. exec.; b. Ipswich, Mass., June 10, 1926; s. Robert and Isabel (Nutt) B.; m. Calypso Giantis, Apr. 21, 1974; children—Sandra, Shiela, Robert, William, Deidre, Tracy. B.S. in Chem. Enging, Worcester Poly. Inst., 1949, M.S., 1950. Research engr. Lever Brothers Co., Cambridge, Mass., 1950-52; mem. sr. staff Arthur D. Little, Inc., Cambridge, 1952-74; pres. Bamford Assos., Inc., Ipswich, 1974-79; v.p. research and devel. FMC Corp., Chgo., 1979—; dir. IMRX, Inc., Phila.; asso. prof. mgmt. of tech. U. N.H., 1971-72. Author: Executive Zoo, 1974. Served with USN, 1944-46. Mem. Indsl. Research Inst. Clubs: Mid-Am., Courtside, Ft. Myers Racquet. Address: FMC Corp 200 E Randolph St Chicago IL 60601

BAMPTON, JAMES WILLIAM, retired rubber and plastic products company executive; b. Lakewood, Ohio, Aug. 15, 1909; s. Samuel Wesley and Henrietta Frances (Hunt) B.; m. Lois Irene Thomasson, June 23, 1937 (dec. Aug. 1974); children: Robin Ann, James William, Barbara; m. Tiami J. Padwick, Sept. 13, 1976; 1 dau., Pamela Padwick Crutcher. A.B., Hobart Coll., 1932, LL.D., 1968; M.B.A., Harvard U., 1934. Sales exec. Goodyear Tire & Rubber Co., Akron, Ohio, 1934-44; spl. rep. U.S. Bd. Econ. Welfare, Australia and N.Z., 1943-44; dir. advt. promotion and comml. research James Lees & Sons Co., Bridgeport, Pa., 1944-48; pres. Theodore Presser Co., Bryn Mawr, Pa., 1948-51; asst. to pres. Charles Lachman Co., Phoenixville, Pa., 1951-53; pres. Krylon, Inc., 1953-67; pres., dir. Thomasson of Pa., Inc., 1956-61; pres., chief exec. officer Globe Rubber Products Corp., Phila., 1970-72; pres., owner A.Z. Bogert Co. Inc., Balt., 1974-82; cons. Borden, Inc., 1966-69. Trustee Hobart and William Smith Colls. Clubs: Harvard (N.Y.C. and Phila.); Union League, Phila. Aviation Country (Phila.); St. David's Golf, Delray Dunes Golf, Seagate Beach, Sons of St. George. Home: 4906 S Lake Dr Delray Dunes Boynton Beach FL 33436

BANCHOFF, THOMAS FRANCIS, mathematics educator; b. Trenton, N.J., Apr. 7, 1938; s. Thomas Francis and Ann Maria (Scarborough) B.; m. Lynore Wilhelmina Gause, July 6, 1963; children: Thomas Francis III, Ann Wilhelmina, Mary Lynn. A.B., U. Notre Dame, 1960; M.A., U. Calif., Berkeley, 1962, Ph.D., 1964; M.A. ad eundem, Brown U., 1970. Benjamin Peirce Instr. Harvard U., Cambridge, Mass., 1964-66; research assoc. Universiteit van Amsterdam, The Netherlands, 1966-67; asst. prof. Brown U., Providence, R.I., 1967-70, assoc. prof., 1970-75, prof. math., 1975—, acting dean student affairs, 1970-71; vis. prof. I.H.E.S., Bures-sur-Yvette, France, 1980-81; pres. Banchoff-Strauss Prodns., Providence, 1977-83, Thomas Banchoff Prodns., 1983—; editorial cons. various pub. cos. Author: Linear Algebra through Geometry, 1983, Cusps of Gauss Mappings, 1983; assoc. editor: Am. Math. Monthly, 1981—; writer, dir. computer animated film: The Hypercube; Projections and Slicing, 1978 (Prix de la Recherche Fundamentale, B). Woodrow Wilson fellow, 1959; Danforth Found. fellow, 1960; NSF research fellow, 1967—; Office Naval Research fellow, 1983—; recipient sr. citation Brown U., 1976. Mem. Am. Math. Soc., Math. Assn. Am., Soc. Values in Higher Edn. (bd. dirs. 1978-84). Democrat. Roman Catholic. Club: Art (Providence) (bd. mgrs. 1979-80). Home: 18 Colonial Rd Providence RI 02906 Office: Brown U Math Dept Providence RI 02912 *One idea, the fourth demension, has provided me the most challenge and fascination and has introduced me and my students to remarkable people and their creations, from Edwin Abbott and his Flatland to Salvador Dali and his CorpusHypercubus. Our own computer graphics films are contributions in the same spirit, to challenge all to see in new ways.*

BANCROFT, ALEXANDER CLERIHEW, lawyer; b. N.Y.C., Feb. 6, 1938; s. Harding F. and Jane (Northrop) B.; m. Margaret A. Armstrong, Mar. 14, 1964; 1 dau., Elizabeth. A.B., Harvard U., 1960, LL.B., 1963. Mem. Shearman & Sterling, N.Y.C., 1964—, ptnr., 1973—. Home: 15 E 91st St New York NY 10128 Office: 53 Wall St New York NY 10005

BANCROFT, ANNE (MRS. MEL BROOKS), actress; b. N.Y.C., Sept. 17, 1931; d. Michael and Mildred (DiNapoli) Italiano; m. Mel Brooks, 1964; 1 son. Broadway stage appearances include Two for the Seesaw, 1958; Anne Sullivan in: The Miracle Worker, 1959-60; Golda, 1977-78; motion pictures include The Pumpkin Eater, 1964, The Graduate, 1967, The Turning Point, 1977, The Elephant Man, 1980; TV appearances include Kraft Music Hall; dir., writer, star: TV spl. Annie-The Woman in the Life of Men, 1970 (Emmy award 1970). Recipient Acad. award for performance in The Miracle Worker, 1962. Address: care 20th Century Fox Studios PO Box 900 Beverly Hills CA 90213

BANCROFT, GEORGE MICHAEL, chemical physicist, educator; b. Saskatoon, Sask., Can., Apr. 3, 1942; s. Fred and Florence Jean B.; m. Joan Marion MacFarlane, Sept. 16, 1967; children: David Kenneth, Catherine Jean. B.Sc., U. Man., 1963; M.Sc., 1964; Ph.D., Cambridge (Eng.) U., 1967, M.A., 1970, Sc.D. (E.W. Staecie fellow), 1979. Univ. demonstrator Cambridge U.; then teaching fellow Christ Coll.; mem. faculty U. Western Ont., London; now prof. chem. physics, also dir. Centre Chem. Physics. Author: Mössbauer Spectroscopy, 1973; also articles in photoelectron spectroscopy; revs. Mössbauer Spectroscopy. Recipient Harrison Meml. prize, 1972, Meldola medal, 1972, Rutherford Meml. medal, 1980; Guggenheim fellow, 1982-83. Fellow Royal Soc. Can.; mem. Royal Soc. Chemistry, Can. Chem. Soc., Can. Geol. Soc., Can. Physics Soc. Mem. United Ch. Can. Clubs: Curling, Tennis (London). Office: Chemistry Dept U Western Ont London ON N6A 5B7 Canada *

BANCROFT, HARDING FOSTER, newspaper executive; b. N.Y.C., Dec. 29, 1910; s. Francis Sidney and Beatrice F. (Jordan) B.; m. Jane Northrop, July 2, 1936; children: Alexander, Mary Jane Bancroft Collins, Harding F., Catherine. A.B., Williams Coll., 1933, LL.D., 1981; LL.B., Harvard U., 1936; LL.D., Wilmington Coll., 1968. Atty. Searle James & Crawford, N.Y.C., 1936-41, OPA, Washington, 1941-43, Lend Lease Adminstrn., 1943; chief div. UN Polit. Affairs, Dept. State, 1945; later dir. Office UN Polit. and Security Affairs; U.S. dep. rep. UN Collective Measures Com., with personal rank of minister, 1950-53; legal adviser ILO, Geneva, 1953-56; sec. New York Times Co., 1956-63, exec. v.p., 1963-74, vice-chmn., 1974-76, also dir., 1961-76; Mem. U.S. del. to 21st UN Gen. Assembly; with rank of ambassador. Bd. dirs. Greer Children's Community, 1969-78, Ralph Bunche Inst. UN; trustee Williams Coll., 1968-81, Sarah Lawrence Coll., 1960-70, Carnegie Endowment for Internat. Peace, 1964-81; vice-chmn. Carnegie Endowment for Internat. Peace, 1970-78; trustee Carnegie Corp. N.Y., 1966-78, vice-chmn., 1974-78; pres. bd. trustees Clark Art Inst., Found. Center, 1975-79; bd. mgrs. N.Y. Bot. Garden; mem. adv. bd. WNET/13 Ednl. TV; bd. govs. N.Y.C. Center Music and Drama, 1975-77. Served as lt. USNR, 1943-45. Mem. Council Fgn. Relations, Fgn. Policy Assn. (dir. 1969-77). Club: Century Assn. Home: Verbank Rd Millbrook NY 12545

BANCROFT, HARRY ALLEN, mfg. co. exec.; b. Detroit, June 11, 1927; s. Harry S. and Anna (Peterson) B.; m. Ann Margaret Dailey, Feb. 23, 1952; children—James M., Patrick A., Mark W., Ann L., Susan L. B.S.M.E., Mich. State U., 1951; postgrad., Sloan Sch. Mgmt., M.I.T., 1980. With Aeroquip Corp., 1951—, plant mgr. indsl. div., Van Wert, Ohio, 1967-69, v.p., gen. mgr., 1969-74, group v.p. U.S. ops., Jackson, Mich., 1974-79, exec. v.p., chief operating officer, 1979-80, pres., chief operating officer, 1980—; dir. All Am. Ins. Co., Central Mut. Ins. Co. Served with U.S. Army, 1945-47. Mem. Soc. Automotive Engrs., Am. Soc. Metals. Club: Elks. Office: 300 S East Ave Jackson MI 49203

BANCROFT, JAMES RAMSEY, business executive, lawyer; b. Ponca City, Okla., Nov. 13, 1919; s. Charles Ramsey and Maude (Viersen) B.; m. Jane Marguerite Oberfell, May 28, 1944; children: John Ramsey, Paul Marshall, Sara Jane. A.B., U. Calif., Berkeley, 1940, M.S. in Bus. Adminstrn, 1941; J.D., Hastings Coll. Law, 1949. Bar: Calif. 1950; C.P.A., Calif. With McLaren, Goode, West & Co., C.P.A.s, San Francisco, 1946-50; partner firm Bancroft, Avery & McAlister, San Francisco, 1950—; pres. Madison Properties, Inc., San Francisco, 1967—, Adams Properties, Inc., 1969-79, Adams-Western Inc., 1969-78; chmn. bd. UNC Resources, 1978-82, United Nuclear Corp., Falls Church, Va., 1972-82; dir. Recortec Inc., Mountain View, Calif. Former pres. Suisun Conservation Fund; former dir. Suisun Resource Conservation Dist.; trustee Dean Witter Found.; pres. Harvey L. Sorensen Found. Served to lt. USNR, 1942-46. Mem. Am. Bar Assn., Phi Beta Kappa. Clubs: Bohemian, Pacific-Union, Olympic (San Francisco). Office: 601 Montgomery St Suite 800 San Francisco CA 94111

BANCROFT, JOHN BASIL, virologist, educator; b. Vancouver, B.C., Can., Dec. 31, 1929; s. John Stanley and Marjorie (White) B.; m. Mary Cairine Ross, Aug. 28, 1954; children: Leslie Anne, Ian David, Graham John, Jane Elizabeth. B.A., U. B.C., 1952; Ph.D., U. Wis., 1955. Mem. faculty Purdue U., 1955-70, prof. plant pathology, 1964-70; head dept. virology John Innes Inst., Norwich, Eng., 1970-73; prof. plant sci. U. Western Ont., London, 1973—, chmn. dept., 1973-78, dean sci., 1979—; fellow virus research unit Cambridge (Eng.) U., 1965. Author papers in field; mem. editorial bds. profl. jours. Recipient Ruth Allen award, 1970, McCoy award, 1971; sr. postdoctoral fellow NSF, 1965. Fellow Royal Soc. Can., Am. Phytopath. Soc.; mem. Soc. Gen. Microbiology, Am. Soc. Virology, Sigma Xi, Phi Kappa Phi. Home: 21 Scarlett Ave London ON N6G 1Z3 Canada Office: Dean's Office Natural Scis Centre U Western Ont London ON N6A 5B7 Canada

BANCROFT, THEODORE ALFONSO, statistics educator emeritus; b. Columbus, Miss., Jan. 2, 1907; s. Frank Hammond and Laura Louise (Cox) B.; m. Lenore Springer, Dec. 1, 1933; children: Alice Muriel, Lenore Louise. B.A., U. Fla., 1927; M.A., U. Mich., 1934; Ph.D., Iowa State U., 1943. Teaching asst. math. Vanderbilt U., 1937-38; head math. dept. Mercer U., 1938-41; asso. prof. math. U. Ga., 1946-47; dir. statis. lab. Auburn U., 1947-49; asso. prof. Iowa State U., Ames, 1949, prof., 1950-77, prof. emeritus, 1977—, dir., head statis. lab., dept. stats., 1950-72; UN assignment, Middle East, India, 1954, Mexico, 1955, Univ. tng. command, Italy, 1945, Japan Soc. Promotion Sci. vis. prof., 1973; vis. prof. U. Philippines, 1973, Cath. U., Chile, 1975; Disting. vis. prof. San Diego State U., 1980. Author: (with R.L. Anderson) Statistical Theory in Research, 1952, Topics in Intermediate Statistical Methods, vol. 1, 1968; Editor: (with Kempthorne, Gowen, Lush) Statistics and Mathematics in Biology, 1954, 64; statistical papers in Honor of George W. Snedecor, 1971, (with C.P. Han) Statistical Theory and Inference in Research, 1981; Contbr. articles to profl. jours., article to Ency. Americana. Recipient Wilton Park award Iowa State U., 1976. Fellow Am. Statis. Assn. (pres. 1970), Inst. Math. Statistics, AAAS; mem. Internat. Statis. Inst., Biometric Soc. (mem. council, past pres.), NRC, Sigma Xi, Phi Kappa Phi, Mu Sigma Rho (nat. dir.). Home: 3515 Woodland St Ames IA 50010

BANDEEN, ROBERT ANGUS, ry. exec.; b. Rodney, Ont., Can., Oct. 29, 1930; s. John Robert and Jessie Marie (Thomson) B.; m. Mona Helen Blair, May 31, 1958; children—Ian Blair, Mark Everett, Robert Derek, Adam Drummond. B.A., U. Western Ont., 1952, LL.D. (hon.), 1975; Ph.D., Duke U., 1959; LL.D. (hon.), Dalhousie U., 1978, D.C.L., Bishop's U., 1978. Asst. economist Can. Nat. Rys., Montreal, Que., 1955-56, research statistician, 1956-58, staff officer planning, 1958-60, chief costs and stats., 1960, chief devel. planning, 1960-66, dir. corp. planning, 1966-68, v.p. corp. planning and fin., 1968-71, v.p. Great Lakes region, 1971-72, exec. v.p. fin. and adminstrn., 1972-74; pres., chief exec. officer Can. Rys. System, 1974—; chmn. bd., dir. Grand Trunk Corp., Central Vt. Ry., Duluth Winnipeg & Pacific Ry., Grand Trunk Western R.R., CN, France, Detroit Toledo & Ironton Ry., CNCP Telecommunications; dir. Crown Life Ins. Co., Mortgage Ins. Co. Can., Sport Participation Can., Intercast S.A., Eurocan. Shipholdings Ltd.; chancellor Bishop's U.; Mem. Brit.-N.Am. Com., Howe Inst. Policy Analysis Com.; bd. dirs. Concordia Center Mgmt. Studies, Festival Lennoxville. Mem. adv. com. Can. Ski Council; hon. v.p. Que. council Boy Scouts Can.; senator Stratford Shakespearean Festival Found. Decorated knight Order St. John; officer Order of Can. Mem. Can. Ry. Club, Can. Transp. Research Forum, Nat. Freight Traffic Assn., Toronto Ry. Club. Clubs: Montreal Amateur Athletic Assn., Mount Royal, Saint James's (Montreal). Home: 3120 Daulac Rd Montreal PQ H3Y 2A2 Canada Office: Crown Life Ins Co 120 Bloor St E Toronto ON Canada M4W IB8

BANDER, MYRON, physics educator, university dean; b. Belzyce, Poland, Dec. 11, 1937; came to U.S., 1949, naturalized, 1955; s. Elias and Regina (Zielonka) B.; m. Carol Heimberg, Aug. 20, 1967. B.A., Columbia U., 1958, M.A., 1959, Ph.D., 1962. Postdoctoral fellow CERN, 1962-63; research assoc. Stanford Linear Accelerator Center, 1963-66; mem. faculty U. Calif., Irvine, 1966—, prof. physics, 1974—, dean phys. scis., 1980—. Sloan Found. fellow, 1967-69. Fellow Am. Phys. Soc. Office: U Calif Irvine CA 92717

BANDLER, JOHN WILLIAM, electrical engineering educator; b. Jerusalem, Nov. 9, 1941. B.Sc., Imperial Coll. Sci. and Tech., London, 1963, Ph.D., 1967; D.Sc., U. London, 1976. With Mullard Research Labs., Eng., 1966-67; postdoctoral fellow, sessional lectr. U. Man., Can., 1967-69; asst. prof. McMaster U., Hamilton, Ont., Can., 1969-71, assoc. prof., 1971-74, prof. elec. enging., 1974—, chmn. dept., 1978-79, dean faculty, 1979-81; coordinator Group on Simulation, Optimization and Control, 1973-83. Fellow Inst. Elec. Engrs. U.K., IEEE; mem. Assn. Profl. Engrs. Province of Ont. Office: McMaster U Dept Elec and Computer Enging Hamilton ON L8S 4L7 Canada

BANDO, SALVATORE LEONARD (SAL BANDO), professional baseball player; b. Cleve., Feb. 13, 1944; m. Sandra Fortunato, Feb. 8, 1969; children: Salvatore Leonard, Santino Luke. Student, Ariz. State U., Tempe. With Oakland Athletics (Am. League), 1967-76, Milw. Brewers, 1977-81, spl. asst. to gen. mgr., 1982—. Named All-Am. 3d baseman Ariz. State U., 1965; named to Am. League All-Star Team, 1969, 72, 73, 74. Address: care Milw County Stadium Milwaukee WI 53214 *

BANDOW, DOUGLAS LEIGHTON, magazine editor, columnist, policy consultant; b. Washington, Apr. 15, 1957; s. Donald E. and Donna J. (Losh) B. A.A., Okaloosa-Walton Jr. Coll., Niceville, Fla., 1974; B.S. in Econsn., Fla. State U., 1976; J.D., Stanford U., 1979. Bar: Calif. 1979. Sr. policy analyst Reagan for Pres. Com., Los Angeles, 1979-80, Arlington, Va., 1979-80, Office of Pres. Elect, Washington, 1980-81; spl. asst. to the Pres. for policydevel. White House, Washington, 1981-82; editor Inquiry Mag., Washington, 1982—; sr. policy cons. Cato Inst., Washington, 1982—; nat. columnist Copley News Service, San Diego, 1983—; contbg. editor Socioecon. Studies Newsletter, 1983—. Contbr. articles to periodicals. Recipient Freedom Leadership award Freedoms Found., Valley Forge, Pa., 1977, cert. for polit. and journalistic activities Freedoms Found., Valley Forge, Pa., 1979; named N.Y. State Coll. Republican of Yr. N.Y. State Coll. Reps., 1982; recipient Nat. Young Am. award Boy Scouts Am., 1977. Mem. Calif. Bar Assn., ABA, Nat. Press Club, Washington Ind. Writers, Nat. Writers Club. Home: 8478 Magic Tree Ct Springfield VA 22153 Office: Inquiry Magazine 1320 G St SE Washington DC 20003

BANDROFCHECK, JOSEPH, mfg. co. exec.; b. Hunker, Pa., Sept. 1, 1920; s. Paul and Catherine (Kukla) B.; m. Mary Kay Wesbecher, Oct. 27, 1951; children—Charles Paul, Susan Kathleen, Mark Joseph. Extension student, U. Pitts. With Robertshaw Controls Co., Richmond, Va., 1941—, asst. controller, 1959-69, treas., 1969—. Served with USNR, 1944-46. Mem. Nat. Assn. Accts. (past pres.), Fin. Execs. Inst. (past pres.), Budget Execs. Inst. (past pres.). Republican. Roman Catholic. Office: 1701 Byrd Ave Richmond VA 23261 *

BANDT, CARL LEE, periodontist, educator; b. Wisconsin Rapids, Wis., Mar. 22, 1938; s. Lawrence Edward and Ethel Marie (Schultz) B.; m. Mary Virginia Rice, June 22, 1963; children—Laura Marie, Mary Louise, Daniel Michael, Matthew Phillip. Student, U. Wis., 1956-57; B.S., U. Minn., 1960, D.D.S., 1962, M.S.D., 1966, M.S., 1968. Instr. Sch. Dentistry, U. Minn., 1966-68, asso. prof., dir. clin. periodontology, 1968-70, asso. prof., dir. clin. systems, 1970-74, prof., 1974—, asst. dean clin. affairs, 1974-78, chmn. dept. periodontology, 1978—; cons. in field. Contbr. articles to profl. jours. Mem. ADA, Am. Acad. Periodontology, Internat. Assn. Dental Research, Am. Assn. Dental Schs., Minn. State Dental Soc., Mpls. Dist. Dental Soc., Phi Eta Sigma, Omicron Kappa Upsilon. Office: Sch Dentistry Univ of Minn Minneapolis MN 55455

BANDURA, ALBERT, psychologist; b. Mundara, Alta., Can., Dec. 4, 1925; came to U.S., 1949, naturalized, 1956; m. Virginia Varns; 2 children. B.A., U. B.C., 1949, D.Sc. (hon.), 1979; M.A. in Psychology, U. Iowa, 1951, Ph.D., 1952. Prof. psychology Stanford U., 1953—, David Starr Jordan prof. social sci. in psychology, 1973—. Author: (With R.H. Walters) Adolescent Aggression, 1959, Social Learning and Personality Development, 1963, Principles of Behavior Modification, 1969, Aggression, 1973, Social Learning Theory, 1977; Editor: Psychological Modeling: Conflicting Theories, 1971. Guggenheim fellow, 1972. Fellow Am. Acad. Arts and Scis.; mem. Am. Psychol. Assn. (Disting. Scientist award div. 12 1972, Disting. Sci. Contbn. award 1980, pres. 1974), Calif. Psychol. Assn. (Disting. Scientist award 1973), Western Psychol. Assn. (pres. 1980), Internat. Soc. Research on Aggression (Disting. Contbn. award 1980), Soc. Child Devel. Office: Dept Psychology Bldg 420 Jordan Hall Stanford U Stanford CA 94305

BANDURRAGA, PETER LOUIS, museum director, historian; b. Los Angeles, Apr. 2, 1944; s. Luis Cipriano and E. Lillian (Slingsby) B.; m. Diane Elizabeth Nassir, Mar. 4, 1979. B.A., Stanford U., 1966; M.A., U. Calif.-Santa Barbara, 1968; Ph.D., U. Calif.Santa Barbara, 1977. Instr. Chapman Coll., Orange, Calif., 1977-78; research librarian Ventura County Hist. Mus., Ventura, Calif., 1978-81; dir. Nev. Hist. Soc., Reno, 1981—; mem. Nev. State Adv. Council on Libraries, 1981—, State Hist. Records Adv. Bd., 1981—; adj. prof. U. Nev.-Reno, 1981—. Co-author: Ventura County's Yesterdays today, 1980. Mem. Downtown Found., Reno, 1983—. Mem. Am. Assn. State and Local History (state chair, awards com. 1981). Democrat. Methodist. Club: Stanford (Reno) (v.p. 1983—). Office: 1650 N Virginia St Reno NV 89503

BANDY, MARY LEA, mus. ofcl.; b. Evanston, Ill., June 16, 1943; d. DeWitt Clinton and Ruth (Coale) Gibson; m. Gary Bandy, June 3, 1967. B.A., Stanford U., 1965. Asst. editor Harry N. Abrams, Inc., N.Y.C., 1966-73; asso. editor publs. Mus. Modern Art, N.Y.C., 1973-76, asso. coordinator exhbns., 1976-78, adminstr. dept. film, 1978-80, dir. dept. film, 1980—. Office: 11 W 53d St New York NY 10019

BANDY, MOE, country music recording artist; b. Meridan, Miss. Former mem., Mission City Playboys band; founder, leader, The

Mavericks band, until 1974; rec. artist for, GRC, 1973-76, Columbia, 1976—; (with Joe Stampley) albums include Just Good Ol' Boys (Recipient (with Joe Stampley) Acad. of Country Music award for top vocal group.). Office: care Blake Mevis 1609 Hawkins St Nashville TN 37203 *

BANE, CHARLES ARTHUR, lawyer; b. Springfield, Ill., May 1, 1913; s. Fred Weller and Frances (Tilley) B.; m. Eileen Blackwell, Jan. 17, 1942; children: Susan Magary, Janet Richardson, Peter, Charles. A.B., U. Chgo., 1935; LL.M., Harvard, 1938; B.A. in Jurisprudence (Rhodes scholar), Oxford U., 1937. Bar: N.Y. 1939, Ill. 1949. Assoc. Sullivan & Cromwell, N.Y.C., 1939-42, 46-48; mem. firm Bishop, Mitchell & Burdett, Chgo., 1949-50, Mitchell, Conway & Bane, 1950-52, Isham, Lincoln & Beale, 1953—; vis. prof. law, dir. continuing legal edn. U. Miami Sch. Law, Coral Gables, Fla., 1979-82; lectr. U. Chgo. Law Sch., 1954, 58; dir. Central Ill. Public Service Co.; sr. atty. Lend Lease Adminstrn., 1942-43; chief counsel emergency crime com. Chgo. City Council, 1952; sec. Crime Detection Inst., 1957-60; chmn. Ill. adv. com. Fed. Civil Rights Commn., 1958-61; mem. Rhodes Scholarship Selection Com. Author: The Electrical Equipment Conspiracies: The Treble Damage Actions, 1973; Editor-in-chief: Chgo. Bar Record, 1966-68; mem. bd. editors: Am. Bar Assn. Jour, 1968-70; chmn., 1970-76; Contbr. articles to profl. publs. Pres. United Charities Chgo., 1961-63; nat. chmn. plaintiff's counsel steering com. Elec. Equipment Antitrust Litigation; chmn. Am. Found. Temple Bar, 1976-79; nat. co-chmn. Lawyers Com. Civil Rights Under Law, 1977-79; bd. dirs. Community Fund, Chgo.; bd. dirs., exec. com. United Cerebral Palsy of Chgo.; mem. cancer research bd. U. Chgo.; trustee Cancer Research Found. Served as lt. USNR, 1943-45. Fellow Am. Bar Found. (Ill. chmn.); mem. ABA (council public utility sect. 1958-61), Ill. Bar Assn., Chgo. Bar Assn. (bd. mgrs.), Am. Law Inst., Council Fgn. Relations (pres. 1956-58), Family Service Assn. Am. (v.p. 1966—, dir.), English-Speaking Union (pres. Chgo. br. 1964-66), Phi Beta Kappa, Phi Kappa Sigma. Clubs: Economic, Commercial, Saddle and Cycle (pres. 1965-67), Tavern, Casino (Chgo.); Internat. House (pres. 1967-69); Wig and Pen (London); Harvard (N.Y.C.); Bath and Tennis, Everglades (Palm Beach, Fla.). Home: 207 Pendleton Palm Beach FL 33480 Office: 3 First National Plaza Chicago IL 60602

BANEN, DAVID MERTON, physician; b. Kiev, Russia, June 1, 1904; came to U.S., 1906, naturalized, 1935; s. Harry and Lena (Hecht) B.; m. Ruth N. Schwartz, May 7, 1939; 1 dau., Elsa Harriet (Mrs. Revan A.F. Tranter). B.S., U. Ill., 1926, M.D., 1930. Diplomate: Am. Bd. Psychiatry and Neurology. Intern Cook County Hosp., Chgo., 1930-32; served as col., M.C. U.S. Army, 1935-38, 41-47, USPHS, 1938-41; chief of staff VA, Brockton, Mass., 1947-66; supt. Cushing Hosp., Mass. Dept. Mental Health, Framingham, 1966-75; asst. clin. prof. psychiatry Tufts U., 1953; del. White House Conf. on Aging, 1961, 71; mem. Calif. Gov.'s Council on Aging, 1976. Contbr. articles to profl. jours. Cons. Jewish Vocat. Service.; Mem. Mass. Commn. on Aging, 1968. Decorated Purple Heart, Bronze Star. Fellow Am. Geriatric Soc., N.E. Soc. Gerontologic Psychiatry, Am. Psychiat. Assn. (life); mem. AMA (life), No. Calif. Psychiat. Soc. Jewish (pres., chmn. bd. temple). Home: 3118 Terra Granada 1 Walnut Creek CA 94595

BANERJEE, (BIMAL), artist; b. Calcutta, India, Sept. 4, 1939; s. Dashurathee and Madhabilata B. Baccalaureate with 1st class honors, Indian Coll. Art, Calcutta, 1960; student, Coll. Art, New Delhi, 1965-67, Atelier 17, Paris, 1967-69, Ecole des Beaux-Arts, Paris, 1967-70, Pratt Inst., N.Y.C., 1969-72; Ed.M., M.A., Columbia U., 1978. Lectr. Bloomfield (N.J.) Coll., 1980-81, Parsons Sch. Design/New Sch., N.Y.C, 1979-83, NAD, N.Y.C., other; art therapist St. John's Epis. Hosp., Queens, N.Y., 1981-83. Multi-media performance artist shows include, Columbia U., 1979, Hofstra U., Just Above Midtown Gallery, N.Y.C., 1977, 78, Bertha Urdang Gallery, N.Y.C., 1976, Fremar Gallery, L.I., N.Y., 1974, Galerie Haut-pave, Paris, 1968-69, Mcpl. Galeria, Levanto, Italy, 1968, Kumar Gallery, New Delhi, 1970, Arts & Prints Gallery, Calcutta, 1963, 64, numerous others; internat. biennials in Paris, Tokyo, Rejika, Miami, Hawaii, Bradford, Eng., others; exhibited in one-man shows in, U.S., Europe and India; Contbr. articles, poetry, short stories, children's lit. to profl. jours. French Govt. grantee, 1967-70; Indian Govt. grantee, 1965-67; recipient awards Hawaii Biennial, 1971, 73, 79; Arthur Kaplan award, 1978; award Painters and Sculptors Soc., 1972; Nat. award Nat. Art Acad., India, 1967, 70; State Acad. award Bengal State, 1967, Punjab State, 1967; Statue of Victory world cultural prize Nat. Center Study and Research, 1984; numerous others. Mem. Mus. Modern Art, Found. for Community of Artists of N.Y.C., Coll. Art Assn., World Print Council, Smithsonian Instn. Introduced new media Fumage and Carbontransfer. Home: Loft #2C 106 Ridge St. New York NY 10002

BANERJEE, SUBIR KUMAR, geophysicist; b. Jamshedpur, India, Feb. 19, 1938; s. Benoy Krishna and Nirmala (Roy-Chowdhury) B.; m. Karin-Christa Barbara Saur, June 15, 1963; children: Sujata, Claire, Rekha. B.Sc. with honors, Calcutta U., 1956; M.Tech., Indian Inst. Tech., 1959; Ph.D. in Geophysics, Cambridge U., 1963. Research fellow Mullard Research Lab., Redhill, Surrey, Eng., 1963-64; sr. research asso., lectr. geophysics U. Newcastle-upon-Tyne, 1964-69; sr. staff scientist Franklin Inst. Research Labs., Phila., 1969-71; asso. prof. geophysics U. Minn., Mpls., 1971-74, prof., 1974—; adj. prof. middle Eastern and Islamic studies, 1976—. Author: (with F.D. Stacey) The Physical Principles of Rock Magnetism, 1974; Contbr. articles to profl. jours. Mem. Am. Geophys. Union. Office: Dept Geology and Geophysics 310 Pillsbury Dr SE Minneapolis MN 55455

BANERJI, RANAN BIHARI, mathematics and computer science educator; b. Calcutta, India, May 5, 1928; came to U.S., 1961, naturalized, 1969; s. Bijan Bihari and Setabja (Chatterji) B.; m. Purnima Purkayastha, July 8, 1954; children: Anindita, Sunandita. B.S., Patna U., 1947; M.S., Calcutta U., 1949, D.Phil., 1956. Research scholar Calcutta U., 1950-53, lectr., 1956; vis. asst. prof. Pa. State U., 1953-55; maintenance engr. Indian Statis. Inst., 1956-58; mem. faculty Case Western Res. U., 1958-74, prof. computer sci., 1968-74, Temple U., Phila., 1974-82; prof. math. and computer sci. St. Joseph's U., Phila., 1983—; asst. prof. engring. U. N.B., Can., 1959-61; cons. in field. Author: Theory of Problem Solving, 1969, Artificial Intelligence, 1980; also articles. Gold medalist univs. Patna and Calcutta. Sr. mem. IEEE; mem. Assn. Computing Machinery, Pattern Recognition Soc., Math. Assn. Am., Soc. Indsl. and Applied Math., Mensa, Common Cause, ACLU. Quaker. Home: 7612 Woodlawn Av Melrose Park PA 19126 Office: Dept Math and Computer Sci St Joseph's U 5600 City Ave Philadelphia PA 19131 *It is my belief that the only successful actions by men and women are those done in selfless service to God. The rest, however laudable, are risky at best.*

BANES, DANIEL, govt. ofcl., chemist, author; b. Chgo., Apr. 19, 1918; s. David and Fanny (Bornstein) B.; m. Helen Mae Richter, Apr. 6, 1941; children—Susan Penny Banes Harris, Elisabeth Ann Banes Bell, Sally Rachel. B.S., U. Chgo., 1938, M.S., 1940; Ph.D., Georgetown U., 1950. With FDA, 1939-73, asso. commr. for sci., 1968-69, dir. pharm. research and testing, 1969-73; dir. drug standards div. U.S. Pharmacopeia, 1973-79; cons. drug analysis and control; adj. prof. chemistry Am. U., 1951—. Author: Introduction to Regulatory Drug Analysis, 1965, Principles of Regulatory Drug Analysis, 1968, Chemist's Guide to Regulatory Drug Analysis, 1974, Provocative Merchant of Venice, 1975, Shakespeare, Shylock and Kabbalah, 1978. Served with USAAF, 1942-46. Recipient Distinguished Service award HEW, 1964, Harvey W. Wiley award, 1968. Fellow AAAS; mem. Am. Chem. Soc., Acad. Pharm. Scis., AAAS. Home: 805 Malcolm Dr Silver Spring MD 20901 Office: 805 Malcolm Dr Silver Spring MD 20901

BANET, CHARLES HENRY, college president, clergyman; b. Ft. Wayne, Ind., Dec. 8, 1922; s. Henry Alexander and Cecilia Marie (Henry) B. B.A., St. Joseph's Coll., 1950; M.L.S., U. Mich., 1951; student, St. Charles Sem., 1949. Ordained priest Roman Catholic Ch., 1949. Librarian St. Joseph's Coll., Rensselaer, Ind., 1952-65, exec. v.p., 1964-65, pres., 1965—, also bd. dirs. Assoc. editor: Philosophy Today, 1957—; author: Our Lady of Precious Blood in Art, 1961. Mem. Assn. Colls. Ind. (sec.-treas. 1973, exec. com.), Ind. Colls. and Univs. Ind. (chmn. 1975-76), Cath. Library Assn. (v.p. 1964-65). Home and Office: St Joseph's Coll Rensselaer IN 47978

BANEY, JOHN EDWARD, insurance company executive; b. Pitts., May 27, 1934; s. James V. and Mathilde M. (McGary) B.; m. Joan A. McGrath, June 14, 1958; children: Jay E., Diane L., Timothy J. B.A., U. Pa., 1957; grad. Advanced Mgmt. Program, Harvard U., 1980. With trust dept. First Pa. Bank & Trust, Phila., 1957-58, Remington Rand, 1958-62; brokerage cons. Conn. Gen. Life Ins. Co., Phila., 1962-68, brokerage mgr., Detroit, 1968-72, dir. agys., Hartford, 1972-73; v.p. brokerage div. Hartford, 1973-77, v.p. br. div., 1977-82; pres. bd. dirs. CG Equity Sales Co., Bloomfield, Conn., 1973-82, sr. v.p. adminstrv. services, 1982-83; pres. broker div. INA a CIGNA Co., Phila., 1983—; exec.-in-residence Baylor U., 1976. Mem. port affairs com. Delaware Valley Council, Phila., 1960-68; mem. exec. com. Hartford Whalers hockey team, 1982-83; pres. Simsbury Little League, Conn., 1976-78; bd. dirs. Birmingham YMCA, Mich., 1970-71, Found. New Am. Music, 1982—;; trustee Hartford Grad. Ctr., 1981-83. Served with U.S. Army Res., 1958-64. Mem. Am. Council Life Ins., C.L.U. Assn. Republican. Roman Catholic. Clubs: Hopmeadow Country,. Home: 220 Ivy Ln Haverford PA 19041 Office: INA 1600 Arch St Philadelphia PA 19103

BANFIELD, EDWARD CHRISTIE, political science educator; b. Bloomfield, Conn., Nov. 19, 1916; s. Edward Christie and Helen (Adams) B.; m. Laura Fasano, Sept. 24, 1938; children: Laura, Elliott. A.B., Conn. State Coll., 1938; Ph.D., U. Chgo., 1951. Jr. adminstrv. asst. U.S. Forest Service, Boston, 1939-40; sec. N.H. Farm Bur. Fedn., Concord, 1940-41; successively info. specialist U.S. Farm Security Adminstrn. in, Upper Darby, Pa., Indpls., Washington and San Francisco, 1941-47; from instr. to assoc. prof. polit. sci. U. Chgo., 1948-59; Henry Lee Shattuck prof. urban govt. Harvard U., 1959-72, prof. govt., 1976—, George D. Markham prof. govt., 1976—; Kenan prof. pub. policy and polit. sci. U. Pa., 1973-76. Author: Government Project, 1951, The Moral Basis of a Backward Society, 1958, Political Influence, 1961, Big City Politics, 1965, Unheavenly City: The Nature and the Future of Our Urban Crisis, 1970, 2d edit., 1974, (with Martin Meyerson) Politics, Planning and the Public Interest, 1955, (with Morton Grodzins) Government and Housing in Metropolitan Areas, 1958, (with James Q. Wilson) City Politics, 1963, (with Meyerson) Boston: The Job Ahead, 1966, The Democratic Muse, 1984; editor: (with Meyerson) Urban Government: Reader in Administration and Politics, 1961, 2d edit., 1969. Address: Littauer Center Harvard U Cambridge MA 02138

BANGDIWALA, ISHVER SURCHAND, educator, statistician; b. Surat, Gujarat State, India, Jan. 9, 1922; came to U.S., 1948, naturalized, 1960; s. Surchand D. and Kamala (Jariwala) B.; m. Pushpa Sukhadia, May 2, 1947; 2 sons, Dweepkumar I., Shrikant I. B.S., U. Bombay, 1943, M.S., 1946, LL.B., 1946; M.S., U. N.C., 1950, Ph.D., 1958. Head stats. sect. and legal adviser K.A. Pandit (cons. actuary), Bombay, India, 1944-48; statistician, head stats. dept. Agrl. Expt. Sta., U. P.R., 1952-58; dir. research Superior Ednl. Council, U. P.R., Rio Piedras, 1958-66; lectr. statistics Inst. Statistics U.P.R., part-time 1953-67; prof. U. P.R., 1966-82, prof. emeritus, 1982—; hon. prof. U. P.R. Med. Sch., 1969—; cons. stats. and research to nat. and internat. agys. Author books on stats. and research methods.; Contbr. articles profl. jours. Trustee El Hogar del Nino, Cupey Alto, 1963—. Fellow Am. Statis. Assn. (pres. P.R. chpt.), Intercontinental Biog. Assn. Internat. Statis. Inst.; mem. Inst. Math. Statistics, Biometric Soc., AAAS, P.R. Tchrs. Assn., Am. Ednl. Research Assn., P.R. Assn. Ex-alumnae U. N.C., N.Y. Acad. Sci., Internat. Platform Assn., P.R. Statis. Soc. (founder, pres. 1968-70), Am. Acad. Polit. and Social Scis., Sigma Xi, Pi Mu Epsilon, Phi Delta Kappa, Gamma Sigma Delta. Lodge: Lions (pres.). Address: Calle Cisne 792 Urb Dos Pinos Rio Piedras PR 00923 *Patience, persistence and unselfishness are essentially the guiding principles for a successful career and the general way of life. These characteristics help create love for everyone and everything one engages in. Hoping for the best and being prepared for the worst gives one comprehension and tolerance about eventualities of life that are not under one's own control.*

BANGERT, RICHARD ELMER, banker; b. Buffalo, June 28, 1920; s. George H. and Jane (Harris) B.; m. Betty Jane Boswell, May 26, 1943; 1 son, Richard Elmer, II. B.S. in Econs, Wharton Sch., U. Pa., 1942; grad., Pacific Coast Banking Sch., 1952. Asst. v.p. Seattle-First Nat. Bank, 1945-55; ptnr. Foster & Marshall Co., Seattle, 1955-59; v.p. surety Safeco Ins. Co., Seattle, 1959-67; v.p. Seattle-First Nat. Bank, 1967-72; exec. v.p. Pacific Nat. Bank Wash. (now First Interstate Bank Wash.), Seattle, 1972-73, pres., 1973-81, chief exec. officer, 1974-81, chmn. bd., 1977—; dir. Pacific Bank Internat., Tacsea, Inc., Fred S. James & Co., Inc., Chgo., Farmers Group, Inc., Los Angeles, Farmers New World Life Ins. Co., Mercer Island, Wash., King Broadcasting Co., Seattle, Seattle Pacific Sales Co. Bd. dirs. or trustee N.W. Kidney Center, Cardio-Pulmonary Rehab. Inst., Virginia Mason Research Center, Seattle Found., Evergreen Safety Found., Pacific N.W. Aviation Hist. Found. Served to maj. USAAF, 1943-46; PTO. Decorated Army Commendation ribbon. Mem. NCCJ.; Mem. Wash. Bankers Assn. (past pres.), Downtown Seattle Devel. Assn. (pres. 1977), Assn. Res. City Bankers, Ind. Colls. Wash., Seattle C. of C., Econ. Devel. Council Puget Sound, Phi Delta Theta. Clubs: Rainier, Harbor (pres. 1977), Seattle Golf, Wash. Athletic (trustee), Tacoma, University. Home: 2615 42d W Seattle WA 98199 Office: PO Box 160 Seattle WA 98111

BANGERTER, NORMAN HOWARD, state legislator, building contractor; b. Granger, Utah, Jan. 4, 1933; s. William Howard and Isabelle (Bawden) B.; m. Colleen Monson, Aug. 18, 1953; children: Garrett, Ann, Jordan, Blair, Alayne, Adam, Erdman (foster son). Student, U. Utah, 1956-57, Brigham Young U., 1951-55. Vice-pres. B and H Real Estate Co., West Valley City, Utah, 1970—; sec. Dixie-Six Land Devel., West Valley City, Utah, 1980—; pres. Bangerter and Hendrickson Co., West Valley City, Utah, 1970—, NHB Construction Co., 1983—. Mem. Utah Ho. of Reps., 1974—, speaker, 1981-84, majority leader, 1977-78; chmn. task force for alternative forms of govt. West Valley City, 1982. Recipient Outstanding Legislator award VFW, 1981, Disting. Service award Home Bldg. Industry; named Outstanding Businessman West Valley C. of C. Mormon. Home: 4059 Montaia Dr West Valley City UT 84119 Office: NHB Construction 3251 W 4100 South West Valley City UT 84119

BANGS, F(RANK) KENDRICK, educator; b. Lostant, Ill., May 17, 1914; s. Mark Howard and Mary Hay (Henning) B.; m. Elizabeth Jane Paisley, May 19, 1944; children—John Kendrick, James Paisley. B.E., Ill. State Normal U., 1936; M.P.S., U. Colo., 1946; Ed.D., Ind. U., 1952. Tchr. bus. Rosiclare (Ill.) High Sch., 1936-37, Carmi (Ill.) High Sch., 1937-42; asst. prof. bus. adminstrn. U. Colo., Boulder, 1946-58, asso. prof., 1958-64, prof., 1964—, chmn. gen. bus. div., 1964-79; vis. prof. Coll. Bus., Ill. State U., Normal, 1979-80, U. Tex-Austin, 1982, Southwestern La U., Lafayette, 1983; cons. adminstrv. mgmt., small bus. Chmn. fin. stability bd. Colo. Pvt. Schs. Assn., 1977—. Contbr.: articles to Jour. Bus. Edn. Served with inf. U.S. Army, 1942-46. Decorated Bronze Star; recipient Robert L. Stearns award U. Colo. Alumni, 1976; John Robert Gregg award Gregg div. McGraw-Hill Pub. Co., 1978. Mem. Mountain-Plains Bus. Edn. Assn. (pres. 1958-59, Leadership award 1967-68), Nat. Bus. Edn. Assn. (co-editor yearbook 1975, nat. pres. 1967-68), Adminstrv. Mgmt. Soc. (pres. Denver chpt. 1963-64, Diamond Merit award 1967), Colo. Bus. Edn. Assn. (pres. 1956-57), Beta Gamma Sigma, Delta Pi Epsilon (nat. pres. 1968-69, pres. Research Found. 1979—). Presbyterian. Club: Rotary (Boulder). Home: 1025 6th St Boulder CO 80302 Office: Coll Bus PO Box 419 U Colo Boulder CO 80309

BANGS, JOHN KENDRICK, lawyer, chem. co. exec.; b. Fairfield, Iowa, Nov. 7, 1920; s. William Henry and Edna (Weller) B.; m. Elizabeth Harlow, Dec. 16, 1944; children—John Harlow, Amy Elizabeth, Gregory William. A.B., U. Iowa, 1942; LL.B., Columbia, 1948. Bar: N.J. bar 1948. Asso. firm Crummy & Consodine, Newark, 1948-52; atty. W.R. Grace & Co., N.Y.C., 1952-59, asst. sec., 1956-59; atty. Shulton, Inc., Clifton, N.J., 1959-73, sec., gen. counsel, 1963-73, v.p., 1967-73; also dir.; sec. exec. com., asst. sec. Am. Cyanamid Co., Wayne, N.J., 1973-78, sec., 1978—. Served to lt. USNR, 1942-45. Mem. Sigma Nu. Republican. Lutheran. Home: 42 Hawthorne Pl Summit NJ 07901 Office: 659 Berdan Ave Wayne NJ 07470

BANISTER, RONALD KITCHENER, construction company executive; b. Okotors, Alta., Can., Jan. 16, 1917; s. Harold and Laura (Brice) B.; m. Inez A. Thorson, May 11, 1938; children: Laureen, Rodger, Harold, Mary. Sr. matriculation, Okotors High Sch., Alta., 1935. Pres., chmn. bd. Banister Continental Ltd. and predecessors, Edmonton, Alta., 1948—. Served to lt. RCAF, 1942-45. Decorated D.F.C., Can. Medal. Mem. Pipeline Contractors Assn. (pres. 1954-55), Internat. Pipeline Contractors Assn. (dir. 1980), Canadian Pipeline Contractors Assn. (dir. 1948-58). Clubs: Edmonton Pete (pres. 1954); Lyford Cay (Nassau); Farmington (Charlottesville, Va.). Home: PO Box N 4903 Nassau Bahamas Office: Banister Continental Ltd 9910 39th Ave PO Box 2408 Edmonton AB Canada T5J 2R4

BANK, MERRILL LEE, paper products co. exec.; b. Balt., Feb. 5, 1915; s. Simon P. and Rose (Fox) B.; m. Helen Shapiro, Nov. 29, 1936; children—Herbert, Phyllis, Marjorie. Student, Balt. City Coll., 1932. With Md. Cup Corp., Owings Mills, Md., 1949—, exec. v.p., 1961—, vice chmn. bd., 1961-77, chmn. bd., 1977—; dir. Sweetheart Plastics Ltd., Fareham, Eng.; Strike-Rite Matches, Ltd., London, Ont., Can., Sweetheart Monocon Corp., Gruenlo, Holland. Bd. dirs. St. Mary's Hosp., West Palm Beach, Fla. Mem. Chief Exec. Forum. Clubs: Palm Beach (Fla.); Country (dir., v.p.). Home: 44 Cocoanut Row Palm Beach FL 33480 Office: Maryland Cup Corp Owings Mills MD 21117

BANK, STEVEN BARRY, educator; b. N.Y.C., Mar. 14, 1939; s. Abraham and Yetta (Slovis) B.; m. Connie Jane Thomas, June 16, 1972; 1 son, Seth Robert. A.B., Columbia Coll., 1959; Ph.D., Columbia U., 1964. Instr. U. Ill., Urbana-Champaign, 1964-66, asst. prof., 1966-68, asso. prof., 1968-71, prof. math., 1971—; prin. investigator NSF grants, 1976—. Contbr. articles to math. jours. Mem. Am. Math. Soc. Home: 2109 Easy St Urbana IL 61801 Office: Dept Math U Ill 1409 W Green St Altgeld Hall Urbana IL 61801

BANKHEAD, PORTER LEE, computer company executive; b. Hickory Grove, S.C., Sept. 28, 1941; s. Robert Odell and Helen Dorothy B. B.S. in Math., S.C. State Coll., 1963. Mathematician NASA Goddard Space Flight Ctr., Greenbelt, Md., 1966; dep. chief of staff for logistics U.S. Army, Reford, Va., 1966-67; mem. tech. staff Computer Scis. Corp., Silver Spring, Md., 1967-69; programmer-analyst AVCO Corp., Wilmington, Mass., 1969-73; pres. Systems and Applied Scis. Corp., Vienna, Va., 1973—. Bd. dirs. Democratic Bus. Council, Washington, 1983; mem. Dem. Nat. Conv. Arrangements Com., Washington, 1983. Served to lt. U.S. Army, 1963-65. Mem. Armed Forces Communications and Electronics Assn., Air Force Assn., Nat. Space Club, Kappa Alpha Psi. Home: 7928 16th St NW Washington DC 20012 Office: Systems and Applied Scis Corp 1577 Springhill Rd Vienna VA 22180

BANKHEAD, WALTER WILL, lawyer; b. Jasper, Ala., July 21, 1897; s. John H. and Musa (Harkins) B.; m. Emelil Crumpton, June 5, 1920 (dec.); children—Blossom B. Dill, Marion B. (Mrs. W.A. Grant), Barbara B. (Mrs. John T. Oliver, Jr.), John H.; m. Faustine Driver. A.B., U. Ala., 1919, LL.B., 1920. Bar: Ala. bar 1920. Practiced in, Jasper.; Formerly chmn. bd. TRI W Broadcasting, Inc., Franklin Broadcasting, Inc., Bankhead Broadcasting-Fayette, Inc.; dir. First Nat. Bank, Jasper. Mem. U.S. Ho. of Reps., 1941. Mem. Sigma Alpha Epsilon. Methodist. Clubs: Mason (Shriner), Musgrove Country (Jasper)). Home: 811 8th Ave Jasper AL 35501 Office: PO Box 2385 Jasper AL 35501

BANKOFF, SEYMOUR GEORGE, chem. engr., educator; b. N.Y.C., Oct. 7, 1921; s. Jacob and Sarah (Rashkin) B.; m. Elaine K. Forgash; children—Joseph, Elizabeth, Laura, Jay. B.S., Columbia U., 1940, M.S., 1941; Ph.D. in Chem. Engring, Purdue U., 1952. Research engr. Sinclair Refining Co., East Chicago, Ind., 1941-42; process engr. du Pont Manhattan project U. Chgo., Richland, Wash., Arlington, N.J., 1942-48; asst. prof. dept. chem. engring. Rose Poly. Inst., Terre Haute, Ind., 1948-52, asso. prof., 1952-54, prof., chmn. dept. chem. engring., 1954-58; NSF fellow Calif. Inst. Tech., Pasadena, 1958-59; prof. chem. engring. Northwestern U., Evanston, Ill., 1959—, Walter P. Murphy prof. chem., mech. and nuclear engring., 1971—, chmn. energy engring. council, 1975-80; vis. scientist Centre d'Etudes Nucléaires, Commissariat d'Energie Atomique, Grenoble, France, 1980; cons. to U.S. Nuclear Regulatory Commn., Argonne (Ill.) Nat. Lab., Los Alamos Sci. Lab., 1974—; Mem. adv. council Ams. for Energy Independence, Washington, 1978—. Mem. editorial adv. bd.: Internat. Jour. Multiphase Flow, 1975—; editor 6 vols. on heat transfer; contbr. 140 articles on research in heat transfer and control theory to profl. jours. Named Disting. Engring. Alumnus Purdue U., 1971; Guggenheim fellow, 1966; Fulbright fellow, 1967. Mem. Am. Inst. Chem. Engring. (chmn. edn. com. 1968-71), ASME, Am. Nuclear Soc. Office: Chem Engring Dept Northwestern Univ Evanston IL 60201

BANKS, ARTHUR SPARROW, political scientist, educator; b. Quincy, Mass., May 30, 1926; s. Gordon Thaxter and Miriam (Goodspeed) B. B.A., Cornell U., 1951; M.A., George Washington U., 1954, Ph.D., 1967. Lectr. govt. dept. U. N.H., 1959-61; research asso. Internat. Devel. Research Center, Ind. U., 1963-65; asst. prof., research asso. George Washington U., 1966-68; assoc. prof. dept. polit. sci., dir. Center for Comparative Polit. Research, SUNY, Binghamton, 1968-76; prof. dept. polit. sci., sr. fellow Center for Social Analysis, 1976—, chmn. dept. polit. sci., 1980—. Author: A Cross-Polity Survey, 1963, Cross-Polity Time-Series Data, 1971, Political Handbook of the World, 1975, 76, 77, 78, 79, 80, 81, 82, Economic Handbook of the World, 1981, 82; contbr. articles to profl. jours. Served with USMC, 1943-45. Wenner-Gren Found. grantee, 1961; NSF grantee, 1969-71; Mellon Found. grantee, 1982; Ford Found. granteee, 1982. Mem.

Am. Polit. Sci. Assn., N.Y. Polit. Sci. Assn., Peace Research Soc., Internat. Studies Assn., Pi Gamma Mu, Pi Sigma Alpha. Home: Center Rd Shirley MA 01464 Office: Center for Social Analysis SUNY Binghamton NY 13901

BANKS, BILLY WAYNE, oil field service company executive; b. Howe, Tex., Jan. 18, 1928; s. John Thomas and Virginia (Pirtle) B.; m. Ruby Jean Young, Nov. 3, 1946; Robert M., Richard A., Paul G. Student in Bus. Adminstrn., So. Methodist U., 1952. C.P.A.,Tex. Asst. div. controller Dresser Industries Inc., Dallas, 1952-63; controller Lone Star Boat Co., Plano, Tex., 1963-65; controller, treas. Tex. Aluminum Co., Rockwell, Tex., 1965-73; sr. v.p. Gearhart Industries, Inc., Fort Worth, 1973—. Mem. Am. Inst. C.P.A.s, Tex. Soc. C.P.A.s. Republican. Methodist. Club: Petroleum (Ft. Worth). Home: 4605 Ramsgate Ct Arlington TX 76013 Office: Gearhart Industries Inc 1100 Everman Rd Fort Worth TX 76140

BANKS, DAVID FRANKLIN, banker, business executive; b. Columbus, Ga., Jan. 25, 1943; s. Edward Henry and Martha Catherine (Lanier) B.; m. Christina Gay Carlson, Dec. 30, 1966; children: Geoffrey Dylan, Jessica Catherine. A.B., Kenyon Coll., 1965; J.D., U. Fla., 1968. With Chase Manhattan Bank, N.Y.C., 1968-84, v.p., asst. gen. mgr. London br., 1976-79, v.p., group exec., 1979-80; sr. v.p. Global Specialized Industries, 1980—; dir. M & M Minerals Inc. Pres. bd. trustees Internat. Ctr. Photography; trustee Kenyon Coll., Gambier, Ohio. Democrat. Episcopalian. Clubs: Am. Yacht (Rye, N.Y.); Union (N.Y.C.); Turf (London). Home: 41 Holly Ln Rye NY 10580 Office: One Chase Manhattan Plaza New York NY 10005

BANKS, DAVID RUSSELL, health care executive; b. Arcadia, Wis., Feb. 15, 1937; s. J.R. and Cleone B.; (m), Oct. 20, 1979; children: Melissa, Michael. B.A., U. Ark., 1959. Vice pres. Dabbs, Sullivan, Trulock, Ark., 1963-74; chmn., chief exec. officer Leisure Lodges, Ft. Smith, Ark., 1974-77; registered rep. Stephens Inc., Little Rock, 1974-79; pres., chief operating officer Beverly Enterprises, Pasadena, Calif., 1979—; dir. Nat. Council Health Centers, Pulaski Bank, Little Rock. Served with U.S. Army. Office: 873 S Fair Oaks Ave Pasadena CA 91105 *

BANKS, EDWIN MELVIN, biological sciences educator; b. Chgo., Mar. 21, 1926; s. David Louis and Eleanor (Johnson) B.; m. Hilda Markoff, June 20, 1950; children—Daniel, Ronald, Ellen. Ph.B., U. Chgo., 1948, B.S., 1949, M.S., 1950; Ph.D., U. Fla., 1955. Asst. prof. biology U. Ill., 1955-60, asso. prof., 1960-63, prof. ethology, head dept., 1965—; asso. prof. zoology U. Toronto, 1963-65. Author: Vertebrate Social Organization, 1977, Animal Behavior, 1977; author articles in field. Served with USNR, 1943-46. H.F. Guggenheim Found. grantee, 1977-78. Fellow AAAS, Animal Behavior Soc. (pres. 1972); mem. Am. Soc. Zoologists, Am. Soc. Mammalogists, Ecol. Soc. Am., Internat. Ethological Soc., Soc. Study of Aggression, Sigma Xi. Jewish. Club: Rotary. Office: 515 Morrill Hall University of Illinois 505 Goodwin Ave Urbana IL 61801

BANKS, EPHRAIM, educator; b. Norfolk, Va., Apr. 21, 1918; s. Israel and Ada (Gesunsky) B.; m. Libby Kohl, Mar. 17, 1945; children—Thomas Israel, Jay Lewis. B.S., Coll. City N.Y., 1937; Ph.D., Bklyn. Poly. Inst., 1949. Various positions to jr. metallurgist U.S. Naval Shipyard, Bklyn., 1938-46; with Poly. Inst. Bklyn. (now Poly. Inst. N.Y.), 1946—, prof., 1958—, head dept. chemistry, 1968-76; Cons. chemistry and electronics to corps. Editor: (with others) Structure Reports, 1963; asso. editor of: Jour. Electrochem. Soc, 1957—; editorial bd. of: Jour. Solid State Chemistry, 1969—. Served with USNR, 1944-46. Weizmann fellow, 1963-64; NSF faculty fellow, 1971-72. Fellow AAAS, N.Y. Acad. Sci.; mem. Am. Chem. Soc., Am. Phys. Soc., Am. Crystallog. Assn., Mineral. Soc., Electrochem. Soc. Research on solid state chemistry, crystal growth, magnetic materials, luminescence. Home: 2307 Stuart St Brooklyn NY 11229

BANKS, ERNEST (ERNIE BANKS), baseball exec.; b. Dallas, Jan. 31, 1931; s. Eddie B.; m. Eloyee Ector, Apr. 6, 1953. Grad. high sch.; student, Grad. Sch. Bus., Northwestern U. Player with Kansas City Monarchs (Negro Am. League), 1950-51, 53; shortstop, then 1st baseman Chgo. Cubs, 1953-71, now mgr. group sales; formerly co-owner, v.p. Bob Nelson-Ernie Banks Ford, Inc., Chgo. Author: (with Jim Enright) Mr. Cub. Past mem. bd. Chgo. Transit Authority.; Active Boy Scouts Am., YMCA. Served with AUS, 1951-53; Europe. Named most valuable player Nat. League, 1958, 59; recipient awards from Fans, 1969, Press Club, 1969, Jr. C. of C., 1971; named Nat. League Most Valuable Player award, 1958, 59, to Tex. Sports Hall Fame, 1971, Baseball Hall of Fame, 1977. Played in 13 All Star Games; holds nat. record for Grand Slam home runs. Address: PO Box 10613 Chicago IL 60610

BANKS, HARVEY OREN, consultant civil engineer; b. Chaumont, N.Y., Mar. 29, 1910; s. Harry Roseboom and Carrie Ethel (Halliday) B.; m. Mary Ida Morgan, Dec. 14, 1934; children—Robert Stephen, Philip Oren, Kimball Morgan. B.S.C.E. magna cum laude, Syracuse (N.Y.) U., 1930; M.S., Stanford U., 1955. Diplomate: Am. Acad. Environ. Engrs. Asst. state engr., then state engr. State of Calif., 1953-56, dir. water resources, 1956-60; v.p., pres., then chmn. Leeds, Hill & Jewett, Inc. (cons. engrs.), San Francisco, 1961-69; pres., owner Harvey O. Banks, Cons. Engr., Inc., Belmont, Calif., 1970-76; pres. water resources div. Camp Dresser & McKee Inc.; environ. consultants Walnut Creek, Calif., 1977-82; pres., owner Harvey O. Banks, Cons. Engr., Inc., 1983—; chmn. bd. dirs. Systems Assocs., Inc., 1970-76; bd. dirs. Belmont County Water Dist., 1972-80; cons., lectr. in field. Served with U.S. Army, 1942-45. Recipient George Arents Pioneer medal Syracuse U., 1961. Fellow Am. Cons. Engrs. Council, ASCE (hon., Royce J. Tipton award 1973, Julian Hinds award 1976); mem. Nat. Acad. Engring., Am. Water Works Assn. (hon.), Water Pollution Control Fedn., Am. Water Resources Assn. (Ikbo Iben award 1980). Methodist. Home and Office:: 3 Kittie Ln Belmont CA 94002

BANKS, HENRY H., physician, dean; b. Boston, Mar. 9, 1921; s. Isaac and Bessie B.; m. Judith Epstein, June 1945; children—Nancy (Mrs. Curt Civin), Betsy (Mrs. David Epstein), Steven. A.B. cum laude, Harvard U., 1942; M.D., Tufts U., 1945. Diplomate: Am. Bd. Orthopedic Surgery (pres. 1978-79, exec. dir. 1979—). Surg. intern Beth Israel Hosp., Boston, 1945-46, asst. resident in surgery, 1947-49; asst. resident orthopedic lab. and pathology Children's Hosp., Boston, 1949-50, asst. resident orthopedic surgery, 1950-51, Mass. Gen. Hosp., Boston, 1951-52; chief resident orthopedic surgery Peter Bent Brigham Hosp., Boston, 1952, Children's Hosp. Med. Center, 1952-53; practice medicine, specializing in orthopedic surgery, Boston, 1953—; prof., chmn. orthopedic surgery Tufts U. Sch. Medicine, 1970—, asso. dean, 1972—, sr. assoc. dean med. affairs, 1982, acting med. dean, then med. dean, 1983—; dir. orthopedic surgery Boston City Hosp., 1970-74; orthopedic surgeon-in-chief New Eng. Med. Center Hosps.; mem. Am. Bd. Med. Spltys. Editor: The Pediatric Clinics of North America-Musculoskeletal Disorders I, 1967; guest editor: Clinical Orthopedics and Related Research, 1968, Orthopedic Clinics of North America, 1976, 78; Contbr. articles to profl. jours. Trustee Kennedy Meml. Hosp., Boston, Mass. chpt. Arthritis Found. Served with M.C. AUS, 1945-47. Mem. Assn. Orthopedic chairmen, Am. Orthopedic Assn., Am. Acad. Orthopedic Surgeons, AMA, A.C.S., Am. Acad. Cerebral Palsy (pres.), Eastern Orthopedic Assn., Mass. Med. Soc., New Eng. Surg. Soc., Internat. Soc. Orthopedic Surgery and Traumatology, Boston Orthopedic Club (pres.), Pediatric Orthopedic Soc. Clubs: Harvard, Aesculapian, University (Boston). Home: 15 Radcliffe Rd Weston ME 02193 Office: 171 Harrison Ave Boston MA 02111

BANKS, JAMES ALBERT, educator; b. Marianna, Ark., Sept. 24, 1941; s. Matthew and Lula (Holt) B.; m. Cherry Ann McGee, Feb. 15, 1969; children: Angela Marie, Patricia Ann. A.A., Chgo. City Coll., 1963; B.E., Chgo. State U., 1964; M.A. (NDEA fellow 1966-69), Mich. State U., 1967, Ph.D., 1969. Tchr. elementary sch. Joliet, Ill., 1965, Francis W. Parker Sch., Chgo., 1965-66; asst. prof. edn. U. Wash., Seattle, 1969-71, assoc. prof., 1971-73, prof., 1973—, chmn. curriculum and instrn., 1982—; vis. prof. edn. U. Mich., 1975; Disting. scholar lectr. Kent State U., 1978, U. Ariz., 1979, Ind. U., 1983; vis. scholar Brit. Acad., June 1983; mem. com. examiners (social studies) Ednl. Testing Service, 1974-77; mem. nat. adv. council on ethnic heritage studies U.S. Office Edn., 1975-78; chmn. Nat. Council for Social Studies Task Force on Ethnic Studies Curriculum Guidelines, 1975-76. Author: Teaching Strategies for Ethnic Studies, 1975, 2d edit., 1979, 3d edit., 1983, Teaching Strategies for the Social Studies, 1973, 2d edit., 1977, Black Self-Concept, 1972, Teaching the Black Experience, 1970, Multiethnic Education: Practices and Promises, 1977, (with Cherry Ann Banks) March Toward Freedom: A History of Black Americans, 1970, 2d edit., 1974, rev. 2d edit., 1978, (with others) Curriculum Guidelines for Multiethnic Education, 1976, Multiethnic Education: Theory and Practice, 1981, We Americans: Our History and People, 2 vols., 1982; editor: Teaching Ethnic Studies: Concepts and Strategies, 1973, (with William W. Joyce) Teaching Social Studies to Culturally Different Children, 1971, Teaching the Language Arts to Culturally Different Children, 1971, Education in the 80's: Multiethnic Education, 1981; editorial bd.: Rev. of Edn, 1974—, Council Interracial Books for Children Bull; contbr. articles to profl. jours. Recipient Outstanding Young Man award Wash. State Jaycees, 1975; Spencer fellow Nat. Acad. Edn., 1973-76; Kellogg fellow, 1980-83; Rockefeller Found. fellow, 1980. Mem. Nat. Council Social Studies (dir. 1973-74, 82—, v.p. 1980, pres.-elect 1981, pres. 1982), Assn. Supervision and Curriculum Devel. (dir. 1976-79), Social Sci. Edn. Consortium (dir. 1976-79), Am. Ednl. Research Assn., Phi Delta Kappa, Phi Kappa Phi. Home: 1333 NW 200th St Seattle WA 98177 *One of the greatest strengths of our nation is its tremendous ethnic, racial, and cultural diversity. A major goal of my career is to increase understanding and communication across different ethnic and racial groups and to make it possible for each ethnic and racial group to make its greatest contribution to the nation. My belief that the public school can play a major role in improving race relations in our nation has greatly influenced my life and career.*

BANKS, JEFFREY, fashion designer. Student, Parsons Sch. Design, N.Y.C. Menswear designer Concorde Internat.; creator's men's fur collection for Alixandre; designer for B. Glanzrock, Lakeland, Merona Sports, 1981, Oxford Industries, Jeffrey Banks div., 1982—. Recipient Saga Mink awards, Coty award, 1982. Mem. Fashion Inst. Tech. (bd. dirs.). Office: Jeffrey Banks Ltd 126 Fifth Ave New York NY 10011 *

BANKS, JOHN HOUSTON, educator; b. Ripley, Tenn., Feb. 9, 1911; s. Roderick Stanton and Ella Celestine (Sinclair) B.; m. Mary Rhea Fowler, Mar. 11, 1933; children—John Fowler, Betty Rhea. B.S., Tenn. Poly. Inst., 1935; M.A., George Peabody Coll. Tchrs., 1938, Ph.D., 1949. Tchr. Tenn. pub. schs., 1934-42; instr. 133d Army Tng. Detachment, 1942-44; dean East Central Jr. Coll., Decatur, Miss., 1944-46; prof. math. Florence (Ala.) State Coll., 1946-49; asso. prof. math. George Peabody Coll. Tchrs., Nashville, 1949-58, prof. math., 1958-79, prof. emeritus, 1979—; chmn. dept., 1959-75; vis. prof. edn. Auburn U., 1956, New Brunswick (Can.) U., 1960; Adviser Am. Council Edn., 1960; cons. AID/ROCAP Textbook Project in C.Am., 1964-70. Author: Elements of Mathematics, 3d edit, 1969, Learning and Teaching Arithmetic, 2d edit, 1964, (with A. Wheeler) Teachers Question and Answer Book on Arithmetic, 1960, (with F.L. Wren) Elements of Algebra, 1962, (with M. Sobel) Algebra: Its Elements and Structure, 1965, 3d edit., 1977, (with Butler and Wren) The Teaching of Secondary Mathematics, 5th edit., 1970, (with others) Geometry: Its Elements and Structure, 1972, 2d edit., 1977. Mem. Tenn. Math. Tchrs. Assn. (pres. 1954), Nat. Council Tchrs. Math. (dir. 1960-63), Tenn. Acad. Scis., Nat., Tenn. edn. assns., Math. Assn. Am., Sigma Xi, Kappa Delta Pi, Phi Delta Kappa, Pi Mu Epsilon. Home: 3708 Lealand Ln Nashville TN 37204 *A love of mathematics, its esthetic appeal, and an overriding compulsion to share it have dominated every major decision in my professional life.*

BANKS, J(OSEPH) EUGENE, investment economist; b. Kirksville, Mo., Jan. 26, 1908; s. Charles and Etta May (Dille) B.; m. Ruth Henckler, Oct. 1, 1932; m. Barbara H. Vietor, Apr. 21, 1956; 1 foster dau., Diana V. Mundy. B.S., Washington U., 1930. Investment analyst Boatmen's Nat. Bank, St. Louis, 1930-31; mgr. pvt. investment funds, St. Louis, 1932-37; market analyst Merrill Lynch, Pierce, Fenner & Beane, N.Y.C., 1938-42; investment economist Brown Bros. Harriman & Co., N.Y.C., 1942, 45-80, asst. mgr., 1950-57, mgr., 1957-61, partner, 1962—, head instnl. div., 1950-77. Author: Guides to Stock Market Policy, 1949, Institutional Investment Guides, 1955, Guides to Growth Stock Investing, 1959; also articles in field. Trustee Tchrs. Coll. Columbia U.; bd. dirs. St. Margaret's House, N.Y.C. Served to lt. comdr. USCGR, 1942-45. Mem. Mil. Order World Wars, Navy League, Pilgrims, Theta Xi. Episcopalian. Clubs: University, Downtown Assn. (N.Y.C.). Home: 880 Fifth Ave New York NY 10021 also Long Beach Rd Saint James NY 11780 Office: 59 Wall St New York NY 10005

BANKS, LLOYD J., insurance company executive; b. Indpls., Dec. 9, 1923; s. Estille and Bernice (Jackson) B.; m. Phyllis Ann Burns, Jan. 31, 1951; children: David Lloyd, Cheri Janeen. Student, Morehead (Ky.) State U., 1941-42, Miami U., Oxford, Ohio, 1944, 46-47, U. Mich., 1955-56. Investigator Retail Credit Co., 1947-49; with Blue Cross-Blue Shield Ind., Indpls., 1949—, group v.p., then exec. v.p., 1974-76, pres., 1976—; chmn., chief exec. officer Regional Mktg. Inc.; chmn. bd., chief exec. officer Alexander Nat. Group Inc.; chmn. bd. Assos. Life Ins. Inc., Alexander Nat. Life Ins. Inc.; dir. Mut. Hosp. Ins., Inc., Ind. Nat. Bank, Internat. Fin. Services Inc. Served with USNR, 1942-46. Mem. Ind. C. of C. (bd. dirs.). Clubs: Columbia, Meridian Hills Country, Masons, Shriners, Rotary. Home: 1210 Willow Way Noblesville IN 46060 Office: 120 W Market St Indianapolis IN 42604

BANKS, LOUIS LAYTON, editor, educator; b. Pitts., June 17, 1916; s. Louis Layton and Laura S. (Shrom) B.; m. Mary Margaret Campbell, Apr. 21, 1945; children—Robert, William, Theodore, Margaret Czekaj. A.B., U. Calif. at Los Angeles, 1937, postgrad., 1938-40; D.H.L., Rollins Coll., 1968, Wilkes Coll., 1980, Harvard U., 1969-70. Corr., editor Time mag., 1945-61; asst. mng. editor Fortune mag., 1961-65, mng. editor, 1965-70; editorial dir. Time Inc., 1970-73, dir., Harvard Mag., Foote, Cone & Belding Communications Inc.; Carroll Ford Found.; vis. prof. Bus. Sch., Harvard, 1973-76; adj. prof. mgmt. Sloan Sch. Mgmt. Mass. Inst. Tech., 1976—. Served as naval aviator USNR, 1941-45. Mem. N.Y.C. Council on Fgn. Relations. Clubs: Naples (Fla.) Yacht; Indian Creek Country (Kilmarnock, Va.); St. Botolph's (Boston). Home: Naples FL 33940 Office: Sloan Sch Mgmt Mass Inst Tech Cambridge MA 02139

BANKS, PETER MORGAN, educator; b. San Diego, May 21, 1937; s. George Willard and Mary Margaret (Morgan) B.; m. Paulett M. Behanna, May 21, 1983; children by previous marriage: Kevin, Michael, Steven, David. M.S. in E.E, Stanford U., 1960; Ph.D. in Physics, Pa. State U., 1965. Postdoctoral fellow Institut d'Aeronomie Spatiale de Belgigue, Brussels, Belgium, 1965-66; prof. applied physics U. Calif., San Diego, 1966-76; prof. physics Utah State U., 1976-81, head dept. physics, 1976-81; prof. elec. engring. Stanford U., 1981—, vis. asso. prof., 1972-73; vis. scientist Max Planck Inst. for Aeronomie, Ger., 1975; pres. La Jolla Scis. Inc., 1973-77, Upper Atmosphere Research Corp., 1978-82. Author: (with G. Kockarts) Aeronomy, 1973, (with J.R. Doupnik) Introduction to Computer Science, 1976; Assoc. editor Jour.: Geophys. Research, 1974-77, Planetary and Space Sci, 1977—; regional editor, 1983—; Contbr. (with J.R. Doupnik) numerous articles in field to profl. jours. Mem. space sci. adv. council NASA, 1976-80. Served with U.S. Navy, 1960-63. Recipient Appleton prize Royal Soc. London, 1978; Space Sci. award Am. Inst. Aeros. and Astronautics, 1981. Mem. Am. Geophys. Union, Internat. Union Radio Sci. Episcopalian. Clubs: Am. Youth Soccer Assn., Cosmos. Home: 23 Peter Coults Circle Stanford CA 94305 Office: Elec Engring Dept Stanford U Stanford CA 94305

BANKS, ROBERT BLACKBURN, univ. pres.; b. Wichita, Kans., Oct. 12, 1922; s. Bernard T. and Georgia (Corley) B.; m. Gunta Matisons, Dec. 25, 1960; children—Steven, Erik. B.S., Northwestern U., 1947, M.S., 1948; Ph.D. (Hilp fellow), U. Calif., 1951; D.I.C., U. London, 1952. Research engr. U. Calif., 1949-51, Infilco, Inc., Tucson, 1952-54; asso. prof. civil engring. Northwestern U., 1954-59, chmn. sci.-engring. com., 1955-57, chmn. dept. civil engring., 1956-59, asst. dean research and grad. studies, prof. engring. sci., 1959-61; dir. research Asian Inst. Tech., Bangkok, Thailand, 1961-63; dean engring. U. Ill., Chgo., 1963-67; adviser sci. and tech. Ford Found., Mex. and C.Am., 1967-76; prof. Grad. Sch. Engring., Nat. U. Mex., 1967-76; v.p., provost Asian Inst. Tech., Bangkok, 1976-77, pres., 1977—. Served from ensign to lt. USNR, 1943-46. Fulbright fellow U. London, 1951-52. Mem. ASCE, AAAS, Internat. Assn. for Hydraulic Research, Am. Geophys. Union, Am. Soc. Engring. Edn., Sigma Xi, Tau Beta Pi, Pi Mu Epsilon, Delta Nu Alpha, Sigma Chi. Home: 34 Soi 19 Sukumvit Bangkok Thailand Office: Asian Inst of Technology Box 2754 Bangkok Thailand

BANKS, ROBERT LOUIS, research chemist; b. Piedmont, Mo., Nov. 24, 1921; s. James Arthur and Maude Lelia (McAllister) B.; m. Mildred Kathleen Lambeth, Aug. 30, 1947; children: Susan Lee, Mary Kathleen, Melissa Ann. Student, S.E. Mo. State Coll., 1940-42; B.S. in Chem. Engring, U. Mo., Rolla, 1944, 1976; M.S., Okla. State U., 1953. Process engr. Coop. Refinery, Coffeyville, Kans., 1944-45; research chemist Phillips Petroleum Co., Bartlesville, Okla., 1946-66, research asso., 1967-80, sr. research asso., 1980—. Recipient Okla. Chemist award, 1974; award Am. Inst. Chemists, 1981. Mem. Am. Chem. Soc. (award in petroleum chemistry 1979, mem. adv. bd. for petroleum research fund 1981—), N. Am. Catalysis Soc. Methodist. Clubs: Masons, Elks, Hillcrest Country, Sunset Country and Golf. Pioneer initial process for producing high density polyethylene; discoverer chem. reaction, olefin metathesis disproportionation. Patentee/crystalline polypropylene. Office: Phillips Petroleum Co Bartlesville OK 74004

BANKS, ROBERT SHERWOOD, lawyer; b. Newark, Mar. 28, 1934; s. Howard Douglas and Amelia Violet (Del Bagno) B.; m. Judith Lee Henry; children—Teri, William; children by previous marriage—Robert, Paul, Stephen, Roger, Gregory, Catherine. A.B., Cornell U., 1956, LL.B., 1958. Bar: N.J. bar 1959, N.Y. State bar 1968. Practice law, Newark, 1958-61; atty. E.I. duPont, Wilmington, Del., 1961-67; with Xerox Corp., Stamford, Conn., 1967—, v.p., gen. counsel, 1976—; Adv. com. Center for Law and Econs. Studies, Columbia U., N.Y.C.; exec. com. Center for Public Resources, N.Y.C. Div. chmn. Tri-State United Way, 1982. Mem. Am. Bar Assn., Am. Arbitration Assn., Practicing Law Inst., Fed. Bar Council, Cornell Law Assn., Am. Corporate Counsel Assn. (chmn.), Tau Kappa Epsilon. Club: Aspetuck Valley Country. Home: 29 Laurel Rd New Canaan CT 06840 Office: Xerox Corp Stamford CT 06904

BANKS, RUSSELL, chemical company executive; b. N.Y.C., Aug. 2, 1919; s. Thomas and Fay (Cowen) B.; m. Janice Reed, July 19, 1949; 1 son, Gordon L. B.B.A., CCNY, 1936-40; J.D., N.Y. Law Sch., 1960. Bar: N.Y. 1961. Sr. acct. Selverne, Davis Co., N.Y.C., 1940-45; pvt. practice as C.P.A., N.Y.C., 1945-61; exec. v.p. Met. Telecommunications Corp., Plainview, N.Y., 1961-62; pres., chief exec. officer Grow Group, Inc. (formerly Grow Chem. Corp.), N.Y.C., 1962—, also dir.; dir. Bainco Corp. Editor: Managing the Small Company. Recipient award of achievement Sch. of Bus. Alumni Soc. of CCNY, 1977; Winthrop-Sears medal Chem. Industry Assn., 1980. Mem. Am. Mgmt. Assn. (gen. mgmt. planning council 1966—), Conf. Bd. (regional council, Phi Delta Phi.). Clubs: Met. (N.Y.C.); Annabel's (London). Home: 1000 Park Ave New York NY 10028 also Pawling NY 12564 Office: 200 Park Ave New York NY 10166

BANKS, SAMUEL ALSTON, college president; b. Frostproof, Fla., May 16, 1928; s. Samuel Alston and Mary Gatewood (Pulliam) B.; m. Joanne Trautmann; children: Samuel Andrew, Lisa Hughes, Piers. A.B., Duke U., 1949; M.Div., Emory U., 1952; Ph.D., U. Chgo., 1971; D. Litt., Coll. Charleston, 1976. Ordained to ministry Meth. Ch., 1951; minister various chs., 1950-59; asst. prof. Drew U., Madison, N.J., 1959-62; asst. prof. psychiatry, sr. chaplain U. Fla. Coll. Medicine, 1963-70, assoc. prof., chief div. social sci. and humanities, 1970-75; pres. Dickinson Coll., Carlisle, Pa., 1975—, chmn. bd. dir. Aardvark, Inc.; Cons. humanities programs in colls. of medicine. Pres. Dist. V Mental Health Bd., Fla., 1973-74; Trustee Thomas Jefferson U., Bethune-Cookman Coll., Dickinson Coll.; mem. founders bd. Transylvania U.; mem. higher edn. adv. com. Pa. Public TV Network; bd. dirs. Inst. Human Values in Med. Edn., Milton Helpern Library Legal Medicine; mem. Gen. Pub. Utilities Nuclear Safety Adv. Bd., 1982. Co-editor: The Health of a Rural County, 1976; Contbr. chpts. to books, articles to profl. jours. Mem. univ. senate United Meth. Ch., 1977—, pres. univ. senate, 1982—; mem. Pa. Humanities Council; bd. consultants Nat. Endowment for Humanities; mem. Pa. Humanities Council, 1979-82. Recipient Liberty Bell award Pa. Bar Assos., 1978; Ann. award Soc. Health and Human Values; Fla. Endowment for Humanities grantee, 1975; Nat. Endowment for Humanities grantee, 1974-75. Fellow Soc. for Values in Higher Edn.; mem. Am. Acad. Religion, Soc. for Health and Human Values (pres. 1972-73), Am. Assn. Colls. (commn. curriculum and faculty devel.), Pa. Assn. Colls. and Univs. (exec. com. 1976-83), Soc. Am. Magicians, Internat. Brotherhood of Magicians, Carlisle C. of C. (hon.), Phi Beta Kappa, Phi Kappa Psi, Omicron Delta Kappa, Phi Eta Sigma, Psi Chi. Clubs: Players, Met., Univ. (N.Y.C.); Union League (Phila.); Rotary (hon.). Home: 212 W High St Carlisle PA 17013

BANKS, SEYMOUR, educator; b. Chgo., Oct. 3, 1917; s. Louis and Dorothy (Hass) B.; m. Miriam Gollub, Jan. 30, 1949; children: Hannah L., Joel A., David E. Student, No. Ill. State Tchrs. Coll., 1934-36; B.S. in Chem. Engring, Ia. State Coll., 1939; M.B.A., U. Chgo., 1940; Ph.D. (Swift Consumer Preference Measurement and Laminated Paperboard fellows), U. Chgo., 1949. Elec. testing asst. Prest-O-Lite Storage Battery, Speedway, Ind., 1939-40; metall. observer Gary Works, Carnegie-Ill. Steel Corp., 1940-42; asso. prof. De Paul U. Coll. Commerce, Chgo., 1946-51; with research and media depts. Leo

Burnett U.S.A., Chgo., 1951-80, v.p., 1955-80; prof. Université des Sciences Sociales de Grenoble, France, 1981—; lectr. U. Chgo., 1960-78; vis. prof. advt. Mich. State U., U. Ill., 1970. Author: Experimentation in Marketing, 1965; also articles. Vice chmn. Hyde Park-Kenwood Community Conf., 1962-65; pres. Ray Sch. PTA, Chgo., 1965-67; mem. citizens com. U. Ill., 1970-80; pres. Hyde Park Coop. Soc., 1951-54, 59-61, 70-71. Served with AUS, 1942-46. Mem. Am. Mktg. Assn. (pres. Chgo. chpt. 1954-55, v.p. mktg. research div. 1964-65, chmn. ethics com. 1969—, v.p. pub. policy and issue div. 1976-77), Chgo. Ednl. TV Assn. (trustee 1978-81), Am. Statis. Assn., Am. Psychol. Assn., Advt. Research Found. (dir. 1974-79, chmn. tech. com.). Home: 5625 S Blackstone Ave Chicago IL 60637 Office: BP47X 38040 Grenoble Cedex France

BANKS, VIRGINIA, artist; b. Norwood, Mass., Jan. 12, 1920; d. Henry Lewis and Ottilie (Rietzel) B.; m. Arthur W. Freidinger, Jan. 1, 1946. A.B., Smith Coll., 1941; M.A., State U. Iowa, 1944. Instr. art State U. Iowa, 1942-47, Albright Art Sch., 1947-48, U. Buffalo, 1947-48, N.Y. State Tchrs. Coll., 1947-48, U. Wash., 1949, Cornish Art Sch., Seattle, 1951-52; Area chmn. capital campaign Smith Coll., 1968-70. One-woman shows include, Grand Central Moderns, N.Y.C., 1950, 52, 56, 59, 65, Dusanne Gallery, Seattle, 1952, 58, Collectors Gallery, Bellevue, Wash., 1965, Foster-White Gallery, Seattle, 1977, 80, exhibited nat. and internat. shows, 1946—, represented in permanent collections, U. Ill., Seattle Art Mus., IBM Coll., U. Oreg., San Francisco Mus. Art, Springfield (Mo.) Art Mus., Davenport (Iowa) Municipal Art Gallery, Plattsburg (N.Y.) State Tchrs. Coll., State U. Iowa, U. Notre Dame, Cornell U., Rainier Nat. Bank, Peoples Nat. Bank, Seattle, Pacific NW Bell collection, Seattle, U. Wash. Med. Sch., Seattle, Duxbury (Mass.) Art Complex, Mass. Sheldon Meml. Art Gallery, U. Nebr., Lincoln, Ency. Brit. Collection Contemporary Am. Painting, Safeco Ins. Hdqrs., Seattle. Recipient award Pepsi-Cola Competition, 1948, Hallmark Internat. Art award, 1949. Mem. Alpha Phi Kappa Psi, Pi Lambda Theta. Clubs: Smith Coll. (Seattle) (pres. 1960-61, hon. bd. mem. 1967-68. Address: 3879 51st Ave NE Seattle WA 98105

BANKS, WARREN EUGENE, lawyer, finance educator; b. Hot Springs, Ark., Feb. 1, 1929; s. Warren Eugene and Helen Frances (Shaw) B.; m. Carolyn Beth Duty, Dec. 27, 1952; children—Karen Marie, Keith Randolph. B.S. in Bus. Adminstrn, U. Ark., 1950, J.D., 1953, M.B.A., 1960, Ph.D., 1968. Bar: Ark. bar 1953, U.S. Supreme Ct. bar 1956. Practiced in, Hot Springs, 1953; investigator GAO, 1955-57; mem. faculty U. Ark., Fayetteville, 1957—, prof. fin., 1970-82, chmn. dept., 1978-82; disting. prof. fin., Harold A. Dulan prof., 1982—; mem. part-time faculty Law Sch., 1957—; of counsel firm Kincaid, Horne & Trumbo, Fayetteville, 1965—. Author articles in field. Vestryman St. Paul's Epis. Ch., Fayetteville, 1964-66, 69-71, lay reader, 1964, treas. bldg. fund, 1962, clk. of vestry, 1962-63. Served to 1st lt. USAF, 1953-55. Recipient Faculty Achievement award U. Ark. Alumni Assn., 1973. Mem. Am. Trial Lawyers Assn., Ark. Bar Assn., Am. Bus. Law Assn., Am. Fin. Assn., Fin. Mgmt. Assn., Omicron Delta Kappa, Beta Gamma Sigma, Beta Alpha Psi, Alpha Kappa Psi, Phi Alpha Delta, Sigma Pi. Office: Coll Bus Adminstrn U Ark Fayetteville AR 72701 also Walker-Stone House 207 W Center St Fayetteville AR 72701

BANKSON, DOUGLAS HENNECK, creative writing educator, playwright; b. Valley, Wash., May 13, 1920; s. Russell Arden and Ella Etna (Henneck) B.; m. Beverly Olga Carlson, June12, 1943; children: Jon Douglas, Daniel Duke, Barbro Sloan. B.A., U. Wash., 1943, M.A., 1949, Ph.D., 1954. Reporter, columnist Seattle Star, 1942-43, 46; account exec., copywriter Beatty Stevens Agy., Seattle, 1946-50; freelance advt. agt., Seattle, 1950-51, 52-54; dir. research Frye Art Mus., Seattle, 1951-52; instr. English and humanities U. Idaho, 1955-57; asst. prof. English U. Mont., 1957-59, assoc. prof. drama, assoc. dir. theater, resident playwright, 1956-65; prof. playwriting U. B.C., Vancouver, 1975—, head dept. creative writing, 1976-83; dir. Masquer Summer Theatre, Missoula, Mont., 1961-65. Author: plays Shellgame, 1960, Mr. Magoo, 1960, The Waterwitch, 1960, The Ball, 1961, Nature in the Raw is Seldom, 1962, Fallout, 1963, Shootup, 1963, Resthome, 1965, The Ants Go Marching One by One, 1966, Many Happy Returns, 1969, Stonehenge, 1972, Lenore Nevermore, 1972, Sigmore Lizard, 1974, Whistle, 1977, The Schweinhuf Quarter, 1978, Ella, 1981, Felicity, 1982. Served as lt. (j.g.) USNR, 1943-46; PTO. Mem. Can. Assn. Univ. Tchrs., Guild Can. Playwrights, Faculty Assn. U. B.C., New Play Centre (pres. bd. 1970-82), Green Thumb Players (v.p. bd. 1978-82). Home: 4722 W 2d Ave Vancouver BC Canada V6T 1B9 Office: Univ BC Creative Writing Dept Vancouver BC Canada V6T 1W5

BANKSTON, ARCHIE MOORE, JR., lawyer, utility executive; b. Memphis, Oct. 12, 1937; s. Archie M. and Elsie Bernice (Shaw) B.; m. Emma Ann Dejan, Apr. 16, 1966; 1 dau., Alice. B.A., Fisk U., 1959; LL.B., Washington U., St. Louis, 1962, M.B.A., 1964. Bar: Mo. bar 1963, N.Y. State bar 1966. Asst. div. counsel Gen. Foods Corp., White Plains, N.Y., 1964-67; product mgr. Maxwell House div., 1967-69; asst. sec. and corp. counsel PepsiCo, Inc., Purchase, N.Y., 1969-72; div. counsel Xerox Corp., Stamford, Conn., 1973; sec. and asst. gen. counsel Consol. Edison Co. of N.Y. Inc., N.Y.C., 1974—; Bd. dirs. Mental Health Assn. Westchester County. Former bd. dirs. Urban League of Westchester; mem. 100 Black Men, Inc., N.Y.C. Recipient Black Achievers in Industry award Harlem br. YMCA, 1971, Merit award Black Exec. Exchange Program Nat. Urban League, 1974. Mem. Am. Soc. Corp. Secs. (dir., chmn. budget com., mem. edn. com. 1974—), Stockholder Relations Soc. N.Y. (past dir.), Am. Bar Assn., Phi Delta Phi, Sigma Pi Phi, Alpha Phi Alpha. Club: Westchester Clubmen. Home: Consolidated Edison Co 4 Irving Place New York NY 10003 Office: 4 Irving Pl New York NY 10003

BANKSTON, GENE CLIFTON, oil and gas company executive; b. McAlester, Okla., Aug. 22, 1924; s. Charles Clifton and Olus (Ritter) B.; m. Jo Earle Roberts, Aug. 2, 1943; children: Ronald, Karen. B.S. in Petroleum Engring., U. Okla., 1949. Registered profl. engr., Tex. With Shell Oil Co., 1949-80, regional exploration and prodn. v.p., Houston, 1966-72; head office prodn., v.p. Houston, 1972-80; pres., dir. Moran Energy Inc., Houston, 1980-84; exec. v.p., dir. Kaneb Services, Inc., Houston, 1984—; pres. Moran Energy div. Kaneb Services, Inc., Houston, 1984—; dir. First City Bank-North Belt, Houston. Served with USAAF, 1943-45. Decorated Air medal with 4 oak leaf clusters. Mem. Internat. Assn. Drilling Contractors, Soc. Petroleum Engrs., Am. Petroleum Inst., Houston C. of C. (past dir.). Republican. Methodist. Clubs: Ramada, Lakeside Country. Home: 11610 Shady Grove Ln Houston TX 77024 Office: 14141 Southwest Freeway Houston TX 77487

BANNAN, BERNARD JEROME (BARNEY BANNAN), gear co. exec.; b. San Francisco, Aug. 26, 1920; m. Catherine McNamara, Sept. 1, 1945; 10 children. B. Mech. Engring. cum laude, U. Santa Clara, 1942. With Western Gear Corp., Seattle, 1945-50, Lynwood, Calif., 1950—, exec. v.p., 1958-63, pres., 1963-71, chmn., 1971—; dir. Jacobs Engring. Group, Inc., Pasadena, Calif., Aerochem, Inc., Orange, Calif., Miller Printing Equipment Corp., Pitts. Trustee, chmn. bd. Loyola-Marymount U., Los Angeles. Served to maj., ordnance U.S. Army, 1942-45. Mem. Shipbuilders Council Am. (dir.), Machinery and Allied Products Inst. (exec. bd.), Conf. Bd., Aerospace Industries Assn. Am., Am. Def. Preparedness Assn., Ireland-U.S. Council (dir. West Coast chpt.). Clubs: Burning Tree (Washington); Bohemian (San Francisco); Eldorado Country (Palm Desert, Calif.); Calif. (Los Angeles); Annandale Golf (Pasadena, Calif.); San Gabriel (Calif.) Country; Newport Harbor Yacht (Newport Beach, Calif.). Office: Western Gear Corp PO Box 182 Lynwood CA 90262

BANNARD, WALTER DARBY, artist, art critic; b. New Haven, Sept. 23, 1934; s. Homes and Janet (Darby) B. B.A., Princeton U., 1956. Lectr. in field, 1969—; vis. prof. Princeton U., 1974,; curator Hans Hoffman, Hirshhorn Mus., 1976; mem. internat. exhbn. com., 1976-78; co-chmn. internat. panel for visual arts Nat. Endowment for Arts, 1979-81; mem. art adv. com. Phillips Exeter Acad., 1977—. Contbr. articles and revs. on modern painting to profl. jours.; contbg. editor: Artforum, 1973-74; One-man shows, Tibor de Nagy Gallery, N.Y.C., 1965, 66, 67, 68, 69, Kasmin Gallery, London, 1965, 68, 69, 70, 72, Richard Feigen Gallery, Chgo., 1966, Nicholas Wilder Gallery, Los Angeles, 1967, Bennington (Vt.) Coll., 1969, David Mirvish Gallery, Toronto, Ont., Canada, 1969, 70, 75, 78, Lawrence Rubin Gallery, N.Y.C., 1970, 72, 73, Joseph Helman Gallery, St. Louis, 1970, Neuendorf Gallery, Cologne, Germany, 1971, Newport Harbor Art Mus., Newport Beach, Calif., 1972, Balt. Mus. Art, 1973, Pasadena (Calif.) Art Mus., Watson-De Nagy, Houston, 1973, 75, 77, 79, 81, Knoedler Contemporary Art, N.Y.C., 1974, 75, 76, 77, 78, 79, 80, 81, 82, numerous group shows include, Chgo. Art Mus., 1965, Mus. Modern Art, N.Y.C., 1965, 66, 72, 75, U. Pa., Phila., 1965, 66, 70, Whitney Mus. Art, N.Y.C., 1967, 71, 72, Prospect 68, Dusseldorf, Germany, 1968, Lee Gallery, Dallas, 1967, 69, 72, 75, Aldrich Mus. Contemporary Art, 1969, 72, 76, Balt. Mus. Art, 1971, Mus. d'Art Contemporain, Montreal, Can., 1973, Mus. Fine Arts, Houston, 1974, U. Va., U. Miami, 1976, Los Angeles County Mus., So. Meth. U., 1977, Guggenheim Mus., 1979, 81, represented in permanent collections at, Mus. Modern Art, N.Y.C., Balt. Mus., Nat. Gallery of Victoria, Australia, Whitney Mus. Am. Art, N.Y.C., Fogg Art Mus., Boston, Oberlin (Ohio) Coll., Newark (N.J.) Mus., Cleve. Mus., Houston Mus. Fine Arts, Met. Mus. Art, others; juror numerous competitions, 1969—. Recipient Nat. Found. Arts award, 1968-69; John Simon Guggenheim Meml. Found. fellow, 1968. Home: PO Box 1157 Princeton NJ 08540

BANNER, BOB, television producer-dir.; b. Ennis, Tex., Aug. 15, 1921; s. Robert James and Viola (Culbertson) B.; m. Alice Jane Baird, Jan. 14, 1946; children—Baird Allen, Robert James, Charles Moore. B.B.A., So. Meth. U., 1943; M.A., Northwestern U., 1948. Faculty Northwestern U. Dir.: Garroway-at-Large, NBC-TV; producer, dir.: Fred Waring Show, CBS-TV; dir.: Omnibus; TV producer, pres., Bob Banner Assos.; TV shows include Features-Warning Shot; series Don Ho Show series; children's series Jr. Almost Anything Goes; movies for TV If Things Were Different; TV series Solid Gold (Recipient Emmy award for best direction TV.). Mem. Acad. of TV Arts and Scis. Presbyn. Home: Beverly Hills CA Office: Pacific Design Center 8687 Melrose Ave Suite M-20 Los Angeles CA 90069

BANNER, DONALD WITTE, lawyer; b. Chgo., Feb. 23, 1924; s. Edward Benjamin and Bertha (Witte) B.; m. Ruth Stein, Feb. 28, 1942; children: Peggy, Donald, Brian, Mark, Pamela. B.S. in Elec. Engring., Purdue U., 1948; J.D., U. Detroit, 1952; M.P.L., John Marshall Law Sch., 1956, LL.D. (hon.), 1979. Bar: Mich. 1953, Ill. 1953, Va. 1979, D.C. 1980. Patent agt. Square D Co., Detroit, 1948-52; patent atty. Borg-Warner Corp., Chgo., 1953-63, gen. patent counsel, 1964-78; U.S. commr. patents and trademarks, Washington, 1978-79; with firm Schuyler, Banner, Birch, McKie & Beckett, Washington, 1980—; adj. prof. law John Marshall Law Sch., Chgo., 1958-78, Disting. prof. law, 1978—; mem. tech. adv. bd. U.S. Dept. Commerce, 1966-71; Mem. U.S. del. Washington Diplomatic Conf. on Patent Cooperation Treaty, 1970. Trustee John Marshall Law Sch., 1968-78. Served with USAAF, 1942-46. Mem. ABA (del. Vienna Diplomatic Conf. on Trademark Registration Treaty 1973, chmn. sect. patent, trademark and copyright law 1972-73), Ill. Bar Assn., Mich. Bar Assn., Am. Patent Law Assn. (pres. 1977-78), Patent Law Assn. Chgo., Assn. Corp. Patent Counsel (pres. 1970-71), Internat. Patent and Trademark Assn. (pres. 1980—), Licensing Execs. Soc. Lutheran. Clubs: Union League (Chgo.); University of Washington. Home: 6800 Fleetwood Dr Apt 320 McLean VA 22101 Office: Schuyler Banner Birch McKie Beckett 1000 Connecticut Ave Washington DC 20036

BANNER, WILLIAM AUGUSTUS, philosophy educator; b. Phila., Sept. 18, 1915; s. Zacharias and Nannie Beatrice (Perry) B.; m. Beatrice Vera Suggs, June 7, 1941; children: Beatrice Anne, William Perry. B.A., Pa. State U., 1935; M.Div., Yale U., 1938; M.A., Harvard U., 1944, Ph.D. (Sheldon traveling fellow), 1947. Instr. philosophy Bennett Coll., Greensboro, N.C., 1938-43; asst. to asso. prof. Sch. Religion, Howard U., Washington, 1945-55, asso. prof. philosophy, 1955-58, prof., 1958-81; assoc. dean Coll. Liberal Arts, 1971-75, chmn. dept. philosophy, 1976-81, grad. prof. philosophy, 1981—; vis. prof. philosophy Yale U., 1964-65; disting. vis. prof. U. Rochester, 1970; mem. com. of examiners for advanced philosophy test Grad. Record Exams., 1978-82. Author: Ethics: An Introduction to Moral Philosophy, 1968, Moral Norms and Moral Order: The Philosophy of Human Affairs, 1981; contbg. author: Greece: 478-336 B.C. Handbook, 1982. Bd. dirs. Hospice Care of D.C., 1980-82. Fellow Soc. Values in Higher Edn.; mem. Am. Philos. Assn., Guild Scholars of Episcopal Ch., Nat. Humanities Faculty. Club: Harvard (Washington). Home: 5719 1st St NW Washington DC 20011

BANNERMAN, ROBIN MOWAT, physician, educator; b. Alton, Eng., Feb. 2, 1928; came to U.S., 1963; s. Robert George and Charlotte (Mowat) B.; m. Franca Angela Eleonora Vescia, Oct. 31, 1953; children—Catherine Eleanora, Francesca Mowat, Isabella Bianca. B.A., Christ Ch. Coll., Oxford (Eng.) U., 1949, B.M., B.Ch., 1952, M.A., D.M., 1960; postgrad., St. Thomas' Hosp. Med. Sch., London, Eng., 1949-52. House officer St. Thomas' Hosp., London, 1952-54, med. registrar, 1955-57; fellow in medicine Washington U., St. Louis, 1957-58, Johns Hopkins U. Hosp., Balt., 1958-59; lectr. medicine, med. tutor Radcliffe Infirmary, Oxford (Eng.) U., 1960-63; asso. prof. medicine State U. N.Y. at Buffalo, 1963-70, prof. medicine, 1970—, prof. pediatrics, 1976—; vis. prof. hematology St. Thomas' Hosp., 1971. Author: Thalassemia, A Survey, 1961. Mem. nat. med. adv. bd. Cooley's Anemia Found., 1964—, March of Dimes Western N.Y., 1966—, others. Radcliffe traveling fellow, 1957-58; recipient Mod. Med. Monographs prize, 1961. Fellow A.C.P., Royal Coll. Physicians (London); mem. Brit., Am., Internat. socs. hematology, Central Soc. Clin. Research, Am. Soc. Human Genetics, Soc. Exptl. Biology and Medicine, Am. Fedn. Clin. Research, Brit. Med. Assn., AAAS. Home: 657 Auburn Ave Buffalo NY 14222 Office: 100 High St Buffalo NY 14203

BANNING, ELIZABETH (MRS. CHARLES PERRY DAVIES), color consultant; b. Waterloo, Iowa, Sept. 11, 1908; d. Evert Alonzo and Odessa Rebecca (Fogleman) Hollenbeck; m. William Clyde Morehead, Aug. 15, 1942; m. Charles Perry Davies, July 17, 1956. Student, Chgo. Art Inst., 1928-29, Northwestern U., 1930, 1932-35. As color technician and archtl. color cons. established office and lab. under name Elizabeth Banning, San Francisco, 1936; color cons. for many orgns., including A.T. & S.F. R.R., W.P. Fuller & Co., Mannings, Inc. (Petroleum Exhibitors), Spreckles Sugar Co., Standard Oil of Calif., Fred Harvey, and architects for Ford Motor Co. Collector Modern French and Am. Fine Art. Mem. Marin County Park Commn. Mem. Am. Soc. Interior Designers. Republican. Home: Rural Route 1 Box 72 Kailua-Kona HI 96740

BANNISTER, DAN WESLEY, ins. co. exec.; b. Erie, Pa., May 13, 1921; s. Earl F. and Hortense (Ashley) B.; m. Audrey M. Shell, May 20, 1944; children—Dan Wesley, Shelley, James E. B.S., Ind. U., 1942; J.D. cum laude, Albany (N.Y.) Law Sch., 1946. Bar: N.Y. bar 1947. Practiced in Rochester, 1946-49; controller Vaisey Bristol Shoe Co., Rochester, 1949-51; financial control dir. Allstate Ins. Co., Skokie, Ill., 1951-61; v.p. Security Ins. Group, New Haven, 1961-62; chief exec. officer companies in Horace Mann Ins. Group, Springfield, Ill., 1963-75; sr. v.p. ins. services, Comml. Credit Co., Balt., 1976-79; pres., chief exec. officer Gulf Ins. Cos., 1979; adv. dir. Ill. Nat. Bank Springfield. Gen. chmn. United Fund Campaign of, Springfield and Gen. chmn. United Fund Campaign of, Sangamon County, 1965-66; v.p. Springfield Central Area Devel. Assn., 1966, pres., 1967; v.p. United Community Services Springfield, 1967-68, pres., 1968-70, bd. dirs., 1967-73; chmn. Capital City R.R. Relocation Authority, 1967-75; mem. Springfield Human Relations Commn., 1973-75; trustee Lincoln Acad., 1971-74. Served with USAAF, 1942-45. Recipient Copley Press First Citizen of Springfield award, 1971. Mem. Soc. Chartered Property and Casualty Underwriters, Ill. Life Ins. Council (pres. 1971-73), Am. Acad. Actuaries, Casualty Actuarial Soc. Episcopalian. Club: Sangamo (Springfield) (pres. 1972-73). Office: 3015 Cedar Springs Dallas TX 75219

BANNISTER, ROBERT CORWIN, JR., educator; b. Bklyn., June 4, 1935; m. Robert C. and Ruth (Allen) B.; m. Joan Turner, June 8, 1958; children: Robert Stanley, Emily E., Paul Andrew, James Peter. B.A., Yale U., 1955; B.A., M.A., Oxford U., Eng., 1957, 61; Ph.D., Yale U., 1961. Intr. history Yale U., New Haven, 1960-62; asst. to full prof. Swarthmore Coll., Pa., 1962—; Bicentennial prof. U. Helsinki, Finland, 1977-78; mem. advanced placement program Ednl. Testing Service, Princeton, N.J., 1963-79. Author: Ray Stannard Baker, 1966; editor: American Values in Transition, 1972; author: Social Darwinism: Science and Myth, 1978. Mem. Am. Studies Assn., Am. Hist. Assn., Orgn. Am. Historians. Democrat. Office: Swarthmore Coll Swarthmore PA 19081

BANNISTER, WALTER S., land development and housing company executive; b. Winnipeg, Man., Can., Dec. 24, 1922; s. Walter and Adeline Ellen B.; m. Margery Jean Anderson, June 12, 1942; children: Bruce, Judith, Eric, Neal. B.S. in Mining Engring, Mich. Technol. U., 1947. Various mine engring. mgmt. positions, 1947-63; v.p. prodn. Inland Cement Industries Ltd., 1963-70, pres., chief exec. officer, 1973-77; pres., gen. mgr. Argentine Portland Cement, Buenos Aires, 1970-73; exec. v.p. Genstar Ltd. (now Genstar Corp.), San Francisco, 1977—; pres. Genstar Devel. Inc., San Francisco, 1978—. Served to capt. Canadian Army, 1942-45. Mem. Assn. Profl. Engrs. Alta. Clubs: Engineers (San Francisco); Peninsula Golf and Country (San Mateo, Calif.). Office: Genstar Devel Inc 2500 Three Embarcadero Center San Francisco CA 94111

BANNISTER, WILLIAM ROWLAND, II, assn. exec.; b. Meriden, Conn., Feb. 18, 1927; s. Rowland Higby and Frances (Stoney) B.; m. Genevieve Leach, Aug. 28, 1948; children—Linda Ann, William Rowland. Student, U. Nebr., 1944. With Flint (Mich.) Police Dept., 1954-76, capt. patrol bur., 1974-76; labor cons. State of Mich. F.O.P., Flint, 1977, nat. sec., 1973—. Editor: Nat. Jour. F.O.P, 1973—; editor: Shrine Temple Mag, 1978-79. Chmn. Genesee County Community Action Agy., 1973-74; mem. Mich. Law Enforcement Officers Tng. Council, 1972-77, chmn., 1973-74. Served with U.S. Army, 1944-52. Republican. Presbyterian. Clubs: Masons, K.T., Royal Order Jesters. Home: G-3094 Bertha St Flint MI 48504

BANNON, JACK, actor; b. Los Angeles, June 14; s. Jim and Bea Benadaret B. B.A., U. Calif., Santa Barbara. Appeared in: films Rabbit Test, Airport '77; TV films Amelia Earhart, Tail Gunner Joe; regular on TV series Lou Grant, 1977—; other TV appearances include Delvechhio, Daniel Boone, Green Acres, The Beverly Hillbillies, Petticoat Junction, Barney Miller, Kojak, Quincy, The Rockford Files, Charlie's Angels; appeared on stage Beginner's Luck, Steambath, Waiting for Godot, The Three Sisters, The Lion in Winter; Appeared in actor in indsl. films. *

BANOWSKY, WILLIAM SLADE, university president; b. Abilene, Tex., Mar. 4, 1936; s. Wade Lowell and Thelma (Slater) B.; m. Gay Constance Barnes, Sept. 7, 1956; children: David Wade, Britton Barnes, William Slater, Baxter Ward. B.A., Lipscomb Coll., 1958; M.A., U. N. Mex., 1959; Ph.D., U. So. Calif., 1963. Dean students Pepperdine U., Los Angeles, 1962-63, asst. to pres., 1959-61, exec. v.p., 1968, chancellor, 1969-70, pres., U. Okla., Norman. Author: It's A Playboy World, 1969. Recipient Liberty Bell award ABA, 1968. Lodge: Rotary. Office: Office of the Pres U Okla Norman OK 73019 *

BANSE, ROBERT LEE, lawyer; b. Phila., Mar. 11, 1927; s. Robert John and Esther Elizabeth (Warren) B.; m. Anne Windels, Dec. 17, 1955; children—Robert L., Amy L., John W. B.S., U. Pa., 1949; LL.B. cum laude, Washington and Lee U., 1953. Bar: N.Y. bar, Pa. bar. Mem. firm Townsend & Lewis, 1953-55; with Merck & Co., Inc., Rahway, N.J., 1955—, counsel, 1960-73, sr. counsel, 1973-75, gen. counsel, 1975—, v.p., 1977—. Mem. ABA, Assn. Bar City N.Y., Pharm. Mfrs. Assn. (chmn. law sect. 1977-78), N.J. Gen. Counsel's Group, Assn. Gen. Counsel. Clubs: Phila. Cricket, Eagles Mere Country, Springdale Golf. Home: Meadowgate PO Box 6147 Lawrenceville NJ 08648 Office: PO Box 200 Rahway NJ 07065

BANTA, HENRY DAVID, physician; b. Electra, Tex., Mar. 3, 1938; s. Henry Eugene and Hazel (Rippy) B.; m. Sandra Lesquier Smith, Sept. 23, 1967; children: Elizabeth Christian, Barbara Shawn, Michael David, Heather Alexandra. Student, Duke U., 1956-59, M.D., 1963; M.P.H., Harvard U., 1968, M.S. in Hygiene, 1969. Intern, resident in medicine U. Wash., 1963-65; tng. program officer Center for Disease Control, Atlanta, 1965-67; asst. prof. dept. community medicine Mt. Sinai Sch. Medicine, N.Y.C., 1969-74, assoc. prof., 1974-75; research dir. health program Office of Tech. Assessment, U.S. Congress, Washington, 1975-77; mgr. health program Office of Tech. Assessment, 1978-81; asst. dir. Office Tech. Assessment, 1981-83; dep. dir. Pan Am. Health Orgn., 1983—; sr. med. advisor Nat. Center for Health Services Research, HEW, 1977-78; cons. Pan Am. Health Orgn., OECD, WHO. Author: (with C. Behney and J. Willems) Toward Rational Technology in Medicine, 1981; editor 2 books in field.; mem. editorial bd.: Jour. Community Health, Health Care Mgmt. Rev; book review editor: Jour. Community Health; contbr. articles to profl. jours. Served with USPHS, 1965-67, 77-78. Milbank Faculty asso. fellow, 1970-73; Robert Wood Johnson Health Policy fellow, 1974-75. Fellow Am. Coll. Preventive Medicine, Am. Public Health Assn.; mem. Assn. Tchrs. Preventive Medicine, Inst. Medicine, Nat. Acad. Scis., Phi Beta Kappa, Alpha Omega Alpha. Home: 310 G St Washington DC 20003 Office: Pan Am Health Orgn 525 23d St NW Washington DC 20037

BANTA, JAMES ELMER, physician, educator, university dean; b. Tucumcari, N.Mex., July 1, 1927; s. James Elmer and Edna Mae (Murnahan) B.; m. Ellen Clara Fera, Apr. 21, 1973. M.D., Marquette U., 1950; M.P.H., Johns Hopkins U., 1954; diploma, U.S. Naval Med. Sch., 1952. Med. officer USN, 1950-60; commd. med. officer USPHS,

1960-69; dir. med. program Peace Corps, 1963-65; dir. Office Internat. Health, HEW, 1967-68; prof. public health U. Hawaii, 1970-73; dep. dir. Office Health, AID, State Dept., Washington, 1973-75; dean, prof. Sch. Public Health and Tropical Medicine, Tulane U., New Orleans, 1975—. Co-author: How to Travel the World and Stay Healthy, 1969, Year-round Travelers' Health Guide, 1978; Contbr. articles on epidemiology, microbiology and health to profl. jours. Served with USN, 1944-46. Recipient Outstanding Service award Georgetown U., 1965. Fellow Am. Coll. Preventive Medicine, Royal Soc. Health (U.K.), Am. Public Health Assn., Am. Heart Assn., AAAS, Am. Coll. Epidemiology, Coll. Phys. Phila.; mem. ACLU, Common Cause, Environ. Action, AAUP, Assn. Schs. Public Health (pres. 1979-31), Sigma Xi, Phi Sigma, Delta Omega. Clubs: Internat. (Washington); Internat. House, Plimsol (New Orleans); Bay Waveland Yacht (Bay St. Louis, Miss.). Office: 1430 Tulane Ave New Orleans LA 70112

BANTLE, LOUIS FRANCIS, tobacco co. exec.; b. Bridgeport, Conn., Nov. 22, 1928; s. Louis A. and Marie E. (Baisenberger) B.; m. Virginia Clark, Jan. 20, 1961; children—Robert C., Terri Ann. B.S., Syracuse (N.Y.) U., 1951. Vice pres. U.S. Tobacco Co., Greenwich, Conn., 1966-73, dir., 1967—, chmn. bd., pres., 1973—; dir. State Nat. Bank Conn. Trustee Fairfield U.; bd. dirs. Greenwich Boy Scouts Am. Served to capt. USMC, 1951-53. Decorated knight of the North Star, Sweden, 1976; named Young Exec. of Year Tobacco Industry, 1966. Mem. Tobacco Inst. (dir.), Nat. Assn. Tobacco Distbrs. (treas., dir. Exec. Mgmt. div.). Republican. Roman Catholic. Clubs: Winged Foot Country, Wee Burn Country. Office: 100 W Putnum Ave Greenwich CT 06830 *

BANYARD, ALFRED LOTHIAN, bishop; b. Merchantville, N.J., July 31, 1908; s. Lothian Rupert and Emma May (Irwin) B.; m. Sarah Alice Hammer, Sept. 1, 1938; 1 son, Richard David. A.B., U. Pa., 1929; student, Gen. Theol. Sem., 1929-31, S.T.B., 1933, S.T.D., 1946; postgrad., Phila. Div. Sch., 1932, D.D., 1947. Ordained to ministry Episcopal Ch., N.J., 1931; pastor St. Lukes Ch., Westville, N.J., 1932-36; rector Christ Ch., Bordentown, N.J., 1936-43; archdeacon Episcopal Diocese N.J., 1943-55; suffragan bishop, 1945-55, bishop of N.J., 1955-73, ret., 1973; Mem. Bd. Examining Chaplains, 1938-55, chmn., 1941-55; dep. to provincial synod, 1940-46; sec. Ho. of Bishops, 2d Province, 1945-48; trustee Diocesan Found., 1941-43, ex-officio, 1945—, pres., 1955—, Procter Found., 1955—; master of Young Men's Conf., 1936-37, dean, 1941; mem. Bd. Religious Edn., 1939-41, 43-46, Bd. Social Service, 1940-42, 44-46; field, publicity dept., 1943-45; trustee Burlington Coll., 1945-53, v.p., 1946-53; Bd. mgrs. St. Martins Ho. of Retreats, Bernardsville, N.J., 1948—; trustee, Evergreens, Moorestown, pres., 1955; v.p. Corp. for Relief Widows and Orphans of Clergymen, 1945—; pres. Mission Advancement, 1955—; trustee Phila. Div. Sch. Mem. Newcomen Soc., Philomathean Soc. of U. Pa. (scriba 1929), Phi Beta Kappa, Eta Sigma Phi. Republican. Home: The Evergreens Moorestown NJ 08057

BANZHAF, CLAYTON HARRIS, retired merchandising company executive; b. Buffalo, Dec. 24, 1917; s. Joseph Maxmillian and Elizabeth (Harris) B.; m. Dolores J. Gavins, Dec. 30, 1962; children by previous marriage: Barbara Banzhaf Grimmett, Debra Banzhaf York, William Clay. M.B.A., U. Chgo., 1954. With Sears, Roebuck & Co., 1936-81, corp. asst. treas., 1958-60, sr. asst. treas., Chgo., 1961-74, treas., 1975-81, v.p., 1976-81, also dir.; pres., chief exec. officer Sears Roebuck Acceptance Corp., Wilmington, Del., 1963-72, dir., 1972-81; former treas. Fleet Maintenance Inc., Lifetime Foam Products, Inc., Sears Finance Corp., Sears Internat. Finance Co., Sears Roebuck Internat. Inc., Sears Roebuck Overseas, Inc., Sears Roebuck de P.R. Inc., Terminal Freight Handling Co., Tower Ventures, Inc.; dir. Barclays Am. Corp.; former dir. Banco de Credito Internacional S.A., Homart Devel. Co., Lake Shore Land Assn., Inc., Sears Overseas Finance N.V., Western Forge Corp.; former officer other subs. Mem. com. banking, monetary and fiscal affairs U.S. C. of C., 1969-74; mem. exec. com. Chgo. Area council Boy Scouts Am., 1963-68, adv. bd., 1969-81; bd. dirs. Council Community Services, Chgo., 1975-77, United Way Met. Chgo., 1977-81; trustee Elmira (N.Y.) Coll., 1975-81; mem. com. on allied health evaluation and accreditation AMA, 1978—; mem. bus. adv. council U. Ill., Chgo., 1978-81. Served to maj. AUS, 1941-46. Decorated Army Commendation medal. Mem. Fin. Execs. Inst. (pres. Chgo. 1972-73, nat. dir., exec. com. 1975-78, Midwest area v.p. 1977-78), Am. Assembly Collegiate Schs. Bus. (continuing accreditation com.), U. Chgo. Alumni Assn. (dir. 1966-67, v.p. 1968, pres. 1969, alumni council Grad. Sch. Bus. 1969, pres. 1972-75). Republican. Presbyterian. Clubs: Hound Ears, Long boat Key, Sarabay Country, Medinah Country. Home: Hound Ears Club Box 188 Blowing Rock NC 28605 also Banyan Bay Club Unit 507 5270 Gulf of Mexico Dr Longboat Key FL 33548

BANZHAF, JOHN F., III, lawyer, organization executive; b. N.Y.C., July 2, 1940; s. John F., Jr. and Olga (Mischenko) B.; m. Ursula Maag, 1971. B.S. in Elec. Engring, M.I.T., 1962; J.D. magna cum laude, Columbia U., 1965. Civilian research asst. Signal Corps Engring. Labs., 1957; research engr., cons. Lear Siegler Corp., 1959-62; editor Columbia Law Rev., 1964-65; research fellow Nat. Municipal League, 1965; law clk. to U.S. Dist. Judge Spottswood W. Robinson III, 1965-66; asso. firm Watson, Leavonworth, Kelton & Taggart, N.Y.C., 1967; founder, exec. dir. Action on Smoking and Health, Washington, 1968—, Inst. Legal Activism, 1980—; prof. law and legal activism Nat. Law Center, George Washington U., 1968—; exec. dir. Action on Safety and Health, 1971-80, Open America, 1975-80; project dir. Nat. Center for Law and the Deaf, 1975-80; Bd. dirs. Consumers Union, 1971. Recipient 17th ann. Sat. Rev. award distinguished TV programming in pub. interest, 1969; Advt. Age award, 1967, 68; those who made advt. news, 1967, 68; Benjamin Franklin Lit. and Med. Soc. award, 1981. Mem. Sigma Xi, Eta Kappa Nu, Tau Beta Pi. Home: 2810 N Quebec St North Arlington VA 22207 Office: 2013 H St NW Washington DC 20006 *Despite the increasing complexity of society, and the seemingly overwhelming power of large institutions both public and private, one determined individual can still have a significant and beneficial impact on society. (I was responsible, as an individual, for over 200 million dollars worth of free radio and television time for "anti-smoking commercials" which led to the ban on cigarette commercials.)*

BARABAS, SILVIO, chemist, research adminstr.; b. Sarajevo, Yugoslavia, June 10, 1920; emigrated to Can., 1951, naturalized, 1956; s. Samuel and Sarah (Kabiljo) B.; m. Louise Sofonio, Sept. 12, 1959; children—Allen, Bertrand. D. Phys. and Chem. Scis., U. Padua, Italy, 1950. Chief chemist Noranda Research Centre, 1953-66; mng. dir. Technicon Corp., Tarrytown, N.Y., Montreal, 1966-71; head analytical research Can. Centre Inland Waters, Burlington, Ont., 1972-74; mgr. WHO collaborating centre on surface and ground water quality; editor-in-chief Water Quality bull., 1974—. Contbr. articles to profl. jours. Mem. Chem. Inst. Can., Am. Chem. Soc., Spectroscopy Soc. Can., ASTM, Nat. Geog. Soc. Patentee. Home: 428 Breckonwood Rd Burlington ON L7L 2T7 Canada Office: Canada Centre Inland Waters PO Box 5050 Burlington ON L7R 4A6 Canada

BARABBA, VINCENT PASQUALE, bus. exec.; b. Chgo., Sept. 6, 1934; s. John and Elvira (Tucci) B.; m. Sheryl Gae Brock, Dec. 10, 1966; children—Heather Anne, Jason Vincent. B.B.A., Woodbury Bus. Coll., 1954; B.S., Calif. State U. at Northridge, 1962; M.B.A., U. Calif. at Los Angeles, 1964. Pres. Datamatics, Inc.; chmn. bd. Decision Making Info.; dir. Bur. Census, Dept. Commerce, Washington, 1973-76, 79-81; former mgr. market research Xerox Corp., Rochester, N.Y.; dir. market intelligence Eastman Kodak Co., Rochester, N.Y., 1981—; dir. Central Bank Glendale, Calif.; former instr. Calif. State U. at Northridge. Served with USAF, 1954-58. Fellow Am. Statis. Assn. (v.p.); mem. Am. Mktg. Assn. (v.p.), Blue Key, Beta Gamma Sigma. Home: 522 Stone Rd Pittsford NY 14534 Office: Eastman Kodak Co Rochester NY 14650

BARACH, PHILIP G., shoe company executive; b. Boston, 1930; (m); 3 children. Ed., Boston U., 1951, Harvard Grad. Sch. Bus. Adminstrn., 1955. Pres., chmn. bd. U.S. Shoe Corp., 1972—; dir. Fifth Third Union Trust Co. Home: 7600 Willow Brook Ln Cincinnati OH 45237 Office: One Eastwood Dr Cincinnati OH 45227

BARAGWANATH, ALBERT KINGSMILL, curator; b. Lima, Peru, July 20, 1917; s. John Gordon and Leila Radcliff (Morris) B.; m. Eileen Mary Flanagan, Sept. 1, 1943; children—Joan Baragwanath Shaw, Janice, John Blackburn, Patricia. Grad., Hill Sch., Pottstown, Pa., 1936; B.A., Princeton, 1940; M.A. in Am. History, Columbia, 1952. With traffic and sales dept. Eastern Air Lines, N.Y.C., 1946-50; librarian Mus. City N.Y., 1952-58, curator prints and portraits, 1959—, sr. curator, 1963-79, sr. curator emeritus, 1980—; mem. N.Y.C. Mayor's Task Force on Municipal Archives, 1966; mem. adv. com. Mus. Am. Folk Art, 1969—. Author: More Than a Mirror to the Past: The First Fifty Years of the Museum of the City of New York, 1973, 50 Currier & Ives Favorites, 1978, 100 Currier & Ives Favorites, 1978; contbr.: New York City Guide, 1964, Currier and Ives, Chronicles of America, 1968. Served from pvt. to capt. AUS, 1941-46; ETO; Served from pvt. to capt. AUS; PTO. Decorated Combat Inf. badge. Mem. Am. Hist. Print Collectors Soc. (dir.). Home: 20 Summit Ave Larchmont NY 10538 Office: 1220 Fifth Ave New York NY 10029

BARAHAL, HYMAN SAMUEL, ret. psychiatrist, hosp. adminstr.; b. Bereznieza, Russia, May 21, 1905; came to U.S., 1914, naturalized, 1923; s. Oscar and Pearl (Rothman) B.; m. Irene Jaffe, Dec. 24, 1939; children—Paul, Susan. M.B., Wayne State U., 1930, M.D., 1931. Diplomate: Am. Bd. Psychiatry and Neurology. Gen. intern Gorgas Hosp., C.Z., 1930-31; staff psychiatrist Kings Park (N.Y.) State Hosp., 1931; then supervising psychiatrist; clin. dir. Pilgrim State Hosp., West Brentwood, N.Y., 1946-53, asso. dir., 1953-58, acting dir., 1958-64; prof. psychiatry N.Y. Sch. Psychiatry, 1955—; founder, dir. Hoch Psychiat. Hosp., 1968—; asso. clin. prof. psychiatry N.Y. State U. Med. Sch. at Stony Brook, 1972—; psychiatrist Catholic Charities. Contbr. numerous articles to profl. jours., chpts. to books. Served to maj., M.C. AUS, 1942-46. Fellow Am. Psychiat. Assn. (life), Acad. Psychoanalysis; mem. Suffolk County Med. Soc. (chmn. com. on mental health, alcoholism and drug addiction). Home and Office: 130 S Bay Ave Brightwaters NY 11718 *The greatest blessing is to be involved in a line of work which is, above all, pleasurable.*

BARAKA, IMAMU AMIRI (LEROI JONES), author; b. Newark, Oct. 7, 1934; s. Coyette LeRoi and Anna Lois (Russ) J.; m. Hettie Roberta Cohen, Oct. 13, 1958 (div. Aug. 1965); children—Kellie Elisabeth, Lisa Victoria Chapman; m. Amina Robinson, Aug. 1966; children—Obalaji Malik Ali, Ras Jua Al Aziz, Shani Isis, Amiri Seku, Ahi Mwenge. B.A., Howard U., 1954. Mem. faculty New Sch. Social Research, N.Y.C.; dir. Spirit House; also spiritual leader Temple Kawaida, Newark.; vis. prof. San Francisco State U.; founder Yugen Mag. and Totem Press, N.Y.C., 1958, Black Arts Repertory Theater Sch., Harlem, 1964; coordinator creativity workshops Black Power Conf., 1968. Author: Preface to a Twenty Volume Suicide Note, 1961, Blues People, 1963, The Moderns, 1963, Dutchman and The Slave, 1964 (Obie award), The Dead Lecturer, 1964, The System of Dante's Hell, 1965, Home, 1966, Black Music, 1966, Tales, 1967, Black Art, 1967, Black Magic, 1969, 4 Black Revolutionary Plays, 1969, In Our Terribleness, 1971, Raise Race Rays Raze, 1971, Creation of the New Art; poetry, 1974, A Collection of Critical Essays, 1978; Maj. theatrical prodns. include Dutchman (Off-Broadway award for best Am. play 1964), The Slave, (2d prize Internat. Art Festival, Dakar 1966), The Toilet, The Baptism, Jello, A Black Mass, Sidnee Poet Heroical, 1975. Served with USAF, 1954-57. Whitney fellow, 1960-61; Guggenheim fellow, 1965-66. Mem. Black Acad. Arts and Letters. Address: care CAP 502 High St Newark NJ 07102 *

BARALL, MILTON, govt. ofcl.; b. N.Y.C., Oct. 28, 1911; s. Louis and Rose (Barall) B.; m. Grace Glaberson, Oct. 28, 1940; 1 son, James David. B.S.S., Coll. City N.Y., 1932, M.S., 1933; certificate, U. Grenoble, France, 1932; Ph.D., N.Y.U., 1948; grad., Nat. War Coll., 1957. Tchr. high schs., N.Y.C., 1934-41, 46-48; 2d sec., vice consul Am. embassy, Santiago, Chile, 1948-50; Chilean desk officer, officer charge West Coast affairs, S. Am., Dept. State, 1950-54; 1st sec., then counselor embassy Port-au-Prince, Haiti, 1954-56; counselor for econ. affairs, dep. dir. econ. mission Am. embassy, Madrid, Spain, 1957-60, consul gen., 1960; dep. asst. sec. of state; Bur. Inter-Am. Affairs, 1960-62; v.p., supr. overseas ops. Am. Machine & Foundry Internat., Geneva, Switzerland, 1962-64; dep. U.S. rep. Inter-Am. Com. on Alliance for Progress, 1964-67; dep. asst. adminstr. AID, 1966-67; alternate del. OAS, 1964-67; head Caribbean Study Group with rank ambassador, 1967-69; minister Am. embassy, Buenos Aires, Argentina, 1969-72; cons. OAS, 1972—. Contbr. articles on polit. sci. to profl. publs. Served from capt. to col. AUS, 1941-45. Decorated Croix de Guerre, Medaille de la Reconnaissance, France; Orden de Mayo, Argentina; Superior Honor award U.S. State Dept. Mem. Am. Fgn. Service Assn., Diplomatic and Consular Officers Ret. Club: Internat. (Washington). Home: 4201 Cathedral Ave NW Washington DC 20016

BARANGER, ELIZABETH, university dean. Dean grad. studies Faculty Arts and Scis., U. Pitts. Office: Office of Dean Grad StudiesU Pitts Coll Arts and Scis Pittsburgh PA 15260§

BARANIK, RUDOLF, painter; b. Lithuania, Sept. 10, 1920; m. May Stevens; 1 son, Steven. Student, Art Inst. Chgo., Art Students League, Academie Julien, Paris, Academie Leger, Paris. Prof. Art Students League, N.Y., Pratt Inst.; vis. artist Ball State U., Cornell U., Ithaca, N.Y. Editor: (with others) Attica Book, by Black Emergency Cultural Coalition and Artists and Writers Protest Against the War in Vietnam; Exhibited, Mus. Modern Art circulating exhbn., 1954-55, Whitney Mus. Am. Art, anns., 1958, 61, Am. Acad. Arts-Nat. Inst. Arts and Letters, 1964, 68, 73, Internat. Anti-war Exhibit, Tokyo, 1968, Collage of Indignation, N.Y. Cultural Center, 1969, Am. Collages, Ball State U., 1971, Voices of Alarm, Moravian Coll., Bethlehem, Pa., 1973, Painting and Sculpture Today, Indpls. Mus. Art, 1974, A Patriotic Show, Wright State U. Gallery, Dayton, Ohio, 1977, Art Inst. Chgo., 1979, Brainerd Art Gallery, Pottsdam, Wright State U. Galleries, 1980, Ronald Feldman Gallery, N.Y.C., 1982, Lerner-Heller, N.Y.C., one-man shows include, Galerie Huit, Paris, 1951, ACA Gallery, N.Y.C., 1953, 55, RoKo Gallery, N.Y.C., 1958, 61, 63, Ball State U. Mus., 1963, Pratt Inst., N.Y.C., 1968, Ten Downtown, N.Y.C., 1969, Rutgers U., 1973, Lerner-Heller Gallery, N.Y.C., 1974, 75, 76, 78, 80, Yares Gallery, Phoenix, 1979, Keen Coll., represented in permanent collections, Everson Mus., Syracuse, N.Y., Newark Mus., Mus. Modern Art, N.Y.C., Wichita (Kans.) State U., Joseph Hirshhorn Mus., Washington, Whitney Mus. Am. Art, U. Mass., N.Y. U., Ball State U., Muncie, Ind., Jacksonville (Fla.) Mus., Peabody Mus., Nashville, Colgate U., Meml. Art Gallery, Rochester, N.Y., Moderna Museet, Stockholm, Slater Mus., Norwich, Conn., Queens Mus., N.Y.C., U. Miami, Hampton (Va.) Coll. Mus., Fine Arts Mus., Anchorage, SUNY, Binghamton, pvt. collections. Recipient 1st prize New Eng. Ann., 1958; N.Y. Critics Choice prize, 1960; Raymond Speiser Meml. award Pa. Acad., 1964; Childe Hassam Purchase award Nat. Inst. Arts and Letters, 1968, 73, 76; MacDowell Colony fellow, 1971, 72, 74, 77; Am. Acad. Arts and Letters grantee, 1973; Guggenheim grantee, 1981. Mem. Artists Meeting for Cultural Change, Coll. Art Assn. Address: 97 Wooster St New York NY 10012

BARANOWSKI, FRANK PAUL, energy consultant, former government official; b. Bayonne, N.J., Nov. 1, 1921; s. John G. and Leona (Besser) B.; m. Alma J. Anders, Oct. 12, 1946; children: Jan Teresa, Susan Leona, Michael Paul, Carol Ann, Kristin Marie. B. Chem. Engring., N.Y. U., 1943; M. Chem. Engring., U. Tenn., 1954. Exec. asst. Union Carbide Co., Oak Ridge, 1948-51; with AEC (now Dept. Energy), 1950—, chief isotope separation br., div. prodn., 1954-57, chief chem. processing br., div. prodn., 1957-59, dep. dir. div. prodn., 1959-61, dir. div. prodn., 1961-75, dir. div. nuclear fuel cycle and prodn., 1975-77; v.p. Mech. Tech. Inc., Arlington, Va., 1977-80; pres. Frank P. Baranowski, Inc., energy program mgmt. cons., Great Falls, Va., 1980—; mem. energy research adv. bd. U.S. Dept. Energy, 1983—. Served with C.E.; Served with AUS, 1943-46. Home: 1110 Dapple Grey Ct Great Falls VA 22066

BARANSKI, JOAN SULLIVAN, editor; b. Andover, Mass., Apr. 6, 1933; d. Joseph Charles and Ruth G. (McCormack) Sullivan; m. Kenneth E. Baranski, Apr. 20, 1970. B.S., U. Lowell, Mass., 1955. Tchr. Andover Public Schs., 1955-61; asso. editor sci. and reading sch. dept. Holt, Rinehart and Winston, N.Y.C., 1961-65; promotion coordinator sch. dept. Harcourt Brace Jovanovich, N.Y.C., 1965-74, mgr. div. verifiability and testing, 1974-75; editor-in-chief Teacher mag., Macmillan Co.; profl. mags., Stamford, Conn., 1975-81; editor-in-chief sch. dept. Harper & Row Pubs., N.Y.C., 1981—. Contbg. author: Winston Basic Reading Series, 1963, Little Owl Program, 1964. Home: 250 E 87th St New York NY 10028 Office: 10 E 53 St New York NY 10022

BARASCH, CLARENCE SYLVAN, lawyer; b. N.Y.C., May 20, 1912; s. Morris and Bertha Lydia (Herschdorfer) B.; m. Naomi Bosniak, July 1, 1957; children: Lionel, Jonathan. A.B., Columbia U., 1933, J.D., 1935. Bar: N.Y. 1936. Practice law specializing in litigation of real estate brokerage commns., N.Y.C., 1935—; Lectr. law of real estate brokerage at various real estate bds. Chmn. Columbia U. Law Sch. Class of 1935 Annual Fund, 1965—, Columbia Coll. Class of 1933 Ann. Fund, 1977—; decade chmn. Columbia Coll. Ann. Fund; pres. Jewish Campus Life Fund, Inc. of Columbia U., 1970—. Author: (with Elliot L. Biskind) The Law of Real Estate Brokers, 1969; also cumulative supplements, 1971-83; contbr. numerous articles to profl. jours. Served to capt. Signal Corps AUS, 1942-46. Recipient cert. of appreciation Columbia U., 1981. Mem. Am., N.Y. State bar assns., N.Y. County Lawyers Assn., Real Estate Bd. N.Y. (mem. legis. com. 1970—), Men's Club (dir. 1972—). Jewish (mem. adv. bd. to chaplain Columbia 1950—). Home: 1016 Fifth Ave New York NY 10028 Office: 110 E 59th St New York NY 10022

BARATI, GEORGE, musician; b. Györ, Hungary, Apr. 3, 1913; s. Miksa B. and Regina (Schreiber) B.; m. Ruth Carroll, Oct. 31, 1948; children: Stephen George; by previous marriage), Lorna, Donna. Grad., Royal Hungarian Franz Liszt Conservatory of Music, Budapest, 1935; diploma, State Tchrs. Coll., 1938, 1938; postgrad. study with, Georges Couvreur and Henry Switten, 1938-40, Roger Sessions, 1940-43, Princeton U. Mem., Budapest Concert Orch., 1933-36; first cellist, Budapest Symphony and Municipal Opera House Orch., 1936-38; cellist, founder, Pro Ideale String Quartet, 1935-40; instr. Westminster Choir Coll., Princeton, N.J., 1938-40, Lawrenceville Sch., Princeton, also, N.J. State Tchrs. Coll., 1939-43; condr., founder, Princeton Ensemble, 1940-43; condr., Princeton Choral Union, 1942-43; mem., guest condr., San Francisco Symphony; mem., Calif. String Quartet, 1946-50; musical dir., Barati Chamber Orch. of San Francisco, (formation of Barati Chamber Orch. Soc.), 1950), 1948-52, Honolulu Symphony Orch.; lectr., U. Hawaii, 1950-68, world tours annually; exec. dir., Montalvo Center for the Arts, New York debut conducting, Madame Butterfly, Bklyn. Opera Co., 1961; Compositions: (orchestral) Chamber Concerto, Confluence For Orch., Polarization For Orch., The Ugly Duckling; Compositions Indiana Triptych (4 players), The Dragon and the Phoenix, A Chant to Pele; recorded Columbia Records Cello Concerto; recorded by the London Philharmonic Noelani; chamber music Octet with Harpsichord; solo instruments: others. Branches of Time; Rec. artist, Lyrichord, Decca, Columbia, CRI. Bd. govs. Pacific and Asian Affairs Council. Served with AUS, 1943-46. Naumburg award, composition, 1959; Guggenheim fellow, 1965-66. Mem. Am. Musicol. Soc., Composers Forum, MacDowell Colony, Am. Composers Alliance, Berlioz Soc. Am. (founding mem.), Bruckner Soc. (hon.).

BARATZ, MORTON SACHS, economic consultant, writer; b. New London, Conn., Nov. 18, 1923; s. Moss and Lydia (Sachs) B.; m. Marleigh Morland, Aug. 24, 1952; children—Cynthia Leigh, Mark Everett, Matthew Anatole. B.A., U. Conn., 1947; M.A., Yale, 1949, Ph.D., 1952. Asst. instr., then instr. econs. U. Conn., 1947-48; asst. instr., then instr. Yale, 1948-55; asst. prof. econs. Haverford Coll., 1955-57; asso. prof., then prof. Bryn Mawr Coll., 1957-69, chmn. dept. econs., 1964-69; prof., chmn. dept. econs. Boston U., 1969-72; dir. Urban Inst., 1970-72; vice chancellor acad. affairs U. Md., Baltimore County, 1972-77; gen. sec. AAUP, Washington, 1977-79; vis. research prof. U. Pa., 1965-70, 80; vis. prof. public adminstrn. George Washington U., 1980-81; editor Managed Account Reports, Columbia, Md., 1981—; research cons. Inst. Urban Studies, U. Pa., 1956-58, Office of Mayor, Phila., 1957-60; dir. Franklin Custodian Funds, N.Y.C., 1958-62; nat. research prof. Brookings Instn., 1960-61. Author: The Union and the Coal Industry, 1955, The Economics of the Postal Service, 1962, (with others) Economies of the World Today, 1965, 3d edit., 1976, (with W.G. Grigsby) Meaning and Measurement of Poverty, 1968, The American Business System in Transition, 1970, (with P. Bachrach) Power and Poverty, 1970; Editor: Commodity Money Management Yearbook, vol. II, Commodity Money Management Yearbook, Vol. III.; Contbr. articles to profl. jours. Chmn. Housing Authority, City of New London, 1949-54; chmn. Willistown Twp. (Pa.) Democratic Com., 1956-61; adv. bd. Chester County (Pa.) Bd. Pub. Assistance, 1959-61; mng. dir. MAR/Consultants, Columbia, Md., 1980—. Mem. Am. Econ. Assn., Nigerian Econ. Soc. Home: 20745 New Hampshire Ave Brookeville MD 20833 Office: 5513 Twin Knolls Rd Columbia MD 21045

BARBAGELATA, ROBERT DOMINIC, lawyer; b. San Francisco, Jan. 9, 1925; s. Dominic Joseph and Jane Zeffra (Frugoli) B.; m. Doris V. Chatfield, June 8, 1956; children: Patricia Victoria, Robert Norman, Michael Alan. B.S., U. San Francisco, 1947, J.D., 1950. Bar: Calif. bar 1950, U.S. Supreme Ct. bar 1964. In practice as Barbagelata Law Corp., San Francisco, 1950—; lectr. U. San Francisco Law Sch., Pacific Med. Center. Contbr. to legal jours. Served with USNR, 1943-46. Mem. Calif. State Bar, Calif. Trial Lawyers Assn. (lectr., v.p.), Am. Bd. Trial Advocates (nat. pres. 1981-82), Assn. Trial Lawyers Am., Am. Coll. Trial Lawyers, Internat. Soc. Barristers, San Francisco Lawyers Club. Roman Catholic. Clubs: Press, Commonwealth, South End Rowing. Home: 819 Holly Rd Belmont CA 94002 Office: 109 Geary St San Francisco CA 94108

BARBAN, ARNOLD MELVIN, communications educator; b. San Antonio, Tex., Sept. 17, 1932; s. Sam and Ida Dollie (Wolfson) B.; m. Barbara Marie Fox, June 2, 1955; children: Polly Gwen, Pamela Florence. B.B.A., U. Tex., Austin, 1955, M.B.A., 1959, Ph.D., 1964. Asst. to v.p. Joske's of Tex., San Antonio, 1955-56; asst. prof. U. Houston, 1959-64, U. Ill., Urbana-Champaign, 1964-66, asso. prof., 1966-70, prof., 1970-83, head dept. advt., 1978-83; research prof. Inst. Communications Research, 1972-83; Jesse H. Jones Centennial prof. communication U. Tex., Austin, 1983—; cons. Gulf Oil Corp., Farm Research Inst., Grid Pub. Co. (various advt. agys.). Author: Readings in Advertising and Promotion Strategy, 1968, Essentials of Media Planning, 1976, Advertising Media Sourcebook and Workbook, 2d edit, 1981, Advertising: Its Role in Modern Marketing, 5th edit., 1982; editor: U. Houston Bus. Rev, 1962-64; cons. editor: Jour. Advt, 1979-81; mem. editorial rev. bd.: Current Issues and Research in Advt, 1980—; contbr. articles to profl. jours. Served with U.S. Army, 1956-58. Recipient Outstanding Service award Houston Advt. Club, 1964; U. Tex. summer fellow, 1960-62. Mem. Am. Mktg. Assn. (pres. Central Ill. chpt. 1970-71), Am. Acad. Advt. (pres. 1981-82), Assn. Edn. in Journalism, Assn. Consumer Research, Beta Gamma Sigma, Omicron Chi Epsilon, Kappa Tau Alpha, Phi Kappa Phi, Alpha Delta Sigma. Jewish. Office: Dept Advt U Tex Austin TX 78712

BARBANEL, SIDNEY MANUEL, medical instruments manufacturing company executive; b. Savannah, Ga., Mar. 5, 1936; s. Leon and Ann M. (Kramer) B.; m. Anne Matthias, Mar. 16, 1961; children: Amy Laura, Bonnie Lynne. Student, U.S. Naval Acad., 1956, Coll. Charleston, 1957-58; B.A., Oglethrope U., 1960. Salesman Dunn & Bradstreet, Inc., 1960-64, Purdue Fredrick Co., Atlanta, 1964-68, Medtronic Inc., 1968-69; So. div. mgr. sales and mktg. Cordis Corp., Atlanta, 1969-74; mgr. Arco Med. Products Co. subs. Atlantic Richfield Corp., Pitts., 1974-76; exec. v.p. sales Intermedics, Inc., Freeport, Tex., 1976—; v.p. Intermedics Intraocular, Inc., 1976-78; lectr. in field. Bd. vistors Oglethorpe U., 1979. Served with USN, 1954-56. Named to Pres.'s Club Medtronic, Inc., 1969, Loyalty Club Oglethrope U., 1978; recipient cert. Ga. Heart Assn., 1972. Mem. Assn. Advancement Med. Instrumentation, Am. Mgmt. Assn., N.Am. Soc. Pacing and Electrophysiology, Sales and Mktg. Execs., Citadel Devel. Found., James Edward Oglethrope Soc. Lodge: Masons. Office: Intermedics Inc 240 Tarpon Inn Village Freeport TX 77541

BARBANELL, ROBERT LOUIS, financial executive; b. N.Y.C., June 30, 1930; s. Morris and Leah (Lorentz) B.; m. Carol Zeligson Feld, Nov. 26, 1960 (div.); 1 son, Edward M. Student, Swarthmore Coll., 1948-50; B.S. in Fin, N.Y. U., 1952. With Loeb Rhoades & Co., N.Y.C., 1954-75; chmn., pres. Geon Industries, Inc., Woodbury, N.Y., 1975-77; v.p. fin. Azcon Corp., N.Y.C., 1977-79, Amcon Group, Inc., 1979-80, pres., 1981; sr. v.p. Bankers Trust Co., 1982—. Bd. dirs. Lexington Sch. for Deaf, 1981—. Served with U.S. Army, 1952-54. Republican. Jewish. Club: Sky. Office: 280 Park Ave New York NY 10015

BARBAROSSA, THEODORE COTILLO, sculptor; b. Ludlow, Vt., Dec. 26, 1906; s. Louis Henry and Maddelina (Verimonde) B.; m. Sally Ann Newhall, Nov. 20, 1962; 1 dau., Susan. Student, Mass. Coll. Art, 1927; B.F.A., Yale U., 1931; D.F.A. (hon.), Susquehanna U., Selingsgrove, Pa., 1977. Exhibited in shows at, Whitney Mus., N.Y.C., 1940, Nat. Sculpture Soc., NAD, Allied Artists, Audubon Artists, commns. include sculptures in stone, Catholic Ch. Assumption, Balt., 1957, five relief panels, Mus. Sci., Boston, two chapels and ten figures, Cath. Shrine, Washington, 1962-65, sculptures in stone for, St. Thomas Episcopal Ch., N.Y.C., 1964, Washington Cath. and Episcopal Chs., 1965-75, others, important works include, Uncle Sam Monument, Arlington, Mass., sculptures, Susquehanna U., Nat. Cathedral, Washington, Balt. Cathedral. Served with C.E. AUS, 1942-46. Recipient numerous gold medals and citations for sculpture. Fellow Nat. Sculpture Soc.; mem. Nat. Acad., Internat. Inst. Arts and Letters, Audubon Artists, Allied Artists. Club: Yale (Boston). Home: 12 Randolph St Belmont MA 02178

BARBASH, JACK, educator, economist; b. Bklyn., Aug. 1, 1910; s. Louis and Rose (Titel) B.; m. Kate Hubbelbank, May 27, 1934; children: Louis, Fred, Mark. B.S., NYU, 1932, M.A., 1937. Investigator N.Y. State Dept. Labor, 1937-39; economist NLRB, 1939-40, U.S. Office Edn., 1940-45, WPB, 1943-45, Dept. Labor, 1945-48; research and edn. dir. Amalgamated Meat Cutters Union, 1948-49; economist, staff dir. subcom. labor and labor mgmt. relations U.S. Senate, 1949-53; economist legal dept. CIO, 1953-55; research and edn. dir., indsl. union dept. AFL-CIO, 1955-57; mem. faculty U. Wis., 1957—, prof. econs., 1959—, Bascom prof., 1976—; mem. Salzburg Seminar on Am. Studies, 1962; lectr. cultural affairs U.S. Dept. State, Europe, Asia, Latin Am., 1966—. Author: Labor Unions in Action, 1948, Practice of Unionism, 1956, Labor's Grass Roots, 1961, American Unions, Structure, Government, Politics, 1967, Trade Unions and National Economic Policy, 1972, Job Satisfaction, 1974, Elements of Industrial Relations, 1984; editorial bd.: Jour. Econ. Issues, 1970-75. Mem. Wis. Commn. Status of Women, 1959-62. Recipient Teaching Excellence award U. Wis., 1968. Mem. Indsl. Relations Research Assn. (exec. bd. 1963-68, pres. 1980), Internat. Indsl. Relations Assn. (exec. com. 1979), Assn. Evolutionary Econs. (pres. 1980), AAUP (pres. U. Wis. chpt. 1970-71). Democrat. Home: 1836 Keyes Ave Madison WI 53711 *Maintain a critical outlook on life and refuse to be coopted into ideologies of the left or right, implicit or explicit.*

BARBE, DAVID FRANKLIN, electrical engineer; b. Webster Springs, W.Va., May 26, 1939; s. Damon and Mary K. (Cooper) B.; m. Elizabeth K. Munyon, June 26, 1965; children: John David, Jane Suzanne. B.S. with high honors in Elec. Engring, W.Va. U., 1962, M.S.E.E., 1964; Ph.D. in Solid State Materials and Electronics, Johns Hopkins U., 1968. Instr. elec. engring. W.Va. U., Morgantown, 1962-65; fellow engr. Westinghouse Advanced Tech. Lab, Balt., 1964-71; head functional devices sect. Electronics Div., Naval Research Lab., Washington, 1971-74, head microelectronics br., 1974-79, asst. for electronics and phys. scis., 1979-83, dir. Submarine and ASW Systems, 1983—; Navy mem. adv. group on electron devices Dept. Def., 1971-79; mem. Navy Strategy Com. for Electron Devices, 1977-79; mem. steering com. Internat. Conf. on Charge-Coupled Devices, Edinburgh, 1974, 76, San Diego, 1975; lectr. 1st Internat. NATO Congress on Charge-Coupled Devices, U. Louvain-La Neuve, Belgium, 1975. Contbr. numerous articles on electronics to profl. publs. Westinghouse fellow, 1964-69. Fellow IEEE (asso. editor Electron Devices Newsletter 1975-79, mem. adminstrv. com. Electron Device Soc. 1977—); mem. Am. Phys. Soc., Sigma Xi, Tau Beta Pi, Eta Kappa Nu (charter mem. sr. exec. service). Democrat. Roman Catholic. Patentee in field. Home: 6905 Bradford Ct Laurel MD 20707 Office: Office of Asst Sec Navy for Research Engring and Systems Pentagon Washington DC 20350

BARBE, WALTER BURKE, teacher educator; b. Miami, Fla., Oct. 30, 1926; s. Victor Elza and Edith (Burris) B.; m. Marilyn E. Wood, Feb. 7, 1967; 1 son, Frederick Walter. B.S., Northwestern U., 1949, M.A., 1950, Ph.D., 1953. Tchr. Dade County Bd. Pub. Instrn., 1947; asst. Psycho-Ednl. Clinic, Northwestern U., 1949-50; instr. psychology, dir. reading clinic Baylor U., 1950; asst. prof. elementary edn. Kent State U., 1952-53, pof., head spl. edn. dept., 1960-64; adj. prof. U. Pitts., 1964-72, Ohio State U., 1972—; editor Highlights for Children, 1964—, dir., 1965—; prof. edn., dir. Jr. League Reading Center, U. Chattanooga, 1953-59; dir. Zaner-Bloser, 1972—; Bd. dirs. internat. council Improvement of Reading Inst., 1954-55. Author: Reading Clinic Directory, 1955, (with Ralph Roberts) Teenage Tales, 1957, (with Dorothy Hinman) We Build Our Words, 1957, Educators Guide to Personalized Reading, 1961, Helping Children Read Better, 1970; sr. author: (with Paul Witty) Creative Growth with Handwriting Series, 1975, Personalized Reading Instruction: New Techniques that Increase Reading Skill and Comprehension, 1975, (with Jerry Abbott) Barbe Reading Skills Check Lists, 1975, (with Joseph Renzulli) Teaching through Modality Strengths: Concepts and Practices, 1979; sr. editor: (with Swassing and Milone) Psychology and Education of the Gifted: Readings, 3d edit, 1980, Basic Skills in Kindergarten, 1980, Resource Book for Kindergarten Teachers, 1980; editor: Teaching of Reading; Selections, 1965, (with Edward Frierson) Educating Children with Learning Disabilities, 1967, Compass Points in Literature, Searchlights in Literature, 1969, Helping Children with Special Needs Series, 1974; Author: (with Francis, Braun) Spelling: Basic Skills for Effective Communication, 1982, (with Lucas, Wasylyk) Basic Skills for Effective Communication, 1984, (with others) Handwriting: Basic Skills and Application Series, 1984. Served with AUS, 1944-46. Fellow Am. Psychol. Assn.; mem. Nat. Assn. Gifted Children (pres. 1958). Democrat. Presbyterian. Home: Box 229 RD 1 Beach Lake PA 18405 Office: Highlights for Children Honesdale PA 18431

BARBEAU, ANDRÉ, physician, educator; b. Montreal, Que., Can., May 27, 1931; s. Antonio and Rachel (Jodoin) B.; m. Lise Trudeau, June 16, 1956; children: Claire, Claude, Michel, Dany. B.A., U. Paris, 1948; M.D., U. Montreal, 1956. Intern Hotel Dieu Hosp., Montreal, 1955-56, resident, 1956-57, U. Chgo.-Billings Hosp., 1957-59, Montreal Neurol. Inst., 1959-60; dept. histology U. Montreal, 1960-61, dir. lab. neurology, 1961-67, prof. neurology, 1970—, chmn. dept. neurology, 1976—; dir. dept. neurobiology Clin. Research Inst. Montreal, 1967—; prof. exptl. medicine McGill U., Montreal, 1970—. Editor 28 books; contbr. articles to profl. jours. Recipient Can. Mental Health Assn. award, 1965; United Parkinson Found. award of merit, 1965; Gold medal Can. Parkinson Found., 1965; Research prize Assn. des Medecins de Langue Francaise du Canada, 1974; M. Piché prize, 1979; Pariseau prize French Can. Assn. Advancement Scis., 1980; decorated officer Order of Can. Fellow Royal Coll. Physicians, Royal Soc. Can.; mem. Am. Acad. Neurology, Am. Neurol. Assn. Roman Catholic. Home: 3769 Wilson Ave Montreal PQ H4A 2T7 Canada

BARBER, ALBERT ALCIDE, educator, zoologist; b. Providence, July 13, 1929; s. Benjamin Arthur and Alice (Proulx) B.; m. Mary Lee Sparling, Sept. 1, 1956; children—Bonnie, Bradley. B.S., U. R.I., 1950; M.S., 1952; Ph.D., Duke, 1958. Mem. faculty U. Calif. at Los Angeles, 1958—, prof. zoology, 1968—, chmn. dept., 1968-70, asso. vice chancellor research, 1970-80, vice chancellor, 1980—. Recipient Purkyne medal Czechoslovakian Med. Soc., 1969. Mem. AAAS, Am. Inst. Biol. Scientists, Am. Soc. Zoology, Am. Physiol. Soc., Sigma Xi. Research biology cell membranes. Home: 1044 20th St Santa Monica CA 90403

BARBER, ARTHUR WHITING, communications company executive; b. Meriden, Conn., July 4, 1926; s. Arthur Leslie and Winifred (Whiting) B.; m. Margaret Shorey, Aug. 27, 1949; children: Jeffrey, Christopher, Jonathan Scott, Kimberley Susan, Cynthia. B.A. in Physics, Harvard, 1950. Physicist Air Force Cambridge (Mass.) Research Center, 1950-61, Mitre Corp., 1961-62; dep. asst. sec. internat. security affairs Dept. Def., 1962-67; pres. Inst. Politics and Planning, 1967-70, 1st Communications Co., 1970—. Home: 7600 Hemlock St Bethesda MD 20817 Office: 6917 Arlington Rd Bethesda MD 20814

BARBER, CHARLES FINCH, metals company executive, lawyer; b. Chgo., Feb. 26, 1917; s. Henri Newton and Lillian (Wanner) B.; m. Lois Helen LaCroix, Aug. 30, 1947; children: Charles Bradford, Ann McDonald, Robin Goodhue, Elizabeth Louise. B.S., Northwestern U., 1939; LL.B., Harvard, 1942; M.Phil. (Rhodes scholar), Oxford U., 1948; LL.D. (hon.), Mont. Tech., 1976; D.Eng., Colo. Sch. Mines, 1981. Bar: D.C. bar 1942, N.Y. State bar 1957, U.S. Supreme Ct 1946. Assoc. Covington & Burling, Washington, 1948-54; asst. solicitor gen. U.S., 1954-56; gen. counsel Asarco Inc. (formerly Am. Smelting & Refining Co.), N.Y.C., 1956-63, v.p., 1959-63, exec. v.p., 1963-69, pres., 1969-71, chmn., chief exec. officer, 1971-82, chmn. fin. com., 1982-84, also dir.; dir. Continental Corp., So. Peru Copper Corp., Desarrollo Industrial Minero Mexico, S.A., Burroughs Corp., Lehman Corp., Lehman Investors Fund Inc., Koppers Co., Inc., N.Y. Stock Exchange. Bd. mgr. Swarthmore Coll., 1966-74; bd. dirs. Council of Ams., America's Soc., Center Inter-Am. Relations; chmn. Nat. Legal Center for Public Interest; mem. council Rockefeller U., Woodrow Wilson Internat. Ctr. for Scholars. Served to lt. comdr. USNR, 1941-46. Decorated Legion of Merit. Mem. ABA, Am. Soc. Internat. Law, AIME (assoc.), Council Fgn. Relations; mem. Conf. Bd. (sr. mem.); Mem. Copper Devel. Assn. (chmn. 1977-79, dir. 1971-82), Internat. Copper Research Assn. (dir. 1971-82, vice-chmn.), Am. Mining Congress (dir., chmn. 1980-83), UN Assn. U.S.A. (dir.), Pilgrims, Phi Beta Kappa. Clubs: Wall St., Down Town Assn., Harvard, Mining (N.Y.C.); Metropolitan (Washington); Belle Haven (Greenwich). Home: 66 Glenwood Dr Greenwich CT 06830 Office: 180 Maiden Ln New York NY 10038

BARBER, CLARENCE LYLE, educator; b. Wolseley, Sask., Can., May 5, 1917; s. Richard Edward and Lulu Pearl (Lyons) B.; m. Barbara Anne Patchet, May 10, 1947; children—Paul Edward, Richard Stephen, David Stuart, Alan Gordon. B.A., U. Sask., 1939; M.A., Clark U., 1941; postgrad., U. Minn., 1941-43, Ph.D., 1952. With Stats. Can., 1945-48; mem. faculty McMaster U., 1948-49, U. Man., Winnipeg, Can., 1949—, prof. econs., 1956—, disting. prof., 1982—, head dept., 1963-72; vis. prof. Queen's U., 1954-55, McGill U., 1964-65; Commr. Royal Commn. on Farm Machinery, 1966-71; spl. adviser on nat. income Phillipines Govt., 1959-60; commr. for study welfare policy in Man., 1972; mem. Nat. Commn. on Inflation, 1979, Royal Commn. Econ. Union and Devel. Prospects for Can., 1982. Author: Inventories and the Business Cycle, 1958, The Theory of Fiscal Policy as Applied to a Province, 1966, (with others) Inflation and Unemployment: The Canadian Experience, 1980, Controlling Inflation: Learning from Experience in Canada, Europe and Japan, 1982. Served with RCAF, 1943-45. Can. Council Profl. Leave fellow, 1970-71. Fellow Royal Soc. Can.; mem. Canadian Assn. U. Tchrs. (pres. 1958-59), Canadian Econ. Assn. (pres. 1971-72), Am. Econ. Assn., Royal Econ. Soc., Social Sci. Research Council Can. (mem. exec. 1972-73). Clubs: Winnipeg Winter, U. Man. Faculty (Winnipeg). Home: 320 Kingsway Winnipeg MB R3M 0H4 Canada

BARBER, HENRY P. C. W., lawyer; b. Evanston, Ill., May 28, 1907; s. Charles S. and Alicia B. (Wilson) B.; m. Mary McElwain, Sept. 8, 1934; children: Charles, Mary Stewart. A.B., Princeton U., 1928; J.D., Northwestern U., 1931. Bar: Ill. bar 1931. Since practiced in, Chgo.; assoc. firm Peterson, Ross, Schloerb & Seidel (and predecessors), 1931—, partner, 1944—. Chmn. Evanston Zoning Amendment Com., 1964-71; alderman, Evanston, 1945-53; trustee Nat. Coll. Edn. Republican. Episcopalian. Club: Plaza (Chgo.). Home: 1519 Hinman Ave Evanston IL 60201 Office: 200 E Randolph Dr Chicago IL 60601

BARBER, JAMES DAVID, political scientist, educator; b. Charleston, W.Va., July 31, 1930; s. Daniel Newman and Edith (Naismith) B.; m. Amanda Joan MacKay Smith, Nov. 25, 1972; children: Sara Naismith, Jane Lewis, Luke David, Silas Higginson. B.A., U. Chgo., 1950, M.A., 1955; Ph.D. (Samuel S. Fels fellow), Yale, 1960. Research staff U. Chgo. Indsl. Relations Center, 1951-53, 55; asst. prof. polit. sci. Stetson U., DeLand, Fla., 1955-57; instr. to prof. Yale U., New Haven, 1960-72, dir. grad. studies in polit. sci., 1965-67; dir. Office for Advanced Polit. Studies, 1967-68; prof. chmn. dept. polit. Sci. Duke U., 1972-77, James B. Duke prof., 1977—; dir. Harvard-Yale-Columbia Intensive Summer Studies Program, 1966-67; series editor Harcourt Brace Jovanovich, 1970—; cons. Nat. Indsl. Conf. Bd., Com. on Econ. Devel., Center for Information on Am., Commn. on Year 2000, Twentieth Century Fund.; guest scholar Brookings Instn., 1964-65, 71-72. Author: The Lawmakers: Recruitment and Adaptation to Legislative Life, 1965, Power in Committees: An Experiment in the Governmental Process, 1966, Citizen Politics, 1969, The Presidential Character: Predicting Performance in the White House, 1972, 77; Editor: Political Leadership in American Government, 1964, Power to the Citizen, 1971, Race for the Presidency, 1977, The Pulse of Politics: Electing Presidents in the Media Age, 1980, Erasmus: A Play on Words, 1981; chmn. editorial bd.: Polit. Sci, 1969-71; Contbr. articles to profl. jours. Mem. Charter Commn., Wallingford, Conn., 1959-61, Bd. Finance, 1960-61; chmn. Nat. Coalition for a Responsible Congress, 1970; Bd. Univs. Nat. Anti-war Fund, 1970; bd. dirs. Amnesty Internat., USA, 1981—. Served with U.S. Army, 1953-55. NSF fellow, 1961-63; fellow Center for Advanced Studies in Behavioral Scis., 1968-69; scholar in residence Rockefeller Found. Study and Conf. Center, Bellagio, Italy, 1975. Mem. Am. Polit. Sci. Assn. (council 1976—), AAUP. Democrat. Office: Dept Polit Sci Duke U Durham NC 27706

BARBER, JERRY RANDEL, chemical company executive; b. Killarney, W.Va., Sept. 23, 1940; s. Edward Clay and Nora (Mullins) B.; m. Carrolyn Rae Acree, June 9, 1964; 1 dau., Alyssa Rae. B.S. in Chem. Engring., W.Va. U.-Morgantown, 1962, M.S., Ohio State U.-Columbia, 1964; Ph.D., Ohio State U.-Columbus, 1968. Research engr. Union Carbide Corp., South Charleston, W.Va., 1968-73, group leader research, 1973-77, assoc. dir. research, South Charleston, 1977-81, dir. research, Tarrytown, N.Y., 1981—. Mem. Am. Inst. Chem. Engrs., Tau Beta Pi, Phi Lambda Upsilon. Democrat. Methodist. Home: 64 Stonewall Ct Yorktown Heights NY 10598 Office: Union Carbide Corp Saw Mill River Rd Route 100C Tarrytown NY 10591

BARBER, JOHN CLARK, association executive; b. Liberty, N.C., Jan. 6, 1925; s. Yates Middleton and Emily Lucille (Clark) B.; m. Francene King, June 16, 1951; children: John Clark, Lewis Williams. B.S., N.C. State U., 1950, M.S., 1951; Ph.D., U. Minn., 1961. Research asst. N.C. State Coll., 1950-51; with U.S. Forest Service, 1951-80, br. chief genetics and timber related crops, Washington, 1967-71, asst. to dep. chief for research, 1971-72; dir. So. Forest Experiment Sta., New Orleans, 1972-76, asso. dep. chief state and pvt. forestry, Washington, 1976-80; exec. v.p. Soc. Am. Foresters, Washington, 1980—. Served with U.S. Army, 1943-46. Fellow Soc. Am. Foresters; mem. AAAS, Forest History Soc., Soil Conservation Soc. Am., Council of Engring. and Sci. Soc. Execs., Sigma Xi. Republican. Episcopalian. Office: 5400 Grosvenor Ln Bethesda MD 20814

BARBER, JOHN MERRELL, banker; b. Homer, La., Apr. 11, 1935; s. Howard I. and Sula (Cowser) B.; m. Betty Gunn Hoye, June 15, 1958; children—Craig Scott, Barry Lane. B.S. in Bus. Adminstrn, La. Tech. U., 1958, M.S., Miss. State U., 1961. Engr. Tex. Eastern Transmission Corp., Shreveport, La., 1958-59; engr.-programmer Miss. State U., Starkville, 1959-61; sect. leader United Gas Corp., Shreveport, 1961-67; adminstrv. officer Republic Nat. Bank, Dallas, 1967-69; sr. v.p. Merc.-Safe Deposit and Trust Co. and; dir. planning Merc. Bankshares Corp., Balt., 1969—; lectr. Centenary Coll., Shreveport, 1964, U. Dallas, 1968. Served with AUS, 1958-59. Mem. Am. Mgmt. Assn., N.Am. Soc. Corp. Planning (past treas.), Md. Bankers Assn., IEEE, Kappa Alpha, Tau Beta Pi, Omicron Delta Kappa, Eta Kappa Nu. Baptist. Home: 331 Presway Rd Timonium MD 21093 Office: 2 Hopkins Pl Baltimore MD 21203

BARBER, LLOYD INGRAM, university president; b. Regina, Sask., Can., Mar. 8, 1932; s. Lewis Muir and Hildred (Ingram) B.; m. Muriel Pauline MacBean, May 12, 1956; children: Muir, Brian, Kathleen, David, Susan, Patricia. B.A., U. Sask., 1953, B.Comm., 1954; M.B.A., U. Calif.-, Berkeley, 1955; Ph.D., U. Wash., 1964; LL.D. (hon.), U. Alta., 1983. Hon. chartered acct. Instr. commerce U. Sask., 1955-57, asst. prof., 1957-64, asso. prof., 1964-65, prof., 1965-68, 74-76, dean commerce, 1965-68, v.p., 1968-74; pres. U. Regina (Sask.), also prof. adminstrn., 1976—; Indian claims commr. Govt. of Can., 1969-76; spl. inquirer for Elder Indian testimony, 1977-81; dir. SED Systems Ltd., Bank of N.S., Burns Food, Ltd., The Molson Cos., Husky Oil Ltd., Sinco Devels., CP Ltd.; cons. bus. and govt. Trustee Inst. Research on Public Policy, 1972-79; bd. dirs. Indian Equity Found., 1978-79, Can. Scholarship Trust Fund, Regina United Way, 1977-79, Can. Schenley Football Awards; chmn. Wascana Centre Authority; adv. com. to Rector on pub. affairs award Concordia U., 1983. Decorated officer Order of Can.; recipient Vanier medal, 1978; hon. Sask. Indian Chief Little Eagle. Mem. Am. Inst. Public Adminstrn., Assn. Univs. and Colls. Can. (past pres.), Am., Can. econ. assns., Assn. Commonwealth Univs. (council). Mem. United Ch. Clubs: Masons, Assiniboia, Regina Beach Yacht. Home: 2500 Cross Pl Regina SK S4S 4C7 Canada Office: Pres's Office U Regina Regina SK S4S 0A2 Canada

BARBER, ORION METCALF, II, publishing company executive; b. Troy, N.Y., Oct. 20, 1935; s. Norton and Marcia Lamberton (Stevens) B.; m. Carol Ann Heald, June 29, 1963; children: Nathaniel Hurd, Caleb Julian Norton. A.B., Harvard U., 1957. Trainee, mfg. coordinator Colonial Press, Clinton, Mass., 1960-66; prodn. editor, coll. div. editorial prodn. mgr. D.C. Heath & Co., Boston, Lexington, Mass., 1966-70; mng. editor Stephen Greene Press, Brattleboro, Vt., 1971-78, v.p., 1973-78, pres., 1978-82, sr. v.p., 1982—; dir. West River Trading Co., Brattleboro, 1978—. Served with U.S. Army, 1957-60. Office: Stephen Greene Press Fessenden Rd Brattleboro VT 05301

BARBER, PERRY OSCAR, JR., lawyer; b. Ft. Worth, Aug. 23, 1938; s. Perry Oscar and Laura Lee (Spires) B.; m. Mary Diane Petrella, Oct. 4, 1975; children: Perry Oscar III, Caroline Killough; 1 dau. by previous marriage, Shelley Anne. B.B.A., U. Tex., 1960, J.D., 1963. Bar: Tex. 1963. Law clk. U.S. Ct. Appeals for 5th Circuit, Houston, 1963-64; staff asst. to Pres. of U.S., Washington, 1964-66; asso. firm Baker & Botts, Houston, 1966-71, partner, 1972-77; gen. counsel, dir., mem. exec. com. Pennzoil Co., Houston, 1977-84; ptnr. Baker & Botts, Houston, 1984—; also dir. Mem. adv. bd. Internat. and Comparative Law Center, Southwestern Legal Found.; trustee Houston Legal Found., 1970-71; bd. dirs. Soc. Performing Arts, 1980—; adv. dir. New Century Fund, U. Tex. Law Sch., 1974-75; mem. Harris County Democratic Exec. Com., 1972-73. Mem. Am. Bar Assn., Am. Judicature Soc., Fed. Bar Assn., State Bar Tex., Tex. Bar Found., Houston Bar Found., Houston Bar Assn.; Council on Fgn. Relations, U. Tex. Law Sch. Assn. (dir. 1977-79). Methodist. Clubs: Lakeside Country, Plaza, Athletic, Met. Racquet., Ramada. Office: Baker & Botts 3000 One Shell Plaza Houston TX 77002

BARBER, RAYMOND H., state ednl. adminstr.; b. Sumner County, Tenn., Dec. 3, 1923; s. Charles Joseph and Ruby Ellen (Roberts) B.; m. Leona May Hinton, Feb. 23, 1947; 1 dau., Nancy Lee. B.S., Western Ky. U., 1949, M.S., 1954. Successively tchr. public schs., fed. programs coordinator, high sch. prin., elem. prin., Allen County, Ky.; successively asst. dir. ESEA Title I, Ky.; Dept. Edn., Frankfort, dep. supt. public instrn., now state supt. public instrn.; former adminstrv. asst. for ednl. affairs Gov. Ky., Frankfort. Mem. Ky. Ho. of Reps., 1964-68. Served with U.S. Army, 1943-46. Decorated Meritorious Service award; life cert. in standard adminstrn. and supervision, Ky. Mem. NEA. Democrat. Methodist. Clubs: Rotary, Lions, VFW. Office: Ky Dept Edn Capital Plaza Tower Frankfort KY 40601 *

BARBER, THOMAS KING, dentist; b. Highland Park, Mich., Sept. 26, 1923; s. Thomas Cassius and Allie Estella (King) B.; m. Margot Jaques, July 12, 1947; children: Margaret, Thomas, Robert. B.S., Mich. State Coll., 1945; B.S.D., U. Ill., 1947, D.D.S., 1949, M.S., 1949. Research asst. U. Ill., 1945-49; instr. pedodontics Marquette U., 1950-51, U. Ill. Coll. Dentistry, 1951-53, asst. prof., 1953-58, assoc. prof., 1958-62, lectr. postgrad. studies, 1958, clin. prof. surgery Coll. Medicine, 1958, assoc. head dept. pedodontics, 1961-65, prof., 1962-69, head dept. pedodontics, 1965-69; prof., chmn, div. pediatric dentistry, prof. pediatrics Sch. Dentistry UCLA, 1969—, chmn. div. preventive dental scis., chmn. sect. pediatric dentistry, 1971-78, assoc. dean, 1978-80, 81—, acting dean Sch. Dentistry, Ctr. Health Scis., 1980-81; cons. USPHS, ADA, R.W. Johnson Found., Am. Fund Dental Health, VA. Hosp., Brentwood, Los Angeles, Vets. Hosp., Wadsworth, Los Angeles, 1972—; examiner Nat. Prevention Demonstration Program, 1977-82; spl. cons. Ednl. Testing Service (Princeton), N.J., 1973-82; cons. Avline, Nat. Library Medicine, 1976—; editorial cons. Jour. Dental Edn., 1979—. Editorial bd.: Jour. Dentistry for Children, 1968—; contbr. articles to profl. jours.; author: (with L. Luke) Pedodontics, 1982, (with Stewart, Troutman and Wei) Pediatric Dentistry, 1981. Mem. bd. edn., Bensenville, Ill, 1964-69; pres. Bensenville Recreation Assn., 1968; sec.-treas. White Pines Civic Assn. Served with U.S. Army, 1941-43; served with USN, 1943-44. Recipient Disting. Alumnus award, U. Ill. Coll. Dentistry, 1977; named Dentist of Yr. Am. Soc. Dentistry for Children, 1980. Fellow Am. Coll. Dentists; mem. Am. Acad. Pedodontics (mem. editorial bd. 1974—, chmn. 1977-79, assoc. editor 1978—), Am. Assn. Dental Editors, Am. Soc. Dentistry for Children (mem. research and rev. bd. 1974—), ADA (chmn. pedodontics council on sci. session 1973-74), Internat. Assn. Dental Reaserch, Am. Assn. Dental Schs. (mem. curricular guidelines dental care of handicapped com. 1978-79), Calif. Soc. Pediatric Dentists (exec. bd. 1974-80, pres. 1979-80), Ill. Soc. Dentistry for Children (pres. 1950-51), So. Calif. Soc. Dentistry for Children, Calif. Dental Assn. (council dental edn. 1979-82), Associacion Odontiologica Del Peru, Sociedad Peruana Odontopediatria, Societe Francaise de Pedodontic, Beverly Hills Acad. Dentistry, Sigma Xi, Omicron Kappa Upsilon. Home: 27406 Rainbow Ridge Palos Verde CA 90274 Office: UCLA Sch Dentistry Los Angeles CA 90024

BARBER, WILLIAM JOSEPH, educator, economist; b. Abilene, Kans., Jan. 13, 1925; s. Ward Seymour Henry and Esther (Roop) B.; m. Sheila Mary Marr, Apr. 16, 1955; children: Thomas, John, Charles. A.B., Harvard U., 1949; B.A., Oxford (Eng.) U., 1951, M.A., 1955, D.Phil., 1957; M.A. (hon.), Wesleyan U., Middletown, Conn., 1965. Asst. prof. Kans. State U., 1951-52; lectr. Balliol Coll., Oxford U., 1956; mem. faculty Wesleyan U., Middletown, Conn., 1957—, prof. econs., 1965—, Andrews prof. econs., 1972—; vis. prof. econs. Yale U., 1982-84; Am. sec. Rhodes Scholarship Trust, 1970-80; bd. electors Eastman professorship Oxford U., 1970-81. Author: The Economy of British Central Africa, 1961, A History of Economic Thought, 1967, British Economic Thought and India 1600-1858, 1975; Contbr. to: Asian Drama: An Inquiry into the Poverty of Nations, 1968, Exhortation and Controls, 1975, Energy Policy in Perspective, 1980, Economists in Government, 1982. Served with AUS, 1943-46; ETO. Decorated Order Brit. Empire; Rhodes scholar, 1949-51; Ford Found. Fgn. Area fellow, Africa, 1955-56. Mem. Am. Econ. Assn., Royal Econ. Soc., Am. Assn. Rhodes Scholars, Phi Beta Kappa. Home: 306 Pine St Middletown CT 06457

BARBER, WILLIAM LEE, ins. exec.; b. Easton, Conn., Mar. 1, 1916; s. Fred R. and Clara L. (King) B.; m. Mary S. Higgins, Aug. 22, 1942; children—Carole, Mary Stone, Joan. Student, N.C. State U., 1937; B.S., Central Conn. Coll., 1941. Actuarial trainee Aetna Life Ins. Co., Hartford, Conn., 1943-52; sr. v.p. Union Mut. Life Ins. Co., Portland, Maine, 1952-72; sr. v.p. ins. ops., corp. sec. Am. Mut. Life Ins. Co., Des Moines, 1972-79; 1st sr. v.p., chief actuary Fed. Home Life Ins. Co., Battle Creek, Mich., 1979—; Former chmn. Sch. Com., Cape Elizabeth, Maine.; Enrolled actuary C.L.U. Fellow Soc. Actuaries, Can. Inst. Actuaries; mem. Am. Acad. Actuaries. Clubs: Rotary, Detroit Actuary's. Home: 448 S Moorland Battle Creek MI 49015 Office: 78 W Michigan Mall Battle Creek MI 49016

BARBERA, JOSEPH, motion picture and TV producer, cartoonist; b. N.Y.C. Grad., Am. Inst. Banking. Formerly accountant trust co. Free-lance mag. cartoonist story man, MGM, 1937; creator; co-producer: (with William Hanna) Tom and Jerry; animated cartoon series; partner, Hanna and Barbera Prodn., Hollywood, Calif., 1957—; animated programming series include The Jetsons, The Flintstones, Top Cat, Johnny Quest, 1971-75, The Addams Family, 1973-75; ptnr.: Devlin, 1974-76, Goober and the Ghost Chasers, 1973-75, Hong Kong Phooey, 1974-76, Jeannie, 1973-75, Korg: 70,000 B.C.!, 1974-75, Partridge Family: 2200 A.D, 1976-77, Scooby-Doo, Where Are You?, 1971-72, Speed Buggy, 1973, Superfriends, 1973-79, Valley of the Dinosaurs, 1974, Josie and the Pussycats, 1971-72, 75-76, The New Tom and Jerry/Grape Ape show, 1975, Pebbles and Bamm-Bamm, 1971-72, 75-76, These Are the Days, 1974-76, Dynomutt, 1976-78, Jabberjaw, 1976-77, Mumbly, 1976-77, Captain Caveman, 1977-79, Godzilla, 1978-79, Popeye Hour, 1978-79; live-action The Runaways, 1974, KISS Meets the Phantom of the Park, 1978, The Beasts are in the Street, 1978, C.H.O.M.P.S, 1979, The Gathering, 1977 (best dramatic spl. award), The Gathering, Part 2, 1979, Belle Starr, 1980, The Gymnast, 1980, Heidi's Song, 1981; Recipient (numerous Acad. and Emmy awards for animated cartoons.). Office: Hanna-Barbera Prodns 3400 W Cahuenga Blvd Hollywood CA 90068 *I have a simple goal; make people laugh.*

BARBERO, GIULIO JOHN, physician, educator; b. Mt. Vernon, N.Y., Oct. 13, 1923; s. Armando and Mary (Celoria) B.; m. Margaret Goff, May 30, 1947; children—Paul, Christopher, Mary, Peter, Claudia, David. B.A., U. Maine, 1943; M.D., U. Pa., 1947. Intern Hosp. U. Pa., 1947-49; resident Children's Hosp. Phila., 1949-50, chief resident, 1951-52; mem. faculty U. Pa. Med. Sch., 1953-67, asso. prof. pediatrics, 1963-67; prof., chmn. dept. pediatrics Hahnemann Med. Coll., Phila., 1967-72, U. Mo. Med. Sch., Columbia, 1972—; Chmn. gen. med. and sci. council Nat. Cystic Fibrosis Research Found., 1971-74; mem. Nat. Heart, Lung, Blood Council, 1977-78. Served with AUS, 1950-51; Korea. Decorated Bronze Star; sr. fellow Nat. Polio Found., 1952-54; recipient Bernard Wenrich award for research in cystic fibrosis, 1962. Mem. Phi Beta Kappa, Sigma Xi, Pi Kappa Phi. Home: 408 S Glenwood Ave Columbia MO 65201

BARBIER, GUY, accounting company executive; b. Paris, Sept. 19, 1928; s. Fernand and Berthe (Hugel) B.; m. Helen Bruening, June 18, 1983; 1 dau., Delphine. Grad., Ecole des Hautes Etudes Commerciales, Paris, 1953. Partner Arthur Andersen & Co., Chgo., 1964—, office mng. partner, Paris, 1967-75, co-chmn., 1975-79, mng. ptnr. area, 1980—; adj. prof. Ecole des Hautes Etudes Commerciales, 1960-64. Mem. Automobile Club of France. Office: Arthur Andersen & Co 69 W Washington St Chicago IL 60602

BARBIERI, JOSEPH PETER, publisher; b. New York, Mar. 6, 1923; s. Michael and Katherine (Garbarini) B.; m. Maria Luiza, Nov. 6, 1974; 1 son, Joseph Peter. Student, Princeton U., 1945-47; A.B., U. Miami, Coral Gables, Fla., 1950. With advt. dept. Hearst Mags., N.Y.C., 1953-58; with sales mgmt. dept. Curtis Pub. Co., N.Y.C., 1958-66; pres., pub. performing arts publs. including Kennedy Center and Lincoln Center program mags., Chgo.; Stagebill, Chgo., 1966—; pres. Arts Press, Inc. Served to 1st lt. USAAF, 1944-45. Decorated D.F.C., Air medal with three oak leaf clusters. Republican. Roman Catholic. Club: Princeton (N.Y.C.). Home: 505 N Lake Shore Dr Chicago IL 60611 Office: 500 N Michigan Ave Chicago IL 60611

BARBORIAK, JOSEPH JAN, pharmacologist; b. Kremnica, Slovakia, Feb. 19, 1923; came to U.S., 1953, naturalized, 1959; s. Joseph M. and Amalie (Kostial) B.; m. Gertrude M. Zmarzlak, Sept. 15, 1956; children: Peter N., Daniel P., Eric M. B.S., Slovak Inst. Tech., 1946; Sc.D., Swiss Fed. Inst. Tech., 1953. Research asso. Swiss Inst. Tech., Zurich, 1947-53, Yale Sch. Medicine, New Haven, 1954-59; group leader Mead Johnson & Co., Evansville, Ind., 1959-61; chief biochemistry sect. VA Center, Wood, Wis., 1961—; asst. prof. pharmacology Marquette U. Sch. Medicine (now Med. Coll. Wis.), Milw., 1962-66, asso. prof., 1966-71, prof. pharmacology, 1971—, dir. interdisciplinary nutrition group, 1980—. Contbr. articles to profl. jours. Mem. Am. Inst. Nutrition, Soc. for Exptl. Biology and Medicine, Société de Chimie Biologique (Paris), Am. Acad. Allergy, Internat. Soc. Biochem. Pharm., Am. Soc. Pharm. and Exptl. Therapeutics, Sigma Xi. Address: VA Center Wood WI 53193

BARBOUR, HUGH REVELL, publisher; b. N.Y.C., Nov. 6, 1929; s. William Rinehart and Mary Alice (McKelvey) B.; m. Eva Marie Cox, May 30, 1953; children—Deborah Faith (Mrs. Frank Dietrich), Steven Cox, Constance Revell (Mrs. Steven Morton). Student, Stevens Inst. Tech., 1949-50. With Fleming H. Revell, Old Tappan, N.J., 1953—; now cons. spl. projects; pres. Book Bargains, Inc. Served with USAF, 1950-53. Mem. Evang. Christian Pubs. Assn., Aircraft Owners and Pilots Assn. Club: Hackensack Golf. Home: 164 Mill St Westwood NJ 07675 Office: 184 Central Ave Old Tappan NJ 07675

BARBOUR, IAN GRAEME, physics and religion educator; b. Peking, China, Oct. 5, 1923; s. George Brown and Dorothy (Dickinson) B.; m. Deane Kern, Nov. 29, 1947; children: John Dickinson, Blair Winn, David Freeland, Heather Deane. B.A., Swarthmore Coll., 1943; M.A., Duke U., 1946; Ph.D., U. Chgo., 1950, B.D., 1956. Asst. prof. physics Kalamazoo Coll., 1949-51, asso. prof., chmn. dept., 1951-53; mem. faculty Carleton Coll., Northfield, Minn., 1955—, chmn. dept. religion, 1956-71, prof. religion and physics, 1965—, Winifred and Atherton Bean prof. sci., tech. and soc., 1972—; Lilly vis. prof. sci., theology and human values Purdue U., 1973-74. Author: Christianity and the Scientist, 1960, Issues in Science and Religion, 1966, Science and Religion: New Perspectives on the Dialogue, 1968, Science and Secularity: The Ethics of Technology, 1970, Earth Might Be Fair, 1972, Western Man and Enyironmental Ethics, 1973, Myths, Models and Paradigms, 1974, Finite Resources and the Human Future, 1976, Technology, Environment and Human Values, 1980, Energy and American Values, 1982; editorial bd.: Sci. and Religion; Author numerous articles. Ford Faculty fellow, 1953-54; Kent fellow, 1954-55; recipient Harbison award for disting. teaching Danforth Found., 1963; Am. Council Learned Socs. fellow, 1963-64; Guggenheim and Fulbright fellow, 1967-78; Nat. Endowment Humanities fellow, 1976-77; Nat. Humanities Center fellow, 1980-81. Mem. Phi Beta Kappa, Sigma Xi. Home: 106 Winona St Northfield MN 55057

BARBOUR, MICHAEL G., botany educator, ecological consultant; b. Jackson, Mich., Feb. 24, 1942; s. George Jerome and Mae (Dater) B.; m. Norma Jean Yourist, Sept. 30, 1963 (div. 1981); children: Julie Ann, Alan Benjamin. B.S. in Botany, Mich. State U., 1963, Ph.D., Duke U., 1967. Asst. prof. botany, botany dept. U. Calif., Davis, 1967-71, assoc. prof., 1971-76, prof., 1976—, chmn., 1982—; ptnr. Ecolabs Cons., Davis, 1969—; vis. prof. botany dept. Hebrew U., Jerusalem, 1979-81; vis. prof. marine scis. dept. La. State U., Baton Rouge, 1984. Co-author: Coastal Ecology, Bodega Head, 1973, botany, 6th edit., 1982, Terrestrial Vegetation of California, 1977, Terrestrial Plant Ecology, 1980. Fulbright Found fellow Adelaide, Australia, 1964; Guggenheim Found. fellow, 1978; NSF research grantee, 1968-80. Mem. Ecol. Soc. Am., Brit. Ecol. Soc., Sigma Xi. Democrat. Jewish. Club: Rotary. Office: Botany Dept U Calif Davis CA 95616

BARBOUR, ROSS, singer; b. Columbus, Ind., Dec. 31, 1928; s. Harold L. and Maude (Fodrea) B.; m. Nancy Sue Carson, Dec. 31, 1948; children: Kent, Gary, Kathy. Student, Arthur Jordan Conservatory, Indpls., 1947. Mgr. employee services Fortin Industries Inc., Sylmar, Calif. Mem.: singing group Four Freshmen, 1948-77; rec. artist, Liberty, Capitol labels; Composer: Crazy Bones, 1955, Love Lost, 1959, First Affair, 1960, Tears in Our Eyes, 1963, And So It's Over, 1963. Hon. mem. Tau Kappa Epsilon. Home: 17233 Rayen St Northridge CA 91325 *If you want to be respected, respect! If you want to be trusted, trust! If you want to be loved, love! Because, when you deal with people, you're only going to get what you give.*

BARBOUR, WILLIAM ALBERT, publishing company executive; b. Phila., Apr. 27, 1921; s. William Schreider and Rose (Emilius) B.; m. Anne Katherine Moore, Mar. 29, 1947; children: Michael W., Anne S. B.J., Mont. State U., 1948. Mng. editor Cape May County (N.J.) Gazette, 1948-49, Moorestown (N.J.) News Chronicle, 1950-52; asst. editor Chilton Co., Phila., 1952-53, mng. editor, 1953-59, editor, 1959-61, publisher, 1961-69, pub., v.p., 1969-71, sr. v.p., 1971-72, pres., chief exec. officer, 1972-82, chmn., 1982—; dir. Newton Falls (N.Y.) Paper Mill; chmn., mem. exec. com., dir. Am. Bus. Press, Inc., N.Y.C. Pres.; bd. dirs. Center for Curriculum Devel., Skokie, Ill., 1970—, Bus. Publs. Audit, 1977—. Trustee Pop Warner Little Scholars, 1974. Served with USAAF, 1942-45. Decorated Bronze Star. Mem. Bus. and Profl. Advt. Assn., Sigma Delta Chi. Clubs: Seaview Country; Nat. Press (Washington); Poor Richard (Phila.). Home: 117 E Central Ave Moorestown NJ 08057 Office: Chilton Way Radnor PA 19089

BARBOUR, WILLIAM ERNEST, JR., assn. exec.; b. Evanston, Ill., Nov. 1909; s. William Ernest and Mabel Ridgway (Hair) B.; m. Georgiana Whitney, Dec. 16, 1950; children—Alicia Barbour, Gigi. B.S., Mass. Inst. Tech. Cons. in field indsl. instrumentation, 1933-36; with Raytheon Mfg. Corp., 1936-39, Boston Edison Co., 1939-41; pres. Tracerlab, Inc., Boston, 1946-57, Controls for Radiation, Inc., 1957-58; cons. nuclear and magnetic fields, 1965—; pres. Magnion, Inc., 1960-65; exec. sec. Assn. Nuclear Instrument Mfrs., 1966—; Dir. QSC Industries, Gen. Aircraft Corp.; Cons. tech. utilization NASA.; Mem. New Eng. Govs. Com. on Atomic Energy, also; Atomic Indsl. Forum.; Mem. alumni council Mass. Inst. Tech.; Mem. council atomic energy Nat. Indsl. Conf. Bd., 1955—; mem. So. Regional Edn. Bd. Nuclear Energy Devel. Project, 1955-56. Bd. corporators Emerson Hosp., 1968—. Served with USAAF, 1941-46. Mem. Nat. Aeros. Assn. (dir. 1970—), Am. Standards Assn. (mem. nuclear standards bd.), Am. Inst. Elec. Engrs. (mem. standards com., Geneva observer 1956, chmn. com. nucleonics 1954-57), Am. Nuclear Soc. (dir. 1954-56), Nat. Pilots Assn., Aircraft Owners and Pilots Assn., IEEE (adminstrv. com. group on nuclear sci.), Delta Kappa Epsilon. Clubs: Union, Aero of New England (dir. 1969—), Aero of New England (pres. 1970-71), Concord Country.). Address: Barbour Assos Box 460 Concord MA 01742

BARBOUR, WILLIAM RINEHART, JR., book publisher; b. N.Y.C., Mar. 2, 1922; s. William Rinehart and Mary (McKelvey) B.; m. Mary Munsell, Nov. 17, 1951; children: Bruce R., Elizabeth M., Alan W. Student, Mich. State Coll., 1941-42. With Fleming H. Revell Co., 1944-83, pres., 1968-80, chmn., 1980-83; adv. bd. Old Tappan br. Citizens 1st Nat. Bank, Ridgewood, N.J. Trustee Walter Hoving Home, Grace Ch., Ridgewood; bd. dirs. Christian Overcomers. Served with USAAF, 1942-44. Named Pub. of Year Religious Heritage Am., 1974. Home: 11 Black Oak Ln Mahwah NJ 07430 Office: 184 Central Ave Old Tappan NJ 07675

BARCHAS, JACK DAVID, psychiatrist, educator; b. Los Angeles, Nov. 2, 1935; s. Samuel Isaac and Cecile Margaret (Pasarow) B.; m. Patricia Ruth Corbitt, Feb. 9, 1957; 1 son, Isaac Doherty. B.A., Pomona Coll., 1956; M.D., Yale U., 1961. Intern Pritzker Sch. Medicine, U. Chgo., 1961-62; postdoctoral fellow in biochemistry and pharmacology NIH, 1962-64; resident in psychiatry Stanford Med. Sch., 1964-67, instr., 1966-67, asst. prof., 1967-71, assoc. prof., 1971-76, prof., 1976—, Nancy Friend Pritzker prof. psychiatry and behavioral scis., 1976—; dir. Nancy Pritzker Lab. of Behavioral Neurochemistry, 1976—. Editor; author: Serotonin and Behavior, 1973, Neuroregulators and Psychiatric Disorders, 1977, Psychopharmacology from Theory to Practice, 1977, Catecholamines - Basic and Clinical Frontiers, 1979, Isoquinolines and Beta-Carbolines, 1981; contbr. articles to profl. jours. Served with USPHS, 1962-64. Recipient Psychopharmacology award Am. Psychol. Assn., 1970, Research Scientist award NIMH, 1980—. Fellow Am. Psychiat. Assn., Am. Coll. Neuropsychopharmacology; Mem. Soc. Neurosci., Am. Coll. Neuropsychopharmacology (Daniel Efron award 1978), Am. Soc. Pharmacology and Exptl. Therapeutics, Am. Physiol. Soc., Am. Soc. Neurochemistry, Am. Chem. Soc., Am. Psychosomatic Soc., Psychiat. Research Soc., Soc. Biol. Psychiatry (A.E. Bennett award 1968), Am. Psychopathol. Assn., Inst. Medicine Nat. Acad. Scis. (chmn. bd. Mental Health and Behavioral Medicine). Home: 669 Mirada Ave Stanford CA 94305 Office: Dept Psychiatry Stanford Med Sch 300 Pasteur Dr Stanford CA 94305

BARCHET, STEPHEN, naval officer, physician; b. Annapolis, Md., Oct. 25, 1932; s. Stephen George and Louise (Lankford) B.; m. Marguerite Joan Racek, Aug. 9, 1965. Student, Brown U., 1949-52; M.D., U. Md., 1956. Diplomate: Am. Bd. Ob-Gyn. Commd. ensign M.C. U.S. Navy, 1955, advanced through grades to rear adm., 1978; intern Naval Hosp., Chelsea, Mass., 1956-57, resident in ob-gyn, 1958-61, resident in gen. surgery, Portsmouth, Va., 1957-58; fellow Harvard Med. Sch., 1959-60; obstetrician-gynecologist Naval Hosp., Naples, Italy, 1961-63, Portsmouth, N.H., 1963-64, Beaufort, S.C., 1964-66, Bremerton, Wash., 1967-70, chief ob-gyn, Boston, 1970-73; asst. head, tng. br. Bur. Medicine and Surgery, Washington, 1973, head, 1973-75; dep. spl. asst. to surgeon gen. Navy, 1975; assoc. dean Sch. Medicine, Uniformed Services U. Health Scis., Bethesda, Md., 1976-77, exec. sec. bd. regents, 1976-77; spl. asst. to surgeon gen. for med. dept. edn. and tng. Bur. Medicine and Surgery, Navy Dept., Washington, 1977-79, insp. gen., 1979-80; comdg. officer Naval Health Scis. and Edn. and Tng. Command, Nat. Naval Med. Center, Bethesda, 1977-79; asst. chief planning, resources BUMED, 1980-82; dep. surg. gen., dep. dir. naval medicine Dept. Navy, 1982—; clin. asst. prof. Boston U. Sch. Medicine, 1971—; alt. regent Nat. Library Medicine, Bethesda, 1977-79; adj. prof. health care scis. George Washington U. Sch. Medicine and Health Scis., Washington, 1978—; ex. officio mem. grad. med. edn. nat. adv. com. HEW, 1978-79; chmn. med.-dental com. Interservice Tng. Rev. Orgn., Washington, 1977-79. Contbr. articles to med. jours. Decorated Bronze star, others. Fellow Am. Coll. Obstetricians and Gynecologists; mem. Md. Med. Soc., Med. Alumni Assn. U. Md., Assn. Mil. Surgeons U.S., Soc. Med. Cons. Armed Forces. Home: 18601 SE 64th Way Issaquah WA 98027 Office: Dep Surg Gen OP09313 Navy Dept Pentagon: Washington DC 20350 *Lasting achievements depend not only upon Knowledge well applied, but also upon doing what ought to be done.*

BARCHOFF, HERBERT, bus. exec.; b. N.Y.C., Apr. 3, 1915; s. Abraham and Mollie (Berkowitz) B.; m. Lilyan Blum; children—Michael, Jared Blum. B.S., N.Y. U., 1935, J.D. (Eliot Shepard scholar), 1938. Vice pres. Eastern Brass & Copper Co. (name now Eastern Rolling Mills, Inc.), 1938-45, exec. v.p., sec., 1945-54, pres., 1954—, chmn. bd., 1978—; pres. Tubotron, Inc., 1959; guest lectr. Columbia, Farleigh Dickinson Coll., Pace Coll.; seminar leader conf., program Alliance for Progress, Bogota, Colombia.; Mem. Pres.'s Council Econ. Advisers, 1952; mem. exec. com. Action Com. for Internat. Devel.; dir. United Cerebral Palsy, 1959; nat. commr. Anti-Defamation League, 1968—; asso. chmn. N.Y. appeal, 1971—; Cons. Copper Recovery Corp, 1942; mem. industry adv. com. NPA, 1951-53; survey small plants NATO area, Europe, Mut. Security Agy., 1952; mem. citizens adv. com. on fgn. trade Senate Banking and Currency Com.; nat. adviser SBA; bd. govs. Joint Def. Appeal, 1956; mem. adv. com. small bus. Nat. Dem. Com., 1956; chmn. mgmt. of smaller cos. Am. Mgmt. Assn.; mem. Canadian Am. Nuclear Proliferation Conf., 1967, Am. Assembly Arden House Conf.-Uses of Sea, 1968; vice chmn., then chmn. Com. Release Stockpile Copper, 1973-74; pres. Am. Copper Council, 1975-79, chmn. bd., 1979—. Author: pub. monthly copper letter Sticking My Neck Out; editor: N.Y. U. Law Quar. Rev; Contbr. articles to trade publs. Mem. Nat. Assn. Ind. Bus. (pres.), Copper and Brass Warehouse Assn. (treas., dir. 1951-54, v.p. 1954, pres. 1955), Young Presidents Orgn. (vice chmn. N.Y. chpt. 1959, dir. 1961, dir. Met. Pres.'s Orgn. 1973—), Conf. to Plan Strategy for Peace, Am. Assembly Arms Control, Am. Baseball Acad. (exec. bd. dirs.), Nat. Planning Assn. (nat. council), Theta Sigma Lambda. Club: Copper (dir.). Home: Horseshoe Hill Pound Ridge NY 10576 Office: 505 Park Ave New York NY 10022

BARCKLEY, ROBERT EUGENE, economics educator; b. Page, N.D., Sept. 14, 1922; s. Adelbert Eugene and Frona Elizabeth (McClure) B.; (div.)children: Thomas B., Maureen B. B.Sc., U. N.D., 1948; M.A., Columbia U., 1950; Ph.D., U. Ill.-Urbana, 1957. Instr. N.D. State U., 1950-51; dist. economist Office Price Stblzn., Fargo, N.D., 1951-53; teaching asst. U. Ill.-Urbana, 1953-55; asst. prof. econs. dept. San Diego State, 1955-64, prof., 1964—, chmn. econs. dept., 1981—. Served with AUS, 1943-46. Democrat. Home: 4436 Arizona St San Diego CA 92116 Office: Dept Econs San Diego State U San Diego CA 92182

BARCLAY, H(UGH) DOUGLAS, lawyer, state senator; b. N.Y.C., July 5, 1932; s. Hugh and Dorothy Douglass (Moody) D.; m. Sara Seiter, Aug. 15, 1959; children—Kathryn D., David H., Dorothy G., Susan M., William A. Grad., St. Paul's Sch., Concord, N.H., 1951; B.A., Yale U., 1955; J.D., Syracuse U., 1961,; D.Sc., Clarkson Coll. Tech., 1981. Bar: N.Y. State bar 1962. Asso. firm Hiscock, Lee, Rogers, Henley & Barclay (and predecessor firm), Syracuse, N.Y., 1961—, partner, 1968—; sec., gen. counsel Key Banks Inc. (and subs.), Albany, N.Y., 1971—; dir. Excelsior Ins. Co., Coradian Corp., Giant Portland & Masonry Cement Co., Empire Airlines, Inc., Key Bank of Central N.Y., Syracuse.; Mem. N.Y. State Senate, 1965—; chmn.

Republican Senate Conf., 1979—, Jud. Com., 1979—. Served as lt., arty. AUS, 1955-57. Mem. Am. Bar Assn., N.Y. State Bar Assn. Home: 6871 Port Rd Pulaski NY 13142 Office: Hiscock Lee Rogers Henley & Barclay PO Box 4878 221 S Warren St Syracuse NY 13221

BARCLAY, IAN ANDREW, forest products company executive; b. Montreal, Que., Can., Mar. 7, 1921; s. Hon. Gregor and Jean Gertrude (Fleck) B.; m. Ann Victoria, Sept. 21, 1951; 1 dau. Deborah Ann. Student, Ashbury Coll., 1939; B.C.L., McGill U., 1948; M.P.A., Harvard U., 1949. Bar: Que. 1948. Assoc. Scott, Huggesen, Macklaier, Chisholm & Hyde; dir. indsl. relations Sheraton Hotels (Can.) Ltd.; asst. sec. Can. Chem. and Cellulose Ltd.; v.p., sec. Columbia Cellulose Co. Ltd.; v.p., sec. Brit. Columbia Forest Products Ltd., 1962-67; exec. v.p. Brit. Columbia Forest Products Ltd., 1967-68, dir., 1968—, chmn., chief exec. officer, 1972-76, chmn., 1976—; dir. Hudson's Bay Co., No. Telecom Ltd., Royal Bank of Can. Bd. dirs. Boys' and Girls' Club of Can.; bd. govs. B.C. Lions Football Club. Served with RCNVR, 1940-45. Recipient Newton D. Baker II award. Mem. Kappa Alpha (pres. McGill 1946-47). Office: British Columbia Forest Products Ltd 1050 W Pender St Vancouver BC Canada V6E 2X3

BARCLAY, JAMES RALPH, psychologist, educator; b. Grand Rapids, Mich., May 6, 1926; s. Gordon William and Ruth Margaret (Christensen) B.; m. Lisa Kurcz, Dec. 29, 1954; children: Anne, Robert, Gregory, Christopher. A.B., Sacred Heart Sem., Detroit, 1947; M.A., U. Mich., 1956, Ph.D., 1959. Diplomate: Am. Bd. Profl. Examiners in Psychology. Tchr. Boy's Republic, Detroit, 1952-53; child welfare worker State of Minn., 1953-54; instr. dept. edn. U. Detroit, 1955-58; sch. psychologist Redford Univ. Schs., Detroit, 1956-59; vis. lectr. U. Mich., 1959; asst. prof., asso. prof., prof., dir. U. Counseling Center, Idaho State U., 1959-64; prof., coordinator Sch. Psychology Program, Calif. State Coll. at Hayward, 1964-69; prof., chmn. dept. ednl. psychology and counseling U. Ky., Lexington, 1969—; cons. Idaho Dept. Edn., Oakland Schs., Louisville, U.S. Office Edn. Proposal Rev. Mem. Bd. Psychol. Examiners Idaho, 1962-64; pres. Ednl. Skills Devel., Inc., Lexington. Author: Counseling Psychology and Philosophy, 1968, Controversial Issues in Testing, 1968, Foundations of Counseling Strategies, 1971; editor: Personnel and Guidance Jour, 1978—; editorial cons.: Measurement and Evaluation in Guidance, 1969-73, Sch. Psychology Digest, Jour. Sch. Psychology; Contbr. articles to profl. jours. Fellow Am. Psychol. Assn. (diplomate); mem. Am. Ednl. Research Assn., Am. Personnel and Guidance Assn., Phi Delta Kappa. Home: 1672 Linstead Dr Lexington KY 40504

BARCLAY, KENNETH STUART, diversified manufacturing executive; b. Montreal, Que., Can., 1926. B.A., McGill U., 1949. With Dominion Engineering Ltd., 1949-62, Dominion Bridge Co., Ltd., 1962; chmn. bd., chief exec. officer Amca Internat. Ltd., Amca Internat. Corp., Hanover, N.H. Address: Amca Internat Corp Dartmouth Nat Bank Bldg Hanover NH 03755 *

BARCLAY, RONALD DAVID, chemical company executive; b. Pitts., 1934; s. David Thompson and Olive Stewart (Bietel) B.; m. Gladys Anne Stoudt, July 11, 1959; children—Todd, Dana, Scott. B.B.A., U. Pitts., 1956; M.B.A., Lehigh U., 1965. Market planning asst. Air Products & Chems., Inc., Allentown, Pa., 1956-57, treasury staff asst., 1957-64, asst. treas., 1964-75, treas., 1975-82, v.p., treas., 1982—. Bd. dirs. Lehigh County Gen. Authority, 1978—. Served with USCG, 1957-58. Republican. Presbyterian. Office: PO Box 538 Allentown PA 18105

BARCUS, JAMES EDGAR, educator; b. Alliance, Ohio, Oct. 29, 1938; s. James E. and Mary (Weizenecker) B.; m. Nancy Ellen Bidwell, May 28, 1961; children: Heidi Anne, Jeffrey Thomas, James Hans. B.A., Houghton Coll., 1959; M.A., U. Ky., 1961; Ph.D., U. Pa., 1968. Teaching fellow U. Ky., U. Pa., 1959-63; asst. to personnel mgr., acting personnel mgr. ASTM, 1961-63; vis. prof. Nyack Coll., 1963-64; vis. U. Ky., Lexington, 1966; prof. Houghton Coll., 1964-79, chmn. div. Englishand speech, 1969-79; v.p. acad. affairs, prof. English Trinity Coll., 1979-80; prof., chmn. English dept. Baylor U., 1980—; vis. disting. prof. English Baylor U., Waco, Tex., 1978; evaluator Middle States Accrediting Assn., Susquehanna U., Coll. Misericordia, Geneva Coll.; nat. treas. Conf. on Christianity and Lit., 1970-71, 80-81; mem. task force (Found. Chrestian Higher Edn.), Christian Coll. Consortium, 1977-78; reader for advanced placement exams Ednl. Testing Service, 1976-82. Assoc. editor: Christian Scholar's Rev., 1970-71; mem. editorial bd., 1970-80; editor: The Literary Correspondence of Bernard Barton, 1966, Shelley: The Critical Heritage, 1975; contbr. articles to profl jours. Fellow Nat. Endowment for Humanities, 1977; John Louis Haney fellow, U. Pa., 1963-64; Paul Robert Steese fellow, Houghton Coll., 1958-59. Mem. MLA, Nat. Council Tchrs. English, Conf. Christianity and Lit., Conf. Coll. Tchrs. English (councilor). Baptist. Office: Dept English Baylor Univ Waco TX 76707

BARCZA, PETER JOSEPH, baritone; b. Stockholm, June 23, 1949; emigrated to Can., 1952, naturalized, 1958; s. Joseph and Katherine Elizabeth (Tamasi) B. Diploma in operatic performance, U. Toronto, 1971; postgrad., Sch. of Fine Arts Villa Schifanoia, Florence, Italy, 1971. Appearances with the following opera cos., Guelph (Ont., Can.) Spring Festival, 1970-71, Can. Opera Co., Toronto and, Can. Opera Co., Ottawa, 1971—, Can. Opera Touring Co., 1972-78, Manitoba Opera Assn., Winnipeg, 1975-76, Opera Theatre of Rochester, N.Y., 1976, Opera in Concert, Toronto, 1976-78, So. Alta. Opera, Calgary, 1978, State Opera, Liege, Belgium, Ky. Opera, Opera Memphis, Teheran Symphony, Toronto Symphony, Regina, Symphony, Paris Opera, CBC Radio and TV, repertoire performed professionally includes; Figaro in: Barber of Seville; Marcello, Schaunard in: La Boheme; Sharpless in: Madame Butterfly; Guglielmo in: Cosi fan tutte; Valentin in: Faust; Papageno in the: Magic Flute; Herode in: Herodiade; Oreste in: Iphigenie en Tauride; Count in: Marriage of Figaro; Silvio in: I Pagliacci; Nick Shadow in: The Rake's Progress; Enrico in: Lucia di Lammermoor; Germont in: La Traviata; participant opera workshops various Can. colls. Recipient Jean Chalmers award Can. Opera Co., 1971; regional winner Met. Opera Auditions, 1972; recipient Bruce Yarnell Meml. award San Francisco Opera, 1976; Can. Council grantee, 1971, 77. Mem. Actors Equity Assn., Assn. Can. Radio and TV Artists, Am. Guild Mus. Artists. Home: 17 Strathallan Blvd Toronto ON M5N 1S8 Canada Office: Can Opera Co 35 Front St E Toronto ON Canada

BARD, ALLEN JOSEPH, educator, chemist; b. N.Y.C., Dec. 18, 1933; s. John J. and Dora (Rosenberg) B.; m. Frances Joan Segal, June 15, 1957; children: Edward David, Sara Lynn. B.S. summa cum laude, CCNY, 1955; A.M., Harvard U., 1956, Ph.D. (NSF fellow), 1958. Research chemist Gen. Chem. Co., Morristown, N.J., 1955; faculty U. Tex., Austin, 1958—, prof. chemistry, 1967—, Jack S. Josey prof., 1980-82, Norman Hackerman prof., 1982—; cons. E.I. duPont de Nemours & Co., Wilmington, Del., Tex. Instruments, Dallas; vis. prof. Mich. State U., UCLA, U. N.C.; vis. scholar U. Ga., 1969; Fulbright prof. U. Paris, 1973; Sherman Mills Fairchild scholar Calif. Inst. Tech., 1977. Author: Chemical Equilibrium, 1966; co-author: Electrochemical Methods, 1980; Editor: Electroanalytical Chemistry-A Series of Monographs on Recent Advances, 1966—, Ency. of Electrochemistry of the Elements, 1973—, Jour. Am. Chem. Soc, 1982—; Contbr. articles to profl. jours. Recipient Ward medal, 1955; named Analyst of Year Dallas Soc. Analytical Chemists, 1976. Mem. Am. Chem. Soc. (Harrison Howe award Rochester sect. 1980), Electrochem. Soc. (Carl Wagner Meml. award 1981), AAAS, Nat. Acad. Sci., Internat. Soc. Electrochemistry, Sigma Xi. Research on electrogenerated chemiluminescence; semicondr. electrodes for solar energy conversion; co-discoverer magnetic field effects on solution spectroscopic and chemiluminescent processes; discoverer solar photosynthesis of amino acids on semicondr. powders. Home: 6202 Mountainclimb Dr Austin TX 78731

BARD, JOHN CHAPMAN, trade asociation executive; b. Akron, Ohio, Nov. 22, 1929; s. Eugene Chapman and Louise (Kelley) Bard S.; m. Marjorie Field Jackson, July 28, 1956; children: John Chapman, Elizabeth L., Catherine M., James W. B.S., U.S. Mil. Acad., 1954; B.A., Oxford U., (Eng.), M.A. (hon.), 1960; M.S.E., U. Mich., 1962; M.B.A., George Washington U., 1984. Enlisted U.S. Army, 1946, commd. 2d lt., 1954, advanced through grades to maj. gen., 1979; brig. comdr. 2d Armored Div., Ft. Hood, Tex., 1974-75; exec. to Supreme Allied Comdr.-Europe SHAPE, Mons, Belgium, 1975-77; comdt. cadets U.S. Mil. Acad., West Point, N.Y., 1977-79; ret., 1979; v.p. Internat. Bank, Inc., Washington, 1979-81; pres. Aluminum assn., Inc., Washington, 1981—; dir. Nat. Coop. Materials Property Data System, N.Y.C., 1983—. Trustee Foxcroft Sch., Middleburg, Va., 1977—. Rhodes scholar, 1954. Republican. Clubs: Army and Navy (Washington); Belle Haven Country (Alexandria, Va.). Office: Aluminum Assn Inc 818 Connecticut Ave NW Washington DC 20006

BARD, RICHARD H., pharmaceutical company executive; b. Irvington, N.J., Nov. 30, 1947; s. Irving and Irene (Pearlman) B.; m. Diane Rose Gibson, Sept. 1984; children by previous marriage: Alison, Jonathan, Adam. B.S.C.E., Pa. State U., 1969; M.B.A., Baruch Coll., N.Y.C., 1973. Asst. v.p. Citibank, N.A., N.Y.C., 1970-74; mgr. Midwest region Citicorp Bus. Credit, Inc., Chgo., 1974-76; chief fin. officer LFV, Inc., Chgo., 1976-77; pres. FoxMeyer Corp., Aurora, Colo., 1977—, dir.; dir. Capital Resource Mgmt., Inc., Denver, 1982—, Prime Home Improvement Ctrs., Inc., 1983—, Prudential Bancshares Inc., 1984—. Mem. Nat. Wholesale Druggists Assn. (chmn. fin. com. 1982—), Nat. Assn. Chain Drug Stores. Home: 100 Vine St Denver CO 80206 Office: FoxMeyer Corp 2821 S Parker Rd Aurora CO 80014

BARDACH, JANUSZ, plastic surgeon, educator; b. Odessa, Russia, July 28, 1919; came to U.S., 1972; s. Mark and Ottylia (Neuding) B.; 1 dau., Ewa. Physician, Moscow Med.-Stomatological Inst., 1950, M.D., 1953. Resident Moscow Med.-Stomatological Inst., 1950-54; dept. head, assoc. prof. dept. maxillofacial surgery Lodz Med. Acad., (Poland), 1954-59, docent, 1959-62, prof., 1962-72, dept. head, prof. dept. plastic surgery, 1971-72, assoc. dean Coll. Medicine, 1967-71, dir. ctr. for congential facial deformities, 1962-72; vis. prof. dept. otolaryngology and maxillofacial surgery U. Iowa, Iowa City, 1972-73, prof., 1973—, prof. plastic surgery, dept. surgery U. Iowa Hosps. and Clinics, 1977—, chmn. div. plastic and reconstructive surgery of head and neck, 1973—; vis. prof. dept. plastic surgery univs. Pekin, Kanton, Shanghai, Tientsin and Kuondiou, China, 1966, Oxford U., (Eng.), 1968, Haccettepe U., Ankara, 1971; vis. prof. dept, plastic surgery U. Istanbul, (Turkey), 1971; fellow in gen. plastic surgery, Prague, 1954, Oxford, 1962. Author (six) books; contbr. numerous articles to profl. jours. in English. Polish, Czech, Russian, Franch and German. Recipient Highest Sci. award Ministry of Health, Poland, 1966, 68, Town Council of Lodz, 1970, 3d prize for clin. research in otolaryngology Am. Assn. Ophthalmology and Otolaryngology, 1977; fed. grantee, 1973-75, 76—. Mem. Internat. Soc. Plastic Surgeons, Brit. Assn. Plastic Surgery, Royal Soc. Medicine, Internat. Soc. Maxillofacial Surgery, Am. Soc. Plastic and Reconstructive Surgeons (assoc.), Turkish Soc. Plastic and Reconstructive Surgery (hon.), AMA, Johnson County Med. Assn., Am. Cleft Palate Assn., Am. Acad. Facial Plastic and Reconstructive Surgery. Lodge: Rotary. Home: 328 Highland Dr Iowa City IA 52240 Office: Dept Otolaryngology Head and Neck Surgery Univ Iowa Hosp Iowa City IA 52242

BARDACH, JOAN LUCILE, clinical psychologist; b. Albany, N.Y., Oct. 3, 1919; d. Monroe Lederer and Lucile May (Lowenberg) B. A.B., Cornell U., 1940; A.M. in Psychology, NYU, 1951; Ph.D. in Clin. Psychology, 1957. Supr. clin. psychologist NYU Inst. Rehab. Medicine, 1959-61, dir. psychol. services, 1965-82; research psychologist, mem. faculty N.Y. Med. Coll., 1961-62; clin. prof. rehab. medicine (psychology) NYU, 1976—, supr. postdoctoral program psychoanalysis and psychotherapy, 1970; pvt. practice cline. psychology, N.Y.C., 1957—; mem. adv. bd. Coalition Sexuality and Disability; mem. med. adv. bd. Planned Parenthood; cons. in field. Contbr. articles to profl. jours., chpt. to books. NIMH fellow Inst. Sex Research, U. Ind., 1976. Fellow Am. Orthopsychiat. Assn.; mem. Am. Psychol. Assn., Am. Congress Rehab. Medicine, Sex Info. and Edn. Council U.S., Am. Assn. Sex Educators, Nat. Register Health Counselors and Therapists, Eastern Psychol. Assn., N.Y. Soc. Clin. Psychologists, N.Y. State Psychol. Assn., N.Y. State Assn. Med. Sch. Psychology Dirs. Home & Office: 50 E 10th St New York NY 10003

BARDACH, SHELDON GILBERT, lawyer; b. Holyoke, Mass., Sept. 4, 1937; s. Arthur Everett and Ruth (Goodstein) B.; m. Martha Robson, June 7, 1970; 1 son, Noah Arthur. A.B., Bklyn. Coll., 1958; J.D., UCLA, 1961. Bar: Calif. 1962. Practiced in Beverly Hills, Calif., 1962-67, Century City, Calif., 1967—; sr. mem. law offices Sheldon G. Bardach, Los Angeles, 1970—; dir. Solari Theatrical Corp., Beverly Hills, 1973—, Backstage Prodns., Inc., Los Angeles, 1978—; arbitrator Los Angeles Superior Ct., 1979—; Mem. nat. panel arbitrators Am. Arbitration Assn.; mem. dean's counsel Sch. Law, U. Calif. at Los Angeles, 1968—; Bd. govs. Studio Watts Workshop, 1963-71. Mem. bd. editors: Law in Transition Quar, 1967; Contbr. articles to profl. jours. Recipient Lubin award U. Calif. Sch. Law, 1961; Bancroft-Whitney award, 1961. Mem. State Bar Calif., Am., Beverly Hills (mem. bd. govs. barristers 1964-69), Century City, Los Angeles County bar assns., Am. Trial Lawyers Assn., Comml. Law League Am., Vikings of Scandia, Zeta Beta Tau, Phi Alpha Delta. Democrat. Jewish religion. Office: 1800 Century Park E Los Angeles CA 90067 *The most difficult problems we face require emotional decisions. It is when factors on both sides are intellectually disparate that solutions are easy. It is only when the intellect cannot distinguish between the advantages and disadvantages of making a choice that one deals with truly difficult problems. Then, the only solutions available are emotional.*

BARDACKE, PAUL GREGORY, lawyer; b. Oakland, Calif., Dec. 16, 1944; s. Theodore Joseph and Frances (Woodward) B.; m. Lauren Marble, June 21, 1980; children: Julie, Brynn, Francheska. B.A. cum laude, U. Calif.-Santa Barbara, 1966; J.D., U. Calif.-Berkeley, 1969. Bar: Calif. 1969, N.Mex. 1970. Lawyer Legal Aid Soc., Albuquerque, 1969; assoc. firm Thayer, Browne, Albuquerque, 1970-82; atty. gen. State of N.Mex., Santa Fe, 1982—; adj. prof. N.Mex. Law Sch., Albuquerque, 1973—; mem. faculty Nat. Inst. Trial Lawyers Advocacy, 1978—. Bd. dirs. All Faiths Receiving Home, Albuquerque, Friends of Art, Albuquerque, 1974, Artspace Mag., Albuquerque, 1979-80, Legal Aid Soc., Albuquerque, 1970-74. Reginald Heber Smith fellow, 1969. Mem. ABA, Calif. Bar Assn., N.Mex. Bar Assn. Democrat. Office: PO Drawer 1508 Santa Fe NM 87504

BARDAZZI, PETER, artist; b. N.Y.C., Mar. 5, 1943; s. Alfred and Clementina (Allotta) B.; m. Judy Stein, Dec. 16, 1966. B.F.A., Pratt Inst., 1967; M.F.A., Yale U., 1969. One-man shows, Cordier & Ekstrom Gallery, N.Y.C., 1971, 72, 74, 76, 78, group shows include, Art Assn. Newport, R.I., 1967, Princeton U., 1968, Alpha Gallery, Boston, New Britain (Conn.) Mus. Am. Art, 1969, Whitney Mus. Modern Art, Finch Coll., N.Y., 1971, Cordier and Ekstrom Gallery, 1972, 73, 74, 77, 78, Indpls. Mus. Art, Weatherspoon Gallery, U. N.C., 1973, Am. Acad. Arts and Letters, N.Y.C., U. Tex., 1976, Arte Fiera, Bologna, Italy, 1978, Cordier & Ekstrom, N.Y.C., 1982, Pratt Invitational Alumni Exhbn., N.Y.C., 1983, others, represented in permanent collections, Amstar Corp., Corcoran Gallery, Elder Art Gallery, Kutztown State Coll., Mus. Modern Art, others, also numerous pvt. collections.

BARDEEN, JOHN, physicist, emeritus educator; b. Madison, Wis., May 23, 1908; s. Charles Russell and Althea (Harmer) B.; m. Jane Maxwell, July 18, 1938; children—James Maxwell, William Allen, Elizabeth Ann Bardeen Greytak. B.S., U. Wis., 1928, M.S., 1929; Ph.D., PrincetonU., 1936. Geophysicist Gulf Research & Devel. Corp., Pitts., 1930-33; mem. Soc. Fellows Harvard, 1935-38; asst. prof. physics U. Minn., 1938-41; with Naval Ordnance Lab., Washington, 1941-45; research physicist Bell Telephone Labs., Murray Hill, N.J., 1945-51; prof. physics, elec. engring. U. Ill., 1951-75, emeritus, 1975—; mem. Pres.'s Sci. Adv. Com., 1959-62. Recipient Ballantine medal Franklin Inst., 1952; John Scott medal, Phila., 1955; Fritz London award, 1962; Vincent Bendix award, 1964; Nat. Medal Sci., 1966; Morley award, 1968; medal of honor IEEE, 1971; Franklin medal, 1975; co-recipient Nobel prizes in physics, 1956, 72; Presdl. medal of Freedom, 1977. Fellow Am. Phys. Soc. (Buckley prize 1954, pres. 1968-69); mem. Am. Acad. Arts and Sci., IEEE (hon.), Am. Philos. Soc., Royal Soc. Gt. Britain (fgn. mem.), Acad. Sci. USSR (fgn. mem.), Indian Nat. Sci. Acad. (fgn.), Japan Acad. (fgn.). Office: Dept Physics Univ Ill Urbana IL 61801 *

BARDELL, DONALD JOSEPH, association executive; b. Rochester, N.Y., June 27, 1931; s. Joseph Angele and Clara Filippa (Cassesa) B.; m. Doreen Elizabeth Lytton, Sept. 7, 1957; children: Brian, Lance, Donna, Tracy, Darren. B.A., U. Rochester, 1953; LL.B., Georgetown U., 1959. Bar: N.Y. 1959, D.C. 1959. Atty. NLRB, Washington, Buffalo, 1959-61, Maloy, Pirello & Bardell, Rochester, N.Y., 1962-71; gen. counsel, dep. commr. N.Y. Dept. Motor Vehicles, Albany, 1971-76; exec. dir. Am. Assn. Motor Vehicle Adminstrs., Washington, 1976—; dir. Nat. Commn. Against Drunk Driving, 1983—; exec. com. Traffic Safety div. Nat. Safety Council, Chgo., 1982—, Nat. Com. on Uniform Traffic Laws and Ordinances, 1978—. Contbr. articles to profl. jours. Mgr., head coach Irondequoit Indians, Pop Warner Football, N.Y., 1962-73. Served to 1st lt. USMC, 1953-56. Mem. Am. Soc. Assn. Execs., Washington Soc. Assn. Execs., N.Y. Bar Assn., Internat. Assn. Chiefs Police, Theta Delta Chi. Roman Catholic. Office: Am Assn Motor Vehicle Adminstrs 1201 Connecticut Ave NW Washington DC 20036

BARDES, PAUL METZNER, insurance company executive; b. Wilkinsburg, Pa., July 21, 1929; s. Paul Metzner and Lillian (Schreiber) B.; m. Evelyn Kay Record, Nov. 1, 1976. Student, U. Pitts., 1947-48; B.B.A., Tulane U., 1957, J.D., 1959. Bar: La. bar 1959; C.L.U.; C.P.C.U. Chpt. counselor Sigma Pi Fraternity, Elizabeth, N.J., 1948-51, 53; dist. claims mgr. Allstate Ins. Co., Northbrook, Ill., 1959-67; atty. Erie Ins. Exchange, Erie, Pa., 1967-72; v.p., gen. counsel, sec. Am. States Ins. Cos., Indpls., 1972—; underwriter Am. States Lloyds Ins. Co., Dallas, 1972—; sec.-treas. Ind. Ins. Guaranty Assn.; dir. City Ins. Agy., Inc. Bd. dirs. Young Reps., Allegheny County, Pa., 1950-51. Served with USMC, 1951-53. Mem. Sigma Pi. Club: Rotary. Home: 1730 Cottonwood Ct N Plainfield IN 46168 Office: 500 N Meridian St Indianapolis IN 46207

BARDGETT, JOHN E., lawyer; b. 1927. LL.B., St. Louis U. Bar: Mo. 1951. Justice Mo. Supreme Ct., to 1982; ptnr. Guilford Petzall & Shoemake, St. Louis, 1982. Address: 100 N Broadway Suite 2000 Saint Louis MO 63102

BARDIS, PANOS DEMETRIOS, sociologist, editor, author; b. Lefcohorion, Arcadia, Greece, Sept. 24, 1924; came to U.S., 1948, naturalized, 1958; s. Demetrios George and Kali (Christopoulos) B.; m. Donna Jean Decker, Dec. 26, 1964; children: Byron Galen, Jason Dante. Student, Panteios Supreme Sch., Athens, Greece, 1945-47; B.A. magna cum laude, Bethany (W.Va.) Coll., 1950; M.A., Notre Dame U., 1953; Ph.D., Purdue U., 1955. Mem. faculty Albion Coll., 1955-59; mem. faculty U. Toledo, 1959—, prof. sociology, 1963—; sec.-treas. World Student Relief, Athens, 1946-48; mem. adv. bd. New World Communications, 1980—; U.S. rep. Internat. Congress Social Scis., Spain, 1965, 66, 71, Italy, 1969; participant World Congress Sociology, France, 1966, Bulgaria, 70, Can., 1974, Sweden, 1978; Inst. Internat. de Sociologie, Italy, 1969, Venezuela, 1972, Algeria, 1974, Portugal, 1980, Sociology of Religion, Italy, 1969, Internat. Sci. Congress, Greece, 1973, 77, Internat. Conf. Unity Scis., 1976, 77, 78, 79, 80, 81, Internat. Conf. Sociology of Religion, France, 1977, Lausanne, Switzerland, 1981, Internat. Conf. on Love and Attraction, Swansea, Wales, 1977, Internat. Seminar on Philosophy and Religion, P.R., 1978, 79, Acapulco, Mex., 1980 81, Internat. Conf. World Peace, Taipei, Taiwan, 1980, Internat. Seminar Marxist Theory, 1981, World Peace Acad. Conf., 1979, 80, 81; lectr., Japan, Korea, Taiwan, 1980; Chmn. crime reduction com. Commn. Community Devel., Toledo, 1967-68; trustee Marriage Mus., N.Y.C.; mem. acad. adv. bd. Georgetown U. Inst., 1981—. Author: novel Ivan and Artemis, 1957, The Family in Changing Civilizations, 1967, 69, Encyclopedia of Campus Unrest, 1971, The Future of the Greek Language in the United States, 1975, Studies in Marriage and the Family, 1975, 76, History of the Family, 1975, The Family in Asia, 1978, History of Thanatology, 1981; editor: Social Sci, 1959—, book rev. editor, 1963—; assoc. editor: Indian Sociol. Bull, 1965-71, Indian Psychol. Bull, 1965—, Revista del Instituto de Ciencias Sociales, Spain, 1965—, Internat. Jour. Sociology of Family, 1970—, Internat. Jour. Contemporary Sociology, 1971—, Jour. Polit. and Mil. Sociology, 1972—, Jour. Marriage and the Family, 1975—; book rev. editor Internat. Rev. History and Polit. Sci, India, 1966—, 1968—; asst. Am. editor: Indian Jour. Social Research, 1965—; adv. editor: S.African Jour. Sociology, 1971—, Synthesis: The Interdisciplinary Jour. Sociology, 1973—; Am. editor: Sociology Internat, India, 1967—; mem. editorial bd.: Darshana Internat, India, 1965—, 1974—; Jour. Edn, India, 1965—, Sociologia Religiosa, Italy, 1966—, Poetry Americas, 1981—; co-editor: Internat. Rev. Sociology, 1970-72, Internat. Rev. Modern Sociology, 1972—; editorial cons.: Soc. and Culture, 1972—, Coll. Jour. Edn, 1973—; adv. editor: Sociol. Inquiry, 1981—, Jour. Sociol. Studies, 1979—; editorial adv.: Am. Biog. Inst, 1980—; asso. editor, book rev. editor: Sociol. Perspectives, 1981—; contbr. poems, articles to profl. jours.; Composer 20 songs for mandolin. Recipient Couphos prize Anglo-Am.-Hellenic Bur. Edn., 1949, award for outstanding achievement in edn. Bethany Coll., 1975, Outstanding Teaching award Toledo U., 1975. Fellow Am. Sociol. Assn. (membership com. 1966-71), AAAS, Internat. Inst. Arts and Letters (life), Inst. Internat. de Sociologie (chmn. membership com. 1970—, coordinator for U.S.A. 1974—), World Acad. Scholars, Intercontinental Biog. Assn., AAAS; mem. AAUP, Nat., Ohio councils family relations, Global Congress World Religions, Internat. Sociol. Assn. (research coms. on social change 1972—, sociology of edn. 1972—, family sociology 1974—), Profs. World Peace Acad. (a founder), Conf. Internationale de Sociologie de la Religion, N. Central Sociol. Assn., Inst. Mediterranean Affairs (adv. council 1968—), Internat. Personnel Research (hon. adviser 1971—), Internat. Sci.

Commn. on Family, Am. Soc. Neo-Hellenic Studies (bd. advisers 1969—), Group for Study Sociolinguistics, N.Y. Acad. Scis., Nat. Acad. Econs. and Polit. Sci. (dir. 1959—), Nat. Writers Club, Nat. Assn. Standard Med. Vocabulary (cons. 1963—), Inst. Study Plural Socs. (hon. asso.), Internat. Assn. Family Sociology, Modern Greek Soc., Nat. Soc. Lit. and Arts, Ohio Soc. Poets, Nat. Soc. Published Poets, World Poetry Soc. Intercontinental, Sigma Xi, Alpha Kappa Delta, Pi Gamma Mu, Phi Kappa Phi, Kappa Delta Pi., numerous others. Home: 2533 Orkney St Ottawa Hills Toledo OH 43606 *All knowledge is both exciting and useful. The origin or history of any subject is never irrelevant. Knowledge must be organized systematically and reviewed frequently. Interdisciplinary synthesis is conducive to creativity and originality.*

BARDOLPH, RICHARD, historian, educator; b. Chgo., Feb. 18, 1915; s. Mark and Anna (Veldman) B.; m. Dorothy Corlett, July 28, 1945; children: Virginia Ann (Mrs. George Haskett), Mark III, Richard. B.A., U. Ill., 1940, M.A., 1941, Ph.D., 1944; Litt.D., Concordia Coll., 1968, Concordia Theol. Sem., 1983. Mem. faculty dept. history U. N.C. at Greensboro, 1944—, head dept., 1960—, Jefferson Standard prof., 1970—; dir. Centenary Project, 1980—; Fulbright lectr., Denmark, 1953-54; Mem. regional selection com. Woodrow Wilson Nat. Fellowship Found.; mem. commn. theology and ch. relations Luth. Ch.-Mo. Synod; mem. exec. com. Luth. Council in U.S. Author: Agricultural Literature and Illinois Farmer, 1948, Negro Vanguard, 1959 (Mayflower award 1960), Civil Rights Record, 1849-1970, 1970; Mem. bd. editors: Jour. So. History; Contbr. articles to profl. jours. and encys. Active ACLU, NAACP. Recipient O. Max Gardner award for outstanding contbns. to the human race U. N.C., 1979; Ford Found. fellow Harvard, 1952-53; Guggenheim fellow, 1956-57; sr. fellow Nat. Endowment for Humanities, 1971-72. Mem. Am. Hist. Assn., Orgn. Am. Historians, So. Hist. Assn., N.C. Com. on Humanities, Phi Beta Kappa. Home: 207 Tate St Greensboro NC 27403

BARDON, JACK IRVING, educator, psychologist; b. Cleve., Oct. 24, 1925; s. Isidor and Rose (Greene) B.; m. Carla Helene Wininger, Sept. 12, 1948; children: Janet, Ruth. B.A., Cleve. Coll. of Western Res. U., 1949; M.A., U. Pa., 1951, Ph.D., 1956. Sch. psychologist Princeton (N.J.) Pub. Schs., 1952-60; gen. practice as psychologist, 1954—; asso. prof. Rutgers U., 1960-63, prof. edn., 1963-74, prof. sch. psychology, 1974-76, chmn. dept. psychol. founds., 1968-73; co-dir. Grad. Sch. Applied and Profl. Psychology, 1974-76; Excellence Found. prof. edn. and psychology U. N.C. at Greensboro, 1976—; adj. prof. edn. U. Pa., 1971-74; dir. ednl. cons. Universal Edn. Corp., 1969-71; cons. Tng. Corps, Camp Kilmer, N.J., U.S. Office Edn., Bd. Missions of Meth. Ch.; vis. prof. U. Auckland, N.Z., 1976, Exchange prof., 1979; Profl. adviser N.J. Assn. Retarded Children, 1965-71; Pres. bd. dirs. Jour. Sch. Psychology, 1964-70, editor, 1968-71. Contbr. articles to profl. jours. Served with AUS, 1944-46. Fulbright-Hayes Sr. Research scholar, 1979. Fellow Am. Psychol. Assn. (mem. council of reps. 1967-69, 75-77, bd. profl. affairs 1969-71, 77-80, chmn. 1980, policy and planning bd. 1980-83, pres. div. sch. psychology 1970), Am. Orthopsychiat. Assn. (bd. dirs. 1981-84); mem. Am. Assn. for Counseling and Devel., Assn. for Advancement Psychology (bd. dirs. 1974-76), N.J. Assn. Sch. Psychologists (past pres.), N.J. Psychol. Assn. (exec. bd. 1963-66), Sigma Xi. Home: 902 Greenwood Dr Greensboro NC 27410 Office: Sch Edn U NC Greensboro NC 27412

BARDON, MARCEL, government official; b. Paris, France, Sept. 16, 1927; came to U.S., 1939, naturalized, 1944; s. Jacques and Rachel (Berger) B.; m. Renate M. Hoffmann, May 29, 1964; children: Oliver, Adrian, Roland. Student, Norwich U., 1945; diplome, U. Paris, 1952; M.A., Columbia U., 1956, Ph.D. in Physics, 1961. Instr. Columbia U., N.Y.C., 1959-64, sr. research asso., dep. dir. Nevis Labs., 1964-70; physics program dir. NSF, Washington, 1970-71, head physics sect., 1971-75, dep. dir. div. physics, 1975-77, dir. div., 1977-83, asst. dir., 1983—; Sci. officer U.S. del. to UNESCO, 1979-81. Exhibited one man shows of photography, Corcoran Gallery Art, Washington, 1975, Castelli Gallery, N.Y.C., 1976, 79, 83, Max Protetch Gallery, Washington, 1976, Diane Brown Gallery, 1977; Gilbert Gallery, N.Y.C., 1983; Exhibited one man shows of photography, Galerie Perspectives, Paris, 1980; Exhibited group show, Mus. Modern Art, N.Y.C., 1976; Contbr. articles to profl. jours. Served with Signal Corps AUS, 1946. Fellow AAAS; mem. Am. Phys. Soc., Sigma Xi. Home: 1051 Waverly Way McLean VA 22101 Office: NSF Washington DC 20550

BARDOS, THOMAS JOSEPH, educator, chemist; b. Budapest, Hungary, July 20, 1915; came to U.S., 1946, naturalized, 1952; s. Arthur and Vilma (Brachfeld) B.; m. Mary Jane Choate, Mar. 24, 1951. Diploma in Chem. Engring, Royal Hungarian Tech. U., Budapest, 1938; Ph.D. in Chemistry, U. Notre Dame, 1949. Chem. engr. Vacuum Oil Co., Budapest, 1938-46; research asso. U. Tex., Austin, 1948-51; sect. head Armour & Co., Chgo., 1951-60; prof. med. chemistry and biochem. pharmacology State U. N.Y. at Buffalo, 1960—; cons. chemistry Roswell Park Meml. Inst., Buffalo, 1961—. Contbr. articles sci. jours. Recipient Ebert prize Acad. Pharm. Scis., 1971. Fellow AAAS, N.Y. Acad. Scis.; mem. Am. Chem. Soc. (Schoellkopf medal Western N.Y. sect. 1974), Chem. Soc. (London), Am. Soc. Biol. Chemists, Am. Assn. Cancer Research, Am. Pharm. Assn., Internat. Soc. Chemotherapy, Sigma Xi, Rho Chi. Club: Cosmos (Washington). Patentee in field. Home: 131 Burbank Dr Buffalo NY 14226

BARDUHN, ALLEN JOHN, chemical engineerin educator, cousultant; b. Seattle, Aug. 24, 1918; s. Carl Emil and Blanche (Etta) Barduhn D.; m. Mary Ednah Wickson, Mar. 16, 1946; children: Patricia, Casey. B.S. in Chem. Engring., U. Wash., 1940, M.S., 1942; Ph.D., U. Tex., 1955. Registered profl. engr., Calif. Engr. Tide Water Associated Oil Co., Associated, Calif., 1941-49; assoc. prof. chem. engring. Syracuse U., N.Y., 1954-61, prof., 1961—; vis. prof. U. Ind. De Santander, Bucaramanga, Colombia, 1969-70, Shiraz U., Iran, 1977-78; cons. chem. engring. Contbr. numerous articles to tech. jours., 1946—; inventor eutectic freezing process; mem. editorial bd.: Desalination Jour., 1968—. Fellow Am. Inst. Chem. Engrs.; mem. Am. Chem. Soc., Internat. Inst. Refrigeration (v.p. Commn. IX 1967-74), Sigma Xi, Tau Beta Pi. Office: Dept Chem Engring Syracuse U Hinds Hall Syracuse NY 13210 *

BARDWICK, JUDITH MARCIA, management consultant; b. N.Y.C., Jan. 16, 1933; d. Abraham and Ethel (Krinsky) Hardis; m. John Bardwick, III, Dec. 18, 1954 (div.); children: Jennifer, Peter, Deborah. B.S., Purdue U., 1954; M.S., Cornell U., 1955; Ph.D., U. Mich., 1964. Lectr. U. Mich., Ann Arbor, 1964-67, asst. prof. psychology, 1967-71, asso. prof., 1971-75, prof., 1975-83, asso. dean, 1977-83; pres. In Transition, Inc., 1983—; mem. population research study group NIH, 1971-75. Author: Psychology of Women, 1971, In Transition, 1979; editor: Readings in the Psychology of Women, 1972; mem. editorial bd.: Women's Studies, 1973—, Psychology of Women quar, 1975—; contbr. articles to profl. jours. Mem. social sci. adv. com. Planned Parenthood Am., 1973. Fellow Am. Psychol. Assn.; mem. Midwest Psychol. Assn., N.Y. Acad. Scis., Am. Psychosomatic Soc., Phi Beta Kappa. Office: In Transition Inc 3312-128 Caminito Eastbluff La Jolla CA 92037 *I am particularly grateful to the principle of academic freedom which has allowed me to pursue intellectual questions that I considered important. No other institution would have supported my pursuit of the answers to questions that seemed significant for theoretical or applied reasons before those issues were obviously important to society.*

BARDWIL, JOSEPH ANTHONY, mfg. co. exec.; b. Bklyn., Oct. 29, 1928; s. Najeb B. and Malvina (Galaini) B.; m. Valerie Pavilonis, Feb. 11, 1961; children—Anita, James, David, Joanna. B.S. in Econs, Wharton Sch., U. Pa., 1950; M.B.A., N.Y. U., 1956. Reporter, mgr. Dun & Bradstreet, Inc., N.Y.C., 1950-57; gen. investment mgr. Prudential Ins. Co., 1957-69; v.p., sec. Hartz Mountain Corp., Harrison, N.J., 1969—; mem. adv. bd. First Jersey Nat. Bank, Harrison. Mem. Fin. Analysts Fedn., N.Y. Soc. Security Analysts. Republican. Roman Catholic. Office: 700 S 4th St Harrison NJ 07029

BARE, BRUCE, life insurance company executive; b. Pierson, Iowa, May 26, 1914; s. Edward E. and Myrtle Viola (Sloan) B.; m. Adaline Light, June 14, 1936; children: Bruce, Barbara Bare Loucks, John. B.A., Grinnell (Iowa) Coll., 1935; LL.D. (hon.), Westmont Coll., Santa Barbara, Calif., 1971. C.L.U. With New Eng. Mut. Life Ins. Co., 1935—, gen. agt., Los Angeles, 1946-80, field v.p., 1979-82; Trustee Westmont Coll., chmn., 1965; past pres. Fuller Evangelistic Found., Pasadena, Calif.; chmn. bd. trustees African Enterprise Internat., 1979—. Recipient Farrell award Los Angeles C. of C., 1968; named to Hall of Fame Gen. Agts. and Mgrs. Assn., 1977. Mem. Am. Soc. C.L.U.'s (pres. 1964, trustee 1974), Life Underwriters Assn. (past pres. Los Angeles chpt.), Los Angeles Life Ins. Mgrs. Assn. (past pres.). Congregationalist. Office: 3303 Wilshire Blvd Suite 300 Los Angeles CA 90010 *The important thing is to establish goals a step at a time as you go through life. College diploma, proper job with opportunity, careful discharge of all responsibilities assumed, proper marriage and complete commitment to the Christian way of life. A periodic check on goal and accomplishments should provide incentive for greater goals. Success will be a result of never turning aside from Christian principles in all aspects of life.*

BARE, JOSEPH EDWARD, lawyer; b. Jackson, Miss., Dec. 27, 1923; s. Joseph Edward and Marguerite (Thompson) B.; m. Meta Rose Bramer, Dec. 25, 1947; children: Marguerite, David, James, John, Robert. B.A., U. Rochester, 1947; J.D., Harvard U., 1950. Bar: Calif. 1953. Atty. U.S. High Commn. Germany, Frankfurt, 1950-51, Bad Godesberg, 1951-53; assoc. firm Pillsbury, Madison & Sutro, San Francisco, 1953-63, ptnr., 1963-67, 70—; v.p. Chevron Oil Europe Inc., N.Y.C., 1967-70. Served with AC U.S. Army, 1942-46. Mem. ABA, State Bar Calif., Bar Assn. San Francisco, Phi Beta Kappa. Clubs: Mill Valley Tennis (dir. 1983—); Stock Exchange (San Francisco)). Office: Pillsbury Madison & Sutro 225 Bush St San Francisco CA 94941

BARE, ROBERT JOSEPH (BOBBY BARE), country music singer and songwriter; b. Ironton, Ohio, Apr. 7, 1935; m. Jeannie. Performed in clubs and local radio stas.; TV appearances include Los Angeles, Sta. WSM Grand Ole Opry, Nashville; syndicated, Grand Ole Opry; host: Bobby Bare and Friends, Nashville Network; appeared in film: A Distant Trumpet; rec. artist for, Fraternity, Mercury, RCA, CBS Records; albums include: Drunk and Crazy; songs written include: 500 Miles; (Recipient Grammy award 1963). Served with U.S. Army. Office: care Greilworks 59 Music Sq W Nashville TN 37203 *

BAREISS, ERWIN HANS, mathematician, computer scientist, nuclear engineer, educator; b. Schaffhausen, Switzerland, May 10, 1922; came to U.S., 1951, naturalized, 1957; s. Karl Johann and Helene Fredericke (Kraft) B.; m. Doris Lilly Wicky, June 4, 1960; children: John Frederick, Peter Andrew. Diploma in Math., Physics and Chemistry, U. Zurich, Switzerland, 1949, Ph.D., 1951; M.S. in Applied Mechanics, Lehigh U., 1952. Mathematician U.S. Navy Taylor Research and Devel. Center, Washington, 1952-56, cons., 1956-57; analyst Argonne (Ill.) Nat. Lab., 1957-63, sr. mathematician, 1963-76; sci. lectr. Harvard U., 1964; prof. computer sci. Northwestern U., 1970-71, prof. computer sci. and engring. sci., 1971-76, prof. elec. engring. and computer sci., engring. sci. and applied math. and nuclear engring., 1976—; Bd. dirs. Swiss Benevolent Soc., Chgo., 1958-80, pres., 1969-77, hon. mem., 1980—. Contbr. articles on sci. computation to profl. publs. Janggen-Poehn fellow, 1950-51; K.C. Baldwin research fellow, 1951-52. Mem. Am. Math. Soc., Soc. Indsl. and Applied Maths., Swiss Math. Soc., Swiss Soc. Natural History. Home: 3400 Lake Knoll Dr Northbrook IL 60062 Office: Tech Inst Northwestern U Evanston IL 60201

BARENBOIM, DANIEL, conductor, pianist; b. Buenos Aires, Argentina, Nov. 15, 1942; s. Enrique and Aida (Schuster) B.; m. Jacqueline DuPre, June 15, 1967. Student, Mozarteum, Salzburg, Austria, Accademia Chigiana, Siena, Italy; grad., Santa Cecilia Acad., Rome, 1956. Debut with, Israel Philharm. Orch., 1953, Royal Philharm. Orch., Eng.; debut as pianist, Carnegie Hall, N.Y.C., 1957, Berlin Philharm. Orch., 1963, N.Y. Philharm. Orch., 1964, 1st U.S. solo recital, N.Y.C., 1958, as pianist performed in, N.Am., South Am., Europe, Soviet Union, Australia, New Zealand, Near East; conductor, 1962—; conducted, English Chamber Orch., London Symphony Orch., Israel Philharm. Orch., N.Y. Philharm. Orch., Phila. Symphony, Boston Symphony and, others; musical dir., Orchestre de Paris, 1975—; artistic adviser, Israel Festival, 1971-74, over 100 recordings as pianist and conductor. Recipient Beethoven medal, 1958; Harriet Cohen Paderewski Centenary prize, 1963. Made debut as pianist at age 7, Buenos Aires. Office: care orchestre de la Porte Maillot F-75017 Paris France *

BARENTS, BRIAN EDWARD, marketing executive; b. Pittsfield, Mass., Jan. 2, 1944; s. Gabriel H. and Blanche E. (Sherinian) B.; m. Barbara Ann Harris, Dec. 30, 1972; children: Kimberly Ann, Jennifer Catharine. B.B.A., Western Mich. U., 1966; postgrad., U. Mich., 1966-68; grad., USAF Air War Coll., 1967. Asst. buyer Gen. Motors Corp., Detroit, 1965-67, regional sales mgr., 1967-70; regional dir. Honeywell Info., Detroit, 1970-76; sr. v.p. mktg. Cessna Aircraft Co., Wichita, Kans., 1976—. Served to lt. col. Air N.G., 1966—. Mem. Gen. Aviation Mfrs. Assn. Home: 701 Preston Trail Wichita KS 67230 Office: PO Box 1521 Wichita KS 67201

BARES, W.G., chemical company executive; b. 1941. B.S. in Chem. Engring., Purdue U., 1963; M.B.A., Case Western Res. U., 1969. Process devel. engr. Lubrizol Corp., Wickliffe, Ohio, 1963-67; group leader, pilot plant Lubrizol Corop., Wickliffe, Ohio, 1967-71; asst. dept. ehad Lubrizol Corp., Wickliffe, Ohio, 1971-72, dept. head., 1972-78, asst. to pres., 1978, v.p., 1978-80, exec. v.p., 1980-82, pres., dir., 1982—. Office: Lubrizol Corp 29400 Lakeland Blvd Wickliffe OH 44092 *

BAREUTHER, ERNST ELLIS, financial executive; b. Aurora, Ill., June 24, 1910; s. Ernst and Lucy (Ellis) B.; m. Eleanor Geiler, Apr. 1934; children: Richard, Jean. B.S. in Accountancy with honors, U. Ill., 1933. Treas. home appliance div. Fairbanks Morse, Chgo., 1934-39; chief accountant refrigerating div. Philco Corp., Phila., 1940-44, then of radio div., 1944-47, budget dir., 1947-48, asst. treas., 1948-52, controller, 1952-62, treas., asst. controller, 1962; controller Air Products & Chems. Inc., Allentown, Pa., 1963-65; v.p. finance McCall Corp., N.Y.C., 1965-69; financial cons., 1969—; v.p., treas. Patagonia Corp., Tucson, 1970-73, pres., 1973-75, vice chmn. bd., 1975-81; v.p. finance U.S. Filter Corp., N.Y.C., 1971—. Mem. Fin. Execs. Inst., Nat. Assn. Accountants (Lybrand gold medal 1957), Beta Gamma Sigma, Beta Alpha Psi, Sigma Phi Epsilon. Clubs: Tubac (Ariz.); Valley Country. Home: Tubac Valley Country Club Estates Tubac AZ 85640 Office: Patagonia Corp 5151 E Broadway Tucson AZ 85711

BARFIELD, BOB F., university dean, mechanical engineer; b. Thomaston, Ga., Feb. 8, 1933; s. Jacon Malcome and Nettie Lee B.; m. Marion Janelle Neill, June 25, 1953 (div. Jan. 1980); children: Kimberly Faith, Robert Fredrick; m. Sara de Saussure Davis, Nov. 27, 1981. B.M.E., Ga. Inst. Tech., 1956, M.S.M.E., 1958, Ph.D., 1965. Diplomate: registered profl. engr. Preliminary design engr. AiResearch Corp., Los Angeles, 1957-59; asst. prof. mech. engring. Ga. Inst. Tech., Atlanta, 1959-65; corp. mech. engr. Thomaston Mills Corp., Ga., 1965-67; prof. mech. engring. U. Ala., University, 1967—, dean of engring., 1982—; dir. Quadtech Corp., Tuscaloosa, Al.; dir., sr. adv. Shiraz Tech. Inst., Iran, 1975-77; gen. bd. Assn. Internat. Practical Tng., 1980—; dir. Capstone Engring. Soc., 1982—; mem. Ala. Commn. High Tech. Recipient disting. service award Inperial Orgn. for Social Services, Tehran, Iran, 1980, U. Ala. Faculty Senate, 1980. Mem. Am. Soc. Engring. Edn. (chmn. internat. div.), ASME, Nat. Soc. Profl. Engrs., Ala. Acad. Sci., Tuscaloosa C. of C., Sigma Xi. Presbyterian. Home: 1702 9th St Tuscaloosa AL 35401 Office: PO Box 1968 University AL 35486

BARFIELD, RUFUS LENRO, college president; b. Hickman, Ky., Nov. 14, 1929; s. Cas Low and Katie Marie (Upshaw) B.; m. Emma Jean Crawford, Dec. 24, 1960; children: Rufus Lenro, Sheila Gail, Joselyn Yvette. B.A. in Edn, Ky. State Coll., 1952; M.A. in Ednl. Adminstrn, U. Ky., 1956; M.Ed. equivalent, U. Cin., 1966; postgrad. (NDEA fellow), Ohio State U., 1967; Ph.D. in Ednl. Adminstrn, Miami U., Oxford, Ohio, 1972, U. Wis., 1973, Harvard U. Tchr. English and social studies Lincoln Heights (Ohio) Sch., 1955-56; tchr. Hoffman Sch., Cin., 1956-64; demonstration tchr. Schiel Sch., Cin., 1964-66, adminstrv. asst. prin., 1966-69; prin. Columbian Sch., Cin., 1969, Burton Sch., 1969-71; instr. Miami U., 1971-72; adminstrv. asst. to pres. Ky. State U., 1972-74, prof. edn. and psychology, 1974-77, acting v.p. for acad. affairs, 1974-77; prof. edn. and psychology U. Ark., 1977-78, vice chancellor acad. affairs, 1977-78; pres. Bowie (Md.) State Coll., 1978—; cons. in field. Bd. dirs. Md. Soc. Crippled Children and Adults; trustee Salvation Army, Frankfort, Ky.; v.p. bd. trustees ARC, Frankfort; mem. Ky. Gov.'s Commn. on Higher Edn., 1975. Served with U.S. Army, 1953-54. Recipient certificate of award for outstanding service Corryville Community Council, Cin., 1967; Disting. Service Achievement award Met. chpts. Phi Beta Sigma, 1979; commd. hon. Ky. Col., 1975. Mem. NAACP, NEA, Prince George's C. of C. (bd. dirs.), Nat. Orgn. Legal Problems in Edn., Soc. Research Adminstrs., Am. Assn. Sch. Adminstrs., Am. Assn. Higher Edn., Phi Delta Kappa, Phi Beta Sigma, Alpha Delta Mu, Alpha Kappa Mu, Kappa Delta Pi. Mem. Ch. of Christ. Home: 11801 Chantilly Ln Mitchellville MD 20716 Office: Bowie State College Jericho Park Rd Bowie MD 20715

BARFIELD, THOMAS HARWELL, army officer; b. Lineville, Ala., Jan. 20, 1917; s. Jesse Morton and Janie Isobel (Davis) B.; m. Beri Harrison Young, Aug. 16, 1941; children: Thomas H., Jane Young. Grad., Marion Mil. Inst., 1935; A.B., U. Ala., 1937; M.S., George Washington U., 1962, Nat. War Coll., 1960; L.H.D., Judson Coll., 1980. Commd. 2d lt. U.S. Army, 1938, advanced through grades to maj. gen., 1969; assigned U.S. Forces in S. Pacific, World War II, Gen. Hdqrs. Far East Command in Occupation of Japan; then UN Command in Korea; assigned Army Gen. Staff, 1945-48, 60-62, U.S. Army Air Def. Command, 1952-53, 62-64, 68-71, Joint Chiefs Staff, 1967-68, U.S. Army Air Def. Center, 1953-56, 65-66, 8th U.S. Army, Korea, 1966-67, N. Am. Air Def. Command, 1969-75; pres. Marion Mil. Inst., 1976-83. Decorated Army Commendation medal with oak leaf cluster, Bronze Star, Meritorious Service medal, Legion of Merit with 3 oak leaf clusters, Distinguished Service medal. Mem. Phi Gamma Delta. Home: Lineville AL 36266 Office: Marion Mil Inst 3 College Heights Marion AL 36756

BARFORD, RALPH MACKENZIE, investment executive; b. Toronto, Ont., Can., July 6, 1929; s. Ralph Alexander and Geraldine Edna (MacKenzie) B.; m. Elizabeth June Stevens, June 9, 1951; children: Ralph, Anne, John, Patricia, Elizabeth, Jane. B.Comm., U. Toronto, 1950; M.B.A., Harvard U., 1952. Analyst Am. Research & Devel. Corp., Boston, 1952-54; pres. Nat. Merchandising Corp., Boston, 1954-60, Beatty Bros. Ltd., Fergus, Ont., 1960-62, GSW Ltd., Toronto, 1962-72, chmn., 1973—, Can. Appliance Mfg. Co. Ltd., 1976—; Union Gas Co. Ltd., 1981—; pres. Valleydene Corp. Ltd., Toronto, 1972—; v.p., dir. Nat. Trust Co.; dir. Canadian Gen. Investments, Sonor Investments Ltd., Thiokol Chem. Corp., 6SW Ltd., Union Gas Co. Ltd., Massey-Ferguson Ltd., E-L Fin. Corp. Ltd., DeHavilland Aircraft Ltd., Molson's Industries Ltd., Wosk's Ltd. Mem. premier's adv. com. Province of Ont.; trustee Toronto Symphony Orch., Toronto Gen. Hosp.; bd. dirs. Niagara Inst. Mem. Can. Elec. Mfg. Assn. (pres. 1967-68), Phi Gamma Delta. Mem. United Ch. Can. Clubs: York, Granite, Rosedale Golf (Toronto). Home: 11 Valleyanna Dr Toronto ON Canada Office: 161 Eglinton Ave E Suite 501 Toronto ON Canada

BARGAR, ROBERT SELLSTROM, investor; b. Jamestown, N.Y., Aug. 8, 1919; s. Crawford Nathaniel and May Euenia (Sellstrom) B.; m. JeAnne Griffin, Apr.9, 1969; children: Nancy Gay, David Griffin, Alison May Churchill, Douglas Crawford. B.S. in Econs., U. Pa., 1941; prodn. mgmt. cert., Grad. Sch. Engring. - U. Pa., 1941. Mgmt. trainee S.M. Flickinger Co. Inc., Jamestown, 1946-52, v.p., 1952-70; pres. S. M. Flickinger Co. Inc., 1970-81; cons., asst. to chmn. bd. S.M. Flickinger Co. Inc., Buffalo, 1981—, dir., Jamestown, Jamesway Corp., Secaucus, N.J., 1977—, Bankers Trust of Western N.Y., Jamestown, 1983—; pres. Fluvanna Realty Corp., Jamestown, 1961—. Vice chmn. bd. Chautauqa Found. (N.Y.), 1983—; bd. dirs. Jamestown Civic Auto Ramps, 1983—; chmn. invest com. 1st Presbyn. Ch., Jamestown, 1983—; trustee Chatauqua Instn., 1974-82. Served to lt. comdr. USNR, 1942-46; PTO. Recipient Man of Yr. award Jamestown chpt. NCCJ, 1979. Clubs: Sportsman's (Stow, N.Y.); Town (Jamestown) (dir. 1982—). Home: 304Arlington Ave Jamestown NY 14701 Office: JBC CO 4th and Pine Bldg Jamestown NY 1407 *Persistence has been most responsible for any successes. I have had.I should discount my average talent and adequate education. There are many educated fools and frustrated geniuses*

BARGELLINI, PIER LUIGI, electrical engineer; b. Florence, Itlay, Feb. 7, 1914; came to U.S., 1948, naturalized, 1956; s. Angelo and Giovanna (Cecchi) B.; m. Anna Cioni, Sept. 8, 1941; children: Clara, Angela, Leonard M. Grad., U. Florence, 1933; D.Eng., Poly. Inst., Turin, 1937; M.S. in Elec. Engring., Cornell U., 1949. Engr. Italo Radio Co., Rome, 1937-41; head spl. tests lab. Fivre Co., Florence, 1941-44; researcher microwave physics Inst. It alian Nat. Research Council, 1945-50; mem. faculty U. Pa., Phila., 1950-68; sr. scientist COMSAT Labs., Clarksburg, Md., 1968-83, cons., 1984—; mem. adv. engring. faculty Montgomery County Community Coll., 1970-75, trustee nominating com., 1975-82. Editor: Communications Satellite Systems and Communications Satellite Technology, 1974; contbr. articles to profl. jours.; lectr. internat. univs. Recipient City of Columbus (Ohio) award Inst. Internat. Communications, 1975; Inst. Internat. Edn. fellow, 1948. Fellow IEEE (life), AIAA (assoc. Democrat. Roman Catholic. Home and Office: PO Box 256 Clarksburg MD 20871

BARGER, CECIL EDWIN, advertising agency executive; b. Marshall, Mo., June 19, 1917; s. James Edwin and Jessie (Witcher) B. B.S. in Agrl. Journalism, U. Mo., 1938; postgrad., Columbia U., 1946-47, Northwestern U., 1955-56. Asso. editor Capper Publs., Topeka, 1939-42; copywriter Wildrick & Miller Advt. Agy., N.Y.C., 1945-48, account exec., 1952-54, Aubrey, Moore & Wallace Advt. Agy., Chgo., 1948-51; creative dir. Aubrey, Finley, Marley & Hodgson Advt. Agy., 1954-59; v.p. Compton Advt., Inc., Chgo., 1959-65, Sander Allen Advt. Inc., 1966—; breeder Angus cattle, Arrow Rock, Mo., 1956—. Mem. Nat. Agri-Mktg. Assn. (charter mem., v.p., dir.), Alpha Gamma Rho, Alpha Zeta. Mem. Christian Ch. Clubs: Chgo. Advt. (dir., treas.), Chgo. Farmers, Friends of Arrow Rock. Home: 900 Lake Shore Dr Chicago IL 60611 Office: 101 E Ontario St Chicago IL 60611:

BARGER, JAMES DANIEL, physician; b. Bismarck, N.C., May 17, 1917; s. Michael Thomas and Mayte (Donohue) B.; m. Susie Belle Helm, 1945 (dec. 1951); m. Jane Ray Regan, Apr. 21, 1980; children: James Daniel, Mary Susan, Michael Thomas, Mary Elizabeth. Student, St. Mary's Coll., Winona, Minn., 1934-35; A.B., U. N.D., 1939, B.S., 1939; M.D., U. Pa., 1941; M.S. in Pathology, U. Minn., 1949. Diplomate: Am. Bd. Pathology; registered profl. engr., Calif. Intern. Milw. County Hosp., Wauwatosa, Wis., 1941-42; fellow in pathology Mayo Found., Rochester, Minn., 1941-49; pathologist Pima County Hosp., Tucson, 1949-50, Maricopa County Hosp., Phoenix, 1950-51; chmn. dept. pathology Good Samaritan Hosp., 1951-63; assoc. pathologist Sunrise Hosp., Las Vegas, Nev., 1964-69, chief pathology dept., 1969—; former med. dir. S.W. Blood Bank, Ariz. Served to maj. AUS, 1942-46. Recipient Sioux award U. N.D. Alumni Assn., 1975, disting. physician award NSMA, 1983. Mem. AAAS, Am. Assn. Pathologists, Soc. Advancement Mgmt., Am. Assn. Clin. Chemists, Am. Assn. History Medicine, Coll. Am. Pathologists (gov. 1966-72, sec.-treas. 1971-79, v.p. 1979-81, pres. 1980-81, pathologist of yr. 1977), Nev. Soc. Pathologists, Am. Assn. Blood Banks, Am. Soc. Quality Control, Am. Mgmt. Assn., Am. Soc. Clin. Pathologists, Am. Cancer Soc. (nat. dir. 1974-80), Am. Pub. Health Assn., Sigma Xi. Home: 1307 Canosa Ave Las Vegas NV 89105 Office: Sunrise Hosp PO Box 14157 Las Vegas NV 89114

BARGER, JAMES EDWIN, physicist; b. Manhattan, Kans., Dec. 28, 1934; s. Edgar Lee and Carolyn Marie (Grantham) B.; m. Mary Elizabeth Rupp, Aug. 24, 1957; children—Elaine Marie, Carolyn Ruth, James Rupp, Corinne Elizabeth. B.S., U. Mich., 1957; M.S., U. Conn., 1960; Ph.D., Harvard U., 1964. Teaching asst. Harvard U., Cambridge, 1961-64; v.p. Bolt Beranek & Newman, Inc., Cambridge, Mass., 1965-75, chief scientist, 1975—. Mem. Methods and Procedures Com., Town of Winchester, 1967-71; trustee Winchester Hosp., 1972—; corp. mem. Mt. Vernon House, 1979—. Served with USNR, 1957-63. NSF fellowship, 1960-64. Fellow Acoustical Soc. Am.; mem. Marine Tech. Soc., AAAS, Tau Beta Pi, Pi Tau Sigma. Conglist (deacon). Club: Winchester Country. Home: 3 Lakeview Rd Winchester MA 01890 Office: 50 Moulton St Cambridge MA 02138

BARGER, RICHARD WILSON, hotel executive; b. Cleve., Aug. 16, 1934; s. Harold Wilson and Blanche (Smith) B.; m. Barbara K. Schroeder, July 20, 1963; children—Scott Wilson, Christopher Armon. B.S., Cornell U., Ithaca, N.Y., 1956. Resident mgr. Sheraton Cleve. Hotel, 1964-67; gen. mgr. Sheraton Biltmore Hotel, Providence, 1967-68, Sheraton Peabody Hotel, Memphis, 1968-69, Sheraton Boston Hotel, 1969-72; v.p., regional mgr. Sheraton Corp., Boston, 1972-79; pres. Barger Hotel Corp., Boston, 1979—; v.p., regional mgr. Horizon Hotels Ltd., 1982—; pres. Conf. Environments Corp., 1982—; Cons., lectr. hotel adminstrs. Bd. dirs. Boston Opera Assn.; Active local Jr. Achievement.; mem. council Cornell U., Ithaca, N.Y. Mem. Boston C. of C., Boston Conv. Bur. (dir.), Cornell U. Alumni Fund, Sigma Chi. Republican. Mem. P.E. Ch. Home: 63 Neptune St Beverly Cove MA 01915 Office: Bay 231 Lewis Wharf Boston MA 02110

BARGER, RICHARDS DALE, SR., lawyer; b. Los Angeles, Aug. 10, 1928; s. Chester Hull and Elizabeth (Swarzlender) B.; m. Ann Fenwick, June 24, 1952; children: Richards Dale, James F., John M., Katherine Ann. B.S. in Bus, Ind. U., 1950; LL.B., U. So. Calif., 1958. Bar: Calif. 1954, U.S. Supreme Ct. 1960, D.C. 1972. Practiced in Los Angeles, 1954-68, 72—; ins. commr. State of Calif., 1968-72; partner firm Barger & Wolen, 1972—; commr. uniform state laws, 1973-77; dir. Acad. Ins. Group, Inc., Valley Forge, Pa.; Mut. Ins. Co. Anchor Nat. Life Ins. Co., Phoenix, Physician's & Surgeon's Underwriters Corp., Pasadena, Calif., Lawyers Mut. Ins. Co., Los Angeles.; Mem. adv. com. to sec. HUD on fed. reinsur. matters, 1969-72; chmn. ins. issues com., malpractice com. of sec. HEW, 1971-72. Bd. dirs. San Gabriel Valley council Boy Scouts Am., 1974—. Recipient Silver Beaver award, 1975. Fellow Am. Bar Found.; mem. State Bar Calif., Delta Tau Delta, Phi Delta Phi. Club: Calif. (Los Angeles). Home: 945 San Marino Ave San Marino CA 91108 Office: 9th Floor 530 W 6th St Los Angeles CA 90014

BARGER, ROBERT VINCENT, publishing company financial executive; b. Glendale, W.Va., Oct. 23, 1942; s. Robert Vincent and Elizabeth Lee (Cotton) B.; m. Cynthia R. Thompson, Aug. 29, 1965; children: Jennifer, Rebecca. B.S. in Fin., Lehigh U., 1964, M.B.A., 1965. Fin. mgmt. trainee Gen. Electric Co., Bridgeport, Conn., 1965-69; dir. fin. planning McGraw Hill Systems Co., 1969-73; corp. controller Devon Group, Inc., Los Angeles, 1973-77; dir. fin. planning McGraw Hill Book Co., N.Y.C., 1977-80, v.p.-controller, 1980-82; sr. v.p.-fin. and services McGraw Hill Internat., N.Y.C., 1982—. Home: 34 Dale Ave Wyckoff NJ 07481 Office: McGraw Hill Inc 1221 Ave of Americas New York NY 00012 *Career success depends on intense application of one's energy and talents. Application depends on one's degree of motivation. I have always been highly motivated by the belief that my efforts, day to day, are enchancing the lives of coworkers, and the products I am helping to bring to market are contributing to society in general.*

BARGER, VERNON DUANE, educator, physicist; b. Curllsville, Pa., June 5, 1938; s. Joseph F. and Olive (McCall) B.; m. Annetta McLeod, 1967; children: Victor A., Amy J., Andrew V. B.S., Pa. State U., 1960, Ph.D., 1963. Research asso. U. Wis.-Madison, 1963-65; asst. prof., then asso. prof. physics U. Wis., Madison, 1965-68, prof. physics, 1968-83, J.H. Van Vleck prof., 1983—; vis. prof. U. Hawaii, 1970, 79, 82, U. Durham, 1983; vis. scientist CERN, 1972, Rutherford Lab., 1972, SLAC, 1975. Co-author: Phenomenological Theories of High Energy Scattering; Classical Mechanics. Guggenheim fellow, 1972; recipient Alumni Fellow award Pa. State U., 1974. Fellow Am. Phys. Soc.; mem. Phi Kappa Phi, Tau Beta Pi. Methodist. Club: Masons. Research in elementary particle theory; classification of hadrons as Regge recurrences; analysis of neutrino scattering and oscillations; weak boson and heavy quark prodn. Home: 5711 River Rd Waunakee WI 53597 Office: U Wis Dept Physics Madison WI 53706

BARHAM, CHARLES DEWEY, JR., electric utility executive, lawyer; b. Goldsboro, N.C., July 7, 1930; s. Charles Dewey and Helen Wilkinson (Douglass) Barham H.; m. Margaret Wright Crow, June 17, 1960; children: Margaret Douglass, Charles Dewey III. B.S., Wake Forest U., 1952, J.D., 1954. Bar: N.C. 1954. Asst. atty. gen. N.C. Dept. Justice, Raleigh, 1958-66; assoc. gen. counsel Carolina Power & Light Co., Raleigh, N.C., 1966-73; ptnr. Douglass & Barham, Raleigh, 1974-80; v.p., sr. counsel Carolina Power & Light Co., Raleigh, 1981-82, sr. v.p., gen. counsel, 1982—; chmn. bd., pres. Nuclear Mut., Ltd., Hamilton, Bermuda, 1981—, dir.; gen. counsel World Nuclear Fueld Market, Atlanta, 1975-80, Meredith Coll., Raleigh, 1977-80. Pres. Raleigh YMCA, 1982—. Served to capt. USNR, 1955-58. Mem. ABA, N.C. Bar Assn., Fed. Energy Bar Assn. Democrat. Baptist. Clubs: Raleigh Civitan (dir. 1974-77), Glen Forest (pres. 1977). Office: Carolina Power & Light Co PO Box 1551 Raleigh NC 27602

BARHAM, MACK ELWIN, lawyer, educator; b. Bastrop, La., June 18, 1924; s. Henry Alfred and Lockie Izorie (Harper) B.; m. Ann LeVois, June 3, 1946; children: Bret L., Megan (Mrs. Thomas Richard). J.D., La. State U., 1946; postgrad., U. Colo., 1964-65. Judge City Ct., Bastrop, 1948-61, 4th Jud. Dist. Ct., Parishes of Ouachita and Morehouse, 1961-67, 2d Circuit Ct. of Appeal, 1967-68; assoc. justice La. Supreme Ct., 1968-75; prof. Sch. Law, Tulane, 1975—; counsel Lemle, Kelleher, Kohlmeyer & Matthews, 1975-78; ptnr. Barham & Churchill, 1979—; mem. faculty Am. Acad. Jud. Edn., U. Ala., 1968-73. Chmn. Ouachita Valley council Boy Scouts Am. Recipient award Freedoms Found. at, Valley Forge, 1969; Outstanding Service award ACLU, 1976; Creative Intelligence award Am. Found. Sci., 1976. Mem. La. Juvenile Judges Assn. (past pres.), La. Law Inst. (council), Internat. Acad. Estate and Trust Law, Scribes, Blue Key, Order of Coif, Omicron Delta Kappa, Lambda Chi Alpha, Phi Delta Phi, Phi Alpha Delta. Club: Kiwaniso. Home: 5837 Bellaire Dr New Orleans LA 70124 Office: Barham & Churchill 400 Lafayette St Ste 300 New Orleans LA 70130

BARHAM, RICHARD WENDELL, oil company executive; b. Toccoa, Ga., Apr. 29, 1923; s. Wendell Stacy and Lona Wood (Switzer) B.; m. Elaine Juliet Vieira, Feb. 6, 1944; children: Richard Wendell, Marsha, Carol, Gail, Lawrence. Student, Rice Inst., 1946-47; B.A. with high honors, U. Tex., 1949; M.A., U. Mich., 1950; M.Phil., Ph.D., Columbia U., 1982. Teaching fellow U. Tex., 1950-51; joined U.S. Fgn. Service, 1951; assigned Oslo, Norway, 1952-55, Nicosia, Cyprus, 1955-56, Washington, 1957, Athens, Greece, 1958-63, Commerce Dept., 1964; officer charge Greek affairs State Dept., 1965-66; govt. relations counselor Standard Oil Co., N.J., N.Y.C., 1966-71; sr. govt. relations adviser Esso Eastern Inc., Houston, 1971—. Served to 1st lt. USAAF and; Served to 1st lt. USAF, 1941-45, 51. Decorated Royal Order of Phoenix, (Greece). Mem. Am. Fgn. Service Assn., Am. Acad. Polit. and Social Sci., Phi Beta Kappa. Home: 14839 La Quinta Ln Houston TX 77079 Office: Esso Eastern Inc Houston TX 77024

BARHYTE, DONALD JAMES, business executive; b. Poughkeepsie, N.Y., May 16, 1937; m. Patricia E. Dressler, Dec. 27, 1958; children: Mark, Leslie. Student, U. Ky. Data processing mktg. rep. IBM, 1962-68; with Multimedia, Inc., Greenville, S.C., 1968—, asst. treas., treas., 1971-73, v.p. fin., treas., 1973-77, v.p. fin. and adminstrn., treas., 1977—; dir. S.C. Nat. Bank. Trustee, pres., St. Francis Community Hosp., 1979—; bd. dirs. United Way. Mem. Am. Mgmt. Assn., Fin. Execs. Inst., Am. Newspaper Pubs. Assn., So. Newspaper Pubs. Assn., Greenville C. of C. (v.p. community devel., dir.). Roman Catholic. Clubs: Poinsett, Green Valley Country, Biltmore Forest Country. Office: 305 S Main St Greenville SC 29601

BARIBAULT, RICHARD PFEIFER, aluminum company executive; b. New Haven, Feb. 11, 1924; s. Harry John and Marion (Pfeifer) B.; m. Jule Marie Jones, Aug. 23, 1948; children: Richard J., Kathleen J., Amy R. Harry J. B.S. in Indsl. Adminstrn., Yale U., 1949. With Aluminum Co. Am., Cleve., 1962-70, mktg. mgr., Pitts., 1974-76, v.p., 1974—, ops. mgr., Massena, N.Y., 1976-79; works mgr. Internat. Alloys Ltd., Eng., 1970-74. Bd. dirs. Jr. Achievement S.W. Pa., Inc., Pitts., 1980—, Vocat. Rehab. Ctr., Pitts., 1980-82; committeeman Republican Party, Sewickley, Pa., 1980-83. Capt. USAAF, 1943-46; ETO. Decorated Air medal with oak leaf cluster, Presdl. citation. Mem. Purchasing Mgmt. Assn. Pitts., Nat. Assn. Purchasing Mgmt., Assn. Light Alloy Refiners (chmn. London 1970-74). Roman Catholic. Clubs: Duquesne, Harvard-Yale-Princeton (Pitts.). Office: Aluminum Co Am 1501 Alcoa Bldg Pittsburgh PA 15219

BARICH, DEWEY FREDERICK, ednl. adminstr.; b. Chisholm, Minn., Feb. 19, 1911; s. Eli and Angelia (Erro) B.; m. Verna Arling Eddy, Dec. 29, 1934; children—Judy, Dewey, Barbara, Wendy. Student, Jr. Coll., Hibbing, Minn., 1929-31; B.S. in Indsl. Edn, Stout Inst., Menomonie, Wis., 1933; A.M. in Edn, U. Mich., 1939; Ed.D., Wayne State U., Detroit, 1961; LL.D., Western New Eng. Coll.; L.H.D., Detroit Inst. Tech., 1977. Tchr. indsl. arts Public Schs. Flint, Mich.; also dept. chmn. Longfellow Jr. High Sch.; chmn. Indsl. Survey Com. on Flint Industries and; mem. Indsl. Arts Supr.'s Council, 1936-38; instr. metal trades Trenton (Mich.) High Sch., 1938-39; instr. indsl. arts Central Mich. Coll. Edn., Mt. Pleasant, 1939-40; state supr. Nat. Def. (later War Prodn.) Tng., Mich. State Bd. Control for Vocat. Edn., 1940-42; prof., head indsl. arts dept. Kent State U., 1942; (on mil. leave 1943-45), univ. coordinator vets. affairs, 1945-51; mgr. ednl. affairs dept. Ford Motor Co., 1951-58; pres. Detroit Inst. Tech., 1958-76, chancellor, 1976—. Co-author: Applied Drawing and Sketching; Metal Work for Industrial Arts Shops; Contbr. articles to profl. jours. Mem. Pres. Truman's Conf. Occupational Safety, Pres. Eisenhower's Conf. Occupational Safety; chmn. bd. dirs., schs. and colls. Nat. Safety Council, 1973-76; chmn. occupational safety standards commn. Mich. Dept. Labor, 1969-70; chmn. Mich. Occupational Standards Commn., 1975-76, Dept. State cons. Internat. Adv. Com. on Medium Level Manpower, Ibadan, Nigeria, 1969; mem. State Bd. Control Vocat. Edn. Served as lt. (j.g.) USNR; engring. officer LCI, (L) Flotilla 24 Staff, 1943-45; engring. officer LCI, (L) Flotilla 24 Staff, 21 mos; PTO. Awarded commendation for service by flotilla comdr.; recipient Indsl. Vocat. Edn. Laureate award. Mem. NEA, Am. Vocat. Assn. (speaker; mem. nat. policies and planning com. for indsl. arts edn.), Am., Ohio indsl. arts assns., Soc. Automotive Engrs., Mich. Indsl. Edn. Assn. (speaker), Nat. Assn. Indsl. Tchr. Educators, Engring. Soc. Detroit, Am. Soc. Engring. Edn., Miss. Valley Indsl. Arts Consf., Epsilon Pi Tau, Phi Delta Kappa, Iota Lambda Sigma. Episcopalian. Clubs: Economic, Detroit Athletic, Rotary. Home and Office: 6757 Placita Bella Tucson AZ 85718 *Like so many of my contemporaries, I am a son of immigrant parents who instilled in their children a deep conviction that the United States was, indeed, the land of opportunity. I lived my early years on the "Iron Range" of northern Minnesota, sometimes called the "melting pot of America", where hard work was accepted as a positive way of life, and where there prevailed an atmosphere of high motivation and expectation.*

BARICKMAN, JAMES HALL, advertising agency executive; b. Mpls., Oct. 5, 1924; s. Mary (Barickman); m. Mary Mischler, Jan. 26, 1974; children: Nancy Barickman Greenley, James Hall, Julie King, Robert, Daniel. B.S. in Fin, U. Minn., 1947. With Northwestern Nat. Bank, Mpls., 1947-50; West Coast advt. mgr. Pillsbury Co., 1950-51; account exec. Brewer Advt., Kansas City, Mo., 1951-59; with Barickman Advt., Kansas City, 1959-80, pres., 1959-80; (co. merged with Doyle Dane Bernbach Internat.), 1980, former chmn. bd., now chief exec. officer; dir. Columbia Union Bank, Kansas City.; Adv. bd. Research Med. Center, Kansas City. Pres. Kansas City Jr. C. of C., 1958-59, Kansas City Jr. Achievement, 1963-65. Served with AUS, World War II. Recipient Ann. Silver medal Am. Advt. Fedn., 1976. Mem. Am. Assn. Advt. Agys., Am. Mktg. Assn., Affiliated Advt. Agys. Internat. Republican. Presbyterian. Clubs: Kansas City, Carriage; La Quinta (Calif.); Country; Hillcrest Country (Bartlesville, Okla.); Moss Creek Country (Hilton Head, S.C.); Williams, Friars (N.Y.C.); Indian Hills Country, Wolf Creek Country. Home: 6417 Verona Rd Shawnee Mission KS 66208 Office: 427 W 12th St Kansas City MO 64102

BAR-ILLAN, DAVID JACOB, concert pianist; b. Haifa, Israel, Feb. 7, 1930; came to U.S., 1954, naturalized, 1967; s. Aaron and Zilla (Beilin) Bar-I.; m. Beverly Slater, Mar. 3, 1969; children: Kim, Daniela, Jeremy. Diploma, Juilliard Sch. Music, 1950. Debut, Carnegie Hall, 1954, N.Y. Philharm., 1960; soloist major orchs. in, Europe, Israel, U.S. and, Latin Am., 1960—, recitalist throughout world; artist-in-residence, Coll. Conservatory Music, U. Cin., 1975—. Served with Israeli Army, 1948. Office: care Columbia Artists Mgmt 165 W 57th St New York NY 10019 *

BARINGER, MAURICE EDMUND, state official; b. Arkansas City, Kans., Dec. 4, 1921; s. George William and Ada Maude (Shilling) B.; m. Dorothy Mac Schlensig, Mar. 19, 1948; children: Sandra, James, Debra, David. B.S. in Bus., U. Kans., 1943, Iowa State U., 1948; M.S. in Animal Sci., Iowa State U., 1949. Instr. Iowa State U., 1948-49; dir. nutrition Foxbilt, Inc., Des Moines, 1949-53; engaged in farming, 1953; mgr. Rooster Mills Co., Dubuque, Iowa, 1954-56; dir. nutrition Oelwein Chem. Co., Inc., Iowa, 1956-67; v.p. Midwest Gruel-O-Matic Co., Grimes, Iowa, 1967-68; treas. State of Iowa, 1969-82; adminstr. Iowa Pub. Employees Retirement System, 1983—; chmn. sci. adv. com. Nat. Feed Ingredients Assn., 1949-63, nat. pres., 1964; mem. nutrition council Am. Feed Mfrs. Assn., 1958-67. Mem. Iowa Ho. of Reps., 1961-68, speaker, 1967-68; mem. Iowa Commn. Interstate Coop., 1967-83; mem. council Synod of Lakes and Prairies, United Presbyn. Ch. U.S.A., 1977-82. Served with AUS, 1943-46. Mem. Farmhouse. Republican. Home: Route 1 Woodburn IA 50275 Office: 1000 E Grand Ave Des Moines IA 50319

BARITZ, LOREN, history educator; b. Chgo., Dec. 26, 1928; s. Joseph Harry and Helen (Garl) B.; m. Phyllis L. Handelsman, Dec. 26, 1948; children: Tony, Joseph. B.A., Roosevelt U., 1953; M.A., U. Wis., 1954, Ph.D., 1956. Asst. prof. history Wesleyan U., Middletown, Conn., 1956-62; asso. prof. Roosevelt U., Chgo., 1962-63; prof. U. Rochester, 1963-69, chmn. dept. history, 1964-67; leading prof. SUNY-Albany, 1969-71; exec. v.p. Empire State Coll., SUNY, 1971-75; exec. dir. univ. commn. on purposes and priorities SUNY-Albany, 1975-76; acting vice chancellor for acad. policy SUNY, 1976-77, provost of univ., 1977-79; dir. N.Y. Inst. Humanities; prof. history NYU, 1979-80; provost, vice chancellor for acad. affairs U. Mass., Amherst, 1980-83, prof. history, 1980—; vis. lectr. U. Wis.-Madison, 1959-60; U.S. rep. UNESCO Conf. on Film, Locarno, Switzerland, 1970. Author: City on a Hill, 1964, Servants of Power, 1960, Sources of the American Mind, 2 vols., 1966, The Culture of the Twenties, 1970, The American Left, 1971. Co-chmn. policy council research and service Assembly Univ. Goals, Am. Acad. Arts and Scis., 1969-70; del. Democratic Nat. Conv., 1968; bd. govs. chmn. com. on student affairs Haifa U., 1975—. Research tng. fellow Social Sci. Research Council, 1955-56, grantee, 1960; grantee Am. Council Learned Socs., 1963. Home: Clark Mountain Rd Sunderland MA 01375 Office: U Mass Amherst MA 01003

BARKA, TIBOR, med. educator; b. Debrecen, Hungary, Mar. 31, 1926; came to U.S., 1958, naturalized, 1963; s. Imre and Hajnal (Szekely) B.; m. Katalin Szalay, Mar. 3, 1957. M.D., Debrecen U., 1950. First research asso. dept. morphology Inst. Exptl. Medicine, Hungarian; Acad. Sci., Budapest, 1954-56; research asso. Inst. Cell Research and Genetics, Karolinska Institutet, Stockholm, 1956-58, Mt. Sinai Hosp., N.Y.C., 1958-62, asst. attending pathologist, 1962-64, asso. attending pathologist, 1964—; prof. dept. pathology Mt. Sinai Sch. Medicine, 1968—, prof., chmn. dept. anatomy, 1967—. Author: (with G. Kiszely) Practical Microtechnique and Histochemistry, 1958, Histochemistry, Methods of the Experimental Medicine, 1959, (with P. J. Anderson) Histochemistry: Theory, Practice and Bibliography, 1963; editor-in-chief: Jour. Histochemistry and Cytochemistry, 1965-73; contbr. numerous articles to profl. jours. Mem. Histochem. Soc. (pres. 1979-80), Am. Soc. Exptl. Pathology, Am. Assn. Anatomists, Council Biol. Editors, Am. Soc. Cell Biology. Research in devel. and application of histochem. methods, studies on regulation of cell div. Home: 200 Winston Dr Cliffside Park NJ 07010

BARKAN, ALEXANDER ELIAS, labor union official; b. Bayonne, N.J., Aug. 9, 1909; s. Jacob and Rachel (Perelmen) B.; m. Helen Stickno, May 10, 1942; children: Lois, Carol. Ph.B., U. Chgo., 1933. With Textile Workers Organizing Com., 1937; organizer Textile Workers Union Am., 1938, sub-regional dir., 1938-42, polit. action dir., 1947-55; vets. dir. CIO community services dir., 1945; exec. dir. N.J. CIO Council, 1946; asst. dir. com. polit. edn. AFL-CIO, Washington, 1955-57, dep. dir. com. polit. edn., 1957-63, dir., 1963-81. Served with USNR, 1942-45. Home: 4701 Willard Ave Chevy Chase MN 20015 Office: 2300 9th St S Suite 209 Arlington VA 22204

BARKAN, PHILIP, mech. engr.; b. Boston, Mar. 29, 1925; s. Philip and Blanche (Seifert) B.; m. Hinda Brody, Sept. 5, 1948 (dec. Aug. 1979); children—Ruth, David. B.S.M.E., Tufts U., 1946; M.S.M.E., U. Mich., 1948; Ph.D. in Mech. Engring, Pa. State U., 1953. Asst. prof. engring. research Pa. State U., 1948-51; sect. mgr. applied physics and mech. engring. Gen. Electric Co., Phila., 1953-77; prof. mech. engring. Stanford U., 1977—; vis. prof. Israel Inst. Tech., Haifa, 1971-72; cons. to electric power industry, 1977—. Contbr. numerous articles to profl. publs. Pres. bd. trustees Middletown (Pa.) Free Library, 1959-61; chmn. bd. trustees Sch. in Rose Valley, 1967-68; Democratic candidate for Middletown Twp. Supr., 1959, 61, 63; pres. Middletown Dem. Club, 1960. Served with USN, 1943-46. Recipient 1st Charles P. Steinmetz medal and award Gen. Electric Co., 1973; Electric Power Research Inst. grantee, 1979. Fellow IEEE; mem. ASME, Nat. Acad. Engring., Sigma Xi. Patentee in field. Office: Design Div Dept Mech Engring Stanford U Stanford CA 94305

BARKER, DAVID BENTON, marine corps officer; b. Needham, Mass., Jan. 11, 1930; s. Charles F. and Mildred R. (Benton) B.; m. Priscilla Farrant, Apr. 20, 1953; children—Laurel, Howard, David, Sandra. B.S. in Chemistry and Biology, Tufts Coll., 1951; M.A. in Personnel Adminstrn, George Washington U., 1966. Commd. 2d lt. U.S. Marine Corps, 1951, advanced through grades to maj. gen., 1980; comdg. gen. Marine Corps Base, Camp Lejeune, N.C., 1978-81; dep. chief of staff for tng. Hdqrs. U.S. Marine Corps, Washington, 1981-82; chief of staff Hdqrs. U.S. Forces, Japan, 1982—. Mem. exec. bd. East Carolina council Boy Scouts Am., 1978-81; exec. v.p. Far East council Boy Scouts Am., 1982—; mem. exec. bd. Keep N.C. Beautiful, 1979-81; exec. dir. Mil.-Civilian Community Council, Jacksonville, N.C., 1970-81. Decorated Legion of Merit with combat V and gold star, Navy Commendation medal with combat V. Methodist. Clubs: Semper Fidelis Lodge, Scottish Rite. Home: PSC Box 381 APO San Francisco CA 96328 Office: Chief of Staff Hdqrs US Forces Japan APO San Francisco CA 96328 *An individual's opportunity to succeed is enhanced by self-discipline, a positive outlook on life, establishment of goals and priorities, being professional, persevering, and above all else, honesty and integrity.*

BARKER, DOUGLAS, lawyer, manufacturing company executive; b. Eng., Dec. 26, 1923; emigrated to Can., 1958; s. Arthur and Susan (Vincent) B.; m. Helen Calder, Apr. 28, 1962. B.A. in Econs., Cambridge U., Eng., 1949; LL.B., Eng., 1950; LL.M., Harvard U., 1951. Bar: Eng., B.C. Sole practice, Eng. and Can., 1953-64; treas.

M.F. Inc., Des Moines, 1967-69; dir. fin. M.F. Europe, London, 1959-72; treas. world Massey-Ferguson Ltd., Toronto, Ont., Can., 1972-82, chmn., 1983—; counsel Raymond & Honsberger; bd. dirs. Can.-China Trade Council. Mem. Fin. Execs. Inst. Club: Granite (Toronto). Home: 48 Arjay Crescent Willowdale On Canada M2L 1C7 Office: 85 Richmond St W Toronto ON Canada M5G 2C3

BARKER, EDWIN BOGUE, musician; b. Tucson, Apr. 14, 1954; s. Francis Hustis and MarY Jeanne (Austin) B.; m. Pamela Paikin, 1980. B.Mus. with honors, New Eng. Conservatory Music, 1976. Prin. bass Lake George Opera Orch., 1971, 72; substitute mem. N.Y. Philharm., 1976. Mem., Chgo. Symphony Orch., 1976-77; prin. bass, Boston Symphony, 1977—; mem., Boston Symphony Chamber Players; instr. double bass, New Eng. Conservatory Music, 1977—, Boston Conservatory of Music, 1980—; instr. double bass and chamber music, Berkshire Music Center (Tanglewood), 1978—; rec. artist; Recipient (Benjamin H. Delson award Berkshire Music Center 1975); bass and string clinics, Am. String Tchrs. Assn. and U. Mich., Ann Arbor, 1982, 83; solo appearances with Boston Symphony, New Eng. Conservatory Symphony Orch., Bergen Music Festival (Norway), others. Recipient Benjamin H. Delson award Berkshire Music Center, 1975. Mem. Am. Fedn. Musicians., Internat. Soc. Bassists (dir. 1983). Office: c/o Boston Symphony 251 Huntington Ave Boston MA 02115

BARKER, EMMETT WILSON, JR., trade association executive; b. Humboldt, Tenn., Aug. 30, 1937; s. Emmett Wilson and Rebecca Evelyn (Coble) B.; m. Barbara Anne Ingram, Nov. 25, 1960; children: Melanie Lynn, Emmett Daniel. B.S. in Agr, U. Tenn., Knoxville, 1960. Advt. and sales promotion mgr. Security Mills, Inc., Knoxville, 1960-62; dir. public relations Am. Feed Mfrs. Assn., Chgo., 1962-67; pres. Agrl. Services Assn., Bells, Tenn., 1967-72; spl. asst. to pres. United Foods, Inc., Bells, 1972-73; exec. sec. Farm and Indsl. Equipment Inst., Chgo., 1973-79, pres., 1979—; nat. chmn. Farm-City Council, 1970, bd. dirs., 1981; mem. adv. com. Found. Am. Agr., 1981, Alliance to Save Energy, 1980; mem. exec. com. Nat. Indsl. Council Mfg. Trade Group, 1981. Pub.: Directory of Communicators in Agriculture, 1968. Chmn. Nat. Endowment for Soil and Water Conservation, 1982-84; bd. dirs. Am. Nat. Standards Inst., 1982—. Served with U.S. Army, 1958-64. Recipient Disting. Service award and Hon. Am. Farmers degree Future Farmers Am., 1967, Meritorious Service award Nat. Assn. Farm Broadcasters, 1968; named Man of Year Memphis Agr. Club, 1970. Mem. Am. Soc. Assn. Execs., Public Relations Soc., Am., Agrl. Relations Council, Chgo. Soc. Assn. Execs., Nat. Agrl. Mktg. Assn., Am. Soc. Agrl. Engrs. Republican. Presbyterian. Clubs: Rotary; Union League (Chgo.). Office: 410 N Michigan Ave Chicago IL 60611

BARKER, GREGSON LEARD, business form printing executive; b. Chgo., Jan. 19, 1918; s. Walter R. and Margaret (Gregson) B.; m. D'Arcy Timmons, Aug. 19, 1978; children: Margaret Louise Barker Thompson, John Leard, Eric Walter, William Jordan. With UARCO, Inc., designers, printer bus. forms, Barrington, Ill., 1937—, pres., 1955—; dir. LaSalle Nat. Bank, Hammond Corp., Chgo., First Nat. Bank Barrington, Chgo. Profl. Basketball Corp., Carson Pirie Scott & Co. Mem. Chgo. Crime Commn.; mem. citizens bd. U. Chgo.; bd. dirs., v.p. Jr. Achievement Chgo.; bd. dirs. Infant Welfare Soc. Chgo., Glenwood Sch. Mem. Computer and Bus. Equipment Mfrs. Assn. (dir.), Ill. Mfrs. Assn. (pres., dir.), Chgo. Assn. Commerce and Industry (dir., v.p.), Ill. State C. of C. (dir.), Employers Assn. Chgo. (dir.), Young Pres.'s Orgn., Northwestern U. Assos. Republican. Episcopalian. Clubs: Econ., Comml., Exec., Commonwealth, Chgo., Mid-Am., Racquet, Meadow (Chgo.); Barrington Hills Country; Lyford Cay (Bahamas); Met. (N.Y.C.). Home: 81 Meadow Hill Rd Barrington IL 60010 Office: UARCO Inc Barrington IL 60010

BARKER, HAROLD GRANT, surgeon; b. Salt Lake City, June 10, 1917; s. Frederick George and Jennetta (Stephens) B.; m. Kathleen Butler, July 29, 1949; children—Janet Stephens, Douglas Reid. A.B., U. Utah, 1939, postgrad., 1939-41; M.D., U. Pa., 1943. Diplomate: Am. Bd. Surgery. Intern. Hosp. U. Pa., 1943-44, asst. resident in surgery, 1947-51, sr. resident in surgery, 1951-52, asst. attending surgeon, 1952-53; also asst. instr., research fellow U. Pa., 1946-51, instr., research fellow, 1951-52, assoc. in surgery, 1952-53; asst. prof. surgery, Columbia, 1953-57, assoc. prof., 1957-68, prof., 1968—; asst. attending surgeon Presbyn. Hosp., 1953-57, asso. attending surgeon, 1957-69, attending surgeon, 1969—, dir. med. affairs, 1974-82; practice medicine specializing in surgery, Phila., 1952-53, N.Y.C., 1953—. Contbr. articles med. jours. Served from 1st lt. to capt., M.C. AUS, 1944-46; ETO. Fellow A.C.S.; mem. Soc. U. Surgeons, N.Y. Surg. Soc., Am. Physiol. Soc., Soc. Exptl. Biology and Medicine, A.M.A., Halsted Soc., N.Y. State (chmn. surg. sect. 1961-62), N.Y. County med. socs., Am. Surg. Assn., N.Y. Gastroent. Assn., Sociètè Internationale de Chirurgie, Soc. Surgery Alimentary Tract, Allen O. Whipple Surg. Soc., Am. Assn. History Medicine, Collegium Internationale Chirurgiae Digestivae. Republican. Presbyn. Clubs: Century Assn.; Manursing Island (Rye, N.Y.); Am. Yacht. Home: 1 Forest Ave Rye NY 10580 Office: 161 Ft Washington Ave New York NY 10032

BARKER, HAROLD KENNETH, university dean; b. Louisville, Apr. 14, 1922; s. J.M. and Fannie Mae (Elliott) B.; m. Elizabeth Johns, Mar. 11, 1948; children: Leslie Ann, Glen Lewis.; m. Beverly Williams, Feb. 28, 1984. A.B., U. Louisville, 1948, M.A., 1949; Ph.D., U. Mich., 1959. Instr. Gunfire Prep. Sch., Hanau, Germany, 1946; sch. psychologist, vis. tchr. Bay City (Mich.) Pub. Schs., 1949-52; also instr. Bay City Jr. Coll.; sch. psychologist Ypsilanti (Mich.) Pub. Schs., 1952-53; instr. Eastern Mich. U., 1954-58; asst. dir. Bur. Appointments and Occupational Info., U. Mich., 1954-59; asso. exec. sec. Am. Assn. Colls. Tchr. Edn., Washington, 1959-66, dir., 1972—; dean Coll. Edn., U. Akron, 1966—; Bd. dirs. World U., San Juan, P.R., 1966—, Joint Council Econ. Edn., 1979. Editor: AACTE Handbook of International Education Programs, 1963; contbr. articles to profl. jours. and periodicals. Served with USAAF, 1942-46. Recipient award outstanding profl. service Am. Assn. Colls. Tchr. Edn., 1966. Mem. Phi Delta Kappa (internat. commn. 1962-69). Home: 1811 Brookwood Dr Akron OH 44313

BARKER, HUGH ALTON, electric utility company executive; b. Stillwater, Minn., Nov. 26, 1925; s. George Clarence and Minerva (Register) B.; m. Janet M. Breitenbucher, Mar. 18, 1949; 1 dau., Pamela J. B.B.A. with distinction, U. Minn., 1949. C.P.A., Minn. Prin. Haskins & Sells, C.P.A.s, Mpls., 1949-58; asst. to exec. v.p. Pub. Service Ind., Plainfield, Ind., 1958-60, fin. v.p., 1960-68, exec. v.p., 1968-74, pres., 1974—, chief exec. officer, 1977—, chmn., 1980—, also dir.; dir. 1st Am. Nat. Bank, Plainfield, Am. Fletcher Nat. Bank & Trust Co., Am. Fletcher Corp., Indpls.; mem. Ind. Commn. on Tax and Financing Policy, 1969-73, chmn., 1971-73. Bd. govs. Associated Colls. Ind.; mem. Ind. Local Govt. Property Tax Control Bd., 1973-74, Gov.'s Water Resources Study Commn., 1977-80; trustee Methodist Hosp., Indpls., 1975-81, Butler U., Indpls.; bd. dirs. Edison Electric Inst., 1978-81, 83—, Ind. Legal Found., Inst. for Nuclear Power Operation. Served with AUS, 1944-45; ETO. Mem. Nat. Assn. Electric Cos. (dir. 1974-78, chmn. 1978), Ind. Mfrs. Assn. (dir.), Ind. Electric Assn. (dir., past pres.), Am. Inst. C.P.A.s, Minn. Soc. C.P.A.s, Ind. C. of C. (dir.), Sigma Alpha Epsilon, Beta Gamma Sigma. Clubs: Columbia, Indpls. Athletic; Union League (Chgo.). Home: Plainfield IN Office: 1000 E Main St Plainfield IN 46168

BARKER, JAMES REX, corporate executive; b. Cleve., Aug. 3, 1935; s. William Wardel and Elizabeth Ranghild (Wandler) B.; m. Kaye Elizabeth Schumacher, Aug. 3, 19S7; children: James Arthur. Karen Elizabeth, Mark William. B.A., Columbia U., 1957; M.B.A. with distinction, Harvard U., 1963; D.Sc. (hon.), Maine Maritime Acad., 1978. Planning exec. Pickands Mather & Co., Cleve., 1963-67; v.p. Harbridge House, Boston, 1967-69; exec. v.p. Temple, Barker & Sloane, Wellesley, Mass., 1970-71; chmn. bd., chief exec. officer Moore McCormack Resources, Inc., Stamford, Conn., 1971—; dir. Gen. Telephone and Electronics, Stamford, Gt. No. Nekoosa Corp. Chmn. bd. trustees Stamford Hosp.; bd. trustees YMCA, Stamford; bd. visitors Columbia U.; mem. bus. adv. bd. Northwestern U.; mem. adv. bd. Transp. Center, M.I.T. Mem. Am. Bur. Shipping (bd. mgrs.). Episcopalian. Clubs: Wee Burn Country, Noroton Yacht, N.Y. Yacht., India House, Landmark, Rolling Rock, Union, Harvard, Links. Home: 180 Long Neck Point Darien CT 06820 Office: 1 Landmark Sq Stamford CT 06901

BARKER, JOHN WALTER, JR., historian educator; b. Bklyn., Oct. 7, 1933; s. John Walton and Evelyn (Doty) B.; children: Christopher Neill, Ellen Carla. B.A., Bklyn. Coll., 1955; M.A., Rugers U., 1956; Ph.D., Rutgers U., 1961. Instr. Bklyn. Coll. Night Sch., 1958-59; fellow Dumbarton Oaks Research Ctr., Washington, 1959-62; mem. faculty U. Wis.-Madison, 1962—, prof. history, 1971—; vis. prof. Inst. Research Humanities, 1964-65, Inst. Advancement Study, Princeton U., 1978-79. Author: Justinian and the Later Roman Empire, 1966, Manuel II Palaeologus (1391-1425): A Study of Late Byzantine Statesmanship, 1969; articles, revs., study guides. Guggenheim fellow, 1973-74. Mem. Am. Hist. Assn., Am. Musicol. Soc., Modern Greek Studies Assn., Byzantine Studies Conf., Midwest Medieval Conf. Democrat. Home: 4206 Mandan Crescent Madison WI 53711 Office: Dept History U Wis Madison WI 53706 *To be a human being is to share in vast potentiality qualified by unavoidable flaws. The worst misconceptions about human nature are that it is either all good or all bad; in fact, it is a mix of both, capable of the greatest nobility and the worst viciousness (sometimes simultaneously), the extremes of the one modifying the effects of the other. Yet, it in the infinite diversity of human capacity and achievement that humanity finds it greatest hope. The worst enemy of humanity is fanaticism and doctrinaire rigidity, which believes that being "right" justifies any imposition on others.*

BARKER, JUDY, consumer products executive; b. Burlington, N.C., Feb. 5, 1941; d. William F. and Thelma M. Ferguson;, Nov. 24, 1973; children: Lesa, Lori. Student, Ohio State U., 1958, Franklin U., 1959-60. With Mt. Carmel Hosp., Columbus, Ohio, 1970-72, Children's Hosp., Columbus, 1965-70; with Borden, Inc., 1972—; now dir. corp. social responsibility, pres. Borden Found., Inc., Columbus; chmn. contbns. council Conf. Bd.; corp. adv. services div. Council Better Bus. Burs.; mem. N.Y. Contbns. Adv. Council; mem. contbns. adv. com. United Negro Coll. Fund. Trustee United Way of Franklin County. Mem. Assn. Black Found. Execs. (dir.), Women and Founds. Office: 180 E Broad St Columbus OH 43215

BARKER, LARRY LEE, speech communication educator; b. Wilmington, Ohio, Nov. 22, 1941; s. Milford and Ruth Maxine (Garringer) B.; children: Theodore Allen., Robert Milford. B.A., Ohio U., 1962, M.A., 1963, Ph. D, 1965. Asst. prof. So. Ill. U., Carbondale, 1965-66, Purdue U., West Lafayette, Ind., 1966-69; assoc. prof. Fla. State U., Tallahassee, 1969-71, prof., 1971-75; pres. Spectra Communication Assocs., New Orleans, 1979—. Author: (with R. Kibler) Conceptual Frontiers in Speech Communication, 1969, Behavioral Objectives and Instruction, 1970, Listening Behavior, 1971, Speech Communication Behavior, 1971, Communication Vibrations, 1974, Speech—Interpersonal Communication, 1974, (with R. Edward) Intrapersonal Communication, 1980, (with R. Kibler) Objctives for Instruction and Evaluation, 1981, Communication, 1982, Communication in the Classroom, 1982, (with others) Effective Listening, 1982, (with L. Malandro) Nonverbal Communication, 1983, (with K. Wahlers) Group in Process, 1983; contbr. articles to profl. jours. Recipient outstanding award in discussion Tau Kappa Alpha, 1962, outstanding tchr. award Central States Speech Assn., 1969. Mem. Speech Communication Assn., Internat. Communication Assn. (v.p. 1972-74), Internat. Listening Assn. (chmn. research com. 1979-82), Am. Psychol. Assn., Am. Bus. Communication Assn. Methodist. Home: 540 N College St Auburn Al 36830 Office: Auburn U Auburn AL 36849

BARKER, LILLIAN MENZIES, electric utility company executive; b. Fenelon Falls, Ont., Can., Mar. 27, 1920; s. Archibald and Laura Blanche (Mathewson) Menzies; children—William, Robert, Betty, Bradley. Student, Lindsay Collegiate Inst., 1939, United Bus. Coll., 1941, Washburn U., 1960. Exec. sec. Security Benefit Life Ins. Co., Topeka, Kans., 1956-60; asst. cashier Fidelity State Bank & Trust Co., Topeka, 1960-66; asst. sec. Security Mgmt. Co., Topeka, 1966-74; corp., sec., asst. treas. Kans. Power & Light Co., Topeka, 1974—; dir. Security Equity Fund, Topeka. Bd. dirs. Girls Club Topeka, 1975-80; mem. adv. bd. St. Francis Hosp., 1972-74; precinct committeeman Republican party. Mem. Am. Soc. Corp. Secs., Topeka C. of C. (dir. 1974-78). Presbyterian. Home: Route 2 Box 255-A Lake Wabaunsee Alma KS 66401 Office: 818 Kansas St Topeka KS 66612

BARKER, LYLE JAMES, JR., army officer; b. Columbus, Ohio, July 28, 1932; s. Llyle James and Mabel Lucile (Johnson) B.; m. Maxine Ruth Metcalf, Jan. 15, 1956; children: Llyle J., Daryl Alan. B.S., Ohio State U., 1954; postgrad., U. Wis., 1961; M.S. in Mass Communication, Shippensburg State Coll., 1975. Commd. officer U.S. Army, 1955, advanced through grades to maj. gen.; service in, Korea and W.Ger.; public affairs officer, Hawaii, 1957-59, NORAD, 1961-63, Dept. Army, 1966-69, Seventh Army, 1969-71, Joint Casualty Resolution Center, 1974, European command, 1975-77, U.S. Army Europe, 1979-80; dep. chief info. Dept. Army, 1980-81, chief public affairs, 1981—. Contbr. articles to mil. jours. Decorated Legion of Merit, others. Office: Chief Public Affairs Army Pentagon Washington DC 20310

BARKER, MUHAMMAD ABD-AL-RAHMAN, linguistics educator; b. Spokane, Wash., Nov. 2, 1929; s. Loris T. and Gertrude (Barnhardt) B.; m. Ambereen Khan, 1959. B.A., U. Wash., 1951; Ph.D., U. Calif., Berkeley, 1959. Research fellow, instr. Inst. Islamic Studies, McGill U., Montreal, Que., Can., 1957-59, faculty, 1962-72, prof., 1968-72; reader in linguistics, lang. unit Oriental Coll., Lahore, West Pakistan, 1959-62; prof. U. Minn., Mpls., 1972—, chmn. dept. South Asian studies, dir., Center for South Asian Lang. and Area Studies, 1972-82; cons. lang. grant applications U.S. Office Edn., 1976—; project reader grant applications Shastri Indo-Can. Inst., Montreal, 1972-79, Am. Inst. for Pakistan Studies, 1974-82, Am. Inst. Indian Studies Lang. Programs, 1976-77; cons., evaluator Berkeley Urdu Lang. Program, in Pakistan, 1974—. Author: Klamath Dictionary, 1964, Klamath Grammar, 1964, A Course in Urdu, 1967, 75, An Urdu Newspaper Reader, 1968, 74, An Urdu News-Word Count, 1969, An Urdu Poetry Reader, 1968, A Course in Baluchi, 2 vols., 1969, A Reader of Classical Urdu Poetry, 3 vols., 1977, A Student's Dictionary of Urdu Journalistic Language, 1980; Contbr. articles to profl. jours. Fulbright scholar, India, 1951-52; Am. Council Learned Socs. grantee U. Chgo. Summer Inst. Linguistics, 1954; U. Calif. All-U. fellow, 1955-57; HEW grantee, 1963-69; Shastri Indo-Can. Inst. fellow, India, 1970-71; U. Minn. Grad. Sch. grantee, 1972-73; HEW grantee, 1974-76; Am. Pakistan Found. grantee, 1977; Bush Found. fellow, 1983-84. Mem. Assn. for Asian Studies (chmn. lang. com. South Asia Regional Council 1976-77), Am. Inst. Indian Studies (lang. com.). Home: 118 E Elmwood Pl Minneapolis MN 55419 Office: Dept South Asian Studies 196 Klaeber Ct U Minn Minneapolis MN 55455

BARKER, NANCY NICHOLS, historian educator; b. Mt. Vernon, N.Y., Dec. 26, 1925; m., 1950. B.A., Vassar Coll., 1946; M.A., U. Pa., 1947, Ph.D., 1955. Asst. instr. U. Pa., 1948-49; instr. U. Del., 1949-50, lectr. modern European history, 1955-67; from asst. prof. to assoc. prof. history U. Tex., Austin, 1967-72, prof., 1972—. Author: Distaff Diplomacy: The Empress Eugenie and the Foreign Policy of the Second Empire, 1967; editor: (with others) Diplomacy in an Age of Nationalism: Essays in Honor of Lynn Marshall Case, Martinus Nijhoff, 1971, Recognition, Rapture and Reconciliation, Vol. 1, 1971, Mission Miscarried, Vol. II, 1973; contbr. articles to profl. jours. Tex. Research Inst. Research grantee, 1967-68; recipient Gilbert Chinard prize, 1972, Summerfield C. Roberts award, 1972. Mem. Am. History Assn., Soc. French Hist. Studies. Office: Dept History Univ Texas Austin TX 78712 *

BARKER, NORMAN, JR., banker; b. San Diego, July 30, 1922; s. Norman and Grace (Bolger) N.; m. Sue Keefe, June 27, 1947; children: Peter, Timothy, Michael, Beth. B.A., U. Chgo., 1947, M.B.A., 1953. Asst. cashier Harris Trust & Savs. Bank, Chgo., 1947-55; credit mgr. Am. Can Co., 1955-57; with 1st Interstate Bank of Calif., Los Angeles, 1957—, pres., after 1968; now chmn., also dir.; vice chmn., dir. 1st Interstate Bancorp.; dir. Carter Hawley Hale Stores, Inc., Carnation Co., So. Calif. Edison Co., Lear-Siegler, Inc., Pacific Telesis Group. Trustee Occidental Coll., U. Chgo. Served to lt. USNR, 1944-46, 50-52. Mem. Delta Kappa Epsilon. Office: 707 Wilshire Blvd Los Angeles CA 90017 Mailing address: PO Box 3666 TA Los Angeles CA 90051

BARKER, RICHARD CLARK, electrical engineering educator; b. Bridgeport, Conn., Mar. 27, 1926; s. George Myron and Elizabeth (Leeds) B.; m. Sela Wadhams, Sept. 4, 1948; children: Sela, Kirtland. B.E., Yale U., 1950, M.E., 1951, Ph.D., 1955. Electronics engr. Airadio, Inc., Stamford, Conn., 1947; control systems engr. Allen D. Cardwell Co., Plainville, Conn., 1953-53; faculty Yale U., New Haven, 1952—, prof. elec. engring., 1970—; cons. IBM, 1973-74, AMP Inc., 1972—, Echlin Mfg. Co., 1976—, Hitachi Metals, Ltd., 1980—; vis. scientist fellow Japan Soc. for Promotion Sci., 1972. Served with USN, 1944-46. Recipient Sr. U.S. Scientist award Alexander von Humboldt Found., 1975. Fellow IEEE (1st prize for paper 1961); mem. AAAS, Am. Phys. Soc., Sigma Xi. Office: Yale U 15 Prospect St New Haven CT 06520

BARKER, RICHARD GORDON, research laboratory administrator; b. Rochester, N.Y., Feb.8, 1937; s. Richard I. and Laura (Gordon) B.; m. Nancy Heiligman, Sept. 7, 1957; children: Laurie Frances, Richard, Jonathan David. A.B., Hamilton Coll., 1958; M.S., Inst. Paper Chemistry, 1960, Ph.D., 1963. Research scientist Union Camp Corp., Princeton, N.J., 1962-69, group leader, 1969-71, sect. leader, 1971-74, dir. research and devel. projects, 1974-79, lab. dir., 1979—; vice chmn. Alkaline Pulping Com.; chmn. Tech. program com. Alkaline Pulping Conf. Contbr. articles to profl. jours.; patentee in field. Chmn. adminstrv. bd. Princeton Methodist Ch.; mgr. Little League Baseball, West Windsor, N.J.; coach PAL basketball and Pop Warner football. Mem. Empire State Paper Research Asn. (chmn. research steering com. 1975-82), Empire State Paper Research Assn. (v.p. N.Am. 1982—), TAPPI (bd. dirs., chmn. bd. dirs. publs, com., chmn. research mgmt. com., mem. annmetting com.; mem. API-TAPPI liaison com. to U.S. Forest Products Lab., APA-TAPPI Whole Tree Chip Com.), Inst. of Paper Chemistry Assn. (past chmn., exec. council, past chmn. pulping and bleaching subcom. research adv com.), Princeton C. of C., am. Chem. Soc., Soc. Research Admistrs. Home: 7 Quaker Rd Princeton Junction NJ 08550 Office: Union Camp corp Research and Devel Div PO Box 412 Princeton NJ 08540

BARKER, ROBERT, biochemist, educator; b. Northumberland, Eng., Sept. 21, 1928; came to U.S., 1955, naturalized, 1966; s. Albert E. S. and Hannah M. (Ferry) B.; m. Kazuko Yamanaka, June 18, 1955; children: Hana, Robin. B.A., U. B.C. (Can.), Vancouver, 1952, M.A. (B. C. Sugar Refineries scholar), 1953; Ph.D., U. Calif., Berkeley, 1958. Technician Fisheries Research Bd. Can., 1953-55; Atlas Powder Co.; postdoctoral fellow in chemistry Washington U., St. Louis, 1958-59; vis. scientist NIH, 1959-60; asst. prof. biochemistry U. Tenn., 1960-63, asso. prof., 1963, U. Iowa, 1963-67, prof., 1967-74; prof., chmn. dept. biochemistry Mich. State U., 1974-79; prof., dir. div. biol. scis. Cornell U., 1979—, v.p. research and advanced studies, 1983—; vis. prof. U. Minn., 1968, Duke U., 1970-71; mem. Nat. Bd. Med. Examiners, 1967-79; cons. to govt. agys. Author: Organic Chemistry of Biological Compounds, 1971; contbr. numerous articles to profl. jours. Recipient Career Devel. award NIH, 1965-70. Mem. Am. Soc. Biol. Chemists, Am. Chem. Soc. (chmn. div. biol. chemistry 1978-79). Office: 310 Day Hall Cornell U Ithaca NY 14853

BARKER, ROBERT WHITNEY, lawyer, business executive, church official; b. Ogden, Utah, July 9, 1919; s. George Simon, Jr. and Florence Emily (Dee) B.; m. Amy Vera Thomas, June 30, 1942; children: Amy Ann Barker Wilson, Robert Whitney, Paul Thomas, Philip Dee, Jeffrey Cutler, Brian Thomas. B.S. with honors, U. Utah, 1941; J.D., Georgetown U., 1947, postgrad. Law Ctr.,, 1949-50. Bar: Utah 1948, D.C. 1949, U.S. Supreme Ct 1949. Partner firm Barker & Barker, Ogden, Utah, 1948; asso. Ernest L. Wilkinson, Washington, 1948-50; adminstrv. asst. to U.S. Senator Wallace F. Bennett, 1951-53; partner firm Wilkinson, Cragun & Barker, Washington, 1953-82, Wilkinson, Barker, Knauer & Quinn, 1982—; dir., sec. Barlow Corp., 1969—; sr. v.p., sec., gen. counsel, dir. Bonneville Internat. Corp., 1964—; v.p., sec., gen. counsel Radio N.Y. Worldwide, Inc., 1964—, Radio Skokie Valley, Inc., 1970-76, Bay Area Broadcasting Co., 1976—; dir. WCLR Bldg. Corp., Bonneville Satellite Corp.; Mem. nat. adv. council U. Utah; bd. visitors Brigham Young U. Law Sch., 1971-78; gen. counsel Presdl. Inaugural Com., 1969, 73, chmn. law com., 1981; dir. Honor Am. Day, Am. Hist. and Cultural Soc., 1970—; mem. continuing legal edn. adv. bd. Georgetown U. Law Center, 1979—. Editorial bd.: Georgetown Law Jour, 1947-48. Pres. Weber County (Utah) Young Republican Club, 1948; mem. exec. bd. Nat. Capitol Area Council Boy Scouts Am., 1966-79. Served to maj., F.A. AUS, 1941-46; MTO, ETO. Decorated Bronze Star with two oak leaf clusters. Fellow Am. Bar Found., Am. Coll. Trial Lawyers; mem. ABA (chmn. Indian matters com. Adminstrv. Law sect. 1957-59), Fed. Bar Assn. (dep. chmn. Indian law com. 1966-72), D.C. Bar Assn. (chmn. legis. com. 1963-65, chmn. U.S. Ct. of Claims com. 1965-67), Utah Bar Assn., Fed. Communications Bar Assn. Mem. Ch. of Jesus Christ of Latter-day Saints (bishop 1953-57, 2d counselor Washington Stake presidency 1957-59, first counselor Washington stake presidency 1959-67, regional rep. Council of Twelve 1967-75, 77-79). Home: 9913 Hillridge Dr Kensington MD 20795 Office: 1735 New York Ave NW Washington DC 20006

BARKER, ROBERT WILLIAM, TV personality; b. Darrington, Wash., Dec. 12, 1923; s. Byron John and Matilda Kent (Tarleton) B.; m. Dorothy Jo Gideon, Jan. 12, 1945. B.A., Drury Coll., 1947. Master of ceremonies: Truth or Consequences, Hollywood, Calif., 1957-75, Price is Right, 1972—, Miss Universe Beauty Pageant, 1966—, Miss U.S.A. Beauty Pageant, 1966—, Pillsbury Bake-Off, 1969—; host:

Rose Parade, CBS, 1969—; Master of ceremonies various charity and civic functions. Nat. chmn. Fund for Animals; nat. spokesman Zero Pet Population Growth; bd. dirs. Actors and Others for Animals. Served with USNR, 1943-45. Mem. Am. Guild Variety Artists, AFTRA, Screen Actors Guild. Club: Bel-Air Country. Office: 1888 Century Park E Suite 1616 Los Angeles CA 90067

BARKER, SAMUEL BOOTH, university administrator, educator; b. Montclair, N.J., Mar. 3, 1912; s. Harry and Marion (Booth) B.; m. Justine Rogers, July 31, 1934. Sc.D (hon.), U. Vt., 1984, B.S. cum laude, 1932; student, Yale U., 1932-34; Ph.D., Cornell U., 1936, 1936-41; Sc.D. (hon.), U. Ala., 1979. Mem. faculty U. Tenn. Coll. Medicine, 1941-44; asst. prof. State U. Iowa Coll. Medicine, 1944-46, asso. prof. physiology, 1946-52; prof. pharmacology U. Ala. in Birmingham, 1952-62, prof. physiology-biophysics, 1965—, prof. biology, 1970—, distinguished prof., 1976—; dir. grad. studies, asso. dean Med. Coll. and Sch. Dentistry, 1965-70; dean Grad. Sch., 1970-78, dean emeritus, 1978—; prof. pharmacology Coll. Medicine, U. Vt., 1962-65; Cons. NIH, NSF, 1944—. Author: (with J.H.U. Brown) Basic Endocrinology, 2d edit, 1966. Krichesky fellow, 1951; recipient Career Research award USPHS, 1962-65. Fellow AAAS, Am. Inst. Chemists; mem. Am. Physiol. Soc., Soc. Exptl. Biology and Medicine, Harvey Soc., AAUP (pres. Iowa chpt. 1950), Ala. Acad. Scis. (pres. 1959-60, chmn. bd. trustees 1972—), Am. Fedn. Clin. Research, Endocrine Soc., Am. Chem. Soc. (chmn. Ala. sect. 1957-58), Biochem. Soc. London, N.Y. Acad. Scis., Am. Thyroid Assn. (pres. 1970-71), Phi Beta Kappa, Sigma Xi, Phi Kappa Phi. Also research and publs. in endocrinology and metabolism. Home: 1812 Woodcrest Rd Birmingham AL 35209 Office: University Station Birmingham AL 35294

BARKER, STEPHEN FRANCIS, educator; b. Ann Arbor, Mich., 1927; s. Ernest F. and Emma (Swigart) B.; m. Evelyn Masi, Aug. 28, 1961; children—Charles, George. B.A., Swarthmore Coll., 1949; M.A., Harvard, 1951, Ph.D., 1954. Instr. U. So. Cal., 1954-55; asst. prof. U. Va., 1956-58, asso. prof., 1958-61; prof. Ohio State U., 1961-64, Johns Hopkins, Balt., 1964—; Santayana fellow Harvard, 1955-56. Author: Induction and Hypothesis, 1957, Philosophy of Mathematics, 1964, The Elements of Logic, 1965. Served with USNR, 1945-46. Guggenheim fellow, 1964-65. Mem. Am. Philos. Assn. Home: 4003 Keswick Rd Baltimore MD 21211

BARKER, STONIE, JR., coal mining company executive; b. Chapmanville, W.Va., Apr. 4, 1926; s. Stonie J. and Ella Maude (Berry) B.; m. Eunice Wilson, Feb. 8, 1952; children: Douglas R., Beverly L. B.S., Va. Poly. Inst., 1951. With Island Creek Coal Co., Lexington, Ky., 1951—, pres., 1970—, also dir. Mem. regional exec. com. Boy Scouts Am. Served with AUS, World War II; PTO. Mem. Am. Inst. Mining, Metall. and Petroleum Engrs., Am. Mining Congress (dir.), Nat. Coal Assn. (dir.). Home: 1598 Lakewood Ct E Lexington KY 40502 Office: 2355 Harrodsburg Rd Lexington KY 40504

BARKER, THOMAS CARL, educator; b. Cedar Rapids, Iowa, May 25, 1931; s. Carl Edward and Bertha Olive (Simons) B.; m. Mary Irene Beorkrem, Sept. 1, 1952; children—Cheryl Lynn, Thomas Carl, Laura Ann, David Edward. Student, Loras Coll., 1949-50, Coe Coll., 1950-51; B.S., U. Iowa, 1954, M.A., 1960, Ph.D., 1963. Accountant Wilson & Co., Cedar Rapids, Iowa, 1951-54; contract adminstr. Collins Radio Co., Cedar Rapids, 1956-57; customer relations The Cryovac Co., Cedar Rapids, 1957-58; bus. officer Mercy Hosp., Iowa City, Iowa, 1958-59; research asst. U. Iowa, 1959-60, teaching asst., 1961-63, asst. prof., 1963-64; adminstrv. asso. U. Iowa Hosp., 1960-62; research asso. UAW Internat. Union, Detroit, 1964-67; dir. Mich. Health & Social Security Research Inst., Detroit, 1964-67; lectr. health econs. Wayne State U., Detroit, 1966-67; Arthur Graham Glasgow prof., dir. Sch. Hops. Adminstrn. Med. Coll. Va., Richmond, 1967-71; prof., dean Sch. Allied Health Professions Va. Commonwealth U., Richmond, 1969—; Served as mem. or cons. to various public health services NIH, Health Resources Adminstrn., VA, HEW agys.; Mem. deans com. VA Med. Center, Richmond, 1974—; mem. Central Va. Health Systems Agy., 1976—, pres., chmn. bd., 1978-80. Contbr. articles to profl. jours. Served with USN, 1954-56; capt. Res. Recipient numerous awards. Mem. Am. Health Planning Assn., Am. Hosp. Assn., Am. Public Health Assn., Am. Soc. Allied Health Professions (pres. 1975-76), Assn. Univ. Programs in Health Adminstrn., Va. Acad. Sci., Va. Assn. Allied Health Professions, Va. Hosp. Assn. Catholic. Club: Rotary Internat. Home: 4516 Croatan Rd Richmond VA 23235 Office: 1200 E Broad St Richmond VA 23298 *My goal in life is that upon my passing, members of Society will conclude that they are better off as a direct consequence of my presence.*

BARKER, W. GARDNER, food company executive; b. Brookline, Mass., May 27, 1913; s. Charles Miller and Lila Brookhouse (Rice) B.; m. Milda Allen, June 20, 1935; children: Sue Brookhouse, William Gardner, Elizabeth H., Bruce Allen. A.B., Harvard U., 1935; postgrad., Stanford U., 1936; M.S., M.I.T., 1937. Successively market research analyst, asst. to advt. mgmt., market exploration mgr. Lever Bros. Co., 1937-48, dir. new products, 1948-50; exec. v.p., dir. Simoniz Co., Chgo., 1950-56; v.p. new products Thomas J. Lipton, Inc., Englewood Cliffs, N.J., 1956-57, exec. v.p., dir., 1957-58, pres., chief exec. officer, dir., 1959-72, chmn. bd., chief exec. officer, 1973-78, chmn. fin. com., dir., 1978—; chmn. bd. Thomas J. Lipton, Ltd., Can., now ret.; Mem. devel. com. M.I.T. Corp. Served to lt. (j.g.) USNR, 1943-46. Mem. AIM, Grocery Mfrs. Am (dir. 1966-69), Am. Mktg. Assn., Consumer Research Inst. (dir.), Tea Assn. U.S.A. (dir. 1958-63, pres. 1960-62), Tea Council U.S.A. (dir. 1961—, chmn. 1963-65, 67-69, 71-73, treas. 1969-71, 1977—). Episcopalian. Clubs: Cruising of Am.; N.Y. Yacht, Brook, Sales Execs. (N.Y.C.); Harvard, Country (Boston); Indian Harbor Yacht (Conn.); Pleon Yacht, Eastern Yacht (Marblehead, Mass.). Home: 405 Ocean Ave Marblehead MA 01945 Office: 800 Sylvan Ave Englewood Cliffs NJ 07632

BARKER, WALTER WILLIAM, artist; b. Coblenz, Germany, Aug. 8, 1921; s. Walter William and Selma Rosalie (Zincke) B.; children: Emily Croy, Michael Brendan. B.F.A., Washington U., 1948; M.F.A., Ind. U., 1950. Mem. faculty Sch. Art, Washington U., St. Louis, 1950-63, Bklyn. Mus. Sch., 1963-66; mem. faculty dept. art U. N.C., Greensboro, 1966—, prof., 1984—; Chmn. Venice Com., N.C., 1969—. One-man exhbns. include, Otto Gerson Gallery, N.Y.C., 1959, Albert Landry Gallery, N.Y.C., 1963, Betty Parsons Gallery, N.Y.C., 1966, 69, Webster Coll., St. Louis, 1968, U. N.C., Greensboro, 1977, Washington U., St. Louis, 1955; one-man exhbns. include, U. N.C., Greensboro, 1983; represented in permanent collections, U. Tex., Austin, Mus. Modern Art, N.Y.C., City Art Mus. of St. Louis, Washington U., St. Louis, Los Angeles County Mus., Phila. Mus. Fine Art, Boston Mus. Fine Art; represented in permanent collections, Corcoran Gallery Art; represented in permanent collections, Ark. Art Center, Little Rock, U. Minn., Mpls., U. Mass., Amherst, Hirschhorn Mus., Washington, Library of Congress, Washington, St. Louis U.; columnist art: St. Louis Post Dispatch, 1962-78. Served with AUS, 1942-45. Recipient Disting. Alumni citation Washington U., St. Louis, 1972. Mem. Max Beckmann Gesellschaft. Episcopalian. Club: Southport (Maine) Yacht. Home: 1606 Walker Ave Greensboro NC 27403 also Dogfish Head Rd West Southport ME 04576 Office: 1000 Spring Garden Greensboro NC 27412 *As an artist I have found that search for self can only be undertaken successfully if there is respect for the visual world.*

BARKER, WILEY FRANKLIN, surgeon, educator; b. Santa Fe, Oct. 16, 1919; s. Charles Burton and Bertha (Steed) B.; m. Nancy Ann Kerber, June 8, 1943; children: Robert Lawrence, Jonathan Steed, Christina Lee. B.S., Harvard, 1941, M.D., 1944. Diplomate: Am. Bd. Surgery (bd. dirs. 1964-70). Intern, then resident Peter Bent Brigham Hosp., Boston, 1944-46; Arthur Tracy Cabot fellow Harvard Med. Sch., 1948-49; asst. chief surg. service, then chief surg. sect. Wadsworth VA Hosp., Los Angeles, 1951-54, attending physician, 1951—; mem. faculty U. Calif. at Los Angeles Med. Sch., 1954—, prof. surgery, 1964—, chief div. gen. surgery, 1955-77; cons. Sepulveda VA Hosp., 1966-78, chief of staff, 1978-83; Mem. com. trauma NRC, 1964—. Author: Surgical Treatment of Peripheral Vascular Disease, 1962, Peripheral Arterial Disease, 1966, 2d edit., 1976, also papers, chpts. in books. Served as lt. (j.g.) M.C. USNR, 1946-47. Harvard Nat. scholar, 1937-44. Fellow ACS; mem. Am. Surg. Assn., Soc. Clin. Surgery (pres. 1972-74), Soc. Univ. Surgeons, Soc. Vascular Surgery (pres. 1972-73), Internat. Cardiovascular Soc. (v.p. N.Am. chpt. 1964-65, pres. 1979-80), So. Surg. Assn., Pacific Coast Surg. Assn. (pres. 1982-83), Pan Pacific Surg. Assn. (pres. elect), Am., Calif., Los Angeles County med. assns., Phi Beta Kappa, Sigma Xi, Alpha Omega Alpha. Republican. Episcopalian. Mailing Address: 13216 Dobbins Pl Los Angeles CA 90049 Office: Dept Surgery Univ Calif Sch Medicine Los Angeles CA 90024

BARKER, WILLIAM ALAN, conductor; b. Melbourne, Australia, Feb. 5, 1938; came to U.S., 1978; s. William Frank and Annie Isabel (Wall) B. Diploma of music teaching, U. Melbourne, 1948. Condr. N.Z. Opera, Wellington, 1969; music dir. N.Z. Maori Theatre Trust, 1970; artistic dir. N.Z. Opera, 1971, N.Z. Ballet, 1971; resident condr. Australian Ballet, Melbourne, 1972-78; assoc. condr. Am. Ballet Theatre, N.Y.C., 1978-80, prin. condr., 1980—; music dir. ballet Fundacion Teresa Carreno, Caracas, Venezuela, 1980—. Home: 24 W 69th St New York NY 10023 Office: 890 Broadway New York NY 10003

BARKER, WILLIAM ALFRED, educator; b. Los Angeles, May 9, 1919; s. Lawrence and Natalie (Cole) B.; m. Mary Louise Miller, June 25, 1941; children—Gail (Mrs. Michael Kahle), Patrick Cole, Claire (Mrs. Jeffrey Stewart), Louisa Lawrene (Mrs. Austin Jarvis), Michael Lawrence. B.A., Yale, 1941; M.S., Calif. Inst. Tech., 1949; Ph.D., St. Louis U., 1952. Mem. faculty St. Louis U., 1949-64, Swiss Fed. Inst. Tech., 1953-55; prof. physics U. Santa Clara, 1964—; cons. Argonne Nat. Lab., 1958-64, industry. Contbr. articles to profl. jours. Served with USNR, 1941-45; PTO. Mem. Am. Phys. Soc., Am. Assn. Physics Tchrs., Phi Beta Kappa, Sigma Xi, Pi Mu Epsilon, Alpha Sigma Nu. Roman Catholic. Research on quantum mechs., relativity, statis. physics, nuclear orientation, planetary atmospheres, quantum electronics, cosmology, exclusive interaction. Home: 73 Bay Tree Ln Los Altos CA 94022 Office: Univ Santa Clara Santa Clara CA 95053

BARKER, WILLIAM SHIRMER, II, clergyman, seminary president; b. St. Louis, Dec. 15, 1934; s. Theodore Roosevelt and Nancy (Edwards) B.; m. Kathryn Gail Kern, Dec. 28, 1957; children: Anne Kathryn, Matthew Woods. A.B., Princeton U., 1956; M.A., Cornell U., 1959; B.D., Covenant Theol. Sem., 1960; Ph.D., Vanderbilt U., 1970. Ordained to ministry Presbyn. Ch., 1960; pastor Hazelwood Presbyn. Ch., Mo., 1960-64; asst. prof. history Covenant Coll., Lookout Mountain, Tenn., 1964-69, dean faculty, 1969-72, Covenant Theol. Sem., St. Louis, 1972-77, pres., 1977—. Trustee Covenant Coll., 1973—. Mem. Am. Soc. Ch. History, Conf. Faith and History, Ref. Presbyn. Ch. Evangelical Synod (now Presbyn. Ch. Am.) (moderator 1973), Phi Beta Kappa. Home: 12262 Conway Rd St Louis MO 63141 Office: 12330 Conway Rd St Louis MO 63141

BARKEY, PATRICK TERRENCE, librarian; b. Flint, Mich., Feb. 11, 1922; s. James Daniel and Damie Ann (Terwilliger) B.; m. Mary Ann Schutte, Nov. 18, 1960; children: Susan, Brian, Leslie, Daniel. B.A., Pomona Coll., 1948; M.L.S., U. Mich., 1949. Audio-visual librarian Flint Pub. Library, 1949-57; head circulation dept. U. Notre Dame Library, 1957-60, Eastern Ill. U. Library, 1960-64; head librarian Tex. A. and I. U., Kingsville, 1964-67; dir. libraries U. Toledo, 1967-74, Claremont (Calif.) Coll., 1974—; pres. Claremont Library Cons., Inc., 1983—; dir. OCLC Western Service Center, 1975—. Contbr. articles to profl. jours. Served with USNR, 1942-44. Mem. Am., Calif. library assns. Democrat. Roman Catholic. Club: Zamorano. Home: 582 W Mount Carmel Dr Claremont CA 91711

BARKHORN, HENRY CHARLES, ret. banker; b. Newark, Aug. 25, 1915; s. Henry Charles and Mariette (Gless) B.; m. Helen Butler, Jan. 16, 1943 (dec. 1967); children—Joan Alexandra (Mrs. Hass), Henry Charles, William Butler; m. Jean Davis Cook, May 14, 1971. A.B., Princeton, 1936. With Prudential Ins. Co. Am., 1936-56; with Mut. Life Ins. Co. N.Y., 1956-73, 2d v.p. securities investment, 1957-63, v.p. securities investment, treas., 1963-73; v.p. Chase Manhattan Bank, N.Y.C., 1974-79. Served to lt. (j.g.) USNR, 1944-46. Mem. Phi Beta Kappa. Clubs: Princeton (N.Y.C.); Maidstone (East Hampton, N.Y.). Home: 36 E 72d St New York NY 10021

BARKHORN, JEAN COOK (MRS. HENRY C. BARKHORN), editor; b. N.Y.C., Apr. 3, 1931; d. Francis Howell and Janet (McCord) Cook; m. Henry C. Barkhorn, May 14, 1971. B.A., Vassar Coll., 1953. With Town and Country mag., N.Y.C., 1954—, exec. dir., 1966-68, mng. editor, 1968—. Home: 36 E 72d St New York NY 10021 Office: 1700 Broadway New York NY 10019

BARKHUUS, ARNE, physician; b. Copenhagen, Aug. 24, 1906; U.S., 1937, naturalized, 1972; s. Carl and Alma (Langkilde) B.; m. Anneli von dem Hagen, Jan. 1941 (dec. 1947); m. Adda von Bruemmer, Feb. 1951. B.A., U. Copenhagen, 1926, M.D., 1933; postgrad., London Sch. Hygiene and Tropical Medicine, 1934, 36-37; Dr.P.H., Johns Hopkins U., 1938. Intern, then resident Blegdamshosp., Copenhagen, 1934, 36; med. officer Brit. Red Cross in Ethiopia, 1935-36; adviser Ministry Health, Caracas, Venezuela, 1938-39; lectr. dept. hygiene U. Calif. at Berkeley, 1940-42; mem. Milbank Meml. Fund, 1942-44; pub. health expert U.S. Fgn. Econ. Adminstrn. Mission to Ethiopia, 1944-45; cons. Def. Dept., 1945-46; with UN Dept. Trusteeship, 1946-55; pub. health expert, chief med. officer for Arab refugees, 1948; dir. health services regional office WHO, S.E. Asia, 1955-59, chief pub. health tng. sect., Geneva, 1959-60; sr. pub. health adminstr. African regional office, 1960-62; chief nat. health planning WHO, Geneva, 1962-68; prof. pub. health practice Columbia U., N.Y.C., 1969-73, adj. prof. pub. health, 1973—; cons. AID, Am. Pub. Health Assn. Author: (with Hilleboe and Thomas) Approaches to National Health Planning, 1972; contbr. articles to profl. jours. Mem. Danish Med. Assn., Am. Pub. Health Assn. Club: Explorers. Home: 24 Beall Circle Bronxville NY 10708

BARKIN, BEN, public relations consultant; b. Milw., June 4, 1915; s. Adolph and Rose Dora (Schumann) B.; m. Shirley Hinda Axel, Oct. 19, 1941; 1 son, Coleman. Student pub. schs. Nat. field dir. Jr. B'nai B'rith, 1937-41; cons. war finance dept. U.S. Treasury Dept., 1941-45; pub. relations cons. Ben Barkin & Asso., 1945-52; chmn., chief exec. officer Barkin, Herman, Solochek & Paulsen, Inc. (and predecessor firm), Milw., N.Y.C., pub. relations counsel, 1952—; partner Milw. Brewers Baseball Club, Inc., 1970—; Bd. dirs., v.p., mem. exec. com. Mt. Sinai Med. Center, also chmn. corp. program. Pres. Mt. Sinai Med. Center Found.; chmn. bd. trustees Athletes for Youth, Inc.; corp. mem. Milw. Children's Hosp., Columbia Hosp., United Way; mem. mgmt. adv. com. Milw. Urban League, We-Milwaukeeans, Greater Milw. Com.; bd. dirs. Nat. Com. against Discrimination in Housing, Inc., Mus. African Art, Washington; mem. civil rights exec. com. Anti-Defamation League; mem. Wis. adv. com. U.S. Commn. on Civil Rights, 1980-81; mem. Wis. exec. com. United Negro Coll. Fund, 1981; mem. music adv. panel orch. sect. Nat. Endowment for Arts. Named man of yr., Milw., 1945; recipient Knight of Bohemia award Milw. Press Club, 1978, Headliner award Milw. Press Club, 1983. Mem. Pub. Relations Soc. Am. (Paul Lund award 1978), NCCJ., B'nai B'rith (nat. chmn. youth commn. 1966-68). Home: 1610 N Prospect Ave Milwaukee WI 53202 Office: 777 E Wisconsin Ave Milwaukee WI 53202

BARKIN, MARVIN E., lawyer; b. Winter Haven, Fla., Nov. 9, 1933; s. Isadore and Jean (Epstein) B.; m. Gertrude Parnes, Sept. 20, 1959; children: Thomas I., Michael A., Pamela L. A.B., Emory U., 1955; LL.B. cum laude, Harvard U., 1958. Bar: Fla. 1958. Research aide Dist. Ct. Appeal Fla., Third Dist., Miami, 1958-60; asso., partner firm Fowler, White, Collins, Gillen, Humkey & Trenam, Tampa, 1960-69; partner firm Trenam, Simmons, Kemker, Scharf. Barkin, Frye & O'Neill, Tampa, 1970—; mem. Fla. Bd. Bar Examiners, 1979—, chmn., 1982-83; chmn. corp., banking and bus. law sect. Fla. Bar, 1974-75, chmn. appellate ct. rules subcom., 1972-73. Mem. Am. Law Inst., Fla. Bar, Omicron Delta Kappa. Democrat. Jewish. Home: 1605 Culbreath Isles Tampa FL 33609 Office: 2600 First Florida Tower Tampa FL 33601

BARKIN, ROBERT ALLAN, newspaper executive; b. Toronto, Ont., Can., Sept. 2, 1939; came to U.S., 1940, naturalized, 1950; s. Jacob and Mildred B.; (div.)children: Craig Lewis, Robin Sue, Richard Lawrence. B.A., George Washington U., 1960. From artist to advt. and sales promotion dir. Giant Food Inc., Washington, 1960-69; freelance artist, designer, Washington, 1969-72; v.p. Lawrence Dobrow & Assos., Washington, 1972-73, Taft Communications Corp., Washington and N.Y.C., 1973-74; cons. MacHarmans Assos., Auckland, N.Z., 1975; Freelance cons., Washington, 1976-77; art dir. Washington Post mag., 1977-78, Washington Post, 1978—; tchr. life drawing and anatomy Georgetown U., 1973-76; inst. D.C. St. Acad., 1970. Exhbns. in, Washington, Phila. and Auckland; rep. pvt. and public collections. Recipient Silver Lions award, Venice, Italy, 1975; also awards N.Y.C. Art Dirs. Club, Communications Art Assn., Ad Club Washington, Am. Inst. Graphic Arts. Mem. Art Dirs. Club Washington (Gold medal 1979), Soc. Publ. Designers (awards 1977-82), Soc. Newspaper Designers. Home: 2909 Porter St NW Washington DC 20008 Office: Washington Post 1150 15th St NW Washington DC 20071

BARKIN, SOLOMON, economist; b. N.Y.C., Dec. 2, 1907; s. Julius and Lillian (Kroll) B.; m. Elaine N. Rappaport, Apr. 21, 1940; children: David Peter, Roger Michael, Amy Claire. B.S., CCNY, 1928; M.A., Columbia, 1929, univ. fellow, 1932-33. Instr. CCNY, 1928-31; asst. dir. N.Y. State Commn. on Old Age Security, 1929-33; NRA Labor Adv. Bd., 1933-36; chief labor sect., div. indsl. econs. U.S. Dept. Commerce, 1936-37; dir. research Textile Workers Union Am., 1937-63; dep. dir. manpower and social affairs directorate OECD, 1963-68; prof. econs. U. Mass., Amherst, 1968-78, prof. emeritus, 1978—; vis. prof. econs. Erasmus U., Rotterdam, Netherlands, 1979; adj. prof. indsl. relations, Columbia, 1959-63; labor cons. WPB.; Mem. Am. standard textile safety code, standing adv. com. U.S. Bur. Labor Statistics; vice chmn. com. on research Pres.'s Conf. on Indsl.; Safety chmn. bd. Interunion Inst., Inc.; textile cons. U.K. Mission of ECA.; Specialist Internat. Information Service, U.S. Dept. State; mem. Sec. Labor's Com. on Automation; chmn. com. on redesign Nat. Com. on the Aging; v.p. Joint Council on Econ. Edn.; mem. AFL-CIO Standing Com. on Research; Am. del. Inter-Am. Statis. Congress, to European Productivity Agy. Conf. on Human Relations, Rome, 1956, OEEC Internat. Textile Conf., Milan, 1957; del. ILO, 1961; econ. adviser Internat. Fedn. Textile and Clothing Workers Assns. Author: Toward Fairer Labor Standards, 1948, The Decline of the Labor Movement, 1961, Worker Militancy and its Consequences, 1965-75, 1975, 2d edit., 1983; co-author: Work Duty Charts for Textile Operations, 1951, Textile Workers' Job Primer, 1953, Forms for Calculating the Frequency of Periodic Work Duties, Manpower Policies and Problems in the Netherlands, 1967, Workers' Negotiated Savings Plans for Capital Formation, Manpower Policy in Norway, 1972; Editor: Technical Change and Manpower Planning: Coordination Enterprise Level, 1967; co-editor: International Labor, 1968; mem. editorial bd.: Jour. Econ. Issues. Fulbright scholar, 1981. Fellow div. psychol. and social scis. Gerontol. Soc., Inc.; mem. Indsl. Relations Research Assn. (past pres.), Am. Statis. Assn., Council on Fgn. Relations, Am. Econ. Assn., Nat. Planning Assn. (trustee), Assn. Evolutionary Econs. (Instl. policy adv. com. 1984—), Phi Beta Kappa Assos., Phi Beta Kappa. Home: Long Hill Rd Leverett MA 01054 Office: U Mass Amherst MA 01003

BARKOFSKE, FRANCIS LEE, lawyer, coal company executive; b. Kansas City, Mo., Feb. 4, 1939; s. Francis and Mildred (Wagner) B.; m. Mary Anne Potts, Apr. 4, 1964; children—Peter, John, Paul, Anne. A.B., Rockhurst Coll., 1960; LL.B., St. Louis U., 1963. Bar: Mo. bar 1963, D.C. bar 1963. Asso., then partner firm Keefe, Schlafly, Griesedieck & Ferrell, St. Louis, 1963-72; atty. Mo. Pacific Corp., St. Louis, 1972-79, corp. sec., 1975-79; asst. gen. counsel Mo. Pacific R.R. Co., St. Louis, 1979-80; sr. v.p. legal and pub. affairs Peabody Coal Co., St. Louis, 1980-82; sr. v.p. legal and pub. affairs, sec. Peabody Holding Co., St. Louis, 1983—. Mem. Am., Fed. Energy bar assns., Mo. Bar, Bar. Assn. Met. St. Louis, Am. Soc. Corp. Secs. Roman Catholic. Club: Racquet. Office: 301 N Memorial Dr Saint Louis MO 63166

BARKSDALE, CLARENCE CAULFIELD, banker; b. St. Louis, June 4, 1932; s. Clarence M. and Elizabeth (Caulfield) B.; m. Emily Catlin Keyes, Apr. 4, 1959; children: John Keyes, Emily Shepley. A.B., Brown U., 1954; postgrad., Washington U. Law Sch., St. Louis, 1957-58, Stonier Grad. Sch. Banking, Rutgers U., 1964, Columbia U. Grad. Sch. Bus., 1968; LL.D. (hon.), Maryville Coll., St. Louis, 1976, Westminster Coll., Fulton, Mo. With 1st Nat. Bank, St. Louis, 1958—, asst. cashier, 1960-62, asst. v.p., 1962-64, v.p., 1964, exec. v.p., 1968-70, pres., 1970-76, chief operating officer, 1974—, chmn. bd., chief exec. officer, 1976—; also dir. Centerre Bank NA; chmn., dir. Centerre Bancorp., UMC Industries, Inc., St. Louis Union Trust Co., Allied Bank Internat., Pet Inc., Dillard Dept. Stores, Inc., Wetterau Inc.; dir. Southwestern Bell Telephone Co. Trustee St. Louis U., Mo. Bot. Gardens; bd. dirs. United Fund Greater St. Louis, Arts and Edn. Council Greater St. Louis, Civic Progress Inc.; pres. Served with M.I. AUS, 1954-57. Mem. Am. Bankers Assn., Assn. Res. City Bankers, St. Louis Regional Commerce and Growth Assn. (dir.), Alpha Delta Phi. Clubs: St. Louis, Mo. Athletic, St. Louis Country, Noonday, Brown University, Bogey (St. Louis); Links (N.Y.C.). Office: Centerre Bank NA One Centerre Plaza St Louis MO 63101

BARKSDALE, HIRAM COLLIER, educator; b. Sandersville, Ga., Dec. 4, 1921; s. William Henry and Maude (Smith) B.; m. Jeanne Epp, July 22, 1950; children—Hiram Collier, Beverly Jeanne, Sally Braswell, Addison Andrew. B.B.A., U. Ga., 1948; M.S., N.Y.U., 1949, Ph.D., 1955. Instr. Washburn Municipal U., 1949-51; projects mgr. Advt. Research Found., 1952-56, asst. to pres., 1956-60; mem. faculty N.Y. U., 1956-65, asso. prof., 1956-60, prof., chmn. dept. marketing,

1960-65; prof. Coll. Bus. Adminstrn., U. Ga., Athens, 1965—, chmn. mktg. dept., 1968-76, distinguished prof. mktg., 1973—. Author: The Use of Survey Research Findings as Legal Evidence, 1957, Problems in Marketing Research: In-Basket Simulation, 1963; co-author: Marketing Research, 1966; Editor: Marketing in Progress Patterns and Potentials, 1964, Marketing Change and Exchange, 1964; Book rev. editor: Media/scope mag, 1964-69; Mem. editorial bd.: Jour. of Marketing, 1965-70, So. Jour. of Bus, 1968-72; editorial adv. bd.: Jour. Bus. Research, 1973-76, Jour. Macromktg, 1979—. Served with AUS, 1943-46. Grantee Ford Found., Harvard Bus. Sch., msummer 1957, Carnegie Inst. Tech., summer 1962. Mem. Am. Mktg. Assn., So. Mktg. Assn., A.A.A.S., Soc. for History of Tech., Phi Beta Kappa, Beta Gamma Sigma. Home: 340 Cedar Creek Dr Athens GA 30605

BARKSDALE, JAMES L., air freight company executive. Exec. v.p., chief operating officer Fed. Express Corp. Office: 2990 Airways Blvd Memphis TN 38194§

BARKSDALE, MAURICE LEE, government official; b. Lockhart, Tex., Jan. 7, 1939; s. James Lee and Ada Varnell (Hughes) B.; m. Faye William, Oct. 4, 1955; children: Hamilton Othal, Marness Lynn, Brian Maurice. B.A. in History, U. Tex.-Arlington, 1970. Clk. U.S. Postal Service, Ft. Worth, 1964-68; v.p. Am. Inst. Mktg., Grand Prairie, Tex., 1968-71, Sey & Co., N.Y.C., 1971-74, Citizens Trust Bank, Atlanta, 1974-75; pres. HMB Mgmt. Co., Ft. Worth, 1975-82; dep. asst. sec. HUD, Washington, 1982—; mem. adv. council SBA, 1981-82; cons. Atlanta Life Ins. Co., 1979-80, Am. Fed. Savs. & Loan, Greensboro, N.C., 1981. Dir. Ft. Worth C. of C., 1976, Ft. Worth Econ. Devel. Corp., 1977; bd. regents Tex. So. U., Houston, 1979—; sector coordinator Tarrant County Republican party, 1980. Served with USN, 1958-63. Mem. United Mortgage Bankers (v.p. 1972-82), Alpha Phi Alpha. Lodge: Masons. Home: 905 6th St SW 801 Washington DC 20024 Office: HUD 451 7th St SW Room 6106 Washington DC 20410

BARKSDALE, PHILLIP DUNLAP, JR., banker; b. Jacksonville, Fla., Mar. 7, 1935; s. Phillip Dunlap and Helen Lee (Wilkens) B.; m. Marion Elizabeth Hathaway, Aug. 25, 1956; children—Karen, Kenneth, Judith. B.A. in Econs, U. Va., 1958; postgrad., N.Y. U. Grad. Sch. Bus., 1960-64. With Irving Trust Co., N.Y.C., 1960—, regional v.p., 1970-72, sr. v.p., 1973, exec. v.p., 1974—; pres. Irving One Wall St. Found. Trustee Citizens Budget Commn., 1977—. Served with U.S. Army, 1958-60. Mem. Assn. Res. City Bankers. Clubs: Wall St., Econ. N.Y. Home: Pleasant Valley Farm Brookside NJ 07926 Office: 1 Wall St New York NY 10015

BARKSDALE, RICHARD DILLON, educator; b. Orlando, Fla., May 2, 1938; s. William Spruil and Lucile Dillon B.; m. Bonnie Alice McClung, Nov. 16, 1962; children—Cheryl Lynn, Richelle Denise. A.S., So. Tech. Inst., Marietta, Ga., 1958; B.C.E., Ga. Inst. Tech., 1962, M.S., 1963; Ph.D., Purdue U., 1966. Registered profl. engr., Fla., Ga., S.C., N.C., Ala., Tenn., La. Asst. prof. civil engring. Ga. Inst. Tech., 1965-69, asso. prof., 1969-75, prof., 1975—; v.p. Soil Systems, Inc., Marietta, 1972-79, Soil Systems of the Carolina, 1976-79; spl. lectr. So. Tech. Inst., 1958-60. Contbr. articles in field to profl. jours. NSF grantee, 1966-67; recipient Ga. Engring. Soc. award, 1961. Mem. ASCE (Norman medal 1978, pres. Ga. sect. 1975-76, chmn. nat. com. structural design of roadways), Phi Kappa Phi (pres. Ga. Tech. chpt. 1979). Republican. Baptist. Club: Apalachee Sportsman (pres. 1974—). Home: 1306 Christmas Ln NE Atlanta GA 30329 Office: Sch Civil Engineering Ga Tech Inst Atlanta GA 30332

BARKSDALE, RICHARD KENNETH, educator, university dean; b. Winchester, Mass., Oct. 31, 1915; s. Simon Daniel and Sarah Irene (Brooks) B.; m. Mildred A. White, Apr. 15, 1960; children: Maxine, James, Richard, Calvin. A.B., Bowdoin Coll., 1937; A.M., Syracuse U., 1938; Ph.D., Harvard U., 1951; L.H.D., Bowdoin Coll., 1972. Instr. English So. U., 1938-39; chmn. dept. English Tougaloo Coll., 1939-42; prof. N.C. Central U., 1949-53, dean, 1953-58; prof., chmn. dept. Morehouse Coll., 1958-62; prof. Atlanta U., 1962-67, dean, 1967-71; prof. English U. Ill., 1971—, acting head dept., 1974, asso. dean, 1975—; Mem. bd. overseers Bowdoin Coll., 1974—; mem. admnstrv. bd. Nat. Fellowships Fund for Black Americans; cons. Ford Found., Nat. Endowment for Humanities.; bd. dirs. GRE, Ednl. Testing Service, 1982-86, U. Ill. Press. Author: Langston Hughes: Poet and His Critics, 1977; co-editor: Black Writers of America, 1972; contbr. articles to profl. jours. Mem. Nat. Council Tchrs. English (bd. dirs. 1972-74), Ill. Humanities Council, Coll. Lang. Assn. (pres. 1973-75), Langston Hughes Soc. (pres.), Phi Beta Kappa. Home: 2207 Wyld Dr Urbana IL 61801 Office: 208 English Bldg Grad Coll U Ill Urbana IL 61801

BARKUN, HARVEY, physician., hospital administrator; b. Montreal, Que., Can., May 2. 1928; s. Samuel and Sylvia (Rabinovitch) B.; m. Yvette Granier, July 23, 1955; children: Alan, Jeffrey. B.Sc., McGill U., 1948; M.D., U. Montpellier, 1957. Intern Jewish Gen. Hosp., Montreal, 1955-56; resident in medicine Queen Mary Vets. Hosp., Montreal, 1958-59; med. dir. Queen Mary VA Hosp., 1963-69, Royal Victoria Hosp., Montreal, 1969-72; exec. dir. Montreal Gen. Hosp., 1972—; dir. Que. Profl. Corp. Physicians; asso. dean faculty of medicine McGill U.; pres. Teaching Hosps. Que.; Mem. Corp. Coll. Stanislas, 26296Montreal. Mem. Soc. Med. Adminstrs. Home: 3197 The Boulevard Westmount PQ H3Y 1S4 Canada Office: 1650 Cedar Ave Montreal PQ H3G 1A4 Canada

BARLETTA, JOSEPH FRANCIS, newspaper executive, lawyer; b. Punxsutawney, Pa., Oct. 1, 1936; s. Michael Albert and Vandolyn R. (Raffetto) B.; m. Marilyn M. Minetti, Feb. 23, 1969. A.B., Marietta Coll., 1959; J.D., Duquesne U., 1963. Bar: Pa. 1963, Ill. 1975, N.Y. 1981. Practice law, Ellwood City, Pa., 1963-66; labor relations mgr. Dow Jones & Co., 1966-70; v.p., dir. employee relations, v.p. dir. ops. Chgo. Tribune, 1970-76; exec. v.p., gen. mgr. N.Y. Daily News, Inc., 1977-81; ptnr. firm Seyfarth, Shaw, Fairweather & Geraldson, 1981—; pres. San Francisco Newspaper Agy., 1982—; commr. pub. utilities City and County of San Francisco; dir. Lebhar-Friedman, Inc. Bd. advisers: Jour. Inst. Socioecon. Studies. Trustee U. San Francisco; trustee Marietta Coll.; bd. govs. San Francisco Symphony; mem. Mayor's Fiscal Adv. Com.; bd. dirs. San Francisco Conv. and Visitors Bur.; mem. community bd. St. Mary's Hosp. Clubs: University, Lotos (bd. dirs.), Family, Friars (N.Y.C.); Bankers, Am. Assn. Knights of Malta. Home: 2222 Hyde St San Francisco CA 94109 Office: 925 Mission St San Francisco CA 94103

BARLEY, ROBERT ARTHUR, banker; b. Glendale, Calif., Oct. 12, 1930; s. Frank William and Ruth Ellen (Gransden) B.; m. Polly Latham, June 27, 1953; children: Linda, Susan, Lauren. B.S., Stanford U., 1953; M.B.A., Harvard U., 1957. With United Calif. Bank, Los Angeles, 1957-76; chmn. bd., chief exec. officer First Tulsa Bancorp., 1976—; Trustee U. Tulsa. Served to 1st lt. USAF, 1953-55. Mem. Met. Tulsa C. of C. (chmn. 1981). Clubs: So. Hills Country, Tulsa. Office: First Pl Tulsa OK 74193

BARLOW, ANNE LOUISE, pediatrician, medical research administrator; b. Skipton-in-Craven, Eng., Jan. 28, 1925; came to U.S., 1951, naturalized, 1954; m. Howard Cadwell, May 19, 1951; children: Barbara Anne, John James Stewart; m 2d Alastair Ramsay, Dec. 19, 1969. M.B., B.S., London (Royal Free Hosp.) Sch. Medicine for Women, U. London, 1948; diploma in child health, Royal Colls. Eng., 1950; M.P.H. with honors, Yale U., 1952. House physician North Lonsdale Hosp., Barrow-in-Furness, Lancashire, Eng., 1948-49; house surgeon Royal Infirmary (Glasgow), Scotland, 1949; resident to profl. unit of child health Royal Hosp. for sick children, Glasgow, 1949-50; jr. hosp. med. officer Knightswood Infectious Diseases Hosp., Glasgow, 1950; Rotary Found. Internat. fellow U. Toronto Med. Sch., Ont., Can., 1950-51; research asst. Yale U. Sch. Pub. Health, New Haven, 1952-53; clinic physician in cancer prevention, Arlington, Va., part-time 1953-54; resident, staff physician William H. Maybury Tb Sanatorium, Northville, Mich., 1954-56; research dir. Detroit Feeding Study with the Detroit City Health Dept., 1954-56; research asst., instr. sch. health U. Pitts. Grad. Sch. Pub. Health, 1957-62; pvt. practice medicine, specializing in pediatrics, Pitts., 1959-62; mem. courtesy staff St. Margaret Hosp., Pitts., 1959-62; research assoc. Tice Lab for Tb research, Cook County Hosp., Chgo., Ill., 1962; med. writer product info. Abbott Labs., North Chicago, Ill., 1963-66, med. specialist antibiotic medicine, 1966-68; mgr. clin. devel. pharm. products div. Abbott Lab., North Chicago, Ill., 1968-71; asst. med. dir. Abbott Labs, North Chicago, Ill., 1971-72, mgr. parenteral nutrition hosp. products div., 1972-73; med. dir. Abbott Labs., North Chicago, Ill., 1973-80, v.p. med. affairs hosp. products div., 1980—; cons. maternal, child and sch. health, dir. well baby clinic Lake County (Ill.) Health Dept., 1963-76; pres. Tb Sanatorium Bd. Lake County Health Dept., Ill., 1976-79; dir., pres. Lake County Bd. Health, 1979-82; health officer Village of North Barrington, Ill., 1964-67; physician-adviser Head Start Lake County Community Action Project, 1970—; chmn. profl. adv. com. Lake County Health Dept., 1972—; preceptor Pediatric Nurse Assoc. Program. Contbr. articles on maternal and infant care, pediatrics and nutrition; patentee high calorie solution of low molecular weight glucose polymer mixt tures useful for intravenouse adminstrn. Bd. dirs. Heart Assn. of Lake County, 1979—, chmn. nutrition com., 1980-82, v.p., 1982-83, pres., 1983—; mem. sch. bd. Grant Twp. Community High Sch. (Ill. Dist. 124), 1973-79; sec. to governing bd. Spl. Edn. Dist. of Lake County, 1977-79; assoc. Nat. Coll. Edn., Evanston, Ill., 1976—. Recipient award of merit for outstanding contns. to pub. health Ill. Pub. Health Assn., 1975, award of merit for outstanding community service to Lake County Community Action Project, 1976, award for outstanding and dedicated service as pres. Lake County Tb Sanatorium Bd., 1979. Mem. Am. Med. Women's Assn. (councilor for orgn. and mgmt. 1977-79, treas. 1980, 1st v.p. 1981, pres. 1983), Pharm. Mfrs. Assn. (med. sect.), Lake County Med. Assn., Ill. State Med. Soc., AMA, Chgo. Network, AAAS, Sigma Xi. Home: 1111 S Waukegan Rd Unit 11 Lake Forest IL 60045 Office: D-970 Abbott Park North Chicago IL 60064

BARLOW, CHARLES FRANKLIN, educator, physician; b. Mason City, Iowa, Nov. 10, 1923; s. Frank Richard and Marie Gertrude (McCabe) B.; m. Patricia Keith, June 30, 1953; children—Ellen, John Keith, Margaret Katherine. Student, Coe Coll., 1941-43; S.B., U. Chgo., 1945, M.D., 1947; A.M. (hon.), Harvard, 1963. Intern Johns Hopkins Hosp., 1947-48; jr. asst. resident Boston Children's Hosp., 1948-49; resident neurology, then instr. neurology U. Chgo. Sch. Medicine, 1951-55; asst. prof., then asso. prof. U. Chgo., 1960-63; Bronson Crothers prof. neurology Harvard Med. Sch., 1963—; neurologist-in-chief Children's Hosp. Med. Center, Boston, 1963—, dir. mental retardation research program, 1968—; cons. Peter Bent Brigham Hosp., Boston, 1963—, Beth Israel Hosp., 1966—. Recipient McClintock Teaching award U. Chgo., 1963. Mem. Am. Neurol. Assn., Am. Assn. Neuropathologists, Am. Acad. Neurology. Home: 482 Jerusalem Rd Cohasset MA 02025 Office: 300 Longwood Ave Boston MA 02115

BARLOW, JOEL, retired lawyer; b. Deckerville, Mich., May 15, 1908; s. Luther Stanley and Jae (McKown) B.; m. Eleanor Livingston Poe, Feb. 19, 1936; children: Eleanor Poe, Jae (Roosevelt), Grace (Schneider). A.B., Alma Coll. (Mich.), 1929, LL.D.; LL.B., George Washington U., 1935; LL.D., Norwich U. Bar: D.C. 1935. Partner Covington & Burling, 1934-77; prof. law Columbus U., 1937; lectr. George Washington Law Sch. Author articles on fed. taxation. Trustee George Washington U., Madeira Sch., Greenway, Va.; bd. dirs. Historic Figure. Mem. Nat. Tax Assn-Tax Inst. Am. (pres. 1959, dir.), Am., D.C., N.Y. bar assns., Am. Bar Found., Am. Law Inst., U.S. C. of C. (treas., dir.), Order of Coif, Phi Beta Kappa, Sigma Alpha Epsilon, Phi Delta Phi. Episcopalian. Clubs: Chevy Chase, Ocean of Fla., Country of Fla., Burning Tree, Met. Home: El Cortijo ZBN 1171 N Ocean Blvd Gulfstream FL 33444

BARLOW, MARK, JR., sch. ofcl.; b. Utica, N.Y., June 15, 1925; s. Mark and Henrietta S. (Siegenthaler) B.; m. Jane N. Atwood, Nov. 27, 1954; children—Mark Andrew, Sarah Endicott, Elizabeth Atwood. A.B., Wesleyan U., Middletown, Conn., 1947; M.A., Colgate U., 1952; Ed.D., Cornell U., 1961. Tchr. N.Y. State pub. schs., 1947-49; asst. to dean, 0sst. dir. preceptorial studies, also instr. math. Colgate U., 1949-51; asst. dean. men Cornell U., Ithaca, N.Y., 1951-57, v.p. student affairs, 1965-72, spl. asst. to pres., 1972-79, vice provost, 1973-79; headmaster St. Mark's Sch., Southborough, Mass., 1979—; dean students Wesleyan U., 1957-63, dean coll., 1963-65. Pres. Middletown Council Community Services, 1961-63; vice chmn. com. ind. schs. Episcopal Diocese Conn., 1962—, chmn. com. on coll. work.; Trustee Wesleyan U. Served with USNR, 1943-46. Mem. Nat. Assn. Student Personnel Adminstrs., New Eng. Assn. Colls. and Secondary Schs., New Eng. Assn. Deans. Clubs: Knickerbocker (N.Y.C.); Tavern (Boston). Address: Saint Mark's Sch Southborough MA 01772

BARLOW, ROBERT FRANCIS, educator, economist; b. Cambridge, Mass., May 6, 1927; s. Thomas F. and Ellen Agnes (O'Mahoney) B.; m. Priscilla M. Potier, 1953; children: Ian C., Paul M., Elizabeth A., Mark P.; m. Karen Edith Berg, 1973. B.A., Colby Coll., 1950; student, London (Eng.) Sch. Econs. and Polit. Sci., 1951-52; M.A., Fletcher Sch. Law and Diplomacy, 1951, Ph.D., 1960. Mem. faculty Colby Coll., 1952-55, 56-62, assoc. prof., asst. to pres., 1961-62; instr. U. Del., 1955-56; prof. econs., dean Whittemore Sch. Bus. and Econs., U. N.H., 1962-66, acad. v.p., 1966-70, prof. econs. and adminstrn., 1970—; vis. prof. Royal U. Malta, 1970, 71; Vis. prof. Tel Aviv (Israel) U., 1973, Internat. Tchrs. Program (INSEAD), Fontainbleau, France, 1974; prof. bus. adminstrn. Institut pour l'Etude des Méthodes de Direction d l'Enterprise, Lausanne, Switzerland, 1973-74; commr. Commn. on Instns. Higher Edn., New Eng. Assn. Schs. and Colls., 1981-85; arbitrator Fed. Mediation and Conciliation Service, Mass. Bd. Conciliation and Arbitration.; Chmn. Gov. N.H. Indsl. Adv. Council, 1963-69, N.H. Fgn. Trade Council, 1963-69, Council on Econ. Edn. in N.H., 1969—; mem. voluntary labor dispute tribunal Am. Arbitration Assn.; mem. natural resources, econ. adv. coms. New Eng. Council. Various publs. Bd. dirs. N.H. Heart Assn., 1968-69; trustee Theatre-by-the Sea, Portsmouth, N.H., 1967-69. Fulbright grantee, 1951-52; sr. Fulbright scholar, Montivedeo, Uruguay, 1977. Mem. Nat. Acad. Arbitrators, Am. Econ. Assn., AAUP, Phi Beta Kappa, Phi Kappa Phi. Home: 55 Gates St Portsmouth NH 03801

BARLOW, THOMAS JAMES, industrial company executive; b. Houston, June 22, 1922; s. Thomas Jefferson and Dorothy (James) B.; m. Billye Louise Sears, May 31, 1944; children: Lance, Lynne. B.S., Tex. A&M U., 1943; postgrad., Harvard U., 1962. Trainee Western Cottonoil Co., Abilene, Tex., 1946-47, asst. gen. mgr., 1948-49; constrn. engr. San Joaquin Cottonoil Co., Bakersfield, Calif., 1948; supt. Western Cotton Products Co., Phoenix, 1949-50; prodn. mgr. Nile Ginning Co., Minia, Egypt, 1950-56; prodn. engr. Anderson, Clayton & Co., Houston, 1956-57, v.p., 1961-66, pres., chief exec. officer, 1966-76, chmn. bd-, chmn. exec. com., chief exec. officer, 1976—, also dir.; dir. Central S.W. Corp., Hughes Tool Co. Served from ensign to lt. USNR, World War II; PTO. Club: River Oaks Country (Houston). Office: Anderson Clayton & Co First Internat Plaza 1100 Louisiana Houston TX 77252 *

BARLOW, WALTER GREENWOOD, public opinion analyst, management consultant; b. Liverpool, Eng., Sept. 10, 1917; came to U.S., 1920, naturalized, 1928; s. Walter and Sarah Ellen (Greenwood); m. Hanna Hansen, 1951 (dec. 1974); children: Eric, Francine, Deborah, Alison; m. Joan K. Frahm, June 21, 1980. B.A., Cornell U., 1939. Reporter Washington Daily News, 1940; mem. editorial staff Time mag., 1941; with Opinion Research Corp., 1946-65, pres., 1960-65, Howard Chase Assos., Inc., N.Y.C., 1965-68, Research Strategies Corp., 1966—; Mem. N.J. Bd. Pub. Welfare, 1966-80, vice chmn., 1973-80; mem. adv. council Electric Power Research Inst., 1977-81; Trustee Cornell U., 1968-75, mem. council, 1968—; bd. dirs. A.D. Publs. (formerly Presbyn. Life Mag.), 1968-72, pres., 1970-72; bd. dirs. support agy. United Presbyn. Ch. in U.S.A., 1973-80; bd. dirs. Family Service Assn. Am., 1958-69, v.p., 1964-67, pres., 1967-69; bd. dirs. A.D. Pub., 1970—, v.p., 1973-75, pres., 1976-80; commr. Middle States Assn. Colls. and Schs., 1982—. Served to maj. AUS, 1941-46; ETO. Decorated Bronze Star. Mem. Pub. Relations Soc. Am., Am. Statis. Assn., Am. Marketing Assn., Phi Beta Kappa, Phi Kappa Phi, Sigma Delta Chi. Presbyterian. Club: Cornell of N.Y. Home and Office: 105 College Rd E Princeton NJ 08540

BARLOW, WAYNE BREWSTER, composer, organist, educator; b. Elyria, Ohio, Sept. 6, 1912; s. Edmund Brewster and Josephine (Muenscher) B.; m. Helen Hutzen, Aug. 7, 1937; children: Robert Wayne, Joan Helen. B.M., Eastman Sch. Music, 1934, M.M., 1935, Ph.D. in Composition, 1937. Emeritus prof. composition Eastman Sch. Music; former grad. dean and dir. electronic music studio; former organist, choir dir. St. Thomas Episcopal Ch. and Christ Ch. (Episcopal); Fulbright sr. lectr. Royal U., Conservatory Copenhagen, U. Aarhus, Denmark, 1955-56; Lectr. Composer: Cantata, Zion in Exile, 1977, The Winter's Passed for oboe and strings, 1938, Lyrical Piece for clarinet and strings, 1943, The Twenty-third Psalm for chorus and orch, 1944; commd. for radio Nocturne for chamber orch, 1946; Sonata for Piano, 1947, Mass in G, 1951, Quintet for piano and strings, 1951, Triptych for string quartet, 1954, Night Song for orch, 1957, Poems for Music for soprano and orch, 1958, Intrada for brass ensemble, 1959, Images for harp and orch, 1961, Sinfonia de Camera, 1962, Vistas for orch, 1963, Trio for oboe, viola and piano, 1964, Dynamisms for two pianos, 1967, Elegy for viola and orch, 1967; cantata Wait for the Promise of the Father, 1968; Concerto for saxophone and band, 1970, Soundscapes for orchestra and electronic tape, 1972, Voices of Darkness for reader, instruments and tape, 1974, Voices of Faith for chorus and orch, 1976; for chorus Out of the Cradle Endlessly Rocking; also church, chamber, electronic music.; Author: Foundations of Music, 1953; periodical articles. Awarded Lillian Fairchild Meml. award for outstanding achievement in arts, 1936; Musician of Year award Mu Phi Epsilon, 1972; Fulbright research grantee work electronic music, Belgium and Holland, 1964-65; Exxon Edn. Found. grantee, 1973. Mem. A.S.C.A.P., Phi Beta Kappa (hon.), Phi Mu Alpha Sinfonia. Episcopalian. Club: Rotarian. Home: 95 Elmcroft Rd Rochester NY 14609

BARLOW, WILLIAM EDWARD, publishing company executive; b. Indpls., Dec. 6, 1917; s. Edward Stevens and Eva (Eustis) B.; m. Marguerite Emily Holcombe, Oct. 4, 1943 (div. 1975); children: Gloria Barlow Bernhardt, Christopher, James. B.S., Hamilton Coll., 1940; postgrad., William Coll., 1940. With Pan Am. Airways, 1941-45, Time Internat., 1945-48; founder, pres. Vision Inc., N.Y.C., 1948-75, Middle East Enterprises, 1975-79; owner, pres. MIN Pub., N.Y.C., 1978—. First pres. Council of the Americas, 1963-71, hon. pres.; bd. dirs. Internat. Univ. Found., 1965—; v.p. Interam. Council Commerce and Prodn., 1968-70; bd. dirs. Fund for Multinat. Mgmt. Edn., 1968—. Recipient Maria Moors Cabot Gold Medal award Columbia U. Grad. Sch. Journalism, 1963; Cordier fellow Columbia U. Sch. Internat. Affairs, 1977—. Mem. Council Fgn. Relations, Pan Am. soc. (dir. 1963-75), Ctr. Inter-Am. Relations (dir. 1966-74). Clubs: Racquet and Tennis of N.Y., University of N.Y., Long Island-Wyandanch. Office: 18 E 53d St New York NY 10022

BARLOWE, RALEIGH, economist; b. Lincoln, Idaho, Nov. 10, 1914; s. George Edward and Charlotte (Campbell) B.; m. Jeannette Topp, Oct. 4, 1941; 1 son, Raleigh R.B. B.S., Utah State Agrl. Coll., 1936; M.A., Am. U., 1939; student, USDA Grad. Sch., 1938-40; Ph.D., U. Wis., 1946. Instr. Am. U., 1937-38; asst. Library of Congress, 1937-40; land economist Southwestern Land Tenure Research Project, Fayetteville, Ark., 1942-43; agrl. economist U.S. Dept. Agr., Milw., 1943-47; economist FAO, Washington, 1947; from lectr. to prof. agrl. econs. Mich. State U., 1948-59, prof., 1959-81, disting. prof., 1981-82, adj. prof., 1982—, chmn. dept. resource devel., 1959-71, 80; vis. prof. U. Calif., Riverside, 1982; economist Robert R. Nathan Assn., Bogota, Colombia, 1959; cons. U. P.R., 1958, Govt. Colombia, 1959, U. Nigeria, 1967, Pub. Land Law Rev. Commn., 1969, Korea, 1971-72, Agr. Devel. Council, 1972, Orgn. for European Cooperation and Devel., 1973, Govt. Thailand, 1976-77; mem. U.S. del. to Indo-U.S. Pugwash Conf. on Sci. and Tech., 1974; Mem. Gov.'s Water Com., 1955-56; staff Mich. Tax Study, 1957-58; chmn. tech. com. Lansing Water Adv. Com., 1961-63; staff Mich. Constl. Conv. Prep. Commn., 1961; treas. Mich. Natural Resources Council, 1961-63, chmn., 1963-65; mem. Gov.'s Task Force on Water Rights, Use and Pollution Control, 1964-66. Author: Land Resource Economics, 1958, rev. 1972, 78, (with V. Webster Johnson) Land Problems and Policies, 1954; also numerous article, bulls. Fellow Soil Conservation Soc. Am. (pres. Mich. chpt. 1980-81); Mem. Am. Agrl. Econs. Assn., Am. Econ. Assn., Econ. History Assn., Agrl. History Soc. Home: 907 Southlawn East Lansing MI 48823

BARMANN, LAWRENCE FRANCIS, educator; b. Maryville, Mo., June 9, 1932; s. Francis Lawrence and Clary Weber (LaMar) B. B.A., St. Louis U., 1956, Ph.L., 1957, S.T.L., 1964; M.A., Fordham U., 1960; postgrad., Princeton, 1965-66; Ph.D., Cambridge U., Eng., 1970. Tchr. history St. Louis U. High Sch., 1957-59; asst. prof. history St. Louis U., 1970-73, asso. prof., 1973-78, prof., 1978—; asst. dir. Am. Studies Program, 1981-83, dir., 1983—. Author: Newman at St. Mary's, 1962, Baron Friedrich von Hügel and the Modernist Crisis in England, 1972, The Letters of Baron Friedrich von Hügel and Professor Norman Kemp Smith, 1982; Contbr. articles profl. jours. Recipient research grant Am. Philos. Soc. of Phila., 1971, Beaumont Found., 1977, 82; Nancy McNeir Ring award for outstanding tchr. St. Louis U., 1975; Danforth asso., 1978—. Mem. Cambridge Soc. (founding 1977), Am. Hist. Assn., Am. Assn. U. Profs., Phi Beta Kappa. Home: The Greystone (4-E) 410 N Newstead St Louis MO 63108 Office: 221 N Grand Blvd St Louis MO 63103 *I have found for myself that the meaning of life is the joy of continuous discovery in unending intellectual, emotional and spiritual growth, and the satisfaction which comes from sharing my vision and concerns with the young people who will lead the next generation.*

BARNA, LILLIAN C., educational administrator; m. Eugene A. Barna; children: Craig A., Keith A. B.A. in Fgn. Lang., Hunter Coll.,

1950, postgrad., 1951; postgrad. in edn., long Beach State U., 1952; M.A., San Jose State U., 1970. Cert. life elem. tchr., elem. adminstr., gen. secondary tchr., gen. adminstr., Calif. Adult edn. tchr., jr. high sch. tchr. N.Y.C. Sch. Dist., 1950-52; elem. tchr. Whittier Sch. Dist., Calif., 1952-54, high sch. tchr., Norwalk Sch. Dist., Calif.; presch. tchr. Los Gatos Sch. Dist., Calif., after 1958, Long Beach Sch. Dist., to 1967; supr. presch. program San Jose Unified Sch. Dist., Calif., 1967-68, coordinator early childhood edn., 1968-72, prin. Title I Schs., 1971, supr. TREND, 1972-74, assoc. adminstr. categorical programs, 1974-80, supt. schs., 1980—; mem. com. on minorities in engring. Nat. Acad. Sci.; chmn. bd. dirs. Calif. Assn. Student Councils; mem. Calif. Block Grants Adv. Council; cons. in field. Vice pres. bd. dirs. San Jose Civic Light Opera. Subject of resolution in recognition of contbns. to edn. Calif. Senate; recipient Outstanding Achiefement in Edn. award Calif. State U.-Hayward, Hidalgo de Calificada Nobleza award State N.M., award for contbns. to enhancement of Puerto Rican community in State of Calif. Western Region Puerto Rican Council, award for achieveents in field of edn. Assn. Puerto Rican Profls., award for outstanding community service, award for support and promotion arts in community Music and Arts Found. Sanat Clara County, Calif.; named Woman of Yr. Soroptomist Internat.; named to Hunter Coll. Hall of Fame. Mem. Assn. Calif. Sch. Adminstrs., Nat. Sch. Bds. Assn., San Jose Adminstrs. Assn., Calif. Assn. Women Admistrs., Calif. Reading Assn., Women Leaders in Edn., Individualized Instrn. Assn., North Assn. Puerto Rican Profls., PTA, Nat. Assn. Edn. Young Children, Calif. Assn. Edn. Young Children, Tchrs. of English to Speakers of Other langs., Fgn. Lang. Assn. Santa Clara county, Phi Kappa Phi, Delta Zeata (treas., pres.). Home: 19700 Charters Ave Saratoga CA 95070 Office: San Jose Unified Sch Dist 1605 Park Ave San Jose CA 95126

BARNARD, CHARLES NELSON, editor, author; b. Arlington, Mass., Oct. 5, 1924; s. Charles Nelson and Mae E. (Johnson) B.; m. Diana Lee Pattison, Aug. 6, 1949 (div. Aug. 1970); children: Jennifer Lee, Rebecca, Charles Nelson, Patrick; m. Karen Louise Zakrison, Apr. 18, 1971. B.J., U. Mo., 1949. Editor Dell Pub. Co., N.Y.C., 1949; assoc. editor True mag., Fawcett Publs., N.Y.C., 1949-54, mng. editor, 1954-63; sr. editor Sat. Evening Post, N.Y.C., 1964-65; exec. editor True Mag., 1965-67, editor, 1968-70; travel editor Modern Maturity and Dynamic Years (publs. of Am. Assn. Ret. Persons); editorial cons., freelance writer, 1971—. Author: The Winter People, 1973, 20,000 Alarms, 1974, I Drank the Water Everywhere, 1975, The Money Pit, 1976, It Was a Wonderful Summer for Running Away, 1977; Editor: A Treasury of True, 1957, Official Automobile Handbook, 1959, Anthology of True, 1962; Contbr. to: Ency. Brit. Served from pvt. to sgt. AUS, 1944-46; war corr. Mem. Alpha Tau Omega, Sigma Delta Chi, Kappa Tau Alpha. Home: 225 Valley Rd Cos Cob CT 06807 Office: 215 Long Beach Blvd Long Beach CA 90801

BARNARD, DRUIE DOUGLAS, JR., congressman; b. Augusta, Ga., Mar. 20, 1922; s. Druie Douglas and Lucy B. B.; m. Naomi Elizabeth Holt, 1946; children: Pamela Holt Barnard Chafee, Lucy Irene, Druie Douglas, III. A.B., Mercer U., 1943; LL.B., Walter F. George Sch. Law, Macon, Ga., 1948. With Ga. R.R. Bank & Trust Co., Augusta, 1948-49, Fed. Res. Bank Atlanta, 1949-50; with Ga. R.R. Bank, Augusta, 1950-62, 66-76, exec. v.p., 1972-76; exec. sec. to gov. Ga., 1963-66; mem. 95th-98th Congresses from 10th Dist. Ga.; mem. bd. Ga. Dept. Transp., 1966-76, Augusta Transp. Authority, 1973-76; chmn. Richmond County Democratic Exec. Com., 1955-60; mem. Ga. Dem. Exec. Com., 1963-66; chmn. Star Student Program, 10th Dist. Ga., 1967-74. Served with AUS, 1943-45. Named Alumni of Year, Augusta Coll., 1966. Mem. Blue Key, Phi Delta Theta. Baptist. Club: Kiwanis. Home: Milledge Rd Augusta GA 30904 Office: 236 Cannon House Office Bldg Washington DC 20515

BARNARD, KURT, retailing economist, association executive; b. Hamburg, Germany, Apr. 16, 1927; came to U.S., 1947, naturalized, 1952; s. León and Senta (Künstlinger) Barnard-J.; m. Wendy Holly Love, Dec. 29, 1979. Student, N.Y. U., 1948, N.Y. State U., 1953; grad., New Sch. for Social Research, 1957. N.Y. corr. European and Japanese publs., 1957-60; dir. Latin Am., Far Eastern pub. relations Anglo-Affiliated Corp., N.Y.C., 1955-60, Am. Research Merchandising Inst., Chgo., 1960-67; exec. dir. Nat. Mass Retailing Inst., N.Y.C., 1967-69, exec. v.p., 1969-74, pres., 1974-76; exec. dir. Fedn. Apparel Mfrs., N.Y.C., 1976; cons. on wage price freeze to dir. U.S. Office Emergency Preparedness, 1971-72; lectr. in retailing economics. Organizer Nat. Loss Prevention Council, 1972, Store Thieves and Their Impact, A Study, 1973; named mem. U.S. Govt. Industry Sector Adv. Com., 1978; mem. U.S. Govt. Exporters Adv. Com., 1979; chmn. bd. N.Y. Internat. Fashion Fair, 1980; Leader nat. campaign against fair trade laws. Author: Cargo of Death, 1966, An Untapped Source of Store Profits, 1974, Picture of a Tragedy, 1974, How Chains Succeed With Non-Foods, 1974, Can Supermarkets Capture Non-Food Sales?, 1974, In Retailing: Future Shock is Now, 1975, Guidelines to Effective Marketing Strategies for Self-Service Retailers, 1975; co-author: Mass Merchandisers Guide to Sales and Expense Reporting, 1969; Contbr. articles to mags. and profl. jours. Recipient Disting. Service award U.S.O., 1965, Am. Soc. Assn. Execs. award, 1965; commd. Ky. col., 1975; DuPont Co. grantee, 1971-75. Mem. Pub. Relations Soc. Am., Am. Mktg. Assn., Nat. Assn. Bus. Economists, Mus. Modern Art. Club: Chgo. Press. Home: 25 Sutton Pl S New York NY 10022 Office: 450 7th Ave New York NY 10123

BARNARD, ROLLIN DWIGHT, savings and loan executive; b. Denver, Apr. 14, 1922; s. George Cooper and Emma (Riggs) B.; m. Patricia Reynolds Bierkamp, Sept. 15, 1943; children: Michael Dana, Rebecca Susan (Mrs. Paul C. Wulfestieg), Laurie Beth (Mrs. Kenneth J. Kostelecky). B.A., Pomona Coll., 1943. Clk. Morey Merc. Co., Denver, 1937-40; ptnr George C. Barnard & Co. (gen. real estate and ins.), Denver, 1946-47; v.p. Foster & Barnard, Inc., 1947-53; instr. Denver U., 1949-53; dir. real estate U.S. P.O. Dept., Washington, 1953-55, dep. asst. postmaster gen., bur. facilities, 1955-59, asst. postmaster gen., 1959-61; pres., dir. Midland Fed. Savs. & Loan Assn., Denver, 1962—; dir. Verex Assurance Inc. Pres. Denver Area council Boy Scouts Am., 1970-71, mem. exec. bd., 1962-73; adv. bd. Denver Area council Boy Scouts Am, 1973—; chmn. Planning and Zoning Commn. Greenwood Village, Colo., 1969-73; mem. Greenwood Village City Council, 1975-77; mem. nat. council Pomona Coll., 1963—; bd. dirs. Downtown Denver Improvement Assn., pres., 1965; bd. dirs. Bethesda Found., Inc., 1973-82, treas., 1983—; bd. dirs. Children's Hosp., 1979—, Rocky Mountain Child Health Services, Inc., 1982—; trustee Mile High United Fund, 1969-72, Denver Symphony Assn., 1973-74; mem. bd. Colo. Council Econ. Edn., 1971-80, chmn., 1971-76; trustee, v.p., treas. Morris Animal Found., 1969-81, pres., chmn., 1974-78; trustee emeritus, 1981—. Served to capt. AUS, World War II. Nominated One of Ten Outstanding Young Men in Am. U.S. Jaycees, 1955, 57; recipient Distinguished Service award Postmaster Gen. U.S., 1960; Silver Beaver award Boy Scouts Am., 1969; Outstanding Citizen of Year Sertoma, 1982; Colo. Citizen of Year Colo. Assn. Reactors, 1982. Mem. Denver C. of C. (pres. 1966-67), U.S. Savs. and Loan League (dir. 1972-77), League Savs. Instns. (mem. nat. legis. com., exec. com. 1974-77, pres. 1980-81), Savs. League Colo. (exec. com. 1969-73, pres. 1971-72), Colo. Assn. Commerce and Industry (dir. 1971-76), Fellowship Christian Athletes (Denver area dir. 1963-76), Western Stock Show Assn. (dir. 1971—), Nu Alpha Phi. Republican. Presbyn. Clubs: 26 (pres. 1970), Rotary (dir. 1979-81), Rotary (Denver) (2d v.p. 1980); Mountain and Plains Appaloosa Horse (pres. 1970-71), Roundup Riders of the Rockies (dir. 1980—). Home: 3151 East Rd Littleton CO 80121 Office: 444 17th St Denver CO 80202

BARNARD, WILLIAM CALVERT, news service exec.; b. Corpus Christi, Tex., Feb. 25, 1914; s. W.C. and Eleanor (Erb) B.; m. Julia Lacy Salter, Mar. 25, 1961; children—William Cornell, Diana Eugenia. Student, Tex. Coll. Arts and Industries, Kingsville, 1933-35. Reporter-columnist Corpus Christi Caller-Times, 1935-40; feature editor San Antonio Express-News, 1941-42; writer, state editor AP, Dallas Bur., 1942-50; AP war corr. Korean War, Far East news editor, 1950-54; bur. chief AP, Dallas, 1954-62, gen. exec., N.Y.C., 1962-71, gen. exec. for ten Western states, San Francisco, 1971-81, gen. exec. for 24 Western states, 1981—. Recipient Journalism Forum award for coverage Korean War So. Meth. U., 1954. Presbyterian. Home: 101 Vista Del Grande San Carlos CA 94070 Office: 318 Fox Plaza San Francisco CA 94119

BARNARD, WILLIAM SPRAGUE, manufacturing company executive; b. Hillsboro, Ill., May 20, 1925; s. Kenneth Homes and Sally (Sprague) B.; m. Barbara Richardson, Jan. 10, 1948; children: Susan Richardson, Elizabeth Gorham, William Sprague; m. Leonora Florian, May 3, 1975. B.A., Harvard U., 1946; Ph.D., Princeton U., 1950; grad. fellow, Textile Research Inst., 1950. Research scientist Nat. Lead Co., N.Y.C., 1950-53; with Chicopee Mfg. Co., 1953—, dir. woven fabric research, Chicopee Falls, Mass., 1957-66, dir. research and devel., New Brunswick, N.J., 1966-69, v.p. research, 1969—; chmn. exec. com. Textile Research Inst., 1980—. Served with USNR, 1944-46. Mem. Am. Chem. Soc., Fiber Soc., Am. Assn. Textile Chemists and Colorists, N.Y. Assn. Research Dirs. (councilor 1974-77, pres. 1982-83), Sigma Xi. Unitarian. Home: 326 Ridgeview Rd Princeton NJ 08540 Office: Chicopee Mfg Co PO Box 1151 New Brunswick NJ 08903 *Scientific research has proven to be a rewarding career choice that you never outgrow. Each day brings new insights and discoveries.*

BARNATHAN, JULIUS, broadcasting company executive; b. N.Y.C., Jan. 22, 1927; s. Elias L. and Julia (Amado) B.; m. Lorraine Glogower, Jan. 13, 1952; children: Joyce Linda, Daniel Elias, Jacqueline Frances. A.B., Bklyn. Coll., 1951; A.M. in Math. Statistics, Columbia, 1955; D.Sc. (hon.), Gallaudet Coll., 1982. Actuarial asst. Nat. Council for Compensation Ins., 1951-52; dir. media research, statis. analyst Kenyon & Eckhardt, 1952-54; with ABC, 1954—, dir. research, 1957-59, v.p., 1959, v.p. affiliated stas., 1959-62, v.p., gen. mgr., 1962-65, v.p. charge broadcast ops. and engring., 1965-76, pres. broadcast ops. and engring., 1976—; pres., owner, operator TV stas., 1962; Pres. Bklyn. Coll. Bur. Econ. Research, 1949-50. Served with USNR, 1944-46. Recipient Emmy award for 1976 Summer Olympics; Emmy award for Winter Olympics, 1980; Spl. Commendation award Soc. Motion Picture and TV Engrs.; Engring. award Nat. Assn. Broadcasters, 1982. Mem. Radio-TV Research Council (past pres.), Internat. Radio-TV Soc., Acad. Radio and TV Arts and Scis. (bd. govs.), Am. Statis. Assn., Phi Beta Kappa, Pi Mu Epsilon. Home: 170 Harbor Ln Roslyn Harbor NY 11576 Office: 1330 Ave Americas New York NY 10019

BARNEBEY, KENNETH ALAN, food company executive; b. Fremont, Nebr., Apr. 16, 1931; s. Hoyt F. and Mae S. (Mott) B.; m. Faith Price, May 10, 1969; children: Robert, Mark, Holiday, Cindy, Kendra, Valerie, Bonnie, Laurel, Susan. B.A. in Transp, U. Wash., Seattle, 1953. With Tropicana Products, Inc., Bradenton, Fla., 1955-80, gen. sales mgr., then v.p. mktg. and sales, 1957-77, exec. v.p., 1977, pres., chief adminstrv. officer, 1977-79, chmn. bd., chief exec. officer, 1979-80, also dir.; corp. v.p. Beatrice Foods, Inc., 1979-81; pres., dir., dep. chmn. Am. Agronomics Corp., Tampa, Fla., 1981—; dir. Dependable Ins. Group Inc. Am., Exmart; mem. sch. mktg. program Fla. Citrus Dept., 1973—. Bd. dirs., treas. Am. Acad. Achievement; bd. dirs. Manette Jr. Coll., Asolo State Theatre; mem. Fla. Council of 100.; adv. council Fla. State U. Served with U.S. Army, 1953-55. Mem. Am. Mgmt. Assn. (lectr.), NAM (mktg. adv. com., dir.), Fla. Canners Assn. (mktg. adv. com.), Manatee County C. of C. (dir., chmn. econ. devel. com.). Clubs: Manatee County Exchange (past pres.), Bradenton Country.; Palma Ceia Country (Tampa). Office: PO Box 24778 Tampa FL

BARNEBEY, MALCOLM RICHARD, ambassador; b. Nebr., Nov. 8, 1927; m. June Mandeville. B.A., North Tex. State Coll., 1949, M.A., 1951; postgrad. econs., U. Calif.-Berkeley, 1957-58. Teaching asst. North Tex. State Coll., 1949-50; instr. Weatherford Coll., 1950-52; joined Fgn. Service, Dept. State, 1952; polit. officer, Vienna, Austria, 1952-53; detailed to U.S. Escapee Program, FOA, 1953-55, visa officer, 1955; econ. officer, La Paz, Bolivia, 1955-57, fgn. affairs officer, Washington, 1958-61, dep. prin. officer, Guayaquil, Ecuador, 1961-63; detailed program officer to AID, 1963-64; dep. dir. Office Ecuadorean-Peruvian Affairs, Washington, 1964-65, dir., 1965-67; dep. chief mission, Managua, Nicaragua, 1967-70, dep. chief mission, counselor, La Paz, 1970-72, assigned to, Washington, 1972-73, dep. chief mission, Lima, Peru, 1973-76; dir. policy planning, congl. and pub. affairs Bur. Am. Republic Affairs, Dept. State, Washington, 1976-77; dir. Office Andean Affairs, 1977-80, consul gen., Belize, 1980-81; Chargé d'affaires, Belize, 1981-83, ambassador to Belize, 1983—. Office: Bur Am Republic Affairs Dept State Washington DC 20520

BARNER, CHARLES WILBUR, church official; b. Richfield, Pa., July 19, 1925; s. Elmer Newton and Blanche Ludella (Basom) B.; m. Etta V. Dysle Berger, Mar. 19, 1983; children—Charles Timothy, Rebecca Barner Fenn, Bruce Eric. B.A., Moravian Coll., 1949; postgrad., Moravian Theol. Sem., 1949-50. Ordained to ministry Evang. Congl. Ch., 1948; pastor Williams Twp. Evang. Congl. Ch., Easton, Pa., 1945-47, Reedsville Evang. Congl. Ch., Schuylkill Haven, Pa., 1947-53, St. Matthews Evang. Congl. Ch., Emmaus, Pa., 1953-61, Grace Evang. Congl. Ch., Allentown, Pa., 1961-67, St. Paul's Evang. Congl. Ch., Reading, Pa., 1967-70, First Evang. Congl. Ch., Palmyra, Pa., 1984—; gen. sec. Internat. Soc. Christian Endeavor, Columbus, Ohio, 1970—, World's Christian Endeavor Union, 1972—. Pres. Emmaus PTA, 1958-61. Club: Gahanna Kiwanis. Home: 144 Regal Pl Gahanna OH 43230 Office: 1221 E Broad St PO Box 1110 Columbus OH 43216

BARNES, A. JAMES, government official; b. Napoleon, Ohio, Aug. 30, 1942; s. Albert James and Mary Elizabeth (Morey) B.; m. Sarah Jane Hughes, June 19, 1976; children: Morey Elizabeth, Laura LeHardy. B.A. with high honors, Mich. State U., 1964; LL.B. cum laude, Harvard U., 1967. Asst. prof. bus. adminstrn. Ind. U., 1967-69; trial atty. Dept. Justice, 1969-70, asst. to dep. atty. gen., 1973; asst. to adminstr. EPA, 1970-73; campaign mgr. for Gov. Milliken of Mich., 1974; partner firm Beveridge, Fairbanks & Diamond, Washington, 1975-81; gen. counsel Dept. Agr., 1981-83, EPA, 1983—; adj. prof. Georgetown U. Sch. Bus. Adminstrn. Co-author: Business Law and the Regulatory Environment, 5th edit., 1984, Law for Business, 1980. Del. Ind. Republican Conv., 1968, Mich. Rep. Conv., 1974. Recipient Outstanding Teaching award Ind. U., 1969. Mem. ABA, Fed. Bar Assn., Am. Bus. Law Assn. Club: Cosmos (Washington). Office: EPA Washington DC 20460

BARNES, ANDREW EARL, newspaper editor; b. Torrington, Conn., May 15, 1939; s. Joseph and Elizabeth (Brown) B.; m. Marion Otis, Aug. 26, 1960; children: Christopher Joseph, Benjamin Brooks, Elizabeth Cheney. B.A., Harvard U., 1961. Reporter, bur. chief Providence Jour., 1961-63; from reporter to edn. editor Washington Post, 1965-73; met. editor, asst. mng. editor St. Petersburg (Fla.) Times, 1973-75, mng. editor, 1975-84, editor, pres., 1984—; dir. Times Pub. Co., Poynter Inst., Congl. Quar., Modern Graphic Arts. Trustee Canterbury Sch., St. Petersburg, 1979—. Served with USAR, 1963-65. Alicia Patterson fellow, 1969-70. Mem. AP Mng. Editors Assn. (bd. dirs. 1983—), Fla. Soc. Newspaper Editors (pres. 1980-81), Am. Soc. Newspaper Editors. Home: 4819 Juanita Way S Saint Petersburg FL 33705 Office: 490 1st Ave S Saint Petersburg FL 33731

BARNES, B. DON, state supreme court chief justice; b. Tulsa, Dec. 25, 1924; s. N. Smith and Anna Agnes (Jackson) B.; m. Jean Merrill, July 16, 1946; children: Donald Brent, Ronald Merrill, Elizabeth Ann. LL.B., U. Okla., 1949. Bar: Okla. 1949. Practiced in, Sulphur, 1949-50, Okmulgee, 1953-54, county atty., Murray County, 1951-52; judge Okla. Superior Ct., 1955-69, Okmulgee County Dist. Ct., 1970-71; chief justice Okla. Supreme Ct., 1972—; bd. dirs. Nat. Center State Cts. Pres. Okmulgee United Fund, 1960; pres. Okmulgee Recreation Council, 1962-71. Served with USNR, 1943-46. Mem. Okla. Judicial Conf. (pres. 1964), Nat. Coll. State Judiciary, Am. Judicature Soc., ABA, Okla. Bar Assn., Okmulgee County Bar Assn. (pres. 1970), U. Okla. Alumni Assn. (dir. 1960-62), Phi Alpha Delta, Phi Kappa Psi. Mem. Christian Ch. Clubs: Mason., Rotarian. Office: State Capitol Bldg Oklahoma City OK 73105

BARNES, BENJAMIN SHIELDS, JR., banker; b. Dothan, Ala., Jan. 26, 1919; s. Benjamin Shields and Ruth Graham (Blue) B.; m. Bettye Osborne Withers, Apr. 2, 1948; children—Julia Lee Barnes Reid, Elizabeth Randylyn Barnes Miller, Carole Osborne Barnes Beason, Bettye Graham Barnes Malcolm. B.S., U. Ga., 1941; postgrad., Rutgers U., 1950-52, Harvard, 1968. With Atlantic Refining Co., 1941; with First Nat. Bank of Atlanta, 1946—, asst. cashier., 1948-50, asst. v.p., 1950-54, v.p., 1954-67, exec. v.p., dir., 1967-75, vice chmn. bd., 1975-78; exec. v.p., dir. First Atlanta Holding Corp., 1970-75, vice chmn. bd., 1975-78; pres., dir. 1st Atlanta Internat. Corp., 1971-78; chmn. bd. London Interstate Bank, Ltd., 1975-78, dir., 1970-78; dir., chmn. bd. First Bank of Savannah, Ga., 1978—; dir. Atlanta Gas Light Co.; vice chmn. bd. Munich Am. Reassurance Co.; State of Ga. adv. dir. Investors Nat. Life Ins. Co. Served to lt. USNR, 1941-46; PTO. Recipient Distinguished Service award Alumni Assn. Baylor Sch., Chattanooga, 1969; Distinguished Alumnus award Alumni Assn. Coll. Bus. Adminstrn., U. Ga., 1972. Mem. Chi Phi. Presbyterian. Clubs: Marshwood at the Landings, Oglethorpe, Chatham (Savannah). Home: 6 Blackbeard Ln The Landings on Skidaway Island Savannah GA 31411 Office: First Bank of Savannah 136 Bull St Savannah GA 31401

BARNES, CARLYLE FULLER, manufacturing executive; b. Bristol, Conn., Feb. 16, 1924; s. Fuller Forbes and Myrtle (Ives) B.; m. Elizabeth Anne May, Oct. 1, 1949; children: Lynne Elizabeth, Janis Lee, Joan Wells, Fuller Forbes. A.B., Wesleyan U., 1948. Staff asst. Wallace Barnes Co. div. Barnes Group Inc., 1948-50, gen. mgr., 1951-53, dir., 1951—, pres., 1953-64, chmn. bd., 1964-77, chmn. exec. com., 1977—; dir. United Bank & Trust Co., Kaman Corp., Travelers Ins. Cos., Burndy Corp. Trustee St. Lawrence U., Canton, N.Y. Club: Economic (N.Y.C.). Home: Peacedale St Bristol CT 06010 Office: 123 Main St Bristol CT 06010

BARNES, CHARLES ANDREW, educator, physicist; b. Toronto, Ont., Can., Dec. 12, 1921; came to U.S., 1953, naturalized, 1961; m. Phyllis Malcolm, Sept. 15, 1950; children—Nancy E., Steven. A. B.A., McMaster U., 1943; M.A., U. Toronto, 1944; Ph.D., Cambridge U., 1950. Physicist Joint Brit.-Canadian Atomic Energy Project, 1944-46; asst. prof. physics U. B.C., 1950-53, 55-56; mem. faculty Calif. Inst. Tech., 1953-55, 56—, prof. physics, 1962—; Guest prof. Niels Bohr Inst., Copenhagen, 1973-74. Editor, contbr. to profl. books and jours. NSF sr. fellow, Denmark, 1962-63. Fellow Am. Phys. Soc. Office: Calif Inst Tech Pasadena CA 91125

BARNES, CHARLES DEE, physiologist, educator; b. Carroll, Iowa, Aug. 17, 1935; s. Jack Y. and Gladys R. (Beckwith) B.; m. Leona Gladys Wohler, Sept. 8, 1957; children: Tara Lee, Teagen Yale, Kalee Meion, Kyler Alen. B.S., Mont. State U., 1958; M.S., U. Wash., 1961; Ph.D., U. Iowa, 1962. Asst. prof. dept. anatomy and physiology Ind. U., Bloomington, 1964-68, assoc. prof., 1968-71, prof., Terre Haute, 1971-75; prof., chmn. dept. physiology Tex. Tech. U. Health Scis. Ctr., Lubbock, 1975—; vis. scientist Instituto di Fisiologia Umana della U. di Pisa, Italy, 1968-69. Author: (with L. Eltherington) Drug Dosage in Laboratory Animals, 1964, 2d edit., 1973, (with C. Kircher) Readings in Neurophysiology, 1968, (with Davies) Regulation of Ventilation and Gas Exchange, 1978, (with Hughes) Neural Control of Circulation, 1980, (with Orem) Physiology in Sleep, 1980, (with Crass) Vascular Smooth Muscle, 1982, (with McGrath) Air Pollution-Physiologic Effects, 1982. Recipient NIH Career Devel. award, 1967-72. Mem. AAAS, Am. Inst. Biol. Scis., Am. Physiol. Soc., Am. Soc. Pharmacology and Exptl. Therapeutics, Assn. Chmn. Depts. Physiology, Internat. Brain Research Orgn., Radiation Research Soc., Soc. Exptl. Biology and Medicine, Soc. Neuroscis., Soc. Gen. Physiologists, Sigma Xi. Home: 4707 29th St Lubbock TX 79410 Office: Physiology Dept Texas Technical U NL Health Science Center Lubbock TX 79430

BARNES, CHRISTOPHER KEEN, U.S. attorney; b. Cin., Mar. 10, 1949. B.A., Wake Forest U., 1971; J.D., Chase Coll. Law, Cin., 1975. Bar: Ohio 1975, U.S. Dist. Ct. (so. dist.) Ohio 1975, U.S. Appeals (6th cir.) 1978. Assoc. Croswell & Wells, Cin., 1976; asst. U.S. atty Dept. Justice, Cin., 1976-82, U.S. atty., 1982—. Councilman Village of Mariemont, Ohio, 1973-76. Mem. Cin. Bar Assn., Fed. Bar Assn. Methodist. Office: US Atty's Office 220 US Courthouse and Post Office Bldg Cincinnati OH 45202

BARNES, CHRISTOPHER RICHARD, geology educator; b. Nottingham, Eng., Apr. 20, 1940; m. Susan Miller, Aug. 19, 1983; children: Penny, Joanne, Allison. B.S., U. Birmingham, Eng., 1961; Ph.D., U. Ottawa, 1964. Asst. prof. U. Waterloo, Ont., Can., 1965-70, assoc. prof., 1970-76, prof., chmn. dept., 1976-81; prof., head dept. earth scis. Meml. U. Nfld., St. John's, Can., 1981—; sr. research fellow U. Southampton, Eng., 1971-72. Fellow Royal Soc. Can. (Bancroft award 1982); mem. Geol. Assn. Can. (pres. 1983, past pres. medal 1977), Can. Geol. Found., Can. Geosci. Council (pres. 1979), Council of Chairmen Can. Earth Scis. Depts. (chmn. 1983). Office: Dept Earth Scis Meml U Nfld Elizabeth Ave Saint John's NF Canada A1B 3X5

BARNES, CLIVE ALEXANDER, drama and dance critic; b. London, Eng., May 13, 1927; came to U.S., 1965; s. Arthur Lionel and Freda Marguerite (Garratt) B.; m. Patricia Amy Evelyn Winckley, June 26, 1958; children—Christopher John Clive, Joanna Rosemary Maya. B.A., U. Oxford, Eng., 1951. Co-editor Oxford dance mag. Arabesque, 1950; asst. editor Dance and Dancers, 1950-58, asso. editor, 1958-61, exec. editor, 1961-65, editor, N.Y.C., from 1965; writer music, dance, drama, films Daily Express, London, 1956-65; dance critic The Times, London, 1962-65, The Spectator, 1959-65, N.Y. Times, N.Y.C., 1965-67, drama and dance critic, from 1967—, theatrical editor, from 1977; now drama and dance critic N.Y. Post; adj. prof. dept. journalism. N.Y. U., 1968-75. Author: Ballet in Britain Since the War, 1953,

Frederick Ashton and His Ballets, 1961, (with others) Ballet Here and Now, 1961, Dance Scene, U.S.A, 1967, Inside American Ballet Theatre, 1977; Editor: Best American Plays, 6th and 7th series. Served with R.A.F., 1946-48. Decorated comdr. Order Brit. Empire; knight Order of Dannebrog, Denmark). Mem. Critics Circle London (past sec., chmn. ballet sect.), N.Y. Drama Critics Circle (pres. 1973-75). Office: NY Post 210 South St New York NY 10002 *

BARNES, DAVID JOHN, mgmt. cons.; b. Sale, Cheshire, Eng., July 23, 1942; s. Harold Guy and Florence (Totten) B.; m. Patricia Anne Hebditch, July 26, 1967; children—Kirsten Emma, Alexander John. B.A., Cambridge U., 1963, M.A., 1967; M.S.I.A., Carnegie-Mellon U., 1969. Chartered acct. Carter, Challoner & Kearns, Manchester, Eng., 1963-67; with Boston Cons. Group, 1969—, Milan, 1971-72, Paris, 1972-79, Chgo., 1979—, v.p., 1970—, dir., 1975—. Fellow Inst. Chartered Accts. Eng. and Wales. Office: 200 S Wacker Dr Chicago IL 60606

BARNES, DAVID KENNEDY, chemical company executive; b. Concordia, Kans., Apr. 23, 1923; s. Richard A. and Leiella B. (Hudson) B.; m. Martha Ann Snapp, Dec. 24, 1942; children: David K., John Allen, Katharine Aileen Barnes Wesolowski, Jeffrey C. B.S., Olivet Coll., 1943; Ph.D. in Organic Chemistry, U. Ind., 1947. Chemist Stanolind Oil & Gas Co., Tulsa, 1947-53; sr. chemist E.I. duPont de Nemours & Co., Kinston, N.C., 1953-57; tech. supt., asst. mgr., Seaford, Del., 1957-63, mgr. production, Wilmington, Del., 1963-66, dir. mfg., 1966-67, dir. mfg. indsl. and biochem. dept., 1967-69, asst. gen. mgr. electrochemicals dept., 1969-72, asst. gen. mgr. indsl. chems. dept., 1972-74, v.p., gen. mgr. energy and materials dept., 1974-77, v.p. textile fibers dept., 1977-81, exec. v.p., mem. exec. com., dir., 1981—; dir. Bank of Del. Bd. trustees Olivet Coll.; trustee Wilmington Med. Center; exec. bd. Del-Mar-Va Council Boy Scouts Am., 1976-83; trustee Howard U., First Unitarian Soc. Served with C.E. U.S. Army, 1944-46. Mem. Am. Chem. Soc., Soc. Chem. Industry, Sigma Xi. Republican. Unitarian. Clubs: Wilmington Country, DuPont Country, Wilmington. Patentee in field. Home: 3704 Centerville Rd Wilmington DE 19807 Office: E I duPont de Nemours & Co Inc DuPont Bldg 9000 Wilmington DE 19898

BARNES, DON B., state supreme court justice; b. Tulsa, Dec. 25, 1924; s. N. Smith and Anna (Jackson) B.; m. Jean Merrill; children: Brent, Ronnie, Beth. LL.B., U. Okla., 1949. Justice Okla. Supreme Ct., chief justice, 1983—; bd. dirs. Nat. Ctr. for State Cts. Mem. Phi Alpha Delta, Phi Kappa Psi. Office: Suite 247 State Capitol Oklahoma City OK 73105 *

BARNES, EDWARD LARRABEE, architect; b. Chgo., Apr. 22, 1915; s. Cecil and Margaret Helen (Ayer) B.; m. Mary Elizabeth Coss, Mar. 4, 1944; 1 son, John Cecil. B.S. cum laude, Harvard U., 1938; M.Arch. (Sheldon Travelling fellow), Grad. Sch. Design, 1942. Architect, N.Y.C., 1949—; practice includes design pvt. houses, apts., low-cost housing, camps, campus planning, art museums, bot. gardens, office bldgs., jet plane interiors, visual identification program for Pan Am. World Airways; archtl. design critic Pratt Inst., Bklyn., 1953-54; urban renewal projects in, Sacramento, San Juan P.R.; design critic Yale U., 1957-59, cons. on phys. planning, 1964; design critic Harvard U., 1979-80, U. Va., 1980; Mem. Urban Design Council of N.Y.C., 1972—; Trustee Am. Acad., Rome, 1963-78, v.p., 1972, 1st vice chmn., 1975—; bd. dirs. Municipal Art Soc., 1960, treas., 1961; trustee Mus. Modern Art, N.Y.C., 1976—, N.Y. Studio Sch. Painting and Sculpture, 1976—; mem. Westchester County Planning Bd., 1976—. Prefabricated (with Henry Dreyfuss), house of aluminum for, Consol. Vultee Aircraft Corp., 1948; Work exhibited, Mus. Modern Art., Whitney Mus., Work pub. in various house and archtl. mags. Served as naval architect USNR, 1942-47. Recipient award for distinction in arts Yale, 1959; Arnold Brunner prize Nat. Inst. Arts and Letters, 1959; Progressive Architecture Top-Design award, 1959; silver medal Archtl. League N.Y., 1960; co-recipient Ford Found. grant for devel. theatre project; Progressive Arch. Design award, 1963; 1st Honor award FHA, 1963; Harleston Parker medal Boston Soc. Architects, 1972; citation honor Progressive Architecture, 1974; Certificate of Excellence Urban Design Awards Program, 1978; Louis Sullivan award, 1979. Fellow AIA (medal of honor N.Y. chpt. 1971, collaborative achievement in architecture 1972, Honor award 1972, 77, Archtl. Firm award 1980, Thomas Jefferson award 1981), Am. Acad. Arts and Scis.; mem. Westchester Council Arts, Century Assn., N.A.D. (academician). Home: Wood Rd Mount Kisco NY 10549 Office: 410 E 62d St New York NY 10021

BARNES, FRANK STEPHENSON, electrical engineer, educator; b. Pasadena, Cal., July 31, 1932; s. Donald Porter and Thedia (Schellenberg) B.; m. Gay Dirstine, Dec. 17, 1955; children—Stephen, Amy. B.S., Princeton, 1954; M.S., Stanford, 1955, Ph.D., 1958. Fulbright prof. Coll. Engring., Baghdad, Iraq, 1957-58; research asso. Colo. Research Corp., Broomfield, 1958-59; prof. dept. elec. engring. U. Colo., Boulder, 1959—, chmn. dept., 1964-81, acting dean, 1980-81; mem. G-Ed Adcom, IEEE, 1970-77; pres. IEEE Device Soc., 1974-75; Faculty Research lectr. U. Colo., 1965. Regional editor: Electronics Letters of Brit. Inst. Elec. Engrs, 1970-75. Bd. dirs. ABET, 1980-82. Recipient Curtis W. McGraw Research award, 1965; Robert L. Stearns award, 1980. Fellow AAAS, IEEE (editor Student Jour. 1967-70, v.p. for publ. activities 1974-75, ednl. activities bd. 1976-82), Engrs. Council Profl. Devel. (dir. 1976-82, chmn. com. advanced level accreditation 1976-78). Home: 225 Continental View Dr Boulder CO 80303 *There are always more interesting problems to solve than time to solve them. The trick is to find important problems which can be solved with an effort which is small compared to the value of the results and where one can have a good time learning new ideas at the same time.*

BARNES, FRED J., petroleum and mining equipment company executive; b. Los Angeles, 1940. B.S., UCLA, 1962. Acct. Arthur Andersen & Co., 1963-72; with Smith Internat., Inc., 1972—, controller, chief acctg. officer, until 1975, v.p. fin., treas., 1975-79, group v.p., chief fin. officer, 1979-83, pres., Newport Beach, Calif., 1983—, dir. Office: Smith Internat Inc 4343 Von Karman Ave Newport Beach CA 92660 *

BARNES, FREDERICK WALTER, JR., physician, medical educator; b. Cleve., Mar. 3, 1909; s. Frederick Walter and Susan (Anderson) B.; m. Catherine Gardner Bowden, Apr. 6, 1940; children: William Anderson, Susan Hammond. A.B., Yale U., 1930; M.D., Johns Hopkins Med. Sch., 1934; Ph.D., Columbia U., 1943. Intern Johns Hopkins Hosp., 1934-36; resident Childen's Hosp., Boston, 1936-38; asst. prof. medicine and biochemistry Cin. Med. Sch., 1942-46; assoc. prof. medicine and biochemistry Johns Hopkins Med. Sch., 1946-62; prof. med. sci. Brown U., 1962—, chmn. studies in world interdependence, 1979. Vice pres. Urban League R.I., 1965; bd. dirs. R.I. Tb Assn., 1966—; mem. Urban Coalition, 1969—; bd. dirs. Progress for Providence, 1970; co-chmn. R.I. Nuclear Arms Referendum Com., 1982; mem. State Commn. on Nuclear Arms, 1982. Recipient W.W. Keene award in medicine, 1979. Mem. Am. Soc. Biol. Chemists, Pediatric Research Soc., ACP, N.Y. Acad. Sci., Am. Osler Soc., Assn. Am. Med. Colls. (chmn. group student affairs N.E. 1970-71). Home: 21 George St Providence RI 02906 *Whatever goals one may have must be valued by their true contribution to human life, sought by persistent, careful effort, and continually verified by critical questioning.*

BARNES, GEORGE ELTON, stockbroker; b. Garner, Iowa, Mar. 17, 1900; s. Charles M. and Cora (Staver) B.; m. Florence Herrcke, Oct. 5, 1922; 1 dau., Ruth Adele. Grad., Hamilton U., Mason City, Iowa, 1918. With LaSalle Nat. Bank, Ill., 1918-30; ptnr. A.C. Baur & Co., 1930-31; co-founder, sr. ptnr. Wayne Hummer & Co., 1931—; mem. N.Y. Stock Exchange; bd. govs., chmn. exec. com. Chgo. Stock Exchange, 1946; chmn. bd. Midwest Stock Exchange, 1956-58; trustee Wayne Hummer Money Trust Fund, 1981—. Author: Pay-as-you-go and Other Fed. Tax Plans. Chmn. budget fin. com. Oak Park and River Forest Community Chest, 1941-49, pres., 1950-51; mem. nat. budget com. Community Chests Councils Am., 1956-60; bd. dirs. LaSalle Extension U., 1952-60, Infant Welfare Soc. Chgo., 1956-60; chmn. corporate large gifts div. Chgo. Community Fund, 1946; v.p., bd. govs. Nat. Assn. Stock Exchange Firms, 1942-46; pres. Chgo. Tennis Assn., 1947-48, U.S. Tennis Assn., 1960-61; mem. exec. com. U.S. Tennis Assn., 1958-79; mem. com. on mgmt. 1955 Davis Cup championships; nat. chmn. sponsors com. 1955 Davis Cup; pres. Nat. Tennis Ednl. Found., Inc., 1958-66; bd. dirs. Nat. Tennis Found. Hall of Fame, 1958—; founder, past pres. Chgo. Tennis Patrons, Inc. Named Sportsman of Year Chgo. Press Club, 1961; recipient Hardy award for contbn. to tennis edn. U.S. Lawn Tennis Assn., 1962, 68. Mem. Ill. C. of C. (dir. 1964-68). Clubs: Oak Park Country, River Forest-Tennis; Tavern (Chgo.); Ft. Lauderdale Yacht, Ft. Lauderdale Country. Home: 1005 Bonnie Brae Ave River Forest IL 60305 also 2100 S Ocean Ln Fort Lauderdale FL 33316 Office: Wayne Hummer & Co 175 W Jackson Blvd Chicago IL 60603

BARNES, GEORGE WILLIAM, archtl./engring. co. exec.; b. Lynn, Mass., Nov. 14, 1927; s. Henry Willis and Fern Louise (Britt) B.; m. Jane Alice Dick; children: Robin, Wendy, Henry. B.S. in C.E, U. Me., 1950. With Wright-Pierce (Architects and Engrs.), Topsham, Me., 1950—, pres., 19—; corporator Coastal Savings Bank, 1970—. Author: How to Build Bamboo Fly Rods, 1976, Building Your First Wooden Boat, 1979. Trustee Brunswick Regional Meml. Hosp., 1975—, treas., 1981—; v.p. Me. Div., Am. Trauma Soc., 19—; mem. Archtl./Engring. Task Force of Maine, 1971-78. Mem. Maine C. of C. (bd. dirs. 1981, vice chmn. 1983), ASCE, Nat. Soc. Profl. Engrs., Constrn. Specifications Inst., Cons. Engrs. of Me. (pres. 1975-76), Am. Cons. Engrs. Council (dir. 1972—, treas. 1976-78, pres. 1979-80), Nat. Constrn. Industry Council (treas. 1980-82). Home: RFD 1 South Harpswell ME 04079 Office: 99 Main St Topsham ME 04086

BARNES, HARRY G., JR., ambassador; b. St. Paul, June 5, 1926; (married); 4 children. B.A. summa cum laude, Amherst Coll., 1949; M.A., Columbia U., 1968. Consular officer U.S. Consul, Bombay, India, 1951-53; head U.S. consular sect., Prague, Czechoslovakia, 1953-55; publs. procurement officer Am. Embassy, Moscow, 1957-59; polit. officer Office of Soviet affairs, Dept. State, Washington, 1959-62; dep. chief Am. Mission, Kathmandu, Nepal, 1963-67; dep. chief of mission, Bucharest, Romania, 1968-71; supervisory personnel officer Dept. State, 1971-72, dep. exec. sec., 1972-74; ambassador to, Romania, Bucharest, 1974-77; dir. gen. of Fgn. Service and; dir. personnel Dept. State, 1977-81; ambassador to, India, New Delhi, 1981—. Served with U.S. Army, 1944-46. Office: Am Embassy Shanti Path Chanakypauri 21 New Delhi India *

BARNES, HAZEL ESTELLA, humanities educator; b. Wilkes-Barre, Pa., Dec. 16, 1915; d. Olin James and May (Petersen) B. B.A., Wilson Coll., 1937, D.Litt., 1965; Ph.D., Yale U., 1941; D.Litt., Ripon Coll., 1983; summer study, Columbia U.; D.Litt., Colorado Coll., 1983, U. Hawaii. Instr. classics Woman's Coll. U. N.C., 1941-43; asso. prof. classics Queens Coll., Charlotte, N.C., 1943-45; tchr. and asst. to pres. Pierce Coll., Elleniko, Athens, Greece, 1945-48; asst. prof. classics and philosophy U. Toledo, 1948-51; asst. prof. philosophy Ohio State U., 1951-53; asst. prof. classics U. Colo., 1953-56, asso. prof., 1956-61, prof. classics, 1961-77, prof. integrated studies, 1977—, Robert B. Hawkins Disting. prof. humanities, 1979—, prof. philosophy, 1983—, also chmn. dept. classics, 1965-69, 75-77; vis. prof. philosophy Yale U., 1974, Phi Beta Kappa vis. scholar, 1974-75, 77-78; vis. disting. prof. classics San Diego State U., 1983. Author intro. and translator: (Jean-Paul Sartre) Existential Psychoanalysis, 1953, Being and Nothingness, 1956, Search for a Method, 1963; author: The Literature of Possibility: A Study in Humanistic Existentialism, 1959, (with D. Sutherland) Hippolytus in Drama and Myth, 1960, An Existentialist Ethics, 1967, The University as the New Church, 1970, Sartre, 1973, The Meddling Gods: Four Essays on Classical Themes, 1974, Sartre and Flaubert, 1981; mem. editorial bd.: Philosophy and Literature; Preparer: series Self Encounter, Nat. Ednl. TV, 1962. Guggenheim fellow, 1977-78. Mem. Am. Philos. Assn., Am. Philol. Assn., Am. Soc. Aesthetics, Classical Assn. Middle West and South. Home: 896 17th St Boulder CO 80302

BARNES, HOWARD G., film executive; b. N.Y.C., Dec. 27, 1913; m. Joan Lesavoy, Jan. 9, 1949 (div. Nov. 1957); foster children: Marshall Alan (dec.), Denis Joy; m. Mary Ellena Mock, Dec. 7, 1958 (div.); children: Christie Ann, Paul Louis Lloyd; m. Patricia Lee Sills, August 4, 1965; children: Paxton Louise, Gillian Leigh. A.B., U. Mich., 1935. Announcer radio sta. WIP, Phila., 1935, stas. KYW, WHN, N.Y.C., 1936; producer WOR Mut., 1936-38; exec. producer MCA, 1938; producer, writer, exec. CBS, N.Y.C., 1938-46; v.p. in charge network programs CBS Radio, 1955-60; dir. programs CBS-TV, Hollywood, 1960-63; producing independently, 1946-48; v.p. in charge radio and TV Dorland, Inc., N.Y.C., 1948-51; pres. Gen. Entertainment Corp., 1949-60; TV exec. Ashley Famous Agy., Inc., 1963-66; dir. film prodn. Westinghouse Broadcasting Co., N.Y.C., 1966-67, exec. v.p. Group W Films, 1967-73, also dir. parent co.; ind. producer, 1973—; pres. Ragazza Inc., Washington, Conn., 1980-81; bd. govs. Dramalites, Washington, Conn., 1979—; dir. Trio Films, Ltd., London; partner The Barnes/Sabinson Partnership, 1976—; Exec. dir. Entertainment Hall of Fame Found., 1974-80. Served as lt. USNR, motion picture producer-writer, 1942-45. Home: Lake Dr Lake Waramaug Washington CT 06794

BARNES, IRSTON ROBERTS, educator, economist; b. New Haven, Feb. 14, 1904; s. Niar and Mabel Jane (Roberts) B.; m. Lidorra Holt Putney, June 30, 1936 (dec. Mar. 1983); 1 son, Chaplin Bradford. Ph.B., Yale, 1926, Ph.D. in Econs, 1928. Faculty Yale, 1928-41, asst. prof. polit. economy, 1932-41; fellow Pierson Coll., 1935-41; cons. economist antitrust div. Dept. Justice, 1941-44; dir. econ. bur. CAB, 1944-45, econ. adviser to bd., 1945-48; economist FTC, 1948-52, 54-60, chief div. econ. evidence, 1952-54; professorial lectr. George Washington U., 1954-55; vis. lectr. Columbia Grad. Sch. Bus., 1949-50, prof. polit. economy, 1960-63; econ. cons. antitrust and govt. regulation, 1960—. Author: Public Utility Control in Massachusetts, 1930, Cases on Public Utility Regulation, 1938, The Economics of Public Utility Regulation, 1942; Contbr. articles to profl. jours.; weekly column The Naturalist in Washington Post, 1951-76. Mem. Am. Econ. Assn., Am. Ornithologists Union, Audubon Soc. Central Atlantic States (pres. 1946-61, chmn. bd. 1961-68), Phi Beta Kappa. Clubs: Graduates (New Haven); Cosmos (Washington); Yale (N.Y.C.). Home: 58 N Branford Rd PO Box 578 Wallingford CT 06492

BARNES, JACK WHITTIER, polit. party ofcl.; b. Dayton, Ohio, Jan. 30, 1940; s. Whittier Ira and Catharine Pauline (Smith) B. B.A., Carleton Coll., 1961; postgrad., Northwestern U., 1961-63. Polit. organizer Socialist Workers Party, 1961—, nat. sec., N.Y.C., 1972—. Contbg. author: Towards an American Socialist Revolution, 1971, A Revolutionary Strategy for the 70's, 1972, Dynamics of World Revolution Today, 1974, Prospects for Socialism in America, 1976, The Lesser Evil?, 1977, The Changing Face of U.S. Politics, 1981. Mem. Phi Beta Kappa, Pi Delta Epsilon. Office: 14 Charles Ln New York NY 10014

BARNES, JAMES E., oil company executive; b. Ponca City, Okla., 1934; married. Grad., Okla. State U., Harvard U. With Continental Pipe Line Co., 1956-62, Cherokee Pipe Line Co., 1962-64, Conoco, Inc., Stamford, Conn., 1964—, mgr. gas products div., 1964-65, gen. mgr. natural gas and gas products dept., 1965-70, v.p. purchasing, 1970-75, v.p. supply and trading, 1975-78, exec. v.p. supply and transp., 1978—. Office: Conoco Inc High Ridge Park Stamford CT 06904 *

BARNES, JAMES MILTON, educator; b. Ypsilanti, Mich., July 5, 1923; s. J. Milton and Elsie (Fischer) B.; m. Marjorie Ruth Petersen, Dec. 17, 1949. B.S., Eastern Mich. U., 1948; M.S., Mich. State U., 1950, Ph.D., 1955. Asst. prof. Eastern Mich. U., Ypsilanti, 1955-58, asso. prof., 1958-61, prof., 1961—, head dept. physics and astronomy, 1961-74. Served with AUS, 1942-46. Mem. A.A.A.S. (life), Nat. Sci. Tchrs. Assn. (life), Am. Assn. Physics Tchrs., Sigma Xi, Sigma Pi Sigma, Pi Mu Epsilon. Club: Ann Arbor (Mich.) Country. Home: 4872 Whitman Circle Ann Arbor MI 48103 Office: Eastern Mich U Ypsilanti MI 48197

BARNES, JAMES WOODROW, musician; b. Winslow, Ind., Jan. 14, 1918; s. George W. and Bernice (Gatton) B.; m. Elizabeth J. Woodruff, Nov. 20, 1941; children: Rebecca Ann (Mrs. Byron L. Elmendorf), Susan Lynn (Mrs. Donald R. Adams), James Mark. B.A., Oakland City (Ind.) Coll., 1941; M.A., Ind. State U., 1949; student, UCLA, 1946; Ph.D., Ind. U., 1960. Tchr. music and math. Winslow High Sch., 1941-42; music dir. Oakland City High Sch., 1946-48; mem. faculty Ind. State U., 1948-83; prof. music, 1960—, head music dept., 1964-73; guest condr., adjucator, string clinician, music cons. Condr., Terre Haute Symphony, 1949-71. Served to capt. USAAF, 1942-46. Recipient Mid-West East honor award for outstanding service to music Duquesne U., 1968; Alumnus of Year award Oakland City Coll., 1972. Mem. Am. String Tchrs. Assn. (pres. Ind. 1960-61), Ind. Music Educators Assn. (exec. sec. 1953-56), Music Educators Nat. Conf., Am. Fedn. Musicians, Pi Kappa Lambda, Phi Mu Alpha (Orpheus award 1973). Office: Grad Sch Ind State U Terre Haute IN 47809

BARNES, JHANE ELIZABETH, fashion design company executive, designer; b. Balt., Mar. 4, 1954; d. Richard Amos and Muriel Florence (Chase) B.; m. Howard Ralph Feinberg, Dec. 12, 1981. A.S., Fashion Inst. Tech., 1975. Pres., desingner Jhane Barnes for ME, N.Y.C., 1976-78, Jhane Barnes Inc., 1978—. Recipient Menswear award Coty Am. Fashion Critics, 1980, Contract Textile award Am. Soc. Interior Designers, 1983; named Most Promising Designer Cutty Sark, 1980, Outstanding Designer, 1982, Outstanding Menswear Designer Council of Fashion Designers Am., 1982. Office: Jhane Barnes Inc 21 W 38th St New York NY 10018

BARNES, JOHN DAVID, banker; b. Oil City, Pa., Aug. 23, 1929; s. Alfred David and Rachael Marian (Kerr) B.; m. Suzanne Franklin Robbins, Nov. 26, 1960. B.A., Allegheny Coll., Meadville, Pa., 1951; LL.B., Harvard U., 1954. With credit div. Mellon Nat. Bank & Trust Co., Pitts., 1956-58, asst. v.p., v.p. nat. dept., 1958-72; v.p., sr. v.p. Mellon Nat. Corp. and Mellon Bank, N.A., Pitts., 1972-78; exec. v.p. Mellon Bank, N.A., 1978; then pres., now chmn. bd., also chmn. and chief exec. officer Mellon Nat. Corp., 1981—; chmn., chief exec. officer Local Loan Co., Chgo., from 1976; v.p., sec., dir. Penn's SW Assn.; dir. Diamond Shamrock Corp., Allomon Corp., Mellon Nat. Mortgage Co. of Colo., Mellon Nat. Mortgage Co. of Ohio, Carruth Mortgage Corp. Pres., trustee Ellis Sch., Pitts. Assn. for Improvement of Poor. Served with AUS, 1954-56. Clubs: Duquesne, Harvard-Yale-Princeton, Fox Chapel Golf, Fox Chapel Racquet. Office: Mellon Nat Corp Mellon Sq Pittsburgh PA 15230 *

BARNES, JOHN R., petroleum company executive; b. 1944. B.B.A., Southwestern State U., 1966; M.B.A., U. Tulsa, 1971. Acctg. mgr. Sun Oil Co., 1966-71; mgr. fin. planning Samsonite Corp., 1971-73; v.p., treas. Aztec Oil & Gas Co., 1973-76; pres., chief operating officer, dir. Dorchester Gas Corp., Dallas, 1976—. Office: Dorchester Gas Corp 5735 Pineland Rd Dallas TX 75231 *

BARNES, LEO, fin. educator, economist; b. Denver, Nov. 12, 1910; s. Benjamin and Bertha (Wittenberg) Lazareff; m. Regina Rosiny, May 27, 1932; children—Peter Franklin, Valerie Berta. B.S. cum laude, Coll. City N.Y., 1931; M.A. (Univ. fellow), Brown U., 1933; Johnston scholar, Johns Hopkins U., 1934-36; Ph.D., New Sch. for Social Research, 1948. Editor, analyst Research Inst. Am., Inc., Washington and N.Y.C., 1942-45, dir. econ. research, N.Y.C., 1945-46; lectr. Rutgers U. Sch. Bus. Adminstrn., 1947; chief economist Prentice-Hall, Inc., N.Y.C. and Englewood Cliffs, N.J., 1946-62; lectr. New Sch. for Social Research, N.Y.C., 1948-63; vis. prof. econs. City U. N.Y., 1963-65; prof., chmn. dept. banking, fin. and investments Hofstra U., Hempstead, N.Y., 1965-72, prof., 1972-77; disting. vis. prof. fin. and investments Adelphi U., Garden City, N.Y., 1978—; lectr. Chautauqua (N.Y.) Inst., 1977—; asso. editor Bus. Econs., 1970—. Author: An Experiment That Failed, 1948, Handbook for Business Forecasting, 1950, Your Buying Guide to Mutual Funds, ann. edits, 1956-60, Your Investments, ann. edits, 1954-68, Current Issues on the Frontiers of Financial Analysis, 1970, Handbook of Wealth Management, 1977; contbr. articles to profl. jours. Mem. Am. Econ. Assn., Am. Fin. Assn., Nat. Assn. Bus. Economists, Phi Beta Kappa. Home: 473 West End Ave New York NY 10024 Office: Adelphi Univ Garden City NY 11530

BARNES, MARTIN MCRAE, entomologist; b. Calgary, Alta., Can., Aug. 3, 1920; s. Harry Olan and Vida (Killian) B.; m. Julia Butts, Aug. 31, 1946; children—Wayne, Martin, Delia, Brian. B.S., U. Calif., Berkeley, 1941; Ph.D., Cornell U., 1946. Mem. faculty U. Calif., Riverside, 1946—, prof. entomology, 1962—, entomologist agrl. research expt. sta., 1946—. Contbr. articles to profl. jours. Fellow AAAS; mem. Entomol. Soc. Am. (pres. Pacific br. 1976-77), Entomol. Soc. Can., Entomol. Soc. Mexico, Pacific Coast Entomol. Soc., Sigma Xi. Democrat. Research in deciduous orchard and vineyard entomology. Home: 1946 Prince Albert Dr Riverside CA 92507 Office: Dept Entomology U Calif Riverside CA 92521 *A certain amount of peregrination pays, providing to the perceptive a positive view of the human race in all its rich variations, instilling a thirst for another language and a penetration of another culture, a thirst for an understanding of earth's forms and biota-the best way I have found to find oneself in relation to the universe.*

BARNES, MICHAEL DARR, congressman; b. Washington, Sept. 3, 1943; s. John P. and Vernon (Smith) B.; m. Claudia Fangboner, June 13, 1970; children—Sarah Dillon, Garrett Hatton. B.A., U. N.C., 1965; postgrad., Inst. of Higher Internat. Studies, Switzerland, 1965-66; J.D. with honors, George Washington U., 1972. Bar: D.C. 1973. Spl. asst. to Sen. Edmund S. Muskie, Muskie for Pres. Com., 1970-72; atty. Covington & Burling, Washington, 1972-75; exec. dir. Nat. Democratic Platform Com., Dem. Nat. Conv., 1975-76; commr. Public

Service Commn. of Md., 1975-78; mem. 96th-98th Congresses from 8th Md. Dist., mem. fgn. affairs com., D.C. Com. chmn. Western Hemisphere Subcom.,; chmn. Fed. Govt. Service Task Force. Asst. editor: Democratic Rev. mag, 1974-78. Vice chmn. Washington Met. Area Transit Commn., 1976-78. Served with USMC, 1967-69. Named Distinguished State Ofcl. of 1977 Young Democrats of Md. Office: 1607 Longworth House Office Bldg Washington DC 20515

BARNES, PAUL HOWARD, banker; b. Hazlewood, Ind., Aug. 28, 1916; s. Conard Wilson and Emma (Turner) B.; m. Marilou Muir, Aug. 30, 1945; children: Sandra, Emilou, Paula Felfeli. Grad., U. Wis. Banking Sch., 1958. With Albuquerque Nat. Bank, from 1935, asst. cashier, auditor, 1948-53, asst. v.p., auditor, 1953-56, v.p., auditor, 1956-63, v.p., controller, 1963-65, sr. v.p., controller, 1965-69, sr. v.p., cashier, from 1970; pres. First N.Mex. Bankshare Corp., 1973-81, pres., chief exec. officer, 1974-81, pres., chief exec. officer emeritus, 1981—. Past pres. N.Mex. Conf. Meth. Found.; past trustee Manzano Day Sch., McMurry Coll., Abilene, Tex., Albuquerque Little Theater. Served with AUS, 1941-45; ETO; Served with AUS; PTO. Mem. Bank Adminstrn. Inst. (past state v.p.), Eastern N.Mex. U. Alumni Assn. (hon. life). Methodist (chmn. bd. trustees ch.). Clubs: Albuquerque Petroleum, Albuquerque Country. Office: 1st N Mex Bankshare Corp 303 Roma Ave NW Albuquerque NM 87102

BARNES, PAUL MCCLUNG, lawyer; b. Phila., June 27, 1914; s. Andrew Wallace and Leila Hope (Andrew) B.; m. Elisabeth McClenahan, Dec. 28, 1940; children—Andrew M., Margaret L. Barnes Nessa, James D., John R. (dec.). B.A., Monmouth (Ill.) Coll., 1936; J.D., U. Chgo., 1939. Bar: Colo. bar 1939. Asso. firm Bannister & Bannister, Denver, 1939-40, Foley & Lardner, Milw., 1940-47, partner, 1948—; dir. Wis. Public Service Corp., Kickhaefer Mfg. Co., Attys. Liability Assurance Soc., Ltd.; sec. Sta-Rite Industries, Inc., 1965-73. Mem. adv. bd. Milw. Protestant Home, 1975—. Served with USNR, 1942-45. Mem. Am. Bar Assn., Wis. Bar Assn., Fed. Bar Assn., Fed. Energy Bar Assn., Order of Coif. Republican. Presbyterian. Office: 777 E Wisconsin Ave Milwaukee WI 53202

BARNES, PETER CRAIN, stockbroker; b. Kansas City, Mo., Apr. 29, 1935; s. Frederic Page and Margaret Louise (Ott) B.; m. Kay Baslee, Jan. 1, 1979; children: Page Rixon, Tyler Bryant. B.A., Dartmouth Coll., 1957. Telephone clk. Hayden Stone & Co., N.Y.C., 1959-60; partner HO Peet & Co., Kansas City, Mo., 1962-70, pres., 1970-78; v.p. Kidder Peabody Co., 1978—; dir. Nat. Clearing Corp., N.Y.C., 1970-77, Midwest Stock Exchange Clearing Corp., 1965-70; Trustee Midwest Research Inst., Inc., Kansas City, Mo., 1973—, Research Hosp., 1973—. Served with USNR, 1957-59. Mem. Securities Industry Assn. (dir. 1976), Nat. Assn. Securities Dealers (nat. chmn. 1972), Sigma Alpha Epsilon. Episcopalian. Clubs: Kansas City Country, River, Saddle and Sirloin (Kansas City). Home: 10141 Halsey St Lenexa KS 66215 Office: Charterbank Center 920 Main St Suite 700 Kansas City MO 64105

BARNES, RICHARD GEORGE, physicist, educator; b. Milw., Dec. 19, 1922; s. George Richard and Irma (Ott) B.; m. Mildred A. Jachens, Sept. 9, 1950; children: Jeffrey R., David G., Christina E., Douglas A. B.A., U. Wis., 1948; M.A., Dartmouth Coll., 1949; Ph.D., Harvard U., 1952. Teaching fellow Harvard, 1950-52; asst. prof. U. Del., 1952-55, asso. prof., 1955-56, Iowa State U., 1956-60, prof., 1960—, chmn. dept. physics, 1971-75; sr. physicist Ames Lab., AEC, 1960—, chief physics div., 1971-75; vis. research prof. Calif. Inst. Tech., 1962-63; guest prof. Tech. U. Darmstadt, Germany, 1975-76; vis. prof. Cornell U., 1982-83. Served with USAAF, 1942-43; C.E. AUS, 1944-46. Recipient U.S. Sr. Scientist award Alexander von Humboldt Found., 1975-76. Fellow Am. Phys. Soc.; mem. Sigma Xi. Home: 515 Oliver Circle Ames IA 50010 Office: Dept Physics Iowa State U Ames IA 50011

BARNES, ROBERT, vascular surgeon; b. Chgo., Nov. 9, 1936; s. Broda Otto and Charlotte Edna (Webster) B.; m. Kay Ellen Brockway, Sept. 25, 1960; children: David, Judy, Kathy. B.A. (Regents scholar), U. Colo., 1958; M.D., U. Ill., 1961. Intern U. Ill. Research and Ednl. Hosps., Chgo., 1961-62; resident in surgery U. Wash. Hosps., Seattle, 1962-63, 65-69, fellow in thoracic and cardiovascular surgery, 1969-70, fellow in vascular surgery, 1970-72; instr. surgery U. Wash., Seattle, 1969-72; asst. prof. surgery U. Iowa Hosps. and Clinics, Iowa City, 1972-74, asso. prof., 1974-77, dir. peripheral vascular labs., 1972-77; David M. Hume prof. surgery Med. Coll. Va., Richmond, 1977—, program dir. vascular surgery, 1977—, also dir. Peripheral Vascular Lab.; dir. Peripheral Vascular Lab., VA. Hosp.; prof., chmn. dept. surgery U. Ark. for Med. Scis., Little Rock, 1983—. Author: (with Russell and Wilson) Doppler Ultrasonic Evaluation of Venous Disease: A Programmed Audiovisual Instruction, 1975, (with Wilson) Doppler Ultrasonic Evaluation of Cerebrovascular Disease: A Programmed Audiovisual Instruction, 1975, Doppler Ultrasonic Evaluation of Peripheral Arterial Disease: A Programmed Audiovisual Instruction, 1976, (with Wu and Hoak) Thrombosis Manual, 1976; contbr. numerous articles, abstracts and revs. to profl. jours., chpts. in books; author Films, videotape presentations; presenter profl. meetings. Served to lt. comdr. USPHS, 1963-65. Recipient Physics Achievement award, 1955, ROTC Convair award, 1956, Mosby award, 1960, Mead Johnson award, 1968-71. Fellow Am. Coll. Chest Physicians, Am. Coll. Cardiology, ACS, Am. Coll. Angiology; mem. Am. Heart Assn., Iowa Heart Assn., Johnson County Med. Soc., Internat. Soc. Thrombosis and Haemostasis, AMA, Internat. Cardiovascular Soc., Iowa Acad. Surgery, Am. Surg. Assn., Iowa Clin. Surg. Soc., Am. Fedn. Clin. Research, Assn. Advancement Med. Instrumentation, Am. Inst. Ultrasound in Medicine, Assn. Acad. Surgery, AAAS, Soc. Exptl. Biology and Medicine, Central Soc. Clin. Research, Soc. Vascular Surgery, Soc. Univ. Surgeons, Midwest Vascular Surgery Soc., European Soc. Surg. Research, Richmond Acad. Medicine, Va. Med. Soc., Va. Surg. Soc., Richmond Surg. and Gynecol. Soc., So. Assn. Vascular Surgery, Internat. Soc. Surgery, Phi Beta Kappa, Sigma Xi, Alpha Omega Alpha.

BARNES, ROBERT GOODWIN, publishing consultant; b. Augusta, Ga., Sept. 1, 1914; s. John Andrew and Charlotte R. (Jones) B.; m. Helen Z. Jeffries, June 21, 1941; children: Susan Jeffries, John Andrew II, Frances Goodwin. A.B., Columbia, 1937. With Procter & Gamble, 1937-42, B. Heller & Co., 1946-47; with Doubleday & Co., Inc., N.Y.C., 1947-51, 52-69, v.p., 1964-69; pres., dir. Columbia U. Press, 1969-80; acting exec. dir. Am. Assn. Univ. Presses, 1980-81; prin. Mosley Assos., 1981-83; consultant, 1983—. Served to lt. comdr. USNR, 1942-46, 51-52. Mem. Assn. Am. Pubs. (dir. 1978-80). Clubs: Publ. Lunch (pres. 1977-78), Century Assn. (N.Y.C.)). Home and office:: PO Box 94 Cornwall CT 06753

BARNES, ROBERT MARSHALL, securities firm executive; b. Jersey City, May 3, 1923; s. Frederick Marshall and Mabelle (Sniffen) B.; m. Margaret Carolyn Hickman, July 1, 1944; children: Nancy C., Joanne Barnes Schock, James H., Henry M., William R., Carol M., John H. B.S., U. Pa., 1944, M.B.A., 1944. Registered rep. White Weld & Co., 1947-55; registered rep. Eastman Dillon, Union Securities Co., 1955-61, Midwest mgr. corporate buying dept., Chgo., 1961-63; ptnr. Howe, Barnes & Johnson, Inc., Chgo., 1963-67, chmn. bd., 1968—, chmn. exec. com., 1979—; corporate mem. N.Y. Stock Exchange, 1965—; bd. dirs. Investors' Forum TV series, WGN-TV, Chgo., 1965-67. Trustee United Methodist Homes and Services, Chgo., David C. Cook Found.; exec. v.p., trustee Chgo. Assn. Retarded Citizens; bd. dirs. Holy Family Cath. Ch., Chgo., 1975; bd. govs. Midwest Stock Exchange, Chgo., 1969-70; fin. chmn. Johnson for Mayor, 1979; exec. v.p. Chgo. Assn. Retarded Citizens, 1979-80, pres., 1979-82. Mem. Investment Bankers Assn. Am. (chmn. Central States group 1971-72, nat. bd. govs.), Nat. Assn. Securities Dealers Inc. (nat. bd. govs. 1971-74, chmn. dist. 8 1969, national arbitrator), Bond Club Chgo. (dir.). Methodist (trustee ch. 1971—). Clubs: Pres.'s (U. Chgo.); Bond (pres. 1973), Econ., Union League (Chgo.). Home: 846 Greenwood Ave Glencoe IL 60022 Office: 135 S La Salle St Chicago IL 60603

BARNES, ROBERT MERTON, artist, educator; b. Washington, Sept. 24, 1934. B.F.A., Art Inst., Chgo., 1956, U. Chgo., 1956; postgrad., Columbia U., 1956, Hunter Coll., 1957-60. Vis. artist Ind. U., Bloomington, 1960-61, prof. fine arts, 1965—; vis. artist Kansas City Art Inst., Mo., 1968; vis. U. Wis., Milw., 1968. One-man shows, Allan Frumkin Gallery, N.Y.C., 1963, 65, 66-67,77, 79, 80, 83, Frumkin Struve Gallery, Chgo., 1961-64, 71, 75-78, 81; represented: permanent collections Mus. Modern Art, Whitney Mus. Am. Art, Art Inst. Chgo., Pasadena Mus. Art, N.D. Art Mus., Albrecht Gallery, St. Joseph, Mo., Weatherspoon Art Gallery, Chapel Hill, N.C. Nat. Endowment for Arts grantee, 1982; recipient Child Hassam award Am. Acad. Arts and Letters, 1971, Guri Siever award Art Inst. Chgo., 1963; Fulbright grantee, 1961-63. Home: 731 E University St Bloomington IN 47401 Office: Sch Fine Arts Indiana Univ Bloomington IN 47405 *I have always tried to maintain a direct and honest dialogue with my work. The contemplative nature of this confrontation has prevented me from exhibiting as I would like and in extending the range of its exposure. I enjoy the intimacy of the studio and would change noting except ideas.*

BARNES, RUSSELL C., foreign news analyst; b. Huntington, Ind., Aug. 31, 1897; s. James F. and Lucy A. (Stewart) B.; m. Constance Ingalls, Oct. 1, 1927; children: Lucie J. Barnes Seymour, John J. A.B., U. Mich., 1920. Fgn. corr. Detroit News, 1925-31, 41-53, Washington corr., 1931-32; fgn. news columnist, radio commentator Detroit News Sta. WWJ, 1932-41, London corr., 1941, fgn. news analyst, 1953-70, contbr. articles, 1970—; lectr. fgn., domestic politics Oakland U. Staff radio div. OWI, 1942, dir., 1943; asst. to Am. ambassador to Egypt, 1943; Am. press officer Cairo and Tehran confs., 1943; dir. psychol. warfare bur. Allied Force Hdqrs., Algiers and Caserta, 1944-45. Recipient exceptional Civilian Service medal War Dept. Mem. Phi Delta Theta. Home: 788 Randall Ct Birmingham MI 48009

BARNES, SAMUEL HENRY, political scientist, educator; b. Miss., Jan. 20, 1931; (married); 3 children. B.A., Tulane U., 1952, M.A., 1954; Ph.D., Duke U., 1957; postgrad. (Fulbright scholar), Institut des Hautes Etudes Politiques, Paris, 1956-57. Instr. polit. sci. U. Mich., Ann Arbor, 1957-60, asst. prof. polit. sci., 1960-64, asso. prof., 1964-68, prof., 1968—, James Orin Murfin prof. polit. sci., 1982—, acting chmn. dept. polit. sci., 1968-69, chmn. dept., 1977-82, research assoc. Survey Research Center, 1969-70, program dir. Center for Polit. Studies, 1970—; Fulbright lectr. U. Florence, Italy, 1962-63, U. Rome, 1967-68; fellow Ctr. Advanced Study in Behavioral Scis. Stanford U., 1982-83. Author: Party Democracy: Politics in an Italian Socialist Federation, 1967, Representation in Italy: Institutionalized Traditions and Electoral Choice, 1977, (with Max Kaase and others) Political Action: Mass Participation in Five Western Democracies, 1979; contbr. articles to profl. publs. Served with USN, 1949-50. Mem. Am. Polit. Sci. Assn. (sec. 1972-74), Council Western European Studies (exec. com. 1971-72, steering com. 1975-78), Midwest Polit. Sci. Assn., Internat. Polit. Sci. Assn., Conf. Group for Italian Polit. Studies (v.p. 1975-77, pres. 1977-79). Office: Dept Polit Sci U Mich 5607 Haven Hall Ann Arbor MI 48109

BARNES, STANLEY NELSON, judge; b. Baraboo, Wis., May 1, 1900; s. Charles Luling and Janet (Rankin) B.; m. Anne Fisk, Oct. 18, 1929; children—Janet Anne Hansen, Judith Fisk Melkesian, Joyce Rankin Robinson. A.B., U. Calif., 1922, J.D., 1925, LL.D., 1961; student, Harvard Law Sch., 1923-24. Bar: Cal. bar 1925. Practiced in, San Francisco, 1925-28, Los Angeles, 1928-46; lectr. law U. So. Calif., 1947-52, lectr. forensic medicine, 1949-51; judge Superior Ct. of Los Angeles, 1947-53, presiding judge, 1952-53; asst. atty. gen., U.S.; anti-trust div. Dept. Justice, 1953-56; judge U.S. 9th Circuit Ct. Appeals, 1956-70, sr. judge, 1970—; Mem. Pres.'s Conf. Adminstrv. Proc., 1953; co-chmn. Atty. Gen.'s Nat. Com. Study Antitrust Laws, 1953-55; adv. council appellate rules jud. Conf. U.S., 1963-68; adv. council Practising Law Inst. Bd. dirs. S.W. Mus., Los Angeles, Calif. Inst. for Cancer Research, UCLA Med. Sch., 1949-75; regent U. Calif., 1946-48; trustee Sigma Chi Found., 1955—. Named Alumnus of Year U. Calif., 1966; recipient award Boalt Hall Sch. Law, U. Calif., Berkeley, Boalt Hall Sch. Law, U. Calif., 1967, St. Thomas More award Loyola Law Sch., Los Angeles, 1973; named to Nat. Collegiate Football Hall Fame, 1954, Helms Athletic Found. Hall of Fame, San Diego Hall of Champions; Berkeley fellow, 1969. Fellow Am. Bar Found., Am. Coll. Trial Lawyers, Am. Acad. Forensic Sci.; mem. Fed. Bar Assn. (nat. pres. 1954-55), ABA (chmn. sect. jud. adminstrn. 1966-67), Calif. Bar Assn., San Francisco Bar Assn., Los Angeles Bar Assn. (Shattuck-Price distinguished service award 1971), N.Y.C. Bar Assn., Am. Judicature Soc., Inst. Jud. Adminstrn., Calif. Alumni Assn. (pres. 1946-48), Phi Delta Phi., Sigma Chi (nat. pres. 1952-55, nat. trustee 1950-52). Episcopalian. Clubs: Rotary (hon.), Nat. Lawyers (hon.). Home: 47-331 Abdel Circle Palm Desert CA 92260

BARNES, THOMAS JOSEPH, United Nations official; b. St. Paul, June 18, 1930; s. Ralph Weikert and Helen (O'Connor) B.; m. Mai Tang; children: Ann, Kim, Kevin; children by previous marriage: Christopher, Ross, Karen, Shannon. B.A., U. Minn., 1950, M.A., 1951. With fgn. service, 1957-80, vice consul, Saigon, Vietnam, 1958-60; prin. officer Am. consulate, Hue, Viet Nam, 1960-61; polit. officer, Bangkok, Thailand, 1962-64, Vientiane, Laos, 1964-67, province sr. adviser, Binh Long, Vietnam, 1967-68; country officer for Laos State Dept., 1968-70; prin. officer Am. Consulate, Udorn, Thailand, 1970-71; asso. dir. AID, Nhatrang, Vietnam, 1971-72; consul gen., Tangier, Morocco, 1972-73, Can Tho, Vietnam, 1973, polit. counselor, Bangkok, 1973-75; sr. staff mem. for East Asia Nat. Security Council, 1975-76; student Sr. Seminar in Fgn. Policy, State Dept., 1976-77; regional refugee coordinator, Bangkok, 1977-78; diplomat-in-residence U. Hawaii, 1978-79; dir. Interagy. Working Group on Kampuchea, Dept. State, Washington, 1979-80; with UN High Commn. for Refugees, 1980—, dep. rep., Somalia, 1980-81, chief Southwest Asia sect., Geneva, 1982—. Served to capt. AUS, 1951-56. Recipient Award for Valor, Meritorious Honor award State Dept., Superior Honor award AID. Home: 6 Chemin De La Pie Chambesy 1292 Switzerland Office: UN High Commn for Refugees Centre Wm Rappard 154 Rue de Lausanne 1202 Geneva Switzerland

BARNES, V. LEE, holding company executive. Exec. v.p. Continental Corp. Office: Continental Corp 80 Maiden Ln New York NY 10038§

BARNES, VIRGIL EVERETT, II, physics educator; b. Galveston, Tex., Nov. 2, 1935; s. Virgil Everett and Mildred Louise (Adlof) B.; m. Barbara Ann Green, 1957 (dec. 1964); 1 son, Virgil Everett III; m. Linda Dwight Taylor, 1970; children—Christopher Richard Dwight, Charles Jeffrey, Daniel Woodbridge. A.B. magna cum laude with highest honors (Perkin Elmer prize 1956), Harvard U., 1957; Ph.D. (Marshall scholar 1957-59, NSF predoctoral fellow 1959-62), Gonville and Caius Coll., Cambridge (Eng.) U., 1962. Successively research asso., asst. physicist, asso. physicist Brookhaven Nat. Lab., Upton, N.Y., 1962-69; mem. faculty Purdue U., 1969—, prof. physics, 1979—, asst. dean, 1974-78; cons. in field. Author papers on exptl. high energy particle physics. Mem. Am. Phys. Soc., AAAS, AAUP, N.Y. Acad. Scis., Phi Beta Kappa, Sigma Xi. Home: 801 N Salisbury St West Lafayette IN 47906 Office: Physics Dept Purdue U West Lafayette IN 47907

BARNES, WALLACE, lawyer, manufacturing executive; b. Bristol, Conn., Mar. 22, 1926; s. Harry Clarke and Lillian (Houbertz) B.; m. Audrey Kent, June 14, 1947 (div. Aug. 1962); children: Thomas Oliver, Jarre Ann; m. Mrs. Frederick B. Hollister, Jr. (div. Feb. 1973); 1 adopted son, Frederick Hollister; m. Joan C. Fierri, Mar. 3, 1973. Grad., Deerfield Acad.; B.A., Williams Coll., 1949; LL.B., Yale U., 1952, Advanced Mgmt. Program, Harvard, 1973. Bar: Conn. 1952. Assoc. firm Beach, Calder & Barnes (and predecessor), Bristol, 1952-55, partner, 1956-62; exec. v.p. Asso. Spring Corp. (name changed to Barnes Group Inc.), 1962-64, pres., 1964-76, chmn., chief exec. officer, 1976—; pres. Nutmeg Air Transport, Inc., 1949-55; asst. to treas. Northeast Airlines, Inc., Boston, 1951; dir., mem. exec. com. Aetna Life & Casualty Co.; dir. Insilco Corp., Motalink Ltd., Wiltshire, England, Autoliaisons France S.A., Paris, Conn. Bank & Trust Co., Stece AB Monsteras; v.p. Bowman Products (Can.) Ltd.; v.p., dir. Wallace Barnes, Ltd., Bowman S.A. de C.V., Mexico City, Resortes Mecanicos S.A., Resortes Industriales del Norte S.A., Monterrey; pres., dir. Asso. Spring-Asia, ASC Internat. Ltd., London, Barnes Group, U.K., London; chmn., dir. Barnes Group Found. Inc., BGI Internat., Inc., Central Metal Products, Inc., Windsor Mfg. Co.; officer Stumpp & Schuele GmbH; dir. Motalink (Scotland) Ltd.; treas., dir. Rogers Corp. Pres. Bristol Community Chest, 1956; bd. dirs., mem. exec. com. Bristol Boys Club, pres., 1965-68; trustee Bristol Girls' Club Assn., Conn. Public Expenditure Council; bd. dirs. New Eng. Legal Found., 1976-79, New Eng. Council, Jr. Achievement N. Central Conn.; Nominee for Congress, 1st Congl. Dist. Conn., 1954; town chmn., Bristol, 1953-55; mem. Conn. Senate from 5th Dist., 1958-62, from 8th Dist., 1966-70, minority leader, 1969; Bd. dirs. Community Council of Capital Region, 1975-77, Hartford Symphony Soc., 1971-78, Council on Employment and Fair Taxation, 1978-80, Citizens Crime Commn. of Conn., Bus. Coalition on Health; trustee Am. Clock and Watch Mus., Bristol Regional Environ. Center; Bd. dirs. Bradley Air Mus.; corporator Inst. of Living, Hartford. Served as aviation cadet USAAF, 1944-45. Recipient distinguished service award Bristol Jaycees, Keystone award Boys Clubs of Am., 1967. Mem. Am., Conn. bar assns., Am. Judicature Soc., Am. Arbitration Assn., Bristol, Simsbury hist. socs., Newcomen Soc. N.Am., Conn. Bus. and Industry Assn. (dir.), Am. Legion. Republican. Episcopalian. Clubs: Elk., Economic, Yale, Williams (N.Y.C.); Hundred of Conn.; Union (Cleve.). Home: 75 Hop Brook Rd West Simsbury CT 06092 Office: 123 Main St Bristol CT 06010

BARNES, WALLACE RAY, lawyer, utilities executive; b. Easton, Pa., Nov. 7, 1928; s. Charles Hicks and Erma (Saylor) B.; m. Helen Bartley, July 2, 1958; children: Charles Calvin, Elizabeth McKee, Douglas Wittmer. A.B., Duke U., 1950; LL.B., Harvard U., 1957. Bar: Pa. 1958, Ohio 1973. Atty. Allegheny Ludlum Steel, Pitts., 1957-62, Columbia Gas, Md., N.Y., Pa., Pitts., 1962-73, sec., gen. counsel, Ky., Md., N.Y., Ohio, Pa., Va., W.Va., Columbus, Ohio, 1973-78, sr. counsel, 1978-81, asso. gen. counsel, 1981—; corp. dir. Columbia Gas Ohio, 1973-78, N.Y., 1973-78. Bd. dirs. Pitts. Better Bus. Bur., 1972-74. Served with USN, 1951-54. Mem. Fed. Bar Assn. (pres. chpt. 1961), ABA, Franklin County Bar Assn., Allegheny County Bar Assn., Phi Beta Kappa. Clubs: Fox Chapel Racquet (Pitts.); Racquet, Univ. (Columbus). Home: 2438 Sandover Rd Columbus OH 43220 Office: 200 Civic Center Dr. Columbus OH 43216

BARNES, WILFRED EATON, educator, mathematician; b. Oak Park, Ill., June 3, 1924; s. Guy Leslie and Nellie (Straw) B.; m. Bernice Elizabeth Michaels, Aug. 24, 1946; children: Julia Kathryn, Karen Wanda. S.B., U. Chgo., 1949, S.M., 1950; Ph.D., U. B.C., 1954. From instr. to prof. math. Wash. State U., 1954-66; prof. math. Iowa State U., 1966—. Author: Introduction to Abstract Algebra, 1963, (with others) Fundamental Concepts of Arithmetic, 1963; also articles. Served to 2d lt. USAAF, 1943-46. Mem. Am Math. Soc., Math. Assn. Am., Nat. Council Tchrs. Math., AAAS, Sigma Xi, Phi Kappa Phi. Mem. United Ch. Christ. Home: 511 Oliver Circle Ames IA 50010

BARNES, WILLIAM ARTHUR, III, clinical chemist; b. Chgo., Apr. 19, 1938; s. Willaim Arthur and Olive Frances (Yost) B.; m. Judith Marie Miles, Oct. 7, 1961; children: William Scott, Todd Andrew, Robbin Marie. B.A., Columbia Union Coll., 1966; M.S., Howard U., 1968; Ph.D., Cath. U., 1971. Lab technician FBI, 1960, U.S. Army Watson Army Hosp., 1960-62, Washington Adventist Hosp., Takoma Park, Md., 1962-63, Prince George Gen. Hosp., Cheverly, Md., 1963-67, asst. chief technician, 1967-71, clin. chemist, 1971-78, dir. clin chemistry sec. of pathology dept., 1978—. Mem. Assn. Clin. Chemists, Am. Soc. Clin. Pathologists, Am. Assn. Bioanalysts, N.Y. Acad. Scis., Sigma Xi. Presbyterian. Home: 8414 Red Wing Ln Lanham MD 20706 Office: Prince Georges Gen Hosp. and Med Ctr Pathology Dept Cheverly MD 20785

BARNES, WILLIAM OLIVER, JR., lawyer; b. Balt., Mar. 18, 1922; s. William Oliver and Jane Ann (Krug) B.; m. Marilyn Louise Isenberg, July 13, 1945; children: William Oliver 3d, Patrick Douglas, Timothy Lee, Jefferson Todd. A.B., Hamilton Coll., 1943; J.D., Rutgers U., 1948. Bar: N.J. 1949. Assoc. Judge R. J. Wortendyke, Jr., Newark, 1949-52; pvt. practice specializing trial work, Newark, from 1952; now Sr. ptnr. Barnes & Barnes, P.A.; Chmn. Rutgers U. Bond Com., 1959; pres. Rutgers Sch. Law Alumni Assn., 1960-61, Alumni Fedn., 1962-63, univ. trustee, 1962-69; v.p., asso. counsel N.J. Cancer Soc., 1963-65, pres., asso. counsel, 1965-68, counsel, 1968-76, dir., del., 1971-76. Mem. West Branch (N.J.) Bd. Edn., 1961-64; chmn. South Orange March of Dimes, 1959; pres. Monmouth Players, 1961-62; mem. N.J. Assembly from Essex County, 1952-55, majority leader, 1955; Republican candidate for Congress, 1952; chmn. South Orange Rep. County Com., 1954-58, N.J. Young Reps., 1954-56. Served to lt. (j.g.) USNR, 1943-46. Recipient Gold medal Rutgers U., 1960. Fellow Am. Coll. Trial Lawyers; mem. Am., N.J., Essex County, Monmouth County bar assns., Trial Attys. N.J. (pres. 1971-72, Trial Bar award 1977), Delta Kappa Epsilon, Delta Sigma Rho. Methodist. Clubs: Orange Lawn Tennis, Piedmont; Downtown (Newark); Nassau (Princeton, N.J.); Lord's Valley Country (Hemlock Farms, Pa.); Plantation Golf and Country (Venice, Fla.); Masons, Shriners. Home: 374 C New Bedford Ln Rossmoor-Jamesburg NJ 08831 Office: 1180 Raymond Blvd Newark NJ 07102

BARNES, WILLIAM P., investor, lawyer; b. Marlin, Tex., May 31, 1920; s. William P. and Katharine E. (Horne) B.; m. Sally Temple, Oct. 20, 1950; children: William P., Joseph L., James H., Thomas L. B.A., So. Meth. U., 1947, LL.B., 1949. Bar: Tex. 1949. Practiced law, Dallas, 1949-53; atty. Gen. Am. Oil Co. Tex., 1953-54, v.p., 1955-60, exec. v.p., gen. counsel, 1960-66, dir., 1960-83, pres., 1966-83, chmn. bd., 1978-83, chmn. exec. com., 1978-83; chmn. bd. Meadows Bldg. Corp., 1966-83; dir. Republic Bank Corp., Stockton, Whatley, Davin & Co., 1964-83. Editor in chief: Southwestern Law Jour., 1948. Trustee So. Meth. U., 1976-84, Southwestern Med. Found., 1977—; v.p., bd. dirs. The Meadows Found., 1966-83. Served to maj. AUS, 1942-46.

Mem. Tex. Bar Assn., Kappa Sigma, Phi Alpha Delta, Blue Key. Clubs: Petroleum, City (Dallas).

BARNES, WILLIAM P., mech. engr., educator. B.S. in Mech. Engring. U. Idaho; M.Mech. Engring., Yale; Ph.D. in Mech. Engring, U. Ill. Prof. mech. engring., chmn. nuclear engring. program U. Idaho, Moscow. Office: Dept Mech Engring U Idaho Moscow ID 83843

BARNES, WILSON KING, lawyer, former judge; b. Pocomoke City, Md., Apr. 17, 1907; s. James Upshur and Annie King (Wilson) B.; m. Elizabeth Maxwell Carroll Chesnut, Apr. 30, 1938; children—William Calvin Chesnut, Wilson King. A.B., Western Md. Coll., 1928, LL.D., 1976; LL.B., U. Md., 1931, J.D., 1969. Bar: Md. bar 1931. Law clk. U.S. Dist. Judge W. Calvin Chesnut, 1931-33; practiced law, Balt., 1933-37, asst. city solicitor, 1937-42, dep. city solicitor, 1942-43; partner firm Anderson, Barnes, Coe & King, Balt., 1943-63; asso. judge Supreme Bench, Balt., 1963-64, Ct. of Appeals Md., 1964-74; law practice, Balt., 1974-77; counsel firm Hall, Steinmann & Fronk (P.A.), Balt., 1977—; mem., sec. Md. Bd. Law Examiners, 1944-63; prof. contracts U. Balt. Law Sch., 1963-71. Trustee Western Md. Coll. Recipient Norment Speech prize Western Md. Coll., 1926. Mem. Am., Md. bar assns., Bar Assn. Balt., SAR (chancellor gen. 1976-77, pres. gen. 1977-78). Episcopalian. Clubs: Univ., Barristers. Home: 111 Ridgewood Rd Baltimore MD 21210 Office: 10 E Baltimore St Baltimore MD 21202

BARNES, ZANE EDISON, communications company executive; b. Marietta, Ohio, Dec. 2, 1921; s. Emmett A. and Frances (Canfield) B.; m. Virginia Harris, May 29, 1948; children: Frances Barnes Davis, Zane Edison, Shelley Barnes Donaho. B.S., Marietta Coll., 1947. With Ohio Bell Telephone Co., 1941-60, asst. v.p. operations, Cleve., 1961-63, gen. plant mgr., 1963-64, v.p. personnel, 1965-67; with engring. dept. AT&T, N.Y.C., 1960-61; v.p., gen. mgr. Oreg. area Pacific N.W. Bell Telephone Co., Portland, 1964-65, v.p. operations, 1967-70, pres., Seattle, 1970-73, Southwestern Bell Telephone Co., St. Louis, 1973—; chmn., chief exec. officer Southwestern Bell Corp., St. Louis, 1983—; dir. H & R Block, Inc., Centerre Bancorp., Centerre Bank, Burlington No., Inc., Gen. Am. Life Ins. Co., Reading & Bates Corp., Interco Inc. Mem. Civic Progress; bd. dirs. St. Louis Area council Boy Scouts Am.; bd. dirs. Arts and Edn. Council Greater St. Louis, Jobs for Mo. Grads., Inc., Barnes Hosp., St. Louis Symphony Orch.; trustee Washington U., Mo. Pub. Expenditure Survey, Midwest Research Inst., Jefferson Nat. Expansion Meml. Assn., Brookings Instn.; life assoc. trustee Marietta Coll.; mem. Com. for Econ. Devel. Mem. Round Table (pres. 1979-80). Address: 1010 Pine St Saint Louis MO 63101

BARNESS, AMNON SHEMAYA, financial executive; b. Israel, Oct. 16, 1924; s. Nahum and Lea (Muhlmann) B.; m. Caren Heller, 1978; children: Rena Lahav, Dalia, Danny, Jordan. B.A., Am. U. Cairo, 1947; M.A., Syracuse U., 1950; Ph.D. (hon.), Stonehill Coll., 1974. Pres. Trans-Internat. Mgmt. Corp., 1976—; founder, pres., chmn. bd. Daylin Inc. (now subs. W.R. Grace Co.); chmn. bd. Handy Dan Home Improvement Centers, Inc., Commerce, Calif., 1972—; sr. partner Adam Assocs., Beverly Hills, Calif., 1965—, Adam Fin. Corp., 1966—; chmn. exec. com., dir. PharmaControl Corp. (OTC), Englewood Cliffs, N.J., 1982—; dir. Serpro S.A., Unico Mortgage Bank, Tel Aviv, Israel, Bourguet de Clausade Traders, Paris, JOBA B.V., Amsterdam. Founder, chmn. Fund Higher Edn.; active Israel Bond campaign; pres. Job Corp Grad. Found., 1966—, Juvenile Opportunities Endeavor Found., 1974—; v.p. Brandeis Inst., 1964-70; bd. dirs. Temple Sinai, Los Angeles, 1968-72; bd. govs. Weizman Inst. Sci., 1970—; Andean Pact countries rep. Mecaform, Paris, 1977-82; founder, bd. dirs. European Found. for Scis., Arts, and Culture, Paris, 1982—. Decorated knight comdr. merit Equestrian Order, Order Holy Sepulcher Jerusalem, Israel Prime Minister's medal, others. Address: 1500 Broadway Suite 1900 New York NY

BARNESS, LEWIS ABRAHAM, physician; b. Atlantic City, N.J., July 31, 1921; s. Joseph and Mary (Silverstein) B.; m. Elaine Berger, June 14, 1953; children: Carol, Laura, Joseph. A.B., Harvard U., 1941, M.D., 1944; M.A. (hon.), U. Pa., 1971. Intern Phila. Gen. Hosp., 1944-45; resident Children's Med. Center, Boston, 1947-50; asst. chief, then chief dept. pediatrics Phila. Gen. Hosp., 1951-72; vis. physician U. Pa. Hosp., 1952-57, acting chief, then chief, 1957-72; mem. faculty U. Pa. Sch. Medicine, 1951-72, prof. pediatrics, 1964-72; prof. pediatrics, chmn. dept. U. So. Fla. Med. Sch., Tampa, 1972—. Author: Pediatric Physical Diagnosis Yearbook, edits. 1-5, 1957—; Editor: Advances in Pediatrics, 1976—. Served to capt. AUS, 1945-46. Recipient Lindback Teaching award U. Pa., 1963; Borden award nutrition, 1972; Noer Disting. Prof. award, 1980. Mem. Am. Pediatric Soc. (recorder-editor 1964-75), Soc. Pediatric Research, Am. Acad. Pediatrics (chmn. com. on nutrition 1975—), Am. Inst. Nutrition, AAAS, Sigma Xi, Alpha Omega Alpha. Home: 548 W Davis Blvd Tampa FL 33606 *Most people, when given the opportunity, try to be unselfish and prefer to do good. The human brain is a fantastic instrument, which when exercised, can solve most problems.*

BARNET, ANN BIRNBAUM, physician; b. Chgo., Jan. 18, 1930; d. John Solomon and Rosalie (Friedman) Birnbaum; m. Richard J. Barnet, Apr. 10, 1953; children—Juliana, Beth, Michael. A.B., Sarah Lawrence Coll., 1951; M.D., Harvard U., 1956. Fellow dept. pediatrics Mass. Gen. Hosp., Boston, 1958-61; clin. dir. Child Devel. Clinic, Cambridge, Mass., 1958-61; research asso. div. neuropsychiatry Walter Reed Army Inst. Research, 1961-73; asst. prof., asso. prof. neurology George Washington Med. Sch., 1967—; dir. EEG research evoked response lab. Children's Hosp. Nat. Med. Center, Washington, 1965—; prin. investigator NIH grants, 1964—; mem. adv. group, communicative scis. study sect. NIH, 1973-77; cons. NSF, Nat. Found., FDA. Pres. The Family Place; bd. dirs. Com. of Responsibility, 1969-73. Recipient Research Career Devel. award NIMH, 1970-75; W.T. Grant Found. grantee, 1972-76; Nat. Found. March of Dimes grantee, 1978—. Mem. N.Y. Acad. Sci., Soc. Neurosci., So. Soc. Pediatric Research, D.C. Med. Soc. Home: 1716 Portal Dr NW Washington DC 20012 Office: 111 Michigan Ave NW Washington DC 20010

BARNET, RICHARD JACKSON, author, educator; b. Boston, May 7, 1929; s. Carl J. and Margaret L. (Block) B.; m. Ann Birnbaum, Apr. 10, 1953; children—Juliana, Beth, Michael. A.B. summa cum laude, Harvard U., 1951, LL.B. cum laude, 1954. Bar: Mass. bar 1954. Research fellow Am. Law Inst., 1957-58; asso. firm Choate, Hall & Stewart, Boston; fellow Harvard U. Russian Research Center, 1959-60; spl. asst. Dept. State, 1961; dep. dir. Office of Polit. Research, U.S. ACDA, 1961-62; fellow Center for Internat. Studies, Princeton U., 1963; co-dir. Inst. for Policy Studies, Washington, 1963-77, sr. fellow, 1977—; vis. prof. Yale U., 1970, Nat. U. Mexico, 1973, U. Paris, 1982. Author: Who Wants Disarmament, 1960, (with Marcus Raskin) After Twenty Years, 1965, (with Richard Falk) Security in Disarmament, 1965, Intervention and Revolution, 1968, The Economy of Dearth, 1969, (with Marcus Raskin) An American Manifesto, 1970, Roots of War, 1972, Global Reach, 1974, The Giants, 1977, The Lean Years, 1980, Real Security, 1981, Alliance 1983; Contbg. editor: Sojourners mag, 1979—. Served to 1st lt. JAGC U.S. Army, 1955-57. Recipient Sidney Hillman prize Amalgamated Clothing Workers Am., 1975; U. Mo. Sch. Journalism award, 1981. Mem. World Peacemakers (pres.), Com. for Nat. Security, Council on Fgn. Relations, Com. of Compassion. Home: 1716 Portal Dr NW Washington DC 20012 Office: 1901 Q St NW Washington DC 20009

BARNET, SYLVAN, educator; b. Bklyn., Dec. 11, 1926; s. Philip and Esther (Katz) B. A.B., N.Y. U., 1948; A.M., Harvard, 1950, Ph.D., 1954. Teaching fellow Harvard, 1951-54; mem. faculty Tufts U., 1954—, chmn. dept. English, 1962-67, 80—, Fletcher prof. English, 1963—; editorial cons. Little, Brown and Co. Author: A Short Guide to Writing About Literature, 4th edit, 1978, (with M. Berman and W. Burto) The Study of Literature, 1960, An Introduction to Literature, 6th edit, 1977, A Dictionary of Literary, Dramatic and Cinematic Terms, 2d edit, 1971, A Short Guide to Shakespeare, 1974, A Short Guide to Writing About Art, 1980, (with Marcia Stubbs) Barnet and Stubbs's Practical Guide to Writing, 3d edit, 1980; also essays.; Editor: (with M. Berman and W. Burto) Tragedy and Comedy, 1967, Nine Modern Classics, 1973, Types of Drama, 2d edit, 1977; also other anthologies Types of Drama, 3d edit; gen. editor: Signet Shakespeare, 1963-69. Served with AUS, 1945-46. Mem. MLA, Shakespeare Assn., Renaissance Soc. Home: 29 Ash St Cambridge MA 02138 Office: East Hall Tufts Univ Medford MA 02155

BARNET, WILL, artist, educator; b. Beverly, Mass., May 25, 1911; s. Noah and Sarah (Toahnich) B.; m. Mary Sinclair, Feb., 1935 (div.); children: Peter George, Richard Sinclair, Todd Williams; m. Elena Ona Ciurlys, Mar. 4, 1953; 1 dau., Ona Willa. Student, Boston Mus. Fine Arts Sch., 1927-30, Art Students League, N.Y.C., 1930-33. Instr. painting Art Students League, N.Y.C., 1946—; faculty Cooper Union, N.Y.C., 1945—, prof., 1965—; instr., critic Pa. Acad., Phila., 1967—; faculty Famous Artists Painting Course, Westport, Conn., 1954—, Mont. State Coll., summer 1951, Summer Artists Workshop, Regina Coll., U. Sask., Can., 1957; instr. advanced painting U. Minn. at Duluth, summer 1959, Wash. State U., Spokane, summer 1963, Pa. State U., summer 1965, Des Moines Art Center, summer 1965; distinguished vis. prof. Pa. State U., 1965-66; vis. critic Yale, 1952-53; vis. prof. Cornell U., 1968-69; condr. grand art tour of, Europe, April, 1959, Ford Found. artist in residence program, 1964. Contbr. to: Art Students League Mag; one-man shows, Hudson D. Walker Gallery, 1938, Galerie St. Etienne, 1943, Berthe Schaefer Gallery, Arthur Harlow & Co., Inc., all N.Y.C., 1946, U.S. Nat. Mus., Washington, Bertha Schaefer Gallery, N.Y.C., 1947, 48, Krasner Gallery, N.Y.C., Gallery Trastevere, Rome, 1960, Terry Dintenfass Gallery, N.Y.C., 1982, retrospective, Inst. Contemporary Art, Boston, 1961, Mary Harriman Gallery, Boston, 1963, 64, Va. Mus., Richmond, 1964, Waddell Gallery, N.Y.C., 1965, 66, 68, 70, Des Moines Art Center, 1965, Pa. Acad. Phila., 1969, Fairweather Hardin Gallery, Chgo., 1971, David and David, Phila., 1972, print retrospective, Asso. Am. Artists, N.Y.C., 1972-79, Hirschl & Adler Galleries, Inc., 1973, 76, 81, Essex Inst., Salem, Mass., 1980, painting retrospective, Neuberger Mus., Purchase, N.Y., 1979, Ringling Mus., Sarasota, Fla., 1980, Wichita Art Mus., Wichita, Kans., 1983, exhibited, Art U.S.A., 1959; represented in permanent collections, Minn. Inst. Arts, Met., N.Y.C., Fogg Art Mus., Library of Congress, Art Gallery, U. N.D., U. Art Gallery, Berkeley, Calif., Cin. Art Mus., Duncan Phillip Meml. Mus., Washington, Phila. Art Mus., Honolulu Acad., Mus. Modern Art, Bklyn. Mus., Mont. State Coll., Whitney Mus. Am. Art, Mus. Fine Arts, Boston, Guggenheim Mus., N.Y.C.; exhibited in museums throughout, U. S., including, Art Inst. Chgo., Los Angeles Mus., Portland Mus., John Herron Inst., Carnegie Inst., Virginia Mus. Fine Arts, Columbia (S.C.) Mus. Art (1st Biennial). Recipient bronze medal, 3d prize Corcoran Biennial, 1961; Benjamin Altman 1st prize NAD, 1977. Fellow Royal Soc. Arts; mem. Art Students League (life) (N.Y.C.), NAD (life), Am. Abstract Artists, Soc. Am. Graphic Artists, Inc., Fedn. Modern Painters and Sculptors, Century Assn. Liberal. Unitarian. Home and Studio: 15 Gramercy Park New York NY 10003

BARNETT, ALLEN MARSHALL, electrical engineer; b. Oklahoma City, June 20, 1940; s. Orville Theodore and Lillian B.; m. Marsha Silverman, Aug. 17, 1968; children: Michael Alexander, Charles Anthony, Jeffrey Andrew. B.S., U. Ill., 1962, M.S., 1963; Ph.D., Carnegie Inst. Tech., 1966. With Gen. Electric Electronics Lab., Syracuse, N.Y., 1966-69, Gen. Electric Research and Devel. Center, Schenectady, 1969-71; pres. Xciton Corp., Latham, N.Y., 1971-75; prof. elec. engring. U. Del., Newark, 1976—; dir. Inst. Energy Conversion, 1976-79; chmn. Del. Gov.'s Energy Resource Mgmt. Commn., 1978-82; participant rev. panels (Nat. Energy Policy), 1977—; mem. Senator's Del. Energy Task Force, 1978—, N.C. Gov.'s Energy Inst. Bd. Sci. Advs., 1977-79; cons. strategic bus. planning for high tech. projects. Contbr. tech. articles to profl. jours.; patentee in field. Mem. exec. com. Del-Mar-Va council Boy Scouts Am., 1979-82. Recipient four IR-100 awards for developing new high tech. indsl. products; named Disting. Delawarean, 1978. Mem. AAAS, Internat. Solar Energy Soc., IEEE (photovoltaic specialists conf. com. 1977—, program chmn. 1982, chmn. elect 1984), Commn. European Communities Photovoltaic Solar Energy Conf., Internat. Solar Energy Soc. (internat. conf. sci. com.). Home: 2 Polaris Dr Newark DE 19711 Office: U Del Newark DE 19716 *My primary goal is to contribute to the solution of a specific worthwhile problem. My methodology is to focus on the most important, single subproblems and to then develop a measurable plan to solve them. Adjustments in the plan are made based on the measurement of progress and information sought from others. I work to help in the development of individuals within the organization and to assist people outside the organization. I stress quality and not quantity in my endeavors and the endeavors of others.*

BARNETT, ARTHUR DOAK, political scientist, educator; b. Shanghai, China, Oct. 8, 1921; s. Eugene Epperson and Bertha Mae (Smith) B.; m. Jeanne Hathaway Badeau, Mar. 22, 1954; children: Katherine Hathaway, Stewart Doak, Martha Jeanne. B.A., Yale U., 1942, M.A., 1947, cert. Chinese, 1947; LL.D., Franklin and Marshall Coll., 1967. Fellow Inst. Current World Affairs in China and S.E. Asia, 1947-50, 52-53; corr. Chgo. Daily News, 1947-50, 52-53, 53-55; cons. ECA, 1950-51; consul, pub. affairs officer Am. consulate-gen., Hong Kong, 1951-52; asso. Am. Univs. Field Staff, 1953-55; head dept. fgn. area studies Fgn. Service Inst., Dept. State, 1956-57; research fellow Council Fgn. Relations, 1958-59; program asso. Ford Found., 1959-61; prof. polit. sci. Columbia U., 1961-69; sr. fellow Brookings Instn., 1969-82; prof. Chinese studies Johns Hopkins U. Sch. Advanced Internat. Studies, Washington, 1982—; sr. fellow East-West Center Hawaii, 1976-77; mem. joint com. Contemporary China Social Sci. Research Council and Am. Council Learned Socs., 1963-64, 65-67, 80-81, chmn., 1963-64; sub-com. Chinese govt., 1965-71, mem. steering com. Chinese fgn. policy, 1974-76; exec. com. Internat. Com. Chinese Studies, 1963-65; bd. dirs. Nat. Com. on U.S.-China Relations, 1966—, chmn. bd. dirs., 1968-69; mem. adv. panel on China Dept. State, 1966-69; vis. com. East Asian civilizations Harvard U., 1962-64; chmn. contemporary China studies com. Columbia U., 1961-67; mem. Inst. Current World Affairs, 1958-60, 66-71, bd. govs., 1960-66, 73-79, vice chmn., 1973-74; mem. Liaison Com. Study Contemporary China, 1965-70, Atlantic Council China Study Group, 1982-83; mem. com. on scholarly communication with People's Republic of China, Nat. Acad. Scis.-Am. Council Learned Socs.-Social Sci. Research Council, 1970-76, vice chmn., 1972-75; co-chmn. China council Asia Soc., 1976-79; bd. visitors in East Asian studies U. Mich., 1974-76; mem. U.S.-People's Republic of China Joint Commn. on Sci. and Tech. Cooperation, 1979-81. Author: Communist Economic Strategy: The Rise of Mainland China, 1959, Communist China and Asia: Challenge to American Policy, 1960, Communist China in Perspective, 1962, China on the Eve of Communist Takeover, 1963, Communist China: The Early Years, 1964, Cadres, Bureaucracy and Political Power in Communist China, 1967, China after Mao, 1967, A New U.S. Policy Toward China, 1970, Uncertain Passage: China's Transition to the Post—Mao Era, 1974, China Policy: Old Problems and New Challenges, 1977, China and the Major Powers in East Asia, 1977, China and the World Food System, 1979, China's Economy in Global Perspective, 1981, The FX Decision, 1981, U.S. Arms Sales: The China-Taiwan Tangle, 1982; co-author: The United States, China, and Arms Control, 1975; editor: Communist Strategies in Asia: A Comparative Analysis of Governments and Parties, 1963, United States and China in World Affairs, 1966, Chinese Communist Politics in Action, 1969, (with Edwin O. Reischauer) The United States and China: The Next Decade, 1970; editorial adv. bd.: Fgn. Affairs, 1972—; editorial bd.: China Quar., 1967-81, Asian Survey, 1967—. Served to capt. USMCR, 1942-46. Mem. Am. Polit. Sci. Assn. (chmn. Conf. Communist Studies 1965-66), Assn. Asian Studies (dir. 1962-65), Asia Soc. (council Chinese affairs 1966-71, co-chmn. China council 1976-79), Council Fgn. Relations (steering com. Project on U.S. and China in World Affairs 1962-66), UN Assn. (China panels 1966-67 70-71, 79-80, Japan panel 1973), Phi Beta Kappa. Home: 1023 Shipman Ln McLean VA 22101 Office: Johns Hopkins Sch Advanced Internat Studies 1740 Massachusetts Ave NW Washington DC 20036

BARNETT, BENJAMIN LEWIS, JR., physician, educator; b. Woodruff, S.C., July 22, 1926; s. Benjamin Lewis and Mattie Bernice (Skinner) B.; m. Annalyne Louise Hall, Oct. 25, 1958; children: Benjamin Lewis III, Jane Kristen. B.S., Furman U., 1946, LL.D., 1978; M.D., Med. U. S.C., 1949. Diplomate: Am. Bd. Family Practice (mem. exam. bd. 1975—, dir. 1976-81, exec. com. 1979-81, pres. 1980-81). Intern Protestant Episcopal Hosp., Phila., 1949-50; pvt. practice gen. medicine, Woodruff, 1950-70; assoc. prof. family practice Med. U. S.C., Charleston, 1970-74, prof. family practice, 1974-77, asst. dir. family practice residency program, 1970-75, chief undergrad. curriculum, 1970-77; vice chmn. dept. family practice, 1973-77, asst. dean for student affairs, 1975-77; mem. clin. staff Med. U. Hosp., Charleston County Hosp., 1970-77; Walter M. Seward prof., chmn. dept. family medicine U. Va. Sch. Medicine, 1977—; family medicine physician-in-chief U. Va. Med. Center Hosp., 1977—; chief of staff Woodruff Hosp., 1966-69; vis. lectr. numerous med. schs.; Stoneburner lectr. Med. Coll. Va., 1975; Daniel Drake lectr. U. Cin., 1976; Robert P. Walton lectr. Med. U. S.C., 1978; Goodlark prof. U. Tenn., 1979; vis. scholar U. Mich. Med. Sch., 1984; Health officer, Town of Woodruff, 1950-54; Mem. Spartanburg County Bd. Edn., 1968-70, sec., 1969-70; Trustee Bethea Bapt. Home for Aged, Darlington, S.C., 1972-73. Editor: S.C. Family Physician, 1973-74; contbr. articles to med. jours. and chpts. to textbooks. Served with USNR, 1954-56. Named Citizen of Year Woodmen of World, 1968; recipient Golden Apple award for clin. teaching Student AMA, 1973; Thomas W. Johnson award Am. Acad. Family Physicians, 1976. Mem. AMA (mem. residency rev. com. for family practice 1974-79), Va., Albemarle County med. socs., Soc. Tchrs. Family Medicine (v.p. 1974, sec.-treas. 1975, dir. 1981—, cert. of excellence 1983), Am. Acad. Family Physicians, S.C. Acad. Family Physicians (v.p. 1973, pres. 1975-76), Spartanburg County Med. Soc. (v.p. 1968), Am. Philatelic Soc., Am. Manuscript Soc., Council Acad. Socs., Furman U. Alumni Assn. (dir. 1972-77), Alpha Omega Alpha (faculty councilor), Alpha Kappa Kappa (pres. 1948), Kappa Alpha (v.p. 1944). Baptist (deacon, chmn. bd.). Club: Masons (32 degree). Home: 2406 Northfields Rd Charlottesville VA 22901 *I have found that the only lasting happiness for me has come from trying to be of some value to others. If I have somehow been a catalyst in the lives of my children, patients, and students, I am satisfied.*

BARNETT, BERNARD, accountant; b. N.Y.C., Oct. 14, 1920; s. Abraham L. and Rose (Albert) B.; m. Helen Salla, July 9, 1953; 1 dau., Susan. B.B.A. magna cum laude, CCNY, 1941. C.P.A., N.Y., Mich., La., N.C., Va. Partner Apfel & Englander, C.P.A.s, N.Y.C., 1941-67, Oppenheim, Appel, Dixon & Co., C.P.A.s, 1967-70; partner Seidman & Seidman, C.P.A.s, N.Y.C., 1970, sr. partner, nat. dir. tax practice, 1971-83; pres. Found. Acctg. Edn., 1977-78; adv. commr. IRC; mem. N.Y. State Bd. Public Accountancy; mem. adv. com. Inst. Estate Planning, U. Miami (Fla.) Law Center.; mem. faculty Am. Law Inst./ABA Estate Planning Course, 1978-83; cons. CBS News Ann. Income Tax Program, 1977-83. Co-author: Estate Planning and the C.P.A, 1958, Attorneys Handbook of Accounting, 2d edit, 1979, 3d edit., 1982, Analysis of the Tax Reform Act of, 1969, 1970; editorial adv. bd.: Trusts and Estates, 1979-83, Tax Adviser, 1970-83, Taxation for Accountants, 1973-83. Served with AUS, 1942-46; to maj. USAF, 1951-52. Mem. Nat. Conf. Lawyers and C.P.A.'s (co-chmn. 1978-81), Am. Inst. C.P.A.s (gov. council 1971-80, chmn. Task Force on Estate and Gift Tax Reform 1979-83, chmn. Task Force on Income Taxation of Trusts and Estates 1983—), N.Y. State Soc. C.P.A.s (pres. 1976-77, chmn. joint Am. Inst. C.P.A.s disciplinary trial bd. 1982-83), Accountants Club Am. (pres. 1977-80), Board Room (N.Y.C.). Office: 15 Columbus Circle New York NY 10023

BARNETT, BERNARD HARRY, lawyer; b. Helena, Ark., July 13, 1916; s. Harry and Rebecca (Grossman) B.; m. Marian Spiesberger, Apr. 9, 1949; 1 son, Charles Dawson. Student, U. Mich., 1934-36; J.D., Vanderbilt U., 1940. Bar: Ky. 1940. Sole practice, Louisville, 1940-42; assoc. Woodward, Dawson, Hobson & Fulton, 1946-48; ptnr. Bulitt, Dawson & Tarrant, 1948-52, Greenebaum, Barnett, Wood & Doll, 1952-70, Barnett & McConnell, 1972, Barnett, Greenebaum, Martin & McConnell, 1972-74, Barnett, Alagia, Greenebaum, Miller & Senn, 1974-75, Barnett & Alagia, Louisville, 1975—; dir. Bank of Louisville, Cook United Inc., Fuqua Industries Inc., Hasbro Industries Inc.; mem. adv. group Joint Com. on Internal Revenue Taxation, U.S. Congress, 1953-55, Com. on Ways and Means, U.S. Ho. of Reps., 1956-58. Chmn. Louisville Fund, 1952-53; mem. nat. exec. com., nat. campaign cabinet United Jewish Appeal, 1959—, nat. chmn., 1967-71; chmn. Louisville United Jewish Appeal, 1968-69; mem. Louisville and Jefferson County Republican Exec. Com., 1954-60; chmn. Ky. Rep. Fin. Com., 1955-60; trustee Spalding Coll., Louisville, 1975—, Norton Gallery and Sch. Art, 1980—, Benjamin N. Cardozo Sch. Law, 1979—, Ford's Theatre, 1981. Served as lt. USNR, 1942-45. Mem. ABA, Ky. Bar Assn., Louisville Bar Assn. Home: 355 Coconut Row Palm Beach FL 33480 Office: 17th Floor Kentucky Home Life Bldg louisville KY 40202

BARNETT, BILL MARVIN, publishing company executive; b. Atlanta, Apr. 15, 1931; s. Henry Claude and Ida Belle (Estes) B.; m. Joan Kitchens, May 28, 1952 (div. 1979); 1 dau., Donna Satin; m. Amy Joseph, May 10, 1981. B.A., Auburn U., 1957, M.A., 1960. English instr. Auburn U., Ala., 1958-61; coll. salesman Harcourt Brace Jovanovich, Atlanta, 1961-65, so. regional sales mgr., 1966-70, gen. mgr., San Francisco, 1970-77, dep. dir., San Diego, 1978-81, dir., 1981—. Trustee COMBO, San Diego, 1983—. Served with USAF, 1950-54. Recipient Kirkland Auburn U., 1955. Mem. Phi Eta Sigma, Phi Kappa Phi. Office: College Dept Harcourt Brace Jovanovich 1250 6th Ave San Diego CA 92101

BARNETT, CHARLES EBBERT, III, minerals company executive, lawyer; b. Charleston, W.Va., Sept. 25, 1939; s. Charles Ebbert and Anne Lorentz (Hall) B.; m. Judith Pierrepont Grape, July 11, 1970; children: Christopher Charles, Lindsay Pierrepont, Andrew Ashton. B.A. in Philosophy, U. Mich., 1961, J.D., 1964. Bar: N.Y. 1965, Conn.

bar 1973. Asso. firm Cadwalader, Wickersham & Taft, N.Y.C., 1964-68; asst. counsel Macmillan, Inc., N.Y.C., 1968-70; asst. gen. counsel ASARCO Inc., N.Y.C., 1970-73; asst. gen. counsel, asst. sec. St. Joe Minerals Corp., N.Y.C., 1974, gen. counsel, 1974—, sec., 1977—, v.p., 1979—. Mem. ABA, Assn. Bar City N.Y. Club: Union League (N.Y.C.). Office: St Joe Minerals Corp 250 Park Ave New York NY 10017

BARNETT, DAVID, pianist, composer; b. N.Y.C., Dec. 1, 1907; s. Samuel and Bertha (Margolis) B.; m. Josephine Wolff, Dec. 31, 1929; 1 son, Jonathan. Diploma, Juilliard Sch. Music, 1925, Ecole Normale de Musique, 1928; B.A., Columbia U., 1927; Mus.D., Elon Coll., 1953. Mem. faculty Wellesley Coll., 1935-65, Harvard U., 1955-59, New Eng. Conservatory Music, 1946-65, Columbia U., summers 1946-62; prof. music U. Bridgeport, Conn., 1967—; vis. lectr. Assn. Am. Colls.; lectr. WGBH, Boston; bd. dirs. Boston Old South Meeting House. Pianist on concert tours in the, east and mid-west, also Gt. Britain; recitalist, Carnegie Hall, Town Hall, Jordan Hall, Gardner Mus., Salle Pleyel; soloist with, Boston, St. Louis, Cin., Bridgeport symphony orchs., Orchestre Symphonique de Paris; dir., Wellesley Concert Series, Westport Friends of Music.; Composer: song Rhapsody and Scherzo for Violin and Piano; recorded: (with Josephine Barnett, narrator.) Three Cycles of Robert Schumann; Author: The Performance of Music; Contbr. articles profl. jours. and mags. Mem. Am. Music Centre, Conn. State Music Tchrs. Assn. (pres.), Coll. Music Soc., Am. British socs. aesthetics, Pi Kappa Lambda, Kappa Gamma Psi, Tau Zeta Epsilon. Home: 3 Ledgebrook Ct Weston CT 06883 Office: Music Dept University of Bridgeport Bridgeport CT 06602

BARNETT, DAVID LEON, editor; b. Savannah, Ga., Jan. 21, 1922; s. Jack and Ida (Levy) B.; m. Jeanne Kahn, Dec. 29, 1946; children: Randel, Megan, Jane. B.S. with honors in Govt, Harvard U., 1943; M.S., Columbia U., 1947. Mem. staff Richmond (Va.) News Leader, 1947-54, chief statehouse bur. and polit. corr., 1950-51, asst. city editor, 1951-54; regional corr. Business Week mag., 1951-54; Washington corr. N.Am. Newspaper Alliance, 1954-55, chief Washington bur., columnist, 1955-65; Washington news editor Hearst Newspapers, 1966-76; asst. mng. editor U.S. News & World Report, Washington, 1976—. Contbr. articles to mags. Served with USAAF, 1943-46. Mem. White House Corr. Assn. Clubs: Gridiron, Harvard, Nat. Press, Federal City (Washington). Home: 7218 Beechwood Rd Alexandria VA 22307 Office: 2400 N St NW Washington DC 20037

BARNETT, EDWARD WILLIAM, lawyer; b. New Orleans, Jan. 2, 1933; s. Phillip Nelson and Katherine (Wilkinson) B.; m. Maureen Mauk, Apr. 3, 1933; children: Margaret Ann Barnett Stern, Edward William. B.A., Rice U., 1955; LL.B., U. Tex.-Austin, 1958. Bar: Tex. 1958. Ptnr. Baker & Botts, Houston, 1958—. Fellow Am. Coll. Trial Lawyers; mem. ABA (chmn. sect. antitrust law 1981-82), State Bar Tex., Houston Bar Assn. Clubs: Houston Country, Athletic; Houston Philos (Houston); Headliners (Austin). Office: Baker & Botts 3000 One Shell Plaza Houston TX 77002

BARNETT, FRANK EUGENE, lawyer, former corporation executive; b. Fairport Harbor, Ohio, July 14, 1912; s. George Forrest and Hazel (Roberts) B.; m. Virginia Severens Russ, Sept. 24, 1936 (div. 1953); 1 son, John Severns; m. Wana Allison, Dec. 31, 1954; 1 stepdau., Pamela Allison. A.B., Duke U., 1933; LL.B., Western Res. U., 1936. Bar: Ohio bar 1936, N.Y. bar 1943. Tax lawyer Lybrand, Ross Bros. & Montgomery, 1936-41; asso. Clark, Carr & Ellis, 1942-44, partner, 1945-68; Eastern gen. counsel U.P. R.R., 1951-60, v.p., 1955-60, v.p., gen. counsel, 1961-66, chmn. exec. com., 1967-69; chmn. bd., chief exec. officer Union Pacific Corp., U.P. R.R., 1969-77, O.S.L. R.R. Co., O. W. R.R. & N. Co., L.A. & S.L. R. R. Co., 1969-77, Spokane Internat. R.R. Co., 1971-77, Union Pacific Land Resources Corp., 1971-77, Union Pacific Mining Corp., 1971-77, Upland Industries Corp., 1971-77; chmn. bd. Champlin Petroleum Co., 1970-77; v.p., dir. St. Joseph & Grand Island Ry. Co., Utah Parks Co., 1969-77; of counsel firm Shea & Gould, 1977-80; trustee Seamen's Bank Savs.; Trustee, mem. exec. com. Union Pacific Found. Named R.R. Man of Yr. Modern R.R., 1975; recipient Seley award Seley Found., 1977. Mem. Am. Bar Assn., Assn. Bar City N.Y., Phi Delta Phi. Clubs: Econ. of N.Y., Univ., River (N.Y.C.); Preston Mountain (Kent, Conn.). Home: 1185 Park Ave Apt 15C New York NY 10128 Office: 375 Park Ave New York NY 10152

BARNETT, GEORGE LEONARD, educator; b. Caldwell, N.J., Jan. 18, 1915; s. D'Arcy Cornwell and Adelle S. (Leonard) B.; m. Johanetta Louise Usinger, June 15, 1940; children: George Leonard, Mary D. Barnett. A.B., Randolph-Macon Coll., 1936; A.M., Princeton U., 1939, Ph.D., 1942. Instr. in English, Latin and French, Randolph-Macon Coll., 1939-41; instr., supr. English and corr. in U.S. Naval Tng. Sch., Ind. U., 1942-44, instr. English, 1944-46, asst. prof., 1946-56, asso. prof., 1956-63, prof., 1963-80, prof. emeritus, 1980—; vis. lectr. U. Colo., summer 1962; cons. Ind. U. Press, also profl. jours. Author: (with others) The English Romantic Poets and Essayists: A Review of Research and Criticism, 1957, rev. edit., 1966, Charles Lamb: The Evolution of Elia, 1964; contbg. author: A Study of Charles Lamb's Essays of Elia (Tsutomu Fukuda), 1964; editor: Eighteenth-Century British Novelists on the Novel, 1968, (with others) Nineteenth-Century British Novelists on the Novel, 1971, Charles Lamb, 1976; contbr. articles to profl. jours. Mem. Charles Lamb Soc. (v.p.), MLA, Phi Beta Kappa. Republican. Home: 1615 E University St Bloomington IN 47401

BARNETT, HAROLD JOSEPH, economist, educator; b. Paterson, N.J., May 10, 1917; s. Abraham and Lena (Schiff) B.; m. Mildred Denn, Aug. 4, 1940; children: Peter, Alexander, Katherine. B.S., U. Ark., 1939; M.S., U. Calif. - Berkeley, 1940; M.A. (Social Sci. Research Council fellow), Harvard U., 1948, Ph.D., 1952. Teaching asst. U. Calif., Berkeley, 1939-40; economist Treasury Dept., 1941-42, Dept. State, also Dept. Interior, 1946-52, Rand Corp., Washington, 1952-55; economist, dir. econ. growth studies Resources For Future, Washington, 1955-59, cons., 1959—; prof. econs., chmn. dept. Wayne State U., 1959-63; prof. econs. Washington U., St. Louis, 1963—, chmn. dept., 1963-66; cons. White House Task Force on Communication Policy, NSF, U.S. Office Edn., Com. for Econ. Devel., Nat Acad. Scis.-NRC. Author: Energy Uses and Supplies, 1950, Malthusianism and Conservation, 1959, (with C. Morse) Scarcity and Growth, 1963, Wired City monographs, 1968-73, Population Problems—Myths and Realities, 1971, Energy, Resources, and Growth, 1974, Atomic Energy in U.S. Economy, 1979, also monographs.; Contbr. articles to profl. jours. Served to maj. U.S. Army, 1943-46. Mem. Am. Econ. Assn., Assn. Environ. and Resource Economists, AAUP. Home: 6320 Northwood Dr Clayton MO 63105

BARNETT, HENRY LEWIS, med. educator, pediatrician; b. Detroit, June 25, 1914; s. Lewis and Florence (Marx) B.; m. Shirley Blanchard, Oct. 19, 1940; children—Judith Florence, Martin David. Student, Dartmouth Coll., 1931-32; B.S., Washington U., St. Louis, 1938, M.D., 1938. Instr. dept. pediatrics Washington U. Sch. Medicine, 1941-43; asst. prof. dept. pediatrics Cornell U. Med. Coll., 1946-50; asso. prof., 1950-55; prof., chmn. dept. pediatrics Albert Einstein Coll. Medicine, 1955-72, asso. dean clin. affairs, 1970-72, Univ. prof., 1972-81, prof. emeritus, 1981—; dir. pediatric service Bronx Municipal Hosp. Center, 1955-64; dir. Internat. Study Kidney Disease in Children, 1957-81; med. dir. Children's Aid Soc., 1981—; cons. Appleton-Century-Crofts, 1981—; Mem. WHO Infant Metabolism Team to, Netherlands and Sweden, 1950, WHO Sci. Group Pediatric Research, 1967; adv. bd. Internat. Pediatric Assn., 1969-74; cons. Cento Meeting Pediatric Edn. and Family Planning, Ankara, Turkey, 1972, Nat.Inst. Child Health and Human Devel., 1974—; mem. bd. on maternal, child, and family health research NRC, 1974—; mem. council Found. for Child Devel., 1966—; chmn. med. adv. bd. Am. Council for Emigrees in Professions, 1974—; mem. med. adv. bd. Children's Aid Soc., 1977-81; Felton Bequests vis. prof. Royal Children's Hosp., Melbourne, Australia, 1978; cons. Asian Study Renal Disease in Children, 1978—. Contbr. articles to profl. jours.; Editor: Pediatrics, 15th edit. Served to capt. M.C. AUS, 1943-46. Fellow N.Y. Acad. Sci.; mem. AAAS, Am. Acad. Pediatrics (E. Mead Johnson award 1949), Soc. Pediatric Research (pres. 1959-60), Soc. Exptl. Biology and Medicine, Harvey Soc., Am. Pediatric Soc. (pres. 1981—), Am. Soc. Clin. Investigation, Assn. Am. Physicians, Brit. Pediatric Soc. (hon.), Am. Physiol. Soc., N.Y. Acad. Medicine, Nat. Turkish Pediatric Assn. (hon.), Societe Francaise de Pediatre (corr.), Sigma Xi, Alpha Omega Alpha. Home: 118 W 79th St New York NY 10024 Office: Children's Aid Soc 150 E 45th St New York NY 10017

BARNETT, HOWARD ALBERT, English language educator; b. Dallas, June 14, 1920; s. Carl Harry and Jennie Bess (McHatton) B.; m. Barbara Joan Brandenburg., Sept. 2, 1947; children: Victoria Joan, Gregory Howard. Student, Butler U., also Arthur Jordan Conservatory, 1938-41; B.A., Ind. U., 1947, M.A., 1948, Ph.D., 1959; postgrad., U. Chgo., summers 1950, 51. Asst. prof. English Bridgewater (Va.) Coll., 1948-50, Washington (Md.) Coll., 1950-52, Wis. State Coll., Whitewater, 1957-59; Marshall Evans prof. lit. Morris Harvey Coll., Charleston, W.Va., 1959-65, chmn. dept. English, 1963-65, Lindenwood Colls., St. Charles, Mo., 1965-69, Alice Parker prof. English, 1965-69, v.p., dean, 1969-75, Alice Parker prof., chmn. dept. English, 1975—. Author articles, revs., columnist. Served with USNR, 1941-45. Mem. MLA, Nat. Council Tchrs. English, St. Charles County Hist. Soc. (pres.), Theta Xi, Tau Kappa Alpha. Episcopalian. Office: Lindenwood Coll St Charles MO 63301

BARNETT, JOHN VINCENT, foundation administrator; b. Lapel, Ind., July 23, 1912; s. Harley E. and Vayne (Castor) B.; m. Jane Callane, Feb. 10, 1940,; children: Bonnie Barnett Burdick, John Vincent. Student, Ind. U., 1930-33. Statistician, Ind. Dept. Pub. Welfare, 1934-42; asst. research dir. Ind. C. of C., Indpls., 1942-52, dir. taxation dept., 1952-61, dir. research, 1962, pres., 1962-78; Past pres. Council State Chambers Commerce; mem. Ind. Adv. Council of Career Edn.; mem. adv. com. on polit. edn. Ind. State U.; past chmn. bd., interim pres. Vocat. Tech. Coll.; bd. dirs. Ivy Tech. Found.; treas. Ind. Legal Found., Inc. Mem. Ind. Commerce Execs. Assn. (past pres.), Ind. Soc. Chgo., Ind. U. Alumni Assn. (past pres.). Republican. Presbyterian. Clubs: Press, Meridian Hills Country (Indpls.); Ulen Country (Lebanon); Masons. Home: 8750 Washington Blvd W Dr Indianapolis IN 46240

BARNETT, JONATHAN, architect, city planner; b. Boston, Jan. 6, 1937; s. David and Josephine (Wolff) B.; m. Nory Miller, Mar. 19, 1983. B.A. magna cum laude, Yale U., 1958, M. Arch., 1963; M.A. Mellon fellow, U. Cambridge, Eng., 1960. Designer Haines, Lundberg & Waehler, Archts., N.Y.C., 1963, 64; asso. editor Archtl. Record, N.Y.C., 1964-67; planning cons., N.Y.C.; New City Exhbn. at Mus. Modern Art, 1966, 67; prin. urban designer N.Y.C. Planning Dept., 1967-68, dir. urban design group, 1969-71; prof., dir. grad. program in urban design Coll. City N.Y., 1971—; cons. AIA; South St. Seaport Mus., Arlen Realty & Devel. Corp., Nat. Park Service, Neighborhood Response Project, Louisville, Pitts., Salt Lake City, N.Y., others, 1971—; bd. dirs. N.Y. Landmarks Conservancy. Author: Urban Design as Public Policy, 1974, (with John C. Portman, Jr.) The Architect as Developer, 1976, Introduction to Urban Design, 1982; editor: Perspecta 8, 1962; contbr.: New Zoning, 1970, Collaborations: Artists and Architects, 1981; editorial cons.: Archtl. Record, 1968—; contbr. articles to profl. jours. Mem. adv. bd. Environment and Behavior, 1968-78, Urban Design Internat., 1977—, Process: Architecture, 1977—. Fellow AIA; mem. Am. Inst. Certified Planners, Archtl. League N.Y. (v.p. 1968-70, dir. 1975—, pres. 1977-81), Municipal Art Soc. (dir. 1970-78, 81—), Berzelius Soc. Unitarian. Clubs: Yale, Century Assn. (N.Y.C.); Elizabethan (Yale). Home: 30 Park Ave New York NY 10016 Office: Sch Architecture City Coll New York NY 10031

BARNETT, LESTER ALFRED, surgeon; b. N.Y.C., Mar. 11, 1915; s. Benjamin and Rae Viola (Marcus) B.; m. Jean Wolfe, Apr. 16, 1939; children: Barbara Jane Barnett Grossman, James A. Student, Ohio State U., 1932-35; B.A. with spl. honors, George Washington U., 1936, M.D., 1939. Diplomate: Am. Bd. Surgery. Intern Gallinger Mcpl. Hosp., Washington, 1939-40; resident St. Peter's Gen. Hosp., New Brunswick, N.J., 1940-41, Walter Reed Gen. Hosp., Washington, 1942-43, Grasslands Hosp., Valhalla, N.Y., 1944-46; practice medicine specializing in surgery, Long Branch, N.J., 1945—; mem. staff Monmouth Med. Center, 1946—, dir. dept. surgery, 1961-71, pres. med. staff, 1970-73, trustee, 1975—; bd. mgrs. Monmouth Meml. Sch. Nursing, 1953-65; clin. prof. surgery Hahnemann U., 1970—; assoc. in surgery U. Pa. Sch. Medicine; cons. surgery Jersey Shore Med. Center, Neptune. Author sci. articles. Trustee Monmouth Coll., 1971-78. Served to 1st lt. M.C. AUS, 1942-43. Fellow Am. Coll. Gastroenterology, A.C.S.; mem. N.J. Med. Soc., Monmouth County Med. Soc. (pres. 1959-60). Jewish. Clubs: Hollywood Golf (Deal, N.J.); Ocean Beach (Elberon, N.J.); Masons, B'nai B'rith (past lodge pres.). Home: 675 Ocean Ave West End NJ 07740 Office: 255 3d Ave Long Branch NJ 07740

BARNETT, M. ROBERT, organization consultant; b. Jacksonville, Fla., Oct. 31, 1916; s. Marvin Robinson and Bessie Grace (Groves) B.; m. Sara Ellen Buttorff, Nov. 10, 1941 (div.); children: Alice Sylvia, Robert Ira; m. Marian Weller, May 22, 1965. Student, Fla. Sch. for the Blind, 1935-36; A.B. cum laude, John B. Stetson U., 1940; L.H.D. (hon.), Pfeiffer Coll., 1958, H.H.D., Stetson U., 1964. Pub. relations, instr. in journalism Stetson U., 1940-42; reporter, br. mgr. Daytona Beach News Jour., 1943-44; rehab. specialist for the blind Fla. Council for the Blind, Tampa, 1944-45, exec. dir., 1945-49, Am. Found. for the Blind, Am. Found. for Overseas Blind, 1949-74; internat. cons. Am. Found. for the Blind and Helen Keller Internat., 1975-81; chmn. Am. del., mem. exec. com. World Council Welfare of the Blind, 1951-75; adviser Blinded Vets. Assn.; mem. President's Com. on Employment of the Handicapped, Jacksonville Mayor's Commn. on Goals for Handicapped, 1977-80; repeated and/or continuous service with spl. study groups, research coms. concerned with social ednl., econ. facilities for the visually handicapped, nationwide, regional, 1944—. Recipient Migel medal for outstanding service to blind, 1976. Mem. Nat. Rehab. Assn., Am. Assn. Workers for the Blind, Can. Council for Blind, Pi Gamma Mu, Phi Soc. Democrat. Congregationalist. Clubs: Lions, Elks. Home: 3550 Lenczyk Dr W Jacksonville FL 32211

BARNETT, OLA WILMA, psychology educator; b. Los Angeles, Jan. 26, 1940; d. William and Ruth Carol (Phillips) King; m. Donald Joseph Barnett, Nov. 27, 1941; children: Darlene Ola Blake, Donna Shirley Johnson. B.A., UCLA, 1962, M.A., 1965, Ph.D., 1971. Research asst. UCLA, 1961-67; asst. prof. psychology Calif. State Poly. U., San Luis Obispo, 1967-70; asso. prof. psychology Pepperdine U., Malibu, Calif., 1970-79, prof. psychology, 1979—; sponsor Camp David Gonzales Tutorial Program, 1974-77. Contbr. articles to profl. jours. Recipient Vol. Service award Atascadero State Hosp., 1970; Action grantee, 1972-73. Mem. Am. Psychol. Assn., Nat. Council Crime and Delinquency, Am. Psychology-Law Soc., AAUP, NOW, Common Cause, Nat. Coalition to Ban Handguns, Western Psychol. Assn., Am. Soc. Criminology, Acad. Criminal Justice Scis., Psi Chi. Mem. Ch. of Christ. Research on spouse abuse. Home: 24301 Sylvan Glen Rd Calabasas CA 91302 Office: Social Sci Div Pepperdine U Malibu CA 90265

BARNETT, ROBERT GLENN, lawyer; b. Oxford, Miss., July 30, 1933; s. Arden and Vera (Turner) B.; m. Rae Ragsdale, Apr. 21, 1962; children: Laura Lee, Mary Melissa. B.A., U. Miss., 1959, J.D., 1961. Ptnr. Houston & Barnett, South Haven, Miss., 1961-63, Neal, Houston, Elliott & Barnett, 1963-65, Barnett & Barnett, Jackson, Miss., 1965-70; legal counsel Deposit Guaranty Nat. Bank, Jackson, 1970-79, gen. counsel, sec. to bd., 1979—; adj. prof. U. Miss. Law Sch., Oxford, Miss., 1978-79; banking law course coordinator, lectr. Sch. Banking of the S., Baton Rouge, 1978-79. Pres. Family Services Assn., Jackson, 1970-71; bd. dirs. Community Services Assn., Jackson, 1968-70; bd. govs. Jackson Symphony Orch. Assn., 1981—. Served to lt. (j.g.) USN, 1954-58; served to capt. USNR, 1979. Mem. Miss. Bar Assn. (2d v.p. 1968-69), Jackson Legal Aid Bd. Trustees (pres. 1966-67), Miss. Bankers Assn. (chmn. bank lawyers com.), ABA (banking com.), Miss. Jr. Bar (pres. 1967-68). Baptist (deacon). Club: River Hills Tennis (dir. 1979-82). Home: 2354 Wild Valley Dr Jackson MS 39211 Office: Deposit Guaranty Corp 1 Deposit Guaranty Plaza Jackson MS 39205

BARNETT, ROBERT JAMES, ballet director; b. Okanogan, Wash., May 6, 1925; s. James Gayfield and Vera Inella (Berry) B.; m. Virginia Gleaves Rich, July 20, 1957; children: James Robert, David Michael. Student pub. schs. Tchr. Atlanta Sch. Ballet, Choreographers Conf.; adjudicator Pacific and Southwestern regions Regional Ballet Movement; mem. Nat. Bd. Regional Ballet. Artistic dir., Original Ballet Russe, 1948-49, N.Y. City Ballet, 1950-58, Atlanta Ballet, 1958—; choreographer: Suite Brilliante, Luminesque. Served with USNR, 1943-46. Recipient Performing Arts award Piedmont Arts Festival, Atlanta. Mem. South Eastern Regional Ballet Assn. (pres.). *

BARNETT, ROBERT WARREN, association executive; b. Shanghai, China, Nov. 6, 1911; s. Eugene Epperson and Bertha Mae (Smith) B.; m. Patricia Robertson Glover, Apr. 26, 1940; children: Dickson Glover, Robert Warren, Clare (dec.), Eugenia. A.B., U. N.C., 1933, M.A., 1934; B.A. (Rhodes scholar), Oxford U., 1936, B.Litt., 1937; postgrad. (Gen. Edn. Bd. fellow), Yale U., 1937-39, U. Mich., 1938, Universita per Stranieri, Perugia, Italy, 1935. Mem. staff Inst. Pacific Relations; exec. sec. program com. United China Relief, 1941-42; U.S. mem. econs. and reparations coms. Far Eastern Commn. representing U.S. Dept. State, Japan, 1945-49, officer charge China econ. affairs, 1949-51; charge Western European econ. affairs, 1951-54, charge European econ. orgns., 1954-56; econ. counselor U.S. embassy, The Hague, Netherlands, 1956-60; counselor U.S. Mission European Communities, Brussels, 1960-61; dep. dir. fgn. econ. adv. staff. Dept. State, Washington, 1961-62, dep. asst. sec. state for East Asian and Pacific affairs, 1963-70; dir. Washington Center, Asia Soc., also; v.p., 1970-79; sr. fellow Asia Soc.; resident asso. Carnegie Endowment for Internat. Peace, 1979—. Author: Economic Shanghai: Hostage to Politics, 1941, Orientation Booklet for U.S. Military Personnel in China, 1945; contbr. to: U.S. Economic Foreign Policy, 1948, Day after Tomorrow in the Pacific Region, 1976-82, Pacific Region Interdependencies, 1981. Served from 1st lt. to maj. USAAF, 1943-45; PTO. Decorated Legion of Merit; Order Supreme Merit, Indonesia; Rockefeller Found. fellow, 1940-41; Center Internat. Affairs fellow Harvard U., 1959-60. Mem. Council Fgn. Relations, Assn. Asian Studies, Am. Polit. Sci. Assn., Am. Rhodes Scholar Assn., Washington Inst. Fgn. Affairs, Phi Beta Kappa, Beta Theta Pi. Methodist. Clubs: Cosmos, Chevy Chase (Washington). Home: 1661 Crescent Pl NW Washington DC 20009 Office: Carnegie Endowment 11 DuPont Circle Washington DC 20036

BARNETT, SOLOMON MEYER, retail executive; b. Evansville, Ind., Mar. 28, 1896; s. Samuel and Teresia (Meyer) B.; m. Jeannette Hofheimer, Oct. 18, 1908 (dec. 1983); children: Jane Abraham, Richard Meyer. With Reliable Stores Corp., Balt., 1916-58; pres., Columbia, Md., 1958-80; chmn. Reliable Stores Corp., Columbia, Md., 1980—. Pres. Aaron Straus and Lillie Straus Found. Inc. Served as ensign USN, 1917-21. Republican. Jewish. Club: Woodmont Country (Washington) (bd. dirs. 1958-60). Home: 4201 Cathdral Ave NE Apt 1214W Washington DC 20016 Office: Reliable Stores Corp 6301 Stevens Forest Rd Columbia MD 21045

BARNETT, THOMAS GLEN, multi-industry co. exec.; b. Olney, Ill., Aug. 15, 1946; s. Burl and Florence Ann (Gant) B.; m. Diana Kay O'Dell, Jan. 27, 1968; children—Kevin Thomas, Kelli Lyn. B.S. in Acctg, Millkin U., Decatur, Ill., 1968. C.P.A., Mo., Ill. Staff acct. Arthur Young & Co. (C.P.A.'s), Chgo., 1968-70, sr. acct., 1970-73, audit mgr., 1973-75; dir. internal audit Chromalloy Am. Corp., St. Louis, 1975-76, asst. controller, 1976-78, v.p., controller, 1978-80, exec. v.p. fin., 1980—. Mem. Fin. Execs. Inst., Am. Soc. C.P.A.'s, Mo. Soc. C.P.A.'s. Republican. Presbyterian. Office: 120 S Central St Saint Louis MO 63105

BARNETT, VINCENT MACDOWELL, JR., political science educator; b. Whittier, Calif., Sept. 1, 1913; s. Vincent MacDowell and Ethel (Roper) B.; m. Barbara Brown, June 24, 1939; children: Peter, Deborah Barnett Venman, Stephen, Mary, Wendy. A.B., UCLA, 1935, M.A., 1936; Ph.D., Harvard U., 1938; LL.D., Syracuse U., 1963, Williams Coll., 1963; Litt. D., Union Coll., 1965; L.H.D., Carnegie Inst. Tech., 1965, Hamilton Coll., 1968; D.C.L., Colgate U., 1969. Resident tutor Leverett House and; instr. hist. govt. and econs. Harvard U., 1937-39; instr. polit. sci. Williams Coll., 1939-42, asst. to asso. prof., 1942-48, prof., chmn. dept. polit. sci., 1948-50, David A. Wells prof. polit. sci., 1950-51, A. Barton Hepburn prof. govt., chmn. dept. polit. sci., 1953-62, chmn. grad. center for devel. econs., 1960-62, dean coll., 1957-58; pres. Colgate U., 1963-69; James P. Baxter III prof. public affairs Williams Coll., Williamstown, Mass., 1969—; dir. Harvard U. Devel. Adv. Service, Malaysia Project, Kuala Lumpur, 1971-72, Ford Found. adv. group Ministry of Economy, Cairo, 1976-77; counselor for econ. affairs Am. embassy, Rome, 1958-60; vis. prof. UCLA, summer 1948, Stanford U., summer 1954; exec. dir. Williams Coll. Inst. Am. Studies, 1956-58; tech. dir. 9th Am. Assembly, Columbia U., 1956; project specialist Ford Found., Cairo, 1976-77; spl. asst. to dir. retail trade div. O.P.A., 1942-43; vice chmn. requirements com. W.P.B., 1943-45; chief program div. Spl. Mission to Italy, E.C.A., 1948-50; chief econ. affairs Am. embassy, Rome, 1951-53, counselor for econ. affairs, 1958-60; U.S. mem. FAO, UN Council, 1959-60, alt. del. conf., 1959, U.S. liaison officer, 1958-60; mem. numerous adv. coms. and commns. Trustee Brookings Instn., Edn. and World Affairs. Contbr. to books, profl. jours; editor: The Representation of the U.S. Abroad, 1956, rev. edit., 1965. Recipient Alumni Profl. Achievement award UCLA, 1968; Superior Service medal State Dept., 1960. Mem. Am. Polit. Sci. Assn., Phi Beta Kappa, Pi Gamma Mu, Pi Sigma Alpha.

BARNETT, VIVIAN ENDICOTT, curator; b. Putnam, Conn., July 8, 1944; d. George and Vivian (Wood) Endicott; m. Peter Herbert

Barnett, July 1, 1967; children: Sarah, Alexander. A.B. magna cum laude, Vassar Coll., 1965; M.A., NYU, 1971; postgrad., CUNY, N.Y.C., 1979-81. Research asst. Solomon R. Guggenheim Museum, N.Y.C., 1973-77, curatorial assoc., 1978-79, assoc. curator, 1980-81, research curator, 1981-82, curator, 1982—. Author: The Guggenheim Museum: Justin K. Thannhauser Collection, 1978, Handbook: The Guggenheim Museum Collection 1900-1980, 1980, Kandinsky at the Guggenheim, 1983. Mem. Am. Assn. Museums (curator com.), Internat. Council Museums, Coll. Art Assn. Am. Home: 317 W 83d St New York NY 10024 Office: The Solomon R Guggenheim Museum 1071 Fifth Ave New York NY 10128

BARNETTE, CURTIS HANDLEY, lawyer, steel company executive; b. St. Albans, W.Va., Jan. 9, 1935; s. Curtis Franklin and Garnett Drucella (Robinson) B.; m. Loris Joan Harner, Dec. 28, 1957; children: Curtis Kevin, James David. A.B. with High Honors, W.Va. U., 1956; postgrad. (Fulbright scholar), U. Manchester, 1956-57; J.D., Yale U., 1962; grad. advanced mgmt. program, Harvard U., 1974-75. Bar: Conn. bar 1962, Pa. bar 1968. Mem. Wiggin & Dana, New Haven, Conn., 1962-67; atty. Bethlehem Steel Corp., Pa., 1967-70, gen. atty., 1970-72, asst. sec., 1972-76, asst. gen. counsel, 1972-77, asst. to v.p., 1974-76, sec., 1976—, asst. v.p., 1976-77, v.p., gen. counsel, 1977—; lectr. U. Md., 1958-59; law tutor Yale U., 1962-67; mem. legal adv. com. N.Y. Stock Exchange; mem. adv. council Practising Law Inst.; v.p., dir. Am. Soc. Corp. secs.; dir. Sta. WLVT-TV. Bd. dirs. Yale Law Sch. Fund, Minsi Trails council Boy Scouts Am.; mem. devel. council W.Va. U. Coll. Law; mem. adv. bd. Inst. for Law and Econs., U. Pa. Served with U.S. Army, 1956-57. Mem. Am., Pa., Conn., Fed., Northampton County bar assns., Am. Iron and Steel Inst., Assn. Gen. Counsel, Am. Soc. Corp. Secs. (v.p., dir.), Am. Law Inst., Stockholder Relations Soc. N.Y., Yale Law Sch. Alumni Assn. (exec. com.), Phi Beta Kappa, Beta Theta Pi, Phi Alpha Theta, Phi Delta Phi. Clubs: New Haven, Lawn, Saucon Valley, Bethlehem, Blooming Grove Hunting and Fishing; Yale (N.Y.C.); Nat. Lawyers (Washington). Home: 1112 Prospect Ave Bethlehem PA 18018 Office: Bethlehem Steel Corp Martin Tower Room 2018 Bethlehem PA 18016

BARNEWALL, GORDON GOUVERNEUR, news analyst, educator; b. Warrenton, Va., Feb. 1, 1924; s. William G. and Nancy G. (Jones) B.; m. Sieglinde Gruber, Sept. 21, 1973; 1 dau. by previous marriage—Ann (dec. 1979). B.S., U. Colo., 1947; M.B.A., Ohio State U., 1949, Ph.D., 1953. Mem. faculty George Washington U., 1950-57; chief of mission OEEC Mission, Athens and Beirut, 1957-60; with ABC-TV, Chgo., 1960-65; mem. faculty Sch. Bus., U. Colo., Denver, 1965—, prof. mktg., 1970—; news analyst, commentator KRMA-TV, Denver, 1970—; mktg. cons. TV and radio stas. Served with AUS, 1942-45. Decorated Silver Star (2), Purple Heart (4). Mem. Am. Mktg. Assn. Club: Cactus. Home: Route 5 Box 450 Evergreen CO 80439 Office: U Colo Sch Bus Denver CO 80202

BARNEY, CHARLES RICHARD, transportation company executive; b. Battle Creek, Mich., June 7, 1935; s. Charles Ross and Helena Ruth (Croose) B.; m. Grace Leone Nightingale, Aug. 16, 1958; children: Richard Nolan, Patricia Lynn. B.A., Mich. State U., 1957; M.B.A., Wayne State U., 1961. Fin. analyst Ford Motor Co., Dearborn, Mich., 1958-65; gen. mgr. RentCo div. Fruehauf Corp., Detroit, 1965-72; pres. Evans Trailer Leasing, Des Plaines, Ill., 1973-77; v.p., gen. mgr. U.S. Rwy. Equipment Co., Des Plaines, 1972-77; pres. Evans Railcar div. Evans Trans. Co., 1978—. Served to 1st lt., inf. U.S. Army, 1958. Mem. Ry. Supply Assn. (dir. 1977-80). Congregationalist. Clubs: Meadows, Met., Union League Chgo. Home: 21076 N Tree Rd Kildeer IL 60047 Office: 2550 Golf Rd Rolling Meadows IL 60008

BARNEY, WILLIAM JOSHUA, JR., gen. contractor; b. N.Y.C., Aug. 17, 1911; s. William Joshua and Lilian C. (Warner) B.; m. Priscilla S. Payne, Feb. 10, 1940. Grad., Choate Sch., 1929; B.S., Yale, 1933. Registered profl. engr., N.Y. With W. J. Barney Corp. (gen. contractors), N.Y.C., 1933—, sec.-treas., 1948—, exec. v.p., 1952-71, chmn. bd., 1971—; pres., treas., dir. W. J. Barney Corp. of Conn., 1957—; pres., sec., trustee W. J. Barney Found., Inc., 1958—; chmn., dir. Middlesex Constrn. Corp., 1976—, W.J. Barney Realty Co., Inc., 1977—; dir. Am. Mut. Liability Ins., Co., 1959—, Am. Policyholders Ins. Co., AM Inc., Am. Mut. Ins. Co. Boston. Bd. dirs. Nat. Horse Show Assn. Am., Ltd., 1956—; dir. U.S. Equestrian Team, Inc., 1956—; Bd. mgrs. Am. Soc. Prevention Cruelty to Animals, 1959-77; bd. dirs. N.Y. Heart Assn., Inc., 1959-70, adv. dir., 1970—; trustee Colony Found., 1962—, Allen-Stevenson Sch., 1968—; employer trustee Metal Lather Local 46 Funds, 1952—. Served from lt. (j.g.) to comdr. USNR, 1940-45. Fellow ASCE; mem. Soc. Cin., U.S. Srs. Golf Assn., Soc. Colonial Wars, Am. Horse Shows Assn. Clubs: Yale, Pinnacle, University, Madison Square Garden (N.Y.C.); Country of Fairfield, Fairfield County Hunt (Fairfield, Conn.); Church (N.Y.C.); EKwanoK Country (Manchester, Vt.). Home: 209 Southport Woods Dr Southport CT 06490 Office: 360 Lexington Ave New York NY 10017

BARNHARDT, WILLIAM HORACE, textile company executive; b. Harrisburg, N.C., Feb. 3, 1903; s. John Addison and Sarah E. (McClellan) B.; m. Margaret McLaughlin, Oct. 8, 1927; children: William M., Nancy (Mrs. William D. Thomas), Charles F. (dec. 1975), John David. B.E., N.C. State Coll. Sch. Textiles, Raleigh, 1923. Pres., treas., dir. Barnhardt Bros. Co., Charlotte, N.C., 1938—, Barnhardt Elastic Corp., 1945—, Barnhardt Internat. Corp., 1945—, Am. Textile Corp., Charlotte, Am. Realty Corp., Charlotte, Novelty Yarns Corp.; chmn., dir. So. Webbing Mills, Inc., Greensboro, N.C.; treas., dir. Providence Acres, Inc., Riverview Acres Corp., Univ. Heights, Inc., Carolinas Corp., Providence Assos., Univ. Plantation, all Charlotte; dir. Standard Bonded Warehouse Co., Charlotte; dir. emeritus N.C. Nat. Bank, Charlotte. Asso. pub.: God's Wisdom and The Holy Bible. Pres., treas., dir. Barnhardt Found., Inc.; past pres., chmn. investment com. N.C. Textile Found.; former trustee Barber-Scotia Coll., Concord, N.C.; former trustee, mem. exec. com., chmn. fin. com. Queen's Coll., Charlotte, 1946-75; former trustee, chmn. fin. com. Crossnore (N.C.) Sch., Johnson C. Smith U., Charlotte; former trustee, nat. chmn. patrons fund Protestant Radio and TV Center, Atlanta; life trustee Charlotte Country Day Sch.; former trustee, treas. Greater Charlotte Found.; former chmn. Found. U. N.C. at Charlotte, 1963-66; mem. regional com. Boy Scouts Am.; mem. adv. council Mecklenburg council; past v.p., chmn. capital funds bd. United Community Services; past chmn. exec. and bldg. coms. Hist. Found., Montreat, N.C.; campaign chmn. Charlotte Citizens for Freedom Park; mem. bldg. com., past pres. Charlotte YMCA; former mem. exec. com. Interstate YMCA; former deacon, elder, vice moderator Myers Park Presbyterian Ch. Recipient Silver Beaver award Boy Scouts Am., 1947, Silver Antelope, 1949; Algernon Sydney Sullivan award Queens Coll., 1953; Service Youth award Charlotte YMCA, 1954; NCCJ award, 1966; named Man of South Dixie Bus. Publ. poll, 1973; various bldgs. named in his honor. Mem. N.C. Textile Mfrs. Assn. (past dir.), Royal Soc. Knights Carrousel (governing council, king 1955), Carolina Yarn Assn. (pres. 1946), Newcomen Soc. N.Am., Phi Kappa Phi, Pi Kappa Alpha. Presbyterian. Clubs: Charlotte Textile, Quail Hollow Country (pres. 1963, 64, 65), Executives (pres. 1956), Charlotte City (past v.p.), Charlotte Country (past v.p.); Metropolitan, New York Athletic (N.Y.C.); Travelers Century. Home: 1512 Queens Rd W Charlotte NC 28207 Office: NC Nat Bank Bldg Charlotte NC 28202

BARNHARDT, ZEB ELONZO, JR., lawyer; b. Winston-Salem, N.C., Dec. 28, 1941; s. Zeb Elonzo and Katie Sue (Taylor) B.; m. Jane Elizabeth Black, June 19, 1965; children: Daniel Black, Kathleen Martin. A.B., Duke U., 1964; J.D., Vanderbilt U., 1969. Bar: N.C. bar 1969. Assoc. Womble, Carlyle, Sandridge & Rice, Winston-Salem, 1969-75, partner, 1975—. Mem. alumni admissions adv. com. Duke U., 1970-72; bd. dirs. Industries for Blind, Winston-Salem, 1973—, v.p., Winston-Salem, 1983—; bd. dirs. Goodwill Industries, Winston-Salem, 1973-80, The Little Theatre, Winston-Salem, 1979—; asst. treas. The Little Theatre, 1980, treas., 1981-82, v.p., 1983; adv. bd. Salvation Army, Winston-Salem, 1973—, chmn., 1979-80; com. mem. Winston-Salem Found., 1975—, vice chmn., 1978-80, chmn., 1983—. Served with USN, 1964-66. Recipient Disting. Service award as Young Man of Yr. Winston-Salem Jaycees, 1974; Disting. Alumni award Duke U., 1979. Mem. N.C. Bar Assn., Forsyth County Bar Assn., ABA, Am. Judicature Soc., Winston-Salem Jaycees (pres. 1973-74, life mem.), N.C. Jaycees (regional dir. 1974-75, legal counsel 1975-77), Greater Winston-Salem C. of C. (dir. 1973-74). Democrat. Methodist. Home: 932 Kenleigh Circle Winston-Salem NC 27106 Office: 2400 Wachovia Bldg 301 N Main St Winston-Salem NC 27101

BARNHART, CHARLES ELMER, educator; b. Windsor, Ill., Jan. 25, 1923; s. Elmer and Irma (Smysor) B.; m. Norma McCarty, Dec. 28, 1946 (dec. Dec. 25, 1970); children: John D., Charles E., Norman R.; m. Jean M. Hutton, Jan. 12, 1973. B.S. in Agr, Purdue U., 1945; M.S., Ia. State U., 1948, Ph.D., 1954. Mem. faculty U. Ky., Lexington, 1948—, asso. prof. animal sci., 1955-57, prof., 1957—, also dean, dir. exptl. sta. and coop. extension service, 1969—; Bd. dirs. Ky. Bd. Agr., Ky. State Fair and Expn. Center, Ky. Tobacco Research Bd.; mem. Gov.'s Council on Rural Devel.; pres. So. Assn. Agrl. Scientist, 1982-83. Named Man of Yr. in Ky. Agr. Progressive Farmer, 1962, Man of Yr. for Ky. Agr. Ky. Agrl. Communicators, 1979. Mem. Am. Soc. Animal Sci., Ky. Hist. Soc., Sigma Xi, Epsilon Sigma Phi, Gamma Sigma Delta., Omicron Delta Kappa. Methodist. Club: Mason (32 deg. Shriner). Patentee in field. Home: 1017 Turkey Foot Rd Lexington KY 40502

BARNHART, CLARENCE LEWIS, lexicographer, editor; b. nr. Plattsburg, Mo., Dec. 30, 1900; s. Franklin Chester and Frances Norah (Elliott) B.; m. Frances Knox, Feb. 21, 1931; children: Robert, David. Ph.B., U. Chgo., 1930, postgrad., 1934-37. Editor Scott, Foresman & Co., 1929-45, War Dept., 1943, Random House, 1945-48; founder Clarence L. Barnhart, Inc.; Hon. research asso. Inst. Psychol. Research, Columbia, 1945, 46. Author: (with Leonard Bloomfield) Let's Read: A Linguistic Approach, 1961; author (with R. Barnhart); also pub.: Let's Read 1, 2, 3, 1963, 4, 5, 6, 1964, 7, 8, 1965, 9, 1966, Let's Look series 1-9, 1966, (with S. Steinmetz and R.K. Barnhart) The Barnhart Dictionary of New English from 1963, 1973, The Second Barnhart Dictionary of New English, 1980; Editor: Thorndike Century Junior Dictionary, 1935, 42, Thorndike Century Senior Dictionary, 1941, Dictionary of United States Army Terms, 1943, American College Dictionary, 1947, Thorndike-Barnhart Comprehensive Desk Dictionary, 1951, Thorndike-Barnhart Junior Dictionary, 1952, Thorndike-Barnhart High School Dictionary, 1952, New Century Cyclopedia of Names, 1954, New Century Handbook of English Literature, 1956, Thorndike-Barnhart Advanced Junior Dictionary, 1957, Thorndike-Barnhart Beginning Dictionary, 1964, Thorndike-Barnhart Intermediate Dictionary, 1971; Thorndike-Barnhart Advanced Dictionary, 1973; editor: (with Robert K. Barnhart) The World Book Dictionary, 1976. Recipient War Dept. certificate appreciation, 1946. Mem. Am. Dialect Soc., Linguistic Soc., Modern Lang. Assn., Nat. Council Tchrs. English, Am. Name Soc. (past pres.), Phi Beta Kappa. Clubs: University (N.Y.C.); Century Association; Authors (London). Office: Box 250 1 Stone Pl Bronxville NY 10708

BARNHART, RAY ANDERSON, federal agency administrator; b. Elgin, Ill., Jan. 12, 1928; s. O.E. and Alice B.; m. Jacqueline Price; children: Mrs. Whitney Ziegler, Mrs. Mark Rousselot. B.A., Marietta Coll., 1950; M.A., U. Houston, 1951. Salesman Barmore Ins. Agy., Inc., Pasadena, 1978-81; commnr. Tex. Dept. Hwys. and Public Transp., Austin, 1979-81; fed. hwy. adminstr. U.S. Dept. Transp., Washington, 1981—. Mem. Pasadena City Council, 1965-69; mem. Tex. Ho. Reps., 1973-74; chmn. Harris County Republican Com., 1975-77, Tex. Rep. Com., 1977-79; co-chmn. Tex. Citizens for Reagan, 1976. Served with AUS, 1946-47. Mem. Tex. Turnpike Authority (dir. 1979-81). Office: 400 7th St SW Washington DC 20590

BARNHART, RICHARD MILLEN, JR., art historian; b. Sewickley, Pa., Feb. 4, 1934; s. Richard Millen and Ruth Seymour (White) B.; m. Suzanne Warner, Aug. 27, 1960; children: Cathleen, Amanda; m. Joan C. Panetti, Dec. 16, 1975; children: Clara Elizabeth, Johanna Panetti. Student, U. Pitts., 1960-61, Cin. Art Acad., 1952-53, Pa. Acad. Fine Arts, 1956-59; B.A., Stanford U., 1963; M.A., Princeton U., 1966, Ph.D., 1967; M.A. (hon.), Yale U., 1979. Lectr., Yale U., 1967-68, asst. prof. art history, 1968-73, asso. prof., 1973-75, prof., 1975—, Princeton U., 1975-79; vis. asso. prof. Harvard U. summer sch., 1973; cons. in field; research asso. Met. Mus. Art, 1976-77; spl. cons. Chinese painting Indpls. Art Mus., 1970-71; mem. com. studies of Chinese civilization Am. Council Learned Socs., 1975-76. Author: Marriage of the Lord of the River, 1970, Wintry Forest, Old Trees, 1972, Peach Blossom Spring: Gardens and Flowers in Chinese Painting, 1983, Along the Border of Heaven: Sung and Yuan Paintings from the C.C. Wang Family Collection, 1983; editorial bd.: Archives of Asian Art, 1981—; co-editor, 1983-84; editor, 1984—. Served with U.S. Army, 1953-56. Mem. Phi Beta Kappa. Home: 5 Saint Ronan Terr New Haven CT 06511 Office: Box 2009 56 High St Yale Univ New Haven CT 06520

BARNHART, WILLIAM RUPP, clergyman, educator; b. Saegerstown, Pa., Feb. 7, 1903; s. John L. and Emma A. (Rupp) B.; m. Eleanor Welch Lyles, Sept. 1, 1927 (dec. July 1981); children: Eleanor Hoyle, Joanne Sanford. A.B., Johns Hopkins U., 1923; A.M., Columbia U., 1924; student, Union Theol. Sem., 1923-25, 1926-27; D.D., Pacific U., 1938. Student asst. Madison Ave. Presbyn. Ch., N.Y.C., 1926-27; prof. philosophy and religion Pacific U., Oreg., 1927-30; head dept. religion Hood Coll., Frederick, Md., 1930-47, head dept. religion and philosophy, 1947-58; minister Circular Congregational Ch., Charleston, S.C., 1958-68; minister emeritus Circular Congl. Ch., 1968—; exec. sec. Fedn. of Chs., Washington, 1940-41; ordained to ministry Congl. Ch., 1930; mem. Potomoc Synod of Evang. and Ref. Ch., 1930-58; past mem. Edn. and Research of Fed. Council of Churches of Christ in Am.; mem. Inter-Faith com. on Religious Life in Nation's Capital, 1940-42; lectr. religious emphasis weeks at various univs. and colls.; weekly religious broadcaster, 1958-80; mem. Md.-Del. Council Chs., 1942-58, Univ. Christian Mission Team sent out by Fed. Council Chs. of Christ, 1946-49, preaching mission teams; lectr. ministerial confs. Contbr. articles to religious jours. Bd. dirs. Community Chest, Washington, 1940-42; trustee S.C. State Coll., 1972—. Mem. Am. Philos. Assn., Nat. Assn. Bibl. Instrs., Charleston Ministerial Assn. (pres. 1964). Clubs: University (Balt.); Interchurch (Washington) (pres. 1948-49); Rotary, Charleston Country (Charleston, S.C.). Home: 16 Broughton Rd Charleston SC 29407 *Life has developed three qualities which reveal its purpose. First, the development of personality. Second, the development of intelligence as represented by Socrates and Einstein. Third, the development of love as represented by Jesus. Life is God's venture in developing intelligent, loving personalities. This means we should strive to develop all of the intelligence and love that we can and help others to do likewise. Our imperative need is intelligent good will.*

BARNHILL, HOWARD EUGENE, insurance company executive; b. Nankin, Ohio, Oct. 2, 1923; s. William Wallace and Juliaette (Garver) B.; m. Evelyn Lucille Poorman, Aug. 24, 1944; children: Eric Stephen, Phillip William. B.A., Ashland (Ohio) Coll., 1946; grad., Advanced Mgmt. Program, Harvard U., 1967. C.L.U. With Mut. Ins. Co. N.Y., 1946-72, sr. v.p., 1969-72; pres., chief exec. officer N.Am. Life & Casualty Co., Mpls., 1972-79, chmn. bd., pres., chief exec. officer, 1979—; dir. Nat. City Bank, Mpls., Downtown Devel. Corp. Bd. dirs. Walker Art Center, Mpls., United Way Mpls. Served to lt. USNR, 1943-46, 50-52. Mem. Life Ins. Mktg. Research Assn. (past chmn.), Greater Mpls. Area C. of C. (past chmn.). Mem. Community Ch. Clubs: Minikahda, Minneapolis, Wayzata Country. Office: 1750 Hennepin Ave Minneapolis MN 55403 *

BARNOFF, ROBERT MARK, civil engineering educator; b. Punxsutawney, Pa., Aug. 28, 1926; s. Joseph A. and Ruth A. (Morris) B.; m. Norma Gugliemi; children: Joni, Janice, Mark, Joseph. B.S., Pa. State U., 1951, M.S., 1956; Ph.D., Carnegie Inst. Tech., 1966. Steel detailer Am. Bridge Co., 1951-52; constrn. engr. John Mohr & Sons, 1952-53; bridge designer Gannett Fleming Corddry & Capenter, 1953-55; from instr. to prof. civil engring. Pa. State U., University Park, 1955-79, prof., chmn. dept. civil engring., 1979—; cons. structural and found. engring. Contbr. articles on civil engring. to profl. jours. Served with USNR, 1944-46. NSF sci faculty fellow, 1965-66. Mem. Transp. Research Bd., ASCE, Am. Concrete Inst., Am. Soc. Engring. Edn., ASTM, Sigma Xi, Tau Beta Pi. Office: 212 Sackett Bldg Pa State U University Park PA 16802

BARNOTHY, JENO MICHAEL, physicist; b. Kassa, Hungary, Oct. 28, 1904; came to U.S., 1948, naturalized, 1954; s. Julius Preinreich and Ida (Rupprecht) B.; m. Madeleine Forro, Dec. 24, 1938. Ph.D., Royal Hungarian U., Budapest, 1933. Prof. physics Royal Hungarian U., 1933-48, Barat Coll., Lake Forest, Ill., 1948-53; chief physicist Nuclear Instruments & Chem. Co., Chgo., 1953-55; owner, tech. dir. Forro Sci. Co., Evanston, Ill., 1955—; pres. Biomagnetic Research Found., 1961—. Author: Experimental Physics, 1945; Contbr. numerous articles to profl. jours. Recipient medal Royal Hungarian Acad. Sci., 1938; Eotvos medal, 1947. Mem. Am., German astron. socs., Astron. Soc. Pacific, Internat. Astron. Union, Biophys. Soc., Am. Phys. Soc. Constructed 1st cosmic ray telescope, 1928; developer Fib steady state cosmological theory, gravitational lens explanation of quasars. Patentee nuclear instrumentation. Address: 833 Lincoln St Evanston IL 60201

BARNOUW, ERIK, educator, writer; b. The Hague, Holland, June 23, 1908; came to U.S., 1919, naturalized, 1928; s. Adriaan Jacob and Anne Eliza (Midgley) B.; m. Dorothy Maybelle Beach, June 3, 1939; children—Jeffrey, Susanna, Karen. A.B., Princeton, 1929. Radio writer and dir. Erwin Wasey & Co. (advt.), 1931-35, Arthur Kudner (advt.), 1935-37; writer, editor CBS, 1939-40; script editor NBC, 1942-44; commentator overseas br. OWI, 1943-44; supr. edn. unit Armed Forces Radio Service, War Dept., 1944-45; mem. faculty Columbia, 1946—, prof. dramatic arts in charge film, radio and TV, 1964-69; editor Center for Mass Communication, Columbia U. Press, 1948-72; chief motion picture, broadcasting and recorded sound div. Library of Congress, Washington, 1978-81; fellow Woodrow Wilson Center for Scholars, 1976; cons. communications USPHS, 1947-50. Occasional writer, adapter: radio and TV series Theater Guild, 1945-61; writer, producer: series Decision, Nat. Ednl. TV, 1957-59; Author: 3 act play Open Collars, 1928, Handbook of Radio Writing, 2d edit, 1947, Handbook of Radio Production, 1949, Mass Communication, 1956, The Television Writer, 1962, (with S. Krishnaswamy) Indian Film, 1963, 2d edit., 1980, A History of Broadcasting in The U.S.: A Tower in Babel, vol. 1, 1966, The Golden Web, vol. 2, 1968, The Image Empire, vol. 3, 1970 (Bancroft prize 1971), Documentary: A History of the Nonfiction Film, 1974, rev. edit., 1983, Tube of Plenty: The Evolution of American Television, 1975, rev. edit., 1982, The Sponsor: Notes on a Modern Potentate, 1978, The Magician and The Cinema, 1981; Editor: Radio Drama in Action, 1945. Recipient Gavel award for Decision films Am. Bar Assn., 1959, Eastman-Kodak gold medal, 1982; Fulbright Research fellow, India, 1961-62; Guggenheim fellow, 1969; JDR 3d fellow, 1972; Indo-Am. fellow, 1978-79. Mem. Authors League Am. (sec. 1949-53), Radio Writers Guild (pres. 1947-49), Writers Guild Am. (chmn. 1957-59), Acad. TV Arts and Scis. (bd. govs. 1966-68), Am. Civil Liberties Union, PEN Club, Pub. Affairs Com. (mem. bd.), Internat. Film Seminars (pres. 1960-68), Phi Beta Kappa. Address: 39 Claremont Ave New York NY 10027

BARNS, WILLIAM DERRICK, historian, educator; b. Fayette County, Pa., Apr. 3, 1917; s. William Post and Lida (Williams) B.; m. Doretha Mae Clayton, Sept. 3, 1947. A.B., Pa. State U., 1939, M.A., 1940; Ph.D., W.Va. U., 1947. Instr. history Pa. State U., 1939-40, vis. prof., 1949; mem. faculty W.Va. U., Morgantown, 1940—, prof. history, 1977—; vis. prof. Marshall U., Huntington, W.Va., 1951, McMaster U., Hamilton, Ont., Can., 1957, 59, 61. Author: The Granger and Populist Movements in West Virginia, 1873-1914, 1947, Highlights in West Virginia's Agricultural History, 1863-1963, 1963, The West Virginia State Grange: The First Century, 1873-1973, 1973; also articles. Field agt. Am. Friends Service Com., 1944-46; co-founder, dir. W.Va. Civil Liberties Union, 1970-79, v.p., 1979-81. Mem. Am. Hist. Assn., Orgn. Am. Historians, Agrl. History Soc., AAUP (co-founder W.Va. conf. 1961, dir. 1961-71), W.Va. Hist. Assn. Coll. and Univ. Tchrs. (co-founder 1959, pres. 1962-63, archivist, adv. 1973—), English Speaking Union, Phi Kappa Phi, Phi Alpha Theta, Pi Gamma Mu, Alpha Tau Omega. Libertarian. Mem. Soc. of Friends. Office: Dept History WVA Univ Morgantown WV 26506

BARNSLEY, ALAN GABRIEL *See* **FIELDING, GABRIEL**

BARNSTONE, WILLIS (ROBERT BARNSTONE), language and literature educator, editor; b. Lewiston, Maine, Nov. 13, 1927; s. Robert Carl and Dora E. (Lempert) B.; m. Helle Phaedra Tzalopoulou, June 1, 1949; children: Akiki Dora, Robert Vassilios, Anthony Dimitrios. B.A. cum laude, Bowdoin Coll., Lewiston, 1948, D.Litt. (hon.), 1981; M.A. with high honors, Columbia U., 1956; Ph.D. with distinction, Yale U., 1958. Tchr., Anavrita Acad., Athens, Greece, 1949; instr. French, U. Md. overseas program, Perigueux, France, 1955-56; asst. prof. Spanish, Wesleyan U., 1958-62; mem. faculty Ind. U., Bloomington, 1962—, prof. comparative lit., Spanish, Portuguese,, 1968—, prof. comparative lit. and Latin Am. studies, 1972-75; vis. prof. U. Mass., Amherst, summer 1965, U. Calif., Riverside, 1968-69; O'Conner prof. lit. Colgate U., spring 1971; Fulbright lectr. Professorado de Avenida de Mayo, Buenos Aires, 1975-76, Fgn. Lang. Inst., Peking, 1984-85; vis. prof. Summer Inst. Lit., U. Tex., Austin, summer 1977. Author: From This White Island, 1960, Eighty Poems of Antonio Machado, 1960, Sappho, 1964, Greek Lyric Poetry, 1962, The Poems of Saint John of the Cross, 1969, Spanish Poetry, 1971; A, Day in the Country, 1971, China Poems, 1976, New Faces of China, 1973, Poems of Mao Tse-tung, 1972, The Unknown Light: The Poems of Fray Luis de Leon, 1979, Overheard, 1979, A Snow Salmon Reached The Andes Lake, 1980, Borges at Eighty: Conversations, 1982, A Bird of Paper: Poems of Vicente Aleixandre, 1982, The Poetics of Ecstasy: Variaties of Ekstasis from Sappho to Borges, 1983; others A Snow Salmon Reached The Andes Lake; editor: Modern European Poetry,

1966, Eighteen Texts, 1973; contbg. editor: Books Abroad. Served with U.S. Army, 1954-56. Guggenheim fellow, 1961-62; Am. Council Learned Socs. fellow, 1969-70; NEH fellow, 1979-80; recipient Cecil Hemley Meml. award Poetry Soc. Am., 1969, Lucille Medwick Meml. award, 1978. Mem. PEN. Democrat. Address: Dept Comparative Literature Indiana Univ Bloomington IN 47401

BARNUM, JOHN WALLACE, lawyer; b. N.Y.C., Aug. 25, 1928; s. Walter and Frances (Long) B.; m. Nancy Russell Grinnell, Sept. 13, 1958; children: Alexander Stone, Sarah Kip, Cameron Long. B.A., Yale U., 1949, LL.B., 1957. Analyst 1st Banking Corp., Tangier, Morocco, 1950; rep. Bache & Co., London and Paris, 1951-52; asso. law firm Cravath, Swaine & Moore, N.Y.C., 1957-62, mem., 1963-71; gen. counsel U.S. Dept. Transp., Washington, 1971-73, undersec., 1973-74, dep. sec., 1974-77; resident fellow Am. Enterprise Inst. for Pub. Policy Research, Washington, 1977-78, vis. fellow, 1978—; mem. firm White & Case, Washington, 1978—; Lectr. Practising Law Inst.; U.S. del. Inter-Am. Comml. Arbitration Commn., 1969-71; adv. mem. Council on Wage and Price Stability, 1974-77; mem. council Adminstrv. Conf. U.S., 1973-77; dir. Palmer Nat. Bank, Washington, 1982—. Chmn. bd. Internat. Play Group, 1962-77; bd. dirs., exec. com. N.Y.C. Center Music and Drama, 1969-75. Served as lt. AUS, 1952-54. Mem. Am Arbitration Assn. (bd. dirs., exec. com. 1968—), N.Y. State (exec. com., chmn. antitrust law sect. 1969-70), Am., D.C., Fed. bar. assns., Am. Bar Found., Assn. Bar City N.Y., Union Internationale des Avocats. Clubs: Metropolitan, Fed. City, Nat. Aviation (Washington); Waquoit Bay Yacht, Chevy Chase; Amateur Ski, India House, N.Y. Yacht (N.Y.C.). Home: 5175 Tilden St NW Washington DC 20016 Office: 1747 Pennsylvania Ave NW Washington DC 20006

BARNUM, WILLIAM LAIRD, pedodontist; b. Medford, Oreg., Nov. 12, 1916; s. William Henry and Jessie Amelia (Eifert) B.; m. Amy B. Elliott, June 20, 1937; children: William Laird, Robert Elliott. D.M.D., U. Oreg., 1940; postgrad. in Pedodontics, Coll. Physicians and Surgeons, San Francisco, 1946. Gen. practice dentistry, Portland, Oreg., 1940-45, specializing in pedodontics, Portland, 1945-64, Medford, 1964-80; mem. dental staff Rogue Valley Meml. Hosp., 1964—; dir. Dental Health Program, Portland Pub. Schs., 1946-64; instr. pedodontics and dental hygiene U. Oreg. Dental Sch., Portland, 1945-60. Pres. Adminstrs. and Suprs. Assn. for Portland Pub. Schs., 1958-59; chmn. health div. Portland Community Council, 1961-62. Fellow Internat., Am. colls. dentists; mem. Am. Soc. Dentistry for Children (pres. Oreg. unit 1952-53), ADA (chmn. council on journalism 1952-56), Oreg. Dental Soc. (editor Oreg. Dental Jour. 1949-53), So. Oreg. Dental Soc. (pres. 1969-70), Am. Dental Interfraternity Council (pres. 1971-72), Xi Psi Phi (supreme pres. 1965-67, supreme sec.-treas. 1970—, editor Quar. 1953-58). Republican. Clubs: Masons, Knife and Fork. Home: 245 Yale Dr Medford OR 97504

BAROCCI, ROBERT LOUIS, advertising executive; b. Milw., Feb. 8, 1942; s. Louis F. and Mary H. (Mesich) B.; m. Nancy Gail Brussat, Aug. 22, 1964; children: Robert, Candace. B.S., U. Wis., 1963; M.B.A., Harvard U., 1965. Client services rep. Leo Burnett U.S.A., Chgo., 1965-76, mng. dir., London, 1976-79; regional mng. dir., dir. Leo Burnett Co., Inc., Chgo., 1979-83; pres. Leo Burnett Internat., 1983—. Mem. Phi Beta Kappa. Roman Catholic. Office: Prudential Plaza Chicago IL 60601

BAROFF, GEORGE STANLEY, psychologist; b. Bronx, N.Y., Nov. 27, 1924; s. Irving and Ida (Herman) B.; m. Rose Kislin, June 15, 1952; children—Marina Binet, Roy James. B.S. in Zoology, George Washington U., 1948, M.A. in Clin. Psychology, 1950; Ph.D., N.Y. U., 1955. Research psychologist dept. med. genetics N.Y. State Psychiat. Inst., 1952-60; chief clin. psychologist Vineland (N.J.) Tng. Sch., 1960-63; asso. prof. psychology U. N.C., Chapel Hill, 1963-67, prof., 1967—, dir. devel. disabilties tng. inst., 1964—. Author: Mental Retardation: Nature, Cause and Management, 1974; Contbr. articles to profl. jours. Served with U.S. Army, 1943-45. Mem. Am. Psychol. Assn., Am. Assn. Mental Deficiency, N.C. Psychol. Assn., Am. Assn. Edn. Severly /Profoundly Handicapped. Jewish. Home: 417 Granville Rd Chapel Hill NC 27514 Office: Univ of NC Chapel Hill NC 27514

BARON, CAROLYN, editor, author; b. Detroit, Jan. 25, 1940; d. Gabriel and Viola (Petlanski) Cohn; m. Richard W. Baron, Nov. 14, 1975. B.A. in Liberal Arts, U. Mich., 1961. Editor, editorial prodn. dir. Holt, Rinehart & Winston, N.Y.C., 1965-71; mng. editor E.P. Dutton Co., Inc., N.Y.C., 1971-74, exec. editor, 1974-75; adminstrv. editor Pocket Books, Simon & Schuster, N.Y.C., 1975-78, v.p., editor-in-chief, 1978-79, Crown Pubs., N.Y.C., 1979-81; v.p., pub. Dell Pub. Co., N.Y.C., 1981—. Author: The History of Labor Unions in the U.S, 1971, Re-Entry Game, 1974, Board Sailboats: A Buying Guide, 1977; Contbr. articles to mags. Mem. Women's Media Group. Club: Shelter Island Yacht. Home: New York NY Home: Shelter Island Heights NY Office: 1 Dag Hammarskjold Plaza New York NY 10017

BARON, CHARLES HILLEL, lawyer, educator; b. Phila., Aug. 18, 1936; s. Samuel A. and Rose (Bailinky) B.; m. Irma Elaine Frankel, June 15, 1958; children: Jessica Susan, Ira Benjamin, David Hume. A.B. in Philosophy with honors, U. Pa., 1958, Ph.D., 1972; LL.B., Harvard U., 1961. Bar: Pa. bar 1967, U.S. Supreme Ct. bar 1970, Mass. bar 1972. Asst. prof. law U. Pa., 1965-66; asso. firm Blank Rome Klaus & Comisky, Phila., 1966-68; chief law reform, consumer's adv. Community Legal Services, Inc., Phila., 1968-70; asso. prof. law Boston Coll., 1970-74, prof., 1974—, asso. dean, 1972-74; exec. dir. Resource Center Consumers Legal Services, 1975-77; dir. Omnidentix, Inc. Author: (with M. Saks) The Use, Nonuse, and Misuse of Applied Social Research, 1980; contbr. articles to profl. jours. Chmn. Cheltenham Twp. (Pa.) Democratic Party, 1966-68; mem. Mass. Health Facilities Appeals Bd., 1974-75; chmn. Mass. Gov.'s Adv. Com. on Prepaid Legal Services, 1978—; bd. dirs. CEPA Found. Recipient various community awards; U. Pa. fellow, 1961-63. Mem. Am. Assn. Law Schs., Soc. Am. Law Tchrs., ABA, Am. Soc. Law and Medicine (bd. editors Am. Jour. Law and Medicine 1978—, dir.), Civil Liberties Union Mass. (dir., v.p.), ACLU. Jewish. Home: 60 Grove Hill Ave Newtonville MA 02160 Office: 885 Centre St Newton Centre MA 02159

BARON, JUDSON RICHARD, educator; b. N.Y.C., July 28, 1924; s. Louis and Leah (Berzin) B.; m. Selma Francine Wasserman, Sept. 4, 1949; children—Jason Roberts, Jeffrey Scott. B.Aero. Engring., N.Y. U., 1947; S.M., Mass. Inst. Tech., 1948, Sc.D., 1956. Stress analyst Change Vought Aircraft Co., 1947; mem. research staff Mass. Inst. Tech., 1948-54, research asst., 1954-56, mem. faculty, 1957—, prof. aero. and astronautics, 1957—; cons. in Field, 1957—. Served with AUS, 1943-46. Decorated Bronze Star. Mem. Am. Inst. Aeros. and Astronautics, AAUP, Sigma Xi, Tau Beta Pi. Home: 7 Gould Rd Lexington MA 02173 Office: 77 Massachusetts Ave Cambridge MA 02139

BARON, MARTIN RAYMOND, psychology educator; b. Stamford, Conn., Oct. 27, 1922; s. Harry Isaac and Gertrude (Sondak) B.; m. Shirley Elaine Thalberg, July 28, 1945; children: Carol Ann (Mrs. David Lawrence Quirke), Cynthia Ellen (Mrs. John Adrian Keohane), Marcia Wendy. B.A., Yale U., 1943; M.A., State U. Iowa, 1948, Ph.D., 1949. Asst. prof. psychology Kent (O.) State U., 1949-53, assoc. prof., 1953-58, prof., 1958-71, U. Louisville, 1971—, chmn. dept. psychology, 1971-72, acting dean, 1972-73, asst. v.p. for acad. affairs, 1973-76, asst. exec. v.p. planning, 1976-81. Assoc. Editor: Behavioral Sci, 1973—; Contbr. articles to psychol. publs. Served with AUS, 1943-46. Mem. Am., Midwestern, Southeastern psychol. assns., So. Soc. Philosophy and Psychology, Sigma Xi. Home: 1611 Spring Dr Apt 2C Louisville KY 40205 Office: Dept Psychology U Louisville Louisville KY 40292

BARON, MELVIN LEON, consulting engineer; b. Bklyn., Feb. 27, 1927; s. Frank and Esther (Hirskowitz) B.; m. Muriel Wicker, Dec. 24, 1950; children—Jaclyn Adele, Susan Gail. B.C.E., CCNY, 1948; M.S., Columbia U., 1949, Ph.D., 1953. Lic. profl. engr., N.Y., Mass. Structural designer Corbett-Tinghir Co., N.Y.C., 1949-50; research assoc. civil engring. Columbia U., 1951-53, asst. prof., 1953-57, adj. assoc. prof., 1958-61, adj. prof., 1961—; chief engr. Paul Weidlinger, N.Y.C., 1957-60, assoc., 1960-64, ptnr., dir. research, 1964—; also v.p. Advanced Computer Techniques Corp., N.Y.C., 1962-66; Formerly chmn. adv. panel engring. mechanics program NSF. Author: (with M.G. Salvadori) Numerical Methods in Engineering, 1952; Editor: Jour. Engring. Mechs. Div. ASCE, 1970—; Contbr. articles profl. jours. Recipient Spirit of St. Louis Jr. award Am. Soc. M.E., 1958; J. James R. Croes medal ASCE, 1963; Walter L. Huber Research prize, 1966; Arthur M. Wellington prize, 1969; Nathan M. Newmark medal, 1977. Fellow ACSE (exec. com. engring. mechanics div. 1966-69, 72-76, mem. mgmt. group C engring. mechanics div. 1972-76, mem. tech. activities com. 1974), ASME; mem. N.Y. Acad. Scis., U.S. Nat. Acad. Engring. (chmn. com. computational mechanics), U.S. Nat. Com. on Theoretical and Applied Mechanics, AAAS, Sigma Xi. Home: 3801 Hudson Manor Terr Riverdale Bronx NY 10463 Office: 110 E 59th St New York NY 10022

BARON, RICHARD WARREN, publisher, writer; b. N.Y.C., Apr. 4, 1923; s. Samuel T. and Mabel B.; m. Pamela Stearns, Sept. 4, 1946; children—Susan, Wendy, Vicki; m. Virginia Olsen, Feb. 15, 1963; children—Amy, Richard Thomas; m. Carolyn Cohn, Nov. 14, 1975. Student, U. N.C., 1940-42, N.Y. U., 1943. Vice pres., dir. Royal Paper Corp., 1947-59, Prodn. Research Corp., 1951-53; pres., chmn. Dial Press, Inc., 1958-68; pres., pub. Richard W. Baron Pub. Co., Inc., N.Y.C., 1969—; dir., pub. Subsistence Press, 1975-77; pres. N.Y. Book Pub. Co., 1979—. Author: guide to sailing Raid!: The Untold Story of Patton's Secret Mission. Served to 1st lt., inf. AUS, World War II. Clubs: Players (N.Y.C.); P.E.N., Shelter Island Yacht. Home: New York NY Home: Shelter Island Heights NY 11965

BARON, SALO W., educator; b. Tarnow, Austria, May 26, 1895; came to U.S., 1926; s. Elias and Minna (Wittmayer) B.; m. Jeannette G. Meisel, June 12, 1934; children: Shoshana Baron Tancer, Tobey Baron Gitelle. Ph.D., U. Vienna, 1917, Polit. Sc.D., 1922, Jur.D., 1923; Rabbi, Jewish Theol. Sem., Vienna, 1920; D.H.L., Hebrew Union Coll., Cin., 1944, Spertus Coll., Chgo., 1975, Jewish Theol. Sem. Am., 1983; LL.D., Dropsie U., 1962; Litt.D., Rutgers U., 1963, Columbia U., 1964; golden doctorate Vienna, 1969; Ph.D., U. Tel-Aviv, 1970, Hebrew U., Jerusalem, 1975; L.H.D., Yeshiva U., 1975, Bard Coll., 1979. Lectr. history Juedisches Paedagogium, Vienna, 1919-25; vis. lectr. Jewish Inst. Religion, N.Y.C., 1926, prof. history, acting librarian, 1927-30, dir. dept. advanced studies, 1928-30; prof. Jewish history, lit. and instns. Columbia, 1930-63, prof. emeritus, 1963—, dir., 1950-68, dir. emeritus, 1968—; Rauschenbusch lectr. Colgate-Rochester Div. Sch., 1944; vis. prof. history Jewish Theol. Sem., 1954-71, Hebrew U., Jerusalem, 1958, Rutgers U., 1964-69; vis. prof. dept. religious studies Brown U., 1966-68; Pres. Conf. Jewish Social Studies, 1941-55, 59-68, hon. pres., 1955-59, 68—; pres. Jewish Cultural Reconstrn., Inc., 1947-80; chmn. commn. survey Nat. Jewish Welfare Bd., 1947-49; chmn. library information Am. Jewish Com.; chmn. cultural adv. com. Conf. Jewish Material Claims against Germany, 1953-55; corr. mem. internat. com. for sci. history mankind UNESCO, 1953—. Author: Die Judenfrage auf dem Wiener Kongress, 1920, Die Politische Theorie Ferdinand Lasalle's, 1923, Azariah de Rossi's Attitude to Life, 1927, The Israelitic Population under the Kings (Hebrew), 1933, A Social and Religious History of the Jews, 3 vols, 1937, rev. edit. vols. I-XVIII, 1952-83, Bibliography of Jewish Social Studies, 1938-39, 1941, The Jewish Community, 3 vols, 1942, Modern Nationalism and Religion, 1947, The Jews of the United States, 1790-1840, (with Joseph L. Blau), 3 vols.) The Jews of the United States, 1963, The Russian Jew under Tsars and Soviets, 1964, rev. edit., 1976, History and Jewish Historians, 1964, Ancient and Medieval Jewish History: Essays, 1972, Steeled by Adversity: Essays and Addresses on American Jewish Life, 1971; Editor: Jewish Studies in Memory of G.A. Kohut, 1935, Jewish Social Studies, quar, 1939—, Essays on Maimonides, 1941, (with George S. Wise) Violence and Defense in the Jewish Experience, 1977, (with Isaac E. Barzilay) Jubilee Vol. of American Academy for Jewish Research, 2 vols, 1980; Contbr. articles to various publs. Trustee Jewish Inst. Religion, 1937-55; pres. acad. council Hebrew U., 1940-50; bd. govs. U. Tel-Aviv, 1968—, U. Haifa, 1971—. Decorated knight Order of Merit Republic of Italy, 1972; Salo Wittmayer Baron professorship in Jewish history, culture and society named in his honor Columbia U., 1979; hon. fellow Oxford Ctr. for Postgrad. Hebrew Studies, 1983. Fellow Am. Acad. Jewish Research (pres. 1940-43, 58-63, 67, 69-79, hon. pres. 1980—), Am. Acad. Arts and Scis.; mem. Am. Jewish Hist. Soc. (pres. 1953-55), Am. Hist. Assn., Soc. Bibl. Lit. Honored by publ. Festschriften Essays on Jewish Life and Thought, 1959, Salo Wittmayer Baron Jubilee Vol., 3 vols., 1974. Home: Honey Hill Rd RD 1 Box 473 Canaan CT 06018 Office: 420 W 118th St New York NY 10027

BARON, SAMUEL, flutist; b. Bklyn., Apr. 27, 1925; s. Jacob and Bella (Deutsch) B.; m. Carol Lynn Kitzes, Dec. 21, 1963; children—Pamela Rachel, David Lazar. Student, Bklyn. Coll., 1940-44; B.S., Juilliard Sch. Music, 1948. Flutist N.Y. Woodwind Quintet, 1948-69, 80—, N.Y. Chamber Soloists, 1958-65, Contemporary Chamber Ensemble, 1962-65; flutist Bach Aria Group, 1965—, dir., 1980—; lectr. flute Yale, 1965-67; instr. chamber music U. Wis.-Milw., summers 1955-67; cons. N.Y. State Arts Council, 1964; asst. prof. flute and chamber music State U. of N.Y. at Stony Brook, 1966-67, lectr. in flute, 1966-71, asso. prof., 1972-74, prof., 1974—; performing artist in residence Harpur Coll., 1967-69; prof. chamber music Juilliard Sch., 1971—, tchr. flute, 1976—; vis. prof. Eastman Sch. Music, 1974-75, Sibelius Acad., Helsinki, Finland, summer 1975; cons. music program Nat. Endowment for Arts, Washington, 1973-76; dir. Bach Aria Group, 1980—. Performer, New Coll. Summer Music Festival, 1974—; Transcribed for: chamber music (J. S. Bach) The Art of the Fugue, 1958; Internat. concert tours auspices, State Dept. to, S.Am., 1956, State Dept. to, S.E. Asia and Orient, 1962, State Dept. to, Central and South Am., 1969. Recipient award distinguished in performing arts Sch. Fine Arts, U. Milw., 1964; officer Order Merit Monisaraphon, Cambodia, 1962. Mem. Nat. Flute Assn. (pres. 1977). Address: 321 Melbourne Rd Great Neck NY 11021 *Performing music has been the life experience in which I found the greatest mystery and the highest pitch of self-fulfillment. The answer to the question "How should I live my life?" (which is everyone's question) is found for me in the pursuit, study and teaching of this experience.*

BARON, SAMUEL, microbiologist, physician; b. N.Y.C., July 27, 1928; s. Harry and Gertrude (Lipnick) B.; m. Phyllis G. Baron, Feb. 4, 1951; children: Steven, Clifton, Jeffrey, Jonathan, Jody Lynn. B.A., N.Y. U., 1948, M.D., 1952. Intern Montefiore Hosp., N.Y.C., 1952-53; fellow U. Mich., 1953-55; commd. med. officer USPHS, 1955; unit head virology sect., div. biol. standards NIH, Bethesda, Md., 1955-57, head virology sect., 1957-60; sr. surgeon, med. dir. Nat. Inst. Allergy and Infectious Diseases, 1960-67; head sect. cellular virology Sect. Viral Diseases, 1968-75, ret., 1975; prof., chairperson dept. microbiology U. Tex. Med. Br., Galveston, 1975—. Editor: Texas Reports Symposium on Interferon, 1977, 81, Medical Microbiology, 1982; Contbr. sci. articles to med. jours., chpts. to books on virology. Recipient Meritorious Service award USPHS, 1970, Equal Employment award NIH, 1975, Disting. Faculty Research award, 1978, Sinclair award, 1979. Mem. Am. Assn. Immunologists, Soc. for Exptl. Biology and Medicine, Am. Soc. Microbiology, AAAS, Am. Acad. Microbiology, Infectious Disease Soc. Am., Assn. Med. Sch. Microbiology Chairmen, Soc. Gen. Microbiology., Sigma Xi. Jewish. Home: 2703 Frostwood Circle Dickinson TX 77539 Office: U Tex Med Br Dept Microbiology Galveston TX 77550

BARON, SAMUEL HASKELL, historian; b. N.Y.C., May 24, 1921; s. James and Dinah (Bader) B.; m. Virginia Wilson, Dec. 22, 1949; children—Sheila, Carla, Laura. B.S., Cornell U., 1942; M.A., Columbia U., 1948; Ph.D., 1952. Instr. history U. Tenn., 1948-53; vis. lectr. Northwestern U., 1953-54, U. Mo., 1954-55, U. Nebr., 1955-56; from asst. prof. to prof. Grinnell (Iowa) Coll., 1956-66; prof. U. Calif., San Diego, 1966-72; alumni distinguished prof. history U. N.C., Chapel Hill, 1972—; chmn. Conf. Slavic and E. European History, 1976. Author: Plekhanov: The Father of Russian Marxism, 1963, The Travels of Olearius in Seventeenth Century Russia, 1967, Muscovite Russia: Collected Essays, 1980; Co-editor: Windows on The Russian Past: Essays on Soviet Historiography since Stalin, 1977. Served from pvt. to capt. AUS, 1942-46. Fellow Ford Found., 1958-59, Guggenheim Found., 1970-71, Nat. Endowment Humanities, 1976. Mem. AAUP (council 1962-65), Am. Hist. Assn., Am. Assn. Advancement Slavic Studies. Home: 5 Marilyn Ln Chapel Hill NC 27514 Office: Dept History Univ NC Chapel Hill NC 27514

BARON, SEYMOUR, engineering company executive; b. N.Y.C., Apr. 5, 1923; s. Benjamin and Tillie (Schuster) B.; m. Florence Chill, Aug. 27, 1950; children: Richard Mark, Paul Lawrence. B.S. Engring., Johns Hopkins U., 1944, M.S., 1947; Ph.D., Columbia U., 1950. Lab. researcher U.S. Indsl. Chem. Co., 1944-47; research asst. Columbia U., N.Y.C., 1947-50; chief engr. Burns and Roe, Inc., Oradell, N.J., 1950-64, v.p., 1964-75, sr. v.p., 1975-76, sr. corporate v.p., 1976—, dir., 1967—; bd. dirs. Argonne Assn. Univs.; mem. exec. com., spl. com. for reactor devel., reactor devel. and safety div. Argonne Univs. Assn., 1976—; mem. adv. com., engring. tech. div. Oak Ridge Nat. Lab.; mem. N.J. Commn. on Radiation Protection. Fellow ASME, Am. Nuclear Soc.; mem. Am. Inst. Chem. Engrs., Nat. Acad. Engring. Club: Lions (Oradell). Office: Burns and Roe Inc 700 Kinderkamack Rd Oradell NJ 07649

BARON, SHELDON, research and development company executive; b. Bklyn., May 13, 1934; s. Harry and Edna (Schleifer) B.; m. Doris Earl Rudd, Aug. 11, 1961; 1 son, David. B.S., Bklyn. Coll., 1955; M.A., Coll. William and Mary, 1961; Ph.D., Harvard U., 1966. Simulation engr. USAF-NACA, Hampton, Va., 1955-57; aerospace technologist NASA, Hampton, 1958-65, Cambridge, Mass., 1965-67; mgr., researcher Bolt Beranek & Newman, Cambridge, 1967-71, mgr., prin. scientist, 1971-79, divisional v.p., 1979—; mem. sci. adv. bd. U.S. Army Missile Command, Huntsville, Ala., 1975-77; chmn. working group on human performance modelling Nat. Acad. Scis.-NRC, 1983—. Assoc. editor: Jour. Cybernetics and Info. Scis., Washington, 1976-81, 83-84. Served to 1st lt. USAF, 1955-57. Fellow IEEE; mem. Control Systems Soc. (sec., treas. 1982—), AIAA, Harvard Soc. Engrs. and Scientists (pres. 1976-78). Home: 7 Birch Hill Ln Lexington MA 02173 Office: Bolt Beranek and Newman Inc 10 Moulton St Cambridge MA 02238

BARONDES, SAMUEL HERBERT, psychiatrist; b. Bklyn., Dec. 21, 1933; s. Solomon and Yetta (Kaplow) B.; m. Ellen Slater, Sept. 1, 1963 (dec. Nov. 22, 1971); children—Elizabeth Francesca, Jessica Gabrielle. A.B., Columbia U., 1954, M.D., 1958. Intern, then asst. resident in medicine Peter Bent Brigham Hosp., Boston, 1958-60; sr. asst. surgeon USPHS, NIH, Bethesda, Md., 1960-63; resident in psychiatry McLean and Mass. Gen. hosps., Boston, 1963-66; asst. prof., then asso. prof. psychiatry and molecular biology Albert Einstein Coll. Medicine., Bronx, N.Y., 1966-69; prof. psychiatry U. Calif. Med. Sch., San Diego, 1969—; mem. alcoholism and alcohol problems rev. com. NIMH, 1967-70; neurobiology rev. com. NSF, 1970-73; neurobiology merit rev. bd. VA, 1972-75; bd. dirs. Founds. Fund Research Psychiatry, 1974-76; mem. scholars rev. com. McKnight Found., 1976—; mem. external adv. com. Howard U. Cancer Research Center. Editor: Cellular Dynamics of the Neuron, 1969, Neuronal Recognition, 1976; editor: Current Topics in Neurobiology, 1971—; asso. editor: Jour. Neurobiology, 1970—; mem. editorial bds. profl. jours.; Contbr. numerous articles to profl. publs. Recipient Research Career Devel. award USPHS, 1967; Fogarty Internat. scholar NIH, 1979. Fellow Am. Coll. Neuropsychopharmacology; mem. Am. Soc. Biol. Chemistry, Am. Soc. Cell Biology, Soc. Neurosci., Am. Soc. Neurochemistry (mem. council 1971-74), Internat. Soc. Neurochemistry, Psychiat. Research Soc., Soc. for Complex Carbohydrates, Phi Beta Kappa, Alpha Omega Alpha. Home: 1642 Kearsarge Rd La Jolla CA 92037 Office: Psychiatry (M-003 Univ Calif San Diego)c La Jolla CA 92093

BARONDESS, JEREMIAH ABRAHAM, physician; b. N.Y.C., June 6, 1924; s. Benjamin and Dora (Greenberg) B.; m. Sue Kaufman, Nov. 22, 1953 (dec. 1977); 1 son, James Joseph. M.D., Johns Hopkins U., 1949; D.Sc. (hon.), Albany Med. Coll., Union U., 1978. Diplomate: Am. Bd. Internal Medicine (bd. govs., council gen. internal medicine 1975). Intern, then asst. resident in medicine Osler Med. Service Johns Hopkins Hosp., 1949-51; asst. medicine Johns Hopkins U. Med. Sch., 1950-51; mem. virology sect., research div. Children's Hosp., Phila., also; research fellow virology U. Pa. Med. Sch., 1951-53; asst. resident, then chief resident in medicine N.Y. Hosp.-Cornell U. Med. Center, 1953-55; mem. faculty Cornell U. Med. Coll., 1953—, clin. prof. medicine, 1971-78, prof. clin. medicine, 1978—; mem. staff N.Y. Hosp., 1953—, attending physician., 1971—; chief pvt. med. service, 1973-83, assoc. chmn. dept. medicine, 1983—; asst. vis. physician Bellevue Hosp., 1960-67; cons. medicine Meml. Hosp. Cancer and Allied Diseases, 1972—; Alpha Omega Alpha vis. prof. U. P.R. Med. Sch., 1972; vis. prof. medicine U. Ill. Med. Sch., 1974; U. Va. Med. Sch., 1976, Mayo Clinic and Med. Sch., 1978, U. Iowa Sch. Medicine, 1979; Meyerowitz meml. lectr. U. Rochester Sch. Medicine, 1980; Disting. lectr. U.N.C., 1982; Mem. nat. resources com. Johns Hopkins U., 1965—, trustee, 1977—, chmn. vis. com., 1978—. Author: (with A.M. Harvey and J. Bordley) Differential Diagnosis; Editor: Diagnostic Approaches to Presenting Syndromes, 1971; editorial bd.: Forum on Medicine; Contbr. articles to med. jours. Served with AUS, 1943-46; Served with USPHS, 1951-53. Recipient Wiggers award Albany Med. Coll. Union U., 1978, Albert E. Stengel award, 1983; Named Hon. Alumnus Cornell U. Med. Coll., 1974. Fellow ACP (chmn. bd. govs. 1973-75, mem. bd. regents 1975—, pres. elect 1977-78, pres. 1978-79), Federated Council Internal Medicine, Royal Soc. Medicine, Royal Soc. Health, Royal Coll. Physicians Ireland (hon.); mem. Am. Clin. and Climatol. Assn. (council 1975-78), Am. Osler Soc. (pres. 1983-84), Am. Fedn. Clin. Research., AAAS, Am. Pub. Health Assn., Assn. Am. Physicians, Harvey Soc., N.Y. Heart Assn., Inst. Medicine Nat. Acad. Scis. (council 1979-81), N.Y. Acad. Scis., N.Y. Acad. Medicine, Internat. Soc. Internal Medicine, Phi Beta Kappa,

Alpha Omega Alpha (dir. 1978—). Jewish. Clubs: Century (N.Y.C.); Cosmos (Washington). Home: 544 E 86th St New York NY 10028 Office: 449 E 68th St New York NY 10021

BARONE, JOHN ANTHONY, univ. provost; b. Dunkirk, N.Y., Aug. 30, 1924; s. John A. and Josephine (Audino) B.; m. Rose Marie Pace, Aug. 23, 1947. B.A., U. Buffalo, 1944; M.S., Purdue U., 1948, Ph.D., 1950. Grad. asst. Purdue U., Lafayette, Ind., 1947-48, research fellow, 1948-50; instr. Fairfield (Conn.) U., 1950-51, asst. prof., 1951-56, asso. prof., 1956-62, prof. chemistry, 1962—, dir. research and grad. sci., 1963-66, v.p. planning, 1966-70, provost, 1970—; Mem. rev. and evaluation com. Conn. Regional Med. Program, 1970-76; dir. NSF In-Service Inst., 1961-69; mem. steering com. comprehensive health planning United Community Services; bd. dirs., mem. Corp. Conn. Blue Cross, 1973-77; bd. dirs., mem. exec. com. Blue Cross-Blue Shield Conn., 1977—; project mgr. HUD New Rural Soc. contract, 1972-76; mem. adv. com. on fed. matters Conn. Commn. for Higher Edn., 1974-77; pres. UN Assn. Conn., 1970-72. Contbr. articles profl. jours. Trustee Conn. Council for Sci. Edn., Hall-Brooke Found.; bd. dirs. Jesuit Research Council Am., chmn., 1968-70; bd. dirs. Higher Edn. Center for Urban Studies; trustee Center for Fin. Studies, vice chmn., 1977—; bd. dirs. Health Systems Agy. S.W. Conn., 1977—; mem. Conn. Statewide Health Coordinating Council, 1979—. Served with AUS, 1944-46. NIH cancer research grantee, dir. NSF Undergrad. Research Program, 1961-67. Fellow AAAS; mem. Am. Chem. Soc. (chmn. western Conn. sect. 1966), AAUP (1st pres. Fairfield U. chpt.), Newcomen Soc., Phi Beta Kappa, Sigma Xi, Phi Lambda Upsilon. Democrat. Roman Catholic. Club: Algonquin. Home: 1283 Round Hill Rd Fairfield CT 06430

BARONE, PAUL LOUIS, retired hospital administrator, physician; b. Paterson, N.J., Oct. 11, 1902; s. Joseph and Jennie (Iozia) B.; m. Martha Watkins, Jan. 20, 1940; children: Joe A., Jean Ann. B.S., Alfred U., 1926; M.D., Royal U., Naples, Italy, 1936. Intern St. Joseph (Mo.) Hosp., 1937, resident, 1938-39; practice medicine, specializing in psychiatry, Nevada, Mo., 1939—; staff physician Mo. State Hosp., 1939—, asst. supt., 1943-48, supt., 1948-70, 72-83; clin. dir. Nevada (Mo.) State Hosp., 1970-83, supt., 1972-83, clin. dir., 1975-83. Fellow Am. Geriatric Soc., Am. Psychiat. Assn. (life mem., certified mental hosp. adminstr.); mem. AMA, West Central Mo. Counties Med. Assn., Am. Assn. Psychiat. Adminstrs., Am. Assn. Grads. Italian Med. Schs., Mo. Med. Assn., Mid Continent Psychiat. Assn. (life), Western Mo. Psychiat. Assn. (counselor, past pres.). Clubs: Elks, Rotary. Home: 716 S Main St Nevada MO 64772 Office: Nevada State Hosp PO Box 308 Nevada MO 64772

BARONE, STEPHEN SALVATORE, electronic company executive; b. N.Y.C., June 25, 1922; s. Vincent and Vincenzina (Reina) B.; m. Maria Regina Abbadessa, June 21, 1947; children—Vivian Barone Dewey, Anne Marie Barone Donaldson, Vincent J. A.B. with honors cum laude, Coll. of Holy Cross, 1943; J.D., Columbia U., 1945. Bar: N.Y. bar 1946, U.S. Supreme Ct. bar 1953. With RCA Corp., N.Y.C., 1945—, div. v.p. license ops. internat. div., 1963-67, staff v.p. internat. licensing, 1967-72, v.p. licensing, 1972-79, sr. v.p. licensing, 1979—; dir., pres. Labs. RCA, Ltd., Zurich, Switzerland; chmn. bd. RCA Engring. Labs., Ltd., Tokyo. Mem. Am. Judicature Soc., Japan Soc., Inst. Dirs., Nat. Trust Hist. Preservation, Alpha Sigma Nu, Delta Epsilon Sigma, Phi Delta Phi. Democrat. Roman Catholic. Clubs: Holy Cross (dir. 1971-74, 79-82); Rockefeller Center (N.Y.C.); Plandome Country (Manhasset, N.Y.). Office: 30 Rockefeller Plaza New York NY 10020 *There are two basic relationships in life: One with my God; the other with my fellow-man. In the latter relationship there is a hierarchy with wife and children at the top. I never forget that, after God, people come first. They are more important than wealth or other material things. With these values clearly in mind, one cannot stray from the road to spiritual happiness.*

BARONNER, ROBERT FRANCIS, banker; b. Hollidaysburg, Pa., June 5, 1926; s. Lawrence H. and Elizabeth M. (Maher) B.; m. Jane C. Fickes, Feb. 21, 1952; children: Rebecca Ann, Elizabeth Jane, Robert F. B.S. in Bus. Adminstrn., St. Francis Coll., Loretto, Pa., 1950. Field rep. Gen. Motors Acceptance Corp., Altoona, Pa., 1950-51; asst. bank examiners Pa. Dept. Banking, Pitts., 1951-54; asst. br. mgr. People Union Bank and Trust Co., N.A., McKeesport, Pa., 1954-59; v.p. Peoples Union Bank and Trust Co., N.A., McKeesport, Pa., 1960-67, exec. v.p., 1967-69; sr. v.p. Union Nat. Bank of Pitts., 1969-70, Kanawha Valley Bank, N.A., Charleston, W.Va., 1971-73, exec. v.p., 1973-75, pres., chief exec. officer, 1975—, One Valley Bancorp of W.Va. Inc., Charleston, 1981—. Trustee U. Charleston, 1979-82; pres. Fund for Arts, Charleston, 1982-83; chmn. bd. trustees Charleston Area Med. Ctr., 1982—. Served with USN, 1944-46; PTO. Lodge: Rotary-Charleston. Office: Kanawha Valley Bank NA One Valley Sq Charleston WV 25301

BAROODY, WILLIAM JOSEPH, JR., research inst. exec.; b. Manchester, N.H., Nov. 5, 1937; s. William Joseph and Nabeeha (Ashooh) B.; m. Mary Margaret Cullen, Apr. 23, 1960; children—William Joseph, III, Mary Nabeeha, David, Jo Ellen, Christopher, Andrew, Thomas, Philip, Paul. A.B. in English, Holy Cross Coll., 1959; postgrad. in polit. sci., Georgetown U., 1961-64; LL.D. (hon.), Seattle U., Marist Coll., Assumption Coll., Litt.D., St. Mary of Woods Coll. Legis. asst. and press sec. to Congressman Melvin R. Laird, 1961-68; research dir. House Republican Conf., 1968-69; asst. to Sec. and Dep. Sec. of Def., 1969-73; spl. asst. to Pres. U.S., 1973-74; asst. to Pres., 1974-76; exec. v.p. Am. Enterprise Inst. for Public Policy Research, Washington, 1977-78, pres., 1978—; chmn. bd. Woodrow Wilson Internat. Center for Scholars; bd. dirs. Center for Study of Presidency, St. Anselm Coll., Sem. of St. Gregory the Theologian, John Carroll Soc. Pub.: Public Opinion mag, 1977—, Regulation mag, 1977—, AEI Foreign Policy and Def. Rev, 1977—, The AEI Economist, 1978—. Served with USN, 1959-61. Recipient Disting. Civilian Public Service award Dept. Def., 1973. Republican. Melkite Catholic. Home: 703 Kingston Pl Alexandria VA 22302 Office: 1150 17th St NW Washington DC 20036

BARR, ALFRED LOWELL, state official; b. Rig, W.Va., Jan. 17, 1933; s. Frederick Earl and Leona Lucy (Parsons) B.; m. Eva Jean Elwell, Aug. 9, 1959; children—Belinda Lee, Frederick Earl. A.A., Potomac State Coll., 1953; B.S., W.Va. U., 1955; M.S., U. Ky., 1957; Ph.D., Okla. State U., 1961. Economist Econ. Research Service, Dept. Agr., Washington, 1960-61; asso. prof. agrl. econs. W.Va. U., Morgantown, 1961-70, prof. agrl. econs., dir. div. animal and vet. scis., 1970-80; asso. dir. W.Va. Agr. and Forestry Experiment Sta., 1980—. Active Boy Scouts Am. Mem. Am. Agrl. Econs. Assn., W.Va. Cattleman's Assn., W.Va. Poultry Assn., Alpha Gamma Rho, Gamma Sigma Delta, Alpha Zeta, Phi Kappa Phi. Home: 1080 Windsor Ave Morgantown WV 26505

BARR, DONALD ROY, statistics and operations research educator, statistician; b. Durango, Colo., Dec. 10, 1938; s. Russell Wesely and Elizabeth Joanette (Grommett) B.; m. Loudean Suttle, June 14, 1958; children: Mark Edward, Bryan Michael. B.A., Whittier Coll., 1960, Colo. State U., 1962, Ph.D., 1965. Instr. Colo. State U., 1964-65; asst. prof. math. U. Wis.-Oshkosh, 1965-66; prof. stats. and ops. research Naval Postgrad. Sch., Monterey, Calif., 1966—; liason scientist London br. Office Naval Research, 1982-83. Author: College and University Mathematics, 1968, Finite Statistics, 1968, Probability, 1971, Analytic Geometry: A Vector Approach, 1971, Probability: Modeling Uncertainty, 1981, Statistics by Calculator, 1983; contbr. articles to profl. jours. Mem. Am. Stat. Assn., Math. Assn. Am., Ops. Research Soc. Am., Sigma Xi. Home: 422 Pine Ave Pacific Grove CA 93950 Office: Naval Postgrad Sch Monterey CA 93940

BARR, HARRY GEORGE, fabricated metal products co. exec.; b. Bonanza, Ark., Jan. 15, 1906; s. John Speir and Mary (Jenisch) B.; m. Irene Verola Bolte, Sept. 5, 1931; children—Thomas J., Richard H., Marilyn I., Larry E. Grad. pub. schs.; LL.D. (hon.), Concordia Coll., St. Paul, 1977. Pres. Harry G. Barr Bldg. Specialties, Ft. Smith, Ark., 1931-49; pres. Harry G. Barr Co. Inc., Ft. Smith, 1949-76, chmn. bd., 1976—; dir. Superior Fed. Savs. & Loan Assn., 1955-75, chmn., 1975—; dir. Superior Services Corp., 1972-75, chmn., 1975—. Chmn. Sebastian County chpt. ARC, 1953, Salvation Army Adv. Bd., 1959-60; mem. Ark. Game and Fish Commn., 1946-51, chmn., 1951; Bd. dirs. West Ark. Area council Boy Scouts Am., also South Central Region; trustee Valparaiso U.; vice-chmn., bd. dirs. Lutheran Ch. Mo. Synod, 1965-77, also mem. armed forces commn., 1959-65; bd. advisers St. Edward Mercy Med. Center, Fort Smith, 1975-80, chmn., 1977-79, trustee, 1980—. Recipient Outstanding Citizen's award Ft. Smith, 1954; award of merit Internat. Luth. Laymen's League, 1958; Silver Beaver award Boy Scouts Am., 1960; Crest of Christ award Concordia Coll., Seward, Nebr., 1977; named Hon. Alumnus of Valparaiso U.; Small Bus. Person of Yr. for State of Ark., 1981. Lutheran (pres. Mid-South dist. Lutheran Laymen's League 1947-53, bd. govs. Internat. Luth. Laymen's League 1949-66, pres. 1960-64, mem. Internat. Luth. Hour Operating Com. 1950-60, chmn. 1954-60, mem. bd. appeals Luth. Ch.-Mo. Synod 1955-59). Home: 1415 N Waldron Rd Fort Smith AR 72904 Office: PO Box 26 Fort Smith AR 72904

BARR, IRWIN ROBERT, aeronautical engineer; b. Newburgh, N.Y., May 16, 1920; s. Abraham Herman and Esther (Reibel) B.; m. Florence Lenore Skliar, Oct. 19, 1941 (dec. Feb. 1957); children: Mary Barr Megee, Betty Barr Mackey, Joan Barr Blanco, Alan Howard; m. Dorothy Friendly Weeks, Sept. 20, 1958. Certificate aero. engring., Inst. Aeros., (formerly Casey Jones Sch. Aeros.), 1940; postgrad. engring. mgmt., U. Calif., Los Angeles, 1967. Registered profl. engr., Md. Design group engr. Glenn L. Martin Co., Balt., 1940-50; chief ordnance engr. to pres. and chief exec. officer AAI Corp. (formerly Aircraft Armaments, Inc.), Cockeysville, Md., 1950—; v.p. United Indsl. Corp., N.Y.C., 1979. Author various papers and reports on weapons devel., economics of solar energy. Served with USAAF, 1944-46. Mem. Am. Def. Preparedness Assn. (advisory council), Am. Soc. Heating, Refrigerating and Air-Conditioning Engrs., Assn. U.S. Army, Nat. Security Indsl. Assn., Internat. Solar Energy Soc. Patentee rocket stabilization and control systems, aircraft, weapons, ground vehicles, underwater weapons, wheels, suspensions, bearings, solar energy collectors. Home: 2020 Belfast Rd Sparks MD 21152 Office: PO Box 6767 Baltimore MD 21204

BARR, JACOB DEXTER, banker; b. Jackson, Miss., Nov. 20, 1944; s. Jacob Dexter and Charlene (Vetter) B.; m. Mary Ellen Hale, Aug. 4, 1967; children: Sherry E., Randall D., Shannon L. B.B.A., U. Miss., 1966; postgrad., La. State U. Sch. Banking, 1977, Stonier Grad. Sch. Banking-Rutgers U., 1983. V.p. 1st Nat. Bank, Jackson, Miss., 1973-76; pres. Columbia Bank br. 1st Nat. Bank, Columbia, Miss., 1976-81, sr. v.p., br. coordinator, Jackson, Miss., 1981-83; pres. Citizens Bank br., Hattiesburg, Miss., 1983—. Pres. Am. Cancer Soc., Columbia, 1978; chmn. Boy Scouts Am., Columbia, 1979. Served to lt. USAF, 1966-73. Am. Baptist. Lodge: Lions. Office: PO Box 1071 Hattiesburg MS 39401

BARR, JOHN ROBERT, lawyer; b. Gary, Ind., Apr. 10, 1936; s. John Andrew and Louise (Stentz) B.; m. Mary Suzanne Mills, Aug. 25, 1957 (div. Jan. 1968); children: Mary Louise, John Mills; m. Joan Ruth Worthy, Dec. 28, 1968 (div. Feb. 1983); 1 dau., Jennifer Susan. A.B., Grinnell Coll., 1957; LL.B. cum laude, Harvard U., 1960. Bar: Ill. 1960. Assoc. Sidley & Austin, Chgo., 1960-69, ptnr., 1970—; mem. Ill. Ho. Reps., 1981-83, Commn. on Presdl. Scholars, Washington, 1975-77. Chmn. Ill. Bd. Regents, 1971-77; mem. Ill. Bd. Higher Edn., 1971-77; chmn. Republican Central Com. of Cook County, Chgo., 1978—. Mem. ABA, Ill. State Bar Assn., Chgo. Bar Assn. (chmn. com. on state and mcpl. taxation 1974-75), Law Club, Legal Club Chgo., Selden Soc., Internat. Assn. Assessing Officers, Phi Beta Kappa. Episcopalian. Clubs: Chgo., Monroe City. Home: 1501 Oak Ave Evanston IL 60201 Office: Sidley & Austin 1 First National Plaza Chicago IL 60603

BARR, JOHN WATSON, III, banker; b. Louisville, Mar. 22, 1921; s. John McFerran and Anita L. (Carrington) B.; m. Mary Louise Engelhard, Nov. 10, 1945; children: John McFerran II, Charles Carrington. B.A. in Econs. and Polit. Sci., Princeton U., 1943. With 1st Nat. Bank of Louisville, 1st Ky. Trust Co., 1946—, 1st Ky. Nat. Corp., 1974—, asst. v.p., 1950-53, v.p., 1953-63, sr. v.p., 1963-72, exec. v.p., 1972-73, vice chmn. bd., 1973-74, chmn. bd., 1974—; dir., officer Collins Co., 1st Ky. Nat. Corp., 1st Nat. Bank Louisville, 1st Ky. Trust Co.; dir. and officer Churchill Downs, Inc., Louisville Gas & Electric Co., Dixie Warehouse & Cartage Co., Kitchen Kompact, Inc., Louisville Cement Co., Capital Holding Corp. Bd. dirs. Cave Hill Cemetery Co., Am. Printing House for Blind, Louisville Fund for Arts, Ky. Higher Edn. Assistance Authority, Ky. Ind. Coll. Found., YMCA, Jr. Achievement of Kentuckiana, Old Ky. Home council Boy Scouts Am., Ky. Ctr. for Arts Endowment Fund, Inc.; trustee Centre Coll. of Ky.; pres. bd. overseers U. Louisville, 1976-78, U. Louisville Found. Served to capt. F.A. AUS, 1942-45; ETO. Decorated Air medal, Bronze Star with V. Mem. Am., Ky. bankers assns., Res. City Bankers Assn., Assn. Bank Holding Cos., Bank Adminstrn. Inst., Robert Morris Assocs., Am. Inst. Banking. Presbyterian. Clubs: Rotary, Ducks Unltd., Louisville Country, River Valley (Louisville); University (N.Y.C.). Home: 16 River Hill Rd Louisville KY 40207 Office: 101 S 5th St Louisville KY 40202

BARR, JOSEPH WALKER, corporate director; b. Vincennes, Ind., Jan. 17, 1918; s. Oscar Lynn and Stella Florence (Walker) B.; m. Beth Williston, Sept. 3, 1939; children—Bonnie (Mrs. Michael Gilliom), Cherry, Joseph Williston, Elizabeth Eugenia (Mrs. Andrew LoSasso), Lynn Hamilton (Mrs. Keith Fineberg). A.B., DePauw U., 1939; M.A., Harvard, 1941; LL.D., Vincennes U., 1966, DePauw U., 1967. Partner J&J Co., 1976—; mem. 86th Congress, 11th Ind. Dist.; asst. to sec. of treasury, 1961-64; chmn. FDIC, 1964-65; under sec. of treasury, 1965-68, sec. of treasury, 1968-69; pres. Am. Security & Trust Co., Washington, 1969-72, chmn. bd., 1972-74; dir. 3M Co., Comml. Credit Co., Burlington Industries, Washington Gas Light Co., Control Data Corp., Manor Care. Bd. dirs. Student Loan Marketing Assn.; bd. regents Georgetown U. Served to lt. comdr. USN, 1942-45. Decorated Bronze Star. Mem. Phi Beta Kappa. Democrat. Home: Houyhnhnm Farm Hume VA 22639 Office: 2111 Jefferson Davis Hwy Suite 422 N Arlington VA 22202 *The greatest satisfaction in my life has been the opportunity to serve the United States in a variety of capacities. I only hope that the joys of public service are not eroded for future generations.*

BARR, LLOYD, physiology educator; b. Chgo., Dec. 27, 1929; s. Edward Barton and Florence Lucy (Lewis) Miller. B.S., U. Chgo., 1954; M.S., U. Ill., 1956, Ph.D., 1958. Asst. prof. U. Mich., Ann Arbor, 1958-65, asso. prof., 1965; prof. Med. Coll. Pa., Phila., 1965-70; prof. physiology and biophysics U. Ill., Urbana-Champaign, 1970—; mem. study panels NIH, NSF, 1976—. Fellow AAAS; mem. Soc. Gen. Physiology (treas. 1979-82), Am. Physiol. Soc., Biophys. Soc., Soc. Neurosci., AAUP, Fedn. Am. Scientists. Democrat. Office: Dept Physiology U Ill Urbana IL 61801

BARR, MARTIN, university dean; b. Phila., Nov. 11, 1925; s. Louis and Bella (Moskowitz) B.; m. Nancy Lipschutz, July 15, 1951; children: Lawrence Allen, Richard Andrew, Debra Ann, Steven Bruce. B.Sc. in Pharmacy, Temple U., 1946, M.Sc., Phila. Coll. Pharmacy and Scis., 1947; Ph.D., Ohio State U., 1950. Grad. asst., then instr. Ohio State U. Coll. Pharmacy, 1947-50; from asst. prof. pharmacy to prof. phys. pharmacy and pharm. research Phila. Coll. Pharmacy and Sci., 1950-61; prof. pharmaceutics Wayne State U. Coll. Pharmacy, 1961—, chmn. dept., 1961-63, dean, 1963-72, v.p. spl. assignments, 1972-76, v.p., sec. to bd. govs., 1976-78, sec. to bd. govs., acting v.p. for health affairs, 1978-80, v.p., dep. provost, 1980-82, dean Coll. Pharmacy and Allied Health Professions, 1982—; cons. HEW, 1964-69. Contbg. author: Pharmacy, Compounding and Dispensing, 2d edit, 1956, Remington's Practice of Pharmacy, 11th edit, 1956, 12th edit., 1965; Profl. editor: Mid-Atlantic Apothecary, 1953-64, Apothecary, 1953-64, Central Pharm. Jour, 1961-64. Chmn. Mayor's Com. for Narcotics Rehab., Detroit, 1971-73; pres. Oakland County unit Mich. Heart Assn., 1970-72. Recipient Disting. Service award Alumni Assn. Coll. Pharmacy, Temple U., 1957; named Disting. Alumnus Temple U., 1964; recipient Alpha Zeta Omega award, 1979; Meritorious Service award Wayne State U. Pharm. Alumni Assn.; Ann. Alumus award Phila. Coll. Pharmacy and Sci., 1983. Fellow Am. Coll. Apothecaries, Acad. Pharm. Scis.; mem. Am. Pharm. Assn. (pres. Phila. 1954-55, chmn. sci. sect. 1959-60, Ebert medal 1956), Am. Soc. Hosp. Pharmacists, Mich. State Pharm. Assn. (named Mich. Pharmacist of Yr. 1971), Am. Assn. Colls. Pharmacy (chmn. sect. tchrs. pharmacy 1959-60, chmn. conf. tchrs. pharmacy 1961-62), Sigma Xi, Rho Chi. Home: 20285 Beechaven Dr Southfield MI 48076 Office: Wayne State Univ Detroit MI 48202

BARR, RICHARD DAVID, theatre producer; b. Washington, Sept. 6, 1917; s. David Alphonse and Ruth Nanette (Israel) Baer. A.B., Princeton U., 1938. Formed prodn. co. Theatre 1960 (became Theatre of the Absurd), 1962; pres. League N.Y. Theatres, 1967-83. Appeared with: Orson Welles' Mercury Theatre War of the Worlds Program; exec. asst. to Orson Welles on: Citizen Kane, 1938-41; dir.: Volpone, City Center, N.Y.C., 1948, Richard III, Booth Theatre, N.Y.C., 1949; Arena Theatre prodns. Arms and the Man, 1950-52; producer: Broadway plays Hotel Paradiso; nat. cos. Auntie Mame, 1952-59; off-Broadway shows including Dutchman, Boys in the Band, 1968; others, 1959-64; Broadway show Who's Afraid of Virginia Woolf, 1962-63, Nat. Co., London Co., 1963-64, Paris company, 1964-65; New Playwrights series, Cherry Lane Theatre and Village South Theatre, That Thing at the Cherry Lane; producer on Broadway: Tiny Alice, 1964, Broadway-Malcolm, 1966, A Delicate Balance, 1966-67, Johnny No-Trump, Everything in the Garden, 1968, Boys in the Band, 1968, All Over, 1971, The Grass Harp, 1972, The Last of Mrs. Lincoln, 1972, Noel Coward in Two Keys, 1973, Seascape, 1974, P.S. Your Cat is Dead, 1975, Sweeney Todd, 1979. Served to capt. USAAF, 1941-46. Mem. ANTA (dir. 1969-71). Office: 226 W 47th St New York NY 10036

BARR, ROBERT ALFRED, JR., ednl. adminstr.; b. Cleve., Feb. 14, 1934; s. Robert Alfred and Adelaide Sutphen (Polhemus) B.; m. Eleanor Mary Moore, June 17, 1961; children—Richard Andrew, Jeffrey Robert. A.B., Swarthmore Coll., 1956; M.A., U. Pa., 1961. With Esso Standard Oil Co., 1956-57; asst. dean admissions Swarthmore Coll., 1957-62, dean men, 1962-70, dean of admissions, 1977—; asst. to pres. Chatham Coll., Pitts., 1970-73; dean ednl. services Dickinson Coll., 1973-77. Adv. Com. LWV. Mem. Am. Studies Assn., Pa. Hist. Soc., Omicron Delta Kappa, Phi Kappa Psi. Home: 510 Strath Haven Ave Swarthmore PA 19081

BARR, ROGER TERRY, sculptor; b. Milw., Sept. 17, 1921; s. Clinton Marion and Helen Inez (Barry) B.; m. Helena Brinton May, 1947 (div. 1953); m. Beryl Sharrar, July 4, 1959 (div. 1970); m. Elizabeth Gunn Quandt, Dec. 23, 1971. Student, U. Wis., 1939-41, 42, Nat. U. Mexico, 1941; B.A., Pomona Coll., 1947; M.F.A., Claremont Grad. Sch., 1949; postgrad., Sorbonne, 1962-63. Instr. UCLA, 1950-52, San Francisco Art Inst., 1954-56; founding dir. Coll. Art Study Abroad, Paris, 1959-69; prof. Am. Coll. in Paris, 1962-69; prof., chmn. dept. art Calif. State U., Hayward, 1969-70. Represented in collections at, Hirshhorn Mus. and Sculpture Garden, Smithsonian Instn., Washington, Mus. Fine Arts, Boston, Nat. Art Mus., Goteborg, Sweden, San Francisco Mus. Modern Art, U.S. Steel Corp., Pitts., other public and pvt. collections.; Important works include monumental sculpture in marble, Symposium Forma Viva, Portoroz, Yugoslavia, 1968, fountain/sculpture in welded bronze, Chamber of Commerce Plaza, Santa Rosa, 1975, Arch/Flight One; commn. by, Art in Pub. Bldgs. Program, Office State Architect Calif., 1978-79; stainless steel sculpture; commn. by, State Printing Facility, Salem, Oreg., 1981; fountain/sculpture, Civic/Conv. Ctr., Anchorage, Alaska, 12-piece sculpture, Ravenwood Sch., Eagle River, Alaska, 1983-84; lectr., numerous univs., colls. and schs. art. Served to lt. USNR, 1942-46. Catherwood Found. fellow in Europe, 1956; Djerassi Found. fellow, 1984. Home and Office: 920 McDonald Ave Santa Rosa CA 95404

BARR, THOMAS DELBERT, lawyer; b. Kansas City, Mo., Jan. 23, 1931; s. Harold D. and Emma M. (Sanders) B.; m. Cornelia Harrington, Sept. 26, 1953; children: Daniel C., Phoebe Anne, Robert A., Sara E. B.A., U. Mo., Kansas City, 1953; LL.B., Yale U., 1958. Bar: N.Y. State 1959, U.S. Supreme Ct. 1964. Assoc. firm Cravath, Swaine, & Moore, N.Y.C., 1958-65, partner firm, 1965—; bd. dirs. Salzburg Seminar. Dep. dir. Nat. Commn. on Causes and Prevention of Violence, 1968-70; mem. exec. com. Lawyers' Com. for Civil Rights Under Law, 1968—, nat. co-chmn., 1977-79. Served as lt. USMC, 1953-55. Mem. Am., N.Y. State bar assns., Assn. Bar of City of N.Y., Am. Coll. Trial Lawyers, Internat. Acad. Trial Lawyers, Am. Bar Found. Home: 18 Meadowcroft Ln Greenwich CT 06830 Office: One Chase Manhattan Plaza New York NY 10005

BARRACK, WILLIAM SAMPLE, JR., petroleum company executive; b. Pitts., July 26, 1929; s. William Sample and Edna Mae (Henderson) B. B.S., U. Pitts., 1950; postgrad., Dartmouth Coll. With Texaco, Inc., 1953—, gen. mgr., 1970, asst. to chmn. bd., N.Y.C., 1971, v.p. internat. Europe, 1971-76, v.p. producing Eastern hemisphere, 1976-77, v.p. personnel and corp. services, 1977-80; chmn., chief exec. officer Texaco Ltd., London, Eng., 1980-83; sr. v.p. Texaco Inc., 1983—; pres. Texaco Oil Trading & Supply Co., 1983—; dir. Caltex Petroleum Corp.; Mem. Naval War Coll. Found., Newport, R.I. Trustee Manhattanville Coll.; bd. dirs. Texaco Philanthropic Found., Mary Rose Soc. Served as comdr. USNR, 1951-53. Mem. Fgn. Policy Assn. N.Y. (gov.). Clubs: Ida Lewis Yacht; North Sea Yacht (Belgium); Woodway Country, Ox Ridge Hunt. Office: Texaco Inc 2000 Westchester Ave White Plains NY 10650

BARRACLOUGH, WILLIAM GEORGE, diplomat; b. Chester, Pa., Apr. 25, 1935; s. Arthur Charles and Emma Marie (Walter) B.; m. Beryl Beatrice Brown, Aug. 1, 1959; children—Keith William, Jennifer Alice. B.A., Colgate U., 1957; postgrad., Johns Hopkins U., 1960-62; M.A., Harvard U., 1973. Dep. br. chief Peace Corps, Washington, 1962-63; commd. fgn. service officer Dept. State, 1963, dep. asst. sec.

for internat. trade policy, Washington, 1977-79; minister for econ. and comml. affairs Am. embassy, Tokyo, 1979-82; dep. chief mission U.S. mission to European communities, 1982—. Served with USN, 1957-60. Unitarian. Address: USEC APO New York NY 09667

BARRATT, ERNEST STOELTING, psychologist, educator; b. North Charleroi, Pa., Mar. 31, 1925; s. Robert Duff and Marie Agnes (Stoelting) B.; m. Karen Marie Creel, Dec. 18, 1968; 1 son, Christopher Robert; 1 dau. by previous marriage, Robin Rhein. B.A., Tex. Christian U., 1947, M.A., 1949; Ph.D., U. Tex., 1952. Asst. prof. U. Del., Newark, 1951-57; prof. Tex. Christian U., Fort Worth, 1957-62; prof., chief psychophysiology lab. and psychology sect. U. Tex. Med. Br., Galveston, 1962—. Contbr. articles to profl. jours. Trustee Galveston Ind. Sch. Dist., 1971—. Served with USN, 1943-46. Spl. fellow UCLA Brain Research Inst., 1961-62. Fellow Am. EEG Soc., Am. Psychol. Assn.; mem. Soc. Neurosci., Soc. Psychophysiol. Research, Soc. Biol. Psychiatry. Episcopalian. Home: 2641 Gerol Dr Galveston TX 77551 Office: Dept Psychiatry and Behavioral Scis U Tex Med Br Galveston TX 77550

BARRATT, RAYMOND WILLIAM, educator, biologist; b. Holyoke, Mass., May 4, 1920; s. George A. and Elizabeth (Bretschneider) B.; m. Helen Ruggles, July 1943 (div. 1968); children: Marguerite E., William R.; m. Barbara H. Kellerup, Oct. 16, 1971. B.Sc., Rutgers U., 1941; M.Sc., U. N.H., 1943; Ph.D., Yale, 1948; M.A. (hon.), Dartmouth, 1958. Asst. plant pathology and horticulture U. N.H., 1943-44; research assoc., asst. plant pathologist Conn. Agrl. Expt. Sta., 1944-45; research assoc. biology Stanford, 1948-53, research biologist, acting asst. prof., 1953-54; mem. faculty Dartmouth, 1954-70, prof. botany, 1958-62, prof. biology, 1962-70, chmn. dept., 1965-69, lectr. microbiology, 1962-70; prof. biology, dean of sci. Humboldt State U., 1970-84; mem. vis. staff Vt. Environ. Center, Ripton, summers 1970, 71. Mem. Hanover Sch. Bd., 1964-68, Dresden (N.H.) Sch. Bd., 1964-68; chmn. Dresden (N.H.) Sch. Bd., 1968; Bd. dirs. Fungal Genetics Stock Center, 1970—. Mem. Genetics Soc. Am. (chmn. com. maintenance genetic stocks 1964-68), Sigma Xi, Alpha Zeta, Phi Sigma, Kappa Sigma. Research microbial genetics. Home: 6949 Fickle Hill Rd Arcata CA 95521

BARRE, CHARLES HOWARD, oil company executive; b. Mooringsport, La., Aug. 8, 1922; s. Aubertin Hypolite and Edna Josephine (Brouillette) B.; m. France Lorraine McLain, Mar. 18, 1944 (dec.); children: Herby C., John B.; m. Mary Frances Smithson Wiseley, June 1, 1980. B.S., La. State U., 1943; grad. program in advanced mgmt., Harvard U., 1965. Chief chemist Plymouth Oil Co. subs. Marathon Oil, Texas City, Tex., 1948-55, coordinator mfg., Texas City, 1955-58, plant mgr., 1958-65, mgr. spl. product sales, 1965-67; mng. dir. Deutsche Marathon Petroleum GmbH, Munich, 1967-71; v.p. refining Marathon Oil Co., Findlay, Ohio, 1971-82, dir., 1977—; dir., v.p. Marathon Petroleum Co., Findlay, 1982—; chmn. supervisory bd. Deutsche Marathon Petroleum GmbH, Munich, 1977—; dir. Conpania Iberica Refinadora de Petroleos S.A., Madrid, 1977-83, Citizens Savs. and Loan Assn., Tiffin, Ohio, 1972—. Pres. Marathon Oil Found., Findlay, 1977—; chmn. bd. San Francisco Plantation Found., Garyville, La., 1976—; mem. La. State U. Found., Baton Rouge, 1978—. Recipient cert. of appreciation Am. Petroleum Inst., 1979, Verdienstorden State of Bavaria, 1982. Mem. Nat. Petroleum Refiners Assn. (dir. 1972—, v.p. 1975-78), Am. Petroleum Inst. (gen. com. refining dept. vice chmn. 1975-76, chmn. 1977-78, mem. 25 Yr. Club 1978—). Democrat. Roman Catholic. Club: Lions Internat. (Findlay and Texas City) (pres. 1951-52). Office: Marathon Petroleum Co 539 S Main St Findlay OH 45840

BARRE, STEPHEN ALAN, manufacturing company executive; b. Brattleboro, Vt., Oct. 19, 1938; s. Ernest Vadnais and Gladys Elizabeth (Holden) B.; m. Barbara Jane Bennett, Mar. 21, 1964; children: Christopher, David, Robin. B.E.E., Rensselaer Poly. Inst., 1960; M.B.A., Harvard U., 1962. Sr. engr. Systems Research Labs., Dayton, Ohio, 1965-69, dir. corp. devel., 1969-74, exec. v.p., 1974-81; group v.p. Airco, Inc., Montvale, N.J., 1981—; dir. Servo Corp. Am., Hicksville, N.Y. Bd. dirs. Greene County (Ohio) United Way, 1980—, chmn. bd., 1980; chmn. campaign Greene County (Ohio) United Way, 1979—. Mem. IEEE (chmn. Dayton Sect. 1978), Eta Kappa Nu, Tau Beta Pi. Home: 25 Grist Mill Ln Upper Saddle River NJ 07458 Office: The BOC Group Inc 85 Chestnut Ridge Rd Montvale NJ 07645

BARRERES, DOMINGO, artist, educator; b. Oliva, Valencia, Spain, Feb. 23, 1941; came to U.S., 1957; s. Domingo and Rosario (Agud) B.; m. Jeannine Heyvaert, Dec. 22, 1963 (div. 1975); 1 son, Domingo-Martin. Instr. Sch. Mus. Fine Arts, Boston, 1967—. Exhbns., Sunne Savage Gallery, Boston, 1975-79, Cutler Stavaridis Gallery, Boston, 1979—. Ford Found. scholar, 1980; Clarissa Barlett Traveling scholar, 1982. Democrat. Home: 34 Farnsworth St Boston MA 02210 Office: Sch Mus Fine Arts 230 The Fenway Boston MA 02115

BARRETT, ALAN HILDRETH, educator; b. Springfield, Mass., June 7, 1927; s. Raymond L. and Sibyl (Jesseman) B.; m. Virginia McCulloch, Sept. 3, 1949; children—Richard Alan, Bonnie Jean. B.S., Purdue U., 1950; M.S., Columbia, 1953; Ph.D. in Physics, 1956. Postdoctoral research fellow U.S. Naval Research Lab., Washington, 1956-57; lectr., research asso. U. Mich., 1957-61; asso. prof. Mass. Inst. Tech., Cambridge, 1961-65, prof. elec. engring., 1965-67, prof. physics, 1967—. Mem. editorial bd.: Astrophys. Jour, 1971-74. Served with USNR, 1944-46. Co-recipient Count Rumford award Am. Acad. Scis., 1971; Guggenheim fellow, 1977-78. Mem. Am. Astron. Soc., Internat. Astron. Union, Internat. Sci. Radio Union, Am. Geophys. Union, Am. Acad. Arts and Scis. Home: 342 Hemlock Circle Lincoln MA 01773 Office: Mass Inst Tech 77 Massachusetts Ave Cambridge MA 02130

BARRETT, ARTHUR J., JR., lawyer, retired association executive; b. San Francisco, Sept. 14, 1910; s. Arthur J. and Lydia B. (Hynes) B.; m. Margaret Wise, Mar. 5, 1977; children from previous marriage—Linda (Mrs. James Taylor), Jane (Mrs. Timothy Lane). J.D., U. San Francisco, 1936. Bar: Calif., Colo. Practice law, San Francisco, 1937-56; gen. counsel Woodmen of World, 1956-57, pres., 1957-75, chmn. bd., 1975-81; pres. Assured Investors Life Co., 1969-76, v.p., 1976-81; adv. bd. Capitol Fed. Savs. Mem. regional council United Way. Served with USMC, 1943-45. Mem. Alumni Assn. U. San Francisco, Calif. Bar, Colo. Bar, Denver Bar Assn. Home: 2625 S Wadsworth Blvd Lakewood CO 80227

BARRETT, ARTHUR PAUL, hotel executive; b. Salem, Mass., Feb. 23, 1930; s. Francis T. and Florence I. B.; m. Marjorie P. Graham, Feb. 11, 1956; children: Steven, Amy, Jane, Michael, Mark. B.B.A., U. Mass., 1952. Nat. mdsg. mgr. Cities Service Oil Co., 1954-65; with Howard Johnson Co., N.Y.C., 1965—, v.p. coop. lodges, U.S.A., 1970—, exec. v.p. hotels and motor lodges domestic and internat., Braintree, Mass., 1980—. Served to capt. USAF, 1952-54. Address: Howard Johnson Co 220 Forbes Rd Braintree MA 02184

BARRETT, BILL, sculptor; b. Los Angeles, Dec. 21, 1934; s. H. Stanford and Theodora (Rogers) B.; children: Kevin Stanford, Alexander, Shannon. B.S. in Design, U. Mich., 1958, M.S., 1959, M.F.A., 1960. Instr. Cleve. Inst. Art, 1963-64; assoc. prof. Eastern Mich. U., Ypsilanti, 1960-68; lectr. CCNY, 1970-78; lectr. in sculpture Columbia U., N.Y.C., 1979—. Exhibited one-man shows, Hanamura Galleries, Detroit, 1964, Eastern Mich. U. Gallery, 1965, Kalamazoo Art Ctr., 1966, 10 Downtown Show, N.Y.C., 1969, Benson Gallery, L.I., N.Y., 1969, 70, 72, 74, 77, 80, 81, Latern Gallery, Ann Arbor, Mich., 1970, James Yu Gallery, Katonah, N.Y., 1973, Katonah Art Gallery, 1974, County Exec. Bldgs. Show, White Plains, N.Y., 1975, CUNY Grad. Mall, 1976, Bklyn. Boro Hall, 1976-77, Sarah Y. Rentschler Gallery, N.Y.C., 1978, DeGraaf Forsythe Galleries, Ann Arbor, 1982, Sculpture Ctr., N.Y.C., 1983, group shows include, Gen. Electric Sculpture Show, Fairfield, Conn., 1978, Alexander Milliken Gallery, N.Y.C., Am. Mission Bldg. UN, N.Y.C., 1978-80, Guild Hall Mus., East Hampton, L.I., N.Y., 1980, Sculpture Ctr., 69th St., N.Y.C., Canton Art Ctr., Ohio, 1981, Bot. Gardens outdoor show, sculptor's guild, Bronx, N.Y.C., Sculptural Arts Mus., Atlanta, 1982, Lever House, N.Y.C., Phoenix Bot. Gardens, 1982-83, Sid Deutsch Gallery, N.Y.C., 1983; represented in permanent collections, Cleve. Mus. Art, Norfolk (Va.) Mus. Art, Henry Ford Community Coll., Dearborn, Mich., U. Mich. Mus. Art, Ann Arbor, Guild Hall Mus. Art, Scotsdale (Ariz.) Ctr. for the Arts, U. Hartford, Conn., Hitachi Corp., Kyushu Plant, Kanda, Japan; in books Outdoor Sculpture Object and Environment, Whiteney Library of Design, N.Y. Art Yearbook, 1975-76, Vol. 1, The Process of Sculpture; sculpture commd. for, N.Y.C. Hari IV, 1982. Mem. Sculptors Guild of N.Y., Inc. (pres. 1983—). Home: 11 Worth St New York NY 10013

BARRETT, BRUCE RICHARD, physics educator; b. Kansas City, Kans., Aug. 19, 1939; s. Buford Russell and Miriam Stanley (Adams) B.; m. Gail Louise Geiger, Sept. 3, 1961 (div. Aug. 1969); m. Joan Frances Livermore, May 21, 1979. B.S., U. Kans., 1961; postgrad., Swiss Poly., Zurich, 1961-62; M.S., Stanford U., 1964, Ph.D., 1967. Research fellow Weizmann Inst. Sci., Rehovot, Israel, 1967-68; postdoctoral research fellow, research assoc. U. Pitts., 1968-70; asst. prof. physics U. Ariz., Tucson, 1970-72, assoc. prof., 1972-76, prof., 1976—, assoc. chmn. dept., 977-83; mem. faculty senate U. Ariz, Tucson, 1979-83. Woodrow Wilson fellow, 1961-62; NSF fellow, 1962-66; Weizmann Inst. fellow, 1967-68; Andrew Mellon fellow, 1968-69; Alfred P. Sloan Found. research fellow, 1972-74; Alexander von Humboldt fellow, 1976-77; NSF grantee, 1971—; Netherlands F.O.M. research fellow Groningen, 1980; recipient sr. U.S. scientist award (Humboldt prize) Alexander von Humboldt Found., 1983-84. Mem. Am. Phys. Soc. (publs. com. div. nuclear physics), Phi Beta Kappa, Sigma Xi, Sigma Pi Sigma, Omicron Delta Kappa, Beta Theta Pi. Club: Internat. Folkdancing (Tucson). Office: Dept Physics U Ariz Bldg 81 Tucson AZ 85721

BARRETT, CHARLES CLAYTON, real estate and fin. cons.; b. Milton, Oreg., Mar. 8, 1918; s. Lawrence Clayton and Capitola (Scott) B.; m. Dorothy Grace Smith, Oct. 6, 1942; children—Barbara Lynn, Jeffrey Scott, Pamela Jean, Bradley Clayton, Mark Douglas. Student, U. Oreg., 1936-39; J.D., John Marshall Law Sch., Chgo., 1949. With Percy Wilson Mortgage & Finance Corp., Chgo., 1940-53, v.p., 1948-53, Greenbaum Mortgage Co., Chgo., 1953-55; with Franklin Life Ins. Co., Springfield, Ill., 1955-65, v.p. charge real estate dept., 1965, Continental Ill. Bank and Trust Co., Chicago, 1965-74; pres., dir., chief exec. officer Gt. Lakes Mortgage Corp., Chgo., 1974—; now real estate and fin. cons., Chgo.; dir., mem. exec. com. Republic Realty Mortgage Corp.; dir. Marina City Mgmt. Corp., Royal-Conill Corp., Continental Ill. Realty Advisors Co., Builders Capital Ltd., Can., N. Marina Bldg. Corp., Continental Ill. Properties Advisors, Western Builders Capitol Corp. Ltd., Can. Adv. com. Central Bus. Dist. Assn.; capital funds com. United Community Services. Served to maj. ordnance dept. AUS, 1942-46. Mem. Springfield Assn. Commerce and Industry (dir.), Am. Mortgage Bankers Assn., Chgo. Mortgage Bankers Assn. (pres., dir.), Am. Inst. Banking, Ill. Assn. Commerce and Industry, Chgo. Real Estate Bd., Lambda Alpha. Presbyn. (deacon). Clubs: Bankers; Illini Country (Springfield). Home: 117 Tennyson Rd Wheaton IL 60187 Office: 29 S La Salle St Chicago IL 60603 *My dream is to aid in the realization of Thomas Jefferson's vision and plans to develop and to maintain (at the University of Virginia) a national university of the first rank with a great library unmatched in resources for American studies. Only thus can I repay that great man whose example has so enriched my life.*

BARRETT, CHARLES SANBORN, emeritus metallurgy educator; b. Vermillion, S.D., Sept. 28, 1902; s. Charles H. and Laura (Dunham) B.; m. Dorothy A. Adams, Aug. 2, 1928; 1 dau., Marjorie A. B.S., U. S.D., 1925; fellow, U. Chgo., 1927-28, Ph.D., 1928. With metallurgy dept. Naval Research Lab., 1928-32; metals research lab., dept. metall. engring. Carnegie Inst. Tech., 1932-46; prof. James Franck Inst., U. Chgo., 1946-71, emeritus, 1971—; prof., sr. research engr., adj. prof. physics U. Denver, 1970—; exchange prof. U. Birmingham, Eng., 1951-52; vis. prof. U. Denver, 1961, Stanford, 1963, U. Va., 1968, 70, Ga. Inst. Tech., 1973; Eastman prof. Oxford U., Eng., 1965-66; Mem. nat. com. on crystallography, 1950-54. Author: Structure of Metals, 1943, rev. edits., 1952, (with T.B. Massalski) Structure of Metals, 1966; Co-editor vols.: Advances in X-ray Analysis; Author tech. papers, phys. metallurgy, crystallography. Recipient Mathewson medal Am. Inst. Mining and Metall. Engrs., 1934, 44, 51, Hume-Rothery award, 1975; Howe medal Am. Soc. Metals, 1939; Clamer medal Franklin Inst., 1950; Heyn medal Deutsches Gesellschaft für Metallkunde, 1966; Sauveur medal Am. Soc. Metals, 1966; Gold medal Japan Inst. Metals, 1976; Acta Metallurgica Gold medal, 1982. Fellow Am. Phys. Soc., Am. Soc. Metals (hon. mem., Gold medal 1976), Am. Inst. Mining and Metall. Engrs. (chmn. Inst. Metals div. 1956, hon. mem. 1980); mem. Am. Crystallographic Assn., Nat. Acad. Scis., Inst. Metals (London), Internat. Union Crystallography (editor metals sect. Structure Reports 1949-51), Phi Beta Kappa, Sigma Xi, Delta Tau Delta, Sigma Pi Sigma, Alpha Sigma Mu. Office: Metallurgy Materials Sci Div Denver Research Inst U Denver Denver CO 80208

BARRETT, EDWARD LOUIS, JR., educator; b. Wellington, Kans., Aug. 11, 1917; s. Edward Lewis and Jeannette (Ostlund) B.; m. Beth Lockhart, Jan. 1, 1942; children—Douglas James, Susan Marie, Kent Edward. B.S., Utah State U., 1938; J.D., U. Calif. at Berkeley, 1941. Bar: Calif. bar 1941. Research asst. Calif. Jud. Council, 1941-42; mem. faculty U. Calif. at Berkeley, 1946-64, prof. law and criminology, 1962-64; prof. law, dean Sch. Law, U. Calif. at Davis, 1964-71, prof. law, 1971—; spl. asst. atty. gen., U.S., 1957; Mem. adv. com. criminal rules Jud. Conf. U.S., 1966-71; asso. reporter prearraignment project Am. Law Inst., 1963-66. Author: The Tenney Committee, 1950, (with W. Cohen) Constitutional Law-Cases and Materials, 6th edit, 1981. Served to lt. USNR, 1942-45. Guggenheim fellow, 1964. Fellow Am. Bar Found.; mem. Am. Bar Assn., State Bar Calif., Am. Judicature Soc., Order of Coif. Democrat. Mem. Ch. of Jesus Christ of Latter Day Saints. Home: 518 Antioch Dr Davis CA 95616

BARRETT, FRANK JOSEPH, insurance company executive; b. Greeley, Nebr., Mar. 2, 1932; s. Patrick J. and Irene L. (Printy) B.; m. Ruth Ann Nealon, Aug. 20, 1956; children—Patrick, Mary, Anne, Karen, Thomas. B.S. in Law, U. Nebr., 1957; LL.B., Nebr. Coll. Law, 1959. Bar: Nebr. bar 1959, U.S. Supreme Ct. bar 1976. Asst. gen. counsel, asst. sec. Nebr. Nat. Life Co., 1957-61; dir. ins. State of Nebr., Lincoln, 1961-67; exec. v.p., sec., gen. counsel Central Nat. Ins. Group of Omaha, 1967-75; exec. v.p., chief counsel Mut. of Omaha (and Affiliates), 1975-81; pres., chief exec. officer Central Nat. Ins. Group (of Omaha), 1981—; dir. Omaha Fin. Life Ins. Co. (Mut. of Omaha affiliate); mem. faculty ins. seminar Coll. of Ins. State organizational chmn. 3 Nebr. gubernatorial campaigns. Served in U.S. Army, 1953-55; Korea. Recipient service citation Am. Nat. Red Cross, 1964, 65. Mem. Am., Nebr., Omaha bar assns., Am. Mgmt. Assn., Fedn. Ins. Counsels, Consumer Credit Ins. Assn. (past pres. and dir.), Nat. Assn. Ind. Insurers (gov., past chmn.), Nat. Assn. Ins. Commrs. (past pres.), Newcomen Soc., Am. Legion, Irish-Am. Cultural Soc. Democrat. Roman Catholic. Clubs: K.C., Elks, Happy Hollow Country. Home: 516 S 119th St Omaha NE 68154 Office: Central Nat Ins Group Omaha 105 S 17th St Omaha NE 68102

BARRETT, HARRY OKE, ret. univ. adminstr.; b. Brantford, Ont., Can., Aug. 26, 1908; s. Charles and Elizabeth (Cook) B.; m. Isabel Alford Weddell, Aug. 10, 1946; children—Charles Alexander, Judith Isabel (Mrs. William John McCreery), John William. B.A., U. Toronto, Ont., 1931, B.Paed., 1938, D.Paed., 1948. Asst. prin. St. Paul's Sch. for Boys, Toronto, Ont., 1935-39; head of guidance Eastern High Sch. Commerce, Toronto, 1939-58, North Toronto Collegiate Inst., 1958-62; prof. ednl. psychology U. Toronto, 1962-66, asst. dean, 1966-73, acting dean, 1973-74, dean, 1974, exec. asst., 1974-76; Bd. dirs. Harshman Found. Author: A Job For You, 1960, Status of the Secondary School Teacher in Ontario, 1963, Here and There in Teacher Education, 1974; Editor: book series Student, Subject and Careers, 1972—; author: series book English, 1972, History, 1980; Contbr. numerous articles to profl. jours., popular mags. Served to maj. Can. Army, 1940-46. Fellow Ont. Tchrs. Fedn. (pres. 1959-60); mem. Ont. Secondary Sch. Tchrs. Fedn. (pres. 1959—, life), Ont. Ednl. Research Council (pres. 1961—, sec. 1962—), Can. Psychol. Assn. (life), Faculty Club of U. Toronto. Progressive Conservative. Clubs: Mason, Knight Hospitaller, mem. Order of St. John of Jerusalem. Home: 90 Berkinshaw Crescent Don Mills ON M3B 2T2 Canada

BARRETT, HERBERT, artists management executive; b. N.Y.C., May 31, 1910; s. John and Mollie (Pike) B.; m. Betty Palash, May 29, 1937; children: Nancy, Katherine. B.A., Cornell U., 1930. Pub. relations counsel Cadillac Car Co., N.Y.C., 1934—, Gen. Motors, 1935—; mgr., pres. Herbert Barrett Mgmt. (artists mgmt. assn.), N.Y.C., 1940—; mgr. inaugural Great Performers series Avery Fisher Hall, Lincoln Center for Performing Arts, N.Y.C., 1965; mem. adv. com. Town Hall, N.Y.C., 1970—; mem. recommendation bd. Avery Fisher Artist Program, Lincoln Center Performing Arts; mem. nat. adv. bd. Van Cliburn Internat. Quadrennial Piano Competition. Mem. Little Orch. Soc. (treas. 1970—, mgr. 1967—), Internat. Assn. Festival and Concert Mgrs. (exec. bd. 1969—), Phi Beta Kappa. Home: 15 W 72d St New York NY 10023 Office: 1860 Broadway New York NY 10023

BARRETT, JAMES E., judge; b. Lusk, Wyo., Apr. 8, 1922; s. Frank A. and Alice C. (Donoghue) B.; m. Carmel Ann Martinez, Oct. 8, 1949; children—Ann Catherine Barrett Sandahl, Richard James, John Donoghue. Student, U. Wyo., 1940-42, LL.B., 1949, St. Catherine's Coll., Oxford, Eng., 1945, Cath. U. Am., 1946. Bar: Wyo. 1949. Mem. firm Barrett and Barrett, Lusk, 1949-67; atty. gen., State of Wyo., 1967-71; judge U.S. Circuit Ct. Appeals, 10th Circuit, 1971—; county and pros. atty., Niobrara County, Wyo., 1951-62; atty. Town of Lusk, 1952-64, Niobrara Sch. Dist., 1950-64. Active Boy Scouts Am.; sec.-treas. Niobrara County Republican Central Com.; bd. dirs. St. Joseph's Children's Home, Torrington, Wyo.; trustee ch. Served as cpl. AUS, 1942-45; ETO. Recipient Distinguished Alumni award U. Wyo., 1973. Mem. VFW, Am. Legion. Lodges: Lions; Kiwanis. Office: US Ct of Appeals PO Box 1288 Cheyenne WY 82001

BARRETT, JAMES EMMETT, insurance company executive; b. Omaha, May 30, 1923; s. John C. and Elizabeth M. (Wilson) B.; m. Mary Ann Forsyth, Oct. 20, 1944; children: Mary Margaret Barrett Slye, Susan Elizabeth Barrett Kozlowski, Joanne Barrett Gates, James Emmett. LL.B., Creighton U., 1948. Bar: Nebr. 1948. With Mut. of Omaha Ins. Co., 1948—, v.p., 1959-65, exec. v.p., 1965—; vice chmn. bd. dirs. Tele-Trip Co., Inc., Omaha, 1964—, also dir.; dir. Companion Life Ins. Co., N.Y.C.; Mem. Greater Washington Bd. Trade. Mem. pres.'s council Creighton U., Omaha, 1969—; bd. dirs. USO of Met. Washington, USO of Central Md., USO of Met. N.Y.; immediate past pres. USO, Inc.; conf. chmn. Nat. Multiple Sclerosis Soc., 1976, chmn. bd. trustees Nat. Capital chpt., 1973-78; trustee Behrend Found., Washington, Am. U., Washington; colleague Nat. Assembly Nat. Vol. Health and Social Welfare Orgns., 1979-82; bd. dirs., founding pres. U.S. Sport and Phys. Edn. Found.; bd. dirs. Height Sch., Washington, 1974-78, Marymount Coll. Va., Arlington. Served as officer, inf. AUS, World War II; ETO. Decorated chevalier de grace Ordre Souverain Militaire et Hospitalier de St. Thomas d'Acre, Rome; recipient Com. Service award Sales and Mktg. Execs. of Washington, 1978; Hope Chest award Nat. Multiple Sclerosis Soc., 1980; Four Seasons Internat. award, 1981. Mem. Health Ins. Assn. Am. (dir. 1966-69), Am., Fed., Nebr. bar assns., Nebr. Soc. Washington (gov. 1961-63, pres. 1962), C. of C. U.S. (healthcare com. 1974-79), Washington Inst. Fgn. Affairs, Newcomen Soc., Heroes, Inc. (charter), Delta Theta Phi, Alpha Sigma Nu. Clubs: Capitol Hill, F Street (Washington); Metropolitan. Home: 4813 Sangamore Rd Bethesda MD 20816 Office: 1700 Pennsylvania Ave NW Washington DC 20006

BARRETT, JAMES LEE, screenwriter; b. Charlotte, N.C., Nov. 19, 1929; s. James Hamlin and Anne (Blake) B.; m. Merete Engelstoft, June 1960; children: Jessica, Penelope, Birgitte, Christian, David. Ed., Furman U., Pa. State U., Columbia U., Art Students League. Screenwriter, 1955—. Screenwriter: motion picture D.I. (Marine Corps Combat Corrs. Assn. award), The Greatest Story Ever Told, Bandolero, The Undefeated, Shenandoah, tick. . .tick. . .tick, The Cheyenne Social Club, The Green Berets, Something Big, Fools' Parade, Hank, Smokey and the Bandit; TV film The Awakening Land (Am. Women in Radio and TV cert. commendation), Belle Starr, Stubby Pringle's Christmas (Humanities nomination), The Day Christ Died, Angel City, Mayflower: The Pilgrim Experience; playwright: Shenadoah (Tony award for best musical book). Served with USMC, 1950-52. Mem. Writers Guild Am., Dramatists Guild, Acad. Motion Picture Arts and Scis. Address: PO Box 66 Paso Robles CA 93446

BARRETT, JOHN PATRIC, manufacturing company executive; b. Malone, N.Y., Feb. 5, 1917; s. John Edward and Evelyn (Flangan) B.; m. Joan Ann Warren, July 9, 1966; children: Peter, Paul, Brian. B.S. in Econs., Siena Coll., Loudenville, N.Y., 1959. Mgmt. trainee Chase Manhattan Bank, N.Y.C., 1959-61; asst. cashier Grace Nat. Bank, N.Y.C., 1961-64; with Carrier Overseas Corp., 1964-71, v.p. adminstrv. services, 1968-71; pres. Carrier Overseas Fin. Corp., 1971-72; also chmn. bd. Carrier Distbn. Credit Corp., 1971-72; v.p. chief fin. officer Carrier Corp., 1972-75; exec. v.p. Carrier Internat. Corp., Syracuse, N.Y., 1975-77, pres., 1977—; dir. Marine Midland Bank-Central, Syracuse, N.Y. Bd. regents LeMoyne Coll., Syracuse; bd. assoc. trustees Siena Coll., Loudonville; trustee Onandaga County Indsl. Devel. Corp. Served with U.S. Army, 1960. Recipient Disting. Alumni award Siena Coll., 1976. Clubs: Century, Cavalry, Onondaga Golf and Country, N.Y. Athletic (N.Y.C.). Home: Limberlost Ln Manlius NY 13104 Office: Carrier Internat Corp Carrier Pkwy Syracuse NY 13201

BARRETT, MADIE WARD, educator, college president; b. Stephenville, Tex., June 3, 1920. A.B., Ala. Coll., 1940; M.A., U. N.C., 1946, Ph.D., 1948. Tchr. pub. schs. Ala., 1940-43; asst. prof. fgn. lang. Troy State Coll., 1943-44; Carnegie grant asst. U. N.C., 1946-48; lectr. German and classics N.C. Coll. Women, 1949-53; asst. prof. French and Spanish High Point Coll. (N.C.), 1951-53; chmn. dept. Plymouth State Coll. (N.H.), 1964-80, prof. French and Spanish, 1956—, acting dean, 1981-82, interim dean, 1982-83, interim pres., 1983—. Contbr.: Our Changing Language Phonodisc, 1959. Elizabeth Avery Colton fellow AAUW, 1954-55. Mem. Am. Council Teaching Fgn. Language, MLA, Am. Assn. Tchrs. French. Office: Office of the Pres Plymouth State Coll Plymouth NH 03264 *

BARRETT, MICHAEL HENRY, civil engineer; b. Dove Creek, Colo., June 20, 1932; s. Frank Ace and Carrie Ethel (Snyder) B.; m. Barbara Jane Kreutz, Aug. 7, 1954; children: Robert, Mary, Bonnie, William. B.S. in Civil Engring, U. Colo., 1955, postgrad., 1955-64; M.B.A., U. Denver, 1979. Registered profl. engr., Colo., 8 other states. Design engr., then partner Ketchum & Konkel, Denver, 1955-69; pres. Ketchum, Konkel, Barrett, Nickel, Austin, Denver, 1969-79, chmn. bd., 1979—; dir. Testing Cons., Inc.; mem. faculty U. Colo., 1963-64, U. Denver, 1968-69; lectr. Civil Def., 1962-68. Exec. bd. Denver Area council Boy Scouts Am., 1970—, pres., 1974-75, area v.p., 1976-82, area pres., 1982; mem. Westminster (Colo.) Planning Commn., 1971-72; chmn. bd. dirs. Denver Boys, Inc. Served with USNR, 1951-54. Recipient Lincoln Arc Welding award, 1966, 68, award Am. Inst. Steel Constrn., 1969. Mem. Nat. Soc. Profl. Engrs., ASCE, Am. Concrete Inst., Soc. Exptl. Stress Analysis, Profl. Engrs. Colo. (pres. 1970), Cons. Engrs. Council (1st pl. award 1973, pres. Colo. chpt. 1982), Structural Engrs. Assn. Colo., Am. Arbitration Assn., Harvard Bus. Sch. Club, Denver C. of C., Phi Kappa Tau, Chi Epsilon, Sigma Tau. Clubs: Rotary (dir. 1976-78), Echo Hills Country (Perry Park, Colo.) Patentee in field.

BARRETT, RAYMOND JAMES, ret. fgn. service officer, educator; b. N.Wildwood, N.J., July 22, 1924; s. James A. and Helen Knight (Ozmon) B.; m. Eleanore M. Spring, Sept. 5, 1948; children—Grainger, Cherilyn, Clark, Melanie (Mrs. Preston C. Dockery), Holly. A.B., Columbia U., 1946; M.A., U. Wis., 1959; Ph.D., Trinity Coll., Dublin, Ireland, 1958. Joined U.S. Fgn. Service, 1948; 3d sec. embassy, Mexico City, 1949-51, 2d sec. embassy, Managua, Nicaragua, 1951-53, Dublin, 1954-58, Cairo, UAR, 1959-61; with Office Eastern and So. African Affairs, State Dept., 1961-63; Canadian desk officer State Dept., 1963-65; 1st sec. embassy, Madrid, Spain, 1965-67; dep. chief program staff Office Internat. Confs. Dept. State, 1967-69; dep. chief global plans div. Hdqrs. USAF, 1969-71; State Dept. adviser U.S. Army John F. Kennedy Center for Mil. Assistance, Ft. Bragg, N.C., 1971-73; instr. history N.C. State U., Ft. Bragg, 1971-73; asso. prof. pub. mgmt. Glassboro (N.J.) State Coll., 1973—; sec. U.S. sect. U.S.-Can. Permanent Joint Bd. Def., 1963-65; U.S. sec. U.S.-Can. Joint Civil Emergency Planning Com., 1963-65. Author: Introduction to Management, 1975, 81; Contbr. articles profl. jours. Mem. U.S. Naval Inst. (First prize essay 1972), Am. Mgmt. Assn., Soc. for Preservation and Encouragement of Barbershop Quartet Singing in Am. Episcopalian. Home: RD 3 Box 22 Salem NJ 08079 Office: Div Adminstrv Studies Glassboro State Coll Glassboro NJ 08028

BARRETT, RICHARD DAVID, banker; b. Cin., Sept. 27, 1931; s. Oscar Slack and Helen Rust (Kaiper) B.; m. Pamela P. Soldwedel, Feb. 25, 1971; children: David, Kimball, Randall. Grad., Choate Sch.; B.A., Yale U., 1953; postgrad., George Washington U., N.Y. U. Prodn. control Reynolds Metals Co., 1954-56; v.p. operations Nat. Bank Washington, 1956-66; officer Irving Trust Co., N.Y.C., 1966-70; v.p. mktg. First Am. Bank, N.A., Washington, 1970-74, sr. v.p., 1974—, head internat. div., now exec. v.p., also dir.; mem. internat. bus. devel. com. Met. Washington Bd. Trade. Trustee, mem. exec. com. Meridian House Internat.; past trustee Washington Hosp. Center; bd. dirs. Nat. Capitol Area Health Care Coalition. Served to lt. (j.g.) USNR, 1953-54. Mem. C. of C. of U.S. (past mem. internat. trade subcom.), Washington Internat. Trade Assn. (dir., treas.). Clubs: Yale, Metropolitan (Washington); Chevy Chase (Md.). Home: 1308 29th St NW Washington DC 20007 Office: 15th and H Sts NW Washington DC 20005

BARRETT, ROBERT DAKER, arts center exec.; b. Tulsa, Dec. 3, 1945; s. Charles and Alice (Daker) Lewis; m. Barbara Pilakowsky, Nov. 2, 1968; 1 son, Max. B.F.A. in Painting, Calif. Coll. Arts and Crafts, Oakland, 1968, M.F.A., 1972. Peace Corps vol., Saclepea, Liberia, 1969, visual arts supr., City of Long Beach, 1972-78; lectr. Calif. State U., Long Beach, 1976-78; cultural arts supr., City of Fresno, Calif., 1978-79; exec. dir. Fresno Arts Center, 1980—. Mem. Alliance for Arts (exec. bd.), Fresno City and County C. of C., Friends Meux House, Fresno City and County Hist. Soc. Club: Fresno Rotary. Address: 3033 E Yale Ave Fresno CA 93703

BARRETT, ROBERT JOHN, JR., corporation executive; b. Bayonne, N.J., Dec. 20, 1917; s. Robert John and Neta (Clark) B.; m. Jane Sponseller, Jan. 24, 1942; children—Betsy Stanton, Robin. B.S., Ohio U., 1940; postgrad., U. Calif. at Los Angeles, 1961-62. Mem. staff Price Waterhouse & Co., Cleve., 1940-42; exec. v.p., dir. Leach Relay Co., Los Angeles, 1947-54; dir. adminstrn. Ramo-Wooldridge Corp., Los Angeles, 1954-62; dir. adminstrn. and fin. Northrop Corp., Anaheim, Calif., 1962-65; treas., chief fin. officer Aeronca, Inc., Torrance, Calif., 1965-75, v.p., treas., 1969-75; v.p. adminstrn. and fin., treas. Pacific Am. Industries Inc., Gardenia, Calif., 1975-76; v.p., chief fin. officer Intermark Inc., La Jolla, Calif., 1976-81, v.p., chief adminstrv. officer, 1981-83; v.p., chief fin. officer, asst. sec. Mgmt. Analysis Co., San Diego, 1983—. Served from 2d lt. to maj. AUS, 1942-46. Mem. Fin. Execs. Inst. (past Western area v.p., chpt. pres., nat. dir.), Corp. Fin. Council San Diego (chmn.). Clubs: La Jolla Beach and Tennis; Cuyamaca (San Diego); Breakfast (Palos Verdes) (past pres.). Home: 1829 Caminito Briso La Jolla CA 92037 Office: Mgmt Analysis Co 11095 Torreyana Rd San Diego CA 92121

BARRETT, ROGER WATSON, lawyer; b. Chgo., June 26, 1915; s. Oliver R. and Pauline S. B.; m. Nancy N. Braun, June 20, 1940; children—Victoria Barrett Bell, Holly, Oliver. A.B., Princeton U., 1937; J.D., Northwestern U., 1940. Bar: Ill. bar 1940. Mem. firm Poppenhusen, Johnson, Thompson & Raymond, Chgo., 1940-43; 45-50; charge documentary evidence Nuremberg Trial, 1944-45; regional counsel Econ. Stablzn. Agy., Chgo., 1951-52; partner firm Mayer, Brown & Platt, Chgo., 1952—; dir. John M. Smyth Co. Vice pres. Mus. Contemporary Art, Chgo., 1972—. Served with AUS, 1943-45. Mem. Am. Bar Assn., Am. Coll. Trial Lawyers, Ill. Bar Assn., Chgo. Bar Assn. Clubs: Indian Hill (Winnetka); Commonwealth, Caxton, Confrerie des Chevaliers du Tastevin (Chgo.). Home: 84 Indian Hill Rd Winnetka IL 60093 Office: 231 S LaSalle St Chicago IL 60604

BARRETT, SAMUEL CASSELL, cons., former gas co. exec.; b. Norman, Okla., Feb. 3, 1911; s. Stephen Melvil and Dolly Susan (Cassell) B.; m. Lucille Miriam Shoop, June 8, 1934; children—Miriam Joan (Mrs. Gibson Hazard, Jr.), Margaret Dianne (Mrs. Timothy N. Tinnes). B.S., U. Mo., 1933, M.S., 1939. Tchr. Independence (Mo.) Pub. Schs., 1934-41; engr. Stanolind Oil & Gas Co., Tex.-Okla., 1941-44, supt. gas sales, Tulsa, 1934-53; mgr. gas sales and supply Colo. Interstate Gas Co., Colorado Springs, 1953-54, v.p., 1954-62, sr. v.p., 1962-72; mgmt. cons., 1972—; sr. v.p. Colo. Interstate Corp.; v.p. Trans-Colo. Pipeline Co.; dir. Colo. Oil & Gas Corp.; Nat. chmn. Future Requirements Com., 1960-70; chmn. liaison com. Fed. Power Commn. Future Requirements Com., 1969—. Scoutmaster Kansas City and Tulsa councils Boy Scouts Am., 1937-48; pres. Sch. Bd., 1959-63; Bd. dirs. YW-YMCA; trustee Iliff Sch. Theology, Denver. Mem. Am. Gas Assn., Ind. Gas Assn., Natural Gas Assn., Midwest Gas Assn. (pres.), So. Gas Assn., State Gas Mens Assn. Tex., Okla., Colo. Methodist. Home: 58 Cheyenne Mountain Blvd Colorado Springs CO 80906

BARRETT, TOM HANS, rubber company executive; b. Topeka, Aug. 13, 1930; s. William V. and Myrtle B.; m. Marilyn Dunn, July 22, 1956; children—Susan and Sara (twins), Jennifer. Grad. Chem. Engr., Kans. State U., 1953, Sloan Sch. Mgmt. MIT, 1969. With Goodyear Tire & Rubber Co., various locations, 1953—, pres., chief operating officer, Akron, Ohio, 1982—, also dir.; dir. A.O. Smith Corp. Served with U.S. Army, 1953-55. Decorated officer with crown Order Merite Civil et Militaire, Luxembourg, 1976; recipient Sigma Phi Epsilon citation, 1979. Home: 2417 Covington Rd Akron OH 44313 Office: 1144 E Market St Akron OH 44316

BARRETT, WILLIAM C., educator, philosopher, author; b. N.Y.C., Dec. 30, 1913; s. John Patrick and Delia (Connolly) B. B.A., CCNY, 1933; M.A., Columbia U., 1934, Ph.D., 1938. Fellow CCNY, 1929-33; instr. philosophy U. Ill., 1938-40, Brown U., 1940-42; vice consul U.S. govt., Rome, 1944-45; mem. faculty N.Y.U., from 1948, prof. philosophy, 1950-79, prof. emeritus, 1979—; sr. fellow Nat. Humanities Ctr., from 1982; vis. prof. Pace U., N.Y.C., from 1982. Editor: Partisan Rev., 1946-53; lit. reviewer: Atlantic Monthly, 1961-65; author: What is Existentialism?, 1947, 64, Irrational Man, 1958, Wine and the Music (later pub. as Pieces of Dreams), 1970, Time of Need: Forms of Imagination in the Twentieth Century, 1972, Illusion of Technique, 1978, Truants: Adventures Among the Intellectuals, 1982; co-author: (with Theodore Besterman) Divining Rod, 1967, (with Daniel Yankelovich) Ego and Instinct, 1969; editor: Zen Buddhism, 1956; co-editor: Philosophy in the Twentieth Century, 1961. Fellow U. Chgo., 1936-38, Rockefeller Found., 1946-47. Mem. Am. Philos. Assn., Authors Guild, Phi Beta Kappa. *

BARRICK, NOLAN ELLMORE, educator, architect; b. Pearland, Tex., Oct. 30, 1913; s. Charles Emery and Hester (Harris) B.; m. Rosemary Watkin, Oct. 17, 1938; children: Bruce Watkin, Anne Hester. B.A., Rice Inst., 1935, B.S., 1936, M.A., 1937, traveling fellow, 1937-38. Registered architect, Tex. Gen. practice architecture, 1940—; asst. prof., asso. prof. architecture and archtl. engring. Iowa State Coll., 1945-49; asso. prof. Sch. Architecture, U. Tex., 1949-53, prof., 1953—, head dept. architecture, 1953-76, asso. dean, chmn. div. architecture, 1976-78, Kleinschmidt prof. architecture, 1978-79, prof. emeritus, 1979—; supervising architect Tex. Tech. U., 1953-65; pres. Res: Con, Inc., 1969—; archtl. adv. com. to State Bldg. Com., 1958-66; mem. Lubbock Zoning and Planning Commn., 1967-70, Lubbock Urban Renewal Bd. Commrs., 1971-75, Lubbock Urban Renewal Design Com., 1973—; dir. regional meetings, sec. Assn. Collegiate Schs. Architecture, 1963-65; sec.-treas. Tex. Archtl. Found., 1964; archtl. TV project com. So. Regional Edn. Bd.; dir. Tex. Technol. Coll. Art Inst.; asso. trustee South Plains Mus. Assn. Mem. publs. bds.: Jour. Archtl. Edn. Served as lt. USNR, World War II. Decorated Bronze Star. Fellow AIA (pres. Lubbock chpt. 1964, scholarship com. 1968); mem. Tex. Archtl. Found. (sec. 1964), Am. Soc. Planning Ofcls., Tex. Soc. Architects (v.p. 1968, chmn. edn. com. 1969, profl. devel. com. 1971, mem. planning com. 1977—, mem. task force on document preservation 1978—, com. on fellowships), Tex. Urban Renewal Assn., Theta Xi, Tau Sigma Delta (nat. pres. 1950-58). Home: 4521 22d St Lubbock TX 79407

BARRICK, PAUL LATRELL, chem. engr., educator; b. Villa Grove, Ill., Aug. 22, 1914; s. Glenn L. and Carrie M. (Duncan) B.; m. Mildred Margaret Daub, Mar. 29, 1947; children—Sandra, Paige, Brenda. B.S., U. Ill., 1935; Ph.D., Cornell U., 1939. Research chemist DuPont Exptl. Sta., Wilmington, Del., 1939-48; prof. chem. engring. U. Colo., Boulder, 1948—. Mem. Am. Inst. Chem. Engrs., Am. Chem. Soc., Soc. Plastics Engrs., Am. Soc. Engring. Edn., Sigma Xi, Phi Lambda Upsilon, Phi Kappa Phi. Patentee in field. Home: 360 18th St Boulder CO 80302

BARRIE, BARBARA ANN, actress; b. Chgo., May 23, 1931; d. Louis and Frances Rose (Boruszak) Berman; m. Jay Malcolm Harnick, July 23, 1964; children: Jane Caroline, Aaron Louis. B.F.A., U. Tex., 1953. Appeared with, N.Y. Shakespeare Festival, 1960, 65, 69, Am. Shakespeare Festival, 1958-59; appeared on Broadway in: Wooden Dish, 1955, Company, 1970, Beaux Stratagem, 1960, Prisoner of Second Ave, 1972, Selling of the President, 1971, California Suite, 1976; other plays include The Killdeer, 1974 (Obie award, Drama Desk award 1974); numerous TV appearances including Barney Miller, Two of a Kind, 1982, Barefoot in the Park, 1982; as Mrs. Miller: Backstairs at the White House; appeared in: films One Potato, Two Potato, 1964 (Cannes Festival Acting award 1964), The Caretakers, 1963, Breaking Away, 1979, Private Benjamin, 1980. Active ERA. Mem. Actors Equity, AFTRA, Acad. Motion Picture Arts and Scis., Screen Actors' Guild. Office: care William Morris Agy 150 El Camino Dr Beverly Hills CA 90212

BARRIE, GEORGE, cosmetics co. exec.; b. 1913; m. Georgette Muir, Aug. 1980. Salesman Raymond Labs., Inc., 1938-45; pres. Caryl Richards, Inc., 1945-58; with Faberge, Inc., N.Y.C., 1958—, now chmn. bd., chief exec. officer, pres., dir. Office: Faberge Inc 1345 Ave of Americas New York NY 10019 *

BARRINGER, ANTHONY RENE, oil and mining exploration and research organization executive; b. Bognor Regis, Eng., Oct. 20, 1925; came to Can., 1954, naturalized, 1959; s. Michael Alan and Dorothy Jesse (Allman) B.; m. Jean Margaret Reid, Nov. 5, 1948; children: Christopher, Claire, Roger, Patrick, Elisabeth. B.Sc. in Mining Geology with 1st class honours, Imperial Coll. Sci. and Tech., U. London, 1951, Ph.D. in Econ. Geology, 1954. Registered profl. engr., Ont. Exploration geologist Selco Exploration Co. Ltd., Toronto, 1954-57; mgr. tech. services div., 1957-61; chmn., chief exec. officer Barringer Resources Inc., Toronto and Denver, 1961—; vis. prof. geology Imperial Coll. Sci. and Tech., 1969—. Served with Brit. Army, 1944-47. Hon. fellow Imperial Coll., 1983. Mem. Geol. Assn. Can. (Logan medal 1977), Instrument Soc. Am. (Sperry medal 1971), Canadian Exploration Geophysicist Soc., Canadian Inst. Mining and Metallurgy, Am. Inst. Mining Engrs., Soc. Exploration Geophysicists (Kauffman award 1980), Assn. Exploration Geochemists, European Assn. Exploration Geophysics, IEEE, Am. Inst. Aeros. and Astronautics. Anglican. Patentee in field. Home: 25060 Montane Dr W Golden CO 80401 Office: 1626 Cole Blvd Suite 120 Golden CO 80401

BARRINGER, PAUL BRANDON, II, lumber co. exec.; b. Sumter, S.C., Aug. 22, 1930; s. Victor Clay and Gertrude (Hampton) B.; m. Merrill Underwood, May 27, 1957; children: Merrill U., Victor Clay, Ann Hampton. B.S., U. Va., 1952; postgrad., George Washington U., 1954. With Human Relations Lab., Washington, 1954; with Coastal Lumber Co., Weldon, N.C., 1954—, pres., treas., dir., 1967—; 1st v.p., dir. exec. com. State Record Co., Columbia, S.C., 1966—, Gulf Pub. Co., Biloxi, Miss., 1967; dir. Sun Pub. Co., Newberry Pub. Co., Branch Corp., Wilson, N.C., Branch Banking & Trust Co., State Printing Co., Columbia Newspapers Inc.; mem. N.C. Dist. Export Council, Pres.'s Task Force on Internat. Pvt. Enterprise. Trustee, mem. exec. com. Louisburg Coll.; trustee Brandon Ednl. Found.; mem. St. Catherine's bd. govs., Richmond, Va.; mem. alumni council, U. Va. Served with USAF, 1952-54. Mem. Young Pres. Orgn. (chmn. rebel chpt.), N.C. Forestry Assn. (dir.), NAM (bd. dirs.), N.C. Forestry Found., Zeta Psi, Sigma Delta Psi, Lambda Chi. Episcopalian. Clubs: Sea Pines Plantation, Summitt, Chockyotte Country, Farmington Country, Augusta Athletic, Downtown. Home: Country Club Rd Weldon NC 27890 Office: PO Box 829 Weldon NC 27890 also Coastal Lumber Co Elm St Weldon NC 27890

BARRINGER, PHILIP E., government official; b. Haverford, Pa., Oct. 2, 1916; s. D. Moreau and Margaret (Bennett) B.; m. Sophia F. Hazard, Aug. 10, 1946 (dec. Apr. 1979); children: Thomas H., C. Frances, Paul M. Student, Heidelberg (Germany) Coll., 1934; A.B. cum laude in European History, Princeton U., 1938; LL.B., U. Pa., 1948; grad., Nat. War Coll., 1952. Bar: Pa. 1949. Staff aide Phila. City Charter Com., 1938-39; research asst. Am. Inst. Pub. Opinion, 1939-40; U.S. sec. Legal Directorate, Allied Control Council for Germany, 1945-46; with Office Sec. Def., 1949-64; dep. dir. European region Office Asst. Sec. for internat. security affairs, 1956-64; attaché, politico-mil. affairs Am. embassy, London, Eng., 1964-66; dep. dir. Near East and South Asia region Office Asst. Sec. Def. for internat. security affairs, Washington, 1966-67; dir. fgn. mil. rights Dept. Def., 1967—; mem. numerous U.S. dels.; dir. Barringer Crater Co., Phila., 1947-63, 78-82. Pres. Alexandria (Va.) Civic Orch., 1950-52; pres., chmn. legis. com. Phoebe Hearst Sch. PTA, Washington, 1959-61; co-founder, mem. Cleveland Park Chamber Music Group, 1957—; exec. com. NW Com. Transp. Planning, Washington, 1959-64; trustee All Souls Unitarian Ch., Washington, 1964, 67-70, chmn., 1969-70; del. to Unitarian-Universalist Gen. Assemblies, 1968-80. Mem. Pa. N.G., 1937-40; served to lt. col., arty. AUS, 1941-46; ETO. Decorated Army Commendation ribbon; recipient Meritorious Civilian Service medal Sec. Def., 1975, 81. Mem. Am. Soc. Internat. Law, Internat. Inst. Strategic Studies (London), UN Assn., Washington Urban League. Clubs: Cosmos, Princeton, Cleveland Park, Potomac Appalachian Trail (Washington) (supr. Washington Met. area trails). Home: 3711 Idaho Ave NW Washington DC 20016 Office: Office of Asst Secretary of Defense ISA Washington DC 20301

BARRIO, RAYMOND, author, artist; b. W. Orange, N.J., Aug. 27, 1921; s. Saturnino and Angelita (Santos) B.; m. Yolanda Sanchez, Feb. 2, 1957; children: Angelita, Gabriel, Raymond, Andrea, Margarita. B.A., U. Calif. at Berkeley, 1947; B.F.A., Los Angeles Art Center Coll. Design, 1952. Artist, 1950—. Exhibited nationally; art tchr. various colls., San Francisco area, 1965—; Author: The Big Picture, 1967, Experiments in Modern Art, 1968, Selections from Walden, 1968, The Plum Plum Pickers, 1969, Mexico's Art, 1975, The Devil's Apple Corps, 1976; Columnist: Barrio's Estuary, 1980. Served with arty. AUS, 1943-46. Office: Ventura Press PO Box 1076 Guerneville CA 95446 *"For men are built for something more important and less trifling than the mere gathering of prunes and apricots, hour upon hour, decade upon decade, insensibly, mechanically, antlike. Men are built to experience a certain sense of honor and pride. Or else they are dead before they die."*

BARRIS, IVAN EDWARD, lawyer; b. Detroit, Apr. 2, 1928; s. Lawrence H. and Irene Jennie (Cohen) B.; m. Mercedes H. Menendez, May 5, 1956; children: Bradley P., Roger D. B.A., U. Mich., 1949, J.D., 1951. Bar: Mich. 1951. Staff atty. Ford Motor Co., Dearborn, Mich., 1954; mem. firm Porritt, Freud, Toppin & Louisell, Detroit, 1954-64; partner Louisell & Barris, Detroit, 1964-70, Fenton, Nederlander, Dodge, Barris, Miller, Ritchie & Crehan, 1970-74, Barris, Golob & Pritchard (P.C.), 1975-77, 1977-78, Barris & Golob (P.C.), 1978—; mem. Mich. Jud. Tenure Commn., 1979—, chmn., 1983—; participant criminal law seminars. Bd. mgrs. Downtown YMCA. Served as 1st lt., JAG Corp. AUS, 1951-54. Fellow Am. Coll. Trial Lawyers; mem. State Bar Mich. (pres. 1979-80), Detroit Bar Assn. (dir. 1968—, pres. 1973-74). Club: Thomas M. Cooley (Detroit). Home: 1302 Forest Glen Ct Bloomfield Hills MI 48013 Office: 1930 Buhl Bldg Detroit MI 48226

BARRITT, EVELYN RUTH BERRYMAN, nurse, educator, university dean; b. Detroit, Sept. 4, 1929; d. George C. and Ruby (Mathews) Berryman; m. Ward LeRoy Barritt, Oct. 28, 1951; 1 dau., Kelli Jo. A.A., Graceland Coll., 1949; diploma, Independence (Mo.) Sanitarium and Hosp. Sch. Nursing, 1952; B.S.N., Ohio State U., 1956, M.A., 1962, Ph.D., 1971. Asst. instr. nursing Atlantic City Hosp., 1952-53; staff nurse Shore Meml. Hosp., Somers Point, N.J., 1953-54, Ohio State U. Hosp., Columbus, 1954-55; instr. White Cross Hosp., Columbus, 1955-57; asso. dir. nursing service Riverside Meth. Hosp., Columbus, 1957-64; asst. exec. dir. Ohio Nurses Assn., Columbus, 1964-65; dean Capital U. Sch. Nursing, Columbus, 1965-72, Coll. Nursing, U. Iowa, Iowa City, 1972—, prof. nursing, 1972-80; dean, prof. Sch. Nursing, U. Miami, Fla., 1980—; pres. So. Fla. Perinatal Network, Inc., 1980; mem. State Bd. Ind. and Pvt. Colls. and Univs., 1980. Author: Florence Nightingale: Her Wit and Wisdom, 1975; contbr. articles to profl. jours. Mem. Am. Nurses Assn., Ohio Nurses Assn. (pres. dist. 1966-68), Iowa Nurses Assn., Fla. Nurses Assn., Graceland Coll. Alumni Assn., Am. Assn. Higher Edn., Am. Assn. Colls. Nursing (pres. 1976-78), Independence Hosp. Sch. Nursing Alumnae Assn. Address: 15001 SW 69th Ct Miami FL 33124

BARRO, ROBERT JOSEPH, economics educator, consultant; b. N.Y.C., Sept. 28, 1944; s. Jack and Barbara (Schonfeld) B.; m. Judy Anne Schwarze, June 12, 1965; children: Jennifer, Jason, Elizabeth. B.S., Calif. Inst. Tech., Pasadena, 1965; Ph.D., Harvard U., 1969. Asst. prof. econs. Brown U., Providence, 1968-72, assoc. prof., 1972-73; assoc. prof. econs. U. Chgo., 1972-75, prof., 1982—; prof. U. Rochester, N.Y., 1975-78, John Munro prof., 1978-82; vis. fellow Hoover Inst., Stanford U., 1977-78; research assoc. Nat. Bur. Econs. Research, Cambridge, Mass., 1978—; mem. rev. panel NSF, 1976-78. Author: The Import of Social Security on Private Savings, 1978, (with Herschel Grossman) Money, Employment & Inflation, 1976, Money, Expectations and Business Cycles, 1981, Macroeconomics, 1984; co-editor: Jour. Polit. Economy, 1973-75, 83—; assoc. editor: Econometrica, 1978-81; mem. editorial bd.: Am. Econ. Rev., 1976-79. NSF grantee, 1972—; Guggenheim Found. fellow, 1982. Fellow Econometric Soc.; mem. Am. Econ. Assn. Home: 5731 S Kenwood Ave Chgo IL 60637 Office: Dept Econs U Chgo 1126 E 59th St Chgo IL 60637

BARRON, ALMEN LEO, microbiologist; b. Toronto, Ont., Can., Jan. 19, 1926; came to U.S., 1954, naturalized, 1963; s. Max and Bena (Sussman) B.; m. Shirley Brovender, Sept. 14, 1949; 1 son, Joshua Charles. B.S.A., Ont. Agrl. Coll., U. Toronto, 1948, M.S.A., 1949; Ph.D., Queen's U., Kingston, Ont., 1953. Mem. faculty SUNY, Buffalo, 1954-74, prof. microbiology, 1968-74; dir. Erie County (N.Y.) Virology Lab., 1968-74; prof. microbiology, chmn. dept. microbiology and immunology U. Ark. Med. Sci., Little Rock, 1974—; cons. Little Rock VA Med. Ctr.; vis. prof. Hadassah Med. Sch., Hebrew U., Jerusalem, 1972, Kaohsiung Med. Coll., (Taiwan), 1982. Co-editor: Microbiology: Basic Principles and Clinical Applications, 1983; Author papers, abstracts in field. Recipient Golden Apple award Student AMA, 1975, 77; Fulbright research scholar, Israel, 1964; Commonwealth Fund travel award, 1964. Mem. Am. Soc. Microbiology (pres. South Central br. 1980), Infectious Diseases Soc. Am., Soc. Exptl. Biology and Medicine, Am. Assn. Immunologists, Am. Acad. Microbiology, Am. Venereal Disease Assn. Research on viruses and Chlamydia organisms. Home: 14000 Rivercrest Dr Little

Rock AR 72212 Office: U Ark Med Sci 4301 W Markham St Little Rock AR 72205

BARRON, CHARLES IRWIN, physician; b. Chgo., July 21, 1916; s. Joseph and Jennie (Buyer) B.; m. Iris Louisa Barklow, July 23, 1945; children—Michael Craig, Suzanne Lee, Scott Walter, Cherie Ann. B.S., U. Ill., 1940; M.D., 1942. Diplomate: Am. Board of Preventive Medicine. Rotating intern Los Angeles County Gen. Hosp., 1942-43; resident internal medicine Portland (Oreg.) VA Hosp., 1946-48; surgeon Q.M. depot U.S. Army, Chgo., 1948-50; with Lockheed-Calif. Co., Burbank, 1950-79, med. dir., 1953-79; ret., 1979; spl. work coordinating aerospace and indsl. med. and human engring.; prof. aviation safety div. U. So. Calif., 1954—, U. So. Calif. Med. Sch., 1956—; clin. prof. aerospace pathology U. So. Calif.; lectr. postgrad. avaiation medicine U. Calif. at Los Angeles, 1955; asso. clin. prof. occupational medicine; lectr. postgrad. avaiation medicine Ohio State U., 1960; lectr. aviation safety div. Royal Inst. Tech., Stockholm, Sweden, 1967—; vis. prof. aviation medicine U. Mex. Sch. Medicine, 1980; Mem. com. hearing and bioacoustics NRC, 1955-57; med. adv. council civil air surgeon FAA, 1960-72; chmn. research adv. com. biotech. and human research NASA, 1963-68; chmn. med. adv. council fed. air surgeons, 1964-70; mem. rehab. com. Los Angeles County Heart Assn., 1955—. Author articles in field. Trustee Los Angeles Com. Alcoholism, 1955-59, 1955-59, Sheltered Workshops, 1955—. Served to maj., flight surgeon USAAF, 1943-46. Fellow Indsl. Med. Assn., Aerospace Med. Assn. (exec. council, pres. 1963); mem. Am., Calif., Los Angeles County med. assns., Airlines Med. Dirs. Assn. (past pres.), Internat. Soc. Air Safety Investigations, Internat. Acad. Aviation and Space Medicine. Presbyn. (elder). Home: 19303 Itasca Ave Northridge CA 91324

BARRON, DEAN JAMES, lawyer, retired government official; b. Peoria, Ill., Dec. 21, 1919; s. James and Alberta (Sprague) B.; m. Anna Belle Bristol, July 27, 1940; children: Deanna A., Stephanie G. Student, Bradley U.; J.D., Am. U., 1959. Bar: Va. 1960, Pa. Supreme Ct. 1969, U.S. Supreme Ct 1970, D.C. 1972; C.P.A., Ill. Asso. with Internal Service Treasury Dept., 1942-74, dir. internat. ops., 1959-60, dir. audit div., Washington, 1960-62, regional commr., Phila., 1962-70, asst. commr. data processing, Washington, 1970-71, asst. commr. accounts, collection and taxpayer service, 1971-73, asst. commr. planning and research, 1973-74; ret., 1974, individual practice law, Fairfax, Va., 1975—; Chmn. Phila. Fed. Exec. Bd., 1964. Author article. Mem. Am., Fed., Pa., Phila., Fairfax, D.C. bar assns., Va. State Bar, Ill. Soc. C.P.A.'s. Home: 7857 Willowbrook Rd Fairfax Station VA 22039 Office: 4020 University Dr Suite 201 Fairfax VA 22030 *In my experience, the key to success involves setting an objective(s) and devotion of oneself to achieving that objective. A casual approach either in objective setting or the pursuit of such objective will not suffice; the feeling must be intense.*

BARRON, DEMPSEY J., state senator; b. Andalusia, Ala., Mar. 5, 1922; s. Jessie Carl and Minnie (Brown) B.; m. Louverne Hall, Jan. 27, 1952; children: Stephen D., Stuart J. B.S., Fla. State U.; J.D., U. Fla. Atty. firm Barron, Redding, Boggs & Hughes, 1954—; owner D-Bar ranch.; Mem. Fla. Ho. of Reps., 1956-60; mem. Fla. senate, 1960—, pres. pro tem, 1967-68, pres., 1975-76. Served with USN, 1942-47; PTO, ETO. Mem. Panama City-Bay County C. of C., Fla. Bar, ABA, Nat. Soc. State Legislators. Methodist. Named one of 10 outstanding mems. Fla. legislature by press, 1957-83. Home: 2311 Magnolia Dr Panama City FL 32407 Office: PO Box 1638 Panama City FL 32401

BARRON, DONALD H., educator; b. Flandreau, S.D., Apr. 9, 1905; s. George E. and Mae Louella (Reed) B.; m. Marie Annette La Courciere, Oct. 22, 1932; children—Marie Annette (Mrs. Stephen G. McCarthy), Donna Marie (Mrs. Robert Gomez). A.B., Carleton Coll., 1928; M.S., Iowa State Coll. of Agr. and Mechanic Arts, 1929; Ph.D., Yale, 1932; M.A. (hon.), Cambridge, 1936, D.Sc., 1974. Asst. plant physiology Iowa State Coll., 1928-29; asst. biology Yale, 1929-31, anatomy, 1931-32; instr. anatomy Albany Med. Coll., 1932-33, asst. prof. anatomy, 1934-35; NRC fellow univs. of, Berne and Cambridge, 1933-34; demonstrator anatomy U. of Cambridge, 1935- 36, lectr., 1936-40; fellow St. John's Coll. and dir. med. studies, 1937-40; asst. prof. zoology U. Mo., 1940-42, asso. prof., 1942-43; asso. prof. physiology Yale Sch. of Medicine, 1943-47, prof., 1947-69, prof. emeritus, 1969—, asst. dean sch. medicine, 1945-48; J. Wayne Reitz prof. reproductive biology and medicine U. Fla., Sch. Medicine, Gainesville, 1969—, doctoral research faculty, 1971—; head expdn. to study pregnancy at high altitudes in, Peru, 1958; Linacre lectr. St. John's Coll., Cambridge, Eng., 1966; Sherrington Soc. lectr. St. Thomas' Hosp. Sch. Medicine, London, 1967; chmn. human embryology and devel. study sect. NIH, 1963-67. Contbr. articles to sci. publs.; Mem. editorial bd.: Jour. Comparative Neurology, 1948-69; mng. editor, 1956-69. Recipient Virginia Apgar award Am. Acad. Pediatrics, 1977; Rockefeller Found. travelling fellow, 1937; Sterling fellow Yale U., 1940. Hon. fellow Am. Gynecol. Soc., Am. Acad. Pediatrics (asso.); asso. fellow Am. Coll. Obstetrics and Gynecology; mem. Am. Assn. Anatomists, Physiol. Soc. (Gt. Britain and Ireland) (hon.), Anatomical Soc. (Great Britain and Ireland) (life), Cambridge (Eng.) Philos. Soc., Am. Physiol. Soc., Am. Acad. Arts and Scis., Royal Soc. Medicine London (hon.), Soc. for Gynecologie Investigation (hon.), Blair-Bell Soc. (hon.), Soc. Perinatal Obstetricians (hon.), Phi Beta Kappa, Gamma Sigma Delta, Sigma Xi. Home: 2892 NW 4th Ln Gainesville FL 32601

BARRON, HAROLD SHELDON, lawyer; b. Detroit, July 4, 1936; s. George Leslie and Rose (Weinstein) B.; m. Roberta Yellin, Nov. 17, 1963; children: Lawrence Ira, Jean Louise. A.B., U. Mich., 1958, J.D., 1961. Bar: N.Y. 1963, Mich. 1961. Practice in, N.Y.C., 1962-68, Southfield, Mich., 1968-83, Chgo., 1983—; atty. Hughes Hubbard & Reed, 1962-68; corp. counsel Bendix Corp., 1968-69, sec., assoc. gen. counsel, 1969-72, sec., gen. counsel, 1972-83, v.p., 1974-83; sr. ptnr. Arnstein, Gluck, Lehr, Barron & Milligan, Chgo., 1983—; Mem. nat. adv. council and faculty Practising Law Inst., N.Y.C.; dir. Maccabees Mut. Life Ins. Co., Southfield. Com. visitors U. Mich. Law Sch.; trustee Children's Hosp. Mich., Detroit, 1976—; mem. Census Adv. Com. on Privacy and Confidentiality, 1975-76; mem. governing bd., adv. council Purdue U. Info. Privacy Research Center.; bd. dirs. Citizens Research Council of Mich., 1982-83. Served with AUS, 1961-62. Mem. ABA (com. on corp. law depts., com. corporate law and taxation, internat. bus. law com., com. devels. in bus. financing), Mich. Bar Assn., N.Y. Bar Assn., Ill. Bar Assn., Assn. Bar City N.Y. (com. on corp. law depts.), Am. Arbitration Assn., Am. Soc. Corporate Secs. Clubs: Franklin Hills Country (Franklin, Mich.); Recess (Detroit); Metropolitan, Carlton (Chgo.). Home: 180 E Pearson Chicago IL 60611 Office: 7500 Sears Tower Chicago IL 60606

BARRON, HOWARD ROBERT, lawyer; b. Chgo., Feb. 17, 1930; s. Irwin P. and Ada (Astrahan) B.; m. Marjorie Shapira, Aug. 12, 1953; children: Ellen J., Laurie A. Ph.B., U. Chgo., 1948; B.A., Stanford U., 1950; LL.B., Yale U., 1953. Bar: Ill. 1953. Assoc. Jenner & Block, Chgo., 1957-63, ptnr., 1964—. Contbr. (articles in field to profl. jours.). Mem. then pres. Lake County Sch. Dist. 107 Bd. Edn., Highland Park, 1964-1971; pres. Lake County Sch. Bd. Assn., 1970-71; mem. Lake County High Sch. Dist. 113 Bd. Edn., Highland Park, 1973-77. Served to lt. j.g. USNR, 1953-57. Mem. ABA (chmn. subcom. labor matters, com. corp. counsel litigation sect.), Ill. State Bar Assn. (chmn. antitrust sect. 1968-69), Fed. Bar Assn., Chgo. Bar Assn., Yale Law Sch. Assn. (v.p. 1978-81), Yale Law Sch. Assn. Ill. (pres. 1962). Democrat. Clubs: Standard; Cliff Dwellers (Chgo.). Home: 433 Ravine Dr Highland Park IL 60035 Office: Jenner & Block 1 IBM Plaza Chicago IL 60611

BARRON, KEVIN DELGADO, physician, educator; b. St. John's, Nfld., Can., Apr. 21, 1929; s. S. John Augustine and Mercedes (Delgado) B.; m. Elizabeth E. Grossmann, June 14, 1956; children—Kevin Lawrence, Sheila Christine. Student, Meml. Univ. Coll., St. John's, 1945-47; M.D., C.M., Dalhousie U., Halifax, N.S., Can., 1947-52. Diplomate: Am. Bd. Psychiatry and Neurology. Intern Victoria Gen. Hosp., Halifax, 1951-52, asst. resident in internal medicine, 1952-53, Queen Mary Vets. Hosp., Montreal, Que., Can., 1953-54; asst. resident in neurology Montefiore Hosp., N.Y.C., 1954-55, chief resident in neurology, 1955-56, fellow in neuropathology, 1956-59, adj. attending physician dept. neurology, 1956-59; instr. neurology Columbia U., N.Y.C., 1957-59; asso. in neurology and psychiatry Northwestern U. Med. Sch., Chgo., 1959-61, asst. prof., 1961-63, asso. prof., 1964-67, prof., 1968-69; prof., chmn. dept. neurology, prof. pathology, Albany, N.Y., 1969—; cons. neurologist Beth Abraham Home, N.Y.C., 1957-59; asst. attending neurologist Morrisania City Hosp., N.Y.C., 1958-59; attending neurologist, neuropathologist VA Hosp., Hines, Ill., 1960-62, sect. chief neurology service, dir. electron microscope lab., 1962-64, chief neurology service, dir. neuropathology research service, 1964-69; neurologist-in-chief Albany Med. Center Hosp., 1969—; dir. neuropathology research sect. research service VA Hosp., Albany, 1969—; cons. to numerous hosps.; chmn. medicine search com. Albany Med. Coll., 1980-81, chmn. med. bd., 1980-81, bd. govs., 1980—. Contbr. articles to various publs. Fulbright fellow, 1976. Fellow Am. Acad. Neurology, A.C.P.; mem. Am. Neurol. Assn., Am. Assn. Anatomists, Am. Assn. Neuropathologists, Am. Soc. Neurochemistry, Assn. Univ. Profs. Neurology, Assn. Research Nervous and Mental Diseases, Histochem. Soc., Internat. Soc. Neurochemistry, Soc. Neurosci., Chgo. Neurol. Soc. (v.p. 1967). Office: Albany Med Coll Albany NY 12208

BARRON, MILTON LEON, sociologist, educator; b. Derby, Conn., Feb. 25, 1918; s. Harry Bernard and Anne (Tevlin) B.; m. Matilda Cogan, June 1, 1947; 1 son, Benjamin. A.B., Yale, 1939, A.M., 1942, Ph.D., 1945. Instr. sociology Jr. Coll. Phys. Therapy, New Haven, Conn., 1942; orgns. and propaganda analyst Dept. Justice, Washington, 1943; instr. sociology St. Lawrence U., 1943-44; asst. prof. sociology Syracuse U., 1944-48; asst. prof. sociology and anthropology Cornell U., 1948-54; asso. prof. sociology Coll. City N.Y., 1954-61, prof., chmn. sociology dept., 1961-65, exec. officer Ph.D. program in sociology, 1965-69; prof. sociology Calif. State U. at Fresno, 1969—; dir. study of occupational retirement Social Sci. Research Center, Cornell U.; vis. lectr. (part time) Wells Coll., 1949-50; Fulbright lectr. Bar-Ilan U., Israel, 1962-63. Author: People Who Intermarry, 1946, The Juvenile in Delinquent Society, 1954, American Minorities, 1957, The Aging American, 1961; Co-author: Delinquent Behavior, 1959; Editor: Contemporary Sociology, 1964, Minorities in Changing World, 1967, The Blending American, 1972. Mem. AAUP, Am. Sociol. Soc., Alpha Kappa Delta. Home: 5482 N 9th St Fresno CA 93710 Office: California State Univ Fresno CA 93740

BARRON, NORMAN MACDONALD, lawyer; b. Highland Falls, N.Y., Nov. 1, 1900; s. Alexander Robertson and Emma (Wyant) B.; m. Frances Clifton Byers, Oct. 24, 1930; children: Fraser, Mortimer Byers, Timothy House and Norman Alexander (twins). A.B., Hamilton Coll., 1921; LL.B., Harvard, 1924. Bar: N.Y. 1924. Practiced in, N.Y.C.; asso. Burlingham, Veeder, Masten & Fearey, 1924-29, Burlingham, Veeder, Fearey, Clark & Hupper, 1929-34, Burlingham, Veeder, Clark & Hupper, 1934-43, partner, 1943-52, Burlingham, Hupper & Kennedy, 1952-61; sr. partner Burlingham, Underwood, Barron, Wright & White, 1961-68; counsel Burlingham, Underwood, Wright, White & Lord, 1968-71. Bd. dirs., v.p. YWCA of Oranges and Maplewood (N.J.); also chmn. bldg. campaign YWCA of Oranges and Maplewood; bd. dirs. Planned Parenthood, ARC of Oranges; pres. Hamilton Coll. Alumni Assn. Met. N.Y., also mem. alumni council. Mem. Assn. Bar City N.Y. (admiralty, other coms.), Maritime Law Assn. U.S., Alpha Delta Phi. Presbyterian. Clubs: Farmington Country, Downtown Assn., India House, Univ. Home: 1840 Edgewood Ln Charlottesville VA 22903

BARRON, ROS, artist; b. Boston, July 4, 1933; d. Louis and Ida (Titel) Myers; m. Harris Barron, Apr. 19, 1953; children—Matt Lewis, Nina Rebecca. B.F.A., Mass. Coll. Art, 1954. Fellow Bunting Inst., Harvard U., 1966-68; co-dir. Zone Visual Theater Co., 1970; asso. prof. art U. Mass.-Harbor Campus, Boston, 1974—; bd. dirs. Boston Performance Artists. Producer numerous video performance tapes.; exhbns. include, Whitney Mus. Am. Art, 1967-68, Mus. Modern Art, N.Y.C., 1980, Le Nouveau Musee, Lyon, France, 1979, Montevideo Gallery, Amsterdam, Holland; represented in permanent collections, Mus. Fine Arts, Boston, Harvard U., Smith Coll. Collection, Worcester Art Mus., Addison Gallery Am. Art. Recipient Design award HUD, 1968; N.Y. Found. for Arts grantee, 1972; Guggenheim Found. grantee, 1972; Nat. Endowment Arts grantee, 1975; Rockefeller Found. grantee, 1978-80; Mass. Council Arts grantee for video art, 1981-82. Address: 30 Webster Pl Brookline MA 02146 *I am a visual artist. As a painter and video artist, my work involves how I see and transform reality. My life force feels the ontological mystery, an intense state of wonder, and the endlessness of seeing. Strategies of surrealism and the transformational process provide emotional, intellectual, and metaphysical coherence to my work.*

BARROW, BERNARD ELLIOTT, actor, educator; b. N.Y.C., Dec. 30, 1927; s. Samuel and Sophie (Halpern) B.; m. Joan Kaye, Sept. 15, 1963; children: Susan M., Thomas E. B.S., Syracuse U., 1947; M.A., Columbia U., 1948; Ph.D., Yale U., 1957. Mem. faculty dept. theatre Lincoln U., Pa., 1948-51; mem. faculty Bklyn. Coll., 1955-83, prof., until 1983, prof. emeritus, 1983—. Appeared in: leading roles in TV daytime drama Where The Heart Is, 1969, Secret Storm, 1970-73, Edge of Night, 1974, Ryan's Hope, 1975—; TV, theatre and films. Mem. AAUP, Screen Actors Guild, AFTRA, Actors Equity Assn. Club: Yale. Office: Theatre Dept Brooklyn Coll Brooklyn NY 11210 *

BARROW, CHARLES HERBERT, banker; b. Evanston, Ill., July 23, 1930; s. Franklin and Ardis (Mozingo) B.; m. Patricia Wandelt, Dec. 27, 1952; children: Paula, Carla, Barbara. A.B., Princeton U., 1952; M.B.A., U. Chgo., 1956. With No. Trust Co., Chgo., 1952—, v.p., 1962-68, sr. v.p., 1968-74, exec. v.p., 1974-78, sr. exec. v.p., 1978-81, pres., 1981—, also dir. Bd. dirs. Planned Parenthood Assn., Chgo., 1965-81, pres., 1972-73; Bd. dirs. Rehab. Inst. Chgo., chmn., 1982-83. Presbyterian. Clubs: Chicago, Commercial, University, Commonwealth, Economic, Bankers (Chgo.) (pres. 1979-80); Glen View; Michigan Shores (Wilmette, Ill.). Office: 50 S LaSalle St Chicago IL 60675

BARROW, CHARLES WALLACE, justice Tex. Supreme Ct.; b. Poteet, Tex., Sept. 22, 1921; s. Hunter Denson and Lillie Ozella (Crouch) B.; m. Sugie Williams, Aug. 25, 1943; children—Charles Wallace, John D., David W., James H. J.D., Baylor U., 1943. Bar: Tex. bar 1943, U.S. Supreme Ct. bar 1955. Practice law, San Antonio, 1945-59; mem. firm Moursund Ball Bengstrom & Barrow, 1946-58; judge 45th Jud. Dist., San Antonio, 1959-62; asso. justice 4th Ct. Civil Appeals, San Antonio, 1962-66, chief justice, 1967-77; justice Tex. Supreme Ct., Austin, 1977—. Served to capt. USNR, 1942-45, 50-52. Mem. Tex., San Antonio bar assns. Democrat. Methodist. Clubs: Masons, Kiwanis, Hermann Sons. Home: 2300 Pebble Beach Austin TX 78747 Office: 310A Supreme Ct Bldg Austin TX 78711

BARROW, FRANK PEARSON, JR., retired energy company executive; b. Montgomery, Ala., Nov. 22, 1928; s. Frank Pearson and Kathleen (Hillman) B.; m. Faye Parker, Mar. 1, 1951; children: Frank Pearson, III, Cathy. B.S.C.E., Auburn U., 1951. With Baton Rouge Refinery, Exxon Co., U.S.A., 1951-66, process supt., 1964-65, mech. supt., 1965-66; exec. v.p. Exxon Enterprises, N.Y.C., 1966-72, 74-77; also dir.; exec. v.p. Esso Libya, 1972-74; pres. Exxon Minerals Co., U.S.A., Houston, 1977-80; project exec. Colony Shale Oil Project, Exxon Co. U.S.A., 1980-82. Congregationalist. *I have been fortunate in life to have been exposed to an array of people who can accurately be described as solid achievers. Few have been preoccupied with security. Most have been preoccupied with results.*

BARROW, GEORGE TERRELL, lawyer; b. Wichita Falls, Tex., July 23, 1909; s. George W. and Jena (Magee) B.; m. Margaret Forrest, Nov. 5, 1954; children: David G., Blake W. J.D., U. Tex., 1932. Bar: Tex. 1932. Since practiced in Houston; partner Barrow, Bland & Rehmet (and predecessors), from 1951, now of counsel; mem. Bd. Law Examiners Tex., 1964-80, chmn., 1975-80; dir. Fed. Home Loan Bank, Little Rock, 1965-69. Bd. dirs. Houston Pub. Library, 1974-76. Served to lt. comdr. USNR, 1942-46. Life fellow Am., Tex. bar founds., Am. Coll. Probate Counsel, ABA (ho. of dels. 1972-76); mem. Nat. Conf. Bar Examiners (chmn. 1979-80), Houston Bar Assn. (pres. 1963-64), State Bar Tex. (dir. 1959-62, cert. estate planning and probate law), Coll. State Bar Tex., Am. Judicature Soc., Am. Arbitration Assn., Tex. Soc. SAR, Sons Republic of Tex., Jamestowne Soc., English Speaking Union (pres. Houston br. 1970-72), Navy League U.S., Am. Vets. World War II, Korea and Vietnam, Houston Mus. Natural Sci., Houston Mus. Fine Arts, Zool. Soc. Houston, Inst. Internat. Edn., Friends Houston Pub. Library, Houston Symphony Soc., Army-Navy Assn. Houston, Harris County Heritage Soc., Big Bros. Houston (pres. 1959), Friends Fondren Library Rice U., U. Houston Libraries, Alpha Tau Omega. Democrat. Methodist. Clubs: Forum, Kiwanis, Petroleum (pres. 1969-70), Reading for Pleasure (Houston); Inns of Court, Forest; Columbia Lakes Country (Brazoria County, Tex.); Warwick-Post Oak, Brazos River, The 100. Home: 6151 Bordley Dr Houston TX 77057 Office: 3000 CitiCorp Center 1200 Smith St Houston TX 77002

BARROW, JOHN CURTIS, retired naval officer; b. New Bloomfield, Mo., Dec. 18, 1925; s. Guy Elmer and Eva Elizabeth (Cave) B.; m. Marilyn Anne Cookman, June 4, 1949; children: Patricia Plunkett, John Christopher (dec.), Mary Clark, Jeffrey Curtis, Sarah Alleyne, Rebecca Elizabeth. B.S., U.S. Naval Acad., 1949; M.A., Fletcher Sch. Law and Diplomacy, Medford, Mass., 1962, 1963. Commd. ensign U.S. Navy, 1949, designated naval aviator, 1951, advanced through grades to rear adm., 1975; service in, Vietnam, comdg. officer, 1971-72, 1972-73, dep. dir. politico-mil. policy div., 1973-75, dir., 1975-77, comdr., 1977-78, comdt., Washington, 1978-80, asst. dep. chief naval ops., from 1980, now ret. Decorated Legion of Merit with 3 gold stars, D.F.C., Air medal, Navy Commendation medal with gold star, Def. Superior Service medal; Vietnamese Air Gallantry Cross; Orden al Merito Naval en su Segunda Classe, Venezuela; Ordre Nat. du Merite, France). Mem. Assn. Naval Aviation, U.S. Naval Acad. Alumni Assn. Methodist. Clubs: Army-Navy Country (Arlington, Va.); Wintergreen (Va.). Home: Quarters B Naval Observatory Washington DC 20390 Office: ADCNO Navy Dept Washington DC 20350

BARROW, LIONEL CEON, JR., college dean; b. N.Y.C., Dec. 17, 1926; s. Lionel Ceon and Wilhelmina B.; m. Carmen Torres, 1961; 1 dau., Kristen Erin. B.A. in English, Morehouse U., 1948; M.A. in Journalism, U. Wis.. 1958; Ph.D. in Mass Communications, 1960. Reporter Richmond Afro-Am., Va., 1953-54; teaching and research asst. U. Wis., Madison, 1954-60, chmn. dept. Afro-Am. studies, 1971-72, prof. mass communications and Afro-Am. studies, 1972-75, chmn., 1974-75; asst. prof. dept. communication Mich. State U., Lansing, 1960-61; research project dir. Bur. Advt., N.Y.C., 1961-63; research project supr. Kenyon & Eckhardt Advt. Agy., N.Y.C., 1963-64; head research group Foote Cone & Belding, N.Y.C., 1964-68, asst. research dir., 1968-71; dean sch. communications Howard U., Washington, 1975—; vis. prof. Stanford U., 1971. Author contbr. articles in field. Served with AUS, 1945-47, 50-53. Recipient media citation Journalism Edn. Assn., 1974, radio pioneer award Medgar Evers Coll., 1979. Mem. Journalism Council Inc. (dir. 1970, pres. 1971-79), Fgn. Service (pub. mem.), Nat. Assn. Black Journalists, Nat. Black Media Coalition, Capitol Press Club, Washington Area Media Orgn. Office: Howard Communication 4th St and College St NW Washington DC 20059

BARROW, ROBERT HILLIARD, marine corps officer; b. Baton Rouge, Feb. 5, 1922; s. Robert E. and Mary M (Haralson) B.; m. Patricia Ann Collins Pulliam, Aug. 29, 1953; children: Charles Crenshaw Pulliam, Cathleen Cosley Bassett, Mary Eliza Barrow Hannigan, Barbara Ellen Barrow Turner, Robert Hilliard. Student, La. State U., 1939-42; B.S., U. Md., 1954; postgrad., Tulane U., 1957-60; grad., Nat. War Coll., 1968. Commd. 2d lt. U.S. Marine Corps, 1943, advanced through grades to gen., 1978; served in, China, 1944-46; aide to comdg. gen. Fleet Marine Force, Atlantic, 1946-48; comdg. officer Company A, 1st Bn., 2d Marines, and Company A, 1st Bn., 1st Marines, Marine Corps Hdqrs., 1948-56, also various staff assignments, 1948-56; Bn. exec. officer 2d Bn. 6th Marines, 1956-57; marine officer instr. Tulane U., 1957-60; various staff assignments Marine Corps Edn. Center, Quantico, Va., 1960-63; asst. chief staff, G-3 Task Force-79/III Marine Amphibious Force, 1963-64; asst. G-3, plans officer Fleet Marine Force, Pacific, 1964-68; regimental comdr. 9th Marines, 1968-69; comdg. gen., Marine Corps Base, Camp Smedley D. Butler, Marine Corps Bases, Pacific (Forward), 1969-72, Marine Corps Recruit Depot, Parris Island, S.C., 1972-75; dep. chief staff Manpower, Marine Corps Hdqrs., 1975-76; comdg. gen. Fleet Marine Force, Atlantic, 1976-78; asst. comdt. Marine Corps, 1978-79, comdt., 1979—. Decorated Navy Cross, Army D.S.C., Def. D.S.M., Silver Star, Legion of Merit with two gold stars and combat V, Bronze Star with combat V and one gold star; Joint Service Commendation medal with oak leaf cluster; Cross of Gallantry with palm (2), Vietnam). Episcopalian. Office: Commdt of Marine Corps Hdqrs US Marine Corps Washington DC 20380

BARROW, THOMAS FRANCIS, artist, educator; b. Kansas City, Mo., Sept. 24, 1938; s. Luther Hopkins and Cleo Naomi (Francis) B.; m. Laurie Anderson, Nov. 30, 1974; children—Melissa, Timothy, Andrew. B.F.A., Kansas City Art Inst., 1963; M.S., Ill. Inst. Tech., 1965. With George Eastman House, Rochester, N.Y., 1966-72, asst. dir., 1971-72; assoc. dir. U. N.Mex. Art Mus., Albuquerque, 1973-76, assoc. prof., 1976-81, prof., 1981—; Mass. Nat. Endowment for Arts fellow, 1971, 78. Author: A Letter With Some Thoughts on Photographys Future, 1970, The Art of Photography, 1971, 600 Faces by Beaton, 1970; sr. editor: Reading Into Photography, 1982; Contbr. to: Britannica Ency. Am. Art, 1973, A Hundred Years of Photographic History: Essays in Honor of Beaumont Newhall, 1975; foreward The Valiant Knights of Daguerre, 1978; one-man show, Light Gallery, N.Y.C., 1974-76, 79, 82, group shows include, Nat. Gallery Can., 1970, Pace Gallery, N.Y.C., 1973, Hudson River Mus., Yonkers, N.Y., Internat. Mus. Photography, Rochester, 1975, Seattle Art Mus., 1976,

Mus. Fine Arts, Houston, 1977; represented in permanent collections, Nat. Gallery Can., Mus. Modern Art, Fogg Art Mus., Cambridge. Mem. Soc for Photog. Edn. (chmn. Rocky Mountain region 1973). Office: Dept Art U NMex Albuquerque NM 87131

BARROWS, STANLEY, interior designer, educator; b. Palacios, Tex., Dec. 5, 1914; s. William Stanley and Margaret Stuart (Sartwelle) B. B.A., Washington and Lee U., 1937; diploma in design, Parsons Sch. Design, N.Y. and Paris, 1940. Designer Joseph Platt Assocs., N.Y.C., 1941-42; prof. interior design, dir. European study program Parsons Sch. Design, N.Y.C., 1946-68; prof. interior design specializing in design histor Fashion Inst. Tech., N.Y.C., 1968—, chmn. dept. interior design, 1980—. Contbr. articles, Archtol. Digest, N.Y. Times, Inside Design. Mem. Mayor's com. for promotion of N.Y.C. as center for home furnishings resources, 1980. Served with AUS, 1942-45. Mem. Am. Soc. Interior Designers (edn. affiliate, DeWolfe award 1976), Irish Georgian Soc., Victorian Soc., Nat. Trust for Hist. Preservation, Kappa Phi Kappa. Republican. Presbyterian. Club: Princeton of N.Y. Home: 400 E 52d St New York NY 10022 Office: Dept Interior Design Fashion Inst Tech 227 W 27th St New York NY 10001

BARRY, ALBERT PAUL, government official, former marine officer; b. New Haven, Apr. 12, 1936; s. Alfred Sylvester and Natalie Alberta (Read) B.; m. Beatrice Weldon Ford, June 30, 1962; children: Barbara, Emily, Albert, Kathleen, Eileen, Beatrice, Sarah. B.A. in History and Govt., Tufts U., 1958; M.A. in Communications, Syracuse U., 1975. Commd. 2d lt. U.S. Marine Corps, 1958, advanced through grades to rank of lt. col., 1975; served in Vietnam; comdg. officer Marine Barracks, Vallejo, Calif.; liaison officer U.S. Senate; personnel mgr. Hdqrs. U.S. Marine Corps; ret., 1979; legis. dir. U.S. Senator Bob Packwood, Washington, 1979-80; mgr. Washington office Fiber Materials, Inc., Biddeford, Maine, 1980-81; dep. asst. sec. Dept. Def., Washington, 1981—. Decorated Legion of Merit, Bronze Star, Air Medal. Mem. Marine Corps League, Marine Corps Rex, Officers Assn., Noncommd. Officer Assn., VFW. Roman Catholic. Home: 4007 Rose Ln Annandale VA 22003 Office: Dept Legis Affairs Pentagon Washington DC 20301

BARRY, BRIAN, philosophy educator; b. London, Aug. 7, 1936; U.S., 1976; s. James F. and Doris (Manners) B.; m. Joanna Hill, Aug. 27, 1960; 1 son, Austin K. M.A., Oxford U., Eng., 1958, D. Phil., 1964. Lectr. Univs. in U.K., 1960-66; fellow Nuffield Coll., Oxford U., 1966-69, 1972-75; prof. U. Essex, Colchester, Essex, Eng., 1969-72, U. B.C., Vancouver, Can., 1975-77, U. Chgo., 1977-82, Calif. Inst. Tech., Pasadena, 1982—. Author: Political Argument, 1965, Sociologists, Economists & Democracy, 1970, The Liberal Theory of Justice, 1973; co-editor: Rational Man an Irrational Society, 1982; founding editor: Brit. Jour. Polit. Sci., 1970-72; editor: Ethics, 1979-82. Rockefeller fellow, 1961-62, 1979-80; Am. Council Learned Socs. fellow, 1979-80; Guggenheim fellow, awardee, 1979-80; Center for Advanced Study in Behavioral Scis. fellow, 1975-77. Fellow Am. Acad. Arts and Scis.; mem. Am. Philos. Assn., Am. Econ. Assn., Am. Polit. Sci. Assn., Polit. Studies Assn. (U.K.), Am. Soc. for Legal and Polit. Philosophy. Club: Athenaeum (London). Office: Calif Inst Tech Pasadena CA 91125

BARRY, COLMAN JAMES, religious educator; b. Lake City, Minn., May 29, 1921; s. John and Frances (O'Brien) B. B.A., St. John's U., 1942; M.A., Cath. U. Am., 1950, Ph.D., 1953. Joined Order St. Benedict, 1942; ordained priest Roman Catholic Ch., 1947; sec. Am. Benedictine Rev.; mem. faculty St. John's U., 1953—, prof. history, 1953-64, pres., 1964-71; exec. dir. Inst. Spirituality, 1977—; pres. Hill Monastic Manuscript Library, 1982; summer tchr. San Raphael (Calif.) Coll., 1956-59, Cath. U. Am., 1959-64, dean religious studies, 1973-77; vis. prof. ch. history Yale U., 1973; Commn. Jours. Acad. and Profl., 1958; chmn. Nat. Com. Edn. for Ecumenism, 1965; commr. N. Central Assn. Colls., 1966; pres. Assn. Minn. Colls., 1967; Penfield fellow in Germany, 1950, Soc. Religion in Higher Edn. fellow, 1972. Author: The Catholic Church and German Americans, 1953, The Catholic University of America, IV, 1950, Worship and Work, 1956, Catholic Minnesota, 1958, Readings in Church History, 3 vols, 1959-65, American Nuncio: Cardinal Aloisius Muench, 1969, Upon These Rocks: Catholics in the Bahamas, 1973; also numerous articles; editor: Benedictine Studies, 1958—. Mem. Am. Cath. Hist. Assn. (pres.). Home: Saint John's Abbey Collegeville MN 56321

BARRY, EDWARD GAIL, biology educator; b. Butte, Mont., May 4, 1933; s. Earl Woolfall and Nora Alexandra (Arthur) B.; m. Patricia Lee Zeller, May 18, 1958 (div. 1978); children: Alan Michael, Neil Sheridan. A.B., Dartmouth Coll., 1955; Ph.D., Stanford U., 1961. Postdoctoral researcher Yale U., New Haven, 1960-62; asst. prof. botany U. N.C., Chapel Hill, 1962-67, assoc. prof., 1967-75, prof., 1975-82, prof. biology, 1982—; vis. research prof. Leeds U., Eng., 1969-70, Stanford U., Calif., 1975-76. Mem. Genetics Soc. Am., Genetical Soc. U.K. Home: Dairyland Rd Chapel Hill NC 27514 Office: Dept Biology Coker Hall 010A U NC Chapel Hill NC 27514

BARRY, EDWARD WILLIAM, publisher; b. Stamford, Conn., Nov. 24, 1937; s. Edward and Elizabeth (Cosgrove) B.; m. Barbara Helen Walker, Sept. 14, 1963; children—Wendy Elizabeth, Neil Edward. B.A. with honors, U. Conn., 1960. Pres. The Free Press, N.Y.C., 1972-82, Oxford U. Press Inc., 1982—; sr. v.p. Macmillan Pub. Co., N.Y.C., 1973-82. Mem. Phi Alpha Theta. Home: 62 High Rock Rd Stamford CT 06903 Office: 200 Madison Ave New York NY 10022

BARRY, FRANKLYN STANLEY, JR., toy company executive; b. Binghamton, N.Y., Oct. 26, 1939; s. Franklyn Stanley and Mildred Floy (Clewell) B.; m. Ann B. Searle, Mar. 9, 1962; children—Allison, Kevin, Kathleen. A.B., Harvard U., 1961, M.B.A., 1967. With Fisher-Price Toys, Inc., East Aurora, N.Y., 1967-83, dir. mfg., 1974-76, v.p. research, devel., 1976-78, exec. v.p., 1978-80, pres., 1980-83; regional dir. Marine Midland Bank, Buffalo, 1980—. Bd. dirs. United Way of Buffalo and Erie County, 1980—, Sheehan Emergency Meml. Hosp., Buffalo, 1979—; chmn. Canisius Coll. Council, 1979—. Served with USN, 1961-65. Clubs: Buffalo, Harvard of Western N.Y., Orchard Park Country (all Buffalo). Home: 7 Chase Rd Orchard Park NY 14127

BARRY, GENE, actor; b. N.Y.C., June 4, 1922; s. Martin and Eva (Conn) Klass; m. Betty Claire Kalb, Oct. 22, 1944; children: Michael Lewis, Fredric James, Liza. Student pub. schs., N.Y.C. Actor on Broadway, since 1942; plays include The Perfect Setup, 1962, La Cage Aux Folles, 1983; nightclub performer: motion pictures include Thunder Road; star: TV series Bat Masterson, NBC, 1958, Burke's Law, 1963, Name of the Game, 1969. Formerly active Boy Scouts Am. Mem. Screen Actors Guild (past 1st v.p.). Office: care Internat Creative Mgmt 40 W 57th St New York NY 10019

BARRY, HERBERT, III, psychologist; b. N.Y.C., June 2, 1930; s. Herbert and Lucy Manning (Brown) B. B.A., Harvard U., 1952; M.S., Yale U., 1953, Ph.D., 1957. USPHS-NIMH postdoctoral research fellow Yale U., 1957-59, asst. prof. psychology, 1960-61, U. Conn., Storrs, 1961-63; research assoc. prof. pharmacology U. Pitts., 1963-70, prof., 1970—; mem. alcohol research rev. com. Nat. Inst. Alcohol Abuse and Alcoholism, 1972-76. Author: (with H. Wallgren) Actions of Alcohol, 1970; Editor: (with A. Schlegel) Cross-Cultural Samples and Codes, 1980; Mng. editor: Psychopharmacology, 1974—; Contbr. articles to profl. jours. Recipient NIMH Research Scientist Devel. award, 1967-77. Fellow Am. Psychol. Assn. (council reps. 1975-76, pres. div. psychopharmacology 1980-81), Acad. Pharm. Sci. (chmn. sect. pharmacodynamics and drug disposition 1983-84), AAAS, Am. Anthrop. Assn.; mem. Am. Soc. Pharm. Exptl. Therapeutics, Psychonomic Soc., Phi Beta Kappa, Sigma Xi. Home: 552 N Neville St Apt 83 Pittsburgh PA 15213 Office: 1100 Salk Hall University of Pittsburgh Pittsburgh PA 15261 *I believe that the contrasting behaviors of persistence and innovation both contribute to effective learning and creativity. Awareness of the need for both contrasting behaviors may help people to avoid the failures caused by overemphasis of either one.*

BARRY, JOHN KEVIN, lawyer; b. Akron, Ohio, Mar. 23, 1925; s. John Henry and MaryEllen (O'Hara) B.; m. Ann L. Trainer, June 14, 1952 (div. 1958); children: Mona A., Barry de Sayve; m. Barabara Ann Lacek, Dec. 15, 1973; children: J. Kevin, Nicholas A., Liza M. A.B., Princeton U., 1974; J.D., Northwestern U., 1951. Bar: Ohio 1951, Pa. 1963. Assoc. Brouse, McDowell Inc., Akron, 1951-54; trial atty. IRS, Washington, 1954-57; atty., mem. legal adv. staff U.S. Treasury Dept., Washington, 1957-60, mem. office of tax legis. council, 1960-62; assoc. Reed Smith Shaw & McClay, Pitts., 1962-66, ptnr., 1966—. Bd. dirs. Pitts. Symphony Soc., 1981—; trustee Sewickley (Pa.) Acad., 1982—. Served with USN, 1943-46. Mem. ABA, Fed. Bar Assn., Pa. Bar Assn., Northwestern U. Sch. Law Alumni Assn. (regional v.p. 1979—). Republican. Roman Catholic. Clubs: Allegheny Country (Sewickley Heights, Pa.); Duquesne, Harvard-Yale-Princeton (Pitts.); Columbia Country (Chevy Chase, Md.); Portage Country (Akron). Home: Scaife Rd Sewickley PA 15143 Office: Reed Smith Shaw & McClay 747 Union Trust Bldg Pittsburg PA 15230

BARRY, MARION SHEPILOV, JR., mayor of Washington; b. Itta Bena, Miss., Mar. 6, 1936; s. Marion S. and Mattie B.; m. Effi Barry, 1978; 1 son, Marion Christoper. B.S. in Chemistry, LeMoyne Coll., 1958; M.S., Fisk U., 1960; postgrad., U. Kans., 1960-61, U. Tenn., 1961-64. Dir. ops. Pride, Inc., Washington, from 1967; co-founder, chmn., dir. Pride Econ. Enterprises, Inc., Washington, 1968; mem. Washington (D.C.) Sch. Bd., 1971-74; mem. city council, Washington, 1974-78, mayor, 1979—. First nat. chmn. Student Nonviolent Coordinating Com.; mem. 3d World Coalition Against the War. Office: Office of the Mayor District Bldg 14th and E Sts Washington DC 20004 *If there is a single ideal which has guided and inspired me in both my pvt. and public lives it is the quest for the uniquely Am. prin. of justice and fair play for all men and women. The promise of this elusive goal took me, as a young man, away from my doctoral studies and has since been a major force in the direction my life has taken.*

BARRY, MARY ALICE, fin. exec.; b. Quincy, Mass., Dec. 31, 1928; d. Lawrence Joseph and Alice Mary (Blaisdell) B. B.S., Emmanuel Coll., 1950; postgrad., N.Y. U. With FBI, Boston, 1950-56, Nat. Assn. Investment Cos., N.Y.C., 1958-59, Dreyfus Fund, 1959-62; v.p. Eberstadt Fund Mgmt., Inc.; corp. sec. Chem. Fund Inc., Surveyor Fund, Eberstadt Energy Resources Fund, Eberstadt Internat. Fund, Inc., 1962—. Home: 520 E 81st St New York NY 10028 Office: 61 Broadway New York NY 10006

BARRY, PHILIP SEMPLE, TV and film producer; b. Aug. 8, 1923; s. Philip and Ellen (Semple) B.; m. Patricia A. White, June 11, 1950; children: Miranda Robbins, Stephanie Ann Thankful. B.A., Yale U., 1945. Prodn. mgr. Theatre Guild; v.p. Tomorrow Entertainment, Inc. Producer, John Drew Theatre, East Hampton, N.Y., Palm Beach Playhouse; asso. producer, producer: TV shows, including Gen. Electric Theatre; assoc. producer, producer 15 movies for TV; producer: feature films Sail A Crooked Ship, The Mating Game; exec. producer, ABC-TV, CBS-TV; now ind. producer: TV films Friendly Fire (Emmy award), First You Cry, Father Brown, Kent State. Mem. Mayor's Bicentennial Commn. on Arts, Los Angeles. Served with USNR, 1942-46. Mem. Am. Nat. Theater and Acad. West (past chmn. bd. dirs.), Caucus of Writers and Producers, Producers Guild Am., Writers Guild Am., Acad. TV Arts and Scis. Democrat. Episcopalian. Clubs: Calif. Yacht, Riviera Tennis, Players (N.Y.C.). Home: 144 N Bristol Ave Los Angeles CA 90049

BARRY, RICHARD FRANCIS, retired life insurance company executive; b. N.Y.C., Aug. 28, 1917; s. Thomas Francis and Gertrude Mary (Spillane) B.; m. Irene Patricia Schulties, July 24, 1948. B.B.A., St. John's U., Bklyn., 1948; J.D., Fordham U., 1953. Bar: N.Y. 1954. With Met. Life Ins. Co., N.Y.C., 1937-82, v.p., office of pres., then v.p. human resources, 1979-80, sr. v.p. human resources, 1980-81, sr. v.p. office of chmn., 1981-82, ret. 1982; mem. faculty St. John's U., 1955-60. Bd. dirs. Urban Acad. for Mgmt., Inc., 1979-82, Met. Life Found., 1981-82; sec. Nat. Assn. Drug Abuse Problems, N.Y.C., 1979-82; mem. Coop. Edn. Commn. N.Y.C., 1979-82. Served with AUS, 1943-45. Mem. Adminstrv. Mgmt. Soc. (pres. N.Y.C. chpt. 1972-73), Life Office Mgmt. Assn., Bar Assn. State N.Y., N.Y. C. of C. and Industry. Republican. Roman Catholic. Club: Huntington Country (L.I.). Lodge: K.C. (Bronx, N.Y.). Home: 237 Berry Hill Rd Syosset NY 11791

BARRY, RICHARD FRANCIS, III, newspaper publisher; b. Norfolk, Va., Jan. 18, 1943; s. Richard F. and Mary Margaret (Perry) B.; m. Carolyn Ann Kennett, Aug. 7, 1965; children: Carolyn Michelle, Christopher David. B.A., LaSalle Coll., 1964; J.D., U. Va., 1967. Bar: Va. 1967. Assoc. firm Kaufman, Oberndorfer & Spainhour, Norfolk, 1967-71, partner, 1972-73; corp. sec. Landmark Communications, Inc., Norfolk, 1973-74; pres., gen. mgr. Roanoke (Va.) Times & World-News, 1974-76, The Virginian-Pilot and The Ledger-Star, Norfolk, 1976-78, pub., 1983—; pres., chief operating officer, dir. Landmark Communications, Inc., Norfolk, 1978—, chief exec. officer, 1984—; dir. Greensboro News Co., Times-World Corp., Telecable Corp. Bd. dirs. Norfolk State U. Found., Chrysler Mus.; bd. dirs., pres., campaign chmn. United Way of south Hampton Rds.; mem. Greater Norfolk Corp. Mem. Am. Newspaper Pubs. Assn. (govt. affairs com. 1978—), Colgate Darden Bus. Sch. Sponsors (trustee). Office: 150 W Brambleton Ave Norfolk VA 23510

BARRY, ROBERT RAYMOND, business executive, former congressman; b. Omaha, May 15, 1915; s. Ralph and Ethel (Thomas) B.; m. Anne Rogers Benjamin, July 19, 1945; children: Cynthia Herndon Bidwell, Henry Huttleston Rogers. Student, Hamilton Coll., 1933-36, Dartmouth Coll., 1936-37, Sch. Finance, NYU, 1938, Law Sch., 1946-47. Investment banker Kidder Peabody & Co., 1937-38; with Mfrs. Trust Co., 1938-40; mgr. exec. Bendix Aviation Corp., 1940-44; asst. to pres. Yale & Towne Mfg. Co., 1945-50; pres. Calicopia Corp., 1965—; engaged in ranching and land devel., Coachella Valley, Calif., also in mining, Quincy, Calif.; mem. 86th-88th Congresses from 27th Dist. N.Y.; mem. coms. govt. operations 88th Congress from 25th Dist. N.Y., 1959-61, post office and civil service, 1959-65, fgn. affairs, 1961-65; dir. Vanderbilt Income Fund, Vanderbilt Growth Fund. Former Mem. Nat. council Boy Scouts Am.; Active campaign Dewey for dist. atty., 1937, Willkie presdl. campaign; mem. N.Y. Republican County Com., 1945; del. coordinator, statistician for Dewey, Rep. Nat. Conv.; mem. Rep. Nat. Campaign Com., Washington, 1948; personal staff Eisenhower campaign tour, Denver, Chgo., 1952; chmn. finance com. N.Y. State Congl. Campaign Com., Citizens for Eisenhower, 1954; chmn. Yonkers Citizens Eisenhower Com., 1956; U.S. del. NATO Parliamentarian Conf., 1959, 60, UNESCO Conf., 1963; Rep. nominee for congress 38th Calif. Dist.; mem. Nixon-Agnew Nat. Staff, 1968; dir. Calif. Rep. Central Com., 1966-68; Former mem. bd. dirs. Greater N.Y. YMCA; appointee Pres. Reagan's Peace Corps Adv. Council; active community, civic affairs. Mem. Alpha Delta Phi Internat. (pres.). Presbyterian. Clubs: Eldorado Country (Palm Springs, Cal.); St. Andrews Golf (Hastings, N.Y.); Sierra; Economic of N.Y., Metropolitan (N.Y.C.); Metropolitan, Capitol Hill (Washington). Home: 155 Wildwood Way Woodside CA 94026 also Thunderbird Country Club Rancho Mirage CA 92270 3001 Normanstone Dr NW Washington DC 20008

BARRY, SEYMOUR (SY BARRY), cartoonist, illustrator; b. N.Y.C., Mar. 12, 1928; s. Samuel and Celia Sally (Menchel) B.; m. Selma Kaplan, July 4, 1948; children—Elyse Robin, Joyce Toni, David Allen. Student, Sch. Art and Design, Art Student's League. Formerly free-lance cartoonist and illustrator; lectr. in field. Contbr. to: Pictorial Media; formerly asst. illustrator: Flash Gordon, King Features Syndicate; now illustrator: The Phanton Daily and Sunday strips for, King Features Syndicate. Mem. Newspaper Comics Council N.Y.C. Club: K.P. Home and office: 34 Saratoga Dr Jericho NY 11753

BARRY, THOMAS CORCORAN, investment counsellor; b. Cleve., Feb. 9, 1944; s. Willard Corcoran and Harriet (Mullin) B.; m. Patricia Ryan, Feb. 14, 1976; children: Hannah, Ryan, Oliver Mullin. B.A. in Latin Am. Studies, Yale U., 1966; M.B.A., Harvard U., 1969. Chartered fin. analyst. Market research analyst Corning Glass Works, Brazil and Japan, 1966-67; investment analyst T. Rowe Price Assos., Inc., Balt., 1969-70; dir. T. Rowe Price Assocs., Inc., 1974—; partner Cole, Thompson and Barry, Inc., Cleve., 1971-73; pres. Rowe Price New Horizons Fund, Balt., 1973—, Saratoga Assocs., 1983—; pres., chief exec. officer Rockefeller's Co., 1983—; dir. numerous cos. Trustee Loyola Coll., Balt.; bd. govs. Asso. Yale Alumni. Office: 30 Rockefeller Plaza New York NY 10112 108 E Read St Baltimore MD 21202

BARSALONA, FRANK, theatrical agent; b. S.I., N.Y., Mar. 31, 1938; s. Peter and Mary (Rotunno) B.; m. June Harris, Sept. 1, 1966; 1 dau., Nicole. Student, Wagner Coll., S.I., 1955-58, Herbert Berghof Sch., N.Y.C., 1959-60. Agt. Gen. Artists Corp., N.Y.C., 1960-64; founder, 1964; since pres. Premier Talent Agy., N.Y.C.; co-founder, pres. Phila. Fury, 1980—; lectr., moderator music industry. Bd. govs. T.J. Martell Leukemia Fund. Named Talent Agt. of Year Billboard Publs., 1976, 77. Office: 3 E 54th St New York NY 10022

BARSANTI, JOHN RICHARD, JR., former home furnishings and fashion co. exec., lawyer; b. Davenport, Iowa, July 1, 1928; s. John Richard and Lucille (Banks) B.; m. Nancy Lee Anne Nansen, Oct. 22, 1955; children—Lisa Anne, William B., Lori Anne, Lucy Anne. B.S. in Indsl. Engring, Washington U., St. Louis, 1949, LL.B., 1952. Bar: Mo. bar 1952. Asso. firm Greensfelder, Hemker & Weise, St. Louis, 1952-54; partner Husch, Eppenberge, Donohue, Elson & Cornfield, St. Louis, 1954-67; atty., Kirkwood, Mo., 1960-67; gen. counsel Kellwood Co., St. Louis, 1967-71, sec., 1967-73, dir., to 1981; v.p. Home Fashions, St. Louis, 1973-76; also dir.; pres. Stanfield Group, 1973-76, pres., chief operating officer, 1976-81. Commr., vice chmn. Mo. Air Conservation Commn., 1974-78; bd. dirs. Kirkwood R-7 Sch. Dist., 1965-70, sec., 1967-68, pres., 1969-70; bd. dirs. Mo. Assn. Retarded Children, 1959-67, St. Louis Assn. Retarded Children, 1957-60, United Way Greater St. Louis, Goodwill Industries Mo., 1968—; pres. Goodwill Industries Mo., 1978—; bd. dirs. Washington U. Alumni Fedn., 1965—, pres., 1968-69; trustee Washington U. Mem. Bar Assn. Met. St. Louis (pres. 1966-67), Am. Bar Assn., Mo. Bar, Nat. Conf. Bar Presidents, Kirkwood C. of C. (pres. 1959-60), Regional Commerce and Growth Assn. St. Louis (dir.), Am. Apparel Mfg. Assn. (dir.), Order of Coif, Phi Delta Phi, Omicron Delta Kappa. Clubs: Washington Univ. (pres. 1969-70, gov. 1969-71. Home: 12195 Bell Mead Des Peres MO 63131 Office: Suite 938 120 S Central Saint Louis MO 63105

BARSCHALL, HENRY HERMAN, physics educator; b. Berlin, Germany, Apr. 29, 1915; m. Eleanor A. Folsom; two children. A.M., Princeton U., 1939, Ph.D., 1940; Dr. rer. nat. h.c., U. Marburg (W. Ger.), 1982. Instr. Princeton U., 1940-41, U. Kans., 1941-43; mem. staff Los Alamos Sci. Lab., 1943-46, asst. div. leader, 1951-52; mem. faculty U. Wis., 1946—, prof. physics, 1950—, Bascom prof., 1973—, chmn. dept., 1951, 54, 56-57, 63-64; assoc. div. leader Lawrence Livermore Labs., 1971-73; Vis. prof. U. Calif. at Davis, 1972-73. Assoc. editor: Revs. Modern Physics, 1951-53; Asso. editor: Nuclear Physics, 1959-72; editor: Phys. Rev. C, 1972—; mem. editorial bd.: Jour. Phys. and Chem. Reference Data, 1979-84. Fellow Am. Phys. Soc. (chmn. div. nuclear physics 1968-69, mem. council 1983-86, Bonner prize 1965); mem. Nat. Acad. Sci. (chmn. physics sect. 1980-83), Am. Inst. Physics (chmn. publ. bd 1980-82, governing bd. 1983-86), NRC (assembly math. and phys. scis. 1980-83). Home: 1110 Tumalo Trail Madison WI 53711

BARSELOU, PAUL EDGAR, actor-writer; b. Cohoes, N.Y., May 31, 1922; s. Alfred William and Lydia Nancy (Hebert) B. B.A., SUNY, Albany, 1947, M.A., 1948; postgrad., U. Florence, Italy. Tchr. drama, speech, English, Schenectady and Ft. Plain, N.Y., 1948-52, radio-TV actor-writer, Troy, N.Y., 1952-54, Santa Monica, Calif., 1954-57; editorial supr. Aerospace, 1957-80; free lance actor-writer, 1954—; cons. identification neotropical butterflies. Appeared in: TV shows Three's Company, Bewitched, Icabod and Me, Dennis the Menace, Big Valley; Author: Identification Guide to the Genus Agrias. Served with USAAF, 1943-45. Decorated Air medal with oak leaf cluster. Mem. AFTRA, Screen Actors Guild. Roman Catholic. *Perseverence, tenacity, and a touch of blissful ignorance have helped me achieve success. I seem to do the impossible sometimes, but only because I don't know that what I'm doing can't be done*

BARSHAK, EDWARD JOEL, lawyer; b. Boston, May 21, 1924; s. Samuel and Lillian (Kahn) B.; m. Regina Winder, Feb. 22, 1958; children: Daniella, Rachelle, Joel. A.B., Tufts Coll., 1947; LL.B., Columbia U., 1949. Bar: Mass. Practiced Boston; mem. firm Sugarman, Rogers, Barshak & Cohen, Boston; spl. asst. atty. gen. Served with USN, 1942-45. Mem. ABA, Am. Coll. Trial Lawyers, Mass. Bar Assn., Boston Bar Assn. Democrat. Jewish. Club: St. Botolph (Boston). Home: 93 Dean Rd Brookline MA 02146 Office: 73 Tremont St Boston MA 02108

BARSHOP, SAMUEL EDWIN, motel executive; b. Waco, Tex., Sept. 11, 1929; s. Joseph J. and Mary (Markusfeld) B.; m. Ann Kronish, Dec. 31, 1952; children: Bruce, Steven, Jamie. B.B.A. in Internat. Trade, U. Tex., 1951; postgrad., Law Sch., St. Mary's U., 1952. Self-employed in real estate, office bldgs., shopping centers and land devel., Tex., 1951—; now pres., chmn., chief exec. officer, dir. La Quinta Motor Inns, San Antonio; dir. S.W. Airlines Co., Nat. Bancshares Corp. Tex., Nat. Bank Commerce; lectr. U. Tex.; mem. Motel Days Permanent Com., N.Y.C. Vice chmn. adv. council U. Tex. Coll. Bus., Adminstrn. Found., 1978-79, chmn., 1979-80, also chmn. devel./endowment com. and mem. exec. com. of adv. council; mem. Chancellor's Council and President's Assos., U. Tex.; former mem. coordinating bd. Tex. Coll. and Univ. System; former mem. Tex. Gov.'s Task Force Higher Edn.; bd. dirs. NCCJ, 1972—, San Antonio Econ. Devel. Found., San Antonio Festival; trustee S.W. Research Inst., San Antonio Med. Found.; chmn. parents com. Princeton U., 1972, 73; mem. San Antonio Com. for Arts; mem. devel. bd. U. Tex.

Health Sci. Center, San Antonio; mem. adv. com. Tex. Lyceum. Served to 2d lt. USAF, 1952-54. Named Man of Yr. Motel Brokers Assn. Am., 1978; recipient Disting. Alumnus award Coll. Bus. Adminstrn., U. Tex., 1979; bronze award for lodging industry Wall Street Transcript, 1980, 82. Mem. San Antonio C. of C. (dir. 1979-81). Club: Century (U. Tex. Coll. Bus. Adminstrn.) (dir.). Established Sam Barshop Professorship in Mktg. Adminstrn. and 2 scholarships for minorities in Grad. Sch. Bus., U. Tex., also centennial professorships in nursing adminstrn., and bus., centennial lectureship in bus. Home: 108 Villa Ann St San Antonio TX 78213 Office: 10010 San Pedro Ave San Antonio TX 78216

BARSKY, JAMES, publisher; b. Regina, Sask., Can., Nov. 26, 1925; came to U.S., 1951, naturalized, 1962; s. Morris and Anna (Basin) B.; m. Marilyn Lee Cannon, June 30, 1957; children: Robert Brian, Rosalind Diane. B.A., U. Sask., 1946; M.A., U. Toronto, Ont., Can., 1951; Ph.D., Northwestern U., 1958; postgrad., UCLA, 1958-60. Research fellow dept. public health nutrition Sch. Hygiene, U. Toronto, 1948-51; dept. biochemistry Northwestern U. Med. Sch., 1952-58; postdoctoral fellow U. Calif. Med. Center Brain Research Inst., Los Angeles, 1958-60; mgr. dept. biochemistry, div. research ETHICON Inc., Somerville, N.J., 1960-63; with Acad. Press Inc., N.Y.C., 1963—, v.p. editorial, 1968-73, sr. v.p., 1973-78, pres., 1978—; sr. v.p. Harcourt Brace Jovanovich, Inc.; treas., bd. dirs. Copyright Clearance Center Inc.; mem. tech. adv. com. Nat. Commn. Library and Info. Scis., 1976-77; mem. adv. com. Copyright Office, Library of Congress, 1978-79. Contbr. articles to profl. jours. Mem. AAAS, Am. Assn. Clin. Chemists, Am. Chem. Soc., Am. Inst. Biol. Scis., Biochem. Soc. (U.K.), Chemists Club, N.Y. Acad. Scis., Info. Industry Assn., Sigma Xi. Jewish. Home: 201 Redbud Ln Longwood FL 32779 Office: Academic Press Inc Orlando FL 32887

BARSNESS, RICHARD WEBSTER, management educator, administrator; b. Elbow Lake, Minn., Apr. 26, 1935; s. Russel E. and Joanna (Warga) B.; m. Dorothea L. Gother, Aug. 22, 1964; children: Karen Louise, Erik Richard. B.S., U. Minn., 1957, M.A., 1958, M.A.P.A., 1960, Ph.D., 1963. Budget analyst U.S. Bur. Budget, Washington, 1960-61; instr., asst. Northwestern U., Evanston, Ill., 1962-69, assoc. prof., 1969-78, assoc. dean, 1972-78; dean, prof. Lehigh U., Bethlehem, Pa., 1978—; exec. sec. Lexington Group in Transport History, 1969—; pres. Bus. History Conf., 1981-82; lectr. Transp. Ctr., Evanston, Ill., 1964—; editorial cons. Various pubs. Contbr.: articles to profl. jours.; editor: Lexington Newsletter 1969-75. Adv. Gov.'s Adv. Council State of Ill., 1969-72; gen. chmn. United Way Lehigh U., 1981. Mem. Acad. Mgmt., Transp. Research Forum, Bus. History Conf. (trustee 1978—, pres. 1981-82), Am. Soc. Pub. Adminstrn., Phi Beta Kappa, Beta Gamma Sigma. Republican. Episcopalian. Club: Bethlehem. Home: 769 Apollo Dr Bethlehem PA 18107 Office: Lehigh U Coll Bus and Econs Bethlehem PA 18015

BARSTOW, ROLAND J., savs. and loan exec.; b. Cambridge, Mass., 1919. Studied, U. Ill.; M.B.A., U. Chgo. Chmn., chief exec. officer Bell Fed. Savs. & Loan Assn., Chgo., Bell Savs. Service Corp.; dir. Ill. Savs. & Loan League; past mem. adv. com. Fed. Home Loan Mortgage Corp. Dir. Chgo. Crime Commn.; bd. dirs. Fed. Savs. and Loan Council Ill. Home: 200 Merton Av Glen Ellyn IL 60137 Office: Bell Fed Savings & Loan Assn Monroe and Clark Sts Chicago IL 60603

BARTA, FRANK RUDOLPH, SR., psychiatrist, neurologist; b. Omaha, Nov. 3, 1913; s. Rudolph J. and Anna (Smejkal) B.; m. Mildred K. Ware, Aug. 12, 1939; children—Frank Rudolph, Nancy and Carol (twins), Richard, Matthew, Michael. A.B., Creighton U., 1935; M.D., Johns Hopkins, 1939. Diplomate Am. Bd. Psychiatry and Neurology. Intern Harper Hosp., Detroit, 1939-40; asst. psychiatry Yale Sch. Medicine, 1942-43; resident neurology U. Chgo. Clinics, 1942-43; pvt. practice psychiatry and neurology, 1946—; instr. psychiatry and neurology Creighton U. Sch. Medicine, 1946-49, dir. dept., 1949-56, prof. psychiatry and neurology, 1956—; clin. prof. psychiatry Chgo. Med. Sch., 1970-74; attending psychiatrist St. Joseph's Hosp., St. Catherine's Hosp., 1949-67; cons. in psychiatry A.R.C., VA Hosp., Cath. Charities, SAC, 1949-67; med. dir. Mental Health Center LaSalle County, Ottawa, Ill., 1968-73; clin. dir. Tideland Mental Health Center, Washington, N.C., 1973-75; psychiatrist Gulfport div. VA Center, 1975—. Author: The Moral Theory of Behavior—A New Answer to the Enigma of Mental Illness, 1952; Contbr. articles med. jours. Chmn. personnel bd., City of Omaha, 1959-67. Dir. mental hygiene unit U.S. Army, 1943-46; Fort Bliss, Tex. Fellow A.C.P. (life), Am. Geriatrics Soc., Am. Psychiat. Assn. (life); mem. A.M.A., N.C., Pamlico-Albemarle med. socs., Ill. Psychiat. Soc., Nat. Acad. Religion and Mental Health (charter, life mem.). Roman Catholic. Home: Great Oaks 518 Shore Dr Ocean Springs MS 39564 Office: VA Center Gulfport MS 39501 *To understand, know and appreciate what to seek and what to avoid, first understand, know and appreciate that in every situation things are the way they are because there is no better way for them to be, under the circumstances.*

BARTALINI, C. RICHARD, judge; b. Kincaid, Ill., Sept. 25, 1931; s. Chester Richard and Florinda (Galli) B.; m. Anne M. Evanoff, June 4, 1955; children: Robert Charles, Denise Anne, David Chester. B.A., U. Calif.-Berkeley, 1954; J.D., U. Calif.-San Francisco, 1957. Bar: Calif. 1957. Practice law, Oakland, 1957-66, Alameda, 1966-77; dep. dist. atty. Alameda County, 1957-59; chief def. counsel Transit Casualty Co., 1959-60; chief trial atty. Alameda/Contra Costa Transit Co., 1960-61; asso. Nichols, Williams, Morgan & Digardi, 1961-66; partner Davis, Craig & Bartalini, 1966-77; judge Superior Ct. Calif., 1977—; atty., counselor Supreme Ct. U.S.; del. Calif. Bar Conf., 1963-68. Chmn. Alameda Youth Activities Com., 1958-63, Nat. Council on Mental Health and Retardation, 1965-69; mem. President's Council on Youth Opportunity, 1965-70; pres. Alameda Bd. Edn.; pres., v.p., bd. dirs. Alameda Boys Club; mem. exec. com. Nat. Found. March of Dimes; mem. nat. adv. bd. Closeup Found.-Partners Program. Named Alameda's Young Man of Year, 1965, Outstanding Civic Leader of Am., 1967; recipient Service award Nat. Congress Parents and Tchrs., 1972, Disting. Service award Alameda Unified Sch. Dist., 1972, Man and Boy award Boys Clubs Am., 1975; Bronze Keystone award Boys Club Am., 1979. Mem. ABA, Calif. Bar Assn., Alameda County Bar Assn. (dir.), Criminal Cts. Bar Assn., Am. Trial Lawyers Assn., Alameda County Lawyers Club (past pres.), Calif. C. of C. (past dir.), Alameda Jaycees (past pres.), U.S. Jaycees (past legal counsel), Phi Alpha Delta. Clubs: Elks, Eagles, Kiwanis, Alameda Rod and Gun, Commonwealth. Home: 1224 Bay St Alameda CA 94501 Office: Hall of Justice Hayward CA 94544

BARTEE, THOMAS CRESON, computer scientist; b. Moberly, Mo., Dec. 18, 1926; s. Thomas Monroe and Verna Miller (Tippett) B.; m. Mildred Higdon, Nov. 5, 1954; 1 son, Thomas Quentin. B.A., Westminster Coll., 1949. Mem. staff computer research M.I.T.-Lincoln Lab., Lexington, Mass., 1955-63; Gordon MacKay lectr. in computer engring. Harvard U., Cambridge, Mass., 1963-69, dir. electronic design center, 1969-72, Gordon MacKay prof. computer engring., 1970—; cons. Nat. Acad. Scis., IDA, IBM, Honeywell, Raytheon; IEEE disting. computer sci. lectr., 1972-74. Author: Digital Computer Fundamentals, 5th edit, 1981, Basic Computer Programming, 1981, Introduction to Computer Science, 1972, (with G. Birkhoff) Modern Applied Algebra, 1971; Editor: IEEE-IRE Computer Jour, 1963-66. Recipient Disting. contbn. in computer sci. award Westminster Coll., 1980. Mem. IEEE (chmn. N.E. computer group 1973-74), Am. Math. Soc. Office: Aiken Computation Lab Harvard Univ Cambridge MA 02138

BARTEL, HERBERT HERMAN, JR., engineering educator; b. Dallas, Tex., Mar. 31, 1924; s. Herbert Herman and Freda (Metzger) B.; m. Dorothy Jean Angus, July 19, 1950; children: Peggy Jean and Kathy Jean (twins). B.S. in Civil Engring., So. Meth. U., 1944; M.S., U. Tex., 1950; Ph.D., Tex. A&M U., 1962. From instr. to prof., chmn. dept. civil and environmental engring. So. Meth. U., Dallas, 1946-72; chmn. dept. civil engring. U. El Paso, Tex., 1972-78, prof., 1972—; design engr. Tex. Hwy. Dept., summer 1953, Forrest & Cotton, Inc., summers 1967-68. Commr. Boy Scouts Am., 1952-55. Served as ensign C.E.C., USNR, 1943-46; PTO. NSF faculty fellow, 1960-61; Automotive Safety Found. fellow, 1958-59; recipient Excellence in Engring. Teaching award Gen. Dynamics Corp., 1969. Mem. ASCE, Am. Soc. Engring. Edn. (instl. rep. 1973—), Am. Road Builders Assn., Nat. Soc. Profl. Engrs., Tex. Soc. Profl. Engrs. (Outstanding C.E. Faculty Mem. 1982, Engr. of Year award El Paso br. 1973, dir. El Paso br.). Lutheran (former elder). Clubs: Town North Lions (v.p. 1969-70), Dallas (dir. 1971-72), El Paso Border Volleyball.). Home: 5801 Kingsfield Ave El Paso TX 79912 *I am fortunate to have been born into a fine Christian family where people always meant more than things. At key points in my life there have always been people of great character who have helped me and who have inspired me to do my best. What small degree of success I have achieved is in greatest measure due to their influence. If in my career, I have a similar impact in the shaping of a few lives I shall consider this success indeed.*

BARTEL, ROLAND, educator; b. Hillsboro, Kans., Feb 17, 1919; s. Peter and Anna (Schmidt) B.; m. Nancy Elizabeth (Betty) Long, Oct. 19, 1943; children—David Roland, Brian Leevern (dec.). B.A., Bethel Coll., 1947; Ph.D., Ind. U., 1951. Tchr. pub. schs., Buhler, Kans., 1938-41; mem. faculty, adminstrn. U. Oreg., Eugene, 1951—, asso. prof. English, 1959-64, prof., 1964—, also asst. dean, 1960-64, head dept., 1968-76; dir. Oreg. Council for Advanced Placement, 1960-63. Editor: Johnson's London, 1956, London in Plague and Fire, 1957, Liberty and Terror in England, 1965, (with E.R. Bingham) America through Foreign Eyes, 1956, Biblical Images in Literature, 1975. Ednl. dir. Civilian Pub. Service Camps for consciencious objectors, Fla. and Calif., 1942-45. Strauss fellow Ind. U., 1950-51; recipient Ersted award for distinguished teaching U. Oreg., 1965. Mem. Modern Lang. Assn., Nat. Council Tchrs. English, Fellowship of Reconciliation. Mennonite. Home: 2660 Baker Blvd Eugene OR 97403

BARTELL, GERALD AARON, business executive; b. Chgo., May 20, 1914; s. Benjamin and Lena (Tartakowsky) Beznor; m. Joyce Jaeger, Nov. 2, 1941; children: Jeffrey, Denis, Laura, Jane, Thad and Thomas, (twins). Ph.B., U. Wis., 1937, M.A., 1939, postgrad. Law Sch., 1939-40. Radio actor, dir., producer, 1932-37; faculty dept. radio edn. U. Wis., 1937-47, asso. prof., 1946; founder Bartell Broadcasting Corp., Milw., 1947, pres., 1947-66, Bartell Media Corp., N.Y.C., 1961-63, chmn. bd., 1963-69, chief exec. officer, pub., 1961-68; pres. Emerald Realty Co., Milw., 1965—, Theater Classic Recitals, Ltd., 1976—; chmn. Telstar Corp., Los Angeles, 1981—; founder, former pres. Netherlands Antilles Broadcasting Corp., Curacao and Aruba; founder, chmn., pres. Am. Med. Bldgs., Inc., Milw., 1962-75; past dir. Capital Indemnity Corp., Madison, Milw. Equity Fund, Inc., Continental Mortgage Ins., Inc.; dir. Corp. Entertainment and Learning, N.Y.C. Producer, performer children's radio programs, records, TV movies. Chmn., Wis. Found. for Arts, 1976—; former bd. dirs. Am. Council Arts, N.Y.C.; founding chmn. Wis. Arts Bd., 1975. Served to lt. (j.g.) USNR, 1942-45. Rockefeller fellow NBC, Chgo., 1983. Mem. Phi Kappa Phi. Unitarian. Home: 64 Oak Creek Trail Madison WI 53717 Office: 3800 Regent St Madison WI 53705

BARTELL, LAWRENCE SIMS, educator, chemist; b. Ann Arbor, Mich., Feb. 23, 1923; s. Floyd Earl and Lawrence (Sims) B.; m. Joy Hilda Keer, Aug. 16, 1952; 1 son, Michael Keer. B.S., U. Mich., 1944, M.S., 1947, Ph.D., 1951. Research asst. Manhattan project U. Chgo., 1944-45; mem. faculty Iowa State U., 1953-65, prof. chemistry, 1959-65, U. Mich., 1965—; vis. prof. Moscow (USSR) State U., 1972, U. Paris XI, Orsay, France, 1973, U. Tex., 1978; cons. Gillette Co., Chgo., 1956-62, Mobil Oil Corp., Paulsboro, N.J., 1960—; mem. commn. on electron diffraction Internat. Union Crystallography, 1966-75. Asso. editor: Jour. Chem. Physics, 1963-66; mem. editorial bd.: Jour. Computational Chemistry, 1979—, Chem. Physics Letters, 1981—. Served with USNR, 1945. Recipient Disting. Faculty Achievement award U. Mich., 1981. Mem. Am. Chem. Soc. (petroleum research fund adv. bd. 1970-73), Am. Phys. Soc. (chmn. div. chem. physics 1977-78), Am. Crystallographic Assn., AAAS, Phi Beta Kappa, Sigma Xi, Phi Kappa Phi, Phi Lambda Upsilon, Alpha Chi Sigma. Home: 305 Sumac Ln Ann Arbor MI 48105

BARTELL, LEE, corporation executive; b. Milw., 1910; s. Benjamin and Lena (Beznor) B.; m. Ina Berginn, Jan. 13, 1934; children: Michael, Rusti, Richard. Student, Milw. State Tchrs. Coll., 1932, Marquette U., 1933; LL.B., U. Wis., 1936. Bar: Wis. 1936, Calif. 1960. With Wis. Atty. Gen.'s Office; counsel Wis. Devel. Authority; trial atty. U.S. Govt.; founder Bartell Broadcasting Corp.; former pres. Bartell Media Corp., KCBQ, Inc.; sec., dir. Bartell Broadcasters, Inc., Bartell Broadcasters N.Y., Inc.; pres. McDodd Corp., Interstate 8 Hotel, Inc.; gen. partner Lee Bartell & Assos.; sec. Radio Sta. KMJC, San Diego. Editor: Wis. Law Rev. Bd. visitors U. San Diego Law Sch.; bd. dirs. San Diego Symphony. Served to lt. (j.g.) USNR, 1943-44. Mem. Am. Legion (past post comdr.), Order of Coif. Club: Mason. Office: 543 Hotel Circle S San Diego CA 92138

BARTELS, JOHN P., chem. co. exec.; b. N.Y.C., Feb. 4, 1922; s. John D. and Ann T. (Persson) B.; children—Debra Ann, Jeffrey John. A.B., Columbia U., 1942, B.S. in M.E, 1943. Registered profl. engr., N.Y. With Pfizer Inc., 1951—, pres., N.Y.C., 1971—; chmn. bd. Quigley Co., 1972—; v.p. Material Sci. Products, N.Y.C., 1973—. Pres. Desert Communities United Fund, Calif., 1966. Served with USN, 1943-46. Mem. ASME, Am. Soc. Mining Engrs. Clubs: Union League, Beta Theta Pi. Home: 1 Pine Point Lloyd Harbor NY 11743 Office: 235 E 42 St New York NY 10017

BARTELS, JOHN RIES, judge; b. Balt., Nov. 8, 1897; s. William Nicholas and Louise (Reuter) B.; m. Anne Bell Willson, May 3, 1930; children: John Ries, William Gilpin. A.B cum laude, Johns Hopkins, 1920; LL.B., Harvard, 1923. Bar: N.Y. 1924. Since practiced in, N.Y.C.; justice Supreme Ct. N.Y., 1950-51; mem. firm Bartels & Hartung, 1951-59; judge U.S. Dist. Ct., Bklyn., 1959-73, sr. judge, 1974—; Mem. N.Y. Law Revision Commn., 1945-50, 52-57; spl. referee appellate div. N.Y. Supreme Ct.; ex-counsel fgn. debt readjustment Govt. Ecuador; ex-gen. counsel Gen. Acceptance Corp. (and subsidiaries), The Fyr-Fyter Co. (and subsidiaries), Brilhart Plastics Corp. Dir. Bklyn. Council for Social Planning, 1953-58; mem. Mayor's Com. on Puerto Rican Affairs, N.Y.C., 1955-57; Alumni trustee Johns Hopkins, 1953-54; sec. bd. regents L.I. Coll. Hosp.; former chmn. lay adv. bd. Kings County Hosp. Center; bd. dirs. NCCJ, Brotherhood-in-Action, Bklyn. Boys Club. Named hon. citizen Md., 1958; recipient Johns Hopkins U. Distinguished Alumnus award, 1967. Fellow Am. Coll. Trial Lawyers; mem. Am., N.Y. State, Bklyn. bar assns., Assn. Bar City N.Y., N.Y. County Lawyers Assn., Fundacion Internacional Eloy Alfaro, Am. Law Inst., Fed. Bar Council, Am. Judicature Soc., Inst. Jud. Adminstrn., Squadron A Ex-Mems., Harvard Law Sch. Assn. N.Y.C. (v.p.), Omicron Delta Kappa, Delta Upsilon. Republican (past treas. exec. com. Kings County). Conglist. (trustee). Clubs: Harvard, Down Town Assn., Lawyers, Nat. Lawyers, Inc. (hon.). Office: US Dist Ct Brooklyn NY 11201

BARTELS, MILLARD, lawyer; b. Syracuse, N.Y., Feb. 24, 1905; s. Herman and Jane Agnes (Millard) B.; m. Eulalia Stevens; children—Millard Stevens, Chester Bruce, Jane Lee. A.B., Cornell U., 1927, LL.B., 1929. Bar: Conn. bar 1930. Since practiced in, Hartford; gen. counsel Travelers Ins. Cos., Hartford, 1945-69, chmn. ins. exec. com., dir., 1955-70; dir. Hosp. Corp. Am. Mem. Parole Bd., Conn. State Prison, 1953-55, Town Council of West Hartford, 1939-45; pres. Town Council of West Hartford, 1943-45; Bd. dirs. Health Ins. Inst., chmn., 1966-67; mem. Cornell U. Council; adv. bd. Cornell Law Sch.; trustee Bishop's Fund, Diocese of Conn., Bushnell Meml. Hall Corp.; regent U. Hartford, 1950-58. Mem. Am., Conn., Hartford County bar assns., Assn. Life Ins. Counsel (pres. 1957-58), Health Ins. Assn. Am. (pres. 1960-61). Clubs: Tunxis (pres. 1966, 67), Hartford (pres. 1956-57), Hartford Golf; Ocean Reef (Key Largo, Fla.). Home: 29 Westwood Rd West Hartford CT 06117 Office: 1 American Row Hartford CT 06103

BARTELS, STANLEY LEONARD, corporation executive; b. N.Y.C., Sept. 1, 1927; s. Abraham and Anna (Schultz) B.; m. Linda Lauretz; children: Jonathan Scott, Nancy Merrill, Diane Brooke, Elizabeth Cara. B.S., NYU, 1954, M.B.A., 1956; grad., N.Y. State Maritime Acad., 1947. Examiner Mfrs. Hanover Bank, N.Y.C., 1948-50; security analyst Standard & Poor's Corp., N.Y.C., 1950-53; sr. financial analyst internat. div. Ford Motor Co., N.Y.C., 1953-56; asst. to treas. Grace Line, Inc., N.Y.C., 1956-57; v.p. Tex. McCrary, Inc.; also controller, asst. to pres., N.Y.C., 1957-60; gen. partner J.R. Williston & Beane, N.Y.C., 1960-63; pres., dir. Electrocopy Corp., 1963-66; sr. v.p., dir. Shaskan & Co., Inc.; mem. N.Y. Stock Exchange, 1966-73; pres. J.D. Winer & Co., Inc.; mem. N.Y. Stock Exchange, 1973-74; v.p. L.M. Rosenthal & Co., Inc.; mem. N.Y. Stock Exchange, 1974-75; dir. Patrician Paper Co., Filigree Foods, Inc., chmn., chief exec. officer, 1975-79; pres., dir., chief exec. officer United Grocers Corp., East Rutherford, N.J., 1979-81; Sr. v.p. Weinrich Zitzmann Whitehead, St. Louis, 1981-82; sr. v.p. Laidlaw Adams & Peck, Inc., N.Y.C., 1982—. Served to lt. USNR., 1945-47, 51-53. Mem. N.Y. Soc. Security Analysts, Phi Alpha Kappa. Clubs: Netherland of N.Y., NYU. Home: Farley Rd Short Hills NJ 07078 *Only those projects that are of a beneficial nature to society have the tendency to survive.*

BARTER, ROBERT HENRY, physician, emeritus educator; b. Harvard, Ill., Mar. 15, 1913; s. Francis Albert and Lula Mae (Rowbottom) B.; m. Joanne Rae Blied, Dec. 29, 1948; children: Robert Raymond, James Francis, Mary Joanne. B.S., U. Wis., 1937, M.D., 1940. Intern Cleve. City Hosp., 1940-41; resident Chgo. Lying-In Hosp., 1941-42, Wis. Gen. Hosp., Madison, 1946-48; chief med. officer obstetrics and gynecology Galinger Municipal Hosp., Washington, 1948-50; faculty George Washington U. Sch. Medicine, 1950—, prof., 1958-83, prof. emeritus, 1983—, chmn. dept. obstetrics and gynecology, 1958-67; cons. emeritus surgeon gen. USAF; sr. cons. emeritus Walter Reed Army Med. Center. Served to maj., M.C. AUS, 1942-46. Mem. Am. Gynecol. and Obstet. Soc., Am. Assn. Obstetricians and Gynecologists, A.C.S., Am. Coll. Obstetricians and Gynecologists, Soc. Gynecol. Surgeons, N.Am. Ob-Gyn Soc., So. Gynecol. and Obstet. Soc., Gynecol. Vis. Soc. Gt. Brit. and Ireland (hon.), AMA, Sigma Xi, Alpha Omega Alpha, Nu Sigma Nu, Kappa Sigma. Clubs: Burning Tree, Congressional Country; Hole in the Wall Golf, Port Royal (Naples, Fla.); Rehoboth Beach (Del.) Country. Home: 6406 Goldleaf Dr Bethesda MD 20817 Office: 2141 K St NW Washington DC 20037

BARTH, DAVID KECK, mfg. co. exec.; b. Springfield, Ill., Dec. 7, 1943; s. David Klenk and Edna Margaret (Keck) B.; m. Dian Oldemeyer, Nov. 21, 1970; children—David, Michael, John. B.A. cum laude, Knox Coll., Galesburg, Ill., 1965; M.B.A., U. Calif., Berkeley, 1971. With data processing div. IBM Corp., Chgo., 1966; with No. Trust Co., Chgo., 1971-72; mgr. treasury ops., then treas. fin. services group Borg-Warner Corp., Chgo., 1972-79; treas. W.W. Grainger, Inc., Skokie, Ill., 1979—. Served to lt. USNR, 1966-69. Mem. Beta Gamma Sigma, Phi Delta Theta. Lutheran. Office: 5500 W Howard St Skokie IL 60077

BARTH, EARL E., physician; b. Olivet, S.D., May 1, 1901; s. Albert and Matilda (Boegler) B.; m. Ella M. Jensen, Feb. 26, 1927; 1 dau., Barbara B. Myers. A.B., North Central Coll., Naperville, Ill., 1922, 1968; M.D., Northwestern U., 1928. Diplomate Am. Bd. Radiology (mem. bd. 1958-64). Practice medicine and surgery, 1928—; faculty Northwestern U., 1931—, dir. x-ray dept., 1936—, asso. prof. radiology, 1948-53, prof., 1953-69, emeritus prof., 1969—, chmn. dept. of radiology, 1957-69, acting chmn., 1969-72, cons., 1972—; radiologist Passavant Meml. Hosp., Chgo., 1936—; cons. radiology VA Research Hosp., Commonwealth Edison Co., Peoples Gas, Light and Coke Co., Ill. Bell Telephone Co.; vis. prof. radiology Mayo Clinic, 1960. Contbr. articles med. jours. Mem. radiation com. NRC-Nat. Acad. Scis.; Treas. 5th Inter-Am. Congress Radiology; del., chmn. U.S. delegations to Internat. Congresses Radiology, Montreal, 1962 del., chmn. U.S. delegations to Internat. Congresses Radiology, Rome, 1965 del., chmn. U.S. delegations to Internat. Congresses Radiology, Tokyo, 1969 del., chmn. U.S. delegations to Internat. Congresses Radiology, Madrid, 1973 del., chmn. U.S. delegations to Internat. Congresses Radiology, Goldmedalist, 1973. Served as comdr. M.C. USNR, World War II. Grubbe gold medalist Chgo. Med. Soc., 1967. Fellow Acad. Internat. Medicine; mem. AMA, Chgo., Ill. med. socs., Inst. Medicine of Chgo., Societa Italiana di Radiologia Medica and Medicina Nucleare (hon. mem.), Am. Roentgen Ray Soc. (past v.p. and chmn. exec. council, pres. 1962-63), Radiol. Soc. N.Am., Am. Coll. Radiology (chmn. bd. of chancellors 1957-60, pres. 1960-61, gold medalist 1962), Chgo. Roentgen Soc. (past pres.), Am. Assn. Ry. Surgeons, Inter-Am. Coll. Radiology, Nipon Radiol. Soc. (hon.), Phi Chi, Alpha Omega Alpha. Presbyn. Club: Rotarian. Home: 2258 Lincoln Park W Chicago IL 60614

BARTH, ELMER ERNEST, wire and cable co. exec.; b. Phila., May 15, 1922; s. Paul Adolph and Anna (Miller) B.; m. Ruth Bradstreet Stone, Sept. 18, 1943; 1 dau., Rebecca Ordway. Student, Bentley Sch. Accounting, 1947-51; B.B.A., Northeastern U., 1956. Asst. treas. Hayward Hosiery Co., Ipswich, Mass., 1945-56; v.p. mfg. Rockbestos Co.; Mem. Marmon Group, New Haven, 1956—; sec., treas., dir. Applied Data Processing, Inc., North Haven, 1961—; trustee Ipswich Savs. Bank, 1947-56. Bd. govs., vice chmn. fin. com. Children's Center, Hamden, Conn., 1965-68. Served with USNR, 1942-45. Club: Branford Yacht (commodore 1976). Home: 3 Sandra Dr Branford CT 06405 Office: 285 Nicoll St New Haven CT 06510

BARTH, FRANCES D., artist; b. N.Y.C., July 31, 1946; d. Frank and Helen (Henning) B. B.F.A., Hunter Coll., 1968, M.A., 1970. Instr. Princeton U., 1976-79, Sarah Lawrence Coll., Bronxville, N.Y., 1979—. Exhibited various one-woman shows, N.Y.C., 1974—, Chgo., 1981, group shows, Moore Coll. Art, 1970, Whitney Mus. Am. Art, N.Y.C., 1972-73, Houston Mus. Contemporary Art, 1972, Corcoran Gallery Art, Washington, Bard Coll., Annandale-on-Hudson, N.Y., 1973, Trenton State Coll., 1974, Princeton U. Art Mus., 1975, High

Mus. Art, Atlanta, 1976, Bennington Coll., San Francisco Art Mus., 1978, U. Pa., MIT, (group shows), William Patterson Coll., Wayne, N.J., 1979, group shows, NYU, 1979, Va. Commonwealth U., Richmond, 1980, Sarah Lawrence Coll., 1981, Mus. Modern Art, Cleve. Mus. Art, 1983, others; represented in permanent collections, Akron Art Inst., Albright-Knox Gallery, Am. Can Co., Greenwich, Conn., Amerada Hess Corp., N.Y.C., Chase Manhattan Bank, N.Y.C., Cornell U., IBM Corp., N.Y.C., Mobil Oil Corp., N.Y.C., Prudential Inst. Co., N.J., Whitney Mus. Am. Art, Lehman Bros., N.Y.C. and Chgo., Isham, Lincoln & Beale, Chgo., Security Pacific Nat. Bank, Los Angeles, Swiss Bank Corp., N.Y.C., Cameron Iron Works, Houston, Mus. Modern Art, N.Y.C., Paul Haim Found., Paris, Humana, Inc., Louisville, Coudert Bros., N.Y.C., Met. Mus. Art, N.Y.C., Dallas Mus. Art. Creative Artists Pub. Service grantee, 1973; Nat. Endowment for Arts grantee, 1974, 82; John Simon Guggenheim Meml. fellow, 1977.

BARTH, FRANK R., management educator, university administrator; b. Chgo., Mar. 19, 1918; s. Frank Phillip and Esther (Pedersen) B.; m. Marjorie V. Hove, Sept. 28, 1940; children: Eugene F., Kathryn L., Frank P. II, James A. A.B., Luther Coll., 1940, LL.D., 1969; M.B.A., Northwestern U., 1947. C.P.A., Ill.; cert. mgmt. acctg., Ill. Prof., head dept. econs. Luther Coll., 1946-53; partner Barth & Hayes (C.P.A.s), Decorah, Iowa, 1947-54, Alexander Grant & Co., Washington and Chgo., 1953-59; fin. v.p. Pettibone Corp., Chgo., 1959-69; pres. Westrac Corp., Ft. Worth, 1967-69, Gustavus Adolphus Coll., St. Peter, Minn., 1969-75, CEO Services, Mpls., 1975-77; prof. mgmt. Luther Coll., 1977—, treas., v.p. fin. affairs, 1978—; dir., chmn. audit com. First Fed. Savs. and Loan, Mpls.; mem. audit com. Interstate Power Co., Dubuque, Iowa; dir. Search Inst., Mpls.; financial cons. Post Office Dept., 1953-55. Mem. Lake Forest (Ill.) Bd. Edn., 1964-69, pres., 1966-69; mem. Minn. Gov.'s Commn. on Salaries, 1970, Minn. Gov.'s Com. Community Corrections, 1975-77; mem. coll. scholarship coms. Soo Line R.R. and Geico Corp.; Mpls. alt. del. Republican Nat. Conv., 1952; Bd. dirs. Minn. Pvt. Coll. Fund, pres., 1972-73; bd. dirs. Luth. Ednl. Conf. N. Am., pres., 1974-75; bd. dirs. Sec. Central States Coll. Assn., sec., 1969-72, chmn., 1972-73; bd. regents Luther Coll., 1976-77; pres., bd. dirs. Minn. Valley Restoration Project, 1975-83; bd. dirs. Luth. Youth Encounter, 1973-79, pres., 1977-78. Served as navigator USNR, 1943-46. Decorated Knight first class Order N. Star, Sweden; named Outstanding Young Man Iowa, 1952. Mem. Am. Inst. Accountants, Iowa Soc. C.P.A.s (chmn. com. taxation 1950-51, com. coop. with bankers 1951-52, com. on edn. 1978—), Ill. Soc. C.P.A.s (com. bankers and creditors 1965- 66), Minn. Socs. C.P.A.s, Beta Alpha Psi, Alpha Kappa Psi, Pi Kappa Delta., Omicron Delta Epsilon. Lutheran. Clubs: Lake Forest (bd. dirs., treas. 1957-61), Minneapolis. Home: 715 Ridge Rd Decorah IA 52101

BARTH, JOHN ROBERT, English educator, priest; b. Buffalo, Feb. 23, 1931; s. Philip C. and Mary K. (Eustace) B. A.B., Fordham U., 1954, M.A., 1956; Ph.L., Bellarmine Coll., 1955; S.T.B., Woodstock Coll., 1961-62; Ph.D., Harvard U., 1967. Joined Society of Jesus, Roman Catholic Ch., 1948; tchr. English, French, Latin (Canisius High Sch.), Buffalo, 1955-58; asst. prof. English Canisius Coll., Buffalo, 1967-70, Harvard U., Cambridge, Mass., 1970-74; assoc. prof. English U. Mo.-Columbia, 1974-77, prof., 1977-79, Catherine Paine Middlebush prof. English, 1979-82, prof. English, chmn. dept., 1980—. Author: Coleridge and Christian Doctrine, 1969, The Symbolic Imagination: Coleridge and the Romantic Tradition, 1977 (Book of Yr award, Conf on Christianity and Lit. 1977); editor: Religious Perspectives in Faulkner's Fiction, 1972; mem. editorial bd. cons.: Thought, 1980—; mem. adv. bd.: Studies in Romanticism, 1981—. Bd. advisors Wordsworth Circle, Phila., 1976—; trustee St. Louis U., 1974-79. Recipient Howard Mumford Jones prize Harvard U., 1967; Dexter fellow, 1967; NEH summer grantee, 1969; Am. Council Learned Socs. grantee, 1970; Harvard U. research grantee, 1973; recipient Book of Yr. award (The Symbolic Imagination) Conf. on Christianity and Lit., 1977. Mem. Conv. on Christianity and Lit. (dir. 1980—), MLA (del. assembly 1979-83, exec. com. romantic div. 1975-79, exec. com. religious opp), Wordsworth-Coleridge Assn. (v.p. 1978, pres. 1979), Keats-Shelley Assn., AAUP, English Inst. Home: Newman Center 1701 Maryland Ave Columbia MO 65201 Office: Dept English U Mo 213 Arts and Sci Columbia MO 65211

BARTH, JOHN SIMMONS, author, educator; b. Cambridge, Md., May 27, 1930; s. John Jacob and Georgia (Simmons) B.; m. Harriette Anne Strickland, Jan. 11, 1950; children: Christine Anne, John Strickland, Daniel Stephen; m. Shelly I. Rosenberg, Dec. 27, 1970. B.A., Johns Hopkins U., 1951, M.A., 1952. From instr. to assoc. prof. English Pa. State U., 1953-65; prof. English SUNY, Buffalo, 1965-73; prof. English and creative writing Johns Hopkins U., 1973—. Author: The Floating Opera, 1956, The End of the Road, 1958, The Sot-Weed Factor, 1960, Giles Goat-Boy, 1966, Lost in the Funhouse, 1968, Chimera, 1972 (Recipient Nat. Book award in fiction 1973), Letters, 1979, Sabbatical: A Romance, 1982. Office: Writing Seminars Johns Hopkins U Baltimore MD 21218

BARTH, JOSEPH JOHN, naval officer; b. Bklyn., Oct. 10, 1931; s. Joseph John and Marion Rita (Lucey) B.; m. Gerarde Ann Query, Aug. 3, 1957; children: Joanne, John, Helen, Andrew, Stephen, Marie. B.S. in Natural Sci., Niagara U., 1952. Commd. ensign U.S. Navy, 1954, advanced through grades to rear adm., 1974; comdg. officer USS Forrestal, 1975-77; chief Naval Air Tng., Corpus Christi, Tex., 1978-80; comdr. Carrier Group Three, Alameda, Calif., 1981-82; dir. Strike and Amphibious Warfare Div., Dept. Navy, Washington, 1982—. Decorated Legion of Merit, Bronze Star, D.F.C., Air medal. Lodge: Rotary. Office: Director Strike and Amphibious Warfare Div Dept Navy Washington DC 20350

BARTH, KARL LUTHER, educational adminstrator; b. Milw., Nov. 7, 1924; s. G. Christian and Louise A. (Schneeman) B.; m. Jean L. Kelly, June 8, 1947; children: Linda, Karl, Laurel, Kurt, Lisa. B.A., Concordia Sem., 1945, M.Div., 1947; D.D. (hon.), Concordia Theol. Sem., 1975. Ordained to minstry, Lutheran Ch., 1947. Asst. pastor First English Lutheran Ch., New Orleans, 1947-49; pastor Trinity Evan. Lutheran Ch., Centralia, Ill., 1949-52, St. Paul's Lutheran Ch., West Allis, Wis., 1956-70; pres. So. Wis. Dist. Lutheran Ch. Mo. Synod, Milw., 1970-82, Concordia Sem., St. Louis, 1982—. Contbr. articles to profl. jours. V.p. So. Wis. dist. Lutheran Ch., Mo. Synod, 1966-70; chmn. Com. on Theology and Ch. Relations, St. Louis, 1974-82; denominational rep. Div. Theol. Studies Lutheran Council U.S.A., N.Y.C., 1975-81; mem. adv. bd. Wis. Citizens Concerned for Life, 1976-82. Republican. Home: 1 N Seminary Terr Clayton MO 63105 Office: 801 De Mun Ave Clayton MO 63105

BARTH, MICHAEL CARL, economist; b. Newark, Apr. 3, 1941; s. Abe and Frances (Keller) B.; m. Marilyn Levy, Dec. 11, 1966; children: Christopher Jay, Karen Rebecca. B.A., Harpur Coll., Binghamton, N.Y., 1962; M.A., U. Ill., Champaign, 1963; Ph.D., CUNY, 1971. Research asso. City Coll. Research Found., N.Y.C., 1967-68; lectr. econs. dept. CCNY, 1965-68; economist Pres.'s Commn. on Income Maintenance Programs, Washington, 1968-69, OEO, 1969-73; dir., income sec. policy/analysis HEW, Washington, 1973-75, dep. asst. sec., income, sec. policy, 1977-80; prin. ICF Inc., Washington, 1980—; vis. assoc. prof. U. Wis., 1975-76. Author: (with G. Carcagno and J. Palmer) Toward an Effective Income Support System: Problems, Prospects and Choices, 1974; contbr. articles to profl. jours. Recipient Sec.'s Spl. citation HEW, 1975, Sec.'s Outstanding Achievement award, 1977. Mem. Am. Econ. Assn., Indsl. Relations Research Assn. Home: 3818 Military Rd NW Washington DC 20015 Office: ICF Inc 1850 K St NW Washington DC 20006

BARTH, RICHARD, corp. counsel; b. N.Y.C., May 23, 1931; s. Alexander Haddon and Georgina (Grant) B.; m. Mary Elizabeth McAnaney, June 13, 1959; children—Leanore, Jennifer, Richard, Michele, Alexander. Grad., Hill Sch.; A.B. cum laude, Wesleyan U., Middletown, Conn., 1952; LL.B., Columbia, 1955; student, N.Y.U. Grad. Sch. Law, 1959-62. Bar: N.Y. bar 1958, N.J. bar 1966. Asso. firm Burke & Burke, 1957-65; gen. counsel, sec., mem. mgmt. com. CIBA, 1965-70; v.p., gen. counsel, mem. mng. com., dir. CIBA-GEIGY Corp., 1971—; dir. Radio Shack Corp., 1964-65. Author articles. Mem. substandard housing bd., Summit, N.J., 1968-70. Served with AUS, 1955-57. Mem. Am., N.Y., N.J. bar assns., Phi Delta Phi, Psi Upsilon. Home: 431 Grace Church St Rye NY 10580 Office: 444 Saw Mill River Rd Ardsley NY 10502

BARTHE, RICHMOND, artist, sculptor; b. Bay St. Louis, Miss., Jan. 28, 1901; s. Richmond and Marie Clementine (Raboteau) B. B.A., Xavier U., 1934; D.F.A., St. Francis Coll., 1946. Exhibited one-man shows, William Grant Still Community Art Center, 1978, Inst. Jamaica, 1959, Montclair (N.J.) Art Mus., 1949, Margaret Brown Galleries, Boston, 1947, Grand Central Art Galleries, N.Y.C., Sayville (L.I.) Playhouse, 1945, Internat. Print Soc., DePorres Interracial Ctr., South Side Art Ctr., Chgo., 1942, Arden Galleries, N.Y.C., 1939, Delphic Studios, 1935, U. Wis.-Madison, 1931, 32, 33,, Ranking Art Galleries, Washington, 1931, Women's City Club, Chgo., 1930, Grand Rapids (Mich.) Art Gallery, numerous others, group shows, Met. Mus., Guggenheim Mus., Whitney Mus., Nat. Urban League, Sculptor's Guild, Audubon Artists, all N.Y.C., Phila. Mus. Art, Afro-Am. Hist. and Cultural Mus., both Phila., Los Angeles County Art Mus., Dallas Mus. Fine Arts, Century of Progress, Chgo., High Mus. Art, Atlanta, Bklyn. Mus., Beverly Hilton Hotel, others; represented: in permanent collections maj. Museums, including Met. Mus.; in permanent collections maj. museums, including Whitney Mus. Am. Art, Schomber Collection, Countee Collen Library, IBM, Arthur Brisbane Meml., all N.Y.C., Art Inst. Chgo., Smithsonian Instn., Jamaican Pub. Library, Theosoph. Soc., Va. Mus. Fine Arts, Los Angeles County Art Mus., Gibbs Mus., Oberlin Coll. Mus., Yale U. Mus., Howard U. Gallery of Art, Tuskegee U. Gallery Art, Fisk U. Gallery of Art, Atlanta U. St. Augustines Sem., Coll. St. Mary of the Springs, U. So. Miss., Ch. St. Jude, Montgomery, Ala., Ch. St. Jude, South Bend, Ind., numerous others; commd. bust: Booker T. Washington, Dr. George Washington Carver, Hall of Fame Great Americans, 1976, Social Security Bldg., Washington, Dessalaines Monument, Haitian Govt., others.

BARTHEL, F. ERNEST, insurance company executive; b. Pitts., Jan. 31, 1933; s. Fred and Emma E. (Koehler) B.; m. Maryann I. Titus, Aug. 18, 1956; children—Julie L., Michael E. B.S., Ohio State U., 1958. C.P.A.; C.L.U. Acct. Arthur Young & Co. (C.P.A.s), N.Y.C., 1958-60; audit mgr. Peat, Marwick, Mitchell & Co. (C.P.A.s), Columbus, Ohio, 1960-69; acctg. mgr. Allstate Ins. Co., Northbrook, Ill., 1969-72; treas. Am. States Life Ins. Co., Indpls., 1972—, now also v.p.; treas. Am. States Ins. Co. Tex., 1972—, Am. States Ins. Co., 1972—, Am. Economy Ins. Co., 1972—, Am. Preferred Ins. Co., 1972—, Am. Union Ins. Co. N.Y., 1972—. Served with AUS, 1954-56. Mem. Am. Inst. C.P.A.'s, Fin. Execs. Inst., Am. Soc. C.L.U.'s. Republican. Office: 500 N Meridian St Indianapolis IN 46207 *

BARTHELMAS, NED KELTON, stockbroker; b. Circleville, Ohio, Oct. 22, 1927; s. Arthur and Mary Bernice (Riffel) B.; m. Marjorie Jane Livezey, May 23, 1953; children: Brooke Ann, Richard Thomas. B.S. in Bus. Adminstrn, Ohio State U., 1950. Stock broker Ohio Co., Columbus, 1953-58; pres. First Columbus Corp. (stock brokers and investment bankers), 1958—; pres., dir. Ohio Fin. Corp., Columbis, 1960—; trustee, chmn. Am. Guardian Fin., Republic Fin.; dir. Conditioned Power Corp., Nat. Foods, Medex, Inc., Liebert Corp., Midwest Capital Corp., Lancaster Colony Corp., United Capital Corp., Capital Equity Corp., Franklin Nat. Corp., Midwest Nat. Corp., 1st Columbus Realty Corp., Court Realty Co., all Columbus. Served with Adj. Gen.'s Dept. AUS, 1945-47. Mem. Nat. Assn. Securities Dealers (past vice chmn. dist. bd. govs.), Investment Bankers Assn. Am. (exec. com. 1973), Investment Dealers Ohio (sec., treas. 1956-72, pres. 1973), Nat. Stock Traders Assn., Young Pres.'s Orgn. (pres. 1971), Nat. Investment Bankers (pres. 1973), Columbus Jr. C. of C. (pres. 1956), Ohio Jr. C. of C. (trustee 1957-58), Columbus Area C. of C. (dir. 1956, named an outstanding young man of Columbus 1962), Newcomen Soc., Phi Delta Theta. Clubs: Kiwanis, Execs., Stock and Bond, Columbus, Scioto Country (Columbus); Crystal Downs Country (Frankfort, Mich.). Home: 1000 Urlin Ave Columbus OH 43212 Office: 42 E Gay St Columbus OH 43215

BARTHELME, DONALD, author; b. Phila., 1931; s. Donald and Bechtold B.; m. Marion Knox, May 26, 1978; children: Anne, Katharine. Author: Snow White, 1967; short stories Come Back, Dr. Caligari, 1964, Unspeakable Practices, Unnatural Acts, 1968, City Life, 1970, Sadness, 1972; stories Guilty Pleasures, 1974; novel The Dead Father, 1975; stories Amateurs, 1976, Great Days, 1979, Sixty Stories, 1981, Overnight to Many Distant Cities, 1983. Recipient Nat. Book award, 1972, Nat. Inst. Arts and Letters award, 1972; Guggenheim fellow, 1966. Mem. Authors Guild, Am. PEN, Am. Acad. and Inst. Arts and Letters. Office: care New Yorker Magazine 25 W 43 rd St New York 10036

BARTHELME, DONALD, architect; b. Galveston, Tex., Aug. 4, 1907; s. Fred Bartheleme and Mary (Anderson) Barheleme; m. Helen L. Bechtold, June 21, 1930; children: Donald, Joan Bartheleme Bugbee, Peter, Frederic, Steven. B.Arch., U. Pa., 1930. Pvt. practitioner architecture, Galveston, Tex., 1935-36, Houston, 1940-63; designer various firms, Dallas and Houston, 1936-40; from instr. to prof. U. Houston, 1946-59, 61-73, prof. emeritus, 1973—; William Ward Watkins prof. Rice U., Houston, 1959-61; vis. prof. U. Pa., Tulane U., Rice U. (Archtl. works include) St. Rose of Lima ch. and Sch., Houston, West Columbia Elem. Sch., Tex. (Sao Paulo 2d Biennial 1st award for schs. 1954), Adams Petroleum Ctr., Houston; (included in exhibits) Nat. Gallery, Washington; Mus. Modern Art N.Y.C. and Sao Paulo, Brazil, also Dallas, Houston, Zurich, Switzerland, Berlin and Yugoslavia. Emeritus fellow AIA (Honor awards 1948); mem. Tex. Soc. Architects (Honor award 1952). Home: 9449 Briarforest Dr 5707 Houston TX 77063

BARTHOLDSON, JOHN ROBERT, steel co. exec.; b. N.Y.C., Sept. 9, 1944; s. Nils and Judith (Kvist) B.; m. Carole Marie Duffy, Sept. 7, 1968; children—John Anders, Catherine Leigh, Kristen Elizabeth. B.S., Pa. State U., 1966, M.B.A., 1970; student, Villanova U., 1967-68. Research and devel. engr. Gen. Electric Co., Valley Forge, Pa., 1966-69; treas. Norco Properties, Inc., Jacksonville, Fla., 1970-72, Warner Co., Phila., 1972-78, Lukens Steel Co., Coatesville, Pa., 1978—. Mem. Beta Gamma Sigma. Home: 1950 Standiford Dr Malvern PA 19355 Office: Lukens Steel Co Coatesville PA

BARTHOLOMEW, ALLAN CAMP, retired utility executive; b. Colter, Wyo., Dec. 4, 1915; s. Almon Edward and Evelyn Camp (Stillwell) B.; m. Alice June Fetters, Feb. 2, 1936; children: Allyn (Mrs. Lester Jacobs), Paul Scott. Grad., Advanced Mgmt. Program, Harvard Bus. Sch., 1973. With Pacific Power & Light Co., Portland, Oreg., from 1938, v.p., 1969-71, sr. v.p., mgr. div. ops., from 1971; dir. Black Butte Ranch. Chmn. Oreg. Heart Assn., 1970-73; Councilman City Worland, Wyo., 1948-50; Bd. dirs. McKenzie Willamette Meml. Hosp., Springfield, Oreg., 1958-64, pres., 1960-61. Served to 1st sgt. AUS, 1943-46; PTO. Mem. C. of C. (v.p. 1961-63, bd. dirs. 1956-65), N.W. Electric Light & Power Assn. (pres. 1976), Am. Legion. Republican. Methodist. Lodges: Masons; Elks. Home: PO Box 8014 Black Butte Ranch Sisters OR 97759

BARTHOLOMEW, ARTHUR PECK, JR., accountant; b. Rochester, N.Y., Nov. 20, 1918; s. Arthur Peck and Abbie West (Dawson) B.; m. Mary Elizabeth Meyer, Oct. 4, 1941; children: Susan B. Hall, Arthur Peck III, James M., Virginia L. A.B., U. Mich., 1939, M.B.A., 1940. With Ernst & Whinney, 1940-79, successively jr. accountant, partner charge Eastern dist., Detroit office, 1940-64, successively jr. accountant, partner charge nat. office, Cleve., 1964-65, N.Y. office, 1965-79; also mem. mng. com. (N.Y. office); instr. accounting U. Mich., 1940, George Washington U., 1945-46. Mem. Mich. Gov.'s Task Force for Expenditure Mgmt., 1963-64; mem. 2d Regional Plan Commn. N.Y.; Bd. dirs. Detroit League for Handicapped, 1952-64; treas. Grosse Pointe War Meml. Assn., 1961; bd. dirs., v.p. Greater N.Y. council Boy Scouts Am. Served from pvt. to capt. AUS, 1942-46. Mem. Nat. Assn. Accountants (pres. Detroit 1963-64, nat. pres. 1974-75), The Conf. Bd., Mich., N.Y. socs. C.P.A.s, Am. Inst. C.P.A.s, Phi Beta Kappa, Phi Kappa Phi, Beta Gamma Sigma, Phi Eta Sigma, Beta Alpha Psi, Phi Kappa Sigma. Republican. Presbyn. Clubs: Country (Detroit); Indian Harbor Yacht, Greenwich Country (pres. 1976-78), Wall Street (pres.). Home: 103 Doubling Rd Greenwich CT 06830 Office: 153 E 53d St New York NY 10022

BARTHOLOMEW, GILBERT ALFRED, retired physicist; b. Nelson, C., Can., Apr. 8, 1922; s. Alfred and Anna (Lenzman) B.; m. Rosalie May Dinzey, Apr. 19, 1952. B.A., U. B.C., 1943; Ph.D., McGill U., 1948. With Atomic Energy of Can., Ltd., 1948-83, head neutron physics br., 1962-71, dir. physics div., 1971-83. Contbr. articles to profl. jours. Fellow AAAS, Royal Soc. Can., Am. Phys. Soc.; mem. Can. Assn. Physicists, Sigma Xi. Home: PO Box 1258 Deep River ON K0J 1P0 Canada

BARTHOLOMEW, HARLAND, city planner; b. Stoneham, Mass., Sept. 14, 1889; s. Aden Luther and Harriet Mary (Lewin) B.; m. Lillian R. Barton, Dec. 1911 (dec. Aug. 1954); children: Herbert, Melvin; m. Frances Ball, Nov. 21, 1955 (dec. Jan. 1963); m. Gladys B. Funsten, May 15, 1968 (dec. May 1971). C.E. course, Rutgers Coll., 1921; D.Sc., 1952; LL.B., Carthage Coll., 1978. Formerly cons. engr. City Plan Commn., St. Louis; formerly cons. Mo. State Planning Bd.; prof. civic design U. Ill., now ret.; former chmn. Nat. Capital Planning Commn., Washington; cons. Harland Bartholomew & Assos. (civil engrs., city planners and landscape architects), St. Louis.; Adv. preparation city plans and zoning ordinances numerous, Am. and Canadian cities, including, St. Louis, Washington, Williamsburg, Va., Pitts., Louisville, Ky., Memphis, New Orleans, Omaha, Mpls., Dallas, Los Angeles, Portland, Vancouver, B.C.; Former pres. Am. Inst. Planning, Nat. Conf. on City Planning, Am. Planning and Civil Assn., Urban Am. Author: Urban Land Uses, 1932, Land Uses in American Cities, 1955. Mem. ASCE (hon.), Am. Inst. Cons. Engrs., Am. Soc. Landscape Architects (hon.), Am. Soc. Planning Ofcls., Zeta Psi, Tau Beta Pi. Republican. Congregationalist. Clubs: Engineers, St. Louis, Bellerive Country, University (St. Louis); Cosmos (Washington). Home: 19 Wydown Terr Saint Louis MO 63105 Office: 7745 Carondolet Saint Louis MO 63105

BARTHOLOMEW, LLOYD GIBSON, physician; b. Whitehall, N.Y., Sept. 15, 1921; s. Emerson F. and Minnie (Swinton) B.; m. Elisabeth Thrall, Dec. 27, 1943; children: Suzanne, Lynne, Lloyd Gibson, Deborah, Douglass Thrall. A.A., Green Mountain Jr. Coll., 1939; B.A., Union Coll., Schenectady, 1941; M.D., U. Vt., 1944; M.S. in Internal Medicine (fellow), U. Minn., 1952. Diplomate: Am. Bd. Internal Medicine, subsplty. bd. gastroenterology. Intern Mary Hitchcock Meml. Hosp., Hanover, N.H., 1944-45, resident, 1945-46, 48-49; asst. internal medicine Dartmouth, 1948-49; 1st asst. div. internal medicine Mayo Clinic, Rochester, Minn., 1949-52, asst. to staff div. internal medicine, 1952-53; practice medicine, specializing in gastroenterology, Rochester, 1952—; instr. internal medicine Mayo Found., U. Minn., 1952-58, asst. prof., 1958-63, asso. prof. internat. medicine, 1963-67, prof. medicine, 1967—, Mayo Med. Sch., 1973—; attending physician St. Mary's, Meth. hosps., Rochester, 1952; mem. adv. bd. to surgeons gen. of armed forces and asst. sec. def., 1978—; mem. policy bd. Bush Found. Contbr. articles profl. publs. Served to capt., M.C. AUS, 1946-47; col. Res. Recipient Woodbury prize in medicine, 1944, Carbee prize in obstetrics, 1944, Distinguished Service award U. Vt. Coll. Medicine, 1977. Mem. AMA (sec. gastroenterology sect. 1962-68, vice chmn. gastroenterology sect. 1968-69, chmn. 1969-70, mem. council sci. assembly 1969, chmn. program planning com. 1971-75, chmn. council sci. assembly 1974-76, chmn. council continuing physician edn. 1976-77), Minn. Med. Assn. (del ho. dels. 1964—, chmn. scholarship and loan com. 1967—, alt. del. to AMA 1974-77, del. to AMA 1978—, Pres.'s award 1983), So. Minn. Med. Assn. (pres. 1963-64), Zumbro Valley Med. Soc. (sec.-treas. 1969-70, v.p. 1970-71, pres. 1971-72), Soc. Med. Consultants to Armed Forces, Am. Gastroent. Assn. (com. on procedures 1970-72, presdl. commn. on future of assn. 1973-74, com. on constn. and by-laws 1980—), Soc. Study Liver Diseases, Minn. Soc. Internal Medicine, Sigma Xi. Home: 1201 6th St SW Rochester MN 55901 Office: 200 1st St SW Rochester MN 55901

BARTHOLOMY, JOHN MARTIN, college president; b. May 13, 1935; m. Mary Jo McCabe; children: Lezlee, Matthew, Andrew. Grad., USAF SAC Leadership Sch., 1956; B.S., Western Mich. U., 1962, M.A., 1963; Ph.D., Ohio State U., 1969. Mem. faculty, v.p. univ. services Murray State U., 1974-77; pres. Drury Coll., 1977-80, William Woods Coll., Fulton, Mo., 1980—. Named Outstanding Instr. Ohio U., 1968. Mem. Am. Speech and Hearing Assn., Speech Communications Assn. Office: William Woods Coll Office of Pres Fulton MO 65251

BARTH-WEHRENALP, GERHARD, chemical company executive; b. Teplitz-Schoenau, Czechoslovakia, Oct. 19, 1920; came to U.S., 1951, naturalized, 1957; s. Burghard and Kaethe (Bechert) von B.-W.; m. Waltraut von Weber, Apr. 8, 1952; children: Christian, Gerald, Markus. Student, U. Hamburg, Germany, 1942-43; Ph.D. maxima cum laude, U. Innsbruck, Austria, 1949. Chemist Inst. Beverage Tech., Bad Homburg, Germany, 1943-44, Breganzia Food Corp., Bregenz, Austria, 1945-46; lectr., asst. U. Innsbruck, 1949-51; research asso. Temple U., 1951-52; asst. prof. LaSalle Coll., Phila., 1952-54; research chemist Pennwalt Corp., Phila., 1953-55, group leader, 1955-57, dir. inorganic research, 1957-63, mgr. research, 1963-70, asst. to chmn., 1971, corp. v.p., tech. dir., 1971-74, sr. v.p., 1974-81, cons., 1981—; Austrian rep. to Younger Chemists Internat. Project, Tech. Assistance Program, 1951; chmn. phosphorus-nitrogen chemistry symposium Gordon Research Conf., 1960. Bd. editors: Research Mgmt; contbr. articles to profl. jours. Mem. Am. Com. for Econ. Edn.; bd. dirs. U.S. commn. WHO; mem. pres.'s council LaSalle Coll., Phila. Mem. Am. Chem. Soc., Am. Rocket Soc. (pres. Phila. sect. 1958), Soc. Chem. Industry. Holder U.S., Canadian, British, German, French, Italian patents. Home and Office: 3267 Boca Ciege Dr Naples FL 33962

BARTILUCCI, ANDREW JOSEPH, coll. adminstr.; b. N.Y.C., Nov. 29, 1922; s. Rocco and Philomena (Innello) B.; m. Lucy Ann Fulvio, June 10, 1950; children—Mary Ann, Phyllis, Eugenie. B.S., St. John's U., 1944; M.S., Rutgers U., 1949; Ph.D., U. Md., 1953. Analytical chemist Armed Services Med. Procurement Lab., War Dept., 1947-48; asso. research pharmacist, research and devel. div. Merck & Co., 1949-50; prof. pharmacy. asst. dean St. John's U. Coll. Pharmacy, 1952-56, dean, 1956—, v.p., 1979—; Fellow Am. Found. Pharm. Edn., 1950-52. Served as pharmacist's mate USNR, 1944-46; ensign, 1949-57; Pharmacist dir. USPHS(R), 1957—. Fellow AAAS; mem. Am. Coll. Apothecaries, N.Y. Acad. Scis., N.Y. Acad. Pharmacy, Am. Pharm. Assn., Sigma Xi, Rho Chi, Phi Delta Chi. Home: 115 Roosevelt St Garden City NY 11530 Office: Grand Central and Utopia Parkways Jamaica NY 11439

BARTIZAL, ROBERT GEORGE, computer systems company executive; b. Oak Park, Ill., Aug. 24, 1932; s. George Frank and Mildred (Hoffman) B.; m. Kathleen Elizabeth Dougherty, Apr. 9, 1960; children—Jeffrey Robert, Julia Ann, John Joseph. B.S.B.A., U. Nebr., 1954; postgrad. Advanced Mgmt. Program, Northeastern U., 1973. With IBM, 1954-65, sales rep., Omaha, 1958-63, mktg. mgr., St. Paul, 1963-65, asst. dist. mgr., Mpls., 1965; with Control Data Corp., 1965-75, Central and East European regional mgr., Frankfurt, W. Ger., 1968-71, v.p. edn. services, 1972-73, v.p. govt. bus. mgmt. office, Mpls., 1974-75; with Dataproducts Corp., Woodland Hills, Calif., 1975-80, exec. v.p., 1977-80; also dir.; pres., chief exec. officer, chmn. Logisticon, Inc., Santa Clara, Calif., 1980—; dir. Ferrix Corp., Sunnyvale, Calif., Applied Data Systems, Phoenix. Mem. Woodland Hills Community Ch. Served with U.S. Army, 1954-56. Mem. Sigma Alpha Epsilon. Republican. Congregationalist. Office: 4001 Burton Dr Santa Clara CA 95050

BARTKOWSKI, STEVEN JOSEPH, professional football player; b. Des Moines, Nov. 12, 1952; s. Roman B.; m. Sandee Barkowski; 1 son, Phillip. Student, U. Calif.-Berkeley. Quarterback Atlanta Falcons, NFL, 1975—; player in NFL Pro Bowl, 1980-81. Named Nat. Football Conf. Rookie of Yr., 1975. Office: Atlanta Falcons I 85 at Suwanee Rd Suwanee GA 30174

BARTKUS, RICHARD ANTHONY, mag. pub.; b. Chgo., Mar. 14, 1931; s. Anthony J. and Mary (Petraitis) B.; m. Betty Ann Luetke, Jan. 2, 1954; children—Susan Kimberly, David Richard. Student, U. Ill., 1949-55. Circulation trainee Chgo. Tribune, 1955-58; asst. advt. mgr. Kilner Pub. Co., Chgo., 1958-59; advt. mgr. Cox Publs., Arcadia, Calif., 1959-60, Bond Pub. Co., 1960, Western advt. mgr., advt. dir., 1969-75; pub. Road and Track, Newport Beach, Calif., 1975—; v.p. CBS Publs., 1977—. Served with USMC, 1951-53. Club: Univ. Athletic. Home: 18681 Via Torino Irvine CA 92715 Office: 1499 Monrovia St Newport Beach CA 92663

BARTLETT, ALBERT ALLEN, educator, physicist; b. Shanghai, China, Mar. 21, 1923; s. Willard William and Marguerite (Allen) B.; m. Eleanor Frances Roberts, Aug. 24, 1946; children—Carol Louise, Jane Elizabeth, Lois Jeanne, Nancy Marie. Student, Otterbein Coll., 1940-42; B.A., Colgate U., 1944; M.A., Harvard U., 1948, Ph.D., 1951. Research asst. Los Alamos Sci. Lab., 1944-46; faculty U. Colo., Boulder, 1950—, prof. physics, 1962—, chmn. faculty council, 1969-71; faculty Harvard U. Summer Sch., 1952, 53, 55, 56; vis. research worker Nobel Inst. Physics, Stockholm, Sweden, 1963-64; lectr. on fundamentals of energy crisis. Contbr. articles to profl. jours. Mem. Boulder City Parks and Recreation Adv. Bd., 1967-72, vice chmn., 1969, 70, chmn., 1971; mem. U. Colo. Centennial Commn., 1973-76. Recipient Thomas Jefferson award U. Colo., 1972, Robert L. Stearns award, 1974, service award Girl Scouts Am., 1974, Univ. Gold medal, 1978. Mem. Am. Phys. Soc., Am. Assn. Physics Tchrs. (recipient Disting. Service citation 1970, Robert A. Millikan award 1981, pres. 1978), Phi Beta Kappa, Sigma Xi, Alpha Tau Omega. Clubs: Colo. Mountain, Rocky Mountain Railroad. Home: 2935 19th St Boulder CO 80302

BARTLETT, ARTHUR EUGENE, franchise executive; b. Glens Falls, N.Y., Nov. 26, 1933; s. Raymond Ernest and Thelma (Williams) B.; m. Collette R. Bartlett, Jan. 9, 1955; 1 dau., Stacy Lynn. Student, Long Beach (Cal.) Coll., 1952-53. Dist. sales mgr. Forest E. Olson, Inc., 1960-64; co-founder Four Star Realty, Inc., Santa Ana, Calif., 1964, v.p., sec., 1964-71; co-founder, pres. Comps, Inc., 1971—; pres. Growth Industry Computing Co.; chmn. bd. emeritus Century 21 Real Estate Corp., Irvine, Calif.; chmn. bd., chief exec. officer Mr. Build Internat., Santa Ana, 1981—; chmn. bd., pres. Western Med. Center, Santa Ana; chmn. bd. Triexcellence Inc., Santa Ana. Lodge: Masons. Office: MR Build International 2114 N Broadway Santa Ana CA 92706

BARTLETT, CHARLES LEFFINGWELL, foundation executive, former newspaperman; b. Chgo., Aug. 14, 1921; s. Valentine C. and Marie (Frost) B.; m. Josephine Martha Buck, Dec. 16, 1950; children: Peter B., Michael V., Robert S., Helen B. Student, St. Mark's Sch., Southboro, Mass., 1934-39; A.B., Yale U., 1943. Reporter Chattanooga Times, 1946-63, Washington corr., 1948-63; editor News Focus Service, 1958-63; columnist Chgo. Sun-Times, 1963-75, Chgo. Daily News, 1975-78, Field Syndicate, 1978-81; pres. Jefferson Found., 1982—. Author: (with Edward Weintal) Facing the Brink, 1957. Served as lt. USNR, 1943-46. Recipient Pulitzer prize for nat. reporting, 1955. Roman Catholic. Clubs: Gridiron, Federal City. Home: 4615 W St NW Washington DC 20007 Office: 1019 19th St NW Washington DC 20036

BARTLETT, EDMUND, investment company executive; b. Bklyn., 1910. Ed., Princeton. Pres., dir. Henry Prentiss & Co. Office: care Peck Sprague & Poor PO Box 239 Oyster Bay NY 11771

BARTLETT, HALL, motion picture producer and director; b. Kansas City, Mo., Nov. 27, 1925; s. Paul Dana and Alice (Hiest) B.; children: Cathy, Laurie. Grad., Yale, 1942. Propr. Hall Bartlett Prodn., Los Angeles, 1952—; now pres. Hall Bartlett Films, Inc., Jonathan Livingston Seagull Mcht. Co.; Bd. dirs. Huntington Hartford Theatre; founder Music Center. Producer, dir.: films Navajo, 1952, Crazylegs, Unchained, All the Young Men, Drango, Zero Hour, The Caretakers, Changes, 1969, Sandpit Generals, Jonathan Livingston Seagull, 1973, The Children of Sanchez, 1977; dir., producer, writer: Comeback to Me, 1982; writer: Love is Forever, 1983; producer: films Zubin Mehta Spl; (Recipient 11 Acad. award nominations, Film Festival awards from Cannes 1961, 63, Venice 1959, 65, Edinburgh 1952, San Sebastian 1969, Moscow 1971, Nat. Conf. Christians and Jews 1955, Fgn. Press awards.). Served with USNR, 1942-46. Mem. Motion Picture Acad. Arts and Scis., Acad. TV Arts and Scis., Friends of Library, Cinema Circulus, Phi Beta Kappa. Presbyn. Club: Bel-Air Country (Los Angeles). Home: 861 Stone Canyon Rd Los Angeles CA 90024 Office: Suite 908 9200 Sunset Blvd Los Angeles CA 90069 *Life for me is without meaning unless one has people he loves and respects and who love and respect him. Nearly all the great philosophers of history have come to the belief that love in its fullest sense is at the center of existence. Living in this chaotic world has convinced me that this is the truth.*

BARTLETT, J(AMES) KENNETH, chemist; b. Lynden, Wash., Feb. 2, 1925; s. James Pierce and Hazel Gertrude (Harmelink) B.; m. Patricia Evelyn Curtis, Aug. 21, 1948; 1 dau., Nancy Evelyn. B.S. in Chemistry, Willamette U., 1949; Ph.D., Stanford U., 1954. Instr. U. Santa Clara, Calif., 1953-54; asst. prof. Long Beach (Calif.) State Coll., 1954-56; mem. faculty So. Oreg. State Coll., Ashland, 1956—, prof. chemistry, 1963—, chmn. dept., 1976—; cons. in field. Author: General Chemistry Experiments, 1976, Identification of Chemical Substances, 1978. Served with U.S. Army, 1943-46. DuPont fellow, 1952-53. Mem. Am. Chem. Soc. Republican. Presbyterian. Home: 1313 Woodland Dr Ashland OR 97520 Office: Chemistry Dept So Oreg State Coll Ashland OR 97520

BARTLETT, JAMES LOWELL, III, investment company executive; b. Boston, May 26, 1945; s. James Lowell and Shirley Victoria (Wyatt) B.; m. Shannon Mara McMillion, May 4, 1979; children: James Lowell IV, Zachary Morgan. B.S., U. Calif., Berkeley, 1967, M.B.A., 1968. Staff nat. div. Bank of Am., Los Angeles, 1968; fin. mgr. Psychology Today mag., Del Mar, Calif., 1968-69; pres. Forum Communications Corp.; pub. Cuisine, Politics Today, Volleyball,, N.Y.C., 1970-82; pres. Bartlett, Schlumberger & Co., Inc., 1982—. Republican. Mem. Ch. of Jesus Christ of Latter-day Saints. Office: 575 Madison Ave New York NY 10022

BARTLETT, JAMES VINCENT, engineering consultant, retired naval officer; b. Point Pleasant, W.Va., Oct. 28, 1917; s. Ira Stump and Blanche (Mitchell) B.; m. Betty Vars Baker, Dec. 27, 1941 (dec. June 1961); children: James Vincent, David Mitchell; m. Margaret Herrin Turkington, Aug. 3, 1962; stepchildren—John Edward Turkington, Timothy Turkington, Michael Turkington. B.Sc., U.S. Naval Acad., 1941; B.C.E., Rensselaer Poly. Inst., 1944, M.C.E., 1945. Commd. ensign U.S. Navy, 1942, advanced through grades to rear adm., 1968; comdg. officer (Mobile Constrn. Bn. 4), 1953-55, Chesapeake div. Bur. Yards and Docks, 1965-67; comdr. (3d Naval Constrn. Brigade), Vietnam, 1967-69, vice comdr., 1969—, dep. chief, 1969-72; sr. v.p. Raymond Internat. Builders Inc., Houston, 1972-82. Decorated D.S.M. Mem. Soc. Am. Mil. Engrs., ASCE, Am. Soc. Profl. Engrs., Sigma Xi, Chi Epsilon, Tau Beta Pi. Home: 15 Deer Run Savannah GA 31411 Office: 2801 S Post Oak Rd Houston TX 77027

BARTLETT, JAMES WILLIAMS, psychiatrist; b. Balt., Feb. 2, 1926; s. James Williams and Margaret Baylor (Alexander) B.; m. Nancy Bieszad, May 8, 1954; children—John Alexander, Anne Lee, Thomas Martin. B.A., Harvard U., 1948; M.D., Johns Hopkins U., 1952. Mem. faculty U. Rochester (N.Y.) Med. Center, 1957—, prof. psychiatry, 1968—, prof. health services, chmn. dept., 1968—, asso. dean, 1966—; med. dir. Strong Meml. Hosp., 1967—. Served with USNR, 1944-46. Fellow Am. Psychiat. Assn.; mem. Assn. Am. Med. Coll. (adminstrv. bd. council teaching hosps.), Am. Hosp. Assn. (council mgmt.), AAAS, Soc. Med. Adminstrs., Hosp. Assn. State N.Y. (dir.), Psychoanalytic Assn. N.Y. State, Western N.Y. Psychoanalytic Soc., Rochester Acad. Medicine. Office: Strong Meml Hosp Box 612 601 Elmwood Ave Rochester NY 14642

BARTLETT, JENNIFER LOSCH, artist; b. Long Beach, Calif., 1941. B.A., Mills Coll., 1963; B.F.A., Yale U., 1964, M.F.A., 1965. Instr. Sch. Visual Arts, N.Y.C. One-woman shows include, Mills Coll., Oakland, Calif., 1963, Reese Paley Gallery, N.Y.C., 1972, Paula Cooper Gallery, N.Y.C., 1974, 76, 77, 79, 81, 82, 83, Saman Gallery, Genoa, Italy, 1974, John Doyle Gallery, Chgo., 1975, Contemporary Art Center, Cin., 1976, Dartmouth Coll., Wadsworth Atheneum, Hartford, Conn., 1977, San Francisco Mus. Modern Art, 1978, U. Calif., Irvine, Hansen-Fuller Gallery, San Francisco, Balt. Art Mus., Margo Leavin Gallery, Los Angeles, 1979, 81, 83, U. Akron, 1979, Carleton Coll., Heath Gallery, Atlanta, 1979, 83, Galerie Mukai, Tokyo, 1980, Akron Art Inst., Albright-Knox Art Gallery, Buffalo, Joslyn Art Mus., Omaha, 1982, Tate Gallery, London, McIntosh/Drysdale Gallery, Houston, Gloria Luria Gallery, Bay Harbor Islands, Fla., 1983, Rose Art Mus., Brandeis U., Waltham, Mass., 1984, Long Beach Mus. Art., Calif., Univ. Art Mus., U. Calif.-Berkeley, group exbhns. include, Mus. Modern Art, N.Y.C., 1971, 81, 83, Whitney Mus. Am. Art, N.Y.C., 1972, 77, 79, 81, 82, 83, Walker Art Center, Mpls., 1972, Kunsthaus, Hamburg, Germany, Paula Cooper Gallery, N.Y.C., 1973, 74, 76, 77, 78, 81, 83, 84, Corcoran Gallery Art, Washington, 1975, Art Inst. Chgo., 1976, Kunstmuseum, Dusseldorf, W. Ger., Kassel, W. Ger., 1977, Contemporary Arts Mus., Houston, 1980, Am. Acad. Arts and Letters, N.Y.C., 1983, Sarah Lawrence Art Gallery, Bronxville, N.Y., 1984, Archer M. Hunting Art Gallery, U. Tex.-Austin, Hudson River Mus., Yonkers, N.Y., Tucson Mus. Art, Leo Castelli Gallery, N.Y.C., numerous others; represented in permanent collections, Mus. Modern Art, N.Y.C., Met. Mus. Art, N.Y.C., Whitney Mus. Am. Art, N.Y.C., Phila. Mus. Art, Walker Art Center, Mpls., Yale U. Art Gallery, New Haven, Art Mus. S.Tex., Corpus Christi, R.I. Sch. Design, Providence, Art Gallery S. Australia, Adelaide, Goucher Coll., Balt., Amerada Hess, Woodbridge, N.J., Dallas Mus. Fine Arts, Richard B. Russell Fed. Bldg. and U.S. Courthouse, Atlanta. Recipient Harris prize Art Inst. Chgo., 1976, Creative Arts award Brandeis U., 1983, award Am. Acad. Arts and Letters, 1983; Creative Artists Public Services fellow, 1974; Lucas vis. lectr. award Carleton Coll., 1979. Address: care Paula Cooper Gallery 155 Wooster St New York NY 10012

BARTLETT, JOSEPH WARREN, lawyer; b. Boston, June 14, 1933; s. Charles W. and Barbara (Hastings) B.; m. May Parish, Apr. 28, 1956 (div.); children: Charles, Susan, Henry; m. Barbara Bemis, Sept. 20, 1980. B.A., Harvard U., 1951; LL.B., Stanford U., 1960. Bar: Mass. 1962, D.C. 1969. Law clk. Chief Justice Warren, U.S. Supreme Ct., 1960-61; practice law, Boston, 1961—; partner Gaston Snow Beekman & Bogue, 1966—; counsel Mass. Commn. Adminstrn., 1964-65; gen. counsel, under sec. Dept. Commerce, Washington, 1967-69; prin. adviser on universal social security coverage Sec. of HEW, Washington, 1978-79; acting prof. Stanford U., 1978; dir. Shawmut Bank, Boston. Trustee council U. Mass. Served to 1st lt. U.S. Army, 1956-57. Fellow Am. Bar Found.; mem. Am. Law Inst., Am. Bar Assn., Boston Bar Assn. (pres. 1977-78). Democrat. Episcopalian. Office: Gaston Snow Beekman & Bogue 14 Wall St New York NY 10005

BARTLETT, LEONARD LEE, advertising agency executive; b. Mountain Home, Idaho, May 31, 1930; s. Harold Roberts and Alma Martina (Nixon) B.; m. Sue Ann Kipfer, Nov. 5, 1966; children: Jennifer, Deborah; children by previous marriage: Linda Lee, Cynthia, Nancy, Pamela, William Charles. B.A. in Art, Brigham Young U., Provo, Utah, 1957. Advt. mgr. Steiner Co., Chgo., 1957-59; sr. v.p. Marsteller Inc., Chgo., 1959-67; vice chmn. Cole & Weber, Inc., Seattle, 1966-84; chmn. Cole & Weber Calif., San Francisco, 1984—. Bd. dirs. Western States Arts Found. Served with USAF, 1951-56. Mem. Am. Assn. Advt. Agys. (chmn. Western region 1980). Republican. Mem. Ch. Jesus Christ of Latter-day Saints. Clubs: Rainier, Wash. Athletic (Seattle); Sand Point Country. Home: 62 Wildwood Gardens Piedmont CA 94611

BARTLETT, LYNN CONANT, English literature educator; b. Bethlehem, Pa., Dec. 14, 1921; s. Fay Conant and Marie Agnes (McGuiness) B.; m. Margaret Emma Johnson, June 29, 1946; 1 dau., Anne Elston. B.A., Lehigh U., 1943; A.M., Harvard, 1947, Ph.D., 1957; B. Litt., Oxford U., Eng., 1952. Instr. English Lehigh U., 1946; teaching fellow Harvard, 1948-50; instr. Vassar Coll., 1952-57; asst. prof., 1957-62, asso. prof., 1962-70, prof., 1970—, asst. dean coll., 1958-61, sec. coll., 1966-76. Editor: (with W.R. Sherwood) The English Novel, Background Readings, 1967. Served with AUS, 1943-46. Decorated Bronze Star. Mem. Phi Beta Kappa, Sigma Phi Epsilon. Club: Harvard (N.Y.C.). Home: 170 College Ave Poughkeepsie NY 12603

BARTLETT, MARSHALL KINNE, surgeon; b. New Haven, Jan. 18, 1904; s. Charles Joseph and Genevieve (Kinne) B.; m. Barbara Frazier Hume, Dec. 21, 1935; children—Charles Joseph, Barbara Hume, Susan Bartlett Demb. B.A., Yale U., 1924; M.D., Harvard U., 1928. Diplomate: Am. Bd. Surgery. Intern Mass. Gen. Hosp., 1928-31; pvt. practice surgery, Boston, 1932—; clin. prof. surgery emeritus Harvard U.; sr. surgeon Mass. Gen. Hosp. Contbr. articles to profl. jours. Served as lt. col. M.C. AUS, 1942-46. Decorated Bronze Star. Mem. Boston, New Eng. surg. socs., Mass. Med. Soc., AMA, A.C.S., Am. Surg. Assn. Home: 43 Chestnut St Dedham MA 02026 Office: Mass Gen Hosp Boston MA 02114

BARTLETT, PAUL DOUGHTY, chemist, educator; b. Ann Arbor, Mich., Aug. 14, 1907; s. George Miller and Mary Louise (Doughty) B.; m. Mary Lula Court, June 24, 1931; children: Joanna Court (Mrs. Stephen D. Kennedy), Geoffrey McSwain, Sarah Webster. A.B., Amherst Coll., 1928, Sc.D. (hon.), 1953; M.A., Harvard U., 1929, Ph.D., 1931; Sc.D. (hon.), U. Chgo., 1954, U. Montpellier, 1967, U. Paris, 1968, U. Munich, 1977. NRC fellow Rockefeller Inst., 1931-32; instr. chemistry U. Minn., 1932-34; mem. faculty Harvard U., 1934-75, prof. chemistry, 1946-75, Erving prof. chemistry, 1948-75, Erving prof. emeritus, 1975—, chmn. dept., 1950-53; Robert A. Welch prof. chemistry Tex. Christian U., 1974—; George Fisher Baker lectr. Cornell U., spring 1949; vis. prof. UCLA, 1950; Walker-Ames lectr. U. Wash., 1952; guest lectr. U. Munich, Germany, 1957; speaker 15th Internat. Congress Pure and Applied Chemistry, Paris, France, 1957; Karl Folkers lectr. U. Ill., 1960; Spl. Univ. lectr. U. London, Eng., 1961; lectr. Japan Soc. for Promotion of Sci., 1978; mem. div. com. math., phys. and engring. scis. NSF, 1957-61. Author: Nonclassical Ions, 1965; also chpts. in textbooks, research papers.; Mem. editorial bd.: Jour. Am. Chem. Soc, 1945-55, Jour. Organic Chemistry, 1954-57, Tetrahedron. Recipient award in pure chemistry Am. Chem. Soc., 1938; August Wilhelm von Hofmann gold medal German Chem. Soc., 1962; Roger Adams award organic chemistry, 1963; Willard Gibbs medal, 1963; Theodore William Richards medal, 1966; Nat. Medal of Sci., 1968; James Flack Norris award in phys. organic chemistry Am. Chem. Soc., 1969; John Price Wetherill medal, 1970; Linus Pauling award, 1976; Nichols medal, 1976; James Flack Norris award in teaching chemistry, 1978; Alexander von Humboldt sr. scientist award U. Freiburg, Germany, 1976, U. Munich, 1977; Wilfred T. Doherty award, 1980; Max Tishler award Harvard U., 1981; Robert A. Welch award, 1981; Guggenheim and Fulbright fellow, spring 1957. Hon. fellow Chem. Soc. (London; Centenary lectr. 1969, Ingold lectr. 1975); mem. Swiss Chem Soc. (hon.), Chem. Soc. Japan (hon.), Nat., N.Y. acads. scis., Am. Acad. Arts and Scis., Am. Philos. Soc., Franklin Inst. (hon.), Am. Chem. Soc. (chmn. Northeastern sect. 1953-54), Internat. Union Pure and Applied Chemistry (pres. organic div. 1967-69, program chmn. 23d internat. congress 1971), Deutsche Akademie der Naturforscher Leopoldina, Phi Beta Kappa, Sigma Xi, Phi Lambda Upsilon. Research kinetics and mechanism organic reactions. Office: Dept Chemistry Texas Christian Univ Fort Worth TX 76129 *

BARTLETT, RICHARD JAMES, lawyer, university dean; b. Glens Falls, N.Y., Feb. 15, 1926; s. George Willard and Kathryn M. (McCarthy) B.; m. Claire E. Kennedy, Aug. 18, 1951; children: Michael, Amy. B.S., Georgetown U., 1945; LL.B., Harvard U., 1949; LL.D., Union Coll., 1974. Bar: N.Y. State 1949. Practiced law, Glens Falls, 1949-73; mem. firm Clark Bartlett & Caffry, 1962-73; justice N.Y. State Supreme Ct., 1973-79; chief adminstr. of courts N.Y. State, 1974-79; dean Albany Law Sch., Union U., Albany, 1979—; Mem. N.Y. State Assembly, 1959-66; chmn. N.Y. Commn. on Revision of Penal Law, 1961-70; del. N.Y. Constl. Conv., 1967. Served to capt. USAF, 1951-53. Fellow Am. Bar Found.; mem. Am. Law Inst., Am. Bar Assn., N.Y. State Bar Assn. Republican. Roman Catholic. Clubs: Lake George; Ft. Orange, Univ. (Albany); Harvard (N.Y.C.). Home: Bolton Landing NY 12814 Office: Albany Law Sch Union U 80 New Scotland Ave Albany NY 12208

BARTLETT, ROBERT CARRICK, lawyer; b. Worcester, Mass., Aug. 15, 1915; s. Elwin Irving and Rena Pearl (Carrick) B.; m. Rita Evelyn Fitzgerald, July 24, 1937; children: Beverly A., Robert W., Jeffrey W. B.A., Williams Coll., 1936; LL.B., Chgo. Kent Coll. Law, 1944, LL.M., 1945. Bar: Ill. bar 1944. With Commerce Clearing House, Inc., Chgo., 1939-81, pres., 1959-81; partner Bartlett & Bartlett; dir. Commerce Clearing House, Inc., Gen. Kinetics, Inc., Quabbin Pub. Co. Mem. Am., Internat., Inter-Am. Bar assns., Société de Législation Comparée, Beta Theta Pi. Clubs: Met., Univ. (Chgo.); Williams (N.Y.C.); Nat. Lawyers (Washington). Office: 255 W Old Mill Rd Lake Forest IL 60045

BARTLETT, STEVE, congressman; b. Los Angeles, Sept. 19, 1947; m. Gail Coke, 1969; children: Allison, Courtney, Brian. B.A., U. Tex., 1971. Businessman; mem. 98th Congress from 3d Dist. Tex., mem. exec. com. Rep. study com., co-chmn. edn. policy task force, ranking Rep. select edn. subcom. Mem. Dallas City Council, 1977-81; mem. Bd. Dental Health Programs. Mem. North Dallas C. of C., Neighborhood Housing Services of Dallas, Birthright, Inc. Republican. Office: 1233 Longworth House Office Bldg Washington DC 20515

BARTLETT, THOMAS ALVA, educator; b. Salem, Oreg., Aug. 20, 1930; s. Cleave Wines and Alma (Hanson) B.; m. Mary Louise Bixby, Mar. 20, 1954; children: Thomas Glenn, Richard A., Paul H. Student, Willamette U., 1947-49; A.B., Stanford U., 1951, Ph.D., 1959; M.A. (Rhodes scholar), Oxford U., 1953; L.H.D. (hon.), Colgate U., 1977, Mich. State U., 1978, Union Coll., 1979, D.C.L., U. Ala., 1983. Mem. U.S. Permanent Mission to UN, 1956-63; adv. Gen. Assembly Dels., 1956-63; pres. Am. U. in Cairo, 1963-69, Colgate U., Hamilton, N.Y., 1969-77, Assn. Am. Univs., Washington, 1977-82; chancellor U. Ala. System, 1982—; dir. Security Mut. Life Ins. Co. N.Y.; Mem. UAR-U.S. Ednl. Exchange Commn., 1966-69, U.S.-Egyptian Com. on Cultural Exchanges, 1977—; mem. Task Force on Financing Higher Edn. in N.Y. State (Keppel Commn.), 1972-73; chmn. Commn. Ind. Colls. and Univs. N.Y., 1974-76; bd. dirs. Nat. Assn. Ind. Colls. and Univs., 1975-76; trustee Gen. Theol. Sem., 1977-82, Am. U. in Cairo, 1978—; mem. nat. bd. examining Chaplains Episcopal Ch. Mem. Council Fgn. Relations, Phi Beta Kappa. Clubs: Cosmos (Washington); Century Assn. (N.Y.C.). Home: #9 Pinehurst Tuscaloosa AL 35401 Office: Univ of Alabama System PO Box BT University AL 35486

BARTLETT, VICTOR EVANS, oil company executive; b. Wichita Falls, Tex., Jan. 16, 1926; s. C.E. and Beatrice (Thornton) B.; m. Betty S. Aldridge, Oct. 11, 1953; children: Blane, Darla, Ronny. B.S. in Bus. Adminstrn., East Central State U., Ada, Okla., 1953. Dist. landman Skelly Oil Co., Midland, Tex., 1966-68, dist. exploration mgr., 1968-73; exploration mgr. Skelley Oil Co., Midland, Tex., 1973-77, Getty Oil Co., Tulsa, 1977-80, v.p., gen. mgr. internat. exploration and prodn., Los Angeles, 1980-82, v.p., gen. mgr. central exploration and prodn. div., Tulsa, 1982—. Bd. dirs. Children's Med. Ctr., Tulsa, 1982—; v.p., bd. dirs. Tulsa YMCA, 1982—. Served with AUS, 1945-47; Philippines. Mem. Mid-Continent Oil and Gas Assn. (dir. 1983—, v.p. Kans.-Okla. div. 1983—). Republican. Home: 10653 S 66th East Ave Tulsa OK 74133 Office: Getty Oil Co 1437 S Boulder Tulsa OK 74119

BARTLETT, WILLIAM MCGILLIVRAY, hospital products company executive; b. Rockford, Ill., Sept. 17, 1932; s. Leonard Brown and Elizabeth (McGillvray) B.; m. Janice L. Wessinger, Aug. 10, 1954; children: R. Scott, Eliz Lynn. B.S. in Civil Engring., Duke U., 1954; postgrad. in Mgmt, Northwestern U., 1971. Staff J.L. Clark Mfg. Co., Rockford and Chgo., 1958-68, gen. mgr. housewares div., Chgo., 1966-68, gen. mgr. plastics div., 1968; v.p., pres. surg. V. Mueller instrument div. Am. Hosp. Supply Corp., Chgo., 1968-74, pres. Atlantic Internat. div., 1975-78; corp. v.p., pres. med. products group G.D. Searle & Co., Skokie, Ill., 1978-82; pres., chief exec. officer Kewaunee Sci. Equipment Corp., Chgo., 1982—; asso. prof. mil. sci. Notre Dame U., South Bend, Ind., 1956-58. Served to lt. USNR, 1954-58; China, Korea. Club: Michigan Shores. Home: 503 Orchard Ln Winnetka IL 60093 Office: 1213 Wilmette Ave Suite 203 Wilmette IL 60091

BARTLETT DIAZ, MANUEL, secretary of the interior Mexico; b. Puebla, Mexico, Feb. 23, 1936; s. Manuel Bartlett Bautista. Law degree, Universidad Nacional Autonoma de Mexico, Mexico City; doctorate, Faculty Polit. and Social Scis., 1968; postgrad. in law, U. Paris, 1959-61, U. Victoria, Manchester, Eng., 1967-68. Aux. sec. Partido Revolucianario Institucional, Mexico City, 1964-68; sec. gen. Partido Revolucionario Institucional, Mexico, 1981-82; dir. gen. Sec. of Interior, Govt. of Mexico, Mexico City, 1970-76, dir.-in-chief sec. Fgn. Affairs, 1976-79, counselor, sec. program and budget, 1979-81, sec. of interior, 1982—. Mem. council of adminstrn. Banco Nacional de Fomento Cooperativo, 1976-79; coordinator Miguel de la Madrid campaign for presidency of Mexico, 1981-82. Office: Secretaria de Gobernacion Bucareli 99 Mexico City Mexico 06600

BARTLEY, RICHARD MYERS, oil company executive; b. Washington, Jan. 10, 1928; s. Edward Ross and Pearl (Myers) B.; m. Patsy Jane Hamilton, Nov. 24, 1950; children: Diane Katherine, Patricia Ann, Richard Hamilton. B.S. in Chemistry, Ind. U.-Bloomington, 1949, M.B.A., 1950. Mgr. strategic planning Spencer Chem. Co., Kansas City, Mo., 1959-67; mgr. devel. nuclear fuels Gulf Oil Co., Pitts., 1967-69, mgr. long range planning, 1969-71; divisional v.p. Gulf Oil Chem. Co., Houston, 1971-73, group v.p., 1973-78, sr. v.p., 1978—; dir. Midwest Carbide Corp., Keokuk, Iowa. 1st lt. USAF, 1951-53. Mem. Am. Chem. Soc., N. Am. Planning Soc. Republican. Presbyterian. Clubs: Petroleum, Yacht (Houston). Home: 415 Bayou Knoll Dr Houston TX 77079 Office: Gulf Oil Corp 909 Fannin St Houston TX 77001

BARTLEY, ROBERT LEROY, newspaper editor; b. Marshall, Minn., Oct. 12, 1937; s. Theodore French and Iva Mae (Radach) B.; m. Edith Jean Lillie, Dec. 29, 1960; children: Edith Elizabeth, Susan Lillie, Katherine French. B.S., Iowa State U., 1959; M.S., U. Wis., 1962; LL.D., Macalester Coll., 1982. Reporter Grinnell (Iowa) Herald-Register, 1959-60; staff reporter Wall Street Jour., Chgo., 1962-63, Phila., 1963-64, editorial writer, N.Y.C., 1964-70, Washington, 1970-71, editor editorial page, N.Y.C., 1972-78, editor, 1979—, v.p., 1983—. Trustee NYU, Mayo Found. Served to 2d lt. USAR, 1960. Recipient Overseas Press Club citation, 1977, Gerald Loeb award, 1979, Pulitzer prize for editorial writing, 1980. Mem. Am. Soc. Newspaper Editors, Nat. Conf. Editorial Writers, Am. Polit. Sci. Assn., Council on Fgn. Relations, Sigma Delta Chi. Clubs: Down Town Assn., Heights Casino. Office: 22 Cortlandt St New York NY 10007

BARTLEY, S. HOWARD, psychobiologist, educator; b. Pitts., June 19, 1901; s. Edward G. and Mary Agnes (Byers) B.; m. Velma Himebaugh, Aug. 19, 1924; children: Samuel Howard, Katherine Joyce, Jeanne Antoinette; m. Leola Sarah Vevis, June 25, 1938. B.S., Greenville Coll., 1923; M.A., U. Kans., 1928, Ph.D., 1931. Tchr. Miltonvale Wesleyan Coll., Kans., 1924-25; asst. instr. U. Kans., Lawrence, 1926-31; fellow, research assoc. Washington U., St. Louis, 1931-42; prof., dir. research Dartmouth Eye Inst., Hanover, N.H., 1942-47, Mich. State U., E. Lansing, 1947-71; disting. research prof. Memphis State U., 1972—. Author: Vision: A Study of Its Basis, 1941, Fatigue and Impairment in Man, 1947, Principles of Perception, 1958, Beginning Experimental Psychology, 1960, The Human Organism as a Person, 1967, Perception in Everyday Life, 1972. NRC fellow, 1931-33; recipient Apollo award Am. Optometric Assn., 1970, Prentice medal Am. Acad. Optometry, 1972. Mem. Am. Acad. Optometry, Am. Psychol. Assn., Optical Soc. Am., Am. Physiol. Soc., Sigma Xi, Beta Sigma Kappa. Christian Ch. Home: 177 N Highland Ave Apt 716 Memphis TN 38111 Office: Dept Psychology Memphis State U Memphis TN 38152

BARTLEY, WILLIAM WARREN, III, educator; b. Pitts., Oct. 2, 1934; s. William Warren and Elvina (Henry) B. A.B., Harvard U., 1956, A.M., 1958; Ph.D., London (Eng.) Sch. Econs. and Polit. Sci., 1962. Lectr. logic London Sch. Econs., 1960-63; lectr. history of philosophy of sci. Warburg Inst. U. London, 1961-64; vis. assoc. prof. philosophy U. Calif.-Berkeley, 1963-64; assoc. prof. U. Calif.-San Diego, 1964-67, co.-dir. humanities program, 1965-66; S.A. Cook Bye fellow Gonville and Caius Coll., Cambridge U., 1966-67; assoc. prof. philosophy U. Pitts., 1967-69, assoc. prof., 1967-69, prof. philosophy and history and philosophy of sci., sr. research assoc., assoc. dir. Philosophy of Sci. Center, 1969-73; prof. philosophy Calif. State U. at Hayward, 1970—, Outstanding prof., 1979—; vis. scholar Hoover Instn. War, Revolution and Peace, Stanford U., 1984—; treas. Struction, Inc., 1978—; dir. N.Y. Tribune; staff philosopher, est, ednl. corp., 1975-78; Neil Arnott lectr. Robert Gordon's Inst. Tech., Aberdeen, Scotland, 1981; seminar leader Austrian Coll., Alpbach, 1961, 65, 75, 80, 82; spl. lectr. Royal Inst. Philosophy, London, 1961, 68, Institut für Wissenschaftstheorie U. Salzburg, Austria, 1962; vis. asso. prof. U. Ill., 1964; spl. lectr. U. Karlsruhe, 1965; adj. prof. philosophy L.I.U., 1966; Bd. dirs. Salzburg Seminar in Am. Studies, 1956-58, Bd. dirs. History and Theory, 1960-65; Bd. dirs. Werner Erhard Charitable Settlement, Jersey, Channel Islands, 1976—, est, an ednl. co., Ltd., London, 1977-81, Internat. Conf. on Unity of Scis., 1979—, Inst. on Comparative Polit. and Econ. Systems, Georgetown U., 1980—. Author: The Retreat to Commitment, 1962, 64, 84, Flucht ins Engagement, 1964, Morality and Religion, 1971, Wittgenstein, 1973, 74, 75, 77, 83, Die Notwendigkeit des Engagements, 1974, 77, Wittgenstein e Popper, 1976, Lewis Carroll's Symbolic Logic, 1977, 78, Werner Erhard, 1978; Assoc. editor: History and Theory, 1958-65; editor: Sir. Karl Popper's Postscript, 1982, 83; bd. editors: Soundings, 1967-69, Philos. Forum, 1967—; Contbr. articles profl. jours. Danforth Found. fellow, 1956-61, 66-67; Am. Council Learned Socs. fellow, 1972-73, 79-80; Am. Philos. Soc. fellow, 1979-80; est Found. fellow, 1982-83; DAAD fellow, 1983; Thyssen Found. fellow, 1984; Earhart Found. fellow, 1984; Morris Found. fellow, 1984; Parshad award, 1952, 83; Fulbright award, 1958-60; Dana Reed award, 1956; Bowen prize Harvard, 1958. Mem. Oxford and Cambridge Soc., Signet Soc., Brit. Soc. Philosophy of Sci. (mem. exec. com. 1964), AAUP, Phi Beta Kappa. Clubs: Harvard, Ivy (San Francisco). Office: Hoover Instn Stanford U Stanford CA 94305

BARTLING, THEODORE CHARLES, oil co. exec.; b. St. Louis, Feb. 19, 1922; s. George Reynard and Dorothy (Adams) B.; m. Phyllis McGinness, Aug. 2, 1946; children—Eric C., Pamela A., Theodore A. B.S. in Geology, Ohio State U., 1947. Staff geologist Pitts. Plate Glass Co., 1947-49; exploration mgr. W. C. McBride Inc., 1949-55; founder, pres., dir. Apache Oil Corp., Mpls., 1955-67; pres. Ada Oil Exploration, 1967-70, Bartling Oil Corp., 1971—; founder, 1st pres. Oil Investment Inst. Mem. Assn. Petroleum Geologists, Houston Geol. Soc., Ind. Producer's Assn. Am. (dir.). Home: 11 Inwood Oaks Houston TX 77024 Office: 8550 Katy Freeway Suite 128 Houston TX 77024

BARTNER, MARTIN A., newspaper publisher; b. Newark, Apr. 11, 1930; s. Joseph and Kate (Libman) B.; m. Audrey Mayer, May 20, 1956; children—Douglas, Lisa. B.S., N.Y. U., 1951. Advt. mgr. Jersey Jour., Jersey City, 1951-62; asso. pub. Newark Star-Ledger, 1962—. Bd. dirs. Daus. of Israel Nursing Home, Newark, Newark chpt. ARC; treas. W. Orange Jewish Center; mem. steering com. Black Achievers N.J. Served with AUS, 1953-55. Mem. Advt. Club N.J. (dir.). Office: Star-Ledger Plaza Newark NJ 07101

BARTNICKI-GARCIA, SALOMON, microbiologist, educator; b. Mexico City, May 18, 1935; U.S., 1957; s. Israel Bartnicki and Refugio Garcia; m. Ildiko Nagy, Aug. 10, 1975; children—Linda Laura, David Daniel. Bacteriological Chemist, Inst. Politecnico Nacional, Mexico City, 1957; Ph.D., Rutgers U., 1961. Research asso. microbiology Rutgers U., 1961-62; mem. faculty U. Calif. at Riverside, 1962—, prof. plant pathology and microbiology, 1971—; vis. prof. Organic Chemistry Inst., U. Stockholm, 1969-70. Author research and rev. papers. Grantee NIH, 1963—, NSF, 1971—. Mem. AAAS, Am. Soc. Microbiology, Am. Phytopathol. Soc., Mycol. Soc. Am., Brit. Soc. Gen. Microbiology, Brit. Mycol. Soc., Am. Soc. Biol. Chemists. Home: 1391 Lynridge Riverside CA 92506 Office: Dept Plant Pathology Univ Calif Riverside CA 92521

BARTNIKAS, RAY, electrical engineer, educator; b. Kaunas, Lithuania, Jan. 25, 1936; s. Andrius and Eugenia (Kanisauskas) B.; m. Margaret McLachlan, Aug. 19, 1967; children: Andrea Marie, Thomas Benedict. B.A.Sc. in Elec. Engring, U. Toronto, 1958; M.Eng., McGill U., 1962, Ph.D., 1964. Research engr. Cable Devel. Labs., No. Electric Co., Lachine, Que., Can., 1958-63; mem. sci. staff Phys. Scis. div. Bell-No. Research Labs., Ottawa, Ont., Can., 1963-68; research scientist, sci. dir. materials sci. research div. Hydro-Quebec Inst. Research, Varennes, Que., 1968—; research assoc., lectr. theory of dielectrics McGill U., Montreal, 1968-75; adj. prof., Fleming Found. visitor dept. elec. engring. U. Waterloo (Ont.), 1969—; vis. prof. dept. engring. physics Ecole Polytechnique U. Montreal, 1982—; cons. Cepel Inst. Research, Rio De Janeiro, 1973—. Editor, author: book series on Engineering Dielectrics, 1979—, Elements of Cable Engineering, 1980; contbr. articles on dielectric and discharge loss mechanisms in elec. insulating systems to profl. jours. Fellow IEEE (Thomas Dakin Disting. Sci. Achievement award 1980); mem. ASTM (chmn. elec. insulation com. 1980—), Internat. Electrotech. Commn., IEEE Elec. Insulation Soc. (pres. 1976-78), Order Engrs. Que. Roman Catholic. Office: 1800 Descente Ste-Julie Varennes PQ J0L 2P0 Canada

BARTNOFF, JUDITH, lawyer; b. Boston, Apr. 14, 1949; d. Shepard and Irene F. (Tennenbaum) B.; m. Eugene F. Sofer, Sept. 10, 1978. A.B., Radcliffe Coll., 1971; J.D. (Harlan Fiske Stone scholar), Columbia U., 1974; LL.M., Georgetown U., 1975. Bar: D.C. bar 1975, Barrister Am. Inn of Ct. 1983. Fellow Inst. Public Interest Representation, Georgetown Law Center, Washington, 1974-75; staff atty. Council Public Interest Law, Washington, 1975-77; spl. asst. to asst. atty. gen. criminal div. Dept. Justice, Washington, 1977-78, assoc. dep. atty. gen., 1978-80; spl. asst. U.S. atty. for D.C., 1980-81, asst., 1982—. Bd. dirs. Com. for Public Advocacy, 1977. Mem. D.C. Bar, Women's Legal Def. Fund. Home: 3005 McKinley St NW Washington DC 20015 Office: US Courthouse 3d and Constitution Ave NW Washington DC 20001

BARTOCHA, BODO, government official; b. Wroclaw, Poland, Dec. 26, 1928; came to U.S., 1956, naturalized, 1964; s. Karl and Erna A. (Mevers) B.; m. Elisabeth Kieckhoefer, Nov. 23, 1957. B.S. in Chemistry and Physics, Philipps U., Marburg/Lahn, Germany, 1951, M.S. in Inorganic Chemistry, 1953, Ph.D., 1956; postgrad. (Milton fellow), Harvard, 1956-58. Research fellow chemistry Harvard, 1956-58; head propellant br. U.S. Naval Ordnance Lab., Corona, Cal., 1958-61; dir. research, acting dir. devel. U.S. Naval Propellant Plant, Indian Head, Md., 1961-64; dep. dir. naval scis. Office Naval Research Br. Office, London, Eng., 1964-66; asst. tech. dir. advanced planning and programs Naval Ordnance Sta., Indian Head, 1966-67; with NSF, Washington, 1967—, staff asso., dep. head office planning and policy studies, 1967-70, dep. exec. sec. exec. council, 1970-71, exec. asst. to asst. dir. nat. and internat. programs, 1971, dir. div. internat. programs, 1972—; Cons. in planning, evaluation and tech. forecasting, 1969-71. Author: (with Clinton A. Stone, Francis Narin) The Science of Managing Organized Technology, 1970, Wirtschaftliche und Gesellschaftliche Auswirkungen des Technischen Fortschritts, 1971, The Education of Engineers and Social Responsibility, 1974; Editor: (with M. Cetron) Technology Assessment in a Dynamic Environment, 1970, The Methodology of Technology Assessment, 1972; Contbr.: articles to profl. jours. The Methodology of Technology Assessment. Recipient Superior Achievement awards USN, 1959, 61, 62, Sustained Superior Performance award, 1963, Outstanding Performance Ratings, 1964, 66, Meritorious Civilian Service award, 1966; Outstanding Performance rating NSF, 1967; Disting. Service award, 1978. Fellow AAAS; Mem. Mil. Ops. Research Soc. Patentee in field. Home: 1332 MacBeth St McLean VA 22102 Office: 1800 G St NW Washington DC 20550

BARTOE, OTTO EDWIN, JR., aircraft company executive; b. Paris Island, S.C., Apr. 5, 1927; s. Otto Edwin and Maude Iris (Lamb) B.; m. Mary Kathryn Marvin, Aug. 15, 1952; children: Carolyn, Sally. B.S. in Mech. Engring, U. Colo., 1949, M.S., 1954. With Upper Air Research Lab., Colo. U., 1949-51; with Hughes Aircraft Co., Santa Barbara Research Center; chief design engr. Research Services Labs., Colo. U., 1952-54; chief advanced systems dept., tech. dir., v.p. aerospace div. Ball Bros. Research Corp., Boulder, Colo., 1956-70, pres., 1970-74, Ball-Bartoe Aircraft Corp., Boulder, 1974-78, Skyote Aeromarine Ltd., 1977—, Bartoe Research & Devel., 1982—. Served with USMC, 1945-46. Mem. Am. Inst. Aeros. and Astronautics (Spacecraft Design award), Nat. Geog. Soc. Antique Airplane Assn., Exptl. Aircraft Assn., Royal Order Aerobee Rocketeers, Sigma Pi Sigma, Pi Tau Sigma. Home: PO Box 808 Clark CO 80428

BARTOL, GEORGE E., III, manufacturing company executive; b. Phila., Apr. 20, 1921; s. George E. and Mary (Rush) B.;, June 18, 1943; children: Blair MacInnes, Mary Rush Wolszon, Victoria Vallely, Katherine Lunt. B.A., Princeton U., 1943. With Hunt Mfg. Co., Phila., 1946-83, pres., chief exec. officer, 1957-69, chmn. bd., chief exec. officer, 1969-73, 75-83; exec. dep. sec. commerce Commonwealth of Pa., 1973-75; mem. bd. 3d Dist. Fed. Res. Bank. Bd. dirs. Urban Affairs Partnership, World Affairs Council Phila., Phila. Hist. Soc.; chmn. bd. mgrs. Franklin Inst.; trustee Oldfields Sch., Glencoe, Md., 1966-74; bd. dirs. Phila. Acad. Natural Scis., Phila. Met. YMCA. Served to lt. (j.g.) USN, 1943-45. Mem. Mayflower Soc., Phila. Internat. Steering Com., Writing Instruments Mfrs. Assn. (pres. 1960-62). Clubs: Racquet (Phila.); Princeton, Gulph Mills., Philadelphia. Office: 1405 Locust St Philadelphia PA 19102

BARTOLETTI, BRUNO, conductor; b. Sesto Fiorentino, Italy, June 10, 1926; m. Rosanna Bartoletti; 2 children. Ed., Conservatory Florence. Co-artistic dir. Lyric Opera Chgo., 1964-75. Operatic debut at, Teatro Comunale di Firenze, 1953, symphonic debut at, Maggio Musicale Fiorentino, 1954; condr. opera houses in, Copenhagen, Lisbon, Wiesbaden, Teatro Colon in, Buenos Aires, Am. debut with, Lyric Opera of Chgo.; resident condr., Lyric Opera Chgo., 1956—. Address: care Lyric Opera of Chgo 20 N Wacker Dr Chicago IL 60606

BARTOLINI, ANTHONY LOUIS, lawyer; b. Waterbury, Conn., Nov. 18, 1931; s. Nazzareno and Augusta (Ciuffoli) B.; m. Angela Judith Topazio, July 27, 1957; children: Maria, David, Rachel. B.A., St. Bernard's Sem. and Coll., 1954; postgrad., Cath. U. Am., 1955-56; J.D., Villanova U., 1958. Bar: Pa. 1958. Assoc. Dechert Price & Rhoads, Phila., 1958-64, ptnr., 1964—. Chmn. Villanova Law Sch. Bd. Consultors, 1982—. Mem. Phila. Bar Assn. (chmn. tax sect.), Internat. Fiscal Assn. (chmn. Mid.-Atlantic region 1980-81), ABA. Home: 273 Winthrop Rd Berwyn PA 19312 Office: Dechert Price & Rhoads 3400 Centre Square W 1500 Market St Philadelphia PA 19102

BARTOLINI, R. PAUL, librarian; b. Ladd, Ill., July 21, 1920; s. Romeo and Ersilia (Galletti) B.; m. Myrtle J. File, Dec. 31, 1942; children: Richard Paul, David R., William F., Mary T. B.S., Ill. State U., 1942, U. Ill., 1946, M.S., 1947. Coordinator adult services Free Library of Phila., 1953-56; asst. city librarian ext. services Milw. Public Library, 1956-65; dir. Lake County (Ind.) Public Library, 1965-79, Public Library of Knoxville-Knox County, Tenn., 1979—. Served with U.S. Army, 1942-46. Mem. ALA, Southeastern Library Assn., Tenn. Library Assn., Am. Soc. Public Adminstrn., Kans. Library Assn. (past pres.), Wis. Library Assn. (past pres.). Republican. Roman Catholic. Clubs: Rotary, Italian-Am. Soc. Knoxville. Home: 7140 Dan Rose Ln Knoxville TN 37920 Office: 500 W Church Ave Knoxville TN 37902

BARTOLO, ADOLPH MARION, food company executive; b. Cairo, Apr. 12, 1929; U.S., 1947, naturalized, 1953; s. Edgar Charles and Emma C. (Borrelli) B.; m. Joycelyn Mary Bergeron, June 7, 1950; children: Pamela Bridget, Edgar Charles II, Janice Ann, Mary Elizabeth. B.S. in Chem. Engring., La. State U., 1950. From chem. engr. to asst. supt. Southdown Sugar, Inc., Houma, La., 1951-58; with Imperial Sugar Co., Sugar Land, Tex., 1958—, v.p. refinery ops., from 1968, now exec. v.p., dir.; dir. Cane Sugar Refiners Research Project, 1965—; dir. Sugar Industry Technologists, Inc., pres., 1976-77. Mem. La. State U. Found., 1966-68. Mem. Am. Inst. Chem. Engrs., U.S. Nat. Com. Sugar Analysis. Roman Catholic. Clubs: Lions (Sugar lane) (1960-61); Sugar Creek Country (Sugar Lane); Exchange (Ft. Bend). Home: 303 S Belknap St Sugar Land TX 77478 Office: Imperial Sugar Co Sugar Land TX 77478

BARTOLOME, FRANCISCO MABALAY, food technologist; b. Manila, P.I., Nov. 6, 1939; came to U.S., 1965; s. Fruto Feliciano and Emiliana (Mabalay) B.; m. Linda Gutierrez, Sept. 3, 1955. B.S., U. Philippines, 1962; M.S., Purdue U., 1968, Ph.D., 1971. Product devel. mgr., packaging engr. Procter & Gamble, Manila, 1962-65; group leader product devel. Hunt-Wesson Foods, Inc., Fullerton, Calif., 1971-75; dir. research and devel. Golden Dipt. Co., Millstadt, Ill., 1975-77; mgr. tech. devel. Pillsbury Co., Mpls., 1977—; instr. chem. engring. Manuel L. Quezon U., Manila, 1965; research asst. Purdue U., 1966-71. Dee Chuaun grantee, 1962. Mem. Inst. Food Technologists, Am. Assn. Cereal Chemists, Phi Tau Sigma. Home: 6501 Vernon Ave S Edina MN 55436 Office: 425 Main St SE Minneapolis MN 55414

BARTON, ALAN RAYMOND, utility executive; b. West Haven, Conn., Feb. 6, 1925; s. Alan Raymond and Edith Beatrice (Mulcahy) B.; m. Peggy Finneran, Feb. 11, 1952 (dec. Apr. 1980); children—Alan, Mary Rae, Elizabeth, William. Student, Ga. Inst. Tech., 1944; B.Mech. Engring., Tulane U., 1946; B.E.E., Auburn U., 1948; M.B.A., U. Ala., 1979. With Ala. Power Co., Birmingham, 1948-80, v.p., 1964-69, sr. v.p., 1969-75, exec. v.p., 1975-80, also dir.; pres. Miss. Power Co., Gulfport, 1980—, chief exec. officer, 1981—, also dir.; dir. So. Co., So. Co. Services, So. Electric Internat. Served to lt. (j.g.) USNR, 1943-47. Mem. IEEE. Roman Catholic.

BARTON, ALLEN HOISINGTON, sociologist; b. Greenwich, Conn., Oct. 7, 1924; s. H. Allen and Elizabeth Folwell (Hoisington) B.; m. Judith Schneider, Mar. 11, 1949; children—Stephen, Hugh, Matthew, Julia. A.B., Harvard U., 1947; Ph.D., Columbia U., 1957. Lectr. sociology U. Oslo, Norway, 1948-49; research asst. Bur. Applied Social Research, Columbia U., N.Y.C., 1947-54, research asso., 1957-62, dir., 1962-77, from asst. prof. to asso. prof., 1958-71, prof. sociology, 1972—; asst. prof. U. Chgo., 1954-57; Dir. Roper Center for Public Opinion Research. Author: Studying the Effects of College Education, 1959, Organizational Measurement, 1961, Communities in Disaster, 1969, Opinion-Making Elites in Yugoslavia, 1973, Decentralizing City Government, 1977, Making Bureaucracies Work, 1980. Active Ams. for Democratic Action, 1948—; del. Conn. Democratic Conv., 1968; mem. Democratic Town Com., Greenwich, 1969—. Served with U.S. Army., 1943-46. Social Sci. Research Council grantee, 1949-50; Carnegie Corp. grantee, 1968-71; Ford Found. grantee, 1972-75; also grantee NIMH, NSF. Mem. Am. Sociol. Assn., Am. Assn. Public Opinion Research, AAUP. Democrat. Home: 327 Valley Rd Cos Cob CT 06807 Office: Dept Sociology Columbia U New York NY 10027 *In science it helps to be able to see patterns in confusing sets of observations. In education based on a scientific field, one tries to communicate not only findings, but how a scientist works, how ignorant he or she is much of the time, and how you find things out. It is also important to combine being honest with being considerate and trying to help students or colleagues over difficulties. As a citizen, it is crucial to be concerned with justice and insuring people an equal chance, at which even the American system is not doing as well as it should.*

BARTON, BABETTE B., lawyer, educator; b. Los Angeles, Apr. 30, 1930; d. Milton Vernon and Ruth (Schreiber) Barancik; m. John K. McNulty, Mar. 23, 1978; children: Jeffrey B. Barton, David R. Barton, Baird R. Barton. B.S., U. Calif., Berkeley, 1951, LL.B., 1954. Bar: Calif., U.S. Dist. Ct., U.S. Ct. Appeals 1955. Law clk. to Chief Justice Phil S. Gibson, Calif. Supreme Ct., San Francisco, 1954-55; lectr., acting prof. Sch. of Law, U. Calif., Berkeley, 1961-72, prof. law, 1972—; cons. Calif. Inter Agy. Task Force on Electronic Funds Transfers, 1978-79, Dept. Treasury, 1963; mem. adv. com. Calif. Bd. Legal Specialization, 1980-83. Contbr. chpts. to books in field. Mem. adv. com. Alameda County Dir. Welfare, 1970-73; bd. dirs. Family Service Berkeley, 1967-74, Univ. Students' Coop. Assn., 1966-74. Fellow Am. Law Inst., Am. Bar Found.; mem. Am. Bar Assn. (mem. council Real Property, Probate and Trust sect. 1977-79), Calif. State Bar (chmn. taxation sec. 1976-77), Western Regional Bar Assn. (chmn. 1978-79), Am. Coll. Tax Counsel, San Francisco Tax Club, San Francisco Estate Planning Council. Democrat. Home: 620 Spruce Berkeley CA 94707 Office: Sch of Law Univ of Calif Berkeley CA 94720

BARTON, BRIGID S., museum director; b. Honolulu, June 1, 1943; d. William M. and Ellen Shanahan. B.A., Barnard Coll. Columbia U., 1965; M.A., U. Calif.-Berkeley, 1968, Ph.D. (NEA fellow), 1976. Instr. art Coll. Marin, Kentfield, Calif., 1969-71; asst. prof. art U. Santa Clara, 1976-82, assoc. prof., 1982—; dir. DeSaisset Mus., 1978—. Mem. Assn. Am. Mus., Coll. Art Assn., Calif. Women in Higher Edn., Western Assn. Art Mus. Office: DeSaisset Mus U Santa Clara Santa Clara CA 95053

BARTON, BRUCE WALTER, artist, educator; b. Ottumwa, Iowa, Sept. 2, 1935; s. Harold H. and Edith L. (Nye) B.; m. Beverly Ann

Manassero, Jan. 17, 1959; children—Bric, Peter Bret Charles. B.F.A., San Francisco Art Inst., 1962; M.A., San Diego State U., 1963; cert., U.S. Sch. Photography, 1955. Photographer, illustrator Community Ednl. Resources, San Diego, 1963-64; art dir. Boeing Co., Seattle, 1964-65; mem. faculty dept. art E. Tex. State U., Commerce, 1965-66, U. Man., Winnipeg, Can., 1966-67; faculty art Ohio State U., Columbus, 1967-69, chmn. dept. art, 1968-69; prof. art U. Mont., Missoula, 1969—, project dir. grad. program in Am. Indian arts, 1971-73, chmn. dept. art, 1969-72. Author: The Tree at the Center of the World, 1979; one-man shows, U. Mont., 1975, 76, 77, Va. Commonwealth U., 1977, U. Center Gallery, Richmond, Va., group shows include, Denver Mus. Art, San Diego Mus. Art, Seattle Mus., San Francisco Art Inst., San Diego State U. Served with USN, 1954-58. Recipient Alfred J. Wright award Ohio State U., 1969; U.S. Office Edn. grantee, 1971; OEO grantee, 1971; Nat. Endowment Humanities grantee, 1971. Mem. Am. Anthrop. Soc., Am. Acad. Religion, Am. Cath. Hist. Assn., Soc. for Anthropology of Visual Communication, Erasmus Soc. Democrat. Roman Catholic. Home: 108 Crestline Dr Missoula MT 59801 Office: Dept Art U Mont Missoula MT 59812

BARTON, CARL P., insurance company executive; b. Haverhill, Mass., Dec. 31, 1916. With N.H. Ins. Co., Manchester, 1936—, asst. sec., 1953-56, sec., 1956-60, sec., comptroller, 1960-63, v.p., comptroller, then exec. v.p., 1963-73, pres., 1973—, chief exec. officer, 1977—; chmn. N.H. Ins. Group, 1979—; exec. v.p., dir. Am. Internat. Group, Inc.; chmn., dir. Granite State Ins. Co., Ill. Nat. Ins. Co., Am. Fidelity Co. Office: 90 Main St Nashua NH 03061

BARTON, DAVID IRVING, new business development company executive; b. Meridan, Conn., Oct. 12, 1938; m. Trisha Young; children: Melinda, Jennifer. B.S., U. Conn., 1961; postgrad. Advanced Mgmt. Program, Harvard U., 1978. Corp. v.p., then pres. New Bus. Devel. Group, Loctite Corp., Newington, Conn. Home: 4 Westborough Dr Simsbury CT 06070 Office: Loctite Corp 705 N Mountain Rd Newington CT 06011

BARTON, DAVID KNOX, radar engineer; b. Greenwich, Conn., Sept. 21, 1927; s. Horace Allen and Elizabeth Folwell (Hoisington) B.; m. Ruth Alice Breitenfeld, Mar. 9, 1950 (div. Apr. 1981); children: Nancy, Margaret, Alice, Linda, Frederick, Susan, William, Allen; m. Cynthia Hodgson Butler, Apr. 4, 1981. B.A. in Physics, Harvard U., 1949. Radar engr. Signal Corps Engring. Labs., Ft. Monmouth, N.J., White Sands (N.Mex.) Proving Grounds, 1949-55; electronic engr. missile and surface radar dept. RCA, Moorestown, N.J., 1955-63; cons. scientist Raytheon Co., Wayland, Mass., 1963-70, Missile Systems div. Raytheon Co., Bedford, Mass., 1970—; lectr. radar George Washington U., 1975—. Author: Radar System Analysis, 1964. Served with Signal Corps U.S. Army, 1946-48. Recipient David W. Sarnoff award for outstanding achievement in engring. RCA, 1958. Fellow IEEE; mem. Aerospace and Electronic Systems Soc. (v.p. tech. ops.). Office: Hartwell Rd Bedford MA 01730

BARTON, EVAN MANSFIELD, physician; b. Chgo., Nov. 7, 1903; s. Enos Melancthon and Mary C. (Rust) B.; m. Jane Purvis High, Oct. 16, 1937 (dec. 1980); children—Cynthia, Eric McMillan. Grad., Choate Sch., 1920; A.B., Williams Coll., 1924; M.D., Johns Hopkins, 1929. Intern Presbyn. Hosp., Chgo., 1929-30, resident in pathology, 1931-34; practice medicine, specializing internal medicine, Chgo., 1935—; attending physician Presbyn.-St. Lukes Hosp.; prof. medicine Rush. Med. Coll.; cons. rheumatology VA Hosp., Hines, Ill. Served from maj. to col., M.C. AUS, 1942-46. Fellow A.C.P.; mem. AMA, Am. Rheumatism Assn., Chgo. Rheumatism Soc., Chgo. Soc. Internal Medicine (pres. 1969), Chgo. Pathol. Soc., Phi Beta Kappa, Phi Gamma Delta, Nu Sigma Nu. Republican. Baptist. Club: Quadrangle. Home: 5817 S Blackstone Ave Chicago IL 60637 Office: 1725 W Harrison St Chicago IL 60612

BARTON, GERALD LEE, agricultural company executive; b. Modesto, Calif., Feb. 24, 1934; s. Robert Paul and Alice Lee (Hall) B.; m. Janet Murray, June 24, 1955; children—Donald Lee, Gary Michael, Brent Richard. A.B. with distinction, Stanford U., 1955. Owner, mgr. R.P. Barton Ranch, Escalon, Calif., 1961—; v.p. R.P. Barton Mfg. Co., Escalon, 1963—; chmn. bd. Diamond Walnut Growers Inc., 1976-81, chmn. emeritus, 1981—; chmn. Diamond-Sunsweet Co., Stockton, Calif., 1978-80, Sun Diamond Growers, Inc., 1980-81; vice chmn. Fed. Land Bank, Modesto, Calif., 1976-81; chmn. Growers Harvesting Com., Modesto, 1976-77; mem. pomology research adv. bd. U. Calif., Davis, 1968—, Walnut Mktg. Bd., San Francisco, 1971-73, 77—; dir. Ross Hort. Found.; mem. San Joaquin County U. Calif. Extension Adv. Bd. Chmn. bd. edn. Escalon Unified Sch. Dist., 1963-75; vice chmn. San Joaquin County Sch. Bds. Assn., 1965. Served with AUS, 1956-58. Named Outstanding Young Farmer in San Joaquin County C. of C., 1965, Farmer of Yr. Escalon C. of C. Mem. Stanford U. Alumni Assn., Delta Chi. Republican. Presbyterian. Home: 31110 E Lee St Escalon CA 95320 Office: 22398 S McBride St Escalon CA 95320

BARTON, JACKSON MOUNCE, petroleum company executive; b. Shawnee, Okla., Jan. 12, 1917; s. Jesse Downy and Elizabeth (Mounce) B.; m. Dorothy King Benedict, May 9, 1942; children: Jackson M., Charles D., Elizabeth B. Student, Phillips U., 1934-36; B.S., U. Okla., 1938; postgrad., Yale U., 1939-41. Geologist Magnolia Petroleum Co., 1938-47; div. geologist Coop. Refinery Assn., Kansas City, Mo., 1947-49, chief geologist, 1949-50, exploration mgr., 1950; mgr. geol. dept. Deep Rock Oil Corp., Tulsa, 1950-53; exploration mgr. to v.p., gen. mgr., dir. No. Natural Gas Producing Co., 1953-65; gen. mgr. Glover Hefner Kennedy Oil Co., Oklahoma City, 1965-68; exec. v.p., dir. Royal Resources Corp.; also exec. v.p. Royal Resources Exploration, Inc., 1968-70; exec. v.p., dir. Champlin Petroleum Co., Ft. Worth, 1970-71; cons. geologist, 1971-72; pres., dir. Home-Stake Prodn. Co., Tulsa, 1972-73; v.p. Terra Resources, Inc., 1973-77; asst. to pres. Warrior Drilling & Engring. Co., Inc., 1977-78, v.p. adminstrn., sec. and treas., 1978-80; pres., dir. Carless Resources, Inc., 1980—; dir. Union Pacific Resources Corp., 1970-71, Carless, Capel & Leonard, London, 1984. Contbr. articles to profl. jours. Bd. dirs. Omaha Planned Parenthood, 1963-65; Mem. Westside Community Schs. Bd. Edn., 1955-65, pres., 1962-65; Mem. alumni adv. council Sch. Geology of U. Okla., 1968—. Fellow Geol. Soc. Am., AAAS; mem. Am. Assn. Petroleum Geologists, Am. Inst. Mining and Metall. Engrs., Soc. Exploration Geophysicists, Am. Geol. Inst., Am. Geophys. Union, Am. Inst. Profl. Geologists, Rocky Mountain Oil and Gas Assn. (past pres. Nebr. sect.), Ind. Petroleum Assn. Am., Am. Petroleum Inst., Am. Gas Assn., Ind. Natural Gas Assn., Mid-Continent Oil and Gas Assn., Omaha C. of C. Unitarian (pres. bd. trustees). Home: 604 Canyon Circle N Tuscaloosa AL 35406

BARTON, JAMES DON, JR., ecologist, univ. adminstr.; b. Anna, Ill., Oct. 25, 1929; s. James Don and Allie (Harrelson) B.; m. Grace E. Valentine, June 30, 1967; children—Robert J., Mark C., Peter V., Maral J., Jayne Dee, Diana J. B.S., No. Ill. U., 1952, M.S., 1953; Ph.D., Purdue U., 1956. Instr. sci. Boston U., 1956-58, asst. prof. sci., 1958-63, dir., 1960- 64; asso. prof. Southampton (N.Y.) Coll., 1963-68, dir. div. natural scis., 1963-66, dean of, 1966-68, acting dir., 1963-64; provost, v.p. acad. affairs, prof. biology Alfred (N.Y.) U., 1968-75; adminstrv. leave to build computer data base Donaldson's Woods, 1975; dir. instl. research State U. N.Y. Agrl. and Tech. Coll. at Alfred, 1976—. Author: Forest Phytosociological Techniques, 1958, Land Use and Vegetation Map, Southampton Town, N.Y, 1969; Cons. to conservation commn.: Instructional Sound Film on Ecology, 1961. Radiol. officer Norfolk (Mass.) Civil Def., 1956-63; Trustee L.I. chpt. Nature Conservancy. Recipient Purdue Research Found. grant, 1955. Mem. Ecol. Soc. Am., Ind., Ill. acads. sci., Sigma Xi, Phi Kappa Phi. Home: Rural Delivery 1 Box 180 Alfred Station NY 14803 Office: State U NY Agrl and Tech Coll Alfred NY 14802

BARTON, JAY, university president, biologist; b. Chgo., June 22, 1922; s. Jay and Agnes (Heisler) B.; m. Ann Taylor, Aug. 1, 1946; children: Sarah Barton Feigin, Elizabeth, Peter, Rachel Barton Sabo, Matthew, Mary, Judith. A.B., U. Mo., 1947, M.A., 1948, Ph.D. in Zoology, 1951. Instr. zoology, then asst. prof. Columbia, 1950-55; from asst. prof. to prof. biology St. Joseph's Coll., Rensselaer, Ind., 1955-65, staff biologist commn. undergrad. edn. in biol. scis., 1965-67; prof. biology, chmn. dept. W.Va. U., 1967-69, provost for instrn., 1968-77, v.p. for acad. affairs, 1977-79; pres. U. Alaska, 1979—; asso. investigator Argonne Nat. Lab., 1958; cons. sci. edn. program AAAS, 1965—; cons. NSF; mem. commn. on instns. higher edn. North Central Assn. Colls. and Secondary Schs., 1970—; Bd. dirs., mem. exec. com. Biol. Scis. Curriculum Study, 1969—, chmn. bd., 1978; mem. exec. com. Nat. Assn. State Univs. and Land-Grant Colls., 1982; bd. dirs. Public Service Satellite Corp., 1981—. Served with AUS, 1943-46. AEC fellow, 1949-50; Lalor fellow, 1951-52; NSF fellow and Fulbright scholar, Copenhagen, Denmark, 1961-62. Mem. Nat. Assn. Biology Tchrs. (bd. dirs., exec. com.), Am. Inst. Biol. Scis., AAAS, Alaska C. of C. (dir. 1982), Sigma Xi. Home: 610 Kobuk U Alaska Fairbanks AK 99701

BARTON, JERRY LEE, hardware distributing company executive; b. Hogansville, Ga., Nov. 7, 1937; s. Harry Kendall and Annie Mae (Spradlin) B.; m. Patricia Hollis, Dec. 29, 1956; children: Lee, Hollis, Stuart, Bill. Student, Ga. State U., U. Calif., Berkeley. With Genuine Parts Co., 1955-77, v.p. mktg., 1974-77; pres. Beck & Greeg Industries, 1977-80; pres., chief exec. officer, chmn. bd., dir. Belknap, Inc., Louisville, 1980—; dir. KFC Coop., Potter Industries. Bd. dirs. Louisville Central Area Bd.; div. chmn. Louisville United Way, 1982; trustee Bellarmine Coll., Louisville. Mem. Young Pres. Orgn., Nat. Wholesale Hardware Assn., So. Hardware Assn. Republican. Methodist. Address: Belknap Inc III E Main St Louisville KY 40202

BARTON, JOHN SELBY, corporation executive; b. Boise, Idaho, Mar. 23, 1918; s. Everett H. and Loraine (Selby) B.; m. Irene E. Brooks, Dec. 5, 1942; children: Katherine L. Barton Lucas, John S., Lawrence B., Patricia I. Barton Zils, Halbert E. B.S. in Chemistry, U. Wash., 1940; M.S., Inst. Paper Chemistry, 1942, Ph.D., 1948. Research chemist Crown Zellerbach Corp., Camas, Wash., 1948-50, group leader, 1950-55, mgr. paper research, 1955-56, dir. packaging research, San Leandro, Calif., 1956-60, dir. research central research div., Camas, 1960-69, v.p. research, 1969-74; v.p. research and devel., San Francisco, 1974—; pres. Empire State Paper Research Assos. Served to lt. USNR, 1942-45. Recipient Westboooke Steele Gold medal Inst. Paper Chemistry, 1948. Mem. Am. Chem. Soc., Paper Industry Mgmt. Assn., Indsl. Research Inst., TAPPI, Sigma Xi. Presbyterian (elder). Patentee in field. Home: 21 Dias Dorados Orinda CA 94563 Office: Crown Zellerbach Corp 1 Bush St San Francisco CA 94104:

BARTON, LEON SAMUEL CLAY, JR., architect; b. Orangeburg, S.C., Jan. 9, 1906; s. Leon Samuel Clay and Georgia (Hadley) B.; m. Alice Barbara Mosher, Dec. 2, 1941 (dec. Sept. 3, 1971); 1 dau., Mary Jane (Mrs. Thomas C. Murray). B.S. in Architecture, Clemson U., 1928; postgrad., NYU, 1932-34, Atelier Morgan, N.Y.C., 1932-35, Inst. Effective Speaking & Human Relations, N.Y.C., 1952, N.Y. Med. Coll., 1966, Columbia U., 1970, Eastern Sch. Real Estate, N.Y.C., 1971; cert., U.S. Civil Def. Preparedness Agy., 1974, Summer Seismic Inst., U. Ill., 1978. Registered architect, Colo., Fla., Md., N.J., N.Y., S.C.; certified Nat. Council Archtl. Registration Bds. Designer, draftsman E.R. Squibb & Sons, 1928-35, dir. master planning, asst. to chief exec. engr., 1944-47; partner Barton & Pilafian, Architects & Engrs., Teheran, Iran, also cons. to Iranian Govt., 1935-38; prin. Leon S. Barton, 1939-41; chief architect head archtl. dept. Robert & Co., Inc., Atlanta, 1941-44; naval architect shipbldg. div. Bethlehem Steel Co., 1944; with Vitro Corp. Am., N.Y.C.; chief architect nuclear energy projects U.S. AEC, 1948-54; sr. partner Barton and Pruitt and Assocs. (Architects, Engrs. and Planners), N.Y.C., 1954—; chmn. bd. pres. Walton Resiliant Floors, Inc., N.Y.C., 1968—. Project architect in charge: design Peter Cooper br. Chase Manhattan Bank, Shreve Lamb & Harmon Assocs., N.Y.C., 1947-48; Prin. works include Engring. and Maintenance Facilities Bldg, E.R. Squibb & Sons, New Brunswick, N.J., Vitro Research Lab. Facilities, Silver Spring, Md., Gen. Nuclear Research Lab. Facilities and Radiation Effects Research Lab. Facilities, Lockheed Aircraft Corp., Dawsonville, Ga., U.S. Food and Drug Adminstrn. Research Lab. and Office Facilities, Bklyn.; assoc. architect: (with Gen. Charles B. Ferris, Engrs.) Barnert Meml. Hosp. Center, Paterson, N.J. Recipient First Hon. mention Nat. WGN Broadcasting Theater Competition, 1934; Grand prize Internat. Teheran Stock Exchange (Bourse) Competition, 1935; First Hon. mention Prix de Rome archtl. Competition, 1935; Certificate of Merit for loyal and efficient services during World War II def. projects Robert & Co., Inc., 1944. Mem. AIA (corp. mem., mem. nat. task force for devel. health facilities research 1969-77, mem. publ. com. 1957-58, mem. pub. affairs com. 1967-68, mem. speakers bur. 1967-71, mem. hosp. and health com. 1967—, mem. sch. and coll. archtl. com. 1971-78, mem. urban planning com. 1972-78, mem. LeBrun Scholarship com. 1972-78, mem. criminal justice facilities com. 1974-75, mem. W. Side Hwy. subcom. 1973-75), N.Y. State Assn. Architects (corp. mem., mem. housing and urban devel. planning com. 1971-78, mem. sch. and coll. com. 1971-78, mem. honors and awards com. 1974-75, mem. environmental and community planning com. 1974-78), Am. Arbitration Assn. (nat. panel arbitrators 1970—), Greater N.Y. Hosp. Assn. (engring. adv. com. 1978—). Episcopalian. Home: PO Box 294 537 North Country Rd Saint James NY 11780 Office: 299 Madison Ave New York NY 10017 *The profession of architecture, art and planning are God's given talents and it is to Him that I turn for strength, courage, fortitude, knowledge, wisdom, understanding, guidance, tact, inspiration, diplomacy, comfort, and happiness. It is to Him that I give my daily thanks for His generous provisions which he has thus bestowed upon me.*

BARTON, RICHARD ALAN, holding company executive, lawyer; b. Sedalia, Mo., Oct. 23, 1924; s. Alvin Lester and Ruby Marie (McClure) B.; m. Constance Therese Geary, Apr. 18, 1952; children: Kathryn, Daniel, Richard, Philip, Joan, Constance, Kevin. B.S. in Civil Engring., U. Mo., 1947, J.D., 1949. Bar: Mo. 1949, Ill. 1950. Instr. U. Mo. Coll. Engring., Columbia, 1946-49; asst. counsel Chgo. Bridge & Iron, 1949-64, gen. counsel, Oak Brook, 1964-79; v.p., gen. counsel CBI Industries, Inc., Oak Brook, 1980-82, sr. v.p., gen. counsel, 1983—; lectr. in field. Trustee Village of Oak Brook, 1962-66; chmn. Oak Brook Plan Commn., 1970-78; bd. dirs., officer DuPage Easter Seal Treatment Ctr., Villa Park, Ill., 1970—; bd. dirs. Ill. Easter Seal Soc., Springfield, 1979—, Hospice Vols. of DuPage, Glen Ellyn, Ill., 1980-83, Graue Mill and Mus., Oak Brook, 1983—; scoutmaster Boy Scouts Am., Hinsdale, 1966-68; soccer coach Oak Brook Park Dist., 1976-78. Mem. ASCE, ABA, Ill. Bar Assn., Chgo. Bar Assn. Republican. Club: Oak Brook Bath and Tennis. Office: CBI Industries Inc 800 Jorie Blvd Oak Brook IL 60521

BARTON, RICHARD FLEMING, business administration educator, university administrator; b. Oshkosh, Wis., Sept. 29, 1924; s. Dan Wiley and Margaret (Freeman) B.; m. Nancy Ann Schalk, Oct. 25, 1952 (div. Nov. 2, 1976); children: Ted Steven, Dan Richard, Jean Nancy; m. Barbara J. Dorn, Jan. 1, 1981. B.S., Northwestern U., 1948; Ph.D., U. Calif. at Berkeley, 1961. With Procter & Gamble, 1948-50, Travelers Ins. Co., 1952-58; asst. prof. bus. orgn. and mgmt. U. Nebr., 1961-64; asso. prof. bus. adminstrn. U. Kan., 1964-67; prof. bus. adminstrn. and computer sci. Tex. Tech U., Lubbock, 1967—, dir. planning and analyses, 1968-71, acting computer center dir., 1970-71; vis. prof. mgmt. San Diego State U., 1975-76; lectr., cons. in field, 1961—. Author: A Primer on Simulation and Gaming, 1970, The Imaginit Management Game, 1973, also numerous articles, papers on policy, oligopoly, simulation, mgmt. sci., adminstrn. of higher edn. Served with USAAF, World War II. Ford Found. fellow, 1959-61. Mem. Ops. Research Soc. Am., Inst. Mgmt. Scis., Acad. Mgmt., Am. Inst. Decision Scis., Beta Gamma Sigma, Sigma Iota Epsilon, Alpha Iota Delta. Office: Coll Bus Adminstrn Texas Tech U Lubbock TX 79409

BARTON, RUSSELL WILLIAM, physician, educator, hosp. adminstr.; b. London, Eng., Apr. 21, 1923; s. Charles William and Muriel Marguerite (Hart) B.; m. Katherine Grizel Maitland-Makgill-Crichton, July 24, 1954; children: Karen Elizabeth, Sarah Muriel. M.B., U. London, 1949, B.Surgery, 1949. Diplomate: Am. Bd. Neurology and Psychiatry. House physician, registrar, psychiat. registrar Westminster Hosp., London, 1948-53; registrar Maudsley Hosp., London, 1953-56; physician supt. Severalls Hosp., Colchester, Eng., 1960-71; dir. Rochester (N.Y.) Psychiat. Center, 1970-77; cons. psychiatrist WHO, 1964, Minn. Dept. Pub. Welfare, 1965; dir. edn. Pilgrim State Hosp., Brentwood, N.Y., 1969, 70; clin. prof. psychiatry N.Y. Sch. Psychiatry, N.Y.C., 1968—; asso. clin. prof. U. Rochester, 1971—; mem. select coms. mental hosps., med. edn., psychogeriatrics Ministry Health, London, 1963-66; chmn. Rochester Area Mental Health Com., 1971. Author: Institutional Neurosis, 1959, 3d edit., 1976, transl. into Greek, French, German, Spanish, Dutch, Italian, Japanese, Science and Psychiatry, 1963, Diabetes Insipidus and Obsessional Neurosis, 1965, A Short Practice of Clinical Psychiatry, 1975. Served with Brit. Red Cross, 1945; Belsen Concentration Camp; with Royal Navy, 1948-50. Fellow Royal Coll. Physicians (Can.), Royal Coll. Psychiatrists, Royal Soc. Medicine, Am. Psychiat. Assn., A.C.P.; mem. Royal Coll. Physicians (London). Home and Office: 2322 Clover St Rochester NY 14618 *Human life is brief and precious and needs regulation with fair play and kindness. Industry and intelligence are necessary to support all three.*

BARTON, THOMAS FRANK, SR., geographer, educator, writer; b. Cornell, Ill., Dec. 3, 1905; s. Frank Douglas and Martha (Gamlin) B.; m. Erselia M.A. Monticello, Sept. 26, 1931; 1 son, Thomas Frank Monticello. Diploma, Ill. State U., 1929, B.Ed., 1930, LL.D. (hon.), 1977; Ph.M., U. Wis., 1931; Ph.D., U. Neb., 1935. Rural sch. tchr., 1925-27; grad. teaching asst., dept. geography U. Wis., 1930-32, U. Nebr., 1932-34; asst. prof. geography Memphis State Coll., summers 1933, 34; assoc. prof. social studies Nebr. State Tchrs. Coll., 1934-35; prof. geography, head geography-geology dept. So. Ill. U., 1935-47; prof. vis. prof. geography U. Nebr., summer 1947; assoc. prof. Ind. U., 1947-51, prof. geography, 1951—, on leave, 1955-57; vis. prof. geography and social studies Sri Nakharinwirot U., Bangkok, Thailand, 1955-57; supr. U.S. Airway Weather Sta., So. Ill. U., 1941-47; One of 4 dels. representing U.S. at 6 week UNESCO seminar McDonald Coll., St. Anne de Bellevue, Que., Can., July-Aug. 1950; sec. Internat. Geog. Union Commn. on Teaching of Geography in Schs., 1952-55; ednl. motion picture collaborator and adviser. Mem. Ill. Reserve Militia; ground instr. meterology Civilian Pilot Tng. Program; geography instr. Army A.C. Tng. Program, all 1942-43. Author: Living in Illinois, 1941, Patrick Henry; Boy Spokesman, 1960, John Smith: Jamestown Boy, 1966, Lyndon Baines Johnson: Texas Boy, 1973, (with others) Southeast Asia In Maps, 1970, (with Sidman P. Poole and Clara Belle Baker) Through The Day, 1947, From Season to Season, 1947, In Country and City, 1947, (with Sedman P. Poole and Irving Robert Melbo) The World About Us, 1948; Co-author: Geography of the North American Midwest, 1955, Curriculum Guide for Geographic Education, 1963, Methods of Geographic Instructions, 1968, An Overall Economic Development Study of Southeastern Indiana, 1970, World Geography, 1972, Southeast Asia: Realm of Contrasts, 1974; Senior author: An Economic Geography of Thailand, 1958; Assoc. editor: Jour. of Geography, 1940-45; asst. editor, 1948-50; editor, 1950-65, land surface wall map series 1952, including world, U.S., Europe, S.A., Africa, Eurasia, N.A.; Editor: series maps and globes Pictorial Relief with Emerging Color; Contbr. chpts. tech. publs., articles profl. jours. Recipient Distinguished Alumni award Alumni Assn. Ill. State U., 1975, Rocking Chair award Sigma Delta Chi of Ind. U., 1976, Disting. Service award Geog. Soc. Chgo., 1978. Fellow AAAS, Ind. Sci., Nat. Council Geog. Edn. (distinguished service award 1965), Nat. Council Geography Teachers (pres. 1948); mem. Am. Geog. Soc., Nebr. Council Geography Tchrs. (pres. 1935), Ill. Council Geography Tchrs. (pres. 1939-40), Ind. Council Geography Tchrs. (pres. 1961-62), Ill. Acad. Social Sci., Ind. Acad. Social Sci. (pres. 1972-73), Ill. Edn. Assn., Ind. State Tchrs. Assn., Assn. Am. Geographers, Royal Geog. Soc., AAUP, Sigma Xi, Phi Delta Kappa, Kappa Phi Kappa, Pi Kappa Delta, Kappa Delta Pi, Phi Gamma Mu, Gamma Theta Upsilon. Home: 940 S Jourdan Ave Bloomington IN 47401 *I believe that the functional nature of geographical information can help solve some of the problems of our society; that education is vital for the constructive development of a country; that geographic knowledge and information can help citizens identify, understand and solve their problems and build a better life and society.*

BARTON, THOMAS HERBERT, university dean; b. Sheffield, Eng., May 28, 1926; s. Herbert Ambrose and Annie (Jackson) B.; m. Patricia Leonora Stokes, Mar. 24, 1951. B. Engring, U. Sheffield, 1947, Ph.D., 1949, D. Engring, 1968. Research engr. English Electric Co., Stafford, Eng., 1949-51; lectr. Sheffield U., 1951-57; mem. faculty McGill U., 1957-75, prof. elec. engring., 1965-75, asso. dean, 1972-75; dean Faculty Engring., U. Calgary, Alta., Can., 1975—; cons. in field. Author papers in field. Bd. govs. U. Calgary, 1982-85. Fellow Instn. Elec. Engring., IEEE (chmn. theory subcom. rotating machinery com. 1971-73, chmn. rotating machinery com. 1975-77); mem. Assn. Profl. Engrs., Geologists and Geophysicists Alta., Sigma Xi. Home: 1115 Varsity Estates Rise NW Calgary AB Canada T3B 2X4

BARTON, WILLIAM BLACKBURN, lawyer; b. Pratt, Kan., Aug. 4, 1899; s. William Burnston and Frances (Blackburn) B.; m. Marian Ruth Humphreys, Sept. 25, 1926 (dec. May 12, 1971); children—Sara Ellen, William Blackburn; m. Dorothy Rindge, Dec. 22, 1972. A.B., Northwestern U., 1921; A.M., Columbia, 1924, LL.M., 1938; LL.B., Yale, 1927. Bar: Calif. bar 1928, D.C. bar 1945. Tchr. pub. speaking Danville (Ill.) High Sch., 1920-23, Maywood, Ill., 1924-26; practiced in, Calif., 1928-37; tchr. pub. speaking U. Calif. at Los Angeles, 1927-29; bus. law Los Angeles City Coll., 1932-37; atty., trial examiner NLRB, 1938-44; in charge employer-employee relations C. of C. U.S., 1944-64, mgr. labor relations dept., 1951-53, mgr. labor relations and legal dept., gen. counsel, 1953-64; editor Labor Relations Letter, 1945-53; lectr. labor relations C. of C. insts. Northwestern U., 1954, Mich. State, Houston univs., 1958; now in pvt. practice law, Washington.; Del. Pres.'s Indsl. Safety Conf., 1949; rep. Pres.'s Conf., Minn. and Ore. Govs.' Indsl. Safety Confs., 1950; mem. U.S. employer delegation

Internat. Labor Conf., 1947-53; faculty Silver Bay Conf. Human Relations in Industry, 1956; mem. dept. labor mgmt. adv. com. Labor-Mgmt. Reporting and Disclosure Act of 1959; mem. Pres.'s Com. for Dept. Labor 50th Anniversary Year, Regional Law Com. for D.C., 1966-68. Speaker, writer on labor relations.; Author: pamphlets Labor in Politics. Mem. prep. com. 4th nat. study conf. Nat. Council of Chs.; Trustee, vice chmn. Sibley Meml. Hosp.; trustee emeritus Bauman Bible Telecast. Mem. Am. Bar Assn. (past co-chmn. regional labor law com. for D.C.), Nat. Safety Council (chmn. Marcus A. Dow Meml. award com. 1955-64), Delta Sigma Rho, Delta Theta Phi. Methodist. Clubs: Mason, Lion., Cleveland Park (pres. 1955-56), Yale, Cosmos (bd. mgmt. 1969-72), Nat. Press.). Home: 2501 Calvert St NW Washington DC 20008 Office: 1819 H St NW Washington DC 20006

BARTON, WILLIAM RUSSELL, government official; b. Detroit, Aug. 18, 1925; s. Richard and Dorothy (Miller) B.; m. Helen Ann Wilkes, Sept. 18, 1955; children: James Richard, Ann Elizabeth. B.A., Mich. State U., 1952. Spl. agt. U.S. Secret Service, 1953-64, spl. agt. in charge, Milw., 1964-70, Hdqrs. mgr., Washington, 1970-78, spl. agt. in charge, Los Angeles, 1978-79, asst. to dir., Washington, 1979-82, dep. dir., 1982—. Served to sgt. USMC, 1943-45; PTO. Mem. Internat. Chiefs of Police, Fed. Exec. Inst. Alumni Assn., Sr. Exec. Assn. Republican. Methodist. Home: 3901 Bentwood Ct Fairfax VA 22031 Office: US Secret Service 1800 G St NW Room 800 Washington DC 20223

BARTOO, JAMES BREESE, educator, university official; b. Swanton, Vt., July 2, 1921; s. DeForest and Lina Martha (Douglass) B.; m. Mary Viola Mead, Oct. 5, 1943; children: Janice, Jill, Kim, Scott, Brenda. B.S. in Edn, Edinboro (Pa.) State Coll., 1947; M.S., State U. Iowa, 1949, Ph.D., 1952. Tchr. math., Erie, Pa., 1947; mem. faculty Pa. State U., 1952—, prof. math., head dept., 1960-68, prof. math. statistics, head dept. statistics, 1968-69, dean Grad. Sch.,, 1969-83, acting v.p. for research, 1970-71, interim provost, 1977, acting exec. v.p., 1983—. Served AUS, 1943-46; ETO. Mem. Inst. Math. Statistics, Am. Math. Soc., Math. Assn. Am., Am. Statis. Assn. Home: 706 Windsor Ct State College PA 16801 Office: 201 Old Main Pa State U University Park PA 16802

BARTOSIC, FLORIAN, lawyer, university dean; b. Danville, Pa., Sept. 15, 1926; s. Florian W. and Elsie (Woodring) B.; m. Eileen M. Payne, 1953 (div. 1969); children: Florian, Ellen, Thomas, Stephen. B.A., Pontifical Coll., 1948; B.C.L., Coll. William and Mary, 1956; LL.M., Yale U., 1957. Bar: Va. 1956, U.S. Supreme Ct. 1959. Asst. instr. Yale U., 1956-57; assoc. prof. law Coll. William and Mary, 1957, Villanova U., 1957-59; atty. NLRB, Washington, 1956, 57, 59; counsel Internat. Brotherhood of Teamsters, Washington, 1959-71; prof. law Wayne State U., 1971-80; dean, prof. law U. Calif. at Davis, 1980—; adj. prof. George Washington U., 1966-71, Cath. U. Am., 1960-71; mem. panel arbitrators Fed. Mediation and Conciliation Service, Nat. Mediation Bd., 1972—; hearing officer Mich. Employment Relations Commn., 1972-80, Mich. Civil Rights Commn., 1974-80; bd. dirs. Mich. Legal Services Corp., 1973-80, Inst. Labor and Indsl. Relations, U. Mich., Wayne State U., 1976-80; mem. Steering com. Inst. on Global Conflict and Cooperation, 1982-83; mem. adv. bd. Assn. for Union Democracy Inc., 1980—. Co-author: Labor Relations Law in the Private Sector, 1977; contbr. articles to law jours. Mem. Am. Law Inst., Soc. Profls. in Dispute Resolution (regional v.p. 1979-80), Indsl. Relations Research Assn., Internat. Soc. Labor Law and Social Legis., Internat. Indsl. Relations Assn., Am. Arbitration Assn. (panel), Am. Bar Assn. (sec. sect. labor relations law 1974-75), Nat Bar Assn, Nat Lawyers Guild, ACLU (dir. Detroit chpt. 1976-77), Order of Coif. Home: 235 Ipanema Pl Davis CA 95616 Office: U Calif Law Sch Davis CA 95616

BARTRAM, MAYNARD CLEVELAND, JR., realty company executive; b. Sharon, Conn., Aug. 9, 1926; s. Maynard Clevel and Nina Louise (Juckett) B.; m. Jeannette Gardner Norton, Apr. 18, 1953; children: Carey, Peter, Sarah, Amy. B.S. in Econs, Yale, 1950; postgrad., Advanced Mgmt. Program, Harvard U., 1979. Sec. Conn. Gen. Life Ins. Co., Hartford, 1950-70; v.p. Conn. Gen. Mortgage and Realty Investments, Springfield, Mass., 1970-75, sec., 1970-73, treas., trustee, 1970-81, pres., 1975-81, Congen Realty Adv. Co., Hartford, 1970-81, Interfaith Homes, Inc., Bloomfield, Conn., 1966-78, dir., 1966—; founding dir., chmn. fin. com. Ch. Homes, Inc., Hartford, 1957—; ptnr. Bartram, Gallagher & Co., 1982—; chmn. Yale Real Estate Fund, 1979—. Vice chmn. Bloomfield Bd. Edn., 1967-71; mem. Republican Town Com., Bloomfield, 1963-72. Served with USNR, 1944-46. Mem. Nat. Assn. Real Estate Investment Trusts (pres. 1972-73, chmn. bd. govs. 1972-73, mem. bd. govs. 1970-82), Internat. Real Estate Fedn., Greater Hartford Bd. Realtors (asso.), Soc. Indsl. Realtors (chmn. mortgage and finance com. 1970-71). Conglist. Home: 56 Gun Mill Rd Bloomfield CT 06002 Office: 10 Tower Ln Avon CT 06001

BARTSCHT, HERI BERT, sculptor, educator; b. Breslau, Germany, Aug. 30, 1919; came to U.S., 1952, naturalized, 1959; s. Richard and Emma (Philipp) B.; m. Waltraud Erika Gutensohn, Mar. 31, 1950; 1 son, Martin Donald. Student, Acad. Fine Arts, Munich, Germany, 1946-52. Prof. sculpture U. Dallas, 1961—, head div. art, music, speech and drama, 1965—. Author: Twenty Years of My Sculpture, 1969; One-man shows, including, Dallas, Oklahoma City, Austin, Tex.; exhibited in group shows, 1951—, including, Ball State Tchrs. Coll., Muncie, Ind., 1959, U. Ill., 1961, Cranbrook Acad. Art, Mich., 1969; important works include Pieta, Ch. in Munich, 1952, Stas. of Cross, Jesuit High Sch., Dallas, 1963; library sculpture The Graduate, Tex. A. and M. U., 1968, Crucifix, Catholic Sacred Heart Cathedral, Dallas, sanctuary embellishment, First Meth. Ch., Alexandria, La. Co-chmn. Council for German Day in Tex., 1963; ch. embellishments and sanctuary design St. Rita Cath. Ch., Ft. Worth, 1975; mem. condrs. com. Dallas Symphony, 1963; pres. Dallas Goethe Center. Served with German Army, 1939-45. Mem. Am. Soc. Ch. Architecture, Nat. Art Edn. Assn., Ch. Archtl. Guild, Dallas Fine Arts Assn., Dallas Soc. Contemporary Arts (founder, dir., trustee 1955-61), Guild Religious Architecture. Research on Bronze Casting. Home and studio: 1125 N Canterbury Ct Dallas TX 75208 *The artist-teacher establishes a basis for the individual, apart from the masses. From there the student will be able to climb the ladder and attain the higher levels of art by himself. To observe a student's evolving metamorphosis step by step is the most rewarding experience for the teacher. Art has given me the satisfaction to fill life with excitement. A sound philosophy toward mankind and a strong desire to create visually have established basic directions in my work. Amorphous conditions in art at the present time have affected aesthetic principles. It is my duty to establish objective judgment among those concerned to prevent further decay. I shall continue to insist on genuine values in the arts, and restore professional integrity in sculpture.*

BARTUNEK, ROBERT RICHARD, physician; b. Cleve., Dec. 3, 1914; s. Emil Arthur and Mae (Friedl) B.; m. Clare Elizabeth Lonsway, Dec. 30, 1943 (dec. July 1975); children: Jean Marie, Robert R., Thomas J.; m. Mary Anne Piotrkowski, July 23, 1978. A.B., Case Western Res. U., 1936, M.D., 1940. Diplomate: Am. Bd. Internal Medicine. Intern St. Alexis Hosp., Cleve., 1940-41, resident, 1941-42; fellow in medicine Cleve. Clinic., 1946-48; pvt. practice medicine, specializing in gastroenterology, Cleve., 1949—; mem. staff St. Alexis Hosp., 1948—, dir. gastroenterology, 1949-81, dir. medicine, 1952-61, dir. labs., 1950-62; mem. staff St. Vincent Charity Hosp., Cleve., 1950—, dir. gastroenterology, 1960-83, dir. emeritus, 1983—, dir. medicine, 1966-72, 80-81; asso. mem. staff Metropolitan Gen. Hosp.; cons. Marymount Hosp., Garfield Heights, Ohio; asso. clin. prof. medicine Case Western Res. U. Med. Sch., 1980—. Mem. med. morals adv. bd. Cleve. Catholic Diocese. Served to lt. col. AUS, 1942-46. Decorated Bronze Star. Fellow Am. Coll. Gastroenterology (pres. 1963-64, Samuel Weiss award 1974), ACP, AAAS (council 1963-76); mem. Am. Geriatric Soc., Am. Soc. Gastrointestinal Endoscopy, Assn. Mil. Surgeons, Internat. Congress of Internal Medicine, Am. Soc. Internal Medicine, Cleve. Diabetes Assn. (dir. 1967-70), AMA, Ohio Med. Assn., Cleve. Acad. Medicine, L'Organisation Mondiale de Gastro-Enterologie (U.S. del. 1963-65), Nu Sigma Nu. Eder-Bartunek Gastroscope designed 1947-48 in Smithsonian Inst., 1971. Home: 23446 Letchworth Rd Beachwood Cleveland OH 44122 Office: St Vincent Charity Hosp 2351 E 22d St Cleveland OH 44115

BARTUS, RAYMOND THOMAS, neuroscientist; b. Chgo., May 19, 1947; s. Frank A. and Katherine (Bogus) B.; m. Cheryl Marie Gyure, Feb. 11, 1967; children: Raymond T., Kristin Marie. B.A., Calif. State Coll., 1968; M.S., N.C. State U., 1970, Ph.D., 1972. NRC postdoctoral fellow, research assoc. Naval Med. Research Lab., Groton, Conn., 1972; scientist Parke-Davis Research Labs., Ann Arbor, Mich., 193-75, sr. scientist, 1975-78, Lederle Labs., Am. Cyanamid Co., Pearl River, N.Y., 1978-79, group leader, dir. geriatric discovery program, 1979—; prof. NYU Med. Ctr., 1979—; cons. in field. Contbr. articles on neurosci. to profl. jours., books; editor-in-chief: Neurobiology of Aging, 1980—. Mem. AAAS, Am. Aging Assn. (bd. dirs. 1980—), Am. Psychol. Assn., Gerontol. Soc. Am., Soc. Neurosci. Office: Lederle Labs Dept CNS Research Pearl River NY 10965

BARTY, BILLY JOHN, entertainer; b. Millsboro, Pa., Oct. 25, 1924; s. Albert Steven and Ellen Cecial (Bettegar) B.; m. Shirley Bolingbroke, Feb. 24, 1962; children—Lori Ellen, Braden William. A.A., Los Angeles City Coll., 1946; postgrad., Los Angeles State U., 1948. Actor: films, full length and short features, 1928—, including Mickey McGuire comedies, 1932-34, Alice in Wonderland, A Midsummer Nights Dream, Gift of Gab, The Amazing Dobermans, 1977, Under the Rainbow, 1981; actor: TV prodns., 1949—, including Peter Gunn, 1950, Alfred Hitchcock; artist: Spike Jones, 8 yrs; Contbr. to findings short stature problems. Active various fund raising programs and events, including San Dimas Golf Tournament.; Founder Little People of Am., 1957, Billy Barty, Found., 1975. Recipient Calif. Gov.'s award, 1966, award Pres.' Commn. on Handicapped, 1966, Commn. on Employment of Handicapped. Republican. Mormon. Clubs: Golf, Via Verdes. Office: 10954 Moorpark St North Hollywood CA 91602

BARUCH, EDUARD, management consultant; b. Bklyn., Dec. 19, 1907; s. Emile and Grace (Willis) B.; m. Dorothy Hurd, Sept. 8, 1934; 1 son, Hurd. Student, Rhenania Coll., Switzerland, 1924-26; A.B., Columbia, 1930; postgrad., Law Sch., 1933. Trust adminstr. spl. loan div. Irving Trust Co., N.Y.C., 1933-39; sales exec. Bankers Life Co., Des Moines, 1939-42; v.p. charge sales James H. Rhodes & Co., 1942-47; nat. sales mgr. vending div. Pepsi Cola Co., 1947-49; v.p. Heli-Coil Corp., Danbury, Conn., 1949-55, exec. v.p., 1955-56, pres., 1956-70; corp. cons., 1970—; dir. Barden Corp., Union Trust Co., Stamford, Conn., N.E. Bancorp Inc., New Haven, Savs. Bank of Danbury, Lago Mar Pl., Ft. Lauderdale, Fla. Bd dirs., mem. bd. mgrs. Danbury Hosp. Mem. Soc. Automotive Engrs., Sales Execs., Psi Upsilon, Phi Delta Phi. Congregationalist. Clubs: Mason (Shriner), K.T., Jester., Columbia University, Wings (N.Y.C.); Ridgewood Country (Danbury); Coral Ridge Yacht, Tower, Lago Mar Beach and Tennis (Fort Lauderdale, Fla.). Home: Candlewood Point New Milford CT 06776 also Harbor Beach Fort Lauderdale FL 33316 Office: City Trust Bldg Danbury CT 06810

BARUCH, JORDAN JAY, engineer, consultant; b. N.Y.C., Aug. 21, 1923; s. Solomon L. and Minnie (Kessner) B.; m. Rhoda Wasserman, June 3, 1944; children: Roberta, Marjory, Lawrence. B.S., Mass. Inst. Tech., 1948, M.S., 1948, Sc.D., 1950. Vice pres., dir. Bolt, Beranek & Newman, Inc., Cambridge, Mass., 1949-66, dir., 1949-77, Boston Broadcasters, 1963-77, 81-83; asst. prof. elec. engring. Mass. Inst. Tech., 1950-53, lectr., 1954-70; lectr. bus. adminstrn. Harvard Grad. Sch. Bus. Adminstrn., 1970-74; prof. Amos Tuck Sch. Bus. Adminstrn., also; Thayer Sch. Engring., Dartmouth Coll., Hanover, N.H., 1974-77; asst. sec. sci. and tech. Dept. Commerce, 1977-81; pres. Jordan Baruch Assos. Inc., 1981—; Mem. Sci. Info. Council, NSF; mem. Commn. on Automation, Fed. Council Sci. and Tech.; chmn. evaluation panel Inst. Computer Sci. and Tech., mem. evaluation panel, exptl. tech. incentives program; chmn. com. on tech. and health care NRC. Contbr. articles to books and profl. jours. Served with AUS, 1942-46. Named Outstanding Young Elec. Engr. Eta Kappa Nu, 1956. Fellow Acoustical Soc. Am., IEEE, AAAS, Nat. Acad. Engring., N.Y. Acad. Scis., Am. Acad. Arts and Scis. Club: Mashnee Yacht (Bourne, Mass.). Patentee loudspeakers, acoustical treatments, automotive mufflers. Home: 3025 Ordway St NW Washington DC 20008 Office: 1200 18th St NW Washington DC 20036

BARUCH, RALPH M., communications company executive; b. Frankfurt, Germany, Aug. 5, 1923; came to France, 1933; came to U.S., 1940, naturalized, 1944; s. Bernard and Alice B.; m. Jean Ursell de Mountford, June 9, 1963; children by previous marriage: Eve, Renee, Alice, Michele. Student, Sorbonne, U. Paris. Account exec. SESAC, 1947-50, Dumont TV, 1950-54; Eastern Sales mgr. Enterprises, N.Y.C., 1954-59, v.p. internat. sales, 1959-67, v.p., gen. mgr., 1967-70; group pres. CBS, 1970-71; pres., chief exec. officer Viacom Internat. Inc., N.Y.C., 1971-78, chmn. bd., mem. office of chief exec., 1979—; dir. Orange and Rockland Utilities. Bd. dirs. exec. com. Internat. Rescue Com., N.Y.C., 1975—; mem. Pres.'s Council for Internat. Youth Exchange, 1982. Mem. Internat. Radio and TV Soc. (pres. co-chmn. minority placement com., pres.), Nat. Cable TV Assn. (sec. 1976-78, chmn. pub. policy planning com. 1976—), Internat. Council TV Acad. Arts and Scis. (pres. 1973-76, dir. 1976—), Council for Cable Info. (dir., exec. com.). Clubs: City Athletic, N.Y. Yacht (N.Y.C.); Poor Richards (Phila.). Office: 1211 Ave of Americas New York NY 10036

BARUT, ASIM ORHAN, physicist, educator; b. Malatya, Turkey, June 24, 1926; came to U.S., 1953, naturalized, 1962; m. Pierrette Helene Gervaz, July 2, 1954. Diploma, Swiss Fed. Inst. Tech., 1949, Dr.Sc., 1952. Mem. faculty U. Chgo., 1953-54, Reed Coll., Portland, Oreg., 1954-55, U. Montreal, 1955-56, Syracuse U., 1956-61, U. Calif., Berkeley, 1961-62; prof. physics U. Colo., Boulder, 1962—, Research lectr., 1982; vis. prof. in various countries; prof. physics U. Colo., Boulder, 1962—. Staff mem. Internat. Centre for Theoretical Physics, Trieste, Italy, 1964-65, 68-69, 72-73; vis. prof. in various countries. Recipient Alexander von Humboldt award, 1974-75, 76, medal of sci. (Turkey), 1982; Faculty Research fellow, 1968, 72, 78; Erskine fellow U. Canterbury, N.Z., 1970. Office: Dept Physics U Colo Boulder CO 80309

BARWICK, EUGENE THOMAS, Mfg. co. exec.; b. Lake City, Fla., Dec. 23, 1913; s. T. J. and Etta (Revels) B.; m. Ann McDougall, Aug. 19, 1944; children—Nancy Jean, Avis Ann, Eugene T., Beverly Allison. B.S., U. N.C., 1936. Buyer floor covering Sears, Roebuck & Co., 1936-48; founder, now pres., chmn. bd., chief exec. officer E. T. Barwick Ind., Inc., 1949—; chmn. Monarch Rug Mills, Inc. Presbyn. Clubs: Peachtree Golf, Capital City, Cherokee Town and Country (Atlanta); Lyford Cay, Porcupine (Nassau, Bahamas); Metropolitan (N.Y.C.). Home: 50 Valley Road Atlanta GA 30305 Office: E T Barwick Industries Inc 5775-C Peachtree Dunwoody Rd NE Atlanta GA 30342

BARYSHNIKOV, MIKHAIL, ballet dancer, ballet dir.; b. Riga, Latvia, Jan. 28, 1948; s. Nicholai and Alexandra (Kisselov) B.; 1 dau. Student, Ballet Sch. of Riga, Kirov Ballet Sch., Leningrad, Russia; D.F.A. (hon.), Yale U., 1979. Mem. Kirov Ballet Co., 1969-74; mem. Am. Ballet Theatre, 1974-78, dir. designee, 1979-80, dir., 1980—; mem. N.Y.C. Ballet, 1978-79. Since 1974 guest artist with leading ballet cos. throughout world, including, Nat. Ballet of Can., Royal Ballet, Hamburg (Germany) Ballet, Ballet Victoria, Australia, Stuttgart (W.Ger.) Ballet; appeared at, Covent Garden, Spoleto (Italy) Festival; dances premier danseur roles in the traditional repertory; danced: title role in Le jeune homme et la morte, 1975; danced in: world premiere Vestris, 1969, Medea, 1975, Push Comes to Shove, 1976, Hamlet Connotations, 1976, Other Dances, 1976, Pas de Duke, 1976; motion picture debut in The Turning Point, 1976; numerous TV appearances, including Dance in America, The Nutcracker; choreographer: The Nutcracker Suite, Am. Ballet Theater, John F. Kennedy Center for Performing Arts, 1976; producer, choreographer, dancer, Don Quixote (Basil) Premiere, Kennedy Center, 1978 (Gold Medalist Varna Competition, Bulgaria 1966), Don Quixote (Basil) Premiere, Kennedy Center (First Internat. Ballet Competition, Moscow, USSR 1968), numerous TV appearances, including, Don Quixote (Basil) Premiere, Kennedy Center, 1978 (recipient Nijinsky prize at First Internat. Ballet Competition Paris Acad. Dance 1968). Dance mag. award, 1978. Office: care Edgar Vincent Assos 145 E 52d St New York NY 10023 *The dancer who would grow in his art must seek to explore and develop new phases of his talent, and to expand his performing horizons in terms of both the new and existing repertoire.*

BARZANTI, SERGIO, educator; b. Rome, Oct. 4, 1925; U.S., 1955, naturalized, 1961; s. Domenico and Pierina (Casadei) B.; m. Gabriele A. Stormer, Oct. 24, 1968 (div. 1973); children—Simonetta, Paul, Mark, Lorenzo. Baccalaureat, Liceo, Rome, 1943; Dr. J., U. Rome, 1947; M.A., N.Y. U., 1958, Ph.D., 1962; postgrad., U. Paris, 1959. Mem. faculty Fairleigh Dickinson U., Rutherford, N.J., 1963—, asst. prof., 1964-67, asso. prof., 1967-75, prof. history and internat. studies, 1975—. Author: The Underdeveloped Areas Within the Common Market, 1965. Fulbright grantee, 1965. Home: 540 80th St Brooklyn NY 11209 Office: Dept Social Sciences Fairleigh Dickinson U Rutherford NJ 07070

BARZUN, JACQUES, author, lit. cons.; b. Créteil, France, Nov. 30, 1907; came to U.S., 1920, naturalized, 1933; s. Henri Martin and Anna-Rose B.; m. Mariana Lowell, Aug. 1936 (dec. 1979); children: James Lowell, Roger Martin, Isabel; m. Marguerite Davenport, June 1980. Ed., Lycée Janson de Sailly, Paris; A.B., Columbia U., 1927, M.A., 1928, Ph.D., 1932. Lectr. history Columbia U., 1927, instr., 1929, asst. prof., 1938, asso. prof., 1942, prof., 1945, dean grad. faculties, 1955-58, dean faculties and provost, 1958-67, Univ. prof. emeritus, also spl. adviser on arts, 1967-75; lit. adviser Scribner's, N.Y.C., 1975—. Author: The French Race, 1932, Teacher in America, 1945, Berlioz and the Romantic Century, 1950, 3d edit., 1969, Pleasures of Music, 1951, 2d edit., 1977, God's Country and Mine, 1954, Music in American Life, 1956, Darwin, Marx, Wagner, 1941, The Energies of Art, 1956, Of Human Freedom, 2d edit, 1964, Race: A Study in Superstition, 1937, The Modern Researcher, 1957, 3d edit., 1977, The House of Intellect, 2d edit, 1975, Classic, Romantic and Modern, 1961, Science: The Glorious Entertainment, 1964, The American University, 1968, A Catalogue of Crime, 1971, On Writing, Editing and Publishing, 1971, The Use and Abuse of Art, 1974, Clio and the Doctors, 1974, Simple and Direct, 1975, Critical Questions, 1982, A Stroll With William James, 1983; Editorial bd.: The American Scholar, 1946-76, Ency. Brit, 1979—; editor: Selected Letters of Lord Byron, 1953, Nouvelles Lettres de Berlioz, 1954, The Selected Writings of John Jay Chapman, 1957, Follett's Modern American Usage, 1966. Trustee N.Y. Soc. Library; bd. dirs. Council for Basic Edn., Am. Friends of Cambridge U., Peabody Inst.; adv. council U. Coll. at Buckingham. Decorated Legion of Honor; Extraordinary fellow Churchill Coll., U. Cambridge (Eng.). Fellow Royal Soc. Arts; mem. Am. Hist. Assn., Mass. Hist. Soc. (corr.), Am. Acad. and Inst. Arts and Letters (pres. 1972-75, 77-78), Inst. Arts and Letters, Friends Columbia Libraries, Phi Beta Kappa. Clubs: Authors, Athenaeum (London); Century (N.Y.C.). Address: 597 Fifth Ave New York NY 10017

BASAR, TAMER, electrical engineering educator; b. Istanbul, Turkey, Jan. 19, 1946; came to U.S., 1969; s. Munir and Seniye (Pirilsu) B.; m. Tangul Unerdem, Dec. 27, 1975; children: Gozen, Elif. B.S., Robert Coll., Istanbul, 1969; M.S., Yale U., 1970, M.Phil., 1971, Ph.D., 1972. Research fellow Harvard U., Cambridge, Mass., 1972-73; sr. researcher scientist Marmara Research Inst., Gebze, Kocaeli, Turkey, 1973-80; adj. assoc. prof. Bogazici U., Istanbul, 1974-80; assoc. prof. elec. engring. U. Ill., Urbana, 1980-83, prof., 1983—; cons. Dynamic Systems, Urbana, 1981—. Con-author: Dynamic Noncooperative Game Theory, 1982; contbr. articles to profl. jours.; assoc. editor 4 jours. in control theory. Recipient Young Scientist award in Applied Math. Turkish Nat. Research Council, 1976, Sedat Simavi Found. award, 1979. Fellow IEEE; mem. N.Y. Acad. Scis., AAAS, Sigma Xi. Home: 1114 Scovill Urbana IL 61801 Office: U Ill 1101 W Springfield Ave Urbana IL 61801

BASCH, MICHAEL DEAN, computer company executive; b. Elizabeth, N.J., Oct. 10, 1938; s. Walter Max and Olive (Holmes) B.; m. Diane Schug, July 1, 1961 (div. Mar. 1979); children: Lisa, Jeffrey, Michael; m. Karen Morgan, Oct. 10, 1980. B.B.A., Clarkson Coll. Tech., 1960. Mgr. indsl. engring. United Parcel Service, Phila., 1960-68; assoc. A. T. Kearney-Cons., N.Y.C., 1968-69; assoc. dir. Rapistan, Inc., Grand Rapids, Mich., 1969-72; sr. v.p. Fed. Express Corp., Memphis, 1972-82; bd. chmn. Exec. Computer Center, Inc., Memphis, 1982—; dir. Glassper Internat., Memphis, 1982-83. Inventor teaching machine, 1964. Pres., founder Memphis Uniport Assn., 1980-82; v.p. Memphis Devel. Found., 1981-82. Mem. Nat. Council Phys. Distbn. Mgmt., Soc. Logistics Engrs. Republican. Presbyterian. Home: 1080 Oak River Rd Memphis TN 38119 Office: Exec Computer Center 1233 Park Pl Memphis TN 38119

BASCOM, PERRY BAGNALL, advertising sales executive; b. Bound Brook, N.J., Jan. 24, 1924; s. Perry H. and Katherine B. (Bagnall) B.; m. Kathryn Dawson, Mar. 24, 1945; children: Janet (Mrs. Charles Wheeler), Alan. Real estate appraiser/broker WIP, Phila., 1948-54; sales mgr. WOR-TV, N.Y.C., 1954-56; nat. sales mgr. Westinghouse Broadcasting Co., N.Y.C., 1956-61; gen. mgr. radio sta. KYW, Cleve., 1961-65; gen. mgr. radio sta. WBZ, Boston, 1965-68; pres. Radio Advt. Reps. Inc., (RAR), N.Y.C., 1968-69; v.p. corp. staff Westinghouse Broadcasting Group W, N.Y.C., 1968-69; v.p., gen. mgr. WNBC-AM/WNWS-FM, N.Y.C., 1969-78; v.p., dir. S.E. sales TVB, Atlanta, 1978—. Mem. alumni council Mt. Hermon Northfield Schs. Served with USNR, 1943-46. Mem. N.Y. Radio Market Broadcasters Assn. (bd. dirs.), N.Y. State Broadcasters Assn. (bd. dirs.). Baptist (trustee). Clubs: Greensboro (Vt.); Country and Yacht. Home: 1841 Pine Rd Dacula GA 30211 Office: 3060 Mercer University Dr Altanta GA 30341

BASCOM, WILLARD NEWELL, scientist, engineer; b. N.Y.C., Nov. 7, 1916; s. Willard Newell and Pearle (Boyd) B.; m. Rhoda Nergaard, Apr. 15, 1946; children: Willard, Anitra. Grad., Colo. Sch. Mines, 1942. Registered profl. engr., Fla., D.C. Research engr. U. Calif.-Berkeley, 1945-50, Scripps Inst. Oceanography, 1950-54; exec. sec. Nat. Acad. Scis., Washington, 1954-62; pres. Ocean Sci. & Engring., Inc., Washington, 1962-72; dir. Coastal Water Research Project, Long Beach, Calif., 1973—; cons. to govt. and industry. Author: Waves and Beaches, 1964, A Hole in the Bottom of the Sea, 1961, Deep Water, Ancient Ships, 1976, over 100 articles. Recipient Disting. Achievement medal Colo. Sch. Mines, 1979, Compass Disting. Achievement award Marine Tech. Soc., 1970. Clubs: Explorers (Explorers medal 1980), Adventurers. Patentee deep ocean search/recovery system.

BASH, JAMES FRANCIS, ins. co. exec.; b. Indpls., Aug. 10, 1925; s. Douglas and Pauline C. (Beattey) B. A.B., Butler U., 1946; J.D., Ind. U., 1949. Bar: Ind. bar 1949. With Standard Life Ins. Co. of Ind., Indpls., 1949-81, pres., 1967-81, chmn. bd., 1979-81; also dir., mem. exec., investment coms.; sec., treas. All Funds Mgmt. Corp., 1963-66, v.p., 1966-74, pres., 1974-81, also dir.; bd. dirs. Central Ind. Better Bus. Bur., 1967-73. Sec. bd. trustees full Central Ave. United Meth. Ch., 1954-73, vice chmn. bd., 1974-75, chmn. bd., 1976-80, treas., 1958—. Mem. Am., Ind. bar assns., Nat. Assn. Life Underwriters, Am. Council Life Ins. (state v.p. 1979-81), Ind. Assn. Life Ins. Cos. (pres. 1979-81), Ind. U. Alumni Assn. (exec. council 1975-78, v.p. 1980-81, pres. elect 1981), Sigma Chi (internat. pres. 1977-79, exec. com. 1973-81). Clubs: Indpls. Athletic, Columbia, Meridian Hills Country, Masons. Home: 8160 N Meridian St Indianapolis IN 46260

BASH, PHILIP EDWIN, advertising executive; b. Huntington, Ind., Aug. 13, 1921; s. Philip Purviance and Nell (Johnson) B.; m. Flora Wiley Oberg, Mar. 11, 1944; children: Barbara, Kingsley, Roger, Amy. B.A., DePauw U., 1943. Account exec. Leo Burnett Co., Inc., Chgo., 1947-54; account supr., v.p., sr. v.p. mktg. services Clinton E. Frank Inc., Chgo., 1954-64, pres., 1964-72; also dir.; pres. Barrington Press, Inc., Ill., 1972—. Chmn. bd. trustees Shimer Coll.; trustee Garrett Theol. Sem., 1976. Served to lt. (j.g.) USNR, 1943-46; PTO. Mem. Am. Assn. Advt. Agys. (bd. govs. Chgo. council), Am. Mktg. Assn., Sigma Chi. Methodist (trustee). Clubs: University, Economics (Chgo.); Barrington Hills Country. Home: 209 Oakdene Rd Barrington IL 60010 Office: 200 James St Barrington IL 60010

BASH, YIGAL AMIR, publisher; b. Jerusalem, Israel, Nov. 3, 1938; s. Meir Zvi and Ahuva Deborah (Cohen) B.; m. Lea Zipori, Feb. 28, 1960; children: David D., Tami, Talia. B.S., N.Y. U., 1964, M.S., 1966, postgrad., 1966-69. Registered profl. engr.; registered investment adv. Pres. T.D.T. Devel. Corp., Poughkeepsie, N.Y., 1964-70; pres. Leland Devel. Corp., Poughkeepsie, 1970-76; also dir.; chief exec. officer Transam. Corp., N.Y.C., 1976—; publisher Transam. Pub. Ltd., N.Y.C., 1976—, Transcontinental Pub. Ltd., 1977—, Transam. Advt. Ltd., 1978—, pres., 1981—, Transam. Prodn. Ltd., 1981—; v.p. AME Corp.; dir. Alpha Devel. Corp., Equitable Enterprises Corp., Dynatronics Corp.; partner weekly TV variety show, N.Y.C. Mem. Republican Nat. Com., 1968—, Nat. Rep. Congressional Com., 1972—; Rep. Assembly Campaign Com., 1972—. Served to capt. Israeli Army, 1956-60. Mem. Assn. Physicists Am., Assn. Elec. Engrs., Home Builders Assn. Am., Nat. Assn. Small Bus., Nat. Assn. Architects, Nat. Assn. Pubs. 3701 Twin Lakes Ct Baltimore MD 21207 Office: 9 W 57th St New York NY 10019 also 352 Park Ave S New York NY 10010

BASHFUL, EMMETT WILFORT, univ. chancellor; b. New Roads, La., Mar. 12, 1917; s. Charles and Mary (Walker) B.; m. Juanita Jones, Aug. 16, 1941; 1 dau., Cornell Bashful Nugent. Student, Leland Coll., 1936-37; B.S., So. U., Baton Rouge, 1940; M.A., U. Ill., 1947, Ph.D., 1955. Tchr. Allen Parish (La.) Schs., 1940-41; asst. mgr. Keystone Ins. Co., 1941-42; faculty Fla. A&M U., 1948-58, prof., 1956-58, head dept. polit. sci., 1950-58; prof. polit. sci. So. U., Baton Rouge, 1958-59, dean, 1959-69, v.p. in charge univ., 1969-77, chancellor in charge univ., 1977—. Author: The Florida Supreme Court - A Study in Judicial Selection, 1958. Chmn. John Albert dist. Boy Scouts Am., New Orleans, 1963-65; v.p. New Orleans Area council, 1974-75, bd. dirs., 1963—; bd. dirs. com. on alcoholism Greater New Orleans United Fund Agy., 1965—; mem. La. Youth Commn., 1965-74; bd. dirs. Community Relations Council, 1965; trustee United Way Greater New Orleans, 1969-78, mem. planning com., 1973—; bd. dirs. New Orleans chpt. NCCJ, 1970—, nat. bd., 1979—; bd. dirs. New Orleans chpt. Nat. Found. March of Dimes, 1969-70, Frey Found., 1970-79, S.E. La. dist. Girl Scouts U.S.A., 1974-78, Met. Area Com., 1978—, Internat. Trade Mart, 1978—; hon. mem. bd. Big Bros., 1978—; adv. bd. Goodwill Industries, 1979—. Served to 1st lt. AUS, 1942-46. Recipient Silver Beaver award, 1967; 1Ford Found fellow, 1954-55, citation Fla. Supreme Ct., 1955, Social Action award Alpha Eta chpt. Phi Beta Sigma, 1957, citation SCLC, 1958, Vol. Activist award, 1976, Ten Outstanding Citizens of New Orleans award Inst. Human Understanding, 1978. Mem. Am. Polit. Sci. Assn., So. Polit. Sci. Assn., AAUP, Assn. Social Sci. Tchrs., Alpha Phi Alpha, Alpha Phi Omega, Sigma Rho Sigma, Pi Gamma Mu. Baptist. Home: 5808 Lafaye St New Orleans LA 70122 Office: So Univ of New Orleans 6400 Press Dr New Orleans LA 70126

BASHKOW, THEODORE ROBERT, engineering educator; b. St. Louis, Nov. 16, 1921; s. Maurice Louis and Caroline (Davidson) B.; m. Delphina Brownlee, Sept. 12, 1960; 1 stepdau., Lynn Michele. B.S., Washington U., St. Louis, 1943; M.S., Stanford U., 1947, Ph.D., 1950. Mem. tech. staff David Sarnoff Research Labs., RCA, 1950-52, Bell Telephone Labs., 1952-58; mem. faculty Columbia U., 1958—, prof. elec. engring., 1967-79, prof. computer sci., 1979—, chmn. dept. elec. engring., 1968-71, mgr. Sch. Engring. Computing Center, 1961-64; cons. to industry, 1959—; dir. MSI Inc., Woodside, N.Y., 1961—; chmn. tech. program 1968 Spring Joint Computer Conf.; chmn. sci. sec. Internat. Fedn. Info. Processing Congress, 1965. Author articles, chpts. in books. Served to 1st lt. USAAF, 1943-45. Mem. Assn. Computing Machinery, IEEE, Profl. Group Circuit Theory and Electronic Computers. Home: 92 Jay St Katonah NY 10536 Office: Computer Sci Bldg Columbia U New York NY 10027

BASIL, DOUGLAS CONSTANTINE, educator, author; b. Vancouver, C., Can., May 30, 1923; s. William and Christina (Findlay) B.; m. Evelyn Margaret Pitcairn, 1950; 1 dau., Wendy Patricia. B.Commerce, U. B.C., 1949; B.A., 1949; Ph.D., Northwestern U., 1954; postgrad., London Sch. Econs., 1950. Instr. Marquette U., 1951-54; asst. prof. Northwestern U., 1954-57; asso. prof. U. Minn., 1957-61; prof. mgmt. U. So. Calif., 1961—; cons. mgmt. devel.; lectr., Brussels, Caracas, Bogota, Paris, London, others. Author: Executive Development, 1964, (Paul Cone, John Fleming) Effective Decision Making Through Simulation, 1972, Organacao E Controls Da Pequena Empresa, 1968, La Direccion de la Pequena Empresa, 1969, Managerial Skills for Executive Action, 1970, Leadership Skills for Executive Action, 1971, Women in Management: Performance, Prejudice, Promotion, 1972, Autorite Personnelle et Efficacite des Cadres, 1972, Conduccion y Liderazgo, 1973, Developing Tomorrow's Managers, 1973, Management of Change, 1974, others.; Contbr. articles to profl. jours. Served to capt. Canadian Army, 1943-46. Home: 2201 Warmouth St San Pedro CA 90732 Office: Grad Sch Bus Adminstrn Los Angeles CA 90007

BASILE, RICHARD EMANUEL, management consultant, educator; b. Buffalo, Dec. 24, 1921; s. Giustino Gregory and Minnie (Bailey) B.; m. Mariette Ruth Borocco, Oct. 12, 1946. B.A., Washington and Lee U., 1943; postgrad., U. Mo., 1948-49, Columbia U., 1965; L.H.D., Combs Coll., Phila., 1969. Geologist U.S. Geol. Survey, 1946-47; mgr. St. Clair Country Club, Belleville, Ill., Avelez Hotel, Biloxi, Miss., Carteret Club, Trenton, N.J., 1948-51; instr. U. Mo., 1948-49; head hotel mgmt. dept. Paul Smith's Coll., 1951-57, adminstrv. dean, 1961-66; mgr. Am. Mgmt. Assn. Acad., 1957-61; dir. devel. ARA, Inc., Phila., 1966-67; v.p. purchasing ARA Services, Inc., 1966-68, v.p., 1968-70; prof. U. Nev., Las Vegas, 1970—; pres. Univ. Assocs., Inc., Las Vegas, 1971—; dir. Casablanca Resort Hotel, Las Vegas.; Cons. Indsl. Relations Counselors, Area Redevel. Act, U.S. Govt., XIX and XXI Olympiads, 1968, 76; mem. NRC, 1977-80; com. chmn. XI Internat. Congress on Nutrition, Rio de Janeiro, 1978; U.S. Dept. Commerce tech. rep. Cyprus Internat. Trade Show, Nicosia, 1982; mem. Nev. Employee-Mgmt. Relations Bd., 1981—; cons. to hospitality industry. Contbr. articles to profl. jours. Pres. Saranac Lake (N.Y.) Gen. Hosp., 1960-66; Bd. dirs. Saranac Lake chpt. ARC, Nat. Council on Hotel and Restaurant Edn., Washington; bd. mem. arbitration, mediation and fact finding bd. Los Angeles Employees Relations Bd.; arbitrator Teamsters local 995, Nev. Resort Assn., others. Served with USNR, 1943-46. Paul Harris fellow, 1980—. Mem. Pa. Acad. Fine Arts, Am. Arbitration Assn. (panel arbitrators 1961—), Sigma Phi Epsilon, Alpha Kappa Psi. Clubs: Masons (K.T.), Rotary (pres. 1962-63), Vesper, Peale. Home: 1800 S 14th St Las Vegas NV 89104 Office: 4505 Maryland Pkwy Las Vegas NV 89154 *Success? Is it not in the eye of the beholder? A strong hero worship from childhood days of those selected educators, religious and business leaders who were honest, unselfish, and who enjoyed pure living—not solely materialistic gain. A family who exemplified the work ethic, and a wife who is almost psychic in her ability to keep me from wearing an oversized hat*

BASINSKI, ZBIGNIEW STANISLAW, metal physicist; b. Wolkowysk, Poland, Apr. 28, 1928; emigrated to Can., 1956, naturalized, 1961; s. Antoni and Maria Zofia Anna (Hilferding) B.; m. Sylvia Joy Pugh, Apr. 1, 1952; children—Stefan Leon Hilferding, Antoni Stanislaw Hilferding. B.A., Oxford (Eng.) U., 1951, B.Sc., 1952, D.Phil., 1954, D.Sci., 1966. With div. indsl. cooperation Mass. Inst. Tech., 1954-55; mem. staff Nat. Research Council Can., 1956—, prin. research officer, 1965—; Ford distinguished vis. prof. Carnegie Inst. Tech., 1963-64; Commonwealth vis. prof. and vis. fellow Wolfson Coll., Oxford U., 1969-70; vis. research scientist Cavendish Lab.; also overseas fellow Churchill Coll., both Cambridge (Eng.) U., 1980-81. Contbr. articles to sci. jours. Recipient Canadian Metal Physics medal, 1977. Fellow Royal Soc. London, Royal Soc. Can. Home: 108 Delong Dr Ottawa ON K1J 7E1 Canada Office: Physics Div NRC Ottawa ON K1A 0R6 Canada

BASKA, JAMES LOUIS, lawyer, wholesale grocery company executive; b. Kansas City, Kans., Apr., 1927; s. John James and Stella Marie (Wilson) B.; m. Juanita Louise Carlson, Oct. 10, 1950; children: Steven James, Scott David. B.S. in Bus. Adminstrn, U. Kans., 1949; J.D., U. Mo., 1960. Bar: Kans. Pres., chief exec. officer Baska Laundry Co., Kansas City, Kans., 1949-62; partner firm Rice & Baska, Kansas City, 1962-76; corporate sec., gen. counsel Asso. Wholesale Grocers Inc., Kansas City, 1976-77, v.p., sec., gen. counsel, 1977-79, exec. v.p., chief fin. officer, sec., gen. counsel, 1979—; exec. v.p., sec., gen. counsel, dir. Super Market Developers Inc.; v.p., sec., gen. counsel, dir. Super Market Investment Co. Inc., Grocers Dairy Co. Inc. Served with U.S. Army, 1945-47. Mem. Am., Kans., Johnson County, Wyandotte County bar assns. Republican. Roman Catholic. Home: 17405 W 159th St Olathe KS 66061 Office: 5000 Kansas Ave Kansas City KS 66106 *There is always room at the top and my objectives whatever they may be and no matter how big or wild, are always attainable. The only questions are— am I ready to make the move and willing to pay the price?*

BASKERVILLE, CHARLES ALEXANDER, geologist; b. Jamaica, N.Y., Aug. 19, 1928; s. Charles H. and Annie M. (Allen) B.; m. Susan Platt, July 5, 1979; children: Mark Dana, Shawn Allison. B.S., CCNY, 1953; M.S., N.Y. U., 1958, Ph.D., 1965. Cert. geologist, Maine, Ind.; cert. profl. geologist. Asst. civil engr. N.Y. State Dept. Transp., Babylon, 1953-66; prof. engring. geology CUNY, N.Y.C., 1966-79, dean sch. of gen. studies, 1970-79, prof. emeritus, 1979—; project research geologist U.S. Geol. Survey, 1979—; guest lectr. various colls., 1979—; mem. U.S. Nat. Com. on Tunneling Tech. Nat. Acad. Scis.; cons. IBM, Madigan-Hyland Engrs., Consol. Edison Co. N.Y., others. Author numerous sci. papers. Mem. com. for minority participation in the geosciences U.S. Dept. of Interior, 1972-75; panelist Grad. Fellowship Program, NSF; chmn. Minority Grad. Fellowship Program, 1979-80. Recipient Founders Day award N.Y. U., 1966, 125th Anniversary medal The City Coll., 1973, award for excellence in engring. geology Nat. Consortium Black Profl. Devel., 1978. Ind. Fellow Geol. Soc. Am. (mem. com. on minorities in geoscis.); mem. N.Y. Acad. Scis., Geol. Soc. Washington, Am. Inst. Profl. Geologists, Assn. Engring. Geologists (rep. to nat. bd. dirs. 1973-74, chmn. N.Y.-Phila. sect. 1973-74), Yellowstone-Bighorn Research Assn., Sigma Xi. Office: US Geol Survey 922 National Center Reston VA 22092

BASKETT, THOMAS SEBREE, biologist; b. Liberty, Mo., Jan. 23, 1916; s. William Denny and Maybelle (Grigsby) B.; m. Marjorie Kenison, Feb. 14, 1947; children—Thomas Sebree, Richard K., Jann D. A.B., Central Meth. Coll., Mo., 1937; M.S., U. Okla., 1939; Ph.D., Iowa State U., 1942. Extension specialist in wildlife conservation Iowa State U., Ames, 1941-42, asst. prof. zoology, 1946-47; asst. prof. wildlife mgmt. U. Conn., Storrs, 1947-48; biologist U.S. Bur. Sport Fish and Wildlife; leader Mo. Coop. Wildlife Research Unit; asst. prof., asso. prof., prof. zoology U. Mo., Columbia, 1948-68; chief div. wildlife research Bur. Sport Fish and Wildlife, U.S. Dept. Interior, Washington, 1968-73, biologist, 1973—; prof. fisheries and wildlife U. Mo. at Columbia, 1973—; leader Mo. Coop. Wildlife Research Unit, 1973—. Editor: Jour. Wildlife Mgmt, 1966-68; contbr. articles to profl. jours. Served from ensign to lt. USNR, 1942-46; PTO. Mem. Am. Ornithologists Union, Am. Soc. Ichthyologists and Herpetologists, Wildlife Soc. (pres.), Council Biology Editors. Home: 201 Bittersweet Ct Columbia MO 65201

BASKETTE, FLOYD KENNETH, JR., educator; b. Alamosa, Colo., Oct. 17, 1940; s. Floyd Kenneth and Carol Grace (Albright) B.; m. Judith Ann Heeren, June 18, 1964; children: Jennifer Lynne, Sean Kenneth. B.A., U. Colo., 1963, M.A., 1968. Staff analyst Colo. Com. on Govt. Efficiency and Economy, 1968-69; mgmt. analyst (Budget Mgmt. Office), City of Denver, 1969-71; exec. dir. Colo. Rural Devel. Commn., 1971-73; asst. planning dir., State of Colo., 1973-75; asst. dir. and rural devel. coordinator Colo. Dept. Local Affairs, Denver, 1975-77; fed. co-chmn. Four Corners Regional Commn., Commerce Dept., Washington, 1977-80; asso. adminstr. policy FHA, Dept. Agr., 1980-81; self-employed, 1981—; tchr., coach Bishop Ireton High Sch., 1982—. Bd. dirs. Standing Room Only. Served with USNR, 1963-67. Mem. Am. Soc. Pub. Adminstrn. Democrat. Episcopalian (vestry man). Home: 8441 Porter Ln Alexandria VA 22308

BASKIN, HERBERT BERNARD, computer company executive, educator; b. N.Y.C., Nov. 24, 1933; s. Jackob and Anna B.; 1 dau., Debby Lynne. M.E.E., Syracuse U., 1959. Elec. engr. IBM Devel. Lab., 1956-59, mgr. systems research, 1960-69; prof. elec. engring. and computer scis. U. Calif., Berkeley, 1969—; pres., founder Computer-Lock Systems Corp., Berkeley, 1972-76; v.p. Western Devel. Center, Datapoint Corp., Berkeley, 1976-81; founder, pres. Gen. Parametrics Corp., 1981—; cons. in field. Asso. editor, contbr. articles to profl. publs. Served with USCGR, 1957-58. Mem. IEEE, Assn. Computing Machinery, Soc. Info. Display, Eta Kappa Nu, Sigma Xi. Patentee in field. Home: 264 Yale Ave Berkeley CA 94708 Office: Gen Parametrics Corp 1505 Solano Ave Berkeley CA 94707

BASKIN, JOHN ROLAND, lawyer; b. Cleve., Dec. 23, 1916; s. Roland A. and Frances M. (Schwoerer) B.; m. Madeline Stricker, Feb. 26, 1949 (dec. 1965); 1 dau., Barbara Anne; m. Betty Anne Meyer, May 12, 1967. A.B. magna cum laude, Western Res. U., 1938, LL.B., 1940. Bar: Ohio 1940, FCC 1949, U.S. Supreme Ct. 1955. Practiced in, Cleve., 1940—; asso. firm Baker & Hostetler, 1941-54, partner, 1954—. Served as spl. agt. AUS, CIC, U.S. Atomic Bomb Project, 1942-46; CIC officer Armed Forces Spl. Weapons Project, 1951-52. Mem. Am. Bar Assn., Ohio Bar Assn., Cleve. Bar Assn., Order of Coif, Ct. of Nisi Prius, Phi Beta Kappa, Delta Tau Delta, Delta Theta Phi. Republican. Episcopalian. Clubs: Union, Mayfield Country (Cleve.); University (Washington). Buttonwood Bay Key Largo FL 33037 also East Chop Martha's Vineyard MA 02557 Office: Baker & Hostetler 3200 National City Center Cleveland OH 44114

BASKIN, RONALD JOSEPH, zoologist, physiologist, educator; b. Joliet, Ill., Nov. 25, 1935; s. Mack Robert and Evelyn Josephine (Rudzinski) B.; m. Lydia Olga Lendl, Mar. 29, 1957; children—Ronald James, Thomas William. A.B., UCLA, 1957; M.A., 1959, Ph.D., 1960. Asst. prof. biology Rensselaer Poly. Inst., Troy, N.Y., 1961-64; asst. prof. zoology U. Calif., Davis, 1964-67, asso. prof., 1967-71, prof., 1971—, chmn. dept. zoology, 1971—; Editorial bd. U. Calif. Press. Contbr. articles to sci. publs. Nat. Heart Inst. predoctoral fellow, 1957-60. Mem. Biophys. Soc., Soc. Cell Biology, Am. Physiol. Soc., N.Y. Acad. Scis., Sigma Xi. Office: Dept Zoology U Calif Davis CA 95616

BASKIR, LAWRENCE M., lawyer; b. N.Y.C., Jan. 10, 1938; s. Philip and Florence B.; m. Marna S. Tucker, May 13, 1973; children: Cecily Elizabeth, Micah Tucker. A.B. magna cum laude, Princeton U., 1959; LL.B., Harvard U., 1962. Bar: N.Y. State 1963, D.C. 1964, U.S. Supreme Ct. 1968. Assoc. Weaver and Glassie, 1963-65; counsel Ho. of Reps. Judiciary Com., 1965-66; chief counsel Constl. Rights Subcom., U.S. Senate, 1968-74; dir. Presidential Clemency, Bd., 1974-75; faculty fellow U. Notre Dame, 1975-77; dep. asst. sec. Dept. Treasury, Washington, 1977-79; legis. dir. Sen. Bill Bradley, 1979-80; sole practice, Washington, 1981—; adj. prof. Georgetown Law Center, Cath. U. Law Sch.; cons. U.S. Senate Intelligence Com., ABA. Contbr. articles to profl. jours.; author: Reconciliation After Vietnam, 1977, Chance and Circumstance: The Draft, the War and the Vietnam Generation, 1978. Ford Found. grantee, 1975-77. Mem. ACLU. Office: 1000 Connecticut Ave NW Suite 500 Washington DC 20036

BASLER, WAYNE GORDON, glass manufacturing executive, consultant; b. Cedar Rapids, Iowa, Aug. 16, 1930; m. Betty Jean Lawrence, June 27, 1953; children: Eric, Janelle, Peter. B.S. in Ceramic Engring., Iowa State U., 1953. With Ford Motor Co., 1960-72; dir. tech. devel. Guardian Industries, Detroit, 1972-77; pres. AFG Industries, Inc., Kingsport, Tenn., 1977—. Served to 1st lt. USAF, 1954-56. Republican. Presbyterian. Office: AFG Industries Inc 1400 Lincoln St Kingsport TN 37660

BASOLO, FRED, chemistry educator; b. Coello, Ill., Feb. 11, 1920; s. John and Catherine (Marino) B.; m. Mary P. Nutley, June 14, 1947; children: Mary Catherine, Freddie, Margaret-Ann, Elizabeth Rose. B.E., So. Ill. U., 1940, D.Sc. (hon.), 1984; M.S., U. Ill., 1942, Ph.D. in Inorganic Chemistry, 1943. Research chemist Rohm & Haas Chem. Co., Phila., 1943-46; mem. faculty Northwestern U., Evanston, Ill., 1946—, prof. chemistry, 1958—, Morrison prof. chemistry, 1980—, chmn. dept. chemistry, 1969—; guest lectr. NSF summer insts.; chmn. Gordon Research Conf., 1976; pres. Inorganic Syntheses, Inc., 1979-81; mem. bd. chem. scis. and tech. NRC-Nat. Acad. Scis.; cons. in field; Riley lectr. Notre Dame U.; Welch lectr. U. Tex.; Disting. vis. lectr. U. Iowa; Arthur D. Little lectr. MIT; Zuffanti lectr. Northwestern U.; Krug lectr. U. Ill. Author: (with R.G. Pearson) Mechanisms of Inorganic Reactions, 1958; author: (with R.C. Johnson) Coordination Chemistry, 1964; asso. editor: Chem. Revs, 1960-65, Inorganica Chemica Acta, 1967—, Inorganica Chemica Acta Letters, 1977—; editorial bd.: Jour. Inorganic and Nuclear Chemistry, 1959—, Jour. Molecular Catalysis, Chem. Revs.; mem. adv. bd. 43d edit.: Who's Who in Am.; co-editor: Catalysis; Transition Metal Chemistry; editor: Inorganic Syntheses XVI; contbr. articles to profl. jours. Recipient Ballar medal, 1972, So. Ill. U. Alumni Achievement award, 1974, Dwyer medal, 1976, James Flack Norris award for Outstanding Achievement in Teaching of Chemistry, 1981, Oesper Meml. award, 1983; Guggenheim fellow, 1954-55; NSF fellow, 1961-62; NATO sr. scientist fellow, Italy, 1981. Fellow Nat. Acad. Scis. U.S.A., AAAS (chmn. chemistry sect. 1979), Am. Acad. Arts and Scis.; Mem. Am. Chem. Soc. (asst. editor jour. 1961-64, chmn. div. inorganic chemistry 1970, pres. 1983, bd. dirs. 1982-84, award for research in inorganic chemistry 1964, Disting. Service award in inorganic chemistry 1975, N.E. regional award 1971), Chem. Soc. London, Italian Chem. Soc. (hon.), Sigma Xi, Phi Lambda Upsilon, Alpha Chi Sigma, Phi Kappa Phi, Kappa Delta Phi, Phi Lambda Theta (hon.). Office: Dept Chemistry Northwestern U Evanston IL 60201

BASRI, SAUL ABRAHAM, educator; b. Baghdad, Iraq, Feb. 15, 1926; came to U.S., 1945, naturalized, 1955; s. Abraham Saul and Levana (Mathalone) B.; m. Phyllis Claire Whyte, Feb. 1, 1950 (div. dissolved June 1975); children—Gibor, David. B.S. in Physics, Mass. Inst. Tech., 1948, Ph.D., Columbia, 1953. Asst. prof. Colo. State U., Ft. Collins, 1953-56, asso. prof., 1956-67, prof. physics, 1967—; physicist Nat. Bur. Standards, Boulder, summers, 1956-58; Fulbright lectr. U. Rangoon, Burma, 1956-57, U. Ceylon, Colombo, 1965-66; vis. prof. Technion, Israel, 1973-74. Author: A Deductive Theory of Space and Time, 1966, also articles. Mem. Am. Phys. Soc., Am. Assn. Physics Tchrs. Office: Colorado State U Dept Physics Fort Collins CO 80523 *The main drive in my scientific career has been an intense thirst for basic knowledge and the esthetic pleasure of putting into order seemingly disordered or uncorrelated facts.*

BASS, BARBARA DEJONG, film director; b. Cleve., May 16, 1946; d. Nathan Winthrop and Audrey (DeJong) B. B.A., Smith Coll., 1968. Spl. investigator City of N.Y. Dept. Investigation, 1968-70; free-lance film asst. dir., N.Y.C. and Hollywood, Calif., 1970—. Films, TV shows include Heavy Traffic, 1973, Adventures of Rabbi Jacob, 1973, Jaws, 1974, Little House on the Prarie, 1974, Eric, 1975, Bob Newhart Show, 1975, 76, Tony Randall Show, 1977, Rhoda, 1978, Like Normal People, 1979, The Last Resort, 1979, East of Eden, 1980, Longshot, 1980-81, 9 to 5, 1982-83; also numerous pilots, series episodes, features. Mem. Dirs. Guild Am. Office: care Dirs Guild Am 7950 Sunset Blvd Hollywood CA 90046

BASS, BERNARD MORRIS, psychology educator; b. N.Y.C., June 11, 1925; s. Alexander Matthew and Clara Helen (Abrams) B.; m. Ruth Rothschild, Aug. 23, 1946; children: Robert, Jonathan, Laurie, Audrey. Student, CCNY, 1941-43; B.A., Ohio State U., 1946, M.A., 1947, Ph.D. in Indsl. Psychology, 1949. Prof. psychology La. State U., Baton Rouge, 1949-61; vis. prof. U. Calif. at Berkeley, 1961-62; prof.

psychology and mgmt., dir. Mgmt. Research Center, U. Pitts., 1962-68; prof. U. Rochester, N.Y., 1968-77, State U. N.Y., Binghamton, 1977—, acting dean, 1978-79; pres. Transnat. Programs Corp., Scottsville, N.Y., 1972—; Lectr., dir. workshops, U.S., fgn. countries; vis. scholar SUNY, 1977—. Author: Leadership Psychology and Organizational Behavior, 1960, Organizational Psychology, 1965, 79, Training in Industry, 1966, Man, Work and Organizations, 1972, Assessment of Managers: An International Comparison, 1979, People, Work and Organizations, 1981, Stogdill's Handbook of Leadership, 1981, Interpersonal Communication in Organizations, 1982, Organizational Decision Making, 1983; editor: Objective Approaches to Personality Assessment, 1959; Editor: Leadership and Interpersonal Behavior, 1961, Conformity and Deviation, 1961, Managing for Accomplishment, 1970, Current Perspectives for Managing Organizations, 1970, Studies in Organizational Psychology, 1972. Served with USAAF, 1943-45. Ford Found. Faculty fellow, 1966-67. Fellow Am. Psychol. Assn., Acad. Mgmt.; mem. Internat. Assn. Applied Psychology (pres. div. orgnl. psychology 1978-82). Home: 2135 W Hamton Rd Binghamton NY 13903 *Life would be a bore without the expectation of new challenges and broader horizons ahead.*

BASS, BOB, professional basketball team executive. Gen. mgr. San Antonio Spurs, NBA. Office: Care San Antonio Spurs Hemis Fair Arena PO Box 530 San Antonio TX 78292

BASS, HYMAN, mathematician, educator; b. Houston, Oct. 5, 1932; s. Isador and Fanny (Weiss) B.; m. Mary Ellen Popkin, June 9, 1957 (div. 1978); children: Anne Ruth, Ivan Philip; m. Dorothea Henriette Goldys, Nov. 1, 1979; 1 dau., Gabriella Sierra. B.A., Princeton U., 1955; M.S., U. Chgo., 1956, Ph.D. (NSF grad. fellow), 1959. Ritt instr. math. Columbia U., 1959-62, asst. prof., 1963-64, chmn. dept. math., 1975—; asso. prof., chmn. at Barnard Coll., 1964-65, prof., 1965—; Vis. mem. Inst. Advanced Study, Princeton, 1964, 65-66, Inst. de Hautes Etudes Scientifiques, Paris, 1968-69; vis. prof. Universidad Nacional Autónoma de Mex., 1965, Tata Inst. Fundamental Research, Bombay, 1965-66, 69, 76, 80, U. Paris, 1968, 73, 81, Cambridge U., 1973, Instituto de Matematica Pura e Applicada, Rio de Janeiro, 1977, Bar Ilan U., Israel, 1980; chmn. adv. com. pure mathematics NRC, 1970-71; adv. panel, div. math. NSF, 1973-75. Editorial bd.: Jour. Indian Math. Soc, 1968—, Cambridge Tracts in Pure and Applied Mathematics; 968: Jour. Pure and Applied Algebra, 1970—, Am. Jour. Mathematics, 1971—, North-Holland Math. Library, 1971—, Acad. Press Series in Pure and Applied Math, 1974—. NSF fellow Coll. de France, 1962-63; Sloan fellow, 1964-66; Guggenheim fellow, 1968-69; recipient Van Amridge book prize Columbia, 1969, Cole prize Am. Math. Soc., 1975. Mem. Am. Math Soc. (editorial bd. 1969—, council 1969-72), London Math. Socs., Societé Mathématique de France, Soc. Collaborateurs N. Bourbaki, Math. Assn. Am., AAAS., Am. Acad. Arts and Scis., Nat. Acad. Scis. Home: 435 Riverside Dr New York NY 10025

BASS, JAMES ORIN, lawyer; b. Summer County, Tenn., July 12, 1910; s. Francis Marion and Sadie (Dunn) B.; m. Susanne Warner, June 9, 1937; children: James Orin, Edwin Warner, Francis Marion II, Susan Richardson. B.A., U. of South, 1931; LL.B., Harvard, 1934. Bar: Tenn. bar 1934. Since practiced in, Nashville; partner firm Bass, Berry & Sims, 1937—; Dir. First Am. Nat. Bank Nashville, 1st Am. Corp., Tenn. Natural Gas Lines, Inc. Mem. Tenn. Ho. of Reps. from Davidson County, 1936-38, Tenn. Senate, 1940-42. Served to lt. col. AUS, 1942-45. Mem. Am., Tenn., Nashville bar assns., Am. Coll. Trial Lawyers. Democrat. Presbyn. Home: 4412 Georgian Pl Nashville TN 37215 Office: First Am Center Nashville TN 37238

BASS, JOEL LEONARD, artist; b. Los Angeles, Dec. 23, 1942; s. Herbert and Ethyl (Kaye) B.; m. Sydney Joan Littenberg, Jan. 28, 1979. B.A., Art Center Coll. of Design, Los Angeles, 1967. Instr. Art Center Coll. Design, Los Angeles, 1976—. Exhibited in one man shows at, Michael Walls Gallery, San Francisco, 1970, 71, 72, Reed Coll., Portland, Oreg., 1971, Cusack Gallery, Houston, 1974, John Berggruen Gallery, San Francisco, John Doyle Gallery, Chgo., John Doyle Gallery, Paris, 1975, Galerie Marguerite Lamy, Paris, 1976, Kathryn Markel Fine Arts, N.Y.C., 1977, 78, Janus Gallery, Venice, Calif., 1978-80, Roy Boyd Gallery, Chgo., 1978; exhibited in group shows at, Michael Walls Gallery, 1970, Joslyn Art Center, Omaha, Whitney Mus. Am. Art, N.Y.C., 1971, 73, Oakland (Calif.) Mus., 1971, Govett-Brewster Art Gallery, New Plymouth, N.Z., 1972-73, Pasadena (Calif.) Art Mus., Mus. Modern Art, N.Y.C., 1975, Davison Art Center, Wesleyan Coll., Mendel Art Gallery, Saskatoon, Sask., Can., 1978; represented in permanent collections at, Des Moines Art Center, Ft. Worth Art Center, Greenville (S.C.) County Mus. Art, Whitney Mus. Am. Art, Albright Knox Mus. Art, Buffalo, Mus. Modern Art, San Francisco Mus. Art, Oakland Mus., La Jolla Mus. Contemporary Art. Nat. Endowment for Arts fellow, 1978—. Jewish. Office: Dept Fine Arts Art Center Coll Design Pasadena CA 91103

BASS, JOHN FRED, lawyer; b. Tucumcari, N.Mex., May 25, 1941; s. John M. and Meridith Jean (Patching) B.; m. Mellanie; children: Devon, Stacia, Layla. B.A., Baylor U., 1963; J.D. with honors, U. Tex., 1968. Coordinator, Peace Corps, Bolivia, 1963-65; asso. firm McGinnis, Lockridge & Kilgore, Austin, Tex., 1968-69; with Smith Barney & Co. of N.Y., investment banking, 1969-71; individual practice law, Dallas, 1971—; Tchr. real estate law Richland Coll., Eastfield Coll. Contbr. articles to profl. jours. Democratic precinct conv. chmn., 1974. Mem. Am., Tex., Dallas bar assns., Am., Tex. trial lawyers assns., Am. Judicature Soc., Dallas Christian Legal Soc. (past pres.). Baptist. Lodges: Masons; Shriners. Office: 2525 Ross Ave Dallas TX 75201

BASS, LOUIS NELSON, agronomist, plant physiologist, govt. ofcl.; b. Iola, Kans., Mar. 7, 1919; s. Herbert and Olive (Felker) B.; m. Helen Jane Collins, Nov. 7, 1943; children—Colin David, Nelsa Louise Mullen. B.S., Upper Iowa U., 1940; M.S., U. Iowa, 1943; Ph.D., Iowa State U., 1949. Asst. prof. botany and plant pathology Iowa State U., Ames, 1949-58; plant physiologist Nat. Seed Storage Lab., USDA, Fort Collins, Colo., 1958-70, dir., 1970—, research leader seed viability and storage, 1972—; Mem. grad. faculty Colo. State U., Fort Collins, 1960—. Recipient Alumni Achievement award Upper Iowa U., 1972. Mem. Am. Soc. Agronomy (asso. editor Jour. 1971-74), Soc. Comml. Seed Technologists, Assn. Ofcl. Seed Analysts (Merit award 1975, sci. edn. editor 1962—, pres. 1971-72, mem. pub. service com. 1962—), Crop Sci. Soc. Am. (ex-officio mem. com. for preservation of genetic stocks 1971—), Am. Soc. Hort. Sci., Internat. Seed Testing Assn. (vice chmn. seed moisture and storage com. 1974-80, chmn. seed storage com. 1980—), Am. Type Culture Collection, Sigma Xi, Gamma Sigma Delta, Epsilon Sigma Phi. Research on factors affecting seed viability. Home: 1117 Fairview Fort Collins CO 80521 Office: Nat Seed Storage Lab Colo State Univ Fort Collins CO 80523

BASS, MAX S., chemical company executive; b. Bklyn., July 31, 1928; s. David and Anna B.; m. Harriet Rubin, June 5, 1949; children: Susan, Michael, Fredric. B. Chem. Eng, CCNY, 1950; M.B.A., Fairleigh Dickinson U., 1969. Registered profl. engr., N.Y. State, N.J., Fla., Ky. With M & T Chems. Inc., 1963—, v.p. chems., Rahway, N.J., 1973-77, sr. v.p. ops., Stamford, Conn., 1977-79, pres., chief exec. officer, Woodbridge, N.J., 1979—; grad. bus. instr. Fairleigh Dickinson U., 1969. Contbr. articles on chem. engring. to profl. jours. Mem. Am. Inst. Chem. Engrs., Am. Mgmt. Assn., Chem. Mfrs. Assn., Soc. Plastics Engrs. Office: One Woodbridge Center Woodbridge NJ 07095

BASS, MICHAEL, electrical engineering educator; b. N.Y.C., Oct. 24, 1939; s. Reuben Herman and Mary (Oboler) B.; m. Judith H. Rubin, June 30, 1962; children: Geogre, Meredith. B.S., Carnegie Mellon U., 1960; M.S., U. Mich., 1962, Ph.D., 1964. Acting asst. prof. U. Calif.-Berkeley, 1964-66; research scientist Raytheon Corp., Waltham, Mass., 1966-73; assoc. dir. Ctr. for Laser Studies, dir., prof. elec. engring. U. So. Calif., Los Angeles, 1973—; cons. Aerospace, Los Angeles, 1977—, Allied Corp., Westlake Village, Calif., 1982—, AMP, Harrisburg, Calif., 1977—, Exxon Corp., Richland, Wash., 1974-80. Contbr. articles to profl. jours.; editor: Laser Materials Processing, 1983, Laser Handbook-Vol. IV, 1984. Fellow IEEE, Optical Soc. Am.; mem. Sigma Xi, Tau Beta Pi. Office: U So Calif Center for Laser Studies Los Angeles CA 90089

BASS, NORMAN HERBERT, physician; b. N.Y.C., July 10, 1936; s. Julius and Celia (Annex) B.; (div.)children—Joel Martin, Rebecca Pier, Robert Farrell. B.S. (Ford Found. scholar 1953, N.U. State Regents scholar 1954), Swarthmore (Pa.) Coll., 1958; M.D., Yale U., 1962. Diplomate: Am. Bd. Psychiatry and Neurology. Intern Med. U. Wash. Hosp., Seattle, 1962-63; resident in neurology U. Va. Hosp., Charlottesville, 1963-65; clin. fellow in neurology Mass. Gen. Hosp., Boston, 1965-67; NIH fellow Harvard U. Med. Sch., 1965-67; from asst. prof. to prof. neurology U. Va. Med. Sch., Charlottesville, 1967-79; dir. Clinic Neurosci. Research Center, 1973-79; vis. prof. pharmacology U. Goteborg, Sweden, 1972-73; prof. neurology, chmn. dept. Albert B. Chandler Med. Center, U. Ky., Lexington, 1979—; neurologist in chief Univ. Hosp., 1979—; dir. lab. neurochemistry Sanders-Brown Ky. Research Center Aging, 1979—; cons. neurology VA Med. Center, Lexington; chmn. nat. research program merit rev. bd. in neurobiology VA; mem. bd. sci. advisers Delta Regional Primate Center, Tulane U., 1978-81, chmn., 1979—; chmn. profl. adv. bd. Epilepsy Assn. Ky., 1980-82. Asso. editor: Neurochem. Research Jour; contbr. numerous articles to med. jours. Served to maj. M.C. USAR, 1963-69. Recipient Research Career Devel. award NIH, 1971-75, Nat. Inst. Neurologic Disease and Blindness research fellow in neurochemistry, 1965-67; Markle scholar in acad. medicine, 1969-74. Fellow Am. Acad. Neurology (S. Weir Mitchell research award 1967), AAAS; mem. Am. Assn. U. Profs. Neurology (v.p. 1980-81), Am. Assn. Anatomists, Am. Soc. Neurochemistry, Soc. Neurosci., Internat. Soc. Neurochemistry, Child Neurology Soc., Am. Neurol. Assn., Assn. Research Nervous and Mental Disease, AMA, Nat. Multiple Sclerosis Soc., Alpha Omega Alpha. Home: 747 W Cooper Dr Lexington KY 40502 Office: Dept Neurology Med Center MS 129 Univ Kentucky Lexington KY 40536

BASS, PAUL, pharmacology educator; b. Winnipeg, Man., Can., Aug. 28, 1928; came to U.S., 1958; s. Benjamin and Sarah B.; m. Ruth Zipursky, May 31, 1953; children: Stuart, Susan. B.S. in Pharmacology, U. B.C., 1953, M.A., 1955; Ph.D. in Pharmacology, McGill U., 1957; fellow in Biochemistry, McGill U., 1957-58, Mayo Found., 1958-60. Research asst. Ayerse, McKenna & Harrison, Can., 1956; assoc. lab. dir. Parke, Davis & Co., 1960-70; prof. pharmacology Sch. Pharmacy and Sch. Medicine, U. Wis., Madison, 1970—. Editorial bd.: Am. Jour. Physiology, 1976-79, Jour. Pharmacology and Exptl. Therapeutics, 1980—; contbr. chpts. to books, articles to jours. in field. Mem. Am. Soc. Pharmacology, Soc. Exptl. Biology and Medicine, Pharmacol. Soc. Can., Am. Gastroent. Assn. Home: 153 Nautilus Dr Madison MI 53705 Office: 524 Charter St Madison WI 53706

BASS, PERRY RICHARDSON, petroleum company executive. Chmn. Perry R. Ross, Inc., Ft. Worth. Office: Perry R Bass Inc Fort worth Nat Bank Bldg Fort Worth TX 76102§

BASS, ROBERT OLIN, manufacturing executive; b. Denver, July 22, 1917; s. Olin R. and Cora (Durham) B.; m. Isabelle Cantrell, Mar. 22, 1941; 1 dau., Susan. B.S. in Bus. Adminstrn., U. Denver, 1941. Pres. Eberhardt-Denver Co., 1956; exec. v.p., asst. gen. mgr. Morse Chain Co., Ithaca, N.Y., 1956-58, pres., 1958-66; group v.p. indsl. Borg-Warner Corp., 1966-68, exec. v.p., 1968-75, pres., 1975-79, vice chmn., 1979-82, chief operating officer, 1975-80, dir., 1973-83; dir. SCM Corp., N.Y.C., Raymond Corp., Greene, N.Y. Chmn. metals and machinery sect. Chgo. Met. Crusade of Mercy, 1968; mem. bus. adv. council Coll. Bus. Adminstrn., U. Denver, 1976—; vice chmn., trustee Field Mus. Natural History, Chgo. Mem. Am. Mgmt. Assn. (v.p., chmn. gen. mgmt. planning council 1976-79, trustee 1979-82). Home: 1242 Lake Shore Dr Chicago IL 60610 Office: 200 S Michigan Ave Chicago IL 60604

BASS, SAUL, graphic designer, filmmaker; b. N.Y.C., May 8, 1920; s. Aaron and Pauline (Feldman) B.; m. Elaine Makatura, Sept. 30, 1961; children: Jennifer, Jeffrey. Student, Art Students League, 1936-39, Bklyn. Coll., 1944-45; hon. doctorates, Phila. Mus. Coll. Art, Los Angeles Art Ctr. Coll. Design. Freelance graphic designer, N.Y.C., 1936-46; propr. Saul Bass & Assocs., Inc., Los Angeles, 1946—; leader seminars, lectr. univs., colls., various instns.; mem. exec. bd. Internat. Design Conf., Aspen, Colo.; hon. mem. faculty Royal Designers for Industry, Royal Soc. Arts, Eng., 1965. Dir. short films, TV commls., motion picture titles, prologues, epilogues; spl. sequences for feature films including shower sequence in Psycho, 1960, maj. battle in Spartacus, 1962, all races in Grand Prix, 1968, live action epilogue West Side Story, 1961, animated equilogue Around the World in Eighty Days, 1956; graphic designs Man With the Golden Arm, 1955, Anatomy of a Murder, 1960, Exodus, 1961, Bonjour Triestesse, 1957, Such Good Friends, 1974, That's Entertainment II, 1976, The Shining, 1980; dir.: feature film Phase IV, 1974; represented permanent collections, Mus. Modern Art, N.Y.C., 1974, Library of Congress, Smithsonian Instn., Prague Mus., Stedelijk Mus., Amsterdam; exhibited one-man and group shows, U.S., Europe, S.Am., Far East; designer, developer: numerous corp. identification systems for indsl. enterprises including Bell System, Celanese Corp., United Airlines, Alcoa, Quaker Oats, Rockwell Internat., Warner Communications, Minolta, Girl Scouts U.S.A., United Way; architect, designer worldwide network, Exxon-Esso Gasoline stas., 1983; designer packages for comml. products, Wesson Oil, 1983, Dixie Paper Products, Lawry's Foods, Hunt's Foods, symbol, Pres.'s White House Council for Energy Efficiency, 1981, U.S. Post Office Commorative Stamp for Art and Industry, 1983; contbr. numerous articles to profl. publs. Recipient award for high artistic value in all work Mus. de Arte Moderna, Rio de Janiero, 1959, citation for distinction brough to profession Phila. Mus. Art, 1960; inducted N.Y. Art Dirs. Hall of Fame, 1977; recipient numerous gold medals various nat. and internat. design competitions, Grand award for The Searching Eye Venice Film Festival, Gold Hugo for From Here to There Chgo. Film Festival, Oscar for documentary Why Man Creates, 1969, Gold medal Moscow Film Festival. Mem. Acad. Motion Picture Arts and Scis., Soc. Typog. Arts, Am. Inst. Graphic Arts, Assn. Graphic Designers Sweden, Package Designers Council, Alliance Graphique Internationale. Address: 7039 W Sunset Blvd Los Angeles CA 90028

BASS, WILLIAM MARVIN, III, educator; b. Staunton, Va., Aug. 30, 1928; s. William Marvin II and Jennie Britton (Hicks) B.; m. Mary Anna Owen, Aug. 8, 1953; children—Charles E., William Marvin IV, James O. B.A., U. Va., 1951; M.S., U. Ky., 1956; Ph.D., U. Pa., 1961. Diplomate: Am. Bd. Forensic Anthropology. Instr. phys. anthropology Grad. Sch. Medicine, U. Pa., 1956-59; instr. U. Nebr., 1959-60; mem. faculty anthropology dept. U. Kans., 1960-71, prof., 1967-71; prof., head dept. anthropology U. Tenn., Knoxville, 1971—, Alumni Disting. prof., 1978. Author: Human Osteology: A Laboratory and Field Manual of the Human Skeleton, 1971, 2d edit., 1979, The Leavenworth Site Cemetery: Archaeology and Physical Anthropology, 1971, also numerous articles. Served with AUS, 1951-53. Named Hill Tchr. U. Kans., 1964; recipient H. Bernerd Fink award for excellence in classroom teaching U. Kans., 1965; Alumni Public Service award U. Tenn., 1975. Fellow Am. Assn. Phys. Anthropologists, Am. Acad. Forensic Scis.; mem. Am. Anthrop. Assn. Home: Dept Anthropology Univ Tennessee Knoxville TN 37996

BASSANI, GIUSEPPE, computer company executive; b. Milan, Italy, June 26, 1937; came to U.S., 1980; s. Luigi and Cesira (Rossini) B.; m. Suzanne Murray, Nov. 21, 1966; children: Gisella, Lorenzo. Student, U. Mediterranean, Italy, 1969, Cath. U.-Milan, 1960-64, City of London Coll., 1958-59. Country mgr. NCR, Milan, 1976-80; group v.p. NRC, Dayton, Ohio, 1980—; dean, prof. Faculty Computer Scis., U. Mediterranean, 1970-74. Trustee Dayton Art Inst., 1982-83. Lodges: Rotary (com. chmn.); Lyons-Rome (v.p. 1973-76). Home: 921 Runnymede Rd Dayton OH 45419 Office: 1700 S Patterson Blvd Dayton OH 45479 *This changing world two values never change: honesty and the permanent struggle for excellence. I always have and always will strive towards achieving these values, both in my professional and private life by setting the example.*

BASSETT, CHARLES ANDREW LOOCKERMAN, surgeon, educator; b. Crisfield, Md., Aug. 4, 1924; s. Harold Reuben and Vesta (Loockerman) B.; m. Nancy Taylor Clark, June 15, 1946; children: Susan, David Clark, Lee Sterling. Student, Princeton U., 1941-43; M.D., Columbia U., 1948, Sc.D., 1955. Diplomate: Am. Bd. Orthopedic Surgery. Intern, resident St. Lukes Hosp., N.Y.C., 1948-50; asst. resident orthopedic surgery N.Y. Orthopaedic Hosp., 1950, Annie C. Kane fellow, 1953-55; asst. attending orthopedic surgeon Presbyn. Hosp., 1955-60, asso. attending, 1960-63, attending orthopedic surgeon, 1963—; instr. orthopedic surgery Columbia U., 1955-59, dir. orthopedic research labs., 1957—, asst. prof., 1959-61, asso. prof., 1961-67, prof., 1967-83, prof. emeritus, spl. lectr., 1983—; cons. Naval Med. Research Inst., Bethesda, Md., 1952-54, Presbyn. Hosp., N.Y.C., 1983—; spl. cons. NIH, Nat. Inst. Neurol. Diseases and Blindness, Bethesda, 1959-62; career scientist N.Y.C. Health Research Council, 1961-71; vis. scientist Strangeway Research Lab., Cambridge, Eng., 1965-66; cons. div. med. scis., cons., exec. sec. com. on skeletal system NRC-Nat. Acad. Scis., 1963-71; pres. Sci. Advisors (A/O) Schwerizerischen Abeitsgemeinschaft fur Osteosynthesefragen, 1969—; pres. bd. sci. advisors Inst. Calot, Berck-Plage, France, 1969—; cons. N.Y. State Rehab. Hosp., West Haverstraw, 1968—; cons. on med. devices FDA, HEW, 1970-77; dir. Electrobiology, Inc. Contbr. articles profl. jours., books. Served to lt. (j.g.) USNR, 1950-54. Recipient Nat. award Paralyzed Vet. Am., 1959, Max Weinstein award United Cerebral Palsy, 1960; James Mather Smith prize Columbia Coll. Physicians and Surgeons, 1971. Fellow ACS, N.Y. Acad. Scis.; mem. Am. Acad. Orthopaedic Surgeons, AMA, Am. Orthopaedic Assn., Am. Soc. Cell Biology, Internat. Soc. Orthopedic Surgery and Traumatology (sci. adv. bd. internat. orthopedics), N.Y. State, N.Y. County med. socs., Orthopaedic Research Soc. (pres.), Royal Coll. Medicine (Eng.), Royal Micros. Soc., Tissue Culture Assn., Can. Orthopaedic Research Soc. (hon.), Soc. Exptl. Biology and Medicine, Harvey Soc., S.C. Orthopaedic Assn. (hon.), Société Belge de Chirurgie Orthopédique et de Traumatologie (hon.), Sigma Xi (Ann. award), Alpha Omega Alpha. Pioneer in surgically-non-invasive, pulsing, electromagnetic fields to treat diseases and disorders of humans and animals. Home: 108 Midland Ave Bronxville NY 10708 Office: 630 W 168th St New York NY 10032 *The joy of discovery is superceded only by knowledge that the discovery will improve human experience. In making the discovery, theory must fit the facts, not the facts, theory.*

BASSETT, DOUGLAS GRAEME, broadcasting executive; b. Toronto, Ont., Can., June 22, 1940; s. John White Hughes and Eleanor Moira B.; m. Susan Joan Bemple, Oct. 19, 1968; children: Deborah Elizabeth, Stephanie Alexandra, Jennifer Moira. Student, U. N.B., 1958-61. Pres., chief exec. officer Baton Broadcasting Inc., Toronto, 1979—, CFTO-TV Ltd., Scarborough, Ont., Can., 1979—; v.p. Glen-Warren Prodns. Ltd. and CFGO Radio Ltd.; chmn. Telegram Corp. Ltd., Telegram Syndicate Ltd., Haughton Graphics Ltd., Telfer Packaging Ltd., ABF Bus. Forms Ltd., ABF Formules, d 'Affaires Limitee, Agincourt Prodns. Ltd.; dir. Telegram Corp. Ltd., Telegram Syndicate Ltd., Baton Broadcasting Inc., Aginbourt Prodns. Ltd., CFGO Radio Ltd., CKLW Radio Broadcasting Ltd., CFQC Broadcasting Ltd., Haughton Graphics Ltd., Telfer Packaging Corp. Ltd., Eaton's of Can. Ltd., Can. Imperial Bank of Commerce, Hollinger Argus Ltd., Ravelston Corp. Ltd., Norcen Energy Resources Ltd., Rothmans of Pall Mall Can. Ltd. Trustee Hosp. for Sick Children; bd. govs. Variety Village Sports Tng. and Fitness Centre, Toronto; bd. dirs. Ont. div. Arthritis Soc., Council for Can. Unity, Nat. Ballet Can., Ireland Fund of Can., Olympic Trust of Can., Hosp. for Sick Children Found., Can. Council Christians and Jews, World Wildlife Fund, Can., Can. Soc. for Weizmann Inst. Sci., Can. Robert F. Kennedy Meml. Decrated Comdr. of Order of St. John; decorated Knight Comdr. of Mil. and Hospitaller Order St. Lazarus of Jerusalem, Ordo Constantini Magni. Mem. Young Pres.s Orgn. Clubs: Toronto; York, Badminton and Racquet, Toronto Golf, Albany, Variety, Canadian, Empire, Royal Can. Yacht (Toronto); Mt. Royal (Montreal); North Hatley Sailing (Que.); Rideau (Ottawa); Lyford Cay (Nassau); Granite, Primrose, Muskoka Lakes Golf and Country, Caledon Ski. Home: 118 Forest Hill Rd Toronto ON Canada M4V 2L7 Office: Box 9 Sta O Toronto ON Canada M4V 2M9

BASSETT, EDWARD POWERS, university dean; b. Boston, Feb. 27, 1929; s. Fraser W. and Fanny (Powers) B.; m. Karen Elizabeth Jack, Dec. 21, 1954; children: Sarah Jack Bassett Williams, Laura Powers, Lisa Wightman. A.B., Washington and Lee U., 1951; M.A., U. Mich., 1955; Ph.D., U. Iowa, 1967. Court reporter Louisville Courier-Jour., 1955-56; asst. editor Falmouth (Mass.) Enterprise, 1956-57; city editor Anderson (Ind.) Herald, 1957-58; editorial writer Longview (Wash.) Daily News, 1958-60; lectr. Lower Columbia Jr. Coll., 1959-60; instr., pub. U. Iowa, 1960-67; asst. prof. U. Mich., 1967-70, Acting chmn. dept. journalism, 1969-70; dean Sch. Journalism U. Kans., 1970-74, assoc. vice chancellor acad. affairs, 1974-75; dir. Sch. Journalism U. So. Calif., 1975-80; editor Statesman-Jour., Salem, Oreg., 1980-83; dean Medill Sch. Journalism Northwestern U., Evanston, Ill., 1984—. Trustee William Allen White Found.; bd. dirs. Found. Am. Communications. Served with USMCR. Recipient citation for excellence in state and local reporting Am. Polit. Sci. Assn., 1960. Mem. Assn. Edn. in Journalism and Mass Communication (pres. 1975-76), Am. Assn. Schs. and Depts. Journalism (pres. 1974-75), Sigma Delta Chi, Kappa Tau Alpha., Delta Tau Delta. Republican. Presbyterian. Club: Rotary. Office: Medill Sch Journalism Northwestern U Evanston IL 60201

BASSETT, ELIZABETH (LIBBY) EWING, editor; b. Cleve., July 22, 1937; d. Ben and Eileen Grace (Ewing) B. A.A., Bradford Jr. Coll., Mass., 1957. Girl Friday Time-Life, Prince Mathabelli, Inc., Ferro, Mogubgub & Schwartz L & L Animation Inc., 1957-63; asst. producer, stage mgr. N.Y. State Pavilion at N.Y. World's Fair, 1963-64; writer, reporter, editor AP, N.Y.C., 1965-72; free-lance corr. AP, Newsweek, Voice of America, UNICEF, ABC Radio, Africa, 1972-74; resident corr. ABC News, Ciaro, 1974-77; dir. publs. and communications World Environment Ctr., N.Y.C., 1978—; guest lectr. Am. U., Cairo, Rutgers U., Columbia U., L.I. U. Author: The Growth of Environment in the World Bank. Mem. Fgn. Press Assn., Sigma Delta Chi. Office: 605 3d Ave 17th Floor New York NY 10158 *To conquer my fear of the unknown, I set out to know the world, first through travel, then through writing. I am still learning, thanks to my correspondents around the world who share their knowledge of international enviromental trends and issues. These natural resources issues greatly influence conomics and politics and, in my view are the new measure of national and international security.*

BASSETT, HARRY HOOD, banker; b. Flint, Mich., May 6, 1917; s. Harry Hoxie and Jessie Marie (Hood) B.; m. Florence Schust Knoll, June 22, 1958; children: Harry Hood, George Rodney, Patrick Glenn. B.S., Yale U., 1940. Asst. trust officer First Nat. Bank, Palm Beach, Fla., 1940-42, chmn. bd., 1965-71, also dir.; asst. v.p., Miami, 1947-48, dir., 1947-48, v.p., 1948-56, asst. to pres., 1951—, chmn. exec. com., 1959—, pres., 1962-66, chmn. bd., 1966-76; dir. Wometco Enterprises, Eastern Airlines, Inc.; chmn. bd. S.E. Banking Corp., Inc. Mem. Orange Bowl Com.; chmn. bd. trustees emeritus U. Miami. Served as pilot Civil Coastal Patrol (anti-submarine), 1941-42; 1st lt. USAAF, 1944-46. Decorated Air medal. Episcopalian. Clubs: Bath (Miami Beach); Bankers (Miami); Links, River (N.Y.C.); Lyford Cay (Nassau, Bahamas); Everglades (Palm Beach, Fla.); Biscayne Bay Yacht (Fla.); Bohemian (San Francisco); Metropolitan (Washington). Home: Coconut Grove FL 33133 Office: 100 S Biscayne Blvd Miami FL 33131

BASSETT, JAMES H., landscape architect; b. Lima, Ohio, Oct. 8, 1929; s. Howard Everett and Doris (Griffin) B.; m. JoAnn Vore, Aug. 1, 1954; children: Scott, Steven, Susan. Landscape Architect, Ohio State U., 1952. Registered landscape architect, Ohio, Mich., Fla., Miss. Air installation engr. U.S. Air Force, 1952-54; landscape architect L.G. Linnard, Toledo, Ohio, 1954-56; pvt. practice landscape architecture, Lima, 1954-70, pvt. practice landscape architecture and planning, 1970—. Recipient Outstanding Alumnus award Ohio State U., 1969, Merit award Am. Assn. Nurserymen, 1971, 76. Fellow Am. Soc. Landscape Architects (Merit award 1974, 76, 78, 81); mem. Am. Assn. Zool. Parks and Aquariums. Republican. Mem. Ch. of the Brethren. Office: James H Bassett Inc 4010 Ada Rd Lima OH 45801 *

BASSETT, JOHN WHITE HUGHES, broadcaster; b. Ottawa, Can., Aug. 25, 1915; s. John and Marion (Avery) B.; m. Isabel Glenthorne Macdonald, July 17, 1967. B.A., U. Bishop's Coll., Lennoxville, Que., 1936. Mem. staff The Telegram, Toronto, 1948-71, chmn. bd., pub., 1952-71; chmn. bd. Baton Broadcasting Inc., 1960—, CKLW-Radio, Windsor, Ont., CFGO Radio, Ottawa, CFQC TV and Radio, Saskatoon, CFTO-TV, Toronto; dir. CTV TV Network Ltd. Served to maj. Seaforth Highlanders Royal Canadian Army, World War II. Home: 76 Binscarth Rd Toronto ON M4W 1Y4 Canada Office: 101 Richmond St W Toronto ON M5H 1T1 Canada

BASSETT, LESLIE RAYMOND, composer, educator; b. Hanford, Calif., Jan. 22, 1923; s. Archibald Leslie and Vera (Starr) B.; m. Anita Elizabeth Denniston, Aug. 21, 1949; children—Wendy Lynn (Mrs. Lee Bratton), Noel Leslie, Ralph (dec.). B.A. in Music, Fresno State Coll., 1947; M.Music in Composition, U. Mich., 1949, A.Mus.D., 1956; student, Ecole Normale de Musique, Paris, France, 1950-51. Tchr. music pub. schs., Fresno, 1951-52; mem. faculty U. Mich., 1952—, prof. music, 1965—, chmn. composition dept., 1970; guest composer Berkshire Music Center, Tanglewood, Mass., 1973. Served with AUS, 1942- 46. Fulbright fellow, 1950-51; recipient Rome prize Am. Acad. in Rome, 1961-63; grantee Soc. Pub. Am. Music, 1960, Nat. Inst. Arts and Letters, 1964, Nat. Council Arts, 1966; Guggenheim fellow, 1973-74; recipient Pulitzer prize in music for Variations for Orch., 1966; citation U. Mich. regents, 1966; Walter Naumburg Found. rec. award for Sextet, 1974. Mem. Am. Composers Alliance, Pi Kappa Lambda, Phi Kappa Phi, Phi Mu Alpha. Methodist. Office: Sch Music U Mich Ann Arbor MI 48109

BASSETT, ROBERT COCHEM, lawyer, publisher; b. Sturgeon Bay, Wis., Mar. 2, 1911; s. Clark Patterson and Lillian Catherine (Cochem) B.; m. Frances E. Whiting, Feb. 28, 1942 (dec. Jan. 1945); m. Mary Catherine Holmes, Mar. 28, 1946; children—Robert Andrew, Jane, Pamela, Karen. B.A., U. Wis., 1932; J.D., Harvard, 1935. Bar: Wis. bar 1935, U.S. Supreme Ct. bar 1942. Partner Minahan & Bassett, lawyers, Green Bay, Wis., 1935-46; gen. counsel Wis. Daily Newspaper League, 1936-43; spl. counsel Inland Daily Press Assn., Chgo., 1937-43; labor counsel Hearst Corp., 1946-54, also dir., v.p., 1954-56; pub. Milw. Sentinel, 1954-56, Sphere Mag., 1971-73; pres., dir. Haywood Pub. Co. of, Ill., 1961-63; exec. v.p., dir. Haywood Pub. Co., 1961-63; v.p., dir. Haywood Tag Co., 1961-63; pres., dir. Visual Communications, Inc., 1963-65; chmn., pres. Bassett Pub. Co., 1965—; mktg. dir. Grant/ Jacoby, Inc., 1968-70; exec. v.p., dir., editorial dir. Omnibus Mag., 1965-67; pub. Boxboard Containers Mag., 1961-63; pres. Vertical Mktg., Inc., 1971-73; v.p. Jos. Schlitz Brewing Co., Milw., 1956-61; Pub. mem. shipbldg. stablzn. com. WPB, 1943-46; shipbldg. commn. Nat. War Labor Bd., 1943; mem. nat. Wage Stblzn. Bd., 1952-53; industry del. Internat. Labor Conf., Switzerland, 1953; mem. Sec. Labor's Mgmt. Adv. Com.; bus. mem. Pay Bd., 1971-72. Author: Wisconsin Laws Affecting Newspapers, 1938, Labor Guide for Italy, 1944; Contbr. articles to profl. jours. Regent U. Wis., 1958-61, regent emeritus, 1973—; trustee Nat. SBA; bd. dirs. Better Bus. Chgo., chmn. pub. relations. Served as lt. comdr. USNR, 1942-46. Mem. U.S. C. of C. (dir.), N.A.M. (dir.), Artus, Phi Kappa Phi, Phi Eta Sigma, Delta Sigma Rho, Delta Upsilon, Sigma Delta Chi. Clubs: Lake Barrington Shores Golf; Racquet, Bob O'Link (Chgo.). Home: 483 Valley View LBS Barrington IL 60010 Office: 435 N Michigan Ave Chicago IL 60611 *Many keys open the divergent doors to "success," some of one's own making, some not. Realism compels an admission that virtue and love cannot succeed without a generous measure of good luck. Realism also compels the question: What is "success"*

BASSETT, WILLIAM AKERS, geologist, educator; b. Bklyn., Aug. 3, 1931; s. Preston Rogers and Jeanne Reed (Mordorf) B.; m. Jane Ann Kermes, Sept. 8, 1962; children—Kari Nicalo, Jeffrey Kermes, Penelope North. B.A., Amherst Coll., 1954; M.A., Columbia, 1956, Ph.D., 1959. Research asso. Brookhaven Nat. Lab., 1960-61; Asst. prof. U. Rochester, N.Y., 1961-65, asso. prof., 1965-69, prof. geology, 1969-77, Cornell U., Ithaca, N.Y., 1978—; vis. prof. Brigham Young U., 1967-68; Crosby vis. prof. Mass. Inst. Tech., 1974. NSF grantee. Fellow Geol. Soc. Am., Mineral. Soc. Am., Am. Geophys. Union; mem. Geochem. Soc., AAAS, Am. Phys. Soc., Sigma Xi (pres. Rochester chpt. 1977-78). Research, publs. on the devel. of techniques for investigation of properties of minerals at pressures and temperatures within the earth's interior. Home: 765 Bostwick Rd Ithaca NY 14850 Office: Dept Geol Scis Cornell U Ithaca NY 14853

BASSETT, WOODSON WILLIAM, JR., lawyer; b. Okmulgee, Okla., Nov. 7, 1926; s. Woodson William and Bee Irene (Knerr) B.; m. Marynm Shaw, Dec. 16, 1950; children: Woodson William III, Beverly M., Tod Corbett. J.D., U. Ark., 1949. Bar: Ark. 1949. Employed in New Orleans and Monroe, La., 1949-51; claims examiner Employers Group Ins. Cos., 1949-51; mgr. Light Adjustment Co., 1951-56; v.p. legal dept. Preferred Ins. Cos., 1957-62; sr. partner Bassett, Bassett & Bassett, 1962—; spl. justice Ark. Supreme Ct.; mem. Ark. Bd. Law Examiners. Mem. editorial staff: Ark. Law Review, 9. Pres. Sherman Lollar Boys Baseball League, 1962; v.p. Babe Ruth Baseball Assn., 1968; chmn. bd. dirs. Fayetteville Public Library, 1975-79. Served with AUS, 1950-51. Mem. ABA, Ark. Bar Assn., Washington County Bar Assn. (pres. 1973-74), Am., Ark. trial lawyers assns., Am. Bd. Trial Advs., Def. Law Inst., Ark. Def. Counsel Assn., Delta Theta Phi, Kappa Sigma. Clubs: Elk., Fayetteville Country (dir.). Home: 2210 Manor Dr Fayetteville AR 72701 Office: 19 E Mountain St Fayetteville AR 72701

BASSETTI, FREDERICK FORDE, architect; b. Seattle, Jan. 31, 1917; s. Frederick Michael and Sophia (Forde) B.; m. Moira C. Feeney, June, 1971; children: Ann, Catherine, Margaret, Megan, Michael. B.Arch., U. Wash., 1942; M.Arch., Harvard U., 1946. Partner Bassetti & Morse, Seattle, 1947-62, Fred Bassetti & Co., 1962-79, Bassetti, Norton, Metler, 1980—; cons. Govt. Italy on exptl. housing, 1956-57; vis. prof. Columbia U., U. Wash., Rice U.; mem. jury Sunset mag., Nat. AIA Honor Awards, 1963, 78, Progressive Architecture, Louis Sullivan Honor Awards, 1981, Alaska Regional-City of Anchorage Library Archtl. Competition, 1981. Designer,, Alvar Aalto, Cambridge, Mass., 1945-46; Designer: U.S. Embassy, Lisbon, Portugal, Seattle Fed. Office Bldg., Seattle Aquarium; Author: Solid Shapes Laboratory. Pres., Allied Arts Seattle, 1970-71. Fellow AIA (pres. Seattle chpt. 1967), Tau Sigma Delta. Club: City. Home: 204 Maiden Ln E Seattle WA 98112 Office: 2021 3d Ave Seattle WA 98121

BASSIN, JULES, fgn. service officer; b. N.Y.C., Apr. 16, 1914; s. Abe and Bessie (Brooks) B.; m. Beatrice M. Kellner, Dec. 25, 1938; children—Arthur Jay, Nelson Jay. B.S., CCNY, 1936; J.D., N.Y.U., 1938; student, Criminal Investigation Sch., U.S. Army, 1943, Security Intelligence Sch., 1944, Mil. Govt. Sch., U. Va., 1944, Far East Civil Affairs, Harvard, 1945; grad., Armed Forces Staff Coll., 1960. Bar: N.Y. bar 1939. Dir. law div. Gen. Hdqrs., Supreme Comdr. Allied Powers, Tokyo, Japan, 1945-51; legal attache Am. embassy, Tokyo, 1951-56; also spl. asst. to ambassador for politico-mil. affairs; spl. asst. to ambassador for mut. security affairs Am. Embassy, Karachi, 1956-59; State Dept. faculty adviser Armed Forces Staff Coll., Norfolk, Va., 1960-62; chief titles and rank br. Dept. State, 1962-63, chief functional assignments br., 1963-65, dir. functional personnel program, 1965-67, spl. asst. to dep. undersec. state for adminstrn., 1967-69; dep. rep. of U.S. to European office UN and other internat. orgns.; also dep. chief U.S. mission with personal rank of minister, Geneva, Switzerland, 1969-74; cons. on refugee and migration affairs Dept. State, 1974—; cons. USIA, 1975-76. Served from 2d lt. to maj., Judge Adv. Gen. Corps. AUS, 1942-46; col. Res. Mem. Am. Fgn. Service Assn. Club: American Internat. (Geneva) (exec. com.). Home: 2891 Audubon Terr NW Washington DC 20008 Office: Dept of State Washington DC 20520

BASSIN, MILTON G., college president; b. Bklyn., Nov. 26, 1923; s. Max and Mirian (Berman) B.; m. Bernice Blasenheim, Dec. 20, 1953; children: Lori, Robert. B.M.E., CCNY, 1944; M.M.E., Poly. Inst. Bklyn., 1951. Registered profl. engr., N.Y. Instr. mech. tech. N.Y.C. Community Coll., 1948-50, asst. prof., 1950-56; assoc. prof. N.Y.C. Community coll., 1956-62; chmn. dept. math. N.Y.C. Community Coll., 1962-64, assoc. dean, 1964, dean, 1964-65, dean-in-charge, 1965-66, pres., 1966-71, York Coll., Jamaica, N.Y., 1971—; assoc. sci. staff, mech. engr. Brookhaven Nat. Lab., summers 1960-65; chmn. commn. higher edn. Middle State Assn. Colls. and Secondary Schs., 1977-78; assn. pres. Middle State Assn. Colls. And Secondary Schs., 1982; mem. nat. adv. commn. Am. Coll. Testing Program, 1968-73; mem. adv. com. N.Y. State Regents External Degree; mem. N.Y. State Adv. Council Continuing Higher Edn.; mem. adv. bd. Queens Assn. for Edn. Exceptionally Gifted Children; adviser sub-com. on edn. U.S. Senate Labor Com., 1970; mem. Queens Borough Pres.'s Com. on Med. Edn., Task Force for Study of Feasibility Nat. Service Acad., 1969; bd. dirs., treas. Council on Higher Ednl. Instns. Author: (with Brodsky) Statics and Strength of Materials, 1969; contbr. articles to profl. jours. Bd. dirs. Queens Council Arts, Queens Econ. Devel. Corp., Greater Jamaica Devel. Corp.; mem. Kingsbrook Jewish Med. Ctr.; bd. dirs. Queens chpt. NCCJ, Queens Symphony Orch., Queensborough Council for Social Welfare, Salvation Army Queens, Queensboro Soc. for Prevention of Cruelty to Children, Jamaica Arts Ctr.; mem. exec. bd. Queens Med. and Health Program, Nat. Assn. for Drug Abuse Problems. Served with USNR. Mem. Am. Soc. Engring. Edn., ASME, Jamaica C. of C. (exec. bd.), Queens C. of C. Home: 265 Park Ln Douglaston Manor NY 11363 Office: Office of the Pres York Coll Jamaica NY 11451

BASSIN, ROBERT HARRIS, virologist; b. Washington, May 2, 1938; s. Max Abraham and Sarah (Zitelman) B.; m. Shirley Lois Shooman, Aug. 6, 1961; children: Stuart Howard, Lawrence Alan, David Seth. B.A. cum laude, Princeton, 1959; Ph.D. (USPHS fellow), Rutgers U., 1966. Research assoc. Rutgers U. Inst. Microbiology, New Brunswick, N.J., 1965-66; NIH fellow Imperial Cancer Research Fund, London, Eng., 1966-68; staff virologist Nat. Cancer Inst., NIH, Bethesda, Md., 1968—, acting head, tumor virus sect., 1970-71, head viral biochemistry sect., 1973-82, head biochemistry of oncogenes sect., 1982—; Cons. virologist Univ. Labs., Highland Park, N.J., 1965-66. Mem. Am. Soc. for Microbiology, AAAS, Am. Assn. for Cancer Research, Soc. for Gen. Microbiology, Tissue Culture Assn., Sigma Xi. Home: 5519 Amesfield Ct Rockville MD 20853 Office: NIH Bldg 10 Room 5B46 Bethesda MD 20014

BASSINGTHWAIGHTE, JAMES BUCKLIN, medical researcher; b. Toronto, Ont., Can., Sept. 10, 1929; s. Ewart MacQuarrie and Velma Emeline B.; m. Joan Elizabeth Graham, June 18, 1955; children: Elizabeth Anne, Mary, Alan, Sarah, Rebecca. B.A., U. Toronto, 1951, M.D., 1955; postgrad., Med. Sch. London, 1957-58; Ph.D., Mayo Grad. Sch. Medicine U. Minn., 1964. Intern Toronto Gen. Hosp., 1955-56; physician Internat. Nickel Co., Sudbury and Matheson, Ont., 1956-57; house physician Hammersmith Hosp., London; postgrad. Med. Sch. London, 1957-58; teaching asst. physiology U. Minn., Mpls., 1961-62; fellow Mayo Grad. Sch. Medicine, Rochester, Minn., 1958-64, instr., 1964-67, asst. prof., 1967-69, assoc. prof., 1969-72; vis. prof. Pharmacology Inst., U. Bern, Switzerland, 1970-71; asso. prof. bioengring. U. Minn., 1972-75; prof. physiology Mayo Grad. Sch. Medicine, 1973-75, prof. medicine, 1975; prof. bioengring. and biomath U. Wash., Seattle, 1975—; dir. Center for Bioengring., 1975-80; vis. prof. medicine and physiology McGill U., 1979-81; NIH; study sect. mem., 1970-74, 80-83; chmn. Biotech. Resources Adv. Com., 1977-79, 1st Gordon Research Conf., 1976. Recipient NIH Research Career Devel. award, 1964-74; Louis and Artur Lucian award McGill U., 1979. Mem. Biophys. Soc. (asso. editor Biophys. Jour. 1980-83), AAAS, Am. Heart Assn. (council on circulation 1976—), Biomed. Engring. Soc. (dir. 1971-74, pres. 1977-78), Microcirculatory Soc. (mem. council 1975-78, 80-83), Am. Physiol. Soc. (mem. circulation group, editorial bd. 1972-76, 79-83, mem. edn. com.), Internat. Union Physiol. Scis. (U.S.A. nat. com. 1978—, U.S. del. to council 1980, 83, chmn. 1983—). Research and publs. in cardiovascular physiology and bioengring., biomath. and computer simulation with emphasis on ion and substrate exchange in heart. Home: 3150 E Laurelhurst Dr NE Seattle WA 98105 Office: Center for Bioengring WD-12 Univ Washington Seattle WA 98195

BASSIOUNI, M. CHERIF, lawyer, legal educator; b. Cairo, Egypt, Dec. 19, 1937; came to U.S., 1961, naturalized, 1966; s. Ibrahim and Amina (Khatab) B. A.B., Coll. Holy Family, Cairo, 1955; postgrad., Dijon U. Sch. Law, France, 1955-57, U. Geneva, Switzerland, 1957; LL.B., U. Cairo, 1961; J.D., Ind. U., 1964; LL.M., John Marshall Lawyers Inst., 1966; S.J.D., George Washington U., 1973. Bar: Ill. 1967, D.C. 1967. Practiced in, Chgo., 1967—; prof. law DePaul U., 1964—; Fulbright-Hays vis. prof. internat. criminal law U. Freiburg, Germany, 1970; vis. prof. law N.Y. U., 1971; guest scholar Woodrow Wilson Internat. Center for Scholars, Washington, 1972; cons. Chgo. Bd. Edn., 1965-69, chmn. advisory bd. law in Am. soc. project, 1973-75; mem. Ill. Com. Law and Justice Edn., 1977—; lectr. in field; spl. cons. 5th and 6th UN Congresses Crime Prevention, 1975, 80; bd. dirs., dean Internat. Inst. Advanced Criminal Scis., Italy; bd. dirs., sec.-gen. Internat. Assn. Penal Law, 1974—. Author: Criminal Law and Its Processes, 1969, The Law of Dissent and Riots, 1971, (with V.P. Nanda) International Criminal Law, 2 vols, 1973, (with Eugene Fisher) Storm Over the Arab World, 1972, International Extradition and World Public Order, 1974, International Terrorism and Political Crimes, 1975; Editor: Issues in the Mediterranean, 1976, Citizens Arrest: The Law of Arrest, Search and Seizure, 1977, Substantive Criminal Law, 1978, (with V. Savitski) The Criminal Justice System of the USSR, 1979, International Criminal Law: A Draft International Criminal Code, 1980, International Extradition in U.S. Law and Practice, 2 vols., 1983; Co-editor-in-chief: Revue Internat. de Droit Penal, 1973—; editor: The Globe, 1970-77; bd. editors: Am. Jour. Comparative Law, 1972—; adv. bd.: Jour Internat. Law and Policy. Decorated Order Merit, Egypt; commendatore Order Merit Italy, also grande ufficiale; recipient Outstanding Citizen of Year Citizenship Council Met. Chgo., 1967. Mem. Am. Soc. Internat. Law, Am. Bar Assn. (chmn. com. internat. legal edn. 1976-78, vice chmn. com. internat. criminal law), Ill. Bar Assn. (chmn. sect. internat. law 1972-73), Chgo. Bar Assn., Mid Am. Arab. C. of C. (chmn. 1973-74, 76-77, sec., gen. counsel 1970-77, pres.), Assn. Arab-Am. U. Grads. (bd. dirs. 1967-74, pres. 1969-70), Phi Alpha Delta. Home: 1448 N Lake Shore Dr Chicago IL 60611 Office: 25 E Jackson St Chicago IL 60604 *My philosophy in life is that the attainment of any meaningful goals can only be through a commitment to higher values which find their expression in tangible actions; that true freedom is not freedom from, but freedom for; and that the truly dedicated are those who not knowing what the result of their work may be, nonetheless continue to strive for what they believe in, even when without success.*

BASSLER, ROBERT COVEY, sculptor, educator; b. N.Y.C., Nov. 9, 1935; s. Robert Stein and Joan (Covey) B.; m. Linda Marie Allen, June 14, 1964. Student, Chouinard Art Inst., Los Angeles, 1953; B.A., Bard Coll., 1957; M.F.A., U. So. Calif., 1960. Instr. sculpture Occidental Coll., 1960-64; asst. prof. sculpture Calif. State U., Northridge, 1964-68, assoc. prof., 1969-72, prof., 1972—; artist in residence Calif. Inst. Tech., 1970-71; art film tour Arts Council, Gt. Britain, 1972-73; works represented in numerous public, coll. and univ. collections. One-man shows, Comara Gallery, Los Angeles, 1961, 63, Occidental Coll., Los Angeles, 1961, Bakersfield (Calif.) Coll., 1964, Los Angeles Mcpl. Gallery, Barnsdall Park, 1965, 81, Calif. State U., Northridge, 1965, Santa Barbara (Calif.) Mus. Art, 1968, Molly Barnes Gallery, Los Angeles, 1969, Occidental Coll., 1970, Baxter Art Gallery, Calif. Inst. Tech., 1971, Galerie La Demeure, Paris, 1972, Amerika-Haus, West Berlin; exhibited in group shows, Jewish Mus., N.Y.C., Milw. Art Center, San Francisco Mus., Los Angeles County Mus., Pasadena Mus., Long Beach (Calif.) Mus., LaJolla (Calif.) Mus., San Francisco Mus., Newport Harbor Art Mus., Oakland Mus., Esther Bear Gallery, Santa Barbara, Houston Mus., Ackland Meml. Art Center, Chapel Hill, N.C., Mus. Fine Arts, St. Petersburg, Fla., Jacksonville (Fla.) Art Mus., Musée d'Art Moderne, Paris, Galerie La Demeure, Paris, Redfern Gallery, London, U.S. Embassy, London, Calif. Inst. Tech., Amerika Haus, Berlin, Sculpture in the City, Century City, Calif., Fine Arts Gallery, San Diego, Art Park, Los Angeles.; represented in permanent collections, Wa Assocs. Inc., Los Angeles, Gensler & Assocs., Century City; urban sculpture, Security Pacific Plaza, Los Angeles. Served with AUS, 1959-62. Recipient creativity award Calif. State U., Northridge, 1978. Developed technique for casting clear polyester resin. Address: 8329 Melvin Ave Northridge CA 91324 *My current work explores visual phenomena created by light or physical juxtapositions and their resulting effects upon one's concept of reality. These phenomena represent to me a broader aspect of the limited realities normally experienced, and it is my intention to elevate awareness of these perceptions through my art.*

BASSNETT, PETER JAMES, librarian; b. Sutton Coldfield, Warwickshire, Eng., Nov. 16, 1933; emigrated to Can., 1966; s. Lionel and Phyllis (Mair) B.; m. Ann Gorham, Dec. 12, 1959; children: Madeline Jane, Sarah Catherine. A.Library Assn., N. Western Poly. Sch. Librarianship, London, 1963. Chartered librarian, U.K. Library asst. City of Westminster, London, 1958-61; tech. librarian Cement & Concrete Assn., London, 1963-64; librarian-in-charge London Borough of Haringey, 1964-66; adminstrv. asst. to dir. Calgary Pub. Library Bd., Alta., 1966-72; dir. systems and mgmt. North York Pub. Library Bd., Ont., 1972-75; dir. libraries Scarborough Pub. Library Bd., Ont., 1975—; exec. coordinator Ont. Pub. Libraries Programme Rev., Toronto, 1980-82. Contbr. articles to profl. jours. Chmn. adv. com. on library arts programme So. Alta. Inst. Tech., 1969-72. Fellow Library Assn. (U.K.); mem. Alta. Library Assn. (pres. 1969-70), Ont. Library Assn., Can. Library Assn., Pvt. Libraries Assn. Home: 106 25 Brimwood Blvd Scarborough ON Canada M1V 1E2 Office: 1076 Ellesmere Rd Scarborough ON Canada M1P 4P4

BASSO, KEITH HAMILTON, cultural anthropologist, linguist; b. Asheville, N.C., Mar. 15, 1940; s. Joseph Hamilton and Etolia (Simmons) B.; div. B.A., Harvard U., 1962; M.A., Stanford U., 1965, Ph.D., 1967. Asst. prof. anthropology U. Ariz.-Tucson, 1967-71, assoc. prof., 1972-76, prof., 1977-81; prof. cultural anthropology Yale U., 1982—; mem. Inst. Advanced Study, Princeton, N.J., 1975-76; Weatherhead fellow Sch. Am. Research, Santa Fe, N.M., 1977-78; cons. cultural and historical matters White Mountain and San Carlos Apache Tribes. Author: Portraits of the Whiteman, 1979, The Cibecue Apache, 1970; editor: Meaning in Anthropology, 1976, Western Apache Witchcraft, 1969. Mem. Assn. Am. Indian Affairs (dir. 1978—), Am. Anthropol. Assn., Am. Ethnol. Soc., Linguistic Soc. Am., AAAS. Democrat. Home: 51 Hillhouse Ave New Haven CT 06520 Office: Yale U Dept Anthropology Box 2114 Yale Sta New Haven CT 06520

BASSUK, RICHARD, real estate executive; b. N.Y.C., Jan. 21, 1941; s. Sidney and Jennie (Schatzberg) B.; m. Eslyn Emmer, June 14, 1964; children: Jonathan, Matthew. B.S. in Econs., U. Pa., 1962; LL.B., Harvard U., 1965. Bar: N.Y. 1964. Assoc. Carter, Ledyard & Milburn, N.Y.C., 1956-67; chmn. bd. Side Fund, Inc., N.Y.C., 1967-73; pres., dir. Starrett Housing Corp., N.Y.C., 1973—; dir. HRH Constrn. Corp., Levitt Corp., United Mchts., Mfrs. Bank. Dir. Altro Health and Rehab. Services, Inc., N.Y.C., 1983. Mem. Assn. Bar City N.Y., N.Y. State Bar Assn. Home: 69 Greenacres Ave Scarsdale NY 10583 Office: Starrett Housing Corp 909 3d Ave New York NY 10022

BAST, JAMES LOUIS, manufacturing company executive; b. Balt., Apr. 19, 1936; s. Louis and Evelyn Frances (Alling) B.; m. Mary Margaret Griffin, June 12, 1959; children: Andrew Griffin, James Mark, Cynthia Elizabeth. B.A., Columbia U., 1958, B.S.M.E., 1959;

M.B.A., NYU, 1968. With Pitney Bowes Inc., Stamford, Conn., 1963-72, 73—, chief fin. officer, 1976-82, v.p. fin., controller, 1976-77, sr. v.p. fin. and adminstrn., 1977-82, pres., chief exec. officer Dictaphone Corp. subs., Rye, N.Y., 1982—; div. controller Bunker Ramo Corp., Trumbull, Conn., 1972-73; dir. Perkin-Elmer Corp. Bd. incorporators Stamford Hosp. Served to lt. USN, 1959-63. Home: 120 Pheasant Run Wilton CT 06897 Office: Dictaphone Corp 120 Old Post Rd Rye NY 10580

BAST, RAY ROGER, utility company executive; b. Kutztown, Pa., Mar. 10, 1925; s. George E. and Mamie E. B.; m. Joan M. Bard, July 2, 1948; children: Roger, Steven, Gary. B.S. in Elec. Engring., Lehigh U., 1950. Registered profl. engr., N.J., Pa. Various engring. positions with Pub. Service Electric & Gas Co, Newark, 1950—; gen. mgr. engring. Pub. Service Electric & Gas Co., Newark, 1974—. Served with USN, 1943-46; PTO. Fellow IEEE. Republican. Home: 97 N Hillside Ave Chatham NJ 07928 Office: Pub Service Electric and Gas Co Park Plaza Newark NJ 07101

BASTABLE, CHARLES WILLIAM, JR., educator, cons.; b. Buffalo, Sept. 24, 1917; s. Charles William and Elsie (Fischer) B.; children—Catherine Stewart, William Talbot, Caroline Cory. B.S., Columbia, 1938, M.S., 1939, Ph.D., 1952. Accountant Haskins & Sells (C.P.A.'s), N.Y.C., 1939-41; mem. faculty Columbia, 1946—; dir. Office Facts and Figures, 1961-63, spl. asst. to pres., 1963-64, prof. bus., 1964—; controller Am. Geog. Soc., 1952-65, sec., 1961-65; bus. cons., 1952—. Contbr. profl. jours.; Book editor: Jour. Accountancy, 1973-76. Served to lt. comdr. USNR, 1941-46. Decorated Commendation medal. C.P.A., N.Y. Mem. Am. Accounting Assn. (v.p. 1961), Am. Inst. C.P.A.'s, Financial Execs. Inst. Home: 90 Durie Ave Closter NJ 07624 Office: Columbia Univ New York NY 10027

BASTEDO, PHILIP, lawyer; b. N.Y.C., Dec. 13, 1908; s. Walter A. and Helen Russell Kip (Priest) B.; m. Helen C. Wilmerding, Feb. 4, 1937; children: Philip R., W. Bayard, Cecily, Christopher K. A.B., Princeton U., 1929; J.D., Harvard U., 1932. Bar: N.Y. 1933. Since practiced in, N.Y.C.; mem. firm Wickes, Riddell, Bloomer, Jacobi & McGuire, 1941-70, counsel, 1970-78; Dep. dir. Office Civilian Def., Washington, 1942-43. Trustee Hosp. Spl. Surgery, pres., 1958-72; trustee United Hosp. Fund, chmn., 1978-84; treas., trustee Am. Acad. Rome, 1977—; trustee MacDowell Colony. Served with USNR, OSS, 1943-45. Mem. Council Fgn. Relations, Pilgrims, Bar Assn. City N.Y. Episcopalian. Clubs: River, Century. Home: 925 Park Ave New York NY 10028 also Dublin NH 03444

BASTIAN, DONALD NOEL, bishop; b. Estevan, Sask., Can., Dec. 25, 1925; s. Josiah and Esther Jane (Millington) B.; m. Kathleen Grace Swallow, Dec. 20, 1947; children: Carolyn Dawn, Donald Gregory, Robert Wilfrid, John David. B.A., Greenville Coll., 1953, S.T.D., 1974; B.D., Asbury Theol. Sem., 1956; D.D., Seattle Pacific U., 1965. Ordained to ministry Free Meth. Ch. N.Am., 1954; pastor chs., Lexington, Ky., 1953-56, New Westminster, B.C., Can., 1956-61; pastor College Free Meth. Ch., Greenville, Ill., 1961-74; bishop Free Meth. Ch. N. Am., Toronto, 1974—, mem. bd. adminstrn., 1964—, exec. editor Light and Life mag., 1974—. Author: The Mature Church Member, 1960, Along the Way, 1974, Belonging, 1974; editor: The Joy of Christian Fathering: Five First Person Accounts, 1979. Recipient Disting. Service award Asbury Theol. Sem., 1974; Presdl. award Greenville Coll., 1972. Mem. Canadian Wesleyan Theol. Soc., Meth. Hist. Soc., Nat. Assn. Evangelicals, Canadian Holiness Fedn. (pres. 1977, 78), Christian Holiness Assn. (v.p. 1977-78). Home: 96 Elmbrook Crescent Etobicoke ON Canada M9C 5E2 Office: 4315 Village Centre Ct Mississauga ON Canada L4Z 1S2

BASTIAN, JAMES HAROLD, air transport company executive, lawyer; b. Hannibal, Mo., Nov. 26, 1927; s. Ira Russell and Opal (Maddox) B.; m. Mary Jean Zugel, Feb. 5, 1955; children: Raphael Maria, Marquette Maria, Bartholomew Barnabas, Boniface Benedict. B.S., U. Mo., 1950; J.D. with honors, George Washington U., 1956. Bar: D.C., Va. 1956, U.S. Supreme Ct. 1960, Md. 1975. Since practiced in Washington; asso. Adair, Ulmer, Murchison, Kent & Ashby, 1956-61; v.p., sec. Pacific Corp., 1961-74; sec. Air Am., Inc., 1961-74, Air Asia Co. Ltd., 1973-74; partner Howard, Poe & Bastian, 1965—; sec., dir. Permawick Co., 1974—; v.p., sec., dir. So. Air Transport, Inc., 1974-79, pres., dir., 1979-83, chmn. bd., chief exec. officer, 1983—; pres., dir. Caribbean Air Services, Inc., San Juan, P.R., 1981—. Served with USNR, 1945-46. Mem. Am., Va., Md., D.C. bar assns., Order of Coif. Clubs: Nat. Aviation, Metropolitan (Washington); Aviation Exec. (Miami, Fla.); Congressional Country (Bethesda, Md.). Home: 9000 Congressional Ct Potomac MD 20854 Office: 1701 Pennsylvania Ave NW Washington DC 20006 also Southern Air Transport Inc Miami Internat Airport PO Box 52-4093 Miami FL 33152

BASU, ASIT PRAKAS, statistician; b. Bangladesh, Mar. 17, 1937; U.S., 1962, naturalized, 1979; s. Hari Pada and Himansu Prabha B.; m. Sandra Bergquist; children: Amit K., Shumit K. B.S., Calcutta U., 1956, M.S., 1958; Ph.D., U. Minn., 1966. Asst. prof. stats. U. Wis., Madison, 1966-68; mem. research staff IBM Research Center, Yorktown Heights, N.Y., 1968-70; asst. prof. indsl. engring. and mgmt. sci. Northwestern U., Evanston, Ill., 1970-71; asso. prof. math. U. Pitts., 1971-74; prof. stats. U. Mo., Columbia, 1974—, chmn. dept., 1976-83. Contbr. articles to profl. jours. Fellow Royal Statis. Soc.; fellow Am. Statis. Assn.; mem. Inst. Math. Stats., Calcutta Statis. Assn., Sigma Xi. Home: 3709 W Rollins Rd Columbia MO 65201 Office: Dept Stats Univ Mo Columbia MO 65211

BASYE, PAUL EDMOND, lawyer, educator; b. Nappanee, Ind., Oct. 2, 1901; s. Otto and Carrie C. (Wynekoop) B.; m. Margaret Louise deClercq, June 13, 1931; children—Charles E., John P. A.B., U. Mo., 1923; J.D., U. Chgo., 1926; LL.M., U. Mich., 1943, S.J.D., 1946. Bar: Mo. bar 1926, Calif. bar 1945. Practiced in, Kansas City, Mo., 1926-42, San Francisco, 1944-48, Burlingame, Calif., 1948—; asst. prof. law U. Kansas City, 1938-42; prof. law Hastings Coll. Law, U. Calif. at San Francisco, 1948—; prof. law summer sessions Stanford, 1950, U. Tex., 1956, U. So. Calif., 1963, 65. Author: Clearing Land Titles, 1953, 2d edit., 1970, (with Lewis M. Simes) Problems in Probate Law Including a Model Probate Code, 1946; Contbr. articles legal jours. Mem. Am. Bar Assn. (chmn. sect. real property, probate and trust law 1965-66), State Bar Calif. (lectr. continuing edn. program), Order of Coif, Phi Beta Kappa. Home: 1427 Floribunda Ave Burlingame CA 94010 Office: 20 Park Rd Burlingame CA 94010

BATA, GEORGE L., research institute director; b. Budapest, Hungary, Nov. 18, 1924; m. Judith Eve; 1 dau. B.A.Sc. in Chem. Engring, U. Budapest, 1946, M.Sc. in Chemistry, 1947; tutorial, U. Utah, 1972. Works engr. Monoplast Ltd., Budapest, 1947-49; cons. new product devel. Societe Gentia, Vincennes, France, 1949-50; devel. group leader Arborite Ltd., Lasalle, Que., Can., 1950-53; dir., v.p. Resinous Products Inc., Dorval, Que., 1953-54; research and devel. mgr. Varcum Chems. Ltd., Lindsay, Ont., Can., 1954-55; with Union Carbide Can. Ltd., 1955-78, dir. devel., 1958-68, dir. tech. plastics and chems. div., 1968-72, dir. tech., 1972-78; dir. Indsl. Materials Research Inst., NRC, Can., 1978—, mem. adv. com. biomed. engring., 1976—; gov. Sodalitas Danubiana Found. and Library, Inc., 1974—; past chmn. 25th Can. Chem. Engring. Conf.; Can. del. Internat. Orgn. for Standardization; bd. dirs. Can. Welding Bur., 1980—. Contbr. articles to profl. publs. Mem. Chem. Inst. Can., ASTM, Can. Inst. Mining and Metallurgy, Can. Research Mgmt. Assn. (past chmn.), Soc. Plastics Engrs. (past chmn. com. internat. relations), Can. Soc. Chem. Engring. (past dir. and v.p.), Assn. Sci., Engring. and Tech. Community of Can. (pres. 1981), World Congress Chem. Engring. (treas. 1979), l'Ordre des Chimistes du Quebec (past dir.). Roman Catholic. Research in high polymer physics, material sci. Patentee in field. Home: 43 Maplewood Ave Montreal PQ H2V 2L9 Canada

BATCHELDER, ARDERN R., retail executive; b. San Mateo, Calif., Dec. 7, 1910; s. Edgar B. and Edna M. (Hillebr) B.; m. Marjorie Lee Bowles, July 20, 1935; children: Ardern R., Gabrielle Ann. B.S., U. Calif. at Berkeley, 1933. Formerly chmn. bd. Emporium Capwell Co., San Francisco; exec. v.p., dir. Carter, Hawley Hale Stores, Inc., now hon. dir., cons. Mem. Calif. Retailers (dir.), Am. Retail Fedn. (dir.), Sons of Calif. Pioneers. Clubs: Orinda Country, Pacific Union, Calif. Home: 10 El Sueno Orinda CA 94563 Office: 150 Stockton St San Francisco CA 94108

BATCHELDER, WILLIAM F., state supreme court justice; b. 1926. A.B., U. N.H.; LL.B., Boston U. Bar: N.H. 1952. Former judge N.H. Superior Ct., Laconia and Plymouth; assoc. justice N.H. Supreme Ct., Concord, 1982—. Office: NH Supreme Ct Noble Dr Concord NH 03301 *

BATCHELOR, BARRINGTON DE VERE, civil engineer, educator; b. Lucea, Jamaica, W.I., July 2, 1928; s. Reginald Augustus and Vera Louise (O'Connor) B.; m. Alison Yvonnie Johnston, Sept. 14, 1960; children: Roger, Nicola, Wayne. B.Sc. with honors (Elias Issa scholar), U. Edinburgh, 1956; Ph.D. (Commonwealth scholar), U. London, 1963; postgrad, Nat. Def. Coll. Can., 1982-83. Registered profl. engr., Ont. Asst. engr. Sir William Halcrow & Partners, London, 1956-58; exec. engr. Ministry Edn., Jamaica, 1958-63, sr. exec. engr., 1963-64; partner Franks & Batchelor, cons. engrs., Kingston, Jamaica, 1964-66; asst. prof. civil engring. Queen's U., Kingston, Ont., Can., 1966-68, asso. prof., 1968-72, prof., 1972—; Mem. task force for devel. Ont. hwy. bridge design code Ministry Transp. and Communications. Mem. ASCE, Can. Soc. Civil Engrs., Am. Concret Inst., Instn. Civil Engrs. (U.K.), Instn. Engrs. (Jamaica). Home: 784 Ashley Crescent Kingston ON Canada Office: Dept Civil Engring Queen's U Kingston ON Canada

BATDORF, SAMUEL B(URBRIDGE), physicist; b. Jung Hsien, China, Mar. 31, 1914; s. Charles William and Nellie (Burbridge) B.; m. Carol Catherine Schweiss, July 19, 1940; children: Samuel Charles, Laura Ann. A.B., U. Calif., Berkeley, 1934, A.M., 1936, Ph.D., 1938. Asso. prof. physics U. Nev., 1938-43; aero. research scientist Langley Lab., NACA, 1943-51; dir. devel. Westinghouse Elec. Corp., Pitts., 1951-56; tech. dir. weapons systems Lockheed Missile & Space Co., Palo Alto, Calif., 1956-58; mgr. communication satellites Inst. Def. Analysis, Washington, 1958-59; dir. research in physics and electronics Aeronutronic, Newport Beach, Calif., 1959-62; prin. scientist Aerospace Corp., El Segundo, Calif., 1962-77; adj. prof. engring. and applied sci. UCLA, 1973—. Contbr. articles to profl. jours. Fellow Am. Phys. Soc., Am. Acad. Mechanics (pres. 1982-83), AIAA; mem. ASME (hon.). Republican. Presbyterian. Home: 5536 B Via La Mesa Laguna Hills CA 92653 Office: 6531 Boelter Hall UCLA Los Angeles CA 90024

BATE, GEOFFREY, physicist; b. Sheffield, Eng., Mar. 30, 1929; came to U.S., 1959, naturalized, 1977; s. Robert Henry and Beatrice (Batchford) B.; m. Christine Elinor Porter, Aug. 15, 1953; children: Simon, Matthew, Nicholas, Fiona. B.Sc. in Physics with honors, U. Sheffield, 1949, Ph.D., 1952. Sci. officer Royal Naval Sci. Service, 1953-56; research asso. U. B.C., Can., Vancouver, 1956-57, asst. prof. physics, 1957-59; mgr. rec. physics, gen. products div. IBM, Poughkeepsie, N.Y. and Boulder, Colo., 1959-78; sr. v.p. research and devel. Verbatim Corp., Sunnyvale, Calif., 1978—; mem. affiliate faculty dept. physics Colo. State U. Contbr. chpts. to books, articles to profl. jours. Fellow IEEE (Disting. lectr. Magnetics Soc.); mem. Am. Phys. Soc., Sigma Xi. Episcopalian. Patentee in field. Home: 23344 Camino Hermoso Los Altos Hills CA 94022 Office: 323 Soquel Way Sunnyvale CA 94081

BATE, WALTER JACKSON, English literature educator; b. Mankato, Minn., May 23, 1918; s. William G. and Isabel (Melick) B. A.B., Harvard U., 1939, M.A., 1940, Ph.D., 1942; L.H.D., Ind. U., 1969, U. Chgo., 1973; Litt.D., Merrimack Coll., 1970, Boston Coll., 1971, Rutgers U., 1979, Colby Coll., 1979. Mem. faculty English Harvard, 1946—, prof., 1956—, chmn. dept. history and lit., 1955-56, chmn. dept. English, 1956-63, 66-68, Abbott Lawrence Lowell prof. humanities, 1962-79, Kingsley Porter Univ. prof., 1979—. Author: Negative Capability, 1939, The Stylistic Development of Keats, 1945, From Classic to Romantic, 1946, Criticism: the Major Texts, 1952, The Achievement of Samuel Johnson, 1955, Prefaces to Criticism, 1959, Writings of Edmund Burke, 1960, John Keats, 1963 (Pulitzer Prize 1964), Coleridge, 1968, The Burden of the Past and the English Poet, 1970, Samuel Johnson, 1977 (Pulitzer Prize 1978, Nat. Book Award 1978, Nat. Book Critics Circle award 1978); co-editor: Biographia Literaria for the Collected Works of Coleridge, 1982; Contbg. editor: Bollingen edit. of Collected Coleridge, Yale edit. of Johnson. Guggenheim fellow, 1956, 65. Mem. Am. Philos. Soc., Brit. Acad., Am. Acad. Arts and Scis., Phi Beta Kappa (Christian Gauss award lit. history and criticism 1956, 64, 70). Home: Warren House Harvard U Cambridge MA 02138

BATEMAN, BARRY LYNN, educator; b. Jacksonville, Tex., Sept. 15, 1943; s. William Kermit and Mildred Fay (Johnson) B.; m. Linda Beth Hughes, Mar. 24, 1963; children—Verr Lynn, Walter Kermit. B.A., Tex. A. and M. U., 1965, M.S., 1967, Ph.D., 1970. Asst. dir. computer center U. Southwestern La., Lafayette, 1969-70, head computer sci., 1969-72, acting dir. computer center, 1970-72; asso. prof., chmn. dept. computer sci. Tex. Tech U. at Lubbock, 1972-76, asso. prof. biomed. engring. and computer medicine, 1973-76; prof. computer sci., prof. bus. adminstrn., exec. dir. for computer affairs, also prof. health edn. So. Ill. U., Carbondale, also; So. Ill. U. Sch. Medicine, Springfield, 1976-81; asst. v.p. gen. adminstrn. U. Md. System, Adelphi, 1981—; bd. dirs. State of Ill. Computer Services Adv. Council, 1976—. Co-author 2 computer sci. text books; contbr. articles to profl. jours. NASA traineeship, 1966-69. Fellow Tex. Acad. Sci. (v.p., mem. exec. com. 1975-76); mem. La. Acad. Sci., Soc. Indsl. and Applied Math, Assn. Computing Machinery (bd. dirs. spl. interest group on computer sci. edn. 1973-75, 75-77, chmn. com. on student membership and chpts. 1974-78, chmn. judges for sci. and engring. fair 1977-81, program chmn. spl. interest group on univ. computing centers 1979), Soc. Computer Simulation, Com. Curriculum in Computer Sci., Mid-Ill. Computer Consortium (dir. 1976-80), AAAS (dir. 1978-80), Assn. Instl. Research (dir. 1978-81), Soc. Mgmt. Info. Services (dir. 1978-81), Data Processing Mgmt. Assn. (dir. 1974—), Math. Assn. Am., Nat. Assn. Coll. and Univ. Bus. Officers, Soc. Coll. and Univ. Planning (chmn. membership com. 1978-81), Sigma Xi, Pi Mu Epsilon, Alpha Pi Mu, Upsilon Pi Epsilon (nat. pres. 1972-74, exec. council 1972-77, nat. sec. 1974—). Home: 15104 Narrows Ln Bowie MD 20716 Office: Office of Gen Adminstrn Univ Md 3300 Metzerott Rd Adelphi MD 20743

BATEMAN, DUPUY, JR., indsl. exec.; b. Henderson, Tex., Dec. 19, 1904; s. Dupuy and Lola Bell (Harris) B.; m. Nancy Gay, Apr. 15, 1945; children—Sally, Elizabeth, George, Dupuy III. Student, Rice Inst., 1922-25. With Anderson, Clayton & Co. (or subsidiaries), Houston, 1927-64, v.p., dir., 1945-59, exec. v.p., dir., 1959-64; partner Anderson, Clayton & Fleming, N.Y.C., 1945-64, Golightly & Bateman (mgmt. cons.), 1964-65; v.p., asst. to pres. for corporate devel. Rockwell Internat. Corp. (formerly N.Am. Rockwell Corp.), 1965-68, sr. v.p., dir., 1968-72, adv. dir., 1973-75, cons., 1973-79; dir. Envirotech Corp., Menlo Park, Calif., 1969-76, Collin's Radio Co., Dallas, 1971-74, AVM Corp., Pitts. Mem. standing liturgical commn. P.E. ch., 1960-79, mem. exec. council, 1970-79; chmn. program and budget com. Gen. Conv., 1973, 76; Bd. dirs. St. Francis Gen. Hosp., Pitts. Mem. Hist. Soc. Episcopal Ch. (pres. 1974-75, dir.). Episcopalian. Home: 418 Emerson St Pittsburgh PA 15206 Office: AVM Corp 525 William Penn Pl Pittsburgh PA 15219

BATEMAN, DURWARD FRANKLIN, plant pathologist, educator; b. Tyner, N.C., May 28, 1934; s. Benny Franklin and Grace (Cale) B.; m. Shirley Eugenia Byrum, June 23, 1953; children: Cynthia Anne, Brenda Sue, Diane Mia. B.S., N.C. State Coll., 1956; M.S., Cornell U., 1958, Ph.D., 1960. Asst. prof. dept. plant pathology Cornell U., Ithaca, N.Y., 1960-65, assoc. prof., 1965-69, prof., 1969-70, prof., chmn. dept., 1970-79, tchr. grad. course in area of disease and pathogen physiology, 1963-79, field rep. dept. plant pathology, 1966-69; cons. NIH, 1968; vis. prof. N.C. State U., Raleigh, 1975, assoc. dean; also dir. N.C. Agrl. Research Service, 1979—; vice chmn. So. Agrl. Expt. Sta. Dirs. Assn., 1983; chmn. legis. subcom. of com. on policy So. Agrl. Expt. Sta., 1983; mem. biotech. com. Nat. Assn. State Univs. and Land Grant Colls., 1982—. Contbr. articles to profl. jours. Spl. NIH fellow U. Calif., Davis, 1967. Fellow Am. Phytopath. Soc. (councilor-at-large 1973, sr. councilor-at-large 1974, v.p. 1975, pres. 1977-78); mem. AAAS, Intersoc. Consortium for Plant Protection (exec. com. 1977-80), Internat. Soc. Plant Pathology, Sigma Xi, Phi Kappa Phi, Kappa Phi Kappa, Gamma Sigma Delta. Home: 4026 Glen Laurel Ln Raleigh NC 27612

BATEMAN, FRED WILLOM, judge; b. Roper, N.C., Sept. 18, 1916; s. N.D. and Eloise (Tarkenton) B.; m. Frances M. Sondag, June 12, 1944; 1 son, Michael Stuart. B.A., Wake Forest Coll., 1939; postgrad., Law Sch., U. N.C., 1939-42. Bar: Ill. 1947, Va. 1950, also U.S. Supreme Ct 1950. Pvt. practice, Newport News, Va., 1952-81; judge Circuit Ct., Newport News, 1981—; Mem. Va. Senate from, Newport News, 1960-68; permanent mem. Fed. Jud. Conf. for 4th circuit; mem. Va. Jud. Inquiry and Rev. Commn., 1971-78. Dir. First Va. Bank of Tidewater.; Mem. Va. Bicentennial com., 1971—, Warwick (Va.) Electorial Bd., 1955; mgr. Congl. and Senatorial Democratic campaigns, 1955—; chmn. Jefferson Jackson Dinner, 1965. Served to comdr. USNR; PTO; Res. ret. Fellow Am. Bar Found.; Mem. Va. State Bar (pres. 1964-65), ABA (ho. of dels. 1974-80), Va. Bar Assn., Nat. Conf. Bar Pres. Clubs: Rotary (Paul Harris fellow), Elk, Mason. Home: 23 Cedar Ln Newport News VA 23601 Office: 2501 Huntington Ave Newport News VA 23607

BATEMAN, HERBERT HARVELL, congressman; b. Elizabeth City, N.C., Aug. 7, 1928; m. Laura Yacobi; children: Herbert Harvell, Laura Margaret. B.A., Coll. William and Mary, 1949; J.D., Georgetown U., 1956. Bar: Va. 1956. Practice law, Newport News, Va., 1957—; law clk. U.S. Ct. Appeals for D.C. Cir., 1956-57; mem. firm Jones, Blechman, Woltz & Kelly, 1957-82; mem. Va. Senate, 1968-82, chmn. consumer credit study commn., 1970-74, chmn. milk commn. study commn., 1973-75; mem. 98th Congress from 1st Va. Dist. Mem. adv. bd. Mary Immaculate Hosp. Newport News; pres. Peninsula United Fund, 1966-67; chmn. Peninsula Arena-Auditorium Authority, 1964-68; pres. Newport News Homeownership Assn., 1969-71; commr. Peninsula Ports Authority Va., 1969-74; bd. dirs. Peninsula Econ. Devel. Council, 1968—; coordinator Citizens for Rev. Constrn., 1970; chmn. Heart Fund campaign, Newport News, 1971. Served to 1st lt. USAF, 1951-53. Mem. ABA, Va. Bar Assn., Va. Jaycees (past pres.), U.S. Jaycees (gen. legal counsel 1962-63), Hampton Rds. Jaycees (hon. pres. 1960-63), Peninsula C. of C. (chmn. legis. com. 1970-72), Omicron Delta Kappa, Phi Delta Phi, Pi Kappa Alpha. Republican. Club: Newport News Propellor. Office: Rm 1518 Longworth House Office Bldg Washington DC 20515

BATEMAN, JOHN JAY, classics educator; b. Elmira, N.Y., Feb. 17, 1931; s. Joseph Earl and Etha M. (Edwards) B.; m. Patricia Ann Hageman, July 5, 1952; children: Kristine M., Kathleen A., John Eric. B.A., U. Toronto, 1953; M.A., Cornell U., 1954, Ph.D., 1958. Lectr. Univ. Coll., U. Toronto, 1956-57; lectr., then asst. prof. U. Ottawa, 1957-60; mem. faculty U. Ill., Urbana, 1960—, prof. classics and speech, 1968—, head dept. classics, 1966-73, acting dir. Sch. Humanities, 1973-74. Author articles. Democratic precinct committeeman, 1964-68; sec. Champaign Dem. Central Com., 1965-66. Mem. Am. Philol. Assn. (sec.-treas. 1968-73), Archeol. Inst. Am., Classical Assn. Middle West and South, Renaissance Soc. Am. Home: 706 W Healey St Champaign IL 61820 Office: Fgn Lang Bldg Univ Ill Urbana IL 61801

BATEMAN, JOHN ROGER, investment holding company executive; b. Medford, Oreg., Sept. 21, 1927; s. Joseph Nielson and Bessie Mable (Jackson) B.; children: David, Sally, Susan. Student, U. Redlands, 1944-45, Mont. Sch. Mines, 1945, Colo. Coll., 1945-46, San Deigo State Coll., 1948; B.S. with honors, U. Calif.-Berkeley, 1951, M.B.A., 1952. Acctg. trainee Standard Oil Co. Calif., San Francisco, 1952; sr. acct. Salvik & Ponder, C.P.A.s, Corpus Christi, Tex., 1953-57; chief acct. Coastal States Corp., Corpus Christi, 1957-59, treas., 1959-66, v.p. fin., 1963-66; mng. ptnr. Bateman Investments, Corpus Christi, 1967—, Bateman Luxor Group Ltd., 1972-75; pres., chmn. bd. Bay Fabricators, Inc., 1973-78, dir., 1972-78, pres., chmn. bd., 1975—, Bateman Industries, Inc., 1976—, Bay Heat Transfer Corp., 1977—; ptnr. Bajon Investments, 1980; chmn. bd. Bajon Corp., 1980—; ptnr. Jaro Leasing, 1980—, Act I Properties, 1981—; chmn. bd. Bajon Signs Co., 1982—, Bajon Devel. Corp., 1981-83. Bd. dirs., pres., treas. Little Theatre Corpus Christie, 1964-68; ofcl. bd. 1st United Methodist Ch., 1964-67, 70-73, 78-80; bd. govs. United Way Coastal Bend, 1964-67, 73-83, campaign chmn., 1977, pres., 1981; mem. exec. council USO, 1971-73; bd. dirs. Camp Fire Girls, 1967-69, Tex. Bd. Mental Health and Mental Retardation, 1981—; del. Tex. Republican Com., 1972, 76; Tex. mem. Nat. Rep. Senatorial Com., 1978-81, Rep. Eagles, 1980-81; mem. Rep. Govs. Assn., 1980-81; co-chmn. Tex. Rep. Fin. Com., 1980-81. Served to lt. (j.g.) UNSR, 1945-50. Mem. Tex. Soc. C.P.A.s, Navy League U.S., Confederate Air Force, Pima Air. Mus., Phi Beta Kappa, Beta Alpha Psi, Beta Gamma Sigma, Alpha Lambda Nu. Clubs: Corpus Christi Country, Town, Nueces. Lodge: Rotary. Home: 401 Cape Cod Corpus Christi TX 740 Office: PO Box 2267 Corpus Christi TX 78403 *When disaster strikes, instead of giving up, I just say "Well that's number one," pick myself up, piece the plan back together and keep going until I finally get past defeat number five to final sucess.*

BATEMAN, PAUL TREVIER, educator, mathematician; b. Phila., June 6, 1919; s. Harold John and Anna (Yeager) B.; m. Felice Hilda Davidson, June 25, 1948; 1 dau., Sarah Elizabeth. A.B., U. Pa., 1939, A.M., 1940, Ph.D., 1946. Lectr. Bryn Mawr Coll., 1945-46; instr. Yale, 1946-48; mem. Inst. Advanced Study, Princeton, 1948-50; mem. faculty U. Ill. at Urbana, 1950—, prof. math., 1958—, head dept., 1965-80; vis. prof. U. Pa., 1961-62, City U. N.Y., 1964-65, U. Mich., 1980-81. Sr. Postdoctoral fellow NSF, 1956-57. Mem. Math. Assn. Am., London Math Soc., Am. Math Soc. (assoc. sec. 1966-83, trustee

1971-75, mem.-at-large council 1961-63), AAUP. Home: 108 The Meadows Urbana IL 61801

BATEMAN, ROBERT MCLELLAN, painter; b. Toronto, Ont., Can., May 24, 1930; s. Joseph Wilbur and Anne (McLellan) B.; m. Suzanne Bowermann, June, 1961 (div. 1975); children: Christopher, Robbie. B.A. in Geography with honors, U. Toronto, 1955; D.Sc., Carleton U., Ottawa, 1982; LL.D., Brock U., St. Catherine, Ont., 1982; D.Letters for Fine Arts, McMater U., Hamilton, Ont., 1983. Tchr. Nelson High Sch., Burlington, Ont., 1958-63, 65-69; tchr. geography, Nigeria, 1963-65; art cons. Halton Bd. Edn., Burlington, Ont., 1969-70; tchr. art Lord Elgin High Sch., Burlington, Ont., 1970-76; dir. Art Gallery Ont., Toronto, 1973-74. Represented permanetnt collections, Govt. Ont. Art Collection, permanent collections, Toronto Bd. Trade, H.R.H. The Prince of Wales, The Late Princess Grace of Monaco. Bd. dirs. Elsa Wild Animal Appeal, Toronto, 1975—; commr. Niagara Escarpment Commn., Georgetown, Ont., 1973—. Recipient Queen Elizabeth Silver Jubilee medal Govt. of Can., 1977; named Artist of Yr. Am. Artist Collection, 1980; recipient award of merit Soc. Animal Artisits, 1979, 80, 81; named Master Artist Leigh Yawkey Woodson Mus., Wausau, Wis., 1982. Mem. Northwest Rendezvous Exhbn. (recipient award of merit 1981, 82), Audubon Soc. (hon.), Can. Wildlife Fedn., Burlington Cultural Ctr., Fedn. Ont. Naturalist (dir. 1968-71). Home and Office: 2400 Britannia Rd Rural Route 2 Milton ON Canada L9T 2X6

BATES, ALAN (ARTHUR BATES), actor; b. Derbyshire, Eng., Feb. 17, 1934; s. Harold Arthur and Florence Mary (Wheatcroft) B.; m. Victoria Ward, May, 1970; twin sons. Student, Royal Acad. Dramatic Art, London. Appeared in: stage productions including Hamlet, all in London, Butley, London and N.Y.C., Poor Richard, N.Y.C., Richard III and The Merry Wives of Windsor at, Stratford (Ont.) Festival, Taming of the Shrew at, Stratford-on-Avon, Eng., 1973, Life Class, 1974, Otherwise Engaged, 1975, The Seagull, 1976, Stage Struck, 1979-80, A Patriot for Me, 1983; films include The Fixer (Oscar nominee), Women in Love, The Three Sisters, A Day in the Death of Joe Egg, The Go-Between, Second Best, Impossible Object, Butley, In Celebration, Royal Flash, An Unmarried Woman, The Shout, The Rose, Very Like a Whale, Nijinsky, Quartet, The Return of the Soldier, 1982, The Wicked Lady, 1983; television plays include The Collection, 1977, The Mayor of Casterbridge, 1978, Very Like a Whale, The Trespasser, 1981, A Voyage Round my Father, 1982, A Englishman Abroad, 1983, Separate Tables, 1983, Dr. Fischer of Geneva, 1984. Served with RAF. Recipient Clarence Derwent award Royal Acad. Dramatic Art; Antoinette Perry Best Actor award for Butley, 1973; Evening Standard award, 1972. Office: care Michael Linnit Chatto and Linnit Ltd Globe Theatre Shaftesbury Ave London W 1 England

BATES, BARON KENT, automobile company executive; b. Los Angeles, Oct. 25, 1934; s. Paul L. and Gwendolin (Mann) B.; m. Doris M. Jackson, Nov. 19, 1966 (div.); children: Ned Alexander, Sarah Elizabeth; m. Dorothy May Peltyn, July 24, 1982. B.A., Princeton U., 1956. Pub. relations staff Chrysler Corp., Detroit, 1957-60, Volkswagon of Am., Englewood Cliffs, N.J., 1961-67, pub. relations mgr., 1968-76; dir. pub. relations Volkswagen of Am., Englewood Cliffs, N.J., 1977-79; v.p. pub. relations Chrysler Corp., Detroit, 1980—. Served to 1st lt. U.S. Army, 1957. Mem. Internat. Motor Press Assn., Detroit Press Club, Automobile Hall of Fame. Club: Detroit Athletic. Home: 2026 W Bend Ct West Bloomfield MI 48033 Office: Chrysler Corp 12000 Chrysler Dr Highland Park MI 48203

BATES, CHARLES CARPENTER, oceanographer; b. nr. Harrison, Ill., 1918; s. Carl Albert and Vera Elizabeth (Carpenter) B.; m. Pauline Barta; children: Nancy Ann, Priscilla Jane, Sally Jean. Grad. (Rector scholar 1936-39), DePauw U., 1939; M.A., U. Calif. at Los Angeles, 1944; Ph.D. in Geol. Oceanography, Tex. A. and M. Coll., 1953; student, Cath. U., 1947-48, Johns Hopkins, 1951, George Washington U., 1954. Geophys. trainee Carter Oil Co., 1939-41; spl. asst. to pres. Am. Meteorol. Soc., 1945-46; mem. survey phys. and geol. environment Marshall Is. relative to pending Bikini atomic bomb tests, 1946; with div. oceanography U.S. Navy Hydrographic Office, 1946-57, dept. dir. div., 1953-57; environmental surveillance coordinator Office Devel. Coordinator, Office Naval Research, 1957-60; chief underground nuclear test detection br. Advanced Research Projects Agy., Office Sec. Def., 1960-64; sci. and tech. dir. U.S. Naval Oceanographic Office, 1964-68; sci. adviser to comdt., also chief scientist Office Research and Devel., USCG, 1968-79; environ. cons., 1979—; part-time cons. in field and industry, 1946-52; Mem. bd. experts Civil Service Examiners, 1954-60; mem. adv. com. postdoctoral awards for Fulbright grants NRC, 1957-60, chmn., 1959-60; vis. geoscientist Am. Geol. Inst., 1959-60; mem. meteorology panel, space sci. bd. Nat. Acad. Sci., 1959-61; mem. Mcht. Marine Council, 1968-71, Nat. Transp. Research Bd., 1968-71; mem. sea grant adv. council La. State U. System, 1968-79; co-chmn. U.S.-Japan panel marine facilities U.S.-Japan Natural Resource Program, 1969-71. Author: Geophysics in Affairs of Man, 1982; numerous articles, reports in field.; Editor: meteorol. terms Glossary of Geology and Related Items, 1957. Served to capt. USAAF, 1941-45. Decorated Bronze Star; recipient U.S. Navy Meritorious Civilian award, 1962; U.S. Navy Superior Civilian Service award, 1969; U.S. Dept. Transp. Silver medal, 1973. Mem. Am. Geophys. Union (chmn. com. interaction sea and atmosphere 1950, mem. council 1964-67), Soc. Exploration Geophysicists (council 1963-67, v.p. 1965-66, hon. mem. 1981), Am. Meteorol. Soc. (chmn. com. indsl. bus. and agrl. meteorology 1946-48), Am. Assn. Petroleum Geologists (President's award 1954), Am. Mgmt. Assn. (research and devel. council 1970-79), Sigma Xi. Home: 136 W La Pintura Green Valley AZ 85614 Office: PO Box 191 Green Valley AZ 85622

BATES, CHARLES TURNER, lawyer, broadcast exec.; b. Tarrytown, N.Y., Jan. 3, 1932; s. Harry Cole and Helen Morris (Turner) B. A.B., Hamilton Coll., 1953; LL.B., Yale U., 1958. Bar: N.Y. bar 1958. Atty. firm Townley & Updike, N.Y.C., 1958-69; atty. CBS Inc., N.Y.C., 1969-71, asst. sec., 1971-74, sec., asso. gen. counsel, 1974—; Trustee Hackley Sch., Tarrytown, N.Y., 1972-76, 81—, Hamilton Coll., 1975-79. Served with Ordnance U.S. Army, 1953-55. Mem. Am. Bar Assn., Assn. Bar City N.Y., Am. Soc. Corp. Secs., Stockholders Relations Soc. N.Y., Phi Beta Kappa, Sigma Phi. Republican. Episcopalian. Office: CBS Inc 51 W 52d St New York NY 10019

BATES, DAVID MARTIN, botanist, educator; b. Everett, Mass., May 31, 1934; s. Leslie Mariner and Ann Louise (Gustafson) B.; m. Jayne Sandra Schwarz, Sept. 4, 1956; children: Jonathan David, Leslie Mariner. B.S., Cornell U., 1959; Ph.D., UCLA, 1963. Postdoctoral fellow Brit. Mus., 1962-63; asst. prof. Cornell U., Ithaca, N.Y., 1963-69, assoc. prof., 1969-75, prof., 1975—, dir. L.M. Bailey Hortorium, 1969—. Author: Hortus Third. Served with U.S. Army, 1954-56. NSF fellow; recipient Gold medal Garden Club Am. Mem. Bot. Soc. Am., Am. Soc. Plant Taxonomists, Internat. Assn. Plant Taxonomy, Soc. Econ. Botany, AAAS, Societe de Biogeographie, Northwest Ornamental Hort. Soc. Home: 140 Forest Home Dr Ithaca NY 14853 Office: L H Bailery Hortorium 467 mann Library Cornell U Ithaca NY 14853

BATES, DAVID VINCENT, physician, physiology educator; b. Kent, Eng., May 20, 1922; s. John Vincent and Alice (Dickins) B.; m. Margaret Sutton, Mar. 24, 1948; children—Anne Elizabeth, Joanna Margaret, Andrew Vincent. M.B., B.Ch., Cambridge (Eng.) U., 1945, M.D., 1954. Intern, resident St. Bartholomew Hosp., 1944- 45; sr. lectr. medicine U. London Sch. Medicine, 1953-56; research fellow U. Pa., 1952; physician Royal Victoria Hosp., Montreal, Can., 1967—; asst. prof. medicine McGill U. Sch. Medicine, 1956-72, prof. exptl. medicine, 1965-72, asso. dean grad. studies and research, 1964-67, chmn. dept. physiology, 1967-72; dean, faculty of medicine U. B.C., 1972-77, prof. physiology and medicine, 1972—; dir. respiratory div., joint cardiorespiratory service Royal Victoria, Montreal Childrens hosps., 1957-67; mem. Sci. Council Can., 1973-79. Author: (with Christie) Respiratory Function in Disease, 1965, A Citizens Guide to Air Pollution, 1972; also articles. Fellow Royal Coll. Physicians (London), Royal Coll. Physicians (Can.), Royal Soc. Can., A.C.P.; mem. Am., Canadian socs. clin. investigation, Am., Canadian physiol. socs., Physiol. Soc. London, Sci. Council Can. Home: 4891 College Highroad Vancouver BC V6T 1G6 Canada

BATES, EDWARD BRILL, insurance company executive; b. Lexington, Mo., May 14, 1919; s. Worth and Faye Marvin (Brill) B.; m. Mary Louise Van Sickle; children: Lynn Louise Bates Russell, Stephen Worth. B.A. in Bus. Adminstrn, U. Chgo., 1940; LL.D. (hon.), Trinity Coll., Hartford, Conn., 1974, L.H.D., U. Hartford, 1976. With Conn. Mut. Life Ins. Co., 1946—, gen. agt., Kansas City, 1949-53, Los Angeles, 1953-59, 2d agy. v.p., Hartford, 1960-61, v.p., 1961-62, exec. v.p., 1962-67, pres., 1967-77, chmn., 1977—; dir. Stanley Works, CBT Corp.; trustee N.E. Utilities. Bd. dirs. Inst. Living. Mem. Am. Council Life Ins. (dir.). Clubs: Hartford; Hartford Golf (West Hartford); Country of Fla. (Delray Beach). Home: 46 Ironwood Rd West Hartford CT 06117 Office: 140 Garden St Hartford CT 06115

BATES, G(EORGE) WALLACE, organization executive, lawyer; b. Battle Lake, Minn., May 17, 1908; s. George Wilson and Anna (Burke) B.; m. Frances E. Trump, June 25, 1932 (dec. 1978); children: Elizabeth B. (Mrs. Robert Zenowich), Anne W. A.B., U. Minn., 1928, LL.B., 1930; LL.M., Columbia U., 1931. Bar: Minn. 1930, N.Y. 1936, Mo. 1950. With firm Root, Clark, Buckner & Ballantine, N.Y.C., 1931-43; atty. Am. Tel. & Tel. Co., N.Y.C., 1943-50, gen. atty., 1953-57; gen. counsel Southwestern Bell Telephone Co., St. Louis, 1950-53; v.p., gen. counsel, dir. N.Y. Telephone Co. and Empire City Subway Co., Ltd., 1958-73; pres. Bus. Roundtable, N.Y.C., 1973—. Bd. dirs. Police Athletic League, State Traffic Safety Council N.Y., Center for Public Resources, Inc. Mem. N.Y. C. of C. (exec. com. 1968-70, pres. 1970-71), Am. Law Inst., ABA (ho. of dels. 1973-75), N.Y. State Bar Assn. (v.p. 1974-75, exec. com. 1969-72, ho. of dels. 1972-75), Assn. Bar City N.Y. Clubs: Indian Harbor Yacht (Greenwich); Pinnacle, University (N.Y.C.). Home: Greenwich CT 06830 Office: 200 Park Ave New York NY 10166

BATES, GLADYS EDGERLY, sculptor; b. Hopewell, N.J., July 15, 1896; d. Webster and Edna Reid (Boyts) Edgerly; m. Kenneth Bates, July 12, 1923; children—Kenneth, David Dunlop, Thomas Edgerly. Student, Corcoran Gallery Sch. of Art, 1910-16, Pa. Acad. Fine Arts, 1916-21. Exhibited in one-man show, Pen and Brush Club, N.Y.C., 1945; exhibited in two-man shows, including, Woodmere Gallery, Phila., 1948, Lyman Allyn Mus., New London, Conn., 1952, Madison (Conn.) Art Gallery, 1958, Rowayton (Conn.) Art Gallery, 1961, Noank (Conn.) Arts Club, 1967, group shows including, Art Inst. Chgo., 1934, 39, Tex. Centennial, Dallas, 1936, Carnegie Inst., Pitts., 1938, Archtl. League, N.Y.C., 1941, Addison Gallery, Andover, Mass., 1941, 51, Phila. Mus., 1949, Phila. Art Alliance, 1950, N.J. State Mus., Trenton, 1953; represented in permanent collections including, Met. Mus. Art, N.Y.C., Pa. Acad. Fine Arts, Phila., N.J. State Mus. Recipient awards including Widener Gold medal Pa. Acad. Fine Arts, 1931; nat. assn. medal; Huntingdon prize Nat. Assn. Women Artists, 1934; Fellow Nat. Sculpture Soc. Home: 15 Grove Ave Mystic CT 06355

BATES, HENRY GEORGE, clergyman; b. Snodland, Eng., Nov. 17, 1919; came to U.S., 1929, naturalized, 1947; s. Henry Philippe and Annie (Parker) B.; m. Ruby Maxine Younce, Jan. 27, 1945; children—Maxine Bates Craver, Nancy Bates McGraw, Lillian Bates Mellott, Mary Ellen. Student, Temple U., 1940-41, Park Coll., 1942-43; A.B., Ashland (Ohio) Coll., 1944; B.D., Ashland Theol. Sem., 1946; S.T.M., Gettysburg Luth. Sem., 1948. Ordained to ministry Brethren Ch., 1946; pastor St. James (Md.) Brethren Ch., 1946-48; prof. O.T. and Hebrew Ashland Theol. Sem., 1948-55; pastor North Manchester (Ind.) Brethren Ch., 1955-59, Vinco (Pa.) Brethren Ch., 1959-71, Wayne Heights Brethren Ch., Waynesboro, Pa., 1971—; part-time prof. O.T. and Christian edn. Broadfording Christian Coll., Hagerstown, Md., 1976—; mem. Pa. Dist. Bd. Evangelists; moderator Pa. Dist. of Brethren Ch., 1961, 69, Gen. Conf., 1973; Bd. dirs. Camp Peniel, Brethren Care Retirement Village, Riverside Christian Tng. Sch., 1961-69. Writer: Sunday Sch. Quar, 1952—; Author: Old Testament Hebrew for Beginning Students, 1951, The Old Testament in Perspective, 1953. Home: 124 Strickler Ave Waynesboro PA 17268 Office: 120 Strickler Ave Waynesboro PA 17268

BATES, JAMES EARL, professional college president; b. Ligonier, Pa., Aug. 10, 1923; s. Earl Barrington and Margaret (Kinsey) B.; m. Lauralou Courtney, Apr. 15, 1950; children: Susan Bates Jaren, Sara Bates Hudson, James Barrington, Willa Laurens. D.S.C., Temple U., 1946; D.P.M., Pa. Coll. Podiatric Medicine, 1970; Ed.D. (hon.), Franklin Pierce Coll., 1972. Practice podiatric medicine, Phila., 1946-71; asso. prof. roentgenology Temple U., 1948-60; prof., pres. Pa. Coll. Podiatric Medicine, Phila., 1962—; cons. BHRD Region IX, HEW, San Francisco, 1973-74, Region V, Chgo., 1974-75; del. Nat. Commn. on Certifying Health Manpower; mem. health adv. com. HEW, 1972-73; adv. panel for podiatry Inst. Medicine, Nat. Acad. Scis., 1972-74; adv. council for comprehensive health planning Pa. Dept. Health, 1972-75, health manpower task force edn. com., 1976; mem. task force on health manpower distbn. Nat. Health Council, 1973, mem. com. on manpower, 1976—; mem. Nat. Adv. Council on Health Professions Edn.; cons. team So. Regional Ednl. Bd. Feasibility Study for So. Podiatry Sch., 1975-76; mem. Statewide Profl. Standards Rev. Council, 1976—, Greater Phila. Com. for Med.-Pharm. Scis. Contbr. sci. articles to profl. jours. Trustee First United Meth. Ch. of Germantown, 1965-72, past chmn. fin. com.; v.p. bd. Germantown Businessmen's Assn., 1962-64, Disting. Service award, 1964; chmn. 277th and 278th Ann. Germantown Week, 1958-59; dep. service dir. Phila. CD Council, 1966-73; mem. Health Adv. Commn., Phila., 1976; past pres., bd. mgrs. Germantown YWCA; v.p. Phila. Boosters Assn.; trustee Univ. City Sci. Center, Phila. Served with M.C. AUS, World War II. Recipient citation Pa. Coll. Podiatric Medicine, 1970, Gov. Pa., 1973. Fellow Internat. Acad. Preventive Medicine (dir. 1973-78), Royal Soc. Health (Eng.), Am. Coll. Foot Roentgenologists (pres. 1958-59), Coll. Physicians Phila.; mem. Am. Podiatry Assn. (Merit award 1962, gen. chmn. Region Three Ann. Conv. 1975—), Pa. Podiatry Assn. (pres. 1959-60, Man of Yr. award 1961, Spl. citation 1973), Greater Phila. Podiatry Soc. (pres. 1955-56), Fedn. Assns. Schs. of Health Professions (pres. 1975-76), Am. Assn. Colls. Podiatric Medicine (pres. 1969-72), Pi Epsilon Delta, Pi Delta. Republican. Club: Greate Bay Downtown. Home: 314 S Lawrence Ct Philadelphia PA 19106 Office: Pa Coll Podiatric Medicine Race at 8th Sts Philadelphia PA 19107

BATES, JIM, congressman; b. Denver, July 21, 1941; s. Chester Owen and Asha (East) B.; m. Marilyn Brewer; 1 dau., Jennifer Leigh. B.A., San Diego State U., 1975; Ph.D. in Humane Letters (hon.), U. Humanistic Studies, San Diego, Calif., 1982; L.H.D. (hon.), Nat. U., San Diego, 1983. Loan officer Bank Am., San Diego, 1963-68; adminstr. Rohr, San Diego, 1968, Solar, 1969; mktg. analyst Heavenly Donuts, San Diego, 1970; mem. San Diego City Council, 1971-74; supr. County of San Diego, 1975-82; mem. 98th Congress form 44th Dist. Calif. Chmn. Health Systems Agy. San Diego Region; mem. San Diego Met. Transit Devel. Bd., Calif. Coastal Commn., San Diego; dir. Gov.'s Adv. Council Solar Energy; chmn. Mental Health Task Force, Subcom. Refugees and Undocumented Aliens; mem. Assn. Retarded Citizens. Served with USMC, 1959-63. Recipient Equal Opportunity award Urban League, 1982, Gary Dores Meml. award, Outstanding Service award Mental Health Assn., Outstanding Young Citizen award Jaycees. Democrat. Office: 1632 Longworth House Office Bldg Washington DC 20515

BATES, JOHN BURNHAM, lawyer; b. Oakland, Calif., Mar. 2, 1918; s. Charles David and lucretia Margaret (Burnham) B.; m. Nancy Witter; children: John Burnham, Catherine Bates Hunt, charles W. A.B., Stanford U., 1940; J.D., U. Calif.-Berkeley, 1947. Bar: Calif. 1947, U.S. Supreme Ct. 1953. Assoc. firm Pillsbury, Madison & Sutro, San Francisco, 1947-53; ptnr. Pillsbury, Madison, Sutro, San Francisco, 1953-77; sr. ptnr. Pillsbury, Madison & Sutro, San Francisco, 1977—, chmn. mgmt. com., 1979-83; mem. Am. team Anglo-Am. Legal Exchange, 1973; lectr. continuing edn. of bar, 1953-56. Mem. piedmont City Council (Calif.), 1959-62; bd. dirs. Bay Area Council, 1979—. Fellow ABA; mem. Bar Assn. San Francisco (chmn. jud. com. 1962, chmn. trail practice com. 1963-64), Am. Coll. Trail Lawyers (chmn. Gumpert award com. 1973-78), Am. Coll. Trial Lawyers (regent 1969-73). Clubs: Commonwealth of Calif. (gov. 1973—, pres. 1977. Home: 20 Bellevue Ave Piedmont CA 94611 Office: Pillsbury Madison & Sutro Standard Oil Bldg 225 Bush St San Francisco CA 94104

BATES, JOSEPH CLARK, aluminum company executive; b. Sparta, Ill., June 26, 1920; s. Joseph C. and Anna Ella (Reinhardt) B.; m. Millicent Anne Simonds, June 28, 1947; children: Jan M. Wheeler, Joseph C. III, Maya A. Roderick, Leslie K., Robert W. B.S. in Mech. Engring, U. So. Calif., 1943; post., MIT, 1945-46. With Bates Engring. Co., Newhard Cook, 1946-61; Vice pres., gen. mgr. Aluminum Container Corp., St. Louis, 1961-65; works mgr. Aluminum Co. Am., Richmond, Ind., 1966-68; mng. dir. Alcoa Australia Ltd., Melbourne, 1968-71; gen. mgr. diversified products Aluminum Co, Am., Pitts., 1975-76, v.p. internat., 1976-78, exec. v.p. internat., 1978-82; exec. v.p. allied products Aluminum Co. Am., 1982—. Served with submarines USN, 1941-45. Decorated Silver Star. Mem. ASME. Republican. Presbyterian. Clubs: Allegheny Country, Duquesne, Harvard-Yale-Princeton, Rolling Rock. Home: Blackburn Rd Sewickley PA 15143 Office: 1501 Alcoa Bldg Pittsburgh PA 15143

BATES, JOSEPH HENRY, physician, educator; b. Little Rock, Sept. 19, 1933; s. Henry Ermer and Susan Elizabeth (Wallis) B.; m. Patsy McGinnis, Aug. 6, 1955; children—Patricia, Susan Elizabeth, Joseph Henry, III, Elisabeth Lee. B.S., U. Ark., 1957, M.D., 1957, M.S., 1963. Diplomate: Am. Bd. Internal Medicine (pulmonary disease; mem. exam. bd.). Med. intern U. Ark. Med. Center, 1957-58, resident in internal medicine, 1958-61, fellow in infections diseases, 1961-63; clin. investigator Little Rock VA Med. Center, 1963-66; mem. faculty U. Ark. Med. Center, Little Rock, 1967—, prof. medicine, 1973—, vice chmn. dept., 1978—; chief med. service Little Rock VA Hosp., 1970—; dir. Twin City Bank of North Little Rock. Author research papers in field, chpts. in books. Chmn. Ark. chpt. NCCJ, 1980; chmn. biracial commn. Little Rock public schs., 1977-79; bd. dirs. Am. Lung Assn., 1972—. Served as officer M.C. AUS, 1956-65. Grantee USPHS, 1961-63, NIH, VA, 1963—. Mem. A.C.P. (gov.), Am. Coll. Chest Physicians (gov.), Am. Fedn. Clin. Research, Am. Thoracic Soc., Infectious Disease Soc., So. Soc. Clin. Research. Presbyterian. Home: 5 Glenridge Rd Little Rock AR 72207 Office: 300 E Roosevelt Rd Little Rock AR 72206

BATES, KENNETH ELDON, architect; b. Casper, Wyo., Dec. 16, 1921; s. Boyd Robert and Lee Ora (Renison) B.; m. Frances Jane Johnson, Aug. 10, 1948; children: Barry Alan, Bruce Randall, Kimberly Jane. B.Arch., U. Oreg., 1951. Pvt. practice architecture, Bellevue, Wash., 1954-64; chief architect Engineered Indsl. Systems, Seattle, 1967-70; mng. architect Port Seattle, 1970-78; chief architect Austin Co., Renton, Wash., 1978—. Architect: Boeing ALCM Bldg., Kent, Wash., Valley Office Park, Renton. Mem. Bellevue Bd. Adjustment, 1962-66, Citizens Adv. Com. Bellevue, 1978. Served with USN, 1942-46. Mem. AIA. Office: 800 SW 16th St Renton WA 98055

BATES, MERCEDES A., food company executive; b. 1915. Grad., Oreg. State U., 1936. Supr. home service So. Calif. Gas Co., 1939-46; owner, mgr. food cons. firm, Calif., 1948-60; sr. editor food dept. McCall's Mag., 1960-64; with Gen. Mills, Inc., 1964—; dir. Betty Crocker Kitchens, Mpls., 1964—, v.p., 1966—; v.p., dir. Betty Crocker Food and Nutrition Center, 1977—. Mem. Pres.'s Commn. White House Fellows, 1971-76. Office: Gen Mills Inc 9200 Wayzata Blvd Minneapolis MN 55426

BATES, PETER JOHN STANLEY, librarian; b. Maidenhead, Eng., Dec. 22, 1940; s. Richard Henry and Eleanor (Milson) B.; m. Janet Margaret Clothier, July 1, 1967; children—Alexander Richard, Evan Dafydd. B.Sc. with honors, Chelsea Coll., London U., 1964. Asst. librarian Associated Lead Manufacturers, London, 1964-67; library asst. reference dept. U. Sask. Library, Saskatoon, 1967-68; librarian Research Council Alta., Edmonton, Can., 1968-72; info. specialist research dept. Syncrude Can. Ltd., Edmonton, 1972—. Editor: Index to the Published Literature on the Athabasca Oil Sands, 1970-72, Argon Plasma Spectroscopy in ICP Info. Newsletter, 1976. Mem. Inst. Info. Scientists (asso.), Alta. Info. Retrieval Assn. (dir. 1975—), Soc. Tech. Communication. Office: PO Box 5790 Edmonton AB T6C 4G3 Canada

BATES, REX JAMES, insurance company executive; b. Seattle, Nov. 9, 1923; s. Rex and Lucy Cornelia (Anderson) B.; m. Reva Mae Myers, June 14, 1947; children: Patricia Ann Mattingley, Rex W. Student, Oreg. State U., 1941-42; S.B., U. Chgo., 1947, M.B.A, 1949. Chartered fin. analyst. Ptnr. Stein, Roe & Farnham, Chgo., 1949-72; fin. v.p. State Farm Ins. Cos., Bloomington, Ill., 1972—, dir., 1977—. Bd. dirs. (Met. Housing and Planning Council), Chgo.; trustee (Ill. Wesleyan U.). Served to 1st lt. USAAF, 1942-46. Clubs: Mid Day, University (Chgo.); Bloomington Country. Home: 32 Sunset Rd Bloomington IL 61701 Office: State Farm Ins Cos 1 State Farm Plaza Bloomington IL 61701

BATES, ROBERT HINRICHS, political science educator; b. Bklyn., Dec. 5, 1942; m.; 1 dau. B.A., Haverford Coll., 1964; Ph.D., MIT, 1969. Intern Dept. State, 1963; legis. asst. to Congressman William L. St. Onge, 1964; research asst. dept. polit. sci. MIT, 1966, fellow Ctr. Internat. Studies, 1969; asst. prof. polit. sci. Calif. Inst. Tech., 1969-75, assoc. prof., 1975-79, prof., 1979—; research in field; cons. AID, World Bank. Author: Unions, Parties, and Political Development: A Study of Mineworkers in Zamba, 1971, Rural Responses to Industrialization: A Study of Village Zambia, 1976, States and Markets in Tropical Africa: The Political Basis of Agricultural Policy, 1981, Essays on the Polictical Economy of Rural Africa, 1983; editor: (with Michael F. Lofchie) Agricultural Development in Africa: Issues of Public Policy, 1980; contbr. articles to profl. jours. Woodrow

Wilson fellow, 1964-65; NDEA fellow, 1965-66; grantee Social Sci. Research Council, 1970-71, 76-77, NIH-Mellon Fund, 1971-72, NSF, 1978-80, 83—. Office: Calif Inst Tech Pasadena CA 91125

BATES, ROBERT THOMAS, labor organization executive; b. Glendale, Oreg., Aug. 18, 1927; s. Monte Allen and Elizabeth Beryl (Bunch) B.; m. Elizabeth Lenora Utt, Feb. 13, 1949; children: Frances, Rebecca, Martha. Ed. public schs. With So. Pacific R.R., 1945-63; various positions from signal helper to signal maintainer; chmn. Local 152 Brotherhood R.R. Signalmen, 1957-63; vice gen. chmn. So. Pacific Gen. Com., 1960-63, gen. chmn. com., 1963-67, v.p. Western region, 1967-70, sec.-treas. Brotherhood, 1970-77, pres., 1977—. Served with USNR, 1945-54. Methodist. Lodges: Elks; Masons. Home: 1108 Barberry Ln Mount Prospect IL 60056 Office: 601 W Golf Rd Mount Prospect IL 60056

BATESON, MARY CATHERINE, college dean; b. N.Y.C., Dec. 8, 1939; d. Gregory and Margaret (Mead) B.; m. J. Barkev Kassarjian, June 4, 1960; 1 dau., Sevanne Margaret. B.A., Radcliffe Coll., 1960; Ph.D., Harvard U., 1963. Instr. Arabic Harvard U., 1963-66; asso. prof. anthropology Ateneo de Manila U., 1966-68; sr. research fellow psychology and philosophy Brandeis U., 1968-69; asso. prof. anthropology Northeastern U., Boston, 1969-71; researcher U. Tehran, 1972-74; vis. prof. Northeastern U., 1974-75; prof. anthropology, dean grad. studies Damavand Coll., 1975-77; prof. anthropology, dean social sci. and humanities U. No. Iran, 1977-79; vis. scholar Harvard U., 1979-80; dean faculty, prof. anthropology Amherst Coll., 1980—; pres. Inst. Intercultural Studies, from 1979. Author: Structural Continuity in Poetry: A Linguistic Study of Five Early Arabic Odes, 1970, Our Own Metaphor: A Personal Account of a Conference on Consciousness and Human Adaption, 1972; Co-editor: Approaches to Semiotics: Anthropology, Education, Linquistics, Psychiatry and Psychology, 1964. Ford Found. fellow, 1961-63; NSF postdoctoral fellow, 1968-69. Mem. Am. Anthrop. Assn., Soc. Iranian Studies, Lindisfarne Assn., Phi Beta Kappa. Office: Dean Faculty Amherst Coll Amherst MA 01002

BATESON, RICHARD G., communications company executive; b. Walpole, Mass., Dec. 16, 1923; m. Yvonne Giacopucci, Aug. 26, 1950; children: Richard F., Peter H. A.B., Amherst Coll., 1947; J.D. cum laude, Harvard U., 1951; postgrad. (Fulbright scholar), U. Grenoble, France, 1951-52. Bar: Mass., N.Y., U.S. Supreme Ct. Teaching fellow law Harvard U., 1952-53; legal staff World Bank, 1953-62; sec., gen. counsel, then v.p. ITT Europe, Inc., 1962-68, asst. gen. counsel-internat., then asso. gen. counsel parent corp., N.Y.C., from 1968, v.p., asso. gen. counsel, from 1970, v.p., dep. gen. counsel, dir. legal ops., to 1982; cons., 1982—. Served to cpl. USAAF, 1943-46; ETO. Mem. ABA, N.Y. State Bar Assn., Mass. Bar Assn., Assn. Bar City N.Y., Phi Beta Kappa.

BATH, JAMES EDMOND, entomologist; b. Santa Ana, Calif., May 4, 1938; s. Darrell Averill and Beth (Illingworth) B.; m. Sonja Kirsten Johnson, Jan. 27, 1959; children—David James, Ronald Darrell, Michael Eric. B.S., U. Calif., Davis, 1960; M.S., U. Wis., 1962, Ph.D., 1964. Asst. prof. entomology Mich. State U., 1964-69, asso. prof., 1969-74, prof., 1974—, chmn. dept. entomology, 1974—; acting prin. entomologist Dept. Agr., SEA, Coop. Research, Washington, 1979. Recipient grants from NSF; NIH; EPA; Dept. Agr. Mem. Entomol. Soc. Am., Am. Phytopathol. Soc., AAAS, Soc. Nematologists, Sigma Xi. Research, publs. on mechanisms of insect transmission of plant viruses. Home: 942 Northgate East Lansing MI 48823 Office: Dept Entomology Mich State U East Lansing MI 48824

BATHON, EDWARD GREGORY ANTHONY, advertising agency executive; b. N.Y.C., Oct. 17, 1933; s. Edward Gregory and Mary F. (O'Connor) B.; m. Heidi Tschudy, Sept. 3, 1960; children: Heather, Nina, Nord, Megan. B.A., Hamilton Coll., 1956; postgrad., Harvard U., 1977. Media buyer J. Walter Thompson Co., N.Y.C., 1960-62, account rep., 1962-63, account supr., dir., Belgium, 1963-66, chmn., mng. dir., India, 1966-70, v.p., account supr., N.Y.C., 1970-72, pres., Brazil, 1972-77, exec. v.p., pres. AmPac div., dir., N.Y.C., 1977-82; sr. exec. v.p., pres. J. Walter Thompson Co. U.S.A., 1980-82; dir., exec. v.p. McCann Erickson, Worldwide, 1983—. Served with USN, 1956-60. Mem. Internat. Advt. Assn., Council of Americas, Japan Soc., Philippine C. of C. Club: Bedford Golf and Tennis. Home: Meadow Farm Croton Lake Rd Mount Kisco NY 10549 Office: 420 Lexington Ave New York NY 10017

BATHURST, DAVID CHARLES, auction company executive; b. London, Dec. 15, 1937; U.S., 1977; s. Benjamin and Joan (Krishaber) B. (Vicount and Vicountess Bledisloe); m. Cornelia McCoch, Aug. 25, 1967; children: Arabella, Lucy, Flora. B.A., Magdalen Coll., Oxford U., 1960. Mem. staff Carnegie Inst., Pitts., 1961-62; head impressionist and modern painting dept. Christie's, London, 1963-77, pres., N.Y.C., 1978—. Served with Brit. Army, 1956-58. Club: Brook (N.Y.C.). Office: 502 Park Ave New York NY 10022 *

BATIUK, THOMAS MARTIN, cartoonist; b. Akron, Ohio, Mar. 14, 1947; s. Martin and Verna (Greskovics) B.; m. Catherine L. Wesemeyer, June 26, 1971. B.F.A., Kent (Ohio) State U., 1969, cert. edn., 1969. Tchr. art Eastern Heights Jr. High Sch., 1969-72. Cartoonist: comic strip Funky Winkerbean, Field Newspaper Syndicate, Chgo., 1972—, John Darling for, Field Newspaper Syndicate, Calif., 1979—; author, cartoonist: Funky Winkerbean, 1973, Funky Winkerbean, Play It Again Funky, 1975, Funky Winkerbean, Closed Out, 1977. Mem. Nat. Cartoonists Soc., Newspaper Comics Guild. Address: Field Newspaper Syndicate 1703 Kaiser Ave Irvine CA 92714

BATJER, CAMERON MCVICAR, state justice; b. Smith, Nev., Aug. 24, 1919; s. Robert William and Mary Belle Stuart (McVicar) B.; m. Lura Gamble, May 16, 1942; children—Lura (Mrs. Charles S. Caldwell), Christina, Marybel. B.A., U. Nev., 1941; J.D., U. Utah, 1950. Bar: Utah bar 1950, Nev. bar 1951. Public sch. tchr., Dayton, Nev., 1941-42, McGill, Nev., 1946-47, Fernley, Nev., 1947-49, Carson City, Nev., 1951-52; counsel Utah Senate, 1951; pvt. practice, Carson City, 1952; mem. staff U.S. Senator George W. Malone, 1952-53; dist. atty., Ormsby County, Nev., 1954-59, pvt. practice, Carson City, 1959-67; justice Nev. Supreme Ct., 1967-81, chief justice, 1977-79; commr. U.S. Parole Commn., Washington, 1981—; dep. chmn. Conf. Chief Justices, 1977—. Served with USNR, 1942-46. Mem. Am. Legion, Footprinters, Lambda Chi Alpha, Phi Alpha Delta. Republican. Presbyn. Clubs: Rotary, Elks. Home: 7 Circle Dr Carson City NV 89701 Office: US Parole Commn 5550 Friendship Blvd Chevy Chase MD 20014

BATLIN, ROBERT ALFRED, editor; b. San Francisco, Aug. 24, 1930; S. Philip Alfred and Lavenia Mary (Barnes) B.; m. Diane Elise Giblin, July 4, 1956; children—Lisa, Philippa. B.A., Stanford, 1952, M.A., 1954. Reporter San Bruno Herald, 1952-53; copy editor, then dept. editor San Francisco News, 1956-59; dept. editor San Francisco News-Call Bull., 1959-65; feature editor San Francisco Examiner, 1965-74, arts editor, 1974—. Served with AUS, 1954-56. Mem. Sigma Delta Chi. Home: 91 Fairway Dr Daly City CA 94015 Office: 110 5th St San Francisco CA 94103

BATOGOWSKI, JOSEPH H., department store chain executive. Sr. exec. v.p. Mdse. Group, Sears Roebuck and Co., Chgo. Office: Mdse Group Sears Roebuck and Co Sears Tower Chicago IL 60684§

BATOR, FRANCIS MICHEL, economist, educator; b. Budapest, Hungary, Aug. 10, 1925; came to U.S., 1939, naturalized, 1944; s. Victor and Franciska Elisabeth (Sichermann) B.; m. Micheline Charlotte Martin, June 30, 1949; children: Nina, Christopher Francis. B.S., MIT, 1949, Ph.D., 1956; M.A. (hon.), Harvard U., 1967. Exec. asst. to dir. Center Internat. Studies, MIT, 1951-54; sr. research staff Center Internat. Studies, Mass. Inst. Tech., 1954-63, asst. prof. econs., 1957-60, asso. prof., 1960-63; sr. econ. adviser AID, Dept. State, 1963-64; sr. staff NSC, Washington, 1964-65; dep. spl. asst. to Pres. for nat. security affairs White House, 1965-67; prof. polit. economy John F. Kennedy Sch. Govt., Harvard U., 1967—; Cons. Rand Corp., Inst. Def. Analysis, Office Sec. Treasury, 1961-63, under sec. state for econ. affairs, 1961; U.S. mem. consultative group on econ. projections UN, 1962, on internat. monetary arrangements, 1969; spl. cons. sec. treasury, 1967-69; mem. Pres.'s Adv. Com. Internat. Monetary Arrangements, 1967-69; mem. fgn. affairs task force Democratic Adv. Council Elected Ofcls., 1974-76; mem. nat. adv. bd. Ctr. Nat. Policy, 1981—; mem. vis. com. Ctr. Internat. Studies (MIT). Author: The Question of Government Spending, 1960; co-author: Energy, the Next Twenty Years, 1979, also articles. Served to 1st lt., inf. AUS, 1944-46. Recipient Disting. Service award Treasury Dept., 1968; Guggenheim fellow, 1959. Fellow Am. Acad. Arts and Scis.; mem. Council Fgn. Relations, Am. Econ. Assn., Inst. Strategic Studies, Econometric Soc., Royal Econ. Soc. Club: Century Assn. (N.Y.C.). Home: 17 Farrar St Cambridge MA 02138

BATOR, PAUL MICHAEL, lawyer, educator; b. Budapest, Hungary, July 2, 1929; came to U.S., 1939, naturalized, 1945; s. Victor and Franciska Elisabeth (Sichermann) B.; m. Alice Garrett Hoag, June 2, 1956; children—Thomas Ewing, Michael G., Julia F. Grad., Groton Sch., 1947; A.B., Princeton, 1951; M.A. in History, Harvard, 1953, LL.B., 1956. Bar: N.Y. bar 1958. Law clk. to Supreme Ct. Justice Harlan, 1956-57; asso. firm Debevoise, Plimpton & McLean, N.Y.C., 1957-59; asst. prof. law Harvard Law Sch., 1959-62, prof., 1962—, asso. dean, 1971-75, Bromley prof., 1981—; dep. solicitor gen., Counselor Solicitor Gen. of U.S., 1983—; Vis. prof. law U. Calif., Berkeley, 1966, Stanford U., 1971-72, U. Chgo., 1978-79. Co-author: Hart and Wechsler's Federal Courts and the Federal System, 2d edit, 1973; author: The International Trade in Art, 1983. Mem. Am. Law Inst. Home: 1010 Memorial Dr Cambridge MA 02138

BATOR, PETER ANTHONY, lawyer; b. Budapest, Hungary, July 2, 1929; s. Victor and Franciska (Sichermann) B.; m. Mary C. Bigelow, May 19, 1951 (div. 1967); children: Francesca Bradley Bator Johnson, Anthony Bigelow (dec.); m. Joanna C. Sturges, Sept. 12, 1969; children: Alexa S., Timothy C. A.B. magna cum laude, Harvard U., 1951, LL.B., 1954, Sheldon fellow, 1954-55. Bar: N.Y. 1955. Assoc. Davis Polk & Wardwell, N.Y.C., 1955-61, partner, 1961—; dir. ICI Americas Inc. (and predecessors), N.Y.C., 1969—, Kreutoll Realization Corp., 1969-78. Editor: Harvard Law Rev. Vice pres., trustee N.Y. Infirmary-Beekman Downtown Hosp., N.Y.C., 1972—; mem. alumni standing com. Groton (Mass.) Sch., 1975-77. Mem. Harvard Law Sch. Assn. N.Y.C. (trustee 1974-76), Am., N.Y. State bar assns., Bar Assn. City N.Y., Am. Law Inst., Am. Inst. Internat. Law, Internat. Law Soc., Council Fgn. Relations, Incorporated Proprietors of Nauquitt, Inc. (pres. 1980-82), Phi Beta Kappa. Clubs: Knickerbocker, River, Downtown Assn., Wall St., Meadow Brook (N.Y.C.). Home: 1185 Park Ave New York NY 10028 Office: Davis Polk & Wardwell 1 Chase Manhattan Plaza New York NY 10005

BATSAKIS, JOHN GEORGE, pathology educator; b. Petoskey, Mich., Aug. 14, 1929; s. George John and Stella (Vlahkis) B.; m. Mary Janet Savage, Dec. 28, 1957; children: Laura, Sharon, George. Student, Va. Mil. Inst., 1947, Albion Coll., Mich., 1948-50; M.D., U. Mich., 1954. Am. Bd. Pathology. Intern George Washington Univ. Hosp., Washington, 1954-55; resident in pathology U. Mich. Hosp., Ann Arbor, 1955-59; prof. pathology U. Mich., Ann Arbor, 1969-79; chmn. dept. pathology M.D. Anderson Hosp. U. Tex., Houston, 1981—; Ruth Legett Jones prof. U. Tex., Austin, 1982; cons. Armed Forces Inst. Pathology, 1972—, VA Hosp., Ann Arbor, 1968-79. Author: Tumors of the Head and Neck, 1974; editor: Clinical Lab. Ann., 1981—; editor editorial bd. 13 jours., 1974—; contbr. numerous articles to profl. jours. Served to capt. U.S. Army, 1959-61. Recipient William H. Rorer award Am. Coll. Gastroenterology, 1972. Fellow ACP, Am. Soc. Clin. Patholgists, Am. Acad. Otolaryngology (assoc.), Coll. Am. Pathologists (chmn. commn. sci. resources). Republican. Episcopalian. Home: 6107 Sanford Rd Houston TX 77096 Office: Dept of Pathology MD Anderson Hospital Houston TX 77030

BATSON, BLAIR EVERETT, pediatrician, educator; b. Hattiesburg, Miss., Oct. 24, 1920; s. Claud L. and Mary Eaton (Bryan) B.; m. Blanche Russell Desmond, 1976. B.A., Vanderbilt U., 1941, M.D., 1944; M.P.H., Johns Hopkins U., 1954. Intern Vanderbilt U. Hosp., 1944-45, asst. resident in pediatrics, 1948-49, resident pediatrician, 1949-50, instr. pediatrics Sch. Medicine, 1949-52; asst. resident dept. pediatrics Johns Hopkins Hosp., 1945-46; instr. pediatrics Johns Hopkins Sch. Medicine, 1952-54, asst. prof., 1954-55; instr. public health adminstrn., div. maternal and child health Sch. Hygiene and Public Health, 1952-54, asst. prof. public health adminstrn., 1954-55; prof. pediatrics, chmn. dept. U. Miss. Sch. Medicine, Jackson, 1955—; Chmn. health com., adv. council Miss. Children's Code Commn., 1958-61; chmn. Miss. Conf. on Handicapped Children, 1960-61; nat. adviser on children, public children's bur. HEW; ofcl. examiner Am. Bd. Pediatrics, 1963—; pediatric cons. USAF, 1971—. Trustee Easter Seal Research Found., 1969-74. Served to capt. M.C. AUS, 1946-48. Mem. Am. Acad. Pediatrics (Mead Johnson awards com. 1958-61, exec. com. child devel. sect. 1964-67, charter mem. sect. on community pediatrics 1968, hosp. car com. 1970, nominating com. 1973-74, exec. bd. 1974-80), AMA, So. Soc. Pediatric Research, Am. Assn. Med. Colls., So. Med. Assn. (sec. pediatric sec. 1956-58, pres. 1959), Vanderbilt Alumni Club (pres. chpt. 1960-64), Am. Pediatric Soc., Sigma Chi, Phi Chi. Home: 1417 Poplar Blvd Jackson MS 39202 Office: Univ Miss Med Center 2500 N State St Jackson MS 39216

BATSON, CHARLES A., broadcasting executive; b. Greenville, S.C., Aug. 14, 1916; s. Charles Austell and Bessie (McCauley) B.; m. Margaret Craig Havird, June 29, 1975; 1 son, Reginald Fleming. B.A., Furman U., 1938. Program dir. Sta. WFBC, Greenville, S.C., 1938-41; dir. information Nat. Assn. Broadcasters, Washington, 1946-49, dir. TV, 1950-51; asst. dir. TV Broadcast Advt. Bur., 1949-50; dir. TV Broadcasting Co. of South (now Cosmos Broadcasting Corp.), Columbia, S.C., 1951-53, v.p., 1953, dir., 1953—, sr. v.p., 1965, mem. exec. com., 1965-83, pres., 1968-79, chief exec. chief exec. officer, 1969-81, chmn. bd., 1977-81, chmn., 1969-77; v.p., gen. mgr. sta. WIS-TV, Columbia, 1953-66; sr. v.p., gen. mgr. sta. WTOL-TV, Toledo, 1966-68; dir., mem. profit-sharing com. Liberty Corp., 1969-81; also dir. Liberty Corp. Found.; dir. Cosmos Broadcasting of La., Inc., 1972-77, TV Stations, Inc., 1969-73; Columbia adv. bd. Citizens and So. Nat. Bank S.C., 1968-81, chmn., 1978; bd. dels NBC-TV, 1962-66. Author: series on TV A Report on the Visual Broadcasting Art, 1948-49. Mem. adv. bd. Fedn. Center of Blind, 1971-77; bd. dirs. S.C. Bd. Easter Seal Soc. Crippled Children and Adults, 1970—, v.p., 1976-81, pres.-elect, 1981; bd. dirs. Columbia Urban League, 1975-77, Broadcast Pioneers Found., 1978—; mem. Greater Columbia Community Relations Council, 1972-81, vice chmn., 1974-76, chmn., 1976-78; mem. S.C. adv. com. U.S. Commn. Civil Rights, 1977-80, 81—, S.C. Com. for Humanities, 1978-82. Served with AUS, 1941-46. Recipient Abe Lincoln award So. Baptist Radio and Television Commn., 1971. Mem. S.C. Broadcasters Assn. (pres. 1957, Hall of Fame 1981), Nat. Assn. Broadcasters (copyright com. 1960-61, TV industry adv. com. to Corp. for Public Broadcasting 1969-72, chmn. TV Code Rev. Bd. 1973-74, dir. 1974-78, task force on reorgn. 1976-77, code rewrite com. 1977, mem. by-laws com. 1977-78, congressional liaison com. 1977-78), Assn. Maximum Service Telecasters (bd. dirs. 1978-81), Greater Columbia C. of C. (pres. 1965, dir. and exec. com. 1976-78). Presbyterian (deacon 1963-67, chmn. finance com. 1965). Clubs: Forest Lake (Columbia); The Summit (gov. 1971-77), Kosmos (pres. 1982), Rotary.). Home: 1623 Milford Rd Columbia SC 29206

BATSON, LARRY FLOYD, author; b. Aguilar, Colo., Feb. 17, 1930; s. Ernest C. and Myrtle Mae (Diskin) B.; m. Laurel A. Larson, Apr. 19, 1951; children—Ernest, William, James. Student, U. Nebr. Reporter, news broadcaster, editor Star Herald, Scottsbluff, Nebr.; asst. mng. editor Omaha World Herald; news and sports editor Mpls. Tribune, also columnist. Contbr. articles to mags.; works include The Hills Are Theirs. Served with USAF, 1950. Mem. Sigma Delta Chi. Home: 3501 Buchanan St NE Minneapolis MN 55418 Office: 425 Portland Ave Minneapolis MN 55488

BATSON, RANDOLPH, physician; b. Hattiesburg, Miss., Oct. 26, 1916; s. John O. and Nellie (Nicholson) B.; m. Bennie Wells Shaw, Nov. 18, 1950; children—Bennie Barbara, Nellie Wells, Randolph, Alicia Bond. B.A., Vanderbilt U., 1938, M.D., 1942. Diplomate: Am. Bd. Pediatrics. Intern pediatrics Vanderbilt U. Hosp., 1942- 43, asst. resident, resident, then fellow, 1943-47, dir. polio clin. study center, 1953-63; mem. faculty Vanderbilt U. Sch. Medicine, 1947-78, prof. pediatrics, 1959-78, acting dean, 1962-63, dean, also dir. med. affairs, 1963-72, vice chancellor med. affairs, 1972-73, vice chancellor for med. affairs devel., 1973-74; pres. Charles Henderson Child Health Center, Troy, Ala., 1978—; Mem. Tenn. Commn. Youth Guidance; chmn. Tenn. Subcom. Handicapped Child; nat. adv. com. Tenn. Crippled Children's Service; adv. com. emotionally disturbed children Nashville Mental Heath Assn.; mem. spl. med. adv. group VA; pres. Assn. for Acad. Health Centers, 1971-72; ex officio mem. exec. com. Assn. Am. Med. Colls. Served with AUS, 1944-46. Mem. Am. Acad. Pediatrics (chmn. Tenn. chpt.), A.C.P., Am., So., Pan Am. med. assns., Am., Tenn., Nashville pediatric socs., Am. Acad. Cerebral Palsy, AAAS, Assn. Am. Med. Colls., Am. Coll. Chest Physicians, AAUP, Nashville Acad. Medicine, Nashville C. of C. (dir.), Sigma Chi, Omicron Delta Kappa, Alpha Omega Alpha, Phi Chi. Clubs: Rotarian., Cosmos (Washington); Univ. (Nashville, Chgo.). Home: Route 6 Box 69-D Troy AL 36081 Office: PO Box 928 Troy AL 36081

BATTAGLIA, ANTHONY SYLVESTER, lawyer; b. Binghamton, N.Y., Aug. 21, 1927; s. Sylvester Anthony and Helen B.; m. Catherine Jean, Oct. 1, 1972; children: Christina, Marc Anthony; children by previous marriage—Anthony, Sandra, Brian, Brenda Lee. A.A., U. Fla., 1948, B.A., 1949, LL.B., 1953, J.D., 1967. Bar: Fla. 1953, U.S. Supreme Ct. 1966. Asst. to U.S. dist. atty., So. Dist. Fla., 1953-56; partner firms Parker, Parker & Battaglia, 1953-56, Parker, Battaglia & Ross, 1965-73, Parker, Battaglia, Parker, Ross & Ross, 1973-75, Battaglia, Parker, Ross, Parker & Stolba, 1975-76, Battaglia, Ross & Stolba, 1976-77, Battaglia, Ross, Stolba & Forlizzo, 1977-78, Battaglia, Ross & Forlizzo, 1978-80, Battaglia, Ross, Hastings, Dicus & Andrews, 1980—; mem. Fla. Public Service Commn., 1971—. Republican nat. committeeman, Fla., 1956-64, bd. dirs., Tampa div.; bd. dirs. San Carlo Opera Fla., 1972-74, pres., chmn. bd. dirs., Pinellas County div., 1974-76; bd. dirs. St. Petersburg Opera Co., 1976-77. Mem. ABA, Fla. Bar Assn., St. Petersburg Bar Assn., Fed. Bar Assn. (v.p. Middle Fla. dist.), Internat. Bar Assn., Acad. Fla. Trial Lawyers, Assn. Trial Lawyers Am., Am. Judicature Soc., Supreme Ct. Hist. Soc. Roman Catholic. Clubs: K. of C., Italian-Am. Unico Internat. Home: 430 72d St S Saint Petersburg FL 33707 Office: 980 Tyrone Blvd Saint Petersburg FL 33743

BATTAGLIA, FREDERICK CAMILLO, physician; b. Weehawken, N.J., Feb. 15, 1932; m. Jane B. Donohue; children—Susan Kate, Thomas Frederick. B.A., Cornell U., 1953; M.D., Yale U., 1957. Diplomate: Am. Bd. Pediatrics. Intern in pediatrics Johns Hopkins Hosp., 1957-58; USPHS postdoctoral fellow biochemistry Cambridge (Eng.) U., 1958-59; Joshiah Macy Found. fellow physiology Yale U. Med. Sch., 1959-60; asst. resident, fellow in pediatrics Johns Hopkins Hosp., 1960-61, resident, fellow, 1961-62; USPHS surgeon lab. perinatal physiology NIH, San Juan, P.R., 1962-64; asst. prof., then asso. prof. Johns Hopkins Med. Sch., 1963-65; mem. faculty U. Colo. Med. Sch., Denver, 1965—, prof. pediatrics, prof. Ob-Gyn, 1969—, dir. div. perinatal medicine, 1970-74, chmn. dept. pediatrics, 1974—; attending pediatrician Children's, Denver Gen., Fitzsimons Gen. hosps.; co-dir. newborn center Colo. Gen. Hosp., 1967-74. Asso. editor: Pediatrics, 15th edit; med. progress contbg. editor: Jour. Pediatrics, 1966-74; mem. editorial bd.: European Jour. Ob-Gyn, 1971—; contbr. numerous articles med. jours. Mem. Am. Acad. Pediatrics (E. Mead Johnson award 1969), Soc. Pediatric Research (pres. 1976-77), Perinatal Research Soc. (pres. 1974-75), Western Soc. Pediatric Research, Soc. Gynecol. Investigation, AAAS, Am. Pediatric Soc., Soc. Gynecol. Investigation (council 1969-72), Soc. Exptl. Biology and Medicine, Phi Beta Kappa, Sigma Xi. Home: 2975 E Cedar Ave Denver CO 80209 Office: Dept Pediatrics Univ Colo Health Scis Center 4200 E 9th Ave Denver CO 80262

BATTAN, LOUIS JOSEPH, meteorology educator, scientist; b. N.Y.C., Feb. 9, 1923; s. Anibale and Louise (Webber) B.; m. Jeannette A. Waitches, June 8, 1952; children: Suzette, Paul. Student, CCNY, 1941-43; B.S., N.Y.U., 1946, Harvard, 1944, Mass. Inst. Tech., 1944; M.S., U. Chgo., 1949, Ph.D., 1953. Research meteorologist U.S. Weather Bur., 1947-51; research meteorologist, lectr. U. Chgo., 1951-58; prof. atmospheric scis., dir. Inst. Atmospheric Physics, U. Ariz., 1958—; Cons. NSF, 1964-71, U.S. Weather Bur., 1957-59, USAF, 1963-65, U.S. Army, 1954, NIH, 1965; chmn. com. atmosphere sci. Nat. Acad. Scis., 1973-76; mem. U.S. nat. com. Internat. Union Geodesy and Geophysics, 1974-76, 78—, chmn., 1980—; mem. Nat. Adv. Com. on Oceans and Atmosphere, 1978—; trustee Univ. Corp. Atmospheric Research, 1983—. Author: Radar Meteorology, 1959, The Nature of Violent Storms, 1961, Radar Observes the Weather, 1962, Cloud Physics and Cloud Seeding, 1962, The Unclean Sky, 1966, The Thunderstorm, 1964, (with others) Earth and Space Sciences, 1966, 71, Laboratory Manual for Earth and Space Science, 1966, 71, Harvesting the Clouds, 1969, Radar Observation of the Atmosphere, 1973, Weather, 1974, Fundamentals of Meteorology, 1979, Weather in Your Life, 1983; also numerous articles.; Asso. editor: Jour. Meteorology, 1961, Jour. Atmospheric Sciences, 1962-66; mem. editorial adv. bd.: Britannica Yearbook of Science and the Future, 1969—; cons. editor: Weatherwise, 1978—; mem. editorial com.: Il Nuovo Cimento C, 1978—. Served to capt. USAAF, 1943-46. Fellow Am. Meteorol. Soc. (pres. 1966-68, councilor 1959-61, Meisinger award 1962, Brooks award 1971, Second Half Century award 1975), Am. Geophys. Union (pres. meteorol. sect. 1974-75), AAAS (sec. sect. on atmospheric and hydrospheric scis. 1968-74); mem. Sigma Xi. Roman Catholic. Home: 5141 E Rosewood Ave Tucson AZ 85711

BATTEN, ALAN HENRY, astronomer; b. Tankerton, Kent, Eng., Jan. 21, 1933; emigrated to Can., 1959, naturalized, 1975; s. George Cuthbert and Gladys (Greenwood) B.; m. Lois Eleanor Dewis, July 30, 1960; children: Michael Henry John, Margaret Eleanor. B.Sc. with 1st class honours, U. St. Andrews, Scotland, 1955, D.Sc., 1974; Ph.D., U. Manchester, Eng., 1958. Research asst. astronomy, jr. tutor St. Anselm Residence Hall, U. Manchester, 1958-59; postdoctoral fellow Dominion Astrophys. Obs., Victoria, B.C., Can., 1959-61, mem. staff, 1961—, asso. research officer, 1970-76, sr. research officer, 1976—; part-time lectr. astronomy U. Victoria, 1961-64; guest investigator Vatican Obs., 1970, Inst. de Astronomia y Fisica del Espacio, Buenos Aires, 1972; chmn. nat. orgn. com. Internat. Astron. Union XVII Gen. Assembly, 1975-79. Author: Binary and Multiple Systems of Stars, 1973; Editor: Extended Atmospheres and Circumstellar Matter in Spectroscoscopic Binary Systems, 1973; sr. author: Seventh Catalogue of the Orbital Elements of Spectroscopic Binary Systems, 1978; co-editor: The Determination of Radial Velocities and Their Applications, 1967; translator: L'Observation des Etoiles Doubles Visuelles par P. Couteau, 1981; contbr. articles to profl. jours. Pres. Willows Elementary Sch. PTA, Victoria, 1971-73; mem. Anglican Ch. Can. Diocesan Synod, B.C., 1966-68, 74. Recipient Queen's Silver Jubilee medal, Can., 1977. Fellow Royal Soc. Can. (convenor interdisciplinary sect. 1980-81, mem. council 1980-81), Royal Astron. Soc., Explorers Club; mem. Internat. Astron. Union (pres. commn. 30 1976-79, pres. commn. 42 1982—), Royal Astron. Soc. Can. (pres. 1976-78, editor jour. 1981—), Astron. Soc. Pacific (v.p. 1965-68), Canadian Astron. Soc. (charter, pres. 1972-74), Am. Astron. Socs. Home: 2987 Westdone Rd Victoria BC Canada V8R 5G1 Office: 5071 W Saanich Rd Victoria BC Canada V8X 4M6

BATTEN, FRANK, newspaper publisher, broadcaster; b. Norfolk, Va., Feb. 11, 1927; s. Frank and Dorothy (Martin) B.; m. Jane Neal Parke; children: Frank, Mary, Dorothy. A.B., U. Va., 1950; M.B.A., Harvard U., 1952. Asst. sec., treas., v.p., dir. Norfolk Newspapers, Inc., 1952-54; chmn. bd., chief exec. Landmark Communications, Inc., 1966—; pub. Norfolk Virginian-Pilot, Norfolk Ledger-Dispatch, 1954—, Portsmouth Star, 1954—; chmn. Greensboro (N.C.) Daily News, Greensboro Record, 1965—, WTAR Radio-TV Corp., 1966—, Roanoke Times and World-News, Tele Cable Corp., Landmark Community Newspapers, Inc.; vice chmn. AP, 1977-82, chmn., 1982—, Newspaper Advt. Bur., 1972-74. Chmn., 1957, Internat. Naval Rev., Hampton Roads, Va.; pres. Norfolk Area United Fund, 1964; vice chmn. State Council Higher Edn. for Va., from 1977; chmn. bd. Old Dominion U., 1962-70; trustee, pres. Norfolk Acad.; trustee Hollins Coll., 1969-75. Recipient Norfolk's First Citizen award, 1966. Mem. Norfolk C. of C. (pres. 1961), Delta Kappa Epsilon. Episcopalian. Clubs: Princess Anne Country, Norfolk Yacht (Norfolk). Office: 150 W Brambleton Ave Norfolk VA 23510 *

BATTEN, JAMES KNOX, newspaperman; b. Suffolk, Va., Jan. 11, 1936; s. Eugene Taylor and Josephine (Winslow) B.; m. Jean Elaine Trueworthy, Feb. 22, 1958; children: Mark Winslow, Laura Taylor, Taylor Edison. B.S., Davidson Coll., 1957; M. Pub. Affairs, Princeton, 1962. Reporter Charlotte (N.C.) Observer, 1957-58, 62-65; corr. Washington bur. Knight Newspapers, 1965-70; editorial staff Detroit Free Press, 1970-72; exec. editor Charlotte (N.C.) Observer, 1972-75; v.p. Knight-Ridder Newspapers, Inc., Miami, Fla., 1975-80, sr. v.p., 1980-82; pres., 1982—; dir. AP. Trustee Davidson Coll. (N.C.), U. Miami. Served with AUS, 1958-60. Recipient George Polk Meml. award for regional reporting, 1968; Sidney Hillman Found. award, 1968. Mem. Greater Miami C. of C. (gov., exec. com.). Methodist. Office: One Herald Plaza Miami FL 33101

BATTEN, JOHN HENRY, III, manufacturing executive; b. Chgo., Jan. 16, 1912; s. Percy Haight and Lisa (Stockton) B.; m. Katherine Vernet Smith, June 30, 1938; children: Edmund Peter Smith, Michael Ellsworth, Linda Vernet. Grad., Phillips (Andover) Acad., 1931; A.B., Yale U., 1935; Cert. M.E., U. Wis. Extension, 1949. With Twin Disc, Inc., Racine, Wis., 1935—, dir., 1937—, asst. treas., 1942-43, v.p., asst. gen. mgr., 1943-45, exec. v.p., 1945-48, pres., chief exec. officer, 1948-76, chmn., chief exec. officer, 1976—; chmn., dir. Twin Disc Clutch AG, Vaduz, Liechtenstein, Brit. Twin Disc Ltd., Eng., Twin Disc Pacific, Albury, Australia, Twin Disc, S.Africa, Twin Disc (Far East) Ltd., Singapore, Racine Comml. Airport Corp., Wis.; dir. Twin Disc Internat. S.A., Nivelles, Belgium, Niigata Converter Co., Tokyo, Japan, Walker Forge, Racine, Employers Ins. of Wausau. Mem., Racine, Bd. Edn., 1936-46. Mem. N.A.M. (former Midwest v.p., dir.), Wis. Mfrs. Assn. (past dir.), Soc. Automotive Engrs., Chief Execs. Forum, SAR, Phi Beta Kappa. Episcopalian. Home: 3030 Michigan Blvd Racine WI 53402 Office: 1328 Racine St Racine WI 53403

BATTEN, ROGER LYMAN, educator, curator; b. Hammond, Ind., June 22, 1923; s. Verne Lyman and Mae I. (Anuta) B.; m. Loretta Elizabeth Lepeska, Jan. 29, 1966 (dec. 1981). B.A., U. Wyo., 1948; Ph.D., Columbia, 1955. Geologist U.S. Geol. Survey, Washington, 1954; prof. geology U. Wis., 1955-62, Columbia, N.Y.C., 1962—; also curator Am. Mus. Natural History, N.Y.C., 1962—; cons. McGraw-Hill Book Co. Author: (with R.H. Dott, Jr.) The Evolution of the Earth, 1981. Served with inf. AUS, 1943-45. Decorated Purple Heart. Mem. Paleontol. Soc., Geol. Soc. Am., Soc. Systematic Zoology, Paleontog. Soc. Great Britain, Malacol. Soc. London, Sigma Xi. Home: 171 Newcomb Rd Tenafly NJ 07670 Office: Am Museum Natural History New York NY 10024

BATTEN, WILLIAM MILFRED, stock exchange executive; b. Reedy, W.Va., June 4, 1909; s. Lewis Allen and Gurry Frances (Goff) B.; m. Kathryn P. Clark, Aug. 10, 1935; children: David Clark, Jane Louise. B.S., Ohio State U., 1932, L.H.D., 1977; LL.D., Morris Harvey Coll., 1960, W.Va., U., 1966, Alderson-Broaddus Coll., 1971, W.Va. Wesleyan Coll., 1974, U. Charleston, 1984; L.H.D., Marietta Coll., 1965, Hofstra U., 1978. Formerly sales promotion rep. Kellogg Co., Battle Creek, Mich.; with J. C. Penney Co., Inc., N.Y.C., 1935—, asst. store mgr., 1937-40, tng. dir., 1940-46, zone personnel rep., 1946-51, asst. to pres., 1951-58, v.p., 1953-58, pres., chief exec. officer, 1958-64, chmn. bd., chief exec. officer, 1964-74; chmn. bd. dirs. N.Y. Stock Exchange, 1976—; mem. bd. adv. council Tex. Instruments Inc., Mem. Bus. Council, 1961—, chmn., 1971-72; bd. dirs. Am. Productivity Center. Served to lt. col. AUS, 1942-45. Recipient Gold medal Nat. Retail Mchts. Assn., 1969; Equal Opportunity award Nat. Urban League, 1974; Man of Yr. award Wharton Sch., U. Pa., 1977; Humanitarianism award Fund for Higher Edn., 1979; Trustees' citation Midwest Research Inst., 1981; named to Nat. Bus. Hall of Fame Jr. Achievement, 1980. Clubs: Links, Creek, Recess, Bond, Econ. (N.Y.C.) (pres. 1967-68); North Hempstead Country.). Home: 18 Cherrywood Rd Locust Valley NY 11560 Office: 11 Wall St New York NY 10005

BATTENHOUSE, ROY WESLEY, English educator; b. Nevinville, Iowa, Apr. 9, 1912; s. Henry Martin and Sarah Louise (Krill) B.; m. Marion Gaber, Feb. 2, 1952; 1 dau., Anna. A.B., Albion Coll., 1933; B. Div., Yale U., 1936, Ph.D., 1938; D. Litt. (hon.), Ripon Coll., 1964; L.H.D., St. Michael's Coll., 1974. Instr. English Ohio State U., 1938-40; asst. prof. ch. history Vanderbilt U., 1940-43, assoc. prof., 1943-46; assoc. prof. ch. history Episcopal Theol. Sch., Cambridge, Mass., 1946-49; assoc. prof. English Ind. U., Bloomington, 1950-56, prof. English, 1956-82, prof. emeritus, 1982—; priest-in-charge St. Paul's Episcopal Ch., Franklin, Tenn., 1942-46; pres. Conf. on Christianity and Lit., 1977-82; vis. prof. English U. Western Ont., 1963-64, NYU, U. Notre Dame, U. Wash. Baylor U. Author: Marlowe's Tamburlaine: A Study in Renaissance Moral Philosophy, 1941, Shakespearean Tragedy: Its Art and Its Christian Premises, 1969; editor, contbg. author: A Companion to the Study of St. Augustine, 1955. Guggenheim fellow, 1958; recipient disting. alumni award Albion Coll., 1983; Kent fellow, 1937; Ford faculty fellow, 1954. Mem. Phi Beta Kappa, MLA (chmn. Shakespeare sect. 1951, chmn. drama sect. 1973, chmn. religious approaches to lit. div. 1981). Home: 1216 E 2d St Bloomington IN 47401 Office: Dept English Ind U Bloomington IN 47405

BATTERMAN, BORIS WILLIAM, physicist; b. N.Y.C., Aug. 25, 1930; m. Elfriede Vollrath, June 24, 1953; children: Robert W., William E., Thomas A. Student, Cooper Union Coll., 1949-50, Technische Hochschule, Stuttgart, Germany, 1953-54; S.B., Mass. Inst. Tech., 1952, Ph.D., 1956. Mem. tech. staff Bell Telephone Labs., Murray Hill, N.J., 1956-65; asso. prof. Cornell U., 1965-67, prof. applied and engring. physics, 1967—, dir., 1974-78, Synchrotron Radiation Lab. (CHESS), 1978—; cons. x-ray diffraction; mem. U.S.A. Nat. Com. Crystallography, Nat. Acad. Sci., 1969-72. Asso. editor: Jour. Crystal Growth, 1964-74. Guggenheim fellow, 1971; Fulbright Hayes fellow, 1971; Humboldt fellow, 1983. Fellow Am. Phys. Soc. Office: Cornell U Ithaca NY 14853

BATTERMAN, STEVEN CHARLES, engineering mechanics and bioengineering educator; b. Bklyn., Aug. 15, 1937; s. Jacob and Anna (Abramowitz) B.; m. Judith Wilpon, Mar. 29, 1959; children: Scott David, Risa Karen, Daniel Adam. B.C.E., Cooper Union, 1959; Sc.M. (NSF fellow), Brown U., 1961, Ph.D., 1964; M.A. (hon.), U. Pa., 1971. Mem. faculty U. Pa., 1964—, prof. mech. engring. and applied mechanics, 1974-79, asso. prof. orthopaedic surgery research, 1972-75, prof. orthopaedic surgery research, 1975—, prof. biomechanics in vet. medicine, 1975—, prof. bioengring., 1974—; cons. to govt., industry, ins. cos., attys. Contbr. numerous articles to profl. jours. NSF postdoctoral fellow, 1970-71; NSF grantee, 1964-70; Nat. Inst. Dental Research grantee, 1973-77. Mem. ASCE, ASME, Am. Acad. Mechanics, Am. Soc. Engring. Edn., Biomed. Engring. Soc., Soc. Exptl. Stress Analysis, Soc. Automotive Engrs., Am. Soc. Safety Engrs., Am. Acad. Forensic Scis., Sigma Xi, Tau Beta Pi, Chi Epsilon. Jewish. Patentee apparatus for acoustically determining periodontal health. Home: 109 Charlann Circle Cherry Hill NJ 08003 Office: 285 Towne Bldg U Pa Philadelphia PA 19104

BATTERSBY, HAROLD RONALD, anthropologist, archaelolgist, Linguist; b. Guildford, Surrey, Eng., Nov. 16, 1922; came to U.S., 1960, naturalized, 1972; s. Eric and Lillian (Darnell) B.; m. Betty Yertchenig O'Hannesian, Apr. 22, 1944. B.A. in Modern Near Eastern Studies, U. Toronto, Can., 1960; Ph.D. in Altiac Studies-Anthropology, Ind. U., 1969. Corr. Surrey Times, London-Guildford, 1947-55; adv. dir. Turkish Post, Istanbul, 1949-53; instr. English Istanbul Med. Faculty, 1948-49, Amerikan Lisan vd San'at Dersanesi, Istanbul, 1948-54, Pangalti Ermeni Orta Okulu, 1949-56; coordiantor athletic events USO, Istanbul, 1948-54; asst. Royal Ont. Mus., Toronto, 1957-59; asst. mgr. City of Toronto, 1957-59; research asst. in med. anthropology U. Pitts., 1960-62; asst. Ind. U., Bloomington, 1962-69; assoc. prof. anthropology SUNY-Genesea, 1970—, dir. linguistics program, 1978—. Author: Anatolian Archaeology: A Comprehensive Bibliograph, 2 vols., 1976; sect. editor: Altaic and Uralic Studies, Ultimate Realigy and Meanings, 1982—. Served with RAF Vol. Res., 1939-46. NDEA fellow; Ind. U. grantee; Geneseo Found. grantee, 1973, 77, 78—. Fellow Royal Anthrop. Inst. Gt. Brit. and Ireland, Am. Anthrop. Assn., Royal Asiatic Soc.; mem. Royal Soc. Asian Affairs, Hakluyt Soc., Internat. Soc. Oriental Research, Middle East Inst., Chgo. Anthrop. Soc., Inst. Ency. of Human Ideas on Ultimate Reality and Meaning, Brit. Inst. Archaelolgy at Ankara, Am. Oriental Soc., Am. Soc. for Study of People of Eastern Europe and No. and Central Asia, Linguistic Soc. Am., Niagara Linguistic Soc., N.Y. State Council Linguistics, Soc. Armensian Studies, Zoryan Inst., Ind. U. Alumni Assn. Republican. Episcopalian. Club: Ind. U. Linguistics. Home: PO Box 80 Groveland Station NY 14462 Office: Blake D 114 Linguistics SUNY-Geneseo Geneseo NY 14454

BATTESTIN, MARTIN CAREY, educator; b. N.Y.C., Mar. 25, 1930; s. Martin August and Marion Fleming (Kirkland) B.; m. Ruth Rootes, June 14, 1963; children: David, Catherine. B.A. summa cum laude, Princeton U., 1952, Ph.D., 1958. English master Westminster Sch., Simsbury, Conn., 1952-53; instr. Wesleyan U., Middletown, Conn., 1956-58, asst. prof., 1958-61, U. Va., Charlottesville, 1961-63, assoc. prof., 1963-67, prof., 1967-75, William R. Kenan, Jr. prof. English, 1975—, chmn. dept. English, 1983—; sr. fellow Council of Humanities, Princeton U., 1971; fellow Center for Advanced Studies, U. Va., 1974-75, Clare Hall, Cambridge (Eng.) U., 1972. Author: The Moral Basis of Fielding's Art, 1959, The Providence of Wit, 1974; editor: (Henry Fielding) Joseph Andrews, 1961, Shamela, 1961, Joseph Andrews, 1967, Tom Jones, 1975, Amelia, 1983, Tom Jones: A Collection of Critical Essays, 1968; adv. editor: Publs. MLA, 1982—. Am. Council Learned Socs. fellow, 1960-61, 72; Guggenheim fellow, 1964-65; Nat. Endowment for Humanities fellow, 1975-76. Mem. MLA, S. Atlantic Modern Lang. Assn., Am. Soc. for Eighteenth-Century Studies, Internat. Assn. U. Profs. English, Acad. for Lit. Studies, The Johnsonians. Mem. Ch. of England. Home: 1832 Westview Rd Charlottesville VA 22903 Office: Dept English Wilson Hall U Va Charlottesville VA 22903

BATTEY, CHARLES W., telecommunications corporation executive; b. 1932; (married). B.B.A., U. Nebr., 1954. With Continental Ill. Nat. Bank & Trust Co., Chgo., 1954-70; pres. Commerce Bank of Kansas City, 1970-73; sr. v.p. corp. relations United Telecommunications, Inc., Kansas City, Mo., 1973-75, sr. v.p. staff, 1975-77, exec. v.p., 1977-79, exec. v.p. fin. and adminstrn. and chief fin. officer, 1979-81, pres., chief operating officer, dir.; dir. First Nat. Bank of Kansas City, Kans.-Nebr. Natural Gas Co., Chater Corp. Bd. dirs. Kansas City Crime Commn., Midwest Research Inst., Heart of Am. United Way, Council on Edn.; bd. dirs., past pres. Kansas City Public TV. Office: United Telecommunications Inc Box 11315 Kansas City MO 64112 *

BATTIN, JAMES FRANKLIN, judge, former congressman; b. Wichita, Kans., Feb. 13, 1925; m. Barbara Choate; children—Loyce, Patricia, James Franklin. Student, Eastern Mont. Coll., Billings; J.D., George Washington U., 1951. Bar: D.C. and Mont. bars. Practice in, Washington, 1951-52, now in, Billings; past dep. county atty.; past sec.-counsel City-County Planning Bd.; past asst. city atty., Billings; then city atty.; mem. Mont. Ho. of Reps., 1958-59; mem. 87th-91st congresses 2d Dist., Mont.; resigned when apptd. U.S. dist. judge, Mont. Dist., 1969, chief judge, 1978—. Served with USNR, World War II. Mem. Am. Legion, DeMolay Legion of Honor. Presbyn. Club: Mason (Shriner). Office: Federal Bldg 316 N 26th St PO Box 1476 Billings MT 59103

BATTIN, JOHN W., electronics company executive; b. Elgin, Ill., Aug. 6, 1937; s. Everett L. and Edith M. (Schnieder) B.; m. Evangeline Battin, July 10, 1979; children: Jeffery, Kandice, Michael. B.E.E., Am. Inst. Tech., 1957. Design engr. Motorola Inc., Schaumburg, Ill., 1958-65, engring. mgmt., 1965-72, gen. mgmt., 1972—. Patentee (7) in gen. communications fields. Republican. Home: 126 Ola Oak Dr North Barrington IL 60010 Office: Motorala Inc 1301 E Algonquin Rd Schaumburg IL 60196

BATTIN, RICHARD HORACE, aeronautical engineer; b. Atlantic City, Mar. 3, 1925; s. Horace Leslie and Martha Esther (Scheu) B.; m. Margery Katheryn Milne, Aug. 25, 1947; children: Thomas, Pamela, Jeffrey. B.S., M.I.T., 1945, Ph.D., 1951. Instr. math. M.I.T., 1946-51, research mathematician Instrumentation Lab., 1951-56, adj. prof. aeros. and astronautics, 1979—; sr. staff mem. Ops. Research Group, Arthur D. Little, Inc., Cambridge, Mass., 1956-58; tech. dir. Apollo Mission devel.; assoc. dir. Instrumentation Lab., 1958-73; assoc. head NASA Program dept. Charles Stark Draper Lab., Inc., 1973—, mem. aerospace safety adv. panel, 1980—. Author: (with J.H. Laning, Jr.) Random Processes in Automatic Control, 1956, Astronautical Guidance, 1964; Mem. editorial com.: Celestial Mechanics, 1968-74. Pres. Project Impact, 1981—; Mem. Lexington (Mass.) Town Meeting, 1956—; mem. Lexington Appropriations Com., 1958-64. Served to lt. (j.g.) Supply Corps USNR, 1945-46. Recipient Louis W. Hill Space Transp. award AIAA, 1972, Mechanics and Control of Flight award, 1978; Superior Achievement award Inst. of Navigation, 1980; Teaching award dept. aeros. and astronautics M.I.T., 1981. Fellow Am. Inst. Aeros. and Astronautics (asso. editor jour., chmn. astrodynamics tech. com. 1978-80, dir. tech. 1979-82); mem. Nat. Acad. Engring., Internat. Acad. Astronautics, Celestial Mechanics Inst., Sigma Xi. Club: Hancock Men's (pres. 1974-76). Home: 15 Paul Revere Rd Lexington MA 02173 Office: 555 Technology Sq Cambridge MA 02139

BATTISON, JOHN HENRY, broadcasting exec.; b. Wembley, Eng., Sept. 11, 1915; s. John Charles and Emily Florence (Butler) B.; m. Cicely Church, 1942 (div. 1954); children: Diana Penelope, John Christopher; m. Nancy H. Mackenzie, 1954 (div. 1971); children: Florence Victoria, Jonathon, Mark; m. Sara Bennett, 1971. B.S., U. London, 1936; Sc.D. in Radiocommunications, Fla. State Christian U., 1973. Registered profl. engr., Washington. Research engr. EKCO Radio Co., 1934-37; mem. tech. div. Brit. Air Ministry, 1937-39; tech. dir. Midland Broadcasting Co., 1945-47; asst. chief allocations engr. ABC, 1947-49; asso. editor Tele-Tech. mag., 1949-52; faculty mem. N.Y. U., 1949-52; dir. TV comml. prodn. Dancer Fitzgerald Sample, Inc., 1951; dir. TV Nat. Council Chs., 1951-52; dir. edn. Nat. Radio Inst., Washington, 1952-54; asso. prof. Am. U., 1952-54; gen. mgr., dir. engring. CHCT-TV, Calgary, Alta., Can., 1954-55; pres., gen. mgr., dir. engring. KAVE and KAVE-TV in name of Voice of the Caverns, Inc., Carlsbad, N.Mex.; tech. controller programs A-R Ltd., Eng., 1958-59; pres., dir. Engring. Internat. Telecommunication Cons., Inc., 1959-63; v.p., dir. engring. Nat. Roadar, Inc., 1966—; head Frequency Allocation Group IIT Research Inst., 1963-68; also cons. engr.; mgr. communications, electronics div. Chesapeake Instrument Corp., 1968; chief engr. Saudi Arabian TV, 1968-70; cons. engr. Smith Electronics Inc., 1970-72; dir. engring. radio sta. WINW, Canton, Ohio, 1972-73, Ohio Communications, Inc., 1973-75; pres. Batcom Internat. Inc., Cleve., 1975—; broadcast cons., Washington, 1955—; dir. Engring. Telecommunications Center, Sta. WOSU-TV-AM-FM, Sta. WPBO-TV, Ohio State U. Fawcett Center for Tomorrow, Columbus, 1978—; mem. U.S. del. to World Adminstrv. Radio Conf., Buenos Aires, 1980, Rio de Janeiro, 1981; lectr. Beijing Broadcasting Inst., Peoples Republic of China, 1981, 82. Author 15 books on broadcasting, TV and films.; Contbr. numerous articles to tech. publs. Trustee Annapolis Jr. High Sch. Served as Squadron Leader RAF, 1939-45. Sr. mem. IEEE; mem. Ohio Assn. Broadcasters, Brit. Inst. Radio Engrs., Soc. Motion Picture and TV Engrs., Nat. TV Film Council, Soc. Broadcast Engrs. (founder, past pres.), U.S. Power Squadron, USCG Aux. (ops. officer flotilla 7-1, communications officer div. 7). Anglican. Clubs: Nat. Press, Broadcasters, Army and Navy (Washington); Am. U. Beirut Alumni (Lebanon); RAF (London); Link (Cleve.). Lodge: Rotary (Washington). Home: 890 Clubview Dr N Worthington Hills OH 43085 Office: Office Telecommunications Center Ohio State U 2400 Olentanguy River Rd Columbus OH 43210

BATTISTA, ORLANDO ALOYSIUS, pharmaceutical company executive, author; b. Cornwall, Ont., Can., June 20, 1917; s. James L. and Carmel (Infante) B.; m. Helen Frances Keffer, Aug. 25, 1945; children: William Keffer, Elizabeth Ann. B.Sc., McGill U., Montreal, 1940; Sc.D., St. Vincent Coll., Latrobe, Pa., 1955. With Am. Viscose Corp., Phila., 1940-63, asst. dir. corporate research, 1961-63; asst. dir. central research dept. FMC Corp., Princeton, N.J., 1963-71; v.p. sci. and tech. Avicon, Inc., Ft. Worth, 1971-74; chmn., pres. Research Services Corp., 1974—, O.A. Battista Research Inst.; Editorial cons. McGraw-Hill Book Co., 1970-74; adj. prof. chemistry U. Tex., Arlington, 1979—; editor, pub. Knowledge Mag., 1976—; founder Olympiads of Knowledge Found., 1977—. Author: How to Enjoy Work and Get More Fun Out of Life, 1957, God's World and You, 1957, Fundamentals of High Polymers, 1958, The Challenge of Chemistry, 1959, Commonscience in Everyday Life, 1960, Mental Drugs: Chemistry's Challenge to Psychotherapy, 1960, The Power to Influence People, 1960, Toward the Conquest of Cancer, 1961, Synthetic Fibers in Papermaking, 1964, Dictionary of Quotoons, 1966, Childish Questions?, 1973, Research for Profit, 1974, Microcrystal Polymer Science, 1975, Work For Profit, 1975, People Power, 1977, Speakers' Dictionary of Quotoons, 1977, Olympiads of Knowledge-1984, How to Enjoy Life 365 Days of the Year, 1984; novel, 1981; Contbr. articles to profl. jours. Fellow Am. Inst. Chemists (Chem. Pioneer award 1969, pres., chief exec. officer 1977-79), N.Y. Acad. Scis.; mem. Am. Acad. Achievement (Golden Plate award 1971), Am. Chem. Soc. (James T. Grady Gold Medal award 1973, creative invention award 1983). Patentee in field; discoverer microcrystalline celluluse, collagon hemostat, man-made ivory, disposable contact lenses, bioassimilable prostheses, protein wound and burn dressings, hybird oil fuels. Home: 3725 Fox Hollow Fort Worth TX 76109 Office: 5280 Trail Lake Dr Fort Worth TX 76133

BATTISTA, ROBERT JAMES, lawyer; b. Detroit, July 25, 1939; s. Theodore and Marguerite (Dalton) B. B.A., U. Notre Dame, 1961; J.D., U. Mich., 1964. Bar: Mich. Assoc., then ptnr. Butzel Long Gust Klein & Van Zile, Detroit, 1965—; mem. rep. assembly State Bar Mich., 1977-80, mem. council labor relations law sect., 1975-78, sec.-treas., 1978-79, vice-chmn., 1979-80, chmn., 1980-81. Mem. Founders Soc., Detroit. Served to 1st lt. U.S. Army, 1964-65. Mem. ABA (com. devel. of law under Nat. Labor Relations Act), Detroit Bar Assn., Mich. Bar Assn., Indsl. Relations Research Assn. Roman Catholic. Clubs: Detroit Golf, Detroit Yacht; Renaissance (Detroit). Home: 2058 Shore Hill Ct West Bloomfield MI Office: 1881 First Nat Bldg Detroit MI 48226

BATTISTI, PAUL ORESTE, hosp. adminstr.; b. Herkimer, N.Y., Mar. 16, 1922; s. Oreste and Ida (Fiore) B.; m. Donna Marie Johannes, Nov. 2, 1945; children—Paul J., Cathy (Mrs. D. Capage), Deborah, Thomas, Daniel, Melora, Stephen. Student, Cornell U., Ithaca, N.Y., 1947-48, U. Neb., 1951-52. With VA, 1946—; dir. VA Hosp., Martinez, Calif., 1969-73, Western region dir., San Francisco, 1973—; adminstr. State Vets. Home Calif., 1976—; chmn., chief exec. officer Medam., Inc.; dir. Med. Am. Corp.; Mem. Contra Costa County Comprehensive Health Planning, Health Facilities Task Force; chmn. adv. com. East Bay Med. Program.; Bd. dirs. East Bay Hosp. Conf., Easter Seals Contra Costa County. Served with AUS, 1942-46. Fellow Am. Coll. Hosp. Adminstrs.; mem. Hosp. Conf. of No. Calif. (pres.), Nat. Assn. State Vets. Homes (pres.). Club: Rotary (Martinez) (dir.). Home: 877 Oak Leaf Way Silverado Country Club Napa CA 94558 Office: Vets Home Calif Yountville CA

BATTISTONE, SAM D., owner and president professional basketball team. Owner, pres. Utah Jazz, NBA, Salt Lake City;. Office: The Utah Jazz Exec Offices The Salt Palace 100 South West Temple Suite 206 Salt Lake City UT 84101

BATTLE, ALLEN OVERTON, JR., educator, psychologist; b. Memphis, Nov. 19, 1927; s. Allen Overton and Florence Louise (Castelvecchi) B.; m. Mary Madeline Vroman, June 14, 1952; 1 son, Allen Overton. B.S., Siena Coll., 1949; M.A., Cath. U. Am., 1953, Ph.D., 1961; certificate in clin. psychology, U. Tenn. Coll. Medicine, 1953. Diplomate: in clin. psychology Am. Bd. Profl. Psychology, 1971. Instr. dept. psychiatry U. Tenn. Coll. Medicine, 1956-61, asst. prof., 1961-67, asso. prof., 1966-72, prof., 1972—; chief clin. psychologist U. Tenn. Mental Health Center, 1971-78, chief div. clin. psychology, 1974—; vis. lectr. Southwestern U. at Memphis, 1962—. Author: Clinical Psychology for Physical Therapists, 1975, Suicide and Crisis Intervention Training Manuals, 1978, The Psychology of Patient Care: A Humanistic Approach, 1979; contbr. articles to profl. jours. Cons. USPHS, Suicide and Crisis Intervention Service; mem. Mayor's Commn. on Alcohol and Drug Abuse, 1974-77; Bd. dirs. Runaway House, St. Peter's Home for Children. Recipient Disting. Service award Tenn. Dept. Mental Health, 1971. Mem. Am., Tenn. psychol. assns., Am. Anthrop. Assn., N.Y. Acad. Sci., AAAS, Brit. Soc. Projective Techniques, Sigma Xi. Home: 2220 Washington Ave Memphis TN 38104 Office: 66 N Pauline St Memphis TN 38105

BATTLE, EDWARD GENE, energy resources executive; b. Mont Belvieu, Tex., June 19, 1923; s. Paul E. and Annie-Mae B. B.S., Tex. A&M U., 1954. Pres., dir. Norcen Energy Resources Ltd., Toronto, Ont., Can., 1975—; with Continental Oil Co., Tex., from 1954; evaluation engr. Medallion Petroleums, Ltd., 1957, v.p prodn., 1965, exec. v.p., 1966, pres., from 1973; pres., chief operating officer No. and Central Gas Corp., 1974—; dir. No. and Central Gas Corp. Ltd., Coleman Collieries, Ltd., Gas Metro, Inc., Greater Winnipeg Gas Co. Mem. Assn. Profl. Engrs., Geologists and Geophysicists Alta., Assn. Profl. Engrs. Ont., Soc. Petroleum Engrs., AIME. Clubs: Calgary Golf and Country, Rosedale Golf. Home: 46 Chestnut Park Toronto ON Canada M4W 1W8 Office: 4600 Toronto Dominion Centre Toronto ON Canada M5K 1E5

BATTLE, HYMAN LLEWELLYN, JR., lawyer; b. Rocky Mount, N.C., Jan. 19, 1925; s. Hyman Llewellyn and Mamie (Braswell) B.; children: Craig L., David H., John M., Kemp P. Grad., Choate Sch., 1942; B.A., Princeton U., 1946; LL.B., U. Pa., 1949. Bar: N.Y. bar 1949. Since practiced in, N.Y.C.; partner Battle, Fowler, Jaffin, & Kheel., 1957—; dir. ARCA Found., Chase Bag Co., Melville Corp., Rocky Mount Mills. Trustee Rectory Sch., Pomfret, Conn., 1967-78. Served with USMCR, 1943-46. 51-52. Home: 860 United Nations Plaza New York NY 10017 Office: 280 Park Ave New York NY 10017

BATTLE, JEAN ALLEN, author, former educator; b. Talladega, Ala., June 15, 1914; s. William Raines and Lemerle McLemore (Allen) B.; m. Lucy Troxell, Aug. 25, 1940; 1 dau., Helen Carol Battle Salmon. Student, Birmingham So. Coll., 1932-33; B.S., Middle Tenn. State U., 1937; M.A., U. Ala., 1941; Ed.D., U. Fla., 1952; postgrad., Oxford U., 1980. Dept. chmn., dean students Fla. So. Coll., 1940-55, dean coll., 1956-59; dean Coll. Edn. U. South Fla., Tampa, 1959-71, prof. higher edn., 1971; guest lectr. Rewley House, Oxford U., 1981; editor, pub. Tenn. Valley News.; Mem. Fla. Tchrs. Edn. Adv. Council, Fla. Continuing Edn. Council; mem. courses study com. Fla. Bd. Edn.; mem. Tampa Bay Com. on Fgn. Affairs; adv. com. Hillsborough County Hosp.; bd. dirs. Fla. Univ. System Honduras Program, World Trade Council, Tampa, Poynter Found., St. Petersburg, Fla., Harold Benjamin Found., U. Md.; bd. dirs., v.p. Southeastern Edn. Lab., Atlanta. Author: Culture and Education for the Contemporary World, 1969, (with others) The New Idea in Education, 1974, Choices for an Intelligent and Humane School and Society, 1981, Education: The Fate of Humanity, 1982, rev., 1983; Contbr. papers to tech. lit. Served to capt. USAAF, 1942-46. Recipient Disting. Service awards Fla. So. Coll., 1952, Fla. Citizenship Clearing House, 1957; Outstanding Alumnus award Middle Tenn. State U. Mem. SAR, Fla. Hist. Soc., NEA, Fla. Edn. Assn. (co-chmn. tchr. recruitment com.), Tampa C. of C. (edn. com.), Acad. Polit. Sci., Omicron Delta Kappa, Pi Gamma Mu, Kappa Delta Pi, Phi Delta Kappa, Sigma Alpha Epsilon. Methodist. Club: Carrollwood Village Golf and Tennis. Lodge: Rotarian. Home: 11011 Carrollwood Dr Tampa FL 33618 Office: U South Fla Fowler Ave Tampa FL 33620

BATTLE, KATHLEEN DEANNA, opera singer, soprano; b. Portsmouth, Ohio; d. Grady and Ollie (Layne) B. B.Mus., U. Cin., M.Mus., Dr. Performing Arts (hons.), 1983. Soprano Met. Opera, San Francisco Opera, Chgo. Opera, Salzburg Festival, N.Y. Philharm., Boston Symphony, Phila. Orch., Berlin Philharm., others. Appearances include Pamina Magic Flute; Rosina Barber of Seville; appearances Adina, Elixir of Love; appearances include Pamina Sophie, Der Rosenkavalier; appearances, Werther, Zerlina, Don Giovanni, Zdenka, Arabella. Mem. Delta Omicron. Methodist. Address: 165 w 57th St New York NY 10019

BATTLE, LUCIUS DURHAM, educator, former diplomat; b. Dawson, Ga., June 1, 1918; s. Warren Lazarus and Jewel Beatrice (Durham) B.; m. Betty Jane Davis, Oct. 1, 1949; children: Lynne, John, Laura, Thomas. A.B., U. Fla., 1939, LL.B., 1946; LL.D.; L.H.D., Fla. State U. Mgr. student staff U. Fla. Library, 1940-42; asso. adminstrv. analyst War Dept., 1942-43; fgn. affairs specialist Dept. State, Washington, 1946-49, spl. asst. to sec. of state, 1949-53, 61-64, also exec. sec., 1961-62; asst. sec. of state for ednl. and cultural affairs, 1962-64; 1st sec. Am. Embassy, Copenhagen, 1953-55; dep. exec. sec. NATO, Paris, 1955-56; ambassador to, UAR, 1964-67, asst. sec. state for Nr. Eastern and South Asian affairs, Washington, 1967-68; v.p. corp. affairs Communications Satellite Corp., 1968-73, sr. v.p. corp. affairs, 1974-80; dir. COMSAT Gen. Corp., 1974-80; chmn. Fgn. Policy Inst., Sch. Advanced Internat. Studies, Johns Hopkins U., 1980—; pres. Middle East Inst., Washington, 1973-74; dir. First Am. Bank N.A., Washington, 1982—; Chmn. UNESCO Gen Conf., Paris, 1962; Vice pres. Colonial Williamsburg, Inc., Williamsburg Restoration, Inc., 1956-61; chpt. mem. Protestant Episcopal Cathedral Found., Washington.; Chmn. bd. St. Albans Sch., 1973-76; vice chmn. Meridian House Internat., 1976-77; trustee George C. Marshall Research Found., Am. U., Cairo, 1970-79; chmn. vis. com. Center for Middle Eastern Studies, Harvard, 1973-76; bd. dirs. Middle East Inst., 1973—, Fgn. Policy Assn., 1974—, Sch. Advanced Internat. Studies, 1975—, Internat. Vol. Services, 1975-76, World Affairs Council of Washington, 1980—, Smithsonian Assos., 1981—, Nat. Def. Univ. Found., 1982—; mem. fine arts com. Dept. State, 1973-77; mem. Nat. Study Commn. on Records and Documents Fed. Ofcls., 1975-76; pres. Bacon House Found., 1975—; adv. bd. Center for Contemporary Arab Studies, Georgetown U., 1976—; mem. founders council Inst. for Study of Diplomacy, 1978—; chmn. nat. com. to honor 14th centennial of Islam, 1979—. Served to lt. USNR, 1943-46. Decorated Order of Republic 1st class, Egypt). Mem. Am. Fgn. Service Assn. (pres. 1962-63), Order of Coif, Phi Beta Kappa, Alpha Tau Omega, Phi Delta Phi. Clubs: Met. (Washington); Alibi. Home: 4856 Rockwood Pkwy NW Washington DC 20016 Office: Sch Advanced Nat Studies Johns Hopkins U 1740 Massachusetts Ave NW Washington DC 20036

BATTLE, WILLIAM RAINEY, ins. co. exec.; b. Santa Ana, Tex., July 10, 1924; s. Fred and Margaret (Rainey) B.; m. Jane Nichol Brown, Jan. 6, 1951; children—Rebecca Brown, William Lee. Student, U. Tex. at El Paso, 1941-43; B.A., U. Iowa, 1947, M.S., 1948. Mgr. actuarial dept. Nat. Life & Accident Ins. Co., Nashville, 1948-51; asso. actuary Southwestern Life Ins. Co., Dallas, 1951-58; actuary Shenandoah Life Ins. Co., Roanoke, Va., 1959-62, v.p., actuary, 1962-70, v.p. fin. ops., 1970-71, exec. v.p., 1971-72, pres., chief exec. officer, 1972—, also dir.; dir. Colonial Am. Nat. Bank Roanoke, Chesapeake and Potomac Telephone Co. Va.; Mem. advisory council Coll. Bus., Va. Poly. Inst. and State U., 1973—. Mem. advisory bd. Salvation Army; bd. dirs. Roanoke Valley Community Hosp., 1975—. Served to 1st lt. USAAF, 1943-46. Fellow Soc. Actuaries; mem. Middle Atlantic Actuarial Club (pres. 1967), Am. Acad. Actuaries, Roanoke Valley C. of C. (pres. 1973). Home: 3419 W Ridge Circle SW Roanoke VA 24015 Office: 2301 Brambleton Ave SW Roanoke VA 24015

BATTLE, WILLIAM ROBERT, newspaper executive; b. Nolensville, Tenn., Dec. 25, 1927; s. William Robert and Cleo (Smith) B.; m. Elizabeth Ogilvie, Dec. 23, 1948; children: Valerie Elizabeth, William Robert III. Student, George Peabody Coll., 1946-49. With Nashville Banner, 1943—, police beat, county polit. beat, 1943-53, city editor, 1953-64, mng. editor, 1964-71, exec. editor, 1971-75, asst. to editor, 1975-78, regional editor, 1978-80, sr. editor, 1980—, movie columnist, 1955-72; editor Hurst Constrn. News; corr. Nat. Enquirer, Lantana, Fla.; staff writer Country Style mag.; bd. dirs. Women's Execs. Internat. Appeared as newspaperman in: film Teacher's Pet, 1957, also in Country Music on Broadway, 1963; Contbr. numerous articles to nat. publs. Supt. gates and admissions Tenn. State Fair, 1953-64; pub. relations chmn. Davidson County chpt. Nat. Found., 1958-70; bd. dirs. Goodwill Industries, 1960-64; chmn. publicity Davison County Council for Retarded Children, 1961-66; mem. exec. bd. Middle Tenn. council Boy Scouts Am.; mem. 4-H Club Found.; sec. Nashville Boys Club. Recipient Big Story award NBC-TV, 1956; named Man of Year 4-H Club, 1974, Future Farmers Am., 1975. Mem. Nashville Area C. of C., Tenn. Press Assn., Nat. Screen Council, Sigma Delta Chi (chmn. scholarship com., pres.). Methodist. Clubs: Nashville City, Exec. of Nashville, Capital, Smyrna Country. Lodges: Masons (32 deg.); Shriners (potentate 1976); Jesters (dir.); Elks (former chmn. scholarship com.). Home: 4108 Crestridge Dr Nashville TN 37204 Office: 1100 Broadway St Nashville TN 37202 *Do your best the first time.*

BATTON, DELMA-JANE HECK, librarian; b. Tampa, Fla., Dec. 10, 1915; d. William Claude and Myfanwy (James) Heck; m. James Harold Batton, July 21, 1951; children—David Jeffrey, Nancy Janine, Thomas William. Student, N.J. State Tchrs. Coll., 1935-36, Coll. of William and Mary, 1937-38, U. Pa., summer 1946; B.S. in Library Sci, U. Ill., 1950, postgrad., 1951. Asst. Princeton (N.J.) Public Library, 1930-32; librarian State Home for Girls, Trenton, N.J., 1934-35; asst. acquisitions and circulation Princeton U. Library, 1935-37; asst. children's and adult sects. Free Library of Phila., 1938-43; asst. librarian U.S. Naval Hosp. Library, Phila., 1943-46; order librarian Principia Coll., Elsah, Ill., 1946-48; catalog asst. U. Ill. Library, 1948-51; field cons. State Library Commn., Dover, Del., 1961-68, acting state librarian, 1964-65, 67-68; dir. Dover Public Library, 1968—; mem. State Adv. Council on Right to Read, 1973-79. Ednl. rep. Del. Assn. Retarded Children, 1963-64; pres. Parents-Friends Assn. of Dover Day Care Center for Retarded, 1964-67. Mem. Am. Library Assn. (adv. com. good reading project), Del. Library Assn. (editor Bull. 1965-66, 72-74, pres. 1969-70, pres. public library div. 1970-73), NEA, AAUW, Storytellers League (pres. 1974—). Clubs: Soroptimist of Dover (sec. 1973-74, pres. 1978-79), Nat. Soc. DAR (treas. Col. Haslet chpt. 1979—). Home: 1081 S Bradford St Dover DE 19901 Office: Dover Public Library Dover DE 19901

BATTS, MICHAEL STANLEY, educator; b. Mitcham, Eng., Aug. 2, 1929; s. Stanley George and Alixe Kathleen (Watson) B.; m. Misao Yoshida, Mar. 19, 1959; 1 dau., Anna. B.A. Gen., U. London, 1952, 1953, D.Litt., 1973; Dr. Phil., U. Freiburg, Germany, 1957; M.L.S., U. Toronto, 1974. Mem. faculty U. Mainz, Germany, 1953-54, U. Basel, Switzerland, 1954-56, U. Wurzburg, Germany, 1956-58; instr. German U. Calif., Berkeley, 1958-60; mem. faculty dept. German U. B.C., Can., 1960—, prof., 1967-80, head dept., 1968-80. Author: Die Form der Aventiuren im Nibelungenlied, 1961, Bruder Hansens Marienlieder, 1964, Studien zu Bruder Hansens Marienliedern, 1964, Das hohe Mittelalter, 1969, Das Nibelungenlied-Synoptische Ausgabe, 1971, Gottfried von Strasburg, 1971, A Checklist of German Literature, 1945-75, 1977, The Bibliography of German Literature: An Historical and Critical Survey, 1978; Editor: Seminar, 1970-80. Served with Brit. Army, 1947-49. Alexander von Humboldt fellow, 1964-65; Can. Council sr. fellow, 1964-65, 71-72; Killam fellow, 1981-82. Fellow Royal Soc. Can.; mem. Canadian Assn. Univ. Tchrs. German (pres. 1982-1984), Philol. Assn. Pacific Coast, Modern Humanities Research Assn., Medieval Acad. Am., Humanities Assn. Can., Alcuin Soc. (exec. v.p. 1972-79, pres. 1979-80). Office: German Dept Univ Brit Columbia Vancouver BC Canada V6T 1W5

BATTS, WARREN LEIGHTON, diversified industry executive; b. Norfolk, Va., Sept. 4, 1932; s. John Leighton and Allie Belle (Johnson) B.; m. Eloise Pitts, Dec. 24, 1957; 1 dau., Terri Allison. B.E.E., Ga. Inst. Tech., 1961; M.B.A., Harvard U., 1963. With Kendall Co., Charlotte, N.C., 1963-64; exec. v.p. Fashion Devel. Co., Santa Paula, Calif., 1964-66; dir. mfg. Olga Co., Van Nuys, Calif., 1964-66; v.p. Douglas Williams Assos., N.Y.C., 1966-67; co-founder Triangle Corp., Orangeburg, S.C., 1967, pres., chief exec. officer, 1967-71; v.p. Mead Corp., Dayton, Ohio, 1971-73, pres., 1973—, chief exec. officer, 1978-80; pres., chief operating officer Dart Industries, Inc. div. Dart & Kraft, Inc., Los Angeles, 1980-81, Dart & Kraft, Inc., Northbrook, Ill., 1981—; adj. prof. U. S.C., 1970-71. Author: (with others) Creative Collective Bargaining, 1964. Trustee Ga. Inst. Tech. Found., 1978—, Am. Enterprise Inst., 1980—; trustee Com. for Econ. Devel., 1981—, Art Inst. Chgo., 1983—. Home: 117 Hidden Oak Dr Longwood FL 32750 Office: Dart & Kraft Inc 2211 Sanders Rd Northbrook IL 60062

BATTY, LAUREN H., baking company executive; b. Long Beach, Calif., May 1, 1921; s. George F. and Cloyce I. B.; m. Alyce LeMert; children: Laura Batty Sloan, Larry H. Student, U. Ariz., 1939-41. With J.C. Penney, 1946-48; with ITT Continental Baking Co., 1948—, regional v.p., 1969-72, div. v.p., 1972-73, corp. v.p., 1973-76, exec. v.p. bakery div., 1977-78, pres., chmn., chief exec. officer, 1978—. Pres. Mental Health of Kansas City, 1969-70. Served with USMC, 1941-46, 51-53. Decorated Purple Heart, Silver Star. Mem. Am. Baking Assn. (bd. govs. exec. com.), Am. Inst. Baking (trustee, fin. com.), Bakery Equipment Mfrs. Assn. Republican. 12909 E 58th St Kansas City MO 64133 Office: ITT Continental Baking Co. PO Box 731 Rye NY 10580

BATUZ, artist; b. Budapest, Hungary, May 27, 1933; came to U.S., 1973, naturalized, 1981; s. Sandor and Irma (Bell) Mahr; m. Ute Mattel, May 28, 1961; children: Sasa, Bandy, Dada, Tas. One-man shows of paintings, sculpture and/or prints include, Wildenstein Galleries, Buenos Aires, Argentina, 1970, Museo de Arte de Sao Paulo, Brazil, 1978, The Phillips Collection, Washington, Everson Mus. Art, Syracuse, N.Y., 1981, Kunsthalle, Nuremberg, W. Ger., Mus. Moderner Kunst, Vienna, Austria; group shows include, Hirshhorn Mus. and Sculpture Garden, Smithsonian Instn., Washington, 1977, Nat. Gallery, Berlin, W. Ger., 1981; represented in numerous permanent collections including, Hirshhorn Mus. and Sculpture Garden, Indpls. Mus. Art, Phillips Collection, Washington, Everson Mus. Art, Syracuse, Musee des Beaux Arts, Zurich, Switzerland, Museo Nacional de Bellas Artes, Montevideo, Uruguay, Kunsthalle, Nuremberg, W. Ger., Met. Mus. Art, Miami, Fla., Nat. Gallery, Berlin, W. Ger., Museo de Arte Contemporaneo, Madrid, Spain, Mus. Modern Art, Vienna, Mus. Fine Art, Santiago, Chile, Mus. Modern Art, Buenos Aires, Mus. Fine Art, Caracas, Venezuela, and others. Address: 77 Morningside Dr South Greens Farms CT 06436

BATZEL, ROGER ELWOOD, chemist; b. Weiser, Idaho, Dec. 1, 1921; s. Walter George and Inez Ruth (Klinefelter) B.; m. Edwina Lorraine Grindstaff, Aug. 18, 1946; children: Stella Lynne, Roger Edward, Stacy Lorraine. B.S., U. Idaho, 1947; Ph.D., U. Calif. at Berkeley, 1951. Mem. staff Lawrence Livermore (Calif.) Lab., 1953—, head chemistry dept., 1959-67, asso. dir. for chemistry, 1961-71, asso. dir. for testing, 1961-64, asso. dir. for space reactors, 1966-68, asso. dir. chem. and bio-med. research, 1969-71, dir. lab., 1971—. Served with USAAF, 1943-45. Named to Alumni Hall of Fame U. Idaho, 1972; recipient disting. assoc. award U.S. Dept. Energy, 1982. Fellow Am. Phys. Soc.; mem. Sigma Xi. Club: Commonwealth of Calif. (San Francisco). Home: 315 Bonanza Way Danville CA 94526 Office: PO Box 808 Livermore CA 94550

BATZER, R. KIRK, accountant; b. Bismarck, N.D., Nov. 28, 1915; s. Reinhold K. and Edna (MacLachlan) B.; m. Marjorie M. White, May 5, 1945 (dec. Oct. 1980); children—John L., Barbara W. Batzer Rivers, Susan M. Batzer Reyes, Kirk W., Laura M. Student, Macalester Coll., 1931-34; A.B., Cornell U., 1935; M.S., Syracuse U., 1940. C.P.A., N.Y., N.J., Ill., Okla., Mo. With Coopers & Lybrand (C.P.A.'s), N.Y.C., 1940-78, partner, 1953-78, dir. internat. services, 1964-71; editor CPA Jour., N.Y.C., 1978—; adj. prof. accounting Lehigh U., Bethlehem, Pa., 1976-77. Sec. Inverclyde Bequest Fund, N.Y.C.; bd. dirs. Essex County council Girl Scouts U.S.A., 1961-68; commr. Housing Authority City of Summit, 1968-78. Served to lt. USNR, 1941-45. Mem. Am. Inst. C.P.A.'s, N.Y. Soc. C.P.A.'s (dir. 1955-58). Episcopalian. Clubs: University (N.Y.C.); Canoe Brook Country (Summit, N.J.). Home: 133 Summit Ave Apt 21 Summit NJ 07901 Office: 600 3d Ave New York NY 10016

BAUCH, THOMAS JAY, lawyer, apparel company executive; b. Indpls., May 24, 1943; s. Thomas and Violet (Smith) B.; m. Ellen L. Burstein, Oct. 31, 1982. B.S., U. Wis., 1964, J.D., 1966. Bar: Ill. 1966, Calif. 1978. Assoc. Lord, Bissell & Brook, Chgo., 1966-72; lawyer, asst. sec. Marcor-Montgomery Ward, Chgo., 1973-75; spl. asst. to solicitor Dept. Labor, Washington, 1975-77; dep. gen. counsel Levi Strauss & Co., San Francisco, 1977-81, v.p., gen. counsel, 1981—; mem. U. Wis. Law Review, Madison, 1964-66. Bd. dirs. San Francisco Planning and Urban Research Assn., 1982. Mem. Am. Assn. Corp. Counsel (dir. 1982—), Order of Coif. Democrat. Clubs: Univ. (San Francisco); Racquet (Chgo.). Office: Levi Strauss & Co 1155 Battery St San Francisco CA 94120

BAUCUS, MAX S., U.S. Senator; b. Helena, Mont., Dec. 11, 1941; s. John and Jean (Sheriff) B.; m. Wanda Minge, Apr. 23, 1983. B.A., Stanford U., 1964, LL.B., 1967. Bar: D.C. 1969, Mont. 1972. Staff atty. CAB, Washington, 1967-69; lawyer SEC, Washington, 1969-71, legal asst. to chmn., 1970-71; practiced in Missoula, Mont., 1971—; mem. Mont. Ho. of Reps., 1972-74, 94th-95th congresses from 1st Dist. Mont., mem. com. appropriations, U.S. Senate from Mont., 1979—; mem. judiciary, fin., small bus. and environ. and pub. works coms. U.S. Senate; acting exec. dir., com. coordinator Mont. Constl. Conv., 1972—. Home: Missoula MT Office: 706 Hart Senate Office Bldg Washington DC 20510

BAUE, ARTHUR EDWARD, surgeon, educator; b. St. Louis, Oct. 7, 1929; s. Arthur Christian and Viola (Wegener) B.; m. Rosemary Dysart, Nov. 24, 1956; children—Patricia Sage, Arthur Christian II, William Dysart. A.B. summa cum laude, Westminster Coll., 1950; M.D. cum laude, Harvard, 1954. Diplomate: Am. Bd. Surgery (dir.), Am. Bd. Thoracic Surgery (dir.). Successively intern, resident, chief resident surgery Mass. Gen. Hosp., Boston, 1954-61; asst. prof. surgery U. Mo. Sch. Medicine, 1962-64; asst. prof., then asso. prof. surgery U. Pa. Sch. Medicine, Phila., 1964-67; Harry Edison prof. surgery Washington U. Sch. Medicine, St. Louis, 1967-75; surgeon-in-chief, dir. dept. surgery Jewish Hosp., St. Louis, 1967-75; chief of surgery Yale-New Haven Hosp., 1975—; prof., chmn. dept. surgery Yale, 1975—, Donald Guthrie prof. surgery, 1977—; cons. surgery Nat. Bd. Med. Examiners; chmn. NIH surgery B study sect., 1978-82. Chief editor: Archives of Surgery, 1977—; mem. editorial bd.: Am. Jour. Physiology. Mem. alumni council Westminster Coll. Served to capt. USAF, 1959. John and Mary R. Markle scholar acad. medicine, 1963; recipient Research Career Devel. award USPHS, 1964. Mem. Am. Assn. Thoracic Surgery, Am. Coll. Cardiology, Am. Coll. Chest Physicians, A.C.S., Assn. Acad. Surgery, New Eng. Surg. Soc., Internat. Cardiovascular Soc., Soc. Thoracic Surgeons, Soc. U. Surgeons, Soc. Vascular Surgery, Internat. Soc. Surgery, Am. Assn. Surgery Trauma, Am. Assn. Artificial Internal Organs, Am. Physiol. Soc., AMA (editorial bd. jour.), Am., Central, Western surg. assns., Soc. Surgery Alimentary Tract, Alpha Omega Alpha. Home: 184 Todd St Hamden CT 06514 Office: 333 Cedar St New Haven CT 06510

BAUER, DIETRICH CHARLES, microbiologist, educator; b. Elgin, Ill., July 1, 1931; s. Karl E. and Martha L. (Dietrich) B.; m. Lois Leonard Reed, Nov. 13, 1954. Student, Lake Forest Coll., 1949-51; B.S., U. Ill., 1954; M.S., Mich. State U., 1957, Ph.D., 1959. Postdoctoral fellow Western Res. U., Cleve., 1959-61; asst. prof. microbiology Ind. U. Sch. Medicine, Indpls., 1961-65, asso. prof., 1965-69, prof. microbiology and immunology, 1969—, chmn. microbiology and immunology, 1981; cons. in field. Contbr. articles to profl. jours. Served with U.S. Army, 1954-56. Recipient Disting. Teaching award Ind. U., 1978. Mem. Am. Assn. Immunologists, Am. Soc. Microbiology, AAAS, Sigma Xi. Office: Dept Microbiology and Immunology Ind Univ Sch Medicine Indianapolis IN 46202

BAUER, EDWARD GREB, JR., lawyer, utilities executive; b. Jeannette, Pa., Aug. 10, 1928; s. Edward Greb and Virginia (Euwer) B.; m. Carolyn Large Isbell, May 8, 1954; children: Charlotte Large, Barbara Greb, Edward Greb III. B.A., Princeton U., 1951; LL.B., Harvard U., 1957. Bar: Pa. 1958. Atty. Ballard, Spahr, Andrews & Ingersoll, Phila., 1957-62; exec. asst. to Mayor James H.J. Tate, Phila., 1962-63; city solicitor, Phila., 1963-70; v.p., gen. counsel Phila. Electric Co., 1970—; dir. Susquehanna Power Co., Susquehanna Electric Co., Adwin Realty Co., Adwin Equipment Co., Continental Bank, Eastern Pa. Devel. Co.; Bd. dirs. Phila. Crime Commn. Served with USAF, 1951-54. Mem. ABA, Pa., Phila. bar assns., Pa. C. of C. (dir.). Clubs: Union League (Phila.); Seaview Country, Hershey's Mill Golf, Boca Raton Hotel and Club. Home: 124 Chandler Dr West Chester PA 19380

BAUER, ELAINE LOUISE, ballet dancer; b. Indpls., July 18, 1949; s. Thomas B. and Elenita M. (Bodwell) B.; m. D. David Brown, June 5, 1971. B.A. in Dance magna cum laude, Butler U., 1971. With, Boston Ballet Co., 1971—; soloist, 1972-74; prin. dancer, 1974—; starred (with Rudolf Nureyev in); N.Y.C. debut of La Sylphide. Office: 553 Tremont St Boston MA 02116

BAUER, FREDERICK CHRISTIAN, motor carrier executive; b. Camden, N.J., Feb. 5, 1927; s. John Albert and Lillian (Saar) B.; m. Dorothy Jane Baker, Jan. 24, 1946; children: Susan, Joan, Scott, Christi. B.A., U. N.C., 1948, M.A., 1949. Tchr. R.J. Reynolds High Sch., Winston-Salem, N.C., 1949-51; sales rep. McLean Trucking Co., Winston-Salem, 1951-58, dist. sales mgr., Memphis, 1958-62, market research mgr., Winston-Salem, 1962-63, Western sales mgr., Indpls., 1963-67, v.p. sales, Winston-Salem, 1967-74, exec. v.p. mktg., 1974-82; v.p. mktg. Kenan Transport Co., Chapel Hill, N.C., 1982—. Served with AUS, 1944-46. Mem. Research Inst. Am., Nat. Indsl. Conf. Bd., Am. Trucking Assn. (sales council 1963), Delta Nu Alpha, Sigma Chi. Presbyterian. Home: 1062 Canterbury Ln Chapel Hill NC 27514 Office: Kenan Transport Co PO Box 2729 Chapel Hill NC 27514

BAUER, GARY LEE, government official; b. Covington, Ky., May 4, 1946; s. Stanley Reynolds and Elizabeth Jane (Gossett) B.; m. Carol Hoke, Sept. 9, 1972; children: Elyse, Sarah. B.A., Georgetown U., 1968, J.J.D., 1973; cert., John F. Kennedy Sch. Govt., Harvard U., 1983. Dir. research Republican Nat. Com., Washington, 1972-73; dir. govt. relations Direct Mai 1 Mktg. Assn., Washington, 1973-80; sr. policy analyst White House, Washington, 1981-82, dep. asst. dir. legal policy, 1982; dep. under sec. U.S. Dept. Edn., Washington, 1982—; polit. cons. Congl. Campaigns, 1972-79. Editor: Reupblican Almanac, 1972; editor and pub.: Businessman's Growth Letter, 1981-82. Cook Legal scholar, 1966; named Ky. Col., 1983. Republican. Baptist. Home: 3610 Lida Pl Fairfax VA 22031 Office: Dept Edn 400 Maryland Ave SW Washington DC 20202

BAUER, HENRY HERMANN, college dean; b. Vienna, Austria, Nov. 16, 1931; came to U.S., 1965, naturalized, 1969; s. Martin Josef and Anne (Rafael) B.; m. Myra Lee Levin, June 29, 1958; children: Helen Suzanne, Judith Ann. B.Sc., U. Sydney, 1952, M.Sc., 1953, Ph.D., 1956. Research asso. U. Mich., 1956-58, vis. scientist, 1965-66; lectr., sr. lectr. U. Sydney, 1958-66; asso. prof., prof. U. Ky., 1966-78; vis. prof. Southampton (Eng.) U., 1972-73; prof. chemistry, dean Coll. Arts and Scis., Va. Poly. Inst. and State U., Blacksburg, 1978—. Author: Alternating Current Polarography and Tensammetry, 1963, Electrodics, 1973, Instrumental Analysis, 1978. Fulbright fellow, 1956-58; Japan Soc. fellow for promotion of sci., 1974. Mem. AAUP, Am. Chem. Soc., Soc. Sci. Exploration (founding mem., councillor), Fedn. Australian Univs. Staff Assns., Internat. Soc. Cryptozoology. Unitarian. Home: 1306 Highland Circle Blacksburg VA 24060 Office: Derring Hall Va Poly Inst and State U Blacksburg VA 24061

BAUER, LUDWIG, medicinal chemist; b. Forchheim, Bavaria, Germany, July 27, 1926; came to U.S., 1950, naturalized, 1961; s. Anton and Paula (Sommerich);; s. Anton and Paula (Bauer); m. Ella Bamberger, Oct. 15, 1957; children—Phillip M., Alan J. B.Sc. with 1st class honors, U. Sydney, Australia, 1949, M.Sc., 1950; Ph.D. in Chemistry, Northwestern U., 1952. Research asso. Harvard, 1952, Columbia, 1953, U. Sydney, 1954; mem. faculty Coll. Pharmacy, Med. Center, U. Ill., Chgo., 1955—, prof. medicinal chemistry, 1966—. Mem. Am. Chem. Soc. Research in medicinal chemistry, especially synthesis of compounds with potential pharmacological interest. Home: 504 Maple St Wilmette IL 60091 Office: 833 S Wood St Chicago IL 60612

BAUER, MALCOLM CLAIR, newspaper editor; b. Enterprise, Oreg., Mar. 19, 1914; s. John Jacob and Lucile (Corkins) B.; m. Roberta Moody, July 11, 1937; children—Bette-B, Mary, Kent, Roberta Jean. B.S., U. Oreg., 1935; Nieman fellow, Harvard, 1950-51; Journalism fellow, Stanford U., 1968. News editor Eugene (Oreg.) Register Guard, 1935-36; news editor Pendleton East-Oregonian, 1936; with The Oregonian, Portland, 1936—, city editor, 1941-51, assoc. editor, 1951—, book editor, 1951—, editor editorial page, 1977-79; ret., 1979; lectr. journalism Portland State Coll., 1956—. Author: Profile of Oregon, 1971; Oreg. corr. Christian Sci. Monitor: also London (Eng.) Economist. Oreg. commr. Edn. Commn. States, 1966; bd. dirs. Reed Coll.; chmn. Oreg. Mental Health Bd., 1972—; trustee Mills Coll. Served from 1st lt. to col AUS, World War II. Decorated Bronze Star medal, Legion of Merit with oak leaf cluster Order Brit. Empire. Mem. Am. Soc. Newspaper Editors, Oreg. Hist. Soc. (past pres.), Phi Delta Phi, Phi Beta Kappa, Phi Delta Theta. Home: 1641 SW Englewood Dr Lake Oswego OR 97034 Office: 1320 SW Broadway Portland OR 97201

BAUER, OTTO FRANK, university administrator, communication educator; b. Elgin, Ill., Dec. 1, 1931; s. Otto Leland and Cora Dorothy (Berlin) B.; m. Jeanette L. Erickson, May 27, 1956; children: Steven Mark, Eric Paul. B.S., Northwestern U., 1953, M.A., 1955, Ph.D., 1959. Instr., then asst. prof. English USAF Acad., Colo., 1959-61, dir. debate, 1959-61; instr. to prof. Bowling Green State U., Ohio, 1961-71, dir. grad. admissions and fellowships, 1965-69; asst. dean Grad. Sch. USAF Acad., Colo., 1967-69, asst. v.p., 1970-71; ACE fellow U. Calif.-Berkeley, 1969-70; prof. communication U. Wis.-Parkside, Kenosha, 1971-79; vice chancellor U. Wis. -Parkside, Kenosha, 1971-76; acting chancellor U. Wis.-Berkeley, 1974-75; vis. prof. communication, spl. asst. to chancellor U. Wis., Madison, 1976-77; vice chancellor for acad. affairs, prof. U. Nebr., Omaha, 1979—; commr. North Central Assn. Colls. and Schs., 1975-77; cons. Bishop Clarkson Coll. Nursing, Omaha, 1981—. Author: Fundamentals of Debate, 1966; co-author: Guidebooks for Student Speakers, 1966; editor: Introduction to Speech Communications, 1968. Bd. dirs. United Way, of Kenosha County (Wis.), 1973-79, Kenosha County Council Girl Scouts U.S.A., 1977-79; chmn. speakers bur. United Way of Midlands, Omaha, 1983. Served to 1st lt. USAF, 1956-61. Recipient Faculty Disting. Service award U. Wis.-Parkside, 1978; named Exec. of Yr. Nat. Secs. Assn., Omaha, 1980; Clarion DeWitt Hardy scholar, 1949-53. Mem. Am. Counci on Edn. (exec. com. Council of Fellow 1982—), Speech Communicatio Assn. (legis. assembly 1953—). Club: Rotary (Omaha). Office: U Nebr 60th and Dodge St Omaha NE 68182

BAUER, PAUL DAVID, corporation executive; b. Buffalo, July 25, 1943; s. Norman Thomas and Rita Ann (Maloney) B.; m. Donna Marie Szlosek, May 6, 1967; children: David, Lisa. B.S., Boston Coll., 1965. Supervising sr. Peat, Marwick, Mitchell & Co. (C.P.A.s), Buffalo, 1965-70; with Niagara Frontier Services, Inc., Buffalo, 1970—, treas., 1972—, v.p., 1976-82, sr. v.p., 1982—; pres. Niassociates, Inc., Buffalo, 1973—. Former treas. Studio Theatre Sch., Buffalo; sec. bd. dirs. Amherst Hockey Assn., 1977; mem. council on accountancy Canisius Coll., 1980; mem. pres.'s council D'Youville Coll.; bd. dirs. Jr. Achievement., YMCA of Buffalo and Erie County. Mem. Nat. Assn. Accountants, Fin. Execs. Inst. Clubs: Park Country (Buffalo); Youngstown Yacht. Home: 49 Oakview Dr Williamsville NY 14221 Office: 60 Dingens St Buffalo NY 14206:

BAUER, RICHARD H., clergyman; b. Cin., May 19, 1913; s. Samuel B. and Alice (Helck) B.; m. Eleanor Nye, July 3, 1941. Comml. Engr., U. Cin., 1936; M.Div., Garrett Theol. Sem., 1947; D.D., Ohio No. U., 1962. With Proctor & Gamble Co., 1932-44; ordained to ministry Methodist Ch., 1948; pastor in, Cin., 1942-44, Ashley, Ind., 1944-47, North College Hill, Cin., 1947-53, Bellefontaine, Ohio, 1953-56, dist. supt., 1956-60; exec. sec. interboard com. enlistment for ch. occupations United Meth. Ch., 1960-72, exec. sec. office personnel services, 1973-76, dir. devel. loans and scholarships, 1976-78; nat. field rep. World Hunger Edn./Action Together, United Meth. Ch., 1978—; Del. World Meth. Conf., 1961, 66, 71, 81; mem. World Meth. Council, 1966-71; mem. assembly Nat. Council Chs., 1963-66, 66-69, 70-73, chmn. commn. vocation and enlistment, 1963-76, vice chmn. dept. ministry, 1966-76; sec. Meth. Council Secs., 1964-68; trustee Meth. Home Aged, 1956-60; bd. dirs., pres. Mid-South Career Devel. Center, 1974-78; chmn. Commn. on Vocation and Religion, Nat. Vocat. Guidance Assn., 1980—. Contbr. articles to ch. publs. Mem. Am. Personnel and Guidance Assn., Ch. Career Devel. Council (sec. 1974-78), UN Assn. (pres. Nashville chpt. 1982—), Common Cause, Sigma Chi, Omicron Delta Kappa. Home: 3809 Brighton Ave Nashville TN 37205

BAUER, RICHARD JOHN, oil co. exec.; b. Cuba City, Wis., Dec. 21, 1925; s. Walter Emery and Lelia Gayle (Skaife) B.; m. Jo-Katherine Ogden, Feb. 23, 1946; 1 son, Richard John. B.S. in Mech. Engring, U. Okla., 1946. With Shell Oil Co., 1946—, mech. engr., 1946-58, chief mech. engr., Denver, 1958-66, dir. prodn. research, Houston, 1966-67, gen. mgr. info. and computer services, N.Y.C., 1967-70, v.p. purchasing and gen. services, Houston, 1970—; dir. MESBIC Fin. Corp., Houston. Active United Way campaign. Served with USN, 1943-46. Recipient U.S. Dept. Commerce award excellence, 1976. Mem. Nat. Assn. Purchasing Mgmt., Soc. Petroleum Engrs., Am. Petroleum Inst. Methodist. Clubs: Petroleum, Brae-Burn Country (both Houston). Patentee in field. Home: 13614 Apple Tree Houston TX 77079 Office: Two Shell Plaza Houston TX 77001

BAUER, RICHARD MAX, paper company executive; b. Appleton, Wis., Apr. 30, 1928; s. Max M. and Gladys Marie (Kranhold) B.; m. Mona Lois Jung, Sept. 2, 1950; children: Mark Peter, Joanne Beth, Sarah Anne, Richard Max, Laura Lois. B.S., Lawrence U., Appleton, Wis., 1953. Process engr. Marathon Corp., Menasha, Wis., 1953-56; supr. Marathon div. Am. Can Co., Neenah, Wis., 1956-60, mgr. product devel., asso. dir. research and devel., 1960-70, dir. research and devel. consumer products div., 1970-80, mng. dir. air-forming tech., 1980-83; v.p. absorbent products research James River Corp., 1983—; with Inst. Paper Chemistry, summer 1962. Served with USMC, 1945-47; Served with AUS, 1950-52. Mem. Paperboard Packaging Council (chmn. tech. task force), TAPPI, Indsl. Research Inst. Roman Catholic. Club: Elks. Patentee wax carton coating process. Home: 804 E Forest Ave Neenah WI 54956

BAUER, ROBERT OLIVER, anesthesiologist; b. Chgo., Mar. 2, 1918; s. Walter George and Mable Eliza (Oliver) B.; m. Bernadine S. Feldt, Aug. 22, 1938; children—Susan Karroll, Frederick Bruce, Patrick Ralph. B.S. in Pharmacy, U. Mich., 1940; M.S. in Pharmacology, Wayne State U., 1943, M.D., 1947. Intern Wayne County Gen. Hosp., Eloise, Mich., 1947-48; asst. prof. pharmacology Boston U. Med. Sch., 1948-52; chief pharmacologist Riker Labs., Northridge, Calif., 1952-55; cancer research Roswell Park Meml. Inst., Buffalo, 1955-58; mem. faculty UCLA Med. Sch., 1958—, prof. anesthesiology and pharmacology, 1971—. Author numerous articles in field. Served as flight surgeon USAF, 1953-55. Decorated Meritorious Service medal. Mem. Am. Soc. Anesthesiology, Soc. Exptl. Biology and Medicine, Am. Soc. Pharmacology and Exptl. Therapeutics, Soc. Clin. Pharmacology and Therapeutics, Res. Officers Assn., Am. Rifle Assn., Sierra Club. Office: UCLA CHS-56-125 Los Angeles CA 90024

BAUER, ROBERT PAUL, industrial executive; b. Cin., Oct. 19, 1920; s. Elmer John and Ione (Koehne) B.; m. Alice M. Miller, Sept. 23, 1944; children—Barbara Jo, Peggy Lou, Gus. B.B.A., U. Cin., 1949. C.P.A., Ohio. Pub. accountant Haskins & Sells (C.P.A.'s), Cin., 1947-51; div. controller Baldwin-Lima-Hamilton Corp., Lima, Ohio, 1951-57, gen. controller exec. office, Phila., 1957-61; treas., controller Cessna Aircraft Co., 1961-67, v.p., treas., 1967-69, sr. v.p., 1969-82; pres., chmn. bd. Pvt. Enterprise, Inc., 1982—; dir. chmn., dir. Cessna Finance Co.; also dir. chmn., dir. Cessna Fluid Power Ltd., Scotland; pres., chmn. Cessna Internat. Finance Corp. Named outstanding young man of the year, Lima, 1956. Mem. Am. Inst. C.P.A.s. Home: 642 Longford Ln Wichita KS 67206 Office: 300 W Douglas St Wichita KS 67202

BAUER, ROGER DUANE, univ. dean; b. Oxford, Nebr., Jan. 17, 1932; s. Albert Carl and Minnie (Lueking) B.; m. Jacquelyn True, Aug. 10, 1956; children—Lisa, Scott, Robert. B.S., Beloit Coll., 1953; M.S., Kans. State U., 1957, Ph.D., 1959. Asst. prof. chemistry Calif. State U., Long Beach, 1959-64, asso. prof., 1964-69, prof., 1969—, dean, 1975—. Served with U.S. Army, 1954-56. USPHS fellow, 1966; Am. Council on Edn. fellow, 1971. Mem. Am. Chem. Soc., Radiation Research Soc., Sigma Xi, Phi Lambda Upsilon. Home: 6320 Colorado St Long Beach CA 90803 Office: Coll Natural Sci Calif State U Long Beach CA 90840

BAUER, RONALD CLOYD, univ. pres.; b. Bottineau, N.D., Feb. 27, 1915; s. Frank and Maud (Hyde) B.; m. Ethel B. Church, July 2, 1939; children—Logan, Elena. B.A., State Tchrs. Coll., Valley City, N.D., 1936; M.S., U. N.D., 1944; Ed.D. (fellow in intergroup relations), Columbia U., 1952. Prin., public schs., 1934-35, edn. supr., State of N.D., 1936-39; area dir. Nat. Youth Adminstrn., N.C., 1939-42; asst. area dir. Am. Jr. Red Cross, St. Louis, 1942-45; coll. dean Poly Inst. P.R., San German, 1945-48; instr. Tchrs. Coll. Columbia U., N.Y.C., 1950-53; vis. lectr. Inst. Edn., U. London, 1953-55; pres. Inter-Am. U., San German, P.R., 1955-65; chancellor World U., San Juan, P.R., 1965—, pres., 1968—; Chmn. Internat. Ednl. Devel. Services, Inc.; lectr. Univ. Coll. Gold Coast, Accra, 1954, Maherer Coll., Kampala, Uganda, 1955; mem. exec. com. Univs. and Quest for Peace. Recipient de Hostos award as Citizen of Yr., 1964; Educator of Yr. award P.R., 1981. Mem. NEA, Commn. on Internat. Cooperation Through Edn., Assn. Am. Colls., Comparative Edn. Assn., Am. Assn. Colls. for Tchr. Edn., Internat. Congress U. Adult Edn. (exec. com.), Phi Delta Kappa, Kappa Delta Pi. Clubs: Lions, Rotary. Home: 1004 Park Blvd Punta Las Marias San Juan PR 00909 Office: World U Barbosa and Guayama Hato Rey PR 00917

BAUER, THEODORE JAMES, physician; b. Iowa City, Nov. 18, 1909; s. Charles A. and Anna (Braun) B.; m. Helen Mattes, Sept. 1, 1938; children—Jane Helen, Virginia, Mary, Martha. B.S., U. Iowa, M.D., 1933. Diplomate: Am. Bd. Preventive Medicine and Pub. Health. Intern U.S. Marine Hosp., N.Y., 1933-34; spl. tng. USPHS, 1934-38; regional cons. venereal disease control Dist. 5, San Francisco, 1938-41, veneral disease control officer, Kansas City, 1941-42, chief div. venereal disease, Washington, 1948-52; med. officer in charge Communicable Disease Center, Altanta, 1953-56; asst. surgeon gen., dep. chief Bur. State Services, Washington, 1956-60, chief, 1960-62; veneral disease control officer Chgo. Health Dept.; also med. officer charge Chgo. Intensive Treatment Center, 1942-48; med. dir. Becton, Dickinson and Co., 1962-67, sr. v.p. research and med. affairs, 1967-75, dir., 1965—; asso. prof. bacteriology and immunology Emory U., 1952-57; spl. lectr. on venereal diseases Georgetown U. Sch. Medicine, Washington.; Mem. expert com. on venereal infections, trepinematoses WHO; bd. dirs. Nat. Council, 1972-76; mem. Surgeon Gen.'s Adv. Com. on Community Health Services, Adv. Council on the Chronic Sick of N.J., N.J. Health Care Adminstrn. Bd., 1975—. Editor: Jour. Venereal Disease Info; mem. editorial bd.: Am. Jour. Syphilis, Gonorrhea and Other Venereal Diseases. Recipient Distinguished Service award USPHS, 1962. Fellow ACP, Am. Pub. Health Assn. (chmn. evaluation and standards com.); mem. U.S. Mexico Border Pub. Health Assn., AMA, Am. Social Hygiene Assn., Sci. Research Soc. Am., Assn. Advancement Med. Instrumentation (exec. com. 1973-76), Am. Venereal Disease Assn. (mem. exec. bd.), Sigma Xi. Home: 451 Weymouth Dr Wyckoff NJ 07481 Office: Becton Dickinson & Co Macke Center Paramus NJ 07652

BAUER, VICTOR JOHN, pharmaceutical company executive; b. N.Y.C., May 14, 1935; s. Victor and Ottilie (Wild) B.; m. Sonia Witkowski, Sept. 14, 1957; children: Katherine E., Steven E. B.S., MIT, 1956; Ph.D., U. Wis., 1960. Research fellow Harvard U., 1961; research chemist Lederle Labs., Pearl River, N.Y., 1961-71; with Hoechst-Roussel Pharms. Inc., Somerville, N.J., 1971—, dir. chem. research, 1971-74, v.p. ops., 1974-80, exec. v.p., chief operating officer, 1980—, also dir., 1980—; dir. Asso. Biosci., Inc., Phoenix. Mem. Am. Chem. Soc. Office: Route 202-206 N Somerville NJ 08876

BAUER, WALTER F., computer company executive; b. Wyandotte, Mich., Mar. 21, 1924; s. Walter Ferdinand and Erna Clara (Schotter) B.; m. Donna Bothamley, Aug. 27, 1949; children: Thomas, Randall, John. B.S., U. Mich., 1946, M.S., 1947, Ph.D., 1951. Research engr. U. Mich., 1951-54; dir. computation and data reduction ctr. TRW Corp., Calif., 1954-59, mgr. dept. info. systems, 1959-62; founder, chief exec. officer, chmn. bd. Infromatics Gen. Corp., Woodland Hills, Calif., 1962—. Contbr. articles to profl. jours. Trustee Charles Babbage Inst., Mpls., 1979—; bd. dirs. United Way; mem. Los Angeles Econ. Adv. Council, 1974-77. 1st lt. USAF, 1943-46. Mem. Am. Electronics Assn. (dir. 1981-82), Assn. Data Processing Service Orgns., Phi Kappa Phi. Republican. Club: Regency (Los Angeles). Home: 15935 Valley Vista Encino CA 91436 Office: Informatics Gen Corp 21031 Ventura Blvd Woodland Hills CA 91364

BAUER, WILLIAM JOSEPH, judge; b. Chgo., Sept. 15, 1926; s. William Francis and Lucille (Gleason) B.; m. Mary Nicol, Jan. 28, 1950; children—Patricia, Linda. A.B., Elmhurst Coll., 1949; J.D., DePaul U., 1952. Bar: Ill. bar 1951. Partner firm Erlenborn, Bauer & Hotte, Elmhurst, Ill., 1953-64; asst. state's atty., Du Page County, Ill., 1952-56, 1st asst. state's atty., 1956-58, state's atty., 1959-64; judge Jud. Circuit Ct., 1964-70; U.S. dist. atty. No. Ill., Chgo., 1970-71; judge U.S. Dist. Ct., Chgo., 1971-75, U.S. Ct. Appeals, 7th Circuit, 1975—; instr. bus. law Elmhurst Coll., 1952-59; lectr. criminal trial practice DePaul U., 1978—. Pres. Elmhurst Young Republicans, 1958-59; bd. govs. Du Page Meml. Hosp. Served with AUS, 1945-47. Mem. ABA, Ill. Bar Assn., Du Page County Bar Assn. (pres.), Ill. State's Attys. Assn. (dir.). Roman Catholic. Club: Union League (Chgo.). Home: 213 Grace St Elmhurst IL 60126 Office: 219 S Dearborn St Chicago IL 60604

BAUERS, ELOI, lawyer, association executive; b. Osseo, Minn., Aug. 5, 1890; s. Casper and Anna Frances (Jacomet) B.; m. Mary F. O'Malley, July 27, 1911 (dec. May 31, 1966); children—Catherine A. (Mrs. Richard W. Kimball), Helen M. (Mrs. Richard P. Mahoney), Mary J. (Mrs. J. Austin Boulay). LL.B., U. Minn., 1913. Bar: Minn. 1913. Since practiced in, Mpls.; mem. firm Bauers & Kelly, 1959-74; of counsel Mahoney, Dougherty and Mahoney, 1974—; exec. v.p. Am. Coll. Allergists, 1953-76; field v.p. sales Americana Hotels, 1960-72; gen. counsel Profl. Conv. Mgmt. Assn., 1975—; spl. counsel, conv. cons. USA, Air France, 1972-75, Hyatt Corp., 1972—; mem. adv. bd. Paris Conv. Center, 1972-74; dir. Gen. Securities, Inc., Mpls. Served as 2d lt., F.A. U.S. Army, World War I. Decorated knight comdr. with shell Equestrian Order Holy Sepulchre, Jerusalem, Knight Grand Holy Sepulchre; recipient Bronze Medal Le Bureau du Conseil de Paris, 1975; first recipient Profl. Conv. Mgmt. Assn.; Disting. Service award, 1978. Disting. fellow Am. Coll. Allergists (pub. emeritus Annals of Allergy 1976—); mem. Am., Minn., Hennepin County bar assns., Am. Legion, Phi Delta Phi, Delta Sigma Rho. Roman Catholic. Clubs: Mpls., Athletic. Home: 19 S 1st St Minneapolis MN 55401 Office: 801 Park Ave Minneapolis MN 55404

BAUERSFELD, CARL F., lawyer; b. Balt., June 9, 1916; s. Emil George and Irene Marie (Hulse) B.; m. Ann Yancey, Mar. 3, 1944 (div.); children—Elizabeth Bauersfeld Keiffer, Carl F. Student, George Washington U., 1937-42; LL.B., Am. U., 1937. Bar: D.C. bar 1937, Md. bar 1957. Practiced in, Washington, 1937—; now partner firm Ash, Bauersfeld & Burton (and predecessor firms); lectr. on fed. taxation at various univs. Served with USNR, 1942-46. Mem. Am., Md. bar assns., Bar Assn. D.C., Sigma Nu Phi, Phi Sigma Kappa. Lutheran. Clubs: Congl. Country; Burning Tree (Md.). Office: 4520 East-West Hwy Bethesda MD 20814

BAUGH, JAMES EDWARD, federal government official; b. Lima, Ohio, Dec. 17, 1941; s. Eddie and Bertha (Simpson) B.; m. Veatrice DeWalt, June 29, 1968; children: Kendyl Chyrese, James Randall. B.S., Western Mich. U., 1964; M.A., U. Wis., 1971, Ph.d., 1973. Tchr. Milw. Pub. Schs., 1964-68; asst. to vice chancellor U. Wis., Madison, 1968-74, asst. dir. housing, 1972-73; asst. pror. edn., asst. vice chancellor U. Wis.-Oshkosh, 1974-77; sr. acad. planner U. Wis. System Adminstrn., Madison, 1977-79; exec. dir. Wis. Council on Criminal Justice, Madison, 1979-81; gen. dep. asst. sec. HUD, Washington, 1981—; cons. Office of Edn., 1969-77; mem. faculty U. Iowa, Iowa City, 1973-74. Contbr. articles to profl. jours. Mem. Madison Zoning Appeals Bd., 1973; pres. Police and Fire Commn., Madison, 1977; mem. Patient Compensation Panel, Madison, 1976; bd. dirs. United Way Dane County, Wis., 1980; 1st v.p., bd. dirs. Urban League, Madison, 1978. Named Most Outstanding Tchr. Fulton Jr. High Sch., Milw., 1967; recipient Most Outstanding Achievement award in Edn. Kappa Alpha Psi, 1972, Martin Luther King Humanitarian City of Madison, 1981, Man of Yr. Kappa Alpha Psi, 1973. Mem. Am. Personnel and Guidance Assn., Higher Edn. Execs. Assn., Am. Assn. Higher Edn., Assn. Social and Behavioral Scientists, Nat. Alliance Black Sch. Educators, Nat. Criminal Justice Assn. (exec. com.). Republican. Baptist. Office: HUD 451 7th St SW Washington DC 20410 *My life has been guided by a real dedication to God, family and self.In this context, I have tested new ideas, set realistic goals and worked tirelessly toward the very highest levels of achievement.*

BAUGHMAN, FRED HUBBARD, aeronautical engineer, former naval officer; b. Michigan City, Ind., Feb. 7, 1926; s. Palmer Hubbard and Mary Moore (Munson) B.; m. Marilyn Ann Weaver, June 20, 1947; children: Lynne Ann, Elizabeth Louise, Bruce Palmer, Laura Alice, Julia Ellen, Robert Alan. B.S., U.S. Naval Acad., 1947, U.S. Naval Postgrad. Sch., 1956; M.S. in Nuclear Engring., Iowa State Coll., 1967, MIT, 1967. Commd. ensign U.S. Navy, 1947, designated naval aviator, 1950, advanced through grades to rear adm., 1973; service in Korean conflict, 1950-53, S-3A project mgr., Washington, 1968-73, force material officer staff, San Diego, 1973-76, vice comdr. Naval Air Systems Command, 1976-79, comdr. Pacific Missile Test Center, 1979-82, ret., 1982. Decorated Legion of Merit with two stars, Air medal with star. Asso. fellow AIAA; mem. Internat. Test and Evaluation Assn. (charter sr. mem.), U.S. Naval Inst. (life), Naval Acad. Alumni Assn. (life), Sigma Xi. Episcopalian. Home: 2700 Wild Holly Rd Annapolis MD 21403 Office: Pacific Missile Test Center Point Mugu CA 93042

BAUGHMAN, GEORGE FECHTIG, foundation executive; b. Tampa, Fla., July 19, 1915; s. G. Norman and Mary (Dodds) B.; m. Hazel Ruth Zoerner, Apr. 27, 1940; children: Sharon Ruth, Mary Gaye. B.S. in Bus. Adminstrn, U. Fla., 1937, J.D., 1939, postgrad., 1949-53; student, Am. Inst. Banking, 1941; M.A., George Washington U., 1944; D.Sc., New Eng. Coll. Pharmacy, Boston; D.C.S., NYU, 1962. Bar: Fla. 1939, D.C. 1940-41, U.S. Supreme Ct. 1968; registered real estate broker, Fla. With Nat. Met. Bank, Washington, summers, 1932-39, 39-41; with Phifer State Bank, Gainesville, 1936-38; practiced in, Washington, D.C., 1940-41; faculty Coll. Bus. Adminstrn., U. Fla., 1941-42, asst. bus mgr., 1945-48, v.p. bus. affairs, 1954-55; bus. mgr. N.Y. U., 1955-56, v.p. bus. affairs, treas., 1956-61; pres. New Coll., Sarasota, Fla., 1961-65, Coll. Found., Sarasota, 1966—; dir. First City Fed. Savs. & Loan Assn., Bradenton, Fla.; chmn. bd. Watergate Center Inc. of Saratota, USLIFE Corp., First Environ. Services, Inc., Environ. Devel. Inc., Gen. Telephone Co. Fla., U.S. Life Ins. Co., First Manatee Corp., Bradenton.; Past pres. N.Y. U. Press; co-chmn. Com. on Future Fla. Public Univs.; Bd. dirs. U.S. Navy Supply Corps Found., Athens, Ga. Contbr. to mgmt. and edn. publs. Served to comdr. Supply Corps USNR, 1942-46; rear admiral Res. Hon. fellow New College.; Decorated Legion of Honor, France; Mil. Order Brit. Empire. Mem. Bar State Fla., D.C. Bar Assn., Nat. Assn. Colls. and Bus. Ofcls., So. Assn. Colls. and Bus. Ofcls. (past pres.), U.S. Navy Supply Officers Assn. (past pres.), Hon. Order Ky. Colls., N.Y. U. Hon. Soc., George Washington U. Alumni Assn., U. Fla. Alumni Assn., Sarasota County C. of C., Beta Theta Pi, Phi Kappa Phi, Beta Gamma Sigma, Phi Delta Phi, Pi Gamma Mu, Alpha Kappa Psi. Congregationalist. Clubs: University, University Faculty (N.Y.C.); Wildcat Cliffs Country, Field, Sara Bay Country, Ivy League, University (Sarasota) (dir., chmn. bd. govs.). Home and Office: 460 Pheasant Dr Sarasota FL 33577

BAUGHMAN, J. ROSS, photographer, writer; b. Dearborn, Mich., May 7, 1953; s. Charles T. and Patricia Jane (Hill) B. B.A. cum laude, Kent State U., 1975. Staff photographer, writer Lorain (Ohio) Jour., 1975-77; contract photographer, writer AP in, Africa and Middle East, 1977-78; co-founder Ind. Visions Internat., Inc., 1978; pres. Visions Photo Group, N.Y.C., 1978—; mem. faculty New Sch. for Social Research, N.Y.C., 1979—, NYU, 1980—; co-founder, program dir. Focus Photography Symposiums, N.Y.C., 1981; adj. prof. U. Mo. Grad. Program in Journalism, N.Y.C., 1984—. (Recipient Pulitzer prize in journalism for feature photography 1978); Author: Graven Images: a thematic portfolio, 1976, Forbidden Images: a secret portfolio, 1977. Mem. Nat. Press Photographers Assn., Photographers Gallery, Am. Soc. Mag. Photographers (sustaining 1984—), Sigma Delta Chi. Office: 105 Fifth Ave New York NY 10003 *Many talented people I have known failed to balance these equally important qualities in their work: enthusiasm, mechanical craft, meaningful content and a strategy for the future.*

BAUGHMAN, LEWIS EDWIN, banker; b. Warren, Ohio, Nov. 15, 1923; s. Milton Day and Katherine (Boone) B.; m. Ann Hawkins Buker, Sept. 7, 1946; children—Milton Day, James Lewis. B.Sc. in Bus. Adminstrn, Ohio State U., 1947; grad., Stonier Grad. Sch. Banking, Rutgers U., 1955. With Second Nat. Bank of Warren, 1948—, pres., 1962—, chmn. bd., 1974—; dir. Sommer Electric Co. Chmn. Warren United Appeal campaign, 1959, Warren YMCA bldg. campaign, 1963; past pres. Warren Bd. Edn. Served with AUS, 1943-46. Named Young Man of Year Warren Jaycees, 1954; Man of Year, 1964; recipient Silver Beaver award Boy Scouts Am., 1970; Alumni Citizenship award Ohio State U. Assn., 1975. Mem. Ohio Bankers Assn. (chmn. group 9 1976-78, v.p. 1978, pres. 1979), Phi Kappa Psi, Beta Alpha Psi. Home: 948 Fairway Dr NE Warren OH 44483 Office: 108 Main Ave SW Warren OH 44482

BAUGHMAN, MILLARD DALE, educator; b. Helmsburg, Ind., Dec. 28, 1919; s. Bert Orin and Josephine (Browning) B.; m. D'Lema Louise Smith, Aug. 26, 1950; children—Dala Dee, Dlynn Lea, Brad Dale. B.S., Ind. U., 1946, M.S., 1948, Ed.D., 1955; postgrad., Purdue U., 1948. Tchr., prin. Brown County (Ind.) Schs., 1939-42, 45-46; athletic dir., tchr., coach Boswell (Ind.) High Sch., 1947-49; coach, tchr., prin. Greenwood (Ind.) High Sch., 1949-55; assoc. prof. edn., head of adminstrv. placement U. Ill., Urbana, 1956-66; prof. edn., editor Contemporary Edn., Ind. State U., Terre Haute, 1966-82; recreation dir., Greenwood, ins. investigator, fin. cons. Author: Teachers' Treasury of Stories and Anecdotes, 1958, The Early Adolescent: A Guide for Parents, 1963, Educator's Handbook of Stories, Quotes and Humor, 1963, Administration of the Junior High School, 1966, (with others) Administration and Supervision of the Modern Secondary School; What Do Youth Really Want?, 1972, Baughman's Handbook of Humor in Education, 1974; contbr. articles to profl. jours.; Lectr. as: Hurryin' Hoosier Humorist. Served with USNR, 1942-45; PTO. Recipient Distinguished Service awards Ill. Assn. Sch. Adminstrs., Jr. High Sch. Assn. Ill., Ill. Assn. Jr. High Sch. Prins.; named Terre Haute's Citizen of Day U. Ill., 1969, 71; Hon. Big Bro. Terre Haute chpt. Big Bros., 1969. Mem. Internat. Platform Assn., Nat. Assn. Secondary Sch. Prins., Ednl. Press Assn., Ind. Assn. Supervision and Curriculum Devel., Phi Delta Kappa. Democrat. Lutheran. Club: Rotary. Home: 30 Circle Dr Terre Haute IN 47803

BAUGHMAN, R(OBERT) PATRICK, lawyer; b. Zanesville, Ohio, Nov. 18, 1938; s. Robert G. and Kathryn E. B.; m. Joyce Hall, June 17, 1959; 1 dau., Patricia. B.S., Ohio State U., 1960, J.D., 1963. Bar: Ohio 1963. Assoc. firm Sindell & Sindell, Cleve., 1964-71, Jones, Day, Reavis & Pogue, 1972-73; asst. atty. gen. State of Ohio, Columbus, 1971-72; pres., prin. firm Baughman & Assocs., Cleve., 1973—. Mem. ABA, Ohio Bar Assn., Cuyahoga County Bar Assn., Nat. Council Self-Insurers, Internat. Assn. Indsl. Accident Bds. and Commns., Internat. Platform Assn. Episcopalian. Club: Columbia Hills Country. Home: 220 S Collier Blvd Marco Island FL Office: 55 Public Sq Cleveland OH 44113

BAUGHMAN, ROLLAND LE ROY, construction company financial executive; b. Ashland, Oreg., Aug. 6, 1926; s. George Monteith and Bertha Mae (Place) B.; m. Jean Louise Stapley, Sept. 4, 1948; children: Mark Rolland, Kevin Merrill, Laurie Jean, Kim Arleen. B.S., Oreg. State Coll., 1952; cert. Advanced Mgmt. Program, Harvard U., 1979. With Guy F. Atkinson Co., 1952—; vp., mgr. fin. systems and services, South San Francisco, Calif., 1976-80, v.p., chief fin. officer, 1980-82, sr. v.p., chief fin. officer, 1983—. Active San Mateo Council, Boy Scouts Am., 1954-82; pres. Horizon Home for Handicapped, Belmont, Calif., 1979; cons. Project Bus. Jr. Achievement, San Francisco, 1979-83. Served with USAAF, 1945-46. Republican. Mormon. Office: Guy F Atkinson Co Calif 10 W Orange Ave South San Francisco CA 94080

BAUGHN, JACK AUSTIN, insurance company executive; b. Fayette County, Ohio, Oct. 22, 1923; s. Roy C. and Marjorie L. (Thornton) B.; m. Nancy Ann Devins, Mar. 16, 1952; 1 son, Daniel Casselman. Student, U. Iowa, 1943-44; B.S., Ohio State U., 1947. C.P.C.U. Dir. regional adminstrn. Nationwide Ins. Co., Columbus, Ohio, 1969-72, v.p., regional mgr., Memphis, 1972-77, v.p. personal, Columbus, 1977-81, v.p. property and casualty ins. staff, 1981, sr. v.p. mktg., 1981-83, sr. v.p. ops., 1983—; dir. Colonial Ins. Co., Anaheim, Calif., 1981—, Scottsdale Ins. Co., Ariz., 1982—; chmn. bd. Gates, McDonald & Co., Ins. Intermediaries Inc., Columbus, 1983—. Served with USAAF, 1943-46; PTO. Mem. Soc. C.P.C.U.s, C.L.U.s Assn. Republican. Presbyterian. Office: Nationwide Ins. Cos 1 Nationwide Plaza Columbus OH 43216

BAUGHN, WILLIAM HUBERT, educational administrator; b. Marshall County, Ala., Aug. 27, 1918; s. J.W. and Beatrice (Jackson) B.; m. Mary Madiera Morris, Feb. 20, 1945; children: Charles Madiera, William Marsteller. B.S., U. Ala., 1940; M.A., U. Va, 1941, Ph.D, 1948. Instr. U. Va., 1942-43, asst. prof., 1946-48; asso. prof., then prof. econs. and bus. adminstrn. La. State U., 1948-56; prof. U. Tex., 1956-62, chmn. fin. dept., 1958-60, asso. dean Coll. Bus. Adminstrn., 1959-62; asso. dir. Sch. Banking of South, 1952-66; dean Coll. Bus. and Pub. Adminstrn. U. Mo., 1962-64; dean Coll. Bus. and Adminstrn., U. Colo., 1964—; pres. Am. Assembly Collegiate Schs. Bus., 1973-74; chmn. Big Eight Athletic Conf., 1970-71, 78-79; dir. Stonier Grad. Sch. of Banking, Rutgers U., 1966—; mem. council Nat. Collegiate Athletic Assn., 1983—. Author: (with E.W. Walker) Financial Planning and Policy, 1961; editor: (with C.E. Walker) The Bankers' Handbook, 1966, 78. Served to 1st lt. USAAF, World War II; lt. col. Res. Home: 555 Baseline Rd Boulder CO 80302

BAUHOF, RUDOLF, accountant; b. Canton, Ohio, Jan. 6, 1902; s. Ralph Addison and Florence (Smith) B.; m. Adelaide Cash, July 7, 1965; children—Barbara Sue (Mrs. James L. Barth), Robert Hamilton. A.B., Mt. Union Coll., 1924. C.P.A., Ohio. Indsl. accountant with two cos. now part Republic Steel Corp., 1924-28; asso. Ernst & Ernst. (C.P.A.'s), Cleve., 1928—, partner, 1946—. Mem. Am. Inst. C.P.A.'s, Ohio Soc. C.P.A.'s, Sigma Nu, Psi Kappa Omega, Beta Alpha Psi. Clubs: Union, Country, Mid-day. Home: 19606 Van Aken Blvd Shaker Heights OH 44122 Office: Union Commerce Bldg 925 Euclid Ave Cleveland OH 44115

BAUKHAGES, FREDERICK EDWIN, lawyer; b. Balt., Feb. 6, 1910; s. Frederick Edwin, Jr. and Elizabeth Wallace (Cartwright) B.; m. Dorothy Meier Freeman, Oct. 26, 1935; children: Frederick Edwin IV, Frederick William, Dorothy Elizabeth, Frederick Hilmar Robert. LL.B., U. Va., 1933. Bar: Va. 1932. With So. Ry., 1925-27; pvt. practice, substitute trial justice, Mathews, Va., 1933-34; atty., counsel RFC, Washington, 1935-40; personnel asst. to v.p. operations U.P. R.R., 1941-44; exec. asst. to v.p. finance B.O. R.R., 1944-46, gen. solicitor, 1946-61, v.p. finance, 1961-63; counsel law firm Hunton, Williams, Gay, Powell and Gibson, Richmond, Va., 1963-65, Mathews, 1965—; partner Blair & Baukhages, Washington, 1965-71, Baukhages and Sadler, Mathews, 1982—. Mem. Alpha Chi Rho. Episcopalian. Club: University (Balt.). Home: Arach Landing Mathews VA 23109 Office: Farmers and Fishermen's Bldg Mathews VA 23109

BAUKNIGHT, CLARENCE BROCK, wholesale and retail company executive; b. Anderson, S.C., May 14, 1936; s. John Edward and Theodosia (Brock) B.; m. Harriet League, June 29, 1959; children: Harriet League, Clarence Brock. B.S., Ga. Inst. Tech., 1958. Dist. mgr. Wickes Corp., and predecessor, Atlanta, 1960-65; exec. v.p. Builder Marts Am., Inc., Greenville, S.C., 1965-70, pres., chief exec. officer, 1970—, dir.; chmn. bd. Aid-in-Mgmt. Tel-Man, Inc., Greenville; dir. Ins. Mgmt. Services, Greenville, Parks Lumber Co., Gainesville, Ga., Westwood Lumber Co., Rocky Mount, N.C., Robert L. Head Lumber Co., Blairsville, Ga., Atkin Harper Lumber Co., Asheville, N.C., Bivens Builder Mart, Pickens, S.C., Builderway of Fla. and Tex., Jacksonville, Fla., Thompson Lumber Co., Memphis, Jim White Lumber Co., Bay City, Mich. Mem. nat. adv. bd. Ga. Inst. Tech.; mem. policy adv. bd. Joint Ctr. Urban Studies Harvard U., MIT. Mem. Indsl. Mgmt. Soc., Young Pres. Orgn., Phi Delta Theta. Methodist. Clubs: Greenville Country; Poinsett (Greenville); Wildcat Cliffs, Highlands Country (Highlands, N.C.). Lodges: Masons; Shriners. Home: 111 Rockingham Rd Greenville SC 29607 Office: Builder Marts of Am PO Box 47 Greenville SC 29602

BAUM, BERNARD HELMUT, sociologist; b. Giessen, Germany, Apr. 18, 1926; came to U.S., 1933, naturalized, 1934; s. Theodor and Beatrice (Klee) B.; m. Barbara B. Eisendrath, June 13, 1953; children—David Michael, Jonathan Klee, Victoria Lucille, Lisa Beatrice. Ph.B., U. Chgo., 1948, M.A., 1953, Ph.D., 1959. Qualifications rating examiner, bd. adviser U.S. CSC, Chgo., 1952-54; instr. human relations, psychology Chgo. Police Officers' Coll. Edn. Program, 1955-59; dir. orgnl. analysis Continental Casualty & Continental Assurance Cos., Chgo., 1960-66; asso. prof. mgmt. and sociology U. Ill., Chgo., 1966-69, asso. dean, 1967-68; prof. mgmt. and sociology, 1969—; prof. health resources mgmt. Sch. Pub. Health, U. Ill. Med. Center, 1973—, dir. health resources mgmt., 1977—; lectr. Roosevelt U., 1955-66, U. Chgo., 1961-68, Northwestern U., 1968-70, U. Colo., 1971-76; mem. speaker's bur. Adult Edn. Council Greater Chgo., 1963-76. Author: Decentralization of Authority in a Bureaucracy, 1961, (with others) Basics for Business, 1968; also articles; editor: Intervention: the Management Use of Organizational Research, 1975. Bd. dirs. Selfhelp Home for Aged, Chgo. Served with AUS, 1944-46; col. Res.; ret. Decorated Legion of Merit; recipient Bus. Adminstrn. and Social Sci. Doctoral Dissertation award Ford Found., 1960. Mem. Am. Sociol. Assn., Indsl. Relations Assn. Chgo. (exec. com), Indsl. Relations Research Assn., Am. Acad. Polit. and Social Sci., AAAS, Midwest Bus. Adminstrn. Assn., Acad. Mgmt., Sigma Xi. Home: 1405 Lincoln St Evanston IL 60201 Office: U Ill Med Center Sch Pub Health Chicago IL 60680

BAUM, BERNARD RENE, biosystematist; b. Paris, Feb. 14, 1937; s. Kurt and Martha (Berl) B.; m. Danielle Habib, May 24, 1961; 1 dau., Anat. B.S., Hebrew U., Jerusalem, 1963, M.S., 1963, Ph.D., 1966. Research scientist Agr. Can., Ottawa, Ont., 1966-74, sr. research scientist, 1974-80, prin. research scientist, 1980—. Author: Oats: Wild and Cultivated, 1977, Monograph of Tamarix, 1978, World Registry of Avena Cultivars, 1972. Fellow Acad. Sci.-Royal Soc. Can.; mem. Can. Bot. Assn. (Lawson medal 1979), Am. Soc. Plant Taxonomists, Internat. Assn. Plant Taxonomists, Classification Soc., Linnean Soc. London, Orgn. Plant Taxonomy of the Mediterranean Area. Home: 8 Alderbrook St Nepean ON Canada K2H 5W5 Office: Biosystematics Research Br Research Inst Central Exptl Farm Agriculture Canada Ottawa ON Canada K1A 0C6

BAUM, DAVID BARRY, lawyer; b. Chgo., May 30, 1934; s. Henry and Molly (Levy) B.; m. Marilyn Ruth Josephs, Apr. 25, 1965; children—Nicole Andrea, Justine Lisa. B.S., U. Wis., 1955; LL.B., Northwestern U., 1957. Bar: Calif. bar 1957. Partner Pollock, Pollock, Fay & Baum, Los Angeles, 1957-72, E. Robert Wallach and David B. Baum, Los Angeles, San Francisco, 1972—; faculty Nat. Coll. of Advocacy, 1973—; adv. Am. Bd. Trial Advocates. Author: Art of Advocacy—Preparation of the Case, 1981; contbr. numerous articles to legal publs. Served with U.S. Army, 1957-58. Fellow Internat. Acad. Trial Lawyers; mem. Am. Trial Lawyers Assn. (nat. chmn. basic trial advocacy 1972, nat. chmn. tort sect. 1975, bd. govs. 1972-77, faculty Coll. of Advocacy, vice chmn. edn. dept. 1980, chmn. editorial adv. bd.), Calif. Trial Lawyers Assn. (pres. 1974, bd. govs. 1970-79, amicus curaie com. 1974-79). Home: Mill Valley CA 94941 Office: 2 Boston Ship Plaza San Francisco CA 94111

BAUM, DAVID ROY, research psychologist; b. Kings County, N.Y., Feb. 13, 1946; s. John Harold and Sylvia (Adler) B. B.S., U. Pitts., 1967; M.A., SUNY-Stony Brook, 1969; Ph.D., U. Mich., 1977. Sr. prin. research scientist Honeywell Systems and Research Ctr., Mpls., 1977—, innovator, past dir. human factors internship program, 1978-82; cons. to flying tng. div. Air Force Human Resources Lab. Contbr. articles to profl. jours. Judge 31st Ann. Sci. and Engring. Fair, St. Paul, 1980. Served with USAF, 1969-73. Mem. Human Factors Soc., Am. Psychol. Assn., AAAS, N.Y. Acad. Scis. Office: Honeywell SRC MN17-2318 2600 Ridgway Pkwy Minneapolis MN 55413

BAUM, DWIGHT CROUSE, investment banking executive; b. Syracuse, N.Y., Nov. 21, 1912; s. Dwight James and Katharine Lucia (Crouse) B.; m. Hildagarde Engelhardt, Jan. 17, 1942; children: Dwight J., John E. E.E., Cornell U., 1936; M.B.A., Harvard U., 1938. Chartered fin. analyst. Asst. to v.p. Mine Safety Appliance Co., Pitts., 1938-40; armament supply officer Brit. Air Commn., Washington, 1940-46; asst. to partner Eastman Dillon & Co., Los Angeles, 1946-47; v.p. 1st Calif. Co., Los Angeles, 1947-56; gen. partner Eastman Dillon Union Securities & Co., Los Angeles, 1956-71, sr. v.p., 1971-72; also dir.; sr. v.p. Blyth Eastman Dillon & Co., Inc., Los Angeles, 1972-80, adv. dir., 1980—; sr. v.p. Paine Webber Jackson & Curtis, 1980—; dir. Dominguez Water Corp., Far W. Fin. Corp., Measurex Corp., Far West Savs. and Loan Assn.; chmn. bd. United Cities Gas Co. Mem. Nat. Assn. Securities Dealers (bd. govs. 1976-79), Los Angeles Soc. Fin. Analysts, IEEE, Pacific Coast Stock Exchange, Inc. (vice chmn. 1980-82), N.Y. Stock Exchange (allied mem.), Phi Delta Theta. Clubs: Calif., Bond (Los Angeles). Home: 1011 Oak Grove Ave San Marino CA 91108 Office: 595 E Colorado Blvd Pasadena CA 91101

BAUM, ELEANOR, electrical engineering educator, academic administrator; b. Poland, Feb. 10, 1939; came to U.S., 1942; d. Sol and Anna (Berkman) Kushel; m. Paul Martin Baum, Sept. 2, 1962; children: Elizabeth, Jennifer. B.S.E.E., CUNY, 1959; M.E.E., Poly Inst. N.Y., 1961, Ph.D., 1964. Engr. Sperry Gyrosoope Co., N.Y.C., 1960-61; instr. Poly. Inst. N.Y., N.Y.C., 1961-64; asst. prof. elec. engring. Pratt Inst., N.Y.C., 1964-67, assoc. prof., 1967-71, prof., chmn. dept. elec. engring., 1971—; cons. engring. to various corps.; accreditiation visitor Accreditation Bd. Engring. and Tech., 1983—; organizer career confs. for careers in engring., careers for women, N.Y.C., 1970—; cons. editor Simon & Schuster, Prentice-Hall. Contbr. articles on engring. careers and edn. to profl. publs.; editor: Fourier Analysis, 1969. Bd. dirs. Kensington Civic Assn., N.Y.C. Mem. Soc. Women Engrs. (sr.), IEEE (sr.), Am. Soc. Engring. Edn. (exec. com. 1977—, chairperson Mid-Atlantic sect. 1979-80), Sigma Xi, Eta Kappa Nu, Tau Beta Pi. Home: 4 Arleigh Rd Great Neck NY 11021 Office: Pratt Inst 200 Willoughby Ave Brooklyn NY 11205

BAUM, JOHN, physician; b. N.Y.C., June 2, 1927; s. Louis Israel and Lilian (Treitman) B.; m. Erna Rose Bailis, Jan. 28, 1950; children—Nina, Jane, Carl, Antonia, Theodore. B.A., N.Y. U., 1949, M.D., 1954. Diplomate: Am. Bd. Internal Medicine, mem. test com. for rheumatology, 1971-76. Intern Balt. City Hosp., 1954-55; resident in medicine Lenox Hill Hosp., N.Y.C., 1955-56, VA Hosp., 1956-57; NIH clin. trainee N.Y.U.-Bellevue Hosp., 1957-58; NIH research fellow Rheumatism Research Unit, Taplow, Eng., 1958-59; asst. prof. medicine U. Tex. Southwestern Med. Sch., 1962-68; dir. arthritis clinic Parkland Meml. Hosp., Dallas, 1959-68, dir. med. clinics, 1965-67; co-dir. pediatric arthritis clinic Scottish Rite Hosp., Dallas, 1960-68; mem. faculty U. Rochester (N.Y.) Med. Sch., 1968—; prof. medicine, pediatrics and preventive, family and rehab. medicine, 1972—; dir. arthritis and clin. immunology unit Monroe Community Hosp., 1968—; dir. pediatric arthritis clinic Strong Meml. Hosp., 1970—; mem. drug efficacy panel NRC-Nat. Acad. Sci., 1960-65; mem. research rev. bd. immunology VA, 1970-76; adv. panel U.S. Pharmacopeia, 1975-80; coordinator therapeutics U.S.-USSR Program Rheumatology, 1974—. Author articles in field, chpts. in books; editorial bd.: Acta Rheumatologica, Belgium, Jour. Rheumatology Can. Served with AUS, 1944-46. Fulbright scholar, 1958; clin. scholar rheumatology Arthritis Found., 1964-69. Mem. Am. Rheumatism Assn. (council pediatric rheumatology 1975-80), Heberden Soc., Am. Fedn. Clin. Research, Am. Soc. Human Genetics, Am. Assn. Immunologists, Reticuloendothelial Soc., So. Soc. Clin. Investigation, Tex. Rheumatism Assn., Polish Rheumatol. Soc. (hon.), Sigma Xi. Home: 60 Council Rock Ave Rochester NY 14610 Office: 435 E Henrietta Rd Rochester NY 14603 *If what I have achieved is called success, it is not because it has been my goal. As a clinician, teacher and researcher, I realize that success comes mostly with the latter, but my greatest satisfaction, which must have been my "secret goal," has been with the personal contacts that come through taking care of people and sharing my knowledge with students. The lagniappe of a supportive wife and fascinating children makes achieving the goals more worthwhile.*

BAUM, JULES LEONARD, ophthalmologist; b. N.Y.C., Mar. 13, 1931; s. Sydney H. and Irene (Brodsky) B.; m. Ann Tarnower, Mar. 1967 (div.); children: Jeffrey Stuart, Alison Rachel. A.B., Dartmouth, 1952; M.D., Tufts U., 1956. Intern Maimonides Hosp., Bklyn., 1956-57; NIH fellow in research in ophthalmology N.Y. U., 1958-59, researcher in ophthalmology, 1961-62, asst. prof., 1965-68; resident in ophthalmology Bellevue Hosp., N.Y.C., 1962-64; mem. faculty Tufts U. Med. Sch., 1968—, prof. ophthalmology, 1974—; sr. surgeon New Eng. Med. Center Hosp., Boston, 1973—. Asso. editor: Ophthalmic Lit, 1967—; sect. editor: Investigative Ophthalmology and Vision Sci., 1978-82, Survey of Ophthalmology, 1970-79; contbr. articles to profl. jours. Served to capt. M.C. AUS, 1959-61. Recipient William Warner Hopping award N.Y. Acad. Medicine.; NIH fellow, 1958-59, 64-65; grantee Nat. Eye Inst. Fellow A.C.S.; mem. Am. Acad. Ophthalmology (honor award 1979), Assn. Research Vision and Ophthalmology (trustee 1981—), Castroviejo Soc. (exec. sec.-treas. 1979—), Mass. Ophthalmology Soc. (sec. 1974-76), Phi Beta Kappa. Jewish. Clubs: Confrerie des Chevaliers du Tastevin, Chaine des Rotisseur, Internat. Wine and Food Soc. Office: 171 Harrison Ave Boston MA 02111

BAUM, PAUL FRANK, mathematician; b. N.Y.C., July 20, 1936; s. Mark and Celia (Frank) B.; m. Barbara Alice Bigelow, June 21, 1961; children—Sarah, Michael, Jessica. A.B., Harvard U., 1958; Ph.D., Princeton U., 1963. Asst. prof. math. Princeton U., 1965-67; asso. prof. Brown U., Providence, 1968-71, prof., 1971—; mem. Inst. Advanced Study, 1976-77. NSF fellow, 1963-64. Mem. Am. Math. Soc., Phi Beta Kappa. Home: 45 Boylston Ave Providence RI 02906 Office: Math Dept Brown Univ Providence RI 02912

BAUM, RICHARD THEODORE, engineering company executive; b. N.Y.C., Oct. 3, 1919. B.A., Columbia U., 1940, B.S., 1941, M.S., 1948. Registered profl. engr., Nat. Bur. Engring. Registration, N.Y., 20 other states and D.C. Engr. Electric Boat Co., Groton, Conn., 1941-43; with Jaros, Baum & Bolles, N.Y.C., 1946—, partner, 1958—; Mem. adv. council, faculty of engring. and applied sci. Columbia U., N.Y.C., 1972—. Served to 1st lt. USAAF, 1943-46. Fellow Am. Cons. Engrs. Council, ASME, ASHRAE; mem. Nat. Acad. Engring., Nat. Soc. Profl. Engrs., Nat. Soc. Energy Engrs., Am. Arbitration Assn. (panel of arbitrators 1973—), Council on Tall Bldgs. and Urban Habitat (mem. steering group, chmn. mech., elec. and vertical transp. coms.). Club: Univ. (N.Y.C.). Office: 345 Park Ave New York NY 10154

BAUM, SIEGMUND JACOB, physiologist; b. Vienna, Austria, Nov. 14, 1920; came to U.S., 1939, naturalized, 1943; s. Joseph L. and Marie (Leiser) B.; m. Arline Renee Weber, Apr. 1, 1947; children: Jonathan W., Andrew M., Vicki M., Joseph L., Anthony P. B.A., UCLA, 1949, M.A., 1950; Ph.D., U. Calif., Berkeley, 1959. Sr. project leader radiobiology U.S. Naval Radiol. Def. Lab., San Francisco, 1950-60; group leader physiology and radiobiology Douglass Missile & Space Div., Santa Monica, Calif., 1960-62; div. head Armed Forces Radiobiology Research Inst., Bethesda, Md., 1962-64, chmn. dept. exptl. pathology, 1964-76, chmn. dept. exptl. hematology, 1976-82; lectr. physiology Georgetown U., 1970-71; prof. physiology Sch. Medicine, Uniformed Services U. of Health Scis., Bethesda, 1978—. Contbr. articles to profl. jours. Served with AUS, 1942-45. Recipient 1st ann. award for sci. achievement Naval Radiol. Def. Lab., 1960,

Exceptional Civilian Service awards Def. Nuclear Agy., 1973, 80. Mem. Am. Physiol. Soc., Internat. Soc. Exptl. Hematology, Transplantation Soc., Radiation Research Soc., Sigma Xi. Club: Toastmasters (pres. club 1963-64). Home and Office: 6600 Greyswood Rd Bethesda MD 20817 *As one approaches the senior years of one's professional life, one must begin to realize that scientific achievements which appeared remarkable in earlier years are probably only a small contribution towards the advancement of scientific knowledge. Of much greater importance, is to instill in young people the desire to continue the search for knowledge.*

BAUM, STANLEY, radiologist, educator; b. N.Y.C., Dec. 26, 1929; s. Herman and Fannie (Harris) B.; m. Jeanne Masch, June 29, 1958; children: Richard Arthur, Laura Dianne, Carol Lisa. B.A., N.Y. U., 1951; M.D., U. Utrecht, Holland, 1957. Intern Kings County Hosp., N.Y.C., 1957-58; resident in radiology Grad. Hosp., U. Pa., Phila., 1958-61; trainee Nat. Cancer Inst., Bethesda, Md., 1958-61; fellow cardiovascular radiology Stanford (Calif.) U., 1961-62; instr. radiology U. Pa., Phila., 1962-63, asst. prof., 1963-66, assoc. prof., 1966-70, prof., 1970—, Eugen P. Pendergrass prof. radiology, 1977—, chmn. dept. radiology, 1975—; chmn. med. bd. Hosp. of U. Pa., 1983—; chief cardiovascular radiology Mass. Gen. Hosp., Boston, 1971-75; prof. radiology Harvard Med. Sch., Boston, 1971-75; cons. Radiation Effects Research Found., Hiroshima, Japan, 1975—; cardiovascular rev. bd. Am. Heart Assn., 1970—. Editorial bd.: Investigative Radiology, 1970-80, New Eng. Jour. Medicine, 1975-76, Radiology, 1975—, Gastrointestinal Radiology, 1975-79, Jour. Continuing Edn, 1978-80, Postgrad. Radiology, 1980—. Fellow Am. Coll. Radiology, Am. Coll. Cardiology; mem. Soc. Cardiovascular Radiology (pres. 1974-76), Soc. Chmn. Acad. Radiology Depts. (sec.-treas. 1983—). Home: 401 W Moreland Ave Chestnut Hill PA 19118 Office: 3400 Spruce St Philadelphia PA 19104

BAUM, WARREN C., international financial organization executive; b. N.Y.C., Sept. 1922; s. William and Elsie B.; m. Jessie Scullen, 1946; 2 daus. Ed., Columbia U., Harvard U. With Office Strategic Services, 1942-46, ECA, 1949-51, Mut. Security Agy., 1952-53; economist Rand Corp., 1953-56; chief office network study FCC, 1956-59; economist European dept. World Bank, 1959-62, div. chief, 1962-64, asst. dir. in charge transp. projects dept., 1964-68, dep. dir. projects dept., 1968, assoc. dir., 1968-72, v.p. projects staff, 1972-82, v.p., 1983—, chmn. consultative group on internat. agrl. research, 1974—. Author: The Marshall Plan and French Foreign Trade, 1951, The French Economy and the State, 1956. Office: 1818 H St NW Washington DC 20433

BAUM, WERNER A., meteorologist, university dean; b. Giessen, Germany, Apr. 10, 1923; came to U.S., 1933, naturalized, 1934; s. Theodor and Beatrice (Klee) B.; m. Shirley Bowman, Jan. 20, 1945; children: Janice Michelle, Sandra Roslyn. B.S., U. Chgo., 1943, M.S., 1944, Ph.D., 1948; D.Sc., Mt. St. Joseph Coll., 1971, U. R.I., 1974; D.P.A., Husson Coll., 1972. Cert. cons. meteorologist. Teaching asst. U. Chgo., 1943, instr., 1943-44, 1947, research asst., 1946; research asso., asst. prof. U. Md., 1947-49; asso. prof., head dept. meteorology Fla. State U., 1949-51, prof., head dept., 1951-58, dir. univ. research, 1957-60, dean, 1958-60, dean faculties, 1960-63; v.p. acad. affairs U. Miami, 1963-65; v.p. sci. affairs N.Y.U., N.Y.C., 1965-67; dep. adminstr. Environ. Sci. Services Adminstrn., 1967-68; pres. U. R.I., Kingston, 1968-73; chancellor U. Wis., Milw., 1973-79, chancellor emeritus, 1979—; dean Coll. Arts and Scis., Fla. State U., Tallahassee, 1979—; treas. Assn. Urban Univs., 1976-77; pres. Com. Urban Program Univs., 1977-79, pres. emeritus, 1979—; cons. climatologist USAF, summer 1953; dir. Sta-Rite Industries; mem. exec. res. U.S. Weather Bur., 1958-62; councilor Oak Ridge Inst. Nuclear Studies, 1958-62; cons. Nat. Acad. Scis., 1962-64, mem. climate bd., 1980—; mem. NRC com. on climatology; adv. to U.S. Weather Bur., 1955-57; mem. Nat. Adv. Com. on Oceans and Atmosphere, 1971-73, 76-77, 78-79; trustee Univ. Corp. Atmospheric Research, 1959-63, 65-67, 80—, corp. sec., 1963-67; chmn. adv. com. edn. and manpower U.S. Weather Bur.; chmn. adv. panel atmospheric scis. program NSF, 1965-67; dir. Fund Overseas Research Grants and Edn., 1965-74; mem. sea grant adv. panel Commerce Dept., 1974-78; chmn. Nat. Climate Program Adv. Com., 1979—. Author: Russian-English Dictionary of Meteorological Terms and Expressions, 1950; Contbr. articles to sci. jours. Served with USNR, 1944-46. Fellow AAAS (councilor 1955-56), Am. Geophys. Union, Am. Meteorol. Soc. (councilor 1956-59, 63-66, exec. com. 1976-79, pres. 1977-78, editor-in-chief periodicals 1957-61, spl. award for disting. service 1962, Charles Franklin Brooks award 1975); mem. Phi Beta Kappa, Sigma Xi, Phi Kappa Phi, Beta Gamma Sigma, Chi Epsilon Pi, Phi Sigma Delta. Club: Cosmos (Washington). Home: 2403 Perez Ave Tallahassee FL 32304

BAUM, WILLIAM ALVIN, astronomer; b. Toledo, Jan. 18, 1924; s. Earle Fayette and Mable (Teachout) B.; m. Ester Bru, June 27, 1961. B.A. summa cum laude, U. Rochester, 1943; Ph.D. magna cum laude, Calif. Inst. Tech., 1950. Physicist U.S. Naval Research Lab., Washington, 1946-49; astronomer Mt. Wilson and Palomar observatories, Pasadena, Calif., 1950-65; dir. Planetary Research Center, Lowell Obs., Flagstaff, Ariz., 1965—; adj. prof. astronomy Ohio State U., 1969—; adj. prof. physics No. Ariz. U., 1973—; cons. physics, astronomy, optics; cons. U.S. Army Research Office, Durham, N.C., 1967-74; vis. prof. Am. Astronomy Soc., 1961—; adv. com. Nat. Acad. Sci., 1958—; mem. optical instrumentation panel adv. Air Force, 1967-76; coms. and panels NASA Office Space Scis., 1967—; mem. NASA Viking Orbiter Imaging Team, 1970-79, NASA Space Telescope Camera Team, 1977—. Contbr. articles to tech. publs. Served to lt., jr. grade USNR, 1943-46. Guggenheim fellow, 1960-61. Mem. Am. Astron. Soc. (chmn. div. planetary scis. 1976-77), Royal Astron. Soc., Astron. Soc. Pacific, Internat. Astron. Union, Phi Beta Kappa, Sigma Xi, Theta Delta Chi. Home: PO Box 1269 Flagstaff AZ 86002 Office: Lowell Obs Flagstaff AZ 86002

BAUM, WILLIAM CARDINAL, former archbishop; b. Dallas, Nov. 21, 1926; s. Harold E. and Mary Leona (Hayes) W. Student, Kenrick Sem., St. Louis, 1947-51, U. St. Thomas Aquinas, Rome, Italy, 1956-58, S.T.D., 1958; S.T.L., Muhlenberg Coll., Allentown, Pa., 1957, D.D., 1967; LL.D., Georgetown U., St. John's U., Bklyn. Ordained priest Roman Cath. Ch., 1951, elevated to cardinal, 1976; asso. pastor (St. Aloysius Parish, St. Therese's Parish and St. Peter's Parish), Kansas City, Mo., 1951-56, 61-64, 67-68, adminstr., Sugar Creek, Mo., 1960-61, pastor, Kansas City, Mo., 1968-70, chancellor, 1967-70, bishop of, Springfield-Cape Girardeau, Mo., 1970-73, archbishop of, Washington, 1973-80, prefect, Rome, 1980—; instr., then prof. Avila Coll., Kansas City, Mo., 1954-56, 58-63; Hon. chaplain of the Pope, 1961; peritus 2d Vatican Council, 1962-65; hon. prelate of the Pope, 1968; 1st exec. dir. Bishops' Commn. Ecumenical and Inter-religious Affairs, 1964-67; mem. Joint Working Group; reps. Cath. Ch. and World Council Chs., 1965-69; mem. Mixed Commn.; reps. Cath. Ch. and Lutheran World Fedn., 1965-66; mem. Vatican's Congregations Cath. Edn., Doctrine of Faith and Secretariat for Non Christians, Bishop's Welfare Emergency Relief Com. Author: The Teaching of Cardinal Cajetan on the Sacrifice of the Mass, 1958, Considerations Toward the Theology on the Presbyterate, 1961. Trustee, chancellor Cath. U. Am.; chmn. bd. trustees Nat. Shrine Immaculate Conception. Mem. Nat. Conf. Cath. Bishops (adminstrv. com.). Office: 3 Piazza Pio XII Rome Italy

BAUMAN, ARNOLD, lawyer; b. N.Y.C., July 25, 1914; s. William and Betty (Kraft) B.; m. Bernice Rechtman, Aug. 7, 1938; children—Jane Dorothy (Mrs. James W. Phillips), William Kraft. B.B.A. cum laude, St. Johns U., 1934; J.D., N.Y. U., 1937. Bar: N.Y. bar 1938. Asst. dist. atty., N.Y. County, 1938-41, 45-47, pvt. practice law, N.Y.C., 1947-53; chief counsel U.S. Senate Com. Investigating Crime and Law Enforcement in D.C., 1951-52; chief criminal div. U.S. Atty.'s Office, So. dist. N.Y., 1953-55; chief counsel Joint Legis. Com. on Govt. Ops., N.Y. State Legislature, 1955-58; mem. firm Christy, Bauman & Christy, 1965-68, Bauman & Marcheso, N.Y.C., 1968-72; judge U.S. Dist. Ct., So. dist. N.Y., 1972-74; partner Shearman & Sterling, N.Y.C., 1974—; trustee Practising Law Inst. Served from ens. to lt. comdr. USNR, 1941-45. Fellow Inst. Jud. Adminstrn., Am. Coll. Trial Lawyers; mem. Am., N.Y. State bar assns., Assn. Bar City N.Y. (chmn. com. on judiciary 1974-77), Fed. Bar Council (pres. 1966-68, chmn. bd. trustees 1968-70). Clubs: Univ., Down Town Assn., Broad Street (N.Y.C.); Beach Point (Mamaroneck, N.Y.). Home: 20 Chester Dr Rye NY 10580 Office: 53 Wall St New York NY 10005

BAUMAN, DALE ELTON, nutritional biochemistry educator; b. Detroit, Dec. 26, 1942; s. Elton Blaine and Waneta Mary (Taylor) B.; m. L. Marie Vinande, Aug. 28, 1965; children: Rebecca, Todd, Jeffrey. B.S., Mich. State U., 1964, M.S., 1968; Ph.D., U. Ill., 1969. Asst. prof., assoc. prof. U. Ill.-Urbana, 1969-78; vis. prof. Mich. State U., East Lansing, 1978; assoc. prof., then prof. Cornell U., Ithaca, N.Y., 1979—. Contbr. articles to profl. jours. Leader and scoutmaster Boy Scouts Am., Mich., N.Y., 1978-83. Mem. Am. Dairy Sci. Assn. (nat. student award 1967, nutrition research award 1982), Am. Soc. Animal Sci. (young scientist award 1977), Am. Inst. Nutrition. Methodist. Home: 2 Eagles Head Rd Ithaca NY 14850 Office: Cornell U 262 Morrison Ithaca NY 14853

BAUMAN, EDWARD JOSPEH, company executive; b. Lorain, Ohio, Jan. 7, 1925; s. Henry Elmer and Clara (Haehner) B.; m. Vivien Kelley; children: Jeff, Kim, Jim. B.S. in Mech. Engring., Purdue U., 1950. Div. pres. Hicks-Ponder div. Blue Bell, Inc., El Paso, Tex., 1976-78; exec. v.p. Red Kap Industries div. Blue Bell Inc., Nashville, 1978-79, pres., 1979-82; pres., chief operating officer Blue Bell, Inc., Greensboro, N.C., 1982-83, pres., chief exec. officer, 1983—, dir.; dir. 1st Union Corp., Charlotte, N.C., AAMA, Arlington, Va., Piedmont Industries, Greensboro. Mem. Old Greensborough, Greensboro Devel. Com. Clubs: Country, Greensboro City (Greensboro).

BAUMAN, GEORGE DUNCAN, former newspaper publisher; b. Humboldt, Iowa, Apr. 12, 1912; s. Peter William and Mae (Duncan) B.; m. Nora Kathleen Kelly, May 21, 1938. Student, Loyola U., Chgo., 1930-35; J.D., Washington U., St. Louis, 1948; Litt.D. (hon.), Central Meth. Coll.; LL.D. (hon.), Maryville Coll.; L.H.D. (hon.), Mo. Valley Coll., 1981, St. Louis Rabbinical Coll., 1981. Reporter, Chgo. Herald Examiner, 1931-39; archtl. rep. Pratt & Lambert, Inc., St. Louis, 1939-43; reporter, rewriter, asst. city editor St. Louis Globe-Democrat, 1943-51, personnel mgr., 1951-59, bus. mgr., 1959-67, pub., 1967-84; dir. City Bank St. Louis. Bd. dirs. Boys Clubs Am., 1969—, St. Louis YMCA, 1967-72, St. Louis City Welfare Commn., 1967-70, Better Bus. Bur., 1968-72, St. Louis Mcpl. Theatre Assn., 1968—, St. Louis Symphony Soc., 1968—, Arts and Edn. Council, 1972-83; mem. lay adv. bd. St. Vincent's Hosp., 1952-75, pres., 1957-58; mem. voting membership bd. Blue Shield, 1968-77; mem. nat. citizen's adv. com. Assn. Am. Med. Colls., 1975—; mem. lay adv. bd. DePaul Community Health Center, 1975—; adv. bd. St. Louis Med. Soc., 1976-78; mem. exec. bd. St. Louis council Boy Scouts Am., 1967—; mem. Pres.'s council St. Louis U., 1968—; bd. visitors Mo. Mil. Acad., 1970-78; mem. adv. bd. Newman Chapel, 1964—, pres., 1968; bd. dirs. Policemen and Firemen Fund, St. Louis, 1959—, sec., 1963-69, pres., 1969-70; bd. dirs. Herbert Hoover Boys Club, St. Louis, 1966—, pres., 1968, 76-78; bd. dirs. United Way Greater St. Louis, 1964—, mem. exec. com., 1964, v.p., 1968-71; chmn. exec. com. and regional adv. com. Bi-State Regional Med. Program, 1968-75; bd. dirs. Health and Welfare Council Met. St. Louis, 1960-70, pres., 1965-67; sec. Bd. Election Commrs., St. Louis, 1957-61; bd. dirs. Catholic Charities, 1967-81, pres., 1969-70; bd. dirs. Child Center Our Lady of Grace, 1965-80, pres., 1965-68; bd. dirs. Jr. Achievement Mississippi Valley, 1953-74, v.p., 1968, pres., 1978-80, nat. bd. dirs., 1979—; mem. Conv. and Visitors Bur. of Greater St. Louis, 1968-77, v.p., 1974, pres., 1975-76; bd. dirs. Dismas House, 1964-73, pres., 1968; bd. dirs. Human Life Found., 1973-81, Downtown St. Louis, Inc., 1977-83; trustee Mo. Bapt. Hosp., 1970—, exec. com., 1974—, treas., 1978-79, asst. sec., 1979-80, vice chmn., 1981—; trustee Jefferson Nat. Expansion Meml. Assn., 1968—, Mo. Pub. Expenditure Survey, 1968—, Govtl. Research Inst., 1968—, Freedoms Found. at Valley Forge, 1968-75, David Ranken Jr. Tech. Inst., 1969—, Nat. Jewish Hosp. and Research Center, 1970—, Laclede Sch. Law, 1981—; state chmn. Mo. Com. for Employer Support of Guard and Res., 1981—, mem. exec. com., 1983—; mem. subdist. commn. St. Louis Zool. Park, 1982—. Recipient Silver Beaver award, 1978; Decorated Knight of Malta; recipient Disting. Alumnus citation Washington U., 1972; Bus. Leader of Yr. award Religious Heritage Am., 1973; citation Loyola U. Alumni Assn., 1973; named to Loyola U. Athletic Hall of Fame, 1976; Right Arm of St. Louis award St. Louis Regional Commerce and Growth Assn., 1980; Silver Crown award St. Louis Rabbinical Coll., 1983; Dept. Def. medal for Disting. Pub. Service, 1983; Disting. Communal Service award B'nai B'rith, 1983. Mem. Newspaper Personnel Relations Assn. (past pres.), Mo. C. of C. (dir. 1969-74), St. Louis C. of C. (exec. com. 1969-73, dir. 1969-73), Mo. Acad. Squires, Round Table (exec. com. 1975—, v.p., treas. 1975-76, pres. 1977-79), Bar Assn. St. Louis, Am., Mo. bar assns., Advt. Club of St. Louis (gov. 1972-75). Clubs: Bogey (pres. 1980-82), Mo. Athletic, St. Louis, Media (St. Louis) (dir. 1968—). Home: 6233 Northwood Ave Saint Louis MO 63105

BAUMAN, HOWARD EUGENE, food co. exec.; b. Woodworth, Wis., Mar. 20, 1925; s. Frederick and Signe (Rassmussen) B.; m. Edith Mae Tabbert, Sept. 3, 1948; children—Victoria Lynn, Kay Diane. B.S., U. Wis., 1949, M.S., 1950, Ph.D., 1953. Research asst. U. Wis., 1949-53, teaching asst., 1952-53; with Pillsbury Co., Mpls., 1953—, asso. dir. life scis., then asso. dir. internat. research and devel., 1965-67, dir. corp. research, 1967-69, v.p. sci. and regulatory affairs, 1969—; rep. Indsl. Research Inst.; chmn. nutrition com. Millers Nat. Fedn. Served with AUS, 1943-46. Fellow AAAS, Inst. Food Technologists (pres. 1977), Royal Soc. Health; mem. Am. Acad. Microbiology, Am. Soc. Microbiology, Am. Assn. Cereal Chemists, Am. Chem. Soc., Am. Inst. Biol. Scis., Assn. Food and Drug Ofcls., Brit. Indsl. Biol. Research Assn., Internat. Assn. Microbiol. Socs. (treas. food and hygiene sect.), Minn. Acad. Sci., Nutrition Soc., Sigma Xi, Phi Tau Sigma. Republican. Clubs: St. Louis Park Sportsmen's, Masons. Address: 311 2d St SE Minneapolis MN 55414

BAUMAN, JEROME ALAN, lawyer; b. N.Y.C., July 7, 1931; s. Melville J. and Tillie (Cohn) B.; m. Esme Pamela Joseph, July 4, 1966; children—David Meredith, Oren Reid. B.S. in Chemistry, Queens Coll., 1953; LL.B. cum laude, Harvard U., 1958. Bar: N.Y. bar 1959, Fla. bar 1971. Asso. counsel firm Levin, Rosmarin & Schwartz, N.Y.C., 1958-62, Sperry, Weinberg & Cutler, 1962-64; gen. counsel Inland Credit Corp., N.Y.C., 1964-66; assoc. counsel firm Golenbock & Barell, N.Y.C., 1966-68; assoc. counsel GAC Corp., Allentown, Pa., Miami, Fla., 1968-72; v.p., gen. counsel GAC Properties, Inc., Miami, 1970-72, Gulfstream Land & Devel. Corp., Plantation, Fla., 1972-78; ptnr. firm Bauman, Wurtenberger & Baker, 1981—. Pres. Plantation Jewish Congregation, 1975-79; mem. campaign cabinet Fedn. Jewish Philanthropies New York N.L.D., 1963-65. Served with U.S. Army, 1953-55. Mem. N.Y., Fla. bar assns. Home: 1028 NW 110 Ln Coral Springs FL 33065 Office: 1244 W University Dr Plantation FL 33322

BAUMAN, JON, entertainer; b. Bklyn., Sept. 14, 1947; s. Charles and Bess (Frank) B.; m. Mary Ryerson, Apr. 8, 1971; children: Nora, Eli. B.A., Columbia U., 1968, postgrad. in music theory, 1969. Leading role: as Bowzer, with Sha Na Na singing group and TV series; appeared in: numerous TV shows including Flip Wilson, 1970, The Smothers Brothers, 1973, 100 Years of General Electric, 1974, Midnight Special, 1971-76, others; singing tours in U.S., Europe, Africa and Japan, 1970—; solo TV appearances in various programs including: The Barbara Mandrell Show, 1981, Mike Douglas Show, 1980-81, The Tomorrow Show, 1981, Dance Fever, others; host: We Dare You, 1982, Bowzer's Guide to Summer, 1983, Pop 'n' Rocker Game, 1983; leading role in TV commercials for, Arby's and GAF's Melody Madness, 1980-81; featured singer, Rockefeller Center Xmas Tree Lighting, 1979; appeared as lead singer in: film Grease, 1978; appearances on, Sta. KRLA, Los Angeles, 1978—. Active fund raising campaigns Cerebral Palsy, Los Angeles, 1977—. Recipient Gold medal award Internat. Film and TV Festival of N.Y., 1979. Mem. AFTRA, Am. Fedn. Musicians, Screen Actors Guild. Office: care Shankman De Blasio Inc 185 Pier Ave Santa Monica CA 90405 *I think acting, singing, writing, playing the piano, my involvement in all the arts, springs from the same impulse. All I look for in a project is that it be expressive, have something to say.*

BAUMAN, RICHARD, anthropologist; b. N.Y.C., Oct. 28, 1940; s. Joseph and Zaphrirah Judith (Kremen) B.; m. Beverly J. Stoeltje, Nov. 26, 1977; children: Mark, Andrew, Gretchen, Rachael. B.A. with honors and distinction, U. Mich., 1961; M.A. (Woodrow Wilson fellow 1961-62), Ind. U., 1962; Ph.D., U. Pa., 1968. Postdoctoral fellow U. Tex., Austin, 1967-68, mem. faculty, 1968—, prof. anthropology, 1976—, dir. Folklore Center, 1970—. Author: For the Reputation of Truth, 1971, Verbal Art as Performance, 1977, Let Your Words Be Few, 1983; co-editor: Toward New Perspectives in Folklore, 1972, Explorations in the Ethnography of Speaking, 1974, And Other Neighborly Names, 1981, Working Papers in Sociolinguistics, 1974—. Fulbright fellow, 1963-64; sr. fellow Nat. Endowment Humanities, 1978-79. Fellow Am. Folklore Soc. (exec. sec.-treas. 1972-76, editor jour. 1981—); mem. Semiotic Soc. Am. (pres. 1980-81), Am. Anthrop. Assn., Am. Ethnol. Soc., Tex. Folklore Soc., Calif. Folklore Soc. Office: SSB 3 106 Univ Tex Austin TX 78712

BAUMAN, RICHARD ARNOLD, coast guard officer; b. Fitchburg, Mass., Aug. 16, 1924; s. Frederick Adams and Dorothy Arnold (Farnham) B.; m. Dorothy Helen Schmalz, June 5, 1948; children: Elizabeth Kay, Richard Arnold, Jr., Robert Arthur, William Lawrence. B.S. in Marine Transp, Mass. Maritime Acad., 1976, D.P.A. hon., 1982; student, Armed Forces Staff Coll., Norfolk, Va., 1966-67, Nat. War Coll., Washington, 1974-75. Officer U.S. Mcht. Marine, 1944-57; commd. lt. U.S. Coast Guard, 1957, advanced through grades to rear admiral, 1980; liaison officer to comdr. in chief U.S. Atlantic Fleet, Norfolk, 1968-71; comdg. officer USCG Cutter Ingham, 1971-73; chief info. systems div. Coast Guard Hdqrs., Washington, 1973-74, chief port safety and law enforcement, 1975-78; ops. officer 9th Coast Guard Dist., Cleve., 1978-80; chief Office Navigation, Coast Guard Hdqrs., Washington, 1980-83; comdr. 1st Coast Guard Dist., Boston, 1983—; U.S. commr. Permanent Internat. Assn. Navigation Congresses, 1980—. Decorated Bronze Star Medal with combat V, Meritorious Service medal (2), Coast Guard Commendation medals (3), Joint Service Commendation medal, Navy Commendation medal with combat V, Vietnamese Gallantry Cross with Gold Star. Mem. Boston Marine Soc., U.S. Naval Inst. Club: Mason. Office: 150 Causeway St Boston MA 02114

BAUMAN, ROBERT PATTEN, diversified company executive; b. Cleve., Mar. 27, 1931; s. John Nevin and Lucille (Patten) B.; m. Patricia H. Jones, June 15, 1961; children: John, Elizabeth. B.A., Ohio Wesleyan U., 1953; M.B.A., Harvard Bus. Sch., 1955. Mktg. adminstrn. Maxwell House div. Gen. Foods, White Plains, N.Y., 1958-65, gen. mgr. Post div., 1967, corp. v.p., 1968, exec. v.p., 1968, pres., dir. internat. ops., 1973; dir. Avco Corp., Greenwich, Conn., 1980—, chmn. bd., 1981—, Avco Fin. Services, Newport Beach, Calif., Paul Res. Life Ins. Group, Worcester, Mass., SCM Corp., N.Y. Author: Plants and Pets, 1982. Trustee Ohio Wesleyan U., Spelman Coll.; bd. mgrs. N.Y. Bot. Garden; mem. The Conf. Bd., Council Fgn. Relations. Clubs: Webannet Golf (Kennebunk, Maine) (pres.); Silver Springs (Ridgefield, Conn.); Quail Ridge (Delray Beach, Fla.); Blind Brook (Port Chester, N.Y.). Office: Avco Corp 1275 King St Greenwich CT 06830

BAUMAN, ROBERT POE, physicist, educator; b. Jackson, Mich., May 8, 1928; s. Chester Ernest and Mabel Victoria (Poe) B.; m. Edith Jane Gerkin, Aug. 27, 1949; children: Katherine Jane, David Gordon, Jeffrey Allen, Alice Victoria. B.S., Purdue U., 1949, M.S., 1951; Ph.D., U. Pitts., 1954. Instr. to asso. prof. chemistry Poly. Inst. Bklyn., 1954-67; mem. tech. staff Bell Telephone Labs., Murray Hill, N.J., summer 1966; prof. physics U. Ala. in Birmingham, 1967—, also chmn. dept., 1967-73, dir. project on teaching and learning Univ. Coll., 1975-78; vis. fellow Joint Inst. Lab. Astrophysics, Boulder, Colo., 1980-81. Author: Absorption Spectroscopy, 1962, Introduction to Equilibrium Thermodynamics, 1966. Asso. counselor Ala. Jr. Acad. Sci., 1970-73; Pres. Birmingham Civic Chorus, 1974-75; Mem. Bethpage (N.Y.) Bd. Edn., 1965-67, pres., 1965-66. Mem. Am. Phys. Soc., Am. Assn. Physics Tchrs. (chmn. sect. reps. 1979-81, pres. 1983), Am. Optical Soc., Coblentz Soc. (pres. 1972-74, bd. mgmt.), Ala. Acad. Sci. (vice chmn., v.p. 1968-70). Home: 3535 Rockhill Rd Mountain Brook AL 35223 Office: Univ Alabama Birmingham AL 35294

BAUMANN, CARL A., educator, biochemist; b. Milw., Aug. 10, 1906; s. Edward Carl and Minna (Einwaldt) B. B.S., U. Wis., 1929, Ph.D. in Agrl. Chemistry, 1933. Asst. agrl. chemistry U. Wis., 1929-34, instr. and research asso., 1936-39, asst. prof. biochemistry and cancer research, 1939-46, prof. biochemistry, 1946-76, emeritus, 1976—; Mem. Alsos Mission, 1945; chief party Midwest Univs. Consortium for Internat. Activities mission U. Agraria-La Molina, Lima, Peru, 1966-69. Editorial bd.: Jour. Nutrition; Contbr. articles to profl. jours. Decorated Medal of Freedom; Order Brit. Empire.; Gen. Edn. Bd. fellow, Heidelberg, Cambridge, Copenhagen, 1934-36. Mem. Am. Chem. Soc., Am. Soc. Biol. Chemists, Am. Inst. Nutrition, Am. Assn. Cancer Research, A.A.A.S., Soc. Exptl. Biology and Medicine, Sigma Xi, Phi Beta Kappa. Office: Biochemistry Bldg University of Wisconsin Madison WI 53706

BAUMANN, EDWARD ROBERT, sanitary engineering educator; b. Rochester, N.Y., May 12, 1921; s. John Carl and Lillie Minnie (Roth) B.; m. Mary A. Massey, June 15, 1946; children: Betsy Louise, Philip Robert. B.S.E. in Civil Engring, U. Mich., 1944, U. Ill., 1945, M.S., 1947, Ph.D., 1954; NSF faculty fellow, U. Durham, Eng., 1959-60. Research asso. U. Ill., 1947-53; asso. prof. civil engring. Iowa State U., 1953-56, prof., 1956—, Anson Marston disting. prof. engring., 1972—; cons. Water Quality Office of EPA, Culligan Internat., Lakeside Engring. Co., many cities and industries. Author: Sewerage and Sewage Treatment, 1958; Mem. editorial bd.: Internat. Jour. Air and Water Pollution, London, 1960-67; asst. editor: San. Engr. Newsletter of ASCE, 1962-74; Contbr. articles to profl. jours. Vice pres., treas. Water Found., Inc., 1978—; mem. Iowa Bd. Health, 1975-76, Iowa State U. Research Found., 1975-78, 1983. Served with C.E. AUS, 1944-46. Recipient gold medal Filtration Soc., Eng., 1970; George B. Gascoigne medal Water Pollution Control Fedn., 1962; Bedell award, 1977; Publs. award, 1963, 80; Purification div. award Am. Water Works Assn., 1965; Research award, 1978; named Water Works Man of Year, 1972; Anson Marston medal Iowa Engring. Soc., 1966; Disting. Service award, 1968. Fellow ASCE; mem. Am. Water Works Assn. (internat. dir. 1978—), Assn. Environ. Engring. Profs. (pres. 1967-70, Nalco award), Nat. Soc. Profl. Engrs. (nat. dir.), AAUP, Am. Soc. Engring. Edn., Am. Inst. Chem. Engrs., Sigma Xi, Phi Kappa Phi, Chi Epsilon. Club: Rotarian. Home: 1627 Crestwood Circle Ames IA 50010 *It isn't enough to build a "big pie"; we must also protect its quality and learn how to cut it fairly*

BAUMANN, RICHARD GORDON, lawyer; b. Chgo., Apr. 7, 1938; s. Martin M. and Harriet May (Granof) B.; m. Terrie Bemel, Dec. 18, 1971; children: Michelle, Alison. B.S. cum laude, U. Wis., 1960, J.D., 1964. Bar: Wis. 1964, Calif. 1970, U.S. Supreme Ct. 1973. Congressional intern U.S. Senator Hubert H. Humphrey, 1959; practiced in, Milw., 1964-69, Los Angeles, 1969—; assoc. firm Kohner, Mann & Kailas, Milw., 1964-69, Sulmeyer, Kupetz & Alberts, Los Angeles, 1969-73; mem. firm Sulmeyer, Kupetz, Baumann & Rothman, Los Angeles, 1973—; judge pro tem Los Angeles Mcpl. Ct. Fellow Comml. Law Found.; Mem. Comml. Law League Am. (chmn. Western region members assn.), Los Angeles County Bar Assn. Office: 615 S Flower St 6th Floor Los Angeles CA 90017

BAUMBACH, HAROLD, artist; b. N.Y.C., Jan. 19, 1904; s. Isaac and Anna (Summer) B.; m. Ida Zackheim, Dec. 25, 1930; children: Jonathan, James, Daniel. Student, Pratt Inst., Ednl. Alliance. Instr. painting, drawing Bklyn. Coll., Bklyn. Mus.; artist in residence U. Iowa, Iowa City, 1972-74. One-man shows include, Contemporary Arts Gallery, N.Y.C., 1935-44, ACA Gallery, N.Y.C., 1944, Galerie Mayer, N.Y.C., 1960, Barone Gallery, N.Y.C., 1958-62, Rose Fried Gallery, N.Y.C., 1966, U. Iowa Mus., 1973, SalPeter Gallery, 1945, Cerberus Gallery, 1975, Larcada Gallery, Summit Gallery, N.Y.C., 1979, group shows include, Phila. Art Alliance, St. Paul Art Inst., Met. Mus. Art, Calif. Palace Legion of Honor, Whitney Mus. Am. Art, N.Y.C., 1947, Bklyn. Mus., Chgo. Art Inst., Corcoran Gallery, Washington, 1947, Balt. Mus., Carnegie Art Inst. Internat., Nebr. Art Inst., Des Moines Art Center, Albright Knox Mus.; represented in permanent collections, Hirshhorn Mus., Washington, Bklyn. Mus., Pa. Acad., R.I. Sch. Design, U. Iowa Mus., U. Ga. Mus., U. Ariz. Mus., Whitney Mus. Am. Art, N.Y. U., Chrysler Mus., U. Ga., U. Ariz., also pvt. collections; represented by, Galerie Ninety-Nine, Bay Harbor Islands, Fla. Recipient 1st prize for painting Bklyn. Soc. Painters.; papers included in Archives Am. Art, Smithsonian Instn. Mem. Fedn. Modern Painters and Sculptors. Address: 278 Henry St New York NY 11201

BAUMBACH, JONATHAN, writer, educator; b. N.Y.C., July 5, 1933; s. Harold M. and Ida Helen (Zackheim) B.; m. Georgia Anne Brown, June 14, 1968; children: David, Nina, Noah, Nicholas. A.B., Bklyn. Coll., 1955; M.F.A., Columbia U., 1956; Ph.D., Stanford U., 1961. Asst. prof. English Ohio State U., 1961-64; asst. prof. N.Y. U., 1964-66, Bklyn. Coll., CUNY, 1966-69, asso. prof., 1970-72, prof., 1972—, dir. M.F.A. in creative writing, 1974—; vis. prof. Tufts U., 1969-70, U. Wash., 1978. Author: The Landscape of Nightmare, 1965, A Man To Conjure With, 1965, What Comes Next, 1968, Reruns, 1974, Babble, 1976, The Return of Service, 1979, Chez Charlotte and Emily, 1979, My Father More or Less, 1982; Editor: Writers As Teachers, 1970, (with others) Moderns and Contemporaries, 1965, Statements 2, 1977; Film critic: Partisan Rev, 1974. Recipient Young Writers award, 1961; Woodrow Wilson fellow, 1961; Nat. Endowment of Arts fellow, 1968; Guggenheim fellow, 1978-79. Mem. PEN, Nat. Soc. Film Critics, Fiction Collective. Jewish. Office: Dept English Brooklyn College Brooklyn NY 11210

BAUMER, FRANKLIN L., educator; b. Johnstown, Pa., May 10, 1913; s. Herman E. and Anna (Dibert) B.; m. Margarita Thieler, June 22, 1936 (dec.); children—Constance (dec.), Joanna.; m. Bodil Bruus Fullerton, Mar. 4, 1983. A.B., Yale U., 1934, Ph.D., 1938; student, London (Eng.) U., 1935-36. Prof. history Yale U., New Haven, 1954—, Randolph W. Townsend prof. history, 1963-83, prof. emeritus, 1983—, dir. grad. studies in history, 1951-60. Author: The Early Tudor Theory of Kingship, 1940, 2d edit., 1966, Main Currents of Western Thought, 1952, 4th rev. edit., 1978, Religion and the Rise of Scepticism, 1960, 69, Intellectual Movements in Modern European History, 1965—, Modern European Thought, 1977; Contbr.: articles to profl. jours. Dictionary of the History of Ideas, 1973. Guggenheim fellow, 1945-46; faculty fellow Fund for Advancement Edn., 1953-54. Mem. Am. Hist. Assn., Hist. Sci. Soc. Episcopalian. Home: 9 Hawley Rd Hamden CT 06517 Office: 1541 Pierson Coll Yale U New Haven CT 06517 *My life as a professor of intellectual history has been a joyous participation with my students in high philosophical adventure. I have found the combination of scholarly exercises: research, writing, and teaching: to be not only compatible but highly dynamic.*

BAUMGARDNER, JAMES LEWIS, history educator; b. Bristol, Va., Jan. 26, 1938; s. John Richard and Roxie Katherine (Lewis) B.; children: Ellen Lorena, James Michael. A.A., Bluefield Jr. Coll., 1957; B.A., Carson-Newman Coll., 1959; M.A., U. Tenn.-Knoxville, 1964, Ph.D., 1968. Ordained to ministry Baptist Ch., 1955. Asst. prof. history Carson-Newman Coll., Jefferson City, Tenn., 1964-67, assoc. prof., 1967-73, prof., 1973—, chmn. history-polit. sci,. dept., 1974—. Contbr. articles to learned jours. Interim mem. Jefferson County (Tenn.) Bd. Sch. Commrs., 1978. Served with U.S. Army, 1959-62. Mem. Am. Hist. Assn., Acad. Polit. Sci., Orgn. Am. Historians, So. Hist. Assn., So. Bapt. Hist. Soc., Phi Alpha Theta. Office: Box 1929 Carson-Newman Coll Jefferson City TN 37760

BAUMGARDNER, RUSSELL HOWARD, glass company executive; b. St. Paul, Sept. 4, 1918; s. Raymond Clyde and Pearl Felicia (Boorman) B.; m. Bernice Ann Grimmer, June 21, 1974; 1 son. Mark R.; stepchildren: Gerald, Vicki, Brett, Kirk, Keith Ylinen. Student, U. Minn., 1937, 39, Macalester Coll., 1938; LL.B., St. Paul Coll. law, 1942; LL.D., George Washington U., 1948. Bar: D.C. 1949, Minn. 1950. Gen. practice law, St. Paul, 1950-53; pres. Harmon Glass Co. (succeeded by Apogee Enterprises, Inc. 1963), Mpls., 1952—, chmn., 1963—; chmn. Red Wing Sewer Pipe Corp., 1960-65, Conolly Shoe Co., 1961-67; dir. Westland Capital Corp. Pres. Minn. Assn. Commerce and Industry, 1970-71, bd. dirs., 1963-72; chmn. Bus. Industry Polit. Action Com. Minn. Served to maj. U.S. Army, 1942-46. Decorated Bronze Star. Mem. Mpls. C. of C., Conf. Bd. Assn. Corp. Growth. Republican. Episcopalian. Clubs: Lafayette, Mpls., Decathlon Athletic. Office: 7900 Xerxes Ave S Suite 1944 Minneapolis MN 55431

BAUMGART, NORBERT K., govt. ofcl.; b. Kampsville, Ill., Sept. 4, 1931; s. Karl J. and Esther (Huelskoetter) B.; m. Bernita Y. Riedemann, July 24, 1955; children—Timothy, Susan, Jean. B.A., U. No. Iowa, 1954, M.A., 1958; Ed.D, Ind. U., 1960. Pub. sch. relations counselor, Cedar Falls, Iowa, 1956-58; counselor Ind. U., 1958-60; dean students Wilmington (Ohio) Coll., 1960-63, Mankato (Minn.) State Coll., 1963-68; pres. No. State Coll., Aberdeen, S.D., 1968-76; edn. chief instl. Support br. Region VIII, U.S. Dept. Edn., Denver, 1976—. Contbr. articles to profl. jours. Served with AUS, 1954-56. Mem. Phi Delta Kappa. Home: 3385 Alkire Way Golden CO 80401 Office: US Dept Edn Fed Bldg 1961 Stout St Denver CO 80202

BAUMGARTNER, JOHN H., refining and petroleum products company executive; b. 1936; married. With Clark Oil & Refining Corp., Milw., 1956-81, retail sales rep., 1960-65, dist. mgr., 1965-72, regional mgr., 1972-74, v.p. retail mktg., asst. gen. sales mgr., 1974-75, sr. v.p. mktg., 1975-78, exec. v.p., 1978-81; pres. J.H. Baumgartner Enterprises, Wauwatosa, Wis., 1981—; chmn. bd. Products Terminaling of Wis. Inc., Milw. Served with USMC, 1953-56. Office: 1414 S Harbor Dr Milwaukee WI 53207

BAUMHART, RAYMOND CHARLES, university president; b. Chgo., Dec. 22, 1923; s. Emil and Florence (Weidner) B. B.S., Northwestern U., 1945; Ph.L., Loyola U., 1952, S.T.L., 1958; M.B.A., Harvard, 1953, D.B.A., 1963; LL.D. (hon.), Ill. Coll., D.H.L., Scholl Coll. Podiatric Medicine. Joined Jesuit Order, 1946; ordained priest Roman Catholic Ch., 1957; asst. prof. mgmt. Loyola U., Chgo., 1962-64, dean, 1964-66, exec. v.p., acting v.p. Med. Center, 1968-70, pres., 1970—; research fellow Cambridge Center for Social Studies, 1966-68; dir. Jewel Cos., Inc., Continental Ill. Corp. Author: An Honest Profit, 1968, (with Thomas Garrett) Cases in Business Ethics, 1968, (with Thomas McMahon) The Brewer-Wholesaler Relationship, 1969; Corr. editor: America, 1965-70. Trustee Boston Coll., 1968-71, St. Louis U., 1967-72; bd. dirs. Council Better Bus. Burs. Served to lt. (j.g.) USNR, 1944- 46. Decorated Order of Cavalier, Italy; recipient Râle medallion Boston Coll.; John W. Hill fellow Harvard, 1961-62. Mem. Assn. Jesuit Colls. and Univs. (dir.), Fedn. Ind. Ill. Colls. and Univs. (dir.). Clubs: Commercial, Economic, Mid-America (Chgo.). Home: 6525 N Sheridan Rd Chicago IL 60626

BAUMHEFNER, CLARENCE HERMAN, banker; b. Lester Prairie, Minn., Apr. 1, 1912; s. Walter P. and Clare A. (Jacobs) B.; m. Virginia Haight, May 11, 1941; children—Robert, Bonnie. Grad., Am. Inst. Banking, 1940; student, Grad. Sch. Banking, Rutgers U., 1951. With Bank of Am., 1940—, 1940-43, insp., 1943-47, asst. chief insp., 1947-50, asst. to cashier, 1950-56, cashier and v.p., 1956-65, sr. v.p., cashier, 1965-66, exec. v.p., 1966-70, vice chmn. bd., 1970—. Clubs: Villa Taverna, Merchants Exchange, Bankers Bohemian, Pacific Union (San Francisco). Home: PO Box 940 Aptos CA 95003 Office: 555 California St San Francisco CA 94104

BAUML, FRANZ HEINRICH, educator; b. Vienna, Austria, June 12, 1926; came to U.S., 1942, naturalized, 1945; s. Gustav Heinrich and Josefa (Sam) B.; m. Betty Zeidner, Aug. 28, 1958; children—Carolyn, Mark, Deborah. B.S., Armstrong Coll., 1950; B.A., U. Calif., Berkeley, 1953, M.A., 1955, Ph.D., 1957. Prof. German U. Calif., Los Angeles, 1957—. Author: Rhetorical Devices and Structure in the Ackermann aus Bohmen, 1960, Kudrun: Die Handschrift, 1969, Medieval Civilization in Germany, 800-1273, 1969, A Dictionary of Gestures, 1975, A Concordance to the Nibelungenlied, 1976. Served with AUS, 1944-46; Served with U.S. Army, 1950-51. Mem. Medieval Acad. Am. Home: 12400 Marva Ave Granada Hills CA 91344 Office: Germanic Langs U Calif Los Angeles CA 90024

BAUMOL, WILLIAM JACK, economist, educator; b. N.Y.C., Feb. 26, 1922; s. Solomon and Lillian (Itzkowitz) B.; m. Hilda Missel, Dec. 27, 1941; children: Ellen Frances, Daniel Aaron. B.S.S., CCNY, 1942; Ph.D., London U., 1949; LL.D. (hon.), Rider Coll., 1965; hon. fellow, London Sch. Econs., 1970, Stockholm Sch. Econs., Sweden, 1971, U. Basel, Switzerland, 1973; L.H.D., Knox Coll, 1973. With U.S. Dept. Agr., 1942-43, 46; asst. lectr. London Sch. Econs., 1947-49; asst. prof. Princeton U., 1949-52, assoc. prof., 1952-54, prof., 1954—, N.Y. U., 1971—; joint appointment Princeton U. and N.Y. U., 1971—; assoc. Stockholm Sch. Econs.; mem., past chmn. Econ. Policy Council of N.J., 1967-75. Author: Economic Dynamics: An Introduction, 1951, Welfare Economics and the Theory of The State, 1952, Business Behavior, Value and Growth, 1959, Economic Theory and Operations Analysis, 1960, (with L.V. Chandler) Economic Processes and Policies, 1954, The Stock Market and Economic Efficiency, 1965, (with W.G. Bowen) Performing Arts: The Economic Dilemma, 1966, (with S.M. Goldfeld) Precursors in Mathematical Economics, 1969, (with W. E. Oates) The Theory of Environmental Policy, 1975, Selected Economic Writings of William Jack Baumol, 1976, (with Klaus Knorr) What Price Economic Growth?, 1961, (with W.E. Oates and S.B. Blackman) Economics, Environmental Policy, and the Quality of Life, 1979, (with A.S. Blinder) Economics: Principles and Policy, 1979, 2d edit., 1982, (with J.C. Panzar and R.D. Willig) Contestable Markets and the Theory of Industry Structure, 1982. Past pres. Am. Friends of London Sch. Econs.; Trustee Rider Coll., Lawrenceville, 1960-70. Recipient Townsend Harris medal City U. N.Y., John Commons award Omicron Delta Epsilon.; Guggenheim fellow, 1957-58; Ford Faculty Fellowship, 1965-66. Fellow Econometric Soc.; mem. AAUP (v.p., chmn. com. on econ. status of the profession 1968-70, mem. com. on hon. mems.), Am. Econ. Assn. (mem. exec. com., v.p. 1966-67, pres. 1981), Am. Acad. Arts and Scis., Am. Philos. Soc., Eastern Econ. Assn. (pres. 1978-79), Assn. Environ. and Resource Economists (past pres.), Resources for the Future, Inc. (mem. res. adv. bd.). Home: 61 Jefferson Rd Princeton NJ 08540

BAUMRIN, BERNARD STEFAN HERBERT, lawyer, educator; b. N.Y.C., Jan. 7, 1934; s. David and Regina (Zuckerburg) B.; m. Judith Anne Marti, Dec. 20, 1953; children: Seth, Jeanne, Rachel. Student, Marietta Coll., 1951-52, N.Y. U., 1952-53; B.A., Ohio State U., 1956; Ph.D., Johns Hopkins U., 1960; postgrad., Washington U., St. Louis, 1965-67; J.D., Columbia U., 1970. Dir. forensics Johns Hopkins U., Balt., 1957-59; vis. asst. prof. philosophy Butler U., 1960-61, Antioch Coll., 1961; asst. prof. philosophy U. Del., Newark, 1961-64, Washington U., 1964-67; asso. prof. philosophy Hunter Coll., City U. N.Y., 1967-68, Grad. Sch. and Lehman Coll., Bronx, N.Y., 1968-72, prof., 1972—, treas. univ. faculty senate, 1978-81, exec. com., 1976—; adj. prof. Mt. Sinai Sch. Medicine, 1983—; ptnr. Baumrin, Galub & Vulkomer. Author: Philosophy of Science, 2 vols, 1963, British Moralists, 1964, Hobbes's Leviathan, 1968, Moral Responsibility and the Professions, 1983; contbr. articles to profl. jours. AEC fellow, 1963; U. Del. fellow, 1962; Washington U. Forsyth fellow, 1964-67; City U. N.Y. grantee, 1968, 70; N.Y. Council for Humanities grantee, 1976; Nat. Endowment for Humanities grantee, 1977-79; Mellon Found. grantee, 1980—. Mem. AAAS, Mind Assn., Am. Philos. Assn., AAUP, Soc. for Philosophy and Public Policy, Internat. Assn. Philosophy of Law and Social Philosophy, ACLU, N.Y. Acad. Scis. Office: CUNY Grad Sch 33 W 42d St New York NY 10036 also Lehman College Bronx NY 10468

BAUMRIND, DIANA, research psychologist; b. N.Y.C., Aug. 23, 1927. A.B., Hunter Coll., 1948; M.A., U. Calif., Berkeley, 1951, Ph.D., 1955. Cert. and lic. psychologist, Calif. Project dir. NIMH grant psychology dept. U. Calif., Berkeley, 1955-58, Inst. Human Devel., 1960-66, project dir., 1967-72, prin. investigator, 1972-74, W.T. Grant Found., from 1974; now research psychologist and prin. investigator family socialization and developmental competence project Inst. Human Devel.; lectr. and cons. in field; referee Nat. Inst. Child Health and Human Devel., 1968—; cons. Head Start Evaluation and Demonstration Program, 1969; referee for research proposals NIH, 1970—, NSF, 1970—; mem. Nat. Commn. on Protection of Human Subjects of Biomed. and Behavioral Research. Contbr. numerous articles to profl. jours. and books; author 2 monographs; cons. editor: Developmental Psychology, 1969—, Child Devel, 1970—, Contemporary Psychology, 1974—, Am. Psychologist, 1974—, Personality and Social Psychology Bull, 1974—; editorial bd.: Child Development. NIMH grantee, 1955-58, 60-66; Nat. Inst. Child Health and Human Devel. grantee, 1967-70, 71-74, 74—; MacArthur Found. grantee; Grant Found. grantee, 1967—. Fellow Am. Psychol. Assn.; mem. Soc. Research in Child Devel. Office: Institute for Human Development 1203 Tolman Hall University of California Berkeley CA 94720

BAUR, JOHN IRELAND HOWE, art consultant, former museum director; b. Woodbridge, Conn., Aug. 9, 1909; s. Paul V.C. Bauer and Susan (Whiting) B.; m. Louise W. Chase, Jan. 8, 1938; children: Susan, Arthur M., Jean E. B.A., Yale U., 1932, M.A., 1934. Supr. edn. Bklyn. Mus., 1934-36, curator paintings and sculpture, 1936-52; curator Whitney Mus. Am. Art, N.Y.C., 1952-58, assoc. dir., 1958-66, dir., 1966-74, ret., 1974; cons. Terra Mus. Am. Art, Evanston, Ill., 1979—. Author: 18 books including Revolution and Tradition in Modern American Art, 1951, American Painting in the 19th Century, 1953, Philip Evergood, 1960, Joseph Stella, 1971, The Inlander: Life and Work of Charles Burchfield, 1982; editor: Am. Art Jour. Books, 1980—. Served with U.S. Army, 1944-45. Home: Mount Holly Rd Katonah NY 10536 Office: Whitney Mus of Am Art 945 Madison Ave New York NY 10021

BAUR, WERNER HEINZ, educator, mineralogist; b. Warsaw, Poland, Aug. 2, 1931; came to U.S., 1962; s. Heinrich Ernst and Melanie (Borkowska) B.; m. Renate Grossmann, June 22, 1962; children: Wolfgang, Brigitte. Dr. rer.nat, U. Gottingen, Germany, 1956, privat-dozent, 1961. Sci. officer U. Göttingen, 1956-63; asst. to asso. prof. U. Pitts., 1963-65; asso. prof. to prof. U. Ill.-Chgo., 1965—, head dept. geol. scis., 1967-80, asso. dean Coll. Liberal Arts and Scis., 1978-80; postdoctoral fellow U. Berne, Switzerland, 1957; vis. asso. chemist Brookhaven Nat. Lab., 1962-63; vis. prof. U. Karlsruhe, Germany, 1971-72. Contbr. articles to sci. jours. Fellow Mineral. Soc. Am.; mem. Am. Crystallogical Assn., Am. Geophys. Union. Research on crystal chemistry of minerals and inorganic compounds, crystal structure determination, hydrogen bonding, computer simulation of crystal structures, empirical theories of chem. bonding, predictive crystal chemistry, ionic conductivity. Office: Box 4348 Dept Geol Scis Univ Illinois Chicago IL 60680

BAUSCH, VIRGINIA QUINN, med. assn. exec.; b. Odessa, Tex., June 9, 1945; d. William Francis and Florence Elizabeth (Decker) Quinn; 1 son, Justin. B.A., Mt. Holyoke Coll., 1967. Exec. dir. Am. Acad. Child Psychiatry, Washington, 1973—, Nat. Consortium for Child Mental Health Services, 1973—. Mem. Am. Soc. Assn. Execs. Home: 3151 19th St NW Washington DC 20010 Office: Suite 201A 1424 16th St NW Washington DC 20036

BAUSTIAN, ROBERT FREDERICK, conductor; b. Storm Lake, Iowa, June 4, 1921; s. Alfred A. and Grace E. (Martin) B. B.Mus., Eastman Sch. Music, Rochester, N.Y., 1942, M.Mus., 1948; postgrad., Zurich (Switzerland) Conservatory. Prof. orch. U. Kans., 1957-66; prof. conducting Oberlin (Ohio) Coll. Conservatory, 1966-83; Coach, condr. Zurich Opera, 1949-53; 2d condr. Hessian State Opera, Wiesbaden, Germany, 1953-57; condr., mus. adminstr. Santa Fe Opera, 1957-78; guest condr. in, Germany, Spain, France, Yugoslavia, also N.Y.C. Opera. Guest condr. in, Ariz. Opera, San Francisco Opera, orchs. of, Atlanta, Kansas City, Akron. Served with AUS, 1942-46. Decorated Bronze Star. Mem. Am. Symphony Orch. League, Music Educators Nat. Conf., Nat. Opera Assn., Pi Kappa Lambda. Home: 424 Abeyta St Santa Fe NM 87501

BAVARIA, EDWARD CLETUS, manufacturing company executive; b. Wind Gap, Pa., Aug. 14, 1932; s. Joseph Peter and Jennie Antionette (Tarsi) B.; m. Elizabeth Jane Swank, June 9, 1956; children: Joseph, Celeste, Cynthia, Jennifer. B.S. in Engring, U.S. Mil. Acad., 1954. Commd. 2d lt. USAF, 1954; now Res.; with Gen. Electric Co., mgr. internat. service and sales ops., 1966-79, corp. v.p., London, 1979—. Office: Shortlands Hammersmith London SW6 8BX England *

BAXLEY, WILLIAM JOSEPH, state lieutenant governor; b. Dothan, Ala., June 27, 1941; s. Keener and Lemma Dorcas (Rountree) B.; m. Lucy Richards; 1 son, Louis. B.S., U. Ala., 1962, LL.B., 1964. Bar: Ala. 1964. Law clk. Ala. Supreme Ct., 1964-65; mem. firm Lee & McInish, Dothan, 1966; dist. atty. 20th Jud. Circuit Ala., 1966-71; atty. gen. State of Ala., 1971-79; ptnr. Baxley, Beck, Dillard & Dauphin, Birmingham, Ala., 1979-83; lt. gov. State of Ala., 1983—. Bd. dirs. Dothan Boys Club. Served with USAF, 1965-66. Mem. Houston County Bar Assn. (pres. 1969), United Comml. Travelers, Kappa Sigma, Alpha Kappa Psi, Phi Alpha Delta. Democrat. Methodist. Lodges: Masons; Shriners; Elks; Eagles; Woodmen of World. Office: Office of Lt Gov 201 State Capitol Bldg Montgomery AL 36130 *

BAXTER, ANNE, actress; b. Michigan City, Ind., May 7, 1923; d. Kenneth Stuart and Catherine (Wright) B.; m. John Hodiak, July 7, 1946; 1 dau., Katrina Baxter; m. Randolph Galt, Feb. 18, 1960; children: Melissa, Maginel; m. David Klee, Jan. 30, 1977. Ed. pub. schs., Theodora Irvine's Sch. of the Theater, White Plains, Chappaqua and Bronxville, N.Y., 1934-36, The Lenox Sch., 1937, The Brearley Sch., 1938-39, Studio Sch. Twentieth Century Fox, 1940. Studied with Ouspenskaya, for 3 years; played in: Seen But Not Heard, 1936, There's Always A Breeze, 1937, Madame Capet, 1937, Susan and God, Summer Playhouse, Dennis, Mass., 1938, Spring Meeting Cape Playhouse, 1939; Broadway play The Joshua Tree, London; appeared in: motion pictures All About Eve, 1951 (Acad. award nominee for best actress 1951), Cimarron, 1960, Walk on the Wild Side, 1961, Mix Me a Person, 1962, The Tall Women, 1980, The Busy Body, 1980, Jane Austen in Manhattan, 1980; 5 mos. tour John Browns Body, 1955-56; Noel Coward in Two Keys, 1975; appeared on: Broadway in Applause; appeared in: Theatre Group prodn. of Cause Celebre, 1979-80; TV series Hotel, 1983; Author: Intermission, 1976. Recipient Acad. award for best supporting actress in The Razor's Edge, 1947, Fgn. Press award for the Razor's Edge, 1947. Presbyterian. Office: 25 Knapp St Easton CT 06612

BAXTER, CECIL WILLIAM, JR., college president; b. Stockton, Kans., Aug. 11, 1923; s. Cecil William and Marjorie LaVerne (Fitzpatrick) B.; m. Pat Ann Layman, June 6, 1951; Children: Cecil William, Michael Kent, Patrick Alan. B.A., Kans. Wesleyan U., 1950; M.B.A., U. Denver, 1954; Ph.D., U. Tex., 1967. Secondary edn. tchr., then secondary sch. prin., 1951-60; bus. mgr. Cottey Coll., Nevada, Mo., 1960-65; dean instrn. Kansas City Community Jr. Coll., Kans., 1967-68, Forest Park Community Coll., St. Louis, 1968-70; pres. North Seattle Community Coll., 1970—; mem. faculty U. Wash., 1971; mem. Comm. on Colls. N.W. Assn. Schs. and Colls. Bd. dirs. Sr. Citizens Orgn., Seattle, 1972. Served with AUS, 1944-46. Ford Found. fellow U. Tex.; Kellogg Found. fellow U. Tex. Mem. Phi Delta Kappa. Lodge: Rotary. Office: 9600 College Way N Seattle WA 98103

BAXTER, COLIN IAN WRIGHT, manufacturing company executive; b. Waipawa, N.Z., Oct. 5, 1931; s. Robert and Eileen (Wright) B.; m.

Diane Elaine Cyr, July 6, 1958; children: Lisa M., John A., David H., Simon J. Nat. cert. in mech. engring. Hutt Valley Tech. Coll., 1953; student in process control, McGill U., Montreal, Que., Can., 1957-58. With Foxboro Co., 1956—, gen. mgr., 1972-74, v.p., 1974-78, exec. v.p., Foxboro, Mass., 1978-80, pres., dir., 1980—; dir. B.I.W. Cable Systems, Boston, Fleet Nat. Bank, Providence. Bd. dirs. Cardinal Cushing Sch. and Tng. Center, Hanover, Mass. Anglican. Home: 1 Colonial Rd Dover MA 02030 Office: 38 Neponset Ave Foxboro MA 02035

BAXTER, DONALD WILLIAM, physician, educator; b. Brockville, Ont., Can., Aug. 24, 1926; s. William Robert and Agnes B.; m. Judith Gould, May 20, 1959; children—Jonathan, Nicky. M.D.C.M., Queens U., Kingston, Ont., 1951, M.Sc., 1953. Intern Kingston (Ont.) Gen. Hosp., 1951-52; resident Montreal (Que., Can.) Neurol. Inst., 1952-53, Boston City Hosp., 1953-57; asst. prof. medicine U. Sask., 1957-62; asso. prof. neurology Temple U., Phila., 1962-63; prof. McGill U., Montreal, 1963—, chmn. dept. neurology and neurosurgery, 1979—. Home: 177 Jasper Ave Montreal PQ H3P 1K1 Canada Office: 3801 University St Montreal PQ H3A 2B4 Canada

BAXTER, HARRY STEVENS, lawyer; b. Ashburn, Ga., Aug. 25, 1915; s. James Hubert and Anne (Stevens) B.; m. Edith Ann Teasley, Apr. 4, 1943; children: Anna Katherine Baxter Worley (dec.), Nancy Julia Baxter Sibley. A.B. summa cum laude, U. Ga., 1936, LL.B., 1939; postgrad., Yale U., 1939-40. Bar: Ga. 1941. Instr. U. Ga. Law Sch., Athens, 1941; assoc. Smith Kilpatrick Cody Rogers & McClatchey, Atlanta, 1942-51; ptnr. Kilpatrick & Cody, Atlanta, 1951—; mem. State Bd. Bar Examiners Ga., 1960-66; chmn. State Bd. Bar Examiners, 1961-66; mem. Ga. Jud Qualifications Commn., 1979—; dir. Latex Constrns. Co., Atlanta. Pres. Atlanta Community Chest, 1963; mem. bd. visitors U. Ga. Law Sch., 1965-68, chmn., 1965-66; chmn. alumni adv. com. on reorgn., 1963-64; chmn. chancellor's alumni adv. com. on selection of pres. U. Ga., 1966-67; gen. co-chmn. Joint Ga. Tech.-Ga. Devel. Fund, 1967; trustee U. Ga. Found., chmn., 1973-76; trustee William E. Honey Found., St. Joseph's Hosp., Atlanta. Served with AUS, 1942-45. Recipient Disting. Alumnus award U. Ga. Law Sch., 1967. Fellow Am. Bar Found.; mem. Am. Law Inst., ABA, Ga. Bar Assn., Atlanta Bar Assn., Atlanta C. of C. (dir. 1959-62), Atlanta Legal Aid Soc. (pres. 1956-57), Phi Beta Kappa, Phi Beta Kappa Assocs., Phi Kappa Phi, Omicron Delta Kappa, Phi Delta Phi. Clubs: Capital City (pres. 1965-67), Lawyers (pres. 1958-59), Piedmont Driving, Commerce, University Yacht. Home: 3197 Chatham Rd NW Atlanta GA 30305 Office: Equitable Bldg 100 Peachtree St NW Atlana GA 30043

BAXTER, JAMES WILLIAM, III, investment counsel; b. New Albany, Ind., June 24, 1931; s. James William, Jr. and Beatrice F. (Diedrich) B.; m. Deborah Smith-Artoe, Nov. 26, 1980; 1 son, P. Andrew. B.S., Ind. U., 1953; postgrad., U. Louisville Sch. Bus. With Scudder, Stevens & Clark, 1963—, office dir., Cin., 1972-78, chmn. bd., pres., Chgo., 1978—, dir., N.Y.C., 1978—. Trustee Cin. Symphony Orch., 1975-78, Cin. Union Bethel, 1974-78; bd. dirs. United Cerebral Palsy, 1978—; adv. council Episcopal Ch. Found., 1977—. Served with AUS, 1953-55. Mem. Investment Counsel Assn. Am. Clubs: Tavern, Skyline (Chgo.). Home: 3750 Lake Shore Dr Chicago IL 60613 Office: 111 E Wacker Dr Chicago IL 60601

BAXTER, JOHN DARLING, physician, educator; b. Lexington, Ky., June 11, 1940; s. William Elbert and Genevive Lockhart (Wilson) B.; m. Ethelee Davidson Baxter, Aug. 10, 1963; children: Leslie Lockhart, Gillian Booth. A.B. in Chemistry, U. Ky., 1962; M.D., Yale U., 1966. Intern, then resident in internal medicine Yale-New Haven Hosp., 1966-68; USPHS research assoc. Nat. Inst. Arthritis and Metabolic Diseases, NIH, 1968-70; Dernham sr. fellow oncology U. Calif. Med. Sch., San Francisco, 1970-72, mem. faculty, 1972—, prof. medicine and biochemistry and biophysics, 1979—; dir. endocrine research Howard Hughes Med. Inst., 1973-82; chief div. endocrinology Moffitt Hosp., 1980—, dir. Metabolic Research Unit, 1981—; attending physician U. Calif. Med. Center, 1972—. Editor textbook of endocrinology and metabolism; Author research papers in field; mem. editorial bd. profl. jours. Recipient George W. Thorn award Howard Hughes Med. Inst., 1978, Disting. Alumni award U. Ky., 1980; grantee NIH, Am. Cancer Soc., others. Mem. Am. Chem. Soc., Am. Soc. Clin. Investigation, Am. Thyroid Assn., Assn. Am. Physicians, Am. Fedn. Clin. Research, Endocrine Soc., Western Assn. Physicians, Western Soc. Clin. Research. Office: 671 HSE U Calif Med Sch San Francisco CA 94143

BAXTER, JOHN LINCOLN, JR., manufacturing company executive; b. Brunswick, Maine, Mar. 11, 1920; s. John Lincoln and Constance (French) B.; m. Alice Preston Comee, June 1, 1942; children: John Randolph, Constance Baxter Marlow, Judith. B.A., Bowdoin Coll., 1942. Partner H. C. Baxter & Bros., Brunswick, 1942-65; v.p., dir. Snow Flake Canning Co., Brunswick, 1945-55, pres., dir., 1965-67; asst. gen. mgr., dir. Lamb-Weston, Inc., Portland, Oreg., 1965-67, exec. v.p., gen. mgr., 1967-71, pres., 1971-73; v.p., food group chmn. Amfac, Inc., Honolulu, 1971-74, exec. v.p., food group chmn., 1974-81; assoc. Omnivest Inc., fin. co., Portland, Oreg., 1983—; pres., chmn. bd. Zebron Corp., Tualatin, Oreg., 1981-83; bd. chmn. Reddicop Systems, Portland, 1980-81; dir. Black Butte Ranch Assn., 1981—, chmn., 1982—. Mem. Maine Ho. of Reps., 1958-62, majority leader, 1960-62, vice chmn. exec. council, 1962-64; mem. New Eng. Interstate Water Pollution Control Commn., 1954-56; dir. Associated Oreg. Industries, 1977-81, Associated Industries Maine, 1955-57; pres., dir. Found. Oreg. Research and Edn., 1977-79; dir. Oreg. Grad. Center; trustee Lewis & Clark Coll., 1979-82; mem. Oreg. Ednl. Coordinating Commn., 1982—, chmn., 1983—. Served to 2d lt. Q.M.C. U.S. Army, 1943-45. Mem. Nat. Canners Assn. (dir. 1954-56), Am. Frozen Food Inst. (dir. 1968-72), Frozen Potato Products Inst. (pres. 1970-71), Instant Potato Products Inst. (pres.), Maine Canners and Freezers (pres. 1960), N.W. Food Processors Assn. (pres. 1973), N.W. Packers and Growers Assn. (pres. 1971), Portland C. of C. (dir. 1978-81), Phi Beta Kappa. Republican. Clubs: University (N.Y.C.); (Portland, Oreg.); Oswego Lake Country (Lake Oswego, Oreg.). Office: 4800 SW Macadam Ave Suite 112 Portland OR 97201

BAXTER, MAURICE GLEN, historian, educator; b. Augusta, Ill., Sept. 22, 1920; s. Sterling Roscoe and Anna (Walsh) B.; m. Cynthia Lewis, Jan. 6, 1951; children: Kent, Hugh. A.B., U. Ill., 1941, M.A., 1942, Ph.D., 1948. Prof. history Ind. U., Bloomington, 1948—. Author: Orville Browning, 1957, Teaching American History in High Schools, 1962, Daniel Webster and the Supreme Court, 1966, The Steamboat Monopoly, 1972. Served with USNR, 1942-46. Mem. Orgn. Am. Historians, Am. Hist. Assn. Home: 501 Arbutus St Bloomington IN 47401 Office: History Dept Indiana University Bloomington IN 47405

BAXTER, MICHAEL JOHN, editor; b. Terre Haute, Ind., July 5, 1944; s. Victor LeRoy and Wilda Ione (Davis) B.; m. Joanne Kay Stohlman, July 5, 1966; children: Bradley Scott, Jeffrey John, Michael Victor Martin, Matthew John. B.A., U. Nebr., 1967. Reporter Lincoln (Nebr.) Evening Jour., 1962-68; reporter Miami (Fla.) Herald, 1968, 70-76, city editor, 1976-80, dep. mng. editor, 1981—; staff writer Tropic mag., 1969. Served with USAR, 1967. Recipient George Polk Meml. award L.I. U., 1973, A.P. Mng. Editors' Pub. Service award, 1974; Investigative Reporting award Fla. Soc. Newspaper Editors, 1974; Pub. Service award, 1974; Distinguished Achievement award U. Nebr., 1975; Distinguished Journalist award, 1975. Mem. Kappa Tau Alpha. Home: 13631 SW 103d Ave Miami FL 33176 Office: 1 Herald Plaza Miami FL 33101

BAXTER, RALPH FELIX, chemical company executive; b. Hamburg, Germany, Aug. 31, 1925; came to U.S., 1941, naturalized, 1944; s. Felix and Irmy (Münden) B.; m. Janice Phillips, 1960; children: David P., Eric F., Robert. Student, Rensselaer Poly. Inst., 1943-44, UCLA, 1946-48; B.S. in Mech. Engring, U. Calif.-Berkeley, 1949. Asso. Gen. Air Conditioning Corp., 1949-50; group project mgr. Rheem Mfg. Co., 1950-56; asst. to pres., dir. mfg. Revell, Inc., 1956-59; with Hunt Foods & Industries, Inc., 1959-67, dir. corp. planning. gen. mgr. ops. v.p. ops., 1959-64, v.p. corporate planning and analysis, 1964-67; sr. v.p. Avery Internat. Inc., Marino, Calif., 1967—; instr. div. extension U. Calif. at Los Angeles, 1959-60; Pres. So. Calif. Industry Edn. Council, 1971-73; v.p. Industry Edn. Council of Calif., 1973-81. Mem. White House Fellowship Commn., 1979-81. Served with AUS, 1943-46. Mem. Inst. Mgmt. Scis. (nat. chmn. coll. on planning 1966-68), Am. Arbitration Assn., Nat. Panel Arbitrators, Am. Ordnance Assn. (Walsh Meml. award 1953), Calif. Mfrs. Assn. (dir. 1981—). Home: 1263 N Citrus Dr La Habra CA 90631 Office: 50 N. Orange Grove Blvd. Pasadena CA 91103

BAXTER, RAYMOND CARLOS, chemical company executive; b. Granville, Pa., Sept. 21, 1922; s. Myron I. and Dorothy L. (Gillil) B.; m. Martha A. Edson, June 26, 1944; children—Frederick E., Bruce A., Susan L., Andrew T. B.S. in Chem. Engring, Cornell U., 1944. Chem. engr. Standard Oil Co., Whiting, Ind., 1944-46; project engr. to chief engr. Solvay div. Allied Chem., Syracuse, N.Y., 1941-59, asst. dir. operations, 1959-61, v.p. engr. and constrn. nat. aniline div., 1961-63, v.p. mfg., 1963-66; asst. to exec. v.p. Allied Chem. Corp., 1966-67, v.p. tech. plastics div., 1967, exec. v.p., 1967-68, pres. plastics div., 1968-74, group v.p., Morristown, N.J., 1974-75, sr. v.p., dir., mem. exec. com., 1975-77; pres. Allied-Gen. Nuclear Services, Barnwell, S.C., 1977-80, Impact Assocs. Inc.; pvt. practice cons., 1980—. Mem. Cornell Soc. Engrs., Tau Beta Phi. Home and Office: Box 130 Genesee PA 16923

BAXTER, REGINALD ROBERT, plant food company executive; b. Cushman, Ark., May 14, 1925; s. Remmel M. and Mary (Wilson) B.; 1 son, Sean Lee. B.S. in Chem. Engring., U. Ark., 1948; M.S., Iowa State U., 1949. Plant mgr. Amoniaco del Caribe, Colombia, S.A., 1961-63; project mgr. Esso Research and Engring Co., 1963-65; gen. mgr. First Nitrogen Corp., Donaldsville, La., 1965-67; with CF Industries, Inc. (and predecessor), Chgo., then Long Grove, Ill., 1967—, exec. v.p., 1969-71, pres., 1971—, also chief exec. officer; pres., dir. CF Chems., Inc., Bartow, Fla., also chief exec. officer, Central Phosphate Inc., Plant City, Fla., also chief exec. officer, CF Chems., Ltd., Ont., Can., CF Sales, Inc., Chgo.; chmn. Central Farmers Fertilizer Co., Chgo.; Bd. dirs. Nat. Council Farmer Coops.; mem. exec. council, bd. dirs. Fertilizer Inst., Washington. Bd. sponsors, past chmn. Good Shepherd Hosp., Barrington, Ill. Served with AUS, 1944-46. Mem. Am. Mgmt. Assn. Pesbyterian. Clubs: Masons, Union League (Chgo.). Home: 241 Island View Ln Lake Barrington Shores IL 60010 Office: Salem Lake Dr Long Grove IL 60047

BAXTER, ROBERT HAMPTON, III, insurance executive; b. Glassport, Pa., Mar. 27, 1931; s. Robert Hampton, Jr. and Charlotte (Biddlestone) B.; m. Barbara Miller, Aug. 4, 1956. Student, Carnegie Inst. Tech., 1949-50; A.B., U.S.C., 1954, J.D., 1958. Bar: S.C. bar 1959. Trust officer Citizens & So. Nat. Bank, Charleston, S.C., 1958-60, First Citizens Bank & Trust Co., Charlotte, N.C., 1960-68; with Participating Annuity Life Ins. Co., McLean, Va., 1968-70, Aetna Life & Casualty Co., Atlanta, 1971—. Served to lt. (j.g.) USNR, 1954-57; comdr. USNR; ret. Mem. Am. Bar Assn., Am. Soc. C.L.U., Am. Soc. Pension Actuaries, N.C. Bankers Assn. (pres. trust div. 1966-67), Navy League U.S. (pres. Charlotte 1966-67), Phi Delta Phi. Republican. Presbyn. Club: Willow Springs. Home: 7685 Ball Mill Rd Atlanta GA 30338 Office: 9 Piedmont Center Atlanta GA 30355

BAXTER, STEPHEN BARTOW, educator; b. Boston, Mar. 8, 1929; s. James Phinney 3d and Anne (Strang) B.; m. Ann Sweeney, Aug. 22, 1953; children—Clare, Persis, James Phinney 5th, Nicholas Holden, Stephen Padraic, Michael Philip. B.A., Harvard, 1950; Ph.D., Cambridge (Eng.) U., 1955. Instr. Dartmouth, 1954-57; vis. asst. prof. U. Mo., 1957-58; mem. faculty U. N.C., 1958—, prof. history, 1966—, Alumni Disting. prof., 1968-69, Kenan prof., 1975—; Clark Library prof. U. Calif., Los Angeles, 1977-78; Charles Henry Fiske III scholar Trinity Coll., Cambridge U., 1950-51. Author: The Development of the Treasury, 1660-1702, 1957, William III, 1966; also articles.; Editor: Basic Documents of English History, 1968, England's Rise to Greatness, 1660-1763, 1983. Guggenheim fellow, 1959-60, 73-74. Fellow Royal Hist. Soc.; mem. Am. Hist. Assn., Conf. Brit. Studies. Democrat. Home: 608 Morgan Creek Rd Chapel Hill NC 27514

BAXTER, WILLIAM FRANCIS, lawyer; b. N.Y.C., July 13, 1929; s. William F. and Ruth C. B.; children—William Francis, Marcia, Stuart Carlton. A.B., Stanford U., 1951, J.D., 1956. Bar: Calif. bar 1956, U.S. Supreme Ct 1960. Asst. prof. law Stanford U., 1956-58, prof., 1960—; asst. atty. gen. of U.S. for antitrust, Washington, 1981-83; asso. firm. Covington & Burling, Washington, 1958-60; vis. prof. Yale U. Law Sch., 1964-65; fellow Center for Advanced Study in Behavioral Scis., 1972-73; cons. in field; fellow Brookings Inst., 1968-72; mem. Pres.'s Task Force on Communications Policy, 1968, Pres.'s Task Force on Antitrust Policy, 1968. Author: People or Penguins, An Optimum Level of Pollution, 1974, (with others) Retail Banking in Electronic Age: The Law and Economics of Electronic Funds Transfer, 1977. Served with USN, 1951-54. Mem. Am. Econ. Assn. Home: 42 Mansion Ct Menlo Park CA 94025 Office: Stanford U Law Sch Stanford CA 94305

BAXTER, WILLIAM LESTER, advt. agy. exec.; b. Wheeler, Wis., Aug. 2, 1911; s. Andrew Carl and Augusta Crescent (Krause) B.;, Aug. 27, 1936; children—William Hunt, Barbara Rae Baxter Hill. B.S., Stout State U., Menomonie, Wis., 1934, M.A., 1941. Tchr. Ida Grove (Iowa) High Sch., 1934-36, Mitchell (S.D.) High Sch., 1936-39, Aberdeen (S.D.) High Sch., 1939-43; advt. mgr. K.O. Lee Co., Aberdeen, 1943-46; advt. account exec. Olmstead-Foley Advt. Agy., Mpls., 1947-49; pres. William L. Baxter Advt., Inc., Mpls., 1949—. Mem. Mpls. Advt. Club, Minn. Press Club. Republican. Clubs: Masons, Shriners. Home: 6709 West Shore Dr Edina MN 55435 Office: Suite 100 Foshay Tower Minneapolis MN 55402

BAXTER, WILLIAM MACNEIL, clergyman; b. Halifax, N.S., Can., Oct. 5, 1923; s. William John and Mary Ellen (MacNeil) B.; m. Jean Marlin Taylor, Oct. 25, 1946; children: Nancy Graeme, Gary MacNeil, Rebecca Roberts, Anne Marlin. B.A., Amherst Coll., 1946; M.Div., Va. Theol. Sem., 1951. Advt. salesman Reuben H. Donnelley, Inc., 1947-49; ordained to ministry Episcopal Ch., 1951; curate, asst. minister, St. Louis, 1951-54, rector, Washington, 1954-66; dir. career info. service, also dir. public affairs Peace Corps, 1966-68; pres. Baxter Assos. (cons. edn. and tng.), 1969-70; pres., exec. dir. Marriage and Family Inst. (counseling and ednl. center), Washington, 1971—; spl. cons. to State Dept. on refugee problems in Vietnam; vis. lectr. pastoral theology Va. Theol. Sem., 1960-66, Wesley Theol. Sem., 1979; Luccock lectr. Yale Div. Sch., 1965; mem. faculty field tng. colloquium Chgo. Div. Sch., 1960-64; lectr. Am. U. Law Sch., 1980-81; P.E. del. Nat. Conf. Radiation and Social Ethics, 1963; pres. Diocese of Washington Clergy, 1960-62; candidate for suffragen bishop, Washington, 1963. Contbr. articles to profl. jours. Mem. planning com. White House Conf. to Secure These Rights, 1964; bd. dirs. Capital Hill Community Council; Bd. dirs. Friendship Settlement House, Washington Area Council on Alcoholism, Neighborhood Service Com., Health and Welfare Council. Served with Merchant Marine, 1946. Mem. Am. Assn. for Marriage and Family Therapy (pres. Midatlantic div. 1975—), Chi Psi. Democrat. Club: Cosmos (Washington). Home: 2141 Wyoming Ave NW Washington DC 20008 Office: 1500 Massachusetts Ave NW Suite 732 Washington DC 20005

BAY, ALFRED PAUL, physician, hosp. supt.; b. Chgo., Feb. 2, 1910; s. Jens Christian and Dora (Detjen) B.; m. Gerda Constance Pearson, July 2, 1935; children—John, Dorothy. B.S., U. Ill., 1932, M.D., 1934. Intern Ill. Research and Ednl. Hosp., 1934-35; resident Chgo. State Hosp., 1935-36; practice medicine, specializing in psychiatry, Chgo., 1936-40, Alton, Ill., 1940-47, Manteno, Ill., 1947-54, Topeka, 1954—; physician Chgo. State Hosp., 1935-42; supt. Alton State Hosp., 1942-47, Manteno State Hosp., 1947-53, Topeka State Hosp., 1954-70, Jacksonville (Ill.) State Hosp., 1970-71; cons. NIMH, USPHS, VA Hosp., Topeka; cons. in psychiat. hosp. architecture. Author: (with others) Therapy by Design, 1965, Architecture for the Community Mental Health Center, 1967; Contbr.: articles to profl. jours. Architecture for the Community Mental Health Center. Mem. Mid-Continent Psychiat. Soc., Am. Psychiat. Assn., Golden Belt, Kan. psychiat. socs., Central Neuropsychiat. Assn., AAAS, Chgo. Inst. Medicine, Group Advancement Psychiatry. Address: Route 3 Box 286 Carthage MO 64836

BAY, EUGENE ALBERT, JR., advertising executive; b. June 15, 1933; s. Eugene Albert and Helene (Carlin) B.; m. Deidre Lesage, Apr. 20, 1963; children: Kristine C., Kathryn C., Eric M. B.A., U. Pa., 1956. Salesman, asst. advt. mgr. TV Guide mag. Triangle Publs., Inc., N.Y.C., 1956-72; advt. dir. Good Food mag., 1972-74; mktg. dir. Seventeen mag., 1974; advt. dir. Am. Home Pub. Co., N.Y.C., 1974—; nat. mktg. dir. Field & Stream mag. CBS Publs., N.Y.C., 1975-78, asso. pub., 1978-80, v.p., pub., 1980—; dir. Malba Assn. Commr. Statue of Liberty-Ellis Island Centennial Commn., 1984-86. Served with USMCR, 1957-60. Named TV Guide Salesman of Year, 1962, 68. Clubs: N.Y. Athletic (gov.), Winged Foot Golf.). Home: 8 Summit Pl Malba NY 11357 Office: 1515 Broadway New York NY 10036

BAY, HAROLD GEORGE, JR., advt. agy. exec.; b. Grosse Pointe, Mich., Oct. 18, 1937; s. Harold George and Lucille (Barker) B.;, Nov. 22, 1961; children—Laura, Whitney. B.A., U. Mich., 1960. Copy supr. Campbell Ewald Co., 1960-66; copywriter Young & Rubicam Inc., 1966-68; with D'Arcy-MacManus & Masius, Bloomfield Hills, Mich., 1968—, v.p., then sr. v.p., now pres., chmn. bd. Served with USAF. Mem. Am. Assn. Advt. Agencies (gov. Mich., scholarship chmn. 1980—), Detroit Advt. Assn., Adcraft Club. Clubs: Bloomfield Hills Country, Bloomfield Open Hunt; Renaissance, Recess (Detroit). Office: PO Box 811 Bloomfield Hills MI 48013 *

BAY, HOWARD, stage and film designer; b. Centralia, Wash., May 3, 1912; s. William D. and Bertha A. (Jenkins) B.; m. Ruth Jonas, Nov. 23, 1932; children: Ellen, Timothy. Student, U. Wash., 1928, U. Colo., 1929, Marshall Coll., 1929-30, Carnegie Inst. Tech., 1930-31, Westminster Coll., 1931-32, Chappell Sch. of Art, Denver, 1928-29; study in Europe, 1939. Vis. instr. Purdue U., 1962; instr. Circle-in-the-Square Theatre Sch., 1962-63, C.C.N.Y., 1979; guest designer, dir., instr. Ohio U., 1964; lectr. Cooper-Hewitt Mus., 1976; Andrew W. Mellon guest dir. Carnegie-Mellon U., 1963; dir. theatre, prof. theatre arts Brandeis U., 1965—; also Alan King prof., chmn. theatre arts dept.; vis. prof. Yale, 1966-67; mem. adv. bd. Internat. Theatre Inst. Designed: Food Pavillion, St. Louis Mid-Am. Jubilee, 1956; designer settings for 170 Broadway stage shows; also designer for TV shows; staged and designed: As the Girls Go, 1948; puppets and settings for Pete Roleum film, 1939; resident designer, Bucks County Playhouse, 1941; designer-dir., Universal-Internat. Pictures, 1946-48; designer: My Mother, My Father and Me, 1963; opera Natalia Petrovna, 1964, Man of La Mancha, Odyssey for Broadway, Poor Murderer, Utter Glory of Morrissey Hall, Oedipus Rex, Volpone, Fanny; art dir.: film Balanchine's Midsummer Night's Dream; ballet; television series Mr. Broadway, 1964, Pueblo Incident, 1973; Pal Joey, 1977; Author: U.S. Navy Handbook, Navy on Stage, 1944, Staging and Stage Design sect. Ency. Brit, 1973, Stage Design, 1973, Broadway sect. Contemporary Stage Design U.S.A, 1974. Guggenheim fellow, 1940-41; cited for year's best setting by Donaldson Awards for best designs for musicals, N.Y. stage, 1943-44, 44-45 seasons; Antoinete Perry award for best setting, 1960, 66; Maharam award for best settings, 1966. Mem. United Scenic Artists Am. (pres.), Nat. Soc. Interior Designers (nat. bd.). Club: Players. Home: 159 W 53rd St New York NY 10019

BAYARD, ALEXIS IRÉNÉE DUPONT, lawyer; b. Wilmington, Del., Feb. 11, 1918; s. Thomas F. and Elizabeth (duPont) B.; m. Jane Brady Hildreth, Apr. 24, 1944 (dec. July 10, 1960); children: Alexis Irenee duPont, Eugene H., Richard H., Jane Bayard Curley, John F., William B. B.A., Princeton U., 1940; LL.B., U. Va., 1947. Bar: Del. bar 1948. Since practiced in, Wilmington; sr. partner firm Bayard, Brill & Handelman, 1965—; dir. Girard Bank Del.; mem. Nat. Commn. on Uniform Laws, 1962-71. Chmn. Delaware River and Bay Authority, 1967-69; bd. dirs. Del. Project Hope, 1962—, Blood Bank of Del., 1955-70, Del. region NCCJ, 1964—; bd. overseers Del. Law Sch.; trustee Widener Univ.; state chmn. Nat. Found. March of Dimes, 1966—; lt. gov. State of Del., 1949-53; campaign chmn. Del. Democratic Com., 1954, chmn., 1967-69; chmn. Del. Citizens for Kennedy and Johnson, 1960, Del. Citizens for Johnson-Humphrey, 1964; mem. fin. com. Nat. Dem. Com., 1970—. Served from pvt. to 1st lt. USMCR, 1942-45. Decorated Purple Heart. Mem. Am., Del. bar assns., Am. Judicature Soc., Soc. Mayflower Descs., SAR, Del. Swedish Colonial Soc., Hist. Soc. Del., Marine Res. Officers Assn., Mil. Order World Wars, Am. Road Bldg. Assn., Am. Acad. Polit. and Social Sci. Episcopalian. Clubs: Wilmington, Wilmington Country, Greenville, Univ. Office: 901 Market St Wilmington DE 19801

BAYDA, EDWARD DMYTRO, judge; b. Alvena, Sask, Can., Sept. 9, 1931; s. Dmytro Andrew and Mary (Bilinski) B.; m. Marie-Therese Yvonne Gagne, May 28, 1953; children: Paula, Chrisopher, Margot, Marie-Theresa, Sheila, Kathryn. B.A., U. Sask., 1951, LL.B. cum laude, 1953. Bar: Sask. 1954. Barrister, solicitor, Regina, Sask., 1953-72; justice Ct. Queen's Bench for Sask., Regina, 1972-74, Ct. Appeal for Sask., 1974-81; chief justice Sask., Regina, 1981—. Office: Ct Appeal for Sask Court House 2425 Victoria Ave Regina SK Canada S4P 3V7

BAYER, HERBERT, painter, designer, architect; b. Haag, Austria, Apr. 5, 1900; came to U.S., 1938, naturalized, 1943; s. Maximillian and Rosa (Simmer) B. Studied design with architects Schmidthammer, Emanuel Margold, Darmstadt, Germany, 1920, Bauhaus, Weimar, 1921-23, Kandinsky, 1921, U. Graz, Austria, 1973, Phila. Coll. Art, Art Center Coll. Design, 1979. Tchr. graphic design and typography Bauhaus, Dessau, 1925-28; advt., typography, painting, photography, exhbn. planning, dir. Dorland Studio, Berlin, 1928-38; art dir. Gt. Ideas of Western Man; cons. Aspen Inst. Humanistic Studies, 1949—; chmn. dept. design Container Corp. Am., 1956-65; cons. cons. on architecture, art and design Atlantic Richfield Co., 1965—. As painter represented in museums throughout, U.S., Europe, one-man exhbns. in, N.Y.C., Berlin, Paris, London, San Francisco, and other maj. cities; retrospective exhibit 33 years of Herbert Bayer's work in, Nürnberg, Munich, Zûrich, Amsterdam, Brussels, Berlin; designed: Earth Sculpture, Marble Garden, 1955, Anderson Park, Aspen, Colo., 1973, Double Ascension; fountain sculpture, Los Angeles, 1972, tile mural and park, Phila. Coll. Art, 1976; articulated wall" hwy. constrn. for, 1968 Olympics, Mexico City; archtl. works include bldgs. of Aspen (Colo.) Inst. for Humanistic Studies; indsl. bldgs. for Container Corp. Am; interiors for Atlantic Richfield Co. in, N.Y.C., Los Angeles, Chgo., Denver, Dallas, Newtown Square, Pa.; designed many posters, exhbn. installations including, Bauhaus Exhbn., 1938, Mus. Modern Art Airways to Peace, 1943, traveling shows for coordinator, Inter-Am. Affairs, 1942, traveling exhbn., 50 yrs. Bauhaus, Exhbn., Stuttgart, London, Amsterdam, Paris, Chgo., Toronto, Pasadena, Tokyo, 1968-71; Editor, designer: World Geo-Graphic Atlas, 1953, Herbert Bayer Book of Drawings, 1961; portfolio Bayer, 1965; suite of lithographs, 8 monochromes, 1965, portfolio of 6 silk screens, 1968; pub. portfolios: 10 fotomontages, 10 fotoplastiken, 1936; books of his work The Way Beyond Art, The Work of Herbert Bayer, 1947, Herbert Bayer-Visual Communication, Architecture, Painting, 1967, Herbert Bayer un Concepto Total, 1975. Decorated Austrian Honor Cross; recipient awards including Ambassador's award for excellence, London, 1968; Kulturpreis, Cologne, Ger., 1969; Gold medal for excellence Am. Inst. Graphic Arts, 1970; Adalbert Stifter Preis, Austria, 1971. Hon. fellow Royal Acad. Fine Arts (Netherlands); mem. Art Dirs. Club (Hall of Fame). Has done fundamental work in environ. design and modern typography and new alphabets. Address: 184 Middle Rd Montecito CA 93108

BAYH, BIRCH EVANS, JR., lawyer, former U.S. senator; b. Terre Haute, Ind., Jan. 22, 1928; s. Birch Evans and Leah (Hollingsworth) B.; m. Marvella Hern, Aug. 24, 1952 (dec. Apr. 1979); 1 son, Birch E., III; m. Katherine Halpin, 1981; 1 son, John Christopher. B.S., Purdue U., 1951; J.D., Ind. U., 1960. Bar: Ind. 1961. Engaged in farming, Vigo County, 1952-57; mem. Ind. Ho. of Reps. from Vigo County, 1954-62, minority leader, 1957-58, 61-62, speaker, 1959-60; U.S. senator from, Ind., 1962-81; chmn. intelligence com., mem. appropriations, jud. coms.; sr. partner firm Bayh, Tabbert & Capehart, Indpls. and Washington, 1981—. Chmn. Nat. Commn. on Insanity Def. Hearings, Amtrak Labor-Mgmt. Productivity Council. Named Outstanding Young Man in Ind. Ind. Jr. C. of C., 1959; one of 10 outstanding Reps. in Ind. Gen. Assembly Ind. Newspaper Men and Women Vets., 1961. Democrat. Office: 1 Indiana Sq Suite 1500 Indianapolis IN 46204 also 1575 I St NW Suite 1025 Washington DC 20005

BAYLEN, JOSEPH OSCAR, emeritus history educator; b. Chgo., Feb. 12, 1920; s. Leo and Mary (Lakin) B.; m. Margaret Pringle, June 16, 1979; 1 son, James Leo. A.A., Wright Jr. Coll., 1939; B.E., No. Ill. U., 1941; M.A., Emory U., 1947; Ph.D., U. N.Mex., 1949. Instr. history U. N.Mex., 1948-49; asst. prof. history N.Mex. Highlands U., Las Vegas, 1950-52, asso. prof., 1952-54; prof. history, chmn. div. social sci. Delta State Tchrs. Coll., 1954-57; prof. history Miss. State U., 1957-61, U. Miss., 1961-66, chmn., 1963-66; chmn. dept. history Ga. State U., 1966-78, Regents' prof., 1969-82, emeritus Regents' prof. history, 1983—; vis. asst. prof. U. Md. Overseas Program, Europe, 1952-53; vis. assoc. prof. Agnes Scott Coll., 1953; vis. prof. summers Emory U., 1952, U. Ala., 1960, Georgetown U., 1964, 1965, Tulane U., 1966, 68, U. York, 1979; mem. Miss. Hist. Commn., 1954-57, 63-66; vice chmn. So. Humanities Conf., 1964-65, chmn., 1965-66; mem. Nat. Fulbright Adv. Screening Com., 1962-64, chmn., 1964-65; cons. Nat. Endowment for Humanities, 1969—; mem. Fed. Govt. Regional Archives Com., 1971-74; chmn. adv. com. on history Univ. System of Ga., 1970-72, 76-78; Trustee Victorian Periodicals Research Soc. Author: monographs Mme. Juliette Adam, Gambetta, and the Idea of a Franco-Russian Alliance, 1960, Lord Kitchener and the Viceroyalty of India, 1910, 1965, Soldier-Surgeon; The Crimean War Letters of Dr. D.A. Reid, 1855-1856, 1968, W.T. Stead and the Russian Revolution of 1905, 1969, (with O.S. Pidhainy) East-European and Russian Studies in the American South, 1972; co-editor: (with N.J. Gossman) Biographical Dictionary of Modern British Radicals, 1979—; bd. editors: So. Humanities Rev., Miss. Quar; contbr. articles to profl. jours. Served from pvt. to capt. AUS, 1941-45. Guggenheim fellow, 1958-59; Fulbright-Hays lectr., U.K., 1961-62, 72-73; research fellow Inst. Advanced Studies, Princeton U., 1966; summer fellowships and awards include So. Fellowship Found., 1955, Am. Philos. Soc., 1956, 65, Am. Council Learned Socs., 1961-62; English-Speaking Union, 1978; recipient Most Disting. Alumni award No. Ill. U., 1976, Disting. Prof. award Ga. State U., 1979, Ga. State U. chpt. Omicron Delta Kappa, 1980, Hugh McCall award for disting. achievement in hist. studies, 1982. Fellow Royal Hist. Soc., Royal Commonwealth Soc.; mem. Am. Hist. Assn. (exec. council 1972-75), So. Hist. Assn. (chmn. European history sect. 1972-73, exec. council 1983—), So. Conf. Brit. Studies (chmn. 1977-79), So. Humanities Conf., Popular Culture Assn., AAUP, Phi Kappa Phi, Omicron Delta Kappa, Phi Alpha Theta, Pi Gamma Mu, Kappa Delta Pi, Phi Kappa Tau. Home: 38 Dean Court Rd Rottingdean Brighton East Sussex BNZ 7DJ England

BAYLES, SAMUEL HEAGAN, advertising agency executive; b. Port Jefferson, L.I., N.Y., Nov. 10, 1910; s. Edward Post and Mary Jane (Lerch) B.; m. Gladys Grinnell, Sept. 25, 1933 (dec. Dec. 1980); children: Elizabeth Jane (Mrs. Frederick Joseph Wheeler), Samuel Heagan, Christina Mary (Mrs. William Francis Callahan, III); m. Jane Curry, Feb. 11, 1984. Student, Stony Brook Prep. Sch., 1928; B.A., Dartmouth, 1933. With Ruthrauff & Ryan, Inc., 1933-46, v.p., dir., co-dir. radio and television, 1940-46; a prin., chief exec. officer, chmn. bd. SSC & B, Inc. (formerly Sullivan, Stauffer, Colwell & Bayles, Inc.), N.Y.C., 1946—; mem. policy, ops. coms. SSC & B Lintas Internat., Ltd.; Bd. overseers Hanover Inn, Dartmouth Coll.; chmn. bd. dirs. Advt. Research Found. Author and pub.: Modern Man's Quest for Identity, The Golden Book on Writing, The Power of Intersensory Selling; writer: (forward) Slogans. Mem. Phi Beta Kappa, Psi Upsilon. Clubs: Cloud, Dartmouth (N.Y.C.); North Hempstead Country (Port Washington, N.Y.); North Fork Country (Cutchogue, L.I., N.Y.). Home: Sands Light Sands Point NY 11050 Nassau Point NY 11935 *Here are the five qualities I have found essential to success and happiness: Imagination to enjoy the wonders of life; integrity to report the true or actual facts as seen; courage to face life and be ready to start all over again; compatibility to team up with your fellow man; vision to see things before they are self-evident.*

BAYLESS, CHARLES EDWARD, lawyer, utility executive; b. Dunbar, W.Va., Nov. 2, 1942; s. Charles Henry and Helen Estella (Crouser) B.; m. Alfreda Joan Schulter, June 1, 1968; children: Charles, Lisa. B.S.E.E., W.Va., (Inst. Tech.), 1968; M.S.E.E., W.Va. U., 1972, J.D., 1972; M.B.A., U. Mich., 1977. Bar: W.Va. Mich. Atty. Consumers Power Co., Jackson, Mich., 1972-76; dir. nuclear fuel supply Consumer Power Co., Jackson, Mich., 1976-78; dir. spl. corp. projects Consumers Power Co., Jackson, Mich., 1978-81; fin. v.p. Pub. Service N.H., Manchester, 1981—; mem. fin. com. Edison Electric Inst. Exec. bd. Daniel Webster council, Boy Scouts Am., Manchester; mem. Philmont Ranch com. nat. council Boy Scouts Am. Served with U.S. Army, 1968-72. Mem. ABA (utility fin. com.), Mich. Bar Assn., W.Va. Bar Assn. Home: 47 Hearthside Circle Bedford NH 03102 Office: Public Service of New Hampshire 1000 Elm St Manchester NH 03101

BAYLESS, THEODORE M(ORRIS), medical educator, researcher, physician; b. Atlantic City, Apr. 14, 1931; s. David R. and Fan (Halpern) B.; m. Janet M. Nides, June 22, 1954; children: Jeffrey, Andrew, Neal. Student, U. Pa., 1949-51; B.S., Bucknell U., 1963; M.D., Chgo. Med. Sch., 1957. Intern Cornell div. Bellevue Hosp., also Meml. Cancer Ctr., N.Y.C., 1957-58, 58-60; instr. medicine Johns Hopkins U., Balt., 1964-66, asst. prof., 1966-69, assoc. prof., 1969-81, prof., 1981—, physician Johns Hopkins Hosp., 1964-83; cons. VA Med. Ctr., Perryville, Md., 1967-83. Editor: Current Therapy-Gastroenterology, 1984; co-editor: Lactose Digestion, 1980; sect. editor: Gastroenterology, 1968-76; editorial bd.: Am. Jour. Clin. Nutrition, 1977-83. Served to capt. USAR, 1962-64. Fellow ACP; mem. Am. Soc. Clin. Investigation, Am. Gastroenterology Assn., Alpha Omega Alpha. Jewish. Home: 2206 South Rd Baltimore MD 21209 Office: Johns Hopkins Hosp 600 N Wolfe St Baltimore MD 21205

BAYLESS, VIRGINIA L., retail stores company executive. With A.J. Bayless Markets Inc., Phoenix, 1965—, chmn. bd., 1967—, dir. Office: A.J. Bayless Markets Inc. 111 E Buckeye Rd Phoenix AZ 85036

BAYLEY, CHARLES CALVERT, historian; b. Congleton, Cheshire, Eng., Mar. 5, 1907; s. Harry and Hannah (Calvert) B.; m. Ethel Woolliscroft, Sept. 11, 1936; children—Ann Margaret, Susan Nancy. B.A., U. Manchester, Eng., 1928, M.A., 1929; postgrad., U. Marburg, W. Ger., 1930; Ph.D. (Univ. fellow), U. Chgo., 1937. Lectr. in history U. Toronto, Ont., Can., 1931-32; asst. prof. history Colo. Coll., 1932; lectr. McGill U., Montreal, Que., Can., 1938, asst. prof., 1938-50, asso. prof., 1950-59, prof., 1959-61, Kingsford prof., 1961—. Author: books, most recent being War and Society in Renaissance Florence, 1962, Mercenaries for the Crimea, 1977. Recipient Prix David Province Que.; Guggenheim fellow; Can. Govt. overseas fellow; Can. Council sr. fellow; Killam fellow. Fellow Royal Soc. Can.; mem. Am. Hist. Assn., Renaissance Soc. Am. Home: 3610 McTavish St Montreal PQ H3A 1Y2 Canada Office: Dept History Leacock Bldg McGill U Montreal PQ H3A 1Y2 Canada

BAYLIS, ARTHUR EUGENE, management consultant; b. Colorado Springs, Colo., Apr. 9, 1910; s. Richard Arthur and Viola (Hardin) B.; m. Dorcas Billings, July 11, 1936 (dec. Mar. 1952); 1 dau., Bonnie Alayne Baylis Stevens; m. E. Elizabeth Colwell, May 27, 1955. A.B., Colo. Coll., 1932; M.A., Tufts Coll., 1934. Instr. transp. and econs. Tufts Coll., 1932-34; staff asst. Fed. Coordinator Transp., Washington, 1934-35; asst. to v.p. in charge traffic N.Y.C. R.R., chief clk. office of v.p. in charge traffic, asst. v.p., 1935-42, fgn. freight traffic mgr., 1944-46, asst. gen. freight traffic mgr., 1946-50, gen. freight traffic mgr., 1950-51, asst. v.p. in charge freight traffic, 1952, v.p. in charge freight traffic, 1953-60, v.p. mktg., 1960-65, v.p. staff, 1965-66; pres. Arthur E. Baylis & Co., Inc. (cons.), Scarsdale, N.Y., 1966—; exec. dir. Nat. Com. on Internat. Trade Documentation, 1967-82; asst. dir. ry. transp. div. Office Def. Transp., Washington, 1942-44. Mem. Phi Beta Kappa, Kappa Sigma. Presbyterian. Clubs: N.Y. Traffic; Golf, Town (Scarsdale, N.Y.). Home: 18 Cohawney Rd Scarsdale NY 10583

BAYLIS, ROBERT MONTAGUE, investment banker; b. N.Y.C., Aug. 20, 1938; s. Chester, Jr. and Dorothy Montague (Smith) B.; m. Lois Margaret Wells, Apr. 6, 1963; children: Robert Wells, David Martin, John Chester. A.B., Princeton U., 1960; M.B.A., Harvard U., 1962. Chartered financial analyst. Mng. dir. First Boston Corp., N.Y.C., 1963—; dir. Travellers Asset Mgmt. Corp. Trustee Tchrs. Coll. of Columbia U. Served with M.C. U.S. Army, 1962-63. Mem. Securities Industry Assn., N.Y. Soc. Security Analysts, Nat. Assn. Bus. Economists, New York Stock Exchange. Clubs: Weeburn Country; Wall Street, University (N.Y.C.); Nassau, Cap and Gown. Home: 32 Sunswyck Rd Darien CT 06820 Office: First Boston Corp Park Ave Plaza New York NY 10005

BAYLISS, GEORGE VINCENT, university dean, art educator; b. Washington, Oct. 14, 1931; s. George V. and Rita C. (Meenehan) B.; m. Shirley Lou Case, Feb. 23, 1957; children: Darby Anne, Sean Michael. Student, U. Va., 1952-53; B.A., U. Md., 1955; M.F.A., Cranbrook Acad. Art, 1956. Tchr. Akron (Ohio) Art Inst., 1957-59, Flint (Mich.) Jr. Coll., 1959-62, State U. Coll. at Potsdam, N.Y., 1962-63; tchr., dean Parsons Sch. Design, N.Y.C., 1963-67; chmn. dept. art State U. Coll., Fredonia, N.Y., 1967-72, U. Mich., Ann Arbor, 1972-74, prof., dean Sch. Art, 1974-84; dean Sch. of Art (Temple U.), Phil., PA, 1984—. Exhibited in numerous one man and group shows, throughout U.S., 1949—; designer, mural artist, Smithsonian Instn., Washington, 1956-57. Served with USN, 1951-52. Grantee for creative work in painting Research Found., State U. N.Y., 1971, Rackham Research Found., U. Mich., 1972-73. Mem. Coll. Art Assn., Nat. Assn. Schs. of Art (pres.). Home: 424 Hilldale Dr Ann Arbor MI 48105 Office: Temple University School of Art Philadelphia PA 19122

BAYLOR, DONALD EDWARD, baseball player; b. Austin, Tex., June 28, 1949; s. George Edward and Lillian Joyce B.; m. Aronetta Jo Cash, June 3, 1970; 1 son, Don Edward. Student, Miami-Dade Jr. Coll., Miami, Fla., Blinn Jr. Coll., Brenham, Tex. With Balt. Orioles, 1970-76, Oakland A's, 1976, California Angels, 1976-82; with N.Y. Yankees, 1982—. Chmn. Orange County (Calif.) Cystic Fibrosis group; bd. dirs. Austin (Tex.) Reportory. Named American League's Most Valuable Player, 1979, Sporting News Player of Yr., 1979; mem. All-Star Game. Office: Care NY Yankees Yankee Stadium Bronx NY 10451

BAYLOR, HUGH MURRAY, musician; b. What Cheer, Iowa, Apr. 8, 1913; s. John Thomas and Elizabeth (Murray) B.; m. Elisabeth A. Barbou, Sept. 1, 1937; children: Denis A., Michael G., Stephen M. B.A., U. Iowa, 1934, M.A., 1936, Ph.D., 1950; diplôme d'exécution, Conservatoire Americain, Fontainebleau, France, 1938. Asst. U. Iowa, 1934-37; prof. music, chmn. dept. William Penn Coll., Oskaloosa, Iowa, 1937-42; prof. music Knox Coll., Galesburg, Ill., 1942—, Distinguished Service prof., 1959-80, prof. emeritus, 1980—, chmn. music dept., 1969-76. Composer chamber music, songs and comic opera; editor piano music; contbr. articles to profl. jours. Mem. Phi Beta Kappa, Pi Kappa Lambda. Home: 1187 N Cherry St Galesburg IL 61401

BAYM, GORDON ALAN, physicist, educator; b. N.Y.C., July 1, 1935; s. Louis and Lillian B.; m. Lillian Hartmann; children—Nancy, Geoffrey, Michael. A.B., Cornell U., 1956; A.M., Harvard U., 1957, Ph.D., 1960. Fellow Universitetets Institut for Teoretisk Fysik, Copenhagen, Denmark, 1960-62; lectr. U. Calif.-, Berkeley, 1962-63; prof. physics U. Ill., Urbana, 1963—; vis. prof. U. Tokyo and U. Kyoto, 1968, Nordita, Copenhagen, 1970, 76, Niels Bohr Inst., 1976, U. Nagoya, 1979; vis. scientist Academia Sinica, China, 1979; mem. adv. bd. Inst. Theoretical Physics, Santa Barbara, Calif., 1978-83; mem. subcom. theoretical physics, physics adv. com. NSF, 1980-81, mem. phys. adv. com., 1982—; Mem. nuclear sci. adv. com. Dept. of Energy/NSF, 1982—. Author: Lectures on Quantum Mechanics, 1969, Neutron Stars, 1970, Neutron Stars and the Properties of Matter at High Density, 1977, (with L.P. Kadanoff) Quantum Statistical Mechanics, 1962; assoc. editor: Nuclear Physics. Recipient Alexander von Humboldt Found. sr. U.S. Scientist award, 1983; Fellow Am. Acad. Arts and Scis.; Alfred P. Sloan Found. Research fellow, 1965-68; NSF postdoctoral fellow, 1960-62. Fellow Am. Phys. Soc.; mem. Am. Astron. Soc., Internat. Astron. Union., Nat. Acad. Scis. Office: Loomis Lab Physics U Ill 1110 W Green St Urbana IL 61801

BAYNE, DAVID COWAN, priest, lawyer, educator; b. Detroit, Jan. 11, 1918; s. David Cowan and Myrtle (Murray) B. A.B., U. Detroit, 1939; LL.B., Georgetown U., 1947, LL.M., 1948; M.A., Loyola U., Chgo., 1946, S.T.L., 1953; Scientiae Juris Dr. (grad. fellow), Yale, 1949; LL.D. (hon.), Creighton U., 1980. Bar: Fed. and D.C. bars 1948, Mich. bar 1960, Mo. bar 1963, Iowa bar 1973. Joined Soc. of Jesus, 1941; ordained priest Roman Catholic Ch., 1952; asst. prof. law U. Detroit, 1954-60, acting dean, 1955-59, dean, 1959-60; research asso. Nat. Jesuit Research Orgn., Inst. Social Order, St. Louis, 1960-63; vis. lectr. St. Louis U. Law Sch., 1960-63, prof. law, 1963-67; vis. prof. Mich. Law Sch., 1967, Inst. fur Auslandisches und Internationales Wirtschaftrecht, Frankfurt, 1967; prof. Coll. Law, U. Iowa, Iowa City, 1967—; vis. prof. U. Koln, Germany, 1970, 74. Author: Conscience, Obligation and the Law, 1966; Contbr. articles to profl. jours.; editor legal materials. Mem. Bar State Mich., Iowa, Mo., Am., Fed., D.C. bar assns., Delta Theta Phi, Alpha Sigma Nu. Research corp. law. Office: Coll of Law U Iowa Iowa City IA 52242

BAYNES, ANDREA LORRAINE, television executive; b. Los Angeles, Sept. 27, 1946; d. William Andrew and Lorraine (Harris) Caldwell; m. William Thomas Baynes, May 26, 1973; 1 son, Kevin Thomas. B.A., U. So. Calif., 1968. Dir. program devel. NBC, Burbank, Calif., 1972-76; sr. v.p. Columbia Pictures TV, Burbank, 1976-80; exec. v.p. 20th Century-Fox TV, Los Angeles, 1980—; bd. dirs. Internat. Design Conf. in Aspen, Colo., 1978—. Mem. Hollywood Radio and TV Soc. (dir. 1982—), Nat. Acad. TV Arts and Scis. Office: 20th Century-Fox PO Box Beverly Hills CA 90213 *

BAYNES, HAROLD LOSEY, banker; b. Elmira, N.Y., May 24, 1935; s. Harold Edgar and Helen Brown (Losey) B.; m. Patricia Ann Dent, June 26, 1956 (div. 1973); children—Jennifer Shannon, James Patrick, Megan Elizabeth; m. Sarah Cornelia Warren, Apr. 7, 1973. B.A. in English with distinction, U. Va., 1956; grad., Sch. Bank Mgmt., 1965, Grad. Sch. Bank Adminstrn., 1972. With United Va. Bank, Richmond, 1959—, v.p., cashier, head ops. div., 1968-73; sr. v.p., dep. head services group United Va. Bankshares Inc., 1973-74, sr. v.p., 1976-78, exec. v.p., ops. group exec., mem. policy group, 1978—; faculty Memphis Sch. Banking, 1972-73, Sch. for Bank Adminstrn., 1974-78. Vice pres., treas., bd. dirs. Richmond Area Arthritis Found., 1966-68; co-chmn., treas. Richmond com. Nat. Council Crime and Delinquency, 1967—; pres. Northside FISH, 1969-72; bd. dirs., treas., team capt. Youth Emergency Service, Lewis Ginter Community Bldg., 1970-72; vice chmn. Vol. Service Bur., 1969-74; chmn. Capital dist. Va. Council Social Welfare, 1974-75; dir. Offender Aid and Restoration, 1974-77; chmn. adv. com. Va. Div. of Volunteerism, 1976-79; chmn. Richmond Friendship Force Flight, 1978; chmn. adv. council Va. Voice for Print Handicapped, 1980—; bd. dirs. Old Dominion Eye Bank Found., 1981—. Served with USN, 1956-59. Mem. Soc. Advancement Mgmt., Bank Adminstrn. Inst. (ops. com. 1969-72), Am. Bankers Assn. (exec. com. automation-ops. div. 1972-77, chmn. 1975-76), Am. Inst. Banking, Nat. Automated Clearing House Assn. (pres. 1976-77), Va. Automated Clearing House Assn., Mensa, Richmond 1st Club, Raven Soc., Omicron Delta Kappa, Phi Gamma Delta. Republican. Methodist. Office: PO Box 26665 Richmond VA 23261 *I believe that I am captain of my own destiny and that which happens to me, both good and bad, is primarily my responsibility. Further, I attempt to treat others as I would have them treat me. I believe that the best prescription for success in both personal and business living is contained in a prayer written by Reinhold Neibuhr: "Oh, God, grant me the serenity to accept the things I cannot change; the courage to change the things I can and the wisdom to know the difference."*

BAYNES, THOMAS EDWARD, JR., lawyer, educator; b. N.Y.C., Mar. 19, 1940; s. Thomas Edward and Ann Jane (Burke) B.; m. Maija Eva Kokko, Dec. 30, 1963; children: Cynthia Lynn, Barbara Ann. B.B.A., U. Ga., 1962; J.D., Emory U., 1967, LL.M., 1972; LL.M., Yale U., 1973. Bar: Ga. 1968, U.S. Supreme Ct. 1971, Ct. of Mil. Appeals 1978, Fla. 1981. Dir. Legal Assistance to Inmates Program, Emory U., 1968-69; asst. dean, asst. prof. bus. law Ga. State U., 1969-72; acting regional dir. Nat. Center for State Cts., Atlanta, 1973-74; prof. law and public adminstrn. Nova U. Law Center, Ft. Lauderdale, Fla., 1974-76, 77-81; mem. firm Peterson, Myers, Craig, Crews, Brandon & Mann, Lake Wales, Fla.; jud. fellow U.S. Supreme Ct., 1976-77; speedy trial reporter U.S. Dist. Ct., So. Dist. Fla., 1977-81; State chmn., Ga., Nat. Council on Crime and Delinquency, 1971-72; legal counsel Reorgn. Study Commn. Ga., 1971-72. Author: (with W. Scott) Legal Aspects of Laboratory Medicine in Quality Assurance in Laboratory Management, 1978; Supplement editor: Fla. Real Estate Law and Procedure, 1976, Eminent Domain in Florida, 1979, Mortgage Law in Florida, 1982. Commr. Lake Wales Mus. Served with USN, 1962-66; to comdr. Judge Adv. Gen. Corps, Res. (ret.), 1960-80. Sterling fellow Yale U. Law Sch., 1972-73; Harry J. Loman Found. research fellow, 1979. Mem. Am. Law Inst., Am. Soc. Legal History, Supreme Ct. Hist. Soc., Ga. Bar Assn., Scribes, Omicron Delta Kappa. Democrat. Office: PO Box 1079 Lake Wales FL 33853

BAYS, KARL DEAN, hosp. supply co. exec.; b. Loyall, Ky., Dec. 23, 1933; s. James K. and Myrtle (Criscillis) B.; m. Billie Joan White, June 4, 1955; children: Robert D., Karla. B.S., Eastern Ky. U., 1955, LL.D. (hon.), 1977; M.B.A., Ind. U., 1958; D.C.S. (hon.), Union Coll., Ky., 1971. With Am. Hosp. Supply Corp., 1958—, pres., dir., 1970, chief exec. officer, 1971—, chmn. bd., 1974—; dir. Internat. Harvester Co., Standard Oil Co., Ind., Delta Air Lines, Inc., No. Trust Corp., The No. Trust Co., Jewel Cos., Inc. Trustee Duke, Northwestern U.; life mem. bd. dirs. Lake Forest Hosp.; bd. visitors Duke Med. Center. Served with USMCR, 1955-57. Recipient Trojan M.B.A. Achievement award U. So. Calif., 1972; Horatio Alger award, 1979; Disting. Alumni Service award Ind. U., 1977; named Outstanding Alumnus Eastern Ky. U., 1973; Mktg. Man of Year Sales & Mktg. Execs. Assn. Chgo., 1977; Outstanding Chief Exec. Officer in drug products and hosp. supply industry Financial World, 1975, 81; Outstanding Chief Exec. Officer in drug products and health care industry Wall St. Transcript, 1980. Mem. Pharm. Mfrs. Assn. Clubs: Execs., Econ., Comml., Mid-Am., Chicago (Chgo.); Glen View, Old Elm, Onwentsia. Office: One Am Plaza Evanston IL 60201

BAYS, ROBERT EARL, univ. adminstr., music educator; b. Bonne Terre, Mo., Apr. 8, 1921; s. J.W. and Bertie (Cole) B.; m. Cleis Armour, May 25, 1946; children: Deborah Lynn, Rebecca Ann. B.S., Emporia (Kans.) State U., 1946; M.A., Columbia U., 1949; Ph.D., George Peabody Coll., Nashville, 1953. Prof. Sch. Music, George Peabody Coll., 1953-65; dir. Sch. Music, 1965-69; chmn. dept. music U. Tex., Austin, 1969-74; dir. Sch. Music, U. Ill., Urbana-Champaign, 1974—; cons. in field; mem. academic music adv. panel Office Cultural Presentations, Internat. Communications Agy., 1974-79; mem. grad. commn. Nat. Assn. Schs. Music, 1970-76, v.p., 1976-79, pres., 1979-82; chmn. publs. planning com. Music Educators Nat. Conf., 1970-76. Served with USNR, 1942-45. Mem. Coll. Music Soc. (v.p. 1975-77), Phi Mu Alpha Sinfonia, Pi Kappa Lambda. Home: 56 Lake Park Champaign IL 61820 Office: Sch Music U Ill Urbana IL 61801

BAYSE, DAVID DUKE, chemist; b. Detroit, Apr. 21, 1938; s. Luther Duke and Pearl (Smithwick) B.; m. Gladys Sisco, Aug. 12, 1968. B.S., U. Tenn., 1960, M.S., 1962, Ph.D., 1966. Asso. dir. Clin. Chemistry

Lab., U. Tenn., Memphis, 1966-71; chief Clin. Chemistry Proficiency Lab., Centers for Disease Control, Atlanta, 1971-72, chief analytical biochemistry br., 1972-74, dir., 1974—; bd. dirs. Nat. Registry in Clin. Chemistry; gen. chmn. Conf. on Nat. Understanding for Devel. Reference Materials and Methods for Clin. Chemistry; chmn. Conf. on Nat. Model for Standardization of Neonatal Hypothyroid Screening Programs, Atlanta, 1979, 2d Internat. Conf. on Biomed. Lab. Standardization, 1982. Mem. Am. Assn. Clin. Chemistry, Am. Chem. Soc., Internat. Fedn. Clin. Chemistry (sci. com., co-dir. Office of Reference Materials and Methods). Home: 668 Rollingwood Dr Stone Mountain GA 30087 Office: Centers for Disease Control Atlanta GA 30333

BAZANT, ZDENEK PAVEL, civil engineering educator, scientist, consultant; b. Prague, Czechoslovakia, Dec. 10, 1937; came to U.S., 1968, naturalized, 1976; s. Zdenek and Stepanka (Curikova) B.; m. Iva Marie Krasna, Sept. 27, 1967; children: Martin Zdenek, Eva Stephanie. Civil Engr., Tech. U., Prague, 1960; Ph.D. in Mechanics, Czechoslovak Acad. Sci., 1963; postgrad. diploma in theoretical physics, Charles U., Prague, 1966. Registered structural engr., Ill. Scientist, adj. prof. Bldg. Research Inst., Tech. U., Prague, 1963-67, docent habilitation, 1967; vis. research engr. Centre d'Étude et de Recherche du Bâtiment et des Travaux Publics, Paris, 1967, U. Toronto, 1967-68, U. Calif., Berkeley, 1969; assoc. prof. civil engring. Northwestern U., Evanston, Ill., 1969-73, prof., 1973—, coordinator structural engring. program, 1974-78; dir. (Center for Concrete and Geomaterials), 1981—; cons. Sargent & Lundy, Engrs., Chgo., 1973-77, Argonne Nat. Lab., 1974—, Oak Ridge Nat. Lab., 1975—, Babcock & Wilcox, 1978-80, Sandia Labs., Albuquerque, 1979-80, Portland Cement Assn., Skokie, 1980-82, Ont. Hydro, Toronto, 1980-82, U.S. Forest Products Lab, Madison, Wis., 1981-82, W.R. Grace & Co., 1982—; vis. prof. Royal Inst. Tech., Stockholm, 1977, Politecnicodi Milano, 1982, Swiss Fed. Inst. Tech., Lausanne, 1983; vis. scholar U. Calif., Berkeley, 1978, Calif. Inst. Tech., 1979, ETH, Zurich, Switzerland, 1979; mem. coms. Nat. Acad. Engring., 1977—. Author: Creep of Concrete in Structural Analysis, 1966, (with others) Analysis of Concrete Structures by Finite Element Method, 1978, Inelasticity and Failure of Concrete, 1979, Creep and Shrinkage in Concrete Structures, 1982; editorial bd.: Cement and Concrete Research Internat. Jour, 1970—, Jour. Engring.-Mech. Div. ASCE, 1973-77, Internat. Jour. Numerical and Analytical Methods in Geomechanics, 1979—, Solid Mechanics Archives, 1980—, Materials and Structures, 1981—; contbr. numerous articles to profl. jours. Served with Czechoslovak Army, 1961. Ford Found. fellow, 1967-68; NSF grantee, 1970—; ERDA grantee, 1975-77; AFOSR grantee, 1975-77; Los Alamos Sci. Lab. grantee, 1978-80; EPRI grantee, 1980—; Guggenheim fellow, 1978-79. Fellow Am. Acad. Mechanics (founder), ASCE (chmn. com. properties of materials 1976-78, Walter L. Huber research prize 1976, T.Y. Lin Prestressed Concrete award 1977), Am. Concrete Inst., Internat. Union Testing and Research Labs. in Materials and Structures, Paris, RILEM (gold medal 1975, IR100 award 1982); mem. AAAS, Internat. Assn. Structural Mechanics in Reactor Tech. (coordinator prestressed reactor vessels), ASME, ASTM, Prestressed Concrete Inst., Am. Ceramic Soc., Internat. Assn. Soil Mech. Found. Engring., Internat Assn. Bridge and Structural Engring. (Zurich, Switzerland), CEB (European Concrete Com.), U.S. Olympic Soc. Clubs: Centennial Tennis, Kenilworth Sailing. Patentee in field. Home: 514 Greenwood Ave Kenilworth IL 60043 Office: Dept Civil Engring Northwestern U Evanston IL 60201

BAZE, ROY ALLEN, petroleum management consultant, former oil company executive; b. Snyder, Tex., Nov. 9, 1921; s. Albert A. and Velma (Hester) B.; m. Geleska Jean Harless, Feb. 28, 1944; children: Robert Ernest, Ben Allan. B.S. in Petroleum Engring, U. Okla., 1943. Registered profl. engr., Tex. Engr. prodn. dept. Humble Oil & Refining Co. (now Exxon Co. U.S.A.), 1946-64, mgr. div. products supply and distbn. supply dept., 1964-66, gen. mgr. supply dept., 1966; exec. asst. to pres. Standard Oil Co. (N.J.) (now Exxon Corp), N.Y.C., 1967, coordinator producing activities, 1968-70, v.p. producing, 1970-72, v.p. logistics, 1972-73; sr. v.p. Exxon Co. U.S.A., Houston, 1973-80; now petroleum mgmt. cons.; former dir. Exxon Research and Engring. Co., Plantation Pipeline Co.; dir. Am. Well Servicing Co. Former bd. dirs. Jr. Achievement. Served to capt. U.S. Army, 1943-46. Decorated Purple Heart. Mem. AIME, Am. Petroleum Inst., Nat. Petroleum Refiners Assn. (former dir.), Nat. Assn. Mfrs. (former dir.), Mid-Continent Oil and Gas Assn. (former dir.), Tex. Mid-Continent Oil and Gas Assn. (former dir.), Taxpayers Assn. of Tex. (dir.). Home and Office: 2604 34th St Snyder TX 79549

BAZELL, ROBERT JOSEPH, science correspondent; b. Pitts., Aug. 21, 1945; s. Irving and Beatrice (Robb) B.; m. Ilene Tanz, Sept. 11, 1966 (div.); children: Rebecca, Joshua; m. Margot Weinshel, July 31, 1979. B.A., U. Calif.-Berkeley, 1967; student, U. Sussex, 1968-69; Candidate in Philosophy, U. Calif., 1971. Writer Sci. Mag., Washington, 1971-72; reporter N.Y. Post, N.Y.C., 1972-76; sic. corr. NBC News, N.Y.C., 1976—. Contbr. articles to mags. Mem. Phi Beta Kappa. Office: NBC News 30 Rockefeller Pl New York NY 10020

BAZELON, DAVID LIONEL, judge; b. Superior, Wis., Sept. 3, 1909; m. Miriam M. Kellner, June 7, 1936; children: James A., Richard Lee. B.S. in Law, Northwestern U., 1931, LL.D., 1974; LL.D. (hon.), Colby Coll., 1966, Boston U., 1969, Albert Einstein Coll. Medicine of Yeshiva U., 1972, U. So. Calif., 1977, Syracuse U., 1980, Georgetown U. Law Center, 1980, U. Santa Clara, 1982, Northeastern U. Sch. Law, 1982, John Jay Coll. Criminal Justice, 1982. Bar: practice in Ill 1932. Asst. atty. gen. U.S. Lands Div., 1946-49; judge U.S. Ct. of Appeals for D.C. Circuit, 1949—, chief judge, 1962-78, sr. circuit judge, 1979—; lectr. psychiatry Johns Hopkins U. Sch. Medicine, 1964—; mem. nat. adv. mental health council USPHS, 1967-71; mem. U.S. mission on mental health, USSR, 1967; mem. adv. com. child devel. NRC, 1971-78; adv. bd. div. legal, ethical and ednl. aspects of medicine Inst. Medicine, Nat. Acad. Scis., 1977-78; mem. sci. adv. bd. Salk Inst. Alcohol Research Center, 1979—; bd. dirs. Washington Sch. Psychiatry, Nat. Council Crime and Delinquency. Cons.: Children Today, 1973—. Trustee Salk Inst. for Biol. Studies. Recipient Isaac Ray award Am. Psychiat. Assn., 1960. Hon. fellow Am. Psychiat. Assn. (Distinguished Service award 1975), Am. Coll. Legal Medicine; fellow Am. Acad. Arts and Scis.; mem. Am., Fed., D.C. bar assns., Am. Orthopsychiat. Assn. (pres. 1969-70, dir.), UN Assn. (panel on human rights and U.S. fgn. policy 1978-79), Am. Correctional Assn. (commn. on accreditation for corrections 1980-82), Inst. of Medicine of Nat. Acad. Scis. Democrat. Jewish. Club: Cosmos. Home: 2700 Virginia Ave NW Washington DC 20037 Office: Court of Appeals Washington DC 20001

BAZEMORE, THOMAS CLIFFORD, professional services industry executive; b. Atlanta, Apr. 5, 1922; s. Thomas and Beula (Rodgers) B.; m. Pauline Crane, June 26, 1948; children—David Myrick, Sandra Jane, Karen Anne, James Sanford. Student, Atlanta Jr. Coll., 1938-40; B.S., Ga. Inst. Tech., 1944; postgrad., Harvard, Mass. Inst. Tech., 1944-45. Electronics engr. Naval Research Lab., Boston, 1946-49; group leader Naval Air Devel. Center, Johnsville, Pa., 1949-51, Lincoln Lab., Mass. Inst. Tech., Lexington, 1951-59; mem. tech staff Inst. for Def. Analyses, Washington, 1959-61; founder Flow Gen. Corp., Santa Barbara, Calif., 1961, dir., 1961—, pres., 1965-76, chmn., 1976-83. Served to lt. (j.g.) USNR, 1944-46. Mem. Tau Beta Pi, Phi Kappa Phi, Eta Kappa Nu. Club: Santa Barbara Yacht. Home: 2916 Arriba Way Santa Barbara CA 93105 Office: PO Box 6770 Santa Barbara CA 93160

BAZZAZ, FAKHRI A., plant biology educator, administrator; b. Baghdad, Iraq, June 16, 1933; came to U.S., 1965; s. Abdul-Lalif and Munifa B.; m. Marrib Bazzaz, Aug. 25, 1958; children: Sarar, Ammar. B.S., U. Baghdad, 1953; M.S., U. Ill., 1960, Ph.D., 1963. Prof. U. Ill., Urbana, 1977—, head dept. plant biology, acting dir. Sch. Life Scis., 1983-84; fellow Clare Hall, Cambridge U., Eng., 1981. Editor: Oecologia, 1983. Mem. Ecol. Soc. Am., Brit. Ecol. Soc. Office: Dept Biology U 111 505 S Goodwin Ave Urbana IL 61801

BEACH, CECIL PRENTICE, librarian; b. Knoxville, Tenn., July 12, 1927; s. Frank Alfred and Lillie Maude (Sims) B.; m. Doris Jean Pardue, Apr. 17, 1949; children: Steven Prentice, Rex Arthur, Keven Sanders, Kyle Alfred, Quentin Anthony; m. Marcia Gibson Buckley, June 20, 1969; children: Stephanie Lynn, Shannon Sue. A.B., U. Chattanooga, 1950; M.A., Fla. State U., 1952. Bookmobile librarian Chattanooga Pub. Library, 1948-51; extension librarian Decatur (Ga.)-DeKalb Regional Library, 1952-54; dir. Piedmont Regional Library, Winder, Ga., 1954-60, Gadsden (Ala.) Pub. Library, 1960-64, Tampa(Fla.)-Hillsborough Library System, 1965-72; state librarian State of Fla., Tallahassee, 1972-77; dir. div. libraries Broward County, Ft. Lauderdale, Fla., 1977—; instr. dept. library sci. U. South Fla.; chmn. Fla. Library Study Commn., 1970-72; bd. dirs. Southeastern Library Network; cons. library bldgs. and service. Pres., Gadsden Community Council, 1963; bd. govs. Nova U.; chmn. adv. council Seagull Sch. for Exceptional Children; mem. Fla. Endowment Humanities, 1972—, Ft. Lauderdale Downtown Council; bd. dirs. Easter Seal Soc., 1975—. Served with USNR, 1944-46. Mem. ALA, Southeastern Library Assn. (pres. 1972—), Ala. Library Assn., Ga. Library Assn., Fla. Library Assn. (pres. 1969), Adult Edn. Assn., Tampa C. of C., Greater Ft. Lauderdale C. of C., Fla. State U. Alumni Assn. (pres. 1967). Democrat. Presbyn. Clubs: Mason, Rotarian. Home: 11127 NW 26th Dr Coral Springs FL 33065 Office: PO Box 5463 Fort Lauderdale FL 33310

BEACH, JAMES ELDRIDGE, state govt. ofcl.; b. St. Petersburg, Fla., Aug. 5, 1925; s. William Thomas and Vera Belle B.; m. Ida Hurst, Sept. 15, 1972; children—Tom, Jarrod. B.S., U. Fla., Gainesburg, 1950. Mem. Fla. Hwy. Patrol, 1951—, dir., Tallahassee, 1972—. Served with USMCR, 1943-46; PTO. Decorated Purple Heart; named to U. Fla. Football Hall of Fame, 1978. Mem. Am. Legion, VFW, DAV. Club: Shriners. Office: Fla Hwy Patrol Kirkman Bldg Tallahassee FL 32301

BEACH, LEE ROY, psychologist, educator; b. Gallup, N.Mex., Feb. 29, 1936; s. Dearl and Lucile Ruth (Krumtum) B.; m. Barbara Ann Heinrich, Nov. 13, 1971. B.A., Ind. U., 1957; M.A., U. Colo., 1959, Ph.D., 1961. Aviation psychologist U.S. Sch. Aviation Medicine, Pensacola, Fla., 1961-63; human factors officer Office of Naval Research, Washington, 1963-64; postdoctoral research U. Mich., Ann Arbor, 1964-66; faculty dept. psychology U. Wash., Seattle, 1966—, prof. psychology, 1974—; cons. VA Med. Center, Seattle, 1979—. Contbr. articles to profl. jours.; author: Psychology: Core Concepts and Special Topics, 1973. Served with USN, 1961-64. Recipient Feldman Research award, 1981; NIMH fellow, 1964-66; NIH grantee, 1979—. Fellow Am. Psychol. Assn.; mem. AAAS. Home: 2129 2d Ave W Seattle WA 98119 Office: Dept Psychology NI25 Univ Wash Seattle WA 98195

BEACHAM, WOODARD DAVIS, physician; b. McComb, Miss., Apr. 10, 1911; s. Woodard D. and Ida (Felder) B. B.A., U. Miss., 1932, B.S., 1933; M.D., Tulane U., 1935. Diplomate: Am. Bd. Obstetrics and Gynecology. Intern Charity Hosp. of La., New Orleans, resident in ob-gyn, sr. resident in urology, 1939-40, later sr. vis. surgeon; past pres. surg. staff Charity Hosp., New Orleans, now cons.; prof. clin. gynecology and obstetrics Tulane U. Sch. Medicine, New Orleans, 1949-81, emeritus prof. ob-gyn, 1981—; assoc. staff Tulane Med. Center Hosp., 1976—; obstetrician and gynecologist So. Bapt. Hosp., pres. staff, 1961, chmn. condolence com., 1976; practice medicine specializing in obstetrics and gynecology, 1940—; cons. Beacham Meml. Hosp., Magnolia, Miss., Meth. Hosp., Hotel Dieu Sisters Hosp., New Orleans; chmn. internat. relations com. 10th World Congress of Ob-Gyn, 1982; pres. Beacham Corp.; Surgeon USPHS, 1943-48. Author: (with Robert J. Crossen and Dan. W. Beacham) Synopsis of Gynecology, (5th edit.), (with Dan. W. Beacham) 6-10th edits.) Synopsis of Gynecology,, 1963, 67, 72, 77, 82; Editor for gynecology and obstetrics: Stedman's Med. Dictionary, 23d edit, 1976; Contbr. articles to tech. jours. Chmn. bd. trustees Carrollton United Meth. Ch., 1980, chmn. pastor-parish relations com., 1980, chmn. adminstrv. bd., 1981; mem. planning com. Internat. House, 1983; mem. New Orleans Tourist and Conv. Commn., New Orleans Mus. of Art, Internat. Trade Mart. Recipient John Herr Musser award Tulane U. Sch. Medicine, 1933; Distinguished Service award So. Med. Assn., 1974; Distinguished Alumnus award U. Miss. Alumni Hall of Fame, 1976; Plaque of appreciation So. Bapt. Hosp. Dept. Ob-Gyn, 1979. Fellow ACS (gov. 1955-63, adv. council 1963-67, chmn. 1967, 2d. v.p. 1972-73, Med. Records prize 1943, pres. La. chpt., presiding officer symposium 1983), Am. Gynecol. Soc. (mem. council 1959-60), Am. Assn. Obstetricians and Gynecologists (v.p. 1970-71, mem. Found.), Am. Coll. Obstetricians and Gynecologists (1st pres. 1951-52, com. on liaison with Internat. Fedn. Gynaecology and Obstetrics 1973—, del. VIIIth World Congress Obstetrics and Gynaecology 1976, Distinguished Service award 1976, mem. task force on geriatric gynecology, Silver Badge Club, Silver Badge Club); mem. Am. Gynec-Ob Soc., So. Gynec-Ob Soc. (pres. 1967), AMA (chmn. sect. obstetrics and gynecology 1957-58), So. Med. Assn. (chmn. sect. on obstetrics 1949, mem. council 1961-63, 2d v.p. 1972, 1st v.p. 1973), Internat. House (founder mem., dir., exec. com. 1977—), C. of C., La., Orleans Parish med. socs., New Orleans Grad. Med. Assembly (past pres., adv. council 1965—, chmn. long range planning com. 1976-77), New Orleans Gynecol. and Obstet. Soc. (past pres.), Am. Cancer Soc., Royal Soc. Medicine, Ole Miss. Loyalty Found., Conrad G. Collins Obstetric and Gynecologic Soc. Tulane U. (1st pres.), Central Assn. Obstetricians and Gynecologists (asst. sec. 1950-52), Am. Assn. Med. Colls., Am. Fertility Soc. (charter asso. mem.), Tulane Med. Alumni Assn. (dir. 1970-71, sec. 1971-73, 2d v.p. 1973-74, 1st v.p. 1974-75, pres. 1976-77), Sociedad Peruana De Obstetricia y Gynecologia (corr. fgn. mem.), Sociedad Paraquaya De Ginecologia y Obstetricia (hon.), U. Miss. Alumni Assn. (dir. 1962-65, past pres. New Orleans chpt.), Philippine Obstet. and Gynecol. Soc. (hon.), AAAS, U. Miss. Guardian Soc., Doctors Club Internat., Assn. Profs. Gynecology and Obstetrics, Emeritus Club of Tulane U., Sigma Xi, Alpha Omega Alpha, Phi Chi (grand presiding sr., nat. pres. 1969-73, exec. trustee 1973—), Beta Theta Pi. Clubs: Plimsoll, New Orleans Country, Circumnavigators, Tulane Green Wave. Home: 1257 S Carrollton Ave New Orleans LA 70118 Office: 4240 Magnolia St at Gen Pershing St New Orleans LA 70115

BEACHER, LAWRENCE LESTER, optometrist, homeopathic physician, research scientist, author and lecturer; b. Cherne, Czechoslovakia, Aug. 18, 1905; came to U.S., 1921, naturalized, 1921; s. Frank A. and Jenny (Berger) B.; m. Sylvia Budoff, Jan. 12, 1930; 1 son, Melvin M. O.D., Pa. Coll. Optometry, 1927; D.Ocular Sci. (hon.), Ill. Coll. Optometry, 1937; Ph.D., Phila. Coll. and Infirmary Osteopathy, 1945; Litt.D., Sem. St. Francis of Assisi, 1947; M.D., McCormick Med. Coll., 1948; M.A., Philathea Coll., London, Ont., Can., 1959, L.H.D., 1961, Ph.D., 1962; Sc.D., Dearborn Coll. Physicians and Surgeons, 1946, Studiorum Colegium Academicum, 1967, London (Eng.) Coll. Applied Sci., 1968, Ind. No. U., 1972; LL.D., Nat. Police Acad., 1970, London Coll. Applied Sci., 1970; Ed.D., Ohio Coll. Podiatric Medicine; M.D. (hon.), Homeopathic Med. Coll., S.Africa, 1975. Diplomate: Am. Bd. Examiners in Psychotherapy. Instr. geometrical optics Pa. State Coll. Optometry, 1927-29, asst. prof., 1929-31; chief staff, head ednl. div. Bronx County Optometrical Clin. Service, 1929-31; lectr. contact lens impression methods Optometric Found., 1944-50; prof. psychology Philathea Coll., 1962-72, chancellor, 1967-72, emeritus, 1972—; vis. lectr. Pa. State Coll. Optometry, 1962-71, emeritus, 1971—; also mem. vis. clin. staff; prof. ophthalmology and contact lens therapy McCormick Med. Coll., 1946-52; vis. lectr. Ill. Coll. Optometry, 1944-68, So. Coll. Optometry, 1962-64; vis. prof. Ind. No. U., 1972-73. Author: Ocular Refraction and Diagnosis, 1931, 2d edit., 1980, Practical Optometry, 1934, Contact Lens Technique, 1941, 5th edit., 1974, Your Precious Eyesight, 1952, Corneal Contact Lenses, 1956, A Study of Practical Psychology, 1962, How Can I Improve Myself, 1962, Psychological Manifestations in Ocular Science, 1968, Happiness and Success in Marriage, 1979, also over 100 articles. Served with USAF-CAP, 1945-62; maj. Res.; ret. Decorated grand cross Eloy Alfano Internat. Found. Panama; Maltese Cross Order St. John Jerusalem; recipient Martin Buber award Midway Counseling Center; award Mass. Gov.'s Council, 1971; Wisdom Hall of Fame award Wisdom Soc., 1971; Good Citizenship medal Nat. Soc. SAR, 1971; Archbishop Benjamin C. Eckardt award, 1971; Humanitarian award J.F. Kennedy Library for Minorities, 1978; named to Hall of Fame Nat. Police Acad., Venice, Fla. Fellow Am. Psychotherapy Assn. (pres. 1971-72), Am. Assn. Clin. Physicians and Surgeons, Assn. Social Psychology, Distinguished Service Found. Optometry, Am. Acad. Optometry (diplomate contact lens bd.), AAAS, Philos. Soc. Eng., Am. Coll. Clinic Adminstrs., Internat. Soc. Psychologists (Eng.), Internat. Coll. Ocular Sci. (dir. edn.), Am. Coll. Homeopathic Physicians, Am. Acad. Med. Adminstrs., N.J. Acad. Sci.; mem. Internat. Coll. Physicians and Surgeons (homeopathic), N.Y. Acad. Scis., Essex County Optometric Soc., Am. Optometric Assn., N.Y. State Optometric Assn., N.Y. County Optometric Assn. (hon. life mem.; 50 Yr. Sci. Service award 1977), N.J. Optometric Assn. (past chmn. contact lens sect., sci. achievement award with honor 1975), Hahnemann Med. Soc., Western Homeopathic Med. Soc. Ariz. (hon. life mem.), Fla. Soc. Homeopathic Physicians, Md. State Homeopathic Med. Soc. (pres. 1980-84), Assn. Mil. Surgeons of U.S., La. Psychol. Assn. (life), Circolo Italiano U. Conn. and U. South Fla., Beta Sigma Kappa (chmn., ret. bd. regents sci. sect., gold medal 1976), Phi Delta Alpha. Jewish. Lodges: Masons; Order of Foresters. Home and Office: 63 Whittingham Pl West Orange NJ 07052 *I advocate and practice the "Golden Rule" For doing unto others should be anticipated, to be reflected in what can be done to us in return. One should not expect to receive without giving and giving of himself brings forth happy living. That is success.*

BEACHLEY, MICHAEL CHARLES, radiologist; b. Harrisburg, Pa., Nov. 14, 1940; s. Kenneth Gumbert and Carolyn Elizabeth (Jones) B.; m. Deborah Rowe Samson, July 27, 1963; children: Kenneth, Barbara, William. A.B., Dartmouth Coll., 1962, B.M.S., 1963; M.D., Harvard U., 1965. Diplomate: Am. Bd. Radiology. Intern in surgery Med. Coll. Va., Richmond, 1965-66, resident in radiology, 1966-69; instr. radiology, 1970, faculty, 1972—, acting chmn. dept. radiology, 1976, prof., 1977—, chmn. dept. radiology, 1977-82, prof. radiation scis., 1981—, prof. biophysics, 1980-82, prof. physiology and biophysics, 1982—; cons. McGuire VA Hosp., 1977—; fellow in radiol. pathology Armed Forces Inst. Pathology, Washington, 1969; mem. Commonwealth of Va. Med. Malpractice Rev. Panel. Contbr. chpt. to book, revs. and med. articles to profl. jours. Vice-pres. College Hills Civic Assn., 1975-77. Served as maj. M.C. U.S. Army, 1970-72. Fellow Am. Coll. Radiology (pres. Va. chpt. 1982-83), Am. Coll. Angiology; mem. AMA, Am. Heart Assn., Med. Soc. Va., Richmond Acad. Medicine, Radiol. Soc. N.Am., Assn. U. Radiologists, Am. Roentgen Ray Soc., Richmond Radiol. Soc. (pres. 1981). Clubs: Dartmouth of Central Va. (exec. com.), Harvard of Va.). Home: 202 Ruggles Pl Richmond VA 23229 Office: Box 2 VCU Med Coll Va Richmond VA 23298

BEACHLEY, NORMAN HENRY, mechanical engineer; b. Washington, Jan. 13, 1933; s. Albert Henry and Anna Garnet (Eiring) B.; m. Marion Ruth Iglehart, July 18, 1959; children: Brenda Ruth, Rebecca Sue, Barbara Joan. B.M.E., Cornell U., 1956, Ph.D., 1966. Mem. tech. staff Hughes Aircraft Co., Culver City, Calif., 1956-57; mem. tech. staff Space Tech. Labs., Redondo Beach, Calif., 1959-63; mech. engring. professorial staff U. Wis., Madison, 1966—, prof. mech. engring., 1978—; cons. Lawrence Livermore Labs., 1978—. Co-author: Introduction to Dynamic System Analysis, 1978. Served with USAF, 1957-59. Sci. and Engring. Research Council Gt. Britain fellow, 1981-82. Mem. ASME, Soc. Automotive Engrs., Sigma Xi. Research in field of energy storage powerplants for motor vehicles, 1970. Home: 2332 Fitchburg Rd Verona WI 53593 Office: U Wis 1513 University Ave Madison WI 53706

BEADLE, ALFRED NEWMAN, architect; b. St. Paul, Sept. 23, 1927; s. Fred Lonard and Marie Nicolin (Lonke) B.; m. E. Nancy Leland, June 5, 1948; children—Steven, Nancy, Caren, Gerri, Scott. Food service planner Beadle Equipment Co., Mpls., 1946-49; bldg. contractor, Phoenix, 1949-51; partner-in-charge firm Daily Assos. (Architects), Phoenix, 1951-66; practice architecture, Phoenix, 1966—; Instr. design Ariz. State U., 1968-69. Served with USNR, 1944-46. Recipient numerous design awards. Mem. AIA, ASCE, Am. Fedn. Arts. Clubs: Ariz., Admirals. Address: 3514 E Oregon St Phoenix AZ 85018

BEADLE, GEORGE WELLS, biologist, emeritus educator; b. Wahoo, Nebr., Oct. 22, 1903; s. Chauncey Elmer and Hattie (Albro) B.; m. Marion Cecile Hill, Aug. 22, 1928 (div. 1953); 1 son, David; m. Muriel Barnett, Aug. 12, 1953; 1 stepson, Redmond James Barnett. B.S., U. Nebr., 1926, M.S., 1927, D.Sc., 1949; Ph.D., Cornell U., 1931; M.A., Oxford (Eng.) U., 1958, D.Sc. (hon.), 1959, Yale U., 1947, Northwestern U., 1952, Rutgers U., 1954, Kenyon Coll., 1955, Wesleyan U., 1956, Birmingham U., 1959, Pomona Coll., 1961, Lake Forest Coll., 1962, U. Rochester, 1963, U. Ill., 1963, Brown U., 1964, Kans. State U., 1964, U. Pa., 1964, Wabash Coll., 1966, Syracuse U., 1967, Loyola U., Chgo., 1970, Hanover Coll., 1971, Eureka Coll., 1972, Butler U., 1973, Gustavus Adolphus Coll., 1975, Ind. State U., 1976; LL.D., U. Calif. at Los Angeles, 1962, U. Miami, 1963, Brandeis U., 1963, Johns Hopkins U., 1966, Beloit Coll., 1966, U. Mich., 1969; D.H.L., Jewish Theol. Sem. Am., 1966, DePaul U., 1969, U. Chgo., 1969, Canisius Coll., 1969, Knox Coll., 1969, Carroll Coll., 1971, Roosevelt U., 1971; D. Pub. Service, Ohio No. U., 1970. Teaching asst. Cornell U., 1926-27, experimentalist, 1927-31; NRC fellow Calif. Inst. Tech., 1931-33, instr., 1933-35; guest investigator Institut de Biologie, physico-chimique, Paris, 1935; asst. prof. genetics Harvard U., 1936-37; prof. biology (genetics) Stanford U., 1937-47; prof. biology and chmn. div. biology Calif. Inst. Tech., 1946-60, acting dean faculty, 1960-61; pres., trustee, prof. biology U. Chgo., 1961-68, pres. emeritus, William E. Wrather Distinguished Service prof., hon. trustee, 1969-75, prof. emeritus, 1975; dir. Inst. Biomed. Research, AMA, Chgo., 1968-70; Eastman vis. prof. Oxford U., 1958-59; mem. Pres.'s Sci. Adv. Council, 1960; hon. pres. 12th Internat. Congress Genetics, 1968.

Author: (with Alfred H. Sturtevant) An Introduction to Genetics, 1939, Genetics and Modern Biology, 1963, (with Muriel B. Beadle) The Language of Life, 1966 (Edison award best sci. book for youth 1967). Hon. trustee Mus. Sci. and Industry, Chgo.; trustee Calif. Inst. Tech., 1969-75; adv. bd. Robert A. Welch Found., 1971—. Recipient Lasker award, 1950, Dyer award, 1951, Emil C. Hansen prize, Denmark, 1953; Albert Einstein Commemorative award in sci., 1958; Nobel Prize in medicine and physiology (with Edward L. Tatum and Joshua Lederberg), 1958; Am. Cancer Soc. award, 1959; Kimber Genetics award, 1960; Priestley Meml. award, 1967; Donald Forsha Jones medal, 1972; Order St. Olaf. Mem. Nat. Acad. Scis. (council 1969-72), Am. Philos. Soc., Royal Soc., Japan Acad. (hon.), Instituto Lombardo di Scienze e Lettre (Milan), AAAS (pres. 1946), Am. Acad. Arts and Scis., Genetics Soc. Am. (pres. 1955), Genetical Soc. Gt. Britain, Indian Soc. Genetics and Plant Breeding, Indian Nat. Sci. Acad. (hon.), Chgo. Hort. Soc. (pres. 1968-71, trustee 1971-76), Danish Royal Acad. Scis., Phi Beta Kappa (hon.), Sigma Xi. Research on genetics, cytology and origin Indian corn (Zea), genetics and devel. fruit fly Drosophila, biochem. genetics of bread mold Neurospora. Home: 900 E Harrison D-33 Pomona CA 91767

BEADLE, JOHN GRANT, manufacturing company executive; b. Chgo., Dec. 16, 1932; s. John G. and Katharine (Brady) B.; m. Lee Oliver, Apr. 11, 1955; children: Katharine, John. B.A., Yale U., 1954. Salesman Pure Oil Co., Jacksonville and Tampa, Fla., 1957-59, Kordite Co., Tampa, New Orleans, 1959-61; with Union Spl. Corp., Chgo., 1961—, exec. v.p., 1972-75, pres., chief operating officer, 1975-76, pres., chief exec. officer, 1976—; dir. Rospatch Corp., Grand Rapids, Mich., Portec Corp., Paxall Group; Past pres., bd. dirs. Juvenile Protection Assn.; chmn., bd. dirs. Midwest Indsl. Mgmt. Assn.; chmn. Internat. Council Machinery and Allied Products Inst. Trustee Allendale Sch. for Boys; bd. dirs. Greater N. Michigan Ave. Assn. Served with USAF, 1954-57. Mem. Northwestern U. Assos., Chgo. Com. Republican. Episcopalian. Clubs: Skokie Country, Mchts. and Mfrs., Commonwealth, Comml. Home: 1432 Scott Ave Winnetka IL 60093: Office: 400 N Franklin St Chicago IL 60610

BEAGLE, CHARLES WELLINGTON, civil engineer; b. Media, Pa., Oct. 25, 1910; s. John Andrew and Ella Mae (Hartman) B.; m. Alice Rosa Rigg, July 6, 1946; children: Joann (Mrs. Morris Bricks), Rosana (Mrs. Duncan Brooks McGill), Charles Andrew, Ruth Ella (Mrs. Andrew Jerome). B.S., Pa. State U., 1933, C.E., 1939. Jr. Civil engr. U.S. Forest Service, Pa., 1933-39; chief constrn. engr. Bendix Aviation Corp., Teterboro, N.J., 1940-44; project engr. George M. Brewster, Inc., Bogota, N.J., 1945-49; pres. R.&B. Constrn. Co., South Plainfield, N.J., 1950-55; municipal engr., dir. pub. works, South Plainfield, 1955-60, New Providence, N.J., 1960-62, Woodbridge, N.J., 1962-76, asphalt paving cons., 1976—. Vice chmn. South Plainfield Redevel. Agy., 1967-70. Served with U.S. Army, 1939-40; Served with USNR, 1944-45. Recipient Industry Recognition award Nat. Asphalt Pavement Assn., 1965; Asphalt Leadership award Poly. Inst. Bklyn., 1972; Pioneer award N.J. Asphalt Pavement Assn., 1974; Outstanding Contbn. award Rutgers U. Asphalt Paving Conf., 1976. Mem. Transp. Research Bd., Am. Rd. Builders Assn., Assn. Asphalt Paving Technologists (dir., pres. 1974), Am. Pub. Works Assn. (Pub. Works Man of Year 1966), Nat. Soc. Profl. Engrs., N.J. Soc. Profl. Engrs. (Engr. of Year 1971, Govt. Profl. Devel. award 1974), N.J. Soc. Mcpl. Engrs. (Merit award 1961), Internat. Inst. Community Service (honor roll 1976), Asphalt Inst. Internat. Platform Assn., Water Pollution Control Fedn., Am. Arbitration Assn., Am. Legion, VFW, Alpha Sigma Phi. Club: Elks. Home and Office: 102 W Nassau Ave South Plainfield NJ 07080 *My life's goal is to be of service to God, my family, my country and to honor my citizenship, in that order. . . Time and patience are necessary requirements for anything worth starting, and anything worth starting must be pursued to completion.*

BEAGLE, PETER SOYER, writer; b. N.Y.C., Apr. 20, 1939; s. Simon and Rebecca (Soyer) B.; m. Enid Nordeen, May 8, 1964 (div. 1980); children: Vicki Lynn, Kalisa, Daniel Nordeen. B.A., U. Pitts., 1959; student, Stanford U., 1960-61. Author: A Fine and Private Place, 1960, I See By My Outfit, 1965, The Last Unicorn, 1968, The California Feeling, 1969, (with Pat Derby) The Lady and Her Tiger, 1976, The Fantasy Worlds of Peter Beagle, 1978, The Garden of Earthly Delights, 1982; screenwriter: The Dove, 1974, The Greatest Thing That Almost Happened, 1977, The Lord of the Rings: Part One, 1978, The Last Unicorn, 1982; free-lance writer for: Ladies Home Jour., Saturday Evening Post, Holiday, others. Vice chmn. Santa Cruz chpt. ACLU, 1968-69. Address: 311 E Rianda Rd Watsonville CA 95076

BEAGRIE, GEORGE SIMPSON, dentist, educator, university dean; b. Peterhead, Scotland, Sept. 14, 1925; emigrated to Can., 1968, naturalized, 1973; s. George and Eliza Lawson (Simpson) B.; m. Marjorie McVie, Sept. 30, 1950; children: Jennifer, Lesley, Ailsa, Elspeth. D.D.S., U. Edinburgh, 1966. Prof., chmn. dept. restorative dentistry U. Edinburgh Dental Sch., 1963-68; prof., chmn. dept. clin. scis. U. Toronto Dental Sch., 1968-78, dir. postgrad. div., 1974-78; dean faculty dentistry U. B.C., Vancouver, Can., 1978—; sci. officer grants com. dental scis. Med. Research Council Can., 1971-76, dir. dental tng. grants programme, 1971-78; cons. in field; cons. WHO, 1975—. Contbr. articles dental jours. Mem. United Ch. Can. Served to flight lt. RAF, 1948-50. Fellow Nuffield Found., 1957-58; grantee Med. Research Council U.K., 1962-64, Med. Research Council Can., 1968, Commonwealth Found., 1973. Fellow Royal Coll. Dentists Can. (pres. 1977-79), Am. Coll. Dentists, Internat. Coll. Dentists; Fellow in dental surgery Royal Coll. Surgeons Edinburgh and Eng.; mem. Internat. Assn. Dental Research (pres. 1977-78), Fedn. Dentaire Internat., Can. Dental Assn. (editor tape cassette program 1972-76), Brit. Dental Assn., Ont. Dental Assn., Canadian Acad. Periodontists, Brit., Ont. socs. periodontology, Omicron Kappa Upsilon. Home: 1344 W 47th Ave Vancouver BC Canada V6M 2L8 Office: Faculty Dentistry Univ BC 345-2194 Health Scis Mall Vancouver BC Canada V6T 1W5

BEAHLER, JOHN LEROY, government official, physician; b. Albuquerque, Sept. 10, 1930; s. Lee Edward and Margaret Verona (King) B.; m. Electra C. Carsonis, Feb. 7, 1973. B.A., U. Tex.-El Paso, 1957; M.D., Southwestern Med. Sch., 1961. Fgn. service med. officer Dept. State, 1961-81, dept. med. dir., Washington, 1981—, sr. dep. asst. sec., 1981—; specialist rep. Sr. Fgn. Service Selection Bd., Washington, 1983—. Served to 1st lt. USAF, 1952-56. Mem. Fed. Physicians Assn. (pres. elect 1981-82). Office: Office of Med Services Dept State Washington DC 20520

BEAHRS, OLIVER HOWARD, surgeon; b. Eufaula, Ala., Sept. 19, 1914; s. Elmer Charles and Elsa Kathryn (Smith) B.; m. Helen Edith Taylor, July 27, 1947; children: John Randolf, David Howard, Nancy Ann. B.A., U. Calif., Berkeley, 1937; M.D., Northwestern U., 1942; M.S. in Surgery, Mayo Grad. Sch. Medicine, 1949. Diplomate: Am. Bd. Surgery. Fellow surgery Mayo Grad. Sch. Medicine, Rochester, Minn., 1942, 46-49; prof. surgery, 1966—; asst. surgeon Mayo Clinic, 1949-50, head sect. gen. surgery, 1950—, vice chmn. bd. govs., 1964-75; Bd. dirs. Rochester Meth. Hosp.; trustee Mayo Found.; mem. cancer control and rehab. adv. com. Nat. Cancer Inst., 1975—; mem. Am. Joint Com. on Cancer, 1975-78, exec. dir., 1980—. Editor: Gen. Surgery Update; editorial bd.: Surgery, Surg. Techniques Illustrated; Contbr. articles in field. Bd. dirs. Am. Cancer Soc., 1980—; trustee Rochester Meth. Hosp. Served to lt. comdr. USNR, 1942-46. Mem. A.C.S. (mem. exec. com., bd. govs., chmn. central jud. com., long-range planning com., chmn. bd. govs., bd. regents), Am. Group Practice Assn. (sec.-treas. 1974-75), Minn. Surg. Soc. (pres. 1960-61), AMA, Am. Thyroid Assn., James IV Assn. Surgeons, Am. Surg. Assn. (pres. 1978-79, chmn. com. on issues 1980-83), So. Surg. Assn., Central Surg. Assn., Western Surg. Assn., Soc. Head and Neck Surgeons (pres. 1966-67), Am. Assn. Clin. Anatomists (pres. 1983), Soc. Surgery Alimentary Tract, Soc. Pelvic Surgeons (pres. 1982), Soc. Surg. Oncology, Sigma Xi, Phi Kappa Epsilon, Phi Beta Pi, Theta Delta Chi. Republican. Methodist. Home: Route 1 Box 329 Rochester MN 55902 Office: 200 1st St SW Rochester MN 55905

BEAIRD, BETTY, actress; b. El Paso, Tex.; d. Benjamin Jessup and George Bell (Rowell) B.; children: Marshall Rowell, Benjamin Jay, Honey. B.B.A., U. Tex.; postgrad., U. Hawaii, Columbia, Pepperdine Coll. Radio writer KTBC-TV, Austin, Tex.; prodn. estimator NBC-TV, N.Y.C.; prodn. asst. Arthur Murray Show, N.Y.C.; comml. producer Edward H. Weiss Advt., N.Y.C.; prodn. asst.-writer Goodson Todman, N.Y.C. Appeared in N.Y. Upstairs at the Downstairs, Just for Openers; appeared as Marie Waggedorn NBC-TV series Julia; appeared in: Lily Tomlin Spl; actress: film Incredible Shrinking Woman; TV appearances include Night Swimmers, Boomer, The Skating Rink, Me and Dads New Wife; Comedy writer; profl. photographer; dir. Mem. Actors Studio, Kappa Alpha Theta.

BEAIRD, CHARLES T., publisher; b. Shreveport, La., July 17, 1922; s. James Benjamin and Mattie Connell (Fort) B.; m. Carolyn Williams, Feb. 6, 1943; children: Susan Beaird McCormick, Marjorie Beaird Seawell, John B. B.A., Centenary Coll., 1966; Ph.D. in Philosophy, Columbia U., 1972. Vice pres., asst. gen. mgr. J.B. Beaird Corp., Shreveport, 1946-57; cons. in oil and investments, Shreveport, 1957-59; pres. Beaird-Poulan Inc., Shreveport, 1959-73; chmn. bd. Beaird-Poulan div. Emerson Electric Co., 1973-76; pres., pub. Shreveport Jour., 1976—; dir. Fed. Res. Bank of Dallas, 1972-78, dep. chmn., 1973-78; dir. Westport Devel. Co., Shreveport, Winrock Enterprises, Inc., Little Rock; adj. prof. Centenary Coll., Shreveport, 1969—. Mem. Caddo Parish Police Jury, 1956-60; bd. dirs. Woodrow Wilson Nat. Fellowship Found., Princeton, N.J., 1975-78. Served to capt. USMCR, 1943-46. Clubs: Shreveport, Shreveport Country, Demolselle (Shreveport). Home: 7030 E Ridge Dr Shreveport LA 71106 Office: PO Box 31110 Shreveport LA 71130

BEAK, PETER ANDREW, chemistry educator; b. Syracuse, N.Y., Jan. 12, 1936; s. Ralph E. and Belva (Edinger) B.; m. Sandra J. Burns, July 25, 1959; children: Bryan A., Stacia W. B.A., Harvard U., 1957; Ph.D., Lowa State U., 1961. From instr. to prof. chemistry U. Ill., Urbana, 1961—; cons. Abbott Labs., North Chgo., Ill., 1964—, Monsanto Co., St. Louis, 1969—. Contbr. articles to profl. jours. A.P. Sloan Found. fellow, 1967-69; Guggenheim fellow, 1968-69. Fellow AAAS; Mem. Am. Chem. Soc. (editorial and adv. bds., mem., sect. and div. officer 1980). Home: 505 W Indiana Ave Urbana IL 61801

BEAL, DALLAS KNIGHT, univ. pres.; b. Ashtabula, Ohio, July 29, 1926; s. Ananias Porter and Clara (Blair) B.; m. Elizabeth Walton, June 9, 1951; children—Jeffrey T., Joan B. B.S., Ohio State U., 1950, M.A., 1951; Ed.D., Columbia, 1958. Instr. edn. State U. N.Y. at New Paltz, 1951-52, Tchrs. Coll., Columbia, 1952-54; dir. placement, lectr. edn. Queens Coll., City Univ. N.Y., 1954-58; mem. adminstrn. State Univ. Coll. N.Y. at Fredonia, 1958—, v.p. acad. affairs, 1969-70, acting pres., 1970-72, pres., 1972—; Dir. Liberty Bank, Dunkirk, N.Y.; Adviser, editor N.Y. State Syllabus Reading and Lang. Arts, 1962-63; Mem. N.Y. Regents Task Force Evaluation N.Y.C. Pub. Schs., 1961-63; charter mem. adv. com. higher edn. N.Y. State Tchrs. Assn., 1966-67; com. on performance-based evaluation for certification N.Y. State Dept. Edn., 1968; chmn. com. on ednl. tech. Am. Assn. State Colls. and Univs.; mem. nursing edn. council, mem. telecommunications com. SUNY; chmn. Western N.Y. Consortium Public and Pvt. Colls. Author: (with Dr. H. Mitzel) Research Study of Campus Schools in American Colleges, 1966. Vice chmn. Community Devel. Com.; bd. dirs. Western N.Y. Ednl. TV Sta.; pres. United Fund, No. Chautauqua County, 1968-70; mem. adv. bd. Model Counties Assn., Chautauqua County, 1971-72; adviser bd. edn., Dunkirk, 1968— adviser bd. edn., Fredonia, 1966—; Bd. dirs. Boorady Reading Center, Dunkirk, Brooks Meml. Hosp., Dunkirk. Mem. Southwestern N.Y. Assn. Instructional Improvement (founding pres.), Dunkirk C. of C. (dir.), Fredonia C. of C. (dir.), N.E.A., Torch Club, Kappa Delta Pi, Phi Delta Kappa, Alpha Phi Omega. Office: SUNY Coll Fredonia Fredonia NY 14063

BEAL, GEORGE MELVIN, sociologist; b. Parkdale, Oreg., May 21, 1917; m. Evelyn Frances Miller, June 6, 1944; children: Carolee, Linda, Dirk, David. B.S., Iowa State U., 1943, M.S., 1947, Ph.D., 1953. Mem. faculty Iowa State U., Ames, 1946-77, Charles F. Curtiss distinguished prof. agr., chmn. dept. sociology and anthropology, 1968-76; with Communication Inst., East-West Center, Honolulu, 1977—; with Ford Found., India, 1958; mem. evaluation com. on health, edn. and communications HEW, 1964-65; mem. Surgeon Gen.'s Task Force on Smoking and Health, 1967-68; research Agrl. Devel. Council (Rockefeller), Guatemala, 1964; U.S. rep. to UNESCO com. to develop evaluation plan for literacy programs, 1966. Co-author: Leadership and Dynamic Group Action, 1962, Social Action and Interaction in program planning, 1966, Social Indicators and Societal Monitoring, 1972, Communication Planning Simulation Game, 1979, Communication Planning Methods Handbook, 1981; Co-editor: Sociological Perspective of Domestic Development, 1971; Contbr. chpts. books, 90 monographs, articles to profl. jours. Served to capt. AUS, 1943-46. Mem. Internat. Sociol. Assn. (rep. on council), Am. Sociol. Assn., Rural Sociol. Soc. (pres. 1967), Sigma Delta Chi, Alpha Kappa Delta, Gamma Sigma Delta, Phi Kappa Phi. Current interests: communication planning, knowledge generation, utilization, devel., and farming systems. Address: Communication Inst East-West Center 1777 East-West Rd Honolulu HI 96848

BEAL, JOHN M., physician; b. Starkville, Miss., 1915. M.D., U. Chgo., 1941. Diplomate: Am. Bd. Surgery (chmn. 1970-71). Intern N.Y. Hosp., N.Y.C., 1941-42, asst. resident surgery, 1942-44, 46-47, surgeon, 1947-48, attending surgeon, 1953-63; chmn. tumor bd. and staff surgeon Wadsworth Gen. Hosp., West Los Angeles, 1949-50, chief surg. service, 1950-53; cons. staff St. John's Hosp., Santa Monica, Cal., 1950-53; instr. surgery Cornell U., Ithaca, N.Y., 1948-49, assoc. prof. clin. surgery, 1953-63; instr. surgery UCLA, 1949-50, asst. prof., 1950-53; now J. Roscoe Miller disting. Northwestern U., chmn. dep. surgery, 1963-82; chmn. dept. surgery Chgo. Wesley Meml. Hosp., 1963-69, Northwestern Meml. Hosp., 1973-82; chief surgery Passavant Meml. Hosp., Chgo., 1963-73. Served to capt. M.C. AUS, 1944-46. Fellow ACS (bd. regents 1973-83, pres. 1982-83); mem. Council of Med. Splty. Socs. (sec. 1978-80), Soc. Univ. Surgeons, Soc. Clin. Surgery, AMA, Am. Surg. Assn. Address: Northwestern U Medical School Chicago IL 60611

BEAL, MERRILL DAVID, government official; b. Richfield, Utah, June 26, 1926; s. Merrill Dee and Bessy (Neill) B.; m. Jean Lorraine Wood, Feb. 24, 1947; children: John David, James Merrill. B.A., Idaho State Coll., 1950; M.S., Utah State U., 1952. Park ranger, naturalist Yellowstone Nat. Park, 1953-60; chief park naturalist Grand Canyon Nat. Park, 1960-69; asst. supt. Great Smoky Mountains Nat. Park, Gatlinburg, Tenn., 1969-72; assoc. regional dir. Midwest region Nat. Park Service, Omaha, 1972-75, regional dir., 1975—. Author: Grand Canyon, the Story Behind the Scenery, 1967. Bd. dirs. Grand Canyon Sch., 1964-69. Served with USN, 1944-46. Recipient Meritorious Service award U.S. Dept. Interior, 1975. Mem. AAAS, Wildlife Soc., Nat. Recreation and Park Assn., S.E. parks and Monument Assn. (bd. dirs. 1975—), Sigma Xi. Office: Cades Cove Vistors Center and Open-Air Mus Great Smoky Mountains Nat Park Gatlinburg TN 37738

BEAL, MYRON CLARENCE, osteopathic physician; b. N.Y.C., Dec. 4, 1920; s. Clarence Joseph and Birdice Elvira (Flint) B.; m. Esther Naomi DeLong, Sept. 11, 1948; children: Rebecca Beal Johnson, Myron Flint, Shelley Beal Reese, Julie Beal Wilson, Christina. A.B., U. Rochester, 1942; D.O., Chgo. Coll. Osteo. Medicine, 1945; M.S. in Physiology, U. Chgo., 1949. Asst. dir. clinics Chgo. Coll. Osteo. Medicine, 1946-49; instr. London (Eng.) Coll. Osteopathy, 1949-51; pvt. practice osteo. medicine, Rochester, N.Y., 1951-74; prof. biomechanics Coll. Osteo. Medicine, Mich. State U., East Lansing, 1974-81, prof. family medicine, 1981—, acting chmn. biomechanics, 1975-77; Mem. Nat. Bd. Examiners for Osteo. Physicians and Surgeons, 1960—; mem. N.Y. State Bd. Medicine, 1961-73. Trustee Chgo. Coll. Osteo. Medicine. Fellow Am. Acad. Osteopathy; mem. Am. Osteo. Assn., N.Y. State Osteo. Soc., Mich. Assn. Osteo. Physicians and Surgeons. Presbyterian (elder). Office: West Fee Hall Coll Osteopathic Medicine Mich State U East Lansing MI 48824

BEAL, RICHARD SIDNEY, JR., zoology educator; b. Victor, Colo., May 7, 1916; s. Richard Sidney and Mona (Ballfinch) B.; m. Wilma Juhree Gibbons, June 30, 1941; children: Richard Sidney (dec.), Andrew Alan. B.S., U. Ariz., 1938; Ph.D., U. Calif.-Berkeley, 1951. Asst. prof. biology Westmont Coll., Santa Barbara, Calif., 1947-48; prof. systematic theology Conservative Baptist Theol. Sem., Denver, 1951-56; research entomologist U.S. Dept. Agr., Washington, 1957-58; asso. prof. zoology Ariz. State U., Tempe, 1958-62; prof. zoology No. Ariz. U., Flagstaff, 1962—, dean, 1965-81. Contbr. profl. jours. Scoutmaster Boy Scouts Am., 1964-68, explorer adviser, 1968-70. NSF grantee. Mem. Entomol. Soc. Am., Washington Entomol. Soc., Soc. Systematic Zoology, Sigma Xi. Republican. Baptist. Home: 534 Bertrand St Flagstaff AZ 86001 Office: Box 5640 No Ariz Univ Flagstaff AZ 86011

BEAL, RICHARD SMITH, government official, political scientist, educator; b. Washington, Nov. 27, 1945; s. George Max and Virginia (Smith) B.; m. Ruth Sorensen, Jan. 31, 1969; children: Emily Longstroth, Jason Richard, Trevor Max, Melinda Ruth, Quincy Frodesen. B.A., Brigham Young U., 1970, M.A. (fellow), 1970; Ph.D. (Herman fellow), U. So. Calif., Los Angeles, 1977. Translator and cons. devel. of lang. materials Lang. Tng. Center, Brigham Young U., Provo, Utah, 1968-69, grad. teaching asst. dept. polit. sci., 1969-70, adminstrv. asst. internat. relations program, 1969-70, research assoc., 1971-72, instr. dept. polit. sci., 1970-72, asst. prof. polit. sci., 1975-78, coordinator internat. relations program, 1975-78, 79-80, assoc. prof. internat. relations and polit. sci., 1978-82; spl. asst. to pres. for nat. security affairs, sr. dir. for crisis mgmt. systems and planning Nat. Security Council, Washington, 1983—; polit. analyst and cons. Decision/Making/Info., Santa Ana, Calif., 1972-73; research assoc. Sch. Internat. Relations, U. So. Calif., 1973, project study dir., 1973-75, vis. prof. internat. relations, summer 1977; vis. scholar dept. systems sci. City U. London, 1978; vis. fgn. fellow Indian Inst. Advanced Studies, summer 1979; vis. Fulbright-Hays scholar Jawaharlal Nehru U. Sch. Internat. Studies, New Delhi, 1979; dir. Polit. Info. System, Reagan-Bush Com., Arlington, Va., 1980; asst. dep. dir. planning and evaluation Office of Pres.-elect, Washington, 1980-81; spl. asst. to Pres. U.S. and dir. Office of Planning and Evaluation, White House, 1981-83; cons. compensatory edn. participation project Decima, Inc., U.S. Office Edn., 1977-79; cons. lang. indicators project Lang. Research Center and Eyring Research Inst., 1977—; spl. cons. computing U.S. Senate Select Com. on Intelligence, 1978-79. Author: (with K.P. Misra) International Relations Theory, 1978, Systems Analysis of International Crises, 1979; contbr. numerous articles on internat. relations, internat. politics, edn. and systems analysis of internat. relations to profl. jours. Mem. Am. Polit. Sci. Assn., Internat. Polit. Sci. Assn., Internat. Studies Assn., Phi Kappa Phi, Pi Sigma Alpha. Mem. Ch. Jesus Christ of Latter-day Saints. Office: White House Nat Security Council Room 303 Washington DC 20500

BEAL, W(ALTER) H(ENRY) JACK, artist; b. Richmond, Va., June 25, 1931; s. Walter Henry and Marion Watkins (Baker) B.; m. Sondra Freckelton, Sept. 3, 1955. Student, Norfolk div. Coll. of William and Mary-Va. Poly. Inst., 1950-53, Art Inst. Chgo., 1953-56, U. Chgo., 1955-56. Exhibited in ten year retrospective exhibit at, Va. Mus. Fine Arts, Richmond, Boston U., Mus. Contemporary Arts, Chgo., 1973-74; executed murals, Dept. Labor Bldg., Washington, 1977; vis. artist, U. Wis., Art Inst. Chgo., San Diego State Coll., Md. Inst., N.Y. U., Ind. U., Skidmore, Boston U., Ohio U., San Francisco Art Inst., Fullerton Coll., Syracuse U., Cornell U., Yale U., SUNY, U. Va., Va. Commonwealth U., Del. Art Mus., U. Pa., Beaver Coll., Moore Coll., Queens Coll., others; bd. artists, Artists' Choice Mus., 1978-79. Mem. Youth Bd., Gouverneur, N.Y., 1970-73; bd. govs. Skowhegan (Maine) Sch., 1972-82; bd. visitors Sch. Visual Arts, Boston U. Recipient Neysa McMein Purchase award Whitney Mus., 1965; Nat. Endowment for Arts grantee, 1973; Hermitage Found. fellow, 1953-56. Home: 83A Delhi Stage Oneonta NY 13820 Office: care Allan Frumkin Gallery 50 W 57th St New York NY 10019

BEALE, BETTY (MRS. GEORGE K. GRAEBER), columnist; b. Washington; d. William Lewis and Edna (Sims) B.; m. George Kenneth Graeber, Feb. 15, 1969. A.B., Smith Coll. Columnist Washington Post, 1937-40; reporter and columnist Washington Evening Star, 1945-81; weekly columnist Field Newspaper Syndicate (formerly Publishers Hall Syndicate), 1953—; lectr. Recipient Freedom Found. award, 1969. Mem. Washington Press Club. Address: 2926 Garfield St NW Washington DC 20008

BEALL, BURTCH W., JR., architect; b. Columbus, Ohio, Sept. 27, 1925; s. Burtch W. and Etta (Beheler) B.; m. Susan Jane Hunter, June 6, 1949; children—Brent Hunter, Brook Waite. Student, John Carroll U., 1943; B.Arch., Ohio State U., 1949. Draftsman Brooks & Coddington (Architects), Columbus, 1949-51, William J. Monroe (Architects), Salt Lake City, 1951-53, Lorenzo Young (Architect), 1953-54; prin. Burtch W. Beall, Jr. (Architect), Salt Lake City, 1954—; vis. lectr. Westminster Coll., 1955; adj. prof. U. Utah, 1955-83; treas. Nat. Council Archtl. Registration Bds., 1980-82. Served with U.S. Navy, 1943-45. Fellow AIA; mem. Soc. Archtl. Historians. Methodist. Club: Masons. Home: 4644 Brookwood Circle Salt Lake City UT 84117 Office: 2188 Highland Dr Salt Lake City UT 84106

BEALL, CHARLES CLYDE, JR., banker; b. Oxford, Miss., Mar. 28, 1935; s. Charles Clyde and Jennie (Dale) B.; m. Ines Anne Watts, July 21, 1961; children: Charles Clyde III, Craig Alan. B.B.A., U. Miss., 1957, M.B.A., 1961. With Tex. Commerce Bank, Houston, 1961—, mgr. met. div., exec. v.p., mgr. banking dept., 1974-78, pres., from 1978, chmn., 1983—; vice chmn. Tex. Commerce Bancshares Inc., Houston, 1983—. Served to 1st lt. USAF. Office: Tex Commerce Bank 712 Main St. Houston TX 77002 *

BEALL, DENNIS RAY, artist, educator; b. Chickasha, Okla., Mar. 13, 1929; s. Roy A. and Lois O. (Phillips) B.; 1 son, Garm. Student, Okla.

City U., 1950-52; B.A., San Francisco State U., 1953, M.A., 1958. Registrar Oakland (Calif.) Art Mus., 1958; curator Achenbach Found. for Graphic Arts, Calif. Palace of the Legion of Honor, San Francisco, 1958-1965; asst. prof. art San Francisco State Coll., 1965-69, asso. prof., 1969-76, prof., 1976—. Numerous one-man shows of prints, 1957—, including: Award Exhbn. of San Francisco Art Commn., Calif. Coll. Arts and Crafts, 1978, San Francisco U. Art Gallery, numerous group shows, 1960—, including, Mills Coll. Art Gallery, Oakland, Calif., Univ. Gallery of Calif. State U., Hayward, 1979, Marshall-Meyers Gallery, 1979, 80, Marin Civic Center Art Galleries, San Rafael, Calif., 1980; represented in numerous permanent collections including, Library of Congress, Washington, Mus. Modern Art, N.Y.C., Nat. Library of Medicine, Washington, Phila. Mus., U.S. embassy collections, Tokyo, London and other major cities, San Francisco Mus., Victoria and Albert Mus., London, Fresno (Calif.) Art Center, Starr King Sch. of the Ministry, Berkeley, Calif., Achenbach Found. for Graphic Arts, Calif. Palace of Legion of Honor, San Francisco, Oakland Art Mus., Phila. Free Library, Roanoke (Va.) Art Center, various colls. and univs. in U.S. Served with USN, 1947-50; PTO. Office: Art Dept San Francisco State Univ 1600 Holloway St San Francisco CA 94132

BEALL, DONALD RAY, mfg. co. exec.; b. Beaumont, Calif., Nov. 29, 1938; s. Ray C. and Margaret (Murray) B. B.S., San Jose State Coll., 1960; M.B.A., U. Pitts., 1961; postgrad., U. Calif. at Los Angeles. With Ford Motor Co., 1961-68, fin. mgmt. positions, Newport Beach, Calif., 1961-66, mgr. corp. fin. planning and contracts, Phila., 1966-67, controller, Palo Alto, Calif., 1967-68; exec. dir. corporate fin. planning N.Am. Rockwell, El Segundo, Calif., 1968-69, exec. v.p. electronics group, 1969-71; exec. v.p. Collins Radio Co., Dallas, 1971-74; pres. Collins Radio Group, Rockwell Internat. Corp., Dallas, 1974-76, Electronic Ops., 1976-77; exec. v.p. Rockwell Internat. Corp., Dallas, 1977-79, pres., chief operating officer, Pitts., 1979—, dir., 1978—; mem. Pres.'s Export Council, 1981—; dir. 1st Internat. Bancshares, Dallas. Past Dallas met. chmn. Nat. Alliance Bus.; mem. Dallas Citizens Council; past bd. dirs. United Way of Met. Dallas, So. Methodist U. Found. Sci. and Engring.; bd. dirs. Dallas Council World Affairs, United Way of Allegheny County, Pitts.; trustee U. Pitts.; gen. campaign chmn. Western Pa. affiliate Am. Diabetes Assn. Recipient award of distinction San Jose State U. Sch. Engring., 1980. Mem. Armed Forces Communications and Electronics Assn. (nat. dir.), Electronic Industries Assn., Aerospace Industries Assn. (gov.), Soc. Automotive Engrs., Def. Preparedness Assn., Young Pres.'s Orgn., Navy League of U.S., Sigma Alpha Epsilon, Beta Gamma Sigma. Office: Rockwell Internat Corp 600 Grant St Pittsburgh PA 15219

BEALL, INGRID LILLEHEI, lawyer; b. Cedar Falls, Iowa, June 18, 1926; d. Ingebrigt Larsen and Olive (Allison) Lillehei; m. George Brooke Beall, Dec. 21, 1951 (div. 1971). A.B., U. Chgo., 1945, M.A., 1948, J.D., 1956. Bar: Ill. 1956. Assoc. firm McDermott, Will & Emery, Chgo., 1956-58, Baker & McKenzie, 1958-61, ptnr., Chgo., Brussels and Paris, 1961—. Mem. ABA, Ill. Bar Assn., Chgo. Bar Assn., Internat. Fiscal Assn. Home: 175 Delaware St Chicago IL 60611 Office: Baker & McKenzie 2800 Prudential Plaza Chicago IL 60601

BEALL, PAUL RENSSELAER, educator, communications consultant, editor; b. Des Moines, Aug. 28, 1909; s. Ollie Monroe and Helen May (Paul) B.; m. Helen Minerva Wadsworth, Sept. 18, 1937; children: Helen Wadsworth Beall Gerken, Sarah Evarts Beall Garcia y Vaz, Christopher Wadsworth Paul, Nancy Patch Beall Hendren. A.B., Grinnell Coll., 1932; student law, Harvard U., 1935-36; A.M., U. Mich., 1940; Ph.D., Pa. State U., 1948, spl. courses indsl. engring., 1948-50. Eastern states sales mgr. Morrison-Shults Mfg. Co. (leather products), 1932-39; teaching fellow speech U. Mich., 1939-41; from instr. to assoc. prof. speech and rhetoric Pa. State U., 1941-50, lectr. indsl. engring. extension, 1941-50, summer sch. lectr. in communications problems in mgmt., 1951-57; dir. info., research and devel. bd. Dept. Def., 1950-51; sci. adviser to comdg. gen. Air Research and Devel. Command, 1952, to comdg. gen. for operations USAF, 1953, to comdg. gen. USAF-Far East, 1955, 57, to comdr.-in-chief U.S. Strike Command, 1969; lectr. Joint U.S.-NATO commands, in Europe, intermittently 1955-58; cons. to founding faculty USAF Acad.; communications cons. in indsl. and mil. mgmt. (aerospace projects), 1953—; pres. Oglethorpe Coll., Atlanta, 1964-67; vis. prof. Rollins Coll., 1977-79; cons. to under sec. Dept. Energy, 1979. Contbr. articles to tech. mags. Trustee Aerospace Edn. Found.; cons. Community Welfare Dr., Greater Balt., 1955-57; mem. bd. Annapolis Roads (Md.) Property Owners Assn., 1958, 62; mem. visitors adv. council Grinnell Coll., 1962-67; mem. pres.'s council Rollins Coll., 1968-72; mem. tech. adv. com. Atlanta-Fulton County Econ. Opportunity Authority, 1965-68; bd. dirs. Atlanta chpt. UN Assn. U.S., 1964-67. Mem. Nat. Conf. Adminstrn. Research (pres. 1961), U.S. Air Force Assn., Nat. Space Inst. (charter, life). Episcopalian. Clubs: Masons, Rotary, County (Orlando, Fla.); Cosmos (Washington); Explorers (N.Y.C.); Racquet (Winter Park, Fla.). Home: Randall House 323 Trismen Terr Winter Park FL 32789 *Trust a little. Leave a few things up to God. Cross on green. For tomorrow, prepare and aspire. Of yesterday little can be changed; right a wrong perhaps.*

BEALL, ROBERT JOSEPH, foundation executive; b. Washington, May 19, 1943; s. William Joseph and Louise Rachel (Tayman) B.; m. Mary Ellen O'Connor, June 24, 1967; children: Thomas Joseph, Robert Andrew. B.S., Albright Coll., 1965; M.A., SUNY, Buffalo, 1970, Ph.D., 1970. Asst. prof. dept. physiology Case-Western Reserve U., Cleve., 1971-74, asst. prof., 1972-74; grants asso. div. research grants NIH, 1974-75; program dir. metabolic diseases program Nat. Inst. Arthritis, Metabolism & Digestive Diseases, 1975-79; med. dir. Cystic Fibrosis Found., Rockville, Md., 1980—, nat. dir., 1981—. Recipient Merit award NIH, 1980. Mem. AAAS, N.Y. Acad. Scis., Sigma Xi. Presbyterian. Office: 6000 Executive Blvd Suite 309 Rockville MD 20852

BEALS, LOREN ALAN, association executive; b. Glens Falls, N.Y., Jan. 10, 1933; s. Edgar Vernon and Ruth (Ackley) B.; m. Sandra Gale Campbell, Feb. 26, 1982; children by previous marriage: Vernon Alan, Catherine Ann, Kimberly Ruth; stepchildren: Vicki Lynn Adair, Steven Montgomery Campbell, Gary Britt Campbell. B.A., Colgate U., 1954; M.P.A., Syracuse U., 1955. Intern, City of Richmond, Va., 1955-56, adminstrv. asst., City of Norfolk, Va., 1956; dir. publs., dir. town affiliations Nat. League of Cities, Washington, 1957-59, dir. congl. relations, 1970, dir. fed. affairs, 1971, dep. dir., 1972-75, exec. dir., 1975—; exec. sec. Md. Municipal League, College Park, 1959-65; dir. econ. ops. programs Met. Fund, Detroit, 1965-66; sec. Pub. Ofcls. Adv. Council, Office Econ. Opportunity, Washington, 1966-67, Great Lakes regional dir., Chgo., 1967-70; lectr. govt. and politics U. Md., 1959-65; chmn. Fed. Regional Council, Chgo., 1968-69; lectr. U. So. Calif., Los Angeles, 1977-81; founding trustee Community Found., Silver Spring, Md., 1971-75; bd. dirs. Nat. Tng. and Devel. Service, Washington, 1975-82, chmn., 1976-77; bd. dirs. Nat. Assn. Regional Councils, Washington, 1975-79, Council for Internat. Urban Liaison, 1975—, chmn., 1980-82; bd. dirs. Pub. Tech., Inc., Washington, 1975—, chmn., 1978-80, 83—; bd. dirs. Acad. for State and Local Govt., Columbus, 1975—; chmn. Acad. for Contemporary Problems, 1977-78; bd. dirs. Center for Renewal Resources, 1980-83; mem. adv. com. John F. Kennedy Sch. Govt., Harvard U., Cambridge, 1979—. Contbg. editor: Nation's Cities Weekly, 1970-75; Editor-in-chief, 1975—; editor: Md. Municipal News, 1959-65. Bd. visitors Maxwell Sch. Citizenship and Pub. Affairs, Syracuse U., 1981—. Mem. Am. Soc. Pub. Adminstrn., Nat. Acad. Pub. Adminstrn. (trustee 1978-81), Internat. City Mgmt. Assn. Methodist. Club: Univ. (Washington). Office: 1301 Pennsylvania Ave NW Washington DC 20004

BEALS, RALPH EVERETT, economist; b. Lexington, Ky., Oct. 30, 1936; s. Wendell Everett and Gratia Marie (Burns) B.; m. Mildred Ann Hubbard, Sept. 3, 1961; children—Gerald E., Ellen H. B.S., U. Ky., 1958; M.A., Northwestern U., 1959; Ph.D., Mass. Inst. Tech., 1970; M.A. (hon.), Amherst (Mass.) Coll., 1971. Asst. prof. econs. Amherst Coll., 1962-63, Northwestern U., 1963-66; assoc. prof. Amherst Coll., 1966-71, prof. econs., 1971—, Clarence Francis prof. social scis., 1980—; vis. assoc. prof. mgmt. M.I.T., 1970-71; adviser, vis. fellow, cons. Harvard U. Inst. Internat. Devel., 1973—, project asso., Indonesia, 1980-82; cons. in field. Author: Statistics for Economists: An Introduction, 1972, (with others) Tax and Investment Policies for Hard Minerals: Public and Multinational Enterprises in Indonesia, 1979; also articles. Chmn. bd. Hampshire Community Action Commn., 1969-73. Mem. Am. Econ. Assn., Econometric Soc., Am. Statis. Assn. Home: 87 Woodside Ave Amherst MA 01002 Office: Dept Econs Amherst Coll Amherst MA 01002:

BEALS, RICHARD WILLIAM, educator; b. Erie, Pa., May 28, 1938; s. Robert Manly and Alice Louise (Benemann) B.; m. Anne Gardiner Farwell, June 30, 1962; children—Katharine, Robert, Susannah. B.A., Yale U., 1960, Ph.D., 1964; student, Harvard U., 1960-61. Instr. Yale U., New Haven, 1964-65, prof. math., 1977—; asst. prof. U. Chgo., from 1965, then asso. prof., prof., until 1977; vis. prof. Duke Univ., Durham, N.C., 1974, U. Paris, 1976-77. Author: Topics in Operator Theory, 1971, Advanced Mathematical Analysis, 1973; editor: (with M.S. Baouendi) Communications in Partial Differential Equations, 1976. Mem. Am. Math. Soc., Math. Assn. Am., AAUP. Office: Math Dept Yale Univ Box 2155 Yale Station New Haven CT 06520

BEALS, VAUGHN LEROY, JR., vehicle manufacturing company executive; b. Cambridge, Mass., Jan. 2, 1928; s. Vaughn Leroy and Pearl Uela (Wilmarth) B.; m. Eleanore May Woods, July 15, 1951; children: Susan Lynn, Laurie Jean. B.S., M.I.T., 1948, M.S., 1954. Research engr. Cornell Aero. Lab., Buffalo, 1948-52, M.I.T. Aero Elastic and Structures Research Lab., 1952-55; dir. research and tech. N.Am. Aviation, Inc., Columbus, Ohio, 1955-65; exec. v.p. Cummins Engine Co., Columbus, Ind., 1965-70, also dir.; chmn. bd., chief exec. officer Formac Internat., Inc., Seattle, 1970-75; dep. group exec. Motorcycle Products Group, AMF Inc., Milw., 1975-77, v.p. and group exec. Motorcycle Products Group, Stamford, Conn., 1977-81; chmn. chief exec. officer Harley-Davidson Motor Co., Inc., Milw., 1981—. Club: University (Milw.). Home: 1707 E Fox Ln Fox Point WI 53217 Office: 3700 W Juneau Ave Milwaukee WI 53208

BEAM, CHARLES GRIER, motor transportation executive; b. Cherryville, N.C., Jan. 15, 1906; s. Charles Lefter and Nancy (Carpenter) B.; m. Lena Sue Brawley, June 14, 1936; children: Joel V., Linda Sue. Student, Brevard Coll., 1927-29; B.S., N.C. State U., 1931. Owner, Beam Trucking Co., Cherryville, 1933-37; pres., dir., chief exec. officer, mem. exec. com. Carolina Freight Carriers Corp., Cherryville, 1937—, now chmn. bd. Mem. Gaston County Bd. Commrs., 1951-77, chmn. bd., 1960-77; trustee Brevard Coll., Gaston Coll.; past dir. Children's Home Soc. of N.C., Inc. Named Cherryville Citizen of Yr., 1979; named to N.C. State Agr. Hall of Fame, 1980; recipient Disting. Alumnus award N.C. State U., 1980; Service to Mankind award Gaston County Sertoma Club, 1980; Am. Truck Hist. Soc. award as founder of trucking industry, 1980. Mem. N.C. Motor Carriers Assn. (past pres., dir.), Am. Trucking Assn. (bd. govs. 1965—). Democrat. Methodist. Clubs: Masons, Shriners, Lions. Home: Route 2 Sunbeam Rd Cherryville NC 28021 Office: PO Box 697 Cherryville NC 28021

BEAM, ROBERT THOMPSON, lawyer; b. What Cheer, Iowa, Oct. 27, 1919; s. Clyde O. and Mary Ethel (Thompson) B. B.S., U. Ill., 1951, J.D., 1954; LL.M., NYU, 1956. Bar: Ill. 1954. Assoc. firm Kramer, Marx, Greenlee & Backus, N.Y.C., 1954-57; ptnr. firm Sidley & Austin, Chgo., 1957—; dir. Piamco, Inc., Des Peres, Mo. Served to lt. col. USAAF, 1941-47; ETO; PTO. Mem. ABA, Ill. Bar Assn., Chgo. Bar Assn. Republican. Episcopalian. Clubs: Mid-Day, University. Lodge: Masons. Home: 1781 N Saunders Rd Riverwoods IL 60015 Office: Sidley & Austin One First National Plaza Chicago IL 60603

BEAM, WALTER WILLIS, oil and gas company executive; b. Denison, Tex., July 25, 1921; s. Orville Wray and Lucy Carey (Fischer) B.; m. Margaretta Beam, Sept. 11, 1943; children: Walter W., Chester W. B.S.M.E., Tex. A&M U., 1946; M.S.M.E., Okla. State U., 1952. Design engr. Dow Chem. Co., Freeport, Tex., 1946-47, Freeport Sulphur Co., 1947-48, Conoco, Inc., Ponca City, Okla., 1948—, now v.p. engring. Patentee liquified natural gas. Bd. dirs. Ponca City Opportunity Ctr. Served with USAF, 1943-45; CBI. Decorated D.F.C. with two oak leaf clusters, Air medal with seven oak leaf clusters, others. Mem. Ponca City C. of C., Okla. soc. PLrofl. engrs. (past pres. chpt.), Am petroleum Inst. (past chmn. com. refinery equipment). Democrat. Mem. Ch. of Christ (elder). Lodge: Rotary. Home: 716 W Overbrook St Ponca City OK 74601 Office: PO Box 1267 Ponca City OK 74603

BEAMAN, RICHARD BANCROFT, artist; b. Waltham, Mass., June 28, 1909; s. George Burnham and Mary (Burnham) B.; m. Jeanne Hays, Mar. 12, 1944; children: Peter Hays, Joanna Beaman Whitt, Valerie, Christina. S.B., Harvard U., 1932; M.Div., Union Theol. Sem., 1935. Mem. faculty U. Redlands, 1939-42, 46-55; prof. Carnegie-Mellon U., Pitts., 1955-74, now prof. art emeritus. Exhibited, Carnegie Mus. Art, 1961, Arts and Crafts Center, 1969, Argent Gallerie, N.Y.C., 1938, Pitts. Plan for Art, 1962, 67, 70, 74, 78, Art Complex Mus., Duxbury, Mass., 1977, Zenith Gallery, Pitts., 1981, group shows in, N.Y.C., Los Angeles, Phila., Washington, Pitts. museums and galleries; invited to show, Carnegie Internat., 1958. Served with USNR, 1942-45. Tiffany Travel grantee, 1965; Ford fellow, 1950. Home: Penryn Ln Rockport MA 01966 *Neither mother, bible nor whiskey so much as an impossible hope for wholeness nags me into trying.*

BEAMENT, THOMAS HAROLD, artist; b. Ottawa, Ont., Can., July 23, 1898; s. Herman Joseph Brooker and Lillian (Perkins) B.; m. Ida Lawson McDougall, Oct. 14, 1939; 1 son, Thomas Harold. Student, Law Sch. Upper Can., 1919-22, Ont. Coll. Art, 1922. Bar: Called to Ont. bar 1923. Practiced law, Ottawa, 1923; tchr. Montreal Mus. Fine Arts, 1936-37; judge Newfoundland Govt. Art Competition, 1954, 55, 56, 57; fellow N.S. Coll. Art, 1962. Can. Fine arts rep., Brit. Empire Expn., 1924; free-lance comml. designer, Montreal, 1925-30; executed murals, Seignory Club, 1930-31; represented in permanent collections including, Nat. Gallery, Ottawa, Montreal Mus. Fine Arts, Provincial Art Gallery, Quebec, Art Gallery, Hamilton, Art Gallery of London, Ont., Beaverbrook Gallery, Edmonton, Alta., McGill U., Montreal, Queen's U., Kingston, Ont., Canadian Club, N.Y.C.; designer: Canadian Eskimo stamp, 1955. Served to comdr. Royal Can. Naval Vol. Res., 1917-18, 39-47. Recipient Jessie Dow award Montreal Mus. Fine Arts, 1935; Centennial medal, 1967; Queen's Jubilee medal, 1977. Academician Royal Can. Acad. Arts (pres. 1964-67). Home: 1160 St Mathieu St Apt 208 Montreal PQ H3H 2P4 Canada

BEAMENT, THOMAS HAROLD (TIB BEAMENT), painter, printmaker, educator; b. Montreal, Que., Can., Feb. 17, 1941; s. Thomas Harold and Ida Lawson (McDougall) B. O level cert. (Crerar scholar), Fettes Coll., Edinburgh, Scotland, 1959; diploma, Beaux-Arts Montreal, 1963; student (Italian Govt. scholar), Belle Arti, Rome, 1963-64; postgrad. graphics and teaching cert., U. Quebec, Que., 1969; M.A. in Art Edn, Sir George Williams U., Montreal, 1972. Tchr. art; dir. art dept. Edgars and Cramps Sch., Montreal, 1966-78; lectr. in drawing and design Concordia U.; lectr. in drawing McGill U.; tchr. painting and drawing for adult edn., 1971-75; mem. program com. Montreal Mus. Fine Arts. One-man shows, Galerie Irla Kert, Montreal, 1965, Galeries Place Royale, Montreal, 1966, Gallery 1640, Montreal, 1968, 73, Mitchell Gallery, Toronto, 1970, Poole Gallery, Toronto, 1975, Klinkhoff Gallery, Montreal, 1976, 79, 81, Union Bank of Switzerland, Zurich, 1981, group shows include, 4th Biennial Paris, 1965, Internat. Exhbn. N.W. Printmakers, Seattle, 1st Biennial Graphics, Crakow, Poland, 1966, Internat. Exhbn. Graphics, Montreal, 1971, Internat. Art Fair, Basel, Switzerland, 1974, 2d Biennale de la Peinture, Montreal, 1979, A Canadian Start in Art, Canada House, London, Eng., 1979; represented in permanent collections, Tate Gallery, London, Mus. Modern Art, N.Y.C., Mus. Rio de Janeiro, Brazil, Nat. Gallery Can., Ottawa, Ont., Art Inst. Chgo. Mem. exec. com. bd. dirs. Greenshields Found. Recipient spl. mention Price Fine Arts Awards, 1970; Heinz Jordan award for drawing Internat. Graphics Exhbn., Montreal, 1971; Can. Council grantee, 1966; Que. Govt. grantee, 1966, 73; Greenshields Found. grantee, 1971, 75. Mem. Royal Can. Acad. Arts (council), Accademia Italia delle Arti, Conceil de La Peinture de Quebec, Print and Drawing Council Can. Home and Office: RR 1 Ayers Cliff PQ J0B 1C0 Canada

BEAN, ALAN L., retired astronaut; b. Wheeler, Tex., Mar. 15, 1932; s. Arnold H. B.; children: Clay, Amy. B.S. in Aero. Engring, U. Tex., 1955; grad., USN Test Pilot Sch.; Dr. Sci. (hon.), Tex. Wesleyan U., 1972, U. Akron. Commd. ensign U.S. Navy, 1955, advanced through grades to capt.; test pilot various aircraft, Patuxent, Md., 1960-63; astronaut Manned Spacecraft Center, NASA, 1963—, lunar module pilot Apollo XII, 1969, ret., 1975. Now artist specializing in themes of space exploration. Decorated D.S.M. with cluster, Navy Astronaut Wings; Navy Disting. Service medal with cluster; recipient Man of Yr. award Tex. Press Assn., 1969; Rear Adm. William S. Parsons award, 1970; Disting. Engring. Grad. award U. Tex., 1970; Godfrey L. Cabot award, 1970; Spl. Trustees award Nat. Acad. TV Arts and Scis., 1970; Yuri Gagarin award AIAA, 1974. Fellow Am. Astron. Soc.; mem. Delta Kappa Epsilon. 4th man to walk on moon; comdr. 2d Skylab mission, set record 59 days in space; back-up comdr. Apollo-Soyuz Test Project in 1975; Holds 10 world records in aeros. and astronautics. Home and Studio: 11711 Memorial Dr Unit 267 Houston TX 77024

BEAN, ATHERTON, business exec.; b. New Prague, Minn., Sept. 14, 1910; s. Francis Atherton and Bertha Juanita (Boynton) B.; m. Winifred E. Wollaeger, June 26, 1934; children: Douglas Atherton, Bruce William. Student, Blake Sch.; A.B. summa cum laude, Carleton Coll., 1931; B.A. (Rhodes scholar), Oxford U., 1934; postgrad., Harvard Sch. Bus. Adminstrn., 1931-32. With Upjohn Co., Dallas, 1934-36, duPont Co., Wilmington, Del., 1936-37; price exec. OPA, Washington, 1942-43; joined Internat. Milling Co. (co. name changed to Internat. Multifoods), Mpls., 1937, exec. v.p., 1944-55, pres., 1955-64, chmn., chief exec., 1964-68, chmn. exec. com., 1968—; chmn. bd. 9th dist. Fed. Res. Bank, 1961-65; dir. First Bank Mpls., 1946-60, 66-76, Bus. Internat., 1969-83. Trustee Mpls. Soc. Fine Arts, 1964-78, chmn. bd., 1975-76, vice chmn. bd., 1969-75, 76-78; trustee Mayo Found., Rochester, 1964-78, chmn. bd., 1969-76; trustee Carleton Coll., Northfield, Minn., 1944—, chmn. bd., 1961-68; trustee Mpls. Found., 1961-80, Sci. Mus. Minn., 1972-80; bd. dirs. Nat. Bur. Econ. Research, 1970-79; apptd. by Pres. Nixon to Spl. Task Force on Econ. Growth, 1969, to Presdl. Commn. on Fin. Structure and Regulation, 1970. Served as civilian spl. br. M.I., 1943-44. Home: 1212 Mount Curve Ave Minneapolis MN 55403 Office: 901 Midwest Plaza East Minneapolis MN 55402

BEAN, CHARLES PALMER, biophysicist; b. Buffalo, Nov. 27, 1923; s. Barton Adrian and Theresa (Palmer) B.; m. Elizabeth Harriman, Sept. 13, 1947; children: Katherine G., Bruce P., Margaret E., Sarah H., Gordon T. B.A., U. Buffalo, 1947, M.A., U. Ill., 1948, Ph.D., 1952. Research scientist Gen. Electric Co., Schenectady, 1951—; adj. asso. prof. Renssalear Poly. Inst., Troy, N.Y., 1957-67, adj. prof., 1978—, Disting. prof., 1983—; adj. prof. SUNY, 1978—, Union Coll., Schenectady, 1981—; guest investigator Rockefeller U., N.Y.C., 1973-76. Contbr. articles to profl. jours.; asso. editor: Biophys. Jour., 1974—. Bd. dirs. Dudley Obs., Albany, N.Y., 1975—, pres., 1983—; Bd. dirs. Bellevue Research Found., Schenectady, 1973—. Served with USAAF, 1943-46. Fellow Am. Phys. Soc.; mem. Biophys. Soc., N.Y. State Acad. Scis., Am. Acad. Arts and Scis., Nat. Acad. Sci. Clubs: Fortnightly (Schenectady); Chemists (N.Y.C.). Patentee in field. Home: 2221 Stoneridge Rd Schenectady NY 12309 Office: Box 8 Schenectady NY 12301:

BEAN, GERALD ALAN, publishing executive; b. Peoria, Ill., Mar. 17, 1943; s. Harold Franklin and Shirley Jane (Dreiman) B.; m. Brenda Margreta Carlson, May 28, 1967; children—Scott, Eric. B.S. in Journalism, U. Ill., Urbana, 1966. With Rockford (Ill.) Register Star, 1966-81, gen. mgr., 1978-79, pres., pub., 1979-81; gen. mgr. Gannett Satellite Info. Network, Washington, 1981-82, USA Today, 1982-83; v.p. Gannett West Newspaper Group, 1983—; pub., pres. Sun, San Bernardino, Calif., 1983—. Bd. Dirs. Inland Action, Inc.; bd. dirs. Inland Action Cultural Found., St. Bernardine Hosp. Found.; corp. bd. San Bernardino Hosp. Mem. Am. Newspaper Pubs. Assn., Calif. Newspaper Pubs. Assn. Office: 399 N D St San Bernardino CA 92401

BEAN, JACOB, museum curator; b. Stillwater, Minn., Nov. 22, 1923; s. William Bronson and Lurain (Eichten) B. Student, Harvard U., 1941-45. Chargé de mission Cabinet des Dessins Musée du Louvre, Paris, 1957-60, chargé de mission honoraire, 1960—; asst. curator charge drawings Met. Mus. Art, 1960-62, assoc. curator, 1962, curator, 1963—; adj. prof. fine arts N.Y. U., 1967-80. Author: Les Dessins Italiens de la Collection Bonnat, 1960, 100 European Drawings in the Metropolitan Museum of Art, 1964, Italian Drawings in the Art Museum, Princeton University, 1966, Dessins Français du Metropolitan Museum, 1973, 17th Century Italian Drawings in the Metropolitan Museum of Art, 1979, 15th and 16th Century Italian Drawings in the Metropolitan Museum of Art, 1982; co-author: Drawings from New York Collections I, The Italian Renaissance, 1965, II, The Seventeenth Century in Italy, 1967, III, The Eighteenth Century in Italy, 1971; assoc. editor: Master Drawings mag, 1962—. Clubs: Athenaeum, Turf (London). Office: Met Mus of Art Fifth Ave and 82d St New York NY 10028

BEAN, JOAN P., psychology educator; b. Chgo., Jan. 3, 1933; d. Christopher C. and Loretta A. (Keenan) O'Leary; children: Darcy, Mac, Christopher, Caitlin. B.A., Calif. State U., San Jose, 1966, M.A., 1968; Ph.D., U. Calif.-Berkeley, 1971. Asst. prof. psychology Calif. State U., San Jose, 1967-71; research assoc. U. Calif., Berkeley, 1968-70; asst. prof. psychology U. Mass., 1971-76; dean Wheaton Coll., Norton, Mass., 1976-78, Richard L. Conolly Coll., Bklyn, Center, L.I. U., 1978-80; vis. exec. Dept. Commerce, Am. Council on Edn., 1981; prof. psychology Coll. Liberal Arts, Fairleigh Dickinson U., Teaneck,

N.J., 1981—, dean, 1981-83. Co-editor: Beyond Sex-role Stereotypes: Toward a Psychology of Androgyny, 1976. Office of Edn. fellow, 1966-68; NIH fellow, 1968-71; NSF grantee, 1972; Carnegie Found. fellow, 1974, 75-76; ACE vis. exec., 1981. Mem. Am. Women in Sci., Am. Council Acad. Deans, Am. Psychol. Assn., Am. Ednl. Research Assn. Office: Fairleigh Dickinson Univ 1000 River Rd Teaneck NJ 07666

BEAN, JOHN MALCOLM WILLIAM, educator; b. Bridgend, Glamorgan, Wales, Aug. 25, 1928; came to U.S., 1968; s. William Alfred and Elizabeth (Davies) B. B.A. (A.M.P. Read scholar), Queen's Coll., Oxford U., 1949, D. Phil, 1953. Asst. lectr. U. Manchester, Eng., 1956-59, lectr., 1959-67; prof. Columbia, N.Y.C., 1968—, chmn. dept. history, 1973-80. Author: The Estates of the Percy Family, 1416-1537, 1958, The Decline of English Feudalism, 1215-1540, 1968. Am. Council Learned Socs. fellow, 1976-77. Fellow Royal Hist. Soc. Home: Hildreth Rd Bridgehampton NY 11932 Office: 622 Fayerweather Hall Columbia U New York NY 10027

BEAN, MAURICE DARROW, diplomat; b. Gary, Ind., Sept. 9, 1928; s. Everett Thomas and Vera Mae (Curry) B.; m. Dolores J. Winston, Apr. 9, 1972; children: Linda D., Karen M., Laura L., James W., Jennifer J. B.A. in Govt, Howard U., 1950; M.A. in Social and Tech. Assistance, Haverford Coll., 1953; postgrad., cert., Sch. Advanced Internat. Studies, Johns Hopkins, 1959. With U.S. Bur. Census, 1950-51, AID, 1951-61; with Peace Corps, 1961-66, ops. officer for, Malaysia and Indonesia, 1961-62, regional program officer for, Far East, 1962-63, dep. regional dir., 1963-64, dir., Phillipines, 1964-66, Malaysia and Singapore affairs Bur. East. Asian and Pacific Affairs, Dept. State, 1966-70; mem. Sr. Seminar in Fgn. Policy, 1970-71; Am. consul, Ibadan, Nigeria, 1971-73; dep. chief mission Am. Embassy, Monrovia, Liberia, 1973-76; sr. fgn. service insp., 1976-77, ambassador to, Socialist Republic of Union of Burma, 1977-79; diplomat-in-residence Case Western Res. U., Cleve., 1979-80; State Dept. adv. to comdr. Air U., Maxwell AFB, Ala., 1980—. Active Neighbors, Inc., Washington. Recipient Superior Honor award Dept. State, 1977, Outstanding Service award Gary Host and Hostess Club, 1979, Benjamin Hooks award NAACP, 1980; Named to Roosevelt High Sch. Hall of Fame, 1980; Christopher Reynolds Found. fellow, 1953; William E. Mosher Meml. scholar, 1961. Mem. Am. Fgn. Service Assn., Am. Sch. Assn., Manila Urban League, Omega Psi Phi. Clubs: Royal Bangkok (Thailand); Sports (life). Home: 341 Sequoia Dr Maxwell AFB AL 36113 Office: AU/CAS Bldg 1401 Maxwell AFB AL 36112 *Opportunity does not knock. It must be sought, pursued, developed and, ultimately, utilized to the fullest.*

BEAN, ORSON (DALLAS FREDERICK BURROWS), actor, comedian; b. Burlington, Vt., July 22, 1928; s. George and Marian (Pollard) Burrows; m. Jacqueline De Sibour, July 2, 1956 (div. 1962); 1 dau.; m. Carolyn Maxwell, Oct. 3, 1965; 2 sons, 1 dau. Ed., Cambridge, Mass. Started as night club performer, Blue Angel, N.Y.C., 1952; stage debut in: summer stock The Spider, 1945; later appeared in: Goodbye Again, 1948, Josephine, 1953, The School for Scandal, 1953, The Scarecrow, 1953, Men of Distinction, 1953, Almanac, 1953, Will Success Spoil Rock Hunter?, 1955, Mr. Roberts, 1956, Nature's Way, 1957, Say, Darling, 1959, Subways Are for Sleeping, 1961, Never Too Late, 1961, Home Movies, 1964, I Was Dancing, 1964, Roar of the Greasepaint-Smell of the Crowd, 1965, Ilya Darling, 1969, Promises, Promises, Australia, 1971; film debut in: How To Be Very, Very Popular, 1955; later appeared in: Anatomy of a Murder, 1959, Skateboard, 1978, TV appearances, 1953—; former regular panelist on: To Tell the Truth; also appears other panel, talk shows; voice in: TV cartoon spl. The Hobbitt, 1979; Author: Me and the Orgone, 1971. Founder, adminstrv. dir. Fifteenth St. Sch., sch. for children based on Summerhill model, N.Y.C., 1964—. Served with AUS, 1946-47; Japan. Mem. Actors Equity Assn., AFTRA, Screen Actors Guild. *

BEAN, ROBERT BEVERIDGE, zoologist; b. Oak Park, Ill., Feb. 7, 1933; s. Robert Anderson and Janet (Beveridge) B.; m. Joan Ellen Alderson, May 20, 1954; children: Pamela, Janet, Ellen. Student, U. Fla., Fla. So. Coll. Animal keeper Chgo. Zool. Park, Brookfield, Ill., 1956-61; with Resources Research, lakeland, Fla., 1961-63; staff asst. zool. dept. Busch Gardens, Tampa, Fla., 1963-64; curator animals, asst. dir. Jimmy Morgan Zoo, Birmingham, Ala., 1964-67; zool. dir., zoo mgr. Anheuser-Busch Gardens, Tampa, Fla., 1967-71, gen. mgr., Tampa, 1971-74; dir. Louisville Zool. Gardens, 1974—. Trustee Wild Animal Propagation Trust; mem. Fla. Wildlife Exhibitors Criteria Com. Served with Armed Forces, 1953-55. Recipient Edward H. Bean award, cert. of appriciation for service in futherance conservation of fish and wildlife resources State of Fla. Mem. Louisville C. of C. Lodge: Rotary. Home: 1615 Windsor Pl Louisville KY 40204 Office: Louisville Zool Garden PO Box 37250 Louisville KY 40233

BEAN, VERNALD FLOYD, manufacturing executive; b. Monida, Mont., Aug. 8, 1929; s. Farmer Floyd and Ethel Marie (Blake) B.; m. Patricia Jane Powers, Apr. 24, 1954; children: John J., David J., Thomas E. Ed. pub. schs. With NCR Corp., 1952—, field engr., 1952-66, dir. field engring. services, 1966-71, ops. mgr. internat. mfg., 1971-75, dir. internat. mfg., 1974-77, v.p. components and support div., 1977-80, v.p. corporate field engring., 1980-83, v.p. customer services, 1983—. Served with U.S. Army, 1947-50. Mem. Dayton C. of C. Republican. Roman Catholic. Club: KC. Home: 2925 Lower Bellbrook Rd Spring Valley OH 45370 Office: 1700 S Patterson Blvd Dayton OH 45479

BEAN, WILLIAM BENNETT, physician; b. Manila, Philippines, Nov. 8, 1909; s. Robert Bennett and Adelaide Leiper (Martin) B.; m. Abigail Shepard, June 17, 1939; children: Robert Bennett, Margaret Harvey, John Perrin. B.A., U. Va., 1932, M.D., 1935. Diplomate: Am. Bd. Internal Medicine, Am. Bd. Nutrition. Intern Johns Hopkins Hosp., 1935-36; asst. resident physician Boston City Hosp., 1936-37; sr. med. resident Cin. Gen. Hosp., 1937-38, asst. attending physician, 1941-46, clinician out-patient dept., 1946-48, attending physician, 1946-48; asst. prof. medicine U. Cin. Med. Coll., 1940-47, asso. prof., 1947-48; prof. medicine, head dept. internal medicine U. Iowa Coll. Medicine, 1948-70; physician-in-chief Univ. Hosps., 1948-70, Sir William Osler prof. medicine, 1970—; Kempner prof., dir. Inst. for Med. Humanities (U. Tex. Med. Br.), Galveston, 1974-80, acting head dept. dermatology, 1977-78; vis. prof. medicine and history of medicine U. Va., 1968; Frank and Tommye Rose vis. prof. medicine U. Ala., 1976; sr. med. cons. VA, 1947—. Author: Sir William Osler: From His Bedside Teachings and Writings, 3d edit, 1968, Vascular Spiders and Related Lesions of the Skin, 1958, Aphorisms from Latham, 1962, Rare Diseases and Lesions: Their Contribution to Clinical Medicine, 1967, Walter Reed: A Biography, 1982; Editor: Monographs in Medicine, 1951-52; book review editor of: Archives of Internal Medicine, 1955-62; editor in chief, 1962-67; editorial cons.: Modern Medicine, 1964-67, Stedman's Med. Dictionary, Familiar Medical Quotations; editor: Current Med. Dialog, 1967-75; editor-in-chief: Tex. Reports Biology and Medicine, 1976-80. Bd. regents Nat. Library Medicine, 1957-61, 1965-69; chmn., 1960-61. Served from capt. to lt. col. M.C. AUS, 1942-46. Recipient John Horsley Meml. prize U. Va., 1944; Groedel medal, 1961; Gold-Headed Cane, 1964; McCollum award, 1974; Disting. Head of Medicine award, 1982; named Ky. col.; hon. adm. Tex. Navy. Fellow Am. Coll. Chest Physicians (past gov. Iowa), Am. Med. Writers Assn., AAAS, ACP (past gov. Iowa, master 1971); mem. Am. Coll. Cardiology (past gov. Iowa), Nat. Assn. Standard Med. Vocabulary (dir.), Nockian Soc., AMA, Soc. Exptl. Biology and Medicine, Soc. Med. Cons. to Armed Forces, Am. Coll. Sports Medicine (charter), N.Y. Acad. Scis., Am. Acad. Polit. and Social Sci., Archeology Inst. Am. (pres. Iowa chpt. 1955-57), Am. Clin. and Climatol. Assn. (pres. 1967-68), Am. Assn. Study Liver Diseases (charter), Am. Assn. Med. History, Am. Soc. Tropical Medicine, Am. Heart Assn. (exec. com., sci. council), Iowa Heart Assn. (pres. 1950), Iowa Med. Soc., Assn. Mil. Surgeons, Med. and Jockey Soc. Interior Valley N.Am., Tb and Health Assn., Central Interurban Clin. Club (pres. 1959-61), Am. Soc. Clin. Nutrition (pres. 1962-63), John Fulton Soc. (charter mem.), Iowa Clin. Soc., World Med. Assn., Am. Osler Soc. (charter, 1st pres. 1970—), Assn. Am. Physicians, Central Soc. Clin. Research (councilor 1946-49, pres. 1951), Sociedad Mexicana Historia y Filosofia de Medicina, Phi Beta Kappa, Sigma Xi, Alpha Omega Alpha. Episcopalian. Clubs: Cosmos (Washington); Stuart and Tudor (Johns Hopkins); Artillery (Galveston). Home: 11 Rowland Ct Iowa City IA 52240 *I must express profound indebtedness to parents and family, wife and children for nurture, stimulus, and a good environment for living and learning. Enduring curiosity led me to careers as clinic investigator, physician, teacher, editor, and institute director, most of the time seeing students and patients nearly every day. My essays, book reviews, and scientific monographs have increasingly dealt with moral and ethical aspects of medicine. The ability to laugh, especially at myself, diminishes the likelihood that pride will grow into pomposity. Good fortune in opportunities and health remind me not to underestimate the importance of luck.*

BEANE, ALPHEUS C., investment banker; b. Augusta, Ga., July 10, 1910; s. Alpheus C. and Marian E. (Bignon) B.; m. Jean A. Tegder, Feb. 26, 1938; children: Alpheus C., Mary C., Marian; m. Elizabeth Geren Souchon., Aug. 21, 1956. B.S., Yale, 1931. Clk. Fenner & Beane, N.Y.C., 1931, gen. partner, 1935, Merrill Lynch, Pierce, Fenner & Beane, 1941-58; directing partner J.R. Williston and Beane, N.Y.C., 1958-63; v.p., dir. Walston & Co., 1963-64; partner Reynolds & Co., 1965-71; v.p., mem. exec. com. Reynolds Securities Inc., N.Y.C., 1971-77; v.p. Dean Witter, Reynolds Inc., Delray Beach, Fla., 1977—; Pres. Commodity Club N.Y., 1952-53; Gov. Wool Assos. N.Y. Cotton Exchange, 1952-53; bd. mgrs. Cocoa Exchange, 1958-60; bd. govs. Am. Stock Exchange, 1938-42. Served to maj. with USAAF, 1942-45. Clubs: Round Hill, Stock Exchange Lunch, Gulfstream Golf, Ocean. Home: 67 Spanish River Dr Ocean Ridge FL 33435 Office: 1010 E Atlantic Ave Delray Beach FL 33444

BEAR, CHARLES BENSON, magazine publisher; b. Washington, Iowa, Mar. 12, 1919; s. Charles H. and Grace (Benson) B. B.A., Grinnell Coll., 1939; M.A., Fletcher Sch. Law and Diplomacy, 1940. With Gallup Poll, Am. Inst. Pub. Opinion, Princeton, N.J., 1940-41; adminstrv. asst. Office Govt. Reports, Chgo., 1941-42; bus. mgr. Time-Life Internat., 1945-49, dep. mng. dir., 1960-64, mng. dir., 1965-68; bus. mgr. Fortune mag., 1949-53, assoc. pub., 1953-60; gen. mgr. Archtl. Forum, 1954-60; v.p. internat. Time Inc., 1965-69, adminstrv. v.p., 1969-72; group v.p., sec. 1972—, dir., 1977—; past chmn., now mem. exec. com. Ethics Resource Ctr., Inc. Trustee Grinnell Coll.; mem. exec. bd. Support Ctr.; bd. dirs. Friends of Earth Found.; mem. U.S. Olympic Com. Served from pvt. to capt. USAAF, 1942-45. Mem. Internat. C. of C. (trustee U.S. council), Internat. Mktg. Inst. (bd. dirs.). Home: 127 E 71st St New York NY 10021 also E Mountain Rd N Cold Spring-on-Hudson NY 10516 Office: Time-Life Bldg Rockefeller Center New York NY 10020

BEAR, STANLEY HERMAN, physician, ret. air force officer; b. Newville, Pa., June 6, 1921; s. Samuel Herman and Elsie Claire (Ginter) B.; m. Jacqueline Jarman Silver, Nov. 17, 1951; children—Susan Jarman, Vicki Lee, Nancy Claire, Stanley David. B.S. in Biology, Bucknell U., 1943; M.D., Temple U., 1946. Diplomate: Am. Bd. Otolaryngology. Intern Temple U. Hosp., Phila., 1946-47; resident in otolaryngology Ill. Eye and Ear Infirmary, Chgo., 1952-54, chief resident, 1953-54; commd. 1st lt. USAF, 1947, advanced through grades to brig. gen., 1972; mem. Air Rescue Service staff, Westover AFB, Mass., 1948-49; Flight Surgeon Sch., Randolph AFB, Tex., 1949; chief aviation medicine, Westover AFB, 1949-50; flight surgeon 20th Fighter Bomber Group, England and; Shaw AFB, S.C., 1950-51, chief otolaryngology and aviation medicine, Maxwell AFB, Ala., 1954-59, chief otolaryngology, Wiesbaden, Germany, 1959-61, hosp. comdr., dir. bioastronautics, Edwards AFB, Calif., 1961-66; vice-comdr. Sch. Aerospace Medicine, Brooks AFB, Tex., 1966-67; surgeon 7th Air Force, Vietnam, 1967-68; dep. surgeon Pacific Air Forces, Hawaii, 1968-69; asst. physician to Pres. U.S., Washington, 1969-71; chief med. inspn. Hdqrs. USAF, Norton AFB, Calif., 1971-72; surgeon Mil. Airlift Command, Scott AFB, Ill., 1972-73; ret., 1973; med. dir. U. Redlands, Calif., 1974—; clin. instr. head and neck surgery U. Calif. at Los Angeles, 1974—; dir. otolaryngology San Bernardino County Med. Center, 1974—; Teaching asst. in otolaryngology U. Ill., Chgo., 1952-53; instr., 1953-54; cons. in otolaryngology Surgeon USAF Europe, 1959-61. Chmn. Community Fund Drive, Edwards, Calif., 1963. Decorated D.S.M., Legion of Merit, D.F.C., Air Medals; recipient Distinguished Alumni award Bucknell U., 1976. Fellow Aerospace Med. Assn. (exec. com. 1965), ACS, Internat. Coll. Surgeons, Coll. Preventive Medicine, Am. Acad. Otolaryngology and Opthalomology; mem. AMA, Am. Council Otolaryngology, Soc. USAF Flight Surgeons (pres. 1965), USAF Clin. Surgeons (treas. 1956), Soc. Mil. Otolaryngologists (pres. 1957), Air Force Assn., Bucknell U., Temple U., alumni assns., Otolaryngol. Alumni Assn. U. Ill. (pres. 1965, 73), Delta Upsilon, Phi Chi. Club: Muroc Lake Golf (pres. bd. govs. 1964). Home: 646 Palo Alto Dr Redlands CA 92373 Office: San Bernardino County Med Center 780 E Gilbert San Bernardino CA 92404

BEARCE, JEANA DALE, painter, educator; b. St. Louis, Oct. 3, 1929; d. Clarence Russell and Maria Emily Dale; m. Lawrence F. Rakovan, June 7, 1969; children: Barbara Emily, Luke, Francesca. B.F.A., Washington U., St. Louis, 1951; M.A., N.Mex. Highlands U., 1954. Vis. artist, varipus lectureships, India, Pakistan, 1961-62; founder art dept. U. Maine-Portland, 1965, chmn. and dept. rep., 1965-70, asst. prof. art, 1967-70, assoc. prof., 1970-81, prof., 1982—. Exhibited one-woman show, Portland Mus. Art, Maine, 1958, U. Maine, Orono, 1958, 65, 69, 77, 80, Madras Govt. Mus., India, 1962, Gallery 65, Paris, 1964, Bristol Mus. Art, R.I., 1965, Center Gallery, N.Y.C., 1974, Benbow Gallery, Newport, R.I., 1979, others, group show, Boston Mus. Art, Library of Congress, Phila. Print Club, Springfield Mus., Mo., Birmingham Mus. Art, Ala., others; represented permanent collection, St. Louis Art Mus., U.S. Edn. Found. in India, New Delhi, U. Maine, Orono and Portland, Bklyn. Mus. Art, Cornell U. Mus. Art, Calif. Coll. Arts and Crafts, Sarasota Art Assn., Fla., Bowdoin Coll., Brunswick, Maine; executed murals, N.Mex. Highlands U., Bowdoin Longfellow-Hawthorn Library, Brunswick, sculpture reliefs, St. Bartholomew, Cape Elizabeth, Maine, St. Charles Ch. Brunswick. Mem. artist's com. Maine Art Gallery, 1957-75; mem. Maine com. Skowhegan Sch. Painting and Sculpture, 1972—. Recipient various awards, Fannie Cook award People's Art Ctr., St. Louis, Prix de Paris N.Y. Nat. Competition, 1958, 59. Mem. Bowdoin Coll. Mus. Assocs. Home: 327 Maine St Brunswick ME 04011 Office: U So Maine Coll Ave Gorham ME 04038

BEARD, CHARLES BABCOCK, insurance consultant; b. Niagara Falls, N.Y., Jan. 13, 1936; s. Charles L. and Marion (Babcock) B.; children—Patricia, Joan, Laura. B.A., Denison U., Granville, Ohio, 1958; postgrad exec. program, Stanford U., 1978. C.L.U. With Aetna Life & Casualty Ins. Co., 1958-80, nat. dir. career agys., 1975-78, regional v.p. Mid-Atlantic region, 1978-80; pres., chief operating officer Colonial Life & Accident Ins. Co., Columbia, S.C., 1980-82; cons., Columbia, S.C., 1982—; pres. Maine Assn. Life Underwriters, 1970-71; trustee Maine Ins. Council, 1972-73; bd. dirs. Aetna Life Ins. Co. Ill., 1974-75. Bd. dirs. Jr. Achievement, Hartford, Conn., 1978-80. Mem. Am. Assn. C.L.U.'s. Independent. Episcopalian. Home: 201 Cricket Hill Rd Columbia SC 29206

BEARD, CHARLES IRVIN, research physicist; b. Ambridge, Pa., Nov. 30, 1916; s. Vivian Dangerfield and Sara (See) B.; m. Nancy Lee Jones, June 20, 1948; children: Charles Clifford, William David. B.S. in E.E, Carnegie Inst. Tech., 1938; Ph.D. in Physics, M.I.T., 1948. Engring. asst. Westinghouse Research Labs., Pitts., 1938-39; sr. physicist Magnolia Petroleum Labs., Dallas, 1948-50, Applied Physics Lab., Johns Hopkins U., Laurel, Md., 1950-56; sr. engring. specialist Sylvania Electronic Def. Lab., Mountain View, Calif., 1956-62; mem. staff Boeing Sci. Research Lab., Seattle, 1962-71; research physicist Naval Research Lab., Washington, 1971-82. Asso. editor: Radio Sci, 1973-75; contbr. articles to profl. jours. Served to maj. Signal Corps U.S. Army, 1941-46. Fellow IEEE (John Bolljahn Meml. award 1962), Am. Phys. Soc., AAAS, Internat. Sci. Radio Union (chmn. Commn. F. 1970-73, U.S. nat. com. 1974-76), Sigma Xi, Tau Beta Pi, Phi Kappa Phi, Theta Tau, Kappa Sigma. Unitarian. Patentee in field. Home: 4309 Ann Fitz Hugh Dr Annandale VA 22003

BEARD, DAVID BREED, physicist, educator; b. Needham, Mass., Feb. 1, 1922; s. Daniel Breed and Anne (Curran) B.; m. Eileen Mona Hersey, Mar. 5, 1945 (div. June 15, 1973); children: Lawrence Bennett, Jonathan Breckenridge, Valerie Curran, Dian Beard Curran. B.S., Hamilton Coll., 1943; postgrad., Calif. Inst. Tech., 1943-44; Ph.D., Cornell U., Ithaca, N.Y., 1951. Instr. Cath. U. Am., Washington, 1950-51, U. Conn., Storrs, 1951-53; asst. prof. U. Calif.-Davis, 1953-56, 58-59, asso. prof., 1959-62, prof., 1962-64; staff scientist Lockheed Missiles & Space Co., Palo Alto, Calif., 1956-58; chmn. dept. physics and astronomy U. Kans., Lawrence, 1964-77, prof. physics, 1964-77, univ. disting. prof., 1977—; Cons. pvt. cos., govt. agys. Author: Quantum Mechanics, 1963, Quantum Mechanics With Applications, 1970; Contbr. articles to profl. jours. Nat. Acad. Sci.-NRC fellow, 1962, 63, 68; Fulbright scholar; Guggenheim fellow, U.K., 1965-66; NATO sr. postdoctoral fellow, 1972; U.K. SRC sr. fellow Imperial Coll., 1978-79. Fellow Am. Phys. Soc., AAAS; mem. AAUP, Am. Geophys. Union, Fedn. Am. Scientists, Sigma Xi, Sigma Pi Sigma. Home: 1203 W 20th St Terr Lawrence KS 66044

BEARD, ELIZABETH LETITIA, physiologist, educator; b. New Orleans, Apr. 2, 1932; d. Howard Horace and Irene (Handley) B. B.A. in Biology, Tex. Christian U., 1952, B.S. in Med. Tech, 1953, M.S., 1955; postgrad., Smith Coll., 1953-54, Vanderbilt U., 1954-55; Ph.D. in Animal Physiology (Libby Research fellow), Tulane U. Sch. Medicine, 1961. Instr. dept. biol. scis. Loyola U., New Orleans, 1955-58, asst. prof., 1958-62, chmn. premed. com., 1978—; research asso. dept. physiology Tulane U. Sch. Medicine, New Orleans, 1960-63, asso. prof., 1962-68, prof., 1969—, prof. biology med. reinforcement and enrichment program, 1968—; vis. prof. dept. physiology and biophysics Harvard Med. Sch., 1983-84. Contbr. articles on research in physiology to profl. publs. Mem. project rev. com. New Orleans Health Planning Council, 1974-77, bd. dirs., 1975-78; soprano soloist Christ Ch. Cathedral and Holy Name of Jesus Ch., 1967—; pres. sch. bd. Holy Name of Jesus Ch., 1976-79; mem. Met. Mus. Art, N.Y.C., 1974—, New Orleans Mus. Art, 1975—; grad. research com. La. chapter Am. Heart Assn., 1970-72, 81—, undergrad. research com., 1978-81. NIH grantee, 1962-64, 67-69; La. Heart Assn. grantee, 1966-67; Edward Schleider Found. grantee, 1974-77; New Orleans Cancer Assn. grantee. Mem. Am. Inst. Biol. Scis., Assn. Southeastern Biologists, AAUP, AAAS, N.Y. Acad. Scis., Am. Physiol. Soc., Soc. Exptl. Biology and Medicine, Sigma Xi. Home: 6127 Garfield St New Orleans LA 70118 Office: 6363 St Charles Ave New Orleans LA 70118

BEARD, JAMES ANDREWS, author, food cons.; b. Portland, Oreg., May 5, 1903; s. Jonathan A. and Mary Elizabeth (Jones) B. Student, Reed Coll., 1920-21, D.H.L., 1976, U. Wash., 1931, Carnegie Inst. Tech., 1931-32. Pvt. tchr. cooking, Portland, 1932-37, tchr. country day sch., N.J., 1938; co-propr. Hors d'Oeuvre, Inc., N.Y.C., 1938-44; asso. dairy and vegetable farm, Reading, Pa., 1943; established clubs for United Seamen's Service throughout world, 1943-46; lectr., cooking demonstrator before groups, 1949—, food cons., 1956; propr. James Beard Cooking Classes., N.Y.C., 1955—. Active amateur theatrical group, Portland; appeared: on stage with Walter Hampden in revivals of Cyrano de Bergerac, 1924, 25, Othelo, 1925; radio, San Francisco and Portland, 1927-32; then as announcer for food commls.; featured on: TV food program Elsie Presents, 1946-47; guest on TV shows in, U.S., France and Eng., 1947-55; Author: Hors d'Oeuvre Canapes, 1940, Cook it Outdoors, 1941, Fowl and Game Cookery, 1944, Fireside Cookbook, 1949, James Beard's Fish Cookery, 1954, The Complete Book of Barbecue and Rotisserie Cooking, 1954, The Complete Cookbook for Entertaining, 1954, Jim Beard's New Barbecue Cookbook, 1958, James Beard's Treasury of Outdoor Cooking, 1960, The James Beard Cookbook, 1961; autobiography Delights and Prejudices, 1964, (with Alexander Watt) Paris Cuisine, 1952, (with Helen E. Brown) The Complete Book of Outdoor Cookery, 1955, (with Sam Aaron) How to Eat Better for Less Money, 1956, rev. edit., 1971, James Beard Cook Book, 1959, rev. edit., 1971, James Beard's Menus for Entertaining, 1965, How To Eat (and Drink) Your Way Through A French (or Italian) Menu, 1971, James Beard's American Cooking, 1972, Beard on Bread, 1973, Beard on Food, 1974, The Cooks Catalogue, 1975, New Fish Cookery, 1976, Theory and Practice of Good Cooking, 1977; weekly food column syndicated by, Universal Press Syndicate. Served with AUS, 1942-43. Decorated chevalier du Merite Agricole, France). Address: 167 W 12th St New York NY 10011

BEARD, JAMES FRANKLIN, educator; b. Memphis, Feb. 14, 1919; s. James Franklin and Anna (Shipley) B.; m. Eleanor Mary Williams, May 26, 1946; children: Anne S., Mary W. A.B., Columbia U., 1940, M.A., 1941; Ph.D., Princeton U., 1949. Instr. English Princeton U., 1943-48; instr. Dartmouth Coll., 1948-51, asst. prof., 1951-55; asst. prof. English Clark U., Worcester, Mass., 1955-57, assoc. prof., 1957-61, prof., 1961—, chmn. dept., 1980—. Editor: The Letters and Journals of James Fenimore Cooper, Vol. I and II, 1960, Vols. III, IV, 1964, Vols. V, VI, 1968; editor-in-chief: the Writings of James Fenimore Cooper, 1980—. Guggenheim fellow, 1952-53, 58-59; Nat. Endowment Humanities sr. fellow, 1967-68; grantee, 1971-72. Mem. Am. Antiquarian Soc., MLA, N.Y. State Hist. Assn., AAUP, Am. Studies Assn., Bibliog. Soc. Am., Phi Beta Kappa (hon.). Democrat. Home: 108 Winifred Ave Worcester MA 01602 Office: Dept English Clark Univ Worcester MA 01610

BEARD, JEAN MILLER, assn. exec.; b. Harrisonburg, Va., May 21, 1930; d. William B. and Edna F. (McMullen) Miller; m. Dan J. Beard, Aug. 20, 1949; children—Elizabeth Anne, Kathryn Sue, Steven Miller, John William, Barbara Leigh. Student public schs, Harrisonburg. With Nat. Extension Homemakers Council, Harrisonburg, 1978—, nat. sec., 1978-80, nat. v.p., 1981—; beauty advisor Merle Norman Cosmetics, 1980—; lectr. in field. Bd. dirs. Harrisonburg/Rockingham chpt. Am.

Cancer Soc., 1975-79; Linville-Edom 4-H project leader, 1965-70; co-chmn. extension homemakers dept. County Fair, 1970-75, bd. dirs., 1980—; bd. dirs. Va. Agribus. Council, 1975-79; coordinator planning dist. VI Family Forum, White House Conf. on Families, 1980; del. to Pres.'s Com. on Employment of Handicapped, 1979; Pres.'s Cons. with Rural Am. Women, 1980; deacon Presbyn. Ch., 1977-78, sec., pres. Sunday sch. clases, 1968-69, 70-71. Address: 95 Perry St Harrisonburg VA 22801

BEARD, LEO ROY, civil engineer; b. West Baden, Ind., Apr. 6, 1917; s. Leonard Roy and Barbara Katherine (Frederick) B.; m. Marian Janet Wagar, Oct. 21, 1939 (dec.); children: Patricia Beard Huntzicker, Thomas Edward, James Robert; m. Marjorie Elizabeth Pierce Wood, Aug. 30, 1974. A.A., Pasadena City Coll., 1937; B.S., Calif. Inst. Tech., 1939. Engr. U.S. Army C.E., Los Angeles, 1939-49; engr. Office Chief of Engrs., Washington, 1949-52; chief of Reservoir Regulation, Sacramento, 1952-64; dir. Hydrologic Engring. Center, Davis, Calif., 1964-72; prof. civil engring. U. Tex., Austin, 1972—; dir. (Center for Research in Water Resources), 1972-80; cons. Espey, Huston & Assos., Austin, 1980—; v.p. Internat. Commn. of Water Resource Systems; mem. NRC Water Sci. and Tech. Bd. Editor-in-chief: Water International; Editor: Jour. of Hydrology. Served with USNR, 1945-46. Recipient Meritorious Civilian Service award U.S. Army C.E., 1972. Fellow ASCE (water resources exec. com., Julian Hinds award 1981); mem. Internat. Water Resources Assn. (exec. bd.), Am. Water Resources Assn. (hon.), Am. Geophys. Union (pres. hydrology sect.), Nat. Soc. Profl. Engrs., Internat. Assn. Hydrol. Scis., World Meteorol. Orgn. (chmn. com. on hydrol. design data), U.S. Com. on Irrigation, Drainage and Flood Control, Univs. Council on Water Resources (exec. bd.), Nat. Acad. Engring. Home: 606 Laurel Valley Austin TX 78746 Office: PO Box 519 Austin TX 78767

BEARD, PAT, b. Waco, Tex., June 22, 1925; s. Hever Samuel and Irna (Jones) B.; m. Martha Sue George, Jan. 25, 1954; children: Carey, Michael, Bramlet, Joseph, Robert. A.B., Baylor U., 1947; LL.B., Harvard U., 1950. Bar: Tex. 1951. Ptnr. H.W. Beard, Waco, 1951-54, Beard, Kultgen & Beard, 1954-63, Beard & Kultgen, 1963—; mem. adv. com. rules of civil procedures Tex. Supreme Ct., 1975—; dir. Am. Inoome Life Ins. Co., Waco, State Nat. Bank, West, Tex., First Nat. Bank, McGregor, Tex., InterFirst Bank of Temple, N.A., Tex. Trustee Tex. Scottish Rite Hosp., Dallas, Scottish Rite Found., Tex., Tex. Scottish Rite Ednl. Found. Served with U.S. Army, 1944-46. Mem. ABA, State Bar Tex., Waco-McLennan County Bar Assn. (pres.). Democrat. Baptist. Clubs: Masons, Shriners. Home: 3200 Inverness Waco TX 76710 Office: Beard & Kultgen 1229 N Valley Mills Waco TX 76710

BEARD, RICHARD LEONARD, educator; b. Findlay, Ohio, Dec. 10, 1909; s. Jesse William and Mae (Leonard) B.; m. Reva Leona Coleman, July 3, 1937; children: Elaine Louise Beard Pinkerton, John Coleman. A.B., Findlay Coll., 1936; M.A., Bowling Green State U., 1936; Ph.D., Ohio State U., 1943. Tchr. English Elida (Ohio) Pub. Schs., 1936-37; head English dept. Whitmer High Sch., Toledo, 1937-42; asst., then instr. Ohio State U., 1942-43; asst. prof. edn. Iowa State Tchrs. Coll., 1946-48; prof. edn. Marshall U., Huntington, W.Va., 1948-52; asso. prof. edn. U. N.C., Chapel Hill, 1952-57; head counselor tng. N.C. Coll. at Durham, 1952-56; chmn., prof. edn., counselor edn. dept. U. Va., Charlottsville, 1957-72, prof. edn., 1972-80, prof. emeritus, 1980—, acting chmn. dept., 1977-78; lectr. Sta. KXEL, Waterloo, Iowa, 1947-48; TV instr. WUNC, Chapel Hill, N.C., 1954-57; ednl. cons. Served to 1st lt. AUS and USAAF, 1943-46; CBI. Career Service award Va. Personnel and Guidance Assn., 1967. Mem. Am. Personnel and Guidance Assn., Am. Assn. Counselor Edn. and Supervision, Nat. Vocational Guidance Assn., Assn. for Humanistic Edn. and Devel., Phi Delta Kappa. (Disting. Service award Va. chpt. 1966). Club: Colonnade. Home: 20 Sutton Ct Charlottesville VA 22901

BEARD, RODNEY RAU, physician, educator; b. Guinda, Calif., Dec. 27, 1911; s. Aiton Holmes and Mathilda Anne (Rau) B.; m. Marion Lucile Harper, July 3, 1938; children—Julie-Anne, Philip, Marian, Edin. A.B., Stanford U., 1932, M.D., 1938; M.P.H., Harvard U., 1940. Diplomate: Am. Bd. Preventive Medicine (trustee 1961-70), Am. Bd. Indsl. Hygiene. Intern Gorgas Hosp., C.Z., 1937-38; asst. resident Stanford U. Hosps., 1938-39; Rockefeller fellow in med. sci., 1939-40; med. officer Pacific-Alaska div. Pan Am. Airways, 1940-49; instr. med. sch. Stanford U., 1940-42, asst. prof., 1942-45, asso. prof., 1945-49, prof., chmn. dept. preventive medicine, 1949-69, prof. family, community and preventive medicine, 1969-77, prof. emeritus, 1977—; dir. rehab., 1955-60; med. cons. W. P. Fuller & Co., 1952-60; clin. prof. occupational health U. Calif. at Berkeley, 1952-64, lectr., 1964-72; vis. prof. U. Occupational and Environ. Health Sch. Medicine, Japan, 1980; cons. surgeon gen. U.S. Army, 1941-45, 54-75, USAF, 1966-69, Calif. Dept. Pub. Health, 1952—, VA, 1954-67; vis. prof. Clinica del Lavoro, U. di Milano, 1960-61. Author: (with W.P. Shepard et al) Essentials of Public Health, 2d edit, 1952, (with Joseph T. Noe) Patty's Industrial Hygiene and Toxicology, 1981, 2d edit., 1982; contbr. also papers; editorial bd.: Archives Environ. Health, 1973—. Chmn. health council San Francisco Community Chest, 1941-44; pub. health com. San Francisco C. of C., 1951-54, San Francisco Bd. Health, 1954-59; mem. commn. A. com. aviation medicine NRC, 1942-45; mem. commn. environ. hygiene Armed Forces Epidemiol. Bd., 1954-55, dir., 1955-66, 67-73; mem. nat. adv. heart council NIH, HEW, 1957-61; mem. nat. adv. council Nat. Inst. Environ. Health Scis., 1971-74; mem. nat. adv. council pub. health tng. USPHS, 1965-69; mem. hearing bd. San Francisco Bay Area Air Quality Mgmt. Dist., 1973—; mem. tech. adv. com. Calif. Air Resources Bd., 1969-72; mem. subcom. on atherosclerosis of peripheral vascular disease study group Inter-Soc. Commn. for Heart Disease Resources, 1969-76; mem. joint residency rev. com. for preventive medicine AMA-Am. Bd. Preventive Medicine, 1971-76, chmn., 1972-76. Fellow Am. Coll. Preventive Medicine (v.p. 1967), Am. Pub. Health Assn., Am. Occupational Medicine Assn. (sec. Western sect. 1945-46, pres. 1949), AAAS, Am. Acad. Occupational Medicine; mem. AMA (sec. sect. preventive medicine 1964-69, chmn. 1970-72, mem. com. occupational toxicology 1969-72), Permanent Commn. and Internat. Assn. Occupational Health, Am. Indsl. Hygiene Assn. (dir. 1956-60), Assn. Tchrs. Preventive Medicine (pres. 1958-59), Am. Heart Assn., Soc. Occupational and Environ. Health, Oceanic Soc., Calif. Acad. Medicine, ACLU, Airline Med. Dirs. Assn. (hon.), Calif. Acad. Preventive Medicine, Sigma Xi, Delta Omega. Unitarian. Home: 511 Gerona Rd Stanford CA 94305 Office: Dept Family Community and Preventive Medicine Stanford U Sch Medicine Stanford CA 94305

BEARD, THOMAS REX, economics educator; b. Baton Rouge, Aug. 12, 1934; s. Rex and Gertrude Louise (Hampton) B.; m. Sharon Virginia Petty, Dec. 21, 1957; children: Thomas Randolph, Sharon Elizabeth. B.S., La. State U., 1956, M.A., 1958; Ph.D., Duke, 1963. Asst. prof. La. State U., Baton Rouge, 1961-64, asso. prof., head econs. dept., 1965-68, prof., head econs. dept., 1969-71, prof., 1972—; economist Fed. Res. Bd. of Govs., Washington, 1964-65; 4th Nat. Bank Distinguished prof. Wichita State U., 1968-69; exec. dir. La. Council Econ. Edn., 1972-77; cons. La. Coordinating Council for Higher Edn., 1970,. Author: U.S. Treasury Advance Refunding, 1966, Financing Government in Louisiana, 1974; Editor: The Louisiana Economy, 1969; asso. editor: Social Sci. Quar, 1966-70; editorial bd.: Public Finance Quar, 1972-74, Rev. of Regional Econs. and Bus, 1980—; Contbr. articles profl. jours. Chmn. La. Gov.'s Council Econ. Advisors, 1975-77, mem., 1973-80. Earhart Found. fellow, 1957-58; Ford Found. fellow, 1960; James B. Duke fellow, 1958-60; La. State U. Parents Assn. grantee, 1983. Mem. Am. Econ. Assn., So. Econ. Assn. (mem. exec. com. 1967-69), Western Econ. Assn., Southwestern Econ. Assn. (pres. 1969-70), Am. Fin. Assn., Nat. Tax Assn., Phi Beta Kappa, Kappa Alpha, Omicron Delta Kappa, Phi Kappa Phi. Methodist. Home: 5952 Hibiscus Dr Baton Rouge LA 70808

BEARDALL, JAMES C., lumber company executive; b. Springville, Utah, Sept. 6, 1939; s. W. Clyde and Florence (Lloyd) B.; m. LaRue Whiting, Sept. 9, 1960; children: Laurie Kae, Stacy Lyn, Michael James. B.S. in Acctg, Brigham Young U., Provo, Utah, 1962. C.P.A., Calif., Utah. With Haskins & Sells (C.P.A.s), Los Angeles, 1962-66; with Anderson Lumber Co., Ogden, Utah, 1966—, v.p., 1977-79, pres., chief operating officer, 1979—, chief exec. officer, 1980—, also dir.; pres., dir. Pioneer Wholesale Supply Co.; mem. adv. bd. First Security Bank; chmn. adv. council Sch. Bus. Weber State Coll. Mem. Am. Inst. C.P.A.s, Mountain States Lumber and Bldg. Material Assn. (pres. 1981-82), Utah Soc. C.P.A.'s, Ogden C. of C. (officer, dir. 1979—). Republican. Mormon. Club: Ogden Golf and Country. Lodge: Ogden Rotary (pres. 1983-84). Address: 1100 First Security Bank Bldg Ogden UT 84401

BEARDEN, ALAN JOYCE, biophysicist; b. Balt., Nov. 23, 1931; s. Joyce Alvin and Lillian Lavonia (Singleton) B. A.B., Johns Hopkins U., 1950, Ph.D., 1958. Asst. prof. physics Cornell U., Ithaca, N.Y., 1960-64; asst. prof. chemistry U. Calif., San Diego, 1966-68, from lectr. to asso. prof. div. med. physics, Berkeley, 1969-76, prof. biophysics, 1976—, chmn. div. med. physics, 1978-79, chmn. dept. biophysics and med. physics, 1979—. Served with USN, 1950-54. NIH career devel. awardee, 1970-74; NIH fellow U. Calif., San Diego, 1964-66; Pollard lectr. Yale U., 1976. Fellow Am. Phys. Soc. (chmn. div. biol. physics 1978-79); mem. Biophys. Soc., Am. Soc. Photobiology, AAAS. Research in photosynthesis, laser radiation, bioenergetics, energy transfer in biology. Office: Dept Biophysics and Med Physics U Calif Berkeley CA 94720

BEARDEN, HAROLD IRWIN, bishop; b. Atlanta, May 8, 1910; s. LLoyd and Mary (DaCosta) B.; m. Lois Minerva Mathis, June 12, 1931; children—JoAnn, Harold Irwin, Gloria, Lloyd, Sharon, Richard. A.B., Morris Brown Coll., Atlanta, 1933, D.D. (hon.), 1962; B.D., Turner Theol. Sem., Atlanta, 1951; D.D. (hon.), Campbell Coll., 1949, Kittrell Coll., 1963, LL.D., Daniel Payne Coll., 1949, Monrovia Coll., 1955, Wilberforce (Ohio) U., 1964. Ordained deacon A.M.E. Ch., 1930, elder, 1931, consecrated bishop, 1964; pastor chs. in, Ga., 1928-64; acting presiding elder A.M.E. Ch., 1960-62, pres. bishop's council, 1972-73, presiding bishop, Atlanta, 1976-80, spl. assignment, 1980—; chmn. trustees Morris Brown Coll., 1976-80, Turner Theol. Sem., 1976-80. Bd. dirs. Atlanta U. Center, 1976—; pres. Atlanta br. NAACP, 1958-59; trustee Southview Cemetery, Atlanta, 1979—. Recipient Religious Achievement award Morris Brown Coll., 1964, citation Bd. Commrs. Fulton County, Ga., 1978; named Outstanding Citizens Ga. Senate, 1978. Mem. Phi Beta Sigma. Democrat. Club: Masons (33 degree). Home: 644 Skipper Dr NW Atlanta GA 30318 Office: 1475 Ezra Church Dr NW Atlanta GA 30314

BEARDEN, JAMES HUDSON, university official, business executive; b. Marion, Ala., Sept. 25, 1933; s. Joseph N. and Lula (Worrell) B.; m. Pauline Larkins, Mar. 31, 1961; children: James Hudson, Pauline Larkins. B.S., Centenary Coll. La., 1956; M.A., East Carolina Coll., 1959; Ph.D., U. Ala., 1966. Bus. mgr. Marion Inst., 1959; mem. faculty East Carolina U., Greenville, N.C., 1959—, prof. bus. adminstrn., 1964—, dir. bur. bus. research, 1964, dean, 1968-83, asst. to chancellor, dir. BBJT Ctr. for Mgmt. Devel., 1983—; Dir. Planters Bank, Hackney Industries. Author articles in field. Former trustee Campbell U.; Trustee N.C. Council Econ. Edn. Served with AUS, 1956-58. Grad. fellow U. Ala., 1961; grantee Nat. Assn. Purchasing Agts., 1962; fellow Birmingham Sales Execs., 1961. Mem. AAUP, Am., So. mktg. assns., Assn. Edn. Internat. Bus., So. Bus. Adminstrn. Assn., Beta Gamma Sigma. Lodge: Rotary (dir. Greenville). Home: 106 Crown Point Rd Greenville NC 27834

BEARDEN, JOYCE ALVIN, educator; b. Greenville, S.C., Oct. 19, 1903; s. Joseph Sylvester and Annie (Haley) B.; m. Lillian S. Singleton, June 6, 1923; 1 son, Alan Joyce. A.B., Furman U., 1923; Ph.D., U. Chgo., 1926; D.Sc., Furman U., 1951. Fellow U. Chgo., 1925, asst., 1926, instr. physics, 1926-29; asso. physics Johns Hopkins, 1929-32, asso. prof., 1932-39, prof., 1939—; chmn. dept. physics, 1947; physicist Applied Physics Lab., Washington, 1942-46; dir. Radiation Lab., Johns Hopkins, 1943-55; physicist Carnegie Instn., Washington, 1941-42; cons. Nat. Def. Research Com., 1940-42. Col. U.S. Army on tech. mission to, 1944-45; European Theater. Fellow Am. Physics. Soc., AAAS; mem. Am. Phys. Soc. (mem. council 1946-50), Phi Beta Kappa, Sigma Xi. Research in X-rays, physical constants, solid state. Home: 214 Lambeth Rd Baltimore MD 21218 Office: Johns Hopkins University Baltimore MD 21218

BEARDEN, ROMARE HOWARD, artist; b. Charlotte, N.C., Sept. 2, 1914; s. Howard R. and Bessye (Johnson) B.; m. Nanette Rohan, Sept. 4, 1954. B.S., N.Y. U., 1935; postgrad., Art Students League, 1937; Dr. Arts (hon.), Pratt Inst., Bklyn., 1973, Carnegie-Mellon U., Pitts., 1975. Art dir. Harlem Cultural Council.; Vis. lectr. African and Afro-Am. art and culture Williams Coll., 1969. Exhibited in one-man shows at, Kootz Gallery, N.Y.C., 1945-47, Niveau Gallery, N.Y.C., 1949, Barone Gallery, N.Y.C., 1955, Michel Warren Gallery, N.Y.C., 1960, Cordier-Ekstrom, N.Y.C., 1961, 64, 67, 69, 73, 75, 77, Corcoran Gallery, Washington, 1965, Carnegie Inst. Tech., 1966, Bundy Mus., Vt., Mus. Modern Art, 1971, Albert Loeb Gallery, Paris, 1975; exhibited in, Mint. Mus. Art, Charlotte, N.C., 1981, Balt. Mus., Mus. State Va., Bklyn. Mus., two-man show, Phila. Art Alliance, 1971; exhibited numerous group shows in, Europe, S.Am.; Author: (with Carl Holty) The Painter's Mind, 1969, (with Harry Henderson) 6 Black Masters of American Art. Served with AUS, 1942-45. Recipient award Nat. Inst. Arts. and Letters, 1966, purchase award Am. Acad. Arts and Letters, 1970; Gov.'s medal State of N.C., 1976; Guggenheim fellow, 1970-71. Mem. Nat. Inst. Arts and Letters. Office: Cordier & Ekstrom 417E 75th St 357 Canal St New York NY 10021 *

BEARDMORE, GLENN EVERETT, university administrator; b. Elmdale, Kans., Apr. 22, 1930; s. Everett L. and Eulah L. (Merritt) B.; m. Gwendolyn Loree Whitfield, Nov. 12, 1950; children—David Eugene, Stephen Leroy. A.A., Mesa Coll., 1967; B. Tech., Tex. State Tech. Inst., 1971; B. Tech. Edn., Nat. U., 1972; M.A., U.S. Internat. U., 1974; Ed.D., Nova U., 1979. Propr. Mt. Hope Produce Co., Kans., 1948-50; enlisted U.S. Navy, 1950, advanced through grades to master chief petty officer; ret., 1973; v.p. adminstrn. Nat. U., San Diego, 1972—, chancellor, 1981—; past chmn. evaluation team for approval of schs. to offer degrees State of Calif.; past mem. planning adv. council Regional Employment and Tng. Consortium; mem. pres.'s assocs. Nat. U. Past bd. dirs. Copley YMCA, 1979; bd. dirs. Lifeline Corp.; hon. dep. sheriff San Diego County.; adv. bd. Econ. Edn. Found. Recipient Silver Knight of Mgmt. award, 1980, Gold Knight of Mgmt. award, 1983. Fellow Am. Biog. Inst. Research Assn. (life); mem. Am. Soc. Personnel Adminstrn., Western Assn. Coll. and Univ. Bus. Officers, Coll. and Univ. Personnel Assn., Personnel Mgmt. Assn. (pres. 1978), Calif. Assn. Fin. Aid Adminstrs., Pacific Assn. Collegiate Registrars and Admission Officers, North San Diego County Navy League (pres. 1982-83), Fleet Res. Assn., Am. Soc. Trainers and Developers, El Cajon Blvd. Assn. (pres. 1978-79), Navy League U.S. (life), Vista C. of C. (treas.), Nat. Assn. Student Personnel Adminstrs., Nat. Mgmt. Assn. (chpt. pres. 1980-81, nat. dir.), Nat. U. Alumni Assn. (life mem., asso. dir. 1974—), AAUP. Club: Rotary (Paul Harris fellow). Home: 5556 Nokomis St La Mesa CA 92041 Office: 4141 Camino del Rio South San Diego CA 92108

BEARDMORE, HARVEY ERNEST, physician, educator; b. Windsor, Ont., Can., Feb. 4, 1921; s. Harold and Marjorie (Harvey) B.; m. Frances Seymour Barnes, Sept. 1, 1945; children: Richard, Anne Beardmore Psaila, Patricia Beardmore Muldoon, Ian, Carol, Diane. B.Sc., McGill U., Montreal, Que., Can., 1946, M.D., 1948, C.M., 1948. Cert. in pediatric surgery Am. Bd. Surgery. Intern Montreal Gen. Hosp., 1948-49; resident Queen Mary Vets. Hosp., Montreal, 1949-51; teaching fellow Tufts U., Boston, 1951-52; chief resident Montreal Children's Hosp., 1952-54, mem. staff, 1954—; practice medicine specializing in pediatric surgery, Montreal, 1954—; assoc. prof. surgery McGill U., 1954—. Served with Princess Patricias Canadian Light Inf., 1943-45; Italy, N.W. Europe. Fellow Am. Acad. Pediatrics (chmn. sect. surgery 1972), A.C.S., Royal Coll. Surgeons Can.; mem. Can. Assn. Paediatric Surgeons (founding pres. 1967-72), Am. Pediatric Surg. Assn. (pres 1974), World Fed. Assn. Pediatric Surgeons (first pres. 1974-77). Club: Chevalier de la Chaine des Rotisseurs. Home: 4501 Sherbrooke St W Apt 6E Montreal PQ Canada H32 1E7 Office: Montreal Children's Hosp 2300 Tupper St Montreal PQ H3H 1P3 Canada

BEARDSLEE, WILLIAM ARMITAGE, educator, clergyman; b. Holland, Mich., Mar. 25, 1916; s. John Walter, Jr. and Frances Eunice (Davis) B.; m. Kathryn Quinby Walker, June 11, 1941 (dec. Nov. 1982); children—Joy Walker (dec.), William Rigby. A.B., Harvard U., 1937; B.D., New Brunswick Theol. Sem., 1941; M.A., Columbia U., 1948; Ph.D., U. Chgo., 1951. Ordained to ministry Reformed Church in Am., 1941; minister Ref. Church in Am., Queens Village, N.Y., 1941-45; asst. prof. Bible Emory U., 1947-52, assoc. prof., 1952-56, prof. religion, 1956-80, Charles Howard Candler prof. religion, 1980—; dir. Grad. Inst. Liberal Arts, 1957-61; acting dean Coll. Arts and Scis., 1958. Author: (with E. H. Rece) Reading Bible: A Guide, 1952, 2d edit., 1964, Human Achievement and Divine Vocation in The Message of Paul, 1961, (with J. Boozer) Faith to Act, 1967, Literary Criticism of the New Testament, 1970, House for Hope, 1972; Editor: American and the Future of Theology, 1967, The Poetics of Faith (Semeia 12 and 13), 1978. Mem. rev. standard version Bible com. Nat. Council Chs. Fulbright Sr. Research grant U. Bonn. Germany, 1961-62; vis. prof. Pomona Coll., spring 1969; fellow Center Bibl. Research, Soc. Bibl. Lit., Claremont, Calif., 1976-77; Honored by Festschrift Orientation by Disorientation (Richard A. Spencer, editor), 1980; recipient Meth. Scholar-Tchr. award Emory U., 1981. Mem. Am. Acad. Religion (asso. editor 1961-69), Soc. Bibl. Lit. (pres. So. sect. 1957-58, editor Semeia Supplements 1974-79, assoc. editor 1979-82), Archeol. Inst. Am., AAUP, Phi Beta Kappa. Home: 1728 Vickers Circle Decatur GA 30030

BEARDSLEY, MONROE CURTIS, educator, author; b. Bridgeport, Conn., Dec. 10, 1915; s. Samuel Birdsey and Esther (Carney) B.; m. Elizabeth Bobette Lane, June 29, 1940; children: Philip, Mark. A.B., Yale U., 1936, Ph.D., 1939. Instr. Yale U., 1940-44; asst. prof. Yale, 196-47, Mt. Holyoke Coll., 1944-46; mem. faculty Swarthmore (Pa.) Coll., 1947-69, prof. philosophy, 1959-69; faculty Temple U., Phila., 1969—. Author: Practical Logic, 1950, (with Elizabeth Beardsley) Philosophical Thinking, 1965, Invitation to Philosophical Thinking, 1972, Aesthetics: Problems in the Philosophy of Criticism, 1958, 2d edit., 1981, Aesthetics from Classical Greece to the Present: A Short History, 1966, 2d edit., 1969, Thinking Straight, 4th edit, 1975, The Possibility of Criticism, 1970, The Aesthetic Point of View, 1982; editor: (with Robert Daniel and Glenn Leggett) Theme and Form, 4th edit, 1978, Foundations of Philosophy series; mem. bd. advisers, contbr.: Ency. Philosophy; editorial bd.: Philosophy Research Archives; sec.: Jour. History of Ideas; book rev. editor: Jour. Aesthetics and Art Criticism. Guggenheim fellow, 1950-51. Fellow Am. Acad. Arts and Scis.; mem. AAUP, Am. Soc. Aesthetics (trustee, pres. 1967-68), Am. Philos. Assn. (past pres. Eastern div.), Am. Soc. Polit. and Legal Philosophy, ACLU (past dir. Greater Phila., pres. 1967-70), NAACP (sec. Chester br. 1965-69). Home: 1916 Delancey Pl Philadelphia PA 19103 Office: Dept Philosophy Temple U Philadelphia PA 19122

BEARDSLEY, ROBERT EUGENE, microbiologist, educator; b. Walton, N.Y., June 11, 1923; s. Harrison R. and Margaret (Sliter) B.; m. Philomena E. Pecora, Aug. 28, 1948; children: Luisa M., Margaret R., Robert E. B.S., Manhattan Coll., 1950; A.M., Columbia U., 1951, Ph.D., 1960. Instr. Manhattan Coll., 1951-54, asst. prof., 1954-58, asso. prof., 1958-68, prof., 1968-77, dir., 1962-69, head dept. biology, 1969-77; prof. Iona Coll., New Rochelle, N.Y., 1977—, dean, 1977-83; vis. investigator Inst. Pasteur, Paris, 1966-67; Co-chmn. Scientists Com. Radiation Info., 1960. Contbr. articles to profl. jours. Served with AUS, 1943-46. Guggenheim fellow, 1966. Mem. Am. Inst. Biol. Scis., Am. Soc. Microbiologists, AAAS, Sigma Xi, Epsilon Sigma Pi. Home: 242 Mountaindale Rd Yonkers NY 10710 Office: Iona Coll New Rochelle NY 10801 *In retrospect, I find that I have lived with the illusion of being guided by a desire to make some contribution toward a better world for all members of the human family. However, like all other people, I have only done what my unique combination of heredity, environmental programming and ego have compelled me to do.*

BEARDSLEY, THEODORE S(TERLING), JR., association executive; b. E. St. Louis, Ill., Aug. 26, 1930; s. Theodore Sterling and Margaret (Kienzle) B.; m. Lenora J. Fierke, May 26, 1955; children: Theodore Sterling III, Mark A., Mary Elizabeth. B.S., So. Ill. U., 1952; M.A. (Max Bryant fellow), Washington U., St. Louis, 1954; postgrad., U. Heidelberg, Germany, 1955-56; Ph.D., U. Pa., 1961; linguistic research, Inst. Caro y Cuervo, Bogota, Colombia, summer 1973. Asst. in English Lycee Wilson, Chaumont, France, 1952-53; mem. faculty Rider Coll., 1957-61, chmn. dept. modern lang., 1959-61; asst. prof. Spanish So. Ill. U., 1961-62, U. Wis., 1962-65; dir. Hispanic Soc. Am., N.Y.C., 1965—; adj. prof. N.Y. U., 1967-69, 80, Adelphi U., 1966, 68, Columbia, 1969; Fulbright lectr., Ecuador, 1974; Chmn. Museums Council N.Y.C., 1972-73; spl. cons. Hispanic bibliography Library of Congress, fall 1973, N.J. State Dept. Edn., spring 1975, Nat. Endowment for Humanities, 1978—. Narrator Spanish lang. recorded tours, Nat. Gallery Art; Met. Mus., Mus. Natural Sci., Boston Sci. Mus., Smithsonian Instn.; continuing series on Caribbean popular music in U.S, WBGO-FM, 1979; Xavier Cugat, 1980, USA Latino, 1981; Author: Hispano-Classical Translations, 1482-1699, 1970, Tomas Navarro Tomas, A Tentative Bibliography, 1908-1970, 1971; also articles; Recordings Charla con Camilo José Cela, 1966, Visita a la Hispanic Society, 1969; narrator-author: 4 part series Hispanic Immigration to the United States (text pub. 1976), CBS-TV, 1972; Librettist: Ponce de Leon, 1973; mem. adv. bd.: Hispanic Rev., Studia humanitatis, Boletín de ANLE. Served with AUS, 1954-56. Decorated Orden de Mérito Civil, Spain).; Fulbright grantee, 1952-53; Jusserand traveling fellow, 1962; research grantee Am. Council Learned Socs., 1964; travel grantee, 1974; Recipient Premio Bibliofilia, Barcelona, Spain, 1973. Mem. Hispanic Soc. Am., Renaissance Soc. Am. (exec. council, acting dir. 1981-82), ASCAP, Academia Norteamericana de la lengua española, Internat. Inst. (Madrid, Spain), Sigma Delta Pi, Sigma Tau Gamma; corr. mem. Royal Spanish Acad., Real Academia de Bellas Artes de San Carlos (Valencia), Academia Guatemalteca de la Lengua. Club: Grolier. Office: 613 W 155th St New York NY 10032

BEARE, GENE KERWIN, company director; b. Chester, Ill., July 14, 1915; s. Nicholas Eugene and Minnie Cole (St. Vrain) B.; m. Doris Margaret Alt, Dec. 11, 1943 (dec.); children: Gail Kathryn, Joanne St. Vrain; m. Patricia Pfau Cade, Sept. 12, 1964. B.S. in Mech. Engring, Washington U., 1937; M.B.A., Harvard, 1939. Registered profl. engr., Ill. With Automatic Electric Co., Chgo., 1939-58, successively asst. to v.p. and gen. mgr., asst. to pres., mgr. internat. affiliated cos., gen. comml. mgr., 1939-54, v.p. prodn., 1954-58, dir., 1956-61; pres., dir. Automatic Electric Internat., Inc., 1958-61; chmn., dir. Automatic Electric (Can.), Ltd., Automatic Electric Sales (Can.), Ltd., 1958-61; pres., dir. Sylvania Internat., 1959-60; pres. Gen. Telephone & Electronics Internat., Inc., 1960-61, dir., 1960-72, also dir. numerous subs. in, Colombia, Mex., Venezuela, Argentina, Switzerland, Panama, Brazil, Belgium, Can., Italy; dir. Am. Research and Devel. Corp., 1967-74, Canadian Ltd., 1972-75; pres. Sylvania Electric Products, Inc., 1961-69, dir., 1961-72; exec. v.p. mfg., dir. Gen. Telephone & Electronics Corp., 1969-72; exec. v.p., dir. Gen. Dynamics Corp., St. Louis, 1972-77; pres. Gen. Dynamics Comml. Products Co., 1972-77; chmn. Asbestos Corp. Ltd., 1974-77; dir. Arkwright-Boston Mut. Ins. Co., Westvaco Corp., Emerson Electric Co., St. Joe Minerals Corp., Am. Maize-Products Corp., Datapoint Corp. Served to lt. USNR, 1942-45. Mem. Pan Am. Soc., Nat. Elec. Mfrs. Assn. (bd. govs. 1963-72, v.p. 1964, pres. 1965-66), Armed Forces Communications and Electronics Assn., Nat. Security Indsl. Assn. (trustee 1969-72). Clubs: Wee Burn (Darien, Conn.) (gov. 1963-68); Union League, Econ. (N.Y.C.); St. Louis (dir. 1979—); Old Warson (Ladue, Mo.) (dir. 1979—). Home: 801 S Skinker Blvd Saint Louis MO 63105 Office: Pierre Laclede Center 7701 Forsyth Blvd Suite 545 Saint Louis MO 63105

BEARE, JOHN ALAN, state official, physician; b. Modesto, Calif., Mar. 12, 1932; s. William and Bernice (Humphrey) B.; m. Marjorie May McMullen, Aug. 23, 1953; children: Cheryl Ann, Kenneth Alan, David John. B.S., Seattle Pacific Coll., 1953; M.D., U. Oreg., 1960; M.P.H., U. Calif., Berkeley, 1964. Intern, Drs. Hosp., Seattle, 1960-61; resident Wash. State Dept. Health, 1961-63; with health div. Wash. Dept. Social and Health Services, Olympia, 1964—, chief office community support, 1971-73, acting asst. sec., 1973, asst. sec., 1973-74, dir. div., 1974—. Served with AUS, 1954-56. Mem. Am., Wash. State public health assns. Home: 2520 Vista Ave Olympia WA 98501 Office: Mail Stop ET-21 Olympia WA 98504

BEARMAN, TONI CARBO, information scientist; b. Middletown, Conn., Nov. 14, 1942; d. Anthony Joseph and Theresa (Bauer) Carbo; m. David A. Bearman, Nov. 14, 1970; 1 dau., Amanda Carole. A.B., Brown U., 1969; M.S., Drexel U., 1973, Ph.D., 1977. Bibliog. asst. Am. Math. Soc., Math. Revs., 1962-63; Coordinator public services Phys. Scis. Library, Brown U., Providence, R.I., 1963-66, 67-71; subject specialist Engring. Library, U. Wash., Seattle, 1966-67; teaching and research asst. Drexel U., 1971-74; exec. dir. Nat. Fedn. Abstracting and Indexing Services, Phila., 1974-79; cons. for strategic planning and new product devel. Instn. Elec. Engrs., London, 1979-80; exec. dir. Nat. Commn. on Libraries and Info. Sci., Washington, 1980—; trustee Engring. Index, Inc. Contbr. articles to profl. jours; mem. editorial bds. profl. jours. Bd. dirs. Center for Literacy, Phila. Fellow AAAS (chmn. sect. T nominating com.); Mem. Am. Soc. Info. Sci., Spl. Interest Group on Library Automation and Networks (dir., chmn. networking com.), Spl. Libraries Assn. (Watson Davis award 1983), ALA, Soc. Scholarly Publishing, Assn. Am. Trust for Brit. Libraries. Home: 907 E Capitol St SE Washington DC 20003 Office: Suite 3122 GSA ROB 7th and D Sts SW Washington DC 20024

BEARN, ALEXANDER GORDON, physician, pharmaceutical company executive; b. Surrey, Eng., Mar. 29, 1923; came to U.S., 1951; s. Edward Gordon and Rose (Kay) B.; m. Margaret Slocum, Dec. 20, 1952; children: Helen Elliot, Gordon Clarence Frederic. Ed., Epsom Coll.; M.B., B.S., Guy's Hosp., U. London, Eng., 1946; M.D., 1951; M.D. Dr. honoris causa, U. René Descartes, Paris, 1974. House physician Guy's Hosp., 1946-47; house physician, registrar Postgrad. Med. Sch., London, 1948-51; mem. staff Rockefeller Inst., N.Y.C., 1951-64, asso. prof., 1957-64, prof., sr. physician, 1964-66; prof. medicine Cornell U., 1966—, Stanton Griffis Distinguished med. prof., 1976-80, chmn. dept., 1966-77; physician-in-chief N.Y. Hosp., 1966-77; med. dir., bd. dirs., sec.-treas. Russell Sage Inst. of Pathology, 1967-79; sr. v.p. for med. and sci. affairs Merck, Sharp & Dohme Internat., Rahway, N.J., 1979—; Lilly lectr., 1973, Lettsomian lectr., 1976; bd. sci. cons. Sloan Kettering Inst., 1967-74; mem. Commn. Human Resources, Nat. Acad. Scis., 1974-77; chmn. div. med. scis. Assembly Life Scis., 1978—; bd. sci. counselors Nat. Inst. Arthritis, Metabolism and Digestive Diseases, 1976-80; mem. Space Sci. Bd., 1978-79; cons. genetics tng. com., div. gen. med. scis. USPHS, 1961-65, cons. genetics study sect., 1966-70; pres. Royal Soc. Medicine Found., Inc., 1976-78; now dir.; mem. bd. sci. overseers Jackson Lab., Bar Harbor; mem. Inst. Medicine, Nat. Acad. Scis. Editor: Am. Jour. Medicine; co-editor: Progress in Medical Genetics, 1962—; asso. editor: Cecil-Loeb Textbook of Medicine; Contbr. articles to profl. jours. Trustee Rockefeller U., Helen Hay Whitney Found. Served as med. officer RAF, 1947-49. Fellow AAAS, Royal Coll. Physicians (Edinburgh, Scotland), Royal Coll. Physicians (London, Eng.); mem. Nat. Acad. Scis., Am. Philos. Soc., Assn. Am. Physicians, Am. Soc. Clin. Investigation, Am. Soc. Human Genetics (pres. 1971), Genetics Soc. Am., Am. Soc. Biol. Chemists, Soc. Exptl. Biology and Medicine, Harvey Soc. (pres. 1972-73, Harvey lectr. 1975), Harveian Soc. London (Council 1959), Assn. Physicians Great Britain and Ireland, Med. Research Soc. Great Britain, Med. Soc. London, Am. Assn. History Medicine, Sigma Xi (pres. Rockefeller chpt. 1962-63); fgn. asso. Norwegian Acad. Sci. and Letters; hon. mem. Sociedad Medica de Santiago, Sociedad de Biologia de Santiago. Presbyterian. Clubs: Century Assn., Grolier (N.Y.C.); Crail Golf (Scotland). Home: 1225 Park Ave New York NY 10028 Office: Merck and Co Inc PO Box 2000 Rahway NJ 07065

BEARY, JOHN FRANCIS, III, physician, government official; b. Melrose, Iowa, Dec. 14, 1946; s. John F. and Dorothy (McGarth) B.; m. Bianca E. Mason, May 6, 1972; children: John Daniel, Vanessa. B.S. summa cum laude, U. Notre Dame, 1969; M.D., Harvard U., 1973. Diplomate: Am Bd. Internal Medicine. Research fellow Cornell Med. Sch., N.Y.C., 1978-80; asst. prof. Georgetown Med. Sch., Washington, 1980-81; prin. dept. asst. sec. health affairs Dept. Def., Washington, 1981—. Editor: Manuel of Rheumatology, 1981. Bd. dirs. Scleroderma Found., Washington, 1982; mem. Am. Irish Found., San Francisco, 1981. Served to capt. USAF, 1974-77. Recipient Polechek N.Y. Arthrities Found., 1979. Fellow ACP; mem. AMA, Res. Officers Assn., John Hopkins Med. and Surg. Assn. Republican. Roman Catholic. Office: Dept Def Health Affairs The Pentagon Washington DC 20301

BEASLEY, B. REX, judge; b. Tulsa, Aug. 29, 1934; s. O. Rex and W. S. B.; m. Donna Knight, Sept. 3, 1954; children: Bradley, Brenda, Barry. B.S. with honors, U. Tulsa, 1959, J.D., 1967; grad., Nat. Jud. Coll., 1977. Bar: Okla. 1967. Asst. dist. atty., Tulsa County, 1968-71, chief prosecutor, McAlester, Okla., 1971-73, assoc. dist. judge, Tulsa, 1973—; chief juvenile judge Tulsa County Dist. Ct. Okla., Tulsa, 1981—; Lectr. Okla. Hwy. Patrol Acad., Oklahoma City, 1971—; Okla. Jud. Council, 1979, 80; leader Nat. Jud. Coll., 1978; co-chmn. Tulsa County Ct. Fund. Mem. Tulsa Safety Council.; chmn. State Foster Care Rev. Adv Bd., 1983—; Mem. Okla. Commn. on Children and Youth. Mem. Am., Okla. bar assns., Okla. Jud. Conf. (v.p. 1978, 79), Nat. Council Juvenile Judges, Kappa Sigma. Methodist (adminstrv. bd.). Club: Lion. Home: 8519 E 32d St Tulsa OK 74145 Office: 312 W 5th Tulsa OK 74103

BEASLEY, BRUCE MILLER, sculptor; b. Los Angeles, May 20, 1939; s. Robert Seth and Bernice (Palmer) B.; m. Laurence Leaute, May 21, 1973; children: Julian Bernard, Celia Beranice. Student, Dartmouth Coll., 1957-59; B.A., U. Calif. at Berkeley, 1962. Sculptor in metal and plastic, one man shows at, Everett Ellin Gallery, Los Angeles, Kornblee Gallery, N.Y.C., Hansen-Fuller Gallery, San Francisco, David Stuart Gallery, Los Angeles, Andre Emmerich Gallery, N.Y.C., De Young Mus., San Francisco, Santa Barbara Mus. Art, Fine Arts Gallery, San Diego; exhibited in group shows at, Mus. Modern Art, N.Y.C., Guggenheim Mus., N.Y.C., Albright Knox Gallery, Buffalo, LaJolla (Calif.) Art Mus., Musée d'Art Modern, Paris, San Francisco Mus. Art, Krannert Art Mus. at U. Ill., Jewish Mus., N.Y.C., Luxembourg Gardens, Paris, Calif. Palace of Legion of Honor, De Young Mus., Santa Barbara Art Mus., others; represented in permanent collections, Mus. Modern Art, Guggenheim Mus., Musée d'Art Modern, Paris, Los Angeles County Art Mus., Univ. Art Mus., Berkeley, Oakland (Calif.) Mus., Wichita (Kans.) Art Mus., San Francisco Art Commn., Santa Barbara Art Mus., Dartmouth Coll., others; major sculpture commns. include, State of Calif., 1967, Oakland Mus., 1972, City of San Francisco, 1976, U.S. govt., City of Eugene, Oreg., 1974, City of Salinas, Calif., 1977, Miami Internat. Airport, Fla., 1978, San Francisco Internat. Airport, 1981, Stanford U., 1982, Los Angeles Olympic Stadium, 1984. Recipient Andre Malraux purchase award Biennale de Paris, 1961. Home: 322 Lewis St Oakland CA 94607

BEASLEY, CECIL ACKMOND, JR., lawyer; b. Birmingham, Ala., Nov. 30, 1912; s. Cecil Ackmond and Louise Adeline (Renfro) B.; m. Parthenia Virginia Stubblefield, Oct. 29, 1942 (dec. Mar. 1976); children—Virginia Beasley Otis, Cynthia Beasley Garten. A.B. cum laude, Princeton U., 1935; LL.B., Yale U., 1939. Bar: D.C. bar 1939. Law clk. to chief justice U.S. Ct. Claims, 1939-40; pvt. practice, Washington, 1940—; mem. firm Mills & Kilpatrick, 1941-43, Kilpatrick, Ballard & Beasley, 1943-65, Ballard & Beasley, 1965—; spl. cons. transp. div. ECA, 1950-51; dir. So. Airways, Atlanta, 1949-79, Republic Airlines, Inc., Mpls., 1979—. Bd. govs. St. Albans Sch. Boys, Washington, 1950-57, chmn., 1956-57; bd. govs. Nat. Cathedral Sch. Girls, Washington, 1958-64, chmn., 1960-64. Fellow Am. Coll. Trial Lawyers; mem. ABA (standing com. aero. law 1969-75, adv. com. to standing com. aero. law 1975-78, chmn. 1975-78), D.C. Bar Assn. (chmn. com. on aero. law 1952-53, 61-63, 67-68), Fed. Power Bar Assns., Am. Judicature Soc., Barristers (pres. 1963-64), St. Albans Sch. for Boys Alumni Assn. (pres. 1948-49), Order of Coif, Phi Delta Phi. Clubs: Metropolitan, Nat. Lawyers, Nat. Aviation, Princeton (Washington); Chevy Chase (Md.); Colonial (Princeton); Corbey Court (Yale). Home: 3825 52d St NW Washington DC 20016 Office: Suite 505 1700 K St NW Washington DC 20006

BEASLEY, ROBERT LAWRENCE, farm supply cooperative executive; b. Poplar Bluff, Mo., Mar. 6, 1929; s. C. F. and Zula Mae (McAllister) B.; m. Betty Lou Lepp, July 21, 1951; children: Rob, Ann. B.A. in Journalism, U. Mo., 1952. Reporter, photographer, editor Columbia (Mo.) Tribune, 1951-54, Dubuque (Iowa) Herald, 1954-56, Madison (Wis.) State Jour., 1956-57; with Farmland Industries Inc., Kansas City, Mo., 1957—, v.p., 1971—. Chmn. bd. govs. Kansas City YMCA; bd. dirs. Cablevision of Kansas City. Mem. Coop. League U.S.A. (chmn. 1974-76, 83-84, vice-chmn. 1980), Internat. Coop. Alliance Econ. Bur. (vice chmn. 1980). Office: 3315 N Oak Trafficway Kansas City MO 64116

BEASLEY, THEODORE PRENTIS, retired life insurance executive; b. Mt. Ayr, Iowa, June 29, 1900; s. Clarence H. and Ada (Prentis) B.; m. Beulah F. Porter, June 21, 1921 (dec. Dec. 1969); children: Ronald Rex, Betty Jean; m. Mary Evans Carsey, Sept. 9, 1972. Student pub. schs., Iowa, Kans.; LL.D., Tex. Christian U., 1968. Organized Joplin Life Ins. Co., Mo., 1928; sec., gen. mgr. Public Nat. Life Ins. Co., Little Rock, 1935-37; pres. Republic Nat. Life Ins. Co., Dallas, 1937-61, chmn. bd., from 1961, now ret.; dir. Merc. Nat. Bank Dallas. Trustee Tex. Christian U.; mem. bd. Nat. City Christian Ch. Corp., Washington; past v.p. Greater Dallas Council Chs.; life dir. Dallas met. bd. YMCA; former U.S. mem. World's Council, mem. nat. com., U.S. and Can.; past mem. and chmn. adv. bd. Salvation Army, Dallas Citizens Council, Greater Dallas Planning Council; mem. Greater Dallas Community of Chs.; past dir. Dallas Community Chest.; Hon. life trustee, past vice chmn. George Williams Coll. Served from pvt. to sgt. U.S. Army, 1918-20. Recipient Lay Churchman of Year award, 1952; Nat. Brotherhood citation NCCJ, 1965. Mem. Oak Cliff C. of C. (past pres.), Dallas C. of C. (past dir.), Am. Life Ins. Assn., Tex. Life Ins. Assn., Ins. Econ. Soc. Am. (past v.p.), Health Ins. Assn. Am., Life Insurers Conf. Mem. Christian Ch. Clubs: Masons (32 deg., 33 deg.), Shriners, Kiwanis, Dallas Country, Lancers, Dallas, Brook Hollow Golf, Austin. Home: 3525 Turtle Creek Blvd Dallas TX 75219

BEASLEY, WALLACE ROLAND, petrochemical company executive; b. Archer City, Tex., Apr. 9, 1936; s. Wallace David and Ella Lou (Burnam) B.; m. Jean Ann Puddy, Aug. 24, 1957; children: Shelly E., Julie E., Lori J., Rebecca D. B.S. in Chem. Engring., Tex. A&M U., 1958; A.M.P., Harvard U., 1977. Mgr. coordination Arco Polymers, Phila., 1974-78, bus. center mgr., 1978-80; exec. v.p. ops. No. Petroleum Co., Omaha, 1980-81, v.p., gen, mgr., 1981-82, pres., chief operating officer, 1982—, dir. Bd. dirs. Omaha Symphony Assn, 1983—. Served to 1st lt. U.S. Army, 1958-59. Mem. Am. Chem. Soc., Soc. Plastics Engrs., Am. Inst. Chem. Engrs. Republican. Mem. Ch. of Christ. Club: Omaha.

BEASLEY, WILLIAM HOWARD, III, holding company executive; b. Dallas, Oct. 1, 1946; s. William Howard, Jr. and Doris Ann (Waddell) B.; m. Jean Childers, June 10, 1972; children: William Howard, IV, Scott Childers. A.B. with distinction (Scholar-Athlete award 1966), Duke U., 1968; M.B.A., U. Tex., Austin, 1969, Ph.D., 1971. Interviewer disting. execs. Nat. Ednl. TV, Austin, 1969; mem. faculty U. Tex., 1968-71; spl. asst. to sec., dep. sec. Treasury Dept., 1971-73; dir. Republican staff U.S. Senate com. on banking, housing, and urban affairs, 1973-75; spl. asst. to pres. N.W. Industries, Inc., Chgo., 1975-78; vice chmn. bd. Velsicol Chem. Corp., Chgo., 1978-79, pres., chief exec. officer, 1979-81; pres., chief exec. officer Beasley Enterprises, Inc., Dallas, 1979—. Dir. The Acorn Fund; chmn. adv. lod. Ctr. for Corp. Economics and Strategy, Duke U.; adv. council Coll. Bus. Adminstrn., U. Tex., Austin; corp. adv. council World Wildlife Fund-U.S.; chmn. exec. com., com. foreign affairs Chgo. Council Foreign Relations; mem. internat. sponsor's council Howard U., Washington; mem. Beta Gamma Sigma Dirs. Table, U. Tex., Austin; trustee Northwestern U., Evaston, Ill.; mem. N.Y. Council Foreign Relations. Served with USAF, 1968-70. Mem. Young Pres.' Orgn. Republican. Presbyterian. Clubs: Union League (Chgo.); Chicago. Home: 61 W Burton Pl Chicago IL 60610 Office: 6300 Sears Tower Chicago IL 60606

BEASON, AMOS THEODORE, investment banker; b. Birmingham, Ala., Aug. 24, 1940; s. Edward Early and Alma Pauline (Kirby) B.; m. Ann Pauline Hutchinson, Aug. 10, 1963; children: Amos Nathaniel, Edward Lewis. B.A., Vanderbilt U., 1961. With Morgan Guaranty Trust Co., N.Y.C., 1961-83; v.p. pub. fin. First Boston Corp., 1983—. Treas., trustee Overlook Hosp., Summit, N.J., 1977—; trustee N.Y.C. Citizens Budget Commn., 1979—. Mem. Dealer Bank Assn. (founding dir., past pres.). Home: 26 Ox Bow Ln Summit NJ 07901 Office: 23 Wall St New York NY 10015

BEASON, ROBERT GAYLE, writer; b. Prescott, Kans., May 21, 1927; s. Henry M. and Ruth (Herman) B.; m. Sylvia Elizabeth Toulouse, Nov. 18, 1950; 1 son, Drew. Student. U. Nebr., 1945-46; B.J., U. Mo., 1949, B.A., 1950. News editor Rolla (Mo.) Daily Herald, 1950; sports editor Moberly (Mo.) Monitor-Index, 1950-51; reporter, then copy editor Kansas City Star, 1951-54; promotion editor, then asst. editor Mechanix Illus. mag., 1955-60; editor Electronics Illus. mag., 1960-63, Mechanix Illus. and Electronics Illus. mags. (mags. merged to Mechanix Illus. 1972), N.Y.C., 1963-79; free-lance writer, editor, 1980—. Author: novel Hanging on, 1984. Served with USNR, 1945-46. Mem. Electronics Press Club (pres. 1965-67), Inst. High Fidelity (pubs. com.), Internat. Motor Press Assn. (pres. 1977-78), Am. Soc. Mag. Editors, Tau Kappa Epsilon, Sigma Delta Chi. Democrat. Congregationalist. Club: Madison Ave. Sports Car Driving and Chowder Soc. Home: Chestnut Hill Rd Stamford CT 06903

BEATHARD, BOBBY, professional football team executive; b. Zanesville, Ohio, Jan. 24, 1937; m. Christine Beathard; children: Kurt, Jeff, Casey, James. Student, Calif. Poly. Inst. Scout Kansas City Chiefs, Am. Football League, 1963-68, Atlanta Falcons, NFL, 1968-72; dir. player personnel Miami Dolphins, NFL, 1972-78; gen. mgr. Washington Redskins, NFL, 1978—. Office: care Washington Redskins PO Box 17247 Dulles Airport Washington DC 20041 *

BEATLEY, CHARLES EARLE, JR., city ofcl.; b. Urbana, Ohio, May 17, 1916; s. Charles Earle and Alice Elizabeth (Carson) B.; m. Marjorie Perry, Nov. 10, 1945; children—Elizabeth, Christopher, Timothy. B.A., Ohio State U., 1938, M.B.A., 1947. Capt. United Airlines, 1943-76; mayor City of Alexandria, Va., 1967-76, 79—; owner, operator Warrenton Air Park Inc., Va., 1977—. Pres. Seminary Hill Citizens Assn., 1955-58, Minnie Howard Elem. Sch. PTA, 1961; commr. No. Va. Transp. Commn., 1966-76, 79—; mem. Alexandria City Council, 1966-76, Va. Airport Authority, 1977-80, Va. Aviation Commn., 1980—; bd. dirs. Washington Met. Area Transit Authority, 1970-72, 74-76, 79—, No. Va. Park Authority, 1970-72. Mem. Air Line Pilots Assn. (1st v.p. 1955-57), Capital Airlines Assn. (pres. 1981), Met. Washington Council Govts. (dir. 1967-76, chmn. health and environ. protection policy com. 1972-73, pres. 1972), Va. Mcpl. League (chmn. urban sect. 1979-80, mem. exec. com. 1979-80). Democrat. Presbyterian. Home: 4875 Maury Ln Alexandria VA 22304 Office: Warrenton Air Park Inc Warrenton VA 22186

BEATLEY, JANICE CARSON, biologist, educator; b. Columbus, Ohio, Mar. 18, 1919; d. Charles Earle and Alice Elizabeth (Carson) B. B.A. cum laude (Mary S. Muellhaupt fellow), Ohio State U., 1940, M.S., 1948, Ph.D., 1953. Instr., then asst. prof. Ohio State U., U. Tenn., N.C. State Coll., Raleigh, 1953-60; asst., then asso. research ecologist Lab. Nuclear Medicine and Radiation Biology, UCLA, 1960-73; asso. prof., now prof. biol. scis. U. Cin., 1973—. Contbr. articles on desert and forest ecology to profl. jours. Fellow AAAS, Ohio Acad. Sci.; mem. Am. Inst. Biol. Scis., Ecol. Soc. Am., Am. Soc. Plant Taxonomists, Calif. Bot. Soc., Soc. Range Mgmt., Tenn. Acad. Sci., AAUP, Nat. Wildlife Fedn., Sierra Club, Friends of the Land, Nature Conservancy, NOW, Phi Beta Kappa, Sigma Xi. Home: 3469 Statewood Dr Cincinnati OH 45239 Office: Department of Biological Sciences University of Cincinnati Cincinnati OH 45221

BEATON, ROY HOWARD, nuclear industry executive; b. Boston, Sept. 1, 1916; s. John Howard and Mary Beaton (LaVoice) B.; children: Constance Beaton Reinholz, Roy Howard. B.S., Northeastern U., 1939, D.Sc. (hon.), 1967; D.Eng., Yale U., 1942. With E.I. DuPont, 1942-45, plant tech. supr., 1944-45; assoc. prof. chem. engring. U. Kans., Lawrence, 1946; with Gen. Electric Co., 1946—, v.p., gen. mgr. electronics systems div., Syracuse, N.Y., 1968-74, v.p., gen. mgr. energy systems and tech. div., Fairfield, Conn., 1974-75, v.p., gen. mgr. nuclear energy systems div., San Jose, Calif., 1975-77, v.p., group exec. nuclear energy group, 1977-79, sr. v.p. group exec. nuclear energy group, 1979—. Chmn. industry div. United Way Campaign, Santa Clara County, Calif., 1978-79. Mem. Am. Inst. Chemists, AAAS, nat. Acad. Engring., Am. Ordnance Assn., Am. Nuclear Soc., Am. Inst. Chem. Engrs., IEEE, AIAA, Navy League U.S., Air Force Assn., Soc. Mil. Engrs., Santa Clara County Mfg. Group, Sigma Xi, Tau Beta Pi. Home: PO Box 1018 Saratoga CA 95070 Office: 175 Curtner Ave San Jose CA 95125

BEATTIE, ANN, author; b. Washington, Sept. 8, 1947; d. James and Charlotte (Crosby) B.; m. David Gates, June 5, 1973; 1 son, Rufus. B.A., Am. U., 1969; M.A., U. Conn., 1970. Vist. asst. prof. U. Va., Charlottesville, 1976-77, vis. writer, 1980; Briggs Copeland lectr. English Harvard U., 1977. Author: Chilly Scenes of Winter, 1976, Distortions, 1976, Secrets and Suprises, 1979, Falling In Place, 1980, Jacklighting, 1981, The Burning House, 1982. Recipient Disting. Alumnae award Am. U., 1980, award in lit. Am. Acad. and Inst. Arts and Letters, 1980; Guggenheim fellow, 1977. Mem. PEN, Authors Guild. Office: care Lynn Nesbit Internat Creative Mgmt 40 W 57 St New York NY 10019

BEATTIE, DIANA SCOTT, biochemistry educator; b. Cranston, R.I., Aug. 11, 1934; d. Kenneth Allen and Lillian Francis (Barton) Scott; m. Benjamin Howard Beattie, June 30, 1956 (div. 1975); children: Elizabeth, Sara, Rachel, Ruth; m. Robert Nathan Stuchell, Feb. 6, 1976. B.A., Swarthmore Coll., 1956; M.S., U. Pitts., 1958, Ph.D., 1961. Research assoc. U. Pitts., 1961-67, VA Hosp., Pitts., 1967-68; faculty Mt. Sinai Sch. Medicine, N.Y.C., 1968—, prof. biochemistry, 1976—; mem. grad. faculty biomed. scis. CUNY, 1968—, biochemistry, 1971—, biology, 1974—; vis. prof. U. Louvain, Belgium, 1983; mem. ad hoc biochemistry study sect. NIH, 1976-77, 79-81, mem. phys. biochemistry study sect., 1981—, chmn. phys. biochemistry study sect., 1983—. Contbr. articles to profl. jours.; Mem. editorial bd.: Archives of Biochemistry and Biophysics, 1975-78, Jour. Bioenergetics, 1975—. Recipient award Met. N.Y. chpt. Assn. for Women in Sci., 1979; NIH grantee, 1966—; NSF grantee, 1970—; Fogarty internat. fellow, 1983. Mem. Am. Soc. Biol. Chemists, Am. Soc. Cell Biology, Biophysics Soc., Gerontol. Soc. Home: 141-21 33d Ave Flushing NY 11354 Office: Dept Biochemistry Mt Sinai Sch Medicine Fifth Ave and 100th St New York NY 10029

BEATTIE, DONALD A., energy scientist, research and development administrator; b. N.Y.C., Oct. 30, 1929; s. James Francis and Evelyn Margaret (Hickey) B.; m. Ann Mary Kean, Mar. 27, 1973; children: Thomas James, Bruce Andrew. A.B., Columbia U., 1951; M.S., Colo. Sch. Mines, 1958. Regional geologist Mobil Oil Co., 1958-63; Apollo lunar expts. program mgr. NASA, 1963-72, dir. NASA energy systems div., Washington, 1978-82; v.p. Houston ops. BDM Corp., 1983—; dir. advanced energy research and tech. NSF, 1973-75; dep. asst. adminstr. ERDA, 1975-77; acting asst. sec. Dept. Energy, Washington, 1977-78; solar energy coordinator U.S./USSR Coop. in Sci. and Tech.; U.S.

rep. Vienna Inst. for Comparative Econ. Studies Workshop on Energy; mem. engring. techs. adv. com. Montgomery Coll. Contbr. numerous articles on lunar sci., energy to profl. jours. Active Boy Scouts Am., 1958-71. Served with AC USN, 1951-56. Recipient Exceptional Service medal NASA, 1971, Sr. Exec. Service and Outstanding Performance award, 1980; Superior Achievement award Dept. Energy, 1978. Mem. Geol. Soc. Am., Am. Astron. Soc., Internat. Solar Energy Soc., AAAS. Office: BDM Corp 3100 S Gessner Suite 303 Houston TX 77063 *

BEATTIE, DONALD SHERMAN, labor union exec.; b. Canisteo, N.Y., May 20, 1921; s. Leo Milton and Catherine (Cornish) B.; m. Virginia Anna Maguire, May 6, 1943; children—James Milton, Thomas Michael, Donald Sherman. B.S., Cornell U., 1951. Dir. research Brotherhood Locomotive Engrs., 1951-62; exec. sec.-treas. Ry. Labor Execs. Assn., 1962-70, dir. govtl. affairs, 1975—; exec. sec. Congress Ry. Unions, 1970-75. Chmn. labor union research com. Presdl. R.R. Commn., 1960-62; mem. exec. bd. and mgmt. com. Internat. Transport Workers Fedn., 1962-77; mem. U.S. nat. com. Pan Am. Ry. Congress. Served with AUS, 1942-46. Mem. Brotherhood Locomotive Engrs., United Transp. Union. Club: Mason. Home: 827 Empress Ct Alexandria VA 22308 Office: 400 1st St NW Washington DC 20001

BEATTIE, EDWARD JAMES, surgeon, educator; b. Phila., June 30, 1918; m. Nicole Mary; 1 son, Bruce Stewart. B.A., Princeton U., 1939; M.D., Harvard U., 1943. Diplomate: Am. Bd. Surgery, Am. Bd. Thoracic Surgery (mem. bd. 1960-69, chmn. bd. 1967-69). Intern, surg. resident Peter Bent Brigham Hosp., Boston, 1942-46; Mosely traveling fellow (Harvard) to U. London, Eng., 1946-47; surg. fellow, Markle scholar George Washington U., 1947-52; chief thoracic surgery Presbyn. Hosp., 1952-54; chmn. dept. surgery Presbyn.-St. Luke's Hosp., 1954-65; cons. thoracic surgery Hines VA Hosp., 1953-65, Chgo. Tb San., 1954-65, Ill. Research and Edn. Hosp., 1956-65, Rockefeller U. Hosp., 1978—; prof. surgery U. Ill., 1955-65, Cornell U., 1965-83, emeritus, 1983—; prof. surgery, prof. oncology U. Miami, Fla., 1983—; chief thoracic surgery Meml. Hosp., N.Y.C., 1965-75, chmn. dept. surgery, 1966-78, chief med. officer, 1966-83, emeritus, 1983—, gen. dir., chief operating officer, 1975-83. Editorial bd.: Jour. Thoracic and Cardiovascular Surgery, 1962—, Pediatric Digest, 1962—, Jour. Surg. Oncology, 1972—, Cancer Clin. Trials, 1977, Internat. Advances in Surg. Oncology, 1977. Fellow A.C.S.; mem. Am. Assn. Thoracic Surgery, Am. Surg. Assn., Soc. Vascular Surgery, AMA, Chgo. Surg. Soc., Central, Western surg. assns., Internat. Soc. Surgery, Soc. Clin. Surgery, James Ewing Soc., Am. Radium Soc., Soc. Thoracic Surgeons, Transplantation Soc., Am. Assn. Med. Colls., Pan Am. Med. Assn., Am. Cancer Soc., Am. Fedn. Clin. Research, Pan Pacific Surg. Assn. Republican. Home: 2575 S Bayshore Dr Coconut Grove FL 33133 Office: C-400 Jackson Mem Hosp 1611 NW 12th Ave Miami FL 33136

BEATTIE, HERBERT WILSON, basso; b. Chgo., Aug. 23, 1926; s. Herbert W. and Myrtle W. (Sloan) B.; m. Elma M. Feltner, Jan. 11, 1947 (div. 1975); children—Kurt, Lynn, Mark, Dawn, Cameron; m. Laurie Lynn Lorck, July 12, 1975. B.A., Colo. Coll., 1948, Ph.D. (hon.), 1978; M.A., Westminster Choir Coll., 1950; postgrad., Mozarteum, Salzburg, Austria, 1955. Instr. Syracuse U., 1950-52; asst. prof. music Pa. State U., 1952-53; asst. prof. Buffalo U., 1953-59; prof. Hofstra U., 1959—; mem. N.Y.C. Opera, 1958-69, 80-81, Central City Colo. Opera, 1959-65, San Francisco Opera, 1960-66. Concert artist, U.S., Netherlands, Brussels; rec. artist. Served with USN, 1943-45. Recipient Sullivan Found. award, 1959; Rockefeller scholar, 1959-60. Mem. AAUP, Am. Guild Mus. Artists, Actors Equity, Can. Actors Equity, Phi Mu Alpha. Democrat. Episcopalian. Office: Hofstra U Fulton St Hempstead NY 11550

BEATTIE, NORA MAUREEN, ins. co. exec., actuary; b. Bklyn., July 10, 1925; d. Robert G. and Eileen (Geaney) B. B.A. summa cum laude, St. John's U., 1947, M.S., 1949. Asst. actuary N.Y. Life Ins. Co., N.Y.C., 1960-63, asso. actuary, 1963-67, actuary, 1967-71, 2d. v.p., 1971-74, v.p., actuary, 1974—. Fellow Am. Acad. Actuaries, Soc. Actuaries; mem. Bus. and Profl. Women's Club (treas. Wall St. Br. 1969-71, Woman of Yr., N.Y. br. 1968), N.Y. Guarantee Assn. (treas. 1981—). Club: N.Y. Actuaries. Office: NY Life Ins Co 51 Madison Ave New York NY 10010

BEATTY, JACK J., magazine editor; b. Cambridge, Mass., May 15, 1945; s. John J. and Frances C. (Parks) B.; m. Lois Masor, Sept. 3, 1976; 1 son, Aaron. Lit. editor The New Republic, Washington, 1978-83; sr. editor The Atlantic, Boston, 1983—. Poynter fellow Yale U., 1980. Mem. Nat. Book Critics Circle. Democrat. Roman Catholic. Home: 5 Kendall St Brookline MA 02146 Office: Care The Atlantic 8 Arlington St Boston MA 02116

BEATTY, JAMES RUSSELL, psychologist, statistician, educator; b. Huntsville, Ala., Nov. 8, 1943; s. Russell and Thelma (Wells) B.; m. Ann lynn Childs, Aug. 31, 1963; children: Kimberly Ann, Lynn Michelle, Susannah Elizabeth. B.A., Franklin Coll. Ind., 1965; M.S., Ind. State U., 1968; Ph.D., U. No. Colo., 1973; postgrad., Calif. Sch. Profl. Psychology, 1975. Accredited personnel diplomate. Counselor Ind. Dept. Corrections, 1965-67; exec. dir. Community Action Program, 1968; asst. prof. psychology Mt. Union Coll., 1968-70; clin. psychologist dir. Union Hosp. Mental Health Clinic, 1969-70; asst. prof., head dept. psychology St. Meinrad Coll., 1970-71; from asst. prof. to prof. dept. mgmt. San Diego State U., 1973—, chmn. dept. mgmt., 1980—; vis. prof. Econs. Inst., U. Colo., 1978-82; seminar leader Am. Compensation Assn., 1982—; internat. speaker, workshop coordinator, expert witness, cons. Contbr. articles to profl. jours., chpts. to textbooks, papers to meetings. Mem. citizens adv. com. Hardy Sch. Dist.; mgr. Little League, pres., 1983; coach Crusader's Youth Soccer; elder College Park Presbyn. Ch., San Diego. Doctoral fellow U. No. Colo. Mem. Am. Psychol. Assn., Am. Soc. Personnel Adminstrs., Am. Inst. Decision Scis. (program co-chmn., v.p. western div. 1980), Acad. Mgmt., Am. Soc. Clin. Hypnosis, Western Acad. Mgmt., Western Psychol. Assn. Home: 5144 Manhasset Dr San Diego CA 92115 Office: Dept Mgmt San Diego State U San Diego CA 92182

BEATTY, JOHN CABEEN, JR., judge; b. Washington, Apr. 13, 1919; s. John Cabeen and Jean (Morrison) B.; m. Clarissa Hager, Feb. 8, 1943; children: John Cabeen III, Clarissa Jean. A.B., Princeton, 1941; J.D., Columbia, 1948. Bar: Oreg. bar 1948. Practiced in, Portland, 1948-70; ptnr. Dusenbery, Martin, Beatty, Bischoff & Templeton, 1956-70; judge circuit ct., 1970—; mem. Oreg. Bd. Bar Examiners, 1953-54; chmn. legis. com. Oreg. Jud. Conf., 1976-82; mem. Oreg. CSC, 1962-64, Oreg. Law Enforcement Council, 1974-77; vice chmn. Oreg. Commn. Jud. Br., 1979—. Mem. legis. com. Nat. Sch. Bds. Assn., 1966-68, chmn. council large city sch. bds., 1967-68; counsel Democratic Party Oreg., 1956-58; co-chmn. Oreg. for Kennedy Com., 1968; chmn. bd. dirs. Portland Public Schs., 1967, 69. Served to capt. AUS, 1941-46; ETO. Decorated Bronze Star medal; recipient City Club of Portland award, 1967. Mem. Am., Oreg., Multnomah County bar assns., Am. Judicature Soc., Oreg. Hist. Soc. (dir. 1973—). Clubs: City (past pres., bd. govs.), Yacht, Racquet (Portland). Home: 2958 SW Dosch Rd Portland OR 97201 Office: 512 Multnomah County Courthouse Portland OR 97204

BEATTY, JOHN JOSEPH, III, corporate executive, lawyer; b. Washington, June 19, 1924; s. John Joseph and Helen (Simpson) B.; m. Mary Shipe, May 29, 1948; children: Patricia Beatty Abell, John J. Student, Duke U., 1943-44; B.S., Georgetown U., 1947, J.D., 1949. Bar: D.C. 1950, Md. 1952. Counsel Kraft Inc., Washington, 1965-76, v.p. govt. relations, 1976—; bd. dirs. B. Frank Joy Co., Blandensburg, Md., Hurley Machine & Boiler Works, Washington, Charles Boteder Ins. Co. Active Bus.-Govt. Relations Council, Washington; trustee Nat. Spinal Cord Injury Found., Washington. Served to lt. USN, 1944-46. Mem. ABA, D.C. Bar Assn., Delta Theta Phi. Clubs: Columbia Country (Chevy Chase, Md.); Univ. (Washington); Frenchman's Creek (West Palm Beach, Fla.); Farmington Country (Charlottesville, Va.). Home: 5412 Albia Rd Bethesda MD 20816 Office: Kraft Inc 1100 17th St NW Washington DC 20816

BEATTY, JOHN LEE, scenic designer; b. Palo Alto, Calif., Apr. 4, 1948; s. Shelton Lee and Caroline Dorothea (Burtis) B. B.A., Brown U., 1970; M.F.A., Yale U., 1973. Designer for Broadway, off-Broadway, regional theatre, opera and TV, 1973—; prof. theatrical design Bklyn. Coll., 1979—. Prodns. designed include Talley's Folly, 1980 (Tony award, Outer Critics Circle, Joseph Jefferson, Los Angeles Drama Critics awards), A Life in The Theatre, 1977, Ashes, 1977, Ain't Misbehavin', 1978, Knock, Knock, 1980, Fifth of July, 1980 (Tony nomination), Crimes of the Heart, 1981, Angels Fall, 1982, Alice in Wonderland, 1982. Recipient Obie award, 1975, Maharam award, 1976, 78. Mem. United Scenic Artists. Democrat. Congregationalist. Address: 107 W 86th St New York NY 10024

BEATTY, KENNETH ORION, JR., chemical engineer; b. East Lansdowne, Pa., Dec. 18, 1913; s. Kenneth Orion and Ada Pearl (Marshall) B.; m. Mary Catharine Carter, Aug. 18, 1936; children—Susan Jenifer, Prudence Carter, Lucy Margaret. B.S., Lehigh U., 1935, M.S., 1937; Ph.D., U. Mich., 1946. Registered profl. engr., N.C. Raybestos-Manhattan fellow Lehigh U., 1935-37; chem. engr. Dow Chem. Co., Midland, Mich., 1937-39; asst. prof. chem. engring. U. R.I., Kingston, 1939-44; research asso. U. Mich., 1944-46; asso. prof. N.C. State U., Raleigh, 1946-48, prof., 1948—, acting head dept. chem. engring., 1959-60, R.J. Reynolds Industries prof. chem. engring., 1961—, spl. cons. in engring. edn., 1982—; dir. Carolina Cons. Scientists and Engrs., 1979—; vis. prof. chem. engring. Ohio State U., summer 1949; vis. engr. Pratt & Whitney Co., Middletown, Conn., summer 1957; resident cons. engr. Nat. Lead Co. of Ohio, Fernald, summer 1959; mem. Max Jakob Award Com., 1963-67, chmn., 1966; mem. Nat. Heat Transfer Conf. Coordinating Com., 1965-71, chmn., 1967; coordinating chmn. 9th Nat. Heat Transfer Conf., Seattle, 1967; U.S. founding del. Assembly for Internat. Heat Transfer Conf., 1967-72; mem. sci. council Internat. Center for Heat and Mass Transfer, Yugoslavia, 1971—. Contbr. articles to profl. jours. Mem. N.C. Gov.'s Sci. Adv. Com. Recipient research grants from NASA, NSF, Wright Air Devel. Center, AEC, Am. Soc. Refrigerating Engrs., others.; Univ. fellow Princeton U., 1967-68. Fellow Am. Inst. Chem. Engrs.; mem. Am. Thermographic Soc., AAAS, Am. Assn. Engring. Edn., Am. Chem. Soc., University Park Homeowners Assn. (dir.). Home: 323 Shepherd St Raleigh NC 27607 Office: Dept Chem Engring NC State U Raleigh NC 27650

BEATTY, NED, actor; b. Louisville, July 6, 1937; s. Charles William and Margaret (Lennis) B.; m. Dorothy Adams Lindsay, June 28, 1979. Student pub. schs., Ky. Actor, Barter Theatre, Abingdon, Va., 1957-66, Arena Stage, Washington, 1963-71; film appearances include Deliverance, 1972, The Thief Who Came to Dinner, 1972, Nashville, 1975, W.W. and The Dixie Dancekings, 1975, Network, 1976, All the Presidents Men, 1976, The Big Bus, 1976, Micky and Nicky, 1976, Silver Streak, 1976, Exorcist II: The Heretic, 1977, Superman, 1978, Gray Lady Down, 1978, Promises in the Dark, 1979, The Incredible Shrinking Woman, 1981, Superman II, 1981, The Toy, 1983; TV films include The Execution of Private Slovik, 1974, The FBI Story: The FBI Versus The Ku Klux Klan, 1975, The Deadly Tower, 1975, Hunter, 1976, Friendly Fire, 1979; title role: TV series Szysznyk, 1977. Office: care Jack Field & Assos 9255 Sunset Blvd Suite 1105 Los Angeles CA 90069

BEATTY, PATRICIA JEAN, author; b. Portland, Oreg., Aug. 26; d. Walter Marcus and Jessie Pauline (Miller) Robbins; m. Carl G. Uhr, July 31, 1977; 1 dau. by previous marriage, Ann Alexandra Beatty Stewart. B.A., Reed Coll., 1944. Tchr. English and history Coeur d'Alene (Idaho) High Sch., 1947-50; librarian DuPont Co., Wilmington, Del., 1952-53; mem. library staff Riverside (Calif.) Public Library, 1953-57; tchr. creative writing UCLA, 1968-69, U. Calif., Riverside, 1967-68. Author: (with John Louis Beatty) At the Seven Stars, 1965, Campion Towers, 1966, (with others) Who Comes to King's Mountain, 1975, Hail Columbia, 1970, A Long Way to Whiskey Creek, 1971, Red Rock Over the River, 1973, Something to Shout About, 1976, By Crumbs, It's Mine, 1976, I Want My Sunday, Stranger, 1977, Wait for Me, Eula Bee, 1978, Lacy Makes a Match, 1979, That's One Ornery Orphan, 1980, Lupita Manana, 1981, Eight Mules From Monterey, 1982, Jonathan Down Under, 1982, Melinda Takes a Hand, 1983, Turn Homeward, Hannalee, 1984. Recipient 9 awards for books. Mem. Soc. Children's Book Writers. Democrat. Club: Zonta. Home and Office: 5085 Rockledge Dr Riverside CA 92506

BEATTY, RICHARD SCRIVENER, lawyer; b. Washington, May 6, 1934; s. John Joseph and Helen Louise (Simpson) B.; m. Barbara Boyd, July 14, 1956; children—Charles, Alexandra, Nicholas. B.A., Williams Coll., 1955; LL.B., Georgetown U., 1962. Bar: D.C. bar 1962. Trial atty. Dept. Justice, Washington, 1962-66; asso. chief counsel Office U.S. Comptroller of Currency, 1966-67; partner firm Alston, Miller & Gaines, Washington, 1968—; dir. Washington Corp., Women's Nat. Bank, Washington. Chmn. devel. council Williams Coll.; sr. warden St. Patricks Episcopal Ch., 1980—. Served with U.S. Army, 1956-59. Mem. Am. Law Inst., Am. Bar Assn., D.C. Bar Assn., Delta Psi. Clubs: Metropolitan (D.C.); Williams (N.Y.C.). Home: 5068 Sedgwick St NW Washington DC 20016 Office 1800 M St NW Suite 1000 Washington DC 20036

BEATTY, SAMUEL ALSTON, state justice; b. Tuscaloosa, Ala., Apr. 23, 1923; s. Eugene C. and Rosabelle (Horton) B.; m. Maude Applegate, Jan. 19, 1949; children—Rosa Beatty Lord, Eugene A. B.S. in Commerce and Bus. Adminstrn, U. Ala., 1948, J.D., 1953; LL.M., Columbia U., 1959, J.S.D., 1964. Bar: Ala. bar 1953. Pvt. practice, Tuscaloosa, 1953-56; mem. faculty U. Ala. Law Sch., 1955-70, prof. law, 1963-70, asst. dean, 1959-63; vis. prof. law U. Cin. Law Sch., 1966-67; asso. dir. Ala. Defender Project, 1967-70; dean, prof. law Mercer U. Law Sch., 1970-72, adj. prof., 1972-74; v.p., trust officer First Nat. Bank & Trust Co., Macon, Ga., 1972-74; asst. atty. gen., chief civil div. State of Ala., 1974; partner firm Henley & Beatty, Tuscaloosa, Northport, Ala., 1975-76; asso. justice Ala. Supreme Ct., 1976—; adj. prof. U. Ala. Grad. Sch., since 1975; speaker, lectr. in field. Contbr. legal jours. Served to maj. USAAF, 1942-45; PTO. Decorated Air medal with 9 oak leaf clusters. Mem. Am., Ala., Tuscaloosa County bar assns., Nat. Orgn. Legal Problems Edn., Farrah Order Jurisprudence, Order of Coif, Phi Alpha Delta. Democrat. Methodist. Address: PO Box 218 Montgomery AL 36101

BEATTY, WARREN, producer, actor; b. Richmond, Va., Mar. 30, 1938; s. Ira O. and Kathlyn (MacLean) B. Student, Northwestern U., 1956, Stella Adler Theatre Sch., N.Y.C., 1957. Film appearances include Splendor in the Grass, 1961, The Roman Spring of Mrs. Stone, 1962, All Fall Down, 1962, Lilith, 1963, Mickey One, 1965, Promise Her Anything, 1965, Kaleidoscope, 1966, Bonnie and Clyde, (also producer), 1967, The Only Game in Town, 1969, McCabe and Mrs. Miller, 1971, Dollars, 1971, The Parallax View, 1974, The Fortune, 1975; producer, co-screenwriter, actor: Shampoo, 1975; producer, co-dir., co-screenwriter, actor: Heaven Can Wait, 1978; appearance on Broadway: in play A Loss of Roses, 1960. Office: care Dirs Guild Am 7950 Sunset Blvd Hollywood CA 90046 *

BEATTY, WILLIAM LOUIS, federal judge; b. Mendota, Ill., Sept. 4, 1925; s. Raphael H. and Teresa A. (Collins) B.; m. Dorothy Jeanne Starnes, June 12, 1948; children: William S., Steven M., Thomas D., Mary C. Student, Washington U., St. Louis, 1945-47; LL.B., St. Louis U., 1950. Bar: Ill. 1950. Gen. practice law, Granite City, 1950-68; circuit judge 3d Jud. Circuit Ill., 1968-79; U.S. dist. judge So. Dist. Ill., 1979—. Served with AUS, 1943-45. Mem. Am. Bar Assn., Ill. Bar Assn., Madison County Bar Assn., Tri-City Bar Assn. Roman Catholic. Office: 501 Belle St Alton IL 62002

BEATY, HARRY NELSON, internist, educator, university dean; b. Brookfield, Mo., June 25, 1932; s. William Harry and Agnes Marie (Walton) B.; m. Georgia Kay Luther, July 30, 1955; children: Dean, Kara Lynn. Student, U. Wash., 1950-54, M.D., 1958. Intern in medicine U. Minn., Mpls., 1958-59; resident in medicine U. Wash., Seattle, 1962-63; NIH fellow in medicine, 1963-65; instr. medicine U. Wash., 1965-67, asst. prof., 1967-71, assoc. prof., 1971-75, prof., 1975-77; prof., chmn. dept. medicine U. Vt., Burlington, 1977-83; prof., dean Med. Sch. Northwestern U., Chgo., 1983—; head infectious diseases Harborview Med. Ctr., Seattle, 1968-73; med. dir. Providence Med. Ctr., Seattle, 1973-77; chief med. service Med. Ctr. Hosp. Vt., Burlington, 1977-83; investigator Howard Hughes Med. Inst., 1965-66. Contbr. articles on infectious disease to med. to profl. jours., chpts. to med. textbooks. Served to lt. USN, 1959-63. Fellow ACP (sec. treas. Wash. chpt. 1975-76); mem. Assn. Profs. Medicine (chmn. task force manpower needs 1980-83), Infectious Diseases Soc. Am. (councillor 1979-82, publs. com. 1979—), Am. Soc. Lin. Investigation, Alpha Omega Alpha. Office: Northwestern U Med Sch 303 E Chicago Ave Chicago IL 60611

BEATY, ORREN, JR., assn. exec.; b. Clayton, N.Mex., June 13, 1919; s. Orren and Edith (Mason) B.; m. Mary Ethel Turner, Dec. 30, 1944; children—Orren III, Laura Leigh, Susan Ray. B.A., N.Mex. State U., 1940; postgrad., U. Houston, 1951-52. Mng. editor Las Cruces (N.Mex.) Sun-News, 1946-47; reporter, polit. writer, columnist Ariz. Republic, Phoenix, 1948-55; adminstrv. asst. to Rep. Stewart L. Udall, 1956-61; asst. to Sec. Dept. Interior, Washington, 1961-67; fed. co-chmn. Four Corners Planning Commn., Econ. Devel. Adminstrn., Dept. Commerce, Washington, 1967-69; asso. editor Congl. Quar., 1969-70; legislative asst. to Rep. Mike McCormack, Washington, 1971; dir. congl. relations Nat. R.R. Passenger Corp. (AMTRAK), Washington, 1971-74; pres. Nat. Assn. R.R. Passengers, Washington, 1974-79; asst. gen. mgr. Western Fuels Assn., 1979—. Democratic candidate from 3d Ariz. dist. to Ho. of Reps., 1970. Served to 1st lt. AUS, 1942-46; Served to 1st lt. USAF, 1950-52. Home: 1784 Proffit Rd Vienna VA 22180 Office: 1225 19th St NW Washington DC 20036 *Pure chance, I believe, plays a major role in helping us attain our ambitions. At age nine, I thought I wanted wanted to be in government—in the legislative area. To do that required becoming a lawyer, I thought. Yet, interest in journalism and military duty prevented that. Still, by a series of chances, I became a congressional aide and later an official in the executive branch. Not exactly what I planned, but satisfying. No amount of work or planning could have achieved what chance provided.*

BEAUBIEN, PHILIPPE DE GASPE, II, communications executive; b. Montreal, Que., Can., Jan. 12, 1928; m. Nan Bowles O'Connell, Jan. 29, 1956; children: Philippe III, Nanon, Francois. B.A., Montreal U., 1952; M.B.A., Harvard U., 1954; hon. degree in law, York U., 1979. Founding pres. Beaubien Distbrn., Montreal, 1960-63; mayor Expo '67, Montreal, 1963-67; pres. Telemedia Que. Ltd., Montreal, 1968-71; chmn., chief exec. officer Telemedia Inc., Montreal, 1971—; chmn., pub. exec. officer TV Guide (Hebdo), Toronto, Ont., 1976—; dir. Can. Devel. Corp., Can. Satellite Communications, Bombardier Inc., Reitman's Can. Ltd., McDonalds Restuarants Can. Ltd., Toronto Dominion Bank. Dir. Banff Sch. Continuing Edn.; mem. York U. adv. bd.; hon. chmn. Parcipaction. Decorated Order Of Can.; dir. Can. Centennial medal; decorated Govt. Czechoslovakia Gold medal; recipient B'nai Brith Award of Merit. Mem. Chief Exec. Orgn. (dir.). Clubs: Mount Royal (Montreal); York (Toronto). Office: Telemedia Inc 1010 Sherbrooke S W Suite 1610 Montreal PQ Canada H3A 2R7

BEAUCHAMP, JACQUES, gas company executive; b. Montreal, Que., Can., July 28, 1926; s. Rosario and Lucienne (Bourdeau) B.; m. Pierrette Mainville, Sept. 9, 1946; 1 dau., Elise. Student, Levis Coll., 1934, 43, LaSalle Extension U., 1941-48, Sir George Williams U., 1958-59. Vice pres. fin., treas. Gaz Metropolitain, Inc., Montreal, 1970-73, group v.p. fin., treas., 1973-75, exec. v.p., 1975-76, pres., 1976-81, also dir.; dir. No. and Central Gas Corp., Ltd. Bd. dirs. U. Que., Montreal, Montreal Symphony Orch. Mem. Fin. Exec. Inst., Conf. Bd. in Can., Canadian, Am. gas assns., Canadian Tax Found., Montreal Bd. Trade. Roman Catholic. Clubs: St. James, St. Denis, Laval-sur-le-Lac Golf Course, Mt. Royal.

BEAUCHAMP, JOHN ROBERT, painter; b. Denver, Nov. 19, 1923; s. John and Rilla (Bevans) B.; m. Nadine Valenti, Sept. 9, 1967; 1 son, Michael. B.F.A., Cranbrook Art Acad., 1950; postgrad., Hofmann Art Sch., 1950-53, Denver U., 1950. Mem. faculty Cooper Union, N.Y. Sch. Visual Arts, U. Calif., San Diego, SUNY, New Paltz, Syracuse, U. Ga., 1980—. Exhibited works in 34 one-man shows, 1953—; exhibited in 32 group shows, 1953—, works in collections at, Met. Mus. Modern Art, Whitney Mus. Am. Art, others. Served with U.S. Navy, 1943-46. Guggenheim fellow, 1974; Fulbright grantee, 1959; Nat. Endowment for Arts grantee, 1964. Mem. Artists Equity Assn. N.Y. Home: 463 West St New York NY

BEAUCHAMP, RONALD A., manufacturing company executive; b. Oakland, Calif., Oct. 2, 1938; s. Wendell G. and Lucille M. (Colambatto) B.; m. Carol M. Mele, Sept. 18, 1964; children: Stephen T., Kathryn M. B.S. in Chemistry, Ariz. State U., 1960; M.B.A., Stanford U., 1967. Prodn. mgr. Procter & Gamble, Dallas, 1960-65; gen. mgr. Boise Cascade Corp., St. Louis, 1967-70, ops. mgr., Hazelwood, Mo., 1970-71, v.p., gen. mgr., 1971—. Mem. lay bd. DePaul Community Hosp., St. Louis, 1974—; bd. dirs. Jr. Achievement of Mississippi Valley, St. Louis, 1976—. Served to 1st lt. USAR, 1960-68. Mem. Aircraft Owners and Pilots Assn. Republican. Home: 149 Bellington Ln Creve Coeur MO 63141 Office: Boise Cascade Corp 13300 Interstate Hazelwood MO 63042

BEAUCHAMP, WILLIAM ELLSWORTH, retired foreign service officer; b. Bklyn., Aug. 30, 1912; s. William Ellsworth and Mary (Klingmann) B.; m. Kathryn Goodman, June 11, 1933; 1 son, William Edward; m. Veronica Ellen Klimek, July 14, 1943; children: Danielle Marie, Mary Anne. Student, Bklyn. Poly. Inst., 1929-31, U. Md., 1953-56, George Washington U., 1956-57. With N.Y. Telephone Co., 1928-42; chief tripartite mil. permit officer for Germany, Prague, 1946, Berne, 1946-49, Paris, 1949-50; attaché Am. Embassy, Paris, 1951-54; mem. U.S. del. NATO meeting, 1953; 2d sec., consul, Paris, 1954, polit. officer, 1955-56; prof. Fgn. Service Inst., 1956-58, mgmt. officer,

1958-61; 1st sec., consul, Belgrade, Yugoslavia, 1961-64; 1st sec., consul and chief adminstrv. sect. Am. Embassy, Algiers, Algeria, 1964-66; fgn. service insp. Dept. State, 1966-69; adminstrv. counselor Am. Embassy, Taipei, Taiwan, 1969-72, ret.; meeter and expediter fgn. guests Washington Internat. Center, 1976-78. Sec. local No. 7 Telephone Employees Union, 1938-40; sub-area chmn. United Givers Fund, Washington, 1956-61; co-founder, v.p. Alexandria (Va.) Soc. Retarded Children, 1958-61; v.p. Minnie Howard PTA, Alexandria, 1959; bd. dirs. No. Va. Sheltered Occupational Tng. Center, 1959-60, No. Va. Assn. Retarded Citizens, 1974-77; chmn. govt. affairs com. No. Va. Assn. Retarded Citizens, 1974-76, now mem.; chmn. residential services com. Va. Assn. Retarded Citizens, 1976-77; mem. adv. council Alexandria Ret. Sr. Vol. Program, 1980-83; mem. governing bd. City of Alexandria Community Mental Health Ctr., 1983—; mem. Mental Health, Mental Retardation, and Substance Abuse Bd. City of Alexandria, 1982—, mem. Pub. Health Adv. Commn., 1982—, mem. Pub. Health Adv. Commn., 1982—, mem. Mental Health, Mental Retardation Community Services Bd., 1982—; chmn. bd. Embassy Shop, Embassy Civilian Fund, both Taipei, 1969-72. Served to capt. AUS, 1942-47; ETO. Mem. Am. Fgn. Service Assn., Diplomatic and Consular Officers Ret., Am. Assn. Ret. Persons (bd. dirs. Alexandria chpt. 1980—), Nat. Assn. Ret. Fed. Employees. Home: 925 N Van Dorn St Alexandria VA 22304

BEAUCHEMIN, ROGER OLIVIER, consulting engineer; b. Donnacona, Que., Can., May 20, 1923; s. Jules Arm and Marie Anne (Gervias) B.; m. Andree Decarie, June 29, 1950; children: Francois, Denys, Anne-Marie, Roger. Bach. Applied Scis., Ecole Polytechnique, U. Montreal, Que., 1950. Engr., tech. sales dept. Canada Cement Co. Ltd., Montreal, 1950-55; partner Beauchemin-Beaton-Lapointe (Cons. Engrs.), Montreal, 1956—; pres. Arrowby Cons.'s, Inc.; dir. Can. Marconi Co., Nat. Westminster Bank Can., Stablex Inc.; chmn. bd. The United Provinces Ins. Co. Councillor Municipality of Mont-Tremblant, Que., 1965-74; pres. Chambre de Commerce du Dist. de Montreal, 1969-70; vice-chair and mem. exec. com. Montreal Port Authority, 1971-76; chmn. Montreal Heart Inst., 1976-78; chmn., chief exec. officer Montreal Port Authority, 1977-80; chmn. Montreal Heart Inst. Research Fund, 1981—; bd. dirs. Found. Fournier Ethier. Recipient Canadian Design of Merit citations, 1966; award Grad. Soc. of Ecole Polytechnique, 1978; decorated knight Order St. Lazarus of Jerusalem. Mem. Order Engrs. Quebec, Assn. Cons. Engrs. Can., Inst. Transp. Engrs. (pres. Canadian sect. 1971), Canadian Transp. Research Forum. Roman Catholic. Clubs: St. Denis, Mount Royal, Mt. Bruno Country. Chmn. project exec. com. for writing and publishing Manual of Geometric Design for Canadian Roads and Sts. Home: 4345 Westmount Ave Westmount PQ H3Y 1W4 Canada Office: 1134 Ste Catherine West Montreal PQ H3B 1H4 Canada

BEAUDET, ROBERT ARTHUR, chemistry educator; b. Woonsocket, R.I., Aug. 18, 1935; s. Ralph Edgar and Blanche L. (Pelchat) B.; m. Julia Maria Hughes, Sept. 14, 1957; children: Susan, Donna, Debra, Stephanie, Michelle, David, Nicole. B.S., Worcester Poly. Inst., 1957; M.A., Harvard U., 1960, Ph.D., 1962. Research scientist Jet Propulsion Lab., Pasadena, Calif., 1961-62; asst. prof. chemistry U. So. Calif., Los Angeles, 1962-66, assoc. prof., 1966-71, prof., 1971—, chmn. dept. chemistry, 1979-83; cons. in field. Served to 1st lt. U.S. Army, 1961-62. Recipient Alexander von Humboldt Spl. award, 1974-75; fellow NSF, 1957-61, Nat. Bur. Standards, 1961-62, A.P. Sloan Found., 1967-71. Mem. Am. Chem. Soc., Am. Phys. Soc., Sigma Xi, Tau Beta Pi a. Home: 887 Vallombrosa Dr Pasadena CA 91107 Office: U So Calif Dept Chemistry Los Angeles CA 90089

BEAUDOIN, GÉRALD-A(RMAND), lawyer, educator; b. Montreal, Apr. 15, 1929; s. Arm and Aldea (St.-Arnaud) B.; m. Renée Desmarais, Sept. 11, 1954; children—Viviane, Louise, Denise, Françoise. B.A. summa cum laude, U. Montreal, Que., Can., 1950, LL.L. magna cum laude, 1953, M.A. in Law, 1954; postgrad. in comparative law (Carnegie scholar), U. Toronto, Ont., Can., 1954-55; D.E.S.D. cum laude, U. Ottawa, Ont., 1958. Bar: Called to Que. bar 1954, created queen's counsel 1969. Practiced law with Paul Gérin-Lajoie, Montreal, 1955-56; adv. counsel Dept. Justice, Ottawa, 1956-65, sr. adv. counsel, 1960-65; asst. parliamentary counsel Ho. of Commons of Can., Ottawa, 1965-69; civil law dean Faculty of Law, U. Ottawa, 1969-79, prof. constl. law, 1969—; mem. Goldenberg Com. on Constn., 1967, La Commission des Services Juridiques du Québec, 1972-73, Task Force on Can. Unity, 1977-79. Author: Essais sur la Constitution, 1979, Le partage des pouvoirs, 1980, 2d edit., 1982, (with others) Mecanismes pour une nouvelle constitution, 1981; Co-editor: La Charte canadienne des droits et libertes, 1982; contbr. numerous articles to Can. and fgn. law revs.; mem.: (with others) Themis Law Rev, 1951-52. Mem. Can. Bar Assn. (nat. chmn. sect. constl. and internat. law 1971-73), Can. Inst. Public Affairs, Inst. Public Adminstrn. (Can.), Can. Law Deans (chmn. 1972-73), Que. Law Deans (chmn. 1975-76), Nat. Gallery Can., Can. Assn. Comparative Law (exec. 1974). Roman Catholic. Club: Cercle Universitaire d'Ottawa. Home: 4 St-Thomas Hull PQ J8Y 1L4 Canada Office: 57 Copernicus Ottawa ON K1N 6N5 Canada

BEAUDOIN, LAURENT, industrial, recreational and transportation company executive; b. Laurier Station, Que., Can., May 13, 1938; s. P.A. and Yvonne (Rodrigue) B.; m. Claire Bombardier, Aug. 29, 1959; children—Nicole, Pierre, Elaine, Denise. B.A., Ste. Anne U., N.S., Can., 1957; M. Commerce, Sherbrooke U., 1960, D. Bus. Adminstrn. (hon.), 1971. Partner firm Beaudoin, Morin, Dufresne & Assos., Quebec, Que., 1961-63; comptroller Bombardier Ltd., Valcourt, Que., 1963-64, gen. mgr., 1964-66, pres., 1966—; chmn., chief exec. officer Bombardier, Inc., Montreal, Que., 1979—; dir. Bombardier-Rotax GmbH, Gunskirchen, Austria, Entreprises de J.-Armand Bombardier, Valcourt, Bombardier Corp. Inc., Duluth, Minn., Banque Nationale du Canada, B.C. Forest Products Ltd., Can. Devel. Corp. Mem. Can. Council Christians and Jews; hon. v.p. Que, Provincial council Boy Scouts Can.; Bd. govs. Faculté d'Adminstrn., U. Sherbrooke, Que. Decorated officer Order Can. Mem. Inst. Chartered Accountants, Young Presidents' Orgn., C. of C. Que. (gov.). Home: Westmount PQ Canada Office: Bombardier Inc 800 Dorchester West Suite 1520 Montreal PQ H3B 1X9 Canada

BEAUDOUIN, JOHN TYRELL, editor; b. Hartford, Conn., Oct. 16, 1920; s. Harry Edward and Margaret (King) B.; m. Patricia Ann Curtin, June 7, 1942 (dec. Nov. 1970); children: Lisa King Beaudouin Bauer, Stephanie Beaudouin Piper, John Curtin, Mark Tyrell; m. Maria Steele, Oct. 9, 1971; step-children: Jonathan Charles Steele, Juliana Steele. B.A., Columbia U., 1941. Asso. editor Reader's Digest, Pleasantville, N.Y., 1947-50, dir., v.p., 1965-82; asso. editor Reader's Digest Condensed Books, 1950-54, mng. editor, 1954-58, exec. editor, 1958-64, editor-in-chief, 1964-82. Author: (with Everett Mattlin) The Phrase-Dropper's Handbook, 1976. Chmn. bd. trustees Chappaqua (N.Y.) Library, 1964-67; bd. dirs. Norwalk (Conn.) Symphony Soc., 1973-77. Served to 1st lt. AUS, 1942-46. Mem. Assn. Am. Pubs. (past dir.), Phi Beta Kappa, Phi Kappa Psi. Clubs: Century, Dutch Treat, Publishers Lunch (N.Y.C.); Woodway (Darien, Conn.).

BEAUDREAU, DAVID EUGENE, dentist, educator; b. Plummer, Idaho, May 30, 1929; s. Arthur T. and Ada B.; m. Leah LaVerne Hardin, Dec. 17, 1950; children: Gary, Brian, Ron. Student, Eastern Wash. Coll., 1947-49; D.D.S., U. Washington, 1954; M.S.D., U. Pa., 1965; D.Sc. (hon.), Georgetown U., 1981. Practice dentistry specializing in restorative dentistry, 1956—; instr. fixed partial dentures and operative dentistry U. Wash., Seattle, 1956-58, clin. instr. operative dentistry, 1958-61; asst. prof. fixed partial dentures U. Pa., Phila., 1963-66, asso. prof., 1966-68, dir. postgrad. perio-prosthesis, 1968, chmn. dept. fixed prosthesis, 1963-68; prof. restorative dentistry Med. Coll. Ga. Sch. Dentistry, Augusta, 1972-77, prof. periodontics, 1975-77, asso. dean, 1972-75; prof. pediodontics and fixed prosthesis Sch. Dentistry, Georgetown U., Washington, 1977—, dean Sch. Dentistry, 1977-81; cons. U.S. Army, 1966-77, VA Hosp., Augusta, Ga., 1968-77, ADA, 1973—, VA, Phila., 1966-68. Author: Atlas of Fixed Partial Prosthesis, 1975; contbg. author: Clinical Dentistry, 1975. Trustee Am. Fund for Dental Health, 1977—. Served to lt. USN, 1954-56. Fellow Am. Coll. Dentists, Internat. Coll. Dentists, D.C. Acad. Gen. Dentistry (hon.), Am. Acad. Gold Foil Operators; mem. ADA (chmn. council dental materials, instruments and equipment 1979—), Am. Acad. Periodontology, Acad. Restorative Dentistry, Am. Acad. Crown and Bridge Prosthesis, Internat. Assn. Dental Research, Ga. State Dental Assn., Eastern Dist. Dental Soc., Omicron Kappa Upsilon. Presbyterian. Home: 4356 Deerwood Ln PO Box 335 Evans GA 30809 Office: 4250 Washington Rd PO Box 335 Evans GA 30809

BEAUDRY, RENE LUC, gastroenterologist, educator; b. Joliette, Que., Can., Apr. 7, 1937; s. J. Donat and Aline (Morand) B.; m. Thislaine Landreville, June 24, 1960; children: Marc, Jules, Claude, Alain. B.A., U. Montreal, Que., 1956, M.D., 1961; M.D., U. Minn., 1964. Asst prof. medicine U. Sherbrooke, Que., 1967-70, assoc. prof., 1970-78, prof., 1978—, chief service gastroenterology, 1970—. Fellow Royal Coll. Physicians Can.; mem. Assn. des Medecines de langue Francaise, Can. Assn. Gastroenterology, Royal Coll. Physicians and Surgeons (dir. program 1970). Office: Faculty Medicine U Sherbrooke Sherbrooke PQ Canada J1H 5N4

BEAUFORT, JOHN DAVID, journalist; b. Edmonton, Alta., Can., Sept. 23, 1912; came to U.S., 1922, naturalized, 1943; s. Ernest and Margaret Mary (Crawley) B.; m. Francesca Bruning, June 28, 1940. Student, Boston U., 1930-33, 35-39, Rollins Coll., 1933-35. With The Christian Science Monitor, Boston, 1930-33, 35—, asst. reviewer, 1937-39, N.Y.C. drama and film critic, 1939-43, war corr. for Pacific, 1943-46, chief N.Y.C. news bur., 1946-50, arts and mag. editor, 1950-51, N.Y.C. drama and film critic, 1951-58, 59-61, arts-entertainment editor, 1959-61, chief London bur., 1962-65, feature editor, Boston, 1965-70, N.Y.C. drama critic, 1971-74, contbg. drama critic, feature writer, 1975—. Author: 505 Theatre Questions Your Friends Can't Answer; BBC European Service panelist, 1962-65. Recipient Critics award Dirs. Guild Am., 1961. Mem. N.Y. Drama Critics Circle, Am. Theatre Critics Assn., New Drama Forum Assn., Critics Circle of London (hon.), Nat. Theatre Conf. (hon.). Christian Scientist. Club: Players (N.Y.C.). Home: 424 E 52d St New York NY 10022 *Adult education is learning to live and living to learn and sharing what life has taught you. This is more than compound interest. It is enrichment without depletion.*

BEAULIEU, ROGER LOUIS, lawyer; b. Montreal, Que., Can., Sept. 26, 1924; s. Guillaume A. and Eulalie (Galibert) B.; m. Andrée Prieur, Mar. 5, 1955; children: Marc, Nicole, Michèle. B.A., Brébeuf Coll., 1944; B.C.L., McGill U., 1947; M.B.A., Harvard Bus. Sch., 1949. Bar: Called to bar 1947, Queen's counsel 1959. Partner firm Martineau Walker, 1949—; Dir. Provident Gen. Ins., The Laurentian Mut. Ins., Can. Permanent Trust Co., Télémedia Communications Ltd., Can. Permanent Mortgage Corp., Netcom Inc., Cara Ops. Ltd., Dominion Electric Protection Co., BBC Brown Boveri Can. Inc., Pirelli Can. Inc., B.C. DisFrick Telegraph Co. Ltd.; Lectr. corp. law U. Montreal, 1960-70. Pres. Montreal Citizen's Com., 1959-60; chmn. Montreal adv. bd. Can. Permanent Trust, Montreal Corp. Hdqrs. Com.; bd. dirs. Montreal Heart Inst.; mem. Arts Council, M&L Urban Community. Mem. Can. Bar Assn. Clubs: Univ., St. Denis, Mt. Royal. Home: 3044 St Sulpice Rd Montreal PQ Canada Office: 3400 Stock Exchange Tower 800 Victoria Sq Montreal PQ H4Z 1E9 Canada

BEAULNES, AURELE, physician, research inst. adminstr.; b. Montreal, Que., Can., Aug. 7, 1928; s. Lucien and Berthe (Courteau) B.; m. Rita Archambault, June 16, 1953; children—Pierre, Marie-Helene, Genevieve. B.A., U. Montreal, 1946, M.D., 1953. Intern Notre Dame, St. Justine, St. Jean-de-Dieu, Montreal, 1952-53; resident Notre Dame Hosp., 1953; asst. prof. pharmacology U. Montreal Faculty Medicine, 1957-59, asso. prof., 1959-62, prof., 1962-66, head dept. pharmacology, 1959-66, vice dean, 1962-64; prof., head dept. pharmacology, dir. basic scis. div. U. Sherbrooke Faculty Medicine, 1966-67; vis. prof. U. Ottawa, Ont., 1967-68; prof. pharmacology and therapeutics, Med. Research Council asso. McGill U., Montreal, 1968-71; sec. Can. Ministry of State for Sci. and Tech., Ottawa, 1971-74, 1971-74; dir. Armand-Frappier Inst., Laval-des-Rapides, Que., 1974—; cons. WHO, 1969-71; MacLaughlin vis. prof. McMaster U. Med. Sch., 1970-71. Author: Le Centre Medical Universitaire, 1966; contbr. articles on pharmacology, physiology, med. health and sci. policy to profl. publs. Decorated Queen Elizabeth II Commemorative medal; knight Order St. Lazarus of Jerusalem; John and Mary R. Markle scholar, 1957-62. Mem. La Corporation professionnelle des medeċins du Quebec (license), Pharmacol. Soc. Can., Am. Soc. Pharmacology and Exptl. Therapeutics, Can. Soc. Clin. Investigation, Clin. Research Club Que., Can. Found. Advancement Clin. Pharmacology. Office: 531 Des Prairies Blvd Laval-des-Rapides PQ H7N 4Z3 Canada

BEAUMONT, PAMELA JO, food and drug company executive; b. Valentine, Nebr., July 30, 1944; d. William Henry and Phyllis Faye (Zersen) Bostrom (Mott); m. Fred H. Beaumont, Apr. 17, 1971 (div. May 1981). B.S. in Bus., U. Colo., 1966, M.B.A., 1968. Asst. product mgr. Ore-Ida Foods, Boise, Idaho, 1969-71, product mgr., 1971-73, sr. product mgr., 1973-75, gen. mgr. sales and mktg. services, 1975; v.p. consumer affairs Albertson's Inc., Boise, 1975-76, v.p. mktg., 1976—. Bd. dirs. Jr. Achievement, Boise, 1973; mem. adv. com. Boise State U. M.B.A. Program, 1974-78; chmn. Albertson's United Way Drive, Boise, 1976; mktg. adviser Idaho Park Found., Boise, 1978-79. Democrat. Home: 5140 Mountain View Dr Boise ID 83704 Office: Albertson's Inc 250 Parkcenter Blvd Boise Id 83726

BEAVEN, WINTON HENRY, college dean; b. Binghamton, N.Y., Jan. 26, 1915. Student, Hamilton Coll., 1933-35; B.S. in History and Internat. Relations, Atlantic Union Coll., 1937, M.A., Clark U., 1938; Ph.D. in Speech, U. Mich., 1950. Instr. history Madison Coll., Tenn., 1938-40; instr. speech and English, dean of men Atlantic Union Coll., South Lancaster, Mass., 1940-43; asst. prof. Union Coll., Lincoln, Nebr., 1943-45, assoc. prof., 1945-47, prof. speech, 1947-50, chmn. dept. speech, 1943-50; asst. prof. U. Mich., Ann Arbor, 1950-52, assoc. prof., 1952-53; assoc. sec. Internat. Commn. for Prevention of Alcoholism, Washington, 1953-57; dean Grad. Sch. Potomac U., Washington, 1956-59; dean acad. adminstrn. Columbia Union Coll., Takoma Park, Md., 1959-65, pres., 1965-70; dean Kettering Coll. Med. Arts, Ohio, 1970—; v.p. edn. Kettering Med. Ctr., 1972—; v.p., lectr. Internat. Commn. for Prevention of Alcoholism; pres. Nat. Com. for Prevention of Alcoholism; bd. dirs., past chmn. Western Ohio Regional Alchoholism Council; past. pres. Dayton Area Council on Alcholism and Drug Abuse. Pres. Am. Bus. Men's Research Found.; chmn. bd., v.p. Dayton-Miami Valley Consortium; bd. dirs. Miami Valley Health Systems Agy., Inc.; bd. dirs., chmn. health div. United Way. Mem. Assn. Higher Edn., Speech Communication Assn., Religious Speech Communication Assn. Adventist. Lodge: Rotary. Office: Kettering Med Ctr 3737 Southern Blvd Kettering OH 45429

BEAVER, BONNIE VERYLE, veterinarian, educator; b. Mpls., Oct. 26, 1944; d. Crawford F. and Gladys I. Gustafson; m. Larry J. Beaver, Nov. 25, 1972. B.S., U. Minn., 1966, D.V.M., 1968; M.S., Tex. A&M U., 1972. Instr. vet. surgery and radiology U. Minn., 1968-69; instr. vet. anatomy Tex. A&M U., College Station, 1969-72, asst. prof., 1972-76, assoc. prof., 1976-82; prof. Tex A&M U., College Station, 1982—. Contbr. articles to profl. jours.; mem. editorial bd.: Applied Animal Ethology, 1981-82. Vice pres. Brazos Valley Regional Sci. and Engring. Fair, 1974—; bd. dirs. Brazos Valley unit Am. Cancer Soc., 1976—, v.p., 1977—. Named Citizen of Week The Press, 1981. Mem. AVMA, Tex. Vet. Med. Assn., Women's Vet. Med. Assn., Brazos Valley Vet. Med. Assn., Am. Animal Hosp. Assn., Am. Soc. Vet. Ethology, Am. Assn. Vet. Clinicians, Vet. Computer Soc., Assn. Am. Vet. Med. Colls., Phi Sigma, Sigma Epsilon Sigma, Phi Zeta, Phi Delta Gamma. Home: RFD 3 Box 354 College Station TX 77840 Office: Coll Vet Medicine Dept Vet Anatomy Tex A&M Univ College Station TX 77843

BEAVER, PAUL CHESTER, parasitologist, educator; b. Glenwood, Ind., Mar. 10, 1905; s. John Chester and Blanche Emma (Murphy) B.; m. Lela E. West, Oct. 16, 1931; 1 dau., Paula Jean Beaver Chipman. A.B., Wabash Coll., 1928, D.Sc. (hon.), 1963; M.S., U. Ill., 1929, Ph.D., 1935. Diplomate: Am. Bd. Microbiology. Asst. zoology U. Ill., 1928-29, 31-34; instr. zoology U. Wyo., 1929-31; instr. biology Oak Park Jr. Coll., 1934-37; asst. prof. biology Lawrence Coll., 1937-42; biologist Wis. Dept. Health, summer 1940, Ga. Dept. Pub. Health, 1942-45; asst. prof. parasitology Tulane U. Med. Sch., 1945-47, asso. prof., 1947-52, prof., 1952—, head dept. parasitology, 1956-71, William Vincent prof. tropical diseases and hygiene, 1958-76, prof. emeritus, 1976—; dir. Internat. Center Med. Research and Tng. in Colombia, 1967-76; vis. prof. Eastern Mont. Normal Sch., summers 1935-37, Colo. State Coll., 1941, U. Mich., 1954-56, 58, U. Natal Med. Sch., Durban, South Africa, 1957; hon. vis. prof. Universidad del Valle, Cali, Colombia, 1970-76; cons. Ga. Dept. Pub. Health, 1946-53, USPHS Hosp., New Orleans, 1949-72, WHO, 1960-77; mem. com. standards and exams. Am. Bd. Microbiology, 1960-67; mem. commn. parasitic diseases Armed Forces Epidemiol. Bd., 1953-73, dir. commn. parasitic diseases, 1967-73; mem. Am. Found. Tropical Medicine, 1960-66; microbiology fellowships rev. panel NIH, 1960-63; mem. WHO expert com. on intestinal helminths, 1963, temp. adv., 1960, 61, 65, 66, 80, 81, WHO expert panel on parasitic diseases, 1963-77; bd. sci. counselors Nat. Inst. Allergy and Infectious Diseases, NIH, 1966-68; mem. NIH parasitic diseases panel U.S.-Japan Coop. Med. Sci. Program, 1965-69; mem. adv. sci. bd. Gorgas Meml. Inst. Tropical and Preventive Medicine, 1970—. Co-author: Animal Agents and Vectors of Human Disease, rev. edit, Craig & Faust's Clinical Parasitology, rev. edit.; contbg. author: Mitchell-Nelson's Pediatrics; editorial bd.: Am. Jour. Tropical Medicine and Hygiene, 1958-60, 67-70; editor-in-chief, 1960-66, 72—; asso. editor: Am. Jour. Hygiene, 1961-64, Jour. Parasitology, 1965-76, Am. Jour. Epidemiology, 1966—; editorial bd.: Transactions of Am. Micros. Soc, 1966-73, Ceskoslovenska Parasitologie, 1966-72; contbr. articles to profl. jours. Fellow Am. Acad. Microbiology (bd. govs. 1966-75), AAAS; mem. Internat. Filariasis Assn., Am. Soc. Tropical Medicine and Hygiene (councilor 1956-57, v.p. 1958, pres. 1969), Royal Soc. Tropical Medicine and Hygiene, Am. Soc. Parasitologists (councilor 1952-54, 56-59, pres. 1968), Am. Micros. Soc. (v.p. 1953, exec. com. 1955-59, 61-62), Am. Pub. Health Assn., Société Belge de Medicine Tropicale de Parasitologie et de Mycologie, Société de Pathologie Exotique (France; hon.), Sociedad Mexicana de Parasitologia (hon.), New Orleans Acad. Sci., Brazilian Soc. Tropical Medicine (hon.), Sigma Xi, Delta Omega, Alpha Omega Alpha (hon.). Club: Round Table (New Orleans). Home: 1416 Cadiz St New Orleans LA 70115 Office: 1430 Tulane Ave New Orleans LA 70112

BEAVER, ROBERT PIERCE, clergyman, educator; b. Hamilton, Ohio, May 26, 1906; s. Joseph Earl and Caroline (Neusch) B.; m. Wilma Manessier, Aug. 22, 1927; children: Ellen (dec.), David Pierce, Stephen Robert. A.B., A.M., Oberlin Coll., 1928; Ph.D., Cornell U., 1933; student, U. Munich, Yale U. Div. Sch., Coll. Chinese Studies at Peking, Union Theol. Sem., Columbia U.; D.D. (hon.), Concordia Sem., 1972. Ordained to ministry Evang. and Ref. Ch. (now United Ch. Christ), 1932; pastor Evang. Ref. Ch. of Oakley, Cin., 1932-36, Huber Meml. Ch., Balt., 1936-38; mem. China Mission Evang. and Ref. Ch., 1938-47; prof. Central China Union Theol. Sem., 1940-42; prof. missions and ecumenics Theol. Sem. of Evang. and Ref. Ch., Lancaster, Pa., 1944-48; dir. Missionary Research Library, N.Y.C.; research sec. div. fgn. missions Nat. Council Chs., 1948-55; lectr. Union Theol. Sem., 1949-55; prof. missions Bibl. Sem., N.Y.C., 1950-55; prof. missions Div. Sch. U. Chgo., 1955-71, now prof. emeritus; dir. Overseas Ministries Study Center, Ventnor, N.J., 1973-76; adj. prof. Fuller Theol. Sem., Pasadena, Calif., 1974—; vis. lectr. Princeton Theol. Sem., 1974-76; vis. prof. Christian Theol. Sem., Indpls., 1981. Author: American Protestant Women in World Mission, 1980, Mission Today and Tomorrow, Introduction to Native American Church History, 1983; editorial bd.: Jour. Ch. and State; editor: World Christian Mission Books; contbr. articles to profl. publs. Trustee Found. for Theol. Edn. in S.E. Asia, Cook Christian Tng. Sch. Mem. Am. Soc. Ch. History, S.E. Asia Soc. Ch. History and Ecumenics (hon. pres. 1968—), Am. Soc. Missiology (exec. com. 1972-76, chmn. bd. publs. 1979—), Assn. Profs. Missions (pres. 1956-58), Deutsche Gesellschaft für Missionswissenschaft, Phi Beta Kappa, Phi Kappa Phi. Home: 766 La Huerta Green Valley AZ 85614

BEAVER, WILLIAM HENRY, accounting educator; b. Peoria, Ill., Apr. 13, 1940; s. John W. and Ethel M. (Kostka) B.; m. Suzanne Marie Hutton, May 22, 1965; children: Marie, Sarah, David. B.B.A., U. Notre Dame, 1962; M.B.A., U. Chgo., 1965, Ph.D., 1965. C.P.A., Ill. Asst. prof. U. Chgo., 1965-69; assoc. prof. acctg. Stanford U., 1969-72, prof., 1972—, Thomas D. Dee II prof., 1977—; adv. com. on corp. disclosure SEC, 1976-77; cons. Fin. Acctg. Standards Bd., 1980—. Author: Financial Reporting: An Accounting Revolution, 1981; editorial bd.: The Acctg. Rev., 1977-80, Jour. Acctg. Research, 1968—, Jour. Acctg. and Econs., 1978—, Fin. Analysts Jour., 1979—; contbr. articles to profl. Jours. Recipient literary award Jour. Accountancy, 1978, faculty excellence award Calif. Soc. C.P.A.s, 1978, Graham and Dodd award Fin. Anaylsts Fedn., 1979, notable contbn. to acct. lit. award, 1969, 79, 83, outstanding research award Inst. Quantitative Research in Fin., 1981, nat. acctg. award Alpha Kappa Psi Found., 1982. Mem. Am. Inst. C.P.A.s, Am. Fin. Assn., Western Fin. Assn., Am. Acctg. Assn. (v.p. 1981-83, disting. internat. lectr. in acct. 1979, Manuscript award 1967). Home: 949 Wing Pl Stanford CA 94305 Office: Stanford U Grad Sch Bus Stanford CA 94305

BEAVERS, ALVIN HERMAN, educator; b. Addington, Okla., Jan. 1, 1913; s. Orlando Franklin and Willie (Morris) B.; m. Edith Sarah Moody, Dec. 24, 1940; children—James Franklin, John Alvin, Nancy Ann. B.S., N.Mex. State U., 1940; M.S. in Soil Sci; grad. asst., U. Mo., 1948, Ph.D., 1950. Soil scientist U.S. Dept. Agr., 1941-43; asst. prof. soil mineralogy and chemistry U. Ill., 1950-58, asso. prof., 1958-63, prof., 1963—; cons. Served with U.S. Army, 1943-46. NSF grantee, lectr., 1967. Mem. Am. Soc. Agronomy, Sigma Xi, Alpha Zeta, Gamma Sigma Delta. Methodist. Home: 2505 Stanford Dr Champaign IL 61820 Office: N507 Turner Hall U Ill Urbana IL 61801

BEAVERS, ELLINGTON MCHENRY, chem. co. exec.; b. Atlanta, Jan. 29, 1916; s. Reuben Willis and Bessie Mae (Sorrow) B.; m. Lorraine Eve Matulewicz, Oct. 12, 1957; 1 son, Cary Donald. B.S. with honors, Emory U., 1938; M.S., 1939; Ph.D.; Textile Research Found. fellow 1939-40, Rockefeller Found. fellow 1940-41, U. N.C., 1941. With Rohm & Haas Co., Phila., 1941-81, dir. research, 1969-70, v.p. charge research and corporate health protection, 1970-74, sr. v.p., 1974-77, group v.p., 1977-81, also dir.; founder, pres. Embarc, Inc., 1981—. Contbr. articles to sci. jours. Mem. Am. Chem. Soc. (chmn. Phila. sect. 1961), AAAS, Am. Inst. Chemists, Acad. Natural Scis. (dir.), Nat. Cath. Edn. Assn. (dir.), Sigma Xi, Alpha Chi Sigma. Republican. Roman Catholic. Patentee in field. Home: 931 Coates Rd Meadowbrook PA 19046 Office: Embarc Inc PO Box 428 Fort Washington PA 19034

BEAZLEY, BERNARD JOSEPH, lawyer, manufacturing company executive; b. Chgo., Apr. 27, 1926; s. Robert J. and Bernice C. (Eckert) B.; m. A. Kathleen Sullivan, May 15, 1948; children: William, Thomas, Timothy, Mary Jane, David, Sara, John, Elizabeth, Edward. J.D., Loyola U., Chgo., 1950. Bar: Ill. 1950, Pa. 1961, U.S. Supreme Ct. 1962. Asst. trust officer Exchange Nat. Bank, Chgo., 1950-54; counsel Armour Research Found., Chgo., 1954-55, ADA, 1955-60; gen. counsel Dentsply Internat. Inc., York, Pa., 1960—, sec., 1963—, v.p., 1969-80, sr. v.p. profl. relations, 1980—, dir., 1971—; dir., sec., sr. v.p. Dentsply Holdings Inc. Trustee, adviser Am. Fund for Dental Health; adv. counsel Diocese of Harrisburg, Pa., 1978—. Served with USAAF, 1943-45. Mem. Am., Pa., York County bar assns., Am. Dental Trade Assn. (chmn. profl. and lab. relations com.), ADA (hon.), Chgo. Dental Soc. (hon.), Internat. Coll. Dentists (hon.). Roman Catholic. Home: 15 N Harlan St York PA 17402 Office: 570 W College Ave York PA 17405

BEBER, ROBERT H., lawyer, manufacturing company executive; b. N.Y.C., Aug. 17, 1933; s. Morris and Martha (Pollock) B.; m. Joan Parsons, June 14, 1957; children: Andrea, Judith, Deborah. A.B. in Econs, Duke U., 1955, J.D., 1957. Bar: N.Y., N.C. With Everett, Everett & Everett, N.C., 1957-58; atty. SBA, Washington, 1961-63; with RCA, 1963-81; sr. v.p., gen. counsel, sec. GAF Corp., N.Y.C., 1981-83, exec. v.p., dir., 1983—, dir. subs. Chmn. bd. Health Care Plan N.J., 1975-78; v.p. South Jersey C. of C., 1974-77. Served with U.S. Army, 1958-61. Mem. ABA, Am. Soc. Corp. Secs. Republican. Jewish. Home: 2 Lords Hwy Weston CT 06883 Office: 140 W 51st St New York NY 10020

BECHANAN, WILLIAM BRYAN, electric utility co. exec.; b. Hodgenville, Ky., Oct. 18, 1925; s. Lucien Bryan and Ruby Jane B.; m. Ann L. Goins, May 10, 1947; children—Gary, Karen. B.S. in Elec. Engring, U. Ky., 1949. Asst. v.p. Ky. Utilities Co., Lexington; then v.p., now pres., v.p. Old Diminion Power Co., now pres.; dir. 1st Security Nat. Bank, Electric Energy, Inc., Edison Electric Inst., Ohio Valley Electric Corp. Mem. IEEE. *

BECHER, JOHN C., actor; b. Milw.; s. John and Katherine (Schmidt) B.; m. Margaret Becher, Aug. 7, 1945. B.S., Milw. State Tchrs. Coll., 1938; B.F.A., Goodman Sch. Theatre, Chgo., 1941. Appeared in: numerous Broadway plays including Mame, 1966-69, Gypsy, 1974; appeared in: numerous films including Up the Sandbox, 1972, Crazy Joe, 1973, Deathwish, 1974, Next Stop Greenwich Village, 1975, Great Bank Hoax, 1979, Below the Belt, 1980, Honky Tonk Freeway, 1981; television films include Ohms, 1979; You Can't Go Home Again, 1979, Too Far to Go, 1979; television series Three's Company, Remington Steele, Different Strokes, others. Served to capt. AUS, 1941-46. Mem. Actors Equity, Screen Actors Guild, AFTRA. *I have found that always telling the truth and not ever inflating past performances, (such as elevating my billing from "bit part" to "co-star"), has not only made me feel better but has given me a standing and respectability in the entertainment community.*

BECHER, PAUL RONALD, publishing executive; b. Columbus, Ohio, Oct. 16, 1934; s. Charles Clevel and G. Irene (Smith) B.; m. Leitsa Pauline Katsampes, Aug. 9, 1965; children: Lori Sue, Lynne Marie. B.F.A., Ohio State U., 1956. Textbook salesman Charles E. Merrill Pub. Co., Columbus, 1960-61, product mgr. bus. and econ. series, 1962-67, mgr. book prodn., 1967-69, editor-in-chief coll. div., 1970, dir. coll. div., 1971-72, exec. v.p. pub., 1973—. Mem. adv. bd.: Personnel Mgmt. Abstracts Jour., 1964—. Mem. Upper Arlington Civic Assn.; mem. adv. bd. Friends Ohio State U. Libraries, 1976—. Served to 1st lt. USAF, 1957-59. Mem. Assn. Am. Pubs., Sigma Chi. Clubs: Scioto Country, City, Upper Arlington Swim (dir. 1982—). Home: 2080 Cheshire Rd Columbus OH 43221 Office: 1300 Alum Creek Dr Columbus OH 43216

BECHER, WILLIAM DON, electrical engineer, university dean; b. Bolivar, Ohio, Nov. 26, 1929; s. William and Eva Vernette (Richardson) B.; m. Helen Norma Hager, Aug. 31, 1950; children: Eric Alan, Patricia Lynn. B.S. in R.E, Tri-State U., 1950; M.S.E. in Elec. Engring, U. Mich., 1961, Ph.D., 1968. Registered profl. engr., Mich., N.J. Project engr. Bogue Electric, Paterson, N.J., 1950-53; sr. devel. engr. Goodyear Aircraft Corp., Akron, Ohio, 1953-57; sr. systems engr. Beckman Instruments, Fullerton, Calif., 1957-58; engring. supr. Bendix Aerospace Systems, Ann Arbor, Mich., 1958-63; research engr. U. Mich., Ann Arbor, 1963-68, adj. prof. elec. engring., 1978-79, 81—, prof. elec. engring., Dearborn, 1968-78, chmn., 1971-76; engring. dept. mgr. Environ. Research Inst. Mich., Ann Arbor, 1977-79, assoc. dir., 1981—; dean (Coll. Engring.); prof. elec. engring. N.J. Inst. Tech., Newark, 1979-81; pres. WIDBEC Engring., Ann Arbor, 1976—; engring. cons., 1968—. Author: Courses in Continuing Education for Electronics Engineers, 1975, 76, Logical Design Using Integrated Circuits, 1977. Served with U.S. Army, 1953-55. Gen. Electric Co. fellow, 1962-63. Mem. IEEE (sr.), Am. Soc. Engring. Edn., Nat. Soc. Profl. Engrs. (N.J.), Order of Engr., Sigma Xi, Alpha Sigma Lambda, Eta Kappa Nu, Phi Kappa Phi, Tau Beta Pi. Patentee in field. Office: 691 Spring Valley Ann Arbor MI 48105 *

BECHERER, HANS WALTER, agricultural equipment manufacturing executive; b. Detroit, Apr. 19, 1935; s. Max and Mariele (Specht) B.; m. Michele Beigbeder, Nov. 28, 1959; children: Maxime, Vanessa. B.A., Trinity Coll., Hartford, Conn., 1957; student, Munich U., Germany, 1958; M.B.A., Harvard U., 1962. Exec. asst. office of chmn. Deere & Co., Moline, Ill., 1966-69; gen. mgr. John Deere Export, Manheim, Germany, 1969-73; dir. export mktg. Deer & Co., Moline, Ill., 1973-77, v.p., 1977-83, sr. v.p., 1983—; dir. U.S.-Yugoslav Econ. Council, 1978—; mem. industry sector adv. com. U.S. Dept. Commerce, 1975-81. Vice pres., trustee St. Katharine's-St. Mark's Sch., Bettendorf, Iowa, 1983. Served to 1st lt. USAF, 1958-60. Republican. Roman Catholic. Clubs: Rock Island Arsenal Golf (Ill.); Davenport (Iowa). Home: 788 25th Ave Ct Moline IL 61265 Office: Deere & Co John Deere Rd Moline IL 61265

BECHTEL, STEPHEN DAVISON, engineer, constructor; b. Aurora, Ind., Sept. 24, 1900; s. Warren A. and Clara (West) B.; m. Laura Adaline Peart, Sept. 7, 1923; children: Stephen Davison, Barbara Bechtel Davies. Student engring., U. Calif., LL.D. (hon.), 1954, Loyola U., 1958, Golden Gate U., 1976; D.Eng., U. Pacific, 1966, Washington U., 1976, Carroll Coll., 1983; D.Pub. Service, U. San Francisco, 1982. Registered profl. engr., Calif. Gen. constrn. bus. with father, 1919; with W.A. Bechtel Co., v.p., 1925-36, pres., 1936; 1st v.p., dir. Six Cos., Inc. (builders), Hoover Dam, 1931-36; co-organizer, dir. Bechtel-McCone Corp., 1937-46; during World War II, chmn. Calif. Shipbldg. Corp., Wilmington; dir. Marinship Corp., Sausalito, Calif.; now sr. dir. Bechtel Group; pres., dir. Lakeside Corp.; adv. com. Export-Import Bank U.S., 1969-74; mem. dirs. adv. council Morgan Guaranty Trust Co. N.Y.; mem. Bus. Adv. Council, U.S. Dept. Commerce, 1950-60, chmn., 1958-59, mem. bus. council, 1961—. Mem. Pres.'s Adv. Com. on Nat. Hwy. Program, 1954-55; sr. mem. The Conf. Bd.; bd. dirs. emeritus Stanford Research Inst.; trustee Ford Found., 1960-70; chmn. San Francisco Bay Area Council, 1961-63, trustee, 1946—. Served with 20th Engrs., AEF, U.S. Army, World War I. Decorated Order of Cedar (Lebanon), knight Order of St. Sylvester (Holy See), knight comdr. Ct. Honor, officer Am. Soc. Order St. John of Jerusalem; recipient John Fritz gold medal and cert., 1961, Nat. Def. Transp. award, 1960, Achievement award Bldg. Industry Conf. Bd., San Francisco, 1951; Moles award for outstanding achievement in constrn., 1952; Alumni Assn. award, 1951; Alumnus of Yr., U. Calif., 1952; 1st Internat. Achievement award World Trade Club, 1970; 1st Outstanding Alumnus award U. Calif. Bus. Adminstrn. Alumni Assn., 1970; Golden Beaver award for mgmt., 1963; Forbes Mag. award, 1977; named Calif. Industrialist of Yr., Calif. Mus. Sci. and Industry, 1968; Berkeley citation U. Calif. Coll. Engring., 1975; Golden Plate award Am. Acad. Achievement, 1976; Narariya Star of Merit, Govt. Indonesia, 1976; William F. Knowland Meml. award New Oakland Com., 1978; Good Scout award Boy Scouts Am., 1978; Man of Yr. award Brazilian-Am. C. of C., 1981; named to Nat. Bus. Hall Fame, 1976, Internat. Exec. of Yr., Brigham Young U. Sch. Mgmt., 1978, Humanitarian of Yr. Easter Seal Soc. of Alameda County, 1984. Mem. Am. Petroleum Inst., ASCE, Soc. Naval Architects and Marine Engrs., Cons. Constructors Council Am., World Affairs Council No. Calif., Calif. Inst. Assocs., Moles, Beavers, Beta Theta Pi. Republican. Methodist. Clubs: Pacific Union, Commonwealth, Press and Union League, Engineers, Stock Exchange, Bohemian (San Francisco); California (Los Angeles); Claremont Country (Oakland, Calif.); Cypress Point (Monterey Peninsula, Calif.); Links, Sky (N.Y.C.). Lodges: Masons (33 deg.); Shriners. Home: 244 Lakeside Dr Oakland CA 94612 Office: 155 Sansome St San Francisco CA 94104

BECHTEL, STEPHEN DAVISON, JR., engineering company executive; b. Oakland, Cal., May 10, 1925; s. Stephen Davison and Laura (Peart) B.; m. Elizabeth Mead Hogan, June 5, 1946; 5 children. Student, U. Colo., 1943-44; B.S., Purdue U., 1946, Dr. Engring. (hon.), 1972; M.B.A., Stanford, 1948; D.Sc. (hon.), U. Colo. Registered profl. engr., N.Y., Mich., Alaska, Calif., Md., Hawaii, Ohio, D.C., Va., Ill. Engring. and mgmt. positions Bechtel Corp., San Francisco, 1941-60, pres., 1960-73, chmn. of cos. in Bechtel group, 1973-80; chmn. Bechtel Group, Inc., 1980—; dir. IBM Co., Santa Fe-So. Pacific Co.; Mem., former vice chmn. Bus. Council; life councillor, past chmn. Conf. Bd.; mem. policy com. Bus. Roundtable; mem. Labor-Mgmt. Group, Nat. Action Council on Minorities in Engring., 1974—. Trustee, mem. bldg. and grounds com. Calif. Inst. Tech.; mem. pres.'s council Purdue U. Served with USMC, 1943-46. Decorated officer French Legion of Honor; recipient Disting. Alumnus award Purdue U., 1964, U. Colo., 1978; Ernest C. Arbuckle Disting. Alumnus award Stanford U., 1974; Man of Yr. Engring. News-Record, 1974; Outstanding Achievement in Constrn. award Moles, 1976; Disting. Engring. Alumnus award U. Colo., 1979; Herbert Hoover medal, 1980. Fellow ASCE (Engring. Mgmt. award 1979), Instn. Chem. Engrs. (U.K.) (hon.); mem. Nat. Acad. Engring. (chmn.), Am. Inst. Metall. Engrs., Calif. Acad. Scis. (hon. trustee), Chi Epsilon, Tau Beta Pi. Clubs: Pacific Union (San Francisco); Claremont Country (Oakland, Calif.); Cypress Point (Monterey Peninsula, Calif.); Thunderbird Country (Palm Springs, Calif.); Vancouver (B.C.); Ramada (Houston); Bohemian, San Francisco Golf (San Francisco); Links, Blind Brook (N.Y.C.); Met. (Washington); Augusta (Ga.) National Golf; York (Toronto); Mount Royal (Montreal). Office: 50 Beale St San Francisco CA 94105

BECHTLE, LOUIS CHARLES, U.S. district judge; b. Phila., Dec. 14, 1927; s. Charles R. and Gladys (Kirchner) B.; m. Margaret Beck, Sept. 5, 1978; children: Barbara, Nancy, Amy; stepchildren: Joanne, Tara, Samuel. B.S., Temple U., 1951, LL.B., 1954. Bar: Pa. 1954. Asst. U.S. atty. U.S. Dept. Justice, Phila., 1957-59, U.S. atty., 1969-72; pvt. practice law Jacoby & Maxmin, Phila., 1959-62; pvt. practice Wisler, Pearlstine, Talone, Gerber, Norristown, Pa., 1962-69; U.S. dist. judge U.S. Dist. Ct., Phila., 1972—; mem. adj. faculty Temple U., Phila., 1974—. Served with U.S. Army, 1946-47. Mem. Montgomery County Bar Assn., Fed. Bar Assn. Republican. Presbyterian. Club: St. Davids Golf. Office: US Dist Ct Eastern Dist Pa 601 Market St Philadelphia PA 19106

BECHTLE, ROBERT ALAN, artist, educator; b. San Francisco, May 14, 1932; m. Nancy Elizabeth Dalton, 1963; children: Max, Robert, Anne Elizabeth. B.A., Calif. Coll. Arts and Crafts, Oakland, 1954, M.F.A., 1958; postgrad., U. Calif.-Berkeley, 1960-61. Graphic designer Kaiser Industries, Oakland, 1956-59; instr. Calif. Coll. Arts and Crafts, 1957-61, assoc. prof. to prof.; lectr. U. Calif.-Berkeley, 1965-66; vis. artist U. Calif.-Davis, 1966-68; assoc. prof. San Francisco State U., 1968-76, prof., 1976—. Exhibitor one man shows, Mus. of Art, San Francisco, 1959, 64, Berkeley Gallery, 1965, Richmond Art Ctr. (Calif.), U. Calif.-Davis, 1967, O.K. Harris Gallery, N.Y.C., 1971, 74, 76, group shows, San Francisco Art Inst., 1966, Whitney Mus. N.Y.C., 1967, Milw. Art Ctr., 1969, Mus. Contemporary Art, Chgo., 1971, Serpentine Gallery, London, 1973, Toledo Mus. Art, 1975, San Francisco Mus. Modern Art, 1976, Pushkin Fine Arts Mus., Moscow, 1978, Pa. Acad. Fine Arts, Phila., 1981, San Antonio Mus. Art, Tucson Mus. Art; represented in permanent collections, Achenbach Found. for Graphic Arts, San Francisco, Chase Manhattan Bank, N.Y.C., E.B. Crocker Art Gallery, Sacramento, Gibbes Art Gallery, Library of Congress, Washington, Lowe Art Mus.-U. Miami, Coral Gables, Fla., Mills Coll., Oakland, Neue Gal der Stadt Aachen, West Germany, Univ. Art Mus.-U. Calif-Berkeley, U. Nebr.-Lincoln, Whitney Mus., N.Y.C., Guggenheim Mus., N.Y.C. Served with U.S. Army, 1954-56. Recipient James D. Phelan award, 1965; Nat. Endowment for Arts grantee, 1977. Office: San Francisco State U Dept Arts and Industry Bldg San Francisco CA 94132 *

BECHTOL, WILLIAM MILTON, educator; b. Arcamum, Ohio, Nov. 26, 1931; s. Owen S. and Maudie B. (Mendenhall) B.; m. Mildred A Isaacs, Sept. 6, 1952; children: William Milton, Susan, Robert. B.S., Miami U., Oxford, Ohio, 1953, M.Ed., 1956, Ed.D., 1970. High school tchr. Reily, Ohio, 1953-54, Tipp City, 1954-56; prin. Nevin Coppock Elem. Sch., 1956-66; dir. ungraded project Tipp City Schs., 1966-67, asst. supt. schs., 1967-69; dirs. Ctr. Mgmt. Ednl. Systems-S.W. Minn. State Coll., Marshall, 1969-73, chmn. div. edn., 1973-74, coll. dir., 1974-77; prof., chmn. dept. edn. S.W. Tex. State U., San Marcos, 1977—. Author: Developing Skills for Individualizing Instruction, 1972, Individualizing Instruction and Keeping Your Sanity, 1973, Individually Guided Social Studies, 1976; mem. publ. bd.: Assn. Individually Guided Edn. Jour., 1975—. Vice chmn. Alamo Area Tchr. Ctr., 1977-81. Mem. Assn. for Individually Guided Edn. (pres. 1980-81), Tex. Assn. Individualized Schooling (pres. 1979-80), Tex. Assn. Tchr. Educators, Assn. Tchr. Educators, Assn. Supervision and Curriculum Devel., Ohio Edn. Assn., Phi Delta Kappa, Delta Chi. Methodist. Lodge: Rotary. Home: 124 Ridgeway St San Marcos TX 78666 Office: Southwest Tex State U Dept Edn San Marcos TX 78666

BECK, AARON TEMKIN, psychiatrist; b. Providence, July 18, 1921; s. Harry S. and Elizabeth (Temkin) B.; m. Phyllis Whitman, June 4, 1950; children: Judith, Daniel, Alice, Roy. B.A., Brown U., 1942, Dr.Med.Sci. (hon.), 1982; M.D., Yale U., 1946. Mem. faculty U. Pa. Med. Sch., 1954—, prof. psychiatry, 1971—, Univ. prof., 1983—; dir. Center Cognitive Therapy, 1965—; mem. rev. panel NIMH, 1965—, chmn. task force suicide prevention in 70s, 1969-70; bd. dirs. West Philadelphia Community Mental Health Consortium, 1975-77. Author: Depression: Causes and Treatment, 1972, Diagnosis and Management of Depression, 1973, Prediction of Suicide, 1973, Cognitive Therapy and the Emotional Disorders, 1976, Cognitive Therapy of Depression, 1979. Served as officer M.C. U.S. Army, 1952-54. Recipient award research R.I. Med. Soc., 1948, ann. award Am. Psychopathol. Assn., 1983. Mem. Am. Acad. Psychoanalysis (trustee 1970-75), Soc. Psychotherapy Research (pres. 1975-76), Am. Psychiat. Assn. (prize research psychiatry 1979), Royal Coll. Psychiatry, Psychiat. Research Soc., Am. Coll. Psychiatrists, Am. Acad. Psychoanalysis, Assn. Advancement Behavior Therapy, Phila. Soc. Clin. Psychologists (ann. award 1978). Office: 133 S 36th St Room 602 Philadelphia PA 19104

BECK, ABE JACK, ret. business exec., ret. air force officer; b. Dallas, May 24, 1914; s. Jacob S. and Mollie (Pollock) B.; m. Anne Gilaire Michlin, Oct. 21, 1945; children—Stephanie Jo, Melanie Gilaire, Darcy Jane, John Dallas. LL.B., So. Meth. U., 1939. Bar: Tex. bar 1939. Pvt. practice law, Dallas, 1939-40; joined USAAF, 1940; grad. Flying Sch., 1941; commd. 2d lt. USAAF, 1941; advanced through grades to maj. gen. USAF, 1963; tactical officer, engring. officer, also pilot instr. Air Cadet Advanced Flying Sch., Luke Field, Ariz., 1941-42; aide Hdqrs. (5th Air Force, later), operation officer, New Guinea, 1942-43, asst. chief staff, also ops. officer, and later asst. chief staff, SW Pacific, 1943-45, student, 1945, officer charge classification and assignment br., San Francisco, 1946, resigned, and returned to civilian life, 1946-47; rejoined USAF, 1947; staff legal officer, later asst. staff judge adv. Hdqrs. 8th Air Force, Ft. Worth, 1947-48; chief air judge adv. sect., personnel and adminstrn. SAC, Andrews AFB, Md., 1948, chief air judge adv. sect., personnel and adminstrn., also project officer, command sect. Hdqrs., Offutt AFB, Omaha, 1948-52; dep. comdr., then comdr. (3902d Air Base Wing), Offutt AFB, 1952-54, comdr., Sedalia AFB, Mo., 1954-57, Goose AFB, Labrador, 1957-59, chief staff, command sect., SAC, Westover AFB, Mass., 1959-61; comdr. (817th Air Div.), Pease AFB, N.H., 1961-63; insp. gen. Hdqrs. SAC, Offutt AFB, 1964, dir. materiel, 1964-66; sr. air force mem. weapon systems evaluation group, directorate def. research and engring. (Office Sec. Def.), 1966-68, comdr., 1968-72, ret., 1972; exec. v.p. Morris Industries, Inc., Omaha, 1972-74; v.p. Zale Corp., Dallas, 1974-78, sr. v.p., 1978-80. Decorated D.S.M., Legion of Merit with 2 oak leaf clusters, D.F.C., Air medal with 3 oak leaf clusters, Air Force Commendation medal; British Mil. Cross, Australia). Home: 6510 Forestshire Dallas TX 75230

BECK, ADRIAN ROBERT, pediatric surgeon; b. N.Y.C., June 8, 1932; s. Alexander George and Frances (Price) B.; m. Marcia Perlmutter, Aug. 18, 1963; children—Adrienne, David. B.S., Union Coll., 1954; M.D., Albany Med. Coll., 1958. Diplomate: Am. Bd. Surgery. Intern Beth Israel Hosp., N.Y.C., 1958-59; asst. resident surgery Mt. Sinai Hosp., N.Y.C., 1959-63, Dazian fellow in surg. research, 1960-61, chief resident, 1963-64; chief resident pediatric surgery Buffalo Children's Hosp., 1964-66; practice medicine specializing in pediatric surgery, N.Y.C., 1968—; clin. prof. surgery Mt. Sinai Sch. Medicine, N.Y.C., 1966-78, clin. prof., 1978—; asso. attending surgeon, asso. dir. div. pediatric surgery Mt. Sinai Hosp.; asso. attending surgeon City Hosp. at Elmhurst; attending surgeon, dir. div. pediatric surgery Beth Israel Med. Center. Contbr. articles to profl. jours., chpt. to book. Fellow Am. Bd. Surgery, Am. Acad. Pediatrics, A.C.S.; mem. Am. Pediatric Surg. Assn., N.Y. Acad. Sci., N.Y. Pediatric Soc., Harvey Soc., N.Y. Soc. Pediatric Surgery, N.Y. Surg. Soc., Soc. Surgery Alimentary Tract. Home: 4919 Goodridge Ave Riverdale NY 10471 Office: 112 E 83 St New York NY 10028

BECK, CHARLES BEVERLEY, botany educator; b. Richmond, Va., Mar. 26, 1927; s. Charles Bryan and Elizabeth (Coleman) B.; m. Janice Luck Milburn, Dec. 21, 1961; children: Ann, Sara. B.A., U. Richmond, 1950; M.S., Cornell U., 1952, Ph.D., 1955. Teaching asst. botany Cornell U., 1951-54, pre-doctoral instr., 1954-55; Cornell-Glasgow Exchange fellow U. Glasgow, Scotland, 1955-56; instr. botany U. Mich., 1956-57, asst. prof., 1957-60, asso. prof., 1960-65, prof., 1965—, chmn. dept., 1971-75, 77-79, curator Mus. Paleontology, 1980—; mem. panel cons. to program in systematic and evolutionary biology NSF, 1970-73. Editor: Origin and Early Evolution of Angiosperms, 1976; mem. editorial bd.: Am. Jour. Botany; Contbr. numerous articles to sci. jours. Served with AUS, 1945-46. NSF Sr. Postdoctoral fellow U. Reading, Eng., 1964. Mem. Mich. Acad. Sci. Arts and Letters (chmn. botany sect. 1966-67), Bot. Soc. Am. (chmn. paleobotan. sec. 1968-69, rep. paleobotan. sect. to Am. Jour. Botany 1969-71), Am. Inst. Biol. Scis., AAAS, Internat. Orgn. Paleobotany, Internat. Assn. Plant Taxonomists, Internat. Soc. Plant Morphologists, Sigma Xi, Phi Kappa Phi. Home: 3075 Provincial Dr Ann Arbor MI 48104

BECK, CURT WERNER, chemist, educator; b. Halle/Saale, Germany, Sept. 10, 1927; came to U.S., 1950, naturalized, 1955; s. Curt Paul and Clara (Fischer) B.; m. Lily Yallourakis, Feb. 10, 1953; children—Curt Peter, Christopher Paul. Student, U. Munich, 1946-48; B.S., Tufts U., 1951; Ph.D., Mass. Inst. Tech., 1955. Instr. Franklin Tech. Inst., Boston, 1955-56; asst. prof. Roberts Coll., Istanbul, Turkey, 1956-57; lectr. Vassar Coll., Poughkeepsie, N.Y., 1957-59, asst. prof., 1959-62, asso. prof., 1962-66, prof. chemistry, 1966—, Matthew Vassar Jr. prof., 1970—. Co-editor: Art and Archaeology Tech. Abstracts, 1966—; sect. editor: Chem. Abstracts, 1967—; editor: Archaeological Chemistry, 1974; mem. editorial bd.: Jour. Field Archaeology, 1975—, Jour. Archaeol. Sci, 1979—. Mem. Zoning Bd. Appeals, La Grange, N.Y., 1965—, chmn., 1974—; mem. Dutchess County council Boy Scouts Am., 1965-67; Candidate supr., La Grange, 1967. Recipient Research award Mid-Hudson sect. Am. Chem. Soc., 1965. Fellow Royal Soc. Arts, Internat. Inst. for Conservation Historic and Artistic Works (London); mem. Am. Chem. Soc. (past sect. chmn.), Chem. Soc. (London), Gesellschaft Deutscher Chemiker, Archeol. Inst. Am., Internat. Union Prehistoric and Protohistoric Scis. (chmn. com. study of amber), Assn. for Field Archaeology, Sigma Xi. Home: Skidmore Rd La Grange Pleasant Valley NY 12569 Office: Vassar Coll Poughkeepsie NY 12601

BECK, DONALD, businesss executive; b. Cleve., Mar. 24, 1928; s. Harold Graf and Dorothy Margaret (Disser) B.; m. Shirley Louise Swope, Apr. 11, 1953; children: Jonathan Alan, David Andrew. B.A., Yale U., 1950. With Pickands Mather & Co., Cleve., 1951-73, treas., 1973-74, Moore McCormack Resources Inc., Stamford, Conn., 1974-78, v.p. and treas., 1978—. Bd. dirs. United Way, Stamford, 1975-80; v.p. bd. dirs. Easter Seal Rehab. Ctr., Stamford, 1975—. Served with U.S. Army, 1950-51. Club: Woodway Country (Darien, Conn.). Office: Moore McCormack Resources Inc 1 Landmark Sq Stamford CT 06901

BECK, DONALD LEE, airline executive; b. Hutchinson, Kans., Aug. 25, 1926; s. Helen (Farrell) B.; m. Susan K. King, Dec. 4, 1982; children: Gary, Larry, Julie, Shanna. Sales rep., supr., agt. Ry. Express Agy., Los Angeles, 1944-57; sales rep. Continental Airlines, 1957-59, dist. sales mgr., N.Y.C., 1959-62, Chgo., 1962-68, regional dir., Kansas City, 1968-69, field v.p. sales and services, Los Angeles, 1969-72; regional v.p. Air Micronesia, Saipan, Marianas Islands, 1972-73, v.p. sales and service, 1973-79, v.p. passenger market devel., 1979-80, pres., Los Angeles, 1980-81; sr. v.p. service Western Airlines, Los Angeles, 1983—. Mem. exec. bd. Gt. Western Council Boy Scouts Am., Los Angeles, 1981-83. Served with USN, 1944-46. Home: 2713 Elm St Manhattan Beach CA 90266 Office: Western Airlines 6060 Avion Dr Los Angeles CA 90009

BECK, EARL RAY, history educator; b. Junction City, Ohio, Sept. 8, 1916; s. Ernest Ray and Mary Frances (Helser) B.; m. Marjorie Culbertson, Nov. 7, 1944; children: Ann, Mary Sue. A.B., Capital U., 1937; M.A., Ohio State U., 1939, Ph.D., 1942. Instr. Capital U., 1942-43, Ohio State U., 1946-49; asst. prof. Fla. State U., Tallahassee, 1949-52, assoc. prof., 1952-60, prof. history, 1960—, chmn. dept. history, 1967-72, chmn. grad. studies, 1982—; summer vis. prof. La. State U., 1955, Tulane U., 1959, Duke U., 1966. Author: Verdict on Schacht, 1956, The Death of the Prussian Republic, 1959, Contemporary Civilization I, 1959, On Teaching History in Colleges and Universities, 1966, Germany Rediscovers America, 1968, A Time of Triumph and of Sorrow: Spanish Politics During the Reign of Alfonso XII, 1874-1885, 1979. Served with AUS, 1946-49. Mem. Am. Hist. Assn. (del. European history sect. 1983—), So. Hist. Assn. (vice chmn. European history sect. 1982-83), Conf. Group for Central European History, Soc. Spanish and Portuguese History. Presbyterian. Home: 2514 Killarney Way Tallahassee FL 32308

BECK, EDWARD WILLIAM, lawyer; b. Atchison, Kans., Aug. 19, 1944; s. Russell Niles and Lucille Mae (Leighton) B.; m. Marshia Ablon, June 24, 1966; children: Michael Adam, David Gordon. B.A. cum laude, Yale Coll., 1967, J.D., Harvard U., 1972. Bar: Calif. bar 1972. Asso. firm Pillsbury, Madison & Sutro, San Francisco, 1972-77; gen. counsel Pacific Lumber Co., San Francisco, 1977—, sec., 1978—, v.p., 1980—. Mem. Calif. Forest Protective Assn. (chmn. govt. and legal affairs com.), Calif. C. of C. (property rights subcom.), Am. Bar Assn., Calif. Bar Assn., San Francisco Bar Assn., Am. Soc. Corp. Secs. Office: 500 Washington St San Francisco CA 94111

BECK, GEORGE WILLIAM, industrial engineer; b. Dayton, Ohio, Aug. 31, 1921; s. George A. and Florence I. (Hosket) B.; m. Elizabeth A. Thatcher, Apr. 14, 1945; children: Bruce, Christine, William. B. Indsl. Engring., Gen. Motors Inst., 1946. Registered profl. engr., Ohio. Sales rep. Inland Mfg. div. Gen. Motors Corp., Dayton, 1946-53, sr. project engr., 1953-56, staff engr., 1956, asst. chief engr., 1956-62, chief engr., 1962-80, dir. engring., 1980—. Trustee Met. YMCA, 1964-71; chmn. bd. mgmt. Kettering YMCA, 1966-70; mem. Centerville City Sch. Dist. bd. edn., from 1968, also past v.p. Served to lt. (j.g.) USNR, 1943-45. Mem. Soc. Automotive Engrs., Dayton C. of C. Presbyterian. Club: MVMA Sycamore Creek Country. Inventor automotive products; patentee in field (9). Home: 887 Cranbrook Ct Dayton OH 45459 Office: PO Box 1224 Dayton OH 45401

BECK, JAMES (HENRY BECK), art historian, author; b. N.Y.C., May 14, 1930; s. Samuel and Margareth (Weisz) B.; m. Darma Tercinod, Apr. 9, 1956; children: Eleonora M., Lawrence C. B.A., Oberlin Coll., 1952; M.A., N.Y. U., 1954; Ph.D., Columbia U., 1963. Asst. prof. U. Ala., Tuscaloosa, 1958-59; asst. prof. Ariz. State U., Tempe, 1959-61; faculty Columbia U., N.Y.C., 1961—, prof. art history, 1972—; vis. asso. prof. Princeton U., 1970. Author: Mariano di Jacopo detto il Taccola, 'Liber tertius', 1969, Jacopo della Quercia e San Petronio, 1970, Michelangelo: A Lesson in Anatomy, 1975, Raphael, 1976, Masaccio, the documents, 1978, Leonardo's Rules of Painting: An unconventional approach to modern art, 1979, Italian Renaissance Painting, 1981. Recipient grants-in-aid Am. Philos. Soc., 1969, 72, 75; Herodotus fellow Inst. for Advanced Study, Princeton U., 1967; fellow Harvard U. Center for Italian Renaissance Studies, 1967-68, 72; vis. scholar Harvard U. Center for Italian Renaissance Studies, 1983; Guggenheim fellow, 1973-74. Mem. Renaissance Soc. Am., Mediaeval Acad. Am., Coll. Art Assn. Home: 435 Riverside Dr N.Y.C. NY 10025 Office: 815 Schermerhorn Hall Columbia U New York NY 10027

BECK, JAY VERN, emeritus microbiology educator; b. American Fork, Utah, Jan. 15, 1912; s. James Vern and Gladys (Johnson) B.; m. Faye Ellison, June 13, 1931; children: Dorthene Beck Richardson, Patricia Lynn Beck McEwan, Jacqueline Beck Foutz, David E., Bonnie Beck Studdert, John C. A.B., Brigham Young U., 1933, A.M., 1936; Ph.D., U. Calif., Berkeley, 1940. Assoc. chemist FDA, 1939-44; asst. prof. chemistry U. Idaho, 1944-46; assoc. prof. bacteriology Pa. State Coll., 1947-51; prof. bacteriology Brigham Young U., Provo, Utah, 1951-77, prof. emeritus, 1977—; 10th ann. Disting. Faculty lectr., 1972-73; mem. Nat. Sci. Bd., 1982—. Recipient Maeser Research award, 1967; Guggenheim fellow Sheffield U., 1957-58; USPHS fellow, 1965. Fellow Am. Acad. Microbiology; mem. Soc. Gen. Microbiology (London), Am. Soc. Microbiology (pres. Intermountain br. 1955), Am. Chem. Soc., AAAS, Utah Acad. Sci. (pres. 1963-64), Sigma Xi, Phi Kappa Phi. Home: 1305 Elm Ave Provo UT 84604

BECK, JOAN WAGNER, journalist; b. Clinton, Iowa, Sept. 5, 1923; d. Roscoe Charles and Mildred (Noel) Wagner; m. Ernest William Beck, Sept. 9, 1945; children—Christopher, Melinda. B.J. cum laude, Northwestern U., 1945, M.S. in Journalism, 1947. Radio script writer O.W.I. Voice of Am., 1945-46; copy writer Marshall Field & Co., 1947-50; feature writer Chgo. Tribune, 1950—, writer syndicated column about young people, 1956-61, syndicated column about children, 1961-72, editor daily features sect., 1972-75, mem. editorial bd., 1975—; syndicated editorial page columnist, 1974—. Author: How to Raise a Brighter Child, 1967, (with Dr. Virginia Apgar) Is My Baby All Right?, 1973, Effective Parenting, 1976, Best Beginnings, 1983. Hon. chmn. Mother's March of Met. Chgo. chpt. Nat. Found. March of Dimes, 1970-75; trustee Ill. Children's Home and Aid Soc., 1971—; mem. Women's Bd. Northwestern U. Recipient Helen Baker Cody award Chgo. Welfare Pub. Relations Bd., 1955; Trans-World Airlines Travel Feature award, 1954; Portal House award Chgo. Com. on Alcoholism, 1955; AP award for best newspaper feature series award, Ill., 1964; best feature, 1966; Alumni Merit award Northwestern U., 1965, 77; Alumnae award, 1977; Nat. award of Achievement Alpha Chi Omega, 1966; 1st place award Penney-U. Mo., 1973; Woodrow Wilson Found. vis. fellow, 1983. Mem. Chgo. Press Club, Chgo. Network, Chgo. Headline Club, Theta Sigma Phi, Alpha Chi Omega. Methodist. Clubs: Northwestern, Lake Forest. Home: 905 Castlegate Ct Lake Forest IL 60045 Office: Chgo Tribune 435 N Michigan Ave Chicago IL 60611 *"You shall know the truth and the truth shall make you free" has been a guiding principle and purpose of my life as a journalist. For I believe that a democracy cannot exist without an informed people and that it is primarily the responsibility of the newspaper to provide information as accurately, fairly, and interestingly as possible.*

BECK, JOHN CHRISTIAN, physician, educator; b. Audubon, Iowa, Jan. 4, 1924; s. Wilhelm and Marie (Brandt) B. M.D., McGill U., 1947, M.Sc., 1951. Diplomate: Am. Bd. Internal Medicine (dir.). Intern Royal Victoria Hosp., Montreal, 1947-48, sr. asst. resident, 1948-49; practice medicine, specializing in endocrinology, Montreal, 1964-74; physician-in-chief Royal Victoria Hosp.; dir. Univ. Clinic; chmn. dept. medicine McGill U.; prof. medicine U. Calif., San Francisco, 1974-79; dir. Robert Wood Johnson Clin. Scholars Program, 1974-79; prof. medicine, dir. multicampus div. geriatric medicine UCLA, 1979—; pres. Am. Bd. Med. Spltys. Fellow A.C.P., Royal Coll. Physicians (Can.), Royal Coll. Physicians (London), Royal Soc. Can., Inst. of Medicine. Home: 1562 Casale Rd Pacific Palisades CA 90272 Office: Multicampus Div Geriatric Medicine U Calif Los Angeles CA 90024

BECK, JOHN HARRIS, communications executive; b. Cody, Wyo., Nov. 23, 1949; s. George Washington and Frances Josephine (Harris) B. B.A., Harvard Coll., 1971. Night supr. sta. WGBH-FM-TV, Boston, 1968-71, asst. to bus. mgr., 1971-72, radio program dir., 1972-75, radio mgr., 1975-80; pres. Eastern Pub. Radio Network, Boston, 1977-79, chmn., 1979-80; dir. communications service City of N.Y. (Sta. WNYC AM-FM-TV), 1980—; Founding bd. dirs. Am. Pub. Radio Assocs., 1982. Mem. Internat. Radio-TV Soc. Democrat. Episcopalian. Club: City (N.Y.C.). Office: Sta WNYC One Centre St New York NY 10007 *Life in the world today has more problems and more possibilities than ever before. For those who enjoy challenge, it is the very best time to be alive.*

BECK, JULIAN, dir., writer, scenic designer, actor, producer; b. N.Y.C., May 31, 1925; s. Irving and Mabel (Blum) B.; m. Judith Malina, Oct. 30, 1948; 1 son, 1 daughter. Student, Yale, 1942-43, City Coll., N.Y., 1946-49. Mem. Actors quity Assn., N.Y. Com. for Gen Strike for Peace, 1961-63. A founder: (with wife) The Living Theatre; designer: The Thirteenth God, 1951; producer, designer: Doctor Faustus Lights the Lights, 1951, Ladies Voices, 1951, He Who Says Yes and He Who Says No, 1951, Childish Jokes, 1951, Dialogue of the Manikin and the Young Man, 1951; producer, designer, dir.: Beyond the Mountains, 1951, An Evening of Bohemian Theatre, 1952, Faustina, 1952, The Heroes (also acted in) and Ubi Roi, 1952, Desire Trapped by The Tail, Ladies Voices, Sweeny Agonistes, 1952, Ticklish Acrobat, 1954; producer, designer, actor: The Age of Anxiety, 1954, The Spook Sonata, 1954, Orpheus', 1954, The Idiot King, 1954, Tonight We Improvise, 1955, Phedre, 1955; dir.: The Young Disciple, 1955; designer: operas Voices for a Mirror and the Curious Fern, 1957, Dances Before a Wall, 1958; designer, producer, dir.: Many Loves, 1959, The Cave at Machpelah, 1959, The Connection, 1959, Tonight We Improvise; also acted in, 1959, The Marrying Maiden and The Women of Trachis, 1960, The Election, 1960, In The Jungle of the Cities, 1960, The Mountain Giants, 1961, The Apple, 1961, Man is Man, 1962, The Brig, 1963, Mysteries and Smaller Pieces, 1964, The Maids, 1965, Frankenstein, 1965, Antiqone, 1967, Paradise Now, 1968, The Legacy of Cain, 1970, 71, 73, 74, 75, Seven Meditations on Political Sadomasochism, 1973, Six Pubic Acts, 1975, European tour of some prodns., 1961, 62, 64-70, 75-80, The Money Tower, 1975, Prometheus, 1978, Antigone, 1979, Masse Mensch, 1980; film performances The Brig (Venice documentary prize 1964), Narcissus, 1957, Living and Glorious, 1965, Amore, Amore, 1966, Agonia, 1967, EdipoRe, 1967 (Living Theatre has received Lola D'Annunzio award 1959, Page One award Newspaper Guild N.Y. 1960, Obie award 1960, 64, 69, 75, Brandeis U. Creative Arts Award 1961, Grand Prix de Theatre de Nations, Paris 1961, medallion Paris Theatre Critics Circle 1961, Prix de 'lUniversite, Paris 1961, New Eng. Theatre Conf. award. 1962, Olympio award (Italy) 1967, Maharam award (stage design) 1969); Author: poems Songs of the Revolution 1-35, 1963, 36-89, 1974, Paradise Now, 1971, The Life of The Theatre, 1972, Seven Meditations on Political Sadomasochism, 1977, others. Vice chmn. U.S. com. for Justice to Latin Am. Political Prisoners, 1973-74; sponsor Am. Friends of Brazil. Address: 800 West End Ave New York NY 10025 also Via Gaeta 79 Rome 00185 Italy

BECK, LOWELL RICHARD, lawyer, association executive; b. Peoria, Ill., June 5, 1934; s. George R. and Hazel F. (McMeen) B.; m. Myrna K. Kohl, Oct. 1, 1961; children: Richard, Jonathan, Lori. B.S., Bradley U., 1956; LL.B., Northwestern U., 1958. Bar: Ill. 1960. Staff dir. Am. Bar Assn. Jr. Bar Conf., Chgo., 1959-60; assoc. dir. Washington office Am. Bar Assn., 1961-67, dir. div. pub. service activities, Chgo., 1967-68; exec. dir. Nat. Urban Coalition Action Council, Washington, 1968-70, Common Cause, 1970-72; assoc. exec. dir. ABA, Chgo., 1972-76, dep. exec. dir., 1976-80; exec. v.p. Nat. Assn. Ind. Insurers, Des Plaines, Ill., 1980-81, pres.-elect, 1981-82, pres., 1982—. Contbr. articles to profl. jours. Chmn. United Methodist. Served with U.S. Army, 1958-59, 61-62. Fellow Am. Bar Found.; mem. ABA (mem. exec. com. ABA-Am. Law Inst. joint com. continuing legal edn.), Am. Law Inst., Property and Casualty Ins. Council, Common Cause (former mem. nat. governing bd.), Ins. Inst. Hwy. Safety (bd. dirs.), Omicron Delta Kappa, Pi Sigma Alpha, Pi Kappa Delta, Phi Delta Phi, Lambda Chi Alpha. Republican. Clubs: Ruth Lake Country, Salt Creek. Home: 17 E Walnut Street Hinsdale IL 60521 Address: Nat Assn Ind Insurers 2600 River Rd Des Plaines IL 60018

BECK, MARGIT, artist; b. Tokay, Hungary; came to U.S., 1932, naturalized, 1938; d. Samuel and Johanna (Blau) B.; m. Sidney Schwartz; children: Joan, John. Student, Art Inst. Oradeamare, Rumania, 1929-32, Art Student League, N.Y.C., 1945-46. Theatrical scenic designer, 1934-36; formerly mem. art faculty Hofstra U.; now adj. asst. prof. art faculty NYU; now asst. prof. art faculty Empire State Coll., N.Y. State U. Exhibited works in one man shows, Contemporary Arts, N.Y.C., 1955, 58, 59, San Joaquin Mus., Stockton, Calif., 1956, Hofstra Coll., L.I., 1958, Mus. Fine Arts, Greenville, S.C., 1959, Babcock Gallery, N.Y.C., 1962, 64, 66, 68, 71, 72, 75, Phila. Art Alliance, 1968, Mansfield (Pa.) State Coll., 1965, Queens Coll., N.Y.C., 1973, Port Washington (N.Y.) Library, 1978; exhibited in group shows, Whitney Mus. Ann., Corcoran Biennial, Art Inst. Chgo. Ann., Pa. Acad. Ann., Allentown (Pa.) Mus. Fine Arts, Lehigh U., Bethlehem, Pa., Bklyn Mus. Internat. W.C. Biennial, NAD Ann., Butler Inst. Ann., U. Nebr. Ann., Springfield (Mass.) Mus., Akron Art Inst., Am. Acad. Arts and Letters, N.Y.C., Am. Soc. Contemporary Artists, Riverside Mus., N.Y.C., Southeby Parke Bernet, N.Y.C., Art U.S.A., Ringling Mus., Davenport (Iowa) Municipal Gallery, São Paulo Mus., N.Y. World's Fair, Am. Fedn. Arts Internat, travelling exhbns. include State Dept. sponsored exhbns., Am. embassies and museums abroad; represented in permanent collections, Peabody Mus., Cambridge, Mass., Speed Mus., Louisville, Morse Mus., Rawlins Coll., Hofstra Coll., Hunter Coll., Herbert Lehman Coll., N.Y.C., Miami U., Oxford, Ohio, Norfolk (Va.) Mus., Sheldon Meml. Mus., Lincoln, Nebr., Glichtenstein Mus., Safaad, Israel, Lyman Allen Mus., New London, Conn., Mansfield (Pa.) State Coll., Whitney Mus., others, also many pvt. collections and pub. bldgs. Recipient Gold medal oil Hofstra Coll., 1954; Purchase prize watercolor, 1955; Silver medal, 1956; Gold medal, 1957; Medal of Honor Nat. Assn. Women Artists, 1956; watercolor award, 1957, 63; oil award, 1958, 64; Winsor and Newton oil award, 1959; others; MacDowell Found. Residence fellow, 1957, 59, 60, 75; Walker award oil Audubon Artists, 1965; Medal Honor, 1968, 71; Henry Ward Ranger Fund Purchase award N.A.D., 1965, 73; Andrew Carnegie award, 1973; Child Hassam award Am. Acad. Arts and Letters, 1968, 69, 72. Mem. Artists Equity Assn. (past mem. exec. bd.), Audubon Artists (v.p. 1968-71, Stephen Hirsch award 1975, annual exhibit award 1981), NAD (full academician, Edwin Palmer award 1975), Coll. Art Assn. Am., Women in Arts. Address: 22 Florence St Great Neck NY 11023 *From the beginning life always has had the tendency to grow, to expand, and mature, to express great potentialities. Within all of us there is an infinite number of intelligence and creativity. We are all striving for happiness and fulfillment. Through my work as an artist I am hoping to express the positive aspect of life. I believe we must all share the responsibilities to help, to struggle, and to achieve man's inherent freedom and equality on this earth.*

BECK, MARILYN MOHR, columnist; b. Chgo., Dec. 17, 1928; d. Max and Rose (Lieberman) Mohr; m. Roger Beck, Jan. 8, 1949 (div. 1974); children: Mark Elliott, Andrea; m. Arthur Levine, Oct. 12, 1980. A.A., U. So. Calif., 1948. Freelance writer nat. mags. and newspapers, Hollywood, Calif., 1959-63; Hollywood columnist Valley Times and Citizen News, Hollywood, 1963-65; West Coast editor Sterling Mags., Hollywood, 1963-74; freelance entertainment writer Los Angeles Times, 1965-67; Hollywood columnist Bell-McClure Syndicate, 1967-72, chief, 1967-72; Hollywood columnist NANA Syndicate, 1967-72; syndicated Hollywood columnist N.Y. Times Spl. Features, 1972-78, 1978-80, United Press abroad, 1978-80, Editors News and Features, Internat., Chgo. Tribune/N.Y. Daily News Syndicate, 1980-82. Creator, host: Marilyn Beck's Hollywood Outtakes spls, NBC, 1977, 78; host: Marilyn Beck's Hollywood Hotline, Sta. KFI, Los Angeles, 1975-77; Hollywood reporter: Eyewitness News, Sta. KABC-TV, Los Angeles, 1981; TV program PM Mag., Sta. KABC-TV, 1983—; Author: Marilyn Beck's Hollywood, 1973. Recipient Citation of Merit Los Angeles City Council, 1973. Club: Hollywood Women's Press. Address: Box 11079 Beverly Hills CA 90213 *Being the best isn't everything; it's the only thing. "Life is too short to be little." (Disraeli).*

BECK, PAUL ADAMS, metallurgist, educator; b. Budapest, Hungary, Feb. 5, 1908; came to U.S., 1928, naturalized, 1944; s. Philip O. and Laura (Bardos) B.; children—Paul John, Philip Odon. M.S., Mich. Coll. Mining and Tech., 1929; M.E., Royal Hungarian U. Tech. Scis., 1931; Dr.Min. (hon.), Leoben Inst. Tech., 1979. Metallurgist Am. Smelting & Refining Co., Perth Amboy, N.J., 1937-41; chief metallurgist Beryllium Corp., Reading, Pa., 1941-42; supt. metall. lab. Cleve. Graphite Bronze Co., 1942-45; faculty U. Notre Dame, 1945—, prof. metallurgy, 1949—, head dept. metallurgy, 1950-51; research prof. phys. metallurgy U. Ill., 1951-76. Co-author: The Physics of Powder Metallurgy, 1951, Metal Interfaces, 1952, Recrystallization, Grain Growth and Textures, 1966; Editor: Theory of Alloy Phases, 1956, Electronic Structure and Alloy Chemistry of Transition Elements, 1963; co-editor: Magnetic and Inelastic Scattering of Neutrons by Metals, 1968, Magnetism In Alloys, 1972. Recipient U.S. Scientist award Humboldt Found., 1978, Heyn Meml. award German Metall. Soc., 1980. Fellow Metall. Soc. of AIME (Mathewson Gold Medal award 1952, ann. lectr. 1971, Hume-Rothery award 1974), Am. Soc. Metals (Sauveur Achievement award 1976), Am. Phys. Soc., Hungarian Phys. Soc. (hon.); mem. Nat. Acad. Engring. Office: Metallurgy Bldg U Ill Urbana IL 61801

BECK, PAUL ALLEN, political science educator; b. Logansport, Ind., Mar. 15, 1944; s. Frank Paul and Mary Elizabeth (Flanegin) B.; m. Maria Teresa Marcano, June 14, 1967; children: Daniel Lee, David Andrew. A.B., Ind. U., 1966; M.A., U. Mich., 1968, Ph.D., 1971. Asst. prof. U. Pitts., 1970-75, assoc. prof., 1976-79; prof. Fla. State U., Tallahassee, 1979—, chmn. dept., 1981—. Co-author: Policical Socialization Across the Generations, 1975, Individual Energy Conservation Behaviors, 1980. Chmn. council Inter-Univ. Consortium for Polit. and Social Research, 1982-83, mem., 1980-83. Mem. Am. Polit. Sci. Assn. (exec. council 1981-82, book review editor 1976-79), Midwest Polit. Sci. Assn, So. Polit. Sci. Assn. (editorial bd. 1982—), Am. Assn. Pub. Opinion Research. Democrat. Home: 3704 Galway Dr Tallahassee FL 32308 Office: Dept Polit Sci Fla State U Tallahassee FL 32306

BECK, ROBERT ARTHUR, insurance company executive; b. N.Y.C., Oct. 6, 1925; s. Arthur C. and Alma (Wickware) B.; m. Frances Theresa Kenny, Aug. 7, 1948; children: Robert Arthur, Arthur Francis, Kathleen Ann, Stephen Duncan, Theresa Frances. B.S. summa cum laude, Syracuse U., 1950. Financial analyst Ford Motor Co., Detroit, 1950-51; salesman Prudential Ins. Co. of Am., 1951-56, mgr., Cin., 1956-57, dir. agy., Jacksonville, Fla., 1957-63, exec. gen. mgr., Newark, 1963-65, v.p., 1965-66, sr. v.p., Chgo., 1966, Newark, 1967-70, exec. v.p., 1970-73, pres., 1974-78, chmn., chief exec. officer, 1978—, also dir.; dir. Campbell Soup Co., Xerox Corp. Trustee Syracuse U., Com. Econ. Devel.; vice chmn. Bus. Council; mem. Bus. Roundtable, also chmn. task force on social security; mem. Nat. Commn. on Social Security Reform; mem. exec. com. Pres. Reagan's Pvt. Sector Survey on Cost Control; past pres. N.J. Hist. Soc.; vice-chmn. Kennedy Center Corp. Fund Bd., Nat. Center State Cts.; chmn. United Way Am., Am. Coll.; trustee Renaissance Newark, Inc. Decorated knight of Malta, Million Dollar Round Table Found. Mem. Am. Council Life Ins. (chmn.), Health Ins. Assn. Am. (past chmn.), Life Ins. Mktg. and Research Assn. (past chmn.), Mt. Vernon Ladies' Assn. (chmn. capital devel. campaign), Econ. Club of N.Y. (trustee), Beta Gamma Sigma (pres., chief exec. officer Dir.'s Table). Clubs: Navesink, Essex, Seabright, Ocean Reef, Boca Grande. Lodge: Knights of Malta. Office: Prudential Plaza Newark NJ 07101

BECK, ROBERT NELSON, philosophy educator, author; b. Ft. Dodge, Iowa, Sept. 27, 1924; s. Victor E. and Elizabeth (Nelson) D.; m. Gladys E. Johnson, Mar. 28, 1942; children: Margaret E. (Mrs. Richard B. Knowlton), JoAnne M. (Mrs. John H. Gottcent), Ronald N. B.A., Clark U., 1947; A.M., Boston U., 1948, Ph.D., 1950. Prof. philosophy Clark U., 1948—, chmn. dept., 1957—, Univ. prof., 1980—; Carnegie intern Yale, 1955-56; prof. philosophy U. So. Calif., 1967-68; Moderator Town of Leicester, Mass., 1953-67; trustee Leicester Jr. Coll., 1966-68, Upsala Coll., 1975—. Author: The Meaning of Americanism, 1956, Perspectives in Philosophy, 1961, American Ideas, 1963, C.J. Bostrom's Philosophy of Religion, 1962, Perspectives in Social Philosophy, 1967, Ethical Choice, 1970, Ideas in America, 1970, (with R.H. Lineback) Page Composition Costs of Philosophy Journals, 1976, Handbook in Social Philosophy, 1979; Founder, editor: Idealistic Studies. Served with AUS, 1943-46. Mem. Am. Philos. Assn., Assn. Philosophy Jour. Editors (pres. 1972-80), Metaphys. Soc. Am. (sec.-treas. 1965-68), Phi Beta Kappa. Lutheran (exec. bd. New Eng. Synod). Home: 25 Brentwood Dr Holden MA 01520 Office: Clark Univ Worcester MA 01610

BECK, ROSEMARIE, painter; b. N.Y.C., July 8, 1924; d. Samuel and Margit (Weisz) B.; m. Robert Phelps, Sept. 14, 1945; 1 son, Roger. A.B., Oberlin Coll., 1944; student, Inst. Fine Arts, N.Y.U., 1944-45, Columbia, 1945, Atelier of Robert Motherwell, 1950. Tchr. Vassar Coll., 1957-55, 61-62, 63-64, Middlebury (Vt.) Coll., 1958, 60, 63, Queens Coll., 1968—. One-man shows include, Peridot Gallery, N.Y.C., 1953, 55, 56, 59, 60, 63, 65, 66, 68-70, 72, Vassar Coll., 1957, 61, Wesleyan U., Middletown, Conn., 1960, State U. N.Y. at New Paltz, 1962, Zachary Waller Gallery, Los Angeles, 1971, Duke, Kirkland Coll., 1972, Washburn Gallery, Poindexter Gallery, 1975, 80, Middlebury (Vt.) Coll., 1979, Ingber Gallery, 1980, Witherspoon Gallery, Cornell U., group shows include, Chgo. Art Inst., 1962, Pa. Acad. Fine Arts, 1954, 66, Whitney Mus., 1955-57, 58, Tate Gallery, London, Eng., 1958, Butler Inst., Indpls., 1962, Kootz Gallery, N.Y.C., 1951, Felix Landau Gallery, Los Angeles, 1962, Nat. Inst. Arts and Letters, 1968, 75, 78, 79. Grantee Ingram Merrill Found., 1966, 79. Address: 6 E 12th St New York NY 10003

BECK, STANLEY CLIFTON, air force officer; b. Gilbert, Ariz., Jan. 21, 1929; s. Clifton Lewis and Thelma (Flowers) B.; m. Betsy Frost, June 13, 1954; children: Daniel Wayne, Hal Eric, Leslie Jean. B.S.,

U.S. Mil. Acad., 1954; student, Air Command and Staff Coll., 1963-64; M.S., George Washington U., 1964; postgrad., Nat. War Coll., 1970-71. Commd. 2d lt. USAF, 1954, advanced through grades to maj. gen., 1980; crew comdr. Squadron Ops. officer, Loring AFB, Maine, 1957-63; staff USAF Acad., 1964-68; ops. officer DaNang Air Base, Vietnam, 1969-70; vice-comdr. (410th Bomb Wing), K.I. Sawyer AFB, 1971-72, comdr., Robins AFB, 1972, Thailand, 1972-73, Barksdale AFB, 1973-74; head USAF ROTC; prof., head aerospace studies U. Tenn., Knoxville, 1974-75; comdt. cadets USAF Acad., Colo., 1975-78; comdt. Air Command and Staff Coll., Maxwell AFB, Ala., 1978-79; comdr. (57th Air Div.), Minot AFB, 1979, Guam, 1980-82, Calif., 1982—. Decorated Legion of Merit, Bronze Star, numerous service, unit medals. Mem. Air Force Assn., Order of Daedalians. Episcopalian. Home: 171 Baucom Riverside CA 92508 Office: Vice Comdr 15th Air Force March AFB CA 92518

BECK, STANLEY DWIGHT, entomology educator, researcher; b. Portland, Oreg., Oct. 17, 1919; s. Dwight William and Eunice (Dodd) B.; m. Isabel Helene Stalker, Aug. 29, 1943; children: Bruce Dwight, Diana Helene, Karen Christine, Marianne Elizabeth. B.S., Wash. State U., 1942; M.S., U. Wis., 1947, Ph.D., 1950; D.Sc., Luther Coll., 1972. Asst. prof. entomology U. Wis., Madison, 1950-57, assoc. prof., 1957-64, prof., 1964-69, W.A. Henry Disting. prof., 1969—; chmn. cotton study team Nat. Acad. Sci., Washington, 1973-75; mem. editorial com. Annual Rev. Entomology, 1975-79. Editor, Wis. Acad. Scis., Arts and Leters, 1957-60; author: Simplicity of Science, 1959, Animal Photoperiodism, 1963, Insect Photoperiodism, 1968, (2d edit.) Insect Photoperiodism, 1980, Modern Science and Christian Life, 1970. Chmn. Madison Lutheran Campus Ministry, Wis., 1967-72; mem. Council of So. Wis. Dist., Am. Luth. Am., 1968-70, mem. Task Force on Ethical Issues in Medicine, 1975-76; mem. Task Force on Ch. and Disabilities Wis. Conf. Chs., 1980-82. Served to lt. USNR, 1942-45. AAAS fellow, 1964; recipient Founders Meml. award Entomol. Soc. Am., 1962, Disting. Achievement award Wash. State U. Almuni Assn., 1981. Mem. AAAS, Entomol. Soc. Am. (pres. 1981-82), Am. Soc. Zoologists, Phi Beta Kappa. Lutheran. Home: 6100 Gateway Green Monona WI 53716 Office: Dept Entomology U Wis Madison WI 53706

BECK, TONI, choreographer; b. N.Y.C., Oct. 4, 1925; d. Samuel and Margaret (Wise) B.; m. Bob Glatter, Dec., 1952 (div. 1965); 1 dau., Lesli; m. Paul Bosner, 1969. B.A., Oberlin Coll., 1946; M.A., Columbia U., 1949; postgrad., Harvard U., 1972. Asst. prof. dance Washington U., St. Louis, 1949-51; lectr. So. Meth. U., Dallas, 1959-60, asst. prof., 1960-63, assoc. prof., 1963-65, prof. dance, 1965-82; exec. dir. The Greenhouse, Arlington, Tex., 1982—; tchr. Modern Ballet Studio, Dallas, 1954-68, Rubin Acad. Music, Jerusalem, 1971, Bat Dor Studios, Tel Aviv, Israel, 1972, Internat. Ballet Center, Copenhagen, 1976, Utah Repertory Co., 1974; tchr., choreographer Scapino Ballet, Amsterdam, Netherlands, 1976, choreographer, 1977, Bat Dor Dance Co., Tel Aviv, 1972, 74, 77, Irish Ballet Co., Cork; mem. adv. bd. to arts Dallas Ind. Sch. Dist., 1981-84; lectr. Am. Cultural Center, Tokyo, 1981. Choreographer: mus. piece Konstallationen, Graz, Austria, 1975, Romeo and Juliet, Ernani, both for Dallas Civic Opera, 1981; Author: Fashion Your Figure, 1971, Focus Your Figure, 1973; contbr. articles to mags. including, Vogue, Harper's, Cosmopolitan; chpt. on arts to The Book of Dallas, 1976. Named One of Most Outstanding Profs. So. Meth. U., 1976-77; One of Top Ten Newsshapers of Yr. Dallas Times Herald, 1978; Ford Found. grantee, 1951-52; So. Meth. U. grantee, 1964, 81; Danforth grantee, 1964-65. Mem. Actors Equity, AFTRA, Am. Coll. Sports Medicine, AAUP. Home: 3327 Mockingbird Ln Dallas TX 75205 *The need to constantly re-evaluate one's own work, whether it be in teaching, choreographing or dealing with others: and with this re-evaluation, to have the courage to change one's work patterns and risk the results. This is my key for keeping aware, alert, and never satisfied with what has been done. Living in the past is dangerous; seeking out the demands of the present and future keeps me always questioning and questing.*

BECKEDORFF, DAVID LAWRENCE, computer scientist, investment manager; b. Ft. Lewis, Wash., Oct. 29, 1940; s. Lawrence LeRoy and Helen Emily (Sekerak) B.; m. Barbara Anne Rissel, June 16, 1963; children: Thomas, Carolyn. A.B., Princeton U., 1962; M.A., Harvard U., 1963, postgrad., 1964-67. Analyst Boston Co., 1967-68, investment officer, 1968-69, v.p., 1971-74, sr. v.p., 1974-83, sr. portfolio mgr., 1980-83; pres. DLB Computer Systems, Inc., Wellesley, 1983—. Patentee programmable appliance controller, 1981. Sec. Wellesley United Soccer Club, 1977-78, pres., 1979-80. Republican. Methodist. Home: 57 Emerson Rd Wellesley MA 02181

BECKEL, CHARLES LEROY, physics educator; b. Phila., Feb. 7, 1928; s. Samuel Mercer and Katherine (Linsky) B.; m. Josephine Ann Beck, June 27, 1958; children—Amanda S., Sarah K. Nicholson, Timothy C., Andrea C. B.S., U. Scranton, 1948; Ph.D., Johns Hopkins, 1954. Asst. prof. physics Georgetown U., 1953-59, asso. prof., 1959-64; research staff mem. Inst. for Defense Analyses, Arlington, Va., 1964-66; asso. prof. physics U. N.Mex., 1966-69, prof., 1969—, asst. dean, 1971-72, acting v.p. research, 1972-73; acting dir. Inst. Social Research and Devel., 1972; vis. prof. theoretical chemistry Oxford U., 1973; Fulbright lectr. U. Peshawar, Pakistan, 1957-58, Cheng Kung U., Tainan, Taiwan, 1963-64; phys. sci. officer U.S. Arms Control and Disarmament Agy., 1980-81; cons. Ballistics Research Lab., Aberdeen Proving Ground, Md., 1955-57, Dikewood Corp., Albuquerque, 1967-72, 74-80, Albuquerque Urban Obs., 1969-71, Inst. Def. Analyses, 1962-64, 66-69, U.S. ACDA, 1981—. Pres. Kidney Found. of N.Mex. Inc., 1968-72, del. trustee, 1972-73, 76-80, exec. com., 1974-80, 83—; v.p. Kidney Foundat. of N.Mex. Inc., 1982-83; bd. dirs. Nat. Capitol area Nat. Kidney Found., 1965-66, N.Mex. Combined Health Appeal, 1972-73; mem. edn. subcom. Navajo Sci. Com., 1975-82. Mem. Am. Phys. Soc., Bioelectromagnetics Soc., Am. Assn. Physics Tchrs., Internat. Soc. Quantum Biology, Fulbright Alumni Assn. (publs. adv. bd. 1978-79), Sigma Xi. Home: 7212 Dellwood Rd NE Albuquerque NM 87110

BECKEL, WILLIAM EDWIN, univ. pres.; b. Kingston, Ont., Can., Apr. 11, 1926; s. Elmer Earnest and Beatrice Mary (Driver) B.; m. Dorothy Kathleen Brown, Sept. 3, 1953; children—John, Meg. Julia, Millie. B.A., Queen's U., 1949; M.S., U. Iowa, 1953; Ph.D., Cornell U., 1955. With Nat. Def. Research Bd., 1949-55; research scientist Can. Dept. Agr., 1955-56; prof. zoology U. Toronto, Ont., 1956-68; v.p. U. Lethbridge, Alta., Can., 1968-72, pres., 1972-79, Carleton U., Ottawa, Ont., 1979—. Contbr. sci. and ednl. articles to profl. jours. Mem. Can. Soc. Zoologists, Can. Soc. Cell Biology, others. Office: Office of Pres Carleton U Ottawa ON K1S 5B6 Canada

BECKEN, BRADFORD ALBERT, engineering laboratory executive; b. Providence, Oct. 5, 1924; s. Albert R. and Ruth M. (Stephenson) B.; m. Gaynelle M. Lane, Nov. 30, 1946; children: Bradford Albert, Brian A., Christian L., Ann Tracey. Student, U. R.I., 1942-43; B.S., U.S. Naval Acad., 1946, U.S. Naval Postgrad. Sch., 1952; M.S., UCLA, 1953, Ph.D., 1961. Commd. officer USN, advanced through grades to comdr.; cons. Airtronics-Spl. Warfare Lab., 1967; mgr. systems engrng. lab. submarine signal div. Raytheon Co., Portsmouth, R.I., 1967-70, mgr. Portsmouth Engrng. Lab. Author: Advanced in Hydroscience, 1964. Bd. dirs. Newport chpt. ARC, 1976—; trustee Newport Hosp., 1977, chmn. bd., 1979—. Recipient Asst. Chief Bur. Ships award, 1963. Fellow Acoustical Soc. Am.; mem. Am. Def. Preparedness Assn. (v.p. sea systems), Naval War Coll. Found., U.S. Naval Inst., Newport C. of C. (chmn. naval affairs council 1977), U.S. Naval Acad. Alumni Assn. Episcopalian. Home: 260 Fischer Circle Portsmouth RI 02871 Office: 1847 W Main Rd Portsmouth RI 02871

BECKENSTEIN, MYRON, journalist; b. Cleve., Mar. 11, 1938; s. Irwin and Rachel (Miller) B.; m. Charlotte Hunt, Oct. 17, 1970; 1 dau., Stacey Amanda. B.S., Northwestern U., 1959, M.S., 1960. Mem. staff Chgo. Daily News, 1959-78, Balt. Sun, 1978—. Served with AUS, 1961-64. Mem. Upper Patuxent Archeol. Group, Sigma Delta Chi. Home: 6281 Tufted Moss Columbia MD 21045 Office: 501 N Calvert St Baltimore MD 21278

BECKER, DAVID VICTOR, physician; b. N.Y.C., May 24, 1923; s. Albert and Miriam R. B.; m. Naomi Isaacson, Feb. 20, 1949 (dec. 1974); children: Daniel F., Susan B. A.B., Columbia U., 1943, M.A., 1944; M.D., N.Y. U., 1948. Diplomate: Am. Bd. Nuclear Medicine. Research fellow, Damon Runyon clin. cancer fellow Sloan-Kettering Inst., 1950-52; founder, dir. clin. isotope unit Brooke Army Hosp., Ft. Sam Houston, Tex.; also chief radioisotope lab. surg. research unit Brooke Army Med. Center, 1952-54; asst. resident dept. medicine N.Y. Hosp., 1954-55, attending radiologist, 1971—, attending physician, 1975—; dir. div. nuclear medicine N.Y. Hosp.-Cornell Med. Center, 1955—; prof. radiology Cornell U. Med. Coll., 1972—, prof. medicine, 1975—; vis. investigator Jackson Meml. Labs., Bar Harbor, Maine, 1962-67; mem. tech. adv. com. on radiation to Health Commr., N.Y.C., 1963—; chmn. radiosotope com. N.Y. Hosp.-Cornell Med. Center, 1966—; mem. steering com. USPHS Nat. Coop. Thyrotoxicosis Follow-up study, 1968—; mem. adv. com. on med. uses of radioactive materials N.Y. State Dept. Health, 1973-76; mem. sci. coms. Nat. Council on Radiation Protection and Measurements, 1973—; cons. Pan Am. World Health Orgn., 1975—; cons. med. dept. Brookhaven Nat. Lab., 1980—; mem. com. environ. health N.Y. Acad. Medicine, 1980—; mem. task force on short-lived radionuclides Bur. Radiol. Health, FDA, 1975-78; chmn. spl. liaison com. between Soc. Nuclear Medicine and World Fedn. Nuclear Medicine and Biology, 1976-78; cons. Bur. Radiol. Health, FDA, 1976—; mem. med. radiation adv. com. FDA, 1981—; mem. Nat. Coop. Thyroid Cancer Treatment Study Group, 1978—. Contbr. articles on thyroid physiology, clin. thyroid disease, nuclear medicine and radiation effects to profl. jours., chpts. in books. Fellow A.C.P.; mem. Am. Thyroid Assn. (1st v.p. 1976-81, pres.-elect 1981, pres. 1982-83, chmn. edn. com. 1977-79, chmn. environ. hazards com. 1980-81), Soc. Nuclear Medicine (pres. Greater N.Y. chpt. 1978, trustee 1978-82, 82—, publs. com. 1981—), Am. Fedn. Clin. Research, Endocrine Soc. Office: 525 E 68th St New York NY 10021

BECKER, DON CRANDALL, newspaper executive; b. Sacramento, Dec. 31, 1933; s. Edwin Archibald B. and Georgiana (Holt) English; m. Maureen Ann Maguire, 1961; children: James Crandall, Brian Edward. A.B., San Jose State U., 1957. Reporter Santa Cruz (Calif.) Sentinel, 1957-58; reporter, editor UPI, San Francisco, 1958-59, corr., mgr., Singapore, 1960-62, Manila, 1962-67, San Juan, P.R., 1969-72, Miami, 1972-73; dep. commr. Nat. Profl. Soccer League, N.Y.C. and San Francisco, 1967-68; dir. corp. relations Knight-Ridder Newspapers, Miami, 1973-78; pub., chmn. Gary (Ind.) Post-Tribune, 1978-79; pres. Detroit Free Press, 1979—; exec. sec. Fgn. Corrs. Assn. S.E. Asia, Singapore, 1961-62; pres. Manila Overseas Press Club, 1963-64. V.p. mktg. Detroit Symphony, 1982-83. Served to cpl. U.S. Army, 1954-56. Mem. Am. Newspaper Pubs. Assn., Greater Detroit C. of C. (vice-chmn. 1983). Clubs: Country of Detroit (Grosse Pointe, Mich.); Athletic Detroit. Office: Detroit Free Press 321 W Lafayete St Detroit MI 48226 *It is better to be lucky than smart but you have to be smart enough to be ready. A positive attitude is a gift like good looks or a good family and even more enduring. Burning bridges is a luxury even the richest should avoid. The right perspective reminds us how life is.*

BECKER, DONALD RAYMOND, surgeon, educator; b. Rochester, N.Y., Mar. 29, 1923; s. Arthur A. and Mildred (Cohen) B.; m. Diane Lynn Decillis, Aug. 20, 1974; children: Stephen, Barbara, Laurie. A.B., U. Pa., 1944; M.D., Syracuse U., 1949; postgrad., U. Pa., 1944. Diplomate: Am. Bd. Surgery. Intern Meyer Meml. Hosp., Buffalo, 1949-50, asst. resident surgery, 1950-51, 53-55, chief resident surgery, 1955-56; coordinator project med. edn. U. Buffalo, 1959-62; chmn. intro. medicine State U. N.Y., Buffalo, 1959-66, asst. dean, 1963-67, clin. prof. surgery, dir. surg. resident program, 1976-80; chmn. dept. surgery Deaconess Hosp., Buffalo, 1966-80; dir. dept. surgery St. Francis Hosp. Med. Center, Hartford, Conn., 1980—; prof. surgery U. Conn., 1980—. Served with USNR, 1944-45; to 1st lt. M.C. AUS, 1951-53. State U. N.Y. at Buffalo research grantee, 1963; Western N.Y. Heart Assn. grantee, 1968-69. Fellow A.C.S.; mem. Assn. Am. Med. Colls., N.Y. State Soc. Surgeons, N.Y. State, Erie County, Maimonides med. socs., Buffalo Vascular Soc. (founder), Buffalo Surg. Soc. (pres.), N.Y. Acad. Scis., Upstate N.Y. Vascular Soc., Buffalo Acad. Medicine, Hartford County Med. Soc., Internat. Cardiovascular Soc., U. Pa., Syracuse U., SUNY at Buffalo alumni assns., Phi Delta Epsilon. Democrat. Jewish. Home: 40 Woodmont Rd Avon CT 06001 Office: 114 Woodland St Hartford CT 06105 *I have been too often impatient with, and unaccepting of, the frailties and inadequacies of others, assuming that because I could do something, everyone else could also. It has taken many years to begin to learn to accept people as they are. I have been my most severe critic.*

BECKER, DWIGHT LOWELL, physician; b. Mercer County, Ohio, July 21, 1918; s. George and Maude R. (Purdyzz) B.; m. Mary Lauer, Sept. 6, 1942; children—Lawrence, Judith, George Edward. B.A., Ohio State U., 1940, M.D., 1943. Intern Christ Hosp., Cin., 1943-44; gen. practice medicine, Lima, Ohio, 1946-65, emergency room practice, Lima, 1965—; mem. staff Lima Meml. Hosp.; med. dir. Blue Cross of Lima, 1970—; student health dir. Ohio No. U.; chmn. bd. Ohio Med. Indemnity, Inc., Worthington; field med. cons. Ohio Vocat. Rehab.; dir. Met. Bank, Lima. Mem. Allen County Bd. Health, 1952-55. Served to capt. M.C. AUS, 1944-46. Mem. Am. Coll. Emergency Physicians, AMA, Ohio Med. Assn., Phi Beta Kappa. Republican. Clubs: Masons, Shawnee Country. Home: 1559 Bunker St Lima OH 45805 Office: Ohio No U Ada OH 45810

BECKER, EDWARD ROY, judge; b. Phila., May 4, 1933; s. Herman A. and Jeannette (Levit) B.; m. Flora Lyman, Aug. 11, 1957; children: James Daniel (dec. 1969), Jonathan Robert, Susan Rose, Charles Lyman. B.A., U. Pa., 1954; LL.B., Yale U., 1957. Bar: Pa. bar 1957, also all state and fed. cts 1957. Partner Becker, Becker & Fryman, Phila., 1957-70; U.S. dist. judge, 1970—; lectr. law U. Pa. Law Sch., 1978-83. Bd. editors: Manual for Complex Litigation. Mem. Am., Pa., Phila. bar assns., Am. Judicature Soc., Am. Law Inst., Jud. Conf. U.S. (com. on adminstrn. probation system), Phi Beta Kappa. Jewish. Home: 936 Herbert St Philadelphia PA 19124 Office: US Court House Independence Mall W Philadelphia PA 19106

BECKER, EDWIN DEMUTH, chemist, laboratory director; b. Columbia, Pa., May 3, 1930; m., 1953; 2 children. B.S., U. Rochester, 1952; Ph.D. in Chemistry, U. Calif., 1955. Instr. U. Calif., 1955; phys. chemist NIH, Bethesda, Md., 1955—, chief sect. molecular biophysics, 1962-72, chief lab. chem. physics, 1972-80, acting dir. Fogarty Internat. Ctr., Methesda, Md., 1979-80, assoc. dir. for research service, Bethesda, Md., 1980—, mem. faculty Grad. Sch., 1963—; lectr. Georgetown U., 1958—. NSF fellow U. Calif. Mem. Am. Chem. Soc., AAAS. Office: NIH Bldg 1 Room 118 9000 Rockville Pike Bethesda MD 20205 *research in nuclear magnetic resonance, hydrogen bonding, molecular structure, infrared spectroscopy, free radicals*

BECKER, ELEANOR HOLDEN, communications exec.; b. Upland, Pa., Sept. 15, 1924; d. James Minshall and Elizabeth Catherine (Jones) Holden; m. Ernest Lovell Becker, July 14, 1972; 1 son, Frederick Holden Gernerd. B.A., Coll. William and Mary, 1946. Sr. editor Ladies' Home Jour., N.Y.C., 1953-62; fashion dir. B. Altman & Co., N.Y.C., 1962-63; dir. fashion publicity Monsanto Textiles Co., N.Y.C., 1965-66; exec. editor Bride's mag., N.Y.C., 1966-78; treas. E & S Communications, N.Y.C., 1978—; guest lectr. Drexel Inst. Tech., Phila., 1962, Phila. Museum Sch. Art, 1970; instr. creative fashion writing Fashion Inst. Tech., N.Y.C., 1964-65. Recipient Best of Year award for art direction Printing Week Graphics Arts Exhibit, 1959, 62, Key to City, New Orleans, 1967. Mem. N.Y. Fashion Group, Home Fashions League, Assn. Interior Designers, Kappa Alpha Theta. Presbyterian. Clubs: Rose Valley (Pa.) Folk; Meadow (Southampton, N.Y.); River (N.Y.C.); Phila. Art Alliance. Home: 14 Sutton Pl S New York NY 10022

BECKER, ERNEST LOVELL, physician, educator; b. Cin., Jan. 13, 1923; s. Ernest Louis and Sarah (Lovell) B.; m. Margaret Webb Thompson, Oct. 22, 1949 (div. 1970); children—James T., Margaret W., Frank L.; m. Eleanor Holden, July 14, 1972. A.B., Washington and Lee U., 1944; M.D., U. Cin., 1948. Diplomate: Am. Bd. Internal Medicine. Asst. pharmacology U. Cin. Coll. Medicine, 1946-47; intern Christ Hosp., Cin., 1948-49; jr. asst. resident Med. Coll. Va. Hosp., Richmond, 1949-50, sr. asst. resident, 1950-51, asst. medicine, 1950-51; instr. physiology N.Y. U. Coll. Medicine, 1951-53; investigator Mt. Desert Island Biol. Lab., Salisbury Cove, Maine, summers 1951-52, 55; asst. prof. medicine Med. Coll. Va., 1955-57, Cornell U. Med. Coll., 1957-62, asso. prof., 1962-69, prof., 1969-78, adj. prof., 1978—; dir. dept. grad. med. evaluation AMA, 1978—; dir. Eugene F. DuBois Pavilion, N.Y. Hosp.-Cornell Med. Center, 1960-73, chief nephrology and hypertension service, dept. medicine, 1967-73; asst. attending physician 2d Cornell med. div. Bellevue Hosp., 1957-68; clin. asst. medicine Meml. Hosp., 1964-81; dir. medicine Beth Israel Med. Center, N.Y.C., 1981—; cons. U.S. Naval Hosp., St. Albans, N.Y., 1960-73; asst. attending physician N.Y. Hosp., 1957-65, asso. attending physician, 1965-69, attending physician, 1969-78; asst. vis. physician James Ewing Hosp.; Sec.-gen. Internat. Co. Nomenclature and Nosology Renal Disease; mem. research adv. com. Health Research Council N.Y.C., also mem. metabolic study sect., 1965-78; chmn. ad-hoc com. establishing criteria chronic renal disease centers Regional Med. Programs, 1972; sci. adv. com. artificial kidney-chronic uremia program Nat. Inst. Arthritis and Metabolic Diseases, 1971-78; mem. steering com. lisiting program specialized clin. services, chmn. kidney research com. Joint Commn. Accreditation Hosps., 1972-73; chmn. adv. com. renal provisions HR-1, Social Security Adminstrn., 1972-73. Editorial cons.: Am. Jour. Medicine, 1971—, Clin. Nephrology, 1971; editorial adv. bd.: Current Contents, 1972—; Contbr. articles to profl. jours. Pres. Nat. Kidney Found., 1970-73. Served to capt. USAF, 1953-55. Recipient Lederle Med. Faculty award, 1960-63; Markle scholar med. scis., 1955-60; WHO fellow, 1974, 78. Fellow AAAS, Royal Soc. Medicine, N.Y. Acad. Scis., Royal Soc. Tropical Medicine and Hygiene, ACP; mem. Am. Soc. Nephrology (finance chmn.), Am. Heart Assn. (exec. com. renal sect. council circulation 1965-67), N.Y. Heart Assn. (bd. dirs. 1965-70), AMA, Soc. Exptl. Biology and Medicine, N.Y. County Med. Soc., N.Y. Med. and Surg. Soc., Chgo. Med. Soc., Am. Physiol. Soc., Harvey Soc., Am. Clin. and Climatol. Assn., Chgo. Soc. Internal Medicine, So. Soc. Clin. Research, Explorers Club N.Y. (pres. 1975-76), Sigma Xi. Clubs: Century Assn., Union (N.Y.C.); Cosmos (Washington). Home: 14 Sutton Pl S New York NY 10022 Office: Dir Medicine Beth Israel Med Center 10 Nathan D Perlman Pl New York NY 10003

BECKER, FREDERICK FENIMORE, physician; b. N.Y.C., July 23, 1931; s. Louis I. and Ruth (Shurr) B.; m. Mary Ellen Terry, Nov. 23, 1971; 1 dau., Bronwyn Elizabeth. B.A., Columbia U., 1952; M.D., N.Y. U., 1956. Intern Harvard service Boston City Hosp., 1956-57; resident Bellevue Hosp., N.Y.C.; pathology trainee N.Y. U. Sch. Medicine, N.Y.C., 1957-60, prof., dir. pathology, 1962-75; chmn. dept. pathology U. Tex. Cancer Center, M.D. Anderson Hosp. and Tumor Inst., Houston, 1976-79, v.p. research, 1979—. Contbr. numerous articles to various publs. Served with USN, 1960-62. Mem. Am. Assn. Pathologists (pres. 1980-81), Am. Assn. Cancer Research, Am. Soc. Cell Biology, Tex. Med. Assn. Club: Athenaeum (London). Office: MD Anderson Hosp and Tumor Inst 6723 Bertner St Houston TX 77030

BECKER, GARY STANLEY, economist; b. Pottsville, Pa., Dec. 2, 1930; s. Louis William and Anna (Siskind) B.; m. Doria Slote, Sept. 19, 1954 (dec.); children—Judith Sarah, Catherine Jean; m. Guity Nashat, Oct. 31, 1979. A.B., Princeton U., 1951; A.M., U. Chgo., 1953, Ph.D., 1955. Asst. prof. econs. U. Chgo., 1955-57; mem. faculty Columbia U., 1957-70, prof. econs., 1960-70, Arthur Lehman prof. econs., 1968-70; Univ. prof. econs. U. Chgo., 1970-83, Univ. prof. econs. and sociology, 1983—; mem. research staff Nat. Bur. Econs. Research, 1957-80; research asso. Econs. Research Center, Nat. Opinion Research Center, 1980—; Ford Found. vis. prof. U. Chgo., 1969-70; research advisor, center for econ. analysis human behavior and social instns. Nat. Bur. Econ. Research, 1972-78. Author: The Economics of Discrimination, 1957, 2d edit., 1971, Human Capital, 2d edit, 1975, Human Capital and the Personal Distribution of Income, 1967, Economic Theory, 1971, (with Gilbert Ghez) The Allocation of Time and Goods Over the Life Cycle, 1975, The Economic Approach to Human Behavior, 1976, A Treatise on the Family, 1981; editor: (with William Landes) Essays in Economics of Crime and Punishment, 1974, Essays in Labor Economics in Honor of H. Gregg Lewis, 1976; contbr. numerous articles to profl. jours. Recipient W.S. Woytinsky award U. Mich., 1965; John Bates Clark medal Am. Econ. Assn., 1967; Profl. Achievement award U. Chgo., 1968. Fellow Nat. Acad. Sci., Econometric Soc., Am. Acad. Arts and Scis., Am. Statis. Assn.; mem. Nat. Acad. Edn. (founding mem., v.p. 1965-67), Am. Econ. Assn. (v.p. 1974), Mt. Pelerin Soc., Internat. Union Sci. Study Population. Home: 1308 E 58th St Chicago IL 60637 Office: Dept Econs U Chgo Chicago IL 60637

BECKER, GEORGE JAMES, marine life park executive; b. Toledo, Oct. 2, 1934; s. George J. and Anna Lydon (Dillon) B.; m. Sandra E. Martin, Sept. 5, 1955; children: Butch, Steve, David, Kim, Carrie, Jennifer. Student pub. schs., Fremont, Ohio. Mktg. support mgr. Ryan Aero. Co., 1962-69; v.p. Teawell, Inc., 1969-70; asst. dir. mktg. Sea World of San Diego, 1970, v.p. mktg., 1970-71; v.p., gen. mgr. Sea World of Ohio, 1971-74; v.p., gen. mgr., dir. Sea World of Fla., Orlando, 1974-78, pres., 1978—. Bd. dirs. Fla. Symphony, Central Fla. Devel. Council, Com. of 100, Winter Park Meml. Hosp., Tourist Devel. Council. Served with USN, 1955-59. Recipient Gov. Askew's award for appreciation and support of 1978 European efforts, 1978, Gov. of Ohio's award for serving as chmn. Ohio Travel Council, 1979. Fellow Am. Assn. Zool. Parks and Aquaruims, Internat. Oceanographic Found.; mem. Fla. C. of C. (pres. 1983), Orlando C. of C. Republican. Roman Catholic. Club: Arnold Palmers Bay Hill. Office: Sea World of Fla 7007 Sea World Dr Orlando FL 32808

BECKER, GEORGE JOSEPH, educator, author; b. Aberdeen, Wash., Apr. 19, 1908; s. George Joseph and Ella (Fox) B.; m. Marion Kelleher, Aug. 25, 1932; children: John, Dennis, Michael. B.A., U. Wash., 1929, M.A., 1930, Ph.D., 1937. Mem. faculty Immaculate Heart Coll., Los Angeles, 1934-39, Los Angeles City Coll., 1939-42; translator War Dept., 1942-45; mem. faculty Swarthmore Coll., 1945-70, chmn. dept. English, 1953-70, Alexander Griswold Cummins prof. English, 1961-70; mem. faculty Western Wash. U., Bellingham, 1970-74, acting chmn. dept. English, 1973; Fulbright lectr. Am. lit. and civilization U. Bordeaux, U. Lille, 1956-57; Fulbright lectr. Am. lit., Pau, summer, 1963, Chmn. selection com. pre-doctoral Fulbright grants to, Gt. Britain, 1958. Author: John Dos Passos, 1974, Shakespeare's Histories, 1977, Realism in Modern Literature, 1980, D.H. Lawrence, 1980, Master European Realists of the Nineteenth Century, 1982, James A. Michener, 1983; also articles on Am. novelists of social criticism; translator: Jean-Paul Sartre, Anti-Semite and Jew, 1948; editor, translator: Documents of Modern Literary Realism, 1963, Paris Under Siege, 1870-1871, 1969, Paris and The Arts, 1851-1896, 1971. Fulbright research grantee to Spain, 1963-64. Mem. AAUP, Authors Guild, Phi Beta Kappa. Home: 2225 Niagara Dr Bellingham WA 98226

BECKER, HOWARD H., advertising agency executive; b. N.Y.C., May 15, 1927; s. Sam and Fannie (Green) B.; m. Harriet June, May 29, 1950; children: Susan, Mark. B.B.A., CCNY, 1950. Product mgr. B.T. Babbit, N.Y.C., 1950-54; account exec. Grey Advt., N.Y.C., 1954-57; account supr. Richard K. Manoff, N.Y.C., 1957-58; v.p. mgmt. supr. Doyle Dane Bernbach, N.Y.C., 1959-72, Conahay & Lyon, 1972-73; sr. v.p. mgmt. supr. SSC&B Lintas Worldwide US, N.Y.C., 1973—. Served with U.S. Army, 1945-47. Home: 84 Surrey Dr New Rochelle NY 10804 *Since I am a reflection of my deeds, the image of which I am proudest is the good fortune, tempered by a small dose of wisdom, in marrying a good woman and raising a daughter and a son who have all reached the absolute heights of humanity and sensitivity.*

BECKER, ISIDORE A., business executive; b. N.Y.C., May 10, 1926; s. Max and Eva (Chester) B.; m. Adele Sandler, Dec. 20, 1947; children: Steven Richard, Carol Ann. B.A., Bklyn. Coll., 1949. Partner Herbert D. Silver & Co., N.Y.C., 1956-63; fin. v.p., chmn. financial com. Rapid-Am. Corp., N.Y.C., 1966-72, vice chmn. bd., 1967-72, 76—, dir., 1964—, pres., 1972-76; chief financial officer, treas. McCrory Corp., N.Y.C., 1964-70, dir., 1964—; vice chmn. bd., dir. Glen Alden Corp., N.Y.C., 1967-72; chmn. bd., dir. Schenley Industries, Inc., 1968—; pres. Riviera Hotel, Inc., 1973—; chmn. bd. Shaw-Ross Internat. Importers, Inc., 1983—. Vice chmn. bd. Boys Town Jerusalem; founder Albert Einstein Coll. Medicine; asso. chmn., bd. govs. Anti Defamation League B'nai B'rith; chmn. bd. trustees Columbia Grammar Sch.; treas. Rapid-Am. Found., 1961. Served with USMCR, 1944-46. Home: 215 E 68th St New York NY 10021 Office: 888 7th Ave New York NY 10106

BECKER, JASON CHARLES, food company executive; b. Boston, May 28, 1929; s. David I. and Anne R. (Averbuch) B.; m. Carol B. Burtanger, Aug. 28, 1955; children: Laura, Karen, Susan, Deborah. A.B., Brown U., 1950; M.B.A., Harvard U., 1958; postgrad., U. Rochester, 1950-51. Staff accountant Kendall Co., Walpole, Mass., 1955-56; account exec. Benton & Bowles, N.Y.C., 1958-62; mgr. corp. devel., dir. mktg. Gen. Foods Co., White Plains, N.Y., 1962-69; pres., chief exec. officer Am. Consumer Products Co., Greenwich, Conn., 1969-74; v.p. Gen. Mills. Inc., Mpls., 1974-81; pres. Douwe Egberts Superior Co., Northfield, Ill., 1981—. Served to lt. USNR, 1951-55. Home: 625 Sunset Ridge Northfield IL 60093 Office: Douwe Egberts Superior Co One Northfield Plaza Northfield IL 60093

BECKER, JOSEPH, information scientist; b. N.Y.C., Apr. 15, 1923; s. Julius and Bella (Mazer) B.; m. Arlen Berlin, Apr. 17, 1945; children: Jane C., Wendy L., William S., Sara E. B.Aero. Engring., Poly. Inst. Bklyn., 1944; M.S. in L.S., Cath. U. Am., 1955. Library asst. N.Y. Pub. Library, 1939-44; electronic data processing Fed. Govt., 1946-66; v.p. Interuniv. Communications Council, U. Pitts, 1966-70; adj. prof. U. Pitts., 1966-69; adj. prof. library sci. UCLA, 1976—; pres. Becker and Hayes Inc., Santa Monica, Calif., 1969—; lectr. Cath. U. Am., 1960-71; cons. in field. Author: Handbook of Data Processing for Libraries, 1970, Application of Computer Technology to Library Processes, 1973, First Book of Information Science, 1974, A National Approach to Scientific and Technical Information in the U.S., 1976; co-author: (with R.M. Hayes) Information Storage and Retrieval, 1963; editor: Wiley Information Sciences Series, 1963—, Data Processing Equipment in Libraries Series, 1964-65, Interlibrary Communications and Information Networks, 1971, The Information Society, 1979—. Tech. dir. computerized library exhibits World's Fair; mem. Nat. Commn. Libraries and Info. Sci., 1971—, Nat. Archives Adv. Council, 1977—. Served to capt. AUS, 1944-46. Research fellow computer sci. UCLA, 1960. Mem. Assn. Computing Machinery, AAAS (sec. sect. T-info., computers and communications 1972-77), Am. Cybernetics Soc., Am. Soc. Info. Sci. (pres. 1969), ALA (pres. info. sci. and automation div. 1968). Clubs: Army-Navy, George Town, Cosmos (Washington); Los Angeles Athletic. Home: 13585 Romany Dr Pacific Palisades CA 90272 Office: 2800 Olympic Blvd Santa Monica CA 90404

BECKER, MARVIN BURTON, historian; b. Phila., July 20, 1922; s. Benjamin and Florence (Wachs) B.; m. Beatrice Lapayowker, Jan. 16, 1944; children: Wendy, Dana. B.S., U. Pa., 1946, M.A., 1947, Ph.D., 1950. Asst. prof. history U. Ark., 1950-52, Baldwin-Wallace Coll., Berea, Ohio, 1952-56; asso. prof. Western Res. U., 1957-62; prof. U. Rochester, N.Y., 1964-73; prof. history U. Mich., Ann Arbor, 1973—, chmn. dept., 1977-79. Author: Florence in Transition, 2 vols, 1968, Medieval Italy: Constraints and Creativity, 1981. Served with AUS, 1944. Fulbright fellow, 1953-55; fellow Guggenheim Found., 1956-57, Am. Council Learned Socs., 1963-64, Inst. Advanced Study, Princeton, N.J., 1968-69; Harvard fellow I Tatti, 1963-64; sr. fellow Humanities Inst., Johns Hopkins U., 1966-67. Mem. Mediaeval Acad., Renaissance Soc. Am., Am. Hist. Assn., Nat. Humanities Faculty. Jewish. Home: 2335 Hill St Ann Arbor MI 48104 Office: 4609 Haven Hall Ann Arbor MI 48109

BECKER, MICHAEL LEWIS, advertising executive; b. Toledo, Oct. 30, 1940; s. Nathan M. and Carolyn (Strasburger) B.; m. Katherine Riesdorph, Mar. 25, 1966; children: Danielle, Adam, Rachael. B.S., Syracuse U., 1962. Helicopter traffic reporter Radio Sta. WJRZ, Newark, 1962-64; copywriter Papert, Koenig, Lois, N.Y.C., 1965-68; copywriter, copy chief, sr. v.p., group creative dir. Young & Rubicam, N.Y.C., 1968-83; vice-chmn., chief creative officer Ted Bates Worldwide, N.Y.C., 1983—; asso. vis. prof. Pratt U., Bklyn., 1973-79. Served with N.J. N.G., 1970. Recipient numerous awards including; Venice Film Festival Gold and Silver Lions; Internat. Broadcasting awards; CLIO awards; N.Y. Art Dirs. Club awards; N.J. Art Dirs. Club award. Mem. Copy Club of N.Y. Jewish. Office: Ted Bates Co 1515 Broadway New York NY 10036

BECKER, QUINN HENDERSON, army officer, orthopaedic surgeon; b. Kirksville, Mo., June 11, 1930; s. QuinnHenry B. and Sarah Lucille (Henderson) Finley; m. Gladys Marie Roussell, Aug. 11, 1951; children: Quinn E., Terri K., Paul Eric. Grad., N.E. La. State Coll., 1952; M.D., La. State Coll., 1956; student, Armed Forces Staff Coll., 1969-70, Command and Gen. Staff Coll., 1971, U.S. Army War Coll., 1974-75. Diplomate: Am. Bd. Orthopedic Surgery. Commd. 2d lt. U.S. Army, advanced through grades to maj. gen., 1977; intern Tripler Gen. Hosp., 1956-57; resident in orthopedic surgery Confederate Meml. Med. Ctr., Shreveprot, La., 1958-61; orthopedic surgeon, Ft. Gordon, Ga., 1962-63, chief orthopedic service, Ft. Rucker, Ala., 1963-64; comdg. officer 5th Surg. Hosp. (Mobile Army), Heidelberg, W. Ger., 1964-65; surgeon 3d Inf. Div., Wurzburg, W. Ger., 1965-66; chief orthpedic surgery 33d Field Hosp., Wurzburg, 1965; asst. chief orthopedic service Walter Reed Gen. Hosp., 1966-69; chief profl. services 85th Evacuation Hosp., Vietnam, 1970; div. surgeon and bn. comdr. 15th Med. Bn. 1st Cavalry Div., Vietnam, 1970-71; chief orthopedic service and orthopedic residency tng. Tripler Army Med. Ctr., 1971-74; surgeon 18th Airborne Corps., Ft. Bragg, 1975-77, comdr. Med. Activity, 1976-77; dir. health care ops. Office Surgeon Gen., 1977-80; supr. Acad. Health Scis., U.S. Army, Ft. Sam Houston, Tex., 1980-81; dep. surgeon gen., Washington, 1981-83; comdr. 7th Med. Command, Heidelberg, 1983—; asst. prof. orthopedic surgery Howard U., Washington, 1967-69; clin. assoc. prof. Sch. Medicine U. Hawaii, Honolulu, 1973-74. Contbr. papers to publs. and confs. in field. Decorated Legion of Merit, Meritorious Service Medal, Bronze Star with A, Air medal. Fellow Am. Acad. Orthopedic Surgeons (chmn. mil. affairs com. 1981—), ACS. Lodge: Masons. Home: 26 San Jacinto Dr Heidelberg Germany 6900 Office: Hdqrs 7th Med Command Heidelberg Germany 6900

BECKER, RALPH ELIHU, lawyer, diplomat; b. N.Y.C., Jan. 29, 1907; s. Max Joseph and Rose (Becker) B.; m. Ann Marie Watters; children: William Watters, Donald Lee, Pamela Rose, Ralph Elihu. LL.B., St. John's U., 1928; L.L.D., St. Johns U., 1983; LL.D. (hon.), South Eastern U., Washington. Bar: N.Y. 1929, U.S. Supreme Ct. 1940, D.C. 1949. Practice in, Washington, 1948-76; spl. counsel to Landfield, Becker & Green, 1978—; gen. counsel, founding trustee John F. Kennedy Center for Performing Arts, 1958-76, hon. trustee, 1980—; U.S. ambassador to Honduras, 1976-77. Author numerous booklets, articles on constl. law, ins., space law, atomic energy. Chmn. and former bd. dirs., gen. counsel Met. Washington Bd. of Trade, 1964-71; bd. dirs., gen. counsel, sec. Albert Schweitzer Found., 1955; pres. bd. dirs. Voice Found., 1976—, Friends of LBJ Library; adv. com. L.B. Johnson Meml. Grove on the Park; founding dir., former gen. counsel Wolf Trap Found., 1964-76; mem. adv. com. Sec. Interior Wolf Trap Farm Park for Performing Arts; dir. emeritus Nat. Bank Washington; rep. of Pres. L.B. Johnson with rank spl. ambassador Independence Ceremonies, Swaziland, 1968; mem. Arctic Expdn. for polar bears Washington Zoo, 1962, Antarctic-S. Pole Operation Deepfreeze, 1963; nat. chmn. Young Republicans, 1946-49; mem. Rep. Nat. Exec. Com., 1948-51, Pres.'s Inaugural Com., 1953, 57, 69, 73, 80, Vice Pres. Rockefeller Inaugural Medal Com., Rep. Senatorial Inner Circle, fin. com. Rep. Eagle, Presdl. Task Force; charter mem. Nat. Rep. Congl. Com.; donor collection polit. Americana to Smithsonian Instn., Dartmouth Coll., St. Albans Sch., L.B.J. Library, U. Tex., Austin., Strom Thurmond Inst., Clemson U. (S.C.); founder, dir. Inter-Am. Music Festival. Served to capt. AUS, 1942-45; ETO. Decorated Bronze Star medal, U.S.; chevalier Legion of Honor; Croix de Guerre with palm, France; Belgian Fourragere; Order Morazon 1st class, Honduras; chevalier and officer So. Cross of Brazil; Knight's Cross Order of Dannebrog, Denmark; Gt. Cross for Meritorious Services to Austrian Republic; Royal Order de Vasa, Sweden; Netherlands Resistance Meml. Cross; Order Rising Sun, Japan; recipient Smithsonian Instn. Benefactor medal, 1975; Antarctic Service medal; honored with award by OAS, 1968. Fellow Corcoran Gallery Art, Aspen Inst. Humanistic Studies; mem. ABA (mem. maj. coms., del. Internat. Bar Assn. com. meeting Monte Carlo 1954, Oslo, 1956, chmn. Vienna post conv. Am. Bar Assn. meeting London 1957), D.C. Bar Assn., N.Y. State Bar Assn., Internat. Bar Assn., Fed. Bar Assn. (nat. council), Am. Law Inst. (life mem.), 30th Inf. Div. Assn. (pres. 1958), U.S. Capitol Hist. Soc. (founding dir.), N.Y. State Soc. (pres. 1963-64), Columbia Hist. Soc., Arctic Polar Inst. (hon.), Smithsonian Assn. (nat. mem.), Supreme Ct. Hist. Soc. (founding dir., mem. exec. com., chmn. ann. meetings 1978, 79, 80), Am. Fedn. Musicians (hon.), Am. Chamber Orch. Soc. (hon.), Choral Arts Soc. (hon.), Council Am. Ambassadors, Am. Fgn. Service Officers Assn., Am. Fgn. Service Assn., Diplomatic and Consular Officers Ret. Clubs: International, Capitol Hill; Bald Peak Colony (N.H.); Dacor House. Lodge: Masons. Home: 4000 Massachusetts Ave NW Washington DC 20016 Office: 1220 19th St NW Suite 201 Washington DC 20036

BECKER, REX LOUIS, architect; b. St. Louis, May 20, 1913; s. Louis Henry and Elsie (Schroeder) B.; m. Ada Sylva Schmidt, Nov. 20, 1937; children—Susan (Mrs. Robert L. Barley), Kathryn (Mrs. Russell Kisling), Rex Louis, Roger G. B.Arch., Washington U., St. Louis, 1934, M.Arch., 1935. With Johnson & Maack (architects), St. Louis, 1935-42; with C.E. U.S. Army, 1942-45; partner Froese, Maack & Becker (architects), St. Louis, 1946-73; pres. Becker & Flowers (Architects), St. Louis, 1973—. Works include: Luth. Hosp, St. Louis, Civil Engring. Bldg, U. Mo. at Rolla; also math. and computer bldg., engring. sci. labs. Pres. Council Luth. Chs. Greater St. Louis, 1960-61. Fellow AIA (pres. St. Louis 1956, regional dir. 1966-69, treas. 1969-71), Mo. Assn. Registered Architects (pres. 1955), Guild Religious Architecture, Scarab. Clubs: Mo. Athletic (St. Louis) (gov. 1973-76, treas. 1975-76); Engrs. (St. Louis)). Home: 9 Wakefield Saint Louis MO 63124 Office: 611 Olive St Saint Louis MO 63101

BECKER, RICHARD CHARLES, college president; b. Chgo., Mar. 1, 1931; s. Charles Beno and Rose Mildred (Zak) B.; m. Magdalene Marie Kypry, June 19, 1954; children: Richard J., Daniel P., Douglas F., Steven G., Pamela J. B.S. in Elec. Engring, Fournier Inst. Tech., 1953, M.S., U. Ill., 1954, 1956, Ph.D. in Elec. Engring, 1959. Engr. Ill. Bell Telephone Co., Chgo., 1952, Andrew Corp., 1953; research asst. U. Ill. at Urbana, 1954-58, asst. prof., 1959; sr. staff engr. Amphenol Corp., Chgo., 1959-60, sr. research scientist, 1961-64, dir. program mgmt., 1965-67, dir., 1968; group v.p., corporate dir. adminstrn. Bunker Ramo Corp., Oak Brook, Ill., 1968-73; chief exec. officer and chmn. bd. Fortune Internat. Enterprises, Inc., Oak Brook, 1973-76; pres. Ill. Benedictine Coll., Lisle, 1976—; prof. Midwest Coll. Engring., Lombard, Ill., 1968—; dir. Amphenol Tyree Proprietary, Ltd., Australia, Amphetronix, Ltd., India, Oxbow Resources, Ltd., Can. Contbr. articles and chpts. to profl. jours. and books. Gov. Brook Forest Community Assn., 1971-74; del. Oak Brook Caucus, 1970; trustee Arthur J. Schmitt Found., Midwest Coll. Engring., Ill. Benedictine Coll.; bd. dirs. Council West Suburban Colls., Chgo. Met. Higher Edn. Council, Fedn. Ind. Ill. Colls. and Univs. Mem. Am. Phys. Soc., Albertus Magnus Guild., Sigma Xi, Eta Kappa Nu, Tau Beta Pi. Club: Rotary. Home: 19 Ivy Ln Oak Brook IL 60521 Office: Ill Benedictine Coll 5700 College Rd Lisle IL 60532

BECKER, RICHARD STANLEY, music publisher; b. Hillside, N.J., Nov. 9, 1934; s. Nat Edward and Hattie Adele (Perkel) B. Student, U. Miami, Fla., 1953. Pres. Keva Music Corp. Music pub.: Moody River (No. 1 song in nation), Pat Boone, 1961, Anna, Beatles, 1963 (million selling album), You Better Move On, Rolling Stones, 1966 (Gold Record award), December's Children album, Moody River, Frank Sinatra, 1969 (Gold Record award), Cycles album, You Better Move On, Dean Martin, 1974, Moody River, Readers Digest, 1975; mgr., Alex Bradford, star of Broadway show, Don't Bother Me, I Can't Cope, 1975; pub.: musical Your Arm's Too Short to Box with God, 1975; dir. first country music show in history, Madison Sq. Garden, 1964; Contbr.: Moody River to, Colliers Yearbook, 1961, Anna to, Ency. Brit., 1963. Recipient Broadcast Music award, 1961, Key to City Memphis, 1973, Ark. Traveler award, 1973; named Hon. Citizen Tenn., 1973, Hon. lt. col. aide-de-camp George C. Wallace, 1973. Mem. Friars Club, Broadcast Music, Inc. Established Richard S. Becker scholarship Juilliard Sch. Music, 1976. Office: Box 144 Deal NJ 07723

BECKER, ROBERT A., advertising executive; b. Mar. 3, 1920; s. William and Eva (Kats) B.; m. Pearl Pehr, Aug. 22, 1948; 1 son, David Jonathan; m. Nancy Gibbs, 1977. B.S. in Mktg., NYU, 1941; B.S. in Pharmacy, L.I. U., 1949. Copywriter Plough Inc., Memphis, 1940-42, Murray Breese Assos., N.Y.C., 1944-48; copywriter, product mgr. E.R. Squibb & Sons, N.Y.C., 1949-52, profl. advt. mgr., 1955-57; advt. dir. Nepera Pharm. Co., Yonkers, N.Y., 1953-54; v.p. Burdick & Becker Inc., N.Y.C., 1957-61; pres. Robert A. Becker, Inc., N.Y.C., 1961—, Hosp. Publs., Inc., 1963-84, RAB Publs., Inc., 1963—. Recipient Gold Medal Govt. Austria. Mem. Beethoven Soc. (founder, pres.). Clubs: Univ., Union League. Home: 875 Park Ave New York NY 10021 Office: 90 Park Ave New York NY 10016

BECKER, ROBERT CLARENCE, clergyman; b. N.Y.C., June 19, 1927; s. Clarence Henry and Lillian (Butler) B.; m. Harriet Louise Egland, June 23, 1951; children: John, Ruth, Paul, Carol, Joel. Student, Providence Bible Inst., 1944-47, Gordon Coll. Theology and Missions, 1947-48; B.A., Upsala Coll., 1951. Ordained to ministry Baptist Ch., 1951; pastor First Bapt. Ch., Sedgwick, Maine, 1952-54, Ticonderoga, N.Y., 1954-58, Garden View Bapt. Ch., Williamsport, Pa., 1958-67, First Bapt. Ch., Clayton, N.J., 1967-73, sr. minister, Bloomfield, N.J., 1973—; pres. Conservative Bapt. Assn. Am., 1979-82; chmn. Am. Council, Africa Evangelical Fellowship, 1981—. Bd. dirs. Denver Conservative Bapt. Theol. Sem., 1972—, Eastern Conservative Bapt. Sem., 1982—, Northeastern Bible Coll., 1983—. Mem. Nat. Assn. Evangelicals, Conservative Bapt. Fgn. Mission Soc., Conservative Bapt. Home Mission Soc. Home: 13 Berkeley Heights Park Bloomfield NJ 07003 Office: 1 Washington St Bloomfield NJ 07003

BECKER, ROBERT EUGENE, association executive; b. Algona, Iowa, Nov. 9, 1933; s. Carlyle H. Beckr and Orvilla (Gilbertson) B.; m. Vivian J. Bergsrud, Sept. 2, 1961; children: Bruce R., Sarah V. B.S., State U. Iowa, 1956; J.D., Chgo. Kent Coll. Law, 1962. Exec. mktg. mgr. Ill. Bell Telephone Co., Chgo., 1956-68; dir. Am. Coll. Radiology, Chgo., 1968-79, exec. dir., 1979-81, Profl. Photographers Am., Des Plaines, Ill., 1981—. Mem. Mayor's adv. com. San. Dist., Chgo., 1966-69. Mem. Chgo. Soc. Assn. Execs. (dir.), Arts and Sci. Found. Oklahoma City (dir.), Ill.Bar Assn., Am. Soc. Assn. Execs., Chgo. Jaycees (pres. 1966), Internat. Jaycees (chmn. 1967). Clubs: Chgo. Athletic Asn.,. Home: 731 N Douglas St Arlington Heights IL 6004 Office: Profl Photographers of America 1090 Executive Way Des Plaines IL 60018

BECKER, ROBERT JEROME, allergist, health care consultant; b. Milw., May 29, 1922; s. Jacob and Sarah (Saxe) B.; m. June Granof, June 25, 1950; children: Scott M., Jill Becker Wilson, Jon G. B.S., U. Wis.-Milw., 1943; M.D., Med. Coll. Wis., 1949. Intern Michael Reese Hosp., Chgo., 1949-50; resident in internal medicine VA Hosp., Wood, Wis., 1950-53; resident in allergy Roosevelt Hosp., N.Y.C., 1955-56; practice medicine specializing in allergy, Joliet, Ill., 1956-82; founder, pres. HealthCare COMPARE, cons. health care cost containment, 1982—; med. dir. Quad River Found. Med. Care; pres. Am. Assn. Profl. Standards Rev. Orgns., 1980-82; exec. v.p. Joint Council Allergy and Immunology., 1978—. Author articles in field. Pres. bd. edn. Joliet Twp. High Sch. Dist. 204, 1969-70, 75-76. Recipient Clemens von Pirquet award George U. Internat. Interdisciplinary Center Immunology, 1978. Fellow A.C.P., Am. Acad. Allergy, Am. Coll. Allergists, Am. Coll. Chest Physicians; mem. Ill. Soc. Internal Medicine (pres. 1984—), Alpha Omega Alpha, Alpha Sigma Nu. Office: 3077 W Jefferson St Suite 204 Joliet IL 60435 *Whatever success I have achieved has occurred with the following rules of my life: 1) Individual and public accountability for decisions made; 2) Kindness to all persons in my sphere of contact; 3) Hard work; 4) Humility, truth, and respect for human dignity have been uppermost elements in my interpersonal relations; and, 5) I have accepted my humanness when I fall short of these rules.* *

BECKER, ROBERT OTTO, orthopedic surgery educator; b. River Edge, N.J., May 31, 1923; s. Otto and Elizabeth (Blank) B.; m. Lillian J. Moller, Sept. 6, 1946; children: Lisa, Michael, Adam. B.A., Gettysburg Coll., 1946; M.D., NYU, 1948. Am. Bd. Orthopedic Surgery; Nat. Bd. Med. Examiners. Intern Bellevue Hosp., N.Y.C., 1948-49; resident Mary Hitchcock Meml. Hosp., Hanover, N.H., 1950-51, SUNY Downstate Med. Ctr., 1953-56; practice medicine specializing in orthopedic surgery, 1956—; prof. orthopedics SUNY Upstate Med. Ctr., Syracuse, 1966—; clin. prof. orthopedics La. State Coll. Medicine, Shreveport, 1980—. Author: Electromagnetism and Life, 1982; editor: Mechanisms of Growth Control, 1981; patentee electric stimulation of growth, 1983. Served to 1st lt. USMC, 1951-53. Faculty exchange scholar SUNY, 1979; recipient Middletown research award VA, 1960, disting. alumnus award NYU Coll. Medicine, 1966, Nicolas Andry award Assn. Bone and Joint Surgery, 1979. Mem. N.Y. Acad. Scis., AAAS. Republican. Club: Angler's (N.Y.). Home: Star Rt Lowville NY 13367 Office: SUNY Upstate Med Ctr 750 E Adams Syracuse NY 13210 *Any success I have enjoyed in research has been due to the fact that it has been the most exciting and all-consuming endeavor I ever engaged in.*

BECKER, ROBERT RICHARD, educator, biochemist; b. Aitkin, Minn., Feb. 16, 1923; s. Rudolph John William and Hermine Henrietta (Meyer) B.; m. Mary Misko, June 15, 1956; children—Nancy Elizabeth, Janet Maria. Student, Harvard U., 1942-43; B.S., U. N.D., 1948; M.S., U. Wis., 1951, Ph.D., 1952. Mem. faculty Columbia, N.Y.C., 1952-60; biochemist Oak Ridge Nat. Lab., 1960-62; assoc. prof. chemistry Oreg. State U., Corvallis, 1962-67, prof. biochemistry, 1967—, Ritchie Disting. prof., 1980—, chmn. biology program, 1978—; Mem. pathobiol. chemistry study sect. NIH, 1975-77, Chmn. biomed. scis. study sect., 1983. Contbr. articles to tech. jours. Served to 1st. lt. USAAF, 1943-46. Recipient Carter award for teaching, 1967, Ritchie Disting. Prof. award, 1980, Alumni Assn. Disting. Prof. award, 1982; NSF grantee; NIH grantee; AEC grantee; Spl. NIH Postdoctoral fellow Brookhaven Nat. Lab., 1968-69. Mem. Am. Chem. Soc., Chem. Soc. (London), AAAS, Am. Soc. Biol. Chemists, AAUP (chpt. pres. 1970-71), Assn. Oreg. Faculties (pres. 1979), Sigma Xi (chpt. pres. 1973-74), Phi Lambda Upsilon, Gamma Alpha. Home: 3406 Polk Ave NW Corvallis OR 97330

BECKER, SAMUEL, lawyer; b. Milw., Mar. 16, 1903; s. Abraham Isaac and Anna Liby Ida (Zack) B. A.B., U. Wis., 1922; LL.B., Harvard, 1925, S.J.D., 1926. Bar: Wis. 1925, U.S. Supreme Ct. 1935, N.Y. State bar 1938, D.C. bar 1960. Asst. to reporter on Torts Am. Law. Inst., Boston, 1925-26; asst. prof. law Tulane U. Law Sch., New Orleans, 1926-27; counsel to gov. of Wis., Madison, 1931-33; gen. counsel Power div. Pub. Works Adminstrn., Washington, 1934-35; spl. counsel in charge telephone industry investigation FCC, Washington, 1935-37; practiced in, Milw., 1927-41, N.Y.C., 1946—, Washington, 1960—. Contbr. articles to profl. jours. Served to col. AUS, 1941-46. Mem. Am. Judicature Soc., Assn. Bar City N.Y., Chgo., Milw., D.C., State Wis. Bar assns., Am. Law Inst., Phi Beta Kappa. Jewish. Clubs:

City Athletic (N.Y.C.); Standard (Chgo.); Milw. Athletic. Lodge: Elks. Home: The Astor Milwaukee WI 53202 Office: 733 N Van Buren St Milwaukee WI 53202

BECKER, SAMUEL LEO, communications educator; b. Quincy, Ill., Jan. 5, 1923; s. Nathan and Rose (Dicker) B.; m. Ruth Henrietta Salzmann, June 14, 1953; children—Judith Ann, Harold Craig, Anne Louise. B.A., U. Iowa, 1947, M.A., 1949, Ph.D., 1953; postgrad., Columbia, 1958-59. Instr. U. Wyo., 1949-50; from instr. to prof. U. Iowa, 1950—, chmn. dept. communication and theater arts, 1968-82, U. Iowa Found. disting. prof. communications, 1981—; vis. prof. U. Wis., 1956; Fulbright prof. U. Nottingham, Eng., 1963-64. Author: (with H.C. Harshbarger) Television, 1958, (with others) A Bibliographical Guide to Research in Speech and Dramatic Art, 1963, General Speech Communication, 1971, Essentials of General Speech Communication, 1973, Discovering Mass Communication, 1983; Editor: Speech Monographs, 1969-71; Assoc. editor: Jour. Broadcasting, Jour. Applied Communication Research, Critical Studies in Mass Communication; Contbr. articles to profl. jours. Past bd. dirs. Goodwill Industries, SE Iowa. Served with inf. AUS, 1942-45. Decorated Bronze Star.; Mass Media fellow Fund for Adult Edn., 1958-59. Mem. Speech Communication Assn. (1st v.p. 1973, pres. 1974, mem. exec. com., adminstrv. council), Assn. Communication Adminstrn. (exec. com.), Nat. Assn. Ednl. Broadcasters (past dir.), Central States Speech Assn., Internat. Communication Assn., NAACP, AAUP, ACLU, AAAS, Internat. Assn. Mass Communication Research, UN Assn. Home: 521 W Park Rd Iowa City IA 52240

BECKER, SHERBURN M., stockbroker; b. Milw., Nov. 7, 1906; s. Sherburn M. and Irene Smith B.; m. Mildren Vander Poel, Nov. 15, 1928; 1 son, Sherburn M. Grad., Princeton U., 1928. With H.L. Horton Co., 1930-37; with Fahnestock & Co., N.Y.C., 1937—, now sr. partner; pres. Phila. Fund, Inc., Fahnestock Daily Income Fund; dir. emeritus Marine Corp., Milw. Served to lt. comdr. USN, 1942-45. Republican. Clubs: The Brook, Piping Rock, Racquet and Tennis, Univ. of Milw. Office: Philadelphia Fund Inc 110 Wall St S New York NY 10005

BECKER, STEPHEN, writer; b. Mt. Vernon, N.Y., Mar. 31, 1927; s. David and Lillian (Kevitz) B.; m. Mary Elizabeth Freeburg, Dec. 24, 1947; children: Keir, Julia, David. B.A., Harvard U., 1947; student, Yenching U., Peking, China, 1947-48. Free-lance writer, 1948—; tchr. Tsing Hua U., Peking, China, 1947-48; faculty Brandeis U., 1951-52, U. Alaska, 1967, Bennington Coll., 1971, 77-78, U. Iowa Writers Workshop, 1974. Author: The Season of the Stranger, 1951, Shanghai Incident, 1955, Juice, 1959, Comic Art in America, 1959, Marshall Field III, 1964, A Covenant with Death, 1965, The Outcasts, 1967, When the War Is Over, 1969, Dog Tags, 1973, The Chinese Bandit, 1975, The Last Mandarin, 1979, The Blue-Eyed Shan, 1982. Paul Harris Found. fellow, 1947-48; Guggenheim fellow, 1954. Home: British Virgin Islands

BECKER, WESLEY CLEMENCE, university official; b. Rochester, N.Y., Mar. 17, 1928; s. William Henry and Alcey (Cole) B.; m. Barbara Ann Beckel, June 15, 1950 (div. Sept. 1968); children: Jill, Jeffrey, Linda, James; m. Janis Lynn Wetherell, Oct. 14, 1968 (div. May 1972); 1 dau., Karen; m. Julia Lee Molloy, July 20, 1972 (div. Apr. 1980); children: David, Brandin. A.B., Stanford, 1951, M.A., 1953, Ph.D., 1955. Instr. U. Ill., Urbana, 1955-56, asst. prof., 1956-60, asso. prof., 1960-63, prof., 1963-70, U. Oreg., Eugene, 1970-78, assoc. dean Coll. Edn., 1978—; cons. U.S. Office Edn., 1968-78; dir. Oreg. Research Inst., 1977—. Author: Teaching—A Course in Applied Psychology, 1971, An Empirical Basis for Change in Education, 1971, Parents Are Teachers, 1971, Successful Parenthood, 1974, Teaching 1, Classroom Management, 1975, Teaching 2, Cognitive Learning and Instruction, 1975, Teaching 3, Evaluation of Instruction, 1976. Served with AUS, 1946-49. Fellow Am. Psychol. Assn.; mem. Phi Beta Kappa, Sigma Xi. Research in behavior modification, edn. of disadvantaged children. Home: 711 Spyglass Eugene OR 97401 Office: Coll Edn U Oreg Eugene OR 97403

BECKER, WILLIAM HENRY, judge; b. Brookhaven, Miss., Aug. 26, 1909; s. William Henry and Verna (Lilly) B.; m. Geneva Moreton, June 9, 1932; children—Frances Becker Mills, Patricia Becker Hawkins, Nancy Becker Hewes, Geneva Becker Jacks, William Henry III. Student, La. State U., 1927-28; LL.B., U. Mo., 1932. Bar: Miss. bar 1930, Mo. bar 1932, U.S. Supreme Ct. bar 1937. Asso. firm Clark & Becker, Columbia, Mo., 1932-36, mem. firm, 1936-44, 46-61; judge U.S. Dist. Ct. Western Dist. Mo., 1961—, chief judge, 1965-77, sr. judge, 1977—; judge U.S. Temp. Emergency Ct. Appeals, 1977—; spl. master Supreme Ct. of U.S., 1979—; counsel to Gov. Lloyd Stark in Kansas City Criminal Investigation, 1938-39; spl. asst. to dir. econ. stblzn. Office of War Mobilization and Reconversion, Washington, 1945-46; spl. commr. Mo. Supreme Ct., 1954-58; spl. counsel Mo. Ins. Dept., 1936-44; chmn. Mo. Supreme Ct. Com. to Draft Rules of Civil Procedure for Mo., 1952-59, mem. coordinating com. for multiple litigation, 1962-68, vice chmn., 1967-68; mem. jud. panel on multidist. litigation Jud. Conf. U.S., 1968-77, mem. com. on operation of jury system, 1966-68; faculty Fed. Jud. Center seminars and workshops for U.S. Dist. judges, 1968—. Bd. editors: Manual for Complex Litigation, 1968—; chmn., 1977-81. Served as lt. (j.g.) USNR, 1944-45. Decorated Naval Commendation medal. Fellow Am. Bar Found., Am. Coll. Trial Lawyers, Am. Coll. Probate Counsel; mem. Am. Judicature Soc., Am., Fed., Mo., Kansas City bar assns., Lawyers Assn. Kansas City, Order of Coif. Office: US Courthouse 811 Grand Ave Kansas City MO 64106

BECKER, WILLIAM WATTERS, lawyer; b. New Orleans, Apr. 1, 1943; s. Ralph Elihu and Ann Marie (Watters) B.; m. Carol Gevry, Dec. 26, 1967; children: Kirsten Anne, Gevry Danielle. B.A., Dartmouth Coll., 1964, M.B.A., 1965; LL.B., Harvard U., 1968. Bar: Mass. 1968, D.C. 1970, U.S. Supreme Ct. 1978, Md. 1978. Staff atty., Reginald Heber Smith fellow Cambridge, Mass., 1968-69; partner firm Landfield, Becker & Green, Washington, 1972—; gen. counsel, dir. Voice Found., N.Y.C., 1976—; asso. gen. counsel John F. Kennedy Center Performing Arts, Washington, 1977—; gen. counsel Kennedy Center Prodns., Inc., 1972—; dir. Met. Washington Bd. Trade, 1978—, gen. counsel, 1981—. Mem. Mass., D.C. bar assns. Home: 107 Hesketh St Chevy Chase MD 20815 Office: 1220 19th St NW Suite 205 Washington DC 20036

BECKERMAN, BERNARD, English literature educator; b. N.Y.C., Sept. 24, 1921; s. Morris and Elizabeth (Scheftel) B.; m. Gloria Brim, Aug. 21, 1940; children: Jonathan, Michael. B.S.S., CCNY, 1942; M.F.A., Yale U., 1943; Ph.D., Columbia U., 1956. Mem. faculty Hofstra Coll., 1947-65; organizer, dir. Ann. Hofstra Shakespeare Festival, 1950-64, chmn. dept. drama and speech, 1957-65; mem. faculty Columbia U., 1957-60, 65—, prof., chmn. dept. theatre arts, 1965-81, Brander Matthews prof. dramatic lit., 1976—, chmn. dept. English and comparative lit., 1983—, dean, 1972-76; Fulbright lectr. U. Tel-Aviv, 1960-61; Andrew Mellon prof. Tulane U., spring 1983; disting. lectr. Kyoto Am. Studies Seminar, summer 1983. Author: Shakespeare at the Globe, 1599-1609, 1962, Dynamics of Drama, 1970, also articles, revs. Bd. dirs. L.I. Arts Center, 1963-64. Served with inf. AUS, 1943-45; ETO. Decorated Bronze Star; recipient 7th Ann. award Am. Shakespeare Festival Theatre and Acad., 1962. Fellow Am. Theatre Assn.; mem. L.I. Speech Assn. (v.p. 1953-54), N.Y. Dist. Theatre Conf. (pres. 1961-62), ANTA (dir. 1963-68), Am. Soc. Theatre Research (dir., chmn. 1973-79), Nat. Theatre Conf. (trustee), Shakespeare Assn. Am. (trustee, pres. 1981-82). Home: Redwood Rd Sag Harbor NY 11963

BECKERS, WILLIAM KURT, investment banker; b. Elberfeld, Germany, May 2, 1900; came to U.S., 1902, naturalized, 1914; s. William Gerard and Antoinette (Pothen) B.; m. Annadel Kelly, Apr. 20, 1929; children: Antoinette (Mrs. Robert W. Macnamara), Annadel (Mrs. James Timpson). B.A., Yale U., 1924; student, Columbia Grad. Sch. Econs., 1925. Sr. v.p. Shearson Am. Express, Inc., N.Y.C.; dir. A & F Investing Co., W & T Investing Co., Inc., Mohawk Paper Mills, Inc. Bd. govs. N.Y. Stock Exchange, 1938-42, 44-47, vice chmn. bd., 1947-50. Republican. Episcopalian. Clubs: Univ., Maidstone. Home: E Dune Ln East Hampton NY 11937 Office: 100 E 42d St New York NY 10017

BECKETT, JOHN ANGUS, management educator, consultant; b. Portland, Oreg., Apr. 27, 1916; s. John Wallace and Agnes Peacock (Scott) B.; m. Elizabeth Ann DeBusk, June 15, 1940; children: Ann Meredith, Kathleen Scott, John Thomas. B.S., U. Oreg., 1949; M.B.A., Harvard U., 1946; LL.D. (hon.), N.H. Coll., 1981. C.P.A., N.H., Wash., Mass., Ill. Asst. prof. bus. adminstrn. Alfred P. Sloan Sch. Indsl. Mgmt., Mass. Inst. Tech., 1946-52; cons. McKinsey & Co., San Francisco, 1952-54; treas. Spreckels Sugar Co.; also Spreckels Companies, Inc., San Francisco, 1954-56; prin., regional dir. mgmt. services Arthur Young & Co., Chgo., 1956-59; asst. dir. Bur. of Budget U.S. Govt., 1959-61; adminstrv. mgr. Smith, Barney & Co., 1961-62; Forbes prof. mgmt. U. N.H., Durham, 1962-81; vis. prof. Grad. Sch. Bus., U. Chgo., 1967, 69, Grad. Sch. Bus., Columbia, 1968, 70, U. Washington, 1969, U. Hawaii, 1973, 74; mem. Commn. on Instns. Higher Edn., New Eng. Assn. Schs. and Colls. Co-author: Accounting: A Management Approach, 1950; author: Management Dynamics: The New Synthesis, 1970; Editor: Industrial Accountants Handbook, 1953. Rep. to gen. ct. (legislature) N.H., 1970-74. Home: Mill Pond Rd Durham NH 03824

BECKETT, JOHN DOUGLAS, mfg. co. exec.; b. Elyria, Ohio, July 4, 1938; s. Reginald Walter and Mildred Jean (Patterson) B.; m. Wendy Dianne Hunt, Aug. 26, 1961; children—Kirsten, Carolyn, Kevin, Catherine, Jonathan, Joel. B.S., M.I.T., 1960. Engr. Lear-Siegler, Inc., Elyria, 1960-63; v.p. R.W. Beckett Corp., Elyria, 1963-65, pres., 1965—. Mem.: Intercessors for Am. Newsletter, 1976—; contbg. author: New Wine mag, 1976—. Pres. Intercessors for Am., Elyria, 1976—; sec.-treas. The Religious Roundtable, Washington, 1980—. Republican. Office: PO Box 1289 Elyria OH 44036 *Any success I have achieved has been much more the grace of God than my own wisdom or ability.*

BECKETT, SAMUEL, writer; b. Dublin, Ireland, Apr. 13, 1906; s. William Frank and Mary Roe B. B.A., Trinity Coll., Dublin, 1927, M.A., 1931, D.Litt. (hon.), 1959. Lectr. English Ecole Normale Superieure, Paris, 1928-30; lectr. French Trinity Coll., Dublin, 1930-32. Author: poems Whoroscope, 1930, Echo's Bones, 1935, Collected Poems in English and Franch, 1977; essay Proust, 1930; short stories More Pricks Than Kicks, 1934, Four Novellas, 1977; novels Murphy, 1938, Watt, 1944, Company, 1980; novels in French Molloy, 1956, Malone Dies, 1956, The Unnamable, 1949, How It Is, 1961, Imagination Dead Imagine, 1966, First Love, 1973, Mercier and Camier, 1974, Company, 1980, Worstward Ho, 1983; plays in French Waiting for Godot, 1952, Endgame, 1956; plays for radio All That Fall, 1956, Embers, 1958; plays Krapp's Last Tape and Other Dramatic Pieces, 1960, Happy Days, 1961, Play, 1963 (Obie award), Breath and Other Short Plays, 1972, Not I, 1973, Rockaby, 1980; short stories in French Nouvelle et Textes pour Rien, 1958, Poems in English, 1961, Cascando and Other Short Dramatic Pieces, 1964, Film, 1969, Six Residuq, 1979, Ill Seen Ill Said, 1981; radio plays All that Fall, 1957, Words and Music, 1961, No's Knife: Collected Short Prose, 1945-66, 67, Cascando, 1964; television play Ghost Trio and. . .But the Clouds, 1977. Recipient Prix Formentor, 1961; Nobel prize for lit., 1969. Mem. Am. Acad. Arts and Scis. (hon.). Office: care Editions de Minuit 7 Rue Bernard-Palissy Paris 6 France *

BECKETT, THEODORE CHARLES, lawyer; b. Boonville, Mo., May 6, 1929; s. Theodore Cooper and Gladys (Watson) B.; m. Daysie Margaret Cornwall, 1950; children: Elizabeth Gayle, Theodore Cornwall, Margaret Lynn, William Harrison, Anne Marie. B.S., U. Mo., Columbia, 1950, J.D., 1957. Bar: Mo. 1957. Since practiced in, Kansas City; mem. firm Beckett & Steinkamp; instr. polit. sci. U. Mo., Columbia, 1956-57; asst. atty. gen., State of Mo., 1961-64. Former mem. bd. dirs. Kansas City Civic Ballet; mem. City Plan Commn., Kansas City, 1976-80. Served to 1st lt. U.S. Army, 1950-53. Mem. Am., Mo., Kansas City bar assns., Lawyers Assn. Kansas City, Newcomen Soc. N.Am., Order of Coif, Sigma Nu, Phi Alpha Delta. Presbyterian. Clubs: Kansas City, Blue Hills Country (Kansas City, Mo.). Home: 11337 Wornall Rd Kansas City MO 64114 Office: 607 Commerce Bank Bldg PO Box 13425 Kansas City MO 64199

BECKETT, WILLIAM WADE, lawyer; b. Charleston, S.C., Feb. 2, 1928; s. Theodore Ashe and Mary (Scroggs) B.; m. Kathryn Rae Sims, June 4, 1955; children: Kathryn Elizabeth, Nancy Ellen, Mary Sims. B.S., The Citadel, 1948; J.D., George Washington U., 1956. Engr. Am. Bridge Co., Ambridge, Pa., 1948; with Burns, Doane, Benedict & Irons, 1953-60; mem. firm Schuyler, Banner, Birch, McKie & Beckett, 1960—. Trustee Internat. Students, Inc., 1962-65. Served to 1st lt. AUS, 1948-53. Mem. Am., D.C. bar assns., Am. Patent Law Assn., Washington Patent Lawyers Club (pres. 1966-67), Order of Coif, Delta Theta Phi., Tau Beta Pi. Presbyterian (elder). Clubs: Univ., Bethesda (Md.) Country. Home: 9300 Renshaw Dr Bethesda MD 20817 Office: One Thomas Circle Washington DC 20005

BECKHAM, EDGAR FREDERICK, university dean; b. Hartford, Conn., Aug. 5, 1933; s. Walter Henry and Willabelle (Hollinshed) B.; m. Ria Haertl, Aug. 16, 1958; 1 son, Frederick Hollinshed. B.A., Wesleyan U., 1958; M.A., Yale U., 1959, postgrad., 1959-61. Instr. German Wesleyan U., Middletown, Conn., 1961-66, dir. lang. lab., 1963-66, lang. lab. dir., lectr. German, 1967-69, asso. provost, 1969-73, dean, 1973—; lectr. English U. Erlangen, Germany, 1966-67; cons. Nat. Endowment for Humanities; mem. Commn. on Instns. of Higher Edn.; v.p. Rockfall Corp.; dir. Sentry Savs. & Loan Assn.; corporator Liberty Bank for Savs. Chmn. Conn. Humanities Council, 1979-80; mem. Democratic Town Com., Middletown; pres. bd. dirs. Conn. Housing Investment Fund, 1981-83; chmn. bd. dirs. Middlesex Meml. Hosp.; trustee Vt. Acad., Conn. Ednl. Telecommunications Corp. With AUS, 1954-57. Mem. Modern Lang. Assn., Am. Assn. Tchrs. German. Office: Wesleyan U Middletown CT 06457

BECKHAM, ROBERT J., music publisher; b. Stratford, Okla., July 8, 1927; s. William Smith and Lovenia Elizabeth B.; m. Shirley Jo Waters, Feb. 25, 1948; children—Pamela Sue, Debbie Lee, Cindy Kay, Mary Gay. With Lowery Music, Nashville, 1964, Raleigh Music, 1965; with Combine Music Corp., Nashville, 1966—; now pres. Mem. Country Music Assn., Nashville Songwriters Assn., Nashville Music Assn. (pres.). Democrat. Clubs: Hillwood Country, Nashville Golf and Athletics, Ravenwood Country, YMCA Athletic. Office: Combine Music Corp 35 Music Sq E Nashville TN 37203 *

BECKJORD, WALTER EDSON, lawyer; b. St. Paul, Feb. 28, 1922; s. Walter C. and Mary (Hitchcox) B.; m. Mary Jane Morris, Dec. 20, 1947; children—W. Reed, James, John, Alex. B.S. in Indsl. Adminstrn, Yale U., 1943, LL.B., 1949. Practice law, Cin., 1949—, individual practice law, 1972—; with Cin. Gas & Electric Co., 1951-72, v.p., gen. counsel, 1958-72. Mem. Ohio State Bd. Edn., 1st Congl. Dist., 1956-65; mem. Cin. City Council, 1975-81; candidate for U.S. Senate, 1982. Served to 1st lt. F.A., 1943-46; PTO, China. Mem. Am. Bar Assn., Cin. Bar Assn., Fed. Energy Bar Assn., Tau Beta Pi. Republican. Congregationalist. Home: 3683 Kroger Ave Cincinnati OH 45226 Office: 1813 Carew Tower Cincinnati OH 45202

BECKLAKE, MARGARET RIGSBY, physician, educator; b. London, May 27, 1922; d. James Thomas and Dorothy Mabel (Mills) B.; m. Maurice McGregor, Mar. 20, 1949; children: James, Margaret. M.B., B.Ch., U. Witwatersrand, 1944, M.D., 1951, M.D. hon., 1974. Lectr. U. Witwatersrand, 1950-57; asst. prof. exptl. medicine McGill U., 1961-65, prof., 1967—; career investigator Med. Research Council Can., 1968—. Contbr. articles to med. jours. Fellow Royal Soc. Physicians; mem. Am. Thoracic Soc., Can. Thoracic Soc., Am. Physiol. Soc. Home: 532 Pine Ave W Montreal PQ Canada H2W 1S6 Office: McGill U 3775 University St Montreal PQ Canada H3A 2B4

BECKLEY, DONALD K., fund raiser; b. Washington, Mar. 27, 1916; s. Frank Ross and Lila Strock (Kauffman) B.; m. Eugenie E. Smith, Nov. 14, 1942 (div. 1972); m. Flora Mack, June 26, 1980. A.B., Columbia U., 1936, M.S., 1937; Ph.D., U. Chgo., 1948. Dept. store work, 1936-39; instr. retailing Rochester (N.Y.) Inst. Tech., 1939-42; prof. retailing and dir. Prince Sch. Retailing, Simmons Coll., Boston, 1946-58; exec. dir. Boston Center for Adult Edn., 1958-62; dir. devel. ops. and donor relations NYU, 1962-68; cons. Frantzreb & Pray Assos., Inc., 1968-75; devel. coordinator Am. Mus. Natural History, N.Y.C., 1976; coordinator N.Y. State com. Nat. Health Agys. for Fed. Campaigns, N.Y.C., 1977-81. Author: (with Edwina B. Hogadone) Merchandising Techniques, 1942, (with W. B. Logan) The Retail Salesperson at Work, 1948, (with John W. Ernest) Modern Retailing, 1950, (with Wenzil K. Dolva) The Retailer, 1950. Served with USAAF, 1944-45; staff U.S. Armed Forces Inst., U. Chgo., 1942-43; tchr. naval flight prep. Sch. Monmouth (Ill.) Coll., 1943-44. Home: 1680 NE 191st St Apt 300 North Miami Beach FL 33179

BECKLEY, THOMAS MALLOY, railroad executive, lawyer; b. Mpls., Mar. 2, 1922; s. Miles and Rosemary (Malloy) B.; m. Nancy M. Arntsen, 1950; children: Rosemary Beckley Everson, Margaret Beckley Herrmann, Nancy, Kathryn. B.S., Yale U., 1942; LL.B., Harvard U., 1948. Bar: Minn. 1948, Mich. 1955. Practiced law, Mpls., 1948-60; asso. firm Stinchfield, Mackall, Crounse & Moore, 1948-52; gen. counsel, sec. Duluth, South Shore & Atlantic R.R., Mpls., 1953-60; asst. to pres., sec. Soo Line R.R., Mpls., 1961-68, v.p., sec., 1968-78, pres., dir., 1978-83, chmn., chief exec. officer, dir., 1983—; pres., dir. Tri State Land Co., 1979—; dir. First Nat. Bank Mpls., Malt-O-Meal Co. Bd. dirs. Minn. Citizens Council Crime and Justice; trustee Dunwoody Indsl. Inst. Served to 1st lt. Adj. Gen. Dept., AUS, 1943-46. Mem. Assn. Am. R.R.s (dir.), Western R.R. Assn. (dir.). Clubs: Mpls., Minikahda (Mpls.). Office: Soo Line Bldg Minneapolis MN 55440

BECKMAN, ARNOLD ORVILLE, chemist, instrument manufacturing company executive; b. Cullom, Ill., Apr. 10, 1900; s. George W. and Elizabeth E. (Jewkes) B.; m. Mabel S. Meinzer, June 10, 1925; children: Gloria Patricia, Arnold Stone. B.S., U. Ill., 1922, M.S., 1923; Ph.D., Calif. Inst. Tech., 1928; D.Sci. (hon.), Chapman Coll., 1965, LL.D., U. Calif., Riverside, 1969, Loyola U., Los Angeles, 1969, D.Sci., Whittier Coll., 1977, U. Ill., 1982, LL.D., Pepperdine U., 1977, D.H.L., Calif. State U. Research asso. Bell Telephone Labs., N.Y.C., 1924-26; chem. staff Calif. Inst. Tech., 1926-39; v.p. Nat. Tech. Lab., Pasadena, Calif., 1935-39, pres., 1939-40, Helipot Corp., 1944-58, Arnold O. Beckman, Inc., South Pasadena, Calif., 1946-58, Beckman Instruments, Inc., Fullerton, Calif., 1940-65; chmn. bd. Beckman Instruments, Inc. (now SmithKline Beckman Corp.), from 1965; vice chmn. SmithKline Beckman Corp., 1984—; vice chmn. Smithkline Beckman; dir. Security Pacific Nat. Bank, 1956-72, adv. dir., 1972-75; dir. Continental Airlines, 1956-71, adv. dir., 1971-73. Author articles in field. Mem. Pres.'s Air Quality Bd., 1970-74; Chmn. bd. trustees System Devel. Found; chmn. bd. trustees emeritus Calif. Inst. Tech.; hon. trustee Calif. Museum Found.; trustee Calif. Inst. Research Found.; bd. overseers House Ear Inst., 1981—; trustee Scripps Clinic and Research Found., 1971-83, hon. trustee, 1983—; bd. dirs. Hoag Meml. Hosp. Served as pvt. USMC, 1918-19. Benjamin Franklin fellow Royal Soc. Arts. Fellow Assn. Clin. Scientists; mem. Am. Acad. Arts and Scis., Los Angeles C. of C. (dir. 1954-58, pres. 1956), Calif. C. of C. (dir., pres. 1967-68), Nat. Acad. Engring., N.A.M., Am. Inst. Chemists, Instrument Soc. Am. (pres. 1952), Am. Chem. Soc., AAAS, Social Sci. Research Council, Am. Assn. Clin. Chemistry (hon.), Newcomen Soc., Sigma Xi, Delta Upsilon, Alpha Chi Sigma, Phi Lambda Upsilon. Clubs: Jonathan, California, Newport Harbor Yacht, Pacific. Patentee in field. Home: 107 Shorecliff Rd Corona del Mar CA 92625 Office: PO Box C-19600 Irvine CA 92713

BECKMAN, BEN, interior designer; b. N.Y.C., Nov. 7, 1927; s. Max and Bessie (Buchman) B.; m. Amoree Cynthia Garden, May 17, 1953; children: Joel Seth, Karen Eeta, Eric Blair. B.B.A., Coll. City N.Y., 1949; certificate, N.Y. Sch. Interior Design, 1955. Owner Ben Beckman, F.A.S.I.D. (Interior Design Studio), N.Y.C., 1955—; asst. prof. interior design dept. Fashion Inst. Tech., State U. N.Y., N.Y.C., 1975—; mem. adv. council, 1975—. Designer furniture, carpets, men's accessories. Chmn. South Bronx Prospect Ave. Rehab. Coop. Served with U.S. Army, 1945-46. Recipient Presdl. citation Nat. Soc. Interior Designers, 1969, Gold medal, 1970. Fellow Am. Soc. Interior Designers (nat. chmn. bd. 1971, past pres. met. chpt. N.Y., nat. dir.). Home: 555 Kappock St Riverdale NY 10463 Office: 421 E 72d St New York NY 10021

BECKMAN, DONALD, lawyer; b. Phila., Feb. 1, 1932; s. Meyer Robert and Ada Edith (Horwitz) B.; m. Aileen Kohn, July 14, 1952; children: Howard, Bradley. B.A., U. Pa., 1953; LL.B. magna cum laude, 1959. Bar: Pa. 1959. Assoc. Dechert Price & Rhoads, Phila., 1959-65, ptnr., 1965—; dir. Teleflex Inc., Limerick, Pa. Mem. allocation com. United Way, Phila., 1978, 79, 82; pres. Bala Cynwyd Library Assn., Pa., 1974-75, Main Line Reform Temple, Wynnewood, Pa., 1974-76; scout leader Valley Forge council Boy Scouts Am., 1960-71. Served to lt. USN, 1953-56. Mem. ABA, Phila. Bar Assn., Am. Arbitration Assn., Order of Coif. Democrat. Jewish. Club: Phila. Racquet. Home: One Independence Pl Apt 1601 6th St and Locust Walk Philadelphia PA 19106 Office: Dechert Price & Rhoads 3400 Centre Square West 1500 Market St Philadelphia PA 19102

BECKMAN, GAIL MCKNIGHT, legal educator; b. N.Y.C., Apr. 8, 1938; d. Irland McKnight and Elizabeth B. (Hurlock) B. B.A., Bryn Mawr Coll., 1959; M.A., U. Pa., 1966; J.D., Yale U., 1963; cert., Hague (Netherlands) Acad. Internat. Law, 1977. Bar: Pa. 1964, Ga. 1971. Counsellor Legal Aid Soc., Phila., 1961; legal research asst., 1963; asso. firm Morgan, Lewis & Bockius, Phila., 1963-66; lectr. Faculty Law, U. Glasgow, Scotland, 1967-71; mem. faculty Ga. State U., Atlanta, 1971—, prof., 1976—; Fulbright scholar U. Tuebingen, W. Ger., 1960; mem. Fulbright screening com. Inst. Internat. Edn.,

1980; vis. scholar Inst. East Asian and Comparative Law, Harvard U. Law Sch., 1980. Author: Statutes at Large of Pennesylvania, 1680-1700, 1976, Law for Business and Management, 1975, also articles, revs.; editor: Am. Bus. Law Jour, 1972-79. Bd. dirs. Northside Shepherd's Center, Atlanta, 1980—, vice chmn. bd., 1981-82; bd. dirs. N.W. Ga. council Girl Scouts U.S.A., 1976-78, United Way, 1979; mem. Atlanta Council Internat. Visitors, 1975—. Colonial Williamsburg, grantee, 1965; Ga. State U. grantee, 1980. Mem. Internat. Acad. Estate and Trust Lawyers, Am. Bar Assn. (chmn. and/or vice chmn. coms.), Am. Arbitration Assn., State Bar Ga., Ga. Assn. Women Lawyers (pres. 1980-81), Atlanta Bar Assn., Juristic Soc. Phila., Jr. League Atlanta, Nat. Soc. Colonial Dames Am., DAR, St. Andrews Soc. Atlanta (founder 1971). Presbyterian. Club: Commerce. Home: 3747 Peachtree St Atlanta GA 30319 Office: Ga State U Univ Plaza Atlanta GA 30303

BECKMAN, JOHN STEPHEN, life insurance company executive; b. Berwyn, Ill., Apr. 16, 1936; s. Lloyd John and Esther (Hubbard) B.; m. Barbara J. Arado, Dec. 2, 1967; 1 son, John Stephen Jr. B.B.A. with spl. distinction, U. Okla., 1958; M.B.A. with distinction, Harvard, 1963. Asso. McKinsey & Co., Inc. (mgmt. cons.), Chgo., 1963-70, partner, 1970-72; v.p. Continental Investment Corp., Boston, 1972-74; pres. United Investors Life Ins. Co., Kansas City, Mo., 1974—, also dir.; exec. v.p. Waddell & Reed Inc., Kansas City, 1974-82, dir., 1974—. Trustee Coll. for Fin. Planning, 1977—, chmn., 1980-81; mem. exec. council Harvard Bus. Sch. Assn., 1982—. Served as lt. USAF, 1958-61. Mem. Beta Theta Pi, Beta Gamma Sigma. Republican. Club: Carriage (Kansas City). Home: 5502 High Dr Mission Hills KS 66208 Office: 1 Crown Center PO Box 1441 Kansas City MO 64141

BECKMAN, MILLARD WARREN, investment securities co. exec.; b. Lodi, Calif., Jan. 8, 1926; s. Sherwood W. and Christine (Koenig) B.; m. Lucille Stark, May 23, 1948; children—Bruce, Don, Joan. Student, Am. Inst. Banking, also Stockton Jr. Coll., Sacramento Jr. Coll., 1949-60. Founder Beckman & Co., 1954, pres., chmn. bd., 1961-72, pres., dir., 1972—; chmn. bd., v.p. Beckman Capital Corp., 1972—; chmn. bd. Beckman Devel. Corp. (doing bus. as Calif. Cellar Masters, Wineries and Wine Tasting Shops), 1973—. Home: 135 S Fairmont Ave Lodi CA 95240 Office: 212 W Pine St Lodi CA 95240 *The best way to attain success is to work at what you enjoy the most, always maintain a plan, do those things first that you enjoy least, think of others before yourself, and don't be a quitter or ever lose hope.*

BECKMANN, GEORGE M., univ. adminstr.; b. N.Y.C., Aug. 19, 1926; (m); 2 children. A.B., Harvard U., 1948; Ph.D. in History, Stanford U., 1952. Mem. faculty dept. history U. Kans., 1951-67, asso. dean faculties, 1964-66; prof. history (Claremont Grad. Sch.), 1967-69; dir. Far Eastern and Russian Inst. U. Wash., Seattle, 1969-71, dean, 1971-78, provost, 1978—. Author: Making of the Meiji Constitution, 1957, Modernization of China and Japan, 1962; co-author: The Japanese Communist Party, 1922-45, 1968. Program asso. Ford Found., 1961-64. Fulbright research scholar, Japan, 1952-53, 60-61; Ford Found. fgn. area fellow, Japan, 1952-53, Japan and So. Asia, 1956-57. Mem. Assn. Asian Study. Office: Office of the Provost U Wash Seattle WA 98195

BECKMANN, JON MICHAEL, publisher; b. N.Y.C., Oct. 24, 1936; s. John L. and Grace (Hazelton) B.; m. Barbara Ann Efting, June 26, 1965. B.A., U. Pa., 1958; M.A., N.Y. U., 1961. Sr. editor Prentice-Hall Inc., Englewood Cliffs, N.J., 1964-68; v.p., editor Barre Pubs., Mass., 1970-73; dir. Sierra Club Books, San Francisco, 1973—. Contbr. articles, book revs., poetry to publs. Home: 1056 Greenwich St San Francisco CA 94133 Office: 2034 Fillmore St San Francisco CA 94115

BECKMANN, PETR, electrical engineer, educator; b. Prague, Czechoslovakia, Nov. 13, 1924; came to U.S., 1963, naturalized, 1974; s. Rudolf and Katerina (Fischer) B.; m. Irene Muller, May 31, 1965. M.Sc. in Engring, Prague Tech. U., 1949, Ph.D., 1955; Dr.Sc., Czechoslovak Acad. Scis., 1962. Registered profl. engr., Colo. Research scientist at several Czechoslovak instns., 1949-55; head of wave propagation dept. Inst. Radio Engring. and Electronics, Czechoslovak Acad. Scis., 1955-63; vis. prof. U. Colo., Boulder, 1963-64, prof. elec. engring., 1964-81, prof. emeritus, 1982—; editor, pub. monthly Access to Energy, 1973—. Author: A History of Pi, 1970, The Structure of Language, 1972, The Health Hazards of Not Going Nuclear, 1976, several books on electromagnetic and probability theory.; Contbr. sci. articles to profl. jours. Mem. Ronald Reagan's Energy Task Force, 1980; bd. dirs. Freedom Found., Houston, Assn. for Rational Environ. Alternatives, Houston, Center for Free Enterprise, Bellevue, Wash., Coalition for Growth, Washington, Consumer Alert, Stamford, Conn., Reason Found., Santa Barbara, Calif., Intellectual Activist, Riverside, N.Y. Served with 311 Czechoslovak squadron RAF, 1942-45; Britain. Fellow IEEE; mem. Scientists and Engrs. for Secure Energy, Am. Nuclear Soc. Petr Beckmann scholarship established at Wittenberg U. (Ohio), 1977. Office: Elec Engring Dept U Colo Boulder CO 80309

BECKMANN, ROBERT BADER, chem. engr.; b. St. Louis, Sept. 15, 1918; s. Harry Frederick and Lydia Meta (Bader) B.; m. Barbara Jane Lee, Sept. 5, 1942; children—Robert Lee, Mary Lee; m. Grace Hope Todd, July 30, 1957 (dec. Nov. 1973); m. Jean L. Bourque, July 18, 1981. Student, U. Okla., 1936-37; B.S. in Chem. Engring, U. Ill., 1940, Ph.D., U. Wis., 1944. Research chem. engr. Humble Oil & Refining Co., 1944-46; tchr., research chem. engring. dept. Carnegie Inst. Tech., 1946-61; head dept. chem. engring. U. Md., 1961-66, prof., 1961-66, 77—, dean, 1966-77; cons., 1946—; pres. Engrs. Council Profl. Devel., 1974-76; dir. Versar Inc. Contbr. articles to profl. jours. Mem. council Oak Ridge Asso. Univs., 1966-76, bd. dirs., 1976—. Fellow Am. Inst. Chemists, Am. Inst. Chem. Engrs.; mem. Am. Chem. Soc., AAAS, Am. Soc. Engring. Edn., Phi Kappa Phi, Omicron Delta Kappa, Sigma Xi, Phi Eta Sigma, Phi Lambda Upsilon, Tau Beta Pi, Sigma Pi, Phi Kappa Phi. Research on process engring. and design, kinetics and catalysis, solvent extraction and liquid phase mass transfer. Home: 10218 Democracy Ln Potomac MD 20854 Office: Dept Chem Engring U Md College Park MD 20742

BECKNER, DONALD LEE, lawyer; b. New Orleans, Dec. 18, 1935; s. Marion L. and Rose Ann (Lee) B.; m. Paulette White, Apr. 22, 1978; children: Donald Glynn, Kristin Dawn. B.S. in Econs., La. State U., 1959, J.D., 1965; grad., Nat. Coll. Dist. Attys., 1972, Nat. Jud. Coll., U. Nev., 1979. Bar: La., Calif., D.C., U.S. Supreme Ct., U.S. Tax Ct. 1982. Vice pres., gen. mgr. Shells, Inc., 1957-65; partner firm Foil, Gill & Beckner, 1965-69; asst. dist. atty. E. Baton Rouge (La.) Parish, 1969-72; individual practice law, 1972-74, Baton Rouge, 1981—; partner firm Gill, Lindsay, Seago & Beckner, Baton Rouge, 1974-77; U.S. atty. Middle Dist. La., 1977-81; guest speaker various civic orgns. Served with U.S. Army, 1957. Named Man of Year, Asso. Builders & Contractors La., 1981; Baton Rougeon of Yr., 1982. Mem. La. Bar Assn. (Ho. Dels.), Bar Assn. Fifth Fed. Circuit (bd. govs.). Democrat. Club: City (Baton Rouge). Office: 6004 Perkins Rd Suite A-1 Baton Rouge LA 70808

BECKNER, MORTON ORVAN, educator; b. Portales, N.Mex., June 9, 1928; s. Arthur Lee and Ora (Jenkins) B.; m. Jean Howells Watkins, Nov. 20, 1951; children—Holly, Douglas, Victoria. A.B., U. Calif. at Santa Barbara, 1951; M.A., Columbia, 1956, Ph.D., 1957. Instr. philosophy Bklyn. Coll., 1956-57; mem. faculty Pomona Coll., 1957—, prof. philosophy, 1966—, dept. chmn., 1965-71; mem. exec. com. Claremont Colls. Senate, 1969-70. Author: The Biological Way of Thought, 1959; novel Money Plays, 1981; Editor: Approaches to Ethics, 1962; Contbr. articles to profl. jours. Served with USN, 1946-48. Recipient Clarke F. Ansley Publn. award, 1957; NSF fellow, 1964-65. Mem. Internat. Congress Philosophy Sci. (mem. program com. 1971), Am. Philos. Assn. (mem. exec. com. Pacific div. 1969-73, chmn. 1971-72), A.A.U.P. (pres. chpt. 1969-70), A.A.A.S. Home: 132 W 12th St Claremont CA 91711

BECKWITH, CHARLES EMILIO, educator; b. Oberlin, Ohio, June 8, 1917; s. Charles Clifton and Anna (Wilkinson) B.; m. Elizabeth Ungar, Sept. 8, 1951; children—Constance Anne, James Allan, Margaret Andrea; m. Joanne Glossop, Dec. 19, 1971. A.B., U. Calif. at Berkeley, 1948, M.A., 1950; Ph.D., Yale U., 1956. Faculty English Cornell U., 1956-57; mem. faculty Calif. State U. at Los Angeles, 1957—, prof. English, 1964—, chmn. div. lang. arts, 1963-64, chmn. dept. English, 1964-67, 77-80, coordinator Am. studies, 1975-77. Publs. editor: Twentieth Century Interpretations of A Tale of Two Cities, 1971; asst. editor: John Gay Poetry and Prose, 1974. Served to 2d lt. AUS, 1942-45. Mem. Calif. State Employees Assn., United Profs. Calif. Democrat. Unitarian. Office: 5151 State College Dr Los Angeles CA 90032

BECKWITH, CHARLES GATES, architect; b. Allentown, Pa., Dec. 28, 1921; s. Charles Leach and Fannie Lincoln (Kirkman) B.; m. Mary Ann Davis, Mar. 31, 1951; children—Thomas G., Kirkman D., Spencer E. B.Arch., Cornell U., 1949. Designer LaFarge, Knox & Murphy, N.Y.C., 1948-49; designer, renderer Eggers & Higgins, N.Y.C., 1949-57, asso., 1957-63, partner, 1963-71; sr. partner The Eggers Partnership, N.Y.C., 1971—; dir. The Eggers Group, D.C., 1979; pub. speaker, panelist. Contbr. articles profl. jours.; prin. works include Pace Civic Center Campus. Trustee, officer Darien (Conn.) Pub. Library; chmn. Archtl. Adv. Commn.; trustee Darien YMCA. Served to capt. AUS, World War II. Mem. AIA, N.Y. State Assn. Architects, N.Y. Bldg. Congress, Am. Assn. Arbitrators, Zeta Psi. Episcopalian. (vestryman). Club: Wee Burn Country (Darien) (dir.). Home: 269 Hollow Tree Ridge Rd Darien CT 06820 Office: Two Park Ave New York NY 10016

BECKWITH, HERBERT L., educator, architect; b. Midland, Mich., Feb. 4, 1903; s. Herbert W. and Antoinette (Lynes) B.; m. Elizabeth McMillin, 1946; 1 dau., Suzanne. B.Arch., MIT, 1926, M.Arch., 1927. Registered architect, Del., Maine, Md., Mass., Mich., N.J., N.Y., Ohio, Va. Pvt. practice architecture, Boston, 1930—; partner Anderson & Beckwith, 1938—; faculty Mass. Inst. Tech., 1927—, prof. architecture, 1947—, dir. exhibits, 1945-66, acting chmn. dept. architecture, 1956-57; Cons. architect George Mason Coll., U. Va., Copley Hill Devel., Charlottesville, others; Mem. corp. vis. com. Case Inst. Tech.; Served asst. to chmn. dept. physics Princeton and; exec. officer Princeton Sta., Div. 2, Nat. Def. Research Com., 1943-45; Cons. Mass. Civil Def. Agy.; Sec. Nat. Archtl. Accrediting Bd., 1949-54, pres., 1954-56. Works include exec. office bldg., Raytheon Mfg. Co., office bldgs., Town of Brookline, Mass., New Eng. Electric Service Co., Lab. for Life Scis., dormitory for women, Mass. Inst. Tech.; U. Va. bldgs. A.I.U. Bldg, Tokyo; Sci. Bldg., Boston campus, U. Mass., Am. Internat. Office Bldg, Bermuda, Fisk-Meharry Sci. Center, Nashville, Raytheon Hist. Mus; co-designer sci. complex, U. Rochester, swimming pool and radiation lab., John Thompson Dorrance Lab.; asso. architect: Kresge Auditorium and Chapel, Mass. Inst. Tech.; architect also bldgs. designed, Burma, P.I., P.R., Taiwan. Recipient Coll. of Fellows citation AIA, 1955; named hon. alumnus U. Rochester. Fellow AIA (nat. com. on edn. 1953-60, vice chmn. 1959-60, nat. com. on profession 1958—); mem. Boston Soc. Architects, Mass. Assn. Architects, Mus. Modern Art N.Y., Mus. Fine Arts Boston, Marine Hist. Assn. Mystic, Phi Kappa Psi. Episcopalian. Clubs: Somerset (Boston); Century Assn., N.Y. Yacht (N.Y.C.); Royal Bermuda Yacht. Home: Indian Pond Rd Kingston MA 02364

BECKWITH, JONATHAN ROGER, geneticist; b. Cambridge, Mass., Dec. 25, 1935; s. Manuel and Mildred B.; m. Barbara Shutt, Dec. 26, 1960; children—Benjamin Hunter, Anthony Rhys. B.A., Harvard U., 1957, Ph.D., 1961. Mem. faculty Harvard U. Med. Sch., 1965—, prof. genetics, 1969—, Am. Cancer Soc. prof., 1979—, Am. Cancer Soc. research prof., 1980—; mem. Sci. for The People, 1971—. Recipient Eli Lilly award, 1970. Mem. Am. Soc. Exptl. Biologists, Am. Soc. Microbiology, Genetics Soc. Am., AAAS, Nat. Sci. Tchrs. Assn. Research and publs. in bacterial genetics. Home: 8A Appleton Rd Cambridge MA 02138 Office: Harvard Univ Medical Sch Boston MA 02115

BECKWITH, WILLIAM HUNTER, clergyman; b. Noank, Conn., Oct. 8, 1896; s. Walter Howard and Annie Elizabeth (Keddy) B. Mus.B. magna cum laude, N.Y. U., 1929, A.M., 1931, Ph.D., 1936; postgrad., U. Poitiers, France. Organist and choir master Ch. of the Transfiguration, N.Y.C., 1917-18, Trinity Ch., Lenox, Mass., 1918-19, Trinity Chapel (Trinity Parish), N.Y.C., 1919-43; instr. French Washington Sq. Coll., N.Y. U., 1931-36, Hofstra Coll., 1936-38, asst. prof., 1938-39, asso. prof., 1939-40; prof. French and dean of Coll., 1941-48; prof., past dir. div. gen. studies Coll. Agr. and Mechanic Arts, Mayaguez, P.R.; ordained priest Protestant Episcopal Ch. of U.S., 1954; asst. San Andrès Episcopal Mission, Mayaguez; ordained priest Antiochian Orthodox Christian Ch., 1981; priest-in-charge St. Gregory's Orthodox Ch., Clearwater, Fla. Author: The Formation of the Esthetic of Romain Rolland, 1935. Served in U.S. Navy, 1918. Fellow Am. Guild Organists; mem. MLA, AAUP, Eastern Assn. Deans, Phi Beta Kappa. Republican. Orthodox. Home: Highland Terrace 1520 Jefford St Clearwater FL 33516

BECTON, HENRY PRENTISS, JR., broadcasting company executive; b. Englewood, N.J., Oct. 16, 1943; s. Henry Prentiss and Jean Sprague (Coggan) B.; m. Jean Campbell Redpath, Sept. 28, 1968; children: Sara Campbell, Wilson Prentiss. B.A. magna cum laude, Yale U., 1965; J.D. cum laude, Harvard U., 1968. Tchr. Cambridge Sch., Weston, Mass., 1968-69; television producer WGBH Edni. Found., Boston, 1970-73, program mgr., 1974-78, v.p., gen. mgr., 1978—; dir. Henry Prentiss & Co., Click Farms, Inc. Mem. corp. Boston Mus. Sci., 1980—; trustee New Eng. Acquarium, 1981—; dir. Mass. Com. for Prevention of Child Abuse, 1979-81; trustee Boston Ballet, 1976-78, Met. Cultural Alliance, Boston, 1974-76. Mem. Nat. Acad. Television Arts and Scis. (dir. New Eng. chpt.), Mass. Bar Assn., Phi Beta Kappa. Clubs: Somerset (Boston); Kollegewidgwok Yacht (Blue Hill, Maine); Blue Hill (Maine) Country. Office: 125 Western Ave Allston MA 02134

BECTON, JULIUS WESLEY, JR., army officer; b. Bryn Mawr, Pa., June 29, 1926; s. Julius Wesley and Rose Inez (Banks) B.; m. Louise Thornton, Jan. 29, 1948; children: Shirley Becton Hill, Karen Becton Johnson, Joyce Becton Cokley, Renee M., Julius Wesley III. B.S., Prairie View (Tex.) A. and M. Coll., 1960; M.A., U. Md., 1966; grad. mil. schs. Enlisted in U.S. Army, 1943, commd. 2d lt., 1945, advanced through grades to lt. gen., 1978; service in PTO, Korea and, Vietnam, former comdr., Ft. Hood, Tex., 1975-76, comdr., Falls Church, Va., 1976-78, VII U.S. Army Corps (USAREUR), Stuttgart, Ger., 1978-81, Army insp. tng., Ft. Monroe, Va., 1981-83. Decorated Silver Star, Legion of Merit, D.F.C., Bronze Star, Air medal, Army Commendation medal, Purple Heart; knight Mil. and Hospitaler Order St. John Jerusalem; Knight of Malta; mem. Inf. Officer Candidate Sch. Hall of Fame. Mem. U.S. Armor Assn. (exec. bd.). Club: Rocks., Inc. Home: 931 N Van Dorn St Alexandria VA 22304 Office: Dir US Fgn Disaster Assistance AID Washington DC 20523

BEDAR, RUDOLPH, architect; b. Boston, Sept. 26, 1923; s. Harry and Rose (Clayman) B.; m. Selma Reta Katler, Apr. 27, 1946; children: Andrew, Bradford, Pamela, Clifford. Student, Archtl. Assn. Sch. Architecture, London, Eng., 1946, Boston Archtl. Center, 1946-51, Ecole des Beaux Artes Fontain Bleau, France, 1950. Designer Clark F. Merrick (architect), Boston, 1949, Kelly & Gruzen (architects), 1950-56; project mgr. S. Glaser Assos. (architects), Boston, 1956-59; prin. Bedar & Alpers (architects), Boston, 1959—; Vice pres. 1st Engrs., Boston, 1970. Prin. works include Chase Bldg, 1963; master plan for New Seabury, Cape Cod, 1964 Boy Scout Hdqrs, Boston, 1969, Lynn (Mass.) Dist. Courthouse, 1973, Dist. Ct. of Peabody, Mass., 1978. Mem. adv. commn. Norwood (Mass.) Planning Bd., 1971—. Served with USAAF, 1942-46. Boston Soc. Architects Traveling scholar, 1950. Mem. Nat. Council Archtl. Registration Bds., AIA, Boston Soc. Architects (profl. sers. com.), Mass. Charitable Mechanic Assn. Lodge: Masons. Home: 83 Groydon Rd Norwood MA 02062 Office: 10 Langley Rd Newton MA 02159

BEDARD, PATRICK JOSEPH, magazine editor; b. Waterloo, Iowa, Aug. 20, 1941; s. Gerald Joseph and Pearl Leona (Brown) B. B.S. in Mech. Engring, Iowa State U., 1963; M.Automotive Engring., Chrysler Inst. Engring., 1965. Product engr. Chrysler Corp., Highland Park, Mich., 1963-67; tech. editor Car and Driver mag., N.Y.C., 1967-69, exec. editor, 1969-78, editor at large, 1978—; tchr. race driving, cons. in field; free-lance writer. Mem. Soc. Automotive Engrs., Internat. Motor Sports Assn., Sports Car Club Am., Pi Tau Sigma. Republican. Roman Catholic. First driver to win profl. road race in N.Am. in Wankel-powered car, 1973; raced at Indpls. 500, 1983. Home: 165 E 32d St New York NY 10016 Office: 1 Park Ave Suite 721A New York NY 10016

BEDAU, HUGO ADAM, educator; b. Portland, Oreg., Sept. 23, 1926; s. Hugo Adam and Laura (Romeis) B.; m. Jan Lisbeth Peterson Martin (separated 1979), Jan. 19, 1952; children—Lauren, Mark Adam, Paul Hugo, Guy Antony. Student, U. So. Calif., 1944-45; B.A. summa cum laude, U. Redlands, 1949; M.A., Boston U., 1951, Harvard, 1953, Ph.D., 1961. Instr. Dartmouth, 1953-54; instr. Princeton, 1954-57, lectr., 1958-61; asso. prof. Reed Coll., 1962-66; prof. philosophy Tufts U., 1966—. Author: The Courts, The Constitution, and Capital Punishment, 1977; co-author: Victimless Crimes, 1974; Editor: Death Penalty in America, 1964, 3d edit., 1982, Civil Disobedience, 1969, Justice and Equality, 1971; co-editor: Capital Punishment in the U.S, 1976; Contbr. articles and essays on social, polit. and legal philosophy to books and profl. jours. Bd. dirs. Am. League To Abolish Capital Punishment, 1959-72, pres., 1969-72. Served with USNR, 1944-46. Danforth fellow, 1957-58; Liberal Arts fellow law and philosophy Harvard U. Law Sch., 1961-62; vis. fellow Clare Hall, Cambridge U., 1980; vis. lectr. Law Faculty, U. Natal, South Africa, 1981. Mem. Am. Philos. Assn., AAUP, Am. Soc. Polit. and Legal Philosophy, Soc. Philos. and Pub. Affairs. Office: Dept Philosophy Tufts U Medford MA 02155

BEDDALL, THOMAS HENRY, lawyer; b. Pottsville, Pa., Apr. 24, 1922; s. Thomas and Martha Roberta (Gallagher) B.; m. Priscilla Kimball, July 26, 1956; children: Laurence, Frederic, Margaret, and Katherine. A.B., Yale U., 1943; LL.B., U. Va., 1950. Bar: N.Y. 1951, D.C. 1968. Assoc. Sullivan & Cromwell, N.Y.C., 1950-57, Paul Mellon Interests, Washington, 1957—; dir. Carborundum Co., Niagara Falls, N.Y., 1960-78; lectr. U. Va., 1976-79. Chmn. bd. trustees Sheridan Sch., Washington, 1972-74; mem. bldg. com. Va. Mus., 1980—. Served to 1st lt. inf. AUS, 1944-46. Mem. Bar Assn. City N.Y., Mil. Order World Wars, Order of Coif, Raven Soc., Phi Delta Phi, Omicron Delta Kappa, Pi Delta Epsilon, Chi Psi. Clubs: Metropolitan (Washington); Rolling Rock (Ligonier, Pa.). Office: 1729 H St NW Washington DC 20006

BEDDOW, THOMAS JOHN, lawyer; b. Frackville, Pa., Oct. 30, 1914; s. John Edward and Pearl Ethel (Sobey) B.; m. Virginia C. Fenton, Nov. 16, 1940; children: Barbara (Mrs. David J. Nordloh), Thomas Fenton, John Warren, Virginia Ellen (Mrs. John Sedwitz). A.B., Ursinus Coll., 1936, LL.D., 1973; LL.B., U. Pa., 1939. Bar: Pa. 1939, N.J. 1941, D.C. 1941, Md. 1950. Assoc. Arthur T. Vanderbilt (atty.), Newark, 1939-41; mem. firm Gardner, Morrison, Sheriff & Beddow, Washington, 1947-80. Bd. dirs. Ursinus Coll., 1958—; mem. Tequesta Village Council, (Fla.); vice mayor Tequesta, 1982. Served to lt. USNR, 1942-46. Mem. Am., D.C., Pa., Md. bar assns. Episcopalian. (sr. warden). Clubs: Metropolitan, Kenwood Golf and Country (Washington); Tequesta (Fla.) Country (pres. 1980—). Home: 212 Golf Club Circle Tequesta FL 33458

BEDELIA, BONNIE, actress; b. N.Y.C., Mar. 25, 1948; d. Philip and Marian (Wagner) Culkin; m. Kenneth Luber, Apr. 15, 1969; children—Uri, Jonah. Grad., Hunter Coll., N.Y.C. Broadway appearances include Enter Laughing, 1963, The Playroom, 1965, My Sweet Charlie, 1966; film appearances include Gypsy Moths, 1968, They Shoot Horses, Don't They?, 1969, Lovers and Other Strangers, 1970, Between Friends, 1972, The Big Fix, 1978; TV series The New Land, 1974 (Recipient Theatre World award for My Sweet Charlie 1967). Address: care The Artists Agy 190 W Canon Dr Beverly Hills CA 90210 *

BEDELL, BERKLEY WARREN, congressman; b. Spirit Lake, Iowa, Mar. 5, 1921; s. Walter Berkley and Virginia (Price) B.; m. Elinor Healy, Aug. 29, 1943; children: Kenneth, Thomas, Joanne. Student, Iowa State U. Founder, chmn. bd. Berkley and Co. (fishing tackle mfrs.), Spirit Lake, 1921—; mem. 94th-98th congresses from 6th Dist. Iowa. Served with USAAF, 1943-45. Named 1st U.S. Small Businessman of Year SBA, 1964. Democrat. Methodist. Home: Spirit Lake IA 51360 also Office: 2459 Rayburn House Office Bldg Washington DC 20515

BEDELL, CATHERINE MAY, political consultant, former Congresswoman. Mem. U.S. Ho. of Reps. from Wash. State, 1958-70; bd. incorporators Amtrak, Washington, 1970-71; chmn. U.S. Internat. Trade Commn., Washington, 1971-75, 1975-79, 80-81; commr. Internat. Trade Commn., Washington, 1979-80; spl. cons. White House, Pres.' 50 States Project, Washington, 1982—. Bd. dirs. Former Mems. of Congress. Address: 514 Sandpiper Palm Desert CA 92260

BEDELL, GEORGE CHESTER, university administrator; b. Jacksonville, Fla., May 13, 1928; s. Chester and Edmonia (Hair) B.; m. Elizabeth Reed Phillips, Jan. 22, 1983; children—George Chester, Frank Moor, Nathan Gale. B.A., U. of South, Sewanee, Tenn., 1950; B.D., Va. Theol. Sem., Alexandria, 1953; M.A., U. N.C., 1966; Ph.D., Duke, U., 1969. Ordained priest Episcopal Ch.; parish priest Episc. Ch., Lake City, Panama City and Tallahassee, Fla., 1953-64; asst. prof. religion Fla. State U., Tallahassee, 1967-73, asso. prof., 1973-74, courtesy asso. prof., 1974—; dir. humanities and fine arts State U. System of Fla., 1971-72, dir. personnel and faculty relations, 1972-76, asso. vice chancellor, 1976-77, exec. asst. to chancellor, dir. pub. affairs, 1977-79, vice chancellor, 1979-80, interim chancellor, 1980-81, exec. vice chancellor, 1981—; mng. editor AAR Studies in Religion, 1972-76; historiographer Episc. Diocese of Fla., 1968-76. Author:

Kierkegaard and Faulkner: Modalities of Existence, 1972, Religion in America, 1975,82. Mem. Tallahassee City Park Bd., 1972-76, Leon County Democratic Exec. Com., 1970-74. Arthur N. Morris fellow, 1964-67; Duke-Danforth fellow, 1965-67. Mem. Am. Acad. Religion, Modern Lang. Assn., S.Atlantic Modern Lang. Assn., Soc. Sci. Study Religion, Acad. Academic Personnel Adminstrn., Council on Advancement and Support Edn. Home: 1218 Terrace St Tallahassee FL 32303 Office: 107 W Gaines St Tallahassee FL 32304

BEDELL, GEORGE NOBLE, physician, educator; b. Harrisburg, Pa., May 1, 1922; s. George Harold and Elsie Clair (Noble) B.; m. Betty Jane Goldzier, Nov. 4, 1950 (dec. Mar. 1970); children: David, Mark, Barbara, Bruce; m. Mirriel Shields Hummel, Oct. 17, 1970; stepchildren: Judy, Jeffrey, Eric, Deborah, Andrew. B.A., DePauw U., 1944; M.D., U. Cin., 1946. Intern U. Iowa, 1946-47, resident in pathology, 1947-48, resident in internal medicine, 1950-52, research fellow in internal medicine, specializing in cardiology, 1952-54; research fellow physiology Postgrad. Sch. Medicine, U., Pa., 1954-55; asst. prof. dept. medicine Coll. Medicine, U. Iowa, 1955-59, asso. prof. dept. medicine, 1959-68, prof., 1968—; dir. Pulmonary Disease div. Dept. Medicine, 1968-81; cons. VA Hosp., Iowa City, 1954—; mem. staff U. Hosps., Iowa City. Contbr. articles to profl. jours. Mem. Johnson County Democratic Central Com., 1956-69, treas., 1958-64. Served with AUS, 1948-50. NIH Spl. fellow, 1954-55; recipient Career Devel. award, 1960-70, Walter L. Bierring award Am. Lung Assn. Iowa, 1973. Mem. Am. Lung Assn. (dir. 1972-80), Am. Lung Assn. Iowa (dir. 1971-81), Am. Fedn. Clin. Research, Am. Thoracic Soc., Iowa Thoracic Soc. (v.p. 1960-61, pres. 1962-63), Iowa Tb and Health Assn. (dir. 1961-65, 67-71), AMA (vice chmn. sect. council on diseases of chest 1971-73, chmn. sec. council diseases of chest 1974-76, Am. Thoracic Soc. del. to AMA 1979—), Iowa, Johnson County med. socs., Soc. Exptl. Biology and Medicine, Iowa Clin. Soc. Internal Medicine, Central Soc. Clin. Research, Am. Coll. Chest Physicians, Am. Physiol. Soc., Am. Soc. Clin. Investigation, A.C.P., Central Clin. Research Club. Democrat. Unitarian. Home: 327 Blackhawk St Iowa City IA 52240 Office: University Hosps Iowa City IA 52242

BEDELL, RALPH CLAIRON, psychologist, educator; b. Hale, Mo., June 4, 1904; s. Charles E. and Jennie (Eaton) B.; m. Stella Virginia Bales, Aug. 19, 1929 (dec. 1968); m. Ann Barclay Sorency, Dec. 21, 1968 (dec. 1975); m. Myra Jervey Hoyle, Feb. 14, 1976. B.S. in Edn., Central Mo. State U., 1926; A.M., U. Mo., 1929, Ph.D., 1932. Diplomate: Am. Bd. Profl. Psychology. Tchr., Hale Pub. Schs., 1922-24; tchr. sci. and math. S.W. High Sch., Kansas City, Mo., 1926-30, 32-33; asst. prof. ednl. psychology N.E. Mo. State U., 1933-34, prof. ednl. psychology, 1934-37, dir. Bur. Guidance, 1934-37; dean, faculty and student personnel Central Mo. State U., 1937-38; freshman counselor, dir. reading labs., asso. prof. ednl. psychology and measurements U. Nebr., 1938-46, prof., 1946-50; chmn. dept., prof. psychology and edn. Sch. Social Scis. and Pub. Affairs, Am. U., Washington, 1950-52; dir. program planning and review br. internat. div. U.S. Office Edn., HEW, 1952-55; sec.-gen. South Pacific Commn. Noumea, New Caledonia, 1955-58; dir. counseling and guidance insts. br. U.S. Office of Edn., Washington, 1959-66; prof. edn., dir. nat. edn. studies U. Mo.-Columbia, 1967; prof. emeritus U. Mo.—Columbia, 1974—; research asso. Center for Ednl. Improvement, 1974-75; cons. faculty devel. Lincoln U. of Mo., 1976-77; mem. study group to Surinam, 1954; adviser U.S. del. UN, 1953, 62; U.S. del. Caribbean Commn. and West Indian Conf., 1952, 53; cons. Stephens Coll., Columbia, 1974, U.S. Office Edn., 1974; chmn. tech. com. access and retention for master planning Mo. Coordinating Bd. Higher Edn., 1976-78; edn. cons. Prince of Songkla U., Pattani, Thailand, 1980-84. Author several books in field, also textbooks and standardized achievement exams., articles profl. publs. Vice pres., trustee Sigma Tau Gamma Found., 1972-74; dean Sigma Tau Gamma Leadership Inst., 1973. Served as comdr. USNR, 1942-46. Named Honored Alumnus, Central Mo. State U., 1971, Disting. Alumnus Central Mo. State U., 1984; Top Tau, Sigma Tau Gamma, 1970, Soc. of Seventeen, 1980; Outstanding Contbn. cert. Assn. Counselor Edn. and Supervision, 1967; Disting. Contbn. award Assn. Counselor Edn. and Supervision, 1984; award of Merit, Mo. Assn. Sch. Librarians, 1971; U. Mo.-Columbia Alumni Assn. citation for outstanding achievement and meritorious service in edn., 1979; Profl. award Mo. Coll. Personnel Assn., 1982. Fellow Am. Psychol. Assn., Royal Soc. Health; mem. NEA (life), Nat. Soc. for Study Edn. (life), Mil. Order of World Wars (perpetual), Am. Counseling and Devel. Assn. (life), Internat. Soc. Polit. Psychology, Am. Assn. for Higher Edn., N.Y. Acad. Scis., Mo. Tchrs. Assn., Mo. Guidance Assn. (award of merit 1971), Mo. Personnel and Guidance Assn., Kappa Delta Pi, Phi Kappa Phi, Phi Delta Kappa (life). Clubs: Explorers (N.Y.C.); Army and Navy (Washington); Columbia Country. Home: 106 S Ann St Columbia MO 65201 *Those whose knowledge and skill are applied to enable good qualities in themselves and in their associates to emerge, grow, and mature make the most important and lasting contributions to mankind.*

BEDERSON, BENJAMIN, educator; b. N.Y.C., Nov. 15, 1921; s. Abraham Michael and Lena (Waxlowsky) B.; m. Betty Weintraub, Jan. 20, 1956; children: Joshua Benjamin, Geoffrey Adam, Aron Gregory, Benjamin Boris. B.S., CCNY, 1946; M.S., Columbia U., 1948; Ph.D., NYU, 1950. Slp. engring. detachment Los Alamos Sci. Lab., 1944-46; research scientist MIT, Cambridge, 1950-52; mem. faculty dept. physics NYU, 1952—, prof., 1967—, chmn. dept., 1973-76, spl. advisor for sci. to dean Faculty Arts & Scis., 1983—; chmn. Internat. Conf. Physics of Electronic and Atomic Collisions, 1983-85; chmn. vis. panel Ctr. for Absolute Phys. Quantities, Nat. Bur. Standards, 1980-83; chmn. vis. com. physics div. Argonne Nat. Lab., 1977-79. Assoc. editor: Atomic Data and Nuclear Data Jour., 1969—; editor: Phys. Reviews, Am. Phys. Soc., 1978—; contbr. articles to profl. jours.; editor: with D.R. Bates Advances in Atomic and Molecular Physics, 1974—; patentee in field. Served with U.S. Army, 1942-46; PTO. Fellow Am. Phys. Soc., AAAS, N.Y. Acad. Sci. (bd. govs. 1977-79); mem. Sigma Pi Sigma. Home: 8 Hall Ave Larchmont NY 10538 Office: NYU 4 Washington Pl New York NY 10003

BEDFORD, BRIAN, actor; b. Morley, Yorkshire, Eng., Feb. 16, 1935; s. Arthur and Ellen (O'Donnell) B. Student, Royal Acad. Dramatic Art, London. Appeared in: plays A View From the Bridge, 1958, Five Finger Exercise, 1959, The Tempest, 1959, Write Me A Murder, 1962, Lord Pengo, 1962, The Doctor's Dilemma, 1963, The Private Ear, 1963, The Knack, 1964, The Unknown Soldier and His Wife, 1967, 73, Astrakhan Coat, 1967, The Cocktail Party, 1968, The Seven Deceits of Myrtle, 1968, Hamlet, 1969, Private Lives, 1969, Three Sisters, 1969, Blithe Spirit, 1970, The Tavern, 1970, School for Wives, 1971 (Tony award 1971), Jumpers, 1972, Butley, 1973, Measure for Measure, 1975, Twelfth Night, 1975, Equus, 1976, Richard III, 1977, The Guardsman, 1977, As You Like It, 1977, The Winter's Tale, 1978, Uncle Vanya, 1978, Death Trap, 1979, The Seagull, 1980, Much Ado About Nothing, 1980, Whose Life Is It Anyway?, 1980; others; appeared in: films Man of the Moment, 1955, Miracle in Soho, 1957, The Angry Silence, 1960, Number Six, 1961, The Pad and How to Use It, 1966, Grand Prix, 1966, Robin Hood; others; dir.: play Titus Andronicus, 1978; numerous TV appearances. (Recipient Tony award for best actor in School for Wives 1971). Address: care STE Representation Ltd 1776 Broadway New York NY 10019

BEDFORD, CLAY PATRICK, retired aircraft, electronics industry executive; b. Benjamin, Texas, Aug. 25, 1903; m. Catherine Ann Bermingham; children—Clay P. II, Peter, Ann. Grad., Rensselaer Poly. Inst., D.Engring. (hon.), 1971. With Kaiser (and affiliates in heavy constrn., shipbldg., automobiles, aircraft), 1925-75; former pres. Kaiser Aerospace & Electronics Corp.; Served as asst. to dir. def. moblzn., 1951-52, asst. to sec. of def., 1952. Hon. trustee Rensselaer Poly. Inst.; trustee emeritus St. Mary's Coll. Calif. Mem. Civil Engrs. Soc., Alpha Tau Omega. Clubs: Paradise Valley Country, Claremont Country; Royal and Ancient Golf (St. Andrews, Scotland). Home: 5223 E Palo Verde Pl Paradise Valley AZ 85253

BEDFORD, JOHN MICHAEL, medical educator, researcher; b. Sheffield, Eng., May 21, 1932. B.A., Cambridge U., 1955, M.A., Vet. M.B., 1958; Ph.D., U. London, 1965. Jr. fellow surgery Bristol U. Vet. Sch., Eng., 1958-59; research assoc. physiology Worcester Found., Mass., 1959-61, scientist, 1966-67; asst. prof. Royal Vet. Coll., U. London, 1961-66; asst. prof. to assoc. prof. anatomy Columbia U., N.Y.C., 1967-72; prof. reproductive biology, anatomy Cornell U. Med. Coll., N.Y.C., 1972—, now Harold and Percy Uris prof. reproductive biology in ob-gyn., 1981—. Mem. Soc. Reprodn., Am. Assn. Anatomists, Endocrine Soc., Brit. Soc. Study Fertility. Office: Dept Obstetrics and Gynecology Cornell U Med Coll New York NY 10021 *

BEDFORD, NORTON MOORE, educator; b. Mercer, Mo., Nov. 11, 1916; s. Cornelius David and Mary (Moore) B.; m. Helen Grace Horn, Mar. 19, 1943; children—Norton Mark, Martha Ann. B.B.A., Tulane U., 1940, M.B.A., 1947; Ph.D., Ohio State U., 1950. C.P.A., 1950. Faculty Ohio State U., 1947-50, Washington U., St. Louis, 1950-53; prof. U. Ill., Urbana, 1954—, Arthur Young prof., 1974—; prof. Harvard U., 1981—; mgmt. cons.; dir. Anderson Physics Labs., Excel Machinery. Author: Income Determination Theory, 1965, Advanced Accounting, 1961, 2d edit., 1967, 3d edit., 1973, 4th edit., 1979, Introduction to Modern Accounting, 1968, Future of Accounting in a Changing Society, 1970, Extensions in Accounting Disclosures, 1973; Contbr. articles to profl. jours. Trustee Wesley Found. Served with AUS, 1942-46. Named Sch. Bus. Outstanding Alumnus Tulane U., 1963, Accountant of Yr. Beta Alpha Psi, 1976; Weldon Powell prof., 1969; Fulbright scholar, 1972. Mem. Am. Accounting Assn. (pres., named Outstanding Educator 1980), Am. Inst. C.P.A.'s (dir.), Nat. Assn. Accountants (v.p.), Inst. Mgmt. Sci. Club: Rotarian. Home: 1208 Belmeade St Champaign IL 61820 Office: 302 Commerce W U Ill Urbana IL 61801 *Success requires admiration for excellence in all things, concern for the human condition, a willingness to sense and accept change, an interest in being respected by others, great sensitivity to criticism, and a desire to learn and generalize knowledge coupled with a belief in the role and effectiveness of education as a means for developing civilization.*

BEDINI, SILVIO A., historian, author; b. Ridgefield, Conn., Jan. 17, 1917; s. Vincent and Cesira (Stefanelli) B.; m. Gerda Hintz, Oct. 20, 1951; children: Leandra, Peter. Ed., Columbia U., 1935-42; LL.D., U. Bridgeport, 1970. Self-employed, Ridgefield, Conn., 1945-61; curator div. mech. and civil engring. U.S. Nat. Mus., Smithsonian Instn., Washington, 1961-65; asst. dir. Mus. History and Tech., 1965-71, dep. dir., 1971-78, keeper rare books, 1978—; Mem. exec. council Soc. History Tech., 1963—. Author: Ridgefield in Review, 1958, The Scent of Time, 1963, Early American Scientific Instruments and Their Makers, 1964, (with F.R. Maddison) Mechanical Universe, 1966, (with W. Von Braun and F.L. Whipple) Moon, Man's Greatest Adventure, 1970, The Life of Benjamin Banneker, 1972, (with others) The Unknown Leonardo, 1974, Thinkers and Tinkers, 1975, The Spotted Stones, 1978, Declaration of Independence Desk: Relic of Revolution, 1981. Fellow Washington Acad. Scis.; mem. Am. Philos. Soc., Am. Antiquarian Soc., Soc. Am. Historians, Soc. History Discoveries, History Sci. Soc. Club: Grolier. Home: 4303 47th St NW Washington DC 20016 Office: Smithsonian Instn Washington DC 20560

BEDKE, ERNEST ALFORD, retired air force officer; b. Oakley, Idaho, Oct. 16, 1934; s. Herschel McIntosh and Ethel Marie (Alford) B.; m. Marilyn Meils, June 8, 1955; children: Curtis, Michael. B.S. in Bus. Adminstrn., U. Idaho, 1955; grad., Air Command and Staff Coll., 1967, Air War Coll., 1973. Commd. 2d lt. U.S. Air Force, 1955, advanced through grades to maj. gen., 1977; instr. pilot, Reese AFB, Tex., 1957-62, air ops. officer, Chaumont Air Base, France, 1962, fighter pilot, Phalsbourg Air Base, France, 1962-63, Holloman AFB, N.Mex., 1963-66, Da Nang Air Base, Vietnam, 1966, air liaison officer, forward air controller, Cat Lai, Vietnam, 1967-68; ops. staff officer NATO, Ramstein Air Base, W. Ger., 1968-71; chief Europe-NATO, plans & policy, Hdqrs. U.S. Air Force, Wash., 1971-72; dep. comdr. ops., Eglin AFB, Eglin, Fla., 1973-74, comdr., Macdill AFB, Fla., 1975-77, dep. comdr. tng., testing and range facilities, Nellis AFB, Nev., 1977-79, insp. gen. Tactical Air Command, Langley AFB, Va., 1979-80, dep. chief staff ops. and intelligence Hdqrs. Pacific Air Forces, Hickam AFB, HAWAII, 1980-83; ret., 1983, mgmt. cons. Decorated AF D.S.M., Legion of Merit (2), Air medal (20), M.S.M., Air Force Commendation medal. Mem. Air Force Assn., Order of Daedalians. Home: 18509 Turtle Dr Lutz FL 33549

BEDNAR, CHARLES SOKOL, political scientist, educator; b. N.Y.C., Nov. 3, 1930; s. Karel and Anna (Tomcala) B.; m. Beluse Alzbeta Pokorny, Aug. 31, 1959. A.B., Rutgers U., 1951, M.A., 1952; Ph.D., Columbia, 1960. Asso. prof. Lynchburg Coll., 1958-62; prof., chmn. dept. polit. sci., asso. dean of coll. Muhlenberg Coll., 1962—; also adj. prof. grad. program in gen. edn., chmn. social sci. panel Temple U., 1963—. Contbr. articles to profl. jours. Chmn. Lehigh Valley Citizens for Progress, 1972-75; pres. Allentown YMCA, 1979-80. Recipient award Lindback Found., 1965. Mem. Czechoslovak Acad. Arts and Scis. (v.p.), AAUP, Phi Beta Kappa, Delta Phi Alpha, Tau Kappa Alpha, Omicron Delta Kappa, Pi Sigma Alpha. Home: Sheridan Rd Box 382 Coopersburg PA 18036 Office: Muhlenberg Coll 2400 Chew St Allentown PA 18104

BEDNAR, JAMES EDMUND, lawyer; b. Omaha, Oct. 13, 1911; s. James Edmund and Britannia R. (Daughters) B.; m. Rachel A. Hancock, Oct. 15, 1940 (dec. May 1975); 1 dau., Lisa; m. Irene Lowrie, July 31, 1976. A.B., Stanford U., 1932; LL.B., Harvard U., 1935. Bar: Calif. 1936. Practiced law, Los Angeles, 1937—; asso. firm Musick & Burrell, Los Angeles, 1937-49, partner, 1949-53, Jones & Bednar, Los Angeles, 1953—; instr. law Southwestern U., Los Angeles, 1949-65; dir. Lyon Moving & Storage Co., Western Air & Refrigeration Inc., 1953-74, Preferred Theatres Corp., Hamilton Supply Co., 1978—. Served with JAG Dept. AUS, 1943-46. Mem. Los Angeles, Calif., Am. bar assns., Phi Beta Kappa, Phi Gamma Delta. Methodist. Club: Jonathan (Los Angeles). Home: 4200 Via Dolce 230 Marina Del Rey CA 90291 Office: 611 S Catalina St Suite 308 Los Angeles CA 90005

BEDNAREK, ALEXANDER ROBERT, mathematician, educator; b. Buffalo, July 15, 1933; s. Alexander G. and Bertha (Wlodarz) B.; m. Rosemary Anderson, Aug. 29, 1954; children: Robert A., Andrew R., Thomas C., Eugene P. B.S., State U. N.Y. at Albany, 1957; M.A., Buffalo U., 1959, Ph.D., 1961. Sr. mathematician Goodyear Aerospace Corp., Akron, Ohio, 1961-62, cons. info. scis. dept., 1963-65; asst. prof. math. U. Akron, 1962-63, U. Fla., Gainesville, 1963-66, assoc. prof., 1967-69, prof., chmn. dept. math., 1969—, co-dir. Center Applied Math., 1974—; vis. staff mem. Los Alamos Sci. Lab., 1976—; mem. adv. bd. CRC Handbook Math. Tables; Nat. Acad. Scis. exchange prof., Warsaw, Poland, 1972. Author: (with L. Cesari) Dynamical Systems, 1977, Vol. II, 1982; Contbr. to: Ency. of Library and Information Sci., Vol. 3, 1970; Contbr. articles to profl. jours. Served with U.S. Army, 1952-54. Mem. Am. Math. Soc., Math. Assn. Am. (past chmn. Fla. sect.), Polish Inst. Arts and Scis. of Am., Inc., Sigma Xi. Home: 530 NE 7th Ave Gainesville FL 32601

BEDROSIAN, EDWARD, elec. engr.; b. Chgo., May 22, 1922; s. Charles and Hazel (Najarian) B.; m. Evelyn Patricia Gardner, Apr. 16, 1971; children—William C., Barbara A., Charles E., Edward G., Victoria G. B.S., Northwestern U., 1949, M.S., 1950, Ph.D., 1953. Aero. engr. Convair, San Diego, 1942, Hughes Aircraft Co., Culver City, Calif., 1943-44; elec. engr. Motorola, Chgo., 1953-57; sr. scientist Rand Corp., Santa Monica, Calif., 1953—; dir. Altran Electronics Corp.; adj. prof. U. So. Calif., 1968-71. Contbr. articles to profl. jours. Served with USMC, 1944-46. Fellow IEEE, Inst. Advancement Engring.; mem. Sigma Xi, Eta Kappa Nu, Tau Beta Pi. Home: 3923 Sierks Way Malibu CA 90265 Office: 1700 Main St Santa Monica CA 90265

BEDROSIAN, EDWARD ROBERT, photographic company executive; b. Chgo., June 30, 1932; s. Kesrow and Rebecca (Babian) B.; m. Diane Yvonne Morse, Aug. 25, 1956; children: Dawn Eve, Cynthia Sarah, Edward Robert. B.S.C.E., Ill. Inst. Tech., 1954; M.S.C.E., M.I.T., 1955; M.B.A., Harvard U., 1964. Registered profl. engr., Mass. Treas. Eastern Shokcrate Corp., Bound Brook, N.J., 1964-65; treas. Polaroid Corp., Cambridge, Mass., 1965—, now also v.p. Mem. Wellesley (Mass.) Town Meeting; trustee Newton-Wellesley Hosp. Served with USNR, 1955-60. Mem. Fin. Execs. Inst., Treasurers Club of Boston. Conglist. Home: 43 Wingate Rd Wellesley MA 02181 Office: Polaroid Corp Cambridge MA 02139

BEDROSIAN, JOHN CHARLES, health care executive; b. Troy, N.Y., Nov. 21, 1934; s. Charles and Dorothy B.; m. Judith Davidian, Sept. 5, 1960; children: Christopher, Matthew, Karen. B.A., UCLA, 1956; LL.B., U. So. Calif., 1959. Bar: Calif. 1960. Partner firm Baechtold & Bedrosian, Van Nuys, 1960-62, Weitkamp, Riddle & Bedrosian, Granada Hills, 1962-68, Eamer, Bell & Bedrosian, Beverly Hills, 1968-69; co-founder, 1969; since sr. exec. v.p., dir. Nat. Med. Enterprises, Inc., Los Angeles.; dir. Valley State Bank. Bd. dirs. Calif. State Univs. and Colls. Found.; bd. councilors U. So. Calif. Sch. Pub. Adminstrn. Served with USAF, 1959-65. Mem. Fedn. Am. Hosps. (past pres.), Am. Bar Assn., Phi Alpha Delta. Republican. Presbyterian. Office: 11620 Wilshire Blvd Los Angeles CA 90025

BEDROSIAN, SAMUEL DER, electrical and systems engineer, educator; b. Marash, Turkey, Mar. 24, 1921; came to U.S., 1922, naturalized, 1942; s. Sahag Der and Zabel B.; m. Agnes Morjigian, Nov. 24, 1951; children—Camille, Gregory. A.B., SUNY, Albany, 1942; M.E.E., Poly. Inst. Bklyn., 1951; Ph.D., U. Pa., 1961. Project engr. Signal Corps Engring. Labs., Ft. Monmouth, N.J., 1946-49, sect. chief, 1949-54, asst. br. chief, 1954-55; systems engr. Burroughs Research Center, Paoli, Pa., 1955-60; mem. research staff U. Pa., 1960-64, asst. prof. elec. engring., 1964-68; asso. prof., 1968-73, prof. elec. and systems engring., 1973—, chmn. dept. systems engring., 1975-80, dir. dual degree MBA/MSE program for, 1977-82; cons. in field; organizer, gen. chmn. 22d M.W. Symposium on Circuits and Systems at Moore Sch., Phila., 1979; NAVELE Research chair prof. Naval Postgrad. Sch., Monterey, Calif., 1980-81. Contbr. numerous articles to profl. jours. Served to 1st lt., Signal Corps U.S. Army, 1943-46; PTO. Recipient Kabakjian award Armenian Students Assn. U.S.A., 1977. Fellow IEEE (guest editor Transactions on Circuits and Systems 1979); mem. Franklin Inst. (asso. editor jour. 1966—, guest editor spl. issue jour. 1973, 76), Sigma Xi, Eta Kappa Nu. Patentee in field. Home: 35 Bryan Ave Malvern PA 19355 Office: Moore Sch U Pa 200 S 33d St Philadelphia PA 19104

BEDROSSIAN, PETER STEPHEN, lawyer, business executive; b. Hoboken, N.J., Sept. 15, 1926; s. Nishan and Helen (Jamagotchian) B.; m. Jean M. Reynolds, Jan. 1951 (div. Oct. 1962); children: Peter, Alice Marie; m. JoAnn H. Thompson, Nov. 16, 1962; children: Stephanie Ann, Jennifer Ann. B.B.A., St. Johns U., 1949, J.D., 1954. Bar: N.Y. 1954, Calif. 1973. Chief acct. Stauffer Chem. Co., N.Y.C., 1948-58, dir. taxes, 1958-76, asst. treas., 1961-76; mem. firm Dobbs, Doyle & Nielsen, San Francisco, 1976-80; pres. Parrot Ranch Co., San Francisco, 1982—; v.p., dir. Stauffer Chem. Internat., Geneva, Switzerland, 1959-62; Vice chmn. Nitron Inc., Cupertino, Calif.; dir. Kali-Chemie Stauffer, Hannover, Germany, Stauffer Chem. Co. Internat. Served with AUS, 1944-46. Mem. Am., N.Y., Calif. bar assns., Tax Execs. Inst. (pres. N.Y. chpt.), Internat. Assn. Assessing Officers, Am. Electronics Assn., Am. Legion, Phi Delta Phi, Alpha Kappa Psi. Club: N.Y. Athletic. Address: 114 Sansome St San Francisco CA 94104 *No matter what adversity comes before you, think positive and you will sufficiently meet the challenge.*

BEDWELL, THEODORE CLEVELAND, JR., physician, assn. exec.; b. Caddo Mills, Tex., Mar. 31, 1909; s. Theodore Clevel and Mary Rebecca (Gary) B.; m. Blanche Elizabeth Harper, June 1, 1935; 1 dau., Beverly Anne. B.S., So. Meth. U., 1931; M.D., Baylor U., 1933; certificate indsl. medicine, Harvard Sch. Pub. Health, 1941; M.P.H., Johns Hopkins U., 1951. Diplomate: Am. Bd. Preventive Medicine (founders group aviation medicine 1953, occupational medicine 1956). Intern Baylor Hosp., Dallas, 1933-34; gen. practice medicine and surgery, Longview, Tex., 1934-35; commd. 1st lt. M.C. U.S. Army, 1935; advanced through grades to maj. gen. USAF, 1963; staff duties various army hosp., 1935-40, grad., 1940, chief indsl. medicine, 1940-42, grad., 1942, base surgeon, comdg. officer, 1942-46, dep. surgeon, 1946-47, surgeon, 1947-48, staff surgeon, Nagoya, Japan, 1948-50, grad., 1951-52; assigned Office Asst. Sec. Def. Health and Medicine, 1952-53; chief preventive medicine USAF Surgeon Gen.'s Office, 1953-56; dep. surgeon SAC, 1956-59, surgeon, 1959-61; comdr. USAF Aero. Med. Center, 1961, 1961-66; dir. staff Office Dep. Asst. Sec. Def. Health and Medicine, dep. asst. sec. of def., health and med., Washington, 1966-68; ret., 1968; chief med. officer Bur. Health Ins., Social Security Adminstrn., Balt., 1968-75; asst. v.p. sci. and profl. relations, dir. med. relations Pharm. Mfrs. Assn., Washington, 1975-79. Decorated D.S.M., Air Force medal with oak leaf cluster; Republic Korea Presdl. citation; recipient Distinguished Alumnus award So. Meth. U., 1966. Fellow Am. Coll. Preventive Medicine (v.p. aviation medicine 1960-61), Aerospace Med. Aesn. (pres. 1964-65), Royal Soc. Health (Eng.); mem. Soc. USAF Flight Surgeons (pres. 1961-62), Am. Pub. Health Assn., Assn. Mil. Surgeons, Internat. Acad. Aviation and Space Medicine, Phi Chi, Alpha Omega Alpha. Home: 6218 Hardy Dr McLean VA 22101

BEE, ROBERT NORMAN, banker; b. Milw., Mar. 4, 1925; s. Clarence Olson and Norma Pern (Pitt) B.; m. Dolores Marie Cappelletti, Apr. 23, 1955; children: Diane, John, Leslie. Ph.B., Marquette U., 1949; B.S. in Fgn. Service, Georgetown U., 1950, M.A., 1955. With Treasury Dept. (various locations), 1950-65, fin. attache, Stockholm, 1952-54, Ankara, Turkey, 1956-60; chief fin. affairs Am. embassy, Bonn, Germany, 1960-65; dep. dir. AID, Karachi, Pakistan, 1965-67; v.p. 1st Wis. Nat. Bank, Milw., 1967-69, 1st v.p., 1969-71; sr. v.p. Wells Fargo Bank; also pres. Wells Fargo Internat. Investment Corp., San Francisco, 1971-78; mng. dir., chief exec. officer London Interstate Bank Ltd., Eng., 1978—; Sr. fellow Center Internat. Banking Studies, Charlottesville, Va. Chmn. World Affairs Council Milw., 1970-71; chmn. bd. dirs. Adam Smith Inst., London. Served with AUS,

1943-46. Mem. Bankers Assn. for Fgn. Trade (pres. 1977-78). Home: 13 Edwardes Sq London W86HE England Office: Bastion House 140 London Wall London EC2Y 5DN England

BEEBE, CORA PRIFOLD, government official. B.A. in Polit. Sci., U. Mich., M.A. Tchr. pub. schs., Chelsea, Mich.; isntr. George Washington U.; adminstrv. asst. to exec. dir. Am. Polit. Sci. Assn.; from planning and evaluation analyst to prin. dep. asst. sec. Office Elem. and Secondary Edn., U.S. Office of Edn., from 1965; asst. sec. for adminstrn. Dept. Treasury, 1981—; fellow Inst. World Affairs. Recipient Superior Service award HEW, 1979. Mem. Am. Polit. Sci. Assn., Am. Soc. for Pub. Adminstrn., N.Am. Soc. for Corp. Planning, Nat. Trust for Hist. Preservation. Office: Dept Treasury Adminstrv Office 15th and Pennsylvania Ave NW Washington DC 20220 *

BEEBE, JOHN ELDRIDGE, financial executive; b. Freeport, N.Y., Jan. 30, 1923; s. Henry W. and Edna (Eldridge) B.; m. Margaret Sands Hubbell, Sept. 7, 1946; children: John Eldridge, Martha. B.A. cum laude, Princeton U., 1947. Vice pres. Chase Manhattan Bank, 1947-65; sr. v.p. Paine, Webber, Jackson & Curtis, Inc., N.Y.C., 1965-80; v.p. corp. fin. F. Eberstadt & Co., Inc., N.Y.C., 1981-83; dir. corp. fin. Ingalls & Snyder, N.Y.C., 1983—; cons. Electro-Nucleonics, 1981—, Becton-Dickinson & Co., Inc.; dir. Olsten Corp., Westbury, N.Y., Taco Viva, Inc. Served to 1st lt. U.S. Army, 1942-46. Episcopalian. Clubs: University, Wall Street, Bond, Garden City Golf, Cove Neck Tennis.

BEEBE, LEO CLAIR, educator, mgmt. cons.; b. Williamsburg, Mich., July 20, 1917; s. Fred Grant and Rena (Allton) B.; m. Jan Wyss, Mar. 11, 1966; children—Leo Peter, Anne Lorraine. B.S. in Edn, U. Mich., 1939; postgrad., Wayne U., 1942-43. With Ford Motor Co. (various locations), 1945-72; gen. mgr. consumers products div. Philco-Ford, Phila., also exec. v.p., until 1972; prof. mgmt. Glassboro State Coll., 1972—, dean adminstrv. studies, 1977—; dir. K-Tron Internat., 1976—; cons. Nat. Council Better Bus. Burs., 1972—, sec. HEW, 1978-81. Author numerous manuals, articles speeches on refugee and hardcore disadvantaged employment. Vice chmn. Pres. Eisenhower's Com. for Hungarian Refugees; dir. program to resettle 36,000 refugees; dir. Cuban Refugee Center, Miami, 1960; chief exec. Pres. Johnson's Program for Hardcore Employment, 1968; mem. Pres. Johnson's Commn. for Exec. Exchange; chmn. Civic Com. on Sch. Needs, Dearborn, Mich., 1958; pres. Dearborn Boys' Club, 1955-60; chmn. numerous campaigns YMCA, United Fund; bd. dirs. Reading is Fundamental; trustee Va. Union U.; Trustee Misericordia Coll., 1983—. Served with USNR, 1942-45. Recipient Gold plate award for achievement Nat. Acad. Achievement, 1969. Mem. Nat. Alliance Businessmen (founding pres.), Indsl. Audio Visual Assn. (past pres.). Episcopalian. Club: Rotary (past dist. gov.). Mgr. winning Ford Motor racing team culminating in 1st U.S. 1-2-3 victory in 24 hours endurance race, LeMans, France, 1966. Home: 108 Glenn Rd Ardmore PA 19003 Office: Glassboro State Coll Glassboro NJ

BEEBE, RICHARD TOWNSEND, physician; b. Great Barrington, Mass., Jan. 22, 1902; s. John and Louise (Taylor) B.; m. Jean Wickersham, Aug. 10, 1932; children—Nancy Taylor, John Wickersham, Louise Townsend. B.S., Princeton U., 1924; M.D., Johns Hopkins, 1928; D.Sc. (hon.), Albany Med. Coll. of Union U., 1982. Diplomate: Am. Bd. Internal Medicine. Intern Johns Hopkins Hosp., 1928-29, asst. resident physician, 1930-32; residency tng. Thorndike Meml. Lab., Harvard, 1929- 30; asso. medicine Albany Med. Coll., 1932-37, asso. prof. medicine, 1937-48, prof. medicine, dir. dept., 1948-67, Distinguished prof. medicine, 1968—; asst. physician Albany Hosp., 1932-34, clin. asst. medicine, 1934-37, attending physician, 1937-48, dispensary physician in charge, 1941-48, physician in chief, 1948-67, sr. physician, 1967—; cons. internal medicine Albany VA Hosp. Author: Albany Medical College and Albany Hospital, A History: 1839-1982. Fellow ACP (master 1983); mem. AMA N.Y. State, Albany County med. socs., Am. Soc. Clin. Investigation, Am. Clin. and Climatol. Assn., Alpha Omega Alpha. Home: Schuyler Rd Loudonville NY 12211 Office: Albany Med Coll Albany NY 12208

BEEBE, ROBERT PARK, yacht designer; b. Fort McKinley, P.I., Nov. 21, 1909; s. Royden Eugene and Sara Reid (Park) B.; m. Lucy Maude Ord, Oct. 21, 1933 (dec. Dec. 1960); 1 dau., Lucy Cresap Ord (Mrs. R.J. Pawlik); m. Linford B. Donovan, July 6th, 1963. B.S., U.S. Naval Acad., 1931; M.A., Boston U., 1957; grad., Naval War Coll., 1958. Commd. ensign U.S. Navy, 1931, advanced through grades to capt., 1950; comdr. (U.S.S. Sitkoh Bay), 1953, 1942, assigned, 1952, dept. chief staff, J-2 staff comdr. in chief Alaska, 1954-56, chmn. naval warfare, 1957-58, head advanced study group, 1957; dir. Gen. Line and Naval Sci. Sch., U.S. Naval Postgrad. Sch., 1958-61; ret., 1961, designer yachts. Author: Voyaging under Power, 1975; Contbr. articles on yachts and yacht design, also politico-mil. affairs. Mem. U.S. Naval Inst. Club: N.Y. Yacht. Address: Box 1452 Carmel CA 93921

BEEBE, WILLIAM ANDREWS, former electronic manufacturing company executive, private investor, consultant; b. Worcester, Mass., May 11, 1935; s. Edwin Mudget and Mae (Andrews) B.; m. Katharine Laura Fernald, Mar. 8, 1958; children: Christopher, Michael, Harry, Effie Mae. B.S., U. Vt., 1957; M.B.A., Harvard U., 1963. With corporate finance dept. Goldman, Sachs & Co., N.Y.C., 1963-66; exec. v.p. finance, treas., controller Dunkin' Donuts, Inc., Randolph, Mass., 1966-73; exec. v.p. finance and control Cramer Electronics, Inc., Newton, Mass., 1973-75; v.p. fin. Kalso Systemet, Inc., N.Y.C., 1976-77; v.p. finance Advent Corp., Cambridge, Mass., 1977-80; chief operating and exec. officer, dir. Automation Devel., Inc., Stoneham, Mass., 1980-83; pvt. investor, cons., 1983—. Served with USAF, 1957-58. Mem. Financial Execs. Inst., Nat. Investor Relations Inst. Club: Treasurers (Boston). Home: 116 Captain Peirce Rd Scituate MA 02066

BEEBY, KENNETH JACK, lawyer, food company executive; b. Peoria, Ill., May 21, 1936; s. Harold J. and L. and Elizabeth (Otten) B.; m. Shelley Jean Seip, June 14, 1959; children—Kathryn Jean, Sara Jane, Christine Vivian. B.A., Beloit (Wis.) Coll., 1958; J.D., Northwestern U., 1961. Bar: Ind. 1961, Ill. 1961, Mo. 1962, Mass. 1974. Staff atty., asst. to gen. counsel Seven-Up Co., St. Louis, 1961-73; house counsel, then chief legal officer Ocean Spray Cranberries, Inc., Hanson, Mass., 1973-77, v.p., gen. counsel, Plymouth, Mass., 1977—, 1982—. Mem. ABA, Mass. Bar Assn. Office: Ocean Spray Cranberries Inc Water St Plymouth MA 02360

BEEBY, THOMAS H., architect. Architect C.F. Murphy, Chgo., 1965-71; ptnr. Hammond, Beeby & Babka, Chgo., 1971—; mem. faculty dept. architecture Ill. Inst. Tech., Chgo., 1973-80; dir. Sch. Architecture U. Ill.-Chgo. Designs exhibited, Art Inst. Chgo., Mus. Contemporary Art, Chgo., Cooper-Hewitt Mus., N.Y.C., Walker Art Ctr., Mpls., Venice Biennale; contbr. articles to profl. jours. Recipient Progressive Architecture Citation, 1976. Mem. AIA (mem. nat. com. on design, design awards). Office: Hammond Beeby & Babka 1126 N State St Chicago IL 60610 *

BEECHAM, CLAYTON TREMAIN, gynecologist; b. Ladd, Ill., Mar. 1, 1907; s. Horace King and Bessie (File) B.; m. Patricia Anne Miller, Dec. 25, 1979; children: Richard K., Jackson B., Nina Beecham Stratton. B.S., U. Minn., 1930, M.D., 1932. Intern U. Minn. Hosp., 1932-33; resident U. Kans. Hosp., 1933-34, Kensington Hosp. Women, Phila., 1934-36; instr. obstetrics and gynecology U. Pa. Sch. Medicine, 1936-40; prof. obstetrics and gynecology Temple U. Med. Sch., 1940-64, dir. tumor clinic, 1940-64; dir. gynecology and obstetrics Geisinger Med. Center, Danville, Pa., 1965—; pres. Am. Assn. Obstetricians and Gynecologists Found., Inc., 1969—; examiner Am. Bd. Obstetrics and Gynecology, in-tng. exams for residents. Author: (with others) Obstetrics and Gynecology, 3d edit, 1966; editorial bd.: Obstetrics and Gynecology, 1968-71; cons. surgery: Year Book Cancer, 1965—. Bd. dirs. Solebury Sch., New Hope, Pa., 1951-53, Chestnut Hill Acad., Phila., 1955-57. Hon. fellow Kansas City (Mo.), N.J., Pitts., Seattle obstet. and gynecol. socs.; fellow A.C.S., Am. Assn. Obstetricians and Gynecologists (exec. bd. 1960—, editor bull., pres. 1968); mem. Am. Coll. Obstetricians and Gynecologists (exec. bd. 1965-68, commr. edn. 1974—), Obstet. Soc. Phila. (exec. bd. 1963-66, pres. 1964-65), Soc. Pelvic Surgeons, Am. Cancer Soc. (dir. Phila. 1964). Home: Mile Post Rd RD 1 Sunbury PA 17801 Office: Geisinger Med Center Danville PA 17821

BEECHER, JOHN DENNIS, naval officer; b. Galion, Ohio, Aug. 15, 1929; s. John R. and Irene (Cowl) B.; m. Joan Ralph, Dec. 13, 1952; children: John Michael, Karen, Mary Kathleen, Julia Anne. Student, U. Detroit; B.S. in Marine Engrng., U.S. Naval Acad.; B.S.E.E., U.S. Naval Postgrad. Sch.; M.S. in Aeros. and Astronautics, MIT. Registered profl. engr. Commd. officer U.S. Navy, 1952, advanced through grades to rear admiral; various sea tours, 1952-70; dept. head Naval Weapons Lab., Dalgren, Va., 1970-72; dir. engrng. Naval Ship Weapons Systems Engrng. Sta., Port Hueneme, Calif., 1972-76; mgr. FFG Program Naval Sea Systems Command, Washington, 1976-79, dep. comdr. surface combatants, 1979-81, asst. dep. comdr. AAW and surface warfare, 1981—. Recipient John Adolphus Dalgren award Naval Weapons Lab., 1971, Meritorious Service medal with two gold stars U.S. Navy, 1979. Mem. Am. Soc. Naval Engrs. Roman Catholic. Office: Naval Sea Systems Command Washington DC 20362 *

BEECHER, WILLIAM JOHN, zoologist, museum director; b. Chgo., May 23, 1914; s. Edward J. and Anna (Lawlor) B. Ph.B., B.S., U. Chgo., 1947, M.S., 1949, Ph.D., 1954. Zoology asst. Chgo. Natural History Mus., 1937-54; sr. naturalist Conservation Dept., Cook County Forest Preserve Dist., 1955-57; dir. Chgo. Acad. Scis., 1958-82, dir. emeritus, 1982—; Chmn. Chgo. Conservation Council, 1964—; pres. Beecher Research Co., mfg. Beecher Mirage spectacle binocular, 1983—. Author: Nesting Birds and the Vegetation Substrate, 1942, Attracting Birds To Your Backyard, 1954; also articles. Mem. open lands project Welfare Council Met. Chgo.; mem. policy com. Chgo. com. Ill. Sesequicentennial; mem. Ill. Nature Preserves Commn., 1971—, Ill. Endangered Species Commn., 1973—; mem. biology com. Ill. Bd. Higher Edn., 1970—; environmental aspects com. Northeastern Ill. Planning Commn.; Bd. dirs. Chgo. council Girl Scouts U.S.A. Served with AUS, 1942-45; PTO. Annual Sci. award Adult Edn. Soc. Greater Chgo., 1963; Ecology award Chgo. Outdoor Art League, 1970; Environ. Quality award U.S. EPA, 1975; 20 Yrs. Service award Open Lands Project; others. Fellow AAAS, Royal Soc. Arts, Am. Ornithol. Union; mem. Nature Conservancy (vice chmn. Ill. chpt., Green Leaf award 1969), Ecol. Soc. Am., Wilson, Cooper ornithol. socs., Geog. Soc. Chgo. (v.p. 1971—), Am. Soc. Zoologists, Ill. Audubon Soc., Chgo. Audubon Soc. (dir.), Sigma Xi (award for lifelong contbn. to sci. 1981). Clubs: Garden of America (mem. conservation com.), Kennicott, Bandar Log, Adventurers. Spl. research anatomy and classification birds of world, ecologist, conservationist; wildlife photographer; inventor spectacle binocular for bird study. Home: 1960 N Lincoln Park W Chicago IL 60614 Office: 2001 N Clark St Chicago IL 60614 *Man is the only species with an aesthetic appreciation of natural beauty, and his very ability to stand off from nature and look at it deludes him into the view that he is not really part of it, vulnerable if impoverished or polluted ecosystems die.*

BEECHING, CHARLES TRAIN, JR., lawyer; b. Herkimer, N.Y., Aug. 31, 1930; s. Charles Train and Lucina Warner (Thompson) B.; m. Suzanne Bronner, Apr. 6, 1957; children—Barbara, Victoria. B.A., Hamilton Coll., 1952; J.D., U. Chgo., 1955. Bar: N.Y. bar 1958. Asso. firm Dewey, Ballantine, Bushby, Palmer & Wood, N.Y.C., 1955, 57-58; asst. U.S. atty. So. Dist. N.Y., 1959-61; law sec. Justice Charles D. Breitel (Appellate div. Supreme Ct. N.Y.), N.Y.C., 1961-62; mem. firm Bond, Schoeneck & King, Syracuse, 1962—; dir. Syracuse China Corp., Unity Mut. Life Ins. Co., Lincoln First Bank, N.A. Regional Bd. Mem. Gov.'s Jud. Nominating Com., 4th Dept., 1975—; bd. dirs. Blue Shield of Central N.Y. Served with USN, 1957-58. Mem. Am. Law Inst., N.Y. State Bar Assn., Onondaga County Bar Assn. Club: Century (Syracuse). Home: 145 Chatham Rd Syracuse NY 13203 Office: One Lincoln Center Syracuse NY 13202

BEEDLE, LYNN SIMPSON, civil engineering educator; b. Orland, Calif., Dec. 7, 1917; s. Granville L. and Carol (Simpson) B.; m. Ella Marie Grimes, Oct. 20, 1946; children: Lynn, Helen, Jonathan, David, Edward. B.S., U. Calif., 1941; M.S., Lehigh U., 1949, Ph.D., 1952. With Todd-Calif. Shipbldg. Corp., Richmond, Calif., 1941; instr. Postgrad. Sch., U.S. Naval Acad.; officer-in-charge Underwater Explosions Research div. Norfolk (Va.) Naval Shipyard, 1941-47; dir. Lehigh U. Fritz Engrng. Lab., Bethlehem, Pa., 1960—; prof. civil engrng. Lehigh U., 1958-77, Univ. Disting. prof., 1978—, dir. High-Rise Inst., 1983—. Author: Plastic Design of Steel Frames, 1958, (with others) Structural Steel Design, 2d edit, 1974; editor-in-chief: Planning and Design of Tall Buildings, 5 vols, 1978-81; contbr. articles to profl. jours. Served with USNR, 1941-47. Recipient Robinson award Lehigh U., 1952, Hillman award, 1973; E.E. Howard award ASCE, 1963; Research prize, 1956; Silver medal Am. Welding Soc., 1957; Constrn. award Engrng. News Record, 1965, 73; Regional Tech. Meeting award Am. Iron and Steel Inst., 1958; T.R. Higgins award Am. Inst. Steel Constrn., 1973; Engr. of Year award Lehigh Valley sect. Nat. Soc. Profl. Engrs., 1977. Fellow ASCE (hon. mem.; dir. 1974-77, dir. Lehigh Valley sect. 1977—, past chmn. structural div. exec. com., past mem. research com.); mem. Structural Stability Research Council (life mem., chmn. 1966-70, dir. 1970—), Welding Research Council, Am. Inst. Steel Constrn., Nat. Acad. Engrng., Council on Tall Bldgs. and Urban Habitat (chmn. 1970-76, dir. 1976—), Internat. Assn. Bridge and Structural Engrng. (hon.). Presbyn. (elder 1957—). Home: 102 Cedar Rd Hellertown PA 18055 Office: Fritz Engrng Lab Lehigh Univ Bethlehem PA 18015

BEELER, JOHN WATSON, physician, educator; b. Indpls., July 2, 1921; s. Raymond Cole and Myra (Watson) B.; m. Marcella Thorson, Jan. 13, 1951; children: John Cole, Richard Thorson, Thomas Watson. Student, Wesleyan U., Middletown, Conn., 1939-41; B.S., Ind. U., 1942, M.D., 1944; M.S. in Radiology, U. Minn., 1950. Diplomate: Am. Bd. Radiology. Intern Phila. Gen. Hosp., 1945; fellow radiology Mayo Found., 1947-50; pvt. practice radiology, Indpls., 1950-64, 66—; chmn. dept. radiology Methodist Hosp., Indpls., 1963-66, dir. dept., 1964-66; asst. prof. radiology Ind. U. Sch. Medicine, 1960-81, assoc. prof., 1981—; mem. courtesy staff Community Hosp., Indpls., 1956—; radiologist Hancock Meml. Hosp., Greenfield, Ind., 1954—; sec. exec. staff Marion County Gen. Hosp., Indpls., 1956-58; dir. dept. radiology Winona Meml. Hosp., 1970-81; dir. Ind. Blue Shield, 1958—, sec., 1969—. Bd. dirs. Nat. Bd. Med. Examiners, 1977-81. Served with M.C., USAAF, 1945-47; with med. dept. AUS, 1953-54. Fellow Am. Coll. Radiology (councilor for Ind. 1961-66, speaker of council 1967-69, mem. bd. chancellors 1969-75, v.p. 1976-77); mem. AMA (interspecialty adv. bd. 1976-80, alt. del. 1979—, exec. com. 1980—, exec. com. Forum Med. Affairs 1981—), Ind. Med. Assn. (mem. ho. dels. 1958-66, 68-75, speaker 1974-75, pres. 1976-77, exec. com. 1975-79, chmn. 1978), Radiol. Soc. N.Am. (counselor for Ind. 1961-66, 1st v.p. 1969-70, dir. 1970-75, chmn. bd. dirs. 1972—, pres. 1975, councilor to Am. Coll. Radiology 1978—), Ind. Roentgen Soc. (chmn. exec. council 1958, pres. 1961), Marion County Med. Soc. (dir. 1956-58, 68-81, chmn. 1969-70), Am. Roentgen Ray Soc., Council Med. Splty. Socs., Eastern, Rocky Mountain radiol socs., Orgn. State Med. Assn. Pres. (pres. 1977). Clubs: Rotary, Indianapolis Athletic. Home: 7974 N Illinois St Indianapolis IN 46260 Office: 1815 N Capitol Indianapolis IN 46202

BEELER, JOSEPH, JR., paper company executive; b. South Bend, Ind., July 27, 1930; s. Joseph and Catherine Louise (Coleman) B.; m. Muriel Ann Eanos, May 7, 1955; children: Cathy Irene, Joseph III. Pres. Knight Paper Co., Jacksonville, Fla., 1974-77, Grahman Paper Co., Jacksonville, 1977-79; sr. v.p. distbn. Jim Walter Papers, Jacksonville, 1979-82, sr. v.p., Jackonville, 1982—. Served with U.S. Army, 1953-55. Republican. Methodist. Club: River, San Jose Country (Jacksonville). Lodge: Rotary. Office: Jim Walter Papers 5402 W 1st St Jacksonville FL 32205

BEELER, THOMAS JOSEPH, lawyer; b. Marion, Ind., June 5, 1933; s. Thomas James and Margaret B. (Milford) B.; children: Kristin, Mark, Laura. B.S. in Bus. Adminstrn. cum laude, Notre Dame U., 1956; J.D., U. Notre Dame, 1957. Bar: Ind. 1957. Sole practice, Anderson, 1958-61; asst. sec., counsel The Weatherhead Co., Cleve., 1961-68; asst. gen. counsel, corp. sec. A-T-O Inc., Willoughby, Ohio, 1968-74; corp. atty., sec. Outboard Marine Corp., Waukegan, Ill., 1974-76, v.p., gen. counsel, sec., 1976—. Served to 1st lt. AUS, 1957-58. Mem. Am., Ind. bar assns., Am. Soc. Corp. Secs. Home: 701 E Prospect Ave Lake Bluff IL 60044 Office: 100 Sea-Horse Dr Waukegan IL 60085

BEELER, THOMAS TAYLOR, III, publishing co. exec.; b. Oklahoma City, May 22, 1944; s. Thomas Taylor and Virginia (Klein) B.; m. Susan Jane O'Connor, July 24, 1965; children—Ethan Thomas, Emily Susan. B.A., Columbia U., 1966, M.A., 1967, Ph.D. (Jethro Robinson fellow in Am. lit., Woodrow Wilson dissertation fellow), 1974. Cross-reference editor Am. Heritage Pub. Co., N.Y.C., 1968; editorial cons. Garrett Press, N.Y.C., 1968-69, editorial dir., v.p., 1969-71; editor Gregg Press div. G.K. Hall & Co., Boston, 1972-73, exec. editor, 1974-78, also exec. editor, 1973-78; pub. G.K. Hall & Co., 1978—. Co-editor, bus. mgr.: Little Mag, 1965-71. Mem. Modern Lang. Assn., Am. Studies Assn., Bibliog. Soc. Am. Home: King St Hampton Falls NH 03844 Office: 70 Lincoln St Boston MA 02111

BEEM, JACK DARRELL, lawyer; b. Chgo., Nov. 17, 1931. A.B., U. Chgo., 1952, J.D., 1955. Bar: Ill. 1955. Assoc. firm Wilson & McIlvaine, Chgo., 1958-63; ptnr. firm Baker & McKenzie, Chgo., 1963—. Mem. ABA, Chgo. Bar Assn. Home: 175 E Delaware Pl Apt 8104 Chicago IL 60611 Office: Baker & McKenzie Suite 2800 Prudential Plaza Chicago IL 60601

BEEMAN, LYMAN ANDERSON, paper mfg. co. exec.; b. Humbird, Wis., Jan. 12, 1896; s. Edward Monroe and Ivis (Anderson) B.; m. Mary Polly Hoopes, Oct. 1, 1944; children—Lyman A., David E., Barbara Ann. B.S. in Chem. Engrng, U. Wis., 1918. Pulp supt. Kimberly-Clark Corp., 1918-22; with Consol. Water and Power Co., 1922-35, mgr. book paper div., 1935-36; dir. sales Combined Locks Paper Co., 1936-37; gen. supt. printing paper mills, v.p. in charge mfg. paper div. St. Regis Paper Co., N.Y.C., 1937-48; with Finch, Pruyn & Co., Glen Falls, N.Y., 1948—, pres., 1949-71, chmn. bd., 1971—; Bd. trustees State U. Coll. of Forestry, Syracuse; dep. dir. paper div. War Production Bd., 1944. Pres. Finch Pruyn Found.; trustee Hyde Collection Trust, Adirondack Hist. Assn. Served with U.S. Army, 1918. Mem. Empire State Forest Products Assn. (past pres.), Am. Soc. Foresters, TAPPI. Office: Finch Pruyn & Co 1 Glen St Glen Falls NY 12801

BEEMAN, WILLIAM WALDRON, physicist, emeritus educator; b. Detroit, Oct. 21, 1911; s. Joseph John and Mary E. (Waldron) B.; m. Eleanor Mildred Coswell, June 22, 1940; children: Ann Margaret, Richard William, John Michael and David Kevin (twins). Student, Wayne U., 1929-35; B.S. in Math, U. Mich., 1937; Ph.D. in Physics, Johns Hopkins U., 1940. Research physicist Gen. Motors Research Labs., Detroit, 1940-41; instr. physics U. Wis., Madison, 1941-44, asst. prof., 1944-47, asso. prof., 1947-52, prof., 1952—82, prof. emeritus, 1982—, chmn. dept., 1951-52, chmn. grad. com. biophysics, 1956-75, dir. biophysics lab., 1963-70; Sci. adviser to gov. Wis., 1963-64; adv. com. Wis. Dept. Resource Devel., 1963-64; cons. Argonne Nat. Lab., Lemont, Ill., Los Alamos Nat. Lab., 1947-52. Editorial bd.: Rev. Sci. Instruments, 1958-61; Contbr. numerous research articles to profl. publs. Citizen mem. Madison Plan Com., 1957-63; Alderman, Madison, 1955-57; Trustee Madison Gen. Hosp., 1955-57. Fellow Am. Phys. Soc.; mem. Am. Crystallographic Assn., Biophys. Soc., Phi Beta Kappa, Sigma Xi. Home: 5010 Tomahawk Trail Madison WI 53705

BEENE, GEOFFREY, fashion designer; b. Haynesville, La., Aug. 30, 1927; s. Albert and Lorene (Waller) B. Student, Tulane U., 1941-45, Traphagen Sch. Fashion, 1949, Acad. Julien, Paris, France, 1949. Designer for Samuel Winston, 1949-50, Harmay, 1950-57, Teal Traina, 1958-62; pres., designer Geoffrey Beene, Inc., N.Y.C., 1962—. Represented in collection, Costume Inst., Met. Mus. Art. Recipient Nat. Cotton award, 1965, Coty award, 1964, 66, Nieman Marcus award, 1965, Ethel Traphagen award, 1966, Coty Hall of Fame award, 1974, 79, 82, Coty Hall of Fame citation, 1975, Fashion Critics Hall of Fame spl. citation, 1977, Critics Hall of Fame citation, 1979, Coty spl. citation, 1979, 82, Council Fashion Designers Am. award, 1981. Office: 550 7th Ave New York NY 10018 *

BEENE, VERNON A., business executive; b. Joshua, Tex., Oct. 25, 1922; s. Guy A. and Virgie M. (Patterson) B.; m. Zelma Lee Booth, Oct. 25, 1940; 1 dau., Brenda Gail Beene Patrick. Gen. supt. Madsen Chair co., Cleburne, Tex., 1940-48; gen. foreman A. Brandt Co., Ft. Worth, 1948-49; asst. mgr. Madsen Chair Co., Cleburne, 1949-57; purchasing mgr. Roberts Mfg. div. Rangaire Corp., Cleburne, 1957-59, dir. mfg. and purchasing, 1959-62; v.p. and gen. mgr. Harris Electric div. Rangaire Corp., Itasca, Tex., 1962-70; exec. v.p. mfg. Rangaire Corp., Cleburne, 1970—. Served with USAF, 1942-46. Methodist. Home: 1311 Loma Alta Pl Cleburne TX 76031 Office: Rangaire Corp 501 S Wilhite Cleburne TX 76031

BEER, ALAN EARL, physician, educator; b. Milford, Ind., Apr. 14, 1937; s. Theo and Naoma Marguerite (Speheger) B.; m. Dorothy Gudeman, Aug. 17, 1958; children—Michael, Elizabeth, Margaret, Laura. B.S., Ind. U., 1959, M.D., 1962. Diplomate: Am. Bd. Ob-Gyn. Resident in Ob-Gyn Hosp. of U. Pa., Phila., 1965-68; USPHS/Ford Found. fellow Dept. Med. Genetics and Ob-Gyn, U. Pa., Phila., 1968-70; asst. prof. dept. Ob-Gyn, U. Tex. Southwestern Med. Sch., Dallas, 1971-73, asso. prof., 1973-76, prof., 1976-79; prof., chmn. dept. Ob-Gyn, U. Mich., Ann Arbor, 1979—. Asso. editor: Jour. Reproductive Immunology, 1979; contbr. articles to profl. jours. Served with USPHS, 1963-65. Recipient Lalor Found. award, 1969; Carl F. Hartman award Am. Fertility Soc., 1970. Mem. Am. Coll. Obstetricians and Gynecologists, Am. Fertility Soc., Internat. Transplantation Soc., AMA, Soc. for Study of Reprodn., Soc. for

Gynecol. Investigation, Am. Assn. Ob-Gyn. Office: L2120 Womens Hosp Univ of Mich Ann Arbor MI 48109

BEER, CLARA LOUISE JOHNSON, electronics exec.; b. Bisbee, Ariz., Jan. 14, 1918; d. Franklin Fayette and Marie (Sturm) Johnson; m. Philip James McElmurry, May 15, 1937 (div. July 1944); children—Leonard Franklin, Philip James Jr.; m. William Sigvard Beer, July 15, 1945 (dec. Aug. 31, 1977); 1 son, Douglas Lee. Student, Merritt Bus. Sch., Oakland, Calif., 1935, Bus. Instrn. Sch., Palo Alto, Calif., 1955. Sec., artist M.R. Fisher Studios, Oakland, 1936-40; piano, organ instr. Anna May Studios, Palo Alto, 1948-50; pvt. piano, organ instr., Palo Alto, 1949-56; sec. Stanford Electronics Labs., Stanford U., 1955-58; corporate sec. and exec. sec. to chmn. bd. Watkins-Johnson Co., Palo Alto, 1958—; dir., sec. Watkins-Johnson Internat., 1968—, Watkins-Johnson Ltd., 1971—, Watkins-Johnson Assos., 1977—. Mem. Am. Soc. Corp. Secs., Nat. Secs. Assn., Christian Bus. and Profl. Womens Council (sec. 1966-67, adviser 1968). Home: 24157 Hillview Dr Los Altos Hills CA 94022 Office: 3333 Hillview Ave Palo Alto CA 94304

BEÉR, JÁNOS MIKLÓS, engineering educator; b. Budapest, Hungary, Feb. 27, 1923; s. Sandor and Gizella (Trismai) B.; m. Marta Gabriella Csato, Oct. 27, 1944. Dipl. Ing., Jozsef Nador U. Tech., Budapest, 1950; Ph.D., U. Sheffield, Eng., 1960, D.Sc., 1968. Fellowship of Engring., London, 1979. Research engr. Heat Research Inst., Budapest, 1949-56, head combustion div., 1952-56; prin. lectr. combustion Budapest Tech. U., 1953-56; research engr. Babcock & Wilcox Ltd., Renfrew, Scotland, 1956-57; head research sta. Internat. Flame Research Found., Ijmuiden, Holland, 1960-63; prof. fuel sci. Pa. State U., 1963-65; Newton Drew prof., head dept. chem. engring. and fuel tech. U. Sheffield, 1965-76, dean engring., 1973-75; prof. chem. and fuel engring. Mass. Inst. Tech., 1976—; mem. joint com. Internat. Flame Research Found., 1972—, supt. research, 1972—; bd. dirs. Combustion Inst., Pitts., 1974; adv. council research and devel. fuel and power U.K. Dept. Energy, 1973-76; mem. Clean Air Council, Dept. Environ., U.K., 1974-76; mem. chem. tech. com. U.K. Sci. Research Council, 1972-75; mem. combustion sci. com. Italian Nat. Research Council, 1974—. Co-author: Combustion Aerodynamics, 1972; Editor: Fuel and Energy Science Monograph Series, 1972; Co-editor: Heat Transfer in Flames, 1972, Industrial Flames, 1972, Combustion Technology, 1974; Author articles. Recipient Moody award ASME, 1963; Australian Commonwealth fellow, 1973. Sr. fellow Inst. Fuel, London; fellow Instn. Chem. Engrs., Inst. Mech. Engrs., Am. Inst. Mech. Engrs., Am. Inst. Chem. Engrs. Patentee in field. Office: 66-552 Mass Inst Tech Cambridge MA 02139

BEER, JEANETTE MARY AYRES, foreign language educator; b. Wellington, N.Z.; d. Alexander Samuel and Una Doreen (Castle) Scott; m. Colin Gordon Beer, June 27, 1959; children: Stephen James Colin, Jeremy Michael Alexander. B.A., Victoria U., N.Z., 1954, M.A. 1st class, 1955, B.A., Oxford U., Eng., 1958, M.A., 1962; Ph.D. (fellow), Columbia U., 1967. Asst. lectr. French Victoria U., Wellington, 1956; lectrice French and English U. Montpellier, France, 1958-59; instr. French Otago U., Dunedin, N.Z., 1963-64, Barnard Coll., Columbia U., N.Y.C., 1966-68; asst. prof. French Fordham U., Bronx, N.Y., 1968-69, asso. prof., 1969-76, prof., 1976-80; acting asso. dean Thomas More Coll., 1972-73, dir. medieval studies, 1972-80; head dept. fgn. langs. and lits. Purdue U., West Lafayette, Ind., 1980—; mem. nat. bd. cons.'s Nat. Endowment for Humanities, 1977—. Author: Villehardouin—Epic Historian, 1968, A Medieval Caesar, 1976, Narrative Conventions of Truth in the Middle Ages, 1981, Medieval Fables: Marie de France, 1981; gen. editor: Teaching Language through Literature, 1971—; contbr. articles to profl. jours. Nat. Endowment for Humanities grantee, 1975; research fellow, 1980. Mem. MLA, Medieval Acad., Internat. Arthurian Soc., Soc. Rencesvals, Comparative Lit. Assn., Am. Assn. Tchrs. French. Anglican. Home: 256 W Hudson Ave Englewood NJ 07631 Office: Dept Fgn Langs and Lits Purdue U West Lafayette IN 47907

BEER, MICHAEL, educator, biophysicist; b. Budapest, Hungary, Feb. 20, 1926; came to U.S., 1958, naturalized, 1965; s. Paul and Lidia (Pap-Kovacs) B.; m. Margaret Terry Peters, Jan. 22, 1954; children—Nicholas, Suzanne, Wendy. M.A., U. Toronto, 1950; Ph.D., U. Manchester, Eng., 1953. Research asso. U. Mich., 1953-56; research fellow Nat. Research Council Can., 1956-58; mem. faculty Johns Hopkins, 1958—, prof. biophysics, 1964—. Mem. Biophys. Soc. (pres. 1975-76), Electron Microscopy Soc. Am. (pres. 1980). Home: 4623 Wilmslow Rd Baltimore MD 21210

BEER, PETER HILL, judge; b. New Orleans, Apr. 12, 1928; s. Mose Haas and Henret (Lowenburg) B.; m. Roberta Webb, Sept. 20, 1953 (div. 1981); children: Kimberly Beer Bailes, Kenneth, Dana. B.B.A., Tulane U., 1949, LL.B., 1952. Bar: La. 1952. Successively asso., partner, sr. partner Montgomery, Barnett, Brown & Read, New Orleans, 1955-74; judge La. Ct. Appeal, 1974-79; U.S. dist. judge Eastern Dist. La., 1979—; vice chmn. La. Appellate Judges Conf. Bd. mgrs. Touro Infirmary, New Orleans, 1969-74; exec. com. Bur. Govtl. Research, 1965-69; chmn. profl. div. United Fund New Orleans, 1966-69; mem. New Orleans City Council, 1969-74, v.p., 1972-74. Served to capt. USAF, 1952-55. Decorated AF Commendation medal, Bronze Star. Mem. ABA (ho. of dels.), Am. Judicature Soc., Fed. Bar Assn., La. State Bar Assn. Jewish. Clubs: Nat. Lawyers, So. Yacht. Home: 5855 Bellaire Dr New Orleans LA 70124 Office: 500 Camp St New Orleans LA 70130

BEER, REINHARD, planetary astronomer; b. Berlin, Germany, Nov. 5, 1935; came to U.S., 1963, naturalized, 1979; s. Harry Joseph and Elizabet Maria (Meister) B.; m. Margaret Ann Taylor, Aug. 11, 1960. B.Sc. with Honors, U. Manchester, Eng., 1956, Ph.D., 1960. Research asst. physics U. Manchester, 1956-60, sr. asst. astronomy, 1960-63; sr. scientist Jet Propulsion Lab., Pasadena, Calif., 1963-70, group supr. atmospheric radiation, 1970—; pres. Infodem Internat., Inc., 1980—; vis. asso. prof. astronomy U. Tex., Austin, 1974; vis. astronomer Kitt Peak Nat. Obs., 1979-81. Contbr. articles to profl. jours. Hon. Turner and Newall fellow, 1961; recipient medal for exceptional sci. achievement NASA, 1974; NASA group achievement award for Pioneer Venus, 1980. Mem. Am. Astron. Soc., Optical Soc. Am., Internat. Astron. Union, Sigma Xi. Discoverer of extra-terrestrial deuterium (heavy hydrogen), 1972, of carbon monoxide in Jupiter, 1975. Office: 183-301 Jet Propulsion Lab Pasadena CA 91109

BEER, WALTER EUGENE, JR., lawyer; b. N.Y.C., Nov. 17, 1904; s. Walter Eugene and Bella (Nathan) B.; m. Florence Louise Fay, Sept. 2, 1930; children: John Walter, David Wells. Student, Choate Sch., Wallingford, Conn., 1918-22; A.B., Harvard U., 1926, LL.B., 1929. Bar: N.Y. 1929. Assoc. Simpson Thacher & Bartlett, N.Y.C., 1929-41; partner Beer, Richards, Haller and O'Neil (and predecessor firms), 1945-73; Lankenau, Kovner, Bickford & Beer, 1974; counsel Bleakley, Platt, Schmidt & Fritz, 1975-81, Miller, Montgomery, Sogi & Brady, 1981-83, Kelley, Drye & Warren, 1983—; mem. legal staff General Counsel to United States OPM and WPB, 1941-44. Mem. Assn. Bar City N.Y. Clubs: University, Harvard (N.Y.C.); Brooklyn, Heights Casino (Bklyn.); Keene Valley Country, Ausable (Keene Valley, N.Y.). Home: 2 Montague Terr Brooklyn NY 11201 Office: 101 Park Ave New York NY 10178

BEERING, STEVEN CLAUS, university president, medical educator; b. Berlin, Germany, Aug. 20, 1932; came to U.S., 1948, naturalized, 1953; s. Steven and Alice (Friedrichs) B.; m. Catherine Jane Pickering, Dec. 27, 1956; children: Peter, David, John. B.S. summa cum laude, U. Pitts., 1954; M.D., 1958. Intern Walter Reed Gen. Hosp., Washington, 1958-59; resident Wilford Hall Med. Center, San Antonio, Tex., 1959-62, chief internal medicine, edn. coordinator, 1962-69; prof. medicine Ind. U. Sch. Medicine, Indpls., 1969—, asst. dean, 1969-70, assoc. dean, dir. postgrad. edn., 1970-74, dir. statewide med. edn. system, from 1970, dean, 1974-83; chief exec. officer Ind. U. Med. Center, 1974-83; pres. Purdue U., Purdue U. Research Found., West Lafayette, Ind., 1983—; cons. Indpls. VA Hosp., St. Vincent Hosp., Eli Lilly & Co.; Chmn. Ind. Commn. Med. Edn., 1972—, Med. Edn. Bd. Ind., 1974-83. Contbr. articles to sci. jours. Sec. Ind. Atty. Gen.'s Trust., 1974-83. Served to lt. col. M.C. USAF, 1957-69. Fellow A.C.P.; mem. Am. Fedn. Clin. Research, Am. Diabetes Assn., Endocrine Soc., Assn. Am. Med. Colls. (chmn. 1982-83), Soc. Med. Cons. to Armed Forces (chmn. liaison com. on med. edn. 1976-80), Council Med. Deans (chmn. 1981-82), AMA (chmn. sect. on med. schs. 1976-78), Nat. Acad. Sci. Inst. of Medicine, Phi Beta Kappa, Sigma Xi, Alpha Omega Alpha, Phi Rho Sigma (U.S. v.p. 1976—). Presbyn. (elder). Clubs: Indpls. Athletic, Columbia., Skyline, Woodstock, Meridian Hills, University. Home: 575 McCormick Rd West Lafayette IN 47906 Office: purdue univ office of the president west lafayette IN 47907

BEERMAN, HERMAN, physician, editor; b. Johnstown, Pa., Oct. 13, 1901; s. Morris and Fannie (Toby) B.; m. Emma N. Segal, May 13, 1924. A.B., U. Pa., 1923, M.D., 1927, Sc.D. (Med.), 1935. Diplomate: Am. Bd. Dermatology, 1935. Asst. Dept. Agr., Phila., 1925-26; intern Mt. Sinai Hosp., Phila., 1927-28; resident Hosp. U. Pa., 1929-33, asst. chief dermatology clinic, 1938-65, Abbott fellow in chemotherapeutic research, 1932-46; with U. Pa. Sch. Medicine, 1929—, prof. dermatology, 1951-70, prof. emeritus, 1970—, prof., 1947-67, chmn., 1949-67; asso. serology Pepper Lab., 1949—; asst. dir. Inst. Study Venereal Disease, 1939-54; physician out patient dept. Pa. Hosp., 1929-36, hosp. dermatologist, chief, 1935-45, asso. dermatologist, 1946-47, dermatologist, head dept., 1947-67, cons. dermatologist, 1967—; asst. dermatologist radium clinic Phila. Gen. Hosp., 1938-40, dermatologist, 1940-53, active cons. dermatology, 1953-68, hon. cons. in dermatology, 1968—; cons. lab. Children's Hosp., Phila., 1949—; cons. VA Hosp., Phila., 1953-66; cons. pathology U.S. Naval Hosp., Phila., 1954—; cons. dermatology VA Hosp., Coatesville, Pa., 1967-79, USPHS, 1937—; pvt. practice, Phila., 1933—; mem. panel venereal diseases subcom. infectious disease, chemotherapy NRC, 1954—; Sigmund Pollitzer lectr. N.Y. U., 1963; Irving Wershaw Meml. lectr., Israel, 1967; Pusey Meml. lectr. Chgo. Dermatol. Soc., 1968; Ruben Nomland Meml. lectr. U. Iowa, 1968; Samuel M. Bluefarb lectr., Chgo., 1973; treas., trustee Inst. Dermatologic Communication and Education, 1963—. Editorial bd.: Jour. Investigative Dermatology, 1948-53, Am. Jour. Med. Scis., Internat. Jour. Dermatology, Jour. Cutaneous Pathology, 1978—; mem. bd. editors sect.: XIII-Dermatology and Syphilology, Excerpta Medica, 1950-75; contbr. articles to profl. jours. Hon. librarian Coll. Physicians of Phila., 1978, 82. Fellow A.C.P., AAAS, Phila. Coll. Physicians; mem. N.Y. Acad. Scis., Tissue Culture Assn., Med. Club Phila., Am. Acad. Dermatology (dir. 1941-48, 62-67, pres. 1965-67, hon.), Am. Soc. Dermatopathology (hon.; pres. 1965-66), Assn. Profs. Dermatology (dir. 1963-68, pres. 1967-68), Dermatology Found. (past trustee), Am. Dermatol. Assn. (hon.; dir. 1960-65, pres. 1967-68), Pacific (hon.), Phila. Dermatol. Assn., Brit. Assn. Dermatology (hon. fgn. mem.), Swedish Dermatol. Soc., Soc. Française de Dermatologie et Syphiligraphie (fgn. corr.), Finnish Dermatologic Soc. (hon.), Greek Dermatol. and Venereological Union (hon.), Deutsche Dermatologische Gesellschaft (hon.), Med. Soc. Study Venereal Disease (hon.; Eng.), Soc. Investigative Dermatology (ann. Herman Beerman lecture 1960—, past pres., dir., sec.-treas. 1950-65, hon.), AMA, Med. Soc. Pa., AAUP, Soc. Investigation Psychosomatic Problems, John Morgan Soc., La Société Dermatol. Danoise (corr.), Am. Venereal Disease Assn. (Thomas Parran award 1974), Solomon Solis-Cohen Med. Lit. Soc. (pres. 1961), Iranian Soc. Dermatology and Venereology (hon.), Sociedad Venezolana De Dermatologie, Venereologia y Leprologia Carcaras (hon.), Phila. County Med. Soc. (chmn. com. on infectious diseases 1968—), Israeli Dermatol. Soc. (hon.), La Academia Mexicana de Dermatologia (hon.), Academia Espanola de Dermatologie y Sifilografia, Dermatol. Assn. Poland, Internat. Coll. Exptl. Dermatology, Laboratorio de Investigaceione's Leprologicas, Societati Dermatologicae Danicae, Iowa Dermatol. Soc., Asociacion Argentina de Dermatologia (corr.), Am. Acad. Veterinary Medicine (hon.), Royal Soc. Medicine London (hon.; sect. dermatology), Pa. Acad. Dermatology (hon.), Physiol. Soc. Phila., Phila. Art Alliance, Pub. Health Soc. U. Pa., Phila. Rhuematism Soc., Am. Med. Writers Assn., Sigma Xi, Phi Lambda Kappa. Club: Athenaem (Phila.). Home: 2422 Pine St Philadelphia PA 19103

BEERMANN, ALLEN JAY, state official; b. Sioux City, Iowa, Jan. 14, 1940; s. Albert and Amanda (Scheonrock) B.; m. Linda R. Dierking, May 23, 1971; 1 son, Matthew Allen. B.A., Midland Lutheran Coll., Fremont, Nebr., 1962; J.D., Creighton U., Omaha, 1965. Bar: Nebr. 1965. Legal counsel, adminstrv. asst. to sec. state, State of Nebr., 1965-67, dep. sec. state, 1967-71, sec. of state, 1971—; Bd. dirs. NEBRASKAland Found., Tabitha Devel. Corp., Immanuel Med. Center, Omaha. Exec. bd. Cornhusker council Boy Scouts Am. Served to lt. col. USAR. Recipient Distinguished Service plaque Omaha Legal Aid Soc., 1964, Silver Beaver award Boy Scouts Am., 1979; named Outstanding Young Man Lincoln Jaycees, 1975, Nebr. Jaycees, 1975. Mem. Nat. Assn. Secs. State (pres. 1976-77), Am., Nebr. bar assns., Nebr. Press Assn., Am. Legion, Pi Kappa Delta, Phi Alpha Delta. Lutheran. Club: Elks. Address: Office Sec State State Capitol Lincoln NE 68509

BEERS, CHARLOTTE L., advertising agency executive; b. Beaumont, Tex., July 26, 1935; d. Glen and Frances (Bolt) Rice; m. Donald C. Beers, 1971; 1 dau., Lisa. B.S. in Math. and Physics, Baylor U., Waco, Tex., 1958. Group product mgr. Uncle Ben's Inc., 1959-69; sr. v.p., dir. client services J. Walter Thompson, 1969-79; chief operating officer Tatham-Laird & Kudner, Chgo., from 1979, now mng. ptnr. and chief exec officer; dir. Federated Dept. Stores, Chgo. Public TV Channel 11. Named Nat. Advt. Woman of Yr. Am. Advt. Fedn., 1975. Mem. Am. Assn. Advt. Agencies (dir.), Women's Advt. Club Chgo., Chgo. Network. Republican. Episcopalian. Office: 625 N Michigan Ave Chicago IL 60611 *

BEERS, DAVID MONROE, railroad executive; b. Pelham, N.Y., July 12, 1934; s. Ernest Monroe and Jean (Thoman) B.; m. Jean Marie Tubbs, Dec. 28, 1965; children: Terri, Mia. B.A., Wesleyan U., 1955; M.P.A., Syracuse U., 1956, postgrad., 1962-63; postgrad., Yale Div. Sch., 1959-61. Exec. dir. University Hill Corp., Syracuse, 1963-67; dir. Joint Legis. Com. Housing and Urban Devel., N.Y. Legislature, 1968-69; pres. Crouse-Irving Meml. Hosp., Syracuse, 1969-80; pres. Ont. Midland R.R., Ont. Eastern R.R., Ont. Central R.R., Rail Mgmt. Services, Inc., 1979—; former chmn. bd. Va. & Md. R.R., Md. & Del. R.R.; chmn. bd. Health Mgmt. Services Corp. of Central N.Y.; dir. Bank of N.Y., Am. Challenger Inc.; cons. Peace Corps, 1961. Served with AUS, 1957. Methodist. Home: 219 Goodrich Ave Syracuse NY 13210 Office: 736 Irving Ave Syracuse NY 13210

BEERS, ROLAND FRANK, geologist, geophysicist, coll. pres.; b. Owego, N.Y., June 6, 1899; s. Archibald Stephen and Jessie Bevans (Creveling) B.; m. Helen Elizabeth Clark, Oct. 29, 1921; children—Roland F., Barbara Helen. E.E., Rensselaer Poly. Inst., 1921; S.M., Mass. Inst. Tech., 1928, Ph.D., 1943; postgrad., Harvard Grad. Sch. Arts and Scis., 1940-41. Instr. physics and elec. engring. Rensselaer Poly. Inst., Troy, N.Y., 1921-22; devel. engr. Western Electric Co., N.Y.C., 1922-23; mgr. A.S. Beers, Binghamton, N.Y., 1925; devel. engr. Raytheon Mfg. Co., Cambridge, Mass., 1925-26; physicist Submarine Signal Corp., Boston, 1927-28; party chief Geophys. Research Corp., Houston, 1928-31, Geophys. Service, Inc., Dallas, 1931-34, v.p., 1934-36; pres., dir. The Geotechnical Corp., Dallas, 1936—; chmn. bd. and dir., 1947-56; pres., dir. Geotech. Corp. of Can., Ltd., Montreal, 1944-56; partner Beers and Heroy, Dallas, 1946-56; pres., dir. Roland F. Beers, Inc., 1955—; acad. dean Ethan Allen Community Coll., Manchester, Vt., 1973—; also pres., 1977—; cons. U.S. AEC, 1957—; pres. Geodynamics, Inc., Alexandria, Va., 1963—; chmn. bd. Beers & Rodemann, Inc., Alexandria, 1964—; pres. Knox Mining Corp., 1964—; research asso., dept. geol. Mass. Inst. Tech., Cambridge, 1943-46; geophys. cons. U.S. Geol. Survey, Washington, 1943-46; mem. NRC Com. on Measurement of Geologic Time, 1945—, NRC Com. on Seismic Effects of Detonations, 1945-46, com. on sedimentation, 1947—; head dept. fuel resources, prof. geophysics Rensselaer Polytech. Inst., Troy, N.Y., 1948-52; permanent adv. com. geol. dept. So. Meth. U., 1947; mem. adv. com. on geophysics Office of Naval Research; mem. com. on rock mechanics Nat. Acad. Scis.; mem. Vt. Higher Edn. Council. Contbr. tech. publs. Trustee Russell Sage Coll., Albany Med. Coll., Vt. Acad.; Mem. Internat. Geologic Year nat. com. seismology and gravity. Fellow Geol. Soc. Am., AAAS, Am. Acad. Arts and Scis.; mem. Am. Assn. Petroleum Geologists, Soc. Exploration Geophysicists (chmn. best paper award com. 1946-47), Am. Inst. Mining Metall. and Petroleum Engrs., IEEE Am. Geophys. Union, Seismol. Soc. Am., Photog. Soc. Am., Royal Photog. Soc. (London), ASTM, Sigma Xi, Eta Kappa Nu, Tau Beta Pi, Alpha Tau Omega. Presbyn. Clubs: Cosmos (Washington); Harvard (Boston); Mass. Institute Technology (N.Y.C.); Petroleum, Brook Hollow (Dallas). Home: Dorset VT 05251 Office: 310 Main St Manchester Center VT 05255

BEERS, VICTOR GILBERT, editor; b. Sidell, Ill., May 6, 1928; s. Ernest S. and Jean (Bloomer) B.; m. Arlisle Felten, Aug. 26, 1950; children: kathleen, Douglas, Ronald, Janice, Cynthia. A.B., Wheaton Coll., 1950; M.R.E., No. Baptist Sem., 1953, M.Div., 1954, Th.M., 1955, Th.D., 1960; Ph.D., Northwestern U., 1963. Prof. No. Baptist Sem., Chgo., 1954-57; editor Sr. High Publs., David C. Cook Pub. Co., Elgin, Ill., 1957-59, exec. editor, 1959-61, editorial dir., 1961-67; pres. Books for Living Inc., Elgin, 1967—; editor Christianity Today, 1982—; pres. Christianity Today Inc., 1982—. Author: A Child's Treasury of Bible Stories, 4 vols., 1970, Family Bible Library, 10 vols., 1971, The Book of Life, 23 vols., 1980. Dirs. Wheaton (Ill.) Youth Symphony, 1961-63, pres., 1962-63; trustee David C. Cook Found., Elgin, 1965-67, Wheaton Coll., 1975—, Scripture Press Inc., 1975—; bd. dirs. Christian Camps Ind., N.Y.C., 1972—. Home: Route 1 Box 321 Elgin IL 60120 Office: Christianity Today Inc 465 Gunderson Dr Carol Stream IL 60188 *True strength for sucess or adversity is the practice of the presence of God daily. In His strength I seek to carry out the responsibilities that come with success and the opportunities that come with adversity. If I succeed, I will gratefully acknowledge His presence. If I fail, I will soberly seek His wisdom and guidance.*

BEERS, WILLIAM O., food company executive; b. Lena, Ill., May 26, 1914; s. Ernest and Rosa (Binz) B.; m. Mary Elizabeth Holmes (dec.); m. Frances Lemaux Miller, Feb. 17, 1954; children: Marila M. Beers Beatty, Mary Elizabeth, Barbara Ann Beers Guzzardo, Richard W., Duncan R. Miller. Student, U. Wis., 1933-37, LL.D., 1970. With Kraft, Inc., 1937—, dir., 1965—, pres., 1968-73, chmn. bd., 1972-79; pres. Kraft Foods, 1965-68; dir. Sears Roebuck and Co., No. Telecom, Ltd., A.O. Smith Corp., Am. Airlines, U.S. Steel Corp. Past pres. Wis. Alumni. Research Found.; mem. U. Wis. Found. Mem. Bus. Council. Clubs: Links (N.Y.C.); Chicago, Old Elm (Chgo.). Office: Suite 2530 One First Nat Plaza Chicago IL 60603

BEERY, BRUCE ARNOLD, bank executive; b. Paterson., N.J., Mar. 3, 1931; m. Mary Hatcher, Oct. 2, 1954; children: Susanne, Jean, Charles. A.B., Princeton, 1952; M.B.A., Columbia, 1957. Mgr. Price Waterhouse & Co., N.Y.C., 1957-66; controller Internat. Flavors & Fragrances, Inc., N.Y.C., 1966-68, Celanese Plastics Co., Newark, 1968-70; sr. v.p., controller Crocker Nat. Bank, San Francisco, 1970-73; exec. v.p. NCNB Corp., Charlotte, N.C., 1973-82; exec. v.p., treas. Fla. Fed., St. Petersburg, 1982—. Trustee Charlotte Country Day Sch.; bd. dirs., treas. Charlotte Mint Mus. Served to 1st lt. F.A. AUS, 1952-54. Mem. Am. Inst. C.P.A.'s, Am. Bankers Assn. (task force on bank accounting principles), Fin. Execs. Inst. (trustee research found.). Episcopalian. Clubs: Olde Providence Racquet, Princeton (N.Y.); Feather Sound Country. Home: 1238 Brightwaters Blvd NE Saint Petersburg FL 33704 Office: PO Box 1509 Saint Petersburg FL 33731

BEERY, NOAH, actor; b. N.Y.C., Aug. 10, 1916; s. Noah and Marguerite B.; m. Lisa; children: Maxine, Melissa, Bucklind; 3 stepchildren. Attended, North Hollywood (Calif.) High Sch. Appeared in: movies, including The Spikes Gang, The Best Little Whorehouse in Texas, 1982; appeared on: TV series Circus Boy, 1956-58, Riverboat, Hondo, 1967, Doc Elliot, 1973-74, Rockford Files, 1974-80; appeared in: TV mini-series The Bastard, 1978; TV films Savages, 1974, Francis Gary Powers, 1976. Office: care Mishkin Agy Inc 9255 Sunset Blvd Los Angeles CA 90069

BEES, JOHN HENRY, corporation executive; b. Huntington, W.Va., Fab. 25, 1927; s. Joseph Leonard and Catherine (Farley) B.; m. Bonita Jean Nielsen, 1946; children: John Henry, Terrance J., David L. B.S. in Chem. Engring., W.Va. U., 1950, M.S., 1951. Metall. engr. Internat. Nickel Co., Huntington, 1951-52; prodn. engr. Union Carbide, Institute, W.Va., 1952-63, purchasing agt., N.Y.C., 1964-66, mgr. agrl. chems., 1966-75, pres. ethylene oxide glycol div., N.Y.C. and Danbury, Conn., 1975—. Served with U.S. Army, 1944-47. Mem. Am. Inst. Chem. Engrs., Tau Beta Pi, Phi Lambda Upsilon, Sigma Gamma Epsilon (pres. 1950), Sigma Xi (assoc). Republican. Roman Catholic. Home: 17 Fox Run Rd West Redding CT 06896 Office: Union Carbide Corp Old Ridgebury Rd M-3 Danbury CT 06817

BEESLEY, H(ORACE) BRENT, savings bank executive; b. Salt Lake City, Jan. 30, 1946; s. Horace Pratt and Mary (Brazier) B.; m. Bonnie Jean Matheson, Dec. 20, 1980; 1 day., Laura Jean. B.A., Brigham Young U., 1969; M.B.A., Harvard U., 1973, J.D., 1973. Bar: Utah 1973. Adj. prof. U. Utah, Salt Lake City, 1973-78; ptnr. Ray, Quinney & Nebeker, Salt Lake City, 1973-81; chmn. bd., chief exec. officer Pioneer Bank, Salt Lake City, 1978-81; dir. Fed. Savs. and Loan Ins. Corp., Washington, 1981-83; pres. Charter Savs. Corp., Jacksonville, Fla., 1983—; chmn. bd., chief exec. officer First Charter Savs. Bank, St. George, Utah, 1983—; dir. Bonneville, Inc., Salt Lake City, 1970—, Modern Motors, Inc., 1970—; ptnr. Alpine Hills Co., Salt Lake City, 1974—, Utah Valley Land Co., 1977—. Bd. trustees Utah Heritage Found., 1978-81, Utah Arthritis Found., 1978-81. Mem. ABA, Utah State Bar Assn. Club: Alta (Salt Lake City). Home: 1876 River Rd Jacksonville FL 32207 Office: First Charter Savs Bank One Charter Plaza Jacksonville FL 32207

BEESLEY, KENNETH HORACE, educator; b. Salt Lake City, Nov. 14, 1926; s. Alvin Douglas and Theresa (McAllister) B.; m. Donna Deem, Dec. 1, 1950; children—Kenneth Reid, Rulon Deem, Diane,

Tamara, Ellen Christine. Student, Brigham Young U., 1948-49; B.A. with honors, U. Utah, 1952; M.A., Columbia Tchrs. Coll., 1954, Ed.D., 1957. Lectr. health edn. Columbia U., 1954-55; research asso. coop. study tchr. recruitment Tchrs. Coll., 1955-56, coordinator student tours, 1956; asst. coordinator student activities Bklyn. Coll., 1955-57; mem. faculty and staff Columbia Tchrs. Coll., 1957-67, asst. provost, registrar, asst. prof. edn., 1958-66, asst. provost, asst. prof. edn., 1966-67; exec. dean, dir. instl. studies Fresno State Coll., 1967-68, exec. dean, 1968-70; assoc. commr. edn. Ch. Jesus Christ Latter-Day Saints, Salt Lake City, 1970-80; dir. gen. and adminstrv. services Welfare Services Dept., 1980-81, dir. transp. and internat. services, 1981-82; dir. internat. and adminstrv. services Materials Mgmt. Corp., 1982—; mem. Morningside Renewal Council, 1964-67; mem. coordinating council and adv. com. Fresno Interagy. Planning for Urban Edn. Needs, 1968-69; mem. Utah Adv. Council Vocat. and Tech. Edn. Trustee Eastchester (N.Y.) Library, 1961-63. Served with USNR, 1944-46. Mem. Assn. Higher Edn. Mem. Ch. Jesus Christ of Latter Day Saints (bishop Fresno 1st ward Fresno E. stake 1967-70, chmn. adminstrn. com. Sunday Sch. Gen. Bd. 1971-79, high priest group leader 1979-80, high council 1980—). Home: 1457 Wilton Way Salt Lake City UT 84108

BEESON, JACK HAMILTON, composer, educator; b. Muncie, Ind., July 15, 1921; children: Christopher Sigerist (dec.), Miranda. Ed., Eastman Sch. Music, U. Rochester, Columbia; studied with, Bela Bartok, Nora Beate Sigerist. Tchr. Juilliard; assoc. dir. opera workshop, MacDowell prof. music, former chmn. dept. Columbia.; Sec. Alice M. Ditson Fund; chmn. music publ. com. Columbia U. Press.; dir. Composers Recs., Inc. Composer: operas Lizzie Borden (commd. by Nat. Ednl. TV), Jonah, Hello Out There, The Sweet Bye and Bye, My Heart's in the Highlands (commd. by Ford Found.); opera Captain Jinks of the Horse Marines (commd. by Nat. Endowment for Arts); operas Dr. Heidegger's Fountain of Youth (commd. Nat. Arts Club); for orch. Hymns and Dances, Symphony in A, Transformations; chamber music Sonata for Viola and piano; composer: chamber work Interlude, Song, 4th and 5th Piano Sonatas, Two Diversions, Round and Round, Sonata Canonica, Old Hundredth for Organ; Composer: vocal works Six Lyrics and Five Songs; composer: Eldorado, Piazza Piece, Big Crash Out West, Indiana Homecoming, Three Love Songs, Margaret's Garden Aria, To a Sinister Potato; Composer: cycles From a Watchtower; cycle Two by Betjeman; numerous others, also works for voice and string quartet, voice and orch., choral works. Trustee Am. Acad. in Rome. Recipient Rome prize, city of Rochester prize, Marc Blitstein Mus. Theatre award Nat. Inst. Arts and Letters, gold medal for music Nat. Arts Club, 1976, Gt. Tchrs. award Columbia U., 1979; Guggenheim fellow; Fulbright fellow to Italy. Mem. Am. Acad.-Inst. of Arts and Letters (v.p.), A.S.C.A.P. Home: Seaforth Ln Lloyd Neck NY 11743 404 Riverside Dr New York NY 10025 Office: Dept of Music Columbia U New York NY 10027

BEESON, PAUL BRUCE, physician; b. Livingston, Mont., Oct. 18, 1908; s. John Bradley and Martha Gerard (Ash) B.; m. Barbara Neal, July 10, 1942; children: John, Peter, Judith. Student, U. Wash., 1925-28; M.D., C.M., McGill U., 1933, D.Sc., 1971; D.Sc., Emory U., 1968, Albany Med. Coll., 1975, Yale U., 1975, Med. Coll. Ohio, 1979. Asst. Rockefeller Inst., 1937-39, Harvard Med. Sch., 1939-40; asst. prof. medicine Emory U. Med. Sch., 1942-46, prof., chmn. dept., 1946-52; Ensign prof. medicine, chmn. dept. internal medicine Yale Med. Sch., 1952-65; physician-in-chief univ. service Grace-New Haven Community Hosp., 1952-65; Nuffield prof. clin. medicine Oxford (Eng.) U., 1965-74; prof. medicine U. Wash., Seattle, 1974-81. Named Alumnus summa laude dignatus U. Wash., 1968, hon. knight comdr. Brit. Empire, 1973; recipient 50th Anniversary Gold medal Peter Bent Brigham Hosp., 1962; Bristol award Infectious Diseases Soc. Am., 1972; Kober medal Assn. Am. Physicians, 1973; Abraham Flexner award Assn. Am. Med. Colls., 1977; fellow Berkeley Coll., Yale, Magdalen Coll. (hon.), Green Coll. (hon.), Oxford U. Fellow Royal Coll. Physicians (London), Royal Soc. Medicine (hon.); mem. Nat. Acad. Scis., Am. Acad. Arts and Scis., A.C.P. (master, John Phillips Meml. award 1976), Soc. Exptl. Biology and Medicine, Am. Soc. Clin. Investigation, Assn. Am. Physicians (pres. 1967), Assn. Physicians Gt. Britain and Ireland. Episcopalian. Home: 8262 Avondale Rd NE Redmond WA 98052

BEETON, ALFRED MERLE, limnologist, educator; b. Denver, Aug. 15, 1927; s. Charles Frederick and Edna F. (Smith) B.; m. Mary Eileen Wilcox, July 20, 1945; children—Maureen Ann, Heather Ann, Celeste Nadine; m. Ruth Elizabeth Holland, June 4, 1966; children—Jonathan Eugene, Daniel Paul. B.S., U. Mich., 1952, M.S., 1954, Ph.D., 1958. Fishery biologist U.S. Bur. Comml. Fisheries, Ann Arbor, Mich., 1957-65, chief environ. research, 1960-65; prof. zoology U. Wis.-Milw., 1965-76, asst. dir., 1965-69, assoc. dir., 1969-73, assoc. dean, 1973-76; dir. Gt. Lakes and Marine Waters Center; prof. U. Mich., Ann Arbor, 1976—; lectr. biology Wayne State U., 1957-61; lectr. civil engring. U. Mich., 1961-65; mem. research adv. council Wis. Dept. Natural Resources; mem. water quality criteria com. Nat. Acad. Scis.; cons. U.S. Army C.E., 1967-73, Met. San. Dist. Chgo., 1968-76, EPA, 1973-83; adviser to Smithsonian Instn. on projects in, Ghana, Laos, Yugoslavia, 1972-82; to WHO/Pan Am. Health Orgn. in, Venezuela, 1978; mem. environ. studies bd. NRC, 1976-82, internat. environ. program com., 1977-82. Contbr. chpts. to books; articles Ency. Brit. Mem. Internat. Assn. Theoretical and Applied Limnology, Am. Soc. Limnology and Oceanography (treas. 1962-81), Am. Soc. Zoologists, Internat. Assn. Gt. Lakes Research, Sigma Xi. Home: 2761 Oakcleft St Ann Arbor MI 48103 Office: U Mich Ann Arbor MI 48109

BEETS, FREEMAN HALEY, government official; b. Chickasha, Okla., Apr. 17, 1919; s. Daniel Walter and Ida Belle (Alverson) B.; m. Margaret Elizabeth Edwards, Dec. 25, 1941; 1 dau., Susan Belle. B.A. in Journalism, U. Okla., 1946, M.A., 1948, Ed.D., 1954; LL.D., Drury Coll., Springfield, Mo., 1974. Instr. journalism Okla. Bapt. U., 1948, asst. prof. journalism and bus., 1950, dir. night sch., chmn. div. applied arts and sci., 1951-53; asst. exec. sec. edn. commn. So. Bapt. Conv., Nashville, 1953-55; dir. admissions, registrar Hardin-Simmons U., 1955-56; asst. to pres., prof. journalism U. Scis. and Arts Okla., 1956-58, pres., 1958-61; regional rep. div. coll. and unvi. assistance U.S. Office of Edn., 1961-66, regional asst. commr. edn., Kansas City, Mo., 1966-70; dir. div. ednl. sers. U.S. Office Edn., Kansas City, Mo., 1970-80; dep. regional rep. Office of Sec., U.S. Dept. Edn., Kansas City, Mo., 1980—. Served as 1st lt. AUS, 1941-45. Decorated Bronze Star, Purple Heart. Home: 7900 Roe Ave Shawnee Mission KS 66208 Office: Fed Office Bldg 324 E 11th St Kansas City MO 64106

BEETZ, JEAN, Canadian justice; b. Montreal, Que., Mar. 27, 1927; s. Jean and Jeanne (Cousineau) B. B.A., U. Montreal, 1947, LL.L., 1950, LL.D. (hon.), 1977; B.A., Honor Sch. Jurisprudence, Oxford (Eng.) U., 1953, M.A., 1958; LL.D. (hon.), U. Ottawa, 1975, York U., 1983, D.C.L., Windsor U., 1978. Bar: Called to Que. bar 1950. Practiced in, Montreal, 1950-51; mem. faculty U. Montreal Faculty Law, 1953-73, prof. Constl. law, 1966-73, dean, 1968-70; spl. counsel on constl. matters to prime minister Can., 1968-71; justice Que. Ct. Appeals, 1973-74; puisne judge Supreme Ct. Can., 1974—. Contbr. to legal publns. Rhodes scholar, 1951; hon. fellow Pembroke Coll., Oxford U. Fellow Royal Soc. Can. Home: 271 Bal Cross Dr Bal Harbour FL 33154

BEFU, YOSHIRO, landscape architect; b. Santa Maria, Calif., Aug. 2, 1921; s. Juma and Komaki (Shimizu) B.; m. Yasuko Kay Kinoshita, Apr. 19, 1952; children: Jonathan Ken, David Tadao. B.S., Mass. State Coll., 1946; B.Landscape Arch., U. Mass., 1947. Lic. landscape architect, Calif. Landscape drafter Los Angeles County Dept. Parks and Recreation, 1949-50; asst. landscape architect Los Angeles Dept. Recreation and Parks, 1950-52; assoc. landscape architect Calif. Div. Architecture, 1952-55; prin., pres. Peterson and Befu, Inc., Pasadena, Calif., 1955—. Bd. dirs. Pasadena Beautiful Found., 1972-78, pres., 1977-78. Fellow Am. Soc. Landscape Architects (trustee 1972-78); mem. Calif. Council Landscape Architects (treas. 1970, v.p. 1976, Profl. Service award 1982). Democrat. Office: Peterson and Befu Inc 663 N Los Robles Ave Pasadena CA 91101 *

BEG, MIRZA ABDUL BAQI, theoretical physicist; b. Etawah, India, Sept. 20, 1934; came to U.S., 1966; s. Mirza Abdul Hai and Sarah (Khan) B.; m. Nancie Stager Kress, Nov. 7, 1958. B.Sc. with honours; D.J.S., Govt. Sci. Coll., Karachi, Pakistan, 1951; M.Sc., Karachi U., 1954; Ph.D., U. Pitts., 1958. Research fellow U. Birmingham, Eng., 1958-60; research asso. Brookhaven Nat. Lab., 1960-62, cons., 1965—; mem. Inst. Advanced Study, Princeton, 1962-64; mem. faculty Rockefeller U., 1964—, prof. physics, 1968—; vis. positions at U. Calif., Berkeley, Argonne Nat. Lab., Niels Bohr Inst., U. Wash., Scuola Normale Superiore, Pisa, Italy, Stanford; sr. vis. scientist European Center for Nuclear Research, Geneva, Switzerland, 1972. Contbr. articles to profl. jours. Fellow Am. Phys. Soc., N.Y. Acad. Scis. Home: 444 E 82d St New York NY 10028 Office: Rockefeller U 1230 York Ave New York NY 10021

BEGAM, ROBERT GEORGE, lawyer; b. N.Y.C., Apr. 5, 1928; s. George and Hilda M. (Hirt) B.; m. Helen C. Clark, July 24, 1949; children—Richard, Lorinda, Michael. B.A., Yale U., 1949, LL.B., 1952. Bar: N.Y. bar 1952, Ariz. bar 1956. Asso. firm Cravath, Swaine & Moore, N.Y.C., 1952-54; spl. counsel State of Ariz., Colorado River Litigation in U.S. Supreme Ct., 1956-58; partner firm Langerman, Begam, Lewis & Marks, Phoenix, 1958—. Pres. Ariz. Repertory Theater, 1960-66; treas. Ariz. Democratic Party, 1964-70, chief counsel, 1970-76; bd. dirs. Phoenix Theater Center, 1955-60; chmn. Attys. Congl. Campaign Trust, 1979—; trustee Atla Roscoe Pound Found. Served as 1st lt. USAF, 1954-56. Fellow Internat. Soc. Barristers; mem. Assn. Trial Lawyers Am. (pres. 1976-77), Western Trial Lawyers Assn. (pres. 1970), Am. Bd. Trial Advocates. Clubs: Yale (N.Y.C.); Ariz. Biltmore Country (Phoenix); Palmetto Dunes Country (Hilton Head, S.C.). Home: 77 E Missouri No 12 Phoenix AZ 85012 Office: 1400 Ariz Title Bldg Phoenix AZ 85003

BEGANDO, JOSEPH SHERIDAN, former university chancellor, educator; b. Roseland, Kans., Jan. 7, 1921; s. James and Bessie (Barcus) B.; m. Virginia DeVillo Suttee, Aug. 6, 1943; children: DeVillo J. (Mrs. Bill C. Janecek), Dana Ann (Mrs. Neal Dawson), Darcy V. B.S., Pittsburg (Kans.) State U., 1942; M.S., U. Ill., 1947, Ph.D., 1951. Asst. in mktg. U. Ill., 1946-47, instr., 1948-51; instr. commerce Pittsburg State U., 1947-48, asst. prof. econs., summer 1951; asst. prof. mktg. U. Kans., 1951-53; asst. dean, asso. prof. pharmacy adminstrn. U. Ill. Med Center, Chgo., 1953-58, asst. to pres., 1958-61, v.p. U., 1961-66, chancellor, 1966-83, chancellor emeritus, 1983—, prof. health resources mgmt. Sch. Pub. Health, 1982—. Served to lt. (s.g.) USCG, 1942-45. Recipient Meritorious Achievement award Pittsburg State U., 1959, Disting. Service award U. Ill. Alumni Assn., 1983. Mem. Inst. Medicine Chgo., Nat., Ill. leagues nursing, Assn. Acad. Health Centers (pres. 1976-77), Assn. Am. Med. Colls., Pi Omega Pi, Beta Gamma Sigma, Alpha Kappa Psi, Rho Chi, Delta Kappa Sigma, Phi Delta Chi. Clubs: Univ., City, Execs. (Chgo.). Home: 842 Washington St Elmhurst IL 60126 Office: PO Box 6998 Chicago IL 60680

BEGELL, WILLIAM, publisher; b. Wilno, Poland, May 18, 1928; came to U.S., 1947, naturalized, 1953; s. Ferdin and Liza (Kowarski) Beigel; m. Esther Kessler, May 27, 1948; children: Frederick Paul, Alissa Maya. B.Ch.E., Coll. City N.Y., 1953; M.Ch.E., Poly. Inst. Bklyn., 1958; postgrad., Columbia U., 1958-59. Engring. mgr. heat transfer research facility dept. chem. engring. Columbia U., 1953-59; co-founder, exec. v.p. Scripta Technica, Inc., Washington, 1959-74; founder, pres. Hemisphere Publishing Corp., Washington, 1974—; lectr. pub. George Washington U., Washington, also N.Y. U.; cons. Heat Transfer Research Lab., Columbia U.; cons. in field. Editor 7 books; contbr. numerous articles in field of heat transfer to profl. jours. Mem. nat. adv. bd. Center for the Book, Library of Congress; chmn. exec. council Profl. and Scholarly Pubs. Mem. AAAS, Am. Inst. Chem. Engrs., Am. Soc. for Engring. Edn., ASME (policy bd.), Assn. Am. Publishers (dir.), N.Y. Acad. Scis. (publs. bd.), Internat. Centre for Heat and Mass Transfer, Washington Book Publishers (founder), Am. Assn. Engring. Socs. Jewish. Patentee in field. Home: 46 E 91st St New York NY 10028 Office: 1010 Vermont Ave NW Washington DC 20005 also 79 Madison Ave New York NY 10016

BEGG, JOHN MURRAY, real estate investment executive; b. San Jose, Costa Rica, Jan. 5, 1903; s. John William and Blanche Eugenie (Bowns) B.; m. Jeanne Frederique van den Bosch, June 27, 1940. Student, Clifton (Eng.) Coll., 1916-19; A.B., Harvard, 1924; B.A., Magdalen Coll., Oxford, Eng., 1925; M.A., Oxford (Eng.) U., 1965. Pub. relations writer Internat. Tel. & Tel. Co., 1926-27; producer ednl. films, Calif., 1927-28; asst. editor and Far Eastern dir. Fox Movietone News, 1928-30; editor Newsreel Theatres, Radio News and Newsreels, Pathe, 1930-36; v.p. Motion Picture Merchandising Corp., 1936-40; asst. to pres. Phillips Lord, Inc. (radio program producers), 1940-41; with Dept. State, 1941-53, asst. chief cultural relations, 1941, acting chief motion picture and radio div., 1944, chief internat. information div., 1944-46, chief internat. motion pictures div., 1946; alternate U.S. rep. subcom. on edn. Com. for Strengthening Democratic Processes, Far Eastern Commn., 1946; cons. U.S. Delegation, London Preparatory Commn. UNESCO, 1946; asst. dir. (media) Office Internat. Info. and Cultural Affairs, 1947, dir. pvt. enterprise coop. staff internat. inform. adminstrn., 1948-53; vice chmn. U.S. Delegation to Internat. High Frequency Broadcasting Conf., Atlantic City, N.J., 1947; spl. asst. to U.S. ambassador to The Netherlands, 1949; dep. examiner Bd. Examiners for Fgn. Service, 1952-53; dep. dir. Office Pvt. Coop. USIA, 1953-60; pres. Islands Investment Corp. (Realtors), Washington, 1960-76, Begg Disher Assos. Inc., 1966-71; v.p. Begg Internat. Inc. (Realtors), 1973—. Recipient Merit citation Nat. Civil Service League, 1956; Superior Service award USIA, 1956; Wisdom award of honor Wisdom Soc. Mem. U.S. Fgn. Service Assn., Washington, V.I., Nat., Internat. real estate bds., Nat. Steeplechase and Hunt Assn. (sr.). Episcopalian. Clubs: Harvard (N.Y.C.); Metropolitan (Washington); Costa Smeralda Yacht (Sardinia, Italy); Gibson Island (Md.); Marlborough Hunt (Upper Marlboro, Md.); Sprat Bay (V.I.). Home: Roedown Farm 3856 Wayson Rd Davidsonville MD 21035 Office: 2121 Wisconsin Ave NW Washington DC 20007

BEGGS, DONALD LEE, university dean; b. Harrisburg, Ill., Sept. 16, 1941; s. C. J. and Mary (Fitzgerald) B.; m. Shirley Malone, Mar. 19, 1963; children: Brent A., Pamela A. B.S. in Edn., So. Ill. U., 1963, M.S., 1964; Ph.D., U. Iowa, 1966. Prof. So. Ill. U., Carbondale, 1966—, assoc. dean grad. sch., 1970-71, asst. dean edn., 1973-75, acting asst. v.p. acad. affairs, 1975-76, assoc. dean edn., 1975-81, dean Coll. Edn., 1981—; cons. Quincy Pub. Schs., Ill., 1974-79, Chgo. Pub. Schs., 1977-80, Ill. State Bd. Edn., 1966—, Nat. Inst. Edn., Washington, 1983. Author: Measurement and Evaluation in the Schools, Evaluation and Decision Making in the Schools, 1971, Research Design in the Behavioral Sciences, 1969, Nat. Standardized Tests, 1980. Mgr. sports, Carbondale, 1979; active United Way Campaign, 1978, Carbondale Schs. PTA, 1972-83. Named Outstanding Tchr. in Edn. Coll. Edn., 1969; Ill. State Bd. Edn. grantee, 1979; Ill. Supt. Pub. Instrn. grantee, 1968; U.S. Office Edn. grantee, 1969. Mem. Am. Edn. Research Assn. (sec. div. D. 1976-79), Ill. Pub. Sch. Deans of Edn. (chmn. 1982-83), Research and Evaluation Adv. Council Ill. Office Edn. (chmn. 1982-83), Phi Delta Kappa (named one of 75 Young Leaders 1981). Office: So Ill U Carbondale IL 62901

BEGGS, JAMES MONTGOMERY, government official; b. Pitts., Jan. 9, 1926; s. James Andrew and Elizabeth (Mikulan) B.; m. Mary Elizabeth Harrison, Oct. 3, 1953; children—Maureen Elizabeth, Kathleen Louise, Teresa Lynn, James Harrison, Charles Montgomery. Student, So. Meth. U., 1942-44; B.S. in Engring, U.S. Naval Acad., 1948; M.B.A., Harvard U., 1955; LL.D. (hon.), Washington and Jefferson Coll., 1972; Dr. Engr. Mgmt., Embry-Ripple U., 1972; LL.D. (hon.), Salem Coll.; D.Engring., U. Ala.; LL.D., Maryville Coll. Commd. ensign U.S. Navy, 1947, advanced through grades to lt. comdr., 1954; resigned, 1954; various mgmt. positions Westinghouse Electric Corp., 1955-68, v.p. Def. and Space Center, 1968; asso. adminstr. advanced research and tech. NASA, 1968-69; undersec. Dept. Transp., 1969-73; mng. dir. Summa Corp., Los Angeles, 1973-74; exec. v.p., dir. Gen. Dynamics Corp., St. Louis, 1974-81; adminstr. NASA, Washington, 1981—; dir. ConRail, Phila., EMC, Inc., Cockeysville, Md. Vice chmn. bd. Howard County (Md.) Charter Bd., 1966-67. Mem. Md. Bd. Natural Resources, 1966-67. Mem. Nat. Acad. Pub. Adminstrn., Am. Soc. Pub. Adminstrn., AIAA, Am. Soc. Naval Engrs. Clubs: Burning Treel (Bethesda Md.); Met. (Washington); St. Louis, Bellerive Country (St. Louis). Office: NASA 400 Maryland Ave SW Washington DC 20546

BEGHE, RENATO, lawyer; b. Chgo., Mar. 12, 1933; s. Bruno and Emmavve (Frymire) B.; m. Bina House, July 10, 1954; children: Eliza Ashley, Francesca Forbes, Adam House, Jason Deneen. B.A., U. Chgo., 1951, J.D., 1954. Bar: N.Y. bar 1955. Mng. editor U. Chgo. Law Review, 1953-54; since practiced in, N.Y.C.; assoc. Carter, Ledyard & Milburn, 1954-65, ptnr., 1965-83, Morgan, Lewis & Bockius, 1973—; lectr. N.Y. U. Fed. Tax Inst., 1967, 78, U. Chgo. Fed. Tax Conf., 1974, 80, also other confs. Contbr. articles to profl. jours. Mem. ABA, Am. Law Inst., Internat. Bar Assn., Internat. Fiscal Assn., N.Y. State Bar Assn. (chmn. tax sect. 1977-78), Am. Coll. Tax Counsel, Assn. Bar City N.Y. (chmn. art law com. 1980-83), Phi Beta Kappa, Order of Coif, Phi Gamma Delta. Clubs: Wall St. (N.Y.C.); Lakeside Golf (N.Y.); America-Italy Society Inc. (dir 1980—). Home: 300 West End Ave New York NY 10023 Office: 101 Park Ave New York NY 10178

BEGHINI, VICTOR GENE, oil company executive; b. Greensboro, Pa., Oct. 24, 1934; s. Peter Victor and Beatrice Katherine (Minor) B.; m. Anna Mae Wancheck, July 7, 1956. B.S. in Petroleum Engring., Pa. State U., 1956; postgrad. in mgmt. devel., Harvard Bus. Sch., 1974. Registered profl. engr., La. With Marathon Oil Co., various locations, 1956-73, mgr. corp. risk, Findlay, Ohio, 1973-75, mgr. prodn. ops., Cody, Wyo., 1975-77, coordinating mgr. prodn. ops., Findlay, 1977-78, v.p. supply and transp., 1978-82, Marathon Petroleum Co., 1982-83, pres., 1984—, dir., 1982—; dir. Marathon Oil Co., Findlay, 1978—. Trustee Ohio No. U., Ada, 1981—; mem. bus. adv. com. Northwestern U. Transp. Ctr., 1982—. Recipient Chauncey Rose award Rose Poly. Inst., Terre Haute, Ind., 1981. Mem. Soc. Petroleum Engrs., Am. Petroleum Inst., Mid Continent Oil and Gas Assn. Republican. Roman Catholic. Club: Elks. Office: Marathon Petroleum Co 539 Main St Findlay OH 45840

BÉGIN, MONIQUE, Canadian legislator; b. Rome, Italy, Mar. 1, 1936; d. Lucien and Maria Ludovica (Van Havre) Begin (parents Canadian citizens). M.A. in Sociology, U. Montreal; postgrad., U. Paris, McGill U., Montreal; Ph.D. in Law (hon.), St. Thomas U., N.B., 1976. Exec. sec. Royal Commn. Status of Women; adminstrv. research br. CRTC; mem. Ho. of Commons for Montreal-St.-Michel, 1972-79, Ho. of Commons for St. Leonard-Anjou, 1979—; minister nat. revenue, 1976-77, minister nat. health and welfare, 1977-79, 83; del. Commonwealth Conf., 1973, UN Gen. Assembly; head Canadian del. Colombo Plan. Co-chmn. nat. conv. Liberal Party, 1973; v.p. Nat. Liberal Caucus, 1975—; founding mem. Fedn. Que. Women; bd. dirs. Canadian Human Rights Fedn. Address: 5167 est Rue Jean-Talon Suite 330 Montreal PQ H1S 1K8 Canada *

BEGLARIAN, GRANT, composer, foundation executive; b. Tiflis, Georgia, USSR, Dec. 1, 1927; came to U.S., 1947, naturalized, 1954; s. Boghos and Arax (Boghosian) B.; m. Joyce Heeney, Sept. 2, 1950; children: Eve, Spencer. B.M., U. Mich., 1950, M.Mus., 1952, D.M.A.; univ. Regents creative arts fellow, 1958. Ford Found. composer in residence Cleveland Heights (Ohio) Schs., 1959-60; editor Prentice Hall Inc., 1960-61; pres. Music Book Assocs., N.Y.C.; also field rep. and project dir. Ford Found., 1961-68; dean, prof. music Sch. Performing Arts, U. So. Calif., 1969-82; pres. Nat. Found. for Advancement of Arts, 1982—; lectr. and cons. in arts, edn.; adv. for arts in state and nat., public and pvt. sectors; mem. Yale U. Music Council, 1974-76; mem. Princeton U. Music Adv. Council; mem. panel Inst. Internat. Edn., Nat. Endowment for Arts. Compositions include String Quartet, 1947, Violin Sonata, 1949, Cello Sonata, 1952, Divertimento for Orchestra, 1957, Nurse's Song; for chorus and orch., 1960, Sinfonia for Orch, 1961, A Hymn for Our Times; for multiple bands, 1967, Fables... for Cellist and Actor, 1971, Diversions, 1973, Sinfonia for Strings, 1974, To Manitou!, 1976, Elegy for Cellist, 1979. Served with U.S. Army, 1952-54. Recipient Gershwin award Meml. Found., 1959; Ford Found. grantee, 1959, 62, 68. Mem. ASCAP (ann. award 1965—), Internat. Council Fine Arts Deans (pres. 1980-82), Am. Music Center, Coll. Music Soc., Nat. Ad Hoc Forum of Film/ Video Schs., Arts Edn. Consultancy in U.S., Gt. Britain, USSR, Israel, Mex., Japan, Iran. Mem. Armenian Apostolic Ch. Office: National Foundation for Advancement Arts 100 N Biscayne Blvd Miami FL 33132 *As a composer and teacher I am convinced that artists inform, instruct, change, improve and affect society through their work. Art is a product of a person's craft, genius and dreams. It is essentially a private activity. The marvel of art is that this private vision has an enduring public impact.*

BEGLEITER, ALVIN LEON, bank exec.; b. N.Y.C., June 6, 1933; s. Sidney and Sally (Goldberg) B.; m. Muriel Kaplowitz, May 15, 1960; children—Steven, David. B.S., N.Y. U., 1955. C.P.A., N.Y. Accountant Coopers & Lybrand, 1955-56, 58-62; accountant Westvaco Corp., 1962-64; with Irving Trust Co., N.Y.C., 1964—, sr. v.p., comptroller, 1976—. Served with U.S. Army, 1956-58. Mem. Am. Inst. C.P.A.'s, N.Y. State Soc. C.P.A.'s, Lambda Gamma Phi. Office: 1 Wall St New York NY 10015

BEGLEY, MICHAEL J., bishop; b. Mass., Mar. 12, 1909; s. Dennis J. and Anna (Monaham) B. Ed., St. Mary Sem., Emmitsburg, Md. Ordained priest Roman Catholic Ch., 1934; ordained first bishop of, Charlotte, N.C., 1972—. Office: PO Box 3776 Charlotte NC 28203 *

BEGOVICH, NICHOLAS ANTHONY, electrical engineer, consultant; b. Oakland, Calif., Nov. 29, 1921; s. Dinko and Anna (Juka) B.; m. Joan Munson Deopker, Apr. 14, 1944. B.S. in Elec. Engring, Calif. Inst. Tech., 1943, M.S., 1944, Ph.D. (Francis J. Cole scholar 1946), 1948. Research physicist, staff cons., lab mgr., dir. engring. Hughes Aircraft Co., Culver City, Calif., 1948-61, corporate v.p., 1961, asst. group exec. ground systems group, 1961-67, group exec., 1967-70; corporate v.p., pres. Data Systems div. Litton Industries, Van Nuys, Calif., 1970-74; mgmt. cons., 1975—; cons. Applied Physics Lab., Johns Hopkins U., 1976—; Cons. weapons system evaluation group Dept. Def., 1952-57; mem. U.S. Army Sci. Bd., 1983—; spl. work devel. electronic-scan radar, free world air def., command and control systems. Fellow IEEE; mem. Am. Phys. Soc., Ops. Research Soc. Am., Sigma Xi. Home: 136 Miramonte Dr Fullerton CA 92635

BEGUIN, FRED PAUL, environmental acoustics engineer; b. Brussels, Oct. 13, 1909; U.S., 1948, naturalized, 1956; s. Florent C. and Maria (Tuerlinckx) B.; m. Sophie Koubekova, Nov. 6, 1934; 1 dau., Natalie. B.S. in Electronics Navigation, Tech. State Coll., Brussels, 1931; M.S. in Physics, Nat. Radioelectronics Inst., Brussels, 1944; postgrad., Syracuse U., 1941; grad., Profl. Bus. Mgmt. Inst., Gen. Electric Co., 1958; cert. in noise control engring. and audiometry, Colby Coll., 1971. Project and patent engr. compagnie Francaise Thomson-CSF, Paris, 1931-34; Tonmeister engr. Philips Rec. Studios, Eindhoven, Holland, 1934-37; TV and acoustics research physicist Philips Phys. Labs. and tech. dir. Philips Europe Internat. TV Ops., 1937-44; chmn. faculty electroacoustics Nat. Radioelectronics Inst. Belgium, 1944-46; tech. dir. Decca Records of Belgium and France, 1944-46; tech. dir. in Benelux countries for Motorola, Acme Electric, Internat. Harvester, 1946-50; project research and devel. engr. electronics div. Gen. Electric Co., Syracuse, N.Y., 1950-54; audio-cons. with Gen. Electric Co., advanced products devel. for architects and sound equipment mfrs., 1954-59; dir. electroacoustics research and devel. Am. Optical Corp., Southbridge, Mass., 1959-72; dir. Hearing Conservation and Noise Control Center, Harrington Meml. Hosp., Southbridge, Mass., 1972-77; environ. acoustics scientist, Port Charlotte, fla., 1983—; govt. expert in productivity, 1946-54; cons. Mut. Security Adminstrn. tech assistance programs, 1951-52; voting mem., safety industry rep. bioacoustics and noise com. Am. Nat. Standards Inst., 1968-75. Patentee (in field 11). Recipient U.S. Presdl., 1981. Fellow Audio Engring. Soc. (Nat. Sic. Achievement 1970); emeritus mem. N.Y. Acad. Scis.; mem. IEEE (sr. mem., vice chmn. electroacoustics com., life), Am. Inst. Physics, Acoutical Soc. Am., Nat. Soc. Profl. Engrs. (P.E.C., life mem.), Indsl. Safety Equipment Assn. (hon.). Home: 1267 Paxton Terr NE Port Charlotte FL 33652 *Success in my career was the result of decisions made in high school: 1. keep courious about everything happening around me, how things are made, working, costing selling, why, when, by whom on a world-wide basis; 2. do not copy successful ideas or products just for the sake of profit. Many were invented long ago; i.e. do not reinvent the wheel but be original! 3. Do not stay in any job longer than 4 to 8 years, you will rust in and bore. Take new challenges by studying them in advanced an attach more importance to your adaptability in new environments and working methods. Act as if you worked for fun, not for money. Money will follow optimists who dare. 4. do not work too long until health degenerates. Have fun before it is too late! Remember: your wealth will go to hospitals, doctors and tax collectors anyway. Keep in mind the real value of time!*

BEHA, JAMES JOSEPH, lawyer; b. N.Y.C., Oct. 15, 1916; s. James A. and Katharine E. (McMorrough) B.; m. Macy Ann Reilly, Aug. 14, 1948; children—James A. II, Ann Macy. A.B., Williams Coll., 1937; LL.B., Harvard U., 1940. Bar: N.Y. bar 1941. Since practiced in, N.Y.C.; mem. firm Gasser & Hayes, 1949—; pres. Capital Investment Corp. Montreal Ltd., Que., Can.; dir. Stuart-Dean, Inc., Bessemer Trust Co. N.A., N.Y.C. Trustee N.Y. U. Med. Center, Mt. St. Mary Coll., Newburgh, N.Y., N.Y. Hist. Soc. Mem. Am., N.Y. State bar assns., N.Y. County Lawyers Assn. Home: 43 Island Dr Rye NY 10580 Office: 100 Park Ave New York NY 10017

BEHAN, FRANK SOULE, food service company executive; b. Hartford, Conn., Dec. 15, 1933; s. Lewis Wyant and Helen Diane (Soule) B.; m. Helen VanValkenburg, May 24, 1952 (div. 1976); children: Alan, Geraldine, Randall, Nancy; m. Susan Alice Green, Nov.27, 1976; 1 son, Scott. Student exec. bus. program, U. So. Calif., Los Angeles, 1980. Asst. mgr. McDonalds Corp., Boston, 1961-62, mgr., 1962-65, area supr. East Coast, 1965-67, dir. ops., 1967-69, regional mgr., 1969-75, zone mgr., sr. v.p., Bloomfield, Conn., 1975—, bus. cons. to Australia, Oak Brook, Ill., 1978-82. Served with USAF, 1951-55. Republican. Home: 20 Windham Dr Simsbury CT 06070 Office: McDonalds Corp 705 Bloomfield Ave Bloomfield CT 06002

BEHARRIELL, FREDERICK JOHN, educator; b. Toronto, Ont., Can., June 5, 1918; came to U.S., 1946, naturalized, 1958; s. Frederick Roy and Anna Beatrice (Moffatt) B.; m. Barbara Jean McBroom, June 16, 1942; children—Ruth, Shirley. B.A. with honors, U. Toronto, 1939, M.A., 1946; Ph.D., U. Wis., 1950. Lectr. U. Toronto, 1945-46; instr. Ind. U., Bloomington, 1948-53, asst. prof. German, 1953-58, asso. prof., 1958-64, prof., 1964-69; prof. German and comparative lit. SUNY, Albany, 1968—. Contbr. articles to books and profl. jours. Served with RCAF, 1942-45. Guggenheim fellow, 1965; Fulbright sr. research fellow, 1965; fellow Inst. Humanistic Studies, 1977—. Mem. MLA, AAUP, Am. Assn. Tchrs. German, Nat. Assn. Psychoanalytic Criticism, Internat. Arthur Schnitzler Research Assn., Am. Comparative Lit. Assn., Am. Assn. Advancement Humanities, Am. Com. Study of Austrian Lit., Am. Goethe Soc. Home: 1969 Village Rd Schenectady NY 12309 Office: 1400 Washington Ave Albany NY 12222

BEHL, WOLFGANG, sculptor, educator; b. Berlin, Germany, Apr. 13, 1918; came to U.S., 1939, naturalized, 1947; s. C.F.W. and Ellida (Schmidt) B.; m. Lula Marie Brock, June 20, 1948; 1 dau., Elizabeth. Student, Acad. Fine Arts, Berlin, 1936-39, R.I. Sch. Design, 1939-40. Mem. faculty Richmond Profl. Inst., Coll. William and Mary, 1945-53; prof. Hartford Art Sch., U. Hartford, Conn., 1955—; Bd. dirs. Sculptors Guild, N.Y.C.; mem. adv. bd. Internat. Sculptors Conf., Washington. Exhibited in one-man shows at, Bertha Schaefer Gallery, 1950, 55, 63, 68, 73, New Britain Mus. Am. Art, 1969, Rosenfeld Gallery, Phila., 1979, others; exhibited in group shows at, Plastics U.S.A.-USSR, 1960, Carnegie Inst., 1964, Pa. Acad., Fogg Mus., 1966; represented in museum and pvt. collections; Represented in: book Masters of Wood Sculpture, 1980. Nat. Inst. Arts and Letters grantee, 1963.

BEHLEN, HERBERT PETER, retired manufacturing company executive; b. Columbus, Nebr., Oct. 15, 1909; s. Frederick Arthur and Ella Sarah (Benthack) B.; m. Ethel Minnie Russell, Apr. 13, 1940 (dec. Aug. 1946); 1 dau., Donna Lee (Mrs Kenneth Kalkowski); stepchildren: James William, Karen Jean (Mrs. David Senften); m. Lois Viola Hickey, Jan. 24, 1948; 1 son, Frederick Michael. Student, U. Nebr., 1934-35. Co-founder Behlen Mfg. Co., Columbus, 1936; former dir., pres.; pres. G.M.W. Corp., Columbus, 1977—; past pres. Behlen-Wickes Co. Ltd., Brandon, Man., Can.; pres. Columbus Conv. Center, 1972—; dir. Industries Nebr. Pres. bd. Columbus YMCA, 1960; past dir. adv. bd. St. Mary's Hosp., 1961; past trustee Platte Coll. Found., Columbus, Nebr.; past bd. dirs. Doane Coll., Crete, Nebr. Served with USAAF, World War II. Recipient Legion of Merit award Sec. War for design of aircraft tng. aids, 1945; Nebr. Builder citation U. Nebr., 1977. Mem. Columbus C. of C. (past pres.), Am. Legion, Mo. Valley Orchid Soc. (past pres.). Republican. Conglist. Club: Elks Country. Home: 1967 E Camino Real Columbus NE 68601 *"Get maximum exposure to good luck." There are three main requirements for success: A little better than average judgment, a lot of hard work and luck. Number three is the will-o'-the-wisp. She may evade you once or ten times—but continue to court her. Of course, if you lack either of the first two, you're betting on a spavined horse*

BEHLEN, WALTER DIETRICH, metal products mfg. co. exec.; b. Columbus, Nebr., Oct. 16, 1905; s. Fred Arthur and Ella (Benthack) B.; m. Ruby Mae Cumming, 1940; children—Mary Ann (Mrs. Roman Hruska), Kent Walter. Student pub. schs., Columbus; D.Engring. (hon.), U. Nebr., 1959; Sc.D., Midland Coll., 1959; L.H.D., Doane Coll., 1973. Asso. Ry. Express Agy., Columbus, 1925-41; founder, pres. Behlen Mfg. Co., Columbus, 1935-63, chmn. bd., 1963-69; past dir. Columbus Savs. & Loan Assn., First Nat. Bank of Columbus, The Wickes Corp., San Diego, Loup River Public Power Dist., Asso. Industries Neb., Nebr. Indsl. Research Inst.; lectr. on bus. and sci. subjects. Author: Walt Behlen's Universe, 1973. Mem. Nat. UN Day Com., 1968; Trustee U. Nebr. Found., Nebr. Independent Coll. Found., 1959—; bd. dirs. Columbus Conv. Center. Recipient Horatio Alger award, 1968; honoree Nebr. dinner Newcomen Soc. N. Am., 1968; inducted into Metal Building Systems Hall of Fame, 1980. Mem. Columbus Community Concert Assn. (past pres.), Columbus YMCA (dir., past pres.), Mississippi Valley Assn. (past v.p. Nebr.-Iowa div.), Columbus C. of C. (past dir.), Metal Bldg. Mfrs. Assn. (dir. 1956-66), U.S. C. of C. (mem. mfr. and indsl. devel. com. 1957-69), N.A.M. (nuclear energy com.). Clubs: Rotary, Elk, Wayside Country. Patentee hydraulic presses; inventions relating to stressed skin structures, various agrl. machines and equipment. Home: 2555 Pershing Rd Columbus NE 68601 *Experience has convinced me that the most selfish policy in business is complete honesty; it pays the most in the end. And the most selfish way to live is to do what we can for others; it brings us the greatest pleasure of all. The most effective mind is not hampered by existing opinions, beliefs, or theories.*

BEHLER, ERNST HEITMAR, educator; b. Essen, West Germany, Sept. 4, 1928; came to U.S., 1963, naturalized, 1976; s. Philip and Elisabeth (Lammerskoetter) B.; m. Diana Elizabeth Ipsen, Nov. 24, 1967; children—Constantine, Sophia, Caroline. Ph.D., U. Munich, Germany, 1951; postgrad., Sorbonne, Paris, France, 1951-53; Habilitation, U. Bonn, Germany, 1961. Asst. prof. philosophy U. Bonn, 1961-63; prof. Germanics and comparative lit. Washington U., St. Louis, 1963-65; prof. U. Wash., 1965—, chmn. humanities council, 1972-78, chmn. dept. comparative lit., dir. program humanities, 1975—; hon. prof. U. B.C., Can., Vancouver, 1968-73. Author: Die Ewigkeit der Welt, 1965, Friedrich Schlegel, 1968, Japanese transl., 1974, Klassische Ironie, Romantische Ironie, Tragische Ironie, 1972; Editor: Critical Edit. of Friedrich Schlegel, 35 vols, 1958—; Contbr. numerous articles on romantic movement, history of Aristotelianism during Middle Ages, and on lit. criticism to profl. jours. Guggenheim fellow, 1967, 75-76; Am. Philos. Soc. grantee, 1969, 72; Am. Council Learned Socs. fellow, 1970; grantee, 1974. Mem. Am. Comparative Lit. Assn., Ovidianum Societas (Bucharest, Roumania) (honoris causa), Medieval Acad. Am., Am. Soc. Eighteenth Century Studies, Am. Lessing Soc., Modern Lang. Assn. Am. Home: 5525 NE Penrith Rd Seattle WA 98105

BEHLING, CHARLES FREDERICK, psychology educator; b. St. George, S.C., Sept. 8, 1940; s. John Henry and Floy (Owings) B.; 1 son, John Charles. B.A., U. S.C., 1962, M.A., 1964; M.A., Vanderbilt U., 1966, Ph.D., 1969. Asst. dean of students U. S.C., Columbia, 1962-63; asst. state news editor The State Newspaper, Columbia, 1963-64; asst. prof. psychology Lake Forest Coll., (Ill.), 1968-74, assoc. prof., 1974-77, prof., 1977—, chmn. dept. psychology, 1977-84; pvt. practice psychotherapy, Lake Bluff, Ill., 1970—. Contbr. articles to profl. jours. Mem. long-range planning com. Lake Bluff Bd. Edn. Named Outstanding Prof. Underground Guide to Colls., Outstanding Tchr. Lake Forest Coll., 1981; NASA fellow. Mem. Am. Psychol. Assn., Soc. Psychol. Study of Social Issues, Assn. Humanistic Psychology, AAUP, U. S.C. Alumni Assn., Psi Chi, Sigma Delta Chi. Democrat. Home: 116 E Prospect St Lake Bluff IL 60044 Office: Lake Forest College Dept Psychology Lake Forest IL 60045

BEHLKE, CHARLES EDWARD, engring. coordinator, former univ. dean; b. Butte, Mont., Jan. 12, 1926; s. Herman E. and Estelle (Mondloch) B.; m. Jane H. McMullen, Nov. 25,1953; children—Susan, Carol, James. B.S. in Mech. Engring, Wash. State Coll., 1948, M.S. in Hydraulic Engring; Ph.D. in Civil Engring, Stanford, 1957. Instr., then asst. prof. civil engring. U. Alaska, 1950- 54; asso. prof., then prof. civil engring. Oreg. State U., 1956-65; acting dean, then dean (Coll. Math., Phys. Scis. and Engring.), 1967-75; dir. Arctic Environmental Engring. Lab., U. Alaska, 1966-72, 1965-68, dean, 1975-80; coordinator Alaska State Pipeline, 1979—; Cons. in field, 1957—; mem. New Capitol Site Planning Commn., State of Alaska, 1977-80; bd. dirs. Alaska Power Authority, 1979-80. Recipient Carter award for outstanding teaching Sch. Engring., Oreg. State U., 1961. Mem. Am. Soc. Engring. Edn., ASCE, N.Y. Acad. Scis., Sigma Xi. Home: Box 8-2230 College AK 99708

BEHM, FORREST EDWIN, glass mfg. co. exec.; b. Lincoln, Nebr., July 31, 1919; s. Forrest E. and Lisle (Jacobson) B.; m. Ethel E. Groth, Aug. 11, 1943; children—Courtney Ann, Douglas, Brian, Gregory. B.S., U. Nebr., 1941, LL.D., 1965. With Corning Glass Works, N.Y., 1946—; pres. Corning Internat., 1965-75, sr. v.p. staff, 1975-80, sr. v.p., gen. mgr. elec. and electronics products div., 1975—, also dir.; dir. Security N.Y. Corp., Goulds Pumps. Served to maj. AUS, 1942-46. Mem. Nebr. Football Hall of Fame. Mem. Beta Gamma Sigma. Republican. Presbyterian. Clubs: N.Y. Athletic (N.Y.C.); Corning Country, Baltosrol Country. Home: 3 Briarcliff Dr Corning NY 14830 Office: Corning Glass Works Houghton Park Corning NY 14830

BEHN, ROBERT DIETRICH, public policy educator, writer; b. Washington, Sept. 5, 1941; s. Victor Dietrich and Nona (Heffley) B.; m. Judith Howe, May 4, 1968; 1 son, Mark Dietrich. B.S. in Physics, Worcester Poly. Inst., 1963; M.S.E.E., Harvard U., 1965, Ph.D. in Decision and Control, 1969. Research dir. The Ripon Soc., Cambridge, Mass., 1968-69, exec. dir., 1970-72; asst. to gov. Commonwealth of Mass., Boston, 1969-70; lectr. Harvard Bus. Sch., 1972-73; assoc. prof. Inst. Policy Scis. and Pub. Affairs, Duke U., Durham, N.C., 1973—, dir., 1982—; cons. RAND Corp., Santa Monica, 1966, Urban Acad., N.Y.C., 1978-79, Ford Found., 1977. Author: (with others) Quick Analysis for Busy Decision Makers, 1982; editor: The Lessons of Victory, 1969; contbr. articles to mags. and profl. jours. Chmn. Gov.'s Task Force Intercity Transp., Boston, 1970-71; alt. del. Republican Nat. Conv., 1972; mem. Mass. Rep. State Com., 1973; nat. governing bd. Ripon Soc., 1966-79; mem. Mass. adv. com. U.S. Civil Rights Commn., 1971-73, Com. to Study Need for Inpatient Services for Children with Chronic Phys. Disabilities, Raleigh, N.C., 1978; campaign advisor Hatch for Gov. Com., Boston, 1977-78. Mem. Assn. Pub. Policy Analysis and Mgmt. (treas. 1983—), Am. Soc. Pub. Adminstrn., Pub. Policy and Mgmt. Program for Case/Course Devel. (chmn. quantitative methods panel 1982-83). Home: 1607 Cotherstone Dr Durham NC 27712 Office: Policy Sciences and Public Affairs 4875 Duke Station Durham NC 27706

BEHNKE, BRUCE STEPHEN, hospital administrator; b. Detroit, Feb. 10, 1949; s. E. Thomas and Marie (Malje) B. B.A. in Bus. Adminstrn., Wayne State U., 1970; M. of Hosp. Adminstrn., U. Minn., 1972. Asst. hosp. adminstr. Rochester Meth. Hosp., Minn., 1972-74; ast. hosp. adminstr. Kaiser Found. Hosp., Los Angeles, 1974-78; assoc. hosp. adminstr., Fontana, Calif., 1979-83, 83—; clin preceptor various univs., 1980—. Mem. Am. Coll. Hosp. Adminstrs. Episcopalian. Office: Kaiser Found Hosp 9961 Sierra Ave Fontana CA 92335

BEHNKE, ROY HERBERT, physician, educator; b. Chgo., Feb. 24, 1921; s. Harry and Florence Alice (MacArthur) B.; m. Ruth Gretchen Zinszer, June 3, 1944; children: Roy, Michael, Donald, Elise. A.B., Hanover Coll., 1943; Ph.D. (hon.), 1972; M.D., Ind. U., 1946. Diplomate: Am. Bd. Internal Medicine. Intern Ind. U. Med. Center, 1946-47, resident, 1949-51, chief resident medicine, 1951-52; instr. medicine Ind. U. Sch. Medicine, Indpls., 1952-55, asst. prof. medicine, 1955-58, asso. prof., 1958-61, prof., 1961-72; chief medicine VA Hosp., Indpls., 1957-72; prof. medicine, chmn. dept. U. South Fla. Coll. Medicine, Tampa, 1972—; AMA rep. to residency rev. com. in internal medicine, 1970-75; mem. exec. and adv. com. Inter-Soc. Commn. Heart Disease Resources, 1968-72, chmn. pulmonary study sect., 1969-72; chmn. career devel. com. VA, 1980-83. Mem. Met. Sch. Bd. Washington Twp., 1968-72, pres., 1971; bd. dirs. Southside Community Health Center, 1968; trustee Tampa Gen. Hosp. Found., 1979; mem. research com. Am. Lung Assn., 1977-79, chmn., 1979-81. Served with AUS, 1943-45, 47-49. Recipient Clin. Tchr. of Year award Ind. U. Sch. Medicine, 1968, 69, 70, U. South Fla. Coll. Medicine, 1977, Distinguished Tchr., Standard Oil Found. award, 1971; Alumni Achievement award Hanover Coll., 1971; John and Mary Markle scholar, 1952-57. Fellow ACP (gov. Fla.), Am. Coll. Chest Physicians.; mem. AMA, Am. Fedn. Clin. Research, Central Soc. Clin. Research, So. Soc. Clin. Research, Alpha Omega Alpha. Home: 5111 Rolling Hill Ct Tampa FL 33617

BEHNKE, WALLACE BLANCHARD, JR., utility executive; b. Evanston, Ill., Feb. 5, 1926; s. Wallace Blanchard and Dorothea (Bull) B.; m. Joan F. Murphy, Sept. 24, 1949; children: Susan F., Ann B., Thomas W. B.S., Northwestern U., 1945, B.E.E., 1947. With Commonwealth Edison Co., Chgo., 1947—, dist. supt., Crystal Lake, Ill., 1956-58, div. engr., Joliet, Ill., 1958-60, area mgr., Mt. Prospect, Ill., 1960-62, div. v.p., Chgo., 1962-66, asst. to pres., 1966-69, v.p., 1969-72, exec. v.p., 1972-80, vice chmn., 1980—; chmn. bd. Project Mgmt. Corp.; dir. Lake View Trust & Savs. Bank, Commonwealth Edison Co., Tuthill Pump Co., Paxall Group, Inc. Bd. dirs. Robert Crown Center for Health Edn., United Way Met. Chgo.; trustee Protestant Found. Chgo., Northwestern Meml. Hosp., Chgo., Atomic Indsl. Forum, Ill. Inst. Tech., Ill. Inst. Tech. Research. Served to lt. USNR, 1943-46, 50-52. Fellow IEEE; mem. Nat. Acad. Engring., Am. Nuclear Soc., Western Soc. Engrs., Nat. Planning Assn. (trustee), Phi Delta Theta. Clubs: Econ., Chgo., Comml., Hinsdale (Ill.) Golf. Home: 411 S Elm St Hinsdale IL 60521 Office: 1 First Nat Plaza Chicago IL 60690

BEHNKE, WILLIAM ALFRED, landscape architect, planner; b. Cleve., Jan. 7, 1924; s. Walter William and Constance Helen (Ireson) B.; m. Virginia E. Woolever, Sept. 18, 1948; children: Lee, Deborah, Mitchel, Mark. B.Landscape Architecture, Ohio State U., 1951. Designer Grier Riemer Assos., Cleve., 1951-55; prin. William A. Behnke, Cleve., 1955-57; asso. Charles L. Knight, Cleve., 1957-58; partner Behnke, Szynyog & Ness, Cleve., 1958-61, Behnke, Ness & Litten, 1961-70; mng. partner William A. Behnke Assos., Cleve., 1970—; asso. prof. Kent State U., 1973—; pres. Ohio State Bd. Landscape Archtl. Examiners, 1973; vice-chmn. Ohio Bd. Unreclaimed Strip Mined Lands, 1973-74. Mem. Ohio Arts Council, 1983-84. Served with USNR, 1943-46. Named Distinguished Alumnus Ohio State U., 1978. Fellow Am. Soc. Landscape Architects (v.p. 1977-79, pres. 1980-81); mem. Ohio Parks and Recreation Assn. Clubs: Downtown Cleve. Rotary, Cleve. Play House. Home: 5363 SOM Center Rd Willoughby OH 44094 Office: 11001 Cedar Ave Cleveland OH 44106 *I am gratified with the knowledge that my livelihood is achieved from a profession that has as its goal the betterment of mankind.*

BEHR, CARL EDMUND, JR., advertisng executive; b. Bloomington, Ill., Dec. 14, 1925; s. Carl E. and Ethel Jane (Forister) B.; m. Jessie Dolan, Feb. 17, 1951; children: Salley Behr Van Durzen, Carl Frederick. B.A., U. Ill.-Urbana, 1949. Account exec. Needham, Louis & Brorby, Chgo., 1949-54, Leo Burnett Co., 1954-58, Foote Cone & Bleding, 1960-74, sr. v.p., group mgmt. supt., 1974-79; exec. v.p. FCB Internat., 1979—; pres. multinat. bus. Foote, Cone & Bleding, Chgo., 1982—. Pres. Woodlands Homeowners Assn., 1958-60. Mem. Am. Mktg. Assn., Econ. Club Chgo., Mid Century Combine, Internat. Advt. Assn. (dir. Mid-Am. chpt. 1982—), Am. Assn. Advt. Agys. (internat. com. 1981—). Clubs: Exmoor Country, The Tavern. Home: 3098 Greenwood Ave HighlandPark IL 60035 Office: Foote Cone & Belding 401 N Michigan Ave Chicago IL 60611

BEHR, ROBERT MCLEAN, business executive; b. Detroit, Sept. 6, 1921; s. Fred Arthur and Camilla (McLean) B.; m. Margery Ann Peters, May 22, 1948; children: Fred Arthur II, Robert McLean, Peter N. A.B., U. Mich., 1946; M.A., U. Nebr., 1965; grad., Air War Coll., 1965. Commd. 2d lt. USAAF, 1942; advanced through grades to col.; with SAC, 1951-64; mem. Joint Staff, 1966-69; sr. staff mem. NSC, 1969-71, U.S. So. Command, 1971-73; ret., 1973; asst. dir. mil. affairs ACDA, Washington, 1973-77; pres. Pathfinder Assocs. Internat., Inc., 1977—. Decorated Legion of Merit with oak leaf cluster, Air Force Commendation medal with 2 oak leaf clusters, Joint Commendation medal. Mem. Delta Kappa Epsilon. Roman Catholic. Clubs: University (Detroit); Army-Navy Country (Washington). Home: 9109 Hamilton Dr Fairfax VA 22031 Office: Fairfax VA 22031

BEHREND, WILLIAM LOUIS, electrical engineer; b. Wisconsin Rapids, Wis., Jan. 11, 1923; s. Albert and Eva Mae (Barney) B.; m. Manet Louise Whitrock, July 17, 1945; children: Jane Louise, Ann Elizabeth. B.S. in Elec. Engring., U. Wis., 1946, M.S., 1947. Research engr. David Sarnoff Research Ctr., RCA, 1947—, advanced devel. engr. comml. systems div., Meadows Lands, Pa., 1964-66, prelimanary design and systems analyst, 1966—. Contbr. articles on elec. engring. to profl. jours.; patentee in field. Served with USNR, 1944-46. Resident RCA David Sarnoff Research Ctr. award, 1956, 59, 63. Fellow IEEE (Scott Helt award 1971); mem. AAAS, N.Y. Acad. Scis., Sigma Xi.

BEHRENDT, DAVID FROGNER, journalist; b. Stevens Point, Wis., May 25, 1935; s. Allen Charles and Vivian (Frogner) B.; m. Mary Ann Weber, Feb. 4, 1961; children: Lynne, Liza, Sarah. B.S., U. Wis., 1957, M.S., 1960. Reporter Decatur (Ill.) Review, 1957-58; reporter Milw. Jour., 1960-70, copy editor, 1970-71, editorial writer, 1971-84, editorial page editor, 1984—. Recipient Am. Polit. Sci. Assn. award for distinguished reporting pub. affairs, 1963, Nat. Council for Advancement Edn. Writing award for best newspaper series on edn., 1968; Recipient 1st prize for editorial writing Nat. Edn. Reporting award, 1981. Home: 1928 Hillside Ct Delafield WI 53018 Office: PO Box 661 Milwaukee WI 53201

BEHRENS, ALFRED J., beverage co. exec.; b. Des Plaines, Ill., May 13, 1915; m. Margaret Rigge; children—Elisabeth, Barbara, A. John,

Stephen. B.A. in Bus. Adminstrn, Lake Forest Coll., 1938. With Pepsi-Cola Gen. Bottlers, Inc., Chgo., 1940-80, sec., 1949-80, exec. v.p., 1954-80, asst. to chmn., 1973-80, also dir. Past mem. bd. edn. Oak Park-River Forest High Sch. Recipient Disting. Alumnus award North Park Coll., 1976. Presbyterian (elder). Home: 1123 Lathrop Ave River Forest IL 60305

BEHRENS, HILDEGARD, opera singer; b. Oldenburg, W. Ger. Student, Music Conservatory, Freiburg, W. Ger. Opera debut in, Freiburg, 1971; resident mem., Deutsche Opera Am Rhein, Dusseldorf, W. Ger.; appeared with, Frankfurt (W. Ger.) Opera, Teatro Nacional de San Carlo, Lisbon, Portugal, Vienna Staatsoper, Met. Opera., N.Y.C. Office: care Columbia Artists Mgmt Inc 165 W 57th St New York NY 10019 *

BEHRENS, ROBERT H., business executive; b. Jersey City, Oct. 8, 1923; s. Herman H. and Pearl Reynolds (Rhodes) B.; m. Helen Yvonne Kindler, May 5, 1945; children: Christine, Eric, Yvonne, Diane, Peter. B.A., Haverford Coll., 1946, M.A., 1947; Ph.D., U. Tuebingen, 1951. With N.W. Ayer, Phila., 1947; pub. relations Campbell Soup Co., 1948; fgn. service officer Office High Commr. of Germany, 1950-52, USIA, 1952-74; counselor embassy pub. affairs Am. embassy, Vienna, 1968-71, Rabat, Morocco, 1971-74; adviser U.S. delegation SALT, 1970-72; prof. Faculty Law and Econs., Mohammed V U., Rabat, 1975-77; founder Cultural Comml. Exchange, Inc.; Partner Moroccan Electric and Electronic Equipment Co.; co-founder, dir. gen. Morocco Investments (Multitech); Mem. adv. bd. Textile Mus., Washington. Contbr. articles to mags. Served with USNR, 1943-45. Decorated officer Ouissam Alaouite, Morocco; recipient Meritorious Honor award USIA, 1965, Superior Honor award, 1972; City of Salzburg Ring, 1971. Clubs: Cosmos, International (Washington). Home: 12 Place des Alaouites Rabat Morocco

BEHRENS, ROLAND CONRAD, banker; b. St. Louis, June 29, 1898; s. Charles Henry and Emma (Windhorst) B.; m. Ruth Gertrude Barrett, Aug. 7, 1928; 1 dau., Jeanne Elizabeth Behrens Lewi. Ed., St. Louis U. Sch. Law, 1927, extension div. Washington U. With St. Louis Union Trust Co., 1917-24, asst. sec., 1924-30, v.p., 1930-56, sr. v.p., 1956-65; now asso. dir.; dir. Pilot Knob Ore Co., St. Louis. Mem. Mo. Bar Assn., Newcomen Soc. N.Am. Clubs: Media, Univ. (St. Louis). Home: 9 Devondale Ln Frontenac Saint Louis MO 63131 Office: 510 Locust St Saint Louis MO 63101

BEHRENS, WILLIAM WOHLSEN, JR., oceanographer, engr., research company executive, educator, retired naval officer; b. Newport, R.I., Sept. 14, 1922; s. William Wohlsen and Nell (Vasey) B.; m. Betty Ann Taylor, June 22, 1946; children—Elizabeth Behrens Garland, William Wohlsen III, Charles Conrad, Susan Raker. B.S., U.S. Naval Acad., 1943; student, U.S. Submarine Sch., 1943, U.S. Naval Nuclear Power Sch., 1955-56, Nat. War Coll., 1963; M.A., George Washington U., 1964; Sc.D., Gettysburg Coll., 1974. Commd. ensign U.S. Navy, 1943, advanced through grades to vice adm., 1972, ret., 1974; combat duty 6 submarine patrols, Pacific, World War II, comdr. four submarines, 1953-63; founding dir. Navy's Nuclear Power Sch., 1955; AEC qualified nuclear chief reactor operator, 1956; special asst. Atomic Energy Comm., 1956-57; dir. NATO nuclear planning strategic plans Office Chief Naval Ops., 1964-66; dep. asst. sec. state, mem. policy planning council, 1966-67; comdr. Amphibious Force, Vietnam, 1967-69; dir. politico-mil. policy Office Chief Naval Operations, 1969-70; oceanographer of Navy, 1970-72; asso. adminstr. and naval dep. NOAA, 1972-74; sr. v.p. J. Watson Noah Inc., Arlington, Va.; pres. Earth Resources Applications Inst., Inc., Washington; sci. adviser Wheeler Industries, Inc., Washington; adj. prof. dept. marine sci. U. South Fla.; Vice pres. Am. Oceanic Orgn., 1976. Trustee SEA Edn. Assn., Boston, 1974-78; dir. Fla. Inst. for Oceanography; mem. Com. of 100, Pinellas County, Fla.; bd. govs. Sci. Center, Inc., Pinellas County, 1975-81; mem. Port Commn., St. Petersburg; exec. bd. St. Petersburg Progress, Inc. Decorated D.S.M., Silver Star, Legion of Merit with 4 gold stars and combat V, Navy Bronze Star with combat V, Army Bronze Star with combat V, Joint Services Commendation medal, Navy Commendation medal, other U.S. and fgn. decorations. Mem. N.Y. Acad. Scis., U.S. Naval Inst. (life), U.S. Naval Acad. Alumni Assn. (life), U.S. Naval Acad. Found., Navy-Marine Corps-Coast Guard Residence Found., Naval Acad. Athletic Assn., Explorers Club, U.S. Navy League, Soc. Am. Mil. Engrs., Inst. Navigation, Marine Tech. Soc., AAAS, IEEE, Am. Geophys. Union, Internat. Oceanographic Found., Internat. Game Fish Assn., Arctic Inst., Am. Soc. Naval Engrs., Smithsonian Instn. Nat. Assos., Ret. Officers Assn. (life). Clubs: N.Y. Yacht (N.Y.C.); U.S. Naval Sailing Assn. (Annapolis, Md.) (commodore 1975); Nat. Propeller, Army Navy (Washington). Home: 1125 Friendly Way S Saint Petersburg FL 33705 Office: 830 1st St S Saint Petersburg FL 33701 *My life has taught me the everlasting value of the oceans to man, not only in the nurturing of mankind through the ages, but now, more than ever, in providing to our burgeoning world populations the essential transport for communications and much-needed goods, as well as the all-important potential of energy food and other key resources from the sea and the environmental rejuvenation so vitally required.*

BEHRLE, FRANKLIN CHARLES, physician; b. Ansonia, Conn., June 4, 1922; s. Frank Edward and Irene Elizabeth (Bannon) B.; m. Margaret Ann Begley, June 16, 1945; children: Barbara, Susan, Carol, Richard, Robert. A.B., Dartmouth Coll., 1944; M.D., Yale U., 1946. Diplomate: Am. Bd. Pediatrics. Intern Nat. Naval Med. Center, Bethesda, Md., 1946-47; resident U. Kans. Med. Center, Kansas City, 1949-51; from instr. to asso. prof. pediatrics U. Kans. Sch. Medicine, 1951-61; prof., chmn. dept. pediatrics U. Medicine and Dentistry, N.J.-N.J. Med. Sch., Newark, 1961—. Contbr. chpts. to books; Contbr. numerous articles to profl. jours. Served to lt. (j.g.) M.C. USN, 1946-49. Fellow Am. Acad. Pediatrics; mem. Soc. for Pediatric Research, Midwest Soc. for Pediatric Research. Home: 18 Glenside Terr Upper Montclair NJ 07043 Office: 100 Bergen St Newark NJ 07107

BEHRMAN, EDWARD JOSEPH, educator; b. N.Y.C., Dec. 13, 1930; s. Morris Harry and Janet Cahn (Solomons) B.; m. Cynthia Fansler, Aug. 29, 1953; children—David Murray, Elizabeth Colden, Victoria Anne. B.S., Yale, 1952; Ph.D., U. Calif. at Berkeley, 1957. Research asso. biochemistry Cancer Research Inst., Boston, 1960-64; bd. tutors biochem. scis. Harvard, 1961-64; asst. prof. chemistry Brown U., Providence, 1964-65; mem. faculty Ohio State U., Columbus, 1965—, asso. prof., 1967-69, prof., 1969—. Contbr. articles profl. jours. USPHS fellow, 1955-56, 57-60; NSF grantee, 1966-73; NIH grantee, 1973—. Mem. Am. Chem. Soc., Chem. Soc. London, Am. Soc. Biol. Chemists, Phi Beta Kappa, Sigma Xi. Home: 6533 Hayden Run Rd Hilliard OH 43026 Office: 484 W 12th Ave Dept Biochemistry Ohio State U Columbus OH 43210

BEHRMAN, HAROLD RICHARD, medical educator; b. Sask., Can., Nov. 26, 1939; s. Henry Fred and Minne Alice (Waslenko) B.; m. Carol Hope O'Rourke, Aug. 8, 1981; children: Tracy Lee, Terri Lynne, Russell Norman, Kevin Michael, Kathleen Hope. B.S., U. Man., (Can.), 1962, M.A., 1965; Ph.D., N.C. State U., 1967; M.S. (hon.), Yale U., 1982. Research fellow Harvard U. Med. Sch., Boston, 1967-71, asst. prof., 1971-72; dir. reproductive biology Merck Inst., Rahway, N.J., 1972-75; assoc. prof. gynecology and pharmacology Yale U., New Haven, 1975-81, prof. ob-gyn. and pharmacology, 1981—, dir. productive biology sect., 1975—; cons. NIH, 1978-83. Editor: (with others) Methods of Hormone Radioimmunoassay, 1974, 79. Recipient Research award Lalor Found., 1971-72; Fulbright-Hays Disting. prof., 1978; MRC Can. fellow, 1967-70; recipient Alta. Heritage Vis. Prof. award, 1983. Mem. Soc. Exptl. Biology and Medicine, Am. Physiol. Soc., Endocrine Soc., Soc. Study of Reprodn., Soc. Endocrinology, Can. Physiol. Soc., AAAS. Home: 790 Greenhill Rd Madison CT 06443 Office: Dept Ob-gyn Yale U Med Sch 1303A Yale Sta New Haven CT 06520

BEHRMAN, JACK NEWTON, economist; b. Waco, Tex., Mar. 5, 1922; s. Mayes and Marguerite (Newton) B.; m. Louise Sims, Sept. 6, 1945; children: Douglas, Gayle, Andrea. B.S. cum laude with honors in Econs., Davidson Coll., 1943, LL.D. (hon.), 1979; M.A., U. N.C., 1945, Princeton U., 1950, Ph.D., 1952. Research asst. ILO, 1945-46; asst. prof. econs. Davidson Coll., 1946-48; research asst. internat. fin. sect. Princeton U., 1950-52; asso. prof. econs. and polit. sci. Washington and Lee U., 1952-57; prof. econs. and bus. adminstrn. U. Del., 1957-61; asst. sec. for internat. affairs U.S. Dept. Commerce, 1961-62, asst. sec. for domestic and internat. bus., 1962-64; prof. internat. bus. Sch. Bus., U. N.C., 1964-77, Luther Hodges Disting. prof., 1977—; Drexel research prof. Sch. Bus., U. N.C., 1970-71; Thomas Carroll vis. prof. Harvard Bus. Sch., 1967, chmn. M.B.A. Program, 1971-77, assoc. dean acad. programs, 1983—; dir. 1st Union Nat. Bank at Chapel Hill, Troxler Electronics, Inc., Longleaf, Inc.; mem. bd. sci. and tech. for internat. devel. NRC, 1973-75; mem. panel sci. and tech. in internat. econs. and trade Nat. Acad. Sci., 1977; dir. research project Dept. State, 1973-74; sr. research advisor Fund for Multinat. Mgmt. Edn., 1974-82, v.p. research and program devel., 1982—; cons. U.S. Dept. State, Pan Am. Union, Com. Econ. Devel., Econ. Council Can., OAS, Nat. Fgn. Trade Council, So. Regional Council, Nat. Planning Assn., Hudson Inst., Nat. Acad. Sci., U.S. C. of C., UN Ctr. Sci. and Tech. for Devel., UN Ctr. on Transnat. Corps, GAO, N.C. Dept. Agr., also pvt. bus.; prin. investigator Patent, Trademark and Copyright Research Inst., 1955-60, George Washington U., 1955-60; cons. Presdl. Commn. on Internat. Trade and Investments, EPA, UN; mem. adv. com. on fgn. investment State Dept., 1976-77; mem. adv. com. on internat. trade, investment and devel. Undersec. State, 1978—; research sec. for study on multinat. enterprises Council on Fgn. Relations, 1976-77; mem. panel tech. and internat. competitiveness Nat. Acad. Engring., 1978-79; lectr. Am. Mgmt. Assn., Columbia U., Salzburg Seminar, USIA, Motorola Exec. Inst., U. N.C. Exec. Program, Young Execs. Inst., Govt. Exec. Program; mem. Dept. State del. Latin Am. Pre-Ministerial Conf., 1974-75; mem. del. UN Conf. Sci. and Tech. in Devel., Vienna, 1979; bd. dirs. Am. Viewpoint, Inc., Ethics Resource Center. Author: (with Gardner Patterson) Survey of United States International Finance, 3 vols., 1950, 51, 52, (with Wilson E. Schmidt) International Economics, 1957, (with Raymond F. Mikesell) Financing Free World Trade with the Sino-Soviet Bloc, 1958, U.S. Private and Government Investment Abroad, 1962, (with Roy Blough) Regional Integration and the Trade of Latin America, 1968, (with A. Kapoor and J. Boddewyn) International Business-Government Communications, 1975, (with H. Wallender) Transfer of Manufacturing Technology within Multinational Enterprises, 1976, (with W. Fischer) Science and Technology for Development, 1980, Overseas Research and Development Activities of Transnational Companies, 1980; author: Rise of the Multinational Enterprise, 1969, National Interests and the Multinational Enterprise, 1970, U.S. International Business and Governments, 1971, Multinational Production Consortia, 1971, Role of International Companies in Latin American Integration, 1972, Decision Criteria for Foreign Direct Investment in Latin America, 1974, Conflicting Constraints on the Multinational Enterprise, 1974, Toward a New International Economic Order, 1974, Tropical Diseases: Responses of Pharmaceutical Companies, 1980, Industry Ties with Science and Technology Policies in Developing Countries, 1980, Discourses on Ethics and Business, 1981; editor: (with Robert E. Driscoll) International Industrial Integration, 1983; contbr. 100 articles to profl. jours.; mem. editorial bd.: Jour. Internat. Bus. Studies, 1976-82. Fellow Acad. Internat. Bus.; mem. Council Fgn. Relations, Regional Export Expansion Council (vice chmn. 1971-73), Assn. Edn. in Internat. Bus. (sec. 1959-60, pres. 1966-68), N.C. World Trade Assn. (dir.), Sigma Phi Epsilon, Pi Gamma Mu, Alpha Phi Omega, Beta Gamma Sigma. Democrat. Presbyterian (elder). Home: 1702 Audubon Rd Chapel Hill NC 27514

BEHRMAN, JERE RICHARD, economics educator; b. Indpls., Mar. 2, 1940; s. Robert Wilbur and Mary Jane (Krull) B.; m. Barbara Ann Ventresco; 1 son, Kennedy Robert. Student, Russian Lang. Inst., Ind. U., 1960-61; B.A. summa cum laude, Williams Coll., Williamstown, Mass., 1962; Ph.D., Mass. Inst. Tech., 1966. Asst. prof. econs. U. Pa., Phila., 1965-68, asso. prof., 1968-71, prof., 1971—, chmn. dept. econs., 1973-79, research asso. Center for Population Studies, 1979—, William P. Kenan, Jr. prof. econs., 1983—, assoc. dir. Lauder Inst. Mgmt. and Internat. Studies, 1983—; co-dir. Ctr. for Analysis Developing Economies, 1982—, co-dir. Ctr. for Household and Family Econs., 1982—, co-dir. South Asian Studies Ctr., 1983—; mem. personnel adv. com. for dean Wharton Sch., 1972-73; faculty asso. NSF sponsored project, 1965-68; vis. seminar coordinator Universidad Catolica, Santiago, Chile, 1969; vis. lectr. pub. and internat. affairs, Princeton, 1973; research asso. Nat. Bur. Econ. Research, 1975-79; hon. fellow dept. econs. U. Wis., 1976-77; research asso. Center for Latin Am. Devel. Studies, Boston U., 1978-79; Cons. econs. dept. IBRD, Washington, 1966-69, Devel. Research Center, 1972-73; research asso., cons. MIT-ODEPLAN-Ford project Office Nat. Econ. Planning, Santiago, 1968-71; cons. Wharton Econ. Forecasting Assos., Inc., 1970-71, U.S. Treasury, 1972, Brookings-SIECA-BID project on Central Am. Common Market, 1973-78, UN Com. on Trade and Devel. World Commodity Models, 1974, Harvard Inst. Internat. Devel., Central Bank Nicaragua Econ. Modeling Project, 1975, LPES-NBER-UN Project on Short Term Policy in Latin Am. Econs., 1975, AID, 1976-77, Dept. of Treasury, 1977, ECIEL, 1978, Internat. Crops Research Inst. for Semi-Arid Tropics, 1980-83; prin. investigator on NSF project, 1972-75; co-investigator NSF projects, 1973—, AID, 1977-80, Ford-Rockefeller, 1977-78, NIH, 1981-84, Population Council, 1982—, also others. Author books and monographs, also book revs.; Contbr. articles to profl. jours. Recipient Benedict prize as outstanding math. student Williams Coll., 1960, Grosvenor Cup as outstanding mem. class of, 1962; award of merit for outstanding research in agrl. econs. Am. Farm Econ. Assn., 1967; Nat. Merit scholar, 1958-62; Tyng Found. fellow, 1958-64; Carnegie fellow, 1961; Danforth Found. fellow, 1962-66; NSF fellow, 1962-63; Mass. Inst. Tech. Center for Internat. Studies fellow, 1964-65; Ford Found. Faculty fellow, 1971-72; Guggenheim Found. Faculty fellow, 1979-80; Compton Found. Population fellow, 1980-81. Fellow Econometric Soc.; Mem. Am. Econ. Assn., Latin Am. Studies Assn., Population Assn. Am., Soc. for Internat. Devel., Phi Beta Kappa. Home: 424 s 26th St Philadelphia PA 19146 Office: Dept Economics University of Pennsylvania Philadelphia PA 19104

BEHRMAN, RICHARD ELLIOT, pediatrician, neonatologist, university dean; b. Phila., Dec. 13, 1931; s. Robert and Vivian (Keegan) B.; m. Ann Nelson, Aug. 14, 1954; children: Amy Jane, Michael Jameson, Carolyn Ann, Hillary. A.B., Amherst Coll., 1953; J.D., Harvard U., 1956; M.D. (Univ. scholar), U. Rochester, 1960. Intern Johns Hopkins Hosp., Balt., 1960-61, resident in pediatrics, 1963-65; asst. prof. pediatrics U. Oreg. Sch. Medicine, Portland, 1965-67, asso. prof., 1967-68; prof. U. Ill. Coll. Medicine, Chgo., 1968-71; prof., chmn. dept. Columbia U. Coll. Physicians and Surgeons, N.Y.C., 1971-76, Case Western Res. U. Sch. Medicine, Cleve., 1976-81, dean Sch. Medicine, 1980—; dir. dept. pediatrics Rainbow Babies and Children's Hosp., Cleve., 1976-81; chmn. bd. maternal, child and family research Nat. Acad. Sci., NRC, 1977-80; examiner Am. Bd. Pediatrics. Author: Neonatology: Diseases of the Fetus and Infant, 1973, Neonatal-Perinatal Medicine, 1977; editor: Nelson's Textbook of Pediatrics, 1978, 83; mem.: editorial bd., sect. editor fetal and neonatal medicine Jour. Pediatrics, 1970—; asso. editor: Pediatric Research, 1971-80. Served with USPHS, 1961-63. Whipple scholar, 1960-61; Wyeth pediatric fellow, 1963-65. Fellow Am. Acad. Pediatrics; mem. Soc. Pediatric Research (v.p. 1976-77), Inst. Medicine of Nat. Acad. Scis., Am. Pediatric Soc., Inst. Medicine, Assn. Med. Sch. Pediatric Dept., Perinatal Research Soc. (council 1970-73), Pediatric Travel Club, Soc. Gynecol. Investigation, Sigma Xi. Presbyterian. Clubs: Cleve. Racquet, Century Assn. Home: 2871 Courtland Blvd Shaker Heights OH 44122 Office: 2101 Adelbert Rd Cleveland OH 44106

BEHRMAN, SAMUEL JAN, educator, obstetrician and gynecologist; b. S. Africa, Sept. 10, 1920; s. Louis and Betty (Danemann) B.; m. Patrisha Ann McManus, Oct. 14, 1956; children: Michael, Andrea. M.B., Ch.B., U. Cape Town, S.Africa; M.Sc., U. Mich., 1949; postgrad., Postgrad. Sch. Medicine, London, Eng., 1948. Diplomate: Am. Bd. Obstetrics and Gynecology. Rotating intern Johannesburg (S.Africa) Hosp., 1945; surg. resident Brad-Royal Infirmary, Yorkshire, Eng., 1946; resident obstetrics and gynecology Royal Maternity Hosp., Belfast, Ireland, 1946-48; research fellow U. Mich., 1948-49; assoc. dir. clin. research Ortho Research Found., 1949-50; mem. faculty U. Mich. Med. Sch., 1949—, prof. obstetrics and gynecology, 1960-77; dir. Center Research and Tng. in Reproductive Biology, 1956; resident lectr. family planning Sch. Pub. Health, 1956, coordinator obstetrics and gynecology to dept. postgrad. medicine, 1958—; prof. obstetrics and gynecology Wayne State U., 1977—; chmn. dept. obstetrics and gynecology William Beaumont Hosp., Royal Oak, Mich., 1977—; cons. Sinai Hosp., Detroit, 1956, Ypsilanti (Mich.) Hosp., 1954, Wayne County Gen. Hosp., 1962; com. maternal care A.M.A., 1954; spl. com. Nat. Inst. Child health and Devel., 1965; conf. immunological aspects of human reprodn. WHO, 1965—; population service AID, 1969—; sci. adv. com. Human Life Found., 1970—; obstet.-gynecol. adviser FDA, 1973—; mem. immunology task force WHO, 1973—; vis. prof. U. London, 1965, U. Cape Town, 1969. Author 3 textbooks, numerous articles in field.; Editor: Internat. Jour. Fertility, 1960-77; asso. editor: Fertility and Sterility, 1970-76; cons. editor: Hosp. Practice, 1970. Recipient numerous research grants, 1948—; recipient Ortho medal for research, 1967, Galen Sr. award for teaching U. Mich., 1956, Galen Shovel award for teaching, 1963; Wyeth award for research, 1972. Fellow A.C.S., Am., Royal colls. obstetrics and gynecologists, Royal Soc. Medicine; founding fellow Coll. Physicians and Surgeons S. Africa; mem. Internat. Fertility Assn., Internat. Soc. Research Biology Reprodn. (founder, trustee 1967—), Central Assn. Obstetricians and Gynecologists, AMA Am. (bd. dirs.), Pacific Coast fertility socs., Am. Pub. Health Assn., Population Assn. Am., Mid-Eastern Obst. and Gynecol. Travel Soc., Norman F. Miller Gynecol. Soc., Internat. Fedn. Fertility Socs. (pres. 1970-73), Mich. Obstetrics and Gynecology Soc., Washtenaw County Med. Soc., Phi Delta Epsilon. Home: 122 E Brown St Birmingham MI 48011

BEHRMANN, JOHN REYNOLDS, dental/medical manufacturing company executive; b. Scranton, Pa., July 6, 1935; s. John Charles and Josephine Scott (Reynolds) B.; m. Nancy Christine Peregrim; children: Nancy Lorraine Behrmann Littlefield, John Scott. B.S. in Commerce and Fin, Bucknell U., Lewisburg, Pa., 1958, postgrad., 1959. With Price Waterhouse, C.P.A.s, 1959-68, audit mgr., Phila., 1964-65, 67-68, mgr., London, Eng., 1966; v.p. fin. Dentsply Internat. Inc. (dental, med. supplies), York, Pa., 1968-80, sr. v.p., chief fin. officer, dir., 1980—; dir., sr. v.p., chief fin. officer parent co. Dentsply Holdings Inc., 1982—; dir. Dentsply Caulk de Mex. S.A. de C.V., Dentsply Ltd., London, Dentsply Employee Stock Ownership Plan; trustee Dentsply Internat. Employees Pension Trust C.P.A., Pa. Mem. Am. Mgmt. Assn., Am. Inst. C.P.A.'s, Nat. Assn. Accts., Fin. Execs. Inst., Pa. Inst. C.P.A.s, Kappa Delta Rho. Presbyterian. Clubs: Country of York, Lafayette (York); Wynooska (Canadensis, Pa.). Office: 570 W College Ave York PA 17404

BEHRSTOCK, JULIAN ROBERT, publishing consultant, editor; b. Chgo., Dec. 14, 1916; s. Herman and Anne (Joseph) B.; m. Monique Delessert, Sept. 24, 1971; 1 son, Jeremy. B.S. with honors, Northwestern U., 1937. Reporter Paris (France) bur. Time mag. and Paris Herald Tribune, 1937-38; editor Compton's Pictured Ency., Chgo., 1938-41; staff writer Office Emergency Mgmt., Washington, 1941-42; editor U.S. Fgn. Broadcast Info. Service, then successively dir. bur., London, Eng., Hawaii, and, Tokyo, Japan, 1942-47; dir. free flow info. and book devel. UNESCO, Paris, 1948-76; chief editor UNESCO publs., 1971-76; book pub. cons., editor, 1976—; Trustee Am. Coll. in Paris. Organizer, head Internat. Book Year, 1972.; Contbr. articles to mags. Recipient Internat. Book award for outstanding services to cause of books, 1977. Mem. Phi Beta Kappa. Home: 26 rue Defrenoy Paris France Office: 261 Rue St Honoré 75116 Paris France

BEIDELMAN, THOMAS OWEN, anthropology educator; b. Aurora, Ill., Mar. 21, 1931; s. Owen Henry and Caroyl (Book) B. B.A., U. Ill., 1953, M.A., 1956; D. Phil., Oxford U., Eng., 1961. Asst. prof. Harvard U., Cambridge, Mass., 1963-65; assoc. prof. Duke U., Durham, N.C., 1965-67; vis. fellow Ctr. for Advanced Study, Stanford, Calif., 1967-68; assoc. prof. NYU, 1968-71, prof. anthropology, 1971—. Author: Matrilineal Peoples of East-Central Tanzania, 1967, The Kaguru, 1971, W. Robertson Smith, 1974, Colonial Evangelism, 1982. Served with U.S. Army, 1954-56; Korea. Ford Found. fellow, 1961-63; NEH fellow, 1983; Guggenheim Found. fellow, 1983-84. Mem. Royal Anthrop. Inst., Am. Ethnol. Assn. Office: Dept Anthropology NYU 25 Waverly Pl New York NY 10003

BEIDLER, PETER GRANT, educator; b. Bethlehem, Pa., Mar. 13, 1940; s. Paul Henry and Margaret (Grant) B.; m. Anne E. Gilbert, June 15, 1963; children: Paul, Kurt, Gretchen, Nora. B.A., Earlham Coll., 1962; M.A., Lehigh U., 1965, Ph.D., 1968. Asst. prof. English Lehigh U., Bethlehem, Pa., 1968-72, assoc. prof., Bethlehem, 1972-77, prof., 1977—, Lucy G. Moses Disting prof. English, 1978—, acting v.p. for student affairs, 1982-83. Author: Fig Tree John: An Indian in Fact and Fiction, 1977; co-author: bibliography The Indian in American Short Fiction, 1979; editor: John Gower's Literary Transformations, 1982. Served with USAF, 1962-68. Named prof. of yr. Council for Advancement and Support of Edn., 1983. Mem. MLA, Nat. Council Tchrs. English, Medieval Soc. Am. Office: Lehigh U English Dept Bethlehem PA 18015 *A teacher's task is not to convey knowledge, but to set up situations in which students cannot help but learn something. Teachers exist not to tell students what they themselves know, but to find ways to share with students the pure fun of discovery, the sense that learning is only slightly less exciting than falling in love. No teacher can claim anything like success in any of this; a few of us, however, can be proud that we have not failed with every student.*

BEIERWALTES, WILLIAM HENRY, physician, educator; b. Saginaw, Mich., Nov. 23, 1916; s. John Andrew and Fanny (Aris) B.; m. Mary Martha Nichols, Jan. 1, 1942; children: Andrew George, William Howard, Martha Louise. A.B., U. Mich., 1938, M.D., 1941. Diplomate: Am. Bd. Internal Medicine and Nuclear Medicine. Intern, then asst. resident medicine Cleve. City Hosp., 1941-43; mem. faculty U. Mich. Med. Center, 1944—, prof. medicine, 1959—; dir. nuclear medicine, also dir. Thyroid Research Lab., 1952—; mem. exec. com. Inst. Sci. and Tech., 1963; Lectr. Nat. Naval Med. Center, 1964—; adv. panel on radionuclide labeled compounds for tumor diagnosis Internat. AEC, 1974—; mem. Mich. State Radiation Bd., 1980—; co-chmn. Nat. Coop. Thyroid Cancer Therapy Group, 1978-81. Author: Clinical Use of Radioisotopes, 1957, Manual of Nuclear Medicine Procedures, 1971, also numerous articles.; Assoc. editor Jour. Lab. and Clin. Medicine, 1954-60; mem. editorial bd.: Jour. Nuclear Medicine, 1959-64; asso. editor, 1975-81; mem. editorial bd.: Jour. Clin. Endocrinology and Metabolism, 1963. Guggenheim fellow, 1966-67; Commonwealth Fund fellow, 1967; Hevesy Nuclear Medicine Pioneer award, 1982; Disting. Faculty award U. Mich., 1982; Johann-Georg-Zimmerman Trust for Cancer Research Sci. prize for greatest contbn. to treatment of thyroid cancer, 1983. Mem. Am. Fedn. Clin. Research (pres. 1954-55), Soc. Nuclear Medicine (pres. 1965-66), Central Clin. Research Club (pres. 1958-59), Am. Thyroid Assn. (v.p. 1964-65, 66-67, Distinguished Service award 1972), Central Soc. Clin. Research (councillor 1964-67, 67-71), Galens Med. Soc. (prefect 1950-51), Am. Cancer Soc., AMA, Assn. Am. Physicians, A.C.P., Mich. Med. Soc., Am. Endocrine Soc. Co-inventor radiopharms; originator radioimmunodetection, other med. techniques. Home: 1025 Forest Rd Barton Hills Village Ann Arbor MI 48105

BEIGHLE, DOUGLAS PAUL, aerospace company executive; b. Deer Lodge, Mont., June 18, 1932; s. Douglas Paul Beighle and Clarice Janice (Driver) Kiefer; m. Gwendolen Anne Dickson, Oct. 30, 1954; children: Cheryl, Randall, Katherine, Douglas J. B.S. in Bus. Adminstrn., U. Mont., 1954, J.D., 1958; LL.M., Harvard U., 1960. Bar: Mont. 1958, Wash. 1959, U.S. Supreme Ct. 1970. Assoc. Perkins, Coie, Stone, Olsen & Wilson, Seattle, 1960-60, ptnr., 1967-80; v.p. contracts Boeing Co., Seattle, 1980-81, v.p. contracts, gen. counsel, sec., 1981—; chief legal counsel Puget Sound Power & Light Co., Bellevue, Wash., 1970-80, dir., 1981—; dir. Peabody Holding Co., St. Louis. Bd. dirs. Mental Health North, Seattle, 1978—; nat. dir. Jr. Achievement, Conn., 1981—; trustee Mcpl. League Seattle, 1983—, U. Mont. Found., Missoula, 1983—. Served to lst. lt. USAF, 1954-56. Harvard U. Law Sch. fellow, 1959. Mem. ABA; eme. Mont. Bar Assn.; mem. Wash. State Bar Assn. (chmn. advt. law sect. 1959-60), Seattle-King County Bar Assn. Republican. Presbyterian. Clubs: Rainier; Yacht (Seattle). Office: Boeing Company 7755 E Marginal Way S Seattle WA 98124

BEIGIE, CARL EMERSON, economist, research administrator; b. Cleve., Apr. 9, 1940; s. George Carroll and Carol Elizabeth (Chamberlin) B.; m. MaryCatherine Hall, June 3, 1961; children: David Philip, Darin Emerson. A.B., Muskingum Coll., New Concord, Ohio, 1962, M.I.T., 1962-66. Lectr. econs. U. Western Ont., London, 1966-68; asst. v.p. Irving Trust Co., N.Y.C., 1968-71; exec. dir. Pvt. Planning Assn., Montreal, Can., 1971-73, C.D. Howe Inst., Montreal, 1973-78, pres., 1978-82; prof. Faculty Mgmt. Studies U. Toronto, 1983—; dir. Fraser Cos (N.B.), Indsl. Bank Japan (Can.), Can. Found. Econ. Edn., Oakwood Petroleums Ltd.; asso. prof. mgmt. McGill U.; Claude T. Bissell vis. prof. Can.-Am. relations U. Toronto, 1981-82. Editor: (with Alfred O. Hero) Natural Resources in U.S.-Canadian Relations, 1979, 80; author monographs; contbr. numerous articles on econ. policy to profl. jours. Mem. Am. Econs. Assn., Nat. Assn. Bus. Economists (Adolph G. Abramson award 1971). Home: 55 Charles St W Suite 1704 Toronto ON M5S 2W9 Canada Office: U Toronto 252 Bloor St W Room 4-291 Toronto ON Canada MSS 1V4

BEIHL, WILLIAM JAMES, III, financial executive; b. Newark, Aug. 12, 1935; s. William James and Edna (Stevens) B.; m. Lois Lillian Burden, June 28, 1958; children: Gregory William, Wendy Ann, Eric Alan. B.B.A., Pace U., 1958. C.P.A. Sr. acct. Arthur Andersen & Co., N.Y.C., 1962-66; v.p., asst. treas. Benton & Bowles, N.Y.C., 1966-73; v.p. fin., dir. Marsteller, Inc., Chgo., 1973—. Served with USNR, 1958-62. Mem. Am. Inst. C.P.A.s, Fin. Execs. Inst., N.J. Soc. C.P.A.s. Republican. Presbyterian. Clubs: Chgo. Athletic Assn., Chgo. Yacht. (Chgo.). Home: 1300 Hackberry Ln Winnetka IL 60093 Office: 1 E Wacker Dr Chicago IL 60601

BEILENSON, ANTHONY CHARLES, congressman; b. New Rochelle, N.Y., Oct. 26, 1932; s. Peter and Edna (Rudolph) B.; m. Dolores Martin, June 20, 1959; children: Peter, Dayna, Adam. B.A., Harvard Coll., 1954; LL.B., Harvard U., 1957. Bar: Calif. 1957. Mem. Calif. Assembly from 59th Dist., 1963-66, Calif. Senate from 22d Dist., 1967-76, 97th-98th Congresses from 23d Calif. Dist. Democrat. Office: House Office Bldg Washington DC 20515

BEIM, DAVID ODELL, international banker; b. Mpls., June 2, 1940; s. Raymond Nelson and Moana (Odell) B.; m. Elizabeth Lucile Artz, Aug. 29, 1964; children—Amy Marie, Nicholas Frederick. B.A. with honors, Stanford U., 1963; B.Phil. (Rhodes scholar), Oxford (Eng.) U., 1965. With First Boston Corp., N.Y.C., 1966-75, v.p., 1971-75, head project finance, 1973-75; exec. v.p. Export-Import Bank U.S., Washington, 1975-77; head corp. fin. Bankers Trust Co., N.Y.C., 1978—, sr. v.p., 1978-79, exec. v.p., 1979—. Bd. dirs. Vols. Tech. Assistance, Wave Hill, Inc. Mem. Council Fgn. Relations. Home: Dodgewood Rd Riverdale NY 10471 Office: 280 Park Ave New York NY 10017

BEIM, NORMAN, playwright, actor; b. Newark; s. Herman and Freida (Thau) B.; m. Virginia Rapkin (div.). Student, Ohio State U., Hedgerow Theatre Sch., Phila., Inst. Contemporary Art, Washington. Actor: Broadway play Inherit the Wind, 1956-58; off-Broadway play Coriolanus, 1953, Black Visions, 1973; nat. touring production Tribute, 1980; playwright: works include The Deserter, 1979, Sucess, 1983, Pygmalion and Galatea, 1983. Served with F.A. U.S. Army. Mem. Actors Equity Assn., Screen Actors Guild, AFTRA, Dramatists Guild Am. Democrat. Jewish. Home: 425 W 57th St New York NY 10019

BEIMFOHR, EDWARD GEORGE, lawyer; b. Marissa, Ill., Dec. 31, 1932; s. Edwin Erdmann and Alvina (Knecht) B.; m. Joella Jane White, March 26, 1951; children—Catherine Jane, Laurence Edward, Douglas Alan. A.B., Washington U., St. Louis, 1953, LL.B., 1956. Bar: Mo., N.Y., N.J. Legal assoc. firm Thompson, Mitchell, Thompson & Douglas, St. Louis, 1956-57, Sullivan and Cromwell, N.Y.C., 1957-65; partner firm Lane & Mittendorf, N.Y.C., 1965—; lectr. in field William Esty Co., Inc., dir.; lectr. in field; dir. Engelhard Hanovia, Inc., Fulfillment Corp. Am. Editor-in-chief: Washington U. Law Quar, 1955-56; Contbr. articles to profl. jours. Trustee Paper Mill Playhouse, Charles Engelhard Found. Mem. Am., N.Y. State bar assns., Bar Assn. City N.Y., Order of Coif, Phi Beta Kappa, Omicron Delta Kappa, Delta Theta Phi. Conglist. Home: 48 Kenilworth Dr Short Hills NJ 07078 Office: Lane & Mittendorf 26 Broadway New York NY 10004

BEINECKE, FREDERICK WILLIAM, II, lawyer, corporation executive; b. Stamford, Conn., June 3, 1943; s. William S. and Elizabeth (Gillespie) B.; m. Candace Krugman, Oct. 2, 1976; 1 son, Jacob Sperry. B.A., Yale U., 1966; J.D., U. Va., 1972; P.M.D., Harvard U., 1977. Bar: N.Y. 1973. Asso. firm Hughes Hubbard & Reed, N.Y.C., 1972-73; gen. counsel, dep. mng. dir. South Street Seaport Mus., N.Y.C., 1973-75; with Sperry and Hutchinson Co., N.Y.C., 1975-82; pres. Gunlocke Co. subs., 1979-80, corp. v.p., 1977-80, pres., 1980-82, dir., 1977-81; pres. Antaeus Enterprises, Inc., 1982—. Trustee Phillips Acad., Andover, Mass.; dir., treas. N.Y.C. Ballet; trustee Trudeau Inst., Saranac Lake, N.Y., N.Y. Zool. Soc. Served to capt. USMC, 1966-69. Decorated Bronze star. Mem. Am. Bar Assn., Assn. Bar City of N.Y. Clubs: River, Yale, Angler's, Ausable, St. Hubert's. Office: 420 Lexington Ave New York NY 10170

BEINECKE, WILLIAM S., corporate executive; b. N.Y.C., May 22, 1914; s. Frederick William and Carrie (Sperry) B.; m. Elizabeth Barrett Gillespie, May 24, 1941; children: Frederick W. II, John B., Sarah S., Frances G. A.B., Yale U., 1936, M.A. (hon.), 1971; LL.B., Columbia U., 1940; LL.D. (hon.), Southwestern U., 1967, Cath. U. Am., 1972. Former asso. firm Chadbourne, Wallace, Parke & Whiteside; co-founder firm Casey, Beinecke & Chase; became gen. counsel The Sperry and Hutchinson Co., N.Y.C., 1952, v.p., 1954-60, pres., 1960-67, chmn. bd., chief exec. officer, 1967-80; trustee Consol. Edison Co., N.Y.C. Trustee, Am. Mus. Natural History, N.Y.C.; chmn. Central Park Conservancy, N.Y.C.; mem. bd. mgrs. N.Y. Bot. Garden.; chmn. bd. Hudson River Found. for Sci. and Environ. Research Inc. Served to comdr. USNR, World War II. Recipient Alumni medal Alumni Fedn. Columbia U., 1971. Mem. Council Fgn. Relations. Clubs: Yale, The Links (N.Y.C.); Baltusrol Golf (Springfield, N.J.); Eastward Ho, Country (Chatham, Mass.); Blind Brook (Purchase, N.Y.). Home: 21 E 79th St New York NY 10021 Office: 420 Lexington Ave New York NY 10170

BEISE, SETH CLARK, banker; b. Windom, Minn., Oct. 13, 1898; s. Henry C. and Blanche (Johnson) B.; m. Virginia Carter, Jan. 27, 1934; children: Sally Ann, Carter Clark. B.S., U. Minn., 1923; LL.D. (hon.), St. Mary's Coll. of Calif., 1960. Clk. Mpls. Trust Co., 1922-24; nat. bank examiner Office Comptroller of Currency, Washington, 1924-27, 33-36; trust officer Peoples Nat. Bank, Jackson, Mich., 1927-30, Nat. Bank of Jackson, 1930-33; with Bank of Am. Nat. Trust and Savs. Assn., San Francisco, 1936—, sr. v.p., 1951-54, pres., 1954-63, chmn. exec. com., 1963-69, also hon. dir.; mem. Bus. Council, Washington, 1959—; Chmn. San Francisco Bay Area Council, 1963-65. Mem. adv. council San Francisco Planning and Urban Renewal Assn., 1968-75; former hon. chmn. Golden Gate chpt. ARC., now hon. life mem. Served with U.S. Army, World War I. Decorated Order of Merit (Italy); recipient Outstanding Achievement award U. Minn., 1955, Econ. Statesmanship award Seattle U., 1957; named One of Fifty Foremost Businessmen of Am. Forbes Mag., 1957, Calif. Industrialist of Yr. Calif. Mus. Sci. and Industry, 1963. Office: Bank of Am Center San Francisco CA 94104

BEISEL, DANIEL CUNNINGHAM, former newspaper publisher; b. Germantown, Pa., June 30, 1916; s. Fred Cornelius and Margaret Stewart (Cunningham) B.; m. Catherine E. Turnbull, Nov. 6, 1941; children: Jane Ellen, Catherine E., Sarah Turnbull, Margaret A. Student, U. Mich., 1934-36. Traffic rep. Green Bay and Western R.R., 1938-42; with Green Bay (Wis.) Press-Gazette, 1946-80, pub., pres., 1965-80; dir. Peoples Marine Bank, Green Bay Packers, Inc. Bd. dirs. U. Wis.-Green Bay Founders Assn., Green Bay br. Am. Found. Religion and Psychiatry. Mem. Green Bay Area C. of C. (past pres.). Episcopalian. Clubs: Oneida Golf and Riding, Delray Dunes Golf and Country, Delray Beach, Kiwanis. Office:: 435 E Walnut St Green Bay WI 54305

BEISEL, ERVIN EUGENE, cons.; b. Frankfort, Ind., Sept. 22, 1913; s. Ervin N. and Nellie (Miller) B.; m. Mary Martha Raaba. Student, N.Mex. Mil. Inst., 1930-31; Ph.B., U. Chgo., 1933. With F.S. Yantis & Co., 1933-34; from credit mgr. to pres. Old Poindexter Distillery (and predecessor companies), 1934-41, 46-48; pres. Pepsi-Cola Louisville Bottlers, 1949-50, Pepsi-Cola Gen. Bottlers, Inc., Chgo., 1951-71, chmn. bd., chief exec. officer, 1972-74, dir., 1951-80; v.p. manpower resources I.C. Industries, Inc., Chgo., 1975-80. Served from pvt. to maj. F.A., AUS, 1942-46. Decorated Bronze Star medal. Home: 99 Woodley Rd Winnetka IL 60093

BEISER, GERALD J., wood products company executive; b. Hamilton, Ohio, Nov. 11, 1930; s. Ralph M. and Eunice (Platt) B.; m. Delores Joy Reynolds, Oct. 8, 1960; children: Jeffrey Gerald, Jennifer Joy. A.B., Earlham Coll., 1952; M.B.A., U. Mich., 1956. Mgmt. trainee Champion Papers, Hamilton, 1956-60, asst. to v.p. finance, 1960-67; dir. budgets and forecasts U. S. Plywood-Champion Papers Inc. (name later changed to Champion Internat.), 1967-69, spl. asst. to chmn., 1968, dir. fin. planning, 1969-70, treas., 1970-72, v.p., treas., 1972-75, sr. v.p. fin., 1975—; mem. East Side adv. bd. Chem. Bank, N.Y.C., Fairfield County adv. bd. Hartford Nat. Bank, Conn. Trustee, mem. exec. com. St. Luke's Sch., New Canaan, Conn. Served with AUS, 1952-54. Mem. Am. Fin. Assn., Am. Paper Inst. (chmn. fin. mgmt. com. 1978-80), Alpha Kappa Psi. Club: Economic (N.Y.C.). Home: 7 Fraser Rd Westport CT 06880 Office: Champion Internat 1 Champion Plaza Stamford CT 06921

BEISTLINE, EARL HOOVER, mining consultant; b. Juneau, Alaska, Nov. 24, 1916; s. Ralph H. and Catherine (Krinach) B.; m. Dorothy Ann Hering, Aug. 24, 1946; children—Ralph Robert, William Calvin, Katherine Noreen, Lynda Marie. B. Mining Engring., U. Alaska, 1939, E.M., 1947, LL.D., 1969. Mem. faculty U. Alaska, 1946—; dean Sch. Mines, 1949-61, Coll. Earth Sci. and Mineral Industry, 1961-75, provost, 1970-75; dean Sch. Mineral Industry, 1975-82, dean emeritus, prof. mining engring., 1982—. Served to maj. AUS, 1941-46. Fellow AAAS; mem. Am. Inst. Mining and Metall. Engrs., Arctic Inst. N. Am., Am. Soc. Engring. Edn., Pioneers of Alaska., Nat. Soc. Profl. Engrs. Home: Box 80148 Fairbanks AK 99708

BEJA, ANTONIO S., advertising executive; b. Lisbon, Portugal, May 3, 1937; came to U.S., 1981; s. Fernando Sarmento and Branca (Graca) B.; m. Maria Graca Moura, Apr. 15, 1976; 1 son, Antonio. B.Sc., Instituto S. Tecnico, Lisbon. With Norman, Craig & Kummel, Madrid, London, 1966-75; pres. Foote, Cone & Belding-Spain, Madrid, 1975-81; exec. v.p. Foote, Cone & Belding, Chgo., 1981-82, pres. Latin Am.-Pacific, South Africa, 1982—; dir. Eurox SA, Lisbon, 1976—. Served with Armed Forces of Portugal, 1959-63. Roman Catholic. Clubs: Adventurers (Chgo.) (dir. 1983—); Estoril Golf (Lisbon); Moraleja Golf (Madrid). Home: 222 E Chestnut St Chicago IL 60611 Office: Foote Cone & Belding 401 N Michigan Ave Chicago IL 60611

BEKEFI, GEORGE, educator; b. Prague, Czechoslovakia, Mar. 14, 1925; s. Emerich and Klara (Braun) B. B.Sc., U. Coll., London, 1948; M.Sc., McGill U., 1950, Ph.D., 1952. Asst. prof. physics McGill U., Montreal, Can., 1952-57; asso. prof. physics Mass. Inst. Tech., 1958-66, prof., 1966—. Office: Physics Dept Room 36-213 Mass Inst Tech Cambridge MA 02139

BEKER, EROL, chemical company executive; b. Istanbul, Turkey, 1919. B.S., Istanbul U.; M.A., New Sch. With Erol Beker Ltd., from 1938, Nat. Phosphate Corp., 1959-64; mgr. fertilizer div. Hooker Chem. Corp., 1964-66; chmn. bd., pres., chief exec. officer, dir. Beker Industries Corp., Greenwich, Conn., 1971—. Address: Beker Industries Corp 124 W Putnam Ave Greenwich CT 06836 *

BEKEY, GEORGE ALBERT, electrical engineer, educator; b. Bratislava, Czechoslovakia, June 19, 1928; came to U.S., 1945, naturalized, 1956; s. Andrew and Elizabeth B.; m. Shirley White, June 10, 1951; children: Ronald Steven, Michelle Elaine. B.S. with honors, U. Calif., Berkeley, 1950; M.S., UCLA, 1952, Ph.D., 1962. Research engr. UCLA, 1950-54; mgr. computer center Beckman Instruments, Los Angeles and Berkeley, 1955-58; mem. sr. staff, dir. computer center TRW Systems Group, Redondo Beach, Calif., 1958-62; mem. faculty U. So. Calif., 1962—, prof. elec. and biomed. engring. and computer sci., 1968—, chmn. dept. elec. engring. systems, 1978—, dir. Robotics Inst., 1984—; cons. to govt. agys. and indsl. orgns. Author: (with W.J. Karplus) Hybrid Computation, 1968; editor 2 books; mem. editorial bd. (with W.J. Karplus) 3 profl. jours.; contbr. over 100 articles to profl. jours. Served with U.S. Army, 1954-56. Recipient Disting. Faculty award Sch. Engring.; Service award U. So. Calif., 1977. Fellow IEEE; mem. Soc. Computer Simulation, Biomed. Engring. Soc., AAAS, World Affairs Council, Sigma Xi, Tau Beta Pi, Eta Kappa Nu. Patentee in computer field. Office: Dept Elec Engring U So Calif Los Angeles CA 90089

BEKKUM, OWEN D., gas company executive; b. Westby, Wis., Mar. 2, 1924; s. Alfred T. and Huldah (Storbakken) B.; m. Dorothy A. Jobs, Aug. 26, 1950. B.B.A., U. Wis., 1950; postgrad., Northwestern U. C.P.A. With Arthur Andersen & Co., 1951-57, Hertz Corp., 1957-62; with No. Ill. Gas Co., Aurora, 1963—, asst. comptroller, 1966-68, comptroller, 1968-70, adminstrv. v.p., 1970-73, exec. v.p., 1973-76, pres., 1976—, also dir.; dir. NICOR, Inc. Bd. dirs. Jr. Achievement, Chgo., 1975-79, vice chmn., 1976-79; bd. dirs. Protestant Found. Greater Chgo., 1975—, Pace Inst., 1977-83, Andrew Corp., 1980—. Served with AUS, 1943-46. Mem. Am. Mgmt. Assn., Am. Gas Assn. (dir. 1978-82, 83—), Inst. Gas Tech. (dir. 1978-82), Gas Research Inst. (dir. 1982—). Clubs: Economic, Mid-Day (Chgo.). Home: 46 Royal Vale Dr Oak Brook IL 60521 Office: PO Box 190 Aurora IL 60507

BELAFONTE, HARRY, singer, concert artist, actor; b. N.Y.C., 1927; s. Harold George and Melvine (Love) B.; m. Julie Robinson, Mar. 8, 1957; children—Adrienne, Shari, David, Gina. Student pub. schs.; D.H.L. (hon.), Park Coll., Mo., 1968, also hon. doctorate humanities; hon. doctorate liberal arts, hon. doctorate arts, New Sch. Social Research. Pres. Belafonte Enterprises, Inc., N.Y.C. Singer, actor: in Broadway shows John Murray Anderson's Almanac (Tony award 1953), Three for Tonight, 1955; motion pictures Bright Road, 1952, Carmen Jones, 1954, Island in the Sun, 1957, The World, the Flesh and the Devil, 1958, Odds Against Tomorrow, 1959, The Angel Levine, 1969, Buck and the Preacher, 1971, Uptown Saturday Night, 1974; producer: stage play To Be Young Gifted and Black, 1969; appeared in: TV movie Grambling's White Tiger, 1981; producer: TV spls. A Time for Laughter, 1967, Harry and Lena, 1969; TV program Tonight with Belafonte, 1960 (Emmy award); appeared on: German TV spl. I Sing What I See, 1980; concert performances, in Cuba, Jamaica, Europe, 1980, Australia, N.Z., U.S., Europe, 1981, Can., 1982, U.S., Europe and with Can. symphony orchs., 1983; producer: Strolling Twenties-TV. Office: Belafonte Enterprises Inc 157 W 57th St New York NY 10019

BELANGER, FREDERICK BELMAR, lawyer; b. Haverhill, Mass., May 2, 1919; s. Frederick Marcotte and Ruthena Minerva B.; m. Gerd Eriksen Nicolaysen, Oct. 22, 1971; children: Brent Jay, Suzanne Eliot. Student, Lowell (Mass.) Tech. Inst., 1938-41; J.D., Loyola U., Los Angeles, 1955. Bar: Calif. 1955, diplomate: Am. Bd. Trial Advs. Sr. partner firm Schell & Delamer, Los Angeles, Santa Ana, San Diego and Van Nuys, Calif., 1962—; mng. partner Schell & Delmar, 1980—; disciplinary referee State Bar Calif. Ct., 1975—; judge pro tempore Los Angeles Superior Ct., 1965—; lectr. Served in U.S. Army, 1941-46; NATOUSA, ETO. Decorated Purple Heart. Fellow Am. Coll. Trial Lawyers, Am. Bd. Profl. Liability Attys.; mem. Am. Bar Assn., Los Angeles County Bar Assn., State Bar Calif. Clubs: Los Angeles, Sons of Norway. Office: 3333 Wilshire Blvd Suite 500 Los Angeles CA 90010

BELANGER, GERARD, economics educator; b. St. Hyacinthe, Que., Can., Oct. 23, 1940; s. Georges and Cecile (Girard) B.; m. Michele Potvin, Sept. 7, 1964; 1 dau., Marie-Jose. B.A., U. Montreal, 1960; B.So.Sc., Laval U., 1961, M.So.Sc., 1967; M.A., Princeton U., 1966. Asst. prof. econs. Laval U., 1967-71, assoc. prof., 1971-77, prof. econs., 1977—; research coordinator Howe Inst., Montreal, 1977-79; mem. fin. com. Council Univs., Que., 1971-73. Co-author: The Price of Health, 1974, Le Prix du Transport au Quebec, 1978; author: L'economique du secteur public, 1981. Woodrow Wilson scholar, 1964-65; Walter N. Rothchild scholar, 1965-66. Fellow Royal Soc. Can. Home: 3384 Gaspareau Ste-Foy Que Canada G1W 2N2 Office: Laval U Dept Econs Quebec PQ Canada G1K 7P4

BELANGER, JEAN ROBERT, publisher; b. Hull, Que., Can., Aug. 5, 1922; s. Joseph Henri and Agnès (Plouffe) B.; m. Marguerite Léger, Sept. 1, 1947; children: Pierre, Paul, Jean, Claire, Lise, Céline. B.A. in Social Studies, U. Ottawa, 1943, B.Ph., 1943; M.A., 1948. With Le Droit Ltd., Ottawa, Ont., Can., 1944—, treas., mgr. labor relations, 1956-72, pub., gen. mgr., 1972—, pub., pres., 1983—; Chmn. Coll. d'Enseignement Gen. Professionel, 1968-71; Vice chmn. bd. govs. U. Ottawa, 1972—; trustee E.B. Health Centre, 1973-83; chmn. bd. dirs, Foyer du Bonheur, Hull, 1976-80. Mem. Can. Daily Newspaper Pubs. Assn. (chmn.), Can. Press Assn., Ottawa Bd. Trade, Soc. Mgmt. Accts. Roman Catholic. Clubs: Rivermead Golf, Cercle Universitaire Ottawa. Office: 375 Rideau St Ottawa ON K1N 5Y7 Canada *Assuring the happiness of the others is still the best way to assure your own.*

BELANGER, PIERRE ROLLAND, electrical engineering educator; b. Montreal, Que., Can., Aug. 18, 1937; s. Pierre Henri and Lucille R. B.; m. Margaret Mary Clark, Aug. 24, 1963; children: Mark, Suzanne, David. B.Eng., McGill U., 1959; S.M., M.I.T., 1961, Ph.D., 1964. Asst. prof. elec. engring. M.I.T., 1964-65; systems analyst The Foxboro (Mass.) Co., 1965-67; asso. prof. McGill U., 1967-75, prof., chmn. dept. elec. engring., 1975—. Mem. IEEE (v.p. 1981-82), Ordre Ingenieurs du Que. Home: 59 Somerville St Westmount PQ Canada H3Z 1J4 Office: 3480 University Montreal PQ Canada H2A 3A7

BÉLANGER, VALÉRIEN, bishop; b. Valleyfield, Que., Can., Apr. 6, 1902; s. Francois and Valentine (Desrosiers) B. B.A., Petit Séminaire de Valleyfield, 1922; L.Th., Grand Séminaire de Montreal, Que., 1926; Ph.L., Angelicum U., Rome, 1930, J.C.L., 1931, J.C.D., 1932; LL.D. (hon.), U. Montreal, 1956. Ordained priest Roman Catholic Ch., 1926, consecrated bishop, 1956; sec. to Bishop of Valleyfield, 1926-28; prof. theology and canon law Grand Séminaire de Montreal, 1934-44; prof. canon law Laval U., Quebec, Que., 1940-47, U. Ottawa, Ont., Can., 1941-44; vice officialis Diocese of Montreal, 1935-39; officialis Regional Tribunal of Montreal, 1947-57; gen. sec. Can. Conf. Bishops of Can., 1955-56; vicar gen. Archdiocese of Montreal, 1956—. Contbr. numerous articles to ecclesiastical publs. Mem. Canadian Canon Law Soc. of Can. Office: 2000 Sherbrooke St W Montreal PQ H3H 1G4 Canada

BELANGER, WILLIAM JOSEPH, polymer applications consultant; b. Chgo., Mar. 20, 1925; m. Keltah Long, Feb. 1, 1947; children:

William Joseph, Thomas, Kathryn, Michael, Jeanne, Judith, Elizabeth, John, Anne. B.S. in Chemistry, St. Louis U., 1948; Ph.D. in Organic Chemistry, Notre Dame U., 1951. Research chemist duPont Co., 1951-53; research chemist, then tech. service mgr. Devoe & Reynolds Co., 1953-60; tech. mgr. resin devel. Celanese Coatings & Specialties Co., Louisville, 1960-69; v.p. tech. and engring. Celanese Polymer Specialities Co., Jeffersontown, Ky., 1970-79; v.p. Specialties Group, Celanese Plastics & Specialties Co., 1979-82; Splty. polymer applications cons., 1982—; tchr. polymer chemistry U. Louisville, 1957. Vice chmn. Jefferson County Housing Authority, 1975-78; trustee Audubon Hosp., 1979-82. Served with USNR, 1943-45. Mem. Am. Chem. Soc., Nat. Paint and Coatings Assn. Patentee in field. Home and Office: 1208 Creighton Hill Rd Louisville KY 40207

BELCASTRO, PATRICK FRANK, pharm. scientist; b. Italy, June 3, 1920; came to U.S., 1927, naturalized, 1943; s. Samuel and Sarah (Mosca) B.; m. Hanna Vilhelmina Jensen, July 6, 1963; children—Helen Maria, Paul Anthony. B.S., Duquesne U., 1942; M.S. (Am. Found. Pharm. Edn. fellow), Purdue U., 1951; Ph.D. in Pharmacy and Pharm. Chemistry (Am. Found. for Pharm. Edn. fellow), Purdue U., 1953. Instr. pharmacy Duquesne U., 1946-49; asst. prof. pharmacy Ohio State U., 1953-54; prof. indsl. pharmacy Purdue U., 1954—. Author: (with others) Physical and Technical Pharmacy, 1963; contbg. editor: Internat. Phar. Abstracts, 1970—, Pharm. Tech, 1977—; contbr. to: Jour. Pharm. Scis. Served with U.S. Army, 1942-46. Mem. Am. Pharm. Assn., Am. Soc. Hosp. Pharmacists, Am. Assn. Colls. Pharmacy, AAUP, Parenteral Drug Assn., Rho Chi, Phi Lambda Upsilon. Roman Catholic. Home: 327 Meridian St West Lafayette IN 47906 Office: Sch Pharmacy and Pharmacal Scis Purdue U West Lafayette IN 47907

BELCHER, BENJAMIN MOORE, paint manufacturing company executive; b. Montclair, N.J., June 30, 1912; s. Ward C. and Ella (Moore) B.; m. Nancy Knapp, May 19, 1934; 3 sons, 2 daus. Student, U. Va. With Benjamin Moore & Co., 1934—, pres., 1952-70, chmn. bd., chief exec. officer, 1955-84, now chmn. exec. com.; staff Chem. Bur., WPB, 1942-45, chief paint sect., 1942-45; cons. NPA. Mem. Nat. Paint and Coatings Assn. (chmn. 1958, 65, dir., mem. exec. com. 1958, 65, 69-71). Home: Lakeville CT 06039 Office: Benjamin Moore & Co 51 Chestnut Ridge Rd Montvale NJ 07645

BELCHER, DONALD DAVID, manufacturing company executive; b. Kansas City, Mo., Nov. 29, 1938; s. Donald Duy and Elizabeth Jane (Martin) B.; m. M. Marie Langguth, Dec. 29, 1962; children: Devon, Eric, Kristin. B.A., Dartmouth Coll., 1960; M.B.A., Stanford U., 1964. Mktg. mgr. Pillsbury Co., Mpls., 1964-70; pres. Troutdale Ranch, Gravios Mills., Inc., Mo., 1970—, also dir., Gravois Mills, Inc., Mo., 1970—; gen. mgr. various divs. Avery Internat., Azusa, Calif., 1972-77; group v.p. Fasson Europe, Lieden, Holland, 1977-82, group v.p. consumer group, Pasadena, Calif., 1982—. Served to capt. U.S. Army, 1960-62. Home: 273 Monte Pl Arcadia CA 91006 Office: Avery Internat 150 N Orange Grove Blvd Pasadena CA 91103

BELCHER, DONALD JENKS, engr., educator; b. Chgo., Feb. 11, 1911; s. Ova Clifford and Helen (Edson) B.; m. Nancy Foote Davies, July 1, 1954; children—Mrs. Gerald O. Whisman, Mrs. J. Peter Brann, Mathew, Mark, Neil, Helen Stacey (dec.). B.S., Purdue U., 1934, M.S., 1940, Ph.D., 1942. Research engr., asst. prof. civil engring. Purdue U., 1937-46; civilian cons. chief engr. Southwest Pacific area, 1943-44; cons. Alaska Permafrost Investigations, 1945-46; asso. prof. civil engring. Cornell U., 1947-49, prof., 1949-76, prof. emeritus, 1976—; dir. research and devel. in measurement of soil moisture and density by neutron and gamma ray scattering, 1949—; dir. Cornell Center of Aerial Photography, 1950-75, head dept. transp. engring., 1948-57; vis. lectr. Grad. Sch. Design, Harvard, 1963—; spl. lectr. Grad. Sch. Engring. and Applied Physics, 1965-69; pres. Donald J. Belcher & Assos., Inc., 1952—; cons. specializing in engring. geology, 1938—; designer computer-based land use and natural resource inventories N.Y. State, P.R., S. Africa, Australia; prin. adviser Venezuela office Nat. Cadastre and Inventory; chief UN Mission to Iran, 1950; selected site for new capital city, Brasilia, Brazil, cons. to govts., Burma, India, Spain, Colombia, Brazil. Prin. author: Formation, Distribution and Engineering Characteristics of Soils, 1943, The Formation, Distribution and Airphoto Identification of U.S. Soils, 1945. Recipient NRC award, 1944; Sigma Xi award, 1945; UN medal for civilian duty with Armed Forces in combat areas, Korea. Mem. ASCE, Chi Epsilon, Sigma Xi, Tau Beta Pi, Pyramid. Home: 1044 Cayuga Heights Rd Ithaca NY 14850

BELCHER, JOHN CHESLOW, sociologist, educator; b. Tulsa, Feb. 26, 1920; s. John Cheslow and Blanche (Renfrow) B.; m. Patricia Lucile Yates, Nov. 25, 1948; children: Meriwyn, John Christopher, Laura (Mrs. Charles McGee), Matthew, Glenda. B.S., Okla. State U., 1943; M.A., La. State U., 1945; Ph.D., U. Wis., 1950. Asst. prof. sociology U. Miss., Oxford, 1947-49; assoc. prof. rural sociology Okla. State U., Stillwater, 1949-55; prof. sociology U. Ga., Athens, 1955—; vis. prof. sociology U. P.R., Rio Piedras, 1969; Fulbright prof. demography Universidad Nacional Pedro Henriquez Urena, Dominican Republic, 1971-72; Cons. in rural sociology UN Devel. Program, Dominican Republic, 1969; cons. div. physician manpower NIH, 1971-72, Universidad de la Republica, Montevideo, Uruguay, 1978, 79; dir. profl. seminars for ex-grantees U.S. Dept. State, Dominican Republic, 1973, 74, 75, 76, 77, 78, 79, Guatemala, 1978, 79. Author: (with King) 1950, (with Morland, Balswick and Rubin) Social Problems in the United States, 1975; also chpts. in books, articles in profl. jours. Recipient Michael award U. Ga., 1967; Tribute of Appreciation Internat. Communication Agy., 1980; Research grantee Health Info. Found., 1959, U.S. Dept. Agr., 1956-58, So. Appalachian Studies, 1959-60, USPHS, 1964-67, Agrl. Devel. Council, 1966-68, Nat. Inst. Child Health and Human Devel., 1971-73, So. Edn. Found., 1974-75, EPA, 1974-75, Adminstrn. on Aging, HEW, 1975-76; Fulbright research scholar, 1979-80. Mem. Am. Sociol. Assn., Am. Pub. Health Assn., Caribbean Studies Assn., Population Assn. Am., Rural, So. sociol. socs., Torch Club. Home: 195 S Homewood Dr Athens GA 30606 Office: Dept Sociology U Ga Athens GA 30602

BELCHER, LOUIS DAVID, financial executive, mayor; b. Battle Creek, Mich., June 25, 1939; s. Louis George and Josephine (Johnson) B.; m. Myrna Elizabeth Stoll, Jan. 31, 1959; children: Debora Louise, Sheri Lynn, Stacy Elizabeth. Student, Kellogg Community Coll., 1959; B.S., Eastern Mich. U., 1962. With Gen. Motors Corp., Livonia, Mich., 1962; adminstr. U. Mich., Ann Arbor, 1962-63; with NCR, Lansing, Mich., 1963-69, Veda, Inc., Ann Arbor, Mich., 1969-72; owner, v.p., treas. First Ann Arbor Corp., 1972-83; owner, chief fin. officer Third Party Services, Inc. and Data Scan, Inc., Ann Arbor, Mich., 1983—; corp. dir. M.W. Microwave, Inc., Ann Arbor, Environment Tech. Corp. Mem. City Council, Ann Arbor, 1974-78; mayor pro tem, Ann Arbor, 1976-78, mayor, Ann Arbor, 1978—. Served to capt. Air N.G., 1956-70. Recipient outstanding alumni awards Kellogg Community Coll., Eastern Mich. U. Coll. Bus., silver elephant award Republican Party. Mem. Air Force Assn., U.S. Conf. Mayors, Mich. Conf. Mayors (pres.). Republican. Mem. Ch. of Christ. Home: 201 Mulholland Ann Arbor MI 48103 Office: 107 Aprill Dr Ann Arbor MI 48103

BELDEN, DAVID LEIGH, industrial engineer, association executive; b. Mpls., Jan. 9, 1935; m. Lois Marion Lind, June 14, 1956; children: Richard Alan, Grant David. B.Gen. Edn., U. Omaha, 1961; M.S. in Indsl. Engring., Stanford U., 1963, Ph.D., 1969; grad., Indsl. Coll. Armed Forces, 1973. Registered profl. engr., Calif.; rated navigator, aviator. Enlisted U.S. Air Force, 1954, commd. 2d lt., 1956, advanced through grades to col., 1973; service in, Thailand; asst. for procurement mgmt. to Sec. Air Force, Washington; ret., 1976; exec. dir. Inst. Indsl. Engrs., Norcross, Ga., 1976—; adj. prof. Far East div. U. Md., 1970; asso. prof. George Washington U., 1974. Author articles in field. Decorated Legion of Merit, Meritorious Service medal, Commendation medal (3). Fellow Am. Inst. Indsl. Engrs.; mem. Am. Assn. Engring. Socs. (bd. govs.); Mem. Council Engring. and Sci. Soc. Execs. (pres. 1984-85), Council Indsl. Engring., Am. Soc. Engring. Edn., Ga. Soc. Assn. Execs., Am. Soc. Assn. Execs., Australian Inst. Indsl. Engrs. (hon.), Alpha Pi Mu. Republican. Club: Dunwoody Country. Home: 1870 Baynham Dr Dunwoody GA 30338 Office: 25 Technology Park-Atlanta Norcross GA 30092

BELDOCK, DONALD TRAVIS, corporation financial executive; b. N.Y.C., May 29, 1934; s. George and Rosa (Tribus) B.; m. Lucy Geringer, Apr. 23, 1971; children: John Anthony, Gwen Ann, James Geringer Christopher. B.A., Yale U., 1955. Mdse., fin. exec. R. H. Macy & Co., N.Y.C., 1955-60; fin. cons. D. T. Beldock & Co., N.Y.C., 1961-66; chmn. fin. com. Basic Resources Corp., N.Y.C., 1966-69, chmn. bd., pres., chief exec. officer, 1970—; chmn., dir. White Shield Greece Oil Corp.; dir. Automatic Toll Systems, Inc., N.Y.C., Fundamental Properties Corp., Ocean Thermal Corp., CRA, Inc., Phoenix. Trustee, treas. Strang Clinic-Preventive Medicine Inst.; bd. dirs. Renewable Energy Inst.; trustee N.Y. Jr. Tennis League, Am. Symphony Orch.; bd. advs. Colo. Timberline Acad.; chmn. bd. dirs. Teamwork Found.; com. Nat. UN Day. Mem. Am. Mgmt. Assn., Fgn. Policy Assn. Clubs: Lotos, Yale, Westchester Country. Home: 784 Park Ave New York NY 10021 Office: 595 Madison Ave New York NY 10022

BELDON, SANFORD T., publisher; b. Scranton, Pa., Nov. 9, 1932; s. Benjamin and Evelyn (Jacobson) B.; m. Jeanne Sherman, June 25, 1967; children: Mary, Kenneth, Emily. B.B.A., CCNY, 1955; postgrad., N.Y. U. Grad. Sch. Bus., 1956-57. Publicist Prentice-Hall, Inc., N.Y.C., 1956-59; publicity dir. Fawcett Publs., Inc., N.Y.C., 1959-62; asst. dir. public relations Crowell-Collier-Macmillan, N.Y.C., 1963-65; dir. advt. and public relations, edn. group Litton Industries, White Plains, N.Y., 1966-68; dir. promotion Balker & Taylor div. W.R. Grace Co., N.Y.C, Balter & Taylor div. W.R. Grace Co., 1968-71; dir. mktg. Book div. Rodale Press, Inc., Emmaus, Pa., 1971-74; dir. advt. Organic Gardening mag., 1974-78, v.p., 1974—, pub., 1978—. Pres. Allentown (Pa.) City Council Ecology and Adv. Com., 1972-75; bd. dirs. Leghigh Valley Child Care, Allentown, 1974—, pres. bd., 1976-80; bd; dirs. Lehigh Valley Conservancy, Allentown, 1976-77, Planned Parenthood of Lehigh County, Pa., 1977-78. Democrat. Jewish. Office: 33 E Minor St Emmaus PA 18049

BELEN, FREDERICK CHRISTOPHER, lawyer; b. Lansing, Mich., Dec. 25, 1913; s. Christopher Frederick and Elizabeth (Lehman) B.; m. Opal Marie Sheets, Feb. 7, 1943; 1 son, Frederick Christopher. A.B., Mich. State U., 1937, Dr. of Laws (hon.), 1967; J.D., George Washington U., 1942. Bar: Mich. 1945, D.C. 1945, Va. 1976, U.S. Supreme Ct. 1975. Sec. to Hon. Andrew Transue, 75th Congress, Hon. George D. O'Brien, 77th-79th congresses; counsel, chief counsel P.O. and Civil Service Com., Ho. of Reps., 1946-61; asst. postmaster gen. charge bur. operations P.O. Dept., 1961-64, dep. postmaster gen., 1964-69; Dir. spl. investigations personnel mgmt.; dir. spl. studies U.S. Postal Service; mem. U.S. delegations various subcoms. Universal Postal Union. Author congressional com. reports and studies. Pres. Nat. Democratic Club, 1974-75. Served to lt. col. AUS, 1941-46; dep. chief intelligence and security div. Army Transp. Corps. Recipient Benjamin Franklin award, 1963; Alumni Achievement award George Wash. U., 1968; Distinquished Alumni award Mich. State U., 1966; Distinguished Service decoration U.S. Army, 1968. Presbyterian (elder). Club: King and Queen Rod and Gun (pres. 1976-79). Home: 2658 N Upshur St Arlington VA 22207 Office: Suite 710 425 13th St NW Washington DC 20004

BELEW, DAVID OWEN, JR., federal judge; b. Ft. Worth, Mar. 27, 1920; s. David Owen and Mazie Despord (Erskine) B.; m. Marjorie Dale Mitchell; children: Marjorie Dale Belew Peterson, Susan Elizabeth Belew Arnoult, David Mitchell. B.A., U. Tex., 1946, LL.B., 1948. Bar: Tex. 1948. Practice with father, Ft. Worth, 1948-49; asst. U.S. atty. No. Dist. Tex., 1949-52; partner firm Cantey, Hanger, Gooch, Munn & Collins, Ft. Worth, 1952-79; U.S. dist. judge No. Dist. Tex., 1979—. Served with AUS, 1942-45. Decorated Silver Star, Purple Heart (3). Mem. Am. Bar Assn., Fed. Bar Assn., State Bar Tex., Ft. Worth-Tarrant County Bar Assn. (pres. 1970). Home: 4451 Crestline Rd Fort Worth TX 76107 Office: US Dist Ct 203 US Courthouse Fort Worth TX 76102

BELFER, ARTHUR B., petroleum company executive; b. Vodzislow, Poland, May 30, 1907; s. Benjamin and Linda (Plapla) B.; m. Rachelle Anisfeld, Feb. 22, 1931 (dec. 1961); children: Selma (Mrs. Lawrence Ruben), Anita (Mrs. Jack Saltz), Robert A.; m. Diane Endelson, Feb. 7, 1965; children: Kenneth M., Kathi Endelson Belfer. LL.D., U. Wyo.; L.H.D., Yeshiva U., Bar-Ilan U. Pres. Belfer Corp., 1941-59; engaged in mfg. sleeping bags for armed forces, 1942-52, engaged in mfg. foamrubber pillows and mattresses, 1949-51; founder, mng. partner Belfer Natural Gas Co., 1954-59; founder, chmn. bd., pres. Belco Petroleum Corp., N.Y.C., 1953-65, chmn. bd., 1962—, also chief exec. officer; gen. partner 630 3d Av. Assocs., 1957—. Pres. Belfer Found.; bd. overseers Albert Einstein Coll. of Medicine of Yeshiva U.; trustee Am. Jewish Com.; mem. bd. Am. Friends Hebrew U.; trustee Yeshiva U.; also sponsor Belfer Grad. Sch. Sci. of univ. Jewish (v.p. synagogue). Clubs: Old Oaks Country, Palm Beach Country. Office: 1 Dag Hammarskjold Plaza New York NY 10017

BELFORD, LEE ARCHER, clergyman, educator; b. Savannah, Ga., Oct. 14, 1913; s. William Thomas and Minnie (Archer) B.; m. Cora Louise McGee, Apr. 12, 1939; children: Fontaine Maury, Mildred Humphreys Okino. B.A., U. of South, 1935, M.Div., 1938, D.D.; S.T.M., Union Theol. Sem., N.Y.C., 1947; Ph.D, Columbia, 1953; Ph.D., U. of South, 1978. Ordained to ministry Episcopal Ch., 1938; vicar in Douglas and Fitzgerald, Ga., 1938-41; rector, Brunswick, Ga., 1941-43; asso. Ch. of Epiphany, N.Y.C., 1948-80; lectr.-prof. Sch. Edn., N.Y.U., 1949-79, chmn. dept. religious edn., 1954-74, chaplain, 1974-79. Author: The Christian and His Jewish Neighbor, 1959, Introduction to Judaism, 1961; Editor: Religious Dimensions in Literature; Contbr. to: The Catholic Ency. for Sch. and Home, also Ency. Americana; Editor: The Church in Georgia, 1949-53; Trustee, asso. editor: The Churchman, 1958—. Served as chaplain USNR, 1943-46. Mem. Religious Edn. Assn., Nat. Council Chs., Am. Acad. Religion, Soc. Sci. Study Religion, Delta Tau Delta, Sigma Upsilon. Home: 107 NW Deer Creek Dr Leland MS 38756

BEL GEDDES, BARBARA, actress; b. N.Y.C., Oct. 31, 1922; d. Norman and Helen Belle (Sneider) Bel G.; m. Carl Schreuer, Jan. 24, 1944 (div. 1951); 1 dau., Susan; m. Windsor Lewis, Apr. 15, 1951 (dec.); 1 dau., Betsy. Student, Buxton Sch., Putney, Andrebrook. First stage role in School for Scandal, Clinton (Conn.) Playhouse, 1939; made Broadway debut in Out of The Frying Pan, 1940; appeared in: Little Darling, 1942, Nine Girls, 1943, Mrs. January and Mr. X, 1944, Deep Are the Roots, 1945 (Clarence Derwent award), The Moon Is Blue, 1952, The Living Room, 1954, Cat on a Hot Tin Roof, 1955, The Sleeping Prince, 1956, Silent Night, Lonely Night, 1959, Mary, Mary, 1961, The Porcelain Year, 1965, Everything in the Garden, 1967, Finishing Touches, 1973, Ah, Wilderness, 1975; motion pictures include The Long Night, 1946, I Remember Mama, 1948, Blood on the Moon, 1948, Caught, 1949, Panic in the Streets, 1950, Fourteen Hours, 1951, The Five Pennies, 1959, Five Branded Women, 1960, By Love Possessed, 1961, The Todd Killings, 1970, Summertree, 1971; appears regularly as: Eleanor Southward Ewing on TV show Dallas, 1978—(Recipient Theatre World award 1946); Author, illustrator: children's books I Like to Be Me, 1963, So Do I, 1972; designer greeting cards for, George Caspari Co. Office: Agency for Performing Arts Inc 120 W 57th St New York NY 10019 *

BEL GEDDES, JOAN, author; b. Los Angeles, Dec. 2, 1916; d. Norman and Helen (Sneider) Bel G.; m. Barry Ulanov, Dec. 16, 1939 (div. 1968); children—Anne, Nicholas, Katherine. B.A., Columbia U., 1937. Researcher and theatrical asst. to Norman Bel Geddes, Inc., N.Y.C., 1937-41; publicity dir. Compton Advt., Inc., N.Y.C., 1942, new program mgr., 1943-47; pub. info. officer UNICEF, N.Y.C., 1970-76, chief of editorial and publs. services, 1976-79; tchr. of drama Birch Wathen Sch., N.Y.C., 1950; mem. faculty of Inst. on Man and Sci., Rensellaerville, N.Y., 1969. Interviewer-hostess: weekly radio program Religion and the Arts, NBC, 1968; author: Small World: A History of Baby Care from the Stone Age to the Spock Age, 1964, How to Parent Alone: A Guide for Single Parents, 1974, To Barbara With Love—Prayers and Reflections by a Believer for a Skeptic (Catholic Press Assn. award 1974), (with others) Art, Obscenity and Your Children, 1969, American Catholics and Vietnam, 1970, The Future of the Family, 1971, Holiness and Mental Health, 1972, The Children's Rights Movement, 1977, And You, Who Do You Say I Am?, 1981; translator: (with Barry Ulanov) Last Essays of Georges Bernanos, 1955; editor: Magic Motorways (Norman B. Geddes), 1940, Earth: Our Crowded Spaceship (Isaac Asimov), 1974; editor in chief: My Baby mag, 1954-56, Congratulations mag, 1954-56. Mem. Authors League of Am., Nat. Soc. of Lit. and the Arts, Am. Theilard de Chardin Assn., Municipal Arts Soc. N.Y., Am. Film Inst., Thomas More Soc. (pres. 1966), Barnard Coll. Alumnae Assn. (class v.p. 1972-76, pres. 1976—). Roman Catholic. Home: 60 E 8th St New York NY 10003 *The longer I live the more I relish life. People praise and envy youth but, to my great surprise, I find that growing older is even better than being young. Pleasures taken for granted before become valued, enlarged, prolonged. Like a baby chortling joyfully at seeing things for the first time, I marvel at seeing things for the hundredth or last time. I don't think of life as a right one can in any way earn or deserve but as an inexplicably, unbelievably amazing gift to enjoy and to use—so each day is, to me, wondrous, surprising, full of unimagined possibilites.*

BELICA, PAUL, investment banker; b. Czechoslovakia, Sept. 27, 1921; s. Paul and Terezia (Virag) B.; m. Bani T. Bose, July 5, 1977. Student, U. Bratislava, U. Prague. Former mem. Czech Diplomatic Corps; exec. dir. N.Y. State Housing Fin. Agy.; chief exec. officer Mcpl. Bond Bank Agy. N.Y. State, N.Y. State Project Fin. Agy., N.Y. State Med. Care Facilities Fin. Agy., N.Y. State Mortgage Agy.; with Smith Barney Harris Upham & Co. Inc., N.Y.C., 1977—. Bd. mgrs. Isabella Geriatric Center, N.Y.C.; treas. Isabella Home, Isabella Housing Co., Isabella Nursing Home. Mem. Am. Mgmt. Assn. Address: Smith Barney Harris Upham & Co Inc 1345 Ave Americas New York NY 10015 *

BELICH, JOHN PATRICK, photographer; b. Peekskill, N.Y., Dec. 6, 1938; s. John Andrew and Iris Patricia (Brown) B.; m. Louise Daniel, June 4, 1971; children: Mary Louise, John P., Andrew J. Student, N.Y. Inst. Photography, St. Petersburg Jr. Coll. Staff news photographer UPI, 1963-69; So. div. photo mgr. Atlanta, 1969-72; photo editor, dir. photography St. Petersburg Times and Evening Independent, 1972—. Mem. parish sch. bd. Transfiguration Ch., St. Petersburg. Recipient Pres.'s medal Nat. Press Photographers Assn., 1978, citation of excellence, 1979. Mem. Nat. Press Photographers Assn. (dir., chmn. info. com. 1978), Atlanta Press Photographers Assn. (past treas., v.p.), Fla. News Photographers Assn., Nat. Press Photographers Found., Sigma Delta Chi. Roman Catholic. Office: 490 1st Ave S St Petersburg FL 33701

BELIN, DAVID WILLIAM, lawyer; b. Washington, June 20, 1928; s. Louis I. and Esther (Klass) B.; m. Constance Newman, Sept. 14, 1952 (dec. June 1980); children—Jonathan L., James M., Joy E., Thomas R., Laura R. B.A., U. Mich., 1951, M.B.A., 1953, J.D., 1954. Bar: Iowa bar 1954. Since practiced in, Des Moines, ptnr. Herrick & Langdon, 1955-62, ptnr. Herrick, Langdon, Sandblom & Belin, 1962-66; sr. ptnr. Herrick, Langdon, Belin, Harris, Langdon & Helmick, 1966-78, Belin, Harris, Helmick, Heartney & Tesdell, 1978—; counsel President's Commn. on Assassination of President Kennedy (Warren Commn.), 1964; exec. dir. Commn. on CIA Activities within the U.S. (Rockefeller Commn.), 1975. Author: November 22, 1963: You Are the Jury, 1973. Dir. Kemper Mut. Funds.; Bd. dirs. Des Moines Civic Music Assn., 1959-61, Des Moines Community Drama Assn., 1961-64, Des Moines Symphony, 1968-70, U. Mich. Alumni Assn., 1963-66. Served with AUS, 1946-47. Recipient Henry M. Bates Meml. award U. Mich. Law Sch., Brotherhood award NCCJ, 1978; hon. orator U. Mich., 1950. Mem. Soc. Barristers, Order of Coif, Phi Beta Kappa, Phi Kappa Phi, Delta Sigma Rho, Beta Alpha Psi. Club: Michigamua. Home: 1705 Plaza Circle Des Moines IA 50322 Office: 2000 Financial Center Des Moines IA 50309 *Knowledge is important because it leads to wisdom, and wisdom is important because it leads to deed.*

BELIN, GASPARD D'ANDELOT, lawyer; b. Scranton, Pa., May 30, 1918; s. Gaspard d'Andelot and Margery (Jenks) B.; m. Harriet Lowell Bundy, Oct. 11, 1941; children: Harriet Lowell Belin Winkelman, Constance Belin Gibb, Richard, Margaretta, Alletta Belin Farmer. B.A., Yale U., 1939, LL.B., 1946. Bar: Mass. 1947. With firm Choate, Hall & Stewart, Boston, 1947-62, partner, 1955-62, 65—; gen. counsel Dept. Treasury, 1962-65; dir. Bank of New Eng., Bank of New Eng. Corp. Past pres. Yale Univ. Council, Cambridge Civic Assn.; trustee Mus. Sci.; v.p. Boston Athenaeum; trustee Brigham & Women's Hosp.; overseer, v.p. Peter Bent Brigham Hosp.; past city councillor Cambridge. Served to capt. AUS, 1942-45; ETO. Fellow Am. Acad. Arts and Scis.; mem. Am., Mass., Boston bar assns., Am. Law Inst. Episcopalian. Home: 4 Willard St Cambridge MA 02138 Office: 60 State St Boston MA 02109

BELIN, JACOB CHAPMAN, paper co. exec.; b. DeFuniak Springs, Fla., Oct. 28, 1914; s. William Jacob and Addie (Leonard) B.; m. Myrle Fillingim, Nov. 28, 1940; children—Jacob Chapman, Stephen Andrew. Student, George Washington U., 1935-38. Dir. sales St. Joe Paper Co., Fla., 1949-56, v.p., 1956-68, pres., dir., 1968—; v.p., dir. St. Joseph Land & Devel. Co., Jacksonville Properties, Inc., Wakulla Silver Springs; pres., dir. St. Joe Container Co.; chmn. bd., dir. New Eng. Container Co.; dir. St. Josaeph Tel. & Tel. Co., Talisman Sugar Corp. Bd. dirs. Nemours Found., Alfred I. duPont Found.; trustee Edward Ball Wildlife Found., Estate of Alfred I. DuPont. Mem. Kappa Alpha. Baptist. Clubs: Elks, Rotary. Office: St Joe Paper Co PO Box 190 Port Saint Joe FL 32456 *

BELING, WILLARD A., international relations educator, consultant; b. Great Bend, N.D., Mar. 16, 1919; s. Adolph W. and Sadie A. (Warner) B.; m. Betty M. Melberg, Feb. 23, 1947; children: Janna R.,

Kristen L. B.A., UCLA, 1943; Ph.D., Princeton U., 1947. Exec. Arabian Am. Oil Co., 1947-58; mem. faculty Harvard U., Cambridge, Mass., 1958-60; prof. internat. relations U. So. Calif., Los Angeles, 1960—. Author: Pan-Arabism and Labor, 1960, Nationalism and African Labor, 1965; editor, author: The Middle East, 1972, King Faisal, 1980; editor: Maghreb Digest jour., 1961-68, others. Fellow Am. Council Learned Socs., 1947, Social Sci. Research Council, 1948, Harvard U., 1958. Mem. Phi Beta Kappa. Office: Dept Internat Relations U So Calif University Park Los Angeles CA 90007

BELINGER, HARRY ROBERT, corp. exec.; b. Phila., Sept. 16, 1927; s. Harry and Florence (McGovern) B.; m. Jean Marie O'Neill, Nov. 30, 1957; 1 dau., Lizanne. B.S., Temple U., 1957. Reporter Phila. bur. U.P.I., 1957-61; reporter Phila. Daily News, 1961-63, asst. city editor, 1963-66, city editor, 1966-68, 70-71, Phila. Inquirer, 1968-70; city rep., dir. commerce City of Phila., 1972-76; v.p. dir. public affairs ARA Services, Inc., Phila., 1976—; Former ex-officio mem. City Planning Commn.; former v.p. Phila. Indsl. Devel. Corp.; past dir., mem. exec. com. Phila. Port Corp. Mem. sch. bd. Archdiocese of Phila.; past bd. dirs., mem. exec. com. Conv. and Tourist Bur.; past bd. dirs. Phila. Civic Center. Served with inf. AUS, 1950-52. Mem. Phila. Press Assn. (dir. 1964-66). Home: 7030 Sherwood Rd Philadelphia PA 19151 Office: Curtis Bldg Independence Sq Philadelphia PA 19106

BELISLE, GILLES, bishop; b. Clarence Creek, Ont., Can., Oct. 7, 1923; s. Hermile and Clara (Charlebois) B. Ordained priest Roman Catholic Ch., 1950; diocesan pastoral coordinator, aux. bishop Archdiocese of Ottawa, 1977—. Home: 95 Parent Ottawa ON K1N 5K1 Canada Office: 256 King Edward Ottawa ON K1N 7M1 Canada

BELITT, BEN, author, educator; b. N.Y.C., May 2, 1911; s. Lewis and Ida (Lewitt) B. B.A., U. Va., 1932, M.A., 1934, postgrad., 1934-36. Asst. lit. editor Nation, 1936-37; prof. English Bennington (Vt.) Coll., 1938—; mem. faculty dance summer schs. Bennington Coll., Mills Coll., 1939, Conn. Coll., 1948-49. Recipient (Shelley Meml. award in poetry 1936, Oscar Blumenthal award in poetry 1956, Chgo. Civic Arts award 1957, Brandeis Creative Arts award in poetry 1962, Nat. Inst. Arts and Letters award in poetry 1965); Author: poems The Five-Fold Mesh, 1938, Wilderness Stair, 1955, The Enemy Joy; New and Selected Poems, 1964, Nowhere But Light; Poems, 1964-1969, The Double Witness, 1970-75; prose School of the Soldier, 1949; essays Adam's Dream: A Preface to Translation, 1978; Editor and translator: Four Poems by Rimbaud: The Problem of Translation, 1947, Poet in New York (Federico García Lorca), 1955, Selected Poems of Pablo Neruda, 1961, Juan de Mairena and Poems from the Apocryphal Songbooks (Antonio Machado), 1963, The Selected Poems of Rafael Alberti, 1965, Pablo Neruda: A New Decade; Poems, 1958-67, 1969, Poems from Canto General, 1969, To Painting (Rafael Alberti), 1972, Splendor and Death of Joaquín Murieta (Pablo Neruda), 1972, New Poems: 1968-70 (Pablo Neruda), 1972, Five Decades: Poems 1925-70 (Pablo Neruda), 1974 Skystones (Pablo Neruda), 1981; Contbr. to: The Selected Poems of Federico García Lorca, 1955, Cántico, Selections (Jorge Guillén), 1965, Selected Poems (Eugenio Montale), 1965, Jorge Luis Borges: Selected Poems, 1923-67), 1972. Served with AUS, 1942-44. Guggenheim fellow, 1946; Nat. Endowment for the Arts grantee, 1967-68; Ben Belitt lectureship endowment Bennington Coll., 1977; Russell Loines award for poetry Am. Acad. and Inst. Arts and Letters, 1981. Fellow Vt. Acad. Arts and Scis.; mem. P.E.N., Authors Guild, Phi Beta Kappa. Address: Bennington College Bennington VT 05201

BELJAN, JOHN RICHARD, university provost and dean, medical educator; b. Detroit, May 26, 1930; s. Joseph and Margaret Anne (Brozovich) B.; m. Bernadette Marie Marenda, Feb. 2, 1952; children: Ann Marie, John Richard, Paul Eric. B.S., U. Mich., 1951, M.D., 1954. Diplomate: Am. Bd. Surgery. Intern U. Mich., 1954-55, resident in gen. surgery, 1955-59; dir. med. services Stuart div. Atlas Chem. Industries, Pasadena, Calif., 1965-66; from asst. prof. to assoc. prof. surgery U. Calif. Med. Sch., Davis, 1966-74, from asst. prof. to assoc. prof. engring., 1968-74, from asst. dean to assoc. dean, 1971-74; prof. surgery, prof. biol. engring. Wright State U., Dayton, Ohio, 1974-83, dean Sch. Medicine, 1974-81, vice provost Sch. Medicine, 1974-78, v.p. health affairs Sch. Medicine, 1978-81, provost, sr. v.p., 1981-83; provost, v.p. acad. affairs, prof. surgery, biomed. engring., dean Sch. Medicine Hahnemann U., Phila., 1983—; prof. arts and scis., assoc. v.p. med. affairs Central State U., Wilberforce, Ohio, 1976—; trustee Cox Heart Inst., 1975-77, Drew Health Center, 1977-78, Wright State U. Found., 1975-83; trustee, regional v.p. Engring. and Sci. Inst. Hall of Fame, 1983—; bd. dirs. Miami Valley Health Systems Agy., 1975-82; cons. in field. Author articles, revs., chpts. in books. Served with M.C. USAF, 1955-65. Decorated Commendation medal; Braun fellow, 1949; grantee USPHS, 1967—; NASA, 1968—. Fellow A.C.S., Royal Soc. Medicine; mem. Aerospace Med. Assn., AAUP, Inst. Aeros. and Astronautics, AMA (council on sci. affairs 1978—), Assn. Acad. Surgery, Biomed. Engring. Soc., F.A. Coller, Dayton surg. socs., Flying Physicians Assn., Ohio Med. Soc., Greene County Med. Soc., Montgomery County Med. Soc. (councilor 1974—), IEEE, Instrument Soc. Am., Royal Soc. Medicine, Soc. Internat. de Chirurgie, Phi Beta Kappa, Phi Eta Sigma, Phi Kappa Phi, Alpha Kappa Kappa. Clubs: Mich. Alumni (Outstanding Alumnus award 1976), Racquet (Dayton); University of Washington, Oakwood Fur, Fin and Feather. Home: 29 Oriole Way Moorestown NJ 08057 Office: Hahnemann Univ Broad and Vine Sts Philadelphia PA 19102

BELK, IRWIN, corporation executive, past Democratic national committeeman for N.C.; b. Charlotte, N.C., Apr. 4, 1922; s. William Henry and Mary Leonora (Irwin) B.; m. Carol Grotnes, Sept. 11, 1948; children: William Irwin, Irene Belk Miltimore, Marilyn Belk Bryan, Carl Grotnes. Student, McCallie Sch., Davidson Coll.; grad., U. N.C., 1946; Student, Exec. Group. With Belk Enterprises, Inc.; pres. Belk Fin. Co.; officer, dir. Belk Group Stores, Charlotte; pres., dir. PMC, Inc., Raleigh, N.C.; v.p. Belk Stores Services, Inc., Charlotte; chmn. bd. Monroe Hardware Co.; dir. Adams-Millis Corp., High Point, N.C., Fidelity Bankers Life Ins. Co., Richmond, Va., First Union Nat. Bank, Charlotte, 1st Union Corp., Lumbermen's Mut. Casualty, Co., Chgo., Stonecutter Mills, Spindale, N.C.; Past pres. men's council N.C. Synod, Presbyn. Ch.; mem. exec. com. Hist. Found. Presbyn and Reformed Chs. (Montreat), N.C.; mem. Nat. Council on Crime and Delinquency. Past pres. N.C. div. Am. Cancer Soc.; trustee N.C. Symphony Soc.; chmn. U.S. Olympic Com. for N.C.; mem. Gov.'s Commn. to Study Cause and Control of Cancer, Edenton and Chowan County Hist. Commn.; past mem. City of Charlotte Urban Redevel. Com.; mem. N.C. Ho. of Reps., 1959-60, 61-62, N.C. Senate, 1963-66, N.C. Legis. Council, 1963-64, Legis. Research Commn., 1965-66, Democratic nat. committeeman for, N.C., 1969-72; del. Dem. Nat. Convs., 1956, 60, 64, 68, 72; bd. dirs. Med. Found. N.C., N.C. State Bus. Found. N.C., Chapel Hill, Ednl. Found., Chapel Hill, Found. of U. N.C., Charlotte, Sch. of Design, N.C. State U.; bd. dirs., mem. exec. com. N.C. Assn. for Blind; bd. dirs., past pres. N.C. chpt. Nat. Soc. Prevention Blindness; ho. dels. Am. Cancer Soc.; bd. dirs. Charlotte Opera Assn.; bd. govs. U. N.C.; trustee Queens Coll., Charlotte, Presbyn. Coll., Clinton, S.C.; bd. advisors Belk Found.; mem. adv. council Wingate (N.C.) Coll.; bd. visitors Babcock Grad. Sch. Mgmt., Wake Forest U.; former bd. assos. Meredith Coll., Raleigh; bd. counselors Erskine Coll., Due West, S.C.; bd. advisers Western Carolina U., Cullowhee, N.C.; former bd. advisers Campbell Coll., Buies Creek, N.C. Served with USAAF, World War II. Recipient Outstanding Young Man award Charlotte, 1954-57. Mem. N.C. (past pres., dir.), Charlotte mchts. assns., Charlotte C. of C. (exec. com., dir.), N.C. Presbyn. Hist. Soc. (past pres.), Kappa Alpha, Delta Sigma Pi. Democrat. Presbyterian (elder, past deacon). Clubs: Masons, Shriners, Lions (Charlotte, dist. gov.) (past pres.); Charlotte City, Charlotte Country, Charlotte Execs. (past pres.), Charlotte Carrousel (past pres.), Myers Park Country (Charlotte); Sky (N.Y.C.). Home: R2 Box 620 Mooresville NC 28115 Office: PO Box 31788 Charlotte NC 28231

BELK, JOHN BLANTON, educational and cultural organization executive; b. Orlando, Fla., Feb. 4, 1925; s. John Blanton and Jennie (Wannamaker) B.; m. Elizabeth Jane Wilkes, Dec. 11, 1954; children: Virginia Elizabeth, Katherine Wilkes. Student, Davidson Coll., 1943, U. N.C., 1943-45. Congl. aide U.S. Congress, Washington, 1949-50; with Moral Re-Armament (numerous locations), 1950-68, exec. dir., 1966-68; founder, chmn. bd., pres. Up With People, Tuscon, 1968—. One-man shows include, Volcano Art Gallery, Hawaii, 1976. Served to lt. (j.g.) USN, 1943-45; PTO. Decorated letter of commendation, Order Vasco Nunez de Balboa, Panama. Mem. Zeta Psi. Clubs: Mountain Oyster; Old Pueblo (Tucson); Guayamas Yacht (Mexico). Home: 2920 Cerrado los Palitos Tucson AZ 85718 Office: Up With People 3103 N Campbell Ave Tucson AZ 85719

BELK, JOHN MONTGOMERY, dept. store exec.; b. Charlotte, Mar. 29, 1920; s. William Henry and Mary (Irwin) B.; m. Claudia Watkins, Feb. 20, 1971. B.S. in Economics, Davidson Coll., 1941. With Belk Stores Services, Inc., Charlotte, 1941—, pres., 1955—, chmn., 1980—, also dir.; mayor, Charlotte, 1969-77; dir. Wachovia Corp., Charlotte and Winston-Salem, N.C., Coca-Cola Bottling Co. Consol., Charlotte, So. Radio Corp., Charlotte. Mem. exec. bd. S.E. region Boy Scouts Am., 1958—, mem. nat. adv. bd., 1979—, v.p. nat. orgn., 1980-81; trustee Davidson Coll.; bd. dirs. Found. U. N.C., Charlotte, N.C. Research Triangle Found., Tom Haggai & Assos. Found., N.C. Sports Hall of Fame, Mint Mus. Served to capt., U.S. Army; 1943-45, 50-52. Recipient Silver Beaver award Boy Scouts Am., 1955, Silver Antelope award, 1962, Distinguished Eagle Scout award. Mem. Charlotte C. of C. (pres. 1964), Am. Mgmt. Assn. (dir.), Nat. Retail Mchts. Assn. (chmn. 1974), World Bus. Council, Am. Legion, Omicron Delta Kappa. Club: Masons. Home: 435 Hempstead Pl Charlotte NC 28207 Office: 308 E 5th St Charlotte NC 28231

BELKIN, BORIS DAVID, violinist; b. Sverdpovsk, USSR, Jan. 26, 1948; s. David Boris and Anna Alexandre B.; 1 son, Julian. Student, Central Music Sch., Moscow, 1969, Moscow Conservatory, 1969-74; studied with, Yankelevitch and Andrievsky. Violinist; appeared with orchs. throughout world, including, N.Y. Philharm., Israel Philharm., Chgo. Symphony Orch., Los Angeles Philharm., Cleve. Symphony Orch., Boston Symphony Orch., Berlin Philharm., Royal Philharm., Phila. Symphony Orch., Paris National, Vienna Symphony, London Philharm., Pitts. Symphony Orch.; also rec. artist, Decca. Recipient 1st prize Nat. Violin Competition USSR, 1973. Office: car ICM Artists Ltd 40 W 57th St New York NY 10019

BELKNAP, JOHN C., financial executive; b. Colombo, Sri Lanka, Aug. 24, 1946; s. Robert Jackson B. and Elsie (Green) Pearson; m. Ann D. Underhill, Aug. 24, 1974. B.A., Cornell U., 1968, M.B.A., 1970. C.P.A., N.Y. Sr. acct. Arthur Young & Co., N.Y.C., 1970-73; asst. controller Kay Corp., N.Y.C., 1973-74, v.p., chief fin. officer, 1979—; chief fin. officer Kay Jewelers, Inc., Alexandria, Va., 1974-79. Mem. Am. Inst. C.P.A.s, N.Y. Soc. C.P.A.s Republican. Episcopalian. Club: Belle Haven (Greenwich, Conn.). Home: 280 Stanwich Rd Greenwich CT 06830 Office: Kay Corp Wall St Plaza New York NY 10005

BELKNAP, NORTON, petroleum company director; b. Topeka, June 17, 1925; s. Paul Edward and Twila Moffett (Norton) B.; m. Mary Lonam, June 7, 1950; children: Paula Belknap Reynolds, David Barrett, Randall Page. B.S., MIT, 1950, M.S., 1951. Various tech. and supervisory positions Exxon, 1951-60; v.p., dir. Esso, Japan, 1961-65, chmn., mng. dir., Australia, 1966-69; v.p., exec. v.p., dir. Esso Europe, 1969-73; v.p. corporate planning Exxon Corp., N.Y.C., 1973-79; sr. v.p. Exxon Internat., N.Y.C., 1979-82; dir., cons. Lend Lease Petroleum Ltd., Sydney, Australia, 1982—; cons. corp. strategic planning Aneutronix, Inc., 1982—; dir. Haddad & Brooks; cons. Nat. Steel Corp., 1982—. Trustee, chmn. exec. com. Carnegie Hall; mem. Met. Opera Assn.; trustee Mcpl. Arts Soc. Served to 1st lt. USAAF, 1943-46. Decorated Air medal with oak leaf cluster. Mem. Tau Beta Pi. Clubs: Union, Met. Opera (N.Y.C.). Home: 563 Park Ave New York NY 10021 Office: 1251 Ave of the Americas New York NY 10020

BELKNAP, ROBERT LAMONT, educator; b. N.Y.C., Dec. 23, 1929; s. Chauncey and Dorothy (Lamont) B.; m. Josephine E. Hornor, Aug. 20, 1955; children: Lydia, Ellen, Abigail. A.B., Princeton U., 1951; postgrad., U. Paris, 1951-52; M.A., Columbia U., 1954; cert., Russian Inst., 1957, Ph.D., 1960; postgrad., Leningrad U., 1963-64. Instr. in Russian Columbia U., 1957-60, asst. prof., 1960-63, asso. prof., 1963-68, prof., 1968—, chmn. freshman humanities, 1963, 67-68, asso. dean student affairs, 1968-69, acting dean, 1976-77; dir. Russian Inst., 1977-80; vis. asso. prof. Russian Ind. U., 1966, 67; adj. prof. Russian Yale U., 1967. Author: The Structure of the Brothers Karamazov, 1967, (co-author) General Education and The Reintegration of the University, 1977. Pres. bd. dirs. Brearley Sch., N.Y.C. Served with U.S. Army, 1953-55. Home: 440 Riverside Dr New York NY 10027 Office: Columbia U Slavic Dept New York NY 10027 *Students rarely learn anything they are told. They often learn the things they say themselves. Good teaching wrestles them into saying sensible, verifiable, interesting, and sometimes important things.*

BELL, BELDEN HILL, government official; b. Cedar Rapids, Iowa, May 22, 1935; s. Robert P. and Margaret M. (Hill) B.; m. Rae E. Graham, Nov. 25, 1960; children: Rebecca Allyn, Leign Margaret, Heather Anne. B.A., Ind. U., Dartmouth, 1957; J.D., Emory U., 1959. Bar: Ind. 1959, U.S. Supreme Ct. 1967. Legal asst. Caro, Roger Zion, Washington, 1967-75; legal specialist FEA, Washington, 1975; dep. dir. House GOP Study Commn., 1977-80; coordinator Reagan Fgn. Policy Advisors, 1980, State Transition Team, 1980-81; dep. asst. sec. Dept. State, Washington, 1981-83; observer Zimbabwe Elections, 1979-80; mem. German War Art Com., Dept. Army, 1982. Author: (editor) Nicaragua Ally Under Siege, 1978; columnist: Hoosier Viewpoint, 1974-75, Different Drum, 1977-78. Republican nominee for Congress, Ind. 8th Dist., 1976, State Legis., Ind., 1960. Served with USAFR, 1959-65. Recipient cert. of merit FEA, 1975; Eisenhower fellow, 1983. Mem. ABA, Phi Delta Phi. Republican. Clubs: Bull Elephants, Rams. Lodges: Masons; Shriners. Home: 4215 Pickering Pl Alexandria VA 22309 Office: Dept State C St NW Washington DC 20520

BELL, CAROLYN SHAW, economist, educator; b. Framingham, Mass., June 21, 1920; d. Clarence Edward and Grace (Wellington) Shaw; m. Nelson S. Bell, Aug. 26, 1953; 1 dau. by previous marriage, Tova Marie. A.B. magna cum laude, Mt. Holyoke Coll., 1941; Ph.D., London (Eng.) Sch. Econs., 1949; D.H.L. (hon.), Babson Coll., 1983. Economist OPA, 1941-45; research economist London Sch. Econs., 1946-47, Social Sci. Research Council, Harvard, 1950-53; mem. faculty Wellesley Coll., 1950—, prof. econs., 1962—, chmn. dept., 1962-65, 79-82, Katharine Coman prof. econs., 1970—; Pub. mem. Fed. Adv. Council on Unemployment Ins., 1974-77, chairwoman, 1975-77; bd. econ. advisers Pub. Interest Econ. Center; bd. overseers Amos Tuck Grad. Sch. Bus. Adminstrn., Dartmouth, 1973-79; mem. econ. policy council UN Assn., 1976—; trustee Joint Council Econ. Edn., 1975—, Tchrs. Ins. and Annuity Assn., 1977—; mem. NRC Assembly Behavioral and Social Scis., 1977—. Author: (with W.W. Cochrane) Economics of Consumption, 1956, Consumer Choice in the U.S. Economy, 1967, The Economics of the Ghetto, 1970, (with others) Coping in a Troubled Society, 1974; also articles., Radio and television commentator; Mem. bd. editors: Challenge, Jour. Econ. Edn. Trustee Crittenton Hastings House, 1977-83. Mem. Am. Econs. Assn. (chmn. com. on status of women in econs. profession 1972-74, mem. exec. com. 1975-77), AAUP (pres. Wellesley chpt. 1965-66), AAUW (Shirley Farr fellow 1961-62), ACLU, Assn. Evolutionary Econs. (dir. 1973-75), Eastern Econ. Assn. (exec. bd. 1983—), UN Assn. (dir. 1980—), Boston Econ. Club, Phi Beta Kappa (pres. Eta of Mass. chpt. 1978-80). Home: 167 Clay Brook Rd Dover MA 02030 Office: Wellesley Coll Wellesley MA 02181

BELL, CHARLES ANDERSON, hotel exec.; b. New Brighton, Pa., Aug. 30, 1925; s. Charles Anderson and Elizabeth (Pollock) B.; m. Claire Naughton, Oct. 1, 1949; children—Charles Anderson III, Jane Canning. B.S., Cornell U., 1949. Food and beverage controller Caribe Hilton Hotel, San Juan, P.R., 1949, purchasing agt., 1950; food cons. Harris, Kerr, Forster, N.Y.C., 1952-53; chief steward Hotel Plaza, 1953; mgr. coffee house Hotel New Yorker, 1954, food and beverage mgr., 1955-56; asst. dir. food and beverage operations Eastern div. Hilton Hotels Corp., 1957; dir. food and beverage operations Hilton Internat. Co., 1958-61, v.p. adminstrn., 1962-70, sr. v.p. adminstrn., 1970-73; exec. v.p. Western Hemisphere ops. and corp. tech. services, 1973—, also dir. Served with USAAF, 1943-46. Mem. Am. Hotel Assn., Cornell Soc. Hotelmen, Les Amis d'Escoffier Soc., Chevaliers du Tastevin Soc., Commanderie du Bontemps du Medoc et des Graves (grand councilor), Alpha Sigma Phi. Republican. Clubs: Quaker Hill Country (Pawling, N.Y.); Marco Polo, at World Trade Center (N.Y.C.). Home: 29 Washington Sq W New York NY 10011 Office: Waldorf Astoria Hotel 301 Park Ave New York NY 10022

BELL, CHARLES GREENLEAF, author, educator; b. Greenville, Miss., Oct. 31, 1916; s. Percy Bell and Nona Oliver Archer; m. Diana Mason, July 23, 1949; children: Carola M. Birnbaum, Sandra M.; children by previous marriage: Nona D., Charlotte C., Margaret Delia. B.S., U. Va., 1936; B.A., Oxford (Eng.) U., 1938, Litt.B., 1939, M.A., 1966. Instr. English Blackburn Coll., Carlinville, Ill., 1939-40; instr. English Iowa State Coll., Ames, 1940-43, asst. prof., 1943-45, asst. in physics, 1943-45; research asst. in physics, Princeton, 1945, asst. prof. English, 1945-49; asst. prof. humanities U. Chgo., 1949-56; tutor math., sci., langs. Great Books Seminars, St. John's Coll., Annapolis, Md., 1956-67, western br. Sante Fe, 1967—; dir. Grad. Preceptorial on dimensions of history, 1972-73; Lectr. history of western arts adult edn. Springfield (Ill.) Pub. Library, 1939-40; lectr. cultural history Black Mountain Coll., N.C., summer, 1947; guest prof. U. Frankfort, Germany, 1952, U. P.R., Mayaguez, 1955-56, dir. honors program, 1955-56; Fulbright prof. Technische Hochschule Munich, Germany, 1958-59; writer in residence, lectr. modern poetry U. Rochester, N.Y., spring 1967; guest prof. SUNY, 1970. Author: verse Songs for a New America, 1953, rev. edit., 1966, Delta Return, 1956, rev. edit., 1969; novels The Married Land, 1962, The Half Gods, 1968; author: film The Spirit of Rome, 1965; 38 slide-tape studies Symbolic History, The Human Arts: Through Sight and Sound; Contbr. numerous poems to, Harper's mag., New Yorker, Atlantic Monthly and other lit. publs.; contbr. short stories and articles to lit. jours. Rockefeller grantee, 1948; Ford Found. fellow, 1952-53. Home: 1260 Canyon Rd Santa Fe NM 87501 Office: St John's College Santa Fe NM 87501

BELL, CHESTER GORDON, computer engineering company executive; b. Kirksville, Mo., Aug. 19, 1934; s. Roy Chester and Lola Dolph (Gordon) B.; m. Gwendolyn Kay Druyor, Jan. 3, 1959; children: Brigham Roy, Laura Louise. B.S. in E.E, M.I.T., 1956, M.S., 1957. Engr. Speech Communication Lab., M.I.T., 1959-60; mgr. computer design Digital Equipment Corp., Maynard, Mass., 1960-66, v.p. engring., 1972-83; chief tech. officer Encore Computer Corp., Wellesley Hills, Mass., 1984—; prof. computer sci. Carnegie-Mellon U., 1966-72; dir. Inst. Research and Coordination Acoustic Music, 1976-81, Computer Mus., 1982—. Author: (with Newell) Computer Structures, 1971, (with Grason, Newell) Designing Computers and Digital Systems, 1972, (with Mudge, McNamara) Computer Engineering, 1978, (with Siewiorek, Newell) Computer Structures, 1982. Recipient 6th Mellon Inst. award, 1972. Fellow IEEE (McDowell award 1975, Eckert-Mauchly award 1982), AAAS; mem. Nat. Acad. Engring., Assn. Computing Machinery (editor Computer Structures sect. 1972-78), Eta Kappa Nu. Home: Page Farm Rd Lincoln MA 01773 Office: 15 Walnut St Wellesley Hills MA 02181

BELL, C(LYDE) RITCHIE, botany educator; b. Cin., Apr. 10, 1921; s. William Harold and Mary Edith (Spielman) B.; m. Sarah Foushee Fore, Jan. 14, 1943. A.B., U. N.C., 1947, M.A., 1949; Ph.D., U. Calif.-Berkeley, 1953. Instr., U. Ill., 1953-55; asst. prof. U. N.C., Chapel Hill, 1955-59, asso. prof., 1959-66, prof. botany, 1966—; dir. N.C. Bot. Garden, 1960—. Author: (with W.S. Justice) Wild Flowers of North Carolina, 1968, (with others) Manual of the Vascular Flora of the Carolinas, 1968, Vascular Plant Systematics, 1974, (with B.J. Taylor) Florida Wild Flowers and Roadside Plants, 1982. Served to 1st lt. USAAF, 1942-45. Decorated Air medal; recipient Silver Seal award Nat. Council State Garden Clubs, 1979. Fellow AAAS; mem. Am. Inst. Biol. Scis. (governing bd. 1970-73), Commn. Undergrad. Edn. Biol. Scis. (exec. com. 1970), Bot. Soc. Am. (program dir. 1967-69, treas. 1972-76, v.p. 1978), Am. Soc. Plant Taxonomists (sec. 1959-62, council 1962-68, pres. 1976), Soc. Study Evolution, Internat. Assn. Plant Taxonomists, Assn. Southeastern Biologists (exec. com. 1963-65). Office: 406 Coker Hall U NC Chapel Hill NC 27514

BELL, CLYDE ROBERTS, naval officer; b. Balt., Apr. 12, 1931; s. William Cameron and Rachel (Roberts) B.; m. Carol Anne Murphy, June 13, 1980; children: Diane, Nancy, Mary Lynn, Catherine, Robert, Brian, Douglas, Jeffrey. B.S. in Marine Engring, U.S. Naval Acad., 1953; student, Naval Nuclear Power Sch., 1958-59. Commd. ensign U.S. Navy, 1953, advanced through grades to rear adm., 1977; served as div. officer aboard surface ships, 1953-55, trained, served as dept. head aboard diesel submarines, 1955-58, engr. aboard nuclear submarines, 1960-62, exec. officer, 1962-67, comdr., 1970-73, in charge overhaul of shipbd. nuclear power plants in naval shipyard, 1973-75, comdr. squadron nuclear submarines, 1975-76, aide, exec. asst. to under sec. of navy, Washington, 1976-77; dir. naval communications Dept. Navy, Washington, 1977-80; comdr. Submarine Group 8, 1980-82; dir. Force Level Plans Office of Naval Warfare, 1982-84, dep. dir., 1984—; coach, mgr. Navy's Interservice Softball Championship Team, 1955. Bd. dirs. Armed Forces Relief and Benefit Assn.; pres. Stratford Elem. Sch. PTA, Alexandria, Va., 1968. Decorated Legion of Merit with gold star, Meritorious Service medal with 2 gold stars, Navy Commendation medal with 3 gold stars, Navy Achievement medal; named Man of Yr. Bremerton Navy League, 1975. Mem. Armed Forces Communications and Electronics Assn. (dir.), Naval Acad. Alumni Assn., Navy Mut. Aid Assn. (nonresident dir.). Episcopalian. Clubs: Army-Navy, Army-Navy Country. Office: Dep Dir Naval Warfare OP-095B Navy Dept Washington DC 20350

BELL, DANIEL, sociologist; b. N.Y.C., May 10, 1919; s. Benjamin and Anna (Kaplan) B.; m. Nora Potashnick, Sept. 20, 1943; 1 dau., Jordy; m. Elaine Graham, Apr. 3, 1949 (div.); m. Pearl Kazin, Dec. 18, 1960; 1 son, David. B.S., Coll. City N.Y., 1938; Ph.D., Columbia. Staff writer The New Leader, 1939-41, mng. editor, 1941-44, Common Sense, 1945; instr. to asst. prof. social scis. U. Chgo., 1945-48; Labor editor Fortune mag., 1948-58; lectr. sociology, Columbia, 1952-58, prof. sociology, 1958-69, Harvard Univ., 1969-80, Henry Ford II prof. social scis., 1980—; Mem. Pres.'s Commn. on Tech., Automation and Econ. Progress; U.S. rep. D.E.C.D. interfutures project, 1976-79; mem. Pres.'s Commn. for Agenda for 1980's. Author: History of Marxian Socialism in the U.S, 1952, The New American Right, 1955, The End of Ideology, 1960, The Radical Right, 1963, The Reforming of General Education, 1966, Towards the Year 2000, 1968, Confrontation, 1969, Capitalism Today, 1971, The Coming of Post-Industrial Society, 1973, The Cultural Contradictions of Capitalism, 1976, The Winding Passage, 1980, The Social Sciences Since World War II, 1981; Mem. editorial board: Daedalus; co-editor and chmn. publs. com.: The Public Interest; contbg. editor: Partisan Rev.; Contbr. to acad. and tech. jours. Trustee Inst. for Advanced Study, Princeton, N.J. Recipient Center for Advanced Studies in Behavioral Sciences fellowship; Am. Council on Edn. prize, 1966. Fellow Am. Acad. Arts and Sci. (v.p.); mem. Council on Fgn. Relations, Century Assn., Am. Philos. Soc. Home: 65 Francis Ave Cambridge MA 02138

BELL, DANIEL LONG, JR., lawyer, utilities executive; b. Pittsboro, N.C., Sept. 29, 1929; s. Daniel Long and Alice Headen (Peoples) B.; m. Mary Anne Bowns, June 23, 1956; children: Mary Anne, Lila Bowns, Cecilia Bliss. B.S., U. N.C., 1951, J.D., 1954; postgrad., N.Y. U., 1955-56; B.A.M. certificate, U. Va., 1965. Bar: N.Y. State bar 1955, Del. bar 1970, W.Va. bar 1975, Ohio bar 1977, U.S. Supreme Ct. bar 1977. Atty. Office Gen. Counsel, N.Y.C. R.R. System, N.Y.C., 1954-58; atty.-counsel Columbia Gas System Service Corp., N.Y.C., 1958-70, counsel, Wilmington, Del., 1970-73, sr. v.p., 1979—; sec., gen. counsel Columbia Gas Transmission Corp., Charleston, W.Va., 1973-76; pres., dir. Columbia Gas of Ky., Md., N.Y., Ohio, Pa., Va., and W.Va., Inc., 1976-79, Belmont Estates, Ltd., Brit. V.I.; dir. Columbia Hydrocarbon Corp., Inland Gas Co., Inc., Columbia Coal Gasification Corp.; Mem. natural gas pipeline industry group Bus. Adv. Council on Fed. Reports, 1965-76; Chmn. student council U. N.C., 1949-50; treas. Southeastern U.S. Nat. Students Assn., 1950-51; rep. Town Meeting, Greenwich, Conn., 1962-68; pres. Westover Hills Woods Assn., Wilmington, 1971-72. Bd. dirs., vice chmn. bd. Salvation Army, Charleston, until 1976; bd. govs. Riverside Assn., Greenwich, 1960-70; bd. dirs. Children's Hosp., Columbus, Ohio, 1977-79, Columbus Symphony, 1977-79. Mem. ABA (chmn. natural gas com., natural resources sect. 1968-70, bd. editors Natural Resources Law Quar. 1968-70), Fed. Power Bar Assn., Del. Bar Assn., Assn. Bar City N.Y. Clubs: Columbus; Metropolitan (Washington); Greenville Country, Wilmington Country. Home: 6500 Kennett Pike Greenville DE Office: PO Box 3678 Greenville DE 19807 *The trait I have most studiously tried to avoid is arrogance; besides being despicable, it bespeaks mental laziness and an unwillingness to admit to the possibility that the person or the idea spurned may be of value or able to help me. The trait giving greatest strength is a true fidelity among those associated together in work or in living.*

BELL, DAVID ARTHUR, advertising agency executive; b. Mpls., May 29, 1943; s. Arthur E. and Frances (Tripp) B.; m. Gail G. Galvani; children: Jenny L., Jennifer L., Jeffrey D., Ashley Tripp. B.A. in Polit. Sci., Malcalester Coll., 1965. Account exec. Leo Burnett, Chgo., 1965-67; pres. Knox Reeves, Mpls., 1967-74; pres. Atlantic div. Bozell & Jacobs, 1974—, also mem. exec. com.; dir. First Midwest Corp., Mpls. Nat. com. coordinator United Way Am., Minn., 1975—; trustee Macalester Coll., 1970-78. Recipient charter centennial medallion Macalester Coll., 1974; named disting. alumnus Macalester Coll., 1978; recipient Minn. Airman of Yr. award, 1967. Republican. Presbyterian. Club: Minikahda (Mpls., Omaha). Home: 1010 Fifth Ave New York NY 10021 Office: Bozell & Jacobs 1 Dag Hammarskjold Plaza New York NY 10017

BELL, DAVID GUS (BUDDY), professional baseball player; b. Pitts., Aug. 27, 1951; s. Gus B.; m. Gloria Bell; children: David, Michael, Ricky, Kristi Marie. Player in minor leagues, 1969-71; outfielder, 3d baseman Cleve. Indians, Am. League, 1969-71; 3d baseman Tex. Rangers, 1979—. Mem.: Am. League All-Star Team, 1973, 80-82. Recipient Gold Glove award, 1979-82. Address: Care Tex Rangers Arlington Stadium PO Box 1111 Arlington TX 76010 *

BELL, DAVID VICTOR JOHN, political science educator, university dean; b. Toronto, Ont., Can., Apr. 9, 1944; s. Herbert McLean and Violet (Bryan) B.; m. Karen Cambell MacDonald, Aug. 30, 1966; children: Kristin Cassandra, Jason David. B.A., York U., 1965; M.A., Harvard U., 1967, Ph.D., 1969. Teaching fellow, tutor Harvard U., Cambridge, Mas., 1968-69; asst. prof. Mich. State U., East lansing, 1969-71; asst prof. York U., Toronto, 1971-73, assoc. prof., 1973-81, prof. polit. sic., dean grad. studies, 1981—; co-founder, co-editor Can. in Transition Series McClelland & Steward Publs., Toronto, 1979-81; mem. editorial adv. com. Polit. Alerts, 1981—; mem. Task Force Pub. Edn. Addiction Research Found., Toronto, 1979-81. Author: Resistance and Revolution, 1973, Power, Influence and Athority, 1975, (with others) The Roots of Disunity, 1979. Pres. Grindstone Coop. Ltd., 1976-81. Woodrow Wilson fellow Woodrow Wilson Found., 1965; Leave fellow Can. Council, 1976-77. Mem. Can. Assn. Amk. Studies (pres. 1974-76), Can. Polit. Sci. Assn., Assn. Can. TV and Radio Artists. Democrat. Unitarian. Club: Thornhill Minor Socc (pres. 1983—). Home: 5 Shaindell St Thornhill ON Canada L3T 3X5 Office: York Univ 4700 Keele St Downsview ON Canada

BELL, DAVITT STRANAHAN, retired steel manufacturer; b. Maywood, Ill., Nov. 27, 1905; s. Frank Breckenridge and Mary Ewing (Stranahan) B.; m. Marian Whieldon, June 27, 1931; children: Margaret W. (Mrs. William H. Woodwell), Frank B. II, Michael, Susan (Mrs. DeCourcy E. McIntosh). M.E., Lehigh U., 1926. Engr. Weirton (W.Va.) Steel Co., 1926-28; engr. Edgewater Corp., Pitts., 1928-37, asst. to pres., 1937-42, pres., 1942-67, chmn. bd., 1967-82. Bd. dirs. Christmas Seal League, Southwestern Pa.; bd. dirs. Pa. Lung Assn.; bd. trustees Children's Hosp., Pitts. Mem. ASME. Republican. Presbyterian. Clubs: Duquesne, Rolling Rock (Ligonier); Pitts. Golf. Home: 3955 Bigelow Blvd Pittsburgh PA 15213 Office: Edgewater Corp Oakmont PA 15139

BELL, DENNIS D., college president; b. Paulding, Ohio, Dec. 18, 1923; s. Ancel C. and Helen V. (Fogle) B.; m. Carnetta J. Burroughs, Aug. 14, 1971; children: Carnetta Denise, Brian Dennis. A.B., Defiance Coll., 1947; M.A., Ohio State U., 1955, Ph.D., 1965. Tchr. high schs., Antwerp, Ohio, 1947, Cardington, Ohio, 1947-57; supt. Riverdale Schs., Wharton, Ohio, 1957-63; research asst. Ohio State U., 1963-64; dir. Ohio State U. br. Lakewood Campus, 1964-66, coordinator regional campuses, 1966-68; asso. dean Coll. Edn., Ill. State U., 1968-71; v.p. West Chester (Pa.) U., 1971-80; pres. East Stroudsburg (Pa.) State Coll., 1980—. Pres. Greater West Chester Religious Council, 1978-80; bd. dirs. Pa. Spl. Olympics, 1981—. Served to lt. comdr. USNR, 1942-46. Mem. Am. Assn. Sch. Adminstrs., Am. Assn. Univ. Adminstrs., Am. Ednl. Research Assn., Pa. Assn. Colls. and Univs. (exec. com. 1983—), Nat. Soc. for Study of Edn., Ohio Edn. Assn., Phi Delta Kappa. Presbyterian. Club: Rotary. Home: 1 College Circle East Stroudsburg PA 18301 Office: East Stroudsburg U East Stroudsburg PA 18301

BELL, DERRICK ALBERT, univ. dean; b. Pitts., Nov. 6, 1930; s. Derrick Albert and Ada Elizabeth (Childress) B.; m. Jewel Allison Hairston, June 26, 1960; children—Derrick Albert III, Douglass Dubois, Carter Robison. A.B., Duquesne U., 1952; LL.B., U. Pitts., 1957. Bar: D.C. bar 1957, Pa. bar 1959, N.Y. State bar 1966, Calif. bar 1969. Atty. civil rights div. Dept. Justice, Washington, 1957-59; 1st asst. counsel N.A.A.C.P. Legal Defense Edn. Fund, N.Y.C., 1960-66; dep. dir. Office Civil Rights, Dept. HEW, Washington, 1966-68; exec. dir. Western Center on Law and Poverty, 1968-69; lectr. law Harvard, 1969-71, prof. law, 1971-80; dean U. Oreg. Law Sch., 1981—. Author: Race, Racism and American Law, 1973, 2d edit., 1980, Shades of Brown: New Perspectives on School Desegregation, 1980. Served to 1st lt. USAF, 1952-54. Ford Found. grantee, 1972, 75; Nat. Endowment Humanities grantee, 1980-81. Home: 2260 Lincoln St Eugene OR 97405

BELL, DOUGLAS LESLIE DEWEY, Can. govt. ofcl.; b. Moose Jaw, Sask., Can., June 15, 1926; s. Douglas Clarence and Irene Margaret (Dewey) B.; m. Pearl Lavina Gray, Sept. 25, 1946; children—Linda Lesly Bell Syverson, Douglas Bernard Charles, Robert Grant. Student schs., Moose Jaw. Radio operator Dept. Transport (various locations), Alta. and B.C., Can., 1946-57, officer-in-charge, Watson Lake, Yukon, 1957-60, Medicine Hat, Alta., 1960-68, telecommunications area mgr., 1968-75; elected to Whitehorse City Council, 1975-77; apptd. dep. commr. Yukon Govt., 1977-79; apptd. adminstr. Yukon Ter., 1979-80, apptd. commr., 1980—; Alderman City of Whitehorse, 1976-77. Mem. library bd. City of Medicine Hat, 1967-68. Served with RCAF, 1943-45. Mem. Whitehorse C. of C. Mem. United Church. Clubs: Toastmasters (area gov. 1966-68), Photo.). Office: PO Box 2703 Whitehorse YT Y1A 2C6 Canada *Care passionately! And show it! Never, ever stop learning; that is how you grow, in all things. Do this and you will find the circle of life becomes ever the same and ever changing, delightful and delicious.*

BELL, DRUMMOND CRILLEY, chemical company executive; b. Balt., Mar. 13, 1916; s. Crilley Drummond and Ella (Witten) B.; m. Ruth Ann McCarthy, Feb. 3, 1940; children: Drummond Crilley III, Richard James. Student, Loyola Coll., Balt., 1934, Johns Hopkins, 1935-38, U. Balt., 1946. With Montgomery Ward & Co., 1935-56, successively mail order house controller, asst. controller for corp., 1935-53, co; personnel mgr., 1953-56, v.p., personnel dir., 1955-56; asst. to pres. Bridgeport Brass Co., 1956-57, controller, 1957-58, v.p., controller, 1958-61, v.p. fin., 1961-62; v.p. Nat. Distillers & Chem. Corp., 1962-68, exec. v.p., 1968, pres., dir., after 1968, chief exec. officer, 1970—, chmn. bd., 1975—; dir. Continental Corp., Panhandle Eastern Corp., Houston, Almaden Vineyards Inc., Calif., Citytrust, Bridgeport, Conn., Surveyor Fund, Inc., N.Y.C. Mem. Mfg. Chemists Assn. Clubs: Pequot Yacht, Country of Fairfield (Conn.); Union League, Pinnacle (N.Y.C.); Biltmore Forest (N.C.) Country; Mid Ocean (Bermuda). Home: 1680 Hillside Rd Fairfield CT 06430 Office: 99 Park Ave New York NY 10016

BELL, ERNEST LORNE, III, lawyer; b. Boston, June 12, 1926; s. Ernest L. and Ellamay (Currier) B.; m. Margaret Van Nostrand Depue, Apr. 14, 1951; children: David E., Robin E., Roseanne Margaret. B.A. cum laude, Harvard Coll., 1949; J.D., U. Mich., 1952. Bar: N.H. 1952. Individual practice law, Keene, N.H., 1952-78; partner firm Bell, Falk and Norton, P.A., 1972—. Author: An Initial View of Ultra as an American Weapon in World War II. Mem. exec. bd. Daniel Webster council Boy Scouts Am., 1970-79; chmn. bd. advisers Colony House Mus.; trustee, treas. Keene Public Library; del. N.H. Constl. Convs., 1964, 74; mem. Am. Com. on History of World War II; commr. N.H. Aeros. Commn., 1980—. Served with Mil. Intelligence, 1944-45. Recipient Silver Beaver award. Mem. N.H. Bar Assn. (pres. 1978-79), Am. Bar Assn., Cheshire County Bar Assn., Lawyer Pilots Bar Assn. (founding dir. 1972-78), Def. Research Inst. (v.p. 1969-73, sec. 1973-76), Am. Kennel Club (del. 1979—), Standard Schnauzer Club Am. Episcopalian. Clubs: Keene County, Harvard of Boston. Home: 54 School St Keene NH 03431 Office: 8 Middle St Keene NH 03431

BELL, GEORGE EDWIN, insurance company executive, physician; b. Canton, Ohio, Dec. 6, 1923; s. George Edwin and Florence Lea (Clark) B.; m. Evelyn Maxine Adams, Apr. 20, 1946; children: Richard, John, Jeffrey, David. Student, Wooster Coll., 1941-42, Yale U., 1943; M.D., Ohio State U., 1947; postgrad., U. Pa., 1954-55. Am. Bd. Life Ins. Medicine. Intern. Del. Hosp., Wilmington, 1947-48, resident in medicine, 1948-49; resident in pathology Aultman Hosp., Canton, Ohio, 1949-50; resident in medicine Ohio State U. Hosp., Columbus, 1955-56, asst. clin. prof. medicine, 1970—; ltd. practice medicine Central Ohio Med. Group, Columbus, 1971—; dir. med. service Columbus State Hosp., 1958-66, dir. research lab., 1966-69, med. dir., 1968—; v.p. Nationwide Ins. Co., Columbus, 1980—; chmn. dept. medicine Grant Hosp., Columbus, 1975-77; mem. Am. Life Ins. Co., 1980—. Contbr. articles to profl. jours.; programmer computer programs for use in lab. office, 1967—; contbr. abstracts to med. jours. Advisor Columbus Pub. Health Nursing Dept., 1967-79; vol. physician Ecco Family Practice Clinic, 1970-74; bd. dirs. Columbus Council on Alcoholism, 1973-77, League Against Child Abuse, 1979—; ad hoc data processing com. chmn. Columbus Acad. Medicine, 1980-81. Served as med. officer USAF, 1951-53. Fed., state, pvt. research grantee, 1958-59; recipient Vol. Services cert. Ohio Dept. Mental Health, 1981, Service plaques J.C. Penney Co., 1981, Columbus Health and Life Claim Assn., 1983. Fellow ACP, Am. Life Ins. Med. Dirs. Assn.; mem. AMA, Am. Council Life Ins. (membership com. med. sect. 1981—), Acad. Medicine Columbus and Franklin County (history and archives com. 1982—), Kappa Mu Epsilon. Club: Presidents (Ohio State U.). Home: 66 Campusview Blvd Worthington OH 43085 Office: Nationwide Ins Col 1 Nationwide Plaza Columbus OH 43216

BELL, GRAYDON DEE, educator; b. Paducah, Ky., May 5, 1923; s. Urban R. and Hilda (Ober) B.; m. Louise E. Wiley, Dec. 26, 1954; children—Katherine, Stephen, Carolee. B.S., U. Ky., 1949; M.S., Calif. Inst. Tech., 1951, Ph.D., 1957. Instr. U. Ky., summers, 1949-50; asst. prof. physics Robert Coll., Istanbul, Turkey, 1951-54; research fellow Calif. Inst. Tech., 1956; prof. physics, chmn. dept. Harvey Mudd Coll., Claremont, Calif., 1957—; physicist Nat. Bur. Standards, 1963-64; vis. scientist U. Queensland, Brisbane, Australia, 1978-79; cons. Gen. Telephone & Electronics Labs., 1979-81. Mem. sci. adv. com. Calif. Bd. Edn., 1966—. Served with USAAF, 1942-46. NSF Sci. Faculty fellow, 1970. Mem. Am. Phys. Soc., Am. Astron. Soc., Am. Assn. Physics Teachers, AAAS, Phi Beta Kappa, Sigma Xi, Sigma Pi Sigma, Omicron Delta Kappa. Research measurement of absolute f-values for heavy elements. Home: 310 W Radcliffe Dr Claremont CA 91711

BELL, GRIFFIN B., lawyer, former attorney general U.S.; b. Americus, Ga., Oct. 31, 1918; s. A.C. and Thelma (Pilcher) B.; m. Mary Foy Powell, Feb. 20, 1943; 1 son, Griffin B. Student, Ga. Southwestern Coll.; LL.B. cum laude, Mercer U., 1948, LL.D., 1967. Bar: Ga. bar 1947. Practice in, Savannah and Rome, 1947-53; partner firm King and Spalding, Atlanta, 1953-59, mng. partner, 1959-61; U.S. judge 5th Circuit, 1961-76; sr. partner firm King and Spalding, Atlanta, 1976, 79—; atty. gen., U.S., 1977-79; served chief of staff Gov. Vandiver of Ga., 1959-61; chmn. Atlanta Commn. on Crime and Delinquency, 1965-66; Mem. vis. com. Law Sch., Vanderbilt U.; trustee Mercer U.; bd. dirs. Fed. Jud. Center, 1974-76; chmn. Madrid Conf. on Security and Cooperation in Europe, 1980; co-chmn. Nat. Task Force on Violent Crime, 1981. Served to maj. AUS, 1941-46. Mem. Am. Coll. Trial Lawyers, Am. Law Inst., ABA (chmn. div. jud. adminstrn. 1975-76), Order of Coif. Baptist. Office: King & Spaulding 2500 Trust Company Tower Atlanta GA 30303

BELL, HANEY HARDY, III, tobacco company executive; b. Staunton, Va., Aug. 20, 1944; s. Haney Hardy and Maud (Deekens) B.; m. Alice Tester, Feb. 17, 1968; 1 son, Landon D. Grad., Gilman Sch., Balt., 1962; B.A., U. Va., 1966; J.D., U. Wis., 1973. Bar: Va. bar 1974. Group ins. rep. Prudential Ins. Co. Am., Milw., 1969-70; asso. firm Woods, Rogers, Muse, Walker & Thornton, Roanoke, Va., 1973-78; asso. counsel R.J. Reynolds Industries, Inc., Winston-Salem, N.C., 1978-79; sec., gen. counsel RJR Foods, Inc., 1979-80; sr. internat. counsel R.J. Reynolds Tobacco Internat., Inc., 1980—. Served to lt. AUS, 1967-69. Mem. Am. Bar Assn., Va. State Bar, Order of Coif. Clubs: Twin City.; Bermuda Run Country (Winston-Salem); Kiawah Island (Charleston, S.C.). Office: R J Reynolds Industries Inc Reynolds Plaza Winston-Salem NC 27102

BELL, HARRISON BANCROFT, publishing consultant; b. Bangor, Maine, May 9, 1925; s. Charles Edward and Dorrice Clement (Robinson) B.; m. Martha Louise Denton, Aug. 7, 1948; children: Sally R. (Mrs. John A. Fink), Martha (Mrs. Robert A. Bell), Judith, Charles Edward II. B.A., Cornell U., 1949, M.A., 1951. Tchr., Templeton, Mass., 1952-53, Greenwich, Conn., 1953-60; sr. editor Holt, Rinehart & Winston, Inc., N.Y.C., 1960-66; editor-in-chief Noble & Noble Pubs., Inc., N.Y.C., 1966-69; v.p., editor-in-chief Silver Burdett Co., Morristown, N.J., 1969-75; v.p., pub. sch. div. Harper & Row, N.Y.C., 1975-81; editor-in-chief McCormick-Mathers Inc., 1981; asst. to pres. Amsco Sch. Pubs., Inc., 1981-82; ednl. and pub. cons., Glen Ridge, N.J., 1983—. Author: Spelling for You, 1968. Treas., council for bd. edn., Greenwich, Conn., 1957-60. Served with USNR, 1943-46, 51-52. Mem. Phi Delta Kappa. Home: 55 Highland Ave Glen Ridge NJ 07028

BELL, HENRY MARSH, JR., banker; b. Tyler, Tex., Jan. 23, 1928; s. Henry Marsh and Elizabeth (Loftin) B.; m. Dorothy N. Allen, Dec. 8, 1951; children: Henry Marsh III, John Allen. B.S. in Indsl. Adminstrn, Yale, 1948. With First City Nat. Bank of Tyler, 1948—, v.p. and trust officer, 1955-62, sr. v.p., 1962-65, exec. v.p., 1964-67, pres., chmn. bd., chief exec. officer, 1967—; pres. Tyler Clearing House Assn.; dir. First City Bancorp. Tex., Inc. Past chmn. bd. dirs. Smith County chpt. A.R.C.; past bd. dirs. Tyler YMCA, Tyler United Fund, East Tex. Symphony Assn.; bd. dirs., past pres. Tex. Rose Festival Assn., Order of Rose; past pres. Smith County Heart Assn.; mem. exec. com., past pres. Tyler Indsl. Found.; past mem. adv. bd. Mother Frances Hosp.; pres. U. Tex. at Tyler Ednl. Found.; mem. finance com. Tyler Mus. Art; past chmn. exec. bd. East Tex. Hosp. Found.; v.p. U. Tex. Dad's Assn.; chmn. bd. trustees Tchr. Retirement System Tex.; trustee Tex. Chest Found.; past pres. Tyler-Smith County Library Found.; pres. Friends of Library.; trustee, treas. Episcopal Found. Tex. Recipient T.B. Butler award, 1971. Mem. E. Tex. C. of C. (dir.), Tyler C. of C. (dir., mem. exec. com., pres. 1966-67), Robert Morris Assos., Newcomen Soc. N.A. Episcopalian (past vestry, past sr. warden). Clubs: Mason (32 deg.), Shriner, Jester, Rotarian (past pres.), Willow Brook Country (past pres.), Tyler Petroleum (dir., past pres.). Home: 2725 Pecan Dr Tyler TX 75701 Office: 100 E Ferguson St Tyler TX 75702

BELL, HERBERT AUBREY FREDERICK, life insurance company executive; b. Toronto, Ont., Can., Jan. 15, 1921; came to U.S., 1946, naturalized, 1954; s. Kenneth Johnson and Mable Helen (Clarke) B.; m. Gretta Nisbet, May 16, 1946; children: Cathryn Patricia, Thomas Scott, Paul Conway. Student, Tulsa U., 1951-53; C.L. U., 1954. Engaged in life ins. bus., 1947—; v.p. sales Mich. Life Ins. Co., Royal Oak, Mich., 1954-65; with Phila. Life Ins. Co., 1965—, exec. v.p., San Francisco, 1970—; lectr. ins. mgmt. Mich. State U., 1961. Mem. Nat. Assn. Life Underwriters, Am. Soc. C.L.U.'s, Gen. Agts. and Mgrs. Assn., Life Ins. Agy. Mgmt. Assn. Clubs: Rotary (past v.p.), Toastmasters, Diablo Country. Home: 220 Joaquin Dr San Ramon CA Office: Trans Global Ins Corp 875 Mahler Ave Burlingame CA 94010

BELL, HOWARD HUGHES, association executive, lawyer; b. N.Y.C., June 27, 1926; s. George H. and Mary Elizabeth (Hughes) B.; m. Corinne Chandler, Aug. 30, 1947; children: Mary Elizabeth, Jeffery Chandler, Laurinda Louise. B.J., U. Mo., 1948; postgrad., George Washington U., 1954-55; J.D., Catholic U. Am., 1960. Bar: Md. bar 1961. Sales promotion mgr. Evening Star Broadcasting Co., Washington, 1948-51; v.p., asst. to pres., dir. code authority Nat. Assn. Broadcasters, 1951-68; pres. Am. Advtg. Fedn., Washington, 1968—; exec. sec. Assn. for Profl. Broadcast Edn.; instr. sales promotion Am. U.; dir. Advt. Council, Advt. Ednl. Found., Nat. Advt. Rev. Council, Inc., Nat. Yellow Pages Advisory Council. Bd. dirs. U. Mo. Freedom of Info. Center, Marietta Coll. Council. Served with USN, 1944-46. Mem. Am., FCC bar assns., Soc. Assn. Execs., Broadcast Pioneers, Delta Theta Phi (alumni award), Pi Kappa Alpha, Alpha Delta Sigma. Episcopalian. Clubs: Washington Advt., Internat. of Washington, Congressional Country; Sky (N.Y.C.); World Trade (San Francisco). Home: 550 N St SW Apt 5401 Washington DC 20024 Office: 1400 K St NW Washington DC 20005

BELL, HOWARD WILLIAM, petroleum co. exec.; b. Hays, Kans., July 8, 1918; s. Myron Judson and Alice (Chambers) B.; m. Dorothy Leslie Goodrick Crosno, July 3, 1976; children—Brenda Bell Jenner, Sherron Bell Mullin. Student, U. So. Calif., 1937-41. With Standard Oil Co., Calif., 1936—, asst. treas., San Francisco, 1961-67, v.p. fin., 1968—, dir., 1971—; officer Iranian Oil Consortium, Teheran, 1954-61; v.p., sec. Chevron Oil Europe, N.Y.C., 1967-68; Bd. regents St. Mary's Coll., Moraga, Calif., 1978—. Mem. Fin. Officers No. Calif., Nat. Planning Assn., Am. Petroleum Inst. Republican. Clubs: Bankers, Pacific-Union, San Francisco Golf, Stock Exchange (San Francisco). Office: 225 Bush St San Francisco CA 94104

BELL, JAMES ADRIAN, journalist; b. Altoona, Kans., Nov. 12, 1917; s. George Andrew and Fay (Commons) B.; m. Virginia Gray, July 8, 1941; children—Jane Gray, George Edward. Grad., Brent Sch., Baguio, Philippines, 1936; A.B., U. Kans., 1940. Reporter Topeka Daily Capital, 1940-42; corr. Chgo. bur. Time Inc., 1942-48; White House corr. Washington bur., 1948-50; chief N.Y. bur., 1950; war corr. Tokyo bur., 1950, Middle East bur. chief, 1951-54, Central European bur. chief, 1954-56; chief China and Southeast Asia bur., Hong Kong, 1956-59, Africa bur., 1959-61, Central European bur., Bonn, Germany, 1961-66, N.Y. bur., 1966-68, London bur., 1968, Rome bur., 1968-73, Atlanta Bur., 1973-76, sr. corr., 1976—. Served from pvt. to 2d lt., Signal Corps AUS, 1942-45. Decorated Verdienstkruez Fed. Rep., Germany; recipient Distinguished Service citation U. Kans. Mem. Delta Tau Delta. Club: St. Botolph (Boston). Office: Time Magazine 277 Dartmouth St Boston MA 02116

BELL, JAMES BRUGLER, historical society administrator; b. St. Paul, Apr. 17, 1932; married; 4 children. B.A., U. Minn., 1955; M.Div., Episcopal Theol. Sch., 1961; D. Phil., Balliol Coll., Oxford, Eng., 1964. Instr. history Ohio State U., 1964-67; vis. lectr. Coll.

Wooster, 1967; research fellow, lectr. Princeton U., 1967-69; dir., librarian New Eng. Hist. Geneal. Soc., 1973-82; dir. N.Y. Hist. Soc., N.Y.C., 1982—; Nat. Hist. Publ. Commn. fellow, 1967-68; commr. Mass. Hist. Commn., 1974-78. Contbr. articles to profl. jours. and books. Mem. Orgn. Am. Historians, Am. Hist. Assn., Soc. Antiquaries, Am. Antiquarian Soc. Office: NY Hist Soc 170 Central Park W New York NY 10024 *

BELL, JAMES FINLEY, retired telephone company executive; b. London, Ohio, Jan. 12, 1915; s. James Finley and Rowena (Moore) B.; m. Charlotte Engard, Feb. 17, 1940 (div. 1973); children—Stephen Ross, Betsey Ann; m. Gloria Smith, July 21, 1973. A.B., DePauw U., 1936; LL.B., Ohio State U., 1939. Bar: Ohio bar 1939. Practice in, London, 1939-42, Columbus, 1962-70; spl. agt. FBI, 1942-46; judge Ct. Common Pleas, Madison County, Ohio, 1947-54, Supreme Ct., Ohio, 1955-62; gen. counsel Gen. Telephone of Fla., Tampa, from 1970, v.p., after 1973. Active Boy Scouts Am.; pres. Ohio Conf. Tb Workers, 1954-55; Mem. London Bd. Edn., 1940-52; Dem. candidate Ohio Gen. Assembly, 1946. Mem. Am., Fla., Ohio bar assns., London Jr. C. of C. (past pres.), Sigma Chi, Phi Delta Phi. Presbyterian (elder). Club: Rotary (past dist. gov.). Home: 612 Gladstone Ln Holmes Beach FL 33510

BELL, JAMES FREDERICK, physicist, educator; b. Melrose, Mass., Apr. 21, 1914; s. John Joseph and Hester (Walsh) B.; m. Perra Somers, Aug. 30, 1940; children: Jane Elizabeth, Christopher James. B.A., N.Y. U., 1940. Design engr. Arma Corp., 1940-45; prof. solid mechanics Johns Hopkins U., Balt., 1945—; vis. prof. U. Va., summers 1951, 52; sr. visitor dept. applied math., theoretical physics U. Cambridge (Eng.), 1962-63; ricercatore associato Istituto Matematico U. Bologna, Italy, 1970-71; sr. visitor Inst. Math., Rumanian Acad. Sci., 1970; Cons. U.S. Govt. Author: The Physics of Large Deformation of Crystalline Solids, 1968, Experimental Foundations of Solid Mechanics, Handbuch der Physik, vol. VIa/1, 1973; also numerous sci. papers on physics of solids; contbr.: sect. to Grove's Dictionary of Music and Musicians, 1981. Fellow Am. Acad. Mechanics; mem. Chamber Music Soc. (bd. govs. 1957—), Soc. Natural Philosophy, Soc. for Exptl. Stress Analysis (B.J. Lazan award 1974), AAUP. Patentee diffraction gratings and on dialysis. Home: 606 W 40th St Baltimore MD 21211 Office: Johns Hopkins U Baltimore MD 21218

BELL, JAMES FREDERICK, lawyer; b. New Orleans, Aug. 5, 1922; s. George Bryan and Sarah Barr (Perry) B.; m. Jill Cooper Arden, Apr. 14, 1951; children: Bradley Cushing, Sarah Perry, Ashley Arden. A.B. cum laude, Princeton U., 1943; LL.B., Harvard U., 1948. Bar: D.C. 1949. Assoc. firm Pogue & Neal (name changed to Jones, Day, Reavis & Pogue 1967), Washington, 1948-53, partner, 1953—; gen. counsel Conf. State Bank Suprs., 1951—. Chmn. com. on canons and other bus. Episcopal Diocese of Washington, 1960-78; pres. Episc. Center for Children, Washington, 1966-67. Served to lt. USNR, 1943-46. Mem. Am., Fed., D.C. bar assns. Club: Metropolitan (Washington). Home: 2103 R St NW Washington DC 20008 Office: 655 15th St NW Washington DC 20005 *The fragmentation of human thought into an increasing number of disciplines has proliferated standards of judgement as to the "rightness" or "wrongness" of human conduct to a point where consensus as to viable guidelines becomes impossible.*

BELL, JAMES ROBERT, banker; b. Red Oak, Iowa, Aug. 3, 1933; s. James Thomas and Marie Henrietta (Brodd) B.; m. Dolores Fay Siever, Mar. 18, 1967. B.S., U. Kans., 1961; M.A. in Math., Central Mich. U., 1965. Tchr. Shawnee Mission, Kans., 1961-66; bank exec. Fed. Res. Bank of Kansas City, Mo., 1966—. Served with USN, 1953-57. Republican. Home: 4743 Heintz Kansas City MO 64133 Office: Fed Res Bank Kansas City 925 Grand Kansas City MO 64198

BELL, JANE MATLACK, art critic, editor; b. Washington, June 27, 1949; d. Harry H. and Mildred Harriet (Post) B.; m. Douglas Matthew Davis, Dec. 12, 1970; stepchildren: Laura Katharine, Mary Elizabeth; 1 dau., Charlotte Victoria. B.A., Bennington (Vt.) Coll., (1971), Ecole Internat., Geneva, 1967. Public affairs asso. N.Y. Cultural Center, 1973-74, acting dir. dept. public affairs, 1974; revs. editor, then contbg. editor Arts mag., 1973-76; editorial asso. Artnews mag., 1979—; contbg. editor N.Y. Arts Jour., 1978—; asso. editor Art Express, 1980—; sr. editor The Art Economist, 1980—; bd. dirs. Internat. Network Arts, 1979—; founding mem. SoHo TV, 1976-77, Artists TV Network, 1978-80; co-tchr. Advanced Video Workshops, Bklyn. Mus. Art Sch., 1978, SUNY, Purchase, 1979, Phila. Coll. Art, 1979, Pratt Inst., 1979, Osaka U. Arts, 1980, Alexander Mackie Coll., Sydney, Australia, 1980. Grantee Kosciuszko Found., 1976. Mem. Internat. Assn. Art Critics. Democrat. Quaker. Address: 80 Wooster St New York NY 10012

BELL, JOHN CLARKE, lawyer; b. Montgomery, Ala., Oct. 22, 1948; s. Thomas Antrim and Mary Wellborn (Clarke) B.; m. Stephanie Wolf, Nov. 28, 1980. B.S., Auburn U., 1971; J.D., U. Ala.-Tuscaloosa, 1974. Bar: Ala. 1974. Law clk. Supreme Ct. Ala., Montgomery, 1974-75; dep. dist. atty, Montgomery, 1975-81, chief dep. dist. atty, 1981; U.S. atty. Middle Dist. Ala., Montgomery, 1981—. Mem. Mt. Meigs Compus adv. bd. Ala. Dept. Youth Services, Montgomery, 1983-84; mem. Montgomery County Republican Com., 1980-81. Mem. Fed. Bar Assn., Ala. State Bar, Montgomery County Bar Assn. Presbyterian. Lodge: Lions/Montgomery (dir. 1982,84). Office: US Attys Office 15 Lee St Montgomery AL 36104

BELL, JOHN LEWIS, manufacturing executive; b. Marion, Ind., June 5, 1942; s. John Lewis and Laovonnia C. (Kinder) B.; m. Jo-Anne Smith, July 27, 1963; children: John Lewis, Robert. Student, Ind. U., 1960-62; B.B.A., U. Miami, 1965; M.B.A., Ball State U., 1971; M.A., in Psychology, 1977; Ph.D., Purdue U., 1980. Treas. Bell Fibre Products Corp., Marion, 1966-68, pres., treas., 1968-71, pres., chief exec. officer, 1971-81, chmn. bd., chief exec. officer, 1981—; pres. Bell Gallery Photog. Art; chmn. bd. Am. Bank and Trust Co. Marion. Bd. dirs. Lakeview Wesleyan Ch. Mem. Am. Inst. Mgmt., Am. Mgmt. Assn., Soc. Advancement Mgmt., Young Pres.'s Orgn., Alpha Kappa Psi. Clubs: Kiwanis, Meshingomesia Country (Marion). Office: Bell Fibre Products Corp 3102 S Boots St Marion IN 46952

BELL, JOHN MILTON, agricultural science educator; b. Islay, Alta., Can., Jan. 16, 1922; s. Milton Wilfred and Elsie Joyce (Larmour) B.; m. Edith Margaret Joan Smith, Sept. 21, 1944; children: Ada Joyce, Donald Charles Milton, Marion Louise, Douglas Wilfred, Keith Murray. B.Sc. in Agr, U. Alta., 1943; M.Sc., McGill U., 1945; Ph.D. Cornell U, 1948. Asst. prof. animal husbandry U. Sask. (Can.), Saskatoon, 1948-50, asso. prof., 1950-53, prof., 1954—, head dept. animal husbandry, 1954-75, asso. dean research Coll. of Agr., 1975-80, Burford Hooke prof. agrl. sci., 1980—; bd. govs. U. Sask. (Can.), 1976-83, Internat. Devel. Research Centre. Contbr. chpts. to books. Recipient Borden award, 1962; 1st Agrl. Laureate of Can., 1970; Queen's Silver Jubilee medal, 1977. Fellow Royal Soc. Can., Agrl. Inst. Can.; mem. Internat. Union Nutrition Scis., Sask. Sci. Council. Mem. United Ch. Can. Home: 1530 Jackson Ave Saskatoon SK S7H 2N2 Canada Office: Animal Science Bldg Coll Agriculture U Saskatchewan Saskatoon SK S7N 0W0 Canada

BELL, JOHN OSCAR, educator; b. Manila, Philippines, Oct. 4, 1912; s. John Oscar and Frances Earl (Cooley) B.; m. Jeannette Shahan, July 5, 1934 (dec. 1974); children—John Shahan, Patricia, Kathleen; m. Ann Lewis, Jan. 25, 1975. B.S., George Washington U., 1934, J.D., 1939; grad., Nat. War Coll., 1948. Bar: D.C. bar 1938. Joined U.S. Dept. State, 1931; exec. officer Passport Div., 1939-41; chief Air Priorities Sect., 1943-46, Air Transport Sect., 1946; asst. chief Aviation Div., 1946-47, asso. chief, 1947-48, chief, 1948; asso. chief Div. No. European Affairs, 1948; dep. coordinator Mut. Security, 1949; asst. dir. Mut. Def. Assistance Program, 1949, Internat. Security Affairs, 1951; apptd. fgn. service officer, 1951; econ. counselor Am. embassy, Copenhagen; also dep. chief Mut. Security Agy. Mission to Denmark, 1952; dep. chief Am. embassy, Copenhagen and; dir. U.S. Ops. Mission, Denmark, 1954, Karachi, Pakistan, 1955; regional dir. Near East and South Asia, ICA, 1957; dep. coordinator fgn. assistance, 1958-61, U.S. ambassador to, Guatemala, 1962-65; polit. adviser to comdr.-in-chief U.S. Strike Command, 1965-69; lectr. U. South Fla., Tampa, 1969—; Sec. for documentation Internat. Civil Aviation Conf., Chgo., 1944; conf. registration officer UN Conf., San Francisco, 1945; spl. rep. of U.S. State Dept., Aviation Negotiations in, Peru, Ecuador, Chile, Argentina, Uraguay, 1946-47; alt. mem. U.S. Dept. State Loyalty and Security Bd., 1948-50; vice chmn. President's Task Force for Fgn. Aid, 1962. Mem. Am. Fgn. Service Assn., Tampa Bay Com., Fgn. Relations, George Washington U. Law Assn., Alpha Chi Sigma. Club: Democrat. Home: 325 Glen Oaks Ave Temple Terrace FL 33617 Office: U of South Fla Tampa FL 33620

BELL, JOSEPH RAYMOND, lawyer, government official; b. New Orleans, Jan. 7, 1908; s. Harry and Anna B.; m. Jeanne Viner, Dec. 15, 1974; children: Carol Johnston, Bonnie Sauve, Joseph Raymond, Melodie Macklin. Grad., NYU, 1928; LL.B., Atlanta Law Sch., 1930. Bar: N.Y., D.C., Ga. Reporter Georgian-Am., 1928-30, Detroit Times, 1930-33; dir. publicity and advt. Loew's Washington Theatres, 1933-42; Eastern publicity mgr. Metro-Goldwyn-Mayer, N.Y.C., 1942-44; dir. pub. relations Capital Airlines, Washington, 1944-47; v.p. Columbia Pictures Industries, Inc., 1949-72; mem. firm Wyman Bautzer Rothman & Kuchel, 1973; chmn. Fgn. Claims Settlement Commn. U.S., Washington, 1973-77, 81—; dir. MacMillen Ring Free Oil Co., WHDH Corp., Miami Hotel Corp., Palm Beach. Bd. dirs. Palm Beach Symphony; dir. polit. communications Reagan-Bush Com., 1980; chmn., dir. Heart Fund, D.C. Cancer Drive. Recipient Exceptional Service award U.S. Air Force, Patriotic Service award U.S. Army, Good Guy award Am. Legion. Mem. Pub. Relations Soc. Am. (dir., pres. N.Y. chpt., D.C. chpt., nat. v.p., presdl. citation), Air Force Assn. (pres. chpt., Man of Yr.), Advt. Club Washington (v.p.), Bar Assn. City N.Y., Bar Assn. D.C., Ga. Bar Assn., Fed. Bar Assn., ABA. Republican. Methodist. Clubs: Metropolitan, Cosmos, Overseas Press, Nat. Press, Army and Navy, Congressional Country, Pisces; Nat. Lawyers (Washington). Home: 2113 S St NW Washington DC 20008 Office: Fgn Claims Steelement Commn Washington DC 20579

BELL, LARRY STUART, artist; b. Chgo., Dec. 6, 1939; s. Hyman David and Rebecca Ann (Kriegmont) B.; 2 daus. Student, Chouinard Art Inst., Los Angeles, 1957-59. One man exhbns. include, Stedelijk Mus., Amsterdam, 1967, Pasadena Art Mus., 1972, Oakland Mus., 1973, Ft. Worth Art Mus., 1975, Santa Barbara Mus. Art, 1976, Washington U., St. Louis, Art Mus. So. Tex., Corpus Christi, Hayden Gallery, M.I.T., 1977, Hudson River Mus., Yonkers, N.Y., 1981, Newport Harbor Art Mus., 1982, Marian Goodman Gallery, Ruth S. Scchaffner Gallery, Erica Williams, Anne Johnson Gallery, 1982; group exhbns. include, Mus. Modern Art, N.Y.C., 1965, 79, Jewish Mus., N.Y.C., 1966, Whitney Mus. Am. Art, Guggenheim Mus., 1967, Tate Gallery, London, 1970, Hayward Gallery, London, 1971, Detroit Inst. Arts, 1973, Nat. Collections Fine Arts, 1975, San Francisco Mus. Modern Art, 1976, Museo de Arte Contemporaneo de Caracas, Venezuela, 1978, Aspen Center for Visual Arts, 1980, Fruit Market Gallery, Edinburgh, Scotland, Albuquerque Mus., Art Inst. Chgo., 1982, represented in permanent collections, Nat. Collection Fine Arts, Mus. Modern Art, N.Y.C., Whitney Mus. Am. Art, Tate Gallery, Gallery New South Wales, Australia, Albright-Knox Gallery, Art Inst., Chgo., Denver Art Mus., Dallas Mus. Fine Arts, Guggenheim Mus., Los Angeles County Mus., Victoria and Albert Mus., London, San Antonio Mus. Art, others; instr. sculpture, U. South Fla., Tampa, U. Calif., Berkeley, U. Calif., Irvine, 1970-73, Copley Found. grantee, 1962, Guggenheim Found. fellow, 1970, Nat. Endowment Arts grantee, 1975. Home: Box 495 Ranchos de Taos NM 87557 Office: Box 1778 Taos NM 87571

BELL, LOWRY M., JR., retired architect, consultant; b. Birmingham, Ala., June 19, 1929; s. Lowry M. and Jerrie H. (Billups) B.; m. Diana M. Marcanthony, July 25, 1976; children by previous marriage: Brian A., Cynthia Bell Misite. B.S. and B.A. in Architecture, Ga. Inst. Tech., 1952. Architect, bus. mgr. Rufus Nims, Architect, 1954-55; group v.p., architecture, design and constrn. Howard Johnson, Braintree, Mass., 1955-82, ret., 1982; Cons., 1982—. Served to 1st lt. C.E. U.S. Army, 1952-54. Mem. AIA, Boston Soc. Architecture.

BELL, MARION SEDWICK, copper company executive; b. Grayson County, Ky., Apr. 28, 1923; s. John Sedwick and Gladys Elizabeth (Collard) B.; m. Annette Koerner, Dec. 26, 1946; children—Greg, Alexis, Mark. Metall. Engr. Colo. Sch. Mines, 1949. With Phelps Dodge Refining Corp., 1949—, v.p., gen. mgr., 1976-79, pres., N.Y.C., 1979—, Phelps Dodge Copper Products, 1982—. Past pres. United Way El Paso County, Tex., El Paso Indsl. Betterment Council, Jr. Achievement El Paso; past regional v.p. Tex. Assn. Bus. Served to 2d lt. USMCR, 1942-46. Recipient Van Diest Gold medal Colo. Sch. Mines, 1961. Mem. Selenium and Tellurium Devel. Assn. (pres. 1979), Mining and Metall. Soc. Am., Metall. Soc. Republican. Roman Catholic. Clubs: Canadian, Mining (N.Y.C.). Patentee in field. Home: 31 Casino St 4H Freeport NY 11520 Office: 300 Park Ave New York NY 10022

BELL, NORMAN HOWARD, physician, endocrinologist, educator; b. Gainesville, Ga., Feb. 11, 1931; s. Kenneth Rush and Henrietta Maria (Howard Rankin) B.; m. Claude Handy, June 27, 1959 (div. 1967); children: Douglas Howard, Julienne Rankin; m. Mary Virginia Baughman, Aug. 24, 1968 (div. July 1972); m. Ledlie Laird Dinsmore, Dec. 19, 1972; 1 son, Bayard Gardiner. A.B., Emory U., 1951; M.D., Duke U., 1955. Intern Duke U. Med. Ctr., Durham, N.C., 1955-56, resident, 1956-57; clin. assoc. Nat. Inst. Allergy and Infectious Deiseases, NIH, Bethesda, Md., 1957-59; mem. staff clin. endocrinology br. Nat. Heart, Lung and Blood Inst., NIH, Bethesda, 1959-63; asst. prof. medicine Northwestern U. Sch. Medicine, Chgo., 1963-68; assoc. prof. Ind. U.-Indpls., 1968-71, prof., 1971-79; prof. medicine and pharmacology Med. U. S.C., Charleston, 1979—; mem. gen. medicine B study sect. NIH, Bethesda, 1982—. Editorial bd.: Calcified Tissue Internat., 1978-83, Jour. Clin. Endocrinology and Metabolism, 1984—. Served with USPHS, 1957-63. Recipeint Career Devel. USPHS, 1965-68; VA med. investigator, 1979, 81—; recipient Thomas A. Roe Found. S.C. Med. Assn., 1982, William S. Middleton VA, 1983. Mem. Am. Soc. Clin. Investigation, Am. Soc. Bone and Mineral Research (sec.-treas. 1978—), Am. Soc. Pharmacology and Exptl. Therapeutics, Assn. Am. Physicians, Endocrine Soc., Am. Soc. Nephrology, Alpha Omega Alpha. Democrat. Episcopalian. Home: 1 Johnson Rd Charleston SC 29407 Office: VA Med Ctr 109 Bee St Charleston SC 29403

BELL, P. JACKSON, airline executive; b. Portsmouth, Va., Dec. 31, 1941; s. John Henry and Lois Belle (Hendrix) B.; m. Virginia Phillips Inman, Apr. 11, 1981; children by previous marriage: Scarlett Lee, Christopher J. B.S.B.A., Northwestern U., 1963; M.A., U. S.C., 1964. Mgmt. cons. McKinsey & Co., Washington, 1967-73; dir. corp. planning Washington Post Co., 1973-77; asst. to pres. Allegheny Airlines, Washington, 1977-78; v.p.-long range planning USAir Inc, Washington, 1978-83, sr. v.p.-fin., 1983—. Served to capt. USMC, 1964-67; Vietnam. Office: USAir Inc Hangar 11 Washington Nat Airport Washington DC 20001

BELL, PETER MAYO, geophysicist; b. N.Y.C., Jan. 3, 1934; s. Frank Kirkhaugh and Mary Elizabeth (Mayo) B.; m. Norma Joan Erkert, June 20, 1959; children: Peter Mayo, James, Elizabeth, Bradford. B.S., St. Lawrence U., 1956; M.S., U. Cin., 1959; A.M., Harvard U., 1961, Ph.D., 1963. Solid state physicist Office of Aerospace Research, Bedford, Mass., 1963; postdoctoral fellow Carnegie Instn. Washington, 1963-64, staff geophysicist, 1964—; advisor space mission planning NASA, Houston and Washington, 1972-74, lunar sample adviser, 1974-80; mem. adv. bd. Petroleum Research Fund, Washington, 1982—. Author Infrared of Minerals, 1975; editor: EOS, 1980—; mem. editorial bd.: Sci. Mag., 1982-83; mem.: Advances in Geochemistry, 1980—; contbr. articles to profl. jours.; patentee system to make solid H2, 1982. Cub scout leader Nat. Capital area council Boy Scouts Am., 1964-72. Served to 1st lt. U.S. Army, 1957. Recipient medal for Highest Sci. Achievement NASA, 1976; named Guiness Book of Records, Guiness Found., 1981; Guggenheim Found. fellow, 1982; Fairchild Disting. scholar Calif. Inst. Tech., 1983. Fellow Am. Geophys. Union, Am. Mineral Soc.; mem. Geochem. Soc., Geol. Soc. Washington, Potomac Geophys. Soc. (v.p. 1983-84). Republican. Episcopalian. Clubs: Cosmos (Washington); West River Sailing (Galesville, Md.). Home: 7604 Glackens Dr Potomac MD 20854 Office: Carnegie Instn of Washington 2801 Upton St NW Washington DC 20008

BELL, PHILLIP MICHAEL, curator; b. Toronto, Ont., Can., Dec. 31, 1942; s. William Harvey and Alice W. (Stone) B.; m. Natalie Marie Luckyj, Aug. 15, 1977. B.A. with honors, U. Toronto, 1966, M.A., 1967. Dir. Anges Etherington Art Gallery, Kingston, Ont., 1973-78; visual arts officer Ont. Arts Council, Toronto, 1978-79; asst. dir. pub. programs Nat. Gallery Can., Ottawa, Ont., 1979-81, acting dir., Ottawa, 1981; dir. McMichael Canadian Collection, Kleinburg, Ont., 1981—; cons. Nat. Archives, Ottawa, 1974—. Author: Painters in a New Land, 1973 (Gov. Gen.'s award for Non-Fiction), Braves and Buffalo: Plains Indian Life in 1837, 1973, William Goodridge Roberts, Drawings, 1976, William Sawyer: Portrait Painter, 1978. Mem. Can. Hist. Assn. (appraisal bd.), Can. Mus. Assn. (dir. 1983—), Ont. Assn. Art (galleries bd. 1974-78). Office: McMichael Can Collection Islington Ave Kleinburg ON Canada L0J 1C0

BELL, RANDALL WILLIAM, ophthalmic surgeon; b. N.Y.C., Jan. 20, 1938; s. William Randall and Frances Veronica (Dwyer) B.; m. Carole Ann Gilligan, June 6, 1959; children: Randall, Deborah, Kevin, Thomas James. B.S., U. Mil. Acad., 1959; M.D., Cornell U., 1966; grad., U.S. Army War Coll. Diplomate: Am. Bd. Ophthalmology, Nat. Bd. Med. Examiners. Commd. 2d Lt. U.S. Army, 1959, advanced through grades to brig. gen. Res., 1975, intern Walter Reed Gen. Hosp., Washington, 1966-67, resident Walter Reed Gen. Hosp., 1967-70, chief ophthalmology Valley Forge (Pa.) Gen. Hosp., 1970-72; practice medicine specializing in ophthalmology USAR 338th Med. Group, Wayne, Pa., 1972-83, comdg. gen. Walter Reed Gen. Hosp., Washington, 1981—; mem. Surgeon's Gen.'s Adv. Council; mem. staff Scheie Inst., Presbyn. U. Pa. Med. Ctr., Wills Eye Hosp., Phila., Jefferson Hosp., Bryn Mawr (Pa.) Hosp., Sacred Heart Hosp., Norristown, Montgomery Hosp.; asst. prof. Thomas Jefferson U., Phila., 1972-76, U. Pa., 1978. Contbr. articles on ophthalmology to profl. jours. Fellow ACS, Pa. Acad. Opthalmology and Otolaryngology, Am. Acad. Opthalmology, Phila. Coll. Physicians; mem. AMA, Pa. Med. Soc., Del. County Med. Soc., Assn. Research in Vision and Ophthalmology, Soc. Contemporary Ophthalmology, Soc. Mil. Ophthalmologists, Ophthalmic Club Phila. (pres. 1981-83), West Point Soc. Phila. (bd. govs. 1975—, pres. 1981-82), Assn. U.S. Army (life). Clubs: Merion Cricket, Merion Golf, Union League of Phila., Cornell. Home: 124 Bloomingdale Ave Wayne PA 19087

BELL, RICHARD, state supreme court associate justice; b. 1920. B.S., Presbyterian Coll.; LL.B., Emory U. Bar: Ga. 1950. Assoc. justice Ga. Supreme Ct., Atlanta, 1982—. Office: George Supreme Ct State Jud Bldg Atlanta GA 30334 *

BELL, RICHARD CHEVALIER, landscape architect; b. Elizabeth, N.C., Apr. 10, 1928; s. Albet Quentin and Maude Carthine (Price) B.; m. mary Jo Harris (Oct. 29, 1955); children: Sharon Elizabeth, Richard Chevalier, Cassandra Lynn. B.S. in Landscape Architecture, N.C. State U. Lic. real estate broker, N.C. Pres. Bell Design Group-Garden Gallery, Raleigh, N.C., 1955—; pres. N.C. land Use Congress, Raleigh, 1972-73; chmn. Wake County Planning Bd., N.C., 1973-74. (Works include) litchfield Plantation, S.C. (Am. Assn. Nurserymen Honor award 1976); works include water garden, Raleigh (Am. Assn. Nurserymen Honor award 1981), Pullen Park, Raleigh (N.C. chpt. Am. chpt. Am. Soc. Landscape Architects Honor award). Capt. arty. U.S. Army. Recipient 2d Pl. award for Bicentennial Plaza Fed. Hwy. Commn., 1982; Rome Prize fellow, Rome. Mem. Am. Soc. Landscape Architects (pres. N.C. chpt. 1975-76), N.C. Assn. Nurserymen (dir. 1975-80). Democrat. Methodist. Home: 5011 Carteret Raleigh NC 27612 Office: Bell Design Group Garden Gallery Route 8 Raleigh NC 27612

BELL, RICHARD EUGENE, grain co. exec.; b. Clinton, Ill., Jan. 7, 1934; s. Lloyd Richard and Ina (Oglesby) B.; m. Maria Christina Mendoza, Oct. 22, 1960; children—David Lloyd, Stephen Richard. B.S. with honors, U. Ill., 1957, M.S., 1958. Internat. economist Dept. Agr., Washington, 1959-60, dir. grain div., 1969-72; agrl. attache Am. embassies in Ottawa, Can., Brussels, and Dublin, Ireland, 1961-68; asst. sec. agr. internat. affairs and commodity programs, 1973-77; pres. Riceland Foods Inc., Stuttgart, Ark., 1977—; pres., dir. Commodity Credit Corp., also Fed. Crop Ins. Corp., 1975-77; exec. sec. President's Agrl. Policy Com., 1976-77; rep. Internat. Wheat Council, London, 1970-77; adv. World Food Conf., Rome, 1974. Recipient Disting. Service award Dept. Agr., 1975. Mem. Alpha Gamma Rho, Alpha Zeta. Republican. Mem. Christian Ch. (Disciples of Christ). Home: 2001 Beumer St Stuttgart AR 72160 Office: PO Box 927 Stuttgart AR 72160

BELL, ROBERT AUSTIN, utility company executive; b. Dallas, May 13, 1933; s. Robert Hurley and Margie Alice (Hughes) B.; m. Doris Young Messer, Oct. 2, 1953 (div.); m. 2d Susan Claire Smyth, Feb. 20, 1982. B.S.E.E., U. Tex., Austin, 1955, M.S.E.E., 1956, Ph.D., 1963. Registered profl. engr., Tex. Tech. staff Bell Telephone Labs., Whippany, N.J., 1963-68; assoc. prof. elec. engring. U. Tex.-Arlington, 1968-70; dir. research Con Edison N.Y., N.Y.C., 1970-78, asst. v.p., 1978-81, v.p., 1981—; dir. Empire State Electric Research Corp., N.Y.C., 1981—, Lighting Research Inst., 1982—, Metals Properties Council, 1979—; pres. Fuel Cell Users Group Inc., Washington, 1982—. Pres. St. Peters Lutheran Ch., Manhattan, N.Y., 1972-77, chmn. bldg. com., Manhattan, N.Y., 1972-77; chmn. bd. Mid Town Arts Common, N.Y.C., 1977—, Greg Smith Singers, N.Y.C., 1981—. Served to col. USAR, 1982—. Sr. mem. IEEE (chmn. pub. affairs council 1983); mem. Sigma Xi, Eta Kappa Nu. Republican. Home:

510 E 23d St #4E New York NY 10010 Office: Consol Edison NY Inc 4 Irving Pl New York NY 10003

BELL, ROBERT EDWARD, educator; b. New Malden, Eng., Nov. 29, 1918; s. Edward R. and Edith (Rich) B.; m. Jeanne Atkinson, July 5, 1947; 1 dau., Alison Ann. B.A., U. B.C., 1939, M.A., 1941; Ph.D., McGill U., 1948. Radar devel. Nat. Research Council, Ottawa, Can., 1941-45; nuclear research Chalk River Nuclear Labs., 1946-52; prof. physics McGill U., Montreal, Que., 1956—, Rutherford prof., 1960—; dir. Foster Radiation Lab., 1960-69, vice dean arts and sci., 1964-67; dean Faculty Grad. Studies and Research, 1969-70, prin., vice chancellor, 1970-79. Fellow Am. Phys. Soc., Royal Soc. (London), Royal Soc. (Can.) (pres. 1978-81); mem. Canadian Assn. Physicists (pres. 1965-66). Home: 363 Olivier Ave Montreal PQ H3Z 2C8 Canada

BELL, ROBERT EUGENE, educator; b. Marion, Ohio, June 16, 1914; s. Harry Thew and Clara (Stouffer) B.; m. Emily Virginia Merz, Aug. 31, 1938; children—Patricia (Mrs. Paul Lindsey), David Eugene. Student, Ohio State U., 1936-38; B.A. with honors, U. N.M., 1940; M.A., U. Chgo., 1943, Ph.D., 1947. Asst. prof. anthropology U. Okla., 1947-51, asso. prof., 1951-55, prof., 1955-69, George L. Cross Research prof., 1969-80, emeritus, 1980—; chmn. dept., 1947-55, 61-64; head curator Stovall Mus., 1947—; Dir. Miss. Valley Dendochronology Lab. U. Chgo., 1942-43, 46-47, Okla. River Basin Salvage Lab., 1962-78. Author Oklahoma Archaeology: an Annotated Bibliography, 1969, 2d edit., 1978, The Harlan Site, CK-6, A Prehistoric Mound Center in Cherokee County, Eastern Oklahoma. Archaeol. investigations at site of El Inga, Ecuador; Editor: Am. Antiquity, 1966-70, Bull. Okla. Anthrop. Soc, 1963-66. Served with M.C. AUS, 1943-46. Fulbright fellow, New Zealand, 1955-56. Mem. Am. Anthrop. Assn., Am. Assn. Phys. Anthropology, A.A.A.S., Far Eastern Prehist. Assn., Okla. Hist. Soc., Am. Ethnol. Soc., Tree Ring Soc., Soc. Am. Archaeology, Mo., Ark., Tex., Kans., Colo., Mich., Pa. archaeol. socs., Inst. Gt. Plains, Southeastern Archaeol. Conf., Polynesian Soc., Soc. for Hist. Archaeology, New Zealand Archaeol. Assn., Soc. for Conservation Archaeology, Explorers Club, Phi Beta Kappa (hon.), Sigma Xi. Home: 1120 Berry Circle Norman OK 73069

BELL, ROBERT PAUL, university president; b. Charlottesville, Ind., Sept. 28, 1918; s. Paul H. and Emma Adaline (Overman) B.; m. Margaret Cora Strattan, Apr. 3, 1942; children: Paul Strattan, Barbara Ann. B.S. Ball State Tchrs. Coll, Munice, Ind., 1940; M.C.S., Ind. U., 1942, Ed.D., 1952. Tchr. bus. Pendleton (Ind.) High Sch., 1940-41; grad. asst. Sch. Bus., Ind. U., 1941-42; instr. U.S. Naval Tng. Sch., 1942-44, Lab. Sch., Sch. Edn., Ind. U., 1944-47; mem. faculty Ball State U., Muncie, 1947—, prof. head dept. bus., 1954-61, prof. bus. edn., dean div. fine and applied arts, 1961-65; dean Coll. Bus., 1964-73, v.p. bus. affairs, treas., 1972-81, univ. pres., 1981—; Dir. Muncie Fed. Savs. & Loan Assn. Author: Instructional Materials in Accounting, 1948, Instructional Materials in Typewriting, 1953, 2d edit., 1972; also articles.; Editor: Ball State Commerce Jour, 1954—. Div. chmn. Muncie United Fund, 1962-63; Bd. dirs. Delaware County Soc. Crippled, 1963—, United Way, 1973—. Mem. Nat. Bus. Tchrs. Assn. (1st v.p. 1960), N. Central Bus. Edn. Assn. (pres. 1963), Nat. Bus. Edn. Assn. (bd. dirs. 1963), Future Bus. Leaders Am. (Ind. adviser 1954-61), N.E.A., Ind. Tchrs. Assn., Nat. Thrift Com., Blue Key, Delta Pi Epsilon, Pi Omega Pi, Sigma Tau Gamma., Beta Gamma Sigma, Sigma Iota Epsilon. Club: Exchange (pres. Muncie 1962-63). Home: 1009 N Meadow Ln Muncie IN 47304 Office: Office of Pres Ball State U 2000 University Ave Muncie IN 47306

BELL, STEPHEN SCOTT (STEVE BELL), news correspondent, anchorman; b. Oskaloosa, Iowa, Dec. 9, 1935; s. Howard Arthur and Florance (Scott) B.; m. Joyce Dillavou, June 16, 1957; children: Allison Kay, Hilary Ann. B.A., Central Coll., Pella, Iowa, 1959, Ph.D. hon.), 1969; M.S. in Journalism, Northwestern U., 1963. Announcer Radio Sta. KBOE, Oakaloosa, 1955-59; reporter WOI-TV, Ames, Iowa, 1959-60; news writer WGN Radio-TV, Chgo., 1960-61; reporter, anchorman WOW-TV, Omaha, 1962-65; anchorman Radio Sta. WNEW, N.Y.C., 1965-66; corr. ABC News, 1967—, assignments include corr., Vietnam, 1970-71, polit. corr., 1968, 72, chief Asia corr., 1972-73, White House corr., Washington, 1974-75; news anchorman World News This Morning and Good Morning Am., 1975—. Recipient Emmy nominations, 1965, 73, Overseas Press Club award, 1969, Headliner award, 1975. Mem. AFTRA, White House Corrs. Assn., Washington Radio-Television Corrs. Assn., Council on Fgn. Relations. Presbyterian (elder). Office: ABC News 1717 DeSales St Washington DC 20036 *As a journalist, the older I get, the less inclined I am to "play God."*

BELL, STOUGHTON, mathematician, educator; b. Waltham, Mass., Dec. 20, 1923; s. Conrad and Florence Emily (Ross) B.; m. Mary Carroll O'Connell, Feb. 26, 1949 (div. 1960); children: Karen, Mark; m. Laura Joan Bainbridge, May 24, 1963; children: Nathaniel Stoughton, Joshua Bainbridge. Student, Harvard U., 1946-49; A.B., U. Calif., Berkeley, 1950, M.A., 1953, Ph.D., 1955. Mem. staff Sandia Corp., Albuquerque, 1955-66, div. supr., 1964-66; vis. lectr. U. N.Mex., 1957-66, dir. computing center, 1966—, asso. prof. math., 1966-71, prof. math. and computing sci., 1971—; vis. lectr. N.Mex. Acad. Scis., 1965—; nat. lectr. Assn. for Computing Machinery, 1972-74. Co-author: Linear Analysis and Generalized Functions, 1965, Introductory Calculus, 1966, Modern University Calculus, 1966. Served with AUS, 1943-44. Mem. Assn. for Computing Machinery, Am. Math. Soc., Math. Assn. Am., Soc. Indsl. and Applied Math., Am. Statis. Assn., Ops. Research Soc. Am. Office: Computing Center U NMex Albuquerque NM 87131 *

BELL, TERREL HOWARD, sec. of edn.; b. Lava Hot Springs, Idaho, Nov. 11, 1921; s. Willard Dewain and Alta (Martin) B.; m. Betty Ruth Fitzgerald, Aug. 1, 1957; children—Mark Fitzgerald, Warren Terrel, Glenn Martin, Peter Fitzgerald. B.A., So. Idaho Coll. Edn., 1946; M.S., U. Idaho, 1953; Ed.D. (Ford fellow), U. Utah, 1961. Tchr. high sch. chemistry and physics, Eden, Idaho, 1946-47; supt. schs. Rockland (Idaho) Valley Schs., 1947-54, Star Valley Sch. Dist., Afton, Wyo., 1955-57, Weber County (Utah) Sch. Dist., 1957-62; prof. sch. adminstrn. Utah State U., 1962-63; supt. pub. instruction State of Utah, 1963-70; asso. commr. for regional office coordination U.S. Office Edn., HEW, 1970, acting commr. edn., 1970, dep. commr. sch. systems, 1971, commr. edn., 1974-76; supt. Granite Sch. System, Utah, 1971-74; commr. higher edn. State of Utah, Salt Lake City, 1976-81; sec. Dept. Edn., Washington, 1981—; chmn. Utah Textbook Commn., Utah Course Study Commn.; mem. Utah Land Bd.; exec. officer Utah Bd. Edn. Author: novel The Prodigal Pedagogue, 1956, Effective Teaching: How to Recognize and Reward Competence, 1962, A Philosophy of Education for the Space Age, 1963, Your Child's Intellect—A Guide to Home-Based Preschool Education, 1972, A Performance Accountability System for School Adminstrators, 1974, Active Parent Concern, 1976. Served with USMCR, 1942-46; PTO. Mem. Am. Assn. Sch. Adminstrs., Council Chief State Sch. Officers, Phi Delta Kappa. Mem. Ch. Jesus Christ of Latter-day Saints. Office: Office of Sec of Edn 400 Maryland Ave SW Washington DC 20202

BELL, THOMAS R., textile executive; b. 1923. With RCN, from 1942, Dominion Textile USA Inc., N.Y.C., 1945—, group v.p. ops. exec. v.p., 1974, now pres., dir.; chmn. bd. DHJ Industries. Address: Dominion Textile USA Inc 1040 Ave of Americas New York NY 10018 *

BELL, THOMAS ROWE, natural gas transmission co. exec.; b. Chattanooga, Feb. 26, 1928; s. Joseph Sumner and Hattie Bush (Rowe) B.; m. Agnes Louise Slaughter, Dec. 29, 1956; children: Bush A., Thomas Rowe, Mary E., David L. B.S. in Bus., U. Tenn., 1950. With E. Tenn. Natural Gas Co., 1950—, dir. sales devel., asst. treas., 1959-64, v.p., 1964-72; pres. Knoxville, 1973—; chmn. mgmt. com. Knoxville Internat. Energy Expn., 1979—. Bd. dirs. Webb Sch.; past pres. Met. Knoxville YMCA. Served with AUS, 1950-52. Mem. Am. Gas Assn., Ind. Natural Gas Assn., So. Gas Assn. (dir.), Tenn. Gas Assn. (past pres.), Sigma Phi Epsilon. Presbyterian. Office: 8200 Kingston Pike PO Box 10245 Knoxville TN 37919

BELL, VICTOR ALTMARK, JR., financial executive; b. Suffolk, Va., July 28, 1942; s. Victor Altmark and Mary Caroline (Chapman) B.; m. Jean Ann Gould, June 12, 1965; children—Anne Ashley, Eleanor Darden. B.E.E., U. Va., 1965, M.B.A., 1967; J.D., Georgetown U., 1974. Bar: D.C. bar 1975, Va. bar 1974. Mgmt. cons. Price Waterhouse & Co. (C.P.A.'s), Washington, 1969-72; with Potomac Electric Power Co., Washington, 1972-82, asst. to pres., 1974-75, treas., asst. sec., 1976-79, v.p., treas., 1979-82; pres. Comprehensive Benefit Services Corp., 1982—. Bd. dirs. Met. Washington YMCA. Served with U.S. Army, 1967-69. Decorated Army Commendation medal. Mem. Va., D.C., Am. bar assns., Financial Execs. Inst., Met. Washington Bd. Trade. Episcopalian. Home: 1436 Laburnum St McLean VA 22101 Office: 1150 Connecticut Ave NW Washington DC 20036

BELL, WALTER, catalog showroom executive; b. Phila., Feb. 28, 1915; s. Samuel and Anna (Rodkin) B.; m. Dorothy Schwarz, Dec. 25, 1938; children: Fredric J., Joan. Student, Pa. State U., 1933-34, George Washington U., 1934-36. Pres., chmn. bd. W. Bell & Co., Inc., Rockville, Md., 1950. Office: 12401 Twinbrook Pkwy Rockville MD 20852

BELL, WALTER DOUGLAS, insurance executive; b. Elma, Iowa, July 24, 1921; m. Sophia Marianna Mihailina, Mar. 25, 1946; 4 children. B.C.S., Drake U., 1943, J.D., 1949; postgrad., Harvard U., U. Notre Dame. Various positions, home office counsel, v.p. and gen. mgr. for Paul Revere Life Ins. Co., Worcester, Mass., 1949-59; mng. dir. Can. Health Ins. Assn., Toronto, 1959-61; v.p. State Mut. Life Assurance Co. Am., Worcester, 1961-62, v.p., gen. counsel, 1962-68, sr. v.p., gen. counsel, 1968-69, pres., 1969—, chief exec. officer, 1972—, chmn. bd., 1980—; also dir., chmn. exec. and investment coms. Worcester Mut. Ins. Co.; dir. Life Ins. Assn. Mass.; chmn. Calif. Compensation and Fire Co., Hanover Ins. Co., Massachusetts Bay Ins. Co., SMA Life Assurance Co.; dir. Colonial Mgmt. Assn., Inc.; dir. Colonial Growth Shares, Inc., New Eng. Electric System.; dirs. Am. Council Life Ins. Bd. dirs. Worcester Meml. Hosp.; trustee Drake U. Mem. Am. Bar Assn. Clubs: Worcester Economic (past pres.), Worcester, Worcester Country, Masons. Home: 50 Wyndhurst Dr Holden MA 01520 Office: 440 Lincoln St Worcester MA 01605

BELL, WARREN NAPIER, internist, educator, consultant; b. Victoria, B.C., Can., May 8, 1921; came to U.S., 1950; s. Percy George and Peri Gilmore (Warren) B.; m. Marion Elizabeth Irish, Oct. 21, 1950; children: Pamela, Peri, Heather. M.D., U. Man., Can., 1944; D.Sc. in Medicine, U. Pa., 1956. Diplomate: Am. Bd. Internal Medicine. Intern Vancouver Gen. Hosp., B.C., 1944-45, resident, 1945, McGill U., 1948-49, Hosp. of U. Pa., Phila., 1950-52; assoc. in medicine U. Pa., Phila., 1950-53; researcher in medicine U. Cambridge, Eng., 1953-54; assoc. prof. medicine U. Miss., Jackson, 1954-59, prof., chmn. dept. clin. lab. sic., 1959—; cons. in field; dir. Miss. div. Am. Cancer Soc., 1958—. Contbr. articles to med. jours. Served to capt. M.C. Royal Can. Army, 1944-46; ETO. Recipient awards Am. Cancer Soc., 1967; Dept. Def. grantee, 1955; HEW grantee, 1957-63, 60. Fellow Royal Coll. Physicians and Surgeons Can.; mem. Miss. State Med. Assn., AMA. Presbyterian. Home: 3928 Eastwood Dr Jackson MS 39211

BELL, WENDELL, sociologist, educator; b. Chgo., Sept. 27, 1924; s. Wendell and Blanche (Leiferman) B.; m. Lora-Lee Edwards, June 15, 1947; children: Sharon Lee, David Howard. B.A. with highest honors, Calif. State U., Fresno, 1948; M.A., UCLA, 1951, Ph.D., 1952; M.A. (hon.), Yale U., 1963. Asst. prof. sociology, acting dir. survey research facility Stanford U., 1952-54; asso. prof. sociology Northwestern U., 1954-57; from asso. prof. to prof. sociology, dir. West Indies study program UCLA, 1957-63; prof. sociology Yale U., 1963—, chmn. dept., 1965-69, dir. comparative sociology tng. program, 1969-77, dir. undergrad. studies, 1976-83, dir. grad. studies, 1984—; editor Internat. Studies in Polit. and Social Change, Schenkman Pub. Co., 1966-76; cons. editor D.C. Heath and Co., 1971-84. Author: (with E. Shevky) Social Area Analysis, 1955, (with R.J. Hill and C.R. Wright) Public Leadership, 1961, (with I. Oxaal) Decisions of Nationhood, 1964, Jamaican Leaders, 1964; editor, contbr.: The Democratic Revolution in the West Indies, 1967, (with James A. Mau) The Sociology of the Future, 1971, (with Walter Freeman) Ethnicity and Nation-Building, 1973; asso. editor: Am. Sociol. Rev., 1958-61; mem. editorial adv. bd.: Sage Profl. Papers in Internat. Studies, 1972—, Sage Research Papers in Social Sci., Series Social Orgn. of Community, U. Iowa, 1974—, Futurics, 1976—, Cultural Futures Research, 1976—; editorial cons.: Sociometry, 1959-61; mem. editorial bd.: Internat. Studies Quar., 1970-80, Plantation Society in the Americas, 1978—, Political Behavior, 1978-80. Mem. exec. com. div. behavioral scis. NRC, 1968-69. Served as naval aviator USNR, 1943-46; Philippines. Research Tng. predoctoral fellow Social Sci. Research Council, 1951-52; Faculty fellow, 1956-59; research grantee, 1978; Carnegie Corp. N.Y. grantee, 1960-63; fellow Center Advanced Study Behavioral Scis., 1963-64; NSF grantee, 1969-70; NIMH tng. grant dir., 1969-77. Mem. Acad. Polit. Sci., Internat. Sociol. Assn., Am. Sociol. Assn., Eastern Sociol. Assn., Pacific Sociol. Assn. (v.p. 1960-61), Sociol. Research Assn., AAAS (mem. at large sect. K), AAUP, Internat. Studies Assn. (v.p. 1970-71), Caribbean Studies Assn. (v.p. 1978, pres. 1979), World Future Soc., Global Futures Network, Bethany Horsemen's Assn. Home: 364 Sperry Rd Bethany CT 06525 Office: Dept Sociology 1965 Yale Sta Yale U New Haven CT 06520

BELL, WHITFIELD JENKS, JR., historian; b. Newburgh, N.Y., Dec. 3, 1914; s. Whitfield Jenks and Lillian Victoria (Hengstler) B. A.B., Dickinson Coll., 1935, LL.D., 1964; A.M., U. Pa., 1938, Ph.D., 1947; Litt.D., Franklin Coll., 1960; LL.D., Washington Coll., 1981. Instr. history Dickinson Coll., 1937, 38-39, 41-43, asso. prof., 1945-50, prof., 1950-54; vis. prof. Coll. William and Mary, 1953-54; asst. editor Papers of Benjamin Franklin, 1954-56, asso. editor, 1956-61; asso. librarian Am. Philos. Soc., 1961-66, librarian, 1966-80, exec. officer, 1977-83. Author: Needs and Opportunities for Research in the History of Early American Science, 1955, John Morgan, 1965, The Colonial Physician, 1975; editor: Bibliography of the History of Medicine in the U.S. and Canada, 1948-53; vs. editor: William and Mary Quar, 1953-54; editor: (with L. W. Labaree) Mr. Franklin, 1956. Vol. Am. Field Service, Italy, Germany, 1943-45. Hon. fellow Coll. Physicians, Phila. Mem. Am. Antiquarian Soc., Mass. Hist. Soc., Phi Beta Kappa. Clubs: Cosmos (Washington); Franklin Inn (Phila.). Office: Am Philos Soc 104 S 5th St Philadelphia PA 19106

BELL, JR. WILLIAM HENRY, banker; b. Schenectady, Oct. 15, 1918; s. William Henry and Elizabeth (Lambert) B.; m. Alice Creedon, Sept. 13, 1947; children: Susan, Martha, Patricia, Barbara, Alexandra, Madelin. B.A., Princeton U., 1939. With J.P. Morgan & Co., N.Y.C., 1939-49, First Nat. Bank, Jersey City, 1950-52, Heritage Bank, Cherry Hill, N.J., 1953—; pres., dir., chief exec. officer, chmn., Heritage Bancorp., 1971-82, vice chmn., 1982—; vice chmn., dir. Duralith Corp., Millville, N.J., 1980—; chmn. Inst. Med. Research, Camden, 1970—; bd. mgrs. Cooper Med. Ctr., Camden, 1976-78. Pres. Camden (N.J.) Housing Improvement Projects, 1967-74; mem. N.J. Gov.'s Commn. to Evaluate Capital Needs, 1968; treas. Princeton U. Class of 1939, 1969—; mem. Gov.'s Task Force for Inproving N.J.'s Econ. and Regulatory Climate, 1982—. Served to lt. comdr. USNR, 1941-46; PTO. Mem. Assn. Bank Holding Cos. (legis. com. 1976-82), Fed. Res. Assn. (nominating adv. com. 1966-69), N.J. Bankers Assn. (exec. com. 1964,81—, chmn. task force on interstate banking 1982—), Phi Beta Kappa. Republican. Roman Catholic. Clubs: Pine Valley Golf (Clementon, N.J.); Riverton (N.J.) Country. Home: 711 Lippincott Ave Moorestown NJ 08057 Office: 66 E Main St Moorestown NJ 08057

BELL, WILLIAM JACK, educator; b. nr. Norcatur, Kans., Nov. 1, 1915; s. James S. and Ruth (Diefendorf) B.; m. Marjorie May Andrews, May 9, 1942. B.A., B.S., Emporia (Kans.) State Tchrs. Coll., 1937, M.S., 1940; Ph.D., U. Mo., 1949. Tchr. high sch., Colby, Kans., 1937-42; reporter-editor Colby Free Press-Tribune, 1937-42; grad. asst., instr. U. Mo. Sch. Journalism, 1946-49; asst. prof. U. Okla. Sch. Journalism, 1949-51; photographer Daily Oklahoman, Oklahoma City, summer 1951; prof. journalism, head journalism and graphic arts dept. East Tex. State U., Commerce, 1951-53. City commr. Commerce, 1960-64, 74—, mayor pro tem, 1964-66, 74—, mayor, 1967-70; bd. dirs. Sulphur River Municipal Water Dist., 1971-72, chmn. airport adv. bd., 1971-74; Mem. exec. com. NetSeO Trails council Boy Scouts Am., 1953-57. Served with USNR, 1942-45. Recipient Faculty award East Tex. State U., 1976; Named Piper prof., 1982. Mem. Sports Information Dirs., Nat. Assn. Intercollegiate Athletics (pres. 1965-67, coordinator 1968—, named to Hall of Fame 1970), Phi Delta Kappa (historian 1957-69), Sigma Delta Chi, Commerce C. of C. (dir. 1955-57, 59-62, 69-71). Clubs: Lion (pres. Commerce 1959-60, dep. dist. gov. 1962-64. Home: 2500 Washington St Commerce TX 75428 *I believe that if this world is to be a better place to live in, it is my responsibility to serve my community in any way and with whatever talents I may have. In other words, if this world is to be better for my having been here, it must start with me at the local level.*

BELL, WILLIAM JOSEPH, television writer; b. Chgo., Mar. 6, 1927; s. William Jennings and Gertrude (Oteman) B.; m. Lee Phillip, Oct. 23, 1954; children: William James, Bradley Phillip, Lauralee Kristen. Student, U. Mich., 1944, DePaul U., 1947-49. Co-editor Hi-Shopper Pub. Co., Chgo., 1948-49; writer, producer CBS, 1949-53; account exec. McCann-Erickson, advt., 1953-56, Cunningham & Walsh, 1956-57; co-owner NBC-TV show Another World, 1964—; treas., dir. 209 E. Lake Shore Dr. Bldg.; pres. Bell-Phillip TV Prodns., Inc., 1970—, Miss Lee Flowers, Inc., 1972; corp. dir. Graphic Pictures, Inc., Dramatic Serials, Inc.; ptnr. Bell Dramatic Serial Co., 1983—; owner Sunset Ridge Farm, Casa del Suena, Lake Geneva, Wis. Co-author: TV show Guiding Light, 1957, As the World Turns, 1958-67, Our Private World, 1965; story editor, head writer: Days of Our Lives, 1966—; creator, head writer: The Young and the Restless, CBS-TV, 1973—; exec. producer, CBS-TV, 1982. Bd. dirs. Geneva Lake Civic Assn.; trustee Latin Sch., Chgo., De Paul U., Chgo. Served with USNR, 1945-46. Recipient Emmy award for best show, 1974, 83, Award for Best Writer, 1976. Mem. Acad. TV Arts Scis., Sarah Siddons Soc. (bd. govs.). Clubs: Execs., Lake Geneva Country; Beach (Palm Beach, Fla.). Home: 209 E Lake Shore Dr Chicago IL 60611

BELLA, SALVATORE JOSEPH, educator; b. Lawrence, Mass., Dec. 21, 1919; s. Joseph and Theresa (Zinno) B.; m. Dantina Quartaroli, Dec. 30, 1946; children: Theresa, Joseph, Jennifer. B.S., Boston U., 1947, M.A., 1948; Ph.D. (Danforth Found. scholar), Cornell U., 1962. Asst. prof. Alfred U., 1948-55; asst. prof. U. Notre Dame, 1958-63, asso. prof., 1963-68, dir. supervisory devel. program, 1962-82, head dept. bus. orgn. and mgmt., 1964-75, Jesse Jones prof. mgmt., 1968—; dean Inst. Mgmt., Nat. Appliance and Radio-TV Dealers Assn., 1972-83. Contbr. articles to profl. jours. Cons. non-profit agys., police and sch. depts, in areas human and community relations, 1967—. Mem. Am. Econ. Assn., AAUP, Indsl. Relations Research Assn., Urban Coalition, Acad. Mgmt., Phi Kappa Phi, Beta Gamma Sigma. Home: 1029 Clermont Dr South Bend IN 46617 Office: U of Notre Dame Notre Dame IN 46556

BELLACK, ALAN SCOTT, clinical psychologist; b. N.Y.C., Nov. 27, 1944; s. Jack and Yetta B.; m. Barbara Bartlett, Nov. 16, 1969; children: Jonathan, Adam. B.S., CCNY, 1965; M.S., St. John's U., 1967; Ph.D., Pa. State U., 1970. Asst. prof. psychology Pa. State U., 1970; mem. faculty U. Pitts., 1971—, prof. psychology and psychiatry, 1980-82; prof. psychiatry Med. Coll. Pa., Phila., 1982—; cons. in field. Author: Behavioral Assessment: A Practical Handbook, 1976, Behavioral Modification: An Introduction, 1977, Indtroduction to Clinical Psychology, 1980, others; editor: Clin. Psychology Rev., 1981—, Behavior Modification, 1977—; contbr. articles to profl. jours. USPHS fellow, 1968-70. Mem. Am. Psychol. Assn., Assn. Advancement Behavior Therapy. Home: 10 Dauphine Rd Ardmore PA 19003 Office: Med Coll Pa 3300 Henry Ave Philadelphia PA 19124

BELLAH, ROBERT NEELLY, sociologist, educator; b. Altus, Okla., Feb. 23, 1927; s. Luther Hutton and Lillian Lucille (Neelly); m. Melanie Hyman, Aug. 17, 1949; children: Jennifer, Harriet. B.A., Harvard U., 1950, Ph.D., 1955. Research asso. Inst. Islamic Studies, McGill U., Montreal, Can., 1955-57; with Harvard U., Cambridge, Mass., 1957-67, prof., 1966-67; Ford prof. sociology and comparative studies U. Calif., Berkeley, 1967—. Author: Tokugawa Religion, 1957, Beyond Belief, 1970, The Broken Covenant, 1975 (Sorokin award Am. Sociol. Assn. 1976), (with Charles Y. Glock) The New Religious Consciousness, 1976, (with Phillip E. Hammond) Varieties of Civil Religion, 1980. Served with U.S. Army, 1945-46. Fulbright fellow, 1960-61; recipient Harbison award Danforth Found., 1971. Mem. Am. Acad. Arts and Scis., Assn. for Asian Studies, Am. Acad. Religion. Office: Center for Japanese Studies U California Berkeley CA 94720

BELLAK, LEOPOLD, psychiatrist, psychoanalyst, psychologist; b. Vienna, Austria, June 22, 1916; came to U.S., 1938, naturalized, 1942; s. Siegfried and Marie (Weiler) B.; (div.)children: Karola, Katrina. Student, Vienna Med. Sch., 1935-38; M.A., Boston U., 1939, Harvard U., 1942; M.D., N.Y. Med. Coll., 1944. Intern, resident St. Elizabeth's Hosp., Washington, 1944-46; practice medicine specializing in psychiatry and psychoanalysis, Larchmont, N.Y., 1946—; clin. prof. psychology postdoctoral tng. program N.Y. U., 1965—; vis. prof. psychiatry George Washington U., 1970-76; vis. prof. edn. and psychology Tchrs. Coll., Columbia U., 1965-69; clin. prof. psychiatry Albert Einstein Coll. Medicine, 1971—; cons. U.S. Mil. Acad. West Point, Mental Health Assn. Westchester County, 1966—; prin. investigator, project dir. NIMH grants, 1951—; adv. bd. Guidance Center, New Rochelle, N.Y., 1960—. Author books, tests and sci. articles. Served with M.C. AUS, 1942-46. Recipient Ann. Merit award N.Y. Soc. Clin. Psychologists, 1963, award Psychiatry Outpatient Centers Am., 1976. Fellow Am. Psychiat. Assn., Am. Psychoanalytic

Assn., Am. Psychol. Assn., Am. Orthopsychiat. Assn., Royal Soc. Medicine; mem. N.Y. Soc. Projective Techniques (pres. 1952-56), Soc. Projective Techniques (pres. 1957-58), Rorschach Inst., Westchester Psychoanalytic Soc. (pres. 1962), Sigma Xi. Established Trouble Shooting Clinic, Queens, N.Y.C., 1958. Office: 22 Rockwood Dr Larchmont NY 10538

BELLAMY, CAROL, city ofcl.; b. Plainfield, N.J., 1942. B.A. with honors, Gettysburg Coll., 1963; J.D., N.Y. U., 1963. Vol. Peace Corps, Guatemala, 1946-65; asso. firm Cravath, Swaine and Moore, N.Y.C., 1968-71; asst. commr. Dept. Mental Health and Mental Retardation Services, N.Y.C., 1971-72; mem. N.Y. State Senate, 1972; pres. N.Y.C. City Council, 1978—. Office: The New York City Council City Hall 250 Broadway New York NY 10007 *

BELLAMY, JAMES CARL, insurance company executive; b. Detroit, Oct. 15, 1926; s. Robert Maxwell Bellamy and Mamie (Moery) B.; m. Marie Alice Brakebill, Jan. 20, 1951; children: James Carl, Janet Marie. B.S., U. Tenn., 1950. C.L.U. Agt., asst. mgr. Nat. Life & Accident Ins. Co., Chattanooga, Louisville, 1950-58, dist. mgr., Little Rock, Nashville, 1958-73, 2d v.p., Nashville, 1973-78, v.p., 1978-82, sr. v.p., dir., 1982—. Solicitor United Way, Nashville, 1968-74, Boy Scouts Am., Nashville, 1968-74. Served with USNR, 1944-46; PTO. Mem. Nat. Assn. Life Underwriters, Nashville Assn. Life Underwriters (pres. 1970-71), Nashville Gen. Agts. and Mgrs. Assn. (pres. 1967). Republican. Baptist. Club: Hillwood Country (Nashville). Office: Nat Life & Accident Ins Co American General Ctr Nashville TN 37250

BELLAMY, JAMES ERNEST, steel importer; b. Victoria, C., Can., June 12, 1932; s. Donald V. and Jessie W.M. (Dunnett) B.; m. Freda E. Bushell, Mar. 15, 1958; children: Candy Jay, James Ernest. Student, U. B.C., 1950-51, U. So. Calif., 1951-52. Pres. Balfour, Guthrie & Co. Ltd., San Francisco, 1958-80, Ferrostaal Metals Corp., San Mateo, Calif., 1980—. Mem. West Coast Metal Importers Assn. (dir. 1980—). Republican. Club: Peninsula Golf and Country (San Mateo, Calif.). Office: Ferrostaal Metals Corp 2121 S El Camino Real San Mateo CA 99403 *

BELLAMY, JOE DAVID, English educator, author; b. Cin., Dec. 29, 1941; s. Orin Ross and Beulah Pearl (Zutavern) B.; m. Connie Sue Arendsee, Sept. 16, 1964; children: Lael Elizabeth, Samuel Ross Carlos. Student, Duke U., 1959-61; B.A., Antioch Coll., 1964; M.F.A., U. Iowa, 1969. Editor The Antiochian, 1965-67; instr. English Pa. State Coll., Mansfield, 1969-70, asst. prof., 1970-72; asst. prof. English St. Lawrence U., Canton, N.Y., 1972-74, assoc. prof., 1974-80, prof. English, 1980—; pub., editor Fiction Internat. mag. and Press, 1972-83; cons. editor U. Ill. Press, Champaign, Ill., 1974—; program cons. Nat. Endowment Humanities, 1976—; book reviewer Sat. Review, 1975—, N.Y. Times Book Rev., 1975—, Washington Post, 1975—. Editor: Apocalypse: Dominant Comtemporary Forms, 1972, Superfiction, or the American Story Transformed, 1975, Moral Fiction, 1980, New Writers for the Eighties, 1981, Love Stories/Love Poems, 1982, American Poetry Observed, 1984; author: The New Fiction, 1974, Olympic Gold Medalist, 1978. Grantee Nat. Endowment Humanities, 1974. Mem. Nat. Book Critics Circle, Coordinating Council Lit Mags. (pres., chmn. bd. dirs. 1979-81). Home: 14 Jay St Canton NY 13617 Office: St Lawrence Univ Canton NY 13617

BELLAMY, PETER, drama critic, lecturer; b. Cleve., Nov. 9, 1914; s. Paul and Marguerite Scott (Stark) B.; m. Jean Margaret Dessel, Mar. 11, 1939; children: Sheila Bellamy Scrozzari, Stephen Paul, John Stark II, Christopher Aladdin, Nicole Loughman. Student, Harvard U., 1932-36. Comml. editor Des Moines Register, 1936-37; mem. staff Cleve. News, 1938-60, gossip columnist, soc. editor, until 1960; mem. staff Cleve. Plain Dealer, 1960—, entertainment editor, drama critic, 1962—; lectr. Shakespeare and criticism Western Res. U., 1963-64. Author: The Amish, 1971. Trustee Neighborhood Settlement Assn., 1952-64; pres. bd. Glenville Community Center, 1952-54; bd. dirs. Nationalities Service Center, 1961-65, Elinor T. Rainey Inst., 1958-60, Golden Age Center, 1961-64. Served with USNR, 1945-46. Mem. Nat. Council Tchrs. English, Am. Theatre Critics Assn., Cleve. Press Club (pres. 1960-62). Episcopalian (vestryman). Clubs: Lambs (N.Y.C.); Cleve. Play House. Home: 2476 Kenilworth Rd Cleveland Heights OH 44106 Office: 1801 Superior Ave Cleveland OH 44114

BELLAMY, RALPH, actor; b. Chgo., June 17, 1904; s. Charles Rexford and Lilla Louise (Smith) B.; m. Alice Delbridge, 1922 (div. 1930); m. Catherine Willard, 1931 (div. 1945); children: Lynn, Willard; m. Ethel Smith, 1945 (div. 1947); m. Alice Murphy, 1949. Ed. high sch. With: William Owen in Shakespeare and the classics, 1921; appeared in: Old Matt and Wash Gibbs, Chautaupua road company, 1922; with stock companies, Madison, Wis., Evansville, Ind., 1922-23, traveling repertoire, Beach & Jones Co., 1924, John Wininger Repertoire Co., 1925, stock companies in numerous other cities, including, St. Joseph, Mo., Ft. Wayne and Terre Haute, Ind., 1923-28, 30; played leading parts, dir. own co., Des Moines, Nashville, Evanston, Ill., 1926-1930; actor stock cos., Jamestown, Rochester, and Freeport, N.Y., 1929-30; appeared in: N.Y.C. prodns. Roadside, 1930; also appeared in plays: Oh, Men Oh, Women, 1934; starred in: play Sunrise at Campobello, on Broadway, 1958-59; on tour, 1959, 60, in movie based on play, 1960; and has appeared in nearly 100 motion pictures, 1930—; including: The Professionals, 1966, Rosemary's Baby, 1968, Cancel My Reservation, 1970, Oh God, 1977; Trading Places, 1983; appeared in: N.Y. stage prodn. Tomorrow the World, 1943-44, State of the Union, 1945-47, Detective Story, 1949-50; producer, dir.: Pretty Little Parlor, N.Y.C., 1944; weekly TV series Man Against Crime, 1949-54; guest star appearances TV dramatic programs including Climax, Theatre Guild of Air, Playhouse 90, 1954—; radio guest maj. programs; narrator: Victor Record Album Rubaiyat of Omar Khayam and Leaves of Grass by Walt Whitman; starred in: TV series Eleventh Hour, 1963-64; NBC documentary Hope-Ship, Saigon, South Vietnam, 1962; 13 week TV series for, Episcopal Ch., 1965-66 (Emmy award); co-star: TV series The Survivors, 1968-69, The Most Deadly Game series, ABC-TV, 1970—, Hunters, 1971—, Moneychangers; appeared as Franklin D. Roosevelt: TV mini-series The Winds of War; appeared: in TV movies Condominium; also guest star: various TV shows including Aloha Paradise, Wheels, The Millionaire; (Recipient 1st ann. Best Actor award Acad. Radio and TV Arts and Scis. 1950, Antoinette Perry award 1958, Emmy award as narrator series One to One 1962, Delia Austrian award for Sunrise at Campobello); Author: When the Smoke Hit the Fan, 1979. Presdl. appointee nat. bd. U.S.O., 1958-60; mem. Pres.'s Com. on 50th Anniv. Dept. Labor, 1962; vice chmn. nat. campaign. ARC, 1963; chmn. N.Y. Regional NCCJ Brotherhood Week, 1963; founder, past mem. Calif. Arts Commn.; bd. dirs. People-to-People Project Hope, Theatervision, 1972-73. Award of merit State of Israel. Mem. Actors Equity Assn. (pres. 1952-64); mem. Acad. Motion Picture Arts and Scis. (bd. govs. 1982); Mem. Screen Actors Guild (a founder, 1st bd. dirs. 1933, Outstanding Achievement award for fostering the finest ideals of theacting profession 1983), Am. Arbitration Assn. (dir. 1962-64). Clubs: Players (bd. 1958-64), Dutch Treat, Lambs (N.Y.C.) (council 1952-56). Donated career memorabilia to Center for Film and Theater Research, U. Wis, UCLA, Boston U., Acad. Motion Picture Arts and Scis. Home: 8173 Mulholland Terr Los Angeles CA 90046 Office: 116 E 27th St New York NY 10016

BELLAMY, WILLIAM BUTLER, newspaper publisher; b. Little Rock, Nov. 28, 1920; s. William B. and Eva (Lee) B.; m. Carolyn Wright, May 12, 1943; children: William B. III, Linda Carol, Russell Wright. Student, Tulane U., 1939-41; LL.D. (hon.), U. Tex., 1969. With Express Publishing Co., 1946; sports editor San Antonio News, 1947-49, sports dir., 1949-52, Express mng. editor, 1952; News mng. editor, 1953-56; exec. adminstr. Express Publishing Co., KENS, TV and radio, 1956-57, asst. to pres., 1957-62; asst. mng. editor San Antonio Light, 1962-67, mng. editor, 1967; former pub., v.p., now pres. Hearst Corp.; Commr. Fiesta San Antonio Assn. Bd. dirs. San Antonio Zoo, San Antonio council Boy Scouts Am., San Antonio Livestock Show, Mental Health Assn., 1962, Council on Alcoholism, 1963, S.W. Research Inst.; bd. govs. San Antonio Med. Found., S.W. Found. for Research and Edn. Served as test pilot USAAF, 1941-45. Named San Antonian of Year Jr. C. of C., 1950; recipient Latin-Am. Good Neighbor award, 1950, San Antonio Bar Assn. award, 1969; named Most Outstanding Young Texan Texas Jr. C. of C., 1956; A.P. Newspaper award, 1970; Hearst Nat. Writing award, 1971; Editorial award Sigma Delta Chi, 1972; Tex. Headliner award, 1974. Mem. San Antonio Air Force Assn. (squadron comdr.), Am. Athletic Union (1st v.p. S. Tex.), Express-News Athletic Assn. (pres. 1948-62), Greater San Antonio C. of C. (dir.), Sigma Delta Chi. Mem. Christian Ch. (elder 1961-64). Clubs: Kiwanis (dir.), Rotary (dir.), Argyle (dir.), San Antonio Breakfast (pres. 1955), San Antonio Exchange (pres. 1961), San Antonio Exchange (dist. gov. 1962), San Antonio Press (trustee 1963). Office: Hearst Corp McCullough & Broadway San Antonio TX 78206 *Always put yourself in the other person's shoes and act accordingly. In other words, treat another person as you would expect to be treated. It pays dividends* *

BELLARD, EMORY DILWORTH, university football coach; b. Luling, Tex., Dec. 17, 1927; s. P.A. and Louie (Davis) B.; m. Mary Kay Watkins, Aug. 12, 1949; children: Emory D., Debra, Bob. B.S. in Phys. Edn, S.W. Tex. State U., 1949. Asst. football coach Alice (Tex.) High Sch., 1949-52; head coach Ingleside (Tex.) High Sch., 1952-54, Breckenridge (Tex.) High Sch., 1955-59, San Angelo (Tex.) High Sch., 1960-66; offensive backfield coach and coordinator U. Tex., Austin, 1967-71; dir. athletics, head football coach Tex. A&M U., College Station, 1971-78; head football coach Miss. State U., Starkville, 1979—. Recipient Gold Cup award for devel. wishbone formation Acad. Am. Football, 1975; named Coll. Coach of Yr. Sporting News, 1975, Disting. Alumni 1978 S.W. Tex. State U. Mem. Tex. High Sch. Coaches Assn. (dir. 1963-65, pres. 1966, elected to Hall of Honor 1976). Team winner Sunbowl championship, 1976. Team winner Hall of Fame Bowl championship, 1981. Office: Athletic Dept Mississippi State U Mississippi State MS 39762

BELLAVANCE, THOMAS EUGENE, college president; b. Norwich, Conn., Jan. 26, 1934; s. Eugene Theodore and Julia Ann (Savage) B.; m. Elizabeth A. Conti, Aug. 17, 1963; children: Eugene T., Sarah E., Genevieve, Emily C. B.A., U. Conn., 1958; M.A., Northwestern U., 1961; Ph.D., Mich. State U., 1969. Tchr. English high schs., in Conn., 1958-60; tchr. English, chmn. dept. Am. Sch., San Salvador, El Salvador, 1962-63; asst. prof. Am. thought and lang. Mich. State U., 1963-70; dean faculty Urbana (Ohio) Coll., 1970-74; dean, acad. v.p. Framingham (Mass.) Coll., 1974-80; pres. Salisbury (Md.) State Coll., 1980—; trustee Dayton-Miami Valley Consortium, 1972-73; cons. in field. Co-author: American Thought and Language Study Aids, 1964; contbr. poems anthologies. Mem. Md. Commn. on Quality Edn., Gov.'s Adv. Council. Served with AUS, 1954-56. Recipient Superior Teaching award Mich. State U., 1967. Mem. Am. Assn. State Colls. and Univs., Kappa Delta Pi, Alpha Phi Omega., Phi Gamma Mu. Democrat. Roman Catholic. Home: 1301 Camden Ave Salisbury MD 21801 Office: Office President Salisbury State Coll Salisbury MD 21801 *I look to what is, not what ought to be, and spend my energies dealing with that. "Ought" people scare me.*

BELLER, ELDON LEROY, banker; b. Prague, Okla., June 26, 1924; s. Everett and Magnola (Brown) B.; m. Colleen Jones, Feb. 5, 1949; children: Jan, Lisa. B.S. in Bus., Oklahoma City U., 1952. Sales mgr. Western Auto Supply Co., Wichita, 1953-60, C.I.T. Corp., Oklahoma City, 1960-69; exec. v.p. lending First Nat. Bank, Oklahoma City, 1969—; pres., dir. Penn Sq. Bank N.A., Oklahoma City, 1981, also chief adminstrv. officer; now v.p., dir. Ford Enterprises, Inc.; dir. FNB Indsl. Co., FNB Leasing Co., First Okla. Trust Co.; v.p., dir. Ford Enterprises, Oklahoma City. Served with AUS, 1940-45. Decorated Bronze Star (4). Mem. Associated Gen. Contractors Am., Mcpl. Contractors Assn., Oklahoma City C. of C. Baptist. Clubs: Beacon, Walnut Creek. Home: 1210 Brookhaven St Norman OK 73069 Office: 5809 NE Grand Blvd Oklahoma City OK 73126

BELLER, GARY A., financial services company executive; b. N.Y.C., Oct. 16, 1938; s. Charles W. and Jeanne A. B.; m. Carole P. Wrubel, Nov. 22, 1967; 1 dau., Jessie Melissa. B.A., Cornell U., 1960; LL.B., NYU, 1963, LL.M., 1971; postgrad. in Advanced Mgmt., Harvard Bus. Sch., 1967-68. Bar: N.Y. 1963. Various postiions gen. counsel's office Am. Express Co., N.Y.C., 1968-82, exec. v.p. and gen. counsel, 1983—. Editorial bd., Ctr. Pub. Resources (Alternatives), N.Y.C. Bd. dirs. Lenox Hill Neighborhood Assn. Mem. ABA, Bar Assn. City N.Y., N.Y. County Bar Assn. (com. corp. law depts.), Am. Corp. Counsel Assn. (dir.). Clubs: Harvard Bus. Sch., Downtown Athletic (N.Y.C.). Office: American Express Co 125 Broad St New York NY 10004

BELLER, MARTIN LEONARD, orthopaedic surgeon; b. N.Y.C., Apr. 30, 1924; s. Abraham Jacob and Ida (Fishkin) B.; m. Wilma Gertrude Kjelgaard, June 29, 1947; children: Alan Lewis, Beatrice Ann Beller Foreman, Peter James. A.B. with honors, Columbia U., 1944, M.D., 1946. Diplomate: Am. Bd. Orthopaedic Surgery. Intern Mt. Sinai Hosp., N.Y.C., 1946-47; resident in orthopaedic surgery Hosp. Joint Diseases, N.Y.C., 1949-52; practice medicine specializing in orthopaedic surgery, Phila., 1952—; asst. prof. orthopaedic surgery U. Pa. Sch. Medicine, Phila., 1967-72, asso. prof., 1972-80, clin. prof., 1980—; attending orthopaedic surgeon Hosp. U. Pa., 1963—; asso. attending orthopaedic surgeon Albert Einstein Med. Center, Phila., 1960-70, chmn. dept. orthopaedic surgery, 1970-79. Author: (with I. Stein and R. O. Stein) Living Bone in Health and Disease, 1955, (with I. Stein) Clinical Densitometry of Bone, 1970. Served from 1st lt. to capt., M.C. AUS, 1947-49. Am. Orthopaedic Assn. exchange fellow, Gt. Britain, 1963. Fellow A.C.S., Am. Acad. Orthopaedic Surgeons (bd. councilors 1978-81, Pa. rep. commn. on trauma 1984—), Internat. Soc. Orthopaedic Surgery and Traumatology; mem. Am. Orthopaedic Assn., Pa. Orthopaedic Soc. (pres. 1975-77), ACS (chmn. Pa. com. on trauma 1978-82), Orthopaedic Research Soc., Am. Rheumatism Soc., N.Y. Acad. Sci., Phila. Coll. Physicians, Phi Beta Kappa, Alpha Omega Alpha, Phi Delta Epsilon (nat. pres. 1975-76, chmn. bd. trustees 1984—). Republican. Episcopalian (vestryman 1966-70, 71—). Club: Union League of Phila. Home: 301 S 20th St Philadelphia PA 19103 Office: 1936 Spruce St Philadelphia PA 19103

BELLER, RONALD E., university president; b. Cin., Oct. 4, 1935; s. Ervin Charles and Marion (Helen) B.; m. Judith Anne Cline, Feb. 13, 1970; children: Julia, Deborah, Lee Anne, Bradley, James, Elizabeth, Ronald. B.I.E., U. Fla., 1957; M.B.A., Kent State U., 1966; Ph.D., U. Fla., 1971. Head budgeting services, asst. prof. hosp. adminstrn. Hillis Miller Health Center, U. Fla., 1970-71; spl. asst. to pres. U. S. Ala., Mobile, 1972-74, dean fin. and adminstrn., 1974-77; provost for adminstrn. Va. Commonwealth U., Richmond, Va., 1977-79; exec. v.p., 1979-80; pres. East Tenn. State U., Johnson City, 1980—; dir. Bank of Tenn. Contbr. articles to profl. jours. Vice chmn. Emergency Med. Service Council of Forsyth County, N.C., 1971-72; mem. personal health services com. Forsyth County Health Planning Council, 1971-72; chmn. Task Force on Orgn., Mobile Mental Health Center, 1973-74, Task Force on Drug Abuse Program, 1974-76; mem. adv. council 5th Dist. of City Council, City of Richmond, Va., 1977-79; bd. dirs. Johnson City Area United Way; bd. advisors Salvation Army, Johnson City. Mem. Johnson City/Washington County C. of C. (dir.), Am. Assn. Med. Colls., Phi Kappa Phi, Beta Gamma Sigma. Presbyterian. Lodge: Kiwanis. Home: Shelbridge E 11th Ave Johnson City TN 37601 Office: E Tenn State U Johnson City TN 37601

BELLI, MELVIN MOURON, lawyer, lecturer, writer; b. Sonora, Calif., July 29, 1907; s. Caesar Arthur and Leonie (Mouron) B.; m. Betty Ballantine, 1933; children: Richard R., Melvin Mouron, Jean, Susan; m. Joy Maybelle Turney, May 3, 1956; 1 son, Caesar Melvin; m. Lia G.T. Triff, June 3, 1972; 1 dau., Melia. A.B., U. Calif. - Berkeley, 1929; LL.B., Boalt Hall, 1933; J.D. (hon.), New Eng. Sch. Law. Bar: Calif. 1933. Sr. partner Belli Law Offices, San Francisco, 1940—; condr. Belli Seminars in Law, 1953—; pres. Belli Found. Lectrs., 1960—; pròvost Belli Soc.; Mem. Calif. Bldg. Standards Commn.; Bd. dirs. Disability & Casualty Inter-Ins. Exchange, N.W. Affairs Council; mem. exec. bd. Western State U. Coll. Law. Author: Modern Trials and Modern Damages, 6 vols, 1954, abridged edit., 1962, 2d edit., 1981, Ready for the Plaintiff, 1956, Trial and Tort Trends, 14 vols, 1954-62, The Adequate Award, 1953, Demonstrative Evidence and The Adequate Award, 1955, Malpractice, 1955, Modern Trials (student edition), (with Danny Jones) Life and Law in Japan, (with Maurice Carroll) Dallas Justice, 1964, The Law Revolt, 2 vols, 1968, Melvin Belli My Life on Trial, 1976, The Belli Files: Reflections on the Wayward Law, 1983; contbr.: numerous articles, also syndicated column So That's The Law; Asso. editor: Am. Trial Lawyers Assn. Law Jour, 1950—; adv. editor: Negligence and Compensation Service, 1955—; legal adv. bd.: Traumatic Medicine and Surgery for the Atty., 1958—; mem. bd. editors: Trial Diplomacy Jour; mem. editorial bd.: The Common Law Lawyer; bd. dirs.: Am. Jour. Forensic Psychiatry. Named dean emeritus Coll. Law, Riverside U.; decorated grand ofcl. St. Brigidian Order. Fellow Internat. Acad. Trial Lawyers (dir., past dean); mem. Authors Guild, Am. Acad. Forensic Scis., Tuolumne County Hist. Soc., Inter-Am. Bar Assn., ABA, Calif. Bar Assn., San Francisco Bar Assn., Fed. Bar Assn., Internat. Bar Assn. (patron), Internat. Legal Aid Assn., San Diego, Hollywood, Beverly Hills bars, Am. Trial Lawyers Assn. (past pres., chmn. torts sect. 1959), Barristers Club San Francisco (past dir.), La Asociacion Nacional de Abogados Mexico (hon.), Societe Driot (pres.), Phi Delta Phi, Delta Tau Delta. Clubs: Mason (Shriner), Olympic, The Commonwealth, Lawyers (San Francisco). Office: Belli Bldg 722 Montgomery St San Francisco CA 94111 also The Belli Bldg 9952 Santa Monica Bldg Suite 9000 Beverly Hills CA 90212 317 Ash St San Diego CA 92101 The Belli Bldg 405 Forest Ave Pacific Grove CA 93950 The Belli Bldg 215 N San Joaquin Stockton CA 95202

BELLINGER, JOHN DOOLEY, banker; b. Honolulu, May 13, 1923; s. Eustace L. and Lei (Williams) B.; m. Joan Simms, Apr. 7, 1945; children: Dona, Jan, Neil. Student, U. Hawaii, 1941-42, LL.D. (hon.), 1982. With 1st Hawaiian Bank (and predecessor), Honolulu, 1942—, pres., chief exec. officer, 1969—, chmn. bd., 1979—; also dir.; pres. chief exec. officer, chmn. bd. 1st Hawaiian, Inc.; also dir.; chmn., chief exec. officer Hawaii Thrift & Loan Inc., also dir.; chmn., pres., rep. Japan Hawaii Fin. Kabushiki Kaisha; chmn., dir. 1st Hawaiian Leasing, Inc.; dir. Alexander & Baldwin, Honolulu, Matson Nav. Co., Aloha Airlines, Hawaiian Telephone Co., Hawaii Meat Co., Restaurant Suntory, U.S.A., Halekulani Corp. Chmn. Japan-Hawaii Econ. Council; civilian aide to sec. Army for Hawaii; chmn. U.S. Army Civilian Adv. Steering Com.; trustee Francis H.I. Brown Found., Punahou Sch., Japan-Am. Inst. Mgmt. Sci., United Student Aid Funds. Served with AUS, 1946-47. Decorated Disting. Civilian Service Medal Sec. of Army, 1980; recipient Disting. Citizen award Congl. Medal of Honor Soc., 1981; decorated ProPatria award, 1984, Torch of Liberty award Anti-Defamation League of B'nai B'rith, 1984, Businessman of Yr. award Hawaiian bus./Profl. Assn., 1984, numerous others. Mem. C. of C. Hawaii, Assn. U.S. Army, Navy League, Hawaii bankers assns. Clubs: Hawaiian Civic, Oahu Country, Waialae Country (Honolulu) (past pres.); The 200 (treas., past pres.). Home: 1057 Waiholo St Honolulu HI 96821 Office: First Hawaiian Bank King and Bishop Sts Honolulu HI 96813

BELLINO, CARMINE SALVATORE, accountant, government investigator; b. Elizabeth, N.J., July 26, 1905; s. Frank and Frances (Lafaso) B.; m. Santina I. Novello, June 6, 1936 (dec. 1979); children: Francis, Robert, Joseph, Mary Catherine, Mary Joan, Mary Sandra, Maryan Joyce.; m. Catherine Tripodi DiGiacomo, Aug. 20, 1983; stepchildren: Joseph, Michael, Elizabeth, John. B.C.S. with honors in Acctg., NYU, 1928. C.P.A., N.J., D.C., N.Y. Acct. Mills & Co., N.Y.C., 1927-34; spl. agt. acct., also adminstrv. asst. to dir. FBI, 1934-45; asst. dir. RFC, 1945-46, War Assets Adminstrn., 1946-47; pvt. practice acctg., Washington and N.Y.C., 1947-62; resident agt. Wright Long & Co., N.Y.C., 1951-60, resident partner, 1964-70; chief investigator select com. on 1972 presdl. campaign activities U.S. Senate, 1973-74; chief investigator U.S. Senate Judiciary Com., 1979-81; spl. cons. Pres. John F. Kennedy, 1961-64; mem. bd. contract appeals AEC, 1964-70; acct. cons. to various U.S. congressional coms., Washington, 1947-60, 64-74. Served to lt. col. USAAF Res. Mem. Am. Inst. C.P.A.s, D.C. Soc. C.P.A.s, Soc. Former Spl. Agts. FBI. Club: KC (4 deg.). Home: 3303 Aruba Way C-3 Coconut Creek FL 33066

BELLIS, CARROLL JOSEPH, surgeon; b. Shreveport, La.; s. Joseph and Rose (Bloome) B.; m. Mildred Darmody, Dec. 26, 1939; children—Joseph, David. B.S., U. Minn., 1930, M.S. in Physiology, 1932, Ph.D. (fellow), 1934, M.D., 1936, Ph.D. in Surgery, 1941. Diplomate: Am. Bd. Surgery. Resident surgery U. Minn. Hosps., 1937-41; pvt. practice surgery, Long Beach, Calif., 1945—; mem. staff St. Mary's, Community hosps., Long Beach; cons. surgery Long Beach Gen. Hosp.; prof., chmn. dept. surgery Calif. Coll. Medicine, 1962—. Author: Fundamentals of Human Physiology, 1935, A Critique of Reason, 1938, Lectures in Medical Physiology; contbr. numerous articles in field of surgery, physiology to profl. jours. Served to col. M.C. AUS, 1941-46. Nat. Cancer Inst. fellow, 1934; recipient Charles Lyman Green prize in physiology, 1934; prize Mpls. Surg. Soc., 1938; ann. award Mississippi Valley Med. Soc., 1955. Fellow A.C.S., Internat. Coll. Surgeons, Am. Coll. Gastroenterology, Am. Med. Writers Assn., Internat. Coll. Angiology (sci. council); mem. Am. Assn. Study Neoplastic Diseases, Mississippi Valley Med. Soc., N.Y. Acad. Scis., Hollywood Acad. Medicine, Am. Geriatrics Soc., Irish Med. Assn., AAAS., Am. Assn. History Medicine, Sigma Xi, Phi Beta Kappa, Alpha Omega Alpha. Home: South Quail Ridge Rd Rolling Hills CA 90274 Office: 1045 Atlantic Ave Long Beach CA 90801

BELLMAN, RICHARD E, mathematician, educator; b. N.Y.C., Aug. 26, 1920; m. Nina Day. B.A., Bklyn. Coll., 1941; M.A., U. Wis., 1943; Ph.D., Princeton U., 1946; D.sc. hon., U. Aberdeen, Scotland, 1973, LL.D., U. So. Calif., 1974; D.Math., U. Waterloo, Ont., Can., 1975. Asst. prof. math. Princeton U., 1946-48; assoc. prof. math. Stanford U., Calif., 1948-52; mathematician RAND Corp., Santa Monica, Calif., 1953-65; prof. math., elec. engring. and medicine U. So. Calif.,

Los Angeles, 1965—; vis. prof. engring. UCLA, 1956. Author numerous books; Stability Theory of Differential Equations, 1953, Dynamic Programming, 1957, Adaptive Control Processes: A Guided Tour, 1961, An Introduction to the Mathematical Theory of Control Processes,, vol. I, 1968, vol. II, 1971, Can Computers Think? An Introduction to Artificial Intelligence, 1978; researcher numerous publs. in field; editor: book series Mathematics in Science and Engineering, 1962—; Jour. Math. Analysis and Applications, 1962—; inventor dynamic programming, 1953; contbr. (pure and applied math., including in invariant imbedding, quasi-linearization and its applications to system identification, application of math) to medicine and biol. scis. Recipient Norbert Weiner prize in Applied math. Am. Math. Soc. and Soc. Indsl. and Applied Math., 1970, Dickson prize Carnegie-Mellon U., 19701378, John von Neumann Theory award Inst. Mgmt. Scis. and Ops. Research Soc. Am., 1976, Gold medal IEEE, 1978, Heritage medal Am. Council for Control, 1983, ALZA Disting. lectr. biomed. Engring. Soc., 1972; honored in apl. issue IEEE Transactions on Automatic Control, 1981; recipient Bicentennial Salute Human Relations Commn., Los Angeles, 1981. Fellow Soc. Math. Biology; mem. Nat. Acad. Engring., Nat. Acad. Scis. Office: U So Calif Dept Elec Engring University Park Los Angeles CA 90089

BELLONI, ROBERT CLINTON, judge; b. Riverton, Oreg., Apr. 4, 1919; s. John Edward and Della (Clinton) B.; m. Doris A. Adams, Jan. 27, 1946; children—James L., Susan K. B.A., U. Oreg., 1941, LL.B., 1951. Bar: Oreg. bar 1951. Practiced in, Coquille, Oreg., 1951-52, Myrtle Point, Oreg., 1952-57; judge Oreg. Circuit Ct., Coos and Curry Counties, Coquille, 1957-67; U.S. dist. judge Dist. Oreg., 1967—, chief judge, 1971-76. Councilman, Myrtle Point, 1953-57, mayor, 1957; chmn. Coos County Democratic Central Com., 1957; Hon. trustee Boys and Girls Aid Soc. Oreg., 1960. Served to 1st lt. AUS, 1942-46. Robert C. Belloni Boys Forest Ranch dedicated in his honor Coos County Bd. Commrs., 1969. Mem. Am., Oreg. bar assns., Am. Judicature Soc., Oreg. Juvenile Ct. Judges Assn. (pres. 1963), Circuit Ct. Judges Assn. Oreg. (pres. 1966), 9th Circuit Dist. Judges Assn. (pres. 1980-81), Sigma Alpha Epsilon, Delta Theta Phi. Episcopalian. Home: 8079 Sacajawea Way Wilsonville OR 97070 Office: 612 US Courthouse Portland OR 97205

BELLO RUIZ, RAFAEL, archbishop; b. Terpan de Galeana, Mex., Mar. 7, 1926. Ordained priest Roman Catholic Ch., 1950; named bishop Titular Ch. of Segia; bishop, Acapulco, Mex., 1976-83, archbishop, 1983—. Address: Apartado 201 Acapulco Mexico

BELLOTTI, FRANCIS XAVIER, state official; b. Dorchester, Mass., May 3, 1923; s. Peter Vincent and Mary J. (Petrocelli) B.; m. Margarita E. Wang, Feb. 22, 1949; children: Francis X., Kathleen A., Mary E., Nina M., Peter V., Therese A., Margarita E., Joseph R., Thomas, Patricia A., Michael G., Sheila A. A.B., Tufts U., 1947; LL.B. (Univ. fellow), Boston Coll., 1952; J.D. (hon.), New Eng. Sch. Law, 1977, Tufts U., 1979. Bar: Mass. 1952, U.S. Supreme Ct. 1965, U.S. Dist. Ct. 1975. Practiced law, Quincy, Mass., 1952-74; lt. gov. Commonwealth of Mass., 1963-64, atty. gen., 1975—; chmn. Criminal History Systems Bd., Comm. on Criminal Justice, Organized Crime Control Council, Com. on Privacy and Consumer Rights; mem. Mass. Council on Juvenile Behavior, Consumers' Council, Criminal Justice Tng. Council, Select Com. on Jud. Needs (Cox Com.), Motor Vehicle Ins. Merit Rating Bd. Served to lt. (j.g.) USN, 1942-46. Recipient Silver medal VFW, 1978, comdr. in chief gold medal and citation VFW, 1979, Louis C. Wyman award Nat. Assn. Attys. Gen., 1981. Fellow Internat. Acad. Trial Lawyers, Am. Coll. Trial Lawyers; mem. Harvard Inst. Politics, Nat. Coll. Criminal Def. Lawyers, Profl. Journalists, New Eng. Law Inst., Am. Judicature Soc., Justinian Law Soc. Roman Catholic. Home: 120 Hillside Ave Quincy MA 02170 Office: Dept of Atty Gen 1 Ashburton Pl Boston MA 02108

BELLOW, ALEXANDRA, mathematician, educator; b. Bucharest, Roumania, Aug. 30, 1935; d. Dumitru and Florica Bagdasar; m. Cassius Ionescu Tulcea, Apr. 1956 (div. 1969); m. 2d Saul G. Bellow, Oct. 1974. M.S. in Math, U. Bucharest, 1957; Ph.D. in Math., Yale U., 1959. Research assoc. Yale U., New Haven, Conn., 1959-61, U. Pa., Phila., 1961-62, asst. prof., 1962-64; assoc. prof. U. Ill., 1964-67; prof. Northwestern U., Evanston, Ill., 1967—. Author: (with C. Ionescu Tulcea) Topics in the Theory of Lifting, 1969; assoc. editor: Annals of Probability, 1979-83, Advances in Math., 1979—. Fairchild Disting. scholar Cal. Inst. Tech., 1980; NSF grantee. Mem. Am. Math. Soc., N.Y. Acad. Sci., Sigma Xi. Office: Dept Math Northwestern U Evanston IL 60201

BELLOW, DONALD GRANT, mechanical engineering educator; b. Winnipeg, Man., Can., Aug. 5, 1931; s. Walter William and Lillian Christine (Hnappdal) B.; m. Jean Marion Daye, May 18, 1956; children: Jonathan Mark, Denise Gisele. B.A. in Sci., U. B.C., 1956; M.S., U. Alta, 1960; Ph.D., U. Alta., 1963. Registered profl. engr., Alta., Can. Project engr. Can. Industries Ltd., Kingston, Ont., 1956-57, Gen. Motors Diesel Ltd., London, Ont., Can., 1957-58; lectr., asst. prof., assoc. prof., prof. U. Alta., Edmonton, Alta., Can., 1958—, chmn. dept. Recipient L.C. Charlesworth award Assn. Profl. Engrs., Geologists and Geophysicists of Alta., 1982. Mem. ASME, Can. Soc. for Mech. Engring., Soc. for Exptl. Stress Analysis, Assn. Profl. Geologists and Geophysicists of Alta. (2d v.p.). Conservative. Anglican. Office: U Alta Dept Mech Engring Edmonton AB Canada T6G 2G8

BELLOW, SAUL, writer; b. Lachine, Quebec, Can., June 10, 1915; s. Abraham and Liza (Gordon) B.; m. Alexandra Bagdasar; children: Gregory, Adam, Daniel. Student, U. Chgo., 1933-35; B.S., Northwestern U., 1937, Litt.D., 1962; Litt.D., Bard Coll., 1962, Harvard U., 1972, Yale U., 1972, McGill U., 1973, Brandeis U., 1974, Hebrew Union Coll.-Jewish Inst. Religion, 1976, Trinity Coll., Dublin, Ireland, 1976. Tchr. Pestalozzi-Froebel Tchrs. Coll., Chgo., 1938-42; faculty Princeton, N.Y. U., U. Minn.; faculty English dept. U. Chgo., 1963—, mem. com. on social thought, 1963—, chmn. com. on social thought, 1970-76, now Raymond W. and Martha Hilpert Gruiner Distinguished Services prof.; Tanner lectr. Oxford U. Author: Dangling Man, 1944, The Victim, 1947, The Adventures of Augie March, 1953 (Nat. Book award 1953), Seize the Day, 1956, Henderson the Rain King, 1959, Herzog, 1964 (James L. Dow award 1964, Internat. Lit. prize 1965, Nat book award 1965, Soc. Midland Authors Fiction award 1976), Mosby's Memoirs and Other Stories, 1968, Mr. Sammler's Planet, 1969 (Nat. Book award 1970), Humboldt's Gift, 1975 (Pulitzer prize 1976), To Jerusalem and Back, 1976; short stories Him With His Foot in His Mouth, 1984; contbr.: fiction to Esquire and lit. quarterlies; criticisms appear in New Leader, others; short story to Atlantic's 125th Anniversary Edit., 1982. Decorated Croix de Chevalier des Arts et Lettres, France, Comdr. Legion of Honor, France; recipient Nat. Inst. Arts and Letters award, 1952; Friends of Lit. Fiction award, 1960; Communicator of Yr. award U. Chgo. Alumni Assn., 1971; Nobel prize for lit., 1976; Medal of Honor for lit. Nat. Arts Club, 1978; O. Henry prize for short story A Silver Dish, 1980; Guggenheim fellow, 1955-56; Ford Found. grantee, 1959-61. Mem. Am. Acad. Arts and Scis. Address: care Com Social Thought Univ Chicago 1126 E 59th St Chicago IL 60637

BELLOWS, CAROLE KAMIN, lawyer; b. Chgo., May 24, 1935; d. Alfred and Sara (Liebenson) Kamin; m. Jason E. Bellows, June 28, 1958 (dec. June 1980); children: Marcia, Douglas, Daniel. B.A., U. Ill., 1957; J.D., Northwestern U., 1960. Bar: Ill. bar 1960. Ptnr. firm Reuben & Proctor, 1979—; mem. Ill. Commn. Edn. for Law and Justice. Editor: Your Bill of Rights, 1967, 69. Recipient Maurice Weigle award for outstanding service to organized bar, 1970, U. Ill. Mothers Assn. medallion of honor, 1975, Northwestern U. Alumnae award, 1978. Fellow Am. Bar Found. (Ill. chmn. 1979-80); mem. ABA (chmn. sect. individual rights and responsibilities 1975-76, mem. council 1967-77, com. on bar services and activities 1977—, ho. of dels. 1975—, state del. 1978—, vice chmn. fellows 1983-84), Ill. Bar Assn. (gov. 1969—, 2d v.p. 1975-76, pres. elect 1976-77, pres. 1977—), Chgo. Bar Assn. (chmn. constl. revision com. 1973-74), Nat. Conf. Bar Pres.'s (exec. council 1977-79), Ill. Bar Found. (dir. 1977-78), Northwestern U. Law Alumni Assn. (2d v.p.), Ill. Inst. Continuing Legal Edn. (dir. 1977-78), Am. Law Inst., Ill. Trial Lawyers Assn., League Women Voters of Ill., Womens Bar Assn. Ill., Decalogue Soc. Home: 725 LaPorte Ave Wilmette IL 60091 Office: 1 IBM Plaza Chicago IL 60611

BELLOWS, CHARLES SANGER, lawyer; b. Mpls., Oct. 20, 1915; s. Henry Adams and Mary (Sanger) B. A.B., Harvard U., 1937; LL.B., Yale U., 1940. Bar: N.Y. 1941, Minn. 1946. Partner firm Best & Flanagan, Mpls., 1946—. Pres., Mpls. Citizens League, 1952; Pres. Minn. Orch. Assn., 1959-62; chmn. bd. dirs. Abbott Northwest Hosp., 1971-74; bd. dirs. Abbott-N.W. Hosp., 1966-81, Minn. Orch. Assn., 1959—; pres., dir. Met. Opera Upper Midwest, 1983—; hon. trustee Macalester Coll. Served with AUS, 1941-46. Mem. Am., N.Y. State, Minn., Hennepin County bar assns. Office: 4040 IDS Center Minneapolis MN 55402

BELLOWS, HOWARD ARTHUR, JR., hardware products mfg. co. exec.; b. N.Y.C., Mar. 10, 1938; s. Howard Arthur and Rita Jennie (Maffitt) B.; m. Mary Josephine Boyd, Sept. 7, 1968; children—Maffitt Vodrey, Alexander Scott, Hillary Newland, Jennifer Pacheteau. B.A., Princeton U., 1960; M.B.A., Harvard U., 1964. Dir. mktg. Olga Co., Van Nuys, Calif., 1964-66; chmn. bd., co-chief exec. officer Triangle Corp., Stamford, Conn., 1967-71, chmn. bd., pres., chief exec. officer, 1971—. Trustee Western Res. Acad., Hudson, Ohio. Served to lt. (j.g.) USNR, 1960-62. Mem. Young Pres's. Orgn., Hand Tools Inst. (dir., mem. exec. com.). Clubs: River, Racquet and Tennis (N.Y.C.); Field, Stanwich (Greenwich, Conn.). Home: 15 Upper Cross Rd Greenwich CT 06830 Office: Care Triangle Corp 72 Cummings Point Rd PO Box 1881 Stamford CT 06904

BELLOWS, JAMES GILBERT, television editor; b. Detroit, Nov. 12, 1922; s. Lyman Hubbard and Dorothy (Gilbert) B.; m. Keven Ryan; children—Amelia, Priscilla, Felicia, Michael, Justine. A.B., Kenyon Coll., 1946, L.H.D., 1965. Mng. editor Miami (Fla.) News, 1958-61; editor N.Y. Herald Tribune, N.Y.C., 1963-66; asso. editor Los Angeles Times, 1966-74; editor Washington Star, 1974-77, Los Angeles Herald-Examiner, 1977-81. Mng. editor: Entertainment Tonight, Paramount TV, 1981—. Trustee Kenyon Coll. Served to lt. (j.g.) USNR, World War II. Mem. Psi Upsilon, Sigma Delta Chi. Office: 202 N Cannon Dr Beverly Hills CA 90210

BELLOWS, JOHN, ophthalmologist; b. N.Y.C., Aug. 22, 1906; s. Louis G. and Rose (Goldfreed) B.; m. Mary Trueblood, Apr. 4, 1945; children: Randall, Diane, Deborah, Sandra, David. B.S., U. Ill., 1927, M.D., 1930; M.S., Northwestern U., 1935, Ph.D., 1938. Diplomate: Am. Bd. Ophthalmology. Intern Cook County Hosp., Chgo., 1929-30, resident, 1930-33; practice medicine, specializing in ophthalmology, Chgo., 1933—; clin. prof. ophthalmology Chgo. Med. Sch.; asso. prof. ophthalmology Northwestern U.; prof. ophthalmology Cook County Grad. Sch. Medicine, 1946; attending ophthalmologist Cook County Hosp., 1946—, Columbus, Henrotin hosps., 1960—; dir. Mediphone (med. consultation by telephone); vis. prof. U. Central de Venezuela; founder, exec. sec. Soc. for Cryo-surgery; hon. pres. El Consejo Directivo del Instituto de Oftalmologicas, Caracas. Author: Cataract and Anomalies Crystalline Lens, 1944, Cryotherapy of Ocular Diseases, 1966, Contemporary Ophthalmology (honoring Sir Stewart Duke-Elder), 1972, Cataract and Abnormalities of the Lens, 1975, Glaucoma: Contemporary International Concepts, 1980; chief editor: Jour. Ocular Surgery, Annals of Ophthalmology, Glaucoma, Comprehensive Therapy; editorial bd.: Excerpta Medica. Served to lt. col. AUS, World War II; chief eye sect. Wakeman Gen. Hosp.; Ind. Recipient Lucien Howe medal U. Buffalo, 1938. Fellow A.C.S., Internat. Coll. Surgeons; mem. Am. Assn. Research Ophthalmology, N.Y. Soc. Clin. Ophthalmology, Pan Am. Med. Assn., Pan-Pacific Surg. Assn., Internat., Am. acads. ophthalmology, Soc. Cryobiology, Soc. Française D'Ophtalomologie, Am. Assn. Ophthalmology, Academia Ophtalmologica Internationalis, Am. Soc. Contemporary Ophthalmology (dir., founder), Internat. Glaucoma Congress (founder, dir.), Am. Soc. Contemporary Medicine and Surgery (dir., founder), Internat. Assn. Ocular Surgeons (founder, dir. 1981), Royal Soc. Medicine. Patentee in field. Home: 1040 N Lake Shore Dr Chicago IL 60611 Office: 211 E Chicago Ave Suite 1044 Chicago IL 60611

BELLOWS, RANDALL TRUEBLOOD, ophthalmologist, educator; b. Chgo., June 1, 1946; s. John D. and Mary Frances (Trueblood) B. B.S., Northwestern U., 1968, M.D., 1971. Intern Los Angeles County-U. So. Calif., 1972; resident U. Fla., Gainesville, 1972-75; practice medicine specializing in eye surgery and diseases, Chgo., 1975—; assoc. dir. Am. Soc. Contemporary Medicine, Surgery and Ophthalmology, 1975—; chmn., head dept. surgery Henrotin Hosp., 1981—; cons. Chgo. Bd. Edn. Editor: Glaucoma Jour, Annals of Ophthalmology, Jour. Ocular Therapy and Surgery, Comprehensive Therapy; contbr. chpts. to textbooks, articles to profl. jours. Recipient cert. of competence in ophthalmic practice. Mem. AMA (recognition award 1981, 82, 83), Am. Soc. Contemporary Ophthalmology, Am. Soc. Contemporary Medicine and Surgery, AAAS, Am. Acad. Ophthalmology, Am. Intraocular Implant Soc., Chgo. Med. Soc., Ill. Med. Soc., Chgo. Inst. Medicine, Chgo. Ophthmol. Soc., Pan-Am. Assn. Ophthalmology, Internat. Glaucoma Congress, Internat. Assn. Ocular Surgeons. Office: 211 E Chicago Ave #1044 Chicago IL 60611

BELLOWS, THOMAS JOHN, educator; b. Chgo., Aug. 15, 1935; s. Charles Everett and Dorothy (Morrison) B.; m. Marilyn Denise Corbell; children: Scott Anthony, Justin Thomas, Trevor Cullen; children by previous marriage: Roderick Alan, Adrienne Marie, Jeannine Louise, Derek John, Marshall Everett. Student, Am. U., 1956, UCLA, 1956-57; B.A., Augustana Coll., 1957; M.A., U. Fla., 1958, Yale U., 1960, Ph.D., 1968. Asst. prof. polit. sci. West Ga. Coll., Carrollton, 1962-64, 66; asst. prof. to prof. polit. sci. U. Ark., Fayetteville, 1967-81, chmn. dept., 1971-78; dir. Div. Social and Policy Scis., U. Tex., San Antonio, 1981—; Vis. lectr. depts. history, polit. sci. Nanyang U., Singapore, 1965; vis. prof. Nat. Chengchi U., Taiwan, 1979. Author: (with S. Erikson and H. Winter) Political Science: Introductory Essays and Readings, 1971, The People's Action Party of Singapore: Emergence of a Dominant Party System, 1970, (with H. Winter) People and Politics: An Introduction to Political Science, 1985, Taiwan's Foreign Policy in the 1970's, 1976, Proxy War in Asia: A New Communist Strategy, 1979. Mem. Southwestern Social Sci. Assn., Am. Polit. Sci. Assn., Assn. Asian Studies, Phi Beta Kappa, Phi Alpha Theta, Phi Kappa Phi. Methodist. Address: Division Social and Policy Sciences Univ Texas San Antonio TX 78285

BELLPORT, BERNARD PHILIP, cons. engr.; b. LaCrosse, Kans., May 25, 1907; s. Bernard P. and Louise H. (Groves) B.; m. Elsy V. Johnson, June 11, 1931 (dec. Mar. 1954); children—Louise Bellport Garcia, Bernard Philip; m. Mabelle W. Kandolin, Sept. 26, 1955. B.S. in Mining Engring, Poly. Coll. Engring., Oakland, Calif., 1927. Registered profl. engr., Colo. Mining engr. Western U.S., 1927-28; engr.-geologist St. Joseph Lead Co., 1928-31; with Phoenix Utility Co., 1931-32, Mont. Hwy. Commn., 1932-35, Bur. Reclamation, 1936-72; regional dir. region 2, Calif., 1957-59, asso. chief engr., Denver, 1959-63, chief engr., 1963-70, dir. design and constrn., 1970-72; practice as engring. cons., 1972—; arbitrator Constrn. Arbitration Panel, State of Calif. Recipient Distinguished Service award Dept. Interior; Golden Beaver for engring.; named Man of Year Am. Pub. Works Assn., 1970. Mem. Nat. Acad. Engring., U.S. Commn. Large Dams (chmn. 1971-72), Internat. Commn. Irrigation, Drainage and Flood Control, ASCE (pres. Colo. 1966), Am. Arbitration Assn., Rossmoor Engrs. Club, Internat. Water Resources Assn., Hon. Order Ky. Cols., Chi Epsilon (hon.). Episcopalian. Clubs: Masons (32 deg.), Shriners, Round Hill Country. Address: 855 Terra California Dr Apt 4 Walnut Creek CA 94595 *In retrospect, I believe my highest contribution to humanity and our nation was and is without question my thirty odd years tenure with the United States Bureau of Reclamation—namely my assistance and guidance in the development of water resources in the arid West and emerging foreign nations to produce water for human consumption and recreation, production of food and fibre, industrial production and, not least, cleanly produced electrical energy.*

BELLSON, LOUIS PAUL, drummer; b. Rock Falls, Ill., July 6, 1924; s. Louis and Carmen (Bartolucci) B.; m., Nov. 19, 1952; children: Tony, Dee Dee. Student, Augustana Coll., Rock Island, Ill., 1942. With Ted Fio Rito, 1942, Benny Goodman, 1943, 46, Tommy Dorsey, 1947-50, Duke Ellington, 1951-546, Jazz at Philharmonic, 1954; concert artist, 1955—; mem. Big Band Now. Served with AUS, 1943-46. Mem. Musicians Union. Office: care Assoc Booking Corp 1995 Broadway New York NY 10023

BELLUCCI, EDWARD M., labor union executive; b. New Haven, May 9, 1919; s. Michael Gaus and Amelia (Cinquini) B.; m. Bernice Bellucci, Nov. 3, 1945; children: Carol, Edward, David, June. Sec.-treas. Internat. Union Bricklayers and Allied Craftsmen, Washington; investment mgr., advisor gen. funds. and pension funds. Office: Internat Union Bricklayers and Allied Craftsmen 815 15th St NW Washington DC 20005

BELLUSCHI, PIETRO, architect; b. Ancona, Italy, Aug. 18, 1899; naturalized, 1929; s. Guido and and Camilla (Dogliani) B.; m. Helen Hemmila, Dec. 1, 1934 (dec. Mar. 1962); children: Peter, Anthony; m. Marjorie Bruckner, June 25, 1965. Student, U. Rome Sch. Engring., 1919-22; doctor's degree in civil engring.; C.E., Cornell U., 1924; LL.D., Reed Coll., Portland, Oreg., 1950; Sc.D., Christian Bros. Coll., Memphis, 1957; D.F.A. (hon.), U. R.I., 1963, U. Mass., 1967, U. Portland, 1977, Pacific Northwest Coll. Art, 1983, D.Arch., U. Mich., 1967, L.H.D., Oklahoma City U., 1968. Insp. housing devel., Rome, 1923; elec. engr. work Bunker Hill and Sullivan Mining Co., Kellogg, Idaho, 1924-25; draftsman A.E. Doyle (architect), Portland, 1925-27; chief designer A.E. Doyle & Asso. (architects), 1927-42, mem. firm, 1932-42; practice architecture under own name, Portland, 1943—; dean Mass. Inst. Tech. Sch. Architecture and Planning, 1951-65; mem. Nat. Fine Arts Commn., 1950; adviser State Dept. on design fgn. bldgs.; Am. del. conv. Inst. Intellectual Coop. of League of Nations, Madrid, 1934. Past pres. bd. trustees Portland Art Mus. N.A.; past trustee Boston Mus. Fine Arts. Fellow AIA (Gold medal 1972), Danish Royal Acad. Fine Arts, Am. Acad. Arts and Scis., Nat. Inst. Arts and Letters (v.p.); mem. NAD. Address: 700 NW Rapidan Terr Portland OR 97210

BELLVILLE, RALPH EARL, banker; b. Lynn, Mass., June 15, 1925; s. Harold Eugene and Edith Floy (Simpson) B.; m. Crescentia Ranftl, Oct. 16, 1954. A.B., Harvard U., 1950. Asst. mgr. No. Trust Co., Chgo., 1955-60; v.p. United Calif. Bank, Los Angeles, 1960-69; exec. v.p. Security Pacific Nat. Bank, Los Angeles, 1969—; dir. Bank of Canton, Hong Kong, Security Pacific Bank (Panama) S.A., Security Pacific Overseas Finance Inc.; vice chmn. bd. Security Pacific Internat. Bank, N.Y.C.; chmn. Security Pacific Overseas Corp., Security Pacific Overseas Investment Corp., Security Pacific Trading Corp. Served with inf. U.S. Army, 1943-46. Decorated Bronze Star with oak leaf cluster. Mem. Bankers Assn. Fgn. Trade (bd. dirs. 1975-77), Nat. Fgn. Trade Council, Los Angeles Com. on Fgn. Relations. Clubs: Jonathan, Internat., Harvard of So. Calif. (Los Angeles). Office: 333 S Hope St Los Angeles CA 90071

BELMAN, A. BARRY, pediatric urologist; b. Columbus, Ga., Oct. 16, 1938; s. David Joseph and Ruth (Radin) B.; m. Paula Yonover, June 14, 1964; children—Peter, Lisa, Trina, Jessica. B.A. with distinction, U. Ariz., 1960; M.D., Northwestern U., 1964, M.S., 1969. Diplomate: Am. Bd. Urology (exam. com. 1980-84). Intern Passavant Meml. Hosp., Chgo., 1974-75; resident dept. urology Northwestern U. Med. Sch., from instr. to asso. prof. urology, 1969-76; attending pediatric urologist Children's Meml. Hosp., Chgo., 1970-76; prof. urology and child health and devel. George Washington U. Sch. Medicine and Health Scis., 1978—; chmn. dept. pediatric urology Children's Hosp. Nat. Med. Center, 1976—; cons. Nat. Naval Walter Reed Army hosps. Co-author: Genitourinary Problems in Children, 1981; asso. editor: Clinical Pediatric Urology, 1976. Mem. Am. Urol. Assn., Am. Acad. Pediatrics, Soc. Pediatric Urology, A.C.S. Office: 111 Michigan Ave NW Washington DC 20010

BELMONT, AUGUST, investment banker; b. N.Y.C., Dec. 30, 1908; s. August and Alice Wall (de Goicouria) B.; m. Elizabeth Lee Saltonstall, June 16, 1931; children: Alice Lee, August, John Saltonstall, Priscilla; m. Louise Vietor Winston, Feb. 8, 1946. A.B., Harvard U., 1931. With Bonbright & Co., Inc. (investment bankers), N.Y.C., 1932-42, v.p., dir., 1939-42; v.p. Dillon, Read & Co. Inc., 1946-62, pres., 1962-70, chmn., 1971-73, dir., 1952—; pres. Nassau Assos., Inc., 1958-70, chmn., 1971-73; dir. The Ryland Group; past dir. Tex. Gas Transmission Corp., Am. Viscose Corp., U.S. & Fgn. Securities Corp., Rouse Co., Am. Kennel Club (chmn. 1977-79), Cameron Iron Works, Inc., Chemistrand Corp., Congoleum Nairn Co., Great Am. Ins. Co.; spl. asst. to under sec. Navy, 1940. Hon. trustee Presbyn. Hosp., N.Y.C., Am. Mus. Natural History. Served to lt. comdr. USNR, 1942-45; served under comdr. Air Force; Pacific Fleet. Decorated Bronze Star. Clubs: Links (N.Y.C.); Jockey (steward 1978—, chmn. 1982-83. Home: Route 1 Box 564 Easton MD 21601

BELMORE, F. MARTIN, lawyer; b. N.Y.C., Mar. 17, 1944; s. Frederick M. and Charlotte Lee (Munn) B.; m. Suzanne Corkedale, July 24, 1981. A.B., Princeton U., 1966; postgrad., Oxford U., 1966-67; J.D., Harvard U., 1970; LL.M. in Taxation, NYU, 1975. Bar: N.Y. 1971, Ill. 1976. Assoc. Dewey, Ballatine, Bushby, Palmer & Wood, N.Y.C., 1970-75, Mayer, Brown & Platt, Chgo., 1975-77, ptnr., 1978—. Mem. ABA, Assn. Bar City N.Y., N.Y. Bar Assn., Internat. Fiscal Assn. Clubs: Racquet (Chgo.); Princeton (N.Y.C.). Office: Mayer Brown & Platt 231 S LaSalle St Chicago IL 60604

BELNAP, DAVID FOSTER, journalist; b. Ogden, Utah, July 27, 1922; s. Hyrum Adolphus and Lois Ellen (Foster) B.; m. Barbara Virginia Carlberg, Jan. 17, 1947. Student, Weber Coll., Ogden, 1940. Asst. city editor Seattle Star, 1945-47; bur. chief UP Assns., Helena, Mont., 1947-50, Honolulu, 1950-52; regional exec. Pacific N.W., 1952-

55, dir. Latin Am. services, 1955-67; Latin Am. corr. Los Angeles Times, 1967-80, asst. fgn. news editor, Los Angeles, 1980—. Recipient Overseas Press Club Am. award for best article on Latin Am., 1970, Maria Moors Cabot prize, 1973. Mem. Overseas Press Club Am. Clubs: Am. of Buenos Aires; Phoenix of Lima (Peru). Home: 1134 W Huntington Dr Arcadia CA 91006 Office: Times Mirror Sq Los Angeles CA 90053

BELNAP, NORMA LEE MADSEN, musician; b. Tremonton, Utah, Dec. 2, 1927; d. Doyle Franklin and Cleo (Crawford) Madsen; m. H. Austin Belnap, Jan. 19, 1980. Student, Brigham Young U., summer 1947, San Francisco Conservatory of Music, summer 1949; B.S., U. Utah, 1951; postgrad., Aspen Inst. Music, 1953, Music Acad. of West, Santa Barbara, Calif., 1962. Sec.-treas., dir., mem. faculty Treasure Mountain Festival of Arts, 1965, 66; mem. nat. adv. com. Nat. Black Music Colloquium and Competition.; lectr. U. Utah, 1951—, instr., 1965, adj. asst. prof. music, 1969-73, adj. asso. prof., 1973-77, adj. prof., 1977—. Violinist, Utah Symphony, 1944—; asst. concert master, 1977—; mem., Utah Opera Theatre Orch., 1951-54, Utah Ballet Theatre Orch., 1953—, Melody Maids, 4 violins and piano, 1943-49; active in chamber music circles, 1946—; concert mistress, U. Utah Symphony, 1947-58; prin. violist, 1958-62; soloist, Utah Artist Series, 1964; mem., Treasure Mountain String Quartet, Park City, Utah, 1964, 65, 66; appeared as violin soloist, U. Utah Symphony and Ballet Threatre Orch., 1954, 56, 57; 2d violinist (affiliated with Young Audiences, Inc.) Utah String Quartet, 1958-68; Quartet-in-residence U. Utah, 1968—, Idaho State U., 1967; with Bach Festival Orch., Carmel, Calif., 1963, 69, Utah-ASTA Faculty Quartet, 1970-79, tour of Europe with, Utah Symphony, 1966, 77, 81, Utah Symphony, S. and Central Am., 1971, Utah Symphony, Brit. Isles, 1975, Utah Symphony, Hawaii, 1979, concertizing throughout Western states, frequent festival adjudicator. Recipient Tchr. Recognition award Music Tchrs. Nat. Assn., 1971, 72, 73. Mem. Music Educators Nat. Conf., Utah String Tchrs. Assn. (state membership chmn. 1969-73), Utah Music Tchrs. Assn. (state cert. bd.), Utah Fedn. Music Clubs (1st v.p.), Am. String Tchrs. Assn. (dir. U. Utah summer string conf. ann. 1970-79), Mortar Bd., Mu Phi Epsilon (nat. v.p., music adv., province gov. 1954-58, chpt. honoree for 30 yrs. of dedicated service 1981), Alpha Lambda Delta, Phi Kappa Phi, Alpha Xi Delta, Lambda Delta Sigma. Mormon. Home: 1333 Chandler Dr Salt Lake City UT 84103 Office: Music Hall Univ Utah Salt Lake City UT 84112

BELNAP, NUEL DINSMORE, JR., philosophy educator; b. Evanston, Ill., May 1, 1930; s. Nuel Dinsmore and Elizabeth (Dafter) B.; m. Joan Cohde, Oct. 23, 1953; children: Nuel Dinsmore, Christopher William, Mary Jo, Tyler Kristan; m. Gillian Hirth, Apr. 7, 1982. B.A., U. Ill., 1952; M.A., Yale U., 1957, Ph.D., 1960. Instr. philosophy Yale U., New Haven, 1958-60, asst. prof., 1960-63; assoc. prof. philosophy U. Pitts., 1963-66, prof., 1966—, prof. sociology, 1967—, prof. dept. history and philosophy of sci., 1971—; vis. prof. U. Calif.-Irvine, winter 1973; vis. Oscar R. Ewing prof. Ind. U., Bloomington, fall, 1977, 78, 79, Alan Ross Anderson lectr., 1983—; vis. fellow Australian Nat. U., 1976; cons. Office Naval Research, 1960-63, System Devel. Corp., 1961-67, U. Pitts. Knowledge Availability Ctr., 1963-66, Westinghouse Research Lab., 1981. Author: (with Thomas B. Steel) The Logic of Questions and Answers, 1976, (with Alan Ross Anderson) Entailment: The Logic of Relevance and Necessity, vol. I, 1975; mem. editorial bd.: Am. Philos. Quar., 1966-78, Jour. Philos. Logic, 1970—; v.p., 1976—; chmn. bd. govs., 1982—; mem. editorial bd.: Notre Dame Jour. of Formal Logic, 1970, Philosophy of Sci., 1975—, Studia Logica, 1976—, Philos. Research Archives, 1976—; author: computer programs Tester, 1974, Bindex, 1974. Mem. U. Ill. Found., Urbana, 1973—. Served to 1st lt. USAF, 1952-54. Sterling Jr. fellow, 1955-56; Fulbright fellow, 1957-58; Morse Research fellow, 1962-63; Guggenheim fellow, 1975-76; Ctr. for Advanced Study in Behavioral Scis. fellow, 1982-83. Mem. Am. Philos. Assn., Assn. for Symbolic Logic (exec. com. 1970-73), AAAS, Soc. for Exact Philosophy (treas. 1979-80), Mind Assn. (U.S. treas. 1974—). Office: Dept Philosophy Univ Pitts 5th Ave and Bigelow Blvd Pittsburgh PA 15260

BELOK, MICHAEL VICTOR, educator; b. Whiting, Ind., June 22, 1923; s. Michael and Helen (Dobos) B.; m. Georgina Pilkington, July 31, 1965. B.S., Ind. U., 1948; M.A., Ariz. State U., 1953; Ph.D., U. So. Calif., 1958. Lectr. edn. U. So. Calif., 1958; mem. faculty Ariz. State U., Tempe, 1959—, prof. edn., 1968—; editorial cons. Author: Psychological Foundations of Education, 1964, Approaches to Values in Education, 1967, Forming the American Minds: Early Schoolbooks and Their Compilers, 1783-1837, 1973, Explorations in the History and Sociology of Indian Education, 1973, Noah Webster Revisited, 1973, Conflict, Permanency, Change and Education, 1976; Contbg. editor: Internat. Rev. History and Polit. Sci, 1968-73; editor: Rev. Jour. of Philosophy and Social Scis, 1976; guest editor: Parsons and Sociology, 1975; adv. editor: Indian Jour. Social Research, 1965-71, others. Served with AUS, 1943-46. Fellow Nat. Philosophy of Edn. Soc.; mem. History of Edn. Soc., Delta Tau Kappa (region chancellor 1968—), Phi Delta Kappa, Kappa Delta Pi. Home: 1015 W Fairway Dr Mesa AZ 85201

BELOOF, ROBERT LAWRENCE, author, educator; b. Wichita, Kans., Dec. 30, 1923; s. P.A. and Ida (Dungan) B.; m. Ruth Madeleine LaBarre, June 14, 1946 (div. 1972); children: Marshall H., Laird D., Douglas E., Grant L. Student, Haverford Coll., 1944, Swarthmore Coll., 1945; B.A., Friends U., 1946; M.A., Northwestern U., 1948, Ph.D., 1954; M.A., Bread Loaf Sch. English, Middlebury Coll., 1948. Faculty U. Calif., 1948—, lectr., asst. prof., then assoc. prof., 1948-64, prof., 1964—, chmn. dept. speech, 1964-68; Fellow Inst. Advancement Edn., 1951-52, Inst. Creative Arts, 1963-64; Fulbright prof., Italy, 1959-60. Author: The One-Eyed Gunner, 1956, The Performing Voice in Literature, 1966, Good Poems, 1973, The Children of Venus and Mars, 1974; also poetry, articles.; Co-author: The Oral Study of Literature, 1966; Editor record performer of hist. anthology of Am. poetry, 2 vol. LP, 1965. Mem. Speech Communication Assn. Office: Dept Rhetoric U Calif Berkeley CA 94720

BELSER, JESS LAWRENCE, corporate executive; b. Bklyn., Nov. 18, 1924; s. Louis and Mina (Kahane) B.; m. Charlotte Helena Furst, June 18, 1948; children: Steven Michael, Mark David, Douglas Stewart, Ann Leslie. B.S. in Metallurgy, Mass. Inst. Tech., 1952; grad., Advanced Mgmt. Program, Harvard U., 1969. Dep. chief ops. Watertown (Mass.) Arsenal, 1958-61; with Continental Can Co., 1962-73, group v.p., 1973-75; exec. v.p. Continental Group, 1975—; pres. Continental Forest Industries, Greenwich, Conn., 1975-84; dir. Hitchiner Mfg. Co.; v.p. bd. dirs. U. Maine Pulp and Paper Found.; vice chmn. bd. trustees Inst. Paper Chemistry. Bd. dirs. U. Maine Pulp and Paper Found. Served with U.S. Army, 1943-46. Mem. Am. Soc. Metals. Clubs: Economics, Sky (N.Y.C.); Landmark (Stamford); Greenwich Country. Address: Continental Group One Harbor Plaza Stamford CT 06904

BELSHAW, CYRIL SHIRLEY, anthropologist; b. Waddington, N.Z., Dec. 3, 1921; s. Horace and Marion B.; m. Betty Joy Sweetman, Mar. 7, 1943 (dec.); children: Diana Marion, Adrian William. B.A., Auckland (N.Z.) U. Coll., 1942; M.A., U. N.Z., 1945; Ph.D., London Sch. Econs., 1949. Tutor in Western Pacific colonial studies U. London, 1948-49; research fellow Australian Nat. U., 1949-53; prof. anthropology U. B.C. (Can.), Vancouver, 1953—; mem. social sci. working party OECD, Paris, 1973—; USSR Acad. Scis. and Hungarian Acad. Scis. guest, USSR and Hungary, 1976; pres. 43d Internat. Congress of Americanists, 1979; mem. exec. com. Can. Nat. Commn. for UNESCO, 1971-72, mem.-at-large, 1973—. Author books, the most recent being: The Conditions of Social Performance: An Exploratory Theory, 1970; Towers Besieged: The Dilemma of the Creative University, 1974, The Sorcerer's Apprentice: An Anthropology of Public Policy, 1976; contbr. articles to profl. publs.; mem. editorial com.: Pacific Affairs, 1960-78; mem. internat. editorial com.: Ethnography, 1961-64, Anthropol. Lit. Index, 1978—; editor: Current Anthropology, 1974—; cons. editor for anthropology, Pergamon Pub. Co., N.Y.C., 1969-74. Bd. dirs., chmn. rehab. com. Vancouver Epilepsy Centre, 1960-61; mem. council Vancouver Inst., 1960-72, pres., 1961; vice chmn. Can. Univ. Service Overseas, 1961-62. Guggenheim fellow, 1966-66; UN Research Inst. Social Devel. fellow, 1965-66; Can. Council leave fellow, 1972-73, 78-79. Fellow Royal Anthrop. Inst. (hon. life), Royal Soc. Can.; mem. Royal Econ. Soc., Am. Anthrop. Assn. (exec. bd. 1969-70), Assn. Social Anthropologists Brit. Commonwealth, Soc. Applied Anthropology, Polynesian Soc., Can. Inst. Internat. Affairs (exec. Vancouver chpt. 1955-58, 60-62), Can. Sociology and Anthropology Assn. (exec. 1960-62), U. B.C. Faculty Assn. (pres. 1960-61), Soc. Internat. Devel., Social Sci. Research Council Can. (v.p. 1969-71), Pacific Sci. Assn. (hon. life, chmn. sci. com. for social scis. and humanities 1968-76), Internat. Union Anthrop. and Ethnol. Scis. (pres. 1978-83, v.p. 1983—, chmn. Can. del. and Nat. Com. for Permanent Council 1968—), Internat. Union Anthrop. and Ethnol Scis. (del. to Internat. Social Sci. Council 1972—), Internat. Union Anthrop. and Ethnol. Scis. (chmn. fin. com., projects com. and Commn. on Ethnocide and Genocide 1973-83), Internat. Social Sci. Council (v.p. 1976-77), Internat. Fedn. Sci. Editors Assns. (dir. 1978-83, v.p. 1983—), Internat. Assn. Anthropology Editors (organizing chmn. 1978). Office: Dept Anthropology and Sociology U BC 6303 NW Marine Dr Vancouver BC V6T 2B2 Canada

BELSHAW, GEORGE PHELPS MELLICK, bishop; b. Plainfield, N.J., July 14, 1928; s. Harold and Edith (Mellick) B.; m. Elizabeth Wheeler, June 12, 1954; children: Richard, Elizabeth, George. B.A., U. of South, 1951; S.T.B., Gen. Theol. Sem., N.Y.C., 1954, S.T.M., 1959, D.D. hon., 1975. Ordained to ministry, Episcopal Ch., consecrated bishop. Vicar St. Matthew's Ch., Hawaii, 1954-57; fellow, tutor Gen. Theol. Sem., N.Y.C., 1957-59; rector Christ Ch., Dover, Del., 1959-65, St. George's Ch., Rumson, N.J., 1965-75; suffragan bishop Diocese of N.J., Trenton, 1975-83, bishop, 1983—; vis. lectr. Gen. Theol. Sem., 1969, 70, Ctr. Continuing Edn., Princeton Theol. Sem., 1983; governing bd. Episc. Urban Caucus, 1982—; mem. Commn. Peace of Episc. Ch., 1979—. Editor: Lent with Evelyn Underhill, 1964, Lent with William Temple, 1966; contbr. articles to theol. jours. Trustee Gen. Theol. Sem., 1975—, Westminister Choir Coll., 1976-82. Mem. Am. Teilhard de Chardin Assn. (dir.). Office: Diocese of New Jersey 808 W State St Trenton NJ 08618 *

BELSKIE, ABRAM, sculptor; b. London, Mar. 24, 1907; U.S., 1929; s. Max and Sarah (Itovitch) B.; m. Helen Atkinson, Mar. 19, 1930; children: Albert, Victor. D.A., Glasgow Sch. Art, 1927. Assoc. N.Y. Acad. Medicine, N.Y.C., 1938-44; tchr. models-med. sculptor N.Y. Med. Coll., N.Y.C., 1949-56; tchr. modeling and scupture N.Y. Acad. Design, N.Y.C., 1962-65. Exhibited group shows, N.Y. Acad. Medicine, Mus. Natural History, Field Mus., Chgo.; represented permanent collections, Johnson & Johnson, New Brunswick, N.J.; sculptor Presdl. Art Medals, series of 50 medals on History of Medicine, 1968-72; works include life-size bronze The Surgeon, Ethicon Bldg, Somerville, N.J.; garden sculpture Brook Green Gardens, S.C.; sculptor portraits; Medal of Deliverance (Entebbe rescue), Judaic Heritage Soc., N.Y.C., 1976. Recipient Sculptor of Yr.-Sanford Saltus Am. Numismatic Soc.award, 1959, 74. Fellow NAD, Nat. Sculpture Soc. (Lindsay Morris prize 1956); mem. Allied Artists of Am. (Golden Anniversary medal). Democrat. Jewish. Home: 38 Brook St Closter NJ 07624 *Z Art in service of mankind. The desire to create is innate in every one of us. So it is a priviledge to be able to work with one's hands, as sculptors do. In such work lies the secret of man's strength and fortitude—the balance of a confident mind and a stout heart. To work, to dream. . .to hope, to learn. . .to live deep instead of fast. . .to take root and to have borne fruit—this is harmony. This is what a man must live for.*

BELT, EDWARD SCUDDER, sedimentologist, educator; b. N.Y.C., Aug. 4, 1933; s. Charles Banks and Emma Willard (Keyes) B; m. Emily Hillen Macsherry, Feb. 4, 1961; children: Emily H., Anne Banks, Agnes Keyes, Catherine Kilty. B.A., Williams Coll., 1955; A.M., Harvard U., 1957; Ph.D., Yale U., 1963. Asst. prof., Villanova (Pa.) U., 1962-66; asst. prof. geology Amherst (Mass.) Coll., 1966-70, asso. prof., 1970-78, prof., 1978—, chmn. dept. geology, 1971-76; hon. prof. U. St. Andrews, Fife, Scotland, 1972-73; vis. prof. Colo. State U., Ft. Collins, 1979-80; cons. in uranium exploration, 1958, cons. in surface water, 1969, cons. in coal, 1975—; geologist coal resources sect. U.S. Geol. Survey, Denver, 1980—; geologist N.D. Geol. Survey, Grand Forks, 1983, Earth Scis. and Resource Inst., Columbia, S.C., 1983. Contbr. chpts. to books, articles to profl. jours. Served with U.S. Army, 1957-62. Geol. Soc. Am. grantee, 1960-61; NSF grantee, 1961, 64-66, 66-67; Sigma Xi grantee, 1967-68; Am. Philos. Soc. grantee, 1972-73; Nat. Geog. Soc. grantee, 1972-73; Que. grantee, 1970-79. Mem. Am. Assn. Petroleum Geologists, Geol. Soc. Am., Geol. Soc. London, Geol. Assn. Can., Am. Inst. Profl. Geologists, Internat. Assn. Sedimentologists, Soc. Econ. Paleontologists and Mineralogists, Nat. Assn. Geology Tchrs. Republican. Roman Catholic. Home: 116 Alpine Dr Amherst MA 01002 Office: 123 Pratt Museum Amherst Coll Amherst MA 01002

BELT, LARRY REYNOLDS, finance corporation executive; b. Kansas City, Mo., Oct. 1, 1931; s. Raymond Robert and Ruth Elizabeth (Reynolds) B.; m. Sandra Kader, Aug. 1, 1979; children: Larry Reynolds, Judith Lynne. B.S., Mo. U., 1953. Field rep. Redisco Inc. (fin. div. Am. Motors Corp.), Kansas City, 1954-56; pres. indsl. group Borg Warner Acceptance Corp., Chgo., 1956—; pres. Borg Warner Internat. P.R., San Juan, 1982—. Missouri Valley Tennis champion, 1973, 77; Kansas City Open Tennis champion, 1964, 67, 69, 73, 77. Mem. Farm and Indsl. Equipment Inst., Assn. Equipment Lessors. Republican. Club: Leawood Country (Kans.). Home: 4903 W 88th St Prairie Village KS 66207 Office: Borg Warner Acceptance Corp(NL)Suite 370 9300 W 110th St Overland Park KS 66210

BELTAIRE, MARK ANTHONY, III, journalist; b. Detroit, Apr. 9, 1914; s. Mark Anthony and Marion (Waters) B.; m. Beverly Anne Strauss, Nov. 7, 1947; children: Mark Anthony IV, Jeffrey Allan, Barbara Marion, Suzanne Michele. A.B., Princeton U., 1937. Sports writer Detroit News, 1937-42; comml. slide film writer Jam Handy Orgn., Detroit, 1942-44; daily columnist Detroit Free Press, 1945-79; tchr. creative writing U. Detroit, 1946-47. Commentator on, Detroit radio stas. WJR, WXYZ, WKMH, at various times. Bd. dirs. Boys Clubs Met. Detroit, Southeastern Mich. chpt. ARC., Children's Aid Soc. Mem. Detroit Press Club, Players, Box 12, Sigma Delta Chi. Presbyterian. Club: Acanthus. Home: 1227 Yorkshire Rd Grosse Pointe MI 48230

BELTH, JOSEPH MORTON, educator, researcher; b. Syracuse, N.Y., Oct. 22, 1929; s. Irving and Helen Rose (Bright) B.; m. Marjorie Helen Lavine, June 12, 1955; children: Ann Irene, Michael Irving, Jeffrey Edward. A.A.S., Cayuga County Community Coll., 1958; B.S. summa cum laude, Syracuse U., 1958; Ph.D., U. Pa., 1961. C.L.U., C.P.C.U. Asst. purchasing agt. Onondaga Supply Co., Syracuse, N.Y., 1947-53; agt. Continental Am. Life Ins. Co., Syracuse, 1953-58; asst. dir. continuing edn. Am. Soc. Chartered Life Underwriters, Bryn Mawr, Pa., 1961-62; asst. prof. Ind. U., Bloomington, 1962-65, assoc. prof., 1965-68, prof., 1968—. Author: Participating Life Insurance Sold by Stock Companies, 1965, The Retail Price Structure in American Life Insurance, 1966; authur: Life Insurance: a Consumer's Handbook, 1973; editor: newsletter The Ins. Forum, 1974—. Mem. Am. Risk and Ins. Assn. (pres. 1973-74, Elizur Wright award 1966, Jour. Risk and Ins. awards 1962,64,65,67,71,79), AAUP, Beta Gamma Sigma, Phi Kappa Phi. Democrat. Jewish. Home: 5125 N Starnes Rd Bloomington IN 47401 Office: Ind U Bloomington In 47405

BELTRAN, EUSEBIUS JOSEPH, bishop; b. Ashley, Pa., Aug. 31, 1934; s. Joseph C. and Helen Rita (Kozlowski) B. Ed., St. Charles Sem., Overbrook, Pa. Ordained priest Roman Cath. Ch., 1960; consecrated bishop, 1978, pastor chs. in, Atlanta and Decatur, Ga., 1960; notary, then vice officialis Atlanta Diocesan Tribunal, 1960-62; vice chancellor Archdiocese Atlanta, 1962; officialis Archdiocesan Tribunal, 1963-74; pastor chs. in, Atlanta and Rome, Ga., 1963-66; vicar gen. Archdiocese of Atlanta, 1971-78; pastor St. Anthony's Ch., Atlanta, 1972-78; bishop of, Tulsa, 1978—; mem. com. liturgy Nat. Conf. Cath. Bishops; also com. for Am. Coll., Louvain, Belgium; bd. regents Conception Sem.; bd. dirs. St. Gregory's Coll., Shawnee, Okla. Mem. Equestrian Order Holy Sepulchre, NCCJ. Club: K.C. Home: 2151 N Vancouver St Tulsa OK 74127 Office: 820 S Boulder St PO Box 2009 Tulsa OK 74101 *

BELTZ, HERBERT ALLISON, construction executive; b. Grand Forks, N.D., July 1, 1926; s. Eugene Maurice and Helen (Aune) B.; m. Opal D. Thomas, Mar. 6, 1948; children: Michael, Mark. Grad., Minn. Sch. Bus., 1949. C.P.A., Minn. Staff acct. Boulay, Anderson, Waldo & Co., Mpls., 1950-58, partner, 1958-65; sec., controller S.J. Groves & Sons Co., Mpls., 1965-73, v.p., sec., 1973-80, exec. v.p. and sec., 1980—, also dir. Served with U.S. Mcht. Marine, 1945-47. Mem. Am. Inst. C.P.A.s, Minn. Soc. C.P.A.s, Fin. Execs. Inst. Clubs: Moles, Beavers. Office: PO Box 1267 10000 Hwy 55 W Minneapolis MN 55440

BELTZ, LEROY DUANE, univ. dean; b. Pierce, Nebr., Apr. 25, 1924; s. Adolph and Caroline (Rohde) B.; m. Glenda Marie Reese, Jan. 21, 1944; children—Judith Ann, Glen Duane, David Scott, Keith Stuart. B.Sc. in Pharmacy with distinction, U. Nebr., 1951; Ph.D. in Pharm. Chemistry, U. Conn., 1956. Instr. pharmacy U. Conn., 1952-56; asst. prof. pharmacy U. Fla., 1956-58; asso. prof., then prof. Ferris State Coll., 1958-66; prof. pharmacy, dean Coll. Pharmacy, Ohio No. U., Ada, 1966—. Served with USN, 1941-47. Mem. Am., Ohio pharm. assns., Am. Inst. History of Pharmacy, Sigma Xi, Rho Chi, Phi Lambda Upsilon, Beta Beta Beta, Phi Eta Sigma, Phi Kappa Phi, Kappa Psi, Omicron Delta Kappa, Alpha Zeta Omega, Gamma Sigma Epsilon, Phi Delta Chi, Kappa Epsilon. Republican. Mem. Christian Ch. Home: 501 W North St Ada OH 45810

BELTZ, WILLIAM ALBERT, publisher; b. Meriden, Conn., Aug. 24, 1929; s. Albert Henry and Marie Adelade (Heusel) B.; m. Beverly Sawyer, May 31, 1958; children—John, Jane, Kurt, Adam. A.B., Tufts U., 1951. With Bur. Nat. Affairs, Inc., Washington, 1956—, asso. editor, then exec. editor, 1965-80, pres., chief exec. officer, 1980—; dir. Fisher-Stevens, Inc., Totowa, N.J., 1978—. Mem. White House Corrs. Assn., Info. Industry Assn. (dir.). Democrat. Episcopalian. Club: Nat. Press (Washington). Home: 1001 Herbert Springs Rd Alexandria VA 22308 Office: 1231 25th St NW Washington DC 20037

BELYTSCHKO, TED BOHDAN, educator; b. Proskurov, Ukraine, Jan. 13, 1943; came to U.S., 1950; s. Stephan and Maria (Harpinak) B.; m. Gail Eisenhart, Aug. 1967; children: Peter, Nicole, Justine. B.S. in Engring. Sci., Ill. Inst. Tech., 1965, Ph.D. in Mechanics, 1968. Asst. prof. structural mechanics U. Ill., Chgo., 1968-73, assoc. prof., 1973-76, prof., 1976-77; prof. civil and nuclear engring. Northwestern U., Evanston, Ill., 1977—; cons. Argonne Nat. Lab., 1971-83. Editor: Computational Methods for Transient Analysis, 1983; asst. editor: Computer Mehtods in Applications Mech. and Engring., 1979—, Jour. Applied Mechanics, 1979—; editor: Nuclear Engring. and Design, 1980—. NDEA fellow, 1965-68; recipient Thomas Jaeger prize Internat. Assn. Structural Mechanics in Reactor Tech., 1983. Fellow ASME (Pi Tau Sigma Gold medal 1975); mem. ASCE (Walter Huber research prize 1977), Acad. Mechanics. Office: Northwestern Univ 2145 Sheridan Rd Evanston IL 60201

BELZBERG, SAMUEL, banker; b. Calgary, Alta., Can., June 26, 1928; s. Abraham and Hilda (Fishman) B.; m. Frances Cooper; children—Cheryl Rae, Marc David, Wendy Jay, Lisa. B.Comm., U. Alta., Edmonton, 1948. Chmn., chief exec. officer First City Trust Co., Edmonton, 1962—; pres. First City Financial Corp. Ltd., First City Devel. Ltd. Liberal. Jewish. Clubs: Edmonton, Mayfair Golf and Country (Edmonton); Richmond Golf and Country, Vancouver Tennis (Vancouver). Home: 3489 Osler St Vancouver BC V6H 2W4 Canada Office: PO Box 11151 Royal Centre 1055 W Georgia St Vancouver BC Canada

BELZBERG, WILLIAM, financial company executive; b. 1932; married. Vice pres., dir. First City Fin. Corp. Ltd. Can.; pres., chief exec. officer Far West Fin. Corp., Newport Beach, Calif., 1976-80, chmn. bd., 1978—, dir.; chmn. bd., pres., chief exec. officer Far West Sav. and Loan Assn., Newport Beach. Office: Far West Fin Corp 4001 MacArthur Blvd Newport Beach CA 92660 *

BELZER, ALAN, chemical fibers and plastics company executive; b. Bklyn., Nov. 27, 1932; s. Morris and Vera B.; children: Debra, Frances. B.S., N.Y. U., 1953. With Allied Corp., N.Y.C., 1955—, gen. mgr. plastic film bus., 1970-71, pres., 1971-72, v.p. ops., 1972-73, exec. v.p., pres., 1973-75; group v.p. Corp. Office, 1975-79; group v.p., pres. Fibers and Plastics Co., 1979-83, corp. exec. v.p., pres. chem. sector, 1983—. Served with USCGR, 1953-55. Mem. N.Am. Soc. for Corp. Planning (dir. 1968), Opportunity Resources for the Arts (dir. 1981). Home: 50 E 10th St New York NY 10003 Office: 1411 Broadway New York NY 10018

BELZER, FOLKERT OENE, surgeon; b. Soerabaja, Indonesia, Oct. 5, 1930; came to U.S., 1951, naturalized, 1956; s. Peter and Jacoba H. (Gorter) B.;, Aug. 4, 1956; children—Ingrid J., John B., G. Eric, Paul O. A.B., Colby Coll., Waterville, Maine, 1953; M.A., Boston U., 1954, M.D., 1958. Diplomate: Am. Bd. Surgery. Intern Grace-New Haven Hosp., 1958-59; asst. resident 1960-62; chief resident U. Oreg. Med. Sch., 1962-63, instr. surgery, 1963-64; asst. research surgeon U. Calif. Med. Center, San Francisco, 1964, asst. prof. surgery, 1966-69, asst. prof. ambulatory and community medicine, 1966-69; asst. chief Transplant Service, 1967-69, co-chief, 1969-72, chief, 1972-74, asso. prof. surgery, 1969-72, asso. prof. ambulatory and community medicine, 1969-72, prof. surgery, 1972-74; dir. Exptl. Surgery Labs., 1973-74; sr. lectr. Guys Hosp., London, Eng., 1964-66; prof., chmn. dept. surgery U. Wis., Madison, 1974—. Contbr. articles to med. jours. Recipient Samuel Harvey award as outstanding resident, 1960. Mem. A.C.S., Am., Calif. med. assns., Am. Soc. Transplant Surgeons (pres. 1975), Calif. Soc. Transplant Surgeons (pres. 1970-72), Am., Central surg. assns., Calif. Acad. Medicine, Halsted Soc., Howard Surg. Soc., C. Naffziger Surg. Soc., Madison Surg. Soc., Pacific Coast Surg. Soc., San Francisco Surg. Soc. (chmn. program com. 1973-74), Wis. surg. socs), Nat. Kidney Found. (vice chmn. com. on dialysis and transplantation 1974-76), Société Internationale de Chirurgie, Soc. Vascular Surgery, Soc. Surg. Chairmen, Soc. U. Surgeons, Surg. Biology Club III, Transplantation Soc., Whipple Soc. Republican. Developed method and machine for human kidney preservation. Home: 6105 S Highlands Dr Madison WI 53705 Office: U Wis Center for Health Scis 600 N Highland Ave Madison WI 53792

BELZILE, CHARLES HENRI, Canadian armed forces officer; b. Trois Pistoles, Que., Can., Mar. 12, 1933; s. Charles Eugene and Alice (Dionne) B.; m. Janet E. Scott, Aug. 1, 1970; children—Denise, Suzanne. B.A. in Politics, Coll. Ste. Marie, U. Montreal, Que., 1953. Commd. officer Canadian Forces, 1952, advanced through grades to lt. gen.; platoon comdr., Korea, Can., Germany, 1953-59; staff officer, Montreal, 1960-63, comdr. co., Victoria, B.C., Can., 1963-64, Cyprus, 1964-65, staff officer, Germany, 1966-68, comdr. Bn., Quebec, Que., 1968-69, Cyprus, 1969-70, with, Gagetown, N.B., Can., 1972-74, brigade comdr., staff officer, Lahr and Heidelberg, Germany, 1974-77; comdr. Can. Forces Europe, Lahr, 1977-81, (Force Mobile Command), 1981—. Decorated Can. Forces Decoration, comdr. Order Mil. Merit, officer Order St. John of Jerusalem. Mem. Queen's Own Rifles Assn. Roman Catholic. Clubs: Les Chevaliers de Tastevin (Bourgogne, France) (grand officer); Confrerie St. Etienne (Alsace, France) (officer). Address: R-100 Drive St-Hubert PQ J3Y 5T5 Canada

BEMAN, DEANE RANDOLPH, assn. exec.; b. Washington, Apr. 22, 1938; s. Delmar W. and Bertha (Foster) B.; m. Miriam Nancy Orndorff, Nov. 23, 1957; children—Amy, Priscilla, Tracy, Deane Randolph, Valerie; m. Judith N. Dixon, Oct. 17, 1978. Student, U. Md., 1957-60. Amateur golfer, 1960-67; mem. Americas Cup Team, 1960, 62, 64, Walker Cup Team, 1959, 61, 63, 65, World Cup Team, 1960, 62, 64, 66; profl. golfer, 1967—; commr. TPA tour, 1974—; also mem. Hall of Fame selection com.; Dir. World Golf Hall of Fame. Brit. amateur champion. 1959, U.S. amateur champion, 1960, 63, winner Tex. Open, 1969, 2d pl. U.S. Open, 1969, winner Milw. Open, 1970, Quad-Cities Open, 1971, 72, Robinson Open, 1973. Office: TPA Tour Ponte Vedra Beach FL 32082

BEMENT, ARDEN LEE, JR., corporate executive; b. Pitts., May 22, 1932; s. Arden Lee and Edith Ardella (Bigelow) B.; m. Mary Ann Baroch, Aug. 24, 1952; children: Kristine, Kenneth, Vincent, Cynthia, Mark, David, Paul, Mary. E.Met., Colo. Sch. Mines, 1954; M.S. in Metall. Engring., U. Idaho, 1959; Ph.D., U. Mich., 1963. Research metallurgist Hanford Labs., Gen. Electric Co., Richland, Wash., 1954-65; sr. research mgr. Pacific N.W. Lab., Battelle Meml. Inst., Richland, 1965-70; prof. nuclear materials MIT, 1970-76; dir. Office Materials Scis., Def. Advanced Research Projects Agy., Dept. Def., Washington, 1976-79, dep. undersec. for research and advanced tech., 1979-80; v.p. tech. resources TRW, Euclid, Ohio, 1980—; tech. assistance expert to Mexico UNIAEA, 1974-76; cons. NRC, Taiwan, 1975. Author publs. in field; editor: Biomaterials: Structural and Biomedical Bases for Hard Tissue and Soft Tissue Substitues, 1971; co-editor: Dislocation Dynamics, 1968; editorial bd.: Jour. Nuclear Materials, 1970—; contbr. articles to profl. jours. Chmn. bd. Health, Mental Health, Mental Retardation, Benton-Franklin Counties, Wash., 1968-70; pres. Arts Council, Richland, Pasco and Kennewick, Wash., 1968-70; councilman City of Richland, 1968-70; treas. Cleve. Opera Bd., 1982—. Served to lt. col. U.S. Army Res., 1954—. Ford Found. fellow, 1959-60. Fellow Am. Nuclear Soc., Am. Soc. Metals, Am. Inst. Chemists; mem. AIME, Nat. Acad. Engrs., ASTM, Sigma Xi, Tau Beta Pi, Sigma Gamma Epsilon. Republican. Roman Catholic. Home: 509 Zorn Ln Mayfield Village OH 44143 Office: TRW 23555 Euclid Ave Euclid OH 44117

BEMILLER, JAMES NOBLE, biochemist, educator; b. Evansville, Ind., Apr. 7, 1933; s. LaMar N. and Mabel (Gruber) BeM.; m. Paraskevi Mavridis, Aug. 6, 1960; children: Byron N., Philip J. B.S., Purdue U., 1954, M.S., 1956, Ph.D., 1959. Asst. prof. biochemistry Purdue U., 1959-61; asst. prof. biochemistry dept. chemistry and biochemistry So. Ill. U., Carbondale, 1961-65, assoc. prof., 1965-68, prof., 1968—, acting chmn. dept. chemistry and biochemistry, 1966-67, prof. biochemistry, 1971—, asst. dean curriculum Sch. Medicine, 1977-79, acting dean Coll. Sci., 1976-77, chmn. dept. med. biochemistry, 1980—; Cons. A.E. Staley Mfg. Co., Decatur, Ill., 1962-70; pres. U.S. adv. com. Internat. Carbohydrate Symposia, 1982—. Editor: Industrial Gums, 1959, 73, Methods in Carbohydrate Chemistry, 1-8, 1962—, Starch: Chemistry and Technology, Vols. 1 and 2, 1965, 67; Mem. adv. bd.: Carbohydrate Research, 1971—; assoc. editor: Cereal Chemistry, 1975-78. Chmn. Western dist. Egyptian council Boy Scouts Am., 1977-81, exec. bd., 1982—; bd. dirs. Luth. Sch. Theology, Chgo., 1967-73, sec., 1971-73; bd. dirs. ACS group ins. trust, 1974-76, Christ Sem., 1976-79; mem. devel. com. Christ Sem., 1979—; exec. bd. Ill. Synod Luth. Ch. Am., 1978—. Mem. Am. Chem. Soc. (councilor 1967—), Am. Soc. Biol. Chemists, Am. Assn. Cereal Chemists, AAAS, Soc. for Complex Carbohydrates, Internat. Carbohydrate Orgn. (U.S. rep. 1978—), Am. Inst. Chemists (dir. 1982—), AAUP, Ill., N.Y. acads sci., Sigma Xi, Alpha Chi Sigma, Alpha Tau Omega. Home: Route 1 Box 206 Murphysboro IL 62966 Office: Dept Chemistry and Biochemistry So Ill U Carbondale IL 62901

BENACERRAF, BARUJ, physician, educator; b. Caracas, Venezuela, Oct. 29, 1920; came to U.S., 1939, naturalized, 1943; s. Abraham and Henriette (Lasry) B.; m. Annette Dreyfus, Mar. 24, 1943; 1 dau., Beryl. B. es L., Lycee Janson, 1940; B.S., Columbia U., 1942; M.D., Med. Sch. Va., 1945; M.A., Harvard U., 1970; M.D. (hon.), U. Geneva, 1980; D.Sc., NYU, 1981, Va. Commonwealth U., 1981, Yeshiva U., 1982, U. Aix-Marseille, 1982. Intern Queens Gen. Hosp., N.Y.C., 1945-46; research fellow dept. microbiology Columbia U. Med. Sch., 1948-50; charge de recherches Centre National de Recherche Scientique Hospital Broussais, Paris, 1950-56; asst. prof. pathology NYU Sch. Medicine, 1956-58, asso. prof., 1958-60, prof., 1960-68; chief immunology Nat. Inst. Allergy and Infectious Diseases, NIH, Bethesda, Md., 1968-70; Fabyan prof. comparative pathology, chmn. dept. Harvard Med. Sch., 1970—; pres., chief exec. officer Dana-Farber Cancer Inst., 1980; J.S. Blumenthal lectr. in allergy and immunology, 1980; Sci. adviser immunology WHO; mem. immunology study sect. NIH; mem. Am. med. adv. bd. Am. Hosp., Paris; pres. Fedn. Am. Socs. Exptl. Biology, 1974-75; chmn. sci. adv. com. Centre d'Immunologie de Marseille. Editorial bd.: Jour. Immunology. Trustee, mem. sci. adv. bd. Trudeau Found.; mem. sci. adv. com. Children's Hosp. Boston; bd. govs. Weizmann Inst. Medicine; mem. award com. Gen. Motors Cancer Research Found., also chmn. selection com. Sloan prize, 1980. Served to capt. M.C. AUS, 1946-48. Recipient T. Duckett Jones Meml. award Helen Hay Whitney Found., 1976; Rabbi Shai Shacknai lectr. and prize Hebrew U. Jerusalem, 1974; Waterford award for biomed. scis., 1980; Nobel prize for medicine or physiology, 1980. Fellow Am. Acad. Arts and Scis.; mem. Nat. Acad. Scis., Nat. Inst. Medicine, Am. Assn. Immunologists (pres. 1973-74), Am. Assn. Pathologists and Bacteriologists, Am. Soc. Exptl. Pathology, Soc. Exptl. Biology and Medicine, Brit. Assn. Immunology, French Soc. Biol. Chemistry, Harvey Soc., N.Y. Acad. Scis., Scandinavian Immunol. Soc., Internat. Union Immunology Socs. (pres. 1980—), Alpha Omega Alpha. Home: 111 Perkins St Boston MA 02130

BENADE, ARTHUR HENRY, physicist, educator; b. Chgo., Jan. 2, 1925; s. James Martin and Miriam (McGaw) B.; m. Virginia Lee Wassall, June 9, 1948; children: Judith Anne, Martin Daniel. A.B., Washington U., 1948, Ph.D., 1952. Design engr. McDonnell Aircraft, St. Louis, 1952; instr. physics Case Western Res. U., Cleve., 1952-54, asst. prof., 1954-60, asso. prof., 1960-69, prof. physics, 1969—; vis. prof. Indian Inst. Tech., Kanpur, India, 1964-65, U. Mich., 1974; cons. instrumentation, musical and archtl. acoustics. Author: Horns, Strings and Harmony, 1960, Fundamentals of Musical Acoustics, 1976. Pres. Cleve. Chamber Music Soc., 1980-81. Served with USAAF, 1943-46. Fellow Acoustical Soc. Am. (v.p. 1974-75), AAAS; mem. Am. Phys. Soc., Galpin Soc., Catgut Acoustical Soc. (pres. 1969-72), Am. Assn. Physics Tchrs. Home: 3126 Woodbury Rd Shaker Heights OH 44120 Office: Physics Dept Case Western Res U Cleveland OH 44106

BENADE, LEO EDWARD, lawyer, ret. army officer; b. Dubuque, Iowa, July 29, 1916; s. Nicholas A. and Jennie (Bruno) B.; m. Marietta Taylor, Mar. 20, 1943; children—Leonard E., Lawrence M. Student, U. Mich. Sch. Law, 1946; J.D., Am. U., 1952. Bar: Va. bar 1951. Enlisted as pvt. U.S. Army, 1941, advanced through grades to lt. gen., 1972; adj. gen. U.S. Army Europe, 1966-67; dep. asst. sec. def. for personnel policy, Washington, 1968-74; Sr. v.p., gen. counsel United Way Am., Alexandria, Va., 1975—. Decorated D.D.S.M., D.S.M. with 2 oak leaf clusters, Legion of Merit with 2 oak leaf clusters, Commendation medal with 2 oak leaf clusters. Mem. Va. State Bar, Am. Judicature Soc., Va. Trial Lawyers Assn., Am. Bar Assn., Sigma Nu Phi. Club: Army-Navy Country (Arlington, Va.) (chmn. bd. govs. 1970-73, 76). Home: 4031 Justine Dr Annandale VA 22003 Office: United Way of Am 701 N Fairfax St Alexandria VA 22314

BENARDE, MELVIN ALBERT, environmental health specialist, educator; b. Bklyn., June 15, 1924; s. Isidor and Belle (Metz) Bernadsky; m. Anita Elfenbein, Sept. 8, 1951; children: Scott, Andrea, Dana. B.Sc., St. John's U., 1948; M.Sc., U. Mo., 1950; Ph.D., Mich. State U., 1954. Mem. staff U.S. Naval Research and Devel. Facility, Bayonne, N.J., 1954-55, Seafood Processing Lab., U. Md., 1955-60; exec. asst. to v.p. Vita Food Products, Chestertown, Md., 1960-61; with environ. engring. lab. Coll. Engring., Rutgers U., New Brunswick, N.J., 1961-67; prof. epidemiology and community medicine Hahnemann Med. Coll. and Hosp., Phila., 1967—, chmn. dept. community medicine and environ. health, 1981—; mem. hazardous materials adv. com. EPA, Washington, 1971-72; bd. dirs. Am. Council on Sci. and Health, N.Y.C., 1978—; chmn. com. public health significance of water pollution NSF, 1977-79. Author: Race Against Famine, 1968, Disinfection, 1969, Our Precarious Habitat, 1970, The Chemicals We Eat, 1971, The Dictionary of Food Additives, 1981; Host: weekly TV show Environment and Health, ABC-TV, 1966-68. Served with USAAF, 1943-46; Served to lt. comdr. USPHSR. WHO fellow U. London Sch. Hygiene, 1963-64. Fellow Am. Public Health Assn., Royal Soc. Health; mem. Assn. Tchrs. Preventive Medicine, Authors Guild, Assn. Mil. Surgeons U.S., Chemists Club N.Y. Club: Men's Jewish Center (Princeton, N.J.). Office: 235 N 15th St Philadelphia PA 19102

BENARIO, HERBERT WILLIAM, classics educator; b. N.Y.C., July 21, 1929; s. Frederick and Ilse (Kessler) B.; m. Janice M. Martin, Dec. 23, 1957; children: Frederick M., John H. B.A., Coll. City N.Y., 1948; M.A., Columbia U., 1949; Ph.D., Johns Hopkins U., 1951. Instr. Greek and Latin Columbia U., 1953-58; asst. prof. Greek and Latin Sweet Briar Coll., 1958-60; mem. faculty Emory U., 1960—; prof. classics, 1967—, chmn. dept., 1968-73, 76-78; dir. Vergilian Soc. Summer Sch. in, Italy, 1963, 67, 73, 81, asst. dir., 1957, 59; dir. Roman Britain tour, 1977, Roman Germany tour, 1981, Rome and North Italy, 1982; vis. prof. Intercollegiate Center Classical Studies, Rome, spring 1967, U. Colo., summer 1969; mem. Latin achievement test com. Coll. Entrance Exam. Bd., 1963-66; co-prof. in charge Intercollegiate Center Classical Studies, Rome, 1984-85. Author: Tacitus, Agricola, Germany, Dialogue on Orators, 1967, An Introduction to Tacitus, 1975, A Commentary on the Vita Hadriani in the Historia Augusta, 1980, Tacitus Annals 11 and 12, 1983. Served with AUS, 1951-53. Fulbright grantee, 1956; research grantee Am. Philos Soc.; Am. Council Learned Socs. fellow, 1978. Mem. Am. Philol. Assn., Archaeol. Inst. Am. (pres. Atlanta Soc. 1965-66, 67-68), Classical Assn. Middle West and South (pres. 1971-72, pres. So. sect. 1968-70), Classical Soc. of Am. Acad. in Rome (pres. 1965), Vergilian Soc. Am. (trustee 1960-65, 69-73, pres. 1980-82), Soc. Promotion Roman Studies, Am. Classical League, Phi Beta Kappa (pres. Emory U. chpt. 1968- 69). Home: 430 Chelsea Circle NE Atlanta GA 30307 Office: Emory U Atlanta GA 30322

BENATAR, LEO, packaging company executive; b. Atlanta, Feb. 21, 1930; s. Morris H. and Mary (Levy) B.; m. Louise Cure, Sept. 2, 1956; children: Morris L., Ann Marie, Ruth Eileen. B. Indsl. Engring., Ga. Inst. Tech., 1951; postgrad., Rochester Inst. Tech., 1956, Harvard Bus. Sch., 1970. Formerly pres. Mead Packaging Co., Atlanta; now pres., chief exec. officer Engraph, Inc., Atlanta; mem. internat. adv. council Trust Co. Ga., Trust Co. Bank; mem. adv. bd. Arkwright-Boston Ins. Past bd. dirs. Research Atlanta, Jr. Achievement; past mem. bd. visitors Emory U.; past bd. dirs. Nat. Minority Purchasing Council, Keep Am. Beautiful; bd. dirs. ARC; steering com. Nat. Found. Ileitis and Colitis; mem. indsl. mgmt. adv. council, nat. adv. bd. Ga. Inst. Tech.; adv. council Coll. Bus. Adminstrn., Ga. State U.; past chmn. Pvt. Industry Council; past mem. DeKalb Reorgn. Com., Ga. Bd. Industry and Trade. Served with USN, 1951-53. Recipient Archdiocesan medal of St. Paul Greek Orthodox Archdiocese of North and South Am. Mem. Ga. Bus. and Industry Assn. (bd. govs.), Nat. Alliance Bus. (past chmn. Metro Atlanta), Japan-Am. Soc. Ga. (past dir.). Clubs: Atlanta City (dir.), Commerce). Home: 2279 Chrysler Terr NE Atlanta GA 30345 Office: PO Box 32816 Charlotte NC 28232

BENATAR, PAT (PAT ANDREJEWSKI), rock singer; b. Bklyn., 1953; m. Neil Geraldo. Albums include In the Heat of the Night, 1979, Crimes of Passion, 1980, Get Nervous, 1982, Live From Earth, 1983. Recipient Grammy award for best female rock vocal performance, 1981, 82, 83, 84. Office: care Premier Talent Agy 3 E 54th St New York NY *

BENBOW, CHARLES CLARENCE, writer-critic; b. Moore Haven, Fla., Feb. 23, 1929; s. Clarence Oliver and Rosalie Florence (King) B.; m. Lois Chandler, Oct. 10, 1954; children—Margot Britton, Claudia King. B.Applied Arts, U. Fla., 1951; M.S. in Art Edn, Fla. State U., 1961, postgrad., 1965-66. Art dir. sta. WJXT-TV, Jacksonville, Fla., 1955-58; tchr. art Duval County (Fla.) Pub. Schs., 1958-62; instr. humanities U. Fla., 1962-65; writer-critic St. Petersburg (Fla.) Times, 1966—. Co-author Fla. state guide for art in secondary schs.; Contbr. articles to profl. jours. Served with USN, 1951-55. Named Best Architecture Critic in Fla. Fla. Assn. Am. Inst. Architects, 1978, 80. Mem. Fla. Art Edn. Assn. (v.p., treas. 1958-63). Democrat. Presbyn. Home: 205 19th Ave SE Saint Petersburg FL 33705 Office: 490 1st Ave S Saint Petersburg FL 33701

BENBOW, JOHN ROBERT, banker; b. Muncie, Ind., June 1, 1931; s. Robert and Thelma (Parr) B.; m. Marilyn Ann Alhand, Dec. 27, 1958; children: Karen, Susan, Julia. B.S., Ind. U., 1954; LL.D. (hon.), Butler U., 1973. Mgmt. trainee Ind. Nat. Bank, Indpls., 1954-59, exec. v.p., 1963-68, pres., 1971-76, dir., 1971-76; chmn., chief exec. officer Barnett Bank of Miami NA, 1977-80; exec. v.p. Barnett Banks of Fla., Inc., Miami, 1980-83; pres. Fla. Nat. Bank, Miami, 1983—; dir. Overmyer Corp., Muncie, Ind. Trustee United Student Aid Funds, Inc., N.Y.C., 1975—; chmn. Players State Theatre, Coconut Grove, Fla., 1979. Served to 1st lt. USAF, 1954-56. Ind. U. fellow, 1975. Mem. Beta Gamma Sigma. Clubs: Miami Country; Riviera Country (Miami). Home: 7105 SW 115th Terr Miami FL 33156 Office: Florida National Bank 169 Flagler St Miami FL 33131

BENBOW, R. MARK, educator; b. Sioux City, Iowa, May 25, 1925; married; 4 children. B.A., U. Wash., 1947; M.A., Yale U., 1949, Ph.D., 1950. From instr. to prof. English Colby Coll., Waterville, Maine, 1950-71, chmn. dept. English, 1966-73, Roberts prof. English lit., 1971—. Author: Providential Theory of Historical Causation in Holinshed's Chronicles, 1959, Thomas Dekker and Some Cures for the City Gout, 1975, The Merchant Antonio, Elizabethan Hero, 1976; contbr. articles to profl. jours. Mem. MLA. Office: Dept English Colby Coll Waterville ME 04901 *

BENCH, JOHNNY LEE, professional baseball player; b. Oklahoma City, Dec. 7, 1947; s. Ted Bench. Grad. high sch. Catcher, Cin. Reds, Nat. League, 1967-83; propr. bowling alley, Cin. Profl. nightclub singer, from 1970; host: TV interview show MVP-Johnny Bench, until 1976; baseball instructional show The Baseball Bunch, 1981, 82, 83; toured Vietnam with: Bob Hope Christmas Show, 1970, 71; Author: Catch You Later. Named Minor League Player of Year, Sporting News, 1967, Nat. League Rookie of Year, Sporting News, 1968, Baseball Writers Assn. Am., 1968, catcher Nat. League All-Star Fielding Team, 1968, 69, 70, 71, 72, 73, 74, 75, 76, 77, 79, 80, Nat. League All-Star Team, Sporting News, 1968, 69, 70, 72, 73, 74, 75, 76, 77, Most Valuable Player in Nat. League, 1970, 72, Major League Player of Year, Sporting News, 1970, Nat. League Player of Year,, 1970, Most Valuable Player, 1976 World Series; Catcher, All-Star Team, 1976. Ten-time winner Golden Glove award; catcher over 100 games a yr. for 13 consecutive seasons; 21st pl. all-time home run list (389). Address: 800 First Nat Bank Bldg Cincinnati OH 45202

BENCHLEY, PETER BRADFORD, author; b. N.Y.C., May 8, 1940; s. Nathaniel Goddard and Marjorie Louise (Bradford) B.; m. Winifred B. Wesson, Sept. 19, 1964; children—Tracy, Clayton. B.A. cum laude, Harvard U., 1961. Gen. assignment reporter Washington Post, 1963; asso. editor Newsweek mag., 1964-67; staff asst. to Pres. White House, Washington, 1967-69. Free lance writer, 1969—; author: Time and a Ticket, 1964, Jonathan Visits the White House, 1964, Jaws, 1974, The Deep, 1976, The Island, 1979; screenplay Jaws (Ann. award nomination Writers Guild Am., Golden Globe award nomination, Fantasy Film Fans Internat. award 1975); co-author: The Deep, 1976; writer narrator: shows Am. Sportsman, ABC-TV (Golden Eagle award Shark episode 1975); contbr. articles to nat. mags. Served with USMCR, 1962-63. Club: Coffee House (N.Y.C.). Address: care Ashley Famous Agency Inc 1301 Ave of Americas New York NY 10019 *

BENCHOFF, JAMES MARTIN, mfg. co. exec.; b. Hagerstown, Md., May 18, 1927; s. J. Thompson and Marie (Hickey) B.; m. Brigitte R. Puhringer, July 1, 1978; children by previous marriage—Helen Marie, James Martin II. Student, U. Pa., 1944-45. With Grove Mfg. Co. div. Kidde, Inc., Shady Grove, Pa., 1954—, v.p., 1962-66, 1st v.p., 1966, 1st v.p., asst. gen. mgr., 1966-68, exec. v.p., gen. mgr., 1968-69, pres., chief exec. officer, 1969-80, chmn., chief exec. officer, 1980—; pres. Monta Vista, Inc., Waynesboro, Pa., 1959—; dir. 1st Nat. Bank & Trust Co., Waynesboro. Bd. dirs. Waynesboro Hosp. Clubs: Waynesboro Country; Fountain Head Country (Hagerstown, Md); Met. (N.Y.C.). Home: Long Meadow Acres 12514 Old Route 16 Waynesboro PA 17268 Office: P O Box 21 Shady Grove PA 17256

BENDELIUS, ARTHUR GEORGE, engineering firm executive; b. Passaic, N.J., May 21, 1936; s. Arthur Leopold and Lydia Ella (Flach) B.; m. Virginia Brown, June 21, 1958; children: Linda Ellen, Bonnie Sue, Heidi Ann. B.E., Stevens Inst. Tech., 1958, M.M.S., 1966. Registered profl. engr., N.Y., N.J., Minn., Ga., Fla., Tex., Ala., Ky., N.C., S.C., Miss., Tenn., La., Ark., Okla., Md., Utah; lic. pilot. Engr. Syska & Hennessey, N.Y.C., 1958-60, Parson Brinckerhoff Quade & Douglas, Inc., 1960-62; asst. dept. head Parsons Brinckerhoff Quade & Douglas, Inc., N.Y.C., 1963-68, dept. head, 1968-70, project mgr., 1970-73, regional mgr., Atlanta, 1973-76, asst. v.p., 1976-78, v.p., 1978-82, sr. v.p., 1982—; engr. Nat. Fiscuit Co., N.Y.C., 1962-63; condr. seminars, moderator forums in computer usage and environ. design. Co-author: Tunnel Engring. Handbook, 1982; contbr. articles to profl. jours. Pres. Brookside Home Sch. Orgn., Westwood, N.J., 1972-73; co-v.p. Dunwoody Bank Booster Club, Ga., 1975-76, co-pres., Ga., 1976-77. Named Atlanta Engr. of Yr. in Pvt. Practice, 1978; recipient Harold R. Fee Alumni award, 1978. Fellow Soc. Am. Mil. Engrs. (pres. Atlanta post 1978-79); mem. Nat. Soc. Profl. Engrs., Ga. Soc. Profl. Engrs. (dir. 1976-78), Nat. Council Engring. Examiners (cert.), Ga. Engring. Found. (dir. 1977—, sec. 1979, v.p. 1980, pres. elect 1981, pres. 1982, 83), Stevens Alumni Assn., ASME, ASHRAE (chmn. tech. com. 1975-79, research promotion com. 1980-82), Brit. Tunneling Soc., Electric Railroaders Assn., Aircraft Owners and Pilots Assn., Ga. Conservancy, Atlanta C. of C., Sigma Nu (pres. alumni assn. 1966-70, comdr. 1971-73). Lutheran. Clubs: Ansley Golf, Atlanta City, Atlanta Stevens (pres. 1974—). Home: 1220 Witham Dr Dunwoody CA 30338 Office: 148 International Blvd Atlanta GA 30303

BENDER, ALAN SIMON, advertising agency executive; b. N.Y.C., Feb. 20, 1941; s. Leonard Bernard and Mildred Gloria (Brenner) B.; m. Dedorah Sue Laub, Dec. 12, 1971; children: Marc Andrew, David Paul. B.S., Lafayette Coll., 1962; M.B.A., Columbia U., 1963. Asst. product mgr. Colgate Palmolive Co., Inc., N.Y.C., 1963-64; product mgr. Am. Cyanamid Co., Inc., Wayne, N.J., 1964-66; account exec. Grey Advt., Inc., N.Y.C., 1966-68; v.p., mgmt. supr. William Esty Co., Inc., N.Y.C., 1968-78; sr. v.p., mgmt. rep. McCann-Erickson, Inc., N.Y.C., 1979-82; sr. v.p., mgmt. supr. Benton & Bowles, Inc., N.Y.C., 1982-83; exec. v.p., ptnr. Popofsky Advt., Inc., N.Y.C., 1983-84; prin. Martha Ward Assocs. Exec. Search Cons., N.Y.C., 1984—. Mem. student counseling bd. Columbia Grad. Sch. Bus., N.Y.C., 1963—. Recipient Joseph Allen essay award Lafayette Coll., 1961. Home: 24 Wimbleton Ln Great Neck NY 11023 Office: Martha Ward Assocs 71 Park Ave New York NY 10016

BENDER, BETTY WION, librarian; b. Mt. Ayer, Iowa, Feb. 26, 1925; d. John F. and Sadie A. (Guess) Wion; m. Robert F. Bender, Aug. 24, 1946. B.S., N.Tex. State U., Denton, 1946; M.A., U. Denver, 1957. Asst. cataloger N. Tex. State U. Library, 1946-49; from cataloger to head acquisitions So. Meth. U., Dallas, 1949-56; reference asst. Ind. State Library, Indpls., 1951-52; librarian Ark. State Coll., 1958-59, Eastern Wash. Hist. Soc., Spokane, 1960-67; reference librarian, then head circulation dept. Spokane (Wash.) Public Library, 1968-73, library dir., 1973—; vis. instr. U. Denver, summers 1957-60, 63, fall 1959; instr. Whitworth Coll., Spokane, 1962-64; mem. Gov. Wash. Regional Conf. Libraries, 1968, Wash. Statewide Library Devel. Council, 1970-71. Bd. dirs. N.W. Regional Found., 1973-75, Inland Empire Goodwill Industries, 1975-77. Mem. ALA (mem. library adminstrn. and mgmt. assn. com. on orgn. 1980—, chmn. nominating com. 1980-81), Pacific N.W. Library Assn. (chmn. circulation div. 1972-75, conv. chmn. 1977), Wash. Library Assn. (pres. 1977-78), AAUW (pres. Spokane br. 1969-71, rec. sec. Wash. br. 1971-73, fellowship named in honor 1972), Spokane and Inland Empire Librarians (dir. 1967-68), Am. Soc. Pub. Adminstrn. Republican.

Lutheran. Clubs: Zonta (pres. Spokane chpt. 1976-77, dist. conf. treas. 1972. Home: 119 N 6th St Cheney WA 99004 Office: W 906 Main Ave Spokane WA 99201

BENDER, DAVID RAY, library association executive; b. Canton, Ohio, June 12, 1942; s. John Ray and Mary Elizabeth (Witmer) B.; children: Robert Ray, Scott David, Lori Jo. B.S., Kent State U., 1964; M.S. in L.S, Case Western Res. U., 1969; Ph.D., Ohio State U., 1977. Librarian South High Sch., Willoughby, Ohio, 1964-68; cons. sch. library services Ohio Dept. Edn., Columbus, 1969-70; grad. research asso. Ohio State U., Columbus, 1970-72; br. chief sch. library media services Md. Dept. Edn., Balt., 1972-79; exec. dir. Spl. Libraries Assn., N.Y.C., 1979—; lectr. Rutgers U., New Brunswick, N.J.; vis. prof. Townson State U., Balt.; cons., project dir. various state depts. edn. and colls. and univs., profl. assns., also internat., state and local orgns. Author: Learning Resources and the Instructional Program in Community College, 1980, Library Media Programs and the Special Learner, 1981. Recipient award for outstanding service Md. Ednl. Media Orgn., 1980. Mem. ALA, Am. Assn. Sch. Librarians, Spl. Libraries Assn., Internat. Fedn. Library Assns. and Instns., Am. Soc. Assn. Execs., Kappa Sigma, Beta Phi Mu. Republican. Episcopalian. Home: 44 Strawberry Hill Stamford CT 06902 Office: Spl Libraries Assn 235 Park Ave S New York NY 10003

BENDER, GARY NEDROW, television sportcaster; b. Norton, Kans., Sept. 1, 1940; s. Herbert Leo and Helen Dolores (Nedrow) B.; m. Linda Wright, Aug. 4, 1963; children: Trey, Brett. B.A., Wichita State U., 1962; M.A., U. Kans., 1964. Sportcaster WIBW-TV, Topeka, Kans., 1966-68, U. Kans. Network, Lawrence, 1968-70, WKOW-TV, Madison, Wis., 1970-75, KMOX TV-Radio, St. Louis, 1975-80, CBS Network, N.Y.C., 1975—. Bd. dirs. Fellowship Christian Athletes, Kansas City, Mo., 1981—; com. mem. Fiesta Fowl, Phoenix, 1982—. Named State Sportscaster of Yr. Nat. Assn. Sportscasters and Writers, 1973, 74; recipient Emmy for best live telecast Radio-TV Sports Com., 1982. Mem. Pen and Mike Club (pres. 1973-74). Republican. Lodge: Rotary. Home: 6102 E Montecito St Scottsdale AZ 85251 Office: CBS TV Sports 51 W 52d St New York NY 10019

BENDER, JAMES FREDERICK, psychologist, university dean; b. Dayton, Ohio, Apr. 6, 1905; s. Fred Jacob and Bertha (Zimmerman) B.; m. Anne Parsons, June 25, 1925; m. Gertrude Moller, Jan. 21, 1966 (div. 1967); m. Vera E. Sattler, Jan. 21, 1968. B.S., Columbia U., 1928, Ph.D., 1939; D.H.L. (hon.), Adelphi U., 1980. Cert. psychologist, N.Y. Psychol. examiner Personnel Bur., CCNY, 1928-37; lectr., adj. prof. psychology Bklyn. Poly. Inst., 1928-40; chmn. dept. speech, dir. Speech and Hearing Center; chmn. div. lang., lit. and arts Queens Coll., 1937-44; dir. Nat. Inst. Human Relations, 1944-54; pres. James F. Bender Assos., 1954-74; prof. bus. adminstrn. Adelphi U., Garden City, 1960-66, dean, 1964-66, acting dean, 1973-74; dean Center Banking and Money Mgmt., 1974-77, dean spl. programs, 1977—; prof. bus. adminstrn. Pace Coll., 1966-68; prof. C.W. Post Coll. of L.I. U.; dir. Money Mgmt. Inst., 1969-73; lic. psychologist, 1958—; dir. sales tng. Lehigh Nav. Coal Sales Co., 1953—; also dir.; sr. cons. Kimberly-Clark Corp.; dean Kimberly Clark Mktg. Inst., 1958-59; lectr. Columbia U., 1950-57, mem. alumni council, 1950-59; Cons. Adelphi-Suffolk Coll.; dir. Follett Corp., Tech Products, Profit Motivation Service, Inc., First Multifund Inc., First Multifund for Income, Inc., Tapewatchers Fund, Inc.; pres., dir. Enterprise Fund of Adelphi U., Inc.; Chmn. exec. com. Nat. Schs. Com. Econ. Edn., 1965—; chmn. Career Planning Comm. Nassau County, N.Y., 1966-67. Author: (with Victor A. Fields) Voice and Diction, 1944, The Technique of Executive Leadership, 1950, Your Way to Popularity and Personal Power, 1950, How to Sleep, Personality Structure of Stuttering, How to Talk Well, 1949, Salesman's Mispronunciations, Make Your Business Letters Make Friends, 1952, Victory Over Fear, 1952, Profits from Business Letters, 1952, How to Sell Well, 1961, 10 Biggest Mistakes Speakers Make, 1963, Our Mixed and Mixed Up Economy, 1972, (with Judy Thornton Stark) You, 1973; also articles. Trustee Queens Speech and Hearing Service Center, 1941-73, Friends Acad., 1957-62, Human Resources Found., 1965—; chmn. Div. II Tri-State United Way, 1977; hon. chmn. N.Y. March of Dimes Dinner, 1975. Recipient Owl award as outstanding alumnus Sch. Gen. Studies Columbia U., 1973; Disting. Teaching award Am. Econ. Found.; L.I. Bus. Rev. Disting. Leadership award, 1975; Honor award Nassau County council Boy Scouts Am., 1980; James F. Bender endowed professorship named in his honor C.W. Post Center L.I. U., 1975; James F. Bender Vis. Professorship in banking and money mgmt. Adelphi U., 1980. Fellow AAAS, Am. Speech and Hearing Assn.; mem. Am. Speech Correction Assn. (past councillor), N.Y. State Assn. Applied Psychology (exec. com. 1942-44), Am. Psychol. Assn., N.Y. Met. Assn. Psychologists, N.Y. Soc. Clin. Psychologists, Nat. Vocat. Guidance Assn., Nat. Council Family Relations, Emerson Lit. Soc., Acad. Mgmt., Fin. Execs. Inst., Internat. Assn. Fin. Planning, Adelphi U. Alumni Assn. (hon.), Sigma Chi.; Mem. Religious Soc. of Friends. Republican. Clubs: Masons, Columbia Univ., Garden City Country. Home: 54 Thornwood Ln Roslyn Heights NY 11577 *Hard work accompanied by efficient productivity are two powerful foes of inflation.*

BENDER, JOHN CHARLES, lawyer; b. N.Y.C., May 17, 1940; s. John H. and Cecilia B. B.S.M.E., Northeastern U., 1964; J.D., NYU, 1968, LL.M., 1971. Bar: N.Y. 1968, U.S. Dist. Ct. (so. dist.) N.Y. 1972. Atty. Marshall, Bratter, Greene, Allison and Tucker, 1968-69; asst. dir, NYU Ctr. for Internat. Studies, N.Y.C., 1969-71; atty. Freidin Prashker Feldman & Gartner, N.Y.C., 1971-75; spl. counsel Moreland Act Commn. on Nursing Homes and Residential Facilities, N.Y.C., 1975-76; gen. counsel N.Y. State Fin. Control Bd., N.Y.C., 1976-80; v.p., counsel News Am. Pub. Inc., N.Y.C., 1980—. Chmn., trustee Trust for Cultural Resources of the City of New York, 1981—; trustee Village Nursing Home. Mem. ABA, N.Y. State Bar Assn., Assn. Bar City N.Y. (com. on communications law 1981—, spl. com. on edn. and the law 1982—). Home: 393 West End Ave New York NY 10024 Office: News Am Pub Inc 210 South St New York NY 1002

BENDER, MYRON LEE, chemist, educator; b. St. Louis, May 20, 1924; s. Averam Burton and Fannie (Leventhal) B.; m. Muriel Blossom Schulman, June 8, 1952; children: Alec Robert, Bruce Michael, Steven Pat. B.S. with highest distinction, Purdue U., 1944, Ph.D., 1948, D.Sc. honoris causae, 1969; postdoctoral student, Harvard, 1948-49; AEC fellow, U. Chgo., 1949-50. Chemist, Eastman Kodak Co., 1944-45; instr. U. Conn., 1950-51; from instr. to asso. prof. Ill. Inst. Tech., 1951-60; mem. faculty Northwestern U., 1960—, prof. chemistry, 1962—, prof. biochemistry, 1975—; cons. to govt. and industry, 1959—; fellow Merton Coll., Oxford U., 1968; J.S.P.S. vis. lectr., Japan, 1974; vis. prof. U. Queensland, Australia, 1979, Nankai U., China, 1982, univs. Tokyo and Kyoto, Japan, 1982. Recipient Midwest award Am. Chem. Soc., 1972; Sloan fellow, 1959-65; Fulbright Hays disting. prof., Zagreb, Yugoslavia, 1977. Fellow Am. Inst. Chemists; mem. Am. Chem. Soc., AAUP, Chem. Soc. (London), Am. Soc. Biol. Chemists, Assn. Harvard Chemists, AAAS (councilor chemistry sect.), Nat. Acad. Scis., Phi Beta Kappa, Sigma Xi, Phi Lambda Upsilon. Home: 2514 Sheridan Rd Evanston IL 60201

BENDER, RALPH EDWARD, emeritus agricultural educator; b. nr. Waldo, Ohio, Dec. 29, 1910; s. George Edward and Nina Amelia (Allmedinger) B.; m. Harriett Louise Anspaugh, June 10, 1937; children: John Edward, Susan Jane. B.S. in Agr, Ohio State U., 1933, M.A., 1941, Ph.D., 1947. Tchr. vocat. agr. Anna (Ohio) High Sch., 1933-37; instr. dept. agrl. edn. Ohio State U.; also tchr. vocat. agr. Canal Winchester High Sch., 1937-47, asst. prof., 1947-48, asso. prof., 1948-51, chmn. dept. agrl. edn., 1948-78, prof., 1951-78, emeritus prof., 1978—; vis. prof. Auburn U., 1954, U. Calif., Colo. State U., 1959, 61, 68, Cornell U., 1962, Pa. State U., 1964, Kans. State U., 1979; U.S. AID specialist Tchr. Edn. Study in Brazil, 1967, 74; external examiner U. Sierra Leone, 1975; cons. Ohio Adv. Council for Vocat. Edn., 1980—; cons.-specialist div. vocat. edn. U.S. Office Edn., 1969, 70; cons. nat. bd. dirs. Future Farmers Am., 1976-77. Author: The FFA and You-Your Guide to Learning, 1972, 74, 79; co-author: Adult Education in Agriculture, 1972; contbg. author: AVA Yearbook, The Individual and His Education, 1972. Mem. troop com. Boy Scouts; pres. Jr. Fair Bd. Ohio, 1929—; Pres. Bd. of Edn.; Mem. adv. com. Sch. Edn., Cornell U., 1942-67. Named to Ohio Agrl. Hall of Fame, 1982. Mem. Am. Vocat. Assn. (life mem.; nat. v.p. 1967-70, pres. agrl. edn. div. 1967-70, Outstanding Service award 1971), Ohio Vocat. Agrl. Assn. (pres. 1945-46), Am. Assn. Tchr. Educators in Agr. (pres. 1957-58, Distinguished Teaching award 1969), Central Regional Agrl. Edn. Conf. (pres. 1963-64), Ohio Vocat. Assn (pres. 1946-47), Ohio Sch. Bd. Assn., Future Farmers Am. (pres. Ohio 1929-30, nat. v.p. 1930-31, VIP citation 1978), NEA, Nat. Vocat. Agr. Tchrs. Assn., Ohio Safety Council, Ohio Edn. Assn., Ohio Assn. Adult Edn., Farm Bur., Grange, Alpha Zeta, Gamma Sigma Delta, Phi Delta Kappa, Phi Kappa Phi, Phi Eta Sigma. Methodist. Clubs: Mason., Lions (pres. 1959), Ohio State U. Faculty, Pres.'s). Home: 265 Woodsview Dr Canal Winchester OH 43110 Office: Ohio State U Columbus OH 43210

BENDER, RICHARD, architect, university dean; b. N.Y.C., Jan. 19, 1930; s. Edward and Betty (Okun) B.; m. Sue Rosenfeld, Aug. 9, 1956; children—Michael, David. B.C.E., CCNY, 1951; M.Arch., Harvard U., 1956. Architect in offices of Walter Gropius, 1951-53, William Lescaze, 1958-60; with Town Planning Assocs., N.Y.C., 1960-66, partner, 1961-66, prin., 1966—; pvt. practice archtl. design and planning cons., 1966—; lectr. Columbia U., N.Y.C., 1957-60; asst. prof. Cooper Union, 1961; prof. architecture U. Calif., Berkeley, 1969—. chmn. dept., 1974-76; dean Coll. Environ. Design, 1976—; chmn. evaluation panel Center Bldg. Tech., Nat. Bur. Standards; dir. bldg. research adv. bd. Nat. Acad. Sci., Mem. Commn. for Engrng. and Tech. Studies, mem. adv. bd. on the built environment; adv. panels HUD, Nat. Endowment Arts. Author: A Crack in the Rearview Mirror, 1973. Served with AUS, 1954-55. Home: 804 Santa Barbara St Berkeley CA 94707 Office: Coll Environ Design Univ Calif Berkeley CA 94720

BENDER, ROSS THOMAS, clergyman; b. Tavistock, Ont., Can., June 25, 1929; came to U.S., 1960, naturalized, 1965; s. Christian and Katie (Bender) B.; m. Ruth Eileen Steinmann, Dec. 22, 1950; children: Ross Lynn, Elizabeth, Michael, Deborah, Anne. B.A., Goshen Coll., 1954, B.D., 1956; M.A., Yale U., 1961, Ph.D., 1962. Ordained to minstry Mennonite Ch., 1958. Prin. Rockway Mennonite sch., Kitchener, Ont., 1956-60; prof. Christian edn. Goshen Bibl. Sem., Ind., 1962—; dean. Assoc. Mennonite Bibl. Sems., Elkhart, Ind., 1964—. Author: The People of God, 1969. Yale U. fellow, 1960-61, 62; NIMH postdoctoral fellow U. Pa., 1970-71. Mem. Am. Assn. Marriage and Family Counselors. Office: Mennonite Ch 1504 S 8th St Goshen IN 46526

BENDER, SHELDON, professional baseball team executive. V.p. for player personnel Cincinnati Reds, Nat. League. Office: Cincinnati Reds 100 Riverfront Stadium Cincinnati OH 45202

BENDER, THOMAS, history and humanities educator, writer; b. Redwood City, Calif., Apr. 18, 1944; s. Joseph Charles and Catherine Frances (McGuire) B.; m. Sally Hill, June 8, 1966 (div. Oct. 1983); 1 son, David William; m. Gwendolyn Wright, Jan. 14, 1971. B.A., U. Santa Clara, 1966; M.A., U. Calif.-Davis, 1967, Ph.D., 1971. Asst. prof. history and urban studies U. Wis., Green Bay, 1971-74; asst. prof. history NYU, N.Y.C., 1974-76, assoc. prof. history, 1976-77, prof. history, 1977—, Samuel Rudin prof. humanities, 1977-82, Univ. prof. humanities, 1982—. Author: Toward Urban Vision, 1975 (Frederick Jackson Turner prize 1975), Community and Social Change in America, 1978, (with Edwin Rozwenc) The Making of American Society, 1978; editor: Democracy in America, 1981. Bd. dirs. Mcpl. Art Soc. N.Y., N.Y.C., 1983—. Guggenheim fellow, 1980-81. Fellow N.Y. Inst. Humanities; mem. Am. Hist. Assn., Orgn. Am. Historians, Soc. Am. Historians. Democrat. Home: 55 Washington Mews New York NY 10003 Office: NYU Washington Sq New York NY 10003

BENDER, WELCOME WILLIAM, consulting engineer; b. Elizabeth, N.J., Nov. 30, 1915; s. Welcome W. and Bertha (Sauer) B.; m. Mary Virginia Priebe, 1946; children: Deborah, Welcome William, Rebecca, Janet, Heidi, Mary, Gregory. B.S., MIT, 1938, M.S., 1939. Tech. dir. pilotless aircraft sect. Martin Co. (div. Martin-Marietta Corp.), 1939-48, mgr. electromech, dept., 1949-51, chief electronics engr., 1952-55; dir. Research Inst. Advanced Studies (div. Martin Co.), 1955-62; dir. research Martin Co., 1962-73, dir. research space exploration group, 1964-73, project scientist planetary programs, 1966-73; v.p. J. R. Nelson & Assos. (cons. engrs.), 1973—; pres. Custom Engrng. Inc. (subs.), 1975—; mem. Gov.'s Sci. Resources Adv. Bd.; chmn. sci. and engrng. edn. com.; edn. counselor Balt. area MIT. Contbr. numerous tech. papers to sci. lit. Fellow IEEE; assoc. fellow AIAA; mem. Md. Acad. Scis. (sci. council), U. S. C. of C., Balt. Assn. Commerce, Sci. Industry Devel. Council. Patentee in field. Home: 5015 W King Crest Ln Littleton CO 80123 Office: 2805 S Tejon St Englewood CO 80110

BENDET, IRWIN JACOB, biophysics educator; b. N.Y.C., May 9, 1927; s. Julius and Anna (Feldman) B.; m. Roslyn Miller, Dec. 29, 1960; children: David, Elizabeth. B.S., CCNY, 1949; M.A., U. Mich., 1950; Ph.D., U. Calif.-Berkeley, 1954. Research assoc., instr. U. Pitts., 1954-58, asst. prof., 1958-63, assoc. prof., 1963-66, prof. biophysics, 1966—. Assoc. editor: Biophys. Jour., 1970-73. Served with USN, 1945-46. U.S.-Soviet Scientist Exchange, 1968; NATO fellow, 1972. Mem. Biophys. Soc., Electron Microscope Soc. Am., N.Y. Acad. Scis., AAAS, Sigma Xi. Democrat. Jewish. Home: 1321 Cordova Rd Pittsburgh PA 15206 Office: U Pitts 5th Ave and Bigelow Blvd Pittsburgh PA 15260

BENDETSEN, KARL ROBIN, business executive, lawyer; b. Aberdeen, Wash., Oct. 11, 1907; s. Albert M. and Anna (Bentson) B.; m. Billie McIntosh, 1938; 1 son, Brookes McIntosh; m. Maxine Bosworth, 1947; 1 dau., Anna Martha; m. Gladys Ponton de Arce Johnston, 1972. A.B., Stanford U., 1929, J.S.D., 1932. Bar: Calif., Oreg., Ohio, N.Y., Wash., D.C., U.S. Supreme Ct. Practiced law, Aberdeen, Wash., 1932-40, mgmt. counsel, 1946-47; cons. spl. asst. to sec. U.S. Dept. Def., 1948; asst. sec. Dept. Army, 1948-50, under sec., 1950-52; dir. gen. U.S. R.R.s, 1950-52; chmn. bd. Panama Canal Co., 1950-54; counsel Champion Papers, 1952-53, v.p. Tex. div., 1953-55, v.p. ops., 1955-60, chmn. bd., pres., chief exec. officer, 1960-67; chmn., pres., chief exec. officer Champion Internat., 1967-72, chmn. exec. com., 1973-75; spl. U.S. rep. with rank of ambassador to W.Ger., 1956, spl. U.S. ambassador to Philippines, 1956; chmn. adv. com. to sec. Dept. Def., 1962; vice chmn. Def. Manpower Commn., 1974-76. Served to col. U.S. Army, 1940-46; spl. rep. sec. of war to Gen. MacArthur, 1941. Decorated D.S.M. with oak leaf cluster, Silver Star, Legion of Merit with 2 oak leaf clusters, Bronze Star with 3 oak leaf clusters and Combat V, Army Commendation medal with 3 oak leaf clusters, medal of Freedom; Croix de Guerre with Palm; officer Legion of Honor (France); Croix de Guerre with palm (Belgium); mem. Order Brit. Empire; recipient Disting. Civilian Service medal. Mem. Theta Delta Chi. Episcopalian. Clubs: Links, Metropolitan, Brook (N.Y.C.); Chicago; Washington Athletic (Seattle); Bohemian, Pacific Union (San Francisco); Petroleum, Tejas, Bayou (Houston); Washington, F Street, Georgetown (D.C.); Everglades, Bath and Tennis (Palm Beach, Fla.). Directed evacuation of Japanese from West Coast, 1942. Home: 2918 Garfield Terr NW Washington DC 20008 Office: 1850 K St Suite 1185 Washington DC 20006

BENDHEIM, ROBERT AUSTIN, textile executive; b. N.Y.C., Aug. 5, 1916; s. Julius and Cora (Lowenstein) B.; children: Lynn, Kim. A.B., Princeton, 1937; student, Harvard Bus. Sch., 1941-42; L.H.D. (hon.), Fordham U., 1966. Trainee Spartan Mills, Spartanburg, S.C., 1937-38; various positions with M. Lowenstein & Sons, Inc., 1938—, sec. and dir., 1946-47, v.p., 1947-59, exec. v.p., 1959-64, pres., 1964-71, chief exec. officer, 1970—, chmn. bd., 1972—, also dir. Trustee Mount Sinai Hosp., N.Y.C.; trustee, mem. exec. com. Fordham U.; mem. council univ. resources Princeton U. Served as lt. USNR, 1942-46. Clubs: Princeton, Century, Stanwich, Lyford Cay, Union League. Home: Flagler Dr Greenwich CT 06830 Office: 1430 Broadway New York NY 10018

BENDINER, ROBERT, writer, editor; b. Pitts., Dec. 15, 1909; s. William and Lillian (Schwartz) B.; m. Kathryn Rosenberg, Dec. 24, 1934; children: David, William, Margaret. Student, CCNY, 1928-33. Mng. editor The Nation, N.Y.C., 1937-44, assoc. editor, 1946-50, free-lance writer, 1951-68, 78—; lectr., program chmn. Wellesley Summer Inst. Social Progress, 1946-53; mem. Faculty Salzburg Sem. in Am. Studies, 1956; vis. lectr. pub. affairs Wesleyan U. (Conn.), 1983. Contbg. editor: The Reporter, N.Y.C., 1956-60; U.S. corr.: New Statesman, London, 1959-61; mem. editorial bd.: N.Y. Times, 1969-77; author: The Riddle of the State Department, 1942, The White House Fever, 1960, Obstacle Course on Capitol Hill, 1964, Just Around the Corner, 1967, The Policics of Schools, 1969, The Fall of the Wild, 1981, The Rise of the Zoo, 1981, TV documentary NBC White White Paper, The Man in the Middle, The State Legislator, 1961. Served with AUS, 1944-45. Guggenheim fellow, 1962-63; grantee Carnegie Found., Natural Resources Def. Council; Grantee Natural Resources Def. Council; recipient Benjamin Franklin Mag. award U. Ill., 1955, School Bell award NEA, 1960. Mem. Nat. Press Club, PEN Am. Center, Am. Soc. Journalists and Authors (pres. 1964). Club: Coffee House (N.Y.C.). Home and Office: 45 Central Pkwy Huntington NY 11743

BENDITT, EARL PHILIP, educator, medical scientist; b. Phila., Apr. 15, 1916; s. Milton and Sarah (Schoenfeld) B.; m. Marcella Wexler, Feb. 18, 1945; children: John, Alan, Joshua, Charles. B.A., Swarthmore Coll., 1937; M.D., Harvard U., 1941. Intern Phila. Gen. Hosp., 1941-43; resident pathology U. Chgo. Clinics, 1944; mem. faculty U. Chgo. Med. Sch., 1945-57, asso. prof. pathology, 1952-57; asst. dir. research LaRabida Children's Sanitarium, Chgo., 1950-56; prof. pathology U. Wash. Sch. Medicine, 1957—, chmn. dept., 1957-81; mem. sci. adv. bd. St. Jude Children's Research Hosp.; cons. USPHS-NIH, 1957-80; Commonwealth Fund fellow, vis. prof. Sir William Dunn Sch. Pathology, U. Oxford, Eng., 1965, Macy faculty scholar, 1979-80, Litchfield lectr., 1980; chmn. bd. sci. counselors adv. com. Nat. Inst. Environ. Health Scis., 1976-79, council mem., 1971-74. Mem. editorial bds. scis. publs. Recipient Med. Alumni award univ. Chgo., 1968; Rous-Whipple award Am. Assn. Pathologists, 1980; Gold Headed Cane Am. Assn. Pathologists, 1984. Fellow AAAS; mem. Am. Soc. Exptl. Pathology (council 1971-77, sec. treas. 1972-73, pres. 1975-76), Nat. Acad. Scis., Am. Soc. Pathologists and Bacteriologists (council 1972-77), Soc. Exptl. Biology and Medicine, Am. Soc. Cell Biology, Am. Soc. Biol. Chemists, Histochem. Soc. (pres. 1963-64), Phi Beta Kappa, Sigma Xi. Home: 3717 E Prospect St Seattle WA 98112

BENDIX, WILLIAM EMANUEL, equipment mfg. co. exec.; b. Los Angeles, Feb. 24, 1935; s. Emanuel S. and Katharine (Rinkle) B.; m. Joyce McCune, June 7, 1957; children—Bruce, Louise, Linda. B.S. in Engrng, UCLA, 1957; M.B.A. with distinction, Harvard U., 1962. With mfg. and engrng. mgmt. dept. Litton Industries, Calif., 1962-65; prin. Theodore Barry and Assos., Los Angeles, 1965-70; v.p. ops., div. pres., group v.p., dir. Mark Controls Corp., Evanston, Ill., 1970—; dir. Sargent-Welch Sci. Co. Served to lt. (j.g.) USNR, 1957-60. Mem. Tau Beta Pi. Home: 611 Longwood Glencoe IL 60022 Office: 1900 Dempster St Evanston IL 60204

BENDIXEN, HENRIK HOLT, physician; b. Frederiksberg, Denmark, Dec. 2, 1923; came to U.S., 1954, naturalized, 1960; s. Carl Julius and Borghild Nicoline (Holt) B.; m. Karen Skakke, Dec. 20, 1947; children—Nils, Birgitte. C.phil., c.m., c.chir. (laudabilis), U. Copenhagen, 1951. Diplomate: Am. Bd. Anesthesiologists. Postgrad. tng. in surgery and anesthesia in, Denmark and Sweden, 1951-54, also Danish hosp. ship in, Korea; resident in anesthesia Mass. Gen. Hosp., Boston, 1954-57; mem. anesthesia dept. faculty Mass. Gen. Hosp. and Harvard U. Med. Sch., 1957-69; prof. anesthesia, head dept. U. Calif. Med. Sch., San Diego, 1969-73; prof. anesthesiology, chmn. dept. Columbia U. Coll. Phys. and Surg., 1973—; pres. Mass. Soc. Anesthesiologists, 1966; mem. gen. med. research program-project com. NIH, 1967; dir. center research and tng. anesthesiology Harvard U. Med. Sch., 1968; chmn. com. anesthesia NRC, 1970. Author: Respiratory Care, 1965, also articles, revs., abstracts. Mem. Soc. Critical Care Medicine (pres. 1974), Assn. U. Anesthetists, Inst. of Medicine, Am. Soc. Pharmacology and Therapeutics., Am. Physiol. Soc., Assn. Am. Med. Colls., N.Y. Acad. Medicine, N.Y. State, N.Y. County med. socs., AMA, Am. Soc. Anesthesiologists, Am. Heart Assn.; hon. mem. Minn. Surg. Soc., Belgian Soc. Anesthesiologists; corr. mem. Danish Soc. Anesthesiologists. Clubs: Harvard (Boston); University (N.Y.C.). Address: Dept Anesthesiology Columbia Univ Coll Phys and Surg 630 W 168th St New York NY 10032

BENEDICK, RICHARD ELLIOT, ambassador; b. N.Y.C., May 10, 1935; s. Lester and Jean (Shamski) B.; m. Hildegard K.G. Schulz, June 1, 1957 (div.); children: Andreas Peter Anselm, Julianna Valeska.; m. Helen Ruth Freeman, Sept. 10, 1983. A.B. summa cum laude, Columbia U., 1955; M.A., Yale U., 1956; postgrad. (Evans fellow), Oxford U., 1956; D.B.A., Harvard U., 1962. Program economist AID, Dept. State, Washington, 1958, Tehran, Iran, 1959-61, Karachi, Pakistan, 1962-64; adminstr. OECD Secretariat, Paris, 1964-66; 1st sec. Am. embassy, Bonn, W.Ger., 1966-71; dir. Office Devel. Fin., Dept. State, Washington, 1971-75; counselor for econ. and comml. affairs Am. embassy, Athens, Greece, 1975-77; mem. exec. seminar in nat. and internat. affairs Dept. State, 1977-78, coordinator population affairs, 1978—, with rank ambassador, 1979—; lectr. in field. Dir. ad hoc group on population policy Nat. Security Council, 1979—; U.S. rep. UN Population Commn., Asian and Pacific Population Conf., Sri Lanka, 1982; mem. Econ. Commn. for Europe, Bulgaria, 1983; inter-agy. coordinator Internat. Conf. on Population, 1984; bd. dirs. Population Resource Ctr., 1984—. Author: Industrial Finance in Iran, 1964, The High Dam and the Transformation of the Nile, 1979; contbr. articles to profl. jours. Mem. Toenissteiner Kreis (Germany), Phi Beta Kappa. Home: 2154 Military Rd Arlington VA 22207 also Hidden Hills CA Office: US Dept State Room 7825 2201 C St NW Washington DC 20520

BENEDICT, ALVIN, hotel and casino company executive; b. 1924; married. B.S., Rutgers U., 1949. With Armour & Co., 1948-49; owner Free Rock Diner, 1950-52; with Last Frontier Hotel, 1953-55; ptnr. Benedict & Romey, 1955-58; dir. hotel ops. Summa Corp., 1958-69; pres., dir. MGM Grand Hotels, Inc., Las Vegas, Nev., 1969-82, chmn., chief exec. officer, 1982—. Office: MGM Grand Hotels Inc 3645 Las Vegas Blvd S Las Vegas NV 89109 *

BENEDICT, BILL CLIFFORD, manufacturing company executive; b. Dallas, Dec. 30, 1925; s. Willie C. and Gladys (Webb) B.; m. Louise Alford, Mar. 15, 1946; children: Charlotte Ann Benedict Burgess, Dennis Wayne, Donna Jean Benedict Reeder. Engaged in optical industry, 1946-51, comml. flight instr., 1951-56; formerly with Internat. Optical Co., pres.; founder, 1979; since pres., chmn. bd., chief exec. officer Omega Optical Co., Dallas; dir. Omega Energy Co., Marine Maintenance Co. Served with USNR, 1944-46. Mem. Nat. Assn. Mfg. Opticans, Optical Labs. Assn. Club: Brookhollow Country. Office: 13515 N Stemmons Freeway Dallas TX 75234 *

BENEDICT, CLEVE, government official, former congressman, dairy farmer; b. Harrisburg, Pa., Mar. 21, 1935; s. Cooper P. and Laura B.; m. Ann Arthur; children: Cooper, Ruth, Pinckney. B.S., Princeton U., 1957; grad., Graham Sch. for Cattlemen. Owner, operator dairy farm, Greenbrier County, W.Va., 1961—; mem. 97th Congress from 2d W.Va. Dist., mem. energy and commerce com.; dep. asst. sec. Dept. Energy, Washington, 1983—; dir. 1st Nat. Bank of Alderson.; Bd. dirs. W.Va. State Fair, 1972, treas., 1978; chmn. W.Va. Bd. Probation and Parole, 1974-75; commr. fin. and adminstr. State of Va., 1975-77; Chmn. W.Va. Republican Exec. Com. Mem. W.Va. Farm Bur., Greenbrier County Area Herd Improvement Assn., W.Va. Holstein-Friesian Assn., Dairymen, Izaak Walton League Am. Episcopalian. Clubs: Ruritan, Rotary. Office: Dept Energy Oil Gas Shale and Coal Liquids Route 270 Germantown MD 20545 *

BENEDICT, DIRK, actor, singer; b. Helena, Mont., Mar. 1, 1945; s. George Edward and Priscilla Mella (Metzger) Niewoehner. B.F.A., Whitman Coll., 1967; diploma advanced theatre, Oakland U., Rochester, Mich., 1969. Actor in repertory theatres, 1969-71; Broadway appearances include Abelard and Heloise, 1971, Butterflies are Free, 1972; films include Georgia Georgia, 1971, SSSSS, 1973, W, 1973, Battlestar Galactica, 1978, Scavenger Hunt, 1979, Ruckus, 1979, Underground Aces, 1979; tour in, Oklahoma, summer 1979; TV series include Battlestar Galactica, 1978-79, Scruples, 1980, The A-Team, 1983—. Address: care Internat Bus Mgmt 1801 Century Park E Suite 1132 Los Angeles CA 90067 *One is limited by the size of one's dream. If your dream is infinite, then the journey never ends and the joy is infinite.*

BENEDICT, MANSON, chemical engineer, educator; b. Lake Linden, Mich., Oct. 9, 1907; s. C. Harry and Lena I. (Manson) B.; m. Marjorie Oliver Allen, July 6, 1935; children: Mary Hannah (Mrs. Myran C. Sauer, Jr.), Marjorie Alice (Mrs. Martin Cohn). B. Chemistry, Cornell, 1928; M.S., Mass. Inst. Tech., 1932, Ph.D., 1935. NRC fellow chemistry, 1935-36; research asso. geophysics Harvard, 1936-37; research chemist M.W. Kellogg Co., 1938-43; in charge process design gaseous diffusion plant for uranium-235 Kellex Corp., 1943-46; dir. process development Hydrocarbon Research, Inc., 1946-51; tech. asst. to gen. mgr. AEC, 1951-52; prof. nuclear engring. Mass. Inst. Tech., 1951-69, Institute prof., 1969-73, prof. emeritus, 1973—, head dept. nuclear engring., 1958-71; dir. Burns & Roe, Inc., 1979—; sci. adv. Nat. Research Corp., 1951-58, dir., 1962-67; mem. gen. adv. com. AEC, 1958-68, chmn., 1962-64; mem. Mass. Adv. Council on Radiation Protection; dir. Atomic Indsl. Forum, 1966-72; mem. energy research and devel. adv. council Fed. Energy Adminstrn., 1973-75. Co-editor: Engineering Developments in the Gaseous Diffusion Process, 1949; Co-author: Nuclear Chemical Engineering, 1981. Recipient William H. Walker award Am. Inst. Chem. Engrs., 1947, Founders award, 1965; Indsl. and Engring. Chemistry award Am. Chem. Soc., 1962; Perkin medal Soc. Chem. Industry; Robert E. Wilson award in nuclear chem. engring.; Arthur H. Compton award Am. Nuclear Soc.; Fermi award AEC, 1972; John Fritz medal Engring. Founder Socs., 1974; Nat. Medal Sci., 1975; Henry D. Smyth Nuclear Statesman award Atomic Indsl. Forum, 1979; Washington award Western Soc. Engrs., 1982. Fellow Am. Nuclear Soc. (pres. 1962-63), Am. Acad. Arts and Sci., Am. Philos. Soc., Am. Inst. Chem. Engrs.; mem. Nat. Acad. Scis., Nat. Acad. Engring. (Founders award 1976), Sigma Xi. Clubs: Cosmos (Washington); Weston (Mass.) Golf; Country of Naples (Fla.). Home: 2151 Gulf Shore Blvd N Naples FL 33940 Office: Dept Nuclear Engring Mass Inst Tech Cambridge MA 02139

BENEDICT, PAUL, actor; b. Silver City, N.Mex., Sept. 17, 1938; s. Mitchell M. and Alma Marie (Loring) B. A.B. in English, Suffolk U., Boston, 1960. Appeared in: motion pictures The Goodbye Girl, The Man with Two Brains; appearing as Harry Bentley in: television program The Jeffersons; appeared as Buckingham in: Broadway play Richard III, 1979; also Broadway stage prodns. The White House Murder Case; appeared in: mini-series The Blue and the Gray, 1983. Mem. Actors Equity Assn., AFTRA, Screen Actors Guild, Greater Los Angeles Zool. Assn. Office: care The Blake-Glenn Agy Ltd 409 N Camden Dr #202 Beverly Hills CA 90210

BENEDIKT, MICHAEL, educator, author, editor, poet, consultant on arts, economics and business; b. N.Y.C., May 26, 1935; s. John and Helen (Davis) B. B.A. in English and Journalism, N.Y. U., 1956; M.A. in Comparative Lit, Columbia U., 1961. Asso. editor Horizon Press, N.Y.C., 1959-61; N.Y. corr. Art Internat., 1965-67; editorial asso. Art News mag., N.Y.C., 1962-72; asso. prof. Bennington Coll., 1968-69, Sarah Lawrence Coll., 1969-73, Hampshire Coll., 1973-75; Sexton prof. poetry Boston U., 1975, vis. prof. English and creative writing, 1977-79; vis. prof. Vassar Coll., 1976-77; judge Nat. Book award in translation, 1974; judge Coordinating Council of Lit. Mags., 1970, 73, Lamont Poetry awards Acad. Am. Poets, 1970-72; mem. CAPS panel in mixed media, 1976, Mass. Arts and Humanities Found. panel in poetry, 1977. Contbg. editor: Am. Poetry Rev, 1973—; editor: poetry The Paris Rev, 1974-78; Author: The Body, 1968, Sky, 1970, Mole Notes, 1971, Night Cries, 1976, The Badminton at Great Badminton, or Gustave Mahler and the Chattanooga Choo-Choo, 1980, Subject: Benedikt: A Profile, 1978; Editor: drama anthologies Theatre Experiment, 1968, Modern Spanish Theatre, 1968, Post-War German Theatre, 1967, Modern French Theatre, 1965; poetry anthologies The Poetry of Surrealism, 1975; The Prose Poem: An International Anthology, 1976; Guest poetry and fiction editor: Chelsea, 1968; guest poetry editor: Modern Poetry Studies, 1971; Contbr. articles on the arts to numerous critical anthologies, also scholarly and popular mags. Recipient Hokin award for best poems in single year Poetry Mag., 1969; Guggenheim fellow in poetry, 1968-69; Nat. Endowment for Arts prize for single poem, 1970; Fels award for excellence in mag. editing, 1975; CAPS poetry grantee, 1975; Nat. Endowment for Arts fellow in poetry, 1979-80. Mem. MLA, PEN, Poetry Soc. Am., Am. Assn. for Advancement of the Humanities. Home: 315 W 98th St New York NY 10025 *As one desires to do one's best in important things, one appreciates acknowledgements of one's achievements, such as this. Therefore, one comes to require the company of those who desire to do their best in important things; and comes to desire the company of those who have accomplished much, and who also have done that much well. In short, I believe that it behooves us, by acts of will, to seek out the best in ourselves, and in art, life, and society as a whole.*

BENEKE, EVERETT SMITH, mycologist, educator; b. Greensboro, N.C., July 6, 1918; s. Herman H. and Grace (Smith) B. B.S., Miami U., Oxford, Ohio, 1940; M.S., Ohio State U., 1941; Ph.D., U. Ill., 1948. Mem. faculty Mich. State U., East Lansing, 1948—, prof. botany, plant pathology, microbiology and pub. health, 1968—; tech. asst. Escola Superior de Veterinaria, Belo Horizonte, Brazil, OAS, Washington, 1960; vis. prof. Inst. de Botanica, U. Sao Paulo, 1961; FAO-UN cons. U. Nacional de Colombia, Bogata, 1968; WHO fellow med. mycology U. North Sumatra Med. Sch., Medan, 1969; cons. U. Minas Gerais, Belo Horizonte, Brazil, July 1977. Author (with C.J. Alexopoulos) Laboratory Manual for Introductory Mycology), 1962, (with A.L. Rogers) Medical Mycology Manual, 1980. Recipient Rhods Benham award in med. mycology, 1984. Fellow AAAS (council 1972-74); mem. Mycol. Soc. Am. (hon. life; pres. 1961), Am. Assn. Bioanalysis (sci. dir. sci. council 1963-75), Am. Bd. Bioanalysis (chmn. 1968—), Am. Inst. Biol. Sci. (rep. on bd. 1964-72), Internat. Soc. Human and Animal Mycology, Med. Mycology Soc. Ams. (sec.-treas. 1976-79, pres. 1981-82), Am. Soc. Microbiology, Internat. Assn. Microbiol. Socs. (chmn. mycology sect. 1971-78), Sigma Xi (jr. award distinguished research Mich. State U. chpt. 1958, sec.-treas. 1974-75, v.p. 1976-77, pres. 1977-78), Phi Sigma. Research in biology of pathogenicity in fungi; fungi found in aquatic habitats; diagnostic studies of pathogenic fungi and teaching mycology. Home: 1664 Forest Hill St Okemos MI 48864

BENEKE, RAYMOND RUDOLPH, economics educator; b. Laurens, Iowa, Aug. 14, 1919; s. Anton and Theresa Elizabeth (Mefferd) B.; m. Marjorie Laurene Mather, Sept. 4, 1948; children: Janet Sue, Patricia Jane. B.S., Iowa State U., 1940, M.S., 1946; Ph.D., U. Minn., 1949. Research asst. Iowa State Coll., Ames, 1945-46, asst. prof. econs., 1948-53, assoc. prof., 1953-59; prof. Iowa State U., Ames, 1959—; acting head dept. econs. Iowa State Coll., Ames, 1971-72, chmn. dept. econs., 1972—; instr. U. Minn., St. Paul, 1946-48; sec. treas. Iowa Farm Mgr. and Rural Appraisers, 1949-52; research cons. Ministry of Agr., Gov. of Peru, Lima, 1966-67; cons. Ford Found. Agr. Devel., Mex., 1966, 67, 68; trustee, sec. treas. Agr. Found. Iowa State U., Ames, 1978—. Author: Managing the Farm Business, 1955; sr. author: Linear Programming Applications, 1973. Served with U.S. Army, 1942-43. Recipient Outstanding Tchr. award Iowa State U., 1968, Faculty Citation Iowa State U. Alumni Assn., 1975. Mem. Am. Agrl. Econs. Assn. (award for profl. excellence 1968), Phi Kappa Phi, Alpha Zeta, Gamma Sigma Delta, Psi Chi. Democrat. Methodist. Home: 925 Gaskill Dr Ames IA 50020 Office: Dept Econs Iowa State U 266 Heady Hall Ames IA 50011

BENENSON, DAVID MAURICE, educator; b. Bklyn., Jan. 22, 1927; s. Louis and Bella (Hirschcowitz) B.; m. Lydia Kathleen Chapman, June 11, 1957; children—Kathleen Ann, Patricia Janice. S.B., MIT, 1950; M.S., Calif. Inst. Tech., 1953, Ph.D., 1957. Project engr. So. Calif. Coop. Wind Tunnel, Pasadena, Calif., 1950-53; research engr. Westinghouse Research Labs., Pitts., 1957-63; prof. SUNY at Buffalo, 1963—; instr. Carnegie Inst. Tech., Pitts., 1958-63; cons. Bell Aerospace Co., 1969-70, Westinghouse Electric Co., 1963-68; treas. Gaseous Electronics Conf., 1971-73. Served with USNR, 1945-46. NSF grantee, 1964—; Air Force Sci. Research grantee, 1970—; Aero. Research Labs. grantee, 1964-67; Guggenheim fellow in jet propulsion Calif. Inst. Tech., 1953-55. Fellow AIAA (assoc.; chmn. Niagara Frontier sect. 1966-67), IEEE (sr., assoc. editor Trans. Plasma Sci. 1976—, mem. switchgear com. 1971—), Am. Phys. Soc. (mem. exec. com. gaseous electronics conf. 1970—, sec. 1978), Current Zero Club, Sigma Xi. Research on analysis and devel. diagnostic techniques for study of steady-state and time varying plasmas. Home: 53 Andover Ln Wlliamsville NY 14221 Office: 4232 Ridge Lea Rd Amherst NY 14226

BENENSON, EDWARD HARTLEY, realty company executive; b. N.Y.C., Mar. 27, 1914; s. Robert C. and Nettie B.; m. Gladys Steinberg, Apr. 5, 1962; 1 dau., Lisa; children by previous marriage: Thomas Hartley, James Stuart, Amy Roberta. B.A., Duke, 1934. Pres. Benenson & Co., Benenson Funding Corp., Yale Motor Inn, Conn., Yale Inn, Meriden, Conn., Conn. Equities Corp., Benenson Investment Corp., Greenwich Devel. Corp., Sedgefield Realty N.C., Thomas James Corp., Arbee Properties of Fla. Chmn. Urban Redevel. Commn., 1957-58; mem. Mayor's Youth Adv. Group, N.Y.C., 1956-58; chmn. Friends Duke U. Mus. Art; trustee Duke U.; overseer Albert Einstein Coll. Medicine; trustee Bronx Lebanon Hosp.; trustee, governing bd. Am. Ballet Theatre; trustee Fedn. Jewish Philanthropics N.Y., mem. exec. com., 1966-66; trustee Synagogue Council; mem. Republican Nat. Com.; pres. YM-YWHA of Bronx, 1958-63, now bd. dirs.; exec. com. Duke U.; univ. rep. com. Corporate Support for Pvt. Univs. Served to 2d lt. AUS, 1939-43. Decorated Officier Ordre du Merite Agricole, France, Order St. John of Maeta; recipient gold medal Renaissance Francaise, Bronze medal City of Paris. Mem. Real Estate Bd. N.Y., Am. Ballet Theatre, Confrerie des Chevaliers du Tastevin (grand sénéchal N.Y. commanderie, grand Camerlingue of Am.), Culinary Inst. Am. (trustee), Les Amis d'Escoffier Soc., Grand Jury Assn., Commerce and Industry Assn. N.Y., Nat. Bd. Realtors, Internat. Real Estate Fedn. (charter), Order of Lafayette, Croix de Guerre Assn., Profl. Engrs., Soc. France, Fedn. War Vets. (France), Chaine des Rotisseurs (mem. Conseil d'Honneur), Am. Soc. Italian Legions Merit (Cavalier), Les Chevaliers de la Croix de Lorraine (Resistance), Commanderie de Bordeaux, du Bailliage N.Am., Res. Officers Assn. Conseil de la Croix du Combattant de l'Europe. Clubs: Century Country, Harmonie (gov.), Presidents, Paris Am., Wines and Food, Noyac Country., Palm Beach Country, Southampton Golf, Banyan Country. Home: 510 Park Ave New York NY 10022 also Georgica Rd East Hampton NY 11937 also 130 Sunrise Ave Palm Beach FL 33480 Office: 445 Park Ave New York NY 10022

BENENSON, JAMES, JR., industrialist; b. Moultrie, Ga., Mar. 9, 1936; s. James and Mary (Camp) B.; m. Sharen Statler, Aug. 28, 1966; children: James, Clement. B.S., M.I.T., 1958; postgrad., Yale U., 1960. With F. Eberstadt & Co., N.Y.C., 1960-65, Walker, Hart & Co., 1965-68, James Benenson & Co., Inc., 1968—; chmn. bd., pres. Bowline Corp., Bala Cynwyd, Pa., 1974—; also chmn. bd., pres. Vesper Corp., Bala Cynwyd, 1978—; chmn. bd. Arrowhead Holdings Corp., Los Alamitos, Calif., 1983—, Indian Bar Co., Los Alamitos, 1983—; dir. Cleve. Gear Co., 1980—; chmn. bd. Penco Products Inc., Oaks, Pa., 1979—. Served with U.S. Army Chem. Corps, 1959. Woodrow Wilson scholar, 1959-60; Andover Teaching fellow, 1958-59. Mem. Audubon Soc., Sierra Club, N.Y. Bot. Garden, N.Y. Mus. Natural History, Friends of N.Y. Public Library, Friends of City Center. Episcopalian. Clubs: Yale (N.Y.C.); Coffee House, Sag Harbor Yacht, Racquet, Buck's Harbor Yacht, Peale (Phila.); National Arts (N.Y.C.). Office: 301 City Line Ave Bala Cynwyd PA 19004

BENENSON, MARK KEITH, lawyer; b. N.Y.C., Oct. 13, 1929; s. Aaron and Luba (Stein) B.; m. Letizia Pitigliani, Dec. 29, 1959; children: Alexander, Daniela. B.S.S., CCNY, 1951; J.D., Columbia U., 1956. Bar: N.Y. 1956. Atty. Dept. Labor, Washington, 1957-58; practiced in, N.Y.C., 1958—; Bd. dirs. Amnesty Internat. U.S.A., 1966-80, sec., 1966-67, chmn., 1968-71, vice chmn., 1972-73, gen. counsel, 1972-80; pres. Vanguard Found., Inc., 1962—. Contbr. articles to profl. jours., mags. and newspapers. Served with U.S. Army, 1951-53. Mem. N.Y. State Bar Assn., Assn. Bar City N.Y., Nat. Rifle Assn., various other orgns. Home: 585 West End Ave New York NY 10024 also RD 2 Box 312 Mt Bethel Rd Port Murray NJ 07865 Office: 666 3d Ave New York NY 10017

BENENSON, WALTER, nuclear physics educator; b. N.Y.C., Apr. 27, 1936; s. Charles and Sylvia (Ogush) B.; m. Antje Semsrott, Dec. 4, 1969; children: Arleigh Ann, Tanya. B.S., Yale U., 1957; M.S., U. Wis., 1959, Ph.D., 1962. Research assoc. U. Strasbourg, 1962-63; asst. prof. nuclear physics Mich. State U., East Lansing, 1963-68, assoc. prof., 1968-72, prof., 1972—; assoc. dir. Nat. Superconducting Cyclotron Lab., 1980-82; vis. fellow Australian Nat. U., 1968; vis. prof. U. Grenoble, 1970; vis. lectr. Inst. for Nuclear Sci., Moscow, 1975; cons. Lawrence Berkeley Lab., 1979; mem. program com. Argonne Nat. Lab.; participant profl. confs. Contbr. articles to profl. jours., mags. and newspapers. Nat. Acad. Scis. fellow, 1974. Fellow Am. Phys. Soc. (chmn. 6th Internat. Conf. on Atomic Masses 1979, mem. exec. com. div. nuclear physics); mem. Internat. Union Pure and Applied Physics (U.S. del.). Home: 6111 Skyline Dr East Lansing MI 48823

BENERITO, RUTH ROGAN (MRS. FRANK H. BENERITO), chemist; b. New Orleans, Jan. 12, 1916; d. John Edward and Bernadette (Elizardi) Rogan; m. Frank Henshaw Benerito, Aug. 22, 1950. B.S., H. Sophie Newcomb Coll., 1935; postgrad., Bryn Mawr Coll., 1935-36; M.S., Tulane U., 1938, D.Sc. (hon.), 1981; Ph.D., U. Chgo., 1948. Instr. chemistry Randolph-Macon Woman's Coll., Lynchburg, Va., 1940-43, Newcomb Coll., New Orleans, 1943-47; asst. prof. chemistry Tulane U., New Orleans, 1947-53, mem. grad. faculty, 1960—, adj. prof. dept. biochemistry med. sch., 1960—; phys. chemist fat emulsion program So. Regional Lab., U.S. Dept. Agr., New Orleans, 1953-58, supervisory phys. chemist, head phys. chem. investigations natural polymers lab., 1958—. Contbr. articles to profl. publs. Recipient Distinguished Service award Dept. Agr., 1964, 70, New Orleans Fed. Exec. Assn., 1967, Fed. Woman's award U.S. CSC, 1968, Outstanding Profl. award Orgn. Profl. Employees, U.S. Dept. Agr., 1982; named as one of 75 most important Women in U.S. Ladies Home Jour., 1971. Fellow Am. Inst. Chemists (Honor Scroll La. chpt. 1977); mem. Am. Chem. Soc. (So. Chemist award 1968, Garvan medal 1970, S.W. Regional award 1972), Am. Oil Chem. Soc., Am. Assn. Textile Chemists and Colorists, Sci. Research Soc. Am., AAAS, Sigma Xi, Sigma Delta Epsilon, Delta Kappa Gamma (hon.), Iota Sigma Pi (hon.). Home: 4733 Marigny St New Orleans LA 70122 Office: 1100 Robert E Lee St New Orleans LA 70124 *Happiness comes only by contributing to the development and happiness of others; it abounds with selflessness and can be found without travelling to far off places.*

BENES, BARTON LIDICE, artist; b. Westwood, N.J., Nov. 16, 1942; s. Richard Stanley B. and Marie Teffny (Benes) Molinari. Student, Pratt Inst., Beaux Arts, Avignon, France. Exhibited in shows Kathryn Markel Fine Arts Gallery, N.Y.C., 1976—, Fendrick Gallery, Washington, 1975—, Carol Taylor Art Gallery, Dallas, 1981—; Galleriet Lund, Sweden, 1979—; Renate Fassbender, Munich, Germany, 1983—, U. Iowa Mus. Art, Iowa City, 1982, Renwick Gallery-Nat. Collection Fine Arts, Washington, 1977, John Michael Kohler Arts Ctr., Sheboygan, Wis., 1982, Craft and Folk Art Mus., Los Angeles, 1979, Victorial and Albert Mus., London; represented pvt. collections, London; permanent collections Art Inst. Chgo., Bibliotheque Nat., Paris, France, Nat. Gallery of Australia, Princeton U., Fed. Res. Systems, Washington; pub. The Dog Bite, 1970, Excerpts from the Diaries of the Late God, 1968, K Have Found a Cockroach in your Product, 1972. Rcipient St. Gaudens award Met. Mus. Art, N.Y.C., 1960; Caps grant for graphics N.Y. State Council on Arts, 1977; Mixed Media grantee Ariana Found. Arts, 1982; cert. arreciation Fed. Res. Bd., 1982. Mem. Ctr. for Book Arts, Franklin Furnace Archives. Home and Office: 463 West St New York NY 10014

BENESCH, RUTH ERICA, educator; b. Paris, Feb. 25, 1925; U.S., 1947; d. Federic and Helen (Fuerst) Baade; m. Reinhold Benesch, 1946; children: Andrew, Susan. B.Sc., U. London, 1946; Ph.D., Northwestern U., 1951. Ind. investigator Marine Biology Lab., Woods Hole, Mass., 1956-60; research assoc. Columbia Coll. of Physicians and Surgeons, N.Y.C., 1960-64, asst. prof. biochemistry, 1964-72, assoc. prof., 1972-80, prof. biochemistry, 1980—; research assoc. Johns Hopkins U., Balt., 1947-48; demonstrator U. Reading, Eng., 1946-47; fellow in physiol. chemistry Northwestern U. Med. Sch., Chgo., 1948-52; fellow in biochemistry State U. Iowa, 1952-55; fellow Inst. Enzyme Research, U. Wis., Madison, 1955-56. Mem. Am. Chem. Soc., Am. Soc. Biol. Chemists, Am. Soc. Hematology, Am. Biophys. Soc. Home: 5355 Henry Hudson Pkwy Bronx NY 10471 Office: Columbia U Coll Physicians and Surgeons Dept Biochemistry 630 W 168th St New York NY 10471

BENET, THOMAS CARR, newspaperman; b. Paris, France, Sept. 28, 1926; s. Stephen Vincent and Rosemary (Carr) B.; m. Joan Gregory, Aug. 27, 1952; children: Rebecca Benet Sawyer, Alice. B.A., Yale U., 1949. Reporter San Francisco Chronicle, 1950-60, asst. city editor, 1968-78, editorial writer, 1978—. Served with AUS, 1945-47. Recipient Christophers award Christophrs Orgn., 1954. Mem. San Francisco Com. on Fgn. Relations. Office: San Francisco Chronicle 901 Mission St San Francisco CA 94119

BENETAR, DAVID L., lawyer; b. N.Y.C., Nov. 19, 1906; s. Morris and Estella B.; m. Beatrice Dalsimer, June 26, 1934; children: Carol Ann, Richard D. Student, N.Y. U., 1923-25, postgrad. law, 1928-29; LL.B., Bklyn. Law Sch., 1928. Bar: N.Y. 1929. Since practiced in, N.Y.C.; mem. firm Nordlinger, Riegelman, Benetar & Charney, 1933-70; prin. mediation officer, dir. disputes div. 22d region, mem. pub. panel U.S. War Labor Bd., Washington and N.Y.C., 1942-45; mem. firm Aranow, Brodsky, Bohlinger, Benetar & Einhorn, N.Y.C., 1971-78, Benetar Isaacs Bernstein & Schair, 1979—; Mem. Gov.'s Labor-Mgmt. Adv. Panel Mediation Bd. N.Y., 1969-79. Bd. dirs. Econ. Devel. Council N.Y.C., Inc., 1968-79; chmn. bd. edn. Mt. Pleasant Dist. Schs., Hawthorne, N.Y., 1950-56; pres. Jewish Bd. Guardians, 1956-60, chmn. exec. com., 1960-78, hon. pres., 1980—; trustee Fedn. Jewish Philanthropies N.Y., 1956—. Mem. ABA (mem. labor law sect. 1965—), Fed. Bar Assn. (chmn. labor com. Empire State chpt. 1971-77, chpt. pres. 1977-79), N.Y. State Bar Assn. (chmn. com. labor law 1959-63, chmn. task force practices and procedures state human rights div. 1977—), Assn. Bar City N.Y. (mem. exec. com. 1957-60), N.Y. Chamber Commerce and Industry (mem. exec. com. 1958-74, dir. 1974-79), U.S. C. of C. (mem. labor relations com. 1965-69), Edward Corsi Labor-Mgmt. Relations Inst. Pace Univ. (chmn. exec. com. 1969—). Club: Cornell. Home: 35 Sutton Pl New York NY 10022 Office: 950 3d Ave New York NY 10022

BENEVENTANO, THOMAS CARMINE, radiologist; b. Maspeth, N.Y., Mar. 20, 1932; s. Joseph Anthony and Mildred Carmela (Citera) B.; m. Marilyn Louise Rarrick, June 15, 1957; 1 son, Thomas Martin. A.B., N.Y. U., 1953; M.D., SUNY, 1957. Diplomate: Am. Bd. Radiology. Intern Kings County Hosp., Bklyn., 1957-58, resident in radiology, 1960-63; radiologist Montefiore Hosp. and Med. Center, Bronx, N.Y., 1963—; prof. radiology Albert Einstein Coll. Medicine, 1978—. Co-author: Radiologic Examination of the Orohypopharynx and Esophagus, 1977. Served to capt. M.C. U.S. Army, 1958-60. Fellow Am. Coll. Radiology, N.Y. Acad. Gastroenterology, N.Y. Acad. Medicine; mem. Radiol. Soc. N.Am., Am. Roentgen Ray Soc., N.Y. Roentgen Soc. (pres. 1980-81), AMA, N.Y. Med. Soc., Bronx County Med. Soc., Soc. Gastrointestinal Radiologists, Assn. Univ Radiologists. Address: 6 Eastwind Rd Yonkers NY 10710 *Equal parts of ability, applied knowledge, serendipity and good fortune have helped me to achieve some degree of success. A continued desire to help others* *coupled with an innate need to be a friend has shaped the course of my professional career and thus my life. A deep sense of personal satisfaction and an understanding, supportive wife have permitted this philosophy to continue.*

BENEZET, LOUIS TOMLINSON, educator; b. La Crosse, Wis., June 29, 1915; s. Louis Paul and Genevieve (Tomlinson) B.; m. Mildred Jean Twohy, 1940 (dec. 1977); children: Joel (dec.), Laura (Mrs. John Remington), Julia, Barbara, Martha. A.B., Dartmouth, 1936, LL.D., 1966; A.M., Reed Coll., 1939; Ph.D., Columbia, 1942; LL.D., Mt. Union Coll., U. Pitts., Waynesburg Coll., U. Denver, Knox Coll., Loyola U., Chgo., Colo. Coll., U. Colo., U. Calif.; L.H.D., Westminister Coll., Hebrew Union Coll. Instr. The Hill Sch., 1936-38; asso. psychology resident adviser Reed Coll., 1938-40; fellow in psychology Coll. City N.Y., 1941-42; asso. prof. psychology, asst. dir. admissions Knox Coll., 1942-43; asst. dean Univ. Coll., Syracuse U., 1946-47, asst. to chancellor, 1947-48; pres. Allegheny Coll., 1948-55, Colo. Coll., 1955-63, Claremont (Calif.) Grad. Sch. and U. Center, 1963-70, State U. N.Y. at Albany, 1970-75; research prof. human devel. and ednl. policy State U. N.Y., Stony Brook, 1975—; pres. Pa. Assn. of Colls. and Univs., 1951-52; chmn. Ind. Coll. Funds of Am., 1961-62, Rhodes scholar selection com., Calif., Colo., N.Y., 1958-74; spl. cons. Conn. Conf. Ind. Colls., 1980; Mem. Com. on Edn. of Women, 1953-56; adv. com. Vets. Rehab., Edn., VA, Washington, 1955-59; spl. cons. HEW, 1959-60; chmn. univ. relations com. AID, 1966-67; mem. instnl. relations com. NSF, 1967-70, chmn., 1969-70; mem. Calif. Gov.'s Commn. on Tax Reform, 1969, Commrs. Adv. Council on Higher Edn. in N.Y. (State), 1971-75, N.Y. Gov.'s Task Force on Financing Higher Edn., 1972-73, Stony Brook Found., 1977—. Author: General Education in the Progressive College, 1943, Private Higher Education and Public Funding, 1976, College Organization and Student Impact, 1976, Prospects for the Middle Level Liberal Arts, College, 1979, Style and Substance: Leadership in the College Presidency, 1981; editor: Building Bridges to the Public, 1979; contbr. monographs, articles, seminars on coll. orgn., human devel. in coll. Trustee Adelphi U., 1979-83, Aspen Inst. Humanistic Studies, 1956-68. Served as ednl. services officer USNR, 1943-46; edn. officer, 7th Fleet, 1944-45; S.W. Pacific. Mem. Western Coll. Assn. (pres. 1969-70), Assn. Am. Colls. (chmn. commn. acad. freedom and tenure 1955-58, commn. liberal edn. 1959-63), Assn. Colls. Colo. (pres. 1959-60), Am. Council on Edn. (mem. exec. com. 1955-58, bd. dirs. 1961-64, chmn. 1965-66), Phi Beta Kappa. Office: State Univ New York Stony Brook NY 11794

BENFEY, OTTO THEODOR, chemist, writer, historian of science; b. Berlin, Oct. 31, 1925; U.S., 1946, naturalized, 1952; s. Eduard and Lotte (Fleischmann) B.; m. Rachel Elizabeth Thomas, Aug. 28, 1949; children: Stephen, Philip, Christopher. B.Sc., Univ. Coll., London, 1945, Ph.D., 1947. Postdoctoral research fellow Columbia U., 1947-48; from instr. to asso. prof. Haverford Coll., 1948-55; research fellow Harvard U., 1955-56; from asso. prof. to prof. chemistry and history of sci. Earlham Coll., Richmond, Ind., 1956-73; Dana prof. chemistry and history of sci. Guilford Coll., Greensboro, N.C., 1973—, clk. faculty, 1977-79; lectr., cons. in field; U.S. del. Inter-Am. Conf. Chemistry Teaching, Buenos Aires, 1965, U.S.-Japan Chem. Edn. Conf., Berkeley, Calif., 1968, Mpls., 1981, Internat. Symposium Chem. Edn., Sao Paulo, Brazil, 1971; vis. scholar Tokyo U. Author: From Vital Force to Structural Formulas, 1964, Classics in the Theory of Chemical Combination, 1963, The Names and Structures of Organic Compounds, 1966 (also Portuguese transl), Introduction to Organic Reaction Mechanisms, 1971 (also German and Japanese trans.'s), From Intellectual Scaffolding to the Elixir of Life, 1978 (also Japanese translation), Friends and the World of Nature, 1981; also articles, intros. and chpts. books; translator: (Ernst Cassirer): Determinism and Indeterminism in Modern Physics, 1956; editor: Chemistry, 1963-78; editorial bd.: Revista Iberoamericana de Educacion Quimica, 1966-78, Current Contents/Phys. Scis, 1974—. Del. Soc. Friends World Conf., Oxford, Eng., 1952 Del. Soc. Friends World Conf., Guilford, N.C., 1967; pres. Soc. Social Responsibility in Sci., 1951-53. Recipient Doan Distinguished Tchr. Travel award Earlham Coll., 1961; E. Harris Harbison award distinguished teaching Danforth Found., 1967; Chemistry Tchr. award Mfg. Chemists Assn., 1967; Fulbright-Hays research-study award Kwansei Gakuin, Japan, 1970-71. Mem. AAUP, History of Sci. Soc., ACLU, Assn. Harvard Chemists, Assn. Asian Studies, Am. Chem. Soc. (chmn. div. history of chemistry 1966, mem. exec. com. div. chem. edn. 1979—, coordinator chem. edn. program Hawaii Chem. Congress of Pacific Basin 1984, task force on future of chem. edn. 1982-84), Sigma Xi. Home: 801 Woodbrook Dr Greensboro NC 27410

BENFIELD, JOHN RICHARD, surgeon; b. Vienna, Austria, June 24, 1931; came to U.S., 1938, naturalized, 1945; s. Richard and Charlotte Lola (Glatter) B.; m. Joyce A. Cohler, Dec. 22, 1963; children: Richard L., Robert E., Nancy J. A.B., Columbia U., 1952; M.D., U. Chgo., 1955. Intern Columbia-Presbyterian Hosp., N.Y.C., 1955-56; E.H. Andrews fellow in thoracic surgery U. Chgo., 1956-57; chief resident and instr. in surgery U. Chgo. Clinics, 1963-64, resident in surgery, 1956-57, 59-63; asst. prof. surgery U. Wis., 1964-67; asst. prof. UCLA, 1967-69, assoc. prof., 1969-72, prof., 1972-76, clin. prof., 1978—; James Utley prof. surgery, chmn. dept. surgery Boston U., 1977; chmn. surgery City of Hope Nat. Med. Ctr., Duarte, Calif., 1978—; cons. U.S. Naval Med. Ctr., San Diego, 1968—; mem. sr. staff VA Wadsworth Med. Ctr., Los Angeles, 1978—; bd. dirs. Am. Bd. Thoracic Surgery, 1982—. Contbr. numerous articles, chpt. to profl. publs.; editor: Current Problems in Cancer, 1975—; editorial bd.: Annals of Thoracic Surgery, 1979—. Sec., trustee Univ. Synagogue, Los Angeles. Served as capt. M.C. U.S. Army, 1957-59; Korea. Recipient Christopher award Chgo. Surg. Soc., 1958; grantee Life Ins. Med. Research, 1962-66, Am. Heart Assn., 1968-71; USPHS, 1971—. Mem. Am. Surg. Assn., Am. Assn. Thoracic Surgery, Soc. Thoracic Surgeons, Soc. Univ. Surgeons, Pacific Coast Surg. Assn., Soc. Surg. Oncology, Am. Coll. Chest Physicians, ACS (bd. govs. 1982—), Internat. Surg. Soc. Club: Pasadena Athletic. Office: City of Hope Nat Med Center Duarte CA 91010

BENFIELD, MARION WILSON, JR., lawyer, educator; b. Belwood, N.C., July 26, 1932; s. Marion Wilson and Gazzie Cleo (Martin) B.; m. Dalida Quijada, Feb. 21, 1964; children: Marion, Steve, Robin, Rosalina, Christopher, Jeanette, Antonio, Maria. A.A., Gardner-Webb Coll., Boiling Springs, N.C., 1951; A.B. in English, U. N.C., 1953; LL.B., Wake Forest U., 1959; LL.M., U. Mich., 1965. Bar: N.C. 1959. Asst. dir. Inst. Govt. U. N.C., 1959-61; individual practice law, Hickory, N.C., 1961-63; asst. prof. law U. Ga., 1963-65; asso. prof. Case Western Reserve U., 1965-66, U. Ill., 1966-68, prof., 1968—, asso. dean, 1980—; vis. prof. U. Houston, 1976-77, Duke U., 1979, NYU, 1984; mem. Nat. Conf. of Commrs. on Uniform State Laws, 1973—. Reporter, draftsman: The Uniform Land Transactions Act and Uniform Simplification of Land Transfers Act, 1970-77; Author: Social Justice through Law-New Approaches in the Law of Contracts, 1970, (with W.H. Hawkland) Cases and Materials on Sales, 1979; Mem. editorial bd.: Uniform Commercial Code, 1974—, Uniform Land Transactions Act and Uniform Simplification of Land Transactions Act, 1982—. Served with U.S. Army, 1954-56. Mem. Am. Law Inst., Am. Bar Assn. Home: 706 Brighton Dr Urbana IL 61801 Office: College of Law University of Illinois Champaign IL 61820

BENFIELD, WILLIAM AVERY, JR., clergyman; b. Greenville, W.Va., July 5, 1915; s. William Avery and Mamie Etta (Bonds) B.; m. Eunice Byrnside, Aug. 31, 1938; children—William Avery III, Robert Byrnside, John Milne. A.B., Davidson Coll., 1936, D.D., 1949; B.D., Louisville Presbyn. Theol. Sem., 1939, Th.M., 1940; Th.D., So. Bapt. Sem., 1943; D.D., Morris Harvey Coll., 1970; L.H.D., Davis and Elkins Coll., 1979. Ordained to ministry Presbyn. Ch., 1939; pastor Beechmont Presbyn. Ch., Louisville, 1940; prof. Hebrew and old testament Louisville Presbyn. Theol. Sem., 1940-44, v.p., 1945-49; sr. minister Highland Presbyn. Ch., Louisville, 1949-58, First Presbyn. Ch., Shreveport, La., 1958-63, Charleston, W.Va., 1963-80; adj. prof. theology U. Charleston, 1980; Moderator Gen. Assembly Presbyn. Ch. U.S., 1970—; chmn. gen. council, chmn. bd. annuities and relief; mem. exec. com. Consultation on Ch. Union. Co-author: Understanding the Books of the Old Testament, 1944, The Church Faces the Isms, 1958. Trustee Davis and Elkins Coll., Centre Coll., Southwestern at Memphis, Austin Presbyn. Theol. Sem., Louisville Presbyn. Theol. Sem., Union Theol. Sem. Mem. Beta Theta Phi. Democrat. Presbyn. Clubs: Rotarian., Juniper Hunting and Fishing (Astor, Fla.); Southern Cross Fishing (Little Cayman, B.W.I.). Home: 1348 Morningside Dr Charleston WV 25314

BENFORADO, DAVID M., environmental engineer; b. N.Y.C., Nov. 17, 1925; s. Mark Joseph and Mathilde (Abraham) B.; m. Ruth Ann Martin, May 5, 1950; children: Mark Andrew, Marcia Ann, David Dean. B.S. in Chem. Engring., Columbia, 1948; student, CCNY, 1942-44. Registered profl. engr., N.Y. Engr., Skelly Oil Co., Eldorado, Kans., 1948-53; applied research engr. Walter Kidde Nuclear Labs., Garden City, N.Y., 1953-56; heat transfer specialist Trane Co., La Crosse, Wis., 1956-61; mgr. application engring. Penn Brass & Copper, Erie, Pa., 1961-65; product mgr. air pollution control equipment Air Preheater Co., Wellsville, N.Y., 1965-69; sr. environ. engring. specialist 3M Co., St. Paul, 1969—; cons. control odorous indsl. emissions Environ. Research & Applications, Inc., Wilton, Conn., 1969—, also fed. govt.; mem. com. odors from stationary and mobile sources NRC, 1978. Active Boy Scouts Am. Mem. Air Pollution Control Assn. (dir. 1968—, pres. 1972-73, hon. mem. 1981—), Am. Inst. Chem. Engrs., Indsl. Gas Cleaning Inst., Am. Acad. Environ. Engrs. (diplomate, trustee 1981—). Clubs: Woodbury Lions (sec. 1970, dir. 1971—), Woodbury Lions (pres. 1978). Home: 7100 Glenross Rd Woodbury MN 55125 Office: 3M Co 900 Bush Ave Saint Paul MN 55101

BENFORD, GREGORY ALBERT, physicist, author; b. Mobile, Jan. 30, 1941; s. James Alton and Mary Eloise (Nelson) B.; m. Joan Abbe, Aug. 26, 1967; children: Alyson Rhandra, Mark Gregory. B.S., U. Okla., 1963; M.S., U. Calif., San Diego, 1965, Ph.D., 1967. Research asst. U. Calif., San Diego, 1964-67; postdoctoral fellow Lawrence (Calif.) Radiation Lab., 1967-69, research physicist, 1969-71; prof. physics U. Calif., Irvine, 1971—; cons. in field. Author: novels Deeper than the Darkness, 1970, Jupiter Project, 1975, If the Stars are Gods, 1977, In the Ocean of Night, 1977, The Stars in Shroud, 1978, Find the Changeling, 1980, Timescape, 1980, Against Infinity, 1983, Across the Sea of Suns, 1984; also research papers on plasma physics, astrophysics, solid state physics. Woodrow Wilson fellow, 1963-64; grantee Office Naval Research, 1975—, NSF, 1972-76, Army Research Orgn., 1977-82, Air Force Office Sci. Research, 1982—; recipient Brit. Sci. Fiction award, 1981; Australian Ditmar award for internat. novel, 1981; John W. Campbell award for best novel, 1981. Mem. Am. Phys. Soc., Royal Astron. Soc., Sci. Fiction Writers Am. (Nebula award 1975, 81). Home: 1105 Skyline Dr Laguna Beach CA 92651 Office: Physics Dept U Calif Irvine CA 92717

BENFORD, HARRY BELL, naval architect; b. Schenectady, Aug. 7, 1917; s. Frank Albert and Georgia (Rattray) B.; m. Edith Elizabeth Smallman, Apr. 26, 1941; children—Howard Lee, Frank Alfred, Robert James. B.S.E. in Naval Architecture and Marine Engring, U. Mich., 1940. With Newport News Shipbldg. Co., Va., 1940-48; mem. faculty U. Mich., Ann Arbor, 1948-59, 60—, prof. naval architecture, 1959—, chmn. dept. naval architecture and marine engring., 1967-72; exec. dir. maritime research adv. com. NRC, 1959-60. Author 2 books, numerous tech. papers. Fellow Soc. Naval Architects and Marine Engrs. (hon. mem., President's award 1957, Linnard prize 1962, Taylor medal 1976), Royal Instn. Naval Architects; mem. Soc. Engring. Edn., Am. Assn. Cost Engrs., Tau Beta Pi, Phi Kappa Phi. Home: 1710 Shadford Rd Ann Arbor MI 48104 Office: Dept Naval Architecture Ann Arbor MI 48109

BENGLIS, LYNDA, artist, sculptor; b. Lake Charles, La., Oct. 25, 1941; d. Michael A. and Leah Margaret (Blackwelder) B. B.F.A., Sophie Newcomb Coll., 1964. Asst. prof. sculpture U. Rochester, 1970-72; vis. artist Yale-Norfolk, summer 1972; prof. Hunter Coll., 1972-73; vis. artist Calif. Inst. Arts, 1974, 76, Kent State U., 1977, Skowhegan Sch. Painting Sculpture, 1979; vis. prof. Princeton, 1975; asst. prof. Hunter Coll., 1980, prof., 1981, U. Ariz., Tucson, 1981. One-woman shows include, U. R.I., 1969, Paula Cooper Gallery, N.Y.C., 1970, 71, 74, 75, 76, 77, 78, 80, 82, 84, Hayden Gallery, Cambridge, Mass., 1971, Kans. State U., Fuller-Goldeen Gallery, 1972, 73, 74, 77, 79, 82, Portland Center Visual Arts, 1972, 80, Jack Glen Gallery, Corona Del Mar, Calif., 1972, The Clocktower, N.Y.C., 1973, The Tex. Gallery, Houston, 1974, 75, 77, 79, 80, 81, Margo Leavin Gallery, Los Angeles, 1977, 80, 83, Dart Gallery, Chgo., 1979, 81, 82, 83, Real Art Ways, New Haven, 1979, Ga. State U., Atlanta, Galerie Albert Baronian, Belgium, 1979, 81, U. South Fla., Tampa, 1980, Lowe Art Mus., Tampa, David Heath Gallery, Atlanta, Chatham Coll., Pitts., Susanne Hilberry Gallery, Birmingham, Mich., 1980, 83, U. Ariz., 1981, group shows include, Bykert Gallery, N.Y.C., 1969, Detroit Inst. Arts, Milw. Art Center, 1971, Walker Art Center, Mpls., 1971, 81, Balt. Mus. Art, 1975, Mus. Contemporary Art, Chgo., 1977, 80, Stedelijk Mus., Amsterdam, 1978, Mus. Modern Art, N.Y.C., 1979, Palazzo Reale, Milan Italy, Guggenheim Mus., N.Y.C., Contemporary Arts Mus., Houston, 1980, San Diego Mus. Art, Whitney Mus., N.Y.C., 1981; represented in permanent collections, Mus. Modern Art, N.Y.C., Guggenheim Mus., Whitney Mus., Walker Art Center; Olympic Com. artist, 1983. Yale-Norfolk scholar, 1963; Max Beckman scholar, 1965; Guggenheim fellow, 1975; Artpark grantee, 1976; Nat. Endowment for Arts grantee, 1979; recipient Australian Art Council award, 1976.

BENGSTON, CLARENCE WILLIAM, wholesale corp. exec.; b. Kirkland, Wash., Dec. 22, 1921; s. Claes J. and Anna M. (Berglin) B.; m. Martha E. Hahn, May 29, 1948; children—Steven W., Robert A. B.A., U. Wash., 1944, postgrad., 1946-47. C.P.A., Wash. Mgr. Peat Marwick, Mitchell & Co., Seattle, 1947-59; treas. Centennial Mills, Portland, Oreg., 1959-70, Univar Corp., Seattle, 1970—. Troop treas. Boy Scouts, 1967-70; chmn. local sch. com., 1965-67. Served to capt., Q.M. AUS, 1943-46. Mem. Am. Inst. C.P.A.'s, Wash. Soc. C.P.A.'s, Nat. Assn. Accountants, Beta Alpha Psi, Tau Kappa Epsilon. Presbyn. (deacon 1967-69). Club: Harbor (Seattle). Home: 6511-82d Ave SE Mercer Island WA 98040 Office: 1600 Norton Bldg Seattle WA 98104

BENHAM, DAVID BLAIR, civil engineer; b. Ft. Riley, Kans., Nov. 11, 1918; s. Webster Lance and Margaret Lemon (Drake) B.; m. Betty Louise Prichard, June 29, 1950; children: Barbara Lee, Zan, Nancy Ann, David Blair. Student, Oklahoma City U., 1936-37; B.S., 1941; cert. naval architecture, U.S. Naval Acad., 1942. Registered profl. engr., 25 states. Jr. engr. Benham Engring. Co., Oklahoma City, 1946, design engr., jr. ptnr., 1947-52, sr. and mng. ptnr., 1952-64, Benham-Blair-Poppino-Stealy, 1967-74; pres., chmn. bd, chief exec. officer Benham-Blair & Affiliates, Inc., Oklahoma City, 1967-74, chmn. bd., chief exec. officer, 1974-81, The Benham Group, Inc., 1981—; dir. Acad. Computing Corp. Contbr. articles to profl. jours. Ruling elder, trustee Westminster Presbyterian Ch.; mem. Com. of 100 Greater Oklahoma City; trustee U.S. Naval Acad. Found.; mem. nat. adv. bd., chemn. adv. bd. Salvation Army, Okla. and Ark., 1978-79; vice-chmn. Okla. Mental Health Bd., 1958-59; chmn.bd. Okla. Bd. Registration Profl. Engrs., 1964; bd. visitors Cill. Engring., U. of Okla., Okla. State U. Served to lt. comdr. USN, 1941-46. Recipient cert. of qualification Nat. Bur. Engring. Registration, 1956; inducted Engring. Hall of Fame Coll. Engring., Okla. State U., 1973. Diplomate Am. Acad. Environ. Engrs.; fellow Am. Cons. Engrs. Council, ASCE (life mem., past pres. Okla. sect.), Soc. Am. Mil. Engrs. (nat. dir. 1977-79, Outstanding Service award 1961); mem. Nat. Soc. Profl. Engrs., Okla. Soc. Profl. Engrs., Am. Soc. Cons. Planners (life), Am. Water Works Assn., Frontiers of Sci. Found. (Okla. past pres.), Okla. State C. of C. (dir.), Okla. City C. of C. (dir.), Mil. Order World Wars (comdr. Oklahoma City 1979), U.S. Naval Acad. Alumni Assn. (nat. pres. 1975-77), Navy League U.S., Newcomen Soc. N. Am. (honoree 1979). Democrat. Clubs: Queensbury, Economic, Men's Dinner, Oklahoma City Golf and Country, Whitehall, Beacon, Embassy (past pres.), Order of Red, Red Rose. Lodges: Masons (32 deg.); Shriners; Jesters. Home: 6621 Hillcrest N Oklahoma City OK 73116 Office: PO Box 20400 9400 N Broadway Oklahoma City OK 73156

BENHAM, JAMES MASON, mut. fund exec.; b. Joliet, Ill., Nov. 24, 1935; s. Charles Orville and Helen Florence (Mason) B.; m. Maribeth Ann Naughton, Sept. 27, 1962; children—James Anthony, William Charles, Timothy Joseph. B.A., Mich. State U., 1959, M.A., 1961. Asst. bank examiner Fed. Res. Bank San Francisco, 1961-63; account exec. Merrill Lynch, Pierce, Fenner & Smith, San Jose, Calif., 1963-71; pres., chmn. bd. Capital Preservation Fund, Inc., Palo Alto, Calif., 1974-78, chmn. bd., 1978—; lectr. in field. Mem. No. Load Mut. Fund Assn. (gov. 1974—). Address: Capital Preservation Fund Inc 755 Page Mill Rd Palo Alto CA 94304

BENHAM, JOHN FITZHUGH, engineering company executive; b. Kansas City, Mo., Aug. 16, 1921; s. Webster and Margaret (Drake) B.; m. Helen Louise Soper, Aug. 4, 1951. B.S., U. Okla., 1946. Salesman Crane Co., Oklahoma City, 1947-53, sales mgr., 1953-56; adminstrv. asst. Benham Group, Oklahoma City, 1956-67, v.p., 1967-81, dir., 1967—, pres., 1981—. Served with USMCR, 1943-46; PTO. Recipient Post Sec.-Treas. award Soc. Am. Mil. Engrs., Oklahoma City, 1982. Mem. Am. Pub. Works Assn., ASCE (affiliate). Republican. Presbyterian. Clubs: Downtown Optimist (Oklahoma City) (pres. 1964-65); (Disting. pres. award 1965). Home: 3601 N W 66th St Oklahoma City OK 93166 Office: Benham Group 9400 N Broadway PO Box 20400 Oklahoma City OK 93156

BENI, JOHN JOSEPH, publisher; b. Mt. Kisco, N.Y., Feb. 26, 1932; s. John and Carmela (Vasta) B.; m. Joan Raymaster, Oct. 17, 1957; children: Bruce, Brian, Holly, Craig. B.A., Yale U., 1955. With advt. sales Am. Weekly, Hearst Advt. Service, 1955-62, Farm Jour. Co., 1962-64; advt. sales Redbook Mag., N.Y.C., after 1964, then mgr. advt. v.p. advt., v.p., pub., to 1978; pres., chief operating officer Parents' Mag. Enterprises div. Gruner & Jahr USA, N.Y.C., 1978—, dir. parent co., 1979—; pres., chief operating officer Gruner & Jahr USA/Pub. Mem. Mag. Pubs. Assn. (dir. 1981—, chmn. mktg. com.), Hackley Alumni Assn., Yale Alumni Assn. Episcopalian (vestryman). Club: Yale of N.Y.C. Home: PO Box 7232 Ardsley-on-Hudson NY 10503 Office: Parents' Magazine 685 3d Ave New York NY 10017

BENIDICKSON, AGNES, university chancellor. Chancellor Queen's U. at Kingston, ON, Can. Office: Queen's U at Kingston Kingston ON Canada K7L 3N6

BENIDICKSON, WILLIAM MOORE, Canadian senator; b. Dauphin, Man., Can., Apr. 8, 1911; s. Christian and Gertrude (Moore) B.; m. Agnes Richardson, 1947; children—William James, Kristjan, Kathleen. B.A., U. Man., 1932, LL.B., 1936. Mem. Canadian House of Commons from Kenora-Rainy River Dist., 1945-65; parliamentary asst. to minister transp., 1951, to minister finance, 1953-57; mem. Privy Council (minister mines and tech. surveys), Canadian Senate, 1965—. Decorated knight Order Falcon, Iceland). Office: Canadian Senate Room 248-N Ottawa ON Canada K1A OA4

BENINCASA, PIUS A., bishop; b. Niagara Falls, N.Y., July 8, 1913. Grad., Buffalo Diocesan Sem., 1931, Propagation U., Lateran U., Rome, Italy, D.C.L., 1952. Ordained priest Roman Catholic Ch., 1937; parish work, Buffalo, 1937-43; sec. Buffalo Diocesan Tribunal, 1947-50, vice-officialis, 1952-54; served with Papal sec. of state, 1955-64; titular bishop of, Buruni and, aux. bishop, Buffalo, 1964—. Chaplain AUS, World War II. Address: 157 Cleveland Dr Buffalo NY 14215

BENIRSCHKE, KURT, pathologist, educator; b. Glueckstadt, Germany, May 26, 1924; came to U.S., 1949, naturalized, 1955; s. Fritz Franz and Marie (Luebcke) B.; m. Marion Elizabeth Waldhausen, May 17, 1952; children: Stephen Kurt, Rolf Joachim, Ingrid Marie. Student, U. Hamburg, Germany, 1942, 45-48, U. Berlin, Germany, 1943, U. Wuerzburg, Germany, 1943-44; M.D., U. Hamburg, 1948. Resident, Teaneck, N.J., 1950-51, Peter Bent Brigham Hosp., Boston, 1951-52, Boston Lying-in-Hosp., 1952-53, Free Hosp. for Women, Boston, 1953, Children's Hosp., 1953; pathologist Boston Lying-in-Hosp., 1955-60; teaching fellow, asso. Med. Sch. Harvard, 1954-60; prof. pathology, chmn. dept. pathology Med. Sch. Dartmouth, Hanover, N.H., 1960-70; prof. reproductive medicine and pathology U. Calif. at San Diego, 1970—, chmn. dept. pathology, La Jolla, 1976-79; dir. research San Diego Zoo, 1975—; cons. NIH, 1957-70. Served with German Army, 1942-45. Mem. Am. Soc. Pathology, Internat. Acad. Pathology, Am. Coll. Pathology, Teratol. Soc., Am. Soc. Zool. Veterinarians. Home: 8457 Prestwick Dr LaJolla CA 92037 Office: U Calif at San Diego San Diego CA 92110

BENITEZ, MARIO ANTONIO, educator; b. Havana, Cuba, May 4, 1926; s. Jose A. and Ernestina A. (Alamo) B.; m. Carolyn McRee, Sept. 27, 1980; children—Anthony R., Kenneth D., Lydia E., Victoria L. Licenciado en Filosofia, Universidad Pontificia de Comillas, 1951; M.A., Tex. Christian U., 1959; Doctor en Filosofia y Letras, U. Havana, 1960; M.Ed., Tex. Wesleyan Coll., 1962; Ph.D., Claremont Grad. Sch., 1967. Asso. prof. philosophy Tex. Wesleyan Coll., Ft. Worth, 1955-62; tchr. Latin, coordinator fgn. langs. West Covina Unified Sch. Dist., 1962-66; chmn. dept. modern langs. Tex. A. and I. U., Kingsville, 1966-70, v.p. acad. affairs, 1971-76; dir. Bilingual Edn. Center, 1976—; dir. div. bicultural-bilingual studies U. Tex., San Antonio, 1980-83; assoc. prof. curriculum and instrn. U. Tex.-, Austin, 1970-71, prof. curriculum and instrn., 1983—; cons. U.S. Office Edn., Tex. Edn. Agy. Author: La poesia mistica de San Juan de la Cruz, 1960, The Education of the Mexican American: A Selected Bibliography, 1979, Bilingual Education and the Law, 1979. Bd. dirs. Tex. A. and I. U. Credit Union, 1967-69. Mem. Southwestern Philosophy of Edn. Soc. (sec. 1971-73, pres. 1973-74), Modern Lang. Assn., Am. Assn. Tchrs. Spanish and Portuguese, Am. Council for Teaching Fgn. Langs. Club: Rotarian. Office: U Tex Austin TX

BENJAMIN, A. JOE, foods company executive; b. Wilmington, Del., May 12, 1945; s. Park D. and Isabelle (Plato) B.; m. Karen J. Kordt, June 17, 1967; children: Amber Wyn, Nils Reed, Tori Lind. B.S., U.

Del., 1967. With Price Waterhouse & Co., Phila., 1967-69; asst. v.p. fin. Drexel Firestone, Inc., Phila., 1969-74; with Keystone Foods Corp., Bryn Mawr, Pa., 1974—, sr. v.p. fin. and corp. devel., 1980—, also dir. Office: 931 Haverford Rd Bryn Mawr PA 19010

BENJAMIN, ALBERT, III, retired oil company executive, naval officer; b. Dorchester, Mass., June 14, 1904; s. Albert and Etta Melissa (Wolcott) B.; m. Alice Moorhead Jackson, May 25, 1929; 1 son, Albert Jackson. B.S., U.S. Naval Acad., 1926. Commd. ensign U.S. Navy, 1926, advanced through grades to capt., 1943; sr. mil. mem. Army-Navy Mission to Uruguay, 1944; sr. mem. Dept. State-Army-Navy Mission to Argentina, 1945; naval attache, also naval attache for air Am. embassy, Montevideo, Uruguay, 1941-45; asso. editor Am. mag., 1931-41, advt. dir., 1947-51; dir. pub. relations, exec. asst. to exec. v.p. Publ. Corp., N.Y.C., 1951-52; exec. asst. to exec. v.p. newspaper relations This Week mag., N.Y.C., 1952-54, mgr. gen. mktg. div., 1954-56, mgr. sales devel., 1956-59; mgr. Latin Am. div. employee and pub. relations Texaco Inc., N.Y.C., 1959-60, dir. pub. relations worldwide, 1960-69; mem. pub. info. adv. com. U.S. Navy; mem. nat. adv. bd. Am. Security Council. Contbr. to popular mags. Decorated Legion of Merit; recipient Disting. Service medal N.Y. State. Mem. Pub. Relations Soc. Am., U.S. Naval Inst., Navy League, SAR, English Speaking Union, U.S. Naval Acad. Alumni Assn. (mem. info. and recruitment com.), Mil. Order World Wars, Ret. Officers Assn., Assn. Former Intelligence Officers, Nat. Parks and Conservation Assn. Episcopalian. Clubs: Dutch Treat (N.Y.C.); Chevy Chase (Md.); Farmington (Va.); Ponte Vedra (Fla.). Home: 40 Old Farm Rd Bellair Charlottesville VA 22901

BENJAMIN, BURTON RICHARD, TV producer-writer; b. Cleve., Oct. 9, 1917; s. Sam and Ruth (Bernstein) B.; m. Aline L. Wolff, Apr. 5, 1942; children: Ann Norma, Jane Ruth. A.B., U. Mich., 1939. Newspaperman with U.P. and NEA Service, Cleve. and N.Y.C., 1939-42, NEA Service, N.Y.C., 1945-46; writer, producer documentary films RKO-Pathe, N.Y.C., 1946-55; exec. producer series Twentieth Century CBS News, 1957, exec. producer World War I, 1957, exec. producer series The 21st Century, 1967, sr. exec. producer, N.Y.C., 1968-75, exec. producer Evening News, 1975-78; v.p. and dir. news CBS, 1978-81, sr. exec. producer, 1981—; writer dramatic and documentary scripts for network TV, 1955—; Lectr. polit. sci. Manhattanville Coll., Purchase, N.Y.; Howard R. Marsh vis. prof. journalism U. Mich., 1976. Trustee Scarborough Sch. Served to lt. USCGR, 1942-45. Recipient Peabody, Overseas Press Club, Emmy, Ohio State U. awards for Twentieth Century series; Co-winner 1st prize Fund for Republic for documentary script Pepito, 1955; Certificate achievement sec. army, 1962; meritorious pub. service citation sec. navy, 1963; meritorious service certificate sec. air force, 1966; Recipient Emmy and Lasker awards for 21st Century, 1968-69, Emmy, Ohio State and Am. Bar Assn. awards for CBS News Spl., Justice Black and the Bill of Rights Aftermath, Martin Luther King Assassination, 1968, Emmy award for Justice in Am., 1972, Emmy awards for CBS reports The Rockefellers, Solzhenitsyn, 1974. Mem. Writers Guild Am. Club: Century Assn. Home: Holbrook Rd Scarborough NY 10510 Office: CBS News 524 W 57th St New York NY 10019

BENJAMIN, EDWARD BERNARD, JR., lawyer; b. New Orleans, Feb. 11, 1923; s. Edward Bernard and Blanche (Sternberger) B.; m. Adelaide Wisdom, May 11, 1957; children: Edward Wisdom, Mary Dabney, Ann Leith, Stuart Minor. B.S., Yale U., 1944; J.D., Tulane U., 1952. Bar: La. 1952. Since practiced in, New Orleans; partner firm Jones, Walker, Waechter, Poitevent, Carrere & Denegre; chmn. bd. Starmount Co., Greensboro, N.C.; mem. adv. bd. CCH Estate and Fin. Planning Service. Editor-in-chief: Tulane Law Rev, 1951-52. Trustee Hollins Coll., 1965—; vice chmn. bd. trustees Southwestern Legal Found., 1980—; pres. Internat. Acad. Estate and Trust Law, 1976-78; vestryman, chancellor Trinity Episcopal Ch., New Orleans. Served to 1st lt. U.S. Army, 1943-46. Mem. ABA (taxation sect. sec. 1967-68, council 1976-79, real property, probate and trust law sect. council 1978-81), La. Bar Assn. (chmn. sect. taxation 1959-60), New Orleans Bar Assn., Am. Law Inst., La. Law Inst., Am. Coll. Probate Counsel (bd. regents 1980—, sec. 1983-84, v.p. 1984-85), Am. Coll. Tax Counsel. Clubs: New Orleans Country, Greensboro Country, So. Yacht, New Orleans Lawn Tennis, Petroleum. Home: 1837 Palmer Ave New Orleans LA 70118 Office: 225 Baronne St New Orleans LA 70112

BENJAMIN, JOHN FREDERICK, brokerage executive; b. Glencoe, Ill., Dec. 24, 1931; s. Jack A. Banjamin and Alice (Uhlmann) B.; m. Esther Rosenthal, Apr. 3, 1955; children: John Frederick, Sally D. Alan C. B.A., Yale U., 1953. Officer Uhlmann Grain Co., Chgo., 1955-61, Uhlmann & Co., 1961-64; sr. v.p. and ant. commodity sales mgr. H. Hentz & Co., Inc., Chgo., 1965-73; sr. v.p. Drexel Burnham Lambert Inc., Chgo., 1973—. Pres. Highland Park Republican Men's Club, 1960-68; officer young peoples div. Jewish Fedn., Chgo., 1961-62; bd. dirs. Med. Research Inst. of Michael Reese Hosp., Chgo., 1955-64; chmn. Med. Reseach Inst. of Michael Reese Hosp., Chgo., 1963-64; trustee Med. Research Inst. of Michael Reese Hosp., Chgo., 1965—; mem. sustaining fund com. Ravinia Festival Assn., Highland Park, 1968—. Mem. Chgo. Merc. Exchange, N.Y. Futures Exchange. Jewish. Clubs: Lake Shore Country (Glencoe); Standard (Chgo.); (dir. 1979—). Office: Drexel Burnham Lambert Inc 1 S Wacker Dr Chicago IL 60606 Home: 1150 Linden Ave Highland Park IL 60035

BENJAMIN, KARL STANLEY, artist; b. Chgo., Dec. 29, 1925; s. Eustace Lincoln and Marie (Klamsteiner) B.; m. Beverly Jean Paschke, Jan. 29, 1949; children: Beth Marie, Kris Ellen, Bruce Lincoln. Student, Northwestern U., 1943, 46; B.A., U. Redlands, 1949; M.A., Claremont Grad. Sch., 1960. Art. tchr., So. Calif., 1949-77; prof. art, artist in residence Pomona Coll. Traveling exhbns. include New Talent, Am. Fedn. Arts, 1959, 4 Abstract Classicists, Los Angeles and San Francisco museums, 1959-61, West Coast Hard Edge, Inst. Contemporary Arts, London, Eng., 1960, Purist Painting, Am. Fedn. Arts, 1960-61, Geometric Abstractions in Am, Whitney Mus., 1962, Paintings of the Pacific, U.S., Japan and Australia, 1961-63, Artists Environment, West Coast, Amon Carter Mus., Houston, 1962-63, Denver annual, 1965, Survey of Contemporary Art, Speed Mus., Louisville, 1965, The Colorists, San Francisco Mus., 1965, Art Across Am, Mead Corp., 1965-67, The Responsive Eye, Mus. Modern Art, 1965-66, 30th Biennial Exhbn. Am. Painting, Corcoran Gallery, 1967, 35th Biennial Exhbn. Am. Painting, 1977, Painting and Sculpture in California: The Modern Era, San Francisco Mus. Modern Art, 1976-77, Smithsonian Nat. Collection Fine Arts, Washington, Los Angeles Hard Edge: The Fifties and Seventies, Los Angeles County Mus. Art, 1977, Corcoran Gallery, Washington, Cheney Cowles Mus., Spokane, 1980, Calif. State U., Bakersfield, 1982, Henry Gallery, U. Wash., U. Calif., Santa Barbara, 1984; rep. permanent collections, Whitney Mus., Los Angeles County Mus. Art, San Francisco Mus. Art, Santa Barbara (Calif.) Mus. Art, Pasadena (Calif.) Art Mus., Long Beach (Calif.) Mus. Art, La Jolla (Calif.) Mus. Art, Fine Arts Gallery San Diego, U. Redlands, Mus. Modern Art, Israel, Pomona Coll., Scripps Coll., Salk Inst., La Jolla, Univ. Mus., Berkeley, Calif., Wadsworth Atheneum, Nat. Collection Fine Arts, Seattle Mus. Modern Art, Newport Harbor Mus., Denver Mus. Art, Portland Mus. Art. Served with USNR, 1943-46. Address: 675 W 8th St Claremont CA 91711

BENJAMIN, LORNA SMITH, psychologist; b. Rochester, N.Y., Jan. 7, 1934; d. Lloyd Albert and Esther (Tack) Smith; children—Laureen, Linda. A.B., Oberlin Coll., 1955; Ph.D., U. Wis., 1960. NIMH fellow dept. psychiatry U. Wis., 1958-62, clin. psychology intern, 1960-64, asst. prof., 1966-71, asso. prof., 1971-77, prof. psychiatry, 1977—; research asso. Wis. Psychol. Inst., Madison, 1962-66. Contbr. articles to profl. jours. Mem. Am. Psychol. Assn., AAAS, Soc. Psychotherapy Research, Phi Beta Kappa. Office: Dept Psychiatry U Wis 600 Highland Ave Madison WI 53792 *I attribute my success to a high energy level, and to some teachers and friends who supported me in times and places women were unwelcome.*

BENJAMIN, NEAL B. H., civil engineer; b. Santa Cruz, Calif., Oct. 24, 1934; s. Charles Hugh and Mildred Emily (Neal) B.; m. Mary Louise Schroeder, July 6, 1963; children: Charles Edward, Julia Anne, Kathryn Mary. B.S., U.S. Coast Guard Acad., 1956; B.C.E., Rensselaer Poly. Inst., 1962; M.S.C.E., Stanford U., 1967, Ph.D., 1969. Registered profl. engr., Mo. Research asst. Stanford U., 1966-69; asst. prof. civil engring. U. Mo., Columbia, 1969-72, asso. prof., 1972-75, prof., 1975—; coordinator Grad. Program in Constrn. Engring. and Mgmt. Contbr. articles to profl. jours. Served in U.S. Coast Guard, 1956-66. Mem. ASCE (exec. com. constrn. div. 1978-82), Nat. Soc. Profl. Engrs., Mo. Soc. Profl. Engrs, Project Mgrs. Inst., Am. Arbitration Assn. Roman Catholic. Home: 1108 S Glenwood St Columbia MO 65201 Office: 1039 Engineering Bldg U Mo Columbia MO 65211

BENJAMIN, RICHARD, actor; b. N.Y.C., May 22, 1938; m. Paula Prentiss. Attended, Northwestern U. Made: Broadway debut in Star Spangled Girl, 1966; co-star: TV series He and She, 1967; play appearances include The Odd Couple; starred: on Broadway in The Little Black Book, 1972, The Norman Conquest, 1976; film appearances include Good-bye Columbus, 1968, Catch-22, 1970, Diary of A Mad Housewife, 1970, The Marriage of a Young Stockbroker, 1971, The Steagle, 1971, Portnoy's Complaint, 1972, Westworld, 1973, The Last of Sheila, 1973, The Sunshine Boys, 1975, House Calls, 1977, Love At First Bite, 1978, Saturday the 14th, 1982; star: TV series Quark, 1977; Hall of Fame prodn. Arthur Miller play Fame, 1978; dir.: London prodn. Barefoot in the Park; My Favorite Year, 1982. Address: care Phil Gersh Agy Inc 222 N Canon Dr Beverly Hills CA 90210

BENJAMIN, ROBERT SPIERS, foreign correspondent, writer, publicist; b. Bklyn., Aug. 17, 1917; s. Harry Asher and Alice (Spiers) B.; m. Dorothy Calhoun, Apr. 25, 1945 (dec. 1961); children: Robert C., Gordon R. (twins), Geraldine Benjamin Ameriks, Alan; m. Sarah Graves (Nov. 7, 1970); 1 dau., Diana Lee. Student Sch. Journalism, Rutgers U., 1940. Staff writer Panama Star & Herald, 1940; asst. editor Dodd, Mead & Co., 1941; chief publs., office coordinator Inter-Am. Affairs Dept. State, Washington, 1942-43; chief Time-Life Bur., Santiago, Chile, 1946-47, Buenos Aires, Argentina, 1947-48, Mexico City, 1949-51; corr., dir. Latin Am. ops. Vision Mag., 1951-56; stringer N.Y. Times, Mexico, 1951-56; founder, chief exec. officer Robert S. Benjamin & Assocs., Mexico City, 1957—. Author: Call To Adventure, 1934, (several fgn. edits.) Call To Adventure, The Vacation Guide, 1940, The Inside Story, 1940, Europa Para Todos, 1973; editor: Eye Witness, 1940, I'm An American, 1941; assoc. editor: New World Guide to the Latin American Republics, 1943; contbr. numerous articles to various publs.; lectr. on Inter-Am. affairs. Served with CIC U.S. Army, 1943-46. Recipient Honor award Ohio U. Coll. Communications, 1971. Mem. Overseas Press Club (founder, hon. life mem.), Explorers Club, Pub. Relations Soc. Am. (v.p. internat. com. 1971-74, dir. 1975-76), Time-Life Alumni Assn., Interam. Fedn. Pub. Relations Assns. (v.p. 1973-75). Club: University (Mexico) (pres. 1977-78). Home: Cda O'Donoju 19 Mexico 10 DF Mexico Office: Paseo Reforma 449-8P Mexico 5 DF Mexico *Almost all my career has been spent in Latin American communication activities. As early as public school days I had my goal set on writing about the countries "south of the border". I hope that I have been able to contribute to better understanding between peoples of the U.S. and the Latin American Republics*

BENJAMIN, THEODORE SIMON, publishing company executive; b. Jacksonville, Fla., Feb. 3, 1926; s. Roy A. and Phyllis M. (Meyer) B.; m. Barbara Joyce Bloch, Sept. 20, 1964; adopted children: Elizabeth J. Sanders-Hines, Ellen J.; children by previous marriage—Phyllis A., Jill. Student, N.C. State Coll. Agr. and Engring., Raleigh, 1943; B.A., U. Fla., 1948. Mgr. Leitman Assos., Geneva, Switzerland and; Frankfurt/Main, Germany, 1948-49; mgr. Tire Mart, Los Angeles, 1949-53; exec. v.p. Benjamin Co., Inc., N.Y.C., 1954-55, 57-82, pres., 1982—; sales dir. Dell Calif. Corp., Los Angeles, 1956. Democratic Dist. leader, White Plains, N.Y., 1958-64; mem. Dem. City Com., 1960-68, Westchester County Dem. Com., 1964-68. Served with inf. AUS, 1944-46. Decorated Bronze Star medal. Mem. Assn. Am. Pubs., Direct Mail/Mktg. Assn., Premium Mktg. Club of N.Y.C., Nat. Premium Sales Execs., U. Fla. Alumni Assn., Phi Beta Kappa, Phi Kappa Phi, Phi Eta Sigma, Pi Lambda Phi. Home: 21 Dupont Ave White Plains NY 10605 Office: One Westchester Plaza Elmsford NY 10523 *The greatest heritage I have from my parents-and the one which I hope I have successfully passed along to my own children-is consideration and respect for other people. I have always been aware that my actions can affect others. Life is hard enough without adding the artificially created problems that make it even more difficult. Whatever I can individually do to brighten the common journey, with a bit of humor or a helpful hand, provides me with a sense of satisfaction and a feeling that here or there someone may have had a little easier time of it because of something I was able to do or say.*

BENKE, PAUL ARTHUR, college president; b. Michigan City, Ind., May 27, 1921; s. Paul Rol and Virginia (Peterson) B.; m. Beverly Anne Benke, Mar. 14, 1982; children: Janet, Eric. Student, Ind. U., 1941-42; A.B., Ind. State U., Terre Haute, 1948; M.A., U. Chgo., 1951, M.B.A., 1954. Gen. mgr. war prodn. div. Cline Electric Mfg. Co., Chgo., 1951-55; gen. mgr. Paasche Airbrush Co., Chgo., 1955-58; asst. to pres. H.K. Porter Co., 1956-57; gen. mgr. div. Coldform, 1957-58, 1958-63; pres. (Colt's Firearms Div.), Hartford, Conn., 1963-73; v.p. Colt Industries Inc., 1969-73; group exec., marine products group, v.p. AMF Inc., White Plains, N.Y., 1973-81; pres. Jamestown (N.Y.) Community Coll., 1981—. Served to 1st lt. Ordnance Corps U.S. Army, 1942-45; CBI. Mem. Blue Key, Beta Gamma Sigma, Alpha Phi Gamma, Pi Gamma Mu. Home: 636 Winsor St Jamestown NY 14701 Office: Jamestown Community College Jamestown NY 14701

BENKENDORF, BERT, graphic designer; b. Vienna, Austria, Dec. 3, 1923; s. Rudolf E. and Ophelia (Kohn) B.; m. Joanne Koehler, Nov. 17, 1951; children—Judith Lydia, Peter Ralph. Student, Royal Tech. Coll., Salford, Eng., 1939-40, Manchester (Eng.) Sch. Art, 1945-47. Head publs. dept. Royal Textile Inst., Manchester, Eng., 1947-50; mem. publs. dept. Acad. Press, N.Y.C., 1951; editorial art dir. Indsl. Pub. Co., Cleve., 1952-65; dir. graphics Edward Howard & Co., Cleve., 1966-69, v.p., 1969-72, sr. v.p., 1972-77, vice chmn., 1977; vis. artist Cleve. Inst. Art.; Trustee Cleve. Inst. Music, 1962—, Cleve. Area Arts Council, 1970-79, Cleve. Chamber Music Soc., 1978—; vis. com. on arts and humanities Case Western Res. U., 1971-76. Mem. Am. Inst. Graphic Arts, Typophiles. Club: City of Cleve. Office: 1021 Euclid Ave Cleveland OH 44115

BENKESER, ROBERT ANTHONY, chemist, educator; b. Cin., Feb. 16, 1920; s. Carl A. and Teresa B. (Koller) B.; m. Abigail Marie Stone, Oct. 19, 1946; children—Carol (Mrs. Richard Luebke), Robert G., Paul J., Donald E., Kenneth J. B.S., Xavier U., 1942; M.S., U. Detroit, 1944; Ph.D., Ia. State U., 1947. Instr. dept. chemistry Purdue U., 1946-48, asst. prof., 1948-51, asso. prof., 1951-55, prof., 1955—, Hovde disting. service prof., 1980—, head dept. chemistry, 1974-78; Cons. Union Carbide Corp., Ethyl Corp., Firestone Tire & Rubber Co., Gen. Electric Co. Editorial bd.: Jour. Organic Chemistry; author numerous research publs. Recipient F.S. Kipping award, Sigma Xi award, Best Tchr. Sch. Sci. award, Frank D. Martin Teaching award, Standard Oil Outstanding Teaching award, Herbert Newby McCoy award. Mem. Am. Chem. Soc., Brit. Chem. Soc., Sigma Xi, Alpha Chi Sigma, Phi Lambda Upsilon, Phi Kappa Phi. Patentee. Home: 2113 Fairway Ln West Lafayette IN 47906 Office: Dept Chemistry Purdue U West Lafayette IN 47907

BENKO, PAUL CHARLES, chess grandmaster; b. Amiens, France, July 15, 1928; came to U.S., 1957; s. Paul and Elisabeth (Wilhelm) B.; m. Gizela Benko, 1968; children—Palma, David. Student, Economy U., Budapest, Hungary. Mem. U.S. Olympic Chess Team. Author: The Benko Gambit, 1973. Club: New York Athletic. Hungarian chess champion; U.S. open chess champion. Home: 73 Garrison Ave Jersey City NJ 07306

BENKOVIC, STEPHEN JAMES, chemist; b. Orange, N.J., Apr. 20, 1938; s. Stephen and Mary (Zamadics) B.; m. Patricia Doran, June 10, 1961. A.B. in English lit, Lehigh U., 1960, B.S. in Chemistry, 1960; Ph.D. in Organic Chemistry (NIH fellow 1961-63. Teeple fellow 1960-61), Cornell U., 1963. Research asso. U. Calif., Santa Barbara, 1964-65; asst. prof. chemistry Pa. State U., University Park., 1965-67, asso. prof., 1967-70, prof., 1970—, Evan Pugh prof., 1977. Contbr. articles to profl. jours. Alfred P. Sloan Found. fellow, 1968-70; Guggenheim fellow, 1975; recipient NIH career devel. award., 1969-74; Pfizer award in enzyme chemistry Pa. State U., 1977. Mem. Fedn. Am. Biologists., Chem. Soc., Am. Chem. Soc., Sigma Xi., Phi Beta Kappa. Home: 1308 S Pugh St State College PA 16801 Office: 152 Davey Laboratory University Park PA 16802

BEN-MENACHEM, YORAM, radiologist; b. Jerusalem, Sept. 1, 1934; U.S., 1969; s. Haim and Eva (Beisem) Ben-M.; m. Sylvia Tizes, Dec. 24, 1957; children: Tamir, Gadi, Drory. M.D., Hebrew U., Jerusalem, 1960. Diplomate: Am. Bd. Radiology. Physician Israel Def. Forces, 1960-63; med. supt. Lilongwe (Malawi) Gen. Hosp., 1963-66; fellow in vascular radiology Thomas Jefferson U., Phila., 1969-72; prof. radiology U. Tex. Med. Sch., Houston, 1977—, dir. vascular radiology, 1972-83. Author: Angiography in Trauma: A Work Atlas, 1981. Mem. Am. Coll. Radiology, Assn. Univ. Radiologsts, Radiol. Soc. N.Am., Harris County Med. Soc., Houston Radiol. Soc., Tex. Med. Assn., Tex. Radiol. Soc. Jewish. Office: 6431 Fannin St Houston TX 77030

BENN, NATHAN HERMAN, photographer; b. Miami, Fla., June 12, 1950; s. Fred and Helen (Gottlieb) B. Student, Miami-Dade Jr. Coll., 1968-70; B.A., U. Miami, 1972. Photographer Miami News, 1969-70, Palm Beach Post-Times, 1971, Nat. Geog. Soc., Washington, 1972—; Residual photo sales Woodfin Camp Inc., N.Y.C. Contbr. to: Rural America, 1974, We Americans, 1975, Nature's Healing Arts, 1977. Recipient awards Nat. Press Photographers Picture of Year Competition, 1973, 74, 78, 80. Mem. White House News Photographers Assn. Democrat. Jewish. Club: Explorers. Home: 913 E Capitol St SE Washington DC 20003 Office: 17th and M St NW Washington DC 20036

BENNACK, FRANK ANTHONY, JR., publishing company executive; b. San Antonio, Feb. 12, 1933; s. Frank Anthony and Lula W. (Connally) B.; m. Luella M. Smith, Sept. 1, 1951; children: Shelley, Laura, Diane, Cynthia, Julie. Student, U. Md., 1954-56, St. Mary's U., 1956-58. Advt. account exec. San Antonio Light, 1950-53, 56-58, adv. mgr., 1961-65, asst. pub., 1965-67, pub., 1967-74; gen. mgr. newspapers Hearst Corp., N.Y.C., 1974-76, exec. v.p., chief operating officer, 1975-78, pres., chief exec. officer, 1978—; dir. Southwest Forest Industries, Aris, Allied Stores Corp., N.Y.C., Mfrs. Hanover Trust Co. Chmn. bd. San Antonio Symphony, 1973-74; Trustee Our Lady of Lake Coll.; hon. trustee Witte Meml. Mus.; bd. govs. N.Y. Hosp., N.Y.C. Served with AUS, 1954-56. Mem. Tex. Daily Newspaper Assn. (pres. 1973—), Am. Newspaper Pubs. Assn. (dir.), Greater San Antonio C. of C. (pres. 1971—). Club: Rotarian (pres. 1974-75). Office: 959 8th Ave New York NY 10019 *

BENNE, KENNETH DEAN, educator; b. Morrowville, Kans., May 11, 1908; s. Henry and Bertha Alveen (Thrun) B. B.S., Kans. State Coll., 1930; A.M., U. Mich., 1936; Ph.D. (scholar Advanced Sch. Edn.), Columbia U., 1941; L.H.D. (hon.), Lesley Coll., Cambridge, Mass., 1969, Morris Brown Coll., 1971. Tchr. phys. and biol. scis. Concordia (Kans.) High Sch., 1930-35; tchr chemistry Manhattan (Kans.) High Sch., 1935-36; asso. social and philos. founds. edn. Columbia Tchrs. Coll., 1938-41; asso. prof. edn. and research asso. Horace Mann-Lincoln Inst., 1946-48; asst. prof. edn. U. Ill., 1941-46, prof. edn., 1948-53; editor Adult Leadership, 1952-53; Berenson prof. Boston U., 1953-73, prof. emeritus, 1973—; dir. Human Relations Center, 1953-61; pres. Staff and Orgn. Consultation, Inc., 1975—; Vice pres. Boston Adult Edn. Center, 1957-60; exec. bd. New Eng. Adult Edn. Inst., 1958-69. Author: A Conception of Authority, 1943, 71, Education for Tragedy, 1967, From Pedagogy to Anthropogogy, 1981; Co-author: Discipline of Practical Judgement, 1943, Mobilizing Educational Resources, 1943, Group Dynamics and Social Action, 1950, Improvement of Practical Intelligence, 1950, Theoretical Foundations of Education, 1952, Social Foundations of Education, 1955, The Planning of Change, 1961, 69, 76, The University and the National Future, 1966, Philosophy and Educational Development, 1966, Teaching and Learning about Science and Social Policy, 1978, The Social Self, 1983; Co-editor: Reading in Foundations of Education, 2 vols., 1941, Essays for John Dewey's Ninetieth Birthday, 1950, Human Relations in Curriculum Change, 1951, Readings in Social Aspects of Education, 1951, T-Group Theory and Laboratory Method, 1963, The Laboratory Method of Changing and Learning, 1975; editorial bd.: Progressive Edn., 1948-53, Jour. Applied Behavioral Sci., 1963-68; bd. cons. editors: Teachers College Record, 1962-64, Integrativ Therapie, 1973—. Mem. Mayor's Civic Unity Com., Boston, 1954-59; mem. Commn. Human Relations, Boston, 1957-65. Served to lt. comdr. USNR, 1942-46. Recipient Kilpatrick award for disting. contbn. to Am. Philosophy of Edn., 1943; Bode Meml. lectr. Ohio State U., 1961; Centennial prof. social scis. U. Ky., 1965. Fellow Nat. Council Religion in Higher Edn., Internat. Inst. Arts and Letters, AAAS, Am. Edn. Research Assn.; mem. Adult Edn. Assn. (pres. 1955-56, publs. com. 1956-59), Nat. Assn. Intergroup Relations Ofcl., Am. Sociol. Soc., Soc. for Psychol. Study Social Issues, Am. Philos. Assn., Philosophy of Edn. Soc. (pres. 1950-51), Am. Edn. Fellowship (pres. 1949-52), NEA (adj. staff, fellow Nat. Tng. Lab. 1959—, dir. 1959-62, 66-70), Internat. Assn. Applied Social Scientists (chmn. bd. 1971-73), Phi Delta Kappa, Phi Kappa Phi, Kappa Delta Pi. Home: 4000 Cathedral Ave NW Washington DC 20016 also Center Lovell ME 04016

BENNER, BRUCE, JR., banker; b. Chgo., Apr. 26, 1927; s. Bruce and Florence Viola (Granert) B.; m. Margery Ann Wheat, Aug. 28, 1954; children: Douglas, Joan. B.A., Dartmouth Coll., 1949; grad., Stonier Grad. Sch. Banking, 1961. Accountant Gen. Electric Co., 1949-51; v.p. Continental Ill. Nat. Bank & Trust Co., Chgo., 1951-69; pres., chief exec. officer First of Am. Bank, Ann Arbor, Mich., 1969—; v.p. First of Am. Bank Corp., Kalamazoo, 1977—. Trustee Nat. Sanitation Found.; trustee, v.p. Ann Arbor Area Found., 1978-82, pres., 1982-83; mem. Ann Arbor City Council, 1972-74, Ann Arbor Planning Commn., 1973-74. Served with USNR, 1945-46. Mem. Phi Beta Kappa. Clubs: Barton Hills Country, Ann Arbor. Lodge: Rotary. Office: 101 S Main St Ann Arbor MI 48107

BENNET, DOUGLAS JOSEPH, JR., government official; b. Orange, N.J., June 23, 1938; s. Douglas Joseph and Phoebe (Benedict) B.; m. Susanne Klejman, June 27, 1959; children: Michael, James, Holly. B.A., Wesleyan U., Middletown, Conn., 1959; M.A., U. Calif., Berkeley, 1960; Ph.D., Harvard, 1968. Asst. to econ. adv. AID, New Delhi, India, 1963-64; spl. asst. to Am. ambassador to India, 1964-66; asst. to Vice Pres. Hubert H. Humphrey, 1967-69; adminstrv. asst. to U.S. Senator Thomas Eagleton, 1969-73, to U.S. Senator Abraham Ribicoff, 1973-74; staff dir. com. budget U.S. Senate, 1974-77; asst. sec. state congressional relations, 1977-79; adminstr. AID, Washington, 1979-81; pres. Roosevelt Ctr. for Am. Policy Studies, 1981-83; pres., chief exec. officer Nat. Pub. Radio; dir. K.T.I. Corp., Overseas Edn. Fund. Mem. Council Fgn. Relations, North-South Roundtable, Soc. Internat. Devel. Democrat. Home: 3206 Klingle Rd NW Washington DC 20008 Office: National Public Radio 2025 M Street NW Washington DC 20036

BENNETSON, W.J., electric products manufacturing company executive, electrical engineer. B.S.E.E., U. Mo.-Rolla, 1941, prof. engr. cert., 1960; postgrad., Washington U., St. Louis, 1946-50. Transmitter design engr. RCA, 1941-42; instr. elec. engring. U. Mo.-Rolla, 1942-43; with Emerson Electric Co., 1946—, v.p. engring., St. Louis, 1962-68, pres. White Rodgers div., 1968-73, 75-78, pres. Fusite div., Cin., 1973-75, group v.p., St. Louis, 1978-80, corp. v.p. mfg., 1980—. Chmn. Grant dist. Boy Scouts Am., 1968-71; mem. chancellor's devel. council U. Mo.-Rolla, 1978—; dist. chmn. United Fund, St. Louis. Office: Emerson Electric Co 8000 W Florissant Ave PO Box 4100 Saint Louise MO 63136

BENNETT, BETTY T., educational administrator; b. N.J.; children: Peter, Matthew. B.A., Bklyn. Coll., 1962; M.A., NYU, 1963, Ph.D., 1970. Adj. asst. prof. dept. English and comparative lit. Suny-Stony Brook, 1970-75; asst. chmn. comparative lit. SUNY-Stony Brook, 1971-72, asst. to dean Grad. Sch., 1970-79, adj. assoc. prof., 1975-79; assoc. prof. English and humanities Pratt Inst., Bklyn., 1979-81, prof., 1981—, dean Sch. Liberal Arts and Scis., 1979—; Danforth Found. fellowship reader, 1978-79; edn. liaison officer N.Y. State, 1977-80. Author: British War Poetry in the Age of Romanticism: 1793-1815, 1976, The Evidence of the Imagination, 1978, The Letters of Mary Wollstonecraft Shelley, Vol. 1, 1980, The Letters of Mary Wollstonecraft Shelley, Vo. II, 1983. Nat. Endowment Humanities Fellow, 1974-75; Henry E. Huntington Library Fellow, 1976; Am. Council Learned Socs. Fellow, 1977-78; Am. Philos. Soc. grantee, 1979-80. Mem. AAUP, AAUW, Bklyn. Coll. Alumni, Byron Assn., Keats-Shelley Assn., MLA, NYU Alumni Assn., Phi Beta Kappa. Home: 181 Steuben St Brooklyn NY 11205 Office: 200 Willoughby Ave Brooklyn NY 11205

BENNETT, C. LEONARD, research scientist; b. Lowell, Mass., Oct. 5, 1939; s. C. Leonard and Ruth E. (Glow) B.; m. Patricia Ann Derival, Aug. 22, 1966; children: Craig, Dawn Marie. B.S. in Elec. Engring., Lowell Tech. Inst., Mass., 1961; M.S., N.C. State U., Raleigh, 1964; Ph.D., Purdue U., 1968. Registered profl. engr., Mass. Research engr. Purdue U., 1968; mem. tech. staff Sperry Research Ctr., Sudbury, Mass., 1968-73, mgr. systems applications, Sudbury, 1973-83; prin. engr. Raytheon, Wayland, Mass., 1983—; lectr. in field. Contbr. chpts. to books, articles to profl. jours.; patentee field. Chmn. Groton Fin. Com., Mass., 1970-76; treas. Groton Ctr. for the Arts, 1976-78; coach Groton Jr. Hockey, 1979—, Groton Little League Baseball, 1981—. Fellow IEEE; mem. Eta Kappa Nu, Tau Beta Pi, Phi Kappa Phi, Sigma Pi Sigma. Home: 42 Blossom Ln Groton MA 01450 Office: Raytheon Boston Post Rd Sudbury MA 01776

BENNETT, CARL, discount department store executive; b. Greenwich, Conn., Jan. 27, 1920; s. Mayer and Rebecca (Lipsky) B.; m. Dorothy Becker, June 24, 1951; children: Marc Mitchell, Robin Cheryl, Bruce Kenneth. Student, NYU, 1937-38. Wholesale liquor salesman, Conn., 1940-51; pres., chmn. bd. Caldor, Inc. discount store chain, Norwalk, Conn., 1951—; dir. Union Trust Co., N.E. Bancorp. Inc., So. New Eng. Telephone Co. Chmn. bd. Bi-Cultural Day Sch., Stamford, Conn., 1965-67, treas., Stamford, Conn., 1967-68; trustee Stamford Hosp.; trustee, exec. adv. com. Fairfield County area NCCJ. Recipient Amudin award outstanding work Hebrew day schs., 1965. Mem. World Bus. Council, Inc., Young Pres.'s Orgn. (treas. 1964-65, chmn. pub. relations com. 1964-65), Nat. Mass. Retailing Inst. (bd. dirs.), United Jewish Fedn. Stamford (hon. chmn.), LWV (hon. chmn. Stamford chpt.). Jewish. Clubs: Landmark (Stamford, Conn.) (gov.); Rockrimmon Country (gov.)). Home: Green Briar Ln Stamford CT 06903 Office: Caldor Inc 20 Glover Ave Norwalk CT 06852

BENNETT, CHARLES DANA, exec. cons.; b. Syracuse, N.Y., Apr. 20, 1903; s. Charles Frederick and Katherine Frances (Carroll) B.; m. Edith Thoman, Sept. 20, 1924. Student, Columbia U., 1920-23; LL.D. (hon.), Okla. Christian Coll., 1969. Public relations dir. for Gov. George D. Aiken of Vt., 1940; editor Washington Farm Reporter, 1942-45; public relations dir. Nat. Grange, 1942-45, Nat. Coop. Milk Producers' Fedn. Conv., 1942, Nat. Council of Farmer Coops. Conv., 1944-45; mem. forest products coordinating com. WPB, 1944-45; cons. to NBC Am. United Program, 1945; spl. cons. to Found. for Am. Agr., Oak Brook, Ill., Washington, Farm Film Found.; cons. Periodical Pubs. Nat. Com., Nat. Paint, Varnish and Lacquer Assn., 1944-55; owner Charles Dana Bennett Assos.; v.p., treas. Elk Run Farms, Inc., 1948-58; pres., dir. Visual Edn., Inc., 1969—; Trustee Goddard Coll., 1941-48; bd. govs. Okla. Christian Coll.; mem. Sec. Forrestal's Joint Orientation Conf. on Nat. Def.; incorporator Crusade for Freedom; chmn. agrl. com.; dir. citizen's com. for Hoover Report; spl. cons. agrl. com. Contbr. to mags. Mem. adv. council Nat. 4-H Club Found.; mem. Nat. council Boy Scouts Am., 1948-75; vice chmn., dir. Nat. Farm City Council, 1955, dir., mem. exec. com., 1956-59, 69—, chmn. spl. events com., 1959—; participant Naval War Coll. Global Conf., 1953-55, Air War Coll. Conf., 1954; mem. adv. com. Univ. Film Found., 1963-78; v.p., exec. com. Coucil on Internat. Non-Theatrical Events, Inc., 1967-69, trustee, 1957—; chmn. adv. com. agrl. div. Am. Vocat. Assn., 1969-72; Trustee Nat. Safety Council, Keep Vt. Beautiful, Inc.; gov. Agrl. Hall of Fame, 1958-68. Recipient citation Nat. 4-H Club (with Mrs. Bennett), 1956, with Mrs. Bennett) Gold Clover citation, 1972; Hon. Am. Farmer Degree Future Farmers Am., 1953; Silver Buffalo award Boy Scouts Am., 1955; Meritorious Service award Nat. Assn. Farm Broadcasters, 1972; named Ky. col., 1966. Mem. Newcomen Soc. N.Am., Nat. Grange (7th Degree), Vt. Farm Bur. Fedn., Nat. Com. for Traffic Safety, Pres.'s Hwy. Safety Conf. (com. to organize pub. support 1945-53), Intercollegiate Studies Inst. (trustee 1954—), Nat. Assn. Farm Broadcasters (asso.), Alpha Zeta (hon.), Alpha Tau Alpha (hon.), Sigma Chi. Clubs: Chicago, Union League (Chgo.); Nat. Press (Washington). Home: Hedgerow House RD 3 Box 426 Vergennes VT 05491 Office: 1616 H St NW Washington DC 20006

BENNETT, CHARLES EDWARD, congressman; b. Canton, N.Y., Dec. 2, 1910; s. Walter James and Roberta Augusta (Broadhurst) B.; m. Jean Bennett; children: Bruce, James, Lucinda. J.D., U. Fla., 1934; H.H.D. (hon.), U. Tampa, 1950, LL.D., Jacksonville U., 1972. Bar: Fla. 1934. Practiced, Jacksonville; mem. Fla. Ho. of Reps., 1941, 81st-97th Congresses, 3d Fla. Dist.; mem. armed services com., chmn. seapower subcom. 81st-98th Congresses, 3d Fla. Dist. Author: Laudonniere and Fort Caroline, 1964, Settlement of Florida, 1968, Southernmost Battlefields of the Revolution, 1970, Three Voyages, 1974, Florida's French Revolution, 1981; co-author: Congress and Conscience, 1970. Bd. dirs. Boys' Home, ARC, Tb Assn., Council Social Agys., Fla. Children's Home Soc. Served to capt., inf. AUS, 1942-47; overseas in New Guinea and the Philippines, including guerrilla fighting in Luzon. Decorated Silver Star, Bronze Star; Philippine Legion of Honor and Gold Cross, 1968; French Legion of Honor, 1976; recipient Disting. Service award Pres.'s Com. on Employment of Handicapped, 1969. Mem. DAV, Am. Legion, VFW, Fla., Jacksonville bar assns., Jacksonville Jr. C. of C. (pres. 1939), U. Fla. Alumni Assn. (pres.). Democrat. Mem. Disciples of Christ Ch. Clubs: Masons., Lions, Rotary. Office: Federal Bldg Jacksonville FL 32202 also House Office Bldg Washington DC 20515

BENNETT, CHARLES LEO, management consultant; b. Springfield, Mass., Apr. 11, 1920; s. Samuel T. and Bessie (Holmes) B.; children: Judith, Barbara; m. Susan Edmisson, Aug. 18, 1977. Reporter, Oneonta (N.Y.) Daily Star, 1945-46; sports, state, city editor Geneva (N.Y.) Times, 1946-52; city editor Schenectady Union-Star, 1952-54; mng. editor Elyria (Ohio) Chronicle-Telegram, 1954-57, Cin. Enquirer, 1957-60, The Daily Oklahoman, Oklahoma City Times, 1960-74, exec. editor, 1974-77; editor Colorado Springs (Colo.) Sun, 1977-80; pres. Assn. Mgmt., Ltd.; exec. dir. Colorado Springs Auto Dealers Assn., Downtown Colorado Springs, Inc. Mem. Colorado Springs Execs. Assn. Home: 3123 Wesley Ln Colorado Springs CO 80907

BENNETT, DAVID JOEL, architect, educator; b. N.Y.C., Aug. 25, 1935; s. Jacob and Rose (Rothstein) B.; m. Judith Deutsch, Sept. 8, 1957; 1 dau., Sarah Ariel. Student, Cooper Union, 1954-57; B.Arch., U. Minn., 1959. Registered architect, Ariz., Colo., Iowa, Minn., Bebr., Wis., Wyo. Project architect Hammel Green & Abrahamson, Mpls., 1963-65; prin. Myers Anonsen & Bennett, Mpls., 1965-68, Myers & Bennett Architects, 1968-73, Bennett-Ringrose-Wolsfeld-Jarvis-Gardner, Inc. (BRW, Inc.), 1973—; assoc. prof. Sch. Architecture U. Minn., Mpls., 1968—; speaker profl. confs., U.S., Germany, Can. Prin. architect: earth sheltered bldgs. Williamson Hall; prin.: USAF Visitors Ctr., C-ME Bldg., Walker Library, Ft. Snelling Visitor Ctr.; co-author: Making the Scene, 1970; co-inventor passive solar lighting system; patentee. Rep. Gov.'s Commn. Employment of Handicapped, 1962-63; mem. Minn. High Tech. Council. Recipient Energy Conservation Design awards Owens-Corning Fiberglass Co., 1980, 82, Concept Design award NSAF, 1980, Outstanding Civil Engring. Achievement award ASCE, 1983. Fellow AIA. Home: 5715 Clinton Ave S Minneapolis MN 55419 Office: BRW Inc 2829 University Ave SE Minneapolis MN 55414

BENNETT, DONALD WILLIAM, air force officer; b. Buckhannon, W.Va., Aug. 24, 1927; s. Edward Clinton and Pauline Camilus (McWhorter) B.; m. Velma May Smith, Aug. 31, 1948; children: Robert Bruce, Thomas William. B.S. in Mech. Engring, W.Va. U., 1950. Commd. 2d lt. USAF, 1951, advanced through grades to maj. gen., 1980; service in, Germany, Eng. and Viet Nam, insp. gen., 1978-79, dep. chief staff logistics, 1979-81, comdr., Travis AFB, Calif., 1981—. Decorated D.S.M., Legion of Merit, Bronze Star, Meritorious Service medal, Air Force Commendation medal; Honor medal 1st class; Cross of Gallantary with palm, Vietnam). Mem. Air Force Assn., Airlifters Assn., Order of Daedalians, Am. Aviation Hist. Soc. Presbyterian. Office: Hdqrs 22d Air Force Travis AFB CA 94535

BENNETT, EDWARD HERBERT, JR., architect; b. Chgo., Dec. 22, 1915; s. Edward Herbert and Catherine (Jones) B.; 1 son, Edward Herbert III; m. Katharine F. Phillips, Nov. 4, 1960. A.B., Harvard U., 1938, M.Arch., 1950. Mem. firm Schweikher & Elting (architects), Chgo., 1953-54, Elting & Bennett, 1954-56; pvt. practice architecture, Chgo., 1956—; Bd. dirs. Chgo. Regional Planning Assn., 1952-58; vice chmn. Lake County regional planning commn., 1958-60, chmn., 1960-70. Bd. dirs. Lyric Opera of Chgo., 1956-76; trustee Chgo. Art Inst., 1958—, Chicago Symphony Orch., 1969-78. Served to lt. comdr. USNR, 1940-45. Mem. Chgo. Orchestral Assn., AIA. Clubs: Arts, Chgo., Cliff Dwellers (Chgo.). Address: 332 S Michigan Blvd Chicago IL 60604

BENNETT, EDWARD MOORE, educator; b. Dixon, Ill., Sept. 28, 1927; s. J. Frank and Marguerite Marion (Moore) B.; m. Margery Mae Harder, Sept. 3, 1950; 1 son, Michael Dana. B.A., Butler U., 1952; M.A., U. Ill., 1956, Ph.D., 1961. Teaching asst. U. Ill., 1956-60; instr. Tex. A. and M. U., 1960-61, Wash. State U., Pullman, 1961-62, asst. prof., 1962-66, asso. prof., 1967-71, prof. history, 1971—, chmn. faculty exec. com., 1970-71; Ford Found. Community Seminar lectr., 1965; Peace Corps lectr. U. Wis., Milw. (on U.S.-Indian fgn. policy), summer 1967; Adviser on Democratic Party platform planks on fgn. policy for, Whitman County and, State of Wash., 1964-68; Mem. adv. council Wash. Council on Higher Edn., 1970-74; pres. Pacific 8 Athletic Conf., 1973, Pacific 10 Athletic Conf., 1980; mem. Theodore Roosevelt award jury Nat. Collegiate Athletic Assn., 1973-76. Author: (with Howard C. Payne and Raymond Callahan) As The Storm Clouds Gathered: European Perceptions of American Foreign Policy in the 1930's, 1979; Editor: Polycentrism: Growing Dissidence in the Communist Bloc?, 1967, Recognition of Russia: An American Foreign Policy Dilemma, 1970; Co-editor, co-author: Diplomats in Crisis: U.S.-Chinese-Japanese Relations, 1919-1941, 1974; Contbg. editor: Annotated Bibliography American Foreign Relations, 1983—; Contbr.: Ency. Am. Fgn. Policy, 1978. Served with AUS, 1946-47; Served with USAF, 1952-54. Recipient Faculty of Yr. award Wash. State U., 1979. Mem. Am. Hist. Assn. (mem. exec. council Pacific Coast br. 1975-78), Orgn. Am. Historians, AAUP, Soc. for Historians of Am. Fgn. Relations, Tau Kappa Epsilon, Phi Alpha Theta. Club: Elk. Home: NE 1315 Orchard Dr Pullman WA 99163

BENNETT, EDWARD NEVILL, insurance company executive; b. Bonham, Tex., Dec. 26, 1936; s. Edward Pendleton and Mary Merle (Nevill) B.; m. Rosalie Allen, Oct. 1, 1960; children: Julie Maria, Laurie Catherine. B.B.A., U. Mass., 1958; M.B.A., U. Pa., 1960. Investment analyst Conn. Gen. Life Ins. Co., Hartford, 1960-66; investment analyst Hartford Fire Ins. Co., Conn., 1966-67, v.p., treas., 1975-79, sr. v.p., treas., 1980—; dir. Mechanics Savs. Bank, Hartford; chmn. Conn. Investment Adv. Council, 1976-80; Pres. U. Mass. Found., 1977-83. Served with U.S. Army, 1960. Methodist. Home: 7 Meadowbrook Rd Simsbury CT 06070 Office: Hartford Fire Insurance Co Hartford Plaza Hartford CT 06115

BENNETT, EDWARD OWEN, biologist; b. St. Louis, Mar. 16, 1926; s. Edward Owen and Myrtle Louise (Sager) B.; m. Dorothy Louise MacDonald, May 30, 1947; children: James David, Robert Paul. A.A., Lamar Coll., 1947; B.S., U. Houston, 1949; M.S., State U. Iowa Med. Sch., 1951; Ph.D., Baylor Coll. Medicine, 1958. Asst. prof. biology U. Houston, 1951-58, assoc. prof., 1958-63, prof., 1961-64, 79-81, chmn. biology dept., 1964-67, asso. dean Coll. Arts and Scis., 1967-73; Cons. in field. Contbr. articles profl. jours. Gulf Oil Corp. summer faculty fellow, 1961, 62; recipient Wilbur Deutsch Meml. award, 1975, Mfg. and Engring. achievement award, 1976. Fellow Am. Acad. Microbiology; mem. Am. Soc. Microbiology, Soc. Indsl. Microbiology, Am. Soc. Mfg. Engrs., Am. Soc. Lubrication Engrs., Soc. Metal Prodn. World, Sigma Xi, Phi Kappa Phi, Beta Beta Beta. Patentee in field. Office: Dept Biology U Houston 3801 Cullen Blvd Houston TX 77004

BENNETT, ELDEAN, mass communication educator, broadcaster; b. Provo, Utah, Feb. 11, 1928; s. C. Leslie and Leatha (Wright) B.; m. Marilyn Payne, Mar. 21, 1947; children: Terri Anne, Randall Dean, Stephen Dean, Julie Anne, Barbara Anne, Allan Dean. B.A., Brigham Young U., 1951; M.A., Mich. State U., 1969, Ph.D., 1970. Broadcaster KSL Radio-TV, Salt Lake City, 1950-65; dir. info. systems CBS-WEEI, Boston, 1965-66; instr., grad. asst. Mich. State U., East Lansing, 1966-70; asst. prof. Ariz. State U., Tempe, 1970-77, assoc. prof., 1978-79, prof., chmn. dept. journalism and telecommunications, 1979—; prof. mass communication U. Jos., Nigeria, 1977-78; Fulbright lectr. U. Los NTV Stas., Nigeria; TV cons. Republican Party of Ariz., Phoenix, 1974-76, v.p., dir. Ariz. Journalism and Telecommunications Endowment, 1982—. Contbr. articles on mass communication to profl. jours.; narrator films, video tapes. Mem. con. Ingham County Republican Pary, Lansing, Mich., 1966-67; mem. Nat. Football Found., 1962-64. NDEA fellow. Mem. Broadcast Promotion Assn., Broadcast Edn. Assn. (mem. com. 1970-83), Assn. for Edn. in Journalism (mem. com.), Assn. for Edn. in Journalsim (AEJ-APNA coordinating com. 1981—). Mormon. Home: 3308 Mariana Circle Tempe AZ 85282 Office: Ariz State U Tempe AZ 85287

BENNETT, FRED LAWRENCE, educator; b. Troy, N.Y., Apr. 4, 1939; s. Fred A. and Dorothy (Lee) B.; m. Margaret Ann Musgrave, Aug. 25, 1962; children: Matthew Lawrence, Andrew Lee. B.C.E., Rensselaer Poly. Inst., 1961; M.S., Cornell U., 1965, Ph.D., 1965. Registered profl. engr., Alaska, Pa., N.H. Planning and scheduling engr. United Engrs. & Cons. Inc., Phila., 1965-68; assoc. prof. engring. mgmt. U. Alaska, Fairbanks, 1968-74, prof. engring. mgmr., 1974—, asst. to chancellor, 1977-79, vice chancellor acad. affairs, 1979-82, acting v.p. for acad. affairs, 1982-83, head dept. engring. and sci. mgmt., 1969-80, 83—; owner F. Lawrence Bennett, P.E., Engring. and Mgmt. Cons., 1969—. Author: Critical Path Precedence Networks, 1977. Den leader cub master Boy Scouts Am., Anchorage and Fairbanks, 1982—. Fellow ASCE; mem. Am. Soc. Engring. Edn., Am. Soc. Engring. Mgmt., Project Mgmt. Inst., Nat. Soc. Profl. Engrs., Sigma Xi, Phi Kappa Phi, Tau Beta Pi, Chi Epsilon. Republican. Methodist. Lodge: Rotary. Home: PO Box 83009 College AK 99708 Office: Univ Alaska 327 Duckering Bldg Fairbanks AK 99701

BENNETT, GEORGE FREDERICK, investment mgr.; b. Quincy, Mass., Aug. 16, 1911; s. Wallace Cherrington and Lois E. (Williams) B.; m. Helen F. Brigham, Oct. 25, 1935; children—Peter C., George Frederick, Robert B. A.B. cum laude, Harvard, 1933. With First Boston Corp., Boston, 1934-37, Newton, Abbe & Co., 1937-43; with State Street Research & Mgmt. Co., Boston, 1943—, partner, 1946—; chmn. State St. Exchange Fund, Boston; pres. State St. Investment Corp., Boston, Fed. St. Fund, Inc.; dir. Campbell Taggert, Inc., Dallas, Middle South Utilities, Inc., N.Y.C., N.E. Electric System, Hewlett Packard Co., Palo Alto, Calif., Fla. Power & Light Co., Miami, Ford Motor Co., Detroit, John Hancock Mut. Life Ins. Co., Boston, Hanna Mining Co., Cleve. Treas. Harvard U., Harvard-Yenching Inst.; trustee Wheaton (Ill.) Coll., Rockefeller U., Gordon Conwell Theol. Sem., Com. Econ. Devel., Washington. Mem. Pi Eta. Clubs: Harvard (Boston and N.Y.C.); Union (Boston); Links (N.Y.C.). Home: 712 Main St Hingham MA 02043 Office: 225 Franklin St Boston MA 02110

BENNETT, GROVER BRYCE, engineering consultant; b. Shelley, Idaho, Apr. 9. 1921; s. Grover T. and Guila (Young) B.; m. Barbara A. Beedle, July 30, 1944; children—William G., Rebecca I., Alan B. B.S. in Civil Engring, U. Idaho, 1943; M.S. (Research fellow), U. Wash., 1949. Registered profl. engr., Calif., Idaho, Ariz., Wash., Hawaii, Alaska. Constrn. engr. Pan Am. Airways, Seattle, 1943-44; instr. civil engring. Seattle U, 1946-48; asst. prof. U. Idaho, 1949-51; materials engr. Idaho Dept. Hwys., 1951-53, asst. state hwy. engr., 1955-56, state hwy. engr., 1956-64; asphalt mgr. Shell Oil Co., Sacramento, 1953-55; with Internat. Engring. Co., Inc., 1964-83, v.p., gen. mgr., San Francisco, 1967-71, exec. v.p., 1971-83, also dir.; mem. engring. adv. bd. U. Idaho, 1968-74; adv. com. Project Mgmt. Inst., 1976-82. Served with USNR, 1944-46. Fellow ASCE; mem. Cons. Engrs. Assn. Calif. (dir.), Am. Cons. Engrs. Council, Nat. Soc. Profl. Engrs. Club: World Trade (San Francisco). Office: 2680 Skyfarm Dr Hillsborough CA 94010

BENNETT, HAROLD CLARK, clergyman, religious organization administrator; b. Asheville, N.C., July 30, 1924; s. Charles C. and Emily H. (Clark) B.; m. Phyllis Jean Metz, Aug. 17, 1947; children: Jeffery Clark, John Scott, Cynthia Ann Bennett Howard. Student, Asheville Biltmore Jr. Coll., 1946, Mars Hill Coll., 1946-47; B.A., Wake Forest U., 1949; postgrad., Duke U. Div. Sch., 1949-51; M.Div., So. Bapt. Theol. Sem., 1953; LL.D. (hon.), Stetson U., 1968, D.D., Campbell U., 1982. Clk. FBI, Washington, 1942-43; ordained to ministry Baptist Ch., 1948; pastor Glen Royal Bapt. Ch., Wake Forest, N.C., 1948-51; chaplain Ky. State Reformatory, LaGrange, 1951-53, Ky. Woman's Prison, 1951-53; pastor Westpoint (Ky.) Bapt. Ch., 1952; asst. pastor First Bapt. Ch., Shreveport, La., 1953-55; pastor Beech St. Bapt. Ch., Texarkana, Ark., 1955-60; supt. new work Sunday Sch. Dept., Sunday Sch. bd. So. Bapt. Conv., Nashville, Tenn., 1960-62; interim pastor Little West Fork Bapt. Ch., Hopkinsville, Ky., 1960, Two Rivers Bapt. Ch., Nashville, 1962; sec. met. missions home mission bd. So. Bapt. Conv., Atlanta, Ga., 1962-65; dir. missions div. Bapt. Gen. Conv. Tex., Dallas, 1965-67; exec. sec., treas. Fla. Bapt. Conv., Jacksonville, 1967-79, So. Bapt. Conv., Nashville, 1979—; Dir. Bapt Life Ins Co, 1982—; bd. dirs. Religion in Am. Life, 1980—; dir. Bapt. Life Ins. Co. Author Glimpses of Faith, 1983; compiler: God's Awesome Challenge, 1980; Contbr. numerous articles to religious publs.; author: Glimpses of Faith, 1983—. Mem. adv. council Fla. State Alcoholism, 1973-78; trustee Fla. Meml. Coll., Miami, 1967-74. Served with USN Air Corps, 1942-45. Named Ky. Col. Mem. Assn. Bapt. State Exec. Secs. (pres. 1978-79), Assn. Bapt. State Conv. Ch. Bond Plans (pres. 1978-79), Fla. Bapt. State Bd. Missions (sec. 1967-79), Am. Bible Soc. (bd. govs. 1979—). Club: Rotary. Home: 202 Long Valley Rd Brentwood TN 37027 Office: 460 James Robertson Pkwy Nashville TN 37219

BENNETT, HARRY, chem. cons.; b. N.Y.C., May 28, 1895; s. Louis and Esther (Cohen) B.; m. Rose Michaels, Feb. 6, 1921; children—Helene M., Marilyn S. (Mrs. L. Ziegler). B.S. in chem. engring, N.Y. U., 1917. Pres. Bennett-Rosendahl Co., Inc. (cons.), Miami Beach, Fla.; dir. B.R. Lab., Miami Beach, Fla.; Chmn. Chem. Forum, Miami Beach. Compiler and pub.: The Chem. Formulary, 20 vols, 1932—; Author numerous books on chemistry. Mem. Am. Inst. Chemists, Am. Chem. Soc., Am. Assn. Textile Chemists and Colorists, N.Y. Acad. Scis., Soc. Cosmetic Chemists, Inst. Chem. Engrs., Inst. Food Tech., Royal Inst. Chemistry, Oil Chem. Soc., Am. Ceramic Soc., Soc. Plastics Engrs., Am. Inst. Chem. Engrs., Tau Beta Pi. Holder eleven U.S. patents, 1 Canadian, 1 Brit. Home: 4747 Collins Ave Miami Beach FL 33140 Office: 714 W 51st St Miami Beach FL 33140

BENNETT, HARRY LOUIS, coll. ofcl.; b. Ansonia, Conn., Dec. 22, 1923; s. Louis and Florence (Swole) B; m. Claire Davis, July 2, 1949; 1 dau., Lisa Brierley. B.A., Yale, 1944, M.A., 1948, Ph.D., 1954. Welfare investigator, Conn., 1950-51; mem. faculty Quinnipiac Coll., Hamden, Conn., 1951—, prof. history, dean coll., 1956-67, v.p. acad. affairs, 1967-69, 72—, prof., chmn. history, 1969-72, provost, 1972—, acting pres., 1978-79; sec.-treas. Conn. Conf. Community and Jr. Colls., 1955-62, v.p., 1962-64, pres., 1964-65; chmn. standing com. accreditation Conn. Council Higher Edn., 1964-65. Served to 1st lt., inf. AUS, 1944-46; MTO. Mem. Am., New Eng., Am. Catholic hist. assns., Orgn. Am. Historians, Assn. Study Conn. History, Am. Mil. Inst., U.S. Naval Inst., Conn. Hist. Soc., New Haven Colony Hist. Soc. Roman Catholic. Home: 21 Knollwood Rd North Haven CT 06518 Office: Quinnipiac Coll Hamden CT 06518

BENNETT, HARVE (HARVE FISCHMAN), TV producer; b. Chgo., Aug. 17, 1930. Student, U. Calif. at Los Angeles. Asso.producer CBS-TV, then free-lance TV writer; program v.p. ABC-TV, Hollywood, Calif., to 1968. Performer: radio show Quiz Kids; newspaper columnist; drama critic; free-lance writer; producer spl. events, CBS-TV; dir. TV film commls.; co-producer: TV show Mod Squad, 1968; creator-writer: The Young Rebels, 1970; exec. producer: The Six Million Dollar Man, 1973, The Invisible Man, 1975-76, The Bionic Woman, 1976; limited dramatic series Rich Man, Poor Man, 1976, Gemini Man, 1976, American Girls, 1978, From Here to Eternity; mini-series, 1979; A Woman Called Golda, 1982 (Emmy award 1982); TV movie Heatwave, 1974, Gemini Man, 1976, Guilty or Innocent: The Sam Sheppard Murder Case, 1975; film Star Trek II—The Wrath of Khan, 1982. Address: care Paramount Pictures 5555 Melrose Ave Los Angeles CA 90038 *

BENNETT, IRVING, optometrist, editor, publisher; b. Bridgeport, Conn., June 11, 1923; s. Isadora B. and Dorothy Mae (Sheer) B.; m. Trude Friesem, July 5, 1945; children—Linda Mae, Donald Walter. D.Optometry, Pa. State Coll. Optometry, 1944. Practice of optometry, Beaver Falls, Pa., 1946—; pres. Advisory Enterprises, Inc., 1971—, OptiFair, Inc., 1977—. Editor: Jour. of Am. Optometric Assn, 1957-64; American editor: Optica International, 1964-70; editor: Optometric Mgmt, 1971-81; Contbg. collaborator: Dictionary of Visual Science. Mem. Beaver Falls Bd. Edn., 1949-68; pres. Beaver Falls Area Bd. Edn., 1955-68; mem. Beaver Falls Recreation Commn., 1949-59, chmn., 1954-59; pres. United Jewish Community Beaver Valley, 1957-60, 74-76, Beaver County Lighthouse Eye Bank, 1972-83; chmn. United Jewish Appeal Beaver Valley, 1956-57; mem. adv. bd. Beaver br. Pa. State U., 1971—, pres., 1981-83; bd. dirs. Pa. Assn. of Blind, pres., 1972-74; trustee Pa. Coll. Optometry, 1976-80. Served with M.C. USAAF, World War II. Recipient Distinguished Service award Pa. State Coll. Optometry Alumni Assn., 1961; Albert Fitch award for excellence pub. relations paper Pa. State Coll. Optometry, 1944; Disting. Service award Beaver Falls Jr. C. of C., 1955; Nat. Optometrist of Year award, 1973; honoree N.Y. United Jewish-Appeal-Fedn. Jewish Philanthropies. Mem. Better Vision Inst., Vision Conservation Institute, Pa. Optometric Assn. (editor 1952-56), Am. Optometric Assn., Western Pa. Optometric Assn. (sec. 1947-52), Beaver Valley Optometric Assn. (pres. 1958), Am. Acad. Optometry, Am. Optometric Found., Beaver Falls Area C. of C., Am. Legion.; mem. B'nai B'rith. Club: Kiwanian. Home: 3307 7th Ave Beaver Falls PA 15010 Office: 1316 6th Ave Beaver Falls PA

BENNETT, IVAN FRANK, psychiatrist; b. Hartford, Conn., Sept. 6, 1919; s. Frank and Iva (Bacon) B.; m. Audrey Poley, Sept. 23, 1944; children: Ivan Stanley, Judith Anne. B.S., Trinity Coll., 1941; M.D., Thomas Jefferson U., 1944. Diplomate: Am. Bd. Neurology and Psychiatry. Intern Jefferson Hosp., Phila., 1944-45, resident, 1946-46; asst. physician State Hosp., Harrisburg, Pa., 1948-50; asst chief acute intensive treatmentservice, chief physiol. treatment sect. VA Hosp., Coatesville, Pa., 1950-56; chief psychiat. research, psychiatry and neurology service dept. medicine and surgery VA, Washington, 1956-58; physician Lilly Lab for Clin. Research, Eli Lilly & Co., Indpls., 1958-63, sr. physician, 1963-76, clin. investigator, 1976—; instr. psychiatry U. Pa., 1954-56; clin. asst. prof. psychiatry Georgetown U., 1956-58; asst. prof. psychiatry Ind. U., 1958-62, asso. prof., 1962-72, prof., 1972—; mem. pharmacology and therapeutic study sec. div. research grants NIH, 1956-58, mem. behavioral scis. study sect., 1956-58; prof. adv. com. Ind. Mental Health Assn., 1958—; asso. staff physician dept. neurpsychiatry Wishard Meml. Hosp., 1958—; dir. Lilly psychiat. clinic, 1959—; sci.-med. adv. bd. Manfred Sakel Inst., 1960-70; adv. com. on alcoholism Ind. Dept. Mental Health, 1961-69, med. research com., 1962-68, adv. com. div. drug abuse, 1971-72; bd. dirs. Marion County Assn. Mental Health, 1967-73, profl. adv. com., 1967—, exec. com., 1969-73; cons. drug abuse Gen. Bd. Christian Social Concerns of Methodist Ch., 1967—; standing com. to study mental health laws of, Ind., 1968-70; mem. Gov.'s Com. Study Mental Health Laws, 1973-76; adv. com. drug edn. Ind. State Health Commr., 1968-74; cons. Indpls. Family Service Assn., 1966—, personnel com., 1969—; mem. project com. drug abuse programs Ind. Dept. Pub. Instrn., 1970-71; sci. adv. com. Nat. Coordinating Council Drug Edn., 1972-76; controlled substances adv. com., State of Ind., 1973—, mem. exec. com., 1976—; cons. dept. psychiatry Mayo Clinic, Rochester, Minn., 1976—; bd. dirs., exec. com. Community Addiction Services Agy., Indpls., 1971-77; Bd. dirs. U.P. Met. Center, 1974-76; mem. adv. bd. neurosci. program U. Hartford, 1978—; mem. Ind. Bd. Mental Health, 1979—. Contbr. articles profl. jours. Served with AUS, 1946-48. Fellow A.C.P., Am. Psychiat. Assn. (life), Am. Coll. Neuropsychopharmacology (charter); mem. AMA, Ind., Marion County med. socs., Ind. Psychiat. Soc. (pres. 1970-71). Home: 8452 Green Braes N Dr Indianapolis IN 46234 Office: 307 E McCarty St Indianapolis IN 46206

BENNETT, IVAN LOVERIDGE, JR., physician, educator; b. Washington, Mar. 4, 1922; s. Ivan Loveridge and Ruby (Jenrette) B.; m. Martha Rhodes, June 24, 1944; children: Susan, Paul Bruce, Katherine, Jeffrey Ivan. A.B., Emory U., 1943, M.D., 1946. Diplomate: Am. Bd. Internal Medicine, 1954. Intern Grady Meml. Hosp., Atlanta, 1946-47, chief resident physician, 1951-52; fellow in pathology Johns Hopkins Hosp., Balt., 1949-50; asst. resident physician Duke Hosp., Durham, 1950-51; asst. in pathology Johns Hopkins U., 1949-50, asso. prof. medicine, 1954-57, prof., 1957-58, Baxley prof. pathology, dir. dept. pathology, 1958-66; asst. in medicine Emory U., 1951-52; asst. prof. internal medicine Yale U., 1952-54; dep. dir., acting dir. Office Sci. and Tech., Exec. Office of Pres., Washington, 1966-69, cons., 1963-70, 76—; v.p. health affairs N.Y. U., 1969, prof., 1970—, exec. v.p., 1976; dir. Med. Center, 1969-73, provost, 1973-82; dean Sch. Medicine, 1970-82, acting pres. univ., 1979-81; asst. pathologist Johns Hopkins Hosp., 1949-50, physician, cons. in bacteriology, 1954-58, pathologist-in-chief, 1958-68; asso. physician Grace-New Haven Hosp., 1952-54; attending physician West Haven VA Hosp., 1953-54; cons. in medicine Loch Raven VA Hosp., 1955-58, Clin. Center, USPHS, Bethesda, Md., 1955-58, Balt. City Hosps., 1954-58, cons. in pathology, 1958-66; lectr. in field; dir. Technicon Corp., 1974—, Group Health Inc., 1976—; Mem. Pres.'s Sci. Adv. Com., 1966-70, Commn. on Epidemiological Survey, Armed Forces Epidemiology Bd.; research contract dir. Army Chem. Corps; mem. bd. sci. counselors Nat. Inst. for Dental Research; member exec. com. div. med. scis.; mem. bd. sci. advisers Armed Forces Inst. Pathology; mem. bd. medicine Nat. Acad. Scis., 1967-70; mem. panel on Sci. and Tech., Com. on Sci. and Astronautics, U.S. Ho. of Reps., 1969—; mem. def. sci. bd. Dept. Def., 1974-77; mem. numerous profl., sci. adv. groups, coms.; mem. long range planning com. Johns Hopkins U., 1965-66; mem.-at-large exec. planning com. U. Okla., 1967-68, bd. visitors, 1968-70; mem. vis. com. bd. overseers Harvard U., 1974-76; mem. vis. com. U. Mass., 1974-75; bd. dirs. Pub. Health Inst. City of N.Y., Inc., 1969—; trustee Milton Helpern Library of Legal Medicine, 1969-76, chmn., 1971; trustee Med. Library Center N.Y., Better Bellevue Assn., 1969; mem. Health Research Council City of N.Y., 1972—; men's com. Japan Internat. Christian U. Found., 1972—; chmn. interim bd. govs. N.Y. County Health Services Rev. Orgn., 1974-76; adv. bd. Assn. Pathology Chmn., 1977—; med. panel N.Y. State Commn. Jud. Conduct, 1977—; adv. com. health manpower Health Planning Council N.Y., 1977—; adv. com. program sci. and tech. policy Grad. Sch. Pub. Adminstrn., N.Y. U., 1978; adv. council Nat. Hypertension Assn., 1979—; adv. council gt. neglected diseases of mankind program Rockefeller Found., 1978—. Author tech. articles sci. jours.; Editorial bd.: Principles of Internal Medicine, 1954-69, Clin. Research, 1954-56, Bull. Johns Hopkins Hosp, 1960-66, Ann. Rev. Medicine, 1965-66, Jour. Biochem. and Molecular Pathology, 1947-67, Lab. Investigation, 1966-69; editorial adv. bd.: Sci. Year, 1974-77; adv. bd.: Tech. in Soc., An Internat. Jour. Served to lt. (j.g.) USNR, 1947-49. Recipient Francis Gilman Blake award Yale, 1954; Gordon Wilson medal, 1958; Arun Bannerjee medal Calcutta U., 1963; Duke Med. Center Alumni award, 1971; Emory U. Med. Alumni Assn. award, 1972; Abraham Flexner award for disting. service to med. edn., 1978. Fellow A.C.P., N.Y. Acad. Scis. (com. on Office of Tech. Assessment 1978—), Am. Soc. Clin. Pathologists, Am. Coll. Osteopathic Internists (hon.), Am. Acad. Arts and Scis.; mem. Soc. Exptl. Biology and Medicine, Am. Fedn. Clin. Research (pres. 1957-58), Am. Soc. Clin. Investigation, Assn. Am. Physicians, AMA, Biomed. Engring. Soc., Am. Assn. Pathologists and Bacteriologists, Am. Soc. Exptl. Pathology, Am. Clin. and Climatol. Assn., Inst. Medicine (charter, chmn. health policy bd. 1973, fin. com. 1977), Am. Assn. Immunologists, Internat. Acad. of Pathology (council 1964-66), Johns Hopkins Med. Soc. (pres. 1963-64), Research Pathologists Am., Balt. City Med. Soc., Md. Soc. Pathologists (council 1965-66), Am. Council Edn. (dir. 1976-78), Orgn. Univ. Health Center Adminstrs., Mental Health Soc. Westchester County, Med. Soc. County N.Y. (comitia minora 1970—, bd. censors 1971—, del. to ho. of dels. Med. Soc. State N.Y. 1973—, pres. 1975-76, trustee 1976—), Am. Assn. Profs. Pathology, Am. Acad. Polit. and Social Sci., Acad. Polit. Sci., Assn. Am. Med. Colls. (chmn. council deans 1974, chmn. assn. 1976, fin. com. 1976—), Am. Assn. Higher Edn., Tokyo Soc. Internal Medicine (hon.), Am. Pub. Health Assn., N.Y. Cancer Soc., Harvey Soc., Phi Beta Kappa, Sigma Xi, Omicron Delta Kappa, Alpha Omega Alpha, Sigma Chi, Phi Chi. Clubs: Century Assn., Cosmos. Office: NY U Med Center 550 1st Ave New York NY 10016

BENNETT, JACK FRANKLIN, oil company executive; b. Macon, Ga., Jan. 17, 1924; s. Andrew Jackson and Mary Eloise (Franklin) B.; m. Shirley Elizabeth Goodwin, Sept. 17, 1949; children: Jackson Goodwin, Philip Davies, Hugh Franklin, Elizabeth Fraser. B.A., Yale U., 1944; M.A., Harvard U., 1949, Ph.D., 1951. Negotiator Joint U.S.-U.K. Export Import Agy., Berlin, Germany, 1946-47; teaching fellow finance Harvard, 1949-51; spl. asst. to adminstr. Tech. Assistance Program, U.S. Dept. State, Washington, 1951-52; economist U.S. Mut. Security Agy., Washington, 1952-53; sr. economist Presdl. Commn. on Fgn. Econ. Policy, 1954; sr. fgn. exchange analyst Exxon Corp., N.Y.C., 1955-58, dep. European fin. rep., London, 1958-60; treas. Esso. Petroleum Co., Ltd., London, 1960-61; asst. treas. Exxon Corp., N.Y.C., 1961-65, mgr. gen. econs. dept., 1965-66, mgr. coordination and planning dept., 1966-67; gen. mgr. supply depr. Exxon Co., U.S.A., Houston, 1967-69; v.p., dir. Exxon Internat., N.Y.C., 1969-71, sr. v.p., dir., 1975—; dep. undersec. for monetary affairs U.S. Dept. Treasury, Washington, 1971-74, undersec. for monetary affairs, 1974-75; dir. Discount Corp. N.Y. Contbr. articles to profl. jours. Bd. dirs. Am. Nat. Red Cross, 1974-75; trustee Com. Econ. Devel. Served with USNR, 1943-46. Mem. Council Fgn. Relations. Republican. Clubs: University (N.Y.C.); Stanwich (Greenwich, Conn.). Office: 1251 Ave of Americas New York NY 10020

BENNETT, JAMES AUSTIN, educator; b. Taber, Alta., Can., Jan. 29, 1915; came to U.S., 1945, naturalized, 1949; s. William Alvin and Mary (Walker) B.; m. Dolores Buttars, Sept. 18, 1940; children: James Ralph, Carl Robert and Calleen (twins), Marvin Charles and Marilyn (twins). B.S., Utah State U., 1940, M.S., 1941; Ph.D., U. Minn., 1957. Livestock asst. Dominion Dept. Agr., Swift Current, Sask., Can., 1941-45; asst. prof. Utah State U., 1945-50, prof., animal sci., 1950-73, 74—, head dept., 1950-73, 74-76, acting dept. head animal, dairy and vet. scis., 1983—; coordinator sheep research Utah State U.-Ministry Agr. Iran, 1973-74. Contbr. numerous articles on animal breeding and genetics to profl. jours. Mem. AAAS, Am. Soc. Animal Sci., Am. Genetic Assn., Sigma Xi. Home: 714 N 150th W Logan UT 84321

BENNETT, JAMES EDWARD, plastic surgeon, educator; b. Burlington, Wis., May 19, 1925; s. John Francis and Florence (Mauer) B.; m. Ellen MacPherson, June 18, 1956; children: David, Martha, Thomas, Jonathan. Student, Notre Dame U., 1943-44, Mass. Inst. Tech., 1944-45; M.D., Northwestern U., 1950. Diplomate: Am. Bd. Plastic Surgery (dir. 1978-84, chmn. 1983-84, chmn. residency rev. com. 1978-79). Intern Milw. County Hosp., 1949-50; resident in surgery U. Mich. Hosp., 1953-58; gen. practice medicine, Burlington, 1950-51, exchange fellow in plastic surgery, Wales, 1956-57; resident in plastic surgery U. Tex. Sch. Medicine, Calveston, 1958-61; asst. prof. surgery, dir. plastic surgery Ohio State U. Sch. Medicine, 1961-64; prof. surgery, dir. plastic surgery Ind. U. Med. Center, 1964—, Willis D. Gatch prof. surgery, 1981—. Fellow A.C.S.; mem. Plastic Surgery Research Council (chmn. 1970), Frederick A. Coller Surg. Soc. (councillor 1981-83), Am. Soc. Plastic and Reconstructive Surgeons, Am. Assn. Surgery Trauma, Am. Assn. Plastic Surgeons (sec. 1978-81, v.p. 1981-82, pres. 1983-84), Am. Surg. Assn., Phi Rho Sigma. Research wound healing, burns, melanoma. Home: 5865 Hunter Glen Rd Indianapolis IN 46226

BENNETT, JAMES JEFFERSON, university official; b. Owensboro, Ky., June 8, 1920; s. James H. and Amelia (Brownfield) B.; m. Christine Thaxton, Oct. 21, 1942; 1 son, James Jefferson. B.S., U. Ala., 1941, J.D., 1948, LL.D., 1966; D.D., Gen. Theol. Sem., 1974. Bar: Ala. bar 1948. Practice in, Fairhope, 1948-50; asst. prof. law U. Ala., 1950-52, asso. prof., asst. dean, 1952-54, prof., 1953-68, asst. to pres. for devel., 1954-56, adminstrv. asst. to pres., 1956-60, adminstrv. v.p., 1960-68, provost, 1968; asst. adminstr. for legislation and pub. policy Health Services and Mental Health Adminstrn., HEW, 1968-69; exec. dir. Health Edn. Authority of La., New Orleans, 1969-71; pres., vice chancellor U. of South, Sewanee, Tenn., 1971-77; ednl. cons., 1977-78; disting. scholar in residence, asso. dir. Center for Pub. Law and Service, U. Ala., Tuscaloosa, 1978-81; acting asst. to chancellor for acad. program devel. U. Ala. System, University, 1981—; Chmn. regional adv. group Tenn. Mid-South Regional Med. Program; chmn. Tenn. Rhodes Scholar Selection Com., 1974-77; chmn. bd. Assn. Episcopal Colls., 1975-76; mem. exec. com. Tenn. Ind. Colls. Fund; mem. exec. council Commn. on Colls., So. Assn. Colls. and Schs. Served to maj. USMCR, 1942-46. Recipient Algernon Sydney Sullivan award, 1964. Mem. Farrah Order Jurisprudence, Sigma Chi, Omicron Delta Kappa, Phi Delta Phi. Episcopalian. Clubs: Univ. (N.Y.C.); (Tuscaloosa). Office: Box BT University AL 35486

BENNETT, JAMES STARK, broadcasting executive; b. N.Y.C., June 1, 1947; s. Rollin Foote and Jane (Williams) B.; m. Carolyn King Doepke, Sept. 17, 1977; children: Katherine Brooks, Lucy Williams. B.A., U. Calif, Berkeley, 1970; M.B.A., Harvard U., 1972. With planning dept. CBS, Inc., N.Y.C., 1972-73; dir. adminstr. sta. KCBS, CBS, Inc., San Francisco, 1973-74; dir. planning and adminstrn. Sta. WBBM, CBS, Chgo., 1974-76, 76-80; gen. mgr., v.p. KNXT, CBS, Los Angeles, 1980—. Treas. St. Nicholas Theatre, Chgo., 1978-80; bd. dirs. Golden State Minority Found., Los Angeles, 1981—, ARC, Los Angeles, 1982—, W. Alton Jones Found., Charlottesville, Va., 1983—, In the Wings Music Ctr., Los Angeles, 1981—. Recipient Kenneth Priestly award U. Calif.-Berkeley, 1970. Mem. Nat. Acad. TV Arts and Scis. (bd. govs. 1977-80), Calif. Broadcasters Assn. (dir. 1982—), Hollywood Radio and TV Soc. Home: 613 N June St Los Angeles CA 90004 Office: 6121 Sunset Blvd Los Angeles CA 90028

BENNETT, JAY I., cosmetics co. exec.; b. N.Y.C., Nov. 22, 1925; m. Madeleine Miller, June 25, 1950; 1 dau., Bonita. B.S., N.Y. U., 1950. Asst. personnel dir. Schenley Industries, Inc., N.Y.C., 1954-55; sr. v.p. personnel and indsl. relations Revlon, Inc., N.Y.C., 1955—, also dir. Served with U.S. Army, 1945-47. Office: 767 Fifth Ave New York NY 10153

BENNETT, JEROME, cement company executive; b. Greenwood, Miss., Oct. 20, 1922; s. Harry and Jennie (Arenzon) B.; m. Julie M. Boyd, Sept. 6, 1947; children: Jerome, Jack, Henry. B.S., La. State U., 1943; postgrad., Wharton Sch., U. Pa., 1946. With Ford Motor Co., Dearborn, Mich., 1950-65; dep. comptroller ITT, 1965-66; dep. dir. Latin ops. Ford Motor Co., 1966-69; v.p. Office of the pres. Xerox Corp., Stamford, Conn., 1969-75; exec. v.p., chief fin. officer White Motor Corp., Eastlake, Ohio, 1975-76, pres., chief operating officer, 1976-79; sr. v.p., chief fin. officer Lonestar Inc., Greenwich, Conn., 1979—. Served with U.S. Army, 1943-46. Mem. Pa. Inst. C.P.A.s. Clubs: Metropolitan (N.Y.C.); Union, Kirtland Country (Cleve.); Greate Bay (Somers Point, N.J.); John's Island (Fla.); Greenwich Country (Conn.). Home: Pheasant Ln Greenwich CT 06830 Office: 1 Greenwich Plaza Greenwich CT 06830

BENNETT, JIM, univ. ofcl.; b. Las Animas, Colo., Aug. 26, 1921; s. Rex Marion and Margaret (Walker) B.; m. Ernestine Y. Rogers, May 2, 1948 (div. Oct. 1977); children—Steven Roger, Patti Sue, Deanne Lee; m. Luise A. Hanson, Mar. 17, 1978. Student, Okla. A. and M. Coll., 1942, Murray State Tchrs. Coll., 1945, U. Ga., 1945, U. Denver, 1947. Reporter-printer Las Animas Leader, 1939-41; announcer radio sta. KOKO, La Junta, Colo., 1941-42; newsman radio stas. KFEL and KOA, Denver, 1942; circulation mgr. San Fernando (Calif.) Reporter, 1946; news writer NBC, Hollywood, Calif., 1946; news writer, newscaster radio sta. KLZ, Denver, 1947-71, news dir., 1957-71; also reporter-photographer KLZ-TV, 1953-71; dir. univ. communications Colo. State U., Ft. Collins, 1971—, asst. to pres., 1977—. Producer: film The Road to Nowhere (Emmy award, Sigma Delta Chi TV documentary award), 1967 (Edward R. Murrow documentary award). Pres. Sunset Hills Recreation Assn., Westminster, Colo., 1965-66. Served with USNR, 1942-45. Named Outstanding Journalist U. Colo., 1968. Mem. Nat. Press Photographers Assn. (treas. 1960-62, pres. 1963-64, Joseph A. Sprague award 1966, merit award 1961-64, fellowship award 1962), Radio TV News Dirs. Assn. (dir. 1961-64), Colo. Press Assn., Order DeMolay (master councilor 1939), Sigma Delta Chi (pres. Colo. 1959, TV Reporting award 1956). Club: Denver Press (Best Spl. Events Broadcast award 1950). Home: 2719 Aberdeen Ct Fort Collins CO 80525 *Any achievements I may have obtained have been possible only by applying myself to the best of my ability at all times, by being loyal to the people with whom I work, and by being fair and honest as a journalist.*

BENNETT, JOAN, actress; b. Palisades, N.J., Feb. 27, 1910; d. Richard and Adrienne (Morrison) B.; m. John Marion Fox, 1926 (div. Aug. 1928); 1 dau., Diana; m. Gene Markey (writer), Mar. 16, 1932 (div. 1937); 1 dau., Melinda; m. Walter Wanger, 1940 (div. 1965); children: Stephanie, Shelley; m. David Wilde, Feb. 14, 1978. Ed., pvt. schs.-Miss Chandor's and Miss Hopkins, N.Y.C., St. Margaret's, Waterbury, Conn., L'Ermitage, Versailles, France. Lectr. The Bennett Playbill, 1971-73. Made stage debut in Jarnegan with father, 1928; appeared in: films We're No Angels, 1955, There's Always Tomorrow, Desire in the Dust, Suspiria, 1976; TV movies Suddenly Love, 1978, A House Possessed, 1980, Divorce Wars, 1981; stage plays Stage Door, 1938, Love Me Little, Janus, Pleasure of His Company, Fallen Angels, Jane, The Man Who Came to Dinner, The Boy Friend, Butterflies are Free; TV series. also Never Too Late, London, 1963-64; Author: (with Lois Kibbee) The Bennett Playbill, 1970. Home: 67 Chase Rd N Scarsdale NY 10583

BENNETT, JOE CLAUDE, medical educator; b. Birmingham, Ala., Dec. 12, 1933; s. Claude and Clara Lucille (Clark) B.; m. Nancy Miller Bennett, June 17, 1958; children: Katherine Diane, Miller, Clark Barton. A.B., Samford U., 1954; M.D., Harvard U., 1958. Intern Univ. Hosp., Birmingham, 1958-59, resident, 1959-60; practice medicine specializing in rheumatology; with NIH, 1962-64; sr. research fellow div. biology Calif. Inst. Tech., Pasadena, Calif., 1964-65; asst. prof. dept. medicine, asso. prof. dept. microbiology, asst. dir. div. clin. immunology and rheumatology U. Ala. Med. Sch., Birmingham, 1966-70, prof., chmn. dept. medicine, dir. div. clin. immunology and rheumatology, prof., chmn. dept. microbiology, 1970-82, dir. multipurpose arthritis center, disting. faculty lectr., 1979; mem. Nat. Arthritis Adv. Bd., 1977-80; mem. subsplty. bd. rheumatology Am. Bd. Internal Medicine, 1979—. Author: Vistas in Connective Tissue Diseases, 1968; Editor: Arthritis and Rheumatism, 1975-80. John and Mary R. Markle Found. scholar in acad. medicine, 1965-70; recipient Research Career Devel. award NIH; fellow Arthritis Found., arthritis unit Mass. Gen. Hosp., 1960-62. Mem. A.C.P., AAAS, Am. Assn. Immunologists, Am. Fedn. Clin. Research, Am. Rheumatism Assn. (pres. 1981—, Am. Soc. Biol. Chemists), Am. Soc. Clin. Investigation, Am. Soc. Microbiology, Assn. Am. Physicians, Genetics Soc. Am., N.Y. Acad. Sci., Soc. Exptl. Biology and Medicine, So. Soc. Clin. Investigation, Sigma Xi. Home: 4236 Antietam Dr Birmingham AL 35213 Office: U Ala in Birmingham Dept Medicine Univ Station Birmingham AL 35294

BENNETT, JOHN F(REDERIC), educator; b. Pittsfield, Mass., Mar. 12, 1920; s. John Frederick and Lauretta (Simpson) Garrigan; m. Elizabeth Mary Owens Jones, Aug. 20, 1960; children—Catherine Jeremy, Jennifer Nora. B.A., Oberlin Coll., 1947; M.A., U. Wis., 1950, Ph.D., 1956. Instr. English Indiana U., Jeffersonville, 1953-58; asst. prof. Beloit (Wis.) Coll., 1958-59; asso. prof. Rockford (Ill.) Coll., 1959-62, prof., 1962-68, chmn. dept., 1960-68; prof. English St. Norbert Coll., DePere, Wis., 1968-70, Bernard H. Pennings Distinguished prof., 1970—, poet in residence, 1979—; mem. faculty adv. com. Ill. Bd. Higher Edn., 1962-68. Author: Melville's Humanitarian Thought: A Study in Moral Idealism, 1956; poetry The Zoo Manuscript, 1968; Griefs and Exultations, 1970, The Struck Leviathan, 1970, Knights and Squires, 1972, Poems from a Christian Enclave, 1976, Echoes from the Peaceable Kingdom, 1978, Seeds of Mustard, Seeds of Tare, 1979, Fire in the Dust, 1980, Beyond the Compass Rose, 1983; co-editor: poetry Beloit Poetry Jour, 1958-72. Served to 1st lt., arty. AUS, 1942-46; ETO. Recipient Borestone Publs., Devins Meml. award, 1970, Chgo. Book Clinic award, 1970, Printing Industries Am. award, 1970, Midwestern Book of Year award,

1970, Am. Assn. U. Presses Book Competition award, 1970, Soc. Midland Authors Poetry award, 1970, 79. Mem. Melville Soc., Amnesty Internat., Whale Protection Fund., Acad. Am. Poets. Democrat. Episcopalian. Home: 526 Karen Ln Green Bay WI 54301 Office: Dept English St Norbert College DePere WI 54115

BENNETT, JOHN MORRISON, medical oncologist; b. Boston, Apr. 24, 1933; s. Theodore and Gladys B.; m. Carol F. Rosenblum, Dec. 22, 1957; children: Robert, Elizabeth, Douglas. A.B. cum laude, Harvard U., 1955, M.D., Boston U., 1959. Intern Mass. Meml. Hosp., Boston, 1959-60; resident Beth Israel Hosp., Boston, 1960-62; instr. medicine Harvard Med. Sch., 1965-66; head morphology and histochem. sect. clin. pathology dept. NIH, 1966-68; asst. prof. medicine Sch. Medicine Tufts U., 1968-69; dir. outpatient labs. Boston City Hosp., 1968-69; dir. hematology and med. oncology Highland Hosp., Rochester, N.Y., 1969-74; prof. med. oncology U. Rochester Sch. Medicine, 1976—; asso. dir. clin. services U. Rochester Cancer Center, 1978—; head med. oncology unit Strong Meml. Hosp., Rochester, 1974—. Contbr. 120 articles to med. jours.; editor 3 books. Served with USPHS, 1966-68. Mem. ACP, AMA, Am. Assn. Cancer Edn., Am. Soc. Clin. Oncology, Am. Soc. Hematology. Home: 335 Avalon Dr Rochester NY 14618 Office: 601 Elmwood Ave Rochester NY 14642 *The major principle that has guided my academic career has been to treat patients with compassion but also in a setting of clinical trials research. Participation of patients in innovative studies and randomized trials offers the best opportunity for quality care and improved results in the field of oncology.*

BENNETT, JOHN ROSCOE, computer company executive; b. Sparta, N.C., Sept. 14, 1922; s. Walter and Maggie J. (Brooks) B.; 1 son, John Patrick; m. Barbara Wunderle, Sept. 22, 1973. B.S. in Commerce, U. Va., 1949. Nat. accounts mgr. Burroughs Corp., Washington, 1949-58; sales mgr. data systems Collins Radio, Dallas, 1958-65; v.p. mktg. Applied Data Research, Inc., Princeton, N.J., 1965-70, pres., chief exec. officer, 1970—, chmn. bd., 1981—; chmn. bd., dir. ADR Products, Inc., ADR Services, Inc., Mass. Computer Assos., Inc. Served as 1st lt. USAAF, 1943-46. Mem. Assn. Computer Mgmt. Data Processing Mgmt. Assn., Armed Forces Communications and Electronics Assn., Serpentine Club. Clubs: Bedens Brook (Princeton); Pike Brook Country (Belle Mead, N.J.); Crane Creek Country (Stuart, Fla.); Elks. Office: Applied Data Research Inc Route 206 and Orchard Rd Princeton NJ 08540

BENNETT, JOSEPH CLIFFORD, mining engineer; b. Mpls., Aug. 26, 1932; s. Theodore Wood and Josephine (Clifford) B.; m. Gainor Lloyd, Jan. 3, 1958; children: Meridan Wood, Sarah Lloyd. B.S. in Mining Engring, Stanford U., 1954, M.S. in Mineral Econs, 1959. Mining engr., ore trader C. Tennant, Sons. & Co., N.Y.C., 1955-57; mining engr. Hanna Mining Co., Hibbing, Minn., 1959-60, Meriden Engring. Co., Hibbing, 1960-62; v.p., sec., dir. Molycorp., Inc., N.Y.C., 1962-69; v.p. Internat. Mining Corp., N.Y.C., 1962-69; cons., N.Y.C., 1970-71; chmn., chief exec. officer Centennial Devel. Co., Salt Lake City, 1971-74, cons., 1974-75; pres. Clifford Minerals Corp., Salt Lake City, 1975-80; pres., chief exec. officer Fed. Resources Corp., Salt Lake City, 1980-82; self-employed mining engr, Salt Lake City, 1982—; dir. Coeur d'Alene Mines Corp., NSM Resources Ltd., Bell Molybdenum Mines, Ltd., Conwest Exploration Co., Storm King Mines, Inc. Founding dir. Mountain States Legal Found. Mem. AIME (dir., exec. com., past chmn. Utah sec. 1976-77), Am. Mining Congress (past mem. Western div. bd. govs.), Can. Inst. Mining and Metallurgy, Mining and Metall. Soc. Am., Rocky Mountain Coal Mining Inst., Utah Geol. Assn., Utah Mining Assn. (pres. 1977, dir., exec. com.). Clubs: Alta (dir.), Cottonwood (Salt Lake City); Knickerbocker (N.Y.C.); Minneapolis. Home: 4425 Covecrest Dr Salt Lake City UT 84117 Office: 678 East South Temple Salt Lake City UT 84102

BENNETT, KENNETH ALAN, biological anthropologist; b. Butler, Okla., Oct. 3, 1935; s. Kenneth Francis and Lillian Imogene (McDaniel) B.; m. Helen Lucille Maze, Sept. 6, 1959; children—Letitia Arlene, Cheri Lynn. A.S., Odessa Coll., 1956; B.A., U. Tex., 1961; M.A., U. Ariz., 1966, Ph.D., 1967. Asst. prof. anthropology U. Oreg., 1967-70; asso. prof. anthropology U. Wis.-Madison, 1970-75, prof., 1975—. Author: The Indians of Point of Pines, Arizona, 1973, Fundamentals of Biological Anthropology, 1979; Editor: Yearbook of Physical Anthropology, 1976-81; Contbg. editor: Social Biology, 1975-77; revs. editor: Human Biology, 1981—; contbr. articles to profl. jours. Served with U.S. Army, 1956-58. NIH fellow, 1964-67. Mem. Am. Assn. Phys. Anthropologists, Am. Soc. Naturalists, Human Biology Council, Soc. for Study Evolution, Soc. for Study Human Biology, Soc. Systematic Zoology, Sigma Xi. Home: 5718 Hammersley Rd Madison WI 53711 Office: Dept Anthropology U Wis Madison WI 53706

BENNETT, LERONE, JR., magazine editor, author; b. Clarksdale, Miss., Oct. 17, 1928; s. Lerone and Alma (Reed) B.; m. Gloria Sylvester, July 21, 1956; children: Alma Joy, Constance, Courtney, Lerone III. B.A., Morehouse Coll., 1949, D.Letters, 1966; D.Hum., Wilberforce U., 1977; D.Litt., Marquette U., 1979, Voorhees Coll., 1981, Morgan State U., 1981; L.H.D., U. Ill., 1980, Lincoln Coll., 1980, Dillard U., 1980. Reporter Atlanta Daily World, 1949-51, city editor, 1952-53; asso. editor Ebony mag., Chgo., 1953-58, sr. editor, 1958—; vis. prof. history Northwestern U., 1968-69. Author: Before the Mayflower: A History of Black America, 1619-1964, 1962, rev., 1964, 82, The Negro Mood, 1964, What Manner of Man, A Biography of Martin Luther King, Jr, 1964, Confrontation: Black and White, 1965, Black Power U.S.A, 1968, Pioneers in Protest, 1968, The Challenge of Blackness, 1972, The Shaping of Black America, 1975, Wade in the Water, 1979; Contbr. to: New Negro Poets: USA, 1964, American Negro Short Stories, 1966. Bd. dirs. Chgo. Pub. Library; trustee Martin Luther King Jr. Ctr. for Social Change, Morehouse Coll. Recipient Patron Saints award Soc. Midland Authors, 1965; Book of Year award Capital Press Club, 1963; AAAL Acad.-Inst. lit. award, 1978. Mem. Black Acad. Arts and Letters, Phi Beta Kappa, Kappa Alpha Psi., Sigma Delta Chi. Office: Ebony Mag 820 S Michigan Ave Chicago IL 60616

BENNETT, LOUIS LOWELL, social welfare consultant; b. N.Y.C., Jan. 15, 1909; s. Maurice and Sarah (Brown) B.; m. Estelle Goldman, June 8, 1929; children—Peter Charles, Richard. LL.B., St. John's U., 1931, B.S., 1939; M.S., Sch. Social Work, Columbia U., 1941. Bar: N.Y. bar 1931, Fed. bar 1931. Dir. evening session St. John's U., 1927-41; practiced in, N.Y.C., 1931-71; asst. regional dir. U.S. Office Community War Services, N.Y., 1941-45; exec. dir., organizer Vets. Service Center, N.Y.C., 1944-45; cons. to adminstr., regional housing expediter Nat. Housing Agy., Washington, also N.Y.C., 1945-47; asst. exec. dir. Am. Jewish Com., N.Y.C., 1947-49; exec. dir. N.Y. Assn. for New Ams., 1949-52; asst. exec. vice chmn. Nat. United Jewish Appeal, 1952-56; exec. dir. Jewish Child Care Assn. of N.Y., 1956-60; asst. exec. dir. Comm. Council Greater N.Y., 1960-62; regional rep. Office of Aging, HEW, N.Y.C., 1962-65; prin. Welfare Adminstrn. regional rep. Bur. Family Services, 1965-67; dep. regional commr., dep. equal employment opportunities rep. Social and Rehab. Service, 1967-70; prof., dean students, chmn. dept. student personnel services Baruch Coll., City U. N.Y., 1970-72; cons. War Manpower Comm., 1942-44; lectr. Columbia U. Sch. Social Work, 1942-45; lectr., condr. insts. at numerous colls. and univs.; adv. bd. N.Y. State Health Preparedness Commn., 1943; hon. dep. commr. N.Y. State Dept. Social Welfare, 1950; cons. N.Y. State CD Commn., 1950, U.S. Office Edn., 1952-53; chmn. family and child welfare com., chmn., sec. functional planning bd. Community Council Greater N.Y., 1956-60, bd. mem., 1959-60; nominating com. N.Y. State Welfare Conf., 1958-60; bd. dirs. Child Welfare League Am., 1960-62; mem. bd. Assn. Children's Instns. N.Y. State, 1956-60; mem. joint bd. com. Council Social Work Edn.-Nat. Assn. Social Workers, 1960-67; mem. com. psychiat. services for children N.Y.C. Dept. Hosps., 1962-65; mem. examining panel N.Y.C. Civil Service Commn., 1956-72, N.Y. State Civil Service Commn., 1968-72; program chmn. combined asso. group meetings Nat. Conf. Social Welfare, 1957; functional planning com. Fedn. Jewish Philanthropies of N.Y., 1957-60; mem. N.Y. Gov.'s Com. Aging, 1971-72; cons. N.Y. State Office for Aging, 1971; del. 1971 White House Conf. Aging. Contbr. numerous articles to profl. publs. Recipient Superior Service award HEW, 1968. Mem. Nat. Assn. Social Workers (mem. bd. N.Y.C. chpt. 1956-73, Fla. chpt. 1973—, nat. treas., nat. bd. 1959-61), Am. Bar Assn., Am. Public Welfare Assn., Am. Soc. Public Adminstrn. (sr.), Columbia U. Sch. Social Work Alumni Assn. (pres. 1945-48, nominating com., chmn. program com.), Acad. Cert. Social Workers, Council Social Work Edn. (v.p., mem. bd., exec. com.), Nat. Council Juvenile Ct. Judges (asso.), Am. Arbitration Assn., Nat. Conf. Social Work, Nat. Conf. Lawyers and Social Workers (co.-chmn. 1965-70, hon. mem.). Home and Office: 230 174th St Suite 1117 Miami Beach FL 33160

BENNETT, MARION TINSLEY, U.S. court appeals judge; b. Buffalo, Mo., June 6, 1914; s. Philip Allen and Bertha (Tinsley) B.; m. June Young, Apr. 27, 1941; children: Ann Bennett Guptill, William Philip. A.B., Southwest Mo. State U., 1935; J.D., Washington U., 1938. Bar: Mo. 1938, D.C. 1956, U.S. Supreme Ct. 1956, other fed. cts. 1956. Sole practice, 1938-43, Congl. adminstrv. asst. to father, 1941-43; commr. U.S. Ct. Claims, 1949-64, chief commr. trial div., 1964-72; judge Appellate div. Ct. Claims, 1972-82, U.S. Ct. Appeals Fed. Circuit, 1982—. Author: American Immigration Policies, A History, 1963, U.S. Court of Claims, A History, 1976. Mem. Greene County Republican Central Com., 1938-42; mem. 78th-80th Congresses from 6th Mo. Dist. Col. USAF Res.; ret. Decorated Legion of Merit; recipient Outstanding Alumnus award S.W. Mo. State U., 1964. Mem. Fed. Bar Assn. (nat. council 1958-76), ABA, D.C. Bar Assn., Res. Officers Assn., Delta Theta Phi. Republican. Methodist (ofcl. bd.). Clubs: Exchange, Nat. Lawyers. Home: 3715 Cardiff Rd Chevy Chase MD 20815 Office: US Court Appeals Nat Courts Bldg Washington DC 20439

BENNETT, MICHAEL, producer, director, choreographer, writer; b. Buffalo, Apr. 8, 1943; s. Salvatore Joseph and Helen (Ternoff) Di Figlia. Student pub. schs. Choreographer: plays Company, Joyful Noise, Henry Sweet Henry, Promises Promises, Coco; dir. plays: God's Favorite, Twigs; co-dir., choreographer play: Follies; dir., choreographer, writer play: Seesaw; originator, co-producer, choreographer, dir. play: A Chorus Line, 1975 (Pulitzer prize for Drama 1976, N.Y. Drama Desk award 1983, Gold Tony award 1984); producer, dir., choreographer: Ballroom, Dream Girls (Tony award for best choreography 1982); dir.: 3rd Street, Young Playwrights Festival, 1983. Recipient 8 Tony awards, 3 Drama Critic Circle awards, Outer Critic Circle award, Los Angeles Drama Critics award, Boston Theatre Critics award, NAACP Image award, Harkness award, Astaire award for best choreographer, Dance Educators of Am. award. Office: 890 Broadway New York NY 10003

BENNETT, MIRIAM FRANCES, biologist; b. Milw., May 17, 1928; d. Stanley Edward and Dorothy (Wheeler) B. A.B., Carleton Coll., 1950; A.M., Mt. Holyoke Coll., 1952; Ph.D., Northwestern U., 1954; A.M. (hon.), Colby Coll., 1973. Mem. faculty Sweet Briar Coll., 1954-73, prof. biology, 1964-73; prof., chmn. dept. biology Colby Coll., Waterville, Maine, 1973—, Dana prof. biology, 1974-80, William R. Kenan, Jr. prof. biology, 1980—; mem. corp. Marine Biol. Lab. Author book on biol. clocks, also articles biol. rhythmicity and endocrinology. Trustee Kents Hill Sch. NSF fellow, 1961. Fellow AAAS; mem. Am. Soc. Zoologists, Ecol. Soc. Am., N.Y. acads. scis., Am. Inst. Biol. Scis., Am. Micros. Soc., Internat. Soc. Chronobiology, Psychonomic Soc., Maine Biologists Assn., Crustacean Soc., Sigma Xi. Address: Dept ,Biology Colby Coll Waterville ME 04901 *The principles, ideals and aims of a classical liberal arts education are the ones that I have attempted to follow as a student, researcher and teacher. I find it imperative that a person perform as well as he or she can professionally as well as during leisure-time activities.*

BENNETT, NORMAN E., publisher; b. Saugus, Mass., Aug. 15, 1917; s. Elmer A. and Mildred J. (Smith) B.; m. Eleanor Teel, Dec. 3, 1942; children—Roger, Jeffrey, Alison. Student, N.Y. U., 1937-40. Dir. bus. relations, v.p. Nat. Better Bus. Bur., 1946-51; with P.F. Collier Inc., N.Y.C., 1951—, sr. v.p., 1960-65, pres., 1965-68, chmn. bd., 1968-71; v.p. Crowell-Collier & MacMillan, Inc., N.Y.C., 1961-67, sr. v.p., 1968-73; chmn. bd. Merit Students Ency., Inc., 1968-71; pres. P.F. Collier Ltd., Toronto, Ont., Can., 1965-68, chmn., 1968-71; chmn. bd. Crowell Internat., 1970-72. Past mem. at large Nassau County council Boy Scouts Am.; Past trustee Oceanside (N.Y.) Pub. Library. Served to lt. col., ord. dept. AUS, 1941-45. Club: Laconia (N.H.) Country. Home: PO Box 607 Center Harbor NH 03226

BENNETT, OTES, JR., coal company executive; b. Barbour County, W.Va., July 30, 1921; s. Otes and Bertha (Cozad) B.; m. Naomi Ruth Queen, May 5, 1941; children: Barbara (Mrs. Charles R. Hertzler), Rebecca (Mrs. A.J. Beal), Jeffrey. B.S. in Mining Engring, W.Va. U., 1955. Registered profl. engr., W.Va., Ohio, Pa. With N. Am. Coal Co., Cleve., 1955—, v.p., 1961-65, pres., 1965-70, pres., chief exec. officer, 1970-83, chmn., chief exec. officer, 1983—. Served with USAAF, 1942-45; ETO. Decorated Air medal with 4 oak leaf clusters. Mem. Nat. Coal assn. (dir.). Office: 12800 Shaker Blvd Cleveland OH 44120 *

BENNETT, PAUL DAVID, art gallery adminstr.; b. Toronto, Ont., Can., Jan. 30, 1928; s. David Leonard and Grace Winnifred (Maidens) B. B.A., U. Toronto, 1950, B.S.W., 1958, B.Ed., 1961, M.Ed., 1964. Tchr. high sch. art, 1953-58; art adv. Ont. Dept. Edn., 1959-64; dir. Art Inst. Ont., 1964-68; curator Roberts Arts Gallery, Toronto, 1969; dir. Robert McLaughlin Gallery, Oshawa, Ont., 1970-72; exec. dir. Ont. Crafts Council, 1972-78; dir. The Gallery, Stratford (Ont.), 1978—; bd. dirs. Can. Conf. Arts, Ont. Assn. Art Galleries, Visual Arts Ont., Can. Crafts Council. Sr. grantee Can. Council, 1968-69. Mem. United Ch. Can. Home: 433 Erie St Stratford ON N5A 2N3 Canada Office: 54 Romeo St Stratford ON N5A 4S9 Canada

BENNETT, REYNOLD, lawyer; b. Detroit, June 26, 1918; s. Harry S. and Muriel R. (Lynn) B.; m. Dorothy Dyer, May 1, 1953; children—Reynold, Dorothy. B.S., Harvard, 1940; LL.B., Georgetown U., 1948; LL.M., Cambridge (Eng.) U., 1949. Bar: Mich. 1949, N.Y. 1957. Practiced in, Detroit, 1949-51, N.Y.C., 1975—; with Office Judge Adv. Gen., Army Hdqrs., Washington, 1951-54; legal staff Bell System, N.Y., 1954-57; with N.A.M., N.Y.C., 1958-75, dir. creative industry program, 1962-75, v.p., 1967-75. Author, editor: Living Tomorrow—Today!, 1970; Editor: Fed. Bar Jour., 1952-54; Contbr. articles and pamphlets to legal and sci. lit. Mem. Mich. Gov.'s Legal Study Commn., 1949-51; bd. dirs. Pacific Indsl. Property Assn., 1970—, Am. Chamber Orch.; del. Patent Cooperation Treaty Diplomatic Conf., Geneva, Washington, 1970; Bd. dirs. Jr. Engring. Tech. Soc., 1967-70. Served to capt. AUS, 1942-46; PTO, Pentagon. Mem. Am., N.Y., Patent Law, Internat. bar assns., Assn. Internationale pour le Protection de Propriete Industriel, AAAS, Am. Arbitration Assn. (arbitrator 1975—). Unitarian (pres. All Souls N.Y. Laymen's League 1962—). Address: 903 Park Ave New York NY 10021

BENNETT, RICHARD EARLE, corp. exec.; b. N.Y.C., Oct. 6, 1919; s. David L. and Augusta B.; m. Helen Pitsillidis, Nov. 22, 1961; 1 son, Gerald Richard; 1 dau. by previous marriage, Nancy (Mrs. Hervey Friss). B.Mech. Engring., Coll. City N.Y., 1941; grad. student, Stevens Inst. Tech., 1947-49. Mfg. engr. Western Electric Co., 1945-50; owner, operator Fairmount Tool Co., Newark, 1950-51; gen. mgr. various divs. Daystrom, Inc. (later Weston Instruments, Inc.), 1952-64; with Internat. Tel. & Tel. Corp., 1964—, sr. exec. v.p., 1980—, also dir., 1968—; dir. various subsidiaries; chmn. bd. ITT Ind. Can., 1978—. Served with AUS, 1942-44. Club: Mason. Patentee wire wrap tool used in electronic assembly. Home: 18 Laurie Dr Englewood Cliffs NJ 07632 Office: 320 Park Ave New York NY 10022

BENNETT, RICHARD GORDON, chem. co. exec.; b. South Boston, Va., Feb. 14, 1932; s. James Gordon and Lillian Frances (McGahey) B.; m. Dorothy Maude McAuley, June 9, 1956; children—Leslie Anne, Richard Lee, Steven Lambert. B.S. in Physics, Coll. William and Mary, 1952, Ph.D., Yale U., 1956. With E.I. du Pont de Nemours & Co., Inc., Wilmington, Del., 1956—, apptd. mgr. radiation physics lab., 1963, asst. dir. research, central research dept., 1967, dir. research film dept., 1972-76, mgr. filaments and strap products div. plastic products dept. plastic products and resins, 1976-77, asst. dir. div. plastic products, dept. plastic products and resins, 1977-79, dir. corp. automotive market devel., 1979-80, dir. fluoropolymers div., polymer products dept., 1980—. Contbr. numerous articles on molecular spectroscopy, effects of light and ionizing radiation on organic materials to profl. jours., 1957-72. Mem. Phi Beta Kappa, Sigma Xi, Pi Kappa Alpha. Home: 11 Birchknoll Rd Northminster Wilmington DE 19810 Office: Corporate Plans Dept E I du Pont de Nemours Co Inc Wilmington DE 19898

BENNETT, RICHARD JOSEPH, corporate executive; b. Bklyn., Jan. 20, 1917; s. Richard and Gertrude (McGuire) B.; m. Eileen P. O'Neill, May 4, 1946; children: Susan, Richard. A.B., Fordham Coll., 1938, J.D., 1942. Bar: N.Y. 1942. Mem. firm Whedon & Bennett, N.Y.C., 1945-46; staff atty. Schering Corp., 1947-55, asst. sec., asst. gen. counsel, 1955-59, sec., gen. atty., 1959-70, v.p., sec., gen. counsel, 1970-72, Schering-Plough Corp., 1971-73, sr. v.p. adminstrn., 1973-76, pres., 1976-80, chief operating officer, 1976-78, dir., 1976—, chief exec. officer, 1978-82, chmn., 1980-83, chmn. bd., 1983—. Pres. bd. trustees Fordham U.; pres. bd. trustees Found. Coll. Medicine and Dentistry N.J.; vice chmn. bd. trustees Health Corp. of Archdiocese of Newark. Served with USAAF, 1942-45. Mem. Am., N.Y. State bar assns., N.Y. County Lawyers Assn. Office: Schering-Plough Corp Madison NJ 07940

BENNETT, RICHARD KISTLER, retired foundation executive; b. N.Y.C., Dec. 25, 1916; s. John Mills and Emily Barbara (Keller) B.; m. Louisa Anna Mueller, Apr. 17, 1943; 1 dau., Barbara Louise Bennett Shadden. Student, Am. Inst. Banking, 1935-39, Inst. Arts and Scis., Columbia U., 1940, Boston U., 1944-45, Northeastern U., Boston, 1945-46, Harvard U., 1945; hon. doctorate, Thomas Jefferson U., 1981. With N.Y. Sun, 1934-35, Chem. Bank & Trust Co., N.Y.C., 1935-41; with Am. Friends Service Com., Phila., 1946-56, nat. sec. community relations div., 1948-56, mem. nat. bd., 1959-69; spl. asst. dept. social affairs UN, 1949; cons. Phoebe Waterman Found., Phila., 1955-56, dir. welfare projects, 1956-62, exec. dir., 1963-68, Phila. Found., 1958-61, adv. com., 1962-71; v.p. Haas Community Fund, Phila., 1968-72; exec. v.p. William Penn Found., Phila., 1972-79, pres., 1980-81, also dir., corp. mem., mem. exec. com.; mem. program com. Council on Founds., 1971, mem. nat. bd., 1977-83; cons. in field. Author: Race and Conscience in America, 1959, also articles, revs., reports. Mem. charter bd. Nat. Com. Against Discrimination in Housing, 1952-54; nat. panel arbitrators Am. Arbitration Assn., 1952-63; mem. Phila. Manpower Commn., 1960-62, Phila. Mayor's Anti-Poverty Task Force, 1962-63, Nat. Com. U.S.-China Relations, 1970—; automation com. Pa. Dept. Pub. Instrn., 1961; adv. bd., chmn. finance com. Phila. Youth Conservation Commn., 1961-63; chmn., pres., mem. bd. Phila. Council Community Advancement, 1965-68; pres., bd. dirs. Maple Corp., 1968-76; chmn. Pa. Com. U.S. Commn. Civil Rights, 1968-72; bd. dirs. Phila. chpt. ACLU, 1969-70, Phila. Housing Devel. Corp., 1969-73, Walnut St. Theatre, 1970-76, Phila. Fedn. Settlement, 1982, Community Coll. Phila., 1981, Med. Coll. Pa., 1982—; trustee Pretrial Services Agy., U.S. Dist. Ct. Eastern Dist. Pa., 1975—; mem. adv. rev. bd. Sch. Architecture, Temple U., 1980—; trustee Phila. Award, 1976—, chmn. bd. trustees, 1980—; bd. dirs. World Affairs Council, 1982—, Independence Hall Assn., 1982—. Recipient Nat. Carver award Berean Inst., Phila., 1960, Key Achievement award OIC, 1967; Humanitarian award Our Neighbors Civic Assn., 1974; Phila. YWCA award, 1970; Martin Luther King award Haven House, Phila., 1977; Nat. Disting. Service award NAACP, 1981; Greater Phila. Cultural Alliance award, 1981; also numerous citations including Phila. mayor, 1981; Disting. Philanthropic and Civic Service award North City Congress, 1982; Russell H. Conwell award Temple U., 1983. Life mem. NAACP (outstanding service award 1981); mem. Fellowship Reconciliation. Quaker. Club: Peale (Phila.). Home: 1237 Lois Rd Ambler PA 19002 *There can be no justice without peace - no peace without justice. Neither will be secure until love becomes a reality rather than a slogan. There can be a brotherhood of man - and there will be. The question is only that of whether we choose brotherhood in time to avert further great catastrophe.*

BENNETT, ROBERT, financial company executive; b. Bklyn., July 14, 1925; s. Robert and Florence (Haggerty) B.; m. Elizabeth Carroll Simpson, Apr. 12, 1958; children: Robert Porter, Bruce Andrew, Andrew Russell. A.B., Harvard U., 1949, M.B.A., 1954; postgrad., Columbia U., 1949-50. With Wertheim & Co. (investment bankers), N.Y.C., 1954-57, White Weld & Co., 1957-62; asst. treas. Cerro Corp., N.Y.C., 1962-65, treas., 1965-68, v.p. fin., treas., 1968-72; sr. v.p. Fed. Nat. Mortgage Assn., Washington, 1972, exec. v.p., chief fin. officer, 1972-82; pres. Nat. Corp. for Housing Partnerships, Washington, 1983—; trustee Northwestern Mut. Life Mortgage and Realty Investors, Milw., 1980—. Bd. govs. Nature Conservancy, 1973-83. Served with USN, 1943-46; Served with USMC, 1950. Mem. Fin. Execs. Inst., Am. Inst. Mining Engrs., N.Y. Soc. Security Analysts. Clubs: Nantucket (Mass.) Yacht; Metropolitan (Washington); Knickerbocker (N.Y.C.). Home: 6033 Franklin Park Rd McLean VA 22101 Office: 3900 Wisconsin Ave NW Washington DC 20016

BENNETT, ROBERT BARCLAY, banking exec.; b. Midland, Mich., Oct. 23, 1920; s. Earl Willard and Eva Victoria (Barclay) B.; m. Bonita Lowden, Aug. 2, 1941; children—Stephanie, Constance. Student, U. Mich., 1940-42. With Dow Chem. Co., Midland, Mich., 1942-73, treas., 1959-73, dir., 1961-76; chmn. bd. Chem. Bank-Albion, Mich., Chem. Financial Corp., 1973—; dir. Chem. Bank & Trust Co., Midland, Chem. Bank-Marshall. Trustee Northwood Inst. Served with USNR, 1944-46. Clubs: Bohemian, Coral Reef Yacht, Midland Country. Home: 1015 W Sugnet Rd Midland MI 48640

BENNETT, ROBERT FREDERICK, lawyer, former gov. of Kans.; b. Johnson County, Kans., May 23, 1927; s. Otto F. and Dorothy Bess (Dodds) B.; m. Olivia Fisher, July 16, 1971; children: Robert Frederick, Virginia Lee, Cathleen Kay, Patricia Ann. A.B., U. Kans.,

1950, LL.B., 1952. Bar: Kans. 1952, Mo. 1952, U.S. Supreme Ct. 1952. Practiced in, Johnson County, Kans., 1952—; partner firm Bennett, Lytle, Wetzler, Winn & Martin, 1952-74, 79—; gov., Kans., 1975-79; mem. City Council, 1955-57; mayor, Prairie Village, Kans., 1957-65; pres. Kans. League Municipalities, 1959; mem. Kans. Senate, 1965-75, pres., 1973-75; chmn. com. on urban and rural devel. Nat. Gov.'s Conf., 1976, mem. exec. com., 1976-79; vice chmn. Republican Govs.' Conf., 1976-77, chmn., 1977-78. Chmn. nat. com. on child abuse and neglect Edn. Commn. of States, 1975-78; trustee Baker U.; bd. govs. U. Kans. Law Sch.; bd. nominators Am. Inst. for Pub. Service. Served with USMCR, World War II and Korean War. Recipient Disting. Alumni award U. Kans., 1979, Disting. Service citation U. Kans., 1984. Mem. ABA, Mo. Bar Assn., Kans. Bar Assn. (past sec.-treas. exec. council), VFW, Am. Legion. Clubs: Prairie Village Optimists, Masons, Shriners. Office: 5100 W 95th St Prairie Village KS 66208 *A meaningful life is the daily dedication of time and energy to the service of others. I hope mine has been no exception to this rule.*

BENNETT, ROBERT WILLIAM, lawyer; b. Chgo., Mar. 30, 1941; s. Lewis and Henrietta (Schneider) B.; m. Harriet Trop, Aug. 19, 1979. B.A., Harvard U., 1962, LL.B., 1965. Bar: Ill. bar 1966. Legal asst. FCC commr. Nicholas Johnson, 1966-67; atty. Chgo. Legal Aid Bur., 1967-68; asso. firm Mayer, Brown & Platt, Chgo., 1968-69; faculty Northwestern U. Sch. Law, Chgo., 1969—, prof. law, 1974—. Author: (with LaFrance, Schroeder and Boyd) Hornbook on Law of the Poor, 1973. Knox Meml. fellow London Sch. Econs., 1965-66. Mem. Chgo. Council Lawyers (pres. 1971-72), Am. Law Inst., Soc. Am. Law Tchrs. Home: 501 W Armitage Ave Chicago IL 60614 Office: Sch Law Northwestern U 357 E Chicago Ave Chicago IL 60611

BENNETT, RONALD THOMAS, news photographer; b. Portland, Oreg., Nov. 6, 1944; s. E.E. and Donna Mae (Thomas) B.; m. Gardina L. Wyckoff, Jan. 23, 1971 (div. 1982); children: Ronald Thomas, Gardina W. Student, Portland State U., 1964-67, U. Wash., 1965, Multnomah Coll., Portland, 1963-64. Lab. technician, photographer sta. KATU-TV, Portland, 1963-65; staff photographer Oreg. Jour., Portland, 1965-68, UPI Newspictures, Los Angeles, 1968-70; staff photojournalist UPI at White House, 1971—; tchr. photojournalism Portland State U., 1967; past bd. dirs. Los Angeles Press Photographers; Mem. standing com. U.S. Senate Press Photographer Gallery., 1980—. Photographer: Assassination, 1968; one-man exhbns., Lake Oswego, Oreg., 1979, group exhbn., Library of Congress, 1971—. Served with USAFR, 1966-72. Recipient 1st prize World Press Photo Assn., 1969, Calif. Press Photographers, 1968, 69, Gold Seal competition, 1968, 69; nominated for Pulitzer prize, 1968, 76, 77, 78. Mem. White House News Photographers (bd. dirs. photo exhbn. com. 1974-76, 1st prize 1976, 77, 78), Nat. Headliner Club (1st prize 1969, 76, 77, 78, 80, 82), Nat. Press Photographers Assn. (1st prize 1972). Presbyterian. Home: 7203 Early St Annandale VA 22003 Office: 506 Nat Press Bldg Washington DC 20045 also Press Room White House Washington DC

BENNETT, ROY FREDERICK, automotive co. exec.; b. Winnipeg, Man., Can., Mar. 18. 1928; s. Charles William and Gladys Mabel (Matthews) B.; children—Bruce, Brenda Laurie, Lynne Susan. Student, North Toronto Collegiate Inst., 1942-47. C.A., Inst. Chartered Accountants, 1953. With Ford Motor Co. of Can., Oakville, Ont., 1956—, dir., 1966—, pres., 1970, pres., chief exec. officer, 1971-81, chmn., chief exec. officer, 1981—. Mem. Premier's Advisory Com. on Econ. Future, Ont.; policy com. Bus. Council on Nat. Issues; mem. Can.-Am. Com. C.D. Howe Research Inst.; bd. govs. Niagara Inst., York U. Fellow Inst. Chartered Accountants Ont.; mem. Motor Vehicle Mfs. Assn. (dir.). Clubs: Mississauga Golf and Country, Toronto.

BENNETT, RUSSELL ODBERT, lawyer; b. Dexter, Mo., July 11, 1915; s. Corna Lewman and Nelle (Odbert) B.; m. Patricia Birch, June 26, 1948; children: Birch Odbert, Russell Andrew. A.B., U. Okla., 1936; LL.B., Harvard, 1939. Bar: Ill. 1939. Asso. firm Taylor, Miller, Busch & Boyden, Chgo., 1939-41, Leibman, Williams, Bennett, Baird & Minow (and predecessors), 1946-52, partner firm, 1952-72; partner successor firm Sidley & Austin, Chgo., 1972—. Bd. dirs. Lawrence Hall Sch. for Boys, 1949—, pres., 1960-63; bd. dirs. Northwestern U. Settlement, Chgo.; trustee Seabury-Western Theol. Sem., Evanston, Ill. Served to maj. AUS, 1941-46. Mem. Internat., Am., Ill., Chgo. bar assns., Am. Law Inst., Chgo. Council Fgn. Relations, Phi Beta Kappa, Phi Gamma Delta. Republican. Episcopalian. Clubs: Law, Legal, Economic, Tavern, Mid-Day, Attic (Chgo.); Westmoreland Country. Home: 918 Locust Rd Wilmette IL 60091 Office: One First National Plaza Chicago IL 60603

BENNETT, SAUL, public relations agy. exec.; b. N.Y.C., Oct. 21, 1936; s. Philip and Ruth (Weinstein) Ostrove; m. Joan Marian Abrahams, Aug. 15, 1965; children—Sara, Charles, Elizabeth. B.S. in Journalism, Ohio U., Athens, 1957. Engaged in public relations, 1963—; account supr., then v.p. Rowland Co. (public relations), N.Y.C., 1965-74; v.p., then sr. v.p. Robert Marston and Assos., N.Y.C., 1974-78, exec. v.p., 1978—, partner, 1979—. Served with USAR, 1958-59, 61-62. Office: 485 Madison Ave New York NY 10022

BENNETT, THOMAS LEROY, JR., clinical neuropsychology educator; b. Norwalk, Conn., Sept. 25, 1942; s. Thomas LeRoy and Gertrude Upson (Richardson) B.; m. Jacqueline Beekman, Sept. 5, 1972; children: Dean, Shannon, Brian, Laurie. B.A., U. N. Mex., 1964, M.S., 1966, Ph.D., 1968. Diplomate: Diplomate Am. Acad. Behavioral Medicine. Asst. prof. Calif. State U., Sacramento, 1968-70; assoc. prof., then prof. psychology physiology and biophysics Colo. State U., Ft. Collins, 1970—. Author: Brain and Behavior, 1977, The Sensory World, 1978, The Psychology of Learning and Memory, 1979, Exploring the Sensory World, 1979, Introduction to Physiological Psychology, 1982; contbr. articles to profl. jours. Elder Timnath Presbyterian Ch. Mem. Psychonomic Soc., Sigma Xi, Am. Psychol Assn., Rocky Mountain Psychol Assn., Nat. Acad. Neuropsychologists. Home: 213 Camino Real Fort Collins CO 80524 Office: Dept Psychology Colo State U Fort Collins Co 80523 *Always look for something good in everyone you meet.*

BENNETT, THOMAS PETER, biologist, museum administrator; b. Lakeland, Fla., Oct. 8, 1937; s. Thomas Edward and Hazel Dean (Smith) B.; m. Gudrun Dorothea Staub, Sept. 1, 1962; children: Vanessa Hildegard, Alexander Staub. A.B., Fla. State U., 1959; Ph.D., Rockefeller U., 1965. Asst. prof. biology dept. Harvard U., 1967-71; prof. Thomas Hunt Morgan Sch. Biol. Scis., U. Ky., 1971-72; prof., chmn. dept. biol. scis. Fla. State U., 1972-76, spl. asst. to pres., acting exec. v.p., 1975-76, courtesy prof. in biol. scis., 1976—; pres. Acad. Natural Scis. of Phila., 1976—; cons. W.H. Freeman & Co., series editor in biology, 1971. Author: (with E. Frieden) Modern Topics in Biochemistry, 1966, Graphic Biochemistry, 1968, Elements of Protein Synthesis, 1969, (with F. Armstrong) Biochemistry, 1979; contbr. articles to research publs.; co-author: Biology Today, 1972, The Physical Basis of Life, 1972. Bd. mgrs. Wistar Inst.; Bd. dirs. Phila. council Boy Scouts Am., World Affairs Council, Greater Phila. Cultural Alliance; chmn. Pa. Museums Coalition, 1979-81; co-chmn. Sci. Edn. Adv. Council Sch. Dist. Phila. Mem. Mus. Assn. Pa. (chmn. 1979—), Harvey Soc., Linnean Soc., AAAS, Am. Inst. Biol. Scis., Am. Chem. Soc., Assn. Sci. Mus. Dirs., Am. Soc. for Cell Biology, Am. Soc. Zoologists, Explorers Club, Phi Beta Kappa, Sigma Xi, Phi Eta Sigma, Phi Kappa Phi. Clubs: Cosmos, Franklin Inn. Home: 2028 Race St Philadelphia PA 19103 Office: 19th and Parkway Philadelphia PA 19103

BENNETT, TONY, entertainer; b. Long Island City, N.Y., Aug. 3, 1926; s. John and Anna (Suraci) Benedetto; m. Patricia Beech, Feb. 12, 1952 (div. 1971); children: D'Andrea, Daegal; m. Sandra Grant, Dec. 29, 1971; children—Joanna, Antonia. Ed. pub. schs., also Am. Theatre Wing, N.Y.C.; Doctorate, Berkeley Sch. Music. Nightclub entertainer; frequent appearances on TV, in summer stock, in concert. (Recipient gold records for recs. Because of You, I Left My Heart in San Francisco, winner popularity polls, also Cash Box mag. best male vocalist award 1951), Recordings for, Columbia Records; owner, recs. for, Improv Records. Served with inf. AUS, World War II. Recipient Grammy award for best solo vocal and record of year, 1962. *

BENNETT, WILLARD HARRISON, physicist, emeritus educator; b. Findlay, Ohio, June 13, 1903; s. Harry and Elsie Mae (Ward) B.; m. Mona D. Sheets, Sept. 8, 1928; children: Willard Harrison, Barbara, Bruce; m. Helen Mae Sawyer, Oct. 24, 1948; children: Charles, Ward, Rebecca. Student, Carnegie Inst. Tech., 1921-22; A.B., Ohio State U., 1924; M.S., U. Wis., 1926; Ph.D., U. Mich., 1928. NRC fellow Calif. Inst. Tech., 1928-30; from instr. to asst. prof. physics Ohio State U., 1930-38; dir. research Electronics Research Corp., 1938-41; dir. applied research Inst. Textile Tech., 1945; physicist, sect. chief Nat. Bur. Standards, 1945-50; prof. physics U. Ark., 1950-51; br. head, div. cons. U.S. Naval Research Lab., 1951-61; Burlington prof. physics N.C. State U., 1961-76, prof. emeritus, 1976—; cons. Los Alamos Sci. Lab., 1953—. Contbr. articles to profl. jours.; co-author textbook. Served to lt. col. AUS, 1941-45. Fellow Am. Phys. Soc., Washington Acad. Sci. Presbyterian (ruling elder). More than 65 patents in field. Resolved infra-red spectrum of symmetric top molecules; discovered pinch effect; developed 1st negative ion source of any element; inventor first model of tandem accelerator; inventor non-magnetic mass spectrometer, dielectric rod cathode for electron beam research; discovered and modeled radiation belts in a lab. tube before their discovery in space, others. Home: 1609 Glengarry Dr Cary NC 27511

BENNETT, WILLIAM JOHN, government humanities foundation administrator; b. Bklyn., July 31, 1943; m. Mary Elayne Glover, May 29, 1982. B.A., Williams Coll., 1965, LL.D., 1983; Ph.D., U. Tex., 1970; J.D., Harvard U., 1971; Litt. D., Gonzaga U., 1982; H.H.D., Franklin Coll., Ind., 1982; L.H.D., U. N.H., 1982. Asst. to pres. Boston U., 1972-76; exec. dir. Nat. Humanities Ctr., Research Triangle Park, N.C., 1976-79, pres., dir., 1979-81; assoc. prof. N.C. State U., Raleigh, 1979-81, U. N.C., 1979-81; chmn. NEH, Washington, 1981—. Office: Nat Endowment Humanities Old Post Office 1100 Pennsylvania Ave NW Washington DC 20506

BENNETT, WILLIAM M., banker; b. Salem, Ohio, May 4, 1938; s. William Moffatt and Anne (Blaszek) B.; m. Barbara Young, June 18, 1960; children: David, Anne, Marjorie. B.S. cum laude, Ohio State U., 1961; postgrad, Wright State U., 1962-65, U. Cin., 1966-68. Sr. v.p. Winters Nat. Bank, Dayton, Ohio, 1973-76; pres. Euclid Nat. Bank, Cleve., 1976-80; mem. SBA Adv. council, Cleve., 1981—; mem. SBA adv. council, Cleve., 1981—. Trustee St. John West Shore Hosp., Westlake, Ohio, 1982—; chmn. bd. trustees Greater Cleve. chpt. ARC, 1976—; trustee Playhouse Sq. Found., Cleve., 1981—, Northeast Ohio March of Dimes, Cleve., 1977—, Greater Cleve. Voluntary Health Planning Assn., 1982—; bd. govs. United Way Services, Cleve., 1976—. Mem. Leadership Cleve., Greater Cleve. Growth Assn. (trustee), Cleve. Clearing House Assn. (pres. 1982-83), Am. Bankers Assn., Ohio Bankers Assn., Am. Inst. Banking. Clubs: Cleve. Athletic; Union (Cleve.); Shaker Heights Country; Westwood Country (Rocky River). Home: 31408 Narragansett Lane Bay Village OH 44140 Office: Euclid Nat Bank 1255 Euclid Ave Cleveland OH 44115

BENNETT, WILLIAM MICHAEL, physician; b. Chgo., May 6, 1938; s. Harry H. and Helen A. (Kaplan) B.; m. Sandra S. Silen, June 12, 1977; five children. Student, U. Mich., 1956-59; B.S., Northwestern U., 1960, M.D., 1963. Diplomate: Am. Bd. Internal Medicine. Intern U. Oreg., 1963-64; resident Northwestern U., 1964-66; practice medicine specializing in internal medicine, Portland, Oreg. and, Boston; mem. staff Mass. Gen. Hosp., 1969-70; asst. prof. medicine U. Oreg. Health Scis. Center, 1970-74, asso. prof., 1974-78, prof. medicine, head div. nephrology, 1978—. Author: Drugs and the Kidney, 1978, Acute Renal Failure, 1976; contbr. articles to med. jours. Served with USAF, 1967-69. Fellow A.C.P.; mem. Am. Soc. Nephrology, Transplantation Soc., Internat. Soc. Nephrology, Am. Soc. Pharmacology and Exptl. Therapeutics. Office: Health Scis Center U Oreg Portland OR 97201

BENNETT, WILLIAM RALPH, JR., educator, physicist; b. Jersey City, Jan. 30, 1930; s. William Ralph and Viola (Schreiber) B.; m. Frances Commins, Dec. 11, 1952; children: Jean, William Robert, Nancy. A.B., Princeton U., 1951; Ph.D., Columbia U., 1957; M.A. (hon.), Yale U., 1965, D.Sc., U. New Haven, 1975. Research asst. physics Columbia Radiation Lab., 1952-54; mem. Pupin Cyclotron Group, 1954-57; mem. faculty Yale U., 1957-59, 62—, prof. physics and applied sci., 1965-72, Charles Baldwin Sawyer prof. engring. and applied sci., prof. physics, 1972—; fellow Berkeley Coll., 1963-81; master Silliman Coll., 1981—; tech. staff Bell Telephone Labs., Murray Hill, N.J., 1959-62; Cons. Tech. Research Group, Melville, N.Y., 1962-67, Inst. Def. Analysis, Washington, 1963-70; vis. scientist Am. Inst. Physics Vis. Scientist Program, 1963-64; vis. prof. Brandeis Summer Inst. Theoretical Physics, 1969; cons. mem. bd. dirs. Laser Scis. Corp., Bethel, Conn., 1968-71; mem. adv. panels atomic physics and astrophysics Nat. Bur. Standards, 1964-69; cons. CBS Labs., Stamford, Conn., 1967-68, AVCO Corp., 1978-81; mem. lab. adv. bd. for research Naval Research Adv. Com., 1968-78; guest of, Soviet Union, 1967, 69, 79. Author: Introduction to Computer Applications, 1976, Scientific and Engineering Problem Solving with the Computer, 1976, The Physics of Gas Lasers, 1977, Atomic Gas Laser Transition Data: A Critical Evaluation, 1979; Editorial adv. bd.: also Jour. Quantum Electronics, 1965-69; guest editor: Applied Optics, 1965. Recipient Western Electric Fund award for outstanding teaching Am. Assn. Engring. Educators, 1977; Outstanding Patent award Research and Devel. Council N.J., 1977; Sloan Found. fellow, 1963-65; Guggenheim fellow, 1967. Fellow Am. Phys. Soc., Optical Soc. Am., IEEE (Morris Liebmann award 1965); mem. Sigma Xi. Research gas lasers and atomic physics. Co-author basic patents on first several gas lasers. Office: Dunham Lab 10 Hillhouse Ave New Haven CT 06520

BENNETT, WILLIAM RICHARDS, premier British Columbia (Canada); b. Kelowna, C., Can., April 14, 1932; s. William Andrew Cecil and Annie Elizabeth May (Richards) B.; m. Audrey Lyne James, April 16, 1955; children: Brad, Kevin, Stephen, Gregory. Grad., Kelowna high sch. Operator, owner furniture and appliance store, Kelowna, B.C., Can.; elected Legis. Assembly B.C. from S. Okanagan dist., 1973, premier, B.C., 1975—. Mem. Social Credit Party, Kelowna C. of C. (past pres.). Mem. United Ch. Office: Premiers Office Parliament Bldgs Victoria BC V8V 4R3 Canada *

BENNETT, WILLIAM TAPLEY, JR., diplomat; b. Griffin, Ga., Apr. 1, 1917; s. William Tapley and Annie Mem (Little) B.; m. Margaret Rutherfurd White, June 23, 1945; children: William Tapley 3d, John Campbell White, Anne Barclay, Ellen Pierrepont (Mrs. Ralph Godsall), Victoria Ridgely. A.B., U. Ga., 1937; student, U. Freiburg, Germany, 1937-38; J.D., George Washington U., 1948; D.C.L. (hon.), Ind. State U., 1966. Instr. polit. sci. U. Ga., 1937; with Nat. Inst. Public Affairs, 1939-40, Dept. Agr., 1940; asst. to coordinator Office Def. Housing, 1940-41; with State Dept., 1941—, officer charge, 1949-51, 1951, dep. dir., 1951-54; assigned to Nat. War Coll., 1954-55; spl. asst. to undersec. state, 1955-57, counselor embassy, Vienna, 1957-61, Rome, Italy, 1961, counselor with rank of minister, Athens, Greece, 1961-64, U.S. ambassador to, Dominican Republic, 1964-66, to Portugal, 1966-69; State Dept. adv. Air U., 1969-71; dep. U.S. rep. to UN; ambassador UN Security Council, 1971-77; U.S. ambassador to NATO, 1977-83, asst. sec. of state, 1983—; U.S. rep. UN Trusteeship Council, 1971-73, pres., 1972-73; asst. to U.S. del. organizing conf. UN, San Francisco, 1945; adviser U.S. delegation UN Gen. Assembly, N.Y.C., 1950, alternate rep., 1971, 72, U.S. rep., 1973, 74, 75, 76; sec. gen. 4th meeting of fgn. ministers of Am. States, Washington, 1951; mem. U.S. del. to inauguration Pres. Ibáñez of Chile, 1952, Eisenhower mission to S.Am., 1953, U.S. del. 10th Inter-Am. Conf., Caracas, 1954, Internat. Atomic Energy Agy. Confs., Vienna, 1957, 58; chmn. UN vis. mission to Papua New Guinea, Australia, 1972, U.S. del. UN Devel. Conf., Geneva, 1973, 76, Econ. Commn. for Europe, Bucharest, 1974, UN Conf. on Indsl. Devel., Lima, Peru, 1975, Econ. Commn. for Asia and S. Pacific, Bangkok, 1976. Mem. adv. council So. Ctr. for Internat. Studies, Harvard U. Div. Sch. Served as lt. AUS, 1944-46; ETO. Recipient Disting. Pub. Service medal U.S. Dept. Def. Mem. Ga. Bar Assn., Council Fgn. Relations, Am. Council on Germany, Sphinx Soc., Phi Beta Kappa, Phi Kappa Phi, Omicron Delta Kappa, Sigma Chi, Phi Delta Phi. Presbyn. Clubs: Chevy Chase, Metropolitan (Washington). Address: care Dept State Washington DC 20025

BENNETT, WINSLOW WOOD, silver mine executive, mechanical engineer; b. Mpls., Mar. 18, 1925; s. Russell H. and Miriam (Fletcher) B.; m. Adele Wulsin, Oct. 20, 1951; children: Winslow Wood, Peter Wulsin, Frank Babbott, Russell Hoadley II. Grad., Phillips Acad., Andover, Mass., 1943; B.Mech. Engring., U. Minn., 1949. Chmn., dir. Equity Silver Mines Ltd., Vancouver, 1968—; dir. MacDonald Dettwiler; owner Shoderee Ranch, Pincher Creek, Alta. Bd. govs. Vancouver Public Aquarium; pres. B.C. Cancer Found.; bd. dirs. Cancer Control Agy. Served to lt. (j.g.) USNR, 1943-48. Clubs: Vancouver, Vancouver Lawn Tennis. Home: 1341 Matthews Ave Vancouver BC Canada Office: Four Bentall Centre 1055 Dunsmuir St PO Box 49277 Vancouver BC V7X 1L3 Canada

BENNING, GEORGE LOUIS, aeronautical manufacturing corporation executive; b. Glendorf, Ohio, May 26, 1924; s. Henry John and Catherine Anna (Kortekrax) B.; m. Helen Louise Kennedy, May 6, 1961; children. Kathy, Rick, Tom, Ray, Michael, Marry Ann, Jennifer. B.S. in Elec. Engring., U. Notre Dame, 1944; M.S., U. Calif.-Berkeley, 1955. With Collins Radio Co., Cedar Rapids, Iowa, 1955-77, mem. sr. tech. staff advanced engring., applied sci., 1961-64, dept. head, 1964-70, v.p. engring. Collins Avionics, 1970-75, v.p. advanced tech., engring., 1975-77; v.p. advanced tech. and engring. Avionics Group, Rockwell Internat. Corp., Cedar Rapids, 1977—; mem. Bus.-Radio Tech. Commn. for Aeros., Washington, 1975—. Mem. adv. bd. Iowa State U. Coll. Engring., Ames, 1979—; mem. nat. bd. advisors Rose-kHulman Inst. Tech., Terre Haute, Ind., 1979—; mem. adv. bd. U. Iowa, Iowa City, 1982—; mem. Gov.'s High Tech. Task Force, Des Moines, 1982. Served with AUS, 1942-46. Mem. European Orgn. for Civic Avionics Electronics Bus., IEEE (tech. mem., Ted A. Hunter award Cedar Rapids sect. 1983), Cedar Rapids C. of C. Republican. Roman Catholic. Club: Elmcrest Country (Cedar Rapids). Lodge: K.C. Home: 2309 Brookland Dr NE Cedar Rapids IA 52402 Office: Avionics Group Rockwell Internat Corp. 400 Collins Rd NE Cedar Rapids IA 52498

BENNINGHOFF, WILLIAM SHIFFER, educator, plant ecologist; b. Ft. Wayne, Ind., Mar. 23, 1918; s. William Nelson and Edith Esther (Shiffer) B.; m. Gladys Helen Kunst, Apr. 19, 1941 (div. 1968); children: Valerie Anne, Jonathan William; m. Anne Louise Stevenson, June 14, 1969. S.B. magna cum laude, Harvard, 1940; A.M., Harvard U., 1942, Ph.D., 1948. Botanist U.S. Geol. Survey, Washington, 1948-57, chief sect., 1953-57; mem. faculty U. Mich., 1957—, assoc. prof. botany, 1957-60, prof., 1960—, U. Mich. Biol. Sta., Douglas Lake, summers 1957, 61, 63, 66; palynologist Great Lakes Research div. Inst. Sci. and Tech., 1960-63; prof., asst. dir. Bot. Gardens, 1965-66, prof., curator, 1966—, acting dir., 1975, dir., 1977—; Mem. com. on polar research, panel on biol. and med. scis. Nat. Acad. Scis., 1962-75, chmn., 1966-71, 1973-75, mem. polar research bd., 1975-77; chmn. aerobiology panel U.S. Nat. Com. for Internat. Biol. Program, 1967, dir. aerobiology program, 1968-72; convenor Internat. Biol. Program aerobiology working group, 1968-74; mem. working group on biology Sci. Com. on Antarctic Research, 1968-71, 74-82, chmn., 1974-80; sec. commn. on aerobiology Internat. Union Biol. Scis., 1973-82; convenor 1st Gordon Research Conf. on Aerobiology, 1980. Asso. editor: Ecological Monographs, 1965-67; Contbr. numerous articles on Pleistocene biogeography, pollen and spores in atmosphere to sci. jours. Served to lt. USNR, 1942-46; ETO, PTO. Recipient Meritorious Service award Dept. Interior, 1954; medal for distinguished contbns. to natural sci. U. Hiroshima, Japan). Fellow AAAS, Geol. Soc. Am., Arctic Inst. N.Am. (gov. 1957-63, 66-71, chmn. research com. 1964-66, vice chmn. bd. 1967-68); mem. Am. Polar Soc. (bd. govs. 1968—), Bot. Soc. Am., Am. Soc. Limnology and Oceanography, Ecol. Soc. Am., Internat. Soc. Plant Geography and Ecology (v.p. 1963-80), Internat. Assn. for Aerobiology (founding pres. 1974), Sigma Xi. Clubs: Explorers (N.Y.C.); Cosmos (Washington). Office: Dept Botany U Mich Ann Arbor MI 48109

BENNINGTON, NEVILLE LYNNE, biology educator; b. Canton, Ohio, Aug. 8, 1906; s. James William and Leora Bell (Slates) B.; m. Virginia Rebecca Tudor, Apr. 19, 1930; children: James Lynne, Ann Tudor. A.B., Coll. of Wooster, 1928; postgrad., Franz Theodore Stone Inst. Hydrobiology, summers 1928, 29; M.A., Northwestern U., 1930, Ph.D., 1934. Instr. zoology Northwestern, part-time 1934-35, mem. staff summer session, 1948; instr. biology Coll. of Wooster (Ohio), 1936; asst. prof. botany and zoology Beloit (Wis.) Coll., 1937-38, assoc. prof., 1939-40, prof., 1941-42; prof. biology Cornelia Bailey Williams Found., 1943—; Researhist Oceanographic Labs. Friday Harbor, Washington U., summer 1934; mem. stream survey Ohio Div. Conservation, 1936; biologist in charge lake survey So. area Wis. Wis. Conservation Dept., summer 1946; research cons. Parker Pen Co., 1955—; head insts. sect. NSF, 1959-60, cons., 1960—; asst. commr. for profl. edn. state edn. dept. SUNY, 1962-66; div. dir. pre-coll. edn. in sci. NSF, Washington, 1966-68; dir. grants adminstrn. U. Wis., Oshkosh, 1968-73; protocol reviewer Health Scis. Cons. Corp., 1980—. Mem. AAAS, AAUP, Am. Soc. Zoologists, Sigma Xi, Omicron Delta Kappa, Sigma Pi. Research germ cells and reproductive rhythms of fish. Home: 3324 Ptarmigan Dr # 1A Walnut Creek CA 94595

BENNINGTON, WILLIAM JAY, insurance company executive; b. Dayton, Ohio, Apr. 16, 1939; s. Jay G. and Mary Joahnn (Weisner) Kirby; m. Pamela Joan Manus, Oct. 22, 1977; children—J. Bret, J. Brad, J. Brian, J. William. B.A. in Journalism, U. Dayton, 1965. Asst. city editor Dayton Jour. Herald, 1964-66; public relations asst. Pickands Mather & Co., Cleve., 1966-67; public relations dir. Bayless-Kerr Co., Cleve., 1967-69; corp. public relations mgr. Eaton Corp., Cleve., 1969-71; v.p. communications The Allen Group, Melville, N.Y., 1971-77; dir. public info. ITT Corp., N.Y.C., 1977-78; sr. v.p. corp. affairs Colonial Penn Group, Phila., 1978—; dir. Acad. Techs.

Inc., Colonial Penn Ins. Co., Colonial Penn Franklin Ins. Co., Colonial Penn Life Ins. Co. Mem. Pres. Council Gwynedd-Mercy Coll. Served with USMC, 1957-60. Mem. Public Relations Soc. Am. (accredited), Nat. Investor Relations Inst., Internat. Assn. Bus. Communicators (accredited). Clubs: Union League (Phila.); Moorestown Field. Office: 5 Penn Center Plaza Philadelphia PA 19181

BENNION, DOUGLAS NOEL, chem. engr., educator; b. Ogden, Utah, Mar. 10, 1935; s. Noel Lindsay and Mildred Amanda (Holmgren) B.; m. Delores Yvonne Wridge, Sept. 15, 1956; children—Debra, Spencer, Donald, Delores, Edwin, Charles, Daniel. B.S. in Chem. Engring, Oreg. State U., 1957, Ph.D., U. Calif., Berkeley, 1964. With Dow Chem., Pittsburg, Calif., 1957-60; mem. faculty dept. chem. engring. UCLA, 1964-80, prof., 1975-80; mem. faculty dept. chem. engring. Brigham Young U., Provo, Utah, 1980—. Contbr. articles to profl. jours. Served with U.S. Army, 1958. Mem. Electrochem. Soc. (pres. 1977-78), Am. Inst. Chem. Engrs., Am. Chem. Soc. Mormon. Office: Dept Chem Engring 350 CB Brigham Young U Provo UT 84602 *Pay attention to what you are doing. Listen to suggestions and counsel, review performance, and improve. Select projects that are challenging, useful and reasonable for you. Get the training appropriate to the task, and build upon the experience of others. Focus mental concentration to the understanding and resolution of problems. Be honest. Apply significant effort, working more than average. Stay with a project long enough to achieve useful results. Be aware of where and who you are. Develop a relationship to God and perform as He expects.*

BENNISON, CHARLES ELLSWORTH, bishop; b. Janesville, Wis., July 23, 1917; s. Floyd William and Cleo Leona (Wilson) B.; m. Marjorie Elizabeth Haglun, June 16, 1942; children: Charles Ellsworth, Mary, John. Student, Lawrence Coll., 1935-38; B.A., U. Minn., 1939; B.D., Seabury-Western Theol. Sem., 1942, D.D., 1960. Ordained priest Episcopal Ch., 1942; rector, Hastings, Minn., 1942-45, Joliet, Ill., 1945-52, Kalamazoo, 1952-60, bishop, 1960—. Trustee Seabury-Western Theol. Sem. Mem. SAR, Beta Theta Pi. Clubs: Outlook, Torch. Office: Cathedral Ch of Christ the King 2600 Vincent Av Kalamazoo MI 49008

BENOIT, GERMAIN EDMOUR, railroad company executive; b. Montreal, Que., Can., June 19, 1919; s. Ovila Joseph and Louisa Marie (Leduc) B.; m. Edith Diana Beasley, Nov. 5, 1951. B.A., Loyola Coll., Montreal. Trainman, conductor Can. Pacific Ry., Montreal, 1942-47, dist. safety agt., 1947-50, asst. supt., Sherbrooke, Que., 1950-57, 957-61, mgr. Que. Central Ry., Sherbrooke, 1961-63, asst. gen. mgr. Atlantic Region, Montreal, 1963-64, gen. mgr. Atlantic Region, 1964-65, v.p. Atlantic Region, 1965—; pres. Aroostook River R.R. Co., Brunterm Ltd., Compagnie d'Investissement Long Champ Inc., Houlton Br. R.R. Co. of Maine, Internat. Ry. Co. of Maine, Newport and Richford R.R. Co.; dir. Frederiction Ry. Co. Mem. Am. Assn. R.R. Supts., Can. Ry. Club, Can. Traffic Club, Montreal Bd. Trade, Vt. State R.R.s Assn. (past pres.), Commn. d'Initiative et de Deve. Econs. Montreal, New Brunswick Devel. Inst., Safety League Que. (past pres.), Montreal C. of C., Met. Que. C. of C. Club: Meadowbrook Golf. Home: 4583 Earnscliffe Ave Montreal PC Canada H3X 2P1 Office: Can Pacific Ry Suite 1134 Catherine St W Montreal PC Canada H3B 1H4

BENOIT, LEROY JAMES, educator; b. Newton, Mass., Aug. 23, 1913; s. Alexander James and Phoebe Anne (White) B.; m. Edith Doris Meyer, May 26, 1939; children: Peter Allan, Diane (Mrs. J. John Ryan). A.B., Tufts U., 1936; licence, U. Paris, France, 1938; A.M., Harvard U., 1939, Ph.D., 1941; Doctor Honoris Causa, U. Coimbra, Portugal, 1952. Asst. prof. French Harvard, 1938-42; assoc. prof. French Amherst Coll., 1945-47; prof. Romance langs. Johns Hopkins, Balt., 1947-51; cultural attache, Lisbon, Portugal, 1951-54, Brazil, 1954-56; dir. lang. and area studies USIA, Washington, 1956-60; dir. cultural exhibit, USSR, 1960, 63; acad. dir. Def. Lang. Program, Washington, 1963-66; prof. linguistics Cornell U., Ithaca, N.Y., 1966-72; prof. French langs. Ga. State U., Atlanta, 1972—, chmn. dept. fgn. langs., 1972-75; ednl. cons. Dennis-Yarmouth (Mass.) Regional Sch. System, 1975-78; adj. prof. Cape Cod Community Coll., 1976-77; cons. U.S. Office Edn., U.S. Dept. State, Ford Found. Author advanced text in French syntax; 8 texts Scepticisme au XIV Siecle en France; Book editor: Barnstable Patriot, 1977-80; Contbr. articles to profl. jours. Chmn. bd. Heart Fund, Bethesda, Md., 1960-61; v.p. PTA, Bethesda, 1962-63; mem. exec. bd. Elder Services Cape Cod. Served to maj. USAAF, 1942-45; Africa, Italy, USSR. Decorated Purple Heart, D.F.C.; Order Brit. Empire; Legion of Honor, (France). Mem. MLA, Linguistic Soc. Am., Yarmouth Hist. Assn., Hist. Soc. Old Yarmouth (trustee 1981—), South Yarmouth Library Assn., Bass River Harbor Assn. (sec. 1977-79), Cape Cod Power Squadron (edn. officer, instr. celestial nav. 1976-81), UN Assn., Phi Beta Kappa. Clubs: Bass River Yacht; Harvard, Cornell, Tufts (Cape Cod) (program dir. 1983—). Home: 1 Homer Ave South Yarmouth MA 02664

BENOLIEL, PETER ANDRE, chemical company executive; b. Phila., Jan. 18, 1932; s. David Jacques and Katherine (Krauss) B.; m. Felicity Roosevelt, Oct. 22, 1982; children by previous marriage: Leslie H., D. Jeffry, Shawn J., Peter W., Todd A. A.B., Princeton U., 1953; postgrad., U. Pa., 1957. Chemist, product mgr. Quaker Chem. Corp., Conshohocken, Pa., 1957-62, v.p., 1963-66, pres., 1966—, chmn., 1980—; dir. Phila. Nat. Corp., UGI Corp. Bd. dirs. Phila. Commn. Effective Criminal Justice, 1974-80; vice chmn. bd. trustees Camp Tecumseh; trustee Marlboro Sch. Music, Philip H and ASW Rosenbach Found., Phila. Mus. Art; chmn. met. area relations com. United Way, 1974-75, trustee, 1967—, gen. chmn., 1981, vice chmn., 1980; pres. Coshohocken Community Chest, 1964-65; bd. dirs. Greater Phila. Partnership; v.p. Phila. Orch. Assn.; bus. chmn. SE Pa. br. Planned Parenthood, 1976-77; mem. council Friends of Library; also adv. council dept. music Princeton U.; mem. internat. adv. council, bd. overseers Faculty Arts and Scis. Bryn Mawr Coll.; assoc. trustee bd. overseers U. Pa.; chmn. long-range planning com. William Penn Charter Sch. (Phila.); bd. visitors, bd. govs. St. John's Coll. Served with USNR, 1953-56. Mem. Young Pres.'s Orgn., Phila. Com. Fgn. Relations. Home: Saint Davids PA Office: Quaker Chemical Corp Conshohocken PA 19428

BENSCH, KLAUS GEORGE, med. educator; b. Miedar, Germany, Sept. 1, 1928; (married); 3 children. M.D., U. Erlangen, Germany, 1953. Diplomate: Am. Bd. Pathology. Intern U. Hosps. of Erlangen, 1953-54; resident in anat. pathology U. Tex. and; M.D. Anderson Hosp., Houston, 1954-56, Yale, 1956-57; instr. pathology Yale Med. Sch., 1958-61, asst. prof., 1961-64, asso. prof., 1964-68; prof. pathology Stanford Med. Sch., 1968—. Mem. Am. Assn. Pathology and Bacteriology. Office: Dept Pathology Stanford U Med Sch Stanford CA 94305

BENSFIELD, RICHARD EDWARD, television writer/producer; b. Los Angeles, June 18, 1926; s. Edward Samuel and Helen Julia (Blumner) B.; m. Donna Jean Ries, June 18, 1949; children: Jan Louise Bensfield Hefley, Thomas Ries. Student, Los Angeles City Coll., 1951-52. Staff writer: TV show Ozzie and Harriet, 1952-67; writer: TV shows including Disney, (1976) One Day at a Time; producer, 1976-77; exec. producer (1977); (Recipient Christopher award for writing 1956). Served with USAF, 1945-50. Mem. Writers Guild Am., West. Republican. Mormon. Office: 100 Universal City Plaza Bldg 84 Universal City CA 91608

BENSINGER, DAVID AUGUST, dentist, university dean; b. St. Louis, May 14, 1926; s. William and Esther (Lissner) B.; m. Myra Blass, Dec. 24, 1944 (div. June 1972); children: Judith Ann (Mrs. William Thomas Haynes), Scott David; m. Susan Cohn Hartman, May 31, 1975. B.A., Washington U., St. Louis, 1944; D.D.S., St. Louis U., 1948; postgrad. health systems mgmt. Harvard U. Sch. Bus. Adminstrn., 1977. Mem. faculty, adminstrn. Sch. Dentistry Washington U., St. Louis, 1949—, assoc. prof. dept. periodontics Sch. Dentistry, 1956-76, prof. Sch. Dentistry, 1976—, assoc. dean Sch. Dentistry, 1970-76, acting dean Sch. Dentistry, 1976-83, exec. assoc. dean Sch. Dentistry, 1983—; practice dentistry, specializing in periodontics, St. Louis, 1949—; mem. staff Barnes, Jewish hosps., both St. Louis; mem. deans com. VA Hosp.; mem. nat. adv. com. Dental Edn. Rev. Com., NIH, 1969-72; cons. Scott AFB, St. Louis, 1956-62; Mem. adv. council SBA, 1975. Editor: Jour. Greater St. Louis Dental Soc, 1963-70; asso. editor: Jour. Mo. Dental Assn, 1966-73. Mem. exec. bd. Ladue (Mo.) Sch. System, 1964-67. Served to lt. M.C. AUS, 1948-49; to capt. M.C. USAF, 1955-56. Fellow Am. Coll. Dentists, Internat. Coll. Dentists; mem. Am. Dental Assn. (ho. of dels.), Mo. Dental Assn. (pres. 1973-74, jud. council), Greater St. Louis Dental Soc. (dir. 1963-70, recipient service award 1971), Am. Acad. Periodontology, Internat. Assn. Dental Research, Midwest Soc. Periodontology (pres. 1972-73), Pierre Fauchard Acad., Washington U. Alumni Assn. (named alumnus year 1968, Omicron Kappa Upsilon.). Club: University (St. Louis). Home: 7514 Wydown Blvd Clayton MO 63105

BENSINGER, PETER BENJAMIN, consulting firm executive; b. Chgo., Mar. 24, 1936; s. Benjamin Edward and Linda Elkus (Galston) B.; m. Judith S. Bensinger; children: Peter Benjamin, Jennifer Anne, Elizabeth Brooke, Virginia Brette. Grad., Phillips Exeter Acad., 1954; B.A., Yale, 1958; hon. degree, San Marcos U., Peru, 1978. Various mktg. positions Brunswick Corp., Chgo., 1958-65, new products mgr., 1966-68; gen. sales mgr. Brunswick Internat., Europe, 1965-66, spl. products mgr., 1966-69; chmn. Ill. Youth Commn., 1969-70; dir. Ill. Dept. Corrections, Chgo., 1970-73; exec. dir. Chgo. Crime Commn., 1973; adminstr. Drug Enforcement Adminstrn., Washington, 1976-81; pres. Bensinger, DuPont & Assocs., Chicago, 1982—; Cons. various orgns.; del. White House Conf. on Corrections, 1971. Pres. Lincoln Park Zool. Soc., Chgo., 1962—; governing life mem., also mem. men's council Chgo. Art Inst.; mem. Ill. Alcoholism Adv. Council, Ill. Law Enforcement Commn., Ill. Council on Diagnosis and Evaluation Criminal Defendants, Ill. Narcotics Adv. Council; adv. com. Center for Studies in Criminal Justice, So. Ill. U., Center for Studies in Criminal Justice, U. Chgo.; vice chmn. ad hoc adv. com. U.S. Dept. Justice Nat. Inst. Corrections; mem. exec. com. Am. Bar Assn. Nat. Commn. Corrections; chmn. Ill. Task Force on Corrections, 1969; mem. bd. Fed. Prison Industries, Inc.; bd. dirs. Jewish Fedn. Met. Chgo., Council Community Services Met. Chgo., Ill. Commn. on Children; bd. dirs., mem. exec. council Anti-Defamation League; regional bd. dirs. NCCJ; trustee Phillips Exeter Acad.; chmn. nat. law enforcement explorers conf. Boy Scouts Am., 1981; U.S. del. to, Interpol, 1978. Recipient Young Leadership award Jewish Fedn.-Welfare Bds. Met. Chgo., 1969, award for excellence John Howard Assn., 1972; EEO award, 1979. Mem. Am. Correctional Assn. (dir.), Assn. State Correctional Adminstrs. (sec. 1971-72, pres. 1972-73), Internat. Assn. Chiefs of Police (exec. com.), Nat. Sheriffs Assn. (life). Clubs: Chicago City (dir.), Arts; Yale (N.Y.C.); Cosmos (Washington). Office: 20 N Wacker Dr Chicago IL 60606

BENSLEY, EDWARD HORTON, educator; b. Toronto, Ont., Can., Dec. 10, 1906; s. Benjamin Arthur and Ruth (Horton) B.; m. Catharine Speid, Sept. 9, 1944. B.A. (Fulton scholar 1924, Balmer scholar 1924; Blake scholar 1925, Wilson scholar 1926, Bronze medal Brit. Assn. Advancement Sci. 1927), U. Toronto, 1927, M.D. (Gold medal 1930), 1930; D.Sc. (hon.), Acadia U., 1964. Diplomate: licentiate Med. Council Can. Jr. intern Montreal Gen. Hosp., 1930-31, resident pathology, 1931-32, mem. staff, 1932—, dir. dept. metabolism and toxicology, 1947-61, chem. pathologist-in-chief, 1947-61, sec. med. bd., 1951-60, cons. physician, 1962—; hon. cons. Royal Victoria Hosp., 1962-67; mem. faculty McGill U., 1932-34, 41—; asst. dir. Univ. Med. Clinic, 1952-57, vice dean faculty medicine, 1961-67, prof. exptl. medicine, 1965-77, hon. lectr. biochemistry, 1956-69, lectr. in history of medicine, 1968—, prof. medicine emeritus, 1977—, hon. Osler librarian, 1979—; cons. metabolism and toxicology Reddy Meml. Hosp., 1950-61; chmn. nutrition panel Def. Research Bd., 1949-52; mem. Canadian Council Nutrition, 1948-58; cons. nutrition Canadian Forces Med. Council, 1957-60; pres. Nutrition Soc. Can., 1961-62. Contbr. numerous articles in fields metabolic diseases, clin. chemistry, nutrition, toxicology, med. history. Bd. curators, past chmn. Osler Library. Served to maj. M.C. Royal Canadian Army, World War II. Decorated Order Brit. Empire. Fellow A.C.P., Royal Coll. Physicians Can., Chem. Inst. Can.; mem. Canadian Med. Assn. (past chmn. com. nutrition), Canadian Soc. Clin. Chemists (past pres.), Osler Soc. (past hon. pres.), Canadian Fedn. Biol. Socs. (past hon. sec.). Home: 157 Morrison Ave Montreal PQ H3R 1K5 Canada Office: 3655 Drummond St Montreal PQ H3G 1Y6 Canada

BENSLEY, ROBERT RUSSELL, TV producer; b. Chgo., June 12, 1930; s. Robert Daniel and Sylvia (Holton) B.; m. Patricia Bannon, Aug. 16, 1969; children: Robert, Robin, Victoria. B.S. in Journalism, Northwestern U., 1951, M.S., 1952. Writer, producer, WBBM-TV, Chgo., 1951-60; writer, producer, dir., CBS News, N.Y.C., 1960-63; Chgo. bur. mgr., CBS News, 1963-64; producer, CBS Evening News, N.Y.C., 1964-71; exec. producer, CBS Evening News, 1972; dir. spl. events, CBS Evening News, 1972-82; exec. producer, CBS Weekend News, 1982, On the Road, 1983, American Parade, 1984—. Mem. Dirs. Guild Am., Writers Guild Am. Office: 555 W 57th St New York NY 10019

BENSON, ANDREW ALM, biochemistry educator; b. Modesto, Calif., Sept. 24, 1917; s. Carl Bennett and Emma Carolina (Alm) B.; m. Dorothy Dorgan, July 31, 1971; children: Claudia Benson Matthews, Linnea, Bonnie Benson Kumar (dec.). B.S., U. Calif., Berkeley, 1939; Ph.D., Calif. Inst. Tech., 1942; Phil.D. (hon.), U. Oslo., 1965. Instr. chemistry U. Calif., Berkeley, 1942-43, asst. dir. bio.-organic group Radiation Lab., 1946-54, assoc. prof. agrl. biol. chemistry Radiation Lab., 1955-60; prof. Pa. State U., 1960-61; prof.-in-residence biophys./physiol. chemistry UCLA, 1961-62; prof. Scripps Instn. Oceanography, U. Calif., San Diego, 1962—; research assoc. OSRD dept. chemistry Stanford U., 1944-45. Contbr. articles on biochem. research to profl. jours. Trustee Found. for Ocean Research, San Diego; mem. adv. council The Costeau Soc., 1976—. Recipient Sugar Research Found. award, 1950, Ernest Orlando Lawrence Meml. award, 1962; Sr. Queen's fellow, Australia, 1979. Mem. Am. Chem. Soc., Am. Soc. Plant Physiologists (Stephen Hales award 1972), Japan Soc. Plant Physiologists), Am. Soc. Biol. Chemists, Nat. Acad. Sci., Am. Acad. Arts and Scis. Home: 6044 Folsom Dr La Jolla CA 92037 Office: Scripps Instn Oceanography A-002 La Jolla CA 92093

BENSON, CHARLES SCOTT, educator; b. Atlanta, May 20, 1922; s. Marion Trotti and Sallie May (Bagley) B.; m. Dorothy Ruth Merrick, June 8, 1946; children: Michele, Charles Scott, Sally Merrick. A.B., Princeton U., 1943; M.A., Columbia U., 1948, Ph.D., 1950. Mem. faculty Bowdoin Coll., Maine, 1950-55, Harvard U., 1955-64; asso. prof. U. Calif., Berkeley, 1964-68, prof. econs. of edn., 1968—; vis. prof. dept. edn. Stanford U., 1980-81; cons. NAACP, San Francisco, R.I. Spl. Commn. on Edn., Calif. Bd. Edn., Com. Econ. Devel., Conn. Gov.'s Commn. on Tax Reform, Govt. Pakistan Planning Commn., Nat. Acad. Edn; staff dir. N.Y. State Edn. Commn.; mem. Pres.'s Adv. Panel on Financing Elem. and Secondary Edn., 1979—; mem. com. on vocat. edn. Nat. Acad. Scis. Author: The Economics of Public Education, 1961, 3d edit., 1978, The Cheerful Prospect, 1965, The School and the Economic System, 1966, (with others) Planning for Educational Reform: Financial and Social Alternatives, 1974; Editor: Perspectives on the Economics of Education, 1963. Served with USN, 1943-46. Mem. Am. Econ. Assn., Econometric Soc., AAAS, Am. Edni. Fin. Assn. (pres. 1977-78), Phi Delta Kappa. Home: 147 Arlington St Kensington CA 94707 Office: Tolman Hall Univ Calif Berkeley CA 94720

BENSON, DAVID WILLIAM, univ. vice pres.; b. N. Branch, Minn., Oct. 13, 1931; s. Fredolf Ernest and Ruth (Rystrom) B.; m. Betty Juan Broders, Feb. 29, 1952; 1 dau., Mary. B.S., U. Calif. at Los Angeles, 1954, M.S., 1958; Ph.D., U. So. Calif., 1966. Instr. U. Calif. at Los Angeles, 1958-61; asst. prof. to prof. phys. edn., Calif. State U., Northridge, 1961-67, dean acad. planning, dean acad. adminstrn., v.p., 1967—. Served as ensign USNR, 1954-56. Named distinguished tchr. San Ferando Valley State Coll., 1966. Home: 23505 Schoenborn St Canoga Park CA 91304 Office: 18111 Nordhoff St Northridge CA 91324

BENSON, EDWARD M., JR., oil company executive; b. Kansas City, Mo., 1920; s. Edward Munroe and Margretta (Brown) B.; m. Shirley Clymer, Sept. 5, 1942; children: Stuart E., John M., Christine. B.S., U. Calif., Berkeley, 1942. With Atlantic Richfield Co., 1947—, v.p., 1966-73, sr. v.p., from 1972, exec. v.p., 1973-80, vice chmn., 1980—, also dir.; dir. Mission Ins. Group Inc. Trustee Harvey Mudd Coll., 1975—, Southwestern Legal Found.; bd. councillors Sch. Public Adminstrn., U. So. Calif., 1980—. Served to maj. U.S. Army, 1942-46. Fellow Claremont U. Center, 1980—. Mem. Am. Petroleum Inst. (dir.), Inst. for Advancement of Engring. (adv. com.), Western Oil and Gas Assn. (Wildcat com.), Industry Edn. Council Calif. (dir.). Republican. Episcopalian. Clubs: Calif., Virginia Country (Long Beach, Calif.). Office: 515 S Flower St Los Angeles CA 90071

BENSON, GEORGE, guitarist; b. Pitts., Mar. 22, 1943; (married); 4 children. Leader jazz group, 1965—; formerly with, Jack McDuff; recs. include This Masquerade (Grammy award for best record of year 1977); album Breezin' (Grammy award for best instrumental performance, also Grammy award for best engineered rec. 1977), Body Talk, White Rabbitt, Good King Bad, In Flight. Named to Top 10 for a decade Downbeat Record Poll, 1976 *

BENSON, GEORGE STUART, university chancellor; b. Okla. Ter., Sept. 26, 1898; s. Stuart Felix and Emma (Rogers) B.; m. Sallie Ellis Hockaday, July 2, 1925 (dec. 1980); children: Mary Ruth, Fannie Lois.; m. Marguerite O'Banion, Feb. 22, 1983. B.S., Okla. A. and M. Coll., Stillwater, 1924; A.B., Harding Coll., 1925, LL.D., 1932; M.A., U. Chgo., 1931; LL.D., Knox Coll., 1948, Waynesburg Coll., Okla. Christian Coll., 1968, Freed-Hardeman Coll., 1981. Tchr. rural schs., Okla., 1918-21, high sch. prin., 1924-25, missionary and tchr., South China, 1925-36; prof. English Nat. Sun Yat Sen U., Canton, China, 1929-30; editor Oriental Christian, Canton, 1929-36; founder, trustee and pres. Canton Bible Sch., 1930-36; pres. Harding Coll., 1936-65; chancellor Okla. Christian Coll., 1956-67, Ala. Christian Coll., Montgomery, 1975—; Tchr., authority on Oriental religions and philosophy. Writer: syndicated weekly newspaper column Looking Ahead, 1942—; producer: radio program Land of the Free (now Behind the News), 1942—; Contbr. to religious publs. and secular mags. Pres. Ark. Pub. Expenditure Council, 1942-44, 52-56; dir. Nat. Thrift Com., Inc.; Mem. Nat. Com. for Religion and Welfare Recovery, 1939; mem. advisory bd. U.S. Mcht. Marine Acad., Kings Point, N.Y., 1953-56; pres. Nat. Edn. Program, Searcy, Ark., 1942—; chmn. bd. Zambia Christian Secondary Sch., Kalomo, 1966—; mem. nat. adv. bd. Am. Security Council, 1975—; mem. Pres. Reagan's Task Force. Recipient numerous awards Freedoms Found., Horatio Alger award, 1981; named to Okla. Hall of Fame, 1972, Arkansan of Year, 1953-54; others. Mem. Nat. Assn. Sch. Adminstrs., C. of C., AIM, Pi Kappa Delta. Mem. Ch. of Christ. Club: Kiwanian. Home: 25 Harding Dr Searcy AR 72143 Home: Harding U Box 760 Searcy AR 72143

BENSON, JAMES, advt. agy. exec.; b. Bromley, Kent, Eng., July 17, 1925; s. Henry Herbert and Olive (Hutchinson) B.; m. Honoria Margaret Hurley, June 29, 1950; 1 dau., Teresa Jill. B.A. with honors, Cambridge (Eng.) U., also M.A. Mgr. research dept. Kemsley Newspapers Ltd., London, 1949-58; with Mather & Crow Ltd. (changed to Ogilvy Benson & Mather Ltd.), London,; mng. dir., then chmn.; now vice chmn. Ogilvy & Mather Internat., Inc., N.Y.C. Author books on naval history. Served with Brit. Royal Navy, 1943-46. Home: 9 E 79th St New York NY 10021 Office: 2 E 48th St New York NY 10017

BENSON, JAMES DEWAYNE, univ. dean; b. Fairbury, Nebr., June 23, 1925; s. Earl Mark and Cleone Matilda (Wycoff) B.; m. Maran Schueller, May 29, 1948; children—David, Barbara, Mary, Stephen. B.Sc., Creighton U., 1949; M.A., U. Iowa, 1952, Ph.D., 1958. Asst. prof. mktg. Iowa State U., 1952-54, 55-57; asso. prof. So. Ill. U., 1957-62, U. Iowa, 1962-70; dean Coll. Bus. Administrn., No. Ariz. U., 1970-73; dir. corp. mktg. Motorola Inc., Chgo., 1973-75; dean Coll. Bus., No. Ill. U., 1975—; Dir. BeeLine Motor Freight Inc.; Cons. Corn Belt Coop., Benson & Assos., Northwestern Bell Telephone Co. Contbr. articles to profl. jours. Pres. No. Ariz. Social Welfare, 1971-73. Served to 2nd lt., AC AUS, 1943-45. Mem. Am. Mktg. Assn., Midwest Econs. Assn., Midwest Bus. Assn., Am. Assembly Collegiate Schs. Bus. (pres. Mid-continent East region), Western and Mid-Western Deans Colls. of Bus., DeKalb (Ill.) C. of C., Omicron Delta Epsilon, Beta Gamma Sigma, Phi Eta Sigma. Club: Kiwanian. Home: 2 Golf View Pl DeKalb IL 60115

BENSON, JOHN ALEXANDER, JR., physician, educator; b. Manchester, Conn., July 23, 1921; s. John A. and Rachel (Patterson) B.; m. Irene Zucker, Sept. 29, 1947; children—Peter M., John Alexander III, Susan Leigh, Jeremy P. B.A., Wesleyan U., 1943; M.D., Harvard U., 1946. Diplomate: Am. Bd. Internal Medicine (mem. bd. 1969—, sec.-treas. 1972-75), and subsplty. bd. gastroenterology (mem. 1961-66, chmn. 1965-66). Intern Univ. Hosps., Cleve., 1946-47; resident Peter Bent Brigham Hosp., Boston, 1949-51; fellow Mass. Gen. Hosp., Boston, 1951-53; research asst. Mayo Clinic, Rochester, Minn., 1953-54; instr. medicine Harvard, 1956-59; prof. medicine, head div. gastroenterology U. Oreg., 1959-75; pres. Am. Bd. Internal Medicine, 1975—; cons. VA Hosps., Madigan Gen. Army Hosp. Editorial bd.: Am. Jour. Digestive Diseases, 1966-73; Contbr. articles to profl. jours. Mem. Oreg. Drug Adv. Council, 1965-73; Dir. Oreg. Med. Ednl. Found., 1967-73, pres., 1969-72. Served with USNR, 1947-49. Mem. Am. Gastroenterol. Assn. (sec. 1970-73, v.p. 1975-76, pres.-elect 1976-77, pres. 1977-78), Am. Clin. and Climatol. Assn., ACP (master), AMA, Am. Soc. Internal Medicine, Western Assn. Physicians, North Pacific Soc. Internal Medicine, Am. Fedn. Clin. Research, Federated Council for Internal Medicine, Am. Assn. Study Liver Disease, Western Soc. Clin. Investigation, Phi Beta Kappa, Sigma Xi, Alpha Omega Alpha. Home: 222 SW Harrison St #20C

Portland OR 97201 Office: Am Bd Internal Medicine 200 SW Market St Portland OR 97201

BENSON, KENNETH PETER, forest industry executive; b. Vancouver, B.C., Can., Mar. 1, 1927; s. Lawrence and Clara (Peel) B.; m. Joyce Alice Heino, Nov. 4, 1949; children: David, Sally. Chartered acct., U. B.C., Vancouver, 1953. Asst. controller Powell River Co., Vancouver, 1955-62; with B.C. Forest Products Co., Vancouver, 1962, comptroller, 1962, v.p. fin., 1967, dir., 1970, exec. v.p. ops., 1972, sr. exec. v.p., 1974, pres., chief operating officer, 1976-79, pres., chief exec. officer, 1979—; bd. dirs. Pulp & Paper Indsl. Relations Bur., Council Forest Industries, Can. Pulp & Paper Assn., Forest Engring. Research Inst. Can. Home: 6329 Angus Dr Vancouver BC Canada V6M 3P4 Office: BC Forest Products Ltd 1050 W Pender St Vancouver BC Canada V6E 2X3

BENSON, KENNETH SAMUEL, mining, smelting, chemical, fertilizer company executive, barrister, solicitor; b. Vancouver, B.C., Can., Aug. 12, 1937; s. Samuel and Ruby Gertrude (Poole) B.; m. Inara Blums, Aug. 8, 1964. B.Com., U. B.C., 1961, LL.B, 1962. Bar: called to B.C. bar 1963. Articled student-at-law Ellis, Dryer and Co., Vancouver, 1962-63; petroleum landman Atlantic Refining Co., Alta., Can., 1963-65, Corpus Christi and Dallas, Tex., 1963-65; barrister, solicitor Guild, Yule and Co., Vancouver, 1965-68; corp. sec. Bulkey Valley Forest Industries Ltd., Vancouver, 1968-72; barrister, solicitor, asst. corp. sec. Cominco Ltd., Vancouver, 1972-80, corp. sec., 1980—, Pine Point Mines Ltd., 1980—, Vestgron Mines Ltd., 1980—, Kamcon Mines Ltd., 1980—; dir. Canpotex Ltd., Toronto, Ont., Can. Bd. dirs. Vancouver Symphony Soc., 1982—. Mem. Can. Bar Assn., Law Soc. B.C. Club: University (Vancouver). Home: 4250 Yuculta Crescent Vancouver BC Canada V6N 3R5 Office: Cominco Ltd 200 Granville St Vancouver BC Canada V6C 2R2

BENSON, KENNETH VICTOR, manufacturing company executive, lawyer; b. New Lisbon, Wis., Aug. 2, 1929; s. Carl W. and Ottilia (Olson) B.; m. Alice May Drewry, June 23, 1951; children: Jennifer, Elizabeth, Kenneth, Jonathan, Nathan. B.B.A., U. Wis., 1951, J.D., 1957. Bar: Wis. 1957. Sales trainee, sales corr. Marathon Corp., Menasha, Wis., 1953-54; practice law with Benson & Day, Marshfield, Wis., 1957-58; sr. v.p., dir., exec. com. Kohler Co., Wis., 1959-81; v.p. corp. devel., dir. Vollrath Co., Sheboygan, Wis., 1982—; dir. Citizens Bancorp., Wis., Wigwam Mills Inc., Sheboygan. Bd. dirs. Sheboygan United Fund, 1969-75; bd. dirs. Sheboygan YMCA, 1971-79, sec., 1975-76, v.p., 1977-79; pres. Sheboygan Community Players and Civic Orch., 1967-69, bd. dirs., 1963-76; bd. dirs. Sheboygan Retirement Home, 1976—, v.p., 1979-80, pres., 1980-81; bd. trustees Lakeland Coll., 1978—. Served with AUS, 1951-53. Mem. Sheboygan County Bar Assn. (pres. 1972). Episcopalian. Lodge: Kiwanis (dir. 1962-65). Home: Oostburg WI 53070 Office: Vollrath Co 1236 N 18th St Sheboygan WI 53081

BENSON, LARRY DEAN, language and literature educator; b. Sioux Falls, S.D., June 20, 1929; s. Joseph Robert and Elsie (Ellis) B.; m. Margaret Owens, Jan. 5, 1951; children—Cassandra, Gavin, Amanda, Geoffrey. A.B., U. Calif. at Berkeley, 1955, A.M., 1957, Ph.D., 1959. Lectr. English U. Calif. at Berkeley, 1958-59; instr. Harvard, 1959-62, asst. prof., 1962-65, asso. prof., 1966-69, prof., 1969—, chmn. dept. English and Am. lang. and lit., 1980—; Allston Burr sr. tutor Quincy House, 1963-65. Author: Art and Tradition in Sir Gawain and the Green Knight, 1965, (with T.M. Andersson) The Literary Context of Chaucer's Fabliaux, 1971, King Arthur's Death, 1974; editor: The Learned and the Lewed, 1975, Malory's Morte Darthur, 1976, (with J.F. Leyerle) Chivalric Literature, 1980, (with S. Wenzel) Wisdom of Poetry, 1982; Asst. editor: Speculum, 1965—. Served with USMCR, 1946-48, 50-51. Guggenheim fellow, 1965. Fellow Medieval Acad. Am. (asst. exec. sec. 1965-71, assoc. exec. sec. 1971-78), Am. Acad. Arts and Scis. Home: 24 Woodland Rd Lexington MA 02173 Office: 271 Widener Library Harvard Cambridge MA 02138

BENSON, LUCY PETERS WILSON, consultant; b. N.Y.C., Aug. 25, 1927; d. Willard Oliver and Helen (Peters) Wilson; m. Bruce Buzzell Benson, Mar. 30, 1950. B.A., Smith Coll., 1949, M.A., 1955; L.H.D. (hon.), Wheaton Coll., Norton, Mass., 1965, Carleton Coll., 1973, Bucknell U., 1972, Bates Coll., 1982, LL.D., U. Mass., 1969, U. Md., 1972, Amherst Coll., 1974, Clark U., 1975; H.H.D., Springfield Coll., 1981. With jr. exec. tng. program Bloomingdale's, N.Y.C., 1949-50; engaged in pub. relations Smith Coll., 1950-53, Mt. Holyoke Coll., 1955; research asst. dept. Am. studies Amherst Coll., 1956-57; pres. League Women Voters, Amherst, Mass., 1957-58, 59-61, dir., Mass., 1957-61, pres., 1961-63, 63-65, nat. bd. dirs., 1965-66, 2d v.p., 1966-68, nat. pres., 1968-74; sec. human services Commonwealth of Mass., 1975; mem. Spl. Commn. on Adminstrv. Rev., U.S. Ho. of Reps., 1976-77; under sec. state for security assistance, sci. and tech., Washington, 1977-80, now chmn. Nat. News Council. Trustee Northeast Utilities, 1971-74, 76-77; dir. Dreyfus Fund, Dreyfus Liquid Assets, Dreyfus Spl. Income Fund, Continental Group, Inc., Grumman Corp., Sci. Applications Internat. Corp.; Mem. steering com. Urban Coalition, 1968, exec. com., 1970-75, 80—, co-chmn., 1973-75; mem. Gov. Mass. Spl. Com. Rev. Sunday Closing Laws, 1961; mem. spl. commn. Mass. Legislature to Study Budgetary Powers of Trustees U. Mass., 1961-62; mem. Gov. Mass. Com. Rev. Salaries State Employees, 1963, Mass. Adv. Bd. Higher Ednl. Policy, 1962-65, Mass. Bd. Edn. Adv. Com. Racial Imbalance and Edn., 1964-65, Mass. adv. com. U.S. Commn. Civil Rights, 1964-73; vice chmn. Mass. Adv. Council Edn., 1965-68; mem. Mass. Com. Children and Youth Com. to Study Report by U.S. Children's Bur., Mass. Youth Service Div., 1967; mem. pub. adv. com. U.S. Trade Policy, 1968; mem. vis. com. John F. Kennedy Sch. Govt.; mem. Trilateral Commn.; Mem. town meeting, Amherst, 1957-74, finance com., 1960-66; Trustee Edn. Devel. Center, Newton, Mass., 1967-72, Nat. Urban League, 1974-77, Smith Coll., 1975-80, Brookings Instn., 1974-77, Alfred P. Sloan Found., 1975-77; bd. dirs. Catalyst, 1972—; former bd. govs. Am. Nat. Red Cross, Common Cause, Women's Action Alliance. Recipient Achievement award Bur. Govt. Research, U. Mass., 1963; Distinguished Service award Boston Coll., 1965; Smith Coll. medal, 1969; Distinguished Civic Leadership award Tufts U., 1965; Distinguished Service award Northfield Mount Hermon Sch., 1976; Radcliffe fellow Radcliffe Inst., 1965-66, 66-67. Mem. Nat. Acad. Pub. Adminstrn., ACLU, UN Assn., Urban League, NAACP, Council Fgn. Relations, Assn. Am. Indian Affairs, East African Wildlife Soc., Jersey Wildlife Preservation Trust Channel Islands. Home: 46 Sunset Ave Amherst MA 01002 Office: Benson & Assos Inc Suite 511 1611 N Kent St Arlington VA 22209 also 46 Sunset Ave Amherst MA 01002

BENSON, MORTON, educator; b. Newark, Dec. 13, 1924; s. Jacob and Mollie (Ravin) B.; m. Evelyn Rose, July 3, 1955; children—Rebecca J., Miriam E. B.A., N.Y. U., 1947; Certificat, Grenoble U., France, 1948; student, Frankfurt (Germany) U., 1948-50; Ph.D., U. Pa., 1954. Asst. prof. Ohio U., 1954-60; mem. faculty U. Pa., 1960—; prof., chmn. dept. Slavic langs., dir. Slavic Lang. and Area Center, 1966-74; Mem. joint com. on Eastern Europe Am. Council Learned Socs., 1971-73. Author: Dictionary of Russian Personal Names, 2d rev. edit., 1967, Serbocroatian-English Dictionary, 1971, 2d edit., 1979, English-Serbocroatian Dictionary, 2d edit., 1980; asso. editor: Slavic and East European Jour, 1960-70; mem. editorial bd.: Names, 1967-70; mem. adv. bd.: Am. Speech, 1961-62; contbr. articles to profl. jours. Served with AUS, 1943-46, 48-52. Fulbright-Hays research fellow, 1965-66. Mem. Am. Assn. Tchrs. Slavic and East European Langs. (pres. 1964), Linguistic Soc. Am., Assn. Internat. des Langues and Litteratures Slaves (sec. 1963-66), MLA, Dictionary Soc. N.Am. Home: 219 Myrtle Ave Havertown PA 19083 Office: Dept Slavic Langs Univ Pa Philadelphia PA 19104

BENSON, NETTIE LEE, educator; b. Arcadia, Tex., Jan. 15, 1905; d. Jasper William and Vora Ann (Reddell) B. Student, Tex. Presbyn. Coll., 1922-24; B.A., U. Tex., Austin, 1929, M.A., 1935, Ph.D., 1949. High sch. tchr., Monterrey, Mex., 1925-27, pub. sch. tchr., Sinton, Tex., 1927-28, Hartley, Tex., 1930-31, high sch. tchr., Ingleside, Tex., 1932-41; librarian Latin Am. collection U. Tex., Austin, 1942-75, prof. Mexican history, 1962—, prof. library sci., 1964-75; Latin Am. Coop. Acquisition Project agt. for New York Pub. Library and Steebert-Hafner, Inc., 1960-62; pres. Seminar on Acquition Latin Am. Library Materials, 1970-71, Internat. Congress on Mexican Studies, 1972; mem. Task Force on Libraries Info. Resources Internat. Edn., Am. Council Edn., 1974. Author: La Diputacion provincial y el federalismo mexicano, 1955, Mexico and the Spanish Cortes 1810-1822, 1968; Translator: The United States versus Porfirio Diaz, 1964; Mem. editorial bd.: Hispanic Am. Hist. Rev, 1974—; Contbr. articles profl. jours. Recipient S.W. Council on Latin Am. Studies award for distinction in scholarship and teaching, 1968-69; Distinguished Service award Conf. Latin Am. History, Am. Hist. Assn., 1976; Aguila Azteca award Mexican Govt., 1979. Fellow Tex. Hist. Assn.; mem. Am. Hist. Assn., Conf. on Latin Am. Studies, Latin Am. Studies Assn., Sigma Delta Pi, Phi Alpha Theta, Pi Kappa Alpha. Democrat. Presbyn. Home: 2834 Shoal Crest St Austin TX 78705

BENSON, OLIVER EARL, political scientist, educator; b. Guthrie, Okla., Aug. 20, 1911; s. Earl A. and Ivy (Hurley) B.; m. June Tompkins, June 1, 1940 (dec. 1981); children: John, Megan (Mrs. Graydon Hale Doolittle). B.A., U. Okla., 1932; M.A., 1933; Docteur ès sciences politiques, U. Geneva, 1936. Instr. govt. U. Okla., Norman, 1936, asst. prof., 1938-41, asso. prof., 1941-47, prof., 1947-67, George Lynn Cross research prof. polit. sci., 1967-80, emeritus, 1980—; chmn. dept. govt., 1946-51, 59-62; dir. grad. internat. studies, dir. Bur. Govt. Research, 1962-69; Vis. prof. history Peabody Coll., 1940; info. analyst U.S. office war info., 1942; vis. prof. polit. sci. Northwestern U., 1954-55, 68, U. Minn., 1964; vis. prof. govt. U. Tex., 1956-57; dir. Okla. Inst. Internat. Relations, 1947-51; mem. Brookings Instn. Seminar U.S. Fgn. Policy, 1952, Naval War Coll. Global Strat. Discussions, 1955. Author: Through the Diplomatic Looking Glass, 1939, How Vulnerable is Communism, 1952, Policy Making in Communist China, 1959, A Simple Diplomatic Game, The Emergent Nations: Problem for the Sixties, 1963, Oklahoma Votes: 1907-62, 1964, Oklahoma Votes for Congress, 1965, Political Science Laboratory, 1969, El laboratorio de ciencia politica, 1974; also articles.; Editor: Southwestern Social Sci. Quar, 1947-53. Served with USNR, 1942-46. Fellow grad. Inst. Internat. Studies, 1935-36, Social Sci. Found., 1964-65. Mem. Hansard Soc., Am., So., S.W., Midwest polit. sci. assns., AAAS, Am. Soc. Pub. Adminstrn., Am. Acad. Polit. and Social Scis., Internat. Inst. Strategic Studies, Am. Assn. U. Profs., Southwestern Social Sci. Assn. (pres. 1970-71, exec. council 1968-77), Phi Beta Kappa, Phi Eta Sigma. Democrat. Presbyn. Clubs: Faculty (Norman, Okla.); Sierra, Allenspark Men's Dinner, Colorado Mountain. Home: 640 E Boyd St Norman OK 73071 also Kingscourt Allenspark CO 80510

BENSON, ROBERT DALE, mgmt. cons.; b. Little River, Kans., June 4, 1912; s. Leslie Robert and Vernena (Sherer) B.; m. Nelle Malick Payne, Dec. 23, 1933 (dec.); children—Robert Payne, Robin Sherwood; m. Gertrude Marie Trudeau, June 21, 1975. Grad., Hutchinson (Kans.) Jr. Coll., 1932; student, Northwestern U., 1939-40; grad., Army Indsl. Coll., 1944. Chief acct. Associated Dairies, Wichita, Kans., 1933-34; chief acct., comptroller Steffen Ice and Ice Cream Corp., Wichita, 1936; with Spurrier & Wood (C.P.A.s), Wichita, 1935; partner Spurrier, Wood & Benson (accts. and auditors), Hutchinson, 1941-43; with firm P.H. Willems (accts. and auditors), McPherson, Kans., 1937; partner Willems & Benson (accts. and auditors), McPherson, 1937-43; chief fixed price audits, chief spl. audits, chief termination audits brs. Hdqrs. USAAF, 1943-47; chief spl. audits br., asst. chief indsl. audits div. Hdqrs. Army Audit Agy., 1947-48; dep. auditor gen. USAF, 1948-53; dep. for acctg. and fin. mgmt. to asst. sec. Air Force, 1953-58, dep. asst. sec., 1958-69, prin. dep. asst. sec., 1969-71; chmn. bd. dirs. Internat. Finance & Mgmt. Corp., Washington, 1971-72; pres. Robert D. Benson & Assos. (mgmt. cons.), Washington, 1972—; guest lectr. George Washington U., 1953-56. Asso. editor: Future mag, Chgo., 1944. Pres. Kans. Jr. C. of C., 1942-43; bd. dirs. Kans. C. of C., 1942-43; v.p. U.S. Jr. C. of C., 1943-44, treas., 1944-45; mem. Bd. U.S. Civil Service Examiners, 1955-71. Named Outstanding Young Man Kans., 1942; recipient Exceptional Civilian Service decoration Dept. Air Force, 1953, 55, 69, 71. Mem. Am. Acctg. Assn., Air Force Assn., Assn. Govt. Accts., Kans. Soc. Lic. Mcpl. Public Accts., Ordre Des Compagnons Du Bontemps-Medoc et Graves (Bordeaux, France; hon. comdr.), Internat. Wine and Food Soc., Les Amis du Vin, Kans. State Soc. Clubs: Rotary; Kenwood Country (Bethesda, Md.); Manor Country (Rockville, Md.); Nat. Aviation (Washington). Home: 3506 Manor Rd Chevy Chase MD 20815

BENSON, ROBERT ELLIOTT, investment banker; b. Bklyn., June 13, 1916; s. Philip Adolphus and Louise A. (Melville) B.; m. Elena Vittoria, June 13, 1942; children: Elena V. (Mrs. Peter Ganzenmuller), Christine L. (Mrs. Alan Corey III), Robert Elliott, William M., David Philip. S.B., Mass. Inst. Tech., 1937; postgrad., Bklyn. Poly. Inst., 1938-39; M.B.A., Harvard, 1941; grad., Program for Execs., Carnegie Inst. Tech., 1957. Student engr. Consol. Edison Co. N.Y., Inc., N.Y.C., 1937-39; security analyst City Bank Farmers Trust Co., N.Y.C., 1940; asst. engr. L.I. Lighting Co., Mineola, N.Y., 1941-42; security analyst Equitable Life Assurance Soc. U.S., 1946, 2d v.p., 1956-60, v.p., 1960-66; exec. asst. to pres. Internat. Tel. & Tel. Corp., N.Y.C., 1966, v.p., 1967-76; sr. cons. White, Weld & Co. Inc., N.Y.C., 1976-78; v.p. Merrill Lynch, Pierce, Fenner & Smith Inc., 1978—; trustee Dime Savs. Bank N.Y. Pres., trustee YWCA Retirement Fund; trustee McAuley Water St. Mission. Served from 2d lt. to maj. AUS, 1942-46. Decorated Legion of Merit. Republican. Clubs: Beaver Dam Winter Sports (Locust Valley); The Creek, City Midday. Home: Duck Pond Rd Locust Valley NY 11560 Office: One Liberty Plaza 165 Broadway New York NY 10080

BENSON, SIDNEY WILLIAM, chemistry educator; b. N.Y.C., Sept. 26, 1918; m. Ann McElroy (dec.); 2 children. A.B., Columbia Coll., 1938; A.M., Harvard U., 1941, Ph.D., 1941. Research asst. Gen. Electric Co., 1940; research fellow Harvard U., 1941-42; instr. chemistry CCNY, 1942-43; group leader Manhattan Project Kellex Corp., 1943; asst. prof. U.So. Calif., 1943-48; assoc. prof. U. So. Calif., 1948-51, prof. chemistry, 1951-64, dir. chem. physics program, 1962-63, sci. dir. Hydrocarbon Research Inst., 1977—; research assoc. dept. chemistry and chem. engring. Calif. Inst. Tech., 1957-58; vis. prof. UCLA, 1959, U. Ill., 1959; hon. Gliddne lectr. Purdue U., 1961; vis. prof. chemistry Stanford U., 1966-70, 71, 73; mem. adv. panel phys. chemistry Nat. Bur. Standards, 1969-72, chmn., 1970-71; hon. vis. prof. U. Utah, 1971; vis. prof. U. Paris VII and XI, 1971-72, U. St. Andrews, Scotland, 1973, U. Lausanne, Switzerland, 1979; cons. in field. Author: Foundations of Chemical Kinetics, 1960, Thermochemical Kinetics, 1968, 3d edit., 1976, Critical Survey of the Data of the Kinetics of Gas Phase Unimolecular Reactions, 1970, Atoms, Molecules, and Chemical Reactions, 1970, Chemical Calculations, 3d edit., 1971; editor in chief Internat. Jour. Chem. Kinetics, 1967-83; mem. editorial adv. bd. Combustion Sci. and Tech., 1973—; mem. editorial bd. Oxidation Communications, 1978—, Revs. of Chem. Intermediates, 1979—; mem. Hydrocarbon Letters, 1980—; mem. editorial bd. Jour. Phys. Chemistry, 1981—. Guggenheim fellow, 1950-51; NSF fellow, 1957-58, 71-72. Fellow AAAS, Am. Phys. Soc.; mem. Am. Chem. Soc., Faraday Soc., Nat. Acad. Scis., Sigma Xi, Phi Beta Kappa, Pi Mu Epsilon, Phi Lambda Upsilon, Phi Kappa Phi. Home: 533 Palos Verdes Dr W Palos Verdes Estates CA 94072 Office: U So Calif-University Park MC-1661 Los Angeles CA 90089

BENSON, THOMAS QUENTIN, lawyer; b. Grand Forks, N.D., Jan. 9, 1943; s. Theodore Quentin and Helen Marie (Winzenberg) B.; m. Mary Mangelsdorf, Aug. 3, 1968; children: Annemarie C., Thomas Quentin II, Mark W. B.A. U. Notre Dame, 1964; J.D., U. Denver, 1967. Bar: Colo. 1967, N.D. 1967, U.S. Dist. Ct. 1968, U.S. Circuit Ct. Appeals 1974, U.S. Mil. Ct. Appeals 1981. Legal counsel Denver Regional Council Govts., 1968-70; assoc. Schneider, Shoemaker, Wham & Cooke, Denver, 1970-72; prin. Thomas Quentin Benson, Denver, 1972-74, 76—; ptnr. Benson & Vernon, Denver, 1974-76; Mem. bd. Am. Health Planning Assn., 1973-77. Mem. bd. Mayor's Adv. Com. Community Devel., Denver, 1975-78; Republican precinct committeeman, 1972-78; mem. White House Advance for U.S. Pres., 1975; pres. Park Vista-Pine Ridge Homeowners Assn., 1971-73; mem. parish council Ch. of Risen Christ, Roman Catholic, 1978-80, chief lector, 1975-76; pres. M.P.B. Home and Sch. Assn. Served as comdr. JAGC USNR. Cited for Leadership Denver C. of C., 1975-76. Mem. ABA, Colo. Bar Assn. (sect. chmn. 1975-78), Denver Bar Assn., Cath. Lawyers Guild Denver (pres. 1979-80). Republican. Clubs: U. Notre Dame (pres. 1980-81), Univ. Hills Rotary (dir. 1976-78, program chmn. 1978-81), Eastmoor Swim and Tennis (Denver) (dir. 1973-74, 78-80). Office: 1600 S Albion St Suite 400 Denver CO 80222

BENSON, WARREN FRANK, composer, educator; b. Detroit, Jan. 26, 1924; s. Fred William and Ella Alma (Hermenau) B.; m. Patricia Louise Vander Velde, Nov. 19, 1949; children: Erika, Dirk Kirsten, Sonja. Mus. B. in Theory, U. Mich., 1949, Mus.M., 1951. Timpanist Detroit Symphony Orch., 1946, Ford Sunday Evening Hour Orch., 1946. Brevard Music Center Orch., 1949, 53, 54; Fulbright tchr. music Anatolia Coll., Salonica, Greece, 1950-52; dir. orch. and band Mars Hill Coll., 1952-53; prof. music, composer in residence Ithaca Coll., 1953-67; prof. composition Eastman Sch. Music, U. Rochester, N.Y., 1967—, Kilbourn prof. composition, 1980—; guest condr., lectr. at festivals and ednl. centers, U.S., Can., Mex., S.Am., Europe; bd. dirs. Am. Wind Ensemble Library.; Mem. MacDowell Colony, 1955, 63. Author: Creative Projects in Musicianship, 1967; compositions include Concertino for Alto Saxophone, 1954, Trio for Percussion, 1956, Psalm XXIV for womens voices and string orch., 1957, Symphony for Drums and Wind Orch., 1962; The Leaves are Falling for wind ensemble, 1963; compositions include The Solitary Dancer for wind ensemble, 1966, Helix for tuba and wind ensemble, 1966, Bailando, ballet for orch., 1965, The Mask of Night for wind ensemble, 1968; for wind ensemble Shadow Wood, song cycle for soprano and orchestra or wind ensemble, 1968; compositions include String Quartet, 1969, Concerto for Horn and Orch, 1971, The Dream Net for alto saxophone and string quartet, 1972, Five Lyrics of Louise Bogan for mezzo-soprano and flute, 1977, Largo Tah for bass trombone and marimba, 1978, Songs For the End of the World, for mezzo-soprano, horn, and chamber ensemble, 1980, The Man with the Blue Guitar, for orch., 1980, Beyond Winter: Sweet Aftershowers for string orch., 1981, Hills, Woods, Brook: Three Love Songs for soprano and chamber ensemble, 1982, Symphony II-Lost Songs, 1982, The Putcha Putcha Variations for solo singer, 1983, A Score of Praises for acappella chorus, 1983, Concertino for Flute, Strings and Percussion, 1983; commns. include, Nat. Endowment for Arts, N.Y. State Council on Arts, Ohio Music Educators Assn., Charlotte Symphony Orch., Internat. Horn Soc., Baldwin-Wallace Conservatory, Am. Wind Symphony Orch., Rochester Philharm. Orch., Mich. State U., U. Conn., The Cantata Singers. Recipient Lillian Fairchild Meml. prize in arts U. Rochester, 1971; citation of excellence Nat. Band Assn., 1976; Ford Found. grantee, 1963, 65; Warren Benson Disting. Tchr. award established at Ithaca Coll., 1965; Guggenheim fellow, 1981-82. Mem. ASCAP (Serious Music awards 1960—), Pi Kappa Lambda, Phi Mu Alpha (nat. hon. mem., Orpheus award), Kappa Kappa Psi. Home: 10 Reitz Pkwy Pittsford NY 14534 Office: Eastman Sch of Music U Rochester 26 Gibbs St Rochester NY 14604 *My goal is to write music worthy of the best in the art which speaks to the best in my time.*

BENSON, WILLIAM EDWARD BARNES, geologist; b. West Haven, Conn., May 15, 1919; s. John Edward and Lucia Purdy (Barnes) B.; m. Mary Freda Hill, July 11, 1944; children—Sharon (Mrs. J.G. Rachel), Lynn (Mrs. J.D. Walker), William Edward. B.A., Yale, 1940, M.S., 1942, Ph.D., 1952. Geologist Conn. Geol. and Natural History Survey, 1940-42; geologist U.S. Geol. Survey, 1942-54, br. chief, 1953-54; exec. sec. div. earth sci. Nat. Acad. Scis./NRC, 1954-55; chief geologist Manidon Mining Inc., N.D., 1955-56; program dir., sect. head NSF, 1956-75, chief scientist earth sci. div., 1975-79; sci. advisory to Office of Pres., Washington, 1976-77; pvt. cons., 1980—; vis. prof. U. Hawaii, 1980; sr. staff asso. Nat. Acad. Scis., 1980—. Contbr., editor profl. jours. Served with USNR, 1944-45. Yale fellow, 1940-42. Fellow Geol. Soc. Am., Am. Geophys. Union, A.A.A.S. (sec. sect. E 1969-73); mem. Geol. Soc. Washington (v.p. 1958), Pick and Hammer Soc. (chmn. 1970-73), Phi Beta Kappa, Sigma Xi. Office: Nat Acad Scis 2101 Constitution Ave NW Washington DC 20418

BENSTOCK, GERALD MARTIN, uniform manufacturing executive; b. Bay Shore, N.Y., May 7, 1930; s. David Lewis and Jane M. B.; m. Joan Kline, Nov. 18, 1951; children: Susan, Wendy, Michael, Peter. B.S., N.Y. U., 1951. Formerly v.p. Superior Surg. Mfg. Co., Inc., Seminole, Fla., now chmn. bd., pres., chief exec. officer; lectr. in field. Author articles in field. Pres. United Jewish Appeal, Fedn. Jewish Philanthropies, 1965-79; dir. Com. of 100 of Pinellas County. Mem. Textile Rental Services Assn., Am. Hotel Assn., Am. Hosp. Assn., Assn. Contamination Control. Home: 3126 Tiffany Dr Belleair Beach FL 33535 Office: Superior Surg Mfg Co Inc Seminole Blvd at 110th Terr Seminole FL 33542

BENSTON, GEORGE JAMES, accountant, economist; b. N.Y.C., Mar. 18, 1932; s. William and Rose L. B.; m. Alice N. Schwartz, July 28, 1951; children: Kimberly W., Randall Craig. B.A., Queens Coll., 1952; M.B.A., N.Y. U., 1953; Ph.D., U. Chgo., 1963. C.P.A., N.C. Acct. C.P.A. firms, 1952-53; acctg. and tax specialist 1st Nat. Bank of Atlanta, 1956-57; asst. prof. acctg. Ga. State U., 1957-58, U. Chgo., 1962-66; asso. prof. acctg. and fin. U. Rochester, 1961-69, prof. acctg., econs. and fin., 1969—; vis. prof. U. Calif., Berkeley, Grad. Sch. Bus. Studies, London, London Sch. Econs., Hebrew U., Jerusalem; trustee Coll. Retirement Equities Fund; Disting. Internat. Lectr. Am. Acctg. Assn., 1980. Author: Corporate Accounting Disclosure in the UK and the USA, 1976, Contemporary Cost Accounting and Control, 1970, 77; assoc. editor, editorial bd.: Jour. Money and Credit Banking, Jour. Bank Res., Jour. Fin. Res., Jour. Acctg. Pub. Policy, others; contbr. articles to profl. jours. Ford Found., U.S. Steel and Woodrow Wilson fellow, 1958-59. Mem. Am. Acctg. Assn., Am. Fin. Assn., Phi Beta Kappa, Beta Gamma Sigma. Home: 165 Pelham Rd Rochester NY

14610 Office: University of Rochester Graduate School of Management Rochester NY 14627

BENT, ALAN EDWARD, political science educator; b. Shanghai, China, June 22, 1939; came to U.S., 1954, naturalized, 1959; s. Walter J. and Tamara (Rocklin) B.; m. Dawn Bickler, Aug. 13, 1977; 1 son by previous marriage, Ronald Geoffrey. B.S., San. Francisco State U., 1963; M.A., U. So. Calif., 1968, Claremont Grad. Sch., 1970, Ph.D., 1971. Instr. polit. sci. Chapman Coll., Orange, Calif., 1969-70; research assoc. Mcpl. Systems Research, Claremont Grad. Sch., 1970-71; asst. prof. polit. sci., assoc. dir. Inst. Govtl. Studies and Research Memphis State U., 1971-74; assoc. prof., chmn. dept. pub. adminstrn. Calif. State U., Dominguez Hills, 1974-77; prof. polit. sci. U. Cin., 1977-81, 82—, head dept. polit. sci., 1977-81, dean Coll. Arts and Scis., 1981-82; prof. polit. sci. U. No. Colo., Greeley, 1981-82; cons. S.W. Mo. State U., 1980, police agys., govtl. and pvt. instns. Author Escape from Anarchy: A Strategy for Urban Survival, 1972; The Politics of Law Enforcement: Conflict and Power in Urban Communities, 1974, 2d edit., 1976; co-author: Police, Criminal Justice and the Community, 1976, Collective Bargaining in the Public Sector: Labor-Management Relations and Public Policy, 1978; co-editor, contbr. Urban Administration: Management, Politics and Change, 1976, 2d edit. 1977; contbr. articles to profl. jours.; bd. editors: Rev. Pub. Personnel Adminstrn., 1980—, Spectrum, A Jour. of Comparative Politics and Devel., New Delhi, 1984—. Served to capt. USAF, 1964-69. NASPAA fellow, 1981-82. Mem. Am. Polit. Sci. Assn., Am. Soc. Pub. Adminstrn., AAUP. Home: 1004C Celestial St Cincinnati OH 45202 Office: U Cin Dept Polit Sci Cincinnati OH 45221

BENT, DANIEL A., lawyer; b. New Orleans, May 24, 1947; s. Edward and Alberta (Fabacher) B.; m. Maribeth Reader, Mar. 10; children: Laurance Elizabeth, Johnathan Binnings. B.S. in Mech. Engring., La. State U., 1970; J.D., Georgetown U., 1974. Bar: La., D.C., Hawaii, U.S. Supreme Ct., U.S. Ct. Appeals (9th cir.), U.S. Ct. Appeals (5th cir.), U.S. Dist. Ct. (ea. dist.) La., U.S. Dist. Ct. Hawaii, U.S. Patent Office. Patent examiner U.S. Patent Office, Washington, 1970-72; patent adviser Naval Ship Research and Devel. Ctr., Bethesda, Md., 1972-74; asst. U.S. atty. Eastern Dist. La., New Orleans, 1974-77, chief criminal div., 1977, 1st asst. U.S. atty., 1977-78; spl. atty. organized crime and racketeering sect. U.S. Dept. Justice, Honolulu Field Office, 1978—; lectr. Sch. Law U. Hawaii, Fed. Agy. Tng. Sessions; lectr. and instr. Atty. Gen's Advocacy Inst., Washington, 1977—; instr. Hasting Ctr. for Trial and Appellate Advocacy, Civil Advocacy Programs; mem. com. on course content and materials Hastings Ctr. for Trial and Appellate Advocacy, Civil Advocacy Programs; mem. com. on local rules U.S. Dist. Ct., Hawaii; mem. com. on course design and revision Atty. Gen's. Advocacy Inst.; organizer, presenter trial advocacy tng. programs County Prosecutors State of Hawaii; co-organizer, co-instr. Patent Trial Advocacy Inst., 1980; mem. local rules com. U.S. Dist. Hawaii, 1981—; mem. com. on penal code reform, Honolulu, 1983. Rowan Oil Co. scholar, 1969; NSF summer research grantee. Mem. ABA, Assn. Trial Lawyers Am., D.C. Bar Assn., La. Bar Assn., Tau Beta Pi, Pi Tau Sigma. Republican. Club: Rotary. Home: 7539 Muolea Pl Honolulu HI 96826 Office: US Dept Justice 300 Ala Moana Blvd Box 50183 Honolulu HI 96850

BENT, ROBERT DEMO, physicist, educator; b. Cambridge, Mass., Dec. 22, 1928; s. Henry Edward and Florence (Demo) B.; m. Mary Alice Keating, June 9, 1956; children—Lisa Clare, Jason Robert, Alan Demo. Student, U. Mo., 1945-46; B.A., Oberlin Coll., 1950; M.A., Rice U., 1952, Ph.D., 1954. Research asso. Rice U., Houston, 1954-55, Columbia, 1955-58; vis. research asso. Brookhaven Nat. Lab., Upton, N.Y., summer 1955; asst. prof. physics Ind. U., Bloomington, 1958-62, asso. prof., 1962-66, prof., 1966—. Contbr. articles on nuclear physics to profl. jours. Guggenheim fellow Oxford, Harwell, 1962-63. Fellow Am. Phys. Soc. Home: 1315 Longwood Dr Bloomington IN 47401

BENTEL, DWIGHT, emeritus journalism educator; b. Walla Walla, Wash., Apr. 15, 1909; s. Joseph Eugene and Kate (Essler) B.; m. Edna Fuller, Mar. 28, 1934 (div. Apr. 1956); 1 son, David; m. Genieva Record, Sept. 8, 1959. A.B., Stanford U., 1934, A.M., 1935; Ed.D. (Henry W. Sackett scholar 1943), Columbia U., 1950. Newspaperman, San Jose and San Francisco, 1928-34; founder, head dept. journalism and mass communications Calif. State U., San Jose, 1934-69, prof., Journalism, 1947—, distinguished prof., 1968-74, prof. emeritus, 1974—; Mem. staff div. of edn. Am. Mus. Natural History, N.Y.C., 1942-43; lectr. Coll. Notre Dame, Columbia, 1943; mem. editorial staff Editor & Publisher mag., 1944-45, edn. editor, 1946-62; co-founder, dir. San Jose Savs. & Loan Assn.; dir. Am. Bank & Trust Co. Contbr. publs. on newspaper industry and journalism, edn. Mem. Am. Council Edn. for Journalism, 1954-58, Am. Council Radio and TV Journalism, 1958-62. Dwight Bentel Hall of Journalism and Mass Communication named in his honor Calif. State U., San Jose, 1982. Mem. Am. Acad. Advt., Am. Soc. Journalism Sch. Adminstrs. (pres. 1949-50), Nat. Press Photographers Assn., Assn. Edn. in Journalism, Calif. Newspaper Pubs. Assn. (sec. central coast div. 1947—, sec., pres. 1960), Kappa Tau Alpha, Sigma Delta Chi. Home: 1729 Santa Barbara Dr San Jose CA 95112

BENTEL, FREDERICK RICHARD, architect; b. N.Y.C., Jan. 2, 1928; s. Carl August and Mary (Muller) B.; m. Maria L. R. Azzarone, Aug. 16, 1952; children: Paul Louis, Peter Andreas, Maria Elizabeth. B.Arch., Pratt Inst., 1949; grad. fellow, Mass. Inst. Tech., M. Arch., 1950; D.Arch., Technische Hochschule, Graz, Austria, 1953. Registered architect, N.Y., N.J., Va., Vt., Conn., profl. planner, N.J. Architect, partner Bentel & Bentel (AIA), Locust Valley, N.Y., 1957—; pres. Correlated Designs Inc., Locust Valley, 1961—; sec. Azzarone Realty Co. Inc., Mineola, N.Y.; v.p. Azzarone Properties, Inc., 1963—; adj. prof. Sch. Architecture Pratt Inst., 1955-70; prof. architecture N.Y. Inst. Tech., 1969—, also assoc. dir. Author publs. in field. Founding mem. com. Locust Valley Bus. Dist. Planning; adv. bd. Oyster Planning, 1970-73, community planning and devel., 1975—. Served with AUS, 1950-52. Fulbright scholar, 1952-53; recipient awards in field including 1st pl. commn. Islip Bay Shore downtown redevel. competition, 1976, C.W. Post Hillwood Commons, Brookville, N.Y., 1973. Fellow AIA; mem. N.Y. Soc. Architects, Am. Italy Soc., Mass. Inst. Tech. Alumni Assn. Home: 23 Frost Creek Dr Locust Valley NY 11560 Office: 22 Buckram Rd Locust Valley NY 11560

BENTEL, MARIA-LUISE RAMONA AZZARONE (MRS. FREDERICK R. BENTEL), architect; b. N.Y.C., June 15, 1928; d. Louis and Maria-Teresa (Massaro) Azzarone; m. Frederick R. Bentel, Aug. 16, 1952; children: Paul Louis, Peter Andreas, Maria Elisabeth. B.Arch., MIT, 1951; Fulbright scholar, Scuola d'Architettura, Venice, Italy, 1952-53. Registered profl. architect, Conn., N.Y., N.J., Va., Vt.; registered profl. planner, N.J. Partner Bentel & Bentel (Architects), Locust Valley, N.Y., 1955—; pres. Tesstoria Realty Corp., N.Y.C., 1961—; v.p., sec.-treas. Correlated Designs, Inc., Locust Valley, 1961—; partner Cobblestone Enterprises, 1967; founding mem. Locust Valley Bus. Dist. Planning Commn., 1968—; regional vice-chairperson MIT Ednl. Council; adv. mem. MIT Council for the Arts; asso. prof. architecture N.Y. Inst. Tech.; adv. prof. Queensboro Community Coll., Bayside, N.Y., 1971—. Archtl. works include C.W. Post Coll. L.I. U (N.Y. State Assn. Architects award 1975, Gold Archi award L.I. Assn. Architects 1974), Hempstead Bank, Nassau Centre Office Bldg, (L.I. Assn. Architects award 1972, N.Y. State Assn. Architects award 1975), North Shore Unitarian Sch, Plandome, N.Y. (L.I. Assn. Architects Silver Archi award 1967), Plandome, N.Y. (N.Y. State Assn. Architects award 1970), Shelter Rock Library, Searingtown, N.Y. (L.I. Assn. Architects award 1970), St. Anthony's Ch, Nanuet, N.Y. (N.Y. State Assn. Architects award 1972), Kinloch Farm, Va, Steinberg Learning Center-Woodmere (N.Y.) Acad, (N.Y. Library Assn. award 1972, L.I. Assn. Architects award 1975), St. Francis de Sales Ch, Bennington, Vt., Neitlich residence, Oyster Bay Cove, N.Y. (L.I. Assn. Architects Silver Archi award 1971), Oyster Bay Cove, N.Y. (N.Y. Assn. Architects award 1971), Amityville (N.Y.) Pub. Library, (Silver Archi award L.I. Assn. Architects, N.Y. State Assn. Architects award 1973), Jericho (N.Y.) Pub. Library, (N.Y. State Assn. Architects award, Silver Archi award L.I. Assn. Architects 1974), John B. Gambling residence, Lattingtown, N.Y. (Silver Archi award L.I. Assn. Architects 1974), Glen Cove (N.Y.) Boys' Club at Lincoln House, (Silver Archi award L.I. Assn. Architects 1978), Aquatics Component Mitchel Park, Nassau County, N.Y., Salten Hall, N.Y. Inst. Tech (award N.Y. State Assn. Architects 1977), N.Y. Coll. Osteo. Med. at N.Y. Inst. Tech, Old Westbury, Commack Pub. Library, Commack (N.Y. State Assn. Architects award 1977), St. Mary Star of the Sea Ch, Far Rockaway (Queens C. of C. grand prize 1977), Oberlin Residence (N.Y. State Assn. Architects/L.I. Assn. Architects Archi award 1983); Contbr.: religious architecture chpt. to Time Saver Standards (De Chiara and Callender), 1973. Mem. comml. panel Am. Arbitration Assn.; chmn. adv. panel on govt. bldg. projects GSA, 1976; chmn. Inst. Internat. Edn.; nat. adv.-selection com. Fulbright-Hays awards, 1976-78, 80, 82; Chairperson Locust Valley Library Adv. Bd., 1973—. Recipient 1st place award for Islip Downtown Urban Renewal Competition, 1976; named Woman Architect of Year Nassau-Suffolk County, 1976. Fellow AIA (corp. mem., chmn. design com., dir. L.I. chpt.); mem. N.Y. State Assn. Architects (chmn. design awards com.), Nat. Council Archtl. Registration Bds., MIT Alumnae Assn., MIT Alumni L.I. (dir., v.p.). Home: 23 Frost Creek Dr Lattingtown NY 11560 Office: 22 Buckram Rd Locust Valley NY 11560

BENTELE, RAYMOND, corp. exec.; b. 1936; (married). B.S., N.E. Mo. State Coll., 1960. Accountant S.D. Leidesdorf & Co., 1960-65; treas., controller Germania Savs. and Loan Assn., 1965-67; with Mallinckrodt, Inc., St. Louis, 1967—, asst. controller, 1969-71, controller, 1971-74, v.p., 1974-76, v.p. fin. and adminstrn., 1976-77, v.p. internat. group, 1977-78, sr. v.p., group exec., 1978-79, pres., 1979—, also dir. Office: care Mallinckrodt Inc 675 Brown Rd St Louis MO 63134 *

BENTHAM, JAMES MALLORY, railway executive; b. Montreal, Que., Can., Aug. 18, 1922; s. James Emil and Annie H. (Mallory) B.; m. Ila Merle Pettingill, Apr. 3, 1948; children: James Kenneth, Douglas Earl. B.C.E., McGill U., 1947. Bridge insp. Can. Pacific Rwy., Montreal, 1947-48, asst. engr., 1948-55, asst. engr. bridges, 1955-58, engr. of track, 1958-62, mgr. research, 1962-69, v.p. purchases and materials, Montreal, 1969—. Served with Can. Air Force, 1943-45. Home: PO Box 6042 Station A Montreal PQ Canada H3C 3E4

BENTINCK-SMITH, WILLIAM, university administrator; b. Boston, Jan. 22, 1914; s. William Frederick and Marion (Jordan) Bentinck-S.; m. Phebe Keyes, June 26, 1937; children: Michael, Judy, Nancy, Peter. A.B., Harvard U., 1937; M.S., Columbia U., 1938. Reporter Boston Globe, 1938-40; mng. editor Harvard Alumni Bull., 1940-46, editor, 1946-54, editorial adv. com., 1954-76; asst. to pres. Harvard, 1954-71, publ. asso., 1971—; editor Harvard Today, 1957-69, editorial chmn., 1969-72, adv. com., 1971-75; hon. curator type specimens and letter design Harvard Coll. Library. Author: The Harvard Book, 1953, rev., 1982, Building A Great Library, The Coolidge Years At Harvard, 1976. Dir. Cambridge Trust Co.; Sec. Harvard Class of 1937. Served to lt. USNR, 1942-45. Decorated Bronze Star. Mem. Am. Antiquarian Soc., Mass. Hist. Soc., Colonial Soc. Mass., Phi Beta Kappa (hon.). Clubs: Odd Volumes, Tavern, Harvard (N.Y.C.). Home: Peabody St Groton MA 01450 Office: 17 Quincy St Cambridge MA 02138

BENTLEY, ANTOINETTE COZELL, insurance executive, lawyer; b. N.Y.C., Oct. 7, 1937; d. Joseph Richard Cozell and Rose (Lafata Cozell) Vila; m. Robert D. Bentley, Aug. 28, 1960; children: Robert S., Anne W. B.A. with distinction, U. Mich., 1960; LL.B., U. Va., 1961. Bar: N.Y. 1962, N.J. 1971. Asso. Sage Gray, Todd & Sims, N.Y.C., 1961-65; of counsel Farrell, Curtis, Carlin & Davidson, Morristown, N.J., 1971-73; asst. sec. Crum and Forster, N.Y.C., 1973, sec., 1973—, v.p., counsel, 1975—. Trustee Crum and Forster Found., 1979—; Vice pres. Mendham Borough (N.J.) Bd. Edn., 1976-79; trustee N.J. Conservation Found., 1981—, Morris Mus. Arts and Sci., 1982. Mem. ABA, N.J. Bar Assn., Am. Soc. Corp. Secs., Assn. Corp. Counsel N.J. (1st v.p., exec. com. 1982—), Women's Econ. Roundtable, LWV, Order of Coif, Chi Omega. Home: 16 Prospect St Mendham NJ 07945 Office: 305 Madison Ave Morristown NJ 07960

BENTLEY, CHARLES FRED, cons. agrologist; b. Cambridge, Mass., Mar. 14, 1914; s. Charles Fred and Lavina Ann (MacKenzie) B.; m. Helen Signe Petersen, Sept. 16, 1943; children—Ann Catherine (Mrs. Manson), Theodore Carl. B.Sc., U. Alta., 1939, M.S., 1942; Ph.D., U. Minn., 1945. Mem. faculty soil sci. U. Minn., U. Sask., and U. Alta., 1943-79; dean Faculty of Agr., U. Alta., 1959-68; spl. adv. agr. Canadian Internat. Devel. Agy., 1969-70; now cons. agrologist, dir. McAllister Environ. Services, Calgary, Alta., Can.; Chmn. governing bd. Internat. Crops Research Inst. for Semi-Arid Tropics, India, 1972—. Contbr. articles to sci. jours. Mem. Internat. Soc. Soil Sci. (pres. 1974-78), Alta. Inst. Agrologists, Canadian Soc. Soil Sci., Agrl. Inst. Can., Royal Soc. Can., Agrl. Inst. Can., Am. Soc. Agronomy, Soil Sci. Soc. Am. Address: 13103 66th Ave Edmonton AB T6H 1Y6 Canada

BENTLEY, CHARLES RAYMOND, geophysicist; b. Rochester, N.Y., Dec. 23, 1929; s. Raymond and Janet Cornelia (Everest) B.; m. Marybelle Goode, July 3, 1964; children: Molly Clare, Raymond Alexander. B.S., Yale U., 1950; Ph.D., Columbia U., 1959. Research geophysicist Columbia U., 1952-56; Antarctic traverse leader and seismologist Arctic Inst. N.Am., 1956-59; project asso. U. Wis., 1959-61, asst. prof., 1961-63, asso. prof., 1963-68, prof. geophysics, 1968—; mem. council Internat. Antarctic Glaciol. Project; chmn. polar research bd. Nat. Acad. Sci.; U.S. mem. working group on solid earth geophysics Sci. Com. on Antarctic Research., U.S. alt. del. Chmn. bd. asso. editors: Am. Geophys. Union Antarctic Research series. Recipient Bellingshausen-Lazarev medal for Antarctic research Acad. Scis. USSR, 1971; NSF sr. postdoctoral fellow, 1968-69; U.S.-U.S.S.R. Acad. Scis. exchange fellow, 1977. Mem. Am. Geophys. Union, Soc. Exploration Geophysicists, AAAS, Internat. Glaciol. Soc., Seismol. Soc. Am., Geol. Soc. Am., Am. Quaternary Assn., Am. Geol. Inst., Am. Polar Soc., AAUP, Phi Beta Kappa, Sigma Xi. Research on Antarctic glaciology and geophysics, seismic refraction measurements at sea, magnetotelluric exploration of earth structure. Home: 5618 Lake Mendota Dr Madison WI 53705

BENTLEY, CLARENCE EDWARD, savings and loan executive; b. Ranger, Tex., Oct. 9, 1921; s. Clarence Edward and Rosa Estelle (Bryant) B.; m. Gloria Gill, Oct. 9, 1943; children—Jon, Kitty, Perry. Student, McMurry Coll., Abilene, Tex., 1939-42. Pres. Abilene Savs. Assn., 1944-77, Southwestern Group Fin. Co., Houston, 1976-77; pres. United Savs. Assn. Tex., Houston, 1977-80, chmn. bd., 1980—; chmn. bd. United Fin. Mortgage Co., Dallas, United Fin. Group, Inc., Houston, 1980—; dir. Kaneb Services Inc., Investors Mortgage Ins. Co., Boston; past dir. Fed. Home Loan Bank, Little Rock. Contbr. articles to profl. publns. Pres. Abilene Indsl. Found., 1970, United Fund Abilene, 1962; mem. bd. Tex. State Hosps., 1962-64; mem. Tex. Fin. Commn., 1964-76, chmn., 1971. Served with USAAF, 1942-43. Recipient Outstanding Citizen award City of Abilene, 1964, Disting. Alumnus award McMurry Coll., 1971. Mem. Nat. Savs. and Loan League (pres. 1970-71), Tex. Savs. and Loan League (pres. 1970-71), Abilene C. of C. (pres. 1964). Episcopalian. Clubs: Abilene Country (pres. 1951); Preston Trails Golf (Dallas)). Home: 52 Rue Maison Abilene TX 79605 Office: 5251 Westheimer St Houston TX 77056

BENTLEY, CLAUDE, artist; b. N.Y.C., June 9, 1915; m. Frances Julia Norman, Apr. 6, 1957. Student, Northwestern U., 1932-34, Art Inst. Chgo., 1945-49. Instr. Art Inst. Chgo., 1959-61. Designer: Plaza Del Lago Shopping Center, Wilmette, Ill.; Exhbns. include, Corcoran Gallery Art, 1953, 59, San Francisco Mus. Art, 1960, Whitney Mus. Am. Art, N.Y.C., 1955, Art Inst. Chgo., 1941, 48, 50-66, 68, Sarasota (Fla.) Art Assn., 1959; represented in permanent collections, including, U. Ill., Met. Mus. Art, N.Y.C., Denver Art Mus., Art Inst. Chgo., Santa Barbara Mus., Ill. State Mus., Springfield, Santa Fe Art Mus., Albuquerque Mus.; works include: mural at, Hotel De La Borda, Taxco, Mexico, murals at, 3600 Lake Shore Dr., Chgo.; artist in residence, Layton Sch. Art, Milw., 1956-59. Served with AUS, 1941-45. Recipient prizes Govt. France, 1971, Sarasota Art Assn., 1959, Art Inst. Chgo., 1949, 50, 55, 63, Met. Mus. Art, 1952, Denver Art Mus., 1954, 60. Mem. Arts Club Chgo. (profl.). Home: 310 Otero St Santa Fe NM 87501

BENTLEY, ERIC, author, comparative literature educator; b. Eng., Sept. 14, 1916; s. Fred and Laura (Evelyn) B. B.A., Oxford (Eng.) U., 1938, Litt.B., 1939; Ph.D., Yale U., 1941; D.F.A., U. Wis., 1975; Litt.D. (hon.), U. East Anglia, 1979. Brander Matthews prof. dramatic lit. Columbia, 1953-69; dramatic critic The New Republic, 1952-56; Norton prof. poetry Harvard U., 1960-61; artist in residence Ford Found., Berlin, 1964-65; Katharine Cornell prof. theatre SUNY, Buffalo, 1974-82; prof. comparative lit. U. Md., College Park, 1982—. Co-producer of: DMZ, a political Cabaret, 1968; (recipient George Jean Nathan award 1966, Obie award 1978); Author: A Century of Hero-Worship, 1944, The Playwright as Thinker, 1946, Bernard Shaw, 1947, In Search of Theatre, 1953, The Dramatic Event, 1954, What is Theatre?, 1956, The Life of the Drama, 1964, The Theatre of Commitment, 1967, What Is Theatre and Other Reviews, 1968, A Time to Die, 1970, The Red White and Black, 1970, Are You Now?, 1972, The Recantation, 1972, Theatre of War, 1972, Expletive Deleted, 1974, Memoirs of Pilate, 1977, Rallying Cries, 1977, Lord Alfred's Lover, 1978, Wannsee, 1979, The Brecht Commentaries, 1981, Concord, 1981, The Fall of the Amazons, 1982, The Kleist Variations, 1983; author-editor: Thirty Years of Treason, 1971; Editor: The Importance of Scrutiny, 1948, From the Modern Repertoire, 1949-56, The Modern Theatre, 1955-60, The Classic Theatre, 1958-61, The Theory of the Modern Stage, 1968, The Great Playwrights, 1970; Adapter, translator: plays A Man's a Man, 1962, Mother Courage, 1963, others. Guggenheim fellow, 1948-49, 67-68; Fulbright scholar in Yugoslavia, 1980. Mem. Am. Acad. Arts and Scis. Address: 194 Riverside Dr New York NY 10025

BENTLEY, HELEN DELICH (MRS. WILLIAM ROY BENTLEY), international consultant; b. Ruth, Nev.; d. Michael and Mary (Kovich) Delich; m. William Roy Bentley, June 7, 1959. Student, U. Nev., 1941-42, George Washington U., 1943; B.J., U. Mo., 1944; LL.D., U. Md., 1970, U. Alaska, 1973, U. Mich., 1974; D.H.L., Bryant Coll., 1971, U. Portland, 1972, L.I. U., 1976, Goucher Coll., 1979. Reporter Ely (Nev.) Record, 1940-42; polit. campaign mgr. for late Senator James G. Scrugham, White Pine County, Nev., 1942; bur. mgr. UP, Fort Wayne, Ind., 1944-45; reporter Balt. Sun, 1945-53, maritime editor, 1953-69; chmn. FMC, Washington, 1969-75, Am. Bicentennial Fleet, Inc., 1973-76; pres. Internat. Resources & Devel. Corp., Washington, 1976, HDB Internat., Inc., 1977—; pub. relations adviser Am. Assn. Port Authorities, 1958-62, 64-67. TV and film producer world trade and maritime shows, 1950-64; Editor: Ports of Americas, 1961. Bd. dirs., mem. council Ch. Home and Hosp.; bd. dirs. United Seamen's Service, Oceanic Ednl. Found.; mem. council Md. Hist. Soc., Villa Julie Coll., Stevenson, Md., Montessori Soc. Central Md., Slavic-Am. Nat. Assn.; Republican nominee for Ho. of Reps. from 2d Dist. Md., 1980, 82, 84. Recipient numerous honors including awards from AFL-CIO Maritime Port Council Greater N.Y., 1965, Ironworkers and Shipbuilders Council AFL-CIO, 1966, AOTOS award United Seamen's Service, 1971, N.Y. Freight Forwarders and Brokers Assn., 1972, Am. Legion, 1973, Navy League U.S., 1973, Jerry Land medal Soc. Naval Architects and Marine Engrs., 1974; George Washington Honor medal Valley Forge Freedoms Found., 1971, 76; named GOP Woman of Year, 1972. Mem. Greater Balt. Com. (chmn. rail com.). Republican. Greek Orthodox. 1st non-Briton to address and be honored by U.K. Chamber Shipping, 1973. Only woman to trek Northwest Passage on S.S. Manhattan, 1969. Home: 408 Chapelwood Ln Lutherville MD 21093 Office: PO Box 10619 Towson MD 21285-0619 *First of all, I always live by the Golden Rule. Next, I set a goal of leading or doing my best in anything I undertake, but also discipline myself to be able to accept adversities and be a good loser. I demand so much of myself and respect myself that I always command respect. Prayer and talking with God has always been of great help.*

BENTLEY, HERSHEL PAUL, JR., pediatrician, educator; b. Amory, Miss., Oct. 27, 1928; s. Herschel Paul and Frankie Mae (Boozer) B.; children: Paul Crawford, John Franklin, Rhonda Kaye, Valerie Anne. B.S. in Chemistry, Jacksonville (Ala.) State Tchrs. Coll., 1950; postgrad. in Biochemistry, U. Minn., 1960; M.D., Med. Coll. Ala., 1954. Intern in pediatrics U. Ala. Hosp. Clinics, Birmingham, 1954-55, resident in pediatrics, 1955-57; resident in pediatrics, fellow in pediatric hematology U. Minn., Mpls., 1958-59; asst. prof. pediatrics U. Ala., Birmingham, 1960-63, prof., 1963-68, chmn. dept. pediatrics, 1963-68, prof. dentistry dept. pedodontics, 1965-68; prof. pediatrics, asst. to v.p. profl. affairs U. Ark., Little Rock, 1968-70; practice medicine specializing in pediatrics Children's Med. Group, Mobile, Ala., 1970—; prof., pediatrics U. South Ala., Mobile, 1972—, chmn. dept., 1972-78. Contbr. articles to pediatrics jours. Home: 1259 Texas St Mobile AL 36604 Office: 3920 Airport Blvd Mobile AL 36608

BENTLEY, JAMES LUTHER, journalist; b. Panama City, Fla., Jan. 24, 1937; s. Thomas Pierce and Sara Pope (Woodruff) B.; m. Patricia Ann Daniel, July 30, 1965. Student Ga. Inst. Tech, Ga. State U., 1958-61, N.C. State U., 1962. Reporter Atlanta Constitution, 1958-64, asst. city editor, 1964-66, night city editor, 1966-71, city editor, 1971-79; corr. Reuters Ltd., 1967-79; dir. info. TVA, 1979; editor Cox Newspapers Inc., Washington bur., 1979; mng. editor Cox News Service, Washington, 1979—. Served with U.S. Army, 1961-63. Mem. Nat. Press Club; Mem. Sigma Delta Chi. Lutheran. Home: 1017 Columbus Dr Stafford VA 22554 Office: 2000 Pennsylvania Ave NW Suite 10000 Washington DC 20006

BENTLEY, KENTON EARL, electronic research exec.; b. Detroit, June 1, 1927; s. Kenneth and Marion Isabel (Tillman) B.; m. Elizabeth Montrose, Apr. 18, 1953. B.S. in Chemistry, U. Mich., 1950; Ph.D. in Analytical Chemistry, U. N.M., 1959. Research phys. chemist Consol. Electrodynamics Corp., Pasadena, Calif., 1956-57; research scientist Lockheed Calif. Co., Burbank, 1962-63; scientist, task leader Jet Propulsion Lab., Calif. Inst. Tech., Pasadena, 1963-65; head electrochemistry group Hughes Aircraft Co., Culver City, Calif., 1965-67; dir. sci. and applications br., dir. Iran earth resources programs Lockheed Electronics Co., Inc., Houston, 1967—; Vis. prof. chemistry Highlands (N.M.) U., 1959; asst. prof. chemistry Am. U. Beirut, Lebanon, 1959-61. Contbr. numerous articles to profl. jours. Served with USNR, 1945-46. Los Alamos research fellow, 1954-56. Mem. Am. Chem. Soc., AAAS (life), AAUP, Am. Astronautical Soc. (sr.; dir. 1969-73), Nat. Mgmt. Assn., Sigma Xi (life), Alpha Chi Sigma. Home: 15811 Dunmoor Dr Houston TX 77059 Office: 1830 NASA Rd 1 Houston TX 77058

BENTLEY, ORVILLE GEORGE, government official; b. Midland, S.D., Mar. 6, 1918; s. Thomas O. and Ida Marie (Sandal) B.; m. Enolia J. Anderson, Sept. 19, 1942; children: Peter T., Craig E. B.S., S.D. State Coll., 1942; M.S. in Biochemistry, U. Wis., 1947, Ph.D., 1950; hon. degree, S.D. State U., 1974. Asst. prof. animal sci. Ohio Agrl. Expt. Sta.; also mem. dept. animal sci. and dept. agrl. biochemistry Ohio State U., 1950-58; dean Coll. of Agr. and Biol. Scis., S.D. State U., 1958-65, Coll. Agr., U. Ill. at Urbana, 1965-82; asst. sec. agr. for sci. and edn. USDA, Washington, 1982—; Mem. com. animal nutrition NRC-Nat. Acad. Scis., 1958-67; mem. Council U.S. Univs. for Rural Devel. in India, 1967-74; mem. ad hoc adv. com. Ill. Inst. for Environmental Quality, 1971; mem. tech. adv. com. on food and agr. U.S. Dept Agr., Viet Nam, 1966; mem. panel Nat. Acad. Scis. to meet mems. Indonesian Acad. Scis., 1968; co-chmn. Agrl. Research Policy Adv. Com., 1973-77; mem. Bd. for Internat. Food and Agrl. Devel., 1976-80. Editorial bd.: jour. Animal Sci, 1956-59; Contbr. articles to profl. jours. Bd. dirs. Am. U. Beirut, Midwest Univs., Consortium for Internat. Activities, 1966-76; chmn. bd. dirs. Farm Found., 1971-78. Served to maj., chem. warfare service AUS, 1942-45. Named Young Man of Year Wooster Jr. C. of C., 1953; recipient Distinguished Alumnus award S.D. State U., 1967. Fellow Am. Soc. Animal Sci. (v.p. midwestern sect. 1963, Am. feed mfrs. award 1958); mem. Am. Chem. Soc., Am. Inst. Nutrition, Am. Soc. Animal Sci., Am. Dairy Sci. Assn., Internat. Union of Nutritional Scis., Farm House (hon.), AAAS (committeeman-at-large 1971-82), Sigma Xi, Phi Kappa Phi. Club: Rotarian. Home: Concord Ln Rural Route 2 Urbana IL 61801 Office: Dept of Agriculture 14th and Independence Ave SW Washington DC 20250

BENTLEY, PETER, lawyer; b. Jersey City, Sept. 1, 1915; s. Peter and Emma P. B.; m. Signe E. von Krusenstierna, Mar. 15, 1944; 1 dau., Fredrique Ann Bentley Martin. B.A., Princeton U., 1938; LL.B., Yale U., 1941. Bar: Conn. Assoc. Simpson, Thacher & Bartlett, N.Y.C., 1941-52, Maguire, Cole, Bentley & Babson (and predecessors), Stamford, Conn., 1952-54; ptnr. Bentley, Lane, Mosher & Babson, P.C. (and predecessors), Stamford, 1954—; chmn. bd. Aegis Corp., Coral Gables, Fla.; dir. Gilbert and Bennett Mfg. Co., Georgetown, Conn. Rep. Greenwich (Conn.) Town Meeting, 1966-68. Mem. Stamford Bar Assn. (pres. 1971-72), Conn. Bar Assn., ABA. Republican. Quaker. Home: 130 Shore Rd Old Greenwich CT 06870 Office: 1 Atlantic St Stamford CT 06904

BENTLEY, PETER JOHN GERARD, forest industry company executive; b. Vienna, Austria, Mar. 17, 1930; s. Leopold Lionel Garrick and Antoinette Ruth B.; m. Shelia Farrington McGiveran, May 23, 1953; children: Michael Peter, Barbara Ruth, Susan Patricia, Joan Katherine, Lisa Marie. Ed., U. B.C. Sch. Forestry, Banff Sch. Advanced Mgmt. Pres., chief exec. officer, dir. Canfor Corp., Vancouver, B.C., Can. Forest Products Ltd., Canfor Ltd.; pres., dir. Canfor Investments Ltd., Vancouver, B.C.; internat. adv. bd. Chem. Bank; dir. Bank Montreal, Balco Industries Ltd., Intercontintal Pulp Co. Ltd., Prince George Pulp and Paper Ltd., Shell Can. Ltd., Versatile Corp., Westcoast Cellufibre Industries Ltd.; mem. internat. adv. bd. Chem. Bank, N.Y.C.; vice-chmn., dir. Seaboard Lumber Sales Co., Ltd., Seaboard Shipping Co. Ltd.; dir. Forest Indsl. Relations Ltd., Pulp and Paper Indsl. Relations Bur., Forest Labour Relations Council; gov. Olympic Trust Can. Chmn. Vancouver Gen. Hosp. Found.; mem. Bus. Council on Nat. Issues, Ottawa; mem. adv. council to faculty commerce and bus. adminstrn. U. B.C.; trustee B.C. Sports Hall of Fame and Mus.; hon. dir. Can. Profl. Golfers' Assn. Mem. Can. Forestry Assn. B.C. (past pres., hon. life). Clubs: Capilano Golf and Country, Marine Drive Golf, Vancouver, Vancouver Lawn Tennis and Badminton; Thunderbird Country (Palm Springs, Calif.); Royal and Ancient Golf (St. Andrews, Scotland). Office: Canfor Corp 1055 Dunsmuir St Suite 2800 Box 49420 Bentall Postal Sta Vancouver BC Canada V7X 1B5

BENTON, ALLEN HAYDEN, biology educator; b. Ira, N.Y., Sept. 4, 1921; s. Haydon Willey and Pearl Amelia (Diddy) B.; m. Marjorie Lois Hall, Aug. 16, 1947; children: Thomas Hall, Christopher Allen, Holly Anne. B.S., Cornell U., 1948, M.S., 1949, Ph.D, 1952. Jr. wildlife biologist U.S. Fish and Wildlife Service, 1949; asst. prof. biology SUNY-Albany, 1949-57, assoc. prof., 1957-62; prof. biology SUNY-Fredonia, 1962-73, disting. teaching prof., 1973—, faculty exchange scholar, 1975—; vis. prof. Stephen F. Austin Coll., 1957, Concord Coll., Athens, W. Va., 1969-70, U. Minn. Biol. Sta., 1970; cons. Nuclear Fuel Services, Inc., Calspan Inc., Environ. Analysts, Inc., Environ. Def. Fund, Nature Conservatory. Author: (with W.E. Werner Jr.) Field Biology and Ecology, 3rd edit., 1974, Manual for Field Biology and Ecology, 6th edit., 1983; contbr. articles to profl. jours. Served with cav. U.S. Army, 1942-46. Decorated Bronze Star; grantee Research Found. SUNY, 1963, 83; NSF grantee, 1972; E.N. Huyck Found. grantee, 1976-78. Mem. Am. Ornithologists Union, Am. Inst. Biol. Sci., AAAS, Am. Soc. Mammalogists, Ecol. Soc., Wilson Ornithol. Soc., N.Y. Entomol. Soc., Intecol, Fedn. N.Y. State Bird Clubs (pres.), PTA (life), Sigma Xi, Phi Kappa Phi. Home: 292 Water St Fredonia NY 14063 Office: Dept Biology SUNY Fredonia NY 14063

BENTON, FLETCHER, sculptor; b. Jackson, Ohio, 1931. B.F.A., Miami U., Oxford, Ohio, 1956. Mem. faculty Calif. Coll. Arts and Crafts, 1959, San Francisco Art Inst., 1964-67; asst. prof. art Calif. State U., San Jose, 1967-81, prof., 1981—. One-man shows include, San Francisco Mus. Modern Art, 1965, Albright-Knox Mus., Buffalo, 1970, Galeria Bonino, N.Y.C., 1968, Galeria Bonino, Buenos Aires, 1970, Galeria Bonino, Rio de Janiero, 1973, Chgo. Arts Club, 1979, Milw. Art Center, 1980, Suermondt-Ludwig Mus., Aachen, W. Ger., 1981, John Berggruen Gallery, group shows include, San Francisco Art Inst., 1964, San Francisco Mus. Modern Art, 1966, Whitney Mus. Am. Art, N.Y.C., 1966, 68, Los Angeles County Mus., 1967, Phila. Art Mus., Walker Art Center, Mpls., 1968, Art Inst. Chgo., Internat. Mus. Fine Arts, Osaka, Japan, 1970, Hayward Gallery, London, Stanford (Calif.) Mus., 1971, U. Calif., Berkeley, 1973, Denver Mus. Art, 1974, Honolulu Acad. Arts, 1978, Am. Acad. and Inst. Arts and Letters, N.Y.C., 1979; represented in numerous permanent collections, including, Whitney Mus. Art, N.Y.C., Hirschhorn Mus. and Sculpture Garden, Washington, UCLA Sculpture Garden. Served with USN, 1949-50. Recipient award for disting. service to arts Am. Acad. and Inst. Arts and Letters, 1979; Pres.'s Scholar award San Jose State U., 1980. Office: 1072 Bryant St San Francisco CA 94103

BENTON, GEORGE STOCK, educator; b. Oak Park, Ill., Sept. 24, 1917; George and Julia (Davieson) Blumenstock; m. Charlotte Ann Russ, June 21, 1945; children—Sandra Jean, Barbara Lea, Jeffrey George, Lauren Ann. S.B., U. Chgo., 1942, Ph.D. in Meteorology, 1947. With U.S. Weather Bur., Akron, Ohio, also Soil Conservation Service, Washington, 1939-42; instr. meteorology U. Chgo., 1942-45, asst. prof., 1948; ops. analyst USAAF, 1945; mem. faculty Johns Hopkins, Balt., 1948-66, prof. meteorology, 1957-66, acting chmn. dept. civil engring., 1958-60, chmn. dept. mechs., 1960-66; dir. research labs. Environ. Sci. Services Adminstrn., Dept. Commerce, Boulder, Colo., 1966-69; prof. earth and planetary scis. Johns Hopkins U., 1969-70, 81—, chmn. dept., 1969-70, dean faculty arts and scis., 1970-72; v.p. Homewood Divs., 1972-77; assoc. adminstr. NOAA, Dept. Commerce, 1978-81; astrogeophysics U. Colo., 1967-69; U.S. permanent rep. World Meteorol. Orgn., 1978-81. Fellow Am. Meteorol. Soc. (pres. 1969-70), Am. Geophys. Union, AAAS; mem. Sigma Xi, Phi Beta Kappa, Tau Beta Pi (hon.). Home: 3925 Canterbury Rd Baltimore MD 21218

BENTON, JESSE WILSON, JR., insurance executive; b. Danville, Va., Feb. 20, 1921; s. Jesse Wilson and Elizabeth (Osborne) B.; m. Mary Trumble, Mar. 29, 1957; children: Pamela, Patricia, Jesse. Student, Averett Coll., Danville, Va., 1939-41; A.B., Washington and Lee U., 1943, J.D., 1948. With Chubb & Son, Inc., N.Y.C., 1948-61; asst. v.p. Fed. Ins. Co., 1961-68, v.p., 1968-69, sr. v.p., 1969—; v.p. Vigilant Ins. Co., 1963; dir., sr. v.p. Chubb & Son, Inc., 1971—; pres. Chubb Found. Bd. dirs., sec. N.J. Soc. to Prevent Blindness, 1978—; pres. Chatham (N.J.) Emergency Squad, 1979-80; lay speaker, mem. adminstrv. bd. Chatham United Meth. Ch., 1970—; Committeeman Chatham Twp, dir. pub. safety; mem. Planning Bd. Chatham Twp.; bd. dirs. Ctr. Addictive Illnesses, 1980—. Served with USAAF, 1943-46. Mem. ABA, N.Y. Bar Assn., Va. Bar Assn., Internat. Assn. Ins. Counsel, Fedn. Ins. Counsel, Claims Execs. Council Am. Ins. Assn. Clubs: Canoe Brook Country (Summit, N.J.); Chatham Fish and Game. Home: 28 Linden Ln Chatham NJ 07928 Office: 51 John F Kennedy Pkwy Short Hills NJ 07078

BENTON, JOHN BUNYAN, lawyer; b. Sabinal, Tex., Dec. 2, 1932; s. Francis Marian and Willie Mae (Cooner) B.; m. Rosa Marie Guajardo, Nov. 22, 1974; children—Jeffrey Franc, Amy Denise, Marie Denise, Anna Marie. B.B.A., U. Tex., 1958, LL.B., 1959, LL.M. (Humble award 1960), 1963. Bar: Tex. bar 1959, N.Y. State bar 1963. Atty. FTC, Washington, 1960-65; exec. vice chmn. gen. counsel Jewelers Com., N.Y.C., 1965-69; sr. counsel NBC, N.Y.C., 1969-73; asst. gen. counsel Montgomery Ward & Co., Inc., Chgo., 1973-76; v.p., gen. counsel, sec., dir. Gimbel Bros., Inc., N.Y.C., 1976-78; v.p., gen. counsel Howell Corp. and Howell Petroleum Corp., Houston, 1978-83; individual bus. practice, Houston, 1983—. Author articles in field. Democrat candidate for N.Y. State Assembly, 1968. Served with USMC, 1953-56; Korea. Mem. Am. Bar Assn., Tex. Bar Assn., Assn. Bar City N.Y., Houston Bar Assn., Phi Alpha Delta. Unitarian. Clubs: Houston, Nat. Lawyers. Home: 8422 Pine Falls Dr Houston TX 77095 Office: 1200 Milam St Suite 318 Houston TX 77002

BENTON, JOHN FREDERIC, history educator; b. Phila., July 15, 1931; s. Frederic Elmon and Anna Josephine (Moffett) B.; m. Elspeth Baillie Hughes, Dec. 31, 1953; children: Helen Benton Metzler, Josephine J., Anna G., Laura E. A.B., Haverford Coll., 1953; M.A., Princeton U., 1955, Ph.D., 1959. Fulbright fellow U. Dijon, 1956-57; Instr. Reed Coll., 1957-59, U. Pa., 1959-60, asst. prof., 1960-65, Calif. Inst. Tech., Pasadena, 1965-66, assoc. prof., 1966-70, prof. history, 1970—, exec. officer for humanities, 1981-83; Fulbright prof. U. Reims (France), 1972; research assoc. Medieval and Renaissance Center, UCLA, 1977—; prof. history grad. dept. U. So. Calif., Los Angeles, 1973-74. Author: Town Origins, 1968, Self and Society in Medieval France, 1970; contbr. articles to profl. jours. Pres. Westside Community Council, Phila., 1960-61; mem. Pasadena Commn. on Human Need and Opportunity, 1969-70. Guggenheim fellow, 1963-64. Fellow Medieval Acad. Am. (councillor 1969-72), Am. Hist. Assn., Medieval Assn. of Pacific (v.p. 1980-82, pres. 1982-84), Internat. Courtly Lit. Soc. (hon. pres.). Office: Dept History 228-77 Calif Inst Tech Pasadena CA 91125

BENTON, JOHN HEMINGWAY, film and publishing company executive; b. Chgo., May 30, 1942; s. William Burnett and Helen Tallman (Hemingway) B.; m. Melinda Popham, Jan. 9, 1971; children: William Worth, Lillian Hemingway. B.A., Yale, 1963, King's Coll., Cambridge (Eng.) U., 1965. Intern Internat. Inst. for Ednl. Planning, UNESCO, Paris, 1965; prodn. intern Tele-Scolaire, Institut Pedagogique Nationale, Paris, 1966-67; dir. Ency. Brit. Reading Achievement Center, Oak Brook, Ill., 1971; v.p. Internat. Ency. Brit. Ednl. Corp., Chgo., 1972-73; chmn. bd. Ency. Brit. Ednl. Corp., Chgo., 1973—. Bd. dirs. Cradle Soc.; trustee Benton Ednl. Research Fund. Mem. Assn. for Ednl. Communication and Tech., Soc. Motion Picture and TV Engrs. Republican. Clubs: Chgo., Racquet, Arts, Malibu Riding and Tennis.; Intecallié (Paris). Home: 3343 Rambla Pacifico Malibu CA 90265 Office: EBE 425 N Michigan Ave Chicago IL 60611

BENTON, JOSEPH NELSON, JR., journalist, broadcaster; b. Danville, Va., Sept. 16, 1924; s. Joseph Nelson and Margaret Elizabeth (Davis) B.; m. Mildred Carolyn Patterson, May 4, 1944; 1 son, Joseph Nelson III. B.S. in Commerce, U. N.C., 1949. Promotion mgr. radio sta. WSOC, Charlotte, N.C., 1949-52; publicity dir. Jefferson Standard Broadcasting Co., Charlotte, 1952-54; news dir. WBT and WBTV, 1954-60; assignment editor, reporter CBS News, N.Y.C., 1960-63, corr., 1964—. (Emmy award Nat. Acad. TV Arts and Scis. 1974). Served with USAAF, 1942-45. Recipient Nat. Sch. Bell award, 1965. Home: 6124 Stoneham Ln McLean VA 22101 Office: 2020 M St NW Washington DC 20036

BENTON, MARJORIE CRAIG, diplomat; b. Phila., July 26, 1933; d. James Henry and Edith K. (Kinhead) Craig; m. Charles William Benton, June 13, 1953; children: Adrianne, Craig, Scott. Student, Conn. Coll. for Women, 1951-53; B.A., Nat. Coll. Edn., 1967. Chmn. Save the Children Fedn., N.Y.C.; mem. adv. bd. Northwestern Inst. Psychiatry, Chgo.; U.S. commr. Internat. Yr. Child; vice-chmn., trustee Better Govt. Assn., Chgo.; co-chmn. Ams. for SALT; mem. exec. bd. Films, Inc., Wilmette, Ill., Alliance to Save Energy, Washington, Democratic House and Senate Council; bd. dirs. Inst. Policy Studies, Washington, Internat. League Human Rights, N.Y.C.; mem. adv. bd. Cook County Welfare Services Com., Chgo., Nat. Women's Polit. Caucus, Washington, Women's Campaign Fund; hon. trustee Nat. Symphony Orch., Washington, UN Assn., Chgo.; pub. del. U.S. Mission to UN, del., 1978; mem. U.N. Assn. Commn., 1978-79; U.S. rep. to UNICEF, N.Y.C., now U.S. ambassador to; mem. adv. com. AID, 1979; del. Democratic Nat. Conv., 1972, 76; mem. Dem. Nat. Com. Commn. on Del. Selection, 1973, Ill. Dem. Platform Com., 1975, Ill. Dem. Affirmative Action Council, 1975. Recipient Pub. Service award UNICEF, 1978, Alumni Service award Nat Coll. Edn., 1979. Democrat. Unitarian. Office: UNICEF 866 UN Plaza New York NY 10017

BENTON, PHILIP EGLIN, JR., automobile mfg. co. exec.; b. Charlottesville, Va., Dec. 31, 1928; s. Philip Eglin and Orient (Nichols) B.; m. Mary Ann Zadosko, May 23, 1974; children—Katherine Benton Saville, Deborah A., Cynthia J., Philip Eglin, III, Paula R. A.B. in Econs. and Math. magna cum laude, Dartmouth Coll., 1952; M.B.A. in Fin. with highest distinction, Amos Tuck Sch., 1953. With Ford Motor Co., 1953—, v.p. truck ops., 1977-79, v.p., Detroit, 1979-81, v.p. sales ops., 1981—. Chmn. Mayflower dist. Trans-Atlantic council Boy Scouts Am., 1979; active Ford div. United Fund drives. Served with USMCR, 1946-48. Mem. Engring. Soc. Detroit. Clubs: Bloomfield Hills (Mich.) Country; Renaissance, Dartmouth (Detroit); Orleans Yacht. Office: 300 Renraissance Center Detroit MI 48243

BENTON, ROBERT, screenwriter, director; b. Waxahachie, Tex., Sept. 29, 1932. B.A., U. Tex. Former writer, then art dir.: Esquire Mag; screenwriting collaboration with David Newman: numerous films including Bad Company; screenwriter, dir.: Still of the Night, 1982; also dir.: Kramer vs Kramer; libretto plays It's A Bird. It's a Plane. It's Superman; author: sketch Oh, Calcutta; co-author: (with David Newman) The In and Out Book; author numerous children's books. (Recipient Dirs. Guild Am. award for Kramer vs Kramer, Oscar (2) for dir., screenwriter Kramer vs Kramer.). Office: care Sam Con Internat Creative Mgmt 40 W 57th St New York NY 10019 *

BENTON, ROBERT AUSTIN, JR., investment banker, broker; b. Manes, Mo., Mar. 21, 1921; s. Robert A. and Laura (Pridgen) B.; m. Marian Oppenheim, Oct. 2, 1943; 1 son, Robert Austin III. B.S., U. Mo., 1943; postgrad., U. Detroit, 1946-47, Wayne State U., 1947-48. Account exec. Cray, McFawn & Co., Detroit, 1946-47, S.R. Livingstone & Co., 1947-50; account exec. Manley, Bennett & Co., Detroit, 1950-52; gen. partner Manley, Bennett, McDonald & Co., Detroit, 1952—, mng. dir., 1981—, chmn. mgmt. com., mng. partner, 1971-79, sr. partner, 1979-80, chmn. bd. dirs., 1980—, MBM Corp., 1980—; chmn. bd. dirs., pres. MBM Leasing, Inc., 1981—; Allied mem. N.Y. Stock Exchange, 1952—; mem. Midwest Stock Exchange; chmn. Detroit Stock Exchange, 1976—. Chmn. Beverly Hills Retirement System; vice chmn. bd. trustees Presbytery of Detroit. Served with USMCR, 1943-46. Mem. Investment Bankers Assn. Am. (mem. nat. com., past chmn., Service awards 1961, 62), Sales Marketing Execs. (pres. Detroit chpt.), Sales/Mktg. Execs. Internat., Am. Asset Mgmt., Inc. (sec. 1982—), Securities Industry Assn. (gov., mem. exec. com. Great Lakes dist., nat. moderator), Pi Sigma Epsilon (life), Alpha Gamma Rho. Clubs: Kiwanian., Detroit Yacht, Detroit Golf, Bond, Economic (Detroit); Quechee (Vt.); Otsego (Mich.) Ski, Renaissance. Home: 15810 Reedmere Rd Birmingham MI 48009 Office: 100 Renaissance Center Detroit MI 48243 *There is no substitute for integrity. Personal integrity is more valuable than power or profit. Every problem has a solution. I am capable of finding the solution if I maintain confidence that man possesses the ability to eventually select the right and best direction to assure survival and success of an enterprise.*

BENTON, ROBERT DEAN, educational administrator; b. Guthrie Center, Iowa, July 22, 1929; s. John H. and Luella M. (Rawlings) B.; m. Rachel Swanson, July 29, 1951; children: Camille, John, Scott. B.A., U. No. Iowa, 1951, M.A., 1956; Ed.D., U. No. Colo., 1961. Tchr., Ruthven, Ia., 1953-56, Mason City, Iowa, 1956-58, dir. pub. info., coordinator secondary edn., Rapid City, S.D., 1958-61, asst. supt. in charge of instrn., 1961-66, supt. schs., Council Bluffs, Iowa, 1966-72; state supt. pub. instrn. State of Iowa, 1972—; part-time journalism tchr. summer sessions U.No. Colo., 1959-61; Mem. Iowa Adv. Council for Vocat. Edn., 1970—. Hon. chmn., mem. founding com. Friends of Music Community Concert Series, 1967; Bd. dirs. Chanticleer Community Theater, 1968—, Christian Home, 1968—. Served with USMC, 1951-53. Named Boss of the Year Jaycees, Council Bluffs, 1970; Outstanding Young Man of the Year Jr. C. of C., Rapid City, 1965. Mem. N.E.A., C. of C., Phi Delta Kappa, Theta Alpha Phi. Methodist. Club: Rotarian. Office: Grimes Office Bldg Des Moines IA 50319

BENTON, WILLIAM PETTIGREW, automobile company executive; b. Laurinburg, N.C., Nov. 4, 1923; s. William P. and Carlie (Austin) B.; m. Blanche Marilyn Lampke, June 26, 1948; children: Barbara, Mary Anne, Judy, Nancy. Student, U. N.C., 1946. With Ford Motor Co., 1947—, v.p. mktg., 1971-73, v.p. parent co., gen. mgr. Lincoln-Mercury div., 1973-75, v.p. parent co., gen. mgr. Ford div., 1975-77; v.p. sales (Ford of Europe), 1977-81, v.p. parent co., v.p. mktg. worldwide Ford of Europe, 1981. Gen. chmn. Meadowbrook Theatre and Music Festival, Oakland U., Rochester, Mich., 1972; bd. dirs. Sch. Bus. Adminstrn. Sponsors, Inc., Coll. William and Mary, 1976—, Marian High Sch. Dads Club, 1973-76; dir. automotive div. United Fund Campaign, Detroit., 1971; mem. exec. com. Internat. Fedn. Multiple Sclerosis Socs. Served with USAAF, 1943-45. Decorated Bronze Star; Croix de Guerre, France). Mem. Advt. Council (dir. 1983—), Detroit C. of C. (dir. 1983—). Clubs: Econ. Detroit, Detroit Athletic, Renaissance; City (Charlotte N.C.); Orchard Lake. Home: 355 Martell Dr Bloomfield Hills MI 48013

BENTSEN, KENNETH EDWARD, architect; b. Mission, Tex., Nov. 21, 1926; s. Lloyd Millard and Edna Ruth (Colbath) B.; m. Mary Dorsey Bates, Dec. 3, 1953; children: Molly Bates, Elizabeth Jean, Kenneth Edward, William Lloyd. B.S., U. Houston, 1951, B.A., 1952. Pvt. practice architecture, prin. Kenneth Bentsen Assocs., Houston, 1958—. Projects include Jones and Anderson Med. Research Tower, Houston, Agnes Arnold Hall, Philip Hoffman Hall, U. Houston, M.D. Anderson Library, U. Houston, Pan Am. U, Grad. Sch. Bus., U. Tex, M.D. Anderson Environ. Research Center, U. Tex, Learning Ctr., U. Tex. Med. Br., Galveston, Summit, Houston Sports Arena, State Law Ctr, Austin, Tex., Harris County Adminstrn. Bldg, Houston. Mem. Mayor's Com. Bd. Appeals; mem. adv. bd. Blaffer Gallery; bd. dirs. Tex. Children's Hosp.; mem. adv. council U. Tex. Sch. Architecture Found. Recipient numerous design awards. Fellow AIA; mem. Tex. Soc. Architects, Houston C. of C. Office: 2919 Allen Pkwy Suite 1266 Houston TX 77019

BENTSEN, LLOYD, U.S. senator; b. Mission, Tex., Feb. 11, 1921; s. Lloyd M. and Edna Ruth (Colbath) B.; m. Beryl Ann Longino, Nov. 27, 1943; children: Lloyd M. III, Lan, Tina. LL.B., U. Tex., 1942. Bar: Tex. 1942. Practice law, McAllen, Tex., 1945-48, judge, Hidalgo County, Tex., 1946-48; mem. 80th to 83d congresses from 15th Tex. Dist.; pres. Lincoln Consol., Houston, 1955-70; U.S. Senator from Tex., 1971—, mem. fin., environment and public works coms., intelligence com., also Congl. joint econ. com.; chmn. Dem. Senatorial Campaign Com. Served to maj. USAAF, 1942-45. Decorated D.F.C., Air Medal with 3 oak leaf clusters. Home: Houston TX Office: Room 703 Hart Senate Office Bldg Washington DC 20510 also 4026 Fed Bldg 515 Rusk St Houston TX 77002 also 912 Fed Bldg Austin TX 78701 also Earle Cabell Bldg Room 7C30 Dallas TX 75242

BENTZ, DALE MONROE, university librarian; b. York County, Pa., Jan. 3, 1919; s. Solomon Earl and Mary Rebecca (Wonders) B.; m. Mary Gail Menius, June 13, 1942; children: Dale Flynn, Thomas Earl, Mary Carolyn. A.B., Gettysburg Coll., 1939; B.S.L.S., U. N.C. Chapel Hill, 1940; M.S., U. Ill., 1951. With Periodicals dept. U. N.C. Library, Chapel Hill, 1940-41, Serials Dept., Duke U. Library, Durham, N.C., 1941-42; asst. librarian E. Carolina Tchrs. Coll., Greenville, N.C., 1946-48; head processing dept. U. Tenn. Library, Knoxville, 1948-53; assoc. dir. libraries U. Iowa, Iowa City, 1953-70, univ. librarian, 1970—. Editor: U. Tenn. Library lectures, 1952; contbr. articles to profl. jours. Mem. Iowa Library Assn., pres., 1959-60, ALA, pres. Resources and Tech. Services div., 1975-76, AAUP; mem Assn. Coll. and Research Libraries; mem. Beta Phi Mu, pres., 1966-67. Lutheran. Clubs: Triangle (pres. 1958-59), Univ. Athletic (sec. 1979-80). Home: 1615 East College Iowa City IA 52240 Office: Univ Iowa Libraries Iowa City IA 52242

BENTZIN, CHARLES GILBERT, actuary, employee consultant; b. Watertown, Wis., Nov. 29, 1932; s. Alfred and Dorothy Joy Soulen.

B.B.A. with honors, U. Wis., 1954. Actuarial trainee Conn. Gen. Life Ins. Co., Hartford, 1954-57; chief actuary Ariz. Ins. dept., Phoenix, 1959-60; cons. actuary, cons. employee benefits, Phoenix, 1960; pres. Charles G. Bentzin Assocs., Actuaries and Employees Benefit Cons., Inc., Phoenix, 1963—; dir. and-or officer Capital Funding Life Ins. Co., Am. Transcontinental Life Ins. Co., Western Travellers Life Ins. Co., Wellington Life Ins. Co. Contbr. articles to trade jours. Served with AUS, 1957-59. Guest exec. Ariz. State U. Sch. Bus. Adminstrn. Fellow Soc. Actuaries, Fin. Analysts Fedn. (enrolled actuary); mem. Inst. Actuaries (Gt. Britain), Internat. Congress Actuaries, Actuarial Club Pacific States, Am. Acad. Actuaries, Phoenix Soc. Fin. Analysts, Mensa Soc. (local sec. 1971-72), U. Wis. Alumni Club. (pres. Ariz. chpt. 1964). Clubs: Ariz. Actuarial (pres. 1963-65), Arzona (Phoenix)). Lodge: Rotary. Home: 730 W Coronado Rd Phoenix AZ 85007 Office: 234 N Central Ave Suite 646 Phoenix AZ 85004

BENUA, RICHARD SQUIER, nuclear physician, educator; b. Bexley, Ohio, Aug. 11, 1921; s. Albert Ray and Ruth (Squier) B.; m Mary Consilia Ralston, June 15, 1945 (div. 1954); m. Joan McLellan, Oct. 16, 1954; children: David Peter, Daniel Ray, Margaret Ann, Laura Helen. B.S. magna cum laude, Western Res. U., 1942; M.D., Johns Hopkins U., 1946; M.S., U. Minn., 1952. Am. Bd. Nuclear Medicine. Intern N.Y. Polyclinic Hosp., N.Y.C., 1946-47; resident fellow in medicine Mayo Clinic, Rochester, Minn., 1950-53; asst. Sloan-Kettering Inst., N.Y.C., 1955-60, assoc. mem., 1960-66; assoc. prof. medicine and radiology U. Tex. Med. Ctr., Galveston, 1966-70; attending physician, chief nuclear medicine service Meml. Hosp., N.Y.C., 1970—; asst. prof. medicine Cornell Med. Coll., N.Y.C., 1970—, assoc. prof. radiology, 1972—, prof. clin. medicine, 1981—; chmn. adv. bd. Bur. of Labs., N.Y.C., 1976-79. Mem. editorial bd.: Yr. Book of Cancer, 1976. Served to capt. AUS, 1947-49. Recipient Research award Mayo Found., 1962. Mem. Endocrine Soc., Am. Thyroid Assn., Soc. Nuclear Medicine (pres. edn. and research found. 1974-76, pres. Greater N.Y. chpt. 1976-77), Am. Coll. Nuclear Physicians, Phi Beta Kappa, Sigma Xi. Unitarian. Club: Horseshoe Harbor Yacht (Larchmont, N.Y.). Home: 82 Willow Ave Larchmont NY 10538 Office: Meml Sloan-Kettering Cancer Ctr 1275 York Ave New York NY 10021

BENYO, RICHARD STEPHEN, magazine editor, race car driver; b. Palmerton, Pa., Apr. 20, 1946; s. Andrew Joseph and Dorothy Rita (Herman) B.; m. Jill Wapensky, Apr. 29, 1972 (div. 1979). B.A. in English Lit., Bloomsburg (Pa.) State U., 1968. Mng. editor Times-News, Lehighton, Pa., 1968-72; editor Stock Car Racing mag., Alexandria, Va., 1972-77, sr. editor, 1977—; exec. editor Runner's World mag., Mountain View, Calif., 1977—; editorial dir. Skier's mag. and Fit mag., Mountain View, 1980—, Fit mag., 1981—, Anderson World Books, 1980—, Strength Tng. for Beauty mag., 1983—; editor Corporate Fitness Report, Mountain View, 1980—, Nat. Health & Fitness Report, 1982—, Runner's World Quar., 1982—; v.p. J.R. Anderson Enterprizes, Inc., 1982—; pres., pub. Specific Publs., Inc., 1983—; program dir. PTVC-TV, Palmerton, Pa., 1969-72. Author: The Grand National Stars, 1975, The Book of Richard Petty, 1976, Superspeedway, 1977, Return to Running, 1978, The Indoor Exercise Book, 1980, Advanced Indoor Exercise Book, 1981, (with Kym Herrin) Sexercise, 1981, Masters of the Marathon, 1983, (with Elaine LaLanne) Elaine LaLanne's Complete Fitness Diary, 1984; editor: The Complete Woman Runner, 1978, Running for Everybody, 1981. Mem. racing panel of experts Union 76. Recipient 1st pl. award local column Pa. Newspaper Pubs. Assn., 1972. Mem. Am. Auto Racing Writers and Broadcasters Assn. (1st place award for tech. writing), Internat. Motor Press Assn., Athletic Congress, U.S. Ski Writers Assn., N.Y. Road Runners Club, Nat. Sportscasters and Sportswriters Assn., Track and Field Writers of Am., Internat. Sports Press Assn. Democrat. Roman Catholic. Home: PO Box 4432 Mountain View CA 94040 Office: 1400 Stierlin Rd Mountain View CA 94042

BENZ, GEORGE ALBERT, economist, educator; b. St. Louis, Feb. 21, 1926; s. George and Genevieve Beatrice (Klueg) B.; m. Dorris Jean Tabor, Apr. 14, 1951; 1 dau., Lynda Kaye. B.B.A., N. Tex. State U., 1953, M.S., 1955; Ph.D., U. Okla., 1969. Mgmt. trainee Montgomery Ward, 1953-54; tchr. social studies, coach Bryson (Tex.) High Sch., 1954-55; tchr. mathematics, coach Grapevine (Tex.) High Sch., 1955-56; instr. social studies N.W. Mo. State Coll., Maryville, 1956-57; grad. asst. U. Okla., Norman, 1957-59; asst. prof. econs. and sociology Central State Coll., Edmond, Okla., 1959-66; asso. prof. econs. St. Mary's U., San Antonio, 1966-79, prof. econs., 1979—; dir. Univ. Research Center, chmn. dept. urban studies; cons. in field; econ. advisor Greater San Antonio C. of C.; bus. advisor, various small bus. loan orgns.; research dir. Scientific Profit Analysis for Restaurants, 1979—; dir. Urban Adv. Group, 1980—; econ. expert witness in loss of income and anti-trust cases, 1973—; mem. Tex. State adv. com. U.S. Civil Rights Com., 1969-77. Contbr. articles to profl. jours. Campaign treas. various local and nat. candidates. Served with U.S. Army, 1943-49. Decorated Bronze Star, Purple Heart.; Named Tchr. of Yr. St. Mary's U.; KBAT Tex. Star award Sta. KBAT. Mem. Am. Econs. Assn., Southwestern Social Sci. Assn., So. Econ. Assn., Assn. for Evolutionary Econs., Am. Assn. Econ. Profs., San Antonio Bus. and Econ. Soc. Democrat. Unitarian. Home: 206 E Sunshine Dr San Antonio TX 78228 Office: One Camino Santa Maria San Antonio TX 78284

BENZ, HARRY R., business executive; b. Montclair, N.J., Oct. 1, 1937; children—Karen, Sylvia. B.B.A., Upsala Coll., 1962. C.P.A., 1963. Auditor, then cons. Peat, Marwick, Mitchell & Co., 1961-71; asst. treas., then treas. Am. Hoechst Corp., Somerville, N.J., 1971-74, v.p., treas., 1975-79, group v.p., chief fin. officer, from 1980, now exec. v.p., chief fin. officer, from 1980. Office: American Hoechst Corp Route 202-206 North Somerville NJ 08876 *

BENZER, SEYMOUR, scientist, educator; b. N.Y.C., Oct. 15, 1921; s. Mayer and Eva (Naidorf) B.; m. Dorothy Vlosky, Jan. 10, 1942 (dec. 1978); children: Barbara Ann Benzer Freidin, Martha Jane Benzer Goldberg; m. Carol A. Miller, May 11, 1980. B.A., Bklyn. Coll., 1942; M.S., Purdue U., 1943, Ph.D., 1947, D.Sc. (hon.), 1968, Columbia U., 1974, Yale U., 1977, Brandeis U., 1978, CUNY, 1978, U. Paris, 1983. Mem. faculty Purdue U., 1945-67, prof. biophysics, 1958-61, Stuart distinguished prof. biology, 1961-67; prof. biology Calif. Inst. Tech., 1967-75, Boswell prof. neurosci., 1975—; biophysicist Oak Ridge Nat. Lab., 1948-49; vis. asso. Calif. Inst. Tech., Pasadena, 1965-67. Contbr. articles to profl. jours. Research fellow Calif. Inst. Tech., 1949-51; Fulbright Research fellow Pasteur Inst., Paris, France, 1951-52; sr. NSF postdoctoral fellow, Cambridge, Eng., 1957-58; recipient Award of Honor, Bklyn. Coll., 1956; Sigma Xi research award Purdue U., 1957; Ricketts award U. Chgo., 1961; Gold medal N.Y. City Coll. Chemistry Alumni Assn., 1962; Gairdner award of merit, 1964; McCoy award Purdue U., 1965; Lasker award, 1971; T. Duckett Jones award, 1975; Prix Leopold Mayer French Acad. Scis., 1975; Louisa Gross Horwitz award, 1976; Harvey award Israel, 1977; Warren Triennial prize Mass. Gen. Hosp., 1977; Dickson award, 1978. Mem. Nat. Acad. Scis., Am. Acad. Arts and Scis., Am. Philos. Soc., Harvey Soc., AAAS; fgn. mem. Royal Soc. London. Home: 2075 Robin Rd San Marino CA 91108

BENZIGER, PETER HAMILTON, utility exec.; b. N.Y.C., Nov. 28, 1926; s. Alfred Felix and Nannie Merrick (Hamilton) B.; m. Joan Patricia Kelly, June 22, 1971; children—John Mitchell, Elizabeth Roberts. B.S. in Engring, Princeton U., 1949. Registered profl. engr., D.C., Md. With Potomac Electric Power Co., 1949—, sr. v.p. generation, Washington, 1973—. Vice chmn. Princeton Schs. and Scholarship Com., 1962-68. Served with USNR, 1944-46. Mem. ASME, Assn. Edison Illuminating Cos., Met. Washington Bd. Trade. Republican. Roman Catholic. Clubs: Chevy Chase Country, Metropolitan. Home: 5207 Westbard Ave Bethesda MD 20816 Office: 1900 Pennsylvania Ave Washington DC 20068

BEN-ZION, artist; b. Ukraine, Russia, July 8, 1897; came to U.S., 1920, naturalized, 1936; m. Lillian Dubin, 1949. Ed., Art Acad., Vienna, Austria. Prepared for rabbinical career, until 1917, engaged in Hebrew letters, 1917-31, painter, 1931—; art instr. Cooper Union, 1947—. Exhibited in one-man shows at, Balt. Mus., Portland (Oreg.) Mus., Taft Mus., Cin., San Francisco Mus., Iowa U., St. Louis Mus., Smithsonian Inst.; exhibited, Am. Artists Gallery, 1936, East River Gallery, 1937; exhibitor at, Bonestell Gallery, spring 1939, Jewish Mus. N.Y., 1948, 52, 59, Brandeis U., 1969, Nat. Maritime Mus. Haifa, 1975, Haifa Mus., 1978; represented in traveling exhbn. circulated by Am. Fedn. Art, 1953-54, permanent collections, Mus. Modern Art, N.Y.C., Whitney Mus., N.Y.C., Dept. State Art Abroad, Art Inst. Chgo., Duncan Phillips Gallery, Washington, Met. Mus. Art, N.Y.C., Newark Mus., St. Louis Mus., Tel Aviv Mus., Bezalel Mus., Jerusalem, New Art Circle, J.B. Newman and Goodyear collections, Marian Willard Gallery, Bertha Schaefer and Buchholz galleries, exhbns., Duveen-Graham Gallery, 1955-56; author of: poetry, drama and fairy tales in Hebrew Portfolio of Biblical Etchings, 1950; Author of: Portfolio of Prophets, 1953, Portfolio of Ruth, Job, Song of Songs, 1954, Drawings: The Wisdom of the Fathers, 1960, Judges and Kings; portfolio of etchings, 1964, The Life of A Prophet, 1965, The Epic of Gilgamesh and Enkidu, 1967, In Search of Oneself, 1968, The Thirty-Six; portfolio of 36 etchings, 1972, numerous others; author: (poetry) Hebrew Songs of Ben-Zion, vols. I-V, The Thirty-Six Unknown (Hebrew and English); (plays in Hebrew) King Solomon, The Street, Advertisement; (epics in Hebrew) Gilgamesh & Enkidu, In Those Days, Adam Alone, In the Beginning; (essays in English) Reflections on Symbolism, The Abstract, On the Inner Life. Recipient art award Congress for Jewish Culture. Mem. United Am. Artists, Artists Congress. One of founders of The Ten, with whom exhibited in Paris, France, 1937. Home and studio: 329 W 20th St New York NY 10011 *Fashion and art don't mix. Whenever art becomes a victim of fashion, art is perverted and annihilated, and the artist who succumbs to it sells his birthright for a bowl of porridge.*

BERACHA, BARRY HARRIS, brewery executive; b. Bronx, N.Y., Feb. 28, 1942; s. Nissim Macy and Celia Grace (Sides) B.; m. Barbara Marie Capobianco, Dec. 23, 1967; children: Brian, Bradley, Bonnie. B.Chem. Engring., Pratt Inst., 1963; M.B.A., U. Pa., 1965. Ops. researcher Celanese Corp., 1965-67; tech. economist Sun Oil Co., 1964-65; with Anheuser-Busch Cos., Inc., 1967—, v.p. corp. planning, 1974-76, v.p., group exec., 1976—; dir. Dirs. Capital, Inc., N.Y.C., Benham Group, Oklahoma City. Mem. Ops. Research Soc., Engrs. Club, Inst. Mgmt. Scientists. Office: 1 Busch Pl Saint Louis MO 63118

BERADINO, JOHN, actor; b. Los Angeles, May 1, 1917; s. Ignazio and Anna B.; m. Marjorie Ann Binder, Apr. 31, 1972; children—Katherine Ann, John Anthony; children by previous marriage—Antoinette, Cynthia. Student, U. So. Calif., 1936-39. Profl. baseball player, 1937-52; with St. Louis Browns, 1939-47, Cleve. Indians, 1948-51, Pitts. Pirates, 1951-52; actor, 1953—. Star: TV daytime serial Gen. Hosp, 1963—; other TV appearances include Laramie; TV movies Moon of the Wolf; (Nominated as best actor in Daytime Drama 1973, 74, 75). Served with USN, 1942-45. Mem. Screen Actors Guild, Am. Fedn. TV Arts Scis., Writers Guild Am.-West. Republican. Roman Catholic. Office: care Press Relations ABC-TV 1330 Ave of Americas New York NY 10019 *

BERALL, FRANK STEWART, lawyer; b. N.Y.C., Feb. 10, 1929; s. Louis J. and Jeannette F.; m. Christiana Johnson, July 5, 1958 (dec. July 1972); children: Erik Dustin, Elissa Alexandra; m. Jenefer M. Carey, Sept. 1, 1980. B.S., Yale U., 1950, LL.B., 1955; LL.M. in Tax, NYU, 1959. Bar: N.Y. 1955, Conn. 1960. Assoc. firm Mudge, Stern, Baldwin & Todd, N.Y.C., 1955-57, Townley, Updike, Carter & Rodgers, 1957-60; atty. Conn. Gen. Life Ins. Co., Bloomfield, Conn., 1960-65; atty. trust dept. Hartford Nat. Bank & Trust Co., Conn., 1965-67; assoc. firm Cooney & Scully, Hartford, Conn., 1968-70; partner firm Copp, Koletsky & Berall (and predecessor firms), Hartford, 1970—; v.p., sec., dir., gen. counsel John M. Blewer, Inc., Essex, Conn., 1969—; dir. Thomson Gen. Corp., Burlington, Mass., 1969-73, Foods Multinat., Ltd., Hamilton, Bermuda, 1971-72; asst. in instrn. Yale U. Law Sch., 1954-55; lectr. U. Conn. Sch. Ins., 1964-72, Law Sch., 1972-73; instr. estate planning Am. Coll. Life Underwriters, 1968-69; adj. asst. prof. Grad. Tax Program, U. Hartford, 1973-74; cons. Conn. Gov.'s Strike Force for Full Employment, 1971-72, Gov.'s Commn. on Tax Reform, 1972-73, State Tax Commrs. Commn., 1972-75; state co-chmn. Joint Editorial Bd. for Uniform Probate Code, 1972—; lectr. in field. Co-author: A Practitioners Guide to the Tax Reform Act of 1969, 1970, Estate Planning and the Close Corporation, 1970, Planning Large Estates, 1970; Sr. editor: Conn. Bar Jour, 1969—; mem. editorial bd.: Estate Planning mag, 1973—; Contbr. articles to legal publs. Bd. dirs. Bloomfield Interfaith Homes, 1967-71; mem. adv. council U. Hartford Tax Inst., 1970-82; co-chmn. Notre Dame Estate Planning Inst., 1977—. Served to 1st lt., F.A. U.S. Army, 1951-52. Fellow Am. Coll. Probate Counsel (chmn. Conn. chpt. 1975-81, editorial bd. 1975—, chmn. estate and gift tax com. 1976-81, accessions tax com. 1984—, regent 1977-83), Am. Coll. Tax Counsel; mem. Internat. Fiscal Assn., ABA (chmn. com. estate planning, ins., real property, probate and trust sect. 1979—, chmn. membership com. 1977-79, chmn. com. on income of estates and trusts, sect. taxation 1983—, co-founder, convener estate planning seminar group 1972-78), Conn. Bar Assn. (exec. com., estates and probate sect. 1973—, chmn. 1982—, chmn. tax sect. 1969-72, exec. com. 1969—, chmn. com. on specialization 1974-77), Hartford County Bar Assn. (chmn. com. liaison with IRS 1972-74, com. charter and by laws 1975), Am. Law Inst. (tax adv. group 1980—), Internat. Acad. Estate and Trust Law (exec. council 1978-82, mem. Conn.'s adv. com. on tax law clarification), Tax Club of Hartford (pres. 1975-76). Republican. Episcopalian. Home: 9 Penwood Rd Bloomfield CT 06002 Office: 111 Pearl St Hartford CT 06103 *As a tax lawyer, I view my job as helping to keep the system going by seeing to it that my clients pay the government all it is legally entitled to receive in taxes, but no more, and doing pro bono work for the improvement of the entire federal and state tax law system.*

BERANEK, LEO LEROY, business and engineering consultant; b. Solon, Iowa, Sept. 15, 1914; s. Edward Fred and Beatrice (Stahle) B.; m. Phyllis Knight, Sept. 6, 1941 (dec. 11/7/82); children: James Knight, Thomas Haynes. A.B., Cornell Coll., 1936, D.Sc. (hon.), 1946; M.S., Harvard U., 1937, D.Sc., 1940; D.Eng. (hon.), Worcester Poly. Inst., 1971, D.Comml. Sci., Suffolk U., 1979, LL.D., Emerson College, 1982. Instr. physics Harvard, 1940-41, asst. prof., 1941-43, dir. research on sound, 1941-45; dir. Electro-Acoustics and Systems Research Labs., 1945-46; assoc. prof. communications engring. MIT, 1947-58, lectr., 1958-81; tech. dir. Acoustics Lab., 1947-53; pres., dir. Bolt Beranek & Newman, Cambridge, Mass., 1953-69, chief scientist, 1969-71, dir., 1953—; pres., chief exec. officer, dir. Boston Broadcasters, Inc., 1963-79, chmn. bd., 1980-83; part-owner WCVB-TV, Boston, 1972-82; chmn. bd. Mueller-BBM GmbH, Munich, Germany, 1962—. Author: (with others) Principles of Sound Control in Airplanes, 1944, Acoustic Measurements, 1949, Acoustics, 1954, Music, Acoustics and Architecture, 1962; Editor, contbr.: Noise Reduction, 1960, Noise and Vibration Control, 1971; Editor: Noise Control mag, 1954-55; assoc. editor: Sound mag, 1961-63; editorial bd.: Noise Control Engring, 1973-77; Contbr. articles on acoustics, audio and TV communications systems to tech. publs. Mem. Mass. Gov.'s Task Force on Coastal Resources, 1974-77; Charter mem. bd. overseers Boston Symphony Orch., 1968-80, chmn., 1977-80, trustee, 1977—, v.p., 1980-83, chmn. bd. trustees, 1983—; mem. vis. com. Center Behavioral Scis., Harvard U., 1964-70, vis. com. biology and related research facilities, 1971-77, mem. vis. com. physics dept., 1983—; mem. advisory com. mgmt. devel. Harvard Bus. Sch., 1965-71; mem. council for arts Mass. Inst. Tech., 1972—; pres. World Affairs Council Boston, 1975-78, vice chmn. bd., 1979—; trustee Cornell Coll., 1955-71, Emerson Coll., 1973-79; bd. dirs. Boston Opera Co., pres., 1961-63; bd. dirs. Boston 200, 1975-77, United Way Mass. Bay, 1975-80, Flaschner Jud. Inst., 1977-81. Guggenheim fellow, 1946-47; recipient Presdl. certificate of merit, 1948; Cornell Coll. Alumni Citation, 1953; 1st Silver medal le Groupement des Acousticiens de Langue Francaise, Paris, 1966; Abe Lincoln TV award So. Bapt. Conv., 1975; Media award NAACP, 1975. Fellow Acoustical Soc. Am. (Biennial award 1944, exec. council 1944-47, v.p. 1949-50, pres. 1954-55, assoc. editor 1946-60, Wallace Clement Sabine Archtl. Acoustics award 1961, Gold medal award 1975), Nat. Acad. Engring. (dir. marine bd., com. pub. engring. policy, aeros. and space engring. bd.), Am. Acad. Arts and Scis., Am. Phys. Soc., AAAS, Audio Engring. Soc. (pres. 1967-68, Gold medal 1971, gov. 1966-71), IEEE (chmn. profl. group audio 1950-51); mem. Inst. Noise Control Engring. (charter pres. 1971-73, dir. 1973-75), Am. Standards Assn. (chmn. acoustical standards bd. 1956-68, dir. 1963-68), Mass. Broadcasters Assn. (dir. 1973-80, pres. 1978-79, Disting. Service award 1980), Boston Community Media Council (treas. 1973-76, v.p. 1976-77), Cambridge Soc. Early Music (pres. 1963-71, dir. 1961-79), Acad. Disting. Bostonians, Greater Boston C. of C. (dir. 1973-79, v.p. 1976-79, Disting. Community Service award 1980), Acad. Disting. Bostonians (charter), Phi Beta Kappa, Sigma Xi, Eta Kappa Nu. Episcopalian. Clubs: Mass. Inst. Tech. Faculty, Winchester Country, St. Botolph, Harvard. Home and Office: 7 Ledgewood Rd Winchester MA 01890

BERBERICH, WILLIAM D(ORRIS), oil company executive; b. Pitts., Nov. 14, 1937; s. Leo Joseph and Ida Mae (Watson) B.; m. Cecilia Maria Del Mul, Nov. 18, 1967; children: Pamela Joy, Jennifer Jill, Karen Paige. A.B., Columbia U., 1959; B.S., Coll. Engring., Columbia U., 1960; M.B.A., U. Pa., 1965. Analyst Exxon Co. U.S.A., Linden, N.J., 1965-67, sr. analyst, Houston, 1967-72, head tech. dept., Bayonne, N.J., 1972-76; v.p. planning-adminstrn. Belcher Oil Co., Miami, Fla., 1976-78; exec. v.p. Belcher New Eng., Inc., Revere, Mass., 1978-82, Belcher-N.Y., N.J., New Eng., Inc., Maspeth, N.Y., 1982—; bd. dirs. New Eng. Fuel Inst., 1978—, Harris County Water Bd., Tex., 1975. Served to lt. (j.g.) USN, 1960-63; Atlantic. Club: Toastmasters (N.J.) (v.p. 1975-76). Office: Belcher NY NJ & New England Inc Maspeth NY 11378

BERCK, MARTIN GANS, journalist; b. N.Y.C., Feb. 5, 1928; s. Samuel M. and Florence (Gans) B.; m. Lenore Fierstein, July 12, 1953; children—Jonathan, Judith, David. A.B., N.Y. U., 1947; M.S. in Journalism, Columbia U., 1953, Russell Sage fellow, 1968. Newsman AP, 1953-56; successively reporter, polit. writer, UN corr., nat. editor N.Y. Herald Tribune, 1956-66; writer, editor, producer NBC News, 1966-72; editorial writer, UN Bur. chief, fgn. editor Newsday, L.I., N.Y., 1972—; adj. prof. journalism N.Y. U., 1975—. Book editor; contbr. articles to mags. Served with AUS, 1950-52. Mem. UN Corrs. Assn., N.Y. U. Alumni Assn., Columbia U. Alumni Assn., Sigma Delta Chi, Kappa Tau Alpha. Clubs: N.Y. U. Faculty, Oversees Press, Nat. Press, Columbia U. Faculty. Home: 604 Ramapo Rd Teaneck NJ 07666 Office: 235 Pinelawn Rd Melville LI NY 11747

BERCOVITCH, HANNA MARGARETA, editor; b. Chgo., Il., Sept. 5, 1934; d. Sven Victor and Elizabeth (Rubin) Malmquist; m. Sacvan Bercovitch, July 29, 1956; 1 son, Eytan. Student, St. Thomas More Coll., 1960, Sir George Williams Coll., Montreal, 1960-61. Acquisition librarian Honnold Library, Claremont, Calif., 1961-62, acting rare book librarian, 1962-63, spl. project staff, 1963-64; asst. editing Partisan Rev. Congress Monthly, Rutgers U., N.Y.C., 1974-75, 78-80; free lance research assoc. Columbia U., N.Y.C., 1965-80; sr. editor Library of Am. Literary Classics, N.Y.C., 1980—; guest curator Melville Whitman Exhibit, N.Y. Pub. Library, 1982; cons. Parkman Exhibit, N.Y. Hist. Soc., 1983, Henry James and Washington Sq. Exhibit, N.Y. Pub. Library, 1983. Environ. commr. City of Leonia, N.J., 1971-73. Home: 445 Riverside Dr New York NY 10027 Office: Library of Am Literary Classics of US 14 E 60th St New York NY 10022

BERCOVITCH, SACVAN, educator; b. Montreal, Que., Can., Oct. 4, 1933; s. Alexander and Bertha (Avrutick) B.; m. Gila Malmquist, July 29, 1956; 1 son, Eytan. B.A., Sir George William Coll., 1961; M.A., Claremont (Calif.) Grad. Sch., 1963, Ph.D., 1965. Asst. prof. English and Am. lit. Brandeis U., 1966-68; asso. prof. U. Calif., San Diego, 1968-70; prof. English and Am. Lit. Columbia U., 1970-83; prof. English and Am. lit. Harvard U., 1983—; lectr., Kyoto, Japan, Princeton U., U. Pa., U. Toronto, U. Paris, U. Berlin, Oxford U.; adv., cons. in field. Author: Typology and Early American Literature, 1972, The American Puritan Imagination, 1974, The Puritan Origins of the American Self, 1975, The American Jeremiad, 1978; editor: Cambridge History of American Literature. Am. Philos. Soc. fellow, 1968-69; Guggenheim fellow, 1969-70; Am. Council Learned Socs. fellow, 1971-72; Nat. Humanities Inst. fellow, 1975-76; Nat. Endowment for Humanities fellow, 1978-79. Mem. MLA (mem. exec. com. Am. sect. 1976-78), English Inst., Am. Studies Assn. (pres. 1982—). Office: Warren House Harvard U Cambridge MA 02138

BERCZI, ANDREW STEPHEN, univ. dean; b. Budapest, Hungary, Aug. 15, 1934; s. Stephen Andrew and Iren Maria (Bartha) B.; m. Susan Bartok, Aug. 30, 1958; children—Thomas Edgar, Peter Alexander. E.E., U. Tech. Scis., Budapest, 1956; B.Sc., Sir George Williams U., 1961, B.A., 1963; M.B.A., McGill U., 1965, Ph.D., 1971. Engr. Bell Tel. Co., Montreal, 1956-59, mem. hdqrs. staff-planning, 1959-62, computer systems supr., 1962-65; prof. quantitative methods, chmn. dept. quantitative methods Sir George Williams U., 1965-71; dean Faculty of Commerce and Adminstrn., Concordia U., Montreal, 1971-77, Faculty of Grad. Studies, Wilfrid Laurier U., Waterloo, Ont., Can., 1978—; cons. govtl. agys., pvt. industry; lectr. U. Calif. at Berkeley, U. Va., U. Chgo. Author: Exercises in Management Science, 1968, Problems in Managerial Operations Research, Vol. I and II, 1969, The Stock Exchange - A Total System Approach, 1970; Contbr. articles to profl. Jours. McConnell fellow, 1965-66; Canada Council fellow, 1966-67; Quebec Province scholar, 1967-68. Fellow A.A.A.S.; mem. Operations Research Soc. Am., Canadian Operations Research Soc., Inst. Mgmt. Scis., Assn. Systems Mgmt., Data Processing Mgmt. Assn., Assn. Computing Machinery, Am. Statis. Assn. Home: 76 McCarron Crescent Waterloo ON Canada Office: 75 University Ave W Waterloo ON Canada

BERDAHL, ROBERT MAX, historian, educator; b. Sioux Falls, S.D., Mar. 15, 1937; s. Melvin Oliver and Mildred Alberta (Maynard) B.; m.

Margaret Lucille Ogle, Aug. 30, 1958; children—Daphne Jean, Jennifer Lynne, Barbara Elizabeth. B.A., Augustana Coll., 1959; M.A., U. Ill., 1961; Ph.D., U. Minn., 1965. Asst. prof. history U. Mass., Boston, 1965-67; asst. prof. history U. Oreg., Eugene, 1967-72, assoc. prof., 1972-81, prof., 1981—, dean, 1981—; research asso. Inst. for Advanced Study, Princeton, 1972-73. Co-author: Klassen und Kultur, 1981; contbr. articles to profl. jours. Fulbright fellow, 1975-76; Nat. Endowment Humanities fellow, 1976-77. Mem. Am. Hist. Assn. Office: Dean's Office Coll Arts and Scis U Oreg Eugene OR 97403

BERE, JAMES FREDERICK, manufacturing company executive; b. Chgo., July 25, 1922; s. Lambert Sr. and Madeline (Van Tatenhove) B.; m. Barbara Van Dellen, June 27, 1947; children—Robert Paul, James Frederick, David Lambert, Lynn Barbara, Becky Ann. Student, Calvin Coll., 1940-42; B.S., Northwestern U., 1946, M.B.A., 1950. With Clearing Machine Corp. div. U.S. Industries, Inc., 1946-53; gen. mgr. Clearing Machine Corp., 1953-56, Axelson Mfg. Co. div., 1956, pres., 1957-61; pres., gen. mgr. Borg & Beck div. Borg-Warner Corp., Chgo., 1961-64, group v.p., 1964-66, exec. v.p. automotive, 1966-68, pres. corp., 1968—, also chief exec. officer, 1972—, chmn. bd., 1975—; Dir. Abbott Labs., North Chicago, Continental Ill. Nat. Bank & Trust Co. of Chgo., Continental Ill. Corp., Time, Inc., Northwest Industries, Hughes Tool Co., Ill. Bell Telephone Co. Trustee U. Chgo. Served as lt. AUS, 1943-45. Mem. Am. Mgmt. Assn., Bus. Roundtable, Bus. Council, Alpha Tau Omega. Home: 641 Elm St Hinsdale IL 60521 Office: 200 S Michigan Ave Chicago IL 60604

BEREND, ERWIN LEENDERT, liquidators and wholesalers co. exec.; b. Paramaribo, Surinam, Oct. 25, 1925; came to U.S., 1953, naturalized, 1958; s. William and Cecilia B.; m. Horcine Mea Sanches, Feb. 25, 1956; children—Cary F., Alan T. B.B.A. with honors, Hofstra U., 1970. With NMC Corp., 1960—, corporate controller, 1970-73, corporate controller, sec., 1974—. Office: One Penn Plaza Suite 1706 New York NY 10119

BEREND, ROBERT WILLIAM, lawyer; b. Miami Beach, Fla., Dec. 31, 1931; s. George Harry and Miriam (Wagner) B. A.B., N.Y. U., 1952; LL.B., Yale U., 1955. Bar: N.Y. State 1955. Asst. gen. atty. to trustee Hudson & Manhattan R.R., N.Y.C., 1958-61; assoc. firm Delson & Gordon (and predecessors), N.Y.C., 1961-65, partner, 1965-76; dir. Mgmt. Assistance Inc., N.Y.C., 1971-84, sec., 1970—, sr. v.p., gen. counsel, 1976—. Served with U.S. Army, 1956-58. Mem. Am., N.Y. State bar assns., Assn. Bar City N.Y., Phi Beta Kappa. Clubs: Jewish., Yale (N.Y.C.). Home: 132 E 35th St New York NY 10016 Office: 560 Lexington Ave New York NY 10017

BERENDES, HEINZ WERNER, medical epidemiologist, pediatrician; b. Dortmund, Germany, May 1, 1925; came to U.S., 1953; s. Johannes and Swanette (Kayma) B.; children: Christoph Mathias, Andrea Maria. M.D., U. Geottingern, Germany, 1949; Dr. Medicine, U. Mich., 1952; M.H.S., Johns Hopkins U., 1972. Diplomate: Am. Bd. Epidemiology. Intern Abbott Hosp., Mpls., 1954, U. Minn. Hosp., 1954-55, resident, 1955-56; instr. dep. pediatrics U. Minn., Mpls., 1954-59, asst. prof., 1959-60; asst. dir. collaborative research Nat. Inst. Neurology Disorder and Stroke, NIH, Bethesda, Md., 1960; chief perinatal research br. Nat. Inst. Neurology Disorder and Storke, NIH, Bethesda, 1960-73; chief contraceptive eval. br. Nat. Child Health and Human Devel. Nat. Inst. Neurology Disorder and Stroke, NIH, Bethesda, 1974-79, dir. Epidemiology and Biometry Research Program Nat. Inst. Child and Human Devel., 1979—; clin. prof. dept. pediatrics Howard U., Washington, 1961—; sr. assoc. dept. epidemiology Johns Hopkins U., Balt., 1982—; mem. WHO Sci. Adv. Group, Geneva, 1979; cons. fertility and maternal health drug adv. com. FDA, Rockville, Md., 1979—. Editor: (monograph) Pharmacology of Steroid Contraceptive Drugs, 1977. Pres. Watergate Assn., Bethany Beach Del., 1976-79. Recipient NIH Dirs. award NIH, 1979. Fellow Am. Coll. Epidemiology; mem. Soc. Epidemiol. Research. Home: 180 New Mark Esplanade Rockville MD 20850 Office: Epidemiology and Biometry Research Program Nat Inst Child Health and Human Devel NIH Landow Bldg Room 8A-6 7910 Woodmont Ave Bethesda MD 20205

BERENDZEN, RICHARD EARL, university president, astronomer, author; b. Walters, Okla., Sept. 6, 1938; s. Earl Emmanuel and Florine Adora (Harrison) B.; m. Gail Anita Edgar, Nov. 26, 1964; children: Deborah Carol, Natasha Karina. B.S., MIT, 1961; M.A., Harvard U., 1967, Ph.D., 1968; LL.D. (hon.), W.Va. Wesleyan U., 1979, L.H.D., Bridgewater Coll., 1983. Staff scientist Geophysics Corp. Am., 1959-64, Ling-Temco-Vought, 1961-62; teaching fellow Harvard U., 1961-64, lectr., 1964, 66; mem. staff Project Physics, 1965; mem. faculty Boston U., 1965-73, assoc. prof. astronomy, 1971-73, chmn. dept., acting dean, 1971-72; prof. physics, dean Coll. Arts and Scis., Am. U., Washington, 1974-76, univ. provost, 1976-79, pres., 1980—; cons. Space Sci. Bd., Nat. Acad. Scis., 1973-74, mem. panel astron. survey com., 1971-73; cons. acad. affairs Am. Council on Edn., 1973-74, now advisor; cons. to pub. cos.; holder numerous lectureships, including Danforth lectr. U. Mass., 1972; Disting. Scholar lectr. Am. U., 1977, U. Utah, 1978, Kuwait U., 1979; Phi Beta Kappa lectr. Franklin and Marshall Coll., 1979; Am. specialist in Asia Am. Council Edn. and Dept. State; adv. Am. Inst. Physics, Library of Congress, Internat. Communication Agy., UNESCO, Smithsonian Instn., NASA, Nat. Geog. Soc., NSF; chmn. adminstrv. com. Met. Washington Consortium Univs., 1977-78; univ. evaluator Commn. Higher Edn. Middle States Assn. Colls. and Secondary Schs.; chmn. priorities and planning com. Assn. Am. Colls., 1978-80, chmn. pres.'s adv. com., 1977-79; program evaluator U.S. Armed Forces Inst.; mem. rev. panel human resources NRC; lectr. USIA; host spls. on astronomy and higher edn. NBC-TV, 1976-77; frequent guest radio and TV shows; dir. Madison Nat. Bank. Author: Education in and History of Modern Astronomy, 1972, Life Beyond Earth and the Mind of Man, 1973, Man Discovers the Galaxies, 1976; Editor jour.: Cosmic Search; Contbr. numerous articles and revs. to profl. jours. Bd. dirs. Bus. Council for Internat. Understanding, 1980—, Assn. Am. Colls., 1981-83, Linda Pollin Inst. for Med. Crisis Counseling, 1981-83; chmn. Nat. Commn. on Fgn. Student Policy, 1981-82. Fellow Com. Sci. Investigation Claims Paranormal, 1977-78; Named one of top young educators Change: Mag. of Learning, 1978; recipient Mortar Bd. Faculty award, 1977, others. Fellow AAAS; mem. Internat. Astron. Union, Internat. Assn. Univ. President, Am. Astron. Soc. (task group astronomy edn.), Am. Assn. U. Adminstrs., AAUP, Am. Assn. for Higher Edn., Internat. Assn. Univs., Internat. Assn. Univ. Presidents, N.Y. Acad. Scis., Am. Assn. Physics Tchrs., Astron. Soc. Pacific, History of Sci. Soc., Nat. Sci. Tchrs. Assn., Am. Assn. Higher Edn., Am. Conf. Acad. Deans, Washington Inst. Fgn. Affairs, Sigma Xi, Kappa Mu Epsilon, Phi Eta Sigma, Phi Kappa Phi. Clubs: University, Cosmos, Metropolitan (Washington); University (N.Y.C.). Research on cosmology, history of astronomy, sci. and soc., Am. and internat. edn. Home: 3300 Nebraska Ave NW Washington DC 20016 Office: President's Bldg American U Washington DC 20016

BERENS, MARK HARRY, lawyer; b. St. Paul, Aug. 4, 1928; s. Harry C. and Gertrude M. (Scherkenbach) B.; m. Barbara Jean Steichen, Nov. 20, 1954; children: Paul J., Joseph F. (dec.), John M., Stephen M., Thomas M., Michael M., Lisa M., James M., Daniel. B.S.C. in Acctg. magna cum laude, U. Notre Dame, 1950, J.D. magna cum laude, 1951; postgrad., U. Chgo., 1951-53. Bar: Ill. 1951, D.C. 1955, U.S. Supreme Ct. 1971; C.P.A., Ill. James Nelson Raymond grad. research fellow U. Chgo. Law Sch., 1951-53; assoc. Mayer, Brown & Platt (and predecessors), Chgo., 1956-61, ptnr., 1961—; chmn. bd., dir. Attys.' Liability Assurance Soc. Ltd., Hamilton, Bermuda, 1979—; dir. Saginomiya Johnson Controls, Tokyo, 1972-79, Admiral Internat. Enterprises, 1969-73; nat. chmn. Nat. Assn. Law Rev. Editors, 1950-51; mem. nat. adv. com. Office Fgn. Direct Investment, U.S. Dept. Commerce, 1969-71. Contbr. articles to law publs.; editor-in-chief: Notre Dame Law Rev, 1950-51. Served as 1st lt. Judge Adv. Gen. Corps, U.S. Army, 1953-56. Mem. Am. Law Inst., ABA; mem. Internat. Bar Assn.; Mem. D.C. Bar Assn., Chgo. Bar Assn., Am. Assn. Atty.-C.P.A.'s, Japan-Am. Soc. Republican. Roman Catholic. Clubs: Union League, Law, Legal (Chgo.). Home: 1251 Pine St Glenview IL 60025 Office: 231 S LaSalle St Chicago IL 60604

BERENSON, GERALD SANDERS, physician; b. Bogalusa, La., Sept. 19, 1922; s. Meyer A. and Eva (Singerman) B.; m. Joan Seidenbach, Mar. 7, 1951; children—Leslie, Ann, Robert, Laurie. B.S., Tulane U., 1943, M.D., 1945. Intern U.S. Navy Hosp., Great Lakes, Ill., 1945-46; practice medicine specializing in cardiology, New Orleans; mem. staff Charity Hosp., Hotel Dieu; instr. dept. medicine Tulane U., 1949-52; asst. prof. medicine La. State U. Med. Sch., 1954-58, asso. prof., 1958-63, prof., 1963—; dir. Specialized Center Research Arteriosclerosis, New Orleans, 1972—; sr. vis. physician Charity Hosp. La., New Orleans, 1948—; cons. Touro Infirmary, 1967—; cons. medicine Hotel Dieu, 1962—. Contbr. articles to profl. jours. Served with USNR, 1945-48. USPHS fellow U. Chgo., 1952-54. Mem. So. Soc. Clin. Investigation (pres. 1969), La. Heart Assn. (pres. 1971), New Orleans Acad. Internal Medicine (pres. 1966), Musser-Burch Soc. (pres. 1981), Sigma Xi, Alpha Omega Alpha. Home: 505 Northline Metairie LA 70005 Office: Dept Medicine La State U Med Center New Orleans LA 70112

BERENSON, ROBERT LEONARD, advertising agency executive; b. Chgo., Nov. 14, 1939; s. James Morton and Harriet Ruth (Fisher) B.; m. Elizabeth Segal, Sept. 9, 1962; 1 dau., Cindy Elizabeth. B.A., Syracuse U., 1961; M.S.J., Northwestern U., 1962. Mgmt. trainee Grey Advt., Inc., N.Y.C., 1964-67, v.p., account supr., 1967-70, v.p., mgmt. supr., 1970-71, sr. v.p., mgmt. rep., 1971-77, exec. v.p., 1977-82, exec. v.p. adminstrn., 1982—; guest lectr. mktg. U. Conn., Hampshire U., 1974-82. Served to 1st lt. inf. U.S. Army, 1962-64. Mem. LaGuardia Sch. Alumni Assn. (bd. dirs.). Jewish. Home: 7 Farmers Rd Kings Point NY 11024 Office: Grey Advt Inc 777 3d Ave New York NY 10017

BERESFORD, RAPHAEL HENRY, oil company executive; b. Epworth, Iowa, Nov. 13, 1928; s. Alfred Appleby and Marie Elizabeth (Nelson) B.; m. ThelmaAnn Taylor, Aug. 13, 1955; children: Jane Nelson, John Taylor. Student, Loras Coll., 1945-46, 48-49; B.S. in Chem. Engring., State U. Iowa, 1952; M.B.A., Harvard U., 1954. With Exxon Corp., various locations, 1954—, exec. v.p., London, 1976-78, v.p. petroleum products, N.Y.C., 1978—; trustee Exxon Edn. Found. Trustee New Eyes for the Needy. Served with AUS, 1946-48. Mem. Internat. Rd. Fedn. (dir., exec. com.), Am. Petroleum Inst. Republican. Roman Catholic. Clubs: Baltusrol Golf, Short Hills, Univ., Harvard Bus. Sch. Home: 125 Forest Dr Short Hills NJ 07078 Office: Exxon Corp 1251 Ave of Americas New York NY 10020

BERESFORD, SPENCER MOXON, lawyer, computer company executive; b. Los Angeles, Dec. 2, 1918; s. Frank Moxon and Mary Abigail (Fitch) B.; children: Richard, Gail Beresford Anderson, Thomas, Douglas, Annette.; m. Florence Baker Gove, Sept. 5, 1981. Grad., Choate Sch., 1935; S.B. cum laude, Harvard U., 1939, LL.B., 1942, J.D., 1947. Bar: Mass. 1947, D.C. 1956, U.S. Supreme Ct. 1953. Asso. firm Goodwin, Procter & Hoar, 1947-49; partner Bidwell & Beresford, 1949-52; spl. asst. to dep. dir. Fgn. Operations Adminstrn., 1952-57; asst. chief Am. law div., sr. specialist Am. law Legislative Reference Service, Library Congress, Washington, 1957-59; spl. counsel select com. on astronautics and space exploration U.S. Ho. of Reps., Washington, 1958-59, Com. on Sci. and Astronautics, 1959-62; partner vom Baur, Beresford & Coburn, 1962-67, Batzell & Nunn, 1967-69; gen. counsel NASA, Washington, 1969-73; counsel, select com. on coms. Ho. of Reps., Washington, 1973-74; gen. counsel Office Tech. Assessment U.S. Congress, Washington, 1975-76; chmn. Internat. Tech. Services, 1976-83; exec. v.p. Info. Design & Mgmt., Inc., Arlington, Va., 1983—; Instr. U.S. Navy Postgrad. Sch., Washington, 1950-52; Hunsaker lectr. Mass. Inst. Tech., Cambridge, 1970; cons. Dept. Transp., 1967-68; mem. U.S. del. to Gen. Assembly UN, N.Y.C., 1969-73, Pres.'s Com. on Govt. Patent Policy, 1969-73. Author: Public Economic Policy, 1959; Compiler, editor: Air Laws and Treaties of the World, 1961; Contbr. articles to profl. jours. Mem. Town Meeting, Wellesley, Mass., 1948-52. Served with USNR, 1943-46, 50-52. Recipient Letter Commendation Chief Naval Personnel; Downer scholar; Ford Found. grantee internat law, 1962. Mem. Am., Fed. bar assns. Patentee in field. Home: 22 South Trail Narragansett RI 02882 Office: 1225 Jefferson Davis Suite 413 Arlington VA 22202

BERESFORD-HOWE, CONSTANCE ELIZABETH, novelist; b. Montreal, Que., Can., 1922; d. Russell and Marjory Mary (Moore) Beresford-H.; m. Christopher Pressnell, Dec. 31, 1960; 1 son, Jeremy. B.A., McGill U., Montreal, 1945, M.A. (Que. Province scholar), 1946; Ph.D., Brown U., 1950. Lectr. to asso. prof. English McGill U., 1949-69; prof. English Ryerson Poly. Inst., Toronto, Ont., Can., 1971—. Novels include The Unreasoning Heart, 1946, Of This Day's Journey, 1948, The Invisible Gate, 1949, My Lady Greensleeves, 1955, The Book of Eve, 1973, A Population of One, 1977, The Marriage Bed, 1981. Recipient Canadian Booksellers' award; Dodd, Mead Intercollegiate Lit. fellow; Can. Council sr. arts grantee; Ont. Arts Council grantee. Mem. Internat. PEN Club, Assn. Canadian Univ. Tchrs. English, Writers Union Can. Anglican. Home: 16 Cameron Crescent Toronto ON M4G 1Z8 Canada

BERESTON, EUGENE SYDNEY, dermatologist; b. Balt., Feb. 21, 1914; s. Arthur and Sarah Bertha (Hillman) B.; m. Marion Ableman, Jan. 15, 1942 (dec. May 1975); children: Linda Bereston Katz, David, Michael; m. Bertha G. Kaufman, June 7, 1980; stepchildren: Felix Kaufman, Bruce Kaufman. A.B., Johns Hopkins U., 1933; M.D., U. Md., 1937; M.Sc., U. Pa., 1945, D.Sc., 1955. Diplomate Am. Bd. Dermatology. Intern Meml. Hosp., Johnstown, Pa., 1937-38, Mercy Hosp., Balt., 1938-39; resident in dermatology U. Pa., Phila., 1939-40, Montefiore Hosp., N.Y.C., 1940-41; practice medicine specializing in dermatology, Balt., 1946—; faculty U. Md., 1946—, prof. medicine in dermatology, 1972—; instr. dermatology Johns Hopkins U., 1946-60; chief dermatology Mercy Hosp., 1968—; part-time chief dermatology VA Hosp., Washington, 1977—; cons. dermatology VA Hosp. Balt., 1951-76, Spring Grove State Hosp., 1952-82. Bd. dirs., chmn. Religious Sch., Temple Oheb Shalom, 1960-72, trustee, 1977-80. Served to maj. M.C. AUS, 1941-46; PTO. Recipient research grant U.S. Army, 1951-57, award Ner Israel Rabbinical Coll., 1970. Fellow A.C.P., Am. Acad. Dermatology, Royal Soc. Health (Eng.); mem. Am. Legion (comdr. 1971-73), AMA, Soc. Investigative Dermatology, Dermatology Found., Md. Dermatol. Soc., Royal Soc. Medicine (affiliate), Md., Balt. City med. socs. Clubs: Civitan (dir. 1964-78), Johns Hopkins (Balt.); Suburban Country. Home: 7 Slade Ave Apt 221 Baltimore MD 21208 Office: 22 E Eager St Baltimore MD 21202

BERETTA, DAVID, consulting company executive; b. Cranston, R.I., July 16, 1928; m. Serena Shuebruk, Nov. 1954; children: David, Norman, Martha. B.S. in Chem. Engring, U. R.I.; postgrad., R.I. Coll., U. Conn. Research asst. Fram Corp., East Providence, R.I., 1949-51; engr. chem. div. Uniroyal, Inc., Middlebury, Conn., 1953-62, gen. foreman prodn. dept., Naugatuck, Conn., 1962-65, factory mgr., 1965-66, v.p. charge chem. ops. in Can., 1966-68; v.p. mktg. Uniroyal, Ltd., 1968-70; pres. Uniroyal Chem., 1970-72, group v.p. charge footwear, consumer, indsl., chem. and textile ops., 1972-74, operating officer, 1974; pres. Uniroyal, Inc., Middlebury, 1974-77, chmn., chief exec. officer, 1975-83; pres. Exec. Cons. Inc., 1983—; exec.-in-residence U.R.I.; dir. Uniroyal Inc., Biltrite Corp., Internat. Supply Corp. Research Inst., U. Waterloo, Ont. Served with Chem. Corps AUS, 941-53. Mem. Am. Inst. Chem. Engrs., Am. Chem. Soc., R.I. Soc. Profl. Engrs. Office: Uniroyal Inc 1230 Ave of Americas New York NY 10020 *

BEREUTER, DOUGLAS KENT, congressman; b. York, Nebr., Oct. 6, 1939; s. Rupert Wesley and Evelyn Gladys (Tonn) B.; m. Louise Meyer, June 1, 1962; children: Eric David, Kirk Daniel. B.A., U. Nebr., 1961; M.Urban Planning, Harvard U., 1966, M.P.A., 1973; postgrad., Eagleton Inst. Politics, 1975. Urban planner HUD, San Francisco, 1965-66; asst. dir. planning Nebr. Div. Resources, Lincoln, 1966-67; dir. div. state and urban affairs Dept. Econ. Devel., 1967-68, state planning coordinator, 1968-69; dir. State Office of Planning and Programming, coordinator fed.-state relations, 1969-71; asso. prof. U. Nebr., Kans. State U., 1972-78; mem. Nebr. Legislature, 1974-78, 96th-98th Congresses from 1st Nebr. Dist.; Chmn. standing com. on urban devel. Nat. Conf. State Legislatures, 1977-78; mem. Nebr. State Crime Commn., 1969-71. Served as officer U.S. Army, 1963-65. Harvard Littauer fellow, 1972-73. Mem. Am. Planning Assn. (dir., exec. com.), Phi Beta Kappa, Sigma Xi. Republican. Lutheran. Office: 1314 Longworth House Office Bldg Washington DC 20515

BERG, DANIEL, university administrator; b. N.Y.C., June 1, 1929; s. Jack and Hattie (Tannenbaum) B.; m. Frances Helene Ely, Aug. 18, 1956; children: Brian, Laura, Meredith. B.S., CCNY, 1950; M.S., Yale U., 1951, Ph.D., 1953; grad. execs. program, Carnegie-Mellon U., 1971. With Westinghouse Electric Co., Pitts., 1953-77, research div. mgr., then tech. dir., 1976-77; prof. sci. and tech. Carnegie-Mellon U., 1977—, dean Mellon Coll. Sci., 1977-81, univ. provost, 1981-83; v.p. acad. affairs, provost, Inst. prof. sci. and tech. Rensselaer Poly. Inst., Troy, N.Y., 1983—; dir. Duquesne Light, Hy-Tech Tool Co.; mem. Pa. Sci. and Engring. Found., 1975-76; vis. council sci. and engring. Coll. City N.Y., 1980—; mem. Yale U. Council, 1981—; asso. fellow Jonathan Edwards Coll., 1982—, cons. to industry and govt. Author; editor; patentee in field. Fellow IEEE, AAAS, Am. Inst. Chemists; mem. Nat. Acad. Engring., Am. Chem. Soc., Am. Phys. Soc., Phi Beta Kappa, Sigma Xi, Alpha Chi Sigma. Clubs: Cosmos (Washington); Rivers (Pitts.). Home: 352 Hoosick St. Troy NY 12180 Office: Vice Pres Acad Affairs Rensselaer Poly Inst 110 8th St Troy NY 12180

BERG, DAVID, author-artist; b. Bklyn., June 12, 1920; s. Morris Isaac and Bessie (Freidman) B.; m. Vivian Lipman, Mar. 3, 1949; children—Mitchel Ian, Nancy Anne Iva. Student, Cooper Union, Pratt Inst., U. Wis., New Sch., Iona Coll., Rochelle, N.Y., Coll. New Rochelle; Th.D. (hon.), Reconstructionist Rabbinical Coll., 1973. Artist-writer Will Eisner Prodns., N.Y.C., 1940-41; asso. editor Timely Comics, 1945—; artist-writer Fawcett Publs., N.Y.C., 1941—, Warner Books, also Signet Books, 1956—, Mad mag.; also contbr. regular feature Lighter Side of; creative cons. NBC-TV, 1979—; guest tchr. Westchester (N.Y.) Schs., lectr. colls. and univs., 1968—. Author, artist: books My Friend God, 1972, Roger Kaputnik and God, 1974; also series of 11 Mad books, 1964—. Field commr., scoutmaster local Boy Scouts Am., 1950-75; bd. dirs. local Girl Scouts, 1962-66; coach Little League, 1962; recreation commr. New Rochelle, 1967; judge state contest Miss Am. Beauty Contest. Served with USAAF, 1941-45. Recipient B'nai B'rith Youth Services award, 1978; named to Chair of Great Cartoonists UCLA student body, 1975; David Berg Day named by Westchester County, N.Y., May 7, 1978. Mem. Authors League, Writers Guild West, Nat. Cartoonists Soc. Democrat. Jewish. Club: B'nai B'rith. Home: 14021 Marquesas Way Apt 307C Marina Del Rey CA 90291 Office: Mad Magazine 485 Madison Ave New York NY 10022 *To succeed while having a ball: Make your hobby your livelihood.*

BERG, EUGENE PAULSEN, mfg. co. exec.; b. Chgo., May 25, 1913; s. Christian Paulsen and Mae Olive (Mathews) B.; m. Margaret Louise Hughes, Jan. 21, 1939; children—Charles, Paula. B.S. in Mech. Engring, Purdue U., 1937; M.B.A., U. Chgo., 1945. With Link-Belt Co., Chgo., 1937-60, gen. mgr., 1950-60; exec. v.p. Bucyrus-Erie Co., South Milwaukee, Wis., 1960-62, pres., 1962-77, chmn. bd., 1963-77, Ruston Bucyrus, Ltd., Lincoln, Eng., 1962-77, Automatic Spring Coiling Co., 1978—; dir. Interlake Inc., Chgo., Chgo. and Northwestern Transp. Co., Cross & Trecker Corp., Gen. Am. Investors Co., Research-Cottrell Inc. Chmn. Pres.'s Council Purdue U., 1973. Mem. ASME (chmn. Chgo. 1956), Delta Upsilon, Pi Tau Sigma. Clubs: Economic, Yacht (Chgo.); Westmoreland Country (Wilmette, Ill.); Bath and Tennis (Lake Forest); Onwentsia. Home: 24 Shawnee Ln Lake Forest IL 60045 Office: Automatic Spring Coiling Co Chicago IL 60646

BERG, GLEN VIRGIL, educator; b. Mead, Nebr., Dec. 17, 1918; s. Emil Gottfred and Rosella (Gibson) B.; m. Margaret Mary Eaton, Aug. 8, 1941; children—Sylvia, Stephanie, Wendy. B.S., U. Nebr., 1941, M.S., 1955; Ph.D., U. Mich., 1958. Jr. engr. Panama Canal, 1941-43, engr., 1946-48, C. Iber & Sons, Peoria, Ill., 1948-50; partner firm Berg-Hartsfield Co., Lincoln, Nebr., 1950-53; engr. Capital Steel Co., Lincoln, 1953-55; research asso. U. Mich., 1955-58, prof., 1958—, chmn. dept. civil engring., 1969-76; pres. Berg-Hanson Engrs., Inc., Ann Arbor, Mich., 1977—. Served to lt. AUS, 1943-46. Mem. Indian Soc. Earthquake Tech., ASCE, Earthquake Engring. Research Inst., Universities Council Earthquake Engring. Research. Home: 1033 Baldwin Ave Ann Arbor MI 48104

BERG, IRWIN AUGUST, psychology educator; b. Chgo., Oct. 9, 1913; s. Bertil Sigfried and Clara (Anderson) B.; m. Sylvia Maria Taipale, Mar. 4, 1939; 1 dau., Karen Astrid (Mrs. A. C. Kirby). A.B. cum laude, Knox Coll., 1936; A.M., U. Mich., 1940, Ph.D., 1942. Asst. prof. psychology U. Ill., 1942-47; assoc. prof. Pomona Coll., 1947-48, Northwestern U., 1948-55; chmn. dept., prof. psychology La. State U., 1955-65, dean coll. arts and scis. emeritus, prof. psychology, 1965-79; Spl. cons. U.S. Dept. Labor, U.S. VA, La. State Dept. Hosps.; Mem. La. State Commn. on Law Enforcement and Adminstrn. Criminal Justice, 1968-73; mem. La. Bd. Licensing for Sanitarians. Author: Workbook in Psychology, 1961, Response Set and Personality Assessment, 1967; Co-editor: Conformity and Deviation, 1961, An Introduction to Clinical Psychology, 3d edit, 1966. Bd. dirs. Nat. Council on Arts and Scis., 1970-73. Mem. Am. Psychol. Assn. (pres. div. counseling psychology 1964), Southeastern Psychol. Assn. (pres. 1963), Southwestern Psychol. Assn. (pres. 1963-64), AAAS, AAUP, Phi Beta Kappa, Sigma Xi, Phi Kappa Phi, Phi Beta. Home: St James Pl 333 Lee Dr Apt G-17 Baton Rouge LA 70808

BERG, JEAN HORTON, author; b. Clairton, Pa., May 30, 1913; d. Harry Heber and Daisy Belle (Horton) Lutz; m. John Joseph Berg, July 2, 1938; children: Jean Horton, Julie Berg Blickle, John Joel. B.S. in Edn, U. Pa., 1935, A.M. in Latin, 1937. Tchr. creative writing, 1968—; speaker in field of creative writing. Author 50 books for children and young people, 1950—, articles, stories, poems for young people, articles for adults. Former mem. Health and Welfare Bd., Phila.; former chmn. Main Line Parents Council. Recipient U. Pa. Alumni award of merit, 1969; Follett award for beginning-to-read book, 1961; medallion City of Phila.; Friends' Central Sch. Distinguished Alumna award, 1978. Mem. Authors Guild, Authors League, ASCAP, Nat. League of Am. Pen Women, Phila. Childrens Reading Round Table, League Women Voters. Home: 207 Walnut Ave Wayne PA 19087 *I suppose integrity is the most important quality in life; next is love - not a sentimental, but a whole love, including affection. I try each day not to react to all the problems and peculiarities that would prevent my living the life that will make those around me glad I'm with them. I'm glad I'm with them.*

BERG, JEFFREY SPENCER, talent agency executive; b. Los Angeles, May 26, 1947. B.A. in English with honors, U. Calif., Berkeley, 1969. Vice pres., head lit. div. Creative Mgmt. Assos., Los Angeles, 1969-75; v.p. motion picture dept. Internat. Creative Mgmt., Los Angeles, 1975-80, pres., 1980—; dir. Josephsa Internat. Industries. Trustee Calif. Inst. Arts. Mem. U. Calif. Berkeley Alumni Assn. Address: Internat Creative Mgmt 8899 Beverly Blvd Los Angeles CA 90048

BERG, JOSEPH NATHAN, air freight company executive; b. Newport, R.I., 1927. Vice-pres. Circle Air Freight Corp., to 1970; with Air Express Internat. Corp., Darien, Conn., 1955—, pres., chief exec. officer, dir., 1973—. Address: Air Express Internat Corp 120 Tokeneke Rd Darien CT 06820 *

BERG, LEONARD, neurologist, educator; b. St. Louis, July 17, 1927; s. Jacob and Sara (Kessler) B.; m. Gerry Saltzman, Mar. 25, 1948; children: Kathleen, John, Nancy. A.B. cum laude, Washington U., St. Louis, 1945, M.D., 1949. Diplomate: Am. Bd. Psychiatry and Neurology (dir. 1978—). Intern Barnes Hosp., St. Louis, 1949-50, resident, 1950-51, Neurol. Inst., N.Y.C., 1951-53; clin. assoc. Nat. Inst. Neurol. Diseases and Blindness, NIH, 1953-55; mem. faculty Washington U. Med. Sch., 1955—, prof. clin. neurology, 1972—; attending neurologist Barnes, Jewish hosps.; prin. investigator NIMH grant, 1978-83; program dir. NIA grant, 1984—. Co-author: Atlas of Muscle Pathology in Neuromuscular Diseases, 1956. Bd. dirs. Temple Israel, St. Louis, 1972-74, Jewish Center for Aged, St. Louis, 1981—. Mem. AMA, Am. Acad. Neurology, Am. Neurol. Assn. Home: 816 S Hanley Rd Apt 7D St Louis MO 63105 Office: Suite 16304 Barnes Hosp Plaza St Louis MO 63110

BERG, LLOYD, chem. engr.; b. Paterson, N.J., Aug. 8, 1914; s. Olav and Anita (Schneider) B.; m. Edna Barrowclough, Jan. 1, 1938; children—Sally, Charles, John, Ann. B.S.Ch.E., Lehigh U., 1936; Ph.D., Purdue U., 1942. Registered profl. engr., Mont., Pa. Tech. service engr. Sherwin-Williams Co., Newark, 1936-39; research engr. Gulf Research and Devel. Co., Pitts., 1942-46; asso. prof. chem. engring. U. Kans., Lawrence, 1946; prof., head dept. chem. engring. Mont. State U., Bozeman, 1946-79, prof., 1979—; cons. Exxon, Concco, Husky Oil, Phillips Petroleum Co., Champion Internat., U.S. Dept. Energy, Celanese Chem. Co. Contbr. articles to profl. jours. Served with U.S. Army, 1936-42. Fellow Am. Inst. Chem. Engrs.; mem. Am. Soc. Engring. Edn., Am. Chem. Soc., Accreditation Bd. for Engring. and Tech. Patentee in field. Home: 1314 S 3d Bozeman MT 59715 Office: Dept Chem Engring Mont State U Bozeman MT 59717

BERG, NORMAN ALF, conservation consultant; b. Burlington, Iowa, Mar. 14, 1918; s. Alf Fredrick and Mary E. (Rohleder) N.; m. Ruth A. Askegaard, Nov. 20, 1941; children: Susan Berg Morgan, Jane Berg Paulsen, Pamela Ann Berg Lieb, Rebecca Ruth Berg Schroeder. B.S., U. Minn., 1941; M.P.A., Harvard, 1956. With Soil Conservation Service, Dept. Agr., 1943-82, asso. adminstr., 1969-79, chief, 1979-82, ret., 1982; chmn. U.S. sect. U.S.-Can. Reference Group on Land Use Activities, Internat. Joint Commn.-Gt. Lakes Water Quality Bd.; chmn Sec. Agr.'s Exec. Com. on Nat. Land Use Policy. Co-author: Modern Supervisory Practice, rev. edit, 1966. Served with USMCR, 1943-46. Recipient Gold medal Distinguished Service award Dept. Agr., 1973; Presdl. rank of Meritorious Exec., 1980; Ford fellow, 1956. Fellow Soil Conservation Soc. Am.; mem. Pocatello Jaycees (pres. 1949-50), Farm House. Methodist (ofcl. bd.). Home: 133 St Andrews Rd Severna Park MD 21146 Office: American Farmland Trust 1717 Massachusetts Ave NW Washington DC 20036 *Our legacy is to leave for future generations the renewable natural resources they will need to produce adequate supplies of food and fiber.*

BERG, NORMAN ASPLUND, management educator; b. Erie, Pa., Dec. 18, 1930; s. Sverre and Fanny Elfrida (Asplund) B.; m. Cynthia Pearson, Aug. 7, 1965; children: Christopher, Eric. B.S. in Mech. Engring, Case Inst. Tech., 1953; M.B.A., Harvard U., 1958, D.B.A., 1964. Engr. U.S. Steel Corp., Pitts., 1963-64; fin. analyst Tex. Instruments, Inc., Dallas, 1958-59; research asso. IMEDE Mgmt. Devel. Inst., Lausanne, Switzerland, 1959-60; asst. prof. Harvard U. Bus. Sch., Cambridge, Mass., 1963-68, assoc. prof., 1968-72, prof. gen. mgmt., 1972—; dir. Instrumentation Lab., Inc., 1965-83, Am. Bakeries Co., 1969-81, Northland Co.; cons., tchr., adv. on mgmt. to numerous cos., 1964—. Author: (with others) Policy Formulation and Administration, 8th edit., 1980. Served with AUS, 1954-56. Mem. Acad. Mgmt., Tau Beta Pi. Office: Dept Mgmt Harvard U Bus Sch Soldiers Field Boston MA 02163

BERG, NORMAN WALTER, clergyman; b. Saginaw, Mich., Mar. 29, 1920; s. Ehrenfried J. and Lydia (Lehman) B.; m. Eleanor M. Martin, Oct. 6, 1946; children—Peter M., Mary E., John W., Margaret A., Miriam E. Student, Mich. Lutheran Sem., 1937; B.A., Northwestern Coll., Watertown, Wis., 1941; B.D., Wis. Luth. Sem., Mequon, 1944. Ordained to ministry Luth. Ch., 1946; instr. Northwestern Luth. Acad., Mobridge, S.D., 1944-46; pastor in Globe, Ariz., 1946-50, Tucson, 1950-54, Benton Harbor, Mich., 1954-60, Plymouth, Mich., 1960-68; exec. sec. bd. home missions Wis. Evang. Luth. Synod, Milw., 1968—, v.p. Ariz.-Calif. dist., 1954, chmn. bd. information and stewardship, 1955-61, sec., 1961-62, v.p., 1965-68, pres. Mich. dist., 1962-68; moderator Luth. Free Conf., 1964-68; chmn. Evang. Luth. Confessional Forum, 1967—. Home: 2774 N Grant Blvd Milwaukee WI 53210 Office: 2929 N Mayfair Rd Milwaukee WI 53222

BERG, PAUL, biochemist, educator; b. N.Y.C., June 30, 1926; s. Harry and Sarah (Brodsky) B.; m. Mildred Levy, Sept. 13, 1947; 1 son, John. B.S., Pa. State U., 1948; Ph.D. (NIH fellow 1950-52), Western Res. U., 1952; D.Sc. (hon.), U. Rochester, 1978, Yale U., 1978. Postdoctoral fellow Copenhagen (Denmark) U., 1952-53; postdoctoral fellow Sch. Medicine, Washington U., St. Louis, 1953-54, Am. Cancer Soc. scholar cancer research dept. microbiology, 1954-57, from asst. to asso. prof. microbiology, 1955-59; prof. biochemistry Stanford Sch. Medicine, 1959—, Sam, Lula and Jack Willson prof. biochemistry, 1970, chmn. dept., 1969-74; non-resident fellow Salk Inst., 1973; lectr. Weizmann Inst., 1977; disting. lectr. U. Pitts., 1978; Priestly lectr. Pa. State U., 1978; Shell lectr. U. Calif., Davis, 1978; adv. bd. NIH, NSF, M.I.T.; vis. com. dept. biochemistry and molecular biology Harvard U. Contbr. profl. jours.; Editor: Biochem. and Biophys. Research Communications, 1959-68; editorial bd.: Molecular Biology, 1966-69. Served to lt. (j.g.) USNR, 1943-46. Recipient Eli Lilly prize biochemistry, 1959; V.D. Mattia award Roche Inst. Molecular Biology, 1972; Henry J. Kaiser award for excellence in teaching, 1972; Disting. Alumnus award, Pa. State U., 1972; Sarasota Med. awards for achievement and excellence, 1979; Gairdner Found. annual award, 1980; Lasker Found. award, 1980; Nobel award in chemistry, 1980; Sci. Freedom and Responsibility award AAAS, 1982; named Calif. Scientist of Yr. Calif. Museum Sci. and Industry, 1963; Harvey lectr., 1972; Lynen lectr., 1977. Mem. Inst. Medicine, Nat. Acad. Scis. (council 1979), Am. Acad. Arts and Scis., Am. Soc. Biol. Chemists (pres. 1974-75), Am. Soc. Microbiology. Office: Stanford Sch Medicine Stanford CA 94305

BERG, PHILIP JAMES, diversified manufacturing company executive; b. Sewickley, Pa., July 27, 1923; s. John Daniel and Martha Moody (Biggert) B.; m. Elizabeth Jane Buffington, June 24, 1944; children: Elizabeth B., Susan Berg Gross, Margaret Berg Anderson. B.S. in Mech. Engring., Lehigh U., 1944. With Dravo Corp., Pitts., 1946—, group v.p., from 1970, sr. v.p. ops., to 1978, exec. v.p., 1978—. Trustee Lehigh U. Served as lt. (j.g.) Submarine Service, USNR, 1943-46. Mem. Am. Iron and Steel Inst. Home: Fairacres Dr Sewickley PA 15143 Office: Dravo Corp 1 Oliver Plaza Pittsburgh PA 15222

BERG, ROBERT LEWIS, physician, educator; b. Spokane, Wash., Sept. 10, 1918; s. Evan and Rachel Myfanwy (Lewis) B.; m. Florence Mitcham Foster, June 18, 1943; children—Erik Christian, Astri Maren. B.S., Harvard, 1940, M.D., 1943. Successively intern, resident, chief med. resident Mass. Gen. Hosp., Boston, 1944-46, 50, asst. to dir. research and edn., 1951-54, asst., then asso. physician, 1951-58; Moseley travelling fellow Royal Caroline Inst., Stockholm, 1948-49; from instr. to asst. prof. medicine Harvard Med. Sch., 1951-58, Albert D. Kaiser prof., also chmn. dept. preventive, family and rehab. medicine, 1958—; assoc. dean planning Univ. Rochester, 1982—, asso. prof. medicine, 1958-69, prof. medicine, 1969—; sr. asso. physician Strong Meml. Hosp., 1958-69, physician, 1969—; acting adminstr., 1960-61. Mem. NIH Epidemiology and Biometry Tng. Com., 1962-66, 67-71, chmn., 1969-70; mem. U.S. Com. Vital and Health Statistics, 1965-69, chmn., 1967-69. Author: (with M. Roy Brooks, Jr. and Miomir Savicevic) Health Care in Yugoslavia and the United States, 1976; editor: Health Status Indexes, 1973. Trustee Eastman Dental Center, 1971—, chmn., 1975-79. Mem. Am. Pub. Health Assn., Assn. Tchrs. Preventive Medicine (treas. 1963-69, v.p. 1969-70, pres. 1970-72), N.Y. State Med. Soc., Assn. Am. Med. Colls., Internat. Epidemiological Assn. Home: 227 Pelham Rd Rochester NY 14610 Office: 601 Elmwood Ave Box 644 Rochester NY 14642

BERG, ROBERT RAYMOND, geologist, educator; b. St. Paul, May 28, 1924; s. Raymond F. and Jennie (Swanson) B.; m. Josephine Finck, Dec. 22, 1946; children: James R., (dec.), Charles R., William R. B.A., U. Minn., 1948, Ph.D., 1951. Geologist, Calif. Co., Denver, 1951-56; cons. Berg and Wasson, Denver, 1957-66; prof. geology, head dept. Tex. A&M U., 1967—, Michel T. Halbouty prof. geology, 1982—; dir. univ. research Tex. A & M U., 1972—; cons. petroleum geology, 1959—. Contbr. papers in field. Served with AUS, 1943-46. Fellow Geol. Soc. Am.; mem. Am. Assn. Petroleum Geologists (disting. lectr. 1972), Am. Inst. Profl. Geologists (pres. 1971). Home: 414 Brookside Bryan TX 77801 Office: Geology Dept Tex A & M Univ College Station TX 77843

BERG, RODNEY KENNETH, college president; b. Lawen, Oreg., July 5, 1912; s. William H. and Myra May (Farrell) B.; m. E. Marie Van Dyke. B.A., Wash. State Coll., 1934, M.A., 1949; Ph.D., U. Wash., 1958. Tchr., Snohomish, Wash., 1935-41, dir. music, LaGrande, Oreg., 1941-42, 45-48; tchr. Everett (Wash.) Jr. Coll., 1948-55, dean instrn., 1955-60, pres., 1961-66, Highline Coll., Seattle, 1960-61, Coll. of DuPage, Glen Ellyn, Ill., 1966-78, pres. emeritus, 1978—; mem. steering com. Edn. Commn. of States, 1965-67; mem. commn. North Central Assn. Secondary and Higher Schs., 1967-72; N.W. Assn. Secondary and Higher Sch., 1960-66. Bd. dirs. Gen. Hosp., Everett, 1963-66, Central DuPage Hosp., 1970-72, Am. Assn. Community and Jr. Colls., 1965-67, Am. Council Edn., 1976—; lay adminstr. Resurrection Luth. Ch., Plano, Tex., 1983—. Served with AUS, 1942-45. Decorated D.F.C., Air Medal with 8 clusters. Mem. Phi Mu Alpha, Phi Delta Kappa. Lutheran. Home: 2124 Heatherhill Ln Plano TX 75075

BERG, ROY TORGNY, university dean; b. Millicent, Alta., Can., Apr. 8, 1927; s. Erik Petrus and Ellen Signe W. (Jonsson) B.; m. Margaret Violet Baines, Aug. 18, 1951; children: Ruth Ellen, Paula Margaret, Kevin John, Nora Winifred. B.S., U. Alta., 1950; M.S., U. Minn., 1954, Ph.D., 1955. Lectr. U. Alta., Edmonton, 1950-52, asst. prof., 1954-58, assoc. prof., 1958-63, prof., 1963, chmn. animal sci., 1977-82, dean, 1983—. Author: New Concepts of Cattle Growth, 1976. Recipient Animal Genetics medal Can. Soc. Animal Sci., 1981, Merit award Can. Soc. Animal Sci., 1982; fellow Agr. Inst. Can., 1976. Mem. Agrl. Inst. Can. (dir. 1975), Canadian Soc. Animal Sci. (pres. 1962), Am. Soc. Animal Sci., Brit. Soc. Animal Prodn., Am. Genetics Assn. Home: 51012 Rge Rd 210 Sherwood Park AB Canada T8G 1E6 Office: Univ of Alberta 2-14 Agric-Forestry Bldg Edmontonon AB Canada T6G 2P5

BERG, SHERWOOD OLMAN, university president; b. Hendrum, Minn., May 17, 1919; s. Joseph O. and Ida E. (Tommerdahl) B.; m. Elizabeth A. Hall, Aug. 12, 1944; children: Mary E., Bradley J. B.S., S.D. State U., 1947; M.S., Cornell U., 1948; Ph.D., U. Minn., 1951. Head Berg Hatchery, Hendrum, 1936-40; undergrad. research asst. agrl. econs. S.D. State U., 1940-43; instr. (Sch. Agr.), Brookings, S.D., 1946-47; research asst. agrl. econs. Cornell U., 1947-48, U. Minn., 1948-51; U.S. agrl. attache, Yugoslavia, 1951-54, Denmark and Norway, 1954-57; prof., head dept. agrl. econs. U. Minn., 1957-63, dean, 1963-73; resident dir. MUCIA-Indonesian Higher Agrl. Edn. project, 1973-75; pres. S.D. State U., Brookings, 1975—; dir. George A. Hormel & Co., Farmhand, Inc., Nat. Bank of S.D., Brookings Internat. Life Ins. Co., Brookings; cons. econ. research service, mem. econs. research adv. com. U.S. Dept. Agr., 1960-68; personnel cons. ICA; cons. AID, 1977-81; Vice chmn., dir. Experience, Inc., 1963-77; bd. dirs. North Star Research and Devel. Inst., 1963-73, State Capitol Credit Union, 1965-67. Contbr. articles to bulls., profl. jours. Chmn. Nat. Adv. Commn. Food and Fiber, 1965-67; bd. dirs., vice chmn. Minn. Council Econ. Edn., 1962-73; bd. dirs. Westminster Found. Minn., 1962-68; mem. Pres.'s Commn. Income Maintenance Programs, 1968-70; overseer Jamestown (N.D.) Coll.; bd. dirs. Voyageurs Nat. Park Assn., 1965-73; trustee Farm Found., 1967-77, U. Mid-Am., 1977—; mem. adv. panel U.S. Army ROTC, 1976-79; mem. critical choices steering com. Upper Midwest Council, 1976—; chmn. joint com. agrl. devel. Bd. Internat. Food and Agrl. Devel., 1977-79; v.p. Nat. Collegiate Athletic Assn. Council, 1977-80. Served with AUS, 1943-46; ETO; col. Res. Decorated Bronze Star, Combat Inf. badge, Army Commendation ribbon, Meritorious Service medal; recipient Superior Service award Dept. Agr., 1956; Distinguished Alumni award S.D. State U., 1972; Superior Service award Minn. Agrigrowth Council, 1973; Outstanding Achievement award U. Minn. Bd. Regents, 1980; others.; Danforth Found. fellow, 1942; Caleb Dorr research fellow U. Minn., 1948; Greater Univ. grad. fellow, 1949; Kellogg Found. Travel fellow, 1958. Mem. Agrl. History Soc., AAUP, Am. Econ. Assn., Am. Farm Econ. Assn., Am.-Scandinavian Found., Assn. U.S. Army, Internat. Assn. Agrl. Economists (U.S. council), Atlantic Community Council U.S. (sponsor 1963-67), St. Paul-Mpls. Com. on Fgn. Relations, Res. Officers Assn., U. Minn. Sci. Club, Alpha Gamma Rho, Alpha Zeta, Gamma Sigma Delta, Pi Gamma Mu, Phi Kappa Phi. Presbyn. Clubs: Rotary, Cosmos. Office: South Dakota State Univ Office of Pres University Station Brookings SD 57007 *

BERG, THOMAS, business executive; b. Sparta, Wis., Dec. 28, 1914; m. Evelyn Sweet, Nov. 13, 1937; children: Barbara Caryl, James Richard. B.S.E.E., U. Wis., 1937. Engr. Gen. Electric Co., Schenectady, 1937-48; instr. Rensselaer Poly. Inst., Troy, N.Y., 1943-44; pres., owner, welding specialist, application engr. Arcway Equipment Co., Phila., 1948-58; pres. Airco Welding Products div. Air Reduction Co., N.Y.C., 1958-68; pres., chief exec. officer, dir. Friedrich Refrigerators Inc., San Antonio, 1968-75, chmn., 1975—; v.p., dir. Crutcher Resources Corp., Houston; v.p. Wylain Inc.; dir. Universal Bookbindery Inc.; v.p., dir. Ellison Industries Inc.; pres. Ray Ellison Devels. Inc.; bd. dirs., chmn. S.W. Research Inst.; founder Skills Tng. Center, San Antonio, 1971; dir. First Nat. Bank, San Antonio, Jim Berg Publs., Inc.; dir., chmn. exec. com., pres. J.E.T. Properties, Inc., San Antonio. Author: Aim for a Job in Welding, 1967. Adv. dir. Southwest Craft Center, San Antonio, 1975—; mem., dir. fed. policy com. Urban Land Inst., Washington, 1977—; trustee Myra Stafford Pryor chair of free enterprise, St. Mary's U., 1977—; chmn. adv. council Sch. Bus., 1976-77 chmn. adv. council Sch. Bus., San Antonio; chmn. bd. City Pub. Service Bd., San Antonio; bd. dirs. Prevent Blindness of San Antonio., Myasthenia Gravis Found, San Antonio. Named hon. citizen City of San Antonio, 1978. Mem. Am. Welding Soc. (founder annual Airco award 1965), Am. Inst. Elec. Engrs., San Antonio C. of C. (dir. 1972—, chmn. econ. devel. council 1973—), Trinity U. Assos. Presbyterian. Clubs: San Antonio Country, City, Argyle, Univ., Giraud, Plaza, St. Anthony, Rotary (dir.). Featured on front cover of Iron Age Mag., June 1967. Developer universal jeep welder and energizer systems, 1942-44. Office: PO Box 5250 San Antonio TX 78209 *I believe we should have goals of achievement and understanding to improve man's day during our precious life. Goals, small or large, make us stay young, alert, and better citizens.*

BERG, WARREN STANLEY, banker; b. Lynn, Mass., Jan. 17, 1922; s. Carl W. and Gladys (Colburn) B.; m. Marjorie E. Coleman, Mar. 25, 1944; children—Peter C., Carolyn (Mrs. John Spengler), Dana S. B.S., Harvard, 1943; grad. exec. devel. program, Cornell U., 1944. Dir. pub. relations and sales promotion Arthur D. Little, Inc., Cambridge, Mass., 1951-65; with Shawmut Bank of Boston (N.A.), 1965—, sr. v.p., 1969—. Author: History of Harvard Baseball, 1964, History of Massachusetts Institute of Technology Athletics, 1950. Trustee, pres. Museum Sci.; bd. dirs. Freedom House, Freedom Trail; exec. com. Wang Ctr. for Performing Arts. Served to 1st lt. USMCR, 1943-46. Mem. Bank Marketing Assn., Pub. Relations Soc. Am. (presdl. citiation for meritorious service 1962), Assoc. Grantmakers of Mass. (v.p.). Clubs: Harvard, Harvard Varsity (Boston); Winchester Country. Home: 81 Bacon St Winchester MA 01890 Office: One Federal St: Boston MA 02110

BERGAN, JOHN JEROME, vascular surgeon; b. Tampico, Mex., Apr. 4, 1927; s. Ernest and Arva Elizabeth (Yeagley) B.; children: Elizabeth Anne, Margaret Alice, John Widener. B.S., Purdue U., 1950; M.D., Ind. U., 1954. Intern Ind. U. Med. Center, 1954-55; resident in surgery Northwestern U. Med. Sch., Chgo., 1955-59, mem. faculty, 1959—; Magerstadt prof., 1967—, chief div. vascular surgery, 1970—; mem. staff Northwestern Meml. Hosp., VA Lakeside Hosp. Editor: (with James Yao) Venous Problems, 1978, Gangrene and Severe Ischemia of the Lower Extremities, 1978, Surgery of the Aorta, 1979, Surgical Techniques in Vascular Surgery, 1980, Aneurysms, 1981, Cerebrovascular Insufficiency, 1982; editorial bd.: (with James Yao) Surgery, 1977—; contbr. articles to profl. jours. Served with USN, 1946-48. Fellow A.C.S. (dir. internat. transplantation registry 1971-75); mem. Am. Surg. Assn., Central Surg. Assn. (recorder 1976—), Internat. Cardiovascular Soc. (v.p. 1973), Soc. for Vascular Surgery (pres. 1983), Soc. Univ. Surgeons (hon. lectr. 1979), Soc. for Clin. Vascular Surgery (hon.), Midwestern Vascular Surg. Soc. (founding mem., pres. 1978-79), Chgo. Surg. Soc. (v.p. 1972). Home: 910 N Lake Shore Dr Chicago IL 60611 Office: 251 E Chicago Ave Chicago IL 60611

BERGANZA, TERESA, mezzo-soprano; b. Madrid, Mar. 16, 1935; d. Guillermo and Ascension (Vargas) B.; children: Teresa, Javier, Cecilia. Student (Premio Extraordinario, Premio Grande de Lucrezia Arana), Madrid Conservatory. Debut in recital, Madrid; operatic debut as Dorabella in: Cosi fan Tutte, Aix-en-Provence (France) Festival, 1957; debut as Cherubino in: Marriage of Figaro, Glyndebourne (Eng.) Festival, 1958; regular appearances at, Covent Garden, London, La Scala, Milan, La Scala, Italy, La Scala, also in Vienna, La Scala, Madrid, La Scala, Paris and, La Scala, Edinburgh; debut as Cherubino, Met. Opera, 1967, rec. artist. Decorated grand cross Isabel La Católica; recipient Lily Pons award, 1976, Disque Lyrique award; Harriet Cohen award. Address: care Columbia Artists Mgmt 165 W 57th St New York NY 10019 *

BERGÉ, CAROL, author; b. N.Y.C.; d. Albert and Molly Peppis; m. Jack Bergé, June 1955; 1 son, Peter. Asst. to pres. Pendray Public Relations, N.Y.C., 1955; disting. prof. lit. Thomas Jefferson Coll., Allendale, Mich., 1975—; tchr. fiction and poetry U. Calif. extension, Berkeley, 1976-77; asso. prof. U. So. Miss., Hattiesburg, 1977-78; vis. prof. U. N.Mex. Honors Ctr., 1978-79; vis. lectr. Wright State U., 1979, SUNY, Albany, 1980-81; tchr. Poets and Writers, Poets in the Schs. (N.Y. State Council in Arts),. Author: A Couple Called Moebius, 1972, Acts of Love: An American Novel, 1973 (N.Y. State Council on Arts CAPS award 1974), Timepieces, 1977, The Doppler Effect, 1979, Fierce Metronome, 1981, Secrets, Gossip and Slander, 1984; poetry From a Soft Angle: Poems About Women, 1972, The Unexpected, 1976, Rituals and Gargoyles, 1976, A Song, A Chant, 1978, Alba Genesis, 1979, Alba Nemesis, 1979; editor: CENTER Press, 1970-84, Miss Rev, 1977-78; contbg. editor: Woodstock Rev., 1977—, Shearsman mag, 1980—. Nat. Endowment Arts fellow, 1979-80. Mem. PEN, Am. Pen, Authors League and Guild, Poets and Writers, MacDowell Fellows Assn., Poets and Writers, N.Mex. Press Women. Office: care Rhoda Weyr William Morris Agy 1350 Ave Americas New York NY 10019

BERGE, KENNETH GEORGE, physician, educator; b. Wahkon, Minn., Feb. 9, 1926; s. Henry Bertin and Edith Frances (Collin) B.; m. Aline H. Hoyt, Sept. 1, 1948; children: Elizabeth Ann Berge Devine, William Hoyt, Keith Hoyt. B.A. magna cum laude, U. Minn., 1948, B.S., 1949, M.B., 1951, M.D., 1952; M.S. in Medicine, Mayo Grad. Sch. Medicine, 1955. Intern Boston City Hosp., 1951-52; resident Mayo Grad. Sch. Medicine, Rochester, Minn., 1952-55, instr., 1957-62, asst. prof., 1962-69, asso. prof. medicine, 1969-74, prof., 1974—, NW Area Found. prof. community health, 1977—; physician Kennecott Copper Corp., Ray, Ariz., 1952; asst. to staff Mayo Clinic, Rochester, 1955, staff physician, internist, 1955—, head sect. medicine, 1970-79, pres. voting staff, 1976; bd. dirs., mem. exec. com. Rochester Meth. Hosp., 1970-83, chmn. com. clin. pastoral care, 1970-82; mem. epidemiology, biometry adv. com. Nat. Heart and Lung Inst., NIH, 1970-72; mem. policy adv. bd. hypertension detection, follow-up program NIH, 1972-80, vice chmn. steering com. coronary drug project, 1962—. Bd. editors: Minn. Medicine, 1972-74; contbr. articles and chpts. to tech. jours. Mem. policy-data monitoring bd. aspirin myocardial infarction study, 1975-80; Mem. Olmsted County Bd. Health, 1975-81, vice chmn., 1976, chmn., 1977; mem. Minn. Health Adv. Council, 1980-83. Served with USNR, 1944-46. Recipient outstanding tchr. award Internal Medicine Residents, Edn. Com., Mayo Grad. Sch., 1970, 71, 74. Fellow ACP (pres. Minn. chpt. 1980-81); mem. AMA (Billings silver medal 1957), Am. Heart Assn. (program com. council on epidemiology 1980-84), Great Plains Heart Assn. (chmn. profl. edn. com. 1972-74), Sigma Xi, Alpha Omega Alpha, Phi Chi. Methodist (lay leader 1964-66). Clin. researcher in cardiovascular disease and diabetes. Home: 1451 Woodland Dr SW Rochester MN 55902 Office: 200 1st St SW Rochester MN 55901

BERGE, OLE M., trade union executive; b. Swift Current, Sask., Can., July 22, 1921; came to U.S., 1948, naturalized, 1955; s. Thorstein and Thora (Bjorgum) B.; m. Katherine Ann Anderson; children—Katherine Ann, Linda Maureen, Ola Loraine. Grad. trade union program, Harvard U., 1963. Laborer Gt. No. Rwy., 1941; with Brotherhood Maintenance of Way Employees, 1942—, staff asst., Chgo., 1966-73, grand lodge v.p., Detroit, 1973-78, pres., 1978—. Served with Can. Air Force, 1942-45. Mem. Ry. Labor Execs. Assn., RCAF Assn. Lutheran. Office: 12050 Woodward Ave Detroit MI 48203 *

BERGEL, RICHARD, department store chain executive; b. Providence, May 12, 1935; m. Myrna J. Kaplan, Aug. 31, 1958; children: Gary, Mark. A.B., Brandeis U., 1957. With Montgomery Ward & Co., Inc., subs. Marcor, Inc., N.E. U.S. catalog gen. mgr., Albany, N.Y., 1975-80, v.p. catalog field sales and ops., Chgo., 1980-83, sr. v.p. distbn., 1983—. Coach North Colonie Youth Basketball League, Latham, N.Y., 1974; v.p. Latham Babe Ruth League, 1978-79. Home: 939 Suffield Terr Northbrook IL 60062 Office: Montgomery Ward & Co Inc Montgomery Ward Plaza Chicago IL 60671

BERGELL, AARON, tenor; b. Bayonne, N.J., Nov. 13, 1938; s. Charles Kalman and Ruth Cohen Bergle; m. Helene Ruth Kurinsky, June 3, 1958 (div. 1981); children: Lisa Meryl, Charles Stephen, David Ira. B.S. in Music Edn, NYU, 1959; postgrad. (scholar), Juilliard Sch. Am. Opera Center, 1976. Debut as leading tenor, Israel Nat. Opera, Tel Aviv, 1970, State Theatres of Munich and Wiesbaden, Germany, 1972; debut in: Verdi Requiem, Carnegie Hall, N.Y.C., 1973; appeared, throughout U.S. including, Lyric Opera, Phila., 1974, San Francisco Opera, 1976, Va. Opera, Am. Opera Center, Boston Opera, 1977, San Diego Opera, N.Y.C. Opera and Am. Nat. Co., 1982, Houston Opera, 1978, San Antonio Opera; appeared with symphony orchs. including, Sao Paulo (Brazil) Philharmonic, 1976, Milw., 1977, Nat. Opera Teatro Colon, Bogota, Columbia, Vancouver, 1979, Savannah Symphony, 1980, Pacific Opera, Victoria, B.C., Can. Recipient William Mattheus Sullivan Mus. Found. award, 1975, 76, 77. Mem. Am. Guild Mus. Artists. Home: 405 Park Ave Rutherford NJ 07070

BERGEN, CANDICE, actress, photojournalist; b. Beverly Hills, Calif., May 9, 1946; d. Edgar and Frances (Westerman) B.; m. Louis Malle, Sept. 27, 1980. Ed., U. Pa. Model during coll. Films include The Group, The Sand Pebbles, The Day the Fish Came Out, Live for Life, The Magus; films include: Soldier Blue, Getting Straight, The Hunting Party, Carnal Knowledge, T.R. Baskin, The Adventurers, 11 Harrowhouse, Bite the Bullet, The Wind and the Lion, The Domino Principle, The End of the World in Our Usual Bed in a Night Full of Rain, Oliver's Story, Starting Over; Photojournalist credits include articles for Life, Playboy; dramatist: play The Freezer (included in Best Short Plays of 1968). Address: care CMA 8899 Beverly Blvd Hollywood CA 90048 *

BERGEN, DANIEL PATRICK, librarian, educator; b. Albert Lea, Minn., May 25, 1935; s. Francis Joseph and Grace Frances (Donovan) B.; m. Carol Lee Janson, Apr. 11, 1958; children: Mary Clare, Paula Maureen, Brent Daniel, Gregory Joseph. A.B. in History-Philosophy, U. Notre Dame, 1957, M.A. in Polit. Sci., 1962, U. Chgo., 1961, postgrad., 1963; M.A. in Am. Studies, U. Minn., 1968, Ph.D., 1970, postgrad. in. Philosophy, 1973-75, U. Conn. Law Sch., 1977. Bar: cert. advanced study librarianship, R.I. Grad. asst. dept. polit. sci. U. Notre Dame, 1957-58, 61-62; asst. librarian, instr. polit. sci. St. Benedict's Coll., 1962-63; asst. dean, lectr. Sch. Library Sci.-Syracuse U., 1964-65; asst. prof. library sci. U. Miss., 1966-70, assoc. prof. library sci., 1966-70, chmn. dept. library sci., 1966-68; assoc. prof. U. R.I., 1970-75, prof., 1975—, teaching fellow, 1981-82, chmn. faculty senate, 1976-77. Contbr. articles to profl. jours. Mem. bd. trustees Upper Iowa U., Fayette, 1973—, South Kingstown (R.I.) Pub. Library, Peace Dale, R.I., 1973—. Served with USAF, 1958-60. Fellow R.I. Bd. Regents for Edn., 1981; U. Chgo. fellow, 1963; U. Minn. fellow, 1970; U. R.I. teaching effectiveness grantee, 1975. Mem. AAAS, ALA, Am. Studies Assn., Assn. Am. Library Schs., New Eng. Library Assn., R.I. Library Assn. (exec. bd. dirs. 1974-78, pres. 1976-77), Soc. Systems Research, Beta Phi Mu. Home: 41 Highland Ave Wakefield RI 02879 Office: Grad Library Sch U RI Kingston RI 02881 *In the end, there is only this one thing: people and one's love and respect for them*

BERGEN, G.S. PETER, lawyer; b. Mineola, N.Y., Apr. 17, 1936; s. Hugh G. and Helen (Sawin) B.; m. Katherine Guthrie, July 28, 1964; children: Jennifer Guthrie, Anne Sawin, Lydia Kunkle. Geol. engr., Colo. Sch. Mines, 1958; J.D., Columbia U., 1962. Bar: N.Y. 1963, U.S. Dist. Ct. (ea. dist.) N.Y. 1964, U.S. Dist. Ct. (so. dist.) N.Y. 1964, U.S. Ct Appeals (2d cir.) 1966, D.C. 1968, U.S. Ct. Appeals (5th cir.) 1979, U.S. Ct. Appeals (D.C. cir.) 1973, U.S. Supreme Ct. 1968. Served to 2d lt. C.E. U.S. Army, 1958-69. Mem. ABA, N.Y. Bar Assn., Assn. Bar City N.Y., Fed. Energy Bar Assn. Clubs: Mining, Manhasset Bay Yacht. Office: LeBoeuf Lamb Leiby & MacRae 520 Madison Ave New York NY 10022

BERGEN, JOHN VANDERVEER, health edn. adminstr.; b. N.Y.C., Nov. 3, 1934. B.S., Phila. Coll. Pharmacy and Sci., 1956; Ph.D., U. Wis., 1961. Instr. U. Wis., summer 1959; mem. faculty Idaho State U., Pocatello, 1960-68, dean, 1963-68, dir. div. med. arts, 1964-68, prof. pharm. chemistry, 1966-68; lectr. U. Kans., 1968-69; asso. dir. Nat. Formulary, Am. Pharm. Assn., 1969, dir., 1970-74; pres. Phila. Coll. Pharmacy and Sci., 1975-80; dir. allied health professions program Wright State U., Dayton, Ohio, 1980—, prof. allied health scis., 1980—; Mem. Idaho Gov. Adv. Council Comprehensive State Health Planning, 1967-69; mem. pharmacy rev. com. USPHS, 1968-72; mem. U.S. Adopted Names Council, 1970-72; mem. expert adv. panel on internat. pharmacopoeia and pharm. preparations WHO, 1974-79; mem. com. revision U.S. Pharmacopeia, 1975—; dir. Remington's Pharm. Scis., 1975-80. Vice-chmn. West Phila. Corp., 1975-80; bd. dirs. University City Sci. Center, 1976-80. Fellow Acad. Pharm. Scis.; mem. Am. Assn. Colls. Pharmacy (bd. dirs. 1980—), Am. Pharm. Assn., Am. Soc. Allied Health Professions, Ohio Soc. Allied Health Professions, Idaho State Pharm. Assn. (hon., named Pharmacist of Yr. 1967), Sigma Xi, Rho Chi, Phi Lambda Upsilon, Kappa Psi, Alpha Zeta Omega (hon.), Phi Delta Chi (hon.)

BERGEN, JULIUS, ret. found. exec.; b. Chgo., Nov. 7, 1896; s. Sophus Theodor and Marie (Tecklenburg) B.; m. Mary Elizabeth Wood, Feb. 14, 1927; children—Barbara Marie (Mrs. Donald L. Phipps), Ann (Mrs. Malcolm Willard Brawn). Student, Ill. Bus. Coll., also extension courses; D.Bus. Adminstrn. (hon.), U. Nev., 1956. With Fleischmann Co., Chgo., 1912-21, sec. mfg. dept., 1920-21; with Fleischmann Co. and Standard Brands, Inc., N.Y.C., 1921-41, asst. to chmn. bd., 1925-41; bus. mgr., agt. for Max C. Fleischmann enterprises, 1941-51; agt. for estate, also chmn., trustee Max C. Fleischmann Found., Reno, Nev., 1951-80; dir. Security Nat. Bank Reno, Haida Corp., J.V. Oil Corp. Mem. Reno chpt. NCCJ; bd. dirs. Council Founds., Inc.; adv. investment com. U. Nev.; trustee Santa Barbara Mus. Natural History, Western Speleological Inst.; hon. mem. Nev. State Mus. Served with USCGR, World War II. Mem. Reno C. of C., Reno Execs. Club. Republican. Episcopalian (vestry). Clubs: Rotarian, Elk., Channel City (Santa Barbara, Calif.); Hidden Valley Country (Reno). Home: 1140 Fairfield Ave Reno NV 89509

BERGEN, POLLY, actress, business executive; b. Knoxville, Tenn.; d. William and Lucy (Lawhorn) Burgin; m. Freddie Fields, Feb. 13, 1956 (div. 1976); children: Kathy, Pamela, Peter.; m. Jeffrey Endervelt, June 25, 1982. Chmn. bd. Polly Bergen Co., Beverly Hills., Polly Bergen Shoes; pres. Polly Bergen Prodns. Inc.; chmn. The Culinary Co. Inc. (Recipient Emmy award as best actress Nat. Acad. TV Arts and Scis. 1957-58, Fame award Top Ten in TV 1957-58); Author: Fashion and Charm, 1960, Polly's Principles, 1974, I'd Love to, But What'll I Wear, 1977; Motion pictures include Cape Fear, Move Over Darling, Kisses for My President; rec. artist for, Mercury, Columbia records; star: Polly Bergen Show, NBC-TV; other TV appearances include To Tell the Truth, The Winds of War. Mem. Share, Inc.; former bd. dirs. Martha Graham Dance Center; co-chmn. Nat. Bus. Council for Equal Rights Amendment.; bd. dirs. U.S.O. Recipient Troupers award Sterling Publs., 1957; Editors and Critics award Radio and TV Daily, 1958; Outstanding Working Woman award Downtown St. Louis, Inc.; Golden Plate award Am. Acad. Achievement, 1969; Outstanding Mother's award Nat. Mothers' Day Com., 1984; named Best Dressed American Woman Entertainer Costume Designers Guild, 1966; Polly Bergen Cardio-Pulmonary Research Lab., Children's Research Inst. and Hosp., Denver dedicated, 1970. Mem. Screen Actors Guild, Actors Equity, AGVA, AFTRA. Office: 200 E 42d St New York NY 10017

BERGEN, SEYMOUR MAURICE, social psychologist; b. Blyn, Jan. 7, 1928; s. Leo and Bessie Ida (Okun) Berger; m. Sara Marilyn Nappen, Sept. 7, 1952; children: Evelyn Joyce Nancy Faith. B.A., Okla. A&M Coll., 1949; M.A., Columbia U., 1950; Ph.D., Cornell U., 1959. Instr. Trinity Coll., Hartford, Conn., 1958-59; from instr. to assoc. prof. Ind. U., Bloomington, 1959-69; prof. social psychology,, U. Mass., Amherst, 1969—, Chmn. dept. psychology, 1983—. Contbr. articles on social psychology to profl. jours.; mem. editorial bd. (Jour. Personality and Social Psychology), 1979-83. Served with USNR, 1945-46; served with USAF, 1951-55. Fulbright sr. research scholar, 1975-76,83; spl. fellow NIH, 1965-66. Mem. Am. Psychol. Assn., Soc. Exptl. Social Psychology, Eastern Psychol. Assn. Democrat. Jewish. Home: 459 Flat Hills Rd Amherst MA 01003 Office: Dept Psychology U Mass Amherst MA 01003

BERGEN, STANLEY SILVERS, JR., physician, university president; b. Princeton, N.J., May 2, 1929; s. Stanley Silvers and Leah (Johnson) B.; m. Suzanne E. Miller, Nov. 16, 1965; children: Steven Richard, Victoria Elizabeth, Stuart Vaughn; children by previous marriage: Stanley Silvers III, Amy Dorle. A.B., Princeton, 1951; M.D., Columbia, 1955. Resident St. Luke's Hosp., N.Y.C., 1955-58, chief resident, Francis Zabriskie fellow, 1958-59, asst. chief dept. medicine, 1959-60, asst. attending physician, 1962-64; med. dir. Convalescent and Research Unit, Greenwich, Conn., 1962-64; chief medicine Cumberland Hosp., Bklyn., 1964-68; asst. dir. dept. medicine Bklyn.-Cumberland Med. Center, 1964-68, chief community medicine, 1968-70; sr. v.p. N.Y.C. Health & Hosps. Corp., 1970-71; instr. medicine Columbia, 1959-64; asso. prof. medicine Downstate Med. Sch., Bklyn., 1964-71; pres. U. Medicine and Dentistry N.J., 1971—; prof. medicine N.J. Med. Sch., Rutgers Med. Sch., N.J. Sch. Osteo. Med.; prof. community dentistry N.J. Dental Sch. Author articles in field. Mem. Mayor's Commn. Health and Hosps., N.Y.C., 1969-70; mem. N.J. Comprehensive Health Planning Council, 1971—; chmn. N.J. Commn. to Study Structure and Function Dept. Health, 1973, N.J. Abortion Commn., 1975, Adv. Council Grad. Edn. N.J., 1978—; adv. com. mcpl. health service program R.W. Johnson, also, Nat. Conf. Mayors; mem. Bd. Comprehensive Health, Newark, 1976-81, treas., 1972-80; bd. dirs. Cancer Inst. N.J., 1974-78, Ednl. Commn. Fgn. Med. Grads., 1982—; bd. dirs., mem. exec. com. Hastings Center on Biomed. Ethics, 1976—, chmn. devel. com., 1980—; bd. dirs., mem. exec. com. Art Center No. N.J., 1978-82; chmn. N.J. Blood Banks Task Force, 1980—. Served as capt. AUS, 1960-62. Fellow Assn. Am. Med. Colls., Am. Fedn. Clin. Research, Endocrine Soc., Clin. Soc. N.Y., Diabetes Assn. (v.p. 1969-70, chmn. clin. soc. 1968-69), N.Y. Acad. Scis., Am. Inst. Nutrition, A.C.P., Harvey Soc.; mem. Assn. Acad. Health Centers, Am. Diabetes Assn. (bd. dirs. N.J. affiliate), AMA, Am. Soc. Clin. Nutrition, Essex County Med. Soc., Med. Soc. N.J., Assn. Dirs. Med. Edn., Am. Hosp. Assn. (chmn. com. grad. med. edn. 1974-76, mem. council profl. services 1973-76), Greater Newark C. of C. (dir.). Home: 164 Glenwood Rd Englewood NJ 07631 Office: Coll Medicine and Dentistry NJ 100 Bergen St Newark NJ 07103 *My career has taken many significant turns, most of which have improved my ability to lead efforts toward better and more accessible health services. I have been fortunate in the opportunity to lead a variety of activities and to express creativity through institutions and individuals. My successes are due to the extent to which this nation still rewards those willing to work hard and learn from experience, as well as to the many intelligent, compassionate mentors with whose guidance I have been blessed.*

BERGER, BENNETT MAURICE, sociology educator; b. N.Y.C., May 1, 1926; s. Julius and Ethel (King) B.; m. Jean Kirkham, Dec. 9, 1956 (div. 1971); children: Jane, Nora.; m. Chandra Mukerji, Jan. 1981; 1 son, Kenneth. A.B., Hunter Coll., 1950; Ph.D., U. Calif. at Berkeley, 1958. Asst. prof., then asso. prof. sociology U. Ill., 1959-63; mem. faculty U. Calif. at Davis, 1963-73, prof. sociology, 1965-73, chmn. dept., 1963-66, 67-69; prof. sociology U. Calif., San Diego, 1973—, chmn. dept., 1979—. Author: Working-Class Suburb, 1960, Looking For America, 1971, The Survival of A Counterculture, 1981; assoc. editor: Sociometry, 1966-69, Social Problems, 1969-72; editor: Contemporary Sociology, 1974-77; sr. editor: Society, 1983—. Served with USMCR, 1944-46. Fellow Am. Sociol. Assn.; mem. AAUP. Office: Univ California San Diego CA 92039

BERGER, BRUCE, discount book company executive; b. N.Y.C., Mar. 24, 1944; s. Abraham H. and Lee (Marcus) B.; m. Susan H. Schneiderman, June 30, 1968. B.S., NYU, 1966. C.P.A., N.Y. Staff acct. Fox & Co., N.Y.C., 1966-70; controller Milgray Electronics Co., Inc., Freeport, N.Y., 1970, v.p. fin., 1971-82; exec. v.p., chief fin. officer Barnes & Noble Bookstores Inc., N.Y.C., 1982—. Mem. NYU Alumni Assn. (bd. dirs. 1977—). Home: 433 56th St New York NY 10022 Office: 105 Fifth Ave New York NY 10003

BERGER, CHARLES MARTIN, food and services company executive; b. Wilkes-Barre, Pa., May 2, 1936; s. Edward and Sadie (Zwass) B.; m. Jane Elrod Purdy, June 5, 1960; children: Cary John Aaron, Elizabeth Anne, Valerie Ann. A.B., Princeton U., 1958; M.B.A., Harvard U., 1960. Mktg. mgmt. Procter and Gamble Co., Cin., 1960-64; with H.J. Heinz Co., 1964—; gen. mgr. mktg. U.S.A. div. Procter and Gamble Co., Pitts., 1964-69, dir. corp. planning world hdqrs., 1969-70; mktg. dir. Heinz-London, 1970-72; mng. dir. Plasmon Diet Alim., Spa, Milan, Italy subs. H. B. Heinz Co., 1972-78; pres., chief exec. officer Weight Watchers Internat. Inc. sub. H. J. Heinz Co., Manhasset, N.Y., 1978—; lectr. Canrnegie-Mellon Grad. Sch. INdsl. Adminstrn., 1968-69. Chmn. bd. dirs. Am. Sch. of Milan, 1975-78; bd. dirs. Am. C. of C. in Italy, 1976-78. Served with U.S. Army, 1960-61. Mem. Young Pres.'s Orgn. Republican. Jewish. Clubs: Princeton (N.Y.); Concordia (Pitts.); Sands Point Bath and Racquet (N.Y.). Office: Weight Waters Internat 800 Community Dr Manhasset NY 11030

BERGER, CLEMENS RAINER ANTON, educator, researcher; b. Graz, Austria, July 3, 1930; came to U.S., 1955, naturalized, 1963; s. Anton and Marie Margarethe Doris (Schnoor) B.; m. Roberta Marie Johnson, Aug. 9, 1981; children—Wolfgang Christian, Gabriella Marie. Student, U. Cambridge, Eng., 1951-53, U. Kiel., 1953-55; Ph.D., U. Ill., 1960. Research asst. Chemische Industrie Basel (CIBA), Duxford-Cambridge, Eng., 1951-53; research asst. U. Ill., Urbana, 1955-60; staff scientist Gen. Dnamics, Convair Sci. Research Dept., San Diego, 1960-62; asst. prof. UCLA, 1963-68, asso. prof., 1968-74, prof. anthropology, geography and geophysics, 1974—, chmn. archeology, 1980—, chmn. acad. senate coms., 1976—; cons. local, state and fed. govts. Contbr. articles in field to profl. jours.; author: Scientific Methods in Medieval Archaeology, 1970, Radiocarbon Dating, 1979. Recipient Disting. Service award UCLA, 1968; Fulbright scholar, 1955-57; Guggenheim fellow, 1968-69; NSF grantee, 1965—; Wenner-Gren grantee, 1967-68; L.S.B. Leakey Found. grantee, 1976—. Mem. Soc. Archaeol. Scis. (dir. 1977—), AAAS, Geochem. Soc., Am. Anthrop. Soc., Am. Geog. Soc., Am. Chem. Soc., C. of C. (dir. 1968), Explorers Club, Alpha Chi Sigma, Phi Lambda Ypsilon, Sigma Xi. Presbyterian. Home: 20556 Little Rock Way Malibu CA 90265 Office: Inst Geophysics UCLA Los Angeles CA 90024 *THINK! There must be a harder way to do it.*

BERGER, CURTIS JAY, legal educator; b. Rochester, N.Y., Apr. 16, 1926; s. Samuel and Ruth (Taksen) B.; m. Constance Lindau, June 29, 1953 (div.); children: Ellen, John, Cathy, Wendy; m., Vivian O. Adler; June 17, 1973. A.B. with high honors, U. Rochester, 1948; J.D., Yale U., 1951. Bar: N.Y. 1951. Practice in, Rochester, 1951-58; instr. law Yale U. Law Sch., 1958-60, vis. lectr., 1966; asso. prof. U. So. Calif. Law Sch., 1960-62; mem. faculty Columbia U. Law Sch., 1962—, prof. law, 1964—; now Lawrence A. Wien prof. real estate law, chmn. div. urban planning Sch. Architecture Columbia U., 1969-70; spl. cons. Nassau (N.Y.) County, 1964-66; lectr. U. Miss., 1967, Leiden U., Netherlands, 1968, NYU, 1969, Amsterdam U., Netherlands, 1971, 79, Cornell U., 1978; vis. prof. public and internat. affairs Princeton U., 1975-82. Author: Land Ownership and Use, 1968, 2d edit., 1975, 3d edit., 1982, Law and Poverty, 1969, (with Axelrod and Johnstone) Land Transfer and Finance, 1971, 2d edit., 1978; bd. editors: Jour. Real Estate Taxation, Jour. Partnership Taxation; Contbr. profl. jours. Exec. dir. N.J. Commn. to Study Meadowland Devel., 1964-67; chmn. Englewood Redevel. Agy., 1968-69; Democratic candidate for N.Y. State Senate, 1956; Bd. dirs. Citizens Housing and Planning Council; chmn. Adv. Services for Better Housing, 1978-82, D.C. 37 Mcpl. Employees Legal Services Adv. Bd., 1977-82, The Bridge; mem. N.Y. Citizens Adv. Com. on Housing. Served with USNR, 1944-46. Mem. AAUP, Am. Law Inst., Am. Jewish Com., Order of Coif, Phi Beta Kappa, Phi Alpha Delta, Zeta Beta Tau. Club: Columbia Men's Faculty. Home: 20 W 64th St New York NY 10023 Office: Columbia U Law Sch New York NY 10027

BERGER, DAVID, advertising agency executive; b. France, Sept. 22, 1928; s. Louis S. and Henriette (Fischkin) B.; m. Barbara Jean Decker, June 19, 1954; children: Michael, Susan, Deborah, Laura. B.A., Columbia U., 1950; M.B.A., Harvard U., 1955. Asst. to mgr. Datos Co., Caracas, Venezuela, 1955-56; asst. mgr. Indsl. Cons. Orgn., Caracas, 1956-58; with Foote, Cone & Belding Advt. Inc., Chgo., 1959—, research dir., 1970-80, nat. research dir., 1980-81, corp. dir. research worldwide, 1982—; tchr. advt. Northwestern U., 1973-76. Mem. Park Forest (Ill.) Sch. Bd., 1973-74; bd. dirs. Ill. Philharmonic Orch., 1983—. Served with AUS, 1950-53. Mem. Am. Mktg. Assn. Home: 134 Warwick St Park Forest IL 60466 Office: 401 N Michigan Ave Chicago IL 60611

BERGER, ERIC, magazine editor; b. N.Y.C., Dec. 18, 1906; s. David and Mary (Friedenberg) B.; m. Isabelle Gronich, Jan. 5, 1935; 1 son, Neil. Student, N.Y. U., 1924-25; LL.B., St. John's Coll., Bklyn., 1928. Reporter Bklyn. Daily Eagle, 1929-31, Bklyn. Times, 1931-33; editor Nat. Sci. Publs., Inc., N.Y.C., 1934-39; free-lance writer and editor, 1940-41; with Scholastic Mags., Inc., N.Y.C., 1941—; editor Sr. Scholastic, 1941-59, World Week, 1942-43, Lit. Cavalcade, 1948-55; editorial dir. Science World, 1960-70, Science Tchrs. World, 1959-70, dir. sci. dept., 1963-70, editor in chief high sch. div., 1968-70, asso. pub. sch. div., 1970-72, editorial cons., 1973—. Served with AUS, 1943-45. Recipient Freedoms Found. award for articles on democracy, 1953. Mem. Nat. Assn. Sci. Writers, AAAS. Home: 127 W 96th St Apt 9-D New York NY 10025 Office: Scholastic Inc 50 W 44th St New York NY 10036

BERGER, EVELYN MILLER, psychologist; b. Hanford, Calif., Nov. 7, 1896; d. George A. and Margaret (Ross) Miller; m. Jesse Arthur Berger, June 16, 1939 (dec. 1971); m. C. Maxwell Brown, Nov. 24, 1972. Grad., State Normal Sch., San Jose, Calif., 1919; spl. student, Coll. Pacific, 1915-16, 20, U. So. Calif., 1916-17, U. Mexico, summer 1926, Entro de Estudios Historicos, Madrid, 1928; A.B., Stanford U., 1921, A.M., 1930; Ph.D. (Romlett Stevens scholar), Columbia U., 1932; Pd.D. (hon.), U. Pacific, 1961. Diplomate: Am. Bd. Examiners in Psychology. Sch. tchr. and prin., Panama City, Panama, 1918-19; exec. sec. girls' work M.E. Ch., Chile and Argentina, 1921-23; tchr. Spanish, San Jose High Sch., 1923- 30, Coll. Pacific, Stockton, Calif., 1929, 30; dean women, asso. prof. Spanish, Allegheny Coll., 1932-36; dean women U. Idaho, 1936-38, State Coll., San Diego, 1938-49; lectr. adult study groups family relations, child guidance Alameda, Berkeley, Albany schs., 1942-44; pres. Calif. Conf. W.S.C.S. (Meth.), 1940-42; adminstr., dir. East Bay Psychol. Center, Oakland, Calif., 1944—; tchr. counseling, cons. clin. psychology Berkeley Baptist Div. Sch., 1962-69; civilian cons. psychol. problems USAF, 1968-69. Author: Triangle, 1970, The Betrayed Wife, 1971, Writing a Religious Play, 1981; writer on Spanish and ednl. subjects; contbr. articles and short stories to ch. mags. Trustee, Scarritt Coll., 1967-71. Fellow Am. Psychol. Assn., Am. Assn. Marriage Counselors; mem. Internat. Council Psychologists, Cal., Western psychol. assns., Nat. Council Family Relations, P.E.O., Phi Beta Kappa, Kappa Delta Pi, Pi Lambda Theta, Phi Sigma Iota, Gamma Phi Beta. Methodist (mem. TV, radio, film commn.). Club: Calif. Writers. Home: 34 La Salle Ave Piedmont CA 94611 Office: 508 16th St Oakland CA 94612

BERGER, FRANK MILAN, scientist, former pharmaceutical company executive; b. Pilsen, Czechoslovakia, June 25, 1913; came to U.S., 1947, naturalized, 1953; s. Otto and Martha (Weigner) B.; m. Bozena Jahodova, Mar. 15, 1939 (dec. Nov. 1972); children: Franklin Milan, Thomas Jan; m. A. Christine Spade, May 21, 1975. M.D., U. Prague, Czechoslovakia, 1937, SUNY, 1948; D.Sc. (hon.), Phila. Coll. Sci. and Pharmacy, 1966. Research fellow physiology U. Prague, 1934-36, research asst. bacteriology, 1936-38; bacteriologist Czechoslovak State Inst. Health, 1938-39; sr. resident Monsall Hosp. Infectious Diseases, Manchester, Eng., 1941-43; chief pharmacologist Brit. Drug Houses, London, 1945-47; asst. prof. pediatrics U. Rochester, 1947-49; dir. research Carter-Wallace Inc., 1949-55, v.p., 1955-58, pres., Cranbury, N.J., 1958-73; mem. adv. council dept. biology Princeton U., 1961-74, lectr., prof., 1969-74; mem. sci. adv. com. Waksman Inst. Microbiology, Rutgers U., 1960-67; cons. Surgeon Gen., Walter Reed Army Med. Center, Washington, 1974-80; pres. Mario Negri Inst.

Found. for Biomed. Research, Inc., 1973—; prof. psychiatry U. Louisville Med. Sch., 1974—; hon. prof. microbiology Waksman Inst. Microbiology, Rutgers U., 1982. Editorial bd.: Clin. Pharmacology and Therapeutics. Fellow N.Y. Acad. Scis., Am. Coll Neuropsychopharmacology, Royal Soc. Medicine, AAAS; mem. Am., Brit., Can. pharm. socs., Am. Bacteriol. Soc., Soc. Gen. Microbiology, Soc. Exptl. Biology and Medicine, AMA, AAUP, Am. Chem. Soc., Biometric Soc., Eastern Psychiat. Assn., Sigma Xi. Clubs: Cosmos (Washington); Nassau (Princeton); Princeton, N.Y. Athletic (N.Y.C.). Discovered tranquilizer meprobamate, muscle-relaxant mephenesin, pain-reliever carisoprodol, also method purification penicillin. Home: 190 E 72d St New York NY 10021 Office: Dept Psychiatry U Louisville Sch Medicine Louisville KY 40201 *Concentrate on the important, rather than the urgent; try not to do what everybody else is doing; and remember that within limits of reason and decency, it is better to do what you like rather than what is expected of you.*

BERGER, FRANK S., consumer products company executive; b. N.Y.C., Nov. 6, 1936; s. Ernest A. and Anna (Weiss) B.; m. Judith Kugel, Jan. 15, 1966; children: Evan, Stacey. B.A., Queens Coll., 1958; M.B.A., N.Y. U., 1960; postgrad., Law Sch., 1961, IBM Edn. Center, 1960. Supr. mktg. and fin. analysis dept. Lever Bros., 1959-61; v.p. fin. and adminstrn. Pacific Enterprises, 1961-62; corp. mktg. staff Joseph E. Seagram & Sons, Inc., 1962-63; mktg. asst. to central div. mgr. Calvert Distillers, 1964, asst. state mgr., Fla., 1965, state mgr., N.J., 1966-67, asst. Eastern div. mgr., 1967-68, So. div. mgr., 1969-70; v.p., gen. sales mgr. Frankfort Distillers, 1970-71, exec. v.p. mktg. and fin., 1972-73; pres. Gen. Wine & Spirits Co., N.Y.C., 1973-76, Seagram Distillers Co., 1976-77, House of Seagram, 1978-79; dir. Joseph E. Seagram & Sons, Inc., 1974-79; chmn. bd. Quadrillon Investments Inc., 1980—, Hazel Bishop Industries Inc., 1981—, Viceroy Imports, Inc., 1981—. Trustee N.Y. Hall of Sci.; Chmn. N.Y. Lunch-o-Ree Boy Scouts Am., United Jewish Appeal, Gaucho Basketball Assn., Cystic Fibrosis Soc.; exec. com. wine and spirits div. Anti-Defamation League, Pro-Am. tennis sponsor Cerebral Palsy; bd. dirs. Bronfman Found. Served with AUS, 1958. Mem. Am. Mgmt. Assn., Am. Mktg. Assn, N.Y. C. of C., Young Pres.' Orgn., A.I.M. Clubs: Advt. of N.Y., N.Y. Sales Execs. Office: Hazel Bishop Industries Inc 200 Williams Dr Ramsey NJ 07446

BERGER, HAROLD, physicist; b. Syracuse, N.Y., Oct. 7, 1926; s. Joseph H. and Fannie A. (Stein) B.; m. Dawn Marie Beranek, Dec. 27, 1952; children: Susan, Margaret, Thomas, Joseph, Daniel. B.S., Syracuse U., 1949, M.S., 1951. Physicist Gen. Electric Co. x-ray dept., Milw., 1951-59; sr. physicist Battelle Meml. Inst., Columbus, 1959-60; asso. physicist Argonne (Ill.) Nat. Lab., 1960-70, group leader nondestructive testing, 1965-73, sr. physicist, 1970-73; nuclear physicist reactor radiation div. Nat. Bur. Standards, Washington, 1973-75; program mgr. nondestructive evaluation Inst. for Materials Research (now Nat. Measurement Lab.), Nat. Bur. Standards), 1975-78; chief Office Nondestructive Evaluation, 1978-81; pres. Indsl. Quality, Inc., Gaithersburg, Md., 1981—; vis. scientist Centre d'Etudes Nucleaires, Grenoble, France, 1968-69; vis. lectr. U. Grenoble, 1968-69; pres.'s honor lectr. Non-Destructive Testing Soc., G.B., 1971; Mem. Nat. Materials Adv. Bd. ad hoc com. Nondestructive Inspection, 1967-68. Author Neutron Radiography, 1965, Nondestructive Testing (in Understanding the Atom series), 1965; Tech. editor: Materials Evaluation, jour. of Am. Soc. Nondestructive Testing, 1969—; editor: Practical Applications of Neutron Radiography and Gaging, 1976, Nondestructive Testing Standards—A Review, 1977; Contbr. articles to profl. jours. Served with USNR, 1944-45. Recipient spl. achievement award Nat. Bur. Standards, 1976; Silver medal Dept. Commerce, 1979. Fellow Am. Nuclear Soc. (Radiation Industry award 1974), Am. Soc. Nondestructive Testing (nat. dir. 1965-68, mem. editorial bd. jour., Achievement award 1967, Mehl lectr. 1975, award for services as editor 1976, Gold medal award 1982); mem. ASTM, Am. Phys. Soc., Sigma Xi. Home: 9832 Canal Rd Gaithersburg MD 20760 Office: Indsl Quality Inc PO Box 2397 Gaithersburg Md 20879

BERGER, HAROLD, engineer, lawyer; b. Archbald, Pa., June 10, 1925; s. Jonas and Anna (Raker) B.; m. Renee Margareten, Aug. 26, 1951; children: Jill Ellen, Jonathan David. B.S. in Elec. Engring, U. Pa., 1948, J.D., 1951. Bar: Pa. 1951. Since practiced in, Phila.; judge Ct. of Common Pleas, Phila. County, 1971-72; Chmn., moderator Internat. Aerospace Meetings, Princeton, 1965-66; chmn. Western Hemisphere Internat. Law Conf., San Jose, Costa Rica, 1967; chmn. internat. Confs. on Aerospace and Internat. Law, Coll. William and Mary; permanent mem. Jud. Conf. 3d Circuit Ct. of Appeals; mem. County Bd. Law Examiners, Phila. County, 1961-71; chmn. World Conf. Internat. Law and Aerospace, Caracas, Venezuela, 1969, Internat. Conf. on Environ. and Internat. Law, U. Pa., 1974, Internat. Confs. on Global Interdependence, Princeton U., 1975, 79; mem. Pa. State Conf. Trial Judges, Nat. Conf. State Trial Judges; chmn. Pa. Com. for Independent Judiciary, 1973—. Mem. editorial advisory bd.: Jour. of Space Law, U. Miss. Sch. of Law, 1973—; Contbr. articles to profl. jours. Served with Signal Corps AUS, 1946-48. Recipient Alumnus of Year award Thomas McKean Law Club, U. Pa. Law Sch., 1965, Gen. Electric Co. Space award, 1966, Nat. Disting. Achievement award Tau Epsilon Rho, 1972, Spl. Jud. Conf. award, 1981. Fellow Brit. Interplanetary Soc.; mem. Inter-Am. Bar Assn. (chmn. aerospace law com.), Fed. Bar Assn. (nat. chmn. com. on aerospace law, past pres. Phila. chpt., nat. exec. council, nat. chmn. fed. and state jud. com., Presdl. award 1970, Nat. Distinguished Service award 1978), ABA (Spl. Presdl. Program medal 1975, chmn. aerospace law com., mem. state and fed. ct. com., nat. conf. of state trial judges), Phila. Bar Assn. (chmn. jud. liaison com. 1975, chmn. internat. law com. 1977), Assn. U.S. Mems. Internat. Inst. Space Law Internat. Astronautical Fedn. (v.p.), Internat. Acad. Astronautics, Paris. Office: 1622 Locust St Philadelphia PA 19103

BERGER, HERBERT, physician, educator; b. Bklyn., Dec. 14, 1909; s. Louis and Augusta (Feldman) B.; m. Sylvia Berger, Oct. 1934; children: Leland S., Shelby L. (Mrs. William Jakoby). B.Sc., NYU, 1929; M.D., U. Md., 1932. Diplomate: Am. Bd. Internal Medicine. Intern Morrisania City Hosp., Bronx, N.Y., 1932-34; resident U.S. Naval Hosps., 1941-45; practice medicine, 1934—; cons. cardiologist Sea View Hosp., S.I., 1934—; attending physician Flower-Fifth Ave. Hosp., Met. Hosp.; cons. USPHS Hosp.; prof. medicine N.Y. Med. Coll., 1962—; pres. med. staff, dir. medicine emeritus Richmond Meml. Hosp., 1975—; dir. emeritus Group Health Ins., Inc. Contbr. over 175 articles to med. jours., chpts. to med. text books.; Cons. editor: med. lectr. in 65 countries. Internat. Jour. Addictions. Served to comdr. USNR, 1942-45. Recipient Gold medal U. Md., 1978. Fellow ACP, Am. Coll. Chest Physicians; mem. Internat. Coll. Angiology, N.Y. Acad. Medicine (v.p., chmn. sect. on medicine, vice chmn. com. med. edn.), Brit. Soc. Health Edn., Richmond County Med. Soc. (past pres.), N.Y.C. Med. Soc. (past pres.), Med. Soc. State N.Y. (past v.p.), Blood Banks Assn. (past pres.), N.Y. Soc. Internal Medicine (past pres.), Internat. Soc. Study Addictions (past pres.). Republican. Jewish. Clubs: Richmond County Country, Richmond County Yacht, Circumnavigators. Endowed Berger Lecture at U. Md. and N.Y. Acad. Medicine; endowed Chair of Medicine at U. Md. Home: 25 Bloomingdale Rd Staten Island NY 10309 Office: 7440 Amboy Rd Staten Island NY 10307 *As a young student I looked upon the opportunity to practice medicine as one of the foremost activities to which one could aspire. Fifty years later in this profession have not altered my original concepts. It has been exciting, non-repetitive and constantly inspiring; an endless opportunity to do good.*

BERGER, JASON, painter, Printmaker; b. Malden, Mass., Jan. 22, 1924; s. Simon and Frances Alice (Sauel) B.; m. Estela Simoes Couto, Sept. 1, 1978; 1 son by previous marriage: Adam Joseph. Student, Boston Mus. Fine Arts Sch., 1942-43, 46-49, U. Ala., 1943-44, Ossip Zadkine Sch Sculpture, Paris, 1950-52. Vis. prof. SUNY-Buffalo, 1969-70; instr. painting Art Inst., Boston, 1973—. Group shows, Carnegie Inst. Mus., 1954, 55, Mus. Modern Art, 1956, Pa. Acad. Fine Arts, 1962, Silvermine Guild, Providence Art Festival, 1969, others; represented: permanent collections Boston Mus. Fine Arts, Mus. Modern Art, Chase Manhattan Bank, Smith Coll. Mus. Art, Guggenheim Mus. Art, Brandeis U., others. Served with U.S. Army, 1943-46; ETO. Recipient Grand prize Boston Arts Festival, 1955, 1st prize Boston Arts Festival, 1961; Boston Mus. Fine Arts Sch. traveling fellow. Jewish. Home: 40 University Rd Brookline MA 02146 Office: 700 Beacon St Boston MA 02215

BERGER, JOHN HANUS, chem. products mfg. co. exec.; b. Pilsen, Czechoslovakia, May 5, 1919; came to U.S., 1960, naturalized, 1965; s. Otto and Martha (Weigner) B.; m. Magda Jakubovic, Jan. 18, 1953; 1 son, Joseph Abraham. B.S. in Chem. Engring, Prague State Coll., Charles U., Czechoslovakia, 1939; cert. in English, U. Cambridge, Eng., 1944. Asst. plant maintenance engr. Consol. Refinerie Ltd., Brit. Petroleum, London, Eng., 1947-49, Haifa, Israel, 1949-57; prodn. mgr. Resimon-Pinturas Montana (C.A.), Caracas, Venezuela, 1957-60; resin house supr. Glidden Co., Chgo., 1960-63; plant mgr. Hooker Glass & Paint Mfg. Co., Chgo., 1963-68; dir. mfg. Enterprise Paint Mfg. Co., Chgo., 1968-71; cons. to major coating cos., 1970-76; mfg. mgr. bioproducts ops. Beckman Instruments, Inc., Palo Alto, Calif., 1976—. Served with Brit. Army, 1940-45. Decorated Brit. il. Cross, Czechoslovak War Cross.; Recipient Nat. Safety Council award, 1966. Mem. Am. Chem. Soc., Soc. Coating Tech., AAU. Instrumental in first large scale manufacture of peptides; developed fiberglas-polyester resin prodn. methods for boat and furniture industries, also dispersion methods for sand mills. Home: 707 Continental Circle Mountain View CA 94040 Office: 1117 California Ave Palo Alto CA 94304

BERGER, JOSEPH, educator, author, counselor; b. Bklyn.; s. Harry and Rose (Diner) B.; m. Margaret Smith, July 9, 1966; children—Adam, Rachel, Gideon. A.B. magna cum laude, Bklyn. Coll., 1949; M.A., Harvard U., 1952, Ph.D. in Sociology, 1958. Lic. counselor. Instr. sociology Dartmouth, 1954-56, asst. prof., 1956-59, Stanford, 1959-62, asso. prof., 1962-68, prof. sociology, 1968—; dir. Lab. for Social Research, 1968-70, 71-74, chmn. dept. sociology, 1977—. Author: (with others) Types of Formalization in Small Groups Research, 1962, Expectation-States Theory: A Theoretical Research Program, 1974, Status Characteristics and Social Interaction: An Expectation-States Approach, 1977; Editor: Sociological Theories in Progress, Vol. I, 1966, Vol. II, 1972; contbr. articles and papers to profl. jours., books. Served to 1st lt. AUS, 1943-46; ETO. Decorated Bronze Star, Army Commendation medal; NIMH spl. postdoctoral fellow, 1964, 70-71. Mem. Am., Pacific sociol. assns., Am. Assn. for Marriage and Family Therapy, Propylea. Home: 955 Mears Ct Stanford CA 94305

BERGER, KENNETH WALTER, audiologist; b. Evansville, Ind., Mar. 22, 1924; s. Walter P. and Ida (Block) B.; m. Barbara Jane Steadman, Aug. 31, 1946; children—Robert W., Kenna J., Laura M., Karen S. B.A., U. Evansville, 1948; M.A., Ind. State U., 1949; M.S., S. Ill. U., Carbondale, 1960, Ph.D., 1962. Speech and hearing therapist pub. schs., Carmi, Ill., 1955-61; dir. audiology Kent State U., Ohio, 1962—, prof., 1967—; curator hearing aid museum. Author: Speechreading Principles and Methods, 1971, The Hearing Aid: Its Operation and Development, 1974, also monographs; Contbr. articles to profl. jours. Served to capt. U.S. Army, 1943-46; Served to capt. USAF, 1951-55. Fellow Am. Speech and Hearing Assn., Am. Audiology Soc., Acoustical Soc. Am. Home: 647 Longmere Dr Kent OH 44240 Office: Speech and Hearing Clinic Kent State Univ Kent OH 44242

BERGER, MARTIN, petroleum co. exec.; b. N.Y.C., May 23, 1926; s. Harry and Elizabeth (Gotthelf) B.; m. Helin Cherin, Aug. 31, 1947; children—Henry, Susan, Laura. B.S. in Physics, Columbia U., 1949. Research physicist Uniroyal, Detroit, 1950-54; research physicist Chrysler Corp., Detroit, 1954-56; dir. govt. research labs. Exxon Research and Engring. Co., Linden, N.J., 1956-76; pres. Occidental Research Corp., Irvine, Calif., 1976—; v.p. research and devel. Occidental Petroleum Corp., Los Angeles, 1977—. Contbr. articles to profl. jours. Served with USCG, 1943-46; ETO. Mem. Nat. Conf. on Advancement Research, Indsl. Research Inst. *

BERGER, MICHAEL, journalist, film writer; b. San Francisco, Sept. 17, 1936; s. Maurice and Ruth (Wilson) B.; m. Yoshiko Kurashina, Dec. 26, 1966; children—Julia Yayoi, Maki. A.B. in Journalism, U. Calif., Berkeley, 1960. Reporter San Francisco Chronicle, 1963-67, dept. editor, 1977-83; Tokyo Bur. chief McGraw-Hill World News, 1983—; reporter/corr. Pacific Stars & Stripes, Tokyo, 1967-72; documentary film writer/dir./conf. organizer Charles von Loewenfeldt, Inc., San Francisco, 1972-75. Script writer: film series Japan: The Changing Tradition, 1978; writer, dir.: film Growing Up Japanese, 1975 (CINE Golden Eagle award); Contbr. articles to newspapers, mags. Bd. dirs. Japan Soc. San Francisco, 1978-79. Served with USNR, 1960-63. Fulbright research journalist grantee, Tokyo, 1975-76. Office: McGraw-Hill World News Kasumigaseki Bldg Room 1528 Kasumigaseki 3-2-5 Chiyoda-ku Tokyo Japan 100

BERGER, MURRY P., food co. exec.; b. Pitts., Jan. 24, 1926; s. Charles H. and Fannie M. (Buck) B.; m. Helen Walsh, Apr. 23, 1947; children—John Lee, Keith David. B.A., Duquesne U., 1948. Sales mgr. Seapak Corp., 1948-55; pres. Carnation Seafoods from Ocean of the World Eastern, Inc., 1955-81, Seabrook Internat. Foods (formerly Seabrook Foods, Inc.), M.B. Internat. Cons., Inc., 1981—; Past pres. Nat. Fishery Inst.; 1st rep. U.S. food industry at Canton Fair, People's Republic China, 1972; mem. Nat. Com. on U.S.-China Relations; former mem. N.J. Econ. Recovery Commn.; mem. outer continental shelf adv. bd. U.S. Dept. Interior, 1976—. Mem. internat. adv. bd. Columbia U., 1979—; trustee Nat. Frozen Foods Ins. Fund, N.J. Pvt. Colls.; bd. dirs. Nat. Fisheries Inst. Scholarship Fund, Duquesne U., Century Club, Duquesne U., Nat. Council U.S.-China Trade. Served with AUS, 1942-46. Named Man of Year Eastern Frosted Foods Assn., 1974; Decorated Bronze Star. Republican. Jewish. Home: 343 Algonquin Rd Franklin Lakes NJ 02417

BERGER, OSCAR, artist; b. Presov, Eperjes, Czechoslovakia, May 12, 1901; came to U.S., 1928, naturalized, 1955; s. Henry and Regina (Berger) B.; m. Ann Arany I. Varga, Feb. 9, 1937. Art study, in Europe. Cartoonist world celebrities drawn from life; sketched meetings, League of Nations, Geneva, 1925, House of Commons, London, 1935-45, San Francisco Conf. of UN for N.Y. Times and Daily Telegraph, London, 1945, UN confs., 1945-83, UN gen. assemblies, 1946-83; work represented in permanent collections, Library of Congress, Nat. Portrait Gallery, Met. Mus., also pvt. collections and museums.; Author: Tip and Top, 1933, A La Carte, 1948, Aesop's Foibles, 1949, Famous Faces, 1950, My Victims, 1952, I Love You, 1960, The Presidents, 1968; Contbr. Am., European publs. Club: Nat. Press (Washington). Portrait Subjects include: Winston Churchill, Eleanor Roosevelt, Queen Elizabeth II, Prince Philip of Eng., Bernard Shaw, Robert Frost, King Paul I of Greece, Gen. de Gaulle, King Baudouin, King Feisal, Emperor Haile Selassie, Premier Kruschev, Pope Pius XII, Pope Paul VI, Anna Pavlova, Toscanini, Prof. Einstein, Jacqueline Kennedy Onassis, Pres. Pompidou, Alexei Kosygin, Molotov, Brezhnev, Chancellor Brandt, Premier Golda Meir, Pres. Tito, Anwar Sadat, latest 11 U.S. presidents (all portraits drawn from life.). Address: Berkeley House 120 Central Park South New York NY 10019 *Being an artist by profession, I always thought that to be "AWARE"-the ability to observe, to consciously "feel" living and feel being "alive"-and enjoy life's wonders, colors and moods, is the greatest gift of Nature. To be blessed with some sense of humor and some sense of proportion is another gift, because without these, life can be a misery. I try to see both sides of a problem, to face it and act without remorse and regret afterwards. I am still trying...*

BERGER, PATRICIA WILSON, librarian; b. Washington, May 1, 1926; d. Thomas Decatur Wood and Nina Hughes; m. George Hamilton Combs Berger, May 20, 1970. B.A., George Washington U., 1965; M.S. in L.S., Catholic U. Am., 1974. Asst. librarian, ops. research office Johns Hopkins U., Chevy Chase, Md., 1949-51, asst. ops. research analyst, 1951-54; head librarian CEIR, Washington, 1954-55; chief, tech. info. and library services Human Relations Area Files, Yale U., 1955-57; tech. info. officer, chief librarian Inst. for Def. Analyses, Washington, Arlington, Va., 1957-67; dir. tech. info. and security programs Lambda Corp., Arlington, 1967-71; chief librarian U.S. Commn. on Govt. Procurement, Washington, 1971-72; head gen. reference br., later dep. chief librarian U.S. Patent and Trademark Office, Arlington, 1972-76; chief library div. U.S. Nat. Bur. Standards, Gaithersburg, Md., 1976-78; chief info. resources and services U.S. EPA, Washington, 1978-79; chief library and info. services U.S. Nat. Bur. Standards, 1979-83; cons. library, info. and security matters, 1965—; mem. Librarians Exec. Council, Met. Washington Council Govts., 1977-78; del. White House Conf. on Libraries and Info. Service, 1979; bd. dirs. Universal Serial and Book Exchange, 1983-84; chmn. com. library and info. scis. and related pub. practices Am. Nat. Standard Inst., 1981-83. Editorial bd. Sci. and Tech. Libraries, 1979—; contbr. articles to profl. jours. Active Nat. Women's Polit. Caucus, 1975—; bd. dirs. Va. Commn. for Reenactment of Battle First Bull Run, 1960-61. Recipient Internat. Women's Year award Dept. Commerce, 1976, Bronze medal, 1980; H.W. Wilson Pub. Co. award, 1980. Mem. Spl. Libraries Assn. (exec. bd. Washington chpt. 1970-71, pres. Washington chpt. 1977), ALA (pres. Fed. Librarians Roundtable 1983-84), Am. Soc. Info. Sci., AAAS, Chi Omega, Beta Phi Mu. Democrat. Episcopalian. Home: 105 Queen St Alexandria VA 22314 Office: US Nat Bur Standards Washington DC 20234

BERGER, PAUL ERIC, artist, photographer; b. The Dalles, Oreg., Jan. 20, 1948; s. Charles Glen and Virginia (Nunez) B. B.A., UCLA, 1970; M.F.A., SUNY-Buffalo, 1973. Vis. lectr. U. Ill., 1974-78; assoc. prof. art U. Wash.-Seattle, 1978—. Exhibited one-man shows, photographs, Art Inst. Chgo., 1975, Light Gallery, N.Y.C., 1977, Seattle Art Mus., 1980, Light Gallery, N.Y.C., 1982. NEA Photographer's Fellowship awardee, 1979. Mem. Soc. Photographic Edn. (dir.). Office: Sch Art DM-10 U Wash Seattle WA 98195

BERGER, PETER LUDWIG, sociologist; b. Vienna, Austria, Mar. 17, 1929; s. George and Jelka B.; m. Brigitte Kellner, Sept. 28, 1959; children: Thomas, Michael. B.A., Wagner Coll., 1949; M.A., New Sch. Social Research, 1950, Ph.D., 1954; LL.D., Loyola U., 1970; L.H.D., Wagner Coll., 1973. Mem. faculty Women's Coll., U. N.C., 1956-58, Hartford Theol. Sem., 1958-63, New Sch. Social Research, 1963-70, Rutgers U., 1970-79, Boston Coll., 1979-81; Univ. prof. Boston U., 1981—; cons. in field. Author: 11 books including The Social Construction of Reality, 1966, Pyramids of Sacrifice, 1975, The Heretical Imperative, 1979. Served with U.S. Army, 1953-55. Lutheran. Office: Univ Profs Program Boston Univ 745 Commonwealth Ave Boston MA 02215

BERGER, RAOUL, lawyer, educator, biolinist; b. Russia, Jan. 4, 1901; came to U.S., naturalized, 1910; s. Jesse and Anna (Kahn) B.; m. Helen Beck, Aug. 1930 (dec. Sept. 1958); m. Patricia Wolcott, 1967. Student, Inst. Mus. Art, N.Y.C., 1919-21; pupil violin with Franz Kneisel and Carl Flesch, Berlin; A.B., U. Cin., 1932, LL.D., 1975; J.D., Northwestern U., 1935; LL.M., Harvard U., 1938; LL.D., U. Mich., 1978. Soloist Cleve. Orch., 1927; 2d concertmaster Cin. Symphony Orch.; 1st violinist Cin. String Quartet; practiced law, Chgo., 1935-37; with SEC, 1938-40; spl. asst. to atty. gen. U.S., 1940-42; assoc. gen. counsel, then gen. counsel Alien Property Custodian, 1942-46; pvt. practice, Washington, 1946-62; vis. prof. U. Calif.-Berkeley Law Sch., 1962-65; Charles Warren sr. fellow Am. legal history Harvard U. Law Sch., Cambridge, Mass., 1971-76, ret. Author: Congress vs. the Supreme Court, 1969, Impeachment: The Constitutional Problems, 1973, Executive Privelege: A Constitutional Myth, 1974, Government by Judiciary: The Transformation of the Fourteenth Amendment, 1977, Death Penalties: The Supreme Court's Obstacle Course, 1982; contbr. articles to legal jours. Mem. ABA (past chmn. sect. adminstrv. law 1961-62), Order of Coif. Address: 140 Jennie Dugan Rd Concord MA 01742

BERGER, RICHARD LEE, civil and ceramic engineering educator; b. Belleville, Ill., July 31, 1935; s. Joseph Henry and Roma Alice B. B.S., U. Ill., 1958, M.S., 1960, Ph.D., 1965. Research sicentist Am. Cement Corp., 1962-70; assoc. prof. U. Ill., Urbana, 1971-74, prof. depts. civil and ceramic engring., 1974—. Nat. Lead fellow, 1961-62; recipient P.H. Bates award, 1974. Mem. ASTM, Am. Ceramic Soc., Sigma Xi. Office: 3211 NCEL Univ Ill Urbana IL 61801

BERGER, ROBERT MICHAEL, lawyer; b. Chgo., Jan. 29, 1942; s. David B. and Sophia (Mizock) B.; m. Joan B. Israel, Aug. 16, 1964; children—Aliza, Benjamin, David. A.B., U. Mich., 1963; J.D., U. Chgo., 1966. Bar: Ill. bar 1966, U.S. Supreme Ct. bar 1975. Law clk. to circuit judge U.S. Ct. Appeals, 2d Circuit, N.Y.C., 1966-67; atty. Chgo. Legal Aid Bur. Law Reform Unit, 1967-68; mem. firm Mayer, Brown & Platt, Chgo., 1968-72, partner, 1972—; lectr. Northwestern U. Law Sch., 1973; summer inst. faculty mem. Nat. Inst. Law-Focused Edn., Chgo., 1969-74; mem. hearing bd. Ill. Supreme Ct. Atty. Disciplinary System, 1973-79; mem. spl. tax adv. commn. to Ill. Dept. Ins., 1972; mem. bd. dirs., legal counsel Consumer Fedn. Ill., 1967-71; mem. regional consumer adv. council FTC, 1969; bd. dirs., chmn. program com. Legal Assistance Found., Chgo., 1975-78. Comment editor: U. Chgo. Law Rev, 1965-66; author: Law and the Consumer, 1969, 74; contbr. articles to law jours. Mem. Am. Law Inst., Am. Bar Assn. (chmn. subcom. on rev. uniform ltd. partnership act 1981—), Chgo. Bar Assn. (bd. mgrs. 1970-72), Chgo. Council Lawyers (bd. govs. 1969-71), Order of Coif, Phi Beta Kappa, Phi Kappa Phi. Office: 231 S LaSalle St Suite 1955 Chicago IL 60604

BERGER, SUZANNE, political science educator; b. Madison, Wis., Mar. 11, 1939; d. Julius and Hazel (Gordon) B.; m. Kenneth Keniston, Jan. 10, 1976; 1 son, Daniel Eben. B.A., U. Chgo., 1960; M.A., Harvard U., 1963, Ph.D., 1967. Instr. Harvard U., Cambridge, Mass., 1968-69; asst. prof. polit. sci. MIT, Cambridge, 1968-70, assoc. prof., 1971-75, prof., 1975—, assoc. chmn. faculty, 1975-77. Author: Peasants Against Politics, 1972, The French Political System, 1974; co-author: Dualism and Discontinuity in Industrial Societies, 1980;

author, editor: Organizing Interests in Western Europe, 1981; mem. editorial bd.: West European Politics, State e Mercato, Jour. Interdisciplinary History. Bd. dirs. Council Internat. Exchange of Scholars, Washington, 1981—. Guggenheim fellow, 1979-80; grantee Ford Found., 1960, Am. Philos. Soc. Fellow Am. Acad. Arts and Scis.; mem. Council of Fgn. Relations (com. on studies), Am. Polit. Sci. Assn. (bd. dirs. 1976-78), Social Sci. Research Council (chmn. com. on western Europe 1974-77), Phi Beta Kappa. Home: 3 Smith Ct Boston MA 02114 Office: Dept Polit Sci MIT E53-439 Cambridge MA 02139

BERGER, SYDNEY L., lawyer; b. N.Y.C., May 29, 1917; s. Abraham I. and Ruth (Levine) B.; m. Sadelle Kaplan, Aug. 30, 1942; children: Charles Lee, Jeri Beth. B.S., Coll. City N.Y., 1936; J.D., Columbia U., 1940. Bar: N.Y. 1941, Ind. 1947, U.S. Supreme Ct. 1952. Atty. REA, 1941-43; individual practice law, Evansville, Ind., 1946-72; ptnr. firm Berger & Berger, 1972—; adj. instr. law and polit. sci. Ind. State U., Evansville, 1971—; adj. lectr. legal medicine Ind. U. Med. Sch., Evansville, 1973—; adj. prof. law Ind. Law Sch., Indpls., 1974—. Mem. Mayor's Commn. on Human Relations; mem. Gov.'s advisory com. for Evansville State Psychiat. Treatment Center for Children, 1961-68; pres. Legal Aid Soc., Evansville, 1965. Served with AUS, 1943-45. Recipient James Bethel Gresham freedom award, 1971; Human Rights award City of Evansville, 1978. Mem. Am. Judicature Soc., ABA, Ind. Bar Assn. (Presdl. citation 1975, chmn. Ho. of Dels. 1980-81), Evansville Bar Assn. (pres. 1966), Am. Trial Lawyers Assn. (editor law jour. 1959-69, bd. govs. 1968-70), Ind. Trial Lawyers Assn. (pres. 1971-72), Am. Acad. Polit. and Social Sci., Am. Polit. Sci. Assn., Am. Arbitrators Assn. (nat. panel), Wilderness Soc., U. Evansville Acad. Arts and Scis. Home: 430 S Kelsey St Evansville IN 47714 Office: 313 Main St Evansville IN 47708

BERGER, THOMAS LOUIS, author; b. Cin., July 20, 1924; s. Thomas Charles and Mildred (Bubbe) B.; m. Jeanne Redpath, June 12, 1950. B.A. with honors, U. Cin., 1948; postgrad., Columbia, 1950-51. Librarian Rand Sch. Social Sci., N.Y.C., 1948-51; staff mem. N.Y. Times Index, 1951-52; asso. editor Popular Sci. Monthly, 1952-53; film critic Esquire, 1972-73; writer in residence U. Kans., 1974; Distinguished vis. prof. Southampton Coll., 1975-76. Author: novels Crazy in Berlin, 1958, Reinhart in Love, 1962, Little Big Man, 1964, Killing Time, 1967, Vital Parts, 1970, Regiment of Women, 1973, Sneaky People, 1975, Who Is Teddy Villanova?, 1977, Arthur Rex, 1978, Neighbors, 1980, Reinhart's Women, 1981; play Other People, performed 1970. Served with AUS, 1943-46; ETO. Recipient Rosenthal award Nat. Inst. Arts and Letters, 1965, Western Heritage award, 1965; Dial fellow, 1962. Mem. Authors Guild, Phi Alpha Theta (hon.). Office: care Dell Pub Co 1 Dag Hammarskjold Plaza New York NY 10017 *In my work I try to compete with that reality to which I must submit in life.*

BERGER, TOBY, electrical engineer, educator; b. N.Y.C., Sept. 4, 1940; s. Henry and Doris (Goldstein) B.; m. Florence Cohen, Aug. 27, 1961; children: Elizabeth, Lawrence. B.E., Yale U., 1962; M.S., Harvard U., 1964, Ph.D., 1965. Sr. scientist Raytheon Co., Wayland, Mass., 1962-68; mem. faculty dept. elec. engring. Cornell U., Ithaca, N.Y., 1968—, prof., 1976—; cons. Raytheon, Schlumberger, IBM. Author: Rate Distortion Theory, 1971. Recipient Frederick E. Terman award as outstanding young elec. engring. educator Elec. Engring. div. Am. Soc. for Engring. Edn., 1982; Guggenheim Found. fellow, 1975-76; Japan Soc. for Promotion of Sci. fellow, 1980-81; Ministry of Edn., Peoples Republic of China fellow, 1981. Mem. IEEE, IEEE Info. Theory Group (bd. govs. 1974-81, v.p. 1977-78, pres. 1979), AAAS, Sigma Xi, Tau Beta Pi. Office: Phillips Hall Cornell Univ Ithaca NY 14853

BERGERAC, MICHEL C., cosmetic and health care co. exec.; b. 1932; (married). B.A., Sorbonne U., Paris, M.A. in Econs, 1953; M.B.A., U. Calif. at Los Angeles, 1955. Asst. factory mgr. U.S. Divers Corp., Los Angeles, 1956-57; sales rep., then mgr., v.p. internat. Cannon Elec. Co., Los Angeles, 1957-66; chief exec. v.p., then pres. ITT Europe, Inc., 1966-74; pres., chief exec. officer, chmn. bd. Revlon, Inc., N.Y.C., 1974—; dir. Mfrs. Hanover Corp., CBS, Inc. Bd. dirs. World Wildlife Fund-U.S.; bd. overseers Cornell Med. Coll. and Grad. Sch. Med. Scis. Office: Revlon Inc 767 Fifth Ave New York NY 10022

BERGERON, CHARLES EDWARD, business executive; b. Hartford, Conn., July 23, 1945; s. Charles E. and Eileen (Healy) B.; m. Julie Pease, Aug. 18, 1968; children: Corrie, Ali. B.S., Rensselaer Poly. Inst., 1967, M.S., 1970; M.B.A., Columbia U., 1973. Systems engr., account rep. IBM, Albany, N.Y., 1967-69, fin. analyst, mgr. fin. services, Kingston, N.Y., 1973-76, pricing analyst, Harrison, N.Y., 1976; dir. planning and fin. analysis Freightliner Corp., Portland, Oreg., 1976-78, sr. v.p. fin., 1978—, also dir. Mem. Fin. Execs. Inst. Office: PO Box 3849 Portland OR 97208

BERGERON, CLIFTON GEORGE, ceramic engr., educator; b. Los Angeles, Jan. 5, 1925; s. Lewis G. and Rose C. (Dengel) B.; m. Laura H. Kaario, June 9, 1950; children—Ann Leija, Louis Kaario. B.S., U. Ill., 1950, M.S., 1959, Ph.D., 1961. Sr. ceramic engr. A. O. Smith Corp., Milw., 1950-55; staff engr. Whirlpool Corp., St. Joseph, Mich., 1955-57; research asso. U. Ill., Champaign-Urbana, 1957-61, asst. prof., 1961-63, asso. prof., 1963-67, prof., 1967-78, head dept. ceramic engring., 1978—; cons. A. O. Smith Corp., Whirlpool Corp., Ingraham Richardson, U.S. Steel Corp., Pfaudler Corp., Ferro Corp. Editor, Ann. Conf. on Glass Problems. Served in U.S. Army, 1943-46; ETO. NSF grantee, 1961—. Fellow Am. Ceramic Soc.; mem. AAAS, Nat. Inst. Ceramic Engrs., AAUP, KERAMOS, Am. Soc. Engring. Edn., Sigma Xi. Research in crystallization kinetics in glass; high temperature reactions. Invented high temperature catalytic coatings for oxidation. Home: 208 W Michigan St Urbana IL 61801 Office: 105 S Goodwin St Urbana IL 61801

BERGERON, JOHN JOSEPH MARCEL, cell biology and molecular endocrinology educctor; b. Belleville, Ont., Can., Dec. 22, 1946; s. Marcel and Florence Caroll (MacKay) B.; m. Jacqueline Marie-Therese Lanoix, May 1, 1971; children: Natasha, Fabien. B.S., McGill U., 1966; D.Phil., Oxford U., 1969. Research assoc. Rockefeller U., N.Y.C., 1969-71; mem. sci. staff Nat. Inst. Med. Research, Mill Hill, London, 1971-74; asst. prof. McGill U., Montreal, Que., Can., 1974-78, assoc. prof., 1978-82, prof., 1982—; mem. scholarships com. Med. Research Council, Ottawa, Ont., Can., 1979-81; mem. research adv. group, Toronto, 1980—; chmn. career awards Nat. Cancer Inst., 1981, chmn. molecular biology panel, 1982—. Recipient Murray J. Barr award Can. Assn. Anatomnists. Mem. Am. Soc. Cell Biology, Am. Soc. Biol. Chemists, Can. Soc. Cell Biology, Endocrine Soc. Home: 55 Highfield Town of Mount Royal PQ Canada H3P 1C5 Office: Dept Anatomy McGill Univ 3640 University St Montreal PQ Canada H3A 2B2

BERGERON, LAURENT ANDRE, mfg. co. exec.; b. Que., Can., June 28, 1935; s. Real and B.; m. Marcelle, Sept. 19, 1959; 1 dau., Danielle. R.I.A., McGill U., 1960; postgrad., Exec. Devel. Inst., Montreal, 1962-64, RIA Inst., Montreal, 1965-67, Can. Inst. Chartered Accts., 1972-73. Systems and procedures analyst Dominion Textile Co., 1952-60; asst. controller N. Bourassa Ltd., Montreal, 1960-64; chief works acct. Dominion Steel and Coal Corp. Ltd., Contrecoeur, Que., 1964-68; corp. controller Ingersoll-Rand (Can.) Ltd., 1968-74; v.p., chief fin. officer Internat. Paints (Can.) Ltd., Montreal, 1974-77; pres., chief exec. officer Can. Arsenals Ltd., Le Gardeur, Que., 1977—. Mem. C. of C., Am. Def. Preparedness Assn., Fin. Execs. Inst. Home: 202 Mgr de Belmon Boucherville PQ J4B 2K9 Canada Office: 5 Montee des Arsenaux Le Gardeur PQ J5Z 2P4 Canada

BERGERON, R. THOMAS, radiologist, educator; b. Chgo., Mar. 30, 1931. B.A., U. Ill., 1953, B. Medicine, 1954, M.D., 1957. Diplomate: Am. Bd. Radiology. Intern Henry Ford Hosp., Detroit; resident in radiology U. Ill. Research Hosp., Chgo., 1957-58; instr. radiology U. Ill. Coll. Medicine, Chgo., 1963-64; asst. in radiology Columbia U. Coll. Phys. and Surgs., N.Y.C., 1965-67; asst. prof. radiology and neurology U. So. Calif. Sch. Medicine, Los Angeles, 1967-69, assoc. prof., 1969-72, prof., 1972-74; prof. radiology, attending physician NYU Med. Ctr., N.Y.C., 1974—, dir. radiology Univ. Hosp., 1977—. Editor: Head and Neck Imaging, 1984. Served to capt. USAF, 1958-60. Mem. Radiol. Soc. N. Am., Am. Soc. Neuroradiology, Am. Soc. Head and Neck Radiology, Am. Coll. Radiology, Western Neuroradiol. Soc. (co-founder). Office: NYU Med Ctr 560 1st Ave New York NY 10016

BERGERON, VICTOR J., restaurateur; b. Calif., 1902; s. Victor and Marie (Camount) B. Ed. pub. schs., Calif. Opened restaurant Hinky Dink's, Oakland, Calif., 1934, 1938; founder, chmn. other Trader Vic's in cities including, N.Y.C., Chgo., Beverly Hills, Portland, Oreg., Seattle, Denver, Washington, Scottsdale, Ariz., Kansas City, Emeryville, Calif., San Francisco, Tokyo, Japan, Dallas, Houston, St. Louis, Atlanta, Toronto, Ont., Can., Vancouver, B.C., Can. and; London, Eng., Munich, Germany, Singapore. Address: 20 Cosmo Pl San Francisco CA 94109

BERGES, MARSHALL WILLIAM, newspaper columnist; b. Chgo.; s. Charles and Beatrice (Marin) B. Ed., Marquette U., U. Chgo. Columnist Los Angeles Times. Author: Corporations and the Quality of Life, 1972. Bd. dirs. Center Theater Group, Music Center, Los Angeles. Served with USNR. Office: Los Angeles Times Times Mirror Sq Los Angeles CA 90053

BERGESCH, LOUIS WILLIAM (BILL), sports association executive; b. St. Louis, June 17, 1927; s. Louis Woestman and Rose (Schiermeier) B.; m. Virginia Else Kammerer, Mar. 8, 1948; children: Robert, Susan. B.S. in Bus. Adminstrn., Washington U., St. Louis, 1948. Gen. mgr. minor leagues St. Louis Cardinals, 1948-60; asst. gen. mgr. Kansas City Athletics, Mo., 1961; pres. Pioneer Capital, N.Y.C., 1962-77; v.p. New York Yankees, Bronx, 1978—. Mem. N.Y. Housing Authority, Mamaroneck, 1969—, Westchester County Republican Com., N.Y. Methodist. Office: New York Yankees Yankee Stadium Bronx NY 10451

BERGESON, SCOTT, retail executive; b. Logan, Utah, Feb. 7, 1938; s. Harold E. and Reba M. (Butler) B.; m. Elaine Ann Johnson, Sept. 7, 1962; children: Eric S., Todd K., Paula A., Jill E., Amy K., Sean M. B.S., Brigham Young U., Provo, Utah, 1962, M.B.A., 1965. With Skaggs Cos., Inc., 1972-79, corp. sec., 1977-79; v.p., sec. Am. Stores Co., Salt Lake City, 1979-81; pres., chief exec. officer subs. co. Am. Stores Mgmt. Systems Co., 1981—. Democrat. Mormon. Office: 5201 Amelia Earhart Dr Salt Lake City UT 84130

BERGETHON, KAARE ROALD, college president; b. Tromso, Norway, June 8, 1918; came to U.S., 1926, naturalized, 1930; s. Maximilian and Petra Rudd (Olsen) B.; m. Katharine Lind, Apr. 4, 1942; children: Bruce L., Peter R. A.B., DePauw U., 1938; M.A., Cornell U., Ithaca, N.Y., 1940, Ph.D., 1945; Litt.D., Brown U., 1959, Franklin and Marshall Coll., 1959; LL.D., Rutgers U., 1959, Muhlenberg Coll., 1959, Lehigh U., 1959, Waynesburg Coll., 1960, DePauw U., 1961, Gannon Coll., 1978, Lafayette Coll., 1978, Temple U., 1978, Allegheny Coll., 1979, Bloomfield Coll., 1980. With Walter Kidde Constructors Inc., N.Y.C., 1938-39, 41-44; instr. German Syracuse (N.Y.) U., 1945-46, Brown U., 1946-47, asst. prof. German, asst. to chmn. div. modern langs., 1947-52, asso. dean, 1952-55, asso. prof. German, 1953-58, dean, 1955-58, prof. German, 1958; pres. Lafayette Coll., Easton, Pa., 1958-78, pres. emeritus, 1978—; interim chief exec. and cons. Bloomfield (N.J.) Coll., 1979-80; vice chmn. Econ. Devel. Council of N.Y.C., Inc. and; exec. dir. Nat. Alliance of Bus. of N.Y.C., 1980-81; interim pres. New Eng. Coll., Henniker, N.H., 1981-82, pres., 1982—; dir. Am. Home Products Corp. Author: Grammar for Reading German, 1950, alt. edit., 1963, rev. edit., 1979, also articles in profl. publs. Past pres. Presbyn. Coll. Union, Middle States Assn. Colls. and Secondary Schs. Mem. N.H. Coll. and Univ. Council, Pa. Assn. Colls. and Univs., Phi Beta Kappa, Phi Eta Sigma, Phi Kappa Phi, Beta Theta Pi, Sigma Delta Chi, Alpha Phi Omega. Presbyterian. Club: University (N.Y.C.). Home: Box 638 Henniker NH 03242

BERGGREN, RONALD BERNARD, surgeon; b. S.I., N.Y., June 13, 1931; s. Bernard and Florence (Schmidt) B.; m. Mary Beth Griffith, Nov. 25, 1954; children—Karen Ann, Eric Griffith. B.A., Johns Hopkins U., 1953; M.D., U. Pa., 1957. Diplomate Am. Bd. Surgery, Nat. Bd. Med. Examiners, Am. Bd. Plastic Surgery. Asst. instr. surgery U. Pa., 1958-62, instr., 1962-65; gen. surg. resident Hosp. U. Pa., 1958-62, resident plastic surgery, 1963-64, chief resident plastic surgery, 1964-65; sr. resident surgery Phila. Gen. Hosp., 1962-63; asst. prof. surgery Ohio State U. Sch. Medicine, 1965-68, dir. div. plastic surgery, 1965—, asso. prof. surgery, 1968-73, prof. surgery, 1973—; attending staff Ohio State U. Hosps., chief of staff, 1981—; attending staff, dir. div. plastic surgery Children's Hosp., Columbus, Ohio. Trustee Mid Ohio Health Planning Fedn., 1979—, PSRO, 1980—. Fellow A.C.S.; mem. Central, Columbus surg. socs., Am. Soc. Plastic and Reconstructive Surgeons, Ohio Valley Plastic Surg. Soc., Am. Cleft Palate Assn., AMA, Am. Assn. Plastic Surgeons, Franklin County Med. Soc., Soc. Cryosurgery, Plastic Surg. Research Council, Soc. Cryobiology, N.Y. Acad. Scis., Am. Assn. Surgery Trauma, Assn. Acad. Surgery, Am. Burn Assn., Am. Trauma Soc., Am. Soc. Aesthetic Plastic Surgery, Am. Soc. Maxillfacial Surgery, Sigma Xi, Phi Kappa Psi, Alpha Kappa Kappa. Home: 1960 Hampshire Rd Columbus OH 43221 Office: 410 W 10th Ave Columbus OH 43210

BERGGRUEN, JOHN HENRY, art gallery executive; b. San Francisco, June 18, 1943; s. Jeinz and Lillian Z. B. Pres., owner John Berggruen Gallery, San Francisco. Office: John Berggruen Gallery 228 Grant Ave San Francisco CA 94108

BERGHOLD, JOSEPH PHILIP, business executive; b. Allentown, Pa., Mar. 5, 1938; s. Joseph Norton and Cecilia (Boandl) B.; m. Kay Rose Binder, June 11, 1960; children: Karin A., J. Hans, Miles P. B.A., Muhlenberg Coll., 1960; M.B.A., NYU, 1963; postgrad. (Sloan fellow), Stanford U. Sch. Bus. Adminstrn., 1973. Asst. treas. Polymer Corp., Reading, Pa., 1967-69; fin. v.p., dir. Automated Health Systems, Burlingame, Calif., 1969-71; fin. v.p. Six Flags, Inc., Los Angeles, 1972; v.p., treas., group v.p. internat. operations Koracorp Industries, San Francisco, 1973-80; v.p., treas. Levi Strauss & Co., San Francisco, 1980-82; sr. v.p., chief fin. officer Ryan Homes, Inc., Pitts., 1983—; mem. businessmen's adv. bd. Golden Gate U., 1980—, San Francisco State U., 1980—. Trustee Muhlenberg Coll. Mem. Nat. Investor Inst. Republican. Home: Fairway Rd Sewickley Heights PA 15143

BERGIN, DANIEL TIMOTHY, lawyer, banker; b. New Rochelle, N.Y., Mar. 21, 1930; s. Daniel Timothy and Elsie (Dillon) B.; m. Ann Averill Edmunds, July 26, 1958; children: Daniel Hunt, Catherine Ann, Jeffrey Thomas, Brian McCormack. Student, Northwestern U., 1948-49; B.S., U. Ariz., 1952, J.D., 1957. Bar: Ariz. 1957. Practiced in, San Francisco, 1957-58, Phoenix, 1958—; clk. to Richard H. Chambers chief judge U.S. Ct. of Appeals, 9th Judicial Circuit, San Francisco, 1957-58; assoc. Fennemore, Craig, von Ammon & Udall, 1958-63, partner, 1964-72; v.p., counsel So. Ariz. Bank & Trust Co., Tucson, 1973-74; mem. Miller, Pitt & Feldman, Tucson, 1974-76; sr. v.p., gen. counsel Ariz. Bank, Phoenix, 1976—. Mem. Am., Ariz., Maricopa County bar assns., Am. Judicature Soc., Phi Delta Phi, Phi Gamma Delta. Republican. Roman Catholic. Club: Ariz. Country (Phoenix). Home: 2083 E Hermosa Dr Tempe AZ 85282 Office: 101 N 1st Ave Phoenix AZ 85003

BERGIN, JOHN FRANCIS, advertising agency executive; b. New Haven, Conn., Nov. 17, 1924; s. Frank;; s. Celia Leo and (Phillips) B.; m. Constance Horton, Aug. 26, 1950 (div.); children: Constance, Frank, Barbara, Katherine, John. A.B., Amherst Coll., 1950. With Batten, Barton, Durstin and Osborne, N.Y.C., 1950-73; became sr. v.p., asso. creative dir. and corp. dir.; exec. v.p., creative dir., corp. dir. and mem. exec. com. SSC&B, Inc. (Advt.), N.Y.C., 1974-81; vice chmn., dir. Coca-Cola Worldwide, also pres. U.S.A. region, 1981—. Bd. edn., Darien, Conn., 1968-74. Served with USAAF, 1943-46. Mem. Am. Assn. Advt. Agencies. Democrat. Roman Catholic. Club: Wee Burn Country. Office: McCann-Erickson Worldwide 485 Lexington Ave New York NY 10017

BERGIN, ROBERT P., foundation administrator; b. Waterbury, Conn., Aug. 9, 1934; s. Martin F. and Margaret M. (Fitzgerald) B. A.B., Harvard U., 1957, J.D., 1960. Bar: Mass. 1960; chartered financial analyst. Asst. mgr. Brown Bros. Harriman, N.Y.C., 1960-68; portfolio mgr. First Greenwich Co. (Conn.), 1969; assoc. dir. research Ford Found., N.Y.C., 1970-72; treas. Guggenheim Found., N.Y.C., 1973—; dir. corp. YADDO. Mem. N.Y. State Soc. Security Analysts, Financial Analysts Fedn., Inst. Chartered Financial Analysts. Clubs: Harvard (N.Y.C.); Apawamis (Rye, N.Y.). Home: 319 E 53d St New York NY 10022 Office: 90 Park Ave New York NY 10017

BERGLEITNER, GEORGE CHARLES, JR., investment banker; b. Bklyn., July 16, 1935; s. George Charles and Marie (Preitz) B.; m. Betty Van Buren, Oct. 29, 1966; children—George Charles III, Michael John, Stephen William. B.B.A., St. Francis Coll., Bklyn., 1959; M.B.A., Coll. City N.Y., 1961; Ph.D. in Bus. Adminstrn. (hon.), Colo. State Christian Coll. Dir. instl. sales A.T. Brod & Co., N.Y.C., 1965-66; dir. instl. sales Weis, Voisin & Cannon, Inc., N.Y.C., 1966-67, C.B. Richard, Ellis & Co., 1967-68; pres. M.J. Manchester & Co., Fashion & Time, Inc., B.J.B. Graphics, Inc., First Coinvestors, Inc., Smart Fit Foundations, Inc., Jay Co., Computer Holdings Corp., Ltd., Delhi Mfg. Corp.; pres. Delhi Chems., Inc., Walton; chmn. bd., dir. Delhi Industries, Delhi Mfg. Inc.; chmn. bd. Delhi Internat., Inc., Luxembourg.; Mem. Nat. Stock Exchange, N.Y. Merc. Exchange, Phila.-Balt.-Washington Stock Exchange. Chmn. Franciscan Fathers Devel. Program, 1967-71; mem. President's Council, Franciscan Spirit award, 1959—; pres. South Kortright Central Sch.; chmn. No. Catskills Econ. Devel. Council.; Regent St Francis Coll.; bd. dirs. Econ. Devel. Council Delaware County, Printing Trade Sch., Community Hosp., Stamford, N.Y., Western Catskills Community Revitalization Council, Inc. Served with U.S. Army, 1952-55. Recipient St. Francis Coll. Alumni Fund award, 1965; John F. Kennedy Meml. award, 1972; Internat. award for service to investment comm., 1972. Mem. Security Traders Assn. N.Y., Nat. Security Traders Assn., AIM, Cath. War Vets., Assn. Investment Bankers, Honor Legion N.Y.C. Police Dept., Coll. City N.Y. alumni assns. Republican. Clubs: K.C., Rotarian (pres. 1980-81), Moose., Stamford Country. Home: Red Rock Rd Hobart NY 13788 Office: Delhi Bldg South St Stamford NY 12167 *With all affluence, accomplishment, and success goes the responsibility of assistance; economic, social, and physical to the less fortunate of the world.*

BERGLES, ARTHUR EDWARD, mechanical engineering educator; b. N.Y.C., Aug. 9, 1935; s. Edward H. and Victoria (Winkelmann) B.; m. Priscilla Lou Maule, June 19, 1960; children: Eric, Dwight. S.B., S.M., MIT, 1958, Ph.D., 1962. Registered profl. engr., Mass. Research staff Nat. Magnet Lab., Cambridge, Mass., 1962-69; asst. prof. to assoc. prof. mech. engring. MIT, Cambridge, 1963-69, assoc. dir. heat transfer lab., 1966-69; prof. mech. engring. Ga. Inst. Tech., Atlanta, 1969-72; prof., chmn. dept. mech. engring. Iowa State U., Ames, 1972-83, prof., 1983—; U.S. rep. Internat. Heat Transfer Conf., 1978-82; chmn. U.S. group heat transfer/U.S. USSR Agreement, Washington, 1979-82; cons. to industry. Co-author: Two-Phase Flow and Heat Transfer in the Power and Process Industries, 1981; co-editor: Heat Exchangers, 1981, Two-Phase Flow Dynamics, 1981, Low Reynolds Number Flow Heat Exchangers, 1983; editorial adv. bd. 6 jours.; contbr. numerous articles to tech. jours. Scoutmaster Boy Scout Am., Ames, 1976—; bd. dirs. Ames Soc. for Arts, 1975-79; mem. Ames Energy Adv. Com., 1983—. Fulbright fellow Technische Hochschule, Munich, W.Ger., 1958-59; recipient U.S. Sr. Scientist award Alexander von Humboldt Found., U. Hanover, W.Ger., 1979-80, Heat Transfer Meml. award ASME, 1979; Anson Marston Disting. prof. engring. Iowa State U., 1981; Honor lectr. Mid-Am. State Univs. Assn., 1983-84. Fellow ASME (v.p. 1981—, chmn. heat transfer div. 1982-83); mem. Am. Inst. Chem. Engrs., Am. Soc. Engring. Edn., ASHRAE, Theta Chi. Republican. Lutheran. Lodge: Rotary (Ames). Office: Dept Mech Engring Iowa State U Ames IA 50011 *My personal philosophy is to do as many things as I can, always striving for excellence and professionalism.*

BERGLUND, CARL NEIL, electronics company executive; b. Thunder Bay, Ont., Can., July 21, 1938; came to U.S., 1978; s. Anton Robert and Mary (Sideen) B.; m. Evelyn Jean McEvilla, Apr. 1, 1961; children: Cheryl Lynn, Gregory Neil, Carl Anton. B.S. with honors, Queen's U., Kingston, Ont., 1960; M.S. in Elec. Engring., MIT, 1961; Ph.D. in Elec. Engring., Stanford U., 1964. Mem. tech staff Bell Labs., Murray Hill, N.J., 1964-66, supr. semicond. devices, 1966-72; mgr. electronic materials Bell No. Research, Ottawa, 1972-73; v.p. tech. Microsystems Internat., Ottawa, 1973-74; dir. silicon technology Bell No. Research, Ottawa, 1974-78; dir. tech. devel. Intel Corp., Aloha, Oreg., 1978—. Contbr. articles to profl. jours.; patentee (in field). Fellow IEEE; mem. Electron Devices Soc. Home: 5 Cellini Ct Lake Oswego OR 97034 Office: Intel Corp 3585 SW 198th Ave Aloha OR 97034

BERGLUND, ROBIN GUNNAR, real estate development company executive; b. Milw., Oct. 12, 1945; s. Gunnar Emmanuel and Viola June (Huebsch) B.; children: Victoria Suzanne, Christopher Frederick. B.S. in Biochemistry magna cum laude, Mich. State U., 1967; M.B.A., Harvard U., 1971; grad., Corp. Fin. Mgmt. Program, 1981, U. Calif., 1980. Photog. engr. Eastman Kodak Co., Rochester, N.Y., 1967-69; asst. v.p., regional mgr. 1st Nat. Bank of Chgo., Chgo., Los Angeles, 1971-75; v.p., dept. head Wells Fargo Bank, Los Angeles, 1975-77; v.p., treas. Aetna Realty Group, Ponderosa Homes, Aetna Diversified Properties, Irvine, Calif., 1977—; instr. sci., math. Rochester Inst. Tech., 1968-69; instr. real estate investment UCLA, 1977. Bd. dirs. Bob Hope United Service Orgn., Hollywood, Calif., 1973-76. Nat. Merit scholar, 1964-67; Nat. Honor Soc. scholar, 1964-67; NSF research grantee, 1965-66. Mem. Urban Land Inst., Fin. Execs. Inst., Bldg. Industries Assn. (home builders council), Nat. Assn. Corp.

Treas., Blue Key, Phi Kappa Phi, Omicron Delta Kappa, Delta Phi Epsilon, Tau Sigma. Republican. Clubs: Harvard (Los Angeles, Orange County); Jonathan (Los Angeles). Office: Aetna Realty Group Ponderosa Homes 2082 Business Center Dr Irvine CA 92715

BERGMAN, ALAN, lyricist; b. Bklyn., Sept. 11, 1925; s. Sammuel and Ruth (Margulies) B.; m. Marilyn Keith, Feb. 9, 1958; 1 dau., Julie Rachel. Grad., Ethical Culture Sch.; B.A., U. N.C.; postgrad., UCLA. TV dir. CBS, Phila., 1949-53. Wrote for: TV prodn. Shower of Stars; spls. for, Jo Stafford, songs for, Fred Astaire, Marge and Gower Champion; author songs for revues, night clubs, films; stage scores include Ice Capades of 1957; lyricist: songs Ol' MacDonald; songs for films The Promise; albums include Aesop's Fables. Served with AUS, 1943-45. Recipient Acad. award for best song, 1968, 73; Acad. award, Grammy award for The Way We Were, 1974; Emmy award for lyrics for Queen of the Stardust Ballroom, 1975. Mem. ASCAP. Address: care Freedman Kinzelberg & Broder 1801 Ave of Stars Los Angeles CA 90067 *

BERGMAN, DANIEL, retail exec.; b. Chgo., May 3, 1938; s. Harold and Florence B. B.A. in English, Ohio State U., 1960. With Bamberger's, div. R.H. Macy and Co., Inc., Newark, 1964—, sr. v.p., dir. personnel and labor relations, 1973—, dir. stores merchandising and display, 1976—. Office: Bamberger's 131 Market St Newark NJ 07101

BERGMAN, ELLEN SHONG, government official; b. Flint, Mich., Oct. 11, 1947; d. Robert L. and Betty Jane (Fredericks) Shong; m. karl G. Bergman, Apr. 30, 1983. B.S., Mich. State U., 1969; J.D., U. Ariz., 1975. Adminstrv. asst., atty. Tucson Gas & Electric Co., 1973-76; personnel adminstr. Climax Molybdenum Co., Climax, Colo., 1976-77; div. mgr. EEO Affirmative Action (Climax Molybdenum Co.), Greenwich, Conn., 1977, corp. dir. EEO, Greenwich, 1978-81; dir. office of Fed. Contract Compliance Dept. Labor, Washington, 1981—. Republican. Roman Catholic. Office: Dept Labor 200 Constitution Ave NW Washington DC 20210

BERGMAN, ERNST INGMAR, film writer, dir.; b. Uppsala, Sweden, July 14, 1918; m. Ingrid Karlebovon Rosen; 8 children. Ed., Stockholm U. Producer Royal Theatre, Stockholm, 1940-42; producer, writer Swedish Film Co., 1940-44; theatrical dir., Helsingborg, 1944-46, Gothenburg, 1946-49, Malmo, 1952-59. Writer: screenplay Torment, 1943; dir.: films Crisis, 1945, A Ship Bound For India, 1947, Summer Interlude, 1950, Summer with Monika, 1952, Sawdust and Tinsel, 1953, Lesson in Love, 1954, Journey into Autumn, 1955, Smiles of a Summer Night, 1956 (Cannes Film Festival award), Seventh Seal, 1957 (Cannes Film Festival award), So Close to Life, 1958 (Cannes Film Festival award), The Magician, 1958, Wild Strawberries, 1958 (Berlin Film Festival award), The Virgin Spring, 1960 (Acad. award), The Devil's Eye, 1961, Through a Glass Darkly, 1961, Winter Light, 1962, The Silence, 1963, Now About All These Women, 1964, Persona, 1967, Hour of the Wolves, 1968, The Shame, 1969, The Passion of Anna, 1970, The Touch, 1971, Cries and Whispers, 1972, Scenes from a Marriage, Fanny and Alexander, 1983 (Acad. Award Best Foreign Language Film Dir. 1984); also TV, 1974, The Magic Flute, 1975, Face to Face, 1975, The Serpent's Egg, 1977, Autumn Sonata, 1978, Summer Paradise, 1978; head: Summer Paradise, Royal Dramatic Theatre, Stockholm, 1963-66; plays produced Hedda Gabler, Cambridge, 1970, Slow, 1971 (Recipient Netherland's Erasmus award for contbn. to arts 1965, Best dir. award Nat. Soc. Film Critics 1970, Best Film award for Cries and Whispers, N.Y. Film Critics 1972, Goethe prize 1976); Author: Four Stories, 1977 *

BERGMAN, HARRY, physician; b. N.Y.C., Oct. 25, 1912; s. Sam and Pauline (Freedman) B.; m. Tillie Simon, Feb. 16, 1936 (dec. Feb. 1957); m. Mollie Holtzman, Apr. 2, 1958. M.D., U. Buffalo, 1934. Diplomate: Am. Bd. Urology. Intern Lebanon Hosp., N.Y.C., 1934-36; resident Morrisania City Hosp., N.Y.C., became attending urologist, 1958—, now hon. vis. urologist; practice medicine specializing in urology, N.Y.C., 1936-78; attending urologist Bronx Lebanon Hosp. Center, 1953-79, cons., 1979—; staff Jewish Meml. Hosp., 1960-79, cons., 1979—; Flower-Fifth Ave. Hosp., Met. Hosp., all N.Y.C.; past dir. urology Hebrew Home for Aged, Riverdale, N.Y., to 1978; cons. staff St. Clare-St. Elizabeth's Hosp. Assn.; clin. prof. urology N.Y. Med. Coll., 1966—, U. Miami Med. Sch., 1983—. Numerous publs. in urol. lit.; Editor-in-chief: The Ureter, 1967, 2d edit., 1981; co-editor: column Urologic-Radiologic Revs. in N.Y. State Jour. Medicine; Contbr.: to book Current Operative Urology, 1973, 2d edit., 1984, Current Urologic Therapy, 2d edit.; urologic book reviewer: N.Y. State Jour. Medicine; Jour. AMA. Recipient Honor award Bronx physicians div. State of Israel-Fedn. Jewish Philenthropies, 1969; citation Am. Cancer Soc. Fellow A.C.S. (exec. com. 1962—, pres. Bronx chpt. 1965—), Am. Urol. Soc., N.Y. Acad. Medicine; mem. AMA, Am. Trauma Soc. (founder), Bronx County Med. Soc., Am. Soc. Clin. Urologists, New York State Soc. Surgeons (dir.), Am. Geriatric Soc., Pan. Am. Med. Assn. (hon. life mem. sect. urology), Met. Med. Alumni U. Buffalo (pres. gen. alumni 1958—), Magicians Guild Am., Physicians Square Club Am., Alpha Omega Alpha. Lodge: Masons. Research and publs. on cancer of ureter; new radiol. sign for cancer ureter called Bergman's Sign. Designer cancer biopsy instrument, 1947, and new prostate catheter, 1958. Home: 4200 Hillcrest Dr Apt 219 Bldg 24 Hollywood FL 33021 *Ethics must be respected, and one's responsibility must come above all things—equal to love of family. Success by competance must be the rule.*

BERGMAN, JULES VERNE, broadcast journalist; b. N.Y.C., Mar. 21, 1929; s. Irving and Ruth B.; m. Joanne, Jan. 11, 1953; children: David, Beth, Karen. Student, CCNY, 1946, Ind. U., 1947, Columbia U., 1948-50; postgrad. (Sloan-Rockefeller Advanced Sci. Writing fellow), Sch. Journalism, 1960-61. News desk asst. CBS News, N.Y.C., 1947-48; writer trainee Time mag., N.Y.C., 1948-50; asst. news dir. Sta.-WFDR, N.Y.C., 1950-51; jr. writer ABC News, N.Y.C., 1953, sr. writer, reporter, 1955-59, sci. editor, 1961—; tech. adv. Inst. Sports Medicine and Athletic Trauma, Lenox Hill Hosp. Author: 90 Seconds to Space, 1962, Anyone Can Fly, 1965, rev. edit., 1978; writer, narrator: documentary Fire, 1974 (Emmy award 1975), Weekend Athletes, 1975, Danger in Sports, 1975, Dupont, 1982, Crashes, Illusions of Safety, 1975, Asbestos: The Way to Dusty Death, 1978. Mem. Nat. Assn. Sci. Writers., Aviation Writers Assn. Club: Wings (v.p. 1976). Office: ABC News 7 W 66th St New York NY 10023 *

BERGMAN, KLAUS, lawyer, electric utility holding company executive; b. b., Nurnberg, Ger., May 24, 1931; came to U.S., 1936; s. Ludwig and Else (Wartheimer) B.; m. Barbara E. Redman, Jan. 30, 1954; children: Nicole V.F., Cathryn L. A.B., Columbia U., 1953, LL.B., 1955. Bar: N.Y. Assoc. Mudge Rose Guthrie & Alexander, N.Y.C., 1959-65; asst. gen. counsel Am. Electric Power Service Corp., N.Y.C., 1965-71; v.p. Allegheny Power System, Inc., N.Y.C., 1971-78, exec. v.p., 1982—, dir. various subs.; dir. Ohio Valley Electric Co., N.Y.C. Served to lt. USCGR, 1956-59. Jewish. Office: Allegheny Power System Inc 320 Park Ave New York NY 10022

BERGMAN, MARILYN KEITH, author, lyricist; b. Bklyn., Nov. 10; d. Albert A. and Edith (Arkin) Katz; m. Alan Bergman, Feb. 9, 1958; 1 dau., Julie Rachel. B.A., NYU. Numerous revues, songs for night clubs and films, numerous TV prodns. for Shower of Stars; spls. for, Jo Stafford, songs for, Fred Astaire, Marge and Gower Champion; stage scores include Ice Capades of 1957; lyricist: songs Marriage-go-Round; film Ol' MacDonald, You Don't Bring Me Flowers; title song for film In the Heat of the Night; other songs for films Same Time Next Year; Broadway lyrics include Ballroom; albums include Aesop's Fables. Recipient Acad. Award nominations for fils songs: What Are You Doing the Rest of Your Life, Pieces of Dreams, All His Children, Marmalade, Molasses and Honey, The Last Time I Felt Like This, I'll Never Say Goodbye, Acad. Award for The Windmills of Your Mind, 1968, Acad. Award for The Way We Were, 1974, Golden Globe award for Windmills of Your Mind, 1968, Grammy award for The Way We Were, 1974, Emmy award for Queen of the Stardust Ballroom, 1975, Acad. Award for best film score adaptation for Yentl, 1984; Am. Film Inst. grantee, 1976. Mem. ASCAP. Address: care Freeman Kinzelberg & Broder 1801 Ave of Stars Los Angeles CA 90067 *

BERGMAN, ROBERT GEORGE, chemist; b. Chgo., May 23, 1942; s. Joseph J. and Stella (Horowitz) B.; m. Wendy L. Street, June 17, 1965; children: David R., Michael S. B.A. cum laude in chemistry, Carleton Coll., 1963; Ph.D. (NIH fellow), U. Wis., 1966. NATO fellow in chemistry Columbia U., N.Y.C., 1966-67; Arthur Amos Noyes instr. chemistry Calif. Inst. Tech., Pasadena, 1967-69, asst. prof. chemistry, 1969-71, asso. prof. chemistry, 1971-73, prof., 1973-77; prof. chemistry U. Calif. at Berkeley, 1977—, Miller Research prof., 1982-83; cons. DuPont Co, 1981—; vis. asso. prof. Stanford U., 1972; vis. prof. Iowa State U., 1975; vis. faculty asso. IBM Research Corp., San Jose, 1974; Sherman Fairchild Disting. scholar Calif. Inst. Tech., 1984; Disting. vis. lectr. U. Tex., 1983; Dains Meml. lectr. U. Kans., 1983; mem. panel NIH bioinorganic and metallobiochemistry study sect. NIH, 1977-80. Mem. editorial bd.: Organometallics, Jour. Organic Chemistry, Chem. Revs.; contbr. articles to profl. jours. Alfred P. Sloan Found. fellow, 1970-72; recipient Camille and Henry Dreyfus Found. Tchr. Scholar award, 1970-75; Excellence in Teaching award Calif. Inst. Tech., 1978. Mem. N.Y. Acad. Scis., Phi Beta Kappa, Sigma Xi, Phi Lambda Upsilon. Home: 501 Coventry Rd Kensington CA 94707 Office: Dept Chemistry U Calif Berkeley CA 94720

BERGMAN, ROBERT PAUL, museum administrator, art historian, educator, lecturer; b. Bayonne, N.J., May 17, 1945; s. Abe and Ethel (Leitner) B.; m. Marcelle Posnak, June 30, 1971. B.A., Rutgers U., 1966; M.F.A., Princeton U., 1969, Ph.D., 1972. Asst prof. history of art U. Rochester, N.Y., 1971-72; asst. prof. history of art Princeton U., N.J., 1972-76; assoc. prof. Harvard U., Cambridge, 1976-81; prof. Johns Hopkins U., Balt., 1981—; dir. Walters Art Gallery, Balt., 1981—; vis. instr. Lincoln U., fall 1968. Author: The Salerno Ivories, 1980; cons. editor: Art Bull.; contbr. articles and revs. in art field. Vol. various mayoral coms., Balt., fundraiser various causes, Balt. Guggenheim fellow; Dumbarton Oaks fellow; Fulbright fellow; Henry Rutgers scholar. Fellow Am. Acad. in Rome; mem. Assn. Art Mus. Dirs., Coll. Art Assn., Internat. Ctr. of Medieval Art (dir.), AAUP, Soc. Archtl. Historians. Office: The Walters Art Gallery 600 N Charles St Baltimore MD 21201

BERGMAN, WILLIAM I., consumer products co. exec.; b. Reading, Pa., Sept. 28, 1931; s. Norman L. and Mary L. (Beck) B.; m. Donna K. Rupert, May 7, 1955; children—Kathryn L., Eric W., David W., Susan G. B.B.A., Drexel U., Phila., 1954; grad., Advanced Mgmt. Program, Harvard U., 1976. With Richardson-Vicks Inc., 1954—; pres. Vicks health care div. USA, 1977-80, corp. exec. v.p., Wilton, Conn., 1980—. Served to 1st lt. AUS, 1955-56. Mem. Proprietary Assn. (exec. com.). Republican. Lutheran. Home: 31 Norfield Rd Weston CT 06883 Office: 10 Westport Rd Wilton CT 06897

BERGMANN, BARBARA ROSE, economics educator; b. N.Y.C., July 20, 1927; d. Martin and Nellie (Wallenstein) Berman; m. Fred H. Bergmann, July 14, 1965; children: Sarah Nellie, David Martin. B.A., Cornell U., 1948; M.A., Radcliffe Coll.-Harvard U., 1955, Ph.D., 1959. Economist U.S. Bur. Labor Stats., N.Y.C., 1949-53; sr. staff ecomomist, cons. Council Econ. Advisors, Washington, 1961-62; mem. sr. staff Brookings Inst., Washington, 1963-65; sr. econ. advisor AID, Washington, 1966-67; assoc. prof. U. Md., College Park, 1965-71, prof. econs., 1971—. Author: (with Chinitz and Hoover) Projection of A Metropolis, 1961, (with George W. Wilson) Impact of Highway Investment on Development, 1966, (with David E. Kaun) Structural Unemployment in the U.S., 1967; mem. bd. editors: Am. Econ. Rev., 1970-73, Challenge, 1978—, Signs, 1978—; colomnist econ. affairs, N.Y. Times, 1981-82. Mem. Economists for McGovern, 1977; mem. panel econ. advisors Congl. Budget Office, Washington, 1977—; mem. price adv. com. U.S. council on Wage and Price Stability, Washington, 1979-80. Mem. Am. Econ. Assn. (v.p. 1976, adv. com. to U. S. Census Bur. 1977-82), Eastern Econ. Assn. (pres. 1974), AAUP (council mem. 1980-83), Phi Beta Kappa. Democrat. Home: 6700 Selkirk Dr Bethesda MD 20817 Office: Dept Econs U Md College Park MD 20742

BERGMANN, FRED HEINZ, scientist, govt. ofcl.; b. Feuchtwangen, Germany, Jan. 26, 1928; came to U.S., 1939; s. Milan and Meda (Bernet) B.; m. Barbara R. Berman, July 16, 1965; children—Sarah, David. B.S., Mass. Inst. Tech., 1951, M.S., 1951; Ph.D., U. Wis., 1957. Jr. biochemist Ethicon Sutures Labs., New Brunswick, N.J., 1951-53; fellow Washington U., St. Louis, 1957-59, Brandeis U., 1959-61; research chemist Nat. Dental Inst., NIH, Bethesda, Md., 1961-63, Nat. Heart Inst., 1963-65; program adminstr. Nat. Inst. Gen. Med. Scis., 1965-72, program dir. genetics program, 1972—; professorial lectr. George Washington U., 1966-67. Mem. Am. Soc. Human Genetics, Sigma Xi. Home: 6700 Selkirk Dr Bethesda MD 20817 Office: Genetics Program Nat Inst Med Scis NIH 5333 Westbard Ave Bethesda MD 20205

BERGMANN, FREDRICK LOUIS, english educator; b. Tecumseh, Kans., Sept. 27, 1916; s. Curt and Minna (Herrmann) B.; m. Jean Marshall, July 6, 1941; children: Juliann, John Fredrick. A.B., Washburn Coll., 1937; M.A., State Coll. Wash., 1939; postgrad., Columbia, 1941; Ph.D., George Washington U., 1953. Asst. Washburn Coll., 1939-40; instr. English DePauw U., 1940-43, asst. prof., 1943-46, asso. prof., 1946-54, prof., 1954-82; prof. emeritus Depauw U., 1982—; head dept. English DePauw U., 1956-78; dir. Conf. Am. Studies, 1956-78, James Whitcomb Riley prof. English lit., 1969—, also chmn. internat. edn. com. Author: (with R.W. Pence) Writing Craftsmanship, 1956, Paragraph Rhetoric, 1967, Sentence Rhetoric, 1969, Essays: Method, Content, Conscience, 1970, Essays 2, 1975, (with H.W. Pedicord) The Plays of David Garrick, 7 vols, 1979-82; contbr. articles to profl. jours. Founder Greencastle Summer Theater, 1962; pres. English dept. chmn. Gt. Lakes Colls. Assn., 1968-69. Fellow Folger Shakespeare Library, 1951, Grad. Council George Washington U. Mem. Ind. Coll. English Assn. (pres. 1956, 63), Modern Lang. Assn., Am. Soc. 18th Century Studies, Societe francaise d'Etude du XVIIe Siecle, Am. English-Speaking Union, Sigma Delta Chi (Leather Medal award for greatest service to DePauw U. 1962), Delta Chi. Episcopalian. Home: 205 N Arlington Ave Greencastle IN 46135

BERGMANN, PETER GABRIEL, research physicist, educator; b. Berlin, Germany, Mar. 24, 1915; came to U.S., 1936, naturalized, 1942; s. Max and Emmy Miriam (Grunwald) B.; m. Margot Eisenhardt, May 23, 1936; children: Ernest, John. Student, Prague, Czechoslovakia, 1933; Dr.rer.-nat., 1936; Dr.rer.-nat. h.c., Tech. U. Dresden, 1979. Research asst. to Prof. A. Einstein, Inst. Advanced Study, 1936-41; asst. prof. physics Black Mountain Coll., 1941, Lehigh U., 1942-44; war work Columbia, also Woods Hole Oceanographic Inst., 1944-47; asso. prof. physics Syracuse U., 1947-50, prof. physics, 1950—; adj. prof. Poly. Inst. Bklyn., 1947-57; vis. prof. physics Yeshiva U., 1959-63, 70-78; prof. physics, chmn. dept. physics Belfer Grad. Sch. Sci., 1963-64; vis. faculty King's Coll., London, also; Stockholm, 1958; summer Inst. Italian Math., 1958; lectr. Internat. Center for Sci. Culture, Erice, Sicily, 1975, 77, course dir., 1979; vis. pres. NYU, 1982-83; Mem. Internat. Commn. on Relativity and Gravitation, 1959—,, pres., Mem., 1977-80, dep. pres., 1980—. Author: grad. texts on relativity, introduction to theoretical physics, also The Riddle of Gravitation; Contbr. research articles to various jours.; articles on spl. and gen. relativity in Ency. Brit; Asso. editor profl. jours. Trustee New Lincoln Sch., 1963-70. Recipient Pregel award for research in physics N.Y. Acad. Scis., 1970. Fellow Am. Phys. Soc., AAAS; mem. Am. Math. Soc., German Physics Soc., Fedn. Am. Scientists (chmn. 1964), European Phys. Soc., Sigma Xi. Office: Dept Physics Syracuse U Syracuse NY 13210

BERGMANN, ROBERT LEWIS, banker; b. St. Louis, Jan. 21, 1926; s. William G. and Elvera (Baum) B.; m. Dorothy E. Thoma, July 24, 1954; children: Laura A., Alice M., Thomas C., Karen S. B.S. in Commerce, St. Louis U., 1949. C.P.A., Mo. Sr. auditor Arthur Andersen & Co., St. Louis, 1949-55; mgr. adminstrv. data processing McDonnell Aircraft Corp., St. Louis, 1955-64; v.p. data processing Merc. Trust Co., N.A., St. Louis, 1964-73, sr. v.p., 1973-77, sr. v.p. data processing and ops. depts., 1977-80, exec. v.p., 1980—; dir., mem. exec. com. Payment and Adminstrv. Communications Corp.; dir., treas., mem. exec. com. Payment and Telecommunications Services Corp.; chmn. bd. Payment and Adminstrv. Communication Services Corp., 1980-83, dir., Monetary Transfer System. Served with AUS, 1944-45. Mem. Assn. Systems Mgmt. (Achievement award 1982, Merit award 1974), Data Processing Mgmt. Assn., Am. Inst. C.P.A.s. Roman Catholic. Club: Mo. Athletic (St. Louis). Office: PO Box 524 Saint Louis MO 63166

BERGOLD, HARRY EARL, JR., diplomat; b. Olean, N.Y., Nov. 11, 1931; s. Harry Earl and Juniata V. (Glosser) B.; m. Karlene G. Knieps. B.A., Yale U., 1953, M.A., 1957. Commd. fgn. service officer Dept. State, 1957, Econ. officer, 1958-60; 3d. sec. embassy, Tegucigalpa, Honduras, 1960-62, 2d sec. embassy, Mexico City, 1962-64; polit. officer Dept. State, 1964-67; polit. mil. counsellor U.S. Embassy, Madrid, Spain, 1967-72; polit. counsellor Am. Embassy, Panama, 1972; dep. asst. sec. def. for NATO/European affairs Dept. Def., Washington, 1973-75, prin. dep. asst. sec. def. for legis. affairs, 1976-77; asst. sec of energy for internat. affairs Dept. Energy, Washington, 1977-79; Am. ambassador to Hungary, Budapest, 1980-84, Nicaragua, Managua, 1984—. Served with U.S. Army, 1954-56. Address: US Embassy - Nicaragua APO Miami FL 34021

BERGONIA, R. DAVID, lawyer; b. Spring Valley, Ill., May 21, 1951; s. Raymond A. and Elva M. (Bernadini) B. B.B.A., U. Notre Dame, 1973; J.D., Harvard U., 1976. Bar: Ill. 1976, U.S. Dist. Ct. (no. dist.) Ill. 1976. Assoc. Winston & Strawn, Chgo., 1976-79; legal counsel, sec. Heizer Corp., Chgo., 1979—; dir. Vacation Resorts, Inc., Aspen, Colo., Vacation Resorts Holdings, Inc. Treas. Wrigthwood Dayton Condominium Assn., 1982, 83. Recipient Elijah Watts Sells award Am. Inst. C.P.A.s, 1973. Mem. ABA, Chgo. Bar Assn. Home: 842 W Wrightwood Apt 3 Chicago Il 60614 Office: Heizer Corp 20 N Wacker Dr Chicago IL 60606

BERGONZI, CARLO, tenor; b. Vidalenzo, Italy, July 13, 1924; m. Adele; 2 children. Studied at, Arrigo Boito Conservatory, Parma, Italy. Operator hotel-restaurant, Busseto, Italy. Debut in opera as baritone in: The Barber of Seville; as Figaro, Lecce, Italy, 1948; debut as tenor in title role of: Andrea Chenier, Teatro Petruzelli, Bari, Italy, 1951, Am. debut, Lyric Opera Chgo., 1955; Met. Opera debut as Radames in: Aida, 1956; appeared in maj. opera cos. through, Europe, North and South Am., including, La Scala, Vienna State Opera, Hamburg (Germany) Opera, Rome Opera, Phila. Grand Opera, Teatro Colon. Office: care Herbert H Breslin Inc 119 W 57th St New York NY 10019

BERGQUIST, GREGORY DAVID, home furnishings manufacturing company executive; b. Spokane, Wash., Nov. 20, 1945; s. George W. and Eleanor W. (Woods) B.; m. Sarah H. Stephens, Aug. 7, 1976; children: John Randol, Ann Warren, S. Parrish. B.A., Whitman Coll., 1968; M.B.A., Dartmouth, 1970. Second v.p. Chase Manhattan Bank, N.Y.C., 1972-73; 2asst. treas., asst. sec. Simmons Co., 1973-74, treas., sec., Atlanta, 1975—, v.p., 1978—; pres. Meadowcraft, Inc., 1979—. Office: Box 1357 Birmingham AL 35201

BERGQUIST, ROBERT LOUIS, army officer; b. Whitinsville, Mass., May 7, 1931; s. Harold George and Edna Katherine B.; m. Marcia Alice Johnston, Nov. 26, 1955; children: Paul Roberts, Katherine Tracy. A.B., Providence Coll., 1954; M.B.A., Wharton Sch., U. Pa., 1969; grad., Armed Forces Staff Coll., 1968, Indsl. Coll. Armed Forces, 1971. Commd. 2d lt. U.S. Army, 1954, advanced through grades to lt. gen., 1977; comdr. co., Germany, 1957-59, project mgr., Detroit, 1964-67, research and devel. staff officer, Vietnam, 1963, ops. research analyst, Washington, 1971-73, comdr. Anniston (Ala.) Army Depot, 1973-76, comdr. Army Depot System Command, Chambersburg, Pa., 1977-79, dep. comdr. U.S. Army Materiel Devel. and Readiness Command, Washington, 1979-83, comdr. U.S. Army Logistics Ctr., Ft. Lee, Va, 1983—. Decorated Legion of Merit with 2 oak leaf clusters, Army Commendation medal with 3 oak leaf clusters; recipient Personal Achievement award Providence Coll., 1977, Community Involvement award Anniston C. of C., 1975; State of Ala. named Aug. 20, 1976 Bob Bergquist Day. Mem. Assn. U.S. Army, Am. Def. Preparedness Assn., Army Aviation Assn. Home: 338 Buna Rd Fort Lee VA 23801 Office: US Army Logistics Ctr Fort Lee VA 23801

BERGSMA, DANIEL, medical foundation executive; b. Wallington, N.J., Apr. 4, 1909; s. Chris and Henrietta (Hengeveld) B.; m. Nellie Dorothy Arnold, June 1937; children: Donald Roy, Claire. A.B., Oberlin Coll., 1932; M.D., Yale, 1936; M.P.H., U. Mich., 1946. Diplomate: Am. Bd. Preventive Medicine and Pub. Health. Chief bur. venereal disease control N.J. Dept. Health, 1940-42, dep. dir., 1946-48, state commnr. health, 1948- 59; asso. dir. med. care Nat. Found., 1959-64, dir. med. dept., 1964-69, v.p. for med. services, 1968-69, dir. profl. edn. dept., v.p. for profl. edn., 1969-78; clin. prof. pediatrics Tufts U. Sch. Medicine, Boston, 1975—. Editor: Birth Defects: Original Article Series, 1965-78, Birth Defects Atlas and Compendium, 1973-83, Birth Defects: Syndrome Identification, 1973—; sr. cons. editor: Jour. Clin. Dysmorphology, 1983—. Mem. Interstate San Commn., N.Y., Conn., N.J., 1951-59, Fed. Water Pollution Control Adv. Bd., 1954-57; conf. dir. 2d Internat. Conf. Congenital Malformations, 1963; former mem. adv. bd. state ofcls. AEC; chmn. adv. com. div. occupational health USPHS, 1958, past mem. nat. research pub. health study sect.; Past pres., chmn. bd. dirs. Christian Health Care Center, Wyckoff, N.J. Served from capt. to col. M.C. AUS, 1942-46. Decorated Legion of Merit. Mem. Am. Social Hygiene Assn. (hon. life), Am. Mgmt. Assn. (past pres. N.J. div.), AMA. Mem. Christian Ref. Ch. (elder 1959—, v.p. 1973-81). Home: 98 Suncrest Ave North Haledon NJ 07508

BERGSMA, WILLIAM LAURENCE, composer; b. Oakland, Calif., Apr. 1, 1921; s. William Joseph and Helen Margaret (Doepfner) B.; m. Nancy Nickerson, 1946. Student, Stanford U., 1938-40; teaching fellow, Eastman Sch. Music, 1942-44; A.B., U. Rochester, 1942, Mus.M., 1943. Faculty Juilliard Sch. Music, 1946—, chmn. composition dept., also chmn. dept. lit. and materials of music, assoc. dean, N.Y.C., 1961-63, prof., 1963—; dir. Sch. Music, U. Wash., Seattle, 1963-71; vis. prof. Bklyn. Coll., CUNY, 1972-73. Composer: ballet Gold and the Señor Commandante, 1942, First Quartet, 1942, Symphony for Chamber Orchestra, 1942; Music on a Quiet Theme, 1943; Composer Second Quartet, 1944; Composer: Six Songs, 1945, Suite from Children's Film, 1945, Symphony, 1949; string orch. The Fortunate Islands, 1947, rev. 1956; piano solo Tangents, 1951; Third Quartet, 1953; orch. A Carol on Twelfth Night, 1953; 3 act opera The Wife of Martin Guerre, 1955, rev. 1958; 3 choruses Riddle Me This, 1956; band March with Trumpets, 1957; Concerto for Woodwind Quintet, 1958; orch. Chameleon Variations, 1960; viola and piano Fantastic Variations, 1961; orch. In Celebration: Toccata for the Sixth Day, 1962; Confrontation from the Book of Job; orch. Documentary One, 1963; Serenade to Await the Moon, 1965, Concerto for Violin and Orchestra, 1966, The Sun, The Soaring Eagle, The Turquoise Prince; chorus, brass, percussion The God, 1967; Orch. Documentary Two, 1967; clarinet, percussion Illegible Canons, 1969, 1969; Fourth Quartet, 1970, rev., 1974; solo woodwind quintet, harp, percussion, strings Changes, 1971; Changes for Seven, 1971; cello, percussion Clandestine Dialogues, 1972; two-act opera The Murder of Comrade Sharik, 1973; chorus, instruments Wishes, Wonders, Portents, Charms, 1974; soprano, instruments In Space, 1975; chorus and orch. Second Symphony: Voyages for Soloists, 1976; solo viola and orch. Sweet Was the Song the Virgin Sung/Tristan Revisited, 1977; trombone and percussion Blatent Hypotheses, 1977; 3 instruments, percussion Four All, 1979; Quintet for Flute and String Quartet, 1979, The Voice of the Coelacanth, 1980; oboe concertante, 2 bassoons and strings In Campo Aperto, 1981; medium voice, clarinet, bassoon and piano Four Songs, 1981; Fifth Quartet, 1982. Recipient Town Hall commn. for Symphony for Chamber Orch., 1942; Bearns prize for String Quartet No. 1, 1943; Koussevitzky Found. commn., 1943-44; grant AAAL and Nat. Inst. Arts and Letters, 1945; award Soc. for Publ. Am. Music, 1945; Guggenheim fellow, 1946, 51; Collegiate Chorale commn., 1946; commn. from Carl Fischer, Inc., for 25th anniversary of League of Composers, 1947; Juilliard Found. commn., 1953-62; Louisville commn., 1953; Elizabeth Sprague Coolidge commn., 1956; Collegiate Chorale of Ill. Wesleyan U. commn., 1956; 1st ann. Edwin Franco Goldman Meml. commn., 1957; Harvard Mus. Soc. commn., 1961; Portland Jr. Symphony commn., 1960; Mid-Am. Chorale commn., 1963; Mus. Arts Soc. La Jolla commn., 1965; Phi Beta commn., 1966; Am. Choral Dirs. Assn. commn., 1967; Kansas City Youth Symphony commn., 1967; U. Ala. for Cadek Quarter, 1970; Poncho and Brechemin Family Found. commn., 1971; New Dimensions in Music, 1972; Nat. Chorale and N.Y. State Council on Arts commn., 1974; Gt. Falls Symphony and Symphonic Choir, Mont. Bicentennial Adminstrn., 1975; Seattle Symphony Orch. commn., 1977; Chamber Music Soc. of Lincoln Center commn., 1980; Nat. Endowment Arts fellow, 1979. Mem. Am. Inst. Acad. Arts and Letters, Phi Beta Kappa, Phi Mu Alpha. Address: 2328 Delmar Dr E Seattle WA 98102

BERGSON, ABRAM, economist, educator; b. Balt., Apr. 21, 1914; s. Issac Burk and Sophia (Rabinovich) B.; m. Rita S. Macht, Nov. 5, 1939; children: Judith, Emily, Lucy. A.B., Johns Hopkins U., 1933; Ph.D., Harvard U., 1940; LL.D., U. Windsor, 1979. Instr. econs. Harvard U., 1937-38, 39-40; asst. prof. econs. U. Tex., 1940-42; economist various agys. Fed. Govt., 1942-46; mem. U.S. delgation Moscow Reparations Conf., summer, 1945; asso. prof. econs. Columbia U., 1946-50, prof., 1950-56; prof. econs. Harvard U., 1956-71, George F. Baker prof. econs., 1971—; dir. The Russian Research Center, Harvard U., 1964-68, 77-80; cons. Rand Corp., 1948—. Author: Structure of Soviet Wages, 1944, Economics of Soviet Planning, 1964, Essays in Normative Economics, 1966, Planning and Productivity under Soviet Socialism, 1968, Productivity and the Social System, 1978, Welfare, Planning, and Employment, 1982; also other books, and various articles in profl. econ. jours.; Co-editor: Economic Trends in the Soviet Union, 1963, The Soviet Economy: Toward the Year 2000, 1983. Mem. social sci. advisory bd. ACDA, 1966-73, chmn., 1972-73. Fellow Econometric Soc., Am. Acad. Arts and Scis.; mem. Am. Philos. Soc., Nat. Acad. Scis., Am. Econ. Assn., Social Sci. Research Council (dir.-at-large 1963-69). Jewish. Home: 334 Marsh St Belmont MA 02178

BERGSON, MARIA, designer; b. Vienna, Austria; came to U.S., 1940, naturalized, 1944; d. Egon F. and Therese (Schey) B.; m. Thomas L. Brunner, Jan. 1, 1942. Entered field of indsl. and interior design, specializing in planning and design of offices, banks, hotels, hosps., stores, other comml. interiors, also product design, fabrics, displays and graphic arts; exhibited, Phila. Art Alliance, 1948, Archtl. League, 1954, various travelling exhibits, U.S. and abroad. Recipient Ann. Merit award Chgo. Bldg. Congress, 1964; Food Service Honor award Instns. mag., 1964. Fellow Internat. Inst. Arts and Letters; mem. Archtl. League N.Y., Mus. Modern Art, N.Y.C. Postal Council, Indsl. Designers Inst. Episcopalian. Home and Office: 140 E 72d St New York NY 10021

BERGSTEIN, HARRY BENJAMIN, psychology educator; b. Sag Harbor, N.Y., Dec. 30, 1916; s. Joseph and Sarah (Baer) B.; m. Evelyn M. Berg, June 25, 1950; children: Mary, Paul, David. A.B., SUNY, 1939, M.A., 1947; Ed.D., NYU, 1960. Tchr., counselor various schs., L.I., N.Y., 1945-60; guidance dir. Huntington (L.I.) Pub. Schs., 1960-67; vis. prof. CUNY, 1967-68; mem. faculty SUNY-Oneonta, 1968—, prof. ednl. psychology, 1968—, chmn. dept. ednl. psychology, 1978-82; cons. sch. psychologist to area pub. schs., 1970-82. Served with AUS, 1941-45. NYU teaching fellow, 1959-60. Mem. Am. Psychol. Assn., Am. Personnel and Guidance Assn. (life), NEA, Phi Delta Kappa. Home: 41 Union St Oneonta NY 13820 Office: SUNY Oneonta NY 13820

BERGSTEN, C. FRED, economist; b. Bklyn., Apr. 23, 1941; s. Carl Alfred and Lois Halkaline (Kirk) B.; m. Virginia Lee Wood, June 16, 1962; 1 son, Mark. A.B., Central Methodist Coll., Fayette, Mo., 1961; M.A., Fletcher Sch. Law and Diplomacy, Medford, Mass., 1962, M.A. in law and Diplomacy, 1963, Ph.D., 1969. Internat. economist Dept. State, 1963-67; vis. fellow Council Fgn. Relations, 1967-68; asst. for internat. econ. affairs NSC, 1969-71; sr. fellow Brookings Instn., 1972-76; asst. sec. treasury internat. affairs, 1977-81; sr. asso. Carnegie Endowment Internat. Peace, 1981; dir. Inst. Internat. Econs., 1981—; bd. dirs. Consumers Union, 1976-77, Atlantic Inst., 1973-77, Atlantic Council, 1982—, Overseas Devel. Council, 1974-77, Central Meth. Coll., 1982—, Center Law and Social Policy, 1973-77, Worldwatch Inst., 1975-77; Dir. Overseas Pvt. Investment Corp., 1977-81, U.S.-Israel Binat. Research and Devel. Found., 1977-81; U.S. coordinator U.S.-Saudi Arabia Joint Econ. Commn., 1977-81. Author: The Future of the International Economic Order: An Agenda for Research, 1973, Toward a New World Trade Policy, 1975, World Politics and International Economics, 1975, Toward a New International Economic Order: Selected Papers of C. Fred Bergsten, 1972-74, 1975, The Dilemmas of the Dollar: The Economics and Politics of United States International Monetary Policy, 1976, American Multinationals and American Interests, 1978, Managing International Economic Interdependence: Selected Papers of C. Fred Bergsten, 1975-1976, 1977, the International Economic Policy of the United States, 1980, The World Economy in the 1980s, 1981, The United States in the World Economy: Selected Papers of C. Fred Bergsten, 1981-82, 1983; Editorial bd.: Fgn. Affairs, 1972-77, Internat. Orgn, 1973-77, Jour. Internat. Econs, 1977-80. Recipient Meritorious Honor award Dept. State, 1965; Distinguished Alumnus award Central Meth. Coll., 1975; Exceptional Service award Treasury Dept., 1980. Mem. Am. Econ. Assn., Council Fgn. Relations., Washington Inst. Fgn. Affairs. Home: 4106 Sleepy Hollow Rd Annandale VA 22003 Office: Inst Internat Econs 11 DuPont Circle NW Washington DC 20036

BERGSTRAND, WILTON EVERET, clergyman; b. Bloomington, Ill., July 16, 1909; s. Rev. John Ivard and Esther (Jernberg) B.; m. Dolores Youngren, Oct. 17, 1953; children—John Wilton, Paul William, Lori Esther. B.A., Gustavus Adolphus Coll., 1930, D.D., 1949; B.D., Augustana Theol. Sem., 1935. Ordained to ministry Lutheran Ch., 1935; prof. English, speech Gustavus Adolphus Coll., 1930-32; pastor Gloria Dei Luth. Ch., Duluth, 1935-38; youth dir. Augustana Luth. Ch., Mpls., 1938-63, chaplain hdqrs., 1942-63, lectr., tchr. Bible, camp program dir., 1963-64; pastor Luth. Ch. of Holy Trinity, Jamestown, N.Y.; dir. internat. youth confs., leadership schs., Bible camps. Producer filmstrip series.; Author: Stitch in Time, 1940, Luther League Scrapbook, 1942, All Smiles, 1943, Centennial Programs, 1945, The Bugles are Calling, 1946, God's Outstretched Hand, 1947, Good Counsel for Counselors, 1956, Leadership, 1956, Youth Round the World, 1958, Youth's Favorite Chuckles, 1958, Christ Unites Us; co-author: Public Speaking Question-ette, 1942, To Light A Candle, 1946, Open Doors, 1949, Who Will Go?, 1947, Luther League Handbook, 1950, A Leaders Guide, 1950, Dynamic District Leagues, 1950, Living High in High School, 1953, Banquet Lore, 1954, Adventuring with Christ in Church Staff Vocations, 1955, Bible Camp Check List, 1956, Bible Study Notes, 1956; Co-editor: The Bible and the Devotional Life, 1972, Home Altar, 1972, 75—, Counsels of Faith and Courage, 1973, Our Flag Speaks, 1973, Independence—Dependence—Interdependence, 1974, Keep the Freedom Bells Ringing, 1975, Disciplined Christian Living, 1976, Studies in Matthew, 1980, also numerous mag. articles. Chmn. commn. young peoples work Am. Luth Conf., 1943-48; del. World Conf. Christian Youth, Oslo, Norway, 1947; Augustana rep. orgn. meeting Luth. World Fedn., Lund, Sweden, 1947. Recipient Our Flag Speaks award Freedoms Found., 1974. Mem. Bd. College Edn., Luth. Church in Am., Greater Gustavus Assn. (pres.), Am. Scandinavian Found., World Council Christian Edn., World Council Chs. (youth dept.). Home: 620 Smith Ave Jamestown NY 14701 Office: 825 Forest Ave Jamestown NY 14701

BERGSTROM, DEDRIC WALDEMAR, paper company executive; b. Neenah, Wis., Aug. 21, 1919; s. D. Waldemar and Agnes (Forsythe) B.; m. Jane Katherine Gibson, June 14, 1941; children—Dedric Waldemar IV, John F., Richard A., Jennifer M., William L. Grad., Northwestern Mil. and Naval Acad., Lake Geneva, Wis., 1936; student, Lawrence Coll., Appleton, Wis., 1936-38, U. Minn., 1939. With Bergstrom Paper div. P.H. Glatfelter Co., Neenah, Wis., 1936—, successively gen. mill, office work, purchasing agt., 1945-50, treas., 1950-56, dir., 1950—, dir. purchases, 1950-71, dir. prodn. planning and scheduling, 1957-71, v.p., sec., 1956-62, exec. v.p., 1962-75, pres., chief operating officer, 1975-80; pres., chief executive officer Bergstrom div., 1980—; dir. Twin City Savs. and Loan Assn. Vice pres. Bergstrom Found., 1962-80, pres., 1980—; bd. regents Campion High Sch., 1968-72. Served to maj. AUS, 1942-45. Mem. Wis. Paper & Pulp Mfrs. Traffic Assn. (dir. 1967-72). Roman Catholic. Club: Bergstrom Paper Management. Home: 835 River Ln Neenah WI 54956 Office: PH Glatfelter Co Bergstrom Div Bergstrom Rd Neenah WI 54956

BERGSTROM, RICHARD NORMAN, civil engineer; b. Chgo., Dec. 11 1921; s. Carl William and Ellen Amanda Victoria (Anderson) B.; m. Patricia Ann Chessman, Apr. 19, 1947; children: George Norman, James Donald, Laura Ann, Martha Jean. B.S. in Civil Engring, Ill. Inst. Tech., 1942, M.S., 1952. Registered profl. engr., Ill., 17 other states. Design engr. Carnegie-Ill. Steel Corp., Gary, Ind., 1942; with Sargent & Lundy (engrs.), Chgo., 1946—, partner, 1966-81, mgr. tech. services dept., 1977—; mem. nuclear standards mgmt. bd. Am. Nat. Standards Inst., 1975—. Contbr. to profl. publs. Stated clk. Presbyn. Ch., Barrington, Ill.; bd. dirs. Presbyn. Home, Evanston, Ill. Served to lt. USNR, 1942-46. Decorated Purple Heart. Fellow ASCE, Am. Cons. Engrs. Council; mem. ASME, Am. Nuclear Soc., Am. Concrete Inst., Am. Inst. Steel Constrn., Western Soc. Engrs., Ill. Cons. Engrs. Council (dir.), Tau Beta Pi, Chi Epsilon. Clubs: Union League (Chgo.); Barrington Hills Country, Desert Forest Golf, Meadow. Home: 274 Leeds Dr Barrington Hills IL 60010 Office: 55 E Monroe St Chicago IL 60603

BERGSTROM, ROBERT WILLIAM, lawyer; b. Chgo., Nov. 8, 1918; s. C. William and Ellen (Anderson) B.; m. Betty Howard; children: Mark Robert, Philip Alan, Bryan Scott, Cheryl Lee, Jeffrey Alan. M.B.A., U. Chgo., 1947; LL.B., Chgo. Kent Coll. Law, 1940, J.D., 1970. Bar: Ill. bar 1940, U.S. Supreme Ct. bar 1950. Practice in Chgo., 1940—; partner firm Bergstrom, Davis & Teeple (and predecessors), 1951—; founder Statewide Com. on Cts. and Justice, mem. exec. com., 1971—; bd. dirs. Ill. Com. for Constl. Conv., 1969-70; spl. counsel Ill. Joint Legislative Com. to Investigate Met. San. Dist. of Cook County, Ill., 1967, Ill. Senate Mcpl. Corp. Com., 1970. Co-author: The Law of Competition in Illinois, 1962; author numerous articles on antitrust and econs.; Editor: Chgo. Bar Record, 1971-72. Served to lt. USNR, 1944-45. Named Chicagoan of Year in Law Chgo. Jaycees, 1969; recipient Disting. Public Service award Union League Club, 1981. Mem. Ill. Bar Assn., Chgo. Bar Assn. (sec. 1969-71, Am. Bar Assn., co-editor Antitrust Developments 1965-68). Club: Union League (pres. 1971-72). Founding chmn. (1972-75) and counsel (1976-80) Com. for Legis. Reform, which drafted constl. amendment approved 1980, reducing Ill. Ho. of Reps. by 1/3 and abolishing cumulative voting. Office: 39 S LaSalle St Suite 800 Chicago IL 60603

BERICK, JAMES HERSCHEL, lawyer; b. Cleve., Mar. 30, 1933; s. Morris and Rebecca Alice (Gerdy) B.; m. Laura Ruth Greenfield, June 19, 1955; children: Michael, Daniel, Robert, Joshua. A.B., Columbia U., 1955; LL.B., Case Western Res. U., 1958. Assoc. Burke, Haber & Berick, Cleve., 1958-60, ptnr., 1960—, mng. ptnr., 1968-83; dir. Cleve. Browns Inc., Equitable Bancorp., Equitable Bank, N.A., Sandusco, Inc., Realty ReFund Trust, A. Schulman Inc., Tranzonic Cos., S.A. Horvitz Testamentary Trust; lectr. law Case Western Res. U., 1969-78. Trustee Mt. Sinai Hosp., 1971-79, trustee emeritus, 1979—; mem. Shaker Heights (Ohio) Bd. Edn., 1980-83; bd. visitors Columbia Coll., 1983—. Mem. Columbia Coll. Alumni Assn. (dir. 1976—), Order of Coif. Clubs: Princeton of N.Y., Cleve. Skating, Oakwood, Union. Home: 14518 Shaker Blvd Shaker Heights OH 44120 Office: 300 Nat City Bank Bldg Cleveland OH 44114

BERINGER, WILLIAM ERNST, electrical equipment manufacturing company executive, lawyer; b. Madison, Wis., Oct. 24, 1928; s. William and Martha M. (Wupper) B.; children: Amy, Julia, Thomas. B.A. summa cum laude, Lawrence Coll., 1950; J.D. with distinction, U. Mich., 1953. Bar: Mich. bar 1953, Wis. bar 1953, Ill. bar 1955, asso. Ga. bar 1978. Asso. firm Vedder, Price, Kaufman & Kammholz, Chgo., 1953-56; atty. law dept. Swift & Co., Chgo., 1956-71; dir. gen. law dept. Allis-Chalmers Corp., Milw., 1971-77; v.p., gen. counsel, sec. Siemens-Allis, Inc. and Utility Power Corp., Atlanta, 1978—; dir. corp. banking and bus. law sect. Wis. Bar, 1976-78; mem. antitrust and corp. policy com. U.S. C. of C., 1974-80. Editorial bd.: Mich. Law Rev, 1952-53. Bd. dirs. Hinsdale (Ill.) Community Concert Assn., 1969-71, Dupage County (Ill.) Girl Scouts U.S., 1969-71, Clarendon Hills (Ill.) Community Chest, 1968-70; vice chmn. Clarendon Hills Human Relations Commn., 1968-70; mem. Chgo. study team Nat. Commn. on Causes and Prevention Violence, 1968. Mem. Am. Bar Assn., Ga. Bar Assn., Atlanta Bar Assn., Order of Coif. Republican. Congregationalist. Club: Cherokee Town and Country. Home: 9010 River Run Atlanta GA 30338 Office: 223 Perimeter Center Pkwy Atlanta GA 30346

BERIO, LUCIANO, composer, conductor, educator; b. Imperia Oneglia, Italy, Oct. 24, 1925; s. Ernesto Filippo and Ada (Dal Fiume) B.; m. Cathy Berberian, Oct. 1, 1950 (div.); 1 dau., Christina Luisa; m. Susan Oyama, 1964 (div.); children: Marina, Stefano; m. Talia Pecker, 1977; children: Daniel, Jonathan. Student, Liceo Classico, 1936-43; grad. composition and orch. conducting, Conservatorio G. Verdi, Milan, 1951. Tchr. composition Berkshire Festival, 1960, Dartington Summer Sch., 1961, 62, Mills Coll., 1962, 63, Darmstadt Ferienkurse, 1963; tchr. at Juilliard Sch. Music, 1965, also seminars at; Harvard, 1966. Founder, 1954, Studio de Fonologia Musicale, for electronic music at Italian Radio; founder, 1954; musical rev. Incontri Musicali; Composer: Tre Liriche popolari, 1948, Magnificat, 1949-71, Due Pezzi, 1951, 5 Variazioni, 1951, Chamber Music, 1953, Variazioni, 1953, El Mar la Mar, 1952-53, Mimusique 1, 1953, Mimusique 2, 1953, Nones, 1954, Quartetto, 1955, Perspectives, 1956, Allelujah II, 1956-57, Serenata, 1957, Thema, 1958, Sequenza, I, 1958, Allez-Hop, 1952-59, Differences, 1958-59, Tempi Concertati, 1958-59, Circles, 1960, Momenti, 1960, Epifanie, 1959-61, Visage, 1961, Passaggio, 1962, Sequenza II, 1963, Rounds, 1965, Sincronie, 1963-64, Chemins, I, 1965, Sequenza III, IV, V, 1955-56, Folk Songs, 1964, Laborintus, 1965, Gesti, 1966, Chemins II, 1967-68, Chemins III, 1968, Sinfonia, 1968, Questo Vuol Dire Che, 1968-69, Opera, 1970, rev., 1977, Memory, 1971, Bewegung, 1971, Concerto, 1972-73, Still, 1973, A. Ronne, 1974, Chemins IV, 1955, Coro, 1975-76, IL Ritorno degli Snovidenia, 1976, La Vera Storia, 1979, numerous recs. Address: Il Colombaio Radicondoli (Siena) Italy *

BERK, JACK EDWARD, physician, educator; b. Phila.; s. Samuel and Esther (Pill) B.; m. Adeline Elizabeth Alberts, June 26, 1937; children: Philip Howard (dec.), Richard Hanna. B.A., U. Pa., 1932, M.S. in Medicine, 1939, D.Sc. in Medicine, 1943; M.D., Jefferson Med. Coll., 1936; postgrad., Grad. Sch. Medicine, U. Pa., 1937-38. Diplomate: Am. Bd. Internal Medicine (subspecialty bd. gastroenterology). Intern Walter Reed Gen. Hosp., Washington, 1936-37; resident No. div. Albert Einstein Med. Center, Phila., 1938-39; fellow gastroenterology Grad. Hosp., U. Pa., 1939-40; Ross V. Patterson fellow physiology Jefferson Med. Coll., Phila., 1940-41, instr. gastroenterology, 1941-46; asst. prof. medicine Sch. Medicine, Temple U., 1946-54; asst. dir. Fels Research Inst., 1946-54; asso. prof. clin. medicine Coll. Medicine, Wayne State U., 1954-62, prof. clin. medicine, 1962-63; prof. medicine Coll. Medicine, U. Calif., Irvine, 1963-79, prof. emeritus, 1979—, chmn. dept. medicine, 1963-73, head div. gastroenterology, 1963-79, disting. prof., asst. dean, 1979—; vis. lectr. Grad. Sch. Medicine, U. Pa., 1961—; cons. VA Hosp., Long Beach, Calif., 1963—, Cedars-Sinai Med. Center, 1963—, White Meml. Hosp., 1963—, Meml. Hosp., Long Beach, 1964—, Sinai Hosp., Detroit, 1963—. Asso. editor: Gastroenterology (Bockus), 3d edit, 1974; editor: Developments in Digestive Diseases, 8Vol. 1, 1977, Vol. 2, 1979, Vol. 3, 1980; editor-in-chief: Gastroenterology, 4th edit.; Editorial bd.: Current Therapeutic Research, 1959—, Am. Jour. Gastroenterology, 1971—, Practical Gastroenterology, 1976—; Contbr. chpts. to books, 185 articles to med. jours. U.S. Dept. State rep. to S.Am. countries Cultural Exchange Program, 1961. Served to maj. M.C. AUS, 1941-46. Recipient Disting. Service award Mich. Med. Soc., 1959; Rudolf Schindler award Am. Soc. Gastro-intestinal Endoscopy, 1966; Rorer award Am. Coll. Gastroenterology, 1970, 74, 78, 79; Disting. Sci. Achievement award Am. Coll. Gastroenterology, 1982; Faculty Community Service award U. Calif., Irvine Alumni Assn., 1971; Faculty Univ. Service award, 1976; Disting. Achievement award Jefferson Med. Coll. Alumni Assn., 1977; Maimonides award Maimonides Soc., 1984; named Disting. Physician Nat. Found. for Ileitis and Colitis, 1980. Master ACP (gov. So. Calif. region II 1976-80); mem. Nat. Found. for Ileitis and Colitis (nat. sci. bd.), Am. Gastroent. Assn., Am. Soc. Gastrointestinal Endoscopy (pres. 1958-59), Am. Fedn. Clin. Research (past chmn. Eastern sect.), Bockus Internat. Soc. Gastroenerology (pres. 1967-71), Am. Coll. Gastroenterology (pres. 1975-76), AMA (chmn. sect. gastroenterology 1965-66), Detroit Gastroent. Soc. (pres. 1960-61), So. Calif. Soc. Gastroenterology (pres. 1967-68), Los Angeles Acad. Medicine (gov. 1981-84), So. Calif. Soc. Gastrointestinal Endoscopy (hon.), Orange County Acad. Medicine, Orange County Gastroenterology Soc. (pres. 1976-77), Interam. Gastroent. Assn. (hon. pres. 1981—), Sigma Xi, Alpha Omega Alpha; hon. mem. Acad. Med. Ecuador, Peruvian Soc. Gastroenterology; corr. mem. Soc. Gastroenterology Colombia, Soc. Gastrointestinal Endoscopy Colombia, Ecuador, Venezuela and Brazilian Soc. of Gastroenterology and Nutrition. Home: 894-C Ronda Sevilla Laguna Hills CA 92653 Office: U Calif Irvine Med Center 101 The City Dr Orange CA 92668

BERK, MORTON EMMETT, physician; b. Lafayette, Ind., Dec. 28, 1913; s. David Lewis and Ann (Klene) B.; m. Carol Yoshiko Furuike, Aug. 23, 1971; children: Brent, Heather, Scott, Clay. Student, Northwestern U., 1930-34; A.B., U. Louisville, 1938; M.D., 1942. Diplomate: Am. Bd. Internal Medicine, Sub-Bd. Cardiology. Intern Med. Coll. Va., Richmond, 1942-44; resident Queen's Hosp., 1944-45, Stanford (Calif.) U. Hosp., 1949; pvt. practice medicine Honolulu Med. Group, 1945-49, 50-79; clin. prof. medicine John Burns Sch. Medicine, U. Hawaii, Honolulu, 1976—; pvt. practice internal medicine and cardiology, Kailua-Kona, Hawaii, 1979—. Contbr. articles to profl. jours. Pres. Better Bus. Bur. of Honolulu, 1955; v.p. Blood Bank of Hawaii, 1955, bd. dirs., 1953-79. Mem. Asian Pacific Soc. Cardiology (pres.), Internat. Soc. and Fedn. Cardiology (exec. bd.), A.C.P., Am. Coll. Cardiology, Royal Soc. Medicine, Honolulu County Med. Soc., Hawaii Med. Assn. (Physician of Yr. award 1978), AMA, Am. Heart Assn., Hawaii Heart Assn. Republican. Congregationalist. Club: Pacific. Office: PO Box V Kealakekua HI 96750 *In June 1929 I was hired to be a bell-boy in the then new Passavant Memorial Hospital (now Northwestern University Hospital). I was at once impressed by the miraculous work done by so many of the physicians and surgeons on the hospital staff. They served as my pattern for living and caring for people. I could not have chosen better.*

BERK, PAUL DAVID, physician, scientist, educator; b. Bklyn., Apr. 3, 1938; s. Charles and Helen (Goell) B.; m. Aviva Ancona, July 4, 1965; children: Claire, Philip, Edward. B.A., Swarthmore Coll., 1959; cert., U. St. Andrews, Scotland, 1960; M.D., Columbia U., 1964. Am. Bd. Internal Medicine. Intern Columbia-Presbyn. Med. Ctr., N.Y.C., 1964-65, resident, 1965-66, fellow in hematology, 1969-70; clin. assoc. metabolism br. Nat. Cancer Inst., Bethesda, Md., 1966-69, sr. investigator, Bethesda, 1970-73; clin. asst. prof. medicine Georgetown U., Washington, 1971-75; clin. assoc. prof. Nat. Cancer Inst., Bethesda, 1975-77; chief sect. on diseases of the liver Nat. Inst. Arthritis, Metabolism and Digestive Diseases, NIH, Bethesda, 1973-77; Albert and Vera List prof. medicine Mt. Sinai Sch. Medicine, N.Y.C., 1980—, chief div. hematology, 1977—; cons. in liver disease NIH, 1978—. Editor: (with others) Chemistry and Physiology of the Bile Pigments, 1977, Frontiers in Liver Disease, 1981, Myleofibrosis and the Biology of Connective Tissue, 1983; editor-in-chief: Seminars in Liver Disease, 1981—; mem. editorial bd.: Artificial Organs,

1979—; mem.: Liver, 1980—; contbr. articles to profl. jours. Served as sr. surgeon USPHS, 1966-69, 75-77. Recipient Merck award Columbia U., 1964; Fulbright scholar, 1959. Fellow ACP; mem. N.Y. Soc. Study of Blood (pres. 1982—), Nat. Polyothemia Vera Study Group (vice-chmn. 1978—), Am. Soc. Clin. Investigation, Assn. Am. Physicians, Am. Assn. Study of Liver Disease, Am. Soc. for Hematology, Sigma Xi, Phi Beta Kappa, Alpha Omega Alpha. Office: Mount Sinai Sch Medicine 1 Gustave Levy Pl New York NY 10029

BERK, ROGER G., broadcasting exec.; b. Akron, Ohio, Mar. 30, 1923; s. S. Bernard and Viola (Greenhut) B.; m. Marilyn Miller, June 25, 1950; children—Roger G., Ellen M., Robert C. Pres., gen. mgr., dir. Summit Radio Corp., Akron, 1947—; v.p., dir. Rogim, Inc., Akron, 1947—; pres., dir. Radio and TV Center of Akron, Inc., Group One Broadcasting Co., Dayton, Ohio, Group One Broadcasting Co. of Tex., Dallas, Group One Broadcasting Co.-West, Denver, Summit Radio Corp.; sec., treas., dir. Hotelvision, Akron; hon. chmn. Acme-Zip Game; dir. Akron Savs. & Loan Co. Trustee United Found. of Summit County, Bluecoats, Inc., Akron Children's Hosp. Med. Center, Akron Chamber Ballet, Children's Concert Soc. Akron; mem. Ohio adv. bd. Nat. Alliance Businessmen. Served with USAAF, inf.; Served with U.S. Army, 1942-46. Recipient Silver Medal award Am. Advt. Fedn., 1979, Leo E. Dugan Community award, 1980. Mem. NAACP (life), League Ohio Sportsmen, Goals for Greater Akron Area, Fraternal Order Police Assns., Area Progress Bd., Akron C. of C., Stan Hywet Found., Akron Art Inst., Friends of Weathervane Theatre, Radio Advt. Bur. N.Y.C. (dir.), Nat. Assn. Broadcasters. Republican. Jewish. Clubs: Rotary, Akron City, Touchdown, Rosemont Country, Sharon Golf, Hilltoppers (Akron U.); Harvard (past pres.). Office: 853 Copley Rd Akron OH 44320

BERKE, ARNOLD, financial holding company executive; b. Sea Cliff, N.Y., Nov. 15, 1923; s. George and Ella B.; m. Marjorie Cate, Jan. 1, 1953; children: Gregory, Deborah. B.S., NYU, 1947; postgrad., Sch. Bus., 1959-60, Georgetown U., 1943, U. Wis., 1941-42. Vice pres., sec. Standard Shares, Inc., N.Y.C., 1959—. Served with U.S. Army, 1943-45; ETO. Office: Standard Shares Inc 230 Park Ave New York NY 10169

BERKE, JULES, management consultant; b. N.Y.C., Jan. 11, 1926; m. Mildred Weiner, June 26, 1949; children: Paul, Robert, Randy, Michael. B.B.A., Coll. City N.Y.; LL.B., Bklyn. Law Sch.; B.S. in Indsl. Engring, Lawrence Inst. Tech. Bar: N.Y. 1949. Comptroller Eight Mile Rd. plant Chrysler Corp., Detroit; also comptroller Highland Park plant, comptroller, 1952-59; asst. comptroller Foster Wheeler Corp., 1959-62; with ITT Corp., 1962—, exec. asst. for ops. Office of Pres., 1968-69, dir. N.Am. staff, 1969-72, dir. staff ops., 1972-75, v.p., dir. ops. planning, rev. and control, 1975-82; mgmt. cons., 1982—. Served to sgt. U.S. Army, 1944-46. Mem. Fin. Execs. Inst. Home: 16 Linda Ln Westport CT 06880

BERKELEY, MARVIN H., business educator, administrator; b. St. Louis, Oct. 22, 1922; m. Betty L. Berkeley, Feb. 7, 1947; children: Kathryn Berkeley Morton, Barbara, Brian, Janet. B.A., Harris Tchrs. Coll., 1944, Washington U., St. Louis, 1947, J.D., 1952. Research psychologist Personnel Research Lab., San Antonio, 1951-54; dir. research White-Rodgers Co., St. Louis, 1954-57; personnel dir. to corp. personnel dir. Tex. Instruments, Dallas, 1957-73; dean Coll. Bus. North Tex. State U., Denton, 1973-83; dir. Westbridge Capital Corp., Dallas, Insource Corp., Tex. Am. Bank, Dallas; mem. bd. mgmt. Internat. Ins. Seminars, Inc., 1977—, v.p.; dir. Tex. Instruments Found., 1969-73; mem. adv. bd. Nat. Inst. for Work and Learning, 1973-79; bd. dirs. North Tex. Found. for Pub. Broadcasting, KERA-TV, 1968-72; mem. adv. bd. Fed. Exec. Inst., 1968; mem. Commn. on Career Advancement in Fed. Service, 1967-68; pres. bd. edn. Dallas Ind. Sch. Dist., 1967-73; chmn. SW Regional Panel White House Fellows, 1968-70; bd. dirs. Dallas Symphony Orch., 1968-72; mem. Tex. Urban Devel. Commn., 1970-72; chmn. adminstrv. bd. Lover's Lane United Methodist Ch., 1963-65; bd. dirs., past pres. Mental Health Assn., Dallas County, Dallas Council on Alcoholism; mem. exec. com. Big City Bds. of Edn., 1969-73; co-founder, chmn. Tex. Council of Maj. Sch. Dists., 1968-71. Served to lt. (j.g.) USNR, 1943-46; served with USAF, 1951-54. Mem. Tex. Council Collegiate Edn. for Bus. (past pres. 1980), Southwestern Bus. Adminstrn. Assn. (past pres. 1981), Sigma Xi, Beta Alpha Psi, Beta Gamma Sigma, Delta Sigma Pi. Home: 13948 Hughes Ln Dallas TX 75240 Office: North Tex State U Denton TX 76203

BERKENKAMP, FRED JULIUS, management consultant; b. Alma, Wis., Oct. 19, 1925; s. Julius Henry and Elisabeth Helen (Polnick) B.; m. Ruth Ethelyn Taylor; children: Linda, Vicki, Thomas, JoAnne. B.S. in Electron Engring, U. Wyo., 1948; postgrad., U. Syracuse, N.Y., 1951. Quality control mgmt. Gen. Electric Co., Syracuse, 1948-55, corporate cons. mfg. mgmt., N.Y.C., 1955-65, mgr. planning jet engines, Cin., 1966-68, mgr. nuclear fuels mfg., Wilmington, N.C., 1969; corp. exec. v.p., pres. Appliance Group, Roper Corp., Kankakee, Ill., 1970-80; pres., chief exec. officer, dir. Allied Structural Steel Co. subs. MSL Industries/Alleghany Corp., Chicago Heights, Ill., 1980-83; pres. F.J. Berkenkamp & Co., mgmt. cons., 1984—. Trustee Community Coll., 1974-80. Served with USNR, 1944-46. Mem. Assn. Home Appliance Mfrs. (chmn. bd. dirs.), Gas Appliance Mfrs. Assn. (dir.), Kankakee Area C. of C. (dir. 1972-76), Sigma Chi. Home: 12 Island View Ln Kankakee IL 60901

BERKEY, BENJAMIN, photographic company executive; b. Podolsk, Russia, Jan. 1, 1911; came to U.S., naturalized, 1921; s. Isidore and Lena (Pisner) Berkowitz; m. Frances Picon, May 15, 1958; children: Dorothy, Harvey, Joseph, Robert, Gilbert, Belinda, Peter, Nina, David. B.B.A., CCNY, 1932. Chmn. bd. Berkey Photo, White Plains, N.Y., including; Willoughby Camera Stores, Berkeey Mktg. Corp., Berkey Tech. Co., 1933—; chmn. bd. Wall Trading Corp., 1980—; chmn. bd., pres. Bentrose Corp., N.Y.C., 1958—. Chmn. City Coll. Fund, 1979-81, Baruch Coll. Fund, 1975-81, Cancer Dr. of Photo Industry, 1960-81. Named Man of Yr. City Coll., Baruch Coll., James Monroe High Sch., Photog. Industry. Mem. Pioneer Club Camera Industry Japan (charter). Address: Berkey Photo Inc 1 Water St White Plains NY 10601 *

BERKHOFER, ROBERT FREDERICK, JR., history educator; b. Teaneck, N.J., Nov. 20, 1931; s. Robert F. and Elsa (Techow) B.; m. Genevieve Zito, June 9, 1962; 1 son, Robert Frederick. B.A., SUNY, Albany, 1953; M.A., Cornell U., 1955, Ph.D., 1960. Research analyst U.S. Dept. Justice, Washington, 1955-56; instr. history Ohio State U., 1959-60, U. Minn., 1960-62, asst. prof., 1962-65, asso. prof., 1965-69; prof. history U. Wis., 1969-73, U. Mich., Ann Arbor, 1973—, dir. Am. Culture program, 1978—. Author: Salvation and the Savage: An Analysis of Protestant Missions and American Indian Response, 1787-1862, 1965, 72, A Behavioral Approach to Historical Analysis, 1969, 71, The White Man's Indian: Images of the American Indian from Columbus to the Present, 1978, 79; editor: Studies in American Culture and History, 1977-81. Mem. adv. bd. Center for History of Am. Indian, Newberry Library, 1972—. Social Sci. Research Council fellow, 1957-59; NEH Sr. fellow, 1973-74; Guggenheim fellow, 1978-79. Mem. Am. Hist. Assn., Orgn. Am. Historians (exec. com. 1981-84), Social Sci. History Assn. (exec. bd. 1979-81), Am. Studies Assn. (pres. 1980-82). Home: 420 Huntington Dr Ann Arbor MI 48104 Office: Dept History U Mich Ann Arbor MI 48109

BERKLEY, EUGENE BERTRAM, manufacturing company executive; b. Kansas City, Mo., May 28, 1923; s. Eugene Bertram and Caroline (Newburger) Berkowitz; m. Joan Meinrath, Sept. 1, 1948; children: Janet Lynn, William Spencer, Jane Ellen. B.A., Duke U., 1948; M.B.A., Harvard U., 1950. With Tension Envelope Corp., Kansas City, Mo., 1950—, asst. to pres., 1958-60, v.p., 1960-62, pres., 1962—, chmn. bd., chief exec. officer, 1966—; dir. Can. Cellulose Co., 1973-80. Pres. Civic Council Greater Kansas City, 1967-68, v.p., dir., 1981—; trustee U. Kansas City, 1967—, vice chmn., 1981—; trustee Midwest Research Inst., 1969-72, Kans. Com. Prevention of Child Abuse, 1980—; bd. dirs. Menorah Med. Center, 1981—; mem. exec. com. Center for Mgmt. Assistance, 1980—; chmn. bd. Johnson County Library, 1979-80; trustee Starlight Theatre Assn. Kansas City, Inc.; mem. exec. com. Voluntary Action Info. Center; sec. Kansas City chpt. NCCJ, bd. dirs., 1956—; mem. nat. exec. council Am. Jewish Com., 1979—; bd. dirs., chmn. Kansas City chpt., 1958-61; chmn. budget com. Jewish Fedn. and Council Greater Kansas City, 1965, 73, gen. campaign chmn., 1961. Served to 1st lt. U.S. Army, 1943-46, 50-52. Decorated Bronze Star; recipient Mr. Kansas City award C. of C. Greater Kansas, 1972; Brotherhood award Kansas City chpt. NCCJ, 1968; Human Relations award Kansas City chpt. Am. Jewish Com., 1968. Mem. Envelope Mfrs. Assn. (exec. com. 1977-79, vice-chmn. 1981), Am. Paper Inst. (council solid waste council), Nat. Fire Protection Assn. (rep. envelope industry), C. of C. Greater Kansas City (pres. 1968-69). Clubs: Oakwood Country, Homestead Country, Kansas City Racquet. Patentee in field. Home: 6635 Indian Ln Shawnee Mission KS 66208 Office: Tension Envelope Corp 19th and Campbell Sts Kansas City MO 64108

BERKLEY, RICHARD L., mayor. Grad., Harvard U. Sec., treas. Tension Envelope Corp., Kansas City, Mo.; mem. City Council Kansas City, Mo., mayor, 1979—; chmn. Jackson County (Mo.) Republican Com. Office: Office of Mayor City Hall 414 E 12th Kansas City MO 64106 *

BERKMAN, JACK NEVILLE, lawyer, broadcasting company executive; b. London, Eng., Feb. 12, 1905; came to U.S., 1908, naturalized, 1922; s. Hyman L. and Sarah (Hellman) B.; m. Sybiel B. Altman, Aug. 27, 1933 (dec. May 1964); children: Myles P., Monroe E., Stephen L.; m. Lillian Dubon Rojtman, Jan. 26, 1970. A.B., U. Mich., 1926; J.D., Harvard U., 1929. Bar: Ohio 1930. Practiced in, Steubenville, 1930-68; vice chmn. bd., chmn. exec. com., dir. Rust Craft Greeting Cards, Inc., N.Y.C., Boston, until 1979; vice chmn. bd., dir. Rust Craft Broadcasting Co.; operating WSTV-TV-AM-FM, Steubenville, WJKS-TV, Jacksonville, Fla., WRDW-TV, Augusta, Ga., WSOL-AM, Tampa, Fla., WEYI-TV, Saginaw, Flint-Bay City, Mich., until 1979; pres., dir. Rust Craft Broadcasting N.Y., Inc.; operating WROC-TV-AM-FM, Rochester, N.Y., Rust Craft Broadcasting Pa., Inc., WRCP-AM-FM, Phila., WPIT-AM-FM, Pitts., Rust Craft Broadcasting Tenn., Inc., WRCB-TV, Chattanooga, Radio Buffalo, Inc., WWOL-AM-FM, until 1979; chmn., chief exec. officer, dir. Associated Communications Corp., N.Y.C.; operating Stas. WROC-AM-FM, Rochester, WSOL, Tampa, WSTV-AM-FM, Steubenville,; WRCP-AM-FM, Phila., WPIT-AM-FM, Pitts., WWOL-AM-FM, Buffalo, also, Associated Am. Artists, Inc., N.Y.C.; dir. Cardigan Press, Leeds, Eng., Barker Greeting Cards, Cin., Rust Craft, Ltd., Friendship House, Ltd., Volland, Ltd., all Toronto, Can.; Asso. Am. Artists, N.Y.C., until 1979. Author: play Playing God, 1931; short stories, articles. Pres., trustee Sybiel B. Berkman Found., Steubenville; past pres. Temple Beth El; former mem. devel. bd. Retina Found.; now dir. emeritus; formerly chmn. Tri-State Indsl. Devel. Com. Mem. Internat. Bar Assn., ABA, FCC Bar Assn., Ohio Bar Assn., Jefferson County Bar Assn. (past officer, com. chmn.), Am. Soc. for Technion (dir.), Soc. of Friends of Japan House, founding, Am. Judicature Soc., Harvard Law Sch. Assn. N.Y., Radio and TV Execs. Soc. Clubs: Steubenville Country, Culver Parents; Broadcasters (Washington); Harvard-Yale-Princeton, Variety (Pitts.); Friars, Harvard, Harmonie (N.Y.C.). Home: New York NYOffice: 680 Fifth Ave New York NY 10019 also 320 Market St Steubenville OH 43952 *You say: "Everybody has a thousand ideas." I say: "Ideas without people are meaningless. People without ideas are meaningless. Only people plus ideas create and achieve. Only people and ideas make things happen. To sum up: Success is Imagination harnessed."*

BERKMAN, LILLIAN, foundation executive, corporation executive, art collector; b. N.Y.C. B.A. summa cum laude, N.Y. U., 1942, M.A., 1943, H.H.D. (hon.), 1976. Dir. public relations J.I. Case Co., 1957-60; pres. Gen. Alarm Corp., N.Y.C., 1967—; corp. dir., head advt. and public relations Am. Tractor Corp., 1948-56; dir. Allied Stores Corp., 1974—, Mich. Nat. Corp., 1977—, Mich. Nat. Bank, Detroit, 1977—, Mich. Nat. Investment Corp., 1978—, MNC-Western Leasing, 1980—, Capital Corp., 1980—; pres. Rojtman Found., Inc., 1967—; cultural advisor Coca Cola Co., 1978—. Fellow in perpetuity Met. Mus. Art, N.Y.C., 1964—; donor Rojtman Medieval Sculpture Gallery, 1964, trustee medieval art com., 1974—; trustee Am. Wing, 1976—; mem. exec. council Inst. Fine Arts, N.Y. U., 1972—; trustee Poly. Inst. N.Y., 1977—; fellow Pierpont Morgan Library, 1969—; bd. dirs. United Cerebral Palsy Research and Ednl. Found., Inc., 1973—; mem. Met. Opera Nat. Council, 1973—; overseer U. Pa. Mus., 1982—; chmn. Theban expdn. to Valley of the Kings, Egypt, 1977—; cultural advisor to Costa Rica, 1978—; chmn., bd. dirs. Associated American Artists, Inc., 1980—. Recipient Highest Honor award Nat. Indsl. Advertisers Assn., 1956, Pere Marquette award Marquette U., 1966, Philippine Golden Heart Presdl. award for cultural interchange, 1976. Mem. Phi Beta Kappa Assos. Home: 22 E 64th St New York NY 10021

BERKMAN, LOUIS, steel company executive; b. Canton, Ohio, Jan. 15, 1909; s. Hyman L. and Sarah (Galman) B.; m. Sandra Weiss, Apr. 14, 1935 (dec. Aug. 1983); children: Marshall, Donna Berkman Paul. D.B.A. (hon.), Bethany Coll., D. Bus. Sci., U. Steubenville. Pres. Louis Berkman Co., Steubenville, Ohio, 1931—, Parkersburg Steel Corp., W.Va., 1946—, Follansbee Steel Corp., 1954—; chmn. exec. com. Ampco-Pitts. Corp., Pitts., 1979—; chmn. bd., pres. First Fin. Group, Inc., Washington, Pa.; dir. Asso. Communications Corp. Pres., trustee Louis and Sandra Berkman Found., Steubenville, 1952—, Ampco-Pitts. Found.; mem. adv. com. Ft. Steuben Area council Boy Scouts Am. Mem. Steubenville C. of C., Pitts. Symphony Soc., Oglebay Inst.; mem. B'nai B'rith. Clubs: Rotarian, Elk, Steubenville Country; Westmoreland Country (Export, Pa.); Downtown, Concordia (Pitts.). Office: 330 N 7th St Steubenville OH 43952

BERKMAN, MARSHALL L., manufacturing company executive; b. Steubenville, Ohio, 1936; (married). A.B., Harvard U., 1958, M.B.A., 1960, J.D., 1963. Pres. Rust Craft Greeting Cards, Inc., 1967-79; with Ampco-Pitts. Corp., 1979—, chmn., chief exec. officer, 1979—, also dir.; dir. Instrumentation Lab. Inc., 1st Fin. Fed. Group, 1st Fin. Group, Inc., 1st Nat. Bank, Washington, Pa., Louis Berkman Co., Follansbee Steel Corp., Parkersburg Steel Co., Dover Securities. Office: 700 Porter Bldg Pittsburgh PA 15219 *

BERKMAN, WILLIAM ROGER, army reserve officer, lawyer; b. Chisholm, Minn., Mar. 29, 1928; s. Carl and Millie (Mikkelson) B.; m. Betty Ann Klamt, Dec. 17, 1950. A.B., U. Calif., Berkeley, 1950, J.D., 1957. Bar: Calif. 1957, D.C. Ct. Appeals 1957, D.C. 1957. Law clk. to judge U.S. Ct. Appeals 9th Circuit, 1957-58; asso. firm Morrison & Foerster, San Francisco, 1958-67, mem. firm, 1967-79; comdg. gen. 351st Civil Affairs Command, Mountain View, Calif., 1975-79; chief Army Res., Washington, 1979—. Mng. editor: Calif. Law Rev, 1956-57. Pres. Sausalito (Calif.) Bd. Library Trustees, 1973-77. Served as officer U.S. Army, 1952-54. Decorated Meritorious Service medal, Def. Superior Service medal, Army Commendation medal. Mem. Assn. U.S. Army, Res. Officers Assn. U.S., State Bar Calif., Fed. Bar Assn., Am. Bar Assn., Sr. Army Res. Comdrs. Assn. (v.p., exec. com.), Civil Affairs Assn. (pres.), Res. Officers Assn. (judge adv. army sect.). Clubs: World Trade, Commonwealth (San Francisco); International (Washington); Sausalito Yacht, Presidio Yacht, Army and Navy. Home: Quarters 20-B Lee Ave Fort Myer Arlington VA 22211 Office: Pentagon (Arlington) Washington DC 20310

BERKÓ, FERENC, photographer; b. Nagyvárad, Hungary, Jan. 28, 1916; came to U.S., 1947; s. Reno and Maria Theresa (Teleki) B.; m. Mirte Hahn-Beretta, Nov. 5, 1937; children: Nora, Gina. Student, U. London Extension, 1934-35. Free lance documentary photographer and filmmaker, London, 1935-38; film cameraman Bhavnani Prodns., Bombay, India, 1938-39; free lance photographer and filmmaker, Bombay, 1940-44; documentary film dir., staff capt. Brit. Directorate of Kinematography, Bombay, 1944-47; instr. film and photography Inst. Design, Chgo., 1947-48; photographer and filmmaker Container Corp. Am., Chgo., 1949-51; photographer Berko Photography, Aspen, Colo., 1951—; assoc. photographer Aspen Inst. Humanistic Studies, 1949—; photographer Aspen Skiing Corp., 1949—, Mus. Assn. Aspen, 1949—; selected portrait photographer cabinet ministers' photographs Carter Adminstrn., 1980. Contbr. books, mags., publs., 1938—; photographer solo and group exhbns., 1937—; represented permanent collections, Mus. Modern Art, Met. Mus. Art, San Francisco Mus. Art, Gersheim Collection, (Tex.), Ctr. Creative Photgraphy, Tucson, pvt. collections. Home: 223 E Hallam PO Box 360 Aspen CO 81612

BERKOV, WALTER, editor; b. Allentown, Pa., July 19, 1922; s. Hyman and Marion (Lang) B.; m. Janet Louise Smith, June 14, 1949; children—Ellen, Amy. B.A. in Journalism, Pa. State U., 1942. Reporter Bethlehem (Pa.) Globe Times, 1943; newsman United Press, Pitts., 1943-48; reporter Pitts. Post-Gazette, 1949; wire editor Middletown (Ohio) Jour., 1950-52; copy editor Atlantic City Press, 1953; wire editor, Sunday editor Columbus (Ohio) Citizen, 1953-57; copy editor, asst. fgn. and nat. editor Cleve. Plain Dealer, 1957, now book editor. Mem. Nat. Book Critics Circle. Home: 3723 W 230th North Olmsted OH 44070 Office: 1801 Superior Ave Cleveland OH 44114

BERKOVITCH, BORIS S., bank exec., lawyer; b. Odessa, Russia, Feb. 24, 1921; s. Samuel and Pauline B.; m. Barbara E. Sinclair, children—Joanne, Ellen. B.S., N.Y. U., 1947; LL.B., Columbia U., 1949. First dep. supt. banks State of N.Y., 1963-64; partner firm Root Barrett Cohen Knapp & Smith, 1964-66; sr. v.p., gen. counsel J. P. Morgan & Co. Inc. and Morgan Guaranty Trust Co. of N.Y., N.Y.C., 1966—; mem. fin. adv. bd. Town of Harrison, N.Y. Served with USMC, 1942-46, 51-52. Mem. Am. Law Inst., Am. Bar Assn., N.Y. State Bar Assn., Assn. Bar City N.Y. Clubs: India House, Golden's Bridge Hounds. Home: 55 Lincoln Ave Purchase NY 10577 Office: 23 Wall St New York NY 10015

BERKOW, IRA HARVEY, writer, journalist; b. Chgo., Jan. 7, 1940; s. Harold Grosswald and Shirley (Halperin) B.; m. Dolores Case, Apr. 18, 1978. B.A., Miami U., Oxford, Ohio, 1963; M.S. in Journalism, Northwestern U., 1965. Reporter Mpls. Tribune, 1965-67; sports columnist, sports editor Newspaper Enterprise Assn., N.Y.C., 1967-76, N.Y. Times, 1981—. Author: (with Walt Frazier) Rockin' Steady, 1974 (Am. Library Assn. Best Books of Year 1975), Beyond the Dream, 1975, Maxwell Street, 1977, The DuSablePanthers, 1978, (with Rod Carew) Carew, 1980; writer: TV documentary Champions of American Sport, 1983. Recipient Page One award Newspaper Guild, Mpls., 1966, Scipps-Howard Feature award, N.Y.C., 1969, N.Y. Pub. Library commendation, 1978, AP Sports Editors award, 1982. Mem. Baseball Writers Assn. Am., Basketball Writers Assn. Am. Home: 333 E 30th St New York NY 10016 Office: New York Times 229 W 43d St New York NY 10036

BERKOWITZ, LEON, artist; b. Phila., Sept. 14, 1919; s. Bernath and Yetta B.; m. Maureen Byrnes. B.A., U. Pa., 1942. Tchr. art Western High Sch., Washington, 1957-67; prof. art Corcoran Art Sch., 1968-82; co-founder Workshop Art Center, Washington, 1947-55. Exhibited in numerous one man shows in Am. and European museums; represented in numerous museum collections. Home: 2003 Kalorama Rd NW Washington DC 20009 *My concern in my painting has been to convert matter to energy, color to light.*

BERKOWITZ, MARSHALL, distillery exec.; b. Salem, Mass., May 28, 1932; s. Nathan and Rose (Lipschutz) B.; m. Sandra R. Brenner, Oct. 30, 1954; children—Nancy, Howard, Melissa. B.S., Ohio State U., 1954. Mng. dir. Mr. Boston Distiller Corp., Miami, Fla., 1969-74, pres., chief operating officer, 1974-76, Glenmore Sales Co., Miami, 1974-76; pres. Glenmore Distillery Co., Louisville, 1976-77, Am. Distilling Co., N.Y.C., 1977—; pres., chief exec. officer Austin Nichols & Co. Inc., N.Y.C., 1980—. Jewish. Home: 8900 Bay Dr Surfside FL 33154 Office: 1290 Ave of Americas New York NY 10104

BERKOWITZ, MONROE, economist, educator; b. Exeter, Pa., Mar. 9, 1919; s. Edward and Molly (Kaufman) B.; m. Shalvo Schwartz, Mar. 6, 1942; 1 son, Edward. A.B., Ohio U., 1942; A.M., Columbia U., 1946, Ph.D., 1951. Assoc. economist NWLB, 1942-44; mem. faculty Rutgers U., 1946—, prof. econs., 1960—, chmn. dept. econs.; mem. arbitration panels Am. Arbitration Assn., Fed. Mediation and Conciliation Service, N.Y.C. Office Collective Bargaining; cons. U.S. Dept. Labor, HEW, Nat. Cancer Inst. Author: (with others) Economics, Experience and Analysis, 1950, Processing Workmen's Compensation cases, 1969, Public Policy Toward Disability, 1976, Economics of Accidents in New Zealand, 1979. Mem. Nat. Acad. Arbitrators, Am. Econ. Assn., Indsl. Relations Research Assn., Nat. Rehab. Assn., Phi Beta Kappa. Home: 1791 Middlebrook Rd Bound Brook NJ 08805 Office: Dept Econs Rutgers U New Brunswick NJ 08903

BERKWITT, GEORGE JOSEPH, editor; b. Springfield, Mass., Feb. 14, 1921; S. Louis Harry and Lillian B.; m. Gilda King, Oct. 1, 1948; 1 dau., Randi Lynn. B.S. in Journalism, N.Y. U., 1949. Journeyman tool and diemaker Springfield Armory, 1941-44; promotional writer Air Reduction Inc., 1949-53; asso. editor Metalworking mag., 1953-58; indsl. mktg. editor Printer's Ink, N.Y.C., 1958-61; spl. feature editor Mill & Factory mag., N.Y.C., 1961-65; sr. editor Dun's Rev., N.Y.C., 1965-73; exec. editor Modern Industry mag., 1967-69; chief editor Indsl. Distbn. mag., N.Y.C., 1973—; editorial bd. Am. Bus. Press, N.Y.C., 1975-76. Pres. council, mem. bd. dirs. Hudson Guild Settlement House, 1973-75. Served with U.S. Army, 1944-45. Recipient Distinguished Service award. Mem. Soc. Advancement Mgmt. (past pres. N.Y. chpt., Achievement award), Internat. Material Mgmt. Soc. (past pres. N.Y. chpt.). Home: 280 9th Ave New York NY 10001 Office: 875 3d Ave New York NY 10022

BERLAGE, GAI INGHAM, sociologist, educator; b. Washington, Feb. 9, 1943; d. Paul Bowen and Grace (Artz) Ingham; m. Jan Coxe Berlage, Aug. 7, 1965; children: Jan Ingham, Cari Coxe. B.A., Smith Coll., 1965; M.A., So. Meth. U., 1968; Ph.D., NYU, 1979. Tchr. math. Piner Jr. High Sch., Sherman, Tex., 1968-69; asst. prof. sociology Iona

Coll., New Rochelle, N.Y., 1971-83, assoc. prof., 1983—, chmn. dept., 1981—. Author: Experience with Sociology: Social Issues in American Society; contbr. articles to profl. jours. Commr. Wilton Commn. on Aging and Social Services, 1980—, chmn., 1982—; chmn. Wilton Task Force Com. for Outreach Program, 1981-82; mem. Wilton Task Force for Pub. Health Nursing Assn., 1981-82; chmn. Wilton Task Force on Day Care, 1983—; bd. dirs. Wilton Meals on Wheels, 1983—. NSF trainee, 1965-68. Mem. Am. Sociol. Assn., N.Y. State Sociol. Assn., N. Am. Soc. Sociology of Sport, Inst. Sport and Social Analysis, Internat. Com. Sociology of Sport, Wilton Assn. Gifted Edn. (pres. 1980-81), Nat. Council Crime and Delinquency, Westchester Council Crime and Delinquency. Office: Dept Sociology Iona Coll New Rochelle NY 10801

BERLAND, ABEL EDWARD, lawyer, realtor; b. Cin., Aug. 27, 1915; s. Samuel and Ann (Brod) B.; m. Meredith E. Tausig, Aug. 31, 1940; children: Michael Gardner, Richard Bruce, Jay Robert. J.D., DePaul U., 1938, D.H.D., 1975. Bar: Ill. bar 1938. Vice chmn. Arthur Rubloff & Co., Chgo.; dir. Retirement Planning Funds Am., Inc.; real estate cons. Bd. dirs. Civic Fedn., Chgo. Crime Commn. Contbr. articles on real estate to profl. scholarly and trade jours. Trustee, mem. exec. com. and academic affairs com. DePaul U.; v.p. Civic Fedn. Met. Chgo.; spl. gifts com. Northwestern Meml. Hosp. Fellow Brandeis U., 1958—; recipient Nat. Community Service award Jewish Theol. Sem. Am. Mem. Am., Chgo. bar assns., Nat. Assn. Realtors, Realtors Nat. Marketing Inst. (C.C.I.M.), Am. Soc. Real Estate Counselors (pres. 1970), Newberry Library Assos., Pvt. Libraries Assn., Manuscript Soc., Am. Arbitration Assn. (nat. panel arbitrators), Internat. Real Estate Fedn. (counseling com.), Bibliog. Soc. Am., Bibliog. Soc. of U. Va., Shakespeare Soc., Am., Lex Legio, Wabash Avenue Assn. (dir.), Ill. State C. of C. (dir.), Pi Gamma Mu, Pi Kappa Delta, Lambda Alpha, Omega Tau Rau. Clubs: Book of California; Caxton, Mid-Day, Economic, Brandeis University (founder 1949), Brandeis University (pres. 1954), Realty, Standard, Grolier (N.Y.C.); Roxburghe of San Francisco; Philobiblon (Phila.). Home: 251 Sylvan Rd Glencoe IL 60022 Office: 69 W Washington St Chicago IL 60602

BERLAND, JAMES FRED, broadcasting station executive; b. Chgo., July 12, 1943; s. Samuel Jesse and Lillian (Singer) B. Student, Reed Coll., 1961-64, UCLA, 1964-66. Photographer with Elson-Alexandre, 1970-73; free lance journalist, 1970-74; public affairs dir. Sta. KPFK-Pacifica, Los Angeles, 1974-77; news dir., 1977-78; gen. mgr., v.p. Sta. KPFK, Pacificia Found. Radio, 1978—; mem. Calif. State Task Force on Telecommunications Policy. Mem. Assn. Calif. Public Radio Stas. (pres. 1980-82), Californians for Public Broadcasting (chmn. 1980-81, pres. 1981-83), Nat. Fedn. Community Broadcasters, Nat. Assn. Ednl. Broadcasters. Democrat. Unitarian. Office: 3729 Cahuenga Blvd W North Hollywood CA 91604

BERLAND, KENNETH K., retail company executive; b. 1922; m. Gloria Berland; children: Alan Lance, Elizabeth Anne. Grad., CCNY. With Melville Corp., N.Y.C., 1955—, v.p. and treas., 1957-64, corp. controller, 1964-65, treas. and controller, 1965-66, v.p., treas., controller, 1966-76, sr. v.p. fin. and adminstrn., treas., 1976-80, pres., 1980—, also dir.; Chmn. tax com. Volume FootWear Retailers Assn. Address: Melville Corp Harrison Exec Park 3000 Westchester Ave PO Box 677 Harrison NY 10528 *Achieving one's goals is success, providing that the foundation of such growth encompasses the principles of professionalism, diligence, high standards of quality in work, a willingness to change with the times, and above all intellectual and material integrity.* *

BERLANT, ANTHONY, artist; b. N.Y.C., Aug. 7, 1941; s. Emmanuel and Gertrude (Sands) B. Student, U. So. Calif., 1959-60; M.A., UCLA, 1963, M.F.A., 1964. Mem. faculty Am. River Jr. Coll., Carmichael, Calif., 1964, UCLA, 1965-69, Los Angeles State Coll., 1969; co-founder Mimbres Archeol. Center, 1973, Mimbres Found., 1976. Co-author: (with Mary Hunt Kahlenberg) Walk in Beauty-The Navajo and their Blankets, 1977; One-man shows include, David Stuart Gallery, Los Angeles, 1963, 65, 67, Dickson Art Gallery, UCLA, 1964, Hansen Gallery, San Francisco, Mizuno Gallery, Los Angeles, 1971, Wichita Art Mus., Whitney Mus. Am. Art, N.Y.C., 1973, Fourcade and Droll, N.Y.C., Utah Mus. Fine Arts, Salt Lake City, 1974, Phyllis Kind Gallery, Chgo., James Corcoran Gallery, Los Angeles, 1975, 79, Friedlander Gallery, Seattle, 1976, Tex. Gallery, Houston, 1976, 79, Sun Valley (Idaho) Center for Arts and Humanities, 1980, Xavier Fourcade, N.Y.C., 1981, group exhbns. include, Sch. of Visual Arts Mus., N.Y.C., 1977, Oakland (Calif.) Mus., Whitney Mus. Am. Art, Los Angeles County Mus. Art, 1978, U. Calif., Santa Barbara, Inst. Contemporary Art, U. Pa., Phila. *

BERLE, MILTON (REAL NAME MILTON BERLINGER), actor; b. N.Y.C., July 12, 1908; m. Joyce Mathews; 2 children; m. Ruth Cosgrove, Dec. 9, 1953; children—Vicki, Billy. Began profl. work as child actor in silent motion pictures for Biograph; later on stage in vaudeville; appearances on N.Y. legitimate stage include Earl Carroll Varieties, Saluta, Life Begins at 8:40, Ziegfeld Follies, See My Lawyer, I'll Take the High Road, Seventeen, The Goodbye People, Last of the Red Hot Lovers, Norman, Is That You?; later motion pictures include New Faces of 1937, Tall Dark and Handsome, 1941, Sun Valley Serenade, 1941, Over My Dead Body, 1943, Always Leave Them Laughing, 1949, Let's Make Love, 1960, It's a Mad, Mad, Mad, Mad World, 1962, The Oscar, The Loved One, Who's Minding the Mint, Where Angels Go, Trouble Follows, 1968, Can Hieronymus Merkin Ever Forget Mercy Humppe and Find True Happiness?, 1969, Lepke, 1974, The Muppet Movie, 1979; recently conducted radio program; TV actor: TV series Kraft Music Hall, 1958-59, Jackpot Bowling, 1960-61, Doyle Against the House (Emmy nominee), Dick Powell Show, 1961, Chrysler TV Spl, 1962, The Milton Berle Show, 1966, The Legend of Valentino, 1975; appeared in: The Best of Everybody, 1975, cabaret appearences in, Las Vegas, Nev., Miami Beach, Fla.; lyricist: Sam, You Made the Pants Too Long, I'm So Happy I Could Cry, Leave the Dishes in the Sink, Ma. Author: Out Of My Trunk, 1945, Earthquake, 1959, Milton Berle: An Autobiography, 1974; contbr. to: Variety Mag. Recipient Golden award AGVA, 1977, Emmy award, 1979. Mem. ASCAP, Am. Guild Authors and Composers, Grand Street Boys, Friar's (re-elected hon. abbot emeritus 1968) (N.Y.C) *

BERLE, PETER ADOLF AUGUSTUS, foundation executive; b. N.Y.C., Dec. 8, 1937; s. Adolf Augustus and Beatrice (Bishop) B.; m. Lila Sloane Wilde, May 30, 1960; children: Adolf Agustus, Mary Alice, Beatrice Lila, Robert Thomas. B.A. (Knox fellow), Harvard U., 1958, LL.B., 1964; LL.D., Hobart Smith Coll., 1977. Bar: N.Y. Assoc. Paul, Weiss, Rifkind, Wharton & Garrison, N.Y.C., 1964-71; ptnr. Berle, Butzel & Kass, N.Y.C., 1971-76, N.Y. state commr. environ. conservation, 1976-79; ptnr. Berle, Butzel, Kass & Case, N.Y.C., 1979—; trustee Twentieth Century Fund, Inc., N.Y.C., 1971—, vice chmn., sec., 1977—; teaching fellow econs. Harvard Coll., Cambridge, Mass., 1963-64; assoc. adj. prof. Sch. Urban Affairs Hunter Coll., 1974. Author: Does the Citizen Stand a Chance, 1974. Mem. N.Y. State Assembly, 1968-74; chmn. N.Y. Gov.'s Transition Task Force on Environment, 1974-75; commr. N.Y. State Moreland Act Commn. on Nursing Homes, 1975—. Served to 1st lt. USAF, 1959-61. Decorated Commendation medal; named Outstanding Legislator Eagleton Inst. Politics, 1971. Mem. Assn. Bar City N.Y. (mem. environ. law com., profl. responsibility com., energy policy com.), Fedn. Protestant Welfare Agys. (mem. com. on social policy 1974-76), Adirondack Mountain Club (bd. govs. 1972-76). Episcopalian. Home: 530 E 86th St New York NY 10028 Office: Twentieth Century Fund Inc 41 E 70th St New York NY 10021

BERLEANT, ARNOLD, philosopher; b. Buffalo, Mar. 4, 1932; s. Bernard and Elizabeth (Barkun) B.; m. Riva Schiller, Aug. 1, 1958; children—Jared Daniel, Andrea, Anne Nicole. Student, SUNY, Fredonia, 1949-51; B.M., Eastman Sch. Music, U. Rochester, 1953, M.A., 1955; Ph.D., SUNY, Buffalo, 1962. Teaching fellow SUNY, Buffalo, 1958-60, instr., 1960-61, lectr., 1961-62; asst. prof. philosophy C.W. Post Center, L.I. U., 1962-65, asso. prof., 1965-70, prof., 1970—; vis. asso. prof. San Diego State Coll., 1966; mem. social sci. faculty Sarah Lawrence Coll., 1966-68. Author: A Phenomenology of Aesthetic Experience, 1970; Contbr. articles to profl. jours. Served with U.S. Army, 1954-56. Am. Council Learned Socs. grantee, 1972, 76. Mem. Am. Soc. Aesthetics (sec.-treas. 1979—), AAUP, Am. Soc. Value Inquiry, L.I. Philos. Soc. Home: 25 Highfield Rd Glen Cove NY 11542 Office: Dept Philosphy CW Post Center of Long Island Univ Greenvale NY 11548

BERLEKAMP, ELWYN RALPH, computer engineer, educator; b. Dover, Ohio, Sept. 6, 1940; s. Waldo and Loretta (Kimmel) B.; m. Jennifer Wilson, 1966; children: Persis, Bronwen, David. B.S. in Elec. Engring; M.I.T., 1962; M.S., 1962; Ph.D. in Elec. Engring, 1964. Mem. Math. Research Center, Bell Telephone Labs., Murray Hill, N.J., 1967-71; asst. prof. elec. engring. U. Calif., Berkeley, 1964-67, prof. math., elec. engring. and computer sci., 1971—; now pres. Cyclotomics, Inc. Author: Algebraic Coding Theory, 1968, Winning Ways, 1982. Recipient award Eta Kappa Nu, 1972. Fellow IEEE (pres. group on info. theory 1973); mem. Nat. Acad. Engring. Home: Cyclotomics 2120 Haste Street Berkeley CA 94704

BERLIN, ALAN DANIEL, lawyer, oil company executive; b. Bklyn., Oct. 20, 1939; s. Joseph Jacob and Rose (Smith) B.; m. Renee Wellinger, Dec. 22, 1962; children—Nicole Suzanne, Allison Leigh. B.B.A., CCNY, 1960; LL.B., NYU, 1963, LL.M., 1968. Bar: N.Y. 1963. Asso. firm Aranow, Brodsky, Bohlinger, Einhorn & Dann, N.Y.C., 1965-68; asst. counsel Gen. Electric Co., N.Y.C., 1968-70; tax counsel Norton Simon Inc., N.Y.C., 1970-77; sr. v.p., gen. counsel Belco Petroleum Corp., N.Y.C., 1977—; asst. prof. Pace U. Law Sch., 1977—. Author monographs on fed. income tax. Bd. dirs. Mental Health Assn., Westchester; vice chmn. Briarcliff Manor (N.Y.) Peoples Caucus. Served with U.S. Army, 1963-65. Mem. Am. Bar Assn., N.Y. State Bar Assn., Assn. Bar City N.Y. Club: Masons. Office: 1 Dag Hammarskjold Plaza New York NY 10017

BERLIN, IRA, historian, educator; b. N.Y.C., May 27, 1941; s. Louis and Sylvia Toby (Lebwohl) B.; m. Martha L. Chait, Aug, 31, 1963; children—Lisa Jill, Richard Aaron. Ph.D., U. Wis., 1970. Vice pres. I.B. Alan, Inc., 1967-69; book rev. editor Wis. Mag. History, 1969; instr. U. Ill.-Chgo., 1970-72; asst. prof. history Fed. City Coll., Washington, 1972-74; fellow Davis Center Hist. Studies, Princeton U., 1975; prof. history U. Md., 1976—; mem. Columbia U. Seminar, Columbia U. Econ. History Program; editor Freedmen and So. Soc. project Nat. Archives. Author: Slaves Without Masters: Free Negros in the Antebellum South, 1975 (Book prize Nat. Hist. Soc. 1975), Freedom: Documentary History of Emancipation, Slavery and Freedom in the Era of the American Revolution; also articles. Recipient Distinguished Teaching award U. Wis., 1969; Younger Humanist fellow Nat. Endowment Humanities, 1971. Mem. Am., So. hist. assns., Orgn. Am. Historians, Internat. Sociol. Assn. (com. on race and ethnicity). Jewish. Address: Dept History Univ Maryland College Park MD 20742

BERLIN, IRVING, composer; b. Russia, May 11, 1888; came to U.S., 1893; s. Moses and Leah (Lipkin) Baline; m. Dorothy Goetz, Feb. 1913 (dec. July 1913); m. Ellin Mackay, Jan. 4, 1926; children: Mary Ellin Berlin Barrett, Linda Berlin Emmet, Elizabeth Berlin Peters. Ed. pub. schs., N.Y.C.; hon. degrees, Bucknell U., Temple U., Fordham U. Pres. The Irving Berlin Music Corp. Writer, composer popular songs; musical film Easter Parade; Broadway musical Mr. President, 1962; also stage musicals, various others; total songs composed about 800. Served as sgt. Infantry, at; Camp Upton, L.I. Recipient Presdl. Medal of Freedom, 1977, medal of Merit for This Is the Army; Lawrence Langer award for disting. lifetime achievement in Am. theater, 1978; Congl. Gold medal for God Bless America; decorated Legion of Honor (France). Clubs: Masons, Shriners, Elks, Lambs, Friars, City Athletic. Office: 1290 6th Ave New York NY 10104

BERLIN, NATHANIEL ISAAC, physician; b. N.Y.C., July 4, 1920; s. Louis and Gertrude (Sugarman) B.; m. Barbara Ruben, June 14, 1953; children: Deborah Joy, Marc David. B.S., Western Res. U., 1942; M.D., L.I. Coll. Medicine, 1945; Ph.D., U. Calif.-Berkeley, 1949. Intern Kings County Hosp., Bklyn., 1945-46, resident pathologist, 1946-47; Nat. Cancer Inst. postdoctorate research fellow U. Calif., 1948-50, research fellow, 1949-50, research asso., 1950-51, instr., 1951, lectr. and research assoc., 1952-53, lectr., assoc. research med. physicist, 1952-53; Nat. Heart Inst. spl. research fellow Nat. Inst. Med. Research, London, 1953-54; med. officer, analysis br. Effects div. Hdqrs. Armed Forces Spl. Weapons Project, 1954-56; head metabolism service, gen. medicine br. Nat. Cancer Inst., 1956-72, chief gen. medicine br., 1959-61, clin. dir., 1961-71, sci. dir. gen. lab. and clinics, 1969-72, dir. div. cancer biology and diagnosis, 1972-75; dir. Cancer Center, Northwestern U., 1975—, Genevieve B. Teuton prof. medicine, 1975—; vis. scientist Walter Hall Inst. Med. Research, Melbourne, Australia, 1980-81; cons. U.S. Naval Hosp., Bethesda, Md., 1955-65, Armed Forces Spl. Weapons Project, Dept. Def., 1957-59; alumni lectr. Downstate Med. Center, 1966; mem. panel diagnostic applications of radioisotopes in hematology Internat. Com. on Standardization in Hematology, 1964—, chmn., 1974-76; chmn. instnl. rev. bd. Fermi Nat. Lab., 1975—; mem. adv. com. div. blood diseases and resources Nat. Heart, Lung and Blood Diseases Inst., 1975-79; mem. adv. bd. cancer control, State of Ill., 1976—. Editorial adv. bd.: Cancer Letters; mem. editorial bd.: Blood; contbr. articles to med. jours. Mem. med. adv. com. Nat. ARC, 1969-75; trustee Ill. Cancer Council, pres., 1979; bd. dirs. Ill. div. Am. Cancer Soc.; mem. med. adv. bd. Leukemia Research Found., 1976-80; chmn. Leukemia Research Council, 1978-80. Served with AUS., 1943-45; lt. comdr. M.C. USNR, 1954-56; comdr. Res. Recipient Superior Service award HEW; Alumni medal for distinguished service to medicine State U. N.Y. Fellow AAAS, N.Y. Acad. Sci., Internat. Soc. Hematology; mem. Am. Fedn. Clin. Research, Soc. Exptl. Biology and Medicine, Am. Physiol. Soc., Biochem. Soc. (Eng.), Radiation Research Soc., Am. Soc. Hematology (publ. com., pub. issues com.), Assn. Am. Physicians, Am. Soc. Clin. Investigation, Am. Clin. and Climatol. Assn., Western Soc. Clin. Research, Mid-Eastern Soc. Nuclear Medicine (sec.-treas. 1957-60), Am. Soc. Clin. Oncology (legis. liaison com., pub. affairs com.), Am. Soc. Preventive Oncology (pres.), Am. Assn. Cancer Research, Sigma Xi, Alpha Omega Alpha, Zeta Beta Tau, Phi Delta Epsilon. Home: 1448 N Lake Shore Dr Chicago IL 60611 Office: Cancer Center Northwestern U 303 Chicago Ave Chicago IL 60611

BERLIN, OVERTON BRENT, anthropology educator; b. Pampa, Tex., Dec. 20, 1936; s. George Oswald and Goldia Winifred (Norwood) B.; m. Elois Ann Sanner, Mar. 4, 1957; children: Saleena Tam, Andrea Mila. B.A., U. Okla., 1959; M.A. (Woodrow Wilson fellow 1959), Stanford U., 1960, Ph.D., 1964. Instr. Harvard U., 1965; mem. faculty U. Calif., Berkeley, 1966—, prof. anthropology, 1973—, chmn. Ctr. Latin Am. Studies, 1983—; Fellow Center Advanced Study Behavioral Scis., 1969. Author: Tzeltal Numeral Classifiers, 1968; co-author: Basic Color Terms, 1969, Principles of Tzeltal Plant Classification, 1974. Fellow Calif. Acad. Scis.; mem. Nat. Acad. Scis., Am. Acad. Arts and Scis., Am. Anthrop. Assn., AAAS, Linguistic Soc. Am. Home: 803 Craft Ave El Cerrito CA 94530 Office: 2220 Piedmont Univ Calif Berkeley CA 94720

BERLIN, STANTON HENRY, lawyer; b. Chgo., May 24, 1934; s. Jerome S. and Gertrude (Levy) Weiss; m. Elinor R. Berlin, Sept. 2, 1958; children: Robert D., Michael J. B.B.A., U. Mich., 1955, M.B.A., 1956, J.D., 1959. Bar: Ill. 1959. Since practiced in, Chgo.; asso. Bell, Boyd and Lloyd, 1959-67, partner, 1968—. Fellow Am. Bar Found.; mem. Am., Ill., Chgo. bar assns., Legal Club Chgo., Law Club Chgo., Chgo. Mortgage Attys. Assn., U. Mich. Alumni Assn., Order of Coif, Phi Kappa Phi, Beta Alpha Psi, Beta Gamma Sigma, Tau Epsilon Rho, Sigma Alpha Mu. Home: 750 Willow Rd Winnetka IL 60093 Office: 70 W Madison St Chicago IL 60602

BERLIND, BRUCE PETER, educator, poet; b. Bklyn., July 17, 1926; s. Peter Sydney and Mae (Miller) B.; m. Doris Lidz, 1947 (div. 1950); m. Mary Elizabeth Dirlam (div. 1983); children: Lise, Anne, John, Paul, Alexandra. Student, Mercersburg Acad., 1941-43; A.B., Princeton U., 1947; M.A., Johns Hopkins U., 1950, Ph.D., 1958. Instr. English Colgate U., Hamilton, N.Y., 1954-58, asst. prof., 1958-63, asso. prof., 1963-66, prof., 1966—, Charles A. Dana prof. English, 1980—, chmn. dept. English, 1967-72, 80-83; poet in residence U. Rochester, 1966; USIS lectr., Germany, 1963, with Hungarian P.E.N. Translation Program, Budapest, 1977, 79, Fulbright grantee, Hungary, 1983-84. Author: poems Ways of Happening, 1959, Companion Pieces, 1971; translator: Selected Poems of Ágnes Nemes Nagy, 1980; asso. editor: The Hopkins Rev, 1949-53; contbr. poems, essays, revs. to mags. Served to 1st lt. AUS, 1945-46, 50-52. Mem. Poetry Soc. Am., Modern Lang. Assn., AAUP (mem. council, past pres. N.Y. State Conf.). Home: 62 Broad St Hamilton NY 13346

BERLIND, ROGER STUART, theatrical and film producer; b. N.Y.C., June 27, 1930; s. Peter Sydney and Mae (Miller) B.; m. Helen Polk Clark, July 7, 1962 (dec.); 1 son, William Polk; m. Brook Wheeler, May 19, 1979. A.B., Princeton U., 1952. Account exec. Eastman Dillon, Union Securities & Co., N.Y.C., 1956-60; gen. partner Carter, Berlind & Weill, N.Y.C., 1960-65; chmn. exec. com. Cogan, Berlind, Weill & Levitt, Inc., N.Y.C., 1965-69; chief exec. officer Shearson Am. Express, N.Y.C., 1970-74, vice chmn. bd., 1974-75, now dir.; dir. UBZ Corp., ETZ Lavud Ltd., Fin. News Network. Producer: (film) Aaron Loves Angela, 1975; (plays) Rex, 1976; Music Is, 1976, Diversions and Delights, 1977, The Merchant, 1977, The 1940's Radio Hour, 1979, Passione, 1980, The Lady from Dubuque, 1980, Amadeus, 1980, Sophisticated Ladies, 1981, Lydie Breeze, 1981, Nine, 1982, All's Well That Ends Well, 1983, The Real Thing, 1984, The Rink, 1984. Trustee Eugene O'Neill Theater Center, MacDowell Colony, Princeton U., Am. Acad. Dramatic Arts, Fresh Air Fund. Served with CIC U.S. Army, 1952-54. Mem. League N.Y. Theatres and Producers (gov.). Clubs: Princeton (N.Y.C.); Tower (Princeton, N.J.); University. Home: 120 East End Ave New York NY 10028

BERLINER, ALLEN IRWIN, dermatologist; b. N.Y.C., Apr. 18, 1947; s. Joseph Benjamin and Ruth (Kaplan) B. B.A., Queens Coll., 1967; M.D., SUNY-Buffalo, 1971. Diplomate: Am. Bd. Dermatology. Intern Nassau County Med. Ctr., East Meadow, N.Y., 1971-72; resident in dermatology Boston U. Med. Ctr., 1974-76, chief resident, 1976-77; practice medicine specializing in dermatology, Norwood, Mass., 1977—; clin. instr. dermatology Boston U., 1978—; asst. clin. prof. Tufts U., 1980—; active staff Norwood Hosp.; assoc. staff Boston U. Hosp., Boston City Hosp., Tufts-New Eng. Med. Ctr. Served as surgeon USPHS, 1972-74. Mem. Am. Acad. Dermatology, New Eng. Dermatol. Soc., Mass. Acad. Dermatology. Office: 511 Washington St Norwood MA 02602

BERLINER, ERNST, chemistry educator; b. Kattowitz, Germany, Feb. 18, 1915; came to U.S., 1940, naturalized, 1949; s. Joseph and Lucy (Selinger-Ehrenhaus) B.; m. Frances Jean Bondhus, Sept. 11, 1947; 1 dau., Susan Lucy. Student univs., Breslau and Freiburg, Germany, 1935-38; M.A., Harvard U., 1941, Ph.D., 1943. Mem. faculty Bryn Mawr Coll., 1944—, chmn. dept. chemistry, 1951-76, 80-82, prof., 1953—. Contbr. articles profl. jours.; Bd. editors: Jour. Organic Chemistry, 1963-68. Recipient Coll. Chemistry Tchr. award Mfg. Chemists Assn., 1963; Disting. Teaching award Lindback Found., 1975; Guggenheim fellow, 1962. Fellow AAAS; mem. Am. Chem. Soc. (Phila. Sect. award 1971), Chem. Soc. (London, Eng.), Sigma Xi. Home: 219 N Roberts Rd Bryn Mawr PA 19010

BERLINER, HANS JACK, computer scientist; b. Berlin, Germany, Jan. 27, 1929; came to U.S., 1937, naturalized, 1943; s. Paul and Theodora (Lehfeld) B.; m. Araxie Yacoubian, Aug. 15, 1969. B.A., George Washington U., 1954; Ph.D., Carnegie Mellon U., 1975. Systems analyst U.S. Naval Research Lab., 1954-58; group head systems analysis Martin Co., Denver, 1959-60; adv. systems analyst IBM, Gaithersburg, Md., 1960-69; sr. research scientist Carnegie-Mellon U., Pitts., 1974—. Editorial bd.: Artificial Intelligence, 1976—. Served with AUS, 1951-53. Awarded title Internat. Grandmaster Corr. Chess, 1968. Mem. Assn. Computing Machinery, Internat. Joint Conf. Artificial Intelligence, U.S. Chess Fedn., Internat. Computer Chess Assn. Among leading chess players U.S., 1950—, N.Y. State champion, 1953, Southwest Open champion, 1960, So. Open champion, 1949, U.S. Open Corr. Chess champion, 1955, 56, 59, World Corr. Chess champion, 1968-72. Developed 1st computer program to defeat a world champion at his own game (backgammon), 1979. Home: 657 Ridgefield Ave Pittsburgh PA 15216

BERLINER, JOSEPH SCHOLOM, economic educator; b. N.Y.C., Sept. 4, 1921; s. Michael and Yetta (Eisenberg) B.; m. Ann Korenbaum, Nov. 7, 1943; children: Paul, Carl, Nancy. B.A., Harvard U., 1947, Ph.D., 1953. Mem. faculty Syracuse (N.Y.) U., 1956-63; prof. econs. Brandeis U., Waltham, Mass., 1963—. Author: Factory and Manager in the USSR, 1957, Economy, Society and Welfare, 1972, The Innovation Decision in Soviet Industry, 1976. Fellow Social Sci. Research Council, Guggenheim Found., Woodrow Wilson Ctr.; grantee NSF, Nat. Council Soviet and East European Research. Mem. Assn. Comparative Econ. Studies (pres. 1975-76), Am. Assn. Advancement Slavic Studies (pres. 1963-64), Am. Econ. Assn. Democrat. Jewish. Home: 9 Chandler St Lexington MA 02173 Office: Brandeis U Waltham MA 02254

BERLINER, ROBERT WILLIAM, physician, university dean; b. N.Y.C., Mar. 10, 1915; s. William M. and Anna (Weiner) B.; m. Leah Silver, Dec. 21, 1941; children: Robert William, Alice (Mrs. James L. Hadler), Henry J., Nancy. B.S., Yale, 1936; M.D., Columbia, 1939. Intern Presbyn. Hosp., N.Y.C., 1939-41; resident physician Goldwater Meml. Hosp., N.Y.C., 1942-43, research fellow 3d div. research service, 1943-44, research asst., 1944-47; asst. medicine N.Y.U. Coll. Medicine, N.Y.C., 1943-44, instr., 1944-47; asst. prof. medicine Columbia, research assoc. dept. hosps., N.Y.C., 1947-50; chief lab. kidney and electrolyte metabolism Nat. Heart Inst., NIH, Bethesda, Md., 1950-62, dir. intramural research, 1954-68; dir. lab. and clinics NIH, 1968-69, dep. dir. sci., 1969-73; dean Yale U. Sch. Medicine, New Haven, Conn., 1973—; lectr. George Washington U. Sch. Medicine, 1951-73; professorial lectr. Schs. Medicine and Dentistry, Georgetown U., 1964-73. Editorial bd.: Jour. Clin. Investigation, 1954-59, 61-66, Am. Jour. Physiology, 1956-61, Circulation Research, 1958-63, 65-70. Mem. Am. Physiol. Soc. (pres. 1967-68), Soc. Gen. Physiol., Am. Soc. Clin. Investigation (pres. 1959-60), Soc. for Exptl. Biology and Medicine (pres. 1979-81), Am. Acad. Arts and Scis., Washington Acad. Medicine, Philos. Soc. Washington, Assn. Am. Physicians, Nat., Washington acads. scis., Am. Soc. Nephrology (pres. 1968-69), Harvey Soc., Sigma Xi, Alpha Omega Alpha. Office: Office of Dean Yale U Sch Medicine New Haven CT 06510 *

BERLINER, WILLIAM MICHAEL, business educator; b. Aug. 24, 1923; s. Samuel L. and Anna (Josephine) B.; m. Bertha A. Hagedorn, Apr. 27, 1946. B.S., N.Y. U., 1949, M.B.A., 1953, Ph.D., 1956. With Continental Casualty Co., 1941-42 45-46; retail div. mgr. B.F. Goodrich Co., 1949-50; asst. purchasing agt. Cutler-Hammer, Inc., 1950-51; mem. faculty N.Y. U., N.Y.C., 1951—, prof. mgmt. and orgnl. behavior, chmn. dept. mgmt., 1965-74; dir., cons. OTI Services, Inc., 1958—; cons. Mfrs. Hanover Trust Co., 1956—; edn. adviser Am. Inst. Banking sect. Am. Bankers Assn., 1962—; Ford Found. cons. exec. program, N.Y.C. and Met. Area, 1961-65; mem. policy com. regents external degree program Univ. of State of N.Y. Kellogg Found.; cons. exec. program Boys Clubs Am., 1962-67; faculty Stonier Grad. Sch. Banking, 1970—, Bank Personnel Grad. Sch., Am. Bankers Assn., 1980—; ednl. cons. Bank Adminstrn. Inst., 1976-81, Prochnow Grad. Sch. Banking, U. Wis., 1982—, N.Y. State Bankers Assn., 1977—; policy and adv. com. Non-collegiate sponsored instrn. program, SUNY, 1983—. Author: (with F.A. DePhillips and J.J. Cribbin) Management of Training Programs, 1960, (with W.J. McLarney (dec.) Management Practice and Training, Cases and Principles, 1974, Managerial and Supervisory Practice, 1979. Served to 1st lt. USAAF, 1942-45. Decorated D.F.C., Air medal with 6 oak leaf clusters, Purple Heart; Ford Found. grantee, 1960. Mem. Acad. Mgmt., Am. Soc. Personnel Adminstrn. (accredited), Am. Mgmt. Assn., Am. Mktg. Assn., Beta Gamma Sigma, Alpha Kappa Psi. Home: 27 Perkins Rd Greenwich CT 06830 Office: NY U Grad Sch Bus Adminstrn 100 Trinity Pl New York NY 10006

BERLINGER, WARREN, actor; b. Bklyn., Aug. 31, 1937; s. Elias and Frieda (Shapkin) B.; m. Betty Lou Keim, Feb. 18, 1960. Student, Profl. Children's Sch., 1952-55, Columbia, 1958. (Recipient Theatre World award for Blue Denim 1959); Broadway appearances include Annie Get Your Gun, 1946, Happy Time, 1950, Take A Giant Step, 1951, Anniversary Waltz, 1955, Roomful of Roses, 1957, Blue Denim, 1958, Come Blow Your Horn, 1960, Bernardine, 1953; London appearance in How to Succeed in Business Without Really Trying, 1963-64; film appearances include The Long Goodbye, Spinout; TV appearances on Secret Storm, 1955-57, The Funny Side, 1971-72, Touch of Grace, 1973. Named hon. mayor of Chatsworth, Calif., 1968, hon. sheriff, 1975. Address: care Fred Amsel & Assos 321 S Beverly Dr Beverly Hills CA 94712 *

BERLITZ, CHARLES FRAMBACH, linguist, author, archaeologist; b. N.Y.C., Nov. 22, 1913; s. Charles L. and Melicent (Berlitz) Frambach; m. Valerie Anne Seary, Jan. 28, 1950; children—Lin Maria, Marc Daniel. Grad., Riverdale County Sch., 1932; B.A. magna cum laude, Yale U., 1936. Dir. Berlitz Schs. Langs., N.Y.C., Balt., Boston, Chgo., and S.A., 1937- 41, v.p., 1944—, Berlitz Publs., 1947-66, pres., 1966—; v.p. Berlitz Schs. East Asia. Author: Berlitz Method Spanish, 1947, berlitz method English, 1947, berlitz method French, 1954, Berlitz Self Teacher French, 1949, Berlitz Self Teacher Spanish, 1949, Berlitz Self Teacher Italian, 1949, Berlitz Self Teacher German, 1949, 50, Berlitz Self Teacher Russian, 1951, Berlitz Self Teacher English, 1951, Berlitz Self Teacher Portuguese, 1953, Berlitz Self Teacher Hebrew, 1953, Phrase Books and Pocket Dictionaries—French, German, Spanish, Italian, 1954, Berlitz Self-Teaching Record Course: French, 1956, Spanish, 1957, German 1957, Italian, 1958, Language Teaching Films, 1962, World Language Phrase Book, 1962, Navajo, 1965, Atlantis, 1969, Mysteries from Forgotten Worlds, 1973, The Bermuda Triangle, 1974 (Dag Hammarskjold Internat. prize for Lit. 1976). Served as maj., intelligence officer AUS, 1941-46. Mem. Res. Officers Assn., Mil. Order of World Wars. Clubs: Overseas Press, Yale. Office: Doubleday 245 Park Ave New York NY 10017

BERLOWITZ, LAURENCE, university administrator, educator; b. N.Y.C., Oct. 20, 1934; s. Israel and Beatrice (Rothenberg) B.; m. Sandra Kaplan, Jan. 13, 1954; children: Dion, Aviva; m. Leslie Cohen Tuttleton, June 23, 1978; 1 stepdau., Sarah Tuttleton. A.B., U. Calif., Berkeley, 1954, Ph.D., 1965; M.A., UCLA, 1958. Mem. tech. staff Thompson-Ramo-Wooldridge Corp., Los Angeles, 1958-60; human factors scientist Western Devel. Lab., Philco Corp., Palo Alto, Calif., 1960-61; instr. biol. sci. Chabot Coll., 1961-64; research fellow med. research council, epigenetics research group U. Edinburgh, Scotland, 1965-66; asst. prof. biology SUNY, Buffalo, 1966-70, asso. prof., 1970-75, co-chmn. dept., 1968-69; program dir. genetic biology NSF, Washington, 1975-76, spl. asst. biol. directorate, 1976-77; prof. biology, asst. v.p. acad. affairs N.Y. U., N.Y.C., 1977-81; sr. research asso. N.Y. U. Center Sci. and Tech. Policy, 1980—; provost, v.p. acad. affairs, prof. biochemistry Clark U., Worcester, Mass., 1981-83; exec. dir. Mass. Biotech. Research Inst., Worcester, Mass., 1983—. NIH spl. fellow U. Nijmegen, Netherlands, 1972-73; NIH grants asso., 1974-75; recipient John Belling prize U. Calif., 1970. Mem. AAAS, Soc. Developmental Biology. Office: U Mass Med Center Worcester MA 01605

BERMAN, ALAN, physicist; b. Bklyn., Nov. 2, 1925; s. Hyman and Sarah (Levy) B.; m. Charlotte Bernstein, Apr. 28, 1962; children: Julia, Jessica, S. Jonathan, Margaret, James. A.B., Columbia U., 1947, Ph.D., 1952. Research scientist Hudson Labs., Columbia, N.Y.C., 1952-57, assoc. dir., 1957-63, dir., 1963-67; dir. research Naval Research Lab., Washington, 1967-82; dean Sch. Marine and Atmospheric Scis. U. Miami, 1982—; mem. Naval Research Adv. Com., 1982—. Served with AUS, 1944-46. Recipient Superior Civilian Service award Dept. Navy, 1969, Disting. Civilian Service award Dept. Def., 1973, Robert Dextar Conrad award, 1982; named Disting. Sr. Exec. Pres. of U.S., 1980. Fellow Am. Phys. Soc., Acoutical Soc. Am.; mem. Sigma Xi. Home: 6645 SW 118th St Miami FL 33156 Office: 4600 Rickenbacker Causeway Miami FL 33149

BERMAN, ALLAN, psychology educator; b. Boston, Sept. 27, 1940; s. Edward Isadore and Irene (Milesky) B.; m. Jerianne Louise Hoddes, June 21, 1964; children: Jennifer Ann, Andrew Ingram, Michael Ross. B.A., U. Mass., 1962; M.Ed., Boston U., 1964; Ph.D., La. State U., 1968. Diplomate: Am. Bd. Profl. Neuropsychology. Chief psychologist R.I. Dept. Corrections, Cranston, 1968-70; mem. faculty U. R.I., Kingston, 1970—, prof. psychology, 1976—, acting dept. chmn., 1973-75; cons. Gov. Med. Center, Providence, 1969-77, E. Greenwich (R.I.) Sch. Dept., 1971-72; dir. neuropsychology lab. R.I. Tng. Sch., Howard, 1970-74; mem. Gov. R.I. Adv. Council Correctional Services, 1971-75; clin. dir. Delta Cons., Providence, 1977—. Mem. editorial bd.: Jour. Learning Disabilities, 1978—; Contbr. articles to profl. jours. Mem. Am. Psychol. Assn., Eastern Psychol. Assn., New Eng. Psychol. Assn., R.I. Psychol. Assn. (exec. bd. 1971—, pres. 1973-76), Nat. Assn. for Children with Learning Disabilities (ethics com. 1977-80), R.I. Psychol. Assn. (exec. bd. 1975—), R.I. Assn. for Children with Learning Disabilities (profl. adviser, pres. 1978-81). Home: 15 Candle Hill Ct Warwick RI 02886 Office: Psychology Dept 407 Chafee Center Univ RI Kingston RI 02881 also Delta Cons 294 Governor St Providence RI 02906

BERMAN, ARIANE R., artist; b. Danzig, Mar. 27, 1937; m. Mario La Rossa, 1965. B.F.A., Hunter Coll., N.Y.C., 1959; M.F.A., Yale, 1962; AAUW and Found. des Etats-Unis fellow, U. Paris, 1962-63. Juror nat. screening com. Fulbright grants, 1976-77, chmn. screening com., 1977-78. One man shows at, Center Gallery, Conn., 1963, Harry Salpeter Gallery, N.Y.C., 1966, Brentano's Art Gallery, N.Y.C., 1973, Graphic Art Gallery, Tel Aviv, Galleria San Sebastianello, Rome, Eileen Kuhlik Gallery, N.Y.C., 1971, 73, Pub. Mus., Oshkosh, Wis., 1974, Wustum Mus. Fine Arts, Racine, Wis., Fontana Gallery, Pa., 1963, 71, 74, Galleria d'Arte Helioart, Rome, 1974, Munson Gallery, Conn., 1975, Ward-Nasse Gallery, N.Y.C., 1975, 77, 80, Phila. Art Alliance, 1980, Silvermine Guild Artists, Conn., 1976, Kornblee Gallery, N.Y.C., 1982, Babson Coll., Mass., 1983, Northwood Inst., Mich., others; exhibited in group shows at, Galerie Atrium Artis, Geneva, Switzerland, 1975, F 15 Gallery, Norway, 1974, Galeries Raymond Duncan, Paris, 1964, Asso. Am. Artists, N.Y.C., 1971, Circle Galleries Ltd., N.Y.C., 1974, Margo Feiden Galleries, N.Y.C., 1972, Gallery 500, Pa., 1973, Van Straaten Gallery, Chgo., 1974, Genesis Gallery, N.Y.C., 1978, Marymount Coll., N.Y.C., 1983, NYU, 1982, Fairleigh Dickenson U., Allentown Art Mus., Pa., numerous others; represented in permanent collections at, Am. Petroleum Inst., Israel Ministry of Tourism, USIA, McGregor-Doniger, Inc., Shipley Sch., Bryn Mawr, Pa., Readers Digest, N.J. Bd. Edn., Athena Gallery, New Haven, Charles E. Ellis Coll., Newton Square, Pa., Hearst Corp., Met. Mus. Art, Phila. Mus. Art, Phila. Art Alliance, Ms. mag., Seventeen, Redbook, Feminist Press, others. Recipient Yale Painting prize, 1960, Purchase award Purdue U., 1964, Stella Drabkin Meml. award, ACPS Purchase prize, 1973, Catherine Lorillard Wolfe Arts Club Gold medal, 1973, Hon. mention Hudson River Mus., 1974. Mem. Am. Color Print Soc., Nat. Assn. Women Artists, Yonkers Art Assn., Women's Caucus for Art, Met. Painters and Sculptors, Pen and Brush, League of Present Day Artists, Sheffield Art League, Silvermine Guild of Artists, Soc. Women Artists (past corr. sec.), Hunter Coll. Alumni Assn. (Hall of Fame 1974). Home: 161 W 54th St New York NY 10019 *I use art as a means of communicating to people. My work is representational and tries to depict life in all its humor, sorrow, satiric aspects, and dream-like qualities of humanity as I see it. I particularly use color for emphasis in everything I do—paintings, graphics, plastics, and sculpture.*

BERMAN, BARUCH, electrical engineer; b. Israel, Nov. 10, 1925; s. Joseph and Sonia (Leoff) B.; m. Rose S. Goodman, Sept. 22, 1952; children: Sharon J., Orrie A. B.S.E.E., Israel Inst. Tech., 1947, diploma Ingenieur, 1948; M.S.E.E., Columbia U., 1957, postgrad., 1958-60. Chief engr., mgr. engring. and sect. head aerospace and indsl. firms, 1948-66; v.p., asst. gen. mgr. engineered magnetics div. Gulton Industries, Inc., Hawthorne, Calif., 1974-77; mgr. power systems and control advanced tech. div. and energy tech. div. TRW, Redondo Beach, Calif., 1966-74, 77-82; with Space Systems dir. Rockwell Internat., Downey, Calif., 1982—; pres. Berman Engring., Palos Verdes Peninsula, Calif., 1966—. Contbr. articles to profl. jours. Served with Brit. Coast Guard, 1944-45. Fellow IEEE (exec. com. region 6 1981, nat. ethics com.), Inst. for Advancement Engring.; mem. Nat. Soc. Profl. Engrs. (nat. state govs. com.), Calif. Soc. Profl. Engrs. (past state chmn. profl. engr. in industry practice div.), Industry Application Soc., Indsl. Electronics and Control Instrumentation Soc., Magnetic Soc. Patentee transistorized regulators, thyristor light and heat and motor control. Home: 28739 Trailriders Dr Rancho Palos Verdes CA 90274 Office: Rockwell Internat 12214 Lakewood Blvd Downey CA 90241

BERMAN, BENNETT I., lawyer; b. Chgo., Oct. 29, 1918; s. Reuben and Lillian (Diamond) B.; m. Nancy Baer, Nov. 16, 1944; 1 dau., Cynthia Ann Berman Watson. B.S., U. Ill., 1940; LL.B., Harvard U., 1943. Bar: Ill. bar 1947. Gen. counsel Investors Realty & Mgmt. Co., Chgo., 1963-66; chief counsel, v.p. Nat. Tea Co., Rosemont, Ill., 1966—. Contbr. articles to profl. pubs. Served to lt. USNR, 1942-46. Mem. Ill. Bar Assn., Chgo. Bar Assn. (chmn. landlord and tenant subcom., lectr. continuing legal edn., Certificate of Appreciation). Clubs: Harvard of Chgo. (dir.), Quadrangle (Chgo.); Harvard of N.Y. Home: 1640 E 50th St Chicago IL 60615 Office: 9701 W Higgins Rd Rosemont IL 60018

BERMAN, BERNARD ALVIN, pediatric allergist; b. Boston, Mar. 12, 1924; s. Hyman Isaac and Elsie Marion (Dubbs) B.; m. Lois Deborah Landau, Aug. 27, 1955; children: Susan, Steven, Laura. M.D., Tufts U., 1948. Diplomate: Am. Bd. Allergy and Immunology. Am. Bd. Pediatrics (chmn. sect. pediatrics). Intern pediatrics Jewish Hosp., Bklyn., 1949-51; resident pediatrics Children's Hosp., Boston, 1953-55, active staff, 1957—; mem. staff N.E. Med. Center, 1958—; fellow pediatric allergy Jerome Glaser, M.D., Rochester, N.Y., 1956-58; practice medicine specializing in allergy, Brookline, Mass., 1957—; asst. pediatrics sch. medicine Boston U., 1957-67; staff physician Boston Lying-In Hosp., 1957—, Beth Israel Hosp., Boston, 1957—; Mt. Auburn Hosp., Cambridge, Mass., 1957—; cons. pediatrics Chelsea (Mass.) U.S. Naval Hosp., 1959-73; mem. staff St. Elizabeth's Hosp., Boston, 1959—, mem. allergy clinic, 1965—, dir. pediatric allergy, 1966—; mem. staff Boston Floating Hosp., 1959—, pres. alumni, 1973-76; dir. allergy clinic Boston City Hosp., 1966-70; sr. clin. instr. pediatrics sch. medicine Tufts U., Boston, 1957-65, assoc. clin. prof. pediatrics, 1966—; Regional cons. Children's Asthma Research Inst., Denver, 1959—; mem. Pres.' commn. White House Conf. Allergy, 1971; regional cons. Nat. Jewish Hosp., Denver, 1960, nat. trustee, 1975. Contbr. articles to profl. jours. Trustee Krebs Sch., Lexington, Mass., 1970-75. Served to lt. j.g. USNR, 1951-53. Fellow Am. Assn. Clin. Allergy Immunology, Am. Coll. Allergists (pres. 1974-75), Am. Acad. Allergy, Am. Coll. Chest Physicians, Am. Assn. Certified Allergists; mem. New Eng. Pediatric Soc., New Eng. Soc. Allergy, AMA, Mass., Norfolk County med. socs., Nat. Bd. Med Examiners, Greater Boston Med. Soc. (pres.), Brookline Med. Soc. (pres. 1971), Mass. Allergy Soc. (pres. 1980-82), Phi Delta Epsilon Grad. Med. Soc. Boston (pres.), Assn. Asthmatic Convalescent Homes (pres., mem. bd. govs.). Home: 31 Hyslop Rd Extension Brookline MA 02146 Office: 1714 Beacon St Brookline MA 02146

BERMAN, DANIEL LEWIS, lawyer; b. Washington, Dec. 13, 1934; s. Herbert A. and Ruth N. (Abramson) B.; m. Debra Virginia Olsen, Mar. 20, 1978; children: Priscilla Decker, Jane, Katherine Ann, Sara Mark. B.A., Williams Coll., 1956; LL.B., Columbia U., 1959. Bar: N.Y. 1960, Utah 1962. Asso. firm Chadbourne, Parke, Whiteside & Wolff, N.Y.C., 1959-60; asst. prof. law U. Utah, 1960-62; practice, Salt Lake City, 1962—; sr. ptnr. Berman & Anderson, 1981—; vis. prof. U. Utah, 1970, 74, 77; Mem. Utah Coordinating Council Higher Edn., 1965-68. Mem. Salt Lake County Merit Council, 1974-80; trustee Salt Lake Art Center, 1978-80; Democratic candidate for U.S. Senate from Utah, 1980. Mem. Am. Law Inst., Salt Lake Area C. of C. (bd. govs. 1976-79). Democrat. Jewish. Office: 50 S Main St Suite 1250 Salt Lake City UT 84144

BERMAN, EDGAR FRANK, surgeon, writer; b. Balt., Aug. 6, 1915; s. Isaas Isaac and Sarah (Katz) B.; m. Phoebe Rhea, Nov. 22, 1952. M.D., U. Md., 1939. Diplomate: Am. Bd. Surgery. Intern Sinai Hosp., Balt., 1939-40, resident in surgery, Lutheran Hosp., Johns Hopkins Hosp.; cons. surgeon to Albert Schweitzer Hosp., Lambarene, Gabon, 1960, Med. Aspects of Community Devel., Colombia, S.Am., 1961; coordinator rural health projects, Central Am., AID, 1962-65, Nat. Physicians Com. for Johnson and Humphrey, 1964; chief cons. to State Dept., AID on Latin Am. Health, 1962-67; dir. Haiti Med. Pilot Project, 1960-61; cons. to White House Task Force, Medicare, 1962-63; dir. of med. survey southeast Asia, 1960-61; Adviser to the Vice President of U.S., 1965-69. Author: Teilhardian Philosophy, 1966, The Unchanging Woman, 1967, Population and Foreign Policy, 1965, Population and Politics, 969, The Politician Primeval, 1974, The Solid Gold Stethoscope, 1976, Hubert-The Triumph and Tragedy of the Humphrey I Knew, 1979, The Compleat Chauvinist: A Guide for the Bedeviled Male; editor: The Carroll County Times, 1964-70; columnist: N.Am. Nespaper Alliance, 1970-71, USA Today. Bd. dirs. Pub. Welfare Found., Washington, 1960, Care/Medico, N.Y.C.; pres. Care/Medico, 1959-65; bd. dirs. Balt. County Gen. Hosp., 1965, Balt. Symphony Orch. Assn., 1960-65, Balt. Opera Soc., 1962-67, May Inst. of Autistic Children, Chatham, Mass., 1964, Latin Am. Commn., State of Md., 1967, Sino-Am. Center Internat. Sci. Studies, 1982; trustee Md. State Coll. and Univs., 1970—. Served to lt. USN, 1943-46. Recipient Moscow Internat. Fellowship award, 1957; fellowships from various univs., in Germany, 1952-55, U. Basel, Switzerland, 1957, U. Paris, 1957. Fellow A.C.S.; mem. AMA, Nat. Pub. Health Assn., Internat. Coll. Surgeons (regent 1957-62), N.Y. Acad. Scis. Democrat. Jewish. Address: 1116 Valley Rd Lutherville MD 21093

BERMAN, FRED JEAN, art educator; b. Milw., Nov. 3, 1926; s. Ezra and Frances (Heyman) B.; m. Joy Gross, Sept. 3, 1949 (div. Apr. 1966); children: Joseph Ezra, Jonathan Gerrit. B.S., Milw. State Tchrs. Coll., 1948; M.S., U. Wis., 1949. Instr. Layton Sch. Art, Milw., 1949-60; prof. art U. Wis.-Milw., 1960—; exchange lectr. Reading U., Eng., 1966-67. Exhibited one-man shows, Camden Arts. Ctr., London, 1983, U. Reading; works exhibited, Art Inst. Chgo., Corcoran Gallery of Art, Washington; work exhibited, Library of Congress; works exhibited, McRoberts and Tunnard Gallergy, London, Mus. Fine Arts, Boston, Pa. Acad. Art, Phila., Royal Acad. Art, London, San Francisco Mus. Art, Venice Biennale, Italy, Van. Mus. Fine Arts, Richmond, Whitney Mus. Am Art, N.Y.C.; work exhibited, others; work reproduced: Art in Am.; work reproduced in: Art Digest; work reproduced: Art Scene; work reproduced in: Art, Search and Self-Discovery (book), Inst. Contemporary Art Bull., London, Yong Am. of Whitney Mus. Am. Art; work reproduced: pub. and pvt. collections U.S. and abroad. Recipient 30 awards for art including Joseph Eisendrath award Art Inst. Chgo., 1950, awards Milw. Art Inst., 1947, 49, 51, 52, 53, 56, Wis. Salon of Art, U. Wis., 1951, 53, 67, 2 awards 4th Biennial of Paintings and Prints Walker Art Ctr., Mpls., 1954. Home: 3133 N Marietta Ave Milwaukee WI 53211 Office: Art Dept U Wis-Milw Milwaukee WI 53211

BERMAN, HAROLD JOSEPH, legal educator; b. Hartford, Conn., Feb. 13, 1918; s. Saul and Emma Rose (Kaplan) B.; m. Ruth Carol Harlow, June 10, 1941; children: Stephen Harlow, Jean Carol, Susanna, John Kingsley. B.A., Dartmouth Coll., 1938; certificate, London Sch. Econs. and Polit. Sci., 1939; M.A., Yale U., 1942, LL.B., 1947. Asst. prof. law Stanford U., 1947-48; vis. prof. law Harvard U., 1948-49; research assoc. Russian Research Center, 1948-70, mem. exec. com., 1952—, asst. prof. law, 1949-52, prof., 1952-73, Joseph Story prof. law, 1973-76, James Barr Ames prof. law, 1976—; lectr. law Salzburg Seminar Am. Studies, summer 1955, 67; lectr. Soviet Law Inst. des Hautes Etudes Internationale, Geneva, Switzerland, 1956-57; guest scholar Inst. State and Law, USSR Acad. Sci., 1961-62; lectr. Am. law Moscow State U., spring 1962, spring 1982; Frances Lewis scholar-in-residence Washington and Lee Law Sch., spring 1983; chmn. com. on teaching law outside of law schs. Assn. Am. Law Schs., 1955, 56, 63; gen. reporter Internat. Assn. Legal Sci. study of legal aspects East-West trade, 1956-58; del. Econ. Commn. Europe, Geneva, 1956-57; mem. legal com. U.S.-USSR Trade and Econ. Council, 1974—. Author: Justice in U.S.S.R.: An Interpretation of Soviet Law, 1950, rev. edit. enlarged, 1963, Soviet Law in Action: The Recollected Cases of a Soviet Lawyer, (with Boris A. Konstantinovsky), 1953, The Russians in Focus, 1953, Soviet Military Law and Administration, (with Miroslav Kerner), 1955, On the Teaching of Law in the Liberal Arts Curriculum, 1956, The Nature and Functions of Law, 1958, 4th edit, Introduction, The Trial of the U-2, 1960, Soviet Criminal Law and Procedure, 1966, 2d edit., 1972, (with Peter B. Maggs) Disarmanent Inspection under Soviet Law, 1967, The Interaction of Law and Religion, 1974, Law and Revolution: The Formation of the Western Legal Tradition, 1983; Editor, translator: (with Miroslav Kerner) Documents on Soviet Military Law and Administration, 1955, Basic Laws on the Structure of the Soviet State, (with John B. Quigley), 1969, Soviet Statutes and Decisions, vols. 1-5, 1964-69; Editor, co-author: Talks on American Law, 1961, 2d edit., 1971, Soviet-American Trade in a Legal Perspective, 1976; Contbr. articles to legal, and other jours. and mags. Chmn. Newton Sch. Com., 1963-65. Served as sgt. AUS, 1942-45. Decorated Bronze Star.; Rockefeller Found. grantee to study in, Europe, 1956-57; Ford Found. and Am. Council Learned Socs. grantee to study in, USSR, 1961-62; Nat. Humanities Center fellow, 1979-80; Fulbright prof., Moscow, spring 1982. Mem. Am. Assn. Advancement Slavic Studies, Am. Soc. Internat. Law, Am. Soc. Legal History, Am. Legal Studies Assn. (hon.), Order of Coif, Phi Beta Kappa. Home: 7 Chauncy Ln Cambridge MA 02138

BERMAN, HOWARD LAWRENCE, congressman; b. Los Angeles, Apr. 15, 1941; s. Joseph M. and Eleanor (Schapiro) B. B.A., UCLA, 1962, LL.B., 1965. Bar: Calif. 1966. Vol. VISTA, Balt., San Francisco, 1966-67; assoc. Levy, Van Bourg & Hackler, Los Angeles, 1967-72; mem. Calif. State Assembly from 43d Dist., 1972-82 (majority leader), 98th Congress from 26th Calif. Dist. Pres. Calif. Fedn. Young Democrats, 1967-69; mem. exec. bd. Ams. for Democratic Action, Anti-Defamation League B'nai B'rith. Office: Room 1022 Longworth House Office Bldg Washington DC 20955

BERMAN, IRWIN, machinery manufacturing company executive; b. Bronx, N.Y., Oct. 16, 1925; s. Morris and Fannie (Rosen) B.; children: Kenneth Howard, Benjamin Seth. B.S., Coll. City N.Y., 1948; M.S., Stevens Inst. Tech., 1953; Ph.D., Poly. Inst. N.Y., 1959. Head analysis sect. Wright Aero. div. Curtis-Wright Corp., Woodridge, N.J., 1948-54; research asso. Poly. Inst. N.Y., 1954-56; head solid mechanics dept. Foster Wheeler Corp., Livingston, N.J., 1956-76, tech. dir., 1976-78, chmn. tech. directorate, 1978—; adj. prof. mech. engring. N.Y. U., 1960-71; chmn. 8th Internat. Conf. High Energy Rate Fabrication, 1984. Editor: Computer Software in Structural Analysis, 1970, Computer Software-Verification, Qualification, Certification, 1972, Explosive Welding, Forming, Plugging and Compaction, 1980, Computers in Engineering, 1982, Jour. Pressure Vessell Tech, 1973-77; contbr. profl. jours. Served with inf. AUS, 1944-46; ETO. Decorated Purple Heart. Fellow ASME (v.p., chmn. policy bd. communications 1977-81, sr. v.p., chmn. council engring. 1981-85, Centennial medallion 1980, Pressure Vessels and Piping medal 1982); mem. Soc. Exptl. Stress Analysis, Montclair Soc. Engrs., Sigma Xi, Tau Beta Pi, Pi Tau Sigma, Sigma Gamma Tau. Patentee in field. Office: 12 Peach Tree Hill Rd Livingston NJ 07039 *The excitement of life is change, which is the only item of permanence.*

BERMAN, JANIS GAIL, municipal commissioner; b. Los Angeles, Jan. 14, 1946; d. Albert and Beatrice (Krupnick) Axelrod; m. Joel Howard Schwartz, Dec. 14, 1968 (div. 1974); m. Howard Berman, June 24, 1978; children: Brinley Ann, Lindsey Rose. B.S., Calif. State U.-Northridge, 1969. Tchr. Montessori Sch., Santa Monica, Calif., 1972-74; fin. coordinator Democratic Party, Los Angeles, 1975-77; exec. dir. Calif. Consumer Adv. Council, Sacramento, 1977-80, Calif. Mus. Sci. and Industry, 1982, pres., 1981-83; colisium commr. Los Angeles Colisium, 1984. Founder Sacramento Women's Campaign Fund, Sacramento, 1981, Los Angeles Women's Campaign Fund, 1983. Recipient award for service to entertainment community Hollywood Reporter, 1982, award for inspiration Calif. Mus. Found., Los Angeles, 1983. Jewish. Home: 3346 Prospect Ave Washington DC 20007

BERMAN, LAZAR, pianist; b. Leningrad, USSR, Feb. 26, 1930; s. Naum and Anna (Makower) B.; m. Valentina, Dec. 28, 1968; 1 son, Pavel. Grad., Moscow Conservatory, 1953, student master classes, 1953-57. Concert debut, 1934, orch. debut, Moscow Philharmonic, 1940; profl. concert pianist, 1957—, U.S. debut, Miami U., Oxford, Ohio, also Am. Orch., 1976, Carnegie Hall debut with, N.J. Symphony Orch., 1976; recording artist. Mem. Philharmonic Soc. Moscow, USSR-Belgium Friendship Soc. (a founder). Winner 1st prize Internat. Youth Festival, E. Berlin, 1951; 4th pl. Queen Elisabeth of Belgium contest, Brussels, 1951. Office: care Jacques Leiser Artists's Mgmt Dorchester Towers 155 W 68th St New York NY 10023 *

BERMAN, LOUISE MARGUERITE, teacher educator; b. Hartford, Conn., July 6, 1928; d. Jacob and Anna Bertha (Woike) B. A.B., Wheaton Coll., 1950; M.A., Columbia U., 1953, Ed.D., 1960. Instr. Central Conn. State Coll., New Britain, 1954-58; asst. prof., then assoc. prof. curriculum U. Wis., Milw., 1960-65; assoc. sec. Assn. for Supervision and Curriculum Devel., Washington, 1965-67; prof. edn. U. Md., College Park, dir. U. Center for Young Children, 1967-75, prof. dept. adminstrn., supervision and curriculum devel., 1975—, interim chmn. dept., 1978-81, assoc. dean Coll. Edn., 1979-81; vis. prof. U. P.R., summer 1969, U. B.C., summers 1977, 78; Mem. U.S. Nat. Com. for Early Childhood Edn., 1969—. Author: From Thinking to Behaving, 1967, New Priorities in the Curriculum, 1968, Supervision, Staff Development and Leadership, 1971, Beyond Confrontation: An Analysis of Power, 1973, (with Jessie A. Roderick) Curriculum: Teaching the What, How and Why of Living, 1977; Editor: (with Jessie Roderick) Feeling, Valuing, and the Art of Growing: Perspectives on the Affective, 1977, (with Alice Miel) Educating for World Cooperation. Mem. Am. Ednl. Research Assn. (disting. contbr. to curriculum award Div. B), World Council on Curriculum and Instrn. (exec. com. 1971-74, 82, 83, pres. 1979-81), Assn. for Supervision and Curriculum Devel. (dir., pres. Md. unit 1978-79), Common Cause, World Future Soc., Profs. Curriculum, Pi Lambda Theta, Kappa Delta Pi. Presbyterian. Home: 7619 Haines Ct Laurel MD 20707 Office: Coll Edn U Maryland College Park MD 20742 *Living is a combination of reflection on the past, immersion in the moment, and hope for the future. Living involves observing closely, listening responsively, thinking creatively, feeling compassionately, and acting ethically.*

BERMAN, MARLENE OSCAR, neuropsychologist; b. Phila., Nov. 21, 1939; d. Paul Oscar and Elvelyn (Hess) Weizenblut (Oscar); m. Michael Brack Berman, June 23, 1963 (div. Feb. 1980); 1 son, Jesse Michael. B.A., U.Pa., 1961; M.A., Bryn Mawr Coll., 1964; Ph.D., U. Conn., 1968; postgrad., Harvard U., 1968-70. Research assoc. Boston VA Med. Ctr., 1970-72, clin. investigator, 1973-76, research psychologist, 1976—, mem. Com. for Protrection Human Participants in Research, 1970-75, assoc. prpf. neurology, 1975-82, prof. neurology and psychiatry, 1982—, dir. lab. neuropsychology, div. psychiatry, 1981—; affiliate prof. psychology Clark U., Worcester, Mass., 1975—. Contbr. articles to profl. jours. Coordinator Newton Communi ty Schs. (Mass.), 1978-80. Recipient Research Scientist Devel. award Nat. Inst. Alchol Abuse and Alcholism, 1981—, Clin. Investigator award, VA, 1973-76; USPHS and Dept. Health and Human Services grantee, 1964—. Fellow Am. Psychol. Assn. (sec.-treas. 1981-83, awards com. 1980—); mem. Acad. Aphasia, Soc. Neurosci., Internat. Neuropsychol. Soc., Psychonomic Soc., Com. to Combat Huntington's Disease, Internat. Council Psychologists, N.Y. Acad. Scis., Eastern Psychol. Assn. Democrat. Jewish. Home: 115 Cotton St Newton MA 02158 Office: 150 S. Huntington Ave Boston MA 02130 *THTS: the four most significant helpers in my career have been, in alphaetical order, hard work luck, mentors, and a sense of humor.*

BERMAN, MARSHALL HOWARD, polotical science educator, writer; b. Bronx, N.Y., Nov. 24, 1940; s. Murray and Betty (Shur) B.; m. Carole Greenman, June 18, 1969 (div. June 1982); 1 son, Marc (dec. 1980); m. Meredith Tax, July 11, 1982; 1 stepdau., Corey Tax Schwartz. A.B., Columbia U., 1961; B.Litt., Oxford U., (Eng.), 1963; Ph.D., Harvard U., 1968. Tutor govt. Harvard U., 1964-67; prof. polit. sci. CCNY, CUNY, 1967—; vis. prof. polit. sci. Stanford U., 1972-73; vis. prof. Am. studies (U. N. Mex.), 1980. Author: The Politics of Authenticity, 1970, All That is Solid Melts Into Air, 1982; editorial bd.: Dissent mag., 1979—. NEH fellow, 1973-74; Guggenhiem fellow, 1981-82; recipient E.V. DebbsMeml. prize, 1980. Mem. Am. Polit. Sci. Assn., Caucus for a New Polit. Sci. Jewish. Home: 838 West End Ave New York NY 10025 Office: CCNY 138th Ar and Convent Ave New York NY 10031

BERMAN, MARTIN M., TV producer; b. N.Y.C., May 8, 1946; s. Abraham B.; m. Elyse Melnikoff; children: Kimberly, Lauren. With ABC, 1967-74; film editor, producer Eyewitness News, WABC-TV, 1970-72; pres. Maravilla Prodns., 1974-76. Producer network spls., ABC-TV, 1972-75; prodns. include Geraldo Rivera: Good Night America; over 250 segments for Good Morning America; 1st show to air the Zupruder film, numerous others; other prodns. include Tell Me Where Can I Go; producer: Hour Magazine, Group W Prodns., 1980-81; exec. producer, 1981—; co-producer variety spls. for cable TV, 1979. Recipient 5 Emmy awards, George Foster Peabody award, Robert F. Kennedy Journalism award, 3 AP Broadcasters Assn. award, Columbia-du Pont award, award for documentary San Francisco Internat. Film Festival, Chgo. Internat. Film Festival, Scripps-Howard Disting. Journalism award, others. Office: 5800 Sunset Blvd Los Angeles CA 90028

BERMAN, MILTON, history educator; b. N.Y.C., Apr. 18, 1924; s. Morris and Ida (Epstein) B.; m. Barbara Ann Roesch, Aug. 18, 1968. B.A., Hofstra Coll., 1953; A.M., Harvard U., 1954, Ph.D., 1959. Instr. history Harvard U., 1959-61, vis. assoc. prof., summer 1963; fellow Charles Warren Center, 1968-69; asst. prof. U. Rochester, N.Y., 1961-73, assoc. prof., 1963-70, assoc. chmn. history dept., 1966-68, prof. history, 1970—. Author: John Fiske: The Evolution of a Popularizer, 1961. Served with U.S. Army, 1949-50. Mem. Am. Hist. Assn., Orgn. Am. Historians. Democrat. Jewish. Home: 149 Genesee Park Blvd Rochester NY 14619 Office: Dept History Univ Rochester Rochester NY 14627

BERMAN, MIRA, advertising agency executive; b. Danzig, June 1, 1928; d. Max and Riva (Gutman);; d. Max and Riva (Berman); m. Richard D. Freedman, Jan. 23, 1972. Ed., Profl. Children's Sch., Berkshire Music Sch. and Festival, Juilliard Sch. Music, David Mannes Coll. Music, N.Y. U., Columbia. Chief copywriter Girl Scouts Am., 1948-50; sr. copywriter Bamberger's, 1950-52; advt. dir., head women fashions Bond Stores, 1952-55; copy dir., Robert Hall, 1955-56; Advt. copy dir. Gimbels, N.Y.C., 1956-57; dir. pub. relations, fashion Snellenburgs, 1957-59; sr. v.p. pub. relations and advt. Lavenson Bur. Advt., 1959-66; pres. Allerton, Berman & Dean, 1966-76; chairperson, chief exec. officer Gemini Images, Inc., 1976—; mem. faculty master's degree program in tourism and travel adminstrn. New Sch. for Social Research, N.Y.C.; Co-chmn. 1st ann. Internat. Symposium Travel and Tourism, Am. Mgmt. Assn.; co-chmn. 1st ann. Marketing Through Retailers Symposium, 1966-67, staff lectr., 1967-70; condr. Modern Bank Practices Seminars; Am. Assn. Advt. Agencies rep. to Nat. Advt. Rev. Bd. Author: Marketing Through Retailers, 1967, also Spanish and Japanese edits; Travel editor: Woman's Life Mag. Recipient Israel Ministry Tourism award; Fashion Gold medal; Carl V. Cesery award Tile Contractors Assn. Am.; silver award; bronze award; AMITA Sister award; winner Gold medal Internat. Film and TV Festival N.Y., Grand award. Mem. Am. Advt. Fedn. (named one of Ten Top Women in Advt.), Fin. Publicist Assn. Am., The Fashion Group, Pub. Relations Soc. Am. (bd. govs.), Phila. Pub. Relations Assn., Am. Soc. Travel Agts., Soc. Advancement Travel for Handicapped, Africa Travel Assn., International Tourism Assn., Nat. Council Women., Women Execs. Internat. (exec. dir.). Home: 116 Central Park South New York NY 10019 Office: 853 Seventh Ave New YorkCity NY 10019 *Goals, aims and my philosophy always seem to go in the same direction-PEOPLE-in business and in private life to succeed is to try to understand, train, motivate and listen to people around me. Also, to learn from those whose ideals and philosophies have inspired me-and never to forget the opportunities offered me and to be so thankful for where I am today.*

BERMAN, MURIEL MALLIN, retail exec., civic worker; b. Pitts.; d. Samuel and Dora (Coopersman) Mallin; m. Philip I. Berman, Oct. 23, 1942; children—Nancy, Nina, Steven. Student, U. Pitts., 1943, Carnegie Tech. U., 1944-45; B.S., Pa. State Coll. Optometry, 1948; postgrad., U. Pitts., 1950, Muhlenberg Coll., 1954, Cedar Crest Coll., 1953, D.F.A., 1972. Practice optometry, Pitts.; vice-chmn. bd. Hess's Inc., Allentown, Pa.; sec., dir. Fleetways, Inc. (real estate); sec.-treas., dir. Philip and Muriel Berman Found.; sec. D.F. Bast, Inc., Fleet-Power, Inc. Producer: weekly TV show College Speak-Out, 1967—; producer, moderator: TV show Guest Spot. Active in UNICEF, 1959—, ofcl. non-govtl. orgns., 1964, 74; founder, donor Carnegie-Berman Coll. Art Slide Library Exchange; mem. Aspen (Colo.) Inst. Humanistic Studies, 1965 mem. Aspen (Colo.) Inst. Humanistic Studies, Tokyo, 1966; chmn. exhibits Great Valley council Girl Scouts U.S.A., 1966; adminstrv. head, chmn. various events Allentown Bicentennial, 1962; vice-chmn. Women for Pa. Bicentennial, 1976; co-chmn. Lehigh County Bicentennial Bell-Trek, 1976; patron Art in Embassies Program, Washington, 1965—; chmn. Lehigh Valley Ednl. TV, 1966—; program chmn. Fgn. Policy Assn. Lehigh County, 1965-67; treas. ann. ball Allentown Symphony, 1955—; mem. art adv. com. Dieruff High Sch., Allentown, 1966—; chmn. art. com. Episcopal Diocese Centennial Celebration, 1971; mem. Pa. Council on Status of Women, 1968-73; adv. com. U.S. Center, Internat. Women's Year; mem. U.S. del., 1975; chmn. numerous art shows; mem. Art Collectors Club Am., Am. Fedn. Art, Friends of Whitney Mus., Mus. Modern Art, Mus. Primitive Art, Jewish Mus., Kemmerer Mus., Bethlehem, Pa., Univ. Mus., Phila., Archives of Am. Art, Met. Opera Guild, others, Electoral Coll., 1968, Democratic Platform Com., 1972; del. Dem. Nat. Conv., 1972; bd. dirs. Pa. Ballet, Heart Assn. Pa., Hadassah, Allentown Art Mus. Aux., Phila. Chamber Symphony, Baum Art Sch., Lehigh County Cultural Center; trustee Kutztown State Coll., 1960-66, vice-chmn. bd., 1965; trustee, sec. bd. Lehigh Community Coll.; mem. nat. bd. UN-U.S.A., 1977—; trustee Pa. Council on Arts, Smithsonian Art Council, Bonds for Israel. Named Woman of Valor State of Israel, 1965; recipient Centenial Yr. hon. citation Wilson Coll., 1969; Henrietta Szold award Hadassah; Outstanding Woman award Allentown YWCA, 1973. Mem. LWV, Hist. Soc. Lehigh County, Lehigh Art Alliance, Phila. Art Alliance, UN We Believe. Jewish. Club: Wellesley. Good will tour to Latin Am. for U.S. Dept. State, 1965. Address: 20 Hundred Nottingham Rd Allentown PA 18103

BERMAN, NEIL SHELDON, chem. engr.; b. Milw., Sept. 21, 1933; s. Henry and Ella B.; m. Sarah Ayres, June 3, 1962; children—Jenny, Daniel. B.S., U. Wis., 1955; M.S., M.A., U. Tex., Austin, 1961, Ph.D., 1962. Engr. Standard Oil Co. Calif., Los Angeles, 1955-62; research engr. E.I. DuPont Co., Wilmington, Del., 1962-64; from asst. prof. to prof. chem. engring. Ariz. State U., 1964—; cons. air pollution, fluid dynamics. Mem. Phoenix Air Quality Maintenance Area Task Force, 1976-77. Contbr. articles on fluid dynamics of polymer solutions, air pollution, thermodynamics and chem. engring. edn. to profl. jours. Served to capt. M.S.C. USAR, 1956-58. Recipient numerous grants for research in fluid dynamics and air pollution. Mem. Ariz. Council Engring. and Sci. Assns. (chmn. 1980-81), Am. Inst. Chem. Engrs. (chmn. Ariz. sect. 1978-79), ASME, Am. Chem. Soc., Am. Phys. Soc., Am. Soc. Engring. Edn., Ariz. Acad. Sci., Sigma Xi, Tau Beta Pi, Phi Kappa Phi. Home: 418 E Geneva Dr Tempe AZ 85282 Office: Dept Chem Engring Ariz State U Tempe AZ 85287

BERMAN, PANDRO SAMUEL, motion picture producer; b. Pitts., Mar. 28, 1905; s. Harry M. and Julie E. (Epstein) B.; m. Kathryn Hereford, July 20, 1960; children: Harry Michael, Susan Pamela, Cynthia. Student pub. schs. Asst. dir., asst. cutter F.B.O. Studios, Hollywood, Calif., 1923-28; with R.K.O. Studios, Hollywood, 1928-40, producer, 1930-37, head prodn., 1937-40; producer M.G.M. Studios, 1940-67, Twentieth Century Fox Studio, 1967-70. Films include: What Price Hollywood, 1932, Morning Glory, 1933, The Gay Divorcee, 1934, Of Human Bondage, 1934, Roberta, 1935, Alice Adams, 1935, Top Hat, 1935, Winterset, 1936, Stage Door, 1937, Gunga Din, 1939, Hunchback of Notre Dame, 1940, Seventh Cross, 1944, National Velvet, 1944, Dragon Seed, 1944, Portrait of Dorian Gray, 1945, Three Musketeers, 1947, Madame Bovary, 1948, Father of the Bride, 1950, Ivanhoe, 1951, Knights of the Round Table, 1953, Blackboard Jungle, 1954, Bhowani Junction, 1955, Tea and Sympathy, 1956, Something of Value, 1957, Brothers Karamazov, 1958, Reluctant Debutante, 1959, Butterfield 8, 1960, Sweet Bird of Youth, 1962, The Prize, 1963, Patch of Blue, 1965. Mem. Acad. Motion Picture Arts and Scis. (Irving G. Thalberg award 1977). Jewish. Club: Hillcrest Country. Address: 914 N Roxbury Dr Beverly Hills CA 90210

BERMAN, PHILIP I., retail executive, electric company executive; b. Pennsburg, Pa., June 28, 1915; s. Joseph and Dora (Feingold) B.; m. Muriel Mallin, Oct. 20, 1942; children: Nancy M., Nina M., Steven M. LL.D., Ursinus Coll., 1968; D.H.L., Lehigh U., 1969; Ph.D.(h.c.), Hebrew U., 1979. Chmn. bd. Commonwealth Industries, Inc., 1969—; pres. Allen Electric Co., Inc., Allentown, Pa., 1965—, Philip I. Berman/DBA Fleetways, 1962—; chmn. bd., chief exec. officer Hess's Dept. Stores, Inc., Allentown, 1968—; dir., mem. com. pub. relations 1st Nat. Bank Allentown; underwriting mem. Lloyd's of London, 1968—; dir. Crown Am. Corp. Mem. Pa. Electoral Coll., 1964; founding chmn., mem. Citizens for Lehigh County Progress, 1966—; chmn. Allentown Redevel. Authority, 1960-69; Pa. rep. Internat. Exec. Service Corps; del. to 43d meeting ECOSOC, UN, Geneva, 1967; participant State Dept. Art in Embassies Program; active Lehigh U., numerous other cultural, ednl., philanthropic instns.; bd. assos. Muhlenberg Coll.; pres. bd. Philip and Muriel Berman Found., 1955—; bd. dirs. Lehigh Valley Ednl. TV-Channel 39, 1964—, pres., 1973-77; bd. dirs. Allentown Housing Devel. Corp., 1968-80; bd. dirs., pres. Allentown Symphony Assn., Pa. Indsl. Devel. Corp.; mem. Lehigh County-Allentown Community Council, 1979—; bd. dirs., pres. Baum Art Sch., World Jewish Congress; mem. internat. bd. Hebrew U., Jerusalem, 1968—; bd. dirs. Am. Friends Hebrew U., 1968—; chmn. Pa. State Pub. TV Network Commn., 1970—; trustee, chmn. fin. and endowment coms. Ceda Crest Coll., 1965-71; bd. dirs. region Research Better Schs., Phila., 1970-79; bd. govs. Shenkar Coll. Fashion and Textile; mem. exec. bd. Lehigh County council Boy Scouts Am., 1968—; nat. bd. dirs. Am. Jewish Com., Israel Bonds; pres. Am. Friends Bibl. Zoo, 1977; founding chmn., mem. Citizens for Lehigh County Progress, 1966-74. Served with USMCR, 1942-45. Recipient various awards, most recent being; citation U.S. Congress, 1968; fellow Aspen Inst. Humanistic Studies, 1962; Friend of Lehigh award Lehigh U. Alumni Assn., 1969; Am.-Israel C. of C. award, 1969; Disting. Citizen award USMC; Disting. Pennsylvanian award, 1977; Disting. Leadership award Am. Jewish Com., 1983—; George Washington Honor medal Freedoms Found. at Valley Forge, 1984; numerous others. Fellow Pa. Acad. Fine Arts, Met. Mus. Art, Culinary Inst. Am.; mem. Am. Fedn. Arts, Pa. Soc. N.Y., Am. Retail Fedn. (dir. 1975—), Met. Opera Guild, Am. Assn. Mus., Council Consumer Info., Soc. Automotive Engrs., Polar Soc., Explorers Club, Beta Gamma Sigma, Navy League U.S., Marine Corps League, USMC Res. Officers Assn. Clubs: Lehigh Valley, Berkleigh Country, Masons, Shriners; Safari, Union League (Phila.); World Trade Center (N.Y.C.). Home: 20 Hundred Nottingham Rd Allentown PA 18103 Office: 20 Hundred Nottingham rd Allentown PA 18103

BERMAN, ROBERT S., marketing consultant; b. N.Y.C., Apr. 13, 1932; s. Sydney and Beatrice (Lipman) B.; m. Eleanor Rae Greenwald, June 16, 1956 (div. 1973); children: Thomas, Eric, Terry; m. Sherry Rona Frawley, May 29, 1975. B.A., Cornell U., 1953, M.A., 1954; advanced mgmt. certificate, Harvard U., 1964. Vice pres. Marschalk, Inc., N.Y.C., 1962-64, DeGarmo, Inc., 1964-70, exec. v.p., 1970-80, D'Arcy MacManus & Masius, 1980-83; pres. Berman Mktg. Network, N.Y.C., 1983—; instr. Parsons Sch., 1968-70, Pratt Inst., 1974-76; columnist Madison Ave. Mag., N.Y.C., 1968-72. Served to 1st lt. U.S. Army, 1954-56. Named Advt. Accountman of the Yr. N.Y. Advt. Council, 1969. Mem. Civil War Roundtable of N.Y., Komos Aiden Theatrical Assn., Quill and Dagger. Clubs: Cornell, Millbrook. Home: North Clove Rd Verbank NY 12585 Office: 2 Tudor City Pl New York NY 10017

BERMAN, RONALD STANLEY, author; b. N.Y.C., Dec. 15, 1930; s. Herman and Jean (Wolfson) B.; m. Barbara Barr, Aug. 27, 1953; children—Andrew, Julia, Katherine. B.A., Harvard U., 1952; Ph.D., Yale U., 1959; H.H.D., George Washington U., 1974, Colo. Coll., 1975; LL.D., St. Anselm's Coll., 1974; L.H.D., Hebrew Union Coll., 1974, U. Md., 1975; Litt.D., Coll. St. Rose, 1975. Instr. Columbia U., N.Y.C., 1959-61, asst. prof., 1961-62; asso. prof. Kenyon Coll., Gambier, Ohio, 1962-65, U. Calif. at, San Diego, 1965-68, prof. renaissance lit., 1968-71, 77—; chmn. Nat. Endowment for Humanities, Washington, 1971-77, Fedn. Council on Arts and Humanities, 1975-77; adj. scholar Am. Enterprise Inst. for Pub. Policy Research, Washington, 1977. Editorial asso.: Kenyon Rev, 1963-70, Henry King and the 17th Century, 1964, A Reader's Guide to Shakespeare's Plays, 1965, Henry V: A Collection of Critical Essays, 1968, America in the Sixties: An Intellectual History, 1970. Served to lt. USNR, 1952-56. Recipient Gold medal for distinguished service Phi Beta Kappa, Chgo., 1974, medal City of N.Y., 1975. Home: 2965 Ariane Dr San Diego CA 92117 Office: U Calif San Diego CA

BERMAN, SIDNEY, physician; b. Washington, July 31, 1908; s. Saul and Gertrude B.; m. Claire Richardson, Nov. 23, 1935; 1 dau., Sarah Miriam Berman Schlein. B.S., Georgetown U., 1928, M.D., 1932. Diplomate: Am. Bd. Psychiatry and Neurology. Intern D.C. Gen. Hosp., 1932-33; jr. med. officer, resident in psychiatry St. Elizabeth's Hosp., Washington, 1933-35; sr. med. officer VA Hosp., Northport, N.Y., 1935-41; Commonwealth Fund fellow in child psychiatry U. Md. Med. Sch. and Hosp., 1941-42; dir. U. Md. Mental Hygiene Clinic, 1942-43, Washington Inst. Mental Hygiene, 1946-48; clin. prof. psychiatry George Washington U Sch. Medicine, 1948—; Practice medicine specilaizing in child and adult psyciatry and psychoanalysis, Washington, 1948—; sr. adv. staff Chilren's Hosp. Nat. Med. Ctr., Washington, 1948—; tng. and supervising analyst Washington Psychoanalytic Inst., 1957-80, Washington Assn. Psychoanalytic Edn., 1979-81; cons. Walter Reed Gen. Hosp., 1960-71, NIH, 1953—. Contbr. articles to med. jours. Founder Nat. Consortium Child Mental Health Service, 1971; rep. to Congress Mental Health Manpower, 1971-74. Served to maj. M.C. USAAF, 1943-46. Fellow Am. Soc. Physician Analysts (hon.); mem. Am. Acad. Child Psychiatry (pres. 1969-71), Washington Psychoanalytic Soc. (pres. 1963-65), Washington Psychiat. Soc. (pres. 1962), Med. Soc. D.C., AMA, Am. Psychiat. Assn., Group Advancement of Psychiatry, Am. Orthopsychiat. Assn., Am. Psychoanalytic Assn., Internat. Psychoanalytic Assn., Pan-Am. Med. Assn. Jewish. Club: George Washington U. Home: 5534 Warwick Pl Chevy Chase MD 20015 Office: 4301 Massachusetts Ave NW Washington DC 20016 *My ideals were established by the rich experiences of my parents, teachers, wife and friends brought to me with love and warmth. They created in me a strong sense of family, social, civic and professional responsibility. As a clinician my primary responsibility has been to my patients. As an educator I endeavor to share my knowledge as my teachers shared it with me. My organizational activities have been to attain and support the goals and aspirations of my colleagues. Above all else, my life with my wife and family has been an exciting experience; success and friendship rewarding, and adversity a challenge.*

BERMAN, SIMEON MOSES, mathematician, educator; b. Rochester, N.Y., Mar. 28, 1935; s. Jeremiah Joseph and Rose (Rappaport) B.; m. Iona Toby, Dec. 28, 1955; children: Jeremy, Jessica, Daniel, Zachary, Migdana, Tehilah. B.A., CCNY, 1956; M.A., Columbia U., 1958, Ph.D., 1961. Lectr. CCNY, 1957-60; asst. prof. Columbia U., 1961-65; asso. prof. math. N.Y. U., N.Y.C., 1965-77, prof., 1977—. Author: The Elements of Probability, 1969, Mathematical Statistics, 1971, Calculus for the Nonphysical Sciences, 1974; asso. editor: Annals of Probability, 1979—; contbr. over 60 articles to math. jours., 1961—. Prin. investigator NSF grant in math., 1966—, N.Y. U. Challenge Fund grant, 1980—. Fellow Inst. Math. Stats. (mem. nominating com. 1983). Jewish (pres. congregation 1973-78, dir. 1980—). Home: 334 Marlboro Rd Brooklyn NY 11226 Office: 251 Mercer St New York NY 10012

BERMANN, GEORGE ALAN, law educator, lawyer; b. Fall River, Mass., Dec. 2, 1945; s. Sigmund Dressler and Mae (Gordon) B.; m. Sandra Lekas, Dec. 28, 1969; children: Sloan, Suzanne. B.A., Yale U., 1967, J.D., 1971; LL.M., Columbia U., 1975. Bar: N.Y. 1972, U.S. Dist. Ct. (So. Dist.) N.Y. 1980, U.S. Dist. Ct (ea. dist.) N.Y. 1980. Assoc. Davis Polk & Wardwell, N.Y.C., 1970-73; asst. prof. law Columbia U., N.Y.C., 1975-79, assoc. prof., 1979-81, prof., 1981—; vis. prof. law U. Paris and U. Rogen, France, 1981-82; lectr. Internat. Faculty for Teaching Comparative Law, Strasbourg, France, 1975; exec. dir. Columbia Summer Program, Netherlands, 1979-82; cons. Nat. Ctr. Adminstrv. Justice, Washington, 1979-82; internat. comml. arbitrator Am. Arbitration Assn., N.Y.C., 1982—; sec. Am. Acad. Fgn. Law, Stanford, Calif., 1983—. Contbr. chpt. to book, articles to profl. jours.; editor: Am. Jour. Comparative Law, 1976—. Marshall scholar, Sussex, Eng., 1967-68; Jerbey fellow Parker Sch. Fgn. and

Comparative Law, N.Y.C., 1973-75. Mem. Am. Fgn. Law Assn. (bd. dirs. 1983), Deutsch-Amerikanische Juristan Vereingung, ABA, German Am. Law Assn. (bd. dirs. 1979—), Phi Beta Kappa. Home: 118 Cedar Ln Princeton NJ 08540 Office: Columbia U Sch Law 435 W 116th St New York NY 10027

BERMANT, GEORGE WILSON, lawyer; b. Los Angeles, July 2, 1926; s. Ira G. and Josephine (Wilson) B.; m. Laurel Ardyce Knight, Aug. 19, 1950; 1 son, James G.; m. 2d Neely Wagner, Oct. 22, 1970. B.A. magna cum laude, U. So. Calif., 1950; LL.B. cum laude, Yale U., 1953. Bar: Calif. 1954, Colo. 1981. Assoc. Gibson, Dunn & Crutcher, Los Angeles, 1953-61, ptnr., 1962-81, Denver, 1981—; dir. Fin. Corp. Am., Gulfstream Aerospace. Bd. dirs., treas. Hist. Denver, Inc., 1983—. Served with USNR, 1944-46. Mem. ABA, Los Angeles Bar Assn., Colo. Bar Assn., Denver Bar Assn., Fin. Lawyers Conf. Los Angeles. Republican. Home: 1512 Larimer St Apt 33 Denver CO 80202 Office: Gibson Dunn & Crutcher 1801 California St Suite 4200 Denver CO 80202

BERMINGHAM, PETER, museum director; b. Buffalo, Nov. 6; s. Donald Michael and Margaret Anne (Murphy) B.; m. Eleanor Joan Sigborn, Sept. 5, 1964; children: Christopher, Jason, Alexander, Noelle, Nicholas. B.A., U. Md., 1964, M.A., 1968; Ph.D. (Smithsonian Instn. fellow 1971-72), U. Mich., 1972. Teaching asst. U Mich., 1968-71; vis. prof. art history U. Cin., 1972-73; curator edn. Nat. Collection Fine Arts, Smithsonian Instn., 1973-78; dir., chief curator U. Ariz. Mus. Art, Tucson, 1978—; mem. mus. policy panel Nat. Endowment Arts. Author exhbn. catalogues. Served with USAF, 1956-60. Mus. tng. fellow Nat. Endowment Humanities, 1967-68. Mem. Western Assn. Art Museums, Coll. Art Assn. Roman Catholic. Home: 3585 E Thimble Peak Tucson AZ 85718 Office: Univ Ariz Mus Art Tucson AZ 85721

BERMINGHAM, RICHARD P., restaurant and food products company executive; b. Glen Ridge, N.J., 1939. Student, U. Colo. With Arthur Andersen & Co., 1962-67; v.p., sec. fin. Collins Foods Internat., Los Angeles, 1967-73, v.p., sec., gen. mgrs. Collins Food Service div., 1973-81, pres., chief operating officer, dir., 1981—. Office: Collins Foods Internat 12731 W Jefferson Blvd Los Angeles CA 90066 *

BERMUDEZ, EUGENIA M. *See* DIGNAC, GENY

BERNACCHI, RICHARD LLOYD, lawyer; b. Los Angeles, Dec. 15, 1938; s. Bernard and Anne (Belluomini) B.; 1 dau., Vanessa Allison. B.S. with honors in Commerce (Nat. Merit Found. scholar), U. Santa Clara, 1961; LL.B. with highest honors (Legion Lex scholar, Jerry Geisler Meml. scholar), U. So. Calif., 1964. Bar: Calif. 1964. Since practiced in, Los Angeles; partner firm Irell and Manella, 1964—; lectr. Am. Law Inst., 1972-73; lectr. data processing contracts and law U. So. Calif., Los Angeles, 1972, 78, 81; Co-chmn. Regional Transp. Com., 1970-72. Author: (with Gerald H. Larsen) Data Processing Contracts and the Law, 1974; Editor-in-chief: U. So. Calif. Law Rev, 1962-64. Served to capt. AUS, 1964-66; PTO. Mem. Am. Bar Assn. (mem. adv. com. on edn. 1973-74, chmn. subcom. taxation computer systems of sect. sci. and tech. 1976-78), Los Angeles Bar Assn., Computer Law Assn. (dir. 1973—, chmn. preconf. symposium on law and computers 1974-75, West Coast v.p. 1976-79, sr. v.p. 1979-81, pres. 1981-83), Am. Fedn. Info. Processing Socs. (mem. spl. com. electronic funds transfer systems 1974-78), Order of Coif, Scabbard and Blade, Beta Gamma Sigma, Alpha Sigma Nu. Office: 1800 Ave of Stars Los Angeles CA 90067

BERNAL, IGNACIO, archaeologist; b. Mexico City, Feb. 13, 1910; s. Rafael Bernal and Rafaela Garcia Pimentel; m. Sofia Verea, Oct. 14, 1944; children—Ignacio, Rafaela, Carlos, Concha. LL.D., U. Mex., 1949; M.A., Cambridge (Eng.) U., 1975, U. Calif., St. Mary's U., San Antonio, U. Americas. Prof. anthropology U. Mex., 1948-76; dir. Nat. Inst., Mexico City, 1968-71, Mus. Anthropology, 1962-77; vis. prof. anthropology U. Tex., 1954, U. Calif., 1958, Harvard U., 1961, Cambridge U., 1975-76, Sorbonne U., Paris, 1955-56, U. Madrid, 1964, U. Rome, 1966. Contbr. numerous articles on archaeology and history to profl. jours. Decorated officer Royal Order Orange-Nassau, Netherlands, Legion of Honor; comdr. Legion of Honor, France, Order of Merit, Italy; officer Order of Crown, Belgium; comdr. Order of Merit, Ger.; officer Royal Order of Danebrog, Denmark; comdr. Order of Merit, Senegal, Royal Victoria Order, Eng., Star of Yugoslavia. Roman Catholic. Home: 65 Tres Picos México DF 5 México

BERNARD, CHARLES KEITH, commuter rail system exec.; b. Montreal, Que., Can., Nov. 4, 1938; came to U.S., 1968; s. George and Barbara (MacDougall) B.; m. Sandra Elaine Boyd, Nov. 30, 1968; children—Kevin, Brendan. B.Engring., McGill U., Montreal, 1961; M.B.A., U. Calif., Berkeley, 1970; grad. Profl. Program in Urban Transp. (Urban Mass Transp. Adminstrn. fellow), Carnegie Mellon U., 1973. Research and devel. engr. Can. Nat. Rys., Montreal, 1961-63; gen. sales and application engr. Ingersoll Rand (Australia) Pty., Ltd., Sydney, 1963-65; project engr. Can. Corp. for 1967 World Exhbn., 1965-68; planning engr. Bay Area Rapid Transit Dist., Oakland, Calif., 1970—, dir. dept. planning, budgeting and research, 1975-78, gen. mgr., 1979—. Office: 800 Madison St Oakland CA 94607

BERNARD, DAVID GEORGE, marine supply company executive; b. Cambridge, Mass., Oct. 30, 1921; s. Frederick and Fayetta (Smith) B.; m. Edith Barnes, Dec. 10, 1960; 1 son, Andrew; children by prior marriage: Jeffrey, Frederick, Joan, Peter. B.S., Harvard U., 1943, M.B.A., 1947. Gen. sales mgr. Am. Can Co., N.Y.C., 1958-61; sr. v.p. Medusa Corp., Cleve., 1961-63; v.p. Internat. Paper, N.Y.C., 1968-78, Nat. Can Corp., Chgo., 1978-81; exec. v.p. Fischbach Corp., N.Y.C., 1981-83; pres. Delta Marine Supply Corp., N.Y.C., 1983—. Served to lt. USN, 1943-46; PTO. Mem. Am. Chem. Soc., Can Mfrs. Inst., Newcomen Soc. Democrat. Episcopalian. Clubs: Harvard (N.Y.C.); Bay Head Yacht (N.J.). Home: 1075 Park Ave New York NY 10128 Office: 5 Varick St New York NY 10013

BERNARD, KENNETH, educator, playwright; b. Bklyn., May 7, 1930; s. Otis and Mary (Travaglini) B.; m. Elaine Ceil Reiss, Sept. 2, 1952; children: Lucas, Judd, Kate. B.A., CCNY, 1953; M.A., Columbia U., 1956, Ph.D., 1962. Faculty, English dept. L.I. U., N.Y.C., 1959—; now prof. Cons. N.Y. Creative Artists Pub. Service Program, 1973-75, Mass. Arts and Humanities Found., 1975—, Wis. Arts Bd., 1975; v.p. N.Y. Theater Strategy, 1972-79; adv. editor Confrontation, 1973-75, asst. editor, 1976, fiction editor, 1979—; cons. Md. Arts Council, 1978. Author: plays Night Club and Other Plays, 1971, Two Stories, 1973. Served with AUS, 1953-55. Recipient Arvon Poetry Prize, 1980; Office for Advanced Drama research grantee U. Minn., 1971; N.Y. State Creative Artist Pub. Service grantee, 1973, 76; Rockefeller grantee, 1975; Guggenheim fellow, 1972-73; Nat. Endowment for Arts grantee in fiction, 1978. Home: 800 Riverside Dr New York City NY 10032

BERNARD, LOLA DIANE, educator; b. Rockaway Beach, N.Y., Nov. 9, 1928; d. Clark C. and Antoinette (Berger) B. B.A., Roosevelt U., 1949; M.A., U. Houston, 1952; M.S.W., Tulane U., 51954; Ph.D., Bryn Mawr Coll., 1967. Psychometrician counseling and testing dept. Roosevelt U., 1948-49; Rorshach interpreter Dr. Ralph J. Wentworth-Rohr, N.Y.C., 1949-50; psychometrician Dr. J. Sanford Davis Vocational Bur., N.Y.C., 1949-50; psychometrician counseling and testing dept. U. Houston, 1950; psychologist Woman's Fed. Penitentiary, Huntsville, Tex., 1951; social worker M.D. Anderson Hosp. Cancer Research, Houston, 1952; med. social worker Bur. Tb Control, New Orleans, 1954-56; dir. social service dept. Touro Infirmary, New Orleans, 1956-60; instr. Bryn Mawr Coll., 1964-65; field instr. Tulane U., 1958-62, asst. prof., 1965-66, assoc. prof., 1966-69; prof., chmn. dept. social work Fla. State U., 1969-72; acting dean Sch. Social Welfare, 1972-73; dean Sch. Social Work, 1973-78, dir. women's studies, 1978-79; prof. Va. Commonwealth U., 1979—, dir. doctoral program social policy and social work, 1980—; vis. prof. U. WaSh., Seattle, 1978; chmn. nat. commn. on accreditation Council Social Work Edn., 1972-75. Contbr. articles to profl. jours., encys. Mem. manpower study Fla. Bd. Regents, 1971-72; Disaster worker A.R.C., 1965-69; mem. Leon County (Fla.) Assn. Community Services, 1970-79, Leon County Humane Soc., 1970-79, Tallahassee Urban League, 1970-79; Bd. dirs. Home for Incurables, New Orleans, 1966-69, Le Moyne Art Found., Tallahassee, 1970-79. Recipient Outstanding Alumnae award Tulane U. Sch. Social Work, 1977; Nat. Found. Infantile Paralysis grantee, 1952-54; NIMH grantee, 1962-64, 77. Mem. Nat. Assn. Social Workers (mem. nat. commn. casework 1967-69), Council Social Work Edn. (dir. 1975-78), Nat. Conf. Social Welfare, AAUP, So. Regional Ednl. Bd., Psi Chi. Home: 3 N Robinson St Richmond VA 23220 *Helping others to achieve their potential started out as a professional commitment and has become a personal conviction. Time and emotional investment are highly valued and selfishly guarded commodities but they are meaningless unless they are spent. Investment in the life of others has enriched my own. Form, structure and content are empty without the capacity for human relationships.*

BERNARD, LOUIS JOSEPH, surgeon; b. Laplace, La., Aug. 19, 1925; s. Edward and Jeanne (Vinet) B.; m. Lois Jeannette McDonald, Feb. 1, 1976; children—Marie Antonia, Phyllis Elaine. B.A. magna cum laude, Dillard U., New Orleans, 1946; M.D., Meharry Med. Coll., 1950. Diplomate: Am. Bd. Surgery. Instr. surgery Sch. Medicine, Meharry Med. Coll., Nashville, 1958-59, prof., chmn. dept. surgery, 1973—; practice medicine specializing in surgery, 1959-69; mem. clin. faculty U. Okla., 1959-69, asso. prof., vice chmn. dept. surgery, 1969-73. Contbr. articles in field to profl. jours. Mem. Okla. State Bd. Corrections, 1968-69. Served with M.C. U.S. Army, 1951-53. USPHS research fellow NCI, U. Rochester, 1953-54. Fellow A.C.S., Southeastern Surg. Congress; mem. Sigma Pi Phi, Alpha Omega Alpha. Democrat. Roman Catholic. Home: 156 Queens Land Nashville TN 37218 Office: 1005 18th Ave N Nashville TN 37208

BERNARD, MICHAEL MARK, city planning consultant, lawyer; b. N.Y.C., Sept. 5, 1926; s. H.L. and Henryetta (Siegel) B.; m. Laura Jane Pincus, Aug. 28, 1958; 1 dau., Daphne Michelle. A.B., U. Chgo., 1949; J.D., Northwestern U., 1953; M.City Planning, Harvard U., 1959, cert. in arts adminstrn., 1972; studied with Paolo Soleri in urban design consortium, Haystack Sch., Me., 1971. Bar: Ill. bar 1952, N.Y. bar 1955. Gen. practice law, Chgo. and N.Y.C., 1953-55; research Harvard Law Sch., 1955-56; city planning cons., atty.-adviser, Puerto Rico, 1956-58; city planner, legal adviser Chgo. Dept. City Planning, 1960-64; cons. planning and land regulation, 1964—, lectr. in field, 1959—; Mem. exec. faculty Boston Archtl. Center, 1967—; vis. prof. urban and regional planning U. Iowa, 1969-70; mem. faculty Am. Law Inst., 1978—; adv. to gov. on reorgn. Commonwealth Mass., 1968-72; adviser A.I.A. Research Corp., 1974; cons. Mass. Atty. Gen., 1981—; Mem. com. urban devel. and housing World Peace Through Law Center, 1965—; mem. com. transp. law Transp. Research Bd., 1966—; cons. White House Policy Adv. Com. to D.C., 1966; del. World Congress Housing and Planning, Paris, France, 1962, Tokyo, Japan, 1966; fellow Ctr. Advanced Visual Studies, MIT. Exhibited sculpture, Inst. Contemporary Art, Boston, 1971, 72, Boston City Hall, 1971, Soc. Arts and Crafts, Boston, 1974, Carpenter Center Visual Arts, Harvard U., Mass. Coll. Art, 1977, Brockton Art Center, 1979, Boston Visual Artists Union Gallery, 1980; Author: Constitutions, Taxation and Land Policy, 2 vols., 1979-80, Airspace in Urban Development, 1963; co-editor: Policy Studies Jour.; editor, pub.: Reflections on Space; Editorial adviser: Urban Law Ann. of, Washington U. Sch. Law.; Contbr. articles to profl. jours. Patron Hull House Assn., Chgo., 1965; v.p., trustee Cambridge Community Art Center, 1971-73. Served with USN, 1944-46. NRC-Nat. Acad. Scis. grantee, 1964-66. Fellow Lincoln Inst. Land Policy; mem. ABA (various coms. 1961-72), Internat. Fedn. Housing and Planning, Am. Soc. Pub. Adminstrn., Policy Studies Orgn., Am. Planning Assn. (chmn. legislative com. Met. Chgo. sect. 1963-65, state reporter planning and law div. 1980—), Internat. Centre for Land Policy Studies (London), Urban Affairs Assn. (jour. rev. editor), Am. Crafts Council, Mass. Assn. Craftsmen (v.p. 1975-78), Boston Visual Artists Union (sec.-gen. 1971-72), New Eng. Poetry Club, Phi Delta Phi. Unitarian (mem. standing com.). Home: 25 Stanton Ave Newton MA 02166 Office: MIT 40 Massachusetts Ave Cambridge MA 02139 *It seems to me that man's random, specialized intervention in the universe will prove to be the most constant cause for concern in the future. The problem might be seen not so much as how to keep the earth whole, but as how man may keep whole himself: this remains the role and strength of creative, intuitive behavior, the source of everything I find of true value. Hopefully, ours will not become the "Age of the Idiot Savant".*

BERNARD, RICHARD LAWSON, geneticist; b. Detroit, Aug. 12, 1926; s. Clarence Rolla and Ilda Gentry (Lawson) B.; m. Ruth V. Thorne, June 14, 1952 (div. 1975); children: Betty Ruth, Richard Thorne, Alice Jean, Daniel Lawson; m. Norma W. Weaver, Nov. 22, 1980 (div. 1982). Student, U. Mich., 1943-45, Okla. State U., 1947-48; B.S., Ohio State U., 1949, M.S., 1950; Ph.D., N.C. State U., 1960. Research geneticist U.S. Dept. Agr., Champaign, Ill., 1954—; prof. plant genetics U. Ill., Champaign, 1966—. Served with USAF, 1945-47. Democrat. Baptist. Home: 614 Richards Ln Champaign IL 61820 Office: Turner Hall Univ of Ill Urbana IL 61801

BERNARD, SPENCER THOMAS, lt. gov. Okla.; b. Rush Springs, Okla., Feb. 5, 1915; s. Cicero Edgar and Gertrude (Sperling) B.; m. Vivan Opal Dorman, Aug. 3, 1935; 1 dau., Kay Ann Bernard Jones. Farmer, rancher, Rush Springs, Okla.; pres. Bernard Enterprises; mem. Okla. Ho. of Reps., 1960-78, speaker pro tempore, until 1978, vice-chmn., then chmn. soil and water resources com., vice chmn. house rules com.; now lt. gov., State of Okla., 1978—; pres. Fed. Land Bank; v.p. Mid-Continent Farmers Coop.; dir. 1st Nat. Bank of Rush Springs. Mem. Cattlemen's Assn., Farmers Union. Democrat. Mem. Ch. of Christ. Club: Lions (past pres.). Home: Box 158 Rush Springs OK 73082 Office: 211 State Capitol Oklahoma City OK 73105 *

BERNARD, WILLIAM G., union official; b. St. Louis, Dec.28, 1927; s. Jack Lawrence and Florence Margret (Muenich) B.; children: Alta Bernard Miller, Kathleen, William, Elizabeth, Daniel. Student, Central Coll., Fayette, Mo. With Internat. Assn. heat and Frost Insulators and Asbestos Workers, Washington, 1950—, rec. sec. local 1, 1957-60, pres. local 1, 1960-64, fin. sec., bus. rep. local, 1964-72, v.p. internat. assn., 1967-72, gen. sec.-treas., 1972—. Served with USMC. Office: Internat Assn Heat and Frost Insulators and Asbestos Workers 505 Machinists Bldg 1300 Connecticut Ave NW Washington DC 20036

BERNARDI, HERSCHEL, actor; b. N.Y.C., Oct. 30, 1923. Actor appearing in: films including Green Fields, 1937, Crime, Inc, 1945, Miss Susie Slagle's, 1946, Stake Out on Dope Street, 1958, the Savage Eye, 1960, A Cold Wind in August, 1961, Irma La Douce, 1963, the Honey Pot, 1967, No Deposit No Return, 1976, The Front, 1976; TV credits include Peter Gunn; series, 1958-60, Arnie, 1970-71, But I Don't Want to Get Married, 1971, No Place to Run, 1972; Broadway appearances include Fiddler on the Roof as; Tevye. Office: care Pacht Ross Warne Bernhard Sears Inc 1800 Ave of the Stars Suite 500 Los Angeles CA 90067

BERNARDI, MARIO, condr.; b. Kirland Lake, Ont., Can., Aug. 20, 1930; s. Leone and Rina (Onisto) B.; m. Mona Kelly, May 12, 1962. Ed., Coll. Piox, Treviso, Italy, Benedetto Marcello Conservatory, Venice, Italy, Mozarteum, Salzburg, Austria, Royal Conservatory, Toronto. Began career as pianist, Italy; mus. dir. Sadler's Wells Opera Co., 1969—; mus. dir., condr. Nat. Arts Centre, Ottawa, Ont., 1967—; guest condr. with San Francisco Opera Assn., Vancouver Opera, Canadian Broadcasting Co., Canadian Opera Co. Decorated companion Order of Can. Club: Savage. Address: National Arts Centre Ottawa ON Canada *

BERNARDIN, JAMES IRWIN, creative director; b. Moundsville, W.Va., May 23, 1929; s. Thomas Jacob and Leota (O'Neil) B.; m. Ruth Elizabeth Andre, Aug. 10, 1952; children: Thomas L., James Irwin, John A., Robert W. B.S., U. Mich., 1952; postgrad., U. Detroit. Art dir. Kenyon & Eckhardt Inc., Detroit, 1953-55, Benton & Bowles Inc., 1955-57, Campbell-Ewald Co., 1957-64, v.p., creative dir., 1964-71, sr. v.p., creative dir., Warren, Mich., 1971-76, exec. v.p., dir. creative services, Warren, 1976—, dir., 1976—, exec. com., 1976—. Served with USNR. Recipient awards including Clio, N.Y.C., Houston Film Festival, Ad Age 100 Best, N.Y.C., One Show Art Dirs., N.Y.C., Robert E. Healy award Interpub. Group of Co., N.Y.C., Big Apple award, N.Y.C., Internat. Film and TV Festival, N.Y.C. Mem. Acad. Motion Pictures Arts and Scis., Creative Advt. Club of Detroit. Republican. Clubs: Hunters Creek (Metamora, Mich.); Pine Lake Country (Orchard Lake, Mich.). Home: 2922 Interlaken Orchard Lake MI 48033 Office: Campbell-Ewald Co 30400 Van Dyke Warren MI 48093

BERNARDIN, JOSEPH LOUIS CARDINAL, archbishop; b. Columbia, S.C., Apr. 2, 1928; s. Joseph and Maria M. (Simion) B. A.B. in Philosophy, St. Mary's Sem., Balt., 1948; M.Ed., Cath. U. Am., 1952. Ordained priest Roman Catholic Ch., 1952; asst. pastor Diocese of Charleston, S.C., 1952-54, vice chancellor, 1954-56, chancellor, 1956-66, vicar gen., 1962-66, diocesan consultor, 1962-66, adminstr., 1964-65; aux. bishop, Atlanta, 1966-68; pastor Christ the King Cathedral, 1966-68; sec., mem. exec. com. Nat. Conf. Cath. Bishops-U.S. Cath. Conf., gen. sec., 1968-72, pres., 1974-77; archbishop of Cin., 1972-82, of Chgo., 1982—; mem. Sacred Congregation Bishops, 1973-78; del., mem. permanent council World Synod of Bishops, 1974, 77—; mem. Pontifical Commn. Social Communications, Rome, 1970-72, Sacred Coll. Cardinals, 1983—. Mem. adv. council Am. Revolution Bicentennial, 1975, Pres.'s Adv. Com. Refugees, 1975. Mem. Nat. Cath. Edn. Assn. (chmn. bd. 1978-79). Address: 1555 N State Pkwy Chicago IL 60610 *

BERNARDO, CHARLES MICHAEL, consultant; b. Yonkers, N.Y., Sept. 24, 1937; s. Charles Joseph and Rose Marie (Albero) B.; m. Jo-Ann Stockglausner; children: Bradford Mitchell, Alexandra Rose, Darrell Raymond. B.S., N.Y. U., 1959; M.A., Columbia, 1962, Ed.D., 1966; postgrad., Harvard, 1969, U. Pa., 1970. Tchr. pub. schs., Yonkers, 1960-62, Oceanside, N.Y., 1962-64; research asso. Columbia, 1964; exec. sec. Central Sch. Bds. Com. for Ednl. Research, State of N.Y., 1964-66; supt. schs., Oxford, Mass., 1967-69, Pottstown, Pa., 1969-70, Providence, 1970-75, Montgomery County, Rockville, Md., 1975-79; v.p. Pacific Cons.'s, Washington, 1979-80; pres. BSW Mgmt. Corp., 1980-82; gen. ptnr. J. Stock-Mgrs., 1982—; instr. R.I. Coll., 1974-75. Contbr. articles to profl. jours. Dir. R.I. Blue Cross-Blue Shield.; Project chief N.Y.C. Mayor's Temporary Commn. on City Finances, 1964-65; mem. priorities task force United Way of Southeastern New Eng., 1975; Bd. dirs., trustee R.I. Sch. Design; bd. dirs. Providence Central YMCA. Served with USMCR, 1959-60. Mem. Am. Assn. Sch. Adminstrs., Nat. Inst. Fin. Freedom, Kappa Delta Pi. Home and Office: 27 Cherokee Ct Palm Coast FL 32037 *My successful transition from public sector leader to real estate investor and executive resulted from the adaptability gained through upward career mobility. Havens of safety are often self-defeating.*

BERNARDS, SOLOMON SCHNAIR, clergyman, consultant; b. Chgo., May 14, 1914; s. Abraham Jacob and Margaret (Josephman) B.; m. Ruth Segal, Dec. 26, 1948; children—Joel Abba (dec.), Reena Miriam. B.A.S., Lewis Inst., 1938; LL.B., J.D., John Marshall Law Sch., 1937; rabbi, M.H.L., Jewish Theol. Sem., 1942, D.H.L., 1950, D.D. (hon.), 1972, D.H.L., Susquehanna U., 1981. Bar: Ill. bar 1937. Rabbi, 1942; served Kesher Zion, Reading, Pa., 1942-44; Midwest regional dir. United Palestine Appeal, 1946-48; rabbi, Phila., 1949-50, Schenectady, 1950-61; dir. interfaith affairs dept. Anti-Defamation League of B'nai B'rith, N.Y.C., 1961-82, cons. interfaith affairs, 1982-84; nat. dir. Friends of Congregation Mevakshei Derech of Jerusalem, N.Y.C., 1982—; Lectr. Wagner Coll., 1971, B'nai B'rith Wildacres Inst., 1981; dir., originator Acad. Seminars on Jews and Judaism, Princeton Theol. Sem., 1961—, Vanderbilt Div. Sch., 1969-79, Emory U., Trinity Sem., Columbus, Ohio, others. Author, editor: Living Heritage of Passover, 1963, Living Heritage of High Holy Days, 1965, Living Heritage of Hannukah, 1968, Who is a Jew—A Reader, 1969; Contbr. articles to mags. Served with USNR, 1944-46. Mem. Rabbinical Assembly, Am. Acad. Religion, Soc. Bibl. Lit., Assn. Jewish Studies, Religious Edn. Assn., Am. Jewish Hist. Soc., B'nai B'rith. Office: 225 Park Ave S 17th Floor New York NY 10003

BERNAU, SIMON JOHN, mathematics educator; b. Wanganui, N.Z., June 12, 1937; came to U.S., 1969; s. Earnest Lovell and Ella Mary (Mason) B.; m. Lynley Joyce Turner, Aug. 11, 1959; children: Nicola Ann, Sally Jane. B.Sc., U. Canterbury, Christchurch, N.Z., 1958, M.Sc., 1959; B.A., Cambridge (Eng.) U., 1961, Ph.D., 1964. Lectr. U. Canterbury, 1964-65, sr. lectr., 1965-66; prof. math. U. Otago, Dunedin, N.Z., 1966-69; assoc. prof. U. Tex., Austin, 1969-76, prof., 1976—. Researcher numerous publs. in field, 1964—; referee profl. jours., 1965—. Gulbenkian jr. research fellow Churchill Coll., Cambridge U., 1963-64. Mem. Am. Math. Soc. (reviewer 1965—), Math. Assn. Am., London Math. Soc. Home: 7207 Montana Norte Austin TX 78731 Office: Dept Math U Tex Austin TX 78712

BERNAY, BETTI, artist; b. N.Y.C., Sept. 21, 1926; d. David Michael and Anna Gaynia (Bernay) Woolin; m. J. Bernard Goldfarb, Apr. 19, 1947; children: Manette Deitsch, Karen Lynn. Grad. costume design, Pratt Inst., 1946; student, N.A.D., N.Y.C., 1947-49, Art Students League, N.Y.C., 1950-51. Exhibited one man shows, Galerie Raymond Duncan, Paris, France, Salas Municipales, San Sebastian, Spain; represented in permanent collections, Jockey Club Art Gallery, Miami; Exhibited one man shows, Circulo de Bellas Artes, Madrid, Spain, Bacardi Gallery, Miami, Fla., Columbia (S.C.) Mus., Columbus (Ga.) Mus., Galerie Andre Weil, Paris, Galerie Hermitage, Monte Carlo, Monaco, Casino de San Remo, Italy, Galerie de Arte de la Caja de Ahorros de Ronda, Malaga, Spain, Centro Artistico, Granada, Spain, Circulo de la Amistad, Cordoba, Spain, Studio H Gallery, N.Y.C., Walter Wallace Gallery, Palm Beach, Fla., Mus. Bellas Artes, Malaga, Harbor House Gallery, Crystal House Gallery, Internat.

Gallery, Jordan Marsh, Fontainebleau Gallery, Miami Beach, Carriage House Gallery, Galerie 99, Pageant Gallery, Carriage House, Miami Beach, Rosenbaum Galleries, Palm Beach; exhibited group shows, Painters and Sculptors Soc., Jersey City Mus., Salon de Invierno, Mus. Malaga, Salon des Beaux Arts, Cannes, France, Nat. Acad. Gallery, Salmagundi Club, Lever House, Lord & Taylor Art Gallery, Nat. Arts Gallery, Knickerbocker Artists, N.Y.C., Salon des Artistes Independants, Salon des Artistes Francais, Salon Populiste, Paris, Salon de Otono, Nat. Assn. Painters and Sculptors Spain, Madrid, Phipps Gallery, Palm Beach, Artists Equity, Hollywood (Fla.) Mus., Gault Gallery Cheltenham, Phila., Springfield (Mass.) Mus., Met. Mus. and Art Center, Miami, Fla., Planet Ocean Mus., Charter Club, Trade Fair Ams.; represented in permanent collections, Mus. Malaga, Circulo de la Amistad, I.O.S. Found., Geneva, Switzerland, others. Recipient medal City N.Y., Sch. Art Leagues, N.Y.C., Prix de Paris Raymond Duncan, 1958, others. Mem. Nat. Assn. Painters and Sculptors Spain, Nat. Assn. Women Artists, Société des Artistes Francais, Société des Artistes Independants, Fedn. Francais des Sociétés d'Art Graphique et Plastique, Artists Equity, Am. Artists Profl. League, Am. Fedn. Art, Nat. Soc. Lit. and Arts, Met. Mus. and Arts Center Miami. Club: Palm Bay. Address: 10155 Collins Ave Bal Harbour FL 33154 *One must have a bountiful supply of knowledge, skill, patience, sincerity, and the imperatives of high standards and principles to attain any measure of success.*

BERNAYS, EDWARD L., public relations executive; b. Vienna, Austria, Nov. 22, 1891; came to U.S., 1892; s. Ely and Anna (Freud) B.; m. Doris E. Fleischman, Sept. 16, 1922 (dec. July 1980); children: Doris Fleischman Bernays Held, Anne Fleischman Bernays Kaplan. B.S., Cornell U., 1912; Dr. Humanities (hon.), Boston U., LL.D., Babson Coll., 1977. Counsel on pub. relations in partnership with Doris Fleischman Bernays to govt., industries, corps., profl. and trade orgns., individuals, 1919—; instr. 1st course pub. relations N.Y. U., 1923, adj. prof. pub. relations, 1949-50, U. Hawaii, 1950, Sch. Pub. Communications Boston U., 1968-69; fgn. affairs officer, cons. U.S. State Dept. Bur. Ednl. and Cultural Affairs, 1970-75; cons. HEW, 1976, U.S. Dept. Commerce, 1977; former mem. advisory council Sch. Gen. Studies, Columbia U.; mem. Am. advisory council Ditchley Found. Author: Crystalizing Public Opinion, 1923; numerous others, latest being Public Relations, 1952, Your Future in Public Relations, 1961, Biography of an Idea, Memoirs of Public Relations Counsel Edward L. Bernays, 1965; editor: The Engineering of Consent, 1955; co-editor: The Case For Reappraisal U.S. Overseas Information Policies and Programs, 1970; contbr.: articles to publs. work covered in book Public Relations, The Edward L. Bernayses and the American Scene, 1978, Your Future in a Public Relations Career, 1979. Bd. dirs. New Eng. Conservatory Music; hon. mem. bd. dirs. Nat. Multiple Sclerosis; Founder, pres. Edward L. Bernays Found., 1946—; mem. Columbia U. Pub. Communications seminar; mem. adv. bd. pub. relations Suffolk U. Sch. Bus. Adminstrn., Edward R. Murrow Center Pub. Diplomacy, Fletcher Sch. Law and Diplomacy, Tufts U. Awarded Officer of Pub. Instruction, France; King Christian medal, Denmark, 1946; bronze medallion of honor City of N.Y., 1961; Benjamin Franklin fellow Royal Soc. Arts, 1969; Honor award Ohio U., 1970; Distinguished Service award Nat. Pub. Relations Council Health and Welfare Services, 1975; Lincoln award New Eng. chpt. Pub. Relations Soc. Am., 1976; Leadership award Chgo. chpt., 1976; Golden Anvil award, 1976; Pres.'s award Internat. Public Relations Assn., 1979; Public Relations Tchr. award Assn. for Edn. in Journalism, 1980. Mem. Soc. Psychol. Study of Social Issues, Columbia Assos. Clubs: Columbia Men's Faculty, Overseas Press, Cornell (N.Y.C.-Boston); Harvard Faculty, Victorian. Address: 7 Lowell St Cambridge MA 02138

BERNBACH, PAUL, investor; b. N.Y.C., Dec. 31, 1945; s. William and Evelyn (Carbone) B.; m. Therese Dorn, June 24, 1967; children: Elizabeth, Sarah, Matthew. A.B., Columbia U., 1967; J.D., U. Pa., 1970. Bar: N.Y. 1970. Assoc. Simpson, Thacher & Barlett, N.Y.C., 1970-79; asst. to pres., dir. acquisitions Joseph E. Seagram & Sons, Inc., N.Y.C., 1979-81; ptnr. Bernbach & Plotkin, N.Y.C., 1982—; dir. Doyle Dane Bernbach Internat., Inc., N.Y.C., 1982—. Trustee Packer Collegiate Inst., Bklyn., 1983—. Mem. Order of Coif. Club: Heights Casino (Bklyn.). Office: Bernbach & Plotkin 437 Madison Ave New York NY 10022

BERND, DAVID LEMOINE, multi-hospital system executive; b. Milw., Mar. 3, 1949; s. Robert L. and Betty J. B.; m. Helen M. Menge, Mar. 15, 1976; children: Jason David, Jeffrey David. B.A. in History, Coll. William and Mary, 1971; M.H.A., Med. Coll. Va., 1973. Adminstrv. asst. Norfolk Gen. Hosp., (Va.), 1972-73, asst. adminstr., 1974-79, adminstr., 1979-83; pres. Med. Ctr. Hosps., Norfolk, (VA.), 1983—. Bd. dirs. Big Bros. of Tidewater, Norfolk, 1973—; solicitor United Community Fund, Norfolk, 1982-83. Mem. Am. Coll. Hosp. Adminstrs., Med. Coll. Va. Alumni Soc. Presbyterian. Home: 1108 Botetourt Gardens Norfolk VA 23507 Office: Medical Center Hospitals 600 Gresham Dr Norfolk VA 23507

BERND, JOSEPH LAURENCE, political scientist, educator; b. Macon, Ga., Dec. 8, 1923; s. Laurence Joseph and Eva (Bloom) B.; m. Ruth Audrey Brady, July 2, 1960; 1 dau., Alison Ruth. B.A., Mercer U., 1945; M.A., Boston U., 1953; Ph.D., Duke U., 1957. Instr. polit. sci. Boston U., 1952-53; asst. prof., asso. prof. High Point (N.C.) Coll., 1957-59, So. Meth. U., 1959-65; prof. Va. Poly. Inst., Blacksburg, 1965—, dept. chmn., 1965-70; cons. former gov. Ga., 1949-50, 54, U.S. Commn. Civil Rights, 1958, NSF, 1965, Duke U. Press, 1966, Harper and Row (pubs.), 1970, Nat. Broadcasting, 1969-70; plaintiffs brief in Sanders v. Gray U.S. Supreme Ct., 1963, Myer & Rubin (in case on election law); dir. summer confs. Math. Applications in Polit. Sci., 1964, 65, 66, 68; lectr., New Orleans, Vienna, Austria, Atlanta, Lynchburg and Lexington, Va., U.S. Mil. Acad., 1982. Author: Grass Roots Politics in Georgia, 1960; editor: Mathematical Applications in Political Science, Vol. I, co-editor Vols. II-IV, 1965-69, Vols. V-VII, 1970-73; asso. editor: Jour. Politics, 1974-77; editor-in-chief, 1978-82; co-editor: Two Hundred Years of the Republic in Retrospect, 1976; contbr. articles to profl. jours. Founder, Young Peoples League for Better Govt., 1947; wage analyst WSB, 1951. Fellow Social Sci. Research Council, 1956-57, Grad. Council Humanities, So. Meth. U., 1962-63. Mem. Am. Polit. Sci. Assn., So. Polit. Sci. Assn. (mem. exec. com. 1966-69), AAUP. Jewish. Home: 500 Stonegate Dr NW Blacksburg VA 24060 *In success, cultivate a long memory for those who helped make it possible and who deserve to share the credits. In adversity, remember only those things which may serve constructively to assist the work of correction. In victory, magnanimity and good will. In adversity, resolution without rancor. In happiness, share the benefits. In sadness, limit its effects.*

BERND-COHEN, MAX, artist, lectr., critic; b. Macon, Ga., May 7, 1899; s. Max and Ernestine (Golinsky) Bernd-C.; m. Mary Churchill Morgan, June 9, 1941; children: Windreth, Nortina. B.A., Columbia, 1920, LL.B., 1922; studied in leading art schs. of Paris and Madrid; under Fernand Leger; under, Charles Baudouin, Academie Suisse. Instr. Ringling Art Sch., 1932-33; head art dept. Fla. So. Coll. and Stanley E. Jones Found., Lakeland, Fla., 1939-44; dir. Royal Gorge Art Sch., Canon City, Colo., 1947; portrait, landscape and mural painter; guest prof. lectr. Central Sch. Arts and Crafts., London, 1952-53; vis. artist Dartmouth, 1964; vis. artist, sr. lectr. Carlisle (Eng.) Coll. Art, 1964-65, U. Calif. at, San Diego, 1965-66; Founder Fla. So. Art League and Museum, also Colo. Friends of Art.; lectr. on art. Painted: mural The Sermon on the Mount, now at the, First Community Church, Columbus, Ohio.; contbr. to mags.; 12 one-man exhbns. Served in S.A.T.C., World War I; with A.R.C. in Pacific, 1945. Recipient first prize Chester County Art Assn., 1934. Mem. Phila. Art Alliance, Zeta Beta Tau, Delta Sigma Rho. Club: Mason. Selected in open competition to paint mural for Florida Bldg., Chgo. Century of Progress Expn., 1933; chosen to represent Fla. in All States Exhbn. (Heron Art Inst.), 1933. Address: 210 Cowles St W Englewood FL 33533 *The human pattern that tends to persist discovers its emerging nature within the folds of overlaid events resulting from chance, and engendered thereby is the urgency for an ever deeper self-awareness and the need to test the adaptability of personal diversities to the outer world. Growth is not forseeable. But within us potentials demand their ultimacies, and to that end generate the dynamics of emotion, imagination and techniques which extend our incipient time-space configuration from effecting instant-tactile experiences to determining anticipatable continuing-expanding values.*

BERNDT, REXER, coll. pres.; b. Bellefontaine, Ohio, Mar. 9, 1920; m. Geraldine Cowman; children—Elizabeth, Katherine. Pres. Ft. Lewis Coll., Durango, Colo., 1969—. Home: Ft Lewis Coll Durango CO 81301

BERNE, BRUCE J., chemistry educator; b. N.Y.C., Mar. 8, 1940; s. Louis W. and Mildred (Faske) B.; m. Naomi S. Maizel, Aug. 27, 1961; children: David, Michael. B.S., Bklyn. Coll., 1961; Ph.D. (NASA fellow, NSF fellow), U. Chgo., 1964. NATO postdoctoral fellow U. Brussels, Belgium, 1964-65; asst. prof. chemistry Columbia U., N.Y.C., 1966-69, asso. prof., 1969-72, prof., 1972—; vis. prof. U. Tel Aviv, 1972-73; cons. Bell Telephone Labs., IBM Research Labs., Exxon Sci. Labs., Gen. Motors Research Labs.; chmn. adv. panel in chemistry NSF, 1976-79; mem. policy bd. Nat. Resource for Computation in Chemistry, Lawrence Berkeley Labs., 1977-81; mem. com. on chem. scis. Nat. Acad. Scis., 1980-83. Author: (with R. Pecora) Dynamic Light Scattering: With Applications to Biology, Chemistry and Physics, 1976; Editor: Modern Theoretical Chemistry, Equilibrium Statistical Mechanics, 1976, Modern Theoretical Chemistry, Statistical Mechanics of Time Dependent Processes, 1976; mem. editorial bd.: Jour. of Statistical Physics, 1976-79; Contbr. articles to profl. jours. Alfred P. Sloan Found. fellow, 1968-71; John Simon Guggenheim Found. fellow, 1972-73; Petroleum Research Found. grantee, 1973-76; NSF grantee, 1967—; NATO grantee, 1971-74; NIH grantee, 1976—. Fellow Am. Phys. Soc.; mem. Am. Chem. Soc., AAAS, Sigma Xi. Club: New York Road Runners. Home: N Hendrick Ln Irvington-on-Hudson NY 10533 Office: Box 755 Havemeyer Hall Columbia U New York NY 10027

BERNE, ROBERT MATTHEW, physiologist, educator; b. Yonkers, N.Y., Apr. 22, 1918; s. Nelson and Julia (Stahl) B.; m. Beth Goldberg, Aug. 18, 1944; children: Julie, Amy, Gordon, Michael. A.B., U. N.C., 1939; M.D., Harvard, 1943; D.Sc., Med. Coll. Ohio, 1973. Intern Mt. Sinai Hosp., N.Y.C., 1943-44, resident, 1946-48; research fellow Western Res. U. Sch. Medicine, Cleve., 1948-49, instr. physiology, 1949-50, sr. instr., 1950-52, asst. prof., 1952-55, assoc. prof., 1955-61, prof., 1961-66; prof., chmn. dept. physiology U. Va. Sch. Medicine, Charlottesville, 1966—; mem. sci. adv. bd. Alfred I. duPont Inst., 1978-82; mem. evaluation com. on post doctoral fellowships in life scis. Nat. Acad. Scis., 1963-65; mem. physiology tng. com. NIH, 1964-65, mem. heart and vascular disease panel, nat. research and devel. demonstration rev. com., 1973-74; mem. tng. com. Nat. Heart Inst., 1966-70; mem. cardio-pulmonary tng. program VA, 1968-71; mem. physiology test Com. Nat. Bd. Med. Examiners, 1969-70; mem. panel on heart and blood vessel diseases, task force Nat. Heart, Lung, and Blood Inst., 1972, mem. heart and lung program project com., 1975-79, mem. hypertension task force, 1976-79; adminstrv. bd., council acad. socs. Assn. Am. Med. Colls., 1975, chmn. council acad. socs., exec. com., 1977-78, disting. service mem., 1982—; Nathanson Meml. lectr. U. So. Calif., 1973; mem. selection com. award for hypertension CIBA Found, 1975-77; Coordinating com. N.Y. State Doctoral Programs rev., 1982—. Author: (with Matthew N. Levy) Cardiovascular Physiology, 1967, 4th edit., 1981; author, editor: textbook Physiology, 1983; Editor: Circulation Research, 1970-75; Sect. editor: Jour. Applied Physiology, 1964-65; mem. editorial bd.: Circulation Research, 1961-70, 75—, Jour. Molecular and Cellular Cardiology, 1969-71, Proc. Soc. Exptl. Biology and Medicine, 1962-64, Am. Jour. Physiology and Applied Physiology, 1964-65; field editor: Pfluegers Archives, 1980—; mem. editorial com.: Annual Rev. of Physiology, 1976—; assoc. editor, 1980-82; editor, 1983—. Trustee Cleve. Area Heart Soc., 1962-65, pres. sci. council, 1964-65; steering com. Circulation Group Physiol. Soc., 1969-71. Served with M.C. AUS, 1944-46. Recipient Carl J. Wiggers award, 1975. Mem. Am. Physiol. Soc. (mem. council 1970-72, mem. finance com. 1966-70, 75—, pres. 1972-73, publs. com. 1976-80, Perkins Meml. Award com. 1977-80), Am. Soc. for Clin. Investigation, Am. Heart Assn. (com. on med. edn. 1963-66, vice chmn. com. on council basic sci., mem. med. adv. bd. council high blood pressure research 1976—, dir. 1979-80, chmn. publs. com. 1981, award of merit 1978, research achievement award 1979), AAAS, Raven Soc. of U. Va., Cardiac Muscle Club, Assn. Chmn. Depts. Physiology (pres. 1970, teaching award 1976), Microcirculatory Soc. (mem. council 1971-72, liaison com. 1973, chmn. Landis award com. 1977-78), Inst. of Medicine, Phi Beta Kappa, Sigma Xi. Home: 1851 Wayside Pl Charlottesville VA 22903

BERNER, JOSEPH LOUIS, advertising executive; b. Illouska, Hungary, Feb. 1, 1928; U.S., 1930; s. Theodore and Marie (Fay) B.; m. Sheila Marie McDonald, June 30, 1956; children: Kevin, Sarah, Kathleen, Anthony, Vincent. Student, John Carroll U., 1948-49, Am. Acad. Art, Chgo., 1950-52. Art dir. Wade Advt. Co., Chgo., 1958-62; art supr. Needham Louis & Brorby, Chgo., 1962-63; exec. v.p., creative dir. Campbell-Mithun, Chgo., 1964—. Served with U.S. Army, 1946-48. Office: Campbell-Mithun Inc 111 E Wacker Dr Chgo IL 60601

BERNER, LEO DE WITTE, JR., oceanographer; b. Pasadena, Calif., Feb. 11, 1922; s. Leo De Witte and Maude Alena (Wright) B.; m. Arvetta Jo Hankins, June 28, 1947; children: Jo Anne Berner Thomas, Ernestine Elizabeth Berner Ice. B.A., Pomona Coll., 1943; M.S., UCLA-Scripps Instn. Oceanography, 1952, Ph.D., 1957. Fishery biologist U.S. Fish and Wildlife Service, La Jolla, Calif., 1957-58; asst. research biologist Scripps Instn. Oceanography, La Jolla, 1958-60, acting curator marine invertebrates, 1960-61; vis. asst. prof. U. Oreg., Oreg. Inst. Marine Sci., 1961; asso. program dir. NSF, Washington, 1961-65; adminstrv. scientist Tex. A&M U., College Station, 1965-66, asso. prof., 1966-72, asst. dean, 1967-71, asso. dean, 1971—, prof. oceanography, 1972—. Served with USNR, 1943-47. Fellow AAAS; mem. Am. Soc. Limnology and Oceanography, Ecol. Soc. Am., Tex. Ornithol. Soc., Sigma Xi, Assn. Tex. Grad. Schs. (1st v.p. 1981-82, pres. 1982-83). Home: 1108 Neal Pickett Dr College Station TX 77840 Office: Grad Coll Tex A&M U College Station TX 77843

BERNER, NORMAN ARTHUR, clergyman; b. Guelph, Ont., Can., Oct. 8, 1910; s. Ulrich Rudolf and Clara Anna (Nieghorn) B.; m. Ruth Marguerite Ludwig, Apr. 14, 1941; children: Carole, Suzanne, Heather. Grad., Waterloo Lutheran Sem., 1938; B.A., Waterloo Coll., U. Western Ont., 1935; D.D., Waterloo Luth. U., 1972. Ordained to ministry Luth. Ch. Am., 1938; pastor Brantford-Woodstock Parish, 1938-45, Morrisburg Parish, 1945-46; editor United Luth. Publ. House, Phila., 1946-50; mgr. Luth. Ch. Supply Store, Kitchener, Ont., 1950-54; asst. to pres. Evang. Luth. Synod of Can., 1955-62, Eastern Can. Synod, Luth. Ch. Am., Kitchener, 1963-79; vice pastor Zion Luth. Ch., Stratford, Ont., 1979-80; Sec., v.p. Can. Luth. Council, 1954-66; pres. Luth. Council in, Can., 1978-80; exec. dir. Luth. Ch. Can. Found., 1980—; mem. bd. social missions United Luth. Ch. in Am., 1958-62; sec. Can. sect. Luth. Ch. Am., 1969-75; mem. Joint Commn. on Inter-Luth. Relationships, 1969-78, Commn. on Luth. Merger, 1978-81; mem. exec. com. Can. Council Chs., 1968-72, pres., 1972-76; del. Luth. World Fedn. Conf. on Social Responsibility, Vienna, 1969; observer Luth. World Fedn. Assembly, Mpls., 1957, Union Am. Hebrew Congregations Biennial Conv., N.Y.C., 1973; bd. dirs. Can. Luth. World Relief, 1978-80; mem. Luth. Ch. Am. Seminar on Japan., 1972; observer, cons. Gen. Commn. on Ch. Union, Can., 1968-72; fraternal del. World Council Chs. Assembly, Nairobi, 1975, visitor, Vancouver, 1983; synod staff ofcl. Luth. Ch. Am. div. for Mission in N.Am., 1970-79; bd. govs. Waterloo Luth. U., 1960-62. Home: 120 Blueridge Ave Kitchener ON N2M 4E1 Canada

BERNER, ROBERT FRANK, emeritus educator; b. Cleve., Nov. 30, 1917; s. Frank Otto and Marie (Gideon) B.; m. Ruth Harriet Levis, Nov. 6, 1943; children: Robert Frank, Mary Elizabeth, John David, Jean Harriet. B.S., U. Buffalo, 1939, M.B.A., 1948; Ph.D., U. Chgo., 1961. Tchr. Palmyra (N.Y.) High Sch., 1939-41; instr. statistics U. Buffalo, 1946-48, acting chmn. dept., 1948-49, asst. dean, 1949-52, asst. prof. statis., 1952-63; assoc. prof. dept. mgmt. sci. SUNY-Buffalo, 1963-65, prof. mgmt. sci. and ops. analysis, 1965-81, prof. emeritus, 1981—; pres. emeritus Center of SUNY-Buffalo, 1983; chmn. M.B.A. program com., 1976-81; acting dean div. continuing edn., 1952-55, dean, 1955-76; Fulbright prof. Robert Coll., Istanbul, Turkey, 1968-69, U. Nairobi, Kenya, 1975-76. Chmn. adult edn. com. Community Welfare Council Buffalo and Erie County, 1962-64; Dir. Creative Edn. Found., 1969—. Served to capt., F.A. AUS, 1941-45. Decorated Bronze Star, Silver Star. Mem. Assn. Univ. Evening Colls. (past pres.), Nat. Univ. Extension Assn. (v.p.), Am. Council Edn., Assn. Continuing Higher Edn., AAUP, Am. Assn. Univ. Adminstrs., Am. Soc. Tng. Dirs. (chpt. sec. 1952-56), Theta Chi, Beta Gamma Sigma, Alpha Sigma Lambda (past nat. pres.). Episcopalian (warden 1973-74, 76-77, mem. commn. ministry Diocese Western N.Y. 1971—, chmn. commn. on continuing edn. 1974-76). Home: 33 Monarch Dr Amherst NY 14226 Office: Crosby Hall 3435 Main St Buffalo NY 14214

BERNER, ROBERT LEE, JR., lawyer; b. Chgo., Dec. 9, 1931; s. Robert Lee and Mary Louise (Kenney) B.; m. Sheila Marie Reynolds, Jan. 12,. 1957; children: Mary, Louise, Robert, sheila, John. A.B., U. Notre Dame, 1953; LL.B., Harvard U., 1956. Bar: Ill. 1956. Assoc. Petit, Olin, Overmyer & Fazio, Chgo., 1956-63; ptnr. Baker & McKenzie, Chgo., 1963—; mem. vis. com. Northwestern U. Law Sch., 1981—. Mem. adv. bd. Catholic Charities, Chgo., 1971—; mem. vis. com. U. Chgo. Div. Sch., 1972—; mem. legal aid com. United Charities, Chgo., 1971—, bd. dirs., Chgo., 1982—, chmn., Chgo., 1983—; bd. dirs. Link Unltd., Chgo., 1975—; mem. adv. bd. Loyola U., Chgo., 1972—. Mem. ABA, Chgo. Bar Assn., Ill. State Bar Assn., Legal Club Chgo. (pres. 1974-75), Law Club Chgo. Home: 932 Euclid Ave Winnetka IL 60093 Office: Baker & McKenzie 2800 Prudential Plaza Chicago IL 60601

BERNER, T. ROLAND, lawyer, corporation executive; b. N.Y.C., Sept. 23, 1909; s. Irwin Rolston and Cecile (Olin) B.; m. Rosalie Leventritt, Mar. 24, 1938; children: Edgar Rolston, Rosalie, Winifred, Thomas Roland, Richard Olin. B.S., Harvard U., 1931; LL.B., Columbia U., 1935. Bar: N.Y. 1936. Assoc. Gravath, DeGersdorff, Swaine & Wood, N.Y.C., 1935-42; sole practice, N.Y.C, 1946-70; chmn. bd., pres. Curtiss-Wright Corp., Wood Ridge, N.J., 1960—, chief exec. officer, 1965-80; chmn. bd. Dorr-Oliver, Inc.; dir., exec. com. Amerace Corp., GAF Corp. Bd. dirs. Young Audiences, Inc., Edgar M. Leventritt Found.; trustee Marlboro Music Sch. Served to lt. comdr. USNR, 1942-45. Recipient Navy Meritorious Pub. Service citation. Mem. Bar Assn. City N.Y., Am. Ordnance Assn., Air Force Assn., Assn. U.S. Army, Nat. Security Indsl. Assn., Soc. Automotive Engrs. Episcopalian. Clubs: Harvard, Highland Country, Economic (N.Y.C.); Nat. Aviation (Washington). Office: Curtiss-Wright Corp One Passaic St Wood Ridge NJ 07075

BERNEY, JOSEPH HENRY, appliance manufacturing company executive; b. Balt., May 7, 1932; s. Eugene Philip and Blanche (Ney) B.; m. Phyllis Pearlove, Jan. 18, 1956; children: Richard, Philip, Julia, David. B.S., U. Pa., 1953; M.S., Columbia U., 1954. C.P.A., Va., Wis. Staff accountant Touche, Niven, Bailey & Smart, C.P.A.s, N.Y.C., 1954, A.M. Pullen & Co., C.P.A.s, Richmond, Va., 1954-56; pres., dir. Nat. Presto Industries, Inc., Eau Claire, Wis., 1956—; officer, dir. Nat. Holding Investment Co., Master Corp. Tex., Century Metalcraft Corp., World Aerospace Corp., Canton Mfg. Corp., Jackson Sale & Storage, Presto Mfg. Co., Presto Internat. Ltd., Nat. Pipeline Co. Bd. dirs. Outward Bound, Inc., United Fund Eau Claire, U. Wis.-Eau Claire Found., Eau Claire YMCA, Minn. Outward Bound Sch.; past pres. Chippewa Valley council Boy Scouts Am. Mem. Am. Inst. C.P.A.s, Va., Wis. socs. accountants, Beta Gamma Sigma, Delta Sigma Rho. Home: 104 Skyline Dr Eau Claire WI 54701 Office: care Nat Presto Industries Inc Eau Claire WI 54701

BERNFIELD, MERTON RONALD, pediatrician, educator; b. Chgo., Apr. 9, 1938; s. Harry B. and Adeline A. (Fischer) B.; m. Audrey A. Rivkin, Aug. 30, 1959; children: Susan, James, Mark. B.S. in Medicine, U. Ill., 1959; M.S. in Biochemistry; M.D., U. Ill., Chgo., 1961. Intern U. Ill. Research Hosps., Chgo., 1961-62; asst. resident in pediatrics N.Y. Hosp.-Cornell U. Med. Center, N.Y.C., 1962-63; research asso. NIH, Bethesda, Md., 1963-65; research investigator Nat. Inst. Child Health and Human Devel., U. Calif., San Diego, 1965-66; chief resident in pediatrics Stanford U. Med. Center, 1967; asst. prof. pediatrics Stanford U., 1967-70, assoc. prof., 1970-75, prof., 1975—, Josephine Knotts Knowles prof. human biology, 1977—, dir. med. scientist tng. program, 1974-77, chmn. program in human biology, 1977-80; mem. research com. Cystic Fibrosis Found., 1972-76; mem. developmental biology panel NSF, 1976-77; mem. physiol. chemistry research com. Am. Heart Assn., 1979-83; mem. craniofacial anomalies evaluation panel Nat. Inst. Dental Research, 1980-81; mem. health adv. com. Calif. Medfly Eradication Project, 1981-82; mem. sci. adv. bd. Collagen Corp., 1981—; cons. in field. Contbr. articles to profl. jours.; mem. editorial bd.: Archives Biochemistry and Biophysics, 1974-79, Cell Differentiation, 1980—, Jour. Craniofacial Genetics and Devel. Biology, 1980-83, Developmental Biology, 1981—. Served with USPHS, 1963-66. Guggenheim fellow, 1972-73; Josiah Macy scholar, 1980-81. Mem. Am. Acad. Pediatrics, Am. Soc. Biol. Chemists, Am. Soc. Cell Biology, Perinatal Research Soc., Soc. Devel. Biology, Soc. Pediatric Research, Teratology Soc., Western Soc. Pediatric Research (Ross award 1973). Home: 1661 Hamilton Ave Palo Alto CA 94303 Office: Dept Pediatrics Stanford Med Center Stanford CA 94305

BERNHAGEN, LILLIAN FLICKINGER, school health consultant; b. Cleve., Oct. 1, 1916; d. Norman Henry and Bertha May (Rogers) Flickinger; m. Ralph John Bernhagen, Sept. 2, 1940; children: Ralph, Janet Bernhagen Smiley, Penelope Bernhagen Braat. Student, Ohio Wesleyan U., 1934-37; B.S., R.N., Ohio State U., 1940, M.A., 1958; postgrad., LaVerne Coll., 1972-73. Asst. dir. Kiwanis Health Camp for Underprivileged Children, Steubenville, Ohio, summer 1940; asst. dir. nurses Jefferson Davis Hosp., Houston, 1940-41; Red Cross instr.

Ohio State U., 1943, 63, elem. edn. lectr., 1970; dir. health services Worthington (Ohio) City Schs., 1951-76; health edn. instr. Ohio State U., 1976-77; spl. cons. venereal disease and sex edn. Ohio Dept. Health, 1976-82; sch. health cons., 1976—; vice chmn. medicine/edn. com. on sch. and coll. health AMA, 1976-78, chmn., 1978-80. Author: Sex Education: Understanding Growth and Social Development, 1968, What A Miracle You Are-Boys, 1968, rev. edit., 1980, What A Miracle You Are-Girls, 1968, rev. edit., 1980, Toward a Reverance for Life, 1971, Personality, Sexuality and Stereotyping, 1974, (with others) Growth Patterns and Sex Education: A Suggested Curriculum Guide K-12, 1967; contbr. articles to profl. jours., mags. Bd. dirs. Hearing and Speech Center of Columbus and Franklin County, 1954-57, sec., 1957; mem. nat. adv. com. Nat. Center for Health Edn., 1978-82; sec. Ohio Wesleyan U. Class of 38, 1968-78, 83—; bd. dirs. V.D. Hotline Columbus and Franklin County, 1974—, bd. expansion chmn., 1978—. Recipient Centennial award Sch. Nursing, Ohio State U., 1970, Outstanding Alumnae award Ohio State U., 1964. Fellow Am. Sch. Health Assn. (pres. 1976, chmn. health guidance in sex edn. com. 1963-67, 71-77, chmn. sr. adv. council 1983, Disting. Service award 1969, Howe award 1979), Am. Pub. Health Assn. (chmn. com. on urban health problems 1972); mem. NEA, Worthington Edn. Assn. (v.p. 1961-62), Central Ohio Tchrs. Assn. (chmn. sch. health services sect. 1963), Royal Soc. Health, AAUW, Chi Omega (pres. Columbus Alumnae chpt. 1947-49, fin. adv. Ohio Wesleyan U. 1964-76), Pi Lambda Theta (citation award), Sigma Theta Tau, Phi Delta Kappa. Methodist. Clubs: Monnett, Worthington Women's, Ohio State U. Women's Golf (chmn. 1973). Home and Office: 5916 Linworth Rd Worthington OH 43085

BERNHARD, ARNOLD, investment adviser, publisher; b. N.Y.C., Dec. 2, 1901; s. Bernhard and Regina (Steigelfest) B.; m. Janet Marie Kinghorn, Dec. 21, 1929; children: Jean Haxton (Mrs. Edgar M. Buttner), Arnold Van Hoven. B.A., Williams Coll., 1925; LL.D.; L.H.D., Skidmore Coll., U. Bridgeport. Newspaper reporter, 1926-28, securities analyst, 1928-31, investment counsel, 1931—; founder, chief exec. officer Arnold Bernard & Co., Inc., 1935; research chmn. The Value Line Investment Survey, N.Y., 1936—, The Value Line Over-the-Counter Spl. Situations Service, 1951—, The Value Line Convertibles Service, 1967—; pres., portfolio mgr. The Value Line Fund, 1950—, The Value Line Income Fund, 1952—, The Value Line Spl. Situations Fund, 1956—; chmn. The Value Line Leveraged Growth Investors, Inc., 1972—, The Value Line Cash Fund, 1979—, The Value Line Bond Fund, 1981—. Life trustee U. Bridgeport; bd. dirs. Children's Eye Care Found., Nat. Cancer Cytology Found., Friends of Animals. Mem. Phi Beta Kappa, Delta Sigma Rho, Delta Upsilon. Clubs: Met., Williams. Home: Rondelet 21 N Sylvan Rd Westport CT 06880 Office: 711 3rd Ave New York NY 10017

BERNHARD, HENRY PAUL, advertising executive; b. Washington, Nov. 12, 1927; s. Henry Albin and Lucie O. (Karge);; s. Henry Albin and Lucie O. (Bernhard); m. Helen Dorothea Albert, Aug. 9, 1952; children: Karen Irene, Eric Albert, Lisa Karge, David Paul. B.A., Union Coll., Schenectady, 1952. Exec. trainee McCann Erickson Advt., N.Y.C., 1952; mgr. mktg. services Life mag. Time Inc., N.Y.C., 1952-60; with Ogilvy & Mather Inc., N.Y.C., 1960—, chmn. continental European offices and mng. dir., Frankfurt, Germany, 1966-70, vice chmn., N.Y.C., 1971—, also dir.; dir. Ogilvy & Mather Internat., Mktg. Outlooks, Inc., Wasa Rye King Inc. Served with USNR, 1945-47. Club: Tuxedo Park. Office: 2 E 48th St New York NY 10017 *

BERNHARD, JOHN TORBEN, univ. pres.; b. N.Y.C., June 24, 1920; s. Torben Martin and Mary (Nielsen) B.; m. Ramona Bailey, June 2, 1941; children—John Gary, Scott Martin, Randall Lee, Julie Ann. B.S., Utah State U., 1941; M.A., UCLA, 1949, Ph.D., 1951; LL.D., Quincy Coll., 1970, Chungnam Nat. U., Korea, 1975; D.Litt., Central Mich. U. Prof. polit. sci. Brigham Young U., 1959-68, dean humanities and social scis., 1962-68; pres., prof. polit. sci. Western Ill. U., Macomb, 1968-74, Western Mich. U., Kalamazoo, 1974—. Served to lt. (j.g.) USCGR. Mem. Am. Assn. Higher Edn., Am. Polit. Sci. Assn., Pi Sigma Alpha, Pi Gamma Mu, Xi Sigma Pi, Sigma Nu, Sigma Iota Epsilon, Phi Delta Kappa, Phi Kappa Phi, Pi Delta Epsilon. Mem. Ch. Jesus Christ of Latter-day Saints. Home: 1201 Short Rd Kalamazoo MI 49008

BERNHARD, ROBERT ARTHUR, investment banker; b. N.Y.C., May 14, 1928; s. Richard J. and Dorothy (Lehman) B.; m. Frances Wells, Dec. 21, 1949; children: Adele, Michael, Susan, Steven; m. Joan M. Sommerfield, Aug. 1, 1970. B.S., Williams Coll., 1951; M.B.A., Harvard U., 1953. With Lehman Bros., N.Y.C., 1953-62, partner, 1963-70; mng. dir. Lehman Bros., Inc., N.Y.C., 1970-71; gen. partner Abraham & Co., N.Y.C., 1971-72; exec. v.p., dir. Abraham & Co., Inc., N.Y.C., 1972-73; gen. ptnr. Salomon Bros., N.Y.C., 1974—; mng. ptnr. Bernhard Assocs.; dir. Sci. Leasing Corp. Mem. vis. com. 20th century dept. Met. Mus. Art; mem. vis. com. John F. Kennedy Sch. Govt., Harvard, Fogg Mus. Art; trustee Worcester Found. Exptl. Biology, Montefiore Hosp.; bd. dirs. Robert Lehman Found.; bd. overseers Albert Einstein Coll. Medicine; trustee Cooper Union.; bd. govs. Bklyn. Mus.; trustee, vice chmn. Montefiore Hosp. Clubs: Bond of N.Y., Madison Square Garden (N.Y.C.); Century Country (White Plains, N.Y.); City Midday, Harvard Business., N.Y. Yacht. Home: 800 Park Ave New York NY 10021 Office: 1211 Ave of the Americas New York NY 10036

BERNHARD, WILLIAM FRANCIS, thoracic and cardiovascular surgeon; b. Bklyn., Dec. 11, 1924; s. William and Helen (Conroy) B.; m. June Horne, Sept. 17, 1948; children—Susan, William Francis, Christine, Margaret, Catherine, John, Ann, James, Robert, Peter. B.A., Williams Coll., 1946; M.D., Syracuse U., 1950. Intern Syracuse U. Hosp., 1950-51; asst. resident Children's Hosp. Med. Center, Boston, 1951-52; dir. surg. research lab. Children's Hosp., Boston, 1960—, asso. surgeon, 1962-66; sr. asso. in cardiovascular surgery Children's Hosp. Med. Center; asst. resident, Peter Bent Brigham Hosp, Boston, 1952-57, attending staff cardiovascular surgery, 1973—, attending staff, 1974—; resident Bellevue Hosp., Columbia div., N.Y.C., 1957-58, Columbia-Presbyn. Hosp., 1959; attending surgeon thoracic and cardiovascular surgery VA Hosp., West Roxbury, Mass., 1960—; clin. asso. surgery Harvard Med. Sch., 1962-66, asst. clin. prof. surgery, 1966-68, asso. clin. prof. surgery, 1968-71, prof. surgery, 1971—. Mem. A.C.S., New Eng. Surg. Soc. (sr.), Am. Heart Assn., Mass. Med. Soc., Am. Assn. Thoracic Surgery, Soc. Thoracic Surgery, Soc. Univ. Surgeons, Am. Acad. Pediatrics, New Eng. Cardiovascular Soc., Soc. Vascular Surgery, Am. Soc. Artificial Internal Organs, Am. Surg. Assn. Home: 60 Singletary Ln Framingham MA 01701 Office: 300 Longwood Ave Boston MA 02115

BERNHARDT, ARTHUR DIETER, housing consultant; b. Dresden, Germany, Nov. 19, 1937; came to U.S., 1966; s. Rudolf B. and Charlotte (Bernhardt). Dipl. Ing., U. Tech., Munich, W. Ger., 1965; postgrad., U. So. Calif., 1966-67; M. City Planning, MIT, 1969. In various postions with bldg. projects, 1965-68; dir. Program in Industrialization of Housing Sector MIT, 1969-76, pres. Program in Industrialization of Housing Sector, 1977—; internat. housing industry cons., Cambridge, Mass., 1973—; asst. prof. MIT, 1970-76. Author book; contbr. articles to profl. jours. Mem. exec. com. Mass. Gov.'s Adv. Com. on Mobile Homes, 1974-75; NRC del. 8th Gen. Assembly Internat. Council Bldg. Research, 1974. Fed. Republic Germany fellow, 1965, 66, 67, 68; MIT fellow, 1968, 69; MIT grantee, 1970; Fed. Republic Germany grantee, 1965; Alfred P. Sloan Found. grantee, 1970; Dept. Commerce grantee, 1972. Mem. Internat. Council Bldg. Research, Am. Acad. Polit. and Social Sci., Am. Planning Assn., Deutscher Hochschulverband, Am. Judicature Soc. (assoc.). Home: Cambridge MA Office: PO Box 303 Cambridge MA 02141

BERNHARDT, HERBERT NELSON, lawyer, educator; s. Michael Maurice and Rose (Miller) B.; m. Rebecca Mehlman, June 30, 1968; children: Beth Margo, Suzanne Piper (twins). B.S., Cornell U., 1956; LL.B., Yale U., 1961; LL.M., NYU, 1971. Bar: N.Y. 1962, U.S. Supreme Ct. 1965. Inst., research assoc. Rutgers U., 1961-62; asst. prof. law U.S.C., 1962-64; atty. NLRB, 1964-67; Assoc. prof. Dickinson Sch. Law, 1967-63; assoc. prof. law Northeastern U., Boston, 1968-69; prof. law U. Balt., 1971—; labor arbitrator Am. Arbitration Assn., Fed. Mediation and Conciliation Service; hearing examiner EEOC. Contbr. articles to legal jours. NDEA fellow, 1969-71. Mem. ABA, Indsl. Relations Research Assn. (v.p. Balt. chpt.), Soc. Profls. in Sispute Resolution, Internat. Soc. Labor Law and Social Legis., Assn. Am. Law Schs. (nat. sec. labor law sect. 1971-72), Common Cause, Balt. Folk Music Soc. Democrat. Jewish. Club: Balt. Bicycle. Home: 6625 Chrlesway Baltimore MD 21204 Office: U Balt Sch Law Baltimore Md 21201

BERNHARDT, JOHN BOWMAN, banker; b. Norton, Va., Aug. 7, 1929; s. Claude Bowman and Mabel (Dixon) B.; m. Ada Nuckels, Aug. 29, 1952; children: Jared B., J. Carter. B.A., U. Va., 1954, LL.B., 1957; postgrad., Rutgers U., 1967. Exec. v.p. Va. Nat. Bank, Norfolk, 1969-79, pres., 1980—; vice chmn. bd. Sovran Fin. Corp. and Sovran Bank N.A., 1984—; exec. v.p. Va. Nat. Bankshares, 1972-79, pres., 1980-83; dir. Va. Electric and Power Co., Dominion Resources Inc. Trustee Eastern Va. Med. Sch. Found.; bd. dirs. United Communities Fund, pres., 1976; chmn. Greater Hampton Roads Orgn.; mem. Va. Fuel Converson Authority. Mem. Va. Bankers Assn. (pres. 1979), Res. City Bankers, Hampton Rds. Maritime Assn., Am. Bankers Assn., Hampton Roads C. of C. (dir.), Va. C. of C. Presbyterian. Clubs: Norfolk Yacht and Country, Harbor (Norfolk); Cedar Point (Suffolk, Va.). Home: 8020 Quail Hollow Cedar Point Suffolk VA 23433 Office: PO Box 600 Norfolk VA 23501

BERNHARDT, MELVIN, director; b. Buffalo, Feb. 26; s. Max and Kate (Benatovich) Bernhard. B.F.A., U. Buffalo, 1952; M.F.A., Yale U. Sch. Drama, 1955. Asst. prof. Goodman Theatre Sch. Drama, Chgo., 1958-63. Dir.: plays, including The Effect of Gamma Rays on Man-in-the-Moon Marigolds, off-Broadway, 1970 (OBIE award 1970), Early Morning, N.Y.C., 1970, And Miss Reardon Drinks a Little, Broadway, 1971, Other Voices, Other Rooms, Buffalo Studio Arena Theatre, 1973, Children (OBIE award 1976), Manhattan Theatre Club, Da (Tony award 1978, Drama Desk award 1978, Outer Critics Circle award 1978), Broadway, 1978, Hide and Seek, Broadway, 1980, Crimes of the Heart (Obie award, 1980, Tony nominee, 1982), Life After High School?, Hartford Stage Co., 1981; TV serial Another World, NBC-TV, 1974-82; live theater Mr. Roberts, NBC-TV, 1984; Author: stage play Pied Piper of Hamelin, 1963. Jewish.

BERNHEIM, ELINOR KRIDEL (MRS. LEONARD H. BERNHEIM), social welfare volunteer; b. N.Y.C., June 26, 1907; d. Alexander Hayes and Irma (Hernsheim) Kridel; m. Leonard H. Bernheim. B.A., Vassar Coll., 1928; postgrad., N.Y. Sch. Social Work, 1947-48. Mem. bd. and council Assn. for Aid for Crippled Children, 1941—; trustee Fedn. Jewish Philanthropies, N.Y.C., 1942—, v.p., 1955-58, chmn. women's div. fund raising drive, 1943, 44, 49, chmn. women's bd., 1955-58, hon. chmn., 1958—, v.p., 1971—; mem. bd. Jewish Assn. Neighborhood Centers; dir. Nat. Jewish Welfare Bd., 1944—, chmn. women's div., 1954-61, hon. chmn. women's bd., 1961—; mem. bd. com. Nat. Conf. for Social Welfare, 1947-51, v.p., 1949-51, chmn. edn. and recreation div., 1959—; adv. com. vol. services VA, 1947-61; bd. dirs. United Neighborhood Houses of N.Y.C., 1949-53; mem. bd. Nat. Council on Social Work Edn., 1952-54, mem. nat. citizens com. on careers, 1961-65; mem. bd. Nat. Assembly Social Policy and Devel.; pres. bd. Mosholu Montefiore Community Center, 1958-70; bd. dir. Asso. YM and YWHA's of Greater N.Y., 1958-60, asso. chmn., 1960-69, co-chmn., 1970—; pres. Community Council Greater N.Y., 1970-78, chmn. bd., 1978—; adv. bd. Columbia Univ. Sch. Social Work, 1968-78; bd. dirs. Community Service Soc., 1961-78; mem. N.Y. State Welfare Conf., 1961-63, Nat. Conf. Social Welfare, 1963, Gov. N.Y. State Com. Children and Youth, 1963; co-chmn. Dimitri Mitropolous Internat. Music Competition, 1961-63; bd. dirs. Young Concert Artists, 1968—; mem. Mayor's Screening Panel to Bd. Higher Edn., N.Y.C., 1964; v.p. Nat. Jewish Welfare Bd., 1967-71, Columbia Univ. Sch. Social Work, 1968—; mem. N.Y.C. chpt. Nat. Council on Alcoholism; co-chmn. YW-YMHA's of Greater N.Y.; mem. N.Y.C. Mayor's Office for Vol. Action, 1975, Nat. Homemakers Service Council, 1980; founder Elinor K. Bernheim awards, 1980. Author articles in field. Recipient Gen. award N.Y. State Welfare Conf., 1958; Bi-Centennial medal Columbia U., 1956; Frank L. Weil award Nat. Jewish Welfare Bd., 1960; Research Inst. citation Nat. Conf. Jewish Center Workers, 1961; Blanche Ittleson award, 1963; Naomi Lehman Meml. Found. award, 1966; caring New Yorker award Community Council Greater N.Y., 1982; citation of honor Nat. Council Jewish Women. Clubs: Women's City, Cosmopolitan (N.Y.C.). Address: 930 Park Ave New York NY 10028

BERNHEIM, FREDERICK, pharmacologist, educator; b. Long Branch, N.J., Aug. 18, 1905; s. George B. and Alice (Rheinstein) B.; m. Mary Christian Hare, Dec. 17, 1928; 1 dau., Cecily Ann (Mrs. Werner K. Honig). B.S., Harvard, 1925; Ph.D., Cambridge (Eng.) U., 1928. NRC fellow Johns Hopkins Med. Sch., 1929-30; mem. faculty Duke Med. Center, 1930—, prof. pharmacology, 1946—, James B. Duke prof. pharmacology, 1963—; Cons. Smith Kline and French Labs., 1948-67. Author: Interaction of Drugs and Cell Catalysts, 2d edit, 1946, also revs., articles, chpts. in books. Fellow N.Y. Acad. Sci., A.A.A.S.; mem. Am. Soc. Oil Chemists, Am. Soc. Biol. Chemists, Am. Soc. Pharmacology and Exptl. Therapeutics, Am. Soc. Cell Biology, AAUP (pres. Duke chpt. 1951-52), Sigma Xi (pres. Duke chpt. 1939-40). Home: 115 Woodridge Dr Durham NC 27705

BERNHEIMER, MARTIN, music critic; b. Munich, Germany, Sept. 28, 1936; came to U.S., 1940, naturalized, 1946; s. Paul Ernst and Louise (Nassauer) B.; m. Lucinda Pearson, Sept. 30, 1961; children: Mark Richard, Nora Nicoll, Marina and Erika (twins). Mus.B. with honors, Brown U., 1958; student, Munich Conservatory, 1958-59; M.A. in Musicology, N.Y. U., 1962. Free-lance music critic, 1958—; mem. music faculty N.Y. U., 1960-62; N.Y. corr. for Brit. publ. Opera, 1962-65, Los Angeles corr., 1965—; contbg. critic N.Y. Herald-Tribune, 1959-62; asst. music editor Saturday Rev., 1962-65; mng. editor Philharmonic Hall Program, N.Y.C., 1962-65; music editor, chief critic Los Angeles Times, 1965—; faculty Rockefeller program for tng. music critics at U. So. Calif., 1966-71; mem. music faculty UCLA, 1969-75, Calif. Inst. for the Arts, 1975—, Calif. State U., Northridge, 1978—. Contbr. articles newspapers, mags. in field, also liner notes for recordings, radio and TV appearances. Recipient Deems Taylor award ASCAP, 1974, 78, Pulitzer prize for disting. criticism, 1982. Office: Los Angeles Times Times-Mirror Square Los Angeles CA 90053

BERNICK, HOWARD BARRY, manufacturing company executive; b. Midland, Ont., Can., Apr. 10, 1952; came to U.S., 1974, naturalized, 1976; s. Henry and Esther (Starkman) B.; m. Carol Lavin, May 30, 1976; children: Craig, Peter. B.A., U. Toronto, Ont., 1973. Investment banker Wood Gundy Ltd., Toronto, 1973-74, First Boston Corp., Chgo., 1974-77; group v.p. Alberto Culver Co., Melrose Park, Ill., 1977—. Office: 2525 Armitage Ave Melrose Park IL 60160

BERNIER, GEORGE MATTHEW, JR., physician, medical educator; b. Portland, Maine, June 29, 1934; s. George Matthew and Lillian Theresa (Wallace) B.; m. Mary Jane Marron, June 29, 1963; children: George Matthew, III, Elizabeth Wallace. A.B., Boston Coll., 1956; M.D., Harvard U., 1960. Intern Univ. Hosps., Cleve., 1960-61, resident, 1961-62, 65-66, U. Fla. Hosps., Gainesville, 1964-65; fellow in biochemistry U. Fla., 1962-64; instr. Case Western Res. U., 1966-67, asst. prof. medicine, 1967-72, asso. prof., 1972-75, prof., 1975-78; dir. div. med. oncology Univ. Hosps., Cleve., 1974-78; prof., chmn. dept. medicine Dartmouth Med. Sch., Hanover, N.H., 1978—, now Joseph M. Huber prof. medicine. Contbr. articles to profl. jours. Trustee Jackson Labs., Bar Harbor, Maine, 1973—. Served to lt. col. M.C. U.S. Army, 1967-70. Leukemia Soc. Am. scholar, 1970-75. Fellow A.C.P.; mem. Am. Soc. Hematology, Am. Soc. Clin. Oncology, Am. Soc. Clin. Investigation, Am. Assn. Immunologists., Assn. Am. Physicians. Office: 3 Maynard St Hanover NH 03756

BERNIER, JEAN, utility company executive, lawyer; b. Montreal, Que., Can., Feb. 10, 1936. B.A., Coll. Saint-Laurent, Que., 1956; L.L.L., U. Montreal, 1959. Bar: Que. 1960. Solicitor Can. Pacific Rys., Montreal, 1960-61, Hydro-Que., 1962-73; gen. sec. Hydro-Que, Montreal, 1980—; solicitor James Bay Energy Corp., Montreal, 1973-74, dir. human resources, 1974-79, chief legal counsel, sec., 1979-80, sec., 1980—, Hydro-Que. Internat., 1980—. Office: Hydro-Quebec 75 West Blvd Dorchester Montreal PQ Canada H2Z 1A4

BERNIER, ROGER BERTRAND, librarian; b. Drummondville, Que., Can., Sept. 28, 1942; s. Armand W. and Jeanne (Ouellette) B.; m. Denise Marquis, Sept. 26, 1967 (div. Sept. 1977); 1 dau., Helene. B.A., Sem. Sherbrooke., 1964; B.Bibl., U. Montreal, 1965. Cataloguer Sem. Sherbrooke, 1965-67, U. Sherbrooke, 1967-70; head of cataloging dept. Library, U. Que., Montreal, 1970-71; head of Sci. Library, U. Sherbrooke, 1971-73, CEDOBUS, 1974-76, head gen. library, 1976-77; head of Informatheque, Programme de Recherche sur L'Amiante, U. Sherbrooke, 1977-81, head sci. library, 1981—; part-time tchr. Library of Congress; cons. Documentation Center, U. Sherbrooke, 1973, owner of tobacco store, 1974; sailboat dealer, 1981—. Author: Etablissement d'un Catalogue Systematique, 1969, La Classification Library of Congress: Cours et Exercices, 1973; co-author: Abrege de la Classification Library of Congress, 1974. Credit commr. of Caisse Populaire Ste. Jeanne D'Arc, Sherbrooke, 1974—, pres., Sherbrooke, 1983—. Mem. Assn. des Proprietaires de la Plage Southiere (sec. 1982, pres. 1983), Am. Soc. Info. Sci., Bureau de Direction Corp. des Bibliothecaires du Que. (pres. 12th ann. meeting 1981), Assn. pour l'avancement des scis. et des techniques de la documentation, Assn. Canadienne des scis. de l'information. Address: 2500 Blvd Sherbrook PQ Canada J1K 2R1

BERNOTAS, RALPH JOSEPH, automotive engineer; b. Cleve., May 16, 1927; s. Joseph and Tessie (Busher) B.; m. Mary Frances Schneider; children—Robert, Raymond, Ronald, Mary Helen. B.S., Case Western Res. U., 1949, M.S., 1954. Sr. design engr. Euclid Road Machinery Co., Cleve., 1949-53; with Terex div. Gen. Motors Corp., Hudson, Ohio, 1953—, chief engr., 1967-80; v.p. engring. Baker Material Handling, 1980—. Mem. Soc. Automotive Engrs., Constrn. Industry Mfrs. Assn., Tau Beta Pi. Republican. Roman Catholic. Patentee earthmoving machine design. Home: Berkshire Rd Gates Mills OH 44040 Office: Baker Material Handling Tiedeman Rd Cleveland OH

BERNOUDY, WILLIAM ADAIR, architect; b. St. Louis, Dec. 4, 1910; s. Jerome Baudy and Elizabeth (Maddox) B.; m. Gertrude Charlotte Tornofsky, June 14, 1956. Student, Taliesin Fellowship, 1930-36. Registered architect, Mo. Pres. Bernoudy Assocs., Inc., St. Louis, 1947—; v is. artist in residence Am. Acad., Rome, 1982. Trustee St. Louis Art Mus., 1981-83; bd. dirs. Laumier Sculpture Park, 1980—; mem. exec. bd. Mo. Bot. Gardens, 1983. Fellow AIA. Clubs: University (St. Louis); Metropolitan (N.Y.C.). Home: 9590 Litzinger Rd Sanit Louis MO 63141

BERNS, KENNETH IRA, physician; b. Cleve., June 14, 1938; s. Charles and Delnet (Cohn) B.; m. Laura Louise Lawless, June 26, 1964; children: Jonathan Charles, Deborah Louise. Student, Harvard U., 1956-59; A.B., Johns Hopkins U., 1960, Ph.D., 1964, M.D., 1966. Intern Johns Hopkins Hosp., 1966-67; asst. prof. microbiology Johns Hopkins U. Sch. Medicine, 1970-74, asst. prof. pediatrics, 1970-76, asso. prof. microbiology, 1974-76, dir., 1973-76; prof., chmn. dept. immunology and med. microbiology, prof. pediatrics U. Fla. Coll. Medicine, Gainesville, 1976—; Howard Hughes med. investigator, 1970-75; mem. microbiology test com. Nat. Bd. Med. Examiners, 1979-82; mem. Recombinant DNA adv. com. NIH, 1980-83; mem. genetic biology panel NSF, 1981-84; Fogarty sr. internat. fellow virology dept. Wetzmann Inst. Sci., Rehovot, Israel, 1982-83; ad hoc mem. Bd. Sci. Counselors, Nat. Inst. Allergy and Infectious Diseases, 1981-82; del. U.S.-Japan Coop. Program on Recombinant DNA, 1981; mem. Internat. Com. Taxonomy of Viruses, 1981—. Served with USPHS, 1967-70. Recipient faculty research award Am. Cancer Soc., 1975-76; grantee NIH, 1970-76, 80—, NSF, 1973-75, 77-80, Am. Cancer Soc., 1970-72; Shell Oil fellow, 1963-64. Mem. Am. Acad. Microbiology, Am. Soc. Biol. Chemists, Am. Soc. Microbiology (bd. public and sci. affairs), AAAS, Assn. Med. Sch. Microbiology Chmn. (counselor 1980-83, chmn. com. on public policy O41979), Soc. Gen. Microbiology, Soc. Pediatric Research, Fla. Pediatric Soc., Fla. Med. Assn., Alachua County Med. Soc., Phi Beta Kappa, Sigma Xi. Home: 10921 NW 14th Ave Gainesville FL 32601 Office: Box J-266 JHMHC U Fla Gainesville FL 32610

BERNS, WALTER FRED, political scientist, educator; b. Chgo., May 3, 1919; s. Walter Fred and Agnes (Westergard) B.; m. Irene Sibley Lyons, June 16, 1951; children: Elizabeth, Emily, Christopher. B.Sc., U. Iowa, 1941; postgrad., Reed Coll., 1948-49, London Sch. Econs. and Polit. Sci., 1949-50; Ph.D., U. Chgo., 1953. Asst. prof. govt. La. State U., 1953-56; asst. prof. polit. sci., Yale U, 1956-59; mem. faculty Cornell U., 1959-69, prof. govt., chmn. dept., 1963-68; prof. polit. sci. U. Toronto, Ont., Can., 1970-79; John M. Olin disting. scholar in constl. and legal studies Am. Enterprise Inst., 1979—; professorial lectr. Georgetown U., 1979—; mem. Salzburg (Austria) Seminar Am. Studies, 1959. Author: Freedom, Virtue and the First Amendment, 1957, Constitutional Cases in American Government, 1963, The First Amendment and the Future of American Democracy, 1976, For Capital Punishment: Crime and the Morality of the Death Penalty, 1979; co-author: Essays on the Scientific Study of Politics, 1963. Alt. U.S. rep. UN Commn. on Human Rights. Served with USNR, 1941-45. Mem. Am. Polit. Sci. Assn., Nat. Council on Humanities. Episcopalian. Address: 4986 Sentinel Dr Apt 402 Bethesda MD 20816

BERNSTEIN, ALAN ARTHUR, oil company executive; b. Bklyn., Feb. 20, 1944; s. Lawrence and Ida (Slutsky) B.; m. Eleanor Gale Thorner, June 26, 1965; children: Andrew, Adam, Aaron, Aric. B.S. in

Chem. Engring., CUNY, 1965, M.S., U. Pa., 1966; M.B.A., Fairleigh Dickinson U., 1971. Engr. Exxon, Florham Park, N.J., 1966-69; planning engr. Amerada Hess Corp., N.Y.C., 1969-72, mgr. refinery econs., 1972-80, v.p., 1980—. Mem. Am. Inst. Chem. Engrs. Jewish. Office: Amerada Hess Corp 1185 Ave of Americas New York NY 10036

BERNSTEIN, ARTHUR JAY, computer scince educator, consultant; b. N.Y.C., May 28, 1937; s. Jack and Gertrude (Kalz) B.; m. Edith H. Cohen, Dec. 24, 1960; children: Peter S., Karen L., Judith Y. A.B., Columbia U., N.Y.C., 1957, Ph.D., 1962. Asst. prof. Princeton U., 1962-65; info. scientist Gen. Electric Research and Devel., Schenectady, 1965-70; assoc. prof. SUNY-Stony Brook, from 1970; now prof. SUNY-Brook; vis. prof. Technion, Haifa, Israel, 1976. Assoc. editor: Handbook of Electrical and Computer Engring., 1979-81, Jour. on Computing, 1972-77; contbr. articles to profl. jours. Grantee NSF, Air Force Office of Sci. Research. Fellow IEEE (cert of appreciation 1982, disting. visitor Computer Soc.); mem. Assn. Computing Machinery. Office: Dept Computer Sci SUNY Stony Brook NY 11794

BERNSTEIN, BARRY, educator; b. N.Y.C., Nov. 20, 1930; s. Charles Michael and Louise Ruth (Fried) B.; m. Ilse Lewenberg, Aug. 22, 1954; children—Lynn, Jill. B.S. magna cum laude, Coll. City N.Y., 1951; M.A., Ind. U., 1954, Ph.D., 1956. Mathematician Naval Research Lab., Washington, 1951-53, 56-61, Nat. Bur. Standards, 1961-65; vis. asso. prof. Purdue U., 1965-66; prof. math. Ill. Inst. Tech., Chgo., 1966—, acting dir., 1970-76; cons. to industry Nat. Bur. Standards. Recipient award for outstanding achievement Nat. Bur. Standards, 1966. Mem. Rheology Soc., Soc. Indsl. and Applied Mathematics, Am. Math. Soc., Phi Beta Kappa, Sigma Xi. Jewish religion (dir. temple). Research and publs. on large deformations of continuous media, viscoelasticity, math. analysis, biol. applications of mathematics. Home: 1039 N Oak Park Ave Oak Park IL 60302 Office: Illinois Inst Tech Chicago IL 60616

BERNSTEIN, BERNARD, lawyer; b. N.Y.C., Nov. 30, 1908; s. Henry and Annie (Goldstein) B.; m. Bernice Lotwin, Aug. 4, 1938; children: Elinor (Mrs. Sigmund R. Balka), Kate, Anne (Mrs. Harold Chesnin). A.B., Columbia, 1928, J.D. (Kent scholar 1927-30), 1930. Bar: N.Y. 1931, U.S. Supreme Ct. 1936, D.C. bar 1947. Asso. Mitchell, Taylor, Capron & Marsh, N.Y.C., 1930-33; atty. U.S. Treasury Dept., 1933-42, asst. gen. counsel, 1938—; participated in all litigation relating to govt.'s gold and monetary policies, and in internat. financial arrangements of Treasury, 1934-42; mem. com. experts that drafted plans for Inter-Am. Bank, 1939-40; active in adminstrn. fgn. funds control by Treasury Dept., 1940-42; U.S. adviser Inter-Am. conf. on systems of econ. and financial control, 1942; financial adviser N. African Econ. Bd., 1942-43; dir. finance div., dir. div. investigation cartels and external assets U.S. Group Control Commn. for Germany, 1944-45; Legal adviser Am. Jewish Conf., 1946-48; chmn. Working Com. Jewish Orgns. (for treaties with enemy countries), 1946-47; cons. on behalf of Coordinating Bd. Jewish orgns. to ECOSOC, 1949-53; chmn. Kings Point (N.Y.) Bd. Appeals, 1971-75. Editor: Columbia Law Rev, 1928-30. Commd. lt. col. U.S. Army, 1942; promoted col., 1944; financial adviser to Gen. Eisenhower for Civil Affairs and Mil. Govt., 1942-45; ETO, MTO. Decorated Legion of Merit, Legion of Honor, Croix de Guerre with palm, France). Mem. N.Y. County Lawyers Assn. (chmn. com. fgn. law and internat. law 1964-69), Am. Soc. Internat. Law, Mil. Govt. Assn., Am. Bar Assn., Am. Legion, Bar Assn. City N.Y., Am. Fgn. Law Assn., Am. Soc. French Legion of Honor, Tau Delta Phi., B'nai B'rith. Testified before Senate Com. on Mil. Affairs respecting investigation by Mil Govt. of I.G. Farben, 1945. Home: 150 E 69th St New York NY 10021 Office: 230 Park Ave New York NY 10169

BERNSTEIN, CARL, author, journalist; b. Washington, Feb. 14, 1944; s. Alfred David and Sylvia (Walker) B.; m. Nora Ephron, Apr. 14, 1976; children: Jacob Walker, Max Ephron. Student, U. Md., 1961-64; LL.D., Boston U., 1975. From copyboy to reporter Washington Star, 1960-65; reporter Elizabeth (N.J.) Jour., 1965-66, Washington Post, 1966-76; Washington bur. chief ABC, 1979-81; corr. ABC News, N.Y.C., 1981-84. Author: (with Bob Woodward) All the President's Men, 1974, The Final Days, 1976. Served with AUS, 1968. Recipient 1st prize gen. reporting N.J. Press Assn., 1966, 1st prize investigative reporting, 1966; Drew Pearson prize for investigative reporting of Watergate, 1972; George Polk Meml. award; Worth Bingham prize; Heywood Broun award Internat. Newspaper Guild; Sigma Delta Chi Distinguished Service award; Sidney Hillman Found. award; gold medal U. Mo. Sch. Journalism, 1972. Office: 2853 Ontario Rd NW Washington DC 20009

BERNSTEIN, CARYL SALOMON, lawyer; b. N.Y.C., Dec. 22, 1933; d. Gustav and Rosalind (Aron) Salomon; m. Wo;;oa, D. Terry, June 12, 1955 (div. 1967); children: Ellen Deborah, Mark David; m. Robert L. Cole, Jr., Oct. 25, 1970 (div. 1975); m. George K. Berstein, June 17, 1979. B.A. with honors, Cornell U., 1955; J.D., Georgetown U., 1967. Bar: D.C. 1968, U.S. Dist. Ct. D.C. 1968, U.S. Ct. Appeals (D.C. cir.) 1968, U.S. Supreme Ct. 1971.; Atty. Covington & Burling, Washington, 1967-73; staff atty. Overseas Pvt. Investment Corp., Washington, 1973-74, asst. gen. counsel, 1974-77, v.p. for ins., 1977-81; sr. v.p., gen. counsel, sec. Fed. Nat. Mortgage Assn., Washington, 1981-82, exec. v.p., gen. counsel, sec., 1982—; dir. Nat. Housing Conf., 1983—. Contbr. articles to profl. jours.; bd. editors: Georgetown Law Jour., 1966. Mem. Women's Legal Def. Fund, Washington, 1981—. N.Y. Regents scholar, 1951-55. Mem. ABA, Fed. Bar Assn., D.C. Bar Assn., Am. Soc. Internat. Law, Phi Beta Kappa, Phi Kappa Phi. Office: 3900 Wisconsin Ave NW Washington DC 20016

BERNSTEIN, DAVID, surgeon; b. Minsk, Russia, Oct. 20, 1910; came to U.S., 1912, naturalized, 1932; s. George and Anna (Rossoff) B.; m. Dorothy Ashery, Sept. 2, 1937; children—Helen Miriam Berman Young, Herbert Jacob. B.S., N.Y. U., 1930, M.D., 1935. Intern Bellevue Hosp.-N.Y. U., N.Y.C., 1935-37, resident in ear, nose, throat and facial plastic surgery, 1937-39; clin. prof. otorhinolaryngology, chief of plastic surgery N.Y. U. Med. Center, 1966—; chief otolaryngology service Maimonides Med. Center, 1966—; cons. otorhinolaryngol. plastic surgery VA Hosp., N.Y.C.; attending otolaryngologist plastic surgery Bellevue-N.Y. U. Hosp.; pres., exec. com. of med. staff Met. Geriatric Center, 1974-75, mem. joint com. bd. trustees, 1975—; cons. Coney Island Hosp. Contbr. articles to profl. jours., sci. papers to meetings. Served to maj. M.C. AUS, 1944-46. Recipient Meritorious Service award N.Y. U., 1977; named hon. police surgeon, N.Y.C., 1979. Fellow Am. Acad. Ophthalmology and Otolaryngology, Am. Acad. Facial, Plastic and Reconstructive Surgery, Am. Assn. Cosmetic Surgeons, Internat. Coll. Surgeons; mem. N.Y., Vienna acads. medicine, N.Y. U. Med. Sch. Alumni Assn. (pres. 1974-75), N.Y. U. Alumni Fedn. (dir.), Phi Beta Kappa. Jewish (adv. com. to bd. trustees temple). Clubs: N.Y. U., Medallion (pres. 1980). Pioneer surg. techniques in rhinoplastic, otoplastic and maxillofacial surgery. Home and Office: 1342 51st St Brooklyn NY 11219 *What has most inspired me is the thought that life is a continuum with no end. Aside from pure faith, this is supported by Einstein's E-MC squared, which to me means matter and energy are interchangeable and nothing in nature is lost. See you in orbit.*

BERNSTEIN, DAVID W., rubber company executive; b. Chelsea, Mass., 1908. Grad., M.I.T., 1931. With Am. Biltrite Inc. (formerly Am. Biltrite Rubber Co.), Chelsea, Mass., 1932—, v.p., 1954-66, pres., chief exec. officer, 1966-70, chmn., chief exec. officer, 1970-75, chmn. bd., 1975—, also dir.; chmn., mem. exec. com. Am. Synthetic Rubber Co., Louisville. Office: American Biltrite Inc 575 Tech Sq Cambridge MA 02139 *

BERNSTEIN, ELLIOT LOUIS, television executive; b. N.Y.C., May 14, 1934; s. George Rubin and Renee (Horlick) B.; m. Marcy Adrienne Rosen, June 3, 1979; children: Joan, Daniel, Julie. B.A., Bklyn. Coll., 1958. Writer, reporter, editor, TV producer UPI, N.Y.C., 1958-63; with ABC News, N.Y.C., 1963-66, bur. chief, Saigon, 1966-67, Chgo., 1967-69; dir. news KGO TV, San Francisco, 1969-71; asst. news dir. ABC TV, N.Y.C., 1971, weekend news producer, 1972, spl. events producer, 1972-78; news producer CBS, N.Y.C., 1978; adj. faculty Grad. Sch. Journalism, Columbia U. Producer: Sunday Morning, 1978-79, Morning News, 1979-80; exec. producer: Morning with Charles Kuralt, 1980-81; producer: Sixty Minutes, 1981-83; sr. producer: On the Road with Charles Kuralt, 1983—, The American Parade, 1984—. Served with AUS, 1958. Recipient Silver Gavel, 1976, Janus award Am. Mortgage Bankers Assn., 1976. Mem. Writers Guild Am. East. Home: 315 E 72d St New York NY 10021 Office: 555 W 57th St CBS Sixty Minutes New York NY 10019

BERNSTEIN, ELMER, composer, conductor; b. N.Y.C., Apr. 4, 1922; s. Edward and Selma (Feinstein) B.; m. Pearl Glusman, Dec. 21, 1946; children: Peter Matthew, Gregory Eames; m. Eve Adamson, Oct. 25, 1965; children: Emily Adamson, Elizabeth Campbell. Student, N.Y. U. Pres. Young Musicians Found., 1961—. Concert pianist, N.Y.C., Phila., Chgo., 1946-50; composer: music for UN radio shows, 1949; mus. scores, 1950—, including, Man with the Golden Arm, The Ten Commandments, The Magnificent Seven, Summer and Smoke, Walk on the Wild Side, To Kill a Mockingbird (Golden Globe award Hollywood Fgn. Press 1962), The Great Escape, The Birdman of Alcatraz, Hud, Sudden Fear, God's Little Acre, Sweet Smell of Success, Desire Under the Elm, Some Came Running, From the Terrace, Love With the Proper Stranger, Baby the Rain Must Fall, The Caretakers, The Sons of Katie Elder, Cast a Giant Shadow, Hawaii, Seven Women, True Grit, The Shootist, National Lampoon's Animal House, Bloodbrothers, Meatballs, Airplane!, Airplane II, Stripes, Heavy Metal, An American Werewolf in London, Honky Tonk Freeway, The Chosen, Genocide, Five Days One Summer, Ghostbusters; scores for TV include Serpico, Little Women, The Rookies, Guyana Tragedy: The Story of Jim Jones; (Recipient Motion Picture Exhibitor Laurel awards 1956, 57, 62, Emmy award for best music written for TV, Making of a President 1964, Acad. award for best original music score for Thoroughly Modern Millie 1968). Mem. Acad. Motion Picture Arts and Scis. (1st v.p. 1963—), The Thalians (v.p. 1959-62), Screen Composers Assn. (dir.), Composers and Lyricists Guild Am. (pres. 1970—), Nat. Acad. Rec. Arts and Scis. (dir.). Office: care Acad Motion Picture Arts and Scis 8949 Wilshire Blvd Beverly Hills CA 90211 *

BERNSTEIN, EMIL STEVEN, financial executive; b. N.Y.C., Aug. 14, 1946; s. Samuel and Elaine (Wershba) B.; m. Natalie Ann Sharp, Aug. 7, 1971; children: Rachel, Lisa. B.S., Syracuse U., 1968; M.B.A., Harvard U., 1971. C.P.A., Mass. Profl. staff Touche Ross & Co., Boston, 1971-78, ptnr., 1978-81; v.p., fin. and corp. devel. Chelsea Industries, Inc., Boston, 1981—. Mem. Am. Inst. C.P.A.s, Mass. Soc. C.P.A.s. Republican. Jewish. Office: 1360 Soldiers Field Rd Boston MA 02135

BERNSTEIN, EUGENE FELIX, medical educator; b. N.Y.C., Oct. 9, 1930; s. Mayer H. and Sarah (Marmerstein) B.; m. Joan Jordan, Oct. 10, 1954; children: Diane, Steven, Susan. Student, Coll. Arts and Pure Scis., NYU, 1947-50; M.D., Downstate Med. Center, SUNY, 1954; M.S., U. Minn., 1961, Ph.D., 1964. Diplomate: Am. Bd. Surgery, Am. Bd. Thoracic Surgery. Intern King's County Hosp., Bklyn., 1954-55; resident U. Minn., 1957-64; instr. dept. surgery U. Minn. Med. Sch., 1963-64, asst. prof., 1964-67, asso. prof., 1967-69; prof. surgery U. Calif. at San Diego Sch. Medicine, 1969-82, head vascular surgery; surgeon Scripps Clinic and Research Found., La Jolla, Calif., 1982—; cons. Naval Hosp., San Diego; mem. study sect. NIH, 1976-79. Served to capt. M.C. AUS, 1955-57. Postdoctoral research fellow Nat. Heart Inst., 1959-62; Advanced research fellow Am. Heart Assn., 1962-64; John and Mary R. Markle scholar acad. medicine, 1963-68. Mem. A.C.S., Am. Heart Assn., Am. Soc. Artificial Internal Organs (past pres.), Assn. Acad. Surgery, Am., Central, Pacific Coast surg. assns., San Diego Soc. Gen. Surgeons, Internat. Cardiovascular Soc., Soc. Univ. Surgeons, Soc. Clin. Vascular Surgery, Soc. Thoracic Surgery, Soc. Vascular Surgery, Mpls., James E. Moore surg. socs., Beta Lambda Sigma, Alpha Omega Alpha. Research in vascular physiology, rheology of blood, assisted circulation. Home: 2520 Via Viesta La Jolla CA 92037 *A good education, hard work and awareness of opportunity when it knocks, permit the achievement of both professional and personal goals with continuing satisfaction and gratification.*

BERNSTEIN, EUGENE MERLE, educator, physicist; b. Balt., Feb. 13, 1931; s. Isidore and Ethel (Karsh) B.; m. Jean M. Stuesser, Aug. 3, 1960; children—Robert Glen, Lisa Joan. B.S., Duke, 1953, M.A., 1954, Ph.D., 1956. Instr. Duke, 1956-57; instr. U. Wis., 1957-59, lectr., 1960-61; NSF postdoctoral fellow Niels Bohr Inst., Copenhagen, 1959-60; asst. prof. U. Tex., 1961-63, asso. prof., 1963-65, prof., 1967-68; vis. staff mem. Los Alamos Sci. Lab., 1965-67; prof. Western Mich. U., Kalamazoo, 1968—, chmn. physics dept., 1980—; vis. prof. U. Ariz., 1975-76. Fellow Am. Phys. Soc.; mem. N.Y. Acad. Scis., Phi Beta Kappa, Sigma Xi. Home: 2417 Acorn Ln Kalamazoo MI 49008

BERNSTEIN, I. LEONARD, physician, educator; b. Jersey City, Feb. 17, 1924; s. Sydney and Jean B.; m. Miriam Goldman, Aug. 29, 1948; children—David, Susan, Ellen, Jonathan. Student, St. John's U., Bklyn., 1940-41, George Washington U., 1941-43; M.D., U. Cin., 1949. Diplomate: Am. Bd. Internal Medicine, Am. Bd. Allergy and Clin. Immunology. Intern Cin. Gen. Hosp., 1949-50; jr. resident in internal medicine Jewish Hosp., Cin., 1950-51; resident in chest diseases Bellevue Hosp., N.Y.C., 1953-55; fellow in allergy and immunology Northwestern U. Med. Sch., 1955-56; mem. faculty U. Cin. Med. Center, 1956—, clin. prof. medicine, 1971—, dir. allergy clinic, 1971—, dir. allergy tng. program, 1958—, dir., 1958—; trustee faculty council on Jewish affairs U. Cin., 1967—; attending physician Cin. Gen., VA, Jewish hosps. Contbr. articles to med. publns. Trustee Adath Israel Synagogue, 1980—. Served with AUS, 1943-45; as officer M.C. USAF, 1951-53. Grantee Nat. Inst. Allergy and Infectious Disease, 1958—. Fellow Am. Acad. Allergy (pres. 1982—), A.C.P.; mem. Am. Assn. Immunologists, AAAS, Central Soc. Clin. Research, Am. Thoracic Soc., Soc. Occupational and Environ. Health. Home: 3117 Esther Dr Cincinnati OH 45213 Office: 8464 Winton Rd Cincinnati OH 45231 *Productive basic and clinical research requires not only an innovative spark but also patience and unswerving determination. Personal commitment, ability to organize working time and association with intellectually honest colleagues are prerequisites to success in these fields.*

BERNSTEIN, IRVING, organization executive; b. N.Y.C., Aug. 9, 1921; s. Jacob and Ethel (Potasewitz) B.; m. Judith Muniz, Jan. 2, 1952; children: Robert, Joseph. B.S.S., CCNY, 1942; M.A., Columbia U. Tchrs. Coll., 1946. Secondary sch. tchr. N.Y.C. Public Sch. System, 1946; social worker N.Y.C. Dept. Welfare, 1947; field rep. midwest region United Jewish Appeal, 1948-50, West Coast regional dir., 1950-62, nat. asst. exec. vice chmn., 1962-68, nat. exec. vice chmn., 1969-83; founder Inst. for Fund-Raising Jewish Agy., Jerusalem, bd. govs., mem. internat. fundraising com.; chmn. meml. mus. com. Pres.'s Council on Holocaust; bd. dirs. United Israel Appeal, United Jewish Appeal of Greater N.Y., Inst. on Am. Jewish Israeli Relations of Am. Jewish Com.; cons. Internat. Outreach Program for Jewish Edn. World Jewish Congress; chmn. bd. advisors Hornstein Program for grad. studies in Jewish communal services Brandeis U.; also mem. adv. council Center for Modern Jewish Studies, Brandeis U.; Milender fellow in Jewish communal leadership Philip Lown Sch. Near East and Judaic Studies, Brandeis U., 1980; mem. Internat. Ctr. for Univ. Teaching of Jewish Civilization in Jerusalem; bd. regents Inst. Contemporary Jewry of Hebrew U. Contbr. articles to profl. jours. Mem. exec. com. Sch. Jewish Communal Service Hebrew Union Coll., Los Angeles; mem. exec. com. Nat. Jewish Conf., Conf. Jewish Communal Services; mem. Com. for Econ. Growth of Israel, Am. Friends of Internat. Edn. Seminar for Middle Eastern Educators at Harvard U., Jewish Family Center; adv. bd. Am. Jewish Com.; mem. exec. com. of adv. bd. William Petschek Nat. Family Ctr. of Am. Jewish Com.; bd. dirs. Hebrew U., Ben Gurion U., Jerusalem Coll. of Tech., Bezalel Acad. Arts and Design, Jerusalem. Served with USAF, 1942-45. Mem. Nat. Soc. Fundraising Execs. Club: Lambs. Home: One Stoneleigh Rd Scarsdale NY 10583 Office: United Jewish Appeal 1290 Ave of Americas New York NY 10104

BERNSTEIN, ISADORE ABRAHAM, biochemistry educator, researcher; b. Clarksburg, W.Va., Dec 23, 1919; s. William and Rosa B.; m. Claire Bernstein, Sept. 8, 1942; children: Lynne, Amy. A.B., Johns Hopkins U., 1941; Ph.D., Western Res. U., 1952. Research assoc. Case Western Res. U., Cleve., 1951-52, sr. instr., 1952-53; research assoc. Inst. Indsl. Health, U. Mich., Ann Arbor, 1953-56, 59-70, instr. biol. chemistry, 1954-57, asst. prof., 1957-61, assoc. prof., 1961-68, prof. dept. dermatology, 1968-71, assoc. prof. dept. indsl. health, 1961-67, prof., 1967-70, prof. dept. biochemistry, 1971—, prof. dept. environ. and indsl. health, 1970—; assoc. dir. research Inst. Environ. and Indsl. Health, 1978—; vis. prof. Osaka (Japan) U., 1963-64, Rockefeller U., N.Y.C., 1977-78; vis. scientist Hebrew U. Jerusalem, 1978. Contbr. numerous articles to sci. jours., chpts. to books; author 4 sci. books. Served to capt. U.S. Army, 1941-46. Decorated Bronze Star; co-recipient Internat. Meml. award for Psoriasis, 1959; recipient Stephen Rothman Meml. award Soc. Investigative Dermatology, 1981, Disting. Faculty Achievement award U. Mich., 1981. Fellow AAAS; mem. Am. Soc. Biol. Chemists, Am. Chem. Soc., Am. Soc. Microbiology, Soc. Investigative Dermatology, Am. Soc. Cell Biology, Soc. Toxicology, Am. Pub. Health Assn., Radiation Research Soc., Am. Inst. Biol. Sci., N.Y. Acad. Scis., Sigma Xi. Office: U Mich Ann Arbor MI 48109

BERNSTEIN, JOE, retail jewelry company executive; b. Greensboro, N.C., June 29, 1932; s. Joe and Claudia M. B.; m. Judy Lewis, Sept. 5, 1954; children: Michael Steven, Amy Lillian. Student, U. Miami, 1951-53, Gemelogical Inst. Am., 1969. Store mgr. The Jewel Box, Johnson City, Tenn., 1955-63, Zale Jewelers, Indpls., 1963-66; exec. v.p. Gray's Jewelers, Tulsa, 1967-80; pres. J. B. Hudson Jewelers, Mpls., 1980-83; exec. v.p. Kay Jewelers, Alexandria, Va.; Bd. cons. Minnetonka (Minn.) Art Center, 1980—; bd. advs. Project Pride in Living. Served with Signal Corps U.S. Army, 1953-55. Mem. Am. Gem. Soc. Home: 6502 Heather Brook Ct McLean VA 22101 Office: 320 King St Alexandria VA 22314

BERNSTEIN, LEONARD, conductor, pianist, composer; b. Lawrence, Mass., Aug. 25, 1918; s. Samuel Joseph and Jennie (Resnick) B.; m. Felicia Montealegre Cohn, Sept. 9, 1951 (dec. June 1978); children—Jamie, Alexander, Nina. A.B., Harvard, 1939; grad., Curtis Inst. Music, 1941; studied conducting with, Fritz Reiner and Serge Koussevitzky; studied piano with, Helen Coates, Heinrich Gebhard, and Isabella Vengerova. Asst. to Serge Koussevitzky at Berkshire Music Center, 1942; asst. condr. N.Y. Philharmonic Symphony, 1943-44; condr. N.Y.C. Symphony, 1945-48; frequent condr. Israel Philharmonic Orch., 1947—, mus. adviser, 1948-49; faculty Berkshire Music Center, 1948-55, head conducting dept., 1951-55; prof. music Brandeis U., 1951-56; co-condr. with Dimitri Mitropoulos of N.Y. Philharmonic, 1957-58, music dir., 1958-69; Charles Eliot Norton prof. poetry Harvard, 1972-73. Condr. major orchs. of, U.S., Europe in tours, 1946—, opera at, La Scala, Milan, also Met. Opera, N.Y.C. and Vienna State Opera; shared transcontinental tour in, U.S. with, Serge Koussevitzky and Israel Philharmonic, 1951; toured, Europe with, Vienna Philharmonic Orch., 1970, gala Bicentennial tour, Am. and Europe with, N.Y. Philharmonic, 1976; works include Clarinet Sonata, 1942, Seven Anniversaries for Piano, 1942, Song Cycle, I Hate Music, 1943, Four Anniversaries for Piano, 1948, Song Cycle, La Bonne Cuisine, 1949, Symphony No.2-The Age of Anxiety, 1949, Trouble in Tahiti; 1 act opera; also wrote libretto, 1952, Symphony No. 3, Kaddish, 1963; also wrote speaker's text Chichester Psalms; for mixed chorus, boys' choir, orch., 1965; score for musical show On The Town; ballets Fancy Free, 1944, Facsmile, 1946; incidental score for prodn. Peter Pan, 1950, The Lark, 1957; mus. score for Broadway prodn. Wonderful Town, 1953; Broadway mus. Candide, 1956, West Side Story, 1957; film On the Waterfront, 1954; songs Afterthought, Silhouette, 1951, Two Love Songs, 1949, Serenade; for violin and string orch. with percussion, 1954, Five Anniversaries for Piano, 1964, Mass; theatre piece for singers, players and dancers, 1971; ballet score Dybbuk, N.Y.C. Ballet Co., 1974, Dybbuk Variations, Suites No. 1 and 2; from ballet by Jerome Robbins, 1974, Songfest; a cycle of Am. poems for six singers and orch., 1977; overture for orch. Slava!, 1977, Three Meditations, from Mass; for cello and orch., 1977, Divertimento for Orchestra, 1980, A Musical Toast for Orchestra, 1980 (Recipient Emmy award for Young People's Concerts 1960, for Outstanding Classical Music Program, Leonard Bernstein and the N.Y. Philharmonic 1976, The Handel Medallion 1977); Author: The Joy of Music, 1959 (Christopher award), Leonard Bernstein's Young People's Concerts for Reading and Listening, 1962, rev. edit., 1970, The Infinite Variety of Music, 1966, The Unanswered Question: Six Talks at Harvard, 1976. Apptd. laureate condr. Philharmonic for life. Office: 1414 Ave of Americas New York NY 10019

BERNSTEIN, LESTER, editorial consultant; b. N.Y.C., July 18, 1920; s. Isidore and Rebecca (Axelrod) B.; m. Jacqueline Lipscomb, Feb. 6, 1946; children: Lynn, Nina, Paul, Daniel. A.B., Columbia U., 1940. Reporter N.Y. Times, 1940-48; writer, fgn. corr., editor Time mag., 1948-58; dir. info. NBC, 1958-60, v.p. corp. affairs, 1960-62; nat. affairs editor Newsweek, 1963-65, exec. editor, 1965-69, mng. editor, 1969-72, editor, 1979-82; editorial cons., 1982—; v.p. corporate communications RCA Corp., 1973-79. Served with AUS, World War II. Club: Century Assn. Office: 140 W 65th St New York NY 10023

BERNSTEIN, LIONEL MANDEL, systems company executive, former medical research administrator; b. Chgo., Sept. 10, 1923; s. Alick and Celia (Weinberg) B.; m. Joan Zeldes, Aug. 10, 1952; children: Alec, Susan, Molly. B.S., U. Ill., 1944, M.D., 1945, M.S., 1951, Ph.D., 1954. Diplomate: Am. Bd. Internal Medicine. Intern Cook County Hosp., Chgo., 1945-46, resident in internal medicine, 1949-51; then attending physician; research fellow Hektoen Inst. Med. Research, 1948-49; research fellow dept. clin. sci. U. Ill., 1951-52, research assoc. dept. medicine and clin. sci., 1952-53, instr. dept. medicine and physiology, 1953-54; prof. medicine Coll. of Medicine, U. Ill.; former attending physician Research and Edn. Hosp., U. Ill.; chief metabolic research div., med. nutrition lab. Fitzsimons Army Hosp., Denver, 1954-55; physician sr. grade VA Hosp., Sepulveda, Calif., 1955-56, chief gastroenterology sect., Hines, Ill., 1956-57, asst. dir. profl. services for research (title changed to asso. chief of staff for research), 1957-62; chief med. service VA West Side Hosp., Chgo., 1962-66; dir. research service VA Central Office, Washington, 1966-70, acting asst. chief med. dir. for research and edn. in medicine, 1967-68; assoc. dir. for extramural programs Nat. Inst. Arthritis, Metabolism, and Digestive Diseases, NIH, Bethesda, Md., 1970-72, assoc. dir. for digestive diseases and nutrition, 1972-73; spl. asst. to dir. Lister Hill Nat. Center for Biomed. Communications, Nat. Library of Medicine, 1976-77, asst. dep. dir. for research and edn., 1977-78; dir. Lister Hill Nat. Center for Biomed. Communications, 1978-82; pres. Knowledge Systems Inc., Chevy Chase, Md., 1983—; dir. office of program ops. Office Asst. Sec. Health, HEW, 1974, spl. asst. to asst. sec. health, 1975-76. Contbr. over 60 articles to profl. jours. Served with AUS, 1943-45; served to capt. M.C. AUS, 1946-48. Recipient chief med. dir. commendation VA, 1969, USPHS commendation medal, 1978; named Fed. Employee Alumnus of Yr. U. Ill., 1974. Fellow A.C.P.; mem. Central Soc. Clin. Research, Am. Fedn. Clin. Research, Am. Gastroent. Assn., Inst. of Medicine of Nat. Acad. Sci., Sigma Xi, Alpha Omega Alpha. Jewish. *

BERNSTEIN, LOUIS, clergyman; b. N.Y.C., Apr. 2, 1927; s. Sam and Anna (Richman) B.; m. Pearl Moshel, Mar. 13, 1955; children: Sara, David, Sima, Avraham. B.A., Yeshiva Coll., 1947; Hebrew Tchrs. degree, Tchrs. Inst., 1950, Ph.D., 1977; rabbi, Isaac Elchanan Theol. Sem., 1950. Rabbi Glenwood (N.Y.) Jewish Center, 1950-52, Kissena Jewish Center, Flushing, N.Y., 1954-55, Young Israel of Windsor Park, Bayside, N.Y., 1955—; assoc. prof. Erna Michael Coll., Yeshiva U., 1955; mem. edn. staff Camp Massad, N.Y.C., 1946-81, camp dir., 1957-71; Pres. Rabbinical Council Am., 1972-74; chmn. Israel schs., 1960—; mem. exec. com. Queens Jewish Community Council, 1971—; jsec. Hapoel Mizrachi Am., 1954-55; v.p. Religious Zionists Am., 1972-75, pres., 1975-81; exec. World Zionist Orgn., 1978—. Editor, RCA Record, 1954—. Served as chaplain AUS, 1952-54; ETO. Mem. Yeshiva Coll. Alumni Assn. (pres.). Home: 64-52 Bell Blvd Bayside NY 11364 Office: Young Israel of Windsor Park 67-45 215 St Bayside NY 11364

BERNSTEIN, MARVER HILLEL, educator, former university president; b. Mankato, Minn., Feb. 7, 1919; s. Meyer M. and Esther (Alpert) B.; m. Sheva Rosenthal, Sept. 19, 1943. B.A., M.A., U. Wis., 1940; Ph.D. in Politics, Princeton U., 1948; D.H.L., Jewish Theol. Sem., 1975, Northeastern U., 1978, Duquesne U., 1978, Brandeis U., 1983, Hebrew Union Coll., 1984. Budget examiner U.S. Bur. Budget, 1942-46; faculty Princeton U., 1947-72, prof. polit. and pub. affairs, 1958-72,; chmn. dept. politics Ford research prof. govtl. affairs, 1961-64; asso. dir. Woodrow Wilson Sch., 1961-64; dean Woodrow Wilson Sch. Pub. and Internat. Affairs, 1964-69; pres. Brandeis U., Waltham, Mass, 1972-83; Univ. prof. Georgetown U., Washington, 1983—; dir. New Eng. Mchts. Nat. Bank, Bank New Eng. N.A., 1973-83; cons. orgn., adminstrn. state and fed. agys. State Controller of Israel, 1953-57, A.I.A., 1968-70; asso. staff dir. spl. com. fed. conflict of interest laws Assn. Bar City N.Y., 1958-60; mem. Adminstrv. Conf. U.S., 1961-62, Rockefeller Pub. Service Awards Selection Com., 1964-69, Nat. B'nai B'rith Hillel Commn., 1966—, chmn., 1969-75, hon. chmn., 1975—. Author: Regulating Business by Independent Commission, 1955, The Politics of Israel, 1957, The Job of the Federal Executive, 1958, (with Walter Murphy, others) American Democracy, 1951. Chmn. Pub. and Sch. Employees' Grievance Procedure Study, Commn. N.J., 1967; mem. N.J. Apportionment Commn., 1968-69, Mass. Ethics Commn., 1978-82, U.S. Holocaust Meml. Council, 1980—; Trustee Am. Jewish Hist. Soc., 1972—, Joint Distbn. Com., 1978—; bd. dirs. WGBH Ednl. Found., 1972-83; pres. Nat. Fedn. for Jewish Culture, 1982—; bd. dirs. 1972. Fellow Am. Acad. Arts and Scis.; mem. Nat. Acad. Pub. Adminstrn., Am. Polit. Sci. Assn., Am. Soc. Pub. Adminstrn. Clubs: Princeton of N.Y.; Cosmos (Washington). Home: 4201 Cathedral Ave NW Washington DC 20016 office: georgetown univ sch of foreign service 37th and o street washington dc 20057

BERNSTEIN, MERTON CLAY, lawyer, educator; b. N.Y.C., Mar. 26, 1923; s. Benjamin and Ruth (Frederica (Kleeblatt) B.; m. Joan Barbara Brodshaug, Dec. 17, 1955; children: Johanna Karin, Inga Saterlie, Matthew Curtis, Rachel Libby. B.A., Oberlin Coll., 1943; LL.B., Columbia U., 1948. Bar: N.Y. 1948, U.S. Supreme Ct. 1952. Assoc. Schlesinger & Schlesinger, 1948; atty. NLRB, 1949-50, 50-51, Office of Solicitor, U.S. Dept. Labor, 1950; counsel Nat. Enforcement Commn., 1951, U.S. Senate Subcom. on Labor, 1952; legis. asst. to U.S. Sen. Wayne L. Morse, 1953-56; counsel U.S. Senate Com. on R.R. Retirement, 1958-59; spl. counsel U.S. Senate Subcom. on Labor, 1959; lectr., sr. fellow Yale U. Law Sch., 1960-65; prof. law Ohio State U., 1965-75; Walter D. Coles prof. law Washington U., St. Louis, 1975—; prin. cons. Nat. Commn. on Social Security Reform, 1982-83; vis. prof. law Columbia U. Law Sch., 1967-68, Leiden U., 1975-76; mem. adv. com. to Sec. of Treas. on Coordination of Social Security and pvt. pension plans, 1967-68; mem. adv. com. research U.S. Social Security Adminstrn., 1967-68, chmn., 1969-70; cons. Twentieth Century Fund, 1966-67, Dept. Labor, 1966-67, Russell Sage Found., 1967-68, NSF, 1970-71, Center for Study of Contemporary Problems, 1968-71; mem. Bethany (Conn.) Planning and Zoning Commn., 1962-65, Ohio Retirement Study Commn, 1972-75; v.p. Ind. Residents Assn. of Dublin, Ohio, 1974-75. Author: The Future of Private Pensions, 1964, Private Dispute Settlement, 1969; contbr. articles to profl. jours. Bd. dirs. St. Louis Theatre Project, 1981-84; pres. bd. Met. Sch. Columbus, Ohio, 1974-75. Served with AUS, 1943-45. Fulbright fellow, 1975-76. Mem. ABA (sec. sect. labor relations law 1968-69), Internat. Assn. for Labor Law and Social Security (dir. U.S. sect. 1973-83), Fulbright Alumni Assn. (dir. 1976-78), Indsl. Relations Research Assn., Nat. Acad. Arbitrators. Democrat. Jewish. Office: Washington U Sch Law Campus Box 1120 Saint Louis MO 63130

BERNSTEIN, NORMAN RALPH, psychiatrist, educator; b. N.Y.C., Oct. 12, 1927; s. Aaron Moses and Rachel (Hochberg) B.; m. Marilyn Jane Gabe, Aug. 30, 1953; children: Michael, Genya. B.A., Cornell U., 1949; M.D., N.Y. Med. Coll., 1951. Intern Fifth Ave. Hosp., 1951-52; resident Kings County Hosp., 1952-53, Mass. Gen. Hosp., 1953-56; fellow in psychiatry M.I.T., 1954-56; dir psychiatry Shriners Burns Inst., Boston, 1968-77; dir. child psychiatry unit Mass. Gen. Hosp., 1973-77; mem faculty Harvard U. Med. Sch., 1953-79; prof. psychiatry U. Ill. Med. Sch., Chgo., 1977—; cons. U. Chgo. Burn Center, 1979—, Isaac Ray Ctr. Law and Psychiatry, U. Ill. Ctr. on Developmental Disabilities. Editor: Diminished People, 1970, (with J. Sussex) Manual of Child Psychiatry, 1983, (with M.C. Robson) Comprehensive Approaches to the Burned Person, 1983; author: Emotional Problems of Burned and Disfigured, 1976. Served with AUS, 1946-47. Mem. Am. Psychiat. Assn., Am. Coll. Psychiatrists, Am. Burn Assn., Internat. Burn Assn., Nat. Assn. Burn Victims, Acad. Child Psychiatry, Group Advancement Psychiatry, Ill. Psychiat. Soc., Chgo. Council on Child Psychiatry, Chgo. Soc. Adolescent Psychiatry, World Med. Assn., Pan Am. Med. Assn., Royal Soc. Health. Home: 2650 Lakeview Ave Chicago IL 60614 Office: Univ Ill Med Center 912 S Wood St Chicago IL 60612

BERNSTEIN, PAUL, academic dean; b. Phila., Jan. 19, 1927; s. Abraham and Jennie (Geek) B.; m. Irma Shuster, Apr. 10, 1949; children: Jay Ira, Lisa Beth. B.S., Temple U., 1949, M.Ed., 1950; Ph.D., U. Pa., 1955. Tchr. social scis. Phila. pub. schs., 1949-55; prof. European history, chmn. social scis. dept. Lock Haven (Pa.) State Coll., 1955-64, Plattsburg (N.Y.) State U. Coll., 1964-66; dean Coll. Gen. Studies, Rochester Inst. Tech., 1966-76, dean grad. studies, 1976—. Author: (with R. Green) History of Civilization, 2d edit, 1962, Career Education and the Quality of Working Life, 1980; also (with R. Green) articles; mng. editor, Lock Haven Bull., 1959-64. Co-chmn. Citizens for Humphrey, Monroe County, N.Y., 1968. Served with AUS, 1944-47. Grantee Am. Philos. Soc., 1959, Swedish Bicentennial Com., 1980. Mem. Ind. Research Assn., French History Soc., Assn. Gen. and Liberal Studies (exec. bd., pres. 1978—). Democrat. Jewish. Club: Elks. Home: 5 Candlewood Circle Pittsford NY 14534 Office: Rochester Inst Tech Rochester NY 14623

BERNSTEIN, RALPH, electrical engineer, scientist; b. Zweibrucken, Germany, Feb. 20, 1933; came to U.S., 1938; s. Eleazar Lazar and Martha (Uhlfelder) B.; m. Leah Kine, Aug. 23, 1959; children: Elanna, Stuart Neil, Alexander Paul. B.S.E.E., U. Conn., 1956; M.S.E.E., Syracuse U., 1960. Staff engr. Fed. Systems div., IBM, Owego, N.Y., 1956-62, sr. engr., Gaithersburg, Md., 1963-79; staff scientist IBM Sci. Ctr., Palo Alto, Calif., 1980—; cons. space applications adv. com. NASA, 1980-82, 83—; prin. investigator NASA Landsort Program, 1972-75, 82—; mem. space sci. bd. NRC-Nat. Acad. Scis., 1977-81, mem. space applications bd., 1983—. Editor: Digital Image Processing for Remote Sensing, 1978; author 50 papers; contbr. chpts. in books; patentee in field. Pres. Luxmanor Citizens Assn., Rockville, Md., 1972-75. Served with USAF, 1950-53. Recipient medal for exceptional sci. achievement NASA, 1974, Group Achievement NASA, 1972, Outstanding Contbn. IBM, 1974. Fellow IEEE; mem. Am. Astron. Soc. (sr.), Am. Soc. Photogrammetry, Soc. Info. Display, IEEE Geosci. Electronic Group (chmn. cert. 1970). Democrat. Jewish. Home: 1201 Woodview Terr Los Altos CA 94022 Office: IBM Sci Ctr 1530 Page Mill Rd Palo Alto CA 94304

BERNSTEIN, ROBERT, advertising executive; b. Kansas City, Mo., May 21, 1938; s. Lewis and Hattie (Lebrecht) B.; m. Phyliss Wilke, June 7, 1964; children: Steven, Susan, David. B.A. in Journalism, Okla. U., 1960. Producer Ray-Eye Prodns., Kansas City, Mo., 1960-61; with creative dept. Allmayer-Fox Advt. (and successor Potts-Woodbury Advt.), Kansas City, Mo., 1961-64; pres., chmn. bd. Bernstein/Rein Advt., Inc. (and predecessor Bernstein/Rein Advt., Inc.), Kansas City, Mo., 1964; chmn. bd., pres. Las Vegas Electronics, Inc.; chmn. bd. Reno Electronics, Inc.; dir. Mark Twain Empire Bank, Kansas City, Mo. Bd. dirs. Jewish Community Center; bd. dirs. Temple B'Nai Jehudah; chmn. bd. dirs. Jewish Geriatric and Convalescent Center; Bd. dirs. Children's Advocacy Services Center; bd. dirs. Shalom Plaza, Ronald McDonald House; mem. Mayor Kansas City Corps Progress. Mem. Am. Assn. Advt. Agys. (gov., Mem. Kansas City Advt. Club, dir.), Am. Assn. Advt. Agencies (past bd. govs.), Kansas City C. of C., Okla. U. Alumni Assn. (life mem., past pres. Greater Kansas City chpt.). Home: 11403 Holly Ct Kansas City MO 64114 Office: 800 W 47th St Kansas City MO 64112

BERNSTEIN, ROBERT, physician, state ofcl., former army officer; b. N.Y.C., Feb. 20, 1920; s. Morris and Rose (Gordich) B. B.A., Vanderbilt U., 1942; M.D. U. Louisville, 1946. Diplomate: Nat. Bd. Med. Examiners, Am. Bd. Internal Medicine. Commd. 2d lt. U.S. Army, 1942, advanced through grades to maj. gen., 1973; intern Grasslands Hosp., Valhalla, N.Y., 1946-47; resident Walter Reed Army Med. Center, Washington, 1952-55, dep. comdr., 1972-73, comdg. gen, 1973-78; hdep. commr. for spl. health services Tex. Dept. Health, Austin, 1978-80, commr. of health, 1980—; surgeon U.S. Mil. Assistance Command, Vietnam, 1970-72. Contbr. articles to mil. and med. jours. Decorated D.S.M. with oak leaf cluster, Legion of Merit with two oak leaf clusters, Bronze Star with oak leaf cluster, Purple Heart. Fellow A.C.P.; mem. Soc. Med. Consultants to Armed Forces, Internat. Soc. Internal Medicine, Phi Delta Epsilon, Phi Kappa Phi, Alpha Epsilon Pi, Alpha Omega Alpha. Home: 6506 Mesa Dr Austin TX 78731 Office: 1100 W 49th St Austin TX 78756

BERNSTEIN, ROBERT LOUIS, book publishing company executive; b. N.Y.C., Jan. 5, 1923; s. Alfred and Sylvia (Bloch) B.; m. Helen Walter, Nov. 23, 1950; children: Peter Walter, Tom Alfred, William Samuel. Grad., Lincoln Sch., N.Y.C., 1940; B.S., Harvard U., 1944. Gen. sales mgr. Simon & Schuster, Inc., N.Y.C., 1946-57; with Random House, Inc., N.Y.C., 1976—, Helsinki Watch, 1979—; Bd. dirs. Am. Book Pubs. Council, 1967-70, Dr. Seuss Found. Bd. dirs. Dr. Seuss Found., Writers and Scholars Internat., Chamber Music Soc., Lincoln Center; bd. dirs., v.p. Internat. League for Human Rights; trustee Blythedale Children's Hosp.; mem. nat. adv. bd. Amnesty Internat.; chmn. U.S. Helsinki Watch, Fund for Free Expression. Served with USAAF, 1943-46. Recipient Florina Lasker award N.Y. Civil Liberties Union, 1976. Mem. Assn. Am. Pubs. (chmn. 1972-73, chmn. com. Soviet-Am. public relations 1973, com. on internat. freedom to pub. 1975-76), Council on Fgn. Relations, Soc. Fellows N.Y. U. Clubs: Century Assn., Harvard, University (N.Y.C.); Century Country (White Plains, N.Y.); Town (Scarsdale, N.Y.). Office: 201 E 50th St New York NY 10022

BERNSTEIN, SIDNEY, lawyer; b. Bronx, N.Y., May 3, 1938; s. Meyer and Ethel (Sloop) B.; m. Joyce Elaine Blum, July 7, 1963; children: Michael Louis, Sheryl Lyn; m. 2d Andra Jane Schutz, June 6, 1982. B.A., Columbia U., 1960; J.D., Cornell U., 1964. Bar: N.Y. 1966, U.S. Dist. Ct. (we. dist.) N.Y. 1966, U.S. Dist. Ct. (so. dist.) N.Y. 1978, U.S. Ct. Appeals (D.C. cir.) 1980, U.S. Supreme Ct. 1971. Jr. editor Lawyer's Coop. Pub. Co., Rochester, N.Y., 1964-65, asst. mng. editor, 1966-71, editor Case and Comment Mag., 1966-71; sr. mng. editor Matthew Bender & Co., N.Y.C., 1971-75, asst. to pres., 1976—; of counsel Tolmage, Peskin, Harris & Falick, N.Y.C., 1981—; faculty Nat. Coll. Advocacy, 1977—; adj. faculty Sch. Continuing Edn., NYU, 1980—. Mem. editorial bd.: Trial Mag.; mem. editorial adv. bd.: Am. Criminal Law Rev., 1972-74; exec. editor: Nat. Law Rev. Reporter; editor-in-chief: Bell Soc. Internat. Law Jour.; editor: Criminal Defense Techniques, 6 vols., 1977—; contbr. articles to profl. jours. Mem. Roscoe Pound. Found.; trustee Bell Found. Mem. ABA, Am. Law Inst., Am. Soc. Writers on Legal Subjects, Assn. Trial Lawyers Am., N.Y. Trail Lawyers Assn., Nat. Assn. Criminal Def. Lawyers, Am. Judicature Soc. Republican. Jewish. Lodge: Masons. Home: W Shore Towers Apt 6B 101 Gedney St Nyack NY 10960 Office: Tolmage Peskin Harris & Falick 20 Vesey St New York NY 10007

BERNSTEIN, SIDNEY RALPH, editor; b. Chgo., Jan. 29, 1907; s. Charles and Jennie R. (Greenblatt) B.; m. Adele Bass, Oct. 5, 1930; children—Janet Bernstein Wingis, Henry. Student, U. Ill., 1924-25; M.B.A., U. Chgo., 1956. Asso. editor and mng. editor Hosp. Mgmt., Chgo., 1925-31; mng. editor Advt. Age, Chgo., 1932-38, editor, 1939-57, editorial dir., 1958-64, pub., 1964-70; dir. research and promotion Crain Communications Inc.; formerly Advt. Pubs., Inc., Chgo., 1938-39, v.p., 1938-60, exec. v.p., gen. mgr., 1961-64, pres., 1964-73, chmn. exec. com., 1973—; pres. Red Tag News Publs., Chgo., 1971-77; chmn. bd. Crain Automotive Group (name formerly Mktg. Services Inc.), Detroit, 1973—, Am. Trade Mags., Chgo., 1973—; lectr. U. Coll., U. Chgo., Mich. State U., 1950-58; mem. nat. mktg. adv. com. U.S. Dept. Commerce, 1969-71; bd. dirs. Am. Bus. Press, 1970-73, Mag. Pubs. Assn., 1970-76. Author: This Makes Sense to Me, 1976. Named Advt. Man of Year, Chgo.; Post 170 Am. Legion, 1957; Chgo. Federated Advt. Club, 1961; Communications Man of Year, Chgo., Jr. Assn. Commerce and Industry, Chgo., 1962; elected to Distbn. Hall of Fame, Boston Conf. on Distbn., 1962; named Man of Year Nat. Advt. Agy. Network, 1964, Communications Man of Year, Chgo.; Soc. Communicating Arts, 1976, Communicator of Year U. Chgo. Alumni Assn., 1975; recipient Humanitarian award Am. Jewish Com., 1976; Torch of Truth award Advt. Club of Indpls., 1979. Mem. numerous advt. and sales orgns., Am. Mktg. Assn. (dir. 1946-47, v.p. mktg. mgmt. 1963-64), Phi Epsilon Pi, Alpha Delta Sigma, Sigma Delta Chi, Beta Gamma Sigma, Chgo. Press Club. Clubs: Arts, Mid-Am., Tavern (Chgo.); Nat. Press (Washington). Home: 534 Stratford Pl Chicago IL 60657 Office: 740 Rush St Chicago IL 60611

BERNSTEIN, SOL, physician, med. services adminstr.; b. West New York, N.J., Feb. 3, 1927; s. Morris Irving and Rose (Leibowitz) B.; m. Suzi Maris Sommer, Sept. 15, 1963; 1 son, Paul. A.B. in Bacteriology, U. Southern Calif., 1952, M.D., 1956. Diplomate: Am. Bd. Internal Medicine. Intern Los Angeles County Hosp., 1956-57, resident, 1957-60; practice medicine specializing in cardiology, Los Angeles, 1960—; staff physician dept. medicine Los Angeles County Hosp. U. So. Calif. Med. Center, Los Angeles, 1960—, chief cardiology clinics, 1964, asst. dir. dept. medicine, 1965-72; chief profl. services Gen. Hosp., 1972-74; med. dir. Los Angeles County-U So. Calif. Med. Center, 1974—; med. dir. central region Los Angeles County, 1974-78; dir. Dept. Health Services, Los Angeles County, 1978—; asso. prof. medicine U. Southern Calif. Sch. Medicine, Los Angeles, 1968—; cons. crippled Childrens Ser. Calif., 1965—. Contbr. articles on cardiac surgery, cardiology, diabetes and health care planning to med. jours. Served with AUS, 1946-47, 52-53. Fellow A.C.P., Am. Coll. Cardiology; mem. Am. Fedn. Clin. Research, N.Y. Acad. Sci., Los Angeles, Am. heart assns., Los Angeles Soc. Internal Medicine, Los Angeles Acad. Medicine, Sigma Xi, Phi Beta Phi, Phi Eta Sigma, Alpha Omega Alpha. Home: 4966 Ambrose Ave Los Angeles CA 90027 Office: 1200 State St N Los Angeles CA 90033

BERNSTEIN, SYLVIA, artist; b. Bklyn.; d. Charles and Anna (Finkelman) Schwartz; m. Michael C. Bernstein, Mar. 5, 1934; children: Davida, Holly, Deborah. Student, NAD, N.Y.C. Exhibited one-woman shows, Ruth White Gallery, Silvermine Guild Artists, Conn., Galeria Irla Kert, Montreal, Columbia Mus. Art, S.C., New Britain Mus. Am. Art, Conn., Hove Mus., Eng., group shows, Met. Mus. Art, N.Y.C., 1967, Whitney Mus. Am. Art, N.Y.C., Bklyn. Mus., Portland Mus., Maine, Pa. Acad. Fine Arts, Am. Acad. Arts and Letters, Wadsworth Atheneum, Hartford, Conn.; represented permanent collections, Whitney Mus. Am. Art, Bklyn. Mus., Corcoran Gallery, Washington, Denver Art Mus., Norfolk Mus. Arts. and Scis., Va., Hudson River Mus., N.Y., Parrish Mus., Southampton, Columbia Mus., S.C., Wadsworth Atheneum, Hartford, Conn., Springfield Art Mus.; Represented, Okla. Mus. Art; represented, New Britain Mus. Am. Art., Va. Mus. Fine Arts, Richmond, pvt. collections. Recipient N.A.W.A. medal of honor, Alfred Khouri meml. award, Brockton Art Assn. award, Roy W. Johnson award, Grumbacher award Nat. Assn. Women Artists. Home: 8 Circle Rd Scarsdale NY 10853 *Art today exists in an age rampant with doubt and confusion. Recognizable imagery has been sacrificed in the frenzied search for novelty. A strong bond must be created to wed the virtues of abstract to the concrete. One's total experience manifests itself in everything one does and so my work is an expression of my beliefs. I like to think my paintings reach into remembered nostalgic moments, that memory could be yours and mine.*

BERNSTEIN, THEODORE, electrical engineering educator; b. Milw., Dec. 1, 1926; s. Philip and Jennie Ruth (Slate) B.; m. Sandra Gail Weiss, Oct. 21, 1961; children: Dana Robin, Lisa Joy. B.S., U. Wis., 1949, M.S., 1955, Ph.D. in Elec. Engring, 1959. Designer Boeing Airplane Co., Seattle, 1949-52; sr. project engr. AC Sparkplug div., Milw., 1952-56; mem. tech. staff TRW Systems, Redondo Beach, Calif., 1959-62; mem. faculty dept. elec. engring. U. Wis., Madison, 1962—, prof., 1968—; cons. in elec. and lighting safety. Served with U.S. Army, 1945-46. Mem. IEEE (sr.). Home: 5105 Regent St Madison WI 53705 Office: Elec and Computer Engring Dept 1415 Johnson Dr Madison WI 53706

BERNSTEIN, THERESA, artist; b. Phila.; d. Isidore and Anne (Ferber) B.; m. William Meyerowitz, 1919. Student, Pa. Acad., Phila. Sch. Design, Art Students League. Dir. Salons of Am. Ind. Artists, 1924-30; life mem. Grand Central Art Galleries, N.Y. Contbr. articles to mags., newspapers.; one-woman shows, Butler Inst. Am. Art, 1973, Smith Gerard Gallery, Stamford, Conn., 1976, Summit Gallery, N.Y.C., 1979; represented in permanent collections, U.S. Nat. Mus., Washington, Library of Congress, Phillips Meml. Art Gallery, Chgo. Art Inst., Met. Mus. Art, N.Y. Pub. Library, Bklyn. Mus., others; also pvt. collections; represented, Art U.S.A., by painting Jazz Players, exhbns. include, Carnegie Inst., NAD, Cooper Union Mus., Butler Inst. Am. Art, Boston Pub. Library, Phila. Mus. Art, Yose Gallery, Boston, one-man shows, Nat. Mus., Smithsonian Instn., Fitchburg Art Mus., Doll & Richards, Inc., Boston Publick House, Sturbridge, Mass., U. Maine, Orono, 1963, Columbus Mus.; dir. summer art show, Gloucester, Mass., Weston U. Chmn., Meml. Exhibit Cape Ann Festival, 1958—. Recipient Phillips prize for Progressive Painting, 1946; Green traveling fellow; John Sartain scholar; Phila. Bd. Edn. scholar; Robert Dain prize, 1964; hon. mention Soc. Am. Graphic Artists, 1954; Knickerbocker Artists, 1956; Ogunquit Art Center; Carl Matson portrait award Rockport Art Assn., 1967; figure prize for Friends, 1981; New Eng. Artists award, N. Shore Arts Assn, 1967; John A. Johnson award, 1972; Johnson Meml. prize, 1975; Clark Meml. prize, 1977; Cantorella prize Nat. Assn. Women Artists, Nat. Acad., N.Y., 1968; Watson Meml. prize, 1979. Mem. Nat. Assn. Women Artists (jury of awards 1948-50, jury oil painting 1959, Margaret Cooper prize for oil portrait Sarah 1951, Jane Peterson prize 1955, nominating com. 1963-64, Klein Figurative award 1977), Boston Printmakers Assn., Cape Ann Soc. Artists, Nat. Assn. Women Painters and Sculptors (jury of award 1920-29), N.Y. Soc. Woman Artists (chmn. 1935-36, dir. 1959—, hon. dir. 1969—), North Shore Arts Assn. (hon.), Cape Ann Soc. Artists, Conn. Acad. Artists Am. (oil jury 1957-58), Allied Artists Am. (Horgan award 1975), Italian Acad. Fine Arts (hon. mem., Gold medal 1980). Studio: 54 W 74th St New York NY 10023 also 44 Mount Pleasant Ave East Gloucester MA 01930

BERNSTEIN, WILLIAM, film company executive; b. N.Y.C., Aug. 30, 1933; s. Philip and Sadie (Lazar) B.; m. Evelyn P. Schnur, Aug. 3, 1958; children: Marian, Steven. B.A., NYU, 1954; LL.B., Yale U., 1959. Bar: N.Y. 1959. From asst. gen. counsel to sr. v.p. United Artists Corp., 1959-78; exec. v.p. Orion Pictures Corp., N.Y.C., 1978—; mem. N.Y. State Com. Motion Picture and TV Prodn., N.Y.C. Adv Council Motion Picture Prodn. Served with AUS, 1954-56. Mem. ABA. Home: Club Rd Rye NY 10580 Office: 711 Fifth Ave New York NY 10022

BERNT, BENNO ANTHONY, battery manufacturing company executive; b. Bielitz, Austria, Mar. 14, 1931; came to U.S., 1954, naturalized, 1961; s. Victor and Grete (Meissner) B.; m. Constance Smigel, June 22, 1957; children: Karin, Eric, Steve. B.S. in Engring. summa cum laude, Fed. Inst. Tech., Vienna, Austria, 1952; D.C.S. summa cum laude, U. Commerce, Vienna, 1953; M.B.A., Carnegie Mellon U., 1954. Fin. and mfg. exec. Chrysler Corp., 1954-59; mfg. and bus. planning exec., subs. gen. mgr. Whirlpool Corp., 1959-68;

pres. Cissell Mfg. Co., Louisville, 1968-70; gen. mgr. Simonds Abrasive Co., Phila., 1970-73; v.p. fin. ESB Ray-O-Vac Corp., Phila., 1973-76, exec. v.p., dir., 1977-78; pres. Ray-O-Vac Co., Madison, Wis., 1979—. Mem. Regional Planning Commn., Marion, Ohio, 1962-65; pres. Marion Concert Assn., 1963-65; bd. dirs. Internat. House, Phila., Phila. Coll. Performing Arts, 1971-79. Recipient Distinguished Service award and named Outstanding Young Man of Year Ohio Jaycees, 1965. Mem. Young Presidents Orgn., Fin. Execs. Inst., Assn. Corporate Growth. Presbyterian. Clubs: Union League (Phila.); Maple Bluff Country (Madison). Home: 1007 Hillside Ave Madison WI 53705 Office: Ray-O-Vac Co 101 E Washington Ave Madison WI 53703 *We should forever ask ourselves two fundamental questions: How well am I using my own potential? and How well am I serving others? I believe the answers indicate our true success in life.*

BERNTHAL, FREDERICK MICHAEL, federal commissioner; b. Sheridan, Wyo., Jan. 10, 1943; s. Erwin John and Erna Emma (Kregar) B.; 1 son, Justin. B.S., Valparaiso U., 1964; Ph.D., U. Calif.-Berkeley, 1969; postgrad., Yale U., 1969-70, U. Copenhagen, 1976-77. Research staff Yale U., New Haven, 1969-70; prof. Mich. State U., East Lansing, 1970-80; legis. asst. Senator Howard Baker, Washington, 1978-80, chief legis. asst., 1980-83; mem. U.S. Nuclear Regulatory Commn., Washington, 1983—. Contbr. articles to sci. jours. NATO Sr. Scientist fellow, 1976; Congl. Sci. fellow Am. Phys. Soc., 1978-79. Mem. Am. Phys. Soc., Am. Chem. Soc., Sigma Xi. Republican. Lutheran. Office: US Nuclear Regulatory Commn 1717 H St NW Washington DC 20555 *

BERNTHAL, HAROLD GEORGE, health care co. exec.; b. Frankenmuth, Mich., June 11, 1928; s. Wilfred Michael and Olga Bertha (Stern) B.; m. Margaret Hrebek, Jan. 25, 1958; children—Barbara Anne, Karen Elizabeth, James Willard. B.S. in Chemistry, Mich. State U., 1950. Sales rep., then v.p. Am. Hosp. Supply Corp., Evanston, Ill., 1954-72, sr. v.p., 1972-74, pres., 1974—; dir. Bucyrus-Erie Co., Bliss and Laughlin Industries, Nalco Chem. Co., Butler Mfg. Co. Bd. trustees Northwestern Meml. Hosp., Chgo., Valparaiso (Ind.) U., Northwestern U. Assos., Chgo. Hort. Soc.; trustee Luth. Ch.-Mo. Synod. Served with AUS, 1950-52. Mem. Health Industry Mfrs. Assn. (past dir.). Clubs: Chgo., Econ., Comml. (Chgo.); Knollwood. Office: One American Plaza Evanston IL 60204

BERNUTH, ERNEST PATRICK, JR., publisher; b. N.Y.C., Nov. 17, 1939; s. Ernest Patrick and Sophie Josephine (Kilbreth) B. B.A., Princeton U., 1962; M.B.A., Columbia U., 1972. With Fairhurst Tech. Services Internat., Tehran, 1964-67, Sanderson & Porter, mgmt. cons./engrs., N.Y.C., 1968-70; bus. mgr. Field and Stream mag., N.Y.C., 1972-74; editor, gen. mgr. Field and Stream Book Club, N.Y.C., 1974-76; dir. adminstrn. Holt, Rinehart & Winston, N.Y.C., 1976-77; pub. Praeger Pubs., N.Y.C., 1977—. Contbr. to, N.Y. Mag., Washington Post, Nat. Observer. Served with USAR, 1963-64. Mem Assn. Am. Pubs. (exec. com. profl. and scholarly pub. div. 1979-82). Democrat. Episcopalian. Club: Racquet and Tennis (N.Y.C.). Home: 562 West End Ave New York NY 10024 Office: 521 Fifth Ave New York NY 10175

BERO, RONALD ARTHUR, banker; b. Green Bay, Wis., Jan. 23, 1935; s. Arthur J. and Bernie (McAllister) B.; m. Mary Forester, Aug. 7, 1959; children—Ronald Arthur, Richard, Michael, Amy, Suzanne. B.B.A., U. Wis., 1958; M.B.A., Marquette U., 1967. Various positions including asst. v.p. internat. div. First Wis. Nat. Bank of Milw., 1961-70; pres. First Wis. Nat. Bank Brookfield, 1970-73; sr. v.p. First Wis. Corp., Milw., 1973—. Active various fund drives. Served with USN, 1958-61. Republican. Home: 14550 Ridgemoor Dr Elm Grove WI 53122 Office: 777 E Wisconsin Ave Milwaukee WI 53202

BEROL, KENNETH ROSSIN, manufacturing company executive; b. N.Y.C., Apr. 16, 1925; s. Alfred C. and Madeleine (Rossin) B.; m. June Waterous, Aug. 14, 1947; children—John A., Margaret J. B.A. Harvard U, (1948); M.B.A., (1948), 1950. Treas. Eagle Pencil Co., Danbury, Conn., 1956-62, v.p., treas., 1962-72; pres. successor company Berol Corp., Danbury, 1972-79, chmn. bd., 1979—. Mem. Naples (Fla.) U.S. Coast Guard Aux. Clubs: Grolier, Stamford Yacht, Explorers; Harvard (N.Y.C.); Westchester Country; Port Royal, Naples Yacht. (Naples, Fla.); Lyford Cay (Nassau, Bahamas). Home: 3 Dewart Rd Greenwich CT 06830 Office: Berol Corp Danbury CT 06810

BERRA, BRUCE, computer educator; b. Smiths Creek, Mich., Apr. 14, 1935; s. Mike John and Dorothy (Nelson) B.; 1 son from former marriage, Marshall R. B.S., U. Mich., 1958, M.S., 1962; Ph.D., Purdue U., 1968. Sr. engr. Hughes Aircraft Corp., Culver City, Calif., 1958-60; engr., tech. advisor Bendix Corp., Ann Arbor, Mich., 1960-61, 61-63; asst. prof. info. engring. Boston U., 1965-66; assoc. prof. Syracuse U. (N.Y.), 1968-74, 74—, prof., chmn. indsl. engring. and ops. research, 1978-82, prof. elec. and computer engring., 1982—; cons. IBM Corp., 1965, 66, 67, Bell No. Research, ITT, PAR Tech., SCEEE. Gen. chmn., organizer Workshop on Database Machines, 1980-83. USAF Office of Sci. Research univ. resident research fellow, 1982-83. Mem. IEEE (editorial bd.), IEEE Computer Soc. (editor-in-chief CS Press 1981-83, vice chmn. publs. bd. 1984—), Assn. for Computing Machinery (chmn. spl. interest group on info. retrieval 1976-79). Office: Syracuse U Elec and Computer Engring 111 Link Hall Syracuse NY 13210

BERRA, LAWRENCE PETER (YOGI BERRA), profl. baseball coach; b. St. Louis, May 12, 1925; s. Peter and Pauline (Longsoni) B.; m. Carmen Short, Jan. 26, 1949; children—Lawrence A., Timothy Thomas, Dale Anthony. Profl. baseball player with N.Y. Yankees, 1946-63, mgr., 1964, coach, 1975—, N.Y. Mets, 1965-72, mgr., 1972-75; Vice pres. Yoo-Hoo Beverage Co. Served with USNR, 1943-46. Recipient Am. League Most Valuable Player award, 1951, 54, 55; elected to Baseball Hall of Fame, 1972. Clubs: Lion, Elk, Moose. Mem. Am. League All-Star Team, 1948-62; Winner Am. League Pennant, 1964. Office: Yankee Stadium Bronx NY 10451 *

BERRA, ROBERT LOUIS, chemical company executive; b. St. Louis, June 24, 1924; s. Angelo John and Clara Catherine B.; m. Vivian Lorene Miles, Nov. 11, 1944; children—Kathleen Patricia Berra Schrage, Patricia Susan Berra Babcock. B.S. in Econs, St. Louis U., 1947; M.B.A., Harvard U., 1947. Mem. econs. faculty St. Louis U., 1947-51; with Monsanto Co., 1951-70, 74—, v.p. personnel, 1974-80; sr. v.p. adminstrn. St. Louis, 1980—; v.p. personnel and public relations Foremost-McKesson, Inc., San Francisco, 1970-74; dir. Fisher Controls Corp. Internat. Adv. council St. John's Mercy Med. Center, St. Louis; mem. vis. com., personnel com. Harvard Coll.; bd. dirs. Group Health Plan St. Louis.; trustee Maryville Coll. Served to lt. USN, 1942-46. Recipient Alumni Merit award St. Louis U., 1977. Mem. Am. Soc. Personnel Adminstrn. (past pres., Personnel Profl. of Yr. 1983), Indsl. Relations Assn. St. Louis (past pres.), Am. Mgmt. Assn., Conf. Bd., Labor Policy Assn., Human Resources Roundtable Group, Sr. Personnel Execs. Forum. Roman Catholic. Club: Bellerive Country. Address: Monsanto Co 800 N Lindbergh Blvd Saint Louis MO 63166

BERRESFORD, SUSAN VAIL, philanthropic foundation executive; b. N.Y.C., Jan. 8, 1943; d. Richard Case and Katherine Vail (Marsters) Berresford H.; m. David F. Stein (div.); 1 son, Jeremy Vail Stein. Student, Vassar Coll., 1961-63; B.A. cum laude in Am. History, Radcliffe Coll., 1965. Vol. UN Vol. Services, N.Y.C., summer 1962; sec. to Theodore H. White, summer 1964; program officer Neighborhood Youth Corps, N.Y.C., 1965-67; program specialist Manpower Career Devel. Agy., N.Y.C., 1967, human resources adminstrn. specialist, 1968; free-lance cons., writer, Europe and U.S., 1968-70; program officer nat. affairs div. Ford Found., N.Y.C., 1970-80, program officer in charge, 1980-81, v.p., 1981—. Home: 36 E 10th St New York NY 10003 Office: Ford Found 320 E 43d St New York NY 10015

BERRETT, JAMES R., computer company executive. Pres., chief exec. officer Computervision Corp., Bedford, Mass. Office: Computervision Corp. 201 Burlington Rd Bedford MA 01730§

BERREY, ROBERT FORREST, lawyer, supermarket chain exec.; b. Oak Park, Ill., Dec. 7, 1939; s. Rhodes Clay and Regina (Kasprovich) B.; m. Betsy Kate Meyer, Sept. 8, 1968; children—Adam Forrist, Ellen Catherine, Kevin Joseph. A.B., Harvard U., 1962; J.D., U. Chgo., 1968. Bar: Ill. bar 1969. With firm Torshen, Fortes & Eiger, Chgo., 1970-75; atty. Jewel Companies, Inc., Chgo., 1975-76, sec., 1976-80, v.p., sec., gen. counsel, 1980—. Served with AUS, 1962-65. Mem. Am., Ill., Chgo. bar assns. Club: Sunset Ridge Country. Home: 131 Apple Tree Rd Winnetka IL 60093 Office: 5725 N East River Rd Chicago IL 60631

BERRIGAN, DANIEL, clergyman, author; b. Virginia, Minn., May 9, 1921; s. Thomas and Frieda (Fromhart) B. Ed., Woodstock Coll., West Coll. Joined Soc. of Jesus, 1939; ordained priest Roman Catholic Ch., 1952; tchr. St. Peter's Prep. Sch., Jersey City, 1945-49, French and philosophy Bklyn. Preparatory Sch., 1954-57; prof. N.T. studies Le Moyne Coll., Syracuse, N.Y., 1957-63; became dir. United Religious Work Cornell U., 1967; prof. theology Woodstock (N.Y.) Coll.; vis. lectr. U. Man., 1973; Religious dir. Walter Farrell Guild, 1954-57; founder Catholic Peace Fellowship; with OEO, summer 1967; active anti-VietNam War movement. Author: Time Without Number, 1957 (Lamont Prize), The Bow in the Clouds, Man's Covenant with God, 1961, World for Wedding Ring, 1962, No One Walks Waters; poetry, 1966, Consequences: Truth &, 1967, Go From Here, a Prison Journal, Love, Love at the End, 1968, They Call Us Dead Men, 1968, Night Flight to Hanoi, 1968, The Trial of the Catonsville Nine, 1970, False Gods, Real Men, 1969, Trial Poems, 1970, No Bars to Manhood, 1970, Dark Night of Resistance, 1971, America is Hard to Find, 1972, Conversations after Prison, 1972, Jesus Christ, 1973, Prison Poems, 3; Selected and New Poems Lights on in the House of the Dead, 1974, (with Thich Nat Hahn) The Raft is Not the Shore, 1975, A Book of Parables, 1977, Uncommon Prayer, A Book of Psalms, 1978, Beside the Sea of Glass, The Song of the Lamb, 1978, The Discipline of the Mountain, 1979, We Die Before We Live; C, onversations with the Very Ill, 1980, Commandments for the Long Haul, 1981. Served as aux. mil. chaplain, 1954. Convicted in case of destruction of draft records in Catonsville, Md., Balt., 1968.

BERRIGAN, PHILIP FRANCIS, author; b. Two Harbors, Minn., Oct. 5, 1923; s. Thomas William and Frida (Fromhart) B.; m. Elizabeth McAlister; 2 children. A.B. in English, Holy Cross Coll., 1950; B.S. in Secondary Edn, Loyola U. of South, 1959; M.A., Xavier U., New Orleans, 1961. Ordained priest Roman Catholic Ch., 1950; prof. English and religion, also student counselor St. Augustine High Sch., New Orleans; asst. pastor St. Peter Claver Ch., Balt.; worked and demonstrated with So. Christian Leadership Conf., NAACP, CORE, SNCC; co-founder, co-chmn. Cath. Peace Fellowship, Balt. Interfaith Peace Mission; lectr. on race, peace, poverty; active anti-Vietnam War movement. Author: No More Strangers, 1965, Punishment for Peace, 1969, Prison Journals of a Priest Revolutionary, 1970, Widen the Prison Gates, 1974, Of Beasts and Beastly Images, 1979. Served with inf. AUS, World War II; ETO. Convicted in two cases of destruction of draft files; acquitted of conspiracy *

BERRY, BREWTON, author, editor; b. Orangeburg, S.C., Aug. 9, 1901; s. Joseph Andrew and Frances Deborah (Pike) B.; m. Margaret Foley Woods, Sept. 11, 1926; children—Margaret (Mrs. Forrest J. Curtin, Jr.), Deborah (Mrs. Douglas R. Houser). A.B., Wofford Coll., 1922; B.D. (Fogg scholarship, Day fellowship), Yale, 1925; Ph.D., U. Edinburgh, 1930. Asst. prof. sociology and anthropology U. Mo., 1931-37, asso. prof., 1937-45, vis. prof., summer 1950, dir. anthrop. collection, 1932-45; dir. Archeol. Survey Mo., 1932-45; prof., head sociology dept. U. R.I., 1945-46; prof. sociology and anthropology Ohio State U., Columbus, 1946-64. Author: You and Your Superstitions, 1940, 74, (with Seba Eldridge) Fundamentals of Sociology, 1950; Race Relations, 1951, Race and Ethnic Relations, 1958, rev. edit, 1965, 78, Almost White, 1963, rev. edit, 1969, The Education of American Indians, 1968, (with N.P. Gist, others) The Blending of Races, 1972; also articles, essays, short stories.; Editor, Mo. Archaeologist, 1934-45, Ohio Valley Sociologist, 1947-52; assoc. editor, Am. Sociol. Rev., 1953-56; editorial bd., Ohio State U. Press, 1964-78. Julius Rosenwald fellow, 1943-44; recipient Anisfield-Wolf book award, 1952. Fellow Am. Anthrop. Assn., Am. Sociol. Assn.; mem. Mo. Archeol. Soc. (hon. life), Ohio Valley Sociol. Soc. (pres. 1954-55), S.A.R.; Mem. Southcaroliniana Soc. (life), S.C. Hist. Soc., Ohio Hist. Soc.; mem. Phi Beta Kappa (chpt. pres. 1965-66), Sigma Xi. Episcopalian. Clubs: Scioto Country; Torch (chpt. pres. 1967-68), Faculty (Columbus, Ohio); Book and Bond (Yale). Home: 2221 Brixton Rd Columbus OH 43221 Office: 300 Adminstrn Bldg 190 N Oval Mall Columbus OH 43210

BERRY, BRIAN JOE LOBLEY, geographer, urban planner; b. Sedgley, Stafford, Eng., Feb. 16, 1934; came to U.S., 1955, naturalized, 1965; s. Joe and Gwendoline (Lobley) B.; m. Janet Elizabeth Shapley, Sept. 6, 1958; children: Duncan Jeffrey, Carol Anne, Diane Leigh. B.Sc. with honors, U. Coll., London, 1955; M.A., U. Wash., 1956, Ph.D., 1958; A.M. (hon.), Harvard U., 1976. Instr. geography, civil engring. U. Wash., Seattle, 1957-58; asst. prof. geography U. Chgo., 1958-62, asso. prof., 1962-65, prof., 1965-72, Irving B. Harris prof. urban geography, 1972-76, dir. Center for Urban Studies, chmn. dept. geography, 1974-76; Williams prof. urban and regional planning Harvard U., 1976-81, chmn. Ph.D. Program in Urban Planning, dir. Lab. for Computer Graphics and Spatial Analysis, fellow Inst. Internat. Devel., 1976-81, prof. dept. sociology, 1978-81; dean Sch. Urban and Public Affairs, Carnegie-Mellon U., 1981—, prof. public policy, 1981—, Univ. prof. urban studies and pub. policy, 1982—. Author numerous books; contbr. articles to profl. jours. Fellow Univ. Coll., U. London, 1983. Mem. Nat. Acad. Scis., Am. Acad. Arts and Scis., Assn. Am. Geographers (pres. 1978-79), Am. Inst. Cert. Planners, Urban Land Inst., Regional Sci. Assn., Inst. Brit. Geographers, Sigma Xi. Office: Sch Urban and Public Affairs Carnegie-Mellon U Pittsburgh PA 15213

BERRY, CHARLES HORACE, economist; b. Ottawa, Ont., Can., Jan. 6, 1930; came to U.S., 1956, naturalized, 1965; s. F. William and Lucinda B. (Pratt) B.; m. Gisella Erdody, May 15, 1965; children—William, Rachel, Katherine. B.S., McGill U., 1951; M.S., U. Conn., 1953; Ph.D., U. Chgo., 1956. Asst. prof. econs. Yale U., New Haven, 1957-63, dir. undergrad. studies, 1959-62; mem. sr. staff Brookings Instn., Washington, 1963-66; assoc. prof. Princeton (N.J.) U., 1966-71, prof., 1971—; dir. Sloan Found. fellowships in econ. journalism, 1975—; dir. grad. program Woodrow Wilson Sch., 1975-78, assoc. dean, 1975-78, 80—; trustee Princeton Med. Center, 1981—; cons. Revenue Can., IRS, Dept. Justice, Dept. Treasury, Sun Oil Co., Royal Commn. on Health Services. Author: Voluntary Medical Insurance and Prepayment, 1965, Corporate Growth and Diversification, 1975. Mem. Regional Planning Bd. Princeton, 1975, Princeton Hosp. Liason Com., 1975-79. Mem. Nat. Bur. Econ. Research (dir.), Am. Econ. Assn., Cons. in Industry Econs. (dir.). Club: Gatineau Fish and Game. Home: 47 McLean Circle Princeton NJ 08540 Office: 423 Woodrow Wilson Sch Princeton Univ Princeton NJ 08540

BERRY, CHUCK (CHARLES EDWARD ANDERSON BERRY), singer, composer; b. San Jose, Calif., Jan. 15, 1926. Popular artist in rock and roll music, plays guitar, saxophone, piano, Concert, TV appearances, 1955—; rec. artist, Chess Records; appeared in: film Go, Johnny Go; composer: Rock 'n' Roll Music. Address: Bob Knight Agy 185 Clinton Ave Staten Island NY 10304 *

BERRY, EDNA JANET, lawyer, chemist; b. Wheatland, Ind., May 28, 1917; d. William and Edna (Merrell) B. B.S., Purdue U., 1942, Ph.D., 1946; J.D., N.Y. U., 1952. Bar: N.Y. State 1953. Research Chemist, patent asst. Am. Cyanamid Co., Bound Brook, N.J., 1946-48; patent atty. Exxon, Elizabeth, N.J., 1948-53; patent atty., mgr. patent dept. Nat. Distillers & Chem., N.Y.C., 1953-63; individual practice law, N.Y.C., 1963—; patent atty. Research Corp., N.Y.C., 1974-83; sec. bd. dirs. Greenwich House, N.Y.C., 1974—. Trustee Carnegie Mellon U., 1977-83. Recipient alumni award Vincennes U., 1964. Mem. Am. Chem. Soc., Am. Bar Assn., Am. Inst. Chemists (pres. 1980-81), Assn. Cons. Chemists and Chem. Engrs. (past pres.), Am. Patent Law Assn., N.Y. Patent Law Assn., Chemists Club (dir.), Société de Chemie. (dir.). Home: 2 Horatio St New York NY 10014 Office: Suite 401 274 Madison Ave New York NY 10016

BERRY, GUY CURTIS, polymer science educator, researcher; b. Greene County, Ill., May 11, 1935; s. Charles Curtis and Wilma Francis (Wickes) B.; m. Marilyn Jane Montooth, Jan. 26, 1957; children: Susan Jane, Sandra Jean, Scott Curtis. B.S.Ch.E., U. Mich., 1957, M.S. in Polymer Sci., 1958, Ph.D., 1960. Fellow Mellon Inst., Pitts., 1960-65, sr. fellow, 1965—; assoc. prof. chemistry Carnegie-Mellon U., Pitts., 1966-73, prof., 1973—, acting dean, 1981-82, acting head dept. chemistry, 1983—; vis. prof. U. Tokyo, 1973, Colo. State U., Ft. Collins, 1979, U. Kyoto, Japan, 1983. Mem. Am. Chem. Soc., Soc. Rheology, AAAS. Office: Carnegie Mellon U 4400 5th Ave Pittsburgh PA 15213 *

BERRY, HAROLD TOWNSEND, mining company executive; b. Westport, Ont., Can., Dec. 30, 1917; s. George Henry and Margret Louise B.; m. Betty Isabel Colles, Sept. 14, 1942; children: Brian, Michael, Jane. B.Sc. in Metal. Engring, Queens U., 1940. Metall. engr. Cominco, Trail, B.C., 1946-53; with Falconbridge Nickel Mines Ltd., Toronto, 1953-82, sr. v.p. metallurgy and research, 1979-80, pres., chief exec. officer, 1980-82, chmn., 1981-82; dir. Indusmin Ltd.; dir. Falconbridge Dominicana C. por A., Falconbridge Nikkelverk A/S. Served with RCAF, 1942-45. Mem. Assn. Profl. Engrs. Ont., Can. Inst. Mining and Metallurgy, AIME, Inst. Mining and Metallurgy U.K. Clubs: National, Donalda. Office: PO Box 40 Commerce Ct W Toronto ON M5L 1B4 Canada

BERRY, JAMES D., banker; b. Sapulpa, Okla., June 23, 1921; s. James D. and Gertrue (Morrow) B.; m. Mary Evelyn Irby, Oct. 16, 1946; children: Beverly, James D., Robert Neil. B.S., U. Okla., 1943; grad., Rutgers U. Grad. Sch. Banking, 1959, Harvard U., 1963. With Am. Nat. Bank, Sapulpa, 1932-50, asst. v.p., 1948-50; with Republic Nat. Bank, Dallas, 1950-74, sr. v.p., 1961-63, exec. v.p., later vice chmn. bd.; pres. Republic Tex. Corp., Dallas, 1974-77, chmn. bd., chief exec. officer, 1977—; dir. Dynalectron Corp., Taylor Pub. Co., Alexander & Alexander Services, Inc., RepublicBank Dallas. Bd. govs. Dallas County chpt. ARC; bd. dirs. Dallas Summer Musicals. Served to capt. AUS, 1943-46. Mem. Inter-frat. Council, Scabbard and Blade, Beta Theta Pi. Clubs: Mason (33 deg., Shriner), Dallas (dir.), Dallas Country, Chaparral (Dallas) (dir.). Office: RepublicBank Corp Ervay and Pacific Dallas TX 75201

BERRY, JAMES FREDERICK, educator; b. Balt., Nov. 11, 1927; s. James Harvey and Atha Mabel (Harer) B.; m. Catherine Ann Smith, Dec. 27, 1952; children—Barbara, Bonnie, Sarah, Catherine. B.A., Johns Hopkins, 1949; Ph.D., U. Rochester, 1953. Research fellow biochemistry U. Western Ont., 1953-55, lectr., 1955-56; fellow Multiple Sclerosis Soc. Inst. Animal Physiology, Babraham, Cambridge, Eng., 1956-57; fellow physiol. chemistry Johns Hopkins Sch. Medicine, 1958-59, lectr., 1959-61; asso. dir. Biochemistry Research div. Dept. Medicine Sinai Hosp., Balt., 1957-61; asso. prof. neurology U. Minn. Med. Sch., 1961-66, prof., chief neurochemistry sect., 1966—. Active Boys Scouts Am., Girl Scouts U.S.A.; mem. Ind. Dist. 623 Sch. Bd., Roseville, Minn., 1970-76; clk. Intermediate Vo-Tech Dist. 916 Sch. Bd., 1972-76; del. assembly Minn. Sch. Bd. Assn., 1970-76. Recipient Silver Beaver award distinguished service to Boy Scouting, 1962. Fellow A.A.A.S., Am. Inst. Chemists; mem. Minn. Acad. Sci., Am., Internat. socs. neurochemistry, Am. Oil Chem. Soc., Assn. Ofcl. Analytic Chemists, Biochem. Soc., Am. Soc. Biol. Chemists, Sigma Xi. Home: 1059 Woodhill Dr Roseville MN 55113 Office: Mayo Bldg Box 289 Minneapolis MN 55455 *I hope to help alleviate human suffering by trying to understand normal and pathological human processes at a biochemical level and to develop biochemical strategies to counter the pathological processes.*

BERRY, JOHN NICHOLS, III, editor; b. Montclair, N.J., June 12, 1933; s. John Nichols and Marian Petrea (Chase) B.; m. Louise Parker, June 5, 1982; children: Elizabeth Ann, John Nichols IV. A.B. in History, Boston U., 1958; M.S. in L.S, Simmons Coll., Boston, 1960. Youth-reference librarian Reading (Mass.) Pub. Library, 1959-60; reference librarian Simmons Coll., 1960-62, asst. dir. library, 1962-64; lectr. Sch. Library Sci., 1961-64; asst. editor Library Jour., R. R. Bowker Co. (div. Xerox), N.Y.C., 1964-66, editor book editorial dept., 1966-68, editor-in-chief Library Jour., 1969—; Lectr. Sch. Library and Info. Sci. U. Pitts., 1972-73. Contbg. author: Library Issues The Sixties, 1970; Editor: Directory of Library Consultants, 1969, Bay State Librarian, 1962-64 (A.L.A./H. W. Wilson Library Periodical award 1962); Contbr. articles to profl. jours. Served with AUS, 1955-57. Recipient First Annual Alumni Achievement award Sch. Library Sci. Simmons Coll., 1970. Mem. ALA, Spl. Library Assn. (chmn. div. pub. 1969), Archons of Colophon. Democrat. Home: 41 Chester St Stamford CT 06905 Office: RR Bowker Co 205 E 42d St New York NY 10017

BERRY, JOHN WIDDUP, psychologist; b. Montreal, Que., Can., May 20, 1939; s. William Macfarlane and Harriet Evelyn (Huycke) B.; m. Joan Frances Melkman, July 1, 1961; children—Heather Frances, Susan Joan, Michael Widdup. B.A., Sir George Williams U., Montreal, 1963; Ph.D., U. Edinburgh, Scotland, 1966. Lectr. psychology U. Sydney, Australia, 1966-69; mem. faculty Queen's U., Kingston, Ont., Can., 1969—, prof. psychology, 1978—; Fellow Netherlands Inst. Advanced Study, 1974-75. Author: Human Ecology and Cognitive Style, 1976, Multiculturalism and Ethnic Attitudes in Canada, 1977; Co-editor: Handbook of Cross-Cultural Psychology, 1979. Fellow Can. Psychol. Assn.; mem. Internat. Assn. Cross-Cultural Psychology (pres. 1982). Home: 36 Wellington St Kingston ON K7L 3C1 Canada Office: Psychology Dept Queen's U Kingston ON K7L 3N6 Canada

BERRY, JOHN WILLIAM, telephone directory advertising company executive; b. Dayton, Ohio, July 8, 1922; s. Loren Murphy and Lucille (Kneipple) B.; m. Marjorie Louise Wendel, Mar. 5, 1944 (div. Jan. 5, 1959); children: George W., John W., David L., Charles D.; m. Mardell Smith, Mar. 1, 1962; 1 son, Richard L. B.A., Dartmouth Coll., 1944; postgrad., La. State U., 1943-44. With L.M. Berry & Co., Dayton, 1940—, mng. dir., 1960-63, pres., 1963-73, chmn., chief exec. officer, 1973—; chmn., dir. Third Nat. Bank, Dayton, 1972—; dir. ITT World Directories, N.Y.C., Super Food Services, Inc., Dayton, Tech., Inc. Trustee U. Dayton, 1980—, Ohio State U., 1981—; mem. exec. com. Ohio Republican Fin. Com., Columbus. Served in U.S. Army, 1943-46. Recipient hon. recognition Newcomen Soc. N.Am., 1971, Spirit of Life award City of Hope, 1977. Mem. Ind. Telephone Pioneers Am., Bell Telephone Pioneers Am. Episcopalian. Clubs: Moraine Country (Dayton); Bermuda Dunes Country (Calif.). Lodges: Masons; Shriners. Office: LM Berry And Co PO Box 6000 Dayton OH 45401

BERRY, JOYCE CHARLOTTE, university press editor; b. Chgo., Feb. 12, 1937; d. George Carlisle and Myrtle Dorothy (Olsen) B. B.S., U. Colo.; cert., Institute de Touraine and U. Grenoble, France, 1960-61; diploma in French studies, The Sorbonne, Paris, 1962; postgrad., Columbia U., 1964-65. Cartographic map editor Corps Engrs., San Francisco, 1958-60; asst. editor Field Enterprises, Chgo., 1962-63; assoc. editor Grolier, Inc., N.Y.C., 1963-65; sr. editor Oxford U. Press, N.Y.C., 1965—. Vol. Lexington Democratic Club, 1964; copywriter Citizens for Clean Air, 1965-66; editor INFORM, N.Y.C., 1979-80; mem. adoption group Amnesty Internat. U.S.A., 1978—. Mem. Gamma Theta Upsilon. Office: Oxford University Press 200 Madison Ave New York NY 10016

BERRY, KEN, actor; b. Moline, Ill. Appeared on: TV series The Ann Southern Show, 1959-61, Dr. Kildare, 1961-66, Andy Griffith Show, 1967-68; starred in: F-Troop, 1965-67, Mayberry R.F.D, 1968-71, The Ken Berry Wow Show, 1972; films include The Reluctant Heroes, 1971; TV movies Hello Down There, 1969, The Cat From Outer Space, 1978. Office: care STE Reps Ltd 211 S Beverly Dr Suite 201 Beverly Hills CA 90212 *

BERRY, LEONIDAS HARRIS, gastroenterologist, internist; b. Woodsdale, N.C., July 20, 1902; s. Llewellyn L. and Beulah Anne (Harris) B.; m. Opheila Flannagan Harrison, June 27, 1937; 1 dau., Judith Berry Griffin; m. Emma Ford Willis, Aug. 7, 1959; stepchildren: Alvin E. Harrison, Frances W. Jackson. B.S., Wilberforce U., Ohio, 1924, D.Sc. (hon.), 1945; B.S., U. Chgo., 1925, M.D., 1930; M.S. in Pathology, U. Ill., 1933; LL.D. (hon.), Lincoln U., 1983. Diplomate: Am. Bd. Internal Medicine and Gastroenterology. Intern Freedmen's Hosp., Washington, 1929-30; fellow internal medicine, gastroenterology Cook County Hosp., Chgo., 1931-35, sr. attending physician, gastroenterologist, 1946-74, chief gastrointestinal endoscopy service, 1966-74, emeritus, 1975—; courtesy staff Michael Reese Hosp., Chgo., 1946-63, sr. attending physician, 1963—; chmn. div. gastroenterology Provident Hosp., Chgo., 1936-70, sr. attending physician, 1935—, chmn. dept. medicine, 1947-48; spl. dep. for profl.-community affairs, Cook County Hosps, Governing Commn., 1975-79; clin. asst. prof. medicine U. Ill. Med. Sch., 1950-57, clin. asso. prof., 1957-67; prof. gastroenterology and endoscopy Cook County Grad. Sch. Medicine, 1947—; State Dept. Fgn. cultural exchange lectr., 1965, 66, 70; organizer, coordinator med. counseling clinics narcotics Ill. Dept. Health, 1950-59; co-founder, trustee Council Bio-Med. Careers, 1962-72; mem. health com. Chgo. Commn. Human Relations, 1947-65, chmn., 1960-65; organizer Flying Black Medics, Chgo. and Cairo, Ill., 1970; mem. 1st nat. adv. council, regional med. programs heart disease, cancer and stroke HEW, 1966-68. Sr. author: Two Centuries of an Afro-American Minister's Family, 1981; contbr. articles to med. publs., books. Trustee Cook County Grad. Sch. Medicine, 1967—, Mary Thompson Hosp., 1965-73. Served to 1st lt. U.S. Army Med. Res., 1931-41; from capt. to maj. Ill. Res. Militia, 1942-47. Recipient resolution of appreciation HEW, 1968; 50th Anniversary cert. U. Chgo. Med. Sch., Alumni Pub. Service award U. Chgo., 1966, Profl. Achievement award, 1978; Daniel Hale Williams Distinguished Service award Cook County Physicians Assn., 1969. Nat. Bd. Med. Examiners.; Fellow A.C.P., N.Y. Acad. Medicine; mem. AMA, Am. Coll. Gastroenterology (past. gov., trustee), Am. Soc. Gastrointestinal Endoscopy (Rudolf Schindler award 1977), Nat. Soc. Gastroenterology France and Chile S.A., Japan Endoscopy Soc. Nat. Med. Assn. (Distinguished Service award 1958, past pres.), NAACP (life), Assn. Study Afro-Am. Life and History, Original Forty Club Chgo. (Man of Year award 1974), Sigma Xi, Alpha Phi Alpha (life), Alpha Omega Alpha (hon.); Mem. African Methodist Episcopal Ch. (steward, trustee, connectional officer, gen. officer, med. dir. 1948-76, emeritus 1976—, Citation for 40 yrs. service 1977). Home: 5142 S Ellis Ave Chicago IL 60615 Office: Michael Reese Med Center Chicago IL 60616

BERRY, LEVETTE JOE, microbiologist; b. Birmingham, Ala., June 17, 1910; s. Levette J. and Elizabeth (Fitzgerald) B.; m. Virginia Lee Goolsby, May 28, 1934; 1 son, James Goolsby. B.S., S.W. Tex. State Coll., 1930; Ph.D., U. Tex., 1939. Instr. U. Tex., 1939-40; faculty Bryn Mawr Coll., 1940-70, asso. prof., 1946-52, prof., 1952-70, Chmn. dept. biology, 1965-70, sec. faculty, 1964-69, acting provost, 1969-70; prof. U. Tex., Austin, 1970—, chmn. dept. micorbiology, 1970-75; research asso. nutrition clinic Hillman Hosp., Birmingham, 1943-45; cons. infectious diseases com. VA, 1960-71, chmn., 1968-71; cons. bacteriology and mycology study sect. NIH, 1963—, chmn., 1966-67, cons. internat. fellowship rev. com., 1970-73, chmn., 1971-73; cons. bacteriology and mycology Lunar Receiving Lab., NASA Space Center, Houston, 1969-71, chmn., 1971—; adv. com. Army Chem. Corps, 1960-63; cons. life scis. research evaluation com. Office Naval Research, 1970-73; chmn. sci. adv. com. Alfred I. DuPont Inst., 1977—; Found. for Microbiology lectr., 1976-77. Editorial bd.: Infection and Immunity, 1970—, editor Jour. Bacteriology, 1964-68. Fellow Am. Acad. Microbiology (bd. govs. 1969-75, chmn. 1970-71, AAAS, mem., Am. Soc. Microbiology, councilor-at-large, council policy com., chmn. bd. edn. and tng. 1971-81, chmn. bacterial infections and pathogenesis div. 1976-77), Am. Physiol. Soc., Reticuloendothelial Soc. (hon. life; chmn. internat. com.; pres. 1966-68, adv. editorial bd. 1973), Soc. Exptl. Biology and Medicine, Sigma Xi. Home: 4618 Crestway Dr Austin TX 78731 *Success is often attributed to luck but it rarely is. I have always tried to do any job, regardless of its magnitude, to the best of my ability. A job well done usually leads to greater opportunities and challenges. This, in large measure, has been the basis of my success. Most of it has been the outgrowth of previously performed tasks and requests to take on others. This approach coupled with a sensitivity toward people, their motivations and asperations has, in my case, contributed to the good will I extend and receive from most associates.*

BERRY, MARY FRANCES, history and law educator; b. Nashville, Feb. 17, 1938; d. George Ford and Frances Southall (Wiggins) B. B.A., Howard U., 1961, M.A., 1962; Ph.D., U. Mich., 1966, J.D., 1970. Bar: D.C. 1972. Asst. prof. history Central Mich. U., Mt. Pleasant, 1966-68; asst. prof. Eastern Mich. U., Ypsilanti, 1968-69, assoc. prof., 1969-70, U. Md., College Park, 1969-76; acting dir. Afro-Am. studies, 1970-72, dir., 1972-74, acting chmn. div. behavioral and social scis., 1973-74, provost div. behavioral and social scis., 1973-76; prof. history, prof. law U Colo. at Boulder, 1976-80, chancellor, 1976-77; prof. history and law Howard U., Washington, 1980—; asst. sec. for edn. HEW, Washington, 1977-80; commr. U.S. Commn. on Civil Rights, 1980-83; adj. assoc. prof. U. Mich., 1970-71; cons. Office Policy Planning of HUD, Office for Civil Rights of HEW, U.S. Civil Rights Commn., Bd. Afro-Am. Bicentennial Corp. Chairperson Md. Commn. on Afro-Am. and Indian History and Culture, 1974-76. Author: Black Resistance/White Law, 1971, Military Necessity and Civil Rights Policy, 1977, Stability, Security and Continuity, Mr. Justice Burton and Decision-Making in the Supreme Court, 1945-58; asso. editor: Jour. Negro History, 1974-78; contbr. articles, revs. to profl. jours. Bd. dirs. Met. Washington Housing and Planning Assn. Recipient Civil War Round Table Fellowship award, 1965-66. Mem. Nat. Acad. Public Adminstrn., Orgn. Am. Historians (exec. bd. 1974-77), Assn. Study of Afro-Am. Life and History (exec. bd. 1973-76), Am. Hist. Assn., Orgn. Am. Historians, Am. Soc. Legal Historians, Am., Nat., D.C. bar assns. Office: Howard U Dept History 2400 6th St NW Washington DC 20059 *

BERRY, MICHAEL JAMES, chemist; b. Chgo., July 17, 1947; s. Bernie Milton and Irene Barbara (Lentz) B.; m. Julianne Elward, Apr. 28, 1967; children—Michael James, II, Jennifer Anne. B.S. in Chemistry, U. Mich., 1967; Ph.D. (NSF predoctoral fellow), U. Calif., Berkeley, 1970. Asst. prof., then assoc. prof. chemistry U. Wis., Madison, 1970-76; mgr. photon chemistry dept., corp. research center Allied Chem. Corp., Morristown, N.J, 1976-79; Robert A. Welch prof. chemistry, dir. Rice Quantum Inst., Rice U., Houston, 1979—; cons. in field. Author research papers in field. Recipient Phi Lamba Upsilon Fresenius award, 1982; Camille and Henry Dreyfus Found. tchr.-scholar, 1974-76; Alfred P. Sloan research fellow, 1975-76; John Simon Guggenheim Meml. Found. fellow, 1981-82. Mem. Am. Chem. Soc. (pure chemistry award 1983), Am. Phys. Soc., AIAA, Optical Soc. Am., Am. Soc. Photobiology, Inter-Am. Photochem. Soc. Inventor, patentee in field. Home: 378 Litchfield Ln Houston TX 77024 Office: Dept Chemistry Rice U PO Box 1892 Houston TX 77251

BERRY, NANCY MICHAELS, organization executive; b. Kansas City, Mo., Sept. 3, 1928; d. William Wilson and Allene (Hart) Michaels; children: C. Nelson, Michaels C., Christopher N. (dec.), David S. Student, Wellesley Coll., 1945-48; B.A., Okla. U., 1971, M.A., 1978. Exec. dir. Oklahoma City Community Found., 1974-78; v.p. World Neighbors, Oklahoma City, 1978-80; v.p. Project Orbis, N.Y.C., 1980-83; v.p. Nat. Exec. Service Corps, N.Y.C., 1983—. Mem. Jr. League. Democrat. Episcopalian. Home: 71 E 77th St New York NY 10021 Office: 622 3d Ave New York NY 10017

BERRY, NORMAN CHARLES, advertising agency executive; b. London, June 15, 1931; U.S., 1979; s. Charles William and Marjorie B.; (divorced); children: Lucy Elizabeth. Student Brit. schs. With Young & Rubicam Ltd., London, 1952-64, copy chief, 1958-64; founder, pres. Davidson, Pearce, Berry & Spottiswoode, London, 1964-79; exec. v.p., head creative dept. Ogilvy & Mather Inc., N.Y.C., 1979—. Served as officer Brit. Army, 1949-51; Korea. Fellow Inst. Practitioners in Advt. Office: Ogilvy & Mather Inc 2 E 48th St New York NY 10017

BERRY, RICHARD EMERSON, physics educator; b. Washington, N.J., Nov. 11, 1933; s. Vernon Emerson and Estelle Patricia (Peterson) B.; m. Ruth Helen Enger, Sept. 4, 1954; children: Dirk, Arthur, Richard, Marilyn, Robert. B.S., Lafayette Coll., 1954; M.A., Princeton U., 1956, Ph.D., 1958. Asst. prof. physics Lafayette Coll., 1958-67; asso. prof. physics Tex. Tech. Coll., 1962-65; prof., chmn. dept. physics Indiana (Pa.) U., 1965—; NASA researcher Wallops Flight Center, 1980—. Mem. Am. Phys. Soc., Am. Assn. Physics Tchrs., Phi Beta Kappa, Sigma Xi, Sigma Pi Sigma. Home: RD 2 Box 19 Indiana PA 15701

BERRY, RICHARD LOUIS, manufacturing company executive; b. East Liverpool, Ohio, June 26, 1927; s. Wilbur Howard and Dorothy (Smith) B.; m. Rosalyn A. Cironi, Nov. 23, 1949; children: Diane, Lesley, Richard Louis. A.B., Mt. Union Coll., 1948; LL.B., Western Res. U., 1952. Bar: Ohio 1952, U.S. Dist. Ct. (no. dist.) Ohio 1954. Ptnr. Fuller, Seney, Henry & Hodge, Toledo, 1952-66; with Owens-Ill., Inc., Toledo, 1966—, v.p. corp. devel. and asst. to pres., 1975-76, v.p., chief corp. staff, 1976-82, sr. v.p. adminstrn., 1982—; trustee Glass, Pottery, Plastics and Allied Workers-Employers Retiree Trust, Ft. Myers, Fla. Trustee Ohio Found. Ind. Colls., Columbus, Toledo Econ. Planning Council, Riverside Hosp., Toledo, Boys Club Toledo. Served with USN, 1945-46. Mem. Toledo Bar Assn., Phi Alpha Delta. Clubs: Toledo Country (Toledo); Imperial Golf (Naples, Fla.). Office: Owens-Ill Inc One Sea-Gate Toledo OH 43666

BERRY, RICHARD ROWLAND, mfg. co. exec.; b. Chgo., Feb. 17, 1932; s. Richard Benson and Leta Lodema (Rowl) B.; m. Joan Widicus Harrison, Aug. 8, 1954; children—Richard H., Karen L., Scott R. B.S. in Metall. Engring, U. Ill. Engring. trainee brass group Olin Corp., 1954, v.p. mfg. from, 1970; group pres. East Alton, Ill., 1980—. Served with U.S. Army, 1955-57. Mem. Ill. State C. of C. (dir.), Copper Devel. Assn. (dir.), So. Ill. Indsl. Assn. (dir., past pres.). Mem. United Ch. of Christ. Home: 705 Saint Louis St Edwardsville IL 62025 Office: Shamrock St East Alton IL 62024

BERRY, RICHARD STEPHEN, chemist; b. Denver, Apr. 9, 1931; s. Morris and Ethel (Alpert) B.; m. Carla Lamport Friedman, Sept. 4, 1955; children: Andrea, Denise, Eric. A.B., Harvard U., 1952, A.M., 1954, Ph.D., 1956. Instr. Harvard U., 1956-57, U. Mich., 1957-60; asst. prof. Yale U., 1960-64; assoc. prof. chemistry U. Chgo., 1964-67, prof. chemistry, 1967—; Arthur D. Little prof. MIT, 1968; Phillips lectr. Haverford Coll., 1968; cons. Avco-Everett Research Labs., 1964-83, Argonne Nat. Lab., 1976—, Oak Ridge Nat. Labs., 1978-81, Los Alamos Sci. Lab., 1975—; mem. adv. com. theory; vis. prof. U. Copenhagen, 1967, 79; mem. adv. panel for chemistry NSF, 1971-73; mem. rev. com. radiol. and environ. research div. Argonne Nat. Lab., 1970-76; mem. evaluation panel measures for air quality Nat. Bur. Standards; mem. numerical data adv. bd. NRC; mem. steering com. panel on environ. monitoring, mem. com. on atomic and molecular sci., com. on chem. scis. Nat. Acad. Scis.-NRC; mem. adv. panel on health of sci. and tech. enterprise, mem. adv. panel on nat. labs. Office Tech. Assessment; mem. adv. bd. Environ. Health Resource Center; mem. vis. com. div. applied physics Harvard U., 1977—; mem. adv. panel dept. chemistry Princeton U.; Hinshewood lectr. Oxford U., 1980; prof. associé U. Paris, 1979-80. Co-author: The Total Social Cost of Fossil and Nuclear Power, 1979; co-author: Physical Chemistry, 1980, TOSCA, The Social Cost of Coal and Nuclear Power, 1979; assoc. editor Jour. Chem. Physics, 1971-74, Accounts Chem. Research, 1975—; Revs. Modern Physics, 1983—; bd. dirs.: Accounts Chem. Research, Bull. Atomic Scientists; adv. editor: Resources and Energy; contbr. articles to profl. jours. Alfred P. Sloan fellow, 1962-66; Guggenheim fellow, 1972-73. Fellow Am. Phys. Soc., Am. Acad. Arts and Scis.; mem. Am. Chem. Soc., Nat. Acad. Scis. (McArthur Prize fellow 1983), Royal Danish Acad. Arts and Letters (fgn.), Sigma Xi (nat. lectr. 1976, 77). Home: 5317 S University Ave Chicago IL 60615

BERRY, ROBERT, professional hockey coach; b. Montreal, Que., Can., Nov. 29, 1943. Profl. hockey player Montreal Canadiens, Que., Can., 1967, Canadien's minor league, 1968-70, Los Angeles Kings, 1970-77; coach Springfield Indians, 1977-78, Los Angeles Kings, NHL, 1978-80, Montreal Canadiens, NHL, Que., Can., 1981—. Office: Montreal Canadiens 2313 Saint Catherine St W Montreal PQ Canada H3H 1N2 *

BERRY, ROBERT LEE, judge; b. Silex, Mo., Aug. 3, 1907; s. James Henry and Catherine Alma (Lee) B.; m. Helen Renfrew Street, Mar. 22, 1968. Student, Notre Dame U., 1925-27; LL.B., Okla. U., 1931; grad., Judge Adv. Gen.'s Sch., U. Mich., 1943. Bar: Okla. bar 1931. Pvt. practice law, 1931-32; asst. municipal counselor City of Oklahoma City, 1932-39; title atty. Phillips Petroleum Co., 1939-46; mem. legal dept. VA, 1946-61; 1st asst. U.S. atty. Western Dist. Okla., 1961-69; spl. dist. judge Oklahoma County, Okla., 1969-70, asso. dist. judge, 1970-73; U.S. bankruptcy judge, 1973—. Mem. Okla. Heritage Assn., Okla., Allied Arts Found., Okla. Zool. Soc., Okla. Arts Center, Oklahoma City Beautiful. Served with Judge Adv. Gen.'s Div. AUS, 1943-46. Mem. ABA, Fed. Bar Assn. (past nat. v.p.), Okla. Bar Assn., Oklahoma County Bar Assn., Okla. Alumni Assn., Phi Kappa Psi. Democrat. Clubs: Embassy, Mayfair, Men's Dinner, Oklahoma city Golf and Country, Com. of 100 (Oklahoma City). Home: 6400 Centennial Ct Oklahoma City OK 73116 Office: US Courts Bldg Oklahoma City OK 73102

BERRY, ROBERT VAUGHAN, electrical/electronic manufacturing corporation executive; b. Newark, Mar. 24, 1933; s. Harold Silver and Elizabeth Lippincott (Vaughan) B.; m. Victoria Shaw, Mar. 8, 1958; children—Patricia E., Michael V. B.A., Dartmouth Coll., 1954. With Thomas & Betts Corp., Raritan, N.J., 1957—, dir., 1972—, v.p. fin., 1975-83, sr. v.p., 1983—; pres. Thomas & Betts Internat., Inc., 1975. Served as 1st lt. Airborne Corps AUS, 1954-57. Republican. Clubs: Baltusrol Golf (Springfield, N.J.); Rock Spring (West Orange, N.J.); Summerlea Golf and Country (Montreal, Que., Can.); Wentworth (Surrey, Eng.); Mid Ocean (Bermuda); Royal and Ancient Golf of St. Andrews (Scotland). Office: 920 Route 202 Raritan NJ 08869

BERRY, ROBERT WORTH, army officer, lawyer, educator; b. Ryderwood, Wash., Mar. 2, 1926; s. John Franklin and Anita Louise (Worth) B. B.A. in Polit. Sci., Wash. State U., 1950; J.D., Harvard U., 1955; M.A., John Jay Coll. Criminal Justice, 1981. Bar: D.C. 1956, Pa. 1961, Calif. 1967, U.S. Supreme Ct. 1961. Research assoc. Harvard U., 1955-56; atty. Office Gen. Counsel U.S. Dept. Def., Washington, 1956-60; staff counsel Philco Ford Co., Phila., 1960-63, dir. Washington office, 1967-71; gen. counsel U.S. Dept. Army, Washington, 1971-74, civilian aide to sec. army, 1975-77; col. U.S. Army, 1978—; prof., head dept. law U.S. Mil. Acad., West Point, N.Y., 1978—; asst. gen. counsel pub. affairs Litton Industries, Beverly Hills, Calif., 1963-67; resident ptnr. Quarles and Brady, Washington, 1974-78. Served with U.S. Army, 1944-46, 51-53; Korea. Decorated Bronze Star; decortated Legion of Merit; recipient Disting. Service medal U.S. Dept. Army, 1973, 74, Outstanding Civilian Service medal, 1977. Mem. ABA, Fed. Bar Assn., Phi Beta Kappa, Phi Kappa Phi. Methodist. Clubs: Army Navy, Army Navy Country, Nat. Lawyers. Home: 120 A Washington Rd West Point NY 10996 Office: Dept Law US Mil Acad West Point NY 10996

BERRY, SIDNEY BRYAN, state ofcl., ret. army officer; b. Hattiesburg, Miss., Feb. 10, 1926; s. Sidney Bryan and Lois Elizabeth (Hathorn) B.; m. Anne Florine Hayes, June 18, 1949; children—Bryan Hathorn, Lynn Elizabeth, Nan Nissiat. Student, U. Miss., 1943-44; B.S., U.S. Mil. Acad., 1948; M.A., Columbia, 1953; postgrad., Am. U. of Beirut, 1954. Commd. 2d lt. U.S. Army, 1948; advanced through grades to lt. gen.; mil. asst. to Sec. of Def., 1961-64; sr. advisor ARVN Inf. Div., Vietnam, 1965-66; inf. brigade comdr., Vietnam, 1966-67; asst. comdt. U.S. Army Inf. Sch., 1968-70; asst. div. comdr. 101st Airborne Div., Vietnam, 1970-71; dep. chief personnel operations Dept. Army, Washington, 1971; comdr. MILPERCEN, DA, 1972-73, 101st Airborne Div., 1973-74; supt. U.S. Mil. Acad., 1974-77; comdr. V Corps, 1977-80; ret., 1980; commr. public safety State of Miss., 1980. Mem. nat. com. Boy Scouts Am., 1969—. Decorated Silver Star with 3 oak leaf clusters, D.S.M. with oak leaf cluster, D.F.C. with oak leaf cluster, Legion of Merit with 3 oak leaf clusters, Bronze Star, Purple Heart with oak leaf cluster. Mem. Council Fgn. Relations (Army fellow 1967-68). Lutheran. Home: 1027 Northpointe Dr Jackson MS 39211 Office: 958 Jackson MS 39205

BERRY, SPENCER J(ULIAN), biology educator, researcher; b. Quincy, Mass., May 24, 1933; s. Roger L. and Ann D. (Martin) B.; m. Susan Wylie, June 15, 1957; children: Matthew, Peter, Alice. B.A., Williams Coll., 1955; M.A., Wesleyan U., 1957; Ph.D. in Biology, Western Res. U., 1965. Asst. prof. biology Wesleyan U., Middletown, Conn., 1965-70, assoc. prof., 1970-76, prof., 1976—. Contbr. numerous articles to profl. publs. Vice chmn. Middlefield Inland Wetlands Commn., Conn. Recipient Research Career Devel. award NIH, 1970. Mem. Devel. Biology Soc., Internat. Soc. Devel. Biology. Democrat. Congregationalist. Home: 89 Jackson Hill Rd Middlefield CT 06455 Office: Wesleyan U Lawn Ave Middletown CT 06547

BERRY, THOMAS JOSEPH, telephone company executive; b. Boston, Feb. 20, 1925; s. Thomas Frances and Mary Josephine (McDonough) B.; m. Pauline Mary Yonkers, Sept. 27, 1948; children: Thomas J., Paul E., Pamela J., David Y. B.S., Boston U., 1948, postgrad., 1949-51. Gen. mgr. for N.H., New Eng. Tel. & Tel. Co., 1966-67, v.p. fin., controller, 1969-73; asst. comptroller AT&T, 1967-69; exec. v.p Ind. Bell Telephone Co., 1973-80; v.p. fin. and gen. services Bell Telephone Labs. Inc., Murray Hill, N.J., 1980-81; asst. v.p. fin. data systems AT&T, 1981-82; v.p., chief fin. officer Am. Bell, 1983—; bd. advisers Manchester Bank (N.H.). Trustee Indpls. Children's Museum, 1979-80. Served with USNR, 1942-46. Mem. Fin. Execs. Inst. Clubs: Union Boat (Boston); Essex County (Manchester, Mass.); Indpls. Athletic.; Morris Country (Convent Station, N.J.). Office: 100 Southgate Pkwy Morristown NJ 07960

BERRY, WALLACE TAFT, educator, composer, music theorist; b. La Crosse, Wis., Jan. 10, 1928; s. Edward Carl and Louise (George) B.; m. Maxine Cecile Metzner, May 11, 1954. B.Mus., U. So. Calif., 1949, Ph.D., 1956; student, Conservatoire Nat. de Paris, 1953-54. Lectr. music U. So. Calif., 1956-57; instr. U. Mich., 1957-60, asst. prof., 1960-63, asso. prof., 1963-66, prof. music, chmn. dept. music theory, 1966-77; prof., head dept. music U. B.C., Vancouver, Can., 1978—; pub. lectr. ednl. cons. Author: Form in Music, 1966, Eighteenth-Century Imitative Counterpoint, (with E. Chudacoff), 1969, Structural Functions in Music, 1975; contbr. articles to Jour., Music Theory, Perspectives in New Music, Music Theory Spectrum., Mus. Quar., Coll. Music Symposium; Composer piano, choral, chamber and orchestral works; rec. of works include Trio for Piano, Violin and Cello, String Quartet No. 2, Duo for Flute and Piano, Canto Lirico for Viola and Piano, Duo for Violin and Piano, Sonata for Piano. Served with AUS, 1954-56. Fulbright fellow, 1953-54; recipient U. Mich. Distinguished Faculty Service award, 1963; Am. Acad.-Inst. Arts and Letters composer award, 1978. Mem. Coll. Music Soc., Am. Musicol. Soc., Soc. for Music Theory (pres. 1982-85), ASCAP. Office: Univ British Columbia Dept Music 6361 Memorial Rd Vancouver BC Canada V6T 1W5 *The work of the composer-theorist is a pursuit of four supreme values: love, imagination, beauty, and intellectual understanding-values that constitute the critical substance of man's defense against the ultimate futility of existence. For the educator who believes in the significance of learning in enrichment of the human experience, to teach is a demonstration of love and an affirmation of the necessity for understanding. And it is the extraordinary privilege of the musician to be* *surrounded with the fruit and stimulus of imagination, the perfect medium of the beautiful.*

BERRY, WALTER, baritone; b. Vienna, Austria, Apr. 8; s. Franz and Hilde (Jelinek) B.; m. Brigitte Hohenecker, 1973; 1 son by previous marriage, Wolfgang. Ed., Akademie fur Musik und darstellende Kunst, Vienna, 1947-49. Leading baritone Vienna State Opera, 1950—. Appearances throughout Europe and Americas in variety of operatic roles; guest various opera festivals inculding, Salzburg Festival, 1952—, Salzburg Easter Festival, Lucerne Festival, Saratoga Festival, Prager Fruhling, Drottningholm, Stockholm, Festival of Flandern, and other; leading baritone, Met. Opera, N.Y.C., Grand Opera, Paris, Teatro Colon, Buenos-Aires, Covent Garden, London, Lyric Opera, Chgo., Deutsche Opera Berlin, Munich; guest performer, San Francisco Opera, Cologne (W. Ger.) Opera, numerous recordings of stardard opera repertoire, lieder, baroque, and classical religious music, 1949—; made: TV and movie film Cosi fan Tutte and IXth Symphony of Beethoven; TV films Bartered Bride; and others; performed in: Missa Solemnis on Eurovision, 1969. Recipient 1st prize Llangollen, Wales, 1948; prize Mozart Competition, Vienna, 1949; 2d prize Concours Musical, Verviers, Belgium, 1949; named Kammersaenger Govt. of Austria, 1963, Order Arts and Scis. 1st class, 1968; recipient Order Arts and Scis. Govt. of Sweden, 1965. Address: care Thea Dispeker Artists Rep 59 E 54th St New York NY 10022 *

BERRY, WENDELL, educator, poet; b. Henry County, Ky., Aug. 5, 1934; m. Tanya Amyx, May 29, 1957; children—Mary Dee, Pryor Clifford. A.B., U. Ky., 1956, M.A., 1957. Mem. faucity U. Ky., 1964-77, Disting. prof. English, 1971-72. Author: novels Nathan Coulter, 1962, A Place on Earth, 1967, The Memory of Old Jack, 1974; poetry The Broken Ground, 1964, Findings, 1969, Openings, 1968, Clearing, 1977, A Part, 1980, Farming: A Handbook, 1970, The Country of Marriage, 1973; essays The Long-Legged House, 1969, The Hidden Wound, 1970, The Unforseen Wilderness, 1971, A Continuous Harmony, 1972, The Unsettling of America, 1977, Recollected Essays, 1965-1980, 1981, The Gift of Good Land, 1981. Home: Port Royal KY 40058

BERRY, WILLIAM BENJAMIN NEWELL, paleontologist, mus. dir.; b. Boston, Sept. 1,1931; s. John King and Margaret Elizabeth (Newell) B.; m. Suzanne Foster Spaulding, June 10, 1961; 1 son, Bradford Brown. A.B., Harvard U., 1953, A.M., 1955; Ph.D., Yale U., 1957. Asst. prof. geology U. Houston, 1957-58; asst. prof. to prof. paleontology U. Calif., Berkeley, 1958—; curator Mus. of Paleontology U. Calif., Berkeley, 1960-75, dir., 1975—, chmn. dept. paleontology, 1975—; cons. U.S. Geol. Survey. Author: Growth of a Prehistoric Time Scale, 1968; contbr. numerous articles on stratigraphic and paleontol. subjects to profl. jours.; editor publs. in geol. scis. Guggenheim Found. fellow, 1966-67. Mem. Paleontol. Soc., Geol. Soc. Norway, Internat. Platform Assn., Explorers Club. Home: 1366 Summit Rd Berkeley CA 94708 Office: Dept Paleontology U Calif Berkeley CA 94720

BERRY, WILLIAM LEE, manufacturing company executive; b. Auburn, N.Y., Sept. 1, 1927; s. E.L. and Frances E. (Potter) B.; m. Jean E. Campbell, Sept. 1, 1950; children: Peggy, Joan (dec.), Ted. B.A. in Chemistry, Cornell U., 1951; M.S. (Dow fellow 1953-54), U. Mich., 1954, Ph.D., 1955. From tech. dir. pigments div. to v.p. indsl. chems. div. Am. Cyanamid Co., 1971-80, pres. organic chems. div., 1981-82, pres. polymer products div., 1982—; pres. Formica Corp., Wayne, N.J., 1980. Served with AUS, 1946-47. Mem. Am. Mgmt. Assn., Sigma Xi, Phi Lambda Upsilon. Republican. Baptist. Clubs: Copper Hill Country (Flemington, N.J.); Baltusrol (Summit, N.J.); Bankers (Cin.). Patentee in organic chemistry. Home: 545 Steel Gap Rd Bridgewater NJ 08807 Office: Polymer Products Div Am Cyanamid Co Berdan Ave Wayne NJ 07470

BERRY, WILLIAM MARTIN, financial service holding company executive; b. Chgo., June 21, 1920; s. William John and Mary Frances (Martin) B.; m. Julia Vail, Dec. 19, 1972; children: William E., Mary P., Peter D. B.S. summa cum laude, St. Mary's Coll., Winona, 1941; M.A., DePaul U., Chgo., 1949. Div. controller Hughes Aircraft Co., Los Angeles, 1951-55, TRW Co., 1955-58; mgr. mgmt. services Peat Marwick, Mitchel & Co., C.P.A.s, Los Angeles, 1958-61; v.p. Litton Industries Inc., Beverly Hills, Calif., 1961-74; chmn., chief exec. officer NN Corp., Milw., 1974-80, Armco Ins. Group, 1980-81, chmn., 1981—; dir. Marine Corp., Milw., Marine Nat. Exchange Bank, Astronautics Corp. Contbr. articles to profl. jours. Bd. dirs. Columbia Hosp. Served to 1st lt. C.E., AUS, 1941-45; ETO, PTO. Mem. Fin. Execs. Inst. Clubs: Union League (N.Y.C.); Carlton (Chgo.); University (Milw.); Milwaukee, Milwaukee Country. Home: 13800 N Birchwood Ln Mequon WI 53092 Office: Armco Ins Group 731 Jackson St Milwaukee WI 53202

BERRY, WILLIAM WELLS, lawyer; b. Nashville, Sept. 10, 1917; s. Allen Douglas and Agnes Wilkie (Vance) B.; m. Mary John Atwell, May 31, 1941; children: William W., Edith Allen Berry Kain. B.A., Vanderbilt U., 1938, LL.B., 1940. Bar: Tenn. 1940. Practice, Nashville, 1940-42, 46—; ptnr. Bass, Berry & Sims, 1965—; dir. Washington Industries, Inc., Ingram Industries, Inc., Ozburn Hessey Storage Co., Franklin Industries, Inc., Berry Wholesale Drug Co. Mem. Tenn. Inheritance Tax Study Com., 1977, 82; mem. adv. com. dental div. Tenn. Dept. Pub. Health, 1953-57; pres. Bill Wilkerson Hearing and Speech Ctr., 1959-67; bd. dirs. Noel Meml. Found., 1954-68; trustee Tenn. Fed. Tax Inst., 1973-79, pres., 1976-77; trustee Monroe Harding Home, 1971—, Washington Found., 1978—, Nashville Found., 1965-82. Served to capt. AUS, 1942-46. Decorated Air medal with oak leaf cluster. Fellow Am. Coll. Probate Counsel (bd. regents 1979—), Internat. Acad. Trial Lawyers, Am. Bar Found.; mem. ABA, Tenn. Bar Assn., Nashville Bar Assn. (dir. 1969-72, v.p. 1971-72), Am. Judicature Soc., Nashville C. of C., Nashville Srs. Golf Assn. (pres. 1978-80), Nat. Soc. SAR. Democrat. Presbyterian (deacon, elder). Clubs: Belle Meade Country, Cumberland, Capitol City (Nashville); Highlands Country (N.C.). Home: 6 Lynwood Ln Nashville TN 37205 Office: Bass Berry & Sims 2700 First American Ctr Nashville TN 37238

BERRY, WILLIAM WILLIS, utility executive; b. Norfolk, Va., May 18, 1932; s. Joel Halbert and Julia Lee (Godwin) B.; m. Elizabeth Mangum, Aug. 23, 1958; children: E. Preston, John Willis, William Godwin. B.S. in Elec Engring, Va. Mil. Inst., 1954; M.S. in Commerce, U. Richmond, 1964. Registered profl. engr., Va. Engr. Gen. Electric Co., 1954-55; with Va. Electric & Power Co., Richmond, 1957—, v.p. div. ops., then sr. v.p. comml. ops., 1974-78, exec. v.p., 1978-80, pres., chief operating officer, 1980-83, pres. chief exec. officer, 1983—; dir. Va. Nat. Bank, Norfolk, Ethyl Corp., Richmond. Trustee Westminster-Canterbury House, Richmond, United Way Greater Richmond, 1981—, Union Theol. Sem., Richmond. Served to 1st lt. AUS, 1955-57. Mem. Public Utilities Assn. Virginias (pres. 1983). Republican. Clubs: Richmond Kiwanis (past pres.), Commonwealth, Country of Va., Downtown, Norfolk Yacht and Country. Home: 6601 Three Chopt Rd Richmond VA 23226 Office: PO Box 26666 Richmond VA 23261

BERRYHILL, HENRY LEE, JR., geologist; b. Charlotte, N.C., Nov. 6, 1921; s. Henry Lee and Viola Estelle (Johnston) B.; m. Louise Randall Russell, Sept. 13, 1947; children: Stuart Randall, Keith Courtney. B.S., U. N.C., 1947, M.S. in Geology, 1949. With U.S. Geol. Survey, 1948—, chief publs. officer, Denver, 1963-65, research marine geologist, 1965-66, chief marine geology Gulf of Mexico-Caribbean region office, Corpus Christi, Tex., 1967-70; chief Office Marine Geology, Washington, 1970-73, sr. research marine geologist, Corpus Christi, 1973—; Tech. adviser offshore prospecting com. ECAFE, 1972-73; Dept. Interior rep. Fed. Intragy. Com. on Marine Sci. and Engring., 1970-73; program mgr. integrated environ. assessment Outer Continental Shelf, N.W. Gulf of Mexico, 1973—; U.S. rep. marine geology panel U.S.-Japan Coop. Programs in Natural Resources, 1973—; cons. Nat. Center for Geoscis., India, 1981—. Author: Geology and Coal Resources of Belmont County, Ohio, 1963, Geology of the Ciales Area, Puerto Rico, 1965, Coal-Bearing Upper Pennsylvanian and Lower Permian Rocks, Washington Area, Pennsylvania, 1971, The Worldwide Search for Petroleum Offshore-A Status Report for the Quarter Century, 1947-72, 1974; Contbr. articles to sci. publs. Served with USAAF, 1942-45. Decorated D.F.C., Air medal with 3 oak leaf clusters.; Recipient Outstanding Performance award U.S. Geol. Survey, 1969. Fellow Geol. Soc. Am.; mem. Am. Assn. Petroleum Geologists, Soc. Econ. Paleontologists and Mineralogists, AAAS, Sierra Club (chmn. Costal Bend group 1980-81), Sigma Xi. Episcopalian. Home: 231 Rosebud St Corpus Christi TX 78404 Office: US Geol Survey Office Marine Geology PO Box 6732 Corpus Christi TX 78411 *Besides an innate enthusiasm for learning, the greatest single factor that has shaped my life has been the choice of a profession that I could pursue as if it were my hobby.*

BERS, LIPMAN, mathematician, educator; b. Riga, Latvia, May 22, 1914; came to U.S., 1940, naturalized, 1949; s. Isaac and Bertha (Weinberg) B.; m. Mary Kagan, May 15, 1938; children: Ruth, Victor. Dr. Rerum Naturalium, U. Prague, 1938. Research instr. Brown U., 1942-45; asst. prof., asso. prof. Syracuse U., 1945-49; mem. Inst. Advanced Study, 1948-50; prof. N.Y. U., 1950-64, chmn. grad. dept. math., 1959-64; prof. Columbia U., 1964—, chmn. dept. math., 1972-75, Davies prof. math., 1973-82, Davies prof. math. emeritus, 1982, spl. prof., 1982-84; Vis. prof. Stanford U., summer 1955; vis. Miller Research prof. U. Calif. at Berkeley, 1968; chmn. Com. Support on Research on Math. Scis., Nat. Acad. Scis.-NRC, 1966-68; chmn. div. math. scis. NRC, 1969-71; chmn. U.S. Nat. Com. for Math., 1977-81. Author math. books.; Contbr. articles to math. jours. Fulbright fellow, 1959-60; Guggenheim fellow, 1959-60, 79. Fellow Am. Acad. Arts and Scis., AAAS (chmn. math. sect. 1973, 83), Am. Philos. Soc.; mem. Am. Math. Soc. (v.p. 1963-65, Steele prize 1975, pres. 1975-77), Fedn. Am. Scientists (council 1977-79, sponsor 1980—), Nat. Acad. Scis. (chmn. math. sect. 1967-70, chmn. com. on human rights 1979—). Home: 111 Hunter Ave New Rochelle NY 10801 Office: Dept Math Columbia U New York NY 10027

BERSANI, LEO, educator; b. N.Y.C., Apr. 16, 1931; s. Guido and Harriet (Wischer) B. B.A., Harvard U., 1952, Ph.D., 1958. Instr. Wellesley Coll., 1957-60, asst. prof. French, 1960-65, asso. prof., 1965-67; assoc. prof. Rutgers U., 1967-69, prof., 1969-74, U. Calif., Berkeley, 1974—, chmn. dept. French, 1974-82. Author: Marcel Proust, 1965, Balzac to Becket, 1970, A Future for Astyanax, 1976, Baudelaire and Freud, 1978, The Death of Stéphane Mallarmé. Recipient award for essay Nat. Endowment for Humanities, 1968; Guggenheim fellow, 1967-68; Nat. Endowment for Humanities fellow, 1979-80; Am. Council Learned Socs. fellow, 1982-83; Nat. Council Learned Socs. fellow, 1982-83. Mem. MLA. Home: 7061 Devon Way Berkeley CA 94705 Office: Dept French U Calif Berkeley CA 94720

BERSCHE, JOSEPH EDWIN, construction company executive; b. Fairmont, W.Va., Oct. 17, 1931; s. G. Joseph and Jessie Naomi (Darling) B.; m. Barbara Carol Stegmaier, June 9, 1956; children: Craig, Chris, Kimberly Jo, Curt, Barbi Jo. Student, Mich. State Normal Sch., 1949-50, Nyack Coll., 1950-51. Pres. Bersche Constrn. Co., Pontiac, Mich., 1956-66; exec. v.p., dir. Hannan Co., Cleve., 1967-77; pres. Inland Constrn., Inc., Chgo., 1977—; also dir.; pres. Aetna Co.; dir. Christian Publs. Inc., Harrisburg, Pa. Trustee Urban Investment and Devel. Co. Employees Pension Plan; mem. Internat. Council Shopping Centers.; Trustee Nyack (N.Y.) Coll., Alliance Theol. Sem., Stow Alliance Fellowship; mem. governing bd. dirs. Christian and Missionary Alliance; bd. dirs. Shell Point Retirement Village, Ft. Myers, Fla. Served with USN, 1951-55. Mem. Asso. Gen. Contractors Am. Clubs: Hudson Country; Carlton, Execs. (Chgo.). Office: Inland Constrn Inc 845 N Michigan Ave Chicago IL 60611

BERSH, PHILIP JOSEPH, psychologist, educator; b. Phila., Sept. 9, 1921; s. Michael and Sophie (Faggen) B.; m. Jacqueline Edith Fratkin, June 10, 1929; children: Lauren Helene, Marilyn Ellen. A.B., Temple U., 1944; A.M., Columbia U., 1947, Ph.D., 1949. Lectr. Columbia U., 1948-54, research assoc., 1951-54; lectr. U. Wis., 1951; chief intelligence and electronic warfare br. Rome Air Devel. Ctr., N.Y., 1954-62; lectr. Utica Coll., Syracuse U., N.Y., 1958-60, Hamilton Coll., 1961-62; chief combat systems div. U.S. Army Behavioral Sci. Research Lab., Washington, 1962-67, assoc. dir. human performance experimentation, 1966-67; lectr. George Washington U., 1966-67; prof. psychology Temple U., Phila., 1967—; vis. prof. dept. psychology Inst. Psychiatry U. London, 1979; cons. U.S. Army Research Inst. for Behavioral and Social Scis. Cons. editor: JSAS; Catalog Selected Documents in Psychology, 1976-79; mem. editorial bd.: Jour. Exptl. Analysis and Behavior, 1980—; contbr. articles on psychology to profl. jours. Served with AUS, 1942-46; ETO. NRC postdoctoral fellow, 1950. Fellow Am. Psychol. Assn., AAAS; mem. Psychonomic Soc., Eastern Psychol. Assn., Sigma Xi. Office: Dept Psychology Temple U Philadelphia PA 19122

BERSI, ROBERT MARION, university administrator; b. Ark., June 4, 1932; s. Mack M. and Angelina (Perona) B.; m. Ann Brakebill, Nov. 27, 1975; 1 dau., Margaret Ann. B.A., U. of Pacific, 1958; M.A., Stanford U., 1962, Ph.D., 1965. Research assoc. Stanford U., 1964-66; exec. asst. to pres. Calif. State U., Dominguez Hills, 1966-70, prof. edn., 1970-75, dean innovative programs, 1971-73, v.p. instl. devel., 1973-75; pres. Western Conn. State U., Danbury, 1975-81; chancellor U. Nev. System, 1981—; mem. exec. com. Conn. Council on Higher Edn. Author: Restructuring the Baccalaureate, 1973; Mem. editorial adv. bd., Coll. Mgmt. mag., 1973-75; Contbr. articles to profl. publs. Served with U.S. Navy, 1952-54. Recipient award of merit Carson Black Heritage Assn., 1973. Mem. Am. Assn. Sch. Adminstrs., Am. Inst. Pub. Service (bd. nominators), Western Assn. Schs. and Colls., Fed. Edn. Data Acquisition Council, Greater Danbury C. of C. (dir.). Office: U Nev System 405 Marsh Ave Reno NV 89509

BERSOFF, DONALD NEIL, lawyer, psychologist; b. N.Y.C., Mar. 1, 1939; s. Irving and Mina (Cohen) B.; m. Darla Maclean, Jan. 2, 1981; children: David, Judith. B.S., N.Y. U., 1958; M.A., NYU, 1960, Ph.D., 1965; student, U. Va. Law Sch., 1973-74; J.D., Yale U., 1976. Bar: Md. Asst. prof. Ohio State U.; asso. prof. U. Ga., U. Md. Sch. Law; now adj. prof. Johns Hopkins U., Balt. and U. Md. Sch. Law; ptnr. Ennis, Friedman Bersoff & Ewing, Balt.; coordinator joint J.D. and Ph.D. program in law and psychology U. Md. Sch. Law and Johns Hopkins U. Dept. Psychology. Author: Learning to Teach: A Decision-Making System, 1976. Served with USAF, 1965-68. N.Y. State Regents coll. teaching fellow. Mem. Am. Psychology-Law Soc. (pres. 1980-81), Am. Psychol. Assn., ABA, Nat. Health Lawyers Assn. Home: 121 Farmgate Ln Silver Spring MD 20904 Office: 1200 17th St NW Washington DC 20036

BERSON, ELIOT LAWRENCE, ophthalmologist, medical educator; b. Boston, 1937. M.D., Harvard U., 1962. Intern in medicine Calif. Hosp., San Francisco, 1962-63; resident in opthalmology Barnes and McMillan Hosp., St. Louis, 1963-66; clin. assoc. ophthalmologist Nat. Inst. Neurol. Diseases and Blindness, Bethesda, Md., 1966-68; asst. Mass. Eye and Ear Infirmary, Boston, 1968-73, asst. surgeon, 1974-79; assoc. surgeon in ophthalmology Mass. Eye and ear Infirmary, Boston, 1979—; dir. Berman-Gund Lab for Study Retinal Degenerations, Mass. Eye and Ear Infirmary, Boston, 1974—; instr. Harvard U. Sch. Medicine, Boston, 1968-70, asst. prof., 1971-76; assoc. prof. ophthalmology Harvard U. Sch. Medicne, Boston, 1976; present Chatlos prof. ophthalmology Harvard U. Sch. Medicine, Boston. Served as surgeon USPHS, 1966-68. Mem. AMA. Office: Berrman-Gund Lab Mass Eye and Ear Infirmary 243 Charles St Boston MA 02114 *

BERSON, JEROME ABRAHAM, chemistry educator; b. Sanford, Fla., May 10, 1924; s. Joseph and Rebecca (Bernicker) B.; m. Bella Zevitovsky, June 30, 1946; children: Ruth, David, Jonathan. B.S. cum laude, Coll. City N.Y., 1944; M.A., Columbia U., 1947; Ph.D., 1949; Ph.D. NRC postdoctoral fellow, Harvard U., 1949-50. Asst. chemist Hoffmann-LaRoche, Inc., Nutley, N.J., 1944; asst. prof. U. So. Calif., 1950-53, asso. prof., 1953-58, prof., 1958-63, U. Wis., 1963-69, Yale U., 1969-79, Irénée du Pont prof., 1979—, chmn. dept. chemistry, 1971-74, dir. div. phys. sci. and engring., 1983—; vis. prof. U. Calif., U. Cologne, U. Western, Ont.; Fairchild Distinguished scholar Calif. Inst. Tech.; cons. Riker Labs., Goodyear Tire & Rubber Co., Am. Cyanamid Co., IBM; mem. adv. panel for chemistry NSF; mem. medicinal chemistry study sect. NIH, 1969-73. Mem. editorial adv. bd.: Jour. Organic Chemistry, 1961-65, Accounts of Chemical Research, 1971-77, Nouveau Journal de Chimie, 1977—, Chem. Revs., 1980-83; contbr. articles to profl. jours. Served with AUS, 1944-46. CBI. Recipient Alexander von Humboldt award, 1980; John Simon Guggenheim fellow, 1980. Fellow Am. Acad. Arts and Scis.; mem. Nat. Acad. Scis., Am. Chem. Soc. (Calif. sect. award 1963, James Flack Norris award 1978, chmn. div. organic chemistry 1971), Chem. Soc. London, Phi Beta Kappa, Sigma Xi, Phi Lambda Upsilon. Home: 45 Bayberry Rd Hamden CT 06517 Office: Dept Chemistry Yale U PO Box 6666 New Haven CT 06511

BERSTICKER, ALBERT CHARLES, chemical company executive; b. Toledo, Mar. 22, 1934; s. Albert Charles and Lillian (Weston) B.; m. Frances Ploeger, Sept. 15, 1956; children: Steven, Susan, Karen, Cristina. M.S. in Geo-Chemistry, Miami U., Oxford, Ohio, 1957. Chemist Interlake Iron Corp., Toledo, 1956; engr. Mobile Producing Corp., Billings, Mont., 1957-58; with Ferro Corp., Cleve., 1958—, asst. to group v.p. internat., 1973-74, group v.p. internat., 1974-76, exec. v.p. ops., chief operating officer, 1976—, also dir.; dir. Ferro Enamel Espanola, S.A., Castellon, Spain, Metal Portuguesa, S.A.R.L., Lisbon, Duramax, Inc., Nissan Ferro Organic Chem. Co. Ltd., Tokyo, Ferro Far East, Ltd., Hong Kong, Ferro Indsl. Products, Ltd., Oakville, Ont., Can., Ferro Corp. (Aust.) Pty., Ltd., Sydney, Queen City Distbrs., Ltd., Downsview, Ont., Ferro South East Asia Pte., Ltd., Singapore. Editor: Symposium on Salt, 1963. Chmn. Cleve. Area Devel. Council; trustee Cleve. Roundtable. Mem. Am. Ceramics Soc., Spanish Ceramics Soc., Chem. Mfg. Assn., Leadership Cleve. Episcopalian. Office: Ferro Corp One Erieview Plaza Cleveland OH 44114

BERT, CHARLES WESLEY, mechanical engineer, educator; b. Chambersburg, Pa., Nov. 11, 1929; s. Charles Wesley and Gladys Adelle (Raff) B.; m. Charlotte Elizabeth Davis (June 29, 1957); children: Charles Wesley IV, David Raff. B.S. in Mech. Engring, Pa. State U., 1951, M.S., 1956; Ph.D. in Engring. Mechanics, Ohio State U., 1961. Registered profl. engr., Pa., Okla. Jr. design engr. Am. Flexible Coupling Co., State Coll., Pa., 1951-52; aero. design engr. Fairchild Aircraft div. Fairchild Engine and Airplane Corp., Hagerstown, Md., 1954-56; prin. M.E. Battelle Inst., Columbus, Ohio, 1956-61; sr. research engr., 1961-62, program dir., solid and structural mechanics research, 1962-63, cons., 1964-65, assoc. prof., U. Okla, asso. prof., Norman, 1963-66, prof., 1966—; dir. Sch. Aerospace, Mech. and Nuclear Engring., 1972-77, Benjamin H. Perkinson prof. engring., 1978—; instr. engring. mechanics Ohio State U., Columbus, 1959-61; cons. various indsl. firms. Bd. dirs. Midwestern Mechanics Conf., 1971-79, chmn., 1973-75. Editorial bd. Composite Structures, 1982—; Contbr. chpts. to books, articles to profl. jours. Served from 2d lt. to 1st lt. USAF, 1952-54. Fellow AAAS (assoc.); fellow AIAA (nat. tech. com. on structures 1969-72, vice chmn. Central Okla. sect. 1965-66, chmn. 1966-67), Am. Acad. Mechanics (dir. 1979—), ASME (Central Okla. sect. exec. com. 1973-78); mem. Am. Soc. Engring. Edn., ASME (Region X mech. engring. dept. heads com. 1972-77, chmn. 1975-77), Japan Soc. for Composite Materials, Soc. Engring. Sci., N.Y., Okla. acads. scis., Nat., Okla. socs. profl. engrs., Soc. Exptl. Stress Analysis (monograph com. 1978—, chmn. 1980—, sec. mid-Ohio sect. 1958-59, chmn. 1959-60, adv. bd. 1960-63, 82), Scabbard and Blade, Sigma Xi, Sigma Tau, Pi Tau Sigma, Sigma Gamma Tau (Disting. Engr. award), Tau Beta Pi (Disting. Engr. award). Home: 2516 Butler Dr Norman OK 73069 Office: Sch Aerospace Mech and Nuclear Engring U Okla 865 Asp Ave Norman OK 73019 *Set high yet realistic goals, put forth the extra effort to achieve them, and practice the Golden Rule.*

BERTAIN, G(EORGE) JOSEPH, JR., lawyer; b. Scotia, Calif., Mar. 9, 1929; s. George J. and Ellen Veronica (Canty) B.; m. Bernardine Joy Galli, May 11, 1957; 1 son, Joseph F. A.B., St. Mary's Coll. of Calif., 1951; J.D., Cath. U. Am., 1955. Bar: Calif. Assoc. Joseph L. Alioto, San Francisco, 1955-57, 59-65; asst. U.S. atty. No. Dist. Calif., 1957-59; pvt. practice of law, San Francisco, 1966—. Editor-in-chief, Law Rev. Cath. U. Am., 1954-55. Chmn. San Francisco Lawyers Com. for Elections of Gov. Ronald Reagan, 1966, 70, 80, 84; spl. confidential adviser to Gov. Reagan for jud. selection, San Francisco, 1967-74. Recipient De La Salle medal St. Mary's Coll. of Calif., 1951, Signum Fidei award St. Mary's Coll. of Calif., 1976. Mem. ABA, Calif. Bar Assn., Fed. Bar Assn. (del. 9th Circuit Jud. Conf. 1967-76), Am. Judicature Soc., St. Thomas More Soc. San Francisco, Calif. Acad. Scis., Mus. Soc., Assn. Former U.S. Attys. and Asst. U.S. Attys. of No. Calif. (past pres.), Supreme Ct. Hist. Soc., Cath. U. Am. Alumni Assn. (pres. No. Calif.-No. Nev. chpt. 1962-76), St. Mary's Coll. of Calif. Alumni Assn. (dir. 1957-60, 65-76, bd. regents 1980—), Knight of Malta. Republican. Clubs: KC, Commonwealth, Commercial, Olympic. Office: 1250 Alcoa Bldg One Maritime Plaza San Francisco CA 94111

BERTE, NEAL RICHARD, college president; b. May 7, 1940; s. Edward H. and Wenonah Maureen (Stevens) B.; m. Anne; children: Becky, Julie, Mark, Scott. B.S. in Polit. Sci, U. Cin., 1962, M.S. (Ford Found. scholar), 1963, Ph.D., 1966; Rockefeller Found. fellow, Union Theol. Sem., N.Y.C., 1962-63; postgrad., Garrett Theol. Sem., Evanston, Ill., 1966-67, Harvard U., 1967. Asst. dir. Coll. Entrance Exam. Bd., Evanston, 1966-68; exec. asst. to pres., asst. prof. Ottawa (Kans.) U., 1968-70; dean New Coll.; asso. prof. U. Ala., 1970-74; v.p. ednl. devel., dean New Coll., 1974-76; pres. Birmingham-So. Coll., Ala., 1976—; dir. Circle S Industries, Selma, Ala., Parisian, Inc., Birmingham, Ala.; project dir. NSF grants, 1972; chmn. session Internat. Council on Edn. for Teaching World Assembly, Nairobi, Kenya, 1973; mem. faculty Danforth Found. sponsored Community Coll. Inst., Stephens Coll., 1973; mem. steering com. Carnegie Found. funded project Coop. Assessment of Experiential Learning, 1974-77;

mem. Commn. on Ednl. Credit, Am. Council Edn., 1975-81, Danforth Found. exec. com. for Danforth Fellows Program, 1974-75; mem. nat. adv. council for career edn. HEW, Office Edn., 1976—; sec.-treas. So. U. Conf., 1977-80, v.p., 1984—. Contbr. articles to edn. jours. Mem. adminstrv. bd. Canterbury United Methodist Ch., Birmingham, 1977-80; chmn. Univ. United Fund campaign, 1973; bd. dirs., mem. exec. com. United Fund, Tuscaloosa, Ala., 1974-75, chmn. edn. div., 1975; chmn. sect. for pvt. ednl. insts. Jefferson-Shelby-Walker Counties United Appeal, 1977; chmn. pub. employees div. United Way campaign, 1978; v.p. Council for Advancement Pvt. Colls. in Ala., 1977-82, pres., 1982—; chmn. com. to select Man of Year in Birmingham, 1977; chmn. selection com. Rhodes Scholarships for Ala., 1976-80; bd. dirs. Jefferson-Shelby Counties Lung Assn., Ala. Partners for Progress with Guatemala Program, Carraway Meth. Hosp., Brookwood Hosp., 1982—, Neighborhood Housing Service, Birmingham, Birmingham Symphony Assn., Community Action Com., Operation New Birmingham; bd. govs. Relay House Club, Birmingham, 1983—; bd. dirs., chmn. long range planning com., chmn. program for Scout Expn. Jefferson County council Boy Scouts Am., 1977—; mem. exec. com. Men's Com., Birmingham Symphony Assn.; chmn. Birmingham Area United Way, 1983; trustee Advent Episcopal Day Sch., Gorgas Scholarship Found., 1976-77, New Coll.-Sarasota, U. South Fla. Recipient Outstanding Citizens award Lawson State Community Coll., 1977; Outstanding Citizen award in Birmingham Erskine Ramsay Award Com., 1978; Brotherhood award NCCJ, 1984; elected to Ala. Acad. Honor, 1979; named One of 10 Outstanding Community Leaders Birmingham Post-Herald, 1984. Mem. Am. Assn. Univ. Adminstrs. (pres. Alpha chpt. 1978-80), Greater Birmingham Area C. of C. (dir., mem. exec. com. 1978—), Am. Assn. Colls. (pres.'s adv. council 1977—), Young Pres.'s Orgn., Am. Assn. for Higher Edn. (chmn. Southeastern Regional Council 1973, chmn. panel on three-year degree programs 1973, program chmn. 1974, adv. bd. NEXUS Project 1974-75), Assn. for Innovation in Higher Edn. (adv. bd. 1973), Phi Beta Kappa (pres. 1975), Phi Delta Kappa. Clubs: Downtown Birmingham Kiwanis (chmn. Ministers Day 1977, chmn. Youth-of-the-Year selection com. 1977. Home: 816 8th Ave W Birmingham AL 35204 Office: 800 8th Ave W Birmingham AL 35204

BERTELSEN, THOMAS ELWOOD, JR., investment banker; b. Chgo., Feb. 13, 1940; s. Thomas Elwood and Virginia Marie (McKenna) B.; m. Sandra Lee Morgan, May 9, 1970; children: Derek, Page. A.B., U. Kans., 1962; LL.B., Stanford, 1965; M.B.A., Columbia, 1966. With Dean Witter Reynolds Inc., 1966—, mgr. corp. fin. dept., San Francisco, 1974-75, sr. v.p., 1975—, mng. dir. investment banking, 1980—, also dir.; exec. v.p. Sutro & Co. Inc., 1983—. Roman Catholic. Club: Pacific Union (San Francisco). Home: PO Box 397 Ross CA 94957 Office: 201 California San Francisco CA 94111

BERTELSMAN, WILLIAM ODIS, judge; b. Cin., Jan. 31, 1936; s. Odis William and Dorothy (Gegan) B.; m. Margaret Ann Martin, June 13, 1959; children—Kathy, Terri, Nancy. B.A., Xavier U., 1958; J.D., U. Cin., 1961. Bar: Ky. bar 1961. Law clk. firm Taft, Stettinius & Hollister, Cin., 1960-61; mem. firm Bertelsman & Bertelsman, Newport, Ky., 1962-79; judge U.S. Dist. Ct. Eastern Dist. Ky., Covington, 1979—; instr. Coll. Law U. Cin., 1965-72; city atty., prosecutor, Highland Heights, Ky., 1962-69. Contbr. articles to profl. jours. Served to capt. AUS, 1963-64. Mem. No. Ky. C. of C. (pres. 1974, dir. 1969-77), Ky. Bar Assn. (bd. govs. 1978-79), Am. Bar Assn., Campbell County Bar Assn. Republican. Roman Catholic. Club: Optimist. Home: 78 W Vernon Ln Fort Thomas KY 41075 Office: 700 Scott St Covington KY 41012

BERTELSMEYER, JAMES EDGAR, petroleum products company executive; b. St. Louis, 1942; s. Harry T. B.; m. Donna Celeste Dantini, July 25, 1968. B.S., U. Mo.-Rolla, 1966; M.B.A., Memphis State U., 1969. Various engring. ops. mgmr. positions Conoco Pipeline, Houston, 1969-79; with Buckeye Gas Products Co. subs. Penn. Central Corp., Tulsa, 1979—, sr. v.p. supply and distbn., 1979-80, now pres., dir. Served with USMC, 1966-68. Office: Buckeye Gas Products Co 320 S Boston Ave Bldg Tulsa OK 74101 *

BERTHOFF, ROWLAND TAPPAN, historian, educator; b. Toledo, Sept. 20, 1921; s. Nathaniel and Helen (Tappan) B.; m. Tirzah Margaret Park, Aug. 5, 1954; children: Thomas Arthur, Margaret Olivia, Andrew Warner, Clarissa Helen. A.B., Oberlin Coll., 1942; A.M., Harvard U., 1947, Ph.D., 1952. Instr. Princeton U., 1953-57, asst. prof., 1957-62; assoc. prof. Washington U., St. Louis, 1962-65, prof., 1965—, chmn. history dept., 1968-74, 81-82, William Eliot Smith prof. history, 1974—; Fulbright lectr. U. Edinburgh, 1965-66. Author: British Immigrants in Industrial America, 1790-1950, 1953, An Unsettled People, Social Order and Disorder in American History, 1971. Served to 1st lt., inf. AUS, 1942-46. Mem. Orgn. Am. Historians. Home: 7195 Washington Ave Saint Louis MO 63130

BERTHOFF, WARNER BEMENT, educator; b. Oberlin, Ohio, Jan. 22, 1925; s. Nathaniel and Helen (Tappan) B.; m. Ann Rhys Evans, June 29, 1949; children—Rachel, Frederic. B.A., Harvard U., 1947, M.A., 1949, Ph.D., 1954. Teaching fellow Harvard, 1949-51; from asst. to prof. English Bryn Mawr Coll., 1951-67; prof. English Harvard U., 1967—; Vis. prof. U. Catania, Italy, 1957-58, U. Minn., 1961, U. Calif.-Berkeley, 1962-63, U. Warsaw, Poland, 1963, Columbia U., 1964, U. Pa., 1967. Author: American Literature Traditions and Talents, 1960, The Example of Melville, 1962, The Ferment of Realism; American Literature, 1884-1919, 1965, 81, Edmund Wilson, 1968, Fictions and Events, 1971, A Literature Without Qualities: American Writing Since 1945, 1979. Served with USNR, 1943-46. Guggenheim fellow, 1968-69; Fulbright-Hays lectr. Italy, 1972; Soc. for Humanities fellow Cornell U., 1975-76. Home: 14 Thoreau St Concord MA 01742 Office: Dept English Harvard Univ Cambridge MA 02138

BERTHOLD, FRED, JR., educator, clergyman; b. St. Louis, Dec. 9, 1922; s. Fred and Myrtle Bernice (Williams) B.; m. Laura Bell McKusick, Dec. 27, 1945; children—Marjorie Chase, Daniel S., Timothy M., Sarah M. A.B., Dartmouth, 1944; B.D., U. Chgo., 1947, Ph.D., 1954; D.D., Middlebury Coll., 1959, Concord Coll., 1960, U. Vt., 1961. Instr. philosophy Utica Coll. of Syracuse U., 1948-49; ordained to ministry Congl.-Christian Ch., 1949; instr. philosophy Dartmouth, 1949-50, instr. religion, 1950-51, asst. prof. religion, 1951-56, prof., 1956—, chmn. dept., 1951-58, 62—; dean William Jewett Tucker Found., 1957-62, dean for humanities, 1976-80. Author: The Fear of God, 1959; Editor: Basic Sources of the Judaeo-Christian Tradition, 1962; Contbr. to The Future of Empirical Theology, 1969, The Dialogue between Psychology and Theology, 1969. Mem. Soc. for Values in Higher Edn., Am. Acad. Religion, Am. Theol. Soc., Phi Beta Kappa. Home: RFD 115 Norwich VT 05055

BERTIN, JOHN JOSEPH, engineering educator, researcher; b. Milw., Oct. 13, 1938; s. Andrea and Yolanda G. (Pasquali) B.; m. Mary Patricia Sommer, July 28, 1962; children: Thomas Alexander, Randolph Scott, Elizabeth Anne, Michael Robert. B.A., Rice Inst., Houston, 1960, M.S., 1962, Ph.D., 1966. Aerospace technologist NASA Johnson Space Ctr., Houston, 1962-66; prof. U. Tex., Austin, 1966—; cons. McGinnis, Lochridge & Kilgore, Austin, 1978—, Sandia Nat. Labs, Albuquerque, 1980—, BPD Difesa e Spazio, Rome, 1980—. Co-author: Aerodynamics for Engineers, 1979, Engineering Fluid Mechanics, 1984. Pres. Western Hills Little League, Austin, 1975. Recipient Dynamics Teaching award Coll. Engring., Austin, 1978, Tex. Exec. Teaching award Ex-Students Assn. U. Tex., Austin, 1982. Assoc. fellow AIAA (dir. region IV 1983—, disting. lectr. 1978-82); mem. N.Y. Acad. Scis. Office: Dept Aerospace Engring U Texas Austin TX 78712

BERTINO, JOSEPH ROCCO, physician, educator; b. Port Chester, N.Y., Aug. 16, 1930; s. Joseph and Madaleine (Posillipo) B.; m. Mary Patricia Hagemeyer, Sept. 29, 1956; children—Frederick, Amy Marie, Thomas Allen, Paul Phillip. Student, Cornell U., 1947-50; M.D., Downstate Med. Center N.Y., 1954. USPHS Research fellow U. Wash. Sch. Medicine, Seattle, 1958-61; mem. faculty Yale U. Sch. Medicine, 1961—, asso. prof. pharmacology and medicine, 1964-67, prof., 1967—, Am. Cancer Soc. prof., 1975—; cons. USPHS, 1966—; N.Y. State scholar for medicine, 1950-54. Contbr. articles to profl. jours. Mem. Am. Soc. for Clin. Investigation, Am. Soc. Hematology, Biol. Chemists, Pharmacology and Therapeutics. Home: 384 Hill St Hamden CT 06514 Office: 333 Cedar St New Haven CT 06510

BERTLES, JOHN FRANCIS, physician, educator; b. Spokane, Wash., June 8, 1925; s. John Francis and Henrita Swart (Brown) B.; m. Jeannette Winans, 1948 (div. 1978); children: Mark Dwight, Jacquelyn Eve, John Francis.; m. Lila De Paganne, 1981. B.S., Yale U., 1945; M.D., Harvard U., 1952. Diplomate Am. Bd. Internal Medicine. Intern Presbyterian Hosp., N.Y.C., 1952-53, asst. resident in medicine, 1953-55; research fellow in hematology U. Rochester and Strong Meml. Hosp., 1955-56; research fellow in immunohematology Harvard U. Med. Sch. and Mass. Gen. Hosp., Boston, 1956-58, research fellow in hematology, 1958-59; instr. in medicine Harvard U. Med. Sch. at Mass. Gen. Hosp., 1959-61; dir. hematology div. St. Luke's Hosp. Center, N.Y.C., 1962—, asst. attending physician, 1962-64, assoc. attending physician, 1964-71, attending physician, 1971—; sr. research asso. dept. biol. scis. Columbia U., 1970-71, asst. clin. prof. medicine, 1962-67, assoc. clin. prof., 1967-71, assoc. prof., 1971-74, prof., 1974—; vis. prof. medicine Nuffield dept. clin. medicine Radcliffe Infirmary, U. Oxford, Eng., 1977-78; cons. to various govt. agys., including hematology study sect. NIH, 1972-76, 83—, blood research rev. group, 1978-83; mem. dirs. council N.Y. Heart Assn., 1974—; mem. basic research adv. com. Nat. Found. March of Dimes, 1977-80. Contbr. articles to profl. publs. Served to ensign USNR, 1945-46. Fellow A.C.P.; mem. Am. Soc. Clin. Investigation, Am. Physiol. Soc., Am. Soc. Hematology, Am. Fedn. Clin. Research, Am. Chem. Soc., Alpha Omega Alpha. Office: St Luke's Hosp Center New York NY 10025

BERTMAN, RICHARD JAY, architect; b. Cambridge, Mass., Apr. 9, 1934; s. Edward and Bessie (Levine) B.; m. Sandra Lee Borkum, July 5, 1959; children: Jonathan Morris, David Laurence, Louisa Anne. B.A., Harvard U., 1956; B.Arch., M.I.T., 1961; M.Arch., U. Calif.-Berkeley, 1965. Registered architect, Mass. Assoc. David Abrahams & Assocs., Boston, 1961; project mgr. Hugh Stubbin and Assocs., Cambridge, 1962-65; founder, prin. CBT-Childs Bertman Tseckares and Casendino Inc., Boston, 1967—; tchr. Boston Archtl. Ctr., 1961-71; asst. prof. R.I. Sch. Design, 1965-67; sec. Mass. Archtl. Registration Bd., 1977, vice chmn., 1978; chmn. Mass. Archtl. Registration, 1979; mem. rev. com. Nat. Archtl. Accrediting Bd., 1979; mem. exam writing com. Nat. Council Archtl. Registration Bds., 1979—. Trustee Soc. Preservation New Eng. Antiques; mem. City of Boston Environ. Com., Boston Back Bay Archtl. Commn., 1979—; chmn. Boston Back Bay Archtl. Commn., 1982—; bd. dirs. Boston Archtl. Ctr., 1978—, sec., 1982—. Served with U.S. Army, 1958. Winner Mass. Council on Arts and Humanities Search for Young Talent, 1967; recipient 1st honor award Guild Religious Architecture, 1974, Design award HUD, 1974, Spl. Firm award Nat. Trust Hist. Preservation, 1976, Plywood Design award Nat. Plywood Assn., 1976, Honor award Nat. Assn. Home Builders, 1976, Honor award for Design Excellence Boston Soc. Architects, 1978, award for Excellence in Housing, 1981, Excellence award Masonry Inst., 1980. Fellow AIA; mem. Boston Soc. Architects (dir. 1977-79). Office: 306 Dartmouth St Boston MA 02116

BERTOLUCCI, BERNARDO, film dir.; b. Parma, Italy, Mar. 16, 1940; s. Attilio and Ninetta B. Attended, Rome (Italy) U. Dir.: films The Grim Reaper, 1962, Before the Revolution, 1964 (Young Critics award Cannes Film Festival), La Via del Petrolio, 1965, His Partner, 1968, The Conformist, 1969 (Nat. Film Critics Best Dir. award), The Spider's Strategem, 1970, Last Tango in Paris, 1972, Luna, 1979; Author: poems In Search of Mystery, 1962 (Viareggio prize, Italy). Office: Via del Babuino 51 Rome Italy *

BERTON, LEE, editor; b. Bklyn., May 30, 1931; s. Samuel and Rose Bertan; m. Leah Ruth Jacoby, Sept. 5, 1959; children—Laura, Wendy, Jennifer. B.A., N.Y. U., 1956; M.S. in Journalism, Columbia U., 1957. Writer Wall St. Jour., N.Y.C., 1962-69, Mobil Oil Corp., 1969-72; mng. editor Financial World, 1972-75; editor Jour. Accountancy, Am. Inst. C.P.A.'s, N.Y.C., 1975—. Author articles. Recipient Photographers award UPI, 1959; Publs. award U. Hartford Center for Study Profl. Acctg., 1980. Mem. Sigma Delta Chi. Home: 1280 White Oak Rd Westfield NJ Office: 22 Cortlandt St New York NY 07090

BERTON, PIERRE, journalist, author; b. Whitehorse, Yukon, Can., July 12, 1920; s. Francis George and Laura (Thompson) B.; m. Janet Walker, 1946; children: Penny, Pamela, Patricia, Peter, Paul, PeggyAnne, Perri, Eric. B.A., U. B.C., 1941; LL.D. (hon.), U. P.E.I., 1973, Dalhousie U., 1978, U. Brock, 1981; D.Litt., York U., 1974, U. Windsor, 1981, U. Athabasca, 1982, U. Victoria, 1983, McMaster U., 1983, U. Alaska, 1984, Royal Can. Coll., 1984. City editor Vancouver (B.C.) News Herald, 1941-42; feature writer Vancouver Sun, 1946-47; successive positions to mng. editor Maclean's Mag., Toronto, Ont., 1947-58, contbg. editor, 1963; asso. editor, daily columnist Toronto Daily Star, 1958-62; TV panelist Front Page Challenge, CBC; radio commentator CKEY, Toronto; also host weekly TV programs The Great Debate, My Country. Author: 30 books including The Royal Family, 1953, Stampede for Gold, 1955, The Mysterious North, 1956, Klondike Fever, 1958, Just Add Water and Stir, 1959, Adventures of a Columnist, 1960, The New City, 1961, The Secret World of Og, 1961, Fast, Fast, Fast Relief, 1962, Big Sell, 1963, Comfortable Pew, 1965, Smug Minority, 1969, The National Dream, 1970, The Last Spike, 1971, The Impossible Railway, 1972, Drifting Home, 1973, Hollywood's Canada, 1974, My Country, 1976, The Dionne Years, 1977, The Wild Frontier, 1978, The Invasion of Canada, 1812-1813, 1980, Flames across the Border, 1981, Why We Act Like Canadians, 1982, Klondike Quest, 1983, The Promised Land, 1984; Screenwriter, narrator: City of Gold; Contbr. to numerous mags. Past chmn. Heritage Can. Found.; chmn. Can. Nat. Trust. Served to capt. Can. Army, 1942-45. Decorated Order Can.; recipient Gov. Gen.'s award for creative non-fiction, 1956, 58, 72; Stephen Leacock medal for humor, 1959; J.V. McAree award for columnist of year, 1959; Nat. Newspaper awards for feature writing and staff corresponding, 1960; Grand Prix film awards.; Beefeater Club prize for lit., 1982; Can. Booksellers award, 1982; named to Can. Newspaper Hall of Fame, 1982. Mem. Authors League Am., Heritage Can., Assn. Can. Radio and TV Artists (award for integrity in broadcasting 1972, award for pub. affairs 1977), AFTRA, Can. Writers Union. Home: Rural Route 1 Kleinburg ON Canada Office: 21 Sackville St Toronto ON Canada

BERTOS, RIGAS NICHOLAS, art history educator; b. Athens, Greece, July 2, 1929; emigrated to Canada, 1966; s. Nicholas and Hedwig (Schwent) B.; m. Joanna Schwerttner, Jan. 6, 1965; 1 son, Nicholas. M.A., U. Athens, Greece, 1952; Ph.D., U. Munich, 1963. Cultural attache Greek Embassy, Bonn, Germany, 1964-65; asst. prof. McGill U., 1966-71, assoc. prof., 1971—, chmn. dept. art history, 1977—. Author: Jacopo Torriti, 1963; contbr. articles to scholarly jours. Served with Greek Army, 1954-55. Grantee Canada Council, McGill U., German Govt., 1967-82. Mem. Can. Soc. Italian Studies, Can. Soc. Renaissance Studies, Univs. Art Assn. Can. Greek Orthodox. Home: Chateau Maisonneuve 4998 de Maisonneuve W Westmount Que Canada H3Z 1N2 Office: McGill U Dept Art History 853 Sherbrooke St W Montreal Que Canada H3A 2T6

BERTRAM, FREDERIC AMOS, architect; b. Detroit, Oct. 15, 1937; s. Martin Terrance and Majorie Constance (Saunders) B.; m. Virginia Bernice Kopec, Sept. 14, 1963. Student, Ctr. for Creative Studies, Detroit, 1957-58; B.Archtl. Engring., Lawrence Inst. Tech., 1962. Registered architect, Mich., Calif., Hawaii. With Detroit City Plan Commn., 1962-63, Louis G. Redstone Assocs., 1963-65, Ziegelman and Ziegelman, 1965-68, Giffels and Rosseti, 1968-69; v.p. design Rossetti Assocs., Los Angeles, 1969-80, prin. in-charge, 1980—; chmn. design juror awards program Delaware Valley Masonry Inst., 1978; chmn. design juror neon sign competition for students Lawrence Inst. Tech., 1978, juror design competition, 1979, Masonry Inst. Mich., 1979; lectr. in field; vis. design critic Cranbrook Acad. Art, 1977; pres. Frederic A. Bertram, Los Angeles, 1982—. Prin. works, Alcoa Chem. and Metallurgy Bldg., Merwin, Pa. (design), United Airlines Reservation Ctr., Dearborn, Mich. (2 design), Cottonwood Condominiums, Traverse City, Mich., Frederic A. Bertram residence, Lake Orion, Mich. (3 design), Gt. Am. Ins. Co. Office Bldg., Birmingham, Mich. (2 design), Ford Motor Land Devel. Office Bldgs., Dearborn, (design), St. John Fisher Coll., Rochester, Henry Ford Hosp. Ambulatory Ctr., Dearborn (3 design), Rossetti Assocs. Office Bldg., Detroit, Henry Ford Hosp. Edn. and Research, Detroit (design), Mfrs. Bank, Detroit, Bendix Hdqrs., Southfield, Mich., Bon Secour Hosp., Grosse Pointe, Mich. (3 design), Pressure Vessel, Detroit (design), Washington Blvd Mall, Detroit, Monroe City Hall, Mich. Served with N.G., 1956-63. Fellow AIA (nat. com. on design 1977-80, mem. coms. Detroit, mem. Calif. council), Engring. Soc. Detroit. Home and Office: 10485 National Blvd Los Angeles CA 90034 *One thing I realized early in life is if someone becomes overly self-satisfied with his or her achievements, he or she will never progress, they will become stagnant. One must look to the future and improve upon their past and present.*

BERTRAM, JOHN ELWOOD, computer company executive; b. Bedford, Pa., May 3, 1927; s. John Franklin and Mildred Rachel (King) B.; m. Lucy Virginia Keen, June 22, 1952; 1 son, John David. B.S.E.E., Washington U., St. Louis, 1952; M.S., Columbia U., 1955, Ph.D., 1958. Staff engr. Research div. IBM, Yorktown Heights, N.Y., 1958-65, dir. computer sci., 1965-67, assoc. dir. advanced computer systems System Devel. div., Menlo Park, Calif., 1967-68, asst. gen. mgr. Advanced Systems Devel. div., 1968, acting lab. mgr. Systems Lab, Mohansic, N.J., 1968, gen. mgr. Advanced Systems Devel. div., San Jose, 1968-70, dir. engring. programming, White Plains, N.Y., 1970-73, v.p., pres. Advanced Systems div., 1973-75, v.p., pres. Systems Product div., 1975-78, v.p., pres. Data Systems div., 1978-83, v.p., pres. Gen. Products div., San Jose, Calif., 1983—. Office: IBM 5600 Cottle Rd San Jose CA 95193

BERTRAM, VICTORIA ELAINE, dancer; b. Toronto, Ont., Can., Feb. 26, 1946; d. Russell Arthur and Lois Marguerite (McBride) B.; m. Jacques Germain Gorrissen, Jan. 5, 1970; children: Adrian Alexander, Cybele Justine. Grad. with honors, Nat. Ballet Sch., Toronto, 1963. Mem. corps de ballet Nat. Ballet of Can., Toronto, 1963-70, soloist, 1970-80, prin. dancer, 1980—. Office: Nat Ballet of Canada 157 King St E Toronto ON Canada M5C 1G9

BERTRAMSON, B. RODNEY, agronomist; b. Potter, Nebr., Jan. 25, 1914; s. James W. and Gladys D. (Nelson) B.; m. Eleanor Anne Maloney, Aug. 28, 1938; children: James Leitch, Christina MacPherson, Susan M. B.S., U. Nebr., 1937, M.S., 1938, D.Agr. (hon.), 1978; Ph.D., Oreg. State Coll., 1941. Chemist technician, lab. asst. U. Nebr., 1936-37; soil surveyor U.S. Dept. Agr., 1941; instr. soils Colo. State Coll., 1941; asst. prof. soils U. Wis., 1946; asso. soil chemist Purdue U., 1946-49; chmn. dept. agronomy Wash. State U., Pullman, 1949-67; dir. resident instruction Coll. Agr., 1967-79, prof. emeritus, cons., 1982—; cons. U.S. Dept. Agr., 1979-80; project leader U. Nebr.-AID Morocco Project, Casablanca, 1981. Editor, Jour. Agron. Edn., 1973; contbr. articles to profl. jours. Entered U.S. Army, 1941; chief of food and agr. for Rheinland, later for Gross Hessen Mil. Govt., 1945; disch. to Research and Devel., U.S. Army Res. as maj., 1946. Fellow AAAS, Am. Soc. Agronomy (v.p. 1959, pres. 1960); mem. Crop Sci. Soc. Am., Soil Sci. Soc. Am., Soil Conservation Soc. Am., Am. Chem. Soc., Sigma Xi, Phi Kappa Phi, Alpha Zeta, Gamma Sigma Delta. Prepared course outlines for soil analysis and soil chemistry. Home: SE 510 Crestview St Pullman WA 99163 *Hearty approbation and generous praise of fellow man's efforts work magic in getting the job done. I have profited over the years from a friend's advice: "Give bouquets to the living!"*

BERTRAND, ALVIN LEE, rural sociologist; b. Elton, La., July 6, 1918; s. Jacob William and Ludie (Treme) B.; m. Mary Nic Ellis, Aug. 29, 1941; Children—William Ellis, Mary Lynne. B.S., La. State U., 1940, Ph.D., 1948; M.S., U. Ky., 1941. Mem. faculty La. State U., 1940-42, 46-78, prof. rural sociology, Boyd disting. prof., prof. emeritus, 1978—; head levels living sect., farm population and rural life br. Dept. Agr., 1957-58; vis. prof., internat. chair Va. Poly. Inst. and State U.; adj. prof. Tulane U.; mem. nat. sci. adv. com. Nat. Park Service; cons. in field. Author books, monographs, bulls., articles in field. Served with USAAF, 1942-46. Fellow Am. Sociol. Assn.; mem. Rural Social Soc. (Disting. Service award), So. Assn. Agrl. Scientists (Disting. Service award rural sociol. sect.), Southwestern Sociol. Soc., Population Assn. Am., La. Acad. Scis., AAUP, Am. Country Life Assn., La. Hist. Assn., European Congress Rural Sociology, Community Devel. Soc., Assn. Latino-Americana De Sociologia Rural, Internat. Rural Sociol. Assn., Nat. Parks and Conservation Assn., Mid-South Sociol. Assn., Gamma Sigma Delta (merit award), Phi Kappa Phi, Alpha Gamma Rho, Alpha Kappa Delta, Alpha Delta, Alpha Sigma Lambda. Democrat. Baptist. Home: 1046 W Lakeview Dr Baton Rouge LA 70810 Office: Dept Sociology and Rural Sociology La State Univ Baton Rouge LA 70803

BERTRAND, FEDERIC HOWARD, insurance company executive; b. Montpelier, Vt., Aug. 5, 1936; s. George Joseph and Delores Gertrude (Mallory) B.; m. Elinor Maude Pierce, June 11, 1960; children: Kimberly Sue, Michael Scott, John Frederic (dec.). B.S. in Civil Engring. magna cum laude, Norwich U., 1958; postgrad., Georgetown U. Law Sch., 1961-63, Carnegie-Mellon U. Sch. Indsl. Engring., 1967-68; J.D., Coll. William and Mary, 1967. Registered profl. engr., Vt., Vt., Va. Engr.-adminstr. CIA, Washington, 1960-70; asst. counsel, assoc. counsel, counsel Nat. Life Ins. Co., Montpelier, 1970-79, v.p., 1979-80, sr. v.p., 1980-83; exec. v.p., chief operating officer Nat. Life Inc. Co., Montpelier, 1983—; mem. exec. bd. Chittenden Trust Co., Montpelier, 1975—; dir. Union Mut. Fire Ins. Co., New Eng. Guaranty Ins. Co., Montpelier; civilian aide to sec. of army, Washington, 1981—. Chmn. Montpelier Bd. Appeals, 1972-76; chmn.

charter revision com. City of Montpelier, 1973, alderman, 1974-76, pres. city council, 1975-76, mayor, 1976-78; vice chmn. Montpelier Republican Com., 1973-74; mem. Vt. Rep. Com., 1974-76; trustee Kellogg-Hubbard Library, Montpelier, 1978-82, Norvich U., Northfield, Vt., 1979—. Recipient Outstanding Alumnus award Norwich U., 1980. Mem. ABA, Vt. Bar Assn., Va. Bar Assn., Washington County Bar Assn., Theta Chi, Epsilon Tau Sigma. Republican. Roman Catholic. Office: Nat Life Ins Co National Life Dr Montpelier VT 05602

BERTRAND, WATSON CLARK, manufacturing company executive; b. Kansas City, Mo., Dec. 7, 1931; s. Lawrence Walter and Frances Evelyn (Smith) B.; m. Sarah Louise Beals, June 23, 1956; children—Sandra Kay, Mark Steven, Paul Steven. Student, Kalamazoo Coll.; B.A. h honors, Mich. State U., 1957. C.P.A., Calif., Mich. Sr. acct. Price Waterhouse & Co., Detroit, Los Angeles, 1957-62; asst. div. controller Garrett Corp., Los Angeles, 1962-66; sec.-treas., dir. Info. Devel. Co., Santa Ana, Calif., 1966-69; treas., dir., v.p. fin. TRE Corp., Beverly Hills, 1969—. Served with USAF, 1951-55. Mem. Delta Sigma Pi. Episcopalian. Office: 9460 Wilshire Blvd Beverly Hills CA 90212

BERTSCH, FRANK HENRY, furniture mfg. co. exec.; b. Mpls., Oct. 2, 1925; s. Herbert Thomas and Eleanor Emma (Tuscany) B.; m. Barbara Tiffany Mills, Sept. 12, 1953; children—Jeffrey T., Steven H., Carolyn T. B.S. in Mech. Engring, Northwestern U., 1947. With Flexsteel Industries, Inc., Dubuque, Iowa, 1947—, plant engr., 1947-49, plant mgr., 1949-53, v.p., dir. design and devel., 1953-58, pres., 1958—; dir. Retirement Investment Corp., Am. Trust and Savs. Bank, Dubuque, CyCare Systems Inc., Northwestern Mut. Life Ins. Co.; partner Ryan House, hist. home restoration partnership, Dubuque, 1969—, J.M. Cardinal, real estate developers, 1973—. Bd. dirs. United Fund Dubuque, U. Dubuque. Served with USNR, 1944-46. Recipient Distinguished Service award Dubuque C. of C., 1964, Man Behind the Boy award Dubuque Boys Club, 1969. Mem. Am. Legion, Dubuque Shooting Soc. Presbyn. (elder, trustee). Club: Dubuque Golf and Country. Home: 700 Sunset Ridge Dubuque IA 52001 Office: care Flexsteel Industries Inc PO Box 877 Dubuque IA 52001

BERUH, JOSEPH, drama and film producer; b. Pitts., Sept. 27, 1924; s. William Israel and Clara (Parnes) B.; children—David Marshall, William Israel. B.F.A., Carnegie Inst. Tech., 1950. Producer numerous: plays including Leave It to Jane, 1959, Long Days Journey into Night, 1970, Godspell, 1971, Promenade, 1969, Waiting for Godot, 1971, Comedy, 1973, Gypsy, 1975, The Night That Made America Famous, 1976, The Magic Show, 1974, American Buffalo, 1977, N.Y.C., Cat's Pajamas, 1963, Nourish the Beast, 1973, Kittiwake Island, 1960, Young, Gifted and Black, 1965, Trains, 1969, The Enclave, 1974, Blasts and Bravos, Gypsy, London; producer: films including Godspell, 1973, Blue Sunshine, 1977, Squirm, 1976, The Wild Party, 1974, He Knows You're Alone, 1979, The Clairvoyant, 1982; partner, Lansbury/Beruh Prodns., N.Y.C., 1969—. Served with AUS, 1943-46. Mem. League of N.Y. Theatres. Office: 1650 Broadway New York NY 10036

BERWALD, HELEN DOROTHY, educator; b. Lac Qui Parle County, Minn., Mar. 15, 1925. B.A., U. Minn., 1948, B.S., M.A., 1951, Ph.D., 1962. Tchr. Robbinsdale (Minn.) High Sch., 1951-52; mem. faculty Carleton Coll., Northfield, Minn., 1952—; now prof. edn. Mem. Minn. State Adv. Com.; dir. programs in tchr. edn. Asso. Colls. Midwest; dir. Chgo. Urban Semester, Video Tape Project; mem. African Edn. Survey Team; mem. accreditation task force Am. Assn. Colls. Tchr. Edn., exec. com., bd. dirs., 1979—; mem. standards and process com., mem. exec. com., also chmn. appeals bd. Nat. Council Accreditation Tchr. Edn., mem. coordinating bd., 1979—. Pres. Minn. Assn. Colls. Tchr. Edn.; Mem. Nat. Council Tchrs. Social Studies, Assn. Supervision and Curriculum Devel., Phi Beta Kappa, Pi Lambda Theta. Home: 208 Elm St Northfield MN 55057

BESCH, EVERETT DICKMAN, veterinarian, university dean; b. Hammond, Ind., May 4, 1924; s. Ernst Henry and Carolyn (Dieckmann) B.; m. Mellie Darnell Brockman, Apr. 3, 1946; children: Carolyn Darnell, Ceryl Lynn, Cynthia Lee, Charlotte Ann, Everett Dickman. D.V.M., Tex. A&M Coll., 1954; M.P.H., U. Minn., 1956; Ph.D., Okla. State U., 1963. Instr. U. Minn., 1954-56; asst. prof. Okla. State U., 1956-64, prof., head dept. vet. parasitology and pub. health, 1964-68; dean Sch. Vet. Medicine, La. State U., 1968—; sec.-treas. council deans Assn. Am. Vet. Med. Colls., 1974-78, sec.-treas., 1976-80, chmn. council deans, 1980-81; mem. Nat. Adv. Council Health Professions Edn., 1982—. Author articles, chpt. in book. Served with USN, 1942-48. Mem. Assn. Tchrs. Vet. Pub. Health and Preventive Medicine, Am., La. vet. med. assns., Am. Soc. Parasitologists, Conf. Pub. Health Veterinarians, Am. Assn. Food Hygiene Veterinarians (pres. 1976—), Am. Assn. Vet. Parasitologists, Helminthological Soc., Washington, Conf. Research Workers Animal Diseases. Home: 1453 Ashland Dr Baton Rouge LA 70806

BESCH, HENRY ROLAND, JR., pharmacologist, educator; b. San Antonio, Sept. 12, 1942; s. Henry Rol and Monette Helen (Kasten) B.; 1 son, Kurt Theodore. B.Sc. in Physiology, Ohio State U., 1964, Ph.D. in Pharmacology (USPHS predoctoral trainee 1964-67), 1967; USPHS postdoctoral trainee, Baylor U. Coll. Medicine, Houston, 1968-70. Instr. Ob-Gyn Ohio State U. Med. Sch., 1967-68; mem. faculty Ind. U. Sch. Medicine, 1971—; prof. pharmacology and medicine, sr. research asso. Krannert Inst. Cardiology, chmn. dept. pharmacology and toxicology, 1977—, Showalter prof. pharmacology, 1980—; Can. Med. Research Council vis. prof., 1979, investigator fed. grants, mem. nat. panels and coms., cons. in field. Contbr. numerous articles pharm. and med. jours.; mem. editorial bds. profl. jours. Fellow Brit. Med. Research Council, 1970-71; Grantee Showalter Trust, 1975—. Fellow Am. Coll. Cardiology; Mem. AAAS, Am. Assn. Clin. Chemistry, Am. Fed. Clin. Research, Am. Heart Assn., Am. Physiol. Soc., Am. Soc. Biol. Chemists, Am. Soc. Pharmacology and Exptl. Therapeutics, Assn. Med. Sch. Pharmacologists, Biochem. Soc., Cardiac Muscle Soc., Internat. Soc. Heart Research (exec. com. Am. sect.), Nat. Acad. Clin. Biochemistry, N.Y. Acad. Scis., Sigma Xi. Office: 1100 W Michigan St Indianapolis IN 46223

BESCHERER, EDWIN A., JR., business information services company executive; b. Bklyn., Nov. 19, 1933; s. Edwin A. and Dorothy (Herbert) B.; m. Jane Madsen, June 11, 1955; children: John, Timothy, Karen, Katherine. B.S., Purdue U., 1955. With fin. depts. Gen. Electric Co., Fairfield, Conn., 1955-74, mgr. corp. fin. analysis, 1974-78; v.p., controller Dun & Bradstreet Corp., N.Y.C., 1978-82, sr. v.p. fin., 1982—. Mem. Fin. Execs. Inst. Home: 38 English Dr Wilton CT 06897 Office: Dun & Bradstreet Corp 299 Park Ave New York NY 10171

BESEN, STANLEY MARTIN, economist; b. Bklyn., Dec. 17, 1937; s. Moe and Sylvia (Forgang) B.; m. Marlene Dublirer, June 10, 1961; children: Roberta Ann, Elizabeth Rebecca. B.B.A., CCNY, 1958; M.A., Yale U., 1960, Ph.D., 1964. Acting asst. prof. econs. U. Calif., Santa Barbara, 1962-63; economist Inst. Def. Analysis, 1963-65; mem. faculty Rice U., Houston, 1965-80, prof. econs., 1974-79, Cline prof. econs. and fin., 1979-80; co-dir. network inquiry spl. staff FCC, 1978-80; sr. economist Rand Corp., Washington, 1980—; mem. task force nat. telecommunications policy making Aspen Inst. Program Communications and Society, 1977; cons. in field. Author articles in field.; Mem. editorial bds. profl. jours. Fellow Brookings Instn., 1971-72, NSF, 1973-75. Mem. Am. Econ. Assn. Home: 6202 Cromwell Dr Bethesda MD 20816 Office: 2100 M St NW Washington DC 20037

BESHAR, CHRISTINE, lawyer; b. Paetzig, Germany, Nov. 6, 1929; came to U.S., 1952, naturalized, 1957; d. Hans and Ruth (vonKleist-Retzow) von Wedemeyer; m. Robert P. Beshar, Dec. 20, 1953; children: Cornelia, Jacqueline, Frederica, Peter. Student, U. Hamburg, 1950-51, U. Tuebingen, 1951-52; B.A., Smith Coll., 1953. Bar: N.Y. 1960, U.S. Supreme Ct. 1971. Asso. firm Casey, Lane & Mittendorf, N.Y.C., 1960-63; assoc. firm Cravath, Swaine & Moore, N.Y.C., 1964-70, partner, 1971—. Bd. dirs. Catalyst for Women Inc., 1977—; trustee Colgate U., 1978—. Inst. Internat. Edn. fellow, 1952-53; recipient Disting. Alumnae medal Smith Coll., 1974. Fellow Am. Coll. Probate Counsel, Am. Bar Found. (bd. dirs. 1977—); mem. Assn. Bar City N.Y. (exec. com. 1973-75), N.Y. State Bar Assn. (ho. of dels. 1971-80, v.p. 1979-80, bd. dirs. 1977—), UN Assn. (bd. dirs. 1975—), Fgn. Policy Assn. (bd. dirs. 1978—). Presbyterian. Clubs: Wall St., Gipsy Trail, Cosmopolitan. Home: 120 East End Ave New York NY 10028 also Stone House Route 1 Somers NY 10589 Office: 1 Chase Manhattan Plaza New York NY 10005

BESHAR, ROBERT PETER, lawyer; b. N.Y.C., Mar. 3, 1928; m. Christine von Wedemeyer, Dec. 20, 1953; children: Cornelia, Jacqueline, Frederica, Peter. A.B. (Scholar of the House, honors with exceptional distinction), Yale U., 1950, LL.B., 1953. Bar: N.Y. 1954. Asst. gen. counsel Waterfront Commn. N.Y. Harbor, 1954-55; law sec. Hon. Charles D. Breitel, Appellate div. 1st dept. N.Y. Supreme Ct., N.Y.C., 1956-58; spl. hearing officer Justice Dept., 1967-68; dep. asst. sec. Commerce; dir. Bur. Internat. Commerce; nat. export expansion coordinator Commerce Dept., Washington, 1971-72; pvt. practice, N.Y.C., 1972—; Dir. Nat. Semiconductor Corp., Nat. Investor Data Services, Inc.; dir. Deep Ocean Tech., Inc.; mem. bus. adv. panel Nat. Commn. for Rev. of Antitrust Laws, 1978-79; mem. Mcpl. Securities Rulemaking Bd., 1982—. Author: Current Legal Aspects of Doing Business With Sino-Soviet Nations, 1973; Editor: Manhattan Auto Study, 1973; contbg. editor: Boardroom Reports, 1974—. Trustee, treas. United Bd. Christian Higher Edn. in Asia, 1981—. Mem. ABA (chmn. corporate and antitrust law com. 1982—), Internat., N.Y. State bar assns., Assn. Bar City N.Y., Westchester and No. Westchester Bar Assn., N.Y. County Lawyers Assn. (dir.), Phi Beta Kappa. Presbyterian. Clubs: Down Town (N.Y.C.); Gipsy Trail (Carmel, N.Y.); Elizabethean (New Haven). Home: 120 East End Ave New York NY 10028 Office: 63 Wall St New York NY 10005 Office: PO Box 533 Somers NY 10589

BESHEAR, STEVEN L., state official; b. Dawson Springs, Ky., Sept. 21, 1944. A.B., U. Ky., Lexington, 1966, J.D., 1968. Bar: N.Y. 1969, Ky. 1971. Assoc. firm White and Case, N.Y.C., 1968-70; later ptnr. Beshear, Meng and Green, Lexington; atty. gen. State of Ky., Frankfort, 1979-83, lt. gov., 1983—; mem. Ky. Ho. of Reps., 1974-79. Bd. editors, Ky. Law Jour., (1967-68.). Mem. Fayette County Bar Assn., Ky. Bar Assn., ABA, Order of Coif, Phi Beta Kappa, Phi Delta Phi, Omicron Delta Kappa. Office: Office Lt Gov New State Capitol Frankfort KY 40601 *

BESHEARS, CHARLES DANIEL, consultant, former insurance executive; b. Vandalia, Mo., Sept. 6, 1917; s. Charles D. and Anabel (Baker) B.; children: Jacqueline, Charles, Scott (dec.), Melanie. Grad. exec. program bus. mgmt., UCLA, 1968; A.M.P., Harvard U., 1971; grad. diploma courses, Ins. Inst. Am. C.L.U. With Farmers Ins. Group, Los Angeles, 1937-79, v.p., 1966, v.p. charge property and casualty ops., from 1967; pres., dir. Farmers New World Life Ins. Co., Mercer Island, Wash., 1973-79; now cons.; bd. govs. Internat. Ins. Seminars Inc. Mem. bd. electors Ins. Hall of Fame. Served with USAAF, 1942-45. Mem. Assn. M.B.A. Execs., Am. Soc. C.L.U., Internat. Platform Assn. Clubs: Legion, DAV, VFW., Chile.

BESING, RAY GILBERT, lawyer; b. Roswell, N.Mex., Sept. 14, 1934; s. Ray David and Maxine Mable (Jordan) B.; children: Christopher, Gilbert, Andrew, Paul. Student, Rice U., 1952-54; B.A., Ripon Coll., 1957; postgrad., Georgetown U., 1957; J.D., So. Methodist U., 1960. Bar: Tex. bar 1960. Partner firm Geary, Brice, Barron, & Stahl, Dallas, 1960-74; sr. partner Besing, Baker & Glast, Dallas, 1974-77; sr. partner firm Besing, Murphy and Armstrong, Dallas, 1977—; lectr. So. Methodist Sch. of Law, 1966-68, guest lectr. communications law, 1981—. Mng. editor, So. Methodist U. Law Jour., 1959-60. Pres. Dallas Cerebral Palsy Found., 1970; bd. dirs. Dallas Symphony, 1972, Dallas Theatre Center, 1971; trustee Ripon Coll., 1969-76; mem. Tex. Gov.'s Transition Team, 1982. Tex. Moot Ct. champion, 1958. Mem. Tex., Dallas bar assns., Dallas Jr. C. of C. (v.p. 1964), Sigma Chi. Democrat. Episcopalian (mem. exec. council diocese Dallas, 1969-72). Home: 6512 Belmead Dallas TX 75230 Office: 1450 One Main Pl Dallas TX 75250

BESS, GORDON CLARK, cartoonist; b. Richhield, Utah, Jan. 12, 1929; s. Claude Lee and Maude (Clark) B.; m. Joanne Elizabeth Vaught, July 9, 1955; children—Susan, Richard, Deborah. Student, Hailey (Idaho) High Sch. Combat artist 1st div. U.S. Marine Corps, Korea, 1951-52; cartoon editor Leatherneck Mag., Washington, 1953-56; art dir. Crest-Craft Co., Cin., 1957-67; vol. adj. tchr. Boise Pub. Schs. Creator: (1967) syndicated comic strip Redeye, Boise, Idaho. Served with USMC, 1948-56. Recipient Alfred award France) for best humor comic strip, 1976. Mem. Nat. Cartoonists' Soc., Newspaper Comics Council. Office: care King Features Syndicate Inc 235 E 45th St New York NY 10017 *

BESS, JEROME, advertising and public relations executive; b. Bayonne, N.J., Nov. 8, 1922; s. Herman M. and Molly C. Galanter B.; m. Jean Abelson, June 1, 1948,; children: John H., Andrea. B.S. in Bus., Ind. U., 1946. Broadcast advt. mgr. Robert Hall Clothes Inc., N.Y.C., 1950-62; exec. v.p. RKO Gen. Broadcasting, N.Y.C., 1962-67; v.p., gen. mgr. WOR-TV, Channel 9, N.Y.C., 1967-69; pres. Sawdon & Bess Inc., advt., N.Y.C., 1969-79, chmn., 1975-79; pres., chmn. Sawdon & Bess subs. Ted Bat WorldWide, N.Y.C., 1979—, also dir. parent co. Served to 1st lt. USAAF, 1943-46. Mem. Am. Assn. Advt. Agys., Internat. Radio-TV Soc. Clubs: Friars, Mountain Ridge Country. 3800 E Lincoln Dr Phoenix AZ 85018 Office: Sawdon & Bess Advt Inc 444 Madison Ave New York NY 10022

BESSE, RALPH MOORE, lawyer; b. Shadyside, Ohio, Nov. 23, 1905; s. Jesse Allman and Hope (Fish) B.; m. Augusta Woodward Mitchell, Apr. 28, 1934; children: Jean Elizabeth Bessee Minehart, William Truman, Robert Allen. A.B. magna cum laude, Heidelberg Coll., 1926; J.D., U. Mich., 1929; LL.D., Baldwin-Wallace Coll., 1957, Oberlin Coll., 1962, Case Inst. Tech., 1962, Western Res. U., 1963, Cleve. Marshall Law Sch., 1959; L.H.D., Wilberforce Coll., 1963, Ursuline Coll., 1970. Bar: Ohio 1930. Assoc. Squire, Sanders & Dempsey, 1929-40, ptnr., 1940-48, 70—; with Cleve. Electric Illuminating Co., 1948-70, pres., 1960-67, chmn. bd., chief exec. officer, 1967-70; chmn., dir. Nat. Machinery Co., 1962—. Contbr. articles to profl. jours. Mem. adv. bd. Ctr. for the Book, Library of Congress, 1979; trustee Nat. History Day, 1980, Ursuline Coll., 1963, John Huntington Art and Poly. Trust, 1966, John Huntington Fund for Edn., 1966. Recipient Cleve. medal for Pub. service Cleve. C. of C., 1960, Ursula Laurus award Ursuline Coll., 1965, Eisenman award Jewish Community Fedn. Cleve., 1966, Human Relations award NCCJ, 1967, award Cleve. Bus. League, 1967, Univ. medal Case Western Res. U., 1976, Wisdom award of honor Wisdom Soc., 1979, Disting. Service award Ohio Coll. Assn., 1980, Disting. Alumni award U. Mich., 1981, Ralph M. Besse chair in bus. established by Heidelburg Coll., 1979, Ralph M. Besse award for teaching excellence established by Cuyahoga Community Coll., 1980, James Dodman Nobel award Council Human Relations, 1982, numerous other awards. Mem. ABA, Ohio Bar Assn., Bar Assn. Greater Cleve. Club: 50 of Greater Cleve. Home: 2701 Ashley Rd Shaker Heights OH 44122 Office: Squire Sanders & Dempsey 1800 Huntington Bldg Cleveland OH 44115

BESSE, RONALD DUNCAN, publishing company executive; b. Stayner, Ont., Can., Dec. 7, 1938; s. Joe Rubin and Annie Mae (Buie) B.; m. Barbara Jane Low, Jan. 26, 1963; children: Christopher, Alison. Student, Ryerson Poly. Inst., 1957-60. With McGraw-Hill, 1960-70; mng. dir. McGraw-Hill Mex., 1970-73; pres. McGraw-Hill Ryerson, Toronto, Ont., Can., 1973-76; pres., chief exec. officer Consol. Graphics Ltd., Toronto, 1976, Gage Pub. Ltd., Agincourt, Ont., 1977—; chmn. bd. Macmillan of Can., Forkner Pub. Corp. U.S.A., Diffulivre Inc., RDB Capital Corp.; dir. Can. Cablesystems Ltd. Bd. dirs. Westpark Hosp.; mem. adv. com. Ryerson Poly. Inst.; mem. Bd. of Trade. Mem. Can. Book Publs. Assn., Young Pres.'s Orgn. (chmn. 1979-80, internat. dir.). Clubs: Granite, Beaumaris, Bd. of Trade. Home: 8 Lawrence Crescent Toronto ON Canada M4N 1N1 Office: Gage Pub Ltd 164 Commander Blvd Agincourt ON Canada M1S 3C7

BESSETTE, JOSEPH THOMAS, publisher; b. Chgo., May 30, 1925; s. Joseph Michael and Rosalie Elizabeth (Kane) B.; m. Elizabeth Ann Porter, Mar. 15, 1947; children: Daniel Joseph, Michael Thomas, Susan Elizabeth, Chad Porter, Matthew Kane. B.S. in Mktg, U. Ill., 1949. Advt. terr. mgr. Popular Mechanics mag., Chgo., 1949-55; advt. terr. mgr., then nat. sales mgr. Conover-Mast Publs., Chgo. and N.Y.C., 1955-60; nat. sales mgr., then pub. Physicians Mgmt. mag., Evanston, Ill., 1961-72; Eastern office mgr. AMA Publs., N.Y.C., 1972-74; pub. dental div. Dental Econs. and Proofs mag. PennWell Pub. Co., Tulsa, 1975-83; pub. dir. Telecommunications Products and Tech. mag., Tulsa, 1983—. Served with USMCR, 1943-46. Mem. Pharm. Advt. Club. Republican. Unitarian. Club: So. Tennis (Tulsa). Home: 1206 Hazel Blvd Tulsa OK 74114 Office: PO Box 1260 Tulsa OK 74101

BESSEY, EDWARD CUSHING, health care company executive; b. Portland, Maine, Dec. 1, 1934; s. Ronald G. and Esther (Pike) Torrey; m. Susan Goodrich, 1959 (div. 1965); children: Michael Thomas, Peter Andrew; m. 2d Jill Mowlem, May 9, 1970; i dau., Sarah Katheryn. A.B., Dartmouth Coll., 1957, M.B.A., 1961. Buyer Lehn and Fink Products Co., N.Y.C., 1961-64; product mgr. to v.p. mktg. Pfizer Inc., N.Y.C., 1964-72, dir. ops, 1972-77; Pfizer Internat. Brussels, 1977-80; exec. v.p. Pfizer Pharms., N.Y.C., 1980-81; pres., chief exec. officer Howmedica, Inc. div. Pfizer, Inc., N.Y.C., 1981—. Served as ensign USN, 1957-60. Republican. Club: Woodway (Darien, Conn.). Home: 652 Ponus Ridge Rd New Canaan CT 06840 Office: Howmedica Inc 235 E 42d St New York NY 10017

BESSEY, WILLIAM HIGGINS, physicist, educator; b. East Lansing, Mich., Mar. 18, 1913; s. Ernst Athearn and Edith Carleton (Higgins) B.; m. Thelma Moyer Shelly, Sept. 8, 1945; children—Barbara Lynn, Karen Elizabeth. S.B., U. Chgo., 1934; M.S., Carnegie Inst. Tech., 1935, D.Sc., 1940. Teaching asst. Carnegie Inst. Tech., 1934-39, instr., asst. prof., 1942-52; instr. S.D. Sch. Mines, 1939-40, N.C. State Coll., 1940-42; asso. prof., then prof. U. Mo. Sch. Mines and Metallurgy, 1952-56; prof., head dept. physics Butler U., 1956-80; summer instr. New Paltz (N.Y.) State Tchrs. Coll., 1953, Mich. State U., 1954; summer staff IBM Research Lab., Poughkeepsie, 1956. Fellow A.A.A.S.; mem. Am. Phys. Soc., Am. Assn. Physics Tchrs. (pres. Ind. sect.), Ind. Acad. Sci., Phi Beta Kappa, Sigma Xi, Phi Kappa Phi, Tau Kappa Epsilon. Home: 8932 Squire Ct Indianapolis IN 46250

BESSIE, SIMON MICHAEL, publisher; b. N.Y.C., Jan. 23, 1916; s. Abraham and Ella (Brainin) B.; m. Constance Ernst, Sept. 12, 1945; children: Nicholas, Katherine; m. Cornelia Schaeffer, Dec. 21, 1968. B.A. magna cum laude, Harvard U., 1936. Reporter Newark Star Eagle, 1936; research dept. RKO-Radio Pictures, 1936-38; editor Market Research Monthly, 1938; free-lance writer, Europe, Africa, 1938-39; asso. editor, war editor, war corr. Look mag., 1940-42; editor Harper & Bros., 1946-52, gen. editor, 1952-59; co-founder Atheneum Publishers, 1959, pres., 1963-75; sr. v.p. Harper & Row, 1975-81, dir., 1975—; pres. Joshuatown Pub. Assocs., 1981—; co-pub. Cornelia and Michael Bessie Books, 1981—; lectr. English Columbia U., 1953-59; dir. Novel Workshop, New School, 1959-63, Franklin Book programs, 1963-72; bd. overseers vis. com. history dept. Harvard U., 1964-77; chmn. vis. com. Harvard U. Press, 1972-78, bd. dirs., 1980—; dir. Am. Book Publishers' Council, 1964-69, chmn. trade book div. Assn. Am. Publishers, 1970-72, dir., 1972-76, chmn., 1974-75, chmn. freedom to read com., 1975-78, internat. freedom to publish com., 1975—; chmn. lit. panel Nat. Arts Council, 1971-74, chmn. spl. projects panel, 1974-81; chmn. bd. advisers WNET, 1979-83, trustee, 1983—; mem. exec. com. Center for the Book, Library of Congress, 1979—, chmn., 1983—; bd. dirs. Ctr. for Communication, 1981—. Author: Jazz Journalism, 1938; Contbr. numerous articles to mags. Served in, 1943-44; Algiers, Sicily, Italy; chief news bur. psychol. warfare br. Allied Forces hdqrs., 1943-44; Algiers and Naples; chief psychol. warfare combat team, 1944; So. France; dep. dir. USIS, 1944-46; France. Recipient Medal of Freedom, 1946. Mem. Council Fgn. Relations, Assn. Harvard Alumni (dir. 1974-77), Phi Beta Kappa. Clubs: Century Assn., Harvard (N.Y.C.); Federal City (Washington). Home: Joshuatown Rd Lyme CT 06371 Office: 10 E 53d St New York NY 10022

BESSINGER, JESS BALSOR, JR., English educator; b. Detroit, Sept. 25, 1921; s. Jess Balsor and Elaine (Brown) B.; m. Elizabeth Lieber Duvally, July 12, 1956; children: Anthony DuVally, Jess Balsor III. B.A., Rice U., 1943; M.A. Harvard U, 1947; Ph.D., 1952. Teaching asst. M.I.T., 1947-48; teaching fellow, tutor Harvard U., 1948-50; hon. teaching asst. Univ. Coll., London, 1950-52; asst. prof. English Brown U., 1952-56; asso. prof. English Univ. Coll., Toronto, 1956-60, prof., 1960-63; prof. English N.Y. U., 1964—. Author: A Short Dictionary of Anglo-Saxon Poetry, 1960; editor: Procs. of a Literary Data Processing Conference, 1964, Franciplegius: Medieval and Linguistic Studies in Honor of F. P. Magoun, Jr, 1965, Essential Articles for the Study of Old English Poetry, 1968, A Concordance to Beowulf, 1969, Medieval Studies in Honor of L. H. Hornstein, 1976, A Concordance to the Anglo-Saxon Poetic Records, 1978, Approaches to the Teaching of Beowulf, 1983; gen. editor: Harvard Old English Series, 1965—; co-founder, editor: Old English Newsletter, 1966-69. Served with U.S. Army, 1943-46. Fulbright scholar, 1950-52; Can. Council fellow, 1960; Guggenheim Found. fellow, 1963, 74. Mem. Mediaeval Acad. Am., MLA, Internat. Assn. Univ. Profs. English, Medieval Soc. So. Africa. Office: Dept English 19 University Pl New York Univ New York NY 10003

BESSMAN, SAMUEL PAUL, pediatrician, educator; b. Newark, Feb. 3, 1921; s. Edward S. and Sara R. (Greenberg) B.; m. Alice Neuman, July 3, 1945; children: Joel David, Ellen. Student, Coll. William and Mary, 1938-41; M.D., Washington U., St. Louis, 1944. Intern, asst. resident St. Louis Children's Hosp., 1944-45; asst. prof.

pediatrics George Washington U., 1947-54; dir. research Children's Hosp., Washington, 1947-54; asso. prof. pediatrics U. Md., 1954-59, prof. pediatric research, 1959-68, prof. biochemistry, 1962-68; prof., chmn. dept. pharmacology and nutrition U. So. Calif., 1968—, prof. pediatrics, 1969—; dir. research Rosewood State Hosp., Md., 1962-68, Jewish Home for Retarded Children, Washington, 1962-68. Editor: Biochem. Medicine; editorial bd.: Analytical Biochemistry. Pres. 1st Dist. Community Council, Balt., 1965; trustee Robert Lindner Found. Served with USPHS, 1945-47. Recipient Crawford Long award U. Ga., 1963; Creative Scholar award U. So. Calif., 1978; technion Maimonides award, 1979. Fellow Am. Acad. Pediatrics, AAAS; mem. Am. Soc. Biol. Chemists, Soc. Pediatric Research, Am. Inst. Nutrition, Am. Soc. Pharmacology and Exptl. Therapeutics, Sigma Xi, Alpha Omega Alpha. Research on treatment of lead poisoning, theoretical basis of hepatic coma, mechanism of insulin action chemistry mental retardation, genetic basis of malnutrition, artificial implantable pancreas. Home: 7404 Woodrow Wilson Dr Los Angeles CA 90046

BESSOM, MALCOLM EUGENE, writer, editor; b. Boston, Sept. 27, 1940; s. Harold Eugene and Mina (Townley) B. B.Mus., Boston U., 1962, postgrad., 1962-63. Dir. vocal music Pub. Schs., Chelmsford, Mass., 1963-67; asst. editor Allyn & Bacon Inc., Boston, 1967-68, asso. editor, 1968-70; asst. editor Music Educators Jour., Washington, 1970-71, editor, 1971-77, 79-81, Reston, Va., 1975-77, 79-81; dir. publs. Music Educators Nat. Conf., Reston, 1976-77, 79-81; pres. David Allen Press, Washington, 1978-81; participant White House Conf. on Arts Edn., 1976. Author: Supervising the Successful School Music Program, 1969, Teaching Music in Today's Secondary Schools, 1974, 2d edit., 1980, How to Sell Your Songs Like Professionals Do, 1978; contbg. author: This is Music for Today, Books 6, 7, 8, 1970-71; editor: Music in Special Education, 1972, Careers and Music, 1977; contbr. numerous articles, columns, musical arrangements to profl. publs. Recipient Distinguished Achievement award in journalism Ednl. Press. Assn. Am., 1973, 74, 75, 76, 78, 81. Mem. Music Educators Nat. Conf. (exec. staff 1970-77, 79-81), Mass. Music Educators Assn., Washington Edn. Press Assn. (steering com. 1972-74), Pi Kappa Lambda, Phi Mu Alpha Sinfonia. Home and office: 2314 Huidekoper Pl NW Washington DC 20007 *Life is a series of beginnings. Success is becoming an expert in beginnings and in maintaining love, happiness, and humor through each uncertainty and challenge.*

BESSON, MICHEL LOUIS, manufacturing company executive; b. Nancy, France, Mar. 14, 1934; came to U.S., 1980; s. Marcel Louis and Germaine (Savignac) B.; m. Marie Jose Ellie, May 19, 1967; children: Frederique, Pascal, Thomas. Diploma, Ecole Centrale des Arts et Mfrs., Paris, 1959; M.S., M.I.T., 1960. With Cellulose du Pin, 1962-80, plant mgr., 1969-71, dep. chief exec. officer, 1971-73, chief exec. officer, 1973-76, chmn. bd., chief exec. officer, 1976-80; chmn bd., chief exec. officer Pap de Condat, 1975-80; pres., vice chmn., chief exec. officer CertainTeed Corp., Valley Forge, Pa., 1980—; dir. Donohue Co., Ltd., Donohue St. Felicien, Inc., St. Gobain, Inc., Fidelcor, Inc. Bd. dirs. Greater Phila. C. of C., 1981—, Greater Phila. Internat. Network, 1981—; trustee Inst. Internat. Edn., 1982—; corp. ptnr. Phila. Mus. Art, 1981—; French fgn. trade advisor, 1982—; mem. Phila. Com. Fgn. Relations, 1982—; ptnr. Greater Phila. Partnership, 1982—. Served with French Air Force, 1960-62. Recipient Leadership award M.I.T., 1980. Club: Union League. Home: 536 Woodlea Ln Berwyn PA 19312 Office: PO Box 860 Valley Forge PA 19482

BEST, EUGENE CRAWFORD, JR., musician; b. Spartanburg, S.C., June 5, 1939; s. Eugene Crawford and Lucille (Gladney) B.; m. Yvette Marie Blanche Capillon, June 15, 1963; children—Stephanie Ann, Alan Charles. B.A., Duke U., 1961; Mus.M, New Eng. Conservatory of Music, 1963. Faculty Brevard (N.C.) Music Center, 1962, Dartmouth Coll. Congregation of the Arts, Hanover, N.H., 1964-69; prin. bassoonist New Orleans Symphony Orch., 1963—, Santa Fe Opera Co., 1971—, personnel mgr., 1977—; owner Best Bassoon Products, Metairie, La., 1971—; mem. faculty and coordinator adj. music faculty Music Sch., Loyola U., New Orleans, 1972—. Recipient Pi Kappa Lambda Performance award New Eng. Conservatory of Music, 1963; Angier B. Duke scholar, 1957-61. Mem. Internat. Conf. Symphony and Opera Musicians (regional vice-chmn. 1971—, del. 1971-73). Democrat. Home: 311 Magnolia Dr Metairie LA 70005 Office: 203 Carondelet St New Orleans LA 70130

BEST, JACOB HILMER, JR. (JERRY BEST), hotel executive; b. Evanston, Ill., July 21, 1937; s. Jacob Hilmer and Clara (Cornell) B.; m. Janet Patrica Donnelly, June 20, 1959; children—Jacob Hilmer, Peter B., Julie D. B.A. in Hotel Mgmt, Mich. State U., 1959; grad. Exec. Program, Stanford U., 1979. Sales rep. Sheraton Blackstone, Chgo., 1960-61, dir. mktg., 1961-63; asst. midwest regional sales mgr. Sheraton Corp., Chgo., 1961; asst. to owner Camelback Inn, Phoenix, 1963-64; dir. mktg. Marriott's Key Bridge, Washington, 1964-65, Saddle Brook Marriott, N.J., 1965-67, O'Hare Marriott, Chgo., 1967-69; resident mgr. Boston Marriott, 1969-70; gen. mgr. O'Hare Marriott, Chgo., 1970-72, Los Angeles Marriott Hotel, 1972-78; regional v.p. Marriott Hotels, 1978-80, corp. v.p., 1980-83, exec. v.p., 1983—; Bd. dirs., treas., mem. exec. com. Greater Los Angeles Visitors and Conv. Bur. Mem. Internat. Hotel Sales Mgrs. Assn., Calif. Hotel Motel Assn. (dir.), Los Angeles C. of C. Republican. Roman Catholic. Clubs: Palos Verdes Country, Palos Verdes Tennis. Home: 612 Epping Rd Palos Verdes Estates CA 90274

BEST, JAMES KNOWLAND, actor; b. Powderly, Ky., July 26, 1926; s. Armen and Essa B.; children—JoJami Kay, Janeen Jae, Gary Allen. Founder 1st sch. for techniques of motion picture acting, 1962; instr. various acting schs., also U. Miss., 1973-75. Appeared in: plays Goodbye Charlie; appeared in over 80 films since, 1951, including, Firecreek, Hooper, Ode to Billy Joe, The Caine Mutiny, Left-Handed Gun, Ride Lonesome, Black Gold, The President's Lady, Sounder; numerous TV appearances Dukes of Hazzard. Served with USAAF, 1943-47. Named to Hall of Fame U. Miss. Mem. Screen Actors Guild, Screen Dirs. Guild, Actors Equity Fund. Office: 1901 Ave of Stars 500 Los Angeles CA 90067

BEST, JOHN STEVENS, lawyer; b. Arlington Heights, Ill., May 18, 1906; s. Bruce Taylor and Genevieve (Stevens) B.; m. Pamelia Laurence, July 9, 1934 (dec.); children: Pamelia, Bruce, Mary Best Bartelt; m. Helen Meredith. A.B., U. Wis., 1928, LL.B., 1930. Bar: Wis. 1930; C.P.A., Wis. Practiced law, Milw., 1938—; assoc. Lecher, Michael, Whyte & Spohn, 1938-43; mem. firm Michael, Best & Friedrich, and predecessors, Milw., 1943—; income tax counsel, gen. counsel Wis. Tax Commn., 1930-38. Mem. Am., Wis., Milw. bar assns., Sigma Nu, Alpha Kappa Psi, Phi Alpha Delta, Beta Gamma Sigma, Order of Coif. Clubs: Milwaukee, University (Milw.); Madison. Home: Town Line Rd Menomonee Falls WI 53051 Office: 250 E Wisconsin Ave Milwaukee WI 53202

BEST, MELVIN HOLMES M., industrial design consultant, educator; b. Pasadena, Calif., May 8, 1923; s. Virgil Holmes and Clara Marie (Embree) B.; m. Magda Martha Best, Dec. 4, 1971; children: Diana Shulman, Randall Holmes. A.A., Pasadena City Coll., 1946; B.S. in Indsl. Design, U. So. Calif., 1949; M.A. in Sculpture, Calif. State U., 1966. Staff indsl. designer James, Pond & Clark, Pasadena, 1950-52; owner Melvin Best Indsl. Design, Pasadena, 1952-55; pres., founder Melvin Best Assocs., Pasadena, 1955-64; prin. Melvin Best Indsl. Design, Wilminton, Calif., 1964-80; pres. Melvin Best & Assocs., Topanga, Calif., 1980—; instr. indsl. design U. So. Calif., Los Angeles, 1951-56; instr. Pasadena City Coll., 1950-69; head indsl. design program, asst. prof. UCLA, 1965-73; v.p., dir. Build Rehab. Industries, North Hollywood, Calif., 1965-73. Inventor shopping cart, 1960, cordless dictation machine, 1965, folding bicycle, 1976; patentee in field. Mem. Pres.'s Com. for Employment of Handicapped, 1968—. Served as 2d lt. USAAF, 1942-45. Recipient Master Design award Product Engrng. Mag., 1960, Excellence in Indsl. Design award Western Electronics Conv., Los Angeles, 1960, 62, award for Samsonite Silhouette luggage Fashion Found. Am., 1958; Nat. Endowment for Arts grantee, 1981. Fellow Indsl. Designers Soc. Am. (regional v.p. 1975); mem. Soc. Mfg. Engrs., Calif. Assn. Cons. to Mgmt., Inst. Advancement Engrng. Home and Office: Skyridge 23124 Saddle Peak Rd Topanga CA 90290 *My work is my hobby, my hobby is my work. Regardless of day-to-day activity, always take time to plan the future. Use talent but get good education to support that talent.*

BEST, RICHARD LUNDELIUS, electrical engineer; b. Plainfield, N.J., Feb. 24, 1923; s. Fred Heller and Alice B.; m. Beth Arlene Inghraham, July 13, 1945 (div. 1980); children: David, Diane, Gerald, Lucinda; m. Hattie Best, Jan. 8, 1981. B.E.E., Cornell U., 1943; M.S. in Elec. Engring., MIT, 1952. Staff mem. MIT Radiation Lab., Cambridge, 1943-45, MIT Lincoln Lab., Lexington, Mass., 1947-58; chief engr. Digital Equipment, Marynard, Mass., 1959—. Mem. IEEE. Home: 73 Sears Rd Wayland MA 01778 Office: Digital Equipment 146 Main St Maynard MA 01778

BEST, ROBERT MULVANE, insurance company executive; b. Newcomerstown, Ohio, May 9, 1922; s. Chester R. and Beatrice (Mulvane) B.; m. Roselyn Welton, Aug. 12, 1944; children: Eric, Linda, Grant. B.S., Ohio State U., 1947. Agt. Bus. Men's Assurance Co. Am., Columbus, Ohio, 1946-48; mgr. group sales Security Mut. Life Ins. Co., Binghamton, N.Y., 1948-49, asst. supt. agys., 1949-51, dir. sales, 1951-53; asst. mgr. Bus. Men's Assurance Co., Columbus, 1953-61; v.p. in charge agys. Security Mut. Life Ins. Co. N.Y., Binghamton, 1961-66, exec. v.p., 1966-69, pres., 1969—, chief exec. officer, 1972—, also dir., chmn., chief exec. officer, 1977—; dir. Marine Midland Bank, Syracuse, Buckingham Mfg. Co., Binghamton, Utica Mut. Ins. Co., N.Y., Republic Franklin Ins. Co., Columbus, Ohio; mem. exec. com. Life Ins. Guaranty Corp., N.Y.C.; mem. N.Y. Ins. Bd., N.Y. State Adv. Bd. on Life Ins. Exams. Trustee Am. Coll., Bryn Mawr, Pa., Bus. Council N.Y. State, Inc.; bd. dirs., v.p. Valley Devel. Found., Binghamton; bd. dirs., exec. com. mem., Forum Harpur Coll. Found.; mem. council SUNY Forum Harpur Coll. Found.; bd. govs. Internat. Ins. Seminars; bd. dirs. Twin Tier Home Health Care, Inc., Binghamton.; mem. N.Y. State Bd. Regents. Served to lt. (j.g.) USNR, 1942-46. Mem. Am. Soc. C.L.U.'s (regional v.p. 1967-70), Am. Council Life Ins. (dir.), Life Ins. Council N.Y. (dir.), Life Underwriters Assn. Binghamton, Gen. Agts. and Mgrs. Assn., Broome County C. of C. (dir. 1970-75, pres. 1974). Clubs: Binghamton (dir. 1969-73); Oteyokwa Lake (Hallstead, Pa.) (pres. 1970-71); Economic (N.Y.C.)). Home: 41A Crestmont Rd Binghamton NY 13905 Office: Courthouse Sq Binghamton NY 13902

BEST, WILLIS D., international union official; b. Gas City, Ind., July 8, 1923; s. Walter and Lillian Opal (Gillespie) B.; m. Belva Jane Cook, Dec. 13, 1947; children: Kathleen Diane, Steven W., Kevin Dale, Theresa Jane. Student, Miss. State Coll., 1943, Wright Jr. Coll., Chgo., 1963-64, George Meany Center Labor Studies, 1969, 71, 72, 76, 77, 78, 80, 81, 82, 83. Signalman Pa. R.R., 1941-63; grand lodge rep. Brotherhood R.R. Signalmen, Mt. Prospect, Ill., 1963-69, dir. research, 1969-73, v.p., 1973-77, sec.-treas., 1977—; mem. Labor/Mgmt. Com.'s Task Force on Rail Transp., 1972—. Trustee Ill. Council Econ. Edn.; mem. labor research adv. com. Bur. Labor Stats., Dept. Labor. Served with USAAC, 1943-45; ETO, NATOUSA. Mem. Am. Legion. Democrat. Clubs: Rotary (Mt. Prospect); Masons (Logansport, Ind.). Home: 642 F Burgundy Ct Elk Grove Village IL 60007 Office: 601 W Golf Rd Mount Prospect IL 60056

BEST, WINFIELD JUDSON, writer, television producer, public relations consultant; b. Dillon, Mont., Oct. 1919; s. Floyd and Margaret (Pearson) B.; m. Lois Gustafson, 1948; children: Charles, Mark, Constance. B.S. summa cum laude, Northwestern U., 1943. Editorial assoc. Pub. Adminstrn. Clearing House, Chgo., 1946-48; dir. pub. relations Am. Mcpl. Assn., 1948-50; dir. research publs. HHFA, Washington, 1951-52; pub. relations dir. Planned Parenthood Fedn. Am., 1952-63; exec. v.p. Planned Parenthood-World Population, N.Y.C., 1963-69; exec. dir. Businessmen's Ednl. Fund, 1969-72; dir. communications and planning Carolina Population Ctr. U. N.C., Chapel Hill, lectr. population and ecology, 1972-78; founder Winfield Best Communications, 1976; freelance writer; communications and TV producer, cons. Communications Resources Found., 1980—. Author: (with Alan F. Guttmacher and Frederick S. Jaffe) The Complete Book of Birth Control, 1962, Planning Your Family, 1964, Birth Control and Love, 1969, (with Everett S. Lee and David L. Birch) America's Lands and Cities: Challenge of Transition, in press; contbr. numerous articles on population, sex, conservation, bus. mgmt. and corp. communications, problems of youth and aging to nat. mag.; Ency. Brit. Served with AUS, 1943-46. Mem. Nat. Assn. Sci. Writers, Am. Pub. Relations Soc., Population Assn. Am., Phi Beta Kappa, others. Episcopalian. Office: PO Box 148 Chapel Hill NC 27514

BESTHOFF, SYDNEY J., III, drug store company executive. Chmn., pres. K & B, Inc., New Orleans. Office: K & B Inc K & B Plaza Lee Circle New Orleans LA 70130§

BESTOR, CHARLES LEMON, composer, educator; b. N.Y.C., Dec. 21, 1924; s. Arthur Eugene and Jeanette Louise (Lemon) B.; m. Ann Newbold Elder, Nov. 1, 1952; children—Charles Elder, Geoffrey Grant, Phillip Russell, Leslie Ann, Wendy Lynn, Jennifer Lee. Student, Yale U., 1943-44; B.A., Swarthmore Coll., 1948; M.Mus., U. Ill., 1951; B.S., Juilliard Sch. Music, 1951; D.Mus. Arts, U. Colo, 1974. Mem. faculty Juilliard Sch. Music, 1951-53, 56-59, asst. to dean, 1951-53, concert mgr., 1952-59, bus. mgr., 1955-59; mgr. Juilliard Orch. European tour sponsored by U.S. State Dept., ANTA, 1958; asst. prof. music U. Colo., 1959-64; prof., dean Coll. Music, Willamette U., 1964-71; prof., head dept. music U. Ala., 1971-73; prof., chmn. dept. music U. Utah, 1973-77; prof., head music and dance U. Mass., Amherst, 1977—; Mem. exec. council N.W. Regional Inst. for Music in Contemporary Edn., 1966-68; assoc. dir. Peter Britt Music Festival, Jacksonville, Oreg., 1966-71; mem. Gov.'s Adv. Com. Arts and Humanities, 1963-71; vice chmn. Utah Opera Assn., 1974—; mem. grad. commn. Nat. Assn. Schs. Music, 1975-79; spl. cons. to State of Mass. Joint Ho. and Senate Com. on Reorgn. of Higher Edn., 1979—. Composer: Undine, 1951, Three Choruses, 1955, J.B, 1962, Piano Sonata, 1963, Measure for Measure, 1963, A Wind in the Willows, 1964, My Love and I, 1966, Suite for Strings, 1968; Concerto Grosso for Percussion and Orchestra, 1968, Improvisation I for Tape Recorder Alone, 1971, Improvisation II for Tape Recorder and Instruments, 1971, In Memoriam to texts by Malcolm X, 1969, Suite for Recorders, 1970, Poem for Choir and Electronic Synthesizer, 1971, Music for the Mountain, 1972, Concertino for Trumpet and Band, 1973, Variations for Violin and Piano Duo with Electronic Synthesizer, 1973, Twelve Short Movements for String Quartet, 1976, The Second Moom of Venus for Piano and Tape, 1976, Until a Time for orch, 1977, Day of the Lake for flute and tape, 1977, Make a Joyful Noise for choir and organ, 1978, Four Ostinati for tape, 1979, Lyric Variations for Oboe, Viola and Tape, 1980; composer: Overture to a Romantic Comedy for Orch., 1981, Suite for Alto Saxophone and Percussion, 1982. Bd. dirs. Salem Art Assn., 1965-69, Salem (Oreg.) Symphony, 1965-71, Salt Lake Chamber Music Soc., 1974-77, Leroy J. Robertson Found., 1965—; nat. bd. Snowbird Arts Found., 1977—. Served to lt. USNR, 1943-46. Mem. Nat. Assn. Composers (nat. council 1979—), Coll. Music Soc. (nat. council 1974-79), ASCAP, Am. Soc. Univ. Composers, Phi Beta Kappa, Pi Kappa Lambda, Phi Mu Alpha Sinfonia, Phi Kappa Psi (past mem. nat. exec. com.), Theta Alpha Phi, Omicron Delta Kappa. Office: U Mass Dept Music Amherst MA 01003

BESTOR, ROBERT, professional basketball team executive. V.p. for player personnel and mktg. dir. Golden State Warriors, NBA, Oakland, Calif. Office: Golden State Warriors Oakland Coliseum Arena Oakland CA 94621

BETCHER, ALBERT MAXWELL, physician; b. Jersey City, June 22, 1911; s. Jacob and Esther (Popkin) B.; m. Gertrude Weinberger, Sept. 22, 1940; children—Diane Trister Dodge, Peter Andrew, Robert William. B.S., N.Y. U., 1931; M.D., St. Louis U., 1935. Diplomate Am. Bd. Anesthesiology (dir. 1967-75, pres. 1974-75). Rotating intern Jersey City Med. Centre, 1935-36, resident anesthesiology, 1937-38, staff anesthetist, 1938-41, Hosp. Joint Diseases, N.Y.C., 1946—, dir. dept., 1947-76, also sec. med. adv. bd. and asso. editor hosp. jour., 1960-69, pres., 1970-76; dir. dept. anesthesiology, Beth Israel Med. Center, 1978-81, NYA CIC Hosp., 1981—; assoc. dir. profl. and acad. affairs Orthopedic Inst., N.Y.C., 1981—; asst. clin. prof. anesthesiology Albert Einstein Coll. Medicine, 1955-61, asso. clin. prof., 1961-67; prof. anesthesiology; Mt. Sinai Sch. Medicine, City U., N.Y., 1967—. Contbr. articles to profl. jours. Pres., chmn. bd. trustees Wood Library-Mus. Anesthesiology, 1956-69; trustee Anesthesia Found. Served to lt. col. M.C. AUS, 1941-46. Decorated Purple Heart, Bronze Star. Fellow Am. Coll. Anesthesiologists, A.C.P.; mem. Am. Soc. Anesthesiologists (treas. 1958-61, pres. 1962-63, Distinguished Service award 1975), N.Y. Acad. Medicine (sec. 1961-63, chmn. sect. anesthesiology and resuscitation 1963-64, trustee 1979—), N.Y. Soc. Anesthesiologists (pres. 1955, speaker ho. dels. 1956-59), N.Y. State Med. Soc. (chmn. anesthesiology 1959-60), A.M.A. (residency rev. com. for anesthesiology 1969-72, chmn. 1973), N.Y. Acad. Scis., A.A.A.S., Acad. Anesthesiology, World Fedn. Socs. Anesthesiologists (del., chmn. finance com., U.S.A. mem. exec. com). Home: 1435 Lexington Ave New York NY 10028 Office: 301 E 17 St New York NY 10003

BETCHKAL, JAMES JOSEPH, editor; b. Racine, Wis., Mar. 11, 1936; s. Herbert M. and Frances (Cetrano) B.; m. Ann Vernon, June 23, 1956; children: Janet Ann, Mark James. B.S., U. Miami, 1956; postgrad., U. Wis., 1957, Northwestern U., 1959. Asst. editor Actual Specifying Engr., Chgo., 1956-58; mng. editor Nation's Schs. Mag., Chgo., 1959-63; editor The Record, Oak Park, Ill., 1963; exec. editor Pioneer Newspapers, Inc., Oak Park, 1964-68; editor, pub. Am. Sch. Bd. Jour., Evanston, Ill., then Am. Sch. Bd. Jour., Washington, 1968-78; editor-in-chief, pub. The Exec. Educator and asso. exec. dir. Nat. Sch. Bds. Assn., Washington, 1978—; instr. folio Nat. Mag. Conf., 1977-78; instr. Sci. Research Assos., Chgo., 1964, No. Ill. U., DeKalb, summer 1966. Gen. chmn. Schaumburg Twp. (Ill.) United Fund, 1966, Stars and Stripes charity cotillion, 1966; mem. Hoffman Estates (Ill.) Police Commn., 1966-67; bd. dirs. Pathfinder council Boy Scouts Am., 1965. Recipient Editorial award Ill. Press Assn., 1966, award of Merit, Boy Scouts Am., 1966, Assn. Sch. Bus. Ofcls. U.S. and Can., 1960; All-Am. award Ednl. Press Assn. Am., 1970, 71, 72, 75, 76. Mem. Nat. Newspaper Assn., Edn. Writers Assn. Am., Am. Soc. Assn. Execs., Soc. Nat. Assn. Publs. (dir. 1972—, pres. 1977-78). Home: 4927 MacArthur Blvd NW Washington DC 20007 Office: 1680 Duke St Alexandria VA 22314

BETHE, HANS ALBRECHT, physicist, educator; b. Strassburg, Alsace-Lorraine, July 2, 1906; U.S., 1935; s. Albrecht Theodore and Anna (Kuhn) B.; m. Rose Ewald, 1939; children: Henry, Monica. Ed. Goethe Gymnasium, Frankfurt on Main, U. Frankfort; Ph.D., U. Munich, 1928; D.Sc., Bklyn. Poly. Inst., 1950, U. Denver, 1952, U. Chgo., 1953, U. Birmingham, 1956, Harvard U., 1958. Instr. in theoretical physics univs. of Frankfort, Stuttgart, Munich and Tubingen, 1928-33; lectr. univs. of Manchester and Bristol, Eng., 1933-35; asst. prof. Cornell U., 1935, prof., 1937-75, prof. emeritus, 1975—; dir. theoretical physics div. Los Alamos Sci. Lab., 1943-46; Mem. Presdl. Study Disarmament, 1958; mem. President's Sci. Adv. Com., 1956-60. Author: Mesons and Fields, 1953, Elementary Nuclear Theory, 1957, Quantum Mechanics of One-and Two-Electron Atoms, 1957, Intermediate Quantum Mechanics, 1964; Contbr. to: books Handbuch der Physik, 1933, Reviews of Modern Physics, 1936-37, Phys. Rev. Recipient A. Cressy Morrison prize N.Y. Acad. Sci., 1938-40; Presdl. Medal of Merit, 1946; Max Planck medal, 1953; Enrico Fermi award AEC, 1961; Nobel Prize in physics, 1967; Nat. Medal of Sci., 1976. Fgn. mem. Royal Soc. London; mem. Am. Philos. Soc., Nat. Acad. Scis. (Henry Draper medal 1968), Am. Phys. Soc. (pres. 1954), Am. Astron. Soc. Office: Lab Nuclear Studies Cornell U Ithaca NY 14853

BETHELL, JOHN TORREY, editor; b. Montclair, N.J., Aug. 1, 1932; s. John Warren and Elizabeth Torrey (Johnson) B.; m. Helen Marie Delage, Oct. 13, 1962; children: Sara Torrey, Hugh Rhys, Thomas Burke. A.B. magna cum laude, Harvard U., 1954. Reporter, editor Essex County Newspapers, Gloucester, Mass., 1949-54; editor McGraw-Hill, Inc., N.Y.C., 1955-66, Harvard Mag., Cambridge, Mass., 1966—. Pres. Harvard Pierian Found.; mem. Trustees of the Charity of Edward Hopkins. Mem. Signet Assocs., Phi Beta Kappa. Episcopalian. Clubs: Tavern (Boston); Manchester Yacht, Waxahachie (Tex.) Striders, Ware St. A.C. Home: 59 School St Manchester MA 01944 Office: 7 Ware St Cambridge MA 02138

BETHKE, ROBERT HARDER, investment banker; b. Chgo., Mar. 12, 1916; s. William and Florence (Gaumnitz) B.; m. Patricia Davis, Dec. 16, 1939; children: Robert Davis, William Milford. B.S., U. Chgo., 1937. With J.P. Morgan & Co., N.Y.C., 1937-39; with Discount Corp. of N.Y., 1939—, pres., 1974—, chmn. exec. com., dir., 1967—, chmn. bd., 1978-81; ind. counsellor U.S. Steel and Carnegie Pension Fund, N.Y.C.; dir. N.Y. Futures Exchange Inc., Chem. Fund, Inc., Internat. Investors Inc., Discount Corp. N.Y. Futures, Union Cash Mgmt. Fund, Inc., N.Y.C.; speaker in field treasury financing and money markets; mem. financial adv. com. U.S. Postal Service, 1973-77. Mem. planning bd. North Castle, N.Y., 1953-63; Pres., trustee North Castle Free Library, Armonk, N.Y., 1955-60; vice chmn., Greenburgh (N.Y.) Bd. Edn., 1950-52; mem. finance com. N.Y.C. Mission Soc., 1961-78; mem. fin. com. Nat. Council Chs., N.Y.C. Served to lt. col. AUS, 1942-46. Decorated Legion of Merit; recipient Alumni Citation U. Chgo., 1960. Mem. Am. Finance Assn., Am. Econ. Assn., Pub. Fin. Assn., Securities Industry Assn. (past chmn. and mem. U.S. Treasury and fed. agy. com. 1966-80), Assn. Primary Dealers in U.S. Govt. Securities (dir. 1977-80), Pilgrims of Am., Alpha Delta Phi. Clubs: Whippoorwill Country (Armonk); Economic (N.Y.C.). Home: 58 Whippoorwill Rd Armonk NY 10504 Office: 58 Pine St New York NY 10005

BETHUNE, EDWIN R., JR., congressman; b. Pocahontas, Ark., Dec. 19, 1935; m. Lana Douthit; children—Paige, Sam. Student, Little Rock Jr. Coll., 1957-58; B.S., U. Ark., 1961, J.D., 1963. Bar: Ark. bar 1963. Agt. FBI, 1964-68; pros. atty. White County, Ark., 1970-71; practice law, Searcy, Ark., 1972-78; chmn. Fed. Home Loan Bank Bd., 9th Dist., 1973-77; mem. 96th-98th Congresses from 2d Ark. Dist., mem. banking com., budget com.; chmn. procedural com. Ark. Criminal Code Revision Commn., 1970-75. Chmn. bd. 1st United Meth. Ch., Searcy, 1972-74. Served with USMC, 1954-57. Republican. Office: 1535 Longworth House Office Bldg Washington DC 20515

BETKOWSKI, WALTER CHRISTOPHER, computer scientist; b. N.Y.C., Aug. 18, 1939; s. Walter Joseph and Helen (Klozko) B.; children—Anne P., Susan M., Jean M. B.A., Fordham U., 1961; postgrad., UCLA, 1961-62; cert. computer programming, Baruch Coll. CCNY, 1981. Coll. traveler Am. Book Co., Calif., 1961-63; field editor West Coast, 1963-65, humanities editor, N.Y.C., 1965-68; mng. editor adult trade dept. G.P. Putnam Sons, N.Y.C., 1968—; sr. editor David McKay Co., Inc., 1976—; assoc. Paul R. Reynolds Inc., N.Y.C., 1977-82; mgr. quality assurance Info. Sci., Montvale, N.J., 1982—. Mem. L.I. Yacht Racing Assn. Club: Midget Ocean Racing. Home: 4 E 95th St New York NY 10028 Office: 95 Chestnut Ridge Rd Montvale NJ 07645

BETO, GEORGE JOHN, clergyman, educator; b. Hysham, Mont., Jan. 19, 1916; s. Louis H. and Margaret (Witsma) B.; m. Marilynn Knippa, Mar. 5, 1943; children—Dan, Lynn, Mark, Beth. Student, Concordia Coll., Milw., 1930-35, Concordia Sem., St. Louis, 1935-37, 38-39; B.A., Valparaiso U., 1938; M.A., U. Tex., 1944, Ph.D., 1955. Instr. Concordia Coll., Austin, Tex., 1939-49; pres. 1949-59; vis. instr. U. Tex., 1944; pres. Concordia Theol. Sem., Springfield, Ill., 1959-62; dir. Tex. Dept. Corrections, Huntsville, 1962-72; distinguished prof. Sam Houston State U., Huntsville, 1972—. Dir. 1st Nat. Bank, Palestine, Tex. Sec. Tex. Bd. Corrections, 1953-59; mem. Ill. Parole and Pardon Bd., 1961-62, Tex. Youth Council, 1975—; Am. del. UN Conf. on Prevention Crime and Treatment Offender, Kyoto, Japan, 1970 Am. del. UN Conf. on Prevention Crime and Treatment Offender, Geneva, 1975; mem. commn. on correctional facilities and services Am. Bar Assn.; mem. Tex. Constl. Revision Commn., 1973-74. Recipient Tex. Heritage Found. medal for devel. ednl. system Tex. Prison System; Distinguished Alumnus award U. Tex., 1971; E. R. Cass award, 1972. Mem. Am. Correctional Assn. (past pres.), Quarter Horse Assn., Phi Delta Kappa, Alpha Delta Kappa. Lutheran. Club: Citadel (Austin). Home: Wits End Ranch PO Box 1296 Huntsville TX 77340

BETTELHEIM, BRUNO, psychologist, retired educator, author; b. Vienna, Austria, Aug. 28, 1903; came to U.S., 1939, naturalized, 1944; s. Anton and Paula (Seidler) B.; m. Trude Weinfeld, May 14, 1941; children: Ruth, Naomi, Eric. Ph.D., U. Vienna, 1938. Research assoc. Progressive Edn. Assn., U. Chgo., 1939-41; assoc. prof. psychology Rockford (Ill.) Coll., 1942-44; asst. prof. ednl. psychology U. Chgo., 1944-47, assoc. prof., 1947-52, prof., 1952-73, Stella M. Rowley Distinguished Service prof. edn., prof. psychology and psychiatry, 1963-73; head Sonia Shankman Orthogenic Sch., 1944-73. Author: (with Morris Janowitz) Dynamics of Prejudice, 1950, Love is Not Enough: The Treatment of Emotionally Disturbed Children, 1950, Symbolic Wounds, 1954, Truants from Life, 1955, The Informed Heart, 1960, Dialogues with Mothers, 1962, The Empty Fortress, 1967, The Children of the Dream, 1969, A Home for the Heart, 1974, The Uses of Enchantment, 1976, (with Karen Zelan) On Learning to Read: The Child's Fascination with Meaning, 1982, Freud and Man's Soul, 1983, (with Morris Janowitz) Surviving, 1979; Contbr.: articles, essays to popular, profl. publs. Surviving. Fellow Am. Psychol. Assn., Am. Orthopsychiat. Assn.; mem. Am. Philos. Assn., AAUP, Am. Sociol. Assn., Chgo. Psychoanalytic Soc., Am. Acad. Edn. Democrat. Home: 1 Sierra Ln Portola Valley CA 94025 *

BETTENHAUSEN, ELIZABETH ANN, theology educator; b. Mobridge, S.D., July 31, 1942; d. Elmer W. and Dorothy M. (Zwicker) B. Student, Yankton Coll., 1960-61; B.A., U. Iowa, 1964; postgrad., U. Chgo., 1965-66; Ph.D., U. Iowa, 1971. Asst. prof. U. Wis.-Eau Claire, 1971-73; sec. social concerns Lutheran Ch. Am., N.Y.C., 1974-79; assoc., prof. theology Boston U., 1979—; mem. exec. council Luth. Ch. Am, 1980—; mem. Commn. for an New Luth. Ch., 1982—, Luth. (Orthodox Joint Commn.), 1978—, Faith & Order Nat. Council Chs., 1976-80. Author: The Equal Rights Amendment, 1979. Mem. Am. Acad. Religion, Soc. Christian Ethics (dir.), N.Am. Acad. Ecumenists. Lutheran. Office: Boston Univ Sch Technology 745 Commonwealth Ave Boston MA 02215

BETTERSWORTH, JOHN KNOX, educator, writer; b. Jackson, Miss., Oct. 1909; s. Horace Greely and Annie McConnell (Murphey) B.; m. Ann L. Stephens, Oct. 28, 1943; 1 dau., Nancy Elizabeth. B.A. magna cum laude, Millsaps Coll., 1929; Ph.D., Duke U., 1937. Instr. Jackson (Miss.) Central High Sch., 1930-35; grad. fellow Duke U., 1935-37, vis. prof., summer 1940; vis. instr. Asheville (N.C.) Normal, summer 1937; instr. history Miss. State U., Mississippi State, 1937; asst. prof. 1938-42, asso. prof., 1945-48, prof., 1948—, head dept. history and govt., 1948-61; dir. Social Sci. Research Center, 1950-60; asso. dean for liberal arts Sch. Arts and Sci., 1956-61, acad. v.p., 1961-77, dean faculty, 1966-77, spl. cons. to pres., 1977-79, prof. and v.p. emeritus, 1978—; text editor Miss. Hist. Commn., 1948-68; chmn. Miss. Research Clearing House, 1953-55; pres. So. Conf. Deans Faculty and Acad. Vice Pres.'s, 1967-68. Author: The People and Policies of a Cotton State in Wartime, 1943, People's College: A History of Mississippi State, 1953, Mississippi: A History, 1959, Mississippi in the Confederacy: As They Saw It, 1961, Your Old World Past, 1960, Mississippi: Yesterday and Today, 1965, New World Heritage, 1968, Your Mississippi, 1975, People's University: The Centennial History of Mississippi State, 1980, Mississippi: The Land and The People, 1981; co-author: This Country of Ours, 1965, South of Appomattox, 1959; contbg. author: A History of Mississippi, 1973; contbr.: articles to profl. publs.; founder, pub. The Miss. Quar; editor, 1946-56. Pres. Mississippians for ETV, 1972-73; founding pres. Friends of the Arts in Miss., 1977-80; trustee Miss. Dept. Archives and History, 1955—; chmn. Miss. Hist. Preservation Rev. Bd., 1979—; mem. Miss. Commn. on Jud. Performance, 1979—. Served as lt. (j.g.) USNR, 1942-45; instr. Naval Indoctrination Sch.; Tucson. Fellow Internat. Inst. Arts and Letters, mem. Miss. Hist. Soc. (dir. 1953—, v.p. 1955-56, pres. 1961-62), Am., Miss., So. hist. assns., Phi Beta Kappa, Omicron Delta Kappa, Phi Kappa Phi, Phi Alpha Theta, Alpha Tau Omega. Democrat. Episcopalian. Club: Starkville Rotary (pres. 1951-52). Home: 401 Broad St Starkville MS 39759 Office: Drawer B Mississippi State MS 39762

BETTI, JOHN A., automobile manufacturing company executive; b. Ottawa, Ill., Jan. 6, 1931; s. Louis and Ida (Dallari) B.; m. Joan Doyle, Aug. 22, 1953; children: Diane Marie, Denise Marie, Donna Marie, Joan Marie. B.S. in Mech. Engring, Ill. Inst. Tech., 1952; M.S. in Engring, Chrysler Inst. Engring., 1954; postgrad., U. Detroit, 1963. Registered profl. engr., Mich. Student engr. to asst. chief engr. Chrysler Corp., 1952-62; with Ford Motor Co., 1962—, chief light truck engr., chief engine engr., chief car planning mgr., chief car engr., then v.p., gen. mgr. truck ops., 1975-76; v.p. product devel. Ford of Europe, Inc., Warley, Essex, Eng., 1976-79; also dir.; v.p. powertrain and chassis ops. Ford N.Am., 1979—; chmn. bd. Ford Caribbean, Ensite Ltd., 1977-79; dir. Ford of Ger., 1978; past instr. Lawrence Inst. Engring., Wayne State U., Detroit; bd. dirs. Truck Hist. Mus., 1975-76; exec. com. Western Hwy. Inst. Chmn. bd. govs.; Marian High Sch., Detroit, 1971-73. Bd. dirs. Mich. Opera Theatre, 1982. Recipient Alumni Profl. Achievement award Ill. Inst. Tech., 1980; John Morse Meml. scholar. Mem. Soc. Automotive Engrs. (fin. com.), Tau Beta Pi, Pi Tau Sigma, Alpha Sigma Phi. Clubs: Bloomfield Hills (Mich.) Country; Renaissance (Detroit). Home: Bloomfield Hills MI Office: Ford Motor Co NAm Automotive Ops PO Box 1522-A Rotunda Dr at Southfield Rd Dearborn MI 48121

BETTINGHAUS, ERWIN PAUL, univ. dean; b. Peoria, Ill., Oct. 28, 1930; s. Erwin Paul and Paula (Bretscher) B.; m. Carole Irma Overmier, Apr. 5, 1952; children—Karen Lee, Joyce Ann, Bruce Alan. B.A., U. Ill., 1952, Ph.D., 1959; M.A., Bradley U., 1953. Instr. Mich. State U., East Lansing, 1958-60, asst. prof., 1960-64, asso. prof., 1964-69, prof., 1969—, chmn. dept. communication, 1972—; dean Coll. Communication Arts and Scis., 1976—; vis. prof. U. Okla., 1970-71. Author: The Nature of Proof, 1971, Persuasive Communication, 1978. Served with Med. Service Corps U.S. Army, 1953-56. Mem. AAAS, Am. Psychol. Assn., Internat. Communication Assn., Speech Communication Assn., Assn. for Edn. in Journalism. Home: 1200 Bryant Dr East Lansing MI 48823

BETTMANN, OTTO LUDWIG, picture archivist, graphic historian; b. Leipzig, Germany, Oct. 15, 1903; came to U.S., 1935, naturalized, 1939; s. Hans and Charlotte (Frank) B.; m. Anne Clemens Gray, Mar. 4, 1938. Ph.D., U. Leipzig, 1927, M.S. in L.S, 1932. Asso. editor C.F. Peters Co. (music pubs.), Leipzig, 1927-28; editor Axel Juncker Pub., Berlin, 1928-30; curator rare books Prussian State Art Library, Berlin, 1930-33; founder picture library on history civilization, N.Y.C., 1941, propr., pres., 1973-81; founder Picture House Press, Inc., pictorial research pubs., advt. agys., TV producers; picture editor, cons. graphic history, organizer picture filing systems; adj. prof. history Fla. Atlantic U., Boca Raton, 1973-80. Author: (with Bellamy Partridge) As We Were, Family Life in America, 1946, (with John Durant) A Pictorial History of American Sports, 1952, A Pictorial History of Medicine, 1956, (with Van Wyck Brooks) Our Literary Heritage, 1956, (with Paul H. Lang) A Pictorial History of Music, 1960, The Bettmann Portable Archive, 1966, The Good Old Days-They were Terrible, 1974, A Word from the Wise, 1977, The Bettmann Archive Picture History of the World, 1978. Home: 2600 S Ocean Blvd Boca Raton FL 33432 Office: 855 Federal Hwy Boca Raton FL 33432

BETTS, AUSTIN WORTHAM, retired research company executive; b. Westwood, N.J., Nov. 22, 1912; s. Irving Wilcox and Bessie Harris (Boardman) B.; m. Edna Jane Paterson, Dec. 8, 1934; children: Jerry W., Lee W., Lynn P. B.S., U.S. Mil. Acad., 1934; M.S., Mass. Inst. Tech., 1938. Commd. 2d lt. U.S. Army, 1934, advanced through grades to lt. gen., 1966; dist. engr. Bermuda Dist., U.S. Engr. Dept., 1942-43; engr. 14th Air Force, 1944-45; asso. dir. Los Alamos Sci. Lab., 1946-48; chief atomic energy br. G-4, Dept. Army, 1949-52; exec. to chief research and devel. Dept. Army, 1952-54; mil. exec. to spl. asst. of dir. guided missiles Office Sec. Def., 1957-59; dir. Advanced Research Projects Agy., Office Sec. Def., 1959-61; dir. mil. application AEC, 1961-64; dep. chief research and devel. Dept. Army, 1964-66, chief research and devel., 1966-70; retired, 1970; sr. v.p. S.W. Research Inst., San Antonio, 1971-83. Mem. Assn. U.S. Army, Nat. Security Indsl. Assn., Inst. Environ. Scis., Air Pollution Control Assn., Soc. Research Adminstrs., Soc. Am. Mil. Engrs., Am. Inst. Aeros. and Astronautics, Am. Indsl. Preparedness Assn., Sigma Xi. Presbyterian. Club: Masons. Home: 6414 View Point San Antonio TX 78229 *Early in my life I was impressed by an autobiographical sketch of a great leader who commented that his goal in life was simply to leave tracks. I took that guidance for my own and have since tried to orient all my major activities toward service, those services to be of such nature that I can look back with pride at the tracks I have left behind me.*

BETTS, BERT A., former state treasurer; b. San Diego, Aug. 16, 1923; s. Bert A. and Alma (Jorgenson) B.; m. Barbara Lang; children: Terry Lou, Linda Sue, Sara Ellen, Bert Alan, Randy Wayne, LeAnn, John Chauncey, Frederick P., Roby F., Bruce H. B.B.A., Calif. Western U., 1950. C.P.A., Calif. Accountant John R. Gillette, 1946-48; partner Gillette & Betts, 1949-50; pvt. accounting practice, 1951-54; partner Betts & Munden, Lemon Grove, Calif., 1954-57; sr. partner Bert A. Betts & Co., 1958-59; treas. State of Calif., 1958-67; prin. Bert A. Betts & Assos., 1967-77; chief exec. officer Internat. Prodn. Assos., 1968-72; dir. Lifetime Communities Inc.; gen. partner Sacramento Met. Airport Properties 4, Ltd., 1970—. Mem. Lemon Grove Sch. Bd., 1954-57; Calif. chmn. Max Baer Heart Fund; state employees chmn. Am. Cancer Soc., 1962-64, bd. dirs. county br., 1963-69, Sacramento County campaign chmn., mem. exec. com., 1965; pres. Sacramento chpt., 1967-68. Served as 1st lt. USAAF, 1942-45. Decorated D.F.C. Air medal with four clusters; recipient Louisville award Municipal Finance Officers Assn. U.S. and Can., 1963; honored by Calif. Municipal Treas.'s Assn., 1964. Mem. Nat. Assn. State Auditors, Comptrollers and Treas.'s, Municipal Forum N.Y., Calif. Soc. C.P.A.'s, San Diego Squadron Air Force Assn. (past vice comdr.), Am. Legion, VFW, Native Sons Golden West, Foresters, Beta Alpha Psi (hon.), Alpha Kappa Psi (hon.). Presbyn. Clubs: Masons, Eagles; Men's (pres.), Lions (Lemon Grove) (treas.); Commonwealth.). Home: 441 Sandburg Dr Sacramento CA 95819 also Betts Ranch East Levee Rd Elverta CA 95626

BETTS, DAVID ANDERSON, diplomat; b. Clearfield, Pa., Aug. 25, 1928; s. William Wilson and Bernyce (Anderson) B. B.S., U.S. Mil. Acad., 1951. Vice consul Am. embassy, Ankara, Turkey, 1956-58, San Jose, Costa Rica, 1960-62; consul Am. embassy, Budapest, Hungary, 1962-65, Palermo, Italy, 1966-67, Saigon, Vietman, 1968-69; consul gen. Am. embassy, Paris, 1970-73, Manila, 1973-76, Munich, Germany, 1976-78, Montreal, Que., Can., 1978-79, Frankfurt, Germany, 1979—. Served with U.S. Army, 1946-47; to 1st lt., 1951-54. Office: US Consulate General Siesmayerstrasse 21 6000 Frankfurt Am Main Germany

BETTS, DONALD DRYSDALE, university dean, physics educator; b. Montreal, Que., Can., May 16, 1939; s. Wallace Havelock and Mary (Drysdale) B.; m. Vilma Florence Mapp, June 5, 1954 (div. 1980); children: Malcolm Robert, Sylvia Margaret, Eric Kelvin, Douglas Russell. B.S. with first class honors, Dalhousie U., 1950, M.S., 1952; Ph.D., McGill U., 1955. NRC postdoctoral fellow, Edmonton, Alta., Can., 1955-56; asst. prof. physics U. Alta., Edmonton, 1956-61, assoc. prof., 1961-66, dir. Theoretical Physics Inst., 1972-78, prof. physics, 1966-80; dean arts and sci. Dalhousie, Halifax, N.S., Can., 1980—; dir. Theoretical Physics Summer Sch., Banff, Alta., Can., 1968, 76; chmn. Internat. Commn. on Thermodynamics and Statis. Mechanics, 1972-75; sci. commentator Can. Broadcasting Corp., Edmonton, Alta., 1977-80; chmn. organizing com. Statphys 14, Edmonton, 1977-80; bd. dirs. Applied Microelectronic Inst., Halifax, 1981-83. Contbr. articles to profl. jours. Pres. Friends of Can. Peace Research Inst., Edmonton, 1961-62; dir. Sci. for Peace, Toronto, Ont., 1981-83. NRC Can. research operating grantee, 1956-77; USAF Office Sci. Research, research operating grantee, 1967-70; natural Sci. and Engring. Research Council Can., research operating grantee, 1977-83. Fellow Royal Soc. Can.; mem. Can. Assn. Physicists (pres. 1969-70), Sci. Tech. and Engring. Assn. Can. (v.p. 1970). Club: Dalhousie Faculty (Halifax). Home: 8 Simcoe Pl Halifax NS Canada B3M 1H3 Office: Faculty Arts and Sci Dalhousie U Halifax NS Canada B3H 4H6

BETTS, DORIS JUNE WAUGH, author, English educator; b. Statesville, N.C., June 4, 1932; d. William Elmore and Mary Ellen (Freeze) Waugh; m. Lowry Matthews Betts, July 5, 1952; children: Doris LewEllyn, David Lowry, Erskine Moore II. Student, Woman's Coll., U. N.C., 1950-53, U. N.C., 1954. Newspaperwoman Statesville Daily Record, 1950-51, Chapel Hill (N.C.) Weekly and News-Leader, 1953-54, Sanford Daily Herald, 1956-57; editorial staff N.C. Democrat, newspaper, 1961-62; editor Sanford (N.C.) News Leader, 1962; lectr. creative writing, English dept. U. N.C., Chapel Hill, 1966—, dir. Freshman-Sophomore English, 1972-76, assoc. prof., 1974-78, prof., 1978—, Alumni Disting. prof., 1981—, dir. Fellows program, 1975-76, asst. dean Honors program, 1979-81, chmn. faculty, 1983—; vis. lectr. creative writing Duke U., 1971; staff Ind. U. Summer Writers Conf., 1972, 73; mem. bd. Asso. Writing Programs; mem. lit. panel Nat. Endowment for Arts, 1979-81, chmn., 1981. Author: story collections The Gentle Insurrection, 1954, Beasts of the Southern Wild, 1973; novel Tall Houses in Winter, 1957 (Sir Walter Raleigh award for best fiction by Carolinian 1957), Scarlet Thread (Sir Walter Raleigh award 1965), The Astronomer & Other Stories, 1966, The River to Pickle Beach, 1972, Heading West, 1981; Contbr. stories collections, anthologies.; Editor: Young Writer at Chapel Hill, 1968. Mem. N.C. Tercentenary Commn., 1961-62, Sanford City Sch. Bd., 1965-71. Recipient short story prize Mademoiselle mag., booklength fiction prize G. P. Putnam-U. N.C., 1954; N.C. medal for lit., 1975; Guggenheim fellow, 1958-59. Mem. N.C. Writers Assn. Office: Dept English U NC Chapel Hill NC 27514

BETTS, EMMETT ALBERT, psychologist, author; b. Elkhart, Iowa, 1903; s. Albert Henry and Grace L. (Greenwood) B. B.S., Des Moines U., 1925; M.S., U. Iowa, 1928, Ph.D., 1931; LL.D., Sioux Falls (S.D.) Coll., 1972. Vocat. dir. indsl. arts and agr., Orient, Iowa, 1922-24; staff physics dept. Des Moines U., 1924-25; supt. schs., Northboro, Iowa, 1925-29; research asst. U. Iowa, 1929-31; sch. psychologist, elementary prin. Shaker Heights, Ohio, 1931-34; dir. tchr. edn., dir. summer sessions State Tchrs. Coll., Oswego, N.Y., 1934-37; research prof., dir. reading clinic sch. edn. Pa. State U., 1937-45; prof. psychology, dir. reading clinic, dept. psychology Temple U., 1945-54; dir. Betts Reading Clinic, Haverford, Pa., 1954-61; research prof. dept. psychology (Sch. Edn.), Miami U., Coral Gables, Fla., 1961; vis. prof. numerous colls. and univs. U.S., 1930—. Editor,contbr.: My Weekly Reader, 1938-69; editor in chief Education, 1957-69; asso. editor: Jour. Ednl. Research; adv. editor: Highlights for Children; contbg. editor: Jour. Exptl. Edn; reading editor Education, 1948-69; mem. editorial bd., 1948-57, 69—; contbg. editor: Reading Tchr. jour, Internat. Reading Assn., 1971—; author vision tests; Author: Foundation of Reading Instruction, rev. edit, 1957, Betts Basic Readers, 1970; others; contbr. articles to profl. jours. V.p., bd. dirs. Nat. Aerospace Edn. Council, 1956—; Chmn. adv. bd. Winter Haven Lion's Research Found., Inc., 1963—; bd. dirs., chmn. state orgn. com. Internat. Council for Improvement of Reading Instruction; trustee Lake Placid (N.Y.) Edn. Found., 1968—. Recipient Apollo award, 1962; Founders award Internat. Reading Assn., 1971; citation of merit, 1971; Gold medal Phonemic Spelling Council; Crown Circle award Nat. Congress Aerospace Edn.-FAA-NASA-USAF-CAP, 1979; 1977; others. Fellow Am. Psychol. Assn. (diplomate sch. psychology, mem. com. sch. psychol. services for exceptional children), Distinguished Service Found. Optometry, Grad. Soc. Optometry; mem. Soc. Advancement Edn., Nat. Council Research in English (chmn. editorial com.), Nat. Conf. Research Elementary Sch. English (co-founder 1932), Nat. Soc. Study of Edn., Internat. Reading Assn. (life), Nat. Council Tchrs. English, Eastern Psychol. Assn., Internat. Council Exceptional Children (adv. com.), NEA, AAUP, Am. Assn. Sch. Adminstrs. (life), Am. Assn. Applied Psychology, Am. Edn. Research Assn., Nat. Aeronautics Assn., Aircraft Owners and Pilots Assn., AAUS, Silver Wings (hon. life), Assn. Childhood Edn., Fla., Dade County, Pa. psychol. assns., Internat. Council Exceptional Children, Linguistic Soc. Am., N.Y., Pa. acads. sci., Pa. Edn. Research Assn., Greater Miami Aviation Assn., LuLu Flying Squadron, Nat. Pilots Assn., Lafayette Escadrille, Delaware Valley Reading Assn. (hon. life mem.), Nat. Aerospace Edn. Assn. (hon. dir. 1972—), Simpler Spelling Assn. (dir. 1966, pres. 1967-71), Phonemic Spelling Council (pres. 1970—), Phi Delta Kappa, Phi Theta Pi Beta, Sigma Kappa, Psi Chi. Clubs: Masons, Shriners; Jockey (Miami); Lake Region Yacht and Country. Home: 144 Lake Mariam Rd SE Lakewood Estates Winter Haven FL 33880 *My teachers indoctrinated me with the work ethic, the need for both depth and breadth of productive scholarship, the necessity of an abundant library of selected materials relevant to my "new" and unique profession, the value of singleness of purpose, and scientific attitudes basic to ethical conduct.*

BETTS, FORREST RICHARD, guitarist, composer, vocalist; b. West Palm Beach, Fla., Dec. 12, 1943; s. Harold and Sarah Estora (Taylor) B.; m. Paulette Eghiazarian, May 15, 1977; children—Elena Christina, Jessica Leigh, Forrest Duane. Guitarist, Allman Brothers Band, 1969—; leader band, Dickey Betts and Great Southern, 1977-79 (Recipient eight Gold Album awards; four Platinum Album awards; Broadcast Music Inc. Citation of Achievement 1973, 74); Composer: In Memory of Elizabeth Reed, 1970, Blue Sky, 1972, Jessica, 1973, Rambling Man, 1973. Mem. AGVA, AFTRA, Am. Fedn. Musicians. Office: 412 Pleasant Valley Way West Orange NJ 07052

BETTS, HENRY BROGNARD, physician, educator; b. New Rochelle, N.Y., May 25, 1928; s. Henry Brognard and Marguerite Meredith (Denise) B.; m. Monika Christine Paul, Apr. 25, 1970. A.B., Princeton, 1950; M.D., U. Va., 1954. Diplomate: Am. Bd. Phys. Medicine and Rehab. Intern Cin. Gen. Hosp., 1954-55; resident, teaching fellow N.Y.U. Med. Center Inst. Rehab. Medicine, N.Y.C., 1958-63; practice medicine, specializing in phys. medicine and rehab., Chgo., 1963—; staff physiatrist Rehab. Inst. Chgo., 1963-64, asso. med. dir., 1964-65, med. dir., 1965-69, v.p., med. dir., 1969-75, exec. v.p., med. dir., 1975—; chmn. dept. rehab. medicine Northwestern U. Med. Sch., 1967—, prof., 1968—; cons. Northwestern Meml. Hosp., Chgo. Contbr. articles to profl. jours. Mem. steering com. United Cerebral Palsy, 1967—; Mem. med. adv. com. Nat. Paraplegia Found., 1969—; bd. dirs. Nat. Com. Arts for Handicapped, 1981—; mem. Gov.'s High Blood Pressure Adv. Bd., 1977—. Served with USNR, 1956-58. Named Physician of Year Ill. Gov.'s Com., 1964; commended by Ill. Gen. Assembly, 1967; cited for meritorious service Pres.'s Com. on Employment of Handicapped, 1965. Mem. Ill. Med. Soc. (chmn. com. on rehab. services), Assn. Acad. Physiatrist (pres. 1968-69), Am. Congress Rehab. Med. (med. adv. com., pres. 1976-77), Mid-m. Soc. Phys. Med. and Rehab. (pres. 1969). Home: 1727 N Orleans Chicago IL 60614 Office: 345 E Superior St Chicago IL 60611

BETTS, HOWARD M., ins. co. exec.; b. Howard County, Ind., Nov. 6, 1913; s. Frank and Arda (Ritchey) B.; m. Mary Ellen Long, Oct. 10, 1942; children—Marlynn Kay, Dee Ann. Grad., Kokomo (Ind.) Jr. Coll., 1935. With Grain Dealers Mut. Ins. Co., Indpls., 1936—, v.p., 1959-65, pres., 1965-79, chmn. bd., 1979—, also dir.; dir. Companion Ins. Co., Indpls., 1962—, pres., 1965-79, chmn. bd., 1979—; past dir. Am. Mut. Ins. Alliance; charter mem., past pres. Indpls. Fire and Marine Underwriters. Named adm. Nebr. Navy. Mem. Indpls. C. of C. Mem. Christian Ch. Clubs: Columbia (Indpls.); Rotary, Sagamore of the Wabash. Home: 1601 N Whitcomb Ave Indianapolis IN 46224 Office: 1752 N Meridian St Indianapolis IN 46202

BETTS, JAMES FRANKLIN, insurance holding company executive; b. Cleve., Apr. 6, 1932; s. John William and Loas Ann (Rodenhauser) B.; m. Martha Goebel, Dec. 26, 1952; children: Nancy, Susan, Elizabeth. B.S. in Bus. Adminstrn, Washington U., St. Louis, 1957. C.L.U. With New Eng. Mut. Life Ins. Co., 1950-72, v.p. sales, then sr. v.p., 1969-72; pres., chief exec. officer Life Ins. Co. Va., Richmond, 1973-79, chmn. bd., 1980—; v.p. Continental Group, Inc., 1979, exec. v.p., 1980—; pres., chief exec. officer Continental Fin. Services Co.; dir. Investors Mortgage Ins. Co., Va. Electric & Power Co., Central Fidelity Banks, Inc., Central Fidelity Bank, N.A., Lawyers Title Ins. Co., Western Employers, Inc. Mem. bd. visitors Va. Mil. Inst.; bd. dirs. Wolf Trap Found., Richmond Symphony, Richmond Ballet; campaign chmn. United Way Greater Richmond, 1981. Served with AUS, 1954-56. Recipient President's trophy New Eng. Mut. Life Ins. Co. Gen. Agts. Assn., 1969. Mem. Am. Soc. C.L.U.'s (past 1st v.p.), Nat. Assn. Life Underwriters, Forum Club Richmond. Roman Catholic. Club: Country of Va. Office: 6600 W Broad St Richmond VA 23230

BETTS, RICHARD FORREST, guitarist, song writer, vocalist; b. West Palm Beach, Fla., Dec. 12, 1943; s. Harold and Sarah Estora (Taylor) B.; m. Paulette Eghiazarian, May 15, 1977; children: Elena Christina, Jessica Leigh, Forrest Duane. Guitarist, vocalist The Allman Bros. Band, 1969—; band leader Dickey Betts and Great Southern, 1977-79; rec. artist Broadcast Music Inc. (BMI). Composer: song Ramblin Man, Blue Sky, Straight from the Heart, Angeline, Crazy Love. Recipient Citation of Achievement Broadcast Music Inc., 1973, 74, 8 gold albums, 4 platinum albums. Mem. AFTRA. Office: 412 Pleasant Valley Way West Orange NJ 07052

BETTS, ROBERT BUDD, advt. agy. exec.; b. Easton, Pa., Nov. 28, 1922; s. James A. and Vanetta (Rickards) B.; m. Emilie Woehrle, July 15, 1945; children—Dorothy Betts Brooks, Anne Louise, Robert Budd. B.S., Harvard U., 1944. Chmn. bd. William Esty Co., N.Y.C. Author: Along the Ramparts of the Tetons, 1978. Served with U.S. Army. Decorated Bronze Star medal. Clubs: Sleepy Hollow Country (Scarborough-on-Hudson, N.Y.); Lost Tree (North Palm Beach, Fla.); Sky (N.Y.C.); Jackson Hole (Wyo.) Golf and Tennis. Home: 12 Beekman Pl New York NY 10022 Office: William Esty Co 100 E 42d St New York NY 10017

BETZ, CHARLES W., manufacturing company executive; b. Chgo., Jan. 13, 1922; s. John L. and Florence (Jayne) B.; m. Shirley M. Barrett, Apr. 18, 1942; children: Charles W., John S., James E., Frederick L. B.S. in Mech. Engring, Eastern Mich. U., 1954; postgrad., Wayne State U., 1955-56. Project engr. Riley Stoker Corp., 1946-47, Tucker Corp., 1947-49, Kaiser-Frazer Corp., 1950-51; dir. research project Am. Metal Products Co., 1954-57; v.p. sales, dir. Alliance Ware, Inc., 1957-61; exec. v.p., dir. Briggs Mfg. Co., 1961-64; pres. Borroughs Mfg. Co., 1964-66, Lindsay Co. div. Union Tank Car, St. Paul, 1966-72, Acryltech Inc., 1972-74; owner C.W. Betz & Assos., St. Paul, 1974—; dir. Crown San. Pottery Co., Briggs-Ohio Co., Hycroft China Co., Am. Nat. Bank St. Paul, Gen. Marking Co. Bd. dirs. Actors Theatre of St. Paul. Served with AUS, 1942-46; ETO; served to capt. USAF, 1951-54. Mem. Triangle Frat., Stoic Honor Soc. (v.p.), Greater St. Paul C. of C. (dir.). Clubs: Chgo. Athletic Assn., Recess, Park, North Oaks Golf, 15 Grand Legion, St. Paul, Rotary, W. R. Yacht. Address: 2445 Londin Ln Saint Paul MN 55119

BETZ, EUGENE WILLIAM, architect; b. Dayton, Ohio, Jan. 12, 1921; s. Jesse Earl and Elizabeth Freda (Meyer) B.; m. Marjorie Lois Frank, Oct. 30, 1948; children—Douglas William, Gregory Vincent. B.S., U. Cin., 1944. Pres. Eugene W. Betz, Architects, Inc., Dayton, 1956—; Chmn. Bd. Building Standards and Appeals, 1960-63, Kettering Planning Commn., 1957-61. Served with AUS, 1944. Recipient Honor award Architects Soc. Ohio, 1967, 71; Award of Merit, 1968, 77, 78; Nation's Sch. Month award Nat. Council Schoolhouse Constrn., 1967; Nat. Citation Am. Assn. Sch. Adminstrs., 1967, 71; Masonry award of excellence, 1976, 78; Outstanding Health Care Facility award UCLA/Columbia U./Archtl. Record, 1980. Mem. AIA (nat. com. architecture for health), Am. Hosp. Assn., Am. Assn. Hosp. Planning. Clubs: Masons, Rotary. Home: 5561 Lotusdale Dr Dayton OH 45429 Office: 2223 S Dixie Ave Dayton OH 45409

BEUERLEIN, SISTER JULIANA, hospital administrator; b. Lawrenceburg, Tenn., June 19, 1921; d. John Adolph and Sophia (Held) B. R.N., St. Joseph's Sch. Nursing, Chgo., 1945; B.S. in Edn, DePaul U., 1947; M.S. in Nursing Edn, Marquette U., 1954; postgrad., St. Louis U. Operating room supr. St. Joseph's Hosp., Alton, Ill., 1945-48; dir. sch. of nursing and nursing service Providence Hosp., Waco, Tex., 1948-56; dir. sch. nursing and nursing service St. Joseph's Hosp., Chgo., 1956-62, asst. adminstr., 1962-63; adminstrv. asst. St. Mary's Hosp., Evansville, Ind., 1963-65, adminstr., 1965-73, pres. governing bd., 1965-73; adminstr. St. Joseph Hosp., Chgo., 1973-81, pres. governing bd., 1973-75; adminstr. St. Thomas Hosp., Nashville, 1981—; Mem. governing bd. St. Vincent's Hosp., Indpls., 1969-73; mem. governing bd. St. Mary's Hosp., Milw., 1974-75, chmn., 1978-79; mem. governing bd. Providence Hosp., Southfield, Mich., 1975-78, chmn. govering bd., 1977-78; mem. Chgo. Health Systems Agy., 1976-79; mem. governing bd. DePaul Community Health Center, Bridgeton, Mo., 1980—; mem. Am. Hosp. Assn. Commn. on Nursing, 1980—. Fellow Am. Coll. Hosp. Adminstrs. (com. on elections); mem. Cath., Tenn. hosp. assns. Address: 4200 Harding Rd Nashville TN 37205

BEUTEL, WILLIAM CHARLES, television host, news correspondent; b. Cleve., Dec. 12, 1930; s. William Charles and Stella Eileen (Forster) B.; m. Betty Adair Atwell, Sept. 20, 1980; children—Peter, Robin, Colby, Heather. A.B., Dartmouth Coll., 1953; postgrad., U. Mich. Law Sch., 1953-54. Newsman WGAR Radio, Cleve., 1957-59, WEWS-TV, 1959-60, CBS Radio, N.Y.C., 1960-62; newsman ABC-TV, N.Y.C., 1962—, London Bur. chief, 1968-70; anchorman WABC-TV, 1970—; host AM Am., 1975. (Recipient George Foster Peabody award for Eye of the Storm 1970). Served with U.S. Army, 1954-56. Mem. Assn. Radio and TV News Analysts, Nat. Acad. TV Arts and Scis. (bd. govs. N.Y. chpt. 1964, Emmy awards 1964, 65, 66, 67), Sigma Delta Chi, Phi Delta Theta. Club: Leash. *

BEUTLER, ALBERT JACOB, college president; b. Osceola, Ind., Feb. 20, 1929; s. Jacob Richard and Florence May (Enders) B.; m. Barbara Jean Heeter, Sept. 3, 1950; children: Nancy, Stephen, Amy Jean. B.A., Bethel Coll., Mishawaka, Ind., 1951; M.A., Winona Laeke Sch. Theology, 1959; Ph.D., Mich. State U., 1970. Dean of men Bethel Coll., 1951-60, dean of students, 1960-66, pres., 1974—; dean student services Ind. U., South Bend, 1966-74; mem. Student Assistance Commn. of Ind. Author: The Development of a Program of Higher Education in the United Missionary Church, 1959, The Founding and History of Bethel College, 1970. Bd. dirs. United Way of St. Joseph County, Ind., Jr. Achievement, South-Bend-Mishawaka; mem. Michiana Arts and Scis. Council; chmn. Bd. Higher Edn. of the Missionary Ch., Ft. Wayne, Ind., 1969-73; chmn. bd. Salvation Army, Mishawaka, 1971-73; bd. dirs. Urban Coalition St. Joseph County. Named Alumnus of Year Bethel Coll., 1966, Top Joe of St. Joseph County, 1977. Mem. Am. Assn. Higher Edn., Council Advancement Small Colls., Ind. Conf. Higher Edn., Ind. Colls. and Univs. Ind., South Bend-Mishawaka Area C. of C. (dir.), Phi Delta Kappa. Club: Lions (Mishawaka). Office: 1001 W McKinley St Mishawaka IN 46544

BEUTLER, ERNEST, physician, research scientist; b. Berlin, Sept. 30, 1928; U.S., 1936, naturalized, 1943; s. Alfred David and Kaethe (Italiener) B.; m. Brondelle Fleisher, June 15, 1950; children: Steven Merrill, Earl Bryan, Bruce Alan, Deborah Ann. Ph.B., U. Chgo., 1946, B.S., 1948, M.D., 1950. Intern U. Chgo. Clinics, 1950-51; resident in medicine 1951-53; asst. prof. U. Chgo., 1956-59; chmn. div. medicine City of Hope Med. Center, Los Angeles, 1959-78; chmn. dept. clin. research Scripps Clinic and Research Found., 1978—; clin. prof. medicine U. So. Calif., 1964-79, U. Calif., San Diego, 1979—; mem. hematology study sect. NIH, 1970-74; mem. med. adv. com. ARC, 1972-78. Author 8 books, numerous articles in med. jours.; mem. editorial bds. profl. jours. Mem. med. and sci. adv. council Cystic Fibrosis Found., 1976-78. Served with U.S. Army, 1953-55. Recipient Gairdner award, 1975. Mem. Nat. Acad. Scis., Am. Acad. Arts and Scis., Am. Assn. Physicians, Am. Soc. Clin. Investigation, Am. Soc. Hematology (mem. exec. com. 1968-72, v.p. 1977, pres. 1979), Am. Soc. Human Genetics (mem. exec. com. 1968-72). Jewish. Home: 4308 Caminito del Zafiro San Diego CA 92121 Office: 10666 N Torrey Pines Rd La Jolla CA 92037

BEUTLER, FREDERICK JOSEPH, info. scientist; b. Berlin, Oct. 3, 1926; U.S., 1936, naturalized, 1943; s. Alfred David and Kaethe (Italiener) B.; m. Suzanne Armstrong, Jan. 6, 1969; children—Arthur David, Kathryn Ruth, Michael Ernest. S.B., Mass. Inst. Tech., 1949, S.M., 1951; Ph.D., Calif. Inst. Tech., 1957. Mem. faculty U. Mich., Ann Arbor, 1957—, prof. info. and control engring., 1963—, chmn. computer info. and control engring., 1970-71, 77—; vis. prof. Calif. Inst. Tech., 1967-68; vis. scholar U. Calif. at Berkeley, 1964-65. Editorial cons.: Math. Rev, 1965-67, 75—; contbr. articles to profl. jours. and books. Bd. dirs. Ann Arbor Civic Theatre, 1976-78. Served with AUS, 1945-46. NSF research grantee, 1971-75, 76-81; Air Force Office Sci. Research grantee, 1970-74, 75-80; NASA grantee, 1959-69. Fellow IEEE; mem. Soc. Indsl. and Applied Math (council 1969-74, mng. editor Jour. Applied Math. 1970-75, editor Rev. 1967-70), Am. Math. Soc., Inst. Math. Statistics, Am. Soc. Engring. Edn. (exec. com. 1967-70), Am. Arbitration Assn., Econ. Club Detroit. Club: Barton Boat. Home: 1717 Shadford Rd Ann Arbor MI 48104

BEVAN, DONALD EDWARD, marine scientist, university dean; b. Seattle, Feb. 23, 1921; s. Arther and Violette B.; m. Tanya L. Potapova, Sept. 8, 1971. B.S., U. Wash., 1948, Ph.D., 1959; postdoctoral student, Moscow U., 1959-60. Sr. fisheries biologist U. Wash., Seattle, 1955-59, lectr., research asst. prof., 1959-61, research asso. prof, 1961-64, asso. prof., 1964-66, prof., 1966—, asso. dean, 1965-69, dir., 1968-69, asst. v.p. research, 1969-77, adj. prof., 1973, acting dean and prof., 1977, asso. dean and prof. Inst. Marine Studies, 1977-80, adj. prof. Inst. Marine Studies, 1978—, dean Inst. Marine Studies, 1980—; pres., dir. Univ. Book Stores, 1977—; mem. US-USSR Pacific Fisheries Negotiations. Author articles and pamphlets in field. Mem. King County (Wash.) Elections Commn. Served to capt., arty. U.S. Army, World War II. Decorated Purple Heart, Bronze Star. Mem. Pacific Region Fisheries Council (chmn. sci. and statis. com.), N. Pacific Fisheries Council, Marine Tech. Soc., Am. Inst. Fishery Research Biologists, Pacific Fisheries Biologists. Home: 29801 NE Cherry Valley Rd Duvall WA 98019 Office: U Wash Fisheries Center Seattle WA 98195

BEVAN, WILLIAM, foundation executive; b. Plains, Pa., May, 16, 1922; s. William and Elizabeth Merrill (Jones) B.; m. Dorothy Louise Chorpening, Feb. 17, 1945; children: William III, Mark Filbert, Philip Ross. A.B. with honors, Franklin and Marshall Coll., 1942, Sc.D., 1979; M.A., Duke U., 1943, Ph.D., 1948, LL.D., 1972; Sc.D., Fla. Atlantic U., 1968, Emory U., 1974, U. Md., 1981. Instr. psychology Duke U., 1947, William Preston Few prof. psychology, 1974—, provost, 1979-83; instr., then asst. prof. psychology Heidelberg Coll., Tiffin, Ohio, 1946-48; mem. faculty Emory U., 1948-59, prof. psychology, 1958-59; prof. psychology, chmn. dept. Kans. State U., 1959-62, dean arts and scis., 1962-63, v.p. acad. affairs, 1963-66; fellow Center for Advanced Study Behavioral Scis., Stanford, Calif., 1965-66; sr. postdoctoral fellow NSF, 1965-66; v.p., provost Johns Hopkins U., Balt., 1966-70, prof. psychology, 1966-74; exec. officer AAAS, 1970-74, pub. Science, 1970-74; v.p. John D. and Catherine T. MacArthur Found., Chgo., 1983—; mem. adv. bd. Univ. Coll., U. Md., 1978—; bd. govs. Research Triangle Inst., 1979—; cons., mem. adv. bds. of insts., founds. Asso. editor: Am. Psychologist; editorial adv. bd.: Am. Men and Women of Sci., 12th edit, 1972, Social Sci. Citations Index, 1972-77; Contbr. articles to profl. jours. Trustee Human Resources Research Orgn., 1968—, Franklin and Marshall Coll., 1971-76, CREF, 1972—, Center for Creative Leadership, 1972-79, Bioscis. Information Service, 1974-80, Am. Psychol. Found., 1970-77, 83—, Assn. Advancement of Psychology, 1974-78, William T. Grant Found., 1977—. Served with USNR, 1944-46. Fulbright scholar U. Oslo (Norway), 1952-53. Fellow Am. Psychol. Assn. (pres. 1982), AAAS; mem. Inst. Medicine of Nat. Acad. Sci., Psychonomic Soc., So. Soc. Philosophy and Psychology, Am. Ecol. Soc. (assoc.), Phi Beta Kappa, Sigma Xi. Clubs: Cosmos (Washington); Century (N.Y.C.). Home: 666 N Lakeshore Dr Apt 202 Chicago IL 60611 Office: 140 S Dearborn St Suite 700 Chicago IL 60603

BEVER, ELLIS DORWIN, lawyer; b. Sedan, Kans., Jan. 2, 1903; s. Daniel J. and Tessa (Elliott) B.; m. Dorothy Ann Pennington, Apr. 29, 1933; 1 dau., Vicki. Student, U. Kans., 1922-24; LL.B., George Washington U., 1927, A.B., 1930. Bar: Kans. 1927. Asst. atty. U.S. Bd. Tax Appeals, Washington, 1927-33; dir. Kans. Income Tax Dept., Topeka, 1933-37; sr. partner Bever, Dye, Mustard & Belin (specializing in fed. and state tax matters), Wichita, 1937—. Mem. ABA. Club: Rotary (Wichita) (pres. 1951-52). Home: 560 Broadmoor Wichita KS 67207 Office: 713 First Nat Bank Bldg Wichita KS 67202

BEVERIDGE, GEORGE DAVID, JR., newspaperman; b. Washington, Jan. 5, 1922; s. George David and Lillian Agnes (Little) B.; m. Betty Jean Derwent, June 6, 1944; children: Barbara J., Deborah A., David C. Student, George Washington U., 1939. Copy boy Washington Star, 1940, news reporter, 1942-63, editorial writer, 1963-74, asst. mng. editor, 1974-75, ombudsman, 1976-81, assoc. editor, 1980-81; asst. to chmn. Allbritton Communications Co., Washington, 1981. Served to lt. AUS, 1942-46. Recipient Pulitzer prize for reporting in local news category, 1958. Democrat. Presbyterian. Home: 9302 Kingsley Ave Bethesda MD 20814 Office: 800 17th St NW Washington DC 20006

BEVILACQUA, ANTHONY J., clergyman; b. Bklyn., June 17, 1923; s. Louis and Maria (Codella) B. Student, Cathedral Coll., Bklyn., 1941-45, Sem. of Immaculate Conception, Huntington, N.Y., 1945-49; J.D., Gregorian U., Rome, Italy, 1956; M.A. in Polit. Sci, Columbia U., 1962; J.C.D., St. John's U. Sch. Law, 1975. Ordained priest Roman Cath. Ch., 1949; asst. pastor Sacred Heart/St. Stephen's Ch., 1945-50; prof. history Cathedral Prep. Sem., Bklyn., 1950-53; asst. chancellor in Tribunal, Diocese of Bklyn., 1957-65, vice chancellor, 1965-76; prof. canon law Sem. of Immaculate Conception, Huntington, N.Y., 1968-80; adj. prof. law St. John's U. Sch. Law, Queens, N.Y., 1976-80; successively asst. chancellor, vice chancellor, chancellor, aux. bishop, chancellor and dir. Cath. migration and refugee office Diocese of Bklyn., 1957—; chmn. U.S. Bishops Com. on Canonical Affairs, U.S. Bishops Com. on Migration and Tourism. Contbr. articles to profl. jours. Bd. dirs. Mercy Home for Children, Am-Italian Coalition of Orgns.; chmn. Nat. Emergency Com. for Haitian Refugees. Mem. Canon Law Soc. Am., Cath. Theol. Soc. Am., Am. Bar Assn., N.Y. State Bar Assn., Bklyn. Bar Assn., Assn. Immigration and Nationality Lawyers. Home: 378 Clermont Ave Brooklyn NY 11238 Office: PO Box c 75 Greene Ave Brooklyn NY 11202

BEVILACQUA, JOSEPH JOHN, state official, social worker; b. Fulton, N.Y., Oct. 20, 1931; s. John and Grace (Petroro) B.; m. Mary Ann Hlatky, Apr. 8, 1958; children: Christina, Michael, Dominic, Anthony. B.S., Canisius Coll., 1953; M.S. in Social Work, U. Buffalo, 1955; Ph.D., Brandeis U., 1967. Program dir. Father Baker's Home for Boys, Lackawanna, N.Y., 1953-55; social work specialist, Fort Bragg, N.C., 1956-57; clin. social worker 97th Gen. Hosp., Frankfurt, Ger., 1957-59; adoption social worker Our Lady of Victory Infant Home, Lackawanna, N.Y., 1959; clin. social worker VA Hosp., Buffalo, 1959-60, Walter Reed Hosp., Washington, 1960-63, mental hygiene consultation service project officer, 1968-71; chief social work service, Fort Devens, Mass., 1966-67; mem. faculty dept. neuropsychiatry Med. Field Service Sch., Fort Sam Houston, Tex., 1967-68; lectr. Worden Sch. Social Work, Our Lady of the Lake Coll., San Antonio, 1968, Nat. Cath. Sch. Social Service, Cath. U. Am., Washington, 1968-71; asso. prof. Sch. Social Work, Va. Commonwealth U., Richmond, 1971-73; asst. commr. community affairs Va. Dept. Mental Health and Mental Retardation, Richmond, 1971-73, asst. commr. mental health and mental retardation ops., 1973-75; clin. lectr. psychiatry Brown U., Providence, 1976-81; dir. R.I. Dept. Mental Health and Mental Retardation, Cranston, 1975-81; commr. Va. Dept. Mental Health and Mental Retardation, Richmond, 1981—; social planning cons. Bexar County Bd.; mem. Dixon Implementation Monitoring Com., 1980—. Editorial bd.: New Eng. Jour. Human Services, 1980—; contbr. articles on mental health services to profl. publs. Trustee, Mental Health and Mental Retardation, San Antonio, 1967-68; social service cons. Holy Trinity Cath. Sem., Washington, 1969-71; moblzn. designee Office of Surgeon Gen., Dept. Army, 1972—; mem. R.I. Gov.'s Commn. on Nursing Homes and Health Care Facilities, 1978-79, R.I. Gov.'s Council on Mental Health, 1975-81; chmn. Gov.'s Adv. Council on Alcoholism, 1975-80, Gov.'s Permanent Council on Drug Abuse Control, 1975-80, Gov.'s Commn. on Mental Health Ins., 1977-78; mem. Pres.'s Commn. on Mental Health, 1977-79; trustee R.I. Health Services Research, Inc., v.p., 1979—, mem. exec. com., 1975-81. Recipient Robert S. Burgess Community Services award Council for Community Services, 1981; United Italian Am. award, 1979. Mem. Nat. Assn. Social Workers, Council Social Work Edn. (dir. 1982—), Assn. Mental Health Adminstrs., Nat. Assn. State Mental Health Program Dirs. (pres. 1983-84). Roman Catholic. Home: 309 N Rowland St Richmond VA 23220

BEVILL, TOM, lawyer, congressman; b. Townley, Ala., Mar. 27, 1921; s. Herman and Fannie Lou (Fike) B.; m. Lou Betts, June 24, 1943; children: Susan B., Donald H., Patricia Lou. B.S., U. Ala., 1943, LL.B., 1948. Bar: Ala. 1949. Pvt. practice law, Jasper, 1948—; mem. Ala. Ho. of Reps., 1958-66, 90th-98th congresses from 4th Dist. Ala. Mem. ABA, Ala. Bar Assn., Walker County Bar Assn. (past pres.), Am. Judicature Soc. Home: 1600 Alabama Ave Jasper AL 35501 Office: House Office Bldg Washington DC 20515

BEVINGTON, DAVID MARTIN, English literature educator; b. N.Y.C., May 13, 1931; s. Merle Mowbray and Helen (Smith) B.; m. Margaret Bronson Brown, June 4, 1953; children: Stephen, Philip, Katharine, Sarah. B.A., Harvard U., 1952, M.A., 1957, Ph.D., 1959. Instr. English Harvard U., 1959-61; asst. prof. U. Va., 1961-65, asso. prof., 1965-66, prof., 1966-67; vis. prof. U. Chgo., 1967-68, prof., 1968—; vis. prof. N.Y. U. Summer Sch., 1963, Harvard U. Summer Sch., 1967, U. Hawaii Summer Sch., 1970, Northwestern U., 1974. Author: From Mankind to Marlowe, 1962, Tudor Drama and Politics, 1968, Action is Eloquence, Shakespeare's Language of Gesture, 1984; editor: Medieval Drama, 1975, The Complete Works of Shakespeare, 3d edit, 1980. Served with USN, 1952-55. Guggenheim fellow, 1964-65, 81-82; sr. fellow Southeastern Inst. Medieval and Renaissance Studies, summer 1975; sr. cons. and seminar leader Folger Inst. Renaissance and Eighteenth-Century Studies, 1976-77. Mem. MLA, Renaissance Soc. Am., Shakespeare Assn. Am. (pres. 1976-77), AAUP. Home: 5747 S Blackstone Ave Chicago IL 60637

BEVINGTON, E(DMUND) MILTON, electrical machinery manufacturing company executive; b. Nashville, Oct. 31, 1928; s. John Laurence and Mary (Halloran) B.; m. Elizabeth Anne Rickey, Sept. 8, 1951 (dec. June 1962); children: Milton, Rickey, Peter; m. Paula Maureen Lawton, Apr. 24, 1965; children: George, Mary-Laurence, Christian, Charles, Justin. Grad., Canterbury Sch., 1945; S.B. in Chem. Engring, Mass. Inst. Tech., 1949; M.B.A., Harvard, 1951. Plant supr. Dewey & Almey Chem. Co. (name changed to W.R. Grace Co., 1954), Cambridge, Mass., 1951-54, marketing research mgr., 1954-56; merchandising mgr. Westinghouse Electric Co., Staunton, Va., 1956-58, So. zone sales mgr., Atlanta, 1958-59; with The Trane Co., Atlanta and LaCrosse, Wis., 1959—, v.p., gen. mgr. consumer products div., 1969-70, exec. v.p., 1970-73; chmn., pres. Servidyne Inc., Atlanta, 1974—. Mem. corp. devel. com. M.I.T., 1978—; mem. mgmt. adv. council Coll. Mgmt., Ga. Inst. Tech.; trustee Canterbury Sch., New Milford, Ga. Conservancy, Atlanta; bd. dirs. Atlanta Council Boy Scouts Am. Mem. MIT Alumni Assn. (v.p. 1983—), Tau Beta Pi, Sigma Alpha Epsilon. Clubs: Harvard (N.Y.C.); Piedmont Driving, Commerce (Atlanta). Home: 146 W Wesley Rd NW Atlanta GA 30305 Office: 2120 Marietta Blvd Atlanta GA 30377

BEVIS, JOSEPH C., pub. opinion research exec.; b. Harrison, Ohio, Jan. 16, 1910; s. Joseph C. and Helen S. (Norton) B.; m. Betsy Ross, Dec. 9, 1934; children—Joseph Ross, James Norton, Cheryl Ann, Beverly Jean. A.B., Miami U., Oxford, Ohio, 1931; M.A., Northwestern U., 1932; student, Ohio State U., 1931. Made pioneer telephone survey of radio audience, 1932, employe, and in full charge, hardware and farm implement store, Harrison, 1932-34; with research div., as dir. surveys of relief population Fed. Emergency Relief Adminstrn. (and successor orgn. WPA), 1934-40; with Opinion Research Corp., Princeton, N.J., 1940-70, v.p., 1945-57, pres., 1957-60, 65-67, chmn. and chief exec. officer, 1960-70; dir. Roper Orgn., Inc., N.Y.C., 1970—. Mem. Am. Mktg. Assn., Am. Assn. for Pub. Opinion Research, Market Research Council N.Y., Sigma Alpha Epsilon. Home: 1075 SE St Lucie Blvd Stuart FL 33494

BEWKES, EUGENE GARRETT, JR., food company executive; b. Norwood, Mass., Sept. 28, 1926; s. Eugene Garrett and Helen (Van Vlaanderen) B.; m. Marjorie Louise Klenk, Aug. 20, 1949; children: Eugene Garrett III, Jeffrey Lawrence, Robert David. B.A., Colgate U., 1948; J.D., Yale U., 1951. Bar: N.Y. bar 1952. With firm Chapman, Bryson, Walsh & O'Connell, N.Y.C., 1951-55; atty.-adviser also asst. Office Sec. USAF, 1955-57; with Am. Mgmt. Assn., 1957-61, gen. mgmt. div., mgr., 1959-61; gen. counsel, sec., asst. v.p. Reuben H. Donnelley Corp., 1961-67; v.p. law and adminstrn., sec. Canada Dry Corp., 1967-68; v.p. Norton Simon, Inc., N.Y.C., 1968-72, sr. v.p., 1972-73, exec. v.p., 1973-77, vice chmn. bd., 1977-81; chmn., pres., chief exec. officer Am. Bakeries Co., 1982—; dir. Manhattan Life Corp., N.Y.C., A.C. Daily Income Fund, Inc., Paine Webber RMA Money Fund, Inc., Paine Webber Cash Fund, Paine Webber RMA Tax-Free Fund, Inc. Trustee Colgate U., Hamilton, N.Y., Deerfield

(Mass.) Acad. Served to ensign USNR, 1945-46. Mem. Am., N.Y. bar assns., Phi Beta Kappa, Delta Kappa Epsilon, Phi Delta Phi. Club: Yale (N.Y.C.). Home: 2 Ox Ridge Ln Darien CT 06820

BEWLEY, JOHN DEREK, biology researcher, educator; b. Preston, Lancashire, Eng., Dec. 11, 1943; s. Clifford and Marion (Garner) B.; m. Christine E. Nee Kite, Sept. 3, 1966; children: Alexander, Janette Louise. B.Sc., U. London, 1965, Ph.D., 1968, D.Sc., 1983. Asst. prof. U. Calgary, Alta., 1970-73, assoc. prof., 1973-77, prof. biology, 1977—. Recipient C.D. Nelson award Can. Soc. Plant Physiologists, 1978; E.W.R. Steacie Meml. fellow Natural Scis. and Engring.; Research Council of Can. fellow, 1979-81. Fellow Royal Soc. Can.; mem. Can. Soc. Plant Physiologists (sec. 1982—). Home: 5116 Dalham Crescent NW Calgary AB Canada T3A 1L7 Office: Plant Physiology Research Group Dept Biology U Calgary 2500 University Dr NW Calgary AB Canada T2N 1N4

BEWLEY, KINGSLEY GRENVILLE, technical school and educational publishing executive; b. Toronto, Ont., Can., June 26, 1939; came to U.S., 1970; s. Rolph Grenville and Irene Jane (Moxon) B.; m. Patricia Ann Peacock, Aug. 13, 1963; children—John Rolph, Paul Kingsley, Michael Grenville. Chartered acct., Inst. Chartered Accts. Ont., 1964. Sr. auditor Sanders Cooper & Balderson, Toronto, 1959-65; chief acct. Bell & Howell Can. Ltd., Toronto, 1965-69; controller consumer and audio visual group Bell & Howell Co., Chgo., 1970-76, v.p. and gen. mgr. western internat. region, 1976-78; corp. v.p. and chmn. bd. Tng. and Edn. Group Bell and Howell Co., Evanston, Ill., 1978—. Served with Can. Army, 1956-57. Mem. Ont. Inst. Chartered Accts., Can. Inst. Chartered Accts. Episcopalian. Home: 1475 Larchmont Dr Buffalo Grove IL 60090 Office: 2201 W Howard St Evanston IL 60202

BEYCHOK, SHERMAN, biochemist, educator; b. N.Y.C., Sept. 10, 1931; s. Abe and Miriam (Schiffman) B.; m. Martha Marcus, Mar. 25, 1950; 1 dau., Cori Bess. B.S., City Coll. N.Y., 1951; Ph.D., N.Y.U., 1957. Guest chemistry Mass. Inst. Tech., 1956-60; research assoc. Children's Cancer Research Found. and Harvard Med. Sch., 1960-61; mem. faculty Columbia U., 1962—, Alan H. Kempner prof. biol. scis., 1975—, chmn. dept. biol. scis., 1968-79; vis. prof. faculty medicine U. Paris; cons. in field; mem. panel on molecular biology NSF, 1979-82, adv. com. on physiology, 1982—; cons. NIH; Trustee Cold Spring Harbor Lab., 1968-79; mem. Louisa Gross Horwitz Prize com., 1980—. Mem. editorial adv. bd.: Chem. Rubber Co. Handbook; mem. editorial bd.: Internat. Jours., Netherlands; Contbr. articles to profl. jours. Mem. Am. Soc. Biol. Chemists, Harvey Soc., Am. Chem. Soc. Home: 560 Riverside Dr Apt 20m New York NY 10027 Office: Dept Biol Scis Columbia Univ New York NY 10027

BEYER, EUGENE EDWARD, JR., manufacturing company executive; b. New Brunswick, N.J., Aug. 31, 1920; s. Eugene Edward and Sara (McGowan) (Moore) B.; m. Katherine Bozorth, July 15, 1944 (div.); children: William Huntley, Alison Beyer Emmerich, Kristi Beyer Bragg.; m. Jane Whitbread Levin, Dec. 30, 1982. B.A. magna cum laude, Williams Coll., 1941; LL.B., Yale U., 1943. Bar: D.C. 1944, Calif. 1946, N.Y. 1950. Law clk. to Justice Douglas, 1943-44; spl. asst. to atty. gen. tax div. Dept. Justice, 1944-46; assoc. Brobeck, Phleger & Harrison, San Francisco, 1946-47; with RCA, 1947—, staff v.p., gen. atty., 1962-73, v.p., gen. atty., j1973-78, sr. v.p., gen. counsel, 1978-80, exec. v.p., gen. counsel, 1980—. Editor-in-chief: Yale Law Jour, 1942-43. Bd. dirs. Pro Musicis Found. Mem. Assn. Bar City N.Y., ABA, Assn. Gen. Counsel, Am. Corp. Counsel Assn., Order of Coif, Phi Beta Kappa, Phi Delta Phi, Delta Upsilon. Clubs: Rockefeller Center Luncheon, Univ. (N.Y.C.). Home: 333 E 68th St Apt 4C New York NY 10021 Office: 30 Rockefeller Plaza New York NY 10020

BEYER, GORDON ROBERT, foreign service officer; b. Chgo., Oct. 13, 1930; m. Mary Paine Winsor, Feb. 22, 1951; children: Theresa Gordon, Hugh Richard, Thomas Paine. A.B., Harvard Coll.; M.A., Northwestern U.; postgrad., Nat. War Coll., 1971-72. With Pres.'s Commn. on Vets.' Pensions (Bradley Commn.), 1956; commd. fgn. service officer Dept. State, 1957; officer Am. embassy, Bangkok, Thailand, 1957-59, Washington, 1959-61; consul gen., Yokohama, Japan, 1961-64; officer Am. embassy, Somalia, consul, Hargeisa, 1964-67; with Dept. State, Washington, 1967-72; dep. chief of mission Am. embassy, Dar es Salaam, Tanzania, 1972-75; officer U.S. UN, 1975-80; U.S. ambassador to Uganda, Kampala, 1980-83; now with Nat. War Coll.; Bd. dirs. Dar es Salaam Internat. Sch., 1972-75, pres., 1974. Author: monograph Race and National Security. Served to 1st lt. USMC, 1953-55. Recipient meritorious honor awards Dept. State, 1967, 75. Mem. Middle East Inst. (Washington), Am. Fgn. Service Assn. Clubs: Cosmos (Washington); Harvard (N.Y.C.). Office: care Nat. War Coll. 4th and P Sts. SW Washington DC 20319 *

BEYER, JOHN ADRIAN, constrn. co. exec.; b. Horicon, Wis., Aug. 25, 1924; s. Emil Ernst and Jean Adrienne (Karsten) B.; m. R. Virginia Grassl, Feb. 4, 1950; children—Jean, Rebecca, John Adrian. B.S. in C.E, U. Wis., 1948. City engr. small cities, Wis.; also field engr. Grand Coulee Dam, Bur. Reclamation, 1949-50; field engr. to dist. mgr. Seattle dist. Morrison-Knudsen Co., Inc., Boise, Idaho, 1950-64; pvt. cons. major heavy constrn. and r.r. projects, 1964-66; dist. mgr. Morrison-Knudsen Co., Inc., 1966-68, v.p., 1968-71; pres., chief exec. officer Gen. Constrn. Co. (and subsidiaries), Seattle, 1971-80, Beyer Corp. (and subsidiaries), Bellevue, Wash., 1980—; dir. Careage Corp., Bellevue, Wash., Nat. Olivine Corp., Seattle, Howard Cooper Corp., Portland, Oreg., Westcat Internat., U.S.A., Trans-Arabian Rail, Ltd. Bd. regents Seattle U. Served with USNR, World War II. Mem. Phi Gamma Delta. Republican. Roman Catholic. Clubs: Seattle Tennis, Univ., Rainier, Harbor, NW Forum (Seattle). Home: 8636 NE 21st Pl Bellevue WA 98004 Office: 13353 Bel-Red Rd Bellevue WA 98005

BEYER, JOHN REGAN, banker; b. Altoona, Pa., Aug. 23, 1929; s. Millard F. and C. Grace (Hickey) B.; m. Patricia L. Cherry, May 22, 1954; children: John Regan, Ronald B. B.A., Pa. State U., 1951; postgrad., Stonier Grad. Sch. Banking, Rutgers U., 1961-63. Diplomate: Cert. comml. lendr, Am. Bankers Assn. With Mid-State Bank & Trust Co., Altoona, 1953—, now exec. v.p., treas., mem. adv. bd. dir. emeritus Reliance Savs. Assn.; dir. Altoona Enterprises. Author: Field Warehouse Inventory Financing, 1963. Vice chmn. adv. bd. Altoona Campus Pa. State U.; bd. dirs., v.p. Fairview Cemetery Assn.; bd. dirs. Altoona YMCA; mem. Penns Woods council Boy Scouts Am.; liaison officer USAF Acad. Served with USAF, 1951-53; col. Res. Mem. Altoona C. of C. (past pres.), Res. Officers Assn. (pres.), Alpha Kappa Psi. Club: Park Hills Country. Lodges: Masons; Shriners; Rotary. Home: 618 Ruskin Dr Altoona PA 16602 Office: Mid-State Bank 1130 12th Ave Altoona PA 16603

BEYER, KARL HENRY, JR., pharmacologist; b. Henderson, Ky., June 19, 1914; s. Karl H. and Lennie M. (Beadles) B.; m. Camille Slobodzian, Nov. 9, 1979; children by previous marriage—Annette Matilda Beyer Mears, Katherine Louise Beyer Cranson. B.S., Western Ky. State Coll., 1935; Ph.M., U. Wis., 1937, Ph.D., 1940, M.D., 1943, Sc.D. (hon.), 1972. Asst. dir. pharmacol. research Sharp & Dohme, 1943-44, dir. pharmacol. research, 1944-50, asst. dir. research, 1950-56; dir. Merck Inst. Therapeutic Research, West Point, Pa., 1956-58, pres., 1961-66; v.p. life scis. Merck Sharp & Dohme, Research Labs., West Point, 1958-66, sr. v.p. research, 1966-73; lectr. Med. Coll. Pa.; vis. prof., guest lectr. U. Wis., 1958, Swedish U. Med. Schs., 1962, Howard U., 1964, Free U. Berlin, 1966; vis. prof. Milton S. Hershey Med. Center, Pa. State U., 1973—, Vanderbilt U. Sch. Medicine, 1973-79; chmn. Cosmetic Ingredient Rev., 1976; bd. sci. advisers Merck Inst., 1973-77, 78—; chmn. bd. Phila. Assn. Clin. Trials, 1980. Author: Pharmacological Basis of Penicillin Therapy, 1950, Discovery, Development and Delivery of New Drugs, 1978; editorial bd.: Clin. Pharmacology and Therapeutics; contbr. articles to profl. jours. Recipient Gairdner Found. award, 1964; Modern Pioneers in Creative Industry award NAM, 1965; Modern Medicine Distinguished Achievement award, 1967; Am. Pharm. Assn. Found. Achievement award, 1967; Distinguished Service award Wis. Alumni Assn., 1968; Lasker award, 1975; Torald Sollmann award, 1978; Catell award Am. Coll. Clin. Pharmacology, 1980. Fellow A.C.P., AAAS, N.Y. Acad. Scis., Royal Acad. of Medicine; mem. Nat. Acad. Scis., Am. Chem. Soc., Am., Phila. physiol. socs., Soc. for Exptl. Biology and Medicine, Phila. Med. Soc., Am. Soc. for Pharmacology and Exptl. Therapeutics (pres. 1964-65), Fedn. Am. Soc. Exptl. Biology (pres. 1965-66), Internat. Soc. Biochem. Pharmacology, Phila. Coll. Physicians, Am. Therapeutic Soc., Soc. Toxicology, Am. Soc. Nephrology, Am. Heart Assn. (hypertension research award 1979, council circulation and renal sect.), Heart Assn. Southeastern Pa., Biol. Abstracts (trustee; treas. 1965-69), Nat. Acad. Scis. (drug research bd. 1964-70), Canadian Pharm. Soc. Home: Box 387 Penllyn PA 19422

BEYER, MORTEN STERNOFF, airlines executive; b. N.Y.C., Nov. 13, 1921; s. Otto Sternoff and Clara (Mortenson) B.; m. Jane I. Hartman, Sept. 29, 1945; children: Barbara, Nancy (Mrs. James Henry McGinnis), James, William. B.A. with honors, Swarthmore Coll., 1943. Various positions Pan Am. World Airways, 1943-48; asst. to v.p. operations and maintenance Capital Airlines Inc., Washington, 1948-60; sr. v.p. operations, maintenance and sales Riddle Airlines Inc., Miami, Fla., 1960-63; dep. dir. gen., gen. mgr. Saudi Arabian Airlines, Jeddah, Saudi Arabia, 1964-67; exec. v.p. Modern Air Transport, Inc., Miami, 1967-70, pres., 1970-71, Capital Internat. Airways, Inc., Nashville, 1971-72, Phoenix Airlines Inc., Detroit, 1972-73; pres., chief exec. officer Johnson Internat. Airlines, Inc., Missoula, Mont., 1974-75; pres. AVMARK Inc., Arlington, Va., 1975—; also editor AVMARK Newsletter, Comml. Aircraft Fleets, Transport Aircraft Values, other publs.; cons. USAF, 1954-55, Miami, Fla., 1963-64. Democratic candidate U.S. Reps., 1956; pres. Fairfax County Young Democrats, 1956-57. Club: Toastmasters Internat. (pres. 1952-56). Home: Lolo Creek Rd Lolo MT 59847 Office: AVMARK Inc Arlington VA

BEYER, ROBERT THOMAS, physicist, educator; b. Harrisburg, Pa., Jan. 27, 1920; s. James M. and Mary (Gibney) B.; m. Ellen Fletcher, Feb. 14, 1944; children: Catherine E., Margaret A., Richard J., Mary L. A.B., Hofstra U., 1942; Ph.D., Cornell U., 1945; M.A. (hon.), Brown U., 1957. Teaching asst. Cornell U., 1942-45; instr. physics Brown U., 1945-47, asst. prof., 1947- 51, asso. prof., 1951-58, prof., 1958—, exec. officer dept. physics, 1966-68, 81—, chmn. dept., 1968-74; vis. prof. Technische Hochschule, Stuttgart, Germany, 1961-62, U. Birmingham, Eng., 1971, U. Tex., Austin, 1977, Pa. State U., 1982; cons., chmn. Am. Inst. Physics Trans. adv. bd., 1957-77; cons. on underwater sound Raytheon, 1962-72; cons. Office of Naval Research, 1974-75. Editor: Soviet Physics JETP transl. jour, 1955-57, Soviet Physics Acoustics transl. jour, 1974—; Translated (from German): Practical Analysis (F. A. Willers), 1948, Mathematical Foundations of Quantum Mechanics (Johann von Neumann), 1955; translated (from Russian): Molecular Scattering of Light (I.L. Fabelinskii), 1968, Theoretical Foundations of Nonlinear Acoustics (G.O.V. Rudenko and S.I. Soluyan), 1977, Waves in Layered Media (L.M. Brekhovskii), 2d edit, 1979; author: (with A.O. Williams, Jr.) College Physics, 1957, (with Stephen V. Letcher) Physical Ultrasonics, 1969, Nonlinear Acoustics, 1974; editor: transl. from Chinese Acta Physica Sinica, 1966-68. Fellow Fund for Advancement Edn., 1953-54. Fellow Am. Phys. Soc., Acoustical Soc. Am. (pres. 1968-69, treas. 1974—), Internat. Commn. Acoustics (chmn. 1978—), IEEE. Home: 132 Cushman Ave East Providence RI 02914 Office: Physics Dept Brown U Providence RI 02912

BEYERS, WILLIAM BJORN, geography educator; b. Seattle, Mar. 24, 1940; s. William Abraham and Esther Jakobia (Svendsen) B.; m. Margaret Lyn Rice, July 28, 1968. B.A., U. Wash., 1962, Ph.D., 1967. Asst. prof. geography U. Wash., Seattle, 1968-74, assoc. prof., 1974-82, prof., 1982—. Editorial bd.: Annals, Assn. Am. Geographers, 1980—; book rev. editor: Jour. Regional Sci., 1980-83. Trustee Alpine Lakes Protection Soc., Ellenburg, Wash., 1970—. Mem. Assn. Am. Geographers, Regional Sci. Assn., Am. Econs. Assn., Peace Sci. Soc., Western Regional Sci. Assn. Home: 7159 Beach Dr SW Seattle WA 98136 Office: Dept Geography DP 10 Univ Wash Seattle WA 98195

BEYSTER, JOHN ROBERT, engineering company executive; b. Detroit, July 26, 1924; s. John Frederick and Lillian Edith (Jondro) B.; m. Betty Jean Brock, Sept. 8, 1955; children: James Frederick, Mark Daneil, Mary Ann. B.S. in Engring., U. Mich., 1945, M.S., 1948, Ph.D., 1950. Registered profl. engr., Calif. Mem. staff Los Alamos Sci. Lab., 1951-56; chmn. dept. accelerated physics Gulf Gen. Atomic Co., San Diego, 1957-69; pres., chmn. bd. Sci. Applications, Inc., La Jolla, Calif., 1969—; mem. Joint Strategic Target Planning Staff, Sci. Adv. Group, Omaha, 1978—; panel mem. Nat. Measurement Lab. Evaluation panel for Radiation Research, Washington, 1983—; dir. Scripps Bancorp, La Jolla, 1983. Co-author: Slow Neutron Scattering and Thermalization, 1970. Served to lt. comdr. USN, 1943-46. Fellow Am. Nuclear Soc., Am. Phys. Soc. Republican. Roman Catholic. Home: 9321 La Jolla Farms Rd La Jolla CA 92037 Office: sci Applications Inc 1200 Prospect St La Jolla CA 92037

BEYTAGH, FRANCIS XAVIER, college dean, lawyer; b. Savannah, Ga., July 11, 1935. B.A. magna cum laude, U. Notre Dame, 1956; J.D., U. Mich., 1963. Bar: Ohio 1964, Ind. 1972, U.S. Supreme Ct. 1967. Clk. firm Fuller, Seney, Henry & Hodge, Toledo, 1961; sr. law clk. Chief Justice Earl Warren, U.S. Supreme Ct., Washington, 1963-64; asso. firm Jones, Day, Cockley and Reavis, Cleve., 1964-66; asst. to solicitor gen. U.S. Dept. Justice, Washington, 1966-70; prof. law U. Notre Dame, 1970-74, 75-76; vis. prof. law U. Va., Charlottesville, 1974-75; prof., dean Toledo U. Coll. Law, 1976-83; vis. prof. law U. Mich., 1983-84; Cullen prof. law U. Houston, 1984—. Editor in chief: Mich. Law Rev., 1962-63; author: Supplement to Kauper's Constitutional Law: Cases and Materials, 1977, Constitutional Law: Cases and Materials, 5th edit., 1980, supplements, 1981, 82, 84; contbr. articles to profl. jours. Served to capt. USNR; ret. Mem. ABA, Tex. Bar Assn., Houston Bar Assn., Order of Coif. Home: 3033 Westchester Rd Ottawa Hills OH 43615 Office: U Toledo Coll Law Toledo OH 43606

BEZAHLER, DONALD JAY, lawyer; b. Bklyn., Apr. 10, 1932; s. Joel and Hannah B.; m. Suzanne Landau, Dec. 2, 1965; 1 son, David Scott. B.A., Bklyn. Coll., 1953; LL.B., J.D., Harvard U., 1958. Bar: N.Y. 1959. Mem. exec. staff SEC, 1958-61; pvt. practice, N.Y.C., 1961—; partner firm Finley, Kumble, Wagner, Heine, Underberg & Casey, 1978—; officer, dir. Data Systems Analysts, Inc. Served with AUS, 1953-55. Recipient Appeal Leadership award Anti-Defamation League, 1966. Mem. Am. Bar Assn., Bar Assn. City N.Y. Home: 923 Fifth Ave New York NY 10021 Office: 425 Park Ave New York NY 10022

BEZANSON, PETER FLOYD, banking and finance company executive; b. Mpls., Apr. 2, 1915; s. Harry B. and Lilliam M. (Zwicker) B.; m. Lorrayne B. Bing, June 17, 1939; children: Judith Rae, Randall Peter. B.A., U. Wis., 1937; postgrad., Columbia U., 1960. Chmn. bd. MorAm. Fin. Corp., also Morris Plan of Iowa, Cedar Rapids, 1953—; chmn. Bezanson Ins., Inc., Cedar Rapids, 1949-70, MorAm. Capital Corp., 1958—, Lease Am., Inc., Sunnycrest Nursing Facilities, Inc., 1964—; chmn. MorAm. Mktg. Inc., MorAm. Realty Co.; pres., dir. Bezanon Property Inc.; v.p., dir. Allen Supply Co.; dir. Hawkeye Bank Corp., Des Moines; chmn. bd. Am. Indsl. Bankers Assn., 1966-68; bd. govs. Nat. Assn. Small Bus. Investment Assn., 1961-68. Pres. Hawkeye area council Boy Scouts Am., 1976-78; nat. vice chmn. fund drive ARC, 1959-60; trustee U. Colo. Installment Banking Sch., 1962-72, Coe Coll., Cedar Rapids, 1974—. Served with USAAF, 1944-45. Mem. Chi Phi. Presbyterian (elder). Clubs: Masons, Shriners, Elks, Rotary, Cedar Rapids Country. Home: 100 1st St NE 2600 Cedar River Towers Cedar Rapids IA 52401 Office: American Bldg Cedar Rapids IA 52401

BEZDEK, HUGO FRANK, scientific laboratory administrator; b. Washington, Feb. 28, 1936; s. Hugo F. and Louise Bezdel. B.S. in Physics, N.Mex. State U., 1965, Ph.D., U. Colo., 1970. Research scientist Scripps Inst. Oceanography, La Jolla, Calif., 1970-74; dep. dir. Ocean Sci. Research Office Devel., Arlington, Va., 1974-80; dir. Atlantic Oceanographic and Meteorol. Labs., Miami, Fla., 1980—. Contbr. numerous articles to profl. jours. Mem. Acoustical Soc. Am., Am. Geophys. Union. Office: Atlantic Oceanographic and Meteorol Labs 4301 Rickenbacker Causeway Cirginia Key Miami FL 33149

BEZOU, HENRY CHARLES, clergyman, educator; b. New Orleans, Apr. 28, 1913; s. André Ralph and Lydia Marie (Bouligny) B. Ed., St. Aloysius Coll., 1929, St. Joseph Sem., St. Benedict, La., 1932, Notre Dame Sem., New Orleans, 1934, 38; A.M., Cath. U. Am., 1947; Litt.D. (honoris causa), Loyola U. of South, 1952. Ordained priest Roman Cath. Ch., 1938; with Sacred Heart Ch., Montegut, La., 1938-42, St. Charles Ch., Lafourche, La., 1942-43; head Normal Sch., Houma, La., 1940-42; archdiocesan supt. schs., New Orleans, 1943-68, named Papal Chamberlain with title Very Reverend Monsignor, 1949, domestic prelate with title Rt. Rev. Monsignor, 1954; dir. Cath. Com. S. Summer Sch., Loyola U.; pastor St. Patricks Ch., New Orleans, 1951-65, Our Lady Star of the Sea Ch., 1965- 67, St. Francis Xavier, Metairie, La., 1967-83, pastor emeritus, 1983—; spiritual dir. Ozanam Inn, 1955-65; Mem. Archdiocesan Central Council, Soc. St. Vincent de Paul, 1956-66, archdiocesan cons., 1962-77; sec. elementary div. Nat. Cath. Ednl. Assn.; mem. Gov.'s Safety Com. (also other state coms.); co-chmn. Archdiocesan Bicentennial Commn., 1975; chmn. Jefferson Parish Hist. Commn., 1976-78; mem. Archdiocesan Bldg. Commn.; co-chmn. Jefferson Parish Sesquicentennial Commn., 1974-75; mem. Council Devel. French in La., 1981—. Author: articles, pamphlets, monographs and brochures including redaction of Metairie: A Tongue of Land to Pasture, 1973, Lourdes on Napoleon Avenue, 1980. Mem. Mayor's Adv. Coms.; bd. dirs. New Orleans Symphony Soc., New Orleans Tb League, La. Soc. Crippled Children, Community Chest, United Fund; mem schs. com. United Fund; mem. adv. com. Juvenile Ct.; cons. supts.' div., dept. edn. Nat. Cath. Welfare Conf.; mem. coms. State Dept. Edn.; trustee Greater New Orleans Ednl. TV Found.; mem. White House Conf. on Edn., 1955; regional adv. bd. ARC; adv. bd. Cath. Ency. Sch. and Home; dir. Info. Council of Ams. Decorated chevalier Legion of Honor; recipient Palmes Académiques and title Officier d'Académie, 1949. Mem. Am. Cath. Hist. Assn., Fgn. Policy Assn., Nat. Cath. Edn. Assn. (pres. supts. dept.), Jefferson Hist. Soc. La. (dir. 1977—), Am. Soc. Legion of Honor. Address: 448 Metairie Rd Metairie LA 70005

BEZZONE, ALBERT PAUL, structural engineer; b. Sacramento, Calif., June 22, 1931; s. Albert Paul and Angela Edna (Nicolai) B.; m. JoAnn Karslie Walther, Aug. 4, 1951; children: Jeffrey Paul, David Ernest, Judith Eileen. Student, Sacramento City Coll., 1949-50, Calif. State U., 1952-56. Engring. technician, State of Calif., Sacramento, 1950-51, civil engr., County of Sacramento, Calif., 1951-53; with Calif. Dept. Transportation, 1953—, chief, office of structure constrn., constrn. div., 1977—. Contbr. articles to profl. jours. Fellow ASCE; mem. Profl. Engrs. in Calif. Govt. Home: 829 Senior Way Sacramento CA 95831 Office: PO Box 1499 Sacramento CA 95807

BHAGWATI, JAGDISH NATWARLAL, economics educator; b. Bombay, India, July 26, 1934; came to U.S., 1968; s. Natwarlal H. and Saraswati (Amin) B.; m. Padma Kalidas Desai, Oct. 24, 1970. B.Commerce, Bombay U., 1954; B.A., Cambridge (Eng.) U., 1956, M.A., 1961; Ph.D., Mass. Inst. Tech., 1967; B.A., Oxford (Eng.) U., 1959. Research asso. internat. econs. U. Chgo., 1959; research fellow Nuffield Coll., Oxford U., 1959-61; prof. econs. Indian Statis. Inst., 1962-63; prof. internat. trade Delhi U., 1963-68; prof. econs. Columbia U., 1967-68, 80-81, Arthur Lehman prof. econs., 1981—, dir. Internat. Econs. Research Ctr., 1982—; prof. econs. MIT, 1968-80, Ford Internat. prof. econs., 1978-80; cons. UN agencies (govts. Turkey and India.). Author: Economics of Underdeveloped Countries, 1966, The Theory and Practice of Commercial Policy, 1968, Trade, Tariffs and Growth, 1969, Planning for Industrialization: A Study of India's Trade and Industrial Policies, 1970; Editor: Jour. Internat. Econs, 1971—, Am. Econ. Rev, 1970-73; Author and editor 25 books; contbr. articles to profl. jours. Recipient Mahalanobis Meml. medal, 1974. Fellow Econometric Soc., Am. Acad. Arts and Scis.; mem. Am. Econ. Assn. Home: 11 White Pine Ln Lexington MA 02173 Office: Columbia Univ Dept Econs New York NY 10027

BHARATI, AGEHANANDA, anthropologist, Hindu monk, educator, author; b. Vienna, Austria, Apr. 20, 1923; came to U.S., 1956, naturalized, 1968; s. Hans and Margarete Helene (von May) Fischer. A.B. in Ethnology and Indology, Oriental Inst. and Ethnol. Inst., U. Vienna, 1948; Acharya (Ph.D.), Samnyasa Mahavidyalaya, India, 1951. Lectr. in German Delhi (India) U., 1951; hon. reader in philosophy Benares Hindu U., India, 1951-54; guest prof. comparative religion Nalanda (India) Inst. Postgrad. Buddhist Studies, 1954-55; vis. prof. comparative religion Mahamukuta Royal Buddhist Acad., Bangkok, Thailand, 1955-56; Asia Found. vis. prof. U. Tokyo, 1956-57, Kyoto, Japan, 1956-57; research asso. Far Eastern Inst., U. Wash., Seattle, 1957-60; asst. prof. anthropology Syracuse (N.Y.) U., 1961-64, asso. prof., 1964-68, prof., 1968—, chmn. dept. anthropology, 1971—; ordained to Hindu Samnyasi Order of Monks, India, 1951; lectr. various Am. univs., 1956—, U. Goettingen, Germany, 1970, Heidelberg (Germany) U., 1971, U. Stockholm, 1968; Rose Morgan Distinguished vis. prof. U. Kans., Lawrence, 1970; coordinator 9th Internat. Congress of Anthrop. and Ethnol. Scis., Chgo., 1973. Author: The Ochre Robe, 1963, A Functional Analysis of Indian Thought and Its Social Margins, 1964, The Tantric Tradition, 1966, The Asians in East Africa: Jayhind and Uhuru, 1972, The Light at the Center: Context and Pretext of Modern Mysticism, 1976, Great Tradition and Little Traditions: Indological Investigations in Cultural Anthropology, 1978, Hindu Views and Ways and the Hindu-Muslim Interface, 1981; editor: Tibet Soc. Bull, 1974—; co-editor: World Anthropology, 1973; Contbr. numerous book revs. and articles on cultural anthropology, religion and the history of Occidental and Oriental philosophy to lit. mags. and scholarly Am., Brit. and German jours.; contbr. numerous book chpts. on Oriental religion and cultural anthropology. NIMH grantee, 1964; Am. Inst. Ceylonese Studies grantee, 1970-71. Fellow Am. Anthrop. Assn., Soc. Applied Anthropology, Royal Anthrop.

Inst. of Gt. Britain and Ireland; mem. Assn. for Asian Studies, Am. Oriental Soc., Wash. Anthrop. Soc., Soc. Sci. Study of Religion, Mensa Internat., Tibet Soc. (dir. 1975—), Mind Assn. Home: 1209 Harrison St Syracuse NY 13210 Office: 500 University Pl Syracuse NY 13210 *As I postulate that a modern man's mind should operate on many levels, I try to be a scientist and a mystic, as an ascetic and as a eudaimonist—at different times of my schedule. I enjoy the discomfiture of ideologues refuted and rebutted by non-ideologues, and I enjoy the discomfiture of non-ideologues refuted and rebutted by ideologues. By aesthetic choice, I leave my options open to act and think as an ideologue or as a non- and anti-ideologue.*

BHARUCHA-REID, ALBERT TURNER, mathematician, educator; b. Hampton, Va., Nov. 13, 1927; s. William Thaddeus and Mae Elaine (Beamon) Reid; m. Rodabé Phiroze Bharucha, June 5, 1954; children: Kurush Feroze, Rustam William. B.S., Iowa State U., 1949; postgrad., U. Chgo., 1950-53. Research asst. math. biology U. Chgo., 1950-53; research asso. math. stats. Columbia U., 1953-55; asst. research statistician U. Calif., Berkeley, 1955-56; instr., asst. prof. math. U. Oreg., 1956-61; fellow Polish Acad. Scis., 1958-59; from asso prof. math. to prof. Wayne State U., 1961-81, asso. provost, dean grad. studies, 1976-81; prof. math. Ga. Inst. Tech., Atlanta, 1981-83; Disting. prof. math. Atlanta U., 1983—; prof. applied math. Inst. Math. Scis., Madras, India, 1963-64; prof. Math. Research Center, U. Wis., Madison, 1966-67, Ga. Inst. Tech., 1973-74; mem. Grad. Record Exam. Bd., Princeton, N.J., 1978-82; bd. govs. Cranbrook Inst. Sci., Bloomfield Hills, Mich., 1977-80. Author or editor: Markov Processes and Their Applications, 1960 (Russian transl. 1969), Random Integral Equations, 1972, Approximate Solution of Random Equations, 1979, Probabilistic Methods in Applied Mathematics, 3 vols., 1968, 70, 73, Probabilistic Analysis and Related Topics, 3 vols., 1978, 79, 83; editor: Jour. Integral Equations; asso. editor: Bull. Math. Biology, Nonlinear Analysis, Stochastic Analysis and Applications. USAF research grantee, 1954-55; U.S. Army Research Office grantee, 1956-62, 77-81, 81—; NIH research grantee, 1966-69; NSF research grantee, 1969-71. Mem. Am. Math. Soc., AAAS, Inst. Math. Stats., Soc. Indsl. and Applied Math., N.Y. Acad. Scis., Iowa Acad. Scis., Polish Math. Soc., Bernoulli Soc., Soc. Math. Biology, Engring. Soc. Detroit, Nat. Assn. Mathematicians, Assn. Women in Math., London Math. Soc., Sigma Xi. Democrat. Episcopalian. Office: Dept Math Atlanta U Atlanta GA 30314

BHATIA, AVADH BEHARI, physicist; b. India, Aug. 16, 1921; emigrated to Can., 1953, naturalized, 1965. B.Sc., U. Allahabad, 1940, M.Sc., 1942, D.Phil., 1946; Ph.D., U. Liverpool, Eng., 1951. Exhbn. scholar univs. Bristol and Liverpool, 1947-49; prof. theoretical physics Phys. Research Lab., Ahmedabad, 1950-52; Imperial Chem. Industries fellow U. Edinburgh, Scotland, 1952-53; fellow Nat. Research Council Can., Ottawa, 1953-55; mem. faculty U. Alta., Edmonton, 1955—, prof. physics, 1960—; dir. Theoretical Physics Inst., 1964-69; hon. prof. U. Liverpool, 1963-64; U.K. Sci. Research Council sr. vis. fellow Oxford (Eng.) U., 1978-79. Author: Ultrasonic Absorption, 1967, also research papers. Fellow Royal Soc. Can., Am. Phys. Soc.; mem. Can. Assn. Physicists; asso. mem. Acoustical Am. Address: Physics Dept Univ Alta Edmonton AB T6G 2J1 Canada

BHAUMIK, MANI LAL, physicist; b. Calcutta, India, Jan. 5, 1932; came to U.S., 1959, naturalized, 1968; s. Gunadhar and Lolita (Pramanik) B. B.S., U. Calcutta, 1951, M.S., 1953; Ph.D., Indian Inst. Tech., 1958. Fellow U. Calif. at Los Angeles, 1959-63; with Xerox Electro-Optical Systems, Pasadena, Calif., 1961-67, Northrop Corp. Labs., Hawthorne, Calif., 1968—, research dir., 1971-75; mgr. Laser Tech. Lab., Northrop Research and Tech. Center, 1976—; lectr. physics Calif. State Coll., Long Beach, 1967-69. Contbr. articles to profl. jours. Fellow Am. Phys. Soc., IEEE. Patentee in field. Home: 820 Seco St Pasadena CA 91103 Office: Northrop Research and Tech Center: 1 Research Park Palos Verdes CA 90274 *A strong and innate belief in basic human goodness has often pulled me out of hostile circumstances where one is likely to lose faith in humanity.*

BHAVSAR, NATVAR PRAHLADJI, painter; b. Gothava, India, Apr. 7, 1934; came to U.S., 1962; s. Prahladji V. and Babu P. B.; m. Janet Brosious, Jan. 15, 1978; children: Shashin, Ajay, Rajeev. A.M., Bombay (India) State Higher Art Exam., 1958, Govt. Diploma Art, 1959; B.A. in Liberal Arts and English Lit, Gujarat U., Ahmedabad, India, 1960; M.F.A., U. Pa., 1965. Instr. in art U. R.I., 1967, 68, 69. One-man shows include, Max Hutchinson Gallery, N.Y.C., 1970, 71, 72, 74, 77, 78, Max Hutchinson Gallery, in Houston, 1978, Gallery A. Sydney, Australia, 1970, Gallery Chemould, Bombay, Kenmore Gallery, Phila., 1963, 74, Kingspitcher Gallery, Pitts., 1977, Suzette Schochet Gallery, Newport, R.I., Gloria Luria Gallery, Miami, Fla., 1978, Wichita (Kans.) Art Mus., 1979, group shows include, Jewish Mus., N.Y.C., 1970, Whitney Mus. Am. Art, 1970 (2), Indpls. Mus. Art, 1970, 78, U. Sydney, 1970, Columbus (Ohio) Gallery Fine Arts, 1971, U. Rochester, Max Hutchinson Gallery, 1973, Am. Acad. Arts and Letters Art Gallery, N.Y.C., Ruth S. Schaffner Gallery, Los Angeles, 1974, Reed Coll., Rockland Center for Arts, West Nyack, N.Y., 1979, Fifth Triennale, New Delhi, India, 1981; represented in permanent collections, Boston Mus. Fine Arts, Guggenheim Mus., N.Y.C., Chase Manhattan Bank, N.Y.C., Wichita Art Mus. (Kans.), Herbert F. Johnson Mus. at Cornell U., Australian Nat. Gallery, Canberra, Library of Congress, M.I.T., Ulrich Mus. Art, Wichita, Met. Mus. Art, N.Y.C., Lannan Found., Palm Beach, Fla., Power Inst., Sydney, Rose Art Mus. at Brandeis U., U. Mass., Amherst, U. Del., Whitney Mus. Am. Art, N.Y.C., Worcester (Mass.) Mus. John D. Rockefeller III Fund fellow, 1965-66; Guggenheim Meml. Found. fellow, 1975-76. Subject of profl. articles. Home and Studio: 131 Greene St New York NY 10012

BIAGGI, MARIO, congressman; b. N.Y.C., Oct. 26, 1917; s. Salvatore and Mary (Campari) B.; m. Marie Wassil, Apr.20, 1941; children: Jacqueline, Barbara, Richard, Mario II. LL.B., N.Y. Law Sch., 1963. Bar: N.Y. 1963. Detective lt. N.Y.C. Police Dept., 1942-65; community relations specialist, N.Y.C., 1961-63; asst. sec. state N.Y., 1966; mem. 91st-98th Congresses from 10th Dist. N.Y.; mem. edn. and labor com., mcht. marine and fisheries com., chmn. subcom. fed., state and community affairs of select com. on aging, ex-officio mem. select com. on narcotics abuse and control, chmn. subcom. on coast guard and navigation. 91st-97th Congresses from 10th Dist. N.Y. Past 1st v.p., acting pres. Patrolmen's Benevolent Assn.; past bd. dirs. Police Widows Relief Fund, Police Recreation Center, Police Pension Fund, Municipal Credit Union. Recipient medal of honor N.Y.C. Police, 1967; decorated Star of Solidarity, Italy, 1961, Cavaliere Order of Merit, 1965; recipient Pub. Service award Greek Orthodox Archdiocese of N. and S.Am. Mem. Am., Bronx County bar assns., Trial Lawyers Assn., NAACP (life), Navy League, Columbia Assns. in Civil Service (pres. nat. council). Office: 2428 Rayburn House Office Bldg Washington DC 20515 *

BIAGGINI, BENJAMIN FRANKLIN, railroad executive; b. New Orleans, Apr. 15, 1916; s. B.F. and Maggie (Switzer) B.; m. Anne Payton, Sept. 9, 1937; children: Constance Sue (Mrs. Jay Guittard), Marian Anne (Mrs. David M. Krattebol). B.S., St. Mary's of Tex., 1936; grad. Advanced Mgmt. Program, Harvard U., 1955. Former Chmn., chief exec. officer So. Pacific Co.; dir. Santa Fe So. Pacific Corp.; dir. Tenneco Inc., Ticor, Carter Hawley Hale Stores, Inc.; mem. Bus. Council, Nat. Transp. Policy Study Commn., 1976—. Trustee Calif. Inst. Tech., Nat. Safety Council; founder, vice chmn. Calif. Roundtable; bd. dirs. SRI Internat. Mem. Calif. C. of C. (pres. 1973), Conf. Bd. Office: Steuart St Tower 22d Floor One Market Plaza San Francisco CA 94105

BIALER, SEWERYN, political science educator, author, consultant; b. Berlin, Nov. 3, 1926; U.S., 1955; s. Victor and Maria (Kalovski) B.; m. Joan M. Afferica, Dec. 23, 1967. B.A., Acad. Polit. Sci., Warsaw, Poland, 1950; M.A., Inst. Social Sci., Warsaw, 1952, Ph.D. in Econs., 1955, Columbia U., 1966. Assoc. prof. Columbia U., N.Y.C., 1966-70, prof., 1974-80, Ruggles prof. polit. sci., 1980—; bd. dirs. Lehrman Inst., N.Y.C., 1980, Research Inst. Internat. Change; chmn. bd. Transnat. Research Inc., N.Y.C., 1981—; mem. Joint Com. on Soviet Studies, N.Y.C., 1982—. Author: Stalin and His Generals, 1968, Radicalism in the Contemporary Age, 3 vols., 1977, Stalin's Successors; Leadership, Stability and Change in the Soviet Union, 1980, The Soviet Paradox, 1984. Bd. dirs. UN-U.S. Assn., N.Y.C., 1982. MacArthur Found. fellow, 1983-88; Ford Found. fellow, 1964-66; Lehrman Inst. fellow; Internat. Research and Exchanges scholar, 1979. Mem. Am. Assn. Polit. Sci., Am. Assn. Advancement Soviet Studies. Office: Research Inst on Internat Change 420 W 118 St New York NY 10027

BIALKIN, KENNETH J., lawyer, educator; b. N.Y.C., Sept. 9, 1929; s. Samuel and Lillian (Kastner) B.; m. Ann Eskind, Aug. 19, 1956; children: Lisa Beth, Johanna. A.B., U. Mich.-Ann Arbor, 1950; cert. of attendance, London Sch. Econ., 1952; J.D., Harvard U., 1953. Bar: N.Y. 1953, U.S. Dist. Ct. (ea. dist.) N.Y. 1955, U.S. Supreme Ct. 1964, U.S. Dist. Ct. (so. dist.) N.Y. 1972, U.S. Ct. Appeals (2d cir.) 1976. Assoc. Willkie Farr & Gallagher, N.Y.C., 1953-60, ptnr., 1960—; dean U. Soc. Calif., Los Angeles, 1980—; adj. prof. law NYU., 1969—; lectr., commentator legal and fin. symposia; dir. E.M. Warburg, Pincus & Co., Inc., Gulf Resources & Chem. Corp., Shearson-Am. Express Inc., The Mcpl. Assistance Corp. City of N.Y. Editor: The Business Lawyer, 1980; contbr. articles on corp., fin. investment law to profl. jours. Nat. chmn. Anti-Defamation League of B'nai B'rith, 1982; vice chmn., dir. Jerusalem Found., Inc., 1975; mem. distbn. com. Fedn. Jewish Philanthropies of N.Y., 1979-82; bd. govs. Tel-Aviv U., 1979; trustee Am. Friends of the Hebrew U., 1980; bd. dirs. United Jewish Appeal Greater N.Y., 1979; mem. report coordinating group SEC, 1974-77. Mem. ABA (chmn. fed. regulation of securities com. 1974-79, chmn. com. to study fgn. investment in U.S. 1978-80, chmn. sect. of corp. banking and bus. law 1981), N.Y. County Lawyers Assn., Am. Bar Retirement Assn. (dir. 1981—). Club: Harvard. Home: 211 Central Park W New York NY 10024 Office: Willkie Farr & Gallagher One Citicorp Ctr 153 E 53d St New York NY 10022

BIANCHINE, JOSEPH RAYMOND, pharmacologist; b. Albany, N.Y., Sept. 7, 1929; s. Nunzie and Rose (Gallela) B.; m. Josette Woel, Oct. 10, 1956; children: Peter Joseph, Christine Rose. B.S., Siena Coll., 1951; Ph.D., Albany Med. Coll., 1959; M.D., State U. N.Y., Syracuse, 1960. Intern Johns Hopkins Hosp., Balt., 1960-61, resident, fellow, 1960-65; instr. medicine and pharmacology Sch. Medicine, Johns Hopkins U., Balt., 1965-68, asst. prof., 1968-70, asso. prof., 1970-72; prof., chmn. dept. pharmacology, prof. medicine Tex. Tech U., Lubbock, 1972-74, Sch. Medicine, Ohio State U., Columbus, 1974-83; v.p. med. research Hoffmann-LaRoche Inc., Nutley, N.J., 1983—. Contbr. research articles to various jours. Served with USPHS, 1962-63. Mem. Am. Soc. Pharmacology and Exptl. Therapeutics, Am. Fedn. Clin. Research, Am. Assn. Study Headache, Am. Assn. Univ. Pharmacologists, Am. Soc. Clin. Parmacology and Therapeutics, Am. Pharm. Assn., Franklin County Med. Assn., Ohio Med. Assn. Office: Hoffmann-La Roche Inc Nutley NJ 07110

BIANCO, JOSEPH PAUL, JR., department store executive; b. West Pittston, Pa., Sept. 4, 1936; s. Joseph P. and Mary M. (Compitello) B.; m. Lynda Joyce Hetfield, July 11, 1964; children: Anne Margaret, Paul Burke. B.B.A., Gen. Motors Inst. Tech., 1958; M.A. Econ., Georgetown U., 1964; D.B.A. (hon.), Cleary Coll., 1981. With Gen. Motors Corp., 1954-60, Touche, Ross & Co., 1964-68, Marantette & Co. (investment bankers), Detroit, 1968-71, Loeb Rhoades & Co., 1971-76; v.p. civic and govtl. affairs Hudson's Dept. Stores-Dayton Hudson Corp., Detroit, 1977—; lectr. in field. Chmn. bd. Southeastern Mich. Transp. Authority; trustee Pontiac Housing Corp.; bd. dirs. Alcoholic Rehab. Center; mem. Detroit Renaissance Corp.; chmn. bd. Mich. Mchts. Council.; mem. central budget bd. Archdiocese of Detroit; allocations bd. Detroit United Way. Lt. comdr. USCGR. Mem. Econ. Club Detroit, Central Bus. Dist. Assn. (vice chmn.), Conf. Bd., Bus.-Urban Council. Roman Catholic. Address: 1250 Romney Rd Bloomfield Hills MI 48013 *I will always be grateful for my upbringing as a member of a religious and ethnic minority. This experience has helped me to understand the movements toward equality of opportunity for all our citizens. I am convinced that private corporations have the technology, management resources, and finances to play an even larger role in solving urban problems and providing leadership for community challenges.*

BIANCO, RICHARD ANTHONY, marketing executive; b. N.Y.C., Dec. 30, 1947; s. Joseph R. and Antonio (Lobello) B.; m. JoAnn Merola, Oct. 8, 1972; 1 dau., Alessandra. B.B.A., Manhattan Coll., 1969; M.B.A., L.I.U., 1971. With Bankers Trust, N.Y.C., 1971-74; v.p. Morgan Stanley & Co., Inc., N.Y.C., 1975-78; v.p., head internat. trading Morgan Stanley Inc., London, 1978-80; mng. dir. Dillon Read & Co., Inc., N.Y.C., 1980—. Republican. Roman Catholic. Office: 48 Wall St New York NY 10005

BIANCOLLI, LOUIS, writer; b. N.Y.C., Apr. 17, 1907; s. Carmine and Achilla (Montesano) B.; m. Edith Rattner, 1933 (dec. 1957); 1 dau., Margaret (Mrs. Murray Weissbach); m. Jeanne Mitchell, 1958; children—Lucy, Amy. A.B., N.Y. U., 1935, A.M., 1936; postgrad., Columbia U., 1936-38, Am. Council Learned Socs. grant for studies Russian, Intensive Lang. Programs, 1943. Music critic, N.Y. World-Telegram and Sun., 1928-66; annotator, N.Y. Philharmonic Soc., 1941-49; Author: (with Robert Bagar) The Concert Companion, 1947, The Book of Great Conversations, 1948, The Victor Book of Operas, 1949, The Analytical Concert Guide, 1951, (with Mary Garden) Mary Garden's Story, 1951, (with Kirsten Flagstad) The Flagstad Manuscript, 1952, The Opera Reader, 1953, The Mozart Handbook, 1954, (with Herbert F. Peyser) Masters of the Orchestra, 1954, (with Ruth Slenczynska) Forbidden Childhood, 1957, (with Roberta Peters) A Debut at the Met, 1967; Translator: Boris Godounoff libretto from Russian, 1952, 64; in blank verse Dante's Divine Comedy, 1966, (with Thomas Scherman) The Beethoven Companion, 1972; libretto: Italian opera Ezio (Handel), 1972, Poro (Handel), 1977, Introduction to Am. edit. Greek collection of letters of Dimitri Mitropoulos, 1972; Contbr. articles to mags., music brochures. Mem. Music Critics Circle, Phi Beta Kappa. Address: New Preston CT 06777 *Music has been a kind of religious faith to me, a source of deep spiritual refreshment and constant emotional renewal. In my darkest moments, its benign and reassuring voice has saved my sanity, perhaps even my life. In my happiest moments it has been the miraculous outside expression of my great inner joy and excitement over the boundless adventure of life.*

BIAS, FRANK JOHN, communications co. exec.; b. Des Moines, Oct. 1, 1919; s. Emory Lowell and Hazel Ethel (Chambers) B.; m. Jean Elinore Kesting, Aug. 4, 1945; children—Carolyn Gail, Elaine Catherine. B.S in E.E, Iowa State Coll., 1941. With Gen. Electric Co., Syracuse, N.Y., 1941-69; v.p. engring. Tele-Vue Systems, Dublin, Calif., 1969-79; v.p. sci. and tech. Viacom Internat., Inc., N.Y.C., 1979—. Recipient Nat. Cable TV Assn. Outstanding Engring. Achievement award, 1979. Fellow IEEE; mem. Soc. Motion Picture and TV Engrs., Soc. Broadcast Engrs., Soc. Cable TV Engrs. Republican. Presbyterian. Home: 5 Incognito Ln Ossining NY 10562 Office: 1211 Ave of Americas New York NY 10036

BIBB, THOMAS FARRIS, manufacturing company executive; b. Murfreesboro, Tenn., July 26, 1943; s. Charles McLean and Ann (Farris) B.; m. Glenda Lenhardt, Jan. 29, 1983; children from previous marriage: Patrick, Michael, John, Casey, Heather. B.S., U. New Orleans, 1964. C.P.A., Tex., La. With Ernst & Whinney (C.P.A.s (formerly Ernst & Ernst), New Orleans, 1964-67, San Antonio, 1967-69; controller Conroy, Inc., San Antonio, 1969-78, v.p., 1975-78, v.p. fin., 1978-80, exec. v.p. adminstrn., 1980—. Mem. Am. Inst. C.P.A.s, Fin. Exec. Inst., Am. Mgmt. Assn. Home: 9202 Bent Elm Creek San Antonio TX 78230 Office: Suite 201 3355 Cherry Ridge Dr San Antonio TX 78230

BIBBO, MARLUCE, physician, educator; b. Sao Paulo, Brazil, July 14, 1939; d. Domingos and Yolanda (Ranciaro) B. M.D, U. Sao Paulo, 1963, Sc.D., 1968. Intern Hosps. das Clinicas, U. Sao Paulo, 1963; resident in ob-gyn, 1964-66; instr. dept. morphology and ob-gyn U. Sao Paulo, 1966-68, asst. prof., 1968-69; asst. prof. sect. cytology dept. ob-gyn U. Chgo., 1969-73, asso. prof., 1973-77, asso. prof. pathology, 1974-77, prof. ob-gyn and pathology, 1978—; asso. dir. Cytology Lab., Approved Sch. Cytotech and Cytocybernetics, AMA-Am. Soc. Clin. Pathologists, 1970—; Mem. research com. Ill. div. Am. Cancer Soc., 1976—. Contbr. numerous articles to profl. jours. Fellow Internat. Acad. Cytology; mem. Am. Soc. Cytology (exec. com., pres. 1982-83). Home: 400 E Randolph St Apt 2009 Chicago IL 60601 Office: 5841 S Maryland Ave Chicago IL 60637

BIBBY, DOUGLAS EARL, radiologist; b. Cisco, Tex., Aug. 15, 1922; s. Earl Riss and Eunice (Key) B.; m. Elinor Elaine Duncan, May 9, 1945; children—Gayle Elaine, Bonnie Colleen, Lynda Diane. Student, John Tarleton Agrl. Coll., 1940-42; M.D., U. Tex., 1946. Diplomate: Am. Bd. Radiology. Intern Harris Meml. Hosp., Ft. Worth, 1946-47; resident radiology VA Hosp., McKinney, Tex., 1949-51; practice radiology, Temple, Tex., 1951-52, Ft. Worth, 1952—; asst. prof. radiology U. Tex. Southwestern Med. Sch., 1961—; Trustee Am. Registry Radiol. Technicians, 1962-66. Served with M.C. AUS, 1947-49. Fellow Am. Coll. Radiology; mem. A.M.A., Tex. Med. Assn., Tarrant County Med. Soc., Radiol. Soc. N.Am. Home: 3708 Sierra Ct Ft Worth TX 76109 Office: 815 Pennsylvania St Ft Worth TX 76104

BIBERSTEIN, ERNST LUDWIG, veterinary medicine educator; b. Breslau, Germany, Nov. 11, 1922; s. Hans Harry and Erna (Stein) B.; m. Hannah Hahn, June 26, 1949; children—Michael P., Helen R., Anne D., Julie B. B.S., U. Ill., 1947; D.V.M., Cornell U., 1951, M.S., 1954, Ph.D., 1955. Diplomate: Am. Coll. Vet. Microbiology. Practice vet. medicine, Akron, Ohio, 1951-52; acting asso. prof. clin. pathology N.Y. State Vet. Coll., 1955-56; faculty U. Calif. at Davis Sch. Vet. Medicine, 1956—, prof. microbiology, 1966—, chmn. dept., 1969-74; chief microbiology service Vet. Med. Teaching Hosp., 1967-75; Mem. com. animal health, subcom. standards methods for vet. microbiology Nat. Acad. Scis., 1967-72; mem. Internat. Com. on Systematic Bacteriology (sec. haemophilus subcom.), 1966-78, chmn., 1980. Co-translator, editor: (with R.E. Habel) The Fundamentals of the Histology of Domestic Animals, rev. edit, 1957. Served with AUS, 1943-45. Decorated Silver Star.; NIH spl. fellow Moredun Inst., Edinburgh, Scotland, 1963-64, 68-69. Mem. Am. Acad. Microbiology, Am. Vet. Med. Assn., Am. Soc. Microbiology, Path. Soc. Gt. Britain and Ireland, Conf. Research Workers Animal Diseases, Sigma Xi, Gamma Sigma Delta, Phi Zeta, Phi Kappa Phi, Alpha Epsilon Pi, Alpha Zeta. Jewish. Home: 508 12th St Davis CA 95616

BIBLE, FRANCES LILLIAN, mezzo soprano, educator; b. Sackets Harbor, N.Y., Jan. 26; d. Arthur and Lillian (Cooke) B. Student, Juilliard Sch. Music, 1939-47. Artist-in-residence Shepherd Sch. of Music Rice U., Houston, 1975—. Appeared throughout, U.S., Australia, Europe including, Vienna Staatsoper, Karlsruhe Staatsoper, Dublin Opera Co., N.Y.C. Opera, NBC-TV Opera, San Francisco Opera, Glyndebourne Opera, San Antonio Opera Festival, New Orleans Opera, Houston Grand Opera, Miami Opera, Dallas Opera; appeared in concert with major symphonies. Mem. Sigma Alpha Iota (hon.), Beta Sigma Phi (hon.). Republican. Episcopalian. Home: 2225 Bolsover Houston TX 77005 Office: 3002 Huldy Houston TX 77098

BICE, MAX H., broadcaster; b. Toppenish, Wash., Aug. 29, 1916; s. Delmar F. and Edith Emily (Williamson) B.; m. Margaret Jane Burrus, June 29, 1941 (dec. Dec. 1975); children: Kathryn Bice Gallaher, Marilyn J. (dec.), Luann M. Bice Holmes; m. Virginia I. Van Wyhe, 1977. Student, U. Wash., 1935-37. With Sta. KRSC, Seattle, 1937-38, Sta. KMO, Tacoma, 1938-48; with electronics div. Tribune Pub. Co., Tacoma, 1948-74, mgr. radio, 1957-58, mgr. radio and TV, 1958-70, v.p., gen. mgr. div., 1970-74; cons. Pierce County Ednl. TV; gen. mgr. KTNT-TV, Seattle; pres. M.B. Communications, Inc.; treas., dir. C & G Electronics Co., 1977—. Pres. Area Wide Bd. Daffodil Festival, 1966; chmn. Wash. Industry Adv. Com., 1969-72; active United Givers Fund; mem. adv. com. Pierce County Commrs.; bd. dirs. Better Bus. Bur., pres., 1975-76; bd. dirs. Tacoma-Pierce County Safety Council; nat. bd. dirs. USO, also Puget Sound exec. com. Mem. Nat. Assn. Broadcasters (TV code bd., chmn.), Wash. Assn. Broadcasters (pres. 1968-69), IEEE, Soc. Motion Picture and TV Engrs., Radio Pioneers, Quarter Century Wireless Club, Am. Radio Relay League, N. Pacific Marine Radio Council (dir. 1977—, pres. 1979-80), Internat. Radio and TV Soc., Seattle, Tacoma advt. clubs, Coast Guard Aux., Radio Club Tacoma (past pres.), Interclub Boating Assn. Wash. (dir. 1982-85). Clubs: Elks, Kiwanis, Tacoma (past pres.), Gig Harbor Yacht (commodore 1982). Home: 10020 86th Ave NW Gig Harbor WA 98335 Office: 2360 Fawcett Ave Tacoma WA 98402

BICE, SCOTT HAAS, lawyer, educator; b. Los Angeles, Mar. 19, 1943; s. Fred Haas and Virginia M. (Scott) B.; m. Barbara Franks, Dec. 21, 1968. B.S., U. So. Calif., 1965, J.D., 1968. Bar: Calif. bar 1971. Law clk. to Chief Justice Earl Warren, 1968-69; asst. prof., asso. prof., prof. law U. So. Calif., Los Angeles, 1969—, asso. dean, 1971-74, dean, 1980—; vis. prof. polit. sci. Calif. Inst. Tech., 1977; vis. prof. U. Va., 1978-79. Contbr. articles to law jours. Affiliated scholar Am. Bar Found., 1972-74. Mem. Am. Law Inst., Calif. Bar, Los Angeles County Bar Assn., Am. Judicature Soc. Home: 787 S San Rafael Ave Pasadena CA 91103 Office: U So Calif Law Center University Park Los Angeles CA 90007

BICH, MARCEL (BARON BICH), industrialist; b. Turin, Italy, July 29, 1914; s. Aime-Mario and Marie (Muffat de Saint-Amour de Chanaz) B.; m. Louise Chamussy (dec.); children: Claude, Marie-Caroline Bich Martin, Bruno, Francois; m. Laurence Courier de Mere; children: Antoine, Marie Aimee, Marie-Charlotte, Marie-Henriette, Marie-Pauline, Xavier. Ed., Coll. St.-Elme à Arcachon, Faculté de Droit de Paris. Founder, former pres., chmn. bd., now hon. chmn. bd. Bic Co.; chmn. bd. Bic Pen Corp. Decorated chevalier Legion of Honor. Office: Bic Pen Corp Wiley St Milford CT 06460 *

BICKEL, BERTRAM WATKINS, banker; b. Mt. Carmel, Pa., Jan. 26, 1925; s. George Isaac and Edith (Watkins) B.; m. Charis Irene Henry,

June 8, 1946; 1 son, Keith David. Grad. high sch. Head teller Union Nat. Bank, Mt. Carmel, 1946-50; nat. bank examiner, 1951-61; sr. v.p., comptroller Merchants Nat. Bank, Allentown, Pa., 1961-76; comptroller Norton Oil Co., Phillipsburg, N.J.; (and subs.'s.); Accounting adviser Lehigh County Community Coll. Bd. dirs., treas. Allentown YMCA. Served with USNR, 1943-46. Mem. Bank Adminstrn. Inst. (dir.), Am. Legion. Republican. Presbyn. Clubs: Masons; Brookside Country (Macungie, Pa.) (dir.); Livingston, Lehigh Valley (Allentown). Home: 1205 Overlook Rd Apt 8 Whitehall PA 18052

BICKEL, HENRY JOSEPH, electronics co. exec.; b. Vienna, Austria, Mar. 16, 1929; came to U.S., 1946, naturalized, 1946; s. Ernest and Albine B.; m. Rogneda Yakimach, July 4, 1954; children—Nina, Andrew. B.S. in Elec. Engring. magna cum laude, CCNY, 1952; M.S., Columbia U., 1955. Supr. Columbia U. Electronics Research Lab., 1952-57; sr. project engr., then pres. Fed. Sci. Corp., N.Y.C., 1957-73; pres. Nicolet Sci. Corp., Northvale, N.J., 1973—, also dir.; v.p., dir. Nicolet Instrument Corp.; dir. Nicolet Japan Corp. Author. Mem. IEEE, Sigma Xi, Tau Beta Pi, Eta Kappa Nu. Club: Westchester Country. Patentee in field. Home: 49 Northway St Bronxville NY 10708 Office: 245 Livingston St Northvale NJ 07647

BICKEL, HERBERT JACOB, JR., oil company executive; b. Evanston, Ill., Feb. 20, 1930; s. Herbert Jacob and Jean (Meadows) B.; m. Joan Hough, July 17, 1954; children: David Alan, Daniel Wayne, John Douglas. B.S. in Bus. Adminstrn, U. Fla., 1952; M.S. in Indsl. Mgmt, Ga. Inst. Tech., 1955; postgrad., Mass. Inst. Tech., 1955-56. Prin. economist Tex. Eastern Transmission Corp., Houston, 1957-66, treas., 1966-80, v.p., 1971-80; sr. v.p. fin. Saxon Oil Co., Dallas, 1980—; instr. Ga. Inst. Tech., 1955, Centenary Coll., Shreveport, 1958; vis. lectr. Pa. State U., 1964. Author: (with others) National Fuels and Energy Study, Competition and Growth in American Energy Markets, 1947-1985, 1968. Served to 1st lt. AUS, 1952-54. Mem. Fin. Execs. Inst., Soc. Petroleum Engrs., Houston Soc. Fin. Analysts (pres. 1970-71). Club: Chaparral. Home: 9915 Meadowbrook Dr Dallas TX 75220 Office: 717 N Harwood St Dallas TX 75201

BICKEL, PETER JOHN, university dean, statistician; b. Bucharest, Roumania, Sept. 21, 1940; came to U.S., 1957, naturalized, 1964; s. Eliezer and P. Madeleine (Moscovici) B.; m. Nancy Kramer, Mar. 2, 1964; children: Amanda, Stephen. A.B., U. Calif., Berkeley, 1960, M.A., 1961, Ph.D., 1963. Asst. prof. stats. U. Calif., Berkeley, 1964-67, asso. prof., 1967-70, prof., 1970—, chmn. dept., 1976-79, dean phys. scis., 1980—; vis. lectr. math. Imperial Coll., London, 1965-66; fellow J.S. Guggenheim Meml. Found., 1970-71; NATO sr. sci. fellow, 1974. Author: (with K. Doksum) Mathematical Statistics, 1976; Assoc. editor: Annals of Math. Statistics, 1968-76; contbr. articles to profl. jours. Fellow Inst. Math. Stats. (pres. 1980), Am. Statis. Assn., AAAS; mem. Royal Statis. Soc., Internat. Statis. Inst. Office: Dept Statistics Evans Hall Univ of Calif Berkeley CA 94720

BICKEL, ROBERT JOHN, educator; b. Louisville, Nov. 8, 1916; s. Robert G. and Agatha C. (Wesch) B.; m. Evanetta Beuther, Nov. 26, 1942. A.B., U. Louisville, 1937; M.A., Northwestern U., 1941; postgrad., U. Pa., 1946-52; Ph.D., U. Pitts., 1960. Tchr. Louisville Pub. Schs., 1937-41; instr. Drexel U., 1946-47, asst. prof., 1947-52, asso. prof., 1952-60, prof., 1960—, asso. dept. head, 1963-68, acting head, 1968-69, asso. head, 1969—. Served with C.E. AUS, 1941-45. Mem. Am. Math. Soc., Math. Assn. Am., Soc. for Indsl. and Applied Math. (treas. 1955-62). Home: Ellis Woods Rd RD 1 Pottstown PA 19464 Office: Dept Math Drexel U Philadelphia PA 19104

BICKERS, DAVID RINSEY, physician, educator; b. Richmond, Va., Sept. 23, 1941; s. William McKenzie and Helen Virginia (Fitzpatrick) B; m. Melinda-Lee Jaeger, May 30, 1970; 1 dau., McKenzie Winchester. A.B., Georgetown U., 1963; M.D., U. Va., 1967. Intern in medicine U. Iowa Hosps., Iowa City, 1967-68; resident in dermatology skin and cancer unit N.Y.U. Med. Center, 1970-73; NIH tng. fellow, guest investigator Rockefeller U., 1971-73, R.J. Reynolds scholar in clin. medicine, asst. prof., asso. physician, 1976-77; asst. prof. dermatology Columbia U. Coll. Phys. and Surg., 1973-76; asst. attending dermatologist Presbyn. Hosp., N.Y.C., 1973-76; prof. dermatology, chmn. dept. Case Western Res. U. Med. Sch., 1977—; dir. dermatology service Univ. Hosps., Cleve. VA Hosp.; mem. gen. medicine A study sect. NIH, 1980-84, chmn., 1982-84. Author: (with L.C. Harber) Photosensitivity Diseases: Principles of Diagnosis and Treatment, 1981, (with Hazen and Lynch) Clinical Pharmacology of Skin Disease, 1984; mem. editorial bd.: Jour. Am. Acad. Dermatology, 1979—, Physicians Drug Alert, 1982—, Today's Therapeutic Trends, 1983—, Photodermatology, 1983—. Served as officer M.C. USAF, 1968-70. Decorated Air Force Commendation medal. Mem. Am. Soc. Clin. Investigation, Am. Soc. Pharmacology and Exptl. Therapeutics, Am. Fedn. Clin. Research, Am. Soc. Photobiology, Am. Acad. Dermatology, Am. Dermatol. Assn., Soc. Investigative Dermatology, Central Soc. Clin. Research, Pasteur Club (Cleve.). Office: Univ Hosps 2074 Abington Rd Cleveland OH 44106

BICKERS, JAMES FRANKLIN, JR., printing co. exec.; b. Bartlett, Tenn., Mar. 2, 1919; s. James Franklin and Kathryn Pauline (Diefenbach) B.; m. Emily Power, May 3, 1941; children—James Franklin, III, John P., Barbara L. B.F.A., U. Ill., 1941; grad. sr. exec. program, M.I.T., 1968. With R.R. Donnelley & Sons Co., Chgo., 1951—, v.p., then sr. v.p. gen. catalog sales div., 1969-75, group v.p. directories, 1975-81; group v.p. Digital Group R.A. Donnelley's Sons Co., 1981—; adv. council Coll. Commerce, U. Ill.; also lectr. in field. Served with AUS, 1941-45. Mem. Direct Mail/Mktg. Assn., U.S. Ind. Telephone Assn. Republican. Clubs: Tavern (Chgo.); Sunset Ridge Country., Dairymen's Country. Home: 3019 Indian Wood Rd Wilmette IL 60091 Office: RR Donnelley & Sons Co 2223 King Dr Chicago IL 60616

BICKFORD, CHRISTOPHER PENNY, historical society executive; b. Bklyn., Feb. 27, 1943; s. Addison Duncan and Carol Anita (Penny) B.; m. Roberta Robbins, Sept. 18, 1965. B.A., Union Coll., Scchenectady, 1964; M.A., Harvard U., 1965; Ph.D., U. Conn., 1971. Librarian Conn. Hist. Soc., Hartford, 1975-79, asst. dir., 1979-80, dir., 1980—. Author: The Connecticut Historical Society: A Short Illustrated History, 1825-1975 1975. Woodrow Wilson fellow, 1964-65. Mem. Soc. Am. Archivists, Am. Assn. State and Local History, Am. Assn. Mus., New Eng Mus. Assn. Lodge: Rotary. Office: Conn Hist Soc 1 Elizabeth St Hartford CT 06105

BICKFORD, GEORGE PERCIVAL, lawyer; b. Berlin, N.H., Nov. 28, 1901; s. Gershon Percival and Lula Adine (Buck) B.; m. Clara L. Gehring, Apr. 6, 1933; 1 dau., Louise G. Boyd. A.B. cum laude, Harvard, 1922, LL.B., 1926. Bar: Ohio 1926. Since practiced in, Cleve.; asso. firm Arter & Hadden, partner, 1940—; instr. Hauchung U., Wuchang, China, 1922-23; instr. taxation Western Res. Law Sch., 1940-47; lectr. Indian history and culture Cleve. Coll., 1948-50; gen. counsel FHA, Washington, 1958-59; dir. Indsl. Electronic Rubber Co.; hon. consul of India, 1964—; Mem. Cleve. Moral Claims Commn., 1935-37. Mem. Cuyahoga County Rep. Exec. Com., 1948-58, 60—; Trustee Am. U. in Cairo; vis. com. fine arts dept. Harvard, 1962-68, 72—; trustee, former v.p. Cleve. Mus. Art; trustee Cleve. Inst. Art.; mem. Nat. Com. for Festival of India in U.S., 1985. Served with Ohio N.G., 1926-29; from capt. to lt. col. JAG dept. AUS, 1942-46. Decorated Legion of Merit. Mem. Am., Ohio, Cleve. bar assns., Cleve. Council World Affairs (trustee). Episcopalian (standing com. Diocese Ohio 1951-63, chancellor 1962-77). Clubs: Union, Rowfant, Skating (Cleve.); East India (London); Army and Navy (Washington); Harvard (N.Y.C.). Home: 2247 Chestnut Hills Dr Cleveland OH 44106 Office: 1144 Union Commerce Bldg Cleveland OH 44115

BICKFORD, JAMES GORDON, banker; b. Huntingdon, Que., Can., 1928; s. Harold Gordon and Jean Forbes (Stark) B.; m. Jetta Goodger-Hill, Aug. 6, 1951. With Canadian Imperial Bank of Commerce, 1945—, exec. v.p. internat. banking, Toronto, 1982—; dir. numerous subsidiaries cos.; dir. Gt. Lakes Re Mgmt. Corp., Martin Corp. Group Ltd. (Australia), Can. Eastern Fin. Ltd. (Hong Kong), Canlea Ltd. Presbyterian. Clubs: City, Overseas Bankers (London); National (Toronto). Office: Head Office Canadian Imperial Bank Commerce Commerce Ct Toronto ON M5L 1A2 Canada

BICKFORD, JOHN HOWE, banker, business executive; b. Berlin, N.H., July 13, 1905; s. Gershon P. and Lula A. (Buck) B.; m. Dorothy Ann Whealton, May 5, 1967; children: John Howe, Charles G., Lydia. B.S., Dartmouth Coll., 1926. Investment researcher Union Service Corp., N.Y.C., 1929-42, 44-54; with WPB, Washington, 1942-43; fin. v.p. Star Drilling Machine Co., Akron, Ohio, 1943-44; self-employed, 1954—; chmn. bd. Liquid Nitrogen Processing Corp., Malvern, Pa., 1966-76; dir. Morris County Savs. Bank, Morristown, N.J., 1959-81, chmn. bd., 1971-81, Transistor Devices, Inc., Cedar Knolls, N.J., 1965—; pres. Bard Inc. (restaurant and motel), Bernardsville, N.J., 1973-82, Perd, Inc. (restaurant and motel), 1972—. Mem. Morris Twp. Com., 1959-67; mayor of Morris Twp., 1962-63; pres. Morris Mus. Arts and Scis., 1971—; v.p. Family Service Morris County, 1968—. Republican. Episcopalian. Clubs: Morris County Golf; Broad St. (N.Y.C.). Address: Village Rd New Vernon NJ 07976

BICKFORD, JOHN VAN BUREN, coal company executive; b. Roanoke, Va., 1934. Grad., Va. Poly Inst., 1955. Pres. Gen. Coal Co., Phila., dir., Eastern Coal & Coke Co. Office: Gen Coal Co 2500 Fidelity Bldg Philadelphia PA 19109 *

BICKHAM, THOMAS MARION, JR., city official; b. Blanchard, La., Sept. 21, 1915; s. Thomas Marion and Mary Emma (Flowers) B.; m. Mildred Freeman, Mar. 22, 1941; 1 dau., Nancy Elizabeth. Grad., La. State U., 1938; postgrad., Centenary Law Sch., 1948-50. Mem. trust dept. 1st Nat. Bank of Shreveport, 1938-41; mgmt. analyst VA, Shreveport, 1946-51; asst. dir. VA Hosp., 1955-69; mayoral exec. officer, City of Shreveport, 1971—. Served to col. U.S. Army, 1941-46, 51-54. Decorated Legion of Merit, others. Mem. Nat. League Cities, U.S. Conf. Mayors, La. Municipal Assn. Methodist. Lodge: Lions. Office: 1234 Texas Ave Shreveport LA 71130 *

BICKING, JOHN FRANCIS, advt. agy. exec.; b. Gloucester, N.J., June 4, 1934; s. Joseph S. and Thelma E. (Ackroyd) B.; m. Marilyn M. Alashantakus, May 4, 1957. B.S., Fordham U., 1956. Asst. advt. mgr. Union Carbide Corp., N.Y.C., 1956-60; advt. mgr. Nat. Distillers & Chem. Co., N.Y.C., 1960-64; chmn. bd. Warner, Bicking & Fenwick, Inc., N.Y.C., 1964—. Pub.: Madison Ave. mag, 1970-73. Office: 866 United Nations Plaza New York NY 10017 *

BICKMORE, J. GRANT, banker; b. Brigham City, Utah, Nov. 24, 1916; s. William M. and Ida Luella (Olson) B.; m. Marjorie Marshall, June 4, 1940; children—Roger G., William Bradford. Student pub. schs. Asst. Cashier, mgr. Downey State Bank, Idaho, 1934-44, Security First Nat., 1944-46; bank examiner, State of Idaho, 1946-48, Fed. Res. Bank, San Francisco, 1948-50; cashier Idaho Bank & Trust Co., Pocatello, 1950, v.p., dir., exec. v.p., 1953-63, pres., chief exec. officer, 1963—, vice chmn. bd., 1981—; dir. Idaho Power Co., Comml. Security Bank, Ogden, Utah, KID-TV Corp., Idaho Falls. Mem. Gov.'s State Health Planning Council, 1967-70; mem. Idaho Bd. Health, 1966-69; regional dir., pres. Tendoy council Boy Scouts Am., 1966-70; mem. Idaho adv. council Small Bus. Adminstrn.; Trustee Found. for Full Service Banks, 1970-73; mem. adv. bd. Coll. Bus., Idaho State U., Pocatello, chmn., 1968-72; governing bd. St. Anthony Hosp. Mem. Am. Bankers Assn. (v.p. Idaho; treas. 1973-75), Idaho Bankers Assn. (past pres.), Fedn. Rocky Mountain States (dir.), U.S. C. of C. (fiscal policy com.), Idaho C. of C. (pres. 1972-73, dir.), Idaho Assn. Commerce and Industry (chmn. 1980). Clubs: Elks, Rotary. Home: 66 Cedar Hills Dr Pocatello ID Office: PO Box 1788 Pocatello ID 83201

BICKNELL, JOSEPH MCCALL, neurologist; b. Detroit, Dec. 3, 1933; s. Edgar Arnold and Bertha Margaret (McCall) B.; m. Nadyne Lenore Cooke, June 22, 1957; children: Martha Gail, Bruce McCall, Donald Morse, Craig Alan. B.A., U. Mich., 1955, M.D., 1959. Diplomate: Am. Bd. Psychiatry and Neurology. Intern U. Mich., Ann Arbor, 1959-60, resident, 1960-63, instr. in neurology, 1963-65; asst. prof. medicine U. N.Mex., 1965-70, asso. prof. neurology, 1970-73, prof., chmn. dept. neurology, 1973—; cons. to hosps. Contbr. Active Nat. Ski Patrol, Boy Scouts Am. Fellow Council Cerebrovascular Disease; mem. Am. Acad. Neurology, AMA, Am. Assn. Electromyography and Electrodiagnosis, Am. Heart Assn., Soc. Clin. Neurologists, Albuquerque and Bernalillo County Med. Soc., N.Mex. Med. Soc., N.Mex. Neurol.-Neurosurg. Soc., Phi Beta Kappa, Phi Kappa Phi, Alpha Omega Alpha. Home: 8721 LaSala Del Centro NE Albuquerque NM 87111 Office: 2211 Lomas Blvd NE Albuquerque NM 87131

BICKNER, BRUCE PIERCE, agriculture and natural resources executive; b. Chgo., Sept. 21, 1943; s. Arno A. and Dorothy P. (Pierce) B.; m. Joan Alice Johnson, July 29, 1967; children: Brian, Kevin, Julie. B.A., DePauw U., 1965; J.D., U. Mich., 1968. Bar: Ill. 1968, Wis. 1968. Law clk. U.S. Dist. Ct., Milw., 1969; ptnr. Sidley & Austin, Chgo., 1970-75; exec. v.p., dir. DeKalb AgResearch, Inc., Ill., 1976—; dir. Heinold Commodities, Inc., Chgo., Depco, Inc., Denver, Pride Oil Well Service Co., Houston, Lindsay Mfg. Co., Nebr. Mem. ABA. Republican. Mem. Evangelical Covenant Ch. Am. Office: DeKalb AgResearch Inc 3100 Sycamore Rd DeKalb IL 60115

BIDDINGTON, WILLIAM ROBERT, university dean, dental educator; b. Piedmont, W.Va., Mar. 30, 1925; s. William M. and Sadie (Vogtman) B.; m. Dolores E. Berrett, June 14, 1947; 1 son, William Berrett. Student, Potomac State Coll., 1942-43, Hampden-Sydney Coll., 1943-44; D.D.S. cum laude, U. Md., 1948. Diplomate: Am. Bd. Endodontics. Gen. practice dentistry, Balt., 1949-59; instr. Balt. Coll. Dental Surgery, Dental Sch. U. Md., 1949-52, asst. prof., 1952-56, assoc. prof., 1956-59; prof., chmn. dept. endodontics Sch. Dentistry, W.Va. U., Morgantown, 1959-68, asst. dean, 1966-68, dean, 1968—, interim v.p. academic affairs, 1979-80, interim v.p. health scis., 1981-82; Mem. at large, sec., vice chmn., chmn. adminstrv. bd., v.p. council deans Am. Assn. Dental Schs., 1974-78, pres., 1983-84. Served with USNR, 1942-46, 48-49. Fellow Am. Coll. Dentists (regent 1983—), Internat. Coll. Dentists; mem. ADA, W.Va. Dental Assn., Monongahela Valley Dental Soc., Monongalia County Dental Soc. (pres. 1966), Am. Assn. Dental Schs., Internat. Assn. Dental Research, Am. Assn. Endodontists, Gorgas Odontological Soc., Psi Omega, Omicron Kappa Upsilon (pres. supreme chpt. 1965-67). Home: Route 7 Box 720 Morgantown WV 26505 Office: School of Dentistry West Va U Morgantown WV 26505

BIDDLE, FLORA MILLER, art museum administrator. Pres. Whitney Mus. Am. Art, N.Y.C. Office: Whitney Museum Am Art 945 Madison Ave New York NY 10021§

BIDDLE, JAMES, fine arts adminstr.; b. Phila., July 8, 1929; s. Charles John and Katherine (Legendre) B.; m. Louisa Copeland, Apr. 25, 1959 (div. 1981); children—Letitia C., Pamela E., James C. B.A. in Art and Archeology, Princeton U., 1951. With U.S. Govt., 1951-53; with Met. Mus. Art, 1955-67, curator Am. wing, 1963-67; pres. Nat. Trust for Historic Preservation, Washington, 1967-80; sr. v.p. Southeby-Park-Bernet, N.Y.C., 1980—. Trustee Pa. Acad. Fine Arts; mem. Am. Revolution Bicentennial Commn.; former trustee Corcoran Mus., Am. Fedn. Arts. Office: 980 Madison Ave New York NY

BIDDLE, LIVINGSTON LUDLOW, JR., former government official, author; b. Bryn Mawr, Pa., May 26, 1918; s. Livingston Ludlow and Eugenia (Law) B.; m. Cordelia Frances Fenton, Mar. 15, 1945 (dec. May 1972); children: Cordelia Frances, Livingston Ludlow IV; m. Catharina Van Beek Baart, Nov. 3, 1973. A.B., Princeton, 1940; L.H.D. (hon.), Mt. St. Mary's Coll., N.Y., 1978, LL.D., Catholic U., 1979, D.F.A., U. L.I., 1979, U. Cin., 1979, Providence Coll., 1980, U. Notre Dame, 1980, D.L., Drexel U., 1980. Reporter Phila. Evening Bull., 1940-42; with Am. Field Service, Middle East, N. Africa, Italy, France, Germany, 1942-45; spl. asst. to U.S. Senator Claiborne Pell, 1963-65; dep. chmn. Nat. Endowment for Arts, Washington, 1965-67; chmn. div. arts Liberal Arts Coll., Fordham U., Lincoln Center, N.Y.C., 1967-70; spl. asst. to Senator Claiborne Pell, 1973-74; liaison dir. Nat. Endowment for Arts, Washington, 1974-75, chmn., 1977-80; staff dir. subcom. on edn. arts and humanities U.S. Senate, 1975-77. Author: Main Line, 1950, Debut, 1952, The Village Beyond, 1956, Sam Bentley's Island, 1960. Pres. Children's Service, Inc., Phila., 1960-62; chmn. bd. Pa. Ballet, 1971-72. Decorated Order of Leopold II, Belgium; recipient Phila. Athenaeum Best Novel award, 1956. Democrat. Episcopalian. Clubs: Philadelphia, Merion Cricket (Phila.); Century Assn. (N.Y.C.). Home: 2914 P St NW Washington DC 20007 *In my work I am seeking to help develop a climate in which the arts may truly flourish for the betterment of mankind.*

BIDDLE, OLIVER CALDWELL, lawyer; b. Belmont, Mass., Nov. 30, 1921; s. Sydney Geoffrey and Olive (Caldwell) B.; m. Mary Van Sciver, Aug. 5, 1968; children: Christine M., Julia C. Biddle Marvel, Geoffrey R., Theresa A. Crowley, Tate E. Anthony, Olivia P., Claudia deH., Vanessa S. A.B., Harvard U., 1943; LL.B., Columbia U., 1951. Bar: N.Y. 1952, Pa. 1960. Law clk. to judge U.S. Ct. Appeals (3d cir.), 1951-52; trial atty. civil div. Dept. Justice, Washington, 1952-54; assoc. Cravath, Swaine & Moore, N.Y.C., 1955-60; ptnr. Ballard, Spahr, Andrews & Ingersoll, Phila., 1961—. Bd. vistors Columbia Law Sch., 1974; bd. dirs. Phila. Chamber Orch. Soc., 1963-70, Phila. Mus. Acad., 1968-73. Served with USNR, 1942-45. Mem. Am. Law Inst., ABA, Phila. Bar Assn., Columbia Law Sch. Alumni Assn. Clubs: Porcellian, Phila. Cricket. Office: Ballard Spahr et al 30 S 17th St 20th Floor Philadelphia PA 19103

BIDDLE, THEODORE WILLIAM, educator; b. Donora, Pa., Mar. 2, 1906; s. Rev. Richard Long and Mary Jane (Pitcock) B.; m. Ruby Anne Meyer, July 7, 1934; children—Susanna, Theodore Long. B.S., U. Pitts., 1929, Ed.M., 1936; Ed.D., Waynesburg Coll., 1952. Asst. to dean men U. Pitts., 1929-41, acting dean men, 1941-42, dean men, 1942-58; pres. U. Pitts. at Johnstown, 1958-71, pres. emeritus, prof.-at-large, 1971—; Trustee Johnstown Savs. Bank.; Mem. Greater Johnstown Com. Contbr. articles to ednl. jours. Bd. dirs. Johnstown United Community Chest, Met. YMCA, Pitts. Mem. Greater Johnstown C. of C. (dir.), Am. Arbitration Assn., Nat., Eastern assns. (deans and advisers of men), Pitts. Personnel Assn., Nat. Assn. Student Personnel Adminstrs., NEA, Pa. Soc., Assn. Higher Edn., Eastern Assn. Coll. Deans (pres. 1950-52), Alpha Phi Omega, Pi Kappa Alpha, Omicron Delta Kappa, Phi Eta Sigma, Scabbard and Blade, Druids. Presbyterian. Clubs: University, Faculty (Pitts.); Bachelor's (Johnstown); Sunnehanna Country (pres.). Home: 2195 Woodcrest Dr Johnstown PA 15905

BIDELMAN, WILLIAM PENDRY, educator, astronomer; b. Los Angeles, Sept. 25, 1918; s. William Pendry and Dolores (De Remer) B.; m. Verna Pearl Shirk, June 19, 1940; children—Lana Louise Bidelman Stone, Linda Elizabeth Bidelman Holden, Billie Jean Bidelman Little, Barbara Jo Bidelman Talley. Student, U. N.D., 1936-37; S.B., Harvard, 1940; Ph.D., U. Chgo., 1943. Physicist, Aberdeen Proving Ground, Md., 1943-45; instr. astronomy, then asst. prof. Yerkes Obs., U. Chgo., 1945-53; asst. astronomer, then asso. Lick Obs., U. Calif., 1953-62; prof. astronomy U. Mich., 1962-69, U. Tex. at Austin, 1969-70, Case Western Res. U., Cleve., 1970—; chmn. dept., dir. Warner and Swasey Obs., 1970-75; mem. adv. panel astronomy NSF, 1959-62; mem. NRC adv. com. astronomy Office Naval Research, 1964-67. Contbr. profl. jours. Mem. Am. Astron. Soc. (councilor 1959-62, participant vis. prof. program 1961-65), Astron. Soc. Pacific (editor publs. 1956-61), Internat. Astron. Union (mem. commns. 5, 29, 45, pres. commn. 45 1964-67), Phi Beta Kappa. Presbyn. Spl. research spectral classification, astron. data, observational astrophysics. Home: 3171 Chelsea Dr Cleveland Heights OH 44118 Office: Dept Astronomy Case Western Res U Cleveland OH 44106

BIDEN, JOSEPH ROBINETTE, JR., U.S. senator; b. Scranton, Pa., Nov. 20, 1942; m. Neilia Hunter (dec.); children: Joseph Robinette, Robert Hunter, Naomi Christina (dec.); m. Jill Tracy Jacobs, June 17, 1977; 1 dau., Ashley Blazer. A.B., U. Del.; J.D., Syracuse U. Bar: Del. 1968. Practice law, Wilmington, 1968-72, U.S. senator from Del., 1972—; mem. fgn. relations, judiciary, budget and intelligence coms. Mem. New Castle (Del.) County Council, 1970-72. Democrat. Office: 489 Russell Bldg Washington DC 20510

BIDGOOD, BERKELEY CARRINGTON, tobacco corporation executive; b. Richmond, Va., Mar. 18, 1925; s. Charles Young and Mary (Carrington) B.; m. Harriett Bagardus Kirk, May 29, 1950; children: Ruth Kirk, Mary Taylor, Harriet Henley, Berkeley Carrington. Student, Williams Coll., Babson Bus. Inst., Boston. Trainee E.V. Webb Co., Kinston, N.C., 1949-54, Dibrell Bros., Inc., Danville, Va., 1954-61, asst. v.p., 1961-70, v.p., 1970-78, sr. v.p., 1978—, also dir.; dir. Am. Nat. Bank & Trust Co., Danville. Bd. dirs. Danville YMCA, 1976-82. Served with USMC, 1943-46. Republican. Episcopalian. Home: Birnam Wood Danville VA 24540 Office: Dibrell Bros Inc 512 Bridge St Danville VA 24541

BIDLACK, JERALD DEAN, manufacturing company executive; b. Oakwood, Ohio, Nov. 18, 1935; s. Ansel Carol and Vivian Irene (Huff) B.; m. Ruth Heidenescher, Dec. 24, 1953; children: Jeffrey, Cynthia, Timothy, Bethann, Deborah. B.S.M.E., Tri-State U., 1956; postgrad., Wayne State U., 1959. Registered profl. engr., N.Y. Sr. engr. Cadillac Gage Co., Warren, Mich., 1956-63; engring. mgr. indsl. Moog Inc., East Aurora, N.Y., 1963-67; mng. dir. Moog Gmbh., Boeblingen, W.Ger., 1967-69, pres. Moog internat. ops., East Aurora, 1969—; adj. lectr. SUNY-Buffalo, 1979—; dir. Moog Inc., Moog Gmbh, Moog Controls Ltd., Moog Sarl, Moog Japan. Patentee in field. Mem. com. Boy Scouts Am., East Aurora, 1973-76. Mem. Young Pres.'s Orgn. (chpt. chmn. 1981-82), Fluid Power Soc., Nat. Soc. Profl. Engrs., Buffalo and Erie County C. of C. Club: Country of Buffalo. Home:

323 Windsor Ln East Aurora NY 14052 Office: Proner Airport East Aurora NY 14052

BIDLACK, RUSSELL EUGENE, librarian, university dean; b. Manilla, Iowa, May 25, 1920; s. Harold Stanley and Mabel (Thompson) B.; m. Melva Helen Sparks, June 13, 1942; children: Stanley Alden, Martha Sue, Christopher Joel, Harold Wilford. B.A. with honors, Simpson Coll., 1947, Litt.D. (hon.), 1976; A.B. in L.S. with honors, U. Mich., 1948, A.M., 1949, 1950, Ph.D. (L.S.), 1954. Instr. library sci. U. Mich., 1951-56, asst. prof., 1956-60, asso. prof., 1960-65, prof., 1965—, dean, 1969—. Author: The City Library of Detroit, 1817-1837, 1955, Letters Home, the Story of Ann Arbor's Forty-Niners, 1960, John Allen and the Founding of Ann Arbor, 1962, The Yankee Meets the Frenchman, 1965, The ALA Accreditation Process, 1977. Served to master sgt. AUS, 1941-46. Recipient Beta Phi Mu award for distinguished service to edn. for librarianship, 1977; Melvil Dewey medal creative profl. achievement, 1979; Joseph W. Lippincott award for disting. service to librarianship, 1983. Mem. ALA (chmn. subcom. to rewrite Standards accreditation 1969-72, chmn. com. 1974-76, chmn. Melvil Dewey award jury 1973-74, chmn. Am. Library History Roundtable 1973-74, mem. council 1972-76, chmn. nominating com. 1980-81), Mich. Library Assn. (pres. tech. services sect.), Spl. Library Assn., Assn. Am. Library Schs. (chmn. deans and dirs. group 1978-79), Mich. Hist. Soc. Home: 1709 Cherokee Rd Ann Arbor MI 48104

BIDNER, ROBERT DAVID HERBERT, painter, art dir.; b. Youngstown, Ohio, Mar. 14, 1930; s. John and Susannah (Teremy) B.; m. Jo A. Heinritz, Apr. 18, 1959; children—David, Anne, Jenni. B.F.A., Cleve. Inst. Art, 1953. Asst. art dir. G.M. Basford Co., N.Y.C., 1958-59; art dir. Fuller, Smith and Ross Inc., N.Y.C., 1959-65; v.p., sr. art dir. Ted Bates Advt., N.Y.C., 1966—. One man shows, Amel Gallery, N.Y.C., 1963, AM Sachs Gallery, N.Y.C., 1967, 69, Brownstone Gallery, N.Y.C., 1973, Mickelson Gallery, Washington, 1970, 72, 74, 77, 80, Far Gallery, N.Y.C., 1975, 77, 79, Cleve. Inst. Art, 1979, group shows include, Am. Fedn. Art, 1964-65, U. N.C., 1967, Corcoran Mus., Westmoreland Mus., AM Sachs Gallery, 1967, 68, 69, 70, 72, Contemporary Gallery, N.Y.C., 1964, Obelisk Gallery, Boston, 1970-71, Nat. Acad. Design, 1955, 57, 77, 80, Am. Acad. Arts and Letters, 1975, 76, 78, Indpls. Mus., 1976, 78, Hammer Gallery, N.Y.C., 1981, others; represented in permanent collections, Nat. Collection Fine Art, Washington, Am. Acad. Arts and Letters, Cornell U., Fordham U., Notre Dame U., Concordia Coll., Butler Inst. Am. Art, Canton Mus. Art, Nat. Acad. Design, Columbus Mus. Art, Kalamazoo Inst. Arts, also numerous private collections. Served with U.S. Army, 1953-55. Recipient numerous awards. Mem. Visual Artists and Galleries Assn. Democrat. Home: 559 1st St Brooklyn NY 11215 Office: care Ted Bates 1515 Broadway New York NY 10036

BIDWELL, CHARLES EDWARD, sociologist, educator; b. Chgo., Jan. 24, 1932; s. Charles Leslie and Eugenia (Campbell) B.; m. Helen Claxton Lewis, Jan. 24, 1959; 1 son, Charles Lewis. A.B., U. Chgo., 1950, A.M., 1953, Ph.D., 1956. Lectr. on sociology Harvard U., 1959-61; asst. prof. edn. U. Chgo., 1961-65, asso. prof., 1965-70, prof. edn. and sociology, 1970—, chmn. dept. edn., 1978—. Author 2 books in field; Contbr. numerous articles to profl. jours.; editor: Sociology of Edn., 1969-72, Am. Jour. Sociology, 1973-78, Am. Jour. Edn., 1983—. Served with U.S. Army, 1957-59. Guggenheim fellow, 1971-72. Mem. Sociol. Research Assn., Nat. Acad. Edn., Phi Beta Kappa. Office: 5835 Kimbark Ave Chicago IL 60637

BIDWELL, JAMES TRUMAN, JR., lawyer; b. N.Y.C., Jan. 2, 1934; s. James Truman and Mary (Kane) B.; m. 2d Gail S. Bidwell, Mar. 6, 1965; children: Hillary Day, Kimberly Wade, Courtney E. B.A., Yale U., 1956; LL.B., Harvard U., 1959. Bar: N.Y. 1959. Atty. U.S. Air Force, Austin, Tex., 1959-62; assoc. firm Donovan, Leisure, Newton & Irvine, N.Y.C., 1962-68, ptnr., 1968—. Pres. Youth Consultation Service, 1973-78. Mem. ABA, Fed. Bar Assn., N.Y. State Bar Assn., N.Y. County Lawyers Assn. Home: 345 Round Hill Rd Greenwich CT 06830 Office: Donovan Leisure Newton & Irvine 30 Rockefeller Plaza New York NY 10012

BIDWELL, ROGER GRAFTON SHELFORD, biologist, educator; b. Halifax, N.S., Can., June 8, 1927; emigrated to U.S., 1965; s. Roger Edward Shelford and Mary (Bothamly) B.; m. Shirley Mae Rachael Mason, July 1, 1950; children—Barbara, Alison, Roger, Gillian. B.Sc., Dalhousie U., 1947; B.A., Queen's U., 1950, M.A., 1951, Ph.D., 1954. Tech. officer Canadian Def. Research Bd., Kingston, Ont., 1951-56; asst. research officer Nat. Research Council, Halifax, 1956-59; asso. prof. biology U. Toronto, Ont., 1959-65; prof. biology Case Western Res. U., Cleve., 1965-69, chmn. dept., 1966-68; prof. biology Queen's U., Kingston, Ont., Can., 1969-79; Vis. prof. Cornell U., summers 1961-63; vis. scientist Atlantic Regional Lab., Nat. Research Council, Halifax, summer 1966, 76; cons. Faculty Edn., Simon Fraser U., 1966; Canadian Sci. Exchange visitor to People's Republic of China. Author: Plant Physiology, 1974, 79; contbr. over 90 articles to profl. jours., chpts. to textbooks on biochem. mechanisms in plants, protein metabolism, CO2 metabolism in leaves, photosynthesis and metabolism in marine algae. Recipient Queen Elizabeth II Silver Jubilee medal, 1977. Fellow Royal Soc. Can.; mem. Canadian Soc. Plant Physiologists (founder, past sec.-treas., pres. 1972-73, Gold medal 1979), Biol. Council Can. (sec. 1973-76), Am. Soc. Plant Physiology, N.S. Inst. Sci. Office: Rivendell Environ Cons Wallace Rural Route 1 NS B0K 1Y0 Canada

BIEBER, OWEN F., labor union official; b. North Dorr, Mich., Dec. 28, 1939; s. Albert F. and Minnie (Schwartz) B.; m. Shirley M. Van Woerkom, Nov. 25, 1950; children: Kenneth, Linda, Michael, Ronald, Joan. H.H.D., Grand Valley Coll., 1983. Internat. rep. Union UAW, Grand Rapids, Mich., 1961-72, asst. regional dir. Region ID, 1972-74, regional dir Region ID, 1974-80; v.p. Internat. Union UAW, Detroit, 1980-83, pres., 1983—. Chmn. Kent County Dem. Com., Wyoming, Mich., 1964-66, mem. exec. bd., Wyoming, Mich., 1966-80; del. Nat. Dem. Convs., 1968, 76. Named Labor Man of Yr. Kent County AFL-CIO, 1965. Mem. NAACP (life), Grand Rapids Urban League. Roman Catholic. Club: Econ. of Detroit. Office: Internat Union UAW 8000 E Jefferson Ave Detroit MI 48314

BIEBER, SAMUEL, biological sciences educator; b. N.Y.C., Feb. 5, 1926; s. Hyman and Pauline (Sussman) B.; m. Rosalyn Lilah Hewitt, Dec. 18, 1949; children: Susan Ellen, Scott Hewitt. B.A., NYU, 1944, M.S., 1948, Ph.D. (Wellcome Research fellow), 1952. Teaching fellow biology NYU, 1948-51; Wellcome research fellow, then sr. research biologist Wellcome Research Labs., 1952-62; sci. collaborator N.Y. Aquarium, 1952-62; lectr. L.I. U., 1957-59, adj. asst. prof., 1959-62, adj. assoc. prof. biology, 1962, prof. biology, 1962-69, assoc. dean grad. sch., 1962-66; dean Richard L. Conolly Coll., 1966-69; assoc. dean sci. Univ. Coll. Liberal Arts and Sci., 1963-64; campus dean Fairleigh Dickinson U., Teaneck, N.J., 1969-71, provost, 1971-78, acting v.p., 1978-80; v.p. for acad. affairs Old Dominion U., 1980-82; prof. giol. scis. Old Dominiou U., 1980—; vis. scientist Reed Coll., summer 1967; vis. fellow Wolfson Coll., Cambridge U., 1976-77; cons. in field, 1952—, participant numerous seminars, lectr. in field. Mem. adv. councils Westchester County and Rockland County sci. fairs; asst. chief radiol. service, New Rochelle, N.Y., 1955-57. Contbr. articles to profl. jours. Mem. exec. bd. Bergen County NCCJ, Hackensack River Coordinating Com., No. N.J. Comprehensive Health Planning Council, 1973-76; trustee HEW Region II, ALPHA, 1976-80; mem. exec. com. Bergen County council Boy Scouts Am. Served with USNR, 1944-46. Fellow N.Y. Acad. Scis.; mem. Am. Assn. Cancer Research, Soc. Exptl. Biology and Medicine, Soc. Devel., Internat. Soc. Developmental Biologists, Am. Chem. Soc., Am. Soc. Zoologists, AAAS, Bergen County Med. Soc. (laymem. jud. com.), Sigma Xi, Phi Sigma. Clubs: Masons, Odd Fellow, Rotary. Patentee in cancer chemotherapy. Home: 316 Westover Ave Norfolk VA 23507

BIEBUYCK, DANIEL PROSPER, educator, anthropologist; b. Deinze, Belgium, Oct. 1, 1925; came to U.S., 1961; s. Marcel G. and Bertha (Van Laere) B.; m. Laure-Marie de Rycke, Nov. 21, 1950; children: Brunhilde, Anne-Marie, Edwin, Hans, Jean-Christophe, Jean-Marie, Beatrice. Lic. Classics, Ghent U., 1948, Doctorate Philosophy and Letters, 1954; postgrad. anthropology, London U., 1948-49. Research fellow Inst. pour la Recherche Sci. en Afrique Centrale, 1949 57; prof. anthropology Lovanium U., Kinshasa, Zaire, 1957-61; govt. anthropologist, Kinshasa, 1958-60; prof. anthropology U. Del., 1961-64, UCLA, 1964-66; H. Rodney Sharp prof. anthropology and humanities U. Del., 1966—, chmn. dept. anthropology, 1969-72, 74-75; curator African ethnology UCLA, 1964-66; vis. lectr. Liège U., 1956, 57, Yale U., 1968-69, 76, 77; vis. prof. London U., 1960-61, Yale U., 1969-70; adj. prof. NYU, 1971-72. Author: De Hond bij de Nyanga, 1958, Congo Tribes and Parties, 1961, (with K. Mateene) The Mwindo Epic from the Banyanga, 1969, Anthologie de la littérature orale nyanga, 1969, Lega Culture: Art, Initiation, and Moral Philosophy Among a Central African People, 1973, Symbolism of the Lega Stool, 1977, Hero and Chief: The Epic Literature of the Nyanga, 1978, Statuary from the Pre-Bembe Hunters, 1981; editor: African Agrarian Systems, 2d edit., 1965, Tradition and Creativity in Tribal Art, 1969. Guggenheim fellow, 1980-81; Rockefeller fellow, 1979-80. Fellow Internat. Soc. Folk-Narrative Research, Belgian Acad. Royale des Scis. d'Outre-Mer, Inst. des Civilisations Différentes, Pacific Arts Assn. Home: 271 W Main St Newark DE 19711

BIEBUYCK, JULIEN FRANCOIS, anesthesiologist, educator; b. South Africa, Feb. 2, 1935; came to U.S., 1971; s. Lucien Jean and Drix J. B.; m. Jeanette A. Sumner, May 10, 1961; children: Gavin L., Richard M., Clare E. M.B., U. Capetown, 1959; D.Phil., Oxford U., Eng., 1971. Nuffield scholar Oxford U., Eng., 1969-71; asst. prof. anesthesiology Harvard Med. Sch., Mass. Gen. Hosp., Boston, 1971-76; prof., chmn. dept. anesthesia Pa. State U. Coll. Medicine, Hershey, 1977—. Mem. editorial bd.: Internat. Jour. Artificial Organs; contbr. chpts. to books, articles to med. jours. Med. Found. fellow, 1972-74. Mem. Assn. Univ. Anesthetists, AMA, Am. Soc. Anesthesiologists (com. on metabolism and regulation), Pa. Med. Soc., Soc. Acad. Anesthesia Chairmen (pres.-elect), Biochem. Soc. (London), Soc. Parenteral Nutrition, Soc. Neurosurg. Anesthesia. Clubs: Trinity Coll. (Oxford); Harvard (Boston). Home: 436 Laurel Dr Hershey PA 17033 Office: Dept Anesthesia Milton S Hershey Med Center Pa State Univ Coll Medicine Hershey PA 17033

BIEDENHARN, LAWRENCE CHRISTIAN, JR., physicist; b. Vicksburg, Miss., Nov. 18, 1922; s. Lawrence Christian and Willetta (Lyons) B.; m. Sarah Jeffress Willingham, Mar. 25, 1950; children—John David, Sally Willetta. B.S., M.I.T., 1944, Ph.D., 1949. Research asso. M.I.T., 1949-50; physicist Oak Ridge Nat. Lab., 1950-52; asst. prof. Yale U., 1952-54; asso. prof. Rice U., 1954-61; prof. physics Duke U., 1961—; cons. Los Alamos Sci. Lab., Nat. Bur. Standards, Oak Ridge Nat. Lab. Author: (with Pieter Brussaard) Coulomb Excitation, 1964, (with H. Van Dam) Quantum Theory of Angular Momentum, 1965, (with J. D. Louck) Angular Momentum in Quantum Physics: Theory and Application, 1981, The Racah-Wigner Algebra in Quantum Theory, 1981; asso. editor: Jour. Math. Physics, 1964-68, 70-74, 79—; contbr. articles to profl. jours. Served with Signal Corps AUS, 1943-46. Sr. Fulbright fellow, 1958; Guggenheim fellow, 1959; NSF Sr. postdoctoral fellow, 1964-65; Erskine fellow, N.Z., 1973; Alexander von Humboldt sr. U.S. scientist award, 1976. Fellow Am. Phys. Soc. (Jesse Beams award 1979), Inst. Physics, Phys. Soc. Gt. Britain; mem. Swiss, European phys. socs., Am. Assn. Physics Tchrs., N.C. Academy Sci., N.Y. Academy Scis., Internat. Assn. Math. Physics, AAAS, AAUP, Sigma Xi, Kappa Sigma. Office: Dept Physics Duke U Durham NC 27706

BIEDERMAN, BARRON ZACHARY, advertising agency executive; b. N.Y.C., Sept. 1, 1930; s. William and Sophye (Groll) B.; m. Susan Howard, May 13, 1967; children: Rachel, David. B.A. with distinction, Cornell U., 1952; postgrad., Columbia Sch. Journalism, 1953, U. London, 1954. Copy group head Mogul, Williams & Saylor, N.Y.C., 1955-59; sr. writer Lennen & Newell, N.Y.C., 1960-62; v.p., assoc. creative services dir. Cunningham & Walsh, N.Y.C., 1962-64; sr. v.p. Needham, Harper & Steers, N.Y.C., 1964—, exec. creative dir., 1964-74, mgmt. rep., 1974-79, dir., 1981—; mng. dir. NH&S Corporate Futures, 1979—; chmn., chief exec. officer NH&S/Issues & Images, 1981—; pres., chmn. Biederman & Co., Inc., 1984—. Recipient every major advt. creative award; Ford Found. fellow, Eng., India, 1953-55. Mem. Fin. Communications Soc. (dir. 1982—), Internat. Advt. Assn. Club: Liberty (adv. council 1983—). Home: 253 E 71st St New York NY 10021 Office: 909 3d Ave New York NY 10022

BIEDERMAN, CHARLES JOSEPH, artist; b. Cleve., Aug. 23, 1906; s. Joseph and Josephine (Kostinec) B.; m. Mary Katherine Moore, Dec. 25, 1941; 1 dau., Anna. Student, Art Inst. Chgo., 1926-29; D.F.A. (hon.), Mpls. Coll. Art and Design, 1973. Author: Art as the Evolution of Visual Knowledge, 1948, Letters on the New Art, 1951, The New Cezanne, 1958, Search for New Arts, 1979; contbr. articles to art jours.; One-man shows, Matisse Gallery, N.Y.C., 1936, Arts Club, Chgo., 1941, Katherine Kuh Gallery, Chgo., St. Paul Gallery Art, 1954, Columbia U. Sch. Arch., 1963, Ga. Inst. Tech., Atlanta, Walker Art Center, Mpls., retrospective, 1965, Hayward Gallery, London, 1969, Mpls. Inst. Arts, 1976, Rochester (Minn.) Art Center, 1967, Gallery 12, Mpls., 1971, Borgenicht Gallery, N.Y.C., 1980, group shows, Albright-Knox Gallery, Buffalo, 1936, Reinhardt Gallery, N.Y.C., Galerie Pierre, Paris, Mayor Gallery, London, Stedelijk Mus., Amsterdam, 1962, Kunstgewerbemuseum, Zurich, Switzerland, Marlborough Gerson Gallery, N.Y.C., 1964, Carnegie Internat., Pitts., Whitney Ann. Exhbn. Sculpture, N.Y.C., 1964, 66, Walker Biennial Walker Art Center, Mpls., Denver Mus., 1965, Marlborough Gallery Fine Arts, London, 1966, Mus. Contemporary Art, Chgo., 1968, Akron (Ohio) Art Inst., 1971, Zabriskie Gallery, N.Y.C., 1972, Dallas Mus. Fine Arts, Annely Juda Fine Art, London, Univ. Mus., Austin, Tex., 1973, Sheldon Art Mus., Lincoln, Nebr., 1974, Mich. Artrain, 1975, Rutgers U., 1979, Art Inst. Chgo.; group shows, Grace Borgenicht Gallery, N.Y.C., 1980, 82, Matthew Hamilton Gallery, Phila., 1984, Pace Master Prints, N.Y.C., N.J. State Mus., Trenton, Mus. Art, Carnegie Inst., Pitts.; represented in permanent collections, Mus. Modern Art, N.Y.C., Met. Mus., N.Y.C., Whitney Mus., N.Y.C., Albright-Knox Gallery, Buffalo, Dallas Mus., High Mus., Atlanta, Phila. Mus. Art, U. Sask. Art Gallery, Saskatoon, Can., Walker Art Center, Tate Gallery, London, Kroller-Muller Mus., Otterio, Holland, Des Moines Art Center, Art Inst. Chgo., U. East Anglia, Eng., Mpls. Inst. Art, McCrory Found., N.Y.C., Dayton-Hudson Corp., Mpls., Gen. Mills Corp., Mpls., Honeywell Corp., Mpls.; represented in permanent collections, N.J. State Mus., Newark Mus., Phoenix Mus. Recipient Sikkens award Stedelijk Mus., Amsterdam, 1963, Ford Found. award, 1964, Walker Biennial Donor's award, 1966, Nat. Council on Arts award, 1966, award Minn. State Arts Council, 1969, Nat. Found. for Arts award, 1971, Fine Arts award Minn. br. AIA, 1971; Nat. Endowment for Arts award, 1973. Address: Route 2 Red Wing MN 55066

BIEGEL, HERMAN CHARLES, lawyer; b. N.Y.C., Aug. 5, 1909; s. David and Tillie (Nusim) B.; m. Shirley Gubert, June 24,1934; children: Richard, Judy. B.S.S. cum laude, CCNY, 1930; LL.B. (editor Law Jour.), Yale U., 1933. Bar: N.Y. 1933, D.C. 1938. With office chief counsel Bur. Internal Revenue, 1934-37; pvt. law practice, Washington, 1937—; partner firm Alvord & Alvord, 1942-50, Lee, Toomey & Kent, 1950—; Lectr. tax and law insts.; legal counsel Profit Sharing Council Am., 1950—; pension research council Wharton Sch. Finance, U. Pa., 1958—. Contbr. articles law jours., periodicals. Served as lt. comdr. USNR, 1944-46. Mem. ABA, Phi Beta Kappa. Home: 2778 S Ocean Blvd Palm Beach FL 33480 Office: 1200 18th St NW: Washington DC 20036

BIEGING, DAVID ARTHUR, mem. Congressional staff; b. Stillwater, Minn., July 28, 1949; s. Kenneth Harold and Ruth Lillian (Edstrom) B. B.A., Harvard U., 1971; J.D., William Mitchell Coll. Law, 1976. Bar: Minn. bar 1976, D.C. bar 1980. Adminstrv. asst. to majority leader Minn. Ho. of Reps., 1972-75; law clk. Hennepin County Atty.'s Office, Mpls., 1975; legis. asst. Office of U.S. Senator Walter F. Mondale, 1975-77; spl. asst. to Vice-Pres. U.S., Washington, 1977-78; adminstrv. asst. to Rep. Martin O. Sabo, Washington, 1978—. Lutheran. Home: 7613 Range Rd Alexandria VA 22306 Office: 426 Cannon House Office Bldg Washington DC 20515

BIELENBERG, IVAN L., sugar company executive; b. Rockwell City, Iowa, 1927; married. B.S.S., Northwestern U., 1951; M.B.M., U. Chgo., 1956. V.p. Schulze & Berch Biscuit Co., 1955-68; pres. Luzianne Coffee Co., 1968-70; group v.p. I.U. Internat. Corp., 1970-76; sr. v.p. United Brands Co., 1976-78; pres. Hunt Internat. Resources Co., Dallas, 1978—. Served with USAF, 1945-47. Office: Hunt Internat Resources Corp 3600 First Internat Bldg Dallas TX 75270 *

BIELENSTEIN, HANS HENRIK AUGUST, educator; b. Stockholm, Sweden, Apr. 8, 1920; came to U.S., 1961; s. Maximilian August Rudolf Gottfried and Elsbeth Margot Erika (von Gruenewaldt) B.; m. Gabrielle Carter Maupin, Jan. 12, 1954; children—Danielle Erika Mary, Andrea Johanna Gabrielle. Ph.D., Royal U., Stockholm, 1954. Prof. Oriental langs., head Sch. Oriental Studies, Australian Nat. U., Canberra, 1952-61; prof. Chinese history Columbia, 1961—, chmn. dept. East Asian langs. and cultures, 1969-77. Author books and articles on Chinese history, historiography and demography. Served with Swedish Vol. Corps to Finland, 1939-40. Decorated Finnish War medal with swords and clasp; Guggenheim fellow, 1967-68. Corr. mem. Royal Acad. Lit. History and Antiquity (Sweden). Club: Union. Home: 50 Riverside Dr New York NY 10024

BIELER, ANDRE (CHARLES BIELER), painter; b. Lausanne, Switzerland, Oct. 8, 1896; s. Charles and Blanche (Merle d'Aubigne) B.; m. Jeannette Meunier, Apr. 27, 1931; children—Nathalie, Sylvie, Andre, Peter. Student, Stanstaed Acad., 1909-15, Art Students League, Woodstock, N.Y., 1919-20; LL.D. (hon.), Queen's U., Kingston, Ont., Can., 1969. Later head dept. art history, studio classes; instr. summer sch., Banff, Alta., Can., 1940; public lectr. Nat. Gallery Can., Ottawa, Ont., 1941; Can. del. opening Nat. Gallery, Washington, 1941; coordinator 1st Conf. Can. Artists (later called Kingston Conf.). Painter: Island of Orleans, Que., Can., 1926-30; with, Beaver Hall group, Montreal, Que., 1930-36, one-man shows throughout, Can., 1926—; apptd. Resident Artist, Queen's U., Kingston, 1936; commd. murals include works for, Aluminum Co. Can., 1945, Vets.' Bldg., Ottawa, 1954, Aluminum Co., Japan, Tokyo, 1968. Served with Can. Inf., 1915-19. Recipient Centennial medal for service to Can., 1967. Mem. Ont. Soc. Artists, Can. Group Painters, Can. Soc. Painters in Water-Color, Can. Soc. Graphic Art, Royal Can. Acad., Fedn. Can. Artists (1st pres.). Clubs: Queen's, Faculty. Designer, inventor press for use in intaglio/relief printing. Home: 185 Ontario St Apt 621 Kingston ON K7L 2Y7 Canada Office: Queen's U Agnes Etherington Art Centre Kingston ON Canada

BIELER, CHARLES LINFORD, zoo director; b. East Greenville, Pa., May 19, 1935; s. Frederick William and Emma May (Freed) B.; m. Judith L. Goodwin, Feb. 23, 1963; children: Stewart, Beatriz, Christina. B.A., Gettysburg (Pa.) Coll., 1957. Dir. tng. Gen. Motors Corp., 1962-69; mem. staff Zool. Soc. San Diego, 1969—, exec. asst. to dir., 1972-73, dir., 1973—; bd. dirs. San Diego Conv. and Visitors Bur., 1983-84. Served with AUS, 1957-62. Recipient Gettysburg Coll. Disting. Alumni award, 1984. Fellow Am. Assn. Zool. Parks and Aquariums (pres. 1983-84), Internat. Union Dirs. Zool. Gardens. Home: 1915 Sunset Blvd San Diego CA 92103 Office: San Diego Zoo PO Box 551 San Diego CA 92112

BIEN, FRANK NORMAN, utility exec.; b. Phila., Dec. 20, 1919; s. Charles Franklin and Antoinette (deCou) B.; m. Florence Roberts, May 2, 1950; children—Suzanne A., Christopher F. B.S. in Econs, U. Pa., 1941; grad. sr. execs. program, M.I.T., 1962. C.P.A. Acct. Niles & Niles (C.P.A.'s), N.Y.C., 1946-58; acctg. mgr. Ohio Power Co., Newark and Canton, 1958-74, exec. v.p., Canton, 1974-76; vice chmn. ops. Am. Electric Power Service Corp., N.Y.C. and; Columbus, Ohio, 1976—; dir. Am. Electric Power Co., Inc. Served with USCGR, World War II. Mem. Am. Inst. C.P.A.'s. Office: 180 E Broad St Columbus OH 43215 *

BIEN, JOSEPH JULIUS, philosophy educator; b. Cin., May 22, 1936; s. Joseph Julius and Mary Elizabeth (Adams) B.; m. Françoise Neve, Apr. 8, 1965. B.S., Xavier U., 1957, M.A., 1958; D.T.C., U. Paris, 1968; postgrad., Laval Univ., 1958, Emory U., 1961-62, U. Edinburgh, 1962. Asst. prof. philosophy Univ. Tex., Austin, 1968-73; asso. prof. philosophy Univ. Mo., Columbia, 1973-79, prof. philosophy, 1979—, chmn. dept. philosophy, 1976-80, 1981-83; vis. prof. Tex. A&M U., 1980; Pres. Central States Philosophical Assn., 1978-79. Author: History, Revolution and Human Nature: Marx's Philosophical Anthropology, 1984; Trans.: (M. Merleau-Ponty): Adventures of the Dialectic, 1973; editor: Phenoemenology and the Social Sciences, 1978, Political and Social Essays by Paul Ricoeur, 1974. Am. Council Learned Socs. grantee, 1973. Mem. Soc. Social and Polit. Philosophy (pres. 1979-80), Central States Slavic Conf. (sec., treas. 1977). Democrat. Home: 1018 Westwinds Ct Columbia MO 65201 Office: Dept of Philosophy Univ of Missouri Columbia MO 65211

BIEN, PETER ADOLPH, educator, author; b. N.Y.C., May 28, 1930; s. Adolph F. and Harriet (Honigsberg) B.; m. Chrysanthi Yiannakou, July 17, 1955; children: Leander, Alec, Daphne. Student, Harvard U., 1948-50; B.A., Haverford Coll., 1952; M.A., Columbia U., 1957, Ph.D., 1961; postgrad. (Fulbright fellow), Bristol (Eng.) U., 1958-59, Woodbrooke Coll., Eng., 1970-71. Lectr. Columbia U., N.Y.C., 1957-58, 59-61; instr. dept. English Dartmouth Coll., Hanover, N.H., 1961-62, asst. prof., 1963-65, assoc. prof., 1965-68, prof., 1969—, Geisel prof., 1974-79; vis. prof. Harvard U., 1983, U. Melbourne, 1983; Trustee Kinhaven Music Sch., Weston, Vt., 1972-78, 81—; trustee Pendle Hill, Wallingford, Pa., 1977—, presiding clk., 1983—; mem. corp. Haverford Coll., 1974—; pres. bd. trustees Hanover Monthly

Meeting, Soc. Friends, 1977—. Author: L.P. Hartley, 1963, Constantine Cavafy, 1964, Kazantzakis and the Linguistic Revolution in Greek Literature, 1972, (with others) Demotic Greek I, 1972, Demotic Greek II, 1982, Nikos Kazantzakis, 1972, Antithesis and Synthesis in the Poetry of Yannis Ritsos, 1980; translator: The Last Temptation, 1960, Saint Francis, 1962, Report to Greco, 1965 (all by Nikos Kazantzakis), Life in the Tomb (Stratis Myrivilis), 1977; coeditor: Modern Greek Writers, 1972; assoc. editor: Byzantine and Modern Greek Studies, 1975-82, Jour. Modern Greek Studies, 1983—. Recipient E. Harris Harbison award for disting. teaching Danforth Found., 1968. Mem. Modern Greek Studies Assn. (exec. com. 1968—, pres. 1982—), MLA. Democrat. Club: Yale (N.Y.C.). Home: 12 Ledyard Ln Hanover NH 03755 also Terpni Waddell Rd Riparius NY 12862

BIENEN, HENRY SAMUEL, political science educator; b. N.Y.C., May 5, 1939; s. Mitchell Richard and Pearl (Witty) B.; m. Leigh Buchanan, Apr. 28, 1961; children: Laura, Claire, Leslie. B.A. with honors, Cornell U., 1960; M.A., U. Chgo., 1962, Ph.D., 1966. Asst. prof. politics U. Chgo., 1965-66; asst. prof. politics Princeton U., 1966-70, asso. prof., 1970-72, prof., chmn. dept. politics, 1972—, William Stewart Tod prof. politics and internat. affairs; mem. exec. com. Inter-Univ. Seminar on Armed Forces and Soc., 1970; cons. U.S. State Dept., 1972—, Nat. Security Council, 1978-79, World Bank, 1982—; nat. co-dir. Movement for a New Congress, 1970-71; NDEA fellow in Russian studies, 1960-63; fellow Center for Advanced Study in Behavorial Scis. Editor: World Politics, 1970-74, 78—; author: Tanzania: Party Transformation and Economic Development, 1967, 70, Kenya: The Politics of Participation and Control, 1974, Violence and Social Change, 1968, Armies and Parties in Africa, 1978. Mem. Am. Polit. Sci. Assn., Council on Fgn. Relations.

BIENENSTOCK, ARTHUR IRWIN, physicist; b. N.Y.C., Mar. 20, 1935; s. Leo and Lena (Senator) B.; m. Roslyn Doris Goldberg, Apr. 14, 1957; children—Eric Lawrence, Amy Elizabeth, Adam Paul. B.S., Poly. Inst. Bklyn., 1955, M.S., 1957; Ph.D., Harvard U., 1962. Asst. prof. Harvard U., 1963-67; mem. faculty Stanford U., 1967—, prof. applied physics, 1972—, vice provost faculty affairs, 1972-77, dir. synchrotron radiation lab., 1978—; mem. U.S. Nat. Com. for Crystallography, 1983—; lectr., cons. in field. Author papers in field. Bd. dirs. No. Calif. chpt. Cystic Fibrosis Research Found., 1970-73, mem. pres.'s adv. council, 1980—; trustee Cystic Fibrosis Found., 1982—. Recipient Sidhu award Pitts. Diffraction Soc., 1968, Disting. Alumnus award Poly. Inst. N.Y., 1977; NSF fellow, 1962-63. Fellow Am. Phys. Soc.; mem. Am. Crystallographic Assn., AAAS, N.Y. Acad. Scis. Jewish. Home: 967 Mears Ct Stanford CA 94305 Office: Synchrotron Radiation Lab Bin 69 Box 4349 Stanford CA 94305

BIENVENU, BERNARD JEFFERSON, educator; b. St. Martinville, La., Apr. 8, 1925; s. Louis Jefferson and Beatrice (Dur) B. B.S., U. Southwestern La., 1947; M.B.A., Harvard U., 1947, D.B.A., 1956; student, U. Paris, U. Lyon, France, 1959. Engaged in stock brokerage bus., 1947-48; asso. gen. agt. Pan Am. Life Ins. Co., 1948-50; prof. bus. adminstrn., dir. alumni relations U. Southwestern La., 1952-53, prof. bus. adminstrn., 1955—, head dept. mktg., 1955-56, head dept. mgmt., 1956—, Lether Edward Frazer honor prof. mgmt. and adminstrv. studies, 1978—; Ford fellow bus. adminstrn., faculty Harvard U. Grad Sch. Bus., 1954-55; mgmt. cons. to bus., govt., ch. orgns.; lectr. nat. orgns.; vis. prof. Institut Superieur Des Affaires, Centre d'Enseignement Superieur des Affaires de Jouy-en-Josas, France, 1970-71; faculty hwy. mgmt. inst. U. Miss., Va. Bankers Sch. Bank Mgmt., mid-south exec. devel. program La. State U., La. Sch. Supervisory Banking, Savs. and Loan Inst. South; African lecture tour for U.S. State Dept.; mgmt. devel. program for Govt. Haiti; dir., vice chmn. bd. Evangeline Pepper & Foods, Inc., 1963-65. Author: New Priorities in Training-A Guide for Industry, 1969; Contbr. to profl. jours. Area chmn. Radio Free Europe drive, 1963; mem. La. Bd. Commerce and Industry, 1960-64; tng. dir. Lafayette United Givers Fund, 1958-59; mem. La. Labor Mediation Bd., 1966—; Pres. faculty senate U. Southwest La., 1966-67. Served with USNR, 1943-46, 50-52; capt. Res. Mem. So. Mgmt. Assn. (dir. 1964, v.p. 1966-67, pres. 1968-69, Outstanding Service award 1974), Southwest Mgmt. Assn. (pres. 1962-63), AAUP, Am. Acad. Mgmt. (gov. 1968-69), John Henry Cardinal Newman Honor Soc., Phi Kappa Theta (nat. sec. 1956-57), Phi Kappa Phi. Home: 211 N Main St St Martinville LA 70582 Office: PO Box 4-0598 Univ Southwestern Louisiana Lafayette LA 70504

BIERBAUM, J. ARMIN, petroleum company executive; b. Oak Park, Ill., June 29, 1924; s. Armin Walter and Harriett Cornelia (Backmann) B.; m. Janith Turnbull, Apr. 17, 1948; children: Steve, Todd, Charles, Peter, Mark. B.S., Northwestern U., 1945, M.S., 1948. Project engr. Am. Oil Co., Ind., 1948-53; sales engr. Universal Oil Products Co., Des Plaines, Ill., 1953-56; tech. dir. Nat. Coop. Refinery Assn., McPherson, Kans., 1956-58; asst. plant mgr., treas., v.p., dir. Gen. Carbon & Chem. Corp., Robinson, Ill., 1958-61; cons., Williston, N.D., 1962-64; v.p. ops. Midland Coops., Inc., Mpls., 1964-72; sr. v.p. ops. Tosco Corp., Los Angeles, 1972-77; cons., Los Angeles, 1977-78; pres., chief exec. officer Gary Energy Co., Englewood, Colo., 1978, U.S. Ethanol Corp., Englewood, 1978—. Served with USNR, 1942-45. Mem. Nat. Petroleum Refiners Assn. (dir.), Am. Petroleum Inst., Am. Inst. Chem. Engrs., Sigma Xi, Phi Epsilon Pi. Home: 7787 Perry Park Blvd Larkspur CO 80118 Office: 5670 S Syracuse Circle Englewood CO 80111

BIERER, WILLIAM E., banker; b. Uniontown, Pa., Dec. 19, 1929; s. William Edmund and Gertrude (Morley) B.; m. Ruth Sibel, Aug. 22, 1959; children: William E., Nannette. Grad., U. Pitts., 1954, Stonier Grad. Sch. Banking, Rutgers U., 1965. With Westinghouse Electric Corp., Pitts., 1954-61; v.p. Mellon Bank N.A., Pitts., 1961-68; sr. v.p. Equibank, Pitts., 1968-70, exec. v.p., 1970-73, pres., 1973—, chief exec. officer, 1975—, chmn. bd., 1981—; pres. Equimark Corp., 1974—, chief exec. officer, 1979—, chmn. bd., 1981—; dir. Allied Bank Internat.; mem. task force on interstate banking Assn. Bank Holding Cos. Trustee North Hills Passavant Hosp., Children's Hosp. of Pitts.; bd. dirs. United Way of Allegheny County and Southeastern Pa.; mem. Commonwealth, Assn. for Devel. of Interstate Navigability on the Allegheny, Monongahela and Ohio Rivers; bd. trustees U. Pa., Grove City Coll. Served with U.S. Army, 1948-49, 51-53. Mem. Am. Mgmt. Assn. (trustee), Pres.'s Assn., Pitts. C. of C. (dir.). Clubs: Duquesne, Fox Chapel Golf, West Penn Motor (dir.), Pitts. Press, Bankers, Univ., Allegheny, Pitts. Athletic (Pitts.); Laurel Valley Golf. Office: Equimark Corp Equibank Bldg Pittsburgh PA 15222

BIERI, JOHN GENTHER, biochemist; b. Norfolk, Va., May 24, 1920; s. Bernhard Henry and Elsie Mathilda (Genther) B.; m. Shirley J. Bloch, Sept. 19, 1943; children—Roger A., Barbara E., Nancy J. B.S., Antioch Coll., 1943; M.S., Pa. State U., 1944; Ph.D., U. Minn., 1949. Nutritionist U.S. Naval Med. Research Inst., Bethesda, Md., 1944-46; asso. prof. biochemistry and nutrition U. Tex. Med. Br., Galveston, 1949-56; biochemist Nat. Inst. Arthritis, Metabolism and Digestive Diseases, NIH, Bethesda, 1955-82, cons., 1982—. Served with USNR, 1944-46. Recipient Mead Johnson award, 1965; Pa. State U. Alumni fellow, 1975. Mem. Am. Inst. Nutrition (pres. 1974), Am. Soc. Biol. Chemists, AAAS, Soc. Exptl. Biology and Medicine. Office: Nat Inst Arthritis Metabolism and Digestive Diseases NIH Bethesda MD 20205

BIERINGER, WALTER H., plastic and rubber mfg. co. exec.; b. Boston, Mass., Nov. 17, 1899; s. Leo and Sara (Wolfenstein) B.; m. Gertrude Marie Kessel, Aug. 5, 1922; 1 dau., Doris Marie (Mrs. Howard H. Hiatt); m. Annabelle Markson, Mar. 9, 1984. A.B., Harvard U., 1921. Sr. v.p., dir. Plymouth Rubber Co., Canton, Mass., 1921—; pres. Plymouth Rubber Internat. Co., Canton.; Cons., on refugee affairs State Dept., 1956; adviser on refugee affairs Pres. Truman. Past pres. United Service for New Americans; past nat. chmn. United Jewish Appeal; past pres. Urban League Boston; chmn. Gov.'s Commn. on Refugees, 1946—; Trustee Howard U.; bd. overseers Brandeis U. Sch. Social Work; bd. dirs. Joint Distbn. Com., Am. ORT Fedn., United HIAS Service, Inc. Served with AUS, World War I. Mem. World Trade Center Boston. Club: Harvard of Boston. Home: 26 Wolcott Rd Extension Brookline MA 02167 Office: 1000 Revere Rubber St Canton MA 02021

BIERLEY, JOHN CHARLES, lawyer; b. Portsmouth, Ohio, Oct. 12, 1936; s. C. Harold and Mildred R. (Turner) B.; m. Ruth Lykes Webb, Sept. 26, 1964; 1 son, John Charles. B.A., U. Fla., 1958, J.D. (Fla. Law Center Assn. scholar, Bigelow Meml. scholar Am. Legion), 1963. Bar: Fla. 1964. Practiced in Tampa, 1964—; asso. firm Fowler, White, Gillen, Humpkey & Trenam, Tampa, 1964-66; partner Macfarlane, Ferguson, Allison & Kelly, Tampa, 1966—; pres. Internat. Cultural and Econ. Center, Inc., 1975-78; lectr. internat. studies U. South Fla., Tampa, 1964-72; dir. Cayman Nat. Bank & Trust Co., Ltd., 1974—; Chmn. Fla. Council Internat. Devel., 1974-75, Fla. Gov.'s Conf. on World Trade, 1980; pres. Tampa World Trade Council, 1971-73; chmn. hurricane disaster com. ARC, 1968-71; sec. Tampa Bay Area Com. Fgn. Relations, 1972—; trustee U. Fla. Law Center Assn., 1981—. Served to capt. USMCR, 1958-61. Recipient Fla. Blue Key award Fla. Hall of Fame, 1958. Mem. Am. Soc. Internat. Law, Internat. Fiscal Assn., Council Fgn. Relations, Fla. Bar Assn. (chmn. internat. law com. 1972-74), ABA, Inter-Am. Bar Assn. (Council 1982—, Silver medal 1983), Internat. Bar Assn., Phi Delta Phi, Kappa Sigma. Democrat. Presbyterian. Clubs: Ye Mystic Krewe Gasparilla, Univ., Tower, Merrymakers. Home: 4614 San Miguel St Tampa FL 33609 Office: 215 Madison St Tampa FL 33601

BIERLEY, PAUL EDMUND, aeronautical engineer, musician, author; b. Portsmouth, Ohio, Feb. 3, 1926; s. William Frederick and Minnie Genieve (Atkin) B.; m. Pauline Jeanette Allison, Sept. 17, 1948; children: Lois Bierley Walker, John. B.Aero. Engring., Ohio State U., 1953. Aero. engr. Rockwell Internat., Columbus, Ohio, 1953-70, 71-73, Ohio Dept. Mental Hygiene, Columbus, 1971, Ellanef Mfg. Corp., 1973—; bd. advs. Detroit Concert Band, Melbourne Mcpl. Band, Chatfield Brass Band; spl. cons. Internat. Sousa Soc.; cons. MUS-I-COL, 1971-72; assoc. mem., adviser research center com. Am. Bandmasters Assn. Research Center.; curator Louis Sudler Library, John Philip Sousa Meml. Found. Author: John Philip Sousa, A Descriptive Catalog of His Works, 1973, John Philip Sousa, American Phenomenon, 1973, Office Fun, 1976, Hallelujah Trombone, 1982, The Music of Henry Fillmore and Will Hoff, 1982; also numerous articles, radio and TV copy, concert programs and record jackets Office Fun; tubist, Columbus Symphony Orch., 1965—, World Symphony Orch., 1971, Detroit Concert Band, 1973; asst. condr., Rockwell Internat. Concert Band, 1961-76. Served with USAAF, 1944-46. Recipient Edwin Franko Goldman Meml. citation Am. Bandmasters Assn., 1974. Mem. Nat. Band Assn., Am. Sch. Band Dirs. Assn. (asso.), Assn. Concert Bands, Inc., Am. Aviation Hist. Soc., Ohio Hist. Soc., Air Force Assn., Tubist Universal Brotherhood Assn., Sonneck Soc., Windjammers. Methodist. Club: Mason. Home: 3888 Morse Rd Columbus OH 43219 Office: Columbus Symphony Orchestra 101 E Town St Columbus OH 43215

BIERMAN, ARTHUR, educator; b. Vienna, Austria, Oct. 14, 1925; came to U.S., 1939, naturalized, 1944; s. Jacob and Regina (Wenig) B.; m. Enid Sharp, Aug. 29, 1953 (div. Nov. 1971); children—Jessica, Cynthia. Student, Bklyn. Coll., 1942-44; M.A., U. Chgo., 1948, Ph.D., 1954; M.A., Columbia U., 1957. Asst. prof. Coll. City N.Y., 1958-62; sr. research scientist Lockheed Calif. Co., 1962-64; prof. physics Coll. City N.Y., 1969—, acting asso. provost, 1971, dir. planning program for humanistic studies, 1971-73. Contbr. articles physics jours. Served with AUS, 1944-46. Fellow Infantile Paralysis Found., 1954-55; research grantee AEC, 1965-71. Mem. Am. Phys. Soc. Home: 137 W 78th St New York City NY 10024

BIERMAN, CHARLES WARREN, physician, educator; b. Ada, Ohio, May 27, 1924; s. Linn Carl and Margery (Warren) B.; m. Joan Wingate, May 15, 1952; children: Margot Ellen, Karen Linn, Charlotte Joane, Barbara Anne. M.D., Harvard U., 1947. Diplomate: Am. Bd. Pediatrics, Am. Bd. Allergy and Immunology (dir. 1971-77). Intern Lankenau Hosp., Phila., 1947-48; resident in pediatrics Bellevue Hosp., N.Y.C., 1948-49, N.Y. Hosp., 1949-50, fellow in neonatology, 1950, Hosp. Enfants Malades, Paris, 1953-54; resident in allergy U. Wash., Seattle, 1965-67; practice medicine specializing in pediatric and adolescent allergy, Seattle, 1967—; mem. staffs Children's Orthopedic Hosp. and Med. Center, Univ. Hosp., Harborview Hosp.; instr. pediatrics Cornell Med. Sch., 1949-50; clin. instr. pediatrics U. Wash., Seattle, 1958-59, clin. asst. prof., 1959-62, clin. assoc. prof., 1962-70, clin. prof., 1970—, chief div. allergy, dept. pediatrics, 1967—; hon. research fellow, dept. pharmacology, hon. cons. respiratory disease Univ. Coll. London, 1978-79; cons. Wash. State Dept. Social and Health Services, 1979—. Editor: (with D.S. Pearlman) Childhood and Adolescence, 1980; mem. editorial bd.: Pediatrics, 1972-76, Pediatrics in Review, 1977—; contbr. articles to med. jours. Served with USN, 1944-46, 50-51; Served with U.S. Army, 1951-52. Fellow Am. Acad. Allergy (exec. com. 1980-84), Am. Acad. Pediatrics (chmn. allergy sect. 1974-76); mem. AMA, Wash. State Med. Assn. (ho. of dels.), Wash. State Pediatrics Assn., Wash. State Allergy Soc., Puget Sound Allergy Soc., Seattle Pediatric Soc., Am. Pediatric Soc., Western Soc. for Pediatric Research. Episcopalian. Home: 4524 E Laurel Dr NE Seattle WA 98105 Office: 3900 NE 45th St Seattle WA 98205

BIERMAN, EDWIN LAWRENCE, physician, educator; b. N.Y.C., Sept. 17, 1930; s. J.M. and Bella (Smolens) B.; m. Marilyn Joan Soforan, July 1, 1956; children: Ellen M., David J. B.A., Bklyn. Coll., 1951; M.D. (Schepp, Shapiro, Grand St. Boys founds. scholar, Thorne Shaw scholar), Cornell U., 1955. Diplomate: Nat. Bd. Med. Examiners, Am. Bd. Internal Medicine. Intern N.Y. Hosp., N.Y.C., 1955-56, resident, 1959-60; asst. Rockefeller Inst., N.Y.C., 1956-57, asst. prof., 1960-62; asso. prof. medicine U. Wash. Med. Sch., Seattle, 1963-68, prof. medicine, 1968—; chief div. metabolism and gerontology VA Hosp., Seattle, 1967-75, head div. metabolism and endocrinology, 1975—. Editor: Arteriosclerosis, 1980-85; Contbr. numerous articles to profl. jours. Served to capt. M.C. AUS, 1957-59. Mead Johnson postgrad. scholar A.C.P., 1959; Guggenheim fellow, 1972. Fellow A.C.P.; mem. Am. Fedn. Cln. Research, Am. Diabetes Assn., Soc. for Exptl. Biology and Medicine, Western Soc. for Clin. Research, Am. Soc. for Clin. Investigation, Assn. Am. Physicians, Endocrine Soc., Am. Physiology Soc., Gerontological Soc., AAAS, Am. Soc. Clin. Nutrition, Western Assn. Physicians (pres. 1980), Am. Heart Assn. (vice chmn. Council on Arteriosclerosis 1981-83, chmn. 1983-85), Phi Beta Kappa, Sigma Xi, Alpha Omega Alpha. Home: 3517 E Olive St Seattle WA 98122

BIERMAN, HAROLD, JR., business educator; b. N.Y.C., June 17, 1924; s. Harold Stahl and Frieda (Zelezney) B.; m. Florence Merwin Kelso, Feb. 2, 1952; children: James Landon, Harold Scott, Donald Bruce, Jonathan David. B.S., U.S. Naval Acad., 1945; M.B.A., U. Mich., 1949, Ph.D., 1955. With Arthur Young & Co., 1949-50; with Shell Oil Co., 1950; faculty La. State U., 1950-51, U. Chgo., 1955-56; mem. faculty Cornell U., Ithaca, N.Y., 1956—, Nicholas H. Noyes prof. bus. adminstrn., 1969—; cons. Ford Found.; adviser to mgmt. program U. W.Indies. Author: The Capital Budgeting Decision, 1960, rev., 1966, 71, 75, 78, 84, (with Seymour Smidt) Strategic Financial Planning, 1965, Financial Policy Decisions, 1970. Served with USN, 1942-47, 51-53. Mem. Am. Acctg. Assn., Am. Fin. Assn., Fin. Mgmt. Assn. Home: 109 Kay St Ithaca NY 14850

BIERNAT, JOSEPH ANTHONY, financial executive; b. Phila., Sept. 26, 1927; s. John and Felicia (Zlot) B.; m. Mary Lillian Nahumenuk, July 22, 1951; children: Joseph A., Daria Ann, Karen Marie, Mark Allen, Brent Hilary. B.S., Temple U., 1950. Sr. staff accountant Price Waterhouse & Co., Phila., 1952-58; controller Philco Finance Corp., 1958-61, v.p., treas., 1962, pres., treas., 1962-65; also dir.; mem. operating policy com. Philco Corp.; asst. treas. United Aircraft Corp., East Hartford, Conn., 1965-74; pres., treas. UT Credit Corp., Hartford; v.p., treas. United Technologies Corp., Hartford, 1974—; dir. Conn. Nat. Bank, Bridgeport, CNB Equity Corp., Hartford Funds. Dir. devel. council Temple U.; trustee Boys' Club Hartford, Inc.; bd. dirs. United Way Greater Hartford. Served with AUS, 1950-52. Mem. Nat. Assn. Accountants, Inst. Internal Auditors, Am. Accounting Assn., Fin. Execs. Inst., Pa. Soc., Columbia Lakes Assn. Club: Golf (Avon). Home: 30 Hurdle Fence Dr Avon CT 06001 also Route 87 Columbia Lake Columbia CT 06327 Office: United Technologies Bldg Hartford CT 06101

BIERSCHBACH, RAYMOND ANTON, insurance company executive; b. Lemmon, S.D., Feb. 15, 1933; s. Nicholas Bernard and Thelma Ursula (Lewis) B.; m. Margaret Jean Benson, Feb. 22, 1963; children: Daniel M., Kimberly M., Catherine J., Kristin R. B.A., State U. Iowa, 1955, M.S., 1957. With Transamerica Occidental Life, Los Angeles, 1960—, v.p., actuary, 1968-71, exec. v.p., actuary, 1971-73, gen. mgr. European ops., 1973-76, exec. v.p., 1976-83, dir., 1976—; pres. Transamerica Internat. Ins. Services, Inc., 1983—. Bd. dirs. Catholic Big Brothers of Los Angeles, 1969-70. Served to 1st lt. USAF, 1957-60. Fellow Soc. Actuaries; mem. Los Angeles Actuarial Club, Am. Acad. Actuaries (dir. 1979-82), Actuarial Club of Pacific States. Home: 2111 El Monte Ave Arcadia CA 91006 office: Transam Internat Ins Services PO Box 2101 Terminal Annex Los Angeles CA 90051

BIERSTEDT, PETER RICHARD, lawyer, film company executive; b. Rhinebeck, N.Y., Jan. 2, 1943; s. Robert Henry and Betty (MacIver) B.; m. Carol Lynn Akiyama, Aug. 23, 1980. A.B., Columbia U., 1965, J.D. cum laude, 1969; cert., Sorbonne, Paris, 1966. Bar: N.Y. bar 1969, Calif. bar 1977. Atty. with firms in, N.Y.C., 1969-74, individual practice, 1971, 75-76; with Avco Embassy Pictures Corp., Los Angeles, 1977—, v.p., gen. counsel, 1978-80, sr. v.p., 1980—, dir., 1981—; guest lectr. U. Calif., Riverside, 1976, 77. Mem. Motion Picture Assn. Am. (dir.), Acad. Motion Picture Arts and Scis. (exec. br.), Am. Film Inst., N.Y. State Bar Assn., Los Angeles County Bar Assn., Beverly Hills Bar Assn., ACLU., AAAS. Office: 956 Seward St Los Angeles CA 90038

BIERSTEDT, ROBERT, sociologist, author; b. Burlington, Iowa, Mar. 20, 1913; s. Henry F. and Bertha (Strauss) B.; m. Betty MacIver, Dec. 26, 1939; children: Peter, Karen, Robin. A.B., U. Iowa, 1934; A.M., Columbia U., 1935; Ph.D., 1950; fellow, Harvard U., 1936-37. Lectr. philosophy Columbia U., 1937-39, head men's residence halls, 1938-39; instr. social studies Bennington Coll., 1939-40; instr. philosophy Bard Coll., 1940-43; asst. prof. sociology U. Wash., summer 1946; asst. prof. Wellesley Coll., 1946-47, U. Ill., 1947-51, asso. prof., 1951-53; prof., chmn. dept. sociology and anthropology Coll. City N.Y., 1953-59; vis. prof. Stanford U., summer 1959; Fulbright lectr. U. Edinburgh, Scotland, 1959-60; Barnett lectr. Oxford U., 1960; head dept. N.Y. U., 1960-66, prof. sociology, 1960-72; mem. Center Advanced Studies, U. Va., 1972-74, prof. sociology, 1972-82, Commonwealth prof., 1982—, prof. emeritus, 1983—; Fulbright lectr. London Sch. Econs., 1966-67; Bd. dirs. Am. Council Learned Socs., 1979—. Author: The Social Order, 1957, 4th edit., 1974, (with others) Modern Social Science, 1964, Emile Durkheim, 1966, Power and Progress, 1974, American Sociological Theory, 1981; Editor: The Making of Society, 1959, (with others) Florian Znaniecki, 1969; adv. editor: Internat. Jour. Sociology and Social Policy; contbr. articles to profl. lit. jours. Served from lt. (j.g.) to lt. USNR, 1943-46. Mem. Am. Sociol. Assn. (past v.p.), Eastern Sociol. Soc. (past pres.), Sociol. Research Assn., AAUP (pres. City Coll. chpt. 1958-59, council 1963-66), ACLU (dir. 1962-74, nat. adv. council 1975—), Phi Beta Kappa. Club: Harvard, Century Assn. (N.Y.C.). Home: 9 Old Farm Rd Charlottesville VA 22901 summer Chilmark MA 02535

BIERWIRTH, JOHN COCKS, aerospace/transportation manufacturing executive; b. Lawrence, N.Y., Jan. 21, 1924; s. John E. and Alice (Marguerite) B.; m. Marion Moise, June 14, 1946. B.A., Yale U., 1947; J.D., Columbia U., 1950. Bar: N.Y. 1951. Asso. White & Case, N.Y.C., 1950-53; asst. v.p. N.Y. Trust Co. (now Chem. Bank), 1953-57; asst. treas. Nat. Distillers & Chem. Corp., N.Y.C., 1957-58, v.p., 1958-69, head Internat. div., 1963-69, dir., 1966-72, exec. v.p., 1969-72; Grumman Corp., Bethpage, N.Y., 1971—, v.p. finance, 1972, pres., 1972, chief exec. officer, 1974—, chmn. bd., 1976—; dir. Discount Corp., Gen. Reins. Corp.; trustee Atlantic Mut. Ins. Co. Mem. pres.'s com. Smith Coll.; mem. Pres.'s Internat. Pvt. Enterprise Task Force; chmn. L.I. Action Com.; bd. dirs. N.Y. Blood Center, L.I. U.; mem. N.Y. Council Fiscal and Econ. Priorities. Mem. UN Assn., Conf. Bd. Club: Yale (N.Y.C.). Office: Grumman Corp 1111 Stewart Ave Bethpage NY 11714

BIESELE, JOHN JULIUS, biologist, educator; b. Waco, Tex., Mar. 24, 1918; s. Rudolph Leopold and Anna Emma (Jahn) B.; m. Marguerite Calfee McAfee, July 29, 1943; children: Marguerite Anne, Diana Terry, Elizabeth Jane. B.A. with highest honors, U. Tex., 1939, Ph.D., 1942. Fellow Internat. Cancer Research Found., U. Tex., 1942-43, Barnard Skin and Cancer Hosp., St. Louis, also; U. Pa., 1943-44, instr. zoology, 1943-44; temporary research assoc. dept. genetics Carnegie Instn. of Washington, Cold Spring Harbor, 1944-46; research assoc. biology dept. Mass. Inst. Tech., 1946-47; asst. Sloan-Kettering Inst. Cancer Research, 1946-47, research fellow, 1947, assoc., 1947-55, head cell growth sect., div. exptl. chemotherapy, 1947-58, mem., 1955-58, assoc. scientist div., 1959-78; asst. prof. anatomy Cornell U. Med. Sch., 1950-52; assoc. prof. biology Sloan-Kettering div. Cornell U. Grad. Sch. Med. Scis., 1952-55, prof. biology, 1955-58; prof. zoology, mem. grad. faculty U. Tex., Austin, 1958-78, also mem. faculty, 1969-71, prof. edn., 1973-78; cons. cell biology M.D. Anderson Hosp. and Tumor Inst., U. Tex. at Houston, 1958-72; dir. Genetics Found., 1959-78; mem. cell biology study sect. NIH, 1958-63; Sigma Xi lectr. N.Y. U. Grad. Sch. Arts and Scis., 1957; Mendel lectr. St. Peter's Coll., Jersey City, 1958; Mendel Club lectr. Canisius Coll., Buffalo, 1971; mem. adv. com. research etiology of cancer Am. Cancer Soc., 1961-64, pres. Travis County unit, 1966, mem. adv. com. on personnel for research, 1969-73; counsellor Cancer Internat. Research Coop., Inc., 1962—; mem. cancer research tng. com. Nat. Cancer Inst., 1969-72; Gen. chmn. Conf. Advancement Sci. and Math. Teaching, 1966. Author: Mitotic Poisons and the Cancer Problem, 1958; Editorial bd.: Year Book Cancer, 1959-72; editorial adv. bd.: Cancer Research, 1960-

64; asso. editor, 1969-72; cons. editor: Am. Jour. Mental Deficiency, 1966-68; Contbr. articles sci. jours., books. Research Career award NIH, 1962, 67, 72, 77. Fellow N.Y., Tex. acads. scis., AAAS; mem. Am. Assn. Cancer Research (dir. 1960-63), Am. Soc. Cell Biology, Am. Inst. Biol. Scis., Phi Beta Kappa, Sigma Xi (pres. Tex. chpt. 1963-64), Phi Eta Sigma. Home: 2500 Great Oaks Pkwy Austin TX 78756

BIESER, IRVIN GRUEN, lawyer; b. Dayton, Ohio, June 15, 1902; s. Charles William and Flora Sophia (Gruen) B.; m. Catharine Mary French, Apr. 14, 1936; children: Catharine Black, Irvin Gruen. B.S. cum laude, Harvard U., 1924, LL.B., 1927. Bar: Ohio 1927. Since practiced in, Dayton; sr. partner firm Bieser, Greer & Landis (and predecessors), 1932-74, of counsel, 1974—; dir. Midwest Securities Investment, Inc., City Transit Co.; v.p., dir. Everybody's Office Outfitters, Inc., 1931-69; dir. emeritus Dayton Power & Light Co., 1958-73; mem. standing com. on gen. principles of law recognized by community of nations and spl. com. on rev. UN charter World Peace Through Law Center. Author: Origin and Rise of the Republican Party, 1924. Founder, trustee, now trustee emeritus Miami Valley Hosp., pres., 1948-54; trustee emeritus Hosp. Care Corp., S.W. Ohio, 1939—, pres., 1956-58, chmn., 1958-60; trustee Dayton Art Inst., 1954-76, sec., 1956, v.p., 1967; trustee Dayton Philharmonic Orch. Assn., 1963-70, Frank M. Tait Found., 1959—; pres. Frank M. Tait Found., 1980—. Mem. Internat. Bar Assn., ABA, Ohio Bar Assn. (past mem. coms. on taxation, jud. reform), Dayton Bar Assn. (pres. 1957-58), Am. Judicature Soc., Dayton Lawyers Club (trustee), Dayton Law Library Assn. (trustee, pres. 1969-72), Alpha Sigma Phi. Republican. Lutheran. Clubs: Rotary, Dayton Country, Moraine Country, Harvard (past pres.), Racquet (Dayton); Masons. Home: 447 Kramer Rd Dayton OH 45419 Office: 400 Gem Plaza Bldg Dayton OH 45402

BIESTER, EDWARD GEORGE, JR., judge; b. Trevose, Pa., Jan. 5, 1931; s. Edward G. and Muriel (Worthington) B.; m. Elizabeth Ruth Lauffer, Apr. 10, 1954; children—Ann Meredith, Edward George III, James Paul, David Robertson. B.A., Wesleyan U., 1952; LL.B., Temple U., 1955. Bar: Pa. bar 1956. Practiced in, Phila., 1956; mem. firm Biester & Ludwig, 1967-69; asst. dist. atty., Bucks County, Pa., 1958-64; mem. 90th-94th congresses from 8th Dist. Pa.; partner firm La Brum & Doak, Phila.; atty. gen. Commonwealth of Pa., 1979-80; judge Ct. of Common Pleas, 1980—. Mem. Am., Pa., Phila. bar assns. Home: Lower Mountain Rd Furlong PA 18925

BIEWAN, ROBERT L., publishing company executive; b. Austin, Minn., July 15, 1936; s. W.J. and Dona C. Biewen Gahagan; m. Catherine E. Jelinek, June 24, 1967; children: Jennifer, Mary. B.A., St. John's U., Collegeville, Minn., 1958; postgrad., U. Minn., 1958-60. Exec. editor, coll. Harcourt, Brace, Jovanovich, N.Y.C., 1970-72; dir. coll. div. Acad. Press, 1972-76, sr. v.p. mktg., N.Y.C., 1976-78; exec. v.p., chief exec. officer Springer-Verlag N.Y. Inc., N.Y.C., 1978-80; exec. v.p McGraw-Hill Book Co., N.Y.C., 1980—. Mem. Norwalk City Council, Conn., 1977-78. Mem. Assn. Am. Pubs. (exec. council 1982—). Club: Norwalk Yacht. Office: McGraw-Hill Book Co 1221 Ave of Americas New York NY 10020 *

BIGBIE, JOHN TAYLOR, lawyer, banker; b. Lynchburg, Va., Sept. 12, 1923; s. William Bright and Maria Woodson (Taylor) B.; m. Nadine de Coninck, Oct. 6, 1956; children: Astrid, John Eric. B.A., Princeton U., 1944; J.D., U. Va., 1948. Bar: N.Y. 1950. Assoc. Breed, Abbot & Morgan, N.Y.C., 1948-54; counsel Nat. Assn. Life Underwriters, Washington, 1954-61; v.p., sec., trust officer European-Am. Bank & Trust Co., N.Y.C., 1961-72; European rep. Butlers Bank Ltd., London, 1972-73; also dir.; dep. chmn. Antony Gibbs Fin. Services (C.I.) Ltd., 1974-77; internat. atty. and cons., 1978—; dir. Internat. Belgian Trading Soc. Brussels, Belgium, Sentinel Holdings Ltd., Nassau, Bahamas, Sentinel Investments Ltd., Can., Hazel Gen. Trading Co. Ltd. Guernsey Channel Islands, Gemco Ltd. Jersey Channel Islands; cons. Profl. Services Ltd., Switzerland. Served to lt. (j.g.) USNR, 1944-46. Mem. S.R., Soc. Colonial Wars, Pilgrims of Gt. Britain. Episcopalian. Clubs: Links (N.Y.C.); American of London, Lansdowne, Bucks, Overseas Bankers (London). Lodge: Masons (N.Y.C.). Home: 33 Egerton Crescent London SW 3 England Office: 11 Upper Brook St London England W1Y 1PB

BIGELEISEN, JACOB, educator, chemist; b. Paterson, N.J., May 2, 1919; s. Harry and Ida (Slomowitz) B.; m. Grace Alice Simon, Oct. 21, 1945; children: David M., Ira S., Paul E. A.B., NYU, 1939; M.S., Wash. State U., 1941; Ph.D., U. Calif., Berkeley, 1943. Research scientist Manhattan Dist., Columbia, 1943-45; research asso. Ohio State U., Columbus, 1945-46; fellow Enrico Fermi Inst., U. Chgo., 1946-48; sr. chemist Brookhaven Nat. Lab., Upton, N.Y., 1948-68; prof. chemistry U. Rochester, N.Y., 1968-78, chmn. dept., 1970-75, Tracy H. Harris prof., 1973-78; v.p. research, dean grad. studies SUNY, Stony Brook, 1978-80, Leading prof. chemistry, 1978—; vis. prof. Cornell U., 1953; NSF sr. fellow, vis. prof. Eidgen Techn. Hochschule, Switzerland, 1962-63; chmn. Assembly Math. and Phys. Scis., NRC-Nat. Acad. Scis., 1976-80. Mem. editorial bd.: Jour. Phys. Chemistry. Trustee Sayville Jewish Center, 1954-68. Recipient Nuclear award Am. Chem. Soc., 1958, Gilbert N. Lewis lectr., 1963, E.O. Lawrence award, 1964, Disting. Alumnus award Wash. State U., 1983; John Simon Guggenheim fellow, 1974-75. Fellow Am. Phys. Soc., Am. Chem. Soc., AAAS, Am. Acad. Arts and Sci.; mem. Nat. Acad. Scis., Phi Beta Kappa, Sigma Xi, Phi Lambda Upsilon. Research in photochemistry in rigid media, semiquinones, cryogenics, chemistry of isotopes, quantum statistics of gases, liquids and solids. Home: PO Box 217 Saint James NY 11780 *As a youth I became interested in a career in science because it offered the opportunity to test ideas and hypotheses objectively by experiment. This unique aspect of science, which differentiates it from all other branches of learning and knowledge, has been a guiding principle both in my professional and my personal life. My career has included research, teaching, administration and public service.*

BIGELOW, CHARLES CROSS, biochemist, university administrator; b. Edmonton, Alta., Can., Apr. 25, 1928; s. Sherburne Tupper and Helen Beatrice (Cross) B.; m. Elizabeth Rosemary Sellick, Aug. 22, 1977; children: Ann K. Bigelow McLean, David C. B.A.Sc., U. Toronto, 1953, M.Sc., 1955; Ph.D., McMaster U., 1957. Postdoctoral fellow Carlsberg Lab., Copenhagen, 1957-59; assoc. Sloan-Kettering Inst. Cancer Research, N.Y.C., 1959-62; asst. prof. chemistry U. Alta., Can., 1962-64, assoc. prof., 1964-65; vis. prof. Fla. State U., Tallahassee, 1965; assoc. prof. biochemistry U. Western Ont. (Can.), London, 1965-69, prof., 1969-74; prof., head biochemistry Meml. U. Nfld. (Can.), St. John's, 1974-76; dean of sci., prof. chemistry St. Mary's U., Halifax, N.S., Can., 1977-79, U. Man. (Can.), Winnipeg, 1979—; vis. prof. U. Toronto, 1973-74; chmn. Ont. Confedn. Univ. Faculty Assns., 1970-71; pres. Can. Assn. Univ. Tchrs., 1972-73. Contbr. articles on protein structure and denaturation to sci. jours. Pres. N.S. New Democratic party, 1978-79, Man. New Dem. party, 1982—. Grantee NRC Can., Med. Research Bd. govs. U. Western Ont., 1972-73. Council Natural Scis. and Engring. Research Council Can.; fellow Chem. Inst. Can.; mem. Can. Biochem. Soc., Am. Chem. Soc., Am. Soc. Biol. Chemists, AAAS, Sigma Xi. Club: Southwood Golf and Country (Winnipeg). Home: 701 South Dr Winnipeg MB Canada R2G OC2 Office: U Man Winnipeg MB Canada R3T 2N2

BIGELOW, DONALD NEVIUS, educational consultant; b. Danbury, Conn., Aug. 19, 1918; s. Harry R. and Bessie M. (Nevius) B.; m. Louise M. Fournel, Sept. 21, 1957; 1 son, Pierre Nevius. B.A. cum laude, Amherst Coll., 1939, M.A., 1945; Ph.D., Columbia U., 1950. Spl. agt. Inland Marine Ins., North Brit. and Merc. Ins. Co., N.Y.C. and Detroit, 1939-43; with U.S. Engr. Dept., Fairbanks, Alaska, 1942; instr. history Amherst Coll., 1943-45; instr. Columbia U., 1947-50, asst. prof., 1951-55; vis. Fulbright prof. Am. civilization U.S. Ednl. Found., India, U. Baroda, U. Lucknow, 1954-55; asso. prof. Brandeis U., 1955-60; prof. humanities N.Y. Sch. Music, 1949-56; vis. prof. U. So. Fla., 1969; postdoctoral research fellow George Washington U., 1970-71; lectr. U. Va., 1973; adj. prof. Am. U., 1975; chief lang. and area centers program Office Edn., HEW, Washington, 1961-64; head task force NDEA Title XI Inst. Program, 1964-65, dir. div. ednl. personnel tng., 1965-67, dir. div. program adminstrn., 1967-68; dir. div. coll. programs Bur. Ednl. Personnel Devel., 1968-71; dir. Northeast div. Nat. Center for Improvement Ednl. Systems, 1972-74; spl. asst., asso. commr. for Instl. Devel. and Internat. Edn., 1974-76; chief grad. tng. Office of Postsecondary Edn., Dept. Edn., 1976-82; cons. Ford Found., 1957, Carnegie Corp., 1958, U.S. Office Edn., 1959-60; moderator ABC TV series Seminar, 1953-54; asso. dir. com. lang. and area centers Am. Council Edn., 1960-61; book reviewer Nat. Pub. Radio series Options in Education, 1976-77. Author: William Conant Church and the Army and Navy Journal, 1952, (with Joseph Axelrod) Resources for Language and Area Studies, 1960, (with Lyman Legters) Language and Area Centers, 1964, (with others) Non-Western Studies in the Liberal Arts College, 1964; editor: (with Hiram Haydn) Makers of the American Tradition Series, 4 vols., 1953-55, The Annals (The Non-Western World in Higher Education), 1964, The Liberal Arts and Teacher Education: A Confrontation, 1971, Schoolworlds '76, New Directions for Educational Policy, 1976; lectr., contbr. articles to profl. jours. Mem. Am. Hist. Assn., Fed. Mgrs. Assn. (pres. 1979-81). Episcopalian. Club: Univ. (Washington). Home: Flying Point Rd Box 15 Water Mill NY 11976

BIGELOW, JANE ELIZABETH, municipal research bureau adminstrator, former mayor; b. Toronto, Ont., Can., June 9, 1928; d. Edward and Margaret Murns (King) Dillon; children: Ann, David. B.Ph.E., U. Toronto, 1950; postgrad., U. Western Ont., 1966-70. Tchr. high schs., Ottawa, Ont., 1951-53, Hamilton, Ont., 1953-57, Edmonton, Ont., 1962-64; controller City of London, Ont., 1970-71, 80-82, mayor, 1972-78, controller, 1981-82; dir. Bur. Municipal Research, 1974—; mem. Ont. Pub. Utilities Commn., 1972-78, Ont. Police Commn., 1972-78; Bd. govs. U. Western Ont., 1972-78; mem. planning bd., City of London, 1970-76, mem. pub. library bd., 1971, 72, 76. Bd. dirs. Can. Conf. of Arts, 1979, v.p., 1980-81; bd. dirs. Can. Civil Liberties Assn., 1979-81, Women's Community House, London, 1980, London Symphony Orch.; v.p. New Democratic Party, Ont., 1969-72; chmn. Women in Local Govt., 1976; bd. dirs. Theatre London, 1981-82; patron Internat. Yr. of Disabled, 1981; mem. Bicentennial Adv. Com. Province of Ont., 1983-84. Named Woman of Year Quota Club, 1973, London Bus. and Profl. Women's Club, 1976. Home: 203 Sherwood Ave London ON N6A 2E8 Canada

BIGELOW, LEONARD, librarian; b. Lockport, N.Y., June 27, 1920; s. Harold Louis and Luella (Leonard) B.; m. Rose Marie Rongo, Sept. 5, 1942; 1 son, Richard Alan. B.S. in Edn, State U. N.Y., 1953; postgrad., U. Buffalo, 1953, U. Ill., 1955. Information specialist Gen. Elec., Ithaca, N.Y., 1956-60; library mgr. (Honeywell Aerospace Div.), Mpls., 1960-72; mgr. library services Medtronic Inc., Mpls., 1972—. Served with USAAF, 1941-50. Mem. Spl. Libraries Assn., Am. Soc. Information Scis., Soc. for Preservation and Encouragement Barber Shop Quartet Singing Am. Home: 1213 Rhode Island Ave N Minneapolis MN 55427 Office: 3055 Hwy 8 PO Box 1453 Minneapolis MN 55440

BIGELOW, MARTHA MITCHELL, historian; b. Talladega Springs, Ala., Sept. 19, 1921; (div.)children—Martha Frances, Carolyn. B.A., Ala. Coll., Montevallo, 1943; M.A. (tuition fellow, Julius Rosenwald scholar 1943-44, Cleo Hearson scholar, summer 1944, Ency. Brit. fellow 1944-45), U. Chgo., 1944, Ph.D., 1946. Asso. prof. history Miss. Coll., Clinton, 1946-48, Memphis State U., 1948-49, U. Miss., 1949-50; asso. curator manuscripts Mich. Hist. Collections, U. Mich., Ann Arbor, 1954-57; prof. history Miss. Coll., 1957-71, chmn. dept. history and polit. sci., 1964-71; dir. Mich. history div. Mich. Dept. State, sec., also state historic preservation officer, 1971—; coordinator for Mich., Nat. Hist. Publns. and Records Commn., 1974; Amer. asso. state and History fellow, summers 1958, 59. Contbr. articles profl. publns. Mem. Am. Assn. State and Local History (pres. 1979-81), Orgn. Am. Historians, Nat. Assn. State Archives and Records Assn., So. Hist Assn., Mich. Hist. Soc., Miss. Hist. Soc. Home: 223 Cowley St East Lansing MI 48823 Office: 208 N Capitol St Lansing MI 48918

BIGELOW, ROBERT OTIS, electrical engineer, utilities executive; b. Boston, Mar. 28, 1926; s. Robert Payne and Carolyn Evans (Chase) B.; m. Jean Davis, May 8, 1948; children: Margaret Bigelow Jacks, John P., Carol. B.S. in Elec. Engring., M.I.T., 1950, M.S., 1950. With New Eng. Power Service Co., 1950—, asst. chief engr., 1970-73, dir. planning and power supply, 1973-77, v.p. planning and power supply, 1977—; v.p. New Eng. Power Co., 1979—, dir., 1980—; pres. New Eng. Electric Transmission Corp., 1981—. Served with USN, 1944-46. Named Young Engr. of Yr., Mass. Soc. Profl. Engrs., 1960. Fellow IEEE. Home: 15 Granuaile Rd Southboro MA 01772 Office: 25 Research Dr Westboro MA 01581

BIGELOW, WILLIAM R., utility exec.; b. 1928; m. Gloria Moylan Fish, Oct. 25, 1952; 1 son, Robert Lawrence. B.S., U. Calif., 1950. With Pacific Lighting Corp., San Francisco, 1956—, treas., asst. sec., 1966-74, asst. controller, 1974—. Served as 1st lt. USAF, 1951-53. Mem. Calif. Inst. C.P.A.'s, Fin. Execs. Inst. Address: Pacific Lighting Corp 810 S Flower St Los Angeles CA 90017

BIGGAR, EDWARD SAMUEL, lawyer; b. Kansas City, Mo., Nov. 19, 1917; s. Frank Wilson and Katharine (Rea) B.; m. Susan Bagby, July 9, 1955; children: John, Julie, Nancy, William, Martha Susan. A.B., U. Mich., 1938, J.D. with distinction, 1940. Bar: Mo. bar 1940. Assoc. firm Stinson, Mag & Fizzell, Kansas City, 1948-50, ptnr., 1950—; dir. Western Chem. Co., Cereal Food Processors, Inc., Lumber Products Sales Co.; Trustee Sunset Hill Sch., Kansas City, 1970-76; mem. com. of visitors U. Mich. Law Sch., 1977—. Editor: Mich. Law Rev, 1939-40. Pres. Met. Kansas City YMCA, 1979-81, Kansas City (Mo.) unit Am. Cancer Soc., 1968-69, Kansas City (Mo.) Bd. Police Commrs., 1981—; mem. Kansas City (Mo.) Met. Planning Commn., 1974-75; chmn. Citizens Assn. Kansas City (Mo.), 1960-61. Served to 1st lt. AC U.S. Army, 1942-45; New Guinea, Philippines. Named Man of Yr. Phi Delta Theta Alumni Assn., Kansas City, 1968. Mem. Am. Bar Assn., Am. Judicature Soc., Lawyers Assn. Kansas City (pres. 1966-67), Kansas City Bar Assn., Order of Coif, Phi Beta Kappa, Phi Delta Theta, Phi Delta Phi. Republican. Presbyterian. Clubs: Kansas City Country, Mission Hills Country, Univ. of Kansas City, Mercury of Kansas City. Home: 1221 Stratford Rd Kansas City MO 64113 Office: 2100 Charter Bank Center Kansas City MO 64105

BIGGAR, JAMES MCCREA, food company executive; b. Cleve., Dec. 5, 1928; s. Hamilton Fisk and Ruth Carolyn (McCrea) B.; m. Margery Dean Stouffer, Dec. 29, 1950; children—Elizabeth, James, William, David. B.S. in Mech. Engring. and Engring. Adminstrn, Case Inst. Tech., 1950. With Reliance Electric Co., Cleve., 1950-60, mgr. alternating current products, 1955-60; with frozen foods div. Stouffer Corp., Cleve., 1960-70, mktg. v.p., 1960-66, v.p., gen. mgr., 1966-68, pres., 1968-70; v.p. food service group Litton Industries, Solon, Ohio, 1970-72; pres., chmn. bd., dir. Stouffer Corp., Solon, 1972—; pres., chief exec. officer Nestle Enterprises, Inc., 1983—; dir. Nestle Enterprises. Pres. Orange Local Sch. Bd., Pepper Pike, Ohio, 1967-68; v.p. Vocat. Guidances and Rehab. Services, Cleve., 1970-76; bd. dirs. Cleve. Clinic, Greater Cleve. Growth Assn.; trustee Univ. Sch. Mem. Am., Frozen Food Inst. (past chmn., dir.), Phi Kappa Psi, Theta Tau, Beta Gamma Sigma. Presbyterian. Clubs: Cleve. Country, Clevelander, Pepper Pike Country. Home: 31600 Fairmount Blvd Pepper Pike OH 44124 Office: nestle enterprises inc 100 bloomingdale road white plains ny 10605

BIGGAR, ROBERT MCCREA, securities company executive; b. Cleve., Mar. 22, 1932; s. Hamilton Fisk and Ruth Carpenter (McCrea) B.; m. Elizabeth Wade, June 15, 1954; children: Anne McMillan, Sarah Courtney, Robert McCrea. B.S. in Commerce, U. Va., 1954. With Gen. Electric Co., Erie, Pa., Louisville and Cleve., 1954-59; account exec. Hornblower & Weeks-Hemphill, Noyes (name now Shearson Am. Express), Cleve., 1959-69, partner, 1969-71, resident mgr., 1971-74, div. mgr., 1974-78, exec. v.p., dir. domestic sales, 1978-79, exec. v.p., dir., regional officer, dir., 1979—; dir. Hill Acme Co. Pres. City Council, Pepper Pike, Ohio; pres. bd. trustees Hathaway Brown Sch. Mem. Securities Industry Assn. (past gov., chmn. Gt. Lakes Dist. 1975), Nat. Assn. Security Dealers, Inc. Home: 31993 Fairmount Blvd Pepper Pike OH 44124 Office: N Main St Stepnorth Chagrin Falls OH 44020

BIGGER, JOHN THOMAS, JR., physician, educator; b. Cambridge, Mass., Jan. 17, 1935; s. John Thomas and Wilma Rebecca (Rushing) B.; m. Susan T. Harrison, 1982; 1 dau., Deborah Lynn. A.B., Emory U., 1955; M.D., Med. Coll. Ga., 1960. Diplomate: Am. Bd. Internal Medicine. Intern Bellevue Hosp., N.Y.C., 1960-61; resident in internal medicine Columbia U., 1961-64, fellow in cardiology, 1964-67, asst. prof. medicine and pharmacology, 1967-72, asso. prof., 1972-75, prof., 1975—; dir. cardiology Columbia-Presbyn. Med. Center, 1978—; attending physician Presbyn. Hosp., N.Y.C., 1975—; mem. pharmacology study sect. A NIH, 1972-75. Mem. editorial bd.: Circulation, 1970-76, 82—, Jour. Pharmacology and Therapeutics, 1974—, Stroke, 1976-80, Am. Jour. Medicine, 1979—, Pharmacology, 1978—, Jour. Cardiovascular Pharmacology, 1979—; contbr. articles to profl. jours. Served with U.S. Navy, 1962-63. Fellow N.Y. Acad. Scis.; mem. Assn. Univ. Cardiologists, Am. Coll. Cardiology, ACP, Am. Soc. Pharmacology and Exptl. Therapeutics, Am. Physiol. Soc., Biophys. Soc., N.Y. Heart Assn., Am. Heart Assn., Assn. Am. Physicians, Am. Soc. Clin. Investigation, Am. Fedn. Clin. Research, Alpha Omega Alpha. Democrat. Office: 630 W 168th St New York NY 10032

BIGGERS, WILLIAM JOSEPH, corporation executive; b. Great Bend, Kans., Mar. 16, 1928; s. William Henry and Frances (Jack) B.; m. Diane McLaughlin, Feb. 14, 1983; children: Frances, Patricia. B.A., Duke U., 1949. C.P.A., Ga. Pub. acct., 1949-55; sec.-treas. Parker, Helms & Langston, Inc., Brunswick, Ga., 1955-59, Stuckey's, Inc., Eastman, Ga., 1959-60; sec.-treas., v.p. finance Curtis 1000 Inc., 1961-69; v.p. Am. Bus. Products, Inc., Atlanta, 1969-73, pres., chief exec. officer, 1973-83, chmn. bd., pres., chief exec. officer, 1983—; also dir.; trustee ABP Profit Sharing Trust; dir. First Nat. Bank of Cobb County.; Trustee Ga. Council Econ. Edn.; mem. mgmt. adv. com. Emory U. Grad. Sch. Bus.; bd. dirs. Com. Publicly Owned Cos.; bd. visitors Berry Coll. Served with USNR, 1946; Served with AUS, 1950-52. Mem. Am. Inst. C.P.A.s, Ga. Soc. C.P.A.s, Fin. Execs. Inst., Am. Mgmt. Assn., Phoenix Soc. Atlanta, U.S. C. of C., Conf. Bd., NAM, Phi Kappa Psi. Clubs: Capital City, Georgian. Office: 2690 Cumberland Pkwy Suite 500 Atlanta GA 30339

BIGGS, BARTON MICHAEL, investment company executive; b. N.Y.C., Nov. 26, 1932; s. William Richardson and Georgene (Williams) B.; m. Judith Anne Lund, June 12, 1959; children: Wende Hammond, Gretchen G., Barton William. B.A., Yale U., 1955; M.B.A. with distinction, NYU, 1962. Research analyst E.F. Hutton & Co., N.Y.C., 1960-65, asst. to chmn., 1962-65, partner, 1965; co-founder, mng. partner Fairfield Partners, Greenwich, Conn., 1965-73; ptnr. Morgan Stanley & Co., N.Y.C., 1973—, mgr. research dept., 1973-79; chmn., chief investment officer Morgan Stanley Asset Mgmt. Co., N.Y.C., 1980—; dir. Rand McNally & Co., 1975—; Trustee Brookings Inst., Lehrman Inst. Contbr. articles to profl. jours. Served as 1st lt. USMC, 1955-58. Mem. N.Y. Soc. Security Analysts. Clubs: Field (Greenwich); Chevy Chase (Washington). Office: 1251 Ave of the Americas New York NY 10020

BIGGS, DONALD ANTHONY, psychologist, educator; b. South Bend, Ind., Jan. 19, 1936; s. Poss and Helen B.; m. Sara Banks, Mar. 30, 1959; five children. B.S., Ariz. State U., 1958; M.S. in Counseling, Ball State U., 1959; Ed.D., UCLA, 1963. Cons. psychologist Cath. Charities, Omaha, 1962-64; assoc. prof. edn. Creighton U., Omaha, 1962-67, dir. Univ. Counselling Ctr., 1965-67; ast.prof. dept. psychology U. Minn., Mpls., 1967-9, assoc. prof., 1969-73, prof. ednl. psychology, 1973-79, dir. student life studies and planning, 1975-78, asst.l to v.p. student affairs, 1975-78; prof. counseling psychology SUNY-Albany, 1978—, chmn. dept. counseling psychology, Mpls., 1978—; vis. prof. counselor edn. NYU, N.Y.C., summers, 1972-77; vis. Fulbright prof. counselor edn. U. Aston, Birmingham, Eng., 1975-76; vis. prof. counselor edn. McGill U., Montreal, Can., summer, 1974. Author: (with E.G. Williamson) Student Personnel Work: A Program of Developmental Relationships, 1975, (with Donald Blocker) Counseling Psychology in Community Settings; editor: Counseling and Values; coptbr. numerous articles on counseling psycholgy to profl. jours. Mem. Am. Psychol. Assn., Assn. for Religious and Value Issues in Counseling (former pres.). Home: 3 Ashford Dr Alany NY 12203

BIGGS, HUGH LAWRY, lawyer; b. Burns, Oreg., Aug. 28, 1904; s. Dalton and Phebe (Lawry) B.; m. Elra Ware, Mar. 25, 1931; children: Suzanne, Barry Hugh. A.B., U. Oreg., 1927, J.D., 1931; postgrad., U. Wash., 1929-30. Bar: Oreg. 1931. Asst. dean men U. Oreg., 1928-30, acting dean men, 1930-31; dist. atty., Malheur County, Oreg., 1933-34; asst. U.S. atty., Oreg., 1934-35; practiced law, Portland, 1935-43; mem. firm Davies, Biggs, Strayer, Stoel & Boley (and predecessor), Portland, 1943-83; of counsel Stoel, Rives, Boley, Fraser & Wyse, 1983—; gen. counsel S.P. & S. Ry. System, 1960-70; Bd. dirs., sec. Oreg. div. Am. Cancer Soc.; bd. dirs., pres. U. Oreg. Devel. Fund; bd. govs. Nat. Legal Aid Assn., 1958-62; bd. visitors U. Oreg. Law Sch., Northwestern Sch. Law of Lewis and Clark Coll. Fellow Am. Coll. Trial Lawyers, Am. Bar Found.; mem. ABA (ho. dels.), Oreg. Bar Assn. (past gov.), Multnomah Bar Assn. (past pres.), Phi Beta Kappa, Phi Delta Phi, Delta Sigma Rho, Alpha Tau Omega. Democrat. Clubs: Rotary, University (Portland); Arlington, Waverley Country. Home: 6834 SE Reed Coll Pl Portland OR 97202 Office: 900 SW 5th Ave Portland OR 97204

BIGGS, J.O., gen. industry co. exec.; b. Kansas City, Mo., Feb. 17, 1925; s. John Olin and Parilee Catherine (Story) B.; m. Marilyn Frances Sweeney, Dec. 27, 1947; children—Melissa Anne, John Kevin, Brian Sweeney. A.B., U. Kans., 1947, LL.B., 1949. Bar: Kan. bar 1949, Mo. bar 1950, Ia. bar 1953. With legal dept. Kansas City Life Ins. Co., 1950-51; exec. asst. to industry members Regional Wage Stblzn. Bd.,

1951-52; dir. labor relations Meredith Pub. Co., 1952-58; with Gustin-Bacon Mfg. Co. (merger into Certain-teed Products Corp. 1966), 1958—, v.p., asst. to pres., 1962-63; pres., chief exec. officer, 1963-66, exec. v.p., Ardmore, Pa., 1966-69; pres. Thermo-Kinetic Corp., 1969-76; mem. firm Wagner, Leek & Mullins, 1976—; cons. in field. Active Big Bros. of Tucson. Mem. Am., Mo., Kans., Johnson County bar assns., Lawyers Assn. Kansas City, Am. Mgmt. Assn., Sigma Alpha Epsilon, Phi Alpha Phi. Republican. Presbyn. Clubs: Skyline, Country (Tucson); Mission Hills Country (Kansas City). Home: 8743 Riggs Circle Shawnee Mission KS 66212 Office: 4101 W 54th Terr Shawnee Mission KS 66205

BIGGS, JOHN H., university official; b. St. Louis, July 19, 1936; s. Peter Willis and Lillian (Herron) B.; m. Penelope Frances Parkman, June 13, 1959; children: Andrea, Henry. A.B. magna cum laude, Harvard U., 1958. Group underwriting v.p. Gen. Am. Ins. Co., 1965-67, dir. corp. planning, 1967-70, v.p., controller, 1970-77; vice chancellor for adminstrn. and fin. Washington U., St. Louis, 1977—; chmn. Washington U. Tech. Assocs.; First v.p. New City Sch., Inc., 1969-73; dir. Centerre Trust; Bd. dirs., vice chmn. Mo. Coordinating Bd. Higher Edn.; bd. dirs. Mark Twain Summer Inst., Higher Edn. Coordinating Council St. Louis, 1969-77; v.p. Arts and Edn. Council St. Louis; trustee, treas. St. Louis County Day Sch.; trustee, chmn. New Med. Found., St. Louis.; trustee, chmn. fin. com. Mo. Bot. Garden. Fellow Soc. Actuaries; mem. Am. Acad. Actuaries (dir. 1970-73). Club: St. Louis Harvard (pres. 1969-70). Home: 4904 Pershing Pl Saint Louis MO 63108 Office: Washington U Saint Louis MO 63130

BIGGS, ROBERT DALE, educator; b. Pasco, Wash., June 13, 1934; s. Robert Lee and Eleonora Christine (Jensen) B. B.A. in Edn, Eastern Wash. Coll. Edn., 1956; Ph.D., Johns Hopkins U., 1962. Research asso. Oriental Inst., Univ. Chgo., 1963-64; asst. prof. Assyriology, 1964-67, asso. prof., 1967-72, prof., 1972—. Author: SÀ.ZI.GA: Ancient Mesopotamian Potency Incantations, 1967, Cuneiform Texts from Nippur, 1969, Inscriptions from Tell Abu Salabikh, 1974, Inscriptions from al-Hiba-Lagash: The First and Second Seasons, 1976; co-author: Nippur II: The North Temple and Sounding E, 1978; asso. editor: Assyrian Dictionary, 1964—; editor: Jour. Near Eastern Studies, 1972—. Fulbright scholar Univ. Toulouse, France, 1956-57; fellow Baghdad Sch., Am. Schs. Oriental Research, 1962-63. Mem. Am. Oriental Soc., Archaeol. Inst. Am., Am. Schs. Oriental Research, Brit. Sch. Archaeology Iraq. Office: 1155 E 58th St Chicago IL 60637

BIGGS, THOMAS JONES, architect; b. Earle, Ark., Jan. 28, 1912; s. Thomas Jones and Fleda May (Boyers) B.; m. Mary Louise Wallis, Dec. 19, 1938; children—Jane Wallis, Lynn Louise, Mary Elizabeth. B.S. in Architecture, Ga. Inst. Tech., 1933. With various archtl. offices in, Jackson, Miss., Washington and N.Y.C., 1933-40; partner Biggs, Weir (Architects), Jackson, Miss., 1946—; mem. bd. visitors sch. architecture Auburn (Ala.) U., Tulane U., Miss. State U. Served to lt. col. C.E. U.S. Army, 1940-46. Fellow AIA. Episcopalian. Address: 3723 Kings Hwy Jackson MS 39206

BIGGS, WELLINGTON ALLEN, editor, journalist; b. Platteville, Colo., Mar. 9, 1923; s. Wellington H. and Adeline (Brown) B.; m. Laura Jean Mowrey, Dec. 7, 1951; children—Catherine, Joseph, Lorraine, Louise, Jeffrey. B.J., U. Colo., 1949. Asst. editor Brighton (Colo.) Blade, 1949-50; editor Haywood Pub. Co., Chgo., 1950-52; asst. editor Alamosa (Colo.) Daily Courier, 1952, Wyo. State Jour., Lander, 1952; dir. publs. U. Colo., 1952-56; editor Rocky Mountain Teamster, Denver, 1956-61; pub. relations cons. Colo. Freedom to Bargain Com., 1958; dir. pub. relations, editor Internat. Teamster mag., Washington, 1961-81; sr. editor Editorial Consultancy, Silver Spring, Md., 1981—. Precinct committeeman, dist. capt., publicity chmn., pub. relations cons. Boulder County (Colo.) Democratic Party, 1952-61. Served with USNR, 1942-46; PTO. Mem. Sigma Delta Chi, Pi Kappa Alpha. Methodist. Home: 500 Valleybrook Dr Silver Spring MD 20904

BIGGY, MARY VIRGINIA, college dean; b. Boston, Oct. 15, 1924; d. John J. and Mary C. (Dwyer) B. B.S., Boston U., 1945, Ed.M., 1946, Ed.D., 1953. Tchr. bus. edn. Needham (Mass.) High Sch., 1944-45; reading cons. Plainville (Conn.) Public Schs., 1946-47; coordinator elem. edn. Concord (Mass.) Public Schs., 1953-62; dir. N.E. instrnl. TV project, dir. instrnl. TV Eastern Ednl. Network, Boston, 1962-67; asst. supt., supr. Concord Public Schs. and Concord Carlisle Regional Sch. Dist., 1967-69; prof. edn. U. Lowell, Mass., 1969—, dean, 1979—; pres. (Designs for Edn.), 1969—; cons. Corp. Public Broadcasting, Carnegie II Study Public Broadcasting.; mem. Acton Boxborough (Mass.) Regional High Sch. Dist. Sch. Com., 1963-66; chmn. Mass. Bd. Library Commrs., 1973-78; project dir. criteria for funding major initiatives Corp. Pub. Broadcasting, 1981—. Author: Independence in Spelling, 1966, (with others) Spell Correctly, 1965-80. Recipient Ida M. Johnston award Boston U., 1981. Mem. NEA, Am. Assn. Sch. Adminstrs., Am. Ednl. Research Assn., Assn. Supervision and Curriculum Devel., AAUP, Internat. Reading Assn., New Eng. Reading Assn., Pi Lambda Theta (nat. pres. 1961-65, Disting. Pi Lambda Thetan award 1983), others. Democrat. Roman Catholic. Home: 162 Park Ln Concord MA 01720 Office: Coll Edn Univ Lowell Lowell MA 01854

BIGHAM, JAMES JOHN, chemical company executive; b. Waterbury, Conn., Aug. 7, 1937; s. Thomas Francis and Kathryn (Meagher) B.; m. Mary Ellen Jeffries, Feb. 1, 1964; children: Stephen, Helen-Anne, Jonathan, Jennifer. B.S., Fairfield U., 1959; M.B.A., Columbia U., 1961; cert., Harvard U., 1970. Br. mgr. Harris Upham & Co., Waterbury, 1961-66; fin. analyst Hess Oil & Chem. Corp., Perth Amboy, N.J., 1966-67; mgr. money and banking Celanese Corp., N.Y.C., 1967-70, asst. treas., 1970-75, v.p., treas., 1975-81; v.p. fin. and planning Celanese Internat. Co., N.Y.C., 1981—; dir. Celanese Can., Inc., Montreal, Celanese Mexicana, S.A., Mexico City, Polyplastics Co., Ltd., Osaka, Japan. Home: 139 Mimosa Circle Ridgefield CT 06877 Office: Celanese International Co 1211 Ave of Americas New York NY 10036

BIGHINATTI, ENSO VICTOR, American Red Cross official; b. East Berlin, Conn., Dec. 18, 1921; s. Floriano and Palmina (Ferrarino) B.; m. Mildred Felicia Genovese, Oct. 20, 1945. Student, Central Conn. Coll., 1947-50, Springfield Coll., 1950-51. Adminstr. or dir. disaster relief actions in U.S. ARC, 1951-75; cons., adviser disaster orgn. and operations Indonesian Red Cross, 1961; dir. operations Cuban Bay of Pigs prisoner exchange, 1962; adviser State Dept. on forest fires disaster, Parana, Brazil, 1963, organized disaster plan and system mut. aid for, Caribbean countries, 1968; coordinator ARC aid Nigeria-Biafra Civil War, 1968; coordinator Peru earthquakes ARC, 1967, coordinator refugee program, Vietnam, 1969, East Pakistan Cyclone Relief, 1970; dir. relief operations internat. Red Cross Com. in Jordan after civil war, 1970; adviser to Ross Perot's trips to Vietnam in attempt to deliver relief packages to U.S. POW's, 1970; nat. dir. ARC disaster preparedness and relief, 1970—; operations dir. for resettlement of Vietnamese refugees in, U.S., 1975; under sec.-gen. for disaster relief League of Red Cross Socs., Geneva, Switzerland, 1975-81; asst. to pres. ARC, Washington, 1982—; adminstr. Guatemalan earthquake relief League of Red Cross Socs., 1976, Turkish earthquake relief, 1977; dir. S.E. Asia refugee relief and resettlement ops. Internat. Red Cross, 1979; Cons., organizer, lectr. Pan Am. Health Organ. seminar, Santiago, Chile, 1969. Author ARC manuals for disaster preparedness action. Served with USAF, 1942-45; prisoner of war, 1944-45; escaped, 1945. Decorated Air medal with 5 oakleaf clusters, Purple Heart. Home: 1301 Delaware Ave SW Washington DC 20024 Office: Am Red Cross Nat Hdgrs 17th and D Sts NW Washington DC 20006

BIGLER, HAROLD EDWIN, JR., investment company executive; b. N.Y.C., Apr. 27, 1931; s. Harold Edwin and Elizabeth Augusta (Cutler) B.; m. Lorinda Jennings Bailey, June 21, 1980; children by previous marriage: John Stephen, Diane Elizabeth, William Campbell. A.B., Brown U., 1953; M.B.A., Babson Inst., 1957; postgrad., Harvard U. Bus. Sch., 1975. Investment analyst Conn. Gen. Life Ins. Co., 1957-64, asst. sec., 1964, sec., 1964, 2d v.p., 1966-68; v.p. Securities Group, Hartford, 1968-81; chmn. C.G. Investment Mgmt. Co., Inc., 1975-81; pres., dir. Conn. Gen. Fund, Income Fund, Municipal Bond Fund, Money Market Fund, Companion Fund, Companion Income Fund, 1975-81; pres. Bigler Investment Mgmt. Co.; gen. ptnr. Crossroads Fund, Crossroads Capital Fund; dir. Conn. Water Service, Inc., Vantage Computer Systems, Inc.; Chmn. investment advisory com., State of Conn., 1972-78; mem. investment com. Brown U., Providence, R.I., 1968-80. Served as lt. (j.g.) USN, 1953-55. Mem. Am. Council Life Ins. (chmn. securities investment com. 1972-76), Fin. Analysts Fedn. (dir. 1974-76), N.Y. Soc. Security Analysts, Hartford Soc. Fin. Analysts (pres. 1966-67). Republican. Clubs: Hartford, Hartford Golf, Stratton Mountain Country. Home: 14 Thicket Ln W Hartford CT 06107 Office: One State St Hartford CT 06103

BIGLEY, JAMES PHILIP, telephone company executive; b. Viroqua, Wis., July 28, 1912; s. Lawrence A. and Ellen (McCall) B.; m. Dorothy Bent, Aug. 28, 1948 (dec.); m. Betty Lou Simmons, Nov. 17, 1978. Officer, dir. State Bank of LaCrosse, Wis., 1930-47; officer, dir. State Bank of Viroqua, 1947-55, 70—; now chmn. bd.; dir. Viroqua Telephone Co., 1948—, sec., treas., mgr., 1954-62, pres., mgr., 1962—; pres. Viroqua Bldg. Corp., 1966—; dir. Capital Indemnity Corp., Capital Transam Corp.; Chmn. Viroqua Housing Authority, 1970—. Bd. dirs. U. Wis.-La Crosse Found. Inc., 1979—, treas., 1981—; exec. sec. Republican party Wis., 1955-57. Served from pvt. to 1st lt., 32d Div. AUS, 1942-46. Mem. U.S. Ind. Telephone Assn. (dir. 1966—, v.p. 1974-77, pres. 1977-78, treas. 1981), LaCrosse Jr. C. of C. (pres. 1939), 32d Div. Vets. Assn. (nat. pres. 1957-58), Am. Legion, VFW, Wis. Telephone Assn. (pres. 1962-64). Clubs: Elks, Eagles (Wis. pres. 1952-53), Eagles (internat. pres. 1959-60), Eagles (fin. adviser 1962-69, 73-78), Eagles (internat. chmn. program and activities 1969-72). Home: 3 S Washington Heights Viroqua WI 54665 Office: 114 E Court St Viroqua WI 54665

BIGLEY, NANCY JANE, microbiology educator; b. Sewickley, Pa., Feb. 1, 1932; d. William Howard and Frances Jane (Engle) B. B.S., Pa. State U., 1953; M.Sc., Ohio State U., 1955, Ph.D., 1957. Research assoc. Ohio State U., 1957-65, asst. prof. immunology, 1965-68, assoc. prof., 1968-69, U. Health Sci. Chgo. Med. Sch., 1969-72, prof., 1972-76; prof., chmn. dept. microbiology and immunology Wright State U., Dayton, Ohio, 1976—, also program dir. Author: Immunologic Fundamentals, 1975, 2d edit., 1981; mem. editorial bd.: Infection and Immunity, 1977-80. NIH grantee, 1970-76; NSF grantee, 1977-79. Mem. Am. Assn. Immunologists, AAAS, Reticuloendothel Soc., Am. Soc. Microbiology, Am. Acad. Microbiology, Sigma Xi. Presbyterian. Home: 1427 Ticonderoga Ct Xenia OH 45385 Office: 409 Oelman Hall Colonel Glenn Hwy Dayton OH 45435 *The excitment of the adventure into understanding microbial pathogenesis and host immunity was first kindled in me as a child trying to perceive my parents' fear of infectious diseases such as polio. Since then, we have seen a dazzling array of scientific achievements from the effects of antibiotics, to those of gene cloning and monoclonal antibody formation, upon human disease; and yet, new infectious diseases emerge. The opportunity to provide one mere spark of information to the flame of enlightenment continues to exist.*

BIGLEY, THOMAS JOSEPH, naval officer; b. Everett, Mass., Sept. 16, 1927; s. William Charles and Mary Theresa (Burns) B.; m. Ann Harrington, Aug. 28, 1950; children—Ann, Mary, Katherine. B.S., U.S. Naval Acad., 1950; M.A., Am. U., 1968. Commd. ensign U.S. Navy, 1950, advanced through grades to vice adm., 1976; served in destroyers (Korean War), 1950-52, comdg. officer submarine, 1961-63, 1968-70, comdr., 1975-76, dep. comdr.-in-chief, 1976-78, comdr., 1979—. Decorated Legion of Merit (4), Navy Commendation medal. Roman Catholic.

BIGLIARDI, MATTHEW PAUL, bishop; b. Charleroi, Pa., Sept. 14, 1920; s. Achille and Regina (Bonaccinni) B.; m. Jeanne C. Gross, Feb. 19, 1949; 1 child, Aidan. B.S., U. Calif., Berkeley, 1950; M.Div., Ch. Div. Sch. of Pacific, 1953, D.D., 1974. Ordained priest Protestant Episcopal Ch., 1954; curate Trinity Ch., Seattle, 1953-55; vicar Emmanuel Ch., Mercer Island, Wash., 1955-60, rector, 1960-74; bishop Diocese of Oreg., Lake Oswego, 1974—; Chmn. bd. trustees Good Samaritan Hosp., Portland, Oreg., from 1974, Oreg. Episc. Schs., from 1974. Trustee Columbia council Boy Scouts Am., Portland, Oreg. Heart Assn., Ch. Div. Sch. of Pacific, Berkeley, Calif., all 1977-80, Presiding Bishop's Fund for World Relief. Mem. Sigma Xi, Phi Beta Kappa. Office: PO Box 467 Lake Oswego OR 97034

BIGLIERI, EDWARD GEORGE, physician; b. San Francisco, Jan. 17, 1925; s. Ned and (Mignacco) B.; m. Beverly A. Bergesen, May 16, 1953; children: Mark, Michael, Gregg. Student, U. San Francisco, 1942-43, Gonzaga U., 1943-44; B.S. in Chemistry summa cum laude, U. San Francisco, 1948; M.D., U. Calif., 1952. Diplomate: Am. Bd. Internal Medicine (endocrine test com. 1971-76). Intern U. Calif., San Francisco Med. Center, also, VA Hosp., San Francisco, 1952-54, resident, 1954-56; clin. assoc. and research physician NIH, 1956-58; also metabolic unit U. Calif., 1958-61, asst. prof. medicine, 1962-65, assoc. prof., 1965-71, prof., 1971—; program dir. gen. clin. research, also chief endocrinology service San Francisco Gen. Hosp., 1962—; vis. prof. Monash U., Melbourne, Australia, 1967; NATO vis. prof., Italy, 1983; cons. Oak Knoll Naval Hosp., Travis AFB; mem. study sect. NIH, 1971-74. Contbr. articles on endocrinology ahd hormones in hypertension to profl. jours. Served to lt. (j.g.) USN, 1944-46. NIH grantee, 1972-73. Mem. Endocrine Soc., A.C.P., Am. Soc. Clin. Investigation, Am. Heart Assn. (council high blood pressure research), Assn. Am. Physicians, Western Assn. Physicians, Am. Fedn. Clin. Research. Home: 129 Convent Ct San Rafael CA 94901 Office: San Francisco Gen Hosp San Francisco CA 94110 *The opportunity to study an ever-inquiring profession, and an incredibly supportive family, are the essential ingredients for sustained growth in the academic arena.*

BIJOU, SIDNEY WILLIAM, educator; b. Balt., Nov. 12, 1908; s. Leon and Leah (Barbert) B.; m. Janet R. Tobias, Aug. 31, 1934; children: Robert Kenneth, Judith Ann. Student, Lehigh U., 1929-31; B.A., U. Fla., 1933; M.A., Columbia U., 1936; Ph.D., U. Iowa, 1941. Psychologist Del. State Hosp. and Mental Hygiene Clinic, 1937-39; research child psychologist Wayne County Tng. Sch., 1941-42, 46-47; asst. prof. Ind. U., 1946-48; asso. prof., prof., dir. Inst. Child Devel., U. Wash., 1948-65; dir. (Child Behavior Lab.); mem. Inst. Research in Exceptional Children, U. Ill., Champaign, 1965-75; adj. prof. psychology and spl. edn. U. Ariz., Tucson, 1975—; asso. (center for Advanced Study), 1972; cons. NIMH, 1959-63, Nat. Inst. Child Health and Human Devel., 1964-67, Bur. of Edn. for Handicapped, U.S. Office Edn., NSF, 1975—; hon. prof. psychology U. Peruana Cayetano Heredia, Lima, Peru; mem. research adv. bd. Nat. Assn. for Retarded Children, 1965—; chmn. task force research on parent tng.; mem. nat. adv. bd. Ill. Inst. Developmental Disabilities, 1972—; mem. nat. sci. adv. bd. nat. program on early childhood edn. Central Midwest Regional Ednl. Lab., 1969-74; adv. panel on behavior modification therapy Nat. Acad. Scis., NRC, Assembly Life Scis. Div. Med. Scis.; profl. adv. com. Johnny Cake Child Study Center Found.; cons. research Portage Project on Parent Tng.; chmn. com. organizers Symposia on Behavior Modification in Latin-Am. Countries; mem. human relations and ethics com. Ariz. Tng. Program at Tucson, 1977—; Trustee Assn. for Advancement Psychology, 1973-76; bd. dirs. Intermountain Centers for Human Devel., Santa Fe, 1977—. Author: (with D.M. Baer) Behavior Analysis of Child Development, 1978, Child Development: The Universal Stage of Infancy, 1965, Child Development: Readings in Experimental Analysis of Behavior, 1967, (with E. Ribes-Inesta) Behavior Modification: Issues and Extensions, 1972, Child Development: The Basic Stage of Early Childhood, 1978, (with E. Rayek-Zaga) Analisis de la Conducta Appicado a Ensenanza, 1978; editor: Behavior Modification: Contributions to Education, 1980, Jour. Exptl. Child Psychology, 1964-71; asso. editor: Internat. Rev. of Research in Mental Retardation, 1965-75, Jour. Behavior Therapy and Exptl. Psychiatry, 1969—; editorial bd.: Jour. Exptl. Child Psychology, 1971-76, Jour. Abnormal Child Psychology, 1972, Jour. Applied Behavior Analysis, 1975-77, The Psychol. Record, 1977—, Quar. Rev. of Devel, 1980—, Behavior Analyst, 1980—. Served to capt. USAAF, 1942-46. Recipient research award Am. Assn. Mental Deficiency, 1974; cert. of merit U. Veracruz, Mexico, 1974; Career Research Scientist award Am. Acad. Mental Retardation, 1980; Disting. Scientist award Nat. Assn. Retarded Citizens, 1980; NIMH Sr. fellow Harvard U., 1961-62; Japan Soc. for Promotion of Sci. fellow, 1978; Festschrift fellow, 1977; Fullbright-Hays fellow, 1976. Fellow Am. Psychol. Assn. (chmn. commn. on behavior modification, past div. devel. psychology pres. bd. social and ethical responsibility for psychology 1976-78, recipient G. Stanley Hall award in devel. psychology 1980); mem. Psychonomic Soc., Soc. Research in Child Devel., Internat. Soc. for Study Behavior Devel., Assn. Behavior Analysis (pres. 1978), Behavior Therapy and Exptl. Psychiatry, AAUP, Midwestern (council 1975-78), Rocky Mountain, Southwestern psychol. assns., Sigma Xi. Home: 5131 N Soledad Primera Tucson AZ 85718

BIJUR, HERBERT ISAAC, retail exec.; b. N.Y.C., Feb. 6, 1911; s. Nathan I. and Eugenie (Blum) B.; m. Marion Halpert, Feb. 1, 1939; children—Peter, Priscilla, Polly. B.S., Haverford Coll., 1932. With McCall Corp., 1949-70, v.p., 1957-70; pres. McCall Pattern Co.; Asst. to pres. N.Y. Bot. Garden, Bronx.; Pres. Bartlett Aboretum Assn. Home: 1208 Westover Rd Stamford CT 06902

BIKEL, THEODORE, actor, singer; b. Vienna, Austria, May 2, 1924; came to U.S., 1954, naturalized, 1961; s. Josef and Miriam (Riegler) B.; m. Rita Weinberg, 1967. Student, U. London; grad., Royal Acad. Art, London, 1948. Apprentice with, Habimah Theatre, Tel Aviv, 1942-44; a founder, Tel Aviv Chamber Theatre, 1944-46; theatrical prodns. include A Streetcar Named Desire, London, 1950, The Love of Four Colonels, London, 1950-52, Tonight in Samarkand, N.Y.C., 1954, The Lark, N.Y.C., 1955-56, Rope Dancers, N.Y.C., 1957-58, Sound of Music, N.Y.C., 1959-61, Fiddler on the Roof, various cities, 1968, 69, 71, 72, 74, 77, 79, 80, 82, 83, The Rothschilds (nat. co.), 1972, Jacques Brel is Alive and Well and Living in Paris, various cities, 1974-75, The Good Doctor, various cities, 1975, Zorba, various cities, 1976, 78, Inspector Gen., N.Y.C., 1978, Threepenny Opera, Mpls., 1983; The Enemy Below, 1957; motion pictures include African Queen, 1951; The Little Kidnappers, 1951, I Want to Live, 1958, The Defiant Ones, 1958 (Academy award nomination), Blue Angel, 1959, My Fair Lady, 1964, Sands of the Kalahari, 1965, The Russians are Coming, 1966, Sweet November, 1967, My Side of the Mountain, 1969, Darker Than Amber, 1970, The Little Ark, 1971; also numerous TV appearances, 1954—; star: TV prodns. The Eternal Light, 1958, Look Up and Live, 1958-60; host-editor: TV prodn. Directions 61, 1961; weekly radio program At Home with Theodore Bikel, 1958-63; concert folk singer, 1955—, rec. artist for, Elektra and Reprise; Author: Folksongs and Footnotes, 1960. Mem. Nat. Council for Arts, 1977-82; founder arts chpt. Am. Jewish Congress, 1961-63, nat. v.p., 1963-70, chmn. governing council, 1970-80, sr. v.p., 1980, v.p., 1980—; del. Democratic Nat. Conv., 1968. Mem. Acad. TV Arts and Scis. (gov. 1961-65), Actors Equity Assn. (councillor 1961-64, 1st v.p. 1964-73, pres. 1973-82, pres. emeritus 1982—), Acad. Motion Picture Arts and Scis., AFTRA, Screen Actors Guild, Am. Fedn. Musicians. Address: Honey Hill Rd Georgetown CT 06829 *If I am a universalist-and I believe myself to be one-I derive my general standard of humanity from a particularist experience. For, above all and before all else, I am a Jew. That, to me, means a heightened awareness of the human condition and the sad-sweet knowledge that where we stand someone has stood before. It means a mode of living and a method of survival. Spiritually and culturally to be a Jew is to be a man on the road from Jerusalem to Jerusalem. I am an American; this is my home and my daily solace. Jerusalem, however, is my hope and my inspiration.*

BILANIUK, OLEXA MYRON, physicist, educator; b. Ukraine, Dec. 15, 1926; U.S., 1951, naturalized, 1957; s. Petro and Maria (Kunkevytch) B.; m. Larissa T. Zubal, Nov. 14, 1964; children: Larissa, Laada. Student, U. Louvain, 1947-51; M.S., U. Mich., 1953, M.A., 1954, Ph.D., 1957. Postdoctoral fellow U. Mich., 1957-58; research asso., asst. prof. U. Rochester, 1958-64; assoc. prof. physics Swarthmore Coll., 1964-70, prof., 1970-82, Swarthmore Centennial prof., 1980—; vis. scientist Argentine Atomic Energy Commn., Buenos Aires, 1961-62, Institut de Physique Nucléaire, Orsay, France, spring 1980, Laboratorio Nazionale di Frascati, Italy, spring 1984; vis. prof., cons. Delhi U., summer 1966, Shivaji U., Kolhapur, India, summer 1969, Faculté des Sciences, Rabat, Morocco, spring 1978; Fulbright prof., Lima, Peru, summer 1971, Kinshasa, Zaïre, fall 1975. NSF fellow, Germany, 1967-68, France, 1972; Nat. Acad. Sci. exchange scientist, Kiev, USSR, 1976. Mem. Am. Phys. Soc., Am. Assn. Physics Tchrs., Ukrainian Acad. Arts and Scis. in U.S., European Phys. Soc., Société Française de Physique, Phi Beta Kappa, Sigma Xi. Research on nuclear structure; with Deshpande and Sudarshan challenged the view that Einstein's relativity precludes possibility of existence of particles that travel faster than light, 1962. Office: Swarthmore Coll Swarthmore PA 19081 *The most cherished possession of humanity is its spiritual and intellectual heritage. Contributing to the enrichment of this heritage I consider to be man's loftiest goal.*

BILBY, KENNETH W., diversified electronic company executive; b. Salt Lake City, Oct. 7, 1918; s. Ralph W. and Marguerite (Mansfield) B.; m. Joanne Herbert Stroud, Oct. 15, 1978; children by previous marriage: Barbara Windsor, Kenneth Mansfield, Marquerite Mansfield, Robert Bryan. B.A., U. Ariz., 1941. Fgn. corr. Europe and Middle East N.Y. Herald Tribune, 1947-50; pub. relations rep. RCA Victor, Camden, N.J., 1950-54; v.p. pub. relations, exec. v.p. NBC, 1954-60; v.p. pub. affairs RCA, 1960-62, exec. v.p. corporate affairs, 1962—; dir. RCA Global Communications, Inc., N.Y. Bank for Savs.; exec.-in-residence Harvard Bus. Sch., 1982. Author: New Star in the Near East, 1950. Bd. dirs. Boys' Clubs Am.; trustee, exec. com. South Street Seaport Mus. Served to lt. col. AUS, World War II. Decorated Silver Star medal, Legion of Merit, Bronze Star medal, Combat Infantry Badge; Croix de Guerre; recipient Alumni Achievement award U. Ariz., 1960. Mem. Phi Delta Theta. Clubs: Apawamis (Rye, N.Y.); Blind Brook (Purchase, N.Y.); Shinnecock Hill Golf

(Southampton, N.Y.); River (N.Y.C.). Home: 38 Alpine Rd Greenwich CT 06830 Office: 30 Rockefeller Plaza New York NY 10020

BILBY, RALPH WILLARD, lawyer; b. Concho, Ariz., Sept. 15, 1891; s. John and Ann Wallrade (Whipple) B.; m. Marguerite Mansfield, May 16, 1914 (dec. Feb. 1956); children—Ralph M. (dec.), Kenneth W., Margaret Ann (Mrs. William A. Drake), Richard M.; m. Ethel Parker McChesney, June 10, 1957. LL.B., U. Ariz., 1920. Bar: Ariz. bar 1917. Since practiced in, Tucson; mem. firm Bilby, Shoenhair Warnock & Dolph, profl. corp., 1946—; asst. U.S. atty. for Ariz., 1922-23; chmn. Ariz. Oil and Gas Conservation Commn. Del. Republican Nat. Conv., 1928, 48. Recipient U. Ariz. Distinguished Citizen award. Fellow Am. Coll. Trial Lawyers; mem. Am., Pima County bar assns., State Bar Ariz. (pres. 1948-49), Alumni Assn. U. Ariz. (past pres.), Order of Coif, Phi Kappa Phi. Clubs: El Rio Golf and Country (past pres.), Old Pueblo (past pres.), Tucson Country (past pres.), Sunshine Climate (Tucson) (past pres.). Office: Valley Nat Bldg Tucson AZ 85701

BILBY, RICHARD MANSFIELD, fed. judge; b. Tucson, May 29, 1931; s. Ralph Willard and Marguerite (Mansfield) B.; m. Ann Louise Borchert, July 6, 1957; children—Claire Louise, Ellen Markley. B.S., U. Ariz., 1955; J.D., U. Mich., 1958. Bar: Ariz. bar 1959. Since practiced in, Tucson; law clk. to Chief Judge Chambers, 9th Circuit Ct. Appeals, San Francisco, 1958-59; mem. firm Bilby, Thompson, Shoenhair & Warnock, 1959-79, partner, 1967-79; judge U.S. Dist. Ct., Dist. Ariz., Tucson, 1979—; conscientious objector hearing officer Dept. Justice, 1959-62; chmn. (Pima County Med.-Legal panel), 1968-70; Mem. Tucson Charter Revision Com., 1965-70. Chmn. United Fund Profl. Div., 1968, Spl. Gift Div., 1970, St. Joseph Hosp. Devel. Fund Drive, 1970; Republican state chmn. Vols. for Eisenhower, 1956; Rep. county chmn., Pima County, Ariz., 1972-74; Past pres. Tucson Conquistadores; bd. dirs. St. Josephs Hosp., 1969-77, chmn., 1972-75. Served with AUS, 1952-54. Fellow Am. Coll. Trial Lawyers; mem. Ariz. Acad., Town Hall (dir. 1976-79). Home: 4717 Brisa Del Sur Tucson AZ 85718 Office: 55 E Broadway Tucson AZ 85701

BILELLO, JOHN CHARLES, engineer, educator; b. Bklyn., Oct. 15, 1938; s. Charles and Catherine (Buonadonna) B.; m. Mary Josephine Gloria, Aug. 1, 1959; children: Andrew Charles, Peter Angelo, Matthew Jonathan. B.E., NYU, 1960, M.S., 1962; Ph.D., U. Ill., 1965. Sr. research engr. Gen. Telephone & Electronics Lab., Bayside, N.Y., 1965-67; mem. faculty SUNY, Stony Brook, 1967—, asst. prof., 1967-71, asso. prof., 1971-75, prof. engring. dean, 1977—, dean Coll. Engring. and Applied Scis., 1977-81; sr. scientist Brookhaven Nat. Labs., 1975—; vis. prof. Politechnico Di Milano, 1974; project dir. synchroton topography project Univ. Consortium, 1981—. Asso. editor: Materials Letters, 1981—. NATO sr. faculty fellow Enrico Fermi Center, Milan, Italy, 1973. Mem. Am. Phys. Soc., Am. Soc. for Metals. Office: Coll Engring and Applied Scis SUNY Stony Brook NY 11794

BILES, JOHN ALEXANDER, pharmaceutical chemistry educator; b. Del Norte, Colo., May 4, 1923; s. John Alexander and Lillie (Willis) B.; m. Margaret Pauline Off, June 19, 1943; children: Paula M. (Mrs. Patrick Murphy), M. Suzanne. B.S., U. Colo., 1944, Ph.D. (AEC fellow), 1949. Prof. pharm. chemistry Midwestern U., 1949-50; asst. prof. pharmacy Ohio State U., 1950-52; asst. prof. pharm. chemistry U. So. Calif., Los Angeles, 1952-53, asso. prof., 1953-57, prof., 1957-68, dean, prof. pharm. chemistry, 1968—; cons. Allergan Pharms., 1953-68, Region IX, Bur. Health Manpower Edn., Health Resources Adminstrn., 1973, Region X, 1974, Region VI, 1975, VA Central Office Pharmacy Services.; Mem. Nat. Adv. Council, Edn. for Health Professions, 1970—, 1972-75; mem. adv. panel on pharmacy for study costs of educating profls. Nat. Acad. Scis., Inst. Medicine, 1973; mem. interdisciplinary tng. in health scis. com. Bur. Health Manpower Edn., 1972, post constrn. evaluation com., 1972, health facilities survey com., 1971. Reviewer: Jour. of AMA, 1982—. Recipient Lehn and Fink Scholarship award, 1945, S.C. Assos. award for excellence in teaching, 1962. Fellow Acad. Pharm. Scis.; mem. Am., Cal. pharm. assns., Am. Cancer Soc. (mem. sci. adv. com. Los Angeles County), Acad. Pharm. Scis., Am. Assn. Colls. Pharmacy (study commn. on pharmacy 1973—), Nat. Adv. Health Services Council (bur. health services research 1974), Phi Kappa Phi. Home: 400 Surfview Dr Pacific Palisades CA 90272 Office: U So Calif Sch Pharmacy 1985 Zonal Ave Los Angeles CA 90033

BILGER, ROBERT CLARK, educator; b. Ft. Wayne, Ind., Aug. 17, 1926; s. Clark A. and Marion Ellen (Stouder) B.; m. Carolyn Jane Antenen, Aug. 23, 1952; children—Thomas Scott, Melissa Ann, Peter Antenen, Richard Carl. B.S., Purdue U., 1949, M.S., 1951, Ph.D., 1954. Research asso. Central Inst. for Deaf, St. Louis, 1954-58; asst. prof. speech U. Mich., 1958-60; asst. prof. audiology U. Pitts., 1960-61, asso. prof., 1961-74, asso. prof. community medicine, 1961-77, asso. prof. otolaryngology, 1974-77; dir. Bioacoustic Lab. Eye & Ear Hosp., Pitts., 1965-77; prof. speech and hearing sci. U. Ill., Champaign, 1977—, head dept. speech and hearing sci., 1980—; mem. Am. Nat. Standareds Inst., 1964-70, 78—, mem. com. on bioacoustics, 1978—. Author: Implanted Auditory Prostheses, 1977; editor: Jour. Speech and Hearing Research, 1970-74; mem. editorial bd.: AMA Archives of Otolaryngology, 1980—, Hearing Research, 1977—. Mem. exec. com. Allegheny Council Campfire Girls, 1966-70. Served with USAF, 1945-46. Grantee in field. Fellow Am. Speech Lang. and Hearing Assn., Acoustical Soc. Am.; mem. Am. Statis. Assn., Assn. Research in Otolaryngology, Psychonomic and Psychometric Soc. Unitarian. Club: Masons. Home: 1113 Newbury Rd Champaign IL 61820 Office: 901 S 6th St Champaign IL 61820

BILHEIMER, ROBERT SPERRY, clergyman; b. Denver, Sept. 28, 1917; s. Gus Steven and Katherine Elizabeth (Sperry) B.; m. Dorothy Stevenson Dodge, June 13, 1942; children—Robert Edwin, Richard Sperry, Roger Stevenson. B.A., Yale U., 1939, B.D., 1945; D.D. (hon.), Chgo. Theol. Sem., 1954, Butler U., 1954, Hamilton Coll., 1980. Ordained to ministry Presbyn. Ch.; exec. sec. The Inter-sem. Movement, 1945-48; pastor Westminster Presbyn. Ch. of Cedar Manor, N.Y.C., 1947-54; adminstrv. sec. First Assembly World Council Chs., 1948, exec. sec., 1954, program sec. in, N.Am., 1948-54, asso. gen. sec., dir. div. of studies, Geneva, Switzerland, 1954-63; sr. minister Central Presbyn. Ch., Rochester, N.Y., 1963-66; dir. internat. affairs program Nat. Council Chs. of Christ, U.S.A., 1966-73; exec. dir. Inst. for Ecumenical and Cultural Research, Collegeville, Minn., 1974—. Author: What Must the Church Do?, 1947, The Quest for Christian Unity, 1952; Gen. editor: The Interseminary Series (4 vols.), 1947. Home: Rural Route 2 Cold Spring MN 56320 Office: Inst for Ecumenical and Cultural Research Collegeville MN 56321

BILINSKI, DONALD STANLEY, clergyman, museumologist; b. Waite Park, Minn., Dec. 14, 1916; s. Francis and Mary (Knapik) B. B.A., St. Francis Coll., 1934, postgrad., 1935-39; B.L.S., U. Chgo., 1944; postgrad., Lourdes Sem., Cedar Lake, Ind., 1939-41, St. Mary's Sem., Green Bay, Wis., 1941-42, U. Chgo., 1942, Cath. U. Am., Am. U., Harvard U., Loyola U., Chgo. Joined Franciscan Fathers of Assumption; ordained priest, Roman Catholic Ch. Dir. libraries Assumption Province, 1942-69; archivist, curator, dir. Polish Mus. Am., Chgo., 1970—; dir. Assumption Province, Pulaski, Wis., 1954-60, dean of students, 1951-56; chaplain Walworth Correction Ctr., 1969—. Editor: Provincial Union Catalog, 8 vols., 1969, (with others) Autograph Letters of Thaddeus Kosciusko, 1977, Franciscan Librarian Contact, 1945-66. Mem. ABA, Cath. Library Assn. (chmn. sem. sect.), Wis. Library Assn., Wis. Cath. Library Assn., Franciscan Library Assn. (pres., sec.), Am. Midwest Archivist Assn., Polish Hist. Assn. (sec.), Am. Bookplace Assn., Am. Correctional Instn. Chaplains Assn. Home: Saint Francis Friary 503 S Browns Lake Dr Burlington WI 53105 Office: Franciscan Fathers of Assumption Province 1 Pulaski WI 54162

BILINSKY, YAROSLAV, political scientist; b. Lutsk, Ukraine, USSR, Feb. 26, 1932; s. Peter Bilinsky and Natalia (Balabaj) Bilinska; m. Wira Rusaniwskyj, Feb. 18, 1962; children: Peter Yaroslav, Sophia Vera Yaroslava, Nadia Yaroslava, Mark Paul Yaroslav. A.B. magna cum laude, Harvard U., 1954, postgrad. in Soviet affairs, 1956-57; Ph.D., Princeton U., 1958. Asso. Harvard U. Russian Research Center, 1956-58; instr. polit. sci. Douglass Coll., Rutgers U., New Brunswick, N.J., 1958-61; asst. prof. U. Del., Newark, 1961-65, asso. prof., 1965-69, prof., 1969—; vis. instr. U. Pa., 1961; vis. prof. Columbia U., 1976. Author: The Second Soviet Republic: The Ukraine after World War II, 1964. Corr. sec. Peter and Paul Ukrainian Orthodox Ch., Wilmington, Del., 1965-66, trustee, 1967-71. Mem. Am. Polit. Sci. Assn., Am. Assn. Advancement Slavic Studies, Ukrainian Acad. Arts and Scis. in U.S. (1st v.p. 1979—). Home: 2 Mimosa Dr Newark DE 19711 Office: Polit Sci Dept U Del Newark DE 19711 *My favorite quotation is from Shakespeare: "The readiness is all." I have tried to be always prepared to serve my country, my students, and my family. I am ready to live and, if it be God's will, ready to die.*

BILIRAKIS, MICHAEL, lawyer, congressman, business executive; b. Tarpon Springs, Fla., July 16, 1930; s. Emmanuel and Irene (Pikramenos) B.; m. Evelyn Miaoulis, Dec. 27, 1959; children: Emmanuel, Gus. B.S. in Engring., U. Pitts., 1959; student, George Washington U., 1959-60; J.D., U. Fla., 1963. Diplomate: cert. coll. tchr., Fla., Fla. 1964. Atty., small businessman, Pinellas and Pasco Counties, Fla., 1968—; mem. 98th Congress from 9th Dist. Fla. Mem. Republican Task Force on Social Security; founder, charter pres. Tarpon Springs Vol. Ambulance Service; dir. Greek Studies program U. Fla.; bd. devel. Anclote Manor Psychiat. Hosp. Served to sgt. USAF, 1951-55. Named Citizen of Yr. for Greater Tarpon Springs, 1972-73. Mem. Am. Legion (comdr. 1977-79), VFW, Air Force Assn., Greater Tarpon Springs C. of C. (past pres., dir.), Pinellas C. of C. (gov.), West Pasco Bar Assn., Am. Judicature Soc., Fla. Bar Assn., Gator Boosters, Phi Alpha Delta. Lodges: Masons; Shriners; Tarpon Springs Rotary; Elks; Eastern Star; White Shrine of Jerusalem. Office: 319 Cannon House Office Bldg Washington DC 20515

BILJAN, ROBERT, court administrator; b. Yugoslavia, Oct. 26, 1942; s. Mato and Sofia (Heini) B.; m. Marie Angele Pelchat, Oct. 10, 1964; children: Kathleen Angie, Stephen Andrew, Christine Alice. B.A., Carleton U., Ottawa, Ont., Can.; cert. in Mgmt. Studies, Algonquin Coll., Ottawa. Clerk of process appeal div., exec. asst. to chief justice, asst. adminstr. appeal div. and trial div. Fed. Ct. of Can., Ottawa; now adminstr. Fed. Ct. Mem. Can. Assn. Ct. Adminstrs. Roman Catholic. Office: Federal Court of Canada Wellington St Ottawa ON Canada K1A 0H9

BILKA, PAUL JOSEPH, physician; b. N.Y.C., Oct. 12, 1919; s. John and Josephine (Hlavaty) B.; m. Madge Ayres Mussey, Dec. 26, 1943. B.S., Trinity Coll., Hartford, Conn., 1940; M.D., Columbia U., 1943; M.S. in Medicine, U. Minn., 1950. Intern Hartford Hosp., 1944-45; fellow in internal medicine Mayo Found, Rochester, Minn., 1947-50; asst. in rheumatology Mayo Clinic, 1949-50; practice medicine specializing in rheumatology, Mpls., 1950—; mem. staff Met. Med. Center, Abbott-Northwestern Hosp.; clin. prof. medicine U. Minn. Med. Sch.; cons. Mpls. VA Hosp. Author numerous papers in field; also producer films on rheumatology. Served to capt. M.C. AUS, 1945-47. Mem. Am. Rheumatism Assn., Nat. Soc. Clin. Rheumatology. Club: Lafayette (Minnetonka, Minn.). Home: 4384 Manitou Rd Excelsior MN 55331 Office: 63 S 9th St Minneapolis MN 55402

BILL, TONY, actor, producer, dir.; b. San Diego, 1940. Student, Notre Dame U. Founder Bill/Phillips Prodns. (with Julia and Michael Phillips), 1971-73; ind. producer, 1973—; bd. govs. Acad. Motion Picture Arts and Scis. Co-producer: Steelyard Blues, 1973, The Sting, 1973, Going in Style, 1979; producer: Hearts of the West, 1975, Harry and Walter Go to New York, 1976, Boulevard Nights, 1979; exec. producer: The Little Dragons, 1978; dir.: The Ransom of Red Chief, 1977, My Bodyguard, 1980; Film appearances include Come Blow Your Horn, 1963, None but the Brave, 1965, Marriage on the Rocks, 1965, You're a Big Boy Now, 1967, Never a Dull Moment, 1968, Ice Station Zebra, 168, Castle Keep, 1969, Shampoo, 1975, Las Vegas Lady, 1977, The Little Dragons, 1978, Heart Beat, 1980; TV movies Haunts of the Very Rich, 1972, Washington: Behind Closed Doors, 1977, Portrait of an Escort, 1980, Freedom, 1981, Washington Mistress, 1981. Office: care Robinson Luttrell & Assos 132 S Rodeo Dr Beverly Hills CA 90212

BILLEN, THOMAS RAYMOND, brewery executive; b. East St. Louis, Ill., Nov. 8, 1945; s. Harry Arnold B. and Stella Barbara (Billen); m. Rose Marie Petraitis, Nov. 19, 1968. B.A. in Math., So. Ill. U., 1967; M.B.A., St. Louis U., 1971. Asst. to v.p. corp. planning and devel. Anheuser-Busch Cos., St. Louis, 1975-77, dir. planning and analysis, 1977-78, dir. corp. planning, 1979-81, v.p. corp. fin. planning, 1982—; dir. Busch Entertainment Inc., St. Louis, Busch Properties Inc., Anheuser-Busch Inc. Roman Catholic. Office: Anheuser Busch Cos 1 Busch Pl St. Louis MO 63118

BILLER, HENRY BURT, educator, psychologist; b. Providence, Oct. 30, 1940; s. David and Thelma (Rodin) B.; m. Margery Salter, Oct. 7, 1979; children: Jonathan, Kenneth, Cameron, Michael, Benjamin. A.B. magna cum laude, Brown U., 1962; Ph.D. (USPHS fellow), Duke U., 1967. Asst. prof. psychology U. Mass., Amherst, 1967-69, George Peabody Coll., 1969-70; prof. U. R.I., Kingston, 1970—; cons. Northampton (Mass.) Welfare Dept., 1968-69, Protestant Youth Center, Baldwinville, Mass., 1969, Cape Cod (Mass.) Mental Health Center, 1970, Newport County (R.I.) Mental Health Center, 1970-71, VA Hosp., Providence, 1972-76, Emma Pendleton Bradley Hosp., Riverside, R.I., 1970-80, No. R.I. Mental Health Center, Woonsocket, 1980-82, No. R.I. Assn. for Retarded Citizens, 1980-83, John E. Fogarty Ctr., North Providence, 1982—; pvt. practice, Warwick, R.I., 1970—. Author: Father, Child and Sex Role, 1971, Paternal Deprivation, 1974, Father Power,, 1974, The Other Helpers, 1977, Parental Death and Psychological Development, 1982; mem. editorial bd.: Archives of Sexual Behavior, 1975—; cons. editor: Sex Roles, 1979—; asso. editor: Family Relations, 1980-81; contbr. chpts. to books, articles to profl. jours. Fellow Am. Psychol. Assn.; mem. R.I. Psychol. Assn., Phi Beta Kappa, Sigma Xi. Home: 227 Crestwood Rd Warwick RI 02886 Office: Dept Psychology U RI Kingston RI 02881

BILLER, HUGH FREDERICK, medical educator; b. Milw., Sept. 11, 1934; s. Saul E. and Mildred (Wilson) B.; m. Diane Schumacher, July 28, 1958; 1 dau., Heather. M.C., Marquette, 1960. Intern Balt. City Hosps.; resident otolaryngology Johns Hopkins Hosp., 1964-67; asst. prof. Wash. U. Sch. Medicine, 1967-70, asso. prof., 1970-71; prof., chmn. dept. otolaryngology Mt. Sinai Sch. Medicine, N.Y.C., 1972—. Served with AUS, 1962-64. Recipient Harris P. Mosher award, 1972. Mem. Am. Laryngologic Soc., Soc. U. Otolaryngologists, AMA, ACS, Am. Laryngol., Rhinol. and Otol. Soc., Am. Soc. Head and Neck Surgery (pres. 1984-85), Soc. Academic Surgeons, Am. Council Otolaryngology (dir. 1972-74). Office: 100th St and 5th Ave New York NY 10029

BILLER, JOEL WILSON, lawyer, former fgn. service officer; b. Milw., Jan. 17, 1929; s. Saul Earl and Mildred (Wilson) B.; m. Geraldine Pollack, May 1, 1955; children—Sydney, Andrew, Charles. B.A., U. Wis., 1950; J.D., U. Mich., 1953; M.A., Northwestern U., 1959. Bar: Wis. bar 1953. Atty., Milw., 1953-55; vice consul Am. consulate, Le Havre, France, 1956-58; econ. officer Am. Embassy, The Hague, Netherlands, 1959-62; internat. relations officer State Dept., Washington, 1962-66; econ. officer, asst. dir. AID mission, Quito, Ecuador, 1966-69; econ. counselor Am. embassy, Buenos Aires, Argentina, 1969-71,; dir. AID mission, Santiago, Chile, 1971-73; spl. asst. to undersec. state for econ. affairs, Washington, 1973-74, spl. asst. to dep. sec. state, 1974, dep. asst. sec. state for comml. and spl. bilateral affairs, 1974-76, dep. asst. sec. state for transp., telecommunications and comml. affairs, after, 1976, practice of law, Milw., 1980—. Mem. Am. Fgn. Service Assn., Wis. Bar Assn. Address: PO Box 2053 Milwaukee WI 53201

BILLER, MORRIS (MOE BILLER), union executive; b. N.Y.C., Nov. 5, 1915; m. Anne Fiefer, Aug. 24, 1940; children: Michael, Steven. Student, Bklyn. Coll., 1936-38, CCNY, 1946. With U.S. Postal Service, 1937—; active Am Postal Workers Union, 1937—, Manhattan-Bronx Postal Union (N.Y. Metro Area Postal Union), 1959-60, N.E. regional coordinator, 1972-80, gen. pres., 1980—; mem. fed. adv. council occupational safety and health Dept. Labor. Bd. dirs. Assn. Children with Retarded Mental Devel., United Way Internat.; nat. labor chairperson March of Dimes Telethon, 1948; bd. dirs. Fund for Assuring an Ind. Retirement. Served with AUS, 1943-45; ETO. Recipient Disting. Service award N.Y.C. Central Labor Council, 1977, Community Service award N.Y.C. Central Labor Council, 1979, Spirit of Life award City of Hope, 1982, Walter P. Reuther Meml. award Ams. for Democratic Action, 1982. Mem. Combined Fed. Campaign (exec. com.), N.Y.C. Central Labor Council (exec. bd dirs.), Central Labor Council (bd. dirs. central rehab.), Coalition Labor Union Women, NAACP, A. Philip Randolph Inst. Office: Am Postal Workers Union AFL-CIO 817 14th St SW Washington DC 20005

BILLIG, THOMAS CLIFFORD, magazine publisher; b. Pitts., Aug. 20, 1930; s. Thomas Clifford and Melba Helen (Stucky) B.; m. Helen Page Hine, May 14, 1951; children—Thomas Clifford, James Frederick. B.S. in Bus. Adminstrn. summa cum laude, Northwestern U., 1956. Ins. mgr., asst. dir. personnel, asst. to chmn. Butler Bros. (now City Products Corp.), Chgo., 1954-59; market research mgr. R.R. Donnelley & Sons, Chgo., 1959-61; pres., dir. Indsl. Fiber Glass Products Corp., Scottville and Ludington, Mich., 1962-69; cons. mass mktg. mgmr., Mpls., 1969-71; v.p. Mail Mktg. Systems and Services, St. Paul and Bloomington, Minn., 1971-74; pres., dir. Billig and Assos., Mpls., 1979—, NIARS Corp., 1974—, Fins and Feathers Pub. Co., 1977—. Served with USNR, 1948-56. Recipient Samuel Dresner Plotkin award Northwestern U., 1956. Mem. Delta Mu Delta, Beta Gamma Sigma. Office: 318 W Franklin Ave Minneapolis MN 55404

BILLINGHAM, RUPERT EVERETT, zoologist, educator; b. Warminster, Eng., Oct. 15, 1921; s. Albert E. and Helen (Green) B.; m. Jean Mary Morpeth, Mar. 29, 1951; children—John David, Peter Jeremy, Elizabeth Anne. B.A., Oriel Coll., Oxford, Eng., 1943, M.A., 1947, D.Phil., 1950, D.Sc., 1957. Lectr. zoology U. Birmingham, Eng., 1947-51; research fellow Brit. Empire Cancer Campaign; hon. research asso. dept. zoology Univ. Coll., London, 1951-57; mem. Wistar Inst.; Wistar prof. zoology U. Pa., Phila., 1957-65; prof., chmn. dept. med. genetics, dir. Henry Phipps Inst., U. Pa. Med. Sch., 1965-71; prof., chmn. dept. cell biology U. Tex. Health Sci. Center at Dallas, 1971—; mem. allergy and immunology study sect. NIH, 1959-62; mem. transplantation immunology com. Nat. Inst. Allergy and Infectious Diseases, NIH, 1968-70, 71-73, mem. council, 1980-83; mem. sci. adv. bd. St. Jude Children's Research Hosp., Memphis, 1965-70; mem. sci. adv. com. Mass. Gen. Hosp., 1976-79. Contbr. articles to profl. jours.; Editorial bd.: Transplantation, 1980-82; adv. editorial bd.: Placenta, 1980—; asso. editor: Am. Jour. Reproductive Immunology, 1981—; adv. editor: Jour. Exptl. Medicine, 1963—; asso. editor: Jour. Immunology, 1964-72, Cellular Immunology, 1970—, Jour. Exptl. Zoology, 1976-80; hon. editorial bd.: Developmental and Comparative Immunology, 1977—. Served to lt. Royal Navy, 1942-46. Recipient Alvarenga prize Coll. Physicians, Phila., 1963; hon. award Soc. Plastic Surgeons, 1964; Fred Lyman Adair award Am. Gynecol. Soc., 1971. Fellow Royal Soc. (London), N.Y. Acad. Scis., Am. Acad. Arts and Scis.; mem. Am. Assn. Immunologists, Transplantation Soc. (pres. 1974-76), Am. Assn. Transplant Surgeons (hon.). Home: 6181 Preston Haven Dr Dallas TX 75230 Office: Dept Cell Biology U Tex Health Sci Center 5323 Harry Hines Blvd Dallas TX 75235

BILLINGS, BRIAN FRANCIS, wholesale petroleum products company executive; b. Kansas City, Mo., 1939. B.B.A., Rockhurst Coll., 1962; M.B.A., U. Mo., 1967. Various mgmt. and exec. positions Inter North Co., 1964-74; v.p. fin. adminstrn. No. Petrochem. Co., 1970-74; exec. v.p. Williams Exploration Co., 1974-78; pres. LA Resources Co. (subs.), 1975-78; prs. Williams Energy Co., 1978-80; chmn. bd. Buckeye Bas Products Co., Tulsa, 1980—; group pres. Energy Penn Central Corp. Office: Buckeye Gas Products Co 320 S Boston Ave Bldg Tulsa OK 74101 *

BILLINGS, BRUCE HADLEY, physicist, aerospace company executive; b. Chgo., July 6, 1915; s. Thomas H. and Grace (Hadley) B.; m. Sarah Winslow, June 23, 1938 (div.); children: Sally Frances, Bruce Randolph, Jane Winslow, Peter Fayssoux; m. Fannie Hu. A.B., Harvard U., 1936, A.M., 1937; Ph.D., Johns Hopkins U., 1943; hon. Ph.D., China Acad. Tchr. math. sci. Am. Community Sch., Beirut, 1937-40; jr. instr. physics Johns Hopkins U., Balt., 1940-41; physicist Polaroid Corp., Cambridge, Mass., 1941-47; mem. radiol. safety sect. atomic bomb test, Bikini, 1946; dir. research Baird-Atomic, Inc., Cambridge, 1947-63, exec. v.p., 1955-59, v.p. and tech. dir., 1960-63; v.p., gen. mgr. labs. operation Aerospace Corp., Los Angeles, 1963-68, v.p. corp. planning, 1973-74, v.p., Washington, 1974-76; pres. Thagard Research Corp., 1976-80; chmn. bd. Internat. Tech. Assos., Inc., 1977—, dir. research, 1980—; mem. Joint Commn. on Rural Reconstrn.; spl. asst. to Am. ambassador for sci. and tech., Taipei, Taiwan, 1968-73; mem. sci. adv. com. Bell & Howell; dir. Ealing Corp., Diffraction, Ltd., Inc., Altovac Tech., Inc.; mem. Air Force Sci. Adv. Bd., 1962-72; asst. dir. def. research and engring. Dept. Def., 1959-60; U.S. del. Marseille Conf. on Thin Films, 1949; U.S. rep. on UN Adv. Com. on Application of Sci. and Tech. to Devel., 1973—; mem. U.S. nat. com. Internat. Commn. Optics; research asso. Harvard Coll. Obs.; cons. Dept. State, 1973—; dir. Laser Sci., Inc., Milco Internat. Inc. Asso. editor: Inst. Physics Handbook; subject editor: Applied Optics; Contbr. tech. articles to profl. jours. Decorated Order of Brilliant Star, Republic of China). Fellow Am. Acad. Arts and Scis. (sec.), Am. Phys. Soc., Optical Soc. Am. (asso. editor jour. 1956-60, pres. 1971, v.p. internat. commn. of optics 1973); mem. Acoustical Soc. Am., AAAS, Sigma Xi. Club: St. Botolph. Office: 7303 N Marina Pacifica Dr Long Beach CA 90803

BILLINGS, CHARLES EDGAR, physician; b. Boston, June 15, 1929; s. Charles Edgar and Elizabeth (Sanborn) B.; m. Lillian Elizabeth

Wilson, Apr. 16, 1955; 1 dau., Lee Ellen Billings Kreinbihl. Student, Wesleyan U., 1947-49; M.D., N.Y. U., 1953; M.Sc. (Link Found. fellow), Ohio State U., 1960. Diplomate: Am. Bd. Preventive Medicine. Instr. to prof. depts. preventive medicine and aviation Ohio State U. Sch. Medicine, 1960-73, dir. div. environ. health, 1970-73, clin. prof., 1973-83; med. officer NASA Ames Research Center, Moffett Field, Calif., 1973-76; chief Aviation Safety Research Office, 1976-80, asst. chief for research Man-Vehicle Systems research div., 1980-83, sr. scientist, 1983—; cons. Beckett Aviation Corp., 1962-73; surgeon gen. U.S. Army, 1965-77, FAA, 1967-70, 75, 83; asso. adviser USAF Sci. Adv. Bd., 1978—. Contbr. chpts. to books, numerous articles in field to med. jours. Served to maj. USAF, 1955-57. Recipient Air Traffic Service award FAA, 1969; Walter M. Boothby research award, 1972; PATCO Air Safety award, 1979; Disting. Service award Flight Safety Found., 1979; John A. Tamisea award, 1980; Laura Taber Barbour Air Safety medal, 1981; NASA outstanding leadership medal, 1981. Fellow Am. Coll. Preventive Medicine, Aerospace Med. Assn. (pres. 1979-80), Am. Acad. Occupational Medicine; mem. AMA. Clubs: Atlantic Whippet Assn., Am. Whippet; Midland Whippet (Gt. Britain). Home: 10460 Albertsworth Ln Los Altos Hills CA 94022 Office: NASA-Ames Research Center Moffett Field CA 94035

BILLINGS, DOROTHY BAKER, interior designer; b. Columbia, S.C., 1918; d. James Alpheus and Ethel Vivian (Ogg) Baker; m. Robinson Billings, June 11, 1943. A.B., Queens Coll., Charlotte, N.C., 1939; postgrad., N.Y. Sch. Interior Design, 1946. Cryptographer Air Transp. Command., Gt. Falls, Mont., 1942-43; with Irene's Interiors, Charlotte, 1947-48; propr. Dorothy Baker Billings, Inc. (interiors), Charlotte, 1948—; liaison between designers and mgrs., ednl. and pub. relations promotor Am. Inst. Interiors Designers (now Am. Soc. Interior Designers), 1959-73; pres. Carolinas chpt., 1964, 70, nat. bd. govs., 1963-66, chmn. coms., 1959-77, nat. chmn. hist. preservation, 1977—; dir. Hadley Peoples Mfg. Co., 1958—; tchr. interior design Queens Coll., 1967; cons. Hezekian Alexander Restoration, 1967—, Latta Place, Inc., 1975—. Designer: Jefferson Standard Broadcasting Co. rooms, Charlotte, 1960-62; 18th century period room, Mint Mus. Art, Charlotte, 1967, room for, Nat. Home Fashion League, So. Furniture Market Center, High Point, Celanese House, N.Y.C., 1970; Celanese House/South, Charlotte, 1977, N.C., 1969; design work appears in major feature mags. Fellow Am. Soc. Interior Designers; mem. Nat. Home Fashion League, Nat. Parks Assn., Hist. N.C. Preservation Soc., Mus. Early Decorative Arts, Nat. Trust. Presbyterian. Clubs: Charlotte Country; Linville Country, Grandfather Golf and Country (Linville, N.C.); Pinehurst (N.C.); Golf and Country. Address: 4516 Randolph Rd Apt 89 Charlotte NC 28217

BILLINGS, EDWARD ROBERT, accountant; b. Blunt, S.D., Nov. 6, 1913; s. Edward C. and Lydia (Abendroth) B.; m. Paula W. Knickrehm, July 11, 1936; children—Edward A., Bruce P., David W. B.S., U. Ill., 1940, B.A., 1940. Jr. accountant Haskins & Sells (C.P.A.'s), Chgo., 1940-52, partner, 1952-63, mng. partner, 1963-69, partner, exec. officer, N.Y.C., 1969—. Home: 44 Byfield Ln Greenwich CT 06830 Office: 1114 Ave of Americas New York NY 10036 *Always render the highest quality of service that you can possibly render — this means keeping abreast of the latest developments in your profession and adapting them to your client's needs before he or your contemporaries may even be aware of them.*

BILLINGS, FRANKLIN SWIFT, JR., chief justice Vermont Supreme Court; b. Woodstock, Vt., June 5, 1922; s. Franklin S. and Gertrude (Curtis) B.; m. Pauline Gillingham, Oct. 13, 1951; children: Franklin, III, Jireh Swift, Elizabeth, Ann. S.B., Harvard U., 1943; postgrad., Yale U. law Sch., 1945; J.D., U. Va., 1947. Bar: Vt. 1948. With dept. electronics Gen. Electric Co., Schenectady, N.Y., 1943-45; bldg. dept. Vt. Marble Co., Proctor, 1945-46; individual practice law, Woodstock, 1948-52; mem. firm Billings & Sherburne, Woodstock, 1952-66; asst. sec. Vt. Senate, 1949-55, sec., 1957-59; sec. civil and mil. affairs, State of Vt., 1959-61, exec. clk. to gov., 1955-57; judge Hartford Mcpl. Ct., 1955-63; mem. Vt. Ho. of Reps., 1961-66, chmn. jud. com., 1961, speaker of ho., 1963-66; judge Vt. Superior Ct., 1966-75; asso. justice Vt. Supreme Ct., Montpelier, 1975-83, chief justice, 1983—; pres., dir. Woodstock Aqueduct Co. Bd. dirs. Norman Williams Library, Woodstock, 1950—; active, Town of Woodstock, 1948-72. Served as warrant officer 1st class attached Brit. Army, 1944-45. Decorated Purple Heart, U.S.; Brit. Empire medal. Mem. Vt. Bar Assn., Delta Theta Phi. Club: Rotary (past pres.). Office: Vt Supreme Ct Montpelier VT 05602

BILLINGS, HAROLD WAYNE, librarian, editor; b. Cain City, Tex., Nov. 12, 1931; s. Harold Ross and Katie Mae (Price) B.; m. Bernice Schneider, Sept. 10, 1954; children: Brenda, Geoffrey, Carol. B.A., Pan Am. Coll., 1953; M.L.S., U. Tex., 1957. Tchr. Pharr-San Juan-Alamo (Tex.) High Sch., 1953-54; catalog librarian U. Tex., Austin, 1954-57, asst. chief catalog librarian, 1957-65, chief acquisitions librarian, 1965-67, asst. univ. librarian, 1967-72, asso. dir. gen. libraries, 1972-77, acting dir. gen. libraries, 1977-78, dir. gen. libraries, 1978—; sec. Tex. Bd. Library Examiners; trustee Amigos Bibliographic Council, 1980-83, chmn. council acad. research libraries, 1979-81. Author: Edward Dahlberg: American Ishmael of Letters, 1968, A Bibliography of Edward Dahlberg, 1972; editor books in field.; Mem. editorial bd.: Library Chronicle, 1970—. Sec., trustee Littlefield Fund for So. History. Mem. ALA, Tex. Library Assn., Assn. Coll. and Research Libraries, Tex. Council State Univ. Librarians, Collector's Inst., OCLC Users Council. Democrat. Office: Univ of Tex Austin TX 78712

BILLINGS, ROGER LEWIS, oil company executive; b. Tulsa, Okla., Oct. 6, 1932; s. Arthur Lewis and Edra Mae (Duckworth) B.; m. Martha Carol Voight, Aug. 29, 1953; children: Victoria Martha Parks, Mega Laura Ann. B.S. in Geology, U. Okla., 1954, M.S., 1956; M.B.A., Harvard U., 1968. Cert. petroleum geologist. Geologist Exxon, Rock Mountains and S.Am., 1955-66; mgr. planning Union Pacific, Los Angeles, 1968-72; v.p. gas and oil Mont. Power Co., Butte, 1972-78; v.p. exploration and prodn. KNEnergy, Denver, 1979-80; exec. v.p., chief operating officer Home Petroleum Corp., Houston, 1980-82; v.p. eastern region Aminoil Inc., Houston, 1982—. Mem. Am. Assn. Petroleum Geologists, Am. Gas Assn. Office: Aminoil Inc 2800 North Loop West Houston TX 77092

BILLINGS, WILLIAM DWIGHT, ecology educator; b. Washington, Dec. 29, 1910; s. William Pence and Mabel (Burke) B.; m. Shirley Ann Miller, July 29, 1958. B.A., Butler U., 1933; M.A., Duke U., 1935, Ph.D., 1936; D.Sc., Butler U., 1955. Instr. botany U. Tenn., 1936-37; instr. biology U. Nev., 1938-40, asst. prof., 1940-43, asso. prof., 1943-49, prof., chmn. biology dept., 1949-52; asso. prof. botany Duke U., 1952-58, prof., 1958-67, James B. Duke prof., 1967—; mem. adv. panels NSF—AEC, Washington, 1954-58; adj. research prof. Desert Research Inst., U. Nev., 1982—. Author: Plants and the Ecosystem, 1964, 78, Plants, Man and the Ecosystem, 1970, Vegetation and the Environment, 1974, Plants and the Ecosystem, 1978; editor: Ecology, 1952-57, Ecol. Monographs, 1969; contbr. articles to tech. jours.; editorial bd.: Ecol. Studies, 1975—, Arctic and Alpine Research, 1975—82. Fulbright research scholar, N.Z., 1959; recipient Certificate of Merit Bot. Soc. Am., 1960, Mercer award Ecol. Soc. Am., 1962. Fellow Arctic Inst. N.Am., Explorers Club, Am. Acad. Arts and Scis.; mem. Ecol. Soc. Am. (v.p. 1960, pres. 1978-79, Disting. Service award 1981), Brit. Ecol. Soc. (hon. fgn. mem. 1982—), Bot. Soc. Am. (chmn. ecology sect. 1976), Inst. Arctic and Alpine Research (sci. adv. com. 1975—). Research on arctic, alpine and desert ecology. Home: 1628 Marion Ave Durham NC 27705

BILLINGS, WILLIAM HOWARD, judge; b. Kennett, Mo., Aug. 21, 1921; s. James. v. and Leora (Sapp) B. Student naval aviator program, U. Iowa, 1942-43; LL.B., U. Mo., 1952. Bar: U.S. Dist. Ct. (ea. dist.) Mo., U.S. Supreme Ct. Ptnr. McHaney, Billings & Welman, Kennett, 1952-66; judge 35th jud. cir., Kennett, 1966-73, so. dist. Mo. Ct. Appeals, Springfield, 1973-82, Mo. Supreme Ct., Jefferson City, 1982—; lectr. Mo. State Hwy. Patrol, 1971-72. Pres., v.p. bd. curators U. Mo., Columbia, 1965-74. Served to capt. USMCR, 1942-45. Recipient John D. Lawson prize Mo. Law Sch. Found. Mem. Mo. Bar. Assn., Dunklin County (Mo.) Bar Assn., Am. Legion, VFW, Amvets, Order of Coif, Phi Delta Phi, Pi Kappa Alpha. Methodist. Lodges: Lions; Masons. Home: 2123 S Meadowview St Springfield MO 65804 Office: Supreme Ct Mo Supreme Ct Bldg Jefferson City MO 65101

BILLINGSLEY, JAMES RAY, telephone company executive; b. Rome, Ga., Jan. 22, 1927; s. Charles White and Loral Tabitha (Barker) B.; m. Helen Lee Brown, May 7, 1960; children: James Ray, Walter Brown, Ann Barker, John Charles. Student, N. Ga. Coll., 1944-45, N.Y. U., 1945; J.D., U. Miss., 1950. Bar: Miss. bar 1950, N.Y. bar 1958. Atty. U.S. Dept. Labor, Birmingham, Ala., 1950-55, Washington, 1955-56, Western Electric Co., N.Y.C., 1956-60, v.p. regulatory matters, 1973-74; atty. N.Y. Telephone Co., N.Y.C., 1960-67, gen. atty., 1967-70, v.p. revenues, 1970-73; v.p. fed. regulatory matters AT&T, N.Y.C., 1974—; dir. Chesapeake & Potomac Telephone Co., W.Va.; pres., dir. Tolten Corp. Trustee, treas. Henry L. and Grace Doherty Charitable Found. Served with U.S. Army, 1944-47. Mem. ABA, N.Y. Bar Assn. (public utilities com. 1967—). Presbyterian. Clubs: Manursing Island (Rye); Internat., Congressional Country (Washington). Office: 195 Broadway Room 2636 New York NY 10007

BILLINGSLEY, WILLIAM ALLEN, composer, trumpeter, educator; b. Glasgow, Mont., June 28, 1922; s. Clarence James and Macil Cleota (Holley) B.; m. Doris Louise Girdner, June 7, 1947; children: William Allen, David James, Thomas Jeffrey. B.M., Drake U., 1952, M.M., 1953. Prof. music U. Idaho, Moscow, 1954—; dir. Sch. Music, 1977-78. First trumpet, Des Moines Symphony, 1951-53; Compositions include Mr. Nobody, 1960, Paradox, secular contata for solo soprano, speaking chorus and orch., 1974; Compositions include ballet Requiem, 1976; Compositions include Sonata for Flute and Piano, 1977, Somewhen for soprano voice, horn and piano on poems by Dante Gabriel Rossetti, 1979, Concerto for Orch., 1981, Landscape Sketches for Two Pianos based on poems by William Studebaker, 1983. Served with USN, 1942-48. Recipient Spl. 3 Star award of merit Nat. Fedn. Music Clubs, 1976. Mem. Pi Kappa Lambda, Phi Kappa Phi. Home: 108 N Monroe St Moscow ID 83843 Office: School of Music Univ of Idaho Moscow ID 83843 *I believe in setting realistic yet challenging goals for myself, and what I produce today should be better than what I produced yesterday.*

BILLINGTON, WILBUR T., bank exec.; b. Lafayette, Colo., May 10, 1922; s. Charles and Jeannie (Lindsay) B.; m. Marian E. Baller, Sept. 20, 1945; children—Charles J., Paul R., Laura A. B.S., U. Colo., 1945, M.A., 1947; Ph.D., U. Minn., 1952. Instr. econs. U. Colo., 1946-47, Brown U., 1947-48, U. Minn., 1948-50; with Fed. Res. Bank of Kansas City, Mo., 1952—, became officer, 1958; now sr. v.p.; mem. faculty Colo. Grad. Sch. Banking, U. Colo., Boulder.; Mem. Sch. Dist. 110 of Johnson County, Kans.) Bd. Edn., 1962-68, pres., 1964-68; chmn. Johnson County Jr. Coll. Study Com., 1963-66; founding chmn. bd. trustees Johnson County Community Coll., 1967-75; mem. adv. council Kans. Community Jr. Coll., 1965-73, chmn., 1970-72; pres. Kans. Assn. Sch. Bds., 1967; mem. Kans. Gov's Com. on Edn., 1968; chmn. Kans. Master Planning Commn. for Post-Secondary Edn., 1970-72; mem. Kans. Geol. Survey Council, 1977—. Served to capt. USAAF, 1943-46; Served to capt. USAF, 1950-52. Recipient George Norlin award U. Colo., 1981. Mem. Kansas City C. of C., Am. Inst. Banking, Robert Morris Assos., Phi Beta Kappa. Presbyterian. Home: 6435 Outlook Dr Mission KS 66202 Office: 925 Grand Ave Kansas City MO 64198

BILLINGTON, WILLIAM HOWARD, JR., business executive; b. Chgo., Mar. 23, 1924; s. William Howard and Gladys Emily (Waterton) B.; m. Priscilla Armstrong, May 19, 1951; children: Jane, Robert, Brian. B.A. in Commerce, Northwestern U., 1949, M.B.A. in Personnel and Indsl. Relations, 1956. Cons. Hewitt Assos., 1951-53; salary adminstr. Chgo. Title & Trust Co., 1953-55; cons. George Fry & Assos., 1955-59, Booz, Allen & Hamilton, 1960-64; with Billington, Fox & Ellis, Inc., Chgo., 1964—, now sec., chmn. bd. Served to 2d lt. USAAF, 1943-46. Mem. Econ. Club Chgo. Clubs: University, Chgo. Curling, Sheridan Shores Yacht. Office: 20 N Wacker Dr Chicago IL 60606

BILLINTON, ROY, engring., educator; b. Leeds, Eng., Sept. 14, 1935; s. Edwin and Nettie (Billinton); m. Alice Joyce McKenna, July 21, 1956; children—Leslie, Kevin, Michael, Christopher, Jeffrey. B.Sc.E.E., U. Man., 1960, M.Sc., 1963; Ph.D., U. Sask., 1967, D.Sc., 1975. Journeyman electrician McKane Electric, Winnipeg, Man., Can., 1956; mem. system operation dept. and system planning dept. Man. Hydro, from 1960; asst. prof. to prof. elec. engring. U. Sask., Saskatoon, 1964—; now head dept.; pres. PowerComp Assos., cons. Author: Power System Reliability Evaluation, 1970, (with R. J. Ringlee and A. J. Wood) Power System Reliability Calculations, 1973, (with C. Singh) System Reliability Modelling and Evaluation, 1977; also articles. Recipient Sir George Nelson award Engring. Inst. Can., 1965-67, Ross medal, 1972. Fellow IEEE, Royal Soc. Can., Engring. Inst. Can. Home: 3 McLean Crescent Saskatoon SK S7J 2R6 Canada Office: U Sask Saskatoon SK S7N 0W0 Canada

BILLITER, WILLIAM OVERTON, JR., journalist; b. Cin., Sept. 3, 1934; s. William Overton and Laura Louise (Dorsey) B.; m. Maureen Ann Flanagan, June 22, 1962; children—Suzanne, Stephen, Mary, Patrick. B.A., U. Ky., 1956; M.S., U. Louisville, 1970. Reporter New Orleans Times-Picayune, 1959-61; instr. Ohio State U., 1961-62; legis. asst. U.S. Rep. F. Edward Hebert of La., 1962-65; reporter, polit. editor Louisville Courier-Jour., 1965-74; editorial writer, columnist Louisville Times, 1974-77, city editor, 1977-78; reporter Los Angeles Times, 1978—. Served with USAF, 1956-59. Mem. Soc. Profl. Journalists, AAUP. Democrat. Roman Catholic. Home: 9522 Telhan Dr Huntington Beach CA 92646 Office: Los Angeles Times Los Angeles CA 90053

BILLMAN, IRWIN EDWARD, publishing company executive; b. Manhattan, N.Y., July 7, 1940; s. Herman Frank and Ruth (Dutchen) B. B.S. in Econs, Wharton Sch., U. Pa., 1962. Asst. controller Whelan Drug Co., 1965-66; v.p., treas. Curtis Circulation Co., Phila., 1966-71; exec. v.p., chief operating officer Penthouse, Omni and Forum Mags., 1971-81; pres., publisher Oui Mag., N.Y.C., 1981-82; pres. Billman Media Group. Mem. Periodical and Book Assn. Am. (pres. 1977-81). Club: Friars. Home: PO Box 350 N Quarter Rd Westhampton NY 11977 Office: 136 E 55th St New York NY 10022

BILLMEYER, FRED WALLACE, JR., educator, chemist; b. Chattanooga, Aug. 24, 1919; s. Fred W. and Eleanor (Salmon) B.; m. Annette M. Trzcinski, Aug. 4, 1951; children—Fred S., Eleanor A., Dean W., David M. B.S., Cal. Inst. Tech., 1941; Ph.D., Cornell U., 1945. With plastics dept. E.I. du Pont de Nemours & Co., 1945-64; lectr. high polymers dept. chemistry U. Del., 1951-64; Vis. prof. chem. engring. Mass. Inst. Tech., 1960-61; prof. analytical chemistry Rensselaer Poly. Inst., 1964—; Cons. various coms. Internat. Commn. Illumination (CIE), 1964—; mem. U.S. Nat. Com. CIE, 1968—, v.p., 1975-79; Trustee Munsell Color Found., sec., 1975—. Author: Textbook of Polymer Chemistry, 1957, Textbook of Polymer Science, 1961, 2d edit., 1971, Synthetic Polymers, 1972, (with Max Saltzman) Principles of Color Technology, 1966, 2d edit., 1981, (with E.A. Collins and J. Bares) Experiments in Polymer Science, 1973, (with R. N. Kelley) Entering Industry, 1975; also articles.; Editorial adviser: Optical Spectra, 1967-80; editor-in-chief: Color Research and Application, 1976—. Recipient Bruning award Fedn. Socs. Coatings Tech., 1977. Fellow Am. Phys. Soc., Optical Soc. Am., AAAS; mem. Am. Chem. Soc., N.Y. Soc. Coatings Tech., Soc. Plastics Engrs., Am. Assn. Textile Chem. Colorists, Inter-Soc. Color Council (pres. 1968-70, sec. 1970-82, Macbeth award 1978, Service award 1983), Council Optical Radiation Measurements (sec. 1979-83), ASTM, Sigma Xi, Phi Kappa Phi. Home: 2121 Union St Schenectady NY 12309 Office: Rensselaer Poly Inst Troy NY 12181

BILLS, ROBERT EDGAR, educator; b. Nutley, N.J., Dec. 15, 1916; s. Willis Minard and Leah (Condit) B.; m. Annie Tarleton Carley, Dec. 22, 1944; children: Mary Ann, Leah Catherine. B.S., Western Ky. U., 1938; M.A., U. Ky., 1946; Ed.D., Columbia U., 1948. Sci. tchr. Breathitt County (Ky.) Bd. Edn., Jackson, 1938-42; sci. tchr. Anchorage (Ky.) Bd. Edn., 1943-44, prin., 1944-45; critic tchr. sci. U. Ky. Coll. Edn., 1945-46; faculty Coll. Arts and Scis., 1948-56, asst. to assoc. prof. psychology, 1948-56, chmn. div. biol. scis., 1950-51; grad. asst. Columbia Tchrs. Coll., 1947-48; vis. summer prof. U. Fla., 1952, 53; cons. sch. plant planning Mich. State U., summer 1956; prof. psychology, chmn. dept. Auburn U., 1956-61; vis. summer prof. U. Wash., 1963; prof. ednl. psychology U. Ala., 1961-69, asst. dean for research, 1961-63; interim dean Coll. Edn., 1963-65, dean, 1965-69, research prof. edn., 1969-79, research prof. ednl. psychology and dean emeritus, 1979—; cons. in field. Chmn. Ky. Bd. Examiners Psychologists, 1954-56; pres. Ky. Psychol. Assn., 1952-53; mem. council psychol. resources of South So. Regional Edn. Bd., 1953-56; bd. dirs. Southeastern Ednl. Corp., 1966-67; scholar Clemson U. Lecture Series, 1967; sec. Ala. Coalition for Better Edn., 1969-70, pres., 1971-72. Author books, numerous articles, revs., bulls. in field. Served with AUS, 1942-43. Fellow Am. Psychol. Assn. (chmn. membership com. div. teaching psychology 1958-61, 61-62, sec.-treas. 1963-66); mem. Am. Edn. Research Assn, Mid-South Edn. Research Assn. (pres. 1979); mem. Assn. Supervision and Curriculum Devel. (bd. dirs. 1962-64), Phi Delta Kappa, Kappa Delta Pi, Psi Chi, Sigma Xi. Home: 73 Woodland Hills Tuscaloosa AL 35401 Office: Care Dept Behavioral Studies U Ala University AL 35486 *I have a deep faith in the ability of people to solve their own problems when extended a relationship which enables them to explore alternatives, desires, and values to the fullest extent. I have attempted to be as honest in my dealings with people as my perceptions permit me to be; I owe no man, neither is any man under obligation to me.*

BILLS, ROBERT HOWARD, political party eecutive; b. North Conway, N.H., Jan. 13, 1944; s. Howard William and Mary Catherine (Jackson) B.; m. Donna Gail Florian; children: Emily Ida, Katherine Mary. Staff writer Weekly People Newspaper, Bklyn., 1970-74, Weekely People Newspaper, Palo Alto, Calif., 1974-76; nat. sec. Socialist Labor Party, Palo Alto, 1980—, mem. nat. eec. subcom., 1976-79. Office: Socialist Labor Party of Am PO Box 50218 Palo Alto CA 94086

BILLS, SHERYL JEAN, newspaper editor; b. Rushville, Ind., Aug. 4, 1945; d. Robert Jackson and Mary Elizabeth (Kehl) B. B.A., Ind. U., 1968. Mem. staff Cin. Enquirer, 1967-82, asst. mng. editor features, 1979-80, mng. editor, 1980-82; planning editor USA Today, Gannett Newspapers, 1982-83, mng. editor life, 1983—; lectr. in field. Mem. adminstrv. bd. Hyde Park Community United Methodist Ch., 1981. Recipient writing award Ohio Newspaper Women's Assn., 1971, 74, Ohio AP award for enterprise in journalism, 1974, award mag. covers-Outdoor Writers Ohio Ohio Press Photographers Assn., 1976, Penney-Mo. award for newspaper lifestyle sect., 1978, Outstanding Career Woman award Cin. YMCA, 1981, Disting. Alumni award Rushville High Sch., 1983. Mem. Women in Communications, AP Mng. Editors Assn., Am. Soc. Newspaper Editors, Sigma Delta Chi. Office: USA Today PO Box 500 Washington DC 20004

BILLUPS, NORMAN FREDRICK, college dean, pharmacist; b. Portland, Oreg., Oct. 15, 1934; s. John Alexander and Myrtle I. B.; m. Shirley Mae Brooks, July 7, 1956; children: Tamra Mae, Timothy Fredrick. Student, Portland State U., 1952-55; B.S. in Pharmacy, Oreg. State U., 1958, M.S., 1961, Ph.D.; Ph.D. (Am. Found. Pharm. Edn. fellow), 1963. Instr. Oreg. State U., 1958-60, grad. asst., 1960-63; asso. prof. pharmacy U. Ky., 1963-73, prof., 1974-77; dean, prof. pharmacy Coll. Pharmacy, U. Toledo, 1977—; pharmacist, Ohio, Oreg., Ky., 1961—. Author: American Drug Index, ann, 1977—. Recipient Research Achievement award Am. Soc. Hosp. Pharmacists, 1975; NIH research fellow, 1962-63. Mem. Acad. Pharm. Scis., Am. Assn. Colls. Pharmacy (Lyman award 1971), Am. Pharm. Assn., Ohio Pharm. Assn., Toledo Acad. Pharmacy, Council Ohio Colls. Pharmacy (chmn. bd. trustees, chmn. council), Toledo Acad. Pharmacy (dir.), Sigma Xi, Phi Kappa Phi (pres. U. Toledo chpt.), Rho Chi., Phi Lambda Sigma. Methodist. Home: 2507 Middlesex Dr Toledo OH 43606 Office: 2801 W Bancroft Toledo OH 43606

BILOCK, JOHN M., bishop; b. McAdoo, Pa., June 20, 1916. Grad., St. Procopius Coll. and Sem., Ill. Ordained priest Roman Catholic Ch., 1946. Vicar gen. Byzantine archdiocese of Munhall, 1969; ordained titular bishop of Pergamum and Munhall, Pitts., 1973—. Office: 66 Riverview Ave Pittsburgh PA 15214 *

BILOTTI, JOHN D., mayor; b. Kenosha, Wis., Oct. 7, 1944; s. Benjamin M. and Helen M. (Molinaro) B.; m. Judy Bleashka, Oct. 28, 1978. Student, U. Wis., 1962-64; B.S., Carthage Coll., 1966; postgrad., Marquette Grad. Sch. History, 1966-68. Tchr. elem. schs. Kenosha, 1966-71; with office of adminstrn. U. Wis., Milw., 1976-80; alderman 11th dist. City of Kenosha, 1970-76, 79-80, mayor, Wis., 1980—. Originator, author, sponsor weekly radio program: The Peoples Right to Know, 1972-76. Organizer, founding chmn. Concerned Property Owners of Kenosha, 1968; founding chmn. Kenosha Landmarks Commn., 1973; candidate for mayor City of Kenosha, 1976; bd. assocs. Kenosha Meml. Hosp.; mem. Crossing Guard Walkie Talkie Fund Project; mem. steering com. Neighborhood Crime Watch; mem. Joint Services Bd., Spl. Edn./Vocat. Edn. Adv. Bd., Retarded Citizens of Kenosha County; chmn. Fed. Emergency Food and Shelter Program. Mem. Wis. Alliance of Cities (pres.), Wis. Sheriff Assn., Wis. League of Municipalities, Am. Public Works Assn. (Wis. chpt.), Italian Am. Soc. Roman Catholic. Lodges: Eagles.; Elks; Moose. Home: 2208 54th St Kenosha WI 53140 Office: 625 52nd St Kenosha WI 53140

BILPUCH, EDWARD GEORGE, nuclear physicist, educator; b. Connellsville, Pa., Feb. 10, 1927; s. John and Elizabeth (Kochisco) B.; m. Marilyn Jean Strohkorb, Sept. 6, 1952. B.S., U. N.C., 1950, M.S., 1952, Ph.D. (Morehead scholar), 1956. Research assoc. Duke U., 1956-

59, asst. prof., 1960-65, assoc. prof., 1966-70, prof. physics, 1970—; dep. dir. Triangle Univs. Nuclear Lab., Duke Sta., Durham, N.C., 1966-78; dir. Triangle Univs. Nuclear Lab, 1978—; vis. prof. U. Frankfurt (West Germany), 1972, 74, Fudan U., Shanghai, China, spring 1983; chmn. NBS Evaluation Panel for Radiation Research, 1983-85. Contbr. articles to profl. jours. Served with USNR, 1945-46. Sr. U.S. scientist Humboldt awardee Fed. Republic of Germany, 1983-84. Fellow Am. Phys. Soc., Nat. Acad. Scis. (physics survey com.), Phi Beta Kappa, Sigma Xi. Home: 106 Cherokee Circle Chapel Hill NC 27514 Office: Duke U Dept Physics Durham NC 27706

BILS, ROBERT FREDERICK, scientist, educator; b. Harvey, Ill., Jan. 10, 1931; s. Frederick Stephen and Grace Esther (Pohlman) B.; m. Afrodite Konstans, Aug. 8, 1954; children—Lynne, Julie, Lisa. Student, Oberlin Coll., 1949-51; B.S., U. Ill., 1954, M.S., 1958, Ph.D. in Plant Biochemistry, 1960. Research asst. Electron Microscope Labs., U. Ill., Urbana, 1958-60; cons. Delco Battery Co., Muncie, Ind., 1957-59; NIH fellow Mass. Inst. Tech., Cambridge, 1960-61; asst. prof. biology U. So. Calif., Los Angeles, 1961-66; dir. Electron Microscope Lab., 1961—, asso. prof., 1966-70, prof. biol. sci., also cellular and molecular biology, 1970—; asso. dir. Specialized Center of Research Environ. Lung Disease, U. So. Calif.-Rancho Los Amigos Hosp., Downey, 1972-77; cons. Los Angeles Air Pollution Control Dist., 1969-71; cons. to spl. studies sect. Nat. Adv. Environ. Health Sci. Council, 1971-72; vis. prof. Pathologisches Institut; research scientist Lufthygiene Silikose Inst. U. Dusseldorf, W. Ger., 1968-69; vis. prof. research unit for comparative animal respiration U. Bristol, 1976-77. Author: Electron Microscopy, 1974; Contbr. articles to profl. jours. Mem. planning bd. Montebello (Calif.) Unified Sch. Dist., 1966-68. Served with AUS, 1954-56; PTO. Fellow Royal Micros. Soc.; mem. AAAS, Am. Soc. Cell Biology, N.Y. Acad. Scis., Electron Microscopy Soc. Am. (chmn. 30th meeting 1972, exec. council 1973-76, dir. tech. certification program), So. Calif. Soc. for Electron Microscopy (pres. 1965), Sigma Xi, Phi Sigma, Pi Alpha Xi. Presbyterian. Home: 816 Westmoreland Dr Montebelleo CA 90640 Office: Dept Biological Sciences Univ So Calif Los Angeles CA 90007

BILSING, DAVID CHARLES, controller; b. Upper Sandusky, Ohio, Mar. 15, 1933; s. John Reuben and Mary Victoria (Neate) B.; m. Dorothy L. Emerson, Sept. 17, 1955; children—Karen, Michael, Linda. B.S., Ohio U., 1955. C.P.A., Ill. Acct. trainee AMSTED Industries, Chgo., 1955-59, asst. plant controller, 1959-61, div. controller, 1962, mgr. cost acctg., 1963-65, asst. controller, 1965-69; corp. controller Beloit Corp., Wis., 1969-73, Baxter Labs., Deerfield, Ill., 1973-80, Reynolds Metals Co., Richmond, Va., 1980—. Served with AUS, 1956-58. Mem. Ill. Soc. C.P.A.'s, Am. Inst. C.P.A.'s, Nat. Assn. Accts., Fin. Execs. Inst. Home: 1 Broad Run Rd Manakin-Sabot VA 23103 Office: 6603 Broad St Richmond VA 23261

BILSKY, MANUEL, educator, philosopher; b. Bklyn., Mar. 25, 1910; s. Harry and Minnie (Haber) B. M.A., U. Mich., 1947, Ph.D., 1951. Asst. prof. U. Chgo., 1949-58; asso. prof. Roosevelt U., Chgo., 1958-60; prof. philosophy Eastern Mich. U., 1960-80, ret., 1980. Author: Logic and Effective Argument, 1956, Patterns of Argument, 1963, (with H.G. Duffield) Tolstoy and the Critics, 1965; also articles, book revs. Served to 1st lt. AUS, 1942-46. Home: 1820 Alhambra Dr Ann Arbor MI 48103

BILSON, BRUCE, motion picture and television director; b. Bklyn., May 19, 1928; s. George and Hattie (Dratwa) B.; m. Mona Weichman, Aug. 31, 1955 (div. 1976); children: Daniel, Julie; m. Renne Jarrett, Apr. 5, 1981. B.A. in Theatre Arts, UCLA, 1950. Film editor: Groucho Marx show, 1953-54; asst. dir. various TV shows, 1954-64; asso. producer, CBS-TV, 1964-65; dir., 1965—; over 300 TV credits; dir.: motion pictures North Avenue Irregulars, Chattanooga Choo Choo; Recipient (Emmy award for outstanding directorial achievement in comedy 1968). Founder Sponsors for Ednl. Opportunities, Los Angeles. Served with USAF, 1951-53. Mem. Dirs. Guild Am. (dir.), Acad. TV Arts and Scis. (trustee). Office: care Downwind Enterprises Inc 4444 Radford Ave North Hollywood CA 91607 *

BIMSON, CARL ALFRED, financial exec.; b. Berthoud, Colo., Mar. 15, 1900; s. Alfred George and Margaret (Eichman) B.; m. Irene M. Hildreth, Oct. 25, 1927. M.E., Colo. A. & M. Coll., 1923. With Mt. States Tel. & Tel. Co., 1924-30, dist. cashier, Colorado Springs, Colo., dist. sales supr., Pueblo; real estate, investment, property mgmt., Denver, 1931-32; with Valley Nat. Bank, Phoenix, since 1933, mgr. installment loan dept., 1936-39, asst. v.p., 1939-40, v.p., 1940-49, exec. v.p., 1949-53, pres., 1953-62, vice chmn. bd., chmn. exec. com., 1962-70, dir., 1941-70, vice chmn. emeritus, 1970—; pres. Concho Investment Co., Concho Life Ins. Co.; mem. exec com., asst. sec. Valley Nat. Ins. Co.; Mgr. Financial relations F.H.A., Ariz., 1934-36; Dir. Sun Angel Found., Maricopa County Better Bus. Bur.; past pres. Municipal Indsl. Devel. Corp., Mchts. and Mfrs. Credit Bur., Maricopa County chpt. A.R.C., Maricopa County chpt. March Dimes, Ariz. Evang. Council; v.p., dir., mem. adv. com. Phoenix YMCA; past pres. Phoenix Credit Bur.; mem. Phoenix Growth Com; chmn. finance com. Maricopa County Planning Com.; mem. adv. council Ariz. Bus.-Industry-Edn. Council; v.p., mem. bd. Jr. Achievement Met. Phoenix; mem. bd. exec. com. Phoenix Devel. Assn.; mem. dean's adv. council Ariz. State U. Sch. Bus.; mem. bd., treas. Christian Care, Inc.; elder, chmn. bd. trustees 1st Christian Ch., Phoenix. Contbr. articles trade jours. Recipient degree Hon. State Farmer, Future Farmers of America; Significant Sig award Sigma Chi, 1963; Distinguished Achievement award Ariz. State U. Coll. Bus. Adminstrn., 1977. Mem. Future Farmers Am. (v.p. 1959, pres. 1960, mgmt., adminstrv., govt. borrowing coms.), Ariz. Bankers Assn. (past pres.), Am. Bankers Assn. (past pres.), Am. Inst. Banking (life), Nat. Assn. Better Bus. Burs. (past mem. bd. govs.), Financial Pub. Relations Assn. (3d v.p.), Phoenix Clearing House Assn. (past pres.), Nat. Retail Credit Men's Assn. (past dir.), Robert Morris Assos. (life), U.S. C. of C. (finance com.), Phoenix C. of C. (past pres.), Phoenix Thunderbirds, Sigma Chi, Beta Gamma Sigma (hon.). Clubs: Kiwanis, Country (Phoenix); Paradise Valley Country, Kiva, Arizona. Home: 5221 N Saddle Rock Dr Phoenix AZ 85018 Office: Valley Nat Bank Phoenix AZ 85036

BINCER, ADAM MARIAN, educator, physicist; b. Krakow, Poland, Apr. 25, 1930; s. Henryk and Rosa Renata (Landau) B.; m. Bianca Margulies, June 2, 1952 (div. 1961); children: Andrea, Roy; m. Wanda Lawendel, Apr. 2, 1972. B.S. in Physics, M.I.T., 1953, Ph.D. in Theoretical Physics, 1956. Physicist Brookhaven Nat. Lab., L.I., N.Y., 1956-58; research assoc. U. Calif. at Berkeley, 1958-60; asst. prof. U. Wis., Madison, 1960-63, assoc. prof., 1963-68, prof. physics, 1968—. Contbr. articles to profl. jours. Fulbright scholar U. Sao Paulo, Brazil, 1965. Mem. Am. Phys. Soc. Home: 1215 Wellesley Rd Madison WI 53705 Office: Univ Wis Madison WI 53706

BINDER, DAVID A., lawyer, educator; b. 1934. B.A., UCLA, 1956; LL.B., Stanford U., 1959. Bar: Calif. 1960. Ptnr. Brown & Brown, Los Angeles, 1965-69; litigation dir. Western Ctr. on Law and Poverty, 1969-70; faculty UCLA, 1970—, prof. law, 1970—. Author: (with Price) Legal Interviewing and Counseling: A Client-Centered Approach, 1977. Office: UCLA Law Sch 405 Hilgrad Ave Los Angeles CA 90024

BINDER, FREDERICK MOORE, college president; b. Atlantic City, N.J., Nov. 18, 1920; s. Paul Reginald and Kathryn (Moore) B.; m. Grace Irene Brandt, May 27, 1943; children: Janet Binder Houts, Roberta Lynn. B.A., Ursinus Coll., 1942, LL.D., 1960; M.A., U. Pa., 1948, Ph.D., 1955; Litt.D., Wagner Coll, 1964; L.H.D., Rider coll., 1967; Pd.D., Susquehanna U., 1969. Tchr. Somerville (N.J.) High Sch., 1946; asst. registrar Temple U., 1946-47, dept. history, 1947-55; dean, asso. prof. history Thiel Coll., 1955-57, acad. v.p. prof. history, 1957-59, acting pres., 1959; pres. Hartwick Coll., 1959-69; asso. commr. for higher edn. N.Y. State Edn. Dept., 1969-70; pres. Whittier (Calif.) Coll., 1970-75, Juniata Coll., Huntingdon, Pa., 1975—; Mem. N.Y. State Regents Exams. Bd., 1962-68; Fulbright lectr., Yugoslavia, 1967-68. Author: Serbian Assignment, 1971, Coal Age Empire, 1974; Contbr. book revs. and articles to profl. publs. Chmn. Ind. Coll. Funds. Am., 1966-67; bd. dirs. S.W. Mus., 1970-75; trustee Fox Hosp., Oneonta, N.Y., 1975-80; mem. Pa. State Bd. Edn., 1983—. Served at lt. (j.g.) USNR, 1942-45; lt. comdr. Res. Recipient Newcomen award for contbn. to cause of material history Newcomen Soc. in N.Am., 1955. Mem. Am. Assn. Univ. Adminstrs. (v.p. 1981—), Newcomen Soc., Pa. Acad. Deans (chmn. 1959), Orgn. Am. Historians, Empire State Found. for Ind. Liberal Arts Colls. (chmn. 1962-63), Phi Alpha Theta, Alpha Chi Rho (nat. scholarship officer 1957-59). Episcopalian. Clubs: Union League (Phila.); Cosmos, Rotary. Address: Office of President Juniata College Huntingdon PA 16652

BINDER, JOHN, clergyman, religious organization executive; b. Can., Nov. 10, 1930; s. Henry Blinder and Katherine B.; m. Barbara Weisser, Aug. 30, 1960; children: Laurette, Douglas, Brian. Student, Sioux Falls Coll., 1952-54; B.A., Augustana Coll., 1956; B.D., N.Am. Bapt. Sem., 1959; postgrad., No. Ill. U., 1967-69. Ordained to ministry N.Am. Conf.,1959. Pastor Emmanuel Bapt. Ch., Morris, Man., Can., 1959-60; youth dir. N.Am. Bapt. Conf., Forest Park, Ill., 1960-66, editor Bapt. Herald Monthly mag., 1967-71, stewardship and communications sec., 1971-79, exec. dir., Villa Park, Ill., 1979—. Mem. Religious Pub. Relations Council, Chgo. Fund Raising Soc. Office: N Am Bapt Conf 1 S 210 Summit Ave Oakbrook Terrace Villa Park IL 60181

BINDER, LEONARD JAMES, magazine editor; b. Jackson, Mich., June 21, 1926; s. Leonard George and Ethel Cecile (Lilly) B.; m. Margery Elizabeth Rose, Sept. 6, 1950; children: Timothy James, Michael Paul, Douglas Harold. B.S., Central Mich. U., 1952. Editor Wingfoot Clan, Goodyear Tire & Rubber Co., 1952-54, Wayne (Mich.) Eagle, 1954-55; news editor Pontiac (Mich.) Press, 1955-57; editor, newsman AP, 1957-60; state editor Detroit News, 1960-67; editor-in-chief Army mag., Washington, 1967—; corr., book reviewer Nat. Observer, 1962-67; Bd. dirs. Central Mich. U. Devel. Fund. Contbr. articles to various publs. Served with USNR, 1944-46; with USAR, 1950-54. Recipient George Washington Honor medal Freedoms Found., 1975, George Washington award editorial, 1974, 76. Mem. Am. Soc. Mag. Editors, Assn. U.S. Army. Methodist. Clubs: Nat. Press, Detroit Press, Ends of Earth. Home: 304 Lewis St Vienna VA 22180 Office: 2425 Wilson Blvd Arlington VA 22201

BINDER, LUCY SIMPSON, utility exec.; b. Phila., May 12, 1937; d. James G. and C. Lucy (Underwood) Simpson; m. Robert A. Binder, Aug. 12, 1967. B.S. in Bus. Adminstrn, Drexel U., Phila., 1959. With Phila. Electric Co., 1959—, asst. corp. sec., 1977-78, sec., 1978—. Mem. Am. Soc. Corp. Secs. Address: Philadelphia Electric Company 2301 Market St Philadelphia PA 19101

BINDER, MICHAEL BERNARD, librarian; b. Bklyn., Mar. 19, 1943; s. Nathan and Lillian (Bier) B.; m. Nancy Ann Kessler, May 25, 1969; 1 dau., Amy Cheryl. B.A. in History (N.Y. State Regents scholar), N.Y. U., 1965; M.L.S., Rutgers U., 1967, U. Pitts., 1968; Ph.D. in Library and Info. Scis. (U.S. Higher Edn. Act Post Master's fellow), U. Pitts., 1973. Engring. librarian CCNY, 1967; librarian Def. Intelligence Agy., Arlington, Va., 1967; grad. asst. U. Pitts., 1967-68, teaching fellow, 1969-70; dir. library services Bradford campus, 1972-74; head librarian, dir. library sci. program, asst. prof. library sci. Clinch Valley Coll., U. Va., Wise, 1974-78; dir. library, assoc. prof. Fairleigh Dickinson U., Rutherford campus, 1978—; adj. prof. library/media services William Paterson Coll., N.J., 1978—; mem. library adv. com. State Council Higher Edn. for Va., 1974-78; mem. statewide planning com. N.J. State Library, 1979—; del. N.J. Gov.'s Conf. on Library and Info. Services, 1979; alt. White House Conf. on Library and Info. Services, 1979; mem. fin. com. Pa. Area Library Info. Network, 1979-80. Contbr. articles, revs. to profl. jours. Mem. ALA, Assn. Coll. and Research Libraries (pres. N.J. chpt. 1980-81), Am. Soc. Info. Sci. (pres. U. Pitts. chpt. 1968-69), N.J. Library Assn. (editor Directions, adminstrn. sect. 1978-79, mem. sect. exec. bd. 1979-80, pres. coll. and univ. sect. 1980-81, mem. library devel. com. 1979-80), Beta Phi Mu. Office: Messler Library Fairleigh Dickinson U Rutherford NJ 07070

BINDLEY, THOMAS LYNCH, manufacturing company executive; b. Terre Haute, Ind., Nov. 8, 1943; s. William F. and Gertrude L. Bindley B.; m. Kathleen Gleason; children: Aimee, Thomas, Ellen, Katherine. B.S., Georgetown U., 1965; M.B.A., Harvard U., 1969. Treas., chief fin. officer Pryor Corp., Chgo., 1969-77; dir. planning McGraw-Edison Co., Rolling Meadows, Ill., 1977-79, v.p., treas., 1979—. Served to 1st lt. AUS, 1965-67; Vietnam. Clubs: Economic; Harvard Bus. Sch. (Chgo.). Office: McGraw-Edison Co 1701 Golf Rd Rolling Meadows IL 60008

BINFORD, CHAPMAN HUNTER, physician; b. Darlington Heights, Va., Oct. 3, 1900; s. Charles F. and W. Ava (Chilton) B.; m. Thelma Lynette Beauchamp, June 8, 1929; children—Charles C., M. Lynette. A.B., Hampden-Sydney Coll., 1923, D.Sc. (hon.), 1962; M.D., Med. Coll. Va., 1929; D.Sc. (hon.), Va. Commonwealth U., 1979. Diplomate: Am. Bd. Pathology.; Registrar for leprosy Am. Registry Pathology, 1951-75. Commd. officer USPHS, 1930, advanced through grades to med. dir., 1948; cancer investigator Harvard Med. Sch., 1931-32; with Leprosy Research Inst., Honolulu, 1933-36; pathology investigations NIH, 1936-37; pathologist USPHS hosps., 1937-51; rep. USPHS at Armed Forces Inst. Pathology, Washington, 1951-60; ret., 1960; chief geog. pathology div. Armed Forces Inst. Pathology, 1960-62; med. dir. Leonard Wood Meml. (Am. Leprosy Found.), 1963-72; chief spl. mycobacterial diseases br. Armed Forces Inst. Pathology, 1963-74; expert com. leprosy WHO, 1964-77; chmn. U.S. coordinating com. Internat. Com. Socs. Pathology, 1966-69; Maude Abbott lectr. Internat. Acad. Pathology, 1973. Author: (with Emmons Utz and Kwon-Chung) Medical Mycology, 1977; also numerous articles; editor: (with Connor) The Pathology of Tropical and Extraordinary Diseases, 1976. Recipient F.K. Mostofi award Internat. Acad. Pathology, 1978; Damien Dutton award in Leprosy, 1970. Mem. Wash. Soc. Pathologists (pres. 1954-55), Coll. Am. Pathologists, AMA, Am. Assn. Pathologists, Am. Soc. Clin. Pathologists (Ward Burdick award 1968), Internat. Acad. Patholgoy (pres. 1958-59, rep. to internat. intersoc. com. pathology 1962-70, editor bull. 1960- 65), Internat. Leprosy Assn. (hon. v.p. 1973—), Am. Soc. Tropical Medicine and Hygiene, Sociètè Belge de Medecine Tropicale (asso.), Phi Beta Kappa, Sigma Xi, Alpha Omega Alpha. Club: Cosmos. Home: 6046 N 23d St Arlington VA 22205 Office: Armed Forces Inst Pathology Washington DC 20306

BINFORD, THOMAS ORIEL, computer scientist, educator; b. Jefferson Twp., Pa., Apr. 13, 1936; s. Robert J. and Ruth A. (Sandbach) B.; m. Ione Garginee Junqueira, Dec. 30, 1975. B.S., Pa. State U.; Ph.D., U. Wis. With M.I.T., Artificial Intelligence Lab., 1966-70; with Stanford (Calif.) U. Artificial Intelligence Lab., 1970—; prof. computer sci. (research). Assoc. editor: Robotics Research. Office: Computer Sci Dept Stanford U Stanford CA 94305

BING, R.H., educator, mathematician; b. Oakwood, Tex., Oct. 20, 1914; s. Rupert Henry and Lula May (Thompson) B.; m. Mary Blanche Hobbs, Aug. 26, 1938; children—Robert H., Susan Elizabeth, Virginia Gay, Mary Patricia. B.S., S.W. Tex. State Tchrs. Coll., 1935; M.Ed., U. Tex., 1938, Ph.D., 1945. Tchr. high sch., Tex., 1935-42; instr., then asst. prof. math. U. Tex., 1942-47; mem. faculty U. Wis.-Madison, 1947-73, prof. math., 1952-64, research prof., 1964-68, Rudolph E. Langer prof. math., 1968-73, chmn. dept., 1958-60; acting prof. U. Va., 1949-50; vis. prof. U. Tex., 1971-72, prof., 1973—, Ashbel Smith prof. math., 1979—, chmn. dept., 1975-77; dir. Summer Inst. on Set Theoretic Topology, Madison, 1955; mem. Inst. Advanced Study, Princeton, 1957-58, 62-63, 67. Mem. Nat. Sci. Bd. (1968-74, chmn. div. math.), Nat. Acad. Scis., NRC (1967-69), Conf. Bd. Math. Sci. (chmn. 1965-66), Nat. Acad. Scis. (chmn. math. sect. 1970-73, councilor 1977-80), Math. Assn. Am. (pres. 1963-64, vis. lectr. 1954-55, 61-62, chmn. Wis. sect. 1952), Am. Math. Soc. (councilor 1952-54, 58-60, v.p. 1967-68, pres. 1977-78), AAAS (v.p., chmn. sect. A 1959), Pi Mu Epsilon (vice dir. gen. 1960-63). Presbyn. (elder). Office: Dept Math U Tex Austin TX 78712

BING, ROBERT KENDALL, occupational therapist, educator; b. Cambridge, Nebr., Mar. 2, 1929; s. Kenneth Lionel and Ruth Helen (Thomas) B. B.S. in Occupational Therapy, U. Ill., 1952; M.A., U. Md., 1954, Ed.D., 1961. Asst. prof. occupational therapy Va. Commonwealth U., Richmond, 1954-56; dir. ind. therapy Norwich (Conn.) State Hosp., 1956-57; teaching fellow Inst. Child Study, U. Md., 1957-59; instr. psychology Towson (Md.) State U., 1959-60; asso. in psychiatry U. Nebr., Omaha, 1960-61; asst. prof. occupational therapy U. Fla., Gainesville, 1961-63; dir. activity therapy Ill. State Psychiat. Inst.; also asst. prof. U. Ill. Med. Center, Chgo., 1963-65; dir. occupational therapy Sch. Allied Health Scis., U. Tex. Med. Br., Galveston, 1965-66, planning dir., 1966-68, dean, 1968-80, prof. occupational therapy, 1980—; cons. in field. Served with AUS, 1951-53. Fellow Am. Occupational Therapy Assn. (chmn. hist. com. 1963-66, chmn. nat. conf. com. 1965, 69, 75-78, chmn. archives com. 1979—, Eleanor Clarke Slage lectr. 1981, pres. 1983—), Am. Soc. Allied Health Professions, Am. Sch. Health Assn., Tex. Occupational Therapy Assn. (pres. 1970-74, Occupational Therapist of Yr. award 1974), Tex. Hosp. Assn. Republican. Methodist. Office: Sch Allied Health Scis U Tex Med Br Galveston TX 77550

BING, ROLAND EDWARD, JR., jr. coll. pres.; b. Hempstead, Tex., Apr. 21, 1921; s. Roland Edward and Evelyn Ione (Winfree) B.; m. Amanda Josephine Watts, Aug. 21, 1951; children—Donald Wayne, Jerry Ray. B.S., Tex. A&M U., 1942, M.Ed., 1962; Ph.D., U. Tex., Austin, 1953. Mgr. student publs. Tex. A&M U., 1946-53; mem. staff and faculty Victoria (Tex.) Coll., 1954—, dean, 1964-75, pres., 1975—. Trustee DeTar Hosp., Victoria, 1979—. Served to capt. AUS, 1942-46. Decorated Legion of Merit. Mem. Assn. Higher Edn., Am. Personnel and Guidance Assn., Am. Vocat. Assn., Tex. Jr. Coll. Tchrs. Assn., Tex. Assn. Coll. Tchrs., Phi Kappa Phi, Phi Delta Kappa. Presbyterian. Club: Northside Rotary. Home: 1908 E Loma Vista St Victoria TX 77901 Office: 2200 E Red River St Victoria TX 77901

BING, SIR RUDOLF, ret. opera mgr., educator; b. Vienna, Austria, Jan. 9, 1902; naturalized, 1946; came to U.S., 1949; s. Ernest and Stefanie (Hoenigsvald) B.; m. Nina Schelemskaya, Dec. 7, 1929. Student schs. in, Vienna; Mus.D. (hon.), Lafayette Coll.; L.H.D., Temple U., Wagner Coll., Dickinson Coll., N.Y. U.; LL.D., Jacksonville U. Adj. prof. theatre mgmt. and prodn. N.Y. U., 1972—; vis. distinguished prof. music Bklyn. Coll., 1972—; dir. Columbia Artists Mgmt., 1974; lectr. on opera. Author: 5000 Nights at the Opera, 1972; Connected with operatic and concert agys. and opera houses, Germany, 1921-33; gen. mgr., Glyndebourne Festival, Eng., 1934-49; artistic dir., Edinburgh Internat. Festival, 1947-49; gen. mgr., Met. Opera Assn., N.Y.C., 1950-72. Decorated comdr. Order Brit. Empire, knight Order Brit. Empire; chevalier Legion of Honor, France; comdr.'s cross Order of Merit, Germany; Grand Silver medal Honor, Austria; grand officer Order Merit, Italy). Office: Columbia Artists Mgmt Inc 165 West 57th St New York City NY 10019

BINGAMAN, DAVID PAUL, research company executive; b. Danville, Pa., June 30, 1944; s. Adam Phillip and Alta Mildred (Kaufman) B.; m. Sandra I. Hayhurst, Aug. 17, 1968; children: Jennifer, Heather. A.B., Susquehanna U., 1968; M.B.A., Sacramento State U., 1971. Contract adminstr. Anchor Darling Industries, Williamsport, Pa., 1971-73; research adminstr. Lorillard Research Center, Lorillard div. Loew's Theatres, Inc., Greensboro, N.C., 1973-79; dir. personnel Bulova Watch Co. Inc.; subs. Loew's Corp., 1979-80; mgr. mktg. Fidelity Electric Co. Inc., Lancaster, Pa., 1980-82; sr. adminstr. advanced tech. systems AIL div. Eaton Corp., N.Y.C., 1983—. Mem. Soc. Research Adminstrs. Republican. Lutheran. Home: 446 Oak Ln Lititz PA 17543 Office: Walt Whitman Rd Melville NY 11747

BINGAMAN, JEFF, senator; b. Silver City, N.Mex., Oct. 3, 1943; s. Jesse and Beth (Ball) B.; m. Anne Kovacovich, Sept. 13, 1968. Ed., Harvard U., 1965; J.D., Stanford U., 1968. Bar: N.Mex. 1968. Partner firm Campbell, Bingaman & Black, Santa Fe, 1972-78; atty. gen. State of N.Mex., from 1979; now U.S. senator from N.Mex. Democrat. Methodist. Home: PO Box 5775 Santa Fe NM 87501 Office: 502 Hart Bldg Washington DC 20510

BINGEL, JOE, labor union official. Rep. Internat. Typog. Union; chapel sec. N.Y. Typog. Union, No. 6; also chapel chmn. and mem. exec. com.; conv. del. Internat. Typog. Union, Colorado Springs, Colo., second v.p., then first v.p., 1968-78, pres., 1978—. Served with U.S. Army. Mem. N.Y. Herald-Tribunes Horace Greeley Post, Am. Legion. Office: Internat Typographical Union PO Box 157 Colorado Springs CO 80901 *

BINGEMAN, JONAS BYRON, chem. co. exec.; b. South River, Ont., Can., Feb. 21, 1925; came to U.S., 1946, naturalized, 1955; s. Gordon Washington and Mary Edna (Dickson) B.; m. Agnes Kathleen Macdonald, Sept. 11, 1948; children—Grant William, Leslie Kathleen, John Macdonald, Claire Eileen. B.Sc. in Chem. Engring. (Dominion of Can. scholar), Queen's U., 1946; M.S. in Phys. Chemistry, U. Detroit, 1948, U. Minn., 1950, Ph.D., La. State U., 1957. From process engr., econ. analyst to supr. process design Ethyl Corp., Baton Rouge, 1950-60; mgr. process and project engring. Rexall Drug and Chem. Co., Los Angeles, 1960-65; with Allied Chem. Corp., Morristown, N.J., 1965-74, project mgr. fibers div. engring., 1965-66, asst. mgr. nylon heavy deniers plant, 1966-67, project dir. maj. plant expansion, 1967-68, v.p. tech., 1968-70, with corporate div., 1970-74, asst. to pres., 1970-71, dir. ops. corporate research and devel., 1971, dir. corp. research and devel., 1971-73, dir. spl. projects, 1973-74; dir. corp. engring. N.L. Industries, N.Y.C., 1974—. Contbr. articles to profl. jours. Mem. adv. council Va. Tech. Services; mem. Nat. Def. Exec. Res., U.S. Dept. Commerce. Served with Canadian Navy, 1944-46. Mem. Am. Assn. Engring. Socs. (industry rep.), Am. Inst. Chem. Engrs. (chmn. Tidewater sect. 1969, chmn. tech. symposia Los Angeles 1964, Tidewater 1968), Va. C. of C. (chmn. edn. com.). Clubs: Springdale Golf (Princeton, N.J.); Met.,

Can. (N.Y.C.). Patentee in field. Home: 1 Sayre Dr Princeton NJ 08540 Office: NL Industries 1230 Ave of Americas New York NY 10006

BINGER, EUGENE THOMAS, business investment executive; b. St. Paul, Jan. 3, 1923; s. Henry Ernest and Vida (DeBar) B.; m. Gail Cohoe, Dec. 23, 1950; children: Christine, Thomas. A.B., Harvard U., 1947; LL.B., U. Minn., 1950. Bar: Minn. 1950. Practiced in, Hibbing, 1950-55; sec., gen. counsel Pacific Isle Co., Hibbing, 1955-60; pres. Pitts. Pacific Co., Mpls., 1953-63, chmn. bd., 1963—; pres., dir. First Grant Corp., Cleve., 1963-69; chmn., dir. Am. Flyers Airline Corp., Ft. Worth and; Ardmore, Okla.; v.p. fin., treas. Bemis Co., Inc., Mpls., 1969-71, dir., MTS Systems Corp., Mpls., Wheeling-Pitts. Steel Corp.; Bd. dirs. Pitts. Pacific Found. Served to ensign USNR, 1943-45. Home: 2401 Meeting St Wayzata MN 55391 Office: Suite 420 2850 Metro Dr Bloomington MN 55420

BINGER, WILSON VALENTINE, civil engineer; b. Greenwich, N.Y., Feb. 28, 1917; s. George and Blanche (Wilson) B.; m. Barbara Ridgway, May 19, 1947; children—Wilson Valentine, Mary Blanche, Julia Ridgway. A.B. cum laude, Harvard, 1938, M.S. in Engring, 1939. Registered profl. engr., N.Y., Ohio. Soils engr. U.S. Army Engrs., Wilmington, Del., 1939-40; soils and found. engr. Gatun 3d Locks project, Panama Canal, 1940-43; soils engr., resident engr. Parsons Brinckerhoff, Hogan & MacDonald, Caracas, Venezuela, 1945-46, chief soils engr., Buenos Aires, Argentina, 1948-49; chief soils and found. sect. Isthmian Canal Studies, Panama Canal, 1946-47; chief soils br. Mo. River div. U.S. Army Engrs., Omaha, 1947-48; v.p. Porterfield-Binger Constrn. Co., Youngstown, Ohio, 1950-52; regional mgr. Tippetts-Abbett-McCarthy-Stratton, Bogota, Colombia, 1952-56, asso. partner, N.Y.C., 1957-61, partner, 1962—, chmn., 1975—. Author papers in field. Pres., trustee Chappaqua (N.Y.) Library, 1967-69; trustee Robert Coll., Istanbul, Turkey, 1970—, vice chmn., 1974-78. Served to 2d lt. C.E. AUS, 1943-45. Recipient; Distinguished Citizen award Warren (Ohio) Met. Area Assn. Fellow ASCE, Inst. Civil Engrs. (Eng.), Am. Cons. Engrs. Council (v.p. 1973-75); mem. Nat. Acad. Engring., Am. Inst. Cons. Engrs. (councillor 1971-73, pres. 1973), Nat. Soc. Profl. Engrs., Harvard Engring. Soc., U.S. Com. Large Dams (exec. com. 1964-69, sec. 1962-78), Internat. Com. Large Dams (v.p. 1978-81), N.Y. Assn. Cons. Engrs. (v.p., dir. 1964-65), Moles, Internat. Road Fedn. (dir. 1975-82, exec. com. 1975-82), Fedn. Internationale des Ingenieurs Conseils (exec. com. 1976-83, treas. 1976-79, v.p. 1980-81, pres. 1981-83). Congregationalist (chmn. bd. deacons 1960-65). Clubs: Century, Harvard, Univ. (N.Y.C.); St. Stephen's (London). Home: 287 Quaker St Chappaqua NY 10514 Office: 655 3d Ave New York NY 10017

BINGHAM, BARRY, editor; b. Louisville, Feb. 10, 1906; s. Robert Worth and Eleanor (Miller) B.; m. Mary Clifford Caperton, June 9, 1931; children: Worth (dec.), Barry, Sarah, Jonathan (dec.), Eleanor (Mrs. Rowland Miller). Student, Middlesex Sch., Concord, Mass., 1921-23; A.B. magna cum laude, Harvard U., 1928; LL.D., U. Ky., Kenyon Coll., Bellarmine Coll., Ind. U., Spalding Coll., Edgecliff Coll.; Litt.D., U. Louisville, U. Cin., Centre Coll., Alfred U., Berea Coll. With Courier-Jour. and; Louisville Times Co., 1930—, editor, pub., 1945-71, chmn. bd., 1971—; chmn. bd. WHAS, Inc., Standard Gravure Corp. Trustee Berea Coll., 1938-76; trustee Nat. Portrait Gallery; bd. overseers Harvard U.; dir. Asia Found.; chmn. Internat. Press Inst., 1964-66; hon. life mem. Chief of mission to France, ECA, 1949-50; Nat. chmn. Vols. for Stevenson-Kefauver, 1956. Served to comdr. USNR, 1941-45. Decorated comdr. Order Brit. Empire; comdr. Legion of Honor; recipient Sullivan award U. Ky.; William Allen White Journalism award U. Kans.; Roger W. Straus award NCCJ. Mem. English-Speaking Union U.S. (chmn. bd. trustees 1974-77). Democrat. Episcopalian. Clubs: River Valley, Wynn-Stay, Louisville Country, Jefferson (Louisville); Century Assn. Home: Glenview KY 40025 Office: Courier-Journal and Times Louisville KY 40202

BINGHAM, CHARLES TIFFANY, JR., assn. exec.; b. Hartford, Conn., June 19, 1933; s. Charles Tiffany and Kathleen Watson (Howell) B.; m. Alice Berry Condon, June 28, 1958 (div. 1978); children—Eleanor Berry, Grace Bradlee, Charles Tiffany III. B.A., Yale U., 1956. With Am. Snuff Co. (now Conwood Corp.), Memphis, 1960-78, regional sales mgr., 1967-70, asst. v.p., 1971-73, v.p. internat., 1973-78; exec. v.p. Memphis C. of C., 1979—; dir. Conwood Corp., Data Communications Corp. Chmn. Regional Export Council, 1974-75, State of Tenn.-Japan S.E. Council, 1975, Tenn. Gov.'s Jobs Conf., 1979, Tenn. Film Commn., 1981, Memphis Pvt. Industry Council, 1980—. Served to capt. USMC, 1956-60. Mem. Nat. Assn. Tobacco Mfrs., Nat. Chamber Execs., Nat. Indsl. Conf. Bd. Episcopalian. Home: 1876 Vinton Ave Memphis TN 38104 Office: Memphis C of C PO Box 224 Memphis TN 38101

BINGHAM, EULA, university dean; b. Covington, Ky., July 9, 1929. B.S., Eastern Ky. U.; M.S., U. Cin., 1952, Ph.D., 1958. Analytical chemist, Cin., 1951-61; asst. prof. Sch. Medicine, U. Cin., 1961-70, assoc. prof., 1970-77, prof. environ. health, 1981—, v.p., 1981—, univ. dean for grad. studies and research, 1981—; asst. sec. for occupational safety and health Dept. Labor, Washington, 1977-81; mem. study sect. safety and occupational health Nat. Inst. Occupational Safety and Health, 1972-76; mem. Food and Drug Adv. Commn., FDA, Environ. Health Adv. Commn.; sci. adv. bd. EPA, 1976—; mem. Nat. Air Quality Criteria Adv. Commn., 1975-76; mem. ad hoc Lead in Paint Commn., Nat. Acad. Scis., 1974-75; chmn. standards Adv. Commn. on Coke Oven Emissions, Dept. Labor, 1974-75. Adv. Commn. on Carcinogens, 1973—. Office: University of Cincinnati Cincinnati OH 45221 *

BINGHAM, GEORGE BARRY, JR., publishing and broadcasting executive; b. Louisville, Sept. 23, 1933; s. George Barry and Mary Clifford (Caperton) B.; m. Edith Wharton Stenhouse, Nov. 30, 1963; children: Emily Simms, Mary Caperton; adopted children: Philip John, Charles Wharton. A.B., Harvard U., 1956. Mgmt. trainee CBS, N.Y.C., 1958-59; researcher, field producer documentaries NBC, N.Y.C. and; Washington, 1959-62; with Courier-Jour. and; Louisville Times, Standard Gravure Corp., WHAS, Inc., Louisville, 1962—; now editor, pub. Courier-Jour. and; Louisville Times; vice chmn. bd. WHAS, Inc.; Active Actors Theatre Louisville, Greater Louisville Fund for Arts; bd. dirs. Nat. Advt. Bur., Louisville; Orch., Berea Coll., African Wildlife Leadership Found., Isaac W. Bernheim Found. Served to capt. USMC, 1956-58. Clubs: Harvard (N.Y.C.); Louisville Country, River Valley. Home: 4309 Glenview Ave Glenview KY 40025 Office: Louisville Courier Jour 525 W Broadway Louisville KY 40202

BINGHAM, JONATHAN BREWSTER, former congressman, lawyer; b. New Haven, Apr. 24, 1914; s. Hiram and Alfreda (Mitchell) B.; m. June Rossbach, Sept. 20, 1939; children: Sherrell Bingham Downes, June Mitchell Bingham Esselstyn, Timothy Woodbridge, Claudia Rossbach (now Gurunam Bhajan Kaur Khalsa). B.A., Yale U., 1936, J.D., 1939. Bar: N.Y. 1940. Practiced in N.Y.C., 1939-41, 46-51, 53-54, 59-61, 81—; with O.P.A., 1941-42; chief Alien Enemy Control Sect., Dept. State, 1945-46, asst. dir. Office Internat. Security Affairs, 1951; dep. adminstr. Tech. Coop. (Point Four), 1951-53; mem. firm Goldwater & Flynn, 1959-61; sec. to gov. N.Y. State, 1955-58; U.S. rep. in UN Trusteeship Council, 1961-62, pres., 1962; prin. adviser to U.S. ambassador to UN on colonial and trusteeship questions, 1961-62; U.S. rep. with rank ambassador UNECOSOC, 1962-63; also alt. rep. 15th-18th Gen. Assemblies; mem. U.S. mission UN, 1961-64, 89th-92d congresses from 23d Dist. N.Y., 93d-97th congresses from 22d Dist. N.Y.; mem. fgn. affairs and interior and insular affairs com., chmn. subcom. on internat. econ. policy and trade, spl. counsel Pryor, Cashman, Sherman & Flynn, N.Y.C., 1983—; lectr. Columbia U. Sch. Law. Author: Shirt Sleeve Diplomacy-Point 4 in Action, 1954, (with Alfred M. Bingham) Violence and Democracy, 1970; also articles. Bd. dirs. People for Am. Way, UN Devel. Corp., Inst. Internat. Edn., U.S. Com. UNICEF, Population Crisis Com.; co-chmn. FDR Four Freedoms Found.; pres. Bronx County Soc. Mental Health, 1960-62; mem., past pres. Bronx Boys' Club; trustee 20th Century Fund. Served to capt. AUS, 1943-45. Yale Corp. fellow, 1949-51; recipient Staff citation War Dept., 1945. Mem. Bronx County Bar Assn., Assn. Bar City N.Y., Council Fgn. Relations N.Y.C. Club: Century Assn. (N.Y.C.). Home: 5000 Independence Ave Bronx NY 10471 Office: 410 Park Ave New York NY 10022

BINGHAM, MARY CAPERTON (MRS. BARRY BINGHAM), civic worker; b. Richmond, Va., Dec. 24, 1904; d. Clifford R. and Helena (Lefroy) Caperton; m. Barry Bingham, June 9, 1931; children: Robert W. (dec.), G. Barry, Sarah M. Bingham Iovenico, Jonathan W. (dec.), Eleanor M. B.A., Radcliffe Coll., 1928; postgrad. (Charles Eliot Norton fellow), Am. Sch. Classical Studies, Athens, 1929; D.Litt., U. Louisville, 1954. Dir. Courier-Jour.; Vice pres., dir. Louisville Times, WHAS, Inc., 1942—; editor World of Books column Louisville Courier Jour., 1943-67; v.p. Louisville Courier-Jour. Times, 1942—. Bd. dirs. Council Basic Edn., Washington; trustee Radcliffe Coll., 1942-60; mem. vis. com. Harvard Arnold Arboretum, 1980—; mem. Ky. Environ. Commn., 1982—. Mem. Colonial Dames. Clubs: River Valley, Louisville Country (Louisville); Cosmopolitan (N.Y.C.); Glenview Garden. Home: Glenview KY 40025

BINGHAM, WALTER D., clergyman; b. Memphis, June 3, 1921; s. Willie and Lena (Allen) B.; m. Rebecca T. Bingham; stepdau., Gail Elaine Bingham. B.A., Talladega (Ala.) Coll., 1945; M.Div., Howard U., 1948, postgrad., 1948-49; D.D., Christian Theol. Sem., Indpls., 1969; L.H.D., Drury Coll., Springfield, Mo., 1972; LL.D., Translyvania U., Lexington, Ky., 1973. Ordained to ministry Disciples of Christ Ch., 1947; campus minister, instr. religion Jarvis Christian Coll., Hawkins, Tex., 1949-57; minister Pine St. Christian Ch., Tulsa, 1957-61, 3d Christian Ch., Louisville, 1961—; v.p. Christian Ch. Commn. Jefferson County, Ky., 1965-66, pres., 1978-81; mem. gen. bd. Christian Ch. (Disciples of Christ), 1979—, chair council on Christian unity, 1982—; pres. Christian Ch. Ky., 1966-67; moderator Disciples of Christ Ch., U.S. and Can., 1971-73; mem. gov. bd. Nat. Council Ch., 1969-73; Christian Ch. del. Consultation on Ch. Union, 1968-79; mem. nat. steering com. on covenant Christian Ch. (Disciples of Christ)-United Ch. of Christ, 1982—; fraternal visitor for Christian Ch. to Japan, Hong Kong, Thailand, India, 1972; del. 5th Assembly, World Council Chs., Nairobi, Kenya, 1975, 6th Assembly, World Council Chs., Vancouver, B.C., Can., 1983. Mem. Louisville and Jefferson Air Bd. Citizens Com., 1971-74; bd. dirs. Vols. Am., 1965-71; trustee Jarvis Christian Coll., 1971-75, Lexington Theol. Sem., 1969—. Named Ky. Col., 1967; recipient Outstanding Community Leadership award Phi Beta Sigma, 1969; named Pastor of Year Sta. WLOU, 1970, Distinguished Citizen Louisville, 1971. Mem. NAACP, Urban League, Omega Psi Phi. Home: Ky Towers Apt 904 Louisville KY 40202 Office: 3900 W Broadway Louisville KY 40211

BINGHAM, WOODBRIDGE, history educator emeritus; b. Cambridge, Mass., Nov. 24, 1901; s. Hiram and Alfreda (Mitchell) B.; m. Ursula W. Griswold, June 28, 1928; children: Anne Bingham Wright, Clarissa Bingham Junge, Evelyn Bingham Goodman, Marian Bingham Hubbell. A.B., Yale U., 1924; A.M., Harvard U., 1929; Ph.D., U. Calif., 1934. Instr., Yale-in-China, Chang-sha, China, 1924-25; instr. Far Eastern history U. Calif., 1937-40, asst. prof., 1940-46, assoc. prof., 1946-52, prof., 1952-69, prof. emeritus, 1969—, dir. Inst. East Asiatic Studies, 1949-57; vis. prof. Centre of Asian studies, U. Hong Kong, 1970-71. Author: The Founding of the T'ang Dynasty: The Fall of Sui and Rise of T'ang, 1941, (with Hilary Conroy, Frank W. Iklé) History of Asia, vol. I: Formation of Civilizations from Antiquity to 1600, 1964, rev. edit., 1974, vol. II, Old Empires, Western Penetration and the Rise of New Nations, since 1600, 1965, rev. edit., 1974. Served as lt. USNR, 1943-45. Mem. Nat. Com. U.S.-China Relations., Assn. Asian Studies, Am. Hist. Assn., Am. Oriental Soc., Psi Upsilon. Club: University (San Francisco). Home: 4 Greenwood Common Berkeley CA 94708

BINHAMMER, ROBERT JOHN HERMAN, clergyman; b. Normanby Twp., Ont., Can., Dec. 25, 1931; s. Herbert Karl and Marianne (Ratzel) B.; m. Beverly Joan Gibson, Oct. 4, 1958; children: Kristine Patricia, Katherine Elizabeth. B.A., U. Western Ont., 1953; grad., Waterloo Luth., 1953-56; D.D., Wilfrid Laurier U., 1975. Ordained to ministry Luth. Ch., 1956. Pastor St. Luke's Luth. Ch., Ridgewat, Ont., 1956-60, St. Matthew's Luth. Ch., Brantford, Ont., 1960-67, St. Philips Luth. Ch., Islington, Ont., 1967—; pres. Can. sect. Luth. Ch. Am., Weston, Ont., 1981—; mem. exec. bd. Eastern Can. Synod, Kitchener, Ont., 1968-74; dean Central Dist. Eastern Can. Synod, Toronto, Ont., 1977-82; mem. bd. Can. Council Chs., Toronto, 1981—; del. World Council Chs. 6th Assembly, Vancouver, B.C., Can., 1983; bd. govs., chmn. Waterloo Luth. U., 1964-75; bd. govs. Waterloo Luth. Sem., 1979-81; mem. exec. com. Luth. Ch. Am., 1979-81, Luth. Council Can., 1981—, Can. Luth. World Relief, 1981—, Nat. Com. Luth. World Fedn., 1981—; mem. Can. Luth. Merger Commn., 1981—; mem. gen. bd. Can. Council Chs., del. Triennial Assembly, 1982; Luth. del. Inter-Ch. Com., 1981. Bd. dirs. Brantford Family Service Bur., 1964-69; mem. Brantford Red Feather Appeal, 1966-68. Home: 68 Brampton Rd Weston ON Canada M9R 3J7 Office: Luth Ch in America Can Sect 61 W Deane Park Dr Islington ON Canada M9B 2S1

BININGER, CLEM EDWARD, clergyman; b. Frankfort, Ky., Feb. 28, 1910; s. Clem Edward, Sr. and Myrtle Ellen (Wyman) B.; m. Carolyn Blanton Merrell, June 1, 1932; children: Barbara Ann (Mrs. James Richard Hyatt), Carol Elaine (Mrs. James Robert Tillman), Robert Merrell. A.B., Centre Coll. of Ky., 1931, D.D., 1945; A.M., Princeton U., 1934, M.Div., 1934; Th.M., Princeton Sem., 1935; D.D., Waynesburg Coll., 1945; L.H.D., Miami U., Oxford, Ohio, 1960. Student asst. First Presbyn. Ch., Rockaway, N.J., 1932-34; ordained to ministry Presbyn. Ch. in, U.S.A., 1934; stated supply Pierce Meml. Presbyn. Ch., Farmingdale, N.J., 1934-35; pastor Cleveland Heights Ch. (now Forest Hills Presbyn. Ch.), Cleve., 1935-43, Second Presbyn. Ch. of Wilkinsburg, Pitts., 1943-48, Grace Covenant Presbyn. Ch., Richmond, Va., 1948-51, Second Presbyn. Ch., Kansas City, Mo., 1951-57, 1st Presbyn. Ch. Second Presbyn. Ch., Ft. Lauderdale, Fla., 1957-82; interim preacher 1st United Presbyn. Ch., Pompano Beach, Fla., 1982-83; preaching faculty Dubuque U. Extension Dept., 1953. Author: Shepherd Who Stayed with the Sheep, 1950, Seven Last Words of Christ, 1969, also numerous pub. sermons, 1957—; broadcaster cassette tape series Power for Our Problems, 1972, Beliefs That Matter, 1973, Learning How to Pray, 1974, Facing Up to Ourselves, 1975. Participant worldwide broadcast in behalf displaced persons Hollywood Radio City, 1949; guest Faith of Our Children Telecast NBC, 1955; Council Chs. weekly telecast Religion Views the News, NBC; radio and TV chmn. Kansas City Presbytery and Greater Kansas City Council Chs.; moderator Kansas City Presbytery, 1957, South Fla. Presbytery, 1969; North Am. del. World Presbyn. Alliance, 1957-60; trustee Synod of South, 1972—; mem. bd. pensions United Presbyn. Ch., U.S.A., 1967-73; Founder Ft. Lauderdale Oral Sch. for Deaf Children, 1958; mem. Govt. Restudy Commn. Broward County, Fla., 1972; bd. dirs. ARC, United Fund Broward County; trustee Princeton Theol. Sem., Broward Community Coll., Ft. Lauderdale, Park Coll., Johnson C. Smith U., Charlotte, N.C.; founding trustee, vice chmn. bd. Eckerd Coll., St. Petersburg, Fla.; overseer Missouri Valley Coll., Centre Coll.; bd. assos. Westminster Coll. (Mo.); adv. com. dirs. Lindenwood Coll.; chmn. bd. Westminster Found., Presbyn. Student Center, U. Mo. Named one of 25 men of Quarter Century, to Silver Anniversary All-America coll. football team Sports Illustrated mag., 1956; recipient Disting. Am. award Nat. Football Found. Hall of Fame, 1980; Disting. Alumni award Centre Coll. Ky., 1981; Paul Harris fellow Rotary Club, Ft. Lauderdale, 1983. Mem. NFL Alumni (conv. chaplain 1978-79, chaplain 1978—), Ye Round Table, Phi Beta Kappa, Omicron Delta Kappa (1st grad. scholar 1932), Phi Delta Theta (province pres., mem. internat. gen. council, internat. pres. 1960-62). Clubs: Rotary (Ft. Lauderdale) (pres.); Ft. Lauderdale Yacht.). Home: 2456 NE 26th Ave Fort Lauderdale FL 33305 Office: 1st Presbyn Ch 401 SE 15 Ave at Tarpon Bend Fort Lauderdale FL 33301 *I have never accomplished anything without the help of a host of friends, and so accept with enthusiasm the open motto of my fraternity, Phi Delta Theta, which is "One Man is No Man". . . or "We enjoy life by the help and society of others."*

BINION, RUDOLPH, educator, historian; b. N.Y.C., Jan. 18, 1927; s. Stephan Rudolph and May (Bunimowitz) B.; m. Alice Lemée Binion, Aug. 30, 1952. B.A., Columbia, 1945; diplôme, Inst. d'Etudes Politiques, Paris, 1949; Ph.D., Columbia U., 1958. Statis. asst. UNESCO, Paris, 1950-53; instr. Rutgers U., 1955-56, Mass. Inst. Tech., 1956-59; asst. prof., then asso. prof. Columbia U., 1959-67; Leff prof. history Brandeis U., Waltham, Mass., 1967—. Author: Defeated Leaders, 1960, Frau Lou, 1968, Hitler among the Germans, 1976, Soundings, 1981, Introduction à la psychohistoire, 1982. Served with AUS, 1945-46. Recipient Clarke F. Ansley award Columbia U., 1958; George Louis Beer prize Am. Hist. Assn., 1960; Collège de France medal, 1980. Home: PO Box 40 Humarock MA 02047 Office: Brandeis Univ Waltham MA 02254

BINION, WILLIE CLAYTE, JR., newspaper editor; b. Houston, June 7, 1912; s. Willie Clayte and Mattie (Sayers) B.; m. Sara Dell Newsom, Mar. 28, 1937; children: Clayte III, Jack Russell, Emma Lee (Mrs. David V. Wilson), Tommy Sayers. Student, Southwestern U., Georgetown, Tex., 1929-31, Stephen F. Austin Coll., Nacogdoches, Tex., 1931-32, U. Tex., 1932-35. With Lufkin (Tex.) Daily News, 1937-42, 45-48, mng. editor, 1942, 47-48; mem. pub. relations dept. Jefferson Amusement Co., Beaumont, Tex., 1942-43; with sports copy desk Beaumont Enterprise, 1948-49; with Houston Chronicle, 1949—, mng. editor, 1965-71, exec. editor, 1971-77, dir., 1971—; vis. lectr. dept. communications Stephen F. Austin U., 1978—; Mem. journalism jury Pulitzer Prize, 1969, 70; Mem. newspapers editors com. U. Tex. Served with USMCR, 1944-46; PTO. Mem. Nat., Tex. (pres. 1971), UPI editors assns., Nat., Tex. AP (pres. 1969) mng. editors assns), SAR, Sons Republic of Tex., Kappa Sigma, Sigma Delta Chi. Methodist. Clubs: Houston Press; Crown Colony Country (Lufkin). Home: 212 Trailwood Circle Lufkin TX 75901

BINKERD, GORDON WARE, composer; b. Lynch, Nebr., May 22, 1916; s. Archie Abijah and Verna Blanche (Jones) B.; m. Frances Patricia Walker, Sept. 11, 1942. Mus.B., S.D. Wesleyan U., 1937; Mus.M., U. Rochester, 1941; M.A., Harvard U., 1952. Prof. music faculty U. Ill., 1949-71, Ctr. for Advanced Studies asso. mem., 1963. Composer: keyboard music The Young Pianist, Entertainments for Piano, Concert Set for Piano, Piano Miscellany, 5 Pieces for Piano, Essays for the Piano, Suite for Piano, 4 Sonatas for Piano, Concert Set for Piano transcribed for organ, Organ Service, The Temple—7 Meditations for the Organ on Poems of G. Herbert; several individual pieces for organ; chamber music 2 String Quartets, Trio for 3 Strings, Trio for Clarinet, Viola & Cello, Duo for Flute & Oboe, Sonatina for Flute & Piano, Sonata for Cello & Piano, (commd. by Library of Congress) Sonata for Violin & Piano, Portrait Intérieur for Mezzo-soprano, Violin & Cello (based on poems of R. Rilke), 3 Songs for Mezzo-soprano & String Quartet (based on poems of A. Crapsey and R. Herrick), Secret-Love for Mezzo-soprano, Cello & Harp (based on poem of J. Dryden); vocal music 4 Songs for High Soprano (poems of Garrigue, Dickinson, Deutsch and Very), Shut Out that Moon for Soprano (poems of T. Hardy), Heart Songs for Tenor (poems of R. Burns), 3 Songs from the Temple for medium voice (poems of G. Herbert); 18 individual songs; choral music Sung under the Silver Umbrella, 6 pieces for treble voices with piano accompaniment (poems by G. Chesterton, W. Blake, J. Stephens, after Beranger, T. Moore), A Scotch Mist, 3 settings of Burns' poems for mens' chorus, Choral Strands, 4 choruses for mixed voices (texts by R. Shackelford, A. Tennyson and S. Freud), 3 Institutional Canons for mixed voices (texts from pub. bldgs.), To Electra—9 choruses for mixed voices (poetry of R. Herrick), 3 Slumber Songs for mixed voices (folk songs), (commd. by Appleton (Wis.) High Sch. choir) Song of Songs, for double chorus and obbligato horn on a Text by W. Owen, (commd. by Ill. Wesleyan U. choir) Eternitie, for mixed voices on a poem of R. Herrick, (commd. by All Saints Ch., Brookline, Mass.) Remember Now Thy Creator, (commd. by Ford Found. for Mid-Am. Chorale, Des Moines) Aspects of Jesus for mixed voices on poetry of R. Herrick and H. Vaughan; also 100 individual choruses for various groupings, largely unaccompanied; music for large instrumental ensembles The Battle for brass and percussion. Served with USNR, 1942-45. Guggenheim fellow, 1959; recipient award Nat. Inst. Arts and Letters, 1964; prize for Symphony 1 from Chgo. Symphony. Mem. ASCAP. Home: Three Acres Rural Route 2 1705 Highcross Rd Urbana IL 61801 Office: Boosey & Hawkes Inc 24 W 57th St New York NY 10019

BINKERT, ALVIN JOHN, hosp. exec.; b. Ft. Atkinson, Wis., Oct. 20, 1910; s. John and Clara (Burrow) B.; m. Lucile Latton, June 4, 1939; children—Barbara L., Cynthia R. Binkert Elias. B.A., U. Wis., 1931. With Haskins & Sells (C.P.A.'s), N.Y.C., 1931-41; comptroller Presbyn. Hosp., N.Y.C., 1941-48, asst. v.p., 1948-54, v.p., gen. mgr., 1954-57, exec. v.p., 1957-70, pres., 1970—, vice chmn. bd., 1975—, also trustee; trustee Sr. Med. Cons.'s, N.Y.C.; lectr. pub. health, adminstrv. medicine Columbia U., 1954—. Trustee Presbyn. Hosp. Mem. Greater N.Y. Hosp. Assn. (past pres., bd. govs.), Hosp. Assn. N.Y. State (past pres., trustee, del.), Am. Coll. Hosp. Adminstrs. Clubs: Scarsdale (N.Y.); Golf; Univ. (N.Y.C.); Key Biscayne (Fla.) Yacht. Home: 681 Harbor Ln Key Biscayne FL 33149 Office: 622 W 168th St New York City NY 10032

BINKLEY, LUTHER JOHN, educator; b. Wernersville, Pa., Oct. 7, 1925; s. Harry Garfield and Jennie Theresa (Yoder) B.; m. Betty Jane Bowman, June 5, 1964. A.B., Franklin and Marshall Coll., 1945; B.D., Lancaster Theol. Sem., 1947; Ph.D., Harvard, 1950. Instr. philosophy Franklin and Marshall Coll., 1949-51; asst. prof., 1951-56, asso. prof., 1956-62, prof. philosophy, 1962—, chmn. dept. philosophy, 1962-74, dir. humanities program, 1972-74; ordained to ministry Evang. and Ref. Ch., 1949; vis. fellow Cambridge U., 1959-60, Princeton, 1967, 69; tchr. grad. courses Lancaster Theol. Sem., 1963-64, 67-68, Temple U., 1965—, Pa. State U., 1975—. Author: The Mercersburg Theology, 1953, Contemporary Ethical Theories, 1961, Conflict of Ideals; Changing Values in Western Society, 1969. Recipient Lindback

Found. award for distinguished coll. teaching, 1962. Mem. AAUP (pres. chpt. 1962-63), Am. Philos. Assn., Am. Soc. Aesthetics, Inst. of Soc., Ethics and Life Scis., Metaphys. Soc., Soc. Sci. Study Religion, Philosophic Soc. for Study of Sport (pres. 1977-78, Soc. for Health and Human Values), Public Com. for Humanities in Pa., Phi Beta Kappa (pres. Theta chpt. of Pa. 1970-71), Delta Sigma Phi, Pi Gamma Mu. Clubs: Hershey Country, Hershey Racquet, Lancaster Torch (pres. 1956-57); Fullerton (Bryn Mawr, Pa.)). Home: PO Box 150 Hershey PA 17033 Office: Franklin and Marshall Coll Box 3003 Lancaster PA 17604

BINKLEY, MAX ARTHUR, university administrator; b. Dayton, Ohio, May 29, 1920; s. Arnold G. and Ruth (Hart) B.; m. Lois A. Akerstrom, Feb. 23, 1946; children: David, Janice, Sara. B.S., Miami U., Oxford, Ohio, 1942; M.S., U. Ill., 1947, Ph.D., 1953. Instr. Miami U., 1945-46, U. Ill., 1946-50; auditor ECA, W.Ger., 1950-52; staff accountant C F & I Steel Corp., Pueblo, 1953-61, div. controller, 1962-65, controller, Denver, 1965-67; v.p. fin. Colo. State U., Ft. Collins, 1968—. Chmn. budget com. Pueblo Single Fund, 1960-65; mem. bus.-alumni adv. council U. Colo., 1966-67; bd. dirs. Ft. Collins United Way, 1970-75, chmn. budget com., 1972-75. Served with USAAF, 1942-45. Mem. Nat. Assn. Coll. and Univ. Bus. Officers (com. on govtl. relations 1972-78, chmn. subcom. on govt. costing policies 1976-78, editor Audit Info. Exchange 1974-78, costing standards com. 1974-76), Audit Info. Exchange (Neal O. Hines Publs. award 1979). Home: 2618 Shadow Ct Fort Collins CO 80525 Office: Colo State U Fort Collins CO 80523

BINKLEY, OLIN TRIVETTE, clergyman, sem. pres. emeritus; b. Harmony, N.C., Aug. 4, 1908; s. Joseph and Minnie (Trivette) B.; m. Pauline Eichmann, Aug. 24, 1933; children—Pauline Edith, Janet Margaret. A.B. magna cum laude, Wake Forest Coll., 1928; Th.B., So. Baptist Theol. Sem., 1930; D.D., Wake Forest (N.C.) Coll., 1951, U.N.C., 1964; B.D., Yale, 1931, Ph.D., 1933; D.Humanities, Campbell Coll., 1973. Ordained to ministry Bapt. Ch., 1928; asso. pastor Calvary Bapt. Ch., New Haven, 1931-33; pastor Chapel Hill (N.C.) Bapt. Ch., 1933-38; lectr. sociology U. N.C., 1937-38; head dept. religion Wake Forest Coll., 1938-44; asso. prof., acting head dept. ethics and sociology So. Bapt. Theol. Sem., 1944-46, prof., head dept., 1946-52; prof. Christian sociology and ethics Southeastern Bapt. Theol. Sem., 1952—, dean, 1958-63, pres., 1963-74, pres. emeritus, 1974—; vis. fellow Yale Divinity Sch., New Haven, 1951; Dir. Central Carolina Bank.; Pres. N.C. Com. Social Service, 1957-58, recipient Social Service award, 1967; Pres. bd. mgrs. Louisville Children's Agy., 1948-50; trustee Ministry Studies Bd., Children's Homes Soc. N.C., Bapt. Children's Homes N.C., Keesee Ednl. Fund, Davis Hosp. Author: Frontiers for Christian Youth, 1942, From Victory Unto Victory, 1945, The Churches and the Social Conscience, 1948, How to Study the Bible, 1969. Mem. Am. Assn. Theol. Schs. (pres.; commn. research and counsel), Am. Sociol. Soc., So Bapt. Conv. (Christian life and social service commns.), Phi Beta Kappa. Clubs: Rotarian (past pres.), Louisville Torch.). Home: 415 Durham Rd PO Box 311 Wake Forest NC 27587

BINNING, LARRY KEITH, horticulture educator; b. Fond du Lac, Wis., Aug. 29, 1942; s. Keith Wallace and Alice W. (Reschke) B.; m. Dorothy Irene Fisher, Sept. 5, 1964; children: Kimberly Ann, Heather Lyn. B.S., U. Wis., 1965; M.S., Mich. State U., 1967, Ph.D., 1969. Laborer dairy farm, Oakfield, Wis., 1942-64; laborer constrn. Scharschmidt Constrn., Oakfield, 1960-65; asst. prof. horticulture U. Wis., Madison, 1969-73, assoc. prof., 1973-78, prof., 1978—. Mem. Weed Sci. Soc. Am., North Central Weed Control Conf. Office: Dept Horticulture U Wis 1575 Linden Dr Madison WI 53706

BINNION, JOHN EDWARD, emeritus educator; b. Paris, Tex., July 14, 1918; s. Roy Cecil and Johnnie Mary (Garner) B.; m. Doris Lee Campbell, Mar. 30, 1945; children: Margaret Anne, John Edward, Mary Virginia, Dianna Lee. A.A., Chaffey Coll., Ontario, Calif., 1936; B.B.A., U. Tex., 1945; M.A., N.Mex. Highlands U., 1951; Ed.D., Okla. State U., 1953; M.B.A., U. Denver, 1972. C.P.A., Okla., Tex.; cert. adminstrv. mgr. Acct. D&B Emsco Mfg. Co., Dallas, 1945-46; accountant, office mgr. Lumber Dealer's Supply Co., Long Beach, Calif., 1946-47; tchr. Sawyer (Kans.) High Sch., 1947-50; asst. prof. bus. edn. and bus. adminstrn., also supr. USAF clk.-typist program N.Mex. Highlands U., 1951-52; assoc. prof. bus. edn. and acctg. Southwestern State Coll., Weatherford, Okla., 1953-55; prof. bus. edn., chmn. dept. U. Denver, 1955-65; prof. bus. edn. charge grad. program bus. edn. Tex. Tech. U., Lubbock, 1965-68; nat. dir. edn., edn. div. Lear Siegler, Inc., 1968-72; prof., chmn. dept. bus. edn. Cleve. State U., 1972-79, prof. acctg., 1979-81; assoc. dean James J. Nance Coll. Bus. Adminstrn., 1980-81, prof. emeritus, 1980—; pres. Tex. Ednl. and Adminstrv. Mgmt. Systems, Crowell, Tex., 1980—; textbook cons. U.S. Armed Forces Inst., 1955-68; test coordinator, profl. standards program Nat. Assn. Ednl. Secs., 1965-69; mem. Policies Commn. Bus. and Econ. Edn., 1962-66; commr. Accrediting Commn. Assn. Ind. Colls. and Schs., 1963-69; mem. Colo. Adv. Com. Bus. Edn., 1955-65, U.S. Office Edn. Adv. Council Insured Loans to Vocat. Students, 1966-69; cons. Acad. Ednl. Devel., 1965-67, Ednl. Testing Service; mem., chmn. mgmt. com. Inst. Certifying Secs., 1970-73. Author: Equipment Standards for Business Classrooms, 1954, Selected Authorities in Business Education, 1965; co-author: College Accounting for Secretaries, 1971; editor: Western Bus. Rev, 1958-62, Colo. Study Guides for Bus. Edn, 1957-65, Purple Heart Mag, 1980—; contbr. articles to profl. jours. Served to capt. AUS, 1940-44; lt. col. Colo. N.G. Decorated Purple Heart. Mem. Adminstrv. Mgmt. Soc. (Diamond Merit award 1976), Mountain Plains Bus. Edn. Assn. (pres. 1964-65), NEA, Nat. Assn. Bus. Tchr. Edn. (nat. sec. 1957-59), Am. Inst. C.P.A.'s, Tex. Soc. C.P.A.'s, Okla. Soc. C.P.A.'s, Assn. Ind. Colls. and Schs. (recipient award of merit accrediting Commn. 1978), Am. Legion, VFW, Delta Pi Epsilon (nat. treas. 1958-61, nat. exec. sec. 1962-66), Beta Gamma Sigma, Pi Omega Pi, Phi Beta Lambda, Alpha Kappa Psi, Beta Gamme Sigma, Pi Omega Pi, Phi Beta Lambda, Alpha Kappa Psi, Beta Alpha Psi, Kappa Kappa Psi, Delta Tau Delta, Phi Delta Kappa. Democrat. Methodist. Club: Military Order of Purple Heart (nat. comdr. 1973-74). Address: Tex Ednl and Adminstrv Mgmt Systems PO Box 840 Crowell TX 79227

BINNS, JAMES EDWARD, banker; b. Alameda, Calif., Oct. 5, 1931; s. Guy Vivian and Beatrice (Jury) B.; m. Marjean Friesen, Feb. 21, 1951; children: Cheryl Jean Binns Smith, Jana Lee, Lori LeAnn. Student, U. Nev., 1950-51; grad., Sch. Bank Audit and Control, U. Wis., 1963, Am. Inst. Banking, 1964. With Sierra Pacific Power Co., Reno, 1948-50; with First Interstate Bank of Nev., Reno, 1951—, asst. cashier, 1957-63, asst. to cashier, 1963-65, auditor, 1965—, asst. v.p., 1968-75, v.p., 1975—; instr. Am. Inst. Banking. Mem. Am. Inst. Banking (past pres. Sierra-Nev. chpt., past nat. asso. councilman), Bank Adminstrn. Inst. (chartered bank auditor, charter pres. chpt., past state dir.), Data Processing Mgmt. Assn. (charter mem. Sierra-Nevada chpt., past pres.), Inst. Internal Auditors (cert. internal auditor, past pres. chpt.), Reno Jr. C. of C. (past treas.). Club: Lakeridge Tennis. Lodges: Masons; Shriners; Elks; Reno Toastmasters (past pres.). Home: 1720 Allen St Reno NV 89509 Office: PO Box 10026 Reno NV 89510 *A true leader must accept all reasonable challenges being fully cognizant that his and the group's success can only be achieved through the combined efforts of all participants.*

BINNS, JAMES HAZLETT, industrial executive; b. Salida, Colo., Dec. 23, 1912; s. Hazlett C. and May (Lacey) B.; m. Ruamie Hill, Dec. 29, 1936; 1 son, James Hazlett. A.B., U. Denver, 1934. Dir. placement and field work U. Denver, 1934-35; with Armstrong Cork Co. (name changed to Armstrong World Industries, Inc.), Lancaster, Pa., 1935—, successively sales trainee floor div., salesman floor div., Atlanta, acting dist. mgr., dist. mgr., asst. sales mgr., Lancaster, Pa., asst. gen. mgr. munitions div., asst. gen. sales mgr. floor div., gen. sales mgr., 1935-60, v.p., gen. mgr. floor and indsl. operations, 1961-62, sr. v.p., 1962-68, pres., 1968-78, chmn., 1978-82, also dir.; dir. Campbell Soup Co., Woodstream Corp., Lititz, Pa. Mem. NAM (dir., chmn. fin. com.), Newcomen Soc. N.Am., Omicron Delta Kappa, Kappa Sigma. Clubs: Lancaster Country, Hamilton (Lancaster); Skytop (Pa.); Goodyear Golf and Country (Litchfield Park, Ariz.). Home: 402 Steeplehouse Sq 110 N Duke St Lancaster PA 17602

BINSTOCK, ROBERT HENRY, public policy educator, writer, lecturer; b. New Orleans, Dec. 6, 1935; s. Louis and Ruth (Atlas) B.; m. Martha Burns, July 27, 1979; 1 dau., Jennifer. A.B., Harvard U., 1956, Ph.D., 1965. Lectr. Brandeis U., Waltham, Mass., 1963-65, asst. prof., 1965-69, assoc. prof., 1969-72, Stulberg Prof. law and politics, 1972—, dir. Policy Ctr. Aging, 1979—; mem. com. on an Aging soc. Nat. Acad. Scis., Washington, 1982—. Author: America's Political System, 4th edit., 1984, Feasible Planning for Social Change, 1966; editor: International Perspectives on Aging: Population and Policy Changes, 1982, Handbook of Aging and the Social Sciences, 2d edit., 1984. Bd. dirs. White House Task Force on Older Ams., 1967-68; chmn. adv. panel Office Tech. Assessment, U.S. Congress, 1982—; tech. adviser, del. White House Conf. on Aging, 1971, 81; trustee Boston Biomed. Research Inst., 1971—; mem. gov.'s adv. com. Dept. of Elder Affairs Mass., 1974—. Recipient Haak-Lilliefors award Mich. State U., 1979, Research Career Devel. award NIH, 1968-73; Ford Found. fellow, 1959-60. Fellow Gerontol. Soc. Am. (pres. 1975-76, Donald P. Kent award 1981, pres. 1975-76, Brookdale Prize award 1983). Office: Brandeis University Heller Bldg Waltham MA 02254

BINSWANGER, MILTON S., JR., glass company executive; b. Memphis, Apr. 12, 1922; s. Milton S. and Florence (Lesser) B.; m. Lenore Heifetz, May 28, 1943; children: Richard, Lisa, Barbara. Grad., Choate Sch., 1939; student, Dartmouth, 1939-42, Southwestern U., 1943. With Binswanger Glass Co., Memphis, 1946—, exec. v.p., 1967-70, former pres., now chmn.; dir. Binswanger Mirror Co., Hamilton of Ind., Inc., Memphis Bank & Trust Co. and; affiliates, Marx & Bensdorf, Inc. Dir. Opportunity Housing Found., 1967; vice chmn. Shelby United Neighbors, 1967; Bd. dirs. Family Ser. of Memphis, 1955, LeBonheur Children's Hosp., from 1961. Served as capt. USAAF, 1942-46. Mem. Flat Glass Marketing Assn. (past pres.), Memphis C. of C. (dir.), The Memphi. Jewish (pres. temple 1964-66). Clubs: Ridgeway Country, Gun (Memphis) (pres. 1967). Office: 5885 Ridgeway Pkwy Memphis TN 38117 *

BINZEN, PETER HUSTED, journalist; b. Montclair, N.J., Sept. 24, 1922; s. Frederick William and Lucy Beckwith (Husted) B.; m. Elisabeth Virginia Flower, June 12, 1951; children: Lucy Binzen Wildrick, Jennifer Brooke, Jonathan Peter, Katherine Lorna. B.A. in Polit. Sci, Yale U., 1947; postgrad. (Nieman fellow), Harvard U., 1962. Reporter UP, N.Y.C., 1947, Passaic (N.J.) Herald-News, 1947-50; reporter, editor Phila. Bull., 1951-82; reporter Inquirer, 1982—. Author: Whitetown U.S.A, 1970, (with Joseph R. Daughen) The Wreck of the Penn Central, 1971, The Cop Who Would Be King, 1977. Served with U.S. Army, 1943-45. Decorated Bronze Star. Office: Phila Inquirer 400 N Broad St Philadelphia PA 19101

BIONDI, FRANK JOSEPH, JR., broadcasting executive; b. N.Y.C., Jan. 9, 1945; s. Frank Joseph and Virginia (Willia) B.; m. Carol Oughton, Mar. 16, 1974; children: Anne, Jane. A.B., Princeton U., 1966; M.B.A., Harvard U., 1968. Various investment banking and cons. positions, N.Y.C., 1968-74; asst. treas. Children's TV Workshop, N.Y.C., 1974-78; v.p. programming Home Box Office, N.Y.C., 1978-82, exec. v.p., 1982-83, pres., 1983—, dir., 1982; dir., treas. Internat. Radio & TV Found., N.Y.C., 1980. Bd. dirs. Leake-Watts Child Care Agy., Yonkers, N.Y., 1975, Morningside Nursing Home, Bronx, N.Y., 1977; trustee Citizens Budget Commn. Ctr. for Communication. Mem. Internat. Radio and TV Soc. (dir. 1983), Am. Film Inst. Democrat. Roman Catholic. Clubs: Princton (N.Y.C.); Riverdale Yacht (Bronx). Office: Home Box Office Inc 1271 Ave of Americas New York NY 10020

BIONDI, LAWRENCE HUGO, university dean; b. Chgo., Dec. 15, 1938; s. Hugo and Albertina (Marchetti) B. B.A., Loyola U., Chgo., 1962, Ph.L., 1964, M.Div., 1971, S.T.L., 1971; M.S., Georgetown U., 1966, Ph.D. in Socioloinguistics, 1975. Joined Soc. Jesus; ordained priest Roman Catholic Ch., 1970; asst. prof. sociolinguistics Loyola U., Chgo., 1974-79, asso. prof., 1979-81, dean Coll. Arts and Scis., 1980—. Author: The Italian-American Child: His Sociolinguistic Acculturation, 1975, Poland's Solidarity Movement, 1984; editor: Poland's Church-State Relations in the 1980s, 1980, Spain's Church-State Relations, 1982. Trustee Xavier U., 1981—, St. Louis U., 1982—. Mellon grantee, 1974, 75, 76, 82. Mem. Linguistic Soc. Am., MLA, Am. Anthrop. Assn. Democrat. Home and Office: 6525 N Sheridan Rd Chicago IL 60626

BIONDI, MANFRED ANTHONY, scientist, educator; b. Carlstadt, NJ., Mar. 5, 1924; s. Manfred Anthony and Helen (Flaction) B.; m. Elaine Teresa Leitkam, May 12, 1952; children: David Mark, George Philip. B.S. in Physics, MIT, 1944, Ph.D., 1949. Research asso. MIT, Cambridge, 1948-49; with Westinghouse Research Labs, Pitts., 1949-60, adv. physicist, 1952-57, mgr. physics dept., 1957-60; prof. physics U. Pitts., 1960—; also dir. Atomic Scis. Inst., 1968-79; exchange prof. U. Paris, 1976—; Trustee Upper Atmosphere Research Corp.; Mem. adv. com. Army Research Office, Durham, N.C., 1962-64, Nat. Acad. Scis., 1962-64; mem. exec. council Fedn. Am. Scientists, 1966-68; mem. adv. panel physics NSF, 1970-72. Editorial bd.: Jour. Applied Physics, 1966-68. Served with USNR, 1943-46. Fellow Am. Phys. Soc. (chmn. div. electron and atomic physics 1957, chmn. gaseous electronics conf. 1962-64), AAAS. Home: 1375 Hillsdale Dr Monroeville PA 15146 Office: Dept Physics and Astronomy U Pitts Pittsburgh PA 15260

BIONDO, MICHAEL THOMAS, paper company executive; b. N.Y.C., Nov. 2, 1928; s. Thomas and Susan (Battaglia) B.; m. Harriet Young, Mar. 1, 1952; children—Sally Ann, Susan, Amy, Michael Thomas. B.A., Adelphi U., Garden City, N.Y., 1950. With St. Regis Paper Co., 1953—, dir. mktg., than v.p. mktg., 1969-78, sr. v.p. consumer and splty. products group, N.Y.C., 1978-81, sr. v.p. packaging and converted products group, 1981—; past mem. mktg. adv. bd. Columbia U. Grad. Sch. Bus. Past pres. Darien (Conn.) Hist. Soc. Clubs: Union League (N.Y.C.); Woodway Country (Darien). Home: 16 Indian Spring Trail Darien CT 06820 Office: 237 Park Ave New York NY 10017

BIRCH, ALBERT FRANCIS, geophysicist, educator; b. Washington, Aug. 22, 1903; s. George Albert and Mary Clayton (Hemmick) B.; m. Barbara Channing, July 15, 1933; children: Anne Campaspe, Francis Sylvanus, Mary Narcissa. B.S. in Elec. Engring., Harvard U., 1924, M.A., 1929, Ph.D. (John Tyndall scholar 1928-31), 1932, Sc.D. hon., 1982; postgrad. (Am. Field Service fellow), U. Strasbourg, France, 1926-28; Sc.D. (hon.), U. Chgo., 1970. Engr., N.Y. Telephone Co., 1924-26; instr., tutor physics Harvard U., 1931-34, research asso. geophysics, 1932-37, asst. prof., 1937-43, asso. prof., 1943-46, prof., 1946-74, emeritus, 1974—; on leave MIT, 1941-42, Sturgis-Hooper prof. geology, 1948; Sherman Fairchild disting. scholar Calif. Inst. Tech., 1975. Editor: Handbook of Physical Constants. Served to comdr. USNR, 1942-45. Decorated Legion of Merit; recipient Arthur L. Day medal Geol. Soc.; William Bowie medal Am. Geophys. Union, 1960; Nat. medal of Sci., 1968; Vetlesen prize Columbia U., 1969; Bridgman medal AIRAPT, 1983. Fellow Royal Astron. Soc. (gold medal 1973), Am. Phys. Soc., Am. Acad. Arts and Sci., Geol. Soc. Am. (pres. 1964, Penrose medal 1969, Geol. Soc. London); mem. Am. Geophys. Union, Seismol. Soc. Am., Nat. Acad. Sci., Am. Philos. Soc., Sigma Xi. Office: Hoffman Laboratory Harvard Univ Cambridge MA 02138

BIRCH, DANIEL RICHARD, university dean; b. Salt Spring Island, B.C., Can., Sept. 1, 1937; s. George Alfred and Grace Lillian (Poland) B.; m. Rose Arlene McDonald, Oct. 26, 1962; 1 dau., Carol Leah. Diploma in Theology, N.W. Bapt. Sem., Vancouver, 1958, B.R.E., 1960; B.A. in Classics, U. B.C., 1968; M.A. in History, U. B.C., 1968; Ph.D., U. Calif.-Berkeley, 1969. Tchr., vice prin. Maple Ridge (B.C.) Sch. Dist., 1959-65; asst. prof. Simon Fraser U., Burnaby, B.C., 1969-72, assoc. prof., dean edn., 1972-75, prof., assoc. v.p. acad., 1975-80; prof., dean edn. U. B.C., Vancouver, 1981—; visting asst. prof. U. Calif.-Berkeley, 1969, 71; dir. Pueblito, Costa Rica, 1974-78. Author, Asia, 1979, Gandhi, 1969, Life in China, 1969; editor, author: Early Indian Cultures of North America, 1973; author: Culture Realms of the World, 1973; coordinating editor: Growth of a Nation Series, 1974—. Trustee Shaughnessy Hosp., Vancouver, 1981—. Mem. Can. Edn. Assn. (dir. 1983—), Can. Soc. for Study of Edn., Can. Assn. Deans Edn. (sec.-treas. 1974-75,82—). Home: 945 Esquimalt Ave West Vancouver BC Canada V7T 1J9 Office: U BC 125 Main Mall Vancouver BC Canada V6T 1Z5

BIRCH, JACK WILLARD, psychologist; b. Glassport, Pa., Nov. 27, 1915; s. Samuel Rush and Anna (Zimmerman) B.; m. Barbara Jane Roof, June 22, 1940; children: Dee Ann, Barbara Joan. B.S., Calif. State Coll., 1937; M.Ed., Pa. State U., 1941; Ph.D., U. Pitts., 1951. Diplomate: Am. Bd. Psychology. Tchr. pub. schs., Berks and Miflin counties, Pa., 1937-41, psychologist county schs. and cts., supr. spl. edn., Somerset, Pa., 1941-48; dir. spl. edn., ednl. clinic Bd. Edn., Pitts., 1948-58; lectr. dept. psychology Sch. Edn. U. Pitts., 1948—, now prof. psychology, spl. edn. Sch. Edn., assoc. Learning Research and Devel. Ctr. Served from pvt. to 1st lt. AUS, 1943-46. Fellow Am. Psychol. Assn. (ednl. and sch. psychol. sects., mem. Thayer com.), Am. Assn. Mental Deficiency (regional chmn. coms. on psychology, edn., nomenclature and standards); mem. Pa. (chmn. clin. div.), Pitts., pres. 1949) psychol. assns), NEA, N.Y. Acad. Sci., Council Exceptional Children (parliamentarian, asso. editor Exceptional Children; pres.), Found. Exceptional Children (pres.), Sigma Xi, Phi Delta Kappa. Presbyn. Clubs: University (Pitts.); Cosmos (Washington). Home: Sherwood Oaks Mars PA 16046

BIRCH, THOMAS CARL, media research executive; b. Binghamton, N.Y., July 8, 1952; s. Willis D. and Ruth E. (Wahlberg) B.; m. Roseann Fuss, July 13, 1974; 1 dau., Erica Lee. B.S. in Labor Relations, Cornell U., 1974. Music dir. Sta. WHYI, Ft. Lauderdale, Fla., 1975; asst. program dir. Sta. WNOE, New Orleans, 1975; program dir. Sta. KOMA, Oklahoma City, 1976, 77, WQAM, Miami, Fla., 1978, 79; pres., owner Birch Research Corp., Coral Springs, Fla., 1979—. Mem. Am. Mgmt. Assn., Assn. for Corp. Growth, Am. Mktg. Assn., Nat. Assn. Broadcasters. Republican. Presbyterian. Club: President's. Office: Birch Research Corp 3200 N University Dr Coral Springs FL 33065

BIRCHBY, KENNETH LEE, banker; b. Columbus, Ind., Feb. 1, 1915; s. Ernest Lee and Constance Douglas (Pinsent) B.; m. Julia C. Barsch, Apr. 12, 1941; children—Kenneth Lee, John D. LL.B., St. Johns U., 1949; postgrad., Grad. Sch. Banking, Rutgers, 1956. With Brevoort Savs. Bank, Bklyn., 1936-42, comptroller, 1945-48; spl. agt. FBI, 1942-45; auditor, v.p. Jamaica (N.Y.) Savs. Bank, 1948-66; exec. v.p. Hudson City Savs. Bank, Jersey City, 1966-68, pres., 1968—, chmn., chief exec. officer, 1981—; also dir. instr. Grad. Sch. Savs. Banks, Brown U.; adv. counsel Conf. State Bank Suprs. Mem. Mayor's Adv. Com., 1971—; v.p., bd. dirs. Hudson County; chpt. ARC.; past bd. dirs. N.J. Coll. Fund Assn.; past regent St. Peter's Coll. Mem. Savs. Banks Assn. N.J. (pres. 1970-72), New York Assn., Jersey City C. of C. (pres., dir.), Assn. Former FBI Agts., Savs. Banks Auditors and Comptrollers Assn. N.Y. (past pres.), Nat. Assn. Mut. Savs. Banks (com. chmn., pres. 1974-75), C. of C. and Industry No. N.J. (dir.). Clubs: Northampton Colony Yacht (Southampton, L.I.) (dir.); Ridgewood Country, Essex, Bergen Carteret. Home: 12 Pine Tree Dr Saddle River NJ 07458 Office: W 80 Century Rd Paramus NJ 07652

BIRCHER, EDGAR ALLEN, manufacturing company executive; b. Sprinfield, Ohio, Apr. 28, 1934; s. John Clark and Ethel Ann (Speakman) B.; m. Lavinia Brock, Sept. 30, 1978; children: Douglas, Stephen, Todd, Karen. B.A., Ohio Wesleyan U., 1956; J.D., Ohio State U., 1961. Bar: Tex. 1973, Ohio 1962. Assoc. Fuller, Seney, Henry & Hodge, Toledo, 1962-64; with Cooper Industries, Inc., Houston, 1964—; v.p. Cooper Industries, Inc., Houston, 1977—; gen. couns. Cooper Industries, Inc., Houston, 1977—. Served with USAF, 1956-59. Mem. Houston World Trade Assn. (v.p. 1974), ABA, Ohio Bar Assn., Tex. Bar Assn., Phi Delta Theta, Phi Delta Phi. Clubs: Houston, Sugar Creek Country, Bob Smith Yacht. Home: 635 Chevy Chase St Sugarland TX 77478 Office: 4000 First City Tower PO Box 4446 Houston TX 77210

BIRCKHEAD, OLIVER WILLIAM, JR., banker; b. Bklyn., June 20, 1922; s. Oliver William and Ethel G. (Hardy) B.; children: Oliver William III, Randall E. Grad., Nichols Coll., Dudley, Mass., 1942, Stonier Grad Sch. Banking, 1955. With Peoples Nat. Bank, White Plains, N.Y., 1946; asst. nat. bank examiner, 1946-48; with Chem. Bank N.Y. Trust Co., 1948-51, Central Trust Co., Cin., 1951—, exec. v.p., 1967-69, pres., 1969-81, chmn. and chief exec. officer, 1981—, also dir.; pres., dir. Central Bancorp.; dir. Union Central Assurance Corp., Union Central Life Ins. Co. of Cin., Gas & Electric Co., West Shell, Inc.; mem. Cin. Bus. Com. Mem. adv. bd. Cin. Salvation Army; active United Fund Drives; trustee Marietta Coll. Served with USAAF, 1942-46. Mem. Assn. Res. City Bankers, Newcomen Soc. Clubs: University, Tennis, Recess, Cin. Country, Queen City, Commonnwealth, Commercial, Ohio Valley Tennis Assn., Queen City (Cin.). Office: Central Trust Co 5th and Main Sts Cincinnati OH 45202

BIRD, AGNES THORNTON, lawyer; b. Wichita Falls, Tex., Sept. 15, 1921; d. Ernest Grady and Ann McNulty (Renfro) Thornton; m. Frank Babington Bird, Mar. 10, 1946; 1 dau., Patricia Ann. B.S., Tex. Womans U., 1943; M.A., U. Tenn., 1959, Ph.D., 1967, J.D., 1974. Bar: Tenn. bar 1975. Draftsman Humble Oil Co., Wichita Falls, Tex., 1943-45; clk. Aluminum Co. Am., Alcoa, Tenn., 1947-49; tchr. public schs., Blount County, Tenn., 1950-52; instr. polit. sci. U. Tenn., 1961-64; asst. prof. polit. sci. Maryville (Tenn.) Coll., 1969-72; partner firm Bird, Navratil & Bird, Maryville, 1975—; Mem. Tenn. Human Rights Commn., 1965-68; mem. Tenn. adv. com. U.S. Civil Rights Commn., 1963-72, vice chmn., 1968; chmn. Tenn. Commn. on Status of Women,

1977-79; pres. Tenn. Fedn. Democratic Women, 1964-65; parliamentarian Nat. Fedn. Dem. Women, 1974—; mem. Nat. Assn. Dem. State Chairs, 1976—; vice chmn. Tenn. Dem. Party, 1976—; Dem. nat. committeewoman for, Tenn., 1976—; bd. dirs. Blount County Girls Group Home, Nat. Assn. Commns. on Women, 1977-78; mem. adv. council Maryville Coll., 1979—. Recipient Disting. Alumna award Tex. Women's U., 1980; Citizens Research Found. of Princeton; N.J., grantee, 1965. Mem. Am. Bar Assn., Tenn. Bar Assn., Blount County Bar Assn. (treas. 1978-79), Am. Trial Lawyers Assn., Tenn. Trial Lawyers Assn., Am. Polit. Sci. Assn., AAUW (pres. Maryville br. 1967-69, chmn. assn. topic com. 1970-72), ACLU, NOW, LWV, DAR, Common Cause. Unitarian. Club: Chilhowee (pres. 1965-66). Home: Cold Springs Rd PO Box 647 Maryville TN 37801 Office: Box 647 100 N Court St Maryville TN 37801

BIRD, CAROLINE, author; b. N.Y.C., Apr. 15, 1915; d. Hobart Stanley and Ida (Brattrud) B.; m. Edward A. Menuez, June 8, 1934 (div. Dec. 1945); 1 dau., Carol (Mrs. John Paul Barach); m. John Thomas Mahoney, Jan. 5, 1957; 1 son, John Thomas. Student, Vassar Coll., 1931-34; B.A., U. Toledo, 1938; M.A., U. Wis., 1939. Desk editor N.Y. Jour. Commerce, 1943-44; editorial researcher Newsweek mag., N.Y.C., 1942-43, Fortune mag., 1944-46; with Dudley-Anderson-Yutzy, pub. relations, N.Y.C., 1947-68; Froman Disting. prof. Russell Sage Coll., 1972-73; Mather prof. Case-Western Res. U., 1977. Author: The Invisible Scar, 1966, Born Female, 1968, rev. edit., 1970, The Crowding Syndrome, 1972, Everything a Woman Needs To Know To Get Paid What She's Worth, 1973, rev., 1982, The Case Against College, 1975, Enterprising Women, 1976, What Women Want, 1979, The Two-Paycheck Marriage, 1979, The Good Years, 1983; chief writer: The Spirit of Houston, 1978; also articles in nat. mags. Mem. review bd. Dept. State, 1974. Mem. Soc. Journalists and Authors, Am. Sociol. Assn., Women in Communications, NOW, Women's Equity Action League. Home: 60 Gramercy Park New York NY 10010 also 31 Sunrise Ln PO Box 3289 Poughkeepsie NY 12603

BIRD, FRANCIS MARION, lawyer; b. Comer, Ga., Sept, 4, 1902; s. Henry Madison and Minnie Lee (McConnell) B.; m. Mary Adair Howell, Jan. 30, 1935; children—Francis Marion, Mary Adair Bird Kennedy, Elizabeth Howell Bird Hewitt, George Arthur. A.B., U. Ga., 1922, LL.B., 1924; LL.M., George Washington U., 1925; LL.D., Emory U., 1980, U. St. Andrews, 1982. Bar: Ga. bar 1924, D.C. bar 1925. Since practiced in, Atlanta; with U.S. Senator Hoke Smith, 1925; individual practice, 1930-45; mem. firm Bird & Howell, 1945-59, Jones Bird & Howell, 1959-82, Alston & Bird, 1982—; served as part-time U.S. referee in bankruptcy, 1945-54; spl. asst. to U.S. atty. gen. as hearings officer Nat. Selective Service Act.; Mem. commn. for preparation plan of govt. City of Atlanta and county area; mem. permanent rules com. Ga. Supreme Ct.; mem. Met. Atlanta Commn. Crime and Juvenile Delinquency, chmn., 1969-70; formerly Ga. co-chmn. Tech.-Ga. Devel. Fund.; Trustee Young Harris Coll., U. Ga. Found., Atlanta Lawyers Found., Interdenominational Theol. Center; trustee, past mem. exec. com. Emory U., Atlanta.; Chmn. Ga. Bd. Bar Examiners, 1954-61. Mem. permanent editorial bd.: Uniform Comml. Code, 1962-77, Fed. Jud. Conf., 5th Circuit, Fed. Jud. Conf., 11th Circuit, 1960-81, 1981—. Recipient Distinguished Service citation U. Ga. Law Sch.; Distinguished Service award Atlanta Bar Assn., 1977; Pres.'s award Assn. Pvt. Colls. and Univs., 1979. Fellow Am. Bar Found; mem. Am. Judicature Soc. (past dir.), Am. Law Inst. (council 1949-82, emeritus, past chmn. com. membership), ABA, Ga. (past pres.), Atlanta), Am., Ga. (past pres.) bar assns.), Assn. Bar City N.Y., Atlanta C. of C. (past pres., Atlanta Civic Service award 1957), U. Ga. Alumni Assn. (past pres., certificate of merit 1952), George Washington U. Alumni Assn. (achievement award 1965), Phi Kappa Phi, Sigma Chi, Phi Delta Phi. Methodist. Clubs: Peachtree Golf, Atlanta Athletic (past pres.), Kiwanis, Piedmont Driving, Capital City, Lawyers (past pres.), Augusta (Ga.) Nat. Golf (gov.)). Home: 89 Brighton Rd NE Atlanta GA 30309 Office: 1200 The Citizens and So Nat Bank Bldg Atlanta GA 30335

BIRD, GEORGE RICHMOND, educator; b. Bismarck, N.D., Jan. 25, 1925; s. George Francis and Mary Helen (Hoppin) B.; m. Doris Elinor Forgue, June 12, 1948; children—George Peter, Elizabeth Newell, Margaret Alison. A.B., Harvard, 1949, A.M., 1952, Ph.D., 1953. Asst. prof. chemistry Rice U., 1954-58; scientist, mgr. phys. chem. lab. Polaroid Corp., Cambridge, Mass., 1958-69; prof. chemistry Rutgers U., New Brunswick, N.J., 1969—; dir. Sch. Chemistry, 1971-74; Guggenheim fellow in residence Photog. Inst., Fed. Tech. Sch., Zurich, Switzerland, 1974-75. Served from pvt. to 1st lt. AUS, 1943-46. Fellow Soc. Photog. Scientists and Engrs., Optical Soc. Am.; mem. Am. Chem. Soc. Inventor (with Maxfield Parrish, Jr.) wire grid optical polarizer; discoverer of collision-narrowing in optical spectrum of H2. Home: 85 Red Hill Rd Princeton NJ 08540

BIRD, HARRIE WALDO, JR., psychiatrist, educator; b. Detroit, Sept. 21, 1917; s. Harrie Waldo and Ann Josephine (Tossy) B.; m. Della Mae Clemmer, Jan. 4, 1943; children: Harrie Waldo, Kathleen Bird Steinhour, Deborah Bird Hall, Mark Henry, Matthew Alexius, Liza George-Aidan. A.B., Yale U., 1939; postgrad., U. Mich. Med. Sch., 1939-41; M.D., Harvard U., 1943. Intern Phila. Gen. Hosp., 1943-44; resident Menninger Sch. Psychiatry, Topeka, 1946-48; chief infirmary sect. Winter VA Hosp., Topeka, 1946; psychiatrist Adult Psychiat. Clinic, Detroit, 1949, acting dir., 1950; psychiat. cons. Mich. Epilepsy Center, Detroit, 1950-55; clin. instr. psychiatry Wayne State U., Detroit, 1952-55; asso. prof. psychiatry U. Chgo., 1955-56, U. Mich., Ann Arbor, 1956-63; asst. dean Med Sch., 1959-61; prof. psychiatry, asso. dean St. Louis U. Sch. Medicine, 1965-68, clin. prof., 1970—; dir. Family Psychicenter Inc., St. Louis, 1972—; lectr., cons. in field. Bd. dirs. Mich. Epilepsy Ctr., 1956-63, Wayne County Mental Health Soc., 1956-63, Mich. Epilepsy Assn., 1956-63, El Paso Mental Health Assn., 1969-70, Cranbrook Sch., 1961-63. Served with M.C. AUS, 1944-46. Recipient Mental Health Inst. award St. John's U., 1966. Fellow Am. Psychiat. Assn. (life); mem. Am. Family Therapy Assn. (charter), AMA, Group for Advancement Psychiatry, Am. Psychosomatic Soc., Am. Psychopath. Assn., Mo., Med. Soc., St. Louis Med. Soc., Eastern Mo. Psychiat. Soc., Phi Beta Kappa. Home: 62 Conway Ln Saint Louis MO 63124 Office: Family Psychicenter 62 Conway Ln Saint Louis MO 62124

BIRD, JOHN ADAMS, headmaster; b. Winchester, Mass., Apr. 3, 1937; s. Frederic Henry and Dorothy Lucy (Jones) B.; m. Mary Alice Hocker, June 11, 1960; children: Edith Simonton, John Adams, Sarah Hocker. B.A., Bowdoin Coll., 1959; postgrad., Law Sch., U. Va., 1959-60; M.A., George Washington U., 1965. Tchr. history, polit. sci. English Landon Sch., Bethesda, Md., 1960-65; asst. headmaster Lake Forest (Ill.) Country Day Sch., 1965-70; headmaster Ferry Hall Sch., Lake Forest, 1970-74, Holland Hall Sch., Tulsa, 1974-84, Pembroke Hill Sch., Kansas City, Mo., 1984—. Bd. dirs. Community Music Assn., Lake Forest, 1966-68. Mem. Ind. Schs. Assn. Central States, Ind. Schs. Assn. S.W. (pres. 1980-82), Ind. Schs. Assn. Greater Chgo. (pres. 1973-74), Nat. Assn. Ind. Schs. (nat. dir. 1982—), Country Day Sch. Headmasters' Assn., Phi Delta Kappa. Episcopalian (sr. churchwarden 1980-81). Club: Rotary. Home: 400 W 51st St Kansas City MO 64112

BIRD, JOHN ALEXANDER, ret. editor; b. Hays, Kans., Feb. 14, 1910; s. John Sterling and Martha (Henderson) B.; m. Katherine Edna Taylor, Oct. 3, 1930; 1 dau., Judith Ann. Student, Ft. Hays State Coll., 1926-27; B.S. in Journalism, Kans. State Coll., 1932. Asst. to pres. Wheat Farming Co., 1930-31; sr. sec. to congl. rep. 6th Dist. of Kans., 1933-34; asst. chief press sect. A.A.A., Washington, 1934-36; asso. prof. journalism Kans. State Coll., 1936-38; dir. information Fed. Crop Ins. Corp., Washington, 1938-40; prin. writer Office Land Use Coordination, Dept. Agr., 1940-42; asso. editor Country Gentleman mag., 1942-55, Sat. Eve. Post, Phila., 1955-60, sr. editor, 1960-64, editor-at-large, 1964-69; freelance writer, editorial cons., 1969—; editor Dynamic Maturity mag., 1971-75, ret., 1975. Contbr. articles to popular mags. Mem. Citizens Com. for Outdoor Recreation Resources and Rev. Commn., Presdl. Trade mission, Central and, Presdl. Trade mission, So. Europe, 1954; Speech writer Republican Presdl. Campaign, 1952. Served as lt. (j.g.) USNR, 1944-45. Eisenhower exchange fellow, 1956. Mem. Beta Theta Pi, Sigma Delta Chi. Clubs: Springhaven (Wallingford); Quill. Home: 506 Oak Crest Ln Wallingford PA 19086

BIRD, JOHN MALCOLM, geologist; b. Newark, Dec. 27, 1931; s. John Robert and Beryl Elizabeth (Wright) B.; m. Marjorie Ann Kelleher, Apr. 18, 1957 (div. 1982); children: Anne Elizabeth, Marsha Jean. B.S., Union Coll., Schenectady, 1955; M.S., Rensselaer Poly. Inst., Troy, N.Y., 1959, Ph.D., 1961. Grad. asst. Union Coll., 1957-58, Rensselaer Poly. Inst., 1958-61; from instr. to assoc. prof. SUNY-Albany, 1961-70; prof., 1970-72, chmn. dept. geol. scis., 1969-72, vis. research prof., 1972-76; research assoc. Dudley Obs., Albany, 1964-72; sr. research assoc. Lamont-Doherty Geol. Obs., Columbia U., 1970-73; prof. geology Cornell U., Ithaca, N.Y., 1972—; pres., treas. Gamma Prime Corp., 1983—; Nat. Acad. Scis. Vis. scientist, 1967; disting. vis. scientist Am. Geol. Inst., 1971; chmn. Appalachian working group U.S. Geodynamics Com., 1971-73; disting. vis. lectr. Am. Assn. Petroleum Geologists, 1977-78; cons geotech. engring., mineral exploration. Editor: Plate Tectonics, 1981; assoc. editor: Jour. Geophys. Research, 1971-74; contbr. profl. jours. Served with AUS, 1955-57. Research grantee NSF, 1964, 68, 72-84; Nat. Acad. Scis., 1969; Petroleum Research Inst., 1975-77; Office Naval Research, 1978-80; Nat. Geog. Soc., 1977-78, 80. Fellow Geol. Soc. Am. (chmn. N.E. sect. 1975-76), Canadian Geol. Soc., Explorers Club; mem. Am. Geophys. Union, Sigma Xi, Chi Psi. Home: 1187 Ellis Hollow Rd Ithaca NY 14850 Office: Geol Scis Dept Cornell Univ Ithaca NY 14853

BIRD, LARRY JOE, professional basketball player; b. French Lick, Ind., Dec. 7, 1956. Student, Ind. U., 1974, Northwood Inst., West Baden, Ind., 1974; B.S., Ind. State U., 1979. Player Boston, Celtics, NBA, 1979—. Mem. U.S. Gold Medal team World Univ. Games, Sophia, Bulgaria, 1977; named Collegiate Player of Yr. AP, UPI and Nat. Assn. Coaches, 1978-79, Rookie of Yr., 1980, Most Valuable Player NBA All Star Game, 1982. Address: care Boston Celtics North Station Boston MA 02114 *

BIRD, RALPH GORDON, naval officer; b. Highland Park, Mich., Sept. 9, 1933; s. Thurman Elmer and Gladys May (Stephenson) B. B.S., U.S. Naval Acad., 1956; M.S., U.S. Naval Postgrad. Sch., 1969. Commd. ensign U.S. Navy, 1956, advanced through grades to rear adm., 1979; various sea assignments primarily in nuclear powered submarines, 1956-67; comdg. officer USS Archerfish (SSN 678), 1970-74; sr. mem. U.S. Pacific Fleet nuclear propulsion examining bd., 1974-76; sr. instr., chief of naval ops. sr. officers ship material readiness course, Idaho Fall, Idaho, 1976-77; chief of staff, submarine force U.S. Pacific Fleet, Pearl Harbor, Hawaii, 1977-79; dir. logistics and security assistance U.S. Pacific Command, 1979-81; assigned to Naval Material Command, Washington, 1981—. Decorated Legion of Merit. Mem. U.S. Naval Inst. Address: Naval Material Command Washington DC 20360

BIRD, RICHARD MILLER, economics educator; b. Fredericton, N.B., Can., Aug. 22, 1938; s. Robert Bruce and Annie Margaret (Miller) B.; m. Marcia Abbey, May 10, 1958; children—Paul, Marta, Abbey. B.A., U. King's Coll., 1958; M.A., Columbia U., 1959, Ph.D., 1961. Instr. economics Harvard U., 1961-63, lectr., 1966-68; sr. research asso. Columbia U., 1963-64; advisor Ministry of Fin., Colombia, 1964-66; asso. prof. U. Toronto, 1968-70, prof., 1970—; dir. Inst. Policy Analysis, 1980—; chief tax policy div. dept. fiscal affairs Internat. Monetary Fund, Washington, 1972-74. Contbr. articles in field to profl. jours. Recipient Killam award Can. Council, 1969-70. Fellow Royal Soc. Can.; mem. Nat. Tax Assn. Tax Inst. Am. (dir. 1977-83, Internat. Inst. Public Fin., dir. 1973-81), Am. Econs. Assn., Canadian Econs. Assn., Can. Tax Found. Office: Inst Policy Analysis 140 Saint George St Toronto ON M5S 1A1 Canada

BIRD, ROBERT BYRON, chemical engineering educator, author; b. Bryan, Tex., Feb. 5, 1924; s. Byron and Ethel (Antrim) B. Student, U. Md., 1941-43; B.S. in Chem. Engring, U. Ill., 1947; Ph.D. in Chemistry, U. Wis., 1950, U. Amsterdam, 1950-51; D.Eng. (hon.), Lehigh U., 1972, Washington U., 1973, Tech. U. Delft, Holland, 1977, Sc.D., Clarkson U., 1980. Asst. prof. chemistry Cornell U., 1952-53, Debye lectr., 1973; mem. faculty U. Wis., 1951-52, 53—, prof. chem. engring., 1957—, C.F. Burgess distinguished prof. chem. engring., 1968-72, John D. MacArthur prof., 1982—, Vilas research prof., 1972—, chmn. dept., 1964-68; vis. prof. U. Calif., Berkeley, 1977; D.L. Katz lectr. U. Mich., 1971; W.N. Lacey lectr. Calif. Inst. Tech., 1974; K. Wohl Meml. lectr. U. Del., 1977; W.K. Lewis lectr. MIT, 1982; lectr. Lectures in Sci. Humble Oil Co., 1959, 61, 64, 66; lecture tour Am. Chem. Soc., 1958, 75, Canadian Inst. Chemistry, 1961, 65; cons. to industry, 1965—; mem. adv. panel engring. sci. div. NSF, 1961-64. Author: (with others) Molecular Theory of Gases and Liquids, 2d printing, 1964, Transport Phenomena, 30th printing, 1982, Spanish edit., 1965, Czech edit., 1966, Italian edit., 1970, Russian edit., 1974, Een Goed Begin: A Contemporary Dutch Reader, 1963, 2d edit., 1971, Comprehending Technical Japanese, 1975, Dynamics of Polymeric Liquids, Vol. 1, Fluid Mechanics, Vol. 2, Kinetic Theory, 1977; also numerous research publs.; Am. editor: Applied Sci. Research, 1969—; adv. bd.: Indsl. and Engring. Chemistry, 1970-72; editorial bd.: Jour. Non-Newtonian Fluid Mechanics, 1975—. Served to 1st lt. AUS, 1943-46. Decorated Bronze Star; Fulbright fellow, Holland, 1950; Fulbright lectr., 1958; Guggenheim fellow, 1958; Fulbright lectr., Japan, 1962-63, Sarajevo, Yugoslavia, 1972; recipient Curtis McGraw award Am. Assn. Engring. Edn., 1959, Westinghouse award, 1960. Fellow Am. Phys. Soc. (Otto Laporte lectr. 1980), Am. Inst. Chem. Engrs. (William H. Walker award 1962, Profl. Progress award 1965, Warren K. Lewis award 1974), Am. Acad. Arts and Scis.; mem. Am. Chem. Soc. (chmn. Wis. sect. 1966, unrestricted research grant Petroleum Research Fund 1963), Soc. Rheology (Bingham award 1974), Am. Acad. Mechanics, Brit. Soc. Rheology, Dutch Phys. Soc., Royal Inst. Engrs. (Holland), Nat. Acad. Engring., N.Y. Acad. Scis., Am. Acad. Arts and Scis., Wis. Acad. Scis., Arts and Letters, Phi Beta Kappa, Sigma Xi (v.p. Wis. sect. 1959-60), Tau Beta Pi, Alpha Chi Sigma, Phi Kappa Phi, Omicron Delta Kappa, Sigma Tau. Office: Chem Engring Dept 3004 Engring Bldg 1415 Johnson Dr U Wis Madison WI 53706

BIRD, ROBERT JAMES, lawyer; b. Milw., July 3, 1911; s. Robe and Gertrude (Trainor) B.; m. Charla Coleman, July 25, 1940; children: Nancy Bird McKown, Charles Coleman, Barbara Bird Ferguson. B.A., Vanderbilt U., 1934, LL.B., 1937. Bar: Ill. 1938, D.C. 1946. Practiced in, Chgo., 1938-44; atty. U.S. Govt., 1944-46; practice in, Washington, 1946—; partner firm Bird & Tansill, 1972-79; firm Ober, Grimes and Shriver, 1979-81; of counsel firm Ross, Marsh & Foster, Washington, 1981—; Mem. fin. com. Republican Nat. Com., 1970-73. Mem. Am., D.C. bar assns. Roman Cath. Clubs: Chevy Chase, Capitol Hill (Washington). Home: 6629 Fairfax Rd Chevy Chase MD 20015 Office: Ross Marsh & Foster 888 16th St NW Washington DC 20006

BIRD, ROBERT WILSON, lawyer; b. Brady, Mont., Sept. 2, 1918; s. Frank W. and Cora Fannie (Lincoln) B.; m. Hedda M. Cimoli, Dec. 29, 1946; children: Frank A., Robert M., Michael J. J.D., U. Wis., 1943. Bar: Wis. 1943, Ill. 1952. Assoc. Schmitt & Bird, Merrill, Wis., 1947-50; v.p., sec. Oliver Corp., Chgo., 1950-70; v.p., sec., gen. counsel Nat. Car Rental, Mpls., 1971—; mem. labor relations com. Ill. State Commerce Commn., Chgo., 1964-68; v.p., chmn. legal and legis. com. Am. Car Rental Assn., Washington, 1976—; mem. labor relations com. Farm and Indsl. Equipment Inst., Chgo., 1964-68. Bd. dirs. Salvation Army, Mpls., 1975—, Crime Stoppers Minn., Mpls., 1979—; active Nat. Def. Execs. Res., Washington, 1964—. Decorated Bronze Star, Crown of Italy, Order of St. George. Mem. Wis. Bar Assn., Ill. Bar Assn., Order of the Coif, Phi Beta Kappa. Republican. Clubs: Upper Lake Minnetonka Yacht; Lake Zumbra Yacht (Excelsior, Minn.). Home: 5520 Zumbra Ln Excelsior MN 55331 Office: Nat Car Rental System Inc 7700 France Ave S Minneapolis MN 55435

BIRD, ROSE ELIZABETH, chief justice Calif. Supreme Ct.; b. Tucson, Nov. 2, 1936. B.A. magna cum laude, L.I. U., 1958; J.D., U. Calif., Berkeley, 1965. Bar: Calif. bar 1966. Clk. to chief justice Nev. Supreme Ct., 1965-66; successively dep. public defender, sr. trial dep., chief appellate div. Santa Clara County (Calif.) Pub. Defenders Office, 1966-74; tchr. Stanford U. Law Sch., 1972-74; sec. Calif. Agr. and Services Agy., also mem. governor's cabinet, 1975-77; chief justice Calif. Supreme Ct., 1977—; chairperson Calif. Jud. Council, Commn. Jud. Appointments; pres. bd. dirs. Hastings Coll. Law, U. Calif.; bd. councilors U. So. Calif. Law Center, 1975-77; Past mem. Western regional selection panel President's Commn. White House Fellowships; bd. assos. San Fernando Valley Youth Found. Named Most Outstanding Sr. L.I. U., 1958; Ford Found. fellow, 1960. Democrat. Address: 350 McAllister St San Francisco CA 94102 *

BIRDMAN, JEROME M., drama educator, dean; b. Phila., Dec. 4, 1930; s. Morris Schiowitz and Minerva B.; m. Evanira Pereira Mendes, July 1, 1959; children: Julia, Beatrice. B.S., Temple U., 1956; A.M., U. Ill., 1957, Ph.D., 1970. Mem. editorial staff Accent Quar. of New Lit., 1957-58; dir. cultural programming for Am. Forces, U.S. Info. Service, Northeast Italy, 1958-61; mem. faculty theatre dept. So. Ill. U., Edwardsville, 1961-71, acad. program officer, mem. bd. trustees, 1972-73; prof. dramatic arts, dean Coll. Fine Arts, U. Nebr., Omaha, 1973-78, Sch. Fine Arts, U. Conn., Storrs, 1978—; adv. bd. Nebr. Alliance for Arts Edn., 1976-78; lectr. USIS, Brazil, 1964; arts commr. Nat. Assn. State Univs. and Land Grant Colls., 1979—; panelist Nat. Endowment Humanities, 1976—; adv. Conn. Dept. Edn., 1980—; accreditor New Eng. Assn. Schs. and Colls.; cons. to various colls. and univs. in arts adminstrn. Contbr. articles on theatrical art to various profl. publs. Mem. Mayor's Task Force on the Arts, Omaha, 1977-78; bd. dirs. Dance Concert Soc., St. Louis, 1970-73, New Music Circle, St. Louis, 1971-73, Prelude Civic Ballet, Ill., 1971-73, Omaha Opera Co., 1973-75, Omaha Symphony Assn., 1973-78, Met. Arts Council, Omaha, 1976-78, Omaha Children's Mus., 1976-78. Served with U.S. Army, 1952-54. Recipient merit citation Provincia di Vicenza, 1961. Mem. Am. Theatre Assn., Internat. Fedn. Theatre Research, Am. Soc. Theatre Research, Internat. Council Fine Arts Deans (dir.), Soc. Theatre Research Great Britain., Societe d'Histoire du Theatre. Office: School of Fine Arts U-128 Univ of Conn Storrs CT 06268

BIRDSALL, BLAIR, consulting engineer; b. Newark, May 21, 1907; s. William Adams and Carrie Jane (Mulford) B.; m. Helen S. Burnett, Oct. 15, 1931; children: Elizabeth Jane Birdsall Evans, William Blair, James Brewster; m. Elizabeth Figueroa, Nov. 28, 1955; stepchildren: Rodolfo Celis, Jose Roberto Celis, Maria Rosario Wirth. B.S.C.E., Princeton, 1929, C.E., 1930. Engr. Voorhees, Gmelin & Walker, N.Y.C., 1930-31, Port of N.Y. Authority, 1931-32, Wallkill (N.Y.) State Prison, 1932-34, John A. Roebling's Sons Co., Trenton, 1934-65; with Steinman, Boynton, Gronquist & Birdsall, N.Y.C., 1965—, mng. partner, 1976—. Contbr. articles to profl. publs. Com. mem. Am. Nat. Standards Inst. Fellow ASME, ASCE; mem. Internat. Bridge, Tunnel and Turnpike Assn., Internat. Assn. Bridge and Structural Engrs., ASTM, Am. Inst. Steel Constrn. Republican. Presbyterian. Club: Princeton (N.Y.C.). Home: 200 Franklin Turnpike Allendale NJ 07401 Office: 50 Broad St New York NY 10004

BIRDSALL, CHARLES KENNEDY, electrical engineer; b. N.Y.C., Nov. 19, 1925; s. Charles and Irene (Birdsall); m. Betty Jean Hansen, 1949; children: Elizabeth (dec.), Anne, Barbara, Thomas, John. B.S., U. Mich., 1946, M.S., 1948; Ph.D., Stanford U., 1951. Research physicist Hughes Aircraft Co., Culver City, Calif., 1951-55; group leader electron physics group Gen. Electric Co., Palo Alto, Calif., 1955-59; prof. elec. engring. U. Calif., 1959—; founder, 1st chmn. Energy and Resources Com., 1972-74; cons. to industry Lawrence Livermore Lab. of U. Calif.; prof. Miller Inst. Basic Research in Sci., 1963-64; sr. vis. fellow U. Reading (Eng.), summer 1976; research asso. Inst. Plasma Physics, Nagoya (Japan) U., winter 1981; Chevron vis. prof. energy Calif. Inst. Tech., 1982. Author: (with W.B. Bridges) Electron Dynamics of Diode Regions, 1966, (with A.B. Langdon) Plasma Physics via Computer Simulation, 1983; contbr. articles to profl. jours. Served with USNR, 1944-46. U.S.-Japan Coop. Sci. Program grantee, 1966-67. Fellow IEEE, Am. Phys. Soc., AAAS; mem. Sigma Xi, Tau Beta Pi, Eta Kappa Nu. Patentee in field; co-originator many-particle plasma simulations in two and three dimensions using cloud-in-cell methods, 1966. Home: 4050 Valente Ct Lafayette CA 94549 Office: EECS Dept Cory Hall U Calif Berkeley CA 94720 *My doctoral students in plasma theory and simulation are given ready access to professionals and challenging problems. I seldom impose a thesis problem. Their transition from classroom to research student is never easy and may take up to a year before they make a commitment to a problem. Then we jointly question approaches and interpret results, again using professionals. However, the research is really theirs and averages 3 to 5 publications by graduation. Their subsequent successes in fusion research and other areas reinforce my use of this seemingly undirected leadership.*

BIRDSONG, GEORGE YANCY, manufacturing company executive; b. Suffolk, Va., Nov. 8, 1939; s. William McLemore and Yancey (Brooking) B.; m. Sue Benton, June 10, 1961; children—Anne Cabell, David Jefferson, Charles Randolph. B.A., Washington and Lee U., Lexington, Va., 1961; LL.B., U. Va., 1964, diploma basic advanced mgmt, 1968. Bar: Va. bar 1964. Mem. firm Godwin & Godwin, Suffolk, 1964-66; sec.-treas. Birdsong Peanuts div. Birdsong Corp., Suffolk, 1966—, exec. v.p., 1981—. Chmn. Suffolk Redevel. and Housing Authority, 1966—; Pres. Louise Obici Meml. Hosp. Found., Suffolk, 1980—; chpt.; pres. Tri-County Area Planned Parenthood, 1969—; mem. president's adv. council Va. Wesleyan Coll., 1971—. Recipient Disting. Service award Suffolk Jaycees, 1971. Mem. Va. Bar Assn., Suffolk Bar Assn., Suffolk C. of C. Methodist. Clubs: Suffork Sports, Suffolk Tennis Assn., Elks, Rotary (Suffolk). Home: 608 Riverview Dr Suffolk VA 23434 Office: 311 Factory St Suffolk VA 23434

BIRDSONG, WILLIAM HERBERT, JR., retail executive; b. Mayersville, Miss., Mar. 16, 1918; s. William H. and Julia Morgan

(Pearl) B.; m. Onylene Joyce Lepper, Apr. 5, 1941 (dec. Apr. 1970); children: William Herbert, Joyce O. Birdsong Murphy, Mary H. Birdsong Davion; m. Jewel Ott Brick, July 18, 1971. B.S., Miss. State Coll., 1939; grad., Army Inf. Sch., 1940, Command and Gen. Staff Coll., 1950, Armed Forces Staff Coll., 1954, Nat. War Coll., 1958. Commd. 2d lt. U.S. Army, 1939, advanced through grades to brig. gen., 1963; command and staff positions (5th and 1st Inf. Divs.), Europe and U.S., 1939-54, assigned army staff, Pentagon, 1954-57, UN, Korea, 1958-59, Inf. Sch., 1960-62; asst. div. comdr. (3d Inf. Div.), Germany, 1963-65, chief of staff, Turkey, 1965-67, joint staff Pentagon, 1967-70, comdg. gen., Ft. Campbell, Ky., 1970-72, ret., 1972; pres. Brick's Men's Store, Inc., Clarksville, Tenn., 1972—; Pres. USO Operating Council, Clarksville, 1974. Decorated D.S.M., Silver Star, Legion of Merit with oak leaf cluster, Bronze Star with 3 oak leaf clusters, Army Commendation medal with oak leaf cluster, Purple Heart, U.S.; Croix de Guerre, France). Mem. Clarksville C. of C. (chmn. mil. affairs com. 1973, 74, pres. 1976), Sigma Chi. Methodist. Clubs: Masons (32 deg.), Shriners, Sojourners, Clarksville Country, Cole Park Golf. Home: 1011 Sunset Dr Clarksville TN 37040

BIRDWHISTELL, RAY L., educator; b. Cin., Sept. 29, 1918; s. Robert N. and Hattie Queen (Hughes) B.; m. Anne Davison; children—Jill Read Birdwhistell Pierce, Nancy Mead Birdwhistell Rothberg. A.B., Miami U., Oxford, Ohio, 1940; M.A., Ohio State U., 1941; Ph.D., U. Chgo., 1951. Lectr. in anthropology U. Toronto, 1944-46; instr. sociology U. Louisville, 1946-48, asst. prof. anthropology, dept. sociology, 1948-52, asso. prof. anthropology, dept. psychology and sociology, 1952-56; asso. prof. anthropology, dept. anthropology and linguistics U. Buffalo, 1956-59; coordinator Inst. for Research in Human Communication, 1956-59; sr. research scientist Eastern Pa. Psychiat. Inst., 1959-77; prof. research in anthropology, dept. psychiatry Health Scis. Center, Temple U., Phila., 1959-66, clin. prof. psychiatry, dept. psychiatry, adj. prof. anthropology, dept. behavioral sci., 1966-68; vis. prof. communication Annenberg Sch. Communications, U. Pa., 1969-70, prof. communication, 1970-83, prof. folklore and communication, 1983—; vis. lectr. U. Chgo., summer 1951; research asso. Fgn. Service Inst., Dept. State, 1952; research cons. Center for Advanced Study in Behavioral Scis., Palo Alto, Calif., 1956, fellow, 1968-69; vis. prof. dept. anthropology U. B.C., Vancouver, 1968; Cons., dept. psychiatry Western Psychiat. Inst., Pitts., 1957-64, Emory U. Med. Sch., Atlanta, 1963-64, U. Louisville, Syracuse U., SUNY, Worcester (Mass.) State Hosp., VA Hosp., Palo Alto, Langley Porter Clinic, U. Kans., Ind. U., NIMH, U. Ill., U. Mich. Author: Kinesics and Context; co-author: Natural History of an Interview; Adv. editor: Family Processes; Mem. editorial adv. bd.: Miss. Quar; mem. editorial bd.: Communication; Contbr. numerous articles, reviews to profl. jours. Fellow Am. Anthrop. Assn., AAAS, Soc. for Applied Anthropology; mem. Phila. Anthrop. Soc., Am. Acad. Polit. and Social Sci., Phi Beta Kappa, Alpha Kappa Delta, Kappa Pi Epsilon. Home: 1417 E Shore Dr Brigantine NJ 08203 Office: Annenberg Sch Communications U Pa 3620 Walnut St Philadelphia PA 19104 *Nothing never happens.*

BIRDZELL, SAMUEL HENRY, hosp. adminstr.; b. Toledo, Ill., Aug. 12, 1916; s. Walter Raymond and Gertie Mae (Kingery) B.; m. Annabel Ellis, Dec. 13, 1936; children—Marcia (Mrs. Peter McGow), Jeffry. B.S., U. Ill., 1937, M.S., 1944; M.S. in Hosp. Adminstrn, Northwestern, 1960. Athletic dir. Louisville (Ill.) High Sch., 1937-40; with WPA, Herrin, Ill., 1940-41; instr. U. Ill., 1942-44; with VA (various locations), 1946—; dep. regional dir. Region III, 1968-70; hosp. dir. VA Hosp., Omaha, 1970-76, Danville, Ill., 1976—; also med. dir. VA Dist. 25, 1972-76, Dist. 15, 1981—. Contbr. articles to profl. jours. Served with AUS, 1945-46. Fellow Am. Coll. Hosp. Adminstrs.; mem. Am. Soc. Pub. Adminstrn. (v.p. 1959, 64), Fed. Exec. Assn. (pres. chpt. 1974-75), Fed. Alumni Assn., Assn. Mil. Surgeons, Am. Legion. Methodist. Clubs: Mason, Elk, Rotarian. Home: 1711 Devonshire Dr Champaign IL 61821 Office: 1900 E Main St Danville IL 61832

BIRELY, WILLIAM CRAMER, investment banker; b. Thurmont, Md., Nov. 13, 1919; s. Victor Morris and Dorothy Grace (Rouzer) B.; m. Luelle Avis Langness, July 21, 1943. Student, Am. U., 1941-42. With Folger, Nolan, Inc., Washington, 1947-52, v.p., 1950-52; gen. partner Rouse, Brewer & Becker, Washington, 1952-55; exec. v.p., treas. Birely & Co., Washington, 1955-62, pres., 1962-67; also dir.; v.p. Mason & Co. (now Legg, Mason, Wood, Walker, Inc.), 1967-70; investment banker Lang & Co., Washington, 1970—; v.p., dir. Thurmont (Md.) Bank (now subs. Suburban Bancorp.), 1961-73; adv. bd. Farmers & Mechanics Nat. Bank, Thurmont, Md., 1975-76; spl. dep. sheriff, Montgomery County, Md., 1965—; mem. adv. council SBA, 1962-66. Mem. Bd. Appeals Montgomery County, 1965, Montgomery County Council, 1965-66; treas. Young Republican Club of Montgomery County, 1947, pres., 1948; del. Md. Rep. Conv., 1952, 56, 60; mem. gen. inaugural coms. Eisenhower and Nixon, 1953, 57, Nixon and Agnew, 1968, 72, Reagan and Bush, 1980. Served with F.A. AUS, 1943-44. Recipient Gov.'s citation for outstanding service to Md. Mem. Am. Legion; Life mem. Frederick County, Carroll County, Columbia, Montgomery County hist. socs.; Mem. Huguenot Soc. Washington (life mem., former v.p.), S.A.R. (former nat. trustee), Soc. Mayflower Descs., Soc. Colonial Wars, Soc. War 1812. Club: Bond. Home: 900 Ashton Rd Ashton MD 20861 Office: 3414 1st Ave Suite 13 Olney MD 20832

BIRENBAUM, WILLIAM M., university president; b. Macomb, Ill., July 18, 1923; s. Joseph and Rose (Whiteman) B.; m. Helen Bloch, Mar. 8, 1951; children: Susan, Lauren Amy, Charles. Student, Iowa State Tchrs. Coll., 1943; Dr. Law, U. Chgo., 1949; L.H.D., Columbia Coll., Chgo., 1970. Dir. student affairs U. Chgo., 1949-54; mem. faculty social scis. coll of univ., 1950-54; dean students Univ. Coll., 1955-57; dir. research, conf. bd. Asso. Research Councils, Ford Found. project study post-doctoral internat. edn. exchanges, 1954-55; asst. v.p. Wayne State U., 1957-61; dean New Sch. Social Research, N.Y.C., 1961-64; v.p., provost Bklyn. Center, L.I. U., 1964-67; pres. Edn. Affiliate, Bedford-Stuyvesant Devel. & Services Corp., Bklyn, 1967-68, S.I. Community Coll., 1968-76; also leader study mission to People's Republic China, 1973; pres. Antioch U., 1976—; mem. faculty N.Y. U. Grad. Sch. Edn., 1969-70. Author: Overlive: Power, Poverty and the University, 1968, Something for Everybody is Not Enough: An Educator's Search for His Education, 1971; Contbg. author: Student Personnel Work in Urban Colleges. Cons. Austrian Ministry Edn., Vienna, 1969; higher edn. adviser Republic of Zambia, 1972; cons. U. Zambia, 1972; guest lectr. 4th Internat. Congress for Sci. Edn., Sorbonne, Paris, 1973; vis. prof. U. Mass., Amherst, 1974-75; faculty Salzburg Seminar in Am. Studies, 1976; Founder Nat. Student Assn., 1946-48, chmn. nat. faculty bd., 1950-54; pres. Assn. Community Councils Met. Chgo., 1955-57; chmn. Mich. Cultural Commn., 1960-61; founder, original dir. Detroit Adventure, vol. assn. cultural instns., 1958-61; mem. Bd. Edn., dists. 21-22, N.Y.C., 1962-64; bd. dirs. Bklyn. chpt. ACLU, 1967-75, chmn. acad. freedom com., 1967-70; chmn. edn. com. Met. council Am. Jewish Congress, 1967-70, chmn. acad. freedom com., 1967-77; trustee Little Red Schoolhouse on Bleecker St., N.Y.C., 1963-75; bd. adv. Bklyn. Acad. Music, 1965—, Bklyn Inst. Arts and Scis; mem. mass media program com. Religion in Am. Life, 1969-75; mem. adv. council Korean Student Assn., N.Y., 1969-75; adv. bd. ERIC Clearinghouse for Jr. Coll., Los Angeles, 1970-73; mem. commn. on curriculum Am. Assn. Jr. Colls., 1970-73; mem. nat. adv. council Eastern Va. Med. Sch., 1971-74; bd. govs. Rochdale Inst., 1972-76; bd. dirs. Brotherhood-in-Action, 1972-75, Regional Plan Assn., 1972-75; Trustee Friends World Coll., Westbury, N.Y. Mem. Chgo. Bar Assn., Delta Sigma. Home: 108 Willow St Brooklyn NY 11201 Office: Antioch U Yellow Springs OH 45387

BIRGE, ROBERT WALSH, physicist; b. Berkeley, Calif., Jan. 30, 1924; s. Raymond Thayer and Irene Adelaide (Walsh) B.; m. Elizabeth Ann Chamberlain, June 26, 1948; children—Margit Ann, Bettine, Norman Owen. A.B. with honors, U. Calif., 1945; M.A., Harvard U., 1947, Ph.D., 1951. Crew mem. Crocker 60 Cyclotron, Radiation Lab., U. Calif., Berkeley, 1942-45; research asst. Harvard U., Cambridge, Mass., 1947-50; research physicist Radiation Lab., Berkeley, 1950-58; co-group leader physics div. Lawrence Berkeley Lab., 1958-71, staff sr. scientist, 1958—, group leader physics div., 1971-73, asso. dir. physics, computer sci. and math. div., 1973-81; lectr. physics U. Calif., Berkeley, 1958-69; Guggenheim fellow, 1960; OEEC sr. vis. fellow Ecole Polytechnique, Paris, 1961; NATO sr. fellow, vis. scientist Center European Nuclear Research, Geneva, Switzerland, 1971-72. Contbr. articles in field to profl. jours. Served with U.S. Army, 1944-46. Fellow Am. Phys. Soc.; mem. AAAS, Fedn. Am. Scientists, N.Y. Acad. Scis., Phi Beta Kappa, Sigma Xi. Office: Lawrence Berkeley Lab 1 Cyclotron Rd Berkeley CA 94720

BIRINGER, PAUL PETER, electrical engineer; b. Marosvasarhely, Hungary, Oct. 1, 1924; emigrated to Can., 1952, naturalized, 1957; s. Arpad and Eszter (Izsak) B.; m. Barbro E.G. Rengman, Apr. 15, 1952; children: Anne Barbro, Monica Eva. Diploma engring, U. Budapest, 1947, U. Stockholm, 1951; Ph.D., U. Toronto, 1956. Research asso. Royal Inst. Tech., Stockholm, 1947-52; research asso. U. Toronto, 1952-57, mem. faculty, 1957—, prof. elec. engring., 1965—; pres. Elec. Engring. Consociates Ltd., 1968-71; vice chmn. bd. govs. George Brown Coll. Applied Arts and Tech., 1976; cons. in field. Author; patentee in field; inventor magnetic frequency changers. Recipient Pleyel award research, 1950, Son's of Martha medal, 1968; sr. research fellow Nat. Research Council Can., 1967. Fellow IEEE (Centennial medal 1984); mem. Engring. Inst. Can., Assn. Profl. Engrs., Ont., Am. Soc. Engring. Edn., Congress Internat. Grands Reseaux, Internat. Electric Commn. Clubs: Kiwanis, Toronto Lawn Tennis, Empire. Home: 6 Lumley Ave Toronto ON M4G 2X4 Canada Office: U Toronto Toronto ON M5S 1A4 Canada

BIRK, ROGER EMIL, investment broker; b. St. Cloud, Minn., July 14, 1930; s. Emil S. and Barbara E. (Zimmer) B.; m. Mary Lou Schrank, June 25, 1955; children: Kathleen, Steven, Mary Beth, Barbara. B.A., St. John's U., 1952. Mgr. Merrill Lynch, Pierce, Fenner and Smith, Inc., Ft. Wayne, Ind., 1964-66, mgr., Kansas City, Mo., 1966-68, asst. div. dir., N.Y.C., 1968-70, div. dir., 1971-74, pres., N.Y.C., 1974-76, chmn. bd., 1980—; pres. Merrill Lynch & Co., N.Y.C., 1976—, chmn. bd., chief exec. officer, 1981—; dir. N.Y. Stock Exchange, 1981—, vice chmn., 1983—; mem. Bus. Roundtable, 1981—, Pres.'s Commn. on Exec. Exchange, 1981—, Pres.'s Pvt. Sector Survey on Cost Control, 1982—. Chmn. nat. adv. council St. John's U., 1975-76, bd. regents, 1975-78; trustee U. Notre Dame, 1981—. Served with AUS, 1952-54. Mem. Nat. Assn. Securities Dealers (mem. long-range planning com. 1975-78), Council on Fgn. Relations. Club: Navesink Country (Middletown N.J.). Office: Merrill Lynch & Co One Liberty Plaza 165 Broadway New York NY 10006

BIRK, SHARON ANASTASIA, nursing administrator; b. Mpls., July 4, 1937; d. Vincent H. and Ethel C. (Baker) B. B.S. in Nursing, U. Minn., 1960. Asst. head nurse premature nursery Charles T. Miller Hosp., St. Paul, Minn., 1960-61, staff nurse labor and delivery, 1961-63; supr. child devel. study U. Minn., Mpls., 1963-65, research asst. dept. ob-gyn., 1965-66; maternal and infant care project nurse coordinator St. Paul Ramsey Hosp., 1966-67; research asso. dept. ob-gyn. U. Miami (Fla.) Sch. Medicine, 1967-73; asso. ob-gyn. U. Fla. Sch. Medicine, Gainesville, 1974-79; adminstr. dept. practice Nurses Assn. of Am. Coll. Obstetricians and Gynecologists, Chgo., 1979-81, acting dir., 1980-81; asst. dir. nursing ob/gyn services Norfolk (Va.) Gen. Hosp., 1981, dir. splty. nursing, 1982—. Contbr. numerous articles on lipid-carbohydrate metabolism studies and oral contraception to profl. jours. Mem. Va. Soc. Nursing Service Adminstrs., Nat. Perinatal Assn., Nurses Assn. of Am. Coll. Obstetricians and Gynecologists (charter mem., dir. cert. corp. 1980—), Sigma Theta Tau. Office: Norfolk Gen Hosp 600 Gresham Dr Norfolk VA 23507

BIRKELBACH, ALBERT OTTMAR, oil company executive; b. Oak Park, Ill., Feb. 22, 1927; s. August and Ann B.; m. Shirley M. Spandet, Aug. 21, 1948; children: J.A., Lisa M., Grace L. Birkelbach Boland, Ann C. B.S.Ch.E., U. Ill., 1949. Various engring., supervisory and mgmt. positions Globe Oil & Refining Co., Lemont, Ill., 1949-53, Anderson Prichard Oil Corp., Cyril, Okla., 1953-58, Signal Oil & Gas Co., Los Angeles, 1958-64; mng. dir. Raffinerie Belge de Petroles, Antwerp, Belgium, 1964-74; v.p. Occidental Petroleum Corp., London, Eng., 1972-74; cons. in field, 1974-75; pres. ATC Petroleum Inc., N.Y.C., 1975-81, also dir.; pres. Amorient Petroleum Corp., Laguna Niguel, Calif., 1981-84; mgmt. cons., 1984—. Served with USCG, 1945-47. Decorated knight Order Leopold, Belgium). Mem. Am. Inst. Chem. Engrs., Am. Petroleum Inst., Nat. Petroleum Refiners Assn. Clubs: Am., London; N.Y. Athletic (N.Y.C.). Office: 30100 Crown Valley Pkwy Laguna Niguel CA 92677

BIRKELUND, JOHN PETER, investment company banking executive; b. Chgo., June 23, 1930; s. George R. and Ruth (Olsen) B.; m. Constance I. Smiles, Oct. 25, 1958; children: Gwynne, Elizabeth, Constance Olivia, Dianna. A.B., Princeton U., 1952. Cons. Booz Allen & Hamilton, Chgo., 1956; v.p. Amsterdam Overseas Corp., N.Y.C., 1956-71; co-founder, ch., dir. New Court Securities Corp., N.Y.C., 1971-81; pres., dir. Dillon, Read & Co., Inc., N.Y.C., 1981—; dir. Copperweld Corp., Pitts., 1979—, Lenox Corp., Lawrenceville, N.J., 1980—. Pres. Hewitt Sch., N.Y.C., 1978—, 1020 Fifth Ave. Corp., N.Y.C., 1972—. Served to lt. USNR, 1953-55. Mem. Phi Beta Kappa. Clubs: Downtown Assn., Links, University (N.Y.C.); Princeton Cap & Gown. Home: 1020 Fifth Ave New York NY 10028 Office: Dillon Read & Co Inc 46 William St New York NY 10005

BIRKEMEIER, WILLIAM PHILIP, engineering educator, researcher; b. Evanston, Ill., Nov. 10, 1927; s. William Herman and Valley (Schultz) B.; m. Helen Margaret Taggart, Feb. 3, 1951; children: Richard P., James D., Christine A. B.S. in E.E., Northwestern U., 1951, M.S., U. Ark-Fayetteville, 1954; Ph.D., Purdue U., 1959. Registered profl. engr., Wis. Engr. Collins Radio Co., Cedar Rapids, Iowa, 1951-54; instr. elec. engring. Purdue U., 1955-59; assoc. prof. U. Ark., 1959-60, U.Wis.-Madison, 1961-65; prof. U. Wis.-Madison, 1965-80, chmn. dept. elec. and computer engring., 1980—; cons. A.O. Smith,, Giddings & Lewis, Harris Corp. Patentee in field. Served with USN, 1946-48. Grantee in field. Mem. IEEE, Internat. Union of Radio Scientists. Home: 409 Oak Crest Ave Madison WI 53705 Office: Dept Elec and Computer Engring U Wis 1415 Johnson Dr Madison WI 53706

BIRKENHEAD, THOMAS BRUCE, theatre administrator, former educator; b. N.Y.C., Dec. 19, 1931; s. Thomas A. and Florence (Morrison) B.; m. Susan Leslie Arkin, Dec. 3, 1954 (div. 1983); children: Peter Lawrence, David Andrew, Richard James, Alison Jane. B.A., Bklyn. Coll., 1954, M.A., 1958; Ph.D., New Sch. Social Research, 1963. Lectr. econs. Bklyn. Coll., CUNY, 1957-60; instr., 1960-65, asst. prof., 1965-69, asso. prof., 1969-71, prof. econs., 1972-80; dean Sch. Social Scis., 1972-75; asst. gen. mgr. Iron Mountain Prodns., 1978—; gen. mgr. Twyla Tharp on Broadway, 1980—; co. mgr. Do Black Patent Leather Shoes Really Reflect Up?, Present Laughter, Master Harold and the Boys, Children of a Lesser God, Ain't Misbehavin'; gen. mgr. Twyla Tharp on Broadway, 1980, 81; asst. mgr. Chapter Two; econ. cons. Emanuel Azenberg, 1977-; gen. mgr. Cape Cod Melody Tent, Hyannis, Mass., 1969-71, 76; bus. mgr. Theatre II of Glen Cove, N.Y., 1970-74. Mgr.: Ain't Misbehavin'. Mem. Am. Econ Assn., U.S. Inst. Theatre Tech. (dir. 1967-69), Am. Def. Preparedness Assn., Nat. Rifle Assn., Rolls Royce Owners Club. Home: 353 W 44th St Apt 1A New York NY 10036 Office: Iron Mountain Prodns 165 W 46th St New York NY 10036 *Although engaged in intellectual activity, my most memorable moments are physical.*

BIRKENSTOCK, JAMES WARREN, business machine manufacturing company executive; b. Burlington, Iowa, May 7, 1912; s. George Louis and Anna (Flynn) B.; m. Jean Lois Hale, Nov. 30, 1935; children: Robert Hale, Joyce Ann. Student, Burlington Jr. Coll., 1933; B.S., U. Iowa, 1935. With IBM Corp., 1935-72, successively student salesman, jr. salesman, sr. salesman, asst. mgr., St. Louis, br. mgr., Kansas City; spl. sales exec. World Hdqrs.; gen. sales mgr. mgr. future demands, spl. adminstrv. asst. corporate ofcls., exec. asst. to pres., exec. dir. product planning and market analysis div., dir. comml. devel., 1935-58, v.p. comml. devel., 1958-70, v.p. corporate relations, 1971-72; pres. Intercal, Inc., 1973—; dir. Univ. Patents, Inc., Norwalk, Conn., DASI Industries, Inc., Chevy Chase, Md., ECD, Inc., Troy, Mich., Harris Trust Co. of Fla. Trustee Chas. Babbage Inst. Mem. Beta Gamma Sigma, Delta Sigma Pi. Clubs: Country of Fla., Ocean of Fla., Knights of Malta. Office: Village of Golf FL 33436

BIRKERTS, GUNNAR, architect; b. Riga, Latvia, Jan. 17, 1925; came to U.S., 1949, naturalized, 1954; s. Peter and Meria (Shop) B.; m. Sylvia Zvirbulis, July 29, 1950; children—Sven Peter, Andra Sylvia, Erik Gunnar. Diplomingeneur Architekt, Technische Hochschule, Stuttgart, Germany, 1949. Designer Perkins & Will, Chgo., 1950-51, Eero Saarinen & Assos., Bloomfield Hills, Mich., 1951-55; prin. chief designer Minoru Yamasaki & Assos., Birmingham, Mich., 1955-59; pres. Gunnar Birkerts & Assos., Inc., Birmingham, 1959; asst. prof. architecture U. Mich., 1961, asso. prof., 1963-69, prof., 1969—; Graham fellow, 1970; architect in residence Am. Acad. in Rome, 1976; 1st Lawrence J. Plym. disting. prof. architecture U. Ill., 1982—. Prin. works include, Schwartz House, Northville, Mich. (First Honor award AIA 1961); prin. works include: Schwartz House, Northville, Mich. (Merit award Detroit chpt. AIA 1962), Northville, Mich. (Archtl. Record award 1961), Univ. Reformed Ch., Ann Arbor Mich. (award Ch. Archtl. Guild Am. 1964), Peoples Fed. Savs. & Loan Bank, Royal Oak, Mich. (Merit award Detroit chpt. AIA 1962), Fisher Adminstrv. Center, Detroit (award of merit Mich. Soc. Architects 1967), Detroit (Merit award Mich. chpt. AIA 1967), Detroit Inst. Arts addition, 1300 Lafayette Apts., Detroit, Tougaloo (Miss.) Coll. (award of honor Mich. Soc. Architects 1974), Vocational-Tech. Campus, So. Ill. U., Glen Oaks Community Coll. Campus, Centreville, Mich., Lincoln Sch., Columbus, Ind. (AIA First Honor award 1968), Fed. Res. Bank, Mpls. (award excellence Am. Inst. Steel Constrn. 1974), Mpls. (design award Am. Iron and Steel Inst. 1975), IBM Corp. Computer Center, Sterling Forest, N.Y. (honor award Detroit chpt. AIA 1973), Contemporary Arts Mus., Houston (honor award Detroit chpt. AIA 1975), Dance Instructional Facility at Purchase (award honor Mich. Soc. Architects 1977, Honor award Detroit chpt. AIA 1978), Calvary Baptist Ch., Detroit (Honor award Mich. Soc. Architects 1979), Detroit (award of excellence Am. Inst. Steel Constrn. 1979), IBM Office Bldg., Southfield, Mich. (Honor award Mich. Soc. Architects 1980), Southfield, Mich. (energy conservation award Owens Corning Fiberglas Corp. 1977), Duluth Public Library (Honor award Mich. Soc. Architects 1981), Fire Sta., Corning, N.Y., Corning Mus. of Glass, Law Library Addition, U. Mich., U.S. Embassy Bldg., Helsinki, Finland, Coll. of Law Bldg., U. Iowa, Uris Library Addition, Cornell U., Dist. Office Bldg., Green Bay, Wis.; exhbns. include, Akron Inst. Art, 1940, 54, Under 40, U.S.A.-N.Y., Sao Paulo (Brazil) Bienniale, 1962, Architects League, 1965, Mus. Modern Art, N.Y.C., 1971, Notre Dame U., 1973, N.Y. Mus. Modern Art, 1979, Neuberger Mus., Purchase, N.Y., 1981, Am. Acad. and Inst. Arts and Letters, N.Y.C., U. Ill., 1983. Named Young Designer of Year Akron Inst. Art, 1954; recipient 1st prize Internat. Furniture competition, Cantu, Italy, 1955; 3d prize Internat. competition for Cultural Centre, Belgian Congo; Design award Progressive Architecture mag., 1957, 59, 61, 71; award of excellence Archtl. Record, 1968; Nat. Gold medal Tau Sigma Delta, 1971; Gold medal Detroit chpt. AIA, 1975, Mich. Soc. Architects, 1980; Brunner Meml. prize Am. Acad. and Inst. Arts and Letters, 1981. Fellow AIA, Graham Found., Latvian Architects Assn.; mem. Mich. Soc. Architects, Ch. Archtl. Guild, Hon. Order Ky. Cols. Home: 1830 E Tahquamenon Ct Bloomfield Hills MI 48013 Office: 292 Harmon St Birmingham MI 48009

BIRKETT, JOHN HOOPER, textile company executive; b. Montreal, Que., Can., Oct. 16, 1925; s. Leonard Harris and Gertrude (Caughill) B.; m. Joan Louise Macklaier, Dec. 27, 1952; children: Peter, Jennifer, Timothy, Elisa. B.Commerce, McGill U., Montreal, 1949. Dist. supr. Canadian Liquid Air Co., 1949-54; sales service mgr. Canadian Chm. & Cellulose Co., Ltd., Montreal, 1955-57, asst. sec., 1959-61, Columbia Cellulose Co. Ltd., 1958-59, Canadian Chem. Co. Ltd., Montreal, 1962-63, Celanese Can. Inc., 1963-64, sec., 1964-71, v.p., sec., 1971-72, v.p. adminstrn., 1972-79, dir., 1973-79; v.p. adminstrn., sec. Wabasso Inc., Montreal, 1980-83, v.p. fin. and adminstrn., 1983—. Co-chmn. fin. campaign Montreal YMCA, 1969-71, bd. mgmt., 1969—, exec. com., 1970—. Served with Royal Canadian Navy, 1944-45. Mem. Chartered Inst. Secs. and Adminstrs., Swiss Canadian C. of C. (dir. 1975-80), Can. Textile Inst. (dir.). Mem. Anglican Ch. Clubs: St. James's, Royal Montreal Golf, Red Birds Ski (Montreal). Home: 47 North Ridge Rd Ile Bizard PQ Canada Office: 1825 Graham Blvd Montreal PQ Canada

BIRKHEAD, GUTHRIE SWEENEY, JR., polit. scientist, univ. dean; b. Holden, Mo., Oct. 28, 1920; s. Guthrie Sweeney and Yula Donna (Glass) B.; m. Louise Gartner, Aug. 16, 1952; children—Guthrie Sweeney III, Richard Gartner, Evan Clark. A.A., Jefferson City (Mo.) Jr. Coll., 1940; A.B., U. Mo., 1942, A.M., 1947; M.A., Princeton, 1949, Ph.D. in Politics, 1951. Mem. faculty Syracuse U., 1950—, prof. polit. sci., 1960—, chmn. dept., 1959-62, 66-67, dir. met. studies program, 1968-73; asso. dean Maxwell Sch., 1973-77, dean, 1977—; also dir. pub. adminstrn. programs, 1959-62; dir. research UN Inst. Pub. Adminstrn. for, Turkey and; Middle East, 1955-56; cons. Pakistan Adminstrv. Staff Coll., Lahore, 1962-64, Ford Found., Pakistan, 1967-68. Co-author: River Basin Administration and the Delaware, 1960, Science and State Government in New York, 1960, Decisions in Syracuse, 1962; Editor: Administrative Problems in Pakistan, 1966, A Look to the North: Canadian Regional Experience, 1974, Education for Public Service, 1980; Contbr. articles to profl. jours. Chmn. pub. finance com. Community Renewal Plan, Syracuse, N.Y., 1970-72; exec. dir. com. local govt. and home rule N.Y. State Constl. Conv., 1967, Syracuse Charter Commn., 1972-74; mem. Nat. Com. Water Quality Policy Nat. Acad. Scis.-NRC, 1974-76. Served with inf. AUS, 1942-46. Fellow Nat. Municipal League, 1952-53. Mem. AAAS, Am. Soc. Pub. Adminstrn., Nat. Acad. Pub. Adminstrn., Phi Beta Kappa. Home: 220 Lockwood Rd Syracuse NY 13214

BIRKHOFF, ROBERT D., physicist; b. Chgo., Jan. 29, 1925; s. Robert D. and Ellen (Gleason) B.; m. Ariel Frances Jewett, Nov. 4, 1945. B.S., MIT, 1945; Ph.D., Northwestern U., 1949. Asso. prof. U. Tenn., Knoxville, 1949-55, prof. physics and astronomy, 1965—; physicist Oak Ridge Nat. Lab., 1955-81; cons., 1950-55; head radiol. def. State of Tenn., 1952-55. Author: Handbuch der Physik, Vol. 34, 1958, Health Physics, 1967; also articles. Fellow Am. Phys., Soc., Health Physics Soc. Measured cross sects. for plasmon excitation, electron flux in irradiated media, optical properties of metals, liquids, scintillators, electron diffusion in metals, plasmon and bremsstrahlung light from irradiated metals, electronic and optical properties of submicron sizes. Home: Apt 1701 Embassy House Condominium 770 S Palm Ave Sarasota FL 33577

BIRKHOLZ, RAYMOND JAMES, manufacturing company executive; b. Chgo., Nov. 10, 1936; s. Raymond I. and Mary (Padian) B.; m. Judy A. Birkholz, Apr. 23, 1966; children: Raymond J., Scott C., Matthew R. B.S. in M.E., Purdue U., 1958; M.B.A., U. Chgo., 1963. Registered prof. engr., Ill. Vice pres. mfg. and engring. Ogden Corp., N.Y.C., 1980-81; pres. Ogden Indsl. Products Corp., Cleve., 1981—. Address: Ogden Industrial Products Corp 20521 Chagrin Blvd Cleveland OH 44122

BIRKIMER, DONALD LEO, civil engineer; b. New Lexington, Ohio, Sept. 6, 1941; s. Edgar E. and Virginia Eileen (Johnson) B.; m. Edith Marie Lowe, Aug. 25, 1962; children: Mark Austin, Thomas Edgar, Julie Lee. B.S. in Civil Engring, Ohio U., 1963; M.S., U. Cin., 1965, Ph.D., 1968; postgrad. Mgmt. Devel. Program, Harvard U., 1973. Registered profl. engr., Ohio. Research scientist Battelle Meml. Inst., Columbus, Ohio, 1968-69; acting chief constrn. materials br. U.S. Army Constrn. Engring. Research Lab., Champaign, Ill., 1969-71; asst. head advanced weapons dept. Naval Surface Weapons Center, Dahlgren, Va., 1971-75; tech. dir. Coast Guard Research and Devel. Center, Groton, Conn., 1975-81, Naval-Civil Engring. Lab., Port Hueneme, Calif., 1981—; cons. to industry. NASA trainee, 1965-68. Co-author 2 books.; Contbr. articles to profl. jours. Mem. Conn. Academy Scientists and Engrs., Nat. Soc. Profl. Engrs., ASCE, Am. Mgmt. Assn., Am. Concrete Inst. (Wason medal). Club: Harvard (Washington). Office: Naval Civil Engring Lab Port Hueneme CA 93043 *My basic feeling is that all constraints on personal development are self imposed. Personal commitment and drive are the beginning and perserverance is a must.*

BIRKINS, RODNEY MANN, retail company executive; b. Englewood, N.J., Sept. 11, 1930; s. Marshall Edwin and Alma Lynette (Parker) B.; m. Janet Seward, Dec. 12, 1953; children: Rodney Mann, Arthur, William, Kim. B.A., Colgate U., 1954. With J.C. Penney Co. Inc., N.Y.C., 1957—, divisional mdse. mgr., 1976-81, v.p., 1981-82, sr. v.p., 1982—. Served to 1st lt. USAF, 1954-57. Mem. Mail Order Assn. Am. (bd. dirs. 1981—). Presbyterian. Office: JC Penney Co Inc 1301 Ave of Americas New York NY 10019

BIRKS, NEIL, metallurgical engineering educaotr, consultant; b. Sheffield, Eng., Oct. 16, 1935; came to U.S., 1978; s. Henry and May (Street) B.; m. Mary Potts; children: Jane C., David J. B.Metallurgy, Sheffield U., Ph.D. in Metallurgy. Chartered engr. NATO research fellow Max Planck Inst., Gottingen, W. Ger., 1960-62; research investigator United Steel Cos., Sheffield, Eng., 1962-66; lectr. metallurgy U. Sheffield, 1964-72, sr. lectr., 1972-78; prof. metall. engring. U. Pitts, 1978—; cons. in metallurgy, Pitts., 1978—. Co-author: Introduction to High Temperature Oxidation of Metals, 1983. Fellow Instn. Metallurgists London; mem. Metals Soc. London, Am. Soc. Metals, AIMe. Mem. Ch. of England. Home: 840 Ella St Pittsburgh PA 15243 Office: 848 Benedum Hall Univ Pittsburgh Pittsburgh PA 15261

BIRMAN, JOAN S., mathematician; b. N.Y.C., May 30, 1927; d. George and Lilian (Siegel) Lyttle; m. Joseph Leon Birman, Feb. 22, 1950; children—Kenneth, Deborah, David. Student, Swarthmore Coll., 1944-46; B.A., Barnard Coll., 1948; M.A., Columbia U., 1950; Ph.D. in Math, N.Y. U., 1968. Asst. prof. math. Stevens Inst. Tech., 1968-72, asso. prof., 1972-73; prof. math. Barnard Coll., Columbia U., N.Y.C., 1973—, chmn. dept., 1973—. Contbr. articles to profl. jours.; author: Links and Mapping Class Groups, 1974. Sloan Found. fellow, 1974-76. Fellow Japan Soc. for Promotion of Sci.; mem. Am. Math. Soc. (mem. at large council), N.Y. Acad. Scis. (human rights com.), Am. Women in Math. Home: 100 Wellington Ave New York NY 10804 Office: Dept Math Columbia Univ New York NY 10027

BIRMAN, JOSEPH LEON, educator; b. N.Y.C., May 21, 1927; s. Max and Miriam Ida (Meyerson) B.; m. Joan Sylvia Lyttle, Feb. 22, 1950; children: Kenneth, Deborah, David. B.S., CCNY, 1947; M.A., Columbia U., 1950, Ph.D., 1952; Doctorate 'es Sciences honoris causa, U. Rennes, France, 1974. Sr. physicist, head luminescence sect. GTE Research Labs., N.Y., 1952-62; Mary Amanda Wood vis. prof. U. Pa., 1960; asso. prof. physics N.Y. U., 1962-64, prof., 1964-74; Henry Semat prof. physics City Coll., CUNY, 1974—; cons. research labs.; vis. prof. U. Paris (France), Ecole Normale Superieure, 1969-70; Japan Soc. for Promotion of Sci. vis. prof. Research Inst. for Fundamental Physics, U. Kyoto, Japan, 1978, 80; vis. prof. Inst. Hautes Etudes Scientifiques, Bures/Yvette, France, 1976, 78, 80, 82, 83; vis. prof. dept. theoretical physics Oxford (Eng.) U., 1981; Lady Davis vis. prof. Technion, Israel, 1981. Author: Theoretical Physics, 1952, Handbuch der Physik, Vol. 25/2b, 1974 (Russian transl. 1978); Editor: Light Scattering in Solids, 1976, 79; Contbr.: over 200 articles to profl. jours. Served with USNR, 1945-46. Guggenheim fellow, 1980-81; research grantee NSF, Army Research Office, Aerospace Research Labs., 1962—. Fellow Am. Phys. Soc. Home: 100 Wellington Ave New Rochelle NY 10804 Office: Physics Dept City Coll 138th St and Convent Ave New York NY 10031

BIRMELIN, AUGUST ROBERT, artist, art educator; b. Newark, N.J., Nov. 7, 1933; s. August William and Julia (Boll) B.; m. Blair Tillisch, Apr. 28, 1960; children: Lucas, Nicholas. Cert., The Cooper Union Art Sch., N.Y.C., 1951-54; B.F.A., Yale U., 1956, M.F.A., 1960. Asst. prof. art Queens Coll., City U.N.Y., Flushing, 1964-67, assoc. prof., 1967-74, prof., 1974—. Exhibited (onw-man shows numerous art galleries); (works represented) Mus. Modern Art., N.Y.C., Met. Mus. Art., N.Y.C., The Hirschorn Mus., Washington. Served with AUS, 1957-59. Am. Acad. Rome Fellowship awardee, 1961-64; Tiffany Found. grantee, 1974; N.J. Council on Arts grantee, 1981; NEA grantee, 1982. Home: 176 Highwood Ave Leonia NJ 07605 Office: Art Dept Queens Coll City U Flushing NY 11367

BIRMINGHAM, BASCOM WAYNE, retired government official; b. Grand Island, Nebr., June 20, 1925; s. James C. and Stella M. (Sorrels) B.; m. Lois Marie Booth, Sept. 3, 1949; children: Steven W., Janet L. Birmingham Chamberlin. S.B., M.I.T., 1948, S.M., 1951. With Sorrels Supply Co., Poteau, Okla., 1947, Wester Geophys. Soc., Worland, Wyo., 1948, W.R. Holway & Assos., Tulsa, 1948-50; chief processes sect., cryogenics div. Nat. Bur. Standards, Boulder, Colo., 1951-63, chief cryogenics div., 1963-68; dep. dir. Inst. Basic Standards, 1968-77; dir. Boulder Labs., 1977-82; cons. cryogenic engring. Birmingham Assocs., 1982—; Mem. Boulder Zoning Bd., 1964-66; bd. dirs. Community Hosp., 1968-77; v.p. Rocky Mountain Eye Found., 1978—. Author: monograph Technology of Liquid Helium, 1968, Am. editor Cryogenics Jour, 1968-83. Served with USNR, 1944-46. Recipient gold medal service award Commerce Dept., 1953, 71, meritorious service award, 1961, Sci. fellow, 1966-67; Best Paper award Cryogenic Engring. Conf., 1961. Mem. Boulder C. of C. (bd. dirs. 1979-82). Patentee in field. Home: 5440 White Pl Boulder CO 80303

BIRMINGHAM, DONALD JOSEPH, physician; b. Youngstown, Ohio, Aug. 28, 1911; s. Thomas Henry and Anna Veronica (Millsop) B.; m. Louise Van Arnam, June 4, 1966; 1 son, Donald Joseph. B.S., John Carroll U., 1936; M.D., St. Louis U., 1940; postgrad., N.Y. U., 1945-46, 49-51. Diplomate: Am. Bd. Dermatology. Commd. asst. surgeon USPHS, 1941, advanced through grades to med. dir., 1952; med. dir. Cin., 1952-64; mem. faculty Wayne State U., Detroit, 1964—, chmn. dept. dermatology, 1972-80, prof. dept. dermatology, 1980—; cons. to industry on occupational dermatology. Contbr. chpts. to textbooks, articles to profl. jours. Recipient Surgeon Gen.'s Meritorious award, 1964; Rockefeller fellow, 1945-46, 49-51. Fellow A.C.P.; mem. AMA, Am. Acad. Dermatology, Am. Dermatol. Assn., Am. Occupational Medicine Assn., Am. Conf. on Indsl. Hygiene, Am. Indsl. Hygiene Assn. Roman Catholic. Home: 19811 Wedgewood Dr Grosse Pointe Woods MI 48236 Office: 4201 St Antoine Detroit MI 48201

BIRMINGHAM, MARTIN F., banker; b. Rochester, N.Y., Oct. 30, 1921; s. Edward M. and Mary Elizabeth (Egleton) B.; m. Ann Louise Bayer, Sept. 30, 1950; children: Katherine J., Mary L., Mark R., Martin K. Student, Dartmouth Coll., 1961, Columbia, 1963. Vice pres. Abstract & Title Ins. Co. (now div. Title Guarantee Co.), Rochester, 1940-54; with Marine Midland Bank, Rochester, 1954—, 1968-73, pres., 1973—, also dir., exec. v.p., N.Y.C. Bd. dirs. United Way Rochester; bd. dirs. St. John Fishers Coll. Served with USAAF, 1943-45. Clubs: Country of Rochester, Oak Hill Country, Genessee Valley. Office: Marine Midland Bank 1 Marine Plaza Rochester NY 14639

BIRMINGHAM, MATTHEW THOMAS, JR., publishing company executive; b. Boston, Apr. 30, 1920; s. Matthew Thomas B. and Beatrice (Strong) Birmingaham; m. Jane McCrady Gaillard, Nov. 8, 1947; children: Matthew Thomas, III, Elizabeth, Peter, James. B.A., Trinity Coll., 1942. Prodn. dir. Street & Smith Pub. Co., N.Y.C., 1950-60, v.p., 1950-60; exec. v.p. Matthew Bender Co., N.Y.C. and San Francisco, 1965-66, pres., 1966-74, chmn. bd., chief exec, officer, 1974—, also dir.; group v.p. Times Mirror Co., Los Angeles, 1970—, chmn. bd.; chmn. bd. Matthew Bender Co., N.Y.C., 1974—, Times Mirror Mags., Inc.; chmn. bd. dir. Southwestern Co., Nashville; dir. Sporting News. Trustee Vt. Acad., 1974—. Served to lt. USNR, 1942-46. Fellow Albany Inst. Art; mem. Patron Saratoga Performing Arts. Clubs: Union League, Noroton Yacht, Ft. Orange. Office: Times Mirror Mag Inc 380 Madison Ave New York NY 10017

BIRMINGHAM, PATRICK JOSEPH, hotel executive; b. Phila., Apr. 9, 1937; s. Martin Joseph and Margaret Ann (Scanlon) B.; m. Carol Ferrigno, Feb. 17, 1970. Student pub. schs., Phila. Various positions Sheraton Hotels, 1957-69, 69-78; resident mgr. St. Regis Sheraton, N.Y.C., 1969-71; gen. mgr. Sheraton Hotels, 1979-80; v.p., area mgr. Sheraton South Asia, 1981—; sr. v.p. Sheraton Africa, Europe, Middle East and S. Asia, Sri Lanka and; vis. lectr. Cornell U. Served with U.S. Army, 1954-57. Mem. Am. Hotel and Motor Inn Assn. (pres. Detroit 1971, pres. Phila. 1974, pres. Boston 1978), Freedom Found. Roman Catholic. Club: Algonquin (Boston). Address: Sheraton Mgmt Corp Denham Uxbridge Middlesex UB9 5BT England

BIRMINGHAM, STEPHEN, author; b. Hartford, Conn., May 28, 1931; s. Thomas J. and Editha (Gardner) B.; m. Janet Tillson, Jan. 5, 1951 (div.); children: Mark, Harriet, Carey. B.A. cum laude, Williams Coll., 1950; postgrad., Univ. Coll., Oxford (Eng.) U., 1951. Advt. copywriter Needham, Harper & Steers, Inc., 1953-67. Author: Young Mr. Keefe, 1958, Barbara Greer, 1959, The Towers of Love, 1961, Those Harper Women, 1963, Fast Start, Fast Finish, 1966, Our Crowd: The Great Jewish Families of New York, 1967, The Right People, 1968, Heart Toubles, 1968, The Grandees, 1971, The Late John Marquand, 1972, The Right Places, 1973, Real Lace, 1973, Certain People: America's Black Elite, 1977, The Golden Dream: Suburbia in the 1970's, 1978, Jacqueline Bouvier Kennedy Onassis, 1978, Life at the Dakota, 1979, California Rich, 1980, Duchess, 1981, The Grandes Dames, 1982, The Auerbach Will, 1983; contbr. numerous articles to numerous periodicals. Served with AUS, 1951-53. Mem. New Eng. Soc. of City N.Y., Phi Beta Kappa. Democrat. Episcopalian. Club: Coffee House (N.Y.C.). Address: care Brandt & Brandt 1501 Broadway New York NY 10036

BIRN, RAYMOND FRANCIS, historian, educator; b. N.Y.C., May 10, 1935; s. Saul Albert and Celia (Markman) B.; m. Randi Ingebrigtsen, July 18, 1960; children—Eric Stephen, Laila Marie. B.A., N.Y. U., 1956; M.A., U. Ill., 1957, Ph.D., 1961. Mem. faculty U. Oreg., Eugene, 1961—, asso. prof., 1966-72, prof. history, 1972—, head dept., 1971-78. Author: Pierre Rousseau and the Philosophes of Bouillon, 1964, Crisis, Absolutism, Revolution: Europe, 1648-1789/91, 1977; adv. editor: Eighteenth-Century Studies, 1974—, French Hist. Studies, 1977-80; contbr. articles to profl. jours. Mem. adv. screening com. Council for Internat. Exchange of Persons (Fulbright program), 1974-76. Served with AUS, 1959-60. Fulbright research fellow to France, 1968-69; Nat. Endowment for Humanities sr. fellow, 1976-77. Mem. Am. Hist. Assn., Soc. French Hist. Studies, Am. Soc. 18th Century Studies. Home: 2140 Elk Ave Eugene OR 97403

BIRNBAUM, ELEAZAR, educator; b. Nov. 23, 1929; emigrated to Can., 1964, naturalized, 1970; s. Solomon Asher and Irene (Grunwald) B.; m. Rebecca Pardes, May 30, 1962; children: Nathan J., Samuel M., Abraham U., Sarah M., Miriam D. Diploma O.A.S. in Hebrew Palaeography and Epigraphy, U. London, 1949, B.A. in Arabic with honours, 1950, 1953. Asst. librarian Oriental sect. Durham (Eng.) U. Library, 1953-60; Near Eastern bibliographer dept. Near Eastern langs. and lits. U. Mich.; also head Near Eastern and S. Asian unit U. Mich. Library, 1960-64; asso. prof. Middle East and Islamic studies U. Toronto, Can., 1964-70, prof., 1970—, dept. coordinator grad. studies, 1983—; cons. U.S. and Can. research fund granting agys. Author: Books on Asia, from the Near East to the Far East, 1971, The Islamic Middle East, 1975; joint editor, co-author: Introduction to Islamic Civilisation, 1976, the Book of Advice by King Kay-Ka'us ibn Iskandar, the Earliest Old Ottoman Turkish Version of his Kabusname, 1981; Author articles, book revs. Exhibitioner, Royal Asiatic Soc. Gt. Britain, 1951; recipient Can. Council award, 1968, 70, 73, U. Toronto Humanities and Social Scis. research awards, 1967, 71, 74, 76-79, 82-84; Social Scis. and Humanities Research Council Can. research award, 1979-81. Fellow Middle East Studies Assn. N.Am.; mem. Am. Oriental Soc., Am. Research Inst. in Turkey (sec. 1978), Turkish Studies Assn., Middle East Librarians Assn., Assn. Orthodox Jewish Scientists, Oriental Club Toronto (pres. 1977-78). Home: 132 Invermay Ave Downsview ON M3H 1Z8 Canada Office: Dept Middle East and Islamic Studies Univ Toronto Toronto ON M5S 1A1 Canada

BIRNBAUM, HENRIK, educator; b. Breslau, Germany, Dec. 13, 1925; came to U.S., 1961; s. Immanuel and Lucie (Richter) B.; m. Marianna Daisy Laszlo, July 3, 1965; children—Ewa Lucia, Björn Staffan. Fil. kand., Stockholm U., 1949, Fil. mag., 1952, Fil. lic., 1954, Fil. dr., 1958. Docent Stockholm U., 1958-61; vis lectr. Harvard U., 1960; mem. faculty U.Calif. at Los Angeles, 1961—, prof. Slavic langs. and lit., 1964—; dir. Russian and East European Studies Center, 1968-78; cons. RAND Corp., 1962-66; prof. Slavic langs. U. Munich (Germany), 1972-73. Author books and articles Slavic linguistics and lit., Balkan linguistics and linguistic theory, Russian history. Served with Swedish Army, 1948-49. Swedish Govt. fellow, 1961; Guggenheim fellow, 1964-65; Am. Council Learned Socs. grantee, 1969-70. Office: 115 Kinsey Hall U Calif Los Angeles CA 90024

BIRNBAUM, HENRY, librarian; b. Switzerland, Mar. 7, 1917; came to U.S., 1929, naturalized, 1941; s. Isaac and Fanny (Hauser) B. B.A. magna cum laude in Internat. Relations, U. Colo., 1952; M.S. in L.S, Columbia U., 1954, cert. advanced librianship, 1973. Personal service mgr. Hoover Mfg. & Sales Co., N.Y.C., 1936-41; adminstrv. asst. Library of Congress Mission in, Europe, 1945-46; library asst. Library Congress, 1946-47; research analyst Office Chief Counsel War Crimes, Nürnberg, Germany, 1947-48; asst. case editor, 1948-49; asst. acquisition div. Bklyn. Coll. Library, 1952-54, catalog librarian, 1954-57, chief circulation librarian, 1957-61; chief librarian Pace U., N.Y.C., 1961-66, dir. libraries, 1966-76, Univ. librarian, 1977—, sec. senate, 1969—; Mem. regents adv. council Task Force on Libraries and Maj. Facilities, N.Y.C.; Regional Plan for Higher Edn., 1972. Author monograph.; Contbr. articles to profl. jours. Served with AUS, 1941-45. Mem. A.L.A. (chmn. ad hoc com. circulation librarians 1959-60, chmn. circulation services discussion group, library adminstrn. div. 1961-62, chmn. planning and action com. circulation service sect. 1968-70), Assn. Coll. and Research Libraries, N.Y. Tech. Services Librarians (chmn. social com. 1958-59), N.Y. Library Club (mem. council 1963-64, 75-78, treas. 1964-66, v.p., pres.-elect 1971-72, pres. 1972-73), Library Assn. City Colls. N.Y. (del. Bklyn. Coll. to exec. council 1956-59), Archons of Colophon (convener 1966-67), N.Y. Hist. Soc., Phi Beta Kappa, Pi Gamma Mu, Delta Phi Alpha. Club: Univ. (N.Y.C.). Home: 40 E 10th St New York NY 10003 Office: Pace U Pace Plaza New York NY 10038

BIRNBAUM, JOE SAMUEL, computer company executive, computer scientist; b. Bronx, N.Y., Dec. 20, 1967; s. Issac and Estelle (Klotz) B.; m. Linda Ann Berwitz, Sept. 23, 1960 (div. June 1973); children: Julia Anne, Michael Stuart; m. 2d Eileen Sue Nankin, Feb. 2, 1975. B.Eng. Physics, Cornell U., 1960; M.S. in Physics, Yale U., 1961; Ph.D. In Physics, Yale U., 1965. Research staff mem. IBM Research Ctr., Yorktown Heights, N.Y., 1965-69, sr. mgr., 1970-75, dir. computer sci., 1975-80; dir. computer research Hewlett-Packard Co., Palo Alto, Calif., 1980—; mem. Computer Sci. Bd., 1976—. Contbr. articles on computer systems to profl. jours. Mem. IEEE, Assn. Computing Machinery. Jewish. Office: Hewlett-Packard Co 1501 Page Hill Rd Palo Alto CA 94304

BIRNBAUM, NORMAN, author, educator; b. N.Y.C., July 21, 1926; s. Silas Jacob and Jean (Bermen) B.; m. Gudrun Apel, Aug. 21, 1955 (div. July 1970); children: Anna, Antonia. B.A., Williams Coll., 1947; M.A., Harvard, 1951, Ph.D., 1958. Editor OWI, 1943-45; teaching fellow Harvard, 1948-52; tutor Adams House, 1949- 52; asst. lectr. London Sch. Econs. and Polit. Sci., U. London, 1953-55, lectr., 1955-59; fellow Nuffield Coll., Oxford (Eng.) U., 1959-66; vis. prof. faculty letters and human scis. U. Strasbourg, France, 1964-66; prof. grad. faculty New Sch. Social Research, 1966-68; prof. Amherst Coll., 1968—; mem. Inst. Advanced Study, 1975-76; Mellon vis. prof. humanities Georgetown U. Law Center, 1979-81; Univ. prof. Georgetown U., 1981—; cons. Nat. Security Council, Exec. Office Pres., 1978. Author: Sociological Study of Ideology (1940-60), 1962, (with others) Sociology and Religion, 1968, Crisis of Industrial Society, 1969, Towards a Critical Sociology, 1971, Beyond the Crisis, 1977, also articles.; Mem. editorial bd.: Praxis, 1966—, The Nation, 1978—; contbg. editor: Change mag. of higher edn, 1970-74; editorial cons.: Partisan Review, 1971—. Cons. Giovanni Agnelli Found., 1972-75; mem. Wellfleet Psychohistory Conf., 1970—; adviser United Automobile Workers; mem. exec. com. New Democratic Coalition, 1978—, chmn. policy adv. council, 1980—; mem. nat. exec. com. Dem. Socialist Organizing Com., 1973-77, nat. adv. bd., 1980—; Mem. founding editorial bd. New Left Rev., London, 1959; sec. com. sociology religion Internat. Sociol. Assn., 1959—, chmn., 1970-74; adviser Democratic Nat. Campaign, 1976, Edward M. Kennedy campaign, 1979. Guggenheim fellow, 1971. Mem. Am. Sociol. Assn. (council 1979-82). Office: Georgetown U Law Center 600 New Jersey Ave NW Washington DC 20001 *I have always thought that one of the strongest ethical and biological forces propelling us is a concern for our children—for our own children and for the continuation of humanity. This elementary sense of care seems increasingly challenged, by governments (of whatever political complexion) in possession of the capacity to destroy humanity and our earth. My own goals have changed, and they now concentrate on altering these governments before they extirpate us and our children.*

BIRNBAUM, ROBERT, higher education educator; b. N.Y.C., Aug. 6, 1936; s. David and Betty (Risk) B.; m. Doris Gardner, Jan. 21, 1960; children: Steven, Matthew, Ann. B.A., U. Rochester, N.Y., 1958; M.A., Tchrs. Coll. Columbia U., N.Y.C., 1964, Ed.D., 1967. Vice chancellor CUNY, 1967-70, N.J. Dept. Higher Edn., Trenton, 1971-74; chancellor U. Wis.-Oshkosh, 1974-78; prof. higher edn. U. Miami, Coral Gables, Fla., 1978-79, Tchrs. Coll. Columbia U., N.Y.C., 1979—. Author: Creative Academic Bargaining, 1980, Maintaining Diversity in Higher Education, 1983; contbr. articles to profl. jours. Trustee Montclair State Coll., N.J., 1970—. Mem. Am. Ednl. Research Assn., Assn. Study of Higher Edn. (dir. 1982—), AAUP, Indsl. Relations Research Assn. Office: Tchrs Coll Columbia U New York NY 10027

BIRNBAUM, ROBERT JACK, stock exchange exec.; b. N.Y.C., Sept. 3, 1927; s. Joseph M. and Beatrice (Herman) B.; m. Joy E. Mumford, June 2, 1957; children—Gregg Gordon, Julie Beth. B.S., N.Y. U., 1957; LL.B., Georgetown U., 1962. Bar: D.C. bar 1963. Atty. SEC, Washington, 1961-66; with Am. Stock Exchange, N.Y.C., 1967—, pres., 1977—. Served with USCGR, 1945-46. Office: 86 Trinity Pl New York NY 10006

BIRNBAUM, STEPHEN NORMAN, editor, broadcaster; b. N.Y.C., Mar. 28, 1937; s. Louis M. and Ruth L. (Kreisel) B.; m. Alexandra Mayes, Dec. 28, 1972. B.A., Columbia U., 1957. Founder Chamberlain Properties, N.Y.C., 1960-67; creative dir. DePerri Advt., Inc., N.Y.C., 1967-72; mng. editor Fodor's Travel Guides, N.Y.C., London, 1972-75; editor Diversion Mag., Titusville, N.J., 1975-76, editor, pub., N.Y.C., 1976—; travel editor Golf Mag., 1973—, Esquire, 1976-79, N.J. Monthly Mag., 1977; travel commentator CBS Radio Network, 1977—; travel editor Today Show NBC, 1977-79, Good Morning America, ABC, 1982—; editor Stephen Birnbaum Travel Guides pub. by Houghton Mifflin Travel Guides, 1977—; syndicated columnist Chgo. Tribune/N.Y. News Syndicate, 1978—; editorial dir. Sojourn mag., 1978—, Fair Lanes mag., 1979—; Direct mag., 1981—; travel commentator Ind. Network News, 1981; travel editor Playboy mag., 1979-82, Good Housekeeping mag., 1982—. Served with USCG, 1958-66. Mem. Soc. Am. Travel Writers, N.Y. Travel Writers, Golf Writers Am. Office: Diversion Mag 60 E 42d St New York NY 10017

BIRNBAUM, ZYGMUNT WILLIAM, mathematics educator; b. Lwow, Poland, Oct. 18, 1903; came to U.S., 1937, naturalized, 1943; s. Ignacy and Lina (Nebenzahl) B.; m. Hilde Merzbach, Dec. 20, 1940; children: Ann Miriam, Richard Franklin. LL.M., U. Lwow, 1925,

Ph.D. in Math, 1929; postdoctoral research, U. Goettingen, Germany, 1929-31. Math. instr. Gymnasium, Lwow, 1926-29; chief actuary Life Ins. Co. Phoenix in Poland, 1931-36; research biometrician, N.Y.U., 1937-39; mem. faculty U. Wash., Seattle, 1939—, prof. math., 1950—; dir. lab. statis. research, 1948—; vis. prof. Stanford, 1951-52, U. Paris, France, 1960-61, U. Rome, Italy, 1964, Hebrew U., Jerusalem, 1980; cons. Boeing Co., 1956—, HEW, 1963—. Editor: Annals of Math. Statistics, 1967-70. Guggenheim fellow, 1960-61. Fellow Inst. Math. Statistics (pres. 1963-64), Am. Statis. Assn.; mem. Am. Math. Soc., Math. Assn. Am., Soc. Indsl. and Applied Math., Internat. Statis. Inst., AAUP. Office: Math Dept Univ Wash Seattle WA 98195

BIRNEY, (ALFRED) EARLE, author; b. Calgary, Alta., Can., May 13, 1904; s. William George and Martha Stout (Robertson) B.; m. Esther Bull, Mar., 1940 (div. 1978); 1 son, William Laurenson. B.A., U. B.C., 1926; postgrad., U. Calif.-Berkeley, 1927-30; M.A., U. Toronto, 1927, Ph.D., 1936, U. London, 1934-35; LL.D., U. Alta., 1965; D.Litt., McGill U., 1979, U. Western Ont., 1984. Summer sch. lectr. U. B.C., 1927-37; instr. U. Utah, 1930-32, 33-34; lectr. U. Toronto, 1936-40, asst. prof., 1940-42; prof. English U. B.C., 1946-62, head dept. creative writing, 1963-65; writer-in-residence U. Toronto, 1965-67, U. Waterloo, Ont., 1967-68, U. Western Ont., 1981-82; Regents prof. U. Calif. at Irvine, 1968; supr. fgn. lang. broadcasts to Europe Radio Can., 1945-46; vis. prof. creative writing U. Oreg., 1961; lit. adviser Can. Council, 1965-67. Author: poetry David, 1942, Near False Creek Mouth, 1964, Memory No Servant, 1968, Pnomes, Jukollages and other Stunzas, 1969, Rag and Bone Shop, 1971, What's So Big About Green?, 1973, Bear on the Delhi Road, 1973, Collected Poems, 2 vols, 1975, The Rugging and the Moving Times, 1976, Alphabeings; poems-drawings, 1976; selected poems Ghost in the Wheels, 1977; new poems Fall by Fury, 1978, The Mammoth Corridors; selected poems, 1980, others; novels Turvey, 1949, Down the Long Table, 1955; short stories Big Bird in the Bush; play Damnation of Vancouver, 1952; lit. theory The Creative Writer, 1966, The Cow Jumped Over the Moon, 1972; lit. criticism Spreading Time/Remarks on Canadian Writing and Writers, 1980; editor-in-chief: Canadian Poetry mag, 1946-48, Prism Internat, 1963-65; lit. editor: Canadian Forum, 1937-40; adv. editor: Selected Poems of Malcolm Lowry, 1962; lit. criticism New Canadian and Am. Poetry, 1964-68. Served with Canadian Army, 1942-45. Decorated officer Order of Can.; recipient Gov.-Gen.'s medals for poetry, 1943, 46, Stephen Leacock medal for humor, 1949, Borestone Mt. poetry 1st prize, 1951, Pierce medal for lit., 1953, Can. Council medal for services to arts, 1968; Canadian Govt. fellow, France, 1953; Nuffield fellow, Eng., 1958-59; Can. Council travelling fellowships and grants to Latin Am., 1962-63, Australia and; New Zealand, 1968; West and East Africa, 1972; Europe and; South Asia, 1974-75. Subject of documentary by Nat. Film Bd. of Can., "Earle Birney: Portrait of a Poet" (1982); poems have been set to music on three albums by Nexus percussion group (1982); poem, "David", adapted for film drama (1983). Address: care McClelland & Stewart 25 Hollinger Rd Toronto ON Canada M4B 3G2

BIRNEY, DAVID EDWIN, actor; b. Washington, Apr. 23; s. Edwin B. and Jeanne L. (McGee) B.; m. Meredith Baxter, Apr. 10, 1974; children: Theodore, Eva, Kathleen. A.B. with high distinction, English honors, Dartmouth Coll., 1961; M.A., U. Calif., Los Angeles, 1963. Adv. panel Nat. Endowment Arts, 1979. N.Y. debut as Antipholus of Syracuse in Comedy of Errors, N.Y. Shakespeare Festival, 1967; appeared in maj. roles including Cusins in Major Barbara, Barter Theatre in Va., 1965-66, Hartford Stage Co., 1966-67, Am. Place Theatre, 1968, Repertory Theatre of Lincoln Center, 1968-71, Am. Shakespeare Theatre, Stratford, Conn., 1974, Mark Taper Forum, Los Angeles, 1971, Studio Arena Theatre, Buffalo, 1972, appeared in maj. roles including, St. Louis Municipal Opera, 1975; Broadway debut Amadeus, 1983; TV series include Bridget Loves Bernie, 1972-73, The Adams' Chronicles, 1975, Serpico, 1976, Testimony of Two Men, 1977, Heroes of the Bible, 1978, High Midnight, Ohms, Mom, the Wolfman and Me, Bible, St. Elsewhere.; films include Caravan to Vaccares, 1973, Trial by Combat, 1975, Goodbye, See You Monday, 1979, Oh God! Book II, Book II. Served with U.S. Army, 1963-65. Recipient Barter Theatre award, 1965, Clarence Derwent award and Theatre World award for performance in Summertree, 1968, Photoplay Mag. award, 1973, Sixteen Mag. award, 1973, Buffalo Courier Express award for best performance, 1972. Mem. Actors Equity, Screen Actors Guild, Am. Fedn. TV Artists, Acad. TV Arts and Scis., Calif. Confedn. Arts. Club: Players. Office: Mab Prodns Ltd care Zeiderman 10313 W Pico Los Angeles CA 90026 *

BIRNS, MARK THEODORE, physician; b. Bklyn., Sept. 24, 1949; s. Leon and Naomi B.; m. Ann Krieger, Aug. 15, 1976; 1 dau., Samantha Lynn. B.A., Case Western Res. U., 1971; M.D., Albert Einstein Coll. Medicine, 1974. Diplomate: Am. Bd. Internal Medicine, Am. Bd. Gastroenterology. Intern Bronx Mcpl. Hosp. Ctr. Albert Einstein Hosps., 1974-75, resident in medicine, 1975-77; fellow in gastroenterology U. Oreg. Health Scis. Ctr., 1977-79; asst. chief gastroenterology Walter Reed Army Med. Ctr., 1979-83; asst. prof. medicine U. Health Scis., 1980-83; emergecny physician Shady Grove Adventist Hosp., 1980-83, Frederick Meml. Hosp., Washington, 1980-83; paractice gastroenterology, Rockville, Md., 1983—; assoc. staff Shady Grove Adventist Hosp.; courtesy staff Suburban Hosp., Montgomery Gen. Hosp., Frederick Meml. Hosp., Holy Cross Hosp. Served to maj. USAF. Mem. AMA, ACP, Am. Fedn. Clin. Research, Am. Gastroent. Assn., Am. Soc. Gastrointestinal Endoscopy, Md. Soc. Gastrointestinal Endscopy, William Earl Clark Soc. Home: 308 Summit Hall Rd Gaithersburg MD 20877 Office: 9715 Medical Center Dr Suite 200 Rockville MD 20850

BIRO, LASZLO, dermatologist; b. Czechoslovakia, May 31, 1929; came to U.S., 1956; s. Sandor and Margaret (Klein) B.; m. Dolores Macchiaroli, July 9, 1961; children: David, Lisa, Deborah, Michele. M.D., Kossuth U., (Hungary), 1953. Diplomate: Am. Bd. Dermatology. Intern Kings County Hosp., Bklyn., 1957-58; resident Bellevue Hosp., N.Y.C., 1958-60; pvt. practice medicine specializing in dermatology, N.Y.C., 1960-61, Bklyn., 1960—; chief dept. dermatology Bklyn. Hosp., Luth. Med. Ctr.; clin. prof. dermatology SUNY, Downstate Med. Ctr., 1971—. Contbr. articles on skin tumors to profl. jours. Fellow ACP, Am. Acad. Dermatology, N.Y. Acad. Medicine; mem. AMA, Kings County Med. Assn., Bay Ridge Med. Assn., N.Y. Dermatol. Soc., Bklyn. Dermatol. Soc., Internat. Soc. Tropical Dermatology, N.Y. Acad. Scis., Am. Coll. Cryosurgery, Semmelweis Sci. Soc. (pres.). Office: 7502 Ridge Blvd Brooklyn NY 11209

BIRRELL, GEORGE ANDREW, oil company executive; b. Warren, Ohio, Apr. 25, 1921; s. George Henry (Mary Ann);; s. George Henry and Mary Ann (Rook) B.; m. Lelia Torrey Pannill, Aug. 7, 1948; children: Lelia Carter, Amanda Griswold, Ellen Torrey, Laura Tudor, George William. B.A., Yale U., 1942, LL.B., 1947. Bar: N.Y. 1948. Assoc. firm Donovan, Leisure, Newton and Irvine, N.Y.C., 1947-55, partner, 1956-58; with Mobil Oil Corp., 1959—, gen. counsel, 1970—, sec., 1972-75, v.p., 1975—, dir., 1976—; v.p., gen. counsel Mobil Corp., 1976—, dir., 1980—; Mem. Rye (N.Y.) Planning Commn., 1957-60, Rye Bd. Zoning Appeals, 1962-67, mem. city council, 1968-72, acting mayor, 1970-72; Mem. adv. bd. Internat. and Comparative Law Center, Internat. Oil and Gas Ednl. Center, Southwestern Legal Found.; mem. adv. com. law of sea Dept. State. Served to 1st lt. USAAF, 1943-45. Fellow Am. Bar Found.; mem. Am. Bar Assn., Assn. Bar City N.Y., Assn. Gen. Counsel. Republican. Clubs: Masons; Apawamis, Blind Brook, Am. Yacht (Rye); Pinnacle (N.Y.C.). Home: Pecksland Rd Greenwich CT 06830 Office: 150 E 42d St New York NY 10017

BIRREN, JAMES EMMETT, university dean, psychologist; b. Chgo., Apr. 4, 1918; m. Elizabeth S., 1942; children: Barbara Ann, Jeffrey Emmett, Bruce William. Student, Wright Jr. Coll., 1938; B.Ed., Chgo. State U., 1941; M.A., Northwestern U., 1942, Ph.D., 1947; postgrad., U. Chgo., 1950-51. Tutorial fellow Northwestern U., 1941-42; research asst. project for study of fatigue Office Sci. Research and Devel., 1942; research fellow NIH, USPHS, 1946-47; research psychologist gerontology unit NIH, 1947-51; research psychologist NIMH, 1951-53, chief sect. on aging, 1953-64; dir. aging program Nat. Inst. Child Health and Human Devel., Bethesda, Md., 1964-65; dir. Gerontology Center; prof. psychology U. So. Calif., 1965—; dean Davis Sch. Gerontology, 1975—; fellow Center for Advanced Study in Behavioral Scis., Stanford, Calif., 1978-79; Green vis. prof. U. B.C., 1979; vis. scientist Cambridge (Eng.) U., 1960-61; Harold E. Jones meml. lectr. U. Calif., Berkeley, 1965; mem. Los Angeles County Bd. Suprs.' Com. on Aging, 1967—; sr. fellow U. So. Calif. Urban Ecology Inst., 1968-70; mem. Dean's Council, U. So. Calif., 1970—; chmn. aging rev. com. Nat. Inst. Aging, 1974-75; program dir. Integration of Info. on Aging: Handbook Project, 1973-76; mem. steering com. Care of Elderly, Inst. of Medicine, 1976-77; bd. dirs. Sears Roebuck Found., 1977-80; cons. Roche Seminars on Aging Series, 1980—. Author: Psychology of Aging, 1964; editor: Handbook of Aging and the Individual, 1959, (with K.W. Schaie) Handbook of the Psychology of Aging, 1977, (with R.B. Sloane) Handbook of Mental Health and Aging; contbr. articles to books, profl. publs.; bd. collaborators: Gerontologia, 1956—; asst. editor: Jour. Gerontology, 1956-61; assoc. editor, 1961-63; editor-in-chief, 1968-74; chmn. publs. com., 1975—; adv. editorial bd., 1956-69; bd. adv. editors: Devel. Psychobiology, 1967—; adv. editor: Jour. Human Devel, 1957-58. Served with USNR, 1943-46; to scientist dir. USPHS Scientist Corps, 1947-65. Recipient award for research on problems of aging CIBA Found., 1956, Stratton award Am. Psychopathol. Assn., 1960, Sr. 65er award Dist. 65 Retail Workers and Dept. Store Union, AFL-CIO, 1962, medal for meritorious service USPHS, 1965, citation Am. Assn. Ret. Persons, 1970, Am. Pioneers in Aging award U. Mich., 1972, commendation for disting. contbns. to field of gerontology Mayor of Los Angeles, 1968, 74, Merit award Northwestern U. Alumni Assn., 1976; Creative Scholarship and Research award U. So. Calif., 1979; Disting. Educator award Assn. Gerontology in Higher Edn., 1983; USPHS research fellow, 1946-47. Fellow AAAS, Am. Geriatrics Soc. (founding fellow Western div.), Am. Psychol. Assn. (Disting. Sci. Contbn. award 1968, chmn. membership com. 1969, Disting. Contbn. award Div. Adult Devel. and Aging 1978, pres. div. 1955-56, editor newsletter 1951-55), Gerontol. Soc. (pres. 1961-62, chmn. publs. com. 1974-77, award for meritorious research 1966, Brookdale award 1980); mem. Am. Ednl. Research Assn., Am. Physiol. Soc., Internat. Assn. Gerontology (chmn. exec. com. 1966-69, chmn. program com. 1968-69), Psychometric Soc., Psychonomic Soc., Western Gerontol. Soc. (dir. 1965—, pres. 1968-69), Western Psychol. Assn., Sigma Xi, Phi Kappa Phi. Office: Andrus Gerontology Center U So Calif Univ Park MC 0191 Los Angeles CA 90089-0191

BIRSH, ARTHUR THOMAS, publisher; b. Englewood, N.J., Oct. 6, 1932; s. Abraham S. and Mary (Levinsohn) B.; m. Judith Rosenberg, June 29, 1955 (div. 1982); children: Andrew, Philip, Joanne.; m. Joan Alleman, 1983. Grad., Lawrenceville N.J. Sch., 1950; B.A., Yale, 1954. Engaged in sales Western Pub. Co., Poughkeepsie, N.Y., 1956-58; founder Cross Road Press, Hyde Park, N.Y., 1958, pres., 1958-60; with Playbill mag., N.Y.C., 1961—, publisher, 1965—; exec. v.p. Am. Theatre Press, Inc., 1961-68, pres., 1974—; group v.p. Metromedia, Inc., 1968-73. Served with AUS, 1954-56. Home: 7$^{1}/_{2}$ Leroy St New York NY 10014 Office: 100 Ave of Americas New York NY 10013 *I have no philosophy, rather a hodge-podge of ideas and beliefs that keep me going; Nature is a match for nurture; everybody's scared; love is a condition, not a contract; the stupid or silly things I have done usually seemed smart or important at the time; life is a series of moments—wallowing in the lows extends them—clutching the highs destroys them. Most enduring good things that have happened to me resulted from taking chances and making commitments. Luck beats brains!*

BIRTEL, FRANK THOMAS, mathematics educator; b. New Orleans, Apr. 4, 1932; s. Frank N. and Virginia B.; m. Jane Ella C. Moriarty, Sept. 16, 1964; children: Rebecca Anne, Michael Teilhard. B.S., Loyola U. South, 1952; M.S., U. Notre Dame, 1953, Ph.D. in Math., 1960. Instr. Conn. Coll. for Women, New London, 1956-57; lectr. Yale U., 1961-62; asst. prof. Ohio State U., 1960-62; asst. prof. math. Tulane U., 1962-64, asso. prof., 1964-67, prof., 1967—, Univ. prof., 1981—; spl. asst. to pres., 1975-76, dep. provost, 1976-78; acting dean Grad. Sch., 1978, acting provost, 1978, provost, dean, 1977-81; vis. prof. U. Nijmegen, Netherlands, 1968-69. Trustee New Orleans Mus. Art, 1978-80, St. Mary's Dominican Coll., New Orleans, 1977—. Yale U. postdoctoral fellow, 1961-62; sr. Fulbright lectr., Eng., Scotland, Germany, Netherlands, 1968-69. Mem. Am. Math. Soc. (asso. sec. 1977—), AAUP, Math. Assn. Am. Roman Catholic. Home: 1229 Cadiz St New Orleans LA 70115 Office: Tulane U New Orleans LA 70118

BISBEE, ROYAL DANIEL, JR., export information company executive; b. Godhra, India, Feb. 21, 1923; s. Royal Daniel and Pearl Bertha (Gosnell) B.; m. Barbara Beeler, Jan. 7, 1946; 1 dau., Renee D. Bisbee Miller. B.A., U. Wash., 1947; M.A., George Washington U., 1964. Joined U.S. Fgn. Service, 1947; vice consul, Bombay, India, 1947-48, vice consul, adminstrv. officer embassy, New Delhi, India, 1948-50; spl. tng. in South Asian regional affairs U. Pa., 1950-51; chief Hindu unit Voice of Am., 1951; dir. USIS, Lucknow, India, 1952-56, Salonika, Greece, 1956-58, Lahore, Pakistan, 1959-61; program and policy officer for, India, Nepal and, Ceylon, USIA, 1961-63; assigned Nat. War Coll., 1963-64; dir. USIS, Freetown, Sierra Leone, 1964-66, Pretoria, South Africa, 1966-69, dep. dir., Manila, 1970-72; chief IOR/RI USIA, Washington, 1972-79; pres. Washington Export Info. Corp., 1979—, Century 21 Royal Properties, Inc., McLean, Va., 1980—. Author: Tibet: Communist Road to India, 1950, China's Traditional National Interests in the Borderlands of the Himalayas, 1964. Served with AUS, 1943-46. Recipient cert. of commendation State Dept., 1950; Meritorious Honor award USICA, 1978. Address: 450 River Bend Rd Great Falls VA 22066

BISCARDI, CHESTER, composer; b. Kenosha, Wis., Oct. 19, 1948; s. Chester Frank and Anne Rose (Rizzo) B. Student, Università di Bologna (Italy) and Conservatorio di Musica G. B. Martini, Bologna, 1969-70; B.A. in English Lit. with honors, U. Wis.-Madison, 1970; M.A. in Italian Lit. (Ford Found. fellow), U. Wis.-Madison, 1972; M.M. in Composition, U. Wis.-Madison, 1974; M.M.A., Yale U., 1976, D.M.A., 1979. Teaching asst. Italian U. Wis., 1970-73, ad hoc instr. Italian for reading knowledge, 1973-74, teaching asst. theory, 1973-74; teaching fellow Italian for singers Yale, 1975-76; seminar instr. Fed. Correctional Instn. at Oxford, summer 1978; faculty mem. music dept. Sarah Lawrence Coll., 1977—. Composer: numerous compositions including Tartini, 1972, Turning, 1973, Chartres, 1973, Indovinello, 1974, orpha, 1974, Heabakès: Five Sapphic Lyrics, 1974, they had ceased to talk, 1975, Trusting Lightness, 1975, Tenzone, 1975, Music for the Duchess of Malfi, 1975, Trio, 1976, At the Still Point, 1977, Eurydice, 1978, Mestiere, 1979, Trasumanar, 1980, Di Vivere, 1981, Good-bye My Fancy!, 1982—, Music for Witch Dance, 1983—, Chez Vous, 1983—. Recipient Rome prize in musical composition Am. Acad. in Rome, 1976-77; Composer/Librettist grantee Nat. Endowment for the Arts, 1977-78, 80-81; Composers' Conf. fellow, Johnson, Vt., 1974, 75; Wrs. Arts Bd. grantee, 1976; Nat. Acad. and Inst. Arts and Letters Charles E. Ives scholar, 1975-76; Guggenheim fellow, 1979-80; Mellon Found. grantee, 1979; Am. Music Center grantee, 1980; McDowell Colony fellow, 1981; Martha Baird Rockefeller Fund grantee, 1982; Creative Artists Pub. Service Program fellow in music, 1983; others. Mem. Am. Composers Alliance.; mem. Am. Acad. in Rome, Am. Composers Alliance, Am. Music Ctr., Broadcast Music Inc., Guild of Composers. Home: 542 Ave of Americas Apt 4R New York NY 10011

BISCHOFF, CHARLES MICHAEL, accounting executive; b. N.Y.C., Nov. 25, 1927; s. Charles John and Grace (Hurley) B.; m. Marilyn A. Guilmette, Sept. 15, 1951; children: Cheryl Ann, Susan Grace. B.S., Seton Hall U., 1951. C.P.A., N.J. Staff accountant Haskins & Sells (C.P.A.s), Newark, 1951-57, semi sr., 1952-55, sr., 1955-57; financial accountant Houdaille Constrn. Materials, Morristown, N.J., 1957-59; divisional controller R.H. Wright, Inc., Ft. Lauderdale, Fla., 1959-61, (Houdaille Duval Wright div.), Jacksonville, Fla., 1961-62; tax mgr. Houdaille Industries, Inc., Buffalo, 1963-64, corp. controller, Buffalo and Ft. Lauderdale, 1964-79, v.p., controller, 1979—; Mem. accounting council Canisus U., 1967-70. Served with USNR, 1945-48. Mem. Am. Inst. C.P.A.s. Home: 2660 NW 112th Ave Coral Springs FL 33065 Office: One Financial Plaza Fort Lauderdale FL 33394

BISCHOFF, DAVID CANBY, university dean; b. Bellefonte, Pa., May 27, 1930; s. Eugen Carl and Jean Stuart (Canby) B.; m. Patricia A. Halfacre, Aug. 15, 1954; children: Cynthia, Steven, Ingrid. B.S., Pa. State U., 1952, Ph.D., 1958; M.S., U. N.C., 1953. Asst. prof. dept. phys. edn. U. Mass., Amherst, 1957-60, asso. prof., 1960-63, prof., 1963—, asso. provost for profl. schs., 1972-79, dep. provost, 1982—; dean U. Mass. Sch. Phys. Edn., 1973—; vis. prof. Wesleyan U., 1968-69. Past pres. Amherst Community Chest, Amherst Am. Field Service; mem. Amherst Planning Bd., 1958-62. Served with U.S. Army, 1953-55. Mem. AAHPER, Nat. Coll. Phys. Edn. Assn. (past pres.). Office: Boyden Bldg Univ Massachusetts Amherst MA 01003

BISCHOFF, ELMER, artist, educator; b. Berkeley, Calif., July 9, 1916; s. John A. and Elna (Nelson) B. B.A., U. Calif.-Berkeley, 1938, M.A., 1939; D.F.A. (hon), Otis Art Inst., Parsons Sch. Design, 1983. Chmn. grad. program San Francisco Art Inst., 1957-63; instr. art dept. U. Calif.-Berkeley, 1963—. Represented permanent collections, Art Inst. Chgo., Mus. Modern Art, U. Kans. Mus. Art, Whitney Mus. Am. Art, Permanent Collections, Rockefeller Inst., permanent collections, New Sch. Art Ctr., N.Y.C., San Francisco Mus. Art, pvt. collections, permanent exhibit, John Berggruen Gallery, San Francisco, Hirschl and Adler-Modern, N.Y.C. Served with USAAF, 1942-46; ETO. Grantee Ford Found., 1959, Nat. Inst. Arts and Letters, 1963; recipient Disting. Teaching award Coll. Art Assn., 1983. Office: 2571 Shattuck Ave Berkeley CA 94704

BISCHOFF, KENNETH BRUCE, chemical engineer, educator; b. Chgo., Feb. 29, 1936; s. Arthur William and Evelyn Mary (Hansen) B.; m. Joyce Arlene Winterberg, June 6, 1959; children: Kathryn Ann, James Eric. B.S., Ill. Inst. Tech., 1957, Ph.D., 1961. Asst. to asso. prof. U. Tex., Austin, 1961-67; asso. prof., then prof. U. Md., 1967-70; Walter R. Read prof. engring. Cornell U., 1970-76, dir. Sch. Chem. Engring., 1970-75; Unidel prof. biomed. and chem. engring. U. Del., 1976—, chmn. dept. chem. engring., 1978-82; cons. Exxon Research and Engring., NIH, Gen. Foods Corp., W. R. Grace Co., Kappers Co. Author: (with D.M. Himmelblau) Process Analysis and Simulation, 1968, (with G.F. Froment) Chemical Reactor Analysis and Design, 1979; editor: (with R.L. Dedrick and E.F. Leonard) The Artificial Kidney; Contbr. articles to research publs.; Editorial bd.: Advances in Chemistry Series, 1973-76, 78—, Jour. Bioengring, 1976-80, Jour. Pharmacokin. Biopharmacy, 1975—; assoc. editor: Advanced Chem. Engring., 1982—. Mem. council thrombosis Am. Heart Assn., 1971-81. Recipient Ebert prize Acad. Pharm. Scis., 1972, Profl. Progress award Am. Inst. Chem. Engrs., 1976; Shell Found. fellow, 1959; NSF fellow, 1960; U. Ghent, 1960-61. Fellow AAAS, Am. Inst. Chemists; mem. Am. Inst. Chem. Engrs. (dir. 1972-74, chmn. nat. program com. 1978), Am. Chem. Soc., Am. Soc. Engring. Edn., Am. Soc. Artificial Internal Organs, Engrs. Council for Profl. Devel. (dir. 1972-78), Council Chem. Research (governing bd. 1981-84), Catalysis Soc., AAUP, N.Y. Acad. Scis., Sigma Xi, Tau Beta Pi, Phi Lambda Upsilon, Omega Chi Epsilon, Alpha Chi Sigma. Home: Box 81A Benge Rd RD 1 Hockessin DE 19707

BISCHOFF, ROBERT MICHAEL, oil co. exec.; b. Sonoma County, Calif., June 20, 1919; s. Michael Paul and Ethlyn Pauline (Graves) B.; m. Ruth Eleanor Schmeeckle, Dec. 14, 1958; children—David Michael, Cynthia Marie Bischoff Houtman, Bradley Robert, Lisa Louise. B.Eng. in Petroleum Engring, U. So. Calif., 1942. Registered profl. engr., Calif. With Texaco Inc. (and affiliates or subsidiaries), 1944—; mgr. ops. Texaco Oil Co. subs., Trinidad, 1963-68; mgr. Tex. Petroleum Co. subs., Bogota, Colombia, 1969-71, gen. mgr. producing dept. Latin Am., Coral Gables, Fla., 1971-77, v.p. producing dept. Latin Am., 1977-80; v.p. Texaco Inc., 1980—; pres. Texaco Latin Am./West Africa, 1980—. Bd. dirs. YMCA, Bogota, 1968-71. Mem. AIME, Nat. Fgn. Trade Council. Club: Riviera Country (Coral Gables, Fla.). Home: 7720 SW 145th St Miami FL 33158 Office: Latin Am/West Africa 2121 Ponce de Leon Blvd Coral Gables FL 33134

BISEL, HARRY FERREE, oncologist; b. Manor, Pa., June 17, 1918; s. George Culbertson and Mary Stotler (Ferree) B.; m. Sara Louise Clark, Oct. 30, 1954; children: Jane, Clark, Harold. B.S., U. Pitts., 1939, M.D., 1942. Intern U. Pitts. Med. Center, 1942-43; resident U. Pa., 1948-49, Harvard U. Boston City Hosp., 1949-50; resident physician Meml. Sloan Kettering Cancer Center, 1951-53; cancer coordinator medicine U. Pitts., 1953-63; chmn. div. med. oncology Mayo Clinic, Rochester, Minn., 1963-72, sr. cons. div. med. oncology, 1972—; prof. oncology Mayo Med. Sch., 1967—; cons. Nat. Cancer Inst. Served to capt. M.C. USNR, 1943-47. Recipient Philip S. Hench Disting. Alumnus award U. Pitts. Sch. Medicine, 1972. Mem. Am. Soc. Clin. Oncology (past pres.), Soc. Surg. Oncology, Am. Assn. Cancer Edn., Am. Assn. Cancer Research. Presbyterian. Club: Rotary. Qome: 1223 Skyline Dr Rochester MN 55902 Office: Mayo Clinic Rochester MN 55905

BISH, LAWRENCE EDWARD (MIKE BISH), home furnishings company executive; b. Butler, Pa., Nov. 26, 1924; m. Sarah Joan Duffy, Aug. 18, 1950; children: Susan Bish Strittmatter, Kathleen Bish Pigford, Lawrence Edward. B.S. in Chem. Engring., Grove City Coll., 1950; postgrad., U. Pitts., 1961-63. With Armstrong World Industries Inc., 1950—; sr. v.p. mfg. Thomasville Furniture Industries subs., Armstrong World Industries Inc., N.C., 1969-76; exec. v.p., gen. mgr. Thomasville div., Armstrong World Industries Inc., 1976-79; pres. Thomasville Furniture Industries, 1979-82, exec. v.p. corp., Lancaster, Pa., 1982—. Served to sgt. C.E. U.S. Army, 1943-46; PTO. Republican. Presbyterian. Clubs: Lancaster Country; Country of N.C. (Pinehurst); Emerywood Country (High Point, N.C.). Office: Armstrong World Industries Inc Liberty and Charlotte Sts Lancaster PA 17604

BISH, MILAN DAVID, ambassador; b. Harvard, Nebr., July 1, 1929; s. Charles and Mabel E. (Williams) B.; m. Allene Rae Miller, Mar. 17, 1951; children: Cindy, Linda, Charles. B.A., Hastings Coll., 1950. Pres. Bish Machinery Co., 1951-72, Mid-Continent Enterprises, 1974-81; ptnr., Grand Island, Nebr., 1979—; hwy. commr. State of Nebr., Grand Island, 1979-81; U.S. ambassador to Antigua and Barabados, Bridgetown, 1981—; also ambassador to Commonwealth of Dominica, St. Lucia, St. Vincent and the Grenadines; spl. rep. to St. Christopher and Nevis. Chmn. Nebr. Republican Party, 1971-73. Mem. Delta Phi Sigma. Presbyterian. Lodges: Rotary; Masons; Shriners; Elks; Eagles. Office: US Embassy PO Box 302 Bridgetown Barabados

BISHARA, SAMIR EDWARD, orthodontist; b. Cairo, Oct. 31, 1935; U.S., 1968, naturalized, 1976; s. Edward Constantin and Georgette Ibrahim (Kelela) B.; m. Cynthia Jane McLaughlin, July 3, 1975; children—Dina Marie, Dorine Gabrielle, Cherine Noelle. B. Dental Surgery, Alexandria U., Egypt, 1957; diploma in orthodontics, 1967; M.S., U. Iowa, 1970, cert. in orthodontics, 1970, D.D.S., 1972. Diplomate: Am. Bd. Orthodontics. Practice gen. dentistry, Alexandria, 1957-66, specializing in orthodontics, Iowa City, Iowa, 1970—; fellow in clin. pedontics Guggenheim Dental Clinic, N.Y.C., 1959-60; resident in oral surgery Moassat Hosp., Alexandria, 1960-61, mem. staff, 1961-68; asst. prof. dentistry U. Iowa, 1970-73, asso. prof., 1973-76, prof., 1976—; vis. prof. Alexandria U., 1974-75. Contbr. articles profl. jours., chpts. in books. Bd. dirs. Am. Cleft Palate Ednl. Found., 1976-79. Mem. Am. Dental Assn., Egyptian Dental Assn., Iowa Dental Assn., Midwestern Soc. Orthodontists, Am. Assn. Orthodontics, Internat. Dental Fedn., AAAS, Internat. Assn. Dental Research, Am. Cleft Palate Assn., Assn. Egyptian Am. Scholars, Omicron Kappa Upsilon (pres. 1981), Sigma Xi. Home: 1014 Penkridge Dr Iowa City IA 52240 Office: Orthodontic Dept College of Dentistry University of Iowa Iowa City IA 52242

BISHER, JAMES FURMAN, journalist, author; b. Denton, N.C., Nov. 4, 1918; s. Chisholm and Mamie (Morris) B.; (div.)children: Roger, James Furman, Monte. Student, Furman U., 1934-36; A.B. in Journalism, U. N.C., 1938. Editor Lumberton (N.C.) Voice, 1938-39; reporter High Point (N.C.) Enterprise, 1939-40; reporter, state editor Charlotte (N.C.) News, 1940-43, sports editor, 1946-50, Atlanta Constn., 1950-57, Atlanta Jour, 1957—; columnist The Sporting News, St. Louis; moderator weekly TV show, Football Rev., 1950-68; Vice pres. Bisher Hosiery Mill, Denton, N.C. Author: With A Southern Exposure, 1962, Miracle in Atlanta, 1966, Strange But True Baseball Stories, 1966, Arnold Palmer—The Golden Year, 1971, Aaron, 1974, The College Game, 1974, The Masters, 1976, also numerous articles; contbr. to: anthologies including Best Sports Stories of Year, 23 times. Chmn. Ga. Christmas Seal campaign, 1961; charter mem. Atlanta-Fulton County Stadium Authority.; Bd. dirs. Salvation Army Boys Club. Served to lt. Air Corps USNR, 1943-46. Recipient Ga. A.P. Sports Writing award, 18 times; recipient Turf Writing award Fla. Throughbred Breeders Assn., 1972, 75, Sigma Delta Chi awards for best sports commentary, 1982, 83, Bert McGrane award for disting. service to coll. football, 1982; named Ky. col., 1958; hon. Tar Heel, 1961; Distinguished Alumnus of Yr. Furman U., 1978; Jake Wade award Coll. Sports Info. Dirs. Am., 1979. Mem. Nat. Sportscasters and Sportswriters Assn. (pres. 1974-76), Football Writers Assn. Am. (pres. 1959-60), Chi Psi. Presbyterian. Clubs: Canongate Golf, Atlanta Country, Capital City (Atlanta); Brookfield West Country; Gridiron (U. Ga.); Snapfinger Woods Golf. Home: 3135 Rilman Rd NW Atlanta GA 30327 Office: 72 Marietta St NW Atlanta GA 30302 *My good fortune in life is not to be confused with success, whose definition yet remains vague to me. Success is some mythical goal clamored and struggled for, and whose pursuit is never-ending. One level leads to a requirement to seek another. Success, in my mind, must be related to the status of that person who achieves happiness, and yet may never have been outside his county.*

BISHOP, ALBERT BENTLEY, III, industrial engineering educator; b. Phila., Apr. 7, 1929; s. Albert Bentley and Sara LeCompte (DesPortes) B.; m. Louise Boyd Squire, Nov. 17, 1951; children: John Albert, Suzanne Squire, James DesPortes. B.E.E., Cornell U., 1951; M.S., Ohio State U., 1953, Ph.D., 1957. Mem. tech. staff Bell Telephone Labs., Allentown, Pa., 1954; instr. indsl. and systems engring. Ohio State U., Columbus, 1954-57, asst. prof., 1957-60, asso. prof., 1960-65, prof., 1965—, chmn. dept., 1974-82; pres. Albert B. Bishop and Assos.; cons. U.S. Army Sci. Adv. Panel, 1975-77. Author: Introduction to Discrete Linear Controls—Theory and Application, 1975; contbr. articles to profl. jours. Mem. Ohio Citizens Council on Health and Welfare, 1973—; active Cub and Boy Scouts Am., 1965-74; mem. council Cornell U., 1974-80, 81—; trustee Buckeye Boys Ranch, 1976—. Served with USAF, 1951-53. Recipient Tech. Person of Yr. award Columbus Tech. Council, 1983. Fellow Am. Soc. Quality Control, Am. Inst. Indsl. Engrs. (nat. engring. economy research com. 1957-60, chmn. Columbus sect. research com. 1957-59, dir. 1976-78, mem. editorial bd. 1960-67, chmn. council acad. dept. heads 1980-81, dir. acad. affairs 1981-82, mem. task force on new technologies 1982—); mem. IEEE, Ops. Research Soc. Am., Inst. Mgmt. Sci., Am. Soc. Engring. Edn., Mil. Ops. Research Soc. (dir. 1969-72, co-chmn. edn. com. 1970-71, chmn. prize com. 1971-72), Tau Beta Pi (nat. exec. council 1966-70), Eta Kappa Nu, Alpha Pi Mu, Sigma Xi, Phi Kappa Phi, Pi Mu Epsilon, Sigma Pi. Episcopalian (vestryman 1958-60, 72-75, 77-80, 83—, jr. warden 1961-63, sr. warden 1963-65, mem. diocesan council 1968-72, nat. conv. del. 1973, 76, 79, 82). Patentee in field. Home: 1946 W Lane Ave Columbus OH 43221

BISHOP, ANNE, journalist, info. scientist, librarian; b. Amasya, Turkey, May 1, 1912; came to U.S., 1947, naturalized, 1950; d. Kevork and Zabel (Isburian) Avakian; m. Jacques Bruyere, June 6, 1940; 1 son, Christian Georges; m. John Bishop, 1950; children—John, Elizabeth. Student, Oxford U., 1935-37, Sorbonne U., 1937-41, Ecole Univerelle de Paris, 1944, Ecole Orientale, 1946, Calif. State U., Northridge, 1978; D.D. (hon.), Christ U., 1980. Paris Bur. chief London Daily Mirror, 1935; fgn. and war corr. UPI, N.Y. News, Chgo. Tribune, 1935-46; freelance writer Social Studies mag., Life and Time mag., Lit. Tabloid, 8-Ball, Armenian Reporter, Armenian Observer, Nor Gyank, Armenian Mirror, Spectator, 1947—; tchr. French, Spanish, German, Chinese, Russian, and Armenian community colls.; parliamentarian Allied Arts, Inc.; Mem. Armenian Gen. Benevolent Union, 1934—. Author: Franklin in Paris, 1937; opera Hripsime, 1974, Spirit of '76, 1974, Western Spirit of '76, 1975, A Nation of Dreamers, 1975, Queen Elizabeth's Silver Jubilee, 1977, World Who's Who of Armenians, 1977-80, Gerontology Outreach Affiliated Library System, 1978, Volunteers International Education, Adv. Council 5-year Ann, 1974-79, 1980, Upon Attaining Immortality, 1980, The Kingdom of Heaven, 1980, Internat. Sr. Citizen, Gerontologist. Life mem. Los Angeles County Parks and Recreations Sr. Citizen Soc., 1967—; chmn. Republican Party, 1972; pres. Cassel Pl. Sr. Citizens, 1973. Named World's Greatest War Corr. N.Y. News-Chgo. Tribune Syndicate, 1946. Mem. ALA (life), Am. Soc. Composers and Producers, Nat. Trust Historic Preservation, Smithsonian Instn., Nat. Soc. Lit. and Arts, Alliance Française, Women's Internat. Aeros. Soc., Q15 Pioneers, Terpsichorean (pres.), Overseas, Greater Los Angeles (bicentennial com.) press clubs, Alethians, Iota Tau Tau, Alpha Phi Omega, Tau Alpha Epsilon, Alpha Gamma Sigma. Home: 615 S Manhattan Pl Los Angeles CA 90005 Office: 600 N Vermont Ave Los Angeles CA 90029 *At the heart of the cosmic process, I see an all-persuasive unifying, coordinating, ever-adjusting catalysis. Viable at all levels of existence, from mathematics up to man, it is ever-present, omnipotent, omniscient, all-perfect, known under the synonym of God. Expressed on the mathematical level in the universal validity of balance; on the chemical level in formulas like H2O for water, and N2Co for salt; on the physical level in the laws of gravitation and hydraulics; on the biological level in formulas demonstrating the awesome evolution of life from the caveman and the jungle law to human rights and inalienable individual dignity, it becomes one with pure love, a power infinitely greater than gravitation, electricity, magnetism, and all other forces and variations such as night and day, spring and summer, autumn and winter. This all-inclusive truth is the Golden Rule. It is at one principle and Principal, the law of balance permeating all beings as one and the same process whose immortal presence makes it all happen in perfect unison. Such is the invisible key to eternal life everlasting.*

BISHOP, AVERY ALVIN, civil engineer; b. Delta, Utah, Aug. 27, 1913; s. John Avery and Lemira (Walker) B.; m. Anna Beth Reeder, Nov. 10, 1938; children: Alvin Bruce, Janet, Carol Anne Bishop Denniston, Dan Roger. B.C.E., Utah State U., 1934, M.S. in Agrl. Engring, 1938; Ph.D. (NSF fellow), Colo. State U., 1961. Draftsman, topographic engr., irrigation engr., civil engr. various fed. agys., 1934-46; faculty agrl. and irrigation engring. Utah State U., Logan, 1946-71, 74—, prof., 1954-71, 74-79, head dept., 1965-71, 74-79, prof. emeritus, 1979—; sr. water mgmt. specialist AID, Washington, 1971-74; cons. engr. City of Logan, 1948—; irrigation cons. fgn. agrl. service Agr. Dept., 1953, 55, FAO, 1956, 58, 61, Aichi Irrigation Pub. Corp., Japan, 1957, AID, 1965, 66, 68, 70, World Bank, Burma, 1977; cons. AID, Lesotho, 1979, Thailand, 1981, Philippines, 1981, 82, 83; lectr. SEATO Grad. Sch. Engring., Bangkok, Thailand, 1963; planner, condr. Near East-S. Asia Irrigation Practices Seminars; also tech. editor Procs. Seminars, 1966, 68, 70; Utah State U. Faculty honor lectr., 1971, Exchange scientist to, Romania, 1971. Mem. ASCE (life mem., exec. sec. irrigation and drainage div., chmn. exec. com. 1976, editor div. Jour.); mem. Am. Soc. Agrl. Engrs., Am. Soc. Engring. Edn. Home: 1780 East 1030 North Logan UT 84321

BISHOP, BUDD HARRIS, museum administrator; b. Canton, Ga., Nov. 1, 1936; s. James M. and Mary E. (Ponder) B.; m. Julia Crowder, Nov. 30, 1968. A.B., Shorter Coll., Rome, Ga., 1958; M.F.A., U. Ga., 1960. Instr. art Ensworth Sch., Nashville, 1961-63; dir. creative services Transit Advt. Assn., N.Y.C., 1964-66; dir. Hunter Mus. of Art, Chattanooga, 1966-76, Columbus (Ohio) Mus. Art, 1976—; vis. lectr. Vanderbilt U., 1962; Past pres. bd. Intermuseum Conservation Lab., Oberlin, Ohio. Trustee Columbus Acad., Kelton House Restoration, Columbus; chmn. adv. com. civic arts City of Columbus; chmn. Airport Art Selection Panel. Recipient Tenn. Art Commn. Gov. awards, 1971, 73. Mem. Am. Assn. Museums, Assn. Art Mus. Dirs. (trustee), Midwestern Mus. Conf. Club: Rotary. Office: 480 E Broad St Columbus OH 43215

BISHOP, CALVIN THOMAS, landscape architect; b. Alexander City, Ala., Oct. 11, 1929; s. Isaiah Washington and Flora Bernice (Carlton) B.; m. Lenna Graves, Aug. 28, 1950; children: Leigh Carlton, Beverly Lynn, Lane Amanda. B.Landscape Arch., Auburn U., 1951. Landscape architect John F. Highberger, Memphis, 1949-51; planner Auburn Planning Bd., 1951; landscape architect, designer Ralph Ellis Gunn, Houston, 1952-53; partner Bishop & Walker, Houston, 1953—; pres. Bishop Wholesale Greenhouses, Inc., Alexander, Ala.; asst. prof. landscape arch. La. State U., 1965-66. Works include Am. Rose Center, Shreveport, La. Post adviser Boy Scouts Am., 1971-73; chmn. Gov.'s Houston-Gulf Coast Region-10 Year Goals for Tex. planning com., 1970, Houston Am. Bicentennial Commn., 1973—; treas. Richmond Elementary PTO, 1975—; Mem. profl. adv. com. Sch. Environ. Design Tex. A. and M.U. Recipient Houston Mcpl. Arts Environ. Distinguished Achievement awards, 1970-72. Mem. Am. Soc. Landscape Architects (pres. S.W. chpt. 1970-71, nat. v.p. 1973-74, 80, pres. elect 1981-82, Council fellows 1978—, Nat. Honor award for design), Houston C. of C., Houston-Auburn U. Alumni Assn. (pres. 1963-64), Pi Kappa Alpha. Baptist. Club: Rotary (sgt. at arms 1978-79). Home: 6103 Reamer St Houston TX 77036 Office: 3502 Roseland St Houston TX 77006

BISHOP, CHARLES EDWIN, university president, economist; b. Campobello, S.C., June 8, 1921; s. Fred and Hattie Bess (Wall) B.; m. Dorothy Anderkin, Feb. 13, 1943; children: Susan Ann, Mary Catherine, Charles Edwin. B.S., Berea Coll., 1946; M.S., U. Ky., 1948; Ph.D. (Farm Found. fellow 1948-49), U. Chgo., 1952. Research asst. agrl. econs. U. Ky., 1947-48; research assoc. econs. U. Chgo., 1949-50; mem. faculty N.C. State U., 1950-70, prof. agrl. econs., 1956-70, head dept. agrl. econs., 1957-65, head dept. econs., 1965-66, William N. Reynolds disting. prof., 1957-70; v.p. U. N.C., Chapel Hill, 1966-70; exec. dir. Agrl. Policy Inst., 1960-66; chancellor U. Md., College Park, 1970-74; pres. U. Ark., Fayetteville, 1974-80, U. Houston System, 1980—; vis. prof. U. Va., 1961-63; cons. Universidad Agraria, Lima, Peru, 1961-65; mem. Nat. Com. Agrl. Policy, Nat. Planning Assn., 1958-70; agrl. bd. Nat. Acad. Scis., 1963-68; sci. adv. com. to sec. agr., 1962-68; mem. Nat. Manpower Adv. Com., 1962-68; exec. dir. Nat. Adv. Com. on Rural Poverty, 1966-67; mem. food adv. com. Pres. Nixon's Cost of Living Council, 1972; mem. Pres.'s adv. com. White House Conf. on Balanced Nat. Growth and Econ. Devel., 1978. Co-author: Introduction to Agricultural Economic Analysis, 1958. Mem. com. on vet. med. edn. So. Regional Edn. Bd., 1974; trustee Farm Found., 1968-78; bd. dirs. Winthrop Rockefeller Found., 1975-78, Resources for the Future; co-chmn. bd. dirs. Nat. Rural Center, 1975-79; mem. Pres.'s Commn. on Agenda for Eighties, 1980. Mem. Am. Agr. Econs. Assn. (pres. 1967-68), Am. Econ. Assn., Internat. Assn. Agrl. Econs., Alpha Zeta, Phi Kappa Phi, Gamma Sigma Delta. Office: Office of Pres U Houston Houston TX 77004

BISHOP, CHARLES JOHNSON, agrologist; b. Semans, Sask., Can., Jan. 6. 1920; s. Lewis Leander and Nellie Erdine (Illsley) B.; m. Katherine Adele Corey, June 19, 1951; 1 son, John. B.Sc., Acadia U., Wolfville, N.S., Can., 1941, D.Sc. (hon.), 1982; A.M., Harvard U., 1946, Ph.D., 1947. Weather forecaster RCAF, Eastern Can., 1942-45; research scientist, fruit breeding Agr. Exptl. Sta., Kentville, N.S., Can., 1947-52, supt., 1952-58, Summerland, B.C., Can., 1958-59; asso. dir. program, research br. Dept. Agr., Ottawa, Ont., Can., 1959-64; research coordinator for horticulture, research br. Agr. Can., Ottawa, 1964—. Research, publs. in field; chmn. editorial policy bd. for Can. jours. agrl. sci., 1962-65. Served with RCAF, 1945. Decorated Queen's Jubilee medal. Fellow Royal Soc. Can., Am. Soc. Hort. Sci., Agrl. Inst. Can.; mem. Can. Soc. Hort. Sci. (pres. 1957-58), Internat. Soc. Hort. Sci. (council mem. for Can.), Genetics Soc. Can. (pres. 1959-60), Royal Soc. Can., Sci. Acad. (pres. 1968-69). Baptist. Home: 548 Hillcrest Ave Ottawa ON K2A 2M9 Canada Office: Central Exptl Farm Ottawa ON K1A 0C5 Canada

BISHOP, ERNEST EUGENE, JR., cafeteria company executive; b. Swainsboro, Ga., May 5, 1930; s. Ernest Eugene and Clara B. (Davis) B.; m. Melba H. Hooks, Sept. 18, 1949; children: Gene, Nick, Tim, Julie, Laura. Ed. public schs. Began career with Morrison Inc. (various positions), from 1947; including asst. mgr., mgr., v.p., sr. v.p., pres., chief exec. officer; dir. Comml. Guaranty Bank, Mobile. Trustee Julius T. Wright Sch., Mobile; bd. dirs. local chpt. Boy Scouts Am. Baptist. Office: care Morrison Inc PO Box 160266 Mobile AL 36625 *

BISHOP, GENE HERBERT, banker; b. Forest, Miss., May 3, 1930; s. Herbert Eugene and Lavonne (Little) B.; m. Kathy S. Bishop, May 27, 1983. B.B.A., U. Miss., Oxford, 1952. With First Nat. Bank, Dallas, 1954-69, sr. v.p., chmn. sr. loan com., 1963-68, exec. v.p., 1968-69; past pres., dir. SBIC subs. First Dallas Capital Corp.; pres. Lomas & Nettleton Fin. Corp., Dallas, 1969-75, Lomas & Nettleton Mortgage Investors, 1969-75; chmn., chief exec. officer Merc. Nat. Bank, Dallas, 1975-81, Merc. Tex. Corp., 1975—; dir. Lomas & Nettleton Fin. Corp., Lomas & Nettleton Mortgage Investors, Anderson Industries, Inc., Gifford-Hill & Co., Inc., S.W. Airlines Co., Republic Nat. Life Ins. Co., Republic Fin. Services, Inc. Trustee, Baylor Coll. Dentistry; bd. dirs. World Trade Center, Southwestern Med. Found., State Fair Tex., Dallas Zool. Soc.; exec. bd. Maguire Oil and Gas Inst.; trustee, mem. devel. com. Children's Med. Center; trustee, bd. dirs. So. Meth. U.; mem. Dallas Citizens Council, Dallas Council World Affairs; adv. council Dallas Community Chest Trust Fund. Served to 1st lt. USAF, 1952-54. Mem. Assn. Res. City Bankers, Tex. Assn. Bank Holding Cos. (dir.). Methodist. Clubs: Dallas Petroleum, Terpsichorean, Idlewild, Brook Hollow Golf. Office: PO Box 225415 Dallas TX 75265

BISHOP, GORDON BRUCE, journalist; b. Paterson, N.J., Jan. 1, 1938; s. Charles E. and Freda Mary (Romyns) B.; m. Jeanne Ann Reed, June 30, 1962; children: Jennifer, Elizabeth. Student, Am. Acad. Dramatic Arts, 1957; B.A., Rutgers U., 1967; Inst. Internat. Edn. scholar, U. Manchester, Eng., 1972. Reporter, columnist Herald-News, Passaic, N.J., 1959-67; investigative reporter, columnist Star-Ledger, Newark, 1969—; lectr. Rutgers U., Princeton U.; Environ. commr., Eatontown, N.J., 1973-76. Author: (with Frank Papps) The Purple Canary, 1963, Holding onto Nothing, 1969; producer: Public Broadcasting System documentary TV film It's My Home, 1980. Recipient Nat. Environ. awards Scripps-Howard Found., 1971, 72, 73, 74, 75; Nat. Conservation awards Washington Journalism Center, 1971, 72; Conservation award N.J. Audubon Soc., 1973; Man of Year award AABC Congregation, Irvington, N.J.; N.J. Press Assn. awards, 1971, 72, 73, 76, 77, 78, 79, 82; Pub. Service award N.J. Profl. Journalism Soc., 1972, 73, 74, 76, 78, N.J. Soc. Profl. Engrs., 1977; N.J. Conf. Mayors award, 1974; Nat. Recycling award Nat. Recycling Assn., 1973; Gold medal N.J. Garden Club, 1980; award Ballew/McFarland Found., 1981, N.J. Agrl. Soc., 1981. Mem. Rutgers U. Alumni Assn. Office: Star-Ledger Plaza Newark NJ 07101 *The will to live, to learn, and to inspire others flows from a genuine desire to want to work at your best and to share your love with those who seek it. This is our destiny: Work and Love. Without either, you can never realize your full potential as an individual.*

BISHOP, HARRY CRADEN, surgeon; b. N.Y.C., Apr. 1, 1921. A.B., Dartmouth Coll., 1943; M.D., Harvard U., 1945; M.A. (hon.), U. Pa., 1971. Diplomate: Nat. Bd. Med. Examiners, Am. Bd. Surgery. Intern in surgery N.Y. Hosp., 1945-46; asst. resident in surgery, then chief resident Mary Imogene Bassett Hosp., Cooperstown, N.Y., 1948-50; surg. pathologist Presbyn. Med. Center, N.Y.C., 1950; asst. resident in surgery Children's Med. Center, Boston, 1950-51, sr. asst. resident, then chief surg. resident, 1952-54; sr. asst. resident Peter Bent Brigham Hosp., Boston, 1951-52; instr. Harvard U. Med. Sch., 1954; mem. faculty U. Pa. Med. Sch., 1955—, prof. pediatric surgery, 1979—; mem. staff Children's Hosp., Phila., 1954—, sr. surgeon, 1960—, pres. staff, 1971-73; mem. cons. staff Jeanes, Pa. hosps.; med. staff Hosp. U. Pa.; adv. bd. Pa. Blue Shield, 1976—. Editorial bd.: Clin. Pediatrics, 1970-80. Served to capt. M.C. AUS, 1946-48. Fellow A.C.S. (chmn. adv. council pediatric surgery 1980—), Am. Acad. Pediatrics; mem. Am. Pediatric Surg. Assn. (gov. 1979-82), AMA, Phila. County Med. Soc., Phila. Pediatric Soc., Brit. Assn. Pediatric Surgeons, Phila. Acad. Surgery, Coll. Physicians Phila., Lilliputian Surg. Soc., Deutscher Gesellschaft Kinderchirurgie. Home: 636 Winsford Rd Bryn Mawr PA 19010 Office: Children's Hosp 34th St and Civic Center Blvd Philadelphia PA 19104

BISHOP, ISABEL (MRS. HAROLD G. WOLFF), artist; b. Cin., Mar. 3, 1902; d. John Remsen and Anna Bartram (Newbold) B.; m. Harold George Wolff, Aug. 9, 1934. Ed., Wicker Art Sch., Detroit, 1917-18, N.Y. Sch. Applied Design for Women, 1918-20, Art Students League N.Y., 1920-22, 1927-30; A.F.D. (hon.), Moore Inst., Phila.; D.F.A. (hon.), Bates Coll., 1979, Mt. Holyoke Coll., 1982. Instr. life painting and composition Art Students League, N.Y.C., 1936-37; instr. Snowhegan Sch. Painting and Sculpture, 1957, lectr., 1957, 60, 62, 64, 66. Represented in, Mus. Bibliothèque Nationale, Paris, Victoria and Albert Mus., London, Brit. Mus., London, Des Moines Art Center, also art galleries, collections, Paul Sachs, Johnson Collection, others; exhibited at expns., 10 one-man shows in, N.Y.C., also at, Berkshire Mus., Pittsfield, Mass., 1957, retrospective exhbns., Whitney Mus. Art, 1975, U. Ariz., 1974, Wichita (Kans.) State U., group shows, Bklyn. Mus., 1977, Hayward Gallery, N.Y. U., Am. embassy, London, Wichita State U., 1979. Recipient awards including; W.A. Clark prize; Bronze medal Corcoran Gallery, Washington, 1945; Mrs. H. S. Noyes and Am. Artists Group prizes, 1947; Forsythia award Bklyn. Bot. Garden, 1979; Benjamin Franklin fellow Royal Soc. Art, 1965; first Altman prize N.A.D., 1967; asso. mem. N.A.D., 1940; elected Nat. Academician, 1941. Fellow Royal Soc. Arts London; mem. Nat. Inst. Arts and Letters, Am. Acad. Arts and Letters, Am. Soc. Painters, Sculptors and Gravers, Soc. Am. Etchers, Nat. Arts Club, Phila. Water Color Club, Am. Group Cosmopolitan Club. Home: 355 W 246th St Fieldston New York NY 10471 Studio: 41 Union Sq W New York NY 10003

BISHOP, JAMES KEOUGH, foreign service officer; b. New Rochelle, N.Y., July 21, 1938. B.S., Coll. Holy Cross, 1960; grad. exec. seminar in nat. and internat. affairs, Fgn. Service Inst., 1977; M.I.I.P., Johns Hopkins U., 1981. With Fgn. Service, Dept. State, 1960—; press officer Dept. State, 1961-63; vice consul, Auckland, N.Z., 1963-66, econ. officer, Beirut, 1966-68, Yaounde, 1968-70; internat. relations officer Bur. African Affairs, 1970-74; dep. dir. Office West African Affairs, 1974-76; dir. North African Affairs, Dept. State, 1977-79; AEP, Republic of Niger, 1979-81; dep. asst. sec. state African Affairs Bur., 1981—. Office: Office 6236 Dept State Washington DC 20520

BISHOP, JIM, author; b. Jersey City, Nov. 21, 1907; s. John Michael and Jenny Josephine (Tier) B.; m. Elinor Margaret Dunning, June 14, 1930 (dec. Oct. 1957); children—Virginia Lee, Gayle Peggy; m. Elizabeth Kelly Stone, May, 1961; children—Karen, Kathleen. Student, Drakes Secretarial Coll., 1923; Litt.D., St. Bonaventure U., 1958, Belmont Abbey Coll., 1968, St. Peter's Coll., 1978. Copy boy N.Y. News, 1929-30; reporter N.Y. Daily Mirror, 1930-32; asst. to Mark Bellinger, columnist, 1932-34; rewriteman, feature writer Daily Mirror, 1934-43; asso. editor Colliers mag., 1943-44, war editor, 1944-45; exec. editor Liberty mag., 1945-47; dir. lit. dept. Music Corp. Am., 1947-49; founding editor Gold Medal Books, 1949-51; exec. editor Catholic Digest; founding editor Catholic Digest Book Club, 1954-55. Author: The Glass Crutch, 1945, The Mark Hellinger Story, 1952, Parish Priest, 1953, The Girl in Poison Cottage, 1953, The Making of a Priest, 1954, The Day Lincoln Was Shot, 1955, The Golden Ham, 1956, The Day Christ Died, 1957, Go With God, 1958, Some of My Very Best, 1960, The Day Christ Was Born, 1960, The Murder Trial of Judge Peal, 1962, Honeymoon Diary, 1963, A Day in the Life of President Kennedy, 1964, Jim Bishop; Reporter, 1965, A Day in the Life of President Johnson, 1967, The Day Kennedy was Shot, 1968, The Days of Martin Luther King, Jr, 1971, F.D.R.'s Last Year, 1974, the Birth of the United States, 1976, A Bishop's Confession, 1980;

Columnist, King Features Syndicate.; Contbr. nat. mags. Recipient Journalism in Life award Ency. Brit., 1979. Home: 641 West Dr Delray Beach FL 33445 *I knew, from the first adolescent consciousness, that life on its many levels would consist of frustrations, struggles, failures and aspirations, offset at times with brief triumphs and periods of happiness. In order to sustain myself, I borrowed this philosophy from my paternal grandmother, Mary Murphy Bishop: Thy will be done.*

BISHOP, JOSEPH WARREN, JR., lawyer, educator; b. N.Y.C., Apr. 15, 1915; s. Joseph Warren and Edna Priscilla (Dashiell) B.; m. Susan Carroll Oulahan, May 6, 1950; 1 son, Joseph Warren III. Grad, Deerfield Acad., 1932; A.B., Dartmouth Coll., 1936; LL.B., Harvard U., 1940. Bar: D.C. 1941, N.Y. 1954, Conn. 1963. Spl. asst. to undersec. war, 1940-42; with Office Solicitor Gen., Dept. Justice, 1947-50; asst. to gen. counsel U.S. High Commn. Occupied Germany, 1950-52; dep. gen. counsel, acting gen. counsel Dept. Army, 1952-53; pvt. practice law, N.Y.C., 1953-57; prof. law Yale Law Sch., 1957—, Richard Ely prof. law, 1968—; vis. prof. law U. Muenster, West Germany, 1965; faculty Salzburg Seminar Am. Studies, 1967; vis. fellow Clare Hall Cambridge (Eng.) U., 1974; vis. prof. U. Munich, W. Ger., 1980; asst. counsel trustees New Haven R.R., 1961-74; Expert cons. SEC, 1958. Author: Indemnifying and Insuring the Corporate Executive, 2d edit., 1980, Obiter Dicta, 1971, Justice Under Fire: A Study of Military Law, 1974; also articles, book revs. Served with AUS, 1943-46. Recipient Exceptional Civilian Service citation Dept. Army, 1953; Guggenheim fellow, 1974. Club: Century. Home: 83 E Rock Rd New Haven CT 06511 Office: Yale Law Sch Box 401A Yale Station New Haven CT 06520

BISHOP, LEO KENNETH, clergyman, educator; b. Britton, Okla., Oct. 11, 1911; s. Luther and Edith (Scovill) B.; m. Pauline T. Shamburg, Sept. 15, 1935; 1 dau., Linda Paulette. A.B., Phillips U., 1932; L.H.D., 1958; M.A., Columbia U., 1944; M.B.A., U. Chgo., 1957; Litt.D., Kansas City Coll. Osteopathy and Surgery, 1964. Ordained to ministry Christian Ch., 1932; asso. minister Univ. Place Ch., Oklahoma City, 1932-35; minister First Ch., Paducah, Ky., 1935-41, Central Ch., Des Moines, 1941-45; dir. St. Louis office NCCJ, 1945-48, v.p., dir. central div., Chgo., 1949-63; dir. pub. affairs People-to-People, Kansas City, Mo., 1963-66; v.p. Chgo. Coll. Osteopathy, 1966-72; pres. Bishop Enterprises, Colorado Springs, Colo., 1972—; also lectr. Contbr. religious and ednl. jours.; Developed: radio series Storm Warning; TV series The Other Guy, 1954. Cons. Community Social Planning Council, Mayor's Race Relations Com., YMCA, St. Louis; Am. del. Conf. World Brotherhood, Paris, 1950; bd. dirs. Am. Heritage Found. Recipient Paducah Jr. C. of C. Most Useful Citizen award, 1937, Distinguished Service award Dore Miller Found., 1958, Freedom Found. of Valley Forge award, 1961; named Chicagoan of Year, 1960. Clubs: Rotary, Union League. Home: 107 W Cheyenne Rd Colorado Springs CO 80906 Office: PO Box 843 Colorado Springs CO 80901

BISHOP, LUTHER DOYLE, educator; b. Graham, Tex., Oct. 31, 1921; s. Luther Whitfield and Clara Bell (Rowe) B.; m. Nan Alice Schneider, Mar. 15, 1942. Student, Baylor U., 1939-40; B.B.A., U. Tex., 1948, M.B.A., 1950; Ph.D., Ohio State U., 1959. With Clifton Mfg. Co., Waco, Tex., 1940-42, Brown and Root Constrn. Co., Texarkana, Tex., 1942; mgr. vets dormitories U. Tex., 1948-49, instr. mgmt. dept., 1949-51; mem. faculty U. Okla., Norman, 1951—, prof. bus. mgmt., 1959-73, David Ross Boyd prof. mgmt., 1973—, chmn. dept., 1959-68, 70-72; Grad. asst. in bus. orgn. Ohio State U., 1953-54. Served with USNR, 1942-45. Mem. Acad. Mgmt., AAUP, Nat. Rehab. Assn., Soc. Advancement Mgmt., Southwestern Social Sci. Assn., Beta Gamma Sigma. Home: 2715 Aspen Circle Norman OK 73069

BISHOP, RAYMOND HOLMES, JR., retired army officer, physician; b. Fort Bennings, Ga., Apr. 6, 1925; s. Raymond Holmes and Henrietta B.; m. Marjorie Harrell, Sept. 1, 1946; children: Michael, Robert, Stephen, Marilyn. B.A., U. Tex., 1948, M.D., 1952. Diplomate: Am. Bd. Internal Medicine. Commd. 1st lt. M.C. U.S. Army, 1952, advanced through grades to maj. gen., 1978; intern Brooke Gen. Hosp., Fort Sam Houston, Tex., 1952-53, resident in medicine, 1954-58; comdr. 5th Gen. Hosp., Stuttgart, W. Ger., 1971-73, Reynolds Army Hosp., Fort Sill, Okla., 1973-76; comdg. gen. William Beaumont Army Med. Center, El Paso, Tex., 1976-79, Fitzsimons Army Med. Center, Aurora, Colo., 1979-80, U.S. Army Health Services Command, Ft. Sam Houston, Tex., 1980-83. Office: San Antonio State Chest Hosp San Antonio TX 78223

BISHOP, ROBERT, museum director, art educator; b. Readfield, Maine, Aug. 25, 1938; s. Charles and Muriel (Webber) B. Ph.D. in Am. Culture, U. Mich., 1975. Mgr. publs. Greenfield Village and Henry Ford Mus., Dearborn, Mich., 1966-74, mus. editor, 1974-76; adj. prof. art history U. Mich., Dearborn, 1977, Ann Arbor, 1975-77; dir. Mus. Am. Folk Art, N.Y.C., 1976—; adj. prof. art and art edn. N.Y. U., 1980—. Author, designer: Centuries and Styles of the American Chair, 1640-1970, 1973, 83, How to Know American Antique Furniture, 1973, Guide to American Antique Furniture, 1973, American Folk Sculpture, 1974, New Discoveries in American Quilts, 1975; author: The Borden Limner and His Contemporaries, 1976, Treasurers of American Folk Art, 1979; co-author, designer: America's Quilts and Coverlets, 1972, American Painted and Decorated Furniture, 1972, The American Clock, 1976, A Gallery of Amish Quilts, 1976; co-author: World Furniture, 1979, The World of Antiques, Art and Architecture in Victorian America, 1979, Folk Painters of America, 1979, A Gallery of American Weathervanes and Whirligigs, 1980; editor, picture editor other books. Bd. dirs. N.Y.C. Council of Museums, 1978—, Koreshan Unity, Estero, Fla., 1978—, Pioneer Ednl. Found., Estero, 1978—; trustee Opportunity Resources, N.Y.C, 1979—, Grove House, Coconut Grove, Fla., 1977—; chmn. bd. dirs. ISALTA, N.Y.C., 1980—. Recipient Impresario award creative writing Internat. Cultural Soc., 1975, Silver medal Internat. Film and TV Festival, 1978. Home: 213 W 22d St New York NY 10011 Office: 49 W 53d St New York NY 10019

BISHOP, ROBERT LYLE, economist; b. St. Louis, June 4, 1916; s. Lyle Austin and Helen (Craden) B.; m. Joan Frances Fiss, Sept. 12, 1942. A.B., Harvard, 1937, M.A., 1942, Ph.D., 1949; postgrad., Princeton, 1938-39. Instr. econs. Harvard, 1939-42; mem. faculty Mass. Inst. Tech., 1942—, successively instr., asst. prof., asso. prof., 1942-57, prof. econs., 1957—, head dept. econs. and social sci., 1958-65; dean Sch. Humanities and Social Scis., 1964-73; vis. lectr. Harvard; vis. prof. Brandeis U. Mem. Am. Econ. Assn., Econometric Soc., Am. Acad. Arts and Scis., Phi Beta Kappa. Home: 27 Amherst Rd Wellesley MA 02181 Office: Mass Inst Tech Cambridge MA 02139

BISHOP, ROBERT MILTON, stock exchange official; b. Elmira, N.Y., June 5, 1921; s. Milton W. and Florence E. (Crofutt) B.; m. Anne Selene Rowan, Oct. 30, 1943; children—Donald M., Anne Selene (Mrs. Donald R. Bennett), Elizabeth M. (Mrs. Thomas H. Speed), Robert Milton, Regina J.M., Rowan J.S. A.B., Union Coll., Schenectady, 1943; A.M., Trinity Coll., Hartford, Conn., 1955. Asst. dir. pub. relations Union Coll., Schenectady, 1945-47; dir. pub. relations Trinity Coll., 1947-55; mem. staff N.Y. Stock Exchange, 1955—; dir. dept. mem. firms liaison, asst. dir. dept. mem. firms, 1961-63, v.p., asso. dir. dept. mem. firms, 1963-65, v.p., dir. dept. mem. firms, 1965-73, sr. v.p. mem. firm regulation and surveillance group, 1973-81, sr. v.p. regulatory services group, 1982—. Author booklets, securities tng. manuals. Served as pilot USAAF, 1943-45. Episcopalian. Clubs: India House, Stock Exchange Luncheon. Home: 4 Kimball Circle Westfield NJ 07090 Office: NY Stock Exchange 55 Water St New York NY 10041

BISHOP, SIDNEY WILLARD, lawyer; b. Denver, Oct. 28, 1926; s. Sidney W. and Helen (Marihugh) B.; m. Betty Lou Dolan, May 10, 1947; children—Linda, Thomas, Nancy, Joan, Ann, Mary, Elizabeth, Sidney Willard III, Jane. B.S., Regis Coll., Denver, 1949; J.D., U. Denver, 1950. Bar: Colo. bar 1950, Calif. bar 1958. With January & Yegge, Denver, 1949-50; dep. dist. atty., Cheyenne County, Colo., 1951-56, pvt. practice, Cheyenne Wells, Colo., 1950-56; with Prudential Ins. Co. Am., Los Angeles, 1956-61, 64-68; asst. counsel law dept., 1958-61, asst. gen. solicitor, 1964-66, dir. govt. relations, 1966-68; gen. counsel Am. Ins. Assn., N.Y.C., 1968-70; with firm Svenson & Garvin, Van Nuys, Calif., 1970-73; sr. v.p., gen. counsel Beneficial Standard Life Ins. Co., 1973—; confidential asst. to postmaster gen. U.S., 1961, asst. postmaster gen. bur. facilities, 1962-63, dep. postmaster gen., 1963-64. So. Calif. vice chmn. Statewide Water Devel. Com., 1959-60. Served with USNR, 1944-46. Home: 6519 Langdon Ave Van Nuys CA 91406 Office: 3700 Wilshire Blvd Los Angeles CA 90010

BISHOP, STEPHEN, singer, songwriter; b. San Diego, 1952. Began musical career performing with The Weeds, Los Angeles, 1967; songwriter, musician for Art Garfunkel, 1975. Albums include Careless, 1976, Bish, 1978, Red Cab to Manhattan, 1980, Sleeping with Girls, 1984; songs include Everybody Needs Love; wrote, performed: theme songs for films Tootsie, Unfaithfully Yours. Named Best New Male Vocalist Rock Music Awards, 1977. Office: care Trudy Green Mgmt 1800 Marchester Pl Los Angeles CA 90069 *

BISHOP, THOMAS WALTER, educator; b. Vienna, Austria, Feb. 21, 1929; came to U.S., 1940, naturalized, 1944; s. Martin M. and Katherine (Abeles) B.; m. Muriel Hausman, June 30, 1950 (div. 1967); children—Jeffrey Bishop, Katherine; m. Helen Gary, Dec. 15, 1967. A.B., N.Y. U., 1950; A.M., U. Md., Paris, 1951; postgrad., U. Paris, 1950-51; Ph.D., U. Calif., Berkeley, 1957. Asst. in French U. Calif., Berkeley, 1951-55; instr. N.Y. U., N.Y.C., 1956-59, asst. prof., 1959-61, asso. prof., 1961-64, prof., 1964—, Florence Gould prof. French lit., 1975—; dir. La Maison Française, 1959-64, chmn. French dept., 1966-70, chmn. dept. French and Italian, 1970—; chmn. Inst. French Studies, 1978—, Center for French Civilization and Culture, 1978—; vis. prof. Ecole des Hautes en Sciences Sociales, Paris, 1980; cons. Nat. Endowment Humanities, 1980—. Author: Pirandello and the French Theater, 1960, rev. edit., 1970, L'Avant-Garde Théâtrale: French Theater since 1950, 1970, rev. edit., 1975, Huis Clos de Jean-Paul Sartre, 1975, Beckett, 1976, also French TV program on U.S. Trustee French Inst.-Alliance Française NY., 1971—; bd. dirs. French-Am. Found., 1976—; Fellow, mem. exec. com. N.Y. Inst. Humanities; fellow Soc. Fellows N.Y.U. Decorated chevalier Légion d'Honneur, officer Ordre National du Mérite, Palmes Académiques, France; recipient Obie award, 1979; Fulbright fellow, 1965. Mem. MLA, Am. Assn. Tchrs. of French, PEN, Beckett Soc., Société des Professeurs Français en Amérique. Home: 56 Washington Mews New York NY 10003 Office: NY U 19 University Pl New York NY 10003

BISHOP, WARNER BADER, business executive; b. Lakewood, Ohio, Dec. 13, 1918; s. Warner Brown and Gladys (Bader) B.; m. Katherine Sue White, Dec. 15, 1944; children: Susan, Judith, Katharine, Jennifer; m. Barrie Osborn, Feb. 4, 1967 (div. Dec. 1980); children: Wilder, Brooks.; m. Susan Bragg Howard, June 3, 1982. A.B., Dartmouth, 1941; M.B.A., Amos Tuck Grad. Sch., 1942; grad. Advanced Mgmt. Program, Harvard, 1955. With Archer-Daniels-Midland Co., Cleve., 1946-59, successively sales rep., export mgr., sales mgr., divisional gen. mgr., asst. v.p., 1946-56, v.p., 1956-59; pres. Fed. Foundry Supply Co., 1957-59, Wyodak Clay & Chem. Co., 1957-59, Basic, Inc., until 1963, Union Fin. Corp., Cleve., 1963-74, Union Savs. Assn., 1963-74, chmn., 1970—; chmn., pres. Transohio Financial Corp., Cleve., 1974—; dir. TRANSOHIO Savs. Assn.; trustee Med. Cleve. Mut.; dir. Med. Life Ins. Co. Sec. Foundry Ednl. Found., 1956-60. Contbr. articles to trade jours. Gen. campaign mgr. Cleve. Area Heart Soc., bd. chmn., 1960-61; mem. corp. Fenn Coll.; Bd. dirs. Ohio Heart Soc.; chmn. Highland Redevel. Corp., 1963-68; pres. Council High Blood Pressure, 1964-69. Served to lt. USNR, 1942-45; comdg. officer escort vessels. Clubs: Chagrin Valley Hunt; Indian House, Union (N.Y.C.); Meadow (Southampton, N.Y.); Chagrin Valley, Union, Tavern (Cleve.); Bath and Tennis (Palm Beach, Fla.). Home: Two Bratenahl Pl Apt 14D Bratenahl OH 44108 Office: One Penton Plaza Cleveland OH 44114

BISHOP, WAYNE STATON, lawyer; b. Tarboro, N.C., Oct. 30, 1937; s. Lionel Lyston and Lelia Ruth (Staton) B.; children: John, Jeffrey, Scott. A.B., U. N.C., 1959, J.D., 1964. Bar: D.C. 1964, U.S. Supreme Ct. 1968. Appellate litigation atty. NLRB, Washington, 1964-68; pvt. practice law, Washington, 1968—; partner firm Bishop, Liberman, Cook, Purcell & Reynolds, 1980—, chmn. adminstrv. com., 1982—; mem. adv. com. U.S. Trade Rep., 1984. Co-author: Authorization Cards and the National Labor Relations Board, 1969. Transition ofcl. Office of Pres.-Elect Reagan, 1980; Nat. dir. Democrats for Reagan/Bush, 1980; mem. adv. council Am. Productivity Center. Mem. Am. Bar Assn., Fed. Bar Assn., D.C. Bar Assn. Home: 3338 Reservoir Rd Washington DC 20007 Office: 1200 17th St Washington DC 20036

BISHOP, WILLIAM PETER, scientist; b. Lakewood, Ohio, Jan. 18, 1940; s. William Hall and Ethel Laverle (Evans) B.; m. Sarah Gilbert, Sept. 1, 1963. B.A. in Chemistry with honors (Nat. Merit scholar), Coll. Wooster, Ohio, 1962; Ph.D. (NDEA fellow), Ohio State U., 1967. Resident research asso. Ohio State U., 1967-69; mem. staff Sandia Labs., Albuquerque, 1969-75; head nuclear waste program NRC, Washington, 1975-78; dep. dir. environ. observation div. NASA, 1978-81, dep. dir. life scis. div., 1981—; cons. Keystone (Colo.) Center. Author articles in field. Bd. dirs. Opportunities Industrialization Centers, Albuquerque, 1974-75, Cave Research Found., 1967-74. Recipient Meritorious Service award NRC, 1977; Spaceship Earth award NASA, 1981. Fellow Nat. Speleological Soc. (conservation editor bull. 1974-78), Washington Acad. Scis.; Mem. Am. Nuclear Soc., AASA, Am. Geophys. Union, AIAA, N.Mex. Acad. Scis., Sigma Xi, Phi Lambda Upsilon. Office: Mail Code EB-3 Washington DC 20546

BISHOP, WILLIAM WARNER, JR., legal educator; b. Princeton, N.J., June 10, 1906; s. William Warner and Finie Murfree (Burton) B.; m. Mary Fairfax Shreve, July 19, 1947; 1 dau., Elizabeth Shreve. A.B., U. Mich., 1928, J.D., 1931; postgrad., Harvard U., 1928-29, Columbia U., 1938-39. Bar: Mich. 1931, U.S. Supreme Ct 1941. Asst. reporter Harvard Research Internat. Law, 1932-35, mem. exec. com., 1949—; asso. Root, Clark, Buckner & Ballantine, N.Y.C., 1935-36; lectr. politics Princeton, 1936-38; asst. legal adv. Dept. State, 1939-47; vis. prof. internat. law Law Sch., U. Pa., 1947-48, Columbia, 1948; research, teaching asst. Law Sch., U. Mich., 1931-35, prof. law, 1948—; Legal adviser to U.S. delegation Council Fgn. Ministers and Paris Peace Conf., 1946; lectr. Hague Acad. Internat. Law, 1961, 65; mem. Permanent Ct. of Arbitration, 1975-81. Author: International Law Cases and Materials, 1962, 71; Contbr. articles to legal jours.; Bd. editors: Am. Jour. Internat. Law, 1947—; editor-in-chief, 1953-55, 62-70; contbg. editor: Ann. Digest of Pub. Internat. Law Cases, 1931-40. Mem. Mich. State Bar, Am. Soc. Internat. Law (v.p. 1960-61, 65-66, hon. v.p. 1969-82, hon. pres. 1982—), Internat. Law Assn. Home: 1612 Morton Ave Ann Arbor MI 48104

BISHOPRIC, KARL, investment banker, real estate executive, advertising executive; b. Greensboro, N.C., Jan. 5, 1925; s. James Robert Karl and Frances (Farrell) B.; m. Rose Anne Straub, Mar. 4, 1944 (div. Jan. 1972); children—Robert Lewis, James Nelson (dec.), Bruce Graham; m. Carmen Deruth Dunlop, May 26, 1973. B.A., U. N.C., 1945. With Houck & Co., Roanoke, Va. and; Miami, Fla., 1946-54; pres. Houck & Co., Fla., 1948-54, Bishopric-Green-Fielden, Inc., Miami and; N.Y.C., 1954-68, chmn. bd., 1968-73, Lando-Bishopric, Inc., 1973-74; chmn., dir. Advt. & Marketing Internat. Network, Inc., 1972-74; pres. Miami Nat. Bank, 1974-75; asso. Oscar E. Dooly Assos., Inc., 1974-76; prin. 1st Equity Financial Corp., 1975—; pres. 1st Equity Properties, Inc., 1976—. Pres. United Fund Dade County, 1967-68, trustee, 1963—; chmn. Port Action Com., 1969-71; bd. dirs. Community TV Found. S. Fla., 1965-67, v.p., 1969-72; mem. citizens bd. U. Miami, 1968—, pres. citizens bd., 1982-83, trustee, 1983—; bd. dirs. Econ. Soc. S. Fla., 1969-73, Urban Coalition Greater Miami, 1968-72, Urban League Greater Miami, 1956-65; pres. Urban League Greater Miami, 1956-60; chmn. budget leaders conf. United Funds and Community Councils Am., 1968; trustee Mus. of Sci., 1973—. Served to lt. (j.g.) USNR, 1944-46. Recipient Printer's Ink Silver medal. Mem. Greater Miami C. of C. (dir. 1971-74), Alpha Delta Sigma, Beta Theta Pi. Home: 600 Biltmore Way Coral Gables FL 33134 Office: 27th Floor New World Center 100 N Biscayne Blvd Miami FL 33132

BISPING, BRUCE HENRY, photojournalist; b. St. Louis, Apr. 27, 1953; s. Harry and Marian B. B.J., U. Mo., Columbia, 1975. Summer intern Cleve. Press, 1974, The Virginian/Pilot-Ledger Star, Norfolk, 1975; staff photojournalist Mpls. Tribune, 1975-82, Mpls. Star and Tribune, 1982—; freelance photographer Black Star Pub. Co., N.Y.C., 1975—, Sporting News, St. Louis, other nat. and local publs.; past mem. faculty Mo. Photojournalism Workshop. Mem. Nat. Press Photographers Assn. (assoc. dir. Region 5 1981-82, dir. Region 5 1983-86, Nat. Newspaper Photographer of Year award 1976, Regional Newspaper Photographer of Year award 1977), Twin Cities News Photographers Assn. (pres. 1979-80). Address: Minneapolis Tribune 425 Portland Ave Minneapolis MN 55488

BISPLINGHOFF, RAYMOND LEWIS, business executive; b. Hamilton, Ohio, Feb. 7, 1917; s. Roscoe Earl and Isabelle (Lewis) B.; m. Ruth Doherty, June 20, 1944 (div.); children: Ross Lee, Ron Sprague. A.E., U. Cin., 1940, M.Sc., 1942; Sc.D., 1963; Sc.D., Swiss Fed. Inst. Tech., 1957; D.Eng. (hon.), Case Inst. Tech., 1965. Registered profl. engr., Mass., Mo. Engr. Aeronca Aircraft Corp., 1937-40, Wright Field, 1940-41; instr. U. Cin., 1941-43; engr. Bur. Aero., Navy Dept., Washington, 1943-46; asst. prof. Mass. Inst. Tech., 1946-48, asso. prof., 1948-53, prof., 1953-62; dir. Office Advanced Research and Tech., NASA, Washington, 1962-63, asso. adminstr., 1963-65, spl. asst. to adminstr., 1965-66; prof., head dept. aeros. and astronautics Mass. Inst. Tech., Cambridge, 1966-68; dean Coll. Engring., 1968-70; dep. dir. NSF, 1970-74; chancellor U. Mo-Rolla, 1974-77; sci. adviser to Mo. Gov., 1975-77; sr. v.p. for research and devel. Tyco Labs., Exeter, N.H., 1977—, also dir., 1977—; trustee MITRE Corp.; cons. Dept. Def.; adminstr. NASA, FAA; Wright Brothers lectr. Inst. Aero. Scis., 1955; Samuel P. Langley lectr. U. Pitts., 1962; 3d Ann. von Karman lectr. AIAA, 1965; vis. prof. U. Fla.; sr. lectr. M.I.T.; chmn. bd. No. Energy Corp.; dir. Allied Research Assos., Allied Systems Ltd., Gen. Aircraft Corp., Mobil-Tyco Corp., Grinnell Corp., Simplex Wire & Cable Corp.; mem. corp. adv. council Eastern Air Lines; chmn. sci. adv. bd. USAF; mem. Nat. Sci. Bd., Def. Sci. Bd.; pres. Internat. Council Aero. Scis.; chmn. investigative bds. for C-5A and B-1 aircraft USAF. Author: (with others) Aeroelasticity, 1955, Principles of Aeroelasticity, (with H. Ashley), 1962, Solid Mechanics, (with J.W. Mar and T.H.H. Pian), 1966, also numerous profl. papers.; Assos. editor: Jour. of Franklin Inst; cons. editor: McGraw Hill Ency. Technology. Mem. vis. com. Carnegie-Mellon U., Princeton U.; trustee Nathaniel Hawthorne Coll. Recipient certificate of merit USAF; Sylvanus Reed award Inst. Aero. Scis., 1958; Distinguished Service medal NASA, 1967; Extraordinary Service medal FAA, 1968; Carl F. Kayan medal, 1971; Godfrey L. Cabot award, 1972; Distinguished Service award NSF, 1973; Exceptional Civilian Service medal USAF; hon. fellow Truman Library Inst. Fellow Am. Acad. Arts and Scis., AAAS, Inst. Aero. Scis., Am. Astronautical Soc., Am. Inst. Aeros. and Astronautics (pres. 1966), Royal Aero. Soc.; mem. Nat. Acad. Engring. (chmn. aeros. space engring. bd., chmn. com. on transp.), Nat. Acad. Sci., Internat. Acad. Astronautics, Engrs. Council for Profl. Devel. (dir.), Engrs. Joint Council (dir.), Sigma Xi, Phi Kappa Phi, Tau Beta Pi. Clubs: Mason., Cosmos (Washington); Engineers (St. Louis); Explorers (N.Y.C.). Office: Tyco Labs Tyco Park Exeter NH 03833

BISSELL, CHARLES OVERMAN, editorial cartoonist; b. Nashville, June 29, 1908; s. Charles Jay and Adelaide (Overman) B.; m. Lolita Hannah, June 5, 1943; 1 son, Charles William. Ed. pub. schs. Lithographic artist, 1924-45; mem. staff The Tennessean, Nashville, 1943—; art dir. Sunday mag., 1945-70, editorial cartoonist, 1943—. Creator: cartoon feature Bissell's Brave New World, 1962-76. Recipient Cartoon award Nat. Headliners Club, 1963; Distinguished Service award Sigma Delta Chi, 1964; Pub. Service award Nat. Safety Council, 1966. Mem. Assn. Am. Editorial Cartoonists. Home: 4221 Farrar A Nashville TN 37215 *As an editorial cartoonist I have tried most for satire because the more our problems appear to originate in the minds of fantasists the more reasonable it is to hope solutions might spring from the gibes of cartoonists. No matter how big and bad a thing is it becomes a little less so if it can be shown to be also funny.*

BISSELL, CUSHMAN BREMMER, JR., lawyer, foundation executive; b. Lake Forest, Ill., Dec. 13, 1931; s. Cushman and Marion (Bremmer) B.; m. Judith Ann Roddewig, Aug. 20, 1954; children: Dianne, Bradley, Jennifer, Juliet. B.A., Stanford U., 1953; LL.B., Harvard U., 1956. Bar: Ill. 1956. Ptnr. Lord, Bissell & Brook, Chgo., 1956-83; exec. Joyce Found., Chgo., 1978—. Exec. dir. Chgo. Boys Club, 1979, Ravinia Highland Park, Ill., 1979; bd. dirs. Catholic Charities, Chgo., 1983; lay bd. dirs. Loyola U., Chgo., 1983. Mem. ABA, Ill. Bar Assn., Chgo. Bar Assn., Chgo. Estate Planning Council. Republican. Roman Catholic. Clubs: Attic (Chgo.); Indian Hill (Winnetka, Ill.); Skokie Country (Glencoe, Ill.). Office: Joyce Found 135 S LaSalle St Chgo IL 60603

BISSELL, MARSHALL PHILIP, life ins. co. exec.; b. Bloomfield, N.J., June 20, 1914; s. Robert B. and Mary (Campbell) B.; m. Claire Marie Flint; children—Beverley Anne (Mrs. Charles F. Wilson), Robert W., Marilyn B. (Mrs. Dennis W. Fread). B.S., U. Va., 1936. With N.Y. Life Ins. Co., 1936—, beginning as mgr. bank relations successively asst. v.p., sec., 1936-58, v.p., asso. comptroller, 1958-63, v.p., comptroller, 1963-65, sr. v.p., 1965-69, exec. v.p., 1969-72, pres., 1972-80, also dir.; dir. Mgmt. Assistance Inc. Home: 13 Robert Dr Chatham NJ 07928

BISSELL, PATRICK, ballet dancer; b. 1958. Attended, Nat. Acad. Arts, N.C. Sch. Arts, Sch. Am. Ballet. Dancer with Boston Ballet; prin. Am. Ballet Theatre, N.Y.C., 1977-81. Office: care Dubé Zakin Mgmt Inc 1841 Broadway New York NY 10023 *

BISSELL, RICHARD MERVIN, JR., economist; b. Hartford, Conn., Sept. 18, 1909; s. Richard Mervin and Marie (Truesdale) B.; m. Ann Cornelia Bushnell, July 6, 1940; children—Richard Mervin, Ann Harriet, Winthrop Bushnell, William George, Thomas Ericsson. Student, Kingswood Sch., 1916-22, Groton Sch., 1922-28, London Sch. Econs., 1932-33; A.B., Yale, 1932, Ph.D., 1939, M.A. (hon.), 1949. Research asst. Yale, 1934, instr. econs., 1935-39, asst. prof., 1939-42; mem. staff Bur. Fgn. and Domestic Commerce, Dept. Commerce, 1941-42; economist Combined Shipping Adjustment Bd.; asst. to dep. adminstr. War Shipping Adminstrn., 1942-43; U.S. exec. officer Combined Shipping Adjustment Bd., 1942-45, dir. ship requirements, 1943-45; econ. adviser to dir. War Mblzn. and Reconversion, 1945-46, dep. dir., 1946; asso. prof. econs. Mass. Inst. Tech., 1942-48, prof., 1948-52; exec. sec. Pres.'s Com. Fgn. Aid (Harriman Com.), 1947-48; asst. adminstr. program ECA, 1948-51, acting adminstr., Sept.-Dec. 1951; mem. staff Ford Found., 1952-54; spl. asst. to dir. CIA, 1954-59, dep. dir. plans, 1959-62; pres. Inst. for Def. Analyses, 1962-64; dir. marketing and econ. planning United Aircraft Corp., East Hartford, Conn., 1964-74; bus. cons., 1974—; dir. Covenant Mut. Ins. Co. of Hartford.; Cons. to dir. Mut. Security, 1952; cons. various intervals Conn. Pub. Utilities Commn., Fortune Mag., Social Sci. Research Council, Cosmopolitan Shipping Co., U.S. Steel Corp., Scudder, Stevens & Clark, Brightwater Paper Co., Asiatic Petroleum Co. Author articles econ. jours.; Prin. editor, contbr.: (report of President's Com. Fgn. Aid) European Recovery and American Aid. Recipient Nat. Security medal, 1962. Mem. Am. Acad. Arts and Scis., Am. Econ. Assn., Am. Geog. Soc., Econometric Assn., Council on Fgn. Relations, Washington Inst. Fgn. Affairs, Conn. Acad. Arts and Scis. Clubs: Hartford; Graduate Club Assn. (New Haven); Yale (N.Y.C.). Home: 22 Mountain Rd Farmington CT 06032 Office: The Exchange Farmington Ave Farmington CT 06032

BISSELLE, MORGAN FITCH, lawyer; b. N.Y.C., Mar. 25, 1908; s. Luther Cleaveland and Lillian (Jones) B.; m. Lucille Florence Marks, Oct. 21, 1933; children: Philip Morgan, Walter Cleaveland. A.B., Colgate U., 1929; J.D., Yale, 1932. Bar: N.Y. bar 1933, U.S. Supreme Ct. bar 1950. Practiced in, N.Y.C., 1933-35, Utica, N.Y., 1939-53, New Hartford, N.Y., 1953-73, Hamilton, N.Y., 1973—; confidential clk. Asso. Justice Rowland L. Davis Appellate Div., Supreme Ct., 2d Judicial Dept., Bklyn., 1935-38; mem. firm Hart, Senior & Nichols, 1939-43, Tucker & Bisselle, 1943-65; gen. counsel Utica Mut. Ins. Co., 1943-73, sec., 1968-73. Trustee Savs. Bank of Utica.; Mem. Bd. Edn., New Hartford Central Sch., 1946-53, pres., 1952; mem. New Hartford Planning Bd., 1962-68, Hamilton Zoning Bd. Appeals. Mem. ABA, N.Y. State Bar Assn., Oneida County Bar Assn. (past pres.), Sigma Nu, Phi Alpha Delta. Republican. Baptist. Clubs: Mason., Fort Schuyler (Utica). Home: 14 E Pleasant St Hamilton NY 13346

BISSET, ANDREW WALZER, lawyer; b. New London, Conn., Feb. 13, 1919; s. Andrew Gustav and Helen Boas Walzer B.; m. Holly Everly, Feb. 7, 1942; children: Andrew E., M. Douglas, Paul J. A.B., Lafayette Coll., 1941; LL.B., Yale U., 1948. Bar: N.Y. 1948, Conn. 1958. Since practiced in N.Y.C. and Conn., specializing in estates and trusts, 1948—; partner Bisset, Atkins & Saunders, N.Y.C., 1952-82; of counsel LeBoeuf, Lamb et al, Southport, Conn., 1982—. Mem. Town of Westport (Conn.) Bd. Finance, 1951-57, chmn., 1955-57; mem. Town of Fairfield (Conn.) Commn. on Ethics, 1984—; Bd. dirs. Nat. Shut-in Soc., N.Y.C., 1965-70, James C. Penney Found., Inc., 1979—. Served to capt. USMCR, 1941-45. Decorated Bronze Star with Valor. Mem. Am., N.Y. State, Conn. bar assns., Assn. Bar City N.Y. Episcopalian. Clubs: Pequot Yacht (Southport, Conn.); Yale (N.Y.C.). Home: 1111 Pequot Ave Southport CT 06490 Office: 299 Park Ave New York NY 10017 Office: 411 Pequot Ave Southport CT 06490

BISSET, JACQUELINE, actress; b. Weybridge, Eng., Sept. 13, 1946. Ed., French Lycée, London. Made film debut in: The Knack, 1965; other motion pictures include Cul de Sac, 1966, Two for the Road, 1967, Casino Royale, 1967, The Sweet Ride, 1968, The Detective, 1968, Bullitt, 1968, The First Time, 1969, Airport, 1970, The Grasshopper, 1970, The Mephisto Waltz, 1971, Believe in Me, 1971, The Life and Times of Judge Roy Bean, 1972, Stand Up and Be Counted, 1972, The Thief Who Came to Dinner, 1973, Day for Night, 1973, Murder on the Orient Express, 1974, The Spiral Staircase, 1974, End of the Game, 1974, St. Ives, 1975, The Deep, 1976, Le Magnifique, 1977, Sunday Woman, 1977, The Greek Tycoon, 1978, Secrets, 1978, Who is Killing the Great Chefs of Europe?, 1978, Amo Non Amo, 1979, When Time Ran Out, 1980, Inchon, 1982, Class, 1983, Under the Volcano, 1984. Address: care Internat Creative Mgmt 8899 Beverly Blvd Los Angeles CA 90048 *

BISSET, JOHN THOMAS, radio station executive; b. Jersey Shore, Pa., Nov. 27, 1937; s. John Osborne and Barbara Gertrude (Orange) B.; m. Mary Ruth Kennedy, Dec. 29, 1964; children: Christina Ruth, Jon Clifford. A.B., Greenville Coll., 1962, Th.B., 1964; diploma, Moody Bible Inst., 1962; M.A., Johns Hopkins U., 1976, M.L.A., 1968. Staff announcer Sta. WRBS, Balt., 1964-68, sales mgr., 1968-70, gen. mgr., 1970—; Bd. dirs. Peter and John Radio Fellowship, Inc., Balt., 1968-70, mem. exec. com., 1970—. Contbr.: articles to Evang. mags., including Christian Herald; also newspapers. Lilly Found. grantee Johns Hopkins U., 1973-76. Mem. Moody Bible Inst. Alumni Assn. (pres. 1982—). Republican. Home: 1840 Deveron Rd Baltimore MD 21234 Office: 3600 Georgetown Rd Baltimore MD 21227

BISSETT, WILLIAM F., metals company executive. Pres. Huntington Alloys, Inc., W.Va. Office: Huntington Alloys Inc Huntington WV 25720§

BISSEX, WALTER EARL, lawyer, company executive; b. Uvalde, Tex., Feb. 16, 1950; m. Christina J. Shaheen, May 23, 1981. A.B., Princeton U., 1972; J.D., U. Houston, 1975. Bar: Tex. 1975. Staff atty. Browning-Ferris Industries, Inc., Houston, 1975-79; assoc. gen. counsel Lifemark Corp., Houston, 1979-82, v.p., gen counsel, 1982—. Mng. editor: Houston Law Rev., 1974-75. Mem. ABA, State Bar Tex. (council corp., banking and bus. law sect. 1981-83), Am. Soc. Hosp. Attys., Houston Law Rev. ALumni Assn. (dir. 1975-78). Democrat. Mem. Disciples of Christ. Office: Lifemark Corp 3800 Buffalo Speedway Houston TX 77098

BISSON, EDMOND EMILE, mechanical engineer; b. East Barre, Vt., July 16, 1916; s. Eugene and Annabella (Desilets) B.; m. Fernande M. Trottier, May 24, 1947; children: Roland Andre, Colette Marie, Michelle Denise. Student, U. Vt., 1934-35; B.S. with honors, U. Fla., 1938, M.E., 1954. Registered profl. engr., Ohio. Research engr. NACA, Langley Field, Va., 1939-43; successively sect. head, br. chief, asso. chief fluid system components div. Lewis Research Center of NASA, 1943-73; now cons. engr.; adj. prof. Rensselaer Poly. Inst.; tchr. short courses UCLA, Case Western Res. U., U. Tenn., Va. Poly. Inst. and State U. Author: (with W.J. Anderson) Advanced Bearing Technology, 1964; Contbr. articles to profl. jours. Recipient medal for exceptional sci. achievement NASA, 1968, nat. award Am. Soc. Lubrication Engrs., 1967, P.M. Ku medal, 1980, Jacques de Vaucanson medal French Soc. Groupement pour l'Avancement de la Mecanique Industrielle, 1966, Alfred E. Hunt meml. medal Am. Soc. Lubrication Engrs., 1954. Fellow ASME (Mayo D. Hersey award and medal 1981), Am. Soc. Lubrication Engrs. (nat. pres. 1963-64, editor-in-chief 1976—); mem. N.Y. Acad. Scis., Phi Kappa Phi, Tau Beta Pi, Sigma Tau. Roman Catholic. Home: 20786 Eastwood Ave Fairview Park OH 44126

BISSONNETTE, GEORGES LOUIS, clergyman; b. Central Falls, R.I., July 22, 1921; s. George Joseph and Alida (Provost) B. B.A., Assumption Coll., 1943; S.T.B., Laval U., 1947, S.T.L., 1949; M.A., Fordham U., 1953; M.H., Columbia, 1957, Ph.D., 1962. Fellow Russian Inst., Columbia, 1957; Instr. Assumption Coll., 1943-45, 49-51; ordained priest Roman Catholic Ch., 1949; chaplain of Americans in USSR and apostolic adminstr. of USSR, 1953-55; dir. sch. fgn. affairs Assumption Coll., also dean of faculty, prof. polit. sci., 1962-68, 71—, pres., 1968-71, asso. dir. devel., 1971—; lectr.-cons. U.S. Army Command and Gen. Staff Coll., Leavenworth, 1962-68. Author: Moscow Was My Parish, 1956, Leavenworth Lamp, 1968. Recipient 175th Anniversary medal of honor Georgetown U., 1964. Home: 50 Old English Rd Worcester MA 01609 Office: Assumption Coll Worcester MA 01609 *Use the talents you were naturally endowed with for the benefit of those with whom life brings you into contact. Remember that laws are made for man. Whenever the application of a law or a rule would result in harm to one of God's children, you have encountered a case not foreseen by the legislator.*

BISTLINE, JAMES ADAMS, railroad executive, lawyer; b. Newport, Pa., June 18, 1915; s. George P. and Laura (Adams) B.; m. Lillian Hunter, Mar. 12, 1949; children: Scott, Mark. A.B. summa cum laude, Duke, 1937; J.D., Columbia, 1940. Bar: N.Y. bar 1941, D.C. bar 1954. Lawyer Sage, Gray, Todd & Sims, N.Y.C., 1940-42; with So. Ry. Co., 1948—, gen. solicitor, 1965-67, gen. counsel, 1967—, asst. to pres., Washington, 1974—; gen. mgr. steam ops. Norfolk So. Corp., Washington, 1982—; Mem. Administrv. Conf. U.S., 1971-74. Served to maj. AUS, 1942-47; col. Res. Mem. Assn. ICC Practitioners (pres. 1969-70), Judge Adv. Gen. Assn. (dir. 1967—, pres. 1973—), Am., Internat., Inter-Am. bar assns., Phi Beta Kappa. Presbyn. (elder 1962-65, 71-74). Club: Mason. Home: 7711 Ridgecrest Dr Alexandria VA 22308 Office: PO Box 1808 Washington DC 20013

BISTLINE, STEPHEN, justice; b. Pocatello, Idaho, Mar. 12, 1921; s. Ray D. and Martha (Faber) B.; m. Sharon Mooney; children—Patrick, Paul, Arthur, Claire, Susan, Shelley, Diana, Leslie. LL.B., U. Idaho, 1949. Bar: Idaho bar 1949. Individual practice law, Sandpoint, Idaho, 1950-76; justice Idaho Supreme Ct., Boise, 1976—. Served with USN, 1941-45. Office: Supreme Ct Bldg State Capitol Boise ID 83720 *

BITNER, HARRY, law librarian; b. Kansas City, Mo., July 22, 1916; s. Barney and Helen (Samberg) B.; m. Anne Goldstein, Sept. 15, 1940; 1 dau., Lorraine Ellen. B.A., U. Mo. at Kansas City, 1941, J.D., 1939; B.S. in L.S, U. Ill., 1942. Instr. law U. Kansas City, 1942-43, law librarian, 1939-42; reference law librarian Biddle Law Library, U. Pa., 1946; asso. law librarian Columbia Law Sch., 1946-54; librarian Dept. Justice, 1954-57; law librarian Yale Law Sch., 1957-65; law librarian, prof. law Cornell U. Law Sch., Ithaca, N.Y., 1965-76, prof. emeritus, 1976; legal bibliographer Columbia U. Law Library, 1978-81; Project dir. libraries study project Assn. Am. Law Schs., 1967—; trustee South Central Research Library Council, Ithaca, 1974-75. Author: (with Price and Bysiewicz) Effective Legal Research, 4th edit, 1979; contbr. articles to profl. jours. Sec. bd. dirs. New Haven Jewish Community Council, 1962-64, v.p., dir., 1963-65; sec. bd. dirs. New Haven Bur. Jewish Edn., 1960-63, treas., dir., 1963-65, 2d v.p., 1965; bd. dirs. New Haven Jewish Family Service, 1961-65, 2d v.p., 1965. Served with AUS, 1943-46. Mem. Internat. Assn. Law Libraries, Am. Assn. Law Libraries (exec. bd. 1951-54, pres. 1963-64, Joseph L. Andrews Bibliog. award 1971), Am., N.Y. library assns., Spl. Libraries Assn., Council Nat. Library Assns. (vice chmn.), Am. Soc. Legal History, Beta Phi Mu. Jewish (pres. temple 1965). Home: 280 Prospect Ave Hackensack NJ 07601

BITONDO, DOMENIC, indsl. research exec.; b. Welland, Ont., Can., June 7, 1925; came to U.S., 1950, naturalized, 1956; s. Vito Leonard and Vita Maria (Gallipoli) B.; m. Delphine May Dicola, June 11, 1949; children—Michael, Annamarie, David, Marisa. B.Sc., U. Toronto, 1947, M.Sc., 1948, Ph.D., 1950. Aerodynamist, Aerophysics div. N.Am. Aviation Co., Downey, Calif., 1950-51; project engr. to chief of aerodynamics Aerophysics Devel. Corp., Santa Barbara, 1951-59; staff engr. Northrup Corp., Hawthorne, Calif., 1959-60; head test planning and analysis TRW Systems, Inc., El Segundo, Calif., 1960-61; dept. head aeromechanics dept. Systems Research and Planning div. Aerospace Corp., El Segundo, 1961; dir. Reentry Systems Program Office, 1961-63; dir. engring. Aerospace Systems div. Bendix Corp., Ann Arbor, Mich., 1963-69; engring. mgr. Apollo lunar sci. expts., 1966; dir., gen. mgr. Bendix Research Labs., Southfield, Mich., 1969-79; exec. dir. research and devel. Bendix Corp., 1979-80; pres. Bitondo Assos. Inc., Ann Arbor, 1980—; Gordon N. Patterson lectr. U. Toronto, 1976; trustee Central Solar Energy and Research Corp., Detroit, 1978-80; dir. Continental Controls Corp., San Diego.; Def. Research Bd. Can. asst., 1948, NRC asst., 1947. Contbr. tech. articles to profl. jours. Mem. AIAA, Mich. Energy and Resource Research Assn. (trustee), Nat. Mgmt. Assn. (Gold Knight award). Office: 5 Manchester Ct Ann Arbor MI 48104

BITTER, GEHART LEONARD, lawyer; b. Hoisington, Kans., July 27, 1921; s. Fred and Mary C. (Lehning) B.; m. June Eliopouios, June 20, 1945; children: Grant, Lynne, Keith. Student, Golden Gate Coll., San Francisco, 1940-42; LL.B., Lincoln U., 1950. Bar: Calif. 1952. Practiced in San Francisco and Burlingame, 1952—; vice chmn., dir. Associated Food Stores, Inc.; sec.-treas. Laurel Wood Market Inc.; dir. San Francisco Grocery Co.; Pres. San Francisco Grocers Assn.; bd. dirs. Bay Area Grocers Assn., No. Calif. Growers Assn. Chmn. bd. trustees No. Calif. Food Industry Pensions Fund; chmn. bd. No. Calif. Retail Clks. Unions-Employers Vacation Fund; trustee No. Calif. Food Pension Supplementary Payment Fund. Served to lt. (j.g.) USNR, 1942-46; PTO. Mem. ABA, Calif. Bar Assn. Lutheran (pres.). Club: Olympic (San Francisco). Home: 2673 Martinez Dr Burlingame CA 94010 Office: 851 Burlway Rd Burlingame CA 94010

BITTER, JOHN, musician, university dean, businessman; b. N.Y., Apr. 8, 1909; s. Karl and Marie Agnes (Schevill) B.; m. Dorothy Michelson, 1934; 1 dau., Ursula; m. Barbara Pinion, Feb. 22, 1947; children: Robin Simonetta, Noel Lesley, Marietta. Grad., Curtis Inst. Music, Phila., 1931. Condr. Jacksonville (Fla.) Symphony Orch., 1934-36, Fla. State Symphony, 1936-39; asso. condr. Leopold Stokowski's All Am. Youth Orch., 1940-41; condr. symphony orch. U. Miami, 1940-59, dean sch. music, 1951-63, dean emeritus, 1980—; asst. to pres., lectr. humanities, 1963-64; v.p. Keyes Investment Group, 1982—; condr. summer symphony, 1951-63; guest condr. Berlin Philharmonic Orch., Berlin Staatsoper, Hamburg Philharmonic, Radio Italiana, others, 1946-67; Realtor Keyes Co., 1978—; Consul for Germany in, Miami, 1969-78. Served as maj. AUS, 1942-46. Decorated Bronze Star; officer's cross Order of Merit Fed. Republic of Germany, 1972; recipient Allied Arts prize for composition, 1969; Nat. Sales Achievement awards, 1968-72. Mem. Nat. Assn. Schs. Music (v.p. 1959), Phi Mu Alpha Sinfonia (hon.), Phi Kappa Phi. Home: 205 E Rivo Alto Dr Miami Beach FL 33139 *"Use your eyes as if tomorrow you would be struck blind. Use your ears, listen to the harmonies of nature, the sounds of symphonies, as if tomorrow you would become deaf. Taste and touch with relish and enjoyment. Revel in beauty and make the most of every sense."... Helen Keller. I add: the mind and spirit will follow.*

BITTER, KENNETH BARRY, university official; b. Los Angeles, May 3, 1934; s. Kenneth G. and Idylle V. (Lauer) B.; m. Patricia J. Ohre, Jan. 1, 1956; children: Rebecca, Kenneth, Belinda. B.S., San Diego State U., 1957. Dir. fin. planning and analysis Gen. Dynamics Corp., St. Louis, 1961-73; v.p. fin., treas. Falcon Products, St. Louis, 1973-76; mgr. acctg. ops. Dun & Bradstreet Corp., N.Y.C., 1976-78, v.p., treas., 1978-83; dir. treasury ops. Rensselaer Poly. Inst., Troy, N.Y., 1983—. Mem. Fin. Execs. Inst., N.Y. Treas's. Group. Democrat. Lutheran. Office: 2144 Burdett Ave Troy NY 12181

BITTICK, T.W., oil and gas exploration company executive; b. Wichita Fallas, Tex., July 9, 1925; s. Ernest W. and Willie L. (Clark) B.; m. Lora Louise Swegler, Apr. 4, 1947; children: Linda Bittick Scruggs, Marily Bittick Crawford, Susan Bittick Foster. Student, U. Tex.-El Paso, 1946-47, J.D., 1950. Clk., landman, div. landman El Paso Natural Gas, Tex., 1953-57, mgr., dir. land exploration, 1957-74, asst. v.p., 1974-77, v.p., 1977-79; exec. v.p. El Paso Exploration Co., Tex., 1979-81, pres., 1982—. Served to staff sgt. USAF, 1943-46; ETO. Mem. State Bar Tex., Mid-Continent Oil and Gas Assn. (dir. Tex. div.), Okla.-Kans. Oil and Gas Assn. (dir.), Phi Alpha Delta, Alpha Chi. Home: 429 Brown Point Dr El Paso TX 79912 Office: El Paso Exploration Co PO Box 1492 El Paso TX 79978

BITTKER, BORIS IRVING, educator; b. Rochester, N.Y., Nov. 28, 1916; s. Albert and Minnie (Rubens) B.; m. Anne Elizabeth Stern, 1949; children—Susan Emilie, Daniel Albert. B.A., Cornell U., 1938; LL.B., Yale, 1941. Bar: N.Y. bar 1942, Conn. bar 1951. Law clk. to Judge Jerome N. Frank U.S. Ct. Appeals, 2d Circuit, N.Y.C., 1941-42; staff Lend Lease Adminstrn., 1942-43, Alien Property Custodian's Office, 1945-46; faculty Yale Law Sch., 1946—, successively asst. prof., asso. prof., 1946-51, prof., 1951-66, Southmayd prof. law, 1958-70, Sterling prof. law, 1970—; Fulbright lectr. univs. Pavia and Siena, Italy, 1955-56; vis. prof. Stanford Law Sch., U. San Diego, 1979-80, U. Calif., Hastings Coll. of Law, 1981; Ford Disting. Vis. prof. N.Y. U. Sch. Commerce, 1965; Charles Inglis Thomson prof. law U. Colo., 1966. Author: Federal Income Taxation, 1958, 5th edit, (with L. Stone) Federal Income Taxation, 1980, Federal Income Taxation of Corporations and Shareholders, 1959, 4th edit, (with J. Eustice) Federal Income Taxation of Corporations and Shareholders, 1979, Professional Responsibility and Federal Tax Practice, 1965, The Case for Black Reparations, 1973, Federal Taxation of Income, Estates and Gifts, 5 vols, 1981; Contbr. articles to profl. jours. Served with AUS, 1943-45. Mem. Am. Acad. Arts and Scis., Am., Conn. bar assns., Am. Law Inst. Office: Yale Law School New Haven CT 06520

BITTLE, BILLY MCMILLAN, JR., investment co. exec.; b. Tupelo, Miss., Aug. 16, 1921; s. Billy McMillan and Thelma M. (Milstead) B.; m. Mary Barbara Martin, Oct. 9, 1943; children—James M., Susan C. (Mrs. Richard Werhle), Judith A. (Mrs. Stewart Barr), Charles W. Student, Miss. State Coll., 1940. With Woodward Governor Co., Rockford, Ill., 1945-66, gen. mgr., 1958-60, pres., gen. mgr., 1960-66; dir.; pres., owner P.F. Jackson Co., Inc., 1966-76; registered rep. ins. and securities, 1976—; pres., owner Bittle Industries Inc., Laramie, Wyo.; dir. Earth Minerals Inc., Denver. Bd. counselors Rockford (Ill.) Coll. Served to capt., navigator USAAF, World War II. Mem. ASME, Chgo. Presidents Orgn. Clubs: Mason, Shriner, Jester, Elk, Rotarian, Moose., Pyramid, Forest Hills Country (Rockford); Laramie Country. Home: 32-200 S 30 St Laramie WY 82070

BITTLEMAN, ARNOLD, artist, educator; b. N.Y.C., July 4, 1933; s. Max and Jean (Rosenblatt) B.; m. Dolores Dembus, June 8, 1958; children—David, Sarah. B.F.A., Yale U., 1956, M.F.A., 1958. Mem. faculty Yale, 1958-63, Parsons Sch. Design, N.Y.C., 1958-60, Skidmore Coll., 1964-66; prof. art Union Coll., Schenectady, 1966—. One man shows, Kanegis Gallery, Boston, 1958, 61, 65, Schenectady Mus., 1971, 75, 76, Webb & Parsons, Bedford, N.Y., 1974, others, group shows, Genesis Gallery, N.Y.C., 1980, Borgenicht Gallery, N.Y.C., 1959-60, Milliken Gallery, N.Y.C., 1981, Mus. Modern Art, N.Y.C., 1978, Whitney Mus. Am. Art, N.Y.C., 1971, Naples (Fla.) Gallery, 1979-80, Am. Embassy, Moscow; represented in permanent collections, Mus. Modern Art, N.Y.C., Whitney Mus. Am. Art., N.Y.C., Bklyn. Mus., Boston Mus., Fogg Mus., Cambridge, Brandeis U., Waltham, Mass., Addison Gallery Am. Art, Andover, Mass., Munson-Williams-Proctor Inst., Utica, N.Y., Schenectady Mus. Alice Kimball English traveling fellow, 1956-57. Home: RFD Eagle Bridge NY 12057 Office: Union Coll Schenectady NY 12308 *Drawing, free from the convention of drawing as preparation for sculpture, painting, printmaking, has been my primary medium since 1956.*

BITTMAN, WILLIAM OMAR, lawyer; b. Milw., Aug. 6, 1931; s. Omar A. and Lyda (Schneider) B.; m. Carole Jean Chiletti, Aug. 25, 1956; children—Michael John, Barbara Jean, Mary Elizabeth, William Omar, Robert James, Julie Anne, Carrie Lynn. B.S., Marquette U., 1956; student, Law Sch., 1956-57; J.D., DePaul U., 1959. Bar: Ill. bar 1960, D.C. bar 1967. With Dept. Justice, 1960-67, spl. atty., Washington, 1965-67; partner firm Hogan & Hartson, Washington, 1967-74, Pierson, Ball & Dowd, 1974—; lectr. trial techniques, 1962—. Served with USNR, 1951-53. Named one of Chgo.'s 10 outstanding young men, 1964; recipient Sustained Outstanding Performance award Dept. Justice, 1964, Spl. Act. Meritorious Achievement award, 1967. Mem. Am., Fed., D.C., Ill. bar assns. Roman Catholic. Chief prosecutor in govt. trial of James R. Hoffa, 1964, of Robert G. Baker, 1967. Home: 9116 Bradley Blvd Potomac MD 20854 Office: 1200 18th St NW Washington DC 20036

BITTNER, EGON, educator; b. Skrecon, Czechoslovakia, Apr. 16, 1921; came to U.S., 1949, naturalized, 1955; s. Zygmunt and Hermine (Lewkowicz) B.; m. Jean G. Kline, Dec. 24, 1951; children—Thomas J., Debora H. B.A., Los Angeles State Coll., 1955, M.A., 1958; Ph.D., U. Calif. at Los Angeles, 1961. Instr., then asst. prof. sociology U. Calif., Riverside, 1960-63; asst. prof., then asso. prof. U. Calif. Med. Sch., San Francisco, 1963-68; prof. sociology Brandeis U., Waltham, Mass., 1968—. Author: The Functions of the Police in Modern Society, 1970. Mem. Am. Sociol. Assn., Eastern Sociol. Soc., Soc. Study Social Problems, Law and Soc. Assn., AAUP. Jewish. Address: Brandeis Univ Waltham MA 02154

BITTS, TODD MICHAEL, broadcast executive; b. Seattle, Mar. 20, 1946; s. Max Krause and Joye (Kugler) B.; children: Kimberly, Craig, Shaun. Student, Green River Coll., 1965. Account exec. Sta. KVI, 1973-75, account exec., 1975-76; gen. mgr. Sta. KETO, 1974-75; v.p., gen. mgr. Sta. KPLZ, Seattle, 1976—; Mem. exec. com. Seafair, Inc. Mem. Puget Sound Radio Broadcasters Assn. (past pres.). Republican. Roman Catholic. Clubs: Sahalee Golf & Country, Washington Athletic. Home: 1900 Taylor Ave N Seattle WA 98109 Office: WSN TV 2520 Westlake N Seattle WA 98109

BITZER, DONALD LESTER, electrical engineering educator, research laboratory administrator; b. East St. Louis, Ill., Jan. 1, 1934; s. Jess L. and Marjorie (Look) B.; m. Maryann Drost, July 2, 1955; 1 son, David. B.S., U. Ill., 1955, M.S., 1956, Ph.D., 1960. Mem. faculty U. Ill.-Urbana, 1955—, assoc. prof., 1963-67, prof. elec. engring., 1967—, dir. Computer-Based Edn. Research Lab., 1967—; cons. Control Data Corp. Contbr. articles to profl. jours.; pioneer PLATO-large computer-based edn. system; co-inventor plasma display panel. Recipient Bobby C. Connelly Meml. award Miami Valley Computer Assn., 1973. Fellow AAAS, IEEE; mem. Data Processing Mgmt. Assn.

(Computer Sci. Man of Yr. award), Nat. Acad. Engring. (Vladimir K. Zworykin award), Am. Soc. Engring. Edn. (Chester Carlson award), Am. Soc. Elec. Engring., AAUP, Sigma Xi, Phi Kappa Phi, Tau Beta Phi, Eta Kappa Nu. Office: Computer Based Edn Research Lab U Ill 103 S Mathews Ave Urbana IL 61801

BIUNNO, VINCENT P., fed. judge; b. Newark, Feb. 2, 1916; s. James and Margaret (George) B.; m. Mary Ann Zocchi, June 8, 1941. Student, Columbia, 1932-33; LL.B. magna cum laude, N.J. Law Sch., 1937. Bar: N.J. bar 1937. Counselor, 1940; mem. firm Lum, Biunno & Tompkins (and predecessors), Newark, 1937-46, partner, 1946-58, 60-73; judge U.S. Dist. Ct., N.J. Dist., 1973—; Counsel to Gov. N.J., 1958-60; mem. N.J. Gov.'s Study Com. Legalized Games of Chance, 1953-54; counsel Legis. Com. to Revise Law of Evidence, 1955-57, to pres. N.J. Senate, to rules com. N.J. Supreme Ct.; Dir., chmn. exec. com. Prudential Ins. Co. Am., 1960-73; Mem. Glen Ridge Devel. Bd.; Pres., trustee N.J. Law Inst., 1955—; mem. adv. bd. Western Res. U. Sch. Library Sci.; mem. com. indexing statutory law Am. Bar Found.; Mem. N.J. Gov.'s Milk Study Com., 1962-64; mem. N.J. Commn. on Def. of Indigent; N.J. pub. rate counsel, utilities, 1970-73. Editorial bd.: N.J. Law Jour; Author articles on legal research. Served with Signal Corps AUS, 1942-43. Fellow Am. Bar Found.; mem. ABA (mem. com. electronic data retrieval 1958-73, mem. ho. of dels. 1968-73), N.J. Bar Assn. (gen. council 1962-73, chmn. jud. selection com. 1968-73), Essex County Bar Assn. (pres. 1963-64, trustee), Nat. Conf. Bar Pres.'s, Alpha Sigma Phi. Club: Glen Ridge Country. Home: 321 Forest Ave Glen Ridge NJ 07028 Office: Room 411 US Post Office Newark NJ 07102

BIVENS, GORDON ELLSWORTH, educator; b. Nevada, Iowa, Feb. 5, 1927; s. Clarence E. and Hazel (Markl) B.; m. Muriel Katherine Collier, Feb. 14, 1953; children: Dale Mark, Carol Sue, Bruce Alan, Paul Wayne. B.S., Iowa State U., 1950, M.S., 1953, Ph.D., 1957. Instr., asst. prof., asso. prof. Iowa State U., 1954-62; asso. prof., prof. econs., founding dir. Center for Consumer Affairs, U. Wis.-Milw., 1962-68; consumption economist Consumer and Food Econs. Research div. Agrl. Research Service, Dept. Agr., 1967-68; prof. family econs. and agrl. econs. U. Mo. at Columbia, 1968-76; prof. dept. family environment Iowa State U., 1976—, head dept., 1976-80; Mary B. Welch disting. prof. home econs., 1983—; vis. scholar Inst. Behavioral Sci., U. Colo., Boulder, 1974-75; Mem. Consumer Task Force, White House Conf. on Food, Nutrition and Health, 1969; cons. Pres.'s Com. on Consumer Interests, Office Econ. Opportunity, Glick & Lorwin, John Wiley & Sons. Founding editor: Jour. Consumer Affairs, 1967-74. Trustee Am. Home Econs. Assn. Found.; bd. dirs. Consumers Union U.S.; chmn. bd. govs. Center for the Family. Served with USMCR, 1945-46. Mem. Am. Econ. Assn., Am. Home Econs. Assn., Am. Agrl. Econ. Assn., Am. Assn. for Consumer Research, Am. Council on Consumer Interests (past pres.), Tau Kappa Epsilon, Phi Kappa Phi, Alpha Zeta, Gamma Sigma Delta, Omicron Nu., Soc. Friends. Home: 3713 Ross Rd Ames IA 50010

BIXBY, ALLAN BARTON, life insurance company executive; b. Worcester, Mass., May 18, 1936; s. J. Allan and Avis (Barton) B.; m. Geraldine Nancy Annear, Nov. 17, 1957; children: Pamela W., Allan Barton. B.S., Northeastern U., Boston, 1959. With Mass. Mut. Life Ins. Co., Springfield, 1959—, asst. treas., then asso. treas., 1970-75, treas., 1975—, also treas. subsidiaries; treas. MML Equity Investment Co., Mass. Mut. Realty Devel. Corp., MML Pension Ins. Co., MML Holding Co., MML Life Ins., MML Managed Bond Investment Co., Inc., MML Money Market Investment Co., Inc., Four Ambassadors Corp., Inc., MML Bay State, Bay Colony Ariz., Bay Colony Vt., Mass Mut. Asset Mgmt. Co., Inc. Trustee New Salem (Mass.) Acad.; mem. found. Greenfield (Mass.) Community Coll. Served to capt. AUS, 1959-60. Recipient Merit award for paper Ins. Accounting and Statis. Assn., 1977. Mem. Fin. Execs. Inst., Life Office Mgmt. Assn. (cash mgmt. com., electronic funds transfer system coms.). Club: Masons. Home: Twin Brook Acres New Salem MA 01355 Office: 1295 State St Springfield MA 01111

BIXBY, FRANK LYMAN, lawyer; b. New Richmond, Wis., May 25, 1928; s. Frank H. and Esther (Otteson) B.; m. Katharine Spence, July 7, 1951; children—Paul, Thomas, Edward, Janet. A.B., Harvard U., 1950; LL.B., U. Wis., 1953. Bar: Ill. bar 1953. Since practiced in, Chgo.; partner firm Sidley & Austin, 1963—; bd. dirs. Ill. Bar Automatic Research, Fund for Justice. Editor-in-chief: Wis. Law Rev, 1952-53; editorial bd.: Chgo. Reporter, 1973—. Trustee MacMurray Coll., Jacksonville, Ill., 1973—; bd. dirs. Chgo. Urban League, 1962—, v.p., 1972—, gen. counsel, 1972—; bd. dirs. Community Renewal Soc., 1973—; chmn. trustees Unitarian Ch., Evanston, Ill., 1962-63; bd. dirs. Spencer Found., 1967—, chmn., 1975—; mem. dist. 202 bd. edn. Evanston Twp. High Sch., 1975-81, pres., 1977-79. Recipient Man of Year award Chgo. Urban League, 1974. Mem. Am., Ill., Chgo., Wis., Fla. bar assns., Chgo. Council Lawyers, Chgo. Council Fgn. Relations, Order of Coif, Phi Beta Kappa. Clubs: Harvard (pres. 1962-63), Mid-Day (Chgo.)). Home: 1100 Ridge Rd Evanston IL 60202 Office: 1 First National Plaza Chicago IL 60603

BIXBY, HAROLD GLENN, manufacturing company executive; b. Lamotte, Mich., July 14, 1903; s. Charles Samuel and Laura (Schenk) B.; m. Pauline Elizabeth Summy, July 3, 1928; children: Mary Louise and Richard Glenn (twins). A.B., U. Mich., 1927, LL.D. (hon.), 1972. Began in accounting dept. Ex-Cell-O Corp., Detroit, 1928, asst. sec., 1929, controller, 1933, sec., treas. and dir., 1937, became v.p., treas., dir., 1947, pres., gen. mgr., 1951-70, chmn. bd., chief exec. officer, 1970-72, chmn. bd., 1972—, chmn. exec. com., 1973-79; pres. Bixby Industries, Inc., Detroit; chmn. bd., sec., dir. Pure Sealed Dairy, Inc., Ft. Wayne, Ind.; dir. Detrex Chem. Industries, Inc., Mich. Chrome & Chem. Co., Detroit, Karmazin Products Corp., Wyandotte, Mich. Bd. dirs. Detroit Met. Indsl. Devel. Corp., Greater Detroit Area Hosp. Council, Detroit Round Table of Catholics, Jews and Protestants; bd. dirs. U. Mich. Devel. Council.; trustee Kalamazoo Coll., HGH Health System, Harper-Grace Hosps., Detroit. Mem. Greater Detroit Bd. Commerce, Tau Kappa Epsilon. Clubs: Economic, Detroit Athletic, Detroit Golf, Detroit. Home: 18510 Bretton Dr Detroit MI 48223 Office: 18353 McNichols Rd West Detroit MI 48219

BIXBY, JOSEPH R., insurance company executive; b. Apr. 7, 1925; s. Walter Edwin and Angeline I. (Reynolds) B.; m. Marilyn Swartzel, Aug. 28, 1947 (dec.); children: Kathryn Ann Bixby-Haddad, Nancy Lea Bixby Curtis Hudson; m. Margie Morris Vogel, May 11, 1976; 1 son, Lee M. Vogel. Ed., U. Mo. Various positions Kansas City Life Ins. Co., Mo., until 1950, asst. sec., 1950-55, asst. regional supr., 1952-55, v.p., asst. sec., 1955-62, dir., 1957—, adminstrv. v.p., 1962-64, pres., 1964—, chief exec. officer, 1970—, chmn. bd., 1972—; adv. dir. Glasgow Savs. Bank, Mo., dir. Hon. bd. dirs. Kansas City Crime Commn. Served with USAAF, 1944-46. Clubs: Kansas City, River, Saddle and Sirloin, Kansas City Country. Home: 3530 Pennsylvania St Kansas City MO 64111 Office: 3520 Broadway PO Box 139 Kansas City MO 64141

BIXBY, R. BURDELL, lawyer; b. Schenectady, Oct. 11, 1914; s. Raymond O. and Mabel A. (Rumsey) B.; m. Anne M. Hardwick, Oct. 25, 1941; 1 son, Robert Hardwick. A.B., Colgate U., 1936; LL.B., Albany Law Sch., 1940, J.D., 1968. Bar: N.Y. 1940. Partner firm Dewey, Ballantine, Bushby, Palmer & Wood, N.Y.C. and Paris, 1955—; Asst. sec. gov. State N.Y., 1948-50, exec. asst., 1950-52, sec., 1952-54; sec.-treas. N.Y. State Thruway Authority, 1950-60, chmn., sec., treas., 1960-61, chmn., sec., 1961-74; permanent pres. N.Y. State Electoral Coll. of 1972. Trustee Hudson City Savs. Instn., N.Y.; treas. N.Y. State Republican Com., 1959-61; trustee Albany Law Sch. Served with USAAF, 1942-46. Mem. Am., N.Y. State bar assns., Assn. Bar City N.Y., N.Y. County Lawyers Assn., Am. Legion. Clubs: Masons; City Midday (N.Y.C.). Home: 7 Joslen Pl Hudson NY 12534 Office: 140 Broadway New York NY 10005

BIXLER, HARRIS JACOB, chemical company executive; b. Harrisburg, Pa., Dec. 14, 1931; s. Alvin Pray and Elsie (Faxon) B.; m. Elizabeth Ann Blain, June 23, 1957; children: Sarah Ann, Alleson Faxon. S.B., M.I.T., 1953, S.M., 1957, Sc.D., 1959; M.A.Sc., U. Toronto, Ont., Can., 1956. Asst. prof. chem. engring. M.I.T., 1960-64; v.p., dir. research Amicon Corp., Lexington, Mass., 1964-70; pres., dir. research Marine Colloids, Inc., Rockland, Maine, 1970-79; pres. Avco Everett Research Lab., Inc., Mass., 1979-81; v.p., gen. mgr. materials div. Chomerics, Inc., Woburn, Mass., 1981-83; v.p., gen. mgr. Delta Chems., Inc., Searsport, Maine, 1983—; dir. Camden Nat. Bank, Maine, 1974-79; trustee Worcester Found. Exptl. Biology, 1980-83; corporator Woods Hole Oceanographic Inst., 1978—. Trustee Hurricane Island Outward Bound Sch., Rockland, Maine, 1979—. Served with U.S. Army, 1953-55. Mem. Am. Chem. Soc., Am. Inst. Chem. Engrs., AAAS. Home: Browns Head RFD 3 Belfast ME 04915 Office: 77 Dragon Ct Woburn MA 01888

BIXLER, JOHN DONOVAN, lawyer; b. Gary, Ind., Sept. 4, 1933; s. Abraham Overhold and Anne Elizabeth (McClelland) B.; m. Elennis Revethis, Jan. 20, 1974; children: Alexandra, Peter; children by previous marriage: Stephen, Ruth Anne. B.S., Ind. U., 1955, LL.B., 1958. Bar: Ill. 1959. Mem. firm Winston & Strawn, Chgo., 1958—. Governing mem. Art Inst. Chgo., 1973; sec. Cradle Soc., Evanston, Ill., 1974. Fellow Am. Bar Found.; mem. Ill. Bar Assn., Chgo. Bar Assn. Club: Arts (Chgo.). Office: Winston and Strawn One First Nat Plaza Chicago IL 60603

BIXLER, PAUL (HOWARD BIXLER), librarian, editor; b. Union City, Mich., Oct. 27, 1899; s. Miles Fred and Lida (Gillett) B.; m. Norma Hendricks, Oct. 6, 1926; children: Giles Norman, Jolyon, Mark Frederick. A.B., Hamilton Coll., 1922; student, U. Pa., 1922-23; M.A., Harvard U., 1924; B.L.S., Western Res. U., 1933. Instr. English, Ohio Wesleyan U., 1924-26; police reporter Cleve. Press, 1926-27; instr. English, Western Res. U., 1928-35; librarian Antioch Coll., 1935-65, librarian emeritus, 1965—; editorial bd. Antioch Rev., 1941-42, 58—, chmn., 1943-58, editor, 1974-77; library adviser Social Sci. Library, U. Rangoon, Burma, 1958-60; staff Study for Ford Found. Policy and Program, 1949; cons. program library orgn. Ford Found., 1964; vis. scholar Univ. Center, Atlanta, 1963. Author: chpts. The Administration of the College Library, 1944, Mexican Library, 1969, Southeast Asia: Bibliographic Directions, 1974; editor: Antioch Rev. Anthology, 1953, Freedom of Communication, 1954; contbr. articles to profl. jours. Judge Nonfiction Nat. Book Award, 1955; Ford Found. grantee for bibliog. research, S.E. Asia, 1962-63; Ford Found. library cons. Faculty of Exact and Natural Scis., U. Buenos Aires, 1964-71. Mem. Ohio Library Assn. (pres. 1948-49, Hall of Fame 1981), ALA (council 1948-51, 56-58, exec. sec. intellectual freedom com. 1952-56), Am. Coll. and Research Libraries, ACLU. Home: 1345 Rice Rd Yellow Springs OH 45387

BIZZARRI, DANTE VIRGIL, physician; b. N.Y.C., July 8, 1913; s. Anthony and Ida (Proli) B.; m. Rosalie Musacchio, Jan. 1, 1941; children—Alida, Leomora, Marina. M.D., N.Y. Med. Coll., 1942. Diplomate: Am. Bd. Anesthesiology. Intern Met. Hosp., N.Y.C., 1942-43, resident, 1944-46; prof., chmn. anesthesiology N.Y. Med. Coll., Valhalla, N.Y., 1973—; mem. staff Met. Hosp., N.Y.C., 1946—, Westchester County (N.Y.) Hosp., 1968—, Lincoln Hosp., 1978—. Contbr. articles in field. Fellow Am. Coll. Anesthesiology; mem. N.Y. State Soc. Medicine, Am. Soc. Anesthesiology, Internat. Coll. Surgeons. Roman Catholic. Developer esophageal tube and laryngoscope. Home: 16 Van etten Blvd New Rochelle NY 10804 Office: Department of Anesthesiology New York Medical College Elmwood Hall Valhalla NY 10595

BIZZELL, BOBBY GENE, management educator, university administrator; b. Frankston, Tex., Sept. 13, 1940; s. Ferrell Lawrence and Ruby LaVelle (Hanna) B.; children: Laurie Ann, Susan Leigh, Amy Rebecca. B.B.A., U. Tex., 1963, M.B.A., 1964, Ph.D., 1971. Mgr. mfg. Gen. Electric Co., Cin., 1964-65, Schenectady, 1965-67, adminstr. mfg. problems analysis, Oklahoma City, 1967-68; asst. dean Grad. Sch. Bus. U. Tex., Austin, 1968-71; instr. mgmt. Stephen F. Austin State U., Nacogdoches, Tex., 1971—, dir. grad. programs, 1972—, chmn. dept. mgmt., 1982—; cons. to bus. Sec. bd. dirs. Nacogdoches Meml. Hosp.; mem. directing com. United Way, Nacogdoches. Stephen F. Austin State U. faculty research grantee, 1972, 79. Mem. Acad. Mgmt., Am. Inst. Decision Scis., Case Research Assn., Beta Gamma Sigma, Sigma Iota Epsilon, Phi Kappa Phi. Democrat. Mem. Ch. of Christ. Office: Stephen F Austin State U PO Box 9070 Nacogdoches TX 75962

BJERKNES, MICHAEL LEIF, dancer; b. Oak Park, Ill., Dec. 6, 1956; s. Christian Edward and Barbara Ann (Sirkin) B.; m. Pamela Booth, July 15, 1979. Student, Rosary Coll., 1970-73. Dancer Joffrey II, N.Y.C., 1973-74; soloist Chgo. Ballet, 1974-76, Houston Ballet, 1976-78, Joffrey Ballet, N.Y.C., 1978-79, 79-82, union rep., 1980-82, workshop tchr., 1982-84, tchr. sch., 1983-84. Prin. dancer, Royal Winnipeg (Man., Can.) Ballet, 1979, Milw. Ballet, 1984; guest artist, No. Ballet Theatre, Manchester, Eng., 1981, Minn. Dance Theatre, 1982-83, Chamber Ballet, 1984; tchr. various ballet schs., U.S., 1972-79, Ruth Page Found., Chgo., 1982-84. Mem. Am. Guild Musical Artists (bd. dirs. 1980-81), Can. Actor's Equity.

BJERREGAARD-JENSEN, VILHELM HANS *See* **HILLCOURT, WILLIAM**

BJORAKER, WALTER THOMAS, agricultural and vocational education educator; b. Steele County, Minn., Jan. 19, 1920; s. Lewis I. and Mary (Barsness) B.; m. Delores E. Johnson, Feb. 15, 1947; children: Barbara Jeanne, Gary Thomas, Gordon Lee. B.S. with distinction, U. Minn., 1942, M.S., 1948, Ph.D., 1952. Instr. vocat. agr. Harmony (Minn.) High Sch., 1942-43; asst. supr. agrl. edn. Minn. Dept. Edn., 1946; instr. vocat. agr., Rochester, Minn., 1946-48; instr. agrl. edn. U. Minn., 1948-50; prof. continuing and vocat. edn. U. Wis., 1950—, chmn. dept., 1953-77; sec. nat. adv. com. Nat. Center for Advanced Study and Research in Agr., 1965; U. Wis. and U.S. AID Study Team Edn. Feasibility in Nigeria, 1964, 65; cons. on Nigeria UN, 1966; cons. AID, Rio Grande do Sul, Brazil, 1966; cons. on edn. in agr. Govt. of Brazil, 1969. Contbr. articles to profl. jours., bulls. Served with USAAF, 1943-45. Recipient Disting. Service award FAA, 1979, Advisor of Merit award U. Wis. Coll. Agr. and Life Scis., 1980. Mem. Am. Vocat. Assn. (regional research rep. 1958-61, mem. credential and accreditation com. 1966), Wis. Assn. Vocat. Agr. Instrs. (25-yr. service award), Nat. Vocat. Agr. Assn., Wis. Acad. Sci., Rural Edn. Assn., Ygdrasil Lit. Soc., Farm House Frat., Alpha Zeta, Delta Theta Sigma, Gamma Sigma Delta, Phi Delta Kappa, Phi Kappa Phi. Home: 5701 Midmoor Rd Madison WI 53716

BJORHUS, ROBERT EINAR, insurance company executive; b. Honolulu, May 1, 1923; s. Einar and Sigrid (Ericksen) B.; m. Elizabeth Jane Hayes, Dec. 28, 1946; children: Elizabeth Anne (Mrs. E. Raymond French), Elaine (Mrs. J. Gibbs), Robert Einar, Kathleen. B.S., Coll. William and Mary, 1949; Pub. Affairs fellow, Brookings Instn., 1961. With Travelers Corp., Hartford, Conn., 1949—, asst. sec., 1959-62, sec., 1962-66, 2d v.p., 1966-68, v.p., 1968-70, sr. v.p., 1970-80, exec. v.p., 1980—; pres., dir. Travelers Corp. Bermuda; dir. Travelers Life Ins. Co. Can., Travelers Indemnity Co. of Can., Travcan Ltd., Constitution Plaza Inc. Served with U.S. Army, 1942-46; PTO. Mem. Health Ins. Assn. Am., Am. Council Life Ins. Club: Hartford. Home: 22 Diana Ln Windsor CT 06095 Office: 1 Tower Sq Hartford CT 06115

BJORK, GORDON CARL, educator; b. Seattle, Dec. 15, 1935; s. Gordon E. and Florence E. (Bloomberg) B.; m. Susan Jill Serman, Dec. 29, 1960; children: Katharine, Rebecca, Susannah, Anders. A.B., Dartmouth Coll., 1957; B.A. (hon.), Oxford U., 1959, M.A., 1963; Ph.D., U. Wash., 1963. Lectr. econs. U. B.C., Vancouver, Can., 1962-63; asst. prof. econs. Carleton U., Ottawa, Ont., 1963-64; assoc. prof. econs. Columbia U., N.Y.C., 1964-68; pres. Linfield Coll., McMinnville, Oreg., 1968-74; prof. econs. Oreg. State U., Corvallis, 1974-75; Lovelace prof. econs. Claremont McKenna Coll., Claremont Grad. Sch., Calif., 1975—; dir. The Hammond Co., Pomona Service Co. Author: Private Enterprise and Public Interest: The Development of American Capitalism, 1969, Life, Liberty and Property: The Economics and Politics of Land Use Planning and Environmental Control, 1980. Vice chmn. Congl. Homes of So. Calif., Claremont, 1979; mem. selection com. for Marshall Scholarships, San Francisco, 1981—; sec. selection com. for Rhodes Scholarships for Oreg., N.W. U.S., 1969-75; pres. Oreg. Ind. Coll. Assn., Portland, 1972. Served to lt. USCGR, 1960-68. Rhodes scholar, 1957; Battelle Inst. fellow, 1975. Mem. Phi Beta Kappa. Republican. United Ch. of Christ. Home: 473 Blaisdell Dr Claremont CA 91711 Office: Claremont McKenna Coll Claremont CA 91711 *An educator teaches by what he is and what he does. My objective, as a teacher, is to mold the values and conceptual framework of the next generation.*

BJORK, PHILIP REESE, museum director; b. Wyandotte, Mich., Sept. 14, 1940; s. Howard Fredeick and Betty (Reese) B.; m. Joyce L. Melvin, Apr. 25, 1964; children: Tanja, Lara. B.S., U. Mich., 1962, Ph.D., 1968; M.S., S.D. Sch. Mines and Tech., 1964. Asst. prof. U. Wis.-Stevens Point, 1968-74, assoc. prof., 1974-75; assoc. prof. dept. geology and geol. engring. S.D. Sch. Mines and Tech., Rapid City, 1975-80, prof., 1980—, dir. dept. geology and geol. engring., 1975—; dir. Mammoth Site Hot Springs Inc., Hot Springs, S.D., 1976—. Mem. Soc. Vertebrate Paleontology, Paleontol. Soc., Geol. Soc. Am. Clubs: Burnt Toast Toastmasters (past v.p., past pres.), Rapid City Lions). Home: 1322 11th St Rapid City SD 57701 Office: Mus Geology SD Sch Mines and tech 500 E St Joseph St Rapid City SD 57701

BJORK, RICHARD EMIL, college chancellor; b. Astoria, Oreg., Aug. 18, 1930; s. Carl E. and Mildred H. (McHugh) B.; m. Joan I. Pineda, June 13, 1953; children: Alison, Tracy. B.A., Yale U., 1952; M.A., Vanderbilt U., 1953; postgrad., U. Wash., 1954-55; Ph.D., Mich. State U., 1961. Dean of students Austin (Tex.) Coll., 1961-63; dean liberal arts SUNY, Plattsburgh, 1963-66; asst. to pres. Rochester (N.Y.) Inst. Tech., 1966-68; acting pres. Glassboro (N.J.) State Coll., 1968-69; vice chancellor higher edn. State of N.J., Trenton, 1968-70; pres. Stockton State Coll., Pomona, N.J., 1969-78; chancellor Vt. State Colls., Waterbury, 1978—; mem. Nat. Adv. Com. Accreditation and Instl. Eligibility. Mem. corp. Cardigan Mountain Sch., N.H.; mem. nat. adv. council U.S. Army Command and Gen. Staff Coll. Served with USCG, 1953-56. Mem. Am. Polit. Sci. Assn., Am. Soc. Pub. Adminstrn., Am. Assn. Higher Edn., AAAS. Home: 32 Deerfield Dr Montpelier VT 05602 Office: Vt State Colls Waterbury VT 05676

BJORKLUND, FREDERICK, savings and loan association executive; b. St. Paul, Feb. 17, 1913; s. Edward and Hanna (Bodin) B.; m. Doris Dunlap, Aug. 28, 1937. B.B.A., U. Minn., 1935. With Minn. Fed. Savs. & Loan Assn., St. Paul, 1940—, pres., 1959-81, chmn. bd., 1965—; vice chmn., dir. FHLB, Des Moines, 1963-66; past trustee Minn. Mut. Life Co. Bd. dirs. Port Devel. Assn.; pres. Indianhead council Boy Scouts Am., 1968-69; bd. dirs. Charles T. Miller Hosp., 1966-71, St. Paul YMCA, 1960-68, St. Paul Jr. Achievement, 1962-69; trustee Coll. of St. Catherine, 1978—. Served to 2d lt. AUS, World War II. Recipient Silver Beaver award Boy Scouts Am., 1954; Boreas Rex XXXV of St. Paul Winter Carnival, 1971. Mem. U.S. League Savs. Assns. (dir. 1965-67, exec. com. 1976—), Savs. League Minn. (pres. 1974), St. Paul Bd. Realtors (past bd. dirs.), St. Paul Home Builders Assn. (past bd. dirs.), Saint Paul Area C. of C. (pres. 1965-67), Savs. Council Twin Cities (past pres.), Am. Legion. Presbyn. (trustee). Clubs: Mason, Shriner, Kiwanis (past pres.), St. Paul Athletic (past dir.), Town and Country (past pres.), Minnesota (St. Paul) (pres. 1974). Home: 1937 Highland Pkwy Saint Paul MN 55116 Office: 355 Minnesota St Saint Paul MN 55101

BJORKMAN, OLLE ERIK, plant biologist; b. Jonkoping, Sweden, July 29, 1933; came to U.S., 1964, naturalized, 1978; m. Erik Gustaf and Dagmar Kristina (Svensson) B.; m. Monika Birgit Waldinger, Sept. 24, 1955; children: Thomas N.E., Per G.O. M.S., U. Stockholm, 1957; Ph.D., U. Uppsala, 1960, D.Sc., 1968. Asst. scientist dept. genetics and plant breeding U. Uppsala, 1956-61; research fellow Swedish Natural Sci. Research Council, 1961-63; postdoctoral fellow Carnegie Inst. Wash., Stanford, Calif., 1964-65, mem. faculty, 1966—, Stanford U., 1967—, prof. biology by courtesy, 1967—; vis. fellow Australian Nat. U., Canberra, 1971-72, 78; sci. adv. Kettering Found., 1976-77; mem. panel world food and nutrition study NRC, 1976; com. carbon dioxide effects Dept. Energy, 1977-82; competitive grants panel Dept. Agr., 1978. Co-author: Experimental Studies of the Nature of Species V, 1971, Physiological Processes in Plant Ecology, 1980; contbr. articles to profl. publns.; editorial bd.: Plant, Cell and Environ, 1978. Recipient Linneus prize Royal Swedish Physiographic Soc., 1977. Mem. AAAS, Nat. Acad. Scis., Am. Soc. Plant Physiologists, Am. Acad. Arts and Scis. Home: 3040 Greer St Palo Alto CA 94303 Office: 290 Panama St Stanford CA 94305

BJORNSON, EDWARD LEE, confection manufacturing company executive; b. Cleve., Oct. 19, 1931; s. Bjorn Adolf and Roberta Lida (Henniger) B.; m. Frieda Garabedian, Oct. 16, 1954; children: Bjorn Gary, Eric Lee. B.A., Yale U., 1953; M.B.A., Harvard U., 1957. Advt. mgr. Kordite Co. div. Nat. Distillers Co., Macedon, N.Y., 1957-60; sales promotion mgr. Nabisco Confections Inc. subs. Nabisco Inc., Cambridge, Mass., 1960-65, asst. to pres., dir. mktg., 1965-75,, exec. v.p., 1978—; gen. mgr. subs. Fred W. Amend Co., 1975-78, v.p. subs., 1975-78. Served with AUS, 1953-55. Mem. New Mfg. Confectioners Assn., North Andover Hist. Soc. (bd. dirs., v.p. 1974-78), New England Confectioners. Clubs: Harvard Musical Assn., Yale of Boston. Office: Nabisco Confections Inc 810 Main St Cambridge MA 02139

BLACHMAN, NELSON M(ERLE), physicist; b. Cleve., Oct. 1923; s. Harry A. and Sarah G. B.; m. Anne Lefkowitz, Nov. 1953; children—Susan J., Nancy R. B.S. in Physics, Case Sch. Applied Sci., Cleve., 1943; A.M., Harvard U., 1947, Ph.D. in Engring. Scis. and Applied Physics, 1947. Spl. research assoc. underwater sound lab. Harvard U., 1943-45; research assoc. Cruft Lab., 1945-46; assoc. physicist Brookhaven Nat. Lab., Upton, N.Y., 1947-51; physicist math. scis. div.

Office Naval Research, 1951-54; sr. engring. specialist electronic def. lab. Sylvania Electric Products, Inc., 1954-58; liaison scientist Office Naval Research, London, 1958-60, 76-78; sr. scientist Sylvania systems group Gen. Telephone and Electronics Corp., Mountain View, Calif., 1960-76, 78—; sr. Fulbright lectr., Madrid, 1964-65; tchr. off-campus programs U. Md., 1951-52, U. Calif., 1961-63, Stanford U., 1967. Author: Noise and Its Effect on Communication, 1966, 2d edit., 1982; also numerous articles. Recipient Ordnance Devel. award U.S. Navy, 1945; John Tyndall fellow, 1946; Gordon McKay scholar, 1946-47. Fellow IEEE (Info. Theory group gov. 1969-75, v.p. 1970, chmn. com. fellows 1969-73, Communications Soc. prize paper award 1976), AAAS, Instn. Elec. Engrs. London; mem. N.Y. Acad. Scis., Fedn. Am. Scientists, Acoustical Soc. Am., Inst. Math. Stats., Am. Statis. Assn., Soc. Indsl. and Applied Math., Math. Assn. Am., U.S. Nat. Com. of Internat. Union Radio Sci. Address: Bldg VI PO Box 7188 GTE Sylvania Systems Group Mountain View CA 94039 *My field, statistical communication theory, is the study of the effect of random disturbances, such as electrical noise, on electronic communication systems. Every signal is inevitably accompanied by noise because the flow of electrons is always somewhat random. My interest in this field stems from my researches as a child, with my father's screwdriver, into the workings of the family radio and telephone. I recommend screwdrivers for children—even if some of the things they take apart never work again.*

BLACHUT, TEODOR JOSEPH, scientist; b. Czestochowa, Poland, Feb. 10, 1915; s. Alaksander and Helena (Czekanska) B.; m. Fannie Emilie Schawalder, Dec. 28, 1948; children—Jan, Daniel, Piotr. Mgr.Ing., Tech. U., Lwow, Poland, 1938; Dr.sci., Tech.U. Zurich, 1971; hon. Dr., U. Mining and Metallurgy, Crakow, Poland, 1974. Asst. Tech. U. E.T.H., Zurich, 1941-45; engr. Wild Co., Switzerland, 1945-51; with Nat. Research Council of Can., Ottawa, 1951—, head photogrammetric research sect., 1979—; vis. prof. univs.; cons. in field. Prin. author, editor: Urban Surveying and Mapping, 1979; contbr. articles to profl. jours. Served with Polish Army, 1940. Recipient 2 sci. awards Am. Soc. Photogrammetry. Fellow Royal Soc. Can.; mem. Can. Inst. Surveying, Am. Soc. Photogrammetry, Polish Geodetic Soc., Brazilian Cartographic Soc. Roman Catholic. Researcher field of photogrammetry. Developer modern instruments and concepts including analytical plotter, stereo-orthophoto technique, stereocompilers, NRC monocomparator; initiator integrated land info. systems based on cadastre and stereo-ortho photos. Home: 29 Cedar Rd Ottawa ON K1J 6L6 Canada

BLACK, ALEXANDER, lawyer; b. Pitts., Nov. 19, 1914; s. Alexander and Ruth (Hay) B.; m. Jane Mevay McIntosh, Apr. 23, 1955; children: F. Kristin Hoeveler, Kenneth M., Elizabeth H. Black Watson. A.B., Princeton U., 1936; LL.B., Harvard U., 1939. Bar: Pa. 1940, U.S. Ct. Claims 1959, U.S. Ct. Appeals (3d cir.) 1957, U.S. Ct. Appeals (Fed. cir.) 1982, U.S. Supreme Ct. 1955. Law clk. Buchanan, Ingersoll, Rodewald, Kyle & Buerger, P.C., Pitts., 1936-39, assoc., 1939-51, ptnr., 1951—, shareholder, 1980—. Served to lt. USNR, 1942-46; PTO. Mem. ABA, Pa. Bar Assn., Allegheny County Bar Assn., Am. Law Inst., Am. Coll. Trial Lawyers, Am. Coll. Real Estate Lawyers, Am. Bar Found., Am. Judicature Soc. Republican. Presbyterian. Clubs: Harvard/Yale/Princeton; Duquesne (Pitts.); Edgeworth (Sewickley, Pa.). Home: 1309 Beaver Rd Osborne Sewickley PA 15143 Officw: Buchanan Ingersoll 600 Grant St 57th Floor Pittsburgh PA 15219

BLACK, ALLEN DECATUR, lawyer; b. Pitts., July 27, 1942; s. Gerald Richard and Amy Elizabeth (Haymaker) B. A.B., Princeton U., 1963; LL.B. magna cum laude, U. Pa., 1966. Bar: D.C. bar 1967, Pa. bar 1971, U.S. Supreme Ct 1975. Law clk. to Hon. John Minor Wisdom, New Orleans, 1966-67; trial atty. Dept. Justice, 1967-68; asst. prof. law U. N.D., Grand Forks, 1971; practice securities and antitrust litigation law, partner firm Fine, Kaplan & Black, Phila., 1971—; lectr. in law Rutgers U., 1972-77, Temple U., 1978. Served with JAGC USN, 1968-71. Mem. Phila. Bar Assn., Phila. Art Alliance. Republican. Episcopalian. Club: Athenaeum (Phila.). Office: 1845 Walnut St Philadelphia PA 19103

BLACK, ARTHUR LEO, educator; b. Redlands, Calif., Dec. 1, 1922; s. Leo M. and Marie A. (Burns) B.; m. Trudi E. McCue, Nov. 11, 1945; children—Teresa (Mrs. William Townsend), Janet (Mrs. William Carter), Patti. B.S., U. Calif. at Davis, 1948, Ph.D., 1951. Faculty physiol. chemistry Sch. Vet. Medicine U. Calif. at Davis, 1951—, prof., 1962—, chmn. dept. physiol. scis., 1968-75; cons. NIH, 1970-72, U.S. Dept. Agr., 1977-80; chmn. Nutritional Scis. Tng. Com., 1971-72. Contbr. papers to profl. jours. Served to 1st lt. USAAF, 1943-46. Recipient Sci. Faculty award NSF, 1958; Acad. Senate Disting. Teaching award U. Calif., Davis, 1977; Research grantee NSF, NIH, 1952—. Mem. Am. Soc. Biol. Chemists, Am. Physiol. Soc., Am. Inst. Nutrition (Borden award 1963), Sigma Xi, Phi Beta Kappa, Phi Zeta. Home: 891 Linden Ln Davis CA 95616

BLACK, BILLY CHARLESTON, college president, chemistry educator; b. Beatrice, Ala., Feb. 1, 1937; s. Billy C. and V. Oweda (Bradley) B.; m. Helen Ruth Jennings, Aug. 27, 1961; children: James Edward, Marla Jeaninne. B.S., Tuskegee Inst., 1960; M.S., Iowa State U., 1962, Ph.D., 1964. Prof. chemistry Albany State Coll., Ga., 1964—, chmn. div. arts and scis., 1970-80, interim asst. to dean acad. affairs, 1979-80, acting pres., 1980-81, pres., 1981—; cons. NSF, 1966—, NIH, 1966—. Bd. dirs. Chehaw council Boy Scouts Am., Albany, 1980-84, Albany Area Primary Health Care, Inc., 1980-84, United Way Dougherty County, 1980—. Named Black Georgian of Yr., 1980. Mem. Am. Chem. Soc., Am. Oil Chemists Soc., Am. Inst. Chemists, Ga. Acad. Sci., Inst. Food Techonlogists, Omega Psi Phi. Methodist. Home: 811 Holley Dr Albany GA 31705 Office: Albany State Coll 504 College Dr Albany GA 31705

BLACK, BRADY FORREST, ret. newspaper editor; b. Lawrence County, Ky., July 31, 1908; s. Fred Nixon and Melissa (Cornwell) B.; m. Edra Dailey, Sept. 17, 1930; children—Brenda Gayle, Brady Brent, Lisa Anne. Student pub. schs. Sports editor Ashland (Ky.) Ind., 1927-38, city editor, 1938-40; with Cin. Enquirer, 1940-75, beginning as copyreader, promoted through various positions to Ky. corr., 1946, Ohio corr., 1948, mng. editor, 1956-57, editor editorial page, 1957-59, exec. editor, 1959-64, v.p., editor, 1964-75; Kiplinger prof. Ohio State U., 1975-76; cons. No. Ky. U., 1976, 77; syndicated newspaper columnist, 1976-80. Mem. Inter Am. Press Assn., Sigma Delta Chi (pres. Central Ohio profl. chpt. 1955-56). Home: 1009 Park Crest Park Hills KY 41011 *Honesty, integrity and fairness are basic standards which, if observed, can keep one with a conscience clear enough not to be a diversion from attention to performance. Day-to-day quality performance is a source of self satisfaction which is a reward in itself and builds as well a record for judgment by others. Analysis of events in terms of their likely course is helpful as a guide to judgments and decisions which best prepare one to cope with the future.*

BLACK, CATHLEEN PRUNTY, newspaper company executive; b. Chgo., Apr. 26, 1944; d. James Hamilton and Margaret (Harrington) B. B.A., Trinity Coll., 1966. Advt. sales rep. Holiday mag., N.Y.C., 1966-69, Travel & Leisure mag., 1969-70; advt. sales rep. New York mag., 1970-72, assoc. pub., 1977-79, pub., 1979-83; pres. USA Today, 1983—; advt. dir. Ms. mag., 1972-75, assoc. pub., 1975-77. Home: 325 E 72d St New York NY 10021 Office: USA Today PO Box 500 Washington DC 20044

BLACK, CHARLES ALLEN, soil scientist, educator; b. Lone Tree, Iowa, Jan. 22, 1916; s. Guy Cameron and Katharine Lavina (Loehr) B.; m. Marjorie Anderson, June 11, 1939; children: Carol Anne, Richard Allen, Marilyn Jean. B.S. in Chemistry and Agronomy, Colo. State U., 1937; M.S. in Soil Fertility, Iowa State U., 1938, Ph.D., 1942. Mem. faculty Iowa State U., 1939—, prof. soils, 1949—, disting. prof., 1967—; vis. prof. Cornell U., 1955; sr. postdoctoral fellow NSF, 1964-65; research asso. Kearney Found., U. Calif., 1964, U. Calif., 1965. Author: Soil-Plant Relationships, 1957, 2d edit., 1968; Editor-in-chief: Methods of Soil Analysis, 1965; Am. editor: Soils Derived from Volcanic Ash in Japan, 1977. Served with USNR, 1945-46. Recipient award of Merit Gamma Sigma Delta, 1976; Dir.'s award Midwest Agrl. Chems. Assn., 1979; Disting. Service award Am. Agrl. Editors Assn., 1979; Henry A. Wallace award Iowa State U., 1980, nat. award for agrl. excellence Nat. Agri-Mktg. Assn., 1983; named honor alumnus Coll. Agrl. Scis., Colo. State U., 1983. Fellow AAAS, Am. Soc. Agronomy (hon. mem., exec. com. 1961-63, Soil Sci. award 1957, nat. pres. 1970-71, Edward W. Browning Achievement award 1976), Am. Inst. Chemists (hon. mem.), Soil Sci. Soc. Am. (chmn. div. 2 1954, nat. pres. 1962, Bauyoucos Soil Sci. Disting. Career award 1981); mem. Council Agrl. Sci. and Tech. (chmn. bd. 1972, nat. pres. 1973, exec. v.p. 1974—), Internat. Soc. Soil Sci. (sec. commn. 2 1960), Am. Soc. Agrl. Engrs. (hon.). Home: 624 Agg Ave Ames IA 50010

BLACK, CHARLES ALVIN, consulting engineer; b. Gainesville, Fla., July 7, 1920; s. Alvin Percy and Lillian Barnes (Russell) B.; m. Elizabeth Beck, Sept. 12, 1943; children: Charles Russell, Elizabeth Ann. B.S., U. Fla., 1947. Registered profl. engr., Fla., Ga., S.C., Ala., Kans., Pa., Ohio; registered real estate broker. Pres. Black Labs., Inc., Gainesville, 1947-69; pres. Black, Crow & Eidsness of Ga.; sr. v.p. Black, Crow & Eidsness, Inc., Gainesville, 1950—; pres. Black & Assos. Land Planning & Engring. Co., Clearwater, Fla., 1959-69, Engring. Devel. Co., Boca Raton, Fla., 1950-69, Black & Cannon Realty, Inc., 1978—; san. engr. USPHS, 1959—. Contbr. articles to profl. jours. Mem. Fla. Gov.'s Task Force for Water, Crystal River-Homosassa Water Basin Bd.; Bd. dirs. People to People; chmn. Citrus County Indsl. Authority; mem. Withlacoochee Regional Planning Council.; chmn. Com. of 100 Citrus County. Served with AUS, 1944-45. Mem. Am. Water Works Assn. (hon., chmn. water quality div. 1951, chmn. Fla. sect. 1962, nat. dir. 1966-69, v.p. 1969-70, pres. 1971-72, Water Works Man of Year 1961), Cons. Engrs. Council, Cons. Engrs. Fla., ASCE, Royal Soc. Health, Nat. Soc. Profl. Engrs., Am. Pub. Health Assn., Fla. Pollution Control Assn., Soc. Am. Mil. Engrs., Am. Acad. Environ. Engrs., Alpha Tau Omega. Episcopalian. Club: Elks (Crystal River, Fla.). Lodges: Rotary Internat. (pres. chpt., dist. gov.-elect). Home: 2941 NW 21st Ave Gainesville FL 32605 Office: Box 2020 1815 SE Hwy 19 Crystal River FL 32629

BLACK, CHARLES HENRY, industrialist; b. Atlanta, Sept. 12, 1926; s. Charles Henry and Elfrida Elizabeth (Peterson) B.; m. Bonnie Nicksic; children: Charles Henry, Richard Swanton, Laura Branch, Peter Branch. B.S., U. So. Calif., 1950. Engr. Hughes Aircraft Co., Culver City, Calif., 1950-53; mgr. budgets Lockheed Missiles & Space Div., Van Nuys, Calif., 1954-57; dir. fin. control and adminstrn., guidance and control div. Litton Industries, Inc., Beverly Hills, Calif., 1958-65, v.p. fin., profl. services and equipment group, 1965-70, corp. treas., 1971—, v.p., 1976-80; exec. v.p. Great Western Fin. Corp. and Great Western Savs. & Loan Assn., Beverly Hills, Calif., 1980-82; sr. v.p. Kaiser Steel Corp., 1982-84, exec. v.p., dir., 1984—; dir. Investment Co. Am., Fundamental Investors Inc., Interdyne Co.; bd. govs. Pacific Stock Exchange; adv. bd. Corp. Asset Trust Co.; trustee Am. Pathway Fund, Inc. Trustee Brentwood Sch. Served with AC USNR, 1944-46. Mem. Fin. Execs. Inst., Internat. Treas.'s Assn., Phi Kappa Psi. Clubs: Los Angeles Country, California. Home: 351 Alma Real Dr Pacific Palisades CA 90272 Office: 9400 Cherry Ave Fontana CA 92335

BLACK, CHARLES LUND, JR., educator; b. Austin, Tex., Sept. 22, 1915; s. Charles Lunn and Alzada Helena (Bowman) B.; m. Barbara Ann Aronstein, Apr. 11, 1954; children: Gavin Bingley, David Alan, Robin Elizabeth. B.A., U. Tex., 1935, M.A., 1938; LL.B., Yale, 1943; LL.D., Boston U., 1975. Bar: N.Y. 1946, U.S. Supreme Ct. 1946. Practiced, N.Y.C., 1946-47; asst. prof. law Columbia U., 1947-49, asso. prof., 1949-52, prof., 1952-56; Henry R. Luce prof. jurisprudence Yale U., 1956-75, Sterling prof. law, 1975—; mem. cast Yale Repertory Theater, 1976, 78; vis. prof. law U. Tex., 1955; mem. faculty Salzburg Seminar in Am. Studies, 1956; Edward Douglass White lectr. La. State U., 1968; mem. faculty Orientation Program in Am. Law, 1969; Holmes Devise lectr. U. Washington, 1970; Morris Ames Soper lectr. U. Md., 1972; Baum lectr. U. Ill., 1975; Tucker lectr. Washington and Lee U., 1975; Pope John XXIII lectr. Cath. U. Sch. Law, 1976; Dreyfus lectr. Tulane U., 1977; Alumni Disting. lectr. U. Tenn. Coll. Law, 1978; Holmes lectr. Harvard Law Sch., 1979; Phi Beta Kappa vis. scholar, 1980-81, Tex. lectr. on the Humanities, 1983; counsel Supreme Ct. briefs in school segregation, civil rights cases; legal cons. N.A.A.C.P. Legal Def. and Edn. Fund.; Mem. adv. com. on admiralty rules Jud. Conf. U.S., 1960-70. Author: (with Grant Gilmore) The Law of Admiralty, 1957, 2d edit., 1975, The People and the Court, 1960, The Occasions of Justice, 1963, Perspectives in Constitutional Law, 1963, rev. edit., 1970; poetry Telescopes and Islands, 1963; Structure and Relationship in Constitutional Law, 1969, Impeachment: A Handbook, 1974, Capital Punishment: The Inevitability of Caprice and Mistake, 1974, 2d edit., 1981; (with Bob Eckhardt) poetry Tides of Power, 1976, Owls Bay In Babylon, 1980; Decision According to Law, 1981; poetry The Waking Passenger, 1983; also articles and poems in mags. and jours. Named Disting. Alumnus U. Tex., 1975; Conn. Law Rev. award, 1980; Soc. Am. Law Tchrs. award, 1983; Fellow Jonathan Edwards Coll., Yale U.; Bye-fellow Queens' Coll., Cambridge U., 1966-67. Mem. Maritime Law Assn. U.S., Am. Acad. Arts and Scis., Conn. Acad. Arts and Scis., Order of Coif, Phi Delta Phi, Kappa Sigma. Club: Elizabethan (gov. bd. 1971-72). Office: Yale U Law Sch New Haven CT 06520

BLACK, CONRAD MOFFAT, corporate executive; b. Montreal, Que., Can., Aug. 25, 1944; s. George Montegu and Jean Elizabeth (Riley) B.; m. Shirley Gail Hishon. B.A., Carleton U., 1965; LL.L., Laval U., 1970; M.A. in History, McGill U., 1973; LL.D., St. Francis Xavier U., 1979, McMaster U., 1979; Litt.D., U. Windsor, 1979. Chmn., co-owner Eastern Twps. Pub. Co., Ltd., La Societe de Publication de l'Avenir de Brome Missisquoi Inc., Farnham, Que., 1967—; chmn. Sterling Newspapers Ltd., Vancouver, 1971—, Dominion Malting Ltd., Winnipeg, 1976—; chmn. bd., chmn. exec. com. Argus Corp. Ltd., Toronto, 1979—, Norcen Energy Resources Ltd., 1981—, Ravelston Corp. Ltd., 1979—; pres. Western Dominion Investment Co. Ltd.; vice chmn., chmn. exec. com., chief exec. officer Hollinger Argus Ltd.; mem. exec. com., dir. Can. Imperial Bank Commerce, Dominion Stores Ltd., Standard Broadcasting Corp. Ltd., Hanna Mining Co.; dir. CFRB Ltd., Carling O'Keefe Ltd., Confedn. Life Ins. Co., Eaton's of Can. Ltd., T. Eaton Acceptance Co. Ltd., Labmin Resources Ltd. Author: Duplessis, 1977. Decorated knight Mil. and Hospitaller Order of St. Lazarus of Jerusalem. Mem. Trilateral Commn., Americas Soc. Clubs: Toronto, York, Toronto Golf; Univ., Mount Royal (Montreal). Office: 10 Toronto St Toronto ON Canada M5C 2B7

BLACK, CREED CARTER, newspaper publisher; b. Harlan, Ky., July 15, 1925; s. Creed Carter and Mary (Cole) B.; m. Mary C. Davis, Dec. 28, 1947 (div. 1976); children: Creed Carter, Steven D., Douglas S.; m. Elsa Goss, Dec. 9, 1977. B.S. with highest distinction and honors in Polit. Sci., Northwestern U., 1949; M.A., U. Chgo., 1952. Reporter Paducah (Ky.) Sun-Democrat, 1942-43, 46; editor Daily Northwestern, 1947; copy editor Chgo. Sun-Times, 1949, Chgo. Herald-Am., 1950; editorial writer Nashville Tennessean, 1950-57, exec. editor, 1957-59; v.p., exec. editor Savannah (Ga.) Morning News and Savannah Evening Press, 1959-60, Wilmington (Del.) Morning News and Evening Jour., 1960-64; mng. editor Chgo. Daily News, 1964-68, exec. editor, 1968-69; asst. sec. for legislation HEW, 1969-70; editor Phila. Inquirer, 1970-77; chmn. bd., pub. Lexington (Ky.) Herald & Leader, 1977—. Served with 100th Inf. Div. AUS, World War II; ETO. Decorated Bronze Star; recipient Northwestern U. Alumni medal, 1973. Mem. Am. Newspaper Pubs. Assn., So. Newspaper Pubs. Assn. (dir. 1980—), Am. Soc. Newspaper Editors (dir.; pres. 1983), Nat. Conf. Editorial Writers (pres. 1962), Sigma Delta Chi, Kappa Tau Alpha, Lambda Chi Alpha. Methodist. Clubs: Lexington Country, Lafayette, Greenbrier Golf (Lexington). Home: 1932 Blairmore Rd Lexington KY 40502 Office: Lexington Herald & Leader Main and Midland Sts Lexington KY 40507

BLACK, CYRIL EDWIN, educator; b. Bryson City, N.C., Sept. 10, 1915; s. Floyd Henson and Zarafinka (Kirova) B.; m. Corinne Manning, June 30, 1951; children: James Manning, Christina Ellen. Student, U. Besancon, 1934-35, U. Berlin, summer 1935; A.B., Duke U., 1936; A.M., Harvard U., 1937, Ph.D., 1941; Litt.D. (hon.), Ursinus Coll., 1978. Mem. faculty Princeton U., 1939—, asst. prof., 1946-49, asso. prof., 1949-54, prof. history, 1954—; dir. Center Internat. Studies, 1968—; fellow Behavioral Studies Center, 1960-61; officer Dept. State, 1943-44, fgn. service aux. officer assigned, Eastern Europe, 1944-46; mem. U.S. del. UN Commn. Investigation Concerning Greek Frontier Incidents, 1947; adviser, alt. U.S. mem. subcommn. on prevention discrimination and protection minorities, 1949-52, mem. U.S. del. to observe Soviet elections, 1958; civilian faculty Nat. War Coll., 1950; vis. fellow Wilson Center, 1982-83. Author: Establishment of Constitutional Government in Bulgaria, 1943, Twentieth Century Europe: A History, (with E.C. Helmreich), 4th edit., 1972, The Dynamics of Modernization, 1966, (with R.A. Falk, K. Knorr, O.R. Young) Neutralization in World Politics, 1968, (with others) The Modernization of Japan and Russia, 1975, The Modernization of China, 1981; Editor: Challenge in Eastern Europe, 1954, Rewriting Russian History, 1956, The Transformation of Russian Society, 1960, (with T.P. Thornton) Communism and Revolution, 1964, (with R.A. Falk) The Future of the International Legal Order, 4 vols, 1969-72, Comparative Modernization: A Reader, 1975; Contbr. profl. jours. Mem. Am. Hist. Assn., Am. Polit. Sci. Assn., Council Fgn. Relations. Home: 348 Ridgeview Rd Princeton NJ 08540

BLACK, DANIEL JAMES, chem. co. exec.; b. Asbury Park, N.J., Dec. 31, 1931; s. Daniel Joseph and Julia (Palmer) B.; m. Marilyn Russo, Apr. 23, 1960; children—Daniel, Deborah, Peter. Student, Cooper Union, St. John's U., 1950-52; B.S., N.Y. U., 1956. Asst. to treas. Frederick Snare Corp., N.Y.C., 1954-60; pres., chief operating officer Carter-Wallace Inc., N.Y.C., 1960—, also dir., mem. exec. com.; chmn. bd. Frank W. Horner, Ltd., Montreal, Que., Can., 1978—. Mem. adv. council Pace U., 1971—. Served with AUS, 1952-54. Mem. Tax Execs. Inst. (v.p. 1967-71), Fin. Execs. Inst. Roman Catholic. Clubs: Nassau Golf and Country, Wheatley Hills Golf; Met., Univ. (N.Y.C.). Home: 3 Shelter Rock Rd Manhasset NY 11030 Office: Carter Wallace Inc 767 Fifth Ave New York NY 10022

BLACK, DAVID STATLER, lawyer; b. Everett, Wash., July 14, 1928; s. Lloyd Llewelyn and Gladys (Statler) B.; m. Nancy Haskell, July 26, 1952; children: David Lloyd, Andrew Haskell, Kathleen Louise. B.A., Stanford U., 1950; LL.B., U. Wash., 1954. Bar: Wash. 1954, D.C. 1969, Kans. 1979. Assoc. firm Preston, Thorgrimson & Horowitz, Seattle, 1954-57; asst. atty. gen. Wash. State; also counsel Wash. Pub. Service Commn., 1957-61; gen counsel Bur. Pub. Roads, Dept. Commerce, 1961-63; vice chmn. Fed. Power Commn., 1963-66; adminstr. Bonneville Power Adminstrn., 1966-67; undersec. Dept. Interior, 1967-69; v.p. Dreyfus Corp., 1969-70; mem. firm Pierson, Ball & Dowd, Washington, 1970-79; v.p., gen. counsel The Kans. Power & Light Co., Topeka, 1979-82, sr. v.p. law, 1982—. Mem. Wash. State, D.C., Kans., Am. bar assns., Phi Delta Phi, Delta Kappa Epsilon. Office: 818 Kansas Ave Topeka KS 66612

BLACK, DONALD BRUCE, lawyer, arbitrator, fast food executive; b. Los Angeles, June 25, 1932; s. Freeman Carleton and Elizabeth (Bergstrom) B.; children: Jeanine, Debra, Lawrence Bently. A.B., UCLA, 1954; J.D., U. So. Calif., 1960. Bar: Calif. 1960. Mem. firm Shield and Smith, 1960-72, Williams and Black, Los Angeles, 1972-75; individual practice law Donald B. Black, Inc., Los Angeles and Laguna Beach, Calif., 1976—; arbitrator Superior Ct.; regional adviser Am. Arbitration Assn. Pres. Parent-Tchr. Council, 1968-70; sec. Betts Found., 1970—, Elliott Found., 1969—; Panel judge pro tem Los Angeles Mcpl. Ct. Served with USAF, 1955-56. Mem. Am. Bd. Trial Advocates (nat. pres. 1975-76), Assn. So. Calif. Def. Counsel (pres. 1972-73, joint legis. commns. on structure of judiciary 1974-77, tort reform 1977-79), ABA (com. chmn. elect), Phi Delta Phi, Delta Tau Delta. Republican. Presbyterian. Clubs: Jonathan, Calcutta Saddle and Cycle (founding gov. 1971—); Balboa Bay (Newport Beach, Calif.)). Office: Suite 1900 615 S Flower St Los Angeles CA 90017 Village Business Center 301 Forest Ave Laguna Beach CA 92651 *The recognition of opportunity is perhaps life's true reward; with that, direction and purpose seem less happenstance.*

BLACK, EDWIN FAHEY, international business consultant; b. New Orleans, Aug. 17, 1915; s. Edwin Gregory and Lillian (Fahey) B.; m. Margaret Cobey, Nov. 26, 1945; children: Star, Christopher, Noel, Nicholas, Brian, Bruce. B.S. in Civil Engring., U.S. Mil. Acad., 1940; M.A. in Internat. Relations, George Washington U., 1962; grad., Nat. War Coll., 1962. Commd. 2d lt. U.S. Army, 1940, advanced through grades to brig. gen., 1965; with OSS, Europe, World War II; comdg. officer 2d bn. 505th Airborne Inf., 82d Airborne Div., Fort Bragg, N.C., 1950-51, comdg. officer 2d battle group 19 Inf., 25th Div., Schofield Barracks, Honolulu, 1957-58; mil. asst. to dep. sec. Dept. Def., Washington, 1959-61; comdg. gen. U.S. Army Support Command, Thailand, 1967-69; asst. div. comdr. (25th Inf. Div.), Vietnam, 1969; asst. chief of staff U.S. Army Pacific, Honolulu, 1970; ret., 1970; exec. v.p. Freedoms Found., Valley Forge, Pa., 1970-71; dir. bus. plans S.E. Asia LTV Aerospace Corp., Bangkok, Thailand, 1971-74; mng. dir. KRA Canal Survey Office, Bangkok, 1972-76; dir. internat. bus. devel. LTV Corp., 1974-75; dir. indsl. devel. Govt. of Am. Samoa; cons. on econ. devel. Trust Ters. of Pacific Islands, 1976-77; v.p. internat. bus. devel. I.R.A.S. Devel. Corp., White Plains, N.Y., 1980—; spl. asst. to pres. Radiation Tech., Inc., Rockaway, N.J., 1983—. Contbr. articles on polit.-mil. affairs to mags. and profl. jours. Decorated Legion Merit with 2 oak leaf clusters, Bronze Star medal; Order Crown, Thailand, 1969; Cross of Gallantry with palm and star Rep. S. Vietnam). Mem. Council Fgn. Relations. Clubs: Outrigger Canoe, Waialae Country (Honolulu); Royal Bangkok Sports; Army-Navy Country, Army-Navy (Washington). Home: 4910 Kahala Ave Honolulu HI 96816 Office: Suite 244 S Pacific Trade Center Honolulu HI 96813

BLACK, EMILIE ANNABELLE, physician, government medical institute administrator; b. New Haven, Apr. 14, 1919; d. Lewis Albert and Margaret Anna (Knopf) B.; m. Samuel J. Solt, July 19, 1946; 1 dau., Margaret. B.S., George Washington U., 1942, M.D., 1945. Intern Garfield Meml. Hosp., Washington, 1945-46, resident in internal medicine, 1946-47; resident Children's Hosp., Washington, 1947-49; practice medicine specializing in pediatrics, Bethesda, Md., 1949-66; med. officer D.C. Dept. Pub. Health Child Health Clinics, 1963-68; with NIH, Bethesda, Md., 1968—; dep. dir. clin. and physiol. program Nat. Inst. Gen. Med. Scis., 1974-76, program dir., 1976-78; asst. dir. Nat. Inst. Gen. Med. Scis. for Clin. Research, 1978—; clin. instr. pediatrics George Washington U., 1950—; NIH rep. 3d Internat. Congress on Burn Research, Prague, Czechoslovakia, 1970, White House Conf. on Children, 1970; mem. planning com. Internat. Trauma Symposium, 1970, First World Congress on Pain, Florence, Italy, 1975; participant V Internat. Congress on Burn Injuries, Stockholm, 1978, 6th Internat. Congress on Burn Injuries, 1982. Editor and contbr.: numerous studies and presentations including A Trauma Conference Report, 1974, A Consensus Development Conference on Burn Injuries, 1978, 2d Conference on Burn Injuries, 1980. Recipient Harvey Stuart Allen award for Disting. Service Am. Burn Assn., 1982. Mem. Am. Assn. Surgery Trauma, Internat. Soc. Burn Injuries, Am. Burn Assn. (hon.), AAAS, George Washington U. Assn.; founding mem. Am. Trauma Soc., HEW Interagy. Task Force on Burn Centers. Home: 5201 Watson St NW Washington DC 20016 Office: 5333 Westbard Ave Room 925 Bethesda MD 20014 *The achievement of one's goals is not the result of single-minded dedication; it is a blend of one's sense of accomplishment with the inspiration derived from one's family and friends.*

BLACK, EUGENE CHARLTON, historian, educator; b. Boston, Dec. 15, 1927; s. Knox Charlton and Margaret Kirkley (Henely) B.; m. Anne Galt Kirby, Nov. 10, 1948 (div. Dec. 1981); children: Alexander Charlton, Rebecca Galt, Andrew Gavin.; m. Frances G. Malino, Mar. 26, 1983. A.B., Coll. William and Mary, 1948; M.A., Harvard U., 1954, Ph.D., 1958. Teaching fellow history and lit. Harvard U., 1956-58; instr. history Brandeis U., 1958-60, asst. prof., 1960-63, assoc. prof., 1963-69, prof. history, 1969-70, Leff prof. history, 1970-72, Springer prof. history, 1972—, assoc. dean of faculty, 1964-65; dean Grad. Sch. Arts and Sci., 1971-72, acting dean of faculty, 1971-72, chmn. dept. history, 1970-72, 73-82; vis. prof. Boston U., 1969; chmn. panelist, speaker profl. meetings. Author: The Association: British Extraparliamentary Political Organization, 1769-1793, 1963, Posture of Europe, 1815-1940: Readings in European Intellectual History, 1964, European Political History, 1815-1870: Aspects of Liberalism, 1967, British Politics in the Nineteenth Century, 1969, Victorian Culture and Society, 1973, Feminists, Liberalism, and Morality: The Unresolvable Triangle, 1981; contbr. numerous articles to profl. jours. Mem. Wellesley (Mass.) Town Democratic Com., 1964-79. Served to capt. USAFR, 1948-53. Fellow Royal Hist. Soc.; mem. Am. Hist. Assn., Conf. Brit. Studies, Hist. Assn. U.K., Econ. History Soc. U.K., New Eng. Hist. Assn., Bus. History Soc., Victorian Studies Group, Acad. Polit. Sci. Episcopalian. Home: 63 Nehoiden Rd Waban MA 02168 Office: Dept History Brandeis U Waltham MA 02254

BLACK, FISCHER, investment banker; b. Washington, Jan. 11, 1938; s. Fischer Sheffey and Elizabeth (Zemp) B.; children: Alethes, Melissa, Ashley, Paige. A.B., Harvard U., 1959, Ph.D., 1964. Cons. Arthur D. Little, Inc., Cambridge, Mass., 1965-69; owner Assocs. in Fin., Belmont, Mass., 1969-71; prof. fin. U. Chgo., 1971-75, MIT, Cambridge, 1975-84; assoc. Goldman, Sachs & Co., N.Y.C., 1984—. Mem. Am. Fin. Assn. (pres. 1985). Office: Goldman Sachs & Co 85 Broad St New York NY 10004

BLACK, G. MONTEGU, food company executive. Chmn., commn. Dominion Stores Ltd.

BLACK, GEORGE MALCOLM, advertising agency executive; b. Crescent City, Calif., Aug. 28, 1982; s. Leo Raymond and Jane (Kane) B.; m. Birgitta Alvin, May 6, 1962. B.S., Stanford U., 1949; postgrad., Syracuse U., 1951. Retail rep. Time, Inc., 1950; media planner, buyer J. Walter Thompson, San Francisco, 1954-56, account rep., N.Y.C., 1956-57, account dir., creative dir., Frankfurt, Germany, 1957-61, mng. dir., Zurich, Switzerland, 1962-65, Antwerp, Belgium, 1965-67, creative dir., Frankfurt, Germany, 1967-73, mng. dir., 1974-77, chmn., 1977—, also exec. v.p., 1977—; lectr. Unilever Mktg. Seminar, London, 1973-83; dir. Del Norte Co. Served with USAF, 1950-54; ETO. Home: An den Braunmannswiensen Bad Hamburg Germany 6380 Office: J. Walter Thompson GmbH Bockenheimer Landstrasse 104 Frankfurt Fed Republic Germany 0611

BLACK, HILLEL MOSES, publisher; b. N.Y.C., Apr. 8, 1929; s. Isidor and Ida (Feldstein) B.; (div. 1978). B.A., U. Chgo., 1949, M.English and Fgn. Langs., 1952. Copy boy N.Y. Times, N.Y.C., 1952-53; reporter AP, Pitts., Newark and N.Y.C., 1954-58; freelance writer, N.Y.C., 1959-65; editor Saturday Evening Post, N.Y.C., 1966-67; sr. editor William Morrwo & Co., N.Y.C., 1967-77, ediotr-in-chief, 1977-82; pub. gen. books div. Macmillan Pub. Co., N.Y.C., 1982—. Author: The Watch Dogs of Wall Street, Buy Now, Pay Later, The American Schoolbook. Mem. Pubs. Club. Office: Macmillan Pub Co Inc 855 3d Ave New York NY 10022 *

BLACK, HUGO LAFAYETTE, JR., lawyer; b. Birmingham, Ala., Apr. 29, 1922; s. Hugo Lafayette and Josephine Patterson Foster; m. Graham Hobson, June 12, 1947; children: Hugo L., Elizabeth Graham, Margaret Hartley. A.B., U. Ala., 1946; LL.B., Yale U., 1949. Bar: Ala. 1949, Fla. 1962, U.S. Supreme Ct. 1950; cert. civil trial lawyer. Partner firm Kelly, Black, Black & Earle (P.A.), Miami, Fla., 1962—; lectr. Practicing Law Inst., Am. Law Inst.-ABA Trial Seminars. Author: My Father, A Remembrance, 1976. Fellow Am. Bar Found.; mem. ABA, Fed. Bar Assn., Dade County Bar Assn., Internat. Soc. Barristers, Am. Law Inst., Am. Coll. Trial Lawyers. Home: 12305 SW 73d Ave Miami FL 33156 Office: 1400 A I du Pont Bldg 169 E Flagler St Miami FL 33131

BLACK, JAMES HAY, chemical engineering educator; b. Pitts., Aug. 14, 1921; s. Alexander and Ruth (Hay) B.; m. Mary Lucretia Garland, Feb. 4, 1950; children: Ruth Hay Black McKinzey, Alexander Chisholm, Patricia Anne. A.B. in Chemistry, Cornell U., 1943; B.S. U. Pitts, 1948; M.S., 1949; Ph.D., 1954; Ph.D. hon. alumnus, Carnegie-Mellon U., 1954. Registered profl. engr., Pa. Research chemist Koppers Co., Inc., Pitts., 1943; instr. U. Pitts., 1950-52; fellow Mellon Inst. Indsl. Research, Pitts., 1952-54; asst. project engr. Standard Oil Co., Ind., 1954-55; sr. technologist, supervising technologist U.S. Steel Corp., Monroeville, Pa., 1955-62; prof., head chem. engring. U. Ala., 1962—; exec. sec. Am. Assn. Cost Engrs., 1964-71, dir., 1972-74, v.p., 1974, pres., 1975; cons. in field; mem. Nat. Air Pollution Techniques Adv. Com. HEW, Washington, 1969—; cons. Tuscaloosa (Ala.) Environ. Quality Control Com., 1969—; mem. Tuscaloosa Environ. Health Adv. Com.; mem. tech. panel U.S. Office Coal Research, Washington. Co-author: Cost and Optimization Engineering, 1983; Univ. Contbg. author: Environmental Engineer's Handbook, 1973; contbr. articles to profl. jours. Served to 1st lt. AUS, 1943-46. Fellow Am. Inst. Chem. Engrs., Am. Assn. Cost Engrs., Am. Inst. Chemists; mem. Am. Chem. Soc., Soc. History Tech., Sigma Xi, Tau Beta Pi, Sigma Tau, Phi Lambda Upsilon, Omega Chi Epsilon. Episcopalian. Club: University. Home: 96 Arcadia Dr Tuscaloosa AL 35401 Office: PO Box G University AL 35486

BLACK, JAMES T., brewery executive; b. Montreal, July 16, 1925; s. James and Agnes (McCartney) B. With McDonald, Currie and Co., Chartered Accts., Montreal, 1941-49; with Molson's Brewery Ltd., 1949-61, comptroller, 1961; v.p., gen. mgr. Molson's Western Breweries Ltd., 1961, pres., 1966; v.p. ops. Molson Breweries Ltd., 1966-68, dir., 1967; sr. v.p. Brewing group Molson Industries, Ltd.; and pres. Molson Breweries of Can. Ltd., 1968-70; v.p. ops. Molson Industries Ltd., Rexdale, Ont., Can., 1970-72, exec. v.p., 1972-73; pres. Molson Cos. Ltd., 1973-83, chief exec. officer, 1983—; dir. Mut. Life Assurance Co. of Can., Canron, Inc., Rio Algom Ltd., Petro-Can.; Niagara. Chmn. Niagara Inst. Trustee Fraser Inst.; gov. Jr. Achievement Can. Served with RCAF, 1943-45. Mem. Can. Mfrs. Assn. (treas.), Bus. Council Nat. Issues, Council for Can. Unity. Office: Molson Cos Ltd 2 International Blvd Rexdale ON M9W 1A2 Canada *

BLACK, JOHN WILSON, emeritus speech educator; b. Veedersburg, Ind., Feb. 9, 1906; s. George Keys and Hattie Lee (Wilson) B.; m. Helen Harrington, Aug. 21, 1936; children: Caroline (Mrs. Philip Utley), Richard Willis, Constance (Mrs. Dennis Nagle), Charlotte. A.B., Wabash Coll., 1927, D.H.L. (hon.), 1977; M.A., U. Iowa, 1930, Ph.D., 1935; D.Sc. (hon.), Bowling Green State U., 1977, D.H.L., Ohio State U., 1982. Prof. speech and rhetoric Adrian (Mich.) Coll., 1927-35; instr. English Kenyon Coll., Gambier, Ohio, 1935-36; prof. speech, 1936-49, Ohio State U., Columbus, 1949-66, regents prof. speech, 1966-76, emeritus, 1976—; vis. prof. U. Minn., summer 1946, Mich. State U., 1977, Tex. So. U., 1978-79, U. Tex. Health Sci. Center, Houston, 1980; Emons prof. Ball State U., 1976; project dir. voice communication lab. Nat. Def. Research Council, Waco, Tex., 1943-45; exec. sec. Ohio Coll. Assn., 1946-53; cons. Vocat. Rehab. Adminstrn., 1962-66. Author: (with Wilbur C. Moore) Speech: Code, Meaning, and Communication, 1955, American Speech for Foreign Students, 1963, 2d edit., 1983, Multiple-Choice Intelligibility Tests, 1963, (with Ruth B. Irwin) Voice and Diction, 1969, (with others) Language and Hearing Journal Titles, 1954-78, 1979; Editor: Speech Monographs, 1959; mem. editorial bd.: Jour. Speech, 1948-53, Jour. Communications Disorders, 1967—, Folia Phoniatrica, 1970—, Jour. Psycholinguistic Research, 1971—. Recipient Presdl. certificate of merit, 1949; Fulbright scholar, 1954-55; NSF postdoctoral fellow, 1961; Japanese Soc. for Promotion Sci. fellow Chiba U., 1976. Fellow AAAS, Acoustical Soc. Am., Am. Speech and Hearing Assn. (v.p. 1964, certificate of merit 1968); mem. Speech Communication Assn. (pres. 1966), Am. Psychol. Assn., Linguistic Soc. Am., AAUP, Internat. Coll. Exptl. Phonology (pres. 1971), Aerospace Med. Assn., Phi Beta Kappa. (hon.). Home: 1400 Lincoln Rd Columbus OH 43212 Office: Dept Communication Ohio State U Columbus OH 43210

BLACK, JOHN WOODLAND, lawyer; b. Spokane, Sept. 22, 1925; s. Hugh James and Margaret (Woodland) B.; m. Iryne Codon, Sept. 3, 1959; children: John McKenzie, Catherine Louise, Bridget Dianne, James Joseph, Ian Andrew, Timothy Matthugh. Student, U. Colo., 1944-45; A.B., U. Wash., 1947; M. Internat. Affairs, Columbia, 1949; J.D., George Washington U., 1959. Bar: D.C. 1960, Calif. 1971. Intern Dept. State, 1949-50; fgn. service officer, Germany and Haiti, 1950-55; mem. profl. staff, commerce com. U.S. Senate, 1955-61; spl. asst. to sec. commerce, 1961; dept. dir. U.S. Travel Service, 1961-64, named dir., 1965; practiced in, Santa Ana, Calif., 1971—; asst. dean Western State U. Coll. Law, Fullerton, Calif., 1974-78. Mem. Calif. Democratic State Central Com., 1971-74; Dem. nominee U.S. Rep., 1972. Served as ensign USNR, 1945-46. Named Nat. Salesman of Year, 1968. Mem. Am. Bar Assn., Pacific Area Travel Assn. (pres. 1966-67), Internat. Union Ofcl. Travel Orgns. (v.p. 1967-68). Home: 1646 Irvine Ave Newport Beach CA 92660

BLACK, JOSEPH, transportation company executive; b. Plainfield, N.J., Feb. 8, 1924; s. Joseph and Martha (Watkins) B.; children: Joseph Frank, Martha Jo. B.S., Morgan State Coll., 1950; postgrad., Stonn Hall U., summer 1958, Rutgers U., 1959; D.H.D. hon., Shalo Coll. at Detroit, 1974, LL.D., Central State U., Xenia, Ohio, 1977; Litt. Dr., Miles Coll. Birmingham, Ala., 1981; D. Pub. Works, Morgan State U., 1983. Player Balt. Elite Giants, 1944-50, Bklyn. Dodgers, 1951-55, Cin. Reds, 1955-56; tchr. Plainfield Bd. Edn., N.J., 1957-62; exec. with Greyhound Corp., 1962—. Author: Ain't Nobody Better Than You, 1983; syndicated columnist: By The Way, 1969—. Trustee Jackie Robinson Found., 1976—, Miles Coll., 1978—. Named Rookie of Yr. Nat. League Profl. Baseball, 1952; named to N.J. Sports Hall of Fame, 1972, Morgan State Coll. Sports Hall of Fame, 1972. Mem. Nat. Assn. Market Developers (pres. 1967-68, chmn. bd. 1968-69). Presbyterian. Home: 3215 E Mescal Phoenix AZ 85028 Office: Greyhound Corp Greyhound Tower Phoenix AZ 85077

BLACK, JOSEPH BURTON, JR., university dean; b. Princeton, Ind., Mar. 7, 1924; s. Joseph Burton and Gladys E. (Ferree) B.; m. Sue Stone, Nov. 15, 1944; children: Joseph Burton, William Meriweather, James Douglas. A.A., Kemper Mil. Sch., Boonville, Mo., 1942; B.S., Ind. U., 1947, M.B.A., 1956, D.B.A., 1965. Mgr. Black Lumber Co., Bloomington, Ind., 1946-55; mem. faculty Ind. U., Bloomington, 1955-60; assoc. prof. fin. Miami U., Oxford, Ohio, 1960-66; prof. fin., dean Wright State U., Dayton, Ohio, 1966-69; pres. Kemper Mil. Sch. and Coll., Boonville, 1969-73; dean Coll. Bus. Ball State U., Muncie, Ind., 1973—; chmn. exec. com. Black Lumber Co., Inc., 1968—. Co-author nat. econ. and social plan for El Salvador, 1965-69. Mem. Bloomington City Council, 1948-52; bd. dirs. Muncie Transp. System, 1981—; charter mem. Ind. Inst. New Bus. Ventures, Indpls., 1983—. Served to 1st lt. U.S. Army, 1942-46; PTO; to capt. U.S. Army, 1950-51; to col. U.S. Army, 1969-73; col. Res. and Mo. N.G., 1946-66, 69-73; ret. Mem. Beta Gamma Sigma (chpt. pres. 1978-79), Alpha Kappa Psi, Delta Pi Epsilon, Sigma Iota Epsilon, Gamma Iota Sigma. Democrat. Lodges: Rotary; Masons; Elks. Office: College of Business Ball State U Muncie IN 47306 *One alone can do so little. Many together can do so much. This is teamwork and it works if one will but remember that credit and praise are not diminished by sharing with others. Leadership is best when offered by example.*

BLACK, KAREN, actress; b. Park Ridge, Ill., July 1, 1942; d. Norman A. and Elsie (Reif) Zeigler; m. Charles Black (div.),; Robert Burton (div.; 1974); m. L. Minor Carson, July 4, 1975; 1 son, Hunter. Ed., Northwestern U.; studied with, Lee Strasberg. Appeared on Broadway in: The Playroom, 1965, Keep it in the Family, 1968; films include A Gunfight, 1961, You're A Big Boy Now, 1967, Hard Contract, 1969, Easy Rider, 1969, Five Easy Pieces, 1970, Portnoy's Complaint, 1972, Rhinoceros, 1974, The Outfit, 1974, The Great Gatsby, 1974, The Day of the Locust, 1975, Nashville, 1975, Family Plot, 1976, Crime and Passion, 1976, Burnt Offerings, 1976, Capricorn One, 1978, In Praise of Older Women, 1979, Killer Fish, 1979, The Last Word, 1979, Valentine, 1979, Miss Right, 1980; TV film The Strange Possession of Mrs. Oliver, 1977; others. Recipient N.Y. Film Critics award for best supporting actress, 1970 *

BLACK, KENNETH, JR., univ. dean; b. Norfolk, Va., Jan. 30, 1925; s. Kenneth and Virginia (Wolf) B.; m. Mabel Folger, Sept. 20, 1948; children—Kenneth III, Kathryn Anne. A.B., U. N.C., 1948, M.S., 1951; Ph.D., U. Pa., 1953. Partner Colonial Ins. Agy., Chapel Hill, N.C., 1948-50; instr. U. Pa., 1952-53; chmn. ins. dept. Ga. State U., 1953-69, regents' prof. ins., 1959—; dean Coll. Bus. Adminstrn., 1969—; pres., dir. gen. Internat. Ins. Seminars, Inc., 1977—; dir. N.Am. Reins. Corp., N.Am. Reassurance Co., N.Y.C., USLIFE Corp., Cousins Properties, Inc., Computone Systems, Inc., Haverty Furniture Cos., Atlanta, Paul Manners Assos. Author: (with Russell) Human Behavior and Life Insurance, 1963, Human Behavior and Property and Liability Insurance, 1964, (with Keir and Surrey) Cases in Life Insurance, 1965, (with Huebner and Cline) Property and Liability Insurance, 1968, 3d edit., 1982, (with Huebner) Life Insurance, 10th edit., 1982, (with Russell) Human Behavior in Business, 1972, Understanding and Influencing Human Behavior, 1981; Editor: Jour. Am. Soc. C.L.U.'s, 1959—; ins. series for Prentice Hall, Inc, 1959—. Vice chmn. Pres.'s Commn. R.R. Retirement, 1971-73; trustee Village of St. Joseph, 1969-80; exec. dir., trustee Ednl. Found., Inc., 1969—. Served with USNR, 1944-46. Mem. Am. Risk and Ins. Assn. (pres. 1964), Phi Beta Kappa, Beta Gamma Sigma, Omicron Delta Kappa, Alpha Kappa Psi. Roman Catholic. Home: 1762 Nancy Creek Bluff NW Atlanta GA 30327

BLACK, KENT MARCH, electronics company executive; b. Carrollton, Ill., Oct. 25, 1939; s. Kenneth Wilbur and Alta Jane (March) B.; m. Karen Anne Jones, Aug. 5, 1960; children: Elizabeth Anne, Nancy Jane. B.S.E.E., U. Ill., 1962. With Rockwell Internat., 1962—, various engring. mgmt. positions, Cedar Rapids, Iowa, 1962-72, program dir. satellite communications systems Govt. Telecommunications div., 1972-76, v.p., gen. mgr. Collins Telecom Systems div., Dallas, 1976-78, pres. Electronic Systems Group, Anaheim, Calif., 1978-80; exec. v.p. def. electronic ops. Reckwell Internat., Anaheim, Calif., 1980-81; corp. v.p., pres. comml. electronics ops. Rockwell Internat., Dallas, 1981—; dir. InterFirst Bank Galleria, N.A. Bd. dirs. United Way of Met. Dallas, 1982, Dallas County Community Coll. Dist. Found., Inc., Assn. for Higher Edn.; mem. exec. bd. Circle Ten council Boy Scouts Am.; mem. devel. bd. U. Tex.-Dallas, Dallas Citizens Council; chmn. 1982-84 U.S. Savs. Bond Campaign, Dallas. Mem. Nat. Mgmt. Assn. (Silver Knight of Mgmt. award 1980), Young Pres. Orgn. Office: 1200 N Alma Rd Richardson TX 75081

BLACK, LEONARD J., retail store chain exec.; b. Bethlehem, Pa., Apr. 26, 1919; s. Morris and Reba I. (Perlman) B.; m. Betty Glosser, June 21, 1942; children—Susan Eiseman, Jodie Lichtenstein. B.S., U. Pa., 1941. With Glosser Bros., Inc., Johnstown, Pa., 1946—, merchandise mgr. ready to wear, 1954-59, exec. v.p. stores and supermarkets, 1959-69, pres., chief exec. officer, 1969—; v.p. Johnstown Savs. Bank. Bd. dirs. Conemargh Valley Meml. Hosp.; bd. dirs. Greater Johnstown Com. Served to lt. comdr. USNR, 1940-46. Mem. Nat. Mass Retailing Inst. (dir.). Republican. Jewish. Clubs: Sunnehanne Country, High Ridge Country. Home: 2207 Spear Ave Johnstown PA 15905

BLACK, LOIS MAE, psychologist, educator; b. Boston, Nov. 16, 1931; d. Lester and Lillian (Porter) B.; m. John Henning, June 23, 1956 (div. 1977); children: Paul, John, Thomas, Michael; m. Karl Barth, July 31, 1982. B.A., Brown U., 1953; M.A., Yale U., 1955; Ph.D., Cornell U., 1962. Diplomate: lic psychologist, N.Y. Lectr. Rutgers U., New Brunswick, N.J., 1960-62; asst. prof. SUNY, Cortland, 1963-64, Syracuse (N.Y.) U., 1967-68; assoc. prof. Onondaga Community Coll., Syracuse, 1971-74; research assoc. SUNY Coll. Medicine, Syracuse, 1965-78; research assoc. prof. psychology and edn., Syracuse U., 1978—; dir. affirmative action Syracuse U., 1974-82. Contbr. articles to profl. jours. Vestry mem. Grace Episcopal Ch., 1968-70; bd. dirs. Upstate Day Care Ctr., 1968-77, Central N.Y. council Girl Scouts U.S.A., 1981—; co-chmn. council on women's issues United Way, Central N.Y., 1981-83. Fulbright scholar, 1953-54; USPHS fellow, 1959-60; HEW grantee, 1977-80. Mem. Am. Psychol. Assn., Eastern Psychol. Assn., Soc. Research in Child Devel., Sigma Xi. Home: 311 Berkely Dr Syracuse NY 13210

BLACK, MALCOLM CHARLES LAMONT, stage director; b. Liverpool, Eng., May 13, 1928; s. Kenneth and Althea Joan (Berger) B.; children: Duncan, Trevor. Student English schs. Adminstr. Am. Shakespeare Festival Acad., 1959-61; artistic dir. Playhouse Theatre Co., Vancouver, B.C., Can., 1964-67; prof. theatre U. Wash., 1968-70, Queens Coll. of City U. N.Y., 1970-74, York U., Toronto, 1974—; dir. numerous profl. prodns. Author: From First Reading to First Night, 1975. Served to 2d lt. Brit. Army, 1946-48. Recipient Can. Drama award, 1967; Silver Jubilee medal, 1978. Office: Theatre NB PO Box 566 Fredericton NB E3B 5A6 Canada *I believe God puts everybody on this earth with potential and in some cases with specific gifts; it is our responsibility to lead our lives working to our maximum potential. I do not consider the acquisition of wealth to be the reason to be on this earth but I see no virtue in poverty for its own sake. As a man I have to look at myself in the shaving mirror each day; therefore, it is important to be looking at a person who has nothing to hide. I accept with reluctance that I will continue to fail frequently, but I am thankful that I have had some successes.*

BLACK, MAX, philosophy educator; b. Baku, Russia, Feb. 24, 1909; came to U.S., 1940, naturalized, 1948; s. Lionel and Sophia (Divinska) B.; m. Michal Landsberg, Aug. 21, 1933; children: Susan Naomi, Jonathan. B.A., Queens Coll., U. Cambridge, 1930; student, U. Göttingen, 1930-31; Ph.D., U. London, 1939, D.Lit., 1955. Lectr., tutor U. London Inst. Edn., 1936-40; prof. philosophy U. Ill., 1940-46, Cornell U., 1946, Susan Linn Sage prof. philosophy and humane letters, 1954-77; prof. emeritus Cornell, 1977—; chmn. program for Andrew D. White profs.-at-large, 1965-78; dir. Soc. for Humanities, 1965-70; sr. mem. program Sci. Tech. and Soc., 1971—; vis. prof. U. Washington, 1951-52; vis. mem. Princeton Inst. Advanced Study, 1970-71; vis. fellow St. John's Coll., Oxford and Clare Hall, Cambridge, 1978; Tarner lectr. Trinity Coll., Cambridge, Eng., 1978. Author: (with others) Philosophical Studies, 1948, Science and Civilization, 1949, Language and Philosophy, 1949, The Nature of Mathematics, 1950, Critical Thinking, rev. edit., 1952, Translations from the Philosophical Writings of Gottlob Frege, (with P. T. Geach), 1952, Problems of Analysis, 1954, Models and Metaphors, 1962, A Companion to Wittgenstein's Tractatus, 1964, The Labyrinth of Language, 1968, Margins of Precision, 1970, Caveats and Critiques, 1975, The Prevalence of Humbug and Other Essays, 1983; Editor: Philos. Rev, 1946—, Philosophical Analysis, 1950, The Social Theories of Talcott Parsons, 1961, The Importance of Language, 1962, Philosophy in America, 1965, The Morality of Scholarship, 1967, Problems of Choice and Decision, 1975. Guggenheim fellow, 1950-51. Fellow Am. Acad. Arts and Scis.; mem. Am. Philos. Assn. (pres. 1958), Aristotelian Soc., Internat. Inst. Philosophy (v.p. 1970, pres. 1981-84). Home: 408 Highland Rd Ithaca NY 14850

BLACK, NEAL FRANCIS, trade association executive; b. Preston, Iowa, Jan. 14, 1928; s. Edwin B. and Gertrude (Mertens) B.; m. Margaret Gerlach, Jan. 22, 1951; children—Rebecca Ann, John Joseph, Angela Mary, Patrick Neal. B.A., State U. Iowa, 1949. With Waterloo (Iowa) Daily Courier, 1949-57, farm editor, 1953-57; mng. editor Nat. Hog Farmer, St. Paul, 1957-72, editor, 1973-79; pres. Livestock Conservation Inst., South St. Paul, 1980—. Mem. Met. Aircraft Sound Abatement Council, Mpls.-St. Paul, 1969-71; vice chmn. Dakota County (Minn.) Republican Com., 1969-71, chmn., 1971-73. Served with AUS, 1950-52. Mem. Am. Agrl. Editors Assn., Nat. Pork Industry Conf. (sec. 1961-74), Livestock Conservation Inst. (chmn. nat. hog cholera eradication com. 1968-78, chmn. emergency diseases com. 1978-79, chmn. bd. 1975-77), U.S. Animal Health Assn. (vice chmn. animal welfare com. 1982—). Home: 2825 Vilas Ln Saint

Paul MN 55121 Office: 239 Livestock Exchange Bldg South Saint Paul MN 55075

BLACK, NORMAN WILLIAM, judge; b. Houston, Dec. 6, 1931; s. Dave and Minnie (Nathan) B.; m. Berne Rose Efron, Feb. 21, 1959; children: Elizabeth Ann, Diane Rebecca. B.B.A., U. Tex., Austin, 1953, J.D. (Frank Bobbitt scholar 1954), 1955. Bar: Tex. 1955. Law clk. to Houston judge, 1956, asst. U.S. atty., Houston, 1956-58, pvt. practice, 1958-76, U.S. magistrate, 1976-79; U.S. dist. judge So. Dist. Tex., Houston, 1979—; adj. prof. South Tex. Coll. Law. Served with AUS, 1955-56. Mem. Fed. Bar Assn., State Bar Tex., Houston Bar Assn., Houston Philos. Soc. Office: 515 Rusk Ave Suite 10501 Houston TX 77002

BLACK, PATRICIA CARR, museum dir.; b. Sumner, Miss., May 18, 1934; d. Samuel Bismarck and Velma Lewis (Carnathan) Carr; (div.)1 dau., Elizabeth Lewis. B.A., Miss. U. Women, 1955; M.A., Emory U., 1968. Successively librarian, research asst., spl. projects dir. Miss. Dept. Archives and History, 1967-67; catalog and art reference librarian Met. Mus. Art, N.Y.C., 1968-69; research librarian Time, Inc., 1969-70; curator exhibits Miss. State Hist. Mus., Jackson, 1971-75, dir., 1976—; dir. archives and library Miss. Dept. Archives and History, 1975-76; panelist museums program Nat. Endowment Humanities, 1976—; nat. adv. bd. Center Study So. Culture, U. Miss., 1978—; adv. bd. Center So. Folklore, Memphis, 1974—; condr. workshops, cons. in field. Compiler, editor catalogs. Founder, bd. dirs. New State Theatre, Jackson, 1965—; Fellow Nat. Endowment Humanities, 1975. Mem. Am. Assn. State and Local History (chmn. awards com. 1980—), Am. Assn. Museums, Miss. Hist. Soc. (award merit 1980), Miss. Folklore Soc., Miss. Art Mus. Assn. Democrat. Home: 1157 Quinn St Jackson MS 39202 Office: Box 571 Jackson MS 39205

BLACK, PETER, oil company executive, artist; b. Boston, Sept. 4, 1918; s. Percy Gamble and Doris (Taylor) B.; m. Caroline Sears Warren, Feb. 3, 1945; children: Sylvia, Caroline, William Murray. B.S., Harvard, 1942. Vice pres. Harold Cabot and Co., Boston, 1945-51; asst. to dir. Office Devel. Moblzn., 1951-53; v.p. Freeport Sulphur Co., N.Y.C., 1953—; pres., dir. subsidiary Sul-Sulphur Export Corp., 1958-61, Freeport Internat. Inc., 1961-64, Internat. Mktg. & Investment Corp., 1964-65, Delta Mktg. and Shipping Corp., 1965-73; v.p., dir. Sulpetro of Can., Ltd., 1965-74; dir. Freeport McMoran Inc. One-man exhbns., Dayton (Ohio) Art Inst., 1955, Witte Meml. Mus., San Antonio, 1957, Empire Studio, New Canaan, Conn., 1959, Rive Gauche Gallery, Darien, Conn., 1961, Acad. Arts, Easton, Md., 1978, Darien Library Gallery. Chmn. bd. govs. Chesapeake Bay Maritime Museum.; adv. trustee Peabody Mus. Salem. Served to lt. comdr. USNR, 1942-45. Mem. Nature Conservancy (chmn. chpt.). Clubs: N.Y. Yacht, Cruising of Am., Chesapeake Bay Yacht. Home: Southerly Royal Oak MD 21662

BLACK, RALPH, performing arts executive; b. Knoxville, Tenn., July 11, 1919; s. Ernest Watson and Margaret Marie (Caston) B.; m. Eva Landsberger, Aug. 1, 1950; children—Johana, Eric, Ralph II, Dean. Student, Houghton Coll., 1937-41. Gen. mgr. Chattanooga Symphony, 1950-51, Buffalo Philharmonic, 1951-55, Nat. Symphony, Washington, 1955-60, Balt. Symphony, 1960-63, Nat. Ballet, Washington, 1963-73; v.p. Am. Symphony Orch. League, Vienna, Va., 1955-59, exec. dir., 1973—; gen. dir. Shenandoah Valley Music Festival, Woodstock, Va., 1974-78. Author: The Best of Black Notes, 1983. Recipient Louis Sudler award for disting. service to orch. mgmt., 1982. Mem. Assn. Am. Dance Cos. (founding chmn.), Am. Arts Alliance (dir. Washington), Nat. Music Council (dir. N.Y.C.). Club: Congl. Country (Bethesda, Md.). Office: 633 E St NW Washington DC 20004

BLACK, RICHARD BRUCE, office machinery and computer company executive; b. Dallas, July 25, 1933; s. James Ernest and Minerva Iantha (Braden) B.; m. Marieluise; children: Kathryn Braden, Paula Anne, Erica Lynn. B.S. in Engring, Tex. A.&M. U., 1954; M.B.A., Harvard U., 1958; postgrad., Northwestern U., 1960-62. With Vulcan Materials Co., Birmingham, Ala., 1958-62; v.p. fin. Warner Electric Brake & Clutch Co., Beloit, Wis., 1962-67, now dir.; pres. automotive group, exec. v.p. corp. Maremont Corp., Chgo., 1967-70, pres. corp., chief operating officer, 1970-72, pres., chmn., chief exec. officer, 1973-76, chmn., 1976-79; pres., chief exec. officer, dir. Alusuisse of Am., Inc., N.Y.C., 1978-81; chmn., chief exec. officer, dir. AM Internat., Inc., Chgo., 1981-82; chmn. Master Software, Inc., Myrtle Beach, S.C., 1982, ECRM, Boston, 1982—, Data Mgmt., Inc., Wyo., 1982—, IXION Inc., Seattle, 1983—, R. Black & Assocs.; dir. Chung Telecommunications, Verticom Inc., Gabelli Group Inc., Summit Software Tech. Inc., Microtech. Services Inc.; lectr. econs. Beloit Coll., 1964-67. Author: (with Jack Pierson) Linear Polyethylene-Propylene: Problems and Opportunities, 1958. Trustee Beloit Coll. Served to 1st lt. USAF, 1954-56; PTO. Mem. Am. Alpine Club. Clubs: University, Mid-Am. (Chgo.). Home: PO Box 208 Moose WY 83012

BLACK, ROBERT COLEMAN, lawyer; b. Greenville, Ala., July 3, 1934; s. James Monroe and Mabel (Coleman) B.; m. Carolyn Musselwhite, Dec. 20, 1960; children: Elizabeth Anne, Robert C., Carolyn Jane. B.S. in Commerce and Bus. Adminstrn, U. Ala., 1960, LL.B., 1961. Bar: Ala. 1961. Law clk. to justice Ala. Supreme Ct., 1961-62; partner firm Hill, Hill, Carter, Flanco, Cole & Black, Montgomery, Ala., 1968—, spl. asst. atty. gen. Ala., 1969-79; judge Circuit Ct., 1979—; prof. law Jones Law Sch., Montgomery; instr. bus. law U. Ala. at Montgomery, Auburn U.; lectr. continuing legal edn. Ala. Bar Assn.; faculty Ala. Jud. Coll. City chmn. March of Dimes, 1966; Bd. dirs. March of Dimes Found., 1966—, Montgomery YMCA, St. James Parrish Sch.; trustee Ala. Indsl. Sch. Served with USMCR, 1954-57. Mem. ABA, Ala. Bar Assn., Montgomery County Bar Assn. (chmn. exec. com. 1969-70, pres. 1971), Phi Delta Phi, Beta Gamma Sigma. Office: Hill Bldg Montgomery AL 36101

BLACK, ROBERT FREDERICK, former oil company executive; b. Mansfield, Ohio, Jan. 9, 1920; s. Judson Ammi and Pauline (Remy) B.; m. Conita Fay McCoslin, June 25, 1944; children: Ronald Gregory, Peggy Lynn. Student, Miami U., Oxford, Ohio, 1946-47. Asst. mgr. Warner Bros. Theatres, Mansfield, 1935-42; asst. treas. Red Arrow Freight Lines, Inc., Houston, 1947-56; controller, sec. Cactus Petroleum Inc., Houston, 1956-62; project controller Del E. Webb Corp., Clear Lake City, Tex., 1962-65; treas. Mitchell Energy & Devel. Corp., The Woodlands, Tex., 1965-82; dir. Treacy, Caron Systems, Inc., 1983—. Served with USAAF, 1942-46; CBI. Decorated Bronze Star. Mem. Fin. Execs. Inst. (past dir. Houston), Nat. Corp. Cash Mgmt. Assn. Republican. Lodge: Masons. Home: 138 Masters Dr Conroe TX 77304

BLACK, ROBERT LINCOLN, pediatrician; b. Los Angeles, Aug. 25, 1930; s. Harold Alfred and Kathryn (Stone) B.; m. Jean Wilmott McGuire, June 27, 1953; children: Donald J., Douglas L., Margaret S. A.B., Stanford U., 1952, M.D., 1955. Diplomate: Am. Bd. Pediatrics. Intern Kings County Hosp., Bklyn., 1955-58; resident and fellow Stanford U. Hosp., 1958-62; practice medicine specializing in pediatrics, Monterey, Calif., 1962—; Clin. prof. Stanford U., 1962—; cons. Calif. Dept. Health, Sacramento, 1962—. Author: (with others) California Health Plan for Children, 1979. Bd. dirs. Lyceum of Monterey Peninsula, 1963—; mem. Monterey Peninsula Unified Sch., 1965-73, pres., 1968-70; mem. Mid-Coast Health System Agy., Salinas, Calif., 1975-80, pres., Salinas, Calif., 1979-80; bd. dirs. Carmel Bach Festival, Calif., 1972-81. Fellow Am. Acad. Pediatrics; mem. Calif. Med. Assn., Monterey County Med. Soc., Inst. Medicine Nat. Acad. Sci. Democrat. Home: 976 Mesa Rd Monterey CA 93940 Office: 920 Cass St Monterey CA 93940

BLACK, ROBERT PERRY, banker; b. Hickman, Ky., Dec. 21, 1927; s. Burwell Perry and Veola (Moore) B.; m. Mary Rives Ogilvie, Oct. 27, 1951; children: Patty Rives, Robert Perry. B.A., U. Va., 1950, M.A., 1951, Ph.D., 1955. Part-time instr. U. Va., 1953-54; research assoc. Fed. Res. Bank, Richmond, Va., 1954-55, assoc. economist, 1956-58, economist, 1958-60, asst. v.p., 1960-62, v.p., 1962-68, 1st v.p., 1968-73, pres., 1973—; asst. prof. U. Tenn., 1955-56; lectr. U. Va., 1956-57; mem. Gov.'s Adv. Bd. Revenue Estimates, 1976—. Contbr. articles to profl. jours. Mem. adv. bd. Central Richmond Assn.; trustee Collegiate Schs., past chmn.; adv. council Robert E. Lee council Boy Scouts Am., 1977-78; trustee Richmond Eye Hosp., Richmond Meml. Hosp.; past pres. United Way Greater Richmond; bd. dirs., mem. exec. com., chmn. fin. com. Downtown Devel. Unltd.; chmn. adv. com. Ctr. Banking Edn., Va. Union U., 1977-79; bd. dirs., mem. fin. and audit com. Blue Cross-Blue Shield Va., 1983—; trustee E. Angus Powell Endowment for Am. Enterprise, 1980—. Served with AUS, 1946-47. Recipient George Washington Honor medal award Freedoms Found. Valley Forge, 1978. Mem. Am. Econ. Assn., Am. Fin. Assn., Richmond Soc. Fin. Analysts, Am. Inst. Banking, Raven Soc., Phi Beta Kappa (past pres. chpt.), Beta Gamma Sigma, Alpha Kappa Psi, Kappa Alpha. Methodist. Clubs: Country of Virginia (Richmond) (dir. 1980—, v.p., chmn. fin. com. 1981-83); Country of Virginia (Richmond) (pres. 1983—). Home: 10 Dahlgren Rd Richmond VA 23233 Office: Fed Res Bank 701 E Byrd St Richmond VA 23219

BLACK, ROGER ANTRIM, elec. mfg. co. exec.; b. Mansfield, Ohio, July 29, 1905; s. Frank B. and Jessie (Baxter) B.; m. Elizabeth Thomas, Nov. 6, 1931; children—Frank T., R. Gordon, David B., Edith T. Black Humphrey. A.B., Princeton U., 1927. With consular service Dept. State, 1927-30, serving as vice consul, Brisbane, Australia, 1928-30; with Ohio Brass Co., Mansfield, 1930—, beginning as salesman, successively mgr. fgn. trade, gen. factory mgr., v.p., 1930-56, pres., 1956-67, chmn. bd., 1967—; dir. Bank One of Mansfield. Mem. IEEE, Nat. Elec. Mfrs. Assn. Clubs: Union (Cleve.); Princeton (N.Y.C.); Westbrook Country, Rotary (Mansfield). Home: 955 Marion Ave Mansfield OH 44906

BLACK, SAMUEL HAROLD, microbiology and immunology educator; b. Lebanon, Pa., May 1, 1930; s. Harold William and Beatrice Irene (Steckbeck) B.; m. Elisabeth Martha Zandveid, Aug. 16, 1961; children: Vicki Ann, Alisa Jo. Student, Hershey Jr. Coll., 1948-50; B.S., Lebanon Valley Coll., 1952; postgrad., U. Pa., 1952-54; M.S., U. Mich., 1958, Ph.D., 1961. NSF fellow Tech. U. Delft (Netherlands), 1960-61; instr. U. Mich., Ann Arbor, 1961-62; asst. prof. Baylor Coll. Medicine, Houston, 1962-67, assoc. prof., 1967-71, Mich. State U., East Lansing, 1971-73, prof., 1973-75; prof., head dept. med. microbiology and immunology Tex. A&M U., College Station, 1975—; lectr. U. Houston, 1964-66; vis. prof. Swiss Fed. Inst. Tech., Zurich, 1969-70. Served with M.C. U.S. Army, 1954-56. Recipient Alumni Assn. Citation Lebanon Valley Coll., 1981. Fellow Am. Acad. Microbiology; mem. Am. Soc. Microbiology, Am. Soc. Cell Biology, Soc. Gen. Microbiology, Electron Microscope Soc. Am., Soc. Invertabrate Pathology. Home: 1205 King Arthur Circle College Station TX 77840 Office: Dept Med Microbiology and Immunology Coll Medicine Tex A&M U College Station TX 77843

BLACK, SAMUEL PAUL WEST, educator; b. Barbourville, Ky., Dec. 19, 1916; s. Read Postlethwaite and Louise (West) B.; m. Betty Lohman, Dec. 23, 1944; children—Susan Postlethwaite, John Sheldon, Nancy Read, Samuel Paul West. B.S., Yale U., 1940; M.D., Johns Hopkins U., 1943. House officer gen. surgery New Haven Hosp., 1944-47; resident neurol. surgery Yale U., New Haven, 1948-50, instr. neurosurgery, 1950-52, asst. prof., 1952-55; prof. neurosurgery U. Mo., Columbia, 1955—. Contbr. articles to profl. jours. Served with USNR, 1944-46. George H. Knight fellow Yale U., 1947-48. Mem. New Eng. Neurosurg. Soc. (exec. com. 1953-55), Am. Assn. Neurol. Surgeons, A.C.S., Assn. Research in Nervous and Mental Disease, So. Neurosurgical Soc., Mo. Med. Soc., Mo. Neurosurg. Soc. (pres. 1980-81), Sigma Xi. Clubs: Austrian Mountain, Pithotomy; Rotary (Columbia) (pres. 1981-82). Home: 300 S Glenwood St Columbia MO 65201

BLACK, SHIRLEY SHARP, oil company executive; b. Springer Station, Tenn., Nov. 19, 1937; d. Allen W. and Lucy Mae (Hartsfield) Hill; m. James H. Black, Jr., Feb. 28, 1970; children: (by previous marriage) David Allan, Star Maenette Black. B.A. in B.A., U. Va., 1958; postgrad., Bates Sch. Law, 1976. Paralegal Royston, Rayzor, Cook & Vickery, Galveston, Tex., 1964-74; asst. sec. Oceaneering Internat., Inc., Houston, 1974-78; corporate sec. Coral Petroleum Inc., Houston, 1978—, United Refining Co., Warren, Pa., 1978—, Coral Petroleum Devel., Inc., Houston, 1978—; dir. Kakawa Petroleum, Inc., Houston, 1978—. Asst. treas. Coral Petroleum Polit. Action Com., Houston, 1982-83, United Refining Polit. Action Com., Pa., 1982-83. Republican. Baptist. Home: 14136 Misty Meadow Ln Houston TX 77079 Office: PO Box 19666 Houston TX 77024

BLACK, SHIRLEY TEMPLE (MRS. CHARLES A. BLACK), former ambassador, former actress; b. Santa Monica, Calif., Apr. 23, 1928; d. George Francis and Gertrude Temple; m. John Agar, Jr., Sept. 19, 1945 (div. 1949); 1 dau., Linda Susan; m. Charles A. Black, Dec. 16, 1950; children: Charles Alden, Lori Alden. Ed. under pvt. tutelage; grad., Westlake Sch. Girls, 1945. Rep. to 24th Gen. Assembly of UN, 1969-70; U.S. ambassador to, Ghana, 1974-76; chief of protocol White House, 1976-77; mem. U.S. Delegation on African Refugee Problems, Geneva, 1981; mem. public adv. com. UN Conf. on Law of the Sea; dep. chmn. U.S. del. UN Conf. on Human Environment, Stockholm, 1970-72; spl. asst. to chmn. Pres.'s Council on Environ. Quality, 1972-74; del. treaty on environment USSR-USA Joint Commn., Moscow, 1972; mem. U.S. Commn. for UNESCO, from 1973. Began film career at age 3 1/2; played leading roles from the start: first full-length film was Stand Up and Cheer; made pictures for, Paramount Studios and, Twentieth Century-Fox Film Corp., including, Little Miss Marker, Baby Take a Bow, Bright Eyes, Our Little Girl, The Little Colonel, Curly Top, The Littlest Rebel, Captain January, Poor Little Rich Girl, Dimples, Stowaway, Wee Willie Winkie, Heidi, Rebecca of Sunnybrook Farm, Little Miss Broadway, Just Around the Corner, The Little Princess, Susannah of the Mounties, The Blue Bird, Kathleen, Miss Annie Rooney, Since You Went Away, Kiss and Tell, 1945, That Hagen Girl, War Party, The Bachelor and the Bobby-Soxer, Honeymoon, 1947; narrator, actress: TV series Shirley Temple Storybook, NBC, 1958, Shirley Temple Show, NBC, 1960. Dir. Bank of Calif., Fireman's Fund Ins. Co., BANCAL Tri-State Corp., Del Monte Corp.; Mem. Calif. Adv. Hosp. Council, 1969, San Francisco Health Facilities Planning Assn., 1965-69; Republican candidate for U.S. Ho. of Reps. from Calif., 1967; bd. dirs. Nat. Wildlife Fedn., Nat. Multiple Sclerosis Soc., UN Assn. U.S.A.; bd. dirs. exec. com. Internat. Fedn. Multiple Sclerosis Socs. Appointed col. on staff of Gov. Ross of Idaho, 1935; commd. col. Hawaiian N.G.; hon. col. 108th Reg. N.G. Ill.; dame Order Knights Malta, Paris, 1968; recipient Ceres medal FAO, Rome, 1975, numerous other state decorations. Mem. World Affairs Council No. Calif. (dir.), Council Fgn. Relations, Nat. Com. for U.S./China Relations. Club: Commonwealth of Calif. Address: 115 Lakeview Dr Woodside CA 94062 *

BLACK, SUSAN HARRELL, judge; b. Valdosta, Ga., Oct. 20, 1943; d. William H. and Ruth Elizabeth (Phillips) Harrell; m. Louis Eckert Black, Dec. 28, 1966. B.A., Fla. State U., 1964; J.D., U. Fla., 1967. Bar: Fla. 1967. Asst. state atty. 4th Jud. Circuit Fla.; asst. gen. counsel City of Jacksonville, Fla.; judge County Ct. of Duval County, Fla.; judge 4th Jud. Circuit Ct. of Fla.; U.S. dist. judge Middle Dist. Fla., Jacksonville, 1979—; former mem. faculty Nat. Jud. Coll., Reno. Mem. adv. bd., former trustee Jacksonville Hosp. Ednl. Program; mem. Jacksonville Council Citizen Involvement; trustee Law Sch. U. Fla. Mem. Am. Bar Assn., Fla. Bar Assn., Jacksonville Bar Assn., Conf. Circuit Judges (former chmn. edn. com., dean New Judges Coll.). Episcopalian. Office: 311 W Monroe St Jacksonville FL 32202

BLACK, THEODORE MICHAEL, publisher, consultant; b. Bklyn., Oct. 3, 1919; s. Walter Joseph and Elsie (Jantzer) B.; m. Barbara A. Somerville, Nov. 10, 1956; children: Walter Joseph II, Theodore Michael Black; stepchildren: Mrs. Beverly A. Pavlak, Mrs. Dorothy B. Scharkopf. A.B. summa cum laude, Princeton U., 1941; grad., Inf. Officers Candidate Sch., Ft. Benning, Ga., 1943; Litt.D. honoris causa, Siena Coll., Loudonville, N.Y., 1971; LL.D. (hon.), Adelphi U., Garden City, N.Y., 1974, Fordham U., 1978, Pd.D., Hofstra U., Hempstead, N.Y., 1974, D.C.L., Molloy Coll., Rockville Centre, N.Y., 1975, L.H.D., C.W. Post Center, L.I. U., Greenvale, N.Y., 1976, Pace U., 1978. With Walter J. Black, Inc., 1945—, v.p., 1952-58, pres., 1958—, treas., 1958-80, chief exec. officer, 1980—; gen. partner Black's Readers Service Co., 1949-58, pres., 1958-68; pres. The Classics Club, Detective Book Club, Zane Grey Library; trustee Roslyn Savs. Bank, 1973—; dir. Harcourt Brace Jovanovich, Inc. Author: Know Your Stamps, 1934, Democratic Party Publicity in the 1940 Campaign, 1941, How to Organize and Run a Citizens' Committee for Your Candidate, 1964, Straight Talk about American Education, 1982. Alumni pres. Class of 1941 Princeton, 1968-73; area chmn. Mercy Hosp. Ball Com., 1966; chmn. county fund drive Nassau Heart Assn., 1967; mem. Nassau-Suffolk com. USO, 1972; staff publicity div. Democratic Nat. Com., 1940; exec. dir. Citizens for Nixon-Lodge, Nassau County, N.Y., 1960; chmn. Citizens for Congressman S.B. Derounian, 1962-64; del. 1967 Constl. Conv.; mem. Port Washington Rep. Club; chmn. Seldin for Congress, 1968; mem. minority research staff N.Y. State Assembly, 1968; dir. Fair Campaign Practices Com., 1971; del. Rep. Nat. Conv., 1980; mem. North Hempstead Bd. Ethics, Fed. Adv. Panel on Financing Elem. and Secondary Edn., 1979-83; chmn. Congressional Club, 1980; exec. com. Alumni Council, Princeton, 1950-63; mem. N.Y. State Bd. Regents, 1969-80, vice chancellor, 1974, chancellor, 1975-80. Served from pvt. to capt., CIC AUS, 1941-45; lt. col. Army Res. ret., 1967. Decorated Bronze Star with cluster (U.S.) Belgian, French Fourragère; recipient medal SAR; Humanitarian award Am. Jewish Com., 1976; John Jay Higher Edn. Public Policy award, 1980; Disting. Service award Nassau-Suffolk Sch. Bds. Assn., 1973; award Poly. Inst. N.Y., 1974, L.I. Assn. Spl. Edn. Adminstrs., 1975; Man of Yr. award L.I. Advt. Club, 1975; Citizen of Yr. award N.Y. State Soc. Profl. Engrs., 1980; St. John Neumann award, Buffalo, 1980. Mem. Better Bus. Bur. L.I., M.I. Res. Soc. (chmn. res. affairs 1956-59, pres. 1961-62), Res. Officers Assn. U.S., Assn. U.S. Army, Nat. CIC Assn., 3d Armored Div. Assn., Am. Legion, Phi Beta Kappa. Republican. Roman Catholic. Clubs: Elk, Lion., Port Washington (N.Y.) Yacht; Capitol Hill (Washington); L.I. Advt.; Publishers/ Lunch (N.Y.C.). Home: 8 Terrace Dr Port Washington NY 11050 Office: 1075 Northern Blvd Flower Hill Roslyn NY 11576

BLACK, THOMPSON, JR., educator; b. Barwick-upon-Tweek, Eng., Sept. 20, 1909; came to U.S., 1913, naturalized, 1919; s. Thompson and Agnes (Percy) B.; m. Katherine Anntoinette Becker, June 16, 1935; children—Robert Thompson, Virginia, Ruth Ann, Bruce Richard. B.S., U.S. Naval Acad., 1933; M.A., U. Cal. at Los Angeles, 1949, Ph.D., 1954. Commd. ensign U.S. Navy, 1933, advanced through grades to comdr., 1944; asst. prof. naval sci. U. Notre Dame, 1941-43; injured during Anzio campaign, 1944; asso. prof. naval sci. U. Calif. at Los Angeles, 1944-45; exec. officer Naval ROTC, 1945-46; ret., 1947; teaching fellow U. Calif. at Los Angeles, 1948-49; faculty Calif. State Coll. at Los Angeles, 1949—, prof. polit. sci., 1959-67, prof. govt., 1967-74, emeritus, 1974—; chmn. dept. govt., 1955-61, chmn. div. social scis., 1961-64, acting dean letters and sci., 1964, coordinator social scis., 1965-73, dir. coll. found., 1951-66. Chmn. Joint Coll. Fed. Service Council, 1959-60. Decorated Purple Heart. Mem. Assn. Calif. State Coll. Profs. (sec. 1958-61), Am. Soc. Legal History (chmn. Pacific Coast br. 1960), So. Calif. Polit Sci. Assn. (chmn. 1959), Los Angeles World Affairs Council, Calif. Employees Assn., U.S. Naval Inst., Blue Key, Pi Sigma Alpha, Phi Delta Kappa. Home: 2557 Northshore Ln Westlake Village CA 91361

BLACK, WALTER EVAN, JR., judge; b. Balt., July 7, 1926; s. Walter Evan and Margaret Luttrell (Rice) B.; m. Catharine Schall Foster, June 30, 1951; children: Walter Evan III, Charles Foster, James Rider. A.B. magna cum laude, Harvard U., 1947, LL.B., 1949. Bar: Md. 1949. Assoc. Hinkley & Singley, Balt., 1949-53, ptnr., 1957-67; asst. U.S. atty. Dist. Md., Balt., 1953-55, U.S. atty., 1956-57; ptnr. Clapp, Somerville, Black & Honemann, Balt., 1968-82; U.S. dist. judge Dist. Md., Balt., 1982—; Sec.-treas. Parkwood Cemetery Co., Balt., 1967-82; also dir.; sec. So. Mech. Inc., Balt., 1971-82; also dir.; pres. Charles T. Brandt Inc., Balt., 1972-82; also dir. Chmn. Bd. Municipal and Zoning Appeals, Balt., 1963-67; mem. Jail Bd., Balt., 1971-73, Atty. Grievance Commn., 1978-82, Rev. Bd., 1975-78, chmn., 1975-76; mem. Gov.'s Commn. to Revise Annotated Code, 1975-82. Alt. Md. del. Republican Nat. Conv., 1960; chmn. Rep. City Com., Balt., 1962-66; Md. del. Rep. Nat. Conv., 1964; Bd. dirs. Balt. Urban League, 1963-69, 76-82; bd. dirs. Union Meml. Hosp., Hosp. for Consumptives of Md. Mem. Bar Assn. Balt. City, ABA, Md. Bar Assn., Rule Day Club, Lawyers' Round Table. Baptist. Clubs: Speaker's, Harvard-Radcliffe of Md. Office: US Dist Ct 141 W Lombard St Baltimore MD 21201

BLACK, WILLIAM A., electric utility company executive; b. Blackenridge, Pa., 1924; married. B.S., MIT, 1949, M.S. in Elec. Engring., 1950, 1962. With Ohio Power Co., 1950-78; exec. v.p. Ind. & Mich. Electric Co., Ft. Wayne, Ind., 1978-80, pres., chief operating officer, dir., 1980—; dir. Am. Elec. Power Service Corp., Inc.-Ky. Elec. Corp.; v.p., dir. various subs Am. Elec. Power Co. Inc. Served with USMCR, World War II. Office: Ind & Mich Electric Co Inc 2101 Spy Run Ave Fort Wayne IN 46801 *

BLACK, WILLIAM HEATH, investment banker; b. Atlanta, Feb. 23, 1931; s. Eugene Robert and Susette (Heath) B.; m. Nancy C. Cowles, June 19, 1953; children: William Heath, Abigail Black Exter, Daniel Pierce. B.A., Yale U., 1954. With Morgan Stanley & Co., Inc., N.Y.C., 1957—; mng. dir. Morgan Stanley & Co. Inc., N.Y.C., 1967—; mem. mgmt. com. Morgan Stanley & Co.,Inc., N.Y.C., 1974—; chmn. Morgan Stanley Internat. Inc., 1981—; investment officer Internat. Bank for Reconstrn. and Devel., 1963-65; mem. internat. adv. bd. Creditanstalt Bankverein, Vienna, Austria, 1983—. Bd. dirs., mem. exec. com. Nat. Park Found., Washington, 1981—; mem. adv. council Columbia U. Grad. Sch. Bus., N.Y.C., 1980—. Clubs: Meadow; Nat. Golf Links Am. (Southampton, N.Y.) (bd. dirs.); Shinnecock Hills Golf, River, University, Blind Brook, Heights Casino. Office: Morgan Stanley & Co Inc 1251 Ave of Americas New York NY 10020

BLACKADAR, ALFRED KIMBALL, educator, meteorologist; b. Newburyport, Mass., July 6, 1920; s. Walter Lloyd and Harriett (White) B.; m. Beatrice J. Fenner, Mar. 23, 1946; children: Bruce Evan, Russell Lloyd, Thomas Alan. A.B., Princeton U., 1942; Ph.D., N.Y. U., 1950. From instr. to asso. prof. N.Y. U., 1946-56; lectr. climatology Columbia U., 1953-55; mem. faculty Pa. State U., 1956—, prof. meteorology, 1961—, head dept. meteorology, 1967-81; bd. dirs. Univ. Corp. Atmospheric Research, 1962-68, mem. exec. com., 1965-68; mem. exec. com. div. earth scis. NRC, 1966-69. Editor: Meteorological Research Revs, 1957; exec. editor: Weatherwise. Sec. Univ. Christian Assn., 1964-68. Served to maj. USAAF, 1942-46. Recipient Sr. Scientist award Alexander von Humboldt Found., 1973. Fellow A.A.A.S., Am. Meteorol. Soc. (sec. 1965-69, pres. 1971-72, editor monographs 1962-65, chmn. publs. commn. 1978—), Am. Geophys. Union; fgn. mem. Deutsche Meteorologische Gesellschaft. Baptist. Home: 805 W Foster Ave State College PA 16801 Office: Walker Bldg University Park PA 16802

BLACKALL, ERIC ALBERT, language educator; b. London, Oct. 19, 1914; U.S., 1958, naturalized, 1965; s. Frederick and Lillie (Stanger) B.; m. Jean Hargrave Frantz, June 25, 1960; 1 son, Roger Nicholas. Student, Latymer Upper Sch., London; B.A., Gonville and Caius Coll., Cambridge (Eng.) U., 1936, M.A., 1940; Litt. D., Cambridge U., 1960; Ph.D., U. Vienna, Austria, 1938. Lectr. English lang. and lit. U. Bâle, Switzerland, 1938-39; lectr. German Cambridge U., 1939-58; vis. prof. German lit. Cornell U., 1957-58, chmn. dept. German lit., 1958-65, Avalon Found. prof. in humanities, 1965-67, Schurman prof. German lit., 1967—; dir. Soc. for the Humanities, 1981—; vis. prof. U. Heidelberg, Germany, 1968. Author: Adalbert Stifter, 1948, The Emergence of German as a Literary Language, 1959, 2d edit., 1978, Die Entwicklung des Deutschen zur Literatursprache, 1966, Goethe and the Novel, 1976, The Novels of the German Romantics, 1983; articles, revs. German studies. Decorated Cross Honor for Sci. and Art 1st class, Austria, 1973; recipient J.G. Robertson prize in German Studies U. London, 1962; Guggenheim fellow, 1965-66. Fellow Am. Acad. Arts and Scis.; mem. Am. Philos. Soc., Modern Lang. Assn., English Goethe Soc., Am. Assn. Tchrs. German, AAUP, Phi Beta Kappa. Home: 811 Triphammer Rd Ithaca NY 14850 Office: Dept German Lit Cornell U Ithaca NY 14853

BLACKBURN, CHARLES LEE, oil company executive; b. Cushing, Okla., Jan. 9, 1928; s. Samuel and Lillian (Beall) B.; m. Jo Ann Benito, Aug. 20, 1950; children—Kern A., Alan J. B.S. in Engring. Physics, U. Okla., 1952. With Shell Oil Co., 1952—, exploration and prodn. budget coordinator, N.Y.C., 1966-67, New Orleans, 1967-68, gen. mgr. onshore div., 1968-70, v.p. So. region, 1970-73, v.p., gen. mgr. transp. and supplies, Houston, 1973-76, exec. v.p. exploration and prodn., 1976—, also dir.; dir. Anderson, Clayton & Co. Chmn. bd. dirs. WYES-TV, New Orleans, 1972-73; v.p. New Orleans Symphony Soc., 1973. Served with U.S. Army, 1946-48; Korea. Mem. Am. Petroleum Inst. (dir.), Nat. Ocean Industries Assn. (dir.), Soc. Petroleum Engrs., Mid-Continent Oil and Gas Assn., U.S. C. of C. (energy com.), Tau Beta Pi, Sigma Tau. Methodist. Clubs: Houston Country, Coronado. Office: PO Box 2463 Houston TX 77001

BLACKBURN, DOUGLAS BRYAN, government official; b. N.Y.C., Nov. 20, 1918; s. Charles Henry and May Elizabeth (Scofield) B.; m. Frances T. Coleman, May 12, 1943; children: Dolores May, Doreen, Douglas Bryan. B.S. in Adminstrv. Engring., Cornell U., 1939. Registered profl. engr., N.J., N.Y., 13 other states. Field engr. Ethyl Corp., Detroit, 1939-42; asst. mgr. Hormiguero (sugar mill), Las Villas, Cuba, 1946-51; engr. Ford, Bacon & Davis, Inc., N.Y.C., 1951-64, So. P.R. Sugar Co., 1964-65; sr. engr., then v.p. Ford, Bacon & Davis, Inc., 1965-72, pres., 1972-73, chmn. bd., chief exec. officer, 1973-82; dir. Mblzn. Concepts Devel. Ctr., Nat. Def. U., Ft. McNair, Washington, 1982—; dir. Trident Engring. Assos., Stratford Graham Engring. Corp. Served to lt. USNR, 1942-46. Mem. ASME, Am. Mgmt. Assn., Am. Arbitration Assn., Nat. Def. Trans. Assn. (chmn.), Nat., La., Cornell U. socs. profl. engrs., Tau Beta Pi, Pi Kappa Alpha. Republican. Episcopalian. Clubs: Lake Mohawk Country, Lake Mohawk Golf (Sparta); City Midday, University (N.Y.C.); Army Navy Country (Washington); Mariner Sands Country (Stuart, Fla.). Home: 34 S Shore Trail Sparta NJ 07871 1200 N Nash St Arlington VA 22209

BLACKBURN, HENRY WEBSTER, JR., physician; b. Miami, Fla., Mar. 22, 1925; s. Henry Webster and Mary Frances (Smith) B.; m. Nelly Paula Trocme, Jan. 10, 1951; children—John Keith, Katherine Ann, Heidi Elizabeth. Student, Fla. So. Coll., Lakeland, 1942-43; B.S., U. Miami, 1947; M.D., Tulane U., 1948; M.S., U. Minn., 1957. Intern Chgo. Wesley Meml. Hosp., 1948-49; resident in medicine Am. Hosp. Paris, 1949-50; med. officer in charge USPHS, Salzburg, Austria, and; Munich, W. Ger., 1950-53; med. fellow U. Minn., Mpls., 1953-56; research asso. Lab. Physiol. Hygiene, 1956-58; asso. med. dir. Mut. Service Ins. Co., St. Paul, 1956-58; asst. prof. physiol. hygiene U. Minn., 1958-61, asso. prof., 1961-68, prof., 1968—; lectr. medicine, 1956—; dir. lab. physiol. hygiene Sch. Pub. Health, prof. medicine, 1972—; vis. prof. U. Geneva, 1970; cons. in field. Author: Cardiovascular Survey Methods, 1968; Mem. editorial bd.: Jour. Chronic Diseases; contbr. articles to profl. pubs. Adv. bd. Life Ins. Md. Research Fund, 1960-63; bd. mgrs. med. sect. Am. Life Conv.; bd. dirs. Minn. Jazz Sponsors, Inc. Served to lt. (j.g.) USNR, 1942-50. Recipient Thomas Francis award in epidemiology, 1975; Naylor Dana award in preventive medicine, 1976; Louis Bishop award in cardiology, 1979. Fellow Am. Coll. Cardiology, Am. Epidemiol. Soc., Am. Pub. Health Assn.; mem. Belgian Royal Acad. Medicine, Am., Ramsey County med. assns., Am. Heart Assn. (dir. 1971—), Internat. Soc. Cardiology (council epidemiology 1964—), Internat. Epidemiol. Soc., Alpha Omega Alpha., Phi Kappa Phi. Home: 1715 Knox Ave S Minneapolis MN 55403

BLACKBURN, JACK BAILEY, educator; b. Sterling, Okla., Oct. 19, 1922; s. Raymond Wasden and Vonnie Irene (Bailey) B.; m. Janice Ann Keller, Sept. 2, 1949; children—Judith Ann Blackburn Cameron, Jo Ann. B.S., Okla. U., 1947; M.S., Purdue U., 1949, Ph.D., 1955. Grad. asst., research asst., research engr. Joint Hwy. Research Project Purdue U., 1947-55; asso. prof. civil engring., asso. dir. Md. Hwy. Research Program, U. Md., 1955-58; transp. planning engr. Harland Bartholomew and Assos., St. Louis, then Memphis, 1958-60; prof. civil engring., dir. Ariz. Transp. and Traffic Inst., U. Ariz., Tucson, 1960-63; prof., head civil engring. dept. Kans. State U., Manhattan, 1963-72; prof. engring. Ariz. State U., 1972—; Mem. Nat. Acad. Sci./Nat. Acad. Engring. bldg. research adv. bd., 1968-71. Served with AUS, 1943-46. Mem. ASTM (chmn. subcom. on evaluation of data of C-9 com. on concrete 1956-58), Engrs. Council Profl. Devel. (ad hoc visitors list 1964-69), ASCE (chmn. publs. com., urban planning and devel. div. 1971-75, chmn. com. on career guidance 1972-75), Manhattan C. of C. (dir. 1968-71), Nat. Soc. Profl. Engrs. (exec. bd. engrs. in edn. practice sect. 1968-71, sec. 1971—, chmn. 1972-73), Am. Arbitration Assn. Home: 4343 N 84th Pl Scottsdale AZ 85251

BLACKBURN, JOHN OLIVER, economist, consultant; b. Miami, Fla., Sept. 13, 1929; s. Elmer E. and Proxie (Hughes) B.; m. Jeanne Elise Miles, Nov. 29, 1957; children: Katherine Elise, John Parkinson, David Laurence. A.B., Duke U., 1951; postgrad., U. Miami, Fla., 1951-52; Ph.D., U. Fla., 1959. C.P.A., Fla. Asst. prof. econs. Duke U., 1959-61, 62-63, asso. prof., 1963-68, prof. econs., 1968-81, provost, 1970-71, chancellor, 1971-76; asst. prof. bus. adminstrn. Am. U., Beirut, 1961-62; vis. prof. Davidson Coll., 1983. Bd. dirs. Fla. Conservation Found.; chmn. Fla. Solar Coalition; mem. adv. bd. Fla. Solar Energy Ctr. Served with USNR, 1952-55. Mem. Am., So. econs. assns., Phi Beta Kappa, Chi Phi. Democrat. Mem. United Ch. of Christ. Home: 221 Shell Point Rd E Maitland FL 32751

BLACKBURN, JOSEPH EARL, telephone company executive; b. Lynchburg, Va., Sept. 23, 1920; s. Joseph Angus and Mary Estelle (Joynson) B.; m. Anne Reynolds, Mar. 23, 1944; children: Joseph, James, Martha, Katherine. B.A., Lynchburg Coll., 1941; LL.B., Washington and Lee U., 1948. Bar: Va. 1948. Atty. William Robertson Sackett & Blackburn, Lynchburg, 1948-57; gen. atty. Chesapeake & Potomac Telephone Co. of Va., Richmond, 1957-74, v.p., dir., 1983—; v.p. Chesapeake & Potomac Telephone Cos., Washington, 1974-83; dir. Souran Bank, Richmond. Mem. Va. Ho. of Dels., 1954-58. Served to capt. USAF, 1941-45; PTO. John W. Davis scholar Washington and Lee U., 1948. Mem. Va. Bar Assn., Phi Beta Kappa, Omicron Delta Kappa. Presbyterian. Clubs: Congl. (Bethesda, Md.); Country; Commonwealth (Richmond). Home: 9021 Norwick Rd Richmond VA 23229 Office: Chesapeake & Potomac Telephone Co Va 703 E Grace St Richmond VA 23229

BLACKBURN, RICHARD WALLACE, lawyer; b. Detroit, Apr. 21, 1942; s. Wallace Manders and E. Jean (Beetham) B.; m. Dede Frances Reid, Aug. 29, 1964; children: David Thomas, Jeffrey Manders, Megan Louise. Student, Baldwin-Wallace Coll., 1960-62; A.B., Mich. State U., 1964; J.D., George Washington U., 1967. Labor atty. Chesapeake & Potomac Telephone Co., Washington, 1967-70, gen. corp. atty., Richmond, Va., 1970-74; regulatory atty. AT&T, N.Y.C., 1974-76; gen. atty. New Eng. Telephone Co., Boston, 1976-81, v.p., gen. counsel, 1981—. Chmn. Bd. Zoning Appeals, Concord, Mass. Mem. Fed. Communications Bar Assn., Am. Bar Assn., Newcomen Soc. N.Am., Boston Bar Assn. Republican. Episcopalian. Office: 185 Franklin St Boston MA 02107

BLACKBURN, ROBERT MCGRADY, bishop; b. Bartow, Fla., Sept. 12, 1919; s. Charles Fred and Effie Frances (Forsythe) B.; m. Mary Jeanne Everett, Nov. 16, 1943 (dec. May 1977); children: Jeanne Marie (Mrs. Ramon Cox), Robert M., Frances Lucille; m. Jewell Haddock, Sept. 9, 1978. B.A., Fla. So. Coll., 1941; M.Div., Emory U., 1943, LL.D., 1973; D.D. (hon.), LaGrange Coll., 1961. Ordained to ministry Methodist Ch., 1943; pastor United Methodist Ch., Boca Grande, Fla., 1943-44; asso. pastor First Methodist Ch., Orlando, Fla., 1946-48, Mt. Dora, Fla., 1948-53, DeLand, Fla., 1953-60, Jacksonville, Fla., 1960-68, sr. pastor, Orlando, 1968-72; bishop United Methodist Ch., Raleigh, N.C., 1972-80, Va. Conf., 1980—; Mem. program council United Methodist Ch., 1963-72; del. to Meth. Gen. Confs., 1968, 70, 72. Trustee Emory U., Randolph-Macon Coll., Randolph-Macon Woman's Coll., Randolph-Macon Acad., Va. Wesleyan, Shenandoah Coll. and Conservatory of Music, Ferrum Coll., Wesley Sem. Served as chaplain U.S. Army, 1944-46. Home: 10610 Baypines Ln Richmond VA 23233 Office: 4016 W Broad St Richmond VA 23230

BLACKBURN, THOMAS HAROLD, educator; b. Englewood, N.J., May 28, 1932; s. Harold L. and Alice A. (Benton) B.; m. Ann Sharon Leigh, June 15, 1963; children: Adam Leigh, Benton. B.A., Amherst Coll., 1954, Jesus Coll., Oxford U., 1956, M.A., 1961; Ph.D., Stanford, 1963. Instr. Swarthmore (Pa.) Coll., 1961-63, asst. prof., 1963-68, asso. prof., 1968-75, prof. English lit., 1975—, dean, 1975-81; vis. lectr. Bryn Mawr Coll., 1964; vis. tutor St. Edmund Hall, Oxford, 1971. Contbr. articles to profl. jours. Am. Council Learned Socs. fellow, 1965. Mem. Modern Lang. Assn., Milton Soc. Am., Renaissance Soc., Assn. Am. Rhodes Scholars (editorial bd. American Oxonian), Phi Beta Kappa. Home: 609 Elm Ave Swarthmore PA 19081

BLACKBURN, WILLIAM MARTIN, lawyer; b. Shreveport, La., Feb. 17, 1939; s. William M. and Prudence B. (Courtney) B.; m. Patricia Ebaugh, Nov. 24, 1973; children—Victoria Ann, Patricia Lynn, Thomas Merriam. B.A., Tex. Tech. U., Lubbock, 1961; LL.B. with honors, U. Tex., 1964. Bar: Tex. bar 1966. Since practiced in, Dallas; v.p., gen. counsel Star Drilling Co., Inc., 1975-76; asst. spl. counsel to Pres. Lyndon B. Johnson, 1967-69. Asso. editor: Tex. Law Rev, 1963. Mem.-at-large Dallas City Council, 1976-80, mayor pro tem, 1977-80. Served as 1st lt. AUS, 1964-66; capt. Res. Decorated Army Commendation medal. Mem. Am., Dallas bar assns., State Bar Tex., Chancellors, Order of Coif, Phi Delta Phi, Sigma Alpha Epsilon. Presbyterian. Home: 5439 Neola Dallas TX 75209 Office: 2800 Ore Main Pl Dallas TX 75250

BLACKER, HARRIET, publishing company executive; b. N.Y.C., July 23, 1940; d. Louis and Rebecca (Siegel) B.; m. Roland Algrant, Aug. 6, 1970 (div. Jan. 1981). B.A., U. Mich., 1962. Exec. asst. Nat. Book com., N.Y.C., 1965-67; dir. publicity Hawthorn Books, N.Y.C., 1967-69, Coward-McCann & Geoghegan, 1969-74; exec. dir. publicity Random House, N.Y.C., 1974-79; East Coast v.p. Pickwick Maslancky Koenigsberg, N.Y.C., 1980-81; v.p. pub. relations Putnam Pub. Group, N.Y.C, 1981—. Mem. Publishers Publicity Assn. (sec. 1973-75, treas. 1982-83, pres. 1983-85), Women's Media Group. Home: 310 E 75th St New York NY 10021 Office: Putnam Pub Group 200 Madison Ave New York NY 10016

BLACKFORD, ROBERT NEWTON, lawyer; b. Cin., Feb. 5, 1937; s. Robert Criley and Virginia Pendelton (Yowell) B.; m. Margaret Ann Williams, July 22, 1961; children: William Pendleton, John Whitner. B.S. in Bus. Adminstrn, U. Fla., 1960; J.D., Emory U., 1968. Bar: Fla. 1968, Ga. 1968. Assoc. firm Maguire, Voorhis & Wells, P.A., Orlando, Fla., 1968-72, mem., 1972—; dir. Hughes Supply, Inc., Orlando, 1970—, sec., 1972—. Mem. Orlando Mepl. Planning Bd., 1969-75; Mem. Orlando Downtown Devel. Bd., 1972-77, chmn., 1975-77; trustee Chesley G. Magruder Found., Inc., 1981—, pres., 1982—; trustee Loch Haven Art Center, Orlando, 1980-82. Served with U.S. Army, 1954-56. Mem. ABA, Fla. Bar, State Bar Ga., Orange County Bar Assn., Orlando Area C. of C. (pres. 1980, chmn. bd. dirs. 1981), Orange County Hist. Soc. (dir. 1980-83). Democrat. Presbyterian. Clubs: Country of Orlando; University (Orlando); St. Petersburg Yacht, Rotary (dir. 1980-82). Home: 1811 Lorena Ln Orlando FL 32806 Office: 2 S Orange Ave Orlando FL 32801

BLACKLEDGE, WILLIAM WESLEY, lawyer; b. Wichita, Kans., Dec. 15, 1923; s. Haskell Reginald and Mildred (Hockett) B.; m. Wilma Dean Trotter, Oct. 22, 1966; children—Larry Wesley, David Eugene, Stephen Ed, Celia Dianne, Trent Eugene. LL.B., Oklahoma City U., 1954. Bar: Okla. bar 1954, Tex. bar 1966. Asst. traffic mgr. Oklahoma City C. of C., 1948-58; traffic mgr. Okla. Dept. Commerce and Industry, Oklahoma City, 1958-62; pvt. practice law, Oklahoma City, 1962-64, Lubbock, Tex., 1979—; counsellor Plains Cotton Coop. Assn., Lubbock, Tex., 1964-66, sec., counsellor, 1966-78, Amerasia Internat., Ltd., 1970-76, Am. Cotton Growers, 1975-78; sec. Amcot, Inc., 1972—, A.I.I., Ltd., 1976-78. Served with USAAF, 1942-46. Mem. Am., Okla. bar assns., State Bar Tex., Assn. Traffic Clubs, Delta Nu Alpha. Home: 3908 54th St Lubbock TX 79413 Office: Metro Tower Suite 703 Lubbock TX 79401

BLACKLER, ANTONIE WILLIAM CHARLES, biologist; b. Portsmouth, Eng., Oct. 19, 1931; came to U.S., 1964; s. Leslie Guy and Florence (Harris) B.; m. Rochelle Lois Melkin, Mar. 12, 1970; children—Mia Samantha, Joshua Harris. B.S. in Zoology, U. Coll., London, 1953, Ph.D., 1956. Professeur extraordinaire U. Geneva, Switzerland, 1961-64; prof. zoology Cornell U., Ithaca, N.Y., 1964—. Mem. Internat. Soc. Devel. Biology, Swiss Zool. Soc. Research on origins of sex. Home: 14 Nottingham Dr Ithaca NY 14850 Office: 246 Emerson Hall Cornell Univ Ithaca NY 14853

BLACKLIDGE, RICHARD HENRY, former newspaper pub.; b. Kokomo, Ind., June 7, 1914; s. Kent H. and Bernice (Kautz) B.; m. Marian Reinertsen, Jan. 5, 1938. B.S. in Chem. Engring, Purdue U., 1936. With Kokomo Tribune, 1936—, chief exec. officer, pub., 1938-78; exec. com., dir. Union Bank and Trust Co., Kokomo, 1942—; dir. Pub. Service Ind. Served with USAAF, 1944-45. Mem. Inland Daily Press Assn. (pres. 1960-61), Hoosier Press Assn. (past pres., dir.), Am. Newspaper Pubs. Assn. (dir., pres. 1970-72, chmn.; past v.p. and dir. research inst.), Internat. Fedn. Newspaper Editors and Pubs. (v.p. 1970-76), Am. Legion. Clubs: Elk., Kokomo Country (past pres.). Home: 814 Maplewood Dr Kokomo IN 46901 Office: 300 N Union St Kokomo IN 46901

BLACKLOW, ROBERT STANLEY, physician, medical college administrator; b. Cambridge, Mass., June 24, 1934; s. Leo Alfred and Clara Edna (Cumenes) B.; m. Winifred Young, Dec. 7, 1958; children: Stephen Charles, Kenneth Lawrence, David Alan. A.B. summa cum laude, Harvard U., 1955, M.D. cum laude, 1959. Intern Peter Bent Brigham Hosp., Boston, 1959-60, resident, 1960-61, 63-64, 67-68; instr. Harvard U., 1967-70, asst. prof. medicine, 1970-76, asso. prof., 1976-78, asst. to dean faculty of medicine, 1969-73, asso. dean, 1973-78; prof., dean Rush Med. Coll., 1978—; v.p. for med. affairs Rush-Presbyn.-St. Luke's Med. Center, Chgo., 1978—; mem. sci. adv. com. Nat. Fund for Med. Edn., 1981—. Editor: Signs and Symptoms, 1971, 6th edit., 1983. Trustee Chestnut Hill Sch., Newton, Mass., 1970—, Belmont (Mass.) Hill Sch., 1973—, Chgo. chpt. ARC, 1979; mem. Ill. Health Service Corps Task Force, Ill. Dept. Public Health, 1980; corporator Belmont (Mass.) Hill Sch., 1978—. Served with USPHS, 1961-63. Fellow Inst. Medicine Chgo., ACP, Chgo. Soc. Internal Medicine; mem. N.Y. Acad. Scis., Assn. Am. Med. Colls., AAAS, Harvard Musical Assn., Phi Beta Kappa, Alpha Omega Alpha. Clubs: Longwood Cricket, Badminton and Tennis, Harvard (Boston); Harvard (N.Y.C.); Cliff Dwellers, Harvard (bd. dirs.), Literary (Chgo.)). Home: 248 South Ave Glencoe IL 60022 Office: 1753 W Congress Pkwy Chicago IL 60612

BLACKMAN, KENNETH ROBERT, lawyer; b. Providence, May 19, 1941; s. Edward and Beatrice (Wolf) B.; m. Meryl June Rosenthal, June 7, 1964; children: Michael, Susan, Kevin. A.B., Brown U., 1962; LL.B., Columbia U., 1965, M.B.A., 1965. Bar: N.Y. 1966. Law clk. to U.S. Dist. Judge, 1965-66; ptnr. Fried, Frank, Harris, Shriver & Jacobson, N.Y.C., 1966—. Mem. ABA, N.Y. Bar Assn., Assn. Bar City of N.Y., Phi Beta Kappa, Beta Gamma Sigma. Office: Fried Frank Harris Shriver & Jacobson 1 New York Plaza New York NY 10004

BLACKMAN, VERNON HAROLD, physicist; b. Woodbury, N.J., Nov. 11, 1929; s. Edward Diament and Virginia Mildred (Wiest) B.; m. Lynne Jonina Sabin, Apr. 17, 1976; children: Heather, Jonina, Holly, Cory, Ruan, Daemon. B.A. in Physics with highest honors, Colgate U., 1951; M.A., Princeton U., 1953, Ph.D., 1955. Research scientist Giannini Research Corp., Santa Ana, Calif., 1957-58; exec. v.p. MHD Research, Inc., Newport Beach, Calif., 1959-66; ind. cons., 1967-72; v.p. Systems, Sci. and Software, La Jolla, Calif., 1973-74, pres., 1975—; dir. Optical Radiation Corp., Enpex Corp., Megahans Corp., Giannini Inst., RDI Video Systems, Digivision; exec. com. John and Alice Tyler Ecology/Energy Prize, 1980. Author papers on high-temperature fluid flow. Trustee Redlands (Calif.) U., 1966-75. Mem. Soc. Exploration Geophysicists, Am. Phys. Soc., Am. Chem. Soc., Phi Beta Kappa. Home: 13591 Nogales Dr Del Mar CA 92014

BLACKMAR, CHARLES BLAKEY, state justice; b. Kansas City, Mo., Apr. 19, 1922; s. Charles Maxwell and Eleanor (Blakey) B.; m. Ellen Day Bonnifield, July 18, 1943; children—Charles A., Thomas J., Lucy E. Blackmar Alpaugh, Elizabeth S., George B. A.B. summa cum laude, Princeton U., 1942; J.D., U. Mich., 1948. Bar: Mo. bar 1948. Practiced in, Kansas City; mem. firm Swanson, Midgley, Jones, Blackmar & Eager, and predecessors, 1952-66; professorial lectr. U. Mo. at Kansas City, 1949-58; prof. law St. Louis U., 1966-82, prof. emeritus; judge Supreme Ct. Mo., 1982—; spl. asst. atty. gen. Mo., 1969-77, labor arbitrator.; Chmn. Fair Pub. Accommodations Commn. Kansas City, Mo., 1964-66; mem. Commn. Human Relations Kansas City, 1965-66. Author: (with Volz and others) Missouri Practice, 1953, West's Federal practice Manual, 1957, 71, (with Devitt) Federal Jury Practice and Instructions, 1970, 3d edit., 1977; contbr. numerous articles on probate law to profl. publs. Mem. Jackson County Republican Com., 1952-58, Mo. Rep. Com., 1956-58. Served to 1st lt., inf. AUS, 1943-46. Decorated Silver Star, Purple Heart. Mem. Am. Law Inst., Nat. Acad. Arbitrators, Mo. Bar (spl. lectr. insts.), Disciples Peace Fellowship, Order of Coif, Phi Beta Kappa. Mem. Disciples of Christ Ch. Home: 7305 Maryland Ave Saint Louis MO 63130 Office: Supreme Ct Bldg Jefferson City MO 63101

BLACKMER, DONALD LAURENCE MORTON, polit. scientist; b. Boston, July 6, 1929; s. Alan Rogers and Josephine (Bedford) B.; m. Joan Dexter, Aug. 25, 1951; children—Stephen, Alexander, Katherine. A.B. magna cum laude, Harvard U., 1952, A.M., 1956, Ph.D., 1967. Harvard U. Sheldon traveling fellow, 1952-53; exec. asst. to dir. Center for Internat. Studies, Mass. Inst. Tech., Cambridge, 1956-61, asst. dir., 1961-68, lectr., 1960-61, asst. prof. polit. sci., 1961-67, asso. prof., 1967-73, prof., 1973—; asso. dean Sch. Humanities and Social Sci., 1973-81; dir. Program in Sci., Tech. and Soc., 1977-81, head dept. polit. sci., 1981—; research asso. West European studies Harvard U., 1973—. Author: Unity in Diversity: Italian Communism and the Communist World, 1967, (with Annie Kriegel) The International Role of the Communist Parties of Italy and France, 1975; co-author, editor: (with Max F. Millikan) The Emerging Nations: Their Growth and United States Policy, 1961, (with Sidney Tarrow) Communism in Italy and France, 1975. Served with U.S. Army, 1953-55. Mem. Council on Fgn. Relations, Phi Beta Kappa. Home: 2 King Ln Concord MA 01742 Office: E53-473 Mass Inst Tech: Cambridge MA 02139

BLACKMON, LAWRENCE GEORGE, electronics company executive; b. Orlando, Fla., Aug. 16, 1919; s. William Andrew and Louise Elizabeth (Sherouse) B.; m. Louise Armstrong, June 14, 1941; children: Etta, Mary. B.S., Yale U., 1940. Indsl. engr. Carnegie-Ill. Steel Corp., Sharon, Pa., 1940-44; with Nat. Castings Co. (later Midland Ross Corp.), 1947-68, v.p., gen. mgr. Capitol Foundry div. Nat. Castings div., 1962-68; with Microdot, Inc., Greenwich, Conn., 1968—, exec. v.p., 1972-77, pres., 1977-84, chmn. bd., 1984—, also dir.; dir. Dayton Malleable, Inc. Served to 1st lt. AUS, 1944-46. Mem. Am. Iron and Steel Inst. Clubs: Union League (Chgo.); Yale (N.Y.C.); Wee Burn Country (Darien, Conn.). Office: 23 Old Kings Hwy S Darien CT 06820

BLACKMORE, ROBERT LONG, educator; b. Akron, N.Y., Sept. 13, 1919; s. Perry Norris and Margaret Elizabeth (Long) B.; m. Lucia Belding Wicker, Aug. 5, 1941; children—James Chilton, John Allen. B.A., Colgate U., 1941, M.A., 1961; Ph.D., Syracuse U., 1965. Comml. pilot, 1941; flight comdr. Brit. Commonwealth Air Tng. Plan, Chatham, N.B., Can., 1942; test pilot Glenn L. Martin Co., Balt.,

1943; with Life Mag., N.Y.C., 1945-59, merchandising mgr., 1953-56, Life Books mgr., 1956-59; instr. English Colgate U., 1941, 60-63, asst. prof., 1963-66, asso. prof., 1966-70, prof., 1970—, chmn. English dept., 1972-75, acting dir. Humanities div., 1975-78, provost and dean of faculty, 1979-80; dir. Colgate U. Press, 1964—; editor Powys Newsletter, 1970—; radio broadcaster, jazz and classical radio sta. WRCU, Hamilton, N.Y., 1961—. Author: Advice to a Young Poet, 1969; intros. R.D. Blackmore's Lorna Doone, 1966, Springhaven, 1969, John Cowper Powys's Autobiography, 1967, An Englishman Up-State, 1974; Contbr. articles to lit., music jours. Served to lt. USNR, 1943-45. Mem. Modern Lang. Assn., Phi Beta Kappa, Delta Kappa Epsilon. Home: 21 University Ave Hamilton NY 13346 Office: 304 Lawrence Hall Colgate U Hamilton NY 13346

BLACKMUN, HARRY ANDREW, associate justice U.S. Supreme Court; b. Nashville, Ill., Nov. 12, 1908; s. Corwin Manning and Theo H. (Reuter) B.; m. Dorothy E. Clark, June 21, 1941; children: Nancy Clark, Sally Ann, Susan Manning. B.A. summa cum laude in Math, Harvard U., 1929, LL.B., 1932; numerous hon. degrees. Bar: Minn. 1932. Law clk. for John B. Sanborn; judge 8th circuit U.S. Ct. of Appeals, St. Paul, 1932-33; asso. Dorsey, Colman, Barker, Scott & Barber, Mpls., 1934-38, jr. partner, 1939-42, gen. partner, 1943-50; instr. St. Paul Coll. Law, 1935-41, U. Minn. Law Sch., 1945-47; resident counsel Mayo Clinic, Mayo Assn., Rochester, 1950-59, mem. sect. adminstrn., 1950-59; judge 8th Circuit U.S. Ct. of Appeals, 1959-70; assoc. justice U.S. Supreme Ct., 1970—; faculty Salzburg Seminar in Am. Studies, July 1977; Mem. bd. members Mayo Assn. Rochester, 1953-60; mem. adv. com. on jud. activities Jud. Conf., 1969-79; co-moderator seminar on justice, society and the individual Aspen Inst., 1979—. Contbr. articles to legal, med. jours. Bd. dirs., mem. exec. com. Rochester Meth. Hosp., 1954-70; trustee Hamline Univ., St. Paul, 1964-70, William Mitchell Coll. Law, St. Paul, 1959-74; jud. mem. Nat. Hist. Publs. and Records Commn., 1975-82; participant Franco-Am. Colloquium on Human Rights, Paris, 1979. Mem. Am., Minn., Olmsted County, 3d Jud. Dist. bar assns., Phi Beta Kappa. Office: Supreme Ct US Washington DC 20543

BLACKNER, BOYD ATKINS, architect; b. Salt Lake City, Aug. 29, 1933; s. Lester Armond and Anna (McDonald) B.; m. Elizabeth Ann Castleton, June 4, 1955; children: Catherine Blackner Philpot, David, Elizabeth, Genevieve. B.Arch., U. Utah, 1956, B.F.A., 1956. Registered architect, Fla., Utah, Wyo. Asst. landscape architect Nat. Park Service, Mt. Rainier, Wash., 1956; job capt. Cannon, Smith & Gustavson, Salt Lake City, 1957, Hellmuth, Obata & Kassabaum, St. Louis, 1958-59, Caudill, Rowlett & Scott, Houston, 1959-60; project architect Victor A. Lundy, Sarasota, Fla. and; N.Y.C., 1960-63, pvt. practice architecture, Salt Lake City, 1963—; vis. juror, critic Grad. Sch. Architecture U. Utah, 1977; grad. program dept. landscape architecture and environ. planning Utah State U., 1977; mem. region 8 adv. panel archtl. and engring. services GSA, 1977-78. Editorial adv. bd.: Symposia mag, 1977—; Contbr. articles to mags. Vice chmn. Utah Advanced Gift Heart Fund drive, 1964; co-chmn archtl. div. United Fund drive, 1964; mem. Salt Lake City City Walls Com., 1976-77, Salt Lake City Council for Arts, 1977-78, Utah Gov.'s Adv. Com. Low Income Housing, Utah Rev. Panel Emergency Energy Conservation Programs; adv. bd. Utah Citizens for Arts, Utah Soc. Autistic Children.; mem. dinner exec. com. Nat. Jewish Hosp./Nat. Asthma Center, Denver, 1983. Recipient Danforth Honor award, 1951; also numerous AIA awards including; regional design awards for U. Utah Library Fountain, 1970; Westminster Coll. Fountain Plaza, 1972; Nat. award for Kearns/Daynes/Alley Annex, 1978; Western Mountain Region Hist. award of merit for Daynes/Kearns/Alley Annex, 1977; Am. Assn. Sch. Adminstrs. Exhibit award for Wilson Elementary Sch., Green River, Wyo., 1974; Award merit Producers' Council, Inc., 1978; award Nat. Lincoln Arc Welding Found., 1978; Urban Design award 3d Ann. Program, 1979; others. Fellow AIA (dir. Utah chpt. 1968, 71, sec. chpt. 1972-73, chmn. regional conf. 1974, pres. Utah soc. 1975-76, chmn. jury for Wyo. chpt. design awards program 1974, regional rep. to housing com., Nat. Honor award jury 1979, recorder nat. conv. 1982); Mem. Salt Lake Area C. of C. (land use, fine arts, city walls coms.; v.p. 1980-81, chmn. bd. 1982-83). Clubs: Salt Lake Rotary (treas. 1976-77, pres. 1979-80), Alta, Salt Lake Swim and Tennis, Ft. Douglas-Hidden Valley Country. Home: 1460 Military Way Salt Lake City UT 84103 Office: Kearns Bldg Suite A-400 136 S Main St Salt Lake City UT 84101

BLACKSHEAR, A.T., JR., lawyer; b. Dallas, July 5, 1942; s. A.T. and Janie Louise (Florey) B. B.B.A. cum laude, Baylor U., 1964, J.D., 1968. Bar: Tex. 1968, U.S. Ct. Appeals (5th cir.) 1970, U.S. Tax Ct. 1970; C.P.A., Tex. Acct. Arthur Andersen & Co., Dallas, 1964-66; ptnr. Fulbright & Jaworski, Houston, 1969—. Mem. ABA, State Bar Tex., Houston Bar Assn. Baptist. Clubs: Athletic of Houston, Warwick Post Oak. Office: Fulbright & Jaworski Suite 800 Bank of the SW Bldg Houston TX 77002

BLACKSTOCK, LEROY, lawyer; b. El Reno, Okla., Apr. 19, 1914; s. Herbert Austin and Ethel Mae (Gwin) B.; m. Virginia Lee Lowman, Dec. 29, 1939; children: Craig, Priscilla, Birch, Lore, Trena. Grad., Draughon's Bus. Inst., Tulsa, 1933; LL.B., U. Tulsa, 1938. Bar: Okla. 1938. With Phillips Petroleum Co., Tulsa, 1933-41, asst. credit mgr., 1939-41; practiced in, Tulsa, 1941—; now of counsel firm Blackstock Joyce Pollard Blackstock & Montgomery; dir., gen. counsel Tulsa Homebuilders Assn., 1959-68; dir. Fourth Nat. Bank, Tulsa, 1969-76, Owasso 1st State Bank, Okla., 1967-70; pres. Skelly Stadium Corp., 1964—; pres., trustee Gt. Western Investment Trust; mem. nat. adv. com. Practising Law Inst., 1969—; pres. Jud. Reform Inc., 1966—; lectr. law office mgmt., econs. U. Tulsa Coll. Law, 1970—; chmn. Okla. Council on Jud. Complaints, 1974—; Pres. Tulsa Sci. Center, 1968-73; chmn. Tulsa U. Law Schs. Com., 1960-74, Citizens Adv. Com. County Commrs., 1963-66; pres., bd. dirs. Tulsa County Bar Found., 1962-66; patron Okla. Bar Found., trustee, 1966; mem. Gov.'s Acad. for State Govt., 1966-68; chmn. Okla. Supreme Ct. Bar Com., 1966. Author: Managing Partner Approach, Paper Dolls and Lawyers' Fees. Pres. Tulsa council Camp Fire Girls, 1971-72, Tulsa Baptist Laymen's Corp., 1962-66; Bd. dirs. Tulsa County Mental Health Assn., 1963-70, Tulsa Psychiat. Found., 1964-67; pres. Tulsa County Legal Aid Soc., 1961-62, bd. dirs., 1958-66. Served with USNR, 1943-46. Recipient Disting. Citizens award Okla. Psychol. Assn., 1963; Disting. Alumni award U. Tulsa, 1969, 78, Tulsa U. Coll. Law, 1978; Boss of Year award Tulsa County Assn. Legal Secs., 1978. Fellow Am. Coll. Probate Counsel; mem. ABA (ho. dels. 1965-67, mem. spl. com. on nat. coordination of disciplinary enforcement 1969-72, standing com. profl. discipline 1973-77), Okla. Bar Assn. (bd. govs. 1965-67, pres. 1966), Tulsa County Bar Assn. (pres. 1962, Outstanding Atty. award 1961), World Assn. Lawyers (charter mem.), Tulsa County Hist. Soc. (founding mem.), Photog. Soc. Am., Soc. Amateur Cinematographers, Phi Alpha Delta. Republican. Baptist (chmn. deacons 1962, chmn. bldg. com. 1951—). Clubs: Petroleum (dir. 1974—), Summit.). Home: 7213 S Atlanta Tulsa OK 74136 Office: 515 S Main Mall Tulsa OK 74103

BLACKSTONE, GEORGE ARTHUR, lawyer; b. Hastings, Nebr., Sept. 30, 1922; s. George Blanchard and Grace Ida (Brown) B.; m. Rosemary Homer, June 11, 1955; children: Carl H., Amy G. A.B. with high distinction, U. Nebr., 1949; LL.B. magna cum laude, Harvard U., 1948. Bar: Calif. 1949. Asso. firm McCutchen, Thomas, Matthew, Griffiths & Greene, San Francisco, 1948-53; asst. U.S. atty. City of San Francisco, 1953-55; regional adminstr. SEC, San Francisco, 1955-56, asso. dir. div. corp. fin., Washington, 1956-57; asso. firm Heller, Ehrman, White & McAuliffe, San Francisco, 1957-59, partner, 1960—; instr. law Golden Gate U., 1953-55, 83—; vis. prof. Stanford U. Grad. Sch. Bus., 1979—, Stanford Law Sch., 1980; lectr. in field. Mem. editorial bd.: Harvard Law Review, 1947-48. Served to 1st lt. Signal Corps U.S. Army, 1943-46. Mem. Am. Bar Assn., Am. Law Inst., State Bar Calif., San Francisco Bar Assn. Republican. Club: Bohemian (San Francisco). Home: PO Box 2835 Carmel CA 93921 Office: 44 Montgomery St San Francisco CA 94104

BLACKSTONE, HARRY BOUTON, JR., magician, actor; b. Three Rivers, Mich., June 30, 1934; s. Harry Bouton and Mildred Irene (Phinney) B.; m. Arla Gay Blevins, Oct. 14, 1974; children by previous marriage: Harry Bouton, III, Cynthia C., Adrienne Susan, Tracey Irene. Student, Swarthmore Coll., 1951-53; B.A., U. So. Calif., 1958; M.F.A. (Library of Congress fellow), U. Tex., 1961. Appeared as magician in, Australia, Eng., France, Japan, Spain and throughout, Europe and, Far East, 1952—; also in numerous night clubs, theatres, amusement parks and univs. in U.S., including Harrah's Club, Reno and Lake Tahoe; The Sahara-Tahoe, The Nugget, The Flamingo, Caesar's Palace, The Sahara and, The Tropicana, Las Vegas, Las Vegas Hilton, Orch. Hall, Chgo., Houston Music Hall, Van Wezel Performing Arts Hall, Sarasota, Fla., Papst Theatre, Milw., Seattle Opera House, Kansas City Starlight Theatre, Concord Pavillion, Sea World, Magic Mountain and, Disneyworld, Calif. Inst. Tech., San Diego State U., Ind. U., Fla. State U., others. Also appeared on: TV shows Good Morning, America; television spl. Mandrake, The Magician, Magic, Magic, Magic!, Magical Musical Halloween, Magic!; tech. cons., magic coordinator: spl. film for The Great Houdini's, ABC-TV; host: television spl. The Magic Show, BBC; gen. mgr. nat. touring cos. of: Hair; assoc. producer: Smothers Bros. Comedy Hour, CBS, 1969-70; gen. mgr. West Coast cos.: Hair, 1970-72; producer star magic extravaganza at, Harrah's Club, Lake Tahoe, 1971; appeared in: Hocus Pocus at, Fremont Hotel, Las Vegas, 1972; Author: There's One Born Every Minute, 1976; Designer, builder magical effects for ski shows at, Sea World of, Ohio and, Sea World of, Fla. Served with U.S. Army Security Agy., 1953-56. Recipient Star of Magic award, 1979; named U.S. Bicentennial Magician, 1976. Mem. Acad. Magical Arts and Scis. (Magician of Yr. 1979, 82), Internat. Brotherhood Magicians, Soc. Am. Magicians. Episcopalian. Office: care David Belenzon Mgmt Box 15428 San Diego CA 92115 *

BLACKSTONE, HENRY, electrical engineering company executive; b. American Falls, Idaho, Aug. 2, 1915; s. Henry A. and Lena Marie (Walder) B. B.S., Mass. Inst. Tech., 1937, M.S., 1938. Test engr. Gen. Electric Co., 1936; jr. engr. San Diego Gas & Electric, 1938; mem. Hillyer & Blackstone, consultants, 1939-44; dir. electromech. engring. Fairchild Camera & Instrument Co., 1944-46; pres., chmn. bd. Servo Corp. Am., Hicksville, N.Y., 1946—; dir. L.I. Comml. Rev., Plainview, N.Y., Ry. Systems Suppliers, Inc., chmn., 1979-81; mem. guided missile div. NDRC, 1943-46; mem. U.S. Senatorial Bus. Adv. Bd.; Adminstrv. vice chmn. SBA, 1953-67. Trustee Adelphi Coll.; mem. governing bd. Ry. Progress Inst. Mem. IEEE, Inst. Nav. (charter mem.), Chief Execs. Forum, The Conf. Bd., World Bus. Council. Office: 111 New South Rd Hicksville NY 11802

BLACKTON, CHARLES S(TUART), history educator; b. N.Y.C., Oct. 27, 1913; s. James Stuart and Paula Hunt (Hilburn) B.; m. Mary Jane Forri, Aug. 16, 1938 (dec. Aug. 1975); children: John Stuart, Susan Porri Blackton Tallman; m. Margaret Rosalind Hando (Baroness Delacourt-Smith), Dec. 21, 1978. B.A., UCLA, 1936, M.A., 1937, Ph.D, 1939. Teaching fellow UCLA, 1937-39; asst. prof. Adams State Coll., Colo., 1939-42; from instr. to asst. prof. history Colgate U., Hamilton, N.Y., 1946-57, prof., 1957-74, Russell Colgate prof., 1974-82, Russell Colgate prof. emeritus, 1982—, dir. social scis. div., 1961-70; mem. nat. selection com. Inst. Internat. Edn., 1954-56, chmn. India, Australia and Japan coms., 1956-58, mem. selection com. for Australia, 1983; cons., referee Nat. Endowment for the Humanities, 1975-81. Contbr. articles to profl. jours. Served as lt. USNR, 1943-46. Recipient award in Pacific History Am. Hist. Soc., 1940; grantee Social Sci. Research Council, 1951; Fulbright grantee, 1952-53; Fulbright lectr., 1963-64; vis. fellow U. Sri Lanka, 1971, 74, 78. Mem. AAUP, Assn. Asian Studies, Assn. Brit. Studies. Clubs: Army and Navy (Washington); Hamilton. Home: Hantana Farm PO Box 267 Hamilton NY 13346

BLACKWELL, CECIL, assn. exec.; b. Enterprise, Miss., Oct. 29, 1924; s. George Dewey and Neely (Baggett) B.; m. Louise McLendon, May 27, 1944; children—Cecil Carl, Donna Lynn, Gregory Dale. B.S., Miss. State U., 1951; M.S., U. Md., 1955; postgrad., U. Ark., 1953-54. Asst. horticulturist Truck Crops Br. Expt. Sta., Crystal Springs, Miss., 1951; research asst. U. Md., College Park, 1951-52; instr., jr. horticulturist U. Ark., 1952-54; extension horticulturist U. Ga., 1954-56, head extension hort. dept., 1956-59; hort. editor Progressive Farmer, Birmingham, Ala., 1959-65; exec. dir. Am. Soc. Hort. Sci.; pub. Jour. Am. Soc. Hort. Sci. and HortScience, St. Joseph, Mich., 1965-74, Mt. Vernon, Va., 1974-79, ALexandria, Va., 1979—. Author: (with L.A. Niven) Garden Book for the South, 1961. Served with USAAF, 1944-46. Decorated Air medal.; Gen. Edn. Bd. fellow Rockefeller Found., 1951-52. Fellow Am. Soc. Hort. Sci.; mem. Internat., Am. socs. hort. sci., Am. Inst. Biol. Scis., AAAS, Royal Hort. Soc. (hon.), Alpha Zeta. Mem. Ch. of God. Home: 5408 Glenallen St Springfield VA 22151 Office: 701 N Saint Asaph St Alexandria VA 22314 *My parents imparted to me self-confidence, and instilled in me an insatiable hunger for learning and an abiding love and respect for my fellowman and for God. To whatever degree my life and my career have been a success, it has been motivated by a compelling desire to be of service to mankind and to be a creative, productive, useful member of society.*

BLACKWELL, DAVID JEFFERSON, insurance company executive; b. Towson, Md., Mar. 17, 1927; s. Jefferson Davis and Salome Lucille (Love) B.; m. Joan Lou Mumma, June 16, 1949; children—David Jefferson, Robert Allen. Student, U. Minn., 1944, Yale U., 1945; B.A., Haverford Coll., 1949. Asso. dir. Prudential Ins. Co., Newark, Mpls., 1949-67; exec. dir. Ednl. Testing Service, Princeton, N.J., 1967-70; 2d v.p. Mass. Mut. Life Ins. Co., Springfield, 1970-71, v.p., 1971-76, sr. v.p., 1976-81, exec. v.p., 1981—; treas., chmn. mgmt. advisory com. Amdahl Users Group, 1977; instr. ins. U. Minn., 1958-64. Mem. exec. bd. Pioneer Valley council Boy Scouts Am., 1970-75; v.p. Springfield Theatre Arts Assn., 1974-79; trustee Bay Path Jr. Coll., 1974-81. Served with U.S. Army, 1944-46. Mem. Assn. for Computer Machinery, Coll. Life Underwriters, Research Bd., Life Ins. Systems Planning Execs. Republican. Congregationalist. Clubs: Longmeadow Country, Colony. (bd. govs.); Woodstock Country (Vt.)). Home: 132 Rugby Rd Longmeadow MA 01106 Office: 1295 State St Springfield MA 01111

BLACKWELL, EARL, publisher, author; b. Atlanta, May 3, 1913; s. Samuel Earl and Carrie (Lagomarsino) B. Student, Culver Mil. Acad., 1928; A.B., Oglethorpe U., 1933, Columbia U. Co-founder, Celebrity Service Inc. (offices N.Y.C., London, Paris, Rome, Hollywood), pres., 1939—; owner, pub. Celebrity Bull., Theatrical Calendar, Contact Book; pub., co-editor Celebrity Register; contbg. editor Town & Country mag., N.Y.C., 1964—, now editorial cons.; pres. Celebrity Register, Ltd., 1957—, Embassy Found., Inc., 1958-67; radio commentator Celebrity Table, 1955-56; founder, v.p. Doubles Club, N.Y.C.; lectr. on celebrities, 1963—. Author: play Aries is Rising, 1939; novels Crystal Clear, 1978, Skyrocket, 1980; contbr. articles on celebrities to mags. Producer Pres. Kennedy's Birthday Celebration, Madison Sq. Garden, 1962; Founder, pres. Nine O'Clocks of N.Y.; dir. Mayor N.Y.C. Com. for Scholastic Achievement, 1957-65; bd. dirs. Soldiers, Sailors, Airmen's Club, N.Y.C.; organizer, pres. Theater Hall of Fame; organizer Salute to Israel's 25th Anniversary. Decorated Knight of Malta. Mem. Pi Kappa Phi, The Boar's Head. Republican. Roman Catholic. Clubs: N.Y. Athletic (N.Y.C.); Tamboo (Bahamas). Office: 171 W 57th St New York NY 10019 *

BLACKWELL, HENRY BARLOW, II, lawyer; b. Salem, Ill., Feb. 15, 1928; s. Carl G. and Goldie Blanche (Hill) B.; m. Nancy Neckers, June 21, 1952; children: Nancy Anne, James Stokely, Thomas Barlow. B.S., U. Ill., 1952; J.D., Ind. U., 1956. Bar: Ind. 1956, U.S. Supreme Ct. 1961. Asst. auditor Mchts. Nat. Bank, Indpls., 1952-53; indsl. engr., personnel rep., atty. Eli Lilly & Co., 1953-62; atty., asst. sec. Eli Lilly Internat. Corp., 1962-70, sec., asst. gen. counsel, 1970-77, sec., gen. counsel, 1977—. Dir. Indpls. Indians, Inc., baseball team, 1967—, chmn. bd., 1971-75; Mem. exec. council Brebeuf Prep. Sch., Indpls., 1972—; bd. dirs. Happy Hollow Children's Camp, 1964—, pres., 1968-71; bd. dirs., mem. exec. com. Indpls. chpt. ARC, 1975—, chmn. bd. dirs., 1979—, mem. Midwest Adv. Council; bd. dirs. Hoosier Salon Patrons Assn., 1980. Served with USNR, 1946-48. Mem. Am., Ind., Indpls. bar assns., Indpls. Legal Aid Soc., English Speaking Union, Ind. State Mus. Soc., Indpls. Zool. Soc., Indpls. Children's Mus., Ind. State Symphony Soc., U. Ill. Alumni Assn. (pres. 1977, dir), Ind. Hist. Soc., U.S. Trotting Assn., Ind. Trotting and Pacing Horse Assn., Phi Delta Phi, Phi Sigma Kappa. Clubs: Meridian Hills Country, Econ. Indpls., Lawyers. Home: 7240 N Pennsylvania St Indianpolis IN 46240 Office: 307 E McCarty St Indianapolis IN 46206

BLACKWELL, JOHN, educator; b. Oughtibridge, Sheffield, Eng., Jan. 15, 1942; came to U.S., 1967; s. Leonard and Vera (Brook) B.; m. Susan Margaret Crawshaw, Aug. 5, 1965; children: Martin Jonathan, Helen Elizabeth. B.Sc. in Chemistry, U. Leeds, Eng., 1963, Ph.D. in Biophysics, 1967. Postdoctoral fellow SUNY Coll. Forestry, 1967-69; vis. asst. prof. Case Western Res. U., Cleve., 1969-70, asst. prof., 1970-74, asso. prof., 1974-77, prof. macromolecular sci., 1977—; vis. prof. Centre National de Recherche Scientifique, Grenoble, France, 1977, U. Freiburg, W. Ger., 1982; cons. in field. Author: (with A.G. Walton) Biopolymers, 1973; contbr. articles to profl. jours. Recipient award for disting. achievement Fiber Soc., 1981; NIH research career devel. award 1973-77. Mem. AAAS, Am. Chem. Soc., Am. Phys. Soc., Biophys. Soc. (chmn. biopolymer subgroup 1975-76), Fiber Soc., Soc. Complex Carbohydrates. Episcopalian. Home: 16011 Fernway Rd Shaker Heights OH 44120 Office: Dept Macromolecular Sci Case Western Res U Cleveland OH 44106

BLACKWELL, JOHN DAVENPORT, banker; b. Richmond, Va., Nov. 30, 1918; s. Karl S. and Mary (Ball) D.; m. Doris Conway Fleming, Aug. 19, 1950; children—Doris Conway, John Davenport, Carl F., Ellen B. B.A., U. Va., 1941; grad. in trusts, Stonier Grad. Sch. Banking, Rutgers U., 1953. Salesman Va. Paper Co., Richmond and; Charlotte, N.C., 1941-44; with First & Mchts. Nat. Bank, Richmond, 1945—, v.p., trust officer, 1961-66, sr. v.p., trust officer, 1966-72, exec. v.p., sr. trust officer, from 1972; now pres. Grace and Holy Trinity Endowment Fund. Treas. St. Andrews Assn. Mem. Estate Planning Council Richmond, Phi Kappa Sigma. Episcopalian. Clubs: German, Commonwealth, Country of Va. (Richmond). Home: 6124 St Andrews Ln Richmond VA 23226 Office: PO Box 26903 Richmond VA 23261

BLACKWELL, LLOYD PHALTI, forester, employment consultant; b. Lynchburg, Va., Nov. 4, 1910; s. Allen Owen and Mary Elizabeth (Martin) B.; m. Eva Ray Mackey, June 30, 1938; 1 dau., Mary Ellen. B.A., Lynchburg Coll., 1931, Va. collegiate teaching certificate, 1932; M.F., Yale U., 1937. Field and staff asst. U.S. Forest Service, Lynchburg, Va., Elkins, W. Va., Charleston and; Columbia, S.C., 1931-35; forester and woodlands mgr. The Urania Lumber Co. Ltd., La., 1937-46; prof., dir. Sch. Forestry, Coll. Life Scis., La. Tech. U., 1946-76, prof., dir. emeritus, 1976—; chmn. bd. Driggers & Blackwell Personnel, Inc., 1976—; nat. landowner assistance advisor to pres. La. Pacific Corp., 1981—. Author: Selective Land Utilization in the Piedmont Region of South Carolina, 1936, Puerto Rico and Its Forests, 1937; co-author: Effects of Thinning on Yield of Loblolly Pine in Central Louisiana, 1972; editor: Handbook of Trees, Shrubs and Vines along Caroline Dorman Nature Trail, 1978; Compiler, pub.: Louisiana Forest Laws; Contbr. to trade jours, on forestry and related subjects. Permanent sec. Yale Forestry Class, 1937; Pres. Presbyn. Young Peoples Conf. for State of Va., 1928; Chmn. La. Tree Farms System, 1950-55; U.S. del. internat. meeting Soc. of Foresters, Helsinki, 1974. Served with USNR, 1942-45; transport duty; Pacific and Atlantic; personnel duty; Dunkeswell, Eng. Fellow Soc. Am. Foresters (mem. nat. com. of income taxation 1949, chmn. La. chpt. Gulf States sect. 1961-62, Outstanding La. Forester Gulf States sect., 1963); mem. La. Forestry Assn. (bd. dirs., exec. com. 1947—, chmn. N. La. group foresters 1941—), Assn. State Coll. and Univ. Forest Research Orgn. (nat. exec. com., So. regional chmn. 1968-76), Am. Legion (dir. 1947, vice comdr. 1948), Phi Kappa Phi, Tau Kappa Alpha, Alpha Psi Omega. Presbyn. Clubs: Mason., Masquers of Hollywood (hon. mem. 1942-43), Kiwanis (past pres.). Home: 1212 Dubach St Ruston LA 71270

BLACKWELL, LYLE MARVIN, elec. engr., ednl. adminstr.; b. Charleston, W.Va., Jan. 29, 1932; s. James Elvin and Sarah Margaret (Ballard) B.; m. Mary Jean Fitzgerald, June 20, 1953; children—James Lyle, Gerald Grant, Scott Allen, Mary Diane, Matthew Fitzgerald. B.S. in Elec. Engring., W.Va. U., 1954; M.A.E., Chrysler Inst. Engring., 1956; Ph.D. in Elec. Engring; NSF fellow 1964-65, Ohio State U., 1966. Automotive engr. Chrysler Corp., Detroit, 1954-58; mem. faculty W.Va. Inst. Tech., Montgomery, 1960—, prof. elec. engring., 1965—, chmn. dept., 1961-64; dean Sch. Engring., 1966—. Author papers, articles in field. Mem. IEEE (pres. W.Va. sect. 1979-80), Soc. Automotive Engrs., Am. Soc. Engring. Edn., Tau Beta Pi, Eta Kappa Nu. Baptist. Club: Lions. Home: PO Box 185 Gauley Bridge WV 25085 Office: WVa Inst Tech Montgomery WV 25136

BLACKWELL, MENEFEE DAVIS, lawyer; b. Lexington, Mo., Feb. 17, 1916; s. Horace F. and Berrien (Menefee) B.; m. Mary Louise Harris, Apr. 25, 1942; 1 son, Stephen M. (dec.). A.B., U. Mo., 1936; J.D., U. Mich., 1939. Bar: Mo. bar 1939. Since practiced in, Kansas City; ptnr. firm Blackwell, Sanders, Matheny, Weary & Lombardi; dir. Kansas City Title div. Chgo. Title Ins. Co., Inter-State Holdings Inc., Commerce Bancshares, Inc., Interstate Prodn. Co., Continental Potash Co., Commonwealth Theatres, Inc., Percy Kent Bag Co. Bd. dirs. Kansas City Assn. Trusts and Founds., Chas. R. Cook and Minnie K. Cook Found., Starlight Theatre Assn.; trustee William Rockhill Nelson Trust, Nelson Gallery Found., Louetta M. Cowden Found., Jacob L. and Ella C. Loose Found., Midwest Research Inst.; bd. govs. Am. Royal Assn. Served from 2d lt. to maj., 14th Armored Div. AUS, 1942-46. Decorated Silver Star, Bronze Star with cluster, Purple Heart. Mem. Am., Mo., Kansas City bar assns., Order of Coif, Phi Beta Kappa, Phi Delta Theta, Phi Delta Phi. Episcopalian. Clubs: Kansas City Country, Kansas City, River (Kansas City). Home: 1215 W 57th Terr Kansas City MO 64113 Office: Five Crown Center 2480 Pershing Rd Kansas City MO 64108

BLACKWELL, RONALD EUGENE, breed registry exec.; b. Lexington, Okla., Feb. 15, 1933; s. Elight and Vee B.; m. Carolyn Crawford, Jan. 17, 1959; children—Scott, Stacy, Steven, Shanda. B.S. in Animal Sci, Okla. State U., 1954. Hog buyer Wilson Packing Co., Chgo. and; Galesburg, Ill., 1954-55; mng. editor Poland China World, Galesburg, 1955; exec. sec. Tex. Angus Assn., Fort Worth, 1957-60; fieldman, asst. exec. sec. Am. Angus Assn., St. Joseph, Mo., 1960-69; dir. public relations Am. Quarter Horse Assn., Amarillo, Tex., 1969-76, exec. sec. and gen. mgr., 1976—; mem. exec. com. Am. Horse Council, 1976—. Bd. dirs. United Way, Tri-State Fair Assn. Served with C.E. U.S. Army, 1955-57; ETO. Recipient animal sci. grad. of distinction award Okla. State U., 1981. Mem. Nat. Soc. Livestock Record Assns. (past pres.), Am. Soc. Assn. Execs. Republican. Baptist. Office: 2736 W 10 St Amarillo TX 79168

BLACKWELL, THOMAS LEO, artist; b. Chgo., Mar. 9, 1938; s. Steven Thomas and Virginia Harriet (Tankersley) B.; m. Linda Chase, June 6, 1969; 1 stepdau., Leila Knox. One-man shows include, Sidney Janis Gallery, N.Y.C., 1975, Louis K. Meisel Gallery, N.Y.C., 1977, 80, 82, Galerie Le Portail, Heidelberg, Ger., 1976, Dartmouth Coll., Hanover, N.H., 1980, group exhbns. include, Whitney Mus., N.Y.C., 1969, 72, San Francisco Mus. Art, 1973, Tokyo Biennale, 1974, Pa. Acad. Fine Art, 1981, Guggenheim Mus., N.Y.C., One-man shows include, Am. Acad. and Inst. Arts and Letters (purchase prize 1981), Springfield Art Mus., 1982, De Cordova Mus., Lincoln, Mass., Des Moines Art Ctr., Currier Gallery Art, N.H., Fischer Fine Art Ltd., London; represented in permanent collections, Mus. Modern Art, N.Y.C., Guggenheim Mus., N.Y.C., Smithsonian Instn., Washington, Elvehjem Art Center, U. Wis., Madison, U. Ariz. Mus., Tucson, Hood Mus., Dartmouth Coll., Ft. Wayne Mus. Art, Currier Gallery Art, Huntington Mus., Austin, Tex.; artist-in-residence, guest prof., Dartmouth Coll., 1980, U. Ariz., Tucson, 1981. Served with U.S. Navy, 1955-59. Mem. Artists Equity Assn., Artworkers Coalition. Home: RFD 2 Box 87 Peterborough NH 03458 Office: 131 Prince St New York NY 10012 *It seems to me that achieving something as a visual artist involves many small struggles fought daily, alone, without an audience. The recognition comes later, often for things one has outgrown or for the wrong reasons. One has to learn to ignore this and concentrate on the everyday quest for excellence, which is fought for and recognized alone. This is really all one has and it is enough.*

BLACKWOOD, ALLISTER CLARK, emeritus microbiology educator; b. Calgary, Alta., Can., Nov. 22, 1915; s. Allister Chester and Bessie (Saunders) B.; m. Mildred Marsh, May 1, 1943; children: Alan, Marsha, Susan. B.Sc., U. Alta., 1942, M.Sc., 1944; Ph.D., U. Wis., 1949. With Canadian Nat. Research Council, 1944-46, 48-57, sr. research officer, Saskatoon, Sask., 1956-57; prof. microbiology Macdonald Coll., McGill U., 1957-81, prof. emeritus, 1981—; chmn. dept., 1957-68; dean Faculty of Agr., vice prin. coll., 1972-77. Recipient Centennial medal Can., 1967; Queen's Silver Jubilee medal, 1977. Fellow Royal Soc. Can.; mem. Canadian Soc. Microbiologists (pres. 1964-65), Que. Soc. de Microbiologie, Am. Soc. Microbiology, Soc. Gen. Microbiology, Soc. Applied Bacteriology, Sigma Psi, Kappa Sigma. Research microbial physiology and fermentations. Home: 2131 Wenman Dr Victoria BC V8N 2S3 Canada

BLACKWOOD, JAMES WEBRE, gospel singer, clergyman; b. Ackerman, Miss.; s. William Emmett and Carrie Savala (Prewitt) B.; m. Miriam LeGrantham, Apr. 4, 1939; children: James Webre, William Leroy. D. Mus. (hon.), Golden State U., San. Marcos, Calif., 1983. Mgr. Blackwood Bros. Quartet, Memphis, 1934-80; mem. Masters V, 1980—. Author: The James Blackwood Story, 1973. Named to Gospel Music Hall of Fame, 1972; recipient 9 Grammy awards. Mem. Nat. Acad. Rec. Arts. Scis., Gospel Music Assn. (bd. dirs. 1970-80, 7 Dove awards for top male vocalist). Republican. Mem. Assembly of God Ch. Home: 4411 Sequoia Rd Memphis TN 38117 Office: Blackwood Bros 5180 Park Ave Memphis TN 38117

BLACKWOOD, RUSSELL THORN, III, educator; b. Phila., Feb. 6, 1928; s. Russell Thorn and Madeleine (Niesley) B.; m. Elizabeth Langdale Hamilton, Sept. 30, 1950; children: Cynthia Niesley, Rebecca Hamilton. A.B., Dartmouth Coll., 1948; M.A., Colgate U., 1951; Ph.D., Columbia U., 1957. Instr. Colgate U., 1950-51; asst. prof. Hood Coll., 1954-57; asst. prof. philosophy Hamilton Coll., Clinton, N.Y., 1957-62, assoc. prof., 1962-65, prof., 1965-72, John Stewart Kennedy prof., 1972—, chmn. dept. philosophy, 1965-81; lectr. U. Athens, 1979, Tenri U., 1983; editorial and acad. accreditation cons.; panelist-cons. Nat. Endowment for Humanities, Fund for Study of World's Great Religions fellow; N.Y. State Faculty Scholar in Oriental Studies. Co-editor: Language and Value, 1969, Problems in Philosophy: West and East, 1975; contbr. articles to profl. jours. Mem. Am. Philos. Soc., N.Y. State Philos. Soc. (pres. 1966), Soc. Asian and Comparative Philosophy, Phi Beta Kappa. Home: 131 College St Clinton NY 13323

BLADEN, ASHBY, life ins. co. exec.; b. Hartford, Conn., May 3, 1929; s. Ashby Edward and Kathryn (Wehman) B.; m. Virginia Cheatham; children—Ashby Davidson, Virginia, Daphne Ann. B.A., Amherst Coll., 1950; M.A., Columbia U., 1952. Research analyst Conn. Mut. Life Ins. Co., Hartford, 1958-62; asst. to treas. Cornell U., Ithaca, N.Y., 1962-65; head convertible securities research Salomon Bros., N.Y.C., 1965-68; mgr. corp. investments Am. Standard, Inc., N.Y.C., 1968-71; sr. v.p. investments Guardian Life Ins. Co. Am., N.Y.C., 1971-81, Phoenix Mut. Life Ins. Co., Hartford, 1981—. Author: How to Cope with the Developing Financial Crisis, 1980; columnist: Forbes mag. Served in U.S. Army, 1952-54. Office: Phoenix Mutual Life Ins Co One American Row Hartford CT 06115

BLADES, ANN, author, illustrator; b. Vancouver, C., Can., Nov. 16, 1947; d. Arthur Hazelton and Dorothy (Planche) Sager. Teaching cert., U. B.C., 1971; R.N., B.C. Inst. Tech., 1974. Elem. sch. tchr., 1967-71, nurse, summers 1974-80, author, illustrator children's books, 1968—. Author, illustrator: Mary of Mile 18, 1971 (Can. Assn. Children's Librarians Book of Year award 1972), A Boy of Taché, 1973, The Cottage at Crescent Beach, 1977; illustrator: Jacques the Woodcutter, 1977, A Salmon for Simon (Can. Council Children's Lit. award for illustration 1979), 1978 (Amelia Frances Howard-Gibbon award 1979), Six Darn Cows, 1979, Anna's Pet, 1980, Pettranella, 1980; art shows include, Bau Xi Gallery, Vancouver, 1982, 83, Bau Xi Gallery, Toronto. Mem. Writers Union Can. Address: care Writers Union Can 24 Ryerson Ave Toronto ON M5T 2P3 Canada

BLADES, HERBERT WILLIAM, pharm. co. exec.; b. Dubuque, Iowa, Apr. 27, 1908; s. Walter and Nellie (Quilliam) B.; m. Jane Larison Marshall, June 1, 1933; children—John William, William Stoddard. B.S., Northwestern U., 1931. Gen. mgr. John Wyeth and Bro., Can., Ltd., 1935-38; v.p., gen. mgr. Kolynos Co., 1938-43; asst. to pres. Am. Home Products Corp., 1943-46, exec. v.p., 1960—, also dir.; exec. v.p. Wyeth Labs. div., 1946-56, pres., 1956-71, chmn. bd., 1971-73; dir. Carlo Erba, S.p.A., Milan, Italy, Provident Mutual Life Ins. Co. Phila., Phila. Nat. Bank, Phila.; Cons. White House Conf. on Aging, 1961; dir. Pa. Plan to Develop Scientists Med. Research.; Bd. dirs. Bryn Mawr (Pa.) Hosp., Pharm. Mfrs. Assn. Found., Inc.; bd. mgrs. Wistar Inst. Recipient Order of Honneur et Merite, Republic Haiti, 1959. Mem. Pharm. Mfrs. Assn. (dir.), Delta Upsilon. Presbyn. (elder, trustee). Clubs: Racquet (Phila.); St. Davids (Wayne). Home: 3 Fenimore Ln St Davids PA 19087 Office: PO Box 8299 Philadelphia PA 19101

BLAEDEL, WALTER JOHN, educator, chemist; b. N.Y.C., May 26, 1916; s. George L. and Marie T. (Grundler) R.; m. Barbara Jeane Bennett, Feb. 1, 1942; children—Mark Edward, Kenneth Lee, Robert Walter. B.A., U. Calif. at Los Angeles, 1938, M.A., 1939; Ph.D., Stanford, 1942. Instr. Northwestern U., 1941-44; research asso. Manhattan Project, U. Chgo., 1944-46, U. Calif. at Berkeley, 1946-47; mem. faculty U. Wis., 1947—, prof. chemistry, 1957—; Mem. com. postdoctoral fellowships Nat. Acad. Sci., 1964-68, adv. panel 31,000, 1968-70. Author: Elementary Quantitative Analysis, 2d edit, 1963, also articles.; Mem. adv. bd.: Analytical Chemistry, 1966-68. Recipient award OSRD, 1945; Manhattan Project, 1945. Mem. Am. Chem. Soc. (chmn. Wis. sect. 1965-66), Phi Beta Kappa, Sigma Xi, Alpha Chi Sigma, Phi Lambda Upsilon. Home: 25 Larch Circle Madison WI 53705

BLAESSER, WILLARD WILLIAM, educator; b. Cedarburg, Wis., Nov. 11, 1912; s. George William and Lydia (Jochem) B.; m. Helen Ann Geimer, Oct. 4, 1941; children—Ann Marie, Jean Margaret, Brian William. B.S., U. Wis., 1934, M.A., 1940; Rockefeller Found. fellow mental hygiene, Columbia, (summer 1939); Ed.D., George Washington U., 1953. Tchr. high sch., Sheboygan, Wis., 1934-36; asst. dir. div. social edn., instr. edn. U. Wis., 1936-39, asst. dean men, coordinator student personnel, 1939-45; asst. dean students, dir. counseling center U. Chgo., 1945-46; dir. student personnel, asso. prof. edn. U. Mont., 1946-47; dean students, asso. prof. edn. Wash. State U., 1947-50, on leave, 1949-50; head student personnel programs div. higher edn. U.S. Office Edn., 1949-53; dean students, prof. ednl. psychology U. Utah, 1953-62; prof. ednl. psychology, dean students Coll. City N.Y., 1962-68; prof. counseling and psychology Ariz. State U., 1968—; fellow Nat. Tng. Inst. for Applied Behavioral Sci., 1957—; chmn. policy com. Intermountain Group Devel. Lab., 1958-62; v.p. Am. Tng. Labs., 1970—; sr. asso. Leadership Resources, Inc.; Spl. cons., editor war service opportunities Am. Council Edn., 1943, adv. com. Japanese univs. student personnel insts., 1952-57; cons. Haile Selassie I U., 1960; Asia Found. cons. U. Ceylon, 1966-67; mem. adv. com. Scarsdale Adult Edn. Sch., 1963-68; mem. edn. policy com. Dept. of Def., 1950-53. Bd. editors: Personnel and Guidance Jour, 1956-60, Jr. Coll. Student Personnel, 1968-74; cons. editor: Jour. Ednl. Research, 1976—. Pres. Greater N.Y. Council for Fgn. Students, 1963-65; mem. Pres.'s Long Range Planning Commn., 1979-82; bd. dirs. Nat. Tng. Inst. for Applied Behavioral Sci. Fellow Am. Psychol. Assn. (chmn. com. counselor tng., div. counseling and guidance 1950-51); mem. Nat. Assn. Student Personnel Adminstrs. (chmn. internat. relations com. 1964—, mem. exec. com. 1965—), Am. Coll. Personnel Assn. (v.p. 1947-48, exec. council 1943-50, 53-55, pres. 1955-57), Am. Personnel and Guidance Assn. (mem. exec. council 1955-57), Council Guidance and Personnel Assns. (chmn. com. manpower utilization 1950-51), Western Personnel Inst. (chmn. acad. council 1959-61), N.E.A. (ednl. policies commn.), Internat. Assn. Applied Social Scientists (charter). Home: 2335 S Grandview Ave Tempe AZ 85282

BLAGOWIDOW, GEORGE, publishing company executive; b. Czestochowa, Poland, Dec. 5, 1923; came to U.S., 1951, naturalized, 1956; s. Pawel and Tamara (Paszyn) B.; m. Ludmilla Dobjitsky, Nov. 8, 1953; children: Nicholas, Natalie, Catherine. Licencié en Sciences Commerciales, Consulaires et Maritimes, U. Antwerp, Belgium, 1949; M.B.A., N.Y. U., 1953, Ph.D., 1959. Sales mgr. Doubleday & Co., N.Y.C., 1955-62; sales dir. Macmillan Co., N.Y.C., 1962-66; gen. mgr. Funk & Wagnalls Co., N.Y.C., 1966-70; pres. Hippocrene Books, Inc., N.Y.C., 1970—; founder, partner The Compleat Strategist (book store), N.Y.C., 1976—; owner Strategy and Fantasy World (book stores); lectr. mktg. Grad. Sch. Bus. Adminstrn., N.Y. U., 1961-63. Author: Optimum Marketing of Trade Books, 1964; novel The Last Train from Berlin, 1982; Operation Parterre; co-author: Decision Exercises in Marketing, 1963. Home: 86-45 Chelsea St Jamaica NY 11432 Office: 171 Madison Ave New York NY 10016 *

BLAHD, WILLIAM HENRY, physician; b. Cleve., May 11, 1921; s. Moses and Rae (Lichtenstader) B.; m. Miriam Weiss, Jan. 29, 1971; children—Andrea Margery, William Henry, Karen Ruth. Student, Western Res. U., 1939-40, U. Ariz., 1940-42; M.D., Tulane U., 1945. Diplomate: Am. Bd. Nuclear Medicine (chmn. 1982), Am. Bd. Internal Medicine (bd. govs. 1981). Resident in pathology and internal medicine VA Wadsworth Med. Center, 1948-52, ward officer metabolic research ward, 1951-52, asst. chief radioisotope service, 1952-56, chief nuclear medicine service, Los Angeles, 1956—; prof. dept. medicine U. Calif., Los Angeles; cons. nuclear medicine; mem. adv. com. on human uses radioisotopes Calif. Dept. Health Services. Author 3 textbooks on nuclear medicine.; Contbr. numerous articles to med. jours. Served with U.S. Army, 1946-48. Grantee Muscular Dystrophy Assn. Am., 1965-69, Nat. Cancer Inst., 1973-76. Fellow A.C.P., Am. Coll. Nuclear Physicians; mem. Soc. Nuclear Medicine (pres. 1977-78), Health Physics Soc. (pres. So. Calif. chpt. 1964-66), Calif. Med. Assn. (mem. sci. bd. 1975—), Am. Coll. Nuclear Physicians (bd. regents 1974—), Soc. Exptl. Biology and Medicine, AMA, Los Angeles County, Calif. med. assns., Western Assn. Physicians, Am. Fedn. Clin. Research, Western Soc. Clin. Research, Alpha Omega Alpha. Office: Nuclear Medicine Ultrasound Service W115 West Los Angeles VA Med Ctr Los Angeles CA 90073

BLAHUT, RICHARD EDWARD, electrical engineer; b. Orange, N.J., June 9, 1937; s. Edward John and Julia Anna (Chamer) B.; m. Barbara Ann Krachnefels, Aug. 30, 1948; children: Gregory, Kenneth, Janice, Keffrey. B.S. in Elec. Engring., MIT, 1960; M.S. in Physics, Steven Inst. Tech., Hoboken, N.J., 1964; Ph.D. in Elec. Engring., Cornell U., 1972. Engr. Kearfott (GPI), Little Falls, N.J., 1960-64, IBM, Owego, N.Y., 1964—; courtesy prof. elec. engring. Cornell U., 1974—. Author: Theory and Practice of Error Control Codes, 1983. IBM fellow, 1980. Fellow IEEE (pres. info theory group 1982). Republican. Roman Catholic. Home: 276 Ridgefield Rd Endicott NY 13760 Office: IBM Owego NY 13827

BLAIK, EARL HENRY, manufacturing corporation executive; b. Detroit, Feb. 15, 1897; s. William Douglas and Margaret Jane B.; m. Merle McDowell, Oct. 20, 1924; children: William McDowell, Robert McDowell. A.B., Miami U., Oxford, Ohio, 1918, LL.D. (hon.), 1959; B.S., U.S. Mil. Acad., 1920; student, Cav. Sch., Fort Riley, Kans., 1920-21; D.H.L., Dartmouth Coll., 1977. Commd. 1st lt. cav. U.S. Army; served with 8th Cav., 1922-23, resigned, 1923; mem. firm W.D. and E.H. Blaik (builders), Dayton, Ohio, 1923-34; head football coach Dartmouth Coll., 1934-40; part time football coach U.S. Mil. Acad., West Point, 1927-34, dir. athletics, chmn. athletic bd., 1949-58; serving as lt. col. U.S. Army, 1943, col. cav., 1944; v.p., dir. Avco Corp., N.Y.C., 1959-60, dir., chmn. exec. com., 1960—; chmn. exec. com. Blaik Oil Co., Oklahoma City. Author, contbr. to mags. Trustee John F. Kennedy Library; mem. adv. bd. MacArthur Meml. Found.; sponsor Hampton Inst. Named Coach of the Yr., 1946; Coach of Yr. Washington Touchdown Club, 1953; named to Nat. Football Hall of Fame, 1959; State of Va. Sportsman Club award Touchdown Club of N.Y. award, 1958; Gold Medal award Nat. Football Found. and Hall of Fame, 1966. Mem. Assn. Grads. U.S. Mil. Acad. (hon. trustee), Assn. U.S. Army (adv. bd.), Beta Theta Pi, Tau Kappa Alpha. Clubs: Blind Brook, Metropolitan (N.Y.); Burning Tree (Washington); La Quinta (Palm Desert, Calif.). Home: 2735 Springmede Ct Colorado Springs CO 80906

BLAIN, BRADLEY GORDON, art gallery executive; b. Kitchener, Ont., Can., Apr. 3, 1953; s. Gordon Charles and Adelle Mary (Leis) B.; m. Heather Gay McCullough, July 18, 1975. B.A., U. Guelph, Ont., 1975. With Kitchener-Waterloo Art Gallery, Kitchener, 1969—, curator, 1976-80, acting dir., 1980, dir., 1980—. Mem. Ont. Assn. Art Gallaries (pres. 1983-84), Can. Art Mus. Dirs. Orgn. Home: 848 Queen's Blvd Kitchener ON Canada N2M 1A7 Office: Kitchener-Waterloo Art Gallery 101 Queen St N Kitchener ON Canada N2H 6P7

BLAINE, CHARLES GILLESPIE, lawyer; b. N.Y.C., Mar. 12, 1925; s. James G. and Marion (Dow) B.; m. Gloria Beckwith, Dec. 16, 1944; children: Cathryn D. Blaine Muzzy, Susan B. Blaine Nesbitt, Charles Gillespie. Grad., St. Paul's Sch., 1943; student, Amherst Coll., 1946; LL.B., U. Va., 1948. Bar: N.Y. 1949. Since practiced in, Buffalo; now partner firm Phillips, Lytle, Hitchcock, Blaine & Huber; dir. Marine Midland Bank, N.A., Marine Midland Banks, Inc., Monroe Abstract & Title Corp., Niagara Envelope Co., Inc.; Pres., dir. Legal Aid Bur. Buffalo, 1967-68; mem. Bd. Edn. City of Buffalo, 1970-73; bd. dirs. SUNY Coll. at Buffalo, 1965-82; chmn. State U. N.Y. Coll. at Buffalo, 1980—. Author: Federal Regulation of Bank Holding Companies, 1973. Bd. dirs. Children's Aid Soc., 1967-72, Buffalo Fine Arts Acad., 1970-73; chancellor Episcopal Diocese of Western N.Y., 1975—. Served to lt. (j.g.) USNR, 1943-46. Mem. ABA, N.Y. State Bar Assn. (chmn. banking, corp. and bus. law sect. 1966-67), Erie County Bar Assn., Assn. Bar City N.Y., Am. Law Inst., Buffalo and Erie County Hist. Soc., Grosvenor Soc. Episcopalian. Clubs: Buffalo, Marshall, Lawyers (Buffalo); Crag Burn (East Aurora, N.Y.); Metropolitan (Washington); Links (N.Y.C.). Home: 1775 N Davis Rd East Aurora NY 14052 Office: 3400 Marine Midland Center Buffalo NY 14203

BLAINE, NELL WALDEN, painter; b. Richmond, Va., July 10, 1922; d. Harry Wellington and Eudora Catherine (Garrison) B. Student, Richmond Sch. of Art, 1939-42, Hans Hofmann Sch. Fine Arts, N.Y.C., 1942-44, Art Students League, 1943, New Sch. for Social Research, 1952-53; hon. degree, Moore Coll. Art, 1980. Pvt. tchr. of painting, N.Y.C., 1942-49, tchr. adult program Great Neck (N.Y.) pub. schs., 1956; Costume designer Studio Theater, N.Y.C., 1949; costume, set designer for Midi Garth, 1956; artistic adviser for Garth concerts Henry St. Playhouse, 92d St. YM-YWHA Dance Center, N.Y.C., 1951, 54, 55. One-woman-shows include, Jane St. Gallery, N.Y.C., 1945, 48, So. Ill. U., Carbondale, 1949, Tibor de Nagy Gallery, N.Y.C., 1953, 54, Stewart Rickard Gallery, San Antonio, 1961, Phila. Art Alliance, Poindexter Gallery, N.Y.C., 1956, 58, 60, 66, 68, 70, 72, 76, Yaddo, Saratoga Springs, N.Y., 1961, Zabriskie Gallery, Provincetown, Mass., 1963, U. Conn., Storrs, 1973, Va. Mus. Fine Arts, 1947, 55, 73, 79, Stagecoach House Gallery, Gloucester, Mass., 1977, Watson de Nagy Gallery, Houston, Fischbach Gallery, N.Y.C., 1979, 81, Hull Gallery, Washington, 1979-80, Jersey City Mus., 1981, Alpha Gallery, Boston, others; travelling retrospective, N.Y. State, 1974-75; exhibited in group shows including, Art Inst. Chgo., 1944, Va. Mus. of Fine Arts Biennials, Richmond, 1944-53, Riverside Mus., N.Y.C., 1944-57, Va. Mus., 1945, Art of This Century Gallery, Stable Galleries Anns., N.Y.C., 1954-57, San Francisco Mus. Art, 1960, summer festivals on, Cape Ann and Cape Cod, Mass., 1943, 54, 58, Mus. Modern Art, N.Y.C., 1956, 68, 74, Wildenstein Gallery, N.Y.C., 1960, also, Brooks Meml. Art Gallery, Visual Arts Gallery, Corcoran Gallery, Mus. Modern Art, Rome, Mus. Modern Art, Copenhagen, Denmark, Kansas City Art Inst., Smithsonian Instn., Palais des Beaux-Arts de la Ville de Paris, France, Mus. Modern Art, Tokyo, Japan, 1955, Nat. Inst. Arts and Letters, 1967, 70, U. Tex., Austin, 1974, and others; represented in numerous permanent collections including, Whitney Mus. Am. Art, N.Y.C., Met. Mus. Art, N.Y.C., Mus. Modern Art, N.Y.C., Carnegie Inst., Pitts., Ga. Mus. Art, Athens, Va., Mus. Fine Arts, Richmond, State U. of Iowa Mus., Iowa City, Chase Manhattan Bank Collection, N.Y.C., U. Art Mus., U. Calif. at Berkeley, Slater Meml. Mus., Norwich, Conn., Rose Art Mus., Brandeis U., Waltham, Mass., Bklyn. Mus., Hallmark Internat. Award Collection, Kansas City, Mo., Hirshhorn Mus. and Sculpture Garden, numerous others. Recipient 1st prize Norfolk Mus., 1945, Purchase award Whitney Mus., 1958; 1st Gov.'s Art Award of Va., 1979; Va. Mus. fellow, 1943, 46; Ingram Merrill grantee, 1962, 64, 66; Longview grantee, 1964, 70; Cultural Council Found. grantee, 1972; Rothko grantee, 1973; Guggenheim fellow, 1974-75; Nat. Endowment grantee, 1975-76. Mem. Artists Equity Assn., NAD (academician). Address: 210 Riverside Dr New York NY 10025 also 3 Ledge Rd Gloucester MA 01930

BLAIR, BOWEN, investment banker; b. Bar Harbor, Maine, Aug. 4, 1918; s. William McCormick and Helen Haddock (Bowen) B.; m. Joan Halpine Smith, Dec. 9, 1950; children: Joan Bowen, Bowen. B.A., Yale U., 1940; postgrad., Harvard U., 1940-41. With William Blair & Co., Chgo., 1946—, partner, 1950—; chmn. Growth Industry Shares; dir. Mid Con Corp. Trustee Art Inst., Chgo., Chgo. Hist. Soc. Field Mus. Natural History, Graceland Cemetery. Clubs: Chicago; Onwentsia (Lake Forest, Ill.); Racquet and Tennis (N.Y.C.). Home: 3 S Green Bay Rd Lake Forest IL 60045 Office: 135 S LaSalle St Chicago IL 60603

BLAIR, CALVIN PATTON, educator; b. Orange, Tex., Nov. 25, 1924; s. Thomas David and Mary Jane (Patton) B.; m. Eleanor Ruth Davis, Nov. 29, 1946; children—Bonnie Jane, Lisa Jill. Student, Lamar Coll., 1942-43; B.A., U. Tex., 1949, M.A.; Univ. fellow, 1953; Ph.D., 1957; Farmer scholar, Universidad Nacional Autonoma de Mexico, 1950. Instr. to prof. econs. U. Tex., Austin, 1953-56, 67-70; research asso. Bur. Bus. Research, 1958-61; asst. dean Coll. Bus., 1958—, prof. internat. bus., 1956—; vis. prof. Universidad de Nuevo Leon, 1959-60, Instituto Tecnologico, 1963, Harvard U., 1964, Centro de Estudios Monetarios Latinoamericanos, 1965-73, Universidad Nacional Autonoma de Mexico, 1969-70, Laredo State U., 1976, 80; Ford Found. Social Sci. Program adv. for Mexico, 1968-70, cons. Fgn. Service officer exams., Peace Corps evaluation, bus. growth and fin. in Mexico. Author: (with Stanley Arbingast and others) Atlas of Mexico, 1975; Contbr. to: (with Raymond Vernon) Pub. Policy and Pvt. Enterprise in Mexico, 1964, Ency. of Latin America, 1974. Served with USN, 1943-46. Mem. Am. Econ. Assn., Latin Am. Studies Assn., AAUP (chpt. pres. 1976-78), Phi Beta Kappa, Sigma Delta Pi. Home: 2115 W 12th St Austin TX 78703 Office: GSB4 132 U Tex Austin TX 78712

BLAIR, CHARLES MELVIN, manufacturing company executive; b. Vernon, Tex., Oct. 24, 1910; s. Charles Melvin and Sallie (Gilliland) B.; m. Catherine E. Stone, June 12, 1936; children: Charles Melvin, Sally. B.A., Rice U., 1931, M.A., 1932; Ph.D., Calif. Inst. Tech., 1935. Research chemist Petrolite Corp., St. Louis, 1935-43, research dir. for corp., 1943-53, pres., 1953-64; dir. Blair Petroleum Co., Fullerton, Calif., Cyber Systems Inc., Anaheim, Calif.; vice chancellor, treas. Washington U., St. Louis, 1964-67; chmn. bd. Magna Corp., Santa Fe Springs, Calif., 1967—. Author articles on sci. and cultural subjects. Mem. Am. Council Edn., Am. Chem. Soc., AAAS, Am. Petroleum Inst., Soc. Petroleum Engrs., Phi Beta Kappa, Sigma Xi, Phi Lambda Upsilon. Clubs: Hacienda, Los Coyotes, Athenaeum, Petroleum (Los Angeles). Patents and publs. in surface chemistry, corrosion sci., petroleum processing. Home: 5320 Buck Hill Buena Park CA 90621 Office: 11808 S Bloomfield Ave Santa Fe Springs CA 90670

BLAIR, CLAY DREWRY, JR., author; b. Lexington, Va., May 1, 1925; s. Clay Drewry and Marie Louise (Barreto) B.; m. Agnes Kemp Devereux, Nov. 25, 1950 (div. 1969); children—Marie Louise, Clay Drewry III, Joseph Devereux (dec.), Sibyl Devereux, Kemp Devereux, Robert Augustus Drewry, Christopher Ryan; m. Joan Rutledge West, Nov. 11, 1972. Student, Tulane U., 1946-48, Columbia U., 1948-49. Corr. Time mag., 1949-55; mil. corr. Life mag., 1955-57; asso. editor Saturday Evening Post, 1957-61, asst. mng. editor, 1961-62, mng. editor, 1962, editor, 1963-64; v.p., editorial dir. Curtis Pub. Co., 1962, sr. v.p., editor-in-chief, 1963-64, exec. v.p., dir., 1964. Author: The Atomic Submarine and Admiral Rickover, 1954, (with James Shepley) The Hydrogen Bomb, 1954, Beyond Courage, 1955, (for Maj. Ward Millar) Valley of the Shadow, 1955, (with Comdr. William R. Anderson) Nautilus 90 North, 1959, Diving for Pleasure and Treasure, 1960, Always Another Dawn, 1960, The Board Room, 1969, The Strange Case of James Earl Ray, 1969, The Archbishop, 1970, Pentagon Country, 1971, Survive, 1973, Silent Victory: The U.S. Submarine War Against Japan, 1975, (with Joan Blair) The Search for J.F.K., 1976, MacArthur, 1977, Scuba!, 1977, Combat Patrol, 1978, Return from the River Kwai, 1979, Mission Tokyo Bay, 1980, Swordray's First Three Patrols, 1980, (Omar N. Bradley) A General's Life, 1983. Served with USNR, 1943-46. Decorated Submarine Combat insignia. Clubs: Metropolitan (Washington); Chevy Chase (Md.). Address: care Scott Meredith Lit Agy 845 Third Ave New York NY 10022

BLAIR, EDWARD MCCORMICK, investment banker; b. Chgo., July 18, 1915; s. William McCormick and Helen Haddock (Bowen) B.; m. Elizabeth Graham Iglehart, June 28, 1941; children: Edward McCormick, Francis Iglehart. Grad., Groton Sch., 1934; B.A., Yale U., 1938; M.B.A., Harvard U., 1940. With William Blair & Co., Chgo., 1946—, partner, 1950—, mng. partner, 1961-77, sr. partner, 1977—; dir. Gen. Binding Corp., Northbrook, Ill., AccuRay Corp., Columbus, Ohio, World Book-Childcraft Internat., Inc., Chgo., Barber-Greene Co., Inc., Aurora, Ill., Hutzler Bros. Co., Balt., Herman Miller, Inc., Zeeland, Mich. Bd. dirs. George M. Pullman Ednl. Found.; trustee James C. King Home, Evanston, Ill., U. Chgo., Chgo. Dock and Canal Trust.; past chmn. trustees Rush-Presbyn.-St. Luke's Med. Center, Chgo. Served to lt. comdr. USNR, 1941-46. Home: Crab Tree Farm Sheridan Rd Lake Bluff IL 60044 Office: 135 S LaSalle St Chicago IL 60603

BLAIR, ETCYL HOWELL, chemical company executive; b. Wynona, Okla., Oct. 15, 1922; s. Tunice Wilbur and Ruby (Belvin) B.; m. Ruth May Cross, Sept. 4, 1949; children: David, Ronald, Kevin. A.B., Southwestern Coll., 1947, D.Sc. (hon.), 1974; M.S., Kans. State Coll., 1949; Ph.D., Kansas State Coll., 1952. With Dow Chem. Co., Midland, Mich., 1951—, research chemist, 1951-56, group leader, div. leader, 1956-66, asst. dir., dir., 1966-68, mgr., dir., 1968-73, dir., 1973—, v.p., 1978—; bd. dirs., vice chmn. Chem. Industry Inst. of Toxicology, Research Triangle Park, N.C., 1977-83. Author: Chlorodioxins-Origin and Fate, 1973; patentee in field. Chmn. sci. subcom. Matrix: Midland, Midland, 1978—. Served with USAAF, 1943-46. Mem. Am. Chem. Soc. (officer Midland sect., sect. award 1979), AAAS, Sci. Research Soc. Am., Fedn. Am. Scientists, N.Y. Acad. Scis., Soc. Chem. Industry (Am. sect.), Nat. Acad. Environ. Safety, Soc. Ecotoxicology and Environ. Safety. Republican. Methodist. Home: 4 Crescent Ct Midland MI 48640 Office: Dow Chem Co 2020 Dow Ctr Midland MI 48640

BLAIR, FRED EDWARD, association executive; b. Huntington, W.Va., Oct. 6, 1933; s. Fred E. and Pearl Amy (King) B.; m. Lois Ann Thomas, Aug. 16, 1958; children: Lesli Winifred, Annlyn Paige, Carter Thomas. B.B.A., Marshall U., 1955; M.A., U. Iowa, 1965. Adminstrv. asst. Jefferson Med. Coll. Hosp., Phila., 1964-66; asst. adminstr. Barberton (Ohio) Citizen Hosp.; sr. asst. adminstrn. U. Ala. Hosp. and Clinics; presently exec. dir. Ohio Valley Med. Center, Wheeling, W.Va.; pres. Ohio Valley Health Services and Edn. Corp.; Instr. health services mgmt. U. Ala., Birmingham; dir. W.Va. Hosp. Service, Inc. (Blue Cross); preceptor health adminstrn. George Washington U., Med. Coll. Va. Bd. dirs. W.Va. Health Systems Agy., treas., 1978; bd. dirs. W.Va. Heart Assn., Wheeling Country Day Sch.; mem. exec. com. W.Va. Regional Med. Program. Mem. Am. Coll. Hosp. Adminstrs., Am., W.Va. hosp. assns., Nat. League Nursing, Am. Assn. Mental Health Adminstrs., Am. Pub. Health Assn. Elder Vance Meml. Presbyterian Ch. Club: Rotary. Home: 1788 National Rd Wheeling WV 26003 Office: 2000 Eff St Wheeling WV 26003

BLAIR, GEORGE SIMMS, social science educator; b. Homewood, Kans., May 31, 1924; s. William Horace and Mary (Simms) B.; m. Gloria Jean Barnes, Sept. 10, 1949; children: David Lawrence, Rebecca Lynn. A.B., Kans. State Tchrs. Coll., Emporia, 1948, B.S. in Edn, 1948, M.S., 1949; Ph.D., Northwestern U., 1951. Asst. prof. polit. sci. U. Tenn., 1951-53; asst. prof. polit. sci. U. Pa., 1953-56, asso. prof., 1956-60; asso. prof. govt. Claremont (Calif.) Grad. Sch., 1960-64, prof., 1964-72, Elizabeth Helm Rosecrans prof. social sci., 1972—. Author: (with S.B. Sweeney) Metropolitan Analysis, 1958 (Fruin-Colnon award 1959), Cumulative Voting in Illinois, 1960, American Local Government, 1964, El Gobierno Local en Los Estados Unidos, 1966, American Legislatures, 1967, (with H.I. Flournoy) Legislative Bodies in California, 1967, Government at the Grass Roots, 1977, 81; Bd. editors: Western Polit. Quar, 1964-68. Mem. Claremont City Planning Commn., 1964-71, Scholars for Rockefeller, 1960, 68, Scholars for Nixon, 1960, 68, Scholars for Reagan, 1969-70; Bd. dirs. Greater Los Angeles Consortium. Served with AUS, 1943-46; PTO. Mem. Am. Polit. Sci. Assn., Am. Soc. Pub. Adminstrn., Pi Sigma Alpha, Pi Gamma Mu. Republican. Methodist. Home: 509 Bowling Green Dr Claremont CA 91711 *I have tried to follow the old Indian adage that I should never criticize another person until I've walked in his mocassins. While much fun is poked at the "psychic" income of teachers, I find it is for real. The respect of students truly makes a professor's role a happy one.*

BLAIR, GLENN MYERS, psychology educator; b. Portland, Oreg., Oct. 2, 1908; s. Oscar Newton and Bertha (Myers) B.; m. Ruth Virginia Van Ness, June 27, 1934; children: Glenn Myers, Sally Virginia (Mrs. Donald Lee Leach). A.B., Seattle Pacific Coll., 1930; A.M., U. Wash., 1931; Ph.D., Columbia, 1938. Denny fellow U. Wash., 1931-32; instr. math. Sedro-Woolley High Sch., 1932-33; head math. dept. Bremerton (Wash.) High Sch., 1933-36; dir. guidance and research Everett (Wash.) pub. schs., 1936-37; Tchrs. Coll. fellow Columbia, 1937-38; prof. ednl. psychology U. Ill. at Urbana, 1938—, chmn. dept., 1948-52; co-dir. Reading Clinic, 1938-48; vis. prof. ednl. psychology U. Wash., summer 1937, U. Kans., 1938, Stanford, 1950; spl. lectr. U. Chgo., Northwestern U., U. Wis., Syracuse U., U. Miami, U. W.Va., U. Mo. Author: Prediction of Freshman Success in the University of Washington, 1931, Mentally Superior and Inferior Children, 1938, Diagnostic and Remedial Teaching, 2d edit., 1956, Educational Psychology; Its Development and Present Status, 1948, Educational Psychology, 4th edit., 1975, Psychology of Adolescence for Teachers, 1964; Editor: The Words You Use, 1958. Fellow Am. Psychol. Assn. (past mem. exec. com.), Am. Ednl. Research Assn.; mem. Nat. Soc. Coll. Tchrs. Edn., Phi Delta Kappa, Kappa Delta Pi, Psi Chi. Home: 51 Island Way Clearwater FL 33515

BLAIR, JAMES PEASE, photographer; b. Phila., Apr. 14, 1931; s. Jacob Jackson and Dorothy Flagg (Pease) B.; m. Patricia Carol Wohlgemuth, Aug. 13, 1964; children: Matthew Ward, David Alexander. B.S., Ill. Inst. Tech., 1954. Reporter, film photographer Sta. WIIC-TV, Pitts., 1958-59; freelance photojournalist, 1959-62; staff photographer Nat. Geog. Soc., Washington, 1962—; instr. dept. photo-communications Rochester Inst. Tech., 1978. Photographer: Listen With The Eye, 1964, As We Live And Breathe, 1971, Our Threatened Inheritance, 1984; one-man shows in, Pitts., New Haven, Washington, Teheran. Served to (j.g.) U.S. Navy, 1954-56. Poynter fellow Yale U., 1977; recipient Overseas Press Club Best Photog. Reporting from Abroad award, 1977. Mem. White House News Photographers Assn., Nat. Press Photographers Assn. Club: Overseas Press. Home: 1411 30th St NW Washington DC 20007 Office: 1145 17th St NW Washington DC 20036

BLAIR, JAMES WALTER, JR., machinery company executive; b. Douglas, Ariz., Mar. 26, 1936; s. James Walter and Edithe Ann (Watson) B.; m. Jeanne Daily, Aug. 30, 1958; 1 son, James Walter III. M.E., U. Ariz., 1959. With Gen. Electric Co., San Jose, Calif. and Schenectady, 1959-73; group v.p. Handy & Harman, N.Y.C., 1973-84; pres. LeRoy Industries Inc. (N.Y.), 1984—. Mem. Am. Mgmt. Assn. Republican. Presbyterian. Clubs: Mining, Oak Hill Country; Masons (Lynn, Mass.); Shriners (San Francisco). Home: 77 Greenhaven Rd Rye NY 10580 Office: 7921 E Main Rd LeRoy NY 14482

BLAIR, JOHN, electronics company executive; b. Budapest, Hungary, Dec. 5, 1929; came to U.S., 1950, naturalized, 1955; s. Eugene I. and Helen (Benedek) B.; m. Constance Smith Drown, Sept. 10, 1955; children: David E., Jennifer C. B.S., Mass. Inst. Tech., 1954, M.S., 1955, Sc.D., 1960. Engr. Pacific Semiconductors, Inc., Culver City, Calif., 1955-57; instr., asst. prof., asso. prof. elec. engring. dept. Mass. Inst. Tech., 1957-66; dir. research Raytheon Co., Lexington, Mass., 1966—; mem. Army Sci. Bd., 1978—. Mem. Nat. Sea Grant Rev. Panel, NOAA, 1979—. Ford Found. fellow, 1960-61. Mem. IEEE, Am. Phys. Soc. Club: Cosmos. Home: 25 Moore Rd Wayland MA 01778 Office: 141 Spring St Lexington MA 02173

BLAIR, JOHN LOUIS, mail order company executive; b. Warren, Pa., Oct. 29, 1920; s. John Leo and Maude (Hall) B.; m. Orpha Thompson, Nov. 26, 1945; children: John Louis, Wendy Blair Dalgleish. A.B.A., Nichols Coll., Dudley Mass., 1942. With Lake Erie Engring. Corp., Buffalo, 1943-45; v.p. New Process Co., Warren, 1945-61, pres., 1962—, also dir.; dir. Warren Nat. Bank. Clubs: Conewango Valley Country, Conewango (Warren); Wanakah Country (Hamburg, N.Y.); Saturn (Buffalo); Yacht, Gulf Stream Bath and Tennis, Delray Beach (Delray Beach, Fla.). Home: 108 East St Warren PA 16365 Office: 220 Hickory St Warren PA 16366

BLAIR, LACHLAN FERGUSON, urban planner; b. Lakewood, Ohio, Sept. 6, 1919; s. Neil Ferguson and Rebecca Henderson (Gunn) B.; m. Mary Anne Novotny, Dec. 12, 1942; children: Douglas MacLachlan, Marilyn Ruth. Student, Cleve. Sch. Arch., Western Res. U., 1936-40; B., MIT, 1949. Archtl. designer various firms, Cleve., 1940-43; sr. planner Providence City Plan Commn., 1949-51; chief state planning div. R.I. Devel. Council, 1952-56; pres. Blair Assos., Planning Cons., Providence, Syracuse, N.Y. and; Washington, 1957-66; prof. urban and regional planning U. Ill., Urbana, 1966—; Mem. Ill. Hist. Sites Adv. Council, 1969-77; chmn. Urbana Plan Comm., 1973-80; mem. Champaign County Regional Planning Comm., 1974—. Author: Cape Cod 1980, 1962, College Hill: A Demonstration of Historic Area Renewal, 1959, 67, The Distinctive Architecture of Willemstad, 1961. Served with C.E. AUS, 1943-46. EPA Public adminstrn. fellow, 1972-73. Mem. Am. Inst. Cert. Planners (past pres. New Eng. and Ill. chpts.; gov.), Am. Planning Assn., Partners for Livable Places, Nat. Trust Hist. Preservation, Preservation Action. Democrat. Unitarian. Home: 506 W Illinois St Urbana IL 61801 Office: 1003 W Nevada St Urbana IL 61801

BLAIR, LEON BORDEN, historian, educator; b. Dexter, Tex., Oct. 26, 1917; s. George Washington and Mattie Belle (Wheeler) B.; m. Edith Witek; children: Christopher David, Peter Leon, David Irvin, Barbara (Mrs. Raymond Henry Stoudt), Michelle Edith (Mrs. David E. Jones), Matthew Curtis. B.A., Tex. Tech U., 1940; M.A., Rice U., 1949; diploma, U.S. Navy Postgrad. Sch., 1953; Ph.D., Tex. Christian U., 1968; postgrad., U. Mohammed V, Rabat, Morocco, 1970-71. Commd. ensign USN, 1941, advanced through grades to lt. comdr., 1952; mil. asst. adv. group, France, 1953-57, politico-mil. liaison officer, N. Africa, 1957-59; tech. adviser Royal Moroccan Armed Forces, 1960; ret., 1962; instr. Temple (Tex.) Jr. Coll., 1966; mem. faculty U. Tex. at Arlington, 1967-73, asso. prof. history, 1972-73; prof., chmn. dept., history and polit. sci. U. Plano, Tex., 1972-73, dean grad. studies, 1973-74; exec. dir. Gifted Students Inst., 1974-80; adj. prof. history U. Tex. at Arlington, 1974—, Tex. Christian U., 1974—; sr. research fellow U. Dallas Grad. Sch. Mgmt., 1979—; Vice pres., sec., exec. dir. Tex. Bur. for Econ. Understanding, Arlington, 1970—; cons. Peace Corps, 1964, Tex. Ednl. Assn., 1974—. Author: Western Window in the Arab World, 1970; Editor: Essay on Russian Intellectual History, 1971, Essays on Radicalism in Contemporary America, 1972, The Miniature Horse World, 1980-83; others. Decorated Legion Merit, Air medal (3); Medaille Aeronvale; Croix d'or du Combattant de l'Europe, France; recipient George Washington Honor medal Freedoms Found., Valley Forge, 1963, 78, award for excellence in pvt. enterprise edn., 1979; Medaille d'Argent Arts-Scies.-Lettres, 1971, City Paris, 1971. Mem. Tex. Hist. Assn., Tangiers Am. Legation Mus. Soc. (dir. 1977—), Am. Miniature Horse Assn. (pres. 1978, exec. v.p. and treas. 1979—). Mem. Christian Ch. Home: 3604 Kimberly Ln Fort Worth TX 76133 Office: Suite 1119 611 Ryan Plaza Dr Arlington TX 76011 *Any educator who would have an impact must be interesting and interested, and therefore cannot be isolated and insulated in an academic institution away from the real world. The day is past when "professionalism" can be used as an excuse for dullness. The great professor seeks continuous new experience; I aspire to greatness.*

BLAIR, LINDA DENISE, actress; b. St. Louis, Jan. 22, 1959; d. James Fredrick and Elinore (Leitch) B. Student pub. schs., Westport, Conn. Model, then actress on TV commls. Film appearances include: The Sporting Club, 1970, The Way We Live Now, 1969, The Exorcist, 1973, Airport '75, 1974, Sweet Hostage, 1975, Exorcist Part II: The Heretic, 1977, Roller-Boogie, 1979; TV appearances include: Born Innocent, 1974, Sarah T.—Portrait of a Teenage Alcoholic, 1974, Victory at Entebbe, 1976. Recipient Golden Globe, also Peoples Choice awards for Exorcist, 1974; plaque for Sarah T.; 3 Bravo mag. Favorite Actress awards; S. America's Favorite Actress award, 1977. Mem. AFTRA, Screen Actors Guild, Am. Horse Shows Assn. Address: care William Morris Agy Inc 151 El Camino Dr Beverly Hills CA 90212 *

BLAIR, MARDIAN JOHN, hospital administrator; b. Rock Springs, Wyo., Dec. 30, 1931; s. Edmund B. and Bernice A. (Mardian) B.; m. Joan Alece Peters, June 20, 1954; children: Michael, Robyn, Douglas, Beth Ann, John. B.S. in Bus., Union Coll., Lincoln, Nebr., 1954; M.A. in Bus. Orgn., U. Nebr., Lincoln, 1958; M.S. in Hosp. Adminstrn., Northwestern U., 1961. Staff auditor Peat, Marwick, Mitchell & Co., 1958; acct. Hinsdale (Ill.) Sanitorium and Hosp., 1958-59; coordinator devel. Hinsdale (Ill.) San. and Hosp., 1959, asst. to adminstr., 1959, asst. adminstr., 1960-63, adminstr., 1963-70, Portland (Oreg.) Adventist Hosp., 1970-73, pres., 1973-76, N.W. Med. Found., Portland, 1972-79, Fla. Hosp., Orlando, 1979—. Served with U.S. Army, 1955-56. Fellow Am. Coll. Hosp. Adminstrs.; mem. Am. Hosp. Assn., Seventh-day Adventist Hosp. Assn. Home: 1132 Dorchester St Orlando FL 32803 Office: 601 E Rollins St Orlando FL 32803

BLAIR, ROBERT NOEL, artist; b. Buffalo, Aug. 12, 1912; s. Charles Frances and Grace Ethylin (McGonegal) B.; m. Jeannette Kenney, Aug. 8, 1943; children—Jeanne Elizabeth (dec.), David Francis, Bruce Allen. Student, Albright Art Sch., 1931, Sch. Mus. Fine Arts, 1931-33, Art Inst. Buffalo, 1937, U. Buffalo, 1951. Painted western N.Y., no. Vt. subjects, 1933-43; instr. Art. Inst. Buffalo, 1939-42, dir., 1945-49; instr. Buffalo Mus. Sci., 1939-42, U. Buffalo, 1952. Contbg. author: Water Colorists at Work, 1972; one-man shows, Buffalo, 1937-41, 45, 53, N.Y.C., 1938-41, 53, 62, Albright Art Gallery, Buffalo, 1942, 54-55, U. Ala., 1944, others, paintings exhibited, Internat. Water Color Exhibit. Bklyn., Art Inst., Chgo., exhbns., Nat. Gallery, Washington, Fleming Mus., Vt., State U. Coll., Buffalo, 1966, others; painter murals, Fifth area Chapel, Fort McClellan, Ala., 1943, Post Hosp., 1944, Bethlehem Steel Plant, Lackawanna, 1947, Olean (N.Y.) House, Unitarian Ch., East Aurora, N.Y., Lake View Hotel, Lake View, New York, works in permanent collection, Nat. Mus. History and Art, Taiwan, Niagara U., Colgate U., Met. Mus., N.Y.C., Munson Williams Proctor Inst., Utica, Dubuque and Bryn Mawr art assos., Butler Art Inst., Ford Motor Co., Buffalo State U. Coll., U. State N.Y. Served with AUS, 1942-45. Awarded water color prize western N.Y. exhibit, 1940-44, 1947-51; Guggenheim fellowships, 1946-51; Silver and Gold medals Buffalo Soc. Artists, 1947, 50; Ala. Water Color Soc., 1947; water color prize Art Inst. Chgo., 1948; watercolor prize N.Y. State Exhbn., 1950; Waugh prize Buffalo Soc. Artists Ann., 1951, 54; gold medal, 1955, 57-68; silver medal, 1956, 62, 69; water color prize 2d Spring Art Exhibit, Buffalo, 1957; 1st watercolor prize Youngstown (Ohio) Nat., 1953, Western N.Y. Exhbn., 1963, Chautauqua Nat. Exhibit, 1963; watercolor prize Balt. Water Color Club, 1954; Buffalo Soc. Artists ann. painting prize, 1958, 62-65, 70; watercolor prize, 1959; gold medal, 1972; Silvermine Guild watercolor prize, 1958; drawing prize Indsl. Niagara Art Exhbn.; 1st painting prize Cooperstown N.Y. Nat. Exhbn., 1970; 1st Watercolor prize White Mountain Art Festival, Sholow, Ariz., 1970; watercolor prize Chautauqua Nat. Exhbn., 1972; others. Mem. Am. Water Color Soc., Patteran Soc., Buffalo Soc. Artists, Western N.Y. Watercolor League. Address: RFD 1 Olean Rd Holland NY 10021 *Over 48 years I have been a painter. Each time I paint I try to do better. So in a way each time is more difficult—a greater challenge. Sometimes it seems one is starting all over again with the latest painting. To be an artist you must be born again, every day.*

BLAIR, S. ROBERT, oil company executive. Pres., chief exec. officer Nova, an Alberta Corp., Calgary, Can.; chmn. Huskey Oil Ltd., Calgary, Alta., Can. Office: 801 Seventh Ave SW Calgary AB Canada T2P 2N6§

BLAIR, SAMUEL RUFUS, sports columnist; b. Dallas, Sept. 26, 1932; s. James Everette and Edna Glenn (Miller) B.; m. Karen Klinefelter, Oct. 1, 1970; children: Jason Everette, Collin Miller. B.J., U. Tex. at Austin, 1954. Mem. sports staff Dallas Morning News, 1954—, writer, copy editor, 1954-61, 79—, columnist, 1961-64, daily columnist, 1964-78, asst. sports editor, 1966-68, sports editor, 1968-81. Author: Dallas Cowboys: Pro or Con?, 1970, (with Roger Staubach and Bob St. John) Staubach: First Down, Lifetime to Go, 1974, (with Grant Teaff) Grant Teaff: I Believe, 1975, Earl Campbell: The Driving Force, 1980, (with Lee Trevino) Super Men, 1982; works included in ann. nat. anthology Best Sports Stories. Served with USAF, 1955-57. Winner Tex. Sports Writers Competition, 1963, 66, 71, 78, 79, 80, 81, Golf Writers Am. Competition, 1964, 66, 67, 69, 70, 71, 74, 78, 80, UPI Competition, 1975, AP Competition, 1978, Pro Football Writers of Am. Competition, 1978. Mem. Football Writers Am., Golf Writers Am., Baseball Writers Am., Tex. Sports Writers Assn. Methodist. Home: 6843 North Ridge Dallas TX 75214 Office: Communication Center Dallas TX 75265

BLAIR, THOMAS S., steel company executive; b. New Castle, Pa., Apr. 15, 1922; s. George Dike, Jr. and Hazel (Slingluff) B.; m. Phyllis Emmerich, Sept. 17, 1946; children: Joan Dix, George Dike, Hadden Slingluff. A.B., Williams Coll., 1943. With Manhattan Project, 1942-47; asso. editor Iron Age mag., 1947-49; former pres. Blair Strip Steel Co., New Castle, chmn. bd., 1949—; dir. Columbia Gas System, Inc., Columbia Gas Pa., Inc., Columbia Gas Md., Inc., Tuscarora Plastics, Inc., Matflo Corp., Southeastern Plastics Corp. Home: 2906 Old Plank Rd New Castle PA 16105 Office: Blair Strip Steel Co New Castle PA 16103

BLAIR, WARREN EMERSON, lawyer, judge; b. Chgo., June 23, 1916; s. Henry Allan and Mae Idella (Spratt) B.; m. Madeline Mary Sheehan, 1947. J.D., DePaul U., 1940; M.B.A., George Washington U., 1958. Bar: Ill. bar 1940, Republic of Korea bar 1951, U.S. Supreme Ct. bar 1954, Ohio bar 1954, N.Y. State bar 1964. Mem. firm Blair, Chiara & Blair, Chgo., 1940-42; atty. SEC, Cleve., 1947-54, chief enforcement atty. trading and exchanges div., Washington, 1954-60, asst. regional adminstr., N.Y.C., 1960-64, adminstrv. law judge, Washington, 1964-70, chief adminstrv. law judge, 1970—; mem. Adminstrv. Conf. U.S., 1972-74. Served to 1st lt. U.S. Army, 1942-46; to capt., 1950-52; ETO, Korea. Decorated Silver Star, Purple Heart with oak leaf clusters. Mem. ABA, Fed. Bar Assn., Am. Judicature Soc., Fed. Adminstrv. Law Judges Conf., Pi Gamma Mu, Delta Kappa Epsilon. Home: 2440 Virginia Ave NW Washington DC 20037 Office: SEC 450 5th St NW Washington DC 20549

BLAIR, WILLIAM DRAPER, JR., conservationist; b. Charlotte, N.C., May 3, 1927; s. William D. and Mary-Eula (Mason) B.; m. Jane Fraser Coleman, June 25, 1949; children—Jane Coleman, Elizabeth Mason. B.A., Princeton, 1949. Successively reporter, Korean war corr., European corr. Balt. Sunpapers, 1949-53; successively asst. editor, corr., London, chief Bonn (Germany) bur., then chief Paris bur. Newsweek mag., 1953-59; press officer, then dep. dir. Office Spl. Projects State Dept., 1959-62; dir. Office Media Services, 1962-70, dep. asst. sec. for pub. affairs, 1970-80; pres. The Nature Conservancy, 1980—. Served with USMCR, 1945-46. Recipient Meritorious Honor award Dept. State, 1964, Superior Honor award, 1967, Disting. Honor award, 1980. Mem. Am. Fgn. Service Assn., The Nature Conservancy (gov. 1972-80, chmn. bd. govs. 1975-77), Audubon Naturalist Soc. Central Atlantic States (dir. 1966-73, pres. 1968-70). Clubs: Princeton (dir. 1966-69), Metropolitan, 192 S F St., Internat. (Washington) (v.p. 1971-76); Chevy Chase; Univ. Cottage (Princeton, N.J.). Home: 118 E Melrose St Chevy Chase MD 20815 Office: The Nature Conservancy 1800 N Kent St Arlington VA 22209

BLAIR, WILLIAM GRANGER, journalist; b. Chgo., Nov. 17, 1925; s. William Mitchell and Martha (Granger) B.; m. Sue Cunningham, Apr. 19, 1952 (div.); children: Robert, Bruce, Laura; m. Ellen Lopin, Sept. 29, 1970. A.B. cum laude, Princeton U., 1950. Reporter Kansas City (Mo.) Star, 1950-53; mem. staff N.Y. Times, 1953—; fgn. corr., Paris, 1956-62, Jerusalem, 1962-65, London, 1965-67, mgr. employee communications, 1968, mgr. pub. relations, 1969-70, dir. pub. relations, 1970-73, broadcast corr., 1973-79, met. reporter, 1980—. Served with USMCR, 1943-46; PTO. Home: 320 E 52d St New York NY 10022 Office: NY Times 229 W 43d St New York NY 10036

BLAIR, WILLIAM MCCORMICK, JR., lawyer; b. Chgo., Oct. 24, 1916; s. William McCormick and Helen (Bowen) B.; m. Catherine Gerlach, Sept. 9, 1961; 1 son, William McCormick III. A.B., Stanford U., 1940; LL.B., U. Va., 1947. Bar: Ill. 1947, D.C. 1972. Assoc. firm Wilson & McIlvaine, Chgo., 1947-50; adminstrv. asst. to Gov. Adlai E. Stevenson of Ill., 1950-52; partner firm Stevenson, Rifkind & Wirtz, Chgo., 1955-61, Paul, Weiss, Rifkind, Wharton & Garrison, N.Y.C., 1957-61; U.S. ambassador to, Denmark, 1961-64, 1964-67; gen. dir. John F. Kennedy Center, 1968-72; partner firm Surrey Morse, Washington, 1978—; Vice pres. bd. dirs. Albert and Mary Lasker Found., N.Y.C.; bd. dirs. Am.-Scandinavian Found., N.Y.C. Served to capt. USAAF, 1942-46. Decorated Bronze Star, U.S.; officer Order of Crown, Belgium; Order of Sikatuna, Philippines; comdr. cross Order of Dannebrog 1st class, Denmark). Mem. Phi Delta Phi. Clubs: Fed. City (Washington); River (N.Y.C.). Office: 1250 Eye St NW Washington DC 20005

BLAIR, WILLIAM MELLVILLE, newspaper reporter; b. Cleve., June 14, 1911; s. Mellville Clifton and Margaret (O'Grady) B.; m. Helen Stern, Oct. 26, 1936; children—Jonathan Stern, Christopher Jo, Jeffrey William. Student, Ohio State U., 1930-34. With publicity dept. Ohio State U. radio sta. WEAO, 1933-34; reporter-editor Canton (Ohio) Repository, 1934-36, Pitts. Sun-Telegraph, 1936-37; with Pitts., Harrisburg and Phila. burs. AP, 1937-42; mem. staff N.Y. Times, 1942-76; reporter-editor Washington bur., 1953-76. Recipient U.S. Navy commendation, 1946; award Nat. Council Farmer Coops., 1950; J.S. Russell Meml. award Newspaper Farm Editors Assn., 1962; Conservation Service award U.S. Dept. Interior, 1969. Mem. Newspaper Farm Editors Am. (pres. 1974-75), Nat. Press Found. (sec. 1976-79), Sigma Delta Chi. Clubs: Washington Athletic (gov. 1958-61, 63-66, 68-70), Nat. Press (sec. 1962-64), Nat. Press (pres. 1965), Touchdown (Washington)). Home: 5228 SW Anhinga Ave Palm City FL 33490 Office: 1000 Connecticut Ave NW Washington DC 20036

BLAIR, WILLIAM ROBERT, fire commr.; b. Wibaux, Mont., Feb. 19, 1928; s. John Francis and Corrine Constance (Robbins) B.; m. Barbara Jeanne Maxfield, June 28, 1952; children: Sandra Jeanne Blair Spencer, Patricia Lucille Blair Brox, Michael John. Student, Los Angeles Valley Jr. Coll., 1954-57, E. Los Angeles Coll., 1964-68. With Los Angeles City Fire Dept., 1953-80; dep. chief Bur. Support Services, 1978-80; fire commr. City of Chgo., 1980—; lectr. in field. Co-author: A Complete Book on High-Rise Operations for the Los Angeles Fire Department, 1977; author: Fire Survival and Protection, 1983. Active Boy Scouts Am., March of Dimes, ARC; mem. Chgo. Hosp. Council, 1980—, Coordinating Council on Arson for Profit, Chgo., 1980—. Served with U.S. Army, 1950-52. Mem. Internat. Assn. Fire Chiefs, Met. Fire Chief Assn., Ill. Fire Chiefs Assn., Northeastern Ill. Fire Chiefs Assn. Republican. Mem. Ch. Jesus Christ of Latter-Day Saints. Address: 121 N LaSalle St Chicago IL 60602

BLAIR, WILLIAM SUTHERLAND, publisher; b. Glasgow, Scotland, Sept. 18, 1917; came to U.S., 1950, naturalized, 1961; s. Duncan and Ada (Sutherl) B.; m. Mary Seymour Barnes, Feb. 17, 1945; children—Colin Campbell, Fiona Seymour, Sheila Sutherland. B.A., Lincoln Coll., Oxford (Eng.) U., 1940; student, Princeton Grad. Sch., 1940-41. Econs. and statistic officer Internat. Air Transp. Assn., Montreal, 1946-49; v.p. Ogilvy & Mather, N.Y.C., 1950-57; pres. Harper-Atlantic Sales Inc., N.Y.C., 1957-68, Harper's mag., 1968-72; pub. Blair & Ketchum's Country Journal, 1973—. Served with Canadian Army, 1943-46. Home: RD 3 Brattleboro VT 05301 Office: Country Journal 205 Main St Brattleboro VT 05301

BLAIR, WILLIAM TRAVIS (BUD BLAIR), organization executive; b. Canton, Ohio, Dec. 17, 1925; s. George Neely and Helen Irene (Travis) B.; m. Eleanor I. Reid, Mar. 16, 1954; children: Carol Blair Oliver, Timothy R., Anne T. Blair Sisson, Linda S. B.A., Ohio Wesleyan U., 1950; grad., Advance Mgmt. Inst. for Assn. Execs., Mich. State U., 1964. Assoc. dir. legis. affairs Ohio C. of C., Columbus, 1958-61, dir. indsl. devel., 1961-77, dir. social legislation, 1963-77, dir. legis. affairs, 1973-77, exec. v.p., 1977-80, pres., 1980—; sec., mem. exec. com. Ohio Med. Indemnity, Inc., Worthington, 1966-79, also dir. Chmn. bd. mgmt. Central YMCA, Columbus, 1974; bd. trustees Center of Sci. and Industry, Columbus, 1962—. Served with USCG, 1943-46. Mem. Ohio Commodores, Am. C. of C. Execs., C. of C. U.S., Am. Soc. Assn. Execs., Newcomen Soc. N. Am., Council State C. of C. (sec. treas. 1978, vice chmn. 1979, mem. exec. com. 1978-79, chmn. 1980-82), Ohio Trade Assn. Execs. (dir. 1979—), SAR, C. of C. Execs. of Ohio (dir. 1978). Presbyterian. Clubs: Columbus Rotary (dir. 1980), University (dir. 1980-83), University (v.p. 1982-83), Columbus Athletic, York Temple Country, Masons. Home: 138 W Cooke Rd Columbus OH 43214 Office: 17 S High St Columbus OH 43215

BLAIS, JEAN-JACQUES, Canadian government official; b. Sturgeon Falls, Ont., Can., June 27, 1940; s. Rodolphe Gaston and Claire (Rochon) B.; m. Maureen Ann Ahearn, May 20, 1968; children: Stephane, Alexandre, Marie-Josée. B.A., U. Ottawa, 1961, LL.B., 1964.. Partner firm Miller & Blais, 1966-70, Blais, McLachlan & Duchesneau-McLachlan, North Bay, Ont., 1970; elected to Ho. of Commons, 1972, 74, 79, 80; apptd. Parliamentary Sec. to Pres. of Privy Council, 1975, Postmaster Gen., dep. ho. leader, 1976-78, solicitor gen. Can., 1978-79, minister of supply and services, 1980-83, minister nat. def., 1983—. Named Queen's Counsel, 1979. Mem. Canadian, Nipissing bar assns., Law Soc. Upper Can., Ottawa C. of C., Algonquin Regt. (hon.). Mem. Liberal Party of Can. Roman Catholic. Club: Richelieu Internat. Office: House of Commons Room 231 WB Ottawa ON Canada K1A 0A7 *

BLAIS, MADELEINE HELENA, writer; b. Holyoke, Mass., Aug. 25, 1949; d. Raymond J. and Maureen M. (Shea) B.; m. John Strong Miner Katzenbach, May 10, 1980. B.A., Coll. New Rochelle, 1969; M.S., Columbia U., 1970. Reporter Boston Globe, 1971-72, Trenton (N.J.) Times, 1974-76; staff writer Tropic Mag., Miami Herald, 1979—. Recipient Pulitzer Prize, 1980. Office: Tropic Mag Miami Herald Miami FL 33101

BLAISE, CLARK LEE, educator, author; b. Fargo, N.C., Apr. 10, 1940; s. Leo Romeo and Anne Marion (Vanstone) Blais (parents Can. citizens); m. Bharati Mukherjee, Sept. 19, 1963; children: Bart Anand, Berbnard Sudhir. A.B., Denison U., 1961, hon. dectorate, 1979; M.F.A., U. Iowa, 1964. Instr. U. Wis.-Milw., 1964-65; lectr. Sir George Williams U., Montreal, Que., Can., 1966; asst. prof. Concordia U., Montreal, 1967-69, assoc. prof., 1969-73, prof. English, 1973-78; prof. humanities York U., Toronto, Ont., Can., 1978-79; prof. Skidmore Coll., Saratoga Springs, N.Y., 1980—. Author: A North American Education, 1973, Tribal Justice, 1974, (with B. Mukherjee) Day and Nights in Calcutta, 1977, Lunar Attractions, 1979, Lusts, 1983; contbr. stories, articles and revs. to publs. Recipient prize Gt. Lakes Colls. Assn., 1973, St. Lawrence award for fiction St. Lawrence U., 1974, Fels award Coordinating Council Lit. Mags., 1975, Books in Can. mag., 1980; Can. Council Sr. Arts grantee, 1976-77; NEA grantee, 1981. Mem. PEN. Home: 115 Circular St Saratoga Springs NY 12866 Office: English Dept Skidmore Coll Saratoga Springs NY 12866

BLAKE, ALFRED GREENE, mining company executive; b. Pitts., June 22, 1902; s. William F. and Blanche (Johnson) B.; m. Mildred I. Cordeaux, July 27, 1929; children: Johnson C., Phyllis I. C.E., Lehigh U., 1925, D.Engrng. (hon.), 1980; spl. student U. Pa, 1933-34. Spl. rep. Standard San. Mfg. Co., Pitts., 1925-32; mgr. dealer div. Phila. Gas Works Co., 1932-37; mgr. Eastern operations Ruud Mfg. Co., Pitts., 1937-45; partner Rogers & Slade, mgmt. cons., N.Y.C., 1945-50; v.p. Edgar Bros. Co., Metuchen, N.J., 1950-54,, exec. v.p., dir., mem. exec. com., 1954-60, Minerals & Chems. Philipp Corp., 1960-64, pres. chief exec. officer minerals and chems. div., 1964-67; (co. merged with Engelhard Industries to form Engelhard Minerals & Chems. Corp. 1967), exec. v.p., 1967-71, chmn. bd., 1971-75, ret. chmn. bd., 1975—, dir., mem. exec. com., 1967-76, dir. emeritus, 1976—, pres. minerals and chems. div., 1967-69, chmn. div., 1969-71; v.p., dir. Porocel Corp., 1954-67, pres., dir., 1967-70, chmn. bd., 1970-75, ret. chmn. bd., 1975—, dir., 1954-76; v.p., dir. Chemstone Corp., 1955-67, pres., dir., 1967-70, chmn. bd., 1970-75, ret. chmn. bd., 1975—, dir., 1955-76; v.p., dir. Cuyahoga Lime Co., 1955-67, pres., dir., 1967-70, chmn. bd., 1970-75, ret. chmn. bd., 1975—, dir., 1955-76; pres., dir. Eastern Magnesia Talc Co., 1967-70, chmn. bd., 1970-75, ret. chmn. bd., 1975—, dir., 1967-76, Commonwealth Bank of Metuchen, N.J.; mem. adv. bd. First Nat. Bank N.J. Bd. dirs. emeritus Syracuse U. Pulp and Paper Found., pres., 1970-71, mem. exec. com.; dir. operations U.S. Govt. tng. within industry div. War Manpower Commn., 1942-45; trustee Lehigh U., Ind. Coll. Fund N.J. Mem. TAPPI, Lehigh U. Alumni Assn. (dir., mem. exec. com., pres. 1969-70). Home: 970 Glenwood Ave Plainfield NJ 07060 Office: Engelhard Minerals & Chems Corp Menlo Park Edison NJ 08817 *Understanding of people and their motives and a sense of human compassion. Enthusiasm - a consuming interest in the future of business and dedication to achievement. Always seeking progress. Rigid sense of integrity.*

BLAKE, BUD (JULIAN WATSON), cartoonist; b. Nutley, N.J., Feb. 13, 1918; s. George Wilbur and Hazel (Metcalfe) B.; m. Doris Gaskill, Jan. 4, 1941; children: Julian G., Mariana. Student, Nat. Acad. Design, 1935-36. Sketch artist, art dir., exec. art dir. Kudner Agy., N.Y.C., 1937-43, 46-54. Cartoonist: Ever Happen To You, syndicated by King Features; also free lance cartooning for various mags. and ads, 1954-65; cartoonist: syndicated comic strip Tiger, 1965—; Paperback cartoon books include Tiger, Tiger Turns On; others. Served with inf. AUS, 1943-46. Mem. Nat. Cartoonists Soc. (Best Humor Strip award 1971, 78), Newspaper Features Council. Home and Office: PO Box 23 Rumson NJ 07760

BLAKE, DAVID HAVEN, university dean; b. Long Branch, N.J., June 5, 1940; s. Edgar Bond and Haven (Johnstone) B.; m. Virginia E. Richmond, Oct. 30, 1982; children: by previous marriage: David H., Jennifer B., Kimberly D. A.B., Dartmouth Coll., 1961; M.B.A., U. Pitts, 1962; M.A., Rutgers U., 1966, Ph.D., 1968. Project mgr., pub affairs Smith Kline & French, Phila., 1962-63; asst. prof. dept. polit. sci. Wayne State U., Detroit, 1966-69; asst. prof., assoc. prof. Grad. Sch. Bus. U. Pitts., 1969-76, assoc. dean, prof., 1976-80; dean, prof. coll. Bus. Adminstrn. Northeastern U., Boston, 1980-82; dean, prof. Grad. Sch. Mgmt. Rutgers U., 1983—; cons. IBM, Armonk, N.Y., Mex., 1972—, Pub. Affairs Council, Washington, 1974—, AT&T, Basking Ridge, N.Y., 1979—, Marsh & McLennan, N.Y.C., 1981—. Co-author: The Politics of Golbal Economic Relations, 1976-83, Managing the External Relations of MNCS, 1977, The Social and Economic Impacts of MNCS, 1977, Social Auditing: Evaluating the Impact of Corporate Programs, 1976. Mem. adv. com. on internat. investment, tech. and devel. Dept. State, Washington, 1983—; mem. UNESCO Consultative Group on Fgn. Investment, Paris, 1982—. Mem. Acad. Internat. Bus (v.p. 1979-81), Am. Assembly Collegiate Schs. of Bus., Beta Gamma Sigma. Home: 31 Dale Dr Summit NJ 07901 Office: Rutgers State U 92 New St Newark NJ 07102

BLAKE, ELIAS, JR., college president; b. Brunswick, Ga., Dec. 13, 1929; s. Elias and Ruth (Thomas) B.; m. Mona Williams, June 13, 1963; children: Michael, Elias Ayinde. B.A., Paine Coll., 1951; M.A., Howard U., 1954; Ph.D., U. Ill., 1960. Asst. prof. Howard U., Washington, 1959-66; dir. Upward Bound program Inst. for Service to Edn., Washington, 1966-67, pres., 1969-77, Clark Coll., Atlanta, 1977—; past chmn. Nat. Adv. Com. of Black Higher Edn., Carnegie Found. for Advancement of Teaching. Contbr. writings to profl. publs. Served with U.S. Army, 1951-53. Recipient outstanding tchr. award Student Council Coll. Liberal Arts, Howard U., 1964. Mem. Nat. Assn. for Equal Opportunity in Higher Edn., Am. Council on Edn. Office: 240 Chestnut St SW Atlanta GA 30314 *

BLAKE, GERALD RUTHERFORD, banker; b. Knoxville, Tenn., Apr. 2, 1939; s. Roy Carl and Katherine Marie (Rutherford) B.; m. Jeanne Avonne Jones, May 11, 1962; children: Robert Alan, Douglas Mark. Student, U. Tenn., 1957-58, Sch. Bank Adminstrn., U. Wis., 1971-73. With Miller's. Inc., Knoxville, 1959-62; with First Tenn. Bank, Knoxville, 1963—, v.p., purchasing officer, 1973—. Vice-chmn. planning com. Knoxville United Way, 1973—; pres. Ramsey Community Club, 1966-67, Ramsey Elementary Sch. PTO, 1976-80; bd. dirs. Planned Parenthood Assn., 1976-77. Mem. Am. Inst. Banking, Bank Adminstrn. Inst. (pres., dir. Smoky Mountain chpt. 1976-77, state dir. 1977-79, 2d vice-chmn. Tenn. Title XX com.). Baptist. Home: 5233 Strawplains Pike Knoxville TN 37914 Office: 800 Gay St Knoxville TN 37914 *I always seem to be caught between the old and the new-in the middle of change from one accepted method or life-style to the new method or life-style, which has yet to be fully accepted. Perhaps everyone in every age is at the same situation. The time is upon us and the need is clear for a return to individualism and self-reliance, and a return to basic moral and religious principles. In doing so, one may just find the answers to most of life's problems.*

BLAKE, JOHN BALLARD, historian; b. New Haven, Oct. 29, 1922; s. Francis Gilman and Dorothy Palmer (Dewey) B.; m. Jean Place Adams, Apr. 2, 1949; children: Catherine Curtis, John Gilman, Ann Ballard, James Adams. B.A., Yale U., 1943; M.A., Harvard U., 1947, Ph.D., 1954; M.D. (hon.), Conn. State Med. Soc., 1966. Fellow history of medicine Johns Hopkins, 1951-52; research fellow history of medicine Yale, 1952-55; asst. historian Rockefeller Inst. Med. Research, N.Y.C., 1955-57; asso. curator div. med. scis. U.S. Nat. Museum, Smithsonian Instn., 1957-59, curator, 1959-61; chief history medicine div., Nat. Library Medicine, Washington, 1961-82, scholar-in-residence, 1982—. Author: Benjamin Waterhouse and the Introduction of Vaccination: A Reappraisal, 1957, Public Health in the Town of Boston, 1630-1822, 1959; Editor: Medical Reference Works, 1967, Education in the History of Medicine, 1968, Safeguarding the Public, 1970, Centenary of Index Medicus, 1879-1979, 1980; Contbr. articles to profl. jours. Served as 1st lt. USAAF, 1943-46. Garrison lectr. Am. Assn. History of Medicine, 1964; Clendening lectr. U. Kans., 1976; Shyrock lectr. U. Pa., 1978; Regents' award Nat. Library of Medicine, 1982; Merit award NIH, 1982. Mem. Med. Library Assn. (Eliot award 1968), Am. Hist. Assn., History Sci. Soc., Am. Assn. History Medicine (sec.-treas. 1956-67, v.p. 1970-72, pres. 1972-74, Welch medal 1980), Phi Beta Kappa. Home: 3038 Newark St NW Washington DC 20008 Office: Nat Library Medicine Bethesda MD 20209

BLAKE, JOHN FRANCIS, former government agency official, consultant; b. San Francisco, July 10, 1922; s. Richard Daniel and Catherine Genevieve B.; m. Frances Olive Foley, June 25, 1949; children: Kathleen, Barbara, Mary, Joan, Margaret. B.S., U. San Francisco, 1943; M.A., George Washington U., 1965. With CIA, 1947-79, dep. dir. adminstrn., 1974-79; staff dir. U.S. Senate Select Com. on Intelligence, Washington, 1981-82; dir. adminstrn. Electronic Warfare Assocs. Inc., McLean, Va., 1982—. Served in U.S. Army, 1943-46. Recipient Career Service award U.S. Civil Service League, 1978. Mem. Assn. Former Intelligence Officers (dir.), Nat. M.I. Assn. (dir.), CIA Retirees Assn. (chmn. bd. dirs.). Home: 8412 Crown Pl Alexandria VA 22308 Office: 2071 Chainbridge Rd Vienna VA 22180

BLAKE, JOHN LEWIS, mgmt. cons., former banker; b. Providence, June 11, 1921; s. Jacob Stephen and Hortense (Hayes) B.; m. Rose Marie Kornegay, Feb. 13, 1952; children—Kim Renee, Edward Marshall. Student, Mich. State U., 1949-52, B.A., 1961; LL.D., Shaw U., 1972. Tchr. bus. West High Sch., Rochester, N.Y., 1961-66; dep. dir. Monroe County Human Relations Com., Rochester, 1966-67; tng. coordinator Sybron Corp., Rochester, 1967-68; gen. mgr. Rochester Bus. Corp., 1968; asst. sec. Marine Midland Bank, Rochester, 1968-69; dep. manpower adminstr. Dept. Labor, 1969-71; dir. Job Corps, 1971-73; asst. v.p. Marine Midland Bank, Rochester, 1973-76; mgmt. cons., 1976—. Trustee Rochester Inst. Tech., 1970—. Served With USMCR, 1943-46. Recipient award Am. Mgmt. Assn., 1969, Nat. C. of C., 1969, Distinguished Achievement award Dept. Labor, 1972. Mem. Am. Soc. Tng. and Devel., NEA, Kappa Alpha Psi. Home: 680 Claybourne Rd Rochester NY 14618

BLAKE, JUDITH, sociology educator; b. N.Y.C., May 3, 1926; d. Forrest James and Sylvia (Blake) Kincade; 1 dau., Laura Isabelle Davis. B.S., Columbia U., 1950, Ph.D., 1961. Prof. Asst. prof. to asso. prof. dept. demography U. Calif., Berkeley, 1962-69, prof., 1969-72; prof. Grad. Sch. Public Policy, Fred H. Bixby prof. Sch. Public Health and dept. sociology UCLA, 1976—; Rand Grad. Inst. adv. bd.; mem. Assembly of Behavioral and Social Scis., Nat. Acad. Scis., 1978—. Contbr. articles to profl. jours. Population Council fellow, 1954; Guggenheim fellow, 1976-77; Phi Beta Kappa vis. scholar, 1976-77. Fellow AAAS; Mem. Population Assn. Am. (pres. 1980), Am. Sociol. Assn., Sociol. Research Assn. (pres. 1978), Am. Public Health Assn. Home: 457 19th St Santa Monica CA 90402 Office: Sch Public Health UCLA Los Angeles CA 90024

BLAKE, JULES, chemical company executive; b. N.Y.C., July 7, 1924; s. Ralph and Celia B.; m. Barbara Stryker, Apr. 9, 1949; children: Sharon, Judith, Janice. B.S., U. Pa., 1949, M.S. in Chemistry, 1951, Ph.D., 1954. Research supr. E.I. duPont de Nemours, Wilmington, Del., 1954-66; dir. research and devel. Mallinckrodt, Inc., St. Louis, 1966-71; v.p. research and devel. Kendall Co., Boston, 1971-73, Colgate-Palmolive, N.Y.C., 1973—; pres. Indsl. Research Inst., N.Y.C., 1967—; bd. of overseers Sch. Dental Medicine U. Pa., 1980—. Chmn. evaluation panel, analytical chemistry Nat. Bur. Standards, Gaithersburg, Md., 1973. Served with U.S. Army, 1942-46. Mem. Am. Chem. Soc., Soc. Chem. Industry, Assn. Research Dirs. (pres. 1968—), Sigma Xi. Clubs: Chemist, University (N.Y.C.). Office: Colgate-Palmolive 909 River Rd Piscataway NJ 08854

BLAKE, LARRY JAY, institute technology president; b. Kalispell, Mont., Apr. 25, 1930; s. Morris E. and Leah V. (Kemmis) B.; m. H. Jeane Trippet, July 9, 1952; children: Howard, Kathleen, Richard, Larry, Jay. B.S., U. Wash., 1957, M.S., 1960; Ph.D., U. Ariz., 1967. Registered profl. engr., Wash. Div. chmn. Highline Coll., Midway, Wash., 1962-66; dean Seattle Community Coll., 1966-67; pres. Flathead Valley Community Coll., Kalispell, 1967-74, Fraser Valley Coll., Chilliwack, B.C., Can., 1974-79, Oreg. Inst. Tech., Klamath Falls, 1983—; state pres. N.C. Comunity Coll. System, Raleigh, 1979-83; cons. Arab Republic of Egypt, Cairo, 1976—, Alaska Health Dept., Juneau, 1963-64. Author: The Character and Significance of Irrigation Return Flows, 1960, Sanitary Waste Disposal for Navy Camps in Polar Regions, 1962, Elements of Engineering For Non-Majors, 1967, State Master Plan for Montana Community Coll., 1970. Mem. Am. Assn. Community and Jr. Colls. (dir. 1972-75), N.W. Assn. Community Colls. (pres. 1972-73), Mont. Assn. Community Colls. (pres. 1968-74), President's Nat Council for Edn. Professions Devel. (chmn. 1970-73). Office: Oreg Inst Tech Klamath Falls OR 97601

BLAKE, PETER JOST, architect; b. Berlin, Sept. 20, 1920; U.S., 1940, naturalized, 1944. Student, U. London, 1938, Sch. Architecture, Regent St. Poly., London, 1939, Sch. Architecture, U. Pa., 1941; B.Arch., Pratt Inst., 1949. Apprentice to Serge Chermayeff, Architect, London, 1938-39, George Howe, Oskar Stonorov and Louis Kahn, Architects, Phila., 1940-42; curator dept. architecture and indsl. design Mus. Modern Art, N.Y.C., 1948-50; asso. editor The Archtl. Forum, Time, Inc., N.Y.C., 1950-61, mng. editor, 1961-64, editor-in-chief, 1964-72; partner Peter Blake & Julian Neski, Architects, N.Y.C., 1956-60, James Baker & Peter Blake, Architects, 1964-71; contbg. editor New York mag., 1968-76; editor-in-chief Architecture Plus, N.Y.C., 1972-75; chmn. Sch. Architecture, Boston Archtl. Center, 1975-79; chmn. dept. architecture and planning Catholic U. Am., Washington, 1979—; vis. critic, lectr. Harvard U., Yale U., Cornell U., Tulane U., Pratt Inst., Cooper Union, New Sch. for Social Research, Bennington Coll., Columbia U., Ill. Inst. Tech., U. Mich., architecture in, Hamburg, Aachen, Hanover, Braunschweig, Vienna, Maracaibo, and West Berlin; chmn. Alcoa Conf. on Future of Housing, Boca Raton, Fla., 1957, Internat. Design Conf., Aspen, Colo., 1962, bd. dirs., 1965-73; now adv. to bd.; chmn. adv. panel on quality of Iranian housing, urban devel. and new town planning Shah of Iran, 1976; mem. U.S. del. Internat. Conf. on Theater Design, Berlin, 1960; participant Internat. Conf. on Urban Design, New Delhi, 1965, U.S./Yugoslav Conf. on Housing, Zagreb, 1974, Iran Internat. Congress on Architecture, Persepolis, 1974. Author: The Master Builders, 1960, God's Own Junkyard, 1964, Form Follows Fiasco, 1977; Contbr. articles to mags. and newspapers.; Important works include Hollis Unitarian Ch, Queens, N.Y.; offices and warehouse, Queens; Temple Emanu-El, Livingston, N.J., Ford Found. Ideal Theater, Darrow Sch. Library, New Lebanon, N.Y., Berlin-Tegel Airport Project, Manistee (Mich.) Town Planning Project, Max Planck Inst. Project, Berlin, Rehab. Center, Binghamton (N.Y.) State Hosp., Roundabout Theater, Stage One, N.Y.C., Neely Exptl. Theater, Vanderbilt U., Nashville, Puerto Rican Traveling Theater, N.Y.C. Bd. dirs. City Walls, N.Y.C., Boston Archtl. Center; trustee Cosanti Found. Served with AUS, 1944-47; ETO. Recipient Howard Myers award for archtl. journalism, 1960; Graham Found. Advanced Studies in Fine Arts fellow, 1962; Ford Found. grantee, 1960. Fellow AIA (Architecture Critics medal 1975, citation for design of exhibit on U.S. architecture sent to Eastern Europe); mem. Soc. Archtl. Historians, Pub. Arts Council of Mcpl. Arts Soc. N.Y., Deutscher Werkbund. Office: Dept Architecture and Planning Catholic U Am Washington DC 20064

BLAKE, RAN, jazz pianist, composer; b. Springfield, Mass., Apr. 20, 1935; s. Philip Randall and Alison (Powers) B. B.A., Bard Coll., 1960. Tchr. New Eng. Conservatory, Boston, 1967—, chmn. third stream dept., 1973—; mem. faculty Hartford Conservatory Music, 1972-75; music columnist Morningsider, 1960-62. Appearances include, Monterrey Festival, 1962, Antibes (France) Music Festival, 1963, Lake Como (Italy) Jazz, 1977, Nancy (France) Jazz Pulsations Festival, New Eng. Life Hall, Boston, Contemporary Music Festival, So. Meth. U., Peabody Conservatory, Johns Hopkins U., 1978, U. Mass., 1978, 79, Mexico City, 1978, Bogota, Colombia, Buenos Aires, Argentina, Mendoza, Argentina, Rosario, Argentina, Tucuman, Argentina, Festival d'Anjou, Angers, France, Harvard U., N.Y.C., Lulu White's, Boston, Fisk U., 1979, Vanderbilt U., Ala. Sch. Fine Arts, Jonathan Swift's, Boston, 1979, 80, 82, New Eng. Conservatory, 1979, 80, 81, 82, 83, U. Mass., 1979, Black Beans Studio, N.Y.C., Northwestern U.,

Evanston, Ill., Am. Embassy, Winnipeg, Man., Can., Brandon (Man.) U., Painted Bride Arts Center, Phila., McGill U., U. Que., Sweet Basil's, N.Y.C., Theatre du Ranelagh, Paris, 1980, Ch. of the Covenant, Boston, Milan, Italy, West Bank Cafe, N.Y.C., Berlin Jazz Festival, U. Padua, Italy, Bunratty's, Boston, 1981, Rome, Third Stream Festival, Boston, 1982, St. Botolph Club, Boston, Merkin Concert Hall, N.Y.C., 1983, Kivik, Sweden, New Morning Club, Paris, Fed. Res. Bank, Boston, Canteen, London, 1984; appeared on TV shows, Flemish TV, radio, 1963, 66-67, concerts in ten European countries; rec. artist: (with Jeanne Lee) Newest Sound Around, 1962, reissued, 1980; R.B. Plays Solo Piano, 1966, The Blue Potato and Other Outrages, 1969, Breakthru, 1975, Wende, 1976, Open City, 1977, Crystal Trip, 1977, Take One, 1978, Take Two, 1978, Rapport, 1978, Realization of a Dream, 1978, Third Stream Today, 1979, Film Noir, 1980, Third Stream Recompositions, 1980, Improvisations with Jaki Byard, 1982, Duke Dreams, 1982, Portfolio of Doktor Mabuse, 1983; subject of numerous articles; included in books on jazz musicians.; arts columnist: Bay State Banner, 1974—. Mem. Am. Com. For Democracy in Greece, 1967. Recipient RCA Album First prize, Germany, 1963; Prix Billie Holiday, 1980; Guggenheim fellow, 1982; Nat. Endowment Arts fellow in Jazz Composition, 1982; Mass. Arts Found. fellow, 1982. Mem. Met. Cultural Alliance, Mass. Council Arts and Humanities, Am. Assn. Music Therapy, World Jazz Soc., AAUP, Film Soc. N.Y. Address: New Eng Conservatory 290 Huntington Ave Boston MA 02115

BLAKE, ROBERT ROGERS, behavioral science company executive; b. Brookline, Mass., Jan. 21, 1918; s. Charles B. and Margaret B.; m. Mercer Blain, Sept. 4, 1941; children—Brooks Blake, Cary Blake. B.A., Berea Coll., 1940; M.A., U. Va., 1941; Ph.D., U. Tex., 1947. Prof. psychology U. Tex., 1947-64; pres. Sci. Methods, Inc., Austin, Tex., 1961-81, chmn., 1981—; lectr. U. Reading, Eng; clin. psychologist Tavistock Clinic, London; lectr., research asso. Harvard U.; mem. hon. faculty of behavioral sci. Inst. Bus. Adminstrn. and Mgmt., Tokyo. Author: numerous books including The Managerial Grid, 1964, Consultation, 1976, Diary of an OD Man, 1976, Making Experience Work: The Grid Approach to Critique, 1978, The New Managerial Grid, 1978, The Versatile Manager: A Grid Profile, 1980, Grid Approach to Managing Stress, The Academic Administrator Grid: A Guide to Developing Effective Management Teams, The Real Estate Grid, 1981, The Grid for Sales Excellence, 1981, Synergogy, 1981, Productivity: The Human Side, 1983, Grid Approaches to Managerial Leadership in Nursing, 1983, The Secretary Grid, 1983. Served with USAAF, 1942-45. Fulbright scholar, 1949-50. Fellow Am. Psychol. Assn.; mem. Internat. Assn. Applied Social Scientists, Inst. Gen. Semantics (trustee). Home: 3700 Hampton Rd Austin TX 78705 Office: PO Box 195 Austin TX 78767

BLAKE, STEWART PRESTLEY, retired ice cream company executive; b. Jersey City, Nov. 26, 1914; s. Herbert P. and Ethel (Stewart) B.; m. Helen Davis, Nov. 16, 1982; children by previous marriage: Nancy Blake Yanakakis, Benson Prestley. Student, Trinity Coll., 1934-35, LL.D., 1976. Co-founder, 1935; chmn. Friendly Ice Cream Corp. (retail shops 18 states, hdqrs. in Wilbraham, Mass.), to 1979. Chmn. bd. trustees Bay Path Jr. Coll., Longmeadow, Mass. Clubs: Kiwanis, Colony (Springfield); Longmeadow Country. Office: 666 Bliss Rd Longmeadow MA 01106

BLAKE, VINCENT PATRICK, corp. exec.; b. N.Y.C., July 20, 1932; s. Patrick John and Mary Agnes (Blake) B.; m. Barbara C. French, May 9, 1964; children—Christopher, Catherine. B.B.A., Manhattan Coll., 1954. C.P.A., N.Y. Audit mgr. Arthur Andersen & Co., 1954-60; corp. mgr. internal auditing Gen. Dynamics Corp., 1961-64; asst. controller C.I.T. Financial Corp., 1964-68; sec.-treas. Sterling Precision Corp., 1968-72; exec. v.p., chief financial officer USLIFE Corp., N.Y.C., 1973-77; v.p., controller Amax, Inc., 1977—. Past pres., bd. dirs. Eastchester Taxpayers Orgn., Jasper Club of Manhattan Coll., Home Sch. Assn. of Immaculate Conception Sch., Bronxville Manor Civic Assn., Eastchester, N.Y. Mem. Financial Execs. Inst., Am. Inst. C.P.A.'s, N.Y. State Soc. C.P.A.'s, Nat. Assn. Accountants. Clubs: K.C., Ancient Order of Hibernians, Friendly Sons St. Patrick. Home: 130 Siwanoy Blvd Eastchester NY 10707 Office: Amax Center Greenwich CT 06836

BLAKE, WILLIAM HENRY, credit and public relations cons.; b. Jasonville, Ind., Feb. 18, 1913; s. Straude and Cora (Pope) B.; m. Helen Elizabeth Platt, Jan. 2, 1937; children—William Henry, Allen Howard. Student, Knox Coll., 1932-35; B.S., U. Ill., 1936, M.S., 1941, postgrad., 1946; student, N.Y. U., 1950-51, Am. U., 1955-56, 1958; grad., Columbia Grad. Sch. Consumer Credit, 1956, Northeastern Inst., Yale U., 1957. Instr. Champaign (Ill.) Pub. Schs., 1936-41; exec. sec. Ill. Soc. C.P.A.'s, Chgo., 1941-44; dean men, asso. prof. bus. adminstrn. Catawba Coll., 1947-51; dir. research Nat. Consumer Fin. Assn., Washington, 1954-59; exec. v.p. Internat. Consumer Credit Assn., St. Louis, 1959-78; pres. Consumer Trends Inc., also Blake Enterprises, cons., 1978—; cons. Decatur Consumer Credit Assn., 1979—; adminstr. Soc. Cert. Consumer Credit Execs., 1961-78. Author: Good Things of Life on Credit, 1960, rev., 1975, How to Use Consumer Credit Wisely, 1963, rev., 1975, Home Study Courses in Credit and Collections, 1968, Human Relations, 1969, Communications, 1970, Retail Credit and Collections, rev., 1974, Adminstrative Office Management, 1972, Consumer Credit Management, 1974; pub.: Consumer Trends Newsletter. Mem. pres.'s adv. cabinet Southeastern U.; adviser Office Edn. Assn.; chmn. public relations com. Ill. Heart Assn., 1979—; bd. dirs. Salvation Army, Decatur, 1979—; mem. fund raising com. Sch. Edn., U. Ill., 1979—; chmn. bd. trustees Alta Deana div. University City, 1970-73, congressional liaison, 1959-78; trustee Internat. Consumer Credit Assn. Ins. Trust and Retirement Program, 1960-78. Served to lt. USNR, 1944-47; lt. comdr., 1951-54. Named Man of Year Mo. Consumer Credit Assn., 1977. Mem. Credit Grantors Assn. Can. (dir. 1959-72), U.S. C. of C. (banking and currency com. 1968-71, trade assn. com. 1964-67), Am. Soc. Assn. Execs. (dir. 1965-68), Public Relations Soc. Am. (chpt. treas. 1979—), Press Club St. Louis, Internat. Platform Assn., Am. Soc. Assn. Execs., Washington Trade Assn. Execs., Am. Public Relations Assn. (chpt. pres. 1958-59), U. Ill. Alumni Assn., Phi Sigma Kappa. Republican. Presbyterian. Clubs: Capitol Hill, Exchequer (Washington); Rotary. Home and Office: 5 Edgewood Ct Decatur IL 62522

BLAKE, WILLIAM J., professional basketball team executive. V.p. Milw. Bucks, N.B.A. Office: Care Milwaukee Bucks 901 N Fourth St Milwaukee WI 53203

BLAKEBURN, ROY ELLSWORTH, clergyman; b. El Reno, Okla., Aug. 17, 1928; s. John Wesley and Jessie Elizabeth (McCarty) B.; m. Dorothy Willetta Condron, Aug. 16, 1947; children—Larry Alan, Robert Mark, Tony Wayne. B.A., Ark. Poly. Coll., (now Ark. Tech. U.), 1955; B.Div., Cumberland Presbyn. Sem., (now Memphis Theol. Sem.), 1962. Ordained to ministry Cumberland Presbyn. Ch., 1951; pastor chs. in, Okla., Ark. and, Tenn., 1950-60; asso. sec. bd. missions Cumberland Presbyn. Ch., Memphis, 1960-66; pastor First Cumberland Presbyn. Ch., Greeneville, Tenn., 1966—; stated clk. Ewing Presbytery, Cumberland Presbyn. Ch., 1952-53; moderator Ark. Synod, 1953, Ewing Presbytery, 1954-55, Hopewell Presbytery, 1956, E. Tenn. Presbytery, 1966, E. Tenn. Synod, 1968; press reporter Gen. Assembly, Cumberland Presbyn. Ch., 1958-61, mem. denominational bd. missions, 1958-60, 72-75, chmn. commn. gen. assembly office, 1966-72, mem. exec. com., 1975-77, chmn. gen. council, 1975-77, chmn. com. to revise Confession of Faith, 1978-83; moderator 145th Gen. Assembly, 1975; instr. Memphis Theol. Sem., 1963; mem. Presbyn. Appalachian Council, 1966-68, Presbyn. Appalachian Broadcasting Council, 1966-70; rep. uniting council World Alliance Presbyn. and Reformed Chs., Nairobi, Kenya, 1970. Author: The Holy Spirit Comes Through the Word, 1970, The Presence, The People, and the Journey, 1977, also articles, columns.; Editor: Missionary Messenger, 1966. Bd. dirs. Citizens Children Day Care Center, Greeneville, 1968-75, Greene County YMCA, 1970-75, Nolichuckey-Holston Mental Health Center, Greeneville, 1973-77; mem. Greene County Citizens Adv. Com. for Tenn. Dept. Human Services, 1972-77, vice chmn., 1975; trustee Bethel Coll., McKenzie, Tenn. Mem. Greene County Ministerial Assn., Internat. Platform Assn., Nat. Exchange Club. Democrat. Home: 1910 Moore St Greeneville TN 37743 Office: 201 N Main St Greeneville TN 37743 *If someone were asking me for advice about how to be successful, I would tell them: Learn gratitude for the people in your life, all the people in your life.*

BLAKEFIELD, WILLIAM HENRY, army officer, educational administrator; b. Sturgeon Bay, Wis., Dec. 28, 1917; s. Harry William and Vivian (Klinkenberg) B.; m. Doris Fairweather, Feb. 12, 1941; children—Nancy Elizabeth (Mrs. Thomas F. Dooley), William J.S. B.A., Ripon (Wis.) Coll., 1939; postgrad., Command and Gen. Staff Coll., 1950, Armed Forces Staff Coll., 1957, U. Pitts., 1958, Nat. War Coll., 1960. Commd. 2d lt. U.S. Army, 1939, advanced through grades to maj. gen., 1965; comdg. officer 1st BG, 7th Cav., 1st Cav. Div., Korea, 1960-61; mem. staff and faculty U.S. Army Command and Gen. Staff Coll., Ft. Leavenworth, Kans., 1961-64; chief Army sect. Joint U.S. Mil. Mission for Aid to Turkey, Ankara, 1964-66; asst. div. comdr. 3d Inf. Div., Wurzburg, Germany, 1966-67; comdg. gen. U.S. Army Intelligence Command, Ft. Holabird, Md., 1967-70; chief U.S. Army Adv. Group, Korea, 1970; chief of staff 8th U.S. Army, 1970-72, dep. comdg. gen. 1st, Ft. Meade, Md., 1972-76; pres. Kemper Mil. Sch. and Coll., Boonville, Mo., 1976-80. Decorated D.S.M. with oak leaf cluster, Silver Star, Legion of Merit, Bronze Star with V and oak leaf cluster, Joint Service Commmendation medal, Army Commendation medal with three oak leaf clusters, Purple Heart, Combat Inf. badge, U.S.; Order Nat. Security Merit Cheon-Su medal, Korea; Croix de Guerre with star, France). Clubs: Masons (32 deg.), Shriners., Rotary. Home: 3107 Springridge Dr Colorado Springs CO 80906

BLAKELY, FLORENCE ELLA, librarian; b. Clinton, S.C., Sept. 3, 1923; d. Ralph Royd and Lois (Newkirk) B. B.A. magna cum laude, Presbyterian Coll., 1943; B.S. in L.S, George Peabody Coll., 1945, M.A., 1960. Asst. librarian Presbyn. Coll., Clinton, 1943-44; reference librarian Greenville (S.C.) Pub. Library, 1945-47, br. librarian, 1947-48; reference librarian Duke U., Durham, N.C., 1948-56, head reference dept., 1956-79, asst. univ. librarian for collection devel., 1979—; vis. lectr. U. N.C., summer 1962, 78. Council on Library Resources fellow, 1970. Mem. AAUW (br. pres. 1965-67), ALA (life, recipient Isadore Gilbert Mudge citation 1974), Soc. Mayflower Descs., Delta Kappa Gamma, Beta Phi Mu. Episcopalian. Club: Altrusa. Home: 709 W Club Blvd Durham NC 27701 Office: Perkins Library Duke U Durham NC 27706

BLAKELY, LAWRENCE MACE, botanist, educator; b. Los Angeles, Nov. 12, 1934; s. Joseph M. and Faye (Allred) B.; m. Ruth Carol Morris, Jan. 1, 1960; children: Karen Louise, Susan Lynn. B.A. in Botany, U. Mont., 1956, M.A., 1958; Ph.D., Cornell U., 1963. Research asso. Cornell U., Ithaca, N.Y., 1963; asst. prof. Calif. State Poly. U., Pomona, 1963-68, asso. prof., 1968-72, prof., 1973—. Contbr. articles on plant physiology to sci. jours. Mem. Am. Soc. Plant Physiologists, Soc. Devel. Biology, Bot. Soc. Am., Plant Growth Regulator Soc. Am., So. Calif. Acad. Sci., Internat. Assn. Plant Tissue Culture, AAAS, Sigma Xi. Home: 678 Northwestern Dr Claremont CA 91711 Office: Dept Biol Sci Calif State Poly U Pomona CA 91768

BLAKELY, R. M., bank executive. Chmn., chief exec. officer Coast Fed. Savs. & Loan Assn., Los Angeles. Office: Coast Fed Savs & Loan Assn 855 S Hill St Los Angeles CA 90014§

BLAKELY, ROBERT JOHN, writer; b. nr. Ainsworth, Nebr., Feb. 24, 1915; s. Percy Lee and Mary Frances (Watson) B.; m. Alta M. Farr, 1964; 3 children. B.A. with highest distinction, State U. Iowa, 1937; scholar, Harvard Grad. Sch., 1937-38. Editorial writer Chgo. Daily News, 1964-67, editor sch. page, 1967-68; with Register and Tribune, Des Moines, 1938-42, 46-48; asst. to dir. domestic br. O.W.I., 1942-43; charge bur. spl. operations; editorial page editor St. Louis Star Times, 1948-51; mgr. central regional office Fund for Adult Edn., 1951-56, v.p., 1956-61; dean extension State U. Iowa, 1961-62; adj. asso. prof. adult edn. Syracuse U., 1969-77, prof., 1977—; Exec. com. Adult Edn. Council, Des Moines, 1939-41, St. Louis, 1948-51. Appeared numerous radio, TV broadcasts; author scripts for films.; Author: Adult Education in a Free Society, 1958, Toward a Homeodynamic Society, 1965, Knowledge Is the Power to Control Power, 1969, The People's Instrument: A Philosophy for Public Television, 1971, Fostering the Growing Need to Learn, 1974, To Serve the Public Interest, 1979; contbr. chpts. to profl. publs., articles to mags. Served from pvt. to 1st lt. USMCR, 1943-46. Home: 5418 S Blackstone Ave Chicago IL 60615

BLAKEMAN, ROYAL E., lawyer; b. N.Y.C., June 9, 1923; s. Jesse H. and Edythe (Siegel) B.; m. Edith Hughes, Sept. 1, 1945; 1 dau., Carol. B.A., Hofstra Coll., 1941, NYU, 1947. Bar: N.Y. 1947, Calif. 1973. Practiced in, N.Y.C.; partner firm Marshall, Bratter, Greene, Allison & Tucker (specializing in theatrical law), 1953-81; counsel Pryor, Cashman, Sherman & Flynn, 1981—, Nat. Acad. Rec. Arts and Scis.; officer, dir. Goodson-Todman Assoc., Inc., Goodson-Todman Enterprises, Ltd., January Enterprises, Inc. Served with U.S. Maritime Service; Served with USNR, 1942-46. Recipient George M. Esterbrook Disting. Service award Hofstra Alumni Assn., 1966. Mem. Nat. Acad. TV Arts and Scis. (pres., bd. govs. N.Y.C. chpt.; past nat. pres., trustee), Nat. Youth Council. Club: Dad's (Long Beach) (past pres.). Home: 750 Lido Blvd Lido Beach NY 11561 Office: 410 Park Ave New York NY 10022

BLAKEMORE, CLAUDE COULEHAN, banker; b. Los Angeles, Apr. 26, 1909; s. Claude Payne and Agnes C. (Coulehan) B.; m. Violet E. Alt, Aug. 27, 1937; children: Susan Blakemore Daniels, Bruce A. Student, UCLA, 1928-29, U. Iowa, 1929; grad., Stonier Sch. Banking, Rutgers U., 1951. With First Nat. Bank Santa Ana, Calif., 1930-41; comptroller of currency, asst. nat. bank examiner, 1941-42; bank examiner Fed. Res. Bank San Francisco, 1942-45; with First Nat. Bank San Diego, 1945-70, sr. v.p., 1962-64, pres., 1964-70, chief exec. officer, 1966-70; pres., chief exec. officer So. Calif. First Nat. Corp., 1969-71; pres., trustee USF Investors; dir. Rice, Hall, James & Assos., Percy H. Goodwin Co., Western Bldg. Spltys. Bd. dirs. San Diego County Med. Rehab. Center Assn.; bd. dirs., pres. San Diego County council Boy Scouts Am.; bd. dirs., treas., chmn. bd. San Diego Hall of Sci.; bd. dirs. San Diego Symphony. Mem. Am. Bankers Assn. (exec. council), Calif. Bankers Assn. (pres., dir.), Navy League U.S., Sigma Pi. Club: San Diego Country (Chula Vista, Calif.). Home: 1822 Altamira St San Diego CA 92103 Office: 1200 3d Ave Suite 1600 San Diego CA 92101

BLAKEMORE, WILLIAM BARNETT, III, journalist; b. Chgo., Oct. 4, 1944; s. William Barnett and Elizabeth Josephine (Gilstrap) B. B.A., Wesleyan U., 1965. Tchr. Milford (Conn.) Acad., 1965-66; tchr. Am. Community Sch., Beirut, 1966-70; instr. Am. U. Beirut, 1969-70; pres. Am. Repertory Theater of Beirut, 1969-70; soundman, radio reporter, producer ABC News, Middle East, India, 1970-76; reporter ABC Radio, London, 1977; bur. chief, corr. ABC News, Rome, 1978-84; Edward R. Murrow fellow Council on Fgn. Relations, 1984-85; spl. corr. Christian Sci. Monitor, 1975—; lectr. Am. Youth Found., 1975—. Recipient award Overseas Press Club, 1974, 76, 81; award for Best TV News Reporting in 1980 (with Gregg Dobbs) Sigma Delta Chi./Soc. Profl. Journalists; Emmy award for coverage of Italian earthquake, 1981; recipient spl. jury award San Francisco Internat. Film Festival, Gold Hugo award; co-recipient award for ABC spl. America Held Hostage: The Secret Negotiations Dupont-Columbia, Nat. Headliner award for outstanding TV network news reporting of Vatican, 1982. Office: ABC News 7 W 66th St New York NY 10023

BLAKENEY, ALLAN EMRYS, lawyer, Canadian politician; b. Bridgewater, N.S., Can., Sept. 7, 1925; s. John Cline and Bertha (Davies) B.; m. Mary Elizabeth Schwartz, 1950 (dec. 1957); m. Anne Louise Gorham, May 1959; children: Barbara, Hugh, David, Margaret. B.A., Dalhousie U., 1945, LL.B., 1947; B.A.; Rhodes scholar, Oxford U., 1949, M.A., 1955. Bar: N.S. 1950, Sask. 1951. Queen's counsel, 1961; sec. to govt. fin. office Govt. Sask., 1950-55; chmn. Sask. Securities Commn., 1955-58; ptnr. Davidson, Davidson & Blakeney, Regina, Sask., 1958-60, Griffin, Blakeney, Beke, Koskie & Lueck, Regina, 1964-70; premier of, Sask., 1971-82; Mem. Sask. Legislature, 1960—; leader of the opposition Sask. Legislature, 1970-71, 82—; minister of edn., Sask., 1960-61, provincial treas., 1961-62, minister public health, 1962-64. Office: Legislative Bldg Regina SK Canada:

BLAKESLEE, ALTON LAUREN, sci. writer; b. Dallas, June 27, 1913; s. Howard Walter and Marguerite Alton (Fortune) B.; m. Virginia Boulden, July 3, 1937; children—Dennis, Carolyn Sandra. Student, Duke, 1931-33; A.B., Columbia, 1935. Reporter Jour. Every Evening, Wilmington, Del., 1935-39; mem. staff AP, 1939—, journalist, Balt., 1939-42, N.Y. fgn. news staff, 1942-46, sci. reporter, 1946, sci. editor, 1969-78; AP corr. U.S. Navy Antarctic Expdn., 1946-47. Author: Polio and the Salk Vaccine, 1956, What You Should Know About Heart Disease, 1957, Your Heart Has Nine Lives (Blakeslee award Am. Heart Assn. 1964), 1963 (Lasker award 1965). Pres. Am. Tentative Soc., ednl. found., 1974—. Recipient George Westinghouse sci. writing award AAAS, 1952, George Polk award, 1952, Lasker Med. Journalism award, 1954, 62, 64; Bronze medallion, 1954; Howard Blakeslee award Am. Heart Assn., 1963, 64; James T. Grady medal Am. Chem. Soc., 1959; Honor award for distinguished service U. Mo., 1966; Distinguished Service award Sigma Delta Chi, 1965; Sci. Writers' award ADA, 1967; Robert T. Morse Writer's award Am. Psychiat. Assn., 1973; Deadline award N.Y. chpt. Sigma Delta Chi, 1973; Claude Bernard award Nat. Soc. Med. Research, 1976; Disting. Journalism award Am. Heart Assn., 1978; Carr Van Anda award Ohio U., 1978. Fellow Rochester Mus. Arts and Scis.; mem. Nat. Assn. Sci. Writers (pres. 1954-55). Home: 13 Vista Way Port Washington NY 11050

BLAKESLEE, ARTHUR LEOPOLD, III, insurance company executive; b. Washington, Oct. 10, 1927; s. Arthur Leopold and Mary Frances (Weigel) B.; m. Mary Thornton Belt, Aug. 25, 1951; children: Priscilla S., Mary W., Susan S., Arthur Leopold, IV. A.B., Harvard U., 1949, M.B.A. with distinction, 1952, grad. Advanced Mgmt. Program, 1971. With controllers div. Life Ins. Co. Va., Richmond, 1949-50; cons. Bowles, Andrews & Towne, Richmond, 1952-60; v.p., treas. Variable Annuity Life Ins. Co., Washington, 1960-65; ind. mgmt. cons., Washington, 1965-67; exec. v.p., then pres., chief exec. officer Aetna Variable Annuity Life Ins. Co., Falls Church, Va., 1967-73; corp. v.p. Aetna Life & Casualty Co., Hartford, Conn., 1973-76; ind. mgmt. cons., West Hartford, 1976-81; v.p. worldwide life ins. ops. Hartford Ins. Group, 1981—; vis. lectr. Harvard U. Grad. Sch. Bus. Adminstrn., 1978-79; dir. Vantage Computer Systems, Inc., Wethersfield, Conn. Served to 2d lt. USAAF, 1946-47. Home: 53 Stoner Dr West Hartford CT 06107 Office: Hartford Plaza Hartford CT 06115

BLAKESLEE, EDWARD EATON, ins. co. exec.; b. N.Y.C., July 23, 1921; s. Edward Eaton and Ada Rainbow (Harris) B.; m. Janice Callaghan, Mar. 19, 1944; children—Edward, David. LL.B., N.Y. U., 1947, LL.M., 1957; grad. exec. program in bus. adminstrn., Columbia U., 1966. Bar: N.Y. bar 1947. Atty. Mut. Life Ins. Co. N.Y., 1947-59, asst. counsel, 1959-61, tax asso., 1961-64, asso. counsel, 1964-65, asso. gen. counsel, 1965-69, 2d v.p., gen. solicitor, 1969-73, v.p., gen. solicitor, 1973—, gen. counsel, 1974—. Served with USAAF, 1943-46. Mem. Am. Bar Assn., Assn. Bar City N.Y., Assn. Life Ins. Counsel, N.Y. U. Alumni Fedn. (dir.), N.Y. U. Law Alumni Assn. (dir. 1974—). Home: 322 W 57th St New York NY 10019 Office: 1740 Broadway New York NY 10019

BLAKEY, ART, drummer; b. Pitts., Oct. 11, 1919. Drummer with various groups, including Jame Murray, Pitts., early 1940s, Mary Lou Williams, 1942, Fletcher Henderson, 1943-44, Billy Eckstine, 1944-47, Lucky Millinder, 1949, Buddy DeFranco Quartet, 1951-53; founder, drummer The Jazz Messengers, 1955—; toured with Giants of Jazz, 1971-72. Albums include Backgammon, Buhaina, Child's Dance, Gypsy Folk, In My Prime, vol. I, In This Korner, Jazz Messengers, Keystone 3, Night in Tunisia, Reflections in Blue, 'S Make It, Straight Ahead, Thermo with Hubbard, Shorter, Fuller, Art Blakey with Thelonius Monk. Recipient New Star award Down Beat Critics, 1953. Office: Art Blakey and the Jazz Messengers 771 Bleecker St New York NY 10012 *

BLAKEY, RICHARD WATSON, lawyer; b. Rock County, Wis., Oct. 17, 1911; s. Richard Watson and Jean (White) B.; m. Dorothy Jean Jones, May 17, 1941; children: Jean Clare, Richard Watson. B.A., Beloit Coll., 1933; LL.B., U. Wis., 1936. Bar: Wis. 1936, Nev. 1945. Practice in, Beloit, Wis., 1936-42, Reno, 1946-47, 51—; litigation atty. OPA, Nev., 1944-45; dep. city atty., Reno, 1947-51; mem. firm McCarran, Rice, Wedge & Blakey, 1951-55, Woodburn, Wedge, Blakey & Jeppson, 1955—; Mem. adv. com. rules of civil procedure Supreme Ct. Nev., 1951—; Mem. Reno CSC, 1963-76. Trustee Nev. Children's Found., 1947-73, 75—. Mem. ABA, Washoe County Bar Assn. (pres. 1954-55), State Bar Nev. (chmn. bd. bar examiners 1955-63, bd. govs. 1962-72, pres. 1971-72), Am. Judicature Soc., Nat. Assn. R.R. Trial Counsel, Am. Law Inst., Am. Coll. Trial Lawyers, Am. Bd. Trial Advocates. Clubs: Hidden Valley Country, Prospectors (Reno). Home: 2225 Lindley Way Reno NV 89509 Office: 1 E 1st St Reno NV 89501

BLAKLEY, GEORGE ROBERT, JR., mathematician, computer scientist, educator; b. Chgo., May 6, 1932; s. George Robert and Gladys Margaret (Baechle) B.; m. Virginia Clarke, Sept. 7, 1957; children: George Robert III, Cynthia Ellen, Lydia Anne. A.B., Georgetown U., 1954; M.A., U. Md., 1959, Ph.D., 1960. Asst. prof. math. U. Ill. at Urbana, 1962-66; asso. prof. State U. N.Y. at Buffalo, 1966-70; prof. Tex. A&M U., College Station, 1970—, head dept., 1970-78; Office Naval Research postdoctoral research asso. Cornell U., 1960. Nat. Acad. Scis.-NRC postdoctoral fellow Harvard U., 1961.

Mem. IEEE (sr. mem.), AAAS, Am. Math. Soc., Assn. Computing Machinery, Math. Assn. Am., Soc. for Indsl. and Applied Math. (vis. lectr. biomath. 1968-70, vis. lectr. applied math. 1979-83), Inst. Math. Statistics, Sigma Xi, Phi Kappa Phi, Pi Mu Epsilon. Home: 1405 Broadmoor St Bryan TX 77802 Office: Dept Math Tex A and M U College Station TX 77843

BLALOCK, HUBERT MORSE, JR., sociology educator; b. Balt., Aug. 23, 1926; s. Hubert Morse and Helen Dorothy (Welsh) B.; m. Margaret Ann Bonar, Aug. 13, 1951; children: Susan Lynn, Kathleen Ann, James Welsh. A.B., Dartmouth Coll., 1949; M.A., Brown U., 1953; Ph.D., U. N.C., 1954. Instr. sociology U. Mich., Ann Arbor, 1954-57, asst. prof., 1957-61; assoc. prof. Yale U., 1961-64; prof. U. N.C., Chapel Hill, 1964-71, U. Wash., Seattle, 1971—. Author: Social Statistics, rev. 2d edit., 1979, Causal Inferences in Nonexperimental Research, 1964, Theory Construction, 1968, Toward a Theory of Minority Group Relations, 1967, Intergroup Processes, 1979, Black-White Relations in the 1980's, 1979, Conceptualization and Measurement in the Social Sciences, 1982. Served with USN, 1944-46. Fellow Am. Acad. Arts and Scis., Am. Statis. Assn.; mem. Nat. Acad. Sci., Am. Sociol. Assn. (pres. 1978-79). Home: 18425 17th Ave NW Seattle WA 98177 Office: U Wash Seattle WA 98195

BLAN, OLLIE LIONEL, JR., lawyer; b. Ft. Smith, Ark., May 22, 1931; s. Ollie Lionel and Eva Ocie (Cross) B.; m. Allen Conner Gillon, Aug. 19, 1960; children: Bradford Lionel, Elizabeth Ann, Cynthia Gillon. A.A., Ft. Smith Jr. Coll., 1951; LL.B., U. Ark., 1954. Bar: Ark. 1954, Ala. 1959. Research analyst Ark. Legis. Council, 1954-55; law clk. to Judge U.S. Dist. Ct. Ala., 1959-60; assoc. Spain, Gillon, Riley, Tate & Etheredge, Birmingham, Ala., 1960—, ptnr., 1965—; tchr. Am. Inst. Banking, 1965-68. Contbr. articles to legal jours. Treas. Jefferson County Hist. Commn., 1972-81, vice chmn., 1981—; mem. Jefferson County Republican Exec. Com., 1973-76; bd. dirs., sec. World Wide Jewish Missions. Served with USMCR, 1955-58. Mem. ABA, Ark. Bar Assn., Ala. Bar Assn. (com. admissions and legal edn. 1971-74, com. jud. office 1972-76), Birmingham Bar Assn., Ala. Def. Lawyers Assn. (v.p. 1983-84), Am. Life Ins. Assn., Internat. Assn. Ins. Counsel, Def. Research Inst. Am. Baptist. Clubs: Birmingham Tip Off (charter); Relay House. Home: 2100 22d Ave S Birmingham AL 35223 Office: 1700 John A Hand Bldg Birmingham AL 35203 *My desire has been to achieve the highest standard in whatever area of life I am thrust, guided by principles of ethics and morality.*

BLANC, PETER (WILLIAM PETERS BLANC), sculptor, painter; b. N.Y.C., June 29, 1912. B.A., Harvard U.; LL.B., St. Johns U.; postgrad., Corcoran Sch. Art.; M.A., Am. U. Instr. Am. U., Washington, 1950-53. One-man shows include, Passedoit Gallery, 1951, 53, 58, Albert Landry Gallery, N.Y., 1960, La Galeria Escondida, Taos, 1955, Hudson River Mus., 1961, 65, Associated Artists Gallery, Washington, 1962, Amel Gallery, N.Y.C., 1964, Ft. Worth Art Center, 1966, Thomson Gallery, N.Y.C., 1969, Benson Gallery, Bridgehampton, N.Y., Southampton Coll., 1971, Avanti Galleries, N.Y.C., 1974, Elaine Benson Gallery, Bridgehampton, 1979, group shows include, Whitney Mus. Am. Art, 1952, City Art Mus., St. Louis, 1951, Washington Water Color Club, 1949, 51, 52, Riverside Mus., 1950, 54, 58, 64, New Sch. for Social Research, 1956, Springfield Mus. Art, 1952, Nat. Collection Fine Art, Washington, 1953, Balt. Mus. Art, Bklyn. Mus., 1955, Fogg Mus. Art, 1959, N.Y. U., 1960, St. Paul Gallery, 1961, Internat. Gallery N.Y., Fort Worth Art Center, 1963, Asso. Art Gallery, Washington, 1961, Hudson River Mus., 1965, Parrish Art Mus., Southampton, N.Y., Benson Gallery, Bridgehampton, N.Y., 1966, 67, 77, Daniels Gallery, N.Y.C., 1965, East Hampton Guild Hall, N.Y.C., 1966, 67, 73, Southampton (N.Y.) Coll., 1967, 68, 69, 70, 71, 72, Iona Coll., N.Y., 1968, Mercy Coll., N.Y., 1970, Ashawagh Hall, Springs, N.Y., 1971-77, 80, 82, Artists Equity Assn., N.Y.C., 1975, N.Y. Artists, Union Carbide Gallery, N.Y.C., Art Guild, N.Y.C., 1976, Abe Rattner Center for Arts, Sag Harbor, N.Y., 1979, Guild Hall Mus., East Hampton, 1980, U. Del., Rattner Meml. Studio, Sag Harbor. Recipient awards Corcoran Gallery Art, 1949, Soc. Washington Artists, 1951, 53, Washington Water Color Club, 1949, 52. Mem. Spiral Group, N.Y. Artists Equity Assn. (dir. 1963-70), Artists Guild Washington (pres. 1951-53), Soc. Washington Artists, Proto-V Group. Address: 161 W 75th St New York NY 10023

BLANC, WILLIAM ANDRE, pathologist; b. Geneva, Switzerland, Sept. 28, 1922; came to U.S., 1953, naturalized, 1957; s. Marcel J. and Blanche (Probst) B.; m. Corinne Pasche, June 6, 1954; 1 dau., Catherine Lombard. B.A., Coll. Geneva, 1940; M.D., U. Geneva, 1947, D. Med. Sc., 1951. Prof. pathology Columbia Coll. Phys. and Surg., 1966—, head div. devel. pathology, 1963—; formerly career scientist Health Research Council N.Y.; cons. Armed Forces Inst. Pathology, NIH, USPHS, VA. Editor-in-chief: Pediatric Pathology. Mem. Soc. Pediatric Pathology (past pres.), Internat. Pediatric Pathology Assn. (Council). Prin. interest in diseases of placenta, fetus and newborn, cystic fibrosis, tumors, immunity. Home: 11 E 86th St New York NY 10028 Office: 622 W 168th St New York NY 10032

BLANCH, EDWARD JAMES, automotive manufacturing company executive; b. Utica, N.Y., Mar. 16, 1926; s. John Edward and Clara Sophia (Jenny) B.; m. Marilyn Joan Fisher, Aug. 11, 1951; children: Susan Marie Blanch Meister, Edward John, Karen Ann, Mary Clare, Ellen Joan. B.M.E., Rensselaer Poly. Inst., 1946; M.B.A. in Fin. and Production, Harvard U., 1950. With Ford Motor Co., 1952—, div. gen. mgr. indsl. and chem. products, Wixom, Mich., 1971-72, div. gen. mgr. gen. products, Rawsonville, Mich., 1972-73, v.p. fin., Dearborn, Mich., 1973-79; pres. Ford of Europe Inc., 1979-84, chmn., 1982-84. Gen. chmn. Roman Cath. Archdiocese Devel. Fund, Detroit; trustee, chmn. fin. com. St. John Hosp., Detroit; past treas., exec. com., trustee Greater Detroit C. of C. Served with USN, 1943-47. Mem. Motor Vehicle Mfrs. Assn. Clubs: Serra (Dearborn); Economic (Detroit). Office: Ford of Europe Inc Brentwood Essex England

BLANCHARD, ALAN FRANKLIN, investment banker; b. Washington, May 4, 1939; s. Alan Johnston and Elizabeth (Franklin) B.; m. Ann Scott Elliott, May 11, 1968; children: Deborah G., A. Elliott. B.A., Yale U., 1961; M.S., MIT, 1966. Mgmt. cons. McKinsey and Co., N.Y.C., 1966-71; adminstrv. asst. Office of Senator J. Javits, Washington, 1971-72; exec. dir. U.S. Securities and Exchange Commn., Washington, 1972-76; exec. v.p. Pershing & Co., N.Y.C., 1976-78; v.p. Goldman, Sachs & Co., N.Y.C., 1978—. Mem. Pres. Reagan Transition Team, 1980-81. Served with U.S. Navy, 1961-65. Mem. Phi Beta Kappa. Home: 1088 Park Ave New York NY 10028 Office: 85 Broad St New York NY 10004

BLANCHARD, CARL RICHARD, architect; b. New Haven, Mar. 17, 1912; s. Carl Russell and Mary (Dann) B.; m. Rachel Estelle Begor, Jan. 8, 1937; children: Mary Ludia (Mrs. James Bradford Kalloch), Susan Anne (Mrs. Mohamed Ahmed Fadl). Cert. in constrn., Pratt Inst., 1933, cert. design, 1934. Job capt. Fletcher Thompson, Bridgeport, Conn., 1937-40; designer Lorenzo Hamilton, Meriden, Conn., 1935-37; individual practice architecture, New Haven, 1937—; Dir. New Haven Savs. & Loan Assn.; chmn. New Eng. Council Archtl. Registration Bds., 1975-77; Pres. Conn. Archtl. Registration Bd., 1974-77. Mem. Town Plan Commn., North Haven, Conn., 1970-74; trustee Center Church Home for Aged. Fellow AIA. Republican. Mem. United Ch. of Christ. Club: Quinnipiack. Lodges: Kiwanis; Masons. Home: 44 Barton Circle North Haven CT 06473 Office: 74 Forbes Ave New Haven CT 06512:

BLANCHARD, GEORGE SAMUEL, army officer; b. Washington, Apr. 3, 1920; s. George S. and Elizabeth (Blanchard) B.; m. Beth Howard, June 9, 1944; children: Kate E. (Mrs. Ronald Hausner), Marylou C. (Mrs. John Hennessey), Deborah E. (Mrs. Eberhard Roell), Blythe H. (Mrs. Charles Watkins). Student, Am. U., 1938-40; B.S., U.S. Mil. Acad., 1944; M.S., Syracuse U., 1948; grad. Advanced Mgmt. Program, Harvard, 1966. Commd. 2d lt. AUS, 1944, advanced through grades to gen., 1975; served as co. comdr. and staff officer, Europe, 1944-47, adviser, Taiwan, 1955-57, with 82d Airborne Div., U.S., 1958-60, Korea, 1961-62, Vietnam, 1966-68, comdr. 82d Airborne div., Ft. Bragg, N.C., 1970-72, mem. Pentagon staff, 1962-66, 68-70, comdg. gen. VII Corps U.S. Army Europe, 1973-75, comdr. in chief U.S. Army Europe, 1975-79, ret., 1979, now cons.; pres. Gen. Analysis, Inc.; Bd. govs. USO. Contbr. to, Ency. Brit. Decorated D.S.M. with 3 oak leaf clusters, Silver Star with oak leaf cluster, D.F.C., Bronze Star with oak leaf cluster. Mem. Assn. U.S. Army; mem. Ret. Officers Assn. (pres.); Mem. Army Aviation Assn. Episcopalian. Club: Army-Navy Country (Washington). Address: 7713 Lear Rd McLean VA 22102

BLANCHARD, JAMES J., governor; b. Detroit, Aug. 8, 1942; m. Paula Parker; 1 son, Jay. B.A., M.B.A., Mich. State U., Lansing; J.D., U. Minn. Bar: Mich. 1968. Legal aid elections bur. Office Sec. State, State of Mich., 1968-69; asst. atty. gen. State of Mich., 1969-74, adminstrv. asst. to atty. gen., 1970-71, asst. dep. atty. gen., 1971-72; mem. 94th-96th Congresses from 18th Mich. Dist.; gov. State of Mich., 1983—; mem. Pres.'s Commn. on Holocaust. Mem. Oakland County exec. club Mich. State U. Mem. Assn. Asst. Attys. Gen., Ferndale Jaycees, State Bar Mich., Am. Bar Assn., LWV, U. Minn. Law Sch. Alumni Club, U. Detroit Titan Club. Democrat. Office: Office of the Governor State Capitol Lansing MI 48933

BLANCHARD, JONATHAN EWART, geophysicist; b. Truro, N.S., Can., Mar. 22, 1921; s. Aubrey B. and Agnes G. (Blair) B.; m. Mary Helena Sandilands, July 5, 1958; children—Jonathan Sandilands, Megan Blair. B.Sc., Dalhousie U., 1940; M.A., U. Toronto, 1947, Ph.D., 1952. Lectr. dept. physics Dalhousie U., 1949-52, asst. prof., 1952-57, asso. prof., 1957-64, prof., 1964-66; acting dir. Dalhousie Inst. Oceanography, 1964-65; dir. geophysics div. Nova Scotia Research Found., Dartmouth, 1949-66, v.p., 1966-68, pres., 1968—. Served as lt. Royal Can. Navy, 1942-45. Fellow Royal Soc. Can.; mem. Soc. Exploration Geophysicists, Am. Geophysical Union, European Assn. Geophysicists, Canadian Assn. Physicists, Seismol. Soc. Am., Can. Inst. Mining and Metallurgy, N.S. Inst. Sci., Canadian Research Mgmt. Assn. Home: 6470 Coburg Rd Halifax NS B3H 2A7 Canada Office: PO Box 790 100 Fenwick St Dartmouth NS B2Y 3Z7 Canada

BLANCHARD, LAWRENCE ELEY, JR., corporation executive; b. Lumberton, N.C., Mar. 7, 1921; s. Lawrence Eley and Anna Neal (Fuller) B.; m. Frances Hallum, May 6, 1944; children: Lawrence Eley, Neal H. Blanchard Johnson, Sally H. Blanchard Rawls, Charles A. A.B., Duke U., 1942; J.D., Columbia U., 1948. Bar: Va. 1948. Asso., then partner firm Hunton, Williams, Gay, Powell & Gibson, Richmond, 1948-66; exec. v.p., dir., mem. exec. com. Ethyl Corp., Richmond, 1967-80, vice chmn., 1980—; dir. United Virginia Bankshares, Brenco, Inc., Am. Filtrona Co., Overnite Transp. Co., Universal Leaf Tobacco Co. Trustee Va. Episcopal Sch., 1959-65; trustee Colgate Darden Bus. Sch., U. Va., Randolph-Macon Coll.; bd. dirs. Richmond Symphony; mem. fin. com. Union Theol. Sem. Served to lt. USNR, 1942-46. Mem. Richmond C. of C. (exec. com., dir. 1971—, chmn. 1975-76), Phi Beta Kappa, Omicron Delta Kappa. Presbyn. (elder). Clubs: Commonwealth, Country of Va. (Richmond); Sky (N.Y.C.); City (Baton Rouge). Home: 4101 Sulgrave Rd Richmond VA 23221 Office: 330 S 4th St Richmond VA 23217

BLANCHARD, RICHARD FRANK, financial consultant; b. Hartford, Conn., Jan. 21, 1920; s. Maurice L. and Maude Elizabeth (Hurst) B.; m. Margaret Rodgers Lyon, May 15, 1944; children: Margaret Scherer, Anne Freihofer and Elizabeth Oppenheimer (twins). A.B., Dartmouth Coll., 1946, M.C.S., 1947. With Brown Bros. Harriman & Co., 1947-52; with Am. Express Co., 1952-81, exec. v.p., 1968-81; dir. Baker Internat., Imperial Clevite, Trust Funds Liquid Assets, Monchik-Weber, Pincock, Allen & Holt. Served to maj. USAAF, 1940-45. Clubs: India House. (N.Y.C.); Morris County (N.J.) Golf. Home: Canfield Rd Convent Station NJ 07961 Office: AEA Investors 640 5th Ave New York NY 10019

BLANCHARD, ROBERT T., cleaning products manufacturing company executive; b. Camp Shelby, Miss., Oct. 28, 1944; s. John A. B. and Sara S. (Blanchard); m. Sandra L. Andersen, Apr. 7, 1972; children: Jill, Kelly, Laura. B.A. in History, Princeton U., 1967. With Procter & Gamble Co., Cin., 1967—, advtg. mgr., 1977-80, mgr. bar soap and household cleaning products div., 1980-82, v.p. bar soap and household cleaning products div., 1982—. Nat. advtg. dir. Juvenile Diabetes Found., N.Y.C., 1979-83; chmn. 700 Co. Group United Appeal, Cin., 1983. Clubs: Princeton of So. Ohio; Queen City (Cin.). Office: Procter & Gamble Co 301 E 6th St Cincinnati OH 45202

BLANCHARD, ROBERT TREAT, petroleum company executive; b. Boston, Mar. 31, 1937; s. James A. Blanchard II and Cornelia W. Sullivan; m. Mary E. Corbin, Sept. 1, 1962; children: Jill A., Stephanie A. Grad., Kimball Union Acad., Meriden, N.H., 1956; B.S. cum laude, Fla. Atlantic U., 1968; grad., Harvard U. Bus. Sch. Advanced Mgmt. Program, 1982. Mgmt. trainee Union Oil Co. of Calif., 1961-66; supply rep. Phillips Petroleum Co., Bartlesville, Okla., 1968-74; with LaGloria Oil & Gas Co. (a Tex. Eastern Co.), Houston, 1974—, exec. v.p., 1978—. Served with USNR, 1959-61. Republican. Office: PO Box 2521 1221 McKinney St Houston TX 77252

BLANCHARD, TOWNSEND EUGENE, diversified technical services company executive; b. Du Quoin, Ill., Jan. 30, 1931; s. Townsend and Anna Belle (Jackson) B.; m. Norma Louise Barr, Dec. 18, 1960; children: John Barr, Susan Melody, Jayne Ann, Stephen Eugene. B.S., U. Ill., 1952; M.B.A., Harvard, 1957. Cons. Ill. Sch. Cons. Service, Monticello, 1958-62; a founder, treas., chief financial officer Americana Nursing Centers, Monticello, 1962-75; v.p. finance, treas., chief financial officer, chief of staff Cenco, Inc., Chgo., 1975-79; sr. v.p., chief fin. officer Dynalectron Corp., McLean, Va., 1979—. Served to lt. USNR, 1952-55. Decorated Spl. Commendation letter. Mem. Fin. Execs. Inst., Fin. Mgmt. Assn., Delta Sigma Phi (nat. found. bd. 1982—, Harvey H. Hebert award 1975). Presbyn. (elder). Clubs: U. Ill. Alumni, Harvard Bus. Sch. (Washington); Econ. (Chgo.). Home: 1222 Aldebaran Dr McLean VA 22101 Office: 1313 Dolley Madison Blvd McLean VA 22101

BLANCHE, FRED A., JR., judge; b. Baton Rouge, Jan. 18, 1921; s. Fred A. and Amy (Moran) B.; m. Polly Pepper, Dec. 27, 1942; children—Fred A., Elizabeth April (dec.), Lauren, Robert Vincent. B.S., La. State U., 1941, LL.B., 1948. Bar: La. bar 1948, U.S. Supreme Ct. bar 1948. Practice law, Baton Rouge; judge La. Dist. Ct. 19th Jud. Dist., 1960-69, 76-77, La. Ct. of Appeal 1st Circuit, 1969; now asso. justice Supreme Ct. of La. Bd. deacons First Presbyn. Ch. Mem. La. State Law Inst., La. Jud. Coll. (bd. govs.), La. State Bar Assn., La. Dist. Judges Assn. (past pres.), Baton Rouge Power Squadron, Am. Legion, East Baton Rouge Parish Jr. Bar Assn. (past pres.), Kappa Alpha Alumni Assn. Democrat. Presbyterian. Office: Supreme Ct of Louisiana 301 Loyola Ave New Orleans LA 70112

BLANCHET, BERTRAND, bishop; b. Montmagny, Que., Can., Sept. 19, 1932; s. Louis and Alberta (Nicole) B. B.A., Coll. Ste-Anne-de-la Pocatiere, 1952; L.Th., Laval U., 1956, D.Sc., 1975. Ordained priest Roman Catholic Ch., 1956, consecrated bishop, 1973; tchr. biology Coll. and Coll. d'Enseignement Général et Professionnel, La Pocatiere, 1963-73; bishop of Gaspe, Que., 1973—. Mem. Chevaliers de Colomb, Fonds de Recherches Forestieres. Address: 172 Rue Jacques Cartier Caspe PQ G0C 1R0 Canada

BLANCHETTE, OLIVA, philosophy educator; b. Berlin, N.H., May 6, 1929; s. Delphis and Odelia (Morneau) B. A.B. in Philosophy, Boston Coll., 1953, M.A., 1958; Licentiate in Philosophy, Coll. St. Albert de Louvain, Belgium, 1954; Licentiate in Sacred Theology, Weston Coll., 1961; Ph.D. in Philosophy, U. Laval, Que., Can., 1966. Prof. Latin, Greek and English Boston Coll. High Sch., 1954-57; instr. philosophy Boston Coll., 1964-65, asst. prof., 1965-67, asso. prof., 1967-74, prof., 1974—; dean Sch. of Philosophy, 1968-73; dir. Inst. Inst. for Social Thought. Author: Initiative in History: A Christian-Marxist Exchange, 1967, For a Fundamental Social Ethic: A Philosophy of Social Change, 1973; contbr. articles on philosophy of history and social ethics to scholarly jours. Mem. Hegel Soc. Am.; mem. Metaphys. Soc. Am., Am. Philos. Assn., Soc. Phenomenology and Existential Philosophy. Home: 28 Florence St Natick MA 01760 Office: Boston Coll Chestnut Hill MA 02167

BLANCHETTE, ROBERT WILFRED, business executive, lawyer; b. New Haven, July 7, 1932; s. Wilfred H. and Dora R. (deJordy) B.; m. Marna Madelaire Nielsen, May 17, 1969; children: Pierre de Jordy, Valerie Claude. B.A., U. Conn., 1953; Woodrow Wilson fellow, Fulbright scholar, U. Grenoble, France, 1953-54; LL.B. cum laude, Yale U., 1957. Bar: Conn. 1957, D.C. 1977. Partner firm Adams, Blanchette & Evans, 1957-62; gen. counsel N.Y., N.H. & H. R.R., 1963-68; gen. atty. New Eng. Penn Central Co., 1969-70; exec. dir. America's Sound Transp. Rev. Orgn., Washington, 1969-70; counsel to bd. trustees Penn Central Transp. Co., Phila., 1970-74, trustee, 1974—, chmn. bd. trustees, chief exec. officer, 1975-78; partner firm Alston, Miller & Gaines, Washington, 1976-81; adminstr. Fed. R.R. Adminstrn., Washington, 1981-83; pres., chief exec. officer The TGV Co., Washington, 1983—; pvt. practice, Washington, 1983—; tutor Yale U. Law Sch., 1961-68. Editor-in-chief: Yale Law Jour. Trustee Assumption Coll., Worcester, Mass., 1981—. Served to 1st lt. USAF, 1958-60. Mem. ABA, D.C. Bar Assn., Order of Coif. Roman Catholic. Clubs: Yale (N.Y.C.); St. David's Golf (Wayne, Pa.); Columbia Country (Chevy Chase, Md.). Home: 5315 Falmouth Rd Bethesda MD 20816 Office: 1801 K St NW Suite 230 Washington DC 20006

BLAND, EDWARD ALBERT, moving company executive; b. Hamilton, Ont., Can., Apr. 11, 1930; came to U.S., 1979; s. Albert Edward and Gladys (Hulbert) B.; m. Jean H. Ross, Mar. 22, 1947; children: Linda Bland Cosier, Patricia Ann Bland Parsons, Brian Douglas. Student Can. schs. Driver Allied Van Lines Can., Hamilton, 1946-50; regional dispatcher, expediter N.Am. Van Lines, 1950-51; sales mgr., then pres. Fidelity Van & Storage Ltd., Hamilton, 1951-65; sec.-treas., dir. United Van Lines, Can., 1960-65, v.p. mktg., 1965-66; partner Cantin's Moving & Storage, Vancouver, B.C., 1966-70; with Atlas Van Lines, Can., 1970—, pres., 1971—; exec. v.p. Atlas Van Lines, Inc., Evansville, Ind., 1978-80, pres., chief operating officer, 1980—; pres. Delco Investments, Ltd., 1970—, Ace Moving & Storage Ltd., 1975—; dir. Worldways (Can.) Ltd. Served as flying officer RCAF, 1955-58. Mem. Nat. Assn. Corp. Dirs., Can. Movers Assn., Am. Movers Conf. (bd. dirs. 1983—). Episcopalian. Clubs: Oak Meadow Country, Kennel, Petroleum; Oakville (Ont.). Home: 16 Oak Meadow St Evansville IN 47711 Office: 1212 St George Rd Evansville IN 47711

BLAND, EDWARD FRANKLIN, physician; b. West Point, Va., Jan 24, 1901; s. James Edward and Mary L. (Bowden) B.; m. Frances Poinier, Sept. 7, 1935 (dec.); children: Frances B. Youngblood, James Edward (dec.), Robert Poinier. B.S., U. Va., 1923, M.D., 1927; research fellow, Univ. Coll. Hosp., London, 1930-31. Intern Mass. Gen. Hosp., 1927-29, resident, 1929-30, chief cardiac unit, 1949-64; cons. vis. physician, 1960—, pvt. practice specializing in cardiology, Boston, 1932—; sr. vis. physician House of Good Samaritan, Children's Med. Center, 1962—; mem. cons. staff W. Roxbury, VA, Winchester, Malden, Brockton, Framingham, Gloucester hosps.; asso. clin. prof. medicine Harvard Med. Sch., 1954-64, clin. prof. medicine, 1964-67, clin. prof. medicine emeritus, 1967—; civilian cons. to surgeon gen. U.S. Army, 1946-50. Mem. editorial bd.: Cardiology Digest, 1965—. Mem. tng. rev. com. Nat. Heart Inst., 1965—. Served to lt. col., M.C. AUS, 1942-45; MTO. Decorated Bronze Star. Mem. Am. Soc. Clin. Investigation, Am. Clin. and Climatol. Assn., Assn. Am. Physicians, New Eng. Cardiovascular Soc. (past pres.), Am. Heart Assn. (past dir., Paul D. White award 1975), Mass. Heart Assn. (past pres.). Clubs: Aesculapian (Boston); Country (Brookline, Mass.). Home: 232 Woodland Rd Chestnut Hill MA 02167 Office: Zero Emerson Pl Charles River Park Boston MA 02114

BLANDAU, RICHARD JULIUS, educator, physician; b. Erie, Pa., Aug. 5, 1911; s. Richard Albert and Kate (Lubbers) B.; m. Olive Lewellen, Oct. 9, 1937; 1 son, Richard Lewellen. A.B., Linfield Coll., McMinnville, Oreg., 1935; Ph.D. in Biology, Brown U., 1939; M.D. with honor, U. Rochester, 1948. Fellow anatomy and psychobiology NRC Yale, 1937-38; instr. biology Brown U., 1939-42; instr. anatomy Harvard Sch. Medicine, 1942-43; mem. faculty U. Rochester, 1943-49; Buswell fellow urology and surgery Sch. Medicine and Dentistry, 1948-49; prof. anatomy U. Wash., 1949—; asso. dean Sch. Medicine, 1960-64; Harry Burr Ferris lectr. Yale, 1965; Otto A. Mortenson lectr. anatomy U. Wis. Sch. Anatomy, 1973; cons. in histopathology Manhattan Dist., 1947; Solomon Theron DeLee lectr. U. Chgo., 1954; mem. adv. com. population affairs NIH, 1976-80, evaluation of research in endocrinology and metabolic diseases task force, 1978—; mem. Wash. Basic Sci. Exam. Bd., 1951—; cons. Children's Orthopedic Hosp. and Med. Center, Seattle, 1965—; mem. expert adv. panel human reprodn. WHO, 1975; cons. Internat. Childbirth Assn., 1978-80; B.B. Weinstein Meml. lectr. Internat. Found Studies of Reprodn., 1979; Warren O. Johnson Meml. lectr. U. Louisville, 1979; Curso Meml. lectr. U. Pa. Med. Sch., 1980. Asso. editor: Jour. Am. Anatomy, 1961, Am. Jour. Fertility and Sterility, 1963—; editorial bd.: Fertility and Sterility, 1975-80, Gynecol. Survey, 1965-78. Pres. bd. dirs. Barren Found., 1979—. Recipient Vienna Film Festival award, 1959; Barren Found. medal, 1969. Mem. Am. Assn. Anatomists (pres. 1968-69, Henry M. Gray award 1976, blue ribbon commn. 1977-81), Soc. Problems in Growth, Soc. Exptl. Biology and Medicine, Am. Soc. Study Sterility (Isidor Rubin award 1952, Ortho Research award 1956, Ortho medal award 1969), Am. Soc. Cell. Biologists, Am. Soc. Teratologists, Am. Soc. Med. Illustrators (hon.), Los Angeles Surg. Soc. (hon.), Los Angeles Obstet. Assembly (hon.), Am. Fertility Soc. (pres. 1967-68, Ayerst lectr. 1974), Soc. Study Reprodn. (pres. 1973-74), Sigma Xi (nat. lectr. 1971), Alpha Omega Alpha (Borden Research award medicine 1948). Republican. Presbyn. (elder). Home: 540 Edmonds Way Edmonds WA 98020 Office: Univ Wash Med Sch Seattle WA 98195

BLANDFORD, KEITH, steel company executive; b. East Chicago, Ind., Jan. 30 1937; s. Alvin R. and Phyllis E. (Grossman) B.; m. Carol McAdoo, Aug. 23, 1958; children: Douglas, Gregory, Jeffrey. B.S. in Chem. Engring., U. Ill., 1959. Vice pres. ops. planning Keystone Steel and Wire, Peoria, Ill., 1972-75, v.p. ops., 1975-77, v.p. ops. Keystone Group, 1977-79, pres. Keystone Group, 1979-82; pres. KEYCON Industries, Dallas, 1982—. Mem. Am. Iron and Steel Inst., Wire Assn. Office: 4835 LBJ Freeway Sutie 300 Dallas TX 75234

BLANDFORD, SISTER MARGARET VINCENT, infirmary executive; b. Lebanon, Ky., Oct. 27, 1920; d. John Martin and Mary Lyda (O'Daniel) B. R.N., St. Joseph's Sch. Nursing, 1941; B.S. in Nursing Edn, Spalding Coll., 1952; postgrad., Sloan Inst. Hosp. Adminstrn., Cornell U., 1962. Asst. adminstr. St. Joseph's Hosp., Lexington, Ky., 1949-54; adminstr. St. Vincent Infirmary, Little Rock, 1955-61, pres., chief exec. officer trustee, 1971—; hosp. coordinator Hosps. of Sisters of Charity, Nazareth, Ky., 1961-71. Trustee Worthen Bank & Trust Co., 3Little Rock; chmn. bd. govs. Am. Health Congress, 1971-72; mem. exec. com. Ark. Regional Med. Program, 1974-77; mem. U.S. Cath. Health Conf., 1974-77; mem. med. morals com. Diocese of Ark., 1973-76; bd. dirs. Our Lady of Peace Hosp., Louisville, 1973-79; dir. Worthen Bank & Trust Co.; Bd. dirs. United Way Pulaski County, 1978, Central Ark. Radiation Therapy Inst., 1974-82. Named Woman of Year Greater Little Rock, 1960; recipient A. Allen Weintraub award, 1980; 100 Ark. Women of Achievement award, 1980. Fellow Am. Coll. Hosp. Adminstrs.; mem. Ark. Conf. Cath. Hosps. (pres. 1957-59), Little Rock Hosp. Council (pres. 1960-61), Cath. Hosp. Assn. (sec. bd. trustees 1961-65, dir. 1966-71, pres. 1971-72), Ark. Hosp. Assn., Ark. C. of C. (dir. 1978), Little Rock C. of C., Met. C. of C. (dir. 1978). Home: Markham St Little Rock AR 72201 Office: St Vincent Infirmary Markham and University Ave Little Rock AR 72201

BLANDFORD, ROGER DAVID, astronomy educator; b. Grantham, Eng., Aug. 28, 1949; s. Jack George and Janet Margaret (Evans) B.; m. Elizabeth Kellett, Aug. 5, 1972; children: Jonathan, Edward. B.A. in Theoretical Physics with first class honors, Magdalene Coll., Cambridge U., Eng., 1970, M.A., 1974, Ph.D., 1974. Research student Inst. Astronomy, Cambridge U., 1970-73; research fellow St. John's Coll., Cambridge U., 1973-76; asst. prof. astronomy Calif. Inst. Tech., Pasadena, 1976-79, prof., 1979—; mem. Inst. Advanced Study, Princeton, 1974-75. Contbr. articles to profl. publs. W.B.R. King scholar, 1967-70; Charles Kingsley Bye fellow, 1972-73; Alfred P. Sloan research fellow, 1980. Fellow Royal Astron. Soc., Cambridge Philos. Soc.; mem. Am. Astron. Soc. (Warner prize 1982). Office: Calif Inst Tech 130-33 Pasadena Ca 91125

BLANE, JOHN, diplomat; b. Birmingham, Ala., July 15, 1929; s. John and Floy (Steart) B.; m. Elizabeth Kubin, Dec. 26, 1953; children: Sharon, John Patrick; m. 2d Dianne Metzger, Dec. 19, 1970. B.A., U. Tenn.-Knoxville, 1951, M.A., 1956; student, U. Vienna, 1952-53, Northwestern U., 1962-63. Fgn. service officer Dept. of State, 1956—, consular and polit. officer, Mogadishu, 1957, Asmara, 1958-60, Salzburg, 1960-62; polit. officer, Yaounde, 1963-66, country officer, Togo, Dahomey, Chad and Gabon, 1966-68; acting chief of No. and Eastern Africa Bur. Intelligence and Research, 1969; dept. chief of mission, Ft. Lamy, 1969-72; policy planning officer Bur. African Affairs, 1972-75; acting staff dir. Nat. Security Council Interdeptl. Group, 1972-75; dir. blilateral programs div. Office of Internat. Activities, EPA, 1975-77; dep. chief of mission, Nairobi, 1977-80; mem. Exec. Seminar in Nat. and Internat. Affairs Fgn. Service Inst., 1980-81; mem. U.S. delegation to 36th session UN Gen. Assembly, N.Y.C., 1981; spl. projects officer Bur. African Affairs, 1982; U.S. ambassador to Rwanda, 1982—. Served with U.S. Army, 1953-55. Fulbright scholar, 1952-53. Mem. Am. Fgn. Service Assn., Alpha Tau Omega. Episcopalian. Lodge: Kigali Rotary. Home: Greenview IL 62642 Office: American Embassy Kigali Rwanda

BLANK, BLANCHE DAVIS, political science educator; b. N.Y.C.; d. Joseph B. and Mathilda (Markendorff) Davis; m. Joseph S. Blank, Jr., Oct. 10, 1945; children: Laura, Barbara, Alice. B.A., Hunter Coll., 1944; M.A. Univ. fellow, Maxwell Sch., Syracuse U., 1945; Ph.D., Columbia U., 1951. Lectr., City Coll., 1946-49, New Sch. Social Research, 1951-52; instr. Hunter Coll., CUNY, 1956-59, asst. prof., 1960-62, asso. prof., 1963-67, prof. polit. sci., 1968—, dean div. social scis., 1972-77, dir. grad. studies, 1967-68; academic v.p. Yeshiva U., 1977-81; vis. prof. Sarah Lawrence Coll., 1969-70; cons. Coll.-Fed. Agy. Internship Program, 1964-65, to dep. mayor Timothy Costello and Office of City Adminstrn., 1966-71; research asso. Tax Found., 1945; exec. dir. Mayor's Task Force on City Personnel, 1965-66; mem. governing council Urban Affairs Task Force, Am.-Jewish Congress, 1971; mem. Chancellor's Com. on Status of Women, CUNY, 1972, Charter Revision Study Group, 1972; co-chmn. Inst. Trial Judges, 1973—. Author books and articles on Am. govt., polit. parties and pub. adminstrn. Chmn. com. on city mgmt. Citizens Union, 1976-77; bd. dirs. Pub. Interest Pub. Relations, 1976-83; mem. Democratic County Com., Greenburgh, 1956-64; chmn. Greenville Dem. Com., 1960-64; mem. women's com. Muskie Presdl. Campaign, 1972, Udall, Carter campaigns, 1976. Recipient Shuster Faculty awards, 1961, 72; N.Y. Legis. grantee, 1964; Univ. research grantee, 1965; NSF research grantee, 1966. Mem. AAUP, Am. Polit. Sci. Assn., Am. Soc. Pub. Adminstrn., ACLU (free speech com. 1975—), Common Cause (gov. bd. N.Y. State 1975-77), Comparative Adminstrn. Group. Office: 500 W 185th St New York NY 10033

BLANK, HARVEY, physician; b. Chgo., June 21, 1918; s. Dave and Blanche (Heyns) B.; m. Joan Gill, Sept. 14, 1975; children by previous marriage—Virginia L., Michelle G. B.S., U. Chgo., 1939, M.D., 1942. Diplomate: Am. Bd. Dermatology. Mem. faculty U. Pa. Med. Sch., 1947-51, Columbia U. Coll. Phys. and Surg., 1951-55; prof. dermatology U. Miami (Fla.) Med. Sch., 1956—, chmn. dept., 1956—; asso. med. dir. E.R. Squibb & Sons, 1951-55; dir. Commn. Cutaneous Diseases to Armed Forces, 1959-73; chmn. tng. grant com. NIH, 1960-64; chmn. adv. panel FDA, 1974-77; mem. Nat. Adv. Allergy and Infectious Diseases Council, 1980; chmn. Found. Internat. Dermatol. Edn., 1980. Author: Viral and Rickettsial Diseases of Skin, 1955, Fungous Diseases and Their Treatment, 1964; contbr. chpt. on skin to, Merck Manual, 1980, also numerous articles; chief editor: Archives of Dermatology, 1962-63; editorial bd.: Skin and Allergy News. Served to maj. M.C. AUS, 1943-46. Recipient Modern Medicine mag. award, 1970, Outstanding Civilian Service medal U.S., 1973; hon. mem. dermatol. socs., Argentina, Brazil, France, Gt. Britain, Israel, Japan, Mex., Poland, South Africa and; Venezuela. Fellow A.C.P.; mem. Assn. Profs. Dermatology (pres. 1980), Soc. Investigative Dermatology (pres. 1968, Gold medal 1969), Am. Acad. Dermatology and Syphology, Assn. Am. Physicians. Home: 600 Grapetree Dr Key Biscayne FL 33149 Office: Dept Derm U Miami PO Box 016250 Miami FL 33101

BLANK, JONAS LEMOYNE, ret. air force officer, bus. exec.; b. Greensburg, Pa., Apr. 9, 1921; s. Jonas Francis and Sara Adelaide (Potter) B.; m. Kathryn Marguerite Ryan, June 29, 1946; children—Jonas LeMoyne, John H. B.S., U.S. Mil. Acad., 1943; M.B.A., Harvard, 1951; M.I.A., George Washington U., 1963. Commd. 2d lt. USAAC, 1943; advanced through grades to maj. gen. USAF, 1972; exec. to asst. sec. Air Force, 1960-62; sr. U.S. logistics officer SHAPE, 1963-66; comdt. Air Command and Staff Coll., 1968-70; dir. supply and services Hdqrs. USAF, Washington, 1970-73; asst. DCS/S&L, 1973-75; ret., 1975; mgr. ops. Eureka X-Ray Tube Co., Chgo., 1975-80; pres. Blank Enterprises, Alexandria, Va., 1980—. Decorated D.S.M., Legion of Merit, D.F.C., Purple Heart. Clubs: Masons; Century (N.Y.C.); Belle Haven Country. Home and Office: 7414 Park Terrace Dr Alexandria VA 22307

BLANK, MARION SUE, psychologist; b. N.Y.C., Dec. 20, 1933; d. Morris David and Tillie Jean (Sherman) Hersch; m. Martin Blank, July 3, 1955; children: Donna, Jonathan, Ari. B.A., CCNY, 1955, M.D. in Edn, 1956; Ph.D., Cambridge (Eng.) U., 1961. Asst. prof. Albert Einstein Coll. Medicine, 1965-70, asso. prof., 1970-73; prof. dept. psychiatry Rutgers Med. Sch., Piscataway, N.J., 1973-83; mem. adj. faculty dept. psychiatry Columbia Coll. Physicians and Surgeons, N.Y.C., 1983—; dir. reading disabilities research inst., pvt. practice, cons., 1983—. Author: Teaching Learning in the Preschool - A Dialogue Approach; Preschool Language Assessment Institute, 1978, (with Rose and Berlin) The Language of Learning, 1978. Recipient award of commendation N.J. Speech and Hearing Assn., 1979; Pinsent-Darwin fellow, 1960; USPHS Career Devel. awardee, 1965-73. Mem. Am. Psychol. Assn., Eastern Psychol. Assn., Soc. for Research in Child Devel. Home: 171 Van Nostrand Ave Englewood NJ 07631 Office: Dept Psychiatry Columbia U Coll Physicians and Surgeons New York NY 10032 *It is heartening, albeit at times difficult, to live in a period of revolutionary change for women*

BLANK, ROBERT HENRY, political science educator; b. Milw., Mar. 28, 1943; s. Orville Albert and Sylvia (Linnemeier) B.; m. Mallory Scott, July 15, 1967; children: Jeremy, Mai'Ling, Maigin. A.B., Purdue U., 1965; M.A., U. Md., 1969, Ph.D., 1971. Prof. U. Idaho, Moscow, 1971—, chmn. polit. sci. dept., 1977-82; sr. Fulbright lectr. U.S. Edn. Found., Taiwan, 1976-77; scholar-in-residence Center for Biopolit. Research, DeKalb, Ill., 1979-80; summer fellow Center for Advanced Study in Behavioral Scis., Stanford, Calif., 1978; state supr. NBC New Elections, Moscow, 1974-78. Author: Regional Diversity in the United States, 1978, Political Parties: An Introduction, 1980, The Political Implications of Human Genetic Technology, 1981; contbr. articles on polit. sci. to profl. jours. Served to lt. USN, 1965-67; Vietnam. Md. fellow, 1968-71; NEH summer fellow, 1981; Earhart Found. fellow, 1983. Mem. Am. Polit. Sci. Assn., Western Polit. Sci. Assn. (exec. council 1981-83), Pacific Northwest Polit. Sci. Assn. (pres. elect 1983-84), Assn. of Politics and the Life Scis. (mem. editorial bd. 1982—), Policy Studies Assn., Phi Kappa Phi, Phi Sigma Alpha. Home: 635 N Haynes Moscow ID 83843 Office: U Idaho Polit Sci Dept Moscow ID 83843

BLANKENBAKER, RONALD GAIL, physician; b. Rensselaer, Ind., Dec. 1, 1941; s. Lloyd L. and Lovina (Anderson) B. B.S. in Biology, Purdue U., 1963; M.D., Ind U., 1968, M.S. in Pharmacology, 1970. Diplomate: Am. Bd. Family Practice. Intern Meth. Hosp. Grad. Med. Center, Indpls., 1968-69, resident in family practice, 1969-71; med. dir. Indpls. Home for Aged, 1971-77, Am. Mid-Town Nursing Center, Indpls., 1974-77, Home Assn., Tampa, Fla., 1977-79; asst. prof. family practice Ind. U., Indpls., 1973-77, clin. prof., 1980—; prof. dept. family medicine U. South Fla., Tampa, 1977-79, chmn. dept., 1977-79; health commr. State of Ind.; sec. Ind. State Bd. Health, Indpls., 1979—; dir. family practice edn. Meth. Hosp. Grad. Med. Center, 1971-77; family practice editor Reference and Index Services, Inc., Indpls., 1976-77, sr. editor, 1977-79; legis. lobbyist Ind. Acad. Family Physicians, 1973-77; med. advisor New Hope Found. Am., Inc., 1974-79. Bd. dirs. Meals on Wheels, Inc., Peoples Health Center Indpls., Marion County Cancer Soc.; bd. dirs. Ind. Sports Corp.; mem. Ind. Gov.'s Council Phys. Fitness and Sports Medicine; med. coordinator Nat. Sports Festival IV, 1983. Served to lt. col. USAFR, 1971—. Recipient Disting. Service award Ind. Pub. Health Assn., 1984; Decorated Meritorious Service medal; recipient Service to Mankind award Sertoma Club, 1975, Outstanding Alumnus award Mt. Ayr (Ind.) High Sch., 1976, Sen. Lugar's Health Excellence award, 1983, Pub. Health excellence award Marion County Health Dept., 1984; named a Sagamore of the Wabash Gov. of Ind., 1980. Fellow Am. Acad. Family Physicians, Am. Coll. Preventive Medicine, Soc. Prospective Medicine (pres., dir.); mem. AMA, Ind. State Med. Assn., Marion County Med. Soc., Ind. Acad. Family Physicians (v.p. 1977, dir.), Ind. Allied Health Assn. (pres. 1973-74), Ind. Acad. Sci., Ind. Pub. Health Assn., Soc. Tchrs. Family Medicine, Ind. Assn. Pub. Health Physicians, Ind. Arthritis Found. (dir.), Ind. Lung Assn. (dir.), Assn. Am. Med. Colls., Assn. Depts. Family Medicine, Fla. Acad. Family Physicians (dir.). Republican. Office: Indiana Board of Health 1330 W Michigan St Indianapolis IN 46206

BLANKENHEIMER, BERNARD, econ. cons.; b. N.Y.C., July 6, 1920; s. Benjamin and Anna (Barach) B.; m. Rosalind Drescher, Dec. 4, 1943; children—Alan Howard, Susan Leslie. B.A., Bklyn. Coll., 1941; postgrad., N.Y. U., 1941-42; M.A. in Econs, George Washington U., 1950. With U.S. Dept. Commerce, 1942-76, jr. economist European div., 1942, asst. economist, 1945-47, internat. economist Africa sect. Brit. Commonwealth div., 1948-50, chief African sect. Africa-Near East div., 1950-61, dep. dir. Africa div., 1961, dir., 1962-68, U.S. Fgn. Service sr. comml. officer Am. consulate gen., Johannesburg, Republic South Africa, 1968-70; dep. dir. Office Import Programs, Washington, 1970-72, dir., 1973-76; dir. U.S. Trade Mission to, Liberia, Ghana, Sierra Leone, Guinea, 1960, Mission to, Kenya, Uganda, Tanganyika, 1963; adviser U.S. del. 22d session GATT, Geneva, 1965; mem. U.S. observer del. UN Econ. Commn. for Africa Symposium on Industrialization, Cairo, 1966; mem. 9th Sr. Seminar in Fgn. Policy Dept. State, 1966-67; observer U.S. del. Unctad III, Santiago, Chile, 1972; mem. U.S. del UNESCO Meeting of Experts, Geneva, 1973, Internat. Rubber Study Group meetings, 1973, 74, Djakarta, Indonesia, 1975; mem. U.S. del. to 5th Internat. Tin Conf. Negotiations, Geneva, 1975, Unctad Confs. on Tungsten and Copper, 1976, Unctad Consultation on Copper, 1976; asst. dir. econ. cons. services Wolf & Co., 1976-78; v.p. Econ. Cons. Services, Inc., Washington, 1978-79; lectr. African studies Johns Hopkins Sch. Advanced Internat. Studies, 1957-62, Am. U. Sch. Bus. Adminstrn., 1967, Howard U., 1962-68. Contbr. articles to govtl., profl. jours. Served with AUS, 1942-45. Recipient silver medal for distinguished authorship Dept. Commerce, 1960, spl. achievement award, 1972, 75. Fellow African Studies Assn., Royal Geog. Soc. Home and Office: 9508 Wadsworth Dr Bethesda MD 20034

BLANKENHORN, DAVID HENRY, cardiologist; b. Cleve., Nov. 16, 1924; s. Marion Arthur and Martha (Taggart) B.; m. Anne Wood Ramsey, June 15, 1948; children—David, Mary, Susan, John. M.D., U. Cin., 1947. Diplomate: Am. Bd. Internal Medicine. Instr. medicine U. Cin., 1955-57; asst. prof. medicine U. So. Calif., 1957-61, asso. prof., 1961-66, prof, 1966—, dir. cardiology, 1966-80, dir. atherosclerosis research, 1980—; research asst. Rockefeller Inst. Med. Research, 1952-54; pres. Nutrition Sci. Corp. Served as capt. M.C. U.S. Army, 1950-52. Commonwealth fellow. Fellow A.C.P., Am. Coll. Cardiology; mem. Western Assn. Physicians, Am. Heart Assn., Assn. Univ. Cardiologists, Am. Soc. Clin. Nutrition, Alpha Omega Alpha. Home: 1165 Afton St Pasadena CA 91103 Office: 2025 Zonal Ave Los Angeles CA 90033

BLANKLEY, WALTER ELWOOD, manufacturing executive; b. Phila., Sept. 23, 1935; s. George William and Martha Emily (McCord) B.; m. Rosemary Deniken, Aug. 16, 1958; children: Stephen Michael, Laura Ann. B.S.M.E., Princeton U., 1957. Mgr. planning Ametek Hunter Spring, Hatfield, Pa., 1965-66, gen. mgr., 1966-69; asst. to pres. Ametek, Inc., San Francisco, 1969-71; v.p. Ametek, Inc., Watsonville, Calif., 1971-78, group v.p., 1978-82, sr. v.p., 1982—. Mem. Aluminum Extruders Council (pres. 1974-76, dir. 1971-78). Office: Ametek Inc PO Box 351 Watsonville CA 95076

BLANPAIN, JAN EUGENE, physician, educator; b. Diest, Belgium, Feb. 24, 1930; s. Henri and Celine (Dochy) B.; m. Hedwig Van Landeghem, Apr. 7, 1958; children—Kristin, Marianne. M.D. summa cum laude, Leuven U., Belgium, 1956. Lectr., asso. adminstr. Leuven U. Hosp., 1958-61, asso. prof., dir., 1961-65, prof., dir. dept. hosp. adminstrn. and med. care orgn., 1965—; cons. WHO, W.K. Kellogg Found., Rockefeller Found., HEW; vis. prof. Ottawa U., 1968; mem. Nat. Research Council, 1967-76, Nat. Hosp. Council, 1963—, Nat. Health Planning Council, 1974—, WHO Expert Panel on Orgn. of Med. Care, 1974—. Author: Community Health Investment, 1976, National Health Insurance and Health Resources, 1978. WHO fellow, 1961-65; Council of Europe fellow, 1963. Fellow Am. Coll. Hosp. Adminstrs. (hon.); mem. Inst. Medicine, Nat. Acad. Scis., European Assn. Tng. Programs in Health Care Studies (pres. 1978—), Internat. Epidemiological Assn., Internat. Hosp. Fedn. Roman Catholic. Home: 61 Konijnenhoekstraat Oud-Heverlee 3044 Belgium Office: 102 Vital Decosterstraat Leuven 3000 Belgium

BLANTON, EDWARD LEE, JR., lawyer; b. nr. Hope Mills, N.C., Oct. 31, 1931; s. Edward Lee and Margaret M. (Bullard) B.; m. Cathleen Estelle Edwards, Aug. 13, 1960; children: Edward Lee III, Cathleen Estelle, Margaret Ellyn. B.S., Davidson Coll., 1953; M.A., Vanderbilt U., 1954; LL.B., U. Md., 1960. Bar: Md. 1960. Tchr. math. Balt. City Schs., 1956-59; law clk. to judge, Washington, 1960-62, practiced in, Balt., 1962-65, 69—; mem. Adelberg, Rudow & Blanton, Balt., 1969-72, Blanton & McCleary, Towson, Md., 1973—; asst. atty. gen. State of Md., Balt., 1965-68; Dir. Aiken Fund, Inc., County Fuel Co., Inc., United Credit Bur. Am.; chmn. subcom. drafting revision Md. election laws Md. Legis. Council, 1966-67; chmn. subcom. drafting revision Md. income tax laws Hughes Commn., 1966-67. Bd. dirs. United Christian Citizens, 1971—, pres., 1974-75; pres. Central Balt. Ecumenical Sch. Christian Edn., 1971-74, Long Green Valley Assn., 1979—, Historic Long Green Valley, Inc., 1980—; mem. State Republican Central Com., 1982—; mem. citizens adv. com. Md. Tng. Sch. for Boys, 1983—. Served to 1st lt. AUS, 1954-56; capt. Md. N.G., 1957-62. Mem. Am., Fed., Md. bar assns., Bar Assn. Baltimore County, Newcomen Soc. N.Am., Delta Theta Phi. Presbyterian (elder). Clubs: Mchts., Center. Lodges: Masons; Shriners. Home: Avondell Glen Arm MD 21057 Office: Suite 210 Bosley Bldg 210 Allegheny Ave Baltimore MD 21204

BLANTON, HOOVER CLARENCE, lawyer; b. Green Sea, S.C., Oct. 13, 1925; s. Clarence Leo and Margaret (Hoover) B.; m. Cecilia Lopez, July 31, 1949; children: Lawson Hoover, Michael Lopez. J.D., U. S.C., 1953. Bar: S.C. 1953. Assoc. Whaley & McCutchen, Columbia, S.C., 1953-66; ptnr. Whaley & McCutchen Blanton & Rhodes, and precessors, Columbia, 1967—; dir. Legal Aid Service Agy., Columbia, chmn. bd., 1972-73. Gen. counsel S.C. Republican party, 1963-66; pres. Richland County Rep. Conv., 1962; del. Rep. State Conv., 1962, 64, 66, 68, 70, 74; bd. dirs. Midlands Community Action Agy., Columbia, vice chmn., 1972-73; bd. dirs. Wildewood Sch., 1976-78; mem. Gov.'s Legal Services Adv. Council, 1976-77, Commn. on Continuing Legal Edn. for Judiciary, 1977—; ordained deacon Baptist Ch. Served with USNR, 1942-46, 50-52. Mem. S.C. Bar (ho. of dels. 1975-76, chmn. fee disputes bd. 1977-81), ABA, Richland County Bar Assn. (pres. 1980), S.C. Def. Trial Attys. Assn., Def. Research Inst., Assn. Ins. Attys. (state chmn. 1971-77, 80—, exec. council 1977-80), Am. Bd. Trial Advs., Phi Delta Phi. Club: Toastmasters (pres. 1959). Home: 3655 Deerfield Dr Columbia SC 29204 Office: 1414 Lady St Columbia SC 29201

BLANTON, JACK SAWTELLE, oil company executive; b. Shreveport, La., Dec. 7, 1927; s. William Neal and Louise (Wynn) B.; m. Laura Lee Scurlock, Aug. 20, 1949; children: Elizabeth Louise (Mrs. Peter Staub Wareing), Jack Sawtelle, Eddy Scurlock. B.A., U. Tex., 1947, LL.B., 1950. Bar: Tex. 1950. With Scurlock Oil Co., Houston, 1950—, v.p., 1956-58, pres., 1958-83, chmn. bd., 1983—; v.p. Eddy Refining Co.; dir. United Energy Resources, Inc., Southwestern Bell Corp., Tex. Commerce Bank N.A., Gordon Jewelry Corp. Trustee, vice chmn. exec. com. Meth. Hosp.; past chmn. bd. trustees St. Luke's United Meth. Ch., Houston. Named Houston's outstanding young man of year, 1960. Mem. Mid-Continent Oil and Gas Assn. (pres.), Houston C. of C. (life), Sons Rep. of Tex. (past pres. San Jacinto chpt.), Sam Houston Meml. Assn., Nat. Tennis Assn., U.S. Lawn Tennis Assn., Am. Petroleum Inst., Tex. Ind. Oil Producers and Refiners, Ex-Students Assn. U. Tex. (past pres.), Delta Kappa Epsilon, Phi Delta Phi, Phi Alpha Delta. Clubs: Houston (past pres.), River Oaks Country (Houston)). Office: Three Allen Ctr 29th Floor 333 Clay Houston TX 77002

BLANTON, JEREMY, dancer; b. Memphis, Dec. 31, 1939; s. Clarence James and Mahalia Dell (Snavely) B. Grad. high sch. Ballet instr. Acad. Dance Arts, Memphis, 1961, Nat. Acad. Arts, Champaign, Ill., 1973-74; asst. to Bob Fosse on nat. tour, Chicago; ballet instr. and coach Ballet Repertory Co., 1976, 77, 78; assoc. dir. Am. Ballet Theatre II, 1979—. Dancer, Robert Joffrey Ballet, N.Y.C., 1959-60, Met. Opera Ballet, N.Y.C., 1960-61; prin. dancer, Nat. Ballet of Can., Toronto, Ont., 1962-71; guest artist: Jacob's Pillow Dance Festival, Lee, Mass., 1971; prin. dancer, Ballet Repertory Co., N.Y.C., 1972, Bar Harbor (Maine) Festival Ballet, Agnes DeMille's Heritage Dance Theatre, N.Y.C., 1974, Jones Beach Summer Theatre, N.Y.C., 1975; performing artist: Dallas Summer Musicals, 1964, Gen. Motors Announcement Show, 1973-74, appeared on, Canadian Broadcasting Co.; TV spls. Romeo and Juliet, 1966 (Grand Prix award), Swan Lake, 1967, Cinderella, 1968 (Emmy award); prin. dancer: Maurice Ravel Centennial Concert, 1975; appeared: My Fair Lady, Broadway 20th Anniversary Revival, 1976, Milliken Breakfast Show, 1976, Chicago-A Musical Vaudeville, 1977; choreographer: Bus and Truck Co. of Chgo, Casa Manana Theatre, North Stage Dinner Theatre, Chgo., 1980, Chicago, Union Plaza Hotel, Las Vegas, 1982. Order of Chevalier, DeMolay. Mem. AFTRA, Actors Equity Assn., Am. Guild Mus. Artists, Assn. Canadian TV and Radio Artists. Episcopalian. Home: 210 W 19 St New York NY 10011

BLASCH, GEORGE DAVID, banker; b. Glendale, N.Y., Feb. 22, 1929; s. Gustave A. and Freda (Bossert) B.; m. Marianne Logemann, May 2, 1954; children—David, Karen. B.S., N.Y. U., 1965, M.B.A., 1969. With Lincoln Savs. Bank, N.Y.C., 1946-81; pres. Tremont Fed. Savs. & Loan Assn., Bronx, N.Y., 1982—. Elder Glendale Reformed Ch. Mem. N.Y. State Safe Deposit Assn. (pres.), Ridgewood C. of C. (v.p.), Queens County Grand Jurors Assn. Clubs: Kiwanis (pres. 1959), Masons (treas. N.Y. Masonic Youth Found., Inc.), Order DeMolay.). Home: 78-27 64 Pl Glendale NY 11385 Office: 3445 Jerome Ave Bronx NY 10467

BLASCO, ALFRED JOSEPH, business and financial Consultant; b. Kansas City, Mo., Oct. 9, 1904; s. Joseph and Mary (Bevacqua) B.; m. Kathryn Oleno, June 28, 1926; children: Barbara Blasco Mehrer, Phyllis Blasco O'Connor. Student, Kansas City Sch. Accountancy, 1921-25, Am. Inst. Banking, 1926-30; Ph.D. (hon.), Avila Coll., 1969.

From office boy to asst. controller Commerce Trust Co., Kansas City, Mo., 1921-35; controller Interstate Securities Co., Kansas City, 1935-45, v.p., 1945-53, pres., 1953—, chmn. bd., 1961-68; sr. v.p. ISC Fin. Corp., 1968-69, hon. chmn. bd., 1970-77, pres., 1979—; chmn. bd. Red Bridge Bank, 1966-72; Mark Plaza State Bank, Overland Park, Kans., 1973-77; spl. lectr. consumer credit Columbia U., N.Y.C., 1956, U. Kans., Lawrence, 1963-64. Contbr. articles to profl. jours. Pres. Cath. Community Library, 1955-56; Mem. Fair Public Accomodations Com., Kansas City, Mo., 1964-68; ward committeeman, Kansas City, Mo., 1972-76; pres., hon. bd. dirs. Baptist Meml. Hosp., 1970-74; chmn. bd. dirs. St. Anthony's Home, 1965-69; chmn. bd. trustees Avila Coll., 1969—. Decorated papal knight Equestrian Order Holy Sepulchre of Jerusalem, 1957, knight comdr., 1964, knight grand cross, 1966, knight of collar, 1982, lt. No. Lieutenancy U.S., 1970-77, vice gov.-gen., 1977—, Knight of Collar; named Bus. Man of Yr. State of Mo., 1957, Man of Yr. City of Hope, 1973; recipient Community Service award Rockne Club Notre Dame, 1959, wisdom award of honor, 1979; Brotherhood award NCCJ, 1979. Mem. Soc. St. Vincent de Paul (pres. 1959-67), Am. Indsl. Bankers Assn. (pres. 1956-57), Am. Inst. Banking (chpt. pres. 1932-33), Bank Auditors and Controllers Assn., Fin. Execs. Inst. (chpt. pres. 1928-29), Nat. Assn. Accts., Kansas City C. of C. Clubs: Rotary, Kansas City, Hillcrest Country, Serra (pres. 1959-60). Office: 8080 Ward Pkwy Kansas City MO 64114

BLASCO-IBANEZ, ALEC MONTGOMERY, photo-journalist; b. Chgo., Mar. 7, 1929; s. Alejandro Serrat and Dalmyra Burnett (Montgomery) Blasco-I. Student, U. Notre Dame, 1948-49; Ph.B., U. So. Calif., 1957. Sports editor Maywood-Bell Indsl. Post McGiffin Pub. Co., Calif., 1959, editor Bell Gardens Rev. and Post Star, 1959; asst. dir. U. So. Calif. News Bur., 1960-61; spl. sci. corr. Los Angeles Examiner and Pictorial Living mag., 1961-62; combat corr. and photographer covering NATO, SEATO and U.S. Armed Forces in Europe, Africa, Middle East, S.E. Asia and Far East including graduating form mil. paratrooper schs., U.S. Army 8th Inf. Div. (W.Ger.), of Fed. Republic of Germany Fernspach 200 Co., Schoengau, and French Fgn. Legion (Algeria), 1st Los Angeles Herald-Examiner and Hearst Headline Service, 1962-66; adminstrv. asst. Rep. John G. Dow, N.Y., 1967; dir. Dow Peace Mission, S. Vietnam, 1967; travel and mil. affairs editor Los Angeles Herald-Examiner, 1968-80, Calif. Living Mag., 1968-80; travel editor daily radio program Ports of Call-Word on Travel Sta. KFAC, 1975-81, covered Am. Floating Artic ice stas., Artic Ocean, 1960-62; covered No. Alaskan Eskimo whaling hunts U. So. Calif. Artic Research Lab., 1961; deepest Artic Ocean ice-pack penetration U.S.S. Burton Island, 1961, U.S.S. Glacier, Marie Byrd Land, Antarctica, 1961; 2d expdn. to relocate South Magnetic Pole U.S.S. Burton Island, Commonwealth Bay, Marie Byrd Land, Adelie Land, 1962; mem. Chile-Peru trench expedn. U.S.S. Anton Brun, NSF, 1965; 1st to photograph living-fossil Neopolina and possible lost undersea Inca city, 1965; participant Sargasso Sea expdn., 1965; pioneer in deep-sea photography, photographed abyssal sea creature Holothurian Duke U.'s Eastward, 1965; mem. Mayan Sacred Wells (cenotes) expdn., Isla Cozeumel and Yucatan Peninsula, 1965, Inter-Am. Geodetic Survey expdn., Peruvian Andes, 1965, 1st. corr. to search for Che Guevara, Bolivia, 1965-66; mem. native Africa music expdn. Dundo Anthrop. Mus., Angola, 1966; mem. lion-human fear response expdn. Gorangoza Nat. Game Preserve, Mozambique, 1966; mem. Mt. Kilimanjaro ski expdn., Helicopter ski expdns., Nevada del Ruiz, Colombia, S.Am., Columbia Mountains, Can., 1969-76; pres. Silver Spur Enterprise, Los Angeles, 1976—; editor-pub. Horses of the Kings. Mag., The Andalusian World mag.; originator, ediotr-pub. Cowboy mag., 1976—; breeder, trainer, exhibitor Andalusian stallion, Paladin, 1976—. Served with USNR, 1948-53; lt. col. USMCR. Recipient Gold Medal of Merit Govt. of Austria, 1972, Gold Medal Lit. Excellence Internat. Poet's Shrine and Congress Am. Poets, 1972, travel writing award Japanese Govt., 1972, 2d ann. Best Writers award N.Am. and Can. Japanese Nat. Tourist Orgn., 1973, Gen. D. MacArthur Gold Medal, 1974. Mem. USMCR Combat Corrs. Assn. (Outstanding Citizen award 1976), USMCR Officers Assn., Appaloosa Horse Club, Andalusian Horse Assn., Internat. Andalusian Horse Assn., Chief Joseph Trail Ride Soc., Explorers Club, Japan Ukiyo-e Soc. (Tokyo). Club: Safari Internat. (Los Angeles). Office: Silver Spur Enterprises 3963 Wilshire Blvd Suite 357 Los Angeles CA 90010

BLASI, ALBERTO, romance languages and comparative literature educator, writer; b. Buenos Aires, Jan. 21, 1931; s. Alberto B. and Emma (Raffo) B. Diploma en Letras, U. Buenos Aires, 1957, licenciado, 1965; D. Letras, U. La Plata, 1976; postgrad. (fellow), U. Iowa, 1975. Reader U. Buenos Aires, 1965-69; prof. U. Rosario, Argentina, 1969-73; writer-in-residence ctlIowa, 1974-75; assoc. prof. Spanish Bklyn. Coll., CUNY, 1975-79, prof. modern langs, 1979—; prof. Spanish and comparative lit. Grad. Ctr. CUNY, 1979—. Author: Los Fundadores, 1962, Introducción a Lucio López, 1965, La tarea del cuento en Fin de Siglo, 1968, Güiraldes y Larbaud: Una amistad creadora, 1970, Manuel Podestá; editor: Fin de Siglo, 1968, Los Trotadores, 1973, Mama Culepina, 1974, El crimen de Don Magin Casanovas, 1976, Essays on Lucio Victorio Mansilla, 1981, Movinientos literarios del siglo XX en Iberoamérica: Teorí y práctica, 1982; contbr. revs. and articles; mem. editorial bd.: Revista Iberoamericana. Recipient French Govt. award Bourse De Marque, 1972, Soc. Argentine Writers Book award, 1960, CUNY Research Award, 1980-83, Argentine Found. for the Arts award, 1966, 69, Municipality of Buenos Aires Book award, 1967; Fulbright fellow, 1974. Mem. PEN Club Internat., Internat. Assn. Hispanists, Internat. Comparative Lit. Assn., Internat. Inst. Iberoamerican Lit., Am. Comparative Lit. Assn., MLA. Office: Grad Ctr CUNY 33 W 42d St New York NY 10036

BLASINGAME, BENJAMIN PAUL, electronics co. exec.; b. State College, Pa., Aug. 1, 1918; s. Ralph Upshaw and Sue Mae (Combs) B.; m. Ella Mae Perry, Aug. 29, 1942; children—Nancy J. Blasingame Wambach, James P., Margaret A. Blasingame Kramer, John R. B.S. in Mech. Engring, Pa. State U., 1940; Sc.D. in Aero. Engring, M.I.T., 1950. Head astronautics dept. U.S. Air Force Acad., 1958-59; resigned, 1959; gen. mgr. electronics div. Gen. Motors Corp., 1959-70; mgr. Milw. operation Delco Electronics div., 1970-72. Author: Astronautics, 1964. Mgr. Santa Barbara operation, 1972-79; Bd.dirs. Santa Barbara Cottage Hosp., 1977—; chmn. Santa Barbara Metro, Nat. Alliance Bus., 1972-75. Commd. 2d lt. U.S. Air Force, 1941; advanced through grades to col., 1959. Decorated Legion of Merit; recipient Public Service award, NASA, 1969, Public Service medal, 1973. Mem. AIAA, Nat. Acad. Engring., N.Y. Acad. Scis., Internat. Acad. Astronautics, Santa Barbara C. of C. (bd. dirs. 1977—). Unitarian. Club: La Cumbre Country. Patentee in field. Home: 517 Carriage Hill Ct Santa Barbara CA 93110

BLASINGAME, FRANCIS JAMES LEVI, physician, educator; b. Hot Springs, Ark., Jan 17, 1907; s. John Mitchell Coleman and Lillian Adams (White) B.; m. Dorothy Isbel Rugeley, June 8, 1932; children—Mary Lillian, Betty Nan, John Chester, Rebecca Louise, James Edward. A.B., U. Tex., 1929, M.D., 1932. Intern Henry Ford Hosp., Detroit, 1935-36; instr. anatomy, med. br. U. of Tex., 1932-33, adj. prof., 1933-35, asso. prof., 1936-37, lectr. anatomy, 1937-58; mem. staff Rugeley and Blasingame Clinic-Hosp., Wharton, Tex., 1937-58; exec. v.p. Am. Med. Assn., Chgo., 1958-68; pres. Blasingame Assos.; cons. to health field. Chmn. bd. edn. Wharton County Jr. Coll.; pres. state bd. dirs. Blue Cross and Blue Shield of Tex. Contbr. articles to profl. jours. Fellow A.C.S., Am. Coll. Hosp. Adminstrs. (hon.); mem. A.M.A. (trustee), Southwestern Surg. Congress, State Med. Assn. Texas (pres.), Cook County Med. Soc., Phi Chi, Alpha Omega Alpha. Episcopalian. Clubs: Mason (110301ner), Rotarian.). Home: 1350 Astor St Chicago IL 60610

BLASIUS, DONALD CHARLES, appliance company executive; b. Oak Park, Ill., June 10, 1929; s. Ervin A. and Frances C. (Critchfield) B.; m. Carle Ann Forslew, Oct. 11, 1952; children: Douglas Charles, Ann Louise. B.S in Bus. Adminstrn., Northwestern U., 1951. Asst. to v.p. sales McCulloch Corp. (chain saws and outboard motors), 1953-55, accessory sales mgr., 1955-58, distbn. mgr., 1958-60, gen. sales mgr., 1960-62, v.p. sales, 1962-65, v.p., gen. mgr., 1965-68; also dir.; gen. mgr. agrl. equipment div. J.I. Case Co., 1968-70, v.p., gen. mgr. div., 1970-72, sr. v.p., gen. mgr. div., 1972-74; exec. v.p., chief operating officer Tappan Co. (maj. appliances), Mansfield, Ohio, 1974-76, pres., chief exec. officer, dir., 1976-84, chmn. bd., chief exec. officer, 1984; group v.p. Domestic Inc., Bloomington, Ill.; pres., dir. Flymo Inc., Husqvarna Motorcycle Co., San Diego, Getinge Internat, Inc., Lakewood, N.J.; dir. Bank One, Mansfield, Nat. Union Electric Corp., Bloomington, Ill., Ohio Edison Co., Akron., Tecfor, Bensonville, Ill., Team Textile Service Corp., Houston, Dometic Sales Co., Elkhart, Ind., Classic Stove Works, New Britain, Conn. Trustee North Central Tech. Coll., Richland County Found. Served with Spl. Services AUS. Club: Westbrook Country. Home: Heritage Farm 1143 CR 2256 Perrysville OH 44864 Office: Tappan Co Box 606 Mansfield OH 44901

BLASS, BILL, designer apparel, home furnishings; b. Ft. Wayne, Ind., June 22, 1922; s. Ralph Aldrich and Ethyl (Keyser) B. D.F.A. (hon.), R.I. Sch. Design. Asst. designer for David Crystal, 1950-51, Anna Miller & Co., 1951-59; designer Maurice Rentner, Ltd. (now Bill Blass Ltd.), 1959—, v.p., 1963-70; pres. Bill Blass Ltd., 1970—. Served with AUS, World War II. Recipient Coty award Am. Fashion Critics, 1961, 63, 70, 1st Men's Coty award Am. Fashion Critics, 1968, Hall of Fame award, 1970, spl. citation, 1971, 82, 83, Cartier Santos award, Lord & Taylor's Creative Design award, Indpls. Art Commn. award., Chgo. Gold Coast Fashion award, 1965; recipient Cotton Council award, 1965, "Millie" Fashion award Boston Academie, 1969, Neiman-Marcus award, 1969, Print Council award, 1971, Martha award, 1974, Great Am. Designers award I. Magnin, 1974, Am. Fashion awards, 1975, First Annual Ayres Look award, 1978, Man Style award Gentleman's Quarterly mag., 1979, Cutty Sark Hall of Fame award, 1979. Mem. Council Fashion Designers Am. (v.p.). Home: 444 E 57th St New York NY 10021 Office: 550 7th Ave New York NY 10018

BLASS, ELLIOTT MARTIN, psychology educator; b. Bklyn., Sept. 10, 1940; s. Joseph Harry and Edythe (Horner) B.; m. Lorraine Hirsch, June 27, 1966; children: David Mark, Joshua Samuel. B.S., Bklyn. Coll., 1963; M.S., U. Conn., 1964; Ph.D., U. Va., 1967. Postdoctoral fellow U. Pa., 1967-69; asst. prof. psychology Johns Hopkins U., Balt., 1969-75, asso. prof., 1975-79, prof. psychology and psychiatry, 1979—; vis. prof. U. Toronto, 1976-77, Hebrew U., Jerusalem, 1982-83. Editor: The Psychobiology of Curt Richter; cons. editor: Developmental Psychobiology, Behavioral Neurosci., Appetite. USPHS postdoctoral fellow U. Pa.; NIH research grantee; NSF research grantee.; John Simon Gugggenheim Meml. fellow, 1982-83; Fulbright Hays research fellow, 1982-83. Mem. AAAS, Internat. Soc. Devel. Psychology, Animal Behavior Soc., Eastern Psychol. Assn. Office: Dept Psychology Johns Hopkins U Charles and 33d Sts Baltimore MD 21218

BLASS, GERHARD ALOIS, educator; b. Chemnitz, Germany, Mar. 12, 1916; came to U.S., 1949, naturalized, 1955; s. Gustav Alois and Anna (Mehnert) B.; m. Barbara Siegert, July 16, 1945; children—Andrew, Marcus, Evamaria, Annamaria, Peter. Abitur, Oberrealschule Chemnitz, 1935; Dr. rer. nat., Universität Leipzig, 1943. Asst. Instutut für Theoretische Physik, Leipzig, 1939-43; research cons. Siemens & Halske, Berlin, 1943-46; dozent math. and physics Oberrealschule, Nuremberg, 1946-47, Ohm Polytechnikum, 1947-49; prof. physics Coll. St. Thomas, St. Paul, 1949-51, U. Detroit, 1951-81, chmn. dept., 1962-71. Author: Theoretical Physics, 1962. Fellow AAAS; mem. Soc. Asian and Comparative Philosophy, Detroit Astron. Soc., Sigma Pi Sigma. Roman Catholic. Home: 4441 Stewart Rd Metamora MI 48455 *It is a great gift to be alive; and no man can presume ever to repay for all the gifts he has received, but I have tried to express, through my work, my deep gratitude.*

BLASS, JOHN PAUL, physician; b. Vienna, Austria, Feb. 21, 1937; s. Gustaf and Jolan (Wirth) B.; m. Birgit Annelise Knudsen, Dec. 20, 1960; children—Charles, Lisa. A.B. summa cum laude, Harvard U., 1958; Ph.D., U. London, 1960; M.D., Columbia U., 1965. Postdoctoral fellow Am. Cancer Soc., Columbia U., 1962-63; intern Mass. Gen. Hosp., Boston, 1965-66, resident in medicine, 1966-67; research assoc. Nat. Heart and Lung Inst., Bethesda, Md., 1967-70; asst. prof. phychiatry and biol. chemistry UCLA, 1970-76, assoc. prof., 1976-78; mem. staff UCLA Hosps. Clinics, 1970-78; Winifred Masterson Burke prof. neurology, prof. medicine Cornell U. Med. Center, 1978—; attending neurologist N.Y. Hosp.; mem. NBS-1 Rev. Com. NIH, 1981—. Editorial bd. Jour. Neurochemistry, Jour. Neurochem. Pathology; Contbr. articles to profl. jours. Served as asst. surgeon USPHS, 1967-70. Mem. Soc. Neurosci. (chmn. social issues com.), Biochem. Soc., Am. Soc. Biol. Chemists, Soc. Neurochemists (chmn. public policy com.), Internat. Soc. Neurochemistry (chmn. clin. com.), Am. Soc. Clin. Investigation, Am. Geriatrics Soc., Assn. Alzheimers and Related Disease (sci. adv. bd.), Am. Chem. Soc., Phi Beta Kappa, Sigma Xi, Alpha Omega Alpha. Jewish. Home: 1 Orchard Pl Bronxville NY 10708 Office: 785 Mamaroneck Ave White Plains NY 10605

BLASS, NOLAND, JR., architect; b. Little Rock, May 28, 1920; s. Noland and Isabel (Ringelhaupt) B.; m. Elizabeth Weitzenhoffer, Oct. 21, 1947; children: Elizabeth Victoria, Wilhelmina Louise, Wendy Valdez. B.Arch., Cornell U., 1941. Designer-draftsman Blass Chilcote and partners (and predecessor firms), Little Rock, 1946-56, partner, 1956—, pres., 1980—. Pres. Ark. Arts Center, 1972; mem. Little Rock Planning Commn., 1960-69; pres. Pulaski Met. YMCA, 1967-68; mem. Gov.'s Inauguration Com., 1971; pres. Ark. Orch. Soc., 1976; Trustee A.I.A. Ednl. Endowment Fund; bd. dirs. Leo N. Levi Hosp., Mid-Am. Arts Alliance, 1980—; pres. Levi Found., 1983. Served with AUS, 1941-45. Fellow AIA (pres. Ark. 1958-59); mem. Tau Beta Pi, Zeta Beta Tau. Jewish. Club: Masons (33 deg.). Home: 217 Normandy Rd Little Rock AR 72207 Office: 303 W Capitol Little Rock AR 72201

BLATT, BURTON, university dean, teacher educator; b. Bronx, N.Y., May 23, 1927; s. Abraham and Jennie (Starr) B.; m. Ethel Draizen, Dec. 24, 1951; children: Edward Richard, Steven David, Michael Lawrence. B.S., NYU, 1949; M.A., Columbia Tchrs. Coll., 1950; Ed.D., Pa. State U., 1956; L.H.D., Ithaca Coll., 1974. Tchr. mentally retarded children, N.Y.C., 1949-55; grad. scholar, grad. asst. Pa. State U., 1955-56; assoc. prof., coordinator spl. edn. So. Conn. State Coll., 1956-59, prof., chmn. spl. edn. dept., 1959-61; prof., chmn. spl. edn. dept. Sch. Edn. Boston U., 1961-69; Centennial prof., dir. div. spl. edn. and rehab., dir. Center on Human Policy, Syracuse U., 1969-76, dean Sch. Edn., 1976—; former asst. commr. and dir. mental retardation Mass. Dept. Mental Health; former prin. cons. R.I. Commn. to Study Edn. of Handicapped Children; cons. U.S. Dept. Edn.; former mem. adv. bd. Joseph P. Kennedy Jr. Found. Author: (with S. Sarason, K. Davidson) The Preparation of Teachers, 1962, The Intellectually Disfranched: Impoverished Learners and Their Teachers, 1967, (with F. Kaplan) Christmas in Purgatory, 1966, (with Frank Garfunkel) The Educability of Intelligence, 1969, Exodus from Pandemonium, 1970, Souls in Extremis, 1973, Revolt of the Idiots, 1976, (with D. Biklen and R. Bogdan) An Alternative Textbook in Special Education: People, Schools and Institutions, 1977, (with A. Ozolins and J. McNally) The Family Papers, 1979, In and Out of Mental Retardation, 1981, In and Out of the University, 1982, In and Out of Books, 1984, (with R. Morris) Perspectives in Special Education, 1984; also articles and monographs on mental retardation, spl. edn. and higher edn. Past bd. dirs. Epilepsy League Mass.; former chmn. Mass. Task Force on Edn. Mentally Handicapped; past mem. nat. adv. bd. Nat. Soc. Prevention Blindness; past mem. Mass. and N.Y. Govs.' coms. on Services to Children, Conn. Gov.'s Adv. Council Mental Retardation; past pres. and current mem. bd. visitors Syracuse Devel. Center; mem. N.Y. State Doctoral Council. Recipient ann. award Mass. Psychol. Assn., 1967, Mass. Assn. Retarded Citizens, 1968; Newell Kephart Meml. award Purdue U., 1974; award N.Y. State Assn. Tchrs. Mentally Handicapped, 1976, Coll. of New Rochelle, 1980; ann. award Pioneer Devel. Ctr., 1983; Profl. Leadership award Young Adult Inst., 1983. Fellow Am. Assn. Mental Deficiency (past nat. v.p. edn., past editorial staff Am. Jour. Mental Deficiency, Mental Retardation, nat. pres. 1976-77, regional award 1973, nat. award 1974); mem. Council Exceptional Children (past mem. found. bd., past state pres., state dir., div. pres., chpt. award 1980), Assn. for Severely Handicapped, Phi Delta Kappa. Jewish. Home: 106 Cedar Heights Dr Jamesville NY 13078 Office: 150 Huntington Hall Syracuse U Syracuse NY 13210 *Throughout my career, I have been preoccupied with one idea: that people can change in very significant ways. And although I have yet to discover sufficient evidence to support the hypothesis that capability is educable, my work has led me to an even more fundamental comprehension: that there is a design of things, and that the design for all of us holds nothing but good.*

BLATT, GENEVIEVE, state judge; b. East Brady, Pa., June 19, 1913; d. George F. and Clara (Laurent) B. A.B., U. Pitts., 1933, M.A., 1934, J.D., 1937; LL.D., St. Francis Coll., 1959, Villanova U., 1960, St. Joseph's Coll., 1964, Barry Coll., 1966, Seton Hill Coll., 1968, LaSalle Coll., 1970, Elizabethtown Coll., 1974, Dickinson Coll. Law, 1974, York (Pa.) Coll., 1975, St. Charles Sem., 1975, Cedarcrest Coll., 1976, Allentown Coll. of St. Francis de Sales, 1976. Bar: Pa. 1938. Mem. faculty U. Pitts., 1934-38; sec., chief examiner Pitts. CSC, 1938-42; asst. city solicitor, Pitts., 1942-45, dep. state treas., Pa.; exec. dir. State Treasury Dept., 1945-49; sec. internal affairs State of Pa., 1955-67; asst. dir. Pres.'s Office Econ. Opportunity, 1967-68; spl. cons. Shared Services Assn., Daus. of Charity, 1968-71; dir. departmental audits Pa. Auditor Gen.'s Office, 1969; counsel to Morgan, Lewis & Bockius, Attys., 1970-72; judge Commonwealth Ct. Pa., 1972-83, sr. judge, 1983—; Founder, exec. dir. Pa. Intercollegiate Conf. on Govt., 1934-72; mem. Pa. Bd. Pardons, 1955-67; sec. Pa. Indsl. Devel. Authority Bd. and Gen. State Authority Bd., 1956-67; Pa. del. to Interstate Oil Compact Commn., 1955-67, vice chmn., 1959-60; mem. weights and measures adv. com. Nat. Bur. Standards, 1960-67; mem. adv. com. women in armed services Def. Dept., 1964-67; mem. Pres.'s Consumer Adv. Council, 1964-66, Pres.'s Commn. on Law Enforcement and Adminstrn. Justice, 1965-67. Bd. dirs. Center for Research in Apostolate, 1972-75, 80—, vice chmn., 1972-75; mem. adv. council Nat. Conf. Catholic Bishops, 1972-75; mem. Nat. Bishops Bicentennial Com., 1974-76; chmn. Harrisburg Diocesan Bicentennial Com., 1974-76; Sec. Pa. Democratic Com., 1948-70; Dem. nominee for auditor gen. Pa., 1952; pres. Young Dem. Clubs Pa., 1942-50; exec. bd. Pa. Fedn. Dem. Women, 1940-72; del. Dem. Nat. Convs., 1936-68; Dem. nominee for U.S. Senate, 1964; Dem. nat. committeewoman Pa., 1970-72; fellow Harry S Truman Library, Lyndon B. Johnson Library; founder, v.p. James A. Finnegan Fellowship Found., 1960—; bd. mgrs. 41st Internat. Eucharistic Congress, 1975-76. Recipient Disting. Dau. of Pa. award, 1956; named Woman of Year in Govt., Pitts., 1959, Nat., 1963; N2Mother Gerard Phelan gold medal; Marymount Coll., 1965; Elizabeth Seton medal Seton Hill Coll., 1960; Pro Ecclesia et Pontifice medal Pope Paul VI, 1966; Louise de Marillac medal St. Joseph's Coll., 1966; Dubois medal Mount St. Mary Coll., 1970; St. Thomas More legal award, Pitts., 1974; Phila. FAME award Greater Phila. Women's Clubs, 1978; Elizabeth Ann Seton medal St. John's U., 1978—; comdr. Equestrian Order of Knights and Ladies of Holy Sepulchre Vatican, 1978; Benemerenti gold medal Pope John Paul II, 1979; Liberty Under Law award Internat. Aux., Fraternal Order of Eagles, 1980; Govtl. Service citation Pa. Elected Women's Assn., 1983, Woman of Yr. Pa. Fedn. Bus. and Profl. Women's Clubs, 1972. Mem. Am. Bar Found., Am., Pa., Dauphin County bar assns., Am. Judicature Soc., Nat. Assn. Women Judges, Nat. Assn. Women Lawyers, LWV (award 1964), Bus. and Profl. Women, Cath. War Vets. Aux., Nat. Council Cath. Women, Nat. Cath. Women's Union, Mortar Bd., Phi Beta Kappa, Delta Sigma Rho, Pi Tau Phi, Pi Sigma Alpha; hon. mem. Eagles, Soroptimists, Beta Sigma Phi, Delta Kappa Sigma. Office: 517 South Office Bldg Harrisburg PA 17120

BLATT, SIDNEY JULES, psychology educator; b. Phila., Oct. 15, 1928; s. Harry and Fannie (Feld) B.; m. Ethel Shames, Feb. 1, 1951; children: Susan, Judith, David. B.S., Pa. State U., 1950, M.S., 1952; Ph.D., U. Chgo., 1957; postgrad., New Eng. Inst. for Psychoanalysis, 1972. Mem. faculty Yale U., New Haven, 1960—, prof. psychology, 1974—; mem. NIMH Research Fellowship Rev. Panel, 1966-69, NIMH Psychology Tng. Rev. Panel, 1969-74. Author: (with J. Allison and C. Zimet) Interpretation of Psychological Tests, 1968, (with C. Wild) Schizophrenia: A Developmental Analysis, 1976, Continuity and Change in Art: The Development of Modes of Representation, 1984. Fellow Found. Fund Research in Psychiatry, 1961-64; named Disting. Practitioner of Psychology Nat. Acad. Practice, 1982. Fellow Am. Psychol. Assn.; mem. AAAS, AAUP, Soc. Personality Assessment. Office: Yale U 25 Park St New Haven CT 06519

BLATTER, FRANK EDWARD, banker; b. Denver, Jan. 9, 1939; s. Anthony John and Irene Marie (Tobin) B.; m. Barbara E. Drieth, Sept. 6, 1959; children: Dean Robert, Lisa Kay, Paul Kelly. B.S., Regis Coll., Denver, 1961; grad., Colo. Sch. Banking, 1966, Sch. Bank Adminstrn., 1973. C.P.A., Colo. Acct. McMahon, Maddox & Rodriguez (C.P.A.s), Denver, 1960-63, United Bank Denver, 1963-65; with United Banks Colo., Inc., Denver, 1965—, comptroller, then treas., comptroller, 1969-74, v.p., fin., treas., 1974-79, sr. v.p. finance and treas., 1979-80, exec. v.p., 1980—; dir. United Bank Brighton, United Banks Service Co., United Bank Longmont, United Fin. Centers. Treas. Denver Catholic Community Services; Nat. Adv. Council Regis Coll. Mem. Tax Execs. Inst., Am. Inst. C.P.A.s, Colo. Soc. C.P.A.s, Fin. Execs. Inst., Bank Adminstrn. Inst. Roman Catholic. Clubs: Rolling Hills Country, Internat. Athletic. Office: 1700 Broadway Denver CO 80217

BLATTMAN, H. EUGENE, foods corporation executive; b. Kansas City, Mo., Feb. 21, 1936; m. Susan Ann Chandler, Oct. 30, 1954 (div. 1974); m. Virginia May Blattman, Dec. 21, 1974; children: Robert, Beth, Vikki, Keith, Kirk, Lori, Kevin. B.A., Whitman Coll., 1958. Vice pres., gen. mgr. grocery products div. Foremost-McKesson Inc., San Francisco, 1978-80, corp. v.p., gen. mgr. ops. resource group, 1981-83; pres. McKesson Foods Group, 1983—; exec. v.p. C.F. Mueller Co., Jersey City, N.J., 1980-81. San Francisco C. of C. (dir. 1983). Republican. Presbyterian. Home: 1580 La Honda Rd Woodside CA 94062 Office: McKesson Corp 1 Post St San Francisco CA 94104

BLATTNER, DAVID JONES, JR., lawyer; b. Milw., Aug. 21, 1938; s. David Jones and Frances Ellen (Tucker) B.; m. Julie Ellen Meyer, Oct. 6, 1939; children: David Jones III, Katherine Elizabeth. A.B., Harvard U., 1960, LL.B., 1963. Bar: Mass. 1963. Assoc. Rope & Gray, Boston, Washington, 1964-73, ptnr., 1973—. Address: 225 Franklin St Boston MA 02110

BLATTNER, JOSEPH LORNE, JR., insurance company executive; b. Chanute, Kans., July 16, 1945; s. Joseph Lorne and Theresa (Becker) B.; m. Alice Lee Adair Musk, Dec. 27, 1969 (div. 1980); m. Luisa Carotenuto, Apr. 17, 1982; 1 dau., Lisa Therese. B.A., Johns Hopkins U., 1967; M.A., Columbia U., 1969. Tchr. Henley Sch., N.Y.C., 1969-72; actuarial student Met. life Inst. Co., N.Y.C., 1972-75; actuarial student, sr. v.p., chief actuary Capitol Life Ins. Co., 1975—; dir. Capitol Life of Colo., Denver, 1982—, Capitol Life of N.Y., N.Y.C., 1982—; chief actuary Providence Ins. Co., Del., 1982—. Fellow Soc. Actuaries; mem. Am. Acad. Actuaries. Clubs: Actuarial of Pacific States (sec.-treas. 1978-79), Actuarial of Denver (pres. 1979-80). Home: 12484 W 2d Dr Lakewood CO 80228 Office: Capitol Life Ins Co 1600 Sherman St Denver Co 80203

BLATTY, WILLIAM PETER, author; b. N.Y.C., Jan. 7, 1928; s. Peter and Mary (Mouakad) B.; children: Christine Ann, Michael Peter, Mary Joanne. A.B., Georgetown U., 1950, George Washington U., 1954; L.H.D., Seattle U., 1974. Publicity dir. U. So. Calif., 1957-58; public relations dir. Loyola U., Los Angeles, 1959-60. Editor: USIA, 1955-57; author: Which Way To Mecca, Jack?, 1959, John Goldfarb, Please Come Home, 1962, I, Billy Shakespeare, 1965, Twinkle, Twinkle "Killer" Kane, 1966 (Golden Globe award as best movie screen play 1981), The Exorcist, 1970, I'll Tell Them I Remember You, 1973, The Exorcist: From Novel to Film, 1974, The Ninth Configuration, 1978, Legion, 1983; writer screenplays: The Man From the Diner's Club, 1961, John Goldfarb, Please Come Home, 1963, Promise Her Anything, 1962, The Great Bank Robbery, 1967, Gunn, 1967, What Did You Do In The War, Daddy?, 1965, A Shot In The Dark, 1964, Darling Lili, 1968, The Exorcist, 1973. Served to 1st lt. USAF, 1951-54. Recipient Academy award Acad. Motion Picture Arts and Scis., 1973; Gabriel award and blue ribbon for Insight TV series script Am. Film Festival, 1969. Roman Catholic. Office: care Simon & Schuster 1230 Ave of Americas New York NY 10020 *

BLATZ, DURAND BARRETT, manufacturing company executive; b. Ventnor, N.J., July 27, 1918; s. John B. and Ethel (Barrett) B.; m. Joan Ipsen, Mar. 29, 1941; children: Durand Barrett, Ann Galen, Megan Eller, John Balthazar, Estelle Elizabeth. A.B., Cornell U., 1940. Treas. George C. Lewis Co., Phila., 1946-50; gen. controller Crosley and Bendix divs. Avco Mfg. Corp., Cin., 1951-57; with Insilco Corp. (formerly Internat. Silver Co.), Meriden, Conn., 1957—, controller, 1957-59, v.p., treas., 1959-65, pres., 1965-66, pres., chief exec. officer, 1966-76, chmn. bd., pres., chief exec. officer, 1976-80, chmn. bd., chief exec. officer, 1980-82, chmn., 1982—, also dir.; dir. Aetna Life & Casualty Co., Hartford., Geosource, Inc., Times Fiber Communications, Inc., Broad Street Communications, Inc. Served to lt. col. F.A. AUS, 1940-46. Mem. Delta Upsilon. Republican. Episcopalian. Home: 39 Currier Pl Cheshire CT 06410 Office: 1000 Research Pkwy Meriden CT 06450

BLATZ, WILLIAM JOSEPH, manufacturing company executive; b. Windsor, Ont., Can., June 28, 1920; came to U.S., 1924; s. Leo V. and Rose (Hickey) B.; m. Shirley J. Smith, June 19, 1948; children—William R., Linda Jean, Andrew Fielding, Katherine Jane. B.S. in Aero. Engring, U. Detroit, 1942. With Rolls Royce Inc., Detroit, 1941-42; with McDonnell Aircraft Co., St. Louis, 1942—, v.p. engring. tech., 1978—. Chmn. St. Louis Alumni scholarship com. U. Detroit, 1975-80. Served with USNR, 1945-46. Recipient Nat. Air Breathing Propulsion award AIAA, 1978, Tech. Mgmt. award, 1969. Asso. fellow AIAA (chmn. St. Louis 1959-60); mem. Navy League U.S., Am. Def. Preparedness Assn., Tau Beta Pi. Home: 606 Chamblee Ln Creve Coeur MO 63141 Office: PO Box 516 Saint Louis MO 63166

BLAU, HARVEY RONALD, lawyer; b. N.Y.C., Nov. 14, 1935; s. David and Rose (Kuchinsky) B.; m. Arlene Joan Garrett, Mar. 21, 1964; children: Stephanie Elizabeth, Melissa Karen, Victoria Gayle. A.B., N.Y.U., 1957, LL.M., 1965; LL.B., Columbia U., 1961. Bar: N.Y. 1961. Practiced in, N.Y.C., after 1961; sr. partner firm Blau, Kramer, Wactlar & Lieberman, P.C., Jericho, N.Y., 1975—; law sec. to U.S. Dist. Judge Cooper So. Dist. N.Y., 1962-63; asst. U.S. atty. So. Dist. N.Y., 1963-66; sec., dir. Aeroflex Labs. Inc., 1980—; chmn. Grant Industries Inc., Instrument Systems Corp.; dir. Universal Holding Corp., John Adams Life Ins. Co.; chmn. com. corp. and Securities law Fed. Bar Council, 1970-73. Served to capt. JAGC, AUS, 1958-66. Mem. Am., Fed. bar assns., Assn. Bar City N.Y., Bar Assn. Nassau County (mem. corp. law and fed. cts. com. 1977—). Home: 125 Wheatley Rd Old Westbury NY 11568 Office: 100 Jericho Quadrangle Jericho NY 11753

BLAU, MONTE, radiology educator; b. N.Y.C., June 17, 1926; s. Samuel and Rose (Cohen) B.; m. Guitta Drimer, June 30, 1946; children: Saul, Hannah. B.S. in Chemistry, Poly. Inst. Bklyn., 1948; Ph.D. in Phys. Chemistry, U. Wis., 1952. Research chemist Geochronometric Lab. Yale U., 1952-53, div. neoplastic diseases Montefiore Hosp., N.Y.C., 1953-54; cancer research scientist Roswell Park Meml. Inst., Buffalo, 1954-75; prof., chmn. dept. nuclear medicine SUNY, Buffalo, 1975-83; vis. prof. radiology Harvard Med. Sch., Boston, 1983—; mem. USP adv. panel on radiopharms.; chmn. med. adv. com. N.Y. State Bur. Radiol. Health; chmn. isotopes adv. com. Los Alamos Nat. Lab. Mem. editorial bd.: Jour. Nuclear Medicine. Served with U.S. Navy, 1944-46. Mem. Soc. Nuclear Medicine (v.p. 1964, pres. 1972), Am. Chem. Soc., Am. Assn. Physicists in Medicine. Home: PO Box 518 South Well Fleet MA 02663 Office: 75 Francis St Boston MA 02115

BLAU, PETER MICHAEL, sociologist, educator; b. Vienna, Austria, Feb. 7, 1918; came to U.S., 1939, naturalized, 1943; s. Theodor I. and Bertha (Selka) B.; m. Judith R. Fritz, July 31, 1968; 1 dau., Reva T.; 1 dau. by previous marriage, Pamela L. A.B., Elmhurst Coll., 1942, LL.D., 1973; Ph.D., Columbia, 1952; M.A., Cambridge U., 1966. Faculty Wayne State U., 1949-51, Cornell U., 1951-53; asst. prof. U. Chgo., 1953-58, asso. prof., 1958-63, prof. sociology, 1963-70; prof. Columbia, 1970—, Quetelet prof. sociology, 1977—; Disting. prof. SUNY, Albany, 1978—; Social Sci. Research Council predoctoral fellow, 1948-49; fellow Center Advanced Studies Behavioral Scis., 1962-63; sr. postdoctoral fellow NSF, 1962-63; Pitt prof. Am. history and instns. Cambridge (Eng.) U., 1966-67; Fellow Netherlands Inst. for Advanced Study, 1975-76; Bd. dirs. Social Sci. Research Council, 1966-69. Author: The Dynamics of Bureaucracy, 1955, rev. edit., 1963, Bureaucracy in Modern Society, 1956, (rev. (with M.W. Meyer) Bureaucracy in Modern Society, 1971, (with W.R. Scott) Formal Organization, 1962, Exchange and Power in Social Life, 1964, (with Otis Dudley Duncan) The American Occupational Structure, 1967, (with Richard A. Schoenherr) The Structure of Organizations, 1971, The Organization of Academic Work, 1973, On the Nature of Organizations, 1974, Inequality and Heterogeneity, 1977; editor: Approaches to the Study of Social Structure, 1975, (with R. K. Merton) Continuities in Structural Inquiry, 1981, (with J.E. Schwartz) Crosscutting Social Circles, 1983, Am. Jour. Sociology, 1961-67. Served with AUS. Decorated Bronze Star. Fellow Am. Acad. Arts and Scis.; mem. Am. Sociol. Assn. (pres. 1973-74), Internat. Sociol. Assn., Nat. Acad. Scis., AAUP. Office: State U NY at Albany 1400 Washington Ave Albany NY 12222

BLAU, THEODORE HERTZL, psychologist; b. Huntington, W.Va., Mar. 3, 1928; s. Ephraim Joseph and Edith (Tanenhaus) B.; m. Lili Rosenman, June 17, 1950; children: Jeffrey Alan, Richard Michael. B.S., Pa. State U., 1949, M.S., 1949, Ph.D., 1951. Diplomate: Am. Bd. Forensic Psychology (v.p. 1981—), Am. Bd. Profl. Psychology trustee; Spl. Achievement award div. psychotherapy 1967, Spl. Achievement award div. clin. psychology 1973). Psychologist VA Hosp., Perry Point, Md., 1951-53, Byron Harless and Assos., Tampa, Fla., 1953-59; dir. research Anclote Manor, Tarpon Springs, Fla., 1956-59; pvt. practice, Tampa, 1959—; adj. prof. behavioral sci. U. South Fla., 1962-70, prof. med. sch., 1974-79; vis. prof. clin. psychology U.S. Internat. U., 1970—; pres. Programmed Instrn., Inc., 1962-70, Forensic Psychology Assos., Inc., Psychol. Seminars Inc., 1978—; nat. cons. Surgeon Gen., USAF, 1973-78; cons. clin. psychology Surgeon Gen., U.S.A., 1977—; Pres. Am. Psychol. Found., 1982. Author: Private Practice in Clinical Psychology, 1959, The Psychologist as Expert Witness, 1984; Cons. editor: Jour. Selected Documents in Psychology; cons. editor clin. neuropsychology: Contemporary Psychology. Served with USAAF, 1946-47. USAF-Med. Research fellow, 1949-50; Alumni fellow Pa. State U., 1977. Mem. Am. Psychol. Assn. (pres. 1977), Fla. Psychol. Assn. (pres. 1957, Outstanding Achievement award 1976), Soc. Personality Assessment (pres. 1971), Undersea Med. Research Soc., Assn. Air Force Psychologists. Patentee spiral aftereffect apparatus, teaching apparatus. Address: 213 E Davis Blvd Tampa FL 33606

BLAUFOX, MORTON DONALD, physician, educator; b. N.Y.C., July 19, 1934; s. Emanuel and Elizabeth (Rosenblum) B.; m. Paulette Goldberg, Dec. 20, 1958; children: Laurie Beth, Ellen Ruth, Andrew David. Student, Harvard U., 1952-55; M.D., SUNY, 1959; Ph.D., U. Minn., 1964. Diplomate: Am. Bd. Internal Medicine, Am. Bd. Nuclear Medicine. Intern Jewish Hosp. of Bklyn., N.Y.C., 1959-60; fellow in medicine Mayo Found. Med. Edn. and Research, Rochester, Minn., 1960-64; advanced research fellow Am. Heart Assn., 1964-66; research fellow in medicine Harvard Med. Sch., Boston, 1964-66; asst. in medicine and radiology Peter Bent Brigham Hosp., Boston, 1964-66; asst. prof. radiology, also assoc. in medicine Albert Einstein Coll. Medicine, Bronx, N.Y., 1966-71, dir. sect. nuclear medicine, 1966—, dir. unified dept., 1976—, chmn. unified dept., 1983—, assoc. dir. clin. research center, 1968-72, assoc. prof. radiology, 1971-76, prof. radiology, 1976—, assoc. prof. medicine, 1972-78, prof. medicine, 1978—; asst. attending physician Bronx Mcpl. Hosp. Center, 1966-71, assoc. attending, 1972, attending physician, 1972—; dir. div. nuclear medicine Montefiore Med. Center, 1976—, chmn. dept. nuclear medicine, 1983—; cons. kidney disease control program USPHS, 1967-72; mem. adminstrv. council nuclear medicine VA, 1970-73; mem. panel on radiopharmaceuticals U.S. Pharmacopeia, 1970—; mem. hypertension adv. com. N.Y.C. Dept. Health, 1975-76. Editor: Evaluation of Renal Function and Disease with Radionuclides, 1972, Radionuclides in Nephrology, Procs. Internat. Symposium, 1971, 75, PDR for Nuclear Medicine and Radiology, 1972-80, Unilateral Renal Function Studies, 1978; contbr. articles to profl. jours; editorial bd.: Nephron, Uroradiology, 1978—, Jour. Nuclear Medicine and Allied Sci., 1982—; assoc. editor: Barnet's Pediatrics, 1972, Radionuclides in Nephrology, 1980; co-editor: Secondary Hypertension: Current Diagnosis and Management, 1981. Recipient Edward Nobel Found. award, Albert Lasker pub. health service award, 1980. Fellow ACP, Am. Coll. Nuclear Physicians, Council on High Blood Pressure Research; mem. Am. Heart Assn., AMA, Am. Physiol. Soc., Am. Fedn. Clin. Research, Soc. Nuclear Medicine (pres. Greater N.Y. chpt. 1976-77, chmn. acad. council 1976-77, mem. exec. com., mem. sci. com., chmn. publ. com. 1979-82), Internat. Soc. Nephrology, Internat. Hypertension Soc., Council on High Blood Pressure Research (med. adv. bd.), N.Y. Med. Soc., N.Y. Nephrology Soc., Sigma Xi. Research on hypertension, renal function and evaluation of renal function with radioisotopes, renal blood flow and renin secretion. Home: 101 Drake-Smith Ln Rye NY 10580 Office: Eastchester Rd and Morris Park Ave Bronx NY 10461 *My life has been directed toward the acquisition, clarification and dissemination of knowledge in the health sciences. The use of such goals to help train young people embarking on a career, with honesty and integrity, has been a particularly rewarding experience.*

BLAUNER, BOB, sociologist; b. Chgo., May 18, 1929; s. Samuel and Esther (Shapiro) B.; children—Marya, Jonathan. A.B., U. Chgo., 1948; M.A., U. Calif., Berkeley, 1950, Ph.D., 1962. Asst. prof. sociology San Francisco State U., 1961-62, U. Chgo., 1962-63; mem. faculty U. Calif., Berkeley, 1963—, prof. sociology, 1978—. Author: Alienation and Freedom, 1964, Racial Oppression in America, 1972. Grantee Social Sci. Research Council, NIMH, Ford Found., Rockefeller Found. Mem. Am. Sociol. Assn. Office: Dept Sociology U Calif Berkeley CA 94720

BLAUSTEIN, AL, painter, printmaker; b. Bronx, N.Y., Jan. 23, 1924; s. Sydney and Sophie (Silbersher) B.; m. Lotte Heilbrunn, May 5, 1949; 1 son, Marc D. Grad., Cooper Union Art Sch., 1947. Mem. faculty Albright Art Sch., 1949-52, Yale U.-Norfolk Summer Sch., 1954-59, 61-66, Yale U., 1959-62, Skowhegan Sch. Painting, 1969, 70; prof. fine arts Pratt Inst., 1959—; instr. Pratt Graphic Center, 1964-69. One-man shows include, Terry Dintenfass Gallery, N.Y.C., 1969, 72, Phila. Art Alliance and Print Club, 1962, U. Nebr., 1961, Nordness Gallery, N.Y.C., 1959-63, Purdue U., 1979, Sumers Gallery, N.Y.C., 1982, S.W. Mo. State U., 1983, group shows include, Pa. Acad., Met. Mus. Art, Whitney Mus. Am. Art, Bklyn. Mus., NAD; represented in permanent collections, Whitney Mus. Am. Art, N.Y.C., Met. Mus. Art, N.Y.C., Library of Congress, Washington, Boston Mus., Chgo. Art Inst., Pa. Acad., Phila., Butler Art Inst., Wadsworth Athenuem, Hartford, Conn. Fellow Am. Acad. in Rome, 1954-57; Guggenheim fellow, 1958, 61; Am. Inst. Arts and Letters grantee, 1958; Ford Found. artist-in-residence, 1965. Home: 141 E 17th St New York NY 10003 Office: Pratt Inst Ryerson St Brooklyn NY 11205

BLAUSTEIN, MORTON K., petroleum company executive. Chmn. Am. Trading and Prodn. Corp., Balt. Office: Am Trading & Prodn Corp PO Box 238 Baltimore MD 21203§

BLAUVELT, FOWLER, manufacturing company executive; b. Bronxville, N.Y., Feb. 8, 1925; s. Charles and Kate (Garthwaite) B.; m. Norma Emerson, Oct. 3, 1953; children: Whitney, Richard Emerson, Margaret Jane. Sc.B. in Engring, Brown U., 1945; grad., Exec. Devel. Program, Cornell, 1959. With Owens-Corning Fiberglas Corp., 1946—, v.p. central region, 1963-64; v.p. Fiberglas Indsl. Materials div., 1964-68, v.p. mktg., 1968-69, group v.p. textile and indsl. group., 1969-76, dir., 1975—, sr. v.p., 1977-78, exec. v.p., 1978—. Served with USNR, 1945-46. Home: 2450 Underhill Rd Toledo OH 43615 Office: Owens-Corning Fiberglas Corp Toledo OH 43659

BLAUVELT, JOHN CLIFFORD, pharm. co. exec.; b. Nyack, N.Y., Feb. 22, 1920; s. John Clifford and Henrietta Lane (Bower) B.; m. Laura Biddleman, July 29, 1944; children—Laura Lane Tabone, J. Clifford III. B.S., Houghton Coll., 1940; postgrad., N. Tex. State Coll., 1940, N.Y. U., 1946-48. With Am. Cyanamid Co., Wayne, N.J., 1940—, various prodn. positions, 1940-69, corp. controller, 1969-71, pres. agrl. div., 1971-73, corp. v.p., 1973-75, sr. v.p., 1975—, also dir. Served to lt. USN, 1943-46. Home: 1071 E Inlet Dr Marco Island FL 33937 Office: 859 Berdan Ave Wayne NJ 07470

BLAYDES, SOPHIA BOYATZIES, English language educator; b. Rochester, N.Y., Oct. 16, 1933; d. James George and Helene (Bougdanos) Boyatzies; m. David Fairchild Blaydes, June 4, 1961; children: Stephanie Anne, Jeffrey Glenn. B.A., U. Rochester, 1955; M.A., Ind. U., 1958, Ph.D., 1962. Teaching asst. English Ind. U., 1955-62; instr. to asst. prof. Am. Thought and Lang. dept. Mich. State U., 1962-65; instr. to prof. English W.Va. U., Morgantown, 1966—; Co-dir. Literary Discussion Group for Sr. Citizens, 1978—. Author: Christopher Smart as a Poet of His Time: A Re-Appraisal, 1966, (with others) Sir William Davenant, 1981; editor: (with others) Selected Papers from the WV Shakespeare and Renaissance Association, 1976, The Literary Discussion Group, 1982; contbr. articles to profl. jours. Recipient Disting. Manuscript award Mich. State U., 1965; W.Va. U. Found. grantee, 1973; W.Va. Humanities grantee, 1980; Folger fellow, 1981. Mem. Am. Soc. 18th Century Studies, MLA, W.Va. Assn. Coll. English Tchrs. (pres. 1977), Shakespeare and Renaissance Soc. W.Va. (chmn. 1978, 84), Carolinas Symposium on Brit. Studies. Home: 652 Bellaire Dr Morgantown WV 26505 Office: 422 Stansbury Hall West Virginia University Morgantown WV 26506

BLECHMAN, HARRY, oral microbiologist, endodontist, educator; b. Bklyn., Aug. 22, 1918; s. Bernard and Mollie (Shalov) B.; m. Zara Ehrich, Nov. 6, 1943; children—Enid Ellen, Betsy. B.S., Coll. City of N.Y., 1938; student, Bklyn. Coll., 1939-41, John Hopkins Sch. Pub. Health and Hygiene, 1943-44; D.D.S., N.Y.U., 1951; M.A., Hunter Coll., N.Y.C., 1959. Diplomate: Am. Bd. Endodontics (dir., pres. 1975-76). Sr. bacteriologist Harlem Hosp., 1946-47; asst. prof., chmn. dept. microbiology N.Y.U. Coll. Dentistry, 1951-53, prof., chmn. dept., 1960-64, asst. dean, 1964-67; dean Coll. Dentistry, 1967-75, prof., 1964-71, prof. endodontics, 1971—, chmn. dept. endodontics, 1975—, chmn. dept. microbiology, 1964-68, asso. prof. preventive med. and hygiene, dir. clin. pathology lab., 1952-70; Exec. sec. Murry and Leonie Guggenheim Found. Inst. Dental Research, 1953-67. Author: Laboratory Manual in Microbiology, rev. edit, 1960; contbg. author: Textbook on Oral Microbiology, 1973, 3d edit., 1978, Textbook on Current Therapy in Dentistry, 1977. Served as capt. Med. Service Corps AUS, 1943-46; maj. USAR, 1946—. Fellow Am. Acad. Endodontists, Internat., Am. colls. dentists, N.Y. Acad. Scis., Am. Acad. Dental Medicine, Am. Acad. Gen. Dentistry; mem. ADA (chmn. council nat. bd. dental examiners), Am. Assn. Endodontists (v.p. 1976-77, pres. 1978-79), AAAS, Internat. Assn. Dental Research, Soc. Am. Bacteriologists, Harvey Soc., Research Soc. Am., Sigma Xi, Omicron Kappa Upsilon. Home: 110 Bleecker St New York NY 10012

BLECHMAN, R. O., artist, film maker; b. Bklyn., Oct. 1, 1930; s. Samuel and Mae B.; m. Moisha Kubinyi, June 3, 1960; children: Nicholas, Max. B.A., Oberlin Coll., 1952. Pres. R.O. Blechman, Inc., N.Y.C., The Ink Tank, 1979—. Freelance illustrator; producer, designer animated films, N.Y.C.; Author, illustrator: The Juggler of Our Lady, 1952; illustrator: Onion Soup, 1963; exhibited one-man shows, Gallery Delpire, Paris, 1968, Graham Gallery, N.Y.C., 1978, ITC Gallery, 1981; represented in permanent collections, Mus. Modern Art, N.Y.C., Chase Manhattan Bank; executed murals, Mus. Natural History, U.S. Pavilion Expo '67, Folger Shakespeare Library.; films include The Juggler of Our Lady, 1958, Abraham and Isaac, 1971, Exercise, 1974, Simple Gifts, 1978, No Room at the Inn, 1978 (Clio award 1968, 69, 73), L'Histoire du Soldat, 1984. Mem. Alliance Graphique Internat., Am. Inst. Graphic Arts, Cartoonists Assn., Cartoonists Guild, Graphic Artists Guild. Office: 2 W 47th St New York NY 10036

BLECK, MAX EMIL, aircraft co. exec.; b. Buffalo, Apr. 11, 1927; s. Max W. and Dora (Loos) B.; m. Gloria H. Robinson, Apr. 18, 1949; children—Mark E., Cynthia Joanne, Sandra Louise. B.S. in Mech. Engring, Rensselaer Poly. Inst., 1949; postgrad., U. Buffalo, 1950-51. Design engr. Stanley Aviation Corp., Denver, 1950-55, project engr., 1955-57, chief engr., 1957-59, v.p. engring., 1959-62; chief engr. Mil. and Twin div. Cessna Aircraft Co., Wichita, Kans., 1962-66, gen. mgr., 1966-68, v.p., gen. mgr., 1968-72, group v.p., 1972-75; sr. v.p. ops. Piper Aircraft Co., Lockhaven, Pa., 1975-76, exec. v.p., 1976-78, pres., chief operating officer, 1978, pres., chief exec. officer, 1979—. Bd. dirs. Friends' U., 1968-71. Mem. Assn. Industry Kans. (v.p., dir.), Kans. Assn. Industry and Commerce (v.p., dir.), Wichita C. of C., Quiet Birdman, Soc. Automotive Engrs., Exptl. Aircraft Assn., Sigma Chi Epsilon. Republican. Episcopalian. Home: 4596 Pebble Bay S Vero Beach FL 32960 Office: Piper Aircraft Co Lockhaven PA 17745

BLEDSOE, BILLY JOE, pipe line co. exec., accountant; b. Normangee, Tex., Apr. 12, 1929; s. Andy W. and Ida (Venable) B.; m. Beverly A. Watkins, Jan. 21, 1965; children: Robin, Bruce. B.B.A., U. Tex., 1958. With Shell Pipe Line Corp., Houston, 1958—, mgr., 1972-74, treas., 1974—, also dir.; v.p., dir. Cortez Capital Corp.; dir. Olympic Pipe Line Co. Served to capt. USAF, 1951-56. Baptist. Home: 6118 Elmgrove Spring TX 77379 Office: PO Box 2648 Houston TX 77001

BLEDSOE, CARL BEVERLY, state legislator; b. Aroya, Colo., Oct. 6, 1923; s. Carl and Josie (Main) B.; m. Alice Elizabeth Cotellessa, Sept. 14, 1946; children: Robert Carl, Thomas Beverly, Christopher Joel. B.S., Colo. State U., 1949. Self employed rancher Aroya, 1949—; mem. Colo. Ho. of Reps. from 64th Dist., Denver, 1972—, chmn. audit com., 1976-77, speaker of house, 1981—. Mem. Colo. Com. Ednl. Endeavor, 1963-64, Colo. Bd. Vet. Medicine, 1968-72, Colo. Interim Com. State and Locl Fin., 1968; sec. Kit Carson Sch. Bd., Dist. R-1, Cheyenne County, Colo., 1961-69, pres., Cheyenne County, Colo., 1969-71; sec. Cheyenne County Republican Com., 1964-66. Served with AUS, 1942-45. Named to Colo. Assn. Sch. Eds. Honor Roll, 1968. Mem. Colo. Cattleman's Assn. (chmn. bd. 1965-66), Colo. Cattlemen's Assn. (pres. 1967-68, Lobbyist 1969-72), Cheyenne County Cattlemen's Assn., Western Stock Show Assn., Lincoln County Stockmen's Assn. (sec. 1958-62), Colo. Farm Bur., Cheyenne County Farm Bur. (pres. 1962-64), VFW, Farm House, Alpha Zeta. Office of Speaker: Colo Ho of Reps State Capitol Denver CO 80203

BLEDSOE, RALPH CHAMPION, government official, management educator; b. Waco, Tex., Oct. 10, 1933; s. Walker Champion and Gertrude Sallie (Austin) B.; m. Rose Marie Joyce Frechette, Sept. 1, 1958; children: Barbara, Linda, Patricia, Joanna. B.B.A., Tex. A&M U., 1955; M.B.A., UCLA, 1962; M.P.A., U. So. Calif., 1968, D.P.A., 1971. Dept. mgr. System Devel. Corp., Santa Monica, Calif., 1958-71; dir. Sch. Pub. Adminstrn. U. So. Calif., Sacramento, 1971-73; prof. mgmt. Fed. Exec. Inst., Charlottesville, Va., 1973-80; dir. Emergency Mgmt. Inst., Emmitsburg, Md., 1980-81; assoc. dir. Office of Planning and Evaluation The White House, Washington, 1981-82, spl. asst. to Pres., exec. sec. Cabinet Council on Mgmt. and Adminstrn., Office of Policy Devel., 1982—; bd. dirs. Calif. Crime Tech. Research Found., Sacramento, 1972-74; mem. bd. councilors U. So. Calif. Sch. Pub. Adminstrn., Los Angeles, 1983—; cons. exec. devel. N.Y.C. Police Dept., 1976—; cons. Va. Dept. Taxation, Richmond, 1976-80. Editor: Zero-Base Budgeting-Fed. Govt. jour., 1978; bd. editors: The Bureaucrat, 1982; contbr. articles on govt. adminstrn. to profl. jours. Mem. middle sch. evaluation council Albermarle County Schs., Va., 1978; mem. exec. com. Ch. of the Incarnation, Charlottesville, 1976-79. Served to 1st lt. USAFR, 1955-58. Mem. Am. Soc. for Pub. Adminstrn.

(chmn. nat. conf. program 1981, chmn. policy issues com. 1981-82), So. Calif. Assn. Pub. Adminstrn., Am. Acad. Polit. and Social Sci., Ctr. Study of Presidency, Phi Kappa Phi. Republican. Roman Catholic. Home: 11250 Inglish Mill Dr Great Falls VA 22066 Office: Office Policy Devel 17th and Pennsylvania Ave NW Washington DC 20500

BLEDSOE, WOODROW WILSON, mathematics and computer sciences educator; b. Maysville, Okla., Nov. 12, 1921; s. Thomas Franklin and Eva (Matthews) B.; m. Virginia Norgaard, Jan. 29, 1944; children: Gregory Kent, Pamela Nelson, Lance Woodrow. B.S. in Math., U. Utah, 1948, Ph.D., U. Calif., 1953. Lectr. in math. U. Calif.-Berkeley, 1951-53; mathematician, staff mem. Sandia Corp., Albuquerque, 1953-60, head math. dept., 1957-60; mathematician, researcher Panoramic Research Inc., Palo Alto, Calif., 1960-65, pres., 1963-65; prof. math. computer sci. U. Tex., Austin, 1966—, acting chmn. dept. math., 1967-69, chmn. dept. math., 1973-75, Ashbel Smith prof. math. and computer sci., 1981—; gen. chmn. Internat. Joint Conf. Artificial Intelligence, MIT, Cambridge, Mass., 1975-77; trustee Internat. Joint Conf. on Artificial Intelligence, 1978-83; mem. subcom. for computer sci. Adv. Com. Math. and Computer Sci., NSF, 1979-82; vis. prof. MIT, 1970-71, Carnegie-Mellon U., Pitts., 1978. Editor: (with Donald Loveland) Automated Theorem Proving, 1984; bd. editor: Internat. Jour. of Artificial Intelligence, 1972—; also rev. editor, 1973-77; author numerous tech. papers in refereed jours., confs. Vice-pres. Capitol Area council Boy Scouts Am., Austin, 1979-83. Served to capt. U.S. Army, 1940-45; ETO. NSF research grantee, 1972—; NIH research grantee, 1967-72. Mem. Am. Math. Soc., Assn. Computing Machinery, Am. Assn. Artificial Intelligence (pres. 1984-85). Mormon. Home: 3002 Willwood Circle Austin TX 78703 Office: Dept Math U Tex Robert Lee Moore Hall 8 100 Austin TX 78712

BLEE, MYRON ROY, educator, state official; b. Paw Paw, Ill., Feb. 25, 1917; s. Roy T. and Martha (Fox) B.; m. Charlotte Marie Leverenz, Jan. 1, 1941; 1 dau., Kathleen Marie Blee Ashe. B.E., No. Ill. State Tchrs. Coll., 1938; M.A. in Polit. Sci, U. Ill., 1939, Ed.D., 1958. Tchr., also teaching prin. elementary schs., Lake County, Ill., 1939-42; asso. dean men, instr. Am. Govt. No. Ill. State Tchrs. Coll., 1946-48; asst. supt. instruction Community Unit Sch. Dist. 271, Ashton, Ill., 1948-52; asso. dir. Fla Legis. Reference Bur., Tallahassee, 1952-54, Council Study Higher Edn. in Fla., 1954-56; ednl. and research officer Fla. Bd. Control Higher Edn., 1956-62; dir. Fla. Inst. Continuing Univ. Studies, Tallahassee, 1962-65; asso. dean academic affairs Fla. Atlantic U., 1965-66; dep. dir. Office Emergency Planning, Exec. Office of Pres., 1966-67; pres. Jr. Coll. Broward County, Ft. Lauderdale, Fla., 1967-68, Asso. Consultants in Edn., Inc., 1968-74; adj. prof. higher edn. Fla. State U., 1970-73; assoc. dir. for program div. community colls. Fla. Dept. Edn., 1972-82, spl. asst. to commr., 1982—; Mem. Fla. Ednl. TV Commn., 1960-66; Mem. bd. edn. Fla. Ann. Conf. Methodist Ch., 1960-68; trustee Bethune Cookman Coll., Daytona Beach, 1961-68. Served to lt. comdr. USNR, 1942-46; PTO. Mem. Fla., Adult edn. assns., World Future Soc., Council for Advancement of Exptl. Learning (trustee 1980—), Kappa Delta Pi, Phi Delta Kappa. Democrat. Home: 1447 Marion Ave Tallahassee FL 32303 Office: State Dept Edn Tallahassee FL 32301

BLEGEN, JUDITH EYER, opera singer; b. Missoula, Mont., Apr. 27; d. Halward Martin and Dorothy Mae (Anderson) B.; m. Raymond Gniewek, 1977; 1 son by previous marriage, Thomas Christopher Singher. Student, Music Acad. of West, 1962; B.M., Curtis Inst. Music, 1964. Appeared with, Met. Opera, N.Y.C., Vienna State Opera, Royal Opera House Covent Garden, Paris Opera, Chgo., Lyric Opera, San Francisco Opera, Miami Opera, worldwide concert tours. Address: care Met Opera Lincoln Center New York NY 10023 *

BLEIBERG, ROBERT MARVIN, fin. mag. editor; b. Bklyn., June 21, 1924; s. Edward and Frances (DuBroff) B.; m. Harriet Evans, May 1948 (div. Mar. 1953); 1 dau., Ellen; m. Sally Diane Beverly, Oct. 25, 1956; 1 son, Richard Beverly. B.A., Columbia, 1943; M.B.A., N.Y. U., 1950; D.C.Sc., Hillsdale Coll., 1977. V.p. Dow Jones & Co., Inc. Asso. editor: Prudden's Digest of Investment and Banking Opinions, N.Y.C., 1946; asso. editor: Barron's Nat. Bus. and Financial Weekly, N.Y.C., 1946-54; editor, 1955-81; pub., 1980—; editorial dir., 1981—. Served with inf. AUS, 1943-45; PTO. Decorated Purple Heart. Mem. N.Y. Soc. Security Analysts., N.Y. Fin. Writers Assn., Mont Pelerin Soc., Econ. Club N.Y., Phi Beta Kappa, Phi Beta Kappa Assos. Home: 25 Central Park W New York NY 10023 Office: 22 Cortlandt St New York NY 10007

BLEICH, ELI FURIE, motion picture producer and director, political media consultant; b. Bklyn., May 1, 1943; s. Emanuel Edward and Anne (Furie) B.; m. Arlene Messitte, Mar. 13, 1964 (div. 1970); 1 dau., Elizabeth Jamie; m. Melody Lane, Sept. 4, 1972; children: Aaron Furie, Oliver Lane. B.A., NYU, 1964. Pres., chief exec. officer Media Group, Beverly Hills, Calif., 1975—; dir. Rowan, Decker, Sanders & Bleich, San Francisco, 1973—; media cons. Askew for pres., 1983-84, Office of Pres. of Sudan, 1982; creative dir. Carter for pres., 1980; media producer Pres. Perez of Venezuela, 1975. Films include Long Road, 1982, This Man, This Office, 1980, Boy from Kahihi (award 1979), Catch a Wave, 1970 (award 1971). Commr. Conv. and Visitors Bur., Santa Monica, Calif., 1983-84; trustee Santa Monica Synagogue, 1983-85. Recipient Cine Golden Eagle Council Non-Theatrical Events, 1979, Golden medal Atlanta Film Festival, 1971, Creative Excellence U.S. Indsl. Film Festival, 1971, L Age D'Or, Brussels Film Festival, 1968. Mem. Dirs. Guild Am., Internat. Assn. Polit. Cons. (dir. 1972-74). Democrat. Jewish. Home: 418 24th St Santa Monica CA 90402 Office: Media Group 336 N Foothill Rd Beverly Hills CA 90210

BLEICHER, SHELDON JOSEPH, endocrinologist, medical educator; b. N.Y.C., Apr. 9, 1931; s. Max and Fannie (Klieger) B.; m. Anne C. M. Ames, July 28, 1967; children: Erick Max, Phillip Thaddeus Samuel. A.B., NYU, 1951; M.S., Western Ill. U., 1952; M.D., SUNY Downstate Med. Center, Bklyn., 1956. Intern L.I. Jewish Hosp. Ctr., New Hyde Park, N.Y., 1956-57; resident Boston City Hosp., 1959-60; research fellow in medicine Harvard-Thorndike Meml. Lab., Boston, 1960-63; chief metabolic research unit Jewish Hosp. Med. Center, Bklyn., 1963-67, chief div. endocrinology and metabolism, 1967-77; practice medicine specializing in endocrinology and diabetes, Bklyn. and Upper Brookville, N.Y., 1963—; prof. medicine SUNY Downstate Med. Center, 1975—; chmn. dept. internal medicine Bklyn.-Cumberland Med. Center, 1978-83, Bklyn.-Caledonian Med. Ctr., 1983—; cons. IAEA, Vienna, 1966—. Contbr. articles to profl. jours. Vice-pres. Locust Valley Central Sch. Bd., 1981-82, pres., 1982—. Served to capt. M.C. USNR, 1957—. NIH fellow, 1960-63; NIH research career devel. award, 1970-75. Mem. Am. Diabetes Assn. (dir. 1979-85), N.Y. Diabetes Assn. (pres. 1976, 77), L.I. Diabetes Assn. (pres. 1978-81), N.Y. State Soc. Internal Medicine (state bd. dirs., treas. Bklyn. chpt.), Bklyn. Soc. Internal Medicine (treas.), Am. Fedn. Clin. Research, Endocrine Soc., AAAS, Harvey Soc. Jewish. Clubs: Sag Harbor, Sagamore Yacht (L.I.) (fleet surgeon 1983—). Office: 121 DeKalb Ave Brooklyn NY 11201

BLEITZ, DONALD LOUIS, engr., author, ornithologist, naturalist; b. Los Angeles, Oct. 1, 1915; s. Louis Rollin and Violet Mae (Trout) B. Owner, operator photog. mfg. firm, pharm. mfg. plant, various tech. labs. and optical mfg. concerns; founder, pres. Bleitz Wildlife Found., 1952—; Mem. faculty tng. program Vet. Medicine Comml., Pet, and Wild Birds.; mem. adv. bd. Reys Bird Obs., San Francisco Bay Bird Obs. Author: 22 folio vols. in compilation Birds of the Americas; Contbr.: feature articles (in color) Ariz. Hwys, Readers Digest, Saturday Evening Post; also various sci. jours., news media periodicals.; color photographs, descriptive manuscripts over 2500 species birds of N.Am., 1940—; produces and shows slides; lectures sci. ornithol. groups; exhibited traveling show of plates from Birds of Am., at various museums including, San Diego Mus. Natural History, Pacific Grove and Santa Cruz Mus. Natural History, 1973. Mem. Los Angeles County Mus.; pres. San Pedro Heart Found.; bd. dirs. Hollywood Chorale, Hollywood Heritage. Recipient award Am. Acad. Achievement, 1964, award of honor Calif. Conservation Council. Fellow Cleve. Zool. Soc.; mem. Nat. Audubon Soc. (life), Cooper Ornithol. Soc. (life), Wilson Ornithol. Club (life), Am. Ornithologists Union (life), Calif., So. Calif. acads. sci., Internat. Soc. Bird Protection, Western Bird Banding Assn. (life), Eastern Bird Banding Assn., Inland Bird Banding Assn., League of Ams. (bd. dirs., pres.), Hancock Park Art Council, Lepidopterists Soc., Am. Soc. Mammologists, Phila. Zool. Soc. (hon. life), Bromeliad Soc., San Diego Zool. Soc., Am. Orchid Soc., Malibu Orchid Soc., Windsor Sq.-Hancock Park Hist. Soc. (trustee, founding mem.), N.Y. Acad. Scis., Am. Soc. Naturalists, Explorers Club., Avicultural Soc., Pacific Hort. Soc. Clubs: Thunderbird Country, Los Angeles (founder, pres., dir.), Los Angeles Men's Garden (dir.). Patentee in field of optics, emulsions, photog. equipment. Office: 5334 Hollywood Blvd Hollywood CA 90027

BLEIWEISS, HERBERT IRVING, publishing exec.; b. Bklyn., July 26, 1931; s. Oscar and Anna (Fliegel) B.; m. Rachel Newman, Apr. 6, 1973; children—Jeffrey, Richard. Student, Cooper Union, 1948-50. Design cons. Syska & Hennessy Engrs.; tchr. mag. design Parsons Sch. Design, N.Y.C. Designer, Ehrlich, Newirth Advt., N.Y.C., 1952-57; art dir., C.J. Herrick Advt., 1957-59, Irving Serwer Advt., 1959-61, DKG Advt., 1961-62, McCalls mag, 1962-67; exec. art dir.: Ladies Home Jour, N.Y.C., 1967-75; also art dir.: Needle and Craft mag; exec. art dir.: Good Housekeeping mag, N.Y.C., 1975—; art dir.: Country Living; Photographer for: books A Patchwork Point of View, 1975, Redo-It Yourself, 1977, The Pillow Book, 1979. Served with U.S. Army, 1950-52. Recipient numerous Art Dirs. awards and Gold medals N.Y. Art Dirs. Club, Los Angeles Art Dirs. Club, London Art Dirs. Club, Soc. Illustrators. Mem. Soc. Publ. Designers, Art Dirs. Club N.Y. Office: 959 8th Ave New York NY 10019

BLEIWEISS, ROBERT MORTON, religious institute executive, publisher; b. N.Y.C., Apr. 18, 1934; s. George Bernard and Esther (Palter) B.; m. Vida Boyan, July 20, 1961; children—Ellen Terry, Mark Evan. A.B., Colgate U., 1956; postgrad., N.Y. U., 1961-62; M.L.A., U. So. Calif., 1976. Asso. editor, treas. Bus. Internat. Corp., N.Y.C., 1960-64; asst. to pres. Wesleyan U. Press, Middletown, Conn., 1964; pres. C. & S. Info. Publs., Los Angeles, 1970-72; corporate v.p. Cordura Corp., Los Angeles, 1973; pres. Bleiweiss & Co., Los Angeles, 1974-76; sr. v.p. Gousha (Times Mirror), 1976-78; cons. and dir. several cos.; bd. dirs. Brandeis-Bardin Inst., Brandeis, Calif., 1975-78, exec. v.p., 1978-81; owner, chief exec. officer Bleiweiss Communications Inc., 1981—. Pub. Xerox Edn. Publs., Middletown, (1965-70); Author: Marching to Freedom: The Life of Martin Luther King, Jr, 1968, Freedom's Words: A Modern Interpretation of the U.S. Constitution, 1974; Founding pub.: Urban World, 1967, Issues Today, 1968, others.; Editor: Torah at Brandeis Institute, 1976. Pres. Center for Jewish Living and Values in Israel, 1981—. Served to capt. USMCR, 1956-67. Home: 4391 Park Milano Calabasas CA 91302

BLENDEN, DONALD COVEY, veterinary medicine educator; b. St. Louis, Aug. 13, 1929; s. Henry A. and Myra (Covey) B.; m. Patricia Crawford, June 9, 1941; children: Michael Dale, Elizabeth Ann. B.S., U. Mo., 1951, M.S., 1953, D.V.M., 1956. Pvt. practice ve. medicine Kirkwood, Mo., 1956-57; instr. vet. medicine U. Mo., Columbia, 1957-59, asst. prof., 1959-64, assoc. prof., 1964-72, prof., 1972—; cons. in field. Emergency coordinator Am. Radio Relay League, Mo., 1983—; communication warning officer Columbia, Boone Country, Mo., 1977—. Recipient Alumni U. Mo., 1974. Fellow Am. Pub. Health Assn.; mem. AVMA, Am. Soc. Microbiologists, Conf. Pub. Health Vets (past pres.), Assn. Tchrs. Vet. Pub. Health, Am. Coll. Epidemiology, Am. Coll. Vet. Preventive Medicine, Central Mo. Radio Assn. (emergency coordinator). Methodist. Home: 1506 N Circle St Columbia MO 65201 Office: 125 Connaway Hall Columbia MO 65211

BLENDON, ROBERT JAY, foundation executive; b. Dec. 19, 1942; s. Edward and Theresa B.; m. Marie C. McCormick, Dec. 31, 1977. B.A., Marietta (Ohio) Coll., 1964; M.B.A., U. Chgo., 1966; M.P.H., Johns Hopkins U., 1967, D.Sc., 1969. Adminstrv. resident Ind. U. Med. Center, Indpls., 1965-66; instr. dept. med. care and hosps. Johns Hopkins U. Sch. Hygiene and Pub. Health, Balt., 1969-70, also asst. to asso. dean for health care programs Sch. Medicine, 1969-70, asst. prof. dept. med. care and hosps., 1970-71; asst. dir. planning and devel. Office of Health Care Programs, Johns Hopkins Med. Instns., Balt., 1970-71; spl. asst. for health affairs to dep. undersec. for policy coordination HEW, Washington, 1971-72; and spl. asst. for policy devel. to asst. sec. to health and sci. affairs, 1971-72; sr. v.p. Robert Wood Johnson Found., Princeton, N.J.; and vis. lectr. Princeton U., 1972—; sr. policy analyst com. on health services industry Cost of Living Council, Washington, 1971; spl. asst. to asst. sec. health and mental hygiene State of Md., Balt., 1969-70. Contbr. articles to health and med., jours. Bd. overseers U. Pa. Sch. Dental Medicine, 1980—. Mem. Council Fgn. Relations, Inst. Medicine, Nat. Acad. Scis. Home: 724 Rodman St Philadelphia PA 19147 Office: PO Box 2316 Princeton NJ 08540

BLENKINSOPP, JOSEPH, theologian; b. Bishop Auckland, Eng., Apr. 3, 1927; came to U.S., 1964; s. Joseph William and Mary (Lyons) B.; m. Irene Cunningham, Mar. 30, 1968; children—David, Martin. B.A. with honors, U. London, 1948; Ph.D., Oxford (Eng.) U., 1967. Tchr. bibl. studies Heythrop Coll., Oxford U., 1966, Vanderbilt U., Nashville, 1968, Chgo. Theol. Sem., 1968-69, Hartford (Conn.) Sem. Found., 1969-70; asso. prof. theology U. Notre Dame, South Bend, Ind., 1970-75, prof., 1975—; chmn. bd. publs. U. Notre Dame Press, 1974—; performed archaeol. field work in, Israel. Author: Sexuality and the Christian Tradition, 1968, Celibacy, Ministry, Church, 1968, Gibeon and Israel, 1972; contbr. articles to profl. jours. Mem. Am. Acad. Religion, Soc. Bibl. Lit., Assn. Jewish Studies, Council Study of Religion in Higher Edn. Home: 409 E Napoleon South Bend IN 46677 Office: Dept Theology U Notre Dame Notre Dame IN 46556

BLESH, RUDI (RUDOLPH PICKETT BLESH), author, artist; b. Guthrie, Okla., Jan. 21, 1899; s. Abraham Lincoln (M.D.) and Theodora Bell (Pickett) B.; m. Editha Tuttle, Feb. 22, 1925; 1 dau., Editha Hilary; m. Barbara Lamont, July 1939. Student, Dartmouth Coll., 1917-20; B.S. with honors, U. Calif., 1924. Prof. emeritus music Queens Coll.; also prof. emeritus Am. arts NYU. Furniture, archtl., indsl. designer, 1924-43; founder, v.p., Circle Sound Inc., N.Y.C., phonograph documentation pure Afro-American music; one-man show: abstract paintings Art of This Century, N.Y.C., 1946; Author: This is Jazz, 1943, Shining Trumpets: A History of Jazz, 1946, (with Harriet Janis) They All Played Ragtime, 1950, Modern Art USA, 1956, (with Harriet Janis) De Kooning, 1960, Stuart Davis, 1960, (with Harriet Janis) Collage, 1962, Keaton, 1966, Combo USA, 1971; writer, narrator: radio programs Dimensions of Jazz, This Is Jazz, Our Singing Land; editor: (with Harriet Janis) O Susanna, 1960. Mem. Phi Gamma Delta, Pi Delta Epsilon. Home: 38 E 4th St New York City NY 10003 also (summer) Hillforge Gilmanton NH 03237

BLESS, ROBERT CHARLES, astronomy educator; b. Ithaca, N.Y., Dec. 3, 1927; s. Arthur A. and Eva C. (Chantrelle) B.; m. Diane McQueen, June 6, 1970. B.S., U. Fla., 1947; Ph.D. in Astronomy, U. Mich., 1958. Physicist Naval Research Lab., 1947-48; project asso. dept. astronomy U. Wis., Madison, 1958-61, asst. prof. astronomy, 1961-63, asso. prof., 1963-69, prof., 1969—, chmn. dept. astronomy, 1972-76; mem. astronomy adv. com. NSF, 1982-85. Asso. editor: Astro-phys. Jour. Letters, 1971-73. Trustee URA, 1980-81. NRC sr. postdoctoral research fellow Goddard Space Flight Center, 1967-68. Mem. Am. Astron. Soc., Internat. Astron. Union. Research in space astronomy. Office: Astronomy Dept U Wis Madison WI 53706

BLETHEN, JOHN ALDEN, publisher; b. Seattle, July 12, 1918; s. Clarance Bretton and Rae (Kingsley) B.; m. Barbara Prentice, Nov. 27, 1948; children: John Prentice, Alden Joseph. Student, Dartmouth Coll., 1936-39. Former pub. Seattle Times, from 1967; chmn. bd. Seattle Times Co., 1977—, Walla Walla (Wash.) Union-Bull. Office: Seattle Times PO Box 70 Seattle WA 98111 *

BLEVEANS, JOHN, lawyer; b. Danville, Ill., Mar. 29, 1938. B.A., Trinity U., 1960; LL.B., U. Tex., 1965. Bar: Tex. 1965, D.C. 1967, U.S. Supreme Ct. 1969, Ill. 1971. Mem. gen. counsel's office Acacia Mut. Life Ins. Co., Washington, 1967-68; trial and appellate atty., civil rights div. U.S. Dept. Justice, Washington, 1966-67, 69-70; exec. dir. Washington Lawyer's Com., Civil Rights Under Law, 1970-71; chief counsel Lawyer's Com. Civil Rights Under Law, Cairo, Ill., 1971-72; assoc. Mayer, Brown & Platt, Chgo., 1972-74, ptnr., 1974-83; sr. v.p., assoc. gen. counsel Continental Ill. Nat. Bank and Trust Co. of Chgo., 1983—. Aldernab, Evanston, Ill., 1981—. Mem. ABA, Tex. Bar Assn., D.C. Bar Assn. Office: Continental Bank 231 S LaSalle St Chicago IL 60697

BLEVINS, J. DONALD, foreign service officer; b. Itman, W.Va., Dec. 1, 1928; s. James Aaron and Chloe Vastia (Miller) B.; m. Irene Edwards, Apr. 4, 1953; children: Brian Douglas, Kim Elaine. A.B.A., Beckley Coll., 1948; B.S., Am. U., 1951, J.D., 1957; grad., Sr. Seminar in Fgn. Policy, 1977. Bar: Va. 1957. Claims examiner Govt. Employees Ins. Co., 1953-56; investigator CSC, 1956-59; atty. U.S. Passport Office, 1959-65; fgn. service officer U.S. Consulate, Naples, Italy, 1965-68, Rotterdam, Netherlands, 1968-70, Hong Kong, 1970-74; dep. dir. Vis. Office, Washington, 1974-76; consul gen. Am. Consulate Gen., Guadalajara, Mex., 1978—. Served with USN, 1946-48, 51-52. Mem. Va. Bar Assn. Office: 175 Progresso Guadalajara Jalisco Mexico

BLEVINS, ROBERT WINSTON, insurance company executive; b. Dallas, Sept. 5, 1927; s. John L. and Ruby (Henslee) B.; m. Jeanie C. McGilvray, Sept. 6, 1947; children—Janet Lynn, Donald Lee, Jon Scott. Student, U. Tex., 1944-47. With Southland Life Ins. Co., 1952—, v.p. underwriting, 1967-73, sr. v.p. new bus. and benefits div., 1973-79, sr. v.p. govt. and industry affairs, 1979—; chmn. bd. dirs. Med. Info. Bur. Inc.; lifetime mem. Hosp. Ins.-Physicians Joint Adv. Com., Tex.; chmn. for Tex., Health Ins. Council; mem. adv. com. to task force Nat. Assn. Ins. Commrs. for Alcoholism and Drug Abuse. Co-chmn. advanced gifts div. Dallas United Fund, 1968. Served with AUS, 1952-53. Fellow Life Office Mgmt. Assn.; mem. Home Office Life Underwriters Assn. (past pres., exec. council 1977—), Am. Council Life Ins., Health Ins. Assn. Am. (council on consumer and profl. relations, com. value added tax, individual ins. com.). Clubs: Masons, Shriners. Home: 9440 Dartridge Dr Dallas TX 75238 Office: PO Box 2220 Dallas TX 75221

BLEWETT, JOHN PAUL, physicist; b. Toronto, Ont., Can., Apr. 12, 1910; s. George John and Clara Marcia (Woodsworth) B. B.A., U. Toronto, 1932, M.A., 1933; Ph.D., Princeton U., 1936. Mem. staff research lab Gen. Electric Co., Schenectady, 1937-46; with Brookhaven Nat. Lab., Upton, N.Y., 1947—, now cons. to dir. Author: Particle Accelerators; Contbr. articles to profl. jours. Fellow Am. Phys. Soc., IEEE, N.Y. Acad. Scis., AAAS. Home: 310 W 106th St New York NY 10025 Office: Bldg 725 Brookhaven Nat Lab Upton NY 11973

BLEWETT, ROBERT NOALL, lawyer; b. Stockton, Calif., July 12, 1915; s. Stephen Noall and Bess Errol (Simard) B.; m. Virginia Weston, Mar. 30, 1940; children—Richard Weston, Carolyn Blewett Lawrence. LL.B., Stanford U., 1936, J.D., 1939. Bar: Calif. bar 1939. Dep. dist. atty. San Joaquin County, 1942-46; practice law, Stockton, 1946—; mem. firm, pres. Blewett, Garretson & Hachman, Stockton, 1971—. Chmn. San Joaquin County chpt. ARC, 1947-49; v.p. Goodwill Industries, 1967-68; vice chmn. Stockton Sister City Commn., 1969-70; adv. bd. bus. adminstrn. dept. U. Pacific; trustee San Joaquin Pioneer and Haggin Galleries. Fellow Am. Coll. Probate Counsel, Am. Bar Found.; mem. State Bar Calif. (mem. exec. com. of conf. of dels. 1969-72, vice chmn. 1971-72), Am. Bar Assn., Am. Judicature Soc., Am. Law Inst., Stockton C. of C., Delta Theta Phi, Theta Xi. Republican. Clubs: Rotary, Yosemite, San Francisco Comml., Masons, Shriners. Home: 3016 Dwight Way Stockton CA 95203 Office: 141 E Acacia St Stockton CA 95202

BLEY, CARLA BORG (MRS. MICHAEL MANTLER), jazz composer; b. Oakland, Calif., May 11, 1938; d. Emil Carl and Arlene (Anderson) Borg; m. Paul Bley, Jan. 27, 1959 (div. Sept. 1967); m. Michael Mantler, Sept. 29, 1967; 1 dau., Karen. Student public schs., Oakland. Mem. adv. bd. Jazz Composers Orch. Assn. Freelance jazz composer, 1956—; pianist, Jazz Composers Orch., N.Y.C., 1964—, European concert tours, Jazz Realities, 1965-66; founder, WATT, 1973—; toured, Europe with, Jack Bruce Band, 1975; leader, Carla Bley Band, touring, U.S. and Europe, 1977—; Composed, recorded: A Genuine Tong Funeral, 1967, (with Charlie Haden) Liberation Music Orch, 1969; opera Escalator Over the Hill, 1970-71 (Oscar Du Disque De Jazz 1973), Tropic Appetites, 1973; composed: chamber och. 3/4, 1974-75; film score Mortelle Rautonnee, 1983; recorded: Dinner Music, 1976, The Carla Bley Band—European Tour, 1977, Musique Mecanique, 1979, (with Nick Mason) Fictitious Sports, 1980, Social Studies, 1981, Carla Bley Live!, 1982, Heavy Heart, 1984. Named winner internat. jazz critics poll Down Beat mag., 1966, 71, 72, 78, 79, 80, 83; Guggenheim fellow, 1972; Cultural Council Found. grantee, 1971, 79; Nat. Endowment for Arts grantee, 1973. Office: 500 Broadway New York NY 10012

BLEY, PAUL, jazz pianist, composer, producer; b. Montreal, Que., Can., Nov. 10, 1932; s. Joseph and Betty B.; m. Carla Bley (div. 1968). Studied violin and piano, jr. diploma McGill Conservatory at age 11; studied composition, conducting at, Juilliard Sch. Music, 1950-52. Pres. Improvising Artists, Inc. (record co.), 1975, now v.p. Started musical career as leader of high sch. band; organized quartet, Chalet Hotel, Montreal, 1945-48; with, Ozzie Roberts, Clarence Joines; played at, Alberta Lounge, 1949-50; weekly TV show Jazz Workshop, Montreal, 1952; with, Stan Kenton, in movie short dealing with jazz history; played N.Y.C. clubs, midwestern colls., 1955, nightclubs, Los Angeles, 1956-58, also group shows with, Ornette Coleman and, Don Cherry, 1958, coll. concert, Calif., 1957-59; with, Charlie Mingus, 1960, Jimmy Guiffre, 1960-61; toured, Germany, 1961, coll. concerts including, Town Hall and, Lincoln Center, 1962-63; mem., Sonny Rollins' quartet, 1963, tours in, U.S., Europe; also appeared: network show WNDT-TV, concert tour of, Japan, and RCA Victor Recordings, 1964; formed: own trio for Bard Coll. concert, 1964; trio recorded for, E.S.P. Records, 1965, tour, Europe, 1965, 66, 67, tour Eastern U.S. colls., 1967; recorded for, Mercury-Limelight Records, Milestone Records, also for, Douglas Internat. Records, solo piano album, ECM Records; commd. to write and to play for, Norddeutcher Rundfunk, Hamburg, W. Germany, 1969; solo pianist European tour, 1970-74, tour with, Gary Peacock and Barry Altschul, Japan, 1976, Gary Peacock and Barry Altschul, Europe, 1976, 77, numerous TV appearances. (Recipient Composition award Nat. Endowment for Arts 1977). Introduced new keyboard instrument Synthesizer at Philharmonic Hall, 1969. Address: care Improving Artists Inc PO Box 225 Village Station New York NY 10014 *As a pianist, it is my goal to compose as well as I can improvise.*

BLEYLE, JOHN ALLEN, insurance company executive; b. Englewood, N.J., Nov. 9, 1944; s. George Alfred and Caroline (Sweet) B.; m. Jean Howard, July 27, 1967; children: Joanne, Susan, Allen. B.A., Bowdoin Coll., 1966; M.A., Johns Hopkins U., 1968. With casualty facultative dept. Gen. Reins. Corp., Hartford, Conn., 1972-74, Greenwich, Conn., 1974-76, Columbus, Ohio, 1976-82; v.p. treaty Gen. Reins Corp., Greenwich, 1982—. Served to lt. USNR, 1968-71. Home: 12 Salem Rd Westport CT 06880 Office: Gen Reins Corp 600 Steamboat Rd Greenwich CT 06830

BLEYMAIER, JOSEPH SYLVESTER, construction company executive, retired air force officer; b. Austin, Tex., Dec. 31, 1915; s. Jacob and Mary Ann (Frish) B.; m. Rosemary Josephine Mathias, June 25, 1942; children: Joseph Sylvester, Marianne, Theodore, John, Eugene. B.B.A., U. Tex., 1950; grad., Air Command and Staff Sch., 1950, Air War Coll., 1954. Commd. 2d lt. USAAF, 1942, advanced through grades to maj. gen., 1967; chief equipment div. Hdqrs. Air Research and Devel. Command, 1954-56, dep. dir. astronautics, 1956-58; also dir. subsystems devel.; asst. dep. comdr. ballistics missiles Air Force Ballistic Missile Div., 1958-60; dep. for launch vehicles, systems program dir., also dep. comdr. manned systems Hdqrs. Space Systems Div., 1961-65; comdr. Air Force Western Test Range, Vandenberg AFB, Calif., 1965-67; dep. dir. MOL program USAF; also dep. comdr. SSD MOL, Los Angeles, 1967-69; ret., 1969; gen. mgr. CONUS-Morrison-Knudsen Saudi Arabia Consortium, Columbia, Md., 1969—. Decorated Air medal with 10 oak leaf clusters, D.S.M., Legion of Merit; recipient John F. Kennedy Meml. award Arnold Air Soc., 1965. Mem. AIAA (astronautics award 1965), Soc. Mil. Engrs., Air Force Assn., Am. Ordnance Assn., Am. Mgmt. Assn. Roman Catholic. Club: K.C. Address: 10275 W Victory Rd Boise ID 83709 Office: Morrison-Knudsen Co Inc PO Box 7808 Boise ID 83729

BLICKENSTAFF, V. DALE, banker; b. Quinter, Kans., Dec. 18, 1925; m. Gernelda Sprenkel, Aug. 16, 1947; 1 son, Scott. B.S., McPherson Coll., 1950; M.A., Ft. Hays Kans. State Coll., 1964; Ed.D., U. Mo. Colo., 1967. Chmn. acctg. dept. Boise State U., Idaho, 1967-70, dean Sch. Bus., 1970-73; v.p. Idaho First Nat. Bank, Boise, 1973-79, sr. v.p., 1979-80, exec. v.p., 1980—; mem. faculty Pacific Board Banking Sch., Seattle, 1982—. Mem. Gov.'s Econ Research Council, Boise, 1983; treas. Boise Future Found., 1983—; mem. Commn. on Excellence in Edn., Boise, 1983. Mem. Am. Bankers Assn., Am. Inst. C.P.A.s, Idaho Soc. C.P.A.s, Nat. Assn. Accts., Greater Boise C. of C. (bd. dirs. 1983—). Clubs: Crane Creek Country; Arid (Boise). Home: 106 E Curling Dr Boise ID 83702 Office: Idaho First Nat Bank 101 S Capitol Blvd Boise ID 83702

BLICKWEDE, DONALD JOHNSON, retired steel company executive; b. Detroit, July 20, 1920; s. Frederic H. and Laura L. (Johnson) B.; m. Meredith Lloyd, Aug. 23, 1943; children: Karen (Mrs. Kimball J. Knowlton), Jon Frederic. B.S., Wayne U., 1943; postgrad., Stevens Inst. Tech., 1943-45; Sc.D., Mass. Inst. Tech., 1948; postgrad. in bus. adminstrn., Harvard, 1969. Metallurgist Curtiss Wright Corp., 1943-45; head high temperature alloys br. Naval Research Lab., 1948-50; research engr. Bethlehem Steel Corp., Pa., 1950-52, div. head, 1952-63, v.p., 1964-82; Campbell Meml. lectr. Am. Metal Congress, 1968, William Park Woodside Meml. lectr., 1969, Zay Zeffries Meml. lectr., 1970; Andrews Meml. lectr. Porcelain Enamel Inst., 1972. Fellow Am. Soc. Metals (pres.); mem. Am. Inst. Mining and Metall. Engrs., Am. Acad. Engring., Am. Iron and Steel Inst. (chmn. gen. research com. 1971-73), Indsl. Research Inst. (pres. 1975). Club: Saucon Valley Country. Home: RD 4 Bethlehem PA 18015 Office: 437 Main St Suite 310 Bethlehem PA 18018

BLILEY, THOMAS JEROME, JR., congressman; b. Chesterfield County, Va., Jan. 28, 1932; s. Thomas J. and Carolyn F. B.; m. Mary Virginia Kelley, June 22, 1957; children: Mary Vaughan, Thomas Jerome III. B.A., Georgetown U., 1952. Pres. Joseph W. Bliley Funeral Home, 1972-80; mem. Congress from Va.; Vice-mayor Richmond City Council, 1968-70, mayor, 1970-77; past bd. dirs. Nat. League Cities; past pres. Va. Municipal League. Past bd. dirs. Crippled Children's Hosp., St. Mary's Hosp.; bd. visitors Va. Commonwealth U. Served with USN. Republican. Roman Catholic. Office: 214 Cannon House Office Bldg Washington DC 20515

BLIM, RICHARD, pediatrician; b. Kansas City, Mo., Nov. 8, 1927; s. Miles G. and Latha Mae (Daniels) B.; m. Myrle Rae Blim, Apr. 12, 1952; children: Richard David, Carol Rae, John Miles. B.A., U. Kans., 1949, M.D., 1953. Diplomate: Am. Bd. Pediatrics. Intern U. Kans., 1953-54, resident in pediatrics, 1954-56; practice medicine specializing in pediatrics; pres. Pediatric Assocs., Kansas City, Mo., 1956—, Health Plan of Mid-Am., Kansas City, 1983—; Peter T. Bohan lectr. U. Kans., Kansas City, 1978; Max Seham lectr. U. Minn., 1982. Editorial bd.: Mo. Medicine, 1978—, Pediatric Annals, 1982—, Pediatric News, 1983—. Bd. dirs. Marillac Spl. Sch. for Children, 1976-79, Crittenden Treatment Ctr. Adolescents, 1980—. Served to sgt. U.S. Army, 1946-48; PTO. Named Outstanding Med. Alumnus U. Kans. Sch. Medicine, 1976. Fellow Am. Acad. Pediatrics (pres. 1980-81, exec. bd. 1973-80, chmn. Mo. chpt. 1964-67); mem. Jackson County Med. Soc. (pres. 1976), S.W. Pediatric Assn. (pres. Kansas City 1963), Mo. Med. Assn., AMA (del. 1976-80), Inst. of Medicine of Nat. Acad. Sci., Council Med. Specialties Soc. (rep., exec. bd. 1974-80), Kans. U. Med. Alumni (pres. 1973), Alpha Omega Alpha. Republican. Presbyterian. Club: Carriage (Kansas City). Home: 2209 W 68th St Shawnee Mission KS 66208 Office: Pediatric Associates 4400 Broadway Kansas City MO 64111

BLINDER, ABE LIONEL, business consultant; b. Osage, Iowa, Nov 7, 1909; s. Heimer and Fanny (Goldstein) B.; m. Henriette Levin, Oct. 19, 1947; children: Henry David, Jonathan. Ph.B., U. Chgo., 1931. Circulation mgr. Apparel Arts, Chgo., 1932-33; circulation mgr. Esquire, Inc., Chgo., 1933-36, circulation dir., 1936-45, dir., 1945—, v.p., 1945-51, exec. v.p., 1952-61, pres., 1961-77, chmn. bd., 1977-80, chmn. internat. ops., 1980-84; cons., 1984—. Bd. dirs. Alliance for Resident Theatres, N.Y.C.; mem. visual aids com. U. Chgo. Mem. Phi Beta Kappa. Clubs: Harmonie (N.Y.C.); Metropolis Country. Home: 5 Horseguard Ln Scarsdale NY 10583 Office: 488 Madison Ave New York NY 10022

BLINDER, ALAN STUART, educator; b. Bklyn., Oct. 14, 1945; s. Morns and Shirley (Rothers) B.; m. Madeline D. Schwartz, July 9, 1967; children: Scott, William. A.B., Princeton U., 1967; M. Sc., London Sch. Econs., 1968; Ph.D., MIT, 1971. Instr. fin. Rider Coll., Trenton, N.J., 1968-69; instr. econs. Boston State Coll., 1969; asst. prof. econs. Princeton U., 1971-76, assoc. prof., 1976-79, prof., 1979-82, Gordon S. Rentschler Meml. prof. econs., 1982—. Author: Economic Policy and the Great Stagflation, 1979, Toward an Economic Theory of Income Distribution, 1974, Economics: Principles and Policy, 1982; editor: (with William T. Bauwal) Natural Resources, Uncertainty and General Equilibrium Systems: Essays in Memory of Rafael Lusky, 1977. Recipient W.S. Woytinsky award, 1981. Fellow Econometric Soc.; mem. Brookings Panel on Econ. Activity (research assoc.). Office: Dept Econs Princeton Univ 110 Dickinson Hall Princeton NJ 08544

BLINDER, SEYMOUR MICHAEL, chemistry educator; b. N.Y.C., Mar. 11, 1932; s. Morris and Ida (Stuchinsky) B.; m. Frances Ellen Bryant, July 8, 1978; children: Michael Ian, Stephen Earl. A.B., Cornell U., 1953; M.A., Harvard U., 1955, Ph.D., 1958. Sr. physicist Applied Physics Lab., Johns Hopkins U., 1958-61; asst. prof. chemistry Carnegie Inst. Tech., 1961-62; research asso. Harvard U., 1962-63; prof. chemistry U. Mich., 1963—. Author: Advanced Physical Chemistry, 1969, Foundations of Quantum Dynamics, 1974; Mem. bd. editors: Jour. Am. Chem. Soc., 1978-80; contbr. research articles to profl. jours. Guggenheim fellow, 1965-66; NSF sr. postdoctoral fellow, 1970-71. Mem. Am. Phys. Soc., Philos. Soc. Washington, Phi Beta Kappa. Home: 1240 Ferdon Rd Ann Arbor MI 48104 Office: Dept Chemistry U Mich Ann Arbor MI 48109

BLINKEN, DONALD MAYER, investment banker; b. N.Y.C., Nov. 11, 1925; s. Maurice Henry and Ethel (Horowitz) B.; m. Vera Evans, Oct. 15, 1975; 1 son, Antony John. B.A. magna cum laude, Harvard U., 1947. Cons. Marks & Spencer, Ltd., London, 1950-51; pres. Exchange Trading Corp., N.Y.C., 1952-53; v.p. Stein's Stores, Inc., N.Y.C., 1953-58; asso. E.M. Warburg & Co., Inc., N.Y.C., 1959-61, v.p., 1961-72; sr. v.p., chmn. exec. com. E.M. Warburg, Pincus & Co., Inc., N.Y.C., 1970-81, mng. dir., 1981—; dir., chmn. fin. com. Mite Corp.; dir. EMW Ventures, Inc., Warburg Pincus Capitol Corps. Author: Wool Tariffs and American Policy, 1948; mem. publ. com.: Commentary, 1974—. Co-chmn. Concerned Citizens for Arts N.Y. State, 1972-82; mem. Task Force on N.Y. State Arts and Cultural Life, 1974—, Citizens Com. for N.Y.C., 1975—; treas. Friends of Whitney Mus. Am. Art, 1967-69; pres. Bklyn. Acad. Music, 1971-76, Mark Rothko Found., 1976—; trustee Inst. Man and Sci., 1971-74, SUNY, 1976—; chmn. bd. SUNY, 1978—; mem. Nat. Commn. on Higher Edn. Issues, 1981. Served with USAAF, 1944-45. Club: Century Assn. (N.Y.C.). Home: 435 E 52d St New York NY 10022 Office: 277 Park Ave New York NY 10017

BLINKEN, ROBERT JAMES, manufacturing company executive; b. N.Y.C., Apr. 18, 1929; s. Maurice Henry and Ethel (Horowitz) B.; m. Jeanne Pagnucco, Mar. 5, 1955 (div. Jan. 1967); children: Robert James, Rachel; m. Allison Matsner, Dec. 14, 1967; children: Anna, Ingrid. Grad., Horace Mann Sch., N.Y.C., 1946; B.A. cum laude, Harvard U., 1950. Vice pres. Exchange Trading Corp., N.Y.C., 1953-57; pres. Teleprinter Corp., 1954-61; v.p. Mite Corp., New Haven, 1961-63, pres., 1963-75, chmn., 1975—, also dir.; dir. Fifth Ave & 59th Corp., Sherry Netherland Hotel, Supradur Corp. Served to 1st lt. USAF, 1950-53. Home: Matthews Mill Rd Bedford Hills NY 10507 Office: 200 Park Ave New York NY 10017

BLINKOFF, JAMES BLADEN, lawyer; b. Buffalo, Aug. 4, 1941; s. Maurice and Goldene P. (Jacobstein) B.; m. Jeanne E. Eckardt, May 21, 1966; children: Rachel, Andrew. A.B., Princeton U., 1963; LL.B., U. Pa., 1966. Bar: D.C. 1967. Clk. to assoc. justice Pa. Supreme Ct., 1966-67; assoc. Fried, Frank, Harris, Shriver & Kampelman, Washington, 1967-75, ptnr., 1975—. Mem. ABA, D.C. Bar Assn., Bar Assn. D.C., Nat. Assn. Corp. Real Estate Execs., Internat. Council Shopping Ctrs. Home: 10601 Shady Circle Silver Springs MD 20903 Office: Fried Frank Harris Shriver & Kampelman 600 New Hampshire Ave NW 1000 Washington DC 20037

BLINKS, JOHN ROGERS, pharmacology educator; b. N.Y.C., Mar. 21, 1931; s. Lawrence Rogers and Anne Catherine (Hof) B.; m. Doris Marie Chambers, Dec. 28, 1953; children: Susan Mayo, Sarah Russell, Elizabeth Rogers. A.B., Stanford U., 1951; M.D., Harvard U., 1955. Med. house officer Peter Bent Brigham Hosp., Boston, 1955-56; research assoc. Nat. Heart Inst., Bethesda, Md., 1956-58; faculty Harvard Med. Sch., Boston, 1958-68; instr., 1958-61, assoc., 1961-64, asst. prof. pharmacology, 1964-68, John and Mary R. Markle Found. scholar, 1961-66; head dept. pharmacology Mayo Found., Rochester, Minn., 1968—; assoc. prof. pharmacology Mayo Grad. Sch. Medicine, 1968-72; prof., chmn. dept. pharmacology Mayo Med. Sch., 1973—, E.A. and M.F. Guggenheim prof., 1981—; hon. research asst. dept. physiology Univ. Coll., London, 1962-63; vis. lectr. dept. physiology U. Auckland, N.Z., 1974; established investigator Am. Heart Assn., 1965-70, mem. research com., 1975-79, chmn. research com., v.p. for research, 1979; mem. program projects com. Nat. Heart and Lung Inst., 1968-72, mem. cardiology adv. com., 1975-79; chmn. Gordon Research Conf. on Heart Muscle, 1970; mem. external adv. bd. Pa. Muscle Inst., 1975-77. Field editor: cellular pharmacology Jour. Pharmacology Exptl. Therapeutics, 1969-71; mem. editorial bd., 1965-80, Circulation Research, 1970-74. Served with USPHS, 1956-58. Fellow AAAS; Mem. Am. Soc. Pharmacology and Exptl. Therapeutics, Am. Physio. Soc., Biophys. Soc., Cardiac Muscle Soc. (sec.-treas. 1977-79, pres. 1979-81), Internat. Soc. for Heart Research, Soc. Gen. Physiologists. Home: 2715 Salem Rd SW Rochester MN 55902 Office: Dept Pharmacology Mayo Found Rochester MN 55905

BLINN, KEITH WAYNE, legal educator; b. Hutchinson, Kans., July 28, 1917; s. Alonzo Cary and Clifton (Wright) B.; m. Ellen Young, Aug. 31, 1940; children—John Randolph, Stephen David. A.B., Washington and Lee U., 1940; J.D. (Sterling fellow), Yale U., 1951. Bar: Wis. 1941, Tex. 1953, N.Y. 1966, Conn. 1976. Atty. TVA, 1942, NLRB, 1942-46; prof. law U. N.D., 1946-52; vis. prof. law U. Idaho, 1952; sr. v.p., gen. counsel Continental Oil Co., N.Y.C., 1962-77; prof. law U. Houston, 1977—; dir. Commonwealth Oil Refining Co., Haldor Topsoe Inc.; lectr., seminar participant, 1964—; arbitrator Am. Arbitrator Assn., 1961—, Fed. Mediation and Conciliation Ser., 1981—; Atty. adviser OPA, 1951; chmn. regional enforcement commn. WSB, Mpls., 1952. Author: Cases and Materials on Federal Energy Regulations. Mem. bd. zoning appels, Bellaire, Tex., 1957, mem. city council, 1959. Mem. Am. Bar Assn., Assn. Bar City N.Y., Order of Coif, Phi Delta Phi. Episcopalian (vestryman). Clubs: Stamford (Conn.); Yacht; Wee Burn Country (Darien, Conn.); Bristol (R.I.); Yacht. Home: 9 Starlight Irvine CA 92715

BLINN, ROBERT D., banker; b. Oklahoma City, Okla., Aug. 21, 1921; s. Clarence J. and Margaret (Davis) B.; m. Susanne Wells, May 15, 1943; children: Susan (Mrs. Jerry L. Latta), Trudy (Mrs. Martin L. Stewart), Diane (Mrs. Herbert K. Kenney). B.A., Okla. U., 1942; postgrad., Harvard Bus. Sch., 1943; LL.B., Oklahoma City U., 1950. Chief accountant, asst. finance officer VA, Oklahoma City, 1946-55; with Liberty Nat. Bank & Trust Co. Oklahoma City, 1955—, sr. v.p., 1964; dir. Atkinson, Warren & Henley, Oklahoma City, Franklin-Aston-Fair, Roswell, N.M., Fairlawn Cemetary Assn., Oklahoma City.; Chmn. Oklahoma City U. Fund Campaign.; Bd. dirs., Charles Morton Share Trust, Alva, Okla. Served with USNR, 1943-46. Mem. Okla. Bankers Assn. (pres. trust div. 1962-63), Petroleum Club Oklahoma City, Beta Theta Pi. Presbyn. (treas., trustee). Clubs: Quail Creek Golf and Country.; Men's Dinner (Oklahoma City). Home: 6613 NW Grand Blvd Oklahoma City OK 73116 Office: PO Box 1097 Oklahoma City OK 73101

BLISS, ANTHONY ADDISON, lawyer; b. N.Y.C., Apr. 19, 1913; s. Cornelius Newton and Zaidee (Cobb) B.; m. Barbara Field, Dec. 22, 1937 (div. Dec. 1941); 1 dau., Barbara Mestre; m. Jo Ann Sayers, June 9, 1942 (div. July 12, 1967); children—Eileen (Mrs. Eileen Bliss Andahazy), Anthony Addison, John Wheeler; m. Sally Brayley, July 24, 1967; children—Mark Brayley, Timothy Newton. B.A., Harvard, 1936; LL.B., U. Va., 1940. Bar: N.Y. State bar 1943. Cons. mem. firm Milbank, Tweed, Hadley & McCloy, N.Y.C.; bd. dirs., exec. com. Met. Opera Assn., pres., 1956-67, gen. mgr., 1981—; trustee U.S. Trust Co. N.Y.; Chmn. bd. Found. for Joffrey Ballet; bd. dirs. Am. Arts Alliance; trustee Portledge Sch.; hon. chmn. Nat. Corporate Fund for Dance, Inc. Served in USNR, 1942-45. Decorated Air medal. Mem. Am., Internat., N.Y. State, Nassau County bar assns., Assn. Bar City N.Y. Clubs: Creek, Beaver Dam Winter Sports, Cove Neck Tennis. Home: Centre Island Oyster Bay NY 11771 Office: Met Opera Assn Lincoln Center Plaza New York NY 10023

BLISS, CARMAN ARTHUR, univ. dean; b. Olds, Alta., Can., Dec. 10, 1923; came to U.S., 1949, naturalized, 1966; s. Walter Franklin and Minnie (Cheeseman) B.; m. Mary Watson Farmer, Aug. 23, 1952; children—Kevin, Allison. B.Sc. in Pharmacy, U. Alta., 1949, M.S., Purdue U., 1952, Ph.D. in Pharm. Chemistry, 1954. Asst. prof. Coll. Pharmacy, U. So. Calif., 1954-56, asso. prof., 1956-66, Coll. Pharmacy, U. Sask., Can., 1966-69, prof., 1969-70; prof., dean Coll. Pharmacy and Dental Programs, U. N.Mex., Albuquerque, 1970—, acting dir. dental programs, 1973-74. Author: chpt. in Pharmaceutical Chemistry, 1969; also articles on plant chemistry and biochemistry. Served with Canadian Army, 1944-45. Am. Found. Pharm. Edn. fellow, 1952-54. Mem. Am. Pharm. Assn., Sigma Xi (pres. U. So. Calif. chpt. 1961-62), Skull and Mortar, Rho Chi, Phi Lambda Upsilon, Phi Delta Chi, Kappa Sigma. Club: Rotarian. Home: 126 Maria Circle NW Albuquerque NM 87114

BLISS, CHARLES MELBOURNE, retired banker; b. Evanston, Ill., Oct. 9, 1921; s. Charles H. and Hazel (Whitmore) B.; m. Margaret Soule, Jan. 1, 1943; children: Charles Melbourne, Marian (Mrs. William White), Emily (Mrs. Robert L. Crawford). A.B. magna cum laude, Harvard U., 1943; student, Harvard Bus. Sch., 1942-43; M.B.A. with distinction, Northwestern U., 1947. With Harris Trust & Savs. Bank, Chgo., 1944—, pres., dir., 1976—, chief exec. officer, 1977—, chmn., 1980-84; dir. G.D. Searle & Co., Kellogg Co., Fed. Res. Bank Chgo., Chgo.; treas. Chgo. Crusade of Mercy. Trustee Alonzo Mather Found., Evanston, Ill., Chgo. Community Trust, Northwestern U.; bd. dirs. Children's Meml. Hosp.; chmn., bd. dirs. Chgo. Clearing House Assn.; treas., dir. United Way/Crusade of Mercy. Served with AUS, 1943. Mem. Assn. Res. City Bankers (bd. dirs.), Phi Beta Kappa, Beta Gamma Sigma. Episcopalian. Clubs: Casino, Chgo., Comml. (Chgo.); Glen View (Ill.) Golf; Metropolitan (Washington). Office: 111 W Monroe St Chicago IL 60690

BLISS, DOROTHY ELIZABETH, zoologist; b. Cranston, R.I., Feb. 13, 1916; d. Orville Thayer and Sophia Topham (Farnell) B. A.B., Brown U., 1937, Sc.M., 1942, Sc.D. (hon.), 1972; Ph.D., Radcliffe Coll., 1952. Sci. tchr. Milton (Mass.) Acad., 1942-49; teaching fellow biology Harvard, 1947-51, research fellow, 1952-55; asst. curator Am. Mus. Natural History, N.Y.C., 1956-62, asso. curator, 1962-67, curator, 1967-80, curator emerita, 1980—, chmn., curator dept. fossil and living invertebrates, 1974-77; research asst. prof. anatomy Albert Einstein Coll. Medicine, 1956-64, vis. research asso. prof., 1964-66; adj. prof. biology City U. N.Y., 1971-80; adj. prof. zoology U. R.I., 1980—; mem. adv. com. respiration and circulation, biol. handbooks Fedn. Am. Socs. Exptl. Biology, 1968-71; Mem. corp. Bermuda Biol. Sta. for Research, Inc. Author: Shrimps, Lobsters and Crabs; Editor-in-chief: The Biology of Crustacea; Mem. editorial bds.: Natural History Press, 1966-70, Am. Zoologist, 1967-72, Curator, 1968-79, Jour. Exptl. Zoology, 1970-73, Natural History Mag, 1970-79, Gen. and Comparative Endocrinology, 1974-78; Contbr. articles sci. jours. NSF grantee, 1957-78. Fellow AAAS (chmn. sect. biol. scis. 1973, mem. council 1973, mem. com. council affairs 1973-75, chmn. nominating com. 1973-74); Mem. Am. Soc. Zoologists (pres. 1978, chmn. div. invertebrate zoology 1970), Am. Inst. Biol. Scis. (chmn. com. biosci. 1974-75), Assn. for Women in Sci., Crustacean Soc., Phi Beta Kappa., Sigma Xi. Home: Brook Farm Rd Rural Route 5 Wakefield RI 02879

BLISS, LAWRENCE CARROLL, botany educator; b. Cleve., Nov. 29, 1929; s. Laurence and Ada May (Peterson) B.; m. Gweneth Ruth Jones, Mar. 15, 1952; children: Dwight I., Karen L. B.S., Kent State U., 1951, M.S., 1953; Ph.D., Duke U., 1956. Instr. biology Bowling Green State U., 1956-57; instr. botany U. Ill., 1957-58, asst. prof., 1958-61, asso. prof., 1961-66, prof., 1966-68; prof. dept. botany U. Alta., 1968-78, dir. controlled environ. facility, 1968-78; prof. botany U. Wash., 1978—, chmn. dept. botany, 1978—; cons. in field. Author: (with M. Balbach) Laboratory Manual for General Botany, 6th edit., 1977; editor: Truelove Lowland, Devon Island, Canada: A High Arctic Ecosystem, 1977, (with others) Tundra Ecosystems: A Comparative Analysis, 1981; contbr. articles to profl. jours. Fulbright scholar, 1963-64. Mem. Ecol. Soc. Am. (v.p. 1976-77, treas. 1977-81, pres.-elect 1981-82, pres. 1982-83), Am. Inst. Biol. Sci.; fellow AAAS, Arctic Inst. N. Am.; mem. Can. Bot. Assn., Sigma Xi. Republican. Presbyterian. Home: 1226 NW 175th St Seattle WA 98177 Office: Dept Botany U Wash Seattle WA 98195

BLISS, ROBERT HARMS, lawyer; b. Paris, Tex., Nov. 20, 1940; s. Jack Edward and Ruth Eugenia (Harms) B.; m. Juliee Dixie Fuselier, Dec. 29, 1964; 1 dau., Katherine Elaine. B.A., U. Colo., 1964; J.D., U. Tex., 1967. Bar: Tex. 1967; Cert. civil trial specialist. Since practiced in, Dallas, individual practice, 1974; Pres. Bliss & Hughes, P.C., Dallas, 1978—. Contbr. articles to profl. jours. Bd. dirs. Dallas Symphony Orch. Guild, Dallas Classic Guitar Soc., Dallas Democratic Forum.; mem. Gov.'s Task Force on Immigration, 1983—. Mem. ABA, Dallas Bar Assn., Am. Immigration Lawyers Assn., U. Tex. Teaching Quiz-Masters Assn., Phi Delta Phi. Episcopalian. Home: 5806 Walnut Hill Ln Dallas TX 75230 Office: 2777 Stemmons Freeway Suite 1657 Dallas TX 75207

BLISS, ROBERT LANDERS, public relations consultant; b. Binghamton, N.Y., Nov. 19, 1907; s. George Calvin Sherwood and Katherine Barbara (Scheider) B.; m. Friede Smidt, May 16, 1942; children: John Smidt, Friede Sherwood (Mrs. Thomas Mark Brayton). A.B., Cornell U., 1930. With Gen. Tire & Rubber Co., N.Y.C., 1933-36, Arthur B. Treman & Co.; mem. N.Y. Stock Exchange, N.Y.C., 1936-38; asst. chief press Bur. J. Walter Thompson, N.Y.C., 1938-40; asst. to pub. and promotion mgr. PM Newspaper, 1940, Compton Advt., Inc., 1941-46; dir. pub. relations Nat. Assn. Ins. Agts., N.Y.C., 1946-49; exec. v.p. Pub. Relations Soc. Am., N.Y.C., 1949-56; mng. editor pub. Pub. Relations Jour., 1950-56; editor Pub. Relations Register, 1949-56; pres. Robert L. Bliss Inc. (now Robert L. Bliss Assos., Inc.), public relations cons., 1956—; pres. New Canaan Neighborhoods, Inc.; chmn. bd. Helicopter Assocs. Inc.; mem. U.S. Senatorial Bus. Adv. Bd., 1980—, mem. steering com., 1981—; Chmn. Ardn-House on Bus. and Politics, 1959, Am. Bus. Conf. on Practical Local Politics, N.Y., 1960; Mem. Republican town com. New Canaan,

1951-80, chmn., 1951-62; mem. Rep. State Central Com., 1954-56; treas., chmn. Fairfield County Rep. Com., 1960-64; mem. Conn. Senate, 1963-67, Conn. Transp. Authority, 1974-75; founder, mem. Presdl. Task Force; founder, chmn. New Canaan ann. Gridiron Dinner, 1961-80; mem. public relations adv. com. Cornell U. Council. Co-author: Handbook of Public Relations, 2d edit, 1971. Served from 2d lt. to maj. USAAF, 1942-46. Mem. Pub. Relations Soc. Am. (charter), Internat. Pub. Relations Assn. (founding council mem. 1955, chmn. research com., mem. council, v.p., pres. 1965-68, gen. rapporteur 2d World Congress on Pub. Relations, Venice 1961, exec. com., program chmn. 3d World Congress, Montreal, Que. 1964, presiding officer 4th World Congress, Rio de Janeiro, Brazil 1967, emeritus mem. 1980—), Nat. Soc. State Legislators (founder, charter mem., 1st v.p.), Pub. Relations Soc. N.Y., Pub. Relations Soc. Am. (pres. N.Y.C. chpt. 1962-63), SAR, Psi Upsilon. Baptist. Clubs: Woodway Country (Darien, Conn.); Cornell (N.Y.C.). Home: 162 Park St New Canaan CT 06840 Office: 111 Elm St New Canaan CT 06840

BLISS, ROBERT LEWIS, architect, educator; b. Seattle, May 21, 1921; s. Lewis Edward and Gladys Emily (Miller) B.; m. Anna Marie Campbell, Apr. 2, 1949. Student, Black Mountain Coll., 1939-42; B.Arch., M.I.T., 1949. Instr. M.I.T., 1951-52; prin. Bliss and Campbell, Mpls., 1956-63, Salt Lake City, 1963—; asso. prof. Sch. Architecture, U. Minn., 1952-63; dean Grad. Sch. Architecture, U. Utah, 1963—. Served with AUS, 1943-44; Served with U.S. Mcht. Marine, 1944-46. Rotch Scholar, 1950-51; recipient awards Producers Council, 1976, Iron and Steel Inst., 1973, Minn. Soc. Architects, 1960. Fellow AIA; mem. Assn. Collegiate Schs. Architecture (pres. 1967-69), Utah Heritage Found. (pres. 1967-69), Nat. Trust Hist. Preservation, ASSIST, Inc. (pres. 1971-75), Utah Sailing Assn. Democrat. Patentee in field. Home: 27 University St Salt Lake City UT 84102 Office: Univ of Utah Salt Lake City UT 84112

BLISS, SALLY BRAYLEY, ballet dancer, educator, director; b. London, Eng., Sept. 18, 1937; came to U.S., 1962; d. John Wilfred and Zeversa Lorraine (Gibbon) Brayley; m. Anthony A. Bliss, July 24, 1967; children: Mark Brayley, Timothy Newton. Student, Nat. Ballet Sch. Can., Toronto, 1950-62, Am. Sch. Ballet, summer 1953, 62-70, Am. Ballet Theatre Sch., 1962-70, Met. Opera Ballet Sch., 1962-66, Am. Ballet Center, 1966-70. Formed Joffrey II Co. (with Jonathan Watts), 1969, asso. dir., 1969-75, dir., 1975—; adjudicator N.E. Regional Ballet Festival, 1974, S.E. Regional Ballet Festival, Pacific Regional Ballet Assn., 1975; owner Portledge Sch. Classical Ballet, Locust Valley, N.Y., 1973—; guest tchr. throughout U.S., 1970—. Ballet dancer: Canadian Nat. Exhbn. Grandstand Show, 1951; television, Montreal, Que., 1953-54, Television Ballet Co., under direction, Brian McDonald, 1955-62, Melody Fair Summer Stock, North Tonawanda, N.Y., 1959; soloist, Nat. Ballet Can., 1956-62, summer stock, Lenny Debin Circuit, 1961-62; prin. dancer, Met. Opera Ballet, 1962-66, Jacob's Pillow, (with James Clouser), summer 1967; guest artist, Am. Ballet Theatre, 1967; prin. dancer, City Center Joffrey Ballet, 1968, N.Y.C. Opera, 1969. Mem. Nat. Assn. for Regional Ballet (dir.). Mem. Ch. of Eng. Office: Found for Joffrey Ballet 130 W 56th St New York NY 10019

BLISS, WILLIAM STANLEY, JR., manufacturing company executive; b. Evanston, Ill., Aug. 23, 1932; s. William S. and Virginia (Allen) B.; m. Beverly Jean Bailer, June 27, 1959; children: William Bailer, Susan Blair. B.S. in Physics, Miami U., Oxford, Ohio, 1954; M.B.A., Harvard U., 1961. With Leeds & Northrup Co., North Wales, Pa., 1965-79, mfg. dir., North Wales, 1972-75, dir. indsl. relations, 1975-79; pres. Wollard Airport Equipment, Inc., Miami, Fla., 1980—. Pres. North Pa. United Way, Lansdale, 1976-79, v.p., Lansdale, 1973-76; vestryman Ch. of the Messiah, Gwynedd, Pa., 1974-80. Served to lt. USN, 1954-59. Mem. Theta Chi (pres.). Republican. Episcopalian. Club: Red Dragon Canoe.

BLISSETT, WILLIAM FRANK, educator; b. East End, Sask., Can., Oct. 11, 1921; s. Ralph Richardson and Gladys (Jones) B. B.A., U. B.C., 1943; M.A., U. Toronto, 1946, Ph.D., 1950. Lectr dept. English U. Toronto, 1946-50, prof. English, 1965—; assoc. prof. dept. English U. Sask., 1950-57, prof., 1957-60; prof., head dept. English Huron Coll., London, Ont., 1960-65. Editor: U. Toronto Quar., 1965-76; adv. bd.: Ency. of Shakespeare and Music, 1982—, Spenser Ency., 1982—; joint editor: A Celebration of Ben Johnson, 1974; editor: Editing Illustrated Books, 1980; author: The Long Conversation, 1981. Huron Coll. hon. fellow, 1966; Royal Soc. Can. fellow, 1979. Mem. Internat. Assn. Univ. Profs. English, Assn. Canadian Univ. Profs. English, Renaissance Soc. Am. Anglican. Home: 36 Castle Frank Rd Apt 212 Toronto ON Canada M4W 2Z7 Office: Univ Coll Univ Toronto Toronto ON Canada M5S 1A1

BLITCH, JAMES BUCHANAN, architect; b. Charleston, S.C., Sept. 2, 1923; s. Norman Henry and Louise (Buchanan) B.; m. Hilda Goodspeed Mouledoux, Nov. 24, 1945; children: James Buchanan, John Crandell, Ronald Buchanan, Judith Ann (dec.), Courtney Ann, David Alan, Leslie Anne, Lisl Maria. B.Arch., Tulane U., 1950. Owner J. Buchanan Blitch & Assocs., 1958-66; pres. J. Buchanan Blitch & Assoc., Inc., 1966-78; chmn. Blitch Architects, Inc., New Orleans, 1978—; vis. lectr. U. Southwestern La. Sch. Architecture; archdiocesan cons. on facilities for aged. Prin. works include Vatican Pavilion, other New Orleans World's Fair structures; homes for aged, religious, med. and ednl. facilities throughout Gulf South.; contbg. author: Housing for a Maturing Population, Urban Land Inst. Pres. adv. council Jesuit High Sch.; mem. bd. Holy Cross High Sch.; Trustee Assoc. Catholic Charities, St. Mary's Dominican Coll., Schimek Meml. Eye Found.; pres. St. Elizabeth's Home for Girls, East Jefferson Hosp. Found.; chmn. Abita Springs Planning Commn.; pres. St. Tammany Parish Hist. Soc.; mem. panel of arbitrators Am. Arbitration Assn. Served with USNR, 1943-45. Recipient 23 honor awards for design Nat. Guild for Religious Architecture, Gulf States region AIA, Am. Planning Assn., La. Architects Assn.; Named papal Knight of Holy Sepulchre New Orleans Archdiocesan Order of St. Louis. Fellow A.I.A. (regional dir. nat. com. on architecture for health); mem. La. Architects Assn. (pres.), New Orleans C. of C., New Orleans Constrn. Industry Assn. (trustee). Republican. Roman Catholic. Clubs: Lotus, Empire. Pioneer devel. regional archtl. design prins., passive energy conservation procedures. Home: Ahmeek Plantation Abita Springs LA 70420 Office: 1070 Saint Charles Ave New Orleans LA 70130

BLITMAN, HOWARD NORTON, construction company executive; b. N.Y.C., Dec. 9, 1926; s. Charles H. and Anna (Palestine) B.; m. Maureen Lefcort-Winter, 1975. C.E., Rensselaer Poly. Inst., 1950; M.A., New Sch. Social Research, 1973. Registered profl. engr., N.Y., N.J., Conn., Mass. Field engr. Drier Structural Steel Co., N.Y., 1950-51; design engr. Blitman & Tischler, N.Y.C., 1952-60; project engr. Blitman Constrn. Corp., N.Y.C., 1960-61, coordinator, 1961-62, exec. v.p., 1962-69, pres., 1969-81; pres., dir. Blitman Bldg. Corp., 1981—; Mem. housing com. State Constnl. Conv., 1968; mem. N.Y.C. Commn. Investigation Water Main Breaks. Mem. sch. bd. Mt. Pleasant Cottage Sch., Union Free Sch. Dist., Pleasantville, N.Y.; bd. dirs. Jewish Child Care Assn.; v.p. bd. dirs. Beth Israel Med. Center; mem. council Rensselaer Poly. Inst.; chmn. archtl. rev. bd. Town of Scarsdale (N.Y.). Served to 2d lt. Chem. Corps AUS, 1944-47; to 1st lt., 1951-53. Recipient Norman Tishman Human Relations award, 1967. Mem. N.Y. State Soc. Profl. Engrs. (pres. 1978, pres. N.Y. chpt. 1974-75), ASCE, Am. Soc. M.E. Clubs: Mason. Club, Harmonie (N.Y.C.). Home: 3 Elmdorf Dr Scarsdale NY 10583 Office: 1290 Avenue of the Americas Suite 1134 New York NY 10104

BLITZ, STEPHEN MICHAEL, lawyer; b. N.Y.C., July 29, 1941; s. Leo and Dorothy B.; m. Ellen Sue Mintzer, Sept. 23, 1962; children: Catherine Denise, Thomas Joseph. B.A., Columbia U., 1962, B.S. in Elec. Engring., 1963; LL.B., Stanford U., 1966. Bar: Calif. 1967, U.S. Dist. Ct. (cen. dist.) Calif. 1967. Law clk. to judge U.S. Dist. Ct. Central Dist. Calif., 1966-67; ptnr. Gibson, Dunn & Crutcher, Los Angeles, 1967—; adj. prof. law U. West Los Angeles Sch. Law, 1978-80. Mem. ABA, Los Angeles County Bar Assn., Order of Coif. Office: Gibson Dunn & Crutcher 2029 Century Park E Sutie 4100 Los Angeles CA 90064

BLITZER, CHARLES, educational administrator; b. N.Y.C., Aug. 10, 1927; s. Max and Grace (Rosenberg) B. A.B., Williams Coll., 1947; M.A., Harvard U., 1949, Ph.D., 1952. Instr. polit. sci. Yale U., 1950-54, asst. prof., 1954-60; exec. asso. Am. Council Learned Socs., N.Y.C., 1960-65; dir. edn. Smithsonian Instn., Washington, 1965-68, asst. sec. for history and art, 1968-83; pres., dir. Nat. Humanities Center, Research Triangle Center, N.C., 1983—; lectr. New Sch. for Social Research, N.Y.C., 1960-61; vis. prof. City U. N.Y., 1964-65; staff dir. Nat. Commn. on Humanities, 1963-64; Mem. adminstrv. com. for Dumbarton Oaks, Harvard, 1968-75, mem. adv. bd., 1975—, chmn., 1978—; mem. U.S.-India Sub-Commn. on Edn. and Culture, 1974—, chmn. joint mus. com., 1974—; mem. vis. com. Research Center Linguistics and Semiotic Studies, Ind. U., 1980—; mem. vis. scholar com. Phi Beta Kappa, 1979—, mem. senate, 1982—; Alderman New Haven, 1955-60; bd. dirs. Central Atlantic Regional Edn. Lab., 1966-68; chmn. Com. Internat. Exchange Scholars, 1972-78, mem., 1978-81; mem. Nat. Adv. bd. Library of Congress Center for the Book, 1983—; trustee Exploratorium, 1977—, Smith Coll., 1979—. Author: (with C.J. Friederich) The Age of Power, 1957, An Immortal Commonwealth, 1960, The Age of Kings, 1967. Rockefeller Found. fellow, 1955-56; Huntington Library research grantee, 1957. Clubs: Cosmos (Washington); Century (N.Y.C.). Home: 3437 Dover Rd Durham NC 27707 Office: Nat Humanities Center 7 Alexander Dr Research Triangle Park NC 27709

BLIVEN, BRUCE, JR., writer; b. Los Angeles, Jan. 31, 1916; s. Bruce and Rose (Emery) B.; m. Naomi Horowitz, May 26, 1950; 1 son, Frederic Bruce. A.B., Harvard U., 1937. Reporter Manchester (Eng.) Guardian, 1936; editorial asst. New Republic mag., 1937-38; editorial writer N.Y. Post, 1939-42; contbr. to New Yorker (other nat. mags.), 1946—; Tchr. Ind. U. Writers Conf., 1955, 66. Author: The Wonderful Writing Machine, 1954, Battle for Manhattan, 1956, Under the Guns, 1972, Book Traveller, 1975, Volunteers, One and All, 1976, The Finishing Touch, 1978, New York: A Bicentennial History, 1981; juveniles The Story of D-Day, 1956, The American Revolution, 1958, From Pearl Harbor to Okinawa, 1960, From Casablanca To Berlin, 1965, (with Naomi Bliven) New York: The Story of the World's Most Exciting City, 1969. Served from pvt. to capt. F.A. AUS, 1942-45. Decorated Bronze Star with oak leaf cluster. Mem. Am. Soc. Journalists and Authors, Authors Guild (council 1970—), P.E.N., Soc. Am. Historians (exec. bd. 1975—). Office: care The New Yorker 25 W 43d St New York NY 10036

BLIVEN, NAOMI, book reviewer; b. N.Y.C., Dec. 28, 1925; d. Frederic and Minnie (Goodfriend) Horowitz; m. Bruce Bliven, Jr., May 26, 1950; 1 son, Frederic Bruce. A.B., Hunter Coll., 1945. Mem. editorial staff New Republic, 1945-47, Random House, 1949-54; book reviewer New Yorker mag., 1958—. Author: (with Bruce Bliven, Jr.) New York: The Story of the World's Most Exciting City, 1969. Mem. Nat. Book Critics Circle, P.E.N. (exec. bd.), Phi Beta Kappa. Office: care The New Yorker 25 W 43d St New York NY 10036

BLIWAS, RONALD LEE, advertising agency executive; b. Pitts., Dec. 23, 1942; s. Reuben and Freda (Fingeret) B.; m. Linda Prince, Sept. 13, 1964; children: Deborah, Michael. B.S., U. Ariz., 1964. Trainee mktg. H.J. Heinz, Pitts., 1964-65; account exec. Edward Weiss & Co., Chgo., 1965-68; v.p., dir. mktg. Rhodes Pharmacal, Chgo., 1968-70; asst. to pres. and v.p. A. Eicoff & Co., Chgo., 1970-80, pres., 1980—. Mem. Young Pres.'s Orgn. Club: Ill. Athletic (dir. 1983). Home: 365 Lincolnwood Dr Highland park IL 60035 Office: 520 N Michigan Ave Chicago IL 60611

BLIZNAKOV, EMILE GEORGE, scientist; b. Kamen, Bulgaria, July 28, 1926; came to U.S., 1961, naturalized, 1966; s. George P. and Paraskeva B. M.D. Faculty of Medicine, Sofia, Bulgaria, 1953; Dir. Regional Sta. for Hygiene and Epidemiology, chief dist. dept. health, Pirdop, Bulgaria, 1953-55; staff scientist, microbiologist Research Inst. Epidemiology and Microbiology, Ministry of Public Health, Sofia, 1955-59; vis. scientist Gamaleya Research Inst. Epidemiology and Microbiology, Acad. Med. Scis., Moscow, 1958-59; sr. staff scientist, prof. life scis. New Eng. Inst., Ridgefield, Conn., 1961-81, dir. personnel, 1968-74, v.p., 1974-76, pres., 1976-81; exec. dir. research and devel. Libra Research, 1981—; pres., sci. dir. Lupus Research Inst., Rockville, Md., 1981—; dir. Child Safety Corp.; cons. to indsl., pharm. and public relations firms. Contbr. articles to profl. jours. Fannie E. Rippel Found. grantee, 1972-80; G.M. McDonald Found. grantee, 1972-81; Whitehall Found. grantee, 1971-75; Wallace Genetic Found. grantee, 1972-81. Fellow Royal Soc. Tropical Medicine and Hygiene (London); mem. AMA, Am. Fedn. Clin. Research, Am. Soc. Microbiology, N.Y. Acad. Scis., Am. Coll. Toxicology, Am. Soc. Neurochemistry, Reticuloendothelial Soc., Bioelectromagnetic Soc., AAAS. Home: 189 Ledges Rd Ridgefield CT 06877 Office: Lupus Research Inst 1300 Piccard Dr Rockville MD 20850

BLIZNAKOV, MILKA TCHERNEVA, architect; b. Varna, Bulgaria, Sept. 20, 1927; came to U.S., 1961, naturalized, 1966; d. Ivan Dimitrov and Maria Kesarova (Khorozova) Tchernev; m. Emile G. Bliznakov, Oct. 23, 1954 (div. Apr., 1974). Architect-engr. diploma, State Tech. U., Sofia, 1951; Ph.D., Engring.-Structural Inst., Sofia, 1959, Columbia U., 1971. Sr. researcher Ministry Heavy Industry, Sofia, 1950-53; pvt. practice architecture, Sofia, 1954-59; assoc. architect Noal Combrisson, Paris, 1959-61; designer Perkins & Will Partnership, White Plains, N.Y., 1963-67; project architect Lathrop Douglass, N.Y.C., 1967-71; assoc. prof. architecture and planning Sch. Architecture, U. Tex., Austin, 1972-74; prof. Coll. Architecture, Va. Poly. Inst. and State U., Blacksburg, 1974—. Prin. works include Speedwell Ave. Urban Renewal, Morristown, N.J., 1967-69, Wilmington (Del.) Urban Renewal, 1968-70, Springfield (Ill.) Central Area Devel, 1969-71, Arlington County (Va.) Redevel, 1975-77. William Kinne scholar, summer 1970; NEA grantee, 1973-74; Am. Beautiful Found. grantee, 1973; Fulbright Hays research fellow, 1983-84. Mem. Am. Assn. Tchrs. Slavic and E. European Langs., Soc. Archtl. Historians, Nat. Trust Hist. Preservation, Am. Assn. Advancement of Slavic Studies, Assn. Collegiate Schs. of Planning, Assn. Collegiate Schs. of Architecture. Home: 219 Pine Dr Blacksburg VA 24060 Office: Coll Architecture Va Poly Inst and State U Blacksburg VA 24061 *I was in the first grade when my father asked me one evening if I had rather play with my friends or study. When I chose play he took me in his arms and said, "Remember, that when the sun goes down in the evening one day of your precious life ends. The value of that day of life is yours to name. Whatever you choose to do during the day should be worth a day of life. Ask yourself every evening what did you exchange a day of life for? Did you enrich yourself with experiences, knowledge, good deeds or did you throw away a day of life for nothing? These words have guided my entire life.*

BLIZZARD, ALAN, artist; b. Boston, Mar. 25, 1939; s. Thomas and Elizabeth B. Student, Mass. Sch. Art; M.A., U. Ariz.; M.F.A., U. Iowa, 1958. Instr. in art U. Iowa; vis. asst. prof. art Albion Coll., U. Okla.; asso. prof. UCLA; now prof. painting Scripps Coll. and; Claremont Grad. Sch. Represented in permanent collections, Bklyn. Mus., Met. Mus. Art, N.Y.C., Art Inst. Chgo., Denver Art Mus., La Jolla (Calif.) Mus. Art. Office: Scripps Coll Claremont CA 91711

BLIZZARD, ROBERT M., educator; b. East St. Louis, Ill., June 20, 1924; s. Robert Watson and Gertrude (Oechsner) B.; m. Gladys Schmelter, June 24, 1950; children—Janice Lyn, Robert Steven. B.S., Northwestern U., 1949, M.D., 1952. Intern Iowa Meml. Hosp., Des Moines, 1952-53; resident pediatrics Blank Meml. Hosp. Children, Des Moines, 1953-55; postgrad. tng. Johns Hopkins Sch. Medicine, 1955-57; asst. prof. pediatrics and medicine Ohio State U. Sch. Medicine, 1957-60; mem. faculty Johns Hopkins Sch. Medicine, 1960-75, dir. nat. pituitary agy., 1963-67, prof. pediatrics, 1967-74; chmn. dept. pediatrics U. Va. Sch. Medicine, Charlottesville, 1974—; cons. NIH, 1970—. Author med. textbooks, articles. Recipient merit award Northwestern U. as alumnus contbg. health and sci., 1972; Ayerst award Endocrine Soc., 1973. Mem. Am. Thyroid Assn., Soc. Pediatric Research, Am. Pediatric Soc., Am. Fedn. Clin. Research, Endocrine Soc., Lawson Wilkins Pediatric Endocrinology Soc., Sigma Xi. Home: Box 121 Ivy VA 22945

BLOCH, ALAN NEIL, federal judge; b. Pitts., Apr. 12, 1932; s. Gustave James and Molly Dorothy B.; m. Elaine Claire Amdur, Aug. 24, 1957; children: Rebecca Lee, Carolyn Jean, Evan Amdur. B.S. in Econs, U. Pa., 1953; J.D., U. Pitts., 1958. Bar: Pa. 1959. Indsl. engr. U.S. Steel Corp., 1953; pvt. practice, then individual practice, Pitts., 1959-79; U.S. judge Western Dist. Pa., Pitts., 1979—. Contbr. articles to legal publs. Vice chmn. Stadium Authority Pitts., 1970—; bd. dirs. St. John's Gen. Hosp., Pitts., 1975—. Served with AUS, 1953-55. Mem. Am. Bar Assn., Pa. Bar Assn., Allegheny County Bar Assn., Acad. Trial Lawyers Allegheny County. Jewish. Club: Allegheny. Office: 1014 US Post Office and Courthouse Pittsburgh PA 15219

BLOCH, E. MAURICE, art historian, educator; b. N.Y.C.; s. Leonard and Rose (von Auspitz) B. B.F.A., N.Y.U., 1939; student, Harvard, 1941-42; A.M., N.Y. U., 1942, Ph.D., 1957. With Met. Mus. Art, 1943; instr. art history U. Mo., 1943-44; lectr. art history N.Y.U., 1945-46, U. Minn., 1946-47; Keeper drawings and prints, prof. chalcography Cooper Union, 1949-53; prof. art history, dir., curator Grunwald Center for the Graphic Arts, UCLA, 1956-83; Bd. dirs., v.p. Virginia Steele Scott Found., Pasadena, Calif.; bd. dirs. Tamarind Inst., U. N.Mex., Albuquerque, Print Council Am., Lovis Corinth Meml. Found., N.Y., UCLA Art Council, Am. Art Council, Los Angeles County Mus. Art. Author: Evolution of an Artist, 1967, Catalogue Raisonne, 1967, The Drawings of George Caleb Bingham, 1975, also articles, revs., mus. and art gallery publns. Recipient Founders Day award of achievement N.Y.U., 1957, Western Heritage Center award, 1968; Belgian Am. Ednl. Found. traveling fellow, Belgium, 1951; Am. Council Learned Socs. grant-in-aid, 1962. Mem. Coll. Art Assn. Am., Art Historians So. Calif., Art Students League, Manuscript Soc., Hist. Soc. Mo. Home: 2253 Veteran Ave Los Angeles CA 90064

BLOCH, ERICH, electrical engineer; b. Sulzburg, Ger., Jan. 9, 1925; came to U.S., 1948, naturalized, 1952; s. Joseph and Tony B.; m. Renee Stern, Mar. 4, 1948; 1 dau., Rebecca Bloch Rosen. Student, Fed. Poly. Inst., Zurich, Switzerland, 1945-48; B.S. in Elec. Engring, U. Buffalo, 1952. With IBM Corp., 1952—, v.p. gen. mgr., East Fishkill, N.Y., 1975-80, v.p. tech. personnel devel., Armonk, N.Y., 1980—; mem. com. computers in automated mfg. NRC, 1980—; Trustee Marist Coll., Poughkeepsie, N.Y., 1978—. Author. Fellow IEEE; mem. Nat. Acad. Engring., AAAS, Am. Soc. Mfg. Engrs. (hon.). Patentee in field. Office: 1000 Westchester Ave Harrison NY 10604

BLOCH, ERNEST, educator; b. Baden-Baden, Germany, Jan. 29, 1921; came to U.S., 1936, naturalized, 1943; s. Gustave and Dora (Hammel) B.; m. Amy Weiss; 1 son, Geoffrey. B.S., CCNY, 1943; M.A., Columbia U., 1949; Ph.D., New Sch. for Social Research, 1962. Economist Fed. Res. Bank of N.Y., N.Y.C., 1949-60, spl. asst., 1961-62; asso. prof. N.Y. U., 1962-65, prof. fin., 1965, C.W. Gerstenberg prof. fin., N.Y.C., 1966—; cons. Bd. dirs. Chatham Towers Coop., 1977-78; mem. N.Y. U. Senate; mem. budget com. N.Y. U., 1971-74. Author, editor: (with R.A. Schwartz) Impending Changed in Securities Markets, 1979; contbr. articles to profl. publs. Served with U.S. Army, 1942-45. Decorated Bronze Star. Mem. Am. Econ. Assn., Downtown Economist Luncheon Group, Beta Gamma Sigma. Home: 100 Bleecker St New York NY 10012 Office: NY U Washington Sq New York NY 10003

BLOCH, HENRY SIMON, economist; b. County Kehl, Baden, Germany, Apr. 6, 1915; came to U.S., 1937, naturalized, 1943; s. Edward and Claire (Bloch) B.; 1 dau., Miriam Bloch Feuerstein. Dr. Laws (Econs.), U. Nancy, 1937; Dr.h.c. in Econs., Polit. Social Scis, Free U. of Brussels, 1969; fellow, Acad. Internat. Law, The Hague, summer 1937. Research asst. U. Chgo., 1938; lectr. Inst. for Mil. Studies, 1941-42, instr. econs., 1943; research supr. Civil Affairs Tng. Sch. for Army and Navy Officers, 1943-45; cons. Fgn. Econ. Adminstrn., 1945; economist Treasury Dept., 1945-46, mem. Treasury del. for tax treaty negotiations, France, U.K., Benelux, 1946; sect. chief UN, 1947-49, dir. fiscal and financial br., 1955-62; acting dir. Bur. Econ. Affairs, 1958-59; dir. Bur. Tech. Assistance, 1959-62, dep. commr. for tech. assistance, 1961-62; pres. Zinder Internat. Ltd., 1962-66; v.p., dir. E.M. Warburg & Co., Inc., 1966-70; sr. v.p. E.M. Warburg, Pincus & Co., Inc., 1970-75, exec. v.p., 1976-81, mng. dir., 1982—; dir. affiliated cos.; adviser to banks, corps., govts.; vis. prof. econs. Yale, 1955; lectr. law Columbia, 1955-63, adj. prof. law and internat. relations, 1963—; guest prof. U. Chile, summer 1958; adviser UN Consultative Com. for Asian Devel. Bank, Bangkok, 1965; chmn., dir. UNITAR Seminar on Internat. Monetary System, 1972; mem. UN Experts Group for Establishment of a Trade and Investment Bank for ACP Group of States, 1978-79. Author: The Challenge of the World Trade Conference, 1965, Financial Strategy for Developing Nations, 1969, Export Financing Emerging as a Major Policy Problem, 1976, Foreign Risk Judgement for Commercial Banks, 1977; co-author: Yale Law Journal Symposium on World Organization, 1946, Legal-Economic Problems of International Trade, 1961, The Global Partnership, 1968, Financial Integration in Western Europe, 1969; contbg. author: Multinational Banking: Theory and Regulation, 1978; Contbr. to econ., legal jours. Decorated comdr. Order of Leopold II, Belgium).; Asso. fellow Berkeley Coll., Yale U., 1977—. Mem. Am. Econ. Assn., Council Fgn. Relations, Soc. Royale d'Economie Politique de Belgique (hon.). Clubs: Cosmos (Washington); Faculty (Columbia). Office: 277 Park Ave New York City NY 10172

BLOCH, HENRY WOLLMAN, tax preparation company executive; b. Kansas City, Mo., July 30, 1922; s. Leon Edwin and Hortense Bienenstok; m. Marion Ruth Helzberg, June 16, 1951; children: Robert, Thomas M., Mary Jo, Elizabeth Ann. B.S., U. Mich., 1943; D.B.A. (hon.), Avila Coll., 1977, LL.D., N.H. Coll., 1983. Partner United Bus. Co., 1946-55; pres., chief exec. officer, dir. H & R Block, Inc., Kansas City, 1955—; dir. Employers Reins. Corp., Commerce

Bank Kansas City, Nat. Fidelity Life Ins. Co., Southwestern Bell Corp. Bd. dirs., vice chmn. Kansas City Art Inst.; past trustee Clearinghouse for Midcontinent Founds.; bd. dirs. Menorah Med. Center; bd. dirs., past pres. Menorah Med. Center Found.; former mem. president's adv. council Kansas City Philharmonic Assn.; pres. H & R Bloch Found.; trustee U. Mo. at Kansas City, William Rockhill Nelson Gallery Art; former trustee Am. Mus. Assn.; bd. dirs. Jewish Fedn. and Council Greater Kansas City; dir., past pres. Civic Council Greater Kansas City; bd. dirs. St. Luke's Hosp.; former mem. bd. dirs. Council of Fellows of Nelson Gallery Found., Am. Jewish Com.; former mem. bd. govs. Kansas City Mus. History and Sci.; bd. dirs. Midwest Research Inst., Kansas City Symphony, Greater Kansas City Community Found.; gen. chmn. Heart of Am. United Way Exec. Com., 1978; past met. chmn. Nat. Alliance Businessmen; former mem. bd. regents Rockhurst Coll.; former mem. bd. chancellor's assocs. U. Kans. at Lawrence; former mem. bd. dirs. Harry S Truman Good Neighbor Award Found.; bd. dirs. Internat. Relations Council; bd. dirs., v.p. Kansas City Area Health Planning Council; past pres. Found. for a Greater Kansas City. Served to 1st lt. USAAF, 1943-45. Named Mktg. Man of Yr. Sales and Mktg. Execs. Club, 1971, Chief Exec. Officer of Yr. for service industry Fin. World, 1976; Decorated Air medal with three oak leaf clusters.; recipient Disting. Exec. award Boy Scouts Am., 1977, Salesman of Yr. Kansas City Advt. Club, 1978, Civic Service award Hyman Brand Hebrew Acad., 1980, Chancellor's medal U. Mo.-Kansas City, 1980, President's trophy Kansas City Jaycees, 1980, W.F. Yates medal for disting. service in civic affairs William Jewell Coll., 1981, bronze award for service industry Wall Street Transcript, 1981, Disting. Missourian award NCCJ, 1982, Lester A. Milgram Humanitarian award, 1983, Hall of Fame award Internat. Franchise Assn., 1983; named to Bus. Leader Hall of Fame Jr. Achievement, 1980. Mem. Assn. Trusts and Founds., Greater Kansas City C. of C. (past pres.), C. of C. Greater Kansas City (Mr. Kansas City award 1978). Jewish. Clubs: Oakwood Country, River, Racquet (Kansas City); Carriage. Office: 4410 Main St Kansas City MO 64111

BLOCH, HERMAN SAMUEL, chemist; b. Chgo., June 15, 1912; s. Aaron and Esther (Broder) B.; m. Elaine J. Kahn, July 4, 1940; children—Aaron N., Janet L. (Mrs. Daniel Martin), Merry D. (Mrs. Dobroslav Valik). B.S., U. Chgo., 1933, Ph.D., 1936. With UOP, Inc., Des Plaines, Ill., 1936-77, asso. dir. research, 1964-73, dir. catalysis research, 1973-77, cons., 1977—; Chmn. com. phys. scis. Ill. Bd. Higher Edn., 1969-71. Author. Commr. Housing Authority Cook County, 1966—, chmn., 1971—; chmn. Skokie (Ill.) Human Relations Commn., 1965-71; pres. bd. edn. Skokie Sch. Dist. 68, 1962-63; trustee Skokie Library Bd., 1981—. Recipient E.V. Murphree award indsl. and engrng. chemistry Am. Chem. Soc., 1974; Eugene J. Houdry award Catalysis Soc., 1971; I-R 100 award Indsl. Research mag., 1973. Hon. mem. Am. Inst. Chemists (honor scroll 1957); mem. Am. Chem. Soc. (chmn. bd. 1973-77), AAAS (v.p. for chemistry 1970), Nat. Acad. Scis., Soc. Chem. Industry, Nat. Acad. Sci., Ill. Acad. Sci., N.Y. Acad. Sci., Chemists Club Chgo., Phi Beta Kappa (pres. Chgo. 1968-69), Sigma Xi. Patentee petroleum refining, catalysis, petrochems. Home and Office: 9700 Kedvale Ave Skokie IL 60076

BLOCH, KONRAD, biochemist; b. Neisse, Germany, Jan. 12, 1912; came to U.S., 1936, naturalized, 1944; s. Frederick D. and Hedwig (Steimer) B.; m. Lore Teutsch, Feb. 15, 1941; children—Peter, Susan. Chem.Eng., Technische Hochschule, Munich, Germany, 1934; Ph.D., Columbia, 1938. Asst. prof. biochemistry U. Chgo., 1946-50, prof., 1950-54; Higgins prof. biochemistry Harvard, 1954—. Recipient Nobel prize in physiology and medicine, 1964; Ernest Guenther award in chemistry of essential oils and related products, 1965. Fellow Am. Acad. Scis.; mem. Nat. Acad. Scis., Am. Philos. Soc. Office: Dept Biochemistry Harvard U 12 Oxford St Cambridge MA 02138 *

BLOCH, KURT JULIUS, physician; b. Germany, Oct. 17, 1929; s. Max and Mathilde B.; m. Margot Bendit, June 25, 1953; children—Kenneth D., Donald B. B.S., CCNY, 1951; M.D., N.Y. U., 1955. Diplomate: Am. Bd. Internal Medicine, Am. Bd. Allergy and Immunology. Intern, asst. resident Bellevue Hosp., N.Y.C., 1955-57; resident in medicine Mass. Gen. Hosp., Boston, 1960-61; instr. medicine Harvard Med. Sch., Boston, 1963-65, asso. in medicine, 1965-68, asst. prof., 1968-70, asso. prof., 1970-74, prof., 1974—; physician Mass. Gen. Hosp., 1974—, chief clin. immunology and allergy units, 1976—; sr. investigator Arthritis Found., 1964-69. Contbr. articles to profl. jours. Served with USPHS, 1957-60. Mem. Am. Soc. Clin. Investigation. Office: Mass Gen Hosp Boston MA 02114

BLOCH, MARTIN B., electronics company executive; b. Ivja, Poland, Dec. 26, 1935; came to U.S., 1951, naturalized, 1956; s. O. and Sonia B.; children: Jerrold, Helen. B.E.E., CCNY, 1955. Engr. research and devel. staff Bulova Watch Co., Woodside, N.Y., 1955-57, jr. engr., acting chief test engr., dept. head frequency control systems, 1957-59, chief engr. electronics div., 1959-61; pres. Frequency Electronics, Inc., Mitchel Field, N.Y., 1961—; dir. Jaco Electronics, Hauppauge, N.Y. Office: Frequency Electronics Inc 3 Delaware Dr Mitchel Field NY 11553

BLOCH, MILTON JOSEPH, mus. adminstr.; b. Bronx, N.Y., Apr. 1, 1937; s. Seymore Jerome and Evelyn Joliet (Foltz) B.; m. Mary E. Lynn, June 2, 1962; 1 dau., Kimberly Dacia. B.Indsl. Design, Pratt Inst., 1958; M.F.A., U. Fla., 1961. Head art dept. Lake-Sumter Community Coll., Leesburg, Fla., 1961-63; dir. Pesacola (Fla.) Art Center, 1964-65, Mus. of Sci. and History, Little Rock, 1966-68, Monmouth (N.J.) Mus., 1968-76, Mint Mus., Charlotte, N.C., 1976—. Editor: Southeastern Mus. Conf. Jour, 1978—. Served with U.S. Army, 1958-61. Mem. Southeastern Mus. Conf., Am. Assn. Mus., N.C. Mus. Assn. Home: 1824 Asheville Pl Charlotte NC 28203 Office: 501 Hempstead Pl Charlotte NC 28207

BLOCH, PAUL, public relations executive; b. Bklyn., July 17, 1939; s. Edwin Lionel and Antoinette (Greenberg) B. B.B. Polit. Sci., UCLA, 1962. Publicist Rogers & Cowan, Beverly Hills, Calif., 1962-70, v.p., 1970-75, sr. v.p., ptnr., 1975-83, exec. v.p., sr. ptnr., 1983—. Advisor Pres.'s Council on Phys. Fitness and Sports, Washington, 1982—; sr. v.p. Barbara Caan Fund-City of Hope Hosp., Los Angeles, 1981—; asst. Am. Cancer Soc., United Way, Am. Diabetes Assn., UNICEF, 1975—; adv. council Orange County Sheriff's Dept., 1980—. Served with U.S. Army, 1957. Mem. Publicists Guild of Am. (award for publicity campaign for Brian's Song 1972), Country Music Assn. Jewish. Clubs: Touch, Pips. Office: Rogers & Cowan 9665 Wilshire Blvd Suite 200 Beverly Hills CA 90212

BLOCH, RICHARD A., tax preparation company executive; b. 1926; married. B.S., U. Pa. With Stern Bros., 1945-46, Harelette Mfg. Co., 1946-47; ptnr. United Bus. Co., 1947-51; co-founder H & R Block, Inc., Kansas City, Mo., 1955, present chmn. bd. Office: H & R Block Inc 4410 Main St Kansas City MO 64111 *

BLOCH, RICHARD ISAAC, labor arbitrator; b. East Orange, N.J., June 15, 1943; s. Jacques Henry and Hannah (Levi) B.; m. Susan Low, July 11, 1966; children: Rebecca Low, Michael Low. A.B., Dartmouth Coll., 1965; J.D., U. Mich., 1968, M.B.A., 1974. Bar: Mich. 1969, D.C. bar 1975. Asso. firm Seyfarth, Shaw Fairweather & Geraldson, Chgo., 1968; lectr. U. Mich. Grad. Sch. Bus. Adminstrn., 1969-71; asst. prof. law U. Detroit, 1971-75; prin. Richard I. Bloch, P.C. (labor arbitrator), Washington, 1969—; vis. prof. law Wayne State U., summer 1974, George Washington U., 1983; adj. prof. Am. U., 1978; chmn. fgn. service grievance bd. Dept. State, 1977-80; chief umpire United Mine Workers and Bituminous Coal Operators Assn., 1980—; permanent arbitrator Maj. League Baseball, 1983. Author: Arbitration of Discipline Cases, 1979; contbr. articles to law jours. Mem. Dartmouth Coll. Alumni Council, 1974-77. Mem. Mich. Bar Assn., D.C. Bar Assn., Am. Bar Assn., Indsl. Relations Research Assn., Nat. Acad. Arbitrators (exec. sec.-treas.). Home and Office: 4335 Cathedral Ave NW Washington DC 20016

BLOCH, ROBERT ALBERT, author; b. Chgo., Apr. 5, 1917; s. Raphael A. and Stella A. (Loeb) B.; m. Eleanor Alexander, Oct. 16, 1964; 1 dau. by previous marriage, Sally Ann. Student public schs., Maywood, Ill. and Milw. Free lance writer, 1934-42, 53—; copywriter Gustav Marx Advt. Agy., Milw., Wis., 1942-53; lectr. various schs. and community orgns., 1946—. Author numerous books of fantasy and suspense fiction, 1945—; latest being The King of Terrors, 1977; The Best of Robert Bloch, 1977, Out of the Mouths of Graves, 1978, Strange Eons, 1979, Such Stuff as Screams Are Made Of, 1979, There is a Serpent in Eden, 1979, La Boite a Malefices de Robert Bloch, 1981, Mysteries of the Worm, 1981, Psycho II, 1982, Le Scene Finale, 1982, Parlez-moi d'horreur, 1982, Le Demon Noir, 1983, Dr. Holmes Modern Castle, 1983, Twilight Zone-The Movie, 1983, Les Yeux de la Momie, 1984, The Night of the Ripper, 1984; screenplays The Couch, 1960; The Cabinet of Caligari, 1961, Straitjacket, 1963, The Night Walker, 1964, The Psychopath, 1965, (with Anthony Marriott) The Deadly Bees, 1966, Torture Garden, 1967, The House That Dripped Blood, 1970, Asylum, 1972; also numerous radio scripts and teleplays; Contbr. numerous short stories to various mags. and lit. jours.; Editor: The Best of Fredric Brown, 1977. Recipient E.E. Evans Meml. award, 1958, Screen Writer's award, 1960, Inkpot award for Sci. Fiction, 1964, Award for Service to Field of Sci. Fantasy Los Angeles Sci. Fantasy Soc., 1974, Fritz Leiber Fantasy award, 1978, World Sci. Fiction Conv. Hugo award, 1958, Edgar Allan Poe Scroll, 1960, Trieste Film Festival award, 1964, Reims Festival award, 1979. Mem. Writers Guild Am., Sci. Fiction Writers Am., Mystery Writers Am. (pres. 1970-71), Acad. of Motion Pictures Arts and Scis. Office: Shapiro-Lichtman Talent Agy 1800 Ave of the Stars Los Angeles CA 90067 *When writing novels such as Psycho, my primary purpose is to entertain—but there is nothing which prevents an entertainer from expressing more serious concerns. In recent years, I have addressed myself to the question of violence, not merely as subject-matter for fiction, but as it affects us in all-too-grim reality. It is my hope to offer some minor insight into what I believe to be a major problem of our times.*

BLOCK, AMANDA ROTH, artist; b. Louisville, Feb. 20, 1912; d. Albert Solomon and Helen (Bernheim) Roth; m. Maurice Block, Jr., July 15, 1949; 1 son, Joseph G. Wolf. Student, Smith Coll., 1930-31, U. Cin., 1933, Art Acad. Cin., 1933-40; B.F.A., Ind. U., 1960. Instr. Herron Sch. Art, U. Ind., 1969-73; instr. lithography Indpls. Art League, 1974; mem. adv. bd. Indpls. Art League Found., 1979—. One-man shows, 1444 Gallery, Indpls., 1962, Sheldon Swope Art Gallery, Terre Haute, Ind., 1963, 73, Park Avenue Gallery, Indpls., 1964, Harriet Crane Gallery, Cin., 1965, Talbot Gallery, Indpls., 1967, Merida Gallery, Louisville, Herron Mus. Art, Indpls., 1969, Editions Ltd. Gallery, Indpls., 1972, 79, Franklin (Ind.) Coll., 1973, Tucson Mus. Sch., 1977, two-man shows, Jason Gallery, N.Y.C., 1964, Orange County Coll., Middletown, N.Y., Washington Gallery, Frankfort, Ind., 1975, Edits. Ltd. Gallery, Indpls., 1983; exhibited in group shows, Chgo. Art Inst., 1941, Butler Inst. Am. Art, Youngstown, Ohio, Burr Gallery, N.Y.C., Hanover Coll., Wabash, Ind., De Pauw U., Soc. Am. Graphic Artists AAA Gallery, Purdue U., Istan Gallery, Tokyo, Phila. Print Club, Pa. Acad. Fine Arts, 1969, Imprint Gallery, San Francisco, 1972, Van Straaten Gallery, Chgo., 1973, Monay Inst., San Antonio, 1972, Pratt Graphics, N.Y.C., 1976, Ind. State Mus., Indpls. Mus. Art, 1977, Tucson Mus. Art, 1978, internat. traveling exhbn., Soc. Am. Graphic Artists, 1974-75, traveling exhbn., 1977, 78; represented in permanent collections, Continental Ill. Bank, Chgo., De Pauw U., Ind. State Coll., Terre Haute, Ind., Med. Soc., Indpls., Sheldon Swope Art Gallery, Stevens Coll., Boston Public Library, USIA, Lafayette (Ind.) Art Center, Lippman Assos., architects, Indpls., J.B. Speed Mus., Louisville, IBM Bldg., Indpls., Phila Mus. Art, Bklyn. Mus., Cin. Art Mus., N.Y. Public Library, Columbua U. Gallery, N.Y.C., Biodynamics Inc., Indpls., Fidelity Bank, Carmel, Ind., Tuscon Mus. Art. Recipient award Ben and Beatrice Goldstein Found., N.Y.C., 1971. Mem. Soc. Am. Graphic Artists. Jewish. Home: 6000 Spring Mill Rd Indianapolis IN 46208

BLOCK, BERNARD FRANCIS, communications industry executive; b. Louisville, Dec. 24, 1936; s. Edward Francis and May Andrew (Hardesty) B.; m. Anne R. Solgere, Sept. 5, 1959 (div. June 1975); children: David J., Sarah Elizabeth, Mary Susan; m. Christine A. Seelmeyer, Feb. 9, 1980; 1 son, Andrew F. B.A., Bellarmine Coll., Louisville, 1958; M.B.A., Ind. U., 1960. Acct. Gen. Electric Co., Louisville, 1970-76, v.p., 1974-76, pres. subs. DRC, 1976-80, sr. v.p., 1980—, dir., 1980—; dir. WHAS, Inc., Standard Gravure Corp. Chmn. bd. overseers Bellarmine Coll., 1979-81; dir. Better Bus. Bur., Louisville, 1982—; sect. chmn. Met. United Way, 1983. Served with USMC, 1958-59. Mem. Leadership Louisville Found., 1980-81; named Alumnus of Yr. Bellarmine Coll., 1977. Mem. Louisville C. of C. (dir.), Beta Gamma Sigma. Lodge: Louisville Rotary. *

BLOCK, DENNIS JEFFERY, lawyer; b. Bronx, N.Y., Sept. 1, 1942; s. Martin and Betty (Berger) B.; m. Hedy Elizabeth Troupin, Nov. 27, 1967; children: Robert, Tracy, Meredith. B.A., U. Buffalo, 1964; LL.B., Bklyn. Law Sch., 1967. Bar: N.Y. 1968, U.S. Dist. Ct. (ea. dist.) N.Y., U.S. Dist. Ct. (so. dist.) N.Y., U.S. Ct. Appeals (2d and 3d cirs.). Br. chief SEC, Washington, 1967-72; assoc. Weil, Gotshal & Manges, N.Y.C., 1972-74, ptnr., 1974—. Co-editor: The Corporate Counselor's Desk Book, 1982; contbr. articles to profl. jours. Mem. ABA. Home: 22 Maple Dr Port Washington NY 11050 Office: Weil Gotshal & Manges 767 Fifth Ave New York NY 10153

BLOCK, DUANE LLEWELLYN, physician; b. Madison, Wis., Dec. 27, 1926; s. Cecil Jay and Josephine Amanda (Holten) B.; m. Mary Jane Lohrman, Sept. 10, 1949 (dec. Oct. 1980); children: Susan Block Rupe, Jeffrey Holten; m. 2d Kathleen Sylvia Smith, June 5, 1982. B.S., U. Wis., 1949, M.D., 1951. Diplomate: Am. Bd. Preventive Medicine. Intern Harper Hosp., Detroit, 1951-52; resident Gen. Motors Occupational Medicine Tng. Program, 1952; plant physician Cadillac div. Gen. Motors Corp., Detroit, 1952-54; med. dir. Gen. Motors Tech. Ctr., Detroit, 1954-55; physician in charge Rouge Med. Ford Motor Co., Dearborn, Mich., 1955-70, med. dir., 1970—; cons. prof. health scis. Oakland U. Center Health Services, Rochester, Mich., 1978—; clin. asst. prof. Wayne State U. Sch. Medicne, Detroit, 1960—; clin. assoc. prof. U. Wis. Health Scis., 1980—; non-resident lectr. U. Mich. Sch. Pub. Health, Ann Arbor, Mich., 1960—. Trustee Mich. Heart Assn., Detroit, 1971-80; mem. policy council Mich. Cancer Found., Detroit, 1974—; dir. Mental Health Assn. Mich., Detroit, 1982—; trustee Maplegrove-Henry Ford Hosp., Detroit, 1981—; trustee, vice-chmn. Rehab. Inst., Detroit, 1973—. Served with USN, 1945-46. Recipient Pres. award Mich. State Med. Soc., 1969, Weisfeldt Meml. award Med. Coll. Wis., 1976. Fellow Am. Occupational Med. Assn. (pres. 1969, meritorious service award 1972, pres., William S. Knudsen award 1975), Am. Acad. Occupational Medicine (Robert A. Kehoe award 1981), Am. Coll. Preventive Medicine (editorial bd. 1982—); mem. Am. Bd. Preventive Medicine (chmn. 1977), AMA, Mich. State Med. Soc., Wayne County Med. Soc. Republican. Presbyterian. Home: 3699 Brookside Dr Bloomfield Hill MI 48013 Office: Ford Motor Co 900 Parklane Towers W Dearborn MI 48126

BLOCK, EMIL NATHANIEL, JR., air force officer; b. Newark, Ohio, Oct. 3, 1930; s. Emil Nathaniel and Louise Jeanette (Palmer) B.; m. Marian Lou Davis, June 9, 1956; children—Eric, Emil Darin. B.S., U.S. Naval Acad., 1956; M.S.E. in Instrumentation, U. Mich., 1961, U. Mich., 1961, George Washington U., 1966. Commd. 2d lt. U.S. Air Force, 1956, advanced through grades to maj. gen., 1979; spl. asst. for B-1 matters, dep. chief staff for research and devel. Hdqrs. USAF, Washington, 1976-78; chief of staff mil. airlift command, dir. Air Force C-X task force, Scott AFB, Ill., 1978-80; dir. plans Hdqrs. USAF, Pentagon, Washington, 1980-81. Decorated D.S.M. (2), Legion of Merit (3), D.F.C., Bronze Star, Meritorious Service medal (2), Air medal (5); Jimmy Doolittle fellow, 1978. Mem. Air Force Assn.

BLOCK, FRANK EMMANUEL, assn. exec.; b. Ashville, N.C., May 15, 1925; s. Hamilton and Evelyn Gail (Johnson) B.; m. Anne Nimmons Burckhardt, Aug. 31, 1948; children—Frank Emmanuel, Jeannette B. Depoy. B.E. with honors in Mech. Engrng, Yale, 1948, B.S. in Indsl. Adminstrn, 1949; student, London U., Vanderbilt U., U. Ga., Ga. Tech. Vice pres. Citizens & So. Nat. Bank, Atlanta, 1949-70; sr. v.p. Girard Trust Bank, Phila., 1970-73; pres. Studley Shupert & Co., Phila., Inc., 1973; v.p., dir. Model Roland & Co., Inc., 1973-74, Shields Model Roland Inc., 1974-77, Bache Halsey Stuart Shields, 1977-79; mem. Fin. Acctg. Standards Bd., Stamford, Conn., 1979—; Trustee Tchrs. Retirement System of Ga., 1962-70, Fin. Analysts Research Found., 1972-78. Editor: Personel Trust Investment Management, 1969; asso. editor: Fin. Analysts Jour, 1965-79, C.F.A. Digest, 1971-79; Contbr. articles to profl. jours. Served with AUS, 1943-45. Mem. Inst. Chartered Fin. Analysts (pres. 1972-73, Sheppard award 1979), Fin. Analysts Fedn. (pres. 1969-70, Graham and Dodd award 1964, hon. mention 1966, Disting. Service award 1977), Fin. Analysts of Phila., atlanta Soc. Security Analysts (pres. 1963-64), N.Y. Soc. Security Analysts. Episcopalian. Clubs: Piedmont Driving (Atlanta); Yale (N.Y.C.); Yale of Ga. (pres. 1962). Home: 191 South Ave New Canaan CT 06840 Office: Fin Acctg Standards Bd High Ridge Park Stamford CT 06905

BLOCK, GEORGE EDWARD, surgeon; b. Joliet, Ill., Sept. 16, 1926; s. Edward J. and Florence (Hyl) B.; m. Mary Cobb, Nov. 26, 1966; children: George, John, Edward. B.S., Northwestern U., 1947; M.D., U. Mich., 1951, M.S. in Surgery, 1958. Diplomate: Am. Bd. Surgery. Mem. faculty U. Chgo. Med. Sch., 1961—, prof. surgery, pres. med. staff, 1979—, Thomas D. Jones prof. surgery, 1984—, head. surg. oncology, 1970—; cons. U.S. Naval Hosp. Gt. Lakes, Ill. Author articles in field. Served to col. M.C. USAR, 1952-54; Korea. Decorated Bronze Star, Combat Medic badge; recipient McClintock award, 1965, Pybus medal, 1977, Edwin S. Hamilton Teaching award, 1978. Fellow A.C.S.; mem. Am. Surg. Assn., Coller Surg. Soc. (pres. 1971-72), Soc. Surg. Oncology, Soc. Surgery Alimentary Tract (v.p. 1976-77), Western Surg. Assn., Soc. Head and Neck Surgeons, Colegium Internat. Chirurgiae, Central Surg. Assn. (pres. elect 1984), AMA, Ill. Surg. Soc. (pres. 1979-80), Chgo. Surg. Soc. (pres. 1978-79), Ill. Med. Soc., Chgo. Med. Soc., Sigma Xi, Alpha Omega Alpha. Republican. Roman Catholic. Clubs: Chgo. Athletic Assn.; Plimsoll (New Orleans). Home: Route 2 Box 108 Yorkville IL 60560 Office: 950 E 59th St Chicago IL 60637

BLOCK, HASKELL MAYER, educator; b. Chgo., June 13, 1923; s. Abraham M. and Edith (Hymen) B.; m. Elaine Carlin, June 27, 1948 (div. Dec. 1981); children: Randall, Laurie, Linda. A.A., North Park Coll., 1942; A.B., U. Chgo., 1944; A.M., Harvard U., 1947; Doct. d'Univ., U. Paris, 1949. Instr. English Queens Coll., N.Y.C., 1949-52; asst. and asso. prof. comparative lit. U. Wis., 1952-61; prof. comparative lit. Bklyn. Coll., 1961-75, Disting. prof., 1974-75; prof. comparative lit. SUNY-Binghamton, 1975—; H. Fletcher Brown prof. comparative lit. U. Del., 1977-78; prof. comparative lit., exec. officer Doctoral Program in Comparative Lit., City U. N.Y., 1968-71; vis. prof. U. Hawaii, summer 1963, U. Ill., 1966-67, George A. Miller vis. prof., 1983; vis. prof. U. Colo., summer 1967, Harvard U., summer 1968, 72, 83, N.Y. U., summer 1971, 82, 84, U. Düsseldorf, Germany, 1972-73, U. Szeged, Hungary, 1979, U. Antwerp, Belgium, 1981, 83; cons. editor Random House, Inc., N.Y.C., 1961—; mem. selection com. for Western Europe, Fgn. Area Fellowship Program, 1965-68, Camargo Found., 1971—; mem. selection com. Nat. Endowment for Humanities, 1977. Author: (with Herman Salinger) The Creative Vision, 1960, (with Robert G. Shedd) Masters of Modern Drama, 1962, Mallarmé and the Symbolist Drama, 1963, Naturalistic Triptych, 1970, Nouvelles Tendances en Littérature Comparée, 1970. Served with USAAF, 1944-45. Fulbright research scholar U. Cologne, 1956-57, U. Paris, 1968-69; faculty exchange scholar SUNY, 1981—. Mem. Internat. Comparative Lit. Assn. (adv. bd. 1970-76), Am. Comparative Lit. Assn. (pres. 1974-77, adv. bd. 1977-83, del. to Am. Council Learned Socs. 1977-81, 84), Association Internationale des Docteurs de Universités de France (v.p. 1981—), Eastern Comparative Lit. Conf. (chmn. exec. com.), Modern Lang. Assn., Modern Humanities Research Assn., Dante Soc. Am., Soc. French Studies, Am. Soc. Aesthetics, AAUP, Columbia U. Seminar on Theory of Lit., Am. Center PEN, Phi Beta Kappa. Clubs: Harvard Faculty (Cambridge, Mass.); Williams; Andiron, Harvard (N.Y.C.); Quadrangle (Chgo.). Office: State U NY Binghamton NY 13901

BLOCK, HERBERT LAWRENCE (HERBLOCK), editorial cartoonist; b. Chgo., Oct. 13, 1909; s. David Julian and Tessie (Lupe) B. Student, Lake Forest (Ill.) Coll., 1927-29, LL.D. (hon.), 1957, Litt. D., Rutgers U., 1963; L.H.D., Williams Coll., 1969, Haverford Coll., 1977, U. Md., 1977, Art Inst. Chgo., (part time classes). Editorial cartoonist: Chgo. Daily News, 1929-33, NEA Service, 1933-43, U.S. Army, 1943-45; editorial cartoonist: The Washington Post, 1946—; Author: The Herblock Book, 1952, Herblock's Here and Now, 1955, Herblock's Special for Today, 1958, Straight Herblock, 1964, The Herblock Gallery, 1968, Herblock's State of the Union, 1972, Herblock Special Report, 1974, Herblock On All Fronts, 1980. Recipient Pulitzer prizes, 1942, 54, 79; Am. Newspaper Guild award, 1948; Heywood Broun award, 1950; Sigma Delta Chi Nat. Editorial Awards, 1949, 50, 52, 57; Sidney Hillman award (for book), 1953; Reuben Award Nat. Cartoonists Soc., 1957; Lauterbach award for civil liberties, 1959; Florina Lasker award N.Y. Civil Liberties Union, 1960; Disting. Service Journalism award U. Mo., 1961; Golden Key award, 1963; Capital Press Club award, 1963; Bill of Rights award, 1966; Nat. Headliners award, 1976; Power of Printing award, 1977; Nat. Press Club 4th Estate award, 1977; award for human relations NEA, 1979; others. Fellow Am. Acad. Arts and Scis., Sigma Delta Chi; mem. Phi Beta Kappa (hon.). Designed U.S. postage stamp commemorating 175th anniversary Bill of Rights, 1966. Address: The Washington Post Washington DC 20005

BLOCK, IRVING ALEXANDER, artist; b. N.Y.C.; s. Abraham and Frieda (Weinberg) B.; m. Jilda Klein, Mar. 10, 1960; children: Gregory, Francesca. B.S. magna cum laude, N.Y. U., 1933; student, NAD, 1935, Grande Chaumiere, Paris, 1947. Artist, writer major motion picture studios, Hollywood, Calif., 1945-60; prof. art Calif. State U., Northridge, 1962-80, prof. emeritus, 1980—, mem. adj.

faculty, 1980—; vis. prof. various univs. in, Calif. Exhibited works in numerous one-man shows, including, Ankrum Gallery, Los Angeles, 1962-81, Calif. State U., Northridge, 1980; producer: documentary films Goya; World of Rubens. Recipient Disting. Prof. award Calif. State U., Northridge, 1967; Outstanding Prof. award Calif. State Univ. System, 1980; Gold medal Academia Italia delle Arti e Del Lavoro; Hirshhorn Found. grantee, 1970. Mem. Accademia Internazionale Tommaso Campanella, Phi Kappa Phi. Home: 3880 Carpenter Ave Studio City CA 91604 Office: Calif State U Northridge CA 91330

BLOCK, JAMES ALEXANDER, drug company executive; b. N.Y.C., Mar. 29, 1937; s. Melvin A. and Anita (Wangron) B.; m. Barbara Heller, June 12, 1960; children: Valerie, Peter. B.A., Dartmour Coll., 1959. Dir. internat. div. Block Drug Co., Jersey City, v.p., dir. mktg., exec. v.p., now pres. Hon. pres. Asso. YM-YWHA Greater N.Y., pres. Asso. Camps; bd. dirs., mem. exec. com. Fedn. Jewish Philanthropies, Columbia U. Sch. Social Work; bd. dirs. Baron de Hirsl Fund. Mem. Propriatary Assn. Washington (dir.), Phi Beta Kappa. Office: Block Drug Co 257 Cornelison Ave Jersey City NJ 07302 *

BLOCK, JOHN RUSLING, secretary of agriculture; b. Galesburg, Ill., Feb. 15, 1935; m. Suzanne Rathje, June 21, 1958; children: Hans, Cynthia, Christine. B.S., U.S. Mil. Acad., 1959. Farmer, Gilson, Ill., 1960-77; dir. Ill. Dept. Agr., Springfield, 1977-81; sec. agr. U.S. Dept. Agr., Washington, 1981—. Served to 2d lt. U.S. Army, 1958-60. Named Outstanding Young Farmer Am. Jaycees, 1969. Mem. Ill. Farm Bur., Knox County Farm Bur. Office: US Dept Agr Office Sec 14th and Independence Ave SW Washington DC 20250

BLOCK, JOSEPH DOUGLAS, utility exec., lawyer; b. Three Lakes, Wis., Apr. 18, 1919; s. Max and Rose (Chaimson) B.; m. Doris Ruth Schoenewald, Sept. 26, 1958. B.A., U. Wis., 1939, J.D., 1941; LL.M., Harvard, 1946. Bar: Wis. bar 1941, Ill. bar 1947, N.Y. bar 1971. Atty. OPA, Washington, 1942, 45-46; practiced in, Chgo., 1946-70; partner firm Aaron, Aaron, Schimberg & Hess, Chgo., 1957-70; v.p., gen. counsel Consol. Edison Co. N.Y., Inc., N.Y.C., 1970-73, exec. v.p., 1973-80, exec. v.p., gen. counsel, 1980—; spl. asst. atty. gen. Ill., 1951-53. Served with CIC AUS, 1942-45. Mem. Am., N.Y. State, Wis. bar assns., Bar Assn. N.Y.C., N.Y.C. C. of C., Order Coif, Phi Kappa Phi. Club: Westchester Country (Rye, N.Y.). Home: 920 Park Ave New York NY 10028 Office: 4 Irving Pl New York NY 10003

BLOCK, JULES RICHARD, psychologist, educator; b. N.Y.C., Nov. 23, 1930; s. Jules Irving and Elizabeth (Shinkle) B.; m. Elizabeth Ehrenstein, Dec. 21, 1952 (div. Nov. 1978); m. Patricia Clark, Feb. 29, 1980; children—Cheryl, Janet. B.A., Hofstra Coll., 1952; Ph.D., N.Y. U., 1962. Lectr. Hofstra U., Hempstead, N.Y., 1956-60, instr., 1960-62, asst. prof., 1962-66, asso. prof., 1966-70, prof., 1970-79, chmn. dept. psychology, 1968-78, exec. dir. research and resource devel., 1976—; research asst. Human Resources Research and Tng. Inst., Albertson, N.Y., 1957-59, research asso., 1959-61, dir. research, 1961—; Pres. Instrumental Psychol. Methods, Hempstead, Inst. for Research and Evaluation, Hempstead. Contbr. articles to profl. jours. Mem. Nassau County Youth Bd., 1968-70; Exec. dir. Initial Teaching Alphabet Found., 1965-72. Served with USNR, 1952-56. Recipient award for outstanding research in rehab. Nat. Rehab. Council, 1969. Mem. Am. Psychol. Assn. Home: 33 Primrose Ln Hempstead NY 11550 Office: Hofstra U Hempstead NY 11550

BLOCK, KENNETH LEROY, management consultant; b. Newark, May 14, 1920; s. Herman J. and Flora E. (Wihle) B.; m. Margaret Sally Sherratt, Aug. 22, 1947; children: Kenneth Lee, Timothy Douglas, Elizabeth Ann. B.B.A., U. Minn., 1942; B.S., MIT, 1947; M.B.A., U. Mich., 1948. With Honeywell, Inc., 1940, Ford Co., 1941, Chevrolet Aviation Engine Co., 1942; instr. Sch. Bus. Adminstrn. U. Mich., 1947-48; chmn., dir. A.T. Kearney Inc., Chgo., 1948—; dir. Lawter Chems., Northbrook, Ill., Safety-Kleen Corp., Elgin, Ill., Littlefuse, Inc., Des Plaines, Ill., Tracor, Inc., Austin, Tex., Capital Opportunities Fund, Stein, Row & Farnham. Contbg. editor: Prodn. Handbook, 1959; contbr. numerous articles to profl. pubs. Mem. vis. com. U. Chgo. Div. Sch.; trustee, vice chmn. Elmhurst Coll., Evanston Hosp.; bd. dirs. Mid-Am. chpt. ARC, 1965-71, Swedish Covenant Hosp.; past chmn. bd. dirs. Bd. Benevolence, Evang. Convenant Ch. Am.; pres., dir. Chgo. Crime Commn., 1969-72; fire and police commr. Village of Glen Ellyn, 1962-65; bd. dirs. Chgo. Met. YMCA; v.p. exec. bd. dirs. Chgo. council Boy Scouts Am., 1965—; bd. dirs. Community Fund of Chgo., 1969—, Christian Workers Found., Lyric Opera, Chgo., Protestant Found. Greater Chgo., Central DuPage Hosp., 1963-69; pres. Central DuPage Hosp., 1969. Served with USAF, 1942-45. Mem. Assn. Cons. Mgmt. Engrs. (dir. 1969-71), Nat. Inst. Mgmt. Cons. (chmn. 1970-73), Nat. Assn. Citizens Crime Commns. (dir., pres. 1970), Inst. Mgmt. Cons. (pres. 1971-73), Conf. Bd. (dir.), Chgo. Assn. Commerce and Industry (dir.), Beta Gamma Sigma, Delta Sigma Pi, Iron Wedge. Clubs: Chicago Sunday Evening (vice chmn.), Union League (dir., v.p. 1969-71), Union League (pres. 1972-73), Commercial (Chgo.); Indian Hill Country. Home: 11 Woodley Rd Winnetka IL 60091 Office: 100 S Wacker Dr Chicago IL 60606

BLOCK, LAWRENCE, author; b. Buffalo, June 24, 1938; s. Arthur Jerome and Lenore Nathan B.; m. Loretta Ann Kallet, 1960; children—Amy Jo, Jill Diana. Student, Antioch Coll., 1955-59. Editor Scott Meredith Inc., 1957-58. Books include Death Pulls a Double Cross, 1961, The Girl with the Long Green Heart, 1965, The Triumph of Evil, 1971, The Burglar Who Liked to Quote Kipling, 1979. Recipient Nero Wolfe award, 1980. Address: care Kelly Bramball and Ford 463 Commonwealth Ave Boston MA 02115 *

BLOCK, LEONARD NATHAN, drug company executive; b. Bklyn., Dec. 21, 1911; s. Alexander and Tillie (Goetz) B.; m. Adele Goldberg, Oct. 8, 1936; children: Peggy Davis (Mrs. Richard M. Danziger), Thomas Roger. B.S., U. Pa., 1933. With Block Drug Co., Inc., Jersey City, 1933—, chmn. bd., 1963—. Mem. N.Y.C. Com. of Foster Care of Children, 1966-69; mem. Bd. Social Welfare, 1969-77, vice chmn., 1974-77; treas. Child Welfare Info. Services, 1972—; bd. dirs. Welfare Research, Inc., 1980; Bd. dirs. Fedn. Jewish Philanthropies, 1953—, asso. chmn. bd., chmn. distbn. com., 1958-63, chmn. communal planning com., 1964-68; bd. dirs., treas. Lincoln Ctr. for the Performing Arts, 1977-84. Recipient award N.Y. State Welfare Conf., 1972, Naomi and Howard Lehman award, 1974, Disting. Service award Fedn. Jewish Philanthropies, 1984. Clubs: Harmonie, Hollywood Golf, Ocean Beach. Home: 535 Park Ave New York NY 10021 Office: 257 Cornelison Ave Jersey City NJ 07302

BLOCK, MELVIN AUGUST, physician, educator; b. Evansville, Ind., July 2, 1921; s. August William and Alma (Klutey) B.; m. Marcia Jean Jacobs, May 28, 1955; children: Deborah Ann, Christopher Reed. B.S., Ind. U., 1942, M.D., 1944; Ph.D., U. Minn., 1953. Intern Ind. U. Med. Center, 1945; resident Mayo Clinic, Rochester, Minn., 1948-54; chmn. dept. surgery Henry Ford Hosp., Detroit, 1975-79, Scripps Clinic Med. Group, La Jolla, Calif., 1980—; clin. prof. surgery U. Mich. Med. Sch., 1970-80, U. Calif., San Diego Med. Sch., 1980—. Contbr. numerous articles to profl. jours. Served to capt. M.C. AUS, 1945-47. Fellow Royal Coll. Surgeons Can.; mem. ACS (past gov.), Am., Central, Western, Pacific Coast surg. assns., Am. Thyroid Assn., Am. Gastroenterology Assn., Soc. Surg. Alimentary Tract, Soc. Head and Neck Surgeons, Soc. Internationale de Chirurgie, AMA, Calif., San Diego County med. socs., Acad. Surg. Detroit (past pres.), Detroit Surg. Soc. (past pres.), Internat. Assn. Endocrine Surgeons, Am. Assn. Endocrine Surgeons, Sigma Xi, Alpha Omega Alpha. Home: 4575 Excalibur Way San Diego CA 92122 Office: Scripps Clinic Med Group 10666 N Torrey Pines Rd La Jolla CA 92037 *Time is our most valuable possession. It is limited qualitatively and quantitatively. This realization should be implied in most actions.*

BLOCK, MICHAEL KENT, business educator; b. N.Y.C., Apr. 2, 1942; s. Philip and Roslyn (Klein) B.; m. Carole Arline Polansky, Aug. 30, 1965; children: Robert Justin, Tamara Nicole. A.B., Stanford U., 1964, A.M., 1969, Ph.D., 1972. Research analyst Bank of Am., San Francisco, 1965-66; research assoc. Planning Assocs., San Francisco, 1966-67; asst. prof. econs. U. Santa Clara, 1969-72; asst. prof. econs. dept. ops. research and adminstrv. sci. Naval Postgrad. Sch., Monterey, Calif., 1972-74, assoc. prof., 1974-76; research fellow Hoover Instn., Stanford U., 1975-76, sr. research fellow, 1976—; dir. Center for Econometric Studies of Justice System, 1977; ptnr. Block & Nold, cons., Palo Alto, Calif., 1980-81; assoc. prof. mgmt. and econs. U. Ariz., Tucson, 1982—; cons. in field. Author: (with H.G. Demmert) Workbook and Programmed Guide to Economics, 1974, 77, 80, (with James M. Clabault) A Legal and Economic Analysis of Criminal Antitrust Indictments:, 1955-80; contbr. articles to profl. publs. NSF fellow, 1965; Stanford U. fellow. Mem. Am. Econ. Assn., Phi Beta Kappa. Home: 3452 Camino Esplanade Tucson AZ 85715 Office: Coll Bus U Ariz Tucson AZ 85721

BLOCK, MURRAY HAROLD, educational consultant; b. N.Y.C., Feb. 14, 1924; s. Joseph and Rebecca (Wollendler) B.; m. Estelle M. Kleckner, May 27, 1948; children: Richard Neil, Paul Alan, Jo-Carol. B.B.A., City Coll. N.Y., 1945; M.A., Columbia, 1947, Ed.D., 1953. Mem. faculty N.Y.C. Community Coll., 1947-50, dir. eve. div., 1950-60, dean, 1960-62, acting pres., 1962-65; pres. Borough Manhattan Community Coll., 1965-70; dep. to the chancellor SUNY, 1970-83; Bd. dirs. Council Higher Ednl. Instns. N.Y.C., 1965-70; vice chmn. Nassau County Adv. Com. Legislation, 1967-70; pres. Council Community Coll. Pres. N.Y. State, 1967-69; mem Regents Adv. Council Two-Year Edn., 1966—; commn. mem., also chmn. Am. Assn. Jr. Colls., 1965-70. Served with USAAF, 1943-46. Mem. Assn. Higher Edn., Phi Delta Kappa, Delta Pi Epsilon. Home and Office: 9 Heather Ln Delmar NY 12054

BLOCK, PAUL, JR., newspaper pub., chemist; b. N.Y.C., May 11, 1911; s. Paul and Dina (Wallach) B.; m. Eleana Barnes Conley, 1940 (div. 1947); 1 son, Cyrus P.; m. Marjorie McNab Main, May 26, 1948 (dec. Sept. 1960); children—Allan James, John Robinson; m. Mary Gall Petok, 1965; 3 children by previous marriage. Grad., Hotchkiss Sch., Lakeville, Conn., 1929; A.B., Yale, 1933; postgrad., Columbia, 1933-34, Ph.D., 1943, Harvard, 1934-35. Reporter Toledo Blade, 1935, became polit. writer, 1938, asst. editor, 1941, co-pub., 1942, Pitts. Post Gazette, 1944—; fellow Mellon Inst. Indsl. Research, Pitts., 1943-44; hon. fellow dept. pharmacology Yale U., 1948-49. Chmn. Toledo Devel. Com., 1975-79; chmn. bd. trustees Med. Coll. Ohio at Toledo, 1964-70; mem. U.S. Metric Bd., 1978-80. Mem. Am. Chem. Soc., Am. Soc. Newspaper Editors, Internat. Press Inst. (chmn. Am. com. 1958-61), Sigma Xi. Home: 4059 River Rd Toledo OH 43614 Office: Toledo Blade Toledo OH 43660

BLOCK, ROBERT CHARLES, nuclear engineering educator; b. Newark, Feb. 11, 1929; s. George and Sue (Ehrenkranz) B.; m. Rita Adler, June 28, 1952; children: Keith, Robin. B.S. in Elec. Engring, Newark Coll. Engring., 1950; M.A. in Physics, Columbia U., 1953; Ph.D. in Nuclear Physics, Duke U., 1956. Elec. engr. Nat. Union Radio Corp., W. Orange, N.J., 1950-51, Bendix Aviation Co., Teterboro, N.J., 1951; physicist Oak Ridge Nat. Lab., 1955-66; vis. scientist Atomic Energy Research Establishment, Harwell, Eng., 1962-63; prof. nuclear engring. and sci. Rensselaer Poly. Inst., 1966—; Vis. scientist Am. Inst. Physics, 1961-67; vis. prof. Kyoto (Japan) U., 1973-74; cons. Gen. Electric Co., 1968-79; cons., mem. nuclear cross sect. adv. com. AEC, 1969-72; vis. physicist Brookhaven Nat. Lab., 1975, mem. vis. com. nuclear energy dept., 1982-85; founder, v.p., treas. Becker, Block, & Harris, Inc., 1981—; mem. U.S. Nuclear Data Com., 1972-74, NRC panel on low and medium energy neutrons, 1977; dir. Gaerttner Linac Lab. Co-author chpt. in book. Japanese Ministry Edn. research grantee, 1973-74. Fellow Am. Nuclear Soc.; Mem. AAAS, AAUP, Am. Phys. Soc., Sigma Xi, Sigma Pi Sigma, Phi Beta Tau, Tau Beta Pi. Research on neutron physics. Home: 114 3d St Troy NY 12180 Office: Rensselaer Poly Inst Troy NY 12181

BLOCK, RUTH S., insurance company executive; b. N.Y.C., Nov. 7, 1930; d. Albert and Celia (Shapiro) Smolensky; m. Norman Block, Apr. 5, 1952. B.A., Adelphi U., Garden City, N.Y., 1952. With Equitable Life Assurance Soc. U.S., 1952—; Sr. v.p. charge individual life ins. bus., 1977-80, exec. v.p. individual ins. bus., 1980—; chmn., chief exec. officer Equitable Variable Life Ins. Co., 1981—; dir. Equitable Gen. Ins. Co., 1977-80, Equitable Money Market Account; Mobil Co. vis. exec. U. Iowa, 1978. Bd. dirs. Stamford (Conn.) YWCA, 1977-80; nat. chmn. Equitable United Way, 1978. Recipient Disting. Alumni award Adelphi U. Sch. Bus., 1979. Office: 1285 Ave Americas New York NY 10019

BLOCK, S. LESTER, dept. store exec.; b. Trenton, N.J., Jan. 10, 1917; s. Maurice R. and Jeanne (Finkle) B.; m. Ruth Harris, Mar. 21, 1942; children—John D., Richard H. A.B., Princeton, 1938; LL.B., U. Pa., 1941. Bar: N.Y. bar 1945, N.J. bar 1947. Asso. Proskauer, Rose, Goetz & Mendelsohn, N.Y.C., 1945-54; labor atty. R.H. Macy & Co., Inc., N.Y.C., 1954-67, v.p., labor atty., 1967-70, sr. v.p. govt. relations, labor counsel, 1970—; lectr. N.Y. State Sch. Indsl. and Labor Relations.; Chmn. labor-mgmt. law com. Am. Arbitration Assn., 1967, mem. arbitration com., 1959; mem. N.Y. State Bus. Adv. Com. Mgmt. Improvement, 1970—; mem. planning com. N.Y.U. 24th Annual Conf. Labor, 1970; mem. regional adv. conf. adminstrn. NLRB, 1960-63; mem. Fed. Adv. Council Employment Security, 1960-62; chmn. adv. council Office Personnel Services, Princeton U.; mem. exec. bd., adv. council Pace U.-Labor Mgmt. Relations Inst. Mem. Bergen County Jewish Welfare Council, 1958-66, Teaneck (N.J.) Jewish Community Council, 1954-60; sec., trustee Princeton Med. Center. Served from pvt. to capt., Signal Corps AUS, 1941-45. Mem. Assn. Bar City N.Y., Am. Retail Fedn. (exec. com., dir.), Am. Mgmt. Assn., U.S. C. of C. (labor relations com.), N.Y. State C. of C. and Industry (chmn. nat. affairs com.), Indsl. Relations Soc., Nat. Retail Mchts. Assn., Nat. Acad. Arbitrators, Bus. Roundtable, Phi Beta Kappa, Order of Coif. Home: 161 Parkside Dr Princeton NJ 08540 Office: 151 W 34th St New York NY 10001

BLOCK, SEYMOUR STANTON, biochemical engineer; b. N.Y.C., May 16, 1918; s. Mark and Frances (Mantell) B.; m. Gertrude H. Hecht, Sept. 29, 1942; children: Sara Block Morton, Judith Block McLaughlin. B.S., Pa. State U., 1939, M.S., 1941, Ph.D., 1942. Research chemist Joseph Seagram & Sons, Louisville, 1942-44; mem. faculty U. Fla., Gainesville, since 1944, prof. chem. engring., since 1965; cons. to govt. and industry, condr. research projects; mem. com. for approval U.S. Army research NRC, 1976-79. Editor: book series Hazardous and Toxic Substances, Marcel Dekker Pubs., 1978—; Author: Disinfection, Sterilization and Preservation, 2d edit, 1977, 3d edit., 1983, Benjamin Franklin: His Wit, Wisdom and Women, 1975; also numerous articles. Bd. dirs. Civic Action Assn., Gainesville, 1958-62; pres. Citizens Com. Planning and Zoning, Gainesville, 1965-70; chmn. Bikeways Com., U. Fla., 1968-77; mem. credit com. U. Fla. Credit Union, 1978. Am. Tobacco Co. fellow, 1940-42; President's scholar U. Fla., 1977-78; Seymour S. Block award created by Alpha Epsilon Pi, 1967. Mem. Am. Chem. Soc. (pres. Fla. 1950, nat. councilor 1951), AAUP (pres. Fla. 1960, pres. assn. state and regional confs. 1965), Zero Population Growth (dir. 1970), Soc. Indsl. Microbiology (charter, treas. 1965), Sierra Club, Fla. Defenders Environment, Planned Parenthood and World Population, Phi Beta Kappa (hon.), Sigma Xi. Patentee in field. Home: 2906 SW 2d Ave Gainesville FL 32607 Office: 217 Chem Engring Bldg Univ Fla Gainesville FL 32611

BLOCK, STANLEY MARLIN, engineering educator, arbitrator; b. Mpls., Feb. 4, 1922; s. Herman J. and Flora (Wiehle) B.; m. Isabelle Jeanette Kirk, Aug. 15, 1947; children: Patricia Sue (Mrs. Alan Unander), Carol Jean (Mrs. Allan Dalton), Beverly Ann, Priscilla Jo (Mrs. John Eckhardt). B.M.E. with high distinction, U. Minn., 1943, M.B.A., 1950, Ph.D. in Mech. Engring, 1956. Registered profl. engr., Minn. Indsl. engr. Minn. Mining and Mfg. Co., 1947-49; from instr. to asst. prof. U. Minn., 1949-59; prodn. planner Mpls.-Honeywell Co., 1951; time standards engr. Whirlpool Corp., 1952; human engring. cons. USAF, 1953; asso. prof. prodn. mgmt. Grad. Sch. Bus., U. Chgo., 1959-62; prof. indsl. engring. Ill. Inst. Tech., 1962-80, chmn. dept., 1962-70; adj. prof. biomed. engring. Rush Med. Coll., Chgo., 1973-75; prin. S.M. Block and Assos., Winnetka, Ill., 1955-80; pres. Vienna Woods Devel. Corp., Olympia Fields, 1961-69; acad. adviser Student Project for Amity among Nations group to S. Africa, 1957; lectr. Japan Mgmt. Assn., 1964, Nat. Mgmt. and Devel. Found., Johannesburg, S. Africa, 1965. Contbr. articles to profl. jours. Pres. Vienna Woods Landowners Assn., 1962-66; U.S. rep. Internat. Fellowship Evangelical Students, Lausanne, Switzerland, 1966—; Bd. dirs. Inter-Varsity Christian Fellowship, 1958-65, 66-76; pres. Health Care Planning Corp. Greater Chgo., 1973-75, Abundant Life Found., 1968-75. Served to 1st lt. AUS, 1943-46. Mem. Am. Inst. Indsl. Engrs., Fed. Mediation and Conciliation Service (labor arbitrator 1972—), Am. Arbitration Assn. (labor panel 1962—), Nat. Acad. Arbitrators, Am. Sci. Affiliation, Hosp. Mgmt. Systems Soc. (pres. Chgo. chpt. 1974-75), Sigma Xi, Pi Tau Sigma, Tau Beta Pi, Alpha Pi Mu. Mem. Evang. Free Ch. Inventor sequential electronic motion timer and recorder. Home: Rt 3 Box 404 Markesan WI 53946

BLOCK, WILLIAM, newspaper publisher; b. N.Y.C., Sept. 20, 1915; s. Paul and Dina (Wallach) B.; m. Maxine Horton, Mar. 23, 1944; children: William, Karen Block Ayars, Barbara Block Burney, Donald. A.B., Yale U., 1936. With circulation, other depts. Toledo Blade, 1937-39, asst. to gen. mgr., 1939-41; co-pub. Pitts. Post-Gazette and Toledo Blade, 1941—; pres. Post-Gazette; v.p. Toledo Blade. Bd. dirs. Pitts. Regional Planning Assn., Pitts. Communications Found., Pitts. Symphony Soc., Pitts. Ctr. for the Arts, Gateway to Music Inc.; trustee Am. Assembly; sponsor Allegheny Conf. on Community Devel. Served to capt. AUS, 1941-46; served in mil. govt. in, 1945-46; Korea. Mem. Internat. Press Inst., Am. Soc. Newspaper Editors, Soc. Profl. Journalists. Office: 50 Blvd of Allies Pittsburgh PA 15222

BLOCK, ZENAS, business consultant, educator; b. N.Y.C., Dec. 7, 1916; s. Joshua and Celia (Kaplow) B.; m. Lillian Bialek, June 12, 1938; children: Richard, Karen Block Chase, Margaret (Mrs. Knute Walker). B.S., Coll. City N.Y., 1938; postgrad., Bklyn. Poly. Inst., 1939-41. Chemist Clairol Inc., N.Y.C., 1938-39; chief chemist Am. Dietaids Co., Yonkers, N.Y., 1938-48; dir. labs. DCA Food Industries, N.Y.C., 1948-55, v.p. research, 1955-60, pres. bakery div., 1960-64, group v.p., 1964-71, exec. v.p., 1971-77, vice chmn. bd., 1977-79, also dir.; chmn. bd. Nisshin DCA Foods Inc., Tokyo, 1975-79, DCA Industries Ltd., Eng., 1976-79; pres. Haystack Cable Vision Inc., Lakeville, Conn., 1978-80, v.p. and treas., 1980-82; adj. lectr. Grad. Sch. Bus. Adminstrn., U. Conn., 1979-81; adj. prof. mgmt. N.Y. U. Grad. Sch. Bus. Adminstrn., 1980-84, clin. prof., 1984—. Author: It's All on the Label, 1981; contbr. articles to profl. jours. Bd. dirs. N.Y.C. Mission Soc., 1983—, Salisbury Family Services, 1983—. Mem. A.I.M., Am. Soc. Bakery Engrs. (v.p.). Patentee in field. Home and Office: Box 758 Salisbury CT 06068

BLOCKER, JOHN RUFUS, oil company executive; b. San Antonio, Nov. 30, 1922; s. William Bartlett and Lela (Barker) B.; m. Peggy Belcher (div.); children: John Rufus, William B., George L., Bennett L., Peggy L. Blocker Schuette; m. Vivian Jeanne Rossler, Jan. 13, 1972. B.S. in Bus. Adminstrn., Tex. A&M. U. Pres. Dresser Atlad div. Dresser Industries, Houston, 1967-69, pres. Petroleum and Mineral Group, 1969-75, sr. v.p. office of Pres., 1975-76; v.p. market devel. Dresser Atlad Div. Dresser Industries, 1976-77; pres. Choya Drilling Co., Houston, 1977-78; pres., chief exec. officer, chmn. bd. Blocker Energy Corp., Houston, 1978—; dir. InterFirst Bank of Houston, N.A. Bd. dirs. Jr. Achievement S.E. Tex., Inc., 1971-76; mem. campaign com. Grand Opera Assn., Houston, 1974; mem. planning bd. Mgmt. Devel. Ctr. of U. Houston, 1972-75; vice chmn. bd. regents Tex. A&M U., 1983—. 2d lt. inf. AUS, 1942-46; ETO. Decorated Bronze Star medal. Mem. Houston C. of C. Internat. Bus Council, Internat. Assn. Contract Drillers (dir.), Tex. Mid-Continent Oil and Gas Assn., Am. Petroleum Inst. Republican. Club: Nomads Internat. (Houston). Office: Blocker Energy Corp 800 Bering Dr Houston TX 77057

BLODGETT, FRANK CALEB, food company executive; b. Janesville, Wis., Apr. 22, 1927; s. Frank Caleb Pickard and Dorothy (Korst) B.; m. Jean Ellen Fountain, June 23, 1951; children: Caleb J., Barbara F., David K. Grad., Beloit Coll., 1950; postgrad., Advanced Mgmt. Program, Harvard U., 1969. First v.p., dir. Frank H. Blodgett Inc., Janesville, 1947-61, pres., dir., 1961-62; with Gen. Mills Inc., Mpls., 1961—, v.p., dir. mktg., 1967-69, gen. mgr., v.p., 1969-73, group v.p., 1973-76, exec. v.p., 1976-80, vice chmn. bd., 1981—, dir., 1980—; dir. Medtronics, Inc., Northwestern Nat. Life Ins. Co.; bd. dirs. Cereal Inst., 1970-76, chmn., 1973-74; trustee Nutrition Found., 1980—, Gen. Mills Found., 1980—. Trustee Washburn Child Guidance Center, 1972-75, Beloit Coll., 1976—. Served with U.S. Navy, 1944-46; PTO. Mem. Millers Nat. Fedn., Young Millers Orgn. (past pres.), U.S. C. of C. (dir.), Greater Mpls. C. of C. (dir. 1975-76), Phi Kappa Psi (trustee alumni bd. Beloit 1961-62), Phi Eta Sigma. Home: 217 Bushaway Rd Wayzata MN 55391: Office: 9200 Wayzata Blvd Minneapolis MN 55426

BLODGETT, OMER WILLIAM, design consultant; b. Duluth, Minn., Nov. 27, 1917; s. Myron O. and Minnie (Foster) B.; m. Dorothy B. Sjostrom, June 14, 1949; 1 son, Robert W. B.Metall.Engring. with distinction, U. Minn., 1941, M.E., 1976. Registered profl. engr., Ohio. Welding supt. Globe Shipbldg. Co., Superior, Wis., 1941-45; sales engr. Lincoln Electric Co., Cleve., 1945-54, design cons., 1954—; condr. seminars Australian Inst. Steel Constrn., Australia, 1971, 75, 78, South African Inst. Steel Constrn., 1981. Author: Design Weldments, 1963, Design of Welded Structures, 1966, also papers. Fellow ASCE, ASME; hon. mem. Am. Welding Soc. (lectr. 1968, A.F. Davis silver medal 1962, 73, 80, 83); mem. Sigma Xi, Tau Beta Pi. Home: 2013 Aldersgate Dr Cleveland OH 44124 Office: 22801 Saint Clair St Cleveland OH 44117

BLODGETT, RALPH HAMILTON, economist, educator; b. North Adams, Mass., Dec. 25, 1905; s. Charles Raymond and Lillian (Morits) B.; m. Loretta Neunfeldt, June 14, 1930 (dec. Dec. 1957); children: Moyra Loretta (Mrs. James F. Schaeffner), Sandra Elizabeth

(Mrs. Stuart A. McIntosh); m. Margaret Adkins, July 18, 1958. B.S. in Econs, U. Vt., 1927; A.M., Syracuse U., 1928; Ph.D., U. Pa., 1933. Grad. asst. econs. Syracuse U., 1927-28; instr. econs. Valparaiso U., 1928-29; instr., asst. prof. econs. U. Pa., 1929-37; asst. prof. econs. U. Ill., 1937-41, asso. prof., 1941-45, prof., 1945-50; prof. econs. U. Fla., 1950-76, prof. emeritus, 1976—, acting head econs. dept., 1964-65; bd. editors U. Fla. Social Sci. Monograph Series; vis. prof. econs. U. So. Calif., summer, 1949; econ. cons., expert witness various law firms; econ. cons. TVA, 1959-61, NASA, 1964-65, HUD, 1965-67. Author: Cyclical Fluctuations in Commodity Stocks, 1935, Principles of Economics, 1941, rev. edit., 1946, 51, Comparative Economic Systems, 1944, 49, Our Expanding Economy: An Introduction, 1955; co-author: An Economic Question Book, 1931, Contemporary Economic Problems, 1932, Getting and Earning, 1937, Economics: Principles and Problems, 1937, rev. edits., 1942, 48, Current Economic Problems, 1939, 1947, Comparative Economic Development, 1956, Fluctuations in General Business, 1977; Author numerous articles and monographs in econs. Mem. Am. Econ. Assn., So. Econ. Assn., Midwest Econ. Assn. (v.p. 1946-47), AAUP, Univ. Profs. for Acad. Order, Am. Contract Bridge League (life master), AAAS, Phi Beta Kappa, Omicron Delta Epsilon, Sigma Alpha Epsilon, Alpha Kappa Psi, Beta Gamma Sigma. Democrat. Episcopalian. Clubs: U. Fla. Bridge, Gainesville Golf and Country. Home: 2358 NW 13th Pl Gainesville FL 32605

BLODGETT, WILLIAM ARTHUR, corporate executive; b. Detroit, Feb. 19, 1937; s. Arthur Charles and Edwina (McRoy) B.; children: William Arthur, Charles Clark, Matthew Scott, James David, Elyse Chantal. Student, U. Fla., 1959. Columnist, sports editor Tampa Times, Fla., 1959-63; columnist Atlanta Constrn., 1963-64; pub. relations mgr. Gen. Electric Co., Atlanta, 1964-65, Washington, 1965-67, N.Y.C., 1967-69, Schenectady, 1969-79; dir. internat. pub. relations Cie Honeywell Bull, Paris, 1970-74; account exec. Carl Byoir & Assocs., Boston, 1974-77, N.Y.C., 1977; v.p. corp. communications Gulf & Western Industries, Inc., N.Y.C., 1977—. Vice chmn. Nat. Kidney Found.; bd. dirs. Jr. Achievement. Served with U.S. Army, 1958-59. Mem. Pub. Relations Soc. Am. Democrat. Roman Catholic. Club: Overseas Press (N.Y.C.). Office: 1 Gulf and Western Plaza New York NY 10023

BLOEDE, VICTOR GUSTAV, advt. exec.; b. Balt., Jan. 31, 1920; s. Victor Gustav, Jr. and Helen (Yoe) B.; m. Merle Huie, Mar. 11, 1945; children—Victor Gustav, Susan Lohn. Student, St. John's Coll., Annapolis, Md., 1939, U. Md., 1941. Vice pres., copy chief French & Preston, N.Y.C., 1947-50; with Benton & Bowles, Inc., N.Y.C., 1950—, v.p., creative dir., 1957-61, sr. v.p., 1961-62, sr. v.p. charge creative services, 1962-63, exec. v.p., 1963-68, chmn. plans bd., 1963-67, pres., chief exec. officer, 1968-71, chmn. bd., 1971—, chief exec. officer, 1971-74; mem. Nat. Advt. Rev. Bd., 1975-79, mem. steering com., 1976-78. Contbg. author: The Copy Writer's Guide, 1958, Ency. International, 1978. Bd. dirs. Travelers Aid Soc. N.Y., 1966—, Am. Cancer Soc., 1976—; bd. visitors and govs. St. John's Coll., 1972-78, 79—. Served to capt. USAAF, 1942-45. Decorated Air medal with 6 oak leaf clusters. Mem. Am. Assn. Agys. (dir.-at-large, vice chmn. 1972-73, chmn. 1973-74, chmn. adv. council 1975—), Am. Advt. Fedn. (dir., vice chmn. 1977-79), Nat. Outdoor Advt. Bur. (dir.), N.Y.C. C. of C. (public service adv. com. 1979—), Profl. Golf Assn. Am. (nat. adv. com. 1979—), Phi Sigma Kappa. Clubs: Sands Point (L.I.) Golf (gov. 1975-80), Coral Beach (Bermuda); Manhasset Bay Yacht, Cloud, Economic (N.Y.C.). Office: Benton and Bowles Inc 909 3d Ave 29th FL New York NY 10022

BLOEMBERGEN, NICOLAAS, physicist, educator; b. Dordrecht, Netherlands, Mar. 11, 1920; came to U.S., 1952, naturalized, 1958; s. Auke and Sophia M. (Quint) B.; m. Huberta D. Brink, June 26, 1950; children: Antonia, Brink, Juliana. B.A., Utrecht U., 1941, M.A., 1943; Ph.D., Leiden U., 1948; M.A. (hon.), Harvard, 1951. Teaching asst. Utrecht U., 1942-45; research fellow Leiden U., 1948; mem. Soc. Fellows Harvard, 1949-51, assoc. prof., 1951-57, Gordon McKay prof. applied physics, 1957—, Rumford prof. physics, 1974, Gerhard Gade univ. prof., 1980; vis. prof. U. Paris, 1957, U. Calif., 1965, Collège de France, Paris, 1980; Lorentz guest prof. U. Leiden, 1973; Raman vis prof. Bangalore, India, 1979; Fairchild disting. scholar Calif. Inst. Tech., 1984. Author: Nuclear Magnetic Relaxation, 1948, Nonlinear Optics, 1965; also articles in profl. jours. Recipient Buckley prize for solid state physics Am. Phys. Soc., 1958, Dirac medal U. New South Wales (Australia), 1983; Stuart Ballantine medal Franklin Inst., 1961; Half Moon trophy Netherlands Club N.Y., 1972; Nat. medal of Sci., 1975; Lorentz medal Royal Dutch Acad., 1978; Frederic Ives medal Optical Soc. Am., 1979; von Humboldt sr. scientist award, Munich, 1980; Nobel prize in Physics, 1981; Guggenheim fellow, 1957. Fellow Am. Phys. Soc., Am. Acad. Arts and Scis., IEEE (Morris Liebmann award 1959, Medal of Honor 1983); hon. fellow Indian Acad. Scis.; mem. Optical Soc. Am. (hon.), Nat., Royal Dutch acads. scis., Nat. Acad. Engring., Am. Philos. Soc., Deutsche Akademie der Naturforscher Leopoldina, Koninklyke Nederlandse Akademie von Wetenschappen (corr.), Paris Acad. Scis. (fgn. assoc.). Office: Pierce Hall Harvard Univ Cambridge MA 02138

BLOLAND, PAUL ANSON, educator; b. Primrose, Wis., Nov. 15, 1923; s. Arthur George and Sarah (Hustad) B.; m. Ruth Marian Nolte, Apr. 7, 1951; children—Eric Craig, Peter Brian. B.S., U. Wis., 1949, M.S., 1950; Ph.D., U. Minn., 1959. Student activities adviser U. Minn., 1950-51, asso. dir. student activities bur., 1953-55, dir., 1955-60, asst. prof. ednl. psychology, 1959-60; dean of students Drake U., Des Moines, 1960-64; dean of students, asso. prof. edn. U. So. Calif., Los Angeles, 1964-69, v.p. student and alumni affairs, 1969-72, prof. edn., 1970—, chmn. dept. counseling, 1973—. Author: Student Group Advising in Higher Education; editorial bd. Jour. Coll. Student Personnel, 1975-78; Contbr. articles to profl. and mountaineering jours. Served with AUS, 1943-46, 1951-52. Mem. Am. Personnel and Guidance Assn. (senate del. 1962-63, mem. com. br. coordination 1963-64, nat. membership com. 1963-65), Am. Coll. Personnel Assn. (program com. 1960-61, commn. advising fgn. students 1963-64, chmn. nat. membership com. 1964-65, mem.-at-large nat. exec. council 1965-66, 67-70, pres. elect 1969-70, pres. 1970-71), Nat. Assn. Student Personnel Adminstrs. (mem.-at-large and sec. nat. exec. com.), Am. Assn. for Higher Edn., Am. Psychol. Assn., Coll. Student Personnel Inst. (exec. com. 1965-66, bd. dirs. 1965-69, chmn. acad. council 1967-69), Calif. Coll. Personnel Assn. (pres. 1981-82), Nat. Vocat. Guidance Assn., Educare, Sierra Club, Iron Cross, Skull and Dagger, Blue Key, Alpha Phi Omega, Phi Delta Kappa, Delta Epsilon, Psi Chi, Omicron Delta Kappa. Home: 27128 Fond du Lac Rd Rancho Palos Verdes CA 90274 Office: Univ So Calif Los Angeles CA 90007

BLOM, DANIEL CHARLES, lawyer, insurance company executive; b. Portland, Oreg., Dec. 13, 1919; s. Charles D. and Anna (Reiner) B.; m. Ellen Lavon Stewart, June 28, 1952; children: Daniel Stewart, Nicole Jan. B.A. magna cum laude, U. Wash., 1941, postgrad., 1941-42; J.D., Harvard U., 1948, U. Paris, 1954-55. Bar: Wash. bar 1949. Teaching fellow speech U. Wash., 1941-42; law clk. to justice Supreme Ct. Wash., 1948-49; since practiced in, Seattle; asso. Graves, Kizer & Graves, 1949-51; gen. counsel Northwestern Life Ins. Co., 1952-54; partner Case & Blom, 1952-54; asso., partner Ryan, Carlson, Bush, Swanson & Hendel, 1956—; sr. v.p., gen. counsel, dir. Family Life Ins. Co., 1964-77, exec. v.p., gen. counsel, 1977—; v.p., dir. Family Life Bldg. Co.; vice chmn. Wash. Bd. Bar Examiners, 1970-72, chmn., 1972-75; mem. industry adv. com. Nat. Assn. Ins. Commrs., 1966-68; pres. Wash. Ins. Council, also Ins. Fund Found., 1971-73, gen. counsel, 1975-78. Editor: Wash. State Bar Jour, 1951-52; assoc. editor: The Brief, 1975-76; Author: Life Insurance Law of the State of Washington, 1980. Chmn. jury selection Wash. Gov.'s Writer's Day Awards, 1976; bd. dirs. Crisis Clinic; trustee Bush Sch., 1971-79, v.p., 1976-77; trustee, v.p. Frye Mus., Seattle, 1976-82, World Affairs Council Seattle, 1972—, Friends of Freeway Park, 1976—; trustee Friends of Seattle Pub. Library, 1982—. Served to 2d lt. AUS, 1942-45; PTO. Decorated Bronze Star. Mem. Am. (vice chmn. com. on life ins. law, sect. ins., negligence and compensation law 1971-76, chmn. 1976-78, sect. program chmn. 1978-79, mem. council 1979-83), Wash. Bar Assn. (award of merit 1975, chmn. legal edn. liason com. 1977-78), Seattle Bar Assn., Am. Judicature Soc., Assn. Life Ins. Counsel, Harvard Law Sch. Assn., Am. Council Life Ins. (legis. com. 1982—), Am. Arbitration Assn., Harvard Assn. Seattle and Western Wash. (trustee 1976-77), Phi Beta Kappa, Tau Kappa Alpha. Home: 2424 Magnolia Blvd W Seattle WA 98199 Office: Park Pl Seattle WA 98101
I think it is the duty of every person to accomplish the highest achievements of which he is capable. What is significant is not how his achievements compare with those of others but how they compare with his potential. The primary struggle of life is, thus, not against others but against one's own limitations.

BLOMFIELD, RICHARD BEST, management consultant; b. Kamuela, Hawaii, Mar. 24, 1919; s. John Harold Stewart and Eirene Alice (Best) B.; m. Laurel Currey, May 18, 1957; children: John Roe, Christiana Jane, Mary Rachel. A.B. cum laude, U. Hawaii, 1945; postgrad., Harvard U., 1945-46; M.A., Columbia U., 1947. Analyst Amfac, Inc., Honolulu, 1947-50; mgr. salary adminstrn. Union Carbide Corp., N.Y.C., 1950-59; dir. personnel adminstrn. Mack Trucks, Inc., Plainfield, N.J., 1959-61; dir. personnel Am. Standard Inc., N.Y.C., 1961-63; v.p. Am. Mut. Ins. Cos., Wakefield, Mass., 1964-69; sr. v.p., sec., dir., mem. exec. com. Hornblower, Weeks Noyes & Trask, Inc. (name now HWN&T, Inc.), N.Y.C., 1969-80; gen. ptnr. HWN&T, Inc., N.Y.C., 1969-72, sr. v.p., sec., dir., 1980—; pres. Richard B. Blomfield Assos. (mgmt. cons.), Morristown, N.J., 1980—; dir. HWN & T, Inc., Henry Hornblower Fund, Inc.; allied mem. N.Y. Stock Exchange; adj. lectr. NYU Sch. Continuing Edn. Contbr.: How to Prepare for Management Responsibilities, 1962, Leadership in the Office, 1963, The Recruitment Process, 1967, The Development Process; contbr. articles to profl. jours. Adviser Nat. Exec. Inst., Boy Scouts Am.; bd. dirs. Morris County Mental Health Assn.; mem. adv. bd. Am. Cleft Palate Edn. Found., Ins. Inst. Boston U., 1967-69; chmn. Hornblower Pension and Profit Sharing Trust; mem. Lexington (Mass.) Town Meeting, also mem. appropriations com. Served to lt. USNR, 1941-45. Mem. Am. Soc. Tng. and Devel., Assn., Am. Soc. Personnel Adminstrn., Morris Mus. Mineral Soc., Nat. Audubon Soc., Am. Mus. Natural History, Smithsonian Inst., Am. Heritage Soc., N.J., Morris County hist. assns., Friends of Mineralogy, Am. Hemerocallis Soc., Frelinghuysen Arboretum, Ret. Officers Assn., Pi Gamma Mu, Phi Kappa Phi. Episcopalian (vestryman). Club: Downtown Athletic (N.Y.C.). Home: 44 Rolling Hill Dr Morristown NJ 07960

BLOMGREN, PAUL BROWN, coll. adminstr.; b. Winterset, Iowa, Dec. 8, 1920; s. Lawrence L. and Aletha (Brown) B.; m. Aileen Helen Trask, Aug. 21, 1942; children—Paul Brown, Richard H., Barbara A., Robert C. B.A., State U. Iowa, 1942, M.A., 1947; D.B.A., Ind. U., 1952. Instr. econs. DePauw U., 1947-50; from teaching fellow to asso. prof. transp. Ind. U. Sch. Bus., 1950-56; asso. prof. mktg. and transp. Mich. State U., 1956-59; prof. bus. adminstrn., dean Sch. Bus., Mont. State U., 1959-64; dean Sch. Bus. Adminstrn. and Econs., Calif. State U., Northridge, 1964-74, prof. bus. adminstrn., 1977; dean Sch. Bus. Adminstrn., U. Mont., Missoula, 1977—; exec. v.p. Hawaii Pacific Coll., Honolulu, 1974-77; Mem. Gov.'s Com. Econ. Studies, Mont. SBA Adv. Council, Mayor's Com. Econ. Devel., San Fernando Valley Indsl. Assn.; adv. com. Pacific N.W. Econ. Base Study; exec. com. Mo. Basin Research and Devel. Council. Pres. Western Mont. council Boy Scouts Am. Served with USNR, 1942-46. Mem. Am. Econ. Assn., Am. Soc. Traffic and Transp., Order Artus, Beta Gamma Sigma, Theta Xi, Delta Nu Alpha. Office: School of Business Univ of Mont Missoula MT 59812

BLOMQUIST, ALFRED THEODORE, JR., chemical manufacturing company executive; b. Chgo., July 22, 1934; s. Alfred T. and Sara (Moffet) B.; m. Nancy Ann Brockman, Dec. 27, 1956; children: Tenleigh Liza, Carrie Lisa. A.B., Cornell U., 1956, M.B.A., 1957. With Rohm & Haas Co., various locations, 1957-80; chmn., chief exec. officer P.A. Hunt Chem. Co., Palisades Park, N.J., 1980—. Served with AUS, 1957. Office: Roosevelt Place Palisades Park NJ 07650 *

BLOMQUIST, CARL GUNNAR, cardiologist; b. Båraryd, Sweden, Dec. 31, 1931; came to U.S., 1965; s. Arvid Elias and Karin Johanna (Hullman) B.; m. Joan Barre Bakula, 1961; children—Mary Jennifer, Peter Carl. B.M., U. Lund, 1954, M.D., 1960; Ph.D., Karolinska Inst., Stockholm, 1967. Research fellow cardiovascular epidemiology U. Minn. Med. Center, Mpls., 1960-61; resident Karolinska Inst., 1962-65; mem. faculty U. Tex. Health Sci. Center, Southwestern Med. Sch., Dallas, 1966—, prof. medicine and physiology, 1976—; mem. research study com. Am. Heart Assn., 1970-73; mem. applied physiology study sect. NIH, 1974-78. Author articles in field; mem. editorial bds. profl. jours. Mem. Dallas Symphony Orch. Guild. Grantee NIH, NASA; established investigator Am. Heart Assn. Fellow Am. Coll. Cardiology; mem. Internat. Soc. Cardiology, Am. Heart Assn. (fellow council epidemiology), So. Soc. Clin. Research. Home: 4229 Willow Grove Rd Dallas TX 75220 Office: Div Cardiology Southwestern Med Sch Dallas TX 75235

BLOMQUIST, JOHN E., metals company executive; b. Kansas City, Kans., Aug. 22, 1914; s. Arthur and Mary (Meeker) B.; m. Harriet T. Rohner, Sept. 25, 1943; 1 dau., Mary. A.B., U. Mo., Kansas City. With Reynolds Metals Co., 1940—, now vice chmn. bd., chief operating officer, Richmond, Va., also dir. subsidiaries; dir. Robertshaw Controls Co. Served with USNR, 1942-46. Mem. Aluminum Assn. (pres. 1978-80), Soc. Automotive Engrs. Address: Reynolds Metals Co 6601 Broad St Rd Richmond VA 23261

BLOMQUIST, RICHARD FREDERICK, chemist, consultant, retired government official; b. Mankato, Minn., Nov. 25, 1912; s. Hjalmar Frederick and Mathilda M. (Miele) B.; m. Helen Mae Ogburn, Aug. 28, 1937; children: John A., Patricia Blomquist Robinson, Frederick C. B.A., Coe Coll., 1934, D.Sc. (hon.), 1982; M.S., U. Iowa, 1936, Ph.D., 1937. Prof. chemistry Doane Coll., Crete, Nebr., 1937-42; project leader glues and glued products research U.S. Forest Products Lab., Madison, Wis., 1942-66; project leader housing research Southeastern Forest Expt. Sta., Forest Service, U.S. Dept. Agr., Athens, Ga., 1966-76; adj. prof. U. Ga., Athens, 1966-76; chmn. Gordon Research Conf. Adhesion, 1956; chmn. ad hoc com. aerospace adhesives Nat. Materials Adv. Bd., 1972-74; cons. Mexican Forest Service, 1973, Industrias del Peru, Lima, 1978. Contbg. author reference texts, encys.; Chmn. editorial com., Forest Products Research Soc., 1963-68; adv. bd.: Jour. Adhesion, 1971—; Contbr. numerous articles in field to profl. jours. Recipient Adhesives award Am. Soc. Testing and Materials, 1962, Marburg Lecture award, 1963; Sr. research fellow New Zealand Forest Service, 1965. Fellow Internat. Acad. Wood Sci., Am. Inst. Chemists; mem. Forest Products Research Soc. (pres. 1974-75, Gottschalk Meml. award 1972), Am. Chem. Soc., Soc. Wood Sci. and Tech. (vis. scientist 1968-73), Adhesive and Sealant Council (hon.). Clubs: Rotarian., Green Hills Country. Home: 195 Robin Rd Athens GA 30605

BLOMQUIST, ROBERT OSCAR, banker; b. Passaic, N.J., Aug. 19, 1930; s. Oscar and Adeline Louise (Hotaling) B.; m. Audrey M. Korn, Apr. 4, 1954; children: Dana C., Carin E. B.A., Allegheny Coll., Meadville, Pa., 1952; M.S., Columbia, 1953. With Chase Manhattan Bank, N.Y.C., 1957-76, gen. mgr., U.K., 1970, regional exec., U.K., Scandinavia, Africa, 1971, sr. v.p., group exec., Europe and Africa, 1971-74, Nat. Banking Group, 1975-76; pres., dir. Chase Manhattan Leasing Corp., Chase Nat. Services Corp., Chase Manhattan Realty Leasing Corp., 1974-76; chmn. Chase Banks-Internat., Chgo., Los Angeles and Houston, 1974-76; pres., dir. Franklin State Bank, Somerset, N.J., 1976-80; vice chmn., dir. Mercantile Trust Co., St.Louis, 1980—; dir. Luth. Brotherhood Life Ins. Co., Mpls. Contbr. articles to profl. jours. Bd. dirs. Luther Northwest Sem., St. Paul, 1982—. Served to lt. USNR, 1954-59. Clubs: Bellerive Country, University, Mo. Athletic (St. Louis); Internat. (Washington); RAC (London, Eng.). Home: 13309 Kings Glen Saint Louis MO 63131 Office: Mercantile Tower Saint Louis MO 63166

BLOMSTER, RALPH NORMAN, educator; b. Lynn, Mass., May 18, 1931; s. George Alfred and Ranghild (Johnson) B.; m. Merilyn Gay Christenson, May 19, 1962; children—Kirsten Joy, Erik Bjorn, Leif Alan. B.S., Mass. Coll. Pharmacy, 1953; M.S., U. Pitts., 1958; Ph.D., U. Conn., 1963. Instr. U. Pitts., 1958-59, asst. prof., 1963-66, asso. prof., 1966-69; prof., chmn. dept. medicinal chemistry and pharmacognosy U. Md., Balt., 1969—; cons. Amazon Natural Drug Co. Editor: Am. Soc. Pharmacognosy Newsletter, 1968—; asso. editor: Lynn Index. Served with AUS, 1953-55. Fellow AAAS, N.Y. Acad. Scis.; mem. Am. Soc. Pharmacognosy (pres. 1973-74), Am. Assn. Coll. Pharmacy (sec. sect. tchrs. biology and sci. 1966-74), Am. Pharm. Assn., Acad. Pharm. Sci. (chmn. sect. nat. products 1974), AAAS, Soc. Econ. Botany, Am. Inst. Biol. Sci., Sigma Xi, Kappa Psi, Rho Chi. Home: 108 Hillside Rd Catonsville MD 21228 Office: 636 W Lombard St Baltimore MD 21201

BLONSTON, GARY LEE, journalist; b. Cleve., May 14, 1942; s. Edward Preston and Billie Marguerite (Bass) V.; m. Judith Susan Miller, Jan. 15, 1977; children: R. Scott, Nancy L. B.S. in Journalism, Northwestern U., 1963, M.S., 1964. Reporter Miami (Fla.) Herald, 1964-66; reporter, asst. city editor, Washington corr., Sunday editor, exec. news editor Detroit Free Press, 1966-80, exec. news editor, 1980-81, nat. corr., 1981—. Recipient Scripps-Howard Meeman award for excellence in environ. reporting, 1970, Disting. Community Service award Nat. Urban Coalition, 1982. Home and Office: 259 Linden Dr Boulder CO 80302

BLOOD, ARCHER KENT, foreign service officer; b. Chgo., Mar. 20, 1923; s. Francis Earle and Hazel Mary (Brown) B.; m. Margaret Lloyd Millward, May 14, 1948; children: Shirley, Barbara, Peter, Archer. B.A., U. Va., 1943; M.A., George Washington U., 1963. Commd. fgn. service officer Dept. State; vice consul, Thessaloniki, Greece, 1947-48, Munich, Germany, 1949-50, 2d sec., Athens, Greece, 1950-52, vice consul, Algiers, 1953, 2d sec., Bonn, Germany, 1953-55, consul, Dacca, 1960-62, dep. chief of mission, Kabul, 1965-68, polit. counselor, Athens, 1968-70, consul gen., Dacca, 1970-71; dep. dir. personnel Dept. State, Washington, 1972-74; dep. comdt. Army War Coll., 1974-77; dep. chief of mission Am. embassy, New Delhi, India, 1977-80, charge' d' affaires, New Delhi, 1980-81; vis. prof., diplomat-in-residence Allegheny Coll., 1982—. Served with USNR, 1944-46. Mem. Phi Beta Kappa. Presbyterian. Address: Allegheny Coll Meadville PA

BLOOD, WAYLAND FREEMAN, financial company executive; b. Gloucester, Mass., Aug. 19, 1930; s. Wayland Potter and Katharine Day (Freeman) B.; m. Charlean Brooks, Aug. 19, 1956; children—David, Katharine, Cynthia, Daniel. B.A., Hamilton Coll., 1953; M.B.A., Columbia U., N.Y.C., 1957. Portfolio mgr. Gulf Oil Corp., Pitts., 1957-61, Chrysler Corp., Highland Park, Mich., 1961-62; mgr. Ford Motor Co., Dearborn, Mich., 1962-70; treas. Ford Brazil, 1970-73; asst. treas., then treas., v.p. Ford Motor Credit Co., Dearborn, 1974—. Del. Republican State Conv., 1966-68; trustee West Bloomfield Twp., 1966-70; mem. Planning Commn., 1966-70, Gov's. Commn. on Extension Northwestern Hwy., 1975-77. Served with U.S. Army, 1953-55. Republican. Presbyterian. Office: The American Rd Dearborn MI 481212

BLOODGOOD, JOHN DUDLEY, architect; b. N.Y.C., Mar. 5, 1931; s. Dudley Tooker and Helen Ann (Beeck) B.; m. Jeanne Eileen Shannon, Nov. 16, 1953; children: Sally, John D., Jr. B.Arch., Renesselaer Poly. Inst., 1952. Registered architect, Ala., Ariz., Ark., Calif., Colo., Del., Fla., Idaho., Ill., Ind., Ioa, Dans., La., Md., Mass., Mich., Minn., Miss, Mo., Nebr., N.J., N.Y., Ohio, Pa., S.C., Tenn., Tex., Utah, Va., Wash., Wis., Wyo. Bldg. editor Better Homes and Gardens, Des Moines, 1957-65; pres. Bloodgood Architects, Des Moines, 1971—; vice chmn. residential council Urban Land inst., 1979-82; design cons. Profl. Builder Mag., 1971—. Trustee Des Moines Art Ctr., 1972-82; mem. com. Iowa Adv. Bldg. Code, 1972-76; mem. Mayor's Com. for Excellence in Urban Design, Des Moines, 1974-79, Iowa State U. Profl. Adv. Bd., 1978-83. Fellow AIA (chmn. housing com. 1978-79). Republican. Club: Wakonda (mem. future planning com. 1975-76). Lodge: Rotary. Office: Bloodgood Architects PC 3001 Grand Ave Des Moines IA 50312

BLOODWORTH, J. M. BARTOW, JR., physician, educator; b. Atlanta, Feb. 21, 1925; s. J.M. Bartow and Elizabeth (Dimmock) B.; m. Jean Stone, Nov. 26, 1947; children: Lowell Ann, Joyce Lynn, Elizabeth Carol; m. Joan Wiltgen, July 8, 1972; children: Allison Joan, Ellen Lucy. Student, Emory U., 1942-43, M.D., 1948, Stanford U., 1944. Intern, then asst. resident pathology Columbia-Presbyn. Med. Center, N.Y.C., 1948-50; instr. pathology Columbia U., 1949-50; asst. resident medicine U. Iowa Hosp., 1950-51; mem. faculty Ohio State U. Coll. Medicine, 1951-62, prof. pathology, 1960-62, U. Wis., 1962—; chief div. pathologic anatomy Ohio State U. Hosp., 1954-61; pathologist Columbus State Hosp., 1954-57; chief lab. service Madison VA Hosp., 1962—. Author numerous articles in field.; Editor: Endocrine Pathology, 1968, 2d edit., 1981. Served with AUS, 1941-45. Recipient Fight for Sight citation Am. Assn. Research in Opthalmology, 1964. Mem. Am., Wis. med. assns., Dane County Med. Soc., Wis. Soc. Pathologists (pres. 1977-79), Am. Assn. Pathologists. Histochem. Soc., Am. Diabetes Assn. (Lilly award 1963, Profl. Service award Wis. affiliate 1982), So. Wis. Diabetes Assn. (past pres.), Am., Wis. heart assns., Soc. Exptl. Biology and Medicine, Internat. Acad. Pathology, Am. Soc. Clin. Pathology, Am. Assn. Neuropathologists, Nat. Soc. Med. Research, Am. Soc. Cell Biology, Am. Legion, Endocrine Soc., Sigma Nu, Phi Chi. Club: Gyro Internat. (pres. Columbus 1962, Madison 1980). Home: 4514 Crescent Rd Madison WI 53711

BLOOM, ARNOLD SANFORD, lawyer; b. Syracuse, N.Y., Sept. 3, 1942; s. Benjamin and Sarah (Kushner) B.; m. Cirelle Dvorin, July 20, 1967; children: Brooke, Jessica, Evan. B.S., Syracuse U., 1964, M.B.A., 1967, J.D., 1967; LL.M., NYU, 1968. Bar: N.Y. 1967, U.S. Dist. Ct. (so. dist.) N.Y. 1972. Assoc. Marshall, Bratter, Greene, Allison & Tucker, N.Y.C., 1968-74; sr. atty. Kane-Miller Corp., Tarrytown, N.Y., 1974-78, gen. counsel, 1978—, v.p., 1980—. Mem. ABA, N.Y.

State Bar Assn., Am. Meat Inst. (legal Com.), Westchester-Fairfield Corp. Counsel Assn., Order of Coif, Justinian Soc., Beta Alpha Psi, Alpha Kappa Psi. Home: 8 Suzanne Ln Chappaqua NY 10514 Office: Kane-Miller Corp 555 White Plains Rd Tarrytown NY 10591

BLOOM, BARRY MALCOLM, pharmacy company executive; b. Roxbury, Mass., Aug. 12, 1928; s. Morris and Ann (Levine) B.; m. Joan Martha Ensign, June 27, 1956; children—Catherine, Brian, Joanna. S.B., M.I.T., 1948, Ph.D., 1951, postgrad., 1967. Research chemist Pfizer, Inc., Groton, Conn., 1952-63, dir. medicinal chems., research, 1963-71, pres. central research div., 1971, v.p. research, 1971-73; pres. Central Research, dir., 1973—; mem. Congressional Commn. on Fed. Drug Approval Process, Commn. on Drugs for Rare Diseases, Pharm. Mfrs. Assn., chmn. research and devel. sect., 1976; cons. Walter Reed Army Inst. Research, 1969, 75-77, U.S. Congress Office Tech. Assessment, 1976-77; Mem. Conn. High Tech. Commn.; mem. vis. coms. depts. biology and chemistry MIT, U. Conn. Sch. Bus. Adminstrn., Inst. Materials Sci. Mem. editorial bd.: Ann. Reports in Medicinal Chemistry, 1968-70. NRC postdoctoral fellow U. Wis., 1952; Poly. Inst. fellow, N.Y.C., 1980. Mem. Am. Chem. Soc. (chmn. div. medicinal chemistry 1967), N.Y. Acad. Scis., Conn. Acad. Sci. and Engring. Patentee in field. Home: Mackintosh Rd Lyme CT 06371 Office: Pfizer Central Research Eastern Point Rd Groton CT 06340

BLOOM, CLAIRE, actress; b. London, Eng., Feb. 15, 1931; d. Edward Max and Elizabeth (Grew) Blume; m. Rod Steiger, Sept. 19, 1959 (div.); 1 dau., Anna. Student, Badminton Sch., Bristol, Eng., Fern Hill Manor, New Milton, Eng.; pub. schs., N.Y. Appeared as: Ophelia, Stratford-Upon-Avon, 1948; plays include also Ring Around the Moon, London, 1949-51; in: others Romeo and Juliet, for Old Vic; also as Juliet in Old Vic tour of, U.S.; film roles in Three Steps to Freedom, 1960, The Brothers Grimm, The Chapman Report, 1962, The Haunting, 1963, 80,000 Suspects, 1963, Alta Infidelita, 1963, Il Maestro di Vigeuono, 1963, The Outrage, 1964, The Spy Who Came in from the Cold, 1965, A Doll's House, 1973, Islands in the Stream, 1976, Clash of the Titans, 1981; appeared Broadway in: Rashomon, 1959, at Royal Court Theatre, London, in Altona, 1960, A Doll's House, Hedda Gabler, 1971, Vivat! Vivat Reginal, 1972; New York appearance The Innocents, 1976; London appearances A Doll's House, 1973, A Streetcar Named Desire, 1974, Rosmersholm, 1977, The Cherry Orchard, 1981, These are Women, 1982-83; Katherine of Aragon: many roles Brit. and U.S. TV including Henry VIII; Hope Louoff: many roles Brit. and U.S. TV including The Ghost Writer; Miss Cooper: Separate Tables; Lady Marchmain: Brideshead Revisited; author: Limelight and After, 1982. Address: care Michael Linnit Globe Theatre Shaftesbury Ave London W1 England

BLOOM, DAVID RONALD, drug company executive; b. Apr. 20, 1943; s. Sam and Tillie (Weinstein) B.; m. Molly Rosenbloom, May 8, 1966; children: Corinne, Michael. B.Sc. in Pharmacy, U. Toronto, 1967. Franchisee Shoppers Drug Mart, Toronto, 1968-73, dir. ops., 1973-74, v.p. ops., 1975-77, exec. v.p. corp. ops., 1978-83, Central region pres., 1978-83, pres., chief exec. officer, 1983—, also dir.; dir. Imasco Ltd., Pharmaprix. Bd. dirs. Can. Found. Advancement of Pharmacy, Eglinton Equestrian Club, 1980-83. Mem. Ont. Pharmacists Assn. (council 1979-81), Ont. Chain Drug Assn. (pres.). Office: Shoppers Drug Mart Ltd 225 Yorkland Blvd Willowdale ON Canada M2J 4R2

BLOOM, EDWARD ALAN, English educator, author; b. Michigan City, Ind., May 24, 1914; s. Robert and Tillie (Leibovitz) B.; m. Lillian Doris Blumberg, June 17, 1947. B.S. in Journalism, U. Ill., 1936, M.A., 1939, Ph.D. in English, 1947; A.M. (hon.), Brown U., 1957. Newspaper reporter, corr., editor Midwestern Papers & Press Service, 1936-38; also free lance mag. writer; asst., instr. English U. Ill., 1939-42, 46-47; faculty dept. English Brown U., 1947—, prof. English, 1959—, chmn. dept., 1960-67, Nicholas Brown prof. oratory and belles lettres, 1960-67; dir. Nat. Endowment for Humanities Summer Seminars, 1978, 80. Author: Samuel Johnson in Grub Street, 1957, (with C.H. Philbrick, E.M. Blistein) The Order of Poetry, 1961, (with L.D. Bloom) Willa Cather's Gift of Sympathy, 1962, The Order of Fiction, 1964, Joseph Addison's Sociable Animal, 1971, Satire's Persuasive Voice, 1979; also articles on 18th Century and contemporary English and Am. lit. problems.; Editor: Shakespeare 1564-1964, 1964, Frances Burney's Evelina, 1968; editor: English and Am. lit. Blaisdell Pub. Co, 1964-70, (with L.D. Bloom) The Variety of Fiction, 1969, Anthony Collins, A Discourse concerning Ridicule and Irony, 1970, Camilla, 1972, Fanny Burney's Journals and Letters, 1978, Addison and Steele Critical Heritage Series, 1980; co-editor: (with Philbrick and Blistein) The Variety of Poetry, 1964; sr. editor: Novel: A Forum on Fiction, 1967—; Contbr. book reviews short stories to nat. and internat. jours. Served from pvt. to capt. AUS, 1942-46. Decorated Bronze Star.; Huntington Library fellow, 1963-64, 67-68, 72; Guggenheim fellow, 1969-70; Huntington Library-Nat. Endowment for Humanities fellow, 1977-78; Nat. Endowment for Humanities grantee, 1980—; Huntington Library fellow, 1981. Mem. AAUP, MLA, Am. Soc. 18th Century Studies, The Johnsonians (chmn. 1980), Sigma Delta Chi. Home: 82 Laurel Ave Providence RI 02906

BLOOM, FLOYD ELLIOTT, physician, research scientist; b. Mpls., Oct. 8, 1936; s. Jack Aaron and Frieda (Shochman) B.; m. D'Nell Bingham, Aug. 30, 1956 (dec. May 1973); children: Fl'Nell, Evan Russell; m. Jody Patricia Corey, Aug. 9, 1980. A.B. cum laude, So. Meth. U., 1956, M.D., Washington U., St. Louis, 1960; D.Sc. h.c., So. Meth. U., 1983. Intern Barnes Hosp., St. Louis, 1960-61, resident internal medicine, 1961-62; research asso. NIMH, Washington, 1962-64; fellow depts. pharmacology, psychiatry and anatomy Yale Sch. Medicine, 1964-66, asst. prof., 1966-67, asso. prof., 1968; chief lab. neuropharmacology NIMH, Washington, 1968-75, acting dir. div. spl. mental health, 1973-75; commd. officer USPHS, 1974-75; dir. Arthur Vining Davis Center for Behavorial Neurobiology; prof. Salk Inst., La Jolla, Calif., 1975—; mem. Commn. on Alcoholism, 1980-81, Nat. Adv. Mental Health Council, 1976-80. Author: (with J.R. Cooper and R.H. Roth) Biochemical Basis of Neuropharmacology, 1971; editor: Peptides: Integrators of Cell and Tissue Function, 1980; co-editor: Regulatory Peptides. Recipient A. Cressy Morrison award N.Y. Acad. Scis., 1971; A.E. Bennett award for basic research Soc. Biol. Psychiatry, 1971; Arthur A. Fleming award Science mag., 1973; Mathilde Solowey award, 1973; Biol. Sci. award Washington Acad. Scis., 1975; Alumni Achievement citation Washington U., 1980; McAlpin Research Achievement award Mental Health Assn., 1980; Lectr.'s medal College de France, 1979. Fellow Am. Coll. Neuropsychopharmacology (mem. council 1976-78); mem. Nat. Acad. Sci. (chmn. sect. neurobiology 1979-83), Inst. Medicine, Am. Acad. Arts and Scis., Soc. Neurosci. (sec. 1973-74, pres. 1976), Am. Soc. Pharmacology and Exptl. Therapeutics, Am. Soc. Cell Biology, Am. Physiol. Soc., Am. Assn. Anatomists, Research Soc. Alcoholism. Home: 1145 Pacific Beach Dr Apt B405 San Diego CA 92109 Office: Salk Inst La Jolla CA 92037

BLOOM, FRANK, financial executive; b. Bklyn., Dec. 25, 1937; s. Ralph M. and Carrie (Horowitz) B.; m. Sheila D. Berger, Jan. 26, 1960; children: Scott H., Kenneth L., Jeffrey M. B.B.A., Baruch Sch., CCNY, 1961; M.A., NYU, 1968. C.P.A., N.Y. Sr. mgmt. auditor Assoc. Univs., Upton, N.Y., 1968-69, Brookhaven Lab, 1968-69; fin. v.p., sec.-treas. Geon Industries, Inc., Woodbury, N.Y., 1969-76; exec. v.p., chief officer, dir. Hi-Shear Industries, Inc., North Hills, N.Y., 1977—; dir. Raymark Corp., Trumball, Conn. Bd. dirs. Am. Cancer Soc., Melville, N.Y. Mem. Am. Inst. C.P.A.s, Am. Mgmt. Assn., N.Y. Soc. C.P.A.s. Office: Hi-Shear Industries Inc 3333 New Hyde Park Rd North Hills NY 11042

BLOOM, HAROLD, humanities educator; b. N.Y.C., July 11, 1930; s. William and Paula (Lev) B.; m. Jeanne Gould, May 8, 1958; children: Daniel Jacob, David Moses. B.A., Cornell U., 1951; Ph.D., Yale U., 1955; L.H.D., Boston Coll., 1973, Yeshiva U., 1976. Mem. faculty Yale U., 1955—, prof. English, 1965-77, DeVane prof. humanities, 1974-77, prof. humanities, 1977—, sterling prof. humanities, 1983—; vis. prof. Hebrew U., Jerusalem, 1959, Breadloaf Summer Sch., 1965-66, Soc. for Humanities, Cornell U., 1968-69; vis. Univ. prof. New Sch. Social Research, N.Y.C., 1982—. Author: Shelley's Mythmaking, 1959, The Visionary Company, 1961, Blake's Apocalypse, 1963, Commentary to Blake, 1965, Yeats, 1970, The Ringers in the Tower, 1971, The Anxiety of Influence, 1973, Wallace Stevens: The Poems of Our Climate, 1977, A Map of Misreading, 1975, Kabbalah and Criticism, 1975, Poetry and Repression, 1976, Figures of Capable Imagination, 1976, The Flight to Lucifer: A Gnostic Fantasy, 1979, Agon: Towards a theory of Revisionism, 1981, The Breaking of the Vessels, 1981, Freud: Transference and Authority, 1984, Poetics of Influence: New and Selected Criticism, 1984. Recipient John Addison Porter prize Yale U., 1955; Newton Arvin award, 1967; Melville Cane award Poetry Soc. Am., 1970; Zabel prize Am. Inst. Arts and Letters, 1982; Guggenheim fellow, 1962; Fulbright fellow, 1955. Mem. Am. Acad. Arts and Scis. Home: 179 Linden St New Haven CT 06511 *strong poets, and strong readers after them, become great only by striving against an earlier greatness, in the hope that by overcoming precursors, they also overcome what is merely peripheral in themselves.*

BLOOM, HERBERT, editor; b. Boston, Nov. 23, 1930; s. Albert and Rose (Swartz) B.; m. Arlene Perlis, Aug. 17, 1958; children: Sarah, Kenneth. B.A., Brandeis U., 1952; A.M., Harvard U., 1954; M.L.S., Simmons Coll., 1959. Librarian, Lowell (Mass.) State Coll., 1959-63; Librarian So. Ill. U., Carbondale, 1963-67; sr. editor ALA, Chgo., 1969—. Contbr. articles to profl. publs. Served with AUS, 1954-56. Title IIB fellow, 1967-69. Mem. ALA. Club: Harvard of Chgo. Home: 1430 Western Ave Flossmoor IL 60422 Office: 50 E Huron St Chicago IL 60611

BLOOM, HYMAN, artist; b. Latvia, Mar. 29, 1913; U.S., 1920. Ed., West End Community Center, Boston. Instr. Wellesley (Mass.) Coll., 1949-51, Harvard U., Cambridge, Mass., 1951-53. One-man shows, Stuart Gallery, Boston, 1945, Inst. Contemporary Art, Boston, Whitney Mus. Art, N.Y.C., 1968, Albright Knox Art Gallery, Buffalo, 1954, retrospective; represented in permanent collections, Hirshorn Mus., Washington, Mus. Modern Art, N.Y.C., Whitney Mus. Art, Harvard U. Office: Kennedy Galleries Inc 40 W 57th St New York NY 10019

BLOOM, JAMES DAVID, government service administrator; b. Newark, Nov. 13, 1934; s. Canfield D. and Alexandria K. (Butters) B.; m. Constance S. Cappe, Sept. 6, 1958; 1 dau., Elizabeth Anne. A.B., Drew U., 1956; M. Pub. Adminstrn., Ind. U., 1966. Budget analyst Farmer's Home Adminstrn., U.S. Dept. Agr., Washington, 1957-60, Bur. State Services USPHS HEW, 1960-63; project grants officer immunization activities Ctr. Disease Control, Atlanta, 1963-66, asst. exec. officer, 1966-71, exec. officer, 1971—. Nat. Inst. Pub. Affairs fellow, 1966. Mem. Atlanta Assn. Fed. Execs., Amateur Fencing League, Metropolitan Square Dancing Assn. Club: Druid Hillbillies Square Dance. Home: 2700 Hawaii Ct Decatur GA 30033 Office: 1600 Clifton Rd Atlanta GA 30333

BLOOM, JOEL N., science museum director; b. N.Y.C., Aug. 5, 1925; s. Philip M. and Minnie (Shainmark) B.; m. Paula Yakira, Mar. 21, 1948; children: Margo, Ron, Dan. B.S. in Chem. Engring., Poly. Inst. Bklyn., 1949; M.S. in Ops. Research, Columbia U., 1954. Research engr. Ministry Def. Israel, Tel Aviv, 1949-52; engr. Inland Machinery Co., N.Y.C., 1953-54; sr. engr. U.S. Army Ordnance, N.Y.C., 1954-55; chief engr. Aywon Wire & Metal Co., N.Y.C., 1955-58; sr. staff engr. to dir. system sci. dept. Research Labs., Franklin Inst., Phila., 1958-69; v.p., dir. Sci. Mus. and Planetarium, 1969—, mem. mus. and planetarium bd.; mem. adv. council Nat. Mus. Act, 1979-81; mem. adv. com. on sci. edn. NSF, 1978-81; mem. Pa. Gov.'s Transp. Com., 1968-69, Phila. Mayor's Cultural Adv. Council, 1984—; mem. adv. council Parkway Program, 1968-72; cons., mem. mus. adv. panel Nat. Endowment for Arts, 1973-79; cons. Exec. Office of Pres., 1965-68, NEH, 1977—; mem. hwy. research bd. Nat. Acad. Sci., NRC, 1965-69; mem. joint com. on museums Indo-U.S. Subcommn. on Edn. and Culture, 1975-79; mem. U.S. Nat. Commn. for UNESCO, 1981—; co-chmn. Commn. on Museums and the New Century, 1981—; pres. Greater Phila. Cultural Alliance, 1983—. Contbr. articles to profl. jours. Bd. dirs. Lower Delaware County United Jewish Appeal. Served with AUS, 1943-46; ETO. Mem. Assn. Sci. and Tech. Centers (pres., dir.), Assn. Sci. Mus. Dirs. (pres., council mem.), N.E. Conf. Mus. (bd. govs.), Internat. Com. Sci. and Tech. Mus., Internat. Council Mus. (U.S. com., dir., v.p., nat. com. sci. and technol. museums), Am. Assn. Mus. (accreditation commn. 1975-79, legis. com. 1979, v.p. 1982-84), Franklin Inst., Sigma Xi. Jewish (dir. synagogue). Home: 614 Yale Ave Swarthmore PA 19081 Office: 20th St and Benjamin Franklin Pkwy Philadelphia PA 19103

BLOOM, JOHN PORTER, historian, editor, administrator, archivist; b. Albuquerque, Dec. 30, 1924; s. Lansing Bartlett and Maude Elizabeth (McFie) B.; m. Eva Louise Platt, 1954 (div.); children: Katherine Elizabeth Bloom Jassen, John Lansing, Susan Marie; m. Nancy Jo Tice, July 30, 1968. A.B., U. N.Mex., 1947; A.M., George Washington U., 1949; Ph.D., Emory U., 1956; Cert. Pre-meteorology, Reed Coll., 1944. Mem. faculty U. Tex., El Paso, 1952-60, Brenau Coll., 1952-60, No. Ga. Coll., 1952-60; historian, mus. planner, editor Nat. Park Service, Washington, 1960-64; editor Territorial Papers of the U.S., 1964-80; sr. specialist western history Nat. Archives, Washington, 1964-80; dir. Holt-Atherton Pacific Ctr. Western Studies, Stockton, Calif., 1981—; editor Pacific Historian, U. Pacific, Stockton, Calif., 1981—; program com. chmn. Conf. History Am. West, Santa Fe, 1961, 71; cons. NEH div. pub. programs Nat. Hist. Publs. and Records Commn., Va. History and Mus. Fedn., 1976-79; mem. adv. bd. Capitol Studies, U.S. Capitol Hist. Soc., 1971-73. Editor: monograph The American Territorial System, 1973, Territoirial Papers of the U.S., 1969, 71; editor, co-editor: Soldier and Brave and other vols., 1963; book reviewer, contbr. articles to profl. jours. Chmn. Fairfax County Hist. Commn., 1972-73; active Cultural Heritage Bd., Stockton, Calif., 1982—; bd. dirs. Gateway Inc., Alexandria, Va., 1971-75, Homeowners Assn. Chatam Colony, Reston, Va.; sheriff Potomac Corral of the Westerners Internat., 1974; bd. dirs. Joseph Priestly Chapel Assocs. Inc., 1978-81. Served with USAAF, 1943-45. So. Fellowships Fund fellow, 1955-56. Mem. Western History Assn. (pres. 1974, spl. service award 1973, v.p. 1973, Ray Allen Billington award com. 1979-82), Westerners Internat. Inc. (pres. 1981-83), Nat. Council Pub. History (bd. dirs. 1980-83, co-chmn. program com. 1983-84), Westerners Soc. (Golden Spike award 1969), Council Am.'s Mil. Past (bd. dirs. 1982-84), Am. Assn. State and Local History (chmn. awards com. 1976-79), Soc. Am. Archivists, Assn. Documentary Editing, Am. Hist. Assn., Orgn. Am. Historians, Nat. Trust Hist. Preservation, Eastern Nat. Parks and Monuments Assn., Soc. Hist. Archaeology, Assn. Fed. Govt. Historians, So. Hist. Assn., Montana State Hist. Soc., Pioneer Am. Soc., Rio Grande Hist. Found., Colonial N.Mex. Found., Mus. N.Mex. Assoc., Unitarian-Universalist Hist. Soc., Commonwealth (San Francisco). Home: 1629 Academy Ct Stockton CA 95207 Office: Holt-Atherton Pacific Ctr Western Studies U Pacific Stockton CA 95211

BLOOM, JULIUS, performing arts administrator, consultant; b. Bklyn., Sept. 23, 1912; s. Samuel Wolf and Sarah Yochebed (Ferman) B.; m. Emily Leah Spicer, Feb. 16, 1935; children: David Shepherd, Joseph Frederick. B.A., Rutgers U., 1933; postgrad., N.Y. U., 1934-36; L.H.D. (hon.), Buena Vista Coll., 1975. Assoc. editor The Literary World, 1934-35; instr. philosophy Rutgers U., Newark, 1935-36; editor Bklyn. Inst. Arts and Scis., Bklyn., 1936-37, asst. to dir., 1937-39, acting dir., 1939-41, dir., 1941-57; exec. dir. Nat. Inst. Music, N.Y.C., 1957-59; dir. concerts and lectures Rutgers U., 1959-72; exec. dir. Carnegie Hall Corp., N.Y.C., 1960-77, vice chmn. bd., dir. corp. planning, 1977-79, cons., 1979—; Founder, gen. mgr. Bklyn. Symphony Orchestra, 1939-41; pres. Bklyn. Mus. Sch., 1956-62; cons. Cultural Devel. Greater Newark Devel. Council, 1959-66, Bucknell U., 1979—; music cons. Norwegian govt., 1957-61, Office Cultural Affairs, N.Y.C., 1962-65, Mexican govt., 1972—, Fundačao Orchestra Sinfônica Brasileira, 1978—, Columbia Pictures, 1980-82; adminstrv. cons. Center for Public Cinema, Inc., 1979-81, Internat. Fellowship for Arts, Culture and Edn., 1979—, Fundación Teresa Carreño, 1981-82, Beethoven Found., Inc., 1980-82; mktg. cons. Lodiar S.A., Geneva, 1980-82; advisor on community devel. Nat. Assn. Music Mchts., 1982—; cons. on theater design U. Judaism, Los Angeles, 1982—; dir., moderator Northwood Conf. on Creativity, Midland, Mich., 1982—; bd. dirs. Ferruccio Busoni Archives, 1983—. Author: The Year in American Music, 1946-47, 1947; contbg. editor: Metropolis mag., 1979—; Contbr. articles to profl. jours. Decorated officer Ordre des Arts et Lettres, France). Mem. Am. Platform Guild (1st v.p. 1943-46, acting pres. 1946-47), Chamber Music Assos. (founder), Nat. Assn. Concert Mgrs. (exec. sec. 1953-57), Assn. Coll. and Univ. Concert Mgrs. (pres. 1962-64), Phi Beta Kappa. Home and Office: 1207 Dorchester Rd Brooklyn NY 11218

BLOOM, LARY ROGER, mag. editor; b. Cleve., Nov. 13, 1943; s. Abraham William and Helen Miriam B.; 1 dau., Amy. B.S. in Journalism, Ohio U., 1965. Reporter Akron (Ohio) Beacon Jour., 1967-68, mag. writer, 1969-70; editor Beacon mag., 1971-78, Tropic mag. Miami (Fla.) Herald, 1978-81, Hartford Courant mag., 1981—; chmn. editorial bd. Met. Sunday Newspapers, Inc., 1982—. Served with U.S. Army, 1965-67. Office: 179 Allyn St Suite 411 Hartford CT

BLOOM, LAWRENCE S., mfg. co. exec.; b. New Rochelle, N.Y., Apr. 30, 1930; s. Hyman and Eleanor (Bursch) B.; m. Mary Ann Hendricks, Aug. 15, 1959; children—Mark, Julie. B.S. in Commerce and Fin, Bucknell U., Lewisburg, Pa., 1952. Trainee Gimbels, N.Y.C., to 1954; with Warnaco Inc., 1954—; now pres. Thane/Pringle of Scotland div., Altoona, Pa.; dir. Woolknit Assos. Served with AUS, 1952-54. Home: 27 Waverly Dr Hollidaysburg PA 16648 Office: PO Box 1779 Altoona PA 16603

BLOOM, LEE HURLEY, lawyer, public affairs consultant, household products manufacturing executive; b. N.Y.C., June 21, 1919; s. Harry and Harriet (Bresel) B.; m. Mary Louise Tolan, Dec. 15, 1945; children: Daniel, Louise, Douglas. B.S., MIT, 1940; LL.B., Harvard U., 1943. Bar: Mass. 1947, N.Y. 1951. Atty. legal div. Lever Bros. Co., N.Y.C., 1947-67, v.p., sec., gen. counsel, 1968-70, adminstrv. v.p., dir., 1970-82; pres. Unilever U.S., Inc., 1978-82, vice chmn., 1982-83. Chmn. bd. Larchmont (N.Y.) chpt. ARC, 1961-63; Mem. Town of Mamaroneck (N.Y.) Rep. Com., 1957-69; mem. Mamaroneck Planning Bd., 1959-69; mem. Town Bd. Town of Mamaroneck, 1969—, dep. supr., 1982-83. Served to lt. comdr. USNR, 1941-46. Mem. Soap and Detergent Assn. (dir. 1971—, vice chmn. 1978-79, chmn. 1980-82), Internat. C. of C. (trustee U.S. council 1978—, exec. com. 1980—, vice chmn. 1982—). Home: 22 Myrtle Blvd Larchmont NY 10538 Office: Unilever U.S. 10 E 53d St New York NY 10022

BLOOM, MAX SAMUEL, wholesale distributor; b. Chgo., Aug. 2, 1907; s. Samuel and Mary (Becker) B.; m. Carolyn Gumbiner, June 11, 1930 (dec. 1966); children: Donald G., Stephen J., Barbara Kreml; m. Mary Frank Bernstein, Apr. 11, 1967 (dec. 1980). B.A., U. Chgo., 1927. With S. Bloom Inc., Chgo., 1927—, chmn. bd. Chmn. Tobacco div. Combined Jewish Appeal, Chgo. Recipient Am. Jewish Com. Chgo. Human Relations award, Alex Schwartz Meml. award, Chgo. Tobacco Table Stanley Loesser award, Merchandising award Cigarette Merchandise Assn. Mem. Ill. Assn. Tobacco Distributors (founder, past pres., dir.), Nat. Assn. Tobacco Distributors (Tobacco Hall of Fame 1967), Nat. Candy Wholesalers Assn. Club: Cliff Dwellers (Chgo.). Lodge: Rotary. Home: 2933 N Sheridan Rd Chicago IL 60657 Office: S Bloom Inc 5401 S Dansher Rd Chicago IL 60525

BLOOM, MURRAY TEIGH, author; b. N.Y.C., May 19, 1916; s. Louis I. and Anna (Teighblum) B.; m. Sydelle J. Cohen, Apr. 30, 1944; children: Ellen Susan Bloom Lubell, Amy Beth Bloom Moon. B.A., Columbia, 1937, M.S., 1938. Reporter N.Y. Post, 1939; free-lance writer, 1940—; Founder, past trustee United Community Fund Great Neck, N.Y.; founder, past pres. Soc. Mag. Writers (now Am. Soc. Journalists and Authors); corr. Stars & Stripes, Paris-Berlin, 1944-45; dept. head Sch. Journalism Biarritz-Am. U., 1945. Author: Money of Their Own, 1957, The Man Who Stole Portugal, 1966; play Leonora, 1966; The Trouble with Lawyers, 1969, Rogues to Riches, 1972, Lawyers, Clients and Ethics, 1974, The 13th Man, 1977; filmed as Last Embrace, 1979; The Brotherhood of Money, 1983. Served with AUS, 1942-46. Recipient 50th Anniversary award Columbia Grad. Sch. Journalism. Mem. Dramatists Guild of Authors League Am. Address: 40 Hemlock Dr Great Neck NY 11024

BLOOM, MYER, educator; b. Montreal, Que., Can., Dec. 7, 1928; s. Israel and Leah (Ram) B.; m. Margaret Holmes, May 29, 1954; children—David, Margot. B.Sc., McGill U., 1949, M.Sc., 1950; Ph.D., U. Ill., 1954. Research fellow U. Leiden, 1954-56; faculty U. B.C., Vancouver, 1956—, asso. prof., 1960-63, prof. physics, 1963—. Recipient Steacie prize, 1967; Jacob Biely prize, 1968; Gold medal Canadian Assn. Physicists, 1973; Alfred P. Sloan fellow, 1961-65; John Simon Guggenheim fellow, 1964-65; Izaak Walton Killam Meml. scholar, 1978-79. Fellow Royal Soc. Can., Am. Phys. Soc. Research in structure and molecular motion in biol. and model membranes, molecular reorientation in gases, liquids and solids using nuclear magnetic resonance. Home: 5669 King's Rd Vancouver BC V6T 1K9 Canada

BLOOM, PAULINE, author, educator; d. Max and Meta (Landau) B. Student, Bklyn. Coll., Hunter Coll., N.Y.C. Instr. fiction writing Bklyn. Coll., 1951—; dir. Pauline Bloom Workshop Writers (corr. course), 1950—; lectr., critic, cons., 1950—. Author: Toby, Law Stenographer, 1959; Contbr. nat. publs. Mem. Authors Guild (past mem. council), Mystery Writers Am. (past sec., dir.), Nat. League Am. Pen Women (pres. N.Y. State 1965-67, 78-80, pres. Manhattan br. 1970-74). Address: 20 Plaza St Brooklyn NY 11238 *It seems to me the most useful way to spend a life is to spread knowledge. I have been lucky. This is precisely what I have always wanted to do, so that my work - writing and teaching writing - has made me very happy.*

BLOOM, STEPHEN JOEL, distribution vending company executive; b. Chgo., Feb. 27, 1936; s. Max Samuel and Carolyn (Gumbiner) B.; m. Nancy Lee Gillan, Aug. 24, 1957; children: Anne, Bradley, Thomas, Carolyn. B.B.A., U. Mich., 1958. Salesman, then gen. mgr. Cigarette Service Co., Countryside, Ill., 1957-65, pres., chief exec. officer, 1965—; exec. v.p., chief exec. officer S. Bloom, Inc., Countryside; pres., dir. Intercontinental Cons. Corp., Balt., chmn. bd., 1978—; dir. Ford City Bank & Trust Co. Bd. dirs. Clarendon Hills United Fund, Ill., 1975—; fin. chmn. DuPage County Republican Com., 1976. Named Man of Yr. Chgo. Tobacco Table, 1972. Mem. Nat. Automatic Mdsg. Assn. (Minuteman award 1974), Nat. Assn. Tobacco Distbrs. (chmn. nat. legis. com., Young Exec. of Yr. award 1973, dir. 1978), Ill. Assn. Tobacco Distbrs., Yong Pres. Orgn. Club: Chgo. Rotary. Home: 3 Hamill Ln Clarendon Hills IL 60514 Office: S. Bloom Inc 5401 S Dansher Rd Countryside IL 60525

BLOOMBERG, WARNER, JR., urban affairs educator; b. Massillon, Ohio, Mar. 2, 1926; s. Warner Sol and Sara (Brockman) B.; m. Carol Jean Shulan, Mar. 19, 1950; children: Warner S. III, Joel David, Victor Daniel, Jason Michael. Ph.B., U. Chgo., 1947, M.A. in Social Sci, 1950, Ph.D. in Sociology, 1961. With Gary Works, United Steel Corp., 1950-52; with Union Edn. Service, U. Chgo., 1952-53, instr. in coll., 1953-57; asst. prof. Syracuse U., 1957-63; asso. prof. U. Wis.-Milw., 1963-66, prof., 1966-73, chmn. dept. urban affairs, 1967-70; lectr., asso. prof. San Diego State U., 1973-80, prof., 1980—; Bd. govs. Dominican Coll., Racine, Wis., Council U. Insts. Urban Affairs. Author: Suburban Power Structures and Public Education, 1963, Power, Poverty, and Urban Policy, 1968, The Quality of Urban Life, 1969. Served with USNR, 1944-46. Mem. United Profs. Calif., Am. Sociol. Assn., Phi Beta Kappa. Jewish. Home: 1671 Burgundy Rd Levcodia CA 92024 *Education cut off from engagement in the human enterprise is mere schooling. Teachers who care more about subject matter than students are idol worshippers.*

BLOOMER, HENRY HARLAN, educator; b. Roseville, Ill., Aug. 3, 1908; s. Henry M. and Mertie (Harlan) B.; m. Hope Frances Hartwig, Aug. 26, 1941; children—Harlan Hartwig, Thomas Yocom. A.B., U. Ill., 1930; M.A., U. Mich., 1933, Ph.D., 1935. Instr. in English Lincoln Jr. Coll., 1931-32; instr. speech U. Mich., 1935-38, asst. prof., 1939-42, asso. prof., 1942-47, prof. speech, 1947—, prof. otorhinolaryngology, 1962-68, prof. speech pathology, dept. phys. medicine and rehab. Med. Sch. and dept. speech communication and theatre, lit., sci. and arts, 1969—, dir., head speech and hearing sci. sect., phys. medicine and rehab., 1969-74, prof., 1974-77, prof. emeritus, 1977—; adj. prof. Western Ill. U., 1978-80; speech therapist Nat. Speech Improvement Camp, Northport, Mich., summers 1935-38. Asso. editor: Speech Monographs, 1950; editorial cons.: Cleft Palate Jour; contbr. articles on speech to profl. jours. Pres. Ann Arbor Bd. Edn., 1958-59. Served as lt. USNR, 1943-46; lt. comdr. USNR, 1950. Fellow Am. Speech and Hearing Assn. (life mem., pres. 1955, mem. grad. edn. and tng. bd., award 1973); mem. Mich. Speech and Hearing Assn. (award 1973), N.Y. Acad. Scis., Am. Cleft Palate Assn. (life mem., exec. council 1958-61), Speech Assn. Am. (exec. council 1947-50), Mich. Assn. Tchrs. Speech, Mich. Assn. Better Hearing, Am. Congress Rehab. Medicine, Internat. Assn. Logopedics and Phoniatrics, Omicron Kappa Upsilon, Phi Sigma, Phi Eta Sigma, Phi Kappa Phi, Alpha Kappa Lambda. Club: Rotary (pres. Ann Arbor 1962-63). Home: Rural Route 3 Macomb IL 61455

BLOOMFIELD, ARTHUR IRVING, economics educator; b. Montreal, Que., Can., Oct. 2, 1914; came to U.S., 1936; s. Samuel and Hanna Mai (Brown) B. B.A., McGill U., 1935, M.A., 1936; Ph.D., U. Chgo., 1942; M.A. (hon.), U. Pa., 1971. Economist Fed. Res. Bank N.Y., 1942-53, sr. economist, officer, 1953-58; prof. econs. U. Pa., Phila., 1958—; vis. prof. Johns Hopkins U., 1961, Princeton U., 1963, CCNY, 1965, U. Melbourne, 1972; cons. Fgn. Econ. Adminstrn., UN Korean Reconstrn. Agy., U.S. State Dept., Ford Found. Author: Capital Imports and U.S. Balance of Payments, 1950, Banking Reform in South Korea, 1951, Monetary Policy under the International Gold Standard, 1880-1914, 1959. Research Council fellow, 1939-40; Rockefeller fellow, 1957-58; Ford Found. faculty fellow, 1962-63. Mem. Am. Econs. Assn., AAUP, Royal Econ. Soc. Democrat. Jewish. Home: 201 S 18th St Apt 817 Philadelphia PA 19103 Office: Dept Econs Univ Pa 3718 Locust Walk Cr Philadelphia PA 19104

BLOOMFIELD, ARTHUR JOHN, music critic; b. San Francisco, Jan. 3, 1931; s. Arthur L. and Julia (Mayer) B.; m. Anne Buenger, July 14, 1956; children: John, Cecily, Alison. A.B., Stanford U., 1951. Music and art critic San Francisco Call-Bull., 1958-59, San Francisco News Call-Bull., 1962-65; co-music and art critic San Francisco Examiner, 1965-79; corr. Musical America mag., 1958-61, 63-64, Opera mag., 1964—; restaurant critic Focus mag., San Francisco, 1979—; guest reviewer Robert Finigan's Guide to Classical Recordings, 1980-81; Mem. artistic adv. com. Spring Opera San Francisco, 1960-62, San Francisco Chamber Music Soc., 1961-62. Author: The San Francisco Opera, 1923-61, 61, Fifty Years of the San Francisco Opera, 1972, Restaurants of San Francisco, 1975, Guide to San Francisco Restaurants, 1977, The San Francisco Opera 1922-78, 1978, Dairy of a Gastronome, 1984. Served with AUS, 1953-55. Home: 2229 Webster St San Francisco CA 94115

BLOOMFIELD, COLEMAN, insurance company executive; b. Winnipeg, Man., Can., July 2, 1926; came to U.S., 1952, naturalized, 1958; s. Samuel and Bessie (Staniloff) B.; m. Shirley Rosenbaum, Nov. 4, 1948; children: Catherine, Laura, Leon, Diane, Richard. B.Commerce, U. Man., 1948. With Commonwealth Life Ins. Co., Louisville, 1948-51; actuary, sr. v.p. Minn. Mut. Life Ins. Co., St. Paul, 1952-70, exec. v.p., 1970-71, pres., chief exec. officer, 1971—, chmn. bd., 1977—, chief exec. officer; dir. Northwestern Bell Telephone Co., 1st Nat. Bank St. Paul. Bd. dirs. Minn. Orch. Assn.; bd. dirs. St Paul United Way. Fellow Soc. Actuaries; mem. St. Paul C. of C., Am. Council Life Ins. (dir.). Office: Minn Mut Life Ins Co 400 N Robert St Saint Paul MN 55101 *

BLOOMFIELD, DANIEL KERMIT, college dean, physician; b. Cleve., Dec. 14, 1926; s. Joseph Bernard and Henrietta (Namen) B.; m. Frances Aub, June 10, 1955; children: Louis, Ruth, Anne. B.S., U.S. Naval Acad., 1947; M.S., Western Res. U., 1954, M.D., 1954. Intern Beth Israel Hosp., Boston, 1954-55, resident, 1955-56, Mass. Gen. Hosp., Boston, 1956-67; research fellow chemistry Harvard U., 1957-59; hon. asst. registrar cardiology Nat. Heart Hosp., London, 1959-60; sr. instr. medicine Western Res. U., Cleve., 1960-64, sr. clin. instr. medicine, 1964-70; dir. cardiovascular research Community Health Found., Cleve., 1964-66; assoc. medicine Mt. Sinai Hosp., Cleve., 1966-69; prof. medicine U. Ill. Sch. Medicine, Urbana, 1970—; dean Coll. Medicine U. Ill.-Urbana, 1970-84; Investigator Am. Heart Assn., 1960-64; Bd. dirs. East Central Ill. Health Systems Agy. Served with USN, 1947-50. Recipient citation for contbns. to med. edn. Ohio Heart Assn., 1964. Mem. Am. Profs. Peace in Middle East (vice chmn.); Mem. Alpha Omega Alpha. Home: 103 E Michigan St Urbana IL 61801

BLOOMFIELD, LINCOLN PALMER, political scientist, educator; b. Boston, July 7, 1920; m. Irirangi Pamela Coates, 1948; children—Pamela, Lincoln, Diana. S.B., Harvard, 1941, M. Pub. Adminstrn., 1952, Ph.D., 1956. Various positions Dept. State, Washington, 1946-57, spl. asst. to asst. sec. state, 1952-57; mem. staff Center for Internat. Studies, MIT, Cambridge, 1957—, prof. polit. sci., 1963—; in charge global issues Nat. Security Council, Washington, 1979-80; mem. Presdl. Commn. on 25th Anniversary of UN, 1970-71; vis. prof. Grad. Inst. Advanced Internat. Studies, Geneva, 1965, 72, 77, 79; cons. govt. and industry. Author: Evolution or Revolution?, 1957, The United Nations and U.S. Foreign Policy: A New Look at the National Interest, revised edit., 1967, In Search of American Foreign Policy: The Humane Use of Power, 1974, The Foreign Policy Process: A Modern Primer, 1982; co-author, editor: Krushchev and the Arms Race, 1966, Outer Space: Prospects for Man and Society, revised edit., 1968, Controlling Small Wars: A Strategy for the 1970's, 1969, The Power to Keep Peace: Today and in a World Without War, 1971. Bd. dirs. Unitarian-Universalist Assn., 1958-64, World Affairs Council of Boston, UN Assn. of U.S.A., World Peace Found. Served to lt. USNR, 1942-46. Recipient Chase prize Harvard, 1956; Littauer fellow, 1952; Rockefeller fellow, 1954, 75. Mem. Am. Polit. Sci. Assn., Council on Fgn. Relations, Internat. Inst. Strategic Studies. Research in fgn. policy and arms control, policy planning, global interdependence, polit. gaming, computerized conflict-minimizing system. Home: 37 Beach St Cohasset MA 02025 Office: 30 Wadsworth St Cambridge MA 02139 *Stay humble but not falsely so. Trust your deepest instincts, but never stop listening, thinking, learning. Grow along with the young.*

BLOOMFIELD, MORTON WILFRED, educator; b. Montreal, Que., Can., May 19, 1913; came to U.S., 1936, naturalized, 1943; s. Samuel and Hanna Mai (Brown) B.; m. Caroline Lichtenberg, Mar. 16, 1952; children: Micah Warren, Hanna, Samuel. B.A., McGill U., 1934, M.A., 1935; grad. study, U. London, 1935-36; Ph.D., U. Wis., 1938; A.M., Harvard U., 1961; Litt. D., U. Western Mich., 1982. Faculty McGill U., 1934-35, U. Wis., 1938-39, U. Akron, 1939-46; asst. prof. English, Ohio State U., 1946-51, asso. prof., 1951-54, prof. English, 1954-61; prof. English, Harvard U., 1961—, chmn. dept. English, 1968-72, Arthur Kingsley Porter prof. English, 1972—; Henry W. and Albert A. Berg prof. English and Am. lit. Washington Sq. Coll., NYU, 1955-56; Fannie Hurst vis. prof. lit. Washington U., St. Louis, 1977, Brandeis U., 1978; Disting. vis. prof. humanities Stanford U., 1981, 83; Spl. civilian cons. Sec. War, 1945-46; mem. exec. com., trustee Nat. Humanities Center, 1973; chmn. bd. trustees, 1973-76; trustee Center for Applied Linguistics, 1966-68; supervising com. The English Inst., 1975-78. Author: The Seven Deadly Sins, An Introduction to the History of a Religious Concept, 1952, Piers Plowman as a Fourteenth-Century Apocalypse, 1962, (with Leonard Newmark) A Linguistic Introduction to the History of English, 1963, Essays and Explorations, Studies in Language and Literature, 1970; also articles; editor: (with R.C. Elliott) Ten Plays, 1951; rev. as Great Plays: Sophocles to Brecht, 1965, Great Plays: Sophocles to Albee, 1975; (with E. Robbins) Form and Idea, 1953, rev. edit., 1961, The Interpretation of Narrative, 1970, In Search of Literary Theory, 1972, (with E. Haugen) Language as a Human Problem, 1974, (Incipits to Latin Works on the Virtues and Vice), 1979; editorial adv. bd., contbr.: Am. Heritage Dictionary; editorial bd.: Jour. History Ideas, 1976-79; editorial adv. bd.: Viator. Served with AUS, 1942-45. Decorated Bronze Star; Moyse fellow, 1935-36; Guggenheim fellow, 1949-50, 64-65; Elizabeth Clay Howald fellow, 1953-54; hon. research asso. U. Coll., U. London, 1953-54; Am. Council Learned Socs. grantee, 1958-59, 76; fellow Center for Advanced Study in Behavorial Scis., Stanford U., 1967-68, Princeton Inst., 1972; Am. Philos. Soc. grantee, 1973; research fellow Australian Nat. U. Humanities Center, 1978. Fellow Mediaeval Acad. Am. (Haskins medal 1964, v.p. 1975-76, pres. 1976-77), Am. Acad. Arts and Scis. (councillor 1969-72, v.p. 1972-76), Am. Philos. Soc., Brit. Acad. (corr.), Medieval Soc. South Africa (corr.); mem. MLA (exec. com. 1966-69), Renaissance Soc. Am., Am. Dialect Soc., Can. Linguistic Assn., Dante Soc. Am. (mem. council 1971-74, 79—), Internat. Assn. Univ. Profs. English (cons. com. 1962—), Modern Humanities Research Assn. (mem. Am. com. 1976—), Soc. Internationale pour l'étude de la Philosophie Medievale, Linguistic Soc. Am., Phi Beta Kappa (hon.). Home: 13 Kirkland Pl Cambridge MA 02138

BLOOMFIELD, PETER, statistician, educator; b. Farnborough, Hampshire, Eng., Mar. 25, 1946; came to U.S., 1971; s. William John and Margaret Bessie (Saunders) B.; m. Christine Bellis, June 27, 1969 (div. Nov. 1982); children: David, Gareth. B.Sc., Imperial Coll., London, 1967, Ph.D., 1970. Asst. lectr., then lectr. math. Imperial Coll., 1969-71; mem. faculty Princeton U., 1971-83, prof. stats., 1979-83, N.C. State U., Raleigh, 1983—; cons. in field. Author: Fourier Analysis of Time Series, An Introduction, 1976. Fellow Inst. Math. Stats., Royal Statis. Soc.; mem. Am. Statis. Assn. Office: Dept Statistics NC State U Raleigh NC 27650

BLOOMFIELD, VICTOR ALFRED, biochemistry educator; b. Newark, June 10, 1938; s. Samuel G. and Miriam B. (Finkelstein) B.; m. Clara Gail Derber, June 11, 1962. B.S. in Chemistry, U. Calif., Berkeley, 1959; Ph.D., U. Wis., 1962. NSF postdoctoral fellow in chemistry U. Calif., San Diego, 1962-64; asst. prof. chemistry U. Ill., Urbana, 1964-69; asso. prof. U. Minn., St. Paul, 1969-70, asso. prof. biochemistry and chemistry, 1970-74, prof. biochemistry and chemistry, 1974—, head dept. biochemistry, 1979—; mem. biophysics and biophys. study sect. NIH, 1975-79; mem. NSF Biophysics Panel, 1980—. Contbr. articles to profl. jours.; author: (with Crothers and Tinoco) Physical Chemistry of Nucleic Acids, 1974, (with R. Harrington) Biophysical Chemistry, 1975; mem. editorial bd.: Jour. Phys. Chemistry, 1974-78, Ann. Rev. of Phys. Chemistry, 1976-80, Biopolymers, 1977—, Biophys. Jour, 1978-81, Biochemistry, 1980—. Recipient Eastman Kodak award, 1962; A.P. Sloan fellow, 1969-71; NIH Research Career Devel. awardee, 1971-76. Fellow AAAS; mem. Am. Chem. Soc. (sec. biol. chemistry div. 1981-83), Am. Soc. Biol. Chemists, Biophys. Soc. (mem. council 1979—, publs. com. 1981-83). Office: 1479 Gortner Ave Saint Paul MN 55108

BLOOR, W(ILLIAM) SPENCER, electrical engineer, consultant; b. Trenton, N.J., Oct. 16, 1918; s. W. Harry and Evva (Averre) B.; m. Barbara P. Walters, Jan. 19, 1952; children: William G., Robert S. B.S. in Elec. Engring, Lafayette Coll., 1940, D.Eng. (hon.), 1981. Registered profl. engr., Calif., Pa. With Leeds & Northrup Co., 1940-81, product market devel. mgr., Phila., 1966-68, engring. coordination mgr., North Wales, Pa., 1968-69, mgr. steam and nuclear power systems, 1969-81; cons. in pvt. practice, 1981—; assoc. Macro Corp., S.T. Hudson Internat.; adj. prof. Drexel U.; cons. staff Moore Sch., U. Pa., 1982—. Served to lt. USN, 1943-46. Named Engr. of Yr., Delaware Valley, 1980. Fellow AAAS, IEEE (mem. fellows and founders medal coms. 1983—), Instrument Soc. Am. (v.p. publs. 1968-70, pres. 1974, chmn. admissions com. 1980—, editor-in-chief Transactions 1982—); mem. ASME, Nat. Soc. Profl. Engrs., Nat. Acad. Engring., Phi Beta Kappa, Tau Beta Pi, Eta Kappa Nu. Presbyterian. Design and application of control and monitoring systems for electric power generating stas. throughout the world. Home and Office: 1904 Jody Rd Meadowbrook PA 19046

BLOS, JOAN W., author, critic; b. N.Y.C., Dec. 9, 1928; m. Peter Blos, Jr., 1953; 2 children. B.A., Vassar Coll., 1950; M.A., CCNY, 1956. Asso. publs. div., mem. tchr. edn. faculty Bank St. Coll. Edn., N.Y.C., 1958-70; lectr. Sch. Edn., U. Mich., Ann Arbor, 1972-80; U.S. editor Children's Literature in Education, 1976-81. Author: "It's Spring!" She Said, 1968, (with Betty Miles) Just Think!, 1971, A Gathering of Days: A New England Girl's Journal, 1830-32, 1979 (Newbery Medal, ALA, and Am. Book award 1980), Martin's Hats, 1984. Office: care Charles Scribner's Sons 597 Fifth Ave New York NY 10017

BLOSSMAN, ALFRED RHODY, JR., banker; b. Madisonville, La., Oct. 21, 1931; s. Alfred Rhody and Mabel (Perrin) B.; m. Royanne Elaire Hurd, Dec. 28, 1957; children: Alfred Rhody III, Roy Edward, Gary Bennett, Christopher Hurd, David Quintin, John Eric. A.B. in Gen. Bus, La. State U., 1955. Chmn. bd. Parish Nat. Bank, Bogalusa, La.; pres., chmn., chief exec. officer First Nat. Bank, Covington, La., First Nat. Corp.; dir. Blossman Investment Corp., WARB, Inc.; mem. adv. bd. Citicorp, Corr. Resources; mem. future banking adv. bd. Correspondent Resources, Inc. subs. Citicorp. Bd. dirs. River Forest Acad.; mem. adv. bd. Southeastern La. State U. Mem. Phi Delta Theta. Democrat. Roman Catholic. Clubs: Southern Yacht, Covington Country. Home: 129 Riverwood Dr Covington LA 70433 Office: PO Box 808 Covington LA 70434 *My formula for life is shaped by the moral and ethical guidelines of my religious faith and my own personal code of ethics. Strong self discipline has made that possible, as well as channelling my enthusiasm for whatever role I have played; being it business, or hobby; educational, military service, or parent, in the right direction.*

BLOTNER, JOSEPH LEO, educator; b. Plainfield, N.J., June 21, 1923; s. Joseph and Johanna Angela (Slattery) B.; m. Yvonne Wright, Aug. 24, 1946; children—Tracy Willoughby Nichoff, Pamela, Nancy. B.A., Drew U., 1947; M.A., Northwestern U., 1947; Ph.D., U. Pa., 1951. Asst. dir. research services RCA Labs., Princeton, N.J., 1949-53; instr. English U. Ida., 1953-55; asst. prof., asso. prof. English U. Va., 1955-68; prof. English U. N.C., Chapel Hill, 1968-71, U. Mich., Ann Arbor, 1971—; vis. prof. English Trinity Coll., Hartford, Conn., 1962; William Faulkner lectr. U. Miss., 1977; vis. prof. English U. Ariz., 1982; cons. Ency. Brit. Ednl. Corp., Tomorrow Entertainment Inc., Center for Study So. Culture, Miss. ETV Authority. Author: The Political Novel, 1955, (with F.L. Gwynn) The Fiction of J.D. Salinger, 1959, Faulkner in the University, 1959, William Faulkner's Library: A Catalogue, 1964, The Modern American Political Novel: 1900-1960, 1966, Faulkner: A Biography, 2 vols, 1974, Selected Letters of William Faulkner, 1977, Uncollected Stories of William Faulkner, 1979; mem. editorial bd.: So. Humanities Rev, Mich. Quar. Rev., So. Lit. Jour., Faulkner Studies, Faulkner Concordance. Served to 2d lt. USAAF, 1943-45; ETO. Decorated Air medal; Fulbright lectr. Am. lit. U. Copenhagen, 1958-59, 63-64; Guggenheim fellow, 1965, 68; State Dept. grantee, Europe, 1975; Rockefeller Found. research scholar, 1979. Sr. fellow Mich. Soc. Fellows; mem. P.E.N., MLA (chmn. Am. lit. sect. 1981), Phi Beta Kappa, Sigma Phi, Omicron Delta Kappa. Democrat. Presbyn. Club: Racquet of Ann Arbor. Home: 816 Berkshire Rd Ann Arbor MI 48104

BLOTNER, NORMAN DAVID, lawyer, real estate broker; b. Boston, Dec. 6, 1918; s. Leon and Sarah B.; m. Helen I. Whitman, Aug. 13, 1954; 1 son, James B. McClain. A.B., Harvard U., 1940, J.D., 1947. Bar: N.Y. 1948. Mem. firm Spiro, Felstiner, Prager & Treeger, N.Y.C., 1947-52; with Lane Bryant Inc., N.Y.C., 1953-82, sr. v.p., sec., dir., 1968-82, ret., 1982. Bd. dirs. Better Bus. Bur. Met. N.Y., Until 1982. Served with USNR, 1941-46. Mem. Assn. Bar City N.Y. Republican. Clubs: Harvard Varsity, New Rochelle Tennis; Harvard (Westchester). Home: 140 Overlook Rd New Rochelle NY 10804 Office: Cushman & Wakefield 1166 Ave of Americas New York NY 10036

BLOUGH, DONALD S., psychology educator; b. Madison, Wis., Sept. 13, 1929; s. Roy and Marie (Goshorn) B.; m. Patricia Irene McBride, June 19, 1954; children: Douglas Earle, Stephen Richard, Kathryn Marie. B.A., Swarthmore Coll., 1951; M.A., Harvard U., 1954, Ph.D., 1955. Psychologist NIMH, Bethesda, Md., 1954-58; asst. prof. Brown U., 1958-61, asso. prof., 1961-66, prof., 1966—, Edgar J. Marston prof., 1980—, chmn. psychology dept., 1973-77; Mem. psychobiology rev. panel NSF, 1963-67; mem. small grants com. NIMH, 1968-72, mem. exptl. psychology rev. panel, 1975-79, chmn., 1977-79. Author: (with Patricia M. Blough) Experiments in Psychology, 1964; editor: Jour. Exptl. Psychology: Animal Behavior Processes, 1982—. Served with USPHS, 1954-58. Mem. Am., Eastern psychol. assns., Psychonomic Soc., Soc. Exptl. Psychologists, Am. Acad. Arts and Sci., AAAS. Home: 169 Brown St Providence RI 02906 Office: Dept Psychology Brown U Providence RI 02912

BLOUGH, GLENN ORLANDO, author, educator; b. Edmore, Mich., Sept. 5, 1907; s. Levi and Catherine (Thomas) B. Student, Central Mich. Coll. Edn., 1922-24, LL.D., 1950; B.A., U. Mich., 1929, M.A., 1932; postgrad., Columbia, summers 1935-37, U. Chgo., 1938. Tchr. secondary schs., Mich., 1925-27, 29-31; instr. State Tchrs. Coll., Ypsilanti, Mich., 1932-36, asst. prof. sci. edn., Greeley, Colo., 1937-38; instr. U. Chgo., 1939-42; specialist sci. U.S. Office Edn., HEW, Washington, 1947-55; prof. edn. U. Md., 1956—; edn. cons. Nat. Geog. Soc., 1970—. Author: Monkey With A Notion, 1948, Beno The Riverburg Mayor, 1949, The Tree on the Road to Turntown, 1953; Jr. Lit. Guild selections Not Only for Ducks, The Story of Rain, 1954, Lookout for the Forest, 1955, After the Sun Goes Down, 1956, Who Lives in This House, 1957; When You Go to the Zoo, 1957, Young Peoples Book of Science, 1958, Soon After September, 1959, Discovering Dinosaurs, 1959, Who Lives in This Meadow?, 1960, Christmas Trees and How They Grow, 1961, Who Lives at the Seashore, 1962, Bird Watchers and Bird Feeders, 1963, Discovering Plants, 1966, Discovering Insects, 1967, Discovering Cycles, 1973, Elementary School Science and How To Teach It, 1978; also textbooks.; Contbr. numerous articles sci., popular publs. Served as lt. comdr. USNR, World War II. Recipient Disting. Service to Sci. Edn. citation Nat. Sci. Tchrs. Assn., 1971; Spl. Recognition for contbn. to sci. edn. Council Elementary Sci. Internat., 1971; award for contbn. to lit. of natural history Am. Nature Study Soc., 1980. Mem. NEA, Assn. Supervision and Curriculum Devel., Assn. Childhood Edn., AAUP, Nat. Council Elementary Sci. (pres. 1947), Nat. Sci. Tchrs. Assn. (pres. 1957-58, adviser ednl. policies commn.), Elementary Prins. Assn., Phi Delta Kappa, Phi Sigma. Home: 2820 Ellicott St NW Washington DC 20008 Office: U Md College Park MD 20740

BLOUGH, HERBERT ALLEN, virologist, educator; b. Phila., Dec. 18, 1929; s. Coleman Judah and Lena (Mink) B.; m. Racelle Miller, Dec. 19, 1954; children: Linda, Colin, Beth, Lawrence. B.Sc., Pa. State U., 1951; M.D., Chgo. Med. Sch., 1955; postgrad., U. Minn., 1958-61, Cambridge (Eng.) U., 1961-63. Intern Cin. Gen. Hosp., 1955-56; med. fellow U. Minn., 1958-60, USPHS postdoctoral fellow, 1960-63; asst. prof. microbiology U. Pa., 1963-69; asso. prof., head div. biochem. virology and membrane research Scheie Eye Inst. U. Pa., 1970-75, prof., head div. biochem. virology and membrane research Scheie Eye Inst., 1976—; chmn. subcom. virology U. Pa. Cancer Center, 1977-79; vis. prof. biochemistry Helsinki U., 1972; mem. teaching staff 1st Internat. Sch. on Molecular Virology, Capri, Italy, 1982; cons. basic sci. U.S. Naval Hosp., Phila.; mem. ad hoc study sect. virology NIH, 1975—; asso. mem., cons. Armed Forces Epidemiol. Bd. Commn. Influenza, 1969-73; charter mem. sci. and med. adv. bd. Herpes Resource Ctr., 1979-82. Co-editor: Cell Membranes and Viral Envelopes; contbr. articles to profl. jours., chpt. in book. Served to capt. M.C. USNR, 1956-58. USPHS grantee, 1964-67, 74—; contract recipient U.S. Army Med. Research and Devel. Command, 1967-76; sr. research fellow Nat. Multiple Sclerosis Soc., Oxford U. and Helsinki U., 1971-72; grantee Damon Runyon Fund, 1967-70, 73-75; Mary Jennifer Selznick fellow Hereditary Disease Found., 1978—; recipient Most Distinguished Alumnus award Chgo. Med. Sch., 1975.

Mem. Biochem. Soc. U.K., Am. Assn. Immunologists, Am. Soc. Biol. Chemists, AAAS, Am. Soc. Virology, Soc. Med. Cons. to Armed Forces, Sigma Xi. Home: 4119 Kottler Dr Lafayette Hill PA 19444 Office: Scheie Eye Institute University of Pennsylvania Philadelphia PA 19104

BLOUGH, ROY, economist; b. Pitts., Aug. 21, 1901; s. Silas S. and Mary (Wertz) B.; m. Marie Goshorn, May 19, 1923; children: Richard, William, Donald. A.B., Manchester Coll., 1921, LL.D., 1921; A.M., U. Wis., 1922, Ph.D., 1929; L.H.D., Columbia U., 1954. Asst. prof. history and econs. Manchester Coll., Ind., 1922-24, assoc. prof., 1924-25; dir. tax research U.S. Treasury Dept., 1938-46, asst. to sec., 1944-46; prof. econs. and polit. sci. U. Chgo., 1946-52, on leave, 1950-52; mem. Council Econ. Advisers to Pres., 1950-52, Tax. Adv. Mission to Turkish Govt., 1949; prin. dir. Dept. Econ. Affairs UN, 1952-55; prof. internat. bus. Columbia U., N.Y.C., 1955-66, S. Sloan Colt prof. banking and Internat. fin., 1966-70, S. Sloan Colt prof. emeritus, 1970—; disting. vis. prof. fin. U. Fla., 1972; Nixon vis. prof. econ. policy Whittier Coll., 1973; mem. UN Tax Avd. Mission to Govt. of Peru, 1957, 59, UN Adv. Mission to Govt. of Chile, 1959; cons. Com. for Econ. Devel., 1965-73. Author: (with others) Facing the Tax Problem, 1937, Federal Taxing Process, 1952, International Business Environment and Adaptation, 1966, Economics Problems and Economic Advice, 1978, Studies in the Taxation of Foreign Source Income, 1979; editor: Nat. Tax Jour., 1947-50; contbr. articles to profl. jours. Mem. Am. Econ. Assn. (v.p. 1954), Nat. Tax Assn., Am. Fin. Assn., Council on Fgn. Relations, UN Assn. U.S.A. Mem. Ch. of Brethren. Clubs: Nat. Economists, Cosmos (Washington). Home: 3700 Dulwick Dr Silver Spring MD 20906

BLOUNT, DON H., college dean; b. Cape Girardeau, Mo., Mar. 25, 1929; married; 3 children. B.A. in Psychology, U. Mo., 1950, M.A. in Physiology and Pharmacology, 1956, Ph.D., 1958. From instr. to asst. prof. physiology and biophysics U. Vt., Burlington, 1958-61; asst. prof. physiology W.Va. U. Med. Ctr., Morgantown, 1961-67; head physiology div. life scis. labs. Melpar, Inc., Falls Church, Va., 1967-69; scientist, adminstr. Nat. Heart, Lung and Blood Inst., 1969-72, chief cardiac functions br. div. heart and vascular diseases, 1972-79, acting assoc. dir. cardiology, 1978-79, dep. assoc. dir. cardiology, 1979; dean Grad. Sch., vice provost research U. Mo., Columbia, 1979—; assoc. grants bd. NIH, 1977-79. Reviewer: Science; contbr. articles to prof. jours. Served with M.C. U.S. Army, 1951-53. Mem. Am. Physiol. Soc. Office: U Mo 203 Jesse Hall Columbia MO 65211

BLOUNT, JOHN BRUCE, army officer; b. Pawtucket, R.I., Apr. 22, 1928; s. Joseph Hagan and Loretta (Moody) B.; m. Joan Garrett, June 17, 1950; children: Gail L., Carol L., John B., Garrett C. B.S., U. R.I., 1950; M.B.A., U. Miami, 1961; student, Command and Gen. Staff Coll., 1959, U.S. Army War Coll., 1971. Platoon leader and co. comdr. 45th Div., Korea, 1952-53; comdr. U.S. Army Tng. Ctr. and Ft. Jackson, S.C., 1977-79; chief of staff Tng. and Doctrine Command, Ft. Monroe, Va., 1979—, maj. gen. TRADOC. Decorated Silver Star, Legion of Merit, Purple Heart; named to Athletic Hall of Fame U. R.I., 1975. Mem. Assn. U.S. Army, Beta Gamma Sigma. Home: 51 Fenwick Fort Monroe VA 23651 Office: Fort Monroe VA 23651

BLOUNT, MELVIN CORNELL (MEL BLOUNT), football player; b. Vidalia, Ga., Apr. 10, 1948. Student, So. U. Defensive back Pitts. Steelers, 1970—. Played NFL Championship Game, 1974, 75, 78, Pro Bowl, 1975, 76, 78. Office: care Pitts Steelers Three Rivers Stadium 300 Stadium Circle Pittsburgh PA 15212 *

BLOUNT, ROBERT, company executive; b. Newton, Mass., Nov. 30, 1938; s. Robert S. B.; m. Vivian S. Aries, July 1, 1982; children: Bobby, Sharon, Kristin, Stephen. B.S. in Acctg., Babson Coll., 1960. C.P.A. Vice-pres. fin. Am. Home Products, Inc., N.Y.C., 1974-83; sr. v.p. Amk. Home Products, Inc., 1983—; ptnr. Arthur Anderson & Co., N.Y.C. Mem. N.Y. State Soc. C.P.A.s, Am. Inst. C.P.A.s. Home: 420 E 54th St New York NY 10022 Office: Am Home Products Corp 685 3d Ave New York NY 10017

BLOUNT, ROBERT HADDOCK, management consultant, retired naval officer; b. Miami, Fla., Dec. 8, 1922; s. Uriel and Aleve Sadie (Haddock) B.; m. Jeannette Mae Barclay, May 13, 1951; children: Barbara Mae, Jennifer. B.E.E., Mass Inst. Tech., 1947; M.S. in Systems Engring, George Washington U., 1970; student, Naval War Coll., 1958-59. Commd. ensign USNR, 1946; transferred to U.S. Navy, 1947, advanced through grades to rear adm., 1973; comdr. submarines, service in MTO, PTO, Scotland, Panama, chief staff, aide to comdr. Submarine Flotilla 6, 1970-72, comdr. Naval Sta., Naval Base, Charleston, S.C., 1972-73, comdr. U.S. Naval Forces, So. Command, also comdt. 15th Naval Dist., Ft. Amador, C.Z., 1973-75, dir. undersea and strategic warfare div. Office Chief Naval Ops., Washington, 1975-77, dep. dir. research, devel., test and evaluation OPNAV, 1977-78, comdr. Operational Test and Evaluation Force, 1978-82, ret., 1982, industry cons., 1982—. Pres. C.Z. council Boy Scouts Am., 1974. Decorated Meritorious Service medal with star, Navy Expeditionary medal; recipient Scroll of Honor Navy League, 1974. Mem. U.S. Naval Inst. Address: 1516 Blanford Circle Norfolk VA 23505

BLOUNT, STANLEY FREEMAN, educator; b. Detroit, June 12, 1929; s. Harry Alfred and Thelma (Freeman) B.; m. Constance Parker, Aug. 30, 1957; children—Jeffrey Parker, Lori Maria. B.A., Wayne State U., 1952, M.A., 1959; Ph.D., Northwestern U., 1962. Account exec. Jam Handy Corp., Detroit, 1952-54; marketing mgr. Chrysler Corp., Detroit, 1954-58; instr. Northwestern U., 1961-62; asst. prof. U. Ill., 1962-63; asso. prof. Kent State U., 1963-67; prof., dept. chmn. State U. N.Y. at Albany, 1967—, chmn. ednl. policies council, 1970—; distinguished vis. prof. U. of Americas, Mexico, 1966; dir. Femtec Inc. Chmn. sub-com. legis. affairs N.Y. State affiliate Am. Heart Assn., 1974—. Served with AUS, 1946-48. Named Outstanding Faculty Mem. Kent State U., 1964. Mem. Sigma Xi, Gamma Theta Upsilon. Clubs: Essayons, Audubon, Phalanx. Research on environment analysis and preception, digitized land use mapping, land use and resource mgmt. Home: 11 Pheasant Ln Delmar NY 12054 Office: SUNY Albany NY 12222

BLOUNT, WILLIAM HOUSTON, company executive; b. Union Springs, Ala., Jan. 3, 1922; m. Frances Dean. Student, U. Ala., Advanced Mgmt. program, Harvard U. Ptnr. Blount Bros. Corp., Montgomery, Ala.; pres. Southeastern Sand & Gravel Co., Tallassee, Ala., also dir.; v.p. So. Cen-Vi-Ro Pipe Corp., Birmingham; with Vulcan Materials Co., Birmingham, 1957—, exec. v.p. constrn. materials group, 1970-77, pres., 1977—, chief operating officer, 1977-79, chief exec. officerr, 1979—, also dir., mem. exec. com., mem. fin. com.; dir. Blount, Inc., Montgomery, Protective Corp., Birmingham, First Ala. Bancshares, Inc., Montgomery, First Ala. Bank of Birmingham. Mem. Ala. Safety Council; pres. Brimingham Area council Boy Scouts Am., 1977-79, 79; active Jr. Achievement of Jefferson County; bd. trustees YWCA; chmn. ann. awards dinner Nat. Conf. Christians and Jews, 1982; active Am. Cancer Soc.; gen. chmn. United Way Drive, 1975; gen. chmn. ann. fund drive Jr. Achievement, 1981; Ala. chmn. US Olympic Com.'s fund raising drive; active Canterbury United Methodist Ch., Mountain Brook, Ala. Served with Air Corps USN, 1943. Mem. Birmingham Area C. of C. Clubs: Mountain Brook Country (ALa.); Shoals Creek; Linville Golf (N.C.); Willow Point Country, Chgo.; River (N.Y.C.); Relay House, The Club. Office: Vulcan Materials Co 1 Metroplex Dr Birmingham AL 35209

BLOUNT, WINTON MALCOLM, constrn. and mfg. co. exec.; b. Union Springs, Ala., Feb. 1, 1921; s. Winton Malcolm and Clara B. (Chalker) B.; m. Mary Katherine Archibald, Sept. 12, 1942; children—Winton Malcolm III, Thomas A., S. Roberts, Katherine Blount Miles, Joseph W. Student, U. Ala., 1939-41; L.H.D., Judson Coll., 1967; Dr. Humanities, Huntingdon Coll., 1969; LL.D., Birmingham-So. Coll., 1969; D.C.L., Southwestern U., 1969; D.Sc., U. Ala., 1971; D.Pub. Service, Seattle-Pacific Coll., 1971. Pres., chmn. bd. Blount Bros. Corp., Montgomery, Ala., 1946-68; postmaster gen. U.S., Washington, 1969-71; chmn. exec. com. Blount, Inc., 1973—, chmn. bd., chief exec. officer, 1974—; dir. Union Camp Corp., Munford Inc. Chmn. Ala. Citizens for Eisenhower, 1952; Southeastern dir. Nixon-Lodge, 1959-60; Bd. dirs. United Appeal Montgomery; bd. dirs. Montgomery YMCA, also life mem.; former trustee So. Research Inst.; trustee U. Ala., Southwestern U.; bd. visitors Air U., Maxwell AFB, 1971-73; mem. adv. council U.S. Army Aviation Mus., Ft. Rucker, Ala. Served with USAAF, 1942-45. Named one of four Outstanding Young Men Ala., 1956; Man of Year, Montgomery, 1961; recipient citation for distinguished service to City of Montgomery, 1966; Ct. Honor award Montgomery Exchange Club, 1969; Nat. Brotherhood award NCCJ, 1970; Silver Quill award Am. Bus. Press, 1971; Golden Plate award Am. Acad. Achievement, 1980; non-mem. award Outstanding Achievement in Constrn. The Moles, 1980. Mem. Am. Mgmt. Assns. (trustee), Bus. Council, Conf. Bd., NAM (Golden Knight Mgmt. award Ala. Council 1962), U.S. C. of C. (nat. pres. 1968), Ala. C. of C. (pres. 1962-65), Newcomen Soc. N.Am. Presbyn. (deacon). Club: Rotarian. Home: Route 10 Box 43 Vaughn Rd Montgomery AL 36116 Office: Blount Inc Box 949 4520 Executive Park Montgomery AL 36192

BLOUNT, WINTON MALCOLM, III, construction executive; b. Albany, Ga., Dec. 14, 1943; s. Winton M. and Mary Katherine (Archibald) B.; m. Lucy Durr Dunn, June 6, 1970; children: Winton, K. Stuart, William, Judkins. Student, U. Ala., 1962-63; B.A., U. South, 1966; M.B.A., U. Pa., 1968. With Blount Bros. Corp., Montgomery, Ala., 1968-73, project mgr., 1972-73; with Mercury Constrn. Corp., Montgomery, 1973-77, pres., 1975-77; chief exec. officer, chmn. bd. Benjamin F. Shaw Co., Wilmington, Del., 1977—; pres., chief operating officer Blount Internat., Ltd., Montgomery, 1980-83, pres., chief exec. officer, 1983—; dir. Blount, Inc., Benjamin F. Shaw Co., Wilmington, Dunn Inc., Birmingham, Ala. Mem. fin. com. Ala. Republican party; bd. dirs. Montgomery YMCA, Episcopal High Sch., Huntingdon Coll. Mem. Young Pres.'s Orgn., Ala. C. of C. (dir.), Montgomery C. of C. (dir.), Del. C. of C. (dir. 1979-80), NAM (dir.). Episcopalian. Office: PO Box 4577 Montgomery AL 36195

BLOUSTEIN, EDWARD J., college president; b. N.Y.C., Jan. 20, 1925; s. Samuel and Celia (Einwohner) B.; m. Ruth Ellen Steinman, Oct. 6, 1951; children: Elise, Lori. B.A., N.Y. U., 1948; B. Phil. (Fulbright Scholar), Wadham Coll., Oxford (Eng.) U., 1950; Ph.D., Cornell U., 1954, J.D., 1959. Bar: N.Y. 1959, Vt. 1971. Polit. analyst State Dept., 1951-52; instr. logic and philosophy Cornell U., 1954-55; prof. law N.Y. U. Law Sch., 1961-65; pres. Bennington (Vt.) Coll., 1965-71, Rutgers U., 1971—. Address: 1245 River Rd Piscataway NJ 08854

BLOUT, ELKAN ROGERS, biological chemistry educator, university dean; b. N.Y.C., July 2, 1919; s. Eugene and Lillian B.; m. Joan E. Dreyfus, Aug. 27, 1939; children: James E., Susan L., William L. A.B., Princeton U., 1939; Ph.D., Columbia U., 1942; A.M. (hon.), Harvard U., 1962, D.Sc., Loyola U., 1976. With Polaroid Corp., Cambridge, Mass., 1943-62, successively research chemist, assoc. dir. research, 1948-58, v.p., gen. mgr. research, 1958-62; research assoc. Harvard U., 1950-52, 56-60; lectr. on biophysics 1960-62, prof. biol. chemistry, 1962—, Edward S. Harkness prof. biol. chemistry, 1964—, head dept. biol. chemistry, 1965-69; dean for acad. affairs Sch. Public Health, 1978—; research assoc. Children's Hosp. Med. Center, Boston, 1950-52, cons. chemistry, 1952—; mem. conseil de surveillance Compagnie Financière du Scribe, 1975-81; trustee Bay Biochem. Research, Inc., 1973—; mem. exec. com. div. chemistry and chem. tech. NRC, 1972-74, mem. assembly of math. and phys. scis., 1979—; mem. sci. adv. com. Center for Blood Research, Inc., 1972—; also mem. bd. dirs.; mem. research adv. com. Children's Hosp. Med. Center, 1976-80; mem. sci. adv. com. Mass. Gen. Hosp., 1968-71, Research Inst., Hosp. for Sick Children, Toronto, Ont., Can., 1976-79; mem. adv. council dept. biochem. scis. Princeton U., 1974—, mem. adv. council program in molecular biology, 1983—; mem. vis. com. dept. chemistry Carnegie-Mellon U., 1968-72; bd. visitors Faculty Health Scis., SUNY, Buffalo, 1968-70; mem. corp. Mus. Sci.; trustee Boston Biomed. Research Inst.; bd. govs. Weizmann Inst. Sci., Rehovot, Israel, 1978—. Mem. adv. bd.: Jour. Polymer Sci, 1956-62; editorial bd.: Biopolymers, 1963—, Am. Chem. Soc. Monograph Series, 1965-72, Internat. Jour. Peptide and Protein Research, 1978—; editorial adv. bd.: Macromolecules, 1967-70, Jour. Am. Chem. Soc, 1978-82; Contbr. articles to profl. jours. Recipient Princeton Class of 1939 Achievement award, 1970; NRC fellow Harvard, 1942-43. Fellow AAAS, Am. Acad. Arts and Scis. (fin. com. 1977—), N.Y. Acad. Arts and Scis., Optical Soc. Am. (past pres. New Eng. sect.); mem. Nat. Acad. Scis., Inst. Medicine (treas. 1980—, fin. com. 1976—, adv. com. USSR and Eastern Europe 1979—), USSR Acad. Scis. (fgn. mem.), Am. Chem. Soc. (nat. councillor 1958-61), The Chem. Soc., Am. Soc. Biol. Chemists (fin. com. 1973—), Biophys. Soc., Commn. on Phys. Scis., Math., and Resources of NRC, Internat. Orgn. Chem. Scis. in Devel. (council 1981—, chmn. fin. com. 1982—), Fedn. Am. Socs. Exptl. Biology (investments adv. com.). Patentee in field. Home: 1010 Memorial Dr Cambridge MA 02138 Office: Harvard Med Sch Boston MA 02115 also Harvard Sch Public Health Boston MA 02115

BLOYER, JAMES RANDALL, insurance company executive; b. Freeport, Ill., Aug. 4, 1943; s. Randall L. B. and Clarice (Buchwalter); m. Margaret Speyer, June 20, 1965. B.S. in Actuarial Sci., U. Ill., 1965. With Northwestern Nat. Life Ins. Co., Mpls., 1965—, 2d v.p., actuary, 1974-76, v.p., 1976-81, sr. v.p. corp. resources, 1981-82, sr. v.p., 1982—; dir. North Atlantic Life Ins. Co., Jericho, N.Y., No. Life Ins. Co., Seattle, NWNL Reins. Co., Mpls., NWNL Gen. Ins. Co., NWNL Investment Services Corp., NWNL Fin. Corp. Bd. dirs. Sabathani Community Ctr., Mpls., 1979-82; mem. adv. bd. LWV, Mpls., 1982—. Fellow Soc. Actuaries; mem. Am. Acad. Actuaries, Nat. Investor Relations Inst., Am. Council Life Ins. (com. on fin. reporting prins. 1983—), Life Office Mgmt. Assn. (fin. planning and control council 1982—). Club: Calhoun Beach (Mpls.). Office: Northwestern Nat Life Ins Co 20 Washington Ave S Minneapolis MN 55440

BLUDMAN, SIDNEY ARNOLD, theoretical physicist; b. N.Y.C., May 13, 1927; s. Morris Louis and Lena (Saltz) B.; m. Doris Marian Wittenberg, June 26, 1949 (dec. 1968); children—Peter, Joel, Lee. A.B., Cornell U., 1945; M.S., Yale U., 1948, Ph.D., 1951. Asst. prof. Lehigh U., 1950-52; staff physicist Lawrence Radiation Lab., Berkeley, Calif., 1952-61; prof. physics U. Pa., 1961—; cons. Stanford Research Inst., 1958-61; vis. mem. Inst. Advanced Study, 1956-57; lectr. U. Calif. at Berkeley, 1959-60; vis. research fellow Imperial Coll., London, 1967-68; vis. prof. Tel Aviv U., 1971; Lady Davis prof. Hebrew U. Jerusalem, 1976. Contbr. articles on theoretical particle physics and astrophysics to profl. jours. Served with USNR, 1945-46. Fellow Am. Phys. Soc., AAAS. Office: Dept Physics U Pa Philadelphia PA 19114

BLUEFARB, SAMUEL MITCHELL, physician; b. St. Louis, Oct. 15, 1912; s. Sol and Pauline (Brown) B.; m. Grace Parsons, Jan. 1, 1944; 1 son, Richard Alan; m. Leah Rose Vendig Pollock, Jan. 24, 1968; children—Fred, Nancy Pollock. B.S., U. Ill., 1936; M.D., 1937. Diplomate: Am. Bd. Dermatology and Syphilology. Intern Cook County Hosp., Chgo., 1937-38; resident Bellevue Hosp., N.Y.C., 1939-41; practice medicine specializing in dermatology, 1941—; sr. attending dermatologist, chmn. dept. Cook County Hosp., 1952-58; attending dermatologist VA Lakeside Hosp., 1954—; sr. attending staff Chgo. Wesley Meml. Hosp., Passavant Hosp.; prof., chmn. dept. dermatology Northwestern U. Med. Sch., 1962-78. Author books and, articles. Fellow Am. Acad. Dermatology and Syphilology (dir. 1969), ACP; mem. AMA, Ill. Med. Soc. (past pres. dermatol. sect.), Chgo. Med. Soc., Soc. Investigative Dermatology, Chgo. Dermatol. Soc. (past pres.), Am. Dermatol. Assn. Club: Ravisloe Country. Home: 1550 N Lake Shore Dr Chicago IL 60610 Office: 55 E Washington Chicago IL 60602

BLUEMLE, LEWIS WILLIAM, JR., university president; b. Williamsport, Pa., Mar. 9, 1921; s. Lewis William and Ora (Waltz) B.; m. Dolores Isabel Batdorf, July 11, 1953; children: Christopher, Lauren, Susan, Amy. A.B., Johns Hopkins U., 1943, M.D., 1946; ScD. (hon.), Phila. Coll. Pharmacy and Sci., 1980, L.H.D., Washington and Jefferson Coll., 1981. Intern U. Pa. Hosp., 1946-47, resident, 1947-48, clinician-tchr. medicine, 1950, dir., 1960-68, asso. dean, 1965-68; researcher nephrology U. Pa. Sch. Medicine, 1950-69; pres., prof. medicine Upstate Med. Center, SUNY, Syracuse, 1969-74, U. Oreg. Health Scis. Center, Portland, 1974-77; pres. Thomas Jefferson U., Phila.; also prof. medicine Jefferson Med. Coll., 1977—; dir. Girard Bank, Teleflex Inc.; cons. NIH, Office Mgmt. Budget. Contbr. numerous articles med. jours. Chmn. Syracuse Hosp. Exec. Council, 1970-72; bd. dirs. Research Found. of SUNY, 1969-74, Syracuse Symphony Orch., 1971-74, Univ. City Sci. Center, Phila.; bd. overseers U. Pa. Sch. Law., 1977-82. Served to capt. M.C. AUS, 1948-50. Markle scholar; recipient Lindbach award disting. teaching. Fellow ACP, Royal Coll. Physicians Edinburgh, Coll. Physicians Phila. (pres. 1980-82); mem. Am. Soc. Artificial Internal Organs (pres. 1967), Am. Clin. and Climatol. Assn., Am. Soc. Nephrology, Assn. Acad. Health Centers (dir. 1980—), Phila. Assn. Clin. Trials (dir.), Phi Beta Kappa, Alpha Omega Alpha. Clubs: Phila., Union League (Phila.). Patentee artificial kidneys, blood pumps. Office: Thomas Jefferson Univ 11th and Walnut St Philadelphia PA 19107

BLUEMLE, ROBERT LOUIS, lawyer; b. Anderson, Ind., Nov. 6, 1933; s. Orville Wesley and Marguerite (Fadely) B.; children: Tiffany Windsor, Elizabeth Hayden; m. Carol Gillard Bidstrup, Aug. 6, 1979. B.S. with distinction, Ind. U., 1955, M.B.A., 1956; J.D., U. Mich., 1959. Bar: Ariz. 1959, U.S. Supreme Ct 1964. Practiced in, Phoenix, 1961—; partner in charge Phoenix office Furth Fahrner Bluemle, Mason; atty., fin. analyst SEC, Washington, 1959-61; contbg. film critic Phoenix Mag., 1977-80. Past bd. dirs. Scottsdale (Ariz.) Arts Center Assn.; bd. dirs. Valley Shakespeare Theater, 1979—; past bd. dirs., past pres. Greater Phoenix Summer Festival-Images: USA; bd. dirs. Am. Light Opera Co., Washington, 1960, Jr. Achievement, Phoenix, 1970-73, SW Ensemble Theater, 1975, Valley Forward Assn., Phoenix, 1972-76, Friends Mexican Art, Phoenix, 1973, Western Opera Theater, San Francisco, 1975-78; pres. Shakespeare on the Desert, Phoenix, 1968; chmn. Scottsdale Com. on Cable TV, 1979-81. Served with USAF, 1959. Mem. Phoenix Soc. Financial Analysts, English Speaking Union, Newcomen Soc., Fed., Am. bar assns., State Bar Ariz. (chmn., sec. law com. 1969—), Bar Assn. San Francisco. Clubs: Plaza, Ariz., Phoenix, Univ. (Phoenix) (pres. 1967-68). Office: 3443 N Central Ave Phoenix AZ 85012

BLUESTEIN, EDWIN A., JR., lawyer; b. Hearne, Tex., Oct. 16, 1930; s. Edwin A. and Frances Grace (Fly) B.; m. Marsha Kay Meredith, Dec. 21, 1957; children: Boyd, Leslie. B.B.A., U. Tex., 1952, J.D., 1958. Bar: Tex. 1957, U.S. Ct. Appeals (5th cir.) 1960, U.S. Dist. Ct. (so. dist.)Tex. 1959, U.S. Dist. Ct. (ea. dist.)Tex. 1965, U.S. Supreme Ct. 1967, U.S. Ct. Appeals (11th cir.) 1982. Law clk. U.S. Dist. Ct., Houston, 1958-59; assoc. Fulbright & Jaworski, Houston, 1959-65, participating atty., 1965-71, ptnr., 1971—; mem. permanent adv. bd. Tulane Admiralty Law Inst., New Orleans, 1983—; mem. planning com. Houston Marine Ins. Seminar, 1970-76; lectr. profl. seminars. Contbr.: articles to profl. jours. Mem. Tex. Coastal Mgmt. Adv. Com., Austin, 1975-78. Served with U.S. Army, 1952-54. Recipient Yachtsman of Yr. award Houston Yacht Club, 1978. Mem. Tex. Bar Found., Maritime Law Assn. U.S. (mem. exec. com 1980-83), Houston Mariners Club (pres. 1970), Southeastern Admiralty Law Inst. (dir. 1983—), Houston C. of C. (chmn. ports and waterways com. 1978-79), Propeller Club U.S. Methodist. Club: Houston Yacht (commodore 1979-80). Home: 203 Bay Colony Circle La Porte TX 77571 Office: Fulbright & Jaworski 910 Travis St Houston TX 77002

BLUESTEIN, PAUL HAROLD, management engineer; b. Cin., June 14, 1923; s. Norman and Eunice D. (Schullman) B.; m. Joan Ruth Straus, May 17, 1943; children: Alice Sue Bluestein Greenbaum, Judith Ann. B.S., Carnegie Inst. Tech., 1946, B.Engring. in Mgmt. Engring., 1946; M.B.A., Xavier U., 1973. Registered profl. engr., Ohio. Time study engr. Lodge & Shipley Co., 1946-47; adminstrv. engr. Randall Co., 1947-52; partner Paul H. Bluestein & Co. (mgmt. cons.), 1952—, Seinsheimer-Bluestein Mgmt. Services, 1964-70; gen. mgr. Baker Refrigeration Co., 1953-56; pres., dir. Tabor Mfg. Co., 1953-54, Bluejay Corp., 1954—, Blatt & Ludwig Corp., 1954-57, Jason Industries, Inc., 1954-57, Hamilton-York Corp., 1954-57, Earle Hardware Mfg. Co., 1955-57, Hermas Machine Co., 1956—, Panel Machine Co., Ermet Products Corp., 1957—, Tyco Labs., Inc., 1968-69, All-Tech Industries, 1968; gen. mgr. Hafleigh & Co., 1959-60; sr. v.p., gen. mgr. McCauley Ind. Corp., 1959-60; gen. mgr. Am. Art Works div. Rapid-Am. Corp., 1960-63; sec.-treas., dir. Liberty Baking Co., 1964-65; pres. Duguesne Baking Co., 1964-65, Goddard Bakers, Inc., 1964-65; pub. Merger and Acquisition Digest, 1962—; partner Companhia Engenheiros Indsl. Bluestein Do Brasil, 1970—; v.p., gen. mgr. Famco Machine div. Worden-Allen Co., 1974-75; exec. v.p., gen. mgr. Peck, Stow & Wilcox Co., Inc., 1976-77; mem. Joint Engring. Mgmt. Conf. Com., 1971-78. Served with AUS, 1943-46. Mem. ASME, Internat. Inst. Indsl. Engrs., Am. Soc. Engring. Mgmt., N.Am. Mgmt. Council, C.T.O.S.-World Council Mgmt. (dir.). Home: 3420 Section Rd Amberley Village Cincinnati OH 45237 Office: 3420 Section Rd Cincinnati OH 45237

BLUESTEIN, VENUS WELLER, psychologist, educator; b. Milw., July 16, 1933; d. Richard T. and Hazel (Beard) Weller; m. Marvin Bluestein, Mar. 7, 1954. B.S., U. Cin., 1956, M.Ed., 1959, Ed.D., 1966. Diplomate: Am. Bd. Examiners in Profl. Psychology. Psychologist-in-tng. Longview State Hosp., Cin., 1956-58; sch. psychologist Cin. Public Schs., 1958-65; asst. prof. psychology U. Cin., 1965-70, asso. prof., 1970-79, prof., 1979—, dir. undergrad. studies, 1976—, dir. sch. psychology program, 1965-70, 1970-75; cons. child psychologist. Sec., U.S. exec. com. research Children's Internat. Summer Villages, 1964-68; chmn. Ohio Interuniv. Council Sch. Psychology, 1967-68. Editor: Ohio Psychologist, 1961-68; co-editor, 1972-79; Contbr. articles to profl. publs. Mem. Am. Psychol. Assn., Cin. Psychol. Assn. (sec. 1961-62), Ohio Psychol. Assn. (citation 1972, Disting. Service award 1968),

Sch. Psychologists Ohio, AAUP, Forum for Death Edn. and Counseling, Kappa Delta Pi, Sigma Delta Pi, Psi Chi. Office: Dept Psychology Univ Cincinnati Cincinnati OH 45221

BLUFORD, GUION STEWART, JR., astronaut, air force officer; b. Phila., Nov. 22, 1942; s. Guion Stewart and Lolita Harriet (Brice) B.; m. Linda M. Tull, Apr. 7, 1964; children: Guion Stewart, James Trevor. B.S. in Aerospace Engring., Pa. State U., 1964; grad., Squadron Officers Sch., 1971; M.S. in Aerospace Engring., Air Force Inst. Tech., 1974, Ph.D., 1978; D.Sc. hon., Fla. A&M U., 1983. Commd. 2d lt. U.S. Air Force, 1965, advanced through grades to col., 1983, F-4C fighter pilot 12 Tactical Fighter Wing, Cam Ranh Bay, Vietnam, 1966-67, T-38 instr. pilot 3630 Flying Tng. Wing, Sheppard AFB, Wichita Falls, Tex., 1967-72; chief aerodynamics and airframe br. Air Force Flight Dynamics Lab., Wright-Patterson AFB, Dayton, Ohio, 1975-78; NASA astronaut Johnson Space Ctr., Houston, 1978—. Decorated USAF Command Pilot Astronaut Wings, Meritorious Service award, Commendation medal, Air medal with 9 oak leaf clusters, Cross of Gallantry with palm Vietnam; recipient Leadership award Phi Delta Kappa, 1962, Outstanding Flight Safety award Air Tng. Command, USAF, 1970, Mervin E. Gross award Air Force Force Inst. Tech., 1974, Disting. Nat. Scientist award Nat. Soc. Black Engrs., 1979, Group Achievement award NASA, 1980, Disting. Alumni award Pa. State U. Alumni Assn., 1983, Space Flight medal NASA, 1983. Mem. AIAA, Air Force Assn., Tau Beta Pi. Christian Scientist. Home: 16439 Brookvilla Dr Houston TX 77059 Office: Astronaut Office CB Johnson Space Ctr Houston TX 77058

BLUHM, BARBARA JEAN, communications agency executive; b. Chgo., Mar. 5, 1925; s. Maurice L. and Clara (Miller) B. Student Coll. William and Mary, 1943-45; B.S., U. Wis., 1947. Exec. tng. program Carson Pirie Scott & Co., Chgo., 1947-52; home economist Lever Bros. Co., Chgo., 1952-57; field rep. The Merchandising Group, Chgo., 1957-62, v.p., N.Y.C., 1962-82, pres., 1982—. Publicity chmn. James Lenox House Assn., N.Y.C., 1980—. Mem. Home Economists in Bus. (publicity chmn. 1972), Am. Home Econs. Assn., Alpha Gamma Delta. Republican. Presbyterian. Home: 351 E 84th St New York NY 10028 Office: The Merchandising Group 477 Madison Ave New York NY 10022

BLUHM, HEINZ, educator; b. Halle, Germany, Nov. 23, 1907; came to U.S., 1925, naturalized, 1931; s. Fritz and Luise (Henke) B.; m. Helen McClure Berry, Aug. 15, 1938; children—Peter, Louise, Margaret, Christopher. B.A., Northwestern Coll., 1928; M.A., U. Wis., 1929, Ph.D., 1932; postgrad., Yale, 1930-31, M.A. (hon.), 1950. Instr. German U. Wis., 1931-37; instr. German Yale, 1937-39, asst. prof., 1939-44, asso. prof., 1944-50, prof., 1950-67, chmn. dept. Germanic lang., 1954-63, Leavenworth prof. German lang. and lit., 1957-67; prof. Germanic studies Boston Coll., 1967—, dir. Germanic studies, 1967-68, chmn. dept., 1968-76; vis. prof. German U. Minn., 1938, 61, Dartmouth, 1964, U. Calif. at Berkeley, 1968; adj. prof. Boston Theol. Inst., 1976—. Author: Martin Luther, Creative Translator, 1965; contbr. to: Luther for an Ecumenical Age, 1967; Editor: Letters and Diaries of the Goethe Family, 7 vols, 1961-79, Newberry Library, Essays in Language and Literature, 1965, Luther's Essays on Christian Culture and Education, 1968, Das Erlebnis und die Interpretation, 1973; Contbr. articles on Luther and German lit. to profl. periodicals. Decorated Grand Cross of Order of Merit Fed. Republic W. Germany).; Fellow Pierson Coll., Yale; Guggenheim fellow, 1957; Newberry fellow, 1958-60, 80; sr. fellow, 1967; Huntington Library fellow, 1973; Folger Shakespeare Library fellow, 1974; Am. Council Learned Socs. fellow, 1975, 78; Herzog August Bibliothek fellow, 1979. Mem. MLA, Renaissance Soc. Am. Club: Elizabethan. Address: Carney Hall Boston Coll Chestnut Hill MA 02167

BLUHM, NORMAN, artist; b. Chgo., Mar. 28, 1920; m. Carolyn Ogle, May 14, 1961; children: David, Nina. Student, Ill. Inst. Tech., 1936-41, École des Beaux Arts, Paris, 1947-48, Academie de Belle Arte, 1945. One-man exhbns. include, Leo Castelli Gallery, 1957, 60, Corcoran Gallery, Washington, 1969, 77, Martha Jackson Gallery, N.Y.C., 1970-74, Everson Mus., 1973, Vassar Coll., 1974, Contemporary Arts Mus., Houston, 1976, group exhbns. include, Carnegie Inst., 1958, Guggenheim Mus., 1961, Mus. Modern Art, 1966, Large Scale Am. Painting, Jewish Mus., 1967; represented in permanent collections, Dallas Mus. Fine Arts, Dayton Art Inst., Mus. Modern Art, Whitney Mus. Am. Art, Corcoran Gallery., Albright-Knox Mus., Met. Mus. Art, N.Y.C., Mus. Nat. Collection, Washington, Hirshorn Mus., Washington. Served with USAAF, 1941-45. Address: PO Box 1992 East Hampton NY 11937

BLUHM, WILLIAM THEODORE, political scientist, educator; b. Newark, Oct. 13, 1923; s. Frederick Theodore and Charlotte Catherine (Walz) B.; m. Eleanor Elizabeth Kearns, Apr. 22, 1950; children: Catherine Elizabeth, Susanna Marie, Andrew Edward Frederick. B.A., Brown U., 1948; M.A., Tufts U., 1949; Ph.D., U. Chgo., 1957. Instr. polit. sci. U. Rochester, 1952-53, asst. prof., 1957-63, asso. prof., 1963-67, prof., 1967—; instr. polit. sci. Brown U., 1953-57; cons. C.H. Beck Verlag, Munich, 1966-70. Author: Theories of the Political System, 1965, Building an Austrian Nation: The Political Integration of a Western State, 1973, Ideologies and Attitudes, 1974; editor: The Paradigm Problem in Political Science, 1982; contbr. articles profl. jours. Served with Signal Corps AUS, 1943-46. Decorated Bronze Star Medal; U. Rochester research grantee, 1963-64, 68-69; Fulbright research fellow to Austria, 1965-66; NSF summer grantee, 1967, 68; U. Rochester Bridging fellow, 1980-81; Nat. Endowment for Humanities grantee, 1976. Mem. Am. Polit. Sci. Assn., N.E. Polit. Sci. Assn., Am. Soc. Legal and Polit. Philosophy, AAUP, Sigma Nu. Democrat. Roman Catholic. Office: Dept of Political Science University of Rochester Rochester NY 14627

BLUM, BARBARA DAVIS, consultant; b. Hutchinson, Kans., July 6, 1939; d. Roy C. and Jo (Crawford) Davis; children—Davis, Devin, Hunter, Ragan. Student, U. Kans., 1955-56; B.A., Fla. State U., 1958, M.S.W., 1959. Mem. faculty Pediatric Psychiatry Clinic, U. Kans. Med. Center, Lawrence, 1960-62; acting adminstr. Suffolk County (N.Y.) Mental Health Clinic, Huntington, L.I., 1963-64; founder, partner Mid-Suffolk Center for Psychotherapy, Hauppage, L.I., N.Y., 1964-66; v.p. Restaurant Associates of Ga., Inc., Atlanta, 1966-74, Blum's Oxford Road Inc., 1975-76; dep. adminstr. U.S. EPA, Washington, 1977-81, mem. Pres.'s Interagy. Coordinating Council; now pres. Direction Internat.; adv. U.S. Del. to UN Environment Program Governing Council, Nairobi, Kenya, 1978, 79; chairperson U.S. Del., U.S./Japan Environ. Agreement, Tokyo, Japan, 1977-79; head 1st. U.S. Environ. Del. to Peoples' Republic of China, 1979; chmn. Environ. Policy Ctr. Bd. dirs. Environ. Law Inst.; Pres. Save America's Vital Environment, Atlanta, 1972-76, Friends of the River, Inc., Atlanta, 1972-75; vice chairperson Fulton County (Ga.) Planning Commn., 1973-76; dep. polit. dir. Carter Primary Campaign, Atlanta, 1976; dir. ops. Carter/Mondale Transition Team, Washington, 1976-77; chmn. Nat. Adv. Commn. for Resource Conservation and Recovery. Decorated comdr.'s cross Order of Merit, W. Ger.; recipient Disting. Service award Federally Employed Women, 1978, Spl. Conservation award Nat. Wildlife Fedn., 1976, Orgn. of Yr. award Ga. Wildlife Fedn., 1974, Disting. Service award Americans for Indian Opportunity, 1978. Mem. Washington Women's Network (dir., founder). Democrat.

BLUM, FRED ANDREW, electronics company executive, physicist; b. Austin, Tex., Nov. 30, 1939; s. Freddie A. and Margaret E. (Stark) B.; m. Sharon L. Russell, Jan. 1, 1977; children: Craig Houston, Karisa Laine. B.S. in Physics, U. Tex., 1962; M.S. in Physics (NSF fellow), Calif. Inst. Tech., 1963; Ph.D. (Howard Hughes fellow), Calif. Inst. Tech., 1968. Research scientist Gen. Dynamics, Ft. Worth, 1963-64; mem. tech. staff Hughes Research Labs., Malibu, Calif., 1966-68, Lincoln Lab., MIT, Lexington, 1968-73; program mgr. Central Research Labs., Tex. Instruments, Dallas, 1973-75; dir. solid state electronics Rockwell Internat., Thousand Oaks, Calif., 1975-79; v.p. Microelectronics Research and Devel. Center, Rockwell Internat., Anaheim, Calif., 1979-81; pres. GigaBit Logic, Newbury Park, Calif., 1981—. Contbr. numerous articles on solid state electronics to sci. jours.; editorial bd.: Fiber Optics and Integrated Optics, 1977—. Chmn. local adv. council Am. Cancer Soc., 1980-81. Fellow IEEE; Mem. Am. Phys. Soc., Am. Mgmt. Assn., Optical Soc. Am., AAAS, Sigma Xi, Phi Beta Kappa. Home: 4582 Tam O'Shanter Dr Westlake Village CA 91362 Office: 1908 Oak Terrace Ln Newberry Park CA 91320

BLUM, GERALD HENRY, department store executive; b. San Francisco, 1926; s. Abe and Mildred (Loewenthal) B.; children: Shelley, Todd, Ryan, Derek. A.B., Stanford U., 1950. Mdse. trainee Emporium, San Francisco, 1950; with E. Gottschalk & Co., Inc., Fresno, Calif., 1951—, exec. v.p., 1954-82, pres., 1982—. Bd. dirs. Better Bus. Bur., Fresno, 1954-77, Blue Cross, Calif., Fresno Conv. Bur.; mem. adv. com. Fresno County Arts Ctr.; bd. dirs. Fresno County Arts, Ctr., 1958-66; v.p. Fresno County Arts Ctr., 1961; chmn. CARE, Fresno County; mem. Area VII Calif. Vocat. Edn. Com., 1972-75, Mayor's Bi-Racial Com., 1968-69; mem. bus. adv. council Reedley Jr. Coll., 1967-69; founding v.p. Jr. Achievement, Fresno County, 1957-63; bd. dirs. Fresno Boys Club, 1958-62, Central Calif. Employers Council, 1956-62; treas. Central Caif. Employers Council, 1958, Fresno State U. Bulldog Found., 1951-61; bd. dirs. Fresno Philharm. Orch., 1954-58, Salbation Army, Fresno, 1956, Youth Edn. Service, Fresno, 1956, Fresno County Taxpayers Assn., 1954, San Joaquin Valley Econ. Edn. Project, 1953; bd. dirs., bus. adv. council Fresno City Coll., 1955-57; trustee Valley Children's Hosp., 1955-57, United Crusade, Fresno, 1952-62. Served with USAAF, 1944-47; PTO. Mem. Nat. Retail Mchts. Assn. (dir. 1978—), Calif. Retailers Assn. (dir. 1964—), Fresno C. of C. (dir. county, city 1955-57, disting. service award 1959, Boss of Yr., Jr. group 1980), Nat. Secs. Assn. (Boss of Yr. 1978), Fresno County Stanford U. Alumni Assn. (pres. 1952). Clubs: Univ. Sequoia Sunnyside, San Joaquin Country, Downtown (Fresno) (pres. 1978). Office: E Gottschalk & Co Inc PO Box 1872 Fresno CA 93718

BLUM, GERALD SAUL, educator, psychologist; b. Newark, Mar, 8, 1922; s. Benjamin Paul and Augusta (Cohen) B.; m. Myrtle Wolf, Mar. 3, 1946; children—Jeffrey, Nancy. B.S., Rutgers U., 1941; M.A., Clark U., 1942; Ph.D., Stanford, 1948. Clin. psychology intern Palo Alto (Calif.) VA Hosp., 1946-48; mem. faculty U. Mich., 1948-68, prof. psychology, 1959-68; prof. U. Calif. at Santa Barbara, 1968—, chmn. dept., 1969-72; cons. clin. psychology VA, 1949-59. Author: Psychoanalytic Theories of Personality, 1953, A Model of the Mind, 1961, Psychodynamics: The Science of Unconscious Mental Forces, 1966; Cons. editor: Bobbs-Merrill reprint series in psychology. Served with USAAF, 1942-46. Fulbright research scholar, 1954-55; fellow Center Advanced Study Behavioral Scis., 1959-60, Social Sci. Research Council, 1962-63. Fellow Am. Psychol. Assn., AAAS; mem. Phi Beta Kappa, Sigma Xi. Inventor of Blacky Pictures, 1950. Home: 1227 Viscaino Rd Santa Barbara CA 93103

BLUM, IRVING, art dealer; b. N.Y.C., Dec. 1, 1930; s. Harry and Adele (Fern) B.; 1 son, Jason Ferus. Student, U. Ariz., 1949-52. With Ferus Gallery, Los Angeles, 1958-73; ptnr. Blum-Helman Gallery, N.Y.C., 1973—. Mem. Art Dealers Assn. Home: 784 Park Ave New York NY 10021 Office: 20 W 57th St New York NY 10019

BLUM, JACOB JOSEPH, physiologist, educator; b. Bklyn., Oct. 3, 1926; s. Paul and Anna (Brown) B.; m. Ruth Marsey, June 3, 1960; children—Mark, Douglas, Lisa, Laura. B.A., N.Y. U., 1947; M.S., U. Chgo., 1950, Ph.D., 1952. Staff Naval Med. Research Inst., Bethesda, Md., 1953-56; chief biophysics sect. gerontology br. NIH, Balt., 1958-62; prof. physiology Duke U., Durham, N.C., 1962—, James B. Duke prof., 1980—. Served with AUS, 1945-46. Merck postdoctoral fellow, 1952; Guggenheim fellow, 1969. Mem. Am. Physiol. Soc., Biophys. Soc., Soc. for Cell Biology. Home: 2525 Perkins Rd Durham NC 27706

BLUM, JEROME, educator; b. Balt., Apr. 27, 1913; s. Moses and Fannie (Herzfeld) B. A.B., Johns Hopkins U., 1933, Ph.D., 1947. Faculty Princeton U., 1947—, prof. history, chmn. dept., 1961-67, James Madison preceptor, 1952-55, master Grad. Coll., 1958-78, Henry Charles Lea prof. history, 1966-81; Lawrence lectr. Conn. Coll., 1968; Schouler lectr. Johns Hopkins U., 1974. Author: Noble Landowners and Agriculture in Austria, 1815-1848, 1948, Lord and Peasant in Russia from the Ninth to the Nineteenth Century, 1961, The End of the Old Order in Rural Europe, 1978; co-author: The European World, 1966, Civilizations: Western and World, 1975, European Landed Elites in the Nineteenth Century, 1977, Our Forgotten Past, 1981; Bd. editors: Jour. Modern History, 1956-58; editorial bd.: Jour. Econ. History, 1963-68; Contbr. articles to scholarly jours. Pres. bd. mgrs. N.J. State Home for Girls, 1965-69; chmn. Ad Hoc Com. on Children's Services N.J., 1966-68; bd. dirs. Morrow Assn. on Correction, 1968-71, Citizens Commn. for Children N.J., 1971-73; mem. Mercer County Mental Health Bd., 1972-74; trustee Princeton U. Press, 1966-70. Served from pvt. to capt. F.A. AUS, 1942-46. Guggenheim fellow, 1951-52, 71-72; Shreve fellow Princeton U., 1952, 68; Nat. Endowment for Humanities fellow, 1975-76. Fellow Am. Acad. Arts and Scis.; mem. Am. Philos. Soc. (Henry Allen Moe prize in humanities 1982), Am. Hist. Assn. (Herbert Baxter Adams prize 1962, Higby prize 1972), Agrl. History Soc. (pres. 1981-82), Econ. History Assn., Center for Research Libraries (council 1969—). Jewish. Club: Nassau (Princeton). Home: 67 S Stanworth Dr Princeton NJ 08540

BLUM, JOHN CURTIS, agricultural economist; b. Terryville, Conn., July 5, 1915; s. John A. and Marion D. (Curtis) B.; m. Mable L. Brooks, Oct. 21, 1939; children—Joanne M. Blum Kogut, John Curtis, Nancy J. Blum Hufnagle. B.S., U. Conn., 1937, M.S., 1939; postgrad., U. Wis., 1941, Dept. Agr. Grad. Sch., 1946; student, Indsl. Coll. Armed Forces, 1965-66. With Dept. Agr., 1939-75; asst. dir. dairy div. Agrl. Marketing Service, 1960-61, dir. div., 1961-63; economist Office of Adminstr., 1963-64, asst. dept. adminstr., 1964-67, dep. adminstr., 1967-74, asso. adminstr., 1974-75; economist E.A. Jaenke & Assos., Inc., Washington, 1975-83. Violinist Fairfax County (Va.) Symphony Orch., 1957—, bd. dirs., 1957-70, pres., 1959-61, treas., 1965-67; dist. dir. North Va. dist. P.T.A., 1961-63; treas. Va. Congress Parents and Tchrs., 1963-65, regional v.p., 1965-67, chmn. extension com., 1967-69, budget chmn., 1969-71, bd. mgrs., 1961-71. Served to lt. (j.g.) USNR, 1944-46; PTO. Mem. Am. Acad. Polit. and Social Sci., Am. Agr. Econ. Assn., Grange. Home: 11500 Fairway Dr #404 Reston VA 22090

BLUM, JOHN LEO, educator; b. Madison, Wis., May 2, 1917; s. John E. and Kathryn (Cullen) B.; m. Anna M. Raick, Jan. 25, 1947; children—Colette (Mrs. Ronald Meister), Suzanne, Annette. B.S., U. Wis., 1937, M.S., 1939; Ph.D., U. Mich., 1953. From instr. to prof. biology Canisius Coll., Buffalo, 1941-63; mem. faculty U. Wis.-Milw., 1963—, prof. botany, 1966—, asso. dean, 1967-69. Author: The Vaucheriaceae, 1972. Pres. Niagara Frontier chpt. Izaak Walton League, 1959-62. Served with AUS, 1943-45. Cole fellow U. Mich., 1952-53. Fellow A.A.A.S.; mem. Bot. Soc. Am., Phycological Soc. Am., Internat. Phycological Soc., Am. Inst. Biol. Scis., Internat. Assn. Great Lakes Research, Wis. Acad. Sci., Arts and Letters, Sigma Xi. Home: 2961 N Marietta Ave Milwaukee WI 53211

BLUM, JOHN MORTON, historian; b. N.Y.C., Apr. 29, 1921; s. Morton Gustave and Edna (LeVino) B.; m. Pamela Louise Zink, June 28, 1944; children: Pamela, Ann, Thomas Tyler. A.B., Harvard U., 1943, M.A., 1947, Ph.D., 1950, LL.D. (hon.), 1980; M.A., Cambridge (Eng.) U., 1963, Oxford (Eng.) U., 1976; D.H.L. (hon.), Trinity Coll., 1970, LL.D., Colgate U., 1978. Research assoc., then asst. prof. history, assoc. prof. M.I.T., 1948-57; prof. history Yale U., 1957—; Pitt prof. Cambridge U., 1963-64; Harmsworth prof. Oxford U., 1976-77. Author: Joe Tumulty and the Wilson Era, 1951, The Republican Roosevelt, 1954, Woodrow Wilson and the Politics of Morality, 1956, From the Morgenthau Diaries, Vol. I, 1959, Vol. II, 1965, Vol. III, 1967, Yesterday's Children, 1959, The Promise of America, 1966, Roosevelt and Morgenthau, 1970, V Was for Victory, 1976, The Progressive Presidents, 1980; assoc. editor: (with Elting E. Morison) Letters of Theodore Roosevelt (8 vols.), 1951-54; editor: The National Experience, 1963, The Price of Vision, 1973. Trustee Buckingham Sch., 1954-56, Hotchkiss Sch., 1964-70; mem. Andover Alumni Council, 1957-60. Served from ensign to lt. USNR, 1943-46. Fellow Harvard U., 1970-79. Mem. Am. Acad. Arts and Scis., Conn. Acad. Arts and Scis., Am. Hist. Assn., Mass. Hist. Assn., Phi Beta Kappa. Home: 34 Edgehill Rd New Haven CT 06511

BLUM, LAWRENCE PHILIP, educational psychology educator; b. Webster, Wis., Feb. 14, 1917; s. Gustav Henry and Mary (Demuth) B.; m. Lucille A. Bloy, June 6, 1940; children: Karen Lynn, Kristine Ellen. B.S., U. Wis., 1939, M.S., 1943, Ph.D., 1947. High sch. tchr., Phillips, Wis., 1939-41, social worker, Chicago Heights, Ill., 1941-42; asst. prof. edn. Mich. State U., 1946-49; mem. faculty U. Wis.-Milw., 1949-82, prof. ednl. psychology, 1960-82; ret., 1982; vocat. cons. Social Security Adminstrn. Author: (with others) Communication, 1964, Cases and Projects in Communication, 1964; also articles, chpts. in books. Served with USAAF, 1943-46. Named Mental Health Man of Year Wis. Assn. Mental Health, 1966. Mem. Phi Kappa Phi, Phi Delta Kappa. Home: 400 E Lexington Blvd Whitefish Bay WI 53217 Office: Univ Wis Milwaukee WI 53201

BLUM, PETER UWE, chemical company executive; b. Hamburg, Germany, Dec. 5, 1939; s. Ernst and Gertrud (Hartig) B.; m. Renate Gerstgraser, Jan. 8, 1963; children: Beatrice, Patrick Oliver. Alumni, of Insead Fontainebleu, France, 1973; A.M.P., Harvard Bus. Sch., 1980. With Hoechst Aktiengesellscyaft, Frankfurt, W.Ger., 1969; mgr. Fibres dystuffs textiles aux. Hoechst, Hong Kong, 1970-72, dep. mng. dir., 1972-74; mng. dir., chmn. bd. textiles aux. Hoechst, Hong Kong, 1974-75; v.p. worldwide mktg. staff Hoechst Aktiengesellschaft, Frankfurt, 1975-79; pres. indsl. chem. div. Am. Hoechst Corp., Somerville, N.J., 1980-82, group v.p., 1983; pres., chief exec. officer Hoechst Can., Inc., Montreal, Que., 1983—. Mem. Chem. Mfrs. Assn., Soc. Chem. Industry, Canadian Chem. Producers Assn. (dir.). Office: Hoechst Canada Inc 4045 Cote Vertu Montreal PQ Canada H4R 1R6

BLUM, RICHARD HOSMER ADAMS, foundation executive; b. Ft. Wayne, Ind., Oct. 7, 1927; s. Hosmer and Imogene (Heino) B.; m. Eva Maria Spitz, July 6, 1957. A.B. with honors magna cum laude, San Jose State Coll., 1949; Ph.D., Stanford U., 1951. Research dir. Calif. Med. Assn., San Francisco, 1956-58, San Mateo County (Calif.) Mental Health Service, San Mateo, 1958-60; lectr. Sch. Criminology, U. Calif., Berkeley, 1960-62; mem. faculty Stanford (Calif.) U., 1962-78, prof. dept. psychology, 1970-75; mem. faculty Stanford (Calif.) U. Law Sch., 1975-78; chmn. bd. Am. Lives Endowment, Portola Valley, Calif., 1979—; prof. dept. gynecology and obstetrics Santford U., 1982—; chmn. Internat. Research Group on Drug Legis. and Programs, Geneva, 1969—; pres. Bio-Behavioral Research Group, Inc., Palo Alto, 1964—; owner/operator Shingle Mill and Volcano ranches, 1964—; U.S. del. UN Narcotics Commn., 1969-71; asso. psychologist Stanford Research Inst., 1953-56; psychol. intern San Quentin State Prison, 1948; cons. Pres.'s Commn. on Law Enforcement, 1966-67, FDA, 1967-69, NIMH, 1967-69, Nat. Commn. Causes and Prevention of Violence, 1969-70, Calif. Council Criminal Justice, 1969-70, Nat. Commn. Marijuana and Drug Abuse, 1971-72, Drug Abuse Council, Washington, 1972-76, Centro Mexicano de Estudios en Farmacodependencia, Mexico City, 1972-73, U.S. Senate Permanent Subcom. on Investigations, 1981-83; mem. adv. commn. psychotomimetic drugs FDA, 1967-68; expert cons. Law Enforcement Assistance Adminstrn., 1966-69, chmn. small grants rev. com., 1968-69; mem. sci. adv. com. Fed. Bur. Narcotics and Dangerous Drugs, 1969-73, sr. advisor strategic intelligence office, 1969-73; co-chmn. White House Conf. Youth, 1970-71; mem. discliplinary bd. Calif. State Bar, 1975-78; referee Calif. State Bar Cts., 1979—. Author: The Management of the Doctor-Patient Relationship, 1960, (with J. Ezekiel) Clinical Records for Mental Health Services, 1962, A Commonsense Guide to Doctors, Hospitals and Medical Care, 1964, (with others) Utopiates: A Study of the Use and Users of LSD-25, 1964, (with Eva Blum) Health and Healing in Rural Greece, 1965, Alcoholism: Modern Psychological Approaches to Treatment, 1967, (with others) Society and Drugs, 1969, Students and Drugs, 1969, (with Eva Blum) The Dangerous Hour: A Socio-psychological Study of the Lore of Crisis and Mystery in Rural Greece, 1970; editor: Police Selection, 1964; author: Deceivers and Deceived: Observations on Confidence Men and Their Victims, Informants and Their Quarry, Political and Industrial Spies and Ordinary Citizens, 1972, (with others) Horatio Alger's Children: Role of the Family in the Origin and Prevention of Drug Risk, 1972, The Dream Sellers: Perspectives on Drug Dealers, 1972, Surveillance and Espionage in a Free Society, 1972, Drug Dealers - Taking Action: Options for International Response, 1973, Drug Education: Results and Recommendations, 1976, Pharmaceuticals and Health Policy: An International Perspective on Provision and Control of Medicines, 1980; editor: Police Selection, 1964, Controlling Drugs: International Handbook for Psychoactive Drug Classification, 1974; Author: fiction The Late Lt. Dessin and Other Stories, 1967, Death and Festivals, 1968, The Mexican Assassin, 1977, Codename Starlight, 1978, A Whisper of Treason, 1981; contbr. poems and, short stories to lit. jours.; Editor: Bull. of Research Exchange on Prevention of War, 1955-57; asso. editor: Jour. Conflict Resolutions, 1954-64. Served in U.S. Army, 1951-53; Korea. Recipient Meritorious Service award U.S. Dept. Justice, 1969; Pacesetter award Nat. Coordinating Council on Drug Edn., 1972; Sandoz Centenary medal, 1972; Outstanding Service award The Proprietary Assn., 1975. Fellow Am. Psychol. Assn., Am. Sociol. Assn., Am. Public Health Assn., AAAS; mem. Am. Criminol. Assn., Archaeol. Inst. Am., Sigma Xi. Unitarian. Club: Cosmos (Washington). Home: PO Box 4066 Woodside CA 94062 Office: 765 Portola Rd Portola Valley CA 94025 Office: Stanford U Sch Medicine Stanford CA 94305

BLUM, ROBERT EDWARD, business executive; b. Bklyn., May 8, 1899; s. Edward C. and Florence (Abraham) B.; m. Ethel Mildred Halsey, Aug. 15, 1928; children: John Robert Halsey, Alice Elizabeth

Packard (Mrs. Robert H. Yoakum). A.B., Yale, 1921; Litt.D., L.I. U., 1959. Joined Abraham and Straus, Inc., Bklyn., 1922, v.p., 1930-37, 42-64, sec., 1936-60; former dir. Equitable Life Assurance Soc. U.S., Bklyn. Union Gas Co., Church & Dwight Co., Inc.; past trustee Dime Savs. Bank N.Y.; hon. v.p., former pres. Bahamas Nat. Trust; mem. N.Y. State Bd. Social Welfare, 1954-64; former mem. Temp. N.Y. State Commn. on Edn. Finance. Hon trustee Am. Mus. Nat. History; hon. trustee N.Y. Zool. Soc.; former trustee, v.p. Bklyn. Public Library; hon. dir. N.Y. World's Fair Corp., 1964-65; bd. dirs., former pres. Am. Friends of Bahamas Found., Inc.; gen. chmn. Prospect Park Centennial, 1966; mem. Mayor's Com. for Cultural Affairs, N.Y.C., 1967; v.p., dir. Bklyn. War Meml., Inc.; dir. emeritus, past treas. Lincoln Center Performing Arts; vice chmn., mem. Bklyn. Sports Center Authority; mem., past pres. Art Commn. City of N.Y.; mem. distbn. com. N.Y. Community Trust; trustee Coll. of Atlantic, Bar Harbor, Maine, Wendell Gilley Mus. Served as 2d lt. F.A. AUS, World War I; maj. Ordnance Dept. AUS, World War II. Mem. Bklyn. Inst. Arts and Scis. (pres. 1951-60, trustee 1936-72, hon. trustee 1972—, past chmn. governing com. Bklyn. Mus.), Bklyn. C. of C. (past v.p., dir.), Better Bus. Bur. N.Y.C., Downtown Bklyn. Assn. (former pres., dir.). Clubs: Yale (N.Y.C.); Century Assn., Bar Harbor, Pilgrims, Sharon Country. Home: Ore Mine Rd Box 95 Rural Route 1 Lakeville CT 06039 also Indian Point Mount Desert ME 04660

BLUM, ROBERT JOSEPH, paper mfr.; b. Cin., June 1, 1906; s. Henry P. and Marie (McHugh) B.; m. Elizabeth Hickey, June 20, 1933; children—Elizabeth Ann Buse, Robert Joseph, Mary Gay (Mrs. Connolly), Julianne (Mrs. Thesing). Student, U. Cin., 1924. Clk. LaBoiteux Co., 1924, successively salesman, N.Y. office mgr., sales mgr., v.p. and treas., 1924-45; pres. Excello Paper Products div. Mead Corp., 1943-59; exec. v.p. Mead Board Sales, Inc., 1946-57, pres., 1957-70, Piedmont Paper Products, 1950—; ret. v.p. Mead Corp., Dayton, Ohio. Home: 2444 Madison Rd Apt 1510 Cincinnati OH 45208 Office: 2639 Erie Ave Suite 2 Cincinnati OH 45208

BLUM, SEYMOUR L., ceramic engineer; b. N.Y.C., Jan. 10, 1925; s. Henry E. and Helen (Geduld) B.; m. Edith D. Levin, June 20, 1948; 1 son, John B. Student, Bowdoin Coll., 1943-44; B.S., Alfred U., 1948; Sc.D., M.I.T., 1954. Plant engr. Comml. Decal Inc., Mt. Vernon, N.Y., 1948-51; research asst. M.I.T., Cambridge, 1951-54; mgr. advanced materials Raytheon Co., Waltham, Mass., 1954-63; v.p. IIT Research Inst., Chgo., 1963-71; dir. energy and resources planning MITRE Corp., Bedford, Mass., 1971-78; v.p. program devel. Northern Energy Corp., Boston, 1978—; bd. dirs. Corp. for Cleaner Commonwealth, Boston, 1979—; cons. to various orgns. Mem. editorial bd.: Conservation and Recycling, 1976—; contbr. numerous articles in fields of materials, energy and environment. Served with USAAF, 1943-46. Fellow Am. Inst. Chemists, Am. Ceramic Soc. (div. chmn., trustee, v.p.); mem. Boston C. of C., Fedn. of Materials Soc., Nat. Inst. Ceramic Engrs., Nat. Soc. Profl. Engrs., AAAS, Sigma Xi. Club: Cosmos (Washington.). Office: 470 Atlantic Ave Boston MA 02110

BLUM, STELLA, curator, educator; b. Schenectady, Oct. 19, 1916; d. Joseph and Mary (Kiskiel) Biercuk; m. George A. Blum, Oct. 5, 1939; children: Walter B., Eric George. B.F.A., Syracuse U., 1938. With Met. Mus. Art, N.Y.C., 1953—, assoc. curator, 1969-72, curator, 1972—; adj. prof. NYU, 1979—; guest curator Kyoto Costume Inst., Japan, 1975, 79, Kunsthaus Mus., Zurich, Switzerland, 1979, St. Louis Mus. Art, 1979, Victoria Gallery, Melbourne, Australia, 1981. Author: Victorian Fashions and Costumes from Harper's Bazar 1867-1898, 1974, Designs by Erte, 1976, Ackermann's Costume Plates, 1978, Everyday Fashions of the 20s, 1981, 18th Century French Fashion Plates, 1982. Recipient Arents Pioneer award Syracuse U., 1983, citation Pratt Inst., 1983. Mem. Fashion Group (v.p.), Costume Soc. Am. (v.p.), Fashion's Inner Circle (pres.), Internat. Council Mus. (titular head costume com.). Home: 14-10 146th Pl Whitestone NY 11357 Office: Met Mus Art 5th Ave and 82d St New York NY 10028

BLUM, VIRGIL CLARENCE, political science educator emeritus; b. Defiance, Iowa, Mar. 27, 1913; s. John Peter and Elizabeth (Rushenberg) B. Student, Creighton U., 1932-34; A.B., St. Louis U., 1938, M.A., 1945, Ph.D., 1954, U. Chgo., 1950-51. Joined Soc. of Jesus, 1934; ordained priest Roman Catholic Ch., 1947; tchr. Campion High Sch., Prairie du Chien, Wis., 1941-44; asst. prof. Creighton U., 1953-56; mem. faculty Marquette U., 1956—, prof. polit. sci., 1961-78, prof. emeritus, 1978—, chmn. dept., 1961-65, 70-71; dir. Santa Fe Communications Inc. Author: Freedom of Choice in Education, 1958, Freedom in Education, 1965, Education: Freedom and Competition, 1967, Catholic Education: Survival or Demise, 1969, Parent Power for Tuition Grants, 1971, Catholic Parents—Political Eunuchs, 1972, also articles. Chmn. Children's Equal Opportunities Com., 1965-71; mem. exec. com. Citizens for Ednl. Freedom, 1964-76, bd. dirs., 1964—; founder Catholic League for Religious and Civil Rights; pres. Catholic League for Religious and Rights; bd. dirs Thomas J. White Found., 1983—. Mem. Am., Midwest polit. sci. assns., Am. Judicature Soc., Nat. Council on Religion and Pub. Edn. Home: 1404 W Wisconsin Ave Milwaukee WI 53233

BLUM, WALTER J., lawyer, educator; b. Chgo., Aug. 17, 1918; m. Natalie Richter; children: Wendy (Mrs. David R. Coggins, Jr.), Catherine (Mrs. James Dennis Scott). A.B., U. Chgo., 1939, J.D., 1941. Bar: Ill., D.C. Atty. OPA, 1941-43; faculty U. Chgo. Law Sch., 1946—, prof., 1953—, mem. planning com. tax conf., 1947—; legal counsel Bull. Atomic Scientists, 1949—; Mem. steering com. IRS project Adminstrv. Conf. of U.S., 1974-76. Author: (with Harry Kalven, Jr.) The Uneasy Case for Progressive Taxation, 1953, Public Law Perspectives on a Private Law Problem, Auto Compensation Plans, 1964, (with Stanley A. Kaplan) Corporate Readjustments and Reorganizations, 1976; also articles. Trustee Coll. Retirement Equity Fund, 1970-82. Mem. ABA (mem. council tax Sect. 1972-75), Chgo. Bar Assn. (past bd. mgrs.), Am. Law Inst. (cons. fed. income tax project 1974-82), Am. Acad. Arts and Scis., Chgo. Fed. Tax Forum, Order of Coif, Phi Beta Kappa. Club: Law (Chgo.). Home: 5724 S Kimbark Ave Chicago IL 60637

BLUM, WILLIAM LEE, lawyer; b. Cin., Dec. 25, 1920; s. Charles J. and Julia J. (Knock) B.; m. Mary B. Janszen, Feb. 15, 1947; children—Mary Lee Blum Olinger, W. Charles, Christine L., John A., Margaret A. A.B., Georgetown U., 1942; Indsl. Adminstrn., Harvard U., 1943, M.B.A., 1949, J.D., 1949. Bar: Ohio bar 1949. Since practiced in, Cin.; partner firm Dinsmore & Shohl, 1953—, adminstrv. partner, 1978—, chmn. litigation dept., 1974—; dir. Suburban Fed. Savs. & Loan Assn., Brighton Corp., Allen Co., Intercontinental Corp. Pres., chmn. trustees Greater Cin. Community Chest and Council, 1966-69; pres. Cin. Bd. Health, 1970-72; trustee United Appeal, 1965-77, Queen City Found., 1975-79, McDonald Found., 1962-79, Cin. Community Action Commn., 1969-72, Catholic Social Services S.W. Ohio, 1970-83, Athenaeum of Ohio, 1970-83, Cin. Zoo, 1977—; pres. Cin. Zoo, 1980—; trustee St. Xavier High Sch., Cin., 1977—; mem. president's council Georgetown U., 1979. Served to maj. AUS, 1943-46. Decorated Knight of Malta, 1970, Knight of Holy Sepulchre, 1983; recipient Xavier Insignis award, 1976. Mem. Am. Bar Assn., U.S. Cath. Conf. Diocesan Attys. Assn., Ohio Bar Assn., Cin. Bar Assn., Mil. Order Knights Malta., Mil. Order Knights of Holy Sepulchre. Roman Catholic. Clubs: Cin. Country, Bankers, Cin. Athletic, K.C. Home: 7 Grandin Ln Cincinnati OH 45208 Office: 2100 Fountain Sq Plaza 511 Walnut St Cincinnati OH 45202

BLUMBERG, BARUCH SAMUEL, research physician, research institute director; b. N.Y.C., July 28, 1925; s. Meyer and Ida (Simonoff) B.; m. Jean Liebesman, Apr. 4, 1954; children: Anne, George, Jane, Noah. B.S., Union Coll., Schenectady, 1946; M.D., Columbia U., 1951; Ph.D., Balliol Coll., Oxford (Eng.) U., 1957; 14 hon. doctoral degrees. Intern, resident Columbia div. Bellevue Hosp., N.Y.C., 1951-53; fellow in medicine Columbia-Presbyn. Med. Center, N.Y.C., 1953-55; chief geog. medicine and genetics sect. NIH, Bethesda, Md., 1957-64; assoc. dir. clin. research Inst. Cancer Research, Phila., 1964—; Univ. prof. medicine and anthropology U. Pa.; George Eastman vis. prof. Balliol Coll., Oxford U., 1983-84. Contbr. articles to profl. jours. Served to ensign USNR, 1943-46. Recipient Albion O. Berstein, M.D. award Med. Soc. State of N.Y., 1969; Grand Sci. award Phi Lambda Kappa, 1972; Ann. award Eastern Pa. br. Am. Soc. Microbiology, 1972; Eppinger prize U. Freiburg, Germany, 1973; Passano award Williams & Wilkens Co., 1974; Modern Medicine Distinguished Achievement award, 1975; Internat. award Gairdner Found., 1975; Karl Landsteiner Meml. award Am. Assn. Blood Banks, 1975; Nobel prize in physiology or medicine, 1976; Scopus award Am. Friends of Hebrew U., 1977; Strittmatter award Philadelphia County Med. Soc., 1980; Disting. Service award Pa. Med. Soc., 1982. Fellow A.C.P.; mem. Nat. Acad. Scis., Assn. Am. Physicians, Am. Soc. Clin. Investigation, Am. Soc. Human Genetics, Am. Assn. Phys. Anthropologists, John Morgan Soc., Chesapeake and Ohio Canal Soc. Club: Provincetown Yacht. Discover causative agt. hepatitis B. Office: Inst Cancer Research 7701 Burholme Ave Philadelphia PA 19111

BLUMBERG, DAVID, builder, developer; b. Dothan, Ala., Jan 19, 1925; s. Myer and Esther (Orovitz) B.; m. Lee Dickens; children: Philip Flayderman, John Aaron, Matthew. Student, U. Ala., 1940-42, U. N.C, 1942-43; M.B.A., Harvard U., 1947. Pres. Cutler Ridge Devel. Corp., Miami, Fla., 1953—, Fla. Water & Utilities Co., 1953-65, Planned Devel. Corp., Miami, 1969—; chmn. exec. Prestressed Systems, Inc., 1967-73; chmn. bd. FMI Fin. Corp., Miami, 1978-82; dir. Southeast Bank, N.A., Southeast Banking Corp., Fla. Power & Light Co. Trustee, mem. exec. com. U. Miami, 1973—; Trustee Miami United Way, 1972—; bd. dirs. Fla. Council of 100; trustee Temple Israel.; vice chmn. New World Center Com., 1978; mem. Fla. High Speed Rail Com., Bayside Splty. Ctr. Rev. Com. Served with USNR, 1943-46. Recipient Silver medallion NCCJ, 1978; named Miami News Businessman of Year, 1973. Mem. Internat. Council Shopping Centers (past trustee, v.p., treas.), Builders Assn. S. Fla. (spl. adv. to bd. 1977-79), S. Fla. Coordinating Council (exec. com.), Econ. Soc. S. Fla. (past dir.), Dade County Drainage Contractors Assn. (past pres.), Fla. C. of C. (dir., past treas.), Greater Miami C. of C. (pres. 1971-72), Western History Assn., Fla. Trail Assn. Clubs: Miami, Standard, Ocean Reef, Boca Grande, Gables Estate Yacht, City of Miami, Bankers. Home: 1 Arvida Pkwy Miami FL 33156 Office: 1400 Brickell Ave Miami FL 33131

BLUMBERG, GERALD, lawyer; b. N.Y.C., July 25, 1911; s. Saul and Amelia (Abramowitz) B.; m. Rhoda Shapiro, Jan. 6, 1945; children: Lawrence, Rena, Alice, Leda. A.B. cum laude, Cornell U., 1931, J.D., Harvard, 1934. Bar: Mass. 1934, N.Y. 1934. Practiced in, N.Y.C., 1934—; mem. firm Gerald & Lawrence Blumberg; instr. econs. Cornell U., 1931; mem. Harvard Legal Aid Bur., 1934; Mem. nat. urban affairs com. Anti-Defamation League, 1972—; mem. nat. estate affairs com. Cornell U., 1974—, mem. univ. council, 1977—. Bd. dirs., v.p., exec. com. Am. Com. Weizmann Inst. Sci., internat. bd. govs., 1982—. Mem. Am., Internat., Fed., N.Y. State, Westchester, Yorktown bar assns., New York County Lawyers Assn., Phi Beta Kappa, Phi Kappa Phi. Home: Baptist Ch Rd Yorktown Heights NY 10598 Office: 1 Rockefeller Plaza New York NY 10020

BLUMBERG, GRACE GANZ, educator, lawyer; b. N.Y.C., Feb. 16, 1940; d. Samuel and Beatrice (Finkelstein) Ganz; m. Donald R. Blumberg, Sept. 9, 1959; 1 dau., Rachel. B.A., U. Colo., 1960; J.D. summa cum laude, SUNY, 1971; LL.M., Harvard U., 1974. Bar: N.Y. State bar 1971. Confidential law clk. Appellate Div., Supreme Ct., 4th Dept., Rochester, N.Y., 1971-72; teaching fellow Harvard Law Sch., Cambridge, Mass., 1972-74; prof. law SUNY, Buffalo, 1974-81, UCLA, 1981—; cooperating atty. ACLU. Editorial bd.: Am. Jour. Comparative Law, 1977; contbr. articles to profl. jours. Baldy Summer Research fellow in law and social policy, 1977-78; SUNY research Found. summer faculty fellow, 1975. Mem. Am. Soc. Comparative Law, Am. Assn. Law Schs., NOW, ACLU. Address: UCLA Law Sch 405 Hilgard Ave Los Angeles CA 90024

BLUMBERG, JOE MORRIS, physician, retired army officer; b. Balt., June 27, 1909; s. A.W. and Hortense (Morris) B.; m. Catherine Weller, Aug. 29, 1935. B.S., Emory U., 1930, M.D., 1933, D.Sc. (hon.), 1978; M.D. with honors, Yonsei U., Seoul, Korea, 1966. Diplomate: Am. Bd. Pathology. Intern Md. Gen. Hosp., Balt., 1933-34; resident Balt. City Hosp., 1934-36; gen. practice medicine, Balt., 1936-41; commd. 1st lt. U.S. Army, 1935, advanced through grades to maj. gen., 1966; chief lab. service, Ft. Eustis, Va., 1941-44, 115th Gen. Hosp., ETO, 1944-45; pathologist Army Inst. Pathology, Washington, 1945-46; chief Histopath. Center, Oliver Gen. Hosp., Augusta, Ga., 1946-47, chief lab. service, 1947-50; pathologist Walter Reed Gen. Hosp., 1950-53, chief lab. services, 1953; pathologist Army Med. Service Grad. Sch., Washington, 1953-54; comdg. officer 406th Med. Gen. Lab., Tokyo; cons. pathology and lab. service to chief surgeon U.S. Army Forces Far East and 8th Army, 1954-57; dep. dir. Armed Forces Inst. Pathology, 1957; dep. dir., chief lab. services cons. div. Directorate Profl. Service, Office Surgeon Gen., 1957-63, dir., 1963-67; comdg. gen. Med. Research and Devel. Command, Washington, 1967-69; spl. asst. to surgeon gen. research and devel., 1967-69; clin. prof. pathology Sch. Medicine Georgetown U., 1963-80; spl. adviser Republic Korea Army, 1956; spl. adviser, cons. Minister Health Philippines, 1956; med. adviser Am. embassy, Manila, 1956; sci. dir. Am. Registry Pathology, 1959-63. Contbr. articles to profl. jours. Bd. dirs. Gorgas Meml. Inst. Tropical Medicine and Preventive Medicine, 1964-70. Decorated Legion of Merit, D.S.M.; recipient Hektoen Bronze medal AMA, 1961; Stitt award Assn. Mil. Surgeons, 1961; Founders medal, 1964; Seale Harris award So. Med. Assn., 1963; award of honor Med. Alumni Assn. Emory U., 1966; Clin. Scientist of Year, 1968; Ward Burdick award, 1969. Fellow Coll. Am. Pathologists (gov.), Am. Soc. Clin. Pathologists (past v.p., com. chmn.), ACP, AMA, Am. Soc. Cytology; mem. Am. Soc. Exptl. Pathology, Am. Assn. Pathologists and Bacteriologists, AAAS, Assn. Mexican Pathologists (hon.), Am. Med. Soc. Vienna (hon.), Assn. Clin. Scientists (past v.p.), Assn. Mil. Surgeons U.S. (life), Washington Soc. Pathologists (past pres.), Internat. Acad. Pathology, So. Med. Assn. (life). Home: 5007 Jamestown Rd Bethesda MD 20816

BLUMBERG, MARK STUART, health care planner; b. N.Y.C., Nov. 16, 1924; s. Sydney N. and Mollie (Leshrowitz) B.; m. Luba Monasevitch, Oct. 23, 1952; children: Bart David, Eve Luise; m.2d Elizabeth R. Conner, Nov. 1, 1974. Student, Johns Hopkins U., 1942-43, Harvard Coll., 1943-44; D.M.D., Harvard Sch. Dental Medicine, 1948; M.D., Harvard U., 1950, Sch. Public Health, 1955. Intern, children's med. service Bellevue Hosp., N.Y.C., 1950-51; ops. analyst Johns Hopkins U. Ops. Research Office, Chevy Chase, Md., 1951-54; exchange analyst Army Ops. Research Group (U.K.), West Byfleet, Eng., 1953-54; staff Occupational Health Program, USPHS, Washington, 1954-56; asso. ops. analyst to dir. health econs. program Stanford (Calif.) Research Inst., 1956-66; asst. to v.p. adminstrn. to dir. health planning, office of the pres. U. Calif., Berkeley, 1966-70; corp. planning advisor to dir. spl. studies Kaiser Found. Health Plan, Inc., Oakland, Calif., 1970—; dir. Kaiser Found. Health Plan of Conn., Hartford, 1982—; various times cons. Pan Am. Health Orgn., Calif. State Dept. Mental Hygiene, Carnegie Commn. on Higher Edn., various agys. HHS. Contbr. writings to profl. publs. Vol. Grenfell Med. Mission, Harrington Harbour, Que., Can., summer 1948; mem. nat. adv. com. program research and devel. on health care costs Robert Wood Johnson Found., 1983—. Served with USNR, 1943-45; with USPHS, 1954-56. Mem. Ops. Research Soc. Am. (past mem. council, Health Applications sect.), Hosp. Mgmt. Systems Soc. (charter), Inst. of Medicine of Nat. Acad. Scis., Am. Public Health Assn. Home: 6150 Pinewood Rd Oakland CA 94611 Office: 1 Kaiser Plaza Oakland CA 94612

BLUMBERG, NATHAN(IEL) BERNARD, journalist, emeritus educator; b. Denver, Apr. 8, 1922; s. Abraham Moses and Jeannette B.; m. Lynne Stout, June 1946 (div. Feb. 1970); children: Janet Leslie Blumberg Knedlik, Jenifer Lyn Blumberg Loeb, Josephine Laura Blumberg Loewen; m. Barbara Farquhar, July 1973. B.A., U. Colo., 1947, M.A., 1948; D.Phil. (Rhodes scholar), Oxford (Eng.) U., 1950. Reporter Denver Post, 1947-48; assoc. editor Lincoln (Nebr.) Star, 1950-53; asst. to editor Ashland (Nebr.) Gazette, 1954-55; asst. city editor Washington Post and Times Herald, 1956; from asst. prof. to assoc. prof. journalism U. Nebr., 1950-55; asso. prof. journalism Mich. State U., 1955-56; dean, prof. Sch. Journalism, U. Mont., 1956-68, prof. journalism, 1968-78, prof. emeritus, 1978—; vis. prof. Pa. State U., 1964, Northwestern U., 1966-67, U. Calif. at Berkeley, 1970; Dept. State specialist in, Thailand, 1961, in Trinidad, Guyana, Surinam and Jamaica, 1964. Author: One-Party Press?, 1954; also articles in mags. and jours.; founder: Mont. Journalism Rev, 1958—. Served with arty. U.S. Army, 1943-46. Decorated Bronze Star medal. Mem. Assn. Am. Rhodes Scholars, Nat. Conf. Editorial Writers, Kappa Tau Alpha (nat. pres. 1969-70). Home: Box 99 Big Fork MT 59911

BLUMBERG, PHILLIP IRVIN, legal educator; b. Balt., Sept. 6, 1919; s. Hyman and Bessie (Simons) B.; m. Janet Helen Mitchell, Nov. 7, 1945 (dec. 1976); children: William A.M., Peter M., Elizabeth B., Bruce M.; m. Ellen Ash Peters, Sept. 16, 1977. A.B. magna cum laude, Harvard U., 1939, J.D., 1942. Bar: N.Y. 1942, Mass. 1970. Assoc. Wilkie, Owen, Otis, Farr & Gallagher, N.Y.C., 1942-43, Szold, Brandwen, Meyers and Blumberg, 1946-66; pres., chief exec. officer United Ventures Inc., 1962-67; pres., chief exec. officer, trustee Federated Devel. Co., N.Y.C., 1966-68, chmn. fin. com., 1968-73; prof. law Boston U., 1966-74; dean U. Conn. Sch. Law, Hartford, 1974—; dir. Verde Exploration Ltd. Author: Corporate Responsibility in a Changing Society, 1972, The Magacorporation in American Society, 1975, The Law of Corporate Groups Procedure, 1983; bd. editors: Harvard Law Rev., 1940-42; treas., 1941-42; contbr. articles to profl. jours. Mem. White House Conf. Indsl. World Ahead, 1972; chmn. Com. to Rev. Conn. Law of Bus. Corps., 1975-77, Fed. Bankruptcy Judge Merit Screening Com. Conn.; mem. Conn. Gov.'s Commn. to Rev. Jud. Nominations, Essex County (N.J.) Democratic Com., 1956-57; pres., trustee Edward A. Filene Goodwill Found. Served with USAAF, 1943-46; ETO. Decorated Bronze Star. Mem. ABA, Conn. Bar Assn., Conn. Bar Found. (trustee), Am. Law Inst., Phi Beta Kappa, Delta Upsilon. Clubs: Harvard (Boston); University (Hartford). Home: 71 Sycamore Rd West Hartford CT 06117 Office: U Conn Sch Law 55 Elizabeth St Hartford CT 06105

BLUMBERG, RICHARD WINSTON, physician, educator; b. Winston-Salem, N.C., Nov. 10, 1914; s. Alexander Webster and Hortense (Morris) B.; (m). B.S., Emory U., 1935, M.D., 1938. Bar: Diplomate Am. Bd. Pediatrics. Rotating intern Grady Meml. Hosp., Atlanta, 1938-39; intern pediatrics Vanderbilt U. Hosp., 1939-40, resident, 1940-41, chief resident, 1941-42; chief outpatient clinic Children's Hosp., Cin., 1945-47, research assoc., 1945-47; mem. faculty Emory U. Sch. Medicine, 1948—, Francis Winship Walters prof. pediatrics, 1959—, chmn. dept., 1959-81; dir. div. phys. health De Kalb County Health Dept., 1981; chief pediatric service Grady Meml. Hosp., 1959-81. Contbr. to: Cyclopedia Medicine; Author articles in field. Served to maj., M.C. AUS, 1942-45. Mem. Am. Acad. Pediatrics, Am. Pediatric Soc., Soc. Med. Cons. to Armed Forces, Alpha Omega Alpha, Omicron Delta Kappa. Home: 2419 Woodward Way NW Atlanta GA 30305

BLUME, JACK PAUL, ret. lawyer; b. N.Y.C., Jan. 25, 1915; s. Bernard and Carrie (Goldberg) B.; m. Ethel Nelson, Oct. 2, 1941 (dec. 1959); children: Mark (dec.), Laura (Mrs. Marvin Kuperstein). B.S., CCNY, 1934; LL.B., N.Y. U., 1937. Bar: N.Y. 1937, D.C. 1952, also U.S. Supreme Ct. 1952. Pvt. practice, N.Y.C., 1937-42; atty., dep. hearing adminstr. OPA, 1942-46; regional atty. FCC, Chgo., 1946, hearing examiner, 1947-51; sr. partner, counsel Fly, Shuebruk, Blume & Gaguine, Washington, 1951-81; chmn. Inst. For Learning in Retirement, Am. U., 1982—. Co-author: West's Federal Practice Manual, 2d edit, 1970. Bd. dirs. Jewish Social Service Agy., Washington, 1960—; bd. dirs. Washington Lawyers' Com. for Civil Rights, com. on blood research ARC. Mem. Am., Fed., D.C. bar assns., Fed. Communications Bar Assn. (pres. 1974-75), ACLU. Home: 4101 Cathedral Ave Washington DC 20016 Office: 1211 Connecticut Ave Washington DC 20036

BLUME, JOHN AUGUST, consulting engineer; b. Gonzales, Calif., Apr. 8, 1909; s. Charles August and Vashti (Rankin) B.; m. Ruth Clarissa Reed, Sept. 14, 1942. A.B., Stanford, 1932, C.E., 1934, Ph.D., 1966. Constrn. engr. San Francisco-Oakland Bay Bridge, 1935-36; individual practice civil and structural engring., San Francisco, 1945-57; pres. John A. Blume & Assos. (Engrs.), San Francisco, 1957-81, chmn., sr. cons., 1980—; sr. engr./scientist URS Corp., San Mateo, Calif., 1981—; Mem., past chmn. adv. council Sch. Engring., Stanford U.; chmn. adv. com. Earthquake Engring. Research Center, U. Calif. at Berkeley.; cons. prof. civil engring. Stanford U.; Past chmn. adv. council Sch. Engring. Stanford U.; Adv. com. Earthquake Engring. Research Center. Author: A Machine for Setting Structures and Ground into Forced Vibration, 1935, Structural Dynamics in Earthquake Resistant Design, 1958, A Reserve Energy Technique for the Design and Rating of Structures in the Inelastic Range, 1960, Dynamic Characteristics of Multistory Buildings, 1969; co-author: Design of Multistory Reinforced Concrete Buildings for Earthquake Motions, 1961, An Engineering Intensity Scale for Earthquakes and Other Ground Motion, 1970, The SAM Procedure for Site-Acceleration-Magnitude Relationships, 1977; Contbr. articles to profl. jours. John A. Blume Earthquake Engring. Center at Stanford U. named in his honor. Mem. Nat. Acad. Engring., Structural Engrs. Assn. Calif. (pres. 1949), Cons. Engrs. Assn. Calif. (pres. 1959), ASCE (hon.; pres. San Francisco sect. 1960, Moisseiff award 1953, 61, 69, Ernest E. Howard award 1962), Seismol. Soc. Am., N.Y. Acad. Scis. (hon. life), Soc. Am. Mil. Engrs., Internat. Assn. Earthquake Engring. (hon.), Earthquake Engring. Research Inst. (hon.; pres. 1977-81), Sigma Xi, Tau Beta Pi. Home: 85 El Cerrito Ave Hillsborough CA 94010 Office: 130 Jessie St San Francisco CA 94105

BLUME, JUDY SUSSMAN, author; b. Elizabeth, N.J., Feb. 12, 1938; d. Rudolph and Esther (Rosenfeld) Sussman; m. John M. Blume, Aug. 15, 1959 (div. Jan. 1976); children: Randy Lee, Lawrence Andrew. B.A. in Edn, N.Y. U., 1960. Author: fiction books including

Are You There God It's Me, Margaret (selected as outstanding children's book 1970), Then Again, Maybe I Won't, 1971, It's Not the End of the World, 1972, Tales of a 4th Grade Nothing, 1972, Otherwise Known as Sheila the Great, 1972, Deenie, 1973, Blubber, 1974, Forever, 1976, Superfudge, 1980, Tiger Eyes, 1981, Smart Women, 1984, others; novel Wifey, 1978. Mem. Authors League and Guild, Soc. Children's Book Writers. Office: care Harold Ober Assos 40 E 49th St New York NY 10017 *

BLUME, MARTIN, physicist; b. Bklyn., Jan. 13, 1932; s. Julius and Frances (Cohen) B.; m. Sheila Bierman, June 12, 1955; children—Frederick, Janet. A.B., Princeton U., 1954; A.M., Harvard U., 1956, Ph.D., 1960. Fulbright research fellow Tokyo U., 1959-60; research asso. Atomic Energy Research Establishment, Harwell, Eng., 1960-62; with Brookhaven Nat. Lab., Upton, N.Y., 1962—, sr. physicist, 1970, head solid state physics, dep. chmn. physics dept., 1975-79, sci. program head nat. synchrotron light source, 1979—, assoc. dir., 1981—; prof. physics SUNY-, Stony Brook, 1972—. NSF grantee, 1973-78; E.O. Lawrence award Dept. of Energy, 1981. Fellow Am. Phys. Soc. (councillor-at-large, mem. exec. com.); mem. Phi Beta Kappa, Sigma Xi. Home: 284 Greene Ave Sayville NY 11782 Office: Brookhaven National Laboratory Upton NY 11973

BLUME, PETER, artist; b. Russia, Oct. 27, 1906; came to U.S., 1911, naturalized, 1921; s. Harry and Rose (Gopin) B.; m. Grace Douglas Gibbs Craton., Mar. 9, 1931. Student pub. schs., Art Student Ednl. Alliance, N.Y.C., 1919-24, Art Students League, N.Y.C., Beaux Arts. Exhibited at, Daniel Gallery, N.Y.C., 1926-31, Cleve., Columbus, Phila., Detroit, Balt., San Francisco, Buffalo, and Whitney museums, Mus. Modern Art, N.Y.C., Century of Progress Expn., Chgo., Internat. Venice, Italy, Julien Levy Gallery, Currier Gallery, Manchester, N.H., Wadsworth Atheneum, Hartford, Conn., Kennedy Gallery, N.Y.C., 1968, Danenberg Gallery, 1970, Coe Kerr Gallery, 1974, Dinten Fass Gallery, 1980, retrospective exhbn., Wadsworth Atheneum, 1964, Mus. Contemporary Art, Chgo., 1976, New Britain (Conn.) Mus. Am. Art, 1982. Recipient first prize Carnegie Art, 1934, 2d purchase award Artists for Victory Exhbn. Met. Mus. of Art, 1942, for his "South of Scranton Exhbn.", Durlacher Bros., 1947; Guggenheim Found. fellow, 1932, 36. Mem. Am. Acad. Nat. Inst. Arts and Letters, A.N.A. Home: Route 1 Box 158 Sherman CT 06784

BLUMEL, JOSEPH CARLTON, univ. pres.; b. Kansas City, Mo., Mar. 3, 1928; s. Joseph F. and Lillian M. (Spinner) B.; m. Priscilla Bryant, June 16, 1961; children—Christina, Carolyn. B.S., U. Nebr., 1950, M.A., 1956; Ph.D., U. Oreg., 1965; LL.D. (hon.), U. Hokkaido, Japan, 1976. Prof. econs. Portland (Oreg.) State U., 1968, dean undergrad. studies, asso. dean faculty, 1968-70, v.p. acad. affairs, 1970-74, pres., 1974—. Served with U.S. Army, 1951-53. Mem. Am., Western econ. assns., Am., Western finance assns., Alpha Kappa Psi, Beta Gamma Sigma. Home: 11650 SW Military Rd Portland OR 97219

BLUMENFELD, ALFRED MORTON, industrial designer, educator; b. Norfolk, Va., June 7, 1919; s. Max and Sara Anna (Markovitz) B.; m. S. Elaine Angstadt, Jan. 22, 1944; children: Sandra B. Lloyd, Steven Wayne. Student, Phila. Coll. Art, 1937-40; cert., Pratt Inst., 1941, B.Indsl. Design, 1976. With Norman Bel Geddes, Inc., N.Y.C., 1946-47, Raymond Spilman (ID), 1947-48; mem. store planning dept. J.C. Penney Co., N.Y.C., 1948; with Francis Blod Design Assos., N.Y.C., 1948-52; mgr. indsl. design plastics mktg. devel. group Rohm & Haas Co., Phila., 1952-69; self-employed indsl. design cons., specializing in med. and sci. instruments, 1969—, seminar instr.; mem. adj. faculty R.I. Sch. Design, 1970-80; assoc. prof. Pratt Inst., 1970-83; seminar instr., conf. coordinator N.Y. U., 1972-75; instr. plastics seminars Soc. Plastics Engrs., Indsl. Designers Soc. Am., 1978—. Author articles plastics applications, instrument design, lighting; contbg. editor: Indsl. Design mag, 1975—. Served to maj. as pilot USAAF, 1941-46. Fellow Indsl. Designers Soc. Am. (v.p. 1975-77); sr. mem. Soc. Plastics Engrs. Address: 16566 San Tomas Dr San Diego CA 92128

BLUMENFELD, M. JOSEPH, judge; b. South St. Paul, Minn., Mar. 23, 1904; s. David and Lena (Laser) B.; m. Rebecca Meyers, July 29, 1929. B.A. U. Minn, 1925; LL.B., Harvard, 1928. Bar: Conn. bar 1928. Practiced in, Hartford, 1928-61; spl. asst. to U.S. atty., 1942-45; U.S. dist. judge for Conn., Hartford, 1961—, chief judge, 1971-74. Mem. Am., Conn., Hartford County bar assns., Am. Judicature Soc. Home: 377 Simsbury Rd Bloomfield CT 06002 Office: US Dist Court Main St Hartford CT 06103

BLUMENFELD, MICHAEL, govt. ofcl.; b. Bklyn., Nov. 10, 1934; s. David Bernard and Rebecca (Dunn) B.; m. Catherine Ann Eck, May 31, 1960. A.B. cum laude, Harvard U., 1958, M.B.A., 1960. Vice-pres., account supr. Benton & Bowles, N.Y.C., 1960-67; dir. public affairs and edn. U.S. Equal Employment Opportunity Commn., Washington, 1967-69; asst. to v.p. for public affairs Consol. Edison Co. of N.Y., 1969-70; dep. adminstr. N.Y.C. Health Services Adminstrn., 1970-73; dir. public affairs N.Y. U., 1973-77; dep. undersec. Army, Washington, 1977-79, asst. sec. of Army for civil works, 1979-81; chmn. bd. dirs. Panama Canal Commn.; Army rep. U.S. Water Resources Council. Served with U.S. Army, 1953-56. Recipient Disting. Civilian Service award Dept. Army, 1981. Democrat. *I have always felt it important that Americans who have been fortunate enough to receive a good education, and valuable training in the private sector, put those assets to use in public sector service for at least part of their working careers.*

BLUMENSTOCK, DAVID ALBERT, surgeon; b. Newark, Feb. 14, 1927; s. Albert G. and Marion (Dickson) B.; m. Audrey J. Webster, Aug. 2, 1952; children—Mary Beth, David Albert II, Kristen Lee. B.S., Union Coll., 1949; M.D., Cornell U., 1953. Diplomate: Am. Bd. Surgery, Am. Bd. Thoracic Surgery. Intern Mary Imogene Bassett Hosp., Cooperstown, N.Y., 1953-54, resident surgery, 1954-55, 56-58, research surgeon, 1960-63, surgeon in chief, 1963—; resident surgery Columbia-Presbyn Med. Center, N.Y.C., 1955-56; clin. instr. thoracic surgery U. Mich. Sch. Medicine, 1958-60; prof. clin. surgery Columbia Coll. Phys. and Surg., 1963—. Served with AUS, 1946-47; ETO. Recipient Research Career Devel. award USPHS, 1962-63. Fellow A.C.S.; mem. Am. Assn. Thoracic Surgery, Soc. U. Surgeons, Am. Surg. Assn., Transplantation Soc., Sigma Xi, Alpha Omega Alpha. Spl. research biology tissue and organ transplantation, living organs and tissues. Home: Shelterwood RD 2 Cooperstown NY 13326 Office: Mary Imogene Basset Hosp Cooperstown NY 13326

BLUMENTHAL, ANDRE, retired executive; b. N.Y.C., Jan. 23, 1904; s. Sidney and Lucy (Picard) B.; m. Mildred Wimpfheimer, Nov. 23, 1927; children: William, Thomas, Elizabeth. Grad., Ethical Culture Sch., 1921; B.A., Yale U., 1925. With Sidney Blumenthal & Co., Inc., 1926-57, dir., 1930-57, pres., 1953, Norwalk Powdered Metals, Inc., 1958-82; Pres. Textile Research Inst., 1952-53, Conn. Hosp. Planning Commn., 1971-72; pres. Conn. Hosp. Assn., 1956, now hon. mem. Pres. Norwalk Hosp., 1960-62, now hon. trustee; chmn. Conn. Bd. Mental Health, 1957-59; chmn. adv. bd. Conn. Mental Health Center, 1965-69; hon. dir. Greater Norwalk Community Council. Served from lt. to comdr. USNR, World War II. Home: 249 Chestnut Hill Rd Norwalk CT 06851

BLUMENTHAL, HENRY, college dean, historian; b. Graudenz, Germany, Oct. 21, 1911; came to U.S., 1938; s. Edwin and Regina (Cronheim) B. A.B., U. Berlin, 1934; M.A., U. Calif., Berkeley, 1943, Ph.D., 1949. Instr. Rutgers U., Newark, 1949-53, asst. prof., 1953-59, asso. prof., 1959-63, prof., 1963—, dir. div. social scis., 1962-65; dean Coll. Arts and Scis., 1969-71. Author: A Reappraisal of French-American Relations, 1830-1871, 1959, France and The United States: Their Diplomatic Relations, 1789-1914, 1970, American and French Culture, 1800-1900, Interchanges in Art, Science, Literature and Society, 1975; also articles. Served with AUS, 1943-46. Selman A. Waksman fellow, in France; Rutgers research fellow; recipient Outstanding Tchr. award Rutgers Alumni, 1960; Medal for disting. service Rutgers U., 1979. Mem. Am. Hist. Assn., Orgn. Am. Historians, Soc. French Hist. Studies, Phi Beta Kappa. Home: 171 Vose Ave South Orange NJ 07079 Office: Rutgers U Newark NJ 07102 *Honesty and integrity are absolutely essential in all activities in civilized life. Ignoring them spells ultimate disaster.*

BLUMENTHAL, HERMAN BERTRAM, accountant; b. Phila., Sept. 30, 1916; s. Bertram and Florence (Wax) B.; m. Elaine J. Belsinger, May 25, 1941; children—Bonni Ann, Herman Bertram III. Student, Oxford U., Birmingham U., Eng., Edinburgh U., Scotland; B.S., Wharton Sch., U. Pa., 1938. Sr. partner Shestack, Blumenthal & Stein (C.P.A.'s), Phila., 1964—; pres. Harlan Products, Inc., Phila., 1958—; dir. Willem Wirtz, Garden Assos., Inc., Palm Beach, Fla.; former lectr. Cambridge U., Eng. Mem. nat. panel arbitrators Am. Arbitration Assn. Sec., Greater Phila. Council of Temple Brotherhoods.; Chmn. bd. trustees Montgomery County Community Coll., 1969—; bd. dirs. Elkins Park Free Library, Montgomery County March of Dimes; nat. bd. dirs. Assn. Community Coll. Trustees, 1976—. Served to capt. USAAF, 1940-46; ETO. Mem. Mensa (internat. treas. 1970—), Intertel. Jewish (trustee congregation); mem. B'nai B'rith (trustee). Clubs: Mason, Ivy Hill Bridge (past pres.). Home: 8000 High Sch Rd Elkins Park PA 19117 Office: 1001 Chateau Towers 7050 Sunset Dr South Pasadena FL 33707

BLUMENTHAL, HERMAN THEODORE, physician, educator; b. N.Y.C., Apr. 8, 1913; s. Samuel and Jennie (Price) B.; m. Eleonore Gottlieb, Aug. 18, 1940 (dec. 1972); children: Daniels S., Frederic A.; m. Margaret B. Phillips, May 29, 1974; children: Edward P., Shana P. B.S., Rutgers U., 1934; M.S., U. Pa., 1936; Ph.D., Washington U., St. Louis, 1938, M.D., 1942. Resident in pathology Jewish Hosp., St. Louis, 1942-43; dir. labs of various hosps., 1945-65; asso. prof. pathology St. Louis U., 1947-52, adj. prof. community medicine, 1975—; mem. faculty Washington U., 1965—, research prof. gerontology, 1965—; dir. Midwest Med. Lab., 1965—. Author: (with J.G. Probstein) Pancreatitis—A Clinical-Pathological Correlation, 1954; Editor: Cowdry's Arteriosclerosis—A Survey of the Problem, 2d edit, 1967, Medical Aspects of Gerontology, 1962, Interdisciplinary Topics in Gerontology, Vols. 1-8, 1968-71, Handbook of Diseases of Aging, 1981, Dilman's Elevational Hypothalmic Mechanisms in Aging and Disease, 1981; Contbr. articles on aging, transplanation, endocrinology, cancer, pathology to profl. jours.; editor Handbook of Diseases of Aging, 1983. Served to maj. M.C. AUS, 1942-45. Mem. Soc. Exptl. Biology and Medicine, Am. Heart Assn., Am. Diabetes Assn., Am. Assn. Cancer Research, Soc. Pathologists and Bacteriologists, Am. Soc. Exptl. Pathology, Gerontol. Soc., AAUP, Sigma Xi. Home: 6203 Washington Ave St Louis MO 63130

BLUMENTHAL, ROBERT LOUIS, lawyer; b. Houston, Oct. 15, 1930; s. Charles and Lillian (Wolf) B.; m. Beverly Renee Brand, Aug. 30, 1953; children: Pamela Joan, Karen Frances, Brad Brand. B.B.A., U. Tex., 1951, LL.B., 1953; LL.M., Harvard, 1954. Bar: Tex. 1953. Practice in, Houston, 1953, N.Y.C., 1954, Dallas, 1957—; partner firm Carrington, Coleman, Sloman & Blumenthal, 1970—; Dir., sec. Am. Title Co. of Dallas. Bd. dirs. Spl. Care Sch., 1968-74; bd. dirs. West Dallas Community Centers, 1968-74, pres., 1973; bd. dirs. Dallas Home and Hosp. for Jewish Aged, 1969-73, Los Barridos Unidos Community Clinic, 1971-78. Served with USAF, 1954-57. Mem. Am., Dallas bar assns., U. Tex. Ex-Students Assn. (past pres. Dallas chpt.), Am. Judicature Soc., Dallas C. of C. (dir., vice chmn. 1976-78), Tex. Law Rev. Assn. (trustee, pres. 1979). Jewish (pres. temple). Clubs: City, Columbian Country, Chaparral. Address: 6043 Desco Dr Dallas TX 75225 Office: 2500 S Tower Plaza of the Americas Dallas TX 75201

BLUMENTHAL, W. MICHAEL, manufacturing company executive, former secretary Treasury; b. Germany, Jan. 3, 1926; U.S., 1947, naturalized, 1952; s. Ewald and Rose Valerie (Markt) B.; m. Margaret Eileen Polley, Sept. 8, 1951. B.Sc., U. Calif., Berkeley, 1951; M.A., M.P.A., Princeton U., 1953, Ph.D., 1956. Research asso. Princeton U., 1954-57; labor arbitrator, State of N.J., 1955-57; v.p. dir. Crown Cork Internat. Corp., 1957-61; became dep. asst. sec. for econ. affairs Dept. State, 1961; apptd. Pres.'s dep. spl. rep. for trade negotiations with rank of ambassador, 1963-67; pres. Bendix Internat., 1967-70; dir. Bendix Corp., 1967-77, vice chmn., 1970-71, pres., chief operating officer, 1971-72, chmn., pres., chief exec. officer, 1972-77; sec. of Treasury, Washington, 1977-79; dir. Burroughs Corp., Detroit, 1979—, vice chmn., chief exec. officer, 1980-81, chmn., chief exec. officer, 1981—; dir. Equitable Life Assurance Soc. U.S., Pillsbury Co., Chem. N.Y. Corp. and subs. Chem. Bank. Charter trustee Princeton U. Mem. Bus. Council, Am. Econ. Assn., Council Fgn. Relations (dir.), Bus. Com. for Arts (dir.), Rockefeller Found. (trustee), Phi Beta Kappa. Clubs: Princeton, Century (N.Y.C.); Econ. Detroit (dir.). Office: Burroughs Corp care Ms G Oldani 4C 51 Burroughs Pl Detroit MI 48323

BLUMER, FREDERICK ELWIN, college president; b. Glencoe, Okla., Sept. 16, 1933; s. Edward H. and Eva Marie (Forbes) B.; m. Ann Louise Anderson, June 9, 1956; children—Frederick Edward, William Robert. B.A., Millsaps Coll., 1955; B.D., Emory U., 1958, Ph.D. (Cokesbury fellow, Dempster fellow, Rockefeller fellow), 1959-60; postgrad., Georg August U., Goettingen, Germany, 1960-61. Ordained to ministry United Methodist Ch., 1962; chaplain, instr. philosophy and religion Nebr. Wesleyan U., Lincoln, 1962-63, asst. prof., 1963-65, asso. prof., 1965-67, prof., 1967-76, v.p. acad. affairs, 1967-70, provost, v.p. acad. affairs, 1970-76; pres. Lycoming Coll., Williamsport, Pa., 1976—; dean, dir. Graz (Austria) Center, 1972-73. Editor: Nebr. Wesleyan Univ. Press, 1967-76; Contbr. articles to profl. jours. Dir. edn. Lincoln United Way, 1971; bd. dirs. N.E. Lincoln YMCA, 1968-71, Lincoln Symphony Orch., 1971-76, Williamsport/Lycoming United Way, 1976-83, Williamsport Hosp. Recipient Pres.'s award Nebr. Wesleyan U., 1966. Mem. Williamsport-Lycoming C. of C. (dir.), Phi Kappa Phi, Pi Gamma Mu, Theta Phi, Omicron Delta Kappa. Republican. Club: Rotary. Home: 325 Grampian Blvd Williamsport PA 17701 Office: Lycoming Coll Williamsport PA 17701

BLUMER, HERBERT, educator; b. St. Louis, Mar. 7, 1900; s. Richard George and Margaret (Marshall) B.; m. Marguerite Barnett, Aug. 16, 1922; 1 dau. Katherine; m. Marcia Jackson, Aug. 22, 1942; children—Linda, Leslie. A.B., U. Mo., 1921, A.M., 1922, LL.D., 1972; Ph.D., U. Chgo., 1927; D.Sc., So. Ill. U., 1974. Instr. sociology U. Mo., 1922-25; instr. sociology U. Chgo., 1925-30, asso. prof., 1931-47, prof., 1947-52; prof. sociology U. Mich., 1936-37, U. Hawaii, 1939; prof. sociology and chmn. dept. U. Calif. at Berkeley, 1952-75, chmn. social sci. council, 1956-58, dir., 1958-66; distinguished prof. U.S. Internat. U., 1974—; Chmn. bd. dirs. Trans-action.; Mem. research staff Motion Picture Research Council, 1929-31; prin. liason officer between OWI and Bd. Econ. Warfare, Washington, 1943; pub. panel chmn. WLB, 1943-44; permanent arbitrator Armour & Co., 1944-45; chmn. bd. arbitration U.S. Steel Corp., 1945-47. Author sci. books and articles.; Editor: Publs. of Am. Sociol. Soc, 1931-36, Am. Jour. Sociology, 1940-52; editor: Sociology Series, pub. by Prentice-Hall, Inc., 1934—; Chmn. bd. editors: Integrated Edn, 1965—. Mem. Inst. Internat. de Sociologie, Soc. Study Social Problems (pres. 1955), Sociol. Research Assn., Internat. Soc. Sci. Study Race Relations, Am. Sociol. Assn. (pres. 1956), Internat. Sociol. Assn. (v.p. 1962-66), Pacific Sociol. Assn. (pres. 1971-72), Phi Beta Kappa, Delta Sigma Rho. Home: 350 Pine Creek Rd Walnut Creek CA 94598 Office: U Cal Berkeley CA 94720

BLUMOFE, ROBERT FULTON, motion picture producer, association executive; b. N.Y.C.; s. Julius and Fannie (Rosenstein) B.; children: Robert David, Joanna Beth. A.B., J.D., Columbia U. Bar: N.Y., Calif. Mem. legal dept. Paramount Pictures, Hollywood, Calif., 1946-52; producer TV films Revue Prodns. of MCA, Inc., Hollywood, 1952-53; v.p. charge prodn. and West Coast ops. United Artists Corp., Hollywood, 1953-66; ind. motion picture producer, Hollywood, 1966—; guest lectr. univs.; mem. steering com. U. So. Calif. Film Conf.; v.p., trustee, chmn. exec. com. Motion Picture and TV Fund, recipient medallion of honor, 1968; dir. Am. Film Inst., West, Beverly Hills, Calif., 1977-81. Films include Yours, Mine and Ours, 1968, Pieces of Dreams, 1969, Bound for Glory (best picture nomination Acad. Motion Picture Arts and Scis., Christopher award), 1976 (Film Adv. Bd. award). Co-chmn. United Jewish Welfare Fund, 1959; So. Calif. chmn. Am.-Israel Cultural Found., 1963; bd. dirs. Los Angeles Philharmonic, 1964-70; pres. Permanent Charities Com., 1974-75. Served to 1st lt., ordnance AUS, 1943-45. Recipient Samuel Goldwyn Founders award Permanent Charities Com. Entertainment Industries, 1978; John Jay Disting. Alumni award Columbia Coll., 1981. Mem. John Jay Assos., Harlan Fiske Stone Assos., Acad. Motion Picture Arts and Scis. (bd. govs. 1978—), Am. Film Inst., Producers Guild Am. Home: 1100 N Alta Loma Rd Los Angeles CA 90069

BLUMROSEN, ALFRED WILLIAM, lawyer, educator; b. Detroit, Dec. 14, 1928; s. Sol and Frances (Netzorg) B.; m. Ruth L. Gerber, July 3, 1952; children: Steven Marshall, Alexander Bernet. B.A., U. Mich., 1950, J.D., 1953. Bar: Mich. 1953, N.J. 1961, N.Y. 1981. Individual practice law, Detroit, 1953-55; mem. faculty Rutgers Law Sch., Newark, 1955—, prof., 1961—, acting dean, 1974-75; labor arbitrator, 1957—; dir. fed.-state relations, chief of conciliations U.S. EEO Commn., 1965-67; adv. U.S. Dept. Justice, Dept. Labor, Dept. HUD, 1968-72; cons. to chmn. EEOC, 1977-79; of counsel firm Kaye, Scholer, Fierman, Hays & Handler, N.Y.C., 1979-82. Contbr. articles to profl. jours. Mem. U.S. Nat. Com., Internat. Soc. for Labor Law and Social Legislation, Indsl. Relations Research Assn., Am. Bar Assn., Fed. Bar Assn., Order of Coif. Office: Rutgers Law Sch 15 Washington St Newark NJ 07102

BLUNDELL, HARRY, utility executive; b. Salt Lake City, May 1, 1925; s. Henry James and Eliza Ellen (Terry) B.; m. Beverly Mae Martin, Aug. 26, 1944; children: Martin, James, John, Peter, Amy, Ann, Todd. B.S. in Philosophy and Math., U. Utah, 1949; postgrad., U. Mich. With Utah Power & Light Co., Salt Lake City, 1949—, successively asst. treas., treas., v.p., sr. v.p., 1949-76, exec. v.p., 1976-79, pres., chief exec. officer, 1979—, dir., 1965—; dir. 1st Interstate Bank of Utah (formerly Walker Bank & Trust Co.), Ideal Basic Industries, Inc., Denver & Rio Grande R.R.; former pres., dir. N.W. Elec. Light and Power Assn. Pres., United Way; mem. nat. adv. council Utah State U.; mem. instl. council and adv. council Utah Tech. Coll. Served with USNR, 1943-46. Mem. Salt Lake C. of C. (past v.p.), Phi Beta Kappa, Phi Kappa Phi. Mormon. Clubs: Rotary, Alta. Home: 3191 Crestview Dr Bountiful UT 84010 Office: 1407 W N Temple St PO Box 899 Salt Lake City UT 84110

BLUNDELL, WILLIAM EDWARD, journalist; b. N.Y.C., Sept. 23, 1934; s. W. Edward and Anne Elizabeth (Dur) B.; m. Gayle Swango, Oct. 19, 1957; children—Bonnie, Scott. B.S., Syracuse U., 1956; postgrad., U. Kans., 1959-61. Reporter Dallas bur. Wall Street Jour., 1961-63, reporter N.Y. bur., 1963-65, page one writer, 1965-68, chief Los Angeles bur., 1968-78, nat. corr., 1978—; Nat. pres. Ind. Assn. Pubs. Employees, 1965-67. Co-author: Swindled: Great Business Frauds of the 70s, 1976; Editor: anthology The Innovators, 1967. Served to 1st lt. AUS, 1957-59. Recipient Berger award for distinguished met. reporting Columbia U., 1966; Roy Howard award for pub. service Scripps-Howard Found., 1974; Disting. feature writing award Am. Soc. Newspaper Editors, 1982. Mem. Zeta Psi. Episcopalian. Home: 910 Wiladonda Dr La Canada CA 91011 Office: 514 S Shatto Pl Los Angeles CA 90020

BLUNDELL, WILLIAM RICHARD C., electrical equipment manufacturing company executive, engineer; b. Montreal, Apr. 13, 1927; s. Richard C. and Did Aileen (Payne) B.; m. Monique Audet, Mar. 20, 1959; children: Richard, Emily, Michelle, Louise. B.A.Sc., U. Toronto, 1949. Registered profl. engr., Ont. Sales engr. Can. Gen. Electric Co., Toronto, 1949-51, travelling auditor, 1951, various fin. positions, 1951-66, treas., 1966-68, v.p.-fin., 1968-70, v.p., exec. consumer div., 1970-72, v.p., exec. apparatus div., Lachine, Que., 1972-79; pres., chief exec. officer Camco Inc., Weston, Ont., 1979-83; pres., chief operating officer Can. Gen. Electric Co. Ltd., Toronto, 1983—. Home: 45 Stratheden Rd Toronto ON Canada M4N 1E5 Office: Can Gen Electric PO Box 417 Commerce Ct N Toronto ON Canada M5L 1J2

BLUNK, FORREST STEWART, lawyer; b. Doniphan, Mo., July 22, 1913; s. Forest Stanley and Margaret Anna (Stewart) B.; m. Mary Williams, July 10, 1971; children—Scott Stewart, Sally Jo. B.A., U. Mo., 1936; J.D., U. Wyo., 1940. Bar: Ill. bar 1946, Colo. bar 1953. Asso. firm Vogel & Bunge, Chgo., 1946-50; firm January & Yegge, Denver, 1953-55; partner firm Blunk and Johnson, Denver, 1955—; pres., dir. Williams Land & Livestock Co., Tie Siding, Wyo. Served with AUS, 1941-46; ETO. Mem. Fed., Am., Ill., Wyo., Colo., 5th Dist., 10th Circuit bar assns., Colo. Def. Bar Assn. (pres. 1969-70), Lawyer-Pilots Bar Assn., Internat. Assn. Ins. Counsel, Denver Bar, Am. Bd. Trial Advs. (pres. Colo. chpt. 1974-75, nat. sec. 1975-76), Legal Club Chgo. Republican. Clubs: Masons, Elks, Rotary, Ft. Collins Country, Denver Athletic. Home: 2909 Terry Lake Rd Fort Collins CO 80524 Office: 480 S Holly St Suite 1 Denver CO 80222

BLUNT, WILLIAM WILLIAMS, JR., lawyer; b. N.Y.C., Dec. 19, 1936; s. William W. and Helen (Phillips) B.; m. Sara Thompson Conrad, Sept. 8, 1962; children: Dorsey, William. Grad., Phillips Acad., 1954; B.A., Yale, 1958; J.D., Harvard, 1961. Bar: N.Y. 1961, D.C. 1976. Assoc. law firm Simpson, Thacher & Bartlett, N.Y.C., 1961-66; asst. gen. counsel Sperry & Hutchison, N.Y.C., 1966-69; chief counsel Econ. Devel. Adminstrn., U.S. Dept. Commerce, Washington, 1969-71, dep. asst. sec. commerce, 1971-73, asst. sec. commerce for econ. devel., 1973-74; pres. William Blunt Assos., Inc., Washington, 1975-81; sole practice, Washington, 1975—; Dir. Nat. Council Urban Econ. Devel., 1975—; mem. Mayor's Adv. Com. Econ. Devel., Washington, 1975—; exec. com. D.C. Local Devel. Corp., 1981—. Mem. Bar Assn. N.Y.C., Am., N.Y., D.C. bar assns. Home: 3200 P St NW Washington DC 20007 Office: 1101 14th St NW Washington DC 20005

BLUTH, ELIZABETH JEAN CATHERINE, sociologist, educator; b. Phila., Dec. 5, 1934; d. Robert Thomas and Catherine Cecelia (Boxman) Gowl; m. Thomas Del Bluth, Aug. 20, 1960 (dec. Aug. 6, 1980); children: Robert Thomas, Richard Del. B.A. in Sociology (Washington semster fellow), Bucknell U., 1953; M.A., Fordham U., 1960; Ph.D., UCLA, 1970. Teaching fellow in methods of social research Fordham U., 1957-58; reading instr. St. Margaret's High Sch., Tappahannock, Va., 1958-59; instr. history, civics and English, Rosary High Sch., San Diego, 1959-60; successively instr., asst. prof. sociology Immaculate Heart Coll., Los Angeles, 1960-65; prof. sociology Calif. State U., Northridge, 1965—; cons. Immaculate Heart Community, Los Angeles, 1967-69; engring. research NASA Space Sta. design Boeing Aerospace Co., 1982—; mem. Presdl. Citizens Adv. Com. on Space, Council on Nat. Space Policy, Nat. Tech. Com. on Society and Tech., UN team on relevance of space activities to econ. and social devel. Editor: (with others) Search for Identity Reader, Vol. I and II, 1973, (with S. R. McNeal) Update on Space, Vol. I, 1981; contbr. articles to profl. jours. Recipient Alpha Omega Faculty awards, 1966, 74; Disting. Teaching award Calif. State U.-Northridge, 1968; Fellow Inst. Advancement in Teaching and Learning, Calif. State U., 1974. Mem. Am. Sociol. Assn., AIAA (chpt. award for outstanding program 1980, 1980), Am. Astronautical Assn., L5 Soc., Brit. Interplanetary Soc., Am. Soc. Aerospace Edn., Inst. Social Sci. Study of Space (acad. adv. bd.), Space Studies Inst., Internat. Acad. Astronautics (com. on space econs. and benefits), Phi Beta Kappa. Republican. Office: Dept Sociology Calif State Univ Northridge CA 91330 *Is it worth a life to seed the universe with intelligence? I think so, and direct my energy to bringing practical human systems technology to solve problems of human habitation of space. This is based on the view that science can enhance freedom by suggesting alternative ways of solving problems. Ideas can be prisons or vehicles of freedom—knowing the difference makes the difference. My goal is to help develop ways of improving human performance in space with the hope that what is learned can "spin-off" to people on earth. Integrity and hard work, and confidence in the future can be better fuel for this effort.*

BLUTTER, JOAN WERNICK, interior designer; b. London, Eng., July 6, 1929; naturalized, 1948; d. Samuel and Bertha (Cohn) Wernick; m. Melvyn Blutter, Oct. 29, 1948; children—Janet Lesley, Steven Scott. Student, Northwestern U., 1944. Pres. Joan Blutter Designs, Ltd., Chgo., 1955—; partner Designers Collaborative, Chgo., San Francisco, 1975—; design cons. Reed, Ltd., Toronto, Can., Exec. House Ltd., Chgo. Contbr.: articles to Interior Design; others. Fellow Am. Soc. Interior Designers (past pres. Ill. chpt., past nat. sec., nat. chmn. industry 1978-79, nat. chmn. Design Interest program 1981-82, recipient Gold Key award, design award, Presdl. citation, Designer of Year 1979); mem. Nat. Soc. Interior Design (past chpt. pres., sec., bd. chmn.), LWV, Nat. Home Fashions League, Mchts. and Mfrs. Club, Art Inst. Chgo., Mus. Contemporary Art. Home: 2801 N Sheridan Rd Chicago IL 60657 Office: 13-124 Merchandise Mart Chicago IL 60654 also 85 Blvd Berthier Paris 17 France also 250 E 87th St New York NY

BLY, ROBERT ELWOOD, poet; b. Madison, Minn., Dec. 23, 1926; s. Jacob Thomas and Alice (Aws) B.; m. Carolyn McLean, June 24, 1955 (div. 1979); children: Mary, Bridget, Noah Matthew Jacob, Micah John Padma.; m. Ruth Ray, June 27, 1980. Student, St. Olaf Coll., 1946-47; A.B., Harvard, 1950; M.A., U. Iowa, 1956. Editor, pub. Seventies Press, Madison, 1958—; Co-chmn. Am. Writers vs. Vietnam War, 1966—. Author: (poems) Silence in the Snowy Fields, 1962, The Light Around the Body, 1967; (prose poems) The Morning Glory; (poems) Sleepers Joining Hands, 1973, Jumping Out of Bed, 1973, Old Man Rubbing His Eyes, 1975; (criticism) Leaping Poetry, 1975; (prose poems) This Body is Made of Camphor and Gopherwood, 1977; (poems) This Tree Will Be Here for a Thousand Years, 1979; Editor: (prose poems) Forty Poems Touching on Recent American History, 1967; A Poetry Reading Against the Vietnam War, 1966; Author: The Sea and the Honeycomb, 1966, News of the Universe, 1980, Man in the Black Coat Turns, 1981; Translator: (from Swedish) (Selma Lagerlöf) The Story of Gösta Berling, 1962; Gunnar Ekelöf I Do Best Alone at Night, 1968; (from Norwegian) Knut Hamsun Hunger, 1967; (from German) Twenty Poems of Georg Trakl, 1961; (from Spanish) Twenty Poems of Cesar Vallejo, 1963, Forty Poems of Juan Ramon Jimenez, 1967, Twenty Poems of Pablo Neruda, 1967; (from Swedish) Twenty Poems of Tomas Tranströmer, 1972, Night Vision (Tomas Tranströmer), 1972; (from Spanish) Lorca and Jimenez: Selected Poems, 1973; (from Swedish) Friends, You Drank Some Darkness: Three Swedish Poets, Martinson, Ekelöf and Tranströmer, 1975; (from Hindi and English) The Kabir Book: 44 of the Ecstatic Poems of Kabir, 1977; (from Norwegian) Twenty Poems of Rolf Jacobsen, 1977; (with Lewis Hyde) (from Spanish) Twenty Poems of Vincente Aleixandre, 1977; (from German) Selected Poems of Rainer Maria Rilke, 1980; (from Spanish) Time Alone: Selected Poems of Antonio Machado, 1983. Served with USNR, 1944-45. Recipient award Nat. Inst. Arts and Letters, Nat. Book award in poetry, 1968; Fulbright grantee, 1956-57; Amy Lowell fellow, 1964-65; Guggenheim fellow, 1965-66, 72-73; Rockefeller Found. fellow, 1967. Address: 308 1st St Moose Lake MN 55767

BLYHOLDER, GEORGE DONALD, educator; b. Elizabeth, N.J., Jan. 10, 1931; s. Orlando and Lucy Pauline (Ramsey) B.; m. Betty Sue Conrod, Dec. 27, 1955; children: Sylvia Jean, Andrew George, Victoria Elizabeth. B.A., Valparaiso U., 1952; B.S., Purdue U., 1953; Ph.D., U. Utah, 1956. Dupont postdoctoral fellow U. Minn., 1956-57; research asso. Johns Hopkins, 1957-59; asst. prof. U. Ark., 1959-64, asso. prof., 1964-67, prof. chemistry, 1967—, vice chmn. dept., 1968-72; Vis. prof. Oxford U., Eng., 1965-66, Hokkaido U., Japan, 1972-73; vis. prof. Cornell U., 1980. Contbr. articles to profl. jours. Mem. AAUP (pres. U. Ark. chpt. 1977), Am. Chem. Soc. (chmn. U. Ark. sect. 1963, 77), Phi Beta Kappa (pres. U. Ark. chpt. 1976), Sigma Xi, Phi Lambda Upsilon, Sigma Pi Sigma. Home: 1054 Eva Fayetteville AR 72701

BLYTH, JOHN WILLIAM, mgmt. cons.; b. Burlington, Wis., Oct. 27, 1909; s. Robert Bayne and Jane (Broadfoot) B.; m. Renée Fourgous, Aug. 29, 1936. A.B., Haverford Coll., 1931; M.A., U. Iowa, 1932; postgrad., U. Berlin, 1934-35; Ph.D., Brown U., 1936. Faculty Hamilton Coll., 1936-62, asst. to pres., dir., summer session, 1946, dean faculty, 1946-48, prof. philosophy, 1947-62, John Stewart Kennedy prof., 1952-62, coordinator teaching machine project, 1959-61; dir. ednl. systems dept. Diebold Group, Inc., 1962-65; v.p. Argyle Pub. Corp., 1965-68; sr. v.p. Metromedia div. AnaLearn Assos., Inc., 1968-70; pres., treas. Blyth Assos., Inc., Stratford, Conn., 1971—; Vice pres., dir. Hamilton Research Assos., Inc., 1959-62. Author: Whitehead's Theory of Knowledge, Vol. VIII, 1941, A Modern Introduction to Logic, 1957; Co-author: Programmed Text in Logic, 6 vols, 1963; contbr. articles to profl. jours. Ford faculty fellow, 1951-52. Mem. Am. Philos. Assn., Phi Beta Kappa. Co-inventor teaching machine. Address: 1236 County Line Rd Radnor PA 19087

BLYTH, MYRNA GREENSTEIN, editor, author; b. N.Y.C., Mar. 22, 1940; d. Benjamin and Betty (Austin) Greenstein; m. Jeffrey Blyth, Nov. 25, 1962; children: Jonathan, Graham. B.A., Bennington (Vt.) Coll., 1960. Sr. editor Datebook mag., N.Y.C., 1960-62, Ingenue mag., 1962-70; book editor Family Health mag., 1972-73; book and fiction editor, then asso. editor Family Circle mag., N.Y.C., 1974-78, exec. editor, 1978-81; editor-in-chief Ladies Home Jour., 1981—; freelance writer, contbr. mags., 1965—. Author: novels Cousin Suzanne, 1975, For Better and For Worse, 1978. Office: Care Ladies Home Journal 3 Park Ave New York NY 10016 *

BLYTHE, JAMES EDWIN, chemical company executive; b. Toledo, May 22, 1929; s. Roy James and Alma Charlotte (Moser) B.; m. Rowena E. Parker, Dec. 7, 1957; children: Ann E., James S. B.S. in Mech. Engring. with distinction, Purdue U., 1950. Design engr. Libbey-Owens-Ford Glass Co., 1950-54; quality control engr. Gen. Electric Co., 1957; with Mobil Chem. Co., 1957—, mgr. research and devel. films dept., 1965—, gen. mgr. tech. ops. plastics div., Macedon, N.Y., 1969-81, v.p. tech. ops. plastics div., 1981—, also mem. operating com. plastics div. Served with AUS, 1954-56. Mem. Tau Beta Pi, Pi Tau Sigma. Home: 7280 Lake Ave Williamson NY 14589 Office: Mobil Chem Co Macedon NY 14502 *Life is like contract bridge, we are measured by how well we play the cards we are dealt.*

BLYTHE, WILLIAM LEGETTE, author; b. Huntersville, N.C., Apr. 24, 1900; s. William Brevard and Hattye (Jackson) B.; m. Esther Emily Farmer, May 31, 1926; children: William Brevard, Samuel LeGette, Esther Lovelace (Mrs. Joseph C. Pugh). A.B., U. N.C., 1921, LL.D., 1969; Litt.D., Davidson Coll., 1950. Tchr. Greensboro (N.C.) pub. schs., 1921-22; successively reporter, columnist, editorial writer Charlotte (N.C.) News, 1922-24; with N.Y. Eve. Post, 1924; pub. N. Mecklenburg News, Huntersville, 1925-26; editor Mecklenburg Times, Charlotte, 1926-27; successively reporter, columnist, editorial writer, lit. editor Charlotte Observer, 1927-50; full time writer, 1950—; writer in residence U. N.C. at Charlotte, 1967—; Chmn. N.C. Writers Conf., 1965; mem. Gov. N.C. Commn. Library Resources, 1964. Author: The Chatham Rabbit, 1921, Marshal Ney: A Dual Life, 1937, Alexandriana, 1940, Shout Freedom!, 1948, Bold Galilean, 1948, William Henry Belk: Merchant of the South, 1950, A Tear for Judas, 1951, Miracle in the Hills, 1953, Voice in the Wilderness, 1955, James W. Davis: North Carolina Surgeon, 1956, The Crown Tree, 1957, Yes, Ma'am, Miss Gee, 1957, Gift from the Hills, 1958, Call Down the Storm, 1958, Thomas Wolfe and His Family, 1961, Hear Me, Pilate!, 1961, Hornets' Nest: The Story of Charlotte and Mecklenburg County, Echo in My Soul, 1962, Mountain Doctor, 1964, Man on Fire, 1964, Robert Lee Stowe: Pioneer in Textiles, 1965, 38th Evac, 1966, The Hornets' Nest, 1968, Brothers of Vengeance, 1969, Meet Julius Abernethy: Trader and Philanthropist, 1969, When Was Jesus Born?, 1974, The Stableboy Who Stayed at Bethlehem, 1974, First in Freedom, 1975, Thunder in Carolina, 1976, Look to the One Beckoning Star, 1978; also articles, revs., short stories. Commr. gen. assembly Presbyn. Ch. U.S., 1952; moderator Mecklenburg Presbytery, 1955-56; mem. permanent com. hist. matters Presbyn. Synod N.C., 1967—, mem. sesquicentennial observance com., 1963; chmn. Pres. Andrew Johnson Sesquicentennial Commn., 1958; mem. Mecklenburg County Econ. Devel. Commn., 1966—, Huntersville Planning and Zoning Commn., 1967—, Mecklenburg Presbytery Centennial Com., 1968, Mayflower Award Jury, 1938, 47, 52, Charlotte Bicentennial Com., 1968, Charlotte-Mecklenburg Bicentennial Com., 1975-76; bd. dirs. N.C. Boys Home, 1971—. Recipient Mayflower award, 1953, 61; Cannon cup for hist. research, 1961. Mem. N.C. Writers Conf., N.C. Lit. and Hist. Assn., Mecklenburg Hist. Assn., N.C. Folklore Soc.; mem. N.C. Soc.; Mem. Phi Beta Kappa, Omega Delta, Sigma Upsilon, Delta Tau Delta. Democrat. Clubs: Lion., Charlotte Philosophy. Address: Gilead Rd Huntersville NC 28078

BOAG, THOMAS JOHNSON, physician; b. Liverpool, Eng., Apr. 11, 1922; s. John Harvey and Elizabeth (Johnson) B.; m. Lorna Christian Milne, July 1, 1951; children—Peter Thomas, Graham Stewart, Patricia Janet, Alexander Harvey. M.B., Ch.B., U. Liverpool, 1944; Dip. Psychiatry, McGill U., Montreal, 1953. Asst. prof. psychiatry McGill U., Montreal, 1953-61; asst. dir. Allan Meml. Inst., Montreal, 1959-61; prof. psychiatry, chmn. dept. U. Vt. Coll. Medicine, Burlington, 1961-67; prof. psychiatry, head dept. psychiatry Queen's U., Kingston, Ont., Can., 1967-75, dean, 1975-82, v.p. health services, 1983—. Contbr. articles to med. jours. Served to capt. Brit. Army, 1944-47. Fellow Royal Coll. Physicians (Can.), Royal Coll. Psychiatrists; mem. Can. Psychiat. Assn., Ont. Psychiat. Assn., Can. Med. Assn., Ont. Med. Assn., Am. Psychiat. Assn., Can. Psychoanalytic Soc., Ont. Psychogeriatric Soc., Can. Assn. Gerontology, Internat. Psychoanalytic Assn., Am. Assn. Geriatric Psychiatry. Home: 82 Centre St Kingston ON K7L 4E6 Canada Office: Queen's U Kingston ON K7L 3N6 Canada

BOAK, RUTH ALICE, physician, educator; b. Auburn, N.Y., May 25, 1906; d. Spencer J. and Jane (Clark) B.; m. Donald L. Ferris, May 30, 1942; children—Boak J., Don R. B.S., Cornell U., 1927, M.S., 1927, Ph.D., 1929; M.D., U. Rochester, 1940. Research asst. Cornell U., 1927-28; instr. Albany Med. Sch., 1928-30; asso. U. Rochester, 1930-47; house officer Johns Hopkins Hosp., 1940-41; pvt. practice medicine, Greenwich, Conn., 1944; asso. prof. infectious diseases and pediatrics U. Calif. Sch. Medicine, Los Angeles, 1947-57, prof., 1957—, prof. med. microbiology, immunology, pediatrics and pub. health, 1966—; Vis. prof. Airlongga U. Sch. Medicine, Surabaja, Indonesia, 1963-66. Named Woman of the Year in Medicine Los Angeles Times, 1955; recipient Outstanding Citizens award, Woman of Yr., 1972; Fulbright award, 1954-55, 59-60. Fellow Am. Pub. Health Assn., Mexican Border Pub. Health Assn., Med. Research Soc. Los Angeles. Home: 85 Avocado Pl Camarillo CA 93010 Office: Univ of Calif Med Center Los Angeles CA 90024

BOAL, ARTHUR MCCLURE, lawyer; b. Cherry Tree, Pa., Feb. 14, 1889; s. William McClure and Hannah Waller (Camp) B.; m. Sara Elizabeth Metzner, Apr. 2, 1921; children—Elizabeth (Mrs. William R. Hogan), Arthur McClure. A.B., Harvard U., 1914, LL.B., 1916. Bar: Mass. bar 1917, N.Y. bar 1930. Asso. with William J.E. Sander, Boston, 1917, Whipple, Sears & Ogden, 1917-19; admiralty atty. U.S. Shipping Bd., Washington, 1919-23, asst. admiralty counsel, 1923-25, admiralty counsel, 1925-29; mem. Chapman, Snider, Duke & Boal, 1930-32; partner Boal, McQuade & Fitzpatrick (and predecessor firms), 1932-72, Boal, Doti & Larsen, 1972—. Contbr.: Am. part article on admiralty jurisdiction Ency. Brit., 14th edit. Mayor Village of Pelham, N.Y., 1949-53; Chmn. adjudication, arbitration internat. courts Southwestern Legal Found.; Dir. Pelham Community Chest, campaign mgr., 1940-41, pres., 1942-43; chmn. Pelham Red Cross War Fund campaign, 1945-46; vice chmn. Westchester County chpt. A.R.C., 1946-49; mem. Pelham Bd. Edn., 1960-67, pres., 1965-67; Mem. Coast Arty. Sch., 1918. Mem. Maritime Law Assn. U.S. (pres. 1958-60, chmn. com. on Comite Maritime Internat. 1960—, v.p. Comite 1969—), N.Y. Bar Assn., Internat. Law Assn., Assn. Bar City N.Y. (mem. com. on judiciary 1962-64), Royal Soc. Arts and Sci. (London). Clubs: Downtown, Harvard (N.Y.C.); Author's (London, Eng.); Men's (pres. 1943-44), Pelham (N.Y.) Country.). Home: 246 Corona Ave Pelham NY 10803 Office: Suite 8909 One World Trade Center New York NY 10048 *The joy in work is the greatest satisfaction in life. If you enjoy your work, you do not mind those parts of it which are dull and boring, and you will get real satisfaction out of solving the problems which your work presents.*

BOAL, DEAN, broadcasting executive, educator; b. Longmont, Colo., Oct. 20, 1931; s. Elmer C. and L. Mildred (Snodgrass) B.; m. Ellen Christine TeSelle, Aug. 23, 1957; children: Brett, Jed. B.Music, B.Music Edn., U. Colo., 1953; M.Music, Ind. U., 1956; D. Musical Arts, U. Colo., 1959. Mem. faculty Hastings (Nebr.) Coll., 1958-60; head piano dept. Bradley U., Peoria, Ill., 1960-66; dean, pianist Peabody Conservatory, Balt., 1966-70; prof. piano, chair music SUNY, Fredonia, 1970-73; pres. St. Louis Conservatory, 1973-76; dir. radio sta. KWMU, St. Louis, 1976-78; v.p., gen. mgr. Sta. WETA-FM, Washington, 1978-83; dir. arts and performance programs Nat. Pub. Radio, Washington, 1982—. Author: Concepts and Skills for the Piano, Book I, 1969, Book II, 1970; contbr. articles to profl. jours. Served with U.S. Army, 1953-55. Woodrow Wilson teaching fellow, 1983—. Mem. Eastern Public Radio Network (chmn. 1979-82), Coll. Music Soc., Pi Kappa Lambda, Mu Phi Epsilon, Phi Mu Alpha. Presbyterian. Office: Nat Pub Radio 2025 M St NW Washington DC 20036

BOARD, JOSEPH BRECKINRIDGE, JR., political scientist, educator; b. Princeton, Ind., Mar. 5, 1931; s. Joseph Breckinridge and Rachel Eleanor (Unthank) B.; m. Kjersti E. Danielson, Dec. 31, 1955; children: Ian Robert, Annika Caroline, Amanda Anne. A.B. with highest honors, Ind. U., 1953, J.D., 1958, Ph.D., 1962; B.A. (Rhodes scholar 1953-55), Oxford (Eng.) U., 1955, M.A., 1961; Ph.D. honoris causa, Umea U., Sweden, 1973. Teaching fellow govt. Ind. U., 1955-58, lectr. govt., 1958; asst. prof. polit. sci. Elmira Coll., 1959-61; asso. prof. polit. sci., chmn. dept. Cornell Coll., 1961-64; prof. polit. sci., chmn. dept. Union Coll., Schenectady, 1964—, Robert Porter Patterson prof. govt., 1973—, chmn. faculty, 1983—; acad. visitor London Sch. Econs. and Polit. Sci., 1972-73; adj. prof. Albany Law Sch., 1974—; acting prof., chmn. dept. polit. sci. U. Umea, 1979; Mem. Rhodes Scholarship Selection Com. Nebr., 1961-62, Iowa, 1963-64; mem. regional selection com. for Woodrow Wilson Fellowships, 1966—; mem. exec. council Iowa Conf. Polit. Scientists, 1963-65; spl. adv. coll. and univ. affairs Young Citizens for Johnson, 1964; cons. Nat. Endowment Humanities, 1968, N.Y. State Dept. Edn., 1968; mem. polit. sci. adv. com. Fulbright-Hays Program, 1969-73; asso., adv. com. for Western Europe Council for Internat. Exchange of Scholars; chmn. Scandinavian peer rev. com. Linkages Project; mem. U.S. Com. on NATO Fellowships; cons., co-host Nobel Prize broadcast Nat. Pub. Radio, 1976. Author: The Government and Politics of Sweden, 1970. Bd. advisers Schenectady Salvation Army. Fulbright lectr., Sweden, 1968-69; Central Am. fellow Asso. Colls. Midwest, 1962; NDEA postdoctoral fellow in Portuguese, 1963. Mem. Am. Assn. Rhodes Scholars, Am. Polit. Sci. Assn., AAUP, Ind. Bar, Am. Arbitration Assn., Am-Scandinavian Found. (com. on fellowships 1981—), Northeastern Polit. Sci. Assn. (exec. Council 1972), Soc. for Advancement Scandinavian Studies (exec. council 1972), Soc. Letters (Lund U.), Acacia, Phi Beta Kappa. Democrat. Episcopalian. Home: 15 Sunnyside Rd Scotia NY 12302 Office: Union Coll Schenectady NY 12308

BOARD, WILLIAM JESSE, JR., chemical engineer; b. Louisville, Dec. 31, 1936; s. William Jesse Board and Helen Marie (zoeller) Broad; m. Marjorie Lee Alexandaer, Mar. 21, 1958; children; Todd William, Stacey M. B. Chem Engring., U. Louisville, 1959, M. Chem. Engring, 1960; postgrad., MIT, 1967-68. Mgr. sales Monsanto, Atlanta, 1975-76, dir. mktg. home furnishing, 1976-77, dir. planning, carpet, 1977-78, dir. product mgmt. nylon, 1978-79, dir. tech., nylon and support, Pensacola, Fla., 1980—. Contbr. articles to profl. jours.; patentee in field. Pres. Interfaith Chorale, Gulf Breeze, Fla., 1982-83; corp. sec. Symphony Bd., Pensacola, 1983—. Ford Found. scholar, 1954-59; Monsanto fellow, 1960. Mem. Sigma Xi, Phi Kappa Phi. Republican. Presbyterian. Home: 421 Kent Pl gulf Breeze FL 32561 Office: PO Box 12830 Pensacola FL 32575

BOARDMAN, EUGENE POWERS, educator; b. Aurora, Ill., Oct. 5, 1910; s. Charles Watkins and Irmgard (Heth) B.; m. Elizabeth Reynolds Jelinek, June 21, 1940 (div. June 1969); children—Susan, Sarah, Christopher, Erika, Andrew, Benjamin. B.A., Beloit (Wis.) Coll., 1932; M.A., U. Wis., 1937, Harvard U., 1939, Ph.D., 1947. Tchr. English prep. dept. Am. U., Beirut, Lebanon, 1932-35; tchr. social studies, French Delavan (Wis.) High Sch., 1935-36; prof. charge courses, grad. work East Asian history U. Wis., Madison, 1946-81; Lobbyist with U.S. Congress for a New China Policy under auspices Friends Com. Nat. Legislation, 1965-66. Author: Madison, 1952. Served as maj. USMCR, 1941-46. Decorated Legion of Merit. Mem. Assn. for Asian Studies (past program chmn.), Phi Beta Kappa, Sigma Pi, Delta Sigma Rho. Mem. Soc. of Friends. Home: 1926 Sheridan St Madison WI 53704

BOARDMAN, JOHN MICHAEL, mathematics educator; b. Manchester, Eng., Feb. 13, 1938; came to U.S., 1969, naturalized, 1973; s. William Edgar and Carrie (Brown) B.; children: Susan, Andrew. B.A., Trinity Coll., Cambridge U., 1961, Ph.D., 1965. Vis. lectr. U. Chgo., 1966-67; asst. lectr. U. Warwick, Eng., 1967-68; assoc. prof. Johns Hopkins U., Balt., 1969-72, prof., 1972—. Author: Singularities of Differentiable Maps, 1967, (with R.M. Vogt) Homotopy Invariant Algebraic Structures on Topological Spaces, 1973, Stable Homotopy Theory. Served with RAF, 1956-58. Sci. Research Council fellow, 1964-66; NSF grantee, 1970—. Mem. Am. Math. Soc. Quaker. Home: 6217 Northwood Dr Baltimore MD 21212 Office: Dept Math Johns Hopkins U Baltimore MD 21218

BOARDMAN, RICHARD STANTON, paleontologist; b. Oak Park, Ill., July 16, 1923; s. Stanton Knight and Irma (Crouch) B.; m. Phyllis Orwig, Apr. 6, 1946; children—William Richard, James Mark. Student, Denison U., 1943; B.S., U. Ill., 1948, M.S., 1952, Ph.D., 1955. Geologist U.S. Geol. Survey, 1952-57; asso. curator Smithsonian Instn., Washington, 1957-60, now curator. Author papers taxonomy, morphology, evolution of phylum Bryozoa. Served, 1943-46. Mem. Paleontol. Soc. Systemic Zoology, Soc. Econ. Paleontologists and Mineralogists, Sigma Xi. Home: 7004 Richard Dr Bethesda MD 20034 Office: Smithsonian Instn Washington DC 20560

BOARDMAN, SEYMOUR, artist; b. Bklyn., Dec. 29, 1921; s. Joseph and Bessie (Warren) B. B.S.S., CCNY, 1942; postgrad., Ecole des Beaux-Arts, Paris, 1946-47, Atelier Fernand Leger, 1948, Art Students League, N.Y.C., 1949-50, Ecole de la Grande Chaumiere, 1950-51. One-man shows, Galerie Mai, Paris, 1951, Martha Jackson Gallery, N.Y.C., 1955, 56, Stephen Radich Gallery, N.Y.C., 1960-61, 62, A.M. Sachs Gallery, N.Y.C., 1965, 67, 68, Dorsky Gallery, N.Y.C., 1972, Aaron Berman Gallery, N.Y.C., 1978, group shows include, Whitney Mus. Am. Art, 1955, 61, 67, Nebr. Art Assn., 1956, Kunsthalle, Basel, Switzerland, 1964, Santa Barbara Art Mus., Albright-Knox Gallery, Buffalo, 1967, Cornell U., 1971; represented in permanent collections, Whitney Mus. Am. Art, Guggenheim Mus., Walker Art Center, Mpls., Santa Barbara Mus. Art, N.Y. U. Served with USAAF, 1942-46. Longview Found. grantee, 1963; Guggenheim Found. fellow, 1972-73; Adolph and Esther Gottlieb Found. grantee, 1979, 83. Address: 234 W 27th St New York NY 10001

BOARDMAN, WILLIAM PENNIMAN, lawyer; b. Columbus, Ohio, June 22, 1941; s. John King and Eleanor Susan (Penniman) B.; m. Nancy Louise Staby, Apr. 10, 1971; children: Abigail Blair, Anna Neel, Elizabeth Penniman. B.A., Washington and Lee U., 1963, J.D. summa cum laude, 1969. Bar: Ohio 1969. Mgmt. trainee 1st Nat. City Bank, N.Y.C., 1963-64; ptnr. Porter, Wright, Morris & Arthur, Columbus, 1969-81; gen. counsel BancOhio Corp., Columbus, 1981—. Trustee Columbus Festival Theater, Gambier, Ohio, 1982, Franklin County Soc. Autism, Columbus, 1980, Columbus Sch. for Girls, 1981. Served to 1st lt. arty. U.S. Army, 1964-66; Korea. Mem. ABA, Columbus Bar Assn., Ohio Bar Assn. Republican. Episcopalian.

Clubs: Rocky Fork Hunt and Country (trustee 1983); Univ. (Columbus); Golf (New Albany, Ohio). Lodge: Rotary. Home: 9455 Harlem Rd Westerville OH 43081 Office: BancOhio Corp 155 E Broad St Columbus OH 43251

BOARMAN, PATRICK MADIGAN, economics and business adminstration educator, business academic administrator, consultant; b. Buffalo, 1922; children: Thomas Christopher, Jesse, Barbara. A.B., Fordham U., 1943; M.S., Columbia U., 1946; Ph.D. in Econs., Grad. Inst. Internat. Studies, U. Geneva, 1965. Asst. to advt. mgr. Doubleday, N.Y.C., 1944-45; fgn. corr. CBS, Geneva, 1946-48; dir. office cultural affairs Nat. Catholic Welfare Conf., Bonn, W. Germany, 1951-55; asst. prof. econs. U. Wis.-Milw., 1956-62; assoc. prof. Bucknell U., Lewisburg, Pa., 1962-67; prof. L.I.U., N.Y.C., 1967-72; prof. internat. econs., dir. research Ctr. Internat. Bus./Pepperdine U., Los Angeles, 1972-75; prof. econs., chmn. internat. bus. Nat. U., San Diego, 1979—; mgr. econ. research div. employee relations and mgmt. devel. Gen. Electric Co., N.Y.C., 1964-65; mgr. econ. reports div. econ. analysis AT&T, 1969; sr. economist cons. World Trade Inst., N.Y.C., 1971; pres. Patrick M. Boarman Assocs., Internat. Bus. Cons., 1975—; dir. research House Republican Conf., Ho. of Reps., Washington, 1976-78; spl. cons. to Sec. Treasury, Washington, 1970; cons. Econ. Stabilization Bd., Washington, 1971-72; guest lectr. U. Chgo., 1957, 64; Disting. vis. lectr. Denison U., 1959; vis. prof. econs. U. Geneva, 1965-66; Disting. vis. prof. econs. Pitzer Coll., 1977, Clarmeont Coll., 1977; supr. 3d dist. San Diego county (Calif.), 1983—. Author: Union Monopolies and Antitrust Restraints, 1963, Germany's Economic Dilemma-Inflation and the Balance of Payments, 1964; editor: books, most recent (with Hans Schollhammer) Multinational Corporations and Governments, 1975, Trade with China, 1974, (with David G. Tuerck) World Monetary Disorder, 1976; author monographs; author, contbr. numerous articles to profl. and popular jours. Served with U.S. Army, 1943. Decorated Disting. Service Cross, Order of Merit W. Germany; Fulbright fellow U. Amsterdam, 1949-50; Ford Found. fellow in econs. U. Mich., 1958; Gen. Electric Found fellow U. Va., 1965. Mem. Am. Econ. Assn., Royal Econ. Soc., Nat. Assn. Bus. Economists. Home: 6421 Caminito Estrellado San Diego CA 92120 *To learn more and more until the end of my days about this wonderful world I inhabit has been my goal, and even passion, from the beginning. I could live 50 lives, and still not have time enough to do all the reading, writing, exploring and loving I want to do. True wealth is what is in one's head and heart and my stock of it is beyond counting.*

BOAS, RALPH PHILIP, JR., mathematics educator; b. Walla Walla, Wash., Aug. 8, 1912; s. Ralph Philip and Louise (Schutz) B.; m. Mary Elizabeth Layne, June 12, 1941; children: Ralph Layne, Anne Louise, Harold Philip. A.B., Harvard U., 1933, Ph.D., 1937. Nat. Research fellow Princeton U. and; Cambridge U., Eng., 1937-39; instr. Duke U., 1939-41, U.S. Navy Pre-Flight Sch., Chapel Hill, N.C., 1942-43; vis. lectr. Harvard U., 1943-45; exec. editor Math. Revs. Brown U., 1945-50; lectr. M.I.T., 1948-49; prof. math. Northwestern U., Evanston, Ill., 1950-80, prof. emeritus, 1980—, chmn. dept., 1957-72, pres. fellow, 1961-62; Henry S. Noyes prof., 1962—. Author: Entire Functions, 1954, A Primer of Real Functions, 1960, (with R.C. Buck) Polynomial Expansions of Analytic Functions, 1958, Integrability Theorems for Trigonometric Transforms, 1967. John Simon Guggenheim Meml. fellow, 1951-52. Fellow AAAS; mem. Am. Math. Soc. (v.p. 1959-60, trustee 1966-71), Math. Assn. Am. (chmn. undergrad. program in math. 1968-71, pres. 1973-74, editor 1977-81, Disting. Service award 1981), London Math. Soc., Phi Beta Kappa, Sigma Xi. Home: 2440 Simpson St Evanston IL 60201

BOAS, ROBERT SANFORD, investment banker; b. N.Y.C., May 21, 1923; s. Benjamin W. and Ruth (Hirschman) B.; m. Marjorie Marks, June 23, 1946; children—Richard, Susan, Andrew. A.B., Cornell U., 1945, Western State Coll. Law, 1973. Exec. v.p. Carl Marks & Co., Inc., N.Y.C., 1946-53, chmn. bd., 1953—; pres. CMNY Capital Co.; v.p. Carl Marks Found. Trustee North Shore Univ. Hosp., Manhasset, N.Y., 1972—, pres., 1973-77; trustee Brandeis U.; bd. overseers Albert Einstein Coll. Medicine; bd. dirs. Met. Opera, N.Y.C. Opera, United Jewish Appeal, United Cerebral Palsy Research and Ednl. Found. Served with AUS, 1943-44. Mem. Nat. Assn. Securities Dealers, Nat. Securities Traders Assn. Clubs: Fresh Meadow Country, Palm Beach Country, Harmonie, Cornell, Broad St., Masons, Confrérie de la Chaine des Rotisseurs. Home: 25 Harbour Rd Great Neck NY 11024 also 333 Sunset Ave Palm Beach FL 33480 Office: 77 Water St New York NY 10005

BOAST, WARREN BENEFIELD, electrical engineer; b. Topeka, Dec. 13, 1909; s. Charles W. and Lulu (Robinson) B.; m. Ruth J. Hansen, Nov. 28, 1936; children: Richard, Charles, Thomas. B.E.E., U. Kans., 1933, M.S., 1934; Ph.D., Iowa State Coll., 1936. Asst. elec. engring. Iowa State U., 1934, prof., head dept., 1954-75, prof. emeritus, 1975—; Anson Marston distinguished prof. engring., 1964; pres. Nat. Electronics Conf., 1967; U.S. del. Internat. Electrotech. Commn., Aix-les Bains, France, 1964. Author: Illumination Engineering, 1942, 53, Principles of Electric and Magnetic Fields, 1948, 56; Spanish transl. Técnica de la Iluminación Eléctrica, 1965; Principles of Electric and Magnetic Circuits, 1950, 57, Vector Fields, 1964, Japanese transl. parts I and II; contbr. to: McGraw-Hill Ency. Sci. and Tech, 1960, 66, 71, 77, 82, Reinhold Ency. Physics, 1966, 74, Standard Handbook for Electrical Engrs., 11th edit, 1978. Recipient Faculty citation, 1971; Marston medal, 1980. Fellow IEEE (Meritorious award of Edn. Soc. 1978), Illuminating Engring. Soc.; mem. Am. Soc. Engring. Edn., Sigma Xi, Eta Kappa Nu, Tau Beta Pi. Research on electro-acoustic transducers. Patentee (3). Home: 225 Parkridge Circle Ames IA 50010

BOAT, THOMAS FREDERICK, pediatrics educator, academic administrator; b. Oskaloosa, Iowa, Sept. 7, 1939; s. Bert Reuben and Anne Marie (Schoenbohm) B.; m. Barbara Mary Walling, June 9, 1962; children: Sarah Elizabeth, Mary Barbara, Anne Christine. B.A., Central Coll., Pella, Iowa, 1961; M.S., U. Iowa, 1966, M.D., 1966. Diplomate: Am. Bd. Pediatrics. Intern U. Minn. Hosps., Mpls., 1966-67, resident in pediatrics, 1966-68; clin. assoc. NIH, Bethesda, Md., 1968-70; research fellow Case Western Res. U., Cleve., 1970-72, asst. prof. pediatrics, 1972-77, assoc. prof., 1977-81, prof., 1981-82; prof., chmn. dept. pediatrics U. N.C., Chapel Hill, 1982—; chmn. med. adv. com. Cystic Fibrosis Found., 1981-83. Contbr. articles to profl. jours., chpts. to books. Served to surgeon USPHS, 1968-70. Mem. Soc. Pediatric Research (pres. elect), Am. Pediatric Soc., Am. Thoracic Soc. (chmn. pediatrics assembly), N.C. Pediatric Soc., Am. Acad. Pediatrics. Presbyterian. Home: 2025 S Lake Shore Dr Chapel Hill NC 27514 Office: U NC Sch Medicine Chapel Hill NC 27514

BOATNER, JAMES GOWEN, army officer; b. Tientsin, China, Mar. 28, 1930; s. Haydon LeMaire and Dorothy Aline (Gown) B. (parents Am. citizens); m. Catherine I. Schroeter, May 1, 1954; children: James Gowen, Thomas, Michael, Jane, Peter. B.S., U.S. Mil. Acad., 1951; M.P.A., Harvard U., 1959, M.S., 1960; grad., Command and Gen. Staff Coll., 1965, Air War Coll., 1968. Commd. 2d lt. U.S. Army, 1951, advanced through grades to maj. gen., 1978, platoon leader, Ft. Hood, Tex., 1951-52, comdr. co., Korea, 1952-53, co-comdr. and staff officer, Ft. Campbell, Ky., 1953-58, Japan, 1953-58; asst. prof. U.S. Mil. Acad., 1960-64, comdr. bn., Vietnam, 1966-67; div. chief Office Dep. Chief of Staff Ops., 1968-70; mil. asst. to dep. sec. def. Dept. Def., Washington, 1970-72; comdr. 82d Airborne Div. Support Command, 1972-73; dep. comdr. U.S. Army, Ft. Polk, La., 1974-75; comdr. Alaskan Brigade, Ft. Richardson, 1975-78; dir. mil. personnel mgmt. Dept. Army, Washington, 1978; now U.S. comdr. U.S. Army, Berlin. Decorated Legion of Merit with 2 oak leaf clusters, Bronze Star with V device and 2 oak leaf clusters, Meritorious Service medal, Air medal with 4 oak leaf clusters. Mem. Assn. U.S. Army, Assn. Grads. U.S. Mil. Acad., Harvard U. Alumni Assn. Roman Catholic. Office: APO New York 09742

BOATRIGHT, JAMES FRANCIS, air force official; b. Colorado Springs, Colo., May 17, 1933; s. Otis Francis and Marjorie Bell (Caldwell) B.; m. Gloria Jane Sellar, Sept. 29, 1956; children: James Jeffrey, Jennifer Jane, William Sellar. B.S. in Civil Engring., U. Colo., 1956. Registered profl. engr., D.C. Constrn. engr. U.S. Army Corps Engrs., Topeka and Salina, Kans., 1959-61; civil engr. Dept. Army, Ft. Belvoir, Va., 1961-66; various positions with directorate of engring. and services Dept. Air Force, Washington, 1966-76, dep. for installations mgmt., 1976-79, dep. asst. sec. installations, 1979-82, dep. asst. sec. installations, environmnent and safety, 1982—. Deacon Parkwood Baptist Ch., Annandale, Va., 1972—, property chmn., Annandale, Va., 1982—. Served to 1st lt. U.S. Army, 1956-58. Recipient Meritorious Civilian Service award Dept. Air Force, 1976, Exceptional Civilian Service award Dept. Air Force, 1981. Mem. Soc. Am. Mil. Engrs. (awards chmn. 1979-79). Home: 8308 Epinard Ct. Annandale VA 22003 Office: Dept Air Force Washington DC 20330

BOBA, IMRE, educator; b. Gyor, Hungary, Oct. 23, 1919; came to U.S., naturalized, 1956; s. Wladyslaw and Ilona (Faludi) B.; m. Elizabeth Herndon Hudson, Dec. 22, 1954; children—Eleanor, Leslie. Grad., U. Budapest, Hungary, 1946; Ph.D. in History, U. Wash., 1962. Faculty U. Wash., Seattle, 1962—, asso. prof. medieval history, 1967-71, prof. history, Russian and East European studies, 1971—. Author: Nomads, Northmen and Slavs, 1967, History of Moravia Reconsidered, 1971; Contbg. editor: Dictionary of Political Science, 1963. Mem. Am. Hist. Assn., Am. Assn. for Advancement Slavic Studies. Home: 7336 55th Ave NE Seattle WA 98115

BOBB, RICHARD ALLEN, credit company executive; b. Gahanna, Ohio, Oct. 27, 1937; s. Everett Leo and Mary Ennetta (Dunlay) B.; m. Betty Lee Knechtly, Oct. 21, 1960; 1 son, Michael Allen. B.Sc. in Bus, Ohio State U., 1959. With Pure Oil Co., 1963-65, Gen. Electric Co., 1965-79; sr. v.p., dir. mktg. ITT Indsl. Credit Co., St. Paul, 1979—. Served with USNR, 1960-63. Republican. Presbyterian. Office: ITT Indsl Credit Co PO Box 43777 Saint Paul MN 55102 *

BOBBITT, JAMES MCCUE, chemist; b. Charleston, W.Va., Jan. 18, 1930; s. James Sterling and Grace (McCue) B.; m. Jane Ann Hickman, Mar. 15, 1952; children: John Sterling, Ann, Laura. B.S., W.Va. U., 1951; Ph.D., Ohio State U., 1955. Instr. chemistry U. Conn., 1956-59, asst. prof., 1959-63, assoc. prof., 1963-68, prof., 1968—, acting head dept., 1976-77, head dept., 1977-82; postdoctoral fellow Wayne State U., 1955-56; NSF fellow U. Zurich, Switzerland, 1959-60; guest prof. U. East Anglia, 1964-65, U. Kiel, Germany, 1968, Tohoku U., Japan, 1971, La Trobe U., Australia, 1971-72. Author: Thin Layer Chromatography, 1963, (with R.J. Gritter and A.E. Schwarting) Introduction to Chromatography, 1968; editorial bd.: Heterocycles. Mem. Am. Chem. Soc., Chem. Soc. Eng., Electrochem. Soc., Phi Beta Kappa, Sigma Xi, Phi Lambda Upsilon. Democrat. Congregationalist. Home: 24 Olsen Dr Mansfield Center CT 06250 Office: U Conn Storrs CT 06268

BOBBITT, PHILIP CHASE, legal educator, writer; b. Temple, Tex., July 22, 1948; s. Oscar Price and Rebekah Luruth (Johnson) B. A.B., Princeton U., 1971; J.D., Yale U., 1975; Ph.D., Oxford U., 1983. Bar: Tex. 1977. Law clk. to judge U.S. Ct. Appeals for 2d Cir., 1975-76; asst. prof. law U. Tex., Austin, 1976-79, prof., 1979—; assoc. counsel to Pres. White House, 1980-81; vis. research fellow Internat. Inst. Strategic Studies, 1981-82; research fellow Nuffield Coll., Oxford U., 1982—. Author: (with Guido Calabresi) Tragic Choices, 1979, Constitutinal Fate, 1982. Mem. Am. Law Inst., Internat. Inst. Strategic Studies (London), Austin Council Fgn. Affairs (pres. 1983—). Democrat. Baptist. Clubs: Princeton (N.Y.C.); Metropolitan (Washington). Office: U Tex Law Sch 727 E 26th St Austin TX 78705

BOBER, HARRY, humanities-history of art educator; b. N.Y.C., Sept. 2, 1915; s. Hyman and Fannie (Newman) B.; m. Phyllis Barbara Pray, Aug. 11, 1943 (div. 1973); children: Jonathan P., David H. B.A., CCNY, 1955; cert., Institut d'Art et d'Archeologie-U. Paris, 1938, Free U., Brussels, 1939; M.A., Inst. Fine Arts-NYU, 1940, Ph.D., 1949; H.H.D. hon, Oakland U., Rochester, Mich., 1979. Reader, tutor CCNY, 1935-42; instr. Queens Coll., 1947-49; asst. prof. Smith Coll., Northampton, Mass., 1949-50; lectr. Inst. Fine Art-NYU, N.Y.C., 1950-51, assoc. prof., 1954-61, prof., 1961-65, Avalon Found. prof. humanities, 1965—; asst. prof. Washington Sq. Coll., 1950-51, Harvard U., Cambridge, Mass., 1951-54; Disting. vis. prof. humanities Johns Hopkins U., Balt., 1964-65; Disting. prof. CCNY, 1970-71; Messinger lectr. Cornell U., Ithaca, N.Y., 1973-74; mem. vis. coms. medieval dept. and Photog. Library Met. Mus. Art, N.Y.C., 1969—; founder Internat. Found. Art Research, 1968—. Author: The St. Blasien Psalter, 1963, Medieval Art in the Guennol Collection, 1975; editor: Astrological and Mythological Illuminated Manuscripts of the Latin Middle Ages in the English Libraries, 2 vols., 1953, Religious Art in France (Emile Male), English edit., 3 vols., 1978-83. Served to lt. USN, 1942-45; Caribbean. Guggenheim fellow, 1947; fellow Bollingen Found., 1953-58, Am. Council Learned Socs., 1960; research fellow Warburg Inst., U. London, 1949-62. Fellow Warburg. Inst. (hon. life); mem. Internat. Ctr. Medieval Art (founding, dir.), Medieval Acad. Am. (council 1959), Assn. Belgian Am. Found. Fellows (founder, pres. 1963-72), Coll. Art Assn. Am. (dir. 1966-73), Soc. N. Am. Goldsmiths (hon.). Home: 3 Washington Sq Village New York NY 10012 Office: Inst Fine Arts NYU 1 E 78th St New York NY 10012 *Such of my accomplishments as may be more commendable could only have come of nurturing tin the unqualified loving confidence of very dear parents.*

BOBER, JOHN D., corporate executive; b. Jersey City, Apr. 27, 1922; s. Dmitro and Eva (Fickanich) B.; m. Eva Lazorik, May 23, 1948; children: Michaele, John. B.S. in Acctg., L.I. U., 1949. With Purolator, Inc., Rahway, N.J., 1950—, treas., 1959-78, controller, 1959-72, v.p., 1972-78, exec. v.p., 1978-82, vice-chmn. bd., 1982—, pres. Filter div., 1972; dir. Purolator India, Ltd., Stant Mfg. Corp., Connorsville, Ind., Indsl. Workmen's br. City Fed. Savs. & Loan Assn., Rahway, N.J. Bd. dirs. Rahway YMCA, 1965-73. Served with USAAF, 1942-45. Mem. Nat. Assn. Accts., Am. Inst. C.P.A.s.

BOBER, LAWRENCE HAROLD, banker; b. N.Y.C., Mar. 29, 1924; s. Michael N. and Julia (Verschleiser) B.; m. Natalie S. Birnbaum, Aug. 27, 1950; children: Stephen, Marc, Elizabeth. B.S., N.Y. U., 1949; postgrad., Grad. Sch. Bus. Adminstrn., 1949-50. With Hanover Bank, 1941—, asst. sec., 1950-52, asst. treas., 1953-55, asst. v.p., 1955-60, v.p., 1960-71, sr. v.p., 1971—; dir. Fab Industries, Inc. Chmn. fin. com., trustee Inst. on Man and Sci.; mem. pres.'s council Brandeis U. Served to 1st lt. USAAF, 1943-46. Recipient community service award, 1974; Decorated D.F.C. with two oak leaf clusters, Air medal with three oak leaf clusters; recipient Human Relations award Am. Jewish Com., 1968; Community Service award Nat. Jewish Hosp. and Research Center, 1980. Mem. N.Y. Credit and Fin. Mgmt. Assn. (past dir.), Am. Apparel Mfrs. Assn., Credit Men's Frat. (dir.), N.Y. U. Commerce Alumni Assn. Clubs: Harmonie, N.Y. U. (past pres., dir.), 475 Club (N.Y.C.)). Home: 50 E 79th St New York NY 10021 Office: 270 Park Ave New York NY 10017

BOBER, PHYLLIS PRAY, art history educator; b. Portland, Maine, Dec. 2, 1920; d. Melvin Francis and Lea Arlene (Royer) Pray; (div.)children: Jonathan Pray, David Hall. B.A., Wellesley Coll., 1941; M.A., N.Y. U., 1943, Ph.D., 1946. Instr. history of art Wellesley Coll., 1947-49, lectr., 1951-54; curator Farnsworth Art Mus., 1951-54; dir. census of antique works of art to Renaissance artists Warburg Inst., U. London, 1949—; Inst. Fine Arts N.Y. U., 1954-73; chmn. fine arts dept. Univ. Coll., NYU, 1967-73; dean Grad. Sch. Arts and Scis., Bryn Mawr (Pa.) Coll., 1973-80, prof. classical archeology and history of art, 1980—; cons. Nat. Endowment for Humanities, 1972—; mem. Grad. Record Exam. Bd., 1976-80, chmn. services com., 1977-80; mem. exec. com., bd. dirs. Council Grad. Schs. in U.S., 1977-80; Soc. for Humanities sr. fellow Cornell U., 1984. Author: Drawings After the Antique: Sketchbooks of Amico Aspertini, 1957, Renaissance Artists and Antique Sculpture, 1984; Contbr. articles to profl. jours. Bd. visitors for art history Boston U., 1976-81; bd. corporators Med. Coll. Pa., 1979—, chmn. nominating com., 1980-83. Guggenheim fellow, 1979-80. Corr. fellow German Archeol. Inst.; mem. Coll. Art Assn. (dir. 1982—, chmn. art historians com. 1983—, rep. to Am. Council Learned Socs. 1983—), Archeol. Inst. Am., Internat. Assn. for Classical Archeology, Renaissance Soc. Am. (council 1978-81, pres. 1983-84), Pa. Assn. Grad. Deans (pres. 1977-78), Northeast Assn. Grad Deans (pres. 1978-79), N.Y. Mycol. Soc. (Ancient Civilization Seminar Group.). Home: 29 Simpson Rd Ardmore PA 19003 Office: Bryn Mawr Coll Bryn Mawr PA 19010

BOBINSKI, GEORGE SYLVAN, librarian, educator; b. Cleve., Oct. 24, 1929; s. Sylvan and Eugenia (Sarbiewski) B.; m. Mary Lillian Form, Feb. 20, 1953; children-George Sylvan, Mary Anne. B.A., Case Western Res. U., 1951, M.S. in L.S, 1952; M.A., U. Mich., 1961, Ph.D., 1966. Research asst. Bus Info. Bur., Cleve. Pub. Library, 1954-55; asst. dir. Royal Oak (Mich.) Pub. Library, 1955-59; dir. libraries State U. Coll. at Cortland, N.Y., 1960-67; asst. dean, prof. Sch. Library Sci., U. Ky., 1967-70; dean, prof. Sch. Info. and Library Studies, State U. N.Y. at Buffalo, 1970—; cons. Mich. State Library, 1958, 1959-60, Clawson (Mich.) Pub. Library, 1956-57, World Maritime U., Malmo, Sweden, 1982; Fulbright-Hays lectr. in library sci. U. Warsaw, Poland, 1977; Chmn. Conf. State U. N.Y. Head Librarians, 1963-64; treas. Eastern Coll. Librarians, 1963-64; pres. bd. trustees Western N.Y. Library Research Council, 1982. Author: A Brief History of the Libraries of Western Reserve University, 1826-1952, 1955, Carnegie Libraries, Their History and Impact on American Public Library Development, 1969, Dictionary of American Library Biography, 1978, also articles. Served with AUS, 1952-54. Mem. ALA (mem. pub. com., mem. council), N.Y. Library Assn. (dir. coll. and univ. sect. 1964-66), Assn. Am. Library Schs. Home: 69 Little Robin Rd Amherst NY 14228 Office: Sch Information and Library Studies State Univ at Buffalo Buffalo NY 14260

BOBISUD, LARRY EUGENE, educator; b. Midvale, Idaho, Mar. 16, 1940; s. Walter and Ida V. (Bitner) B.; m. Helen M. Meyer, June 15, 1963. B.S., Coll. of Ida., 1961; M.A., U. N.M., 1963, Ph.D., 1966. Vis. mem. Courant Inst. Math. Scis., N.Y.C., 1966-67; prof. math. U. Idaho, Moscow, 1967—. Contbr. articles to profl. jours. Mem. Am. Math. Soc. Home: 860 Eisenhower St Moscow ID 83843 Office: Univ Ida Dept Math Moscow ID 83843

BOBKO, KAROL J., astronaut; b. N.Y.C., Dec. 23, 1937; s. Charles P. and Veronica (Sagatis) B.; m. Frances Dianne Welsh, Feb. 11, 1961; children: Michelle Ann, Paul Joseph. B.S., U.S. Air Force Acad., 1959; grad., U.S. Air Force Aerospece Research Pilot Sch., 1966; M.S., U. So. Calif., 1970. Commd. officer U.S. Air Force, 1959, advanced through grades to col., pilot trainee, 1959-61, F-100 tactical fighter pilot, 1961-63, F-105 tactical fighter pilot, 1963-65, test pilot, 1965-67, astronaut, 1967—, mem. (pilot) 1st mission Space Shuttle Challenger, 1983. Office: NASA Johnson Space Ctr Houston TX 77012

BOBO, DONALD ARTHUR, labor union executive; b. Lawrence, Kans., Sept. 18, 1918; s. Drexel Morgan and Hazel B.; m. Doris Johanna Evers, July 26, 1940; 1 son, Donald Arthur. Student, pub. schs., Galveston, Tex. Local chmn. Santa Fe Systems Div. 61, Order of R.R. Telegraphers, 1952-56, asst. gen. chmn. div., 1956-59, gen. sec.-treas. div., 1959-60, gen. chmn. div., 1960-62; 1st v.p. Order of R.R. Telegraphers, 1962-71; pres. transp. communications employees div., internat. v.p., asst. internat. sec.-treas. Brotherhood of Ry., Airline and Steamship Clks., Freight Handlers, Express and St. Employees, Rockville, Md., 1972-75; internat. sec.-treas. Order of R.R. Telegraphers, Rockville, Md., 1975. Served with U.S. Army, 1944-46. Mem. Am. Legion. Democrat. Office: Brotherhood of Ry Airline and Steamship Clks 3 Research Pl Rockville MD 20850

BOBO, JACK E., association executive; b. S.C.; m. Gladys; 1 son, Glen. Student public schs. C.L.U. Salesman, Stewart Warner Co., Phoenix, to 1956; agt. N.Y. Life Ins. Co., Phoenix, 1956-78; partner Rasmussen/Bobo and Co. Ins., Phoenix, to 1978; trustee Nat. Assn. Life Underwriters, 1970-74, sec., 1975-76, pres.-elect, 1976-77, pres., 1977-78, exec. v.p., Washington, 1979—; charter mem. N.Y. Life Ins. Chairmen's Council; sec. N.Y. Life Ins. Agts. Adv. Council; speaker. Past pres. Phoenix Better Bus. Bur., Washington (Ariz.) Elem. Sch. Dist.; past chmn. ins. div. Phoenix United Fund; assns. div. D.C. Area United Way; past pres. Congregational Ch., Phoenix. Served as fighter pilot USAAF, World War II. Mem. Assn. Advanced Underwiting, Million Dollar Round Table, Am. Soc. C.L.U.s, Central Ariz. Estate Planning Council. Address: 1922 F St NW Washington DC 20006

BOBO, JAMES ROBERT, educator; b. Marion County, Ala., Aug. 16, 1923; s. Robert Lee and Lenora (Vickery) B.; m. Cala Sue Reid, Mar. 27, 1969; 1 dau., Harriet Seretha. B.S., Florence State U., 1950; M.A., George Peabody Coll., 1952; Ph.D., La. State U., 1961. Tchr. East Central Jr. Coll., 1952-58; asst. prof. La. State U. at New Orleans, 1961-63; dean Sch. Bus. of N.E. La. State U., 1963-64; prof. econs., dir. div. research La. State U. at New Orleans, 1964-69, prof. econs., dean Grad. Sch., 1969-78; dean faculties U. South Ala., Mobile, 1978-79, prof. econs., v.p. for acad. affairs, 1979—; on leave as exec. dir. Met. Goals Found. Council, 1970-71; cons. Served with AUS, 1943-46. Mem. Am., So. econ. assns., Regional Sci. Assn., South Western Social Sci. Assn. Home: 1613 Sugar Creek Dr W Mobile AL 36609

BOBROFF, HAROLD, lawyer; b. Bronx, N.Y., Apr. 29, 1920; s. Max and Mary (Platofsky) B.; m. Marion Hemendinger, Nov. 25, 1945; children: Caren Spital, Fredric Jon. B.B.A., City U. N.Y., 1947; J.D., N.Y. Law Sch., N.Y.C., 1951. Bar: N.Y. State 1952. Partner Bobroff & Olonoff (C.P.A.s), 1949-51, 52-61; auditor U.S. Army Audit Agy., N.Y.C., 1951-52; partner firm Bobroff, Olonoff & Scharf, N.Y.C., 1962—; chief dep. county atty., Nassau County, N.Y., 1962-63; chief counsel joint legis. com. on ins. N.Y. State Legislature, 1965-67; chief counsel com. on intergovt. relations N.Y. State Constl. Conv., 1967. Financial sec. Nassau County Democratic Com., 1973; former chmn. bd. Trustees Nassau Community Coll. Served with AUS, 1942-45. Decorated Bronze Star medal with oak leaf cluster, Presdl. Unit citation with oak leaf cluster, Belgium Fouraggere.; Honored by United Jewish Appeal Fedn. Mem. B'nai B'rith. Jewish (past pres. temple). Club: Mason. Home: 795 Hampton Rd Woodmere NY 11598 Office: 122 E 42d St New York NY 10017

BOBROW, DAVIS BERNARD, political science educator; b. Boston, Sept. 2, 1936; s. Robert and Elizabeth (Gelf) B. B.A. in Gen. Edn. (Ford Found. scholar), U. Chgo., 1955, 1956, Queen's Coll., Oxford U., 1958; Ph.D. (Social Sci. Research Council fellow), Mass. Inst. Tech., 1962. Lectr. dept. politics Princeton, 1961-62, asst. prof., 1962-64; sr. social scientist dir.'s div. Oak Ridge Nat. Lab., 1964-68; acting dir. Behavioral Scis. Office, Advanced Research Projects Agy., 1969-70; spl. asst. behavioral and social scis. Office of Dir. Def. Research and Engring., 1968-70; prof. dept. polit. sci. Sch. Pub. Affairs, U. Minn., Mpls., 1970-74; dir. Quigley Center Internat. Studies, 1970-74; prof., chmn. dept. govt. and politics U. Md., College Park, 1974-77, prof., 1977—; vis. Fulbright prof. Tel Aviv U., 1979-80; vis. research prof. Inst. Policy Sci., Saitama U., 1982-83; professorial lectr. Sch. Advanced Internat. Studies, Johns Hopkins, 1970; Mem. Def. Sci. Bd., 1972—; mem. polit. sci. panel NSF, 1976-78; Mem. USAF Sci. Adv. Bd., 1971-76; mem. com. energy and environment Nat. Acad. Scis.-NRC, 1974-77. Author: International Relations: New Approaches, 1972; co-author: Understanding Foreign Policy Decisions: The Chinese Case, 1979; Editor, co-author: Components of Defense Policy, 1965, Weapons System Decisions: Political and Psychological Perspectives on Continental Defense, 1969; co-editor, co-author: Computers and the Policy-Making Community: Applications to International Relations, 1968; asso. editor: Policy Sciences, 1969-80; editorial asso.: Public Opinion Quar, 1963-64; editorial bd.: Jour. Conflict Resolution, 1972—. Home: 256 8th St SE Washington DC 20003

BOCCARDI, LOUIS DONALD, news exec.; b. Bronx, N.Y., Aug. 26, 1937; s. Louis and Delphine (Albanesi) B.; m. Joan M. Quinlan, Jan. 18, 1964; children—Susan, Lynn, Paul, Mark, Lauren. B.A., Fordham Coll., 1958; B.S., Columbia U. Grad. Sch. Journalism, 1959. Reporter/desk editor N.Y. World Telegram & Sun, 1959-64; asst. mng. editor N.Y. World Jour. Tribune, 1966-67; asst. gen. news editor AP, 1967-69, mng. editor, 1969-73, v.p., exec. editor, N.Y.C., 1973—; adj. prof. journalism Fordham Coll., 1966-73; juror Pulitzer Prize, 1975. Served with U.S. Army, 1959-60. Recipient Alumni Achievement award Fordham Coll., 1967, Outstanding Alumnus award Fordham U., 1968. Mem. Council Fgn. Relations, Am. Newspaper Pubs. Assn. (news research com.), Newspaper Readership Council. Office: 50 Rockefeller Plaza New York NY 10020

BOCCARDO, JAMES FREDERICK, lawyer; b. San Francisco, July 1, 1911; s. John H. and Erminia Gemma Ferrando B.; m. Lorraine V. Dimmett, Nov. 21, 1936; children—Leanne (Mrs. Thomas Rees), John H. II. A.B., San Jose State U., 1931; LL.B., J.D., Stanford, 1934. Bar: Calif. bar 1934. Practice law, San Jose, 1934—, San Francisco, 1964, Los Angeles, 1964, Irvine, Calif., 1977—, also Washington; founder, chmn. bd. Community Bank San Jose, 1963—. Mem. Inner Circle of Advocates (co-founder, pres.). Clubs: Elk, Mason (Shriner), Monterey Peninsula Country, San Jose Country, La Rinconada Country, Indian Wells Country; Thunderbird Country (Palm Springs, Calif.). Home: 17020 Wildway Los Gatos CA 95030 also 40941 Tonopah Rd Rancho Mirage CA 92270 also 17-Mile Dr Pebble Beach CA Office: Community Bank Bldg San Jose 111 W St John St San Jose CA 95115

BOCHNER, MEL, artist; b. Pitts., 1940. B.F.A., Carnegie Inst. Tech., 1962. Instr. Sch. Visual Arts. Exhibited one-man shows, Galerie Heiner Friedrich, Munich, Galerie Konrad Fischer, Dusseldorf, Germany, Ace Gallery, Los Angeles, 1969, Galleria Sperone, Torino, Italy, 1970, Galleria Toselli, Milan, Italy, Mus. Modern Art, N.Y.C., 1971, Galerie Sonnabend, Paris, 1972, Sonnabend Gallery, N.Y.C., Lisson Gallery, London, Sonnabend Gallery, N.Y.C., 1973, Galerie Sonnabend, Paris, Galerie Sonnabend, Paris, 1974, U. Art Mus., Berkeley, Calif., Sonnabend Gallery, N.Y.C., 1976, Balt. Mus. Art, Bernier Gallery, Athens, 1977, Gallerie Schema, Milan and Florence, Italy, 1978, Galerie Sonnabend, Paris, Galerie Art in Progress, Dusseldorf, Germany, 1979, Sonnabend Gallery, N.Y.C., 1980, Daniel Weinberg Gallery, San Francisco, 1981, Sonnabend Gallery, N.Y.C., 1982, Centre Internat. de Creation Artistique, Abbaye de Senanque, Gordes, France, Yarlow Salzman Gallery, Toronto, 1983, Daniel WeinbergGallery, San Francisco, Pace Editions, N.Y.C., Sonnabend Gallery, N.Y.C., group shows, Finch Coll. Mus. Art, 1967, Paula Cooper Gallery, N.Y.C., 1968, Seattle Art Mus., 1969, Mus. Modern Art, N.Y.C., 1970, Museo Civico D'Arte Moderna, Turin, Italy, Gallery Nachet St. Stephen, Innsbruck, 1971, Spoleto Festival, Itlay, 1972, Documenta V. Kassel, Germany, Sonnabend Gallery, N.Y.C., Kunstmuseum, Basel, Switzerland, Fogg Mus., Harvard U., Cambridge, Mass., 1973, Seattle Art Mus., Seattle, Whitney Mus. Am. Art, N.Y.C., Princeton Art Mus., 1974, Art Inst. Chgo., Mus. Modern Art, N.Y.C., 1975, Am. Drawings' Mus., Leverkusen, Art Gallery Ont., Mus. Modern Art, N.Y.C., 1976, Chgo. Art Inst., Fort Worth Mus., Detroit Inst. Art, groups shows, Whitney Mus. Am. Art, N.Y.C., 1977, group shows, Mus. Contemporary Art, Chgo., 1977, Sonnabend Gallery, N.Y.C., Phila. Mus. Art, 1978, Leo Castelli Gallery, Whitney Mus. Am. Art, N.Y.C., 1979, Palazzo Reale, Milan, Italy, W Centre Georges Pomipdou, Beauborg, Paris, MIT, 1980, Sonnabend Gallery, N.Y.C., 1981, Beaubourg Centre Nationale d'Art et de Culture, 1981-82, gorup shows, Centre Georges Pompidou, 1981-82, group shows, Chgo. Art Inst., 1982, Yale U. Art Gallery, Whitney Mus. Am. Art, N.Y.C., 1983; represented permanent collections, Los Angeles County Mus., Mus. Nat. d'Art Moderne, Paris; film Walking a Straight Line Through Grand Central Station, 1965, N.Y.C. Windows, 1965, Dorothea in Fifteen Positions Stasis, 1970; contbr. articles in field to profl. jours. Office: Sonnabend Gallery 420 W Broadway New York NY 10012 *

BOCK, EDWARD JOHN, chemical manufacturing company executive; b. Ft. Dodge, Iowa, Sept. 1, 1916; s. Edward J. and Maude (Juday) B.; m. Ruth Kunerth, Aug. 9, 1941; children: Barbara (Mrs. J.E. Lundstrom), Edward, Nancy (Mrs. Stephen Percy), Roger. M.S. in Mech. Engring, Iowa State U., 1940. With Monsanto Co., St. Louis, 1941—, asst. gen. mgr., 1958-60, v.p., gen. mgr., 1960-65, v.p. adminstrn., mem. exec. com., dir., 1965-68, pres., chief exec. officer, chmn. corp. mgmt. and exec. coms., dir., 1968-72; now cons.; chmn. bd., chief exec. officer Cupples Co. (mfrs.), St. Louis, 1975—; dir. Meyer Blanke Co., Harbour Group Ltd., Midcoast Aviation Inc., InterNorth Omaha. Trustee Deaconess Hosp.; chmn. bd. trustees, 1972, Ladue Chapel; bd. govs. Iowa State U. Found. Recipient Silver Anniversary All-Am. Football award Sports Illustrated, 1963; Anston Marston award Iowa State U., 1972; Significant Sig award, 1971; named to All Am. Football Team, 1938; elected to Nat. Football Found. Hall of Fame, 1970. Mem. ASME, Sigma Chi, Tau Beta Pi. Clubs: St. Louis, Old Warson Country (pres. 1972), Bogey.). Home: 7 Huntleigh Woods Saint Louis MO 63131 Office: 7700 Clayton Rd Suite 201 Saint Louis MO 63117

BOCK, JERRY (JERROLD LEWIS), composer; b. New Haven, Nov. 23, 1928; s. George Joseph and Rebecca (Alpert) B.; m. Patricia Faggen, May 28, 1950; children: George Albert, Portia Fane. Student, U. Wis., 1945-49. Writer: score for high sch. mus. comedy My Dream, 1945; score for original coll. musical Big as Life, 1948; wrote: songs for TV show Admiral Broadway Revue, also Show of Shows, 1949-51; composer songs, Camp Tamiment, summers 1950, 51, 53; writer: continuity sketches Mel Torme show, CBS, 1951, 52; writing staff: Kate Smith Hour, 1953-54; writer: original songs for night club performers, including night club revue Confetti; wrote: songs for Wonders of Manhattan (hon. mention Cannes Film Festival 1956); composer: music for Broadway show Catch a Star, 1955, Mr. Wonderful, 1956, (collaborated with Sheldon Harnick on) The Body Beautiful, 1958, Fiorello, 1959 (Pulitzer prize, Drama Critics award, Antoinette Perry award), Tenderloin, 1960, She Loves Me, 1963, The Apple Tree, 1966, The Rothschilds, 1972; London prodn. of She Loves Me, 1964, off-Broadway, 1982; London prodn. of Fiddler on the Roof, 1964 (Tony award); wrote: series of children's songs now pub. under title Sing Something Special; also recorded album, N.Y. Bd. Edn., radio broadcasts, 1961—. Mem. Wilderness Soc., Hort. Soc. N.Y., Broadcast Music Inc., ACLU. *

BOCK, JOSEPH RETO, industrial relations executive; b. Phillipsburg, N.J., June 19, 1929; s. Guy and Anne (Reto) B.; m. Barbara L. Donovan, Feb. 6, 1954. B.S., Seton Hall U., 1950; J.D., Fordham U., 1953; LL.M., Temple U., 1958. Bar: Pa. 1961. Mgmt. cons. C.W. Farmer, Allentown, Pa., 1957-62; labor relations asst. N.J. Zinc Co., N.Y.C., 1962; corp. personnel mgr. Hess Oil & Chem. Co., Perth Amboy, N.J., 1962-64; asst. to dir. indsl. relations Am. House Products Corp., N.Y.C., 1964-67, asst. dir. indsl. relations, 1967-70; assoc. dir. Am. Home Products Corp., N.Y.C., 1970-72, asst. v.p., 1972-77, v.p. indsl. relations, 1977—. Trustee Warren Hosp., Phillipsburg, N.J., 1982—. Served to capt. USMC, 1954-56. Mem. ABA, Pa. Bar Assn., Northampton County Bar Assn. Office: Am Home Products Corp 685 3d Ave New York NY 10017

BOCK, ROBERT HOWARD, university administrator; b. Chgo., Feb. 1, 1932; s. Ralph Edward and Gertrude (Lux) B.; children: Mark, Andrew, Natalie. B.S., Purdue U., 1954, M.S., 1955, Ph.D., 1960. Instr. indsl. adminstrn. Purdue U., 1957-60; asst. prof., asso. prof. Grad. Sch. Bus., Northwestern U., 1960-65; v.p., dean U. Puget Sound, Tacoma, 1965- 69; dean Sch. Bus. Adminstrn., U. Miami, Fla., 1969-72, Grad. Sch. Bus., U. Wis.-Madison, 1972-84. Author: Production Planning and Control, 1963. Bd. dirs. Madison Gen. Hosp. Served with USAF, 1955-57. Club: Rotarian. Home: 3132 Waucheeta Trail Madison WI 53711

BOCK, ROBERT M., univ. dean; b. Preston, Minn., July 26, 1923; s. Glen E. and Hilda (Snyder) B.; m. Ruth Golbien, Sept. 21, 1947; children—Karen, Susan. B.S., U. Wis., 1949, Ph.D. in Chemistry, 1952; postgrad., Calif. Inst. Tech., 1955, Cambridge (Eng.) U., 1961. Mem. faculty U. Wis., Madison, 1952—, prof. molecular biology, 1965—, dean, 1967—; mem. exec. com. Nat. Assn. State U. and Land Grant Colls., 1979, chmn. council on research policy and grad. edn., 1978; chmn. com. on young research faculty in sci. and engring. NRC, 1979. Contbr. profl. jours. Sci. adviser Gov. of Wis., 1969—. Mem. Am. Chem. Soc. (chmn. div. biol. chemistry 1974—), Soc. Exptl. Biologists (chmn. public affairs com.), Assn. Grad. Schs. (pres. 1972-73), Sigma Xi (pres. Wis. Soc. 1972). Home: 4816 Hillview Terr Madison WI 53706

BOCK, RUSSELL SAMUEL, author; b. Spokane, Wash., Nov. 24, 1905; s. Alva and Elizabeth (Mellinger) B.; children: Suzanne Ray, Beverly A. Bock Wunderlich, James Russell. B.B.A., U. Wash., 1929. Part-time instr. U. So. Calif., UCLA, 1942-50; with Ernst & Ernst, C.P.A.s, Los Angeles, 1938; ptnr. Ernst & Ernst (C.P.A.'s), 1951-69, cons., 1969—. Author: Guidebook to California Taxes, annually, 1950—, Taxes of Hawaii, annually, 1964—; also numerous articles. Dir., treas. Community TV So. Calif., 1964-74; dir., v.p., treas. So. Calif. Symphony-Hollywood Bowl Assn., 1964-70; trustee Internat. Center for Ednl. Devel., 1969-72, Claremont Men's Coll., 1964-70; bd. dirs. Community Arts Music Assn., 1974-76, 78—, Santa Barbara Symphony Assn., 1976-78, Santa Barbara Boys Club, 1980—, UCSB Affiliates, 1983—. Mem. Am. Inst. C.P.A.s (council 1953-57, trial bd. 1955-58, v.p. 1959-60), Calif. Soc. C.P.A.s (past pres.), Los Angeles C. of C. (dir. 1957-65, v.p. 1963), Sigma Phi Epsilon, Beta Alpha Psi, Beta Gamma Sigma. Clubs: Birnam Wood Golf, Santa Barbara Yacht. Office: 1398 Plaza Pacifica Santa Barbara CA 93108

BOCK, WALTER JOSEPH, educator; b. N.Y.C., Nov. 20, 1933; s. Paul and Anne (Kalsch) B.; m. Katharine Lippitt, June 29, 1957; children: Katharine Rose, Susan Ruth, Walter David. B.S., Cornell U., 1955; M.A., Harvard U., 1957, Ph.D., 1959. NSF postdoctoral fellow Universität Frankfurt Main, 1959-61; asst. prof. dept. zoology U. Ill., 1961-64, asso. prof., 1964-65; asst. prof. dept. biol. scis. Columbia U., 1965-66, asso. prof., 1966-73, prof., 1973—; research asso. Am. Mus Natural History, 1965—. Author: (with J.J. Morony and J. Farrand) Reference List of the Birds of the World, 1975; Contbr. articles to profl. jours. Pres. Tenafly (N.J.) Nature Center, 1977-80. NSF grantee, 1962-79. Mem. Am. Ornithologists Union (Coues award 1975), Am. Soc. Zoologists, Am. Soc. Naturalists (treas. 1978-80), Soc. Study Evolution, Soc. Systematic Zoology, AAAS, Brit. Ornithologists Union, Deutschen Ornithologen-Gesellschaft. Home: 114 Hudson Ave Tenafly NJ 07670 Office: Dept Biological Sciences Columbia U New York NY 10027 *Humans are not independent of the earth's environment in which they live and of their evolutionary history. As a scholar, I hope to learn about evolutionary and ecological mechanisms; as a teacher I hope to pass this knowledge on to others; and as a person I hope to preserve and enjoy the beauty of nature that exists about us.*

BOCK, WILLIAM RICHARD, JR., insurance company executive; b. Glen Ridge, N.J., Aug. 26, 1939; s. William Richard and Hildegard (Brandt) B.; m. Susan Elizabeth Lambert, Dec. 26, 1960; 1 dau., Lisa Anne. B.S., Ohio State U., 1961; M.B.A., U. Richmond, 1963. Archtl. sales rep. Armstrong Cork Co., Lancaster, Pa., 1963-66; brokerage cons. Conn. Gen. Life Ins. Co., Phila., 1966; prodn. and sales coordinator Container Corp., Oaks, Pa., 1966-67; personnel and operational dir. Lybrand, Ross Bros., Phila., 1967-72; sr. v.p., sec. Home Life Ins. Co., N.Y.C., 1972—; trustee Life Office Mgmt. Assn.; ins. personnel adv. com. Coll. of Ins. of N Coll. of Ins. of N.Y. Mem. bd. Basking Ridge, Republican Com. Served to 1st lt. U.S. Army, 1961-63. Mem. N.Y. Personnel Mgmt. Assn., N.Y. C. of C. and Industry. Club: Merchant's. Office: 253 Broadway New York NY 10007 *

BOCKELMAN, JOHN RICHARD, lawyer; b. Chgo., Aug. 8, 1925; s. Carl August and Mary (Ritchie) B. Student, U. Wis., 1943-44, Northwestern U., 1944-45, Harvard U., 1945, U. Hawaii, 1946; B.S. in Bus. Adminstrn, Northwestern U., 1946; M.A. in Econs, U. Chgo., 1949, J.D., 1951. Bar: Ill. 1951. Atty.-advisor Chgo. ops. office AEC, 1951-52; asso. firm Schradzke, Gould & Ratner, Chgo., 1952-57, Brown, Dashow & Langeluttig, 1957-59, Antonow & Weissbourd, 1959-61; partner firm Burton, Isaacs, Bockelman & Miller, Chgo., 1961-69; individual practice law, Chgo., 1970—; prof. bus. law Ill. Inst. Tech., Chgo., 1950-82; lectr. econs. DePaul U., Chgo., 1952-53; dir., v.p., sec. Secretaries, Inc., Beale Travel Service, Inc; dir., sec. Arlington Engring. Co.; dir., v.p. Universal Distbrs., Inc. Served with USNR, 1943-46. Mem. Am. Bar Assn., Ill. Bar Assn., Chgo. Bar Assn., Cath. Lawyers Guild Chgo., Phi Delta Theta. Clubs: Lake Point Tower, Barclay Ltd., Whitehall, Internat. (Chgo.); Anvil (East Dundee, Ill.). Home: 1212 Lake Shore Dr Chicago IL 60610 Office: 69 W Washington St Chicago IL 60602

BOCKHOFF, FRANK JAMES, educator; b. Tiffin, Ohio, Mar. 26, 1928; s. Cornelius F. and Helen O. (Bormuth) B.; m. Esther I. Camperchioli, Jan. 27, 1951; children—Frank Matthew, Susan Virginia, Celia Marie, James Paul. B.S., Case Inst. Tech., 1950; M.S., Case Western Res. U., 1952, Ph.D., 1959. Registered profl. engr., Ohio. Grad. asst. Case Western Res. U., 1950-51; instr. Fenn Coll., Cleve., 1951-54, asst. prof., 1954-60, asso. prof., 1960-62, chmn. chemistry, 1962-65; prof., chmn. chemistry Cleve. State U., 1965—; Tech. cons. Am. Agile Corp., Bedford, Ohio, 1953-56, asso. dir. research, devel., 1956-61; cons., dir. Signal Chem. Mfg. Co., Bedford, 1960-62, Reox Corp., Cleve., 1962-69; cons. Apex Reinforced Plastics, Cleve., 1961-63. Author: Welding of Plastics, 1959, Elements of Quantum Theory, 1969, 2d edit., 1976; Contbr. articles and revs. profl. jours. Trustee Northeastern Ohio Sci. Fair, 1961-64. Named Outstanding Engring. Tchr. Ohio sect. Am. Soc. E.E., 1960; recipient Tech. Achievement award Cleve. Tech. Soc. Council, 1961; Disting. Faculty award Cleve. State U., 1965; Outstanding Faculty award, 1980. Fellow Am. Inst. Chemists; mem. AAAS, Am. Chem. Soc., Sigma Xi, Tau Beta Pi, Alpha Chi Sigma. Home: Dept of Chemistry Cleveland State Univ Cleveland OH 44115

BOCKHOP, CLARENCE WILLIAM, agrl. engr.; b. Paullina, Iowa, Mar. 28, 1921; s. Fred Henry and Sophie Dorothea (Laue) B.; m. Virginia Buhman, July 9, 1949; children—Barbara Lucille, Nancy Jeanne, Bryan William, Karl David. B.S. in Agrl. Engring, Iowa State U., 1943, M.S., 1955, Ph.D. in Agr. Engring. and Theoretical and Applied Mechanics, 1957. Service and edn. mgr. Stewart Co., Dallas, 1948-53; mem. faculty Iowa State U., Ames, 1953-57, 60-80, prof. agrl. engring., 1960-80, head dept., 1962-80; head dept. agrl. engring. Internat. Rice Research Inst., Los Banos, Philippines, 1980—; prof., head dept. agrl. engineering U. Tenn., 1957-60; vis. prof. U. Ghana, 1969-70. Gen. reporter, VIth Internat. Congress Agrl. Engring., Lausanne, Switzerland, 1964; Author articles in field. Served to capt. AUS, 1943-48. Fellow Am. Soc. Agrl. Engrs. (chmn. Tenn. sect. 1958-59, chmn. mid-central sect. 1960-61, chmn. Iowa sect. 1963-64, chmn. edn. and research div. 1966-67, dir. 1973-75); mem. Am. Soc. Engring. Edn. (chmn. agrl. engring. div. 1966-67), Sigma Xi, Gamma Sigma Delta, Phi Kappa Phi, Phi Mu Alpha, Tau Beta Pi. Lutheran. Office: Internat Rice Research Inst Box 933 Manila Philippines

BOCKMAN, MARILYN MODERN, information executive; b. New Orleans; d. Ruben and Acelie (Nunez) Modern; m. Sigurd S. Bockman, Sept. 13, 1968. B.S., Columbia U., 1951, M.S. in L.S, 1955. Tchr.-librarian Belle Chasse (La.) High Sch., 1951-54; asst. info. specialist Am. Petroleum Inst., N.Y.C., 1955; mgr. info. center Arabian Am. Oil Co., N.Y.C., 1955-59; mgr. info. service Am. Assn. Advt. Agencies, N.Y.C., 1960-65, staff exec., dir., mem. info. service, 1965—, v.p. info., research, internat,, 1978—; mem. U.S. Dept. Commerce-Industry Sector Adv. Com., 1980—. Mem. Spl. Libraries Assn. (pres. N.Y. 1963-64, chmn. advt. and mktg. div. 1969-70), Am. Soc. Info. Sci., Am. Mgmt. Assn., Bank Mktg. Assn., Am. Mktg. Assn., U.S. Council for Internat. Bus., Advt. Women N.Y., Women in Communications, Alpha Xi Delta. Democrat. Roman Catholic. Home: 301 E 66th St New York NY 10021 Office: 666 3d Ave New York NY 10017

BODANSKY, DAVID, physicist, educator; b. N.Y.C., Mar. 10, 1924; s. Aaron and Marie (Syrkin) B.; m. Beverly Ferne Bronstein, Sept. 7, 1952; children: Joel N., Daniel M. B.S., Harvard U., 1943, M.A., 1948, Ph.D., 1950. Instr. physics Columbia U., N.Y.C., 1950-52, asso., 1952-54; mem. faculty U. Wash., Seattle, 1954—, asso. prof. physics, 1958-63, prof., 1963—, chmn. dept., 1976—. Author: (with Fred H. Schmidt) The Energy Controversy: The Fight over Nuclear Power, 1976; Editorial bd.: Rev. Sci. Instruments, 1967-69. Served with AUS, 1943-46. Sloan Research fellow, 1959-63; Guggenheim fellow, 1966-67, 74-75. Fellow Am. Phys. Soc.; mem. Am. Assn. Physics Tchrs., AAAS, Am. Nuclear Soc., Phi Beta Kappa. Research in nuclear physics, nuclear astrophysics and energy policy. Office: Dept Physics U Wash Seattle WA 98195

BODANSZKY, MIKLOS, chemist; b. Budapest, Hungary, May 21, 1915; came to U.S., 1957, naturalized, 1964; s. Lajos and Maria (Friedner) B.; m. Agnes A. Vadasz, Apr. 21, 1950; 1 dau., Eva. Diploma chem. engring, Tech. U. Budapest, 1939, D.Sc., 1949. Sr. lectr. Tech. U. Budapest, 1950-56; research asso. Cornell U. Med. Coll., 1957-59; sr. research asso. Squibb Inst. Med. Research, New Brunswick, N.J., 1959-66; prof. chemistry and biochemistry Case Western Res. U., Cleve., 1966—, Charles Frederic Mabery prof. research in chemistry, 1978—. Author: Peptide Synthesis, 1966, 2d edit., 1976; Editorial bd.: Jour. Antibiotics, 1971—, Internat. Jour. Peptide Protein Research, 1978—. Recipient Pierce award, 1977; Morley medal, 1978; A. von Humboldt award, 1979. Mem. Am., Swiss chem. socs., Am. Soc. Biol. Chemistry, Chem. Soc. London, Antibiotic Research Assn. Japan. Research in Nitrophenyl ester method of peptide synthesis, 1954; first synthesis gastrointestinal hormone secretin, 1966; synthesis vasoactive intestinal peptide, 1973. Office: Dept Chemistry Case Western Res Univ Adelbert Rd Cleveland OH 44106

BODDE, WILLIAM, JR., foreign service officer; b. Bklyn., Nov. 27, 1931; s. William and Georgiana B.; m. Ingrid Oberle, Jan. 16, 1954; children: Barbara, Peter William, Christopher Scott. B.A., Hofstra Coll., Hempstead, N.Y., 1961; postgrad., Johns Hopkins U., 1966-67. Joined U.S. Fgn. Service, 1962; service in, Vienna, Austria, Stockholm, W.Berlin and Bonn, W. Ger.; dir. Office Pacific Island Affairs, Dept. State, 1978-80; ambassador to, Fiji, Tonga and Tuvalu, also minister to, Kiribati, 1980-83, consul gen., Frankfort, W.Ger., 1983—; U.S. rep. South Pacific Commn. Author articles in field. Served with USAR, 1951-54. Recipient Meritorious Honor award Dept. State, 1977. Mem. Am. Fgn. Service Assn. Address: APO New York NY 09757 *

BODDEN, WILLIAM MICHAEL, publishing company executive; b. Lafayette, Ind., Oct. 15, 1929; s. William Albert and Dorothy Catherine (Schlacks) B.; m. Louise-Marie Therese Longpre, June 12, 1951; children—Susan Louise, Michael Peter, Sarah Longpre, Jacob Andrew. B.A., Yale, 1951; M.B.A., U. Pa., 1953. With Houghton Mifflin Co., Boston, 1956—, prodn. mgr., 1963-70, mgr. art and prodn. depts., 1970-74, v.p., 1974—; Lectr. on pub. Harvard Grad. Sch. Bus. Adminstrn., 1968, Radcliffe Coll., 1968, 69; visitor Boston Mus. Fine Arts, 1966. Contbr. articles to bus. and mil. jours. Mem. Town Meeting, Wellesley, Mass., 1972-80; pres. Wellesley Sr. High Sch. P.T.A., 1974-75; trustee Wellesley Free Library, 1969-75, chmn., 1972-74; mem. Friends of Wellesley Free Library, 1964—, pres., 1967-69; Yale class agt., 1975—, alumni schs. com., 1978—; lay mass reader St. Paul's Ch.; vol. instr. Project Bus.; reader Mass. Assn. for Blind. Served to lt. (j.g.) Supply Corps USNR, 1953-56; now comdr. Res. ret. Mem. Soc. Printers Boston (pres. 1972-74), New Eng. Printing and Pub. Council (gen. chmn. 1969-70), Bookbuilders of Boston (pres. 1964-66, William A. Dwiggins award 1974), Am. Inst. Graphic Arts (dir. 1971-74), Assn. Am. Pubs. (chmn. textbook specifications com. 1978-80), Assoc. Grantsmakers of Mass. (bd. dirs. 1983—), Wellesley Tennis Assn. (treas. 1974-77). Republican. Roman Catholic. Home: 23 Cornell Rd Wellesley MA 02181 Office: 1 Beacon St Boston MA 02107

BODDIGER, GEORGE CYRUS, insurance company executive; b. Polo, Ill., July 5, 1917; s. George E. and Bertha Belle (Billig) B.; m. Wilma Helen Ray, May 23, 1943; children: Nancy Boddiger Estrada, Jean Boddiger Petrie, Kathryn Boddiger Jones. B.S., U. Ill., 1939; M.B.A. with distinction, Harvard U., 1943. C.L.U. Various positions Mut. of Omaha, Omaha, 1952-59; pres., dir. Pacific Fidelity Life Ins. Co., Los Angeles, 1959-71, Equitable Life Ins. Co., Washington, 1971—, vice chmn., dir., 1982—; dir. Gulf United Corp., NS&T Bank,

NS&T Bank Shares Inc. Mem. nat. council Pomona Coll.; bd. dirs. Nat. Multiple Sclerosis Soc.; trustee Nat. Capital Multiple Sclerosis Soc.; pres. Internat. Fedn. Multiple Sclerosis Socs.; elder Potomac Presbyterian Ch. Served with AUS, 1943-46. Recipient Hope Chest award Nat. Multiple Sclerosis Soc., Bess Goodman Humanitarian award. Fellow Life Mgmt. Inst.; mem. Harvard Bus. Sch. Club Washington (chmn., dir.), Sigma Alpha Epsilon. Clubs: Congressional Country (Bethesda, Md.); Met. (Washington). Home: 9901 Kentsdale Dr Potomac MD 20854 Office: 8300 Greensboro Dr PO Box 900 McLean VA 22101

BODE, BARBARA, foundation executive; b. Evanston, Ill., Aug. 4, 1940; d. Carl and Margaret Emilie (Lutze) B. B.A. magna cum laude, U. Md., 1962, M.A. Woodrow Wilson Nat. Found. fellow1963-64, 1966; scholar, Ludwig-Maximillians-Universitat, Munich, W. Ger., 1960-61; English Speaking Union scholar, U. London, summer 1964; Bundesrepublik scholar, Goethe Institut, Lubeck, W. Ger., summer 1965; postgrad. NDEA fellow, UCLA, 1966-67. Woodrow Wilson teaching fellow N.C. Central U., Durham, 1965-66; community developer Community Devel. Dept. Prince George's County, Md., 1967-68; field dir. Nat. Council Hunger and Malnutrition in U.S., Washington, 1968-70; pres. Children's Found., Washington, 1970—; mem. food industry adv. commn. Fed. Energy Adminstrn., 1975-76. Author: School Lunch Bag, 1971, Barriers to School Breakfast, 1979; contbr. numerous articles to profl. jours. Mem. Citizens Bd. of Inquiry into Brookside Miners Strike, Harlan, Ky., 1974; mem. nat. adv. com. Food Day, 1975, 76, 77, Rural Am. Women, 1978-80, Project VOTE, 1981—; dir., mem. exec. com. Human Services Inst. for Children and Families, 1973-75; bd. dirs., v.p. Am. Freedom from Hunger Found., 1973-78, U.S. Com. on Refugees, 1976-78; dir. RAINBOW TV Works, 1976—, Nat. Council Women, Works and Welfare, 1976-77, Nat. Com. Responsive Philanthropy, 1975—; bd. dirs. Am. Parents Com., 1974-78, Rural America, Inc., 1975-79, Coalition for Children and Youth, 1975-79, FWR Found., 1982—, Human SERVE Found., 1983—, Women's Campaign Fund, 1984—; cons., mem. steering and adv. coms. commns. and organs in field; convenor Nat. Women's Polit. Caucus, 1971; mem. nat. adv. bd. Women's Campaign Fund, 1975-77; active in press bur. Poor People's Campaign, 1968; mem. planning com. Women's Leadership Conf. Dem. Nat. Com., 1972, vice chmn. com. on regional conf. planning and strategy, 1969-70; active voting and civil rights campaigns, 1961—. Named one of ten Outstanding Young Women of Am. various women's orgns., 1977. Mem. Older Women's League, Women's Equity Action League, Washington Women's Network, Women's Nat. Dem. Club. Episcopalian. Office: 1420 New York Ave NW Washington DC 20005

BODE, CARL, educator, writer; b. Milw., Mar. 14, 1911; s. Paul and Celeste Helene (Schmidt) B.; m. Margaret Lutze, Aug. 3, 1938 (dec.); children: Barbara, Janet, Carolyn; m. Charlotte W. Smith, 1972. Ph.B., U. Chgo., 1933; M.A., Northwestern U., 1938, fellow, 1940-41, Ph.D., 1941. Tchr. Milw. Vocat. Sch., 1933-37; asst. prof. English UCLA, 1946-47; prof. English U. Md., College Park, 1947-82, exec. sec. Am. Civilization program, 1950-57; cultural attache Am. embassy, London, 1957-59 (on leave from U. Md); chmn. U.S. Ednl. Commn. in, U.K., 1957-59; vis. prof. Calif. Inst. Tech., Claremont Colls., Northwestern U., U. Wis., Stanford. Author: poems The Sacred Seasons, 1953, reprinted, 1971, The American Lyceum, 1956 (paperback 1968), The Man Behind You, 1959, The Anatomy of American Popular Culture, 1840-1861, 1959 (repub. as Antebellum Culture, 1970), The Half-World of American Culture, 1965; Mencken, 1969, Highly Irregular (newspaper columns), 1974, Maryland: A Bicentennial History, 1978; poems Practical Magic, 1981; Maryland, 1983; Editor: Collected Poems of Henry Thoreau, 1943, enlarged edit., 1964, The Portable Thoreau, 1947, rev. edit., 1964, American Life in the 1840s, 1967, The Selected Journals of Henry David Thoreau, 1967, (hardcover version The Best of Thoreau's Journals, 1971), Ralph Waldo Emerson, A Profile, 1969, Midcentury America: Life in the 1850's, 1972, The Young Mencken, 1973, The New Mencken Letters, 1977, Barnum, Struggles and Triumphs, 1982; Co-editor: American Heritage, 2 vols., 1955, The Correspondence of Henry David Thoreau, 1958, American Literature, 3 vols, 1966, The Portable Emerson, 1981; Editor and contbr.: The Young Rebel in American Literature, 1959, The Great Experiment in American Literature, 1961; Contbr. articles to encys., poetry and revs. to Brit. and Am. jours.; Columnist: Balt. Evening Sun. Mem. Md. State Arts Council, 1971-79, chmn., 1972-76; mem. Md. Humanities Council, 1981—, Marshall Scholarship Adv. Council, 1960-69. Served with AUS, 1944-45. Ford Found. fellow, 1952-53; Newberry Library fellow, 1954; Guggenheim Found. fellow, 1954-55. Fellow Royal Soc. Lit. U.K. (hon.); mem. AAUP (council 1965-68), Am. Studies Assn. (founder, 1st pres. 1952), Modern Lang. Assn., Thoreau Soc. Am. (dir. 1955-57, pres. 1960-61), Popular Culture Assn. Am. (v.p. 1972-75, pres. 1978-79), Mencken Soc. (founder, 1st pres. 1976-79), Phi Beta Kappa (hon.), Alpha Tau Omega. Democrat. Episcopalian. Clubs: Cosmos (Washington); Hamilton St. (Balt.). Home: 7008 Partridge Pl College Heights Estates Hyattsville MD 20782 Office: Dept English U Md College Park MD 20742

BODE, RICHARD ALBERT, publishing co. exec.; b. Oak Park, Ill., July 26, 1931; s. Charles John and Esther (Burgert) B.; m. Marjorie Ann Lane, July 28, 1962; children—Anne, Julie, John, Ellen, Mary Elizabeth. Student, Loras Coll., 1949-51; B.S.C., DePaul U., 1953; M.B.A., U. Detroit, 1960. C.P.A., Ill. With Baumann, Finney & Co. (pub. accountants), Chgo., 1953-56; staff accountant Nat. Tea Co., Chgo., 1956- 58, divisional controller, Detroit, 1958-62; asst. controller Eagle Food Centers, Rock Island, Ill., 1962-63; comptroller Brinks, Inc., Chgo., 1963-68, treas., 1968-69, v.p., treas., 1970-78; v.p. fin. DLM, Inc., Allen, Tex., 1978—. Mem. Plans Commn. Village of Hinsdale, 1969-75; mem. adv. com. for devel. parish accounting systems Archdiocese of Chgo., 1970. Served with M.C. AUS, 1953-55. Mem. Ill. C.P.A. Soc. (dir. 1976-78). Home: 3321 Hulings Ct Plano TX 75023 Office: One DLM Park Allen TX 75002

BODE, ROBERT W., free-lance art dir., designer, artist; b. N.Y.C., Nov. 20, 1912; s. William L. and Wilhelmina (Talmon) B.; m. Dorothy Lounsbery, Nov. 20, 1937; children—Susan, Glenn. Grad., Sch. Fine and Applied Arts, Pratt Inst., 1933. Art dir. N.Y.C. advt. agencies, 1944-69; now free-lance art designer.; lectr. on art and design. Nat. exhibitor water color shows; designer Davy Crockett, Johnny Appleseed and Energy Conservation stamps for, Post Office Dept. Recipient prizes from nat. and local art shows. Mem. Am. Water Color Soc. (recipient prizes), Soc. Illustrators, Art Dirs. Club N.Y.C. Home: PO Box 917 239 Chatham Rd South Harwich MA 02661

BODEM, DENNIS RICHARD, museum ofcl.; b. Milw., July 27, 1937; s. Frederick William and Helen Margaret (Bandow) B.; m. Beverly Ann Jacobson, Sept. 21, 1963; children—Heather, Dawn, Brent. B.A., Wabash Coll., 1959; postgrad., U. Wis., 1959-61. Asst. archivist Wis. Hist. Soc., Madison, 1961-64; chief, resources div. Buffalo and Erie County Hist. Soc., Buffalo, 1964-66; state archivist Mich. History div. Mich. Dept. of State, Lansing, 1966-72; curator State Mus., 1972-74; dir. Jesse Besser Mus., Alpena, Mich., 1974—; mem. mus. adv. panel Mich. Council Arts, 1976-78. Contbr. articles, revs. to profl. publs. Vice pres. Alpena County unit Am. Cancer Soc., 1978-80; sec. Alpena County Rep. Party, 1979-81. Mem. Soc. Am. Archivists, Am. Records Mgmt. Assn. (founding pres. Mid-Mich. chpt., nat. v.p. region II 1972-74), Nat. Archives (exec. council, chmn. com. Region 5 Adv. Council), Mich. Archival Assn. (exec. council 1970-73), Mich. Museums Assn. (dir. 1975-77, state treas. 1977-79), Hist. Soc. Mich. (trustee 1980—), also nat. and state orgns. Club: Rotary. Home: 121 E White St Alpena MI 49707 Office: 491 Johnson St Alpena MI 49707

BODEMER, CHARLES WILLIAM, scientific historian; b. Denison, Iowa, Jan. 4, 1927; s. Herman and Blanche Orpha (Nicola) B.; m. Sheila Campbell Hedley, June 22, 1948; children: Karen Hedley, Eric Charles, Brett William; m. Susanne Maria Lilja, July 14, 1977. A.A., San Francisco City Coll., 1949; B.A. magna cum laude, Pomona Coll., 1951; M.A., Claremont Grad. Sch., 1952; Ph.D., Cornell U., 1956. Teaching fellow Dartmouth Coll., Hanover, N.H., 1952-53; mem. faculty U. Wash., Seattle, 1956—, prof. biomed. history, 1967—, dir. research tng. program, 1960-65, asso. dean, 1963-67, chmn. dept. biomed. history, 1964—. Author: Modern Embryology, 1968; contbr. articles to profl. jours. Served with USMC, 1944-47. Decorated Purple Heart. Mem. Academie Internationale d'Histoire de la Medecine, Am. Assn. History Medicine (sec.-treas. 1964-71), History Sci. Soc., Am. Assn. Anatomists, Société Internationale d'Histoire de la Medecine, Sigma Xi. Home: 1525 NW 8th St North Bend WA 98045

BODEN, ROBERT FRANCIS, lawyer, educator; b. Milw., June 4, 1928; s. Francis X. and Edith A. (Ebert) B.; m. Patricia M. Gill, July 10, 1954 (dec. Nov. 1979). Ph.B., Marquette U., 1950, J.D., 1952; LL.D., Carthage Coll., 1975. Bar: Wis. bar 1952. Asso. Quarles, Spence & Quarles, Milw., 1952-56; gen. practice, Milw., 1956-63; lectr. Marquette U. Law Sch., 1959-63, asst. prof., 1963-65, asso. prof., 1965-71, prof., 1971—, acting dean, 1965-66, dean, 1966—; editor Wis. Continuing Legal Edn. Jour., 1964-70; Chmn. adminstrn. of justice com. State Bar Wis., 1970-75, research reporter creditor-debtor law revision project, 1971-75; pres. Law Projects, Inc., 1970-76; mem. Gov.'s Spl. Com. on Jud. Orgn., 1971—; Mem. Wis. Judicial Council, 1961-71, chmn., 1963-65; mem. Milw. Police Edn. Study Com., 1967-69; chmn. Wis. Garnishment Law Revision Com., 1968-69, Wis. Supreme Ct. Chief Judge Study Com., 1974-75, Gov.'s Judicial Appointment Adv. Commn., 1978-79. Author: Bankruptcy Practice in Wisconsin, 1966, Wisconsin Creditor-Debtor Law, 1971, Basic Bankruptcy Law, 1973; also contbr. articles to profl. jours. Bd. dirs. Milw. Legal Aid Soc., 1969-74. Fellow Am. Bar Found., mem. (mem. council on legal edn. and bar admission 1970-76, spl. com. on legal assts. 1974-76), Wis. Bar Assn., Milw. Bar Assn., Am. Law Inst., Am. Judicature Soc., Delta Theta Phi, Alpha Sigma Nu. Home: 1404 Lynne Dr Waukesha WI 53186 Office: 1103 W Wisconsin Ave Milwaukee WI 53233 *The law is man's oldest compromise with his own baser animal instincts. A life commitment to the law ought to involve a balanced dedication to reason and precedent and an appreciation that, regardless of the level at which one participates in the system, a meaningful contribution to justice finally depends upon the exercise of right reason, informed by the lessons of history and the jurisprudential wisdom of the past, but applied to modern conditions and the probable requirements of the future. Justice is impossible without good legal scholarship.*

BODENHAMER, WILLIAM TURNER, JR., textile company executive; b. Ty Ty, Ga., Sept. 27, 1937; s. William Turner and Miriam (Brooks) B.; m. Cheryl Dolores Sowell, Sept. 27, 1964; children: William Glynn, Cheryl Elizabeth. Student, Ga. Inst. Tech., 1955-59; postgrad. in bus. adminstrn., Ga. State U., 1980-82. V.p. Barwick Industries, Atlanta, 1967-71; founder, pres. Venture Carpets Ltd., Drummondville, Que., Can., 1971-75; pres. Pioneer Carpet Mills, Morganfield, Ky., 1975-77; sr. v.p. Sweetwater Carpets, Chattanooga, 1977-80; pres., chief exec. officer Harding Carpets Ltd., Toronto, Ont., Can., 1982—; textile and EDP cons. K.S.A., Atlanta, 1966-67; pvt. practice carpet and EDP cons., Chattanooga, 1980-82. Prin. Area Tech. Sch., Marietta, Ga., 1964-66. Mem. Ga. Tech. Edn. Assn. (pres. 1965-66). Baptist. Clubs: Nat. Golf (Toronto); Lookout Mountain (Chattanooga). Home: 1865 Paddock Crescent Mississauga ON Canada L5L 3J5 Office: Harding Carpets Ltd 35 Worcester Rd Rexdale ON Canada M9W 1K9

BODENSTEINER, WAYNE DEAN, naval officer; b. Kansas City, Mo., Oct. 4, 1933; s. Chris and Elsie Anna (Kaeg) B.; m. Sue Green, July 28, 1978; 1 son, Robert Wayne. B.B.A., So. Methodist U., 1954; M.S. in Mgmt., U.S. Navy Postgrad. Sch., Monterey, Calif., 1962-63; Ph.D., U. Tex., 1970. Commd. ensign U.S. Navy, 1954, advanced through grades to rear adm., 1978, comdg. officer Air Antisubmarine Squadron 33, 1970-71; comdg. officer Naval Air Sta., Jacksonville, Fla., 1976-78; dir. undersea welfare and strategic devel. div. Office of Chief of Naval Ops., Dept. Navy, Washington, 1978, now dep. chief naval material acquisition. Author: Infromation Channel Utilization Under Varying Research and Development Project Conditions, 1970. Decorated Air medal. Mem. Exptl. Test Pilot Assn., Phi Kappa Phi, Lambda Chi Alpha. Mem. Ch. of Christ. Home: 5005 King David Blvd Annandale VA 22003 Office: Dept Navy Washington DC 20360

BODEY, GERALD PAUL, physician; b. Hazelton, Pa., May 22, 1934; s. Allen Zartman and Marie Frances (Smith) B.; m. Nancy Louise Wiegner, Aug. 25, 1956; children—Robin Gayle, Gerald Paul, Sharon Dawn. A.B. magna cum laude, Lafayette Coll., 1956; M.D. (Henry Strong Denison fellow), Johns Hopkins, 1960. Diplomate: Nat. Bd. Med. Examiners, Am. Bd. Internal Medicine, also subspecialities oncology and infectious diseases. Intern Osler Med. Service, Johns Hopkins U., Balt., 1960-61, resident, 1961-62; clin. asso. Nat. Cancer Inst., NIH, Bethesda, Md., 1962-65; resident U. Wash., Seattle, 1965-66; internist, prof. medicine U. Tex.-M.D. Anderson Hosp. and Tumor Inst., Houston, 1966—, chief sect. infectious diseases and chemotherapy, 1981—; also med. dir. Cancer Clin. Research Center, 1977-81; prof. medicine U. Tex. Health Sci. Center Grad. Sch. Biomed. Scis., 1969-81, also clin. prof. dental br., 1977—; adj. prof. microbiology, immunology and medicine Baylor Coll. Medicine, Houston, 1969—; prof. medicine and pharmacology U. Tex. Med. Sch., Houston, 1973—; mem. Collaborative Cancer Treatment Research Program, Pan-Am. Health Orgn.; cons. Brooke Gen. Hosp., Brooke Army Med. Center, Fort Sam Houston, Tex., 1971—, Wilford Hall USAF Med. Center, Lackland AFB, Tex., 1975—, Commn. Devel. Comprehensive Cancer Care Center, Panama. Contbr. articles to profl. jours. Leukemia Soc. scholar, 1969-74; NIH grantee, 1966—. Fellow ACP, Royal Soc. Medicine; mem. AMA, Tex. Med. Assn., Harris County Med. Soc., Am. Assn. Cancer Research, Am. Coll. Clin. Pharmacology, Am. Soc. Clin. Oncology, Am. Soc. Hematology, Am. Soc. Microbiology, Infectious Diseases Soc. Am., AAAS, Houston Acad. Medicine, Am. Fedn. Clin. Research, Assn. for Gnotobiotics, S.W. Oncology Group, Am. Soc. Pharmacology and Exptl. Therapeutics, Johns Hopkins Med. and Surg. Assn., Royal Soc. Promotion Health, Internat. Soc. Chemotherapy; Mem. Academia Peruana de Cirugia (hon.), La Asociacion Costarricense de Oncologia (hon.), Sociedade Brasileira de Cancerologia, Am.-Soviet Meetings Cancer Chemotherapy; mem. Phi Beta Kappa., Sigma Xi. Presbyn. Home: 5023 Glenmeadow St Houston TX 77096 Office: MD Anderson Hosp 6723 Bertner St Houston TX 77030 *The ultimate goal of my life is to serve my Lord and Savior, Jesus Christ. I have found the source of an abundant and meaningful life through a personal relationship with God.*

BODIAN, DAVID, educator; b. St. Louis, May 15, 1910; s. Harry and Tillie (Franzel) B.; m. Elinor Widmont, June 26, 1944; children—Helen, Marion, Brenda, Alexander, Marc. B.S., U. Chgo., 1931, Ph.D., 1934, M.D., 1937. Asst. in anatomy U. Chgo., 1935-38; NRC fellow medicine U. Mich., 1938; anatomy Johns Hopkins, 1939- 40; asst. prof. anatomy Western Res. U., 1940-41; research on problems poliomyelitis, faculty dept. epidemiology Johns Hopkins, 1942-57, asso. prof. epidemiology, 1946-57, prof. anatomy, dir. dept., 1957-75, prof. neurobiology dept. otolaryngology, 1975—; tech. com. poliomyelitis vaccine USPHS, 1957-64; vaccine adv. com. Nat. Found., 1956-60; cons. NIH, mem. bd. sci. counselors, div. biol. standards, 1957-59; mem. bd. sci. advisers Nat. Inst. of Neurol. Diseases, 1968—. Author: Neural Mechanisms in Poliomyelitis, 1942; Mng. editor: Am. Jour. Hygiene, 1948-57; mem. editorial bds.: Jour. Comparative Neurology; Contbr. science articles profl. jours. Served as lt. USNR, World War II. Recipient E. Mead Johnson award in pediatrics Am. Acad. Pediatrics, 1941. Mem. Am. Assn. Anatomists (pres. 1971-72), Am. Acad. Arts and Scis., Nat. Acad. Scis., Am. Philos. Soc., A.A.A.S., Am. Physiol. Soc., Neurosci. Soc., Assn. Research Nervous and Mental Diseases, Phi Beta Kappa, Sigma Xi. Researcher on structure and diseases of nervous tissue. Home: 3917 Cloverhill Rd Baltimore MD 21218 Office: 1721 E Madison St Baltimore MD 21205

BODILY, DAVID MARTIN, chemist, educator; b. Logan, Utah, Dec. 16, 1933; s. Levi Delbert and Norma (Christenson) B.; m. Beth Alene Judy, Aug. 28, 1958; children—Robert David, Rebecca Marie, Timothy Andrew, Christopher Mark. Student, Utah State U., 1952-54; B.A., Brigham Young U., 1949, M.A., 1960; Ph.D., Cornell U., 1964. Postdoctoral fellow Northwestern U., Evanston, Ill., 1964-65; asst. prof. chemistry U. Ariz., Tucson, 1965-67; asst. prof. fuels engring. U. Utah, Salt Lake City, 1967-70, asso. prof., 1970-77, prof., 1977—, chmn. dept. mining and fuels engring., 1976—. Contbr. articles to profl. jours. Mem. Am. Chem. Soc. (chmn. Salt Lake sect. 1975), Catalysis Soc. N. Am., Am. Inst. Mining and Metall. Engrs., Sigma Xi. Mormon. Home: 2651 Cecil St Salt Lake City UT 84117 Office: 320 WBB U Utah Salt Lake City UT 84112

BODINE, JAMES FORNEY, civic leader; b. Villanova, Pa., June 16, 1921; s. William Warden and Angela (Forney) B.; m. Jean G. Guthrie, June 25, 1949; children: Jane G., Margaret F., Murray G., Tracy W. B.A., Yale U., 1944; M.B.A., Harvard U., 1948. With First Pa. Bank, Phila., 1948-78, v.p., 1958-63, sr. v.p., 1963-65, exec. v.p., 1965-68, sr. exec. v.p., dir., 1968-72, pres., 1972-77, First Pa. Corp., 1974-78; sec. of commerce, Commonwealth of Pa., 1979-80; mng. partner Urban Affairs Partnership, 1980—. Home: 401 Cypress St Philadelphia PA 19106 Office: 900 Ave of Arts Bldg SE corner Broad and Chestnut Sts Philadelphia PA 19107

BODKIN, HENRY GRATTAN, JR., lawyer; b. Los Angeles, Dec. 8, 1921; s. Henry Grattan and Ruth May (Wallis) B.; m. Mary Louise Davis, June 28, 1943; children: Maureen L. Dixon, Sheila L. Bobrick, Timothy Grattan. B.S. cum laude, Loyola U., Los Angeles, 1943, J.D., 1948. Bar: Calif. 1948. Practiced, Los Angeles, 1948-51, 53—; mem. firm Bodkin, McCarthy, Sargent & Smith (and predecessor), Los Angeles, 1948-51, 53—. Mem. Los Angeles Bd. Water and Power Commrs., 1972-74, pres., 1973-74; Regent Marymount Coll., 1962-67; trustee Loyola-Marymount U., 1967—. Served with USNR, 1943-45, 51-53. Fellow Am. Coll. Trial Lawyers; Mem. Calif. State Bar (mem. exec. com. conf. of dels. 1968-70, vice chmn. 1969-70), Phi Delta Phi. Republican. Roman Catholic. Clubs: Calif., Riviera Tennis, Marina City. Home: 956 Linda Flora Dr Los Angeles CA 90049 Office: Bodkin McCarthy Sargent & Smith 707 Wilshire Blvd Los Angeles CA 90017

BODLE, GEORGE EMERY, lawyer; b. Boise, Idaho, Apr. 12, 1908; s. Joseph Horace and Ada Maude (Neal) B.; m. Rita Wallen, Apr. 5, 1942; children: Mary Stephanie Bodle Kerker, Neal Wallen. A.B., Stanford U., 1930, LL.B., 1933. Bar: Calif. 1934. Practiced in, San Francisco, 1934-37, Los Angeles, 1937—, atty., arbitrator, Los Angeles; gen. counsel Los Angeles County Fedn. Labor, 1948-78; mem. ad hoc com. Nat. Emergency Strikes, 1965-66, 74—, co-chmn., 1974—; fellow Churchill Coll., Cambridge (Eng.) U., mem. faculty law, 1977; lectr. Practising Law Inst., Los Angeles, 1971, Pacific Coast Labor Inst., Seattle, 1974, Inst. Indsl. Relations, UCLA, 1970-74, Stanford Law Sch., 1979-80. Editor: The Courts and the National Labor Relations Act, 1971. Mem. Economy and Efficiency Commn., Los Angeles County, 1973-74, 75—; mem. adv. bd. U. Calif. Extension, 1963-67, chmn., 1980-81; bd. visitors Stanford Law Sch., 1969-72; mem. employee relations bd., City of Los Angeles, 1980—. Served with AUS, 1944-45. Fellow Am. Bar Found.; mem. State Bar Calif. (spl. com. arbitration 1974—), ABA (sect. chmn. labor relations law 1972-73), Los Angeles County Bar Assn. (trustee 1974—), Stanford Law Soc. So. Calif. (pres. 1967). Home: 344 Rossmore Ave S Los Angeles CA 90020 Office: 344 S Rossmore Ave Los Angeles CA 90020

BODMAN, RICHARD STOCKWELL, satellite communications company executive; b. Detroit, Apr. 9, 1938; s. Henry Taylor and Marie Louise (McMillan) B.; m. Helene Kempton Dunn; children: Taylor Stockwell, James Martyn. B.S. in Engring, Princeton, 1959; M.S. in Indsl. Mgmt, Mass. Inst. Tech., 1961. With Touche Ross & Co. (C.P.A.s), San Francisco, 1961-71, partner, 1967-71, chmn. nat. com. services to banks, chmn. long-range plan com. mgmt. con. services, 1969-71; asst. sec. for mgmt. and budget U.S. Dept. Interior, Washington, 1971-73; asst. treas. E.I. duPont de Nemours & Co., Inc., Wilmington, Del., 1973-75, product mgr., 1975, mktg. mgr., 1976, asst. comptroller, 1977-78; sr. v.p. fin. and corp. devel. Communications Satellite Corp., Washington, 1978-80; pres., chief exec. officer Comsat Gen. Corp., Washington, 1980-82; pres. Satellite TV Corp., Washington, 1982—; dir. Emhart Corp., Hartford, Conn.; mem. internat. adv. bd. Am. Security Bank, Washington, 1981—. Bd. dirs. San Francisco Spring Opera Co., 1965-68, Del. Art Mus., 1975-77, Grand Opera House, Wilmington, 1975-77; mem. central selection com. Morehead Found., U. N.C., Chapel Hill., 1972-82; nat. trustee Boys Clubs Am. Clubs: Bohemian (San Francisco); Chevy Chase (Md.) Country; Burning Tree, Met. (Washington). Home: 1336 30th St NW Washington DC 20007 Office: 950 L'Enfant Plaza SW Washington DC 20024

BODMAN, SAMUEL W., III, investment company executive; b. Chgo., Nov. 26, 1938; s. Samuel W. Jr. and Lina (Hervel) B.; children: Elizabeth L., Andrew M., Sarah H. B.S. in Chem. Engring., Cornell U., 1960; Sc.D., MIT, 1964. Tech. dir. Am. Research and Devel., Boston, 1965-70; Prof. and lectr. MIT, Cambridge, Mass., 1964—; v.p. Fieelity Venture Assn., Boston, 1970—, pres., 1974-77, chmn., 1977—; pres. Fidelity Mgmt. and Research Corp., Boston, 1977—, FMR Corp., 1983—; dir. WellTech, Inc., Houston, Addressograph Farrington, Boston, Madrill Inc., Lafayette, La., Modar, Natick, Mass., Continental Cablevision, Boston. Trustee Multiple Sclerosis Soc., Mass. chpt., 1982; corp. mem. Babson coll., Wellesley, Mass., 1982. Mem. Boston C. of C. (dir. 1983). Episcopalian. Home: 22 Longfellow Rd Wellesley MA 02181 Office: Fidelity Mgmt and Research Corp 82 Devonshire St Boston MA 02109

BODMER, ARNOLD RUDOLPH, educator, physicist; b. Frankfurt am/Main, Germany, May 23, 1929; came to U.S., 1963, naturalized, 1978; s. Ernest Julius and Sylvia (Bodmer) B.; m. Doris E. Zerbe, Aug. 14, 1956; children: Edward C.F., Sylvia E., Richard E., Anne D. B.Sc., Manchester (Eng.) U., 1949, Ph.D., 1953. Sci. officer Royal Armament Research and Devel. Establishment, Eng., 1953-56; postdoctoral research fellow Manchester U., 1956-57, lectr., 1958-63; with European Orgn. Nuclear Research, Geneva, Switzerland, 1957-58; physicist, sr. physicist Argonne (Ill.) Nat. Lab., 1963—; prof. physics U. Ill.-Chgo., 1965—; Vis. prof. nuclear physics dept. Oxford (Eng.) U., 1970-71. Contbr. articles to profl. jours. Fellow Am. Phys. Soc. Research in theoretical nuclear physics. Home: 239 55th Pl Downers Grove IL 60516 Office: Dept Physics SES Univ Ill Chicago Chicago IL 60680

BODOR, NICHOLAS STEPHEN, medicinal chemistry researcher, educator, consultant; b. Satu Mare, Transylvania, Romania, Feb. 1, 1939; came to U.S., 1968, naturalized, 1976; s. Miklos Sandor and Berta (Horvath) B.; m. Gyongyver Gorog, Sept. 21, 1961 (div. 1971); 1 son, Miklos; m. Sheryl Lee Reimann, Nov. 26, 1971; children: Nicole, Erik. B.S., M.S. in organic chemistry, Bolyai U., Cluj, Romania, 1959; D. Chemistry, Babes-Bolyai U., Supreme Council of Acad. Sci., Bucharest, Romania, 1965. Prin. investigator Chem. and Pharm. Research Inst., Cluj, 1961-68, 69-70; R.A. Welch postdoctoral fellow U. Tex., Austin, 1968-69, 70-72; sr. research scientist Alza Co., Lawrence, Kans., 1972-73; dir. medicinal chemistry INTERx Research Corp., Lawrence, Kans., 1973-79; adj. prof. U. Kans., 1974-79; prof. medicinal chemistry, chmn. dept. medicinal chemistry U. Fla., Gainesville, 1979-83, grad. research prof. medicinal chemistry, chmn. dept., 1983—; cons. to pharm. cos.; v.p., dir. research Pharmatec, Inc., Arlington Hts., Ill., 1983—. Author numerous publs. in field. Grantee NIH, 1976-83. Fellow Acad. Pharm. Sci.; mem. Am. Chem. Soc., Am. Pharm. Assn. Home: 7211 SW 97th Ln Gainesville FL 32608 Office: Dept Medicinal Chemistry Box J-4 J H M Health Ctr U Fla Gainesville Fla 32610 *A multidisciplinary approach is the key to successful drug design. Basic organic chemistry, pharmacology, physical chemistry, molecular biology, enzymology, and toxicology considerations have to be used simultaneously.*

BODSWORTH, CHARLES FREDERICK, naturalist, author; b. Port Burwell, Ont., Can., Oct. 11, 1918; s. Arthur John and Viola (Williams) B.; m. Margaret Neville Banner, July 8, 1944; children: Barbara (Mrs. Edward Welch), Nancy (Mrs. Richard Hannah), Neville. Student pub. schs., Port Burwell. Reporter St. Thomas (Ont.) Times-Jour., 1940-43; reporter, editor Toronto (Ont.) Daily Star, 1943-46; staff writer, editor Maclean's Mag., Toronto, 1947-56; novelist, 1956—; organizer, leader numerous natural history tours. Author: Last of the Curlews, 1954, The Strange One, 1960, The Mating Call, 1961, The Atonement of Ashley Morden, 1964, The Sparrow's Fall, 1967; also pub. in Eng., fgn. translations The Pacific Coast, Illustrated Natural History of Canada series, 1970; (with others) Wilderness Canada, 1970; editor: Illustrated Natural History of Canada series, 1980-81. Bd. dirs. Natural Sci. of Can., 1980—; hon. bd. dirs. Long Point Bird Obs., 1970—; chmn. bd. trustees James L. Baillie Meml. Fund for ornithol. field research, 1975—. Mem. Fedn. Ont. Naturalists (pres. 1964-66), Canadian Authors Assn., Writers Union of Can. Clubs: Men's Press, Ornithological, Field Naturalists (past pres.), Brodie (Toronto)). Address: 294 Beech Ave Toronto ON M4E 3J2 Canada

BODVARSSON, GUNNAR, educator; b. Reykjavik, Iceland, Aug. 8, 1916; s. Bodvar and Gudrun (Thorsteinsson) Kristjansson; m. Tove Christensen, Aug. 12, 1944; children—Gudrun, Kristjana (Mrs. Charles Kang), Orn. Diploma of engring., Tech. U. Berlin, 1943; Ph.D., Cal. Inst. Tech., 1957. Research engr. Atlas Machinery Co., Copenhagen, 1943-45; head geothermal research dept., Reykjavik, Iceland, 1945-64; prof. math. and oceanography Oreg. State U., Corvallis, 1964—; Cons. geothermal research and engring. UN, 1951—. Mem. Am. Math. Soc., Am. Geophys. Union, Soc. Exploration Geophysicists. Research in theoretical geophysics and devel. geothermal energy resources, Iceland and other countries. Home: 1377 NW Alta Vista Dr Corvallis OR 97330

BOE, ARCHIE R., retired retail and insurance company executive; b. Estherville, Iowa, Feb. 27, 1921; s. Berge B. and Regina B. (Nelson) B.; m. Elaine B. Jansson, May 11, 1973. B.C.S., Drake U., 1941, LL.B. (hon.), 1976; M.B.A., U. Chgo., 1950. With Allstate Ins. Co., 1941—82, v.p., sec., 1960-66, pres., 1966-68, vice chmn., 1968-72; v.p., sec. Allstate Enterprises, Inc., 1960-66, pres., 1966-68, vice chmn., 1968-72; chmn., chief exec. officer Allstate Ins. and Allstate Enterprises, 1972—82; pres. Sears, Roebuck & Co., 1982-84, also dir.; dir. NICOR Inc., Chgo. Bank of Commerce, No. Ill. Gas Co., U.S. Gypsum Co., William Wrigley Jr. Co. Served with USNR, 1942-45. Mem. Newcomen Soc. N.Am. Clubs: Chicago, Commercial, Executives, Economic, Mid-America (Chgo.); Metropolitan, Tavern, Sunset Ridge Country. Office: Wrigley Bldg 400 N Michigan Chicago IL 60611

BOE, DAVID STEPHEN, musician, educator, college dean; b. Duluth, Minn., Mar. 11, 1936; s. Egbert Thomas and Beatrice Ella (Steen) B.; m. Sigrid North, July 23, 1961; children: Stephen, Eric. B.A. magna cum laude, St. Olaf Coll., Northfield, Minn., 1958; M.Mus., Syracuse (N.Y.) U., 1960. Asst. prof. music U. Ga., 1961-62; mem. faculty Oberlin (Ohio) Coll. Conservatory Music, 1962—, prof. organ and harpsichord, 1976—, dean, 1976—; dir. music, organist First Lutheran Ch., Lorain, Ohio, 1962—; organ recitalist, U.S. and Europe, 1962—; mem. advanced placement music com. Coll. Entrance Exam. Bd., 1980-83. Fulbright scholar, W. Ger., 1960-61. Mem. Nat. Assn. Schs. Music (trustee, sec. 1981—), Phi Beta Kappa, Pi Kappa Lambda. (nat. v.p. 1981—). Home: 30 Colony Dr Oberlin OH 44074 Office: Oberlin Coll Conservatory Music Oberlin OH 44074

BOE, NILS ANDREAS, govt. ofcl.; b. Baltic, S.D., Sept. 10, 1913; s. Nils and Sissel C. (Finseth) B. A.B., U. Wis., 1935, LL.B., 1937; LL.D. (hon.), Huron Coll. Bar: Wis. bar 1937, S.D. bar 1938, U.S. Supreme Ct. bar 1944, D.C. bar 1970. Practice in, Sioux Falls, S.D., 1938-65, lt. gov., S.D., 1963-65, gov., 1965-67, 67-69; dir. Office of Intergovtl. Relations, Exec. Office of Pres., Washington, 1969-71; judge U.S. Ct. Internat. Trade, 1971—, chief judge, 1971-77; Mem. S.D. Ho. of Reps., 1951-59, speaker, 1955, 57. Served with USN, 1942-46. Mem. Am. Legion, VFW, Phi Alpha Delta. Republican. Lutheran. Clubs: Elk, Odd Fellow. Home: 71 No Manursing Island Rye NY 10580 Office: US Ct Internat Trade 1 Federal Plaza New York NY 10007

BOEDE, MARVIN J., union official. Pres. United Assn. Journeymen and Apprentices of the Plumbing & Pipe-Fittint Industry, Washington, D.C. Office: United Assn. Journeymen & Apprentices 901 Massachusetts Ave NW Washington DC 20001

BOEDEKER, ALICE VERNELLE, ins. co. exec.; b. Nehawka, Nebr., May 17, 1921; d. Frank A. and Stella Marie (Opp) B. Student, U. Iowa, 1938-39, Creighton U., Omaha, 1939-41. With Fed. Land Bank, Omaha, 1941-44; various positions in acctg., 1944-51; with Central Nat. Ins. Group Omaha, 1951—, sr. v.p., treas., 1980—; v.p., treas. Drum Fin. Corp., 1976—. Mem. Nat. Assn. Ind. Insurers, Omaha-Lincoln Soc. Fin. Analysts, Omaha C. of C. Republican. Club: Omaha Press. Home: 1010 Regency Pkwy Apt 205 Omaha NE 68114 Office: 105 S 17th St Omaha NE 68102

BOEHLE, WILLIAM RANDALL, JR., music educator; b. Waxahachie, Tex., July 1, 1919; s. Wilhelm Reinhold and Ruby (Connally) B.; m. Emma Jean Belk, Dec. 10, 1943; children: Dulcy Jean, Alison Lee. Mus.B., Hardin-Simmons U., 1941; Mus.M., La. State U., 1948; Ph.D., U. Iowa, 1954. Asst. prof. music Chadron (Nebr.) State Coll., 1949-52, chmn. div. fine arts, 1952-60; chmn. dept. music U. N.D., Grand Forks, 1960-77, acting dean Coll. Fine Arts, 1971-73, prof. music, 1977—. Mem. N.D. Council Arts and Humanities, 1966-77; pres. Internat. Music Camp, 1978—. Served with AUS, 1942-46. Mem. Music Tchrs. Nat. Assn. (past nat. chmn. student activities), Nat. Assn. Composers U.S.A., Nebr. Music Tchrs. Assn. (past pres.). Home: 406 22d Ave S Grand Forks ND 58201

BOEHLERT, SHERWOOD LOUIS, congressman; b. Utica, N.Y., Sept. 28, 1936; s. Sherwood John and Elizabeth Monica (Champeaux) B.; m. Marianne Willey; children: previous marriage: Mark Christopher, Tracy Ann, Leslie Jane. B.S. in Pub. Relation, Utica Coll., Syracuse U., 1961. Mgr. pub. relations Wyandotte Chems. Corp., Mich., 1961-64; chief of staff Rep. Alexander Pirnie, Washington, 1964-73, Rep. Donald J. Mitchell, 1973-79; exec. Oneida County, 1979-81; mem. 98th Congress from 25th N.Y. Dist. Author: Telling the Congressman's Story, The Voice of Government, 1968. Served with U.S. Army, 1956-58. Republican. Lodge: Rotary. Office: Room 1641 Longworth House Office Bldg Washington DC 20515

BOEHM, DAVID ALFRED, publisher, producer; b. N.Y.C., Feb. 6, 1914; s. Alfred and Frances (Ehrlich) B.; m. Sylvia Link, Sept. 18, 1965 (dec. 1977); children: Suzanne, Diana, Lincoln, Emily, David Lee.; m. Alva Baxter, Sept. 1, 1983. A.B., Columbia Coll., 1934. Editor Standard Stats Co., 1936-38; pres. Printed Arts Co., 1938-41; asst. prodn. mgr. McGraw-Hill Book Co., 1941-44; editor Cupples & Leon Pubs., 1944-45; sales mgr. Greenberg-Publisher, 1945-49; founder, pres., now chmn. Sterling Pub. Co., N.Y.C., 1949—, editor, pub., 1960—; pres. Printed Arts Co., 1958—, Bold Face Books, Inc., 1958-80, World Record Films, 1975—, Guinness Mus. of World Records and Exhibit Halls, Inc., 1976—, David A. Boehm Prodns. Inc., 1979—; founder, editor Guinness Mag., 1981-82; chmn. Lit. Tours, Inc., 1981—. Author 16 books on stamp collecting, games, fgn. countries. Home: The Penthouse 39 E 79th St New York NY 10021 Office: 2 Park Ave New York NY 10016

BOEHM, ERIC HARTZELL, information management executive; b. Hof, Germany, July 15, 1918; came to U.S., 1934, naturalized, 1940; s. Karl and Bertha (Oppenheimer) B.; m. Inge Pauli, June 5, 1948; children: Beatrice (dec.), Ronald James, Evelyn (dec.), Steven David. B.A., Wooster (Ohio) Coll., 1940, Litt.D. (hon.), 1973; M.A., Fletcher Sch. Law and Diplomacy, 1942; Ph.D., Yale U., 1951. With Dept. Air Force, 1951-58; chmn. bd. ABC-CLIO Info. Services, Santa Barbara, Calif., 1960—, European Bibliog. Center, Clio Press, Ltd., Oxford, Eng., 1970—; chmn. bd. Internat. Acad. at Santa Barbara, 1970—; pub. Environ. Studies Inst., 1971—; planning com. Info. Inst., 1980—; cons. bibliography, information systems. Author: We Survived, 1949; microfilm Policy-making of the Nazi Government, 1969; editor: Historical Abstracts, 1955-83, cons., 1983, America: History and Life, 1964-83, cons., 1983, Bibliographies on International Relations and World Affairs, an Annotated Directory, 1965, Blueprint for Bibliography, a System for Social Sciences and Humanities, 1965, Clio Bibliography Series, 1973—; co-editor: Historical Periodicals, 1961; pub.: Advanced Bibliography of Contents: Political Science, 1969—, ART Bibliographies: Modern, 1972—, Environ. Periodicals Bibliography, 1972—; bd. advisors: CEO Jour. Info. Strategy; contbr. articles to profl. jours. Bd. dirs. UN Assn., Santa Barbara, 1973-77, Santa Barbara's Adv. Bd. Internat. Relationships (Sister Cities), 1974, Friends of Public Library, Friends of U. Calif. at Santa Barbara Library; mem. affiliates bd. U. Calif.-Santa Barbara. Served with USAAF, 1942-46. Mem. AAAS, Am. Soc. Info. Sci., Assn. Bibliography in History, Calif. Library Soc., Nat. Trust Historic Preservation, Santa Barbara Com. Fgn. Relations, Am. Friends of Wilton Park, Santa Barbara C. of C. (dir. 1982-84). Clubs: Rotary, Univ. Office: ABC-Clio Info Services 2070 Alameda Padre Serra Santa Barbara CA 93103 *

BOEHM, FELIX HANS, ldgcator, physicist; b. Basel, Switzerland, June 9, 1924; came to U.S., 1952, naturalized, 1964; s. Hans G. and Marquerite (Philippi) B.; m. Ruth Sommerhalder, Nov. 26, 1956; children: Marcus F., Claude N. M.S., Inst. Tech., Zurich, 1948, Ph.D., 1951. Research assoc. Inst. Tech., Zurich, Switzerland, 1949-52; Boese fellow Columbia U., 1952-53; faculty Calif. Inst. Tech., Pasadena, 1953—, prof. physics, 1961—; Sloan fellow, 1962-64, Niels Bohr Inst., Copenhagen, 1965-66, Cern, Geneva, 1971-72, Laue-Langevin Inst., 1980. Recipient Humboldt award, 1980. Fellow Am. Phys. Soc.; mem. Nat. Acad. Scis. Research on nuclear physics, nuclear beta decay, neutrino physics, atomic physics, muonic and pionic atoms, parity and time-reversal. Home: 2510 N Altadena Dr Altadena CA 91001 Office: Calif Inst Tech Pasadena CA 91125

BOEHM, WERNER WILLIAM, social work educator; b. Oberlangenstadt, Germany, June 19, 1913; came to U.S., 1937, naturalized, 1944; s. Karl and Bertha (Oppenheimer) B.; m. Bernice Roseburg Brower, June 5, 1948; 1 son, Andrew. LL.B., U. Dijon, France, 1936, D.L., 1937; M.S.W., Tulane U., 1941. Prof. social work U. Minn., 1952-63, dir., coordinator U.S. and Canadian social work curriculum study, 1955-58; prof. Grad. Sch. Social Work, Rutgers U., 1963—, dean, 1963-72; dir. Center for Internat. and Comparative Social Welfare, 1973-81; Vice pres. Minn. Welfare Conf., 1954-55; mem. U.S. Com. on Internat. Social Work, 1955-61, 76—; vice chmn. commn. 10th Internat. Conf. Social Work, Italy, 1961, rep., Brazil, 1962; mem. continuing edn. tng. rev. com. NIMH, 1969-72; chmn. Commn. I, XVth Internat. Conf., Manila, 1970; mem. Sr. Fulbright travel grant Italo-U.S. Conf. on Ednl. Exchange in Social Welfare, Rome, 1969; sr. Fulbright appointment, Italy, 1971; vis. scholar Nat. Inst. Social Work Tng., London, 1972-73; U.S. rep. commn. on social devel. XVIII Internat. Conf. on Social Welfare, San Juan, 1976; lectr. internat. meetings Ger., France, 1982, 83. Author: Objectives of the Social Work Curriculum of the Future, 1959, The Social Casework Method in Social Work Education, 1959; author U.S. report for, 19th and 20th Internat. Confs. on Social Welfare, 1978, 80, also seven monographs in field; adv. editor: Social Work Series, Harper & Row, Pubs., 1973-83; editor-in-chief: Internat. Social Work, 1975-81; contbr. articles to profl. jours., chpts. to books. Mem. Gov.'s Council on Aging, 1960; mem. N.J. Crime Commn., 1966-68; mem. nat. exec. council Am. Jewish Com., 1973—. Recipient Cassidy Meml. research award U. Toronto, 1959, Disting. Alumnus award Tulane U., 1981, medal Rutgers U., 1983; named Social Worker of Yr., Nat. Assn. Social Workers, 1983. Mem. AAAS, Nat. Assn. Social Workers (chmn. commn. edn. 1965-68, dir., mem. exec. com. 1966-67), Nat. Commn. for Social Work Careers (dir.), Council Social Work Edn. (mem. exec. com. 1967-69, chmn. commn. on ednl. services 1969-72, chmn. commn. internat. social work 1978—), Nat. Conf. Social Welfare (1st v.p. 1969-70), N.J. Welfare Council (exec. com. 1964-70). Home: 1050 George St New Brunswick NJ 08901 Office: Rutgers U Grad School Social Work New Brunswick NJ 08903

BOEHNE, EDWARD GEORGE, banker, economist; b. Evansville, Ind., May 15, 1940; s. Edward John and Lucy Naomi (Strieter) B.; m. Patricia Graffis, Jan. 24, 1960; children: Lisa Elena, Edward Mark. B.S., Ind. U., 1962, M.B.A., 1963, M.A., 1967, Ph.D. in Econs, 1968. Economist Fed. Res. Bank, Phila., 1968-70, research officer, economist, 1970-71, v.p., dir. research, 1971-73, sr. v.p., 1973-81, pres., 1981—; mem. faculty Bradley U., 1963-65, Ind. U., 1965-67, Temple U., 1969-70. Contbr. numerous articles on bus., fin. to profl. jours. Bd. dirs. Greater Phila. C. of C., Greater Phila. Partnership, Urban League Phila., Baldwin Sch., Bryn Mawr, Pa., Pa. Hosp., Phila., University City Sci. Ctr., Phila., United Way, Global Interdependence Ctr., World Affairs Council. Recipient Lieber award Ind. U., 1967, Gov.'s citation for outstanding service to Pa., 1978. Mem. Am. Econ. Assn., Nat. Assn. Bus. Economists. Club: Sunday Breakfast (Phila). Office: Ten Independence Mall Philadelphia PA 19105

BOEHNING, JOSEPH FREDERICK, architect; b. Albuquerque, Mar. 27, 1931; s. Albert William and Henrietta (Marohn) B.; m. Bonnie Jean Snider, Aug. 6, 1952; children: Joanne, Paula, David Frederick. B.S. in Archtl. Engring, U. N.Mex., 1953, B. Arch., 1961. Registered architect. N.Mex., Ariz., Colo., Okla., Mo., Calif., Wis., Tex.; registered profl. engr., N.Mex. Archtl. designer A.W. Boehning, Albuquerque, 1955-61, prin. firm, 1961-76; pres. Boehning Protz Cook & Pogue, 1980—. Editorial bd.: SYMPOSIA mag, 1968—. Vice pres. Albuquerque Boys Clubs, 1968; mem. Gov.'s Adv. Council on Vocational Edn. Facilities, Santa Fe, 1971-72, Heights Cath. Sch. Bd., Albuquerque, 1969-72. Served to 1st lt. USAF, 1953-55; Korea. Mem. AIA (pres. Albuquerque chpt. 1965, 66, sec.-treas. Western Mountain region 1971—, mem. nat. com. on architecture for arts and recreation 1973, nat. com. on restructure of inst. 1973, com. on architecture for edn. 1975, com. on architecture for justice 1977), N.Mex. Soc. Architecture (pres. 1970), Am. Arbitration Assn. (mem. N.Mex. adv. council 1970—), U. N.Mex. Alumni Assn. (pres. 1969), Sigma Tau. Club: Tennis (Albuquerque) (dir. 1974-76). Home: 4809 Madison Ct NE Albuquerque NM 87110 Office: Suite 500 Sunshine Bldg Albuquerque NM 87102

BOEKE, ROBERT WILLIAM, manufacturing company executive; b. Hubbard, Iowa, July 28, 1925; s. John Henry and Elizabeth A. (Schwartz) B.; m. Roberta Starbuck, Sept. 6, 1947; children: Lee Anne Boeke-Burke, Linda Sue Boeke Day, John Robert. B.S., Iowa State Coll., 1948, M.S., 1950; grad. exec. program, Columbia U., 1966, Aspen (Colo.) Inst., 1976. Instr. Iowa State U., 1947; with Deere & Co., 1951—, mng. dir. Europe, Africa and Middle East, Heidelberg, W. Ger., 1970, v.p. farm equipment and consumer products mfg. U.S. and Can., Moline, Ill., 1972, sr. v.p. components design and mfr., 1979—, also dir.; dir. Banks of Iowa; mem. adv. bd. to dean engring. Iowa State U., 1978—. Pres. Illowa council Boy Scouts Am., 1975—, mem. exec. and adv. bds., 1972-78; pres. United Way Rock Island and Scott Counties, 1977, exec. com., 1978; v.p. Iowa State U. Found., 1977—; trustee Iowa State U. Alumni Achievement Fund, 1972-78. Served with USNR, 1943-45. Mem. Am. Soc. Quality Control, Farm and Indsl. Equipment Inst. Presbyterian. Home: 2895 W Court Bettendorf IA 52722 Office: Deere & Co John Deere Rd Moline IL 61265

BOEKELHEIDE, VIRGIL CARL, chemistry educator; b. Cheslea, S.D., July 28, 1919; s. Charles F. and Eleonora C. (Toennies) B.; m. Caroline Barrett, Apr. 7, 1924; children: Karl, Anne, Erich. A.B. magna cum laude, U. Minn.-Mpls., 1939, Ph.D., 1943. Instr. U. Ill., Urbana, 1943-46; asst. prof. to prof. U. Rochester, 1946-60; prof. dept. chemistry U. Oreg., Eugene, 1960—. Contbr. articles to profl. jours. Recipient Disting. Achievement award U. Minn., 1967, Alexander von Humboldt award W.Ger. Govt., 1974, 82, Centenary Lectureship Royal Soc. G.B., 1983, Coover award Iowa State U., 1981; Disting. scholar designate U.S.-China Acad. Sci., 1981; Fulbright Disting. prof., Yugoslavia, 1972. Mem. Nat. Acad. Sci. Home: 2017 Elk Dr Eugene OR 97403 Office: Dept Chemistry U Oreg Eugene OR 97403

BOEKER, PAUL HAROLD, government official; b. St. Louis, May 2, 1938; s. Victor W. and Marie Dorothy (Bernthal) B.; m. Margaret Macon Campbell, Nov. 25, 1961; children: Michelle Renee, Kent Elliott, Katherine Madison. A.B., Dartmouth Coll., 1960; postgrad., Princeton U., 1961; M.A. in Econs, U. Mich., 1967. Joined Dept. State, 1961; vice consul, Duesseldorf, Germany, 1962-63; 2d sec. Am. embassy, Bogota, Colombia, 1964-66; mem. White House Task Force on Internat. Devel., 1969; dir. Office Devel. Fin., Dept. State, 1970; 1st sec. Am. embassy, Bonn, Germany, 1971-73; mem. policy planning staff Dept. State, 1974, dep. asst. sec. state for internat. fin. and devel., 1975, sr. dep. asst. sec. state for econ. and bus. affairs, 1976; ambassador to, Bolivia, 1977-80; dir. Fgn. Service Inst., Washington, 1980—; mem. Sec.'s Planning Council, Washington, 1983. Recipient Arthur S. Fleming award for outstanding young people in fed. service, 1976. Office: Dept State S/P Washington DC 20520

BOELL, EDGAR JOHN, biology educator; b. Rudd, Iowa, Oct. 30, 1906; s. Albert Emil and Gertrude (Van der Las) B.; m. Mildred Cottingham, June 3, 1932; children—Carl David, Dorothy Eleanor. A.B., U. Dubuque, 1929, D.Sc., 1963; Ph.D., State U. Iowa, 1935; postgrad., Cambridge U., 1937-38; A.M. (hon.), Yale, 1946. Research asso. State U. Iowa, 1934-37; faculty Yale, 1938—, prof. zoology, 1946-47, Ross Granville Harrison prof. exptl. zoology, 1947-75, emeritus, 1975—, sr. research asso. biology, 1975—, chmn. dept. zoology, dir. zool. labs., 1956-62, acting dean Yale Coll., spring 1968-69, fellow Jonathan Edwards Coll., master Jonathan Edwards Coll., 1975-77, exec. sec. corp. search com. for 19th pres., 1977; asso. prof. zoology U. Calif., summer 1941. Cons. editor: Zoology, 1949-62; co-mng. editor: Jour. Exptl. Zoology, 1965—; Contbr. articles on chem. embryology to profl. jours. Bd. dirs. U. Dubuque, 1980—. Fulbright award Carlsberg Lab., 1953-54; Guggenheim Meml. fellow, 1963-64. Fellow Am. Acad. Arts and Scis.; mem. Am. Soc. for Cell Biology, Soc. for Developmental Biology (pres. 1952-53), Internat. Soc. Developmental Biology, Am. Physiol. Soc., Am. Soc. Zoologists (exec. com. 1959-63, mem. organizing com. 16th internat. congress zoology), Conn. Acad. Arts and Scis., Phi Beta Kappa, Sigma Xi (pres. Yale chpt. 1945-46). Home: 577 Skiff St North Haven CT 06473 Office: Osborn Meml Lab Yale U New Haven CT 06520

BOELZNER, GORDON DIX, JR., orchestral conductor, pianist; b. Inglewood, Calif., July 6, 1937; s. Gordon Dix and Angie Irene (Ketchum) Boelzner. Student, Eastman Sch. Music, Rochester, N.Y., 1954-57; B.M., Manhattan Sch. Music, N.Y.C., 1958; pvt. studies with, Arturo Benedetti Michelangeli, Italy, 1957. Condr., solo pianist N.Y.C. Ballet Orch., 1958—; guest appearances as piano soloist and condr., orchs., Am., Europe. Office: NYC Ballet NY State Theatre New York NY 10023

BOENNING, HENRY DORR, JR., investment banker; b. Phila., Oct. 16, 1914; s. Henry Dorr and Clara Virginia (Smith) B.; m. Clare Huston Miller, Feb. 18, 1946; m. Sara Ann Perkins, Aug. 19, 1964. B.S., U. Pa., 1935; postgrad., Harvard Bus. Sch., 1935-37. Partner Boenning & Co., Phila., 1946-70; v.p. Boenning & Scattergood, Inc., 1970—, also dir.; dir. Fluid Energy Process and Equipment, Hatfield, Pa. Served from 2d lt. to maj. AUS, 1939-46. Mem. Phi Gamma Delta. Home: 936 Rock Creek Rd Bryn Mawr PA 19010 Office: 1809 Walnut St Philadelphia PA 19103

BOER, FRANK PETER, chemical company executive, researcher; b. Hungary, Nov. 22, 1940; s. Frank Joseph and Flora Elaine (Pillion) B.; m. Ellen Laurie Strauss, Aug. 9, 1963; children: Alexandra Florence, Andrew Pillion. A.B., Princeton U., 1961; Ph.D., Harvard U., 1965. With Dow Chem. Co., 1965-78, lab. dir., Freeport, Tex., 1973-77, bus. mgr., Midland, Mich., 1977-78; v.p. and gen. mgr. research and devel. Am. Can Co., Greenwich, Conn., 1978-82; corp. v.p., pres. research div. W.R. Grace & Co., Columbia, Md., 1983—; chmn. pub. communications com. Indsl. Research Inst. Contbr. numerous articles to profl. jours. Bd. dirs. Saginaw Valley Montessori Sch., Midland, 1971-73; coach Mid-Fairfield Youth Hockey Assn., Darien, Conn., 1978-81, Chevy Chase Club Hockey, Md., 1983-84. Woodrow Wilson fellow, 1961-62. Mem. Am. Chem. Soc., Chem. Soc. (London), Am. Crystallographic Assn., Phi Beta Kappa, Sigma Xi. Patentee in field. Home: 4710 Woodway Ln NW Washington DC 20016 Office: WR Grace & Co 7379 Route 32 Columbia MD 21044

BOER, ROBERT HENRY, oil company executive; b. Haledon, N.J., Nov. 16, 1926; s. Henry John and Lillian Marie (Nordblom) B.; m. Juanita Eileen Freeborn, Aug. 5, 1949; children: David Stanford, Brain Robert. B.A. in Econs., Stanford U., 1948, M.B.A., 1950. Supr. fin. forecasts Standard Oil Co. Calif., San Francisco, 1957-59, mgr. gen. services, 1965-66, mgr. supply and transp. acctg. western ops., 1966-71; sec., treas. Salt Lake Pipe Line & Refining Cos., Salt Lake City, 1959-61; comptroller Standard Oil Co. Ky., Louisville, 1961-65; treas. P.T. Caltex Pacific Indonesia, Jakarta, 1971-74; v.p., sec.-treas. Eastern div. Chevron Oil Co., perth Amboy, N.J., 1974-77; sec.-treas. Chevron U.S.A., Inc., San Francisco, 1977—. City clk. City of Maryhill Estates, Ky., 1962-65; chmn. troop com. Stanford Area council Boy Scouts Am., 1965-68; pres. Am. Men's Assn., Jakarta, 1972-73. Served with USN, 1944-45. Mem. Stanford Bus. Sch. Alumni Assn., Am. Petroleum Inst., Theta Chi. Republican. Club: Indonesia Petroleum (dir. 1972-74). Office: 575 Market St San Francisco CA 94105

BOERRIGTER, GLENN CHARLES, educational administrator; b. Hickman, Nebr., Aug. 25, 1932; s. John Anthony and Ruth (Hupel) B.; m. Carol Marie Dunker, June 13, 1959; children: Dean Glenn, Kay Anne. A.B., Nebr. Wesleyan U., 1953; M.Ed., U. Neb., 1957, D.Ed., 1960. Prin., tchr., Daykin, Nebr., 1953-55, prin., supt., Atkinson, Neb., 1955-58; instr. U. Nebr., 1958-60; asst. prof. edn. No. State Tchrs. Coll., Aberdeen, S.D., 1960-61; edn. specialist sch. adminstrn. U.S. Office Edn., Washington, 1961-63, coordinator research, 1963-65, chief adminstrn. studies br., 1965-67, dir. div. elementary and secondary research, 1968-71, chief applied studies br., 1971-72, chief research br., 1972-78, chief program improvement br., 1978—; cons. ednl. research matters colls., univs., pub. schs. State Dept. Edn. (profit and non-profit groups, also various fgn. govts.). Contbr.: chpt. to Elementary Teacher Education, 1971; also articles profl. jours. Recipient Superior Service award U.S. Office Edn., 1971. Mem. N.E.A., Am. Ednl. Research Assn., Am. Vocat. Assn., Am. Vocat. Research Assn., Am. Assn. Sch. Adminstrs., Rural Edn. Assn., Horace Mann League, Phi Delta Kappa. Presbyterian (elder). Home: 4 Mel Mara Dr Oxon Hill MD 20745 Office: 400 Maryland Ave Washington DC 20202

BOESCH, FRANCIS THEODORE, electrical engineer, educator; b. N.Y.C., Sept. 28, 1936; s. Victor and Margaret (Wright) B. B.S., Poly. Inst. N.Y., 1957, M.S., 1960, Ph.D., 1963. Instr., then asst. prof. elec. engring. Poly. Inst. N.Y., 1957-63; mem. mil. research staff Bell Telephone Labs., 1963-68, mem. research staff, 1969-79; McKay prof. elec. engring. and computer sci. U. Calif., Berkeley, 1968-69; prof. pure and applied math. and Charles Batchelor prof. elec. engring. and computer sci., head dept. Stevens Inst. Tech., Hoboken, N.J., 1979—. Author: Large-Scale Networks, 1976; editor-in-chief: Networks, 1970-81; editor: Graph Theory, 1978-81; contbr. articles to profl. jours. Vice pres. Fair Haven (N.J.) Little League, 1974; scoutmaster Fair Haven council Boy Scouts Am., 1973-78, dist. commnr. Monmouth council, 1978-80. Fellow IEEE, N.Y. Acad. Scis.; mem. Assn. Computing Machinery, Am. Math. Soc., Sigma Xi, Eta Kappa Nu. Home: 730 Hudson St Hoboken NJ 07030 Office: Stevens Inst Tech Castle Point Station Hoboken NJ 07030

BOESCHENSTEIN, WILLIAM WADE, glass products manufacturing executive; b. Chgo., Sept. 7, 1925; s. Harold and Elizabeth (Wade) B.; m. Josephine H. Moll, Nov. 28, 1953; children: William Wade, Michael M., Peter H., Stephen S. Student, Phillips Acad., 1944; B.S., Yale, 1950. With Owens-Corning Fiberglas Corp., 1950—, br. mgr., Detroit, 1955-59, v.p. central region, 1959-61, v.p. sales br. operations, Toledo, 1961-63, v.p. marketing, 1963-67, exec. v.p., 1967-71, pres., 1971—, chief exec. officer, 1972—, chmn., 1981—, dir., 1967—; dir. Prudential Ins. Co. Am., FMC Corp., Chgo., Hanna Mining Co., Cleve. Trustee Toledo Mus. Art, Phillips Acad., Andover, Mass. Mem. The Bus. Council, The Conf. Bd. Clubs: Links, Econ. (N.Y.C.); Econ. (Detroit); Toledo, Inverness (Toledo); Belmont Country (Perrysburg, Ohio); Augusta (Ga.); Nat. Home: 3 Locust St Perrysburg OH 43551 Office: Owens-Corning Fiberglas Corp Fiberglas Tower Toledo OH 43659

BOESE, GILBERT KARYLE, zoo director; b. Chgo., June 24, 1937; s. Carl H. and Winifred A. B.; m. Wilma Lou Blenz, Dec. 19, 1959; children: Ann Carroll, Peter Austin. B.A., Carthage (Ill.) Coll., 1959; M.S., No. Ill. U., 1965; Ph.D.; NIMH trainee 1970, Johns Hopkins U., 1973. Instr. biology Thornton Community Coll., Harvey, Ill., 1965-67; asst. prof. biology Elmhurst (Ill.) Coll., 1967-69; dep. dir. Chgo. Zool. Park, Brookfield, Ill., 1971-80; dir. Milw. County Zool. Gardens, Milw., 1980—; adj. prof. U. Wis., Milw.; bd. dirs. Riverside Nature Center, 1980. Bd. dirs. Greater Milw. Conv. and Visitors Bur. Grantee, Elmhurst Coll. Alumni Faculty, 1969; Women's Bd. of Brookfield Zoo, 1974. Mem. Am. Assn. Zool. Parks and Aquariums, Adventurers Club, Internat. Union Dirs. Zool. Gardens, Internat. Crane Found., Am. Museum Natural History. Address: 10001 W Bluemound Rd Milwaukee WI 53226

BOESEL, MILTON CHARLES, JR., lawyer, business exec.; b. Toledo, July 12, 1928; s. Milton Charles and Florence (Fitzgerald) B.; m. Lucy Laughlin Mather, Mar. 25, 1961; children—Elizabeth Parks, Charles Mather, Andrew Fitzgerald. B.A., Yale, 1950; LL.B., Harvard, 1953. Bar: Ohio bar 1953, Mich. bar 1953. Of counsel firm Ritter, Boesel, Robinson & Marsh, Toledo, 1956—; pres., dir. Michabo, Inc.; dir. 1st Nat. Bank of Toledo. Served to lt. USNR, 1953-56. Episcopalian. Clubs: Mason., Toledo, Toledo Country. Home: 2268 Innisbrook Rd Toledo OH 43606 Office: 240 Huron St Toledo OH 43604

BOESKY, IVAN FREDERICK, securities company executive; b. Detroit, Mar. 6, 1937; s. William H. and Helen (Silverberg) B.; m. Seema Silberstein, Jan. 7, 1962; children: William Lehman, Marianne S., Theodore Emerson, Johnathan Brandeis. J.D., Detroit Coll. Law, 1964. Bar: Mich. 1962. Law clk. to judge U.S. Dist. Ct., 1964-65; tax acct. Touche, Ross & Co. (C.P.A.'s), Detroit, 1965-66; security analyst L.F. Rothschild Co., N.Y.C., 1966-67, First Manhattan Co., 1968-70; gen. partner Edwards & Hanly, N.Y.C., 1972-75; mng. partner Ivan F. Boesky & Co., 1975—; adj. prof. Grad. Sch. Bus. Adminstrn. N.Y. U., 1977; fellow Brandeis U. Mem. Wall St. coms. Fedn. Jewish Philanthropies, United Jewish Appeal; trustee Albert Einstein Coll. Medicine, Trust for Cultural Resources, Hebrew Union Coll., Eagle Hill Sch., Greenwich, Conn., Temple Sholom, Greenwich; adv. mem. Jewish Theol. Sem. Mem. Am., Mich., Detroit bar assns., N.Y. Stock Exchange (allied), Delta Theta Phi. Democrat. Jewish. Clubs: City Athletic (N.Y.C.); Burning Tree Country. *

BOETTCHER, BYRON KURTH, retired manufacturing company executive, consultant; b. Prairie Farm, Wis., Nov. 24, 1917; s. Arthur Otto and Edna Augusta (Kurth) B.; m. Dorothy Edith Finck, July 6, 1942; children: Barbara Ann, Robert Byron. B.A. in Math, North Central Coll., 1941. Mgr., Dayton office, then dir. central region Avco Corp., 1953-63, Washington rep., 1964, v.p. def. and indsl. products group, 1964-67, v.p., gen. mgr. Avco Precision Products div., Richmond, Ind., 1967-73, v.p. govt. products group, 1973-74, v.p. products and research parent co., 1974-83, ret., 1983, cons., 1983—. Chmn. civic affairs-spl. events com. Dayton Area C. of C., 1960-62; Chmn. def. adv. council, 1962-64; Charter mem. Air Force Mus. Found; mem. Nat. Aviation Hall of Fame, v.p., 1975-80, mem. bd. nominations, 1981—. Served to lt. col. USAAF and USAF, 1941-53; brig. gen. Res. ret. Mem. Armed Forces Mgmt. Assn., Res. Officers Assn., Am. Ordnance Assn. (dir. 1969-77, pres. Cin. chpt. 1972-75), Nat. Def. Transp. Assn., IEEE, Nat. Security Indsl. Assn. (pres. Dayton 1966-67), Assn. U.S. Army, Richmond Area C. of C. (dir. 1968-70). Clubs: Bermuda Dunes Country; Forest Hills Country (Richmond); Carolina Trace (N.C.). Home: 43-400 Lacovia Dr Bermuda Dunes CA 92201 Office: 9841 Airport Blvd Suite 1130 Los Angeles CA 90045 *"Do unto others as you would have them do to you."*

BOETTCHER, HAROLD PAUL, engr.; b. Eagle, Wis., July 24, 1923; s. Emil Ernst and Henrietta (Seefeld) B.; m. Dorothy Strandberg, Feb. 1, 1948; children—David Paul, John Harold, Mark Alan. B.S., U. Wis., 1947, M.S., 1950, Ph.D., 1954. Registered profl. engr., Wis. Instr. mechanics U. Wis., Madison, 1946-54; research dir. electric motor lab. A.O. Smith Corp., Milw., 1954-61; asso. prof. U. Wis., Milw., 1961-65, prof., 1965—, chmn. dept., 1965-69, 74-77. Served with USN, 1944-46. Mem. IEEE (sr.), Am. Soc. Engring. Edn., Sigma Xi. Home: 19285 Lothmoor Dr Lower Brookfield WI 53005 Office: U Wis Milwaukee WI 53201

BOGAN, ELIZABETH CHAPIN, economist, educator; b. Morristown, N.J., Aug. 22, 1944; d. Daryl Muscott and Tirzah (Walker) Chapin; m. Thomas Rockwood Bogan, June 5, 1965; children: Nathaniel Rockwood, Andrew Allerton. A.B., Wellesley Coll., 1966; M.A., U. N.H., 1967; Ph.D., Columbia U., 1971. NSF trainee U. N.H., 1966-67; mem. faculty Farleigh Dickinson U., Madison, N.J., 1971—, prof. econs., 1982—, chmn. merit scholarship com., 1981-82, chmn. dept. econs. and fin., 1981—, reviewer univ. press. Reviewer: Fin. Analyst Jour. Recipient Outstanding Tchr. award Fairleigh Dickinson U., 1979. Mem. Am. Econ. Assn., Women's Econ. Round Table, AAUP, Eastern Econ. Assn. Congregationalist. Clubs: Wellesley, Beacon Hill. Home: 41 Windermere Terr Short Hills NJ 07078 Office: Fairleigh Dickinson U 285 Madison Ave Madison NJ 07940

BOGAN, RALPH A.L., JR., banker; b. Hibbing, Minn., Oct. 31, 1922; s. Ralph A. L. and Ann (Gerzin) B.; m. Peggy Wickman, Apr. 3, 1951; children: Pamela, Sandra, Karen, Diane. B.A., Dartmouth Coll., 1944. Exec. trainee Greyhound Corp., 1946-48; v.p. Chgo. Door Corp., 1948-58; agt. Sylvania Electric Products Co., 1958-59; Blunt, Ellis & Simmons, Chgo., 1959-62; Chgo. mgr., v.p. Dominick & Dominick, Inc., 1962-70; Chgo. mgr., gen. partner W.E. Hutton and Co., Chgo., 1970-72; chmn., dir. Atlanta/LaSalle Corp., Chgo., 1973—; chmn. NW Fin. Corp.; chmn., chief exec. officer Nat. Security Bank Chgo.; dir. OEA, Inc. Clubs: Chicago, Economic. Home: 815 Timberline Dr Glenview IL 60025 Office: 1030 W Chicago Ave Chicago IL 60622

BOGARD, CAROLE CHRISTINE, lyric soprano; b. Cin.; d. Harold and Helen Christina (Whittlesey) Geistweit; m. Charles Paine Fisher, Dec. 30, 1966; children: Christine, Pamela. Student, San Francisco State U. Debuts include: Despina in Cosi fan Tutte (Mozart), San Francisco, 1965, Poppea in Coronation of Poppea (Monteverdi), Netherlands Opera, 1971; other appearances include, Boston Opera, N.E.T., orchs. Boston, Madrid, Minn., Phila., Pitts., San Francisco, summer festivals, Mostly Mozart, N.Y., Tanglewood, Carmel, Aston Magna, Gt. Barrington, Mass.; appeared in concerts throughout Europe and with Smithsonian Chamber Players, 1976—; recorded numerous albums including 1st rec. of songs of John Duke for his 80th birthday, 1979, recital of Groupe des Six; premiered songs of Dominic Argento in, Holland, 1978, songs of Richard Cumming (in collaboration with Donald Gramm); regular participant rec. and scholarly projects, Smithsonian Instn.; judge regional auditions, Boston; tchr., with emphasis on technique as taught in last Century. Mem. Sigma Alpha Iota. Home: 161 Belknap Rd Framingham Center MA 01701 Office: care Cambridge Artists 124 Irving St Framingham MA 01701 *In my career, I've stuck to old-fashioned principles - trying to use my talent according to the standards which place singing technique on a level with the most taxing instruments. I sing for sincere acclaim and demand for my talent and my music, avoiding repertoire which would abuse my voice. I have refrained from pushing myself through "arranged" magazine articles about my hobbies and insipid appearances on TV talk shows. I have done my best rather than my most - by choice.*

BOGARDUS, CARL ROBERT, JR., educator; b. Hyden, Ky., June 26, 1933; s. Carl Robert and Jeannette Wanda (Eversole) B.; m. Norma Gail Shields, June 24, 1956; children—Carl Robert III, Cynthia Gail. B.A., Hanover Coll., 1955; M.D., U. Louisville, 1959. Diplomate: Am. Bd. Radiology, Am. Bd. Nuclear Medicine. Intern Penrose Cancer Hosp., Colorado Springs, Colo., 1959-60, resident, 1960-63; mem. staff U. Okla. Med. Center, 1963—, presently prof., dir. dept. radiation therapy; cons. Okla. hosps. Author: Practical Applied Physics of Radiology and Nuclear Medicine, 1969; contbg. author: Benign and Malignant Tumors of the Bladder, 1971, Radiation Biology for the Physician, 1973; Contbr. profl. jours. Fellow Am. Coll. Radiology; mem. Okla. Soc. Nuclear Medicine (charter pres. 196), Am. Soc. Therapeutic Radiology (nat. sec. 1968-70), S.W. Regions Soc. Nuclear Medicine, Okla. Radiol. Soc. (treas. 1970, pres. 1974—, counselor to Am. Coll. Radiology 1976—), Okla. County Radiol. Soc. (pres. 1974). Home: 3224 Lamp Post Lane Oklahoma City OK 73120 Office: 800 NE 13th St Oklahoma City OK 73190

BOGARDUS, JOHN ARTHUR, JR., insurance company executive; b. N.Y.C., Sept. 15, 1927; s. John Arthur and Elinor Morris (Strong) B.; m. Mary Lela Wood, June 9, 1950; children: John A., R. Stephen, James W., Janet S. B.A., Princeton U., 1950. With Alexander & Alexander Inc., N.Y.C., 1950—, pres., chief exec. officer, dir., 1978-82; chmn., chief exec. officer Alexander & Alexander Services Inc., 1982—; dir. Eurpac Service Inc., U.S. Surg. Corp., Donaldson, Lufkin & Jenrette. Served with USNR, 1945-46, 51-54. Mem. Nat. Assn. Ins. Brokers, Ins. Brokers Assn. N.Y. Office: Alexander & Alexander Services 1211 Ave of Americas New York NY 10036

BOGART, PAUL, director; b. N.Y.C., Nov. 21, 1919; s. Benjamin and Molly (Glass) B.; m. Alma Jane Gitnick, Mar. 22, 1941; children: Peter Gareth, Tracy Katherine, Jennifer Jane. Ed. pub. schs., N.Y.C. Lectr. New Sch. Social Research, 1960, ANTA, 1960, U. Memphis, 1968—, U. Calif., Irvine, 1979, UCLA, 1979, Loyola Marymount, 1981. Puppeteer-actor with, Berkeley Marionettes, 1946-48; TV stage mgr., asso. dir., NBC, 1950-52; free-lance dir., 1952—; TV prodns. include U.S. Steel Hour, Kraft Theatre, Armstrong Circle Theatres Goodyear Playhouse, Hallmark Hall of Fame, 1953-60, The Defenders, 1963, Ages of Man, 1965, Final War of Ollie Winter, 1966, All in the Family, 1975—; films include Marlowe, 1968, Halls of Anger, 1969, Skin Game, 1971, Class of '44, 1973, Mr. Ricco, 1975; (Emmy award for 700 Year-Old-Gang (Defenders), 1964-65, for Dear Friends (CBS Playhouse), 1967-68, for Shadow Game (CBS Playhouse), 1969-70, for All in the Family 1977-78). Served with USAAF, 1944-46. Recipient Christopher award, 1955, 73, 75; Dirs. Guild Am. awards, 1977, 78; Human Arts award Community Relations Conf. So. Calif., 1964; Humanitas award, 1977-78; Golden Globe award, 1977; So. Calif. Motion Picture Council award, 1979; Film Adv. Bd. award, 1979. Mem. Dirs. Guild Am. (nat. dir. 1962, 79, 80-81), Writers Guild Am., Am. Film Inst., Acad. Motion Picture Arts and Scis. (bd. govs.), Acad. TV Arts and Scis. Soc. Stage Dirs. and Choreographers. Home: 1033 N Carol Dr Los Angeles CA 90069 Office: Tiber Prodns Inc 760 N LaCienega Blvd Los Angeles CA 90069

BOGASH, RICHARD, pharmaceutical company executive; b. Phila., Dec. 26, 1922; s. Harry and Anna (Lieberman) B.; m. Bernice Ruth Larner, Feb. 27, 1944; children: Andrea Bogash Adelman, Ilene Bogash Silver. B.S., U. Pa., 1943, M.S., 1947, Ph.D., 1949. Asst. Manhattan Project, Columbia U., 1943-44; test engr. Insinger Machine Co., 1944-46; head product devel. lab. Wyeth Labs., Radnor, Pa., 1947-52, dir. product devel., 1952-60, asst. v.p. research and devel., 1960-67, v.p. charge research and devel., 1968-76, pres., 1976—, chmn. bd., 1978—. Contbr. articles to profl. jours. Mem. Am. Chem. Soc., Am. Pharm. Soc., Sigma Xi, Tau Beta Pi, Sigma Tau. Patentee in field. Home: 101 Cheswold Ln Haverford PA 19041 Office: PO Box 8299 Philadelphia PA 19101

BOGDAN, VICTOR MICHAEL, mathematics educator, scientist; b. Kiev, Ukraine, Jan. 4, 1933; U.S., 1961, naturalized, 1975; s. Michael Andrew and Anastasia (Chikrygin) B.; m. Ulla Eva-Maria Seeger, Nov. 12, 1968; children: Nina Ania, Michael Andrew. B.S., U. Warsaw, 1953, M.S., 1955; Ph.D., Polish Acad. Scis., 1960. Asst. math. U. Warsaw, 1952-55, instr., 1955-60, asst. prof., 1960-61; research asso. U. Md., 1961-62; asst. prof. Georgetown U., 1962-63, asso. prof., 1963-64, Cath. U. Am., 1964-66, prof. math., 1966—; sr. research asso. NASA Johnson Space Center, 1979-80. Editorial bd.: Commentationes Mathematicae, 1959-62; author monographs; contbr. articles to profl. jours. Recipient 1st prize Math. Olimpiad, Poland, 1950, Banach's prize Polish Math. Soc., 1958; award NRC, 1978, 79; NSF research grantee, 1963-64. Mem. Am., Polish, London math. socs., Assn. for Computing Machinery, IEEE (sr.). Theory distbns., almost periodic differential equations, vectorial integration theory, spectral theory operators, optimal control of dynamical systems, computer simulation of random processes. Home: 13012 Pacific Ave Rockville MD 20853 Office: Catholic Univ Washington DC 20064

BOGDANOFF, JOHN LEE, aeronautical engineering educator; b. East Orange, N.J., May 25, 1916; s. Paul George and Louise (Oswald) B.; m. Ruth Franklin Brown, Sept. 9, 1945; children: Sue Carol, Paul Lawson. B.M.E., Syracuse U., 1938; S.M., Harvard U., 1939; Ph.D., Columbia U., 1950. Asst. project engr. Wright Aero. Corp., Paterson, N.J., 1939-46; instr. civil engring. Columbia U., 1946-50; faculty Purdue U., Lafayette, Ind., 1950—, prof. engring. scis., from 1953, now prof. emeritus, former head; treas. Kozin-Bogdanoff & Assos.; cons. to industry, 1950; past v.p., dir. Midwest Applied Sci. Corp., Lafayette. Author articles in field. Fellow ASME, AAAS; mem. Am. Phys. Soc., Nat. Acad. Engring., ASTM, Sigma Xi. Research in dynamics, vibration, fatigue, wear, cumulative damage theory, application of stochastic processes to engring. problems. Home: 327 Laurel Dr West Lafayette IN 47906 Office: Sch Aero Astronautics Engring Purdue U Lafayette IN 47907

BOGDANOFF, LEONARD, musician; b. Phila., June 14, 1930; s. Herman and Tillie (Miller) B.; m. Arlene Sterling, Oct. 31, 1954; children—Adrienne, Sharon. Asst. Music student, Settlement Music Sch., Phila., 1948. Mem. faculty Settlement Music Sch., 1969—. 1st violist, New Orleans Symphony Orch., 1954-55; violist, Phila. Orch., 1955—. Served with USAF, 1951-53. Home: 204 Glen Pl Elkins Park PA 19117

BOGDANOVICH, JOSEPH JAMES, food co. exec.; b. San Pedro, Calif., May 9, 1912; s. Martin Joseph and Antoinette (Simich) B.; m. Nancynell Swaffield, Apr. 3, 1937; children—Martin, Robert, Joseph James. Student, Sch. Commerce, U. So. Calif., 1934. With Star-Kist Foods, Inc., Terminal Island, Calif., 1926—, adminstrv. asst., 1937-44, pres., from 1944; now chmn., dir.; sr. v.p., dir. H.J. Heinz Co.; Mem. Calif. Marine Research Com., 1960-66; ofcl. adviser joint U.S.-Japanese Tuna Conf., 1959, 62. Bd. dirs. Marymount Coll., South Palos Verdes Estates, Calif. Club: Virginia Country (Long Beach, Calif.). Office: Star-Kist Foods Inc 582 Tuna St Terminal Island CA 90731 *

BOGDANOVICH, PETER, movie producer, dir.; b. Kingston, N.Y., July 30, 1939; s. Borislav and Herma (Robinson) B.; m. Polly Platt, Oct. 25, 1962 (div. 1973); children—Antonia, Alexandra Welles. Student, Stella Adler's Theatre Studio, 1956-59. Co-founder Directors Co., 1972; owner Saticoy Prodncs., Inc., Los Angeles, 1968—, Copa de Oro Prodns., 1973—. Actor summer stock, 1955-58, Am. Shakespeare Festival, Stratford, Conn., 1956, Joe Papp's N.Y. Shakespeare Festival, 1958; dir., producer: off-Broadway plays The Big Knife, 1959, Once in a Lifetime, 1964; dir., Phoenicia Playhouse, N.Y.C., 1961; film critic, writer: others N.Y. Mag, 1959—; film dir., writer, producer, actor, 1968—, Targets, 1968; dir., screenwriter: The Last Picture Show, 1971; dir., writer: Directed by John Ford, 1971, Nickelodeon, 1976; dir., producer, writer: What's Up, Doc?, 1972, At Long Last Love, 1975; dir., producer: Paper Moon, 1973; dir.: Saint Jack, 1979; dir., producer: Daisy Miller, 1974 (Recipient N.Y. Film Critics award for best screenplay Last Picture Show 1971, Brit. Acad. award 1972, Writers Guild of America West award for best screenplay What's Up, Doc 1972); Author monographs on, Orson Welles, 1961, Howard Hawks, 1962, Alfred Hitchcock, 1963; books John Ford, 1968, Fritz Lang in America, 1969, Allan Dwan: The Last Pioneer, 1971, Pieces of Time: Peter Bogdanovich on the Movies, 1973, Picture Shows, 1975. Mem. A.F.T.R.A., Dirs. Guild of Am., Writers Guild of Am., Acad. Motion Picture Arts and Scis. Office: Moon Pictures 212 Copa de Oro Rd Los Angeles CA 90077 *

BOGDEN, GEORGE ANDREW, publisher; b. Paterson, N.J., Apr. 15, 1932; s. George John and Rose (Clemis) B.; m. Carolyn Siegle, Nov. 25, 1955 (dec.); children—Margaret, Kathleen, George, Suzanne. B.S. in Bus. Mgmt, Fairleigh Dickinson U., 1955. Editor-in-chief sci. publns. Allyn & Bacon, Boston, 1959-67; co-founder, pub. Bogden & Quigley, Inc., Tarrytown, N.Y. and Belmont, Calif., 1967-74; officer, dir. Springer Verlag N.Y., Inc, N.Y.C., 1974-77; co-founder, pub. K.G. Saur Pub., N.Y., Inc., N.Y.C., 1977-80; pres., chief exec. officer George A. Bogden & Son, Inc. (pubs. and distbrs. sci. and med. publs.), Ridgewood, N.J., 1980—; pres. World-Wide Book Distbrs.., Ridgewood, N.J. Active fund raising Ridgewood Scholarship Com. Served to 1st lt. USMCR, 1955-58. Mem. Sci., Tech. and Med. Pubs., Am. Pubs. Assn., Internat. Fedn. Lit. Assns., N.Y. Library Assn. Club: Benefactor Lituanus. Home: 563 Van Dyke St Ridgewood NJ 07450 Office: P.O. Box 3 Ridgewood NJ 07451

BOGDONOFF, MORTON DAVID, physician, educator; b. N.Y.C., Dec. 8, 1925; s. M. Myron and Minnie (Alpher) B.; m. Jano Segal, July 1, 1951 (div. 1971); children—Reid, Ladd, Jesse, Drue; m. Mary Patton Welt, May 9, 1975. M.D., Cornell U., 1948. Diplomate: Nat. Bd. Med. Examiners, Am. Bd. Internal Medicine. Intern, jr. asst. resident, sr. asst. resident dept. medicine N.Y. Hosp., N.Y.C., 1948-50; sr. asst. surgeon USPHS, Nat. Heart Inst., John Hopkins U., Balt., 1950-52; sr. asst. resident dept. medicine Duke Hosp., 1952-53, Eli Lilly Research fellow div. endocrinology and metabolism, 1953-54, chief resident dept. medicine, 1954-55; attending physician, chief metabolic div. Durham VA Hosp., 1955-56, cons., 1959-62; asso. prof. clin. medicine Med. Sch. U. Miami, 1956-57; asso. dept. medicine Duke U., 1955-56, asst. prof. medicine, 1957-59, asso. prof., 1959-62, prof. med., 1962-69, asst. dean grad. med. edn., 1967-69; prof., chmn. dept. internal medicine U. Ill., Chgo., 1970-75; prof. medicine, exec. asso. dean Med. Coll. Cornell U., 1975—; cons. Ft. Bragg Hosp., 1959-62, VA Hosps., Fayetteville, Durham, West-Side, Chgo.; mem. study sect. health services research NIH, 1966-70. Editor: Clinical Research, 1959-64; chief editor: Archives of Internal Medicine, 1967-77; sci. editor: Drug Therapy, 1978—; Contbr. articles to med. jours. Fellow Center Advanced Study Behavioral Scis., Stanford, 1977-78. Fellow A.C.P.; mem. Am. Fedn. Clin. Research (past pres.), Am., So., Central socs. clin. investigation, Assn. Am. Physicians, AAAS (chmn. Sect. N 1981—), Endocrine Soc., Psychosomatic Soc. (past nat. councillor), Soc. Exptl. Biology and Medicine, AMA, Harvey Soc., Alpha Omega Alpha. Office: Med Coll Cornell U 1300 York Ave New York City NY 10021

BOGDONOFF, SEYMOUR MOSES, aeronautical engineer; b. N.Y.C., Jan. 10, 1921; s. Glenn and Kate (Cohen) B.; m. Harriet Eisenberg, Oct. 1, 1944; children: Sondra Sue, Zelda Lynn, Alan Charles. B.S., Rensselaer Poly. Inst., 1942; M.S., Princeton U., 1948. Asst. sect. head fluid and gas dynamics sect. Langley Meml. Aero. Lab., NASA, 1942-46; research assoc. aero. engring. dept. Princeton U., 1946-53, asso. prof., 1953-57, prof., 1957-63, Henry Porter Patterson prof. aero. engring., 1963—, chmn. dept. mech. and aerospace engring., 1974-83, head gas dynamics lab.; cons. aero. engr.; mem. adv. council NASA; mem. sci. adv. bd. Dept. Air Force, 1958-76, 80—. Recipient Exceptional Civilian Service award Dept. Air Force, 1968. Fellow AIAA (dir., Fluid and Plasma Dynamics award 1983); mem. Internat. Acad. Astronautics of Internat. Astronautical Fedn. (corr.), Nat. Acad. Engring., ASME, Am. Phys. Soc., Sigma Xi, Tau Beta Pi. Home: 39 Random Rd Princeton NJ 08540

BOGEN, SAMUEL ADAMS, consulting electrical engineer; b. N.Y.C., Mar. 15, 1913; s. Louis and Irma Hermina (Goodman) B.; m. Ruth V. Delisky, Apr. 22, 1941; children: Elizabeth, Nicholas, Timothy. B.S., Columbia U., 1932, 1933, M.S. in Elec. Engring, 1934. Pres. Bogen Jenal Engrs. (P.C.), Garden City, N.Y., 1947—; dir. Design Profls. Ins. Co., San Francisco, 1970-75, chmn., 1970-72, pres., 1972-75; v.p. Bogen, Johnston, Lau & Jenal (P.C.), Garden City, 1976-81; adj. prof. elec. engring. Poly. Inst. N.Y., 1950-52. Trustee Port Washington (N.Y.) Sch. Bd., 1969-74. Fellow Am. Cons. Engrs. Council (pres. 1967-68); mem. IEEE (life), Nat. Soc. Profl. Engrs. Home: 20 Reid Ave Port Washington NY 11050 Office: 1225 Franklin Ave Garden City NY 11530

BOGER, GAIL PARSONS GREEN, educator; b. Worthington, Ind., June 8, 1914; d. Byron Tennison and Bula (Taylor) Green; m. Alva B. Parsons, June 8, 1935; children: Donald Alva, Robert Bradley, Gail Marie Parsons Michel, Helen Jean Parsons Czuba. B.S., Ind. U., 1950, M.S., 1959; postgrad., U. Internat., Santandar, Spain, 1968; Ph.D., U. Utah, 1969. Instr. Fresno (Calif.) State Jr. Coll., 1948-54; asst. prof. Purdue U. Extension, Michigan City, Ind., 1955-58; tchr. Jr.-Sr. High Sch., Michigan City, 1954-59; instr. Ind. U., Bloomington, 1959-64; prof. dept. edn. and Sch. Engring. Ohio No. U., Ada, 1964—; chmn. internat. research com. Children's Internat. Summer Villages, Inc., 1980—, chmn. nat. research com., trustee. Contbr. articles to profl. jours. Dupont fellow, 1957; NSF fellow, 1961, 63; NSF-AEC fellow, 1960. Mem. Am. Assn. for Supervision and Curriculum Devel., Am. Assn. Coll. Tchrs. of Edn., AAUP, Nat. Assn. Edn. of Gifted (dir., past v.p.), Nat. Assn. Creative Children and Adults (nat. trustee), Ohio Assn. Gifted Children, NEA, Ohio Edn. Assn., N.W. Ohio Edn. Assn., Ohio Acad. Sci., Gifted Children's Study Club, Kappa Delta Pi, Kappa Sigma Pi, Kappa Phi. Democrat. Episcopalian. Club: Federated Women's. Home: 1703 Wonderlick Rd Lima OH 45805 Office: Ohio No U 315 Dukes Bldg Ada OH 45810 *Nothing in the world can take the place of persistance. Talent will not; nothing is more common than unsuccessful men with talent. Genius will not; unrewarded genius is almost a proverb. Education alone will not; the world is full of educated derelicts. Persistence and determination alone are omnipotent*

BOGER, LAWRENCE LEROY, university president; b. DeKalb County, Ind., Sept. 26, 1923; s. Lester Elmer and Lazeal (Witt) B.; m. Frances June Wilbur, Sept. 2, 1945; children: Richard Lee, Judith Ann. B.S., Purdue U., 1947; student, Harvard U., U. Chgo.; M.A., Mich. State U., 1948, Ph.D., 1950. Faculty dept. agrl. econs. Mich. State U., 1948-77, beginning as instr., successively asst. prof., assoc. prof., 1948-54, prof., head dept., 1954-69, dean coll., 1969-76, univ. provost, 1976-77; pres. Okla. State U., Stillwater, 1977—; cons. U.S. Crop Reporting Service, Dept. Agr., 1953-56, Bur. Census and Statis. Reporting Service, 1965-68; cons. village devel. program for Pakistan govt. Ford Found., 1957, 64, 67; cons. programs econ. assistance Nat. U. of Colombia, S.Am., Kellogg Found., 1959; mem. Nat. Com. on Use of Electronic Data Processing in Farm Mgmt.; dir.-at-large Central Bank for Coops., FCA, 1967-71; mem. joint univ. adv. com. U. Nigeria, 1965-68; guest lectr. Govt. of Taiwan, 1979. Mem. Spl. Commn. on Land Use Planning, 1971—; chmn. Gov.'s Oil and Gas Task Force, 1973; del. White House Conf. on Nutrition, 1969, Chgo. Foothills Conf. on Inflation, 1974, Pres.'s Conf. on Inflation, Washington, 1974; mem. Gov.'s Council on Sci. and Tech., 1983—; trustee Nat. 4-H Council, 1981—. Mem. Am. Econ. Assn., Am. Agrl. Econs. Assn. (v.p. 1960-61), Internat. Assn. Agrl. Econs. (Am. council, participant conf. USSR 1970), Am. Statis. Assn., Okla. State C. of C. (bd. dirs), Stillwater C. of C. (bd. dirs), Blue Key, Sigma Xi, Alpha Zeta, Omicron Delta Kappa, Pi Mu Epsilon, Phi Kappa Phi. Home: 1600 N Washington Stillwater OK 74078

BOGERT, GEORGE TAYLOR, lawyer; b. Ithaca, N.Y., Sept. 20, 1920; s. George Gleason and Lolita Eleanor (Metzger) B.; m. Adelyn Mayo Russell, July 22, 1950; children: Nicholas Snowden, Amy Gleason, Carroll Russell. A.B., Cornell U., 1941; LL.B., Harvard U., 1948. Bar: Ill. 1949. Mem. Hopkins, Sutter, Halls, DeWolfe & Owen, Ill., 1948-51; gen. counsel, asst. to pres. Guardian Electric Mfg. Co., Chgo., 1951-54; mem. Crowell & Liebman, and predecessors, Chgo., 1954-60, ptnr., 1960-66, Mayer, Brown & Platt, 1966—. Co-author, editor: Trust and Trustees, 1959-66; author, 2d rev. edit., 1974. Mem. ABA, Ill. Bar Assn., Chgo. Bar Assn., Am. Law Inst., Chgo. Estate Planning Council, Am. Coll. Probate Counsel, Internat. Acad. Estate and Trust Law. Home: 2440 N Lakeview Ave Chicago IL 60614 Office: Mayer Brown & Platt 231 S LaSalle St Chicago IL 60604

BOGERT, HENRY LAWRENCE, banker; b. N.Y.C., Oct. 7, 1911; s. Henry Lawrence and Elizabeth Blodget (Sanford) B.; m. Margaret Milbank, Apr. 25, 1936; children—Henry Lawrence III, Jeremiah M. Grad., St. Paul's Sch., Concord, N.H., 1930; B.A., Yale U., 1934. With Bankers Trust Co., N.Y.C., 1934-42; with Blyth, Eastman, Paine, Webber Inc. (and predecessors), 1946—, gen. partner, 1948-56, Eastman Dillon, Union Securities & Co., Inc., 1956-71, sr. v.p., dir., 1971-73, sr. subordinated debenture holder, 1973—. Trustee Provident Loan Soc. N.Y.; Hon. trustee Buckley Sch. of N.Y., Boys Club N.Y. Mem. Investment Bankers Assn. Am. (pres. 1966-67, gov.), Soc. of Cincinnati. Clubs: Links, River. (N.Y.C.); Fishers Island Country (N.Y.) (gov., pres. 1957-59); Hobe Sound Country (Fla.) (dir., pres. 1974-78). Office: Blyth Eastman Paine Webber Inc 1221 Ave of Americas New York NY 10020

BOGERT, IVAN LATHROP, sanitary engineer; b. Johnson City, N.Y., Mar. 24, 1918; s. Robert John and Donna Katherine (Sherwood) B.; m. Lorene E. Eakins, Aug. 21, 1942; children—P. Jeffrey, Lawrence R., Carolyn V. C.E., Cornell U., 1939, postgrad., 1940-41. Registered profl. engr., N.J., N.Y., Fla., Conn., Mass., Pa., Ohio, Calif., Va., R.I., Ill., Md.; registered profl. planner, N.J. Inspector, estimator, designer Beckerle & Wright, Pearl River, N.Y., 1939-40; jr. camp sanitarian N.Y. State Dept. Health, Albany, 1940; san. engring. designer Charles H. Hurd, Indpls., 1941, Silas Mason Co., Shreveport, La., 1941; engring. designer Sanborn & Bogert, N.Y.C., 1942-44, Bogert and Childs Engring. Assos., 1946-48; mng. partner Clinton Bogert Assos. (and predecessor firms), N.Y.C. and; Ft. Lee, N.J., 1949—. Served in San. Corps U.S. Army, 1944-46. Decorated Army Commendation Ribbon. Mem. Am. Arbitration Assn., Am. Cons. Engrs. Council, Am. Geophys. Union, Am. Planning Assn., Am. Public Health Assn., Am. Public Works Assn., ASCE, N.J. Assn. Profl. Planners, Am. Soc. Engring. Edn., Am. Soc. Planning Ofcls., Am. Water Works Assn., Am. Soc. Profl. Ecologists, Cornell Soc. Engrs., Internat. Assn. Water Pollution Research, Internat. Water Resources Assn., Internat. Water Supply Assn., Nat. Assn. Regional Councils, Nat. Soc. Profl. Engrs., N.J. Bus. and Industry Assn., Soc. Am. Mil. Engrs., Water Pollution Control Assn., N.J. C. of C., Royal Soc. Health. Unitarian. Clubs: Englewood Field, Knickerbocker Country. Home: 27 Jefferson Ave Tenafly NJ 07670 Office: 2125 Center Ave Fort Lee NJ 07024

BOGERT, JONATHAN, controller; b. Englewood, N.J., Nov. 8, 1941; s. Frank Warner and Elsie Mae (Gilmour) B.; m. Janet R. Schlageter, June 15, 1963; children—Laura Jean, Jonathan Drew, David Christopher. B.A., Yale, 1963; postgrad., Pace U., 1963-67. C.P.A., N.Y. Auditor Price Waterhouse & Co., N.Y.C., 1963-68; corp. controller Sterling Drug Inc., N.Y.C., 1968-77; controller Steuber Co. Inc., N.Y.C., 1977-78, Main Hurdman and Cranstoun, 1978-80; asst. controller Black & Decker Mfg. Co., Towson, Md., 1980-81, controller, 1981—; instr. Fairleigh Dickinson U., 1974-75. Mem. Nat. Assn. Accountants (past pres. E. Bergen-Rockland chpt.), Am. Inst. C.P.A.'s, Fin. Execs. Inst. Home: 13713 Killarney Ct Phoenix MD 21131 Office: 701 E Joppa Rd Towson MD 21204

BOGGESS, MILDRED MORFORD ANDREWS, educator; b. Hominy, Okla., Sept. 25, 1915; d. George Frederick and Clara (Parks) Andrews; m. Rough Adams Boggess, Nov. 21, 1973. Student, Bethany Coll., Lindsborg, Kans., 1933-34; B.F.A., U. Okla., 1937; M.Mus., U. Mich., 1940. Mem. faculty Sch. Music, U. Okla., Norman, 1938—, prof. music, 1953—, David Ross Boyd disting. prof., 1964-76, Davis Ross Boyd prof. emeritus, 1976—; vis. prof. organ Union Theol. Sem., N.Y.C., summers 1963, 66, Episcopal music confs., Evergreen, Colo., 1940-64, Eugene, Oreg., 1965, Sewannee, Tenn., 1960, 62, 65; organ concerts, throughout U.S., 1939—. Author: (with others) Church Organ Method, 1973. Organist-choirmaster St. John's Episcopal Ch., Norman, 1936-64; cons. music and fine arts. Bur. Higher Edn., Wash.; Chmn. Episcopal Diocese Okla. Music Com., 1945-63. Named Outstanding Faculty Woman U. Okla., 1948, One of 10 Outstanding Faculty Mems., 1953, Okla. Musician of Year, 1972; recipient Career Achievement award Profl. Panhellenic Assn.; Distinguished Service citation U. Okla.; named to Okla. Hall of Fame, 1971. Mem. Am. Guild Organists (chmn. Okla. 1962-64, nat. dir. student guild groups 1966—, nat. council 1966-69), Music Tchrs. Nat. Assn. (nat. chmn. organ and ch. music com. 1956-64), Nat. Fedn. Music Clubs (nat. organ chmn. 1956-60), Mortar Bd., Phi Beta Kappa, Mu Phi Epsilon (dist. dir. 1966-68, nat. v.p. 1966—), Pi Kappa Lambda, Alpha Lambda Delta, Delta Kappa Gamma. Home: 704 Mockingbird Ln Norman OK 73071 *Personal and professional discipline will determine any championship.*

BOGGS, CORINNE C. (LINDY BOGGS), congresswoman; b. Brunswick Plantation, La.; m. Thomas Hale Boggs (dec. 1973); children: Barbara Boggs Sigmund, Thomas Hale, Corinne Boggs Roberts. Grad., Sophie Newcomb Coll. Mem. 93d-98th Congresses from 2d La. dist.; mem. appropriations com., 1977—, also mem. select com. on children, youth and families, chmn. task force on crisis intervention, subcoms. on energy and water devel., housing and urban devel., ind. agys., subcom. on legis. br., chmn. joint com. on bicentennial arrangements, 1975-76; mem. exec. com. Dem. Congressional Campaign Com., 1979-82; mem. women's council Dem. Nat. Com., 1979-82. Active numerous civic activities; past pres. Women's Nat. Democratic Club, Dem. Congressional Wives Forum, Congressional Club; head inaugural balls for Pres. Kennedy, 1961, Pres. Johnson, 1965; chairwoman Dem. Nat. Conv., 1976, mem. platform drafting subcom., 1980; Bd. dirs. Am. Bicentennial Adminstrn., 1974-77, La. Council Music and Performing Arts; bd. regents Smithsonian Instn., 1976-77, regent emeritus, 1980—. Mem. Nat. Soc. Colonial Dames, League Women Voters. Roman Catholic. Office: 2353 Rayburn House Office Bldg Washington DC 20515

BOGGS, DANE RUFFNER, educator, physician; b. Orton, W.Va., Apr. 21, 1931; s. Earl R. and Leni (Rohrabaugh) B.; m. Sallie Slaughter, Aug. 14, 1969; children: Dane Ruffner, Keith W., Richard E., J. Eric. B.A., U. Va., 1952, M.D., 1956. Diplomate: Am. Bd. Internal Medicine. Intern U. Va. Hosp., 1956-57; med. resident U. Utah Hosp., 1959-60; instr., then asst. prof. U. Utah Sch. Medicine, 1961-67; asso. prof. Rutgers U. Sch. Medicine, 1967-69; prof. medicine U. Pitts. Sch. Medicine, 1969—, chief div. hematology, 1967-79; dir. Pitts. Sickle Cell Center, 1972-79; Clin. asso. Nat. Cancer Inst., 1957-59; Leukemia Soc. Scholar, 1962-65; Faculty research asso. Am. Cancer Soc., 1965-70. Author: White Cell Manual, 4th edit., 1983, Clinical Hematology, 1974-81; also chpts. in books, articles. Recipient John Horseley Meml. Research award U. Va., 1970. Mem. Am. Soc. Clin. Research, Am. Fedn. Clin. Research, Western Soc. Clin. Research, Am., Internat. socs. hematology, AAAS, Soc. Exptl. Biology and Medicine, Reticuloendothelial Soc., Phi Beta Kappa, Alpha Omega Alpha, Sigma Phi Epsilon. Democrat. Office: Scaife Hall U Pitts Pittsburgh PA 15261

BOGGS, JACK AARON, banker; b. Easley, S.C., July 4, 1935; s. Walter Benston and Bessie Mae (Jones) B.; m. Isabel Thomas Brown, July 7, 1965; children—James Benston, Renee Chaplin, Edward Cunningham. B.S. in Bus. Econs, U.S.C., 1964. Chartered bank auditor; certified internal auditor. Sec.-treas. Cedarpoint Farms Corp., Columbia, S.C., 1963-67; auditor S.C. Nat. Bank, Columbia, 1967-76; exec. dir. S.C. Automated Clearing House Assn., 1976—; instr. S.C. Bankers Sch., 1972—. Mem. Town Council, Arcadia Lakes, S.C., 1977—. Served with USN, 1952-56. Mem. Nat. Assn. Accountants, Inst. Internal Auditors (bd. govs. 1971-74, pres. 1973-74, internat. research com. 1972—, internat. membership com. 1976), Data Processing Mgmt. Assn., Bank Adminstrn. Inst. (1st award 1972), Sigma Delta Pi, Chi Psi. Democrat. Unitarian. Home: 804 Arcadia Lakes Dr Columbia SC 29206 Office: 2009 Park St Columbia SC 29202 *It's not who you are; it's what you do that counts.*

BOGGS, JAMES ERNEST, chemistry educator; b. Cleve., June 9, 1921; s. Ernest Beckett and Emily (Reid) B.; m. Ruth Ann Rogers, June 22, 1948; children: Carol, Ann, Lynne. A.B., Oberlin Coll., 1943; M.S. in Chemistry, U. Mich., 1944, Ph.D., 1953. Asst. prof. dept. chemistry Eastern Mich. U., Ypsilanti, 1949-52; instr. U. Mich. at Ann Arbor, 1952-53; mem. faculty dept. chemistry U. Tex. at Austin, 1953—, assoc. prof., 1958-66, prof., 1966—, asst. dean Grad. Sch., 1958-67, dir. Center for Structural Studies, 1969—, acting dir. Inst. Theoretical Chemistry, 1979-81. Contbr. 140 articles to profl. jours. Mem. Am. Chem. Soc., Am. Phys. Soc., Phi Beta Kappa, Sigma Xi, Phi Lambda Upsilon, Gamma Alpha. Research in structural chemistry, microwave spectroscopy, quantum chemistry. Home: 4603 Balcones Dr Austin TX 78731

BOGGS, JOSEPH DODRIDGE, pediatric pathologist; b. Bellefontaine, Ohio, Dec. 31, 1921; s. Walter C. and Birdella Z. (Coons) B.; m. Donna Lee Shoemaker, June 12, 1964; 1 son, Joseph Dodridge. A.B., Ohio U., 1941, Litt.D., 1966; M.D., Jefferson Med. Coll., 1945. Intern Jefferson Med. Coll. Hosp., Phila., 1945-46; resident Peter Bent Brigham Hosp., Boston, 1946-48, asso. pathologist, 1947-51; instr. pathology Harvard Med. Sch., Boston, 1948-51; with Children's Meml. Hosp., Chgo., 1951—, dir. labs., 1951—; prof. pathology Northwestern U., Chgo., 1952—; dir. BSP Ins. Co., Phoenix. Contbr. articles to profl. jours. Mem. med. adv. bd. Ill. Dept. Corrections, Springfield, 1971-77; bd. dirs. Blood Services, Phoenix, 1972, Community Hosp., Evanston, Ill., 1958-61, Lorreto Hosp., Chgo., 1971-72. Served to capt. M.C. U.S. Army, 1948-51. Mem. Am. Soc. Study of Liver Disease, N.Y. Acad. Scis., Midwest Soc. Pediatric Research, Inst. Medicine, Ill. Soc. Pathologists (pres. 1965), Ill. Assn. Blood Banks (pres. 1969-70). Home: 1448 N Lake Shore Dr Chicago IL 60610 Office: Children's Meml Hosp 2300 Children's Plaza Chicago IL 60614

BOGGS, LINDY *See* **BOGGS, CORINNE C.**

BOGGS, MARCUS LIVINGSTONE, JR., novelist, editor; b. Birmingham, Ala., Dec. 10, 1947; s. Marcus Livingstone and Sarah Alice (McFarland) B.; m. Elizabeth Ruth Bell, June 12, 1977. A.B., Princeton U., 1970. Editor Oxford Univ. Press, N.Y.C., 1977-83, Harcourt Brace Jovanovich, San Diego, 1983—. Author: Scissors, Paper, Stone, 1981. Club: Sierra. Home: 1335 Torrance St San Diego CA 92103 Office: Harcourt Brace Jovanovich 1250 6th Ave San Diego CA 92101

BOGGS, RALPH STUART, lawyer; b. Toledo, June 6, 1917; s. Nolan and Sarah (MacPhie) B.; m. Mary Frances Sharp Wiggins, Sept. 7, 1940; children: Sally Ann Boggs Bashore, William S., Robert A. A.B., Denison U., 1939; LL.B., U. Mich., 1942. Bar: Ohio 1942, U.S. Supreme Ct. 1960. Spl. agt. FBI, 1942-45; practiced in Toledo, 1946—; partner Boggs, Boggs & Boggs (P.A.), 1946-74, now pres., treas., dir.; sec., dir. Master Chem. Corp., Mar-Mil Corp., Cousino Metal Products Inc. Mem. Maumee Bd. Edn., 1953-69; mem. Maumee Recreation Com., 1954-69; v.p. Toledo adv. com. Salvation Army, 1970-81, pres., 1981-83; pres. Maumee Men's Republican Club, 1947-48; former chmn. bd. trustees Presbytery of Maumee, Inc. Mem. X-FBI Agts. Soc., Am., Ohio, Lucas County, Toledo bar assns., Am. Judicature Soc., Assn. Trial Lawyers Am. Presbyterian (elder). Clubs: Masons (Toledo) (33 deg.); Shriners; Heather Downs Country (Toledo) (past pres., dir.). Home: 5920 Swan Creek Dr Toledo OH 43614 Office: 413 Michigan St Toledo OH 43624 *Education, preparation and perseverance are essential to attaining success.*

BOGGS, ROBERT NEWELL, editor; b. Denver, Sept. 14, 1930; s. John Irwin and Rowena Opal (Newell) B.; m. Gwendolyn Carol Lee, June 18, 1955; children: Kerrie Kim and Kristie Kay (twins), Kevin Clarke, Karole Lee. B.S.M.E., U. Colo., 1958. Design engr. Denver Equipment Co., 1958-59; application engr., writer Gates Rubber Co., Denver, 1959-63; asst. editor Design News, Denver, after 1963, then assoc. editor, sr. editor, to 1971, mng. exec. editor, Boston, 1971—; co-founder Busy B Ceramics, 1975. Pres. Franklin Assn. Childhood Edn., Denver, 1969, Cherrywood Ridge Civic Assn., 1969-71; mem. adv. bd., Marshfield, Mass., 1975-77. Served with USAF, 1950-54. Mem. Am. Soc. Bus. Press Editors (founding pres. chpt. 1974-75, dir. 1979-82, 1st v.p. 1983-84), Marshfield Civic Assn. (founding pres. 1973-75). Home: 288 Holly Rd Marshfield MA 02050 Office: 221 Columbus Ave Boston MA 02116

BOGGS, THOMAS HALE, JR., lawyer; b. New Orleans, Sept. 18, 1940; s. Thomas Hale and Corinne (Claiborne) B.; m. Mary Barbara Denechaud, Dec. 27, 1960; g6children—Hale, Elizabeth, Douglas. A.B., Georgetown U., 1961, LL.B., 1965. Bar: D.C. bar 1965. Economist Joint Econ. Com., U.S. Congress, 1961-65; spl. asst. to dir. Office Emergency Planning, 1965-66; practice in, Washington, 1966—; mem. firm Patton, Boggs & Blow, 1966—; mem. Presdl. Commn. on Exec. Exchange, 1979—; Presdl. del. Independence of Solomon Islands, 1978, Trade Mission to People's Republic of China, 1979. Co-author: Private Trade Barriers in the Atlantic Community, 1964. Democratic candidate for U.S. Ho. of Reps. 8th Dist. Md., 1970; mem. Charter Commn. Dem. Nat. Com., 1973. Mem. Am. Judicature Soc., Am. Bar Assn. (com. chmn.), Martime, Fed. bar assns., Delta Theta Phi. Home: 6 E Kirke St Chevy Chase MD 20015 Office: 2550 M St NW Washington DC 20037

BOGGS, WILLIAM BRENTON, computer service company executive; b. Douglas, Ariz., Dec. 18, 1918; emigrated to Can., 1927; s. William Brenton and Catherine Lynn B.; m. Hughene Parkes, Feb. 7, 1948; children: Mary Catherine, William Brenton, Talbot Hugh. B.Mech., McGill U., 1940; Hon. fellow, Can. Sch. Mgmt., Toronto, 1981. Cert. profl. engr., Ont., Que. Asst. supt. maintenance Trans. Can. Airlines, Montreal and Winnipeg, 1945-50; prodn. supt. Canadair Ltd., Montreal, 1950; v.p. Hawker Siddeley Can., Montreal, 1957-65; pres., chief exec. officer De Havilland Aircraft, Toronto, 1965-70, Can. Systems Group, 1971-82, chmn., 1982—; dir. Guardian Ins., Toronto, Montreal Life Ins. Co., Magna Internat. Ltd., Toronto, Kenrod Mfg., Montreal. Pres. Toronto Symphony Orch. Assn., 1982—. Served as squadron leader RCAF, 1940-45. Decorated officer Order of Brit. Empire. Fellow Can. Aircraft and Space Inst.; mem. Can. Aircraft Industry Assn. (pres. Ottawa 1967), Can. Assn. Data Processing Assn. (pres. Montreal 1976), Can. Mfrs. Assn. (chmn. Toronto 1981-82). Conservative. Baptist. Clubs: Granite, Posedale Golf; Queens Tennis (Toronto); Rotary (pres. 1950); Rideau (Ottawa)). Home: 190 Roxborough Dr Toronto ON Canada M4W 1X8 Office: Canada Systems Group Ltd 45 Saint Clair St W Toronto ON Canada M4V 1K9

BOGHOSIAN, VARUJAN YEGAN, sculptor; b. New Britain, Conn., June 26, 1926; s. Mesrop and Baidzar (Saylandzian) B.; m. Marilyn Cummins, Sept. 1, 1953; 1 dau., Heidi. Student, Conn. Tchrs. Coll., 1946-48, Vesper George Sch. Art, 1948-50; B.F.A., Yale U., 19—, M.F.A., 1959; M.A. (hon.), Brown U., 1965, Dartmouth Coll., 1969. Instr. in art U. Fla., 1958-59, Pratt Inst., 1961, Yale U., 1962-64; asst. prof. art Cooper Union Coll., 1959-64; asso. prof. Brown U., 1964-68; artist-in-residence Dartmouth Coll., 1968, prof. art, 1968—, George Frederick Jewett prof. art, 1983—; sculptor in residence Am. Acad. in Rome, 1966-67. Artist: woodcut portfolios Orpheus, 1951, The River Styx, 1971; numerous one-man shows including, Stable Gallery, N.Y.C., 1963, 64, 65, 66, Cordier and Ekstrom, N.Y.C., 1969, 71, 73, 75, 77, 78, 79, 80, Arts Club of Chgo., 1970, group shows include, Obelisk Gallery, Rome, 1953, Mus. Modern Art, N.Y.C., 1956, Hanover Gallery, London, 1966; represented in numerous permanent collections including, Mus. Modern Art, N.Y.C., Whitney Mus. Am. Art, N.Y.C., Addison Gallery Am. Art, Andover, Mass., Worcester Art Mus., Phoenix Art Mus. Served with USN, 1944-46. Recipient award Nat. Inst. Arts, Letters, 1972; Fulbright grantee, 1953; U.S. Specialists grantee, 1961. Club: Century (N.Y.C.). Office: Visual Studies Office Dartmouth Coll HB 6081 Hanover NH 03755

BOGLE, HUGH ANDREW, engineering consultant; b. Lenoir City, Tenn., June 14, 1909; s. Hugh Andrew and Cornelia (Monger) B.; m. Mary Johnson Davis, Nov. 25, 1935 (dec. 1959); 1 son, Edwin Davis; m. Ethel L. Mitchell, July 28, 1961 (div.); m. Denise R. Dupriez, Sept. 6, 1975. B.S. in Chem. Engring, U. Tenn., 1929. With E.I. du Pont de Nemours & Co., Inc., Wilmington, Del., 1929-66, mgr. indsl. engring. cons. sect., 1954-58, cons. engring. and econ. evaluations, 1958-66; chmn. bd. West Chester Chem. Co., Pa., 1966—; exec. v.p. Sealants Internat., Inc., West Chester, 1966—; pres. Bolmar Corp., Roan Industries, West Chester, Bonded Products, Inc.; ASME rep. to Fedn. Mgmt. Oriented Orgns., 1959-66, v.p., 1961-62, pres., 1962; mem. council indsl. engring. Nat. Indsl. Conf. Bd., 1951-67, chmn., 1959; mem. Grantt Medal Award Bd., ASME-Am. Mgmt. Assn., 1960-63, Wallace Clark Award Bd., ASME-Soc. Advancement Mgmt.-Am. Mgmt. Assn.-Am. Soc. Indsl. Engrs., 1962-66. Fellow Soc. Advancement Mgmt.; mem. Am. Inst. Indsl. Engrs. (sr.), ASME (chmn. mgmt. div. 1960), ASTM, Council Internat. Progress Mgmt. (dir. 1962-67, exec. com. 1963-65, sec. 1964-66), Kappa Alpha, Alpha Chi Sigma. Episcopalian. Clubs: Plays and Players (Phila.); Wine and Food Soc. (London); Confrerie des Chevaliers du Tastevin (Dijon); Les Bon Vivants (Media, Pa.). Home: 2216 Monica Pl Sarasota FL 33580 Office: 439 S Bolmar St West Chester PA 19380

BOGLE, JOHN CLIFTON, investment company executive; b. Montclair, N.J., May 8, 1929; s. William Yates, Jr. and Josephine (Hipkins) B.; m. Eve Sherrerd, Sept. 22, 1956; children: Barbara, Jean, John Clifton, Nancy, Sandra, Andrew. A.B., Princeton U., 1951. With Wellington Mgmt. Co., Phila., 1951-74, asst. to pres., 1954-62, sec., adminstrv. v.p., 1962-66, exec. v.p., 1966-67, pres., chief exec. officer, 1967-74; chmn., chief exec. officer Vanguard Group Investment Cos. (Wellington Fund, Windsor Fund, others), Valley Forge, Pa., 1974—; trustee Phila. Sav. Fund Soc., mem. exec. com., 1969—; dir., mem. exec. com. Gen. Accident Group, Penn Gen. Ins. Co., Camden Fire Ins. Co., Potomac Ins. Co.; dir. Mead Corp. Contbr. numerous articles to profl. jours., chpts. to books. Trustee Blair Acad.; adv. council econs. dept. Princeton U.; adv. council Center for Fin. Insts., U. Pa.; bd. dirs. Bryn Mawr (Pa.) Hosp. Mem. Nat. Assn. Securities Dealers (investment cos. com. 1967-74, long-range planning com. 1973-74), Investment Co. Inst. (gov. 1969-81, chmn. 1969-70). Clubs: Merion Cricket, Merion Golf (Haverford); Union League (Phila.). Home: 418 N Rose Ln Haverford PA 19041 Office: PO Box 876 Valley Forge PA 19482

BOGOMOLNY, RICHARD JOSEPH, retail food chain executive; b. Cleve., Jan. 17, 1935; s. Michael and Hilda (Faigin) B.; m. Annette Nathanson, Apr. 5, 1959; children: Michael, Mark, Edward. Student, Harvard U., 1954-55; B.A., Western Res. U., 1957; J.D., Cleve. State U., 1961. Pres., Eagle Ice Cream Co., Cleve., 1955-68; div. v.p. Fisher Foods, Inc., Bedford, Ohio, 1968-70, adminstrv. v.p., 1971-72; v.p. Pick-N-Pay Supermarkets, Cleve., 1972-75, pres., 1975-78, also dir.; chmn. bd., pres., chief exec. officer First Nat. Supermarkets, Inc., Cleve., 1978—. Trustee, Jewish Community Fedn., 1979—, Cleve. Tomorrow Com., 1983—, Cleve. Civic Orch., 1972—. Mem. Food Mktg. Inst. (dir.), Ohio Retail Merchants Assn. (dir.), Cleve. Bar Assn., Cuyahoga County Bar Assn., Ohio State Bar Assn., Greater Cleve. Growth Assn. Home: 3436 Lanark Ln Pepper Pike OH 44124 Office: 17000 Rockside Rd Cleveland OH 44137

BOGOMOLNY, ROBERT LEE, educator; b. Cleve., June 27, 1938; s. Michael and Hilda Faigin (Berkowitz) B.; m. Alice Rogan, Feb. 16, 1961; children—Lara Ann, Lael Michaela, Michael Nathan, Joshua David. A.B., Harvard U., 1960, LL.B., 1963. Bar: Ohio bar 1963, D.C. bar 1967, U.S. Supreme Ct. bar 1967. Asso. firm Burke, Haber & Berick, Cleve., 1963-66; atty. criminal div. Dept. Justice, Washington, 1966-68; asst. chief counsel Bur. Narcotics and Dangerous Drugs, 1968-69, Bur. Drug Abuse Control HEW, 1968; spl. asst. to U.S. atty. for, D.C., 1966-68; asst. dir. Vera Inst. Justice, N.Y.C., 1969-70; prof. law So. Meth. U., 1970-77, dir. criminal justice program, 1970-77; prof. law Cleve. State U., 1977—, dean, 1977—; cons. spl. commn. narcotic and hallucinogenic drug act Nat. Conf. Commrs. Uniform State Law, 1968-69; dir. Continental Steel Corp., IMS Internat., Inc., United Western Corp., First Nat. Supermarkets, Inc. Author: (with M. Sonnenreich and A. Roccograndi) A Handbook on the 1970 Federal Drug Act: Shifting the Perspective, 1975; Editor: Human Experimentation, 1976; Contbr. articles to profl. jours. Bd. dirs. Jewish Vocat. Service, 1978; trustee Human Relations Com., 1981—; Bd. dirs. Free Clinic of Greater Cleve., 1983—. Mem. Am. Bar Assn., Greater Cleve. Bar Assn., Ohio Bar Assn., Legal Aid Soc. Home: 24275 Lyman Blvd Shaker Heights OH 44122 Office: 1801 Euclid Ave Cleveland OH 44115

BOGORAD, LAWRENCE, biology educator; b. Tashkent, U.S.S.R., Aug. 29, 1921; came to U.S., 1922; s. Boris and Florence (Bernard) B.; m. Rosalyn G. Sagen, June 29, 1943; children—Leonard Paul, Kiki M. Lee. B.S., U. Chgo., 1942, Ph.D., 1949. Instr. botany U. Chgo., 1948-51, asst. prof. dept. botany, 1953-57, assoc. prof., 1957-61, prof., 1961-67; prof. biology Harvard U., Cambridge, Mass., 1967—, chmn. dept. biology, 1974-76, dir. Maria Moors Cabot Found., Cambridge, Mass., 1976—, Maria Moors Cabot prof. biology, 1980—; vis. investigator Rockefeller Inst., N.Y.C., 1951-53; mem. com. on sci. and public policy Nat. Acad. Scis., 1977-81; mem. Assembly of Life Scis., NRC; mem. joint council on food and agrl. scis. Dept. Agr., 1978-82. Asso. editor: Bot. Gazette, 1958; editoral com.: Annual Rev. Plant Physiology, 1963-67; editorial bd.: Plant Physiology, 1965-66, Biochimica Biophysica Acta, 1967-69, Jour. Cell Biology, 1967-70, Jour. Applied and Molecular Genetics, 1981—, Plant Molecular Biology, 1981—, Plant Cell Reports, 1981—. Served with AUS, 1943-46. Merck fellow, 1951-53; Fulbright fellow, 1960; recipient Career Research award NIH, 1963. Fellow Am. Acad. Arts and Scis.; mem. Am. Soc. Biol. Chemistry, Am. Soc. Cell Biology, Nat. Acad. Scis. (chmn. botany sect. 1974-77), Am. Soc. Plant Physiologists (pres. 1968-69, Stephen Hales award 1982), AAAS (bd. dirs. 1982), Royal Danish Acad. Scis. and Letters (fgn.), Soc. Developmental Biology (pres. 1984). Office: Dept of Biology Harvard Univ 16 Divinity Ave Cambridge MA 02138

BOGORAD, SAMUEL NATHANIEL, educator; b. New Bedford, Mass., Apr. 7, 1917; s. Sidney and Rebecca (Eisenstadt) B.; m. Ruth Pollack, Sept. 10, 1944. A.B. summa cum laude, Brown U., 1939, A.M., 1941; Ph.D., Northwestern U., 1946. Instr. English Northwestern U., Evanston, Ill., 1942-45; instr. U. Vt., Burlington, 1946-47, asst. prof., 1947-52, asso. prof., 1952-57, prof., 1957—, Frederick Corse prof. English lang. and lit., 1968—, chmn. English dept., 1961-1969; Vis. asst. prof. Brown U., 1948-49; vis. prof. William and Mary Coll., summer 1951, U. Colo., summer 1958. Author: (with J. Trevithick) The College Miscellany, 1952, (with C. Graham) Atlantic Essays, 1958, (with R.G. Noyes) Samuel Foote's Primitive Puppet Shew, 1973. Chmn. planning commn., South Burlington, Vt., 1952-55, town moderator, 1955-61, justice of peace, 1973—; mem. commn. on insts. of higher edn. New Eng. Assn. Colls. and Secondary Schs., 1963-71; commr. New Eng. Bd. Higher Edn., 1973-79. Mem. MLA, Nat. Council Tchrs. English, Coll. English Assn. (pres. New Eng. 1966-67, nat. dir. 1968-71, v.p. 1971-73, pres. 1973), AAUP (pres. U. Vt. chpt. 1954-55), Phi Beta Kappa (pres. New Eng. dist. United chpts. 1961-76, com. on Qualifications United chpts., mem. Senate 1970-76). Home: 1425 Hinesburg Rd South Burlington VT 05401 Office: U Vt Burlington VT 05405

BOGSCH, ARPAD, internat. agy. exec.; b. Budapest, Hungary, 1919; (married); 2 children. Ed. in law, U.S. Bar: bar. Staff mem. copyright div. UNESCO, 1948-54; legal counsel to U.S. Copyright Office, after 1954; with World Intellectual Property Orgn. (and predecessor agy.), 1963—, dir. gen., 1973—. Address: 34 Chemin des Colombettes 1211 Geneva 20 Switzerland

BOGUE, ALLAN G., history educator; b. London, Ont., Can., May 12, 1921; married; 3 children. B.A., U. Western Ont., 1943, M.A., 1946; Ph.D., Cornell U., 1951; LL.D., U. Western Ont., 1973; D.Fil (hon.), U. Uppsala, 1977. Lectr. econs. and history, asst. librarian U. Western Ont., 1949-52; from asst. prof. to prof. history U. Iowa, 1952-64, chmn. dept., 1959-63; prof. history U. Wis.-Madison, 1964-68, chmn. dept., 1972-73, Frederick Jackson Turner prof. history, 1968—; mem. hist. adv. com. Math. Soc. Sci. Bd., 1965-71; Scandinavian-Am. Found. Thord-Gray lectr., 1968; mem. Council Inter-Univ. Consortium Polit. Research, 1971-73; vis. prof. history Harvard U., 1972; dir. Social Sci. Research Council, 1973-76. Author: Money at Interest, 1955, From Prairie to Corn Belt, 1963; co-author, editor: The West of the American People, 1970; co-author, contbr.: The Dimensions of Quantitative Research in History, 1972; editor: Emerging Theoretical Models in History, 1973; co-editor, contbr.: American Political Behavior: Historical Essays and Readings, 1974; co-editor: The University of Wisconsin: One Hundred and Twenty Five Years, 1975; author: The Earnest Men, 1981. Social Sci. Research Council fellow, 1955, 66; Guggenheim fellow, 1970; Sherman Fairchild disting. fellow Calif. Inst. Tech., 1975. Mem. Agr. Hist. Soc. (pres. 1963-64), Orgn. Am. Historians (pres. 1982-83), Am. Hist. Assn., Econ. Hist. Assn. (pres. 1981-82), Social Sci. Hist. Assn. (pres. 1977-78). Office: Dept History U Wis Madison WI 53706 *

BOGUE, PHILIP ROBERTS, university administrator; b. Seattle, Dec. 22, 1924; s. Freeman Snowden and Nina (Reck) B.; m. A. Suzanne Weatherly, June 9, 1951; children: Scott Weatherly, Nancy Sue. B.A., U. Wash., 1947; M.B.A., Harvard U., 1949. C.P.A., Oreg., Wash. With Arthur Andersen & Co. (C.P.A.s), 1949-81, partner, 1956-81, mng. partner, Portland, Oreg., 1961-81; asst. to pres. for univ. relations Portland State U., 1982—; dir. Oreg. Title Ins. Co. Bd. dirs. Oreg. Symphony Assn., World Affairs Council, Burnside Consortium; exec. dir. Portland State U. Found. Served to lt. (j.g.) USNR, 1943-46. Mem. Oreg. Soc. C.P.A.s, Am. Inst. C.P.A.s, Portland C. of C. (dir.), Phi Beta Kappa, Beta Gamma Sigma, Beta Alpha Psi. Republican. Episcopalian. Clubs: City of Portland, Arlington, University (Portland). Lodge: Rotary of Portland. Home: 11519 S W Breyman Ave Portland OR 97219 Office: PO Box 751 Portland OR 97207

BOGUSLAW, ROBERT, sociology educator; b. N.Y.C., June 19, 1919; s. Max and Eva (Zaslavsky) B.; m. Wanda Steinberg, Apr. 23, 1956; children: Chelle, Janet, Lisa. A.B., Bklyn. Coll., 1940, M.A., 1947; Ph.D., NYU, 1954. Sr. staff scientist Rand Corp. and Systems Devel. Corp., Santa Monica, Calif., 1953-65; research prof., sr. social scientist Am. U., Washington, 1965-66; prof. sociology Washington U., St. Louis, 1966—; vis. scholar London Sch. Econs., 1973; cons. Nat. Acad. Sci., 1963, Office Advanced Systems, U.S. Social Security Adminstrn., Washington, 1978-79; mem. adv. panel Office Tech. Assessment, U.S. Congress, 1976-77. Author: Systems Analysis and Social Planning, 1982, The New Utopians, 1965, 81 (C. Wright Mills 1966), Prologue to Sociology, 1977; contbr. articles to profl. jours. Mem. adv. bd. City Community Mental Health Service, Santa Monica, Calif., 1958-63; chmn. Santa Monica Welfare Council, Calif., 1958-59. Served to 1st lt. U.S. Army, 1941-45. Decorated Bronze Star medal; Fulbright fellow, Paris, 1972-73; NEH sr. fellow, 1973-74; Camargo Found. research fellow, 1980-81. Mem. Am. Sociol. Assn., Soc. for Study Social Problems (chmn. com. on internat. tensions 1964-66). Democrat. Jewish. Home: 6330 S Rosebury Ave Clayton MO 63105 Office: Dept Sociology Box 1113 Washington U St Louis MO 63130 *I have learned to be wary of the organizational, political or other labels people wear and to focus on what I think of as fundamental values. Exclusive preoccupation with oneself while ignoring the concerns of others is one of the central pathologies of our time.*

BOGY, DAVID B(EAUREGARD), mechanical engineering executive; b. Wabbaseka, Ark., June 4, 1936; s. Jesse C. and Dorothy (Duff) B.; m. Patricia Lynn Pizzitola, Mar. 28, 1961; children: Susan, Rebecca. B.S., Rice U., 1959, M.S., 1961; Ph.D., Brown U., 1966. Mech. engr. Shell Devel. Co., Houston, 1961-63; asst. prof. mech. engring. U. Calif., Berkeley, 1967-70, asso. prof., 1970-75, prof., 1975—; cons. IBM Research, 1972—. Served with C.E. U.S. Army, 1961-62. Research on static and dynamic elasticity, fluid jets and mechanisms of computer disk files and printers. Home: 8531 Buckingham Dr El Cerrito CA 94530 Office: 6119 Etcheverry Hall U Calif Berkeley CA 94720

BOH, IVAN, philosophy educator; b. Dolenji Lazi, Yugoslavia, Dec. 13, 1930; s. France and Marija (Mihelic) B.; m. Magda Kosnik, Aug. 30, 1957; children: Boris, Marko. B.A., Ohio U., 1954; M.A., Fordham U., 1956; Ph.D., U. Ottawa, Ont., Can., 1958. Instr. Clarke Coll., Dubuque, Iowa, 1957-59, asst. prof., 1959-62; vis. asst. prof. U. Iowa, 1962-63; Fulbright research fellow U. Munich, Germany, 1964-65; asso. prof. Mich. State U., 1966-69; prof. philosophy Ohio State U., 1969—; research in Spanish libraries, 1972-73; MUCIA exchange prof. Moscow State U., 1979-80; Fulbright sr. research fellow U. Ljubljana (Yugoslavia), 1982-83. Contbr. articles to profl. jours. Recipient Evans Latin prize Ohio U., 1954. Mem. Am. Philos. Assn., Am. Catholic Philos. Assn. (v.p.), Medieval Acad. Am. Home: 6171 Middlebury Dr East Worthington OH 43085 Office: Dept Philosophy Ohio State U Columbus OH 43210

BOHAN, MARC, fashion designer; b. Paris, France, Aug. 22, 1926; s. Alfred and Genevieve (Baudoux) B.; m. Dominque Gaborit, Feb. 23, 1950 (dec. June 1962); 1 dau., Marie Anne. Received baccalaureat. Asst. designer at, Piquet, Paris, 1945-49, at Molyneux, 1949-51; designer at, Patou, 1951-58, Christian Dior, London, 1958-60; chief designer, artistic dir., Christian Dior S.A., Paris, 1960—; also designer for theatre and film, Christian Dior S.A., Paris. *

BOHANAN, PAUL JAMES, anthropologist, university administrator; b. Lincoln, Nebr., Mar. 5, 1920; s. Hillory and Hazel (Truex) B.; m. Laura Marie Smith, Mar. 15, 1943 (div. 1975); 1 son, Denis Michael; m. Adelyse D'Arcy, Feb. 28, 1981. B.A., U. Ariz., 1947; B.Sc., Oxford U., Eng., 1949, Ph.D., 1951. Lectr. social anthropology Oxford U., 1951-56; asst. prof. Princeton U., 1956-59; prof. Northwestern U., 1959-75, U. Calif.-Santa Barbara, 1976-82; prof., dean social scis. and communications U. So. Calif., 1982—. Author: Justice and Judgement, 1957, Africa and Africans, 1964, Divorce and After, 1970, All the Happy Families, 1983. Served to capt. U.S. Army, 1941-45. Decorated Legion of Merit. Mem. Am. Anthrop. Assn. (pres. 1979-80), Am. Ethnol. Soc. (dir. 1963-66), African Studies Assn. (pres. 1963-64), Social Sci. Research Council (dir. 1962-64). Office: University of Southern California ADM 200 Los Angeles CA 90089

BOHANNON, DAVID D., community planner and developer; b. San Francisco, May 23, 1898; s. David Eugene and Elizabeth Jane (Bosch) B.; m. Ophelia E. Kroeger, June 7, 1921; children: Frances B. Nelson, Barbara B. Carleton, David E. Ed. public schs. of Calif. Mfr. metal products, until 1925, in real estate bus. and land devel., 1925—; organizer, pres. David D. Bohannon Orgn., community planner and developer, San Mateo, Calif., 1928—; pres. Hillsdale Devel. Co., 1951—; developer Bohannon Indsl. Park, Menlo Park, Bay Center Indsl. Park, San Lorenzo, Mayfair Heights, San Jose, Westwood, Westwood Oaks and Park Westwood, Santa Clara, El Cerrito Manor, Hillsdale, Hillsdale Shopping Center, San Mateo, San Lorenzo Village, Alameda County, Westwood, Napa, Rollingwood, Contra Costa County, Woodside Hills, Woodside, Montgomery Estates and Tahoe Tyrol, Lake Tahoe, all Calif. Mem. Urban Land Inst. (trustee, past pres., mem. past pres.'s adv. bd.), Nat. Assn. Home Builders U.S. (past pres., mem. past pres.'s council, named to Housing Hall of Fame), Nat. Assn. Realtors (past v.p.), San Francisco Bay Area Council, Calif. Assn. Realtors (life dir.), Lambda Alpha. Clubs: Commonwealth (bd. govs., past pres.), Bohemian, Peninsula Golf and Country, Eldorado Country, The Vintage, Sharon Heights Golf and Country, Internat. Order St. Hubert, Mzuri Safari, Shikar-Safari Internat., Game Conservation Internat., Bear River, Ducks Unltd. (sponsor in perpetuity, nat. trustee), Wildlife Preservation Soc. India, No. Calif. Retriever Trial, Rotary (hon.), Kiwanis (hon.). Recipient nat. recognition for wartime housing activities; credited with unusually large number of wartime pvt. houses and dev. of on-site prodn. techniques. Home: 115 Oakford Rd Woodside CA 94062 Office: 60 Hillsdale Mall San Mateo CA 94403-3497

BOHANNON, RICHARD LELAND, physician; b. Dallas, Oct. 11, 1907; s. Llewellyn Macey and Gussie Anna (Umphress) B.; m. Josephine Adelia Read, June 11, 1932; children—Richard Leland, Carol Josephine, Virginia Macey. Student, So. Meth. U.; M.D., Baylor U., 1932. Diplomate: Am. Bd. Preventive Medicine. Intern Parkland Hosp., Dallas, 1932-33; commd. 1st lt. U.S. Army Res., 1932; advanced through grades to lt. gen. USAF, 1965; assigned various posts, U.S., 1933-45, command surgeon, Germany, 1945-47, base surgeon, Castle AFB, Calif., 1948-49; command surgeon 2d Air Force, Barksdale AFB, La., 1949-53, March AFB, Calif., 1953-58, Tokyo, 1958-59, PACAF, Hawaii, 1959-61; dep. surgeon gen. Hdqrs. USAF, Washington, 1961-63, surgeon gen., 1963-67; ret.; dir. profl. services Doctors Hosp., Washington, 1968-71; exec. dir. Inst. Aerobics Research, Dallas, 1971-73, med. cons., 1974—. Recipient Disting. Alumnus award Baylor Med. Coll., 1964, So. Meth. U., 1968. Fellow A.C.P., Aerospace Med. Assn.; mem. Am. Heart Assn., Am. Coll. Preventive Medicine, AMA, Nat. Jogging Assn. (founder), Assn. Mil. Surgeons (life). Methodist. Home: 12040 Tavel Circle Dallas TX 75230 Office: Aerobic Center 12200 Preston Rd Dallas TX 75230 *As I look back over my life, I realize that I have been favored by God and man, despite my shortcomings; and I am thankful. It seems to me that patience and understanding, along with a spirit of helpfulness and cooperation, have enhanced the opportunities presented to me; and for that, too, I am grateful. For daily living, I know of no more satisfying and rewarding philosophy than that embodied in the Christian ethic.*

BOHANON, LUTHER L., U.S. judge; b. Ft. Smith, Ark., Aug. 9, 1902; s. William Joseph and Artelia (Campbell) B.; m. Marie Swatek, July 17, 1933; 1 son, Richard L. LL.B., U. Okla., 1927. Bar: Okla. bar 1927, U.S. Supreme Ct. bar 1927. Gen. practice law, Seminole, Okla. and Oklahoma City, 1927-61, U.S. dist. judge, No., Eastern and Western dists., Okla., 1961-74, sr. judge, 1974—. Mem. platform com. Democratic Nat. Conv., 1940. Served to maj. USAAF, 1942-45. Recipient citations and awards. Mem. Oklahoma City C. of C., Sigma Nu, Phi Alpha Delta. Methodist. Clubs: Mason (Shriner, 32 deg.), K.T., Jester, Kiwanian. Home: 1617 Bedford Dr Oklahoma City OK 73116 Office: US Courthouse 4th and Robinson Sts Oklahoma City OK 73102 *A lawyer must possess and demonstrate integrity and fidelity. He should always treat his client's business as he would if he knew his client was in the ceiling of his office, looking down seeing and hearing everything his attorney does and has to say about his client's business. Do right and fear no man.*

BOHEN, PATRICK JAMES, advt. exec.; b. N.Y.C., May 8, 1929; s. Chester James and Lillian (Curry) B.; m. Maureen A. Kolman, June 9, 1956; children—Mary Helen, Elizabeth Theresa, Patrick James, Peitr Anne, Sean Patrick. A.B., The Citadel, 1951; M.B.A., N.Y. U., 1960. Account supr. Foote, Cone & Belding, N.Y.C., 1959-63; sr. v.p., dir. McCaffrey & McCall, N.Y.C., 1963-69; partner Della Femina, Travisano & Partners, Inc., N.Y.C., 1969-81; pres. South Bay Advt., Melville, N.Y.; dir. Aero Mini Inc. Served to capt. U.S. Army, 1951-54. Decorated Bronze Star. Mem. Am. Mgmt. Assn., Proprietary Assn., Am. Assn. Advt. Agencies. Republican. Roman Catholic. Home: 11 Beaumont Dr Melville NY 11746 Office: 515 Madison Ave New York NY 10022

BOHL, ROBERT WALTER, educator; b. Peoria, Ill., Sept. 29, 1925; s. Francis John and Ella (Ziegenbein) B.; m. Florence Marie Reace, May 30, 1947; children—Nancy (Mrs. Theodore Williams), Betty (Mrs. Vance Kepley, Jr.), Barbara, Robert F. B.S., U. Ill., 1946, M.S., 1949, Ph.D., 1956. Faculty U. Ill., Urbana, 1946—, now prof. metall. and nuclear engring.; cons. Caterpillar Tractor Co., U.S. Steel Co., Argonne Nat. Lab., Battelle Meml. Inst. Contbr. articles profl. jours. Bd. dirs. Univ. YMCA. Fellow Am. Soc. Metals; mem. Am. Soc. Engring. Edn., Am. Inst. Mining, Metall. and Petroleum Engrs., Sigma Xi, Tau Beta Pi, Phi Kappa Phi, Alpha Sigma Mu, Sigma Tau. Home: 2014 G Huff Dr Urbana IL 61801

BOHLE, BRUCE WILLIAM, editor; b. St. Louis, July 21, 1918; s. Edward F. and Emma W. (Fricke) B. B.A., Washington U., St. Louis, 1939. Film critic St. Louis Star-Times, 1946-51, drama and music critic, 1950-51; asst. mgr. St. Louis Symphony Orch., 1951-53; asso. editor Grolier Soc., N.Y.C., 1960-64. Editor: Theatre Arts mag., N.Y.C., 1953-63; usage editor: Am. Heritage Dictionary, Am. Heritage Pub. Co., N.Y.C., 1964—; editor: The Home Book of American Quotations, 1967; Editor: International Cyclopedia of Music and Musicians, 10th edit., 1974, rev., 1984. Served with USAAF, 1942-46; PTO. Recipient Harvard Book prize, 1935. Mem. Phi Beta Kappa. Home: 260 Audubon Ave New York NY 10033 *Make willing synonymous with working.*

BOHLEN, NINA, artist; b. Boston, Mar. 5, 1931; d. Henry Morgan and Margaret (Curtis) B. B.A., Radcliffe Coll., 1953; student drawing and painting, Hyman Bloom, 1952-56. One-woman shows, Siembab Gallery, Boston, 1962, Shore Gallery, Boston, 1968, Tragos Gallery, Boston, 1971, 74, Library Boston Atheneam, 1977, Am. Acad. Arts and Letters Candidates for Awards Exhbn., Far Gallery, N.Y.C., 1978, Mus. Comparative Zoology, Harvard U., 1982, Tichnor Library, Harvard U., 1983, group shows, Swetzoff Gallery, Boston, 1959, Boston Mus. Sch., 1963, Boston Arts Festival, Brockton (Mass.) Mus., 1969, Far Gallery, 1973, Hassam Fund Exhbn. Am. Acad. Arts and Letters, 1978, 81. Recipient award Am. Acad. Arts and Letters, 1977. Address: 55 Hagen Rd Newton MA 02159

BOHLMANN, RALPH ARTHUR, clergyman, church official; b. Palisade, Nebr., Feb. 20, 1932; s. Arthur Erwin and Anne Fredericka (Weeke) B.; m. Patricia Anne McCleary, Apr. 19, 1959; children: Paul, Lynn. Student, St. Johns Coll., Winfield, Kans.; B.A., Concordia Sem., 1953; M.Div., 1956; S.T.M., 1966; Fulbright scholar, U. Heidelberg, 1956-57; Ph.D., Yale U., 1968. Ordained to ministry Lutheran Ch. (Mo. Synod), 1958; instr. history and religion Concordia Coll., 1957-58; pastor Mt. Olive Luth. Ch., Des Moines, 1958-60; prof. systematic theology Concordia Sem., St. Louis, 1960-71, acting pres., 1974-75, pres., 1975-81, Luth. Ch.-Mo. Synod, 1981—; exec. sec. Commn. Theology and Ch. Relations Luth. Ch. Mo. Synod, St. Louis, 1971-74; mem. Faith and Order Commn. Nat. Council Chs., 1973-76. Author: Principles of Biblical Interpretation in the Lutheran Confessions, 1968. Office: 1333 S Kirkwood Rd Saint Louis MO 63122

BOHM, HENRY VICTOR, physics educator; b. Vienna, Austria, July 16, 1929; came to U.S., 1941, naturalized, 1946; s. Victor Charles and Gertrude (Rie) B.; m. Lucy Margaret Coons, Sept. 2, 1950; children: Victoria Rie, Jeffrey Ernst Thompson. A.B., Harvard U., 1950; M.S., U. Ill., 1951; Ph.D., Brown U., 1958. Jr. physicist Gen. Electric Co., 1951, 53-54; teaching, research asst. Brown U., 1954-58, research assoc., summer 1958; staff mem. Arthur D. Little, Inc., Cambridge, Mass., 1958-59; asso. prof. physics dept. Wayne State U., Detroit, 1959-64, acting chmn. physics dept., 1962-63, prof., 1964—, v.p. for grad. studies and research, 1968-71, v.p. for spl. projects, 1971-72, provost, 1972-75, on leave, 1978-83; pres. Argonne Univs. Assn., 1978-83; Vis. prof. Cornell U., 1966-67, U. Lancaster, Eng., summer 1967, Purdue U., spring 1977; cons.-examiner commn. on instns. higher edn. N. Central Assn. Colls. and Schs., 1971-80, mem. commn., 1974-78. Bd. dirs. Center for Research Libraries, Chgo, 1970-75, chmn., 1973; bd. overseers Lewis Coll., Ill. Inst. Tech., 1980-83. Served to lt. (j.g.) USNR, 1951-53. Fellow Am. Phys. Soc. Office: Dept Physics Wayne State U Detroit MI 48202

BOHM, KARL-HEINZ HERMANN, astrophysicist, educator; b. Hamburg, Germany, Sept. 27, 1923; came to U.S., 1968; s. Carl Hermann and Emma (Galonska) B.; m. Erika Helga Vitense, Sept. 19, 1953; children: Hans-Jurgen, Manfred, Helga, Eva. Physik-Diplom, U. Kiel, 1951, Ph.D., 1954. Research astronomer U. Calif., Berkeley, 1955, vis. prof., 1960-61, 63-64; asst. prof., then asso. prof. U. Kiel, 1957-64; prof. theoretical astrophysics U. Heidelberg, 1964-67; prof. astronomy U. Wash., Seattle, 1968—; pres. commn. stellar atmospheres Internat. Astron. Union, 1964-67; Gauss prof. Goettingen (W. Ger.) Acad. Scis., 1976-77. Contbr. articles to profl. jours., books. Recipient Physics prize Goettingen Acad. Scis., 1958, Humboldt prize Fed. Republic Germany, 1974. Mem. Am. Astron. Soc., Astronomische Gesellschaft. Lutheran. Office: Astronomy Dept U Wash Seattle WA 98195 *

BOHMAN, GEORGE VROOM, educator; b. Princeton, Ill., Sept. 24, 1908; s. Oscar William and Rachel Maude (Vroom) B.; m. Gladys Presley, June 22, 1940; children—Robert Presley, Eric James. A.B., Monmouth Coll., 1929; M.A., U. Wis., 1934, Ph.D., 1947. Instr. speech Dakota Wesleyan U., 1930-33, asst. prof., head dept., 1933-37; instr. pub. speaking Dartmouth, 1937-39, asst. prof., 1939-47, chmn. dept. pub. speaking, 1941-45, dir. speech in Naval English V-12 course, 1943-45; prof. speech Wayne State U., Detroit, 1947-78, prof. emeritus, 1978—, grad. chmn., 1947-55, chmn., 1955-73. Co-author: History of the First Presbyterian Church of Princeton, Ill, 1937; editor, author: History of the First Congregational Church, Royal Oak, Mich, 1967; Contbr. articles to speech and hist. jours. Mem. Hanover (N.H.) Democratic Town Com., 1944-47, chmn., 1946-47; Trustee Congl. Found. for Theol. Studies, 1963-70, 71-74, chmn., 1966-70; lectr. Congl. history and polity Congl. Library, 1978. Mem. AAUP, Speech Communication Assn. (chmn. com. on microfilm and microcard materials 1949-50, com. on history Am. pub. address 1952-55, com. on problems in speech edn. in colls. and univs. 1942-45), Eastern Pub. Speaking Conf. (sec.-treas. 1942-45), Central States Speech Assn., Ill., Bureau County (Ill.) hist. socs., Nat. Assn. Congl. Christian Chs. (exec. com. 1955-56, 59-62, chmn. 1961-62, moderator 1957-58), Pi Kappa Delta (nat. council 1934-37), Tau Kappa Alpha, Phi Kappa Phi, Gamma Omicron Mu, Delta Sigma Rho. Conglist. (del. Gen. Council 1954-56; moderator Mich. State Assn. 1961-62, exec. com. Mich. conf. 1962-73, editor Mich. Conglist. 1977—). Home: 1014 Edgewood Royal Oak MI 48067

BOHME, DIETHARD KURT, chemistry educator; b. Boston, June 20, 1941; s. Kurt F. and Maria (Kiesel) B.; m. Shirley Faith Broadway, Dec. 23, 1966; children: Kurt, Kenneth Diethard, Heidi Claire. B.Sc., McGill U., 1962, Ph.D., 1965. Asst. prof. dept. chemistry York U., Downsview, Ont., 1970-74, assoc. prof., Downview, Ont., 1974-77, prof. chemistry, Downsview, Ont., 1977—, dir. grad. program in chemistry, 1979—; mem. chemistry grant selection com. Nat. Scis. and Engring. Research Council of Can., Ottawa, 1983—. Contbr. articles to profl. jours. Nat. Acad. Sci.-NRC postdoctorial research assocs., 1967; A.P. Sloan fellow, 1974; sr. scientist vis. fellow, 1978; recipient Rutherford Meml. Medal in chemistry Royal Soc. Can., 1981. Fellow Chem. Inst. Can. (phys. chemistry div. exec. 1980-83, Noranda lecture award in phys chemistry 1983); mem. Combustion Inst., Am. Soc. Mass Spectrometry. Home: 28 Colonsay Rd Thornhill ON Canada L3T 3E8 Office: York Univ 4700 Keele St Downsview ON Canada M3J 1P3

BOHMONT, DALE WENDELL, agricultural consultant; b. Wheatland, Wyo., June 7, 1922; s. J.E. and Mary (Armann) B.; m. Marilyn J. Horn, Mar. 7, 1969; children: Dennis E., Craig W. B.S., U. Wyo., 1948, M.S., 1950; Ph.D., U. Nebr., 1952; M.P.A., Harvard U., 1959. Registered investment adv., SEC. Pub. sch. tchr., Rock River, Wyo., 1941-42; from research asst. to head plant scis. U. Wyo., 1946-60; assoc. dir. expt. sta. Colo. State U., 1961-63; dean, dir. agr. U. Nev., Reno, 1963-82, dean, dir. emeritus, 1982—; pres. Bohmont Cons. Inc., 1982—; Cons. Devel. & Resources Corp., N.Y.C., 1968—; cons. Frederiksen, Kamine & Assos., Sacramento, 1976; pres. Enide Corp., Reno, 1974-80, Thermal Dynamics Internat., 1983—; co-chmn. research planning (West Div. Agr. Expt. Stas.), 1975; mem. exec. com., council adminstrv. heads agr. Nat. Assn. State Univ. Land Grant Colls., 1975. Contbr. articles to profl. jours.; Editorial bd.: Crops and Soils, 1962—. Served with USAAF, 1942-45. Fellow AAAS, Agronomy Soc.; mem. Western Soc. Weed Scis. (hon.), Western Crop Sci. Soc. (pres. 1962-63), Nat. Expt. Sta. Dirs. Assn. (chmn. 1967-68), Am. Range Mgmt. Soc., Farm House (dir. 1962—), Weed Soc. Am. (hon.), Sigma Xi, Gamma Sigma Delta (pres. 1964-66), Alpha Zeta, Alpha Tau Alpha, Phi Kappa Phi. Home: 280 Island Ave Reno NV 89501 *There is nothing that has been done that could not have been done better; therefore, there is always room for improvement and always room at the top.*

BOHN, RALPH CARL, educator; b. Detroit, Feb. 19, 1930; s. Carl and Bertha (Abrams) B.; m. Adella Stanul, Sept. 2, 1950 (dec.); children—Cheryl Ann, Jeffrey Ralph; m. JoAnn Olvera Butler, Feb. 19, 1977; stepchildren—Kathyrn Jeanne, Kimberly JoAnn, Gregory Edward. B.S., Wayne State U., 1951, Ed.M., 1954, Ed. D., 1957. Part-time instr. Wayne State U., 1954-55, summer, 1956; faculty San Jose (Calif.) State U., 1955—, prof. indsl. arts, 1961—, chmn. dept. indsl. studies, 1960-69, asso. dean ednl. service, 1968-70, dean continuing edn., 1970—; Guest summer faculty Colo. State Coll., 1963, Ariz. State U., 1966, U.P.R., 1967, 74, So. Ill. U., 1970, Oreg. State U., 1971, Utah State U., 1973, Va. Poly. Inst. and State U., 1973, U. Idaho, 1978; cons. U.S. Office Edn., 1965-70, Calif. Pub. Schs., 1960, Nat. Assessment Ednl. Progress, 1968—, Ednl. div. Philco-Ford Corp., 1970-73, Am. Inst. Research, 1969—, Far West Labs for Ednl. Research Devel., 1971—; adv. bd. Center for Vocat. and Tech. Edn., Ohio State U., 1968-74; dir. project Vocat. Edn. Act, 1965-67, NDEA, 1967, 68; co-dir. Project Edn. Profession Devel. Act, 1969, 70; mem. commn. coll. and univ. contracts Western Assn. Schs. and Colls., 1976-78, chmn. spl. com. on off-campus instrn. and continuing edn., 1978—; chmn. continuing edn. accreditation visit U. Santa Clara, 1976; mem. accreditation team for Azusa Pacific Coll., 1975, Portland State U., 1975, Brigham Young U., 1976, Columbia Coll., 1977, Western Wash. U., 1978, Wash. State U., 1980, Chapman Coll., 1980, Calif. State U., Fullerton, 1981; vice chmn. accreditation team for U. Guam, 1978, Pepperdine U., 1979, U. LaVerne, 1980, Azusa Pacific Coll., 1981. Author: (with G.H. Silvius) Organizing Course Materials for Industrial Education, 1961, (with others) Fundamentals of Safety Education, 2d edit, 1973, 3d edit., 1981, (with A. MacDonald) Power-Mechanics of Energy Control, 1970, The McKnight Power Experimenter; 4 lab. manuals, 1970, (with G.H. Silvius) Planning and Organizing Instruction, 1976, (with others) Basic Industrial Arts and Power Mechanics, 1978, Technology and Society: Interfaces with Industrial Arts, 1980; Indsl. arts editor: Am. Vocat. Jour, 1963-66; editor: Jour. Indsl. Tchr. Edn, 1962-64, (with Ralph Norman) Graduate Study in Industrial Arts, 1961. Served to lt. (j.g.) USCGR, 1951-53; capt. Res. ret. Recipient Am. Legion award, 1945; scholar Wayne State U., 1953. Mem. Am. Indsl. Arts Assn. (pres. 1967-68, Ship's citation 1971), Am. Council Indsl. Art Tchrs. Edn. (pres. 1964-66, recipient Man of Year award 1967), Nat. Assn. Indsl. Tchr. Educators (past v.p.), Calif. Indsl. Edn. Assn. (recipient State Ship's citation 1971), Am. Drive Edn. Assn., Nat. Fluid Power Soc., Am. Vocat. Assn. (recipient Service awards 1966, 67), NEA, N.Am. Assn. for Summer Sessions (v.p. western region 1976—), Lutheran Acad. Scholarship, Calif. Employees Assn. (pres. San Jose State Coll. chpt. 1966-67), Western Assn. Summer Session Adminstrs. (Newsletter editor 1970-73, pres. 1974-75), Calif. C. of C. (edn. com. 1969-77), Industry-Edn. Council Calif. (dir. 1974-80), Sci. and Human Values, Inc. (dir. 1974—, chmn. bd. 1976—). Home: 15363 Robin Anne Ln Monte Sereno CA 95030

BOHN, SHERMAN ELWOOD, educator, mathematician; b. New England, N.D., Mar. 11, 1927; s. Paul T. and Josephine (Conradson) B.; m. Dorothy V. Solberg, June 15, 1952; children: Jeffrey Andrew, Corinn Jo, Jon Paul. B.A., Concordia Coll., 1949; M.A., U. Neb., 1951, Ph.D., 1961; student, U. Minn., 1952-53. Aero. research scientist NACA, 1951-52; instr., then asst. prof. Concordia Coll., 1953-56; instr. U. Nebr., 1957-59; asso. prof. Wartburg Coll., 1959-61; asst., then asso. prof. Bowling Green State U., 1961-64; mem. faculty Miami U., Oxord, Ohio, 1964—, prof. math., 1966—, chmn. dept., 1965-71, 73-82. Author articles in field. Mem. Math. Assn. Am. (chmn. elect Ohio sect. 1970-71, chmn. 1971-72, gov. 1973-76), Ohio Acad. Sci. (membership chmn. math. sect. 1968-69, chmn. sect. 1969-70). Home: 416 Sandra Dr Oxford OH 45056

BOHNE, CARL JOHN, JR., accountant; b. Cuero, Tex., Oct. 24, 1916; s. Carl John and Byrd (White) B.; m. Lelon Maurine Brautigam, June 25, 1948; children: Carl John III, Lelon Maurine. B.B.A. with highest honors, U. Tex., 1947, M.B.A., 1948. C.P.A., Tex., Ill. With Arthur Andersen & Co., C.P.A.'s, 1949—, dir. tng., Chgo., from 1956, dir. tng. Center Profl. Devel., St. Charles, Ill., 1970-79, sr. partner, 1979—; instr., then asst. prof. accounting U. Tex., 1947-48; cons. U.S. Army Audit Agy., 1954-58. Asst. treas. Evanston (Ill.) Hosp. Assn., 1956—; chmn. profl. accounts solicitation Chgo. Heart Assn., 1957; bd. dirs. Northwestern Med. Faculty Found., 1981—. Served to maj. AUS, 1941-45. Decorated Purple Heart, Bronze Star medal; recipient Elijah Watts Sells Gold medal for C.P.A. exam, 1948. Mem. Am. Inst. C.P.A.s, Ill. Soc. C.P.A.s (chmn. com. profl. devel. 1957), Tex. Soc. C.P.A.s, Beta Gamma Sigma. Episcopalian (vestryman 1958-60, 66-68, warden 1969-70, 79-80, treas. 1970—). Club: Union League (Chgo.). Home: 711 Oak St Winnetka IL 60093 Office: 69 W Washington St Chicago IL 60602

BOHNER, CHARLES HENRY, educator; b. Wilmington, Del., Nov. 23, 1927; s. Charles Henry and Frances Gilmour (Ramsey) B.; m. Mary Jean Astolfi, Dec. 2, 1961; children—Christine Ramsey, Charles Russell, Catherine Russell. B.A., Syracuse U., 1950; M.A., U. Pa., 1952, Ph.D., 1957. Instr. Syracuse U., 1952-54; instr. U. Del., 1955-58, asst. prof. English, 1958-62, asso. prof., 1962-66, H.F. duPont Winterthur prof., 1966—, chmn. dept., 1969-76; lectr. in field. Author: John Pendleton Kennedy, 1961, Robert Penn Warren, 2d edit, 1981; Contbr. articles to profl. jours. Served with AUS, 1946-47. Am. specialist grantee State Dept., 1964. Mem. Am. Studies Assn., Modern Lang. Assn., AAUP, Sigma Phi Epsilon, Rho Delta Phi, Kappa Delta Pi, Phi Kappa Phi. Home: 61 Kells Ave Newark DE 19711

BOHNERT, HERBERT GAYLORD, educator, philosopher; b. Cleve., Mar. 24, 1918; s. Herbert F. and Margaret (Sharp) B. A.B., U. Chgo., 1940; Ph.D., U. Pa., 1961. Instr. Queen's Coll., 1947-50; asst. mathematician RAND Corp., 1950-51; asst. prof. Swarthmore Coll., 1953-54; computing engr. N.Am. Aviation, 1955-57; sr. scientist Litton Industries, 1958; asso. Planning Research Corp., 1969; mem. research staff IBM Research Center, 1961-68; prof. philosophy Mich. State U., 1968—. Author articles in field. Fulbright lectr. Am. philosophy U. Cuyo, Mendoza, Argentina, 1966. Mem. Am. Philos. Assn., Assn. Symbolic Logic, Philosophy Sci. Assn. Home: 4 Pinecrest Fortuna CA 95540 *My life has been inspired by scientific reason, whose development has transformed the human condition more in a few centuries than had preceding millenia of ritualistic belief.*

BOHNETT, FLOYD NEWELL, restaurant executive; b. Campbell, Calif., May 26, 1923; s. Floyd Oscar and Violet (Morgan) B.; m. Nada Violet Nickoloff, Feb. 24, 1946; children: Nikki Bohnett Marks, Lynda Bohnett Ober, James Newell, Victoria Bohnett Rockey. Student, Santa Barbara State Coll., 1940-42. Sales mgr. Bohnett Inc., Santa Barbara, Calif., 1945-50; sales rep. Fred Griswold Co., Santa Barbara, 1952-56; co-founder Sambo Restaurants Inc., Santa Barbara, 1956, pres., 1965-68, co-chmn. bd. dirs., 1968—; owner Puu Waa Waa Ranch, Hawaii, 1972—. Served with USMCR, 1942-45, 50-52. Decorated D.F.C., Air medal. Home: 44-600 Kaneohe Bay Dr Kaneohe HI 96744 Office: 3760 State St Santa Barbara CA 93105

BOHNING, ELIZABETH EDROP, educator; b. Bklyn., June 26, 1915; d. Percy Tom and Marion Lothrop (Stafford) Edrop; m. William H. Bohning, Aug. 18, 1943; children: Barbara Bohning Young, Margaret Bohning Anderson. B.A., Wellesley Coll., 1936; M.A., Bryn Mawr Coll., 1938, Ph.D., 1943; postgrad., Middlebury Coll., summer 1936, U. Cologne, 1936-37, U. Munich, summer 1955. Faculty Bryn Mawr Coll., 1938-39, Middlebury Coll. (Summer Sch. German), 1956, 58, Grinnell Coll., 1940-41, Stanford U., 1939-40; prof. U. Del., Newark, 1967—, chairperson dept. langs. and lit., 1971-78. Author: The Concept "Sage" in Nibelungen Criticism, 1944; contbr. articles on lit. to profl. jours. Vice-chairperson Del. Humanities Council, 1981-82; pres. Del. Council Internat. Visitors. Recipient Lindback award for excellence in teaching, 1962. Mem. Soc. German-Am. Studies, Am. Assn. Tchrs. German (cert. of merit 1982), Am. Soc. 18th Century Studies, Am. Council Study of Austrian Lit., Middle State Assn. Colls. and Schs. (trustee 1974-80), Phi Beta Kappa, Delta Phi Alpha, Phi Kappa Phi, Alpha Chi Omega. Episcopalian. Clubs: Wellesley Alumnae, Bryn Mawr Alumnae. Home: Box 574 Newark DE 19711 Office: Dept Lang and Lit U Del Newark DE 19711 *Cultivating international friendships is an especially valuable goal: they enable us to see ourselves and our country in perspective, and they help others to understand and appreciate our American way of life and thought.*

BOHNING, RICHARD HOWARD, emeritus college dean; b. Hope Valley, R.I., Sept. 16, 1919; s. Clarence Minot and Annie Delhia (Lewis) B.; m. Evelyn Maxon Bitgood, Oct. 7, 1938; 1 son, Richard Howard. B.S., R.I. State Coll., 1940; M.S., Ohio State U., 1941, Ph.D., 1948. Mem. faculty Ohio State U., 1946—, prof. botany, 1961—, dean, 1969-78, dean emeritus, 1978—. Co-author: Introduction to Plant Physiology, 1960. Served with USNR, 1943-46. NSF Sci. Faculty fellow, 1957. Fellow Ohio Acad. Sci.; mem. Bot. Soc. Am., Am. Inst. Biol. Scis., AAAS, Am. Soc. Plant Physiologists, Sigma Xi, Phi Kappa Phi Epsilon Phi, Alpha Zeta, Gamma Sigma Delta, Gamma Alpha. Home: Pinehaven Dr Wyoming RI 02898

BOHNSACK, KURT KARL, zoologist, educator; b. Stuttgart, Germany, Mar. 23, 1920; came to U.S., 1923, naturalized, 1941; s. Rudolf Otto and Johanna Marie (Mauser) B.; m. Julie Mary Low, June 15, 1946; children: Linda Mae, Richard Carl, Mary Ellen. B.S., Ohio U., 1946; M.S., U. Mich., 1947, Ph.D., 1954. Instr. zoology U. Mich., 1950-51; instr., asst. prof. Swarthmore Coll., 1951-56; from asst. prof. to prof. zoology San Diego State U., 1956—; mem. summer faculty Pa. State U., 1954, 55, Ariz. State U., 1971-73, John Carroll U., 1970, Mich. State U., 1978; researcher Arctic Research Lab., Barrow, Alaska, 1961-64. Mem. editorial bd: Pedobiologia, 1964—; contbr. articles to profl. publs. Trustee San Diego Natural History Soc., 1966-79. Served with U.S. Army, 1942-45. Research grantee Arctic Inst., 1962, 63, Oak Ridge Nat. Lab, 1956, 57. Fellow AAAS; mem. AAUP, Acarological Soc. Am., Entomol. Soc. Wash., Western Soc. Naturalists, Audobon Soc., Arctic Inst. N. Am., Sigma Xi. Democrat. Unitarian. Home: 5130 Mesa Terr La Mesa CA 92041 Office: Zoology Dept San Diego State U San Diego CA 92182

BOHROD, AARON, artist; b. Chgo., Nov. 21, 1907; s. George and Fannie (Feingold) B.; m. Ruth Bush, Dec. 27, 1929; children: Mark, Georgi (Mrs. Stephen Rothe), Neil. Student, Crane Coll., Chgo., 1925-26, Art Inst. Chgo., 1927-29, Art Students League, N.Y.C., 1930-32; D.F.A., Ripon Coll., 1960. Artist in residence So. Ill. U., 1942-43, U. Wis.-Madison, 1948-73; With War Art Unit (South Pacific War Area, on Govt. assignment); served as artist war corr. Life mag., Normandy, Cherbourg, Eng., Luxembourg, Germany, 1943-45. Painted series pictures of Kansas City for, Mo. Documentary Art Project, 1946, series on Pitts. for, Pa. Documentary Art Project, 1947, series on Mich. for, Mich. Documentary Art Project, 1947, series of symbolic still life paintings for, Look mag., Great Religions of America, 1957-60; Represented in permanent collections, Met. Mus. Art, Whitney Mus. Am. Art, N.Y.C., Art Inst. Chgo., Bklyn. Mus., Boston Mus. Art, Pa. Acad. Art, Corcoran Mus., Washington, Swope Gallery Art, Terre Haute, Butler Art Inst., Youngstown, U. Ariz., Walker Art Center, Mpls., Norton Art Inst., Telfair Art Acad., Fla., Davenport (Iowa) Art Inst., Library of Congress, Witte Meml. Mus., San Antonio, Springfield (Mass.) Mus. Fine Arts, New Britain (Conn.) Art Mus., Detroit Inst. Arts, Miller Art Center, Sturgeon Bay, Wis., Wichita State U., Mich. State U., Hartford Gallery Modern Art, Finch Coll., N.Y., Milw. Art Center, Oshkosh Pub. Mus., Madison Art Center, U. Ill., Miami U., Bergstrom Art Center, Neenah, Wis., U. Maine, Ball State U., So. Ill. U., Clinton (Ill.) Art Center, U. Mo., Ohio U., St. Lawrence U., Mac Nider Mus., Albrecht Gallery, St. Joseph, Mo., U. Wyo., Hirschhorn Mus., Washington, Elvejhem Art Center, U. Wis., Wis. Med. Soc., Madison, Beloit (Wis.) Coll., San Diego Mus. (Calif.), permanent collections, State Capitol, Madison, U. Maine; represented in, Cleve. Mus. Art, Detroit Art Inst., Syracuse U.; Author: A Decade of Still Life, 1966; Paintings reproduced in, Time, Life, Fortune, Holiday, Coronet and, Esquire mags.; Illustrator: book drawings) by A Pottery Sketch Book, U. Wis. Press, 1959, Wisconsin Sketches, (with Robert Gard), 1973. Recipient Carr landscape prize, 1935; recipient Tuthill watercolor prize, 1935, Logan prizes and Art Inst. medals, 1937-45, Brower prize Art Inst. Chgo., 1947, 84, hon. mention San Francisco Golden Gate Expn., 1939, Carnegie Internat. Exhbn., 1939, first award of merit Calif. Water Color Soc., 1940, first prize Phila. Water Color Soc., Pa. Acad. Fine Arts, 1942, 5th Purchase prize Artists for Victory Expn., Met. Mus. Art, 1942, Corcoran 2d prize, W.A. Clark prize and silver medal, 1943, prize Am. Nat. Acad., 1951, 53, 1st prize Profl. Art Exhbn., Ill. State Fair, 1955, hon. mention Miami Nat. Ceramic Exhbn., 1956, Saltus Gold medal NAD, 1961; Hassam Purchase award, 1962; Kirk Meml. award, 1965; Fine Arts award Gov. Wis., 1969; Guggenheim fellow in creative art, 1936-37, 37-38; Beloit Coll. Nat. academician. Address: 4811 Tonyawatha Trail Madison WI 53716

BOIES, WILBER H., lawyer; b. Bloomington, Ill., Mar. 15, 1944; s. Wilbur H. and Martha Jane (Hutchison) B.; m. Victoria Joan Steinitz, Sept. 17, 1966; children: Andrew Charles, Carolyn Ursula. A.B., Brown U., 1965; J.D., U. Chgo., 1968. Bar: Ill. 1968, U.S. Dist. Ct. (no. dist.) Ill. 1968, U.S. Dist. Ct. (ea. dist.) Wis. 1973, U.S. Ct. Appeals (7th cir.) 1974, U.S. Ct. Appeals (5th cir.) 1975, U.S. Ct. Appeals (3d cir.) 1977, U.S. Supreme Ct. 1978. Assoc. Altheimer & Gray, Chgo., 1968-71; ptnr. McDermott, Will & Emery, Chgo., 1971—. Contbr. articles to profl. jours. Served with USAR, 1968-74. Mem. Legal Club Chgo., Bar Assn. 7th Fed. Cir., ABA, Chgo. Bar Assn., Chgo. Council Lawyers. Clubs: Chgo. Athletic, Monroe. Office: McDermott Will & Emery 111 W Monroe St Chicago IL 60603

BOILEAU, OLIVER CLARK, aerospace company executive; b. Camden, N.J., Mar. 31, 1927; s. Oliver Clark and Florence Mary (Smith) B.; m. Nan Eleze Hallen, Sept. 15, 1951; children: Clark Edward, Adrienne Lee, Nanette Erika, Jay Marshall. B.S. in Elec. Engring., U. Pa., 1951, M.S., 1953; M.S. in Indsl. Mgmt., MIT, 1964. With Boeing Aerospace Co., 1953-80, mgr. Minuteman, v.p., 1968, pres., 1973-80, Gen. Dynamics Corp., St. Louis, 1980—, also dir. Served with USNR, 1944-46. Sloan fellow, 1963-64. Mem. AIAA, Navy League, Air Force Assn., Am. Def. Preparedness Assn., Assn. U.S. Army, Armed Forces Communications and Electronics Assn., Nat. Aeros. Assn., Nat. Space Club, Naval War Coll. Found., Nat. Acad. Engring. Office: Gen Dynamics Corp Pierre Laclede Center Saint Louis MO 63105

BOILEAU, OLIVER CLARK, JR., aerospace company executive; b. Camden, N.J., Mar. 31, 1927; s. Oliver Clark and Florence Mary (Smith) B.; m. Nan Eleze Hallen, Sept. 15, 1951; children: Clark Edward, Adrienne Lee, Nanette Erika, Jay Marshall. B.S., U. Pa., 1951, M.S. in Elec. Engring, 1953, Mass. Inst. Tech., 1964. Vice pres., gen. mgr. missile div. Boeing Aerospace Co., Seattle, 1969-70, v.p. aerospace group, 1970-73, pres., 1973-80, Gen. Dynamics Corp., 1980—; dir. Pacific NW Bell Co.; Mem. Def. Sci. Bd.; mem. adv. bd. Centerre Bank. Trustee Wash. Mut. Savs. Bank.; mem. vis. com. dept. aeros. and astronautics MIT; trustee St. Louis U.; bd. overseers Sch. Engring., U. Pa., Lawrence Inst. Tech. Corp. Served with USNR, 1944-46. Fellow AIAA; mem. IEEE, Nat. Acad. Engring., Air Force Assn., Navy League, Am. Def. Preparedness Assn., Nat. Space Club, Kent C. of C., Theta Xi, Sigma Tau, Eta Kappa Nu. Office: General Dynamics Corp Pierre Laclede Center Saint Louis MO 63105 *

BOIME, ALBERT ISAAC, social history of art educator; b. St. Louis, Mar. 17, 1933; s. Max and Dorothy (Rubin) B.; m. Myra Block, June 23, 1964; children: Robert, Eric. A.B., UCLA, 1961; M.A., Columbia U., 1963, Ph.D., 1968. Instr. social history of art Columbia U., 1966-67; assoc. prof. SUNY, Stony Brook, 1967-72, prof., chmn. dept., Binghamton, 1972-74, prof., 1974-78; prof. social history of art UCLA, 1978—; art historian in residence Coll. Creative Studies, U. Calif.-Santa Barbara, 1973; judge NEH, Washington, 1975; mem. adv. council N.Y. Acad. Art, N.Y.C., 1981—. Author: The Academy and French Painting in the 19th Century, 1971, Thomas Couture and the

Eclectic Vision, 1981. Served with AUS, 1955-58. Am. Council Learned Socs. fellow, 1970-71; Guggenheim fellow, 1974-75. Mem. Coll. Art Assn., Soc. Fellows Am. Acad. at Rome. Office: Dept Art UCLA 405 Hilgard Ave Los Angeles CA 90024 Z *I am grateful for this opportunity to join with my listing the memory of my dear brother, Jerome Philip Boime, whose rare, provacative mind inspired me with the sheer joy of intellectual pursuit. Whatever present success I may have, I owe to my capacity to thoroughly enjoy my work, to exult in ideas and the unboundedness of scholarly activity, and to commit this love to my developing engagement with political, philosophical and social issues.*

BOIS, PIERRE, medical research organization executive; b. Oka, Que., Can., Mar. 22, 1924; s. Henri and Ethier (Germaine) B.; m. Joyce Casey, Sept. 8, 1953; children: Monique, Marie, Louise. M.D., U. Montreal, Que., 1953, Ph.D., 1957; hon. doctorate, U. Ottawa, Ont., 1982. Research fellow pathology U. Montreal, 1957-58, asst. assoc. prof. dept. pharmacology, 1960-64, prof., head dept. anatomy, 1964-70, dean faculty medicine, 1970-81; pres. Med. Research Council of Can., 1981—; asst. prof. histology, Ottawa, Ont., Can., 1958-60. Contbr. over 130 publs. to profl. jours. Fellow Royal Soc. Can., Royal Coll. Physicians and Surgeons Can.; mem. Am., French Canadian assns. anatomists, N.Y. Acad. Scis., AAAS, Can. Fedn. Biol. Socs., Can. Soc. Clin. Investigation. Research and numerous publs. on morphological effects of hormones, histamine and mast cells in magnesium deficiency, muscular dystrophy, exptl. thymic tumors. Office: Med Research Council Can 20th Floor Jeanne Mance Bldg Tunney's Pasture Ottawa ON K1A 0W9 Canada

BOISFONTAINE, CURTIS RICH, lawyer; b. New Orleans, June 30, 1929; s. Albert Sidney and Margaret (Toomer) B.; m. Cheryl Reynaud; children: Suzanne Baker, Curtis Rich, Eugenie Wright, Stephanie Brett, Arthur Maxwell. B.A., Tulane U., 1951, LL.B., 1952. Bar: La. 1952. Practice in, New Orleans, 1952-53; asso. Porteous & Johnson, New Orleans, 1955-61; partner Sessions, Fishman, Rosenson, Snellings & Boisfontaine, New Orleans, 1961—. Served with Judge Adv. Gen.'s Corps USAF, 1953-55. Fellow Am. Bar Found., Am. Coll. Trial Lawyers; mem. ABA, La. Bar Assn. (pres. 1977-78), New Orleans Bar Assn., Am. Judicature Soc., Internat. Assn. Ins. Counsel, Fed. Ins. Counsel, La. Assn. Def. Counsel (pres. 1972-73), New Orleans Assn. Def. Counsel. Home: 428 Betz Pl Metairie LA 70005 Office: Pan-Am Life Center New Orleans LA 70112

BOISI, JAMES O., banker; b. N.Y.C., Apr. 30, 1919; s. H.L. and Mary Magdalene (Davolio) B.; m. Edith M. Mullen, June 2, 1945; children—James Christopher, Geoffrey, Jeanne Marie Boisi Sheehy, Patricia Boisi Sheehy, Mark, Eileen. B.A., Bklyn. Coll., 1939; J.D., Fordham U., 1942; L.H.D. (hon.), Pace U., 1983. Bar: N.Y. Sr. assoc. firm Amend & Amend, N.Y.C., 1942-56; v.p. real estate N.Y.C. R.R. System, N.Y.C., 1956-64; v.p. Morgan Guaranty Trust Co. N.Y., N.Y.C., 1964-67, sr. v.p., 1967-70, exec. v.p., 1970-79, vice chmn., 1979-84; exec. v.p. J.P. Morgan & Co., Inc., N.Y.C., 1972-79, vice chmn., 1979-84; exec. v.p. (investments) Helmsley Enterprises, Inc., N.Y.C., 1984—; officer Morgan Community Devel. Corp.; chmn. N.Y.C. Community Preservation Corp.; chmn. dept. real estate and ins. Pace U. Bd. dirs. N.Y.C. Housing Partnership; Mem. Old Brookville (L.I.) Planning Bd.; bd. dirs. Greater N.Y. council Boy Scouts Am., Downtown-Lower Manhattan Assn. Mem. Real Estate Bd. N.Y., Inc. Roman Catholic. Club: Nassau Country. Office: Helmsley Enterprises 60 E 42nd St New York NY 10165

BOISSE, JOSEPH ADONIAS, librarian; b. Marlboro, Mass., June 20, 1937; s. Anthony Joseph and Blanche Marie (Demers) B. A.B., Stonehill Coll., 1963; M.A., Brown U., 1965; M.S. in L.S, Simmons Coll., 1967. Asst. librarian Lawrence U., Appleton, Wis., 1968-71; asst. state librarian State of Vt., Montpelier, 1971-73; dir. Library/Learning Center, U. Wis.-Parkside, Kenosha, 1973-79; prof., dir. libraries Temple U., Phila., 1979-83; univ. librarian U. Calif., Santa Barbara, 1983—; bd. govs. Research Libraries Group, Inc., 1980—; cons. in field. Contbr. articles to profl. jours. Named Wis. Librarian of Year Wis. Library Assn., 1978. Mem. ALA, Nat. Librarians Assn., Pa. Library Assn. Office: Library of Univ Calif Santa Barbara CA 93106

BOIVIN, BERNARD, botanist; b. Montreal, Que., Can., June 7, 1916; s. Alexis and Marie L. (Tremblay) B.; m. Cosette Marcoux, Dec. 26, 1946; children—Lilian, Hélène, Jacques. B.A., U. Montreal, 1937, L.Sc., 1941; PH.D., Harvard U., 1943. Botanist Nat. Mus., Ottawa, Ont., Can., 1946-47; research asso. Harvard U., 1947-48; research scientist Can. Agr., Ottawa, 1948-65, 67-81; vis. prof. Laval U., 1965-66, lectr., 1981—; vis. prof. U. Toronto, 1969-70. Author: American Thalictra, 1944, Enumeration des Plantes du Canada, 1967, Flora of the Prairie Provinces, 5 vols, 1967-81, Survey of Canadian Herbaria, 1980. Served with Canadian Army, 1943-46. Guggenheim fellow, 1947-48. Fellow Royal Soc. Can.; mem. New England Bot. Club, Ottawa Field Naturalists Club. Roman Catholic. Home: 380 ch St-Louis Apt 1107 Québec PQ G1S 4M1 Canada Office: Herbier Louis-Marie Pavillon Comtois Cité Universitaire Québec PQ G1K 7P4 Canada

BOK, DEREK, university president; b. Bryn Mawr, Pa., Mar. 22, 1930; s. Curtis and Margaret (Plummer) B.; m. Sissela Ann Myrdal, May 7, 1955; children: Hilary Margaret, Victoria, Tomas Jeremy. B.A., Stanford U., 1951; J.D., Harvard U., 1954; M.A., George Washington U., 1958. Fulbright scholar, Paris, France, 1954-55; faculty Harvard U. Law Sch., Cambridge, Mass., 1958—; prof. Harvard Law Sch., 1961—, dean, 1968-71; pres. Harvard U., Cambridge, 1971—. Editor: (with Archibald Cox) Cases and Materials on Labor Law, 1962; author: (with John T. Dunlop) Labor and the American Community, 1970, (Beyond the Ivory Tower: Social Responsibilities of the Modern University), 1982; contbr. to: In the Public Interest, 1980. Served to 1st lt. AUS, 1956-58. Fellow Am. Acad. Arts and Scis.; mem. Am. Council on Edn., Com. for Econ. Devel. (trustee), Inst. Medicine, Am. Philos. Soc., Phi Beta Kappa, Phi Kappa Sigma. Office: Massachusetts Hall Harvard U Cambridge MA 02138

BOK, JOAN TOLAND, utility executive; b. Grand Rapids, Mich., Dec. 31, 1929; d. Don Prentiss Weaver and Mary Emily (Anderson) Tol; m. John Fairfield Bok, July 15, 1955; children: Alexander Toland, Geoffrey Robbins. A.B., Radcliffe Coll., 1951; J.D., Harvard U., 1955. Bar: Mass. bar 1955. Asso. firm Ropes & Gray, Boston, 1955-61; individual practice law, Boston, 1961-68; atty. New Eng. Electric System, Westborough, Mass., 1968-73, asst. to pres., 1973-77, v.p., sec., 1977-79, vice chmn., dir., 1979-84, chmn., 1984—; vice chmn., dir. New Eng. Power Co., New Eng. Power Service Co., New Eng. Energy Inc.; dir. Norton Co., Mass. Electric Co., Bank New Eng., Narragansett Electric Co. Bd. overseers Harvard U.; trustee Radcliffe Coll. Mem. Am. Bar Assn., Boston Bar Assn., Woods Hole Oceanographic Instn., Am. Antiquarian Soc., Phi Beta Kappa. Unitarian. Home: 53 Pinckney St Boston MA 02114 Office: 25 Research Dr Westborough MA 01581

BOK, JOHN FAIRFIELD, lawyer; b. Boston, Aug. 30, 1930. A.B. magna cum laude, Harvard U., 1952, LL.B. magna cum laude (editor law rev. 1954-55), 1955. Bar: Mass. 1955, N.Y. 1982. Assoc. firm Ropes & Gray, Boston, 1957-62, 64-69; counsel to devel. adminstr. Boston Redevel. Authority, 1962-64; partner firm Csaplar & Bok, Boston, 1969—; instr. law Boston Coll. Law Sch., part-time 1974-75; lectr. Practicing Law Inst., 1974, New Eng. Law Inst., 1973. Pres. Cambridge St. Community Devel. Corp., 1972-75, Citizens Housing and Planning Assn. Met. Boston, 1968-70, Met. Cultural Alliance, 1973-75, Beacon Hill Civic Assn., 1959-61, Beacon Hill Nursery Sch., 1964-65, Peddock's Island Trust, 1982—; chmn. bd. Boston Children's Museum, 1976—; bd. dirs. and/or officer Boston Mcpl. Research Bur., 1976—; trustee Greater Boston Community Devel. Corp., 1969—; bd. dirs. and/or officer Boston Neighborhood Housing Services, 1974-76, Boston Waterfront Devel. Corp., 1970—, Archtl. Conservation Trust for Mass., 1978—, Wheelock Coll., 1980—, Strawberry Banke, Inc., 1981—, United Community Planning Corp., 1982—; active Mass. Housing Fin. Agy., 1969—. Fulbright-Hays scholar, 1976. Mem. Am. Bar Assn., Mass. Bar Assn., Boston Bar Assn. (chmn. land use com. 1971-74), Phi Beta Kappa. Home: 53 Pinckney St Boston MA 02114 Office: 1 Winthrop St Boston MA 02110

BOK, P. DEAN, cell biologist, educator; b. Douglas County, S.D., Nov. 1, 1939; s. Kryn Arie and Rena (Van Zee) B.; m. Audrey Ann Van Diest, Aug. 21, 1964; children: Jonathan, Jeremy, James. B.A., Calvin Coll., 1960; M.A., Calif. State U., Long Beach, 1965; Ph.D., UCLA, 1968. Sci. instr. Valley Christian High Sch., Cerritos, Calif.; now prof. anatomy and Dolly Green prof. ophthalmology UCLA; asso. dir. Jules Stein Eye Inst., 1972-80. Recipient 9 disting. teaching awards UCLA; Nat. Eye Inst. grantee; Nat. Retinitis Pigmentosa Soc. grantee; Wm. and Mary Greve internat. research scholar Research to Prevent Blindness, Inc., 1982. Fellow AAAS; mem. Nat. Eye Inst. (bd. sci. counselors 1980-82), Assn. Research in Vision and Ophthalmology (trustee 1978-82), Am. Assn. Anatomists, Am. Soc. Cell Biology. Home: 2135 Kelton Ave Los Angeles CA 90025 Office: UCLA Los Angeles CA 90024

BOKE, NORMAN HILL, botanist; b. Mobridge, S.D., Mar. 14, 1913; s. Hans Christian and Elenor (Hill) B.; m. Beulah Esther Brown, Sept. 4, 1948; 1 dau., Janice Sue. A.B., U. S.D., 1934; M.S., U. Okla., 1936; Ph.D., U. Calif. at Berkeley, 1939. Instr. biology U. N.Mex., 1941-42, Johns Hopkins U., 1942-44; mem. faculty U. Okla., Norman, 1945—, George Lynn Cross research prof. botany, 1965—. Contbr. articles to profl. jours.; editor: Am. Jour. Botany, 1970-75. Served with USAAF, 1944-45; PTO. Guggenheim Meml. fellow, 1953. Mem. Bot. Soc. Am., Sociedad Mexicana de Cactologia, Torrey Bot. Club, Explorers Club, Phi Beta Kappa, Sigma Xi, Alpha Tau Omega. Author research articles on plant anatomy and morphology, especially Cactaceae. Home: 610 Broad Ln Norman OK 73069 Office: 770 Van Vleet Oval Dept Botany and Microbiology U Okla Norman OK 73019

BOLAN, ROBERT S., association executive; b. New Britain, Conn., Aug. 24, 1941; s. Robert Stuart and Susanne (Humphreys) B.; m. Robin Rice Bolan, Sept. 3, 1972; 1 dau., Carol Susanne. A.B., U. N.C.-Chapel Hill, 1963; M.S., U. So. Calif., 1967, Ph.D., 1976. Placement dir. U. So. Calif., Los Angeles, 1970-71; exec. v.p. Eckman Ctr., Inc., Woodland Hills, Calif., 1971-73; dir. exec. edn. and MBA Field Studies UCLA, 1973-77; dir. govt. affairs Los Angeles Community Coll., 1977-80; exec. v.p. Am. Diabetes Assn., N.Y.C., 1980—; adj. prof. U. San francisco, 1976-80, U. Redlands, 1976-80; acting dean students U. Calif.-Santa Barbara, 1973. Author: The Consulting Process, 1978, Guidebook for Arts management Interns, 1976; author: A Student Guide to Management Field Studies, 1976. Mem. Bd. Edn. Mgmt. Rev. Com., Los Angeles, 1976-77; chmn. YMCA Reorgn. study com., Los Angeles, 1976; cons. ACTION-Peace Corps, Ecuador, 1974. Lt. USN, 1963-70. Decorated Air medal. Mem. Am. Mgmt. Assn., Am. Soc. Tng. and Devel., Am. Soc. Assn. Execs. Home: 121 Beechwood Rd Summit NJ 07901 Office: Am Diabetes Assn 2 Park Ave New York NY 10016

BOLAN, THOMAS ANTHONY, lawyer; b. Lynn, Mass., May 30, 1924; s. Thomas J. and Margaret (Cremin) B.; m. Marie T. Gerst, Nov. 25, 1950; children: Sean, Douglas, Mary, Jacqueline, William. B.A. summa cum laude, St. John's U., 1952, LL.B. summa cum laude, 1950. Bar: N.Y. Assoc. firm Burroughs & Brown, N.Y.C., 1951-53; asst. U.S. atty. Dept. Justice, N.Y.C., 1953-57; assoc. Roy M. Cohn, N.Y.C., 1957-59; mem. firm Saxe, Bacon & Bolan, N.Y.C., 1960-71, counsel, 1972—; lectr. law St. John's U., 1957-61; pres., chmn. bd. 5th Ave. Coach Lines, N.Y.C., 1967-68, Championship Sports, Inc., 1961—; treas., exec. dir. Feature Sports, Inc., 1959-61; chmn. bd. Merc. Nat. Bank, Chgo., 1967-68, Gateway Nat. Bank, 1966-67; sec. Balt. Paint and Chem. Corp., N.Y.C., 1966-68, TelePro Industries Inc., 1966-68; sec., dir. B.S.F. Co., N.Y.C., 1966-68, Defiance Industries, 1966-68; v.p. Am. Steel and Pump Corp., N.Y.C., 1966-68, WRNJ Assocs., Atlantic City, 1961-68, Harrisburg Broadcasting Co., Palmyra, Pa., 1966-68; sec., treas., dir. Berwick Broadcasting Corp., Reading, Pa., 1967-68; dir. Overseas Pvt. Investment Corp. Bd. editors: Nat. Law Jour., 1983—; Contbr. articles to legal jours. Founder, law chmn., mem. exec. com. Conservative Party, N.Y. State, 1962—; chmn. E. Side Conservative Club, N.Y.C., 1973—; v.p. Crusade for Am., Rockville Center, N.Y., 1957-62; bd. regents St. Francis Coll., Bklyn., 1968—; treas. Ednl. Reviewer, 1960—; pres. Cambria Heights (N.Y.) Parish Council, 1968-70; pres., dir. Pro Ecclesia Found., 1972-73; trustee Cambria Heights Boys Club Assn., 1968-72; v.p., dir. Heiser Found., 1955-73; mem. Com. to Restore Internal Security, 1979—; bd. govs. Council for Nat. Policy, 1983—; mem. Am. Council on Germany, 1983—, U.S. Commn. for UNESCO, 1983—; bd. visitors Eureka Coll., 1983—; nat. adv. council Actors Youth Fund, 1982—; mem. U.S. Senator Alfonse D'Amato's Jud. Screening Com., 1982—. Served with USAF, 1943-45. Decorated Air medal with 5 oak leaf clusters; recipient Medal of Honor The 52 Assn., 1981; Bella V. Dodd Meml. award N.Y. County Conservative Party, 1981. Mem. Fed. Bar Council, Am., N.Y. State, N.Y. County bar assns., Am. Judicature Soc., Cath. Lawyers Guild, Nat. Assn. Coll. and Univ. Attys., Cath. War Vets. (judge advocate 1965—, Service award Queens County chpt. 1968, 77, elected to Order St. Sebastian, nat. assn. 1981), Am. African Affairs Assn. (sec., dir. 1975—), Internat. Assn. Jurists, Ret. Officers Assn. (Knickerbocker chpt.). Club: Knights of Malta. Office: 39 E 68th St New York NY 10021

BOLAND, CHRISTOPHER THOMAS, II, lawyer; b. Scranton, Pa., June 10, 1915; s. Patrick J. and Sarah (Jennings) B.; m. Nora Cusick, Jan. 23, 1943; m. Cornelia Bingham Maury, Mar. 1, 1980. B.S.S. cum laude, Georgetown U., 1937; LL.B., Harvard, 1940. Staff dir. Spl. Senate Com. on Atomic Energy, 1945-47; staff dir., counsel Joint Senate-House Com. on Atomic Energy, 1947; practice law, Washington, 1947—; now sr. partner firm Gallagher, Boland, Meiburger & Brosnan; utility specialist Dept. Energy. Served to lt. col., intelligence USAAF, 1941-45. Mem. Fed. Energy Bar Assn. (pres. 1970), ABA, D.C. Bar Assn. Clubs: Congressional Country (pres. 1974), Harvard (Washington); Burning Tree (Bethesda, Md.). Home: 5309 Cardinal Ct Bethesda MD 20016 Office: 821 15th St NW Washington DC 20005

BOLAND, EDWARD P., congressman; b. Springfield, Mass., Oct. 1, 1911. Student, Boston Coll. Law Sch. Mem. Mass. Legislature, 1935-40; register of deeds, Hampden County, Mass., 1941-52; mem. 83d-97th Congresses from 2d Mass. Dist. Served to capt. AUS, World War II; PTO. Democrat. Home: Springfield MA 01101 Office: 2426 Rayburn House Office Bldg Washington DC 20515

BOLAND, EDWARD WARD, physician; b. Redlands, Calif., Dec. 18, 1907; m. Jane Pauline Rooney; children—Paul, Peter, Philip, Patrick, Ann. Student, Santa Clara U., 1926-28; B.S., St. Louis U., 1931, M.D., 1933; M.S. in Medicine, U. Minn., 1938. Diplomate: Am. Bd. Internal Medicine. Intern San Bernardino County (Calif.) Gen. Hosp., 1933-34; resident medicine St. Vincent's Hosp., Los Angeles, 1934-35, chmn. dept. medicine, 1956-61, dir. medicine, 1958-61, pres. staff, 1962-63; mem. attending staff Hosp. of Good Samaritan, Los Angeles County Hosp., 1960—; clin. prof. medicine U. So. Calif.; Mem. adv. bd. Am. Hosp. of Paris, Alumni Assn. Mayo Found. Med. Edn. and Research, v.p., 1966-67, pres., 1968-69, chmn. com. devel., 1976—. Author numerous publs. in field, also chpts. med. textbooks.; Asso. editor: Annals of the Rheumatic Diseases, London, 1948-72; sect. editor: Arthritis and Allied Conditions, 1949—; co-editor: Rheumatism Revs; editorial bd.: Calif. Medicine, 1957-67. Mem. president's council Loyola U., Los Angeles; bd. regents U. Santa Clara, bd. founders, 1968; bd. regents Loyola Marymount U., Los Angeles, 1973—. Served to maj. M.C. AUS, 1942-46. Recipient Outstanding Achievement award U. Minn., 964; Physician Service award Arthritis Found. and Am. Rheumatism Assn., 1973; Fellow in medicine Mayo Clinic, 1935-38. Fellow Am. Geriatric Soc. (founding), A.C.P. (gov. for So. Calif. 1970-73, master 1974); mem. AMA (cons. drugs council), Calif., Am., Internat. socs. internal medicine, Pan-Am. League Against Rheumatism, Ligue Internationale Contre le Rhumatisme, Arthritis and Rheumatism Found. (v.p. 1947-64, chmn. med. and sci. com. 1959-60, gov. 1952—), Brazilian Rheumatism Soc. (hon.), Argentine Rheumatism Assn. (hon.), Am. Heart Assn., Am. Therapeutic Soc., Am. Rheumatism Assn. (pres. 1954-55), Los Angeles Soc. Internal Medicine (pres. 1952), Los Angeles Acad. Medicine (v.p. 1966-67, pres. 1967-68), Mexican Rheumatism Soc. (hon.), Internat. Coll. Physicians, N.Y. Acad. Scis., Calif. Med. Assn., Los Angeles Heart Assn., So. Calif. Rheumatism Assn., Knights of Malta, Sigma Xi, Alpha Omega Alpha, Alpha Sigma Nu. Club: Jonathan (Los Angeles). Office: 321 N Larchmont Blvd Los Angeles CA 90004

BOLAND, JANET LANG, judge; b. Kitchener, Ont., Can., Dec. 6, 1924; d. George William and Miriam Janet (Geraghty) Lang; m. John Brown Boland, Oct. 1, 1949; children: Michael, Christopher, Nicholas. B.A., Waterloo Coll., 1946; law degree, Osgoode Hall, 1950; hon. doctorate of law, Sir Wilfred Laurier U. Bar: Ont. 1950, named Queen's counsel 1965. Mem. firm White, Bristol, Beck & Phipps, Toronto, Ont., 1959-69; partner firm Lang Michener, Toronto, 1969-72; county ct. judge, Toronto, 1972-76; judge Supreme Ct. of Ont., Toronto, 1976—; co-chmn. Penal Reform for Women Joint Com., 1956-58. Mem. Jr. League Toronto. Roman Catholic. Office: Osgoode Hall Queen St Toronto ON Canada *

BOLAND, JOHN, physician; b. Dublin, Ireland, Feb. 16, 1916; came to U.S., 1958; s. John and Hannah (Clarke) B.; m. Kay Turner Norton, Sept. 14, 1968. B.A.M.B. B.Ch., U. Dublin, 1938; M.D., SUNY, 1959. Sci. mem. Med. Research Council, London, 1953-58; prof., chmn. dept. radiotherapy Mt. Sinai Sch Medicine, N.Y.C., 1959-82, disting. service prof., 1982—; chmn. bd. examiners x-ray tech. Dept. Health, State of N.Y., 1970—. Surg. lt. comdr. English Royal Navy, 1940-46. Decorated Dising. Service Cross, 1942. Fellow N.Y. Acad. Medicine, Royal Coll. Surgeons Edinburgy, Royal Coll. Radiologists London; mem. Am. Radium Soc. Episcopalian. Office: Dept Radiotherapy Mt Sinai Sch Medicine of CUNY 1 Gustave L Levy Pl New York NY 10029

BOLAND, JOHN FRANCIS, JR., lawyer; b. Yonkers, N.Y., July 23, 1915; s. John Francis and Celeste (Kinalley) B.; m. Jean Clayton Smith, Sept. 15, 1942; children: John Francis III, Richard P., Christopher J., Katherine B., Patricia, Anne, Pegeen. B.A., Fordham U., 1935, J.D., 1946. Bar: N.Y. 1946, Ariz. 1949. Practiced in, White Plains, N.Y., 1946-48, Tucson, 1949-50, Phoenix, 1951—; asso. McCarthy & Gaynor, 1946-48; partner Boland & D'Antonio, 1949-50, Evans, Kitchel & Jenckes (P.C.), 1951—, pres., 1976—; dir. Apache Powder Co., Tuscon, Cornelia & Gila Bend R.R. Served to capt., Signal Corps AUS, 1941-46. Mem. Am., Ariz., Maricopa County bar assns., AIME, Am. Mining Congress (cons. labor-mgmt. subcommittees). Clubs: Ariz. Yacht, University (Phoenix); Southwestern Yacht (San Diego); Cornell (N.Y.C.). Home: 1102 E Tapatio Dr Phoenix AZ 85020 Office: 2600 N Central Ave Phoenix AZ 85004-3099

BOLAND, LAWRENCE, metals co. exec.; b. Robesonia, Pa., Jan. 3, 1917; s. Thomas N. and Gertrude (Flanagan) B.; m. Anna Louise Lebengood, Apr. 11, 1948; children—Lawrence F., Joseph P., Michael C., Stephen E., Elizabeth Anne. Student, Wharton Sch., U. Pa., 1937-38, Cath. U. Am., 1938-41. Prodn. mgr. Beryllium Corp., Reading, Pa., 1947-52, gen. sales mgr., 1952-56, v.p., 1956-60, exec. v.p., 1960-72; also dir. pres. Intercontinental Wire Co., Inc., 1972—; dir. Nonotuck Mfg. Co., Holyoke, Mass., Chem. Pollution Scis., Inc., Consol. Beryllium, Ltd., London, Eng. Trustee St. Joseph's Hosp., Reading, Pa. Mem. Am. Soc. Metals, Am. Ordnance Assn., Wire Assn., Internat. Copper Devel. Assn., Am. Inst. Aeros. and Astronautics. Clubs: Nat. Dem.; Wyomissing, Berkshire Country (Reading). Home: 1730 Dauphin Ave Wyomissing PA 19610 Office: PO Box 1652: Reading PA 19603

BOLAND, THOMAS EDWIN, banker; b. Columbus, Ga., July 8, 1934; s. Clifford Edwin and Helen Marjorie (Robinson) B.; m. Beth Ann Campbell, May 23, 1959; children—Susan Ann, Thomas Edwin. Student, Emory U., 1952-54; grad., Advanced Mgmt. Program, 1972; B.B.A., Ga. State U., 1957; postgrad., Stonier Grad. Sch. Banking, Rutgers U., 1964-66. With First Nat. Bank of Atlanta, 1954—, v.p., 1968-71, group v.p., 1972-73, sr. v.p., 1974-78, exec. v.p., in charge in credit policy, 1979—; exec. v.p., chief adminstrv. officer, 1981—; v.p. First Atlanta Internat. Corp., 1979—; dir. First Nat. Bank Atlanta, First Atlanta Corp., First Atlanta Leasing, First Atlanta Mortgage Corp., First Financial Life Ins. Co., First Nat. Bldg. Corp., First Nat Bank of Dalton, Tharpe & Brooks, Inc., Gulf Finance Corp.; T & B, P.C.; dir. Woods-Tucker Leasing Corp. of Ga.; mem. investment com. Minbanc Capital Corp., Washington, 1978—. Trustee Atlanta Bapt. Coll., 1970-72; trustee, treas., mem. endowment com., mem. investment com. Ga. Bapt. Found., Atlanta, 1980—; mem. pres.'s council Mercer U., 1980—; bd. visitors Emory U., 1982; mem. exec. bd. Atlanta area council Boy Scouts Am., 1982. Served with AUS, 1975. Recipient Disting. Salesman award Sales and Mktg. Execs., 1968. Mem. Am. Bankers Assn. (cert. comml. lender, bank card com. 1964-66), Robert Morris Assocs. (security dealers relations com. 1974-75, chmn. Met. Atlanta Area 1979—, chmn. and dir. Eastern Group, Southeastern Chpt. 1981, pres. and dir., Southern chpt. 1982), Ga. State U. Alumni Assn. (mem. exec. com. and bd. dirs. 1979—). Club: Cherokee Town and Country (Atlanta). Home: 4986 Buckline Crossing Dunwoody GA 30338 Office: 2 Peachtree St NE Atlanta GA 30302

BOLANDE, ROBERT PAUL, pathologist, educator; b. Chgo., Apr. 16, 1926; s. Herman Asher and Florence (Levy) B.; m. A. Suzanne Hiss, Apr. 1, 1954; children: Deborah, Jennifer, Miriame, Hyam Asher. B.S., Northwestern U., 1948, M.S., 1952, M.D., 1952. Intern Chgo.-Wesley Meml. Hosp., 1952-53; resident in pathology Children's Meml. Hosp., Chgo., 1953-54; resident Inst. Pathology, Case Western Res. U., Cleve., 1954-56, chief pediatric pathology, 1956-66, asso. prof. pathology, 1960-72; dir. labs. Akron (Ohio) Children's Hosp., 1966-72; dir. pathology Montreal Children's Hosp.; prof. pathology McGill U., Montreal, 1972-83, also prof. pediatrics, 1975-83; prof. pathology East Carolina U. Sch. Medicine, Greenville, N.C., 1983—. Author: Cellular

Aspects of Development Pathology, 1967; editor: Perspectives in Pediatric Pathology, 1973-80, Human Pathology, 1979; contbr. articles to profl. jours., also monograph. Served with USNR, 1944-46. Mem. Am. Assn. Pathologists and Bacteriologists, Pediatric Pathology Club, Inc. Home: 1013 E Wright Rd Greenville NC 27834 Office: East Carolina U Sch Medicine Greenville NC 27834

BOLCH, CARL EDWARD, JR., lawyer, corporation executive; b. St. Louis, Feb. 28, 1943; s. Carl Edward and Juanita (Newton) B.; m. Susan Bolch; children: Carl, Allison, Natalie. B.S. in Econs, U. Pa., 1964; J.D., Duke U., 1967. Bar: Fla. 1967. Chmn. bd., chief exec. officer Racetrac Petroleum, Inc., Atlanta, 1967—. Edition editor: Close Corporations, 1967. Mem. ABA, Fla. Bar Assn., Soc. Ind. Gasoline Marketers (dir.). Office: Suite 100 2625 Cumberland Pkwy Atlanta GA 30339

BOLCOM, WILLIAM ELDEN, composer; b. Seattle, May 26, 1938; s. Robert Samuel and Virginia (Lauermann) B.; m. Fay Levine, Dec. 23, 1963 (div. 1967); m. Katherine Agee Ling, June 8, 1968 (div. 1969); m. Joan Morris, Nov. 28, 1975. B.A., U. Wash., 1958; M.A., Mills Coll., 1961; postgrad., Paris Conservatoire de Musique, 1959-61, 64-65; D. Mus. Art, Stanford U., 1964; student piano, Berthe Poncy Jacobson, 1949-58; student composition, George F. McKay, 1949-51, John Verrall, 1951-58, Leland Smith, 1961-64, Darius Milhaud, 1957-61, George Rochberg, 1966. Acting asst. prof. music dept. U. Wash., Seattle, 1965-66; lectr., asst. prof. music Queens Coll., Flushing, N.Y., 1966-68; vis. critic music theater Drama Sch., Yale U., 1968-69; composer in residence Theater Arts Program, N.Y. U., N.Y.C., 1969-71; asst. prof. Sch. Music, U. Mich., 1973, asso. prof., 1977—; mem. jury Nat. Endowment for Arts, 1976-77. Composer symphonies, 1957, 64, String Quartets 1-8, 1950-65, Décalage for cello and piano, 1961-62, Fantasy-Sonata for piano, 1960-62, Concertante for Flute, Oboe, Violin, and Orch, 1960; opera Dynamite Tonite, 1960-61, rev., 1966, Octet, 1962, Concerto-Serenade for Violin and Strings, 1964, Session for Chamber Ensemble, 1965, 12 Etudes for Piano, 1959-66, Fives, Double Concerto for Violin, Piano and Strings, 1966, Morning and Evening Poems, Cantata, 1966, Session II; violin and viola, 1966, Session III; clarinet, violin, cello, piano, percussion, 1967, Session IV; chamber ensemble, 1967, Black Host for organ, percussion and taped sounds, 1967, Piano Rags, 1967-74; opera Greatshot, 1967-69, Praeludium for vibraphone and organ, 1969, Dark Music for tympani and cello, 1969, Duets for Quintet, 1970, Unpopular Songs, 1970, Hydraulis for organ, 1971, Commedia for chamber orch, 1971, Whisper Moon; chamber ensemble, 1971, Frescoes for two pianists, 1971, Novella (string quartet No. 9), 1972, Trauermarsch for trio-sonata ensemble, 1973, Songs of Innocence (Blake), 1974, Seasons for solo guitar, 1974, Open House; cycle on poems by Roethke, 1975, Piano Concerto, 1975-76, Piano Quartet, 1976, Revelation Studies for Carillon, 1976, Mysteries for Organ, 1976, Vocalise for a cappella chorus, 1977; score for stage works Puntila (Brecht), 1977, Man is Man, 1978, Beggar's Opera, 1978, 2d Violin Sonata, 1978, Gospel Preludes for Organ, 1978-79, 81, Humoresk for organ and orch, 1979, Brass Quintet, 1980, Songs of Experience (Blake), 1981, Symphony for Chamber Orchestra, 1979; others.; Pianist in: (with Gerard Schwarz) recs. Cornet Favorites, (with Clifford Jackson, baritone) An Evening with Henry Russell, (with mezzo-soprano Joan Morris) Songs of Leiber and Stoller, (with Joan Morris and Max Morath) These Charming People, (with Joan Morris) The Girl on the Magazine Cover; (with Joan Morris and Lucy Simon) songs of Irving Berlin The Rodgers and Hart Album; others.; Author: (with Robert Kimball) Reminiscing with Sissle and Blake, 1973; contbr.: to Groves Dictionary, 6th edit; contbg. editor: Annals of Scholarship. Recipient Kurt Weill award for composition, 1962, William and Noma Copley award, 1960, Marc Blitzstein award for excellence in mus. theatre Am. Acad. Arts and Letters, 1965; Guggenheim Found. fellow, 1964, 68; Rockefeller Found. grantee, 1965, 69-70; N.Y. State Council awardee, 1971; Nat. Endowment for Arts, 1974, 75; Koussevitzky Found. award, 1974; Henry Russel award, 1977. Mem. Am. Music Center (bd. dirs.), Am. Composer Alliance. Home: 3080 Whitmore Lake Rd Ann Arbor MI 48103

BOLDA, PETER G., electronics company executive; b. Marienwerder, Germany, Aug. 6, 1930; came to U.S., 1961, naturalized, 1967; s. Bruno M. and Frieda L. (Hahn) B.; m. Brigitte E. M. Ludwig, Oct. 11, 1958; children: Kirsten, Karen, Mark, Eric. B.S.E.E., Polytech. Coll., Germany, 1954. Registered profl. engr., Wis. Engr. Brow, Boveri & Co., Germany, 1954-56, Ont. Hydrol, Can., 1956-61; engring. mgr., internat. sales mgr., pres., gen. mgr. Giddings & Lewis, Inc, AMCA Internat., Fond du Lac, Wis., 1961—. Home: 15705 W Timber Ln Libertyville Ill 60048 Office: Giddings & Lewis Inc. 142 Doty St Fond du Lac WI 54935

BOLDEN, CONNIE EDWARD, govt. ofcl.; b. Newton, N.C., Dec. 1, 1933; s. William Dan and Ethel May (Yancey) B.; m. Elizabeth Anne Carlson, July 11, 1970. B.S. in Bus. Adminstrn, U. N.C., 1956, J.D., 1959, M.L.S., 1963. Bar: N.C. bar 1959. Practiced in, Burlington, to 1962; asst. state law librarian State of Wash., Olympia, 1963-65, state law librarian, 1966—; asst. prof. law, law librarian Stetson U., St. Petersburg, Fla., 1965-66. Co-author: American Judge, 1968, Appellate Opinion Preparation, 1978; editor: Law Library Jour, 1967-77. Bd. visitors U. Puget Sound Law Sch., Tacoma, 1972-76. Mem. Internat. Assn. Law Libraries, Am. Assn. Law Librarians (exec. bd. 1971-74, v.p. 1978-79, pres. 1979-80), Spl. Libraries Assn., N.C. Bar Assn. Home: PO Box 1674 Olympia WA 98507 Office: Wash State Law Library Olympia WA 98504

BOLDEN, THEODORE EDWARD, dentist, educator; b. Middleburg, Va., Apr. 19, 1920; s. Theodore D. and Mary E. (Jackson) B. A.B., Lincoln U., 1941, LL.D. (hon.), 1981; D.D.S., Meharry Med. Coll., 1947; M.S. (John Hay Whitney Found. opportunity fellow), 1951; Ph.D. (USPHS fellow), 1958. Diplomate: Am. Bd. Oral Medicine, Am. Bd. Oral Pathology. Instr. operative dentistry, pedodontics and periodontics Meharry Med. Coll., 1948-49; chmn. oral pathology (Sch. Dentistry), 1962-77, dir. research, 1962-75, asso. dean, 1965-70; asst. prof. gen. and oral pathology Seton Hall Coll. Medicine and Dentistry, 1957-60, asso. prof., 1960-62; prof. gen. and oral pathology, dean Coll. Medicine and Dentistry of N.J.-N.J. Dental Sch., Newark, 1977—, dean coll., 1977-78, acting chmn. gen. and oral pathology, 1979-80; cons. in field; trustee Am. Fund for Dental Health. Author: (with John Manhold, Jr.) Outline of Pathology, 1960, Dental Hygiene Examination Review Book, 4th edit, (with E. Mobley and E. Chandler), 1982. Chmn. adv. health com. Montclair (N.J.) Health Dept., 1959-60; commr. urban redevel., Town of Montclair, 1960-62. Served to sgt. U.S. Army, 1942-43, 51-52. Fellow Am. Acad. Oral Pathology, Am. Acad. Oral Medicine, Internat. Coll. Dentistry; mem. Nat. Dental Assn. (editor Quar. NDA 1975-82), Pan Tenn. Dental Assn., Capitol City Dental Soc., Ewell Neil Dental Soc., Internat. Assn. Dental Research, Sigma Xi, Omicron Kappa Upsilon, Kappa Sigma Pi. Baptist. Home: 29 Montague Montclair NJ 07042 Office: 100 Bergen Newark NJ 07103

BOLDREY, EDWIN BARKLEY, neurol. surgeon, educator; b. Morgantown, Ind., July 17, 1906; s. Edwin H. and Florence B. (Barkley) B.; m. Helen B. Eastland, June 16, 1932; children—Nancy J., Edwin E., Susan E. A.B., De Pauw U., 1927; M.A., Ind. U., 1930, M.D., 1932; M.Sc., McGill U., 1936. Diplomate: Am. Bd. Neurol. Surgery (dir. 1958-64). Intern Montreal Gen. Hosp., 1932-34, admitting officer, spl. grad. student pathology, 1934-35; research fellow Montreal Neurol. Inst., 1935-36, 40, house officer neurology and neurol. surgery, 1936-37, fellow neuropathology, 1938, resident neurology and neurol. surgery, 1939; mem. faculty U. Calif. Sch. Medicine, 1940—, instr. surgery, 1940-44, asst. clin. prof. surgery, 1944-47, asst. clin. prof. neurol. surgery, 1947-48, asso. prof. neurol. surgery, 1948-60, prof., 1960-74, prof. emeritus, 1974—, chmn. dept., 1951-56, neurol. surgeon-in-chief of hosps., 1951-56; attending neurol. surgeon Langley Porter Clinic, 1945-74; cons. neurol. surgeon San Francisco Shriner's Hosp. for Crippled Children, 1948—, US Naval Hosp., Camp Pendleton, Calif., VA, Washington, San Francisco Hosp., 1951—, Parks AFB Hosp., 1955-58, May T. Morrison Rehab. Center, 1956-62, Ft. Miley VA Hosp., 1957—, Travis AFB Hosp., 1958—, Barrow Neurol. Inst., Phoenix, Letterman Gen. Hosp., USN Hosp., San Diego; lectr. neurol. surgery Oakland Naval Hosp., 1966—; Cons. Nat. Inst. Neurol. Disease and Blindness, 1960-64; cons. Nat. Inst. Neurol. Disease and Stroke, 1966-73, chmn. research tng. grant com., 1967-70, mem. nat. adv. council, 1973-77; mem. dist. rev. com. Calif. Bd. Med. Examiners, 1969-76; Mem. nat. clin. adv. United Cerebral Palsy, 1953-63, bd. dirs., San Francisco, 1958-78, mem. med. adv. bd., 1961-78; adv. council neurol. surgery A.C.S., 1956-61; cons. USPHS Hosps., 1966—; mem. med. adv. bd. Epilepsy Found., 1966-76; Bd. dirs. Princeton Conf. Cerebrovascular Disease, 1970-74, Neurol. Scis. Found. of Portland, Oreg., 1978—. Author articles; contrbr. med. books, encys. Recipient Royer award, 1970. Fellow A.C.S.; mem. A.M.A., Assn. for Research and Nervous and Mental Disease, Pan Pacific Surg. Assn. (v.p. 1975, 78), Am. Neurol. Assn., Am. Acad. Neurol. Surgery (pres. 1958-59, historian 1970-81), Soc. Neurol. Surgeons (pres. 1965-66, historian 1970—), Am. Assn. Neurol. Pathology, AAAS, Harvey Cushing Soc. (v.p. 1964-65, parliamentarian 1975, 76), N.Y., Calif. acads. sci., Calif. Acad. Medicine, Can. Neurol. Soc., San Francisco Neurol. Soc. (a founder, pres. 1948-49, 80-81), Can. Neurosurg. Soc., Western Neurosurg. Soc. (a founder, pres. 1964-65), Am. Trauma Soc. (founding mem.), Calif. Assn. Neurol. Surgery (founder), N. Calif. Acad. Clin. Oncology, Am. Heart Assn., Phi Delta Theta, Phi Chi, Alpha Omega Alpha. Clubs: Commonwealth, University (San Francisco). Home: 924 Hayne Rd Hillsborough CA 94010 Office: U Calif Med School San Francisco CA 94143 *Work, work, work.*

BOLDT, CHARLES MARTIN, construction company executive; b. Neewah, Wis., July 1, 1950; s. Oscar C. and Patricia (Hamar) B.; m. Linda C. Arntzen, Aug. 31, 1974; children: Andrew C., David M. B.S. in Civil Engring., Bucknell U., 1973, B.A. in Econs., 1973. Registered profl. engr., Wis., Minn., Mich. Project mgr. Boldt Constrn., Appleton, Wis., 1975-80, pres., 1980—. Pres. Casa Clare, Appleton, 1981-82; bd. dirs. YMCA, Goodwill. Served to 2d lt. C.E. U.S. Army, 1973-75. Lodge: Rotary. Home: 1508 S Outagamie St Appleton WI 54914 Office: Oscar J. Boldt Construction PO Box 419 217 S Badger Ave Appleton WI 54912

BOLDT, DAVID RHYS, journalist; b. N.Y.C., Nov. 27, 1941; s. Joseph Raymond and Margaret (Nutting) B.; m. Fereshteh Sarshar, June 11, 1967; 1 son, Thomas Arash. B.A., Dartmouth Coll., 1964. Staff writer The Wall Street Jour., N.Y.C., 1964-65, Staff writer Los Angeles bur., 1967-69; staff reporter The Washington Post, Washington, 1969-72; with Phila. Inquirer, 1973—; editor The Inquirer mag., 1976—; instr. Temple U., 1974-80. Editor: The Founding City, 1976. Served to 1st lt. U.S. Army, 1965-67. Recipient Pulitzer Prize for local reporting (as part of Inquirer staff), 1980, Overseas Press Club citation for excellence, 1980. Unitarian. Club: Franklin Inn (Phila.). Home: 7809 Winston Rd Philadelphia PA 19118 Office: 400 N Broad St Philadelphia PA 19101

BOLDT, GEORGE HUGO, U.S. dist. judge; b. Chgo., Dec. 28, 1903; s. George F. and Christine (Carstensen) B.; m. Eloise Baird, Nov. 17, 1928; children—Joan (Mrs. Hugh C. Sobottka), Virginia (Mrs. T. R. Riedinger), George B. A.B., U. Mont., 1925, LL.B., 1926; LL.D., Coll. Puget Sound, 1954; grad., Command and Gen. Staff Sch., Ft. Leavenworth, 1943; LL.D., U. Mont., 1961. Bar: Mont. bar 1926, Wash. bar 1928. Asso. W.D. Rankin, Helena, Mont., 1926-27; partner firm Ballinger, Hutson & Boldt, Seattle, 1928-45, Metzger, Blair, Gardner & Boldt, Tacoma, 1945-53; U.S. dist. judge (West dist. Wash.), 1953-71, chief judge, 1971, sr. judge, 1971—; spl. asst. atty. gen. State of Wash., 1940, 50; U.S. del. 1st UN Congress on prevention of crime and treatment of offenders, Geneva, 1955; mem. com. on jud. facilities Am. Bar Assn.-A.I.A.; chmn. bd. visitors U. Puget Sound Law Sch.; mem. com. on operations and appraisals Fed. Jud. Center; Jud. Conf. rep. Sec. State Adv. Com. Internat. Law; chmn. Pay Bd., Econ. Stablzn. Program, Office of Pres., 1971-73. Trustee, pres. U. Mont. Found., 1975-76; trustee U. Puget Sound; also chmn. bd. visitors Law Sch. Served as lt. col. AUS, World War II. Mem. Am., Fed., Washington State, Pierce County bar assns., Am. Judicature Soc., Inst. Jud. Adminstrn., Am. Law Inst., Internat. Inst. Juridical Studies (gen. sci. com.), U.S. Jud. Studies (gen. sci. com.), U.S. Jud. Conf. (various coms.), Am. Legion, Phi Delta Phi, Sigma Chi. Republican. Presbyterian. Club: Mason (32 deg., Shriner)

BOLDT, OSCAR CHARLES, construction company executive; b. Appleton, Wis., Apr. 20, 1924; s. Oscar John and Dorothy A. (Bartmann) B.; m. Patricia Hamar, July 9, 1949; children:Charles, Thomas, Margaret. B.S.C.E., U. Wis., 1948. Pres. O.J. Boldt Constrn. Co., Appleton, 1948-79, chmn. bd., chief exec. officer, 1979—; sec. dir. W.S. Patterson Co., 1963—; sec. A.K. Jensen Corp., 1971—; dir. Valley Bank, Valley Bancorp., Pierce Mfg. Co., Midwest Express Airlines. Pres. Appleton Area C. of C., 1967, Appleton YMCA, 1955-57, Appleton Meml. Hosp., 1975-76. Served to 2d lt. USAAF, 1943-45. Recipient Disting. Service award Appleton Jaycees, 1960; Paul Harris fellow, 1979. Republican. Presbyterian. Clubs: Appleton Rotary (pres. 1975-76, Vocat. Service award 1977), Riverview Country (pres. 1968-69). Home: 1715 Reid Dr Appleton MI 54914 Office: Oscar J Boldt Constrn Co 217 S Badger Ave Appleton WI 54914

BOLDUC, ERNEST JOSEPH, association executive; b. Lawrence, Mass., June 11, 1924; s. Ernest Joseph and Ernestine (Mercier) B.; m. Grace Gaydis, June 23, 1945; children: Philip, Richard, Stephen. B.S. in M.E, Northeastern U., 1948. Cert. assn. exec. Market devel. rep. Kawneer Co., Boston and N.Y.C., 1950-55, Kaiser Aluminum, N.Y.C., 1955-58; exec. sec. com. tool steel producers Am. Iron and Steel Inst., N.Y.C., 1958-66; exec. dir. Nat. Council Paper Industry for Air and Stream Improvement, N.Y.C., 1966-83; prin. EJB Assocs., Armonk, N.Y., 1983—. Author: Curtain Wall Do's and Don'ts, 1955, Planning the Successful Meeting, 1959; Editor: Tool Steel Trends, 1961-66. Served with USAAF, 1943-45. Decorated Air medal with 3 oak leaf clusters.; Named Man of Yr. N.Y. Producers Council, 1955. Mem. Am. Soc. Assn. Execs. (awards com. 1978-80), N.Y. Soc. Assn. Execs. (dir. 1979-80, chmn. govt. relations com. 1979-81), Meeting Planners Internat. (bd. dirs. N.Y. chpt. 1979-80), U.S. C. of C. Club: Princeton (N.Y.C.). Office: 2 Sunrise Pl Armonk NY 10504

BOLEN, CHARLES WARREN, univ. dean; b. West Frankfort, Ill., Sept. 27, 1923; s. William and Iva (Phillips) B.; m. Maxine Sheffler, Aug. 1, 1948; children—Ann, Jayne. B. Mus. Edn., Northwestern U., 1948; M.Mus., Eastman Sch. Music, 1950; Ph.D., Ind. U., 1954. Instr. music Eastern Ill. U., 1950-51; chmn. music dept. Ripon (Wis.) Coll., 1954-62; instr. flute Nat. Music Camp, summers 1954-62; dean Sch. Fine Arts, U. Mont., Missoula, 1962-70, Coll. Fine Arts, Ill. State U., Normal, 1970—. Contbr. articles to profl. jours. Chmn. Mont. Arts Council, 1965-70; mem. Pres.' Adv. Council to Arts, Pres.'s Adv. Council to J.F. Kennedy Center for Performing Arts, 1970; cons. Chancellor's Panel on Univ. Purposes, State U. N.Y., 1970, Ednl. Mgmt. Services; pres. Central Ill. Cultural Affairs Consortium, 1975-76. Mem. Music Tchrs. Nat. Assn. (pres. East central div. 1961-62, nat. v.p. states and divs. 1962-65), Music Educators Nat. Conf., Am. Musicol. Soc., Internat. Council Fine Arts Deans (chmn. 1969-70), Fedn. Rocky Mountain States (arts and humanities com. 1966-70), Assn. Western Univs. Home: 1007 Barton Dr Normal IL 61761

BOLEN, DAVID B., corporation executive, former ambassador; b. Dec. 23, 1923; m. Betty Gayden; children: Cynthia, Myra, David B. B.S., U. Colo., 1950, M.S., 1950; M.P.A., Harvard U., 1960; student, Nat. War Coll. Joined Fgn. Service, 1950; adminstrv. asst., Monrovia, Liberia, 1950-52, econ. asst., Karachi, Pakistan, 1952-55; detailed internat. economist Dept. Commerce, Washington, 1955-56, State Dept., 1957-58; desk officer for, Afghanistan, 1958-59; detailed advanced econ. studies Harvard, 1959-60; econ. officer, Accra, Ghana, 1960-62, staff asst., Washington, 1962-64, officer-in-charge Nigerian affairs, 1964-66, detailed Nat. War Coll., 1966-67, econ. and comml. officer, econ. counselor, Bonn, Germany, 1967-72, econ.-comml. counselor, Belgrade, 1972-74, ambassador to, Botswana, Lesotho and Swaziland, 1974-76; dep. asst. sec. state for African affairs Dept. State, Washington, 1976-77; ambassador to, German Democratic Republic, 1977-80; assoc. dir. internat. affairs E.I. duPont de Nemours & Co., Inc., Wilmington, Del., 1981—; dir. Wilmington Trust Co.; dir. trade policy com. Nat. Fgn. Trade Council. Contbg. editor: World Economic Problems and Policies, 1965. Mem. polit. sci. vis. com. MIT; trustee U. Del., 1983. Recipient Robert Russell Meml. award, 1948; Norlin Disting. Alumni award U. Colo., 1969; named to Hall of Honor, 1969, Alumni of Century, 1976; recipient Disting. Service award U. Colo., 1983. Mem. Am. Council on Germany, Nat. War Coll. Alumni Assn., Fgn. Service Assn., Wilmington World Affairs Council (dir.). Mem. U.S. Olympic track and field team, 1948. Home: Wesley Dr Hockessin DE 19707 Office: E I DuPont de Nemours & Co Inc Wilmington DE 19898

BOLENDER, CARROLL HERDUS, retired air force officer, consultant; b. Cin., Nov. 2, 1919; s. Oscar H. and Kathryn L. (Baughman) B.; m. Virginia I. McWilliams, Nov. 7, 1942; children—Carol S. (Mrs. James B. Walden), Robert A. B.S., Wilmington Coll., 1941; M.B.A., Ohio State U., 1949. Commd. 2d lt. USAAF, 1941; advanced through grades to brig. gen. USAF, 1965; dep. chief of staff plans and operations Eglin Air Force Base, Fla., 1963-64; study coordinator Office of Vice Chief of Staff, Hdqrs. USAF, Washington, 1964-65; Apollo Mission dir. NASA, Washington, 1965-67, program mgr. for lunar module, Houston, 1967-69; dep. dir. devel. and acquisition Dep. Chief of Staff Research and Devel., Hdqrs. USAF, Washington, 1969-72; asst. mgr. Hampton (Va.) ops. Systems Devel. Corp., 1972-73, mgr., 1973-78; cons. Engring. Inc., Hampton, 1979-80. Decorated Air Force D.S.M. with oak leaf cluster, Legion of Merit, D.F.C. with oak leaf cluster, Air medal with 8 oak leaf clusters, Air Force Commendation Medal; Croix de Guerre with palm and gold star, France; recipient Apollo Achievement award, exceptional service medal, distinguished service medal, Apollo Program Mgmt. Team award, Group Achievement award all NASA. Home: 111 Bonito Dr Grafton VA 23692

BOLENDER, TODD, choreographer; b. Canton, Ohio, 1919. Student, Hanya Holm, N.Y.C.; enrolled, Sch. American Ballet, N.Y.C., 1936. Joined, Lincoln Kirstein's Ballet Caravan, 1937; Formed, Am. Concert Ballet; choreographed 1st ballet, 1943; also danced with, Ballet Theatre, 1944, and, Ballet Russe de Monte Carlo, 1945; joined, Ballet Soc. (later N.Y.C. Ballet), 1946; prin. dancer, 1947-61; directed opera ballet companies of, Cologne and Frankfurt, 1963-69, numerous freelance choreography assignments; with, Ankara (Turkey) Opera House, Pacific NW Ballet, Seattle, 1975; dir., Istanbul Opera Ballet, 1977; with, Ailvin Ailey Dance Theater; artistic dir., Kansas City Ballet, 1981—. Address: Kansas City Ballet 706 W 42d St Kansas City MO 64111

BOLES, HAROLD WILSON, educator; b. Trafalgar, Ind., July 25, 1915; s. Forest Joseph and Audra (Foster) B.; m. Esther Lucile Bowers, Nov. 2, 1944; children—Sharon Kaye Boles Ames, Deborah Dee Boles Montesano, David Brian, Dennis Ray. B.S., Ind. State U., 1937; M.A., Ohio State U., 1950, Ph.D., 1957; postgrad., U. Colo., 1951, U. Chgo., 1968. Tchr., dept. head Morton Meml. High Sch., Knightstown, Ind., 1937-41; sect. mgr. L.S. Ayres & Co., Indpls., 1946-47; prin. Mad River High Sch., Westville, Ohio, 1947-48; supt. Mad River Schs., Urbana, Ohio, 1948-50, Madison Local Schs., London, Ohio, 1950-51; instr. Ohio State U., 1951-52; supt. Marion Local Schs., Columbus, Ohio, 1952-55; ednl. facilities cons. Joseph Baker & Assocs. (architects), Newark, Ohio, 1955-61; assoc. prof., prof., dept. head Western Mich. U., Kalamazoo, 1961—; vis. lectr. Ariz. State U., 1963, Wash. State U., 1965, U. Guam, 1975; vis. fellow Western Australian Inst. Tech., Perth, 1974-75; cons. sch. bldg. projects, 1955—; cons. Region I Dept. Edn. and Culture Republic of Philippines, 1975. Author textbooks.; Contbr. articles profl. jours. Served with USNR, 1941-46. Mem. Nat. Conf. Profs. Ednl. Adminstrn., Mich. Assn. Profs. Ednl. Adminstrn., Am. Assn. Higher Edn., Phi Delta Kappa. Home: 5123 Ridgebrook Dr Kalamazoo MI 49001 Office: 3112 Sangren Hall Western Mich U Kalamazoo MI 49008

BOLES, ROGER, otolaryngologist; b. Oakland, Calif., Jan. 13, 1928; s. Albert and Julia B.; m. Marianna Reeves, June 16, 1956; children: Martin Reeves, Melissa. A.B., Stanford U., 1949; postgrad., Denver U., 1950-52; M.D. with distinction, George Washington U., 1955. Diplomate: Am. Bd. Otolaryngology. Intern Fitzsimmons Army Hosp., Denver, 1956-57; asst. resident through sr. clin. instr. Mich. U. Hosp., Ann Arbor, 1959-63, faculty dept. otorhinolaryngology, 1963-74, prof., 1973-74; prof., chmn. dept. otoloaryngology U. Calif. San Francisco Sch. Medicine, 1974—; mem. staff San Francisco gen. Hosp., 1974—; pres. med. staff U. Calif. - San Francisco, 1982—; cons. in otolaryngology VA Hosp., Ann Arbor, Wayne County Hosp., Eloise, So. Mich. Prison, Jackson, Fed. Penitentiary, Milan, all Mich., 1963-74, Letterman Gen. Hosp., Presidio of San Francisco, U.S. Naval Hosp., Oakland, Calif., 1974—, Kaiser Hosp., Oakland, 1975, VA Hosp., San Francisco, Naval Regional Med. Center, Oakland, 1975—; cons. in otolaryngology to Surgeon Gen. USAF, 1980—; bd. dirs. Council Med. Splty. Socs., 1981-82, sec., 1982-83; bd. dirs. Am. Acad. Otolaryngology - Head and Neck Surgery, 1981—, coordinator for continuing med. edn., 1980-83; residency rev. com. for otolaryngology Marshall-Hale Hosp., San Francisco, 1975-83, bd. dirs., 1983—; vis. prof. various univ.; participant in confs., convs., workshops, seminars, insts. Contbr. chpts. to books, numerous revs., articles, abstracts to profl. lit. Served with M.C. AUS, 1956-59. Fellow A.C.S. (chmn. adv. council for otolaryngology 1977-80, adv. com. for continuing med. edn. 1982—); mem. AMA (ho. dels. 1975-82, bd. editors Archives Otolaryngology 1975—, mem. reference com. on ins. and med. service 1978—, adv. com. for continuing med. edn. 1981—), Am. Acad. Ophthalmology and Otolaryngology (asso. sec. com. on continuing edn. 1974—, chmn. manuals editorial com. 1977-80, mem.-at-large exec. com. div. otolaryngology 1977—, mem. intersplty. cooperation med. splty. socs. 1978—), Am. Acad. Facial Plastic and Reconstructive Surgery (co-chmn. standards com. 1977—, mem. edn. com. 1979—),

Soc. Univ. Otolaryngologists (sec.-treas. 1973, chmn. com. on undergrad. curriculum 1969-74, mem. exec. council 1968—, pres. 1978), Council Acad. Socs.-Assn. Am. Med. Colls., Assn. Acad. Depts. Otolaryngology (vice chmn. subcom. Nat. Cancer Inst. liaison com. 1977—, chmn. edn., nominating coms. 1978—), Am. Broncho-Esophagological Assn. (mem. council 1981-82), Am. Bd. Otolaryngology (dir. 1974—, exec. com. 1981—, mem. various coms. 1974—, chmn. ad hoc com. for nomination process for membership on bd. dirs. 1976-77), Am. Council Otolaryngology (mem. sumcom. on hearing 1976—, research adv. com. 1977—, pres. 1978-79), Am. Laryngol., Rhinological and Otol. Soc. (mem. editorial bds. transactions 1978—, mem. council 1982—), Soc. Acad. Chmn. in Otolaryngology, Am. Soc. for Neck and Head Surgery, Otosclerosis Study Group, Am. Bd. Med. Spltys., Am. Tinnitus Assn. (sci. adv. bd. 1978-81), Am. Laryngol. Soc. (fellow, chmn. 1977—), Pacific Coast Oto-Ophthal. Soc., Soc. Med. Consultants to Armed Forces, Calif. Med. Assn. (program co-chmn. sects. on allery and otolaryngology, neurology and otolaryngology 1977-78, chmn. adv. council of otolaryngology 1979-80), Calif. Otolaryn. Soc. (pres. 1978-80), U. Calif. San Francisco Sch. Medicine Alumni-Faculty Assn. (pres. 1978-79), Am. Otological Soc., Am. Laryngological Assn. (mem. council 1983—), Alpha Omega Alpha. Office: Dept Otolaryngology Suite 739A U Calif San Francisco 400 Parnassus Ave San Francisco CA 94143

BOLEY, BRUNO ADRIAN, engineering educator; b. Gorizia, Italy, May 13, 1924; came to U.S., 1939, naturalized, 1945; s. Orville F. and Rita (Luzzatto) B.; m. Sara R. Boley, May 12, 1949; children: Jacqueline, Daniel L. B.C.E., CCNY, 1943, D.Sc. hon., 1982; M.Aero. Engring., Poly. Inst. Bklyn., 1945, D.Sc. in Aero. Engring., 1946. Asst. dir. structural research, aero. engring. dept. Poly. Inst. Bklyn., 1943-48; engring. specialist Goodyear Aircraft Corp., 1948-50; asso. prof. aero. engring. Ohio State U., 1950-52; asso. prof. civil engring. Columbia U., 1952-58, prof., 1958-68; Joseph P. Ripley prof. engring., chmn. theoretical and applied mechanics Cornell U., Ithaca, N.Y., 1968-72; dean Technol. Inst., Walter P. Murphy prof. Northwestern U., Evanston, Ill., 1973—; mem. adv. com. George Washington U., Princeton U., Yale U., FAMU/FSU Inst. Engring.; chmn. Midwest Program for Minorities in Engring., 1975—; bd. govs. Argonne Nat. Lab., 1983—. Author: Theory of Thermal Stresses, 1960, High Temperature Structures and Materials, 1964, Thermoinelasticity, 1970, Crossfire in Professional Education, 1976; also articles, numerous tech. papers.; editor-in-chief: Mechanics Research Communications; bd. editors: Jour. Thermal Stresses, Bull. Mech. Engring. Edn., Internat. Jour. Computers and Structures, Internat. Jour. Engring. Sci., Internat. Jour. Fracture Mechanics, Internat. Jour. Mech. Engring. Scis., Internat. Jour. Solids and Structures, Jour. Applied Mechanics, Jour. Structural Mechanics Software, Letters in Applied and Engring. Sci., Nuclear Engring. and Design. Recipient Disting. Alumnus award Poly. Inst. N.Y., 1974; Townsend Harris medal, 1981; NATO sr. sci. fellow, 1964-65.; Fellow AIAA; hon. mem. ASME (exec. com., pres. applied mechanics div. 1975, bd. govs. 1984—); fellow Am. Acad. Mechanics (pres. 1974); mem. Nat. Acad. Engring. (chmn. task force engring. edn. 1979-80), Soc. Engring. Scis. (pres. 1975), Assn. Chairmen Depts. Mechanics (founder, pres. 1970-72), Internat. Assn. Structural Mechanics in Reactor Tech. (adv.-gen. 1979—), Internat. Union Theoretical and Applied Mechanics (sec. Congress com. 1976—), N.Y. Acad. Scis. (named Outstanding Educator of Am. 1971), U.S. Nat. Com. Theoretical and Applied Math. (chmn. 1975—), Ill. Council Energy Research and Devel. (chmn. 1979—). Office: Northwestern U Tech Inst Evanston IL 60201

BOLEY, FORREST IRVING, physicist, educator; b. Ft. Madison, Iowa, Nov. 27, 1925; s. Ira Everett and Olive (Conlee) B.; m. Marjorie Lovell, Dec. 26, 1946 (div. 1969); children—Kathleen, Sandra, Philip, John; m. Barbara Bishop Fellows, Dec. 31, 1969. B.S., Iowa State U., 1946, Ph.D., 1951; M.A. (hon.), Wesleyan U., Middletown, Conn., 1959, Dartmouth, 1967. Faculty Wesleyan U., 1951-61; prof. physics, 1959-61; physicist U. Calif. at Berkeley, 1961-64; prof. physics and astronomy Dartmouth, Hanover, N.H., 1964—. Author: Plasmas-Laboratory and Cosmic, 1966; Editor: Am. Jour. Physics, 1966-73. Served with USNR, 1943-46. Mem. Am. Phys. Soc., Am. Astron. Soc., Internat. Astron. Union. Home: Ely VT 05044

BOLGER, RAY, actor; b. Boston, Jan. 10, 1904; s. James Edward and Anne (Wallace) B.; m. Gwendolyn Rickard, July 9, 1929. Ed. pub. schs., Boston. Sr. cons. U. Conn. Center for Instructional Media and Tech., 1977; lectr., throughout U.S. Began acting career with, Bob Ott Repertory Co., 1923-25, (with Ralph Sanford as) A Pair of Nifties, vaudeville 1925; (with Gus Edwards in) vaudeville Ritz Carton Nights, 1926-28; appeared on Broadway: in Shubert revue The Merry Whirl, 1925; revues Heads Up, 1929, George White's Scandals of 1931, (with Bert Lahr) Life Begins at 8:40, 1934; starred in: On Your Toes, 1936; under MGM picture contract made Rosalie, Sweethearts, Wizard of Oz, 1938-40; starred on Broadway in: Keep Off the Grass, 1940, By Jupiter, 1942; with MGM, 1941-42, 45—; appeared in: The Harvey Girls, 1945; starred in: Three to Make Ready, 1946, and in, Warner Bros.; film Silver Lining; starred on Broadway in: (produced by wife, Gwen Rickard) Where's Charley?, 1948-51; filmed: film Where's Charley?, 1951; co-starred in: April in Paris, 1952; star: motion picture Babes in Toyland, 1961, NBC, That's Dancing, MGM 60th anniversary film, 1984; TV debut Comedy Hour, 1952; filming weekly: Ray Bolger Show, ABC-TV, 1953-55, Washington Square, NBC-TV series, 1956; appeared in: TV series The Partridge Family; starred in: Broadway mus. All American, 1962, Come Summer, 1968-69; summer theatres The Happy Time, 1969; appearing in: one-man show a Musical Comical Concert; various concert halls and nightclubs; appeared: TV programs The Entertainer, 1975, Captains and Kings, 1976, Boston Pops Concert, 1976; appeared in concert with, Sarasota Symphony Orch., Kansas City Philharmonic Orch., Amarillo Symphony Orch., 1977; film The Runner Stumbles, 1979. Recipient Silver medal for Treasury activities during World War II; Antoinette Perry award, 1948-49; 2 Donaldson award for best performances; drama critics poll best musical comedy performance, 1946; N.Y. Newspapers Guild Page One award, 1943, 50; Decency in Entertainment award Notre Dame Club, Chgo., 1967; Medallion of Valor State of Israel, 1970; named to Theatrical Hall of Fame, 1980. Clubs: Players; Bel-Air Country (Calif.); Valley (Montecito); Bohemian (San Francisco); Burlingame Country (Calif.); Swallows (Pebble Beach, Calif.). With U.S.O. Camp Shows entertained soldiers in Caribbean, Brit. Guinea area, 1941; with Little Jack Little entertained in Pacific combat zone, 1943; made 1st war bond tour for Treas. Dept. Home: 618 N Beverly Dr Beverly Hills CA 90210 *When one deals in the business of achieving success by being highly regarded by others, integrity is the primary requisite.*

BOLGER, THOMAS E., telecommunication company executive; b. 1927; married. B.S.E.E., S.D. Sch. Mines, 1949. Chief engr. Northwestern Bell Telephone Co., 1948-55, 57-61; pres. subs. Pacific N.W. Bell Telephone Co., 1961-70, Chesapeake & Potomac Telephone Cos., 1970-74; with AT&T, N.Y.C., 1955-57, 74—, exec. v.p., 1974—; dir. Garfinckel, Brooks Bros., Miller & Rhoads, Inc., Govt. Employees Ins. Co. Office: AT&T 195 Broadway New York NY 10007 *

BOLGER, WILLIAM FREDERICK, U.S. postmaster gen.; b. Waterbury, Conn., Mar. 13, 1923; s. George F. and Catherine E. (Leary) B.; m. Marjorie Tilton, Dec. 17, 1949; children—Catherine, Margaret. Student, George Washington U., Columbus U.; Litt.D. (hon.), St. Bonaventure Coll., 1979. With U.S. Postal Service, 1941—, regional postmaster gen. for N.E. region, 1973-75, dep. postmaster gen., 1975-78, postmaster gen. U.S., Washington, 1978—. Bd. dirs. Boston chpt. ARC, 1971-74, Nat. Council on Alcoholism; trustee Leukemia Soc. Am., Inc., Greater Washington chpt. Leukemia Soc. Am., Inc.; mem. adv. bd. DAR. Served with AUS, 1942-45. Mem. Soc. Logistics Engrs., Am. Mgmt. Assn. Clubs: Rotary, Army-Navy. Office: 475 L'Enfant Plaza SW Washington DC 20260

BOLGIANO, RALPH, JR., electrical engineering educator; b. Balt., Apr. 1, 1922; s. Ralph and Edith (Flitton) B.; m. Mary Elizabeth Sneeringer, Mar. 29, 1948; children: Ralph, Douglas Caldwell, Chrisopher Flitton, Elizabeth Scott. B.S. in Elec. Engring., Cornell U., 1944, B.E.E., 1947, M.E.E., 1949, Ph.D., 1958. Devel. engr. Gen. Electric Co., Syracuse, N.Y., 1949-54; assoc. prof. elec. engring. Cornell U., 1958-65, prof., 1965—; cons. Gen. Electric Co., Syracuse, 1954-62, 68, Rome Air Devel. Ctr., Rome, N.Y., NATO, Paris, 1968-76, NOAA, Boulder, Colo., 1979-80; dir. Univ. Corp. Atmosphere Research, Boulder, Colo., 1961-71; pres. Interunion Commn. Radiometeriology, Brussels, 1966-69. Served with AUS, 1943-46. Gerard Swope fellow, 1955; Guggenheim fellow, 1964; Fulbright fellow, 1965. Fellow AAAS; mem. IEEE, Am. Meterol. Soc., Am. Geophys. Union, Internat. Union Radio Sci. Episcopalian. Club: Ithaca Yacht. Home: 129 Midway Rd Ithaca NY 14850 Office: Sch Elec Engring Ithaca NY 14853 *Conserve the printed page. Publish only when you have something new, substantial to contribute. The many variations on a theme, the refinements of accepted hypothesis, the large asemblages of data, gathered without clear view of the thesis to be proved, only mire the roadway for one's colleagues without adding significantly to their understanding. You have more impact if your name appears infrequently, but in association with major new ideas when it does.*

BOLIN, JOHN RICHARD, investment securities executive; b. Balt., Apr. 18, 1938; s. N. Venay and Evelyn Jane (Biechele) B.; m. Virginia Thayer Mize, Dec. 27, 1959; children: John, Todd, Scott, Patrick. B.A., U. Kans., 1960. Dist. sales mgr. Dow Chem. Co., 1960-66; investment broker Barret, Fitch, North & Co., Kansas City, Mo., 1966-67, Paine Webber Jackson & Curtis, Kansas City, 1967-69; exec. v.p., dir. sales and mktg. A.G. Edwards & Sons, Inc., St. Louis, 1969—, also dir.; past dir. Chgo. Bd. Options Exchange, Inc.; allied mem. N.Y. Stock Exchange, Am. Stock Exchange. Trustee St. Louis Coll. Pharmacy. Mem. Chgo. Bd. Trade, Securities Industry Assn., Chgo. Bd. Options Exchange, Nat. Assn. Securities Dealers, Phi Delta Theta. Republican. Episcopalian. Club: Bellerive Country (St. Louis). Office: 1 N Jefferson St Saint Louis MO 63103

BOLIN, ROBERT ALDINE, insurance company executive; b. Atlanta, Aug. 21, 1917; s. Walter M. and Marie (McCuen) B.; m. Nancy Graham Mobley, Oct. 31, 1941; children: Judith Cotehett Smith, Patricia Bolin Cecil, Margaret Bolin O'Dell. LL.B., John Marshall Law Sch., 1940. Underwriter U.S. Fidelity and Guaranty Co., Atlanta, 1936-48, supt. fidelity and surety dept., 1940-50, spl. agt., 1950-51, mgr., Columbia, S.C., 1951-55, asst. agy. dir., asst. v.p., v.p., Balt., 1955-72, sr. v.p., 1972-82, dir., 1975-82, Fidelity and Guaranty Ins. Underwriting Co., 1978-82. Served to capt. inf. U.S. Army, 1942-46. Home: 1047 Royalist Rd Mount Pleasant SC 29464 Office: 100 Light St Baltimore MD 21203

BOLIN, WILLIAM HARVEY, banker; b. Dallas, Dec. 8, 1922; s. William Harvey and Bertha (Dickey) B.; m. Emma Jane Davis, July 9, 1949; children: Teresa, Patricia. B.A. in Internat. Relations, U. Calif., Berkeley, 1947; student, Nat. U. Mexico, 1948. Joined Bank of Am., N.T. & S.A., San Francisco, 1947, asst. v.p., 1956, mgr., 1957-60, asst. v.p., 1960, v.p., 1961, v.p., head Latin Am. div., 1965-68, sr. v.p., 1968-75, exec. v.p., 1975-81, exec. v.p. world banking div., 1981—, vice chmn., 1982-84; sr. fellow UCLA, 1984—. Bd. dirs. Council Ams. and Ams. Soc.; trustee Pan Am. Devel. Found., Washington, World Affairs Council, Com. for Caribbean, Council of Ams. Served to capt., inf. AUS, 1942-46. Decorated Order Francisco de Miranda, Venezuela). Mem. Pan Am. Soc. San Francisco (pres. 1973), World Trade Assn. San Francisco, Am. Bankers Assn. (chmn. internat. div. 1982-83), Am. Inst. Banking, World Affairs Council No. Calif., Bankers Assn. for Fgn. Trade, World Trade Club San Francisco, Delta Phi Epsilon. Mem. United Ch. Christ. Office: Bank of Am Ctr 555 California St San Francisco CA 94137

BOLINDER, ROBERT DONALD, former supermarket executive; b. Sacramento, Sacramento, Apr. 25, 1931; s. Eldon L. and Rose (Zitting) B.; m. Trudi S. Beer, June 16, 1954; children: Kurt E., Sonia L., Heidi M., Kari Ann, Tina D., Erik J., Remi S., Clint R. B.S., Brigham Young U., 1956; M.B.A., U. Calif. at Berkeley, 1958; grad. advanced mgmt. program, Harvard, 1968. C.P.A. Calif., Idaho. Journalist, typographer No. Sacramento Jour., 1947-50; mgr., accountant Touche, Ross, Bailey & Smart, San Francisco, 1956-65; exec. v.p. adminstrn. and fin., treas. Albertson's Inc., Bosie, Idaho, 1965-72, pres., 1972-80, vice chmn., chief exec. officer, 1974-84; dir. Idaho Power Co.; instr. U. Calif. Extension Sch., Berkeley, 1959-65. Pres. Idaho Taxpayers Assn., Boise, 1974; mem. advisory council Coll. Bus. Brigham Young U.; bd. dirs. Bogus Basin Ski Assn.; chmn. Boise United Way of Ada County, 1965-67. Served with USAF, 1950-54. Mem. Nat. Assn. Accountants (pres.), Am. Inst. C.P.A.'s, Fin. Execs. Inst., Western Assn. Food Chains (dir.), Greater Boise C. of C. (pres. 1972), Idaho Assn. Commerce and Industry (dir.), Phi Kappa Phi, Beta Alpha Psi, Beta Gamma Sigma. Republican. Mem. Ch. of Jesus Christ of Latter-day Saints. *

BOLING, EDWARD JOSEPH, university president; b. Sevier County, Tenn., Feb. 19, 1922; s. Sam R. and Nerissa (Clark) B.; m. Carolyn Pierce, Aug. 8, 1950; children: Mark Edward, Brian Marshall, Steven Clark. B.S. in Accounting, U. Tenn., 1948, M.S. in Statistics, 1950; Ed.D. in Ednl. Adminstrn, Vanderbilt U., 1961. With Wilby-Kinsy Theatre Corp., Knoxville, Tenn., 1940-41, Aluminum Co. Am., 1941-42; instr. statistics U. Tenn., 1948-50; research statistician Carbide & Carbon Chem. Corp., Oak Ridge, 1950, supr. source and fissionable materials accounting, 1951-54; budget dir., Tenn., 1955-59, commr. finance and adminstrn., 1959-61; v.p. U. Tenn., 1961-70, pres., 1970—; Dir. N.Am. Philips Corp., Signal Cos., CSX Corp., Genex Corp., Swan's, United Foods Co., Home Fed. Savs. & Loan Assn.; Mem. So. Regional Edn. Bd., 1957-61, 70-81, 83—, exec. com., 1974-75, 79-81; mem. Edn. Commn. of States, 1970—; trustee, chmn. Am. Coll. Testing Program. Author: (with D. A. Gardiner) Forecasting University Enrollment, 1952, Methods of Objectifying The Allocation of Tax Funds to Tennessee State Colleges, 1961. Mem. Nat. Govs. Conf. Good Will Tour to Brazil and Argentina, 1960; Mem. com. on taxation Am. Council on Edn. Served with AUS, 1943-46; ETO. Mem. Am. Statis. Assn., Assn. Higher Edn., Nat. Assn. Land-Grant Colls. (com. on financing higher edn.), Am. Coll. Pub. Relations Assn. (trustee, chmn. com. taxation and philanthropy), Am. Council on Edn., Knoxville C. of C. (dir.), Am. Legion, L.Q.C. Lamar Soc., Phi Kappa Phi (Scholarship award 1947), Beta Gamma Sigma (charter pres. Alpha chpt. 1948), Phi Delta Kappa, Omicron Delta Kappa. Democrat. Club: Univ. Home: 940 Cherokee Blvd Knoxville TN 37919

BOLING, LAWRENCE H., paper company executive; b. 1923; (married). B.S., U. Cin.; postgrad., Harvard U. Bus. Sch., Carnegie Inst. Tech. Pres. S.D. Warren div. Scott Paper Co., 1947-72; exec. v.p. Consol. Papers Inc., Wisconsin Rapids, Wis., 1972-79, pres., chief operating officer, 1979—, also dir. Office: 231 1st Ave N Box 50 Wisconsin Rapids WI 54494 *

BOLINGER, JOHN C., JR., management consultant; b. Knoxville, Tenn., Feb. 12, 1922; s. John C. and Elsie (Burkhart) B.; m. Helen McCallie, Jan. 26, 1944; children: Janet Marie, John M., Robert B. B.S. in Bus. Adminstrn., U. Tenn., 1943; M.B.A., Harvard U., 1947. Asst. sec. Lehigh Coal & Nav. Co., Phila., 1947-49, asst. to pres., 1949-50, v.p., 1950-54; asst. to pres. Mississippi River Corp., St. Louis, 1954-57; pres. East Tenn. Natural Gas Co., Knoxville, 1957-61; pres., dir. Houston Nat. Bank, 1961-63; exec. v.p., dir. Mississippi River Corp., St. Louis, 1963-67; pres. Mississippi River Transmission (subs.), 1964-67; mgmt. cons., Knoxville, 1967—; chmn., pres. Tenn. Natural Resources; chmn. pres. Nashville Gas Co.; dir. Aladdin Industries, Nashville, Home Fed. Savs. & Loan, Knoxville, Consol. Freightways, Inc., Palo Alto, Calif., Gen. Shale Co.; lectr. U. Tenn.; cons. in field. Served to capt. AUS, 1943-46. Decorated Bronze Star, Purple Heart, Croix de Guerre (France). Address: 1400 Kenesaw Ave SW Apt 130 Knoxville TN 37919

BOLINGER, ROBERT STEVENS, banker; b. Mt. Union, Pa., July 22, 1936; s. J. Morrow and Nell E. (Stevens) B.; m. Reba M. Fleisher, June 17, 1962; children: Todd Wesley, Steven Morrow, Mark Andrew. A.B., Dartmouth Coll., 1958, M.B.A., 1962. Auditor Irving Trust Co., N.Y.C, 1962-63, asst. sec., N.Y.C., 1964866, asst. v.p. Wall St. div., 1966-70, v.p. regional credit officer, 1970-71, v.p. McGraw Hill officer, 1972-75, v.p. Rockefeller Ctr. office, 1975; pres., chief exec. officer, dir. Farmers First Bank, Lititz, Pa., 1976—; pres., chief exec. officer Susquehanna Bancshares, Inc., Lititz, 1982—; dir. Farmers Agcredit Corp., Lititz, Susquehanna Banschares, Inc., Third Dist. Funds Transfer assn., Phila. bd. dirs. United Way of Lancaster County, Pa., 1977—. Served to lt. (j.g.) USN, 1958-61. Mem. Lancaster (Pa.) C. of C. and Industry (dir., treas. 1978-80). Republican. Prebyterian. Club: Masons. Office: Farmers First Bank 9 East Main St Lititz PA 17543

BOLKER, HENRY IRVING, chemist, research institute director, educator; b. Montreal, Que., Can., Feb. 19, 1926; s. Abraham Isaac and Mary (Ballon) B.; m. Estelle Ruth Samuels, Nov. 22, 1953; 1 dau., Louis Ellen. B.A., Queen's U., Kingston, Ont., Can., 1948, M.A., 1950; Ph.D., Yale U., 1952. Research chemist DuPont of Can., Ltd., Kingston, Ont., 1954-60, Pulp and Paper Research Inst. Can., Pointe Claire, Que., 1960-67; sect. head Pointe Claire, 1967-77; div. dir. Pulp and Paper Research Inst. Can., 1977-80, asst. dir. research, 1980-81, assoc. dir. research, 1981—; research assoc. McGill U., Montreal, 1962—. Author: Natural and Synthetic Polymers, 1974; contbr. articles to profl. jours.; patentee in field. Pres. Youth Sci. Found., Ottawa, 1965-66; sec. Lakeshore Chamber Music Soc. Ste. Anne de Bellevue, Que., 1973-74; pres. Lakeshore Dog Tng. Assn., Pointe Claire, 1975-77;. Served with Can. Army, 1944-45. Internat. Acad. Wood Sci. fellow, 1980. Fellow Chem. Inst. Can. (chmn 1979-81), Royal Soc. Chemistry; mem. Am. Chem. Soc., Can. Pulp and Paper Assn.; Fellow Sigma Xi. Home: 110 Spartan Crescent Pointe Claire PQ Canada H9R 3R5

BOLKS, ERVIN JAY, diversified corporation executive; b. Allegan, Mich., Oct. 14, 1941; s. Myron E. and Juella (Maatman) B.; m. Susan Pfleeger, Sept. 11, 1965; children: Heather, Catherine. B.A., Hope Coll., 1964; M.B.A., U. Mich., 1965. Sr. auditor Arthur Andersen & Co., Chgo., 1965-68; div. controller Republic Corp., Century City, Calif., 1968-69, regional controller, 1969-72, group ops. controller, 1972-77, staff v.p., 1977-78, treas., 1978-79, v.p., treas., 1979-83; now v.p., treas. The Wickes Cos., 1983—. Mem. Am. Inst. C.P.A.s, Fin. Execs. Inst., Los Angeles C. of C. (pres.'s council). Republican. Club: Warner Racquet. Home: 19222 Linnet Tarzana CA 91356

BOLL, CHARLES RAYMOND, engine company executive; b. Columbus, Ind., Mar. 29, 1920; s. Charles Raymond and Hestella (Snyder) B.; m. Mary Genevieve Lortz, Nov. 6, 1943; children: Charles Raymond III, Cynthia Ann. B.S. in Elec. Engring, Purdue U., 1941. With Cummins Engine Co., Inc., Columbus, 1941—, sales engr., 1941-42, asst. regional mgr., Cleve., 1947, mgr. engine sales, 1948-52, gen. sales mgr., 1953-55, 55, v.p. sales, 1955-60, exec. v.p. mktg., 1960-64, pres. Internat. div., 1965-66, exec. v.p., 1966—, also dir. Served to 1st lt., Signal Corps AUS, 1943-46. Mem. Soc. Automotive Engrs. Home: 2940 Washington St Columbus IN 47201 Office: 1000 5th St Columbus IN 47201:

BÖLL, HEINRICH, author; b. Cologne, Germany, Dec. 21, 1917; s. Viktor and Maria (Hermanns) B.; m. Annemarie Cech, 1942; children: Christoph (dec.), Raimund, René, Vincent. Student state schs., Cologne, 1924-37. Books include Der Zug war pünktlich, 1949, Wanderer, kommst du nach Spy, 1950, Die schwarzen Schafe, 1951, Wo warst du, Adam?, 1951, Und sagte kein einziges Wort, 1953, Nicht nur zur Weihnachtszeit, 1952, Haus ohne Hüter, 1954, Das Brot der frühen Jahre, 1955, So ward Abend und Morgen, 1955, Unberechenbare Gäste, 1956, Im Tal der donnerden Hufe, 1957, Irisches Tagebuch, 1957, Die Spurlosen, 1957, Dr. Murkes gesammeltes Schweigen, 1958, Billard um halb zehn, 1959, Erzählungen, Hörspiele, Aufsätze, 1961, Ein Schluck Erde, 1962, Ansichten eines Clowns, 1963, Entfernung von der Truppe, 1964, Als der Krieg ausbrach, 1962, Frankfurter Vorlesungen, 1966, Ende einer Dienstfahrt, 1966, Aufsatze, Kritiken, Reden, 1967, Hausfriedensbruch. Aussatz, 1969, Gruppenbild mit Dame, 1971, Gedichte, 1972, Neve politische und Literarische Schriften, 1973, Die verlorene Ehre der Katharina Blum, 1974, Drei Tage im März, 1975, Berichte zur Gesinnungslage der Nation, 1975, Einmischung erwünscht, 1977, Querschnitte, 1977, Werke I-V, 1977, Werke VI-X, 1978, Mein Lesebuch, 1978, Du fährst zu oft nach Heidelberg, 1979, Eine deutsche Erinnerung, 1979, Fürsorgliche Belagerung, 1979, Was soll aus dem Jungen bloss werden? Ode: Irgendwar mit Büchern, 1981, Vermintes Gelände, 1982, Das Vermarchtnis, 1982. Recipient numerous lit. prizes including; Group 47 prize, 1951; Rene Schickele prize, 1952; Kritikerpreis, 1952/53; So. German Narrator prize, 1953; Eduard Van der Heydt prize, 1957; Charles Veillon prize, 1960; Lit. prize Cologne, 1961; Nobel prize for lit., 1972; Carl von Ossietzky Medal, 1974; Premio Latina, 1980; hon. prof. numerous univs. Mem. Am. Acad. Arts and Letters (hon.), German Acad. for Lang. and Poetry, PEN (past pres.). Address: An Der Nüllheck 19 S165 Hürtgenwald-Grosshau Federal Republic of Germany

BOLLE, DONALD MARTIN, educator; b. Amsterdam, Netherlands, Mar. 30, 1933; came to U.S., 1955, naturalized, 1961; s. Maarten C. and Petronella (Kramer) B.; m. Barbara June Girton, Nov. 29, 1957; children—Alan Martin, Thomas Raymond, John Kenneth, Cornelis Adrianus. B.Sc., Durham U., Eng., 1954; Ph.D., Purdue U., 1961; M.A., Brown U., 1966. Asst. prof. elec. engring. Purdue U., 1961-62; NSF postdoctoral fellow dept. applied math. and theoretical physics Cambridge (Eng.) U., 1962-63; asst. prof. engring. Brown U., 1963-66, asso. prof., 1966-70, prof., 1970-80; Chandler-Weaver chair elec. engring. Lehigh U., Bethlehem, Pa., 1980-81, dean, 1981—; Richard Merton vis. prof. Technische Hochschule, Braunschweig, Germany, 1967; cons. in field. Mem. IEEE, AAAS, AAUP, ACLU, Sigma Xi, Tau Beta Pi, Eta Kappa Nu. Home: 1340 Madison Ave Bethlehem PA 18018 Office: Packard Lab 19 Lehigh U Bethlehem PA 18015

BOLLEN, ROGER, cartoonist; b. Cleve., June 27, 1941; s. Roy Price and Beryl Elizabeth (Evans) B.; m. Marilyn June Sadler; 1 dau., Melissa Anne. B.F.A., Kent (Ohio) State U., 1963. Tchr. spl. illustration course art dept. Kent State U. Illustrator comml. art studio, Cleve., 1963-66; first pub.: cartoon strip for Funny Business, Newspaper Enterprise Assos., 1965, Animal Crackers; cartoon strip released, Chgo. Tribune-N.Y. News Syndicate, 1967, Catfish, released, 1973. Home: 36675 Eagle Rd Willoughby Hills OH 44094 Office: Chgo Tribune NY News Syndicate 220 E 42d St New York NY 10017

BOLLES, EDMUND BLAIR, corporation executive; b. St. Louis, Feb. 26, 1911; m. Mona Byrnina Dugas, Apr. 19, 1941; children: Edmund B., Charles DeV., Zoe L., Harry P. Student, Yale U., 1929-30, 31-32. Wrote for newspapers and mags., 1925-32; tchr. Gunston Sch., Centreville, Md., 1930-31; in advt. office Palais Royal Dept. Store, Washington, 1932; reporter Washington Sun, also Washington Herald, 1933; congl. corr. Universal Service, 1934, 34-35; rewrite man. N.Y. Am., 1934; with Washington Star, 1935-44; successively as writer on N.R.A. and A.A.A. diplomatic corps; dir. Washington bur. Fgn. Policy Assn., 1944-51, Washington corr., 1951-53; U.S. editor France Actuelle, 1952-53; European corr. Toledo Blade, 1953-57, assoc. editor, 1957-59; v.p. mktg., dir. water div. Fairbanks, Morse and Co., 1959-64; v.p. govt. relations Colt Industries Inc, 1964-67, 68-77, v.p. internat., 1966-68, adviser to pres., 1977-82, Sr. Rep. Office, 1982—, also chmn. vol. polit. com.; regular contbr. Washingtoniana, Sunday edit. N.Y. Times, 1938; contbr. on fgn. affairs N.Am. Newspaper Alliance; reg. contbr. on polit. affairs Toronto Star Weekly; polit. writer for mags., 1936—; Spl. adviser FAO Conf., UN, Copenhagen, 1946; Chmn. exec. com. Com. for Effective Capital Recovery; chmn. exec. com. Com. for Reform Double Taxation of Investment.; chmn. steering com. Coalition for Uniform Product Liability Law. Author: America's Chance of Peace, 1939, Arctic Diplomacy, 1948, Military Establishment of the United States, 1949, U.S. Military Policy, 1950, Tyrant from Illinois, 1951, How To Get Rich in Washington, 1952, Armed Road to Peace, 1952, The Big Chance in Europe, 1958, Men of Good Intentions, 1960, Corruption in Washington, 1961; Contbr. to nat. mags. Decorated Royal medal of St. Olav, Norway). Mem. Am. Soc. Naval Engrs., A.I.M., Nat. Security Indsl. Assn., Anglo-Am. Press Assn. Paris. Roman Catholic. Clubs: Cosmos (Washington); Yale, Met. (N.Y.). Home: 4831 Linnean Ave Washington DC 20008 also 385 Saint Lucie St Stuart FL 33494 Office: 1901 K St NW Washington DC 20036

BOLLES, RICHARD NELSON, clergyman, author; b. Milw., Mar. 19, 1927; s. Donald Clinton and Frances Fethers (Fifield) B.; m. Janet Lorraine Price, Dec. 30, 1949 (div. 1971); children: Stephen, Mark, Gary, Sharon. Student, M.I.T., 1946-48; B.A. cum laude, Harvard U., 1950; S.T.B., Gen. Theol. Sem., 1955, S.T.M., 1957. Ordained priest Episcopal Ch., 1953; vicar St. James Ch., Ridgefield, N.J., 1955-58; rector St. John's Episcopal Ch., Passaic, N.J., 1958-66; canon pastor Grace Cathedral, San Francisco, 1966-68; provincial sec. for coll. work 8th Province of the Episcopal Ch., 1968-74; dir. Nat. Career Devel. Project, Walnut Creek, Calif., 1974—; fellow, tutor Gen. Theol. Sem., N.Y.C., 1953-55; fellow Coll. Preachers, Washington, 1964. Author: What Color is Your Parachute? A Practical Manual for Job Hunters and Career Changers, 1972, 83, Where Do I Go From Here With My Life, 1974, The Three Boxes of Life and How to Get Out of Them, 1978; Editor: Newsletter about life/work planning, 1974—. Served with USNR, 1945-46. Mem. Am. Soc. Tng. and Devel., Mensa. Home: 2135 Londonderry Ct Walnut Creek CA 94596 Office: PO Box 379 Walnut Creek CA 94597 *As I look back over my life thus far, the motivating force seems to have been: "What kind of person would you like to see more of, in this world?"—and then trying hard to be that kind of person. I wish famous people answered their mail, returned their phone calls, put their address in the books they write, stayed accessible. So, that's what I've tried to do.*

BOLLING, ALEXANDER RUSSELL, JR., retired army officer, business executive; b. Ft. McPherson, Ga., Sept. 11, 1922; s. Alexander Russell and Mary Josephine (Hoyer) B.; m. Frances Bigbee, Dec. 17, 1945; children: Kathryn Josephine (Mrs. Roy B. Woodward), Alexander Russell III. B.S., U.S. Mil. Acad., 1943; grad., Inf. Sch., 1952, Army Command and Gen. Staff Coll., 1956, Army War Coll., 1962. Commd. 2d lt. U.S. Army, 1943, advanced through grades to maj. gen., 1970; brigade comdr. 3d Brig., 82nd Airborne Div., Vietnam, 1968, chief of staff XXIV Corps, 1968-69; with Office of Asst. Chief of Staff for Force Devel., Army Dept., Washington, 1969-71; comdg. gen. Army Tng. Center, Inf. and Ft. Lewis, Wash., 1971-72; chief U.S. Mil. Group, Brazil, 1972-73; ret., 1973; v.p. Planned Mktg. Assos., Inc., Dallas, 1973; pres. TIPS Agy., 1976; mng. partner BLC Group, Inc., Dallas, 1977; pres. APS, Inc., Dallas, 1979—, vice chmn., 1981—; mem. Dallas Manpower Adv. Planning Com., 1973-74, Nat. Alliance Businessmen, 1974-76. Active Boy Scouts Am.; pres. Dallas/Ft. Worth Airport Community Services Bd., 1977. Decorated D.S.M. with oak leaf cluster; Silver Star medal with 2 oak leaf clusters; Legion of Merit with 3 oak leaf clusters; Bronze Star medal with 1 oak leaf cluster; Combat Infantryman's badge; Air medal with 3 silver, 3 bronze oak leaf clusters; Purple Heart, U.S.; grand ofcl. Order Mil. Merit, Brazil; Distinguished Service Order 1st Class; Nat. Order 5th Class; Gallantry cross with palm, Vietnam). Mem. Assn. U.S. Army (pres. Dallas chpt. 1975-76), West Point Soc., Assn. Higher Edn. North Tex. (trustee 1982), Mil. Order World Wars. Episcopalian. Home: 7425 Spring Valley Rd Dallas TX 75240 Office: 3310 Keller Springs Rd #130 Carrollton TX 75006

BOLLING, RICHARD NORMAN, metal company executive; b. Huntington, W. Va., Aug. 6, 1926; s. Carl Levering and Leticia (Simer) B.; m. Ella Juanita Baisden, Feb. 15, 1947; children: Constance Anne, Amy Diane. B.I.E., Ga. Inst. Tech., 1950. Registered profl. engr., Ky. Plant indsl. engr. Am. Sugar Refining Co., Balt., 1950-51; group indsl. engr. Internat. Nicel Co., Huntington, 1951-60; staff chief, indsl. engr. Reynolds Metals Co., Richmond, Va., 1960-68, dir. new product planning and tech. service, 1969, gen. mgr. recycling div., 1969-79, v.p., 1979—; pres., bd. dirs. ALRECO Metals Inc., 1982—, Reynolds Alumnium Recycling Co., 1979—. Bd. dirs. Keep Va. Beautiful, Richmond, 1978—. Served with U.S. Army, 1944-46. Republican. Office: PO Box 27003 6601 W Broad St Richmond VA 23261

BOLLINGER, JOHN GUSTAVE, mechanical engineer; b. Grand Forks, N.D., May 28, 1935; s. Elroy William and Charlotte (Kirchner) B.; m. Heidelore Ladwig, Aug. 16, 1958; children: William, Kristin, Pamela. B.S., U. Wis., Madison, 1957; M.S., Cornell U., 1958; Ph.D., U. Wis., 1961. Asst. prof. U. Wis., Madison, 1961-65, asso. prof. dept. mech. engring., 1965-68, prof., 1968—, Bascom prof., 1973—, chmn. dept., 1975-79, dir. data acquisition and simulation lab., 1972-75, dean, 1981—; chmn., dir. Unico Inc.; dir. Rexnard Inc., Nicolet Instrn. Corp. Contbr. articles to profl. jours. Bd. dirs. Madison Gen. Hosp. Fulbright postdoctoral fellow, Aachen, Ger., 1962; vis. Fulbright prof. Cranfield (Eng.) Inst. Tech., 1980-81. Fellow ASME (Gustus L. Larson Meml. award 1976); mem. Am. Soc. Engring. Edn., Soc. Mfg. Engrs. (Research Medal award 1978), Sigma Xi. Club: Mendota Yacht. Patentee in field. Home: 6117 S Highlands Madison WI 53705 Office: 1513 University Ave Madison WI 53706

BOLLINGER, LEE CARROLL, legal educator; b. Santa Rosa, Calif., Apr. 30, 1946. B.S., U. Oreg., 1968; J.D., Columbia U., 1971. Law clk. U.S. Ct. Appeals (2d cir.), 1971-72, Chief Justice Warren Burger, U.S. Supreme Ct., 1972-73; asst. prof. law U. Mich., Ann Arbor, 1973-76, assoc. prof., 1976-78, prof., 1978—; research assoc. Clare Hall, Cambridge U., Eng., 1983. Author: (with Jackson) Contract Law in Modern Society, 1980. Mem. Rockefeller Humanities Fellowship. Office: U Mich Law Sch 922 Legal Research Bldg Ann Arbor MI 48109

BOLLINGER, LOWELL MOYER, physicist; b. Greene County, Va., Apr. 28, 1923; s. Amsey Floyd and Florence (Moyer) B.; m. Margaret Jeffries, Nov. 5, 1944; children—Lesley, Jeffrey, Priscilla. A.B., Oberlin Coll., 1943; Ph.D., Cornell U., Ithaca, N.Y., 1951. Physicist aircraft engine research lab. NACA, Cleve., 1943-46; nuclear physicist Argonne Nat. Lab., Ill., 1951—, dir. physics div., 1963-72, 74-75, dir. superconducting linac project, 1972—; Guest physicist Atomic Energy Research Establishment, Harwell, Eng., 1961-62. Recipient award for disting. performance at Argonne U. Chgo., 1981. Fellow Am. Phys. Soc. Home: 1741 Prairie Ave Downers Grove IL 60515 Office: Argonne Nat Lab Argonne IL 60439

BOLLINGER, STEPHEN JAMES, government official; b. Louisville, Apr. 11, 1948; s. James Jesse and Marie Constance (Davieau) B.; m. Linette Lou Sprague, 1971; 3 daus., Megan Lou, Heather Marie, Rebecca Lin. B.A., Harvard U., 1970. Legis. asst., Washington, 1970-71; mem. exec. and policy com. Hamilton County Republican Party, Ohio, 1975; chmn. Pres. Ford Campaign, Hamilton, Ohio, 1976; v.p. Caral Corp., Cin., 1973-75; pres. Sta. WNOP, 1976-77; v.p. Laws Ins. Agy. and Finney & Assocs. Products, 1977-81; asst. sec. for community planning and devel. HUD, Washington, 1981—; Alt. del. Republican Nat. Conv., 1976. Office: HUD Bldg 451 7th St SW Washington DC 20410 *

BOLLMAN, MARK BROOKS, JR., advt. exec.; b. Meriden, Conn., Aug. 24, 1925; s. Mark B. and Esther (Stevens) B.; m. Barbara Ann Smith, July 8, 1928; children—Mark Brooks, III, Richard N., Steven A. A.B., Princeton U., 1949; M.B.A., Harvard U., 1951. Sr. v.p. Benton & Bowles Inc., N.Y.C., 1968-70; exec. v.p. Diners Club Inc., N.Y.C., 1970-72; corp. v.p. Magnavox Co., N.Y.C., 1972-75; pres. McDonald & Little Inc., Atlanta, 1975-77; sr. v.p. N.W. Ayer A.B.H. Internat., N.Y.C., 1977—; dir. Dana Perfumes Corp. Served with AUS, 1944-46. Decorated Purple Heart. Republican. Episcopalian. Clubs: University (N.Y.C.); Cherochee Country (Atlanta); Stanwich (Greenwich, Conn.). Home: 20 Rockwood Ln Spur Greenwich CT 06830 Office: 1345 Ave of Americas New York City NY 10019

BOLLMEIER, EMIL WAYNE, manufacturing company executive; b. Hurst, Ill., Jan. 16, 1925; s. Emil Philip and Flossie Louise (Swain) B.; m. Nancy Lee Mercier, Feb. 9, 1972; children—David Wayne, Ann Louise, Paul Wesley. B.S. in Chem. Engring, U. Nebr., 1947; postgrad., U. Minn., 1949-51. With 3M Co., St. Paul, 1947-82, div. v.p. electro products div., 1965-72, group v.p. elec. products group, 1973-83, mem. 3M ops. com.; chief exec. officer, gen. ptnr. C-TEK Ltd. Partnership, 1983—; pres. Dynex Research, Inc., 1983—. Mem. Planning Commn., Mendota Heights, Minn., 1960-65; chmn. Republican Party, Dakota County, Minn., 1965-68. Served with USNR, 1945-46. Fellow IEEE; mem. Nat. Elec. Mfrs. Assn. (bd. govs.), Sigma Xi, Sigma Tau. Presbyterian. Patentee in field. Home: 265 Burlington Rd Saint Paul MN 55119 Office: 3615 29th Ave NE Minneapolis MN 55418

BOLLUM, FREDERICK JAMES, biochemist, educator; b. Ellsworth, Wis., June 14, 1927; s. Frederick Edward and Helen (Buchholz) B.; m. Joan Bachman, July 18, 1948 (div. Sept. 1974); children: Thomas, Jane, Barbara, Susan. B.A., U. Minn., 1949, Ph.D., 1956. Postdoctoral fellow U. Wis., Madison, 1956-58; biochemist Oak Ridge Nat. Lab., 1958-65; prof. biochemistry U. Ky., Lexington, 1965-77; prof. Uniformed Services U. Health Scis., Bethesda, Md., 1977—, chmn. dept. biochemistry, 1977-81; vis. prof. Univ. de Santiago, Chile, 1969, U. Calif. Med. Center, San Francisco, 1973, Johns Hopkins Med. Sch., Balt., 1983; cons. NIH, 1969-73, 75-77, Am. Cancer Soc., 1972-72. Mem. editorial bd.: Jour. Biol. Chemistry, 1966-69, Biochemistry, 1977-80. Served with USCGR, 1945-46; Served with USNR, 1951-53. Recipient K.A. Forster prize, Mainz, 1974; USPHS fellow, 1956-58, 72-73. Mem. Am. Chem. Soc., Am. Soc. Biol. Chemists, AAUP, Sigma Xi. Club: Cosmos (Washington). Home: 5617 Sonoma Rd Bethesda MD 20817 Office: Dept Biochemistry Uniformed Services U Health Scis Bethesda MD 20814

BOLOGNA, JOSEPH, writer, actor; b. Bklyn., 1938; m. Renee Taylor, 1965. Student, Brown U. Writer (with wife); stage play Lovers and Other Strangers, 1968; films) 2, 1966, Lovers and Other Strangers, 1970, Made for Each Other, 1971; TV shows Acts of Love and Other Comedies, 1973, Paradise, 1974; series Calucci's Department, 1973; actor: play Lovers and Other Strangers, 1968; in films Cops and Robbers, 1973, Mixed Company, 1974, The Big Bus, 1976; TV movie Honor Thy Father, 1973, Torn Between Two Lovers, 1979, Chapter Two, 1979; (Recipient Emmy award with wife Acts of Love and Other Comedies 1973). Served in USMC. *

BOLOGNESI, DANI PAUL, virologist, educator; b. Forgaria, Italy, Mar. 19, 1941; s. Carlo and Marina (Iem) B.; m. Sarah Sampson, Aug. 1, 1964; children: James, Michael. B.S., Rensselaer Poly. Inst., 1963, M.S., 1965; Ph.D. in Virology, Duke U., 1967. Research assoc. dept. surgery Duke U., 1967-68; NIH postdoctoral fellow Max-Planck Institut für Virusforschung, Tübingen, W. Ger., 1968-71; asst. prof. surgery, microbiology and immunology Duke U., Durham, N.C., 1971-72, assoc. prof. surgery, asst. prof. microbiology and immunology, 1972-77, prof. surgery, assoc. prof. microbiology and immunology, 1977-81, prof. surgery, prof. microbiology and immunology, 1981—, dir. surg. virology lab., dep. dir. Duke Comprehensive Cancer Center, 1981—; cons. virus cancer program Frederick Cancer Research Center, M.D. Anderson Hosp. and Tumor Inst.; mem. med. and sci. adv. com. Leukemia Soc. Am.; mem. NIH Virology Study Sect. Mem. editorial bd.: Cancer Research, 1978—, Virology, 1978—. Mem. Am. Soc. Microbiology, Sigma Xi. Office: 256 Jones Bldg Research Dr Durham NC 27710

BOLOMEY, ROGER HENRY, sculptor; b. Torrington, Conn., Oct. 19, 1918; s. Henry Albert and Ida (Vurlod) B.; m. Alice Susanne Ryser, June 11, 1948; children: Florence Susanne, Yvonne Marguerite. Student, Acad. Fine Arts, Florence, Italy, 1947, U. Lausanne, Switzerland, 1947-48, Calif. Coll. Arts and Crafts, Oakland, 1948-50. Prof. Herbert H. Lehman Coll., CUNY, 1968-75; prof., chmn. dept. art Calif. State U. at Fresno, 1975—; painter, 1948-60, sculptor, 1960—; mem. adv. bd. Mus. No. Ariz. Art Inst., Flagstaff, 1976-78, Nat. Sculpture Conf., U. Kans., Lawrence, 1971—. Chosen to execute 2 large sculptures for state office bldg., Albany, N.Y., 1967, sculpture for, new Nassau County Supreme Ct. Bldg., 1968, Lehman High Sch., Bronx, N.Y., 1969, Eastridge Mall, San Jose, Cal., 1970, N.Y. State Office Bldg., Hauppauge, N.Y., 1973, others.; one-man shows including, Bolles Gallery, San Francisco, 1960, Royal Marks Gallery, N.Y.C., 1964, 65, numerous group exhbns., 1960—, including, 66th Arm. Exhbn., Chgo. Art Inst., 1962, Salon de Mai, Paris (France) Mus. Art, 1963, 64, Whitney Mus., 1964, Larry Aldrich Mus., Ridgefield, Conn., Carnegie Inst. Internat. Exhbn., Whitney Mus., 1964, 66, Highlights, 1964-65, Larry Aldrich Mus., 1965, Quatrieme Expn. Suisse de Sculpture, Bienne, Switzerland, 1966, Amerikanische Kunst aus Schweizer Besitz, St. Gallen, Switzerland, Contemporary Am. Painting and Sculpture, U. Ill. at Urbana, 1967; represented permanent collections, Mus. Modern Art, San Francisco Mus. Modern Art, Whitney Mus., Slädlische Kunsthalle, Mannheim, W.Ger., Larry Aldrich Mus., Bundy Art Gallery, Waitsfield, Vt., San Francisco Art Inst., Oakland Mus., Los Angeles County Mus., U. Calif. Mus. Art, Berkeley, Chase Manhattan Bank, N.Y.C., also numerous pvt. collections; curator: Forgotten Dimension. Recipient 1st prize, commn. for large mural San Jose (Calif.) State Coll. competition, 1962, 1st prize, purchase award Bundy Art Gallery competition, 1963, Sculpture prize 84th Ann. competition San Francisco Art Inst., 1965. Hon. fellow Royal Acad. Fine Arts (Hague, Netherlands); mem. San Francisco Art Inst., Am. Fedn. Arts. First to use polyurethane from its fluid form as a medium of art. Address: Route 113 North Fryeburg ME 04058 *My ultimate goal is to live a fully creative life with the hope that what I do and the way I live will stimulate others to do the same.*

BOLOOKI, HOOSHANG, cardiac surgeon; b. Langeh, Iran, Mar. 28, 1937; came to U.S., 1960, naturalized, 1976; s. Hossein and Fatima (Arjomand) B.; m. C. Joanne McDonald, Aug. 30, 1975; children: Hooshang Michael, Cyrus William, Andrew John. B.S. cum laude, Alborz Coll., Tehran, 1954; M.D., Tehran U., 1960. Asst. instr. SUNY Med. Center, Bklyn., 1964-69; mem. faculty U. Miami (Fla.) Med. Sch., 1969—, prof. surgery, 1977—; attending surgeon, dir. adult cardiac surgery Jackson Meml. Hosp., 1969—; cons. VA Hosp., Miami, 1977—; mem. adv. panel cardiovascular surgery Ethicon Inc., Davis & Geck Co., Inc. Author: Clinical Application of Intra-Aortic Balloon pump; Contbr. articles to med. publs. Recipient Research Career Devel. award NIH, 1972-77, grantee, 1972-75; recipient Grand award U. Tex. Med. Br. Fellow Royal Coll. Surgeons Can., A.C.S., Am. Coll. Cardiology, Am. Coll. Chest Physicians; mem. Am. Assn. Thoracic Surgery, Soc. Univ. Surgeons, Am. Heart Assn., Thoracic Surg. Soc., AMA (cert. merit), Soc. Internat. de Chirugie, Internat. Cardiovascular Soc., Soc. Vascular Surgery, Am. Soc. Heart Transplantation, Soc. Acad. Surgeons. Republican. Moslem. Clubs: Hillcrest Racquet., Ski. Office: Div Thoracic and Cardiovascular Surgery R-114 U Miami Sch Medicine PO Box 01690 Miami FL 33101

BOLSTER, ARCHIE MILBURN, foreign service officer; b. Ames, Iowa, Apr. 9, 1933; s. Horace Goodwin and Ella Schimpf B.; m. Ann Dorcas Matthews, Mar. 22, 1959; children: Christopher, Matthew, Amy. B.A. in Internat. Relations, U. Va., 1955; M.A. in Public Policy and Adminstrn, U. Wis., 1972. Commd. fgn. service officer Dept. State, 1958; assigned, Phnom Penh, Cambodia, 1959-60, Tabriz, Iran, 1961-63, Tehran, Iran, 1964-66, Bur. Intelligence and Research, 1966-68, Office Fuels and Energy, 1969-71; consul gen., Antwerp, Belgium, 1978-81; dep. dir. Div. Office Security Assistance and Sales, 1981—. Chmn. editorial bd.: Fgn. Service Jour, 1971. Pres. Williamsburg Civic Assn., Arlington, Va., 1969-70. Served with USNR, 1955-58. Mem. Am. Fgn. Service Assn. Home: 2738 N Lexington St Arlington VA 22207 Office: Dept State Washington DC

BOLSTER, ARTHUR STANLEY, JR., educator; b. Bismarck, N.D., Jan. 30, 1922; s. Arthur S. and Gertrude (Pierce) B.; m. Elizabeth Barker Winkfield, Oct. 8, 1949; children: Stephen Clark, Gregory Pierce. A.B., Dartmouth, 1943; M.A., Harvard, 1947, Ph.D., 1954. Tchr. history Grosse Pointe (Mich.) High Sch., 1952-57, Pelham (N.Y.) High Sch., 1957-59; mem. faculty Harvard U., Cambridge, Mass., 1959—, prof. edn., 1967-82, prof. emeritus, 1982—. Author: James Freeman Clarke, Disciple to Advancing Truth, 1954. Served to lt. USNR, 1943-46. Mem. Orgn. Am. Historians, Nat. Council Social Studies, New Eng. History Tchrs. Assn. (pres. 1968-69, Kidger award 1970), Phi Beta Kappa, Phi Delta Kappa. Mem. United Ch. of Christ (deacon). Home: 355 Bennington Ln Lake Worth FL 33463 Office: Longfellow Hall Harvard Grad Sch Edn Cambridge MA 02138

BOLSTER, JAMES, banker; b. N.Y.C., May 23, 1929; s. James and Mary C. (Lunse) B.; m. Jeanne Cinelli, July 14, 1956. B.B.A., CCNY, 1953; cert., Stonier Grad. Sch. Banking, Rutgers U., 1963, 1971. Mgmt. trainee Corn Exchange Bank & Trust Co., N.Y.C., 1945-55; with N.Y. State Banking Dept., N.Y.C., 1955-75, supervising bank examiner, 1970-72, dep. supt. banks, 1971-75; pres., chief exec. officer, chmn. Nassau Trust Co., Glen Cove, N.Y., 1975-80; exec. v.p. Dime Savs. BanK N.Y., N.Y.C., 1981-83; exec. v.p., chief fin. officer Dime Savs. Bank N.Y., N.Y.C., 1983—; dir. Trexar Corp., Woodbury, N.Y., 1981-83. Pres. Nassau County council Boy Scouts Am., 1982-83; bd. govs. Human Resources Ctr., Albertson, N.Y., Sch. Banking and Money Mgmt., Adelphi U., Garden City, N.Y.; chmn. Bishop's Investment Adv. Com., Rockville Centre, N.Y. Mem. Robert Morris Assocs. Club: Nassau Country (Glen Cove, N.Y.). Home: 22 Shady Ln Laurel Hollow NY 11791 Office: Dime Savs Bank NY 589 5th Ave New York NY 10017

BOLSTERLI, MARGARET JONES, educator; b. Watson, Ark., May 10, 1931; d. Grover Clevel and Zena (Cason) Jones; m. Mark Bolsterli, Dec. 30, 1953 (div. Dec. 1964); children: Eric, David. B.A. with honors, U. Ark., 1952; M.A., Washington U., St. Louis, 1953; Ph.D., U. Minn., 1967. Asst. prof. Augsburg Coll., Mpls., 1967-68; prof. English, U. Ark., Fayetteville, 1968—. Author: The Early Community at Bedford Park, 1977, Vinegar Pie and Chicken Bread, 1982; contbr.: articles and stories to Jour. Modern Lit.; others. NEH Younger Humanist grantee, 1970-71; Ark. Endowment for Humanities grantee, 1980, 81. Mem. MLA, S. Central MLA. Democrat. Office: Dept English Univ Arkansas Fayetteville AR 72701

BOLT, BRUCE ALAN, seismology educator; b. Largs, Australia, Feb. 15, 1930; s. Donald Frederick and Arlene (Stitt) B.; m. Beverley Bentley, Feb. 11, 1956; children: Gillian, Robert, Helen, Margaret. B.S. with honors, New Eng. U. Coll., 1952; M.S., U. Sydney, Australia, 1954, Ph.D., 1959, D.Sc. (hon.), 1972. Math. master Sydney (Australia) Boys' High Sch., 1953; lectr. U. Sydney, 1954-61, sr. lectr., 1961-62; research seismologist Columbia U., 1960; dir. seismographic stas. U. Calif., Berkeley, 1963—, prof. seismology, 1963—, chmn. Grad. Council, 1980-82; Mem. com. on seismology Nat. Acad. Scis., 1966-72, mem., 1974-76; also chmn. nat. earthquake obs. com. 1979-81; mem. earthquake and wind forces com. VA, 1971-75; mem. Calif. Seismic Safety Commn., 1978—; earthquake studies adv. panel U.S. Geol. Survey, 1979—, U.S. Geodynamics Com., 1979—. Author, editor textbooks on applied math., earthquakes, geol. hazards and detection of underground nuclear explosions. Recipient H.O. Wood award in seismology, 1967, 72; Fulbright scholar, 1960; Churchill Coll. Cambridge overseas fellow, 1980. Fellow Am. Geophys. Union (mem. geophys. monograph bd. 1971-78, chmn. 1976-78), Geol. Soc. Am., Calif. Acad. Scis. (trustee 1981—, pres. 1982—), Royal Astron. Soc.; mem. Nat. Acad. Engring., Seismol. Soc. Am. (editor bull. 1965-70, dir. 1965-71, 73-76, pres. 1974-75), Internat. Assn. Seismology and Physics Earth's Interior (exec. com. 1964-67, v.p. 1975-79, pres. 1980-83), Earthquake Engring. Research Inst., Australian Math. Soc., Sigma Xi. Club: Univ. Research on dynamics, elastic waves, earthquakes, reduction geophys. observations; inferences on structure of earth's interior; cons. on seismic hazards. Home: 1491 Greenwood Terr Berkeley CA 94708

BOLT, RICHARD HENRY, scientist, business executive; b. Peking, China, Apr. 22, 1911; s. Richard Arthur and Beatrice (French) B.; m. Katherine Mary Smith, June 24, 1933; children: Beatrice Bolt Scribner, Richard Eugene, Deborah Bolt Zieses. A.B. in Architecture, U. Calif.-Berkeley, 1933, A.M. in Physics, 1937, Ph.D. in Physics,

1939. Asso. in physics U. Ill., 1940; NRC fellow in physics M.I.T., Cambridge, 1939-40, research asso., 1941-43, assoc. prof. physics, 1946-54, prof. acoustics, 1954-64, adj. prof. acoustics, 1983—, lectr. polit. sci., 1964-70, dir. acoustics lab., 1946-57; assoc. dir. NSF, 1960-63; prin. cons. biophysics and biophys. chemistry study sect. NIH, Bethesda, Md., 1957-59; chmn. bd. Bolt, Beranek & Newman, Inc. (cons.), Cambridge, 1953-76; chmn. emeritus Bolt, Beranek & Newman, Inc., cons., 1976—; vis. scientist Mass. State Legislature, 1977; guest lectr. Inst. Acoustics, Academia Sinica, Peking and Xian, China, 1981; Sci. liaison officer OSRD, London, 1943-44; chief tech. aide Nat. Def. Research Com., 1944-45; mem. Armed Forces-Nat. Research Council chmn. com. on hearing and bio-acoustics, 1953-55; pres. Internat. Commn. on Acoustics, 1951-57; chmn. com. on sound spectrograms NRC, 1976-79; chmn. adv. panel on White House tapes U.S. Dist. Ct. D.C., 1973-74. Author: (with other) Sonics, 1959; also numerous articles in sound, acoustics, noise control, sci. and public policy. Fellow Center for Advanced Study in Behavioral Sciences, Stanford, 1963-64; Phi Beta Kappa vis. scholar, 1979-80; New Eng. award Engring. Socs. New Eng., 1980. Fellow Acoustical Soc. Am. (pres. 1949-50, Biennial award 1942, Gold medal 1979), IEEE, Am. Acad. Arts and Scis., AAAS (dir. 1969-77), Inst. Noise Control Engring., Nat. Acad. Engring., Mass. Engrs. Council (chmn. 1975-77), Am. Inst. Physics (gov. bd. 1957-63), Phi Beta Kappa, Sigma Xi, Eta Kappa Nu. Club: Cosmos (Washington). Home: Tabor Hill Rd Lincoln MA 01773 Office: 50 Moulton St Cambridge MA 02138

BOLT, ROBERT JAMES, physician, educator; b. Grand Rapids, Mich., Feb. 23, 1920; s. Rhine and Jennie (DuPree) B.;, Apr. 21, 1945; children: Christine, Kathryn Jane, Barbara Ann, Robert James. B.A., Calvin Coll., 1942; M.D., U. Mich., 1945. Intern St. Mary's Hosp., Grand Rapids, Mich., 1945-46; resident Butterworth Hosp., Grand Rapids and Univ. Hosp., Ann Arbor, Mich., 1948-51; fellow in gastroenterology U. Mich., 1951-53, instr., 1953-54, asst. prof. medicine, 1954-57, assoc. prof., 1957-64, prof., 1964-66; prof., chmn. dept. medicine U. Calif., Davis, 1966—; Fulbright lectr. Louvain U., Brussels, 1959-60; Exchange prof. U. Antioquia, Colombia, 1956; vis. prof. Shiraz U., Iran, 1976. Contbr. to books.; Contbr. articles in field to profl. jours. Trustee Ann Arbor (Mich.) Bd. Edn., 1964-66. Served with U.S. Navy, 1946-48. Mem. Am. Gastroenterologic Assn., Western Soc. Clin. Research, Am. Fedn. Clin. Research, Assn. Profs. Medicine. Democrat. Club: Pacific Coast Interurban Clin. Patentee peroral small bowel biopsy instrument. Home: 545 Oak Ave Davis CA 95616 Office: 4301 X St Sacramento CA 95817

BOLT, WILLIAM J., banker; b. Tekamah, Nebr., Jan. 4, 1930; s. William J. and Anna (Lindenmeyer) B.; m. Jane Kenner; children: Thomas Allen, James Andrew, William Kenner. B.S., U. Pa., M.B.A. With Fed. Res. Bd., Phila., 1956—, United Mo. Bank of Kansas City, 1956—; dir. United Mo. Bank-Joplin, United Mo. Bank-Carthage; adv. dir. Overland Park State Bank. Home: 6000 W 90th St Overland Park KS 66207 Office: United Mo Bank Kansas City 10th & Grand Ave Kansas City MO 64106

BOLTÉ, BROWN, investment executive; b. Winnetka, Ill., Dec. 23, 1908; s. John Willard and Jessie (Brown) B.; m. Bernice Nicholson, Jan. 4, 1930 (dec.); 1 dau., Celia (Mrs. John William Griese, Jr.); m. Suzanne Klenk, Apr. 21, 1979. Student, Butler U., 1930, U.S. Army Sch. for Spl. Services, Washington and Lee U., 1943. Western and So. sales mgr. Rytex Co., Indpls., 1930-35; asst. to pres. in charge marketing Scott & Bowne, Inc., Bloomfield, N.J., 1935-41; account exec. Benton & Bowles, Inc., 1941-50, v.p., 1950, exec. v.p., 1955, chmn. plans bd., 1957; pres. Sullivan, Stauffer, Colwell & Bayles, Inc., 1958-60, vice chmn. bd., 1961-65; chmn. bd. Bolté Advt.-Suburban N.Y., Inc., 1965-73, Bolté Advt.-Hartford, Inc., 1965-73; gen. partner Bolté Advt.-Yonkers, N.Y., 1970—, Grebolt Realty Assos., Hartford, Conn., 1973—; chmn. Bolté, Lukin & Assos., Inc., Palm Beach, 1970—; pres. Realty Enterprises Corp., North Palm Beach, Fla., 1973-77; mng. partner Sanders Syndicate, Tucson, 1973—, Bolté Syndicate, 1973—; dir. World of Plastics, Inc., Ft. Pierce, Fla., 1973—; founder, dir. Sani-Sip Drinkware, Inc., Ft. Pierce, 1983—. Also inventor; writer; composer. Trustee Norwalk Hosp. Assn., 1958-65, YMCA, New Canaan, 1967—; bd. dirs. New Canaan chpt. ARC, 1953-54, Eleanor Roosevelt Cancer Found., 1961, Child Welfare League Am., 1962-63, Community Mental Health Center, West Palm Beach, 1970-72; hon. dir. Community Mental Health Center, 1972—; mem. pres.'s adv. council Butler U., Indpls., 1968—; bd. govs. Gulfstream Goodwill Industries, 1973—; trustee, sec. exec. com. Palm Beach-Martin County Med. Center, Inc., Jupiter, Fla., 1974—, life mem., 1977—; bd. dirs., mem. exec. com. Boys Club of Palm Beach County, 1973—. Served from 2d lt. to maj. AUS, 1942-45. Mem. Am. Assn. Advt. Agys. (gov. 1956, chmn. eastern region 1957), Inst. Outdoor Advt. (dir., chmn. bd. 1967-68), Advt. Council (dir. 1966—), Nat. Def. Transp. Assn. (exec. com., chmn. public relations. com. 1956-58), ASCAP, Am. Guild Authors and Composers, SAR, Sigma Chi. Clubs: Lost Tree (Lost Tree Village, Fla.); Sailfish (Palm Beach); Old Port Yacht, Limited. Home: 11174 Turtle Beach Rd 106-C Ocean House S Lost Tree Village North Palm Beach FL 33408 Office: 630 N Federal Hwy North Palm Beach FL 33408

BOLTE, CHARLES GUY, writer, editor, cons.; b. N.Y.C., Jan. 19, 1920; s. Guy Willard and Marian (Stewart) B.; m. Mary Brooks Elwell, Aug. 1, 1943; children: Guy Willard II, John Cox, Brooks. A.B., Dartmouth Coll., 1941, L.H.D., 1970; M.Litt. (Rhodes scholar 1947), Oxford (Eng.) U., 1949. Newspaper reporter, 1937-41; spl. writer O.W.I., 1943-44; organizer, chmn. Am. Vets. Com., 1944-47; mil. corr. The Nation, 1944; staff U.S. Mission to UN, 1949; exec. sec. Am. Book Pubs. Council, 1952; v.p. Viking Press, 1956-61, exec. v.p., 1961-66; v.p. Carnegie Endowment for Internat. Peace, N.Y.C., 1966-71, counsellor, 1971-73; editor Am. Oxonian, 1977; writer, cons., 1973—. Author: The New Veteran, 1945, The Price of Peace: A Plan for Disarmament, 1956, Libraries and the Arts and Humanities, 1977; editor: (Mary Bolté) Portrait of a Woman Down East, 1983. Served as lt. Brit. Army, 1941-43. Home: Dresden ME 04342

BOLTON, ARTHUR K., lawyer, former atty. gen. Ga.; b. Griffin, Ga., May 14, 1922; s. Herbert Alfred and Eunice (Maddox) B.; m. Marion Lee Cashen, Sept. 30, 1946; children: Arthur Key, Marian Lee. Grad., North Ga. Coll., 1941; LL.B., U. Ga., 1943. Practice law, Griffin, 1947—; mem. Ga. Ho. of Reps., 1949-65; floor leader, 1963-65; judge Criminal Ct., Griffin, 1952-65; county adminstr., 1950-65, atty. gen., Ga., 1965-81. Served to capt., inf. AUS, World War II; ETO. Decorated Silver Star, Purple Heart, 3 Battle Stars; recipient Statesmanship award Ga. Gen. Assembly, 1961-62; Pub. Service award Ga. Municipal Assn., 1965; Key Citizenship award, 1970; Man of Yr. award, Griffin, Ga., 1962; Outstanding Alumnus award N. Ga. Coll., 1971; U. Ga. Disting. Service scroll, 1975; Wyman award Nat. Assn. Attys. Gen., 1977; named to N. Ga. Coll. Hall of Fame, 1971, Officers Candidate Sch. Hall of Fame, 1973. Mem. Ga. Law Sch. Alumni Assn. (pres. 1969-70), Ga. State Bar (gov.), VFW, Am. Legion, Phi Delta Phi. Baptist. Clubs: Elks, Kiwanis. Office: Commercial Bank Bldg Suite 525 Griffin GA 30223

BOLTON, EARL CLINTON, lawyer, consultant; b. Los Angeles, Aug. 22, 1919; s. John R. and Hazel A. (Van Order) B.; m. Jean Studley, June 27, 1942; children—Barbara Bolton Poley, Elizabeth Ann Bolton Newell, William Earl. A.B. magna cum laude, U. So. Calif., 1941, J.D., 1948; LL.D. (hon.), U. San Diego, 1963. Bar: Calif. 1949, U.S. Supreme Ct. 1949. Staff, Coordinator Inter-Am. Affairs, N.Y.C., also Washington, 1941; v.p., treas. Nat. Public Discussions, Inc., N.Y.C., 1942; lectr. polit. sci. dept. U. So. Calif., 1946-48, asst. prof., 1948-50, asso. prof. law and v.p. planning, 1952-60; spl. asst. to pres. U. Calif., Berkeley, 1960-61, v.p. univ. relations, 1962-64, v.p. adminstrn., 1964-66, v.p. govtl. relations, 1966-68, v.p. adminstrn., 1968-70; v.p. Booz, Allen & Hamilton, Inc., Chgo., 1970-79; of counsel firm Willis Butler & Scheifly, Los Angeles, 1979-81, Pepper, Hamilton & Scheetz, 1981-84, Earl C. Bonton & Assocs., 1984—. Editorial bd.: Law Rev., U. So. Calif., 1947-48. Mem. Calif. Gov.'s Mental Health Adv. Com., Citizens' Legis. Adv. Com.; past chmn., founding mem. Calif. Scholarship Com. Served to capt. USNR, 1942-46, 50-52. Mem. State Bar Calif., Order of Coif, Phi Beta Kappa, Phi Kappa Phi. Home: 630 S Orange Grove Pasadena CA 91105 Office: 2049 Century Park E Suite 1650 Los Angeles CA 90067

BOLTON, ELLIS TRUESDALE, marine scientist; b. Linden, N.J., May 4, 1922. B.S., Rutgers U., 1943, Ph.D., 1950. Mem. faculty Coll. Marine Studies, U. Del., Newark, 1975—, prof. marine biology, 1975—, dir., 1977—; dir. dept. terrestrial magnetism Carnegie Instn., Washington, 1966-74. Author numerous articles, reports in field. Address: Coll Marine Studies U Del 700 Pilottown Rd Lewes DE 19958

BOLTON, JAMES ROBERT, educator, chemist; b. Swift Current, Sask., Can., June 24, 1937; s. James Linden and Margaret (McFadden) B.; m. Wilma Burdette Hall, Dec. 26, 1959; children: Judith Louise, James Thomas. B.A., U. Sask., 1958, M.A., 1960; Ph.D., Cambridge U., Eng., 1963. Research asso. Columbia, 1962-64; asst. prof. U. Minn., Mpls., 1964-66, asso. prof., 1966-69, prof., asso. chmn. chemistry, 1969-70; prof., dir. photochemistry unit U. Western Ont., London, 1970—. Co-author: Electron Spin Resonance, 1972, Photochemistry, An Introduction, 1974; Editor: Solar Power and Fuels, 1977; co-editor: Biological Applications of Electron Spin Resonance, 1972. Sloan fellow, 1966-68; Noranda lectr. Chem. Inst. Can., 1976. Fellow Chem. Inst. Can.; mem. Internat. Magnetic Resonance Soc., Interam. Photochem. Soc., Am. Chem. Soc., Can. Assn. Univ. Profs., Am. Soc. Photobiology, Solar Energy Soc. Can. (past chmn.), Internat. Solar Energy Soc. (past chmn. biology and chemistry topical div. Am. sect.). Research, publs. on devel. electron spin resonance spectroscopy as tool to provide detailed information about electronic structure of molecules with unpaired electrons; applications of electron spin resonance to problems in photosynthesis and storage of solar energy. Home: 485 Coombs Ave London ON N6G 1J8 Canada

BOLTON, ROBERT HARVEY, banker; b. Alexandria, La., June 19, 1908; s. James Wade and Mary (Calderwood) B.; m. Elsie Elizabeth McLundie, Apr. 14, 1939; children: Robert Harvey Jr., Elizabeth McLundie (Mrs. Robert Conery Hassinger), Mary Calderwood (Mrs. James Kelly Jennings Jr.). B.S., Wharton Sch. Finance and Commerce, U. Pa., 1930. With credit dept. Guaranty Trust Co., N.Y.C., 1930-32; asst. cashier Rapides Bank & Trust Co., Alexandria, 1932-36, cashier, 1936-43, v.p., 1943-47, exec. v.p., 1947-56, pres., 1956—, dir., 1948—; dir. New Orleans br. Fed. Res. Bank Atlanta., 1979-81; Rep. La. to Conf. State Bank Suprs., 1964-71. Mem. La. State U. Found., 1972-80; mem. council fin. steering com. Attakapas council Boy Scouts Am., 1971—; chmn. Rapides Parish chpt. ARC, 1943, Alexandria Little Theatre, 1942; bd. dirs. Rapides United Givers, Indsl. Devel. Bd. Central La.; mem. exec. com. Central Cities Devel. Com.; chmn. fin. com. Emanuel Bapt. Ch. Served with USNR, World War II. Recipient Distinguished Service award Jr. C. of C., 1943. Mem. Mortgage Bankers Assn. (Washington com. 1962—), La. Bankers Assn. (pres. 1950, mem. legislative study com. 1950—, mem. fed. affairs com. 1971—), La. Mortgage Bankers Assn. (pres. 1952, mem. legis. com. 1970—), Bus. and Indsl. Devel. Corp. La. (dir. 1971-73), Council Better La. (dir. 1970—), Alexandria-Pineville C. of C. (pres. 1965, chmn. aviation com. 1972—), Am. Bankers Assn. (pres. state bank div. 1955), Robert Morris Assos. (nat. dir. 1943-45), U.S. C. of C. (fin. com. 1964-71). Baptist (deacon 1934—, chmn. Every Member Canvass 1937-74). Clubs: Mason, Rotarian (pres. Alexandria 1942), Boston, Blenville, Internat. House (New Orleans); Alexandria Golf and Country; City (Baton Rouge); Confrerie des Chevaliers du Tastevin. Home: 3200 Parkway Dr Alexandria LA 71301 Office: PO Box 31 Alexandria LA 71301

BOLTON, ROGER EDWIN, economist, educator; b. Dover, Pa., Nov. 23, 1938; s. Oscar Jacob and Edna Irene (Hughes) B.; m. Julia Carolyn Gooden, June 27, 1964; children: Christopher, Jonathan. A.B., Franklin and Marshall Coll., 1959; Ph.D., Harvard U., 1964. Instr. Harvard U., Cambridge, Mass., 1964-66; asst. prof. econs. Williams Coll., Williamstown, Mass., 1966-69, asoc. prof., 1969-74, prof., 1974—, chmn. dept., 1975-76, 79-81; vis. prof. Wellesley Coll., 1977, U. Pa., 1981-82; mem. assoc. staff Brookings Instn., 1965-68; sr. economist Curran Assocs., 1973-75; research assoc. Joint Ctr. for Urban Studies, 1979-81. Author: Defense Purchases and Regional Growth, 1966; co-author: Regional Diversity, 1981; editor: Defense and Disarmament, 1966; contbr. articles to profl. jours.; mem. editorial bd.: Resources and Conservation, Internat. Regional Sci. Rev., Jour. Regional Sci. Mem. Berkshire County Regional Planning Commn., Mass., 1980-81, 82—, clk., Mass., 1983—; mem. Williamstown Planning Bd., 1983—. Woodrow Wilson fellow, 1959-60; Danforth fellow, 1959-64. Mem. Am. Econ. Assn. (Rigional Sci. Assn.), AAAS, Assn. for Pub. Policy Analysis and Mgmt. Home: 30 Grandview Dr Williamstown MA 01267 Office: Dept Econs Fernald House Williams Coll Williamstown MA 01267

BOLWELL, HARRY JAMES, manufacturing company executive; b. Bloomfield, N.J., May 17, 1925; s. Harry George and Ann Lillian (Seymour) B.; m. Suzanne Ruth Poljacik, Sept. 24, 1949 (dec. 1984); children: Brian, Suzanne. B.S., U. Vt., 1949; M.S., Stevens Inst. Tech., 1952. Gen. mgr. Combustion Engring., Inc., Chattanooga, 1959-61; v.p., gen. mgr. Surface Combustion div. Midland-Ross Corp., Toledo, 1961-65, group v.p. corp., 1965-69, pres., 1969-77, chief exec. officer, Cleve., 1969—, chmn., 1977—; dir. Nat. City Corp., Cleve., Cleve. Cliffs Iron Co., Leaseway Transp. Corp., Provident Life and Accident Ins. Co. Trustee Boys Club Cleve., Cleve. Scholarship Programs, Inc., Laurel Sch. for Girls, NCCJ, Cleve. Council World Affairs. Served to 1st lt. USAAF, 1942-45. Decorated D.F.C., Air Medal. Mem. Ohio, Cleve. chambers commerce, Sigma Alpha Epsilon. Episcopalian (vestryman). Clubs: The Clevelander, The Country, Cleve. Racquet, Pepper Pike, Union. Office: 20600 Chagrin Blvd Cleveland OH 44122

BOLZ, NORMAN ALEXANDER, retired accounting executive; b. Detroit, June 12, 1920; s. Alexander F. and Elsie Ellen (Kneale) B.; m. Betty Jane Sitlington, Feb. 23, 1946; children—Karen Jeanne Haller, Norman Alexander, James Carleton. B.S., Wayne State U., 1942; postgrad., Walsh Inst. Accountancy, 1946, Detroit Coll. Law, 1949-53. Partner, mem. internat. exec. com., vice chmn. internat. ops. Coopers & Lybrand, N.Y.C., From 1942, now ret.; trustee emeritus Walsh Inst. Accountancy. Bd. dirs., chmn. fin. com., treas. Nat. Symphony Orch., Washington. Served with AUS, 1942-46. Mem. Am. Inst. C.P.A.s, Mich. Assn. C.P.A.s, Washington Assn. C.P.A.s, Pitts. Assn. C.P.A.s, Smithsonian Assos., Internat. Mgmt. Devel. Inst., Wolf Trap Farms Soc., Wayne State U. Alumni Assn., Newcomen Soc. N.Am., Alpha Kappa Psi. Clubs: Pitts., Duquesne, Fox Chapel Country (Pitts.); Detroit, Country of Detroit, Grosse Pointe; 1925 F St., Metropolitan, Columbia Country, Capitol Hill (Washington); N.Y. Athletic, Marco Polo, Hemisphere (N.Y.C.). Home: 5112 Cape Cod Ct Bethesda MD 20816 Office: 1156 15th St NW Suite 701 Washington DC 20005

BOLZ, RAY EMIL, retired engineering educator; b. Cleve., Oct. 24, 1918; s. William and Amelia Anne (Waechter) B.; m. Jean Kathryn Hoeft, Oct. 4, 1944; children: Elaine Kathryn, Nancy Jane, Patricia Lynn, Janet Gail. B.S. in Engring, Case Inst. Tech., 1940; M.S., Yale, 1942, D.Engring., 1949; D.Engring., Worcester Poly. Inst., 1984. Research scientist NACA, 1942-46, head jet engine combustion sect., 1944-46; asst. prof. aero. engring. Rensselaer Poly. Inst., 1947-50; faculty Case Western Res. U., 1950-73, prof. aero. engring., coordinator research, 1952-55, head dept. mech. engring., 1956-60, head engring. div., 1960-67, dean, 1967-73; v.p., dean faculty Worcester (Mass.) Poly. Inst., 1973-84, ret., 1984; Cons. to industry, 1950—; mem. adv. panel to engring. div. NSF, 1958-61, adv. panel to course content and improvement sect., 1961-66; applied mechanics reviewer. Adv. com. Air Force Inst. Tech., 1971-74. Trustee Worcester Craft Ctr., 1978—, pres., 1983—. Recipient award for advancement basic and applied sci. Yale U., 1957; Outstanding Alumni award Case Western Res. U., 1968. Fellow ASME (v.p., chmn. policy bd. edn. 1968-70); mem. Am. Soc. Engring. Edn. (mem. bd. engring. coll. council 1975—), Am. Inst. Aero. and Astronautics, Cleve. Engring. Soc. (bd. govs. 1972-73), Engring. Council Profl. Devel. (chmn. region II 1963-68), Sigma Xi. Unitarian (trustee 1964-68, pres. bd. trustees 1967-68). Home: 21 Lantern Ln Worcester MA 01609

BOLZ, SANFORD HEGLEMAN, lawyer, consultant; b. Albany, N.Y., May 3, 1915; s. August Joseph and Etta (Hegleman) B.; m. Joyce Barbara Farbstein, Nov. 24, 1940; children: Diane Miriam, Jody. A.B. with honors, Cornell U., 1935, LL.B., 1938. Bar: N.Y. 1939, U.S. Supreme Ct. 1946, D.C. 1947, Calif. 1961. Research asst. N.Y. State Law Revision Commn., 1938-39; assoc. firm Cohen, Cole, Weiss & Wharton, N.Y.C., 1939-41; appeals atty. NLRB, Washington, 1941-43; enforcement atty. OPA, Washington, 1943-44; chief counsel transp. and shipping Fgn. Econ. Adminstrn., Washington, 1944-46; individual practice law, Washington, 1946-60, 65-68; partner firm Abramson & Bolz, Salinas, Calif., 1960-65; gen. counsel Empire State C. of C., Albany, N.Y., 1969-78, sr. v.p., gen. counsel, 1978-80; employee benefits cons., lectr., labor arbitrator, 1980—; Washington counsel Am. Jewish Congress, 1948-60, Am. Jewish Com., 1965-68. Dem. candidate for Congress from 12th Dist. Calif., 1964. Mem. Am. Bar Assn., N.Y. State Bar Assn., Calif. Bar Assn., Phi Beta Kappa, Phi Kappa Phi, Delta Sigma Rho. Jewish. Home and Office: Bethlehem Terr M-234 Slingerlands NY 12159

BOMAN, JOHN HARRIS, JR., lawyer; b. Anniston, Ala., Mar. 8, 1910; s. John Harris and Myrtle (Creen) B.; m. Marie Askew, Aug. 17, 1935; children: John Harris, Scott A., Proctor C. A.B., Marquette U., 1930; J.D., U. Mich., 1933. Bar: Ga. 1933. Since practiced in Atlanta; asso. firm Crenshaw & Hansell, 1933; sr. mem. Hansell & Post, 1939—; sec., dir. Jackson Packing Co., Miss., 1946—; pres. bd. Atlanta Legal Aid Soc., 1956; sec. Met. Found. of Atlanta, 1952-77. Gen. counsel Atlanta Area council Boy Scouts Am.; trustee Atlanta Lawyers Found. Served to lt. comdr. USNR, World War II. Recipient Silver Beaver award Boy Scouts Am. Fellow Am. Bar Found.; mem. Am., Ga., Atlanta bar assns., Lawyers Club Atlanta (pres. 1950), State Bar Ga., Am. Law Inst. Methodist (steward). Clubs: Capital City, Commerce (Atlanta). Home: 3497 Paces Valley Rd NW Atlanta GA 30327 Office: 1st Atlanta Tower Atlanta GA 30383

BOMBECK, ERMA LOUISE (MRS. WILLIAM BOMBECK), author, columnist; b. Dayton, Ohio, Feb. 21, 1927; d. Cassius Edwin and Erma (Haines) Fiste; m. William Lawrence Bombeck, Aug. 13, 1949; children: Betsy, Andrew, Matthew. B.A., U. Dayton, 1949. Syndicated columnist Newsday Syndicate, 1965-70, Pubs.-Hall Syndicate, 1970,; contbg. editor Good Housekeeping Mag., 1969-74. Author: At Wit's End, 1967, Just Wait Till You Have Children of Your Own, 1971, I Lost Everything In The Post-Natal Depression, 1974, The Grass Is Always Greener Over The Septic Tank, 1976, If Life is a Bowl of Cherries, What Am I Doing in the Pits?, 1978, Aunt Erma's Cope Book, 1979, Motherhood: The Second Oldest Profession, 1983. Mem. Theta Sigma Phi (Headliner award 1969). Office: care News America Syndicate 1703 Kaiser Ave Irvine CA 92714

BOMBERG, THOMAS JAMES, dental educator; b. Curtis, Nebr., May 31, 1928; s. Robert Joseph and Alpha Marie (Fairburn) B.; m. Arthurene Edens, Apr. 29, 1954; children—Bryan Craig, Scott Edens. B.S., U. Denver, 1951; D.D.S., U. Mo., Kansas City, 1961. Pvt. practice dentistry, Colorado Springs, 1961-72; asst. prof. U. Ky. Coll. Dentistry, 1972-73; asso. prof. U. Okla. Coll. Dentistry, 1973-74; prof. U. Colo. Sch. Dentistry, Denver, 1974—, dean, 1977-80. Contbr. articles to dental related jours. Bd. dirs. El Paso County (Colo.) Mental Health Assn., 1967-70. Served with USN, 1946-48; to 1st lt. USAF, 1951-56. Mem. Am. Dental Assn., Am. Assn. Dental Schs. Republican. Episcopalian. Office: 4200 E 9th Ave Denver CO 80262

BOMBERGER, RUSSELL BRANSON, lawyer, educator; b. Lebanon, Pa., May 1, 1934; s. John Mark and Viola (Aurentz) B.; children: Ann Elizabeth, Jane Carmel. B.S., Temple U., 1955; M.A., U. Iowa, 1956, 1961, Ph.D., 1962; M.S., U. So. Calif., 1960; LL.B., J.D., LaSalle U. Bar: Calif. also various fed. cts. Mem. editorial staff Phila. Inquirer, 1952-54; lectr. U. Iowa, 1955-57, U. So. Calif., 1957-58; asst. prof. U.S. Naval Postgrad. Sch., Monterey, Calif., 1958-62, asso. prof., 1963-75, prof., 1975—; practice law, 1970—; free lance writer, 1952—, communications cons., 1963—. Author: broadcast series The World of Ideas; motion picture Strokes and Stamps; Abstracter-editor: Internat. Transactional Analysis Assn. Served to comdr. USNR. Am. Psychol. Found. fellow Columbia U., 1954-55; CBS fellow U. So. Calif., 1957-58. Mem. Am. Bar Assn. Office: PO Box 8741 Monterey CA 93940

BOMBIERI, ENRICO, mathematician; b. Milan, Italy, Nov. 26, 1940; came to U.S., 1977; s. Carlo and Luisa (Cambi) B.; m. Susan Russell, Jan. 21, 1967; 1 dau., Donata. Ph.D., U. Milan, 1963. Prof. U. Cagliari, Italy, 1965, U. Pisa, 1966-74, Scuola Normale Superiore, Pisa, 1974; prof. math. Inst. Advanced Study, Princeton, N.J., 1977—. Recipient Fields medal Internat. Math. Union, Vancouver, B.C., 1974; Balzan prize, Rome, 1981. Mem. Am. Acad. Arts and Scis., Accademia Nazionale Delle Scienze (Italy), Accademia Nazionale dei Lincei (corr. mem., recipient Feltrinelli prize 1976, Balzan prize 1981). Office: Inst Advanced Study Princeton NJ 08540

BOMGARDNER, MARTHA-ANN, librarian; b. Ft. Knox, July 31, 1953; d. Bobby Gene and Barbara-Ann (Auwaerter) B. Student, Ruthers U., France, 1973-74; B.A., U. Ky., 1975, M.S.L.S., 1977. Research asst. Info. for Bus., N.Y.C., 1977; reference librarian Neptune Pub. Library, N.J., 1977-79; librarian U.S. Atty. for Dist. N.J., Newark, 1979-82; head reference Main Library, Dept. Justice, Washington, 1982-83; library dir. Congl. Quar., Washington, 1983—. Mem. Am. Assn. Law Librarians, Law Librarians Soc. Washington, Law Library Assn. Greater N.Y. Club: Scrabble Players. Office: Congressional Quarterly Inc 1414 22d St NW Washington DC 20037

BOMGARDNER, WILLIAM EARL, assn. exec., editor; b. Hershey, Pa., Jan. 28, 1925; s. Howard Snyder and Carrie (Brunner) B.; m. Jean Rupp Ebersole, June 10, 1945; children—Barbara (Mrs. John F.

Elliott), Susan. A.A. in Bus, Hershey Jr. Coll., 1946; B.S. in Bus. Adminstrn, Susquehanna U., 1947. Supr. clerical div. dept. accident and health Conn. Gen. Life Ins. Co., Hartford, 1947-54; salesman Conn. Mut. Life Ins. Co., Hartford, 1954-55; pub. accountant, Hershey, 1955-62; editor Antique Automobile Mag.; exec. dir. Antique Automobile Club of Am., Hershey, 1959—. Treas. Derry Twp. (Pa.) Sch. Bldg. Authority, Hershey, 1973-79. Served to 1st lt. USAAF, 1943-45. Decorated Air medal with four oak leaf clusters, D.F.C.; Charles E. Duryea cup Antique Automobile Club Am., 1974. Mem. Am. Soc. Assn. Execs., Pa. Soc. Assn. Execs., Nat. Watch and Clock Collectors Assn., Phi Mu Delta. Methodist. Clubs: Masons, Shriners (pres. Hershey club 1979), Jesters, Lions. Home: 56 Maple St Hershey PA 17033 Office: 501 W Governor Rd Hershey PA 17033

BOMMARITO, SALVATORE JOHN, management services company executive; b. Bklyn., Jan. 19, 1949; s. Sylvester John and Marie Hosephine (Maiello) B.; m. Constance Marie Jacque, Nov. 29, 1969; children: Steven John, Ann Marie. A.B., U. Notre Dame, 1970; M.B.A., Fordham U., 1973. Vice-pres. Mfrs. Hanover Trust Co., N.Y.C., 1971-80; v.p., treas. Gelco Corp., Eden Prairie, Minn., 1980—. Republican. Roman Catholic. Home: 91 Choctaw Circle Chanhassen MN 55317 Office: Gelco Corp 1 Gelco Dr Eden Prairie MN 55344

BONACCI, DONALD NICHOLAS, petroleum corporation executive; b. N.Y.C., Oct. 2, 1929; s. Daniel John and Fay A. (Giamondi) B.; m. Frances Milanowycz, Sept. 13, 1952; children: Daniel, Michele, Donald, Jr. B.A., N.Y. U., 1951. Personnel mgr. Combusion Engring., Inc., Windsor, Conn., 1955-60; dir. personnel United Nuclear Corp., Elmsford, N.Y., 1961-69; v.p. Orgn. Resources, Inc., Boston, 1969-73; sr. v.p. adminstrn. Commonwealth Oil, Inc., Ponce, P.R., 1973-78; sr. v.p. adminstrn. and human resources Tesoro Petroleum Corp., San Antonio, 1978—. Served as 1st lt. U.S. Army, 1951-53. Mem. Am. Soc. Personnel Adminstrs., Am. Petroleum Inst. Club: Oak Hills Country. Office: Tesoro Petroleum Corp 8700 Tesoro Dr San Antonio TX 78286

BONAN, SEON PIERRE, real estate developer; b. N.Y.C., Feb. 6, 1917; s. Salvator and Matilda (Fox) B.; m. Janet Ross, Apr. 22, 1948; children: Elizabeth Janet (Mrs. Paul A. Bertin-Boussu), Charles Sauveur, Virginia Allegra. B.S., Columbia U., 1938; LL.B., Bklyn. Law Sch., 1946. Bar: N.Y. State 1946. Gen. partner Charles River Park, Boston, 1956—, Capital Place Assos., Trenton, N.J., 1972—, others. Bd. dirs. Jobs for Youth. Served to lt. USNR, 1941-46. Recipient Congressional Record tribute, 1966. Mem. World Bus. Council, Met. Presidents Orgn. Club: Union League (N.Y.C.). A pioneer organizing, financing and constrn. housing devel., urban redevel. projects. Home: Dublin Hill Greenwich CT 06830 Office: 10 W 20th St New York NY 10011

BONANSEA, BERNARDINO MARIA, philosophy educator emeritus, author; b. Pinerolo, Turin, Italy, Sept. 27, 1908; came to U.S., 1950; s. Joseph and Josephine (Savino) B. Grad., Studio Liceale, Casale Monf., Italy, 1927; postgrad., Studio Teologico, Turin, 1927-28; grad., Collegio Internazionale S.Antonio, Italy, 1928-31; M.A., Cath. U. Am., 1952, Ph.D., 1954. Prof. English, religion, music Cath. Middle Sch., Changsha, Hunan, China, 1933-48; prof. Italian Hunan Province Music Sch., Changsha, 1946-47; supt. Cath. Schs., Archdiocese of Changsha, 1940-48; asst. prof. philosophy Siena Coll., Loudonville, N.Y., 1955-57; instr. Cath. U. Am., Washington, 1957, asst. prof., 1958, asso. prof., 1960, prof. philosophy, 1964-74, emeritus, 1974—, sr. lectr. philosophy, 1974-75; lectr. philosophy Villanova (Pa.) U., 1975—; supt. Cath. Hosp., Changsha, 1945-48; prof. English Cath. Nursing Sch., Changsha, 1946-48; vis. prof. St. John's U., Jamaica, N.Y., 1968. Author: The Theory of Knowledge of Tommaso Campanella, 1954, Tommaso Campanella: Renaissance Pioneer of Modern Thought, 1969, God and Atheism: A Philosophical Approach to the Problem of God, 1979, Man and His Approach to God in John Duns Scotus, 1983; co-editor: John Duns Scotus, 1265-1965, 1965; translator, editor: Duns Scotus: The Basic Principles of His Philosophy, 1961, My Conversations with Teilhard de Chardin on the Primacy of Christ, 1971; Contbr. articles to philos. mags. and encyclopedias. Sec. Hunan Province Cath. Relief Com., China, 1945-48; sec. ad interim Apostolic Delegation, Washington, 1954, 60. Recipient Distinguished Service award Cath. U. Am., 1974; named Lector Generalis by Minister Gen. of Order of Friars Minor, 1960. Mem. Am. Cath. Philos. Assn., Internat. Scotistic Assn. Home: 1400 Quincy St NE Washington DC 20017 *My life has been inspired by the ideal of serving God and my fellowmen to the best of my ability.*

BONAPART, ALAN DAVID, lawyer; b. San Francisco, Aug. 4, 1930; s. Benjamin and Rose B.; m. Helen Sennett, Aug. 20, 1955; children—Paul S., Andrew D. A.B. with honors, U. Calif., Berkeley, 1951, J.D., 1954. Bar: Calif. bar 1955, U.S. Tax Ct. bar 1965, U.S. Supreme Ct. bar 1971; Cert. specialist in taxation law, Calif. Bd. Legal Specialization. Asso. firm Ben K. Lerer, 1955-59, Bancroft, Avery & McAlister, San Francisco, 1959-62, partner, 1962—; Trustee BAMAC Found.; mem. adv. com. Estate Planning Inst., U. Miami, Fla. Mem. Internat. Acad. Estate and Trust Law, Am. Bar Assn., Am. Coll. Probate Counsel, Bar Assn. San Francisco, State Bar Calif. Office: 601 Montgomery St Suite 900 San Francisco CA 94111

BONAPARTE, TONY HILLARY, university dean and official; b. Grenada, West Indies, June 13, 1939; came to U.S., 1959; s. Norman and Myra (McClean) B.; 1 dau., Yvette. B.B.A., St. John's U., 1963, M.B.A., 1964; Ph.D., N.Y.U., 1967. Instr., asst. prof. St. John's U., N.Y., 1964-68; assoc. prof., prof., dir. internat. bus. program, assoc. dean Grad. Sch. Pace U., N.Y.C., 1968—, dean Bus. Sch., 1968—, vice provost; dir. World Trade Inst.; prof. bus. adminstrn., Liberia. Editor (with J. Flaherty) Contributions to Business Enterprises, 1970. Fulbright fellow, Liberia. Fellow AAAS; mem. Fulbright Alumni Assn. (pres. 1983), Middle Atlantic Assn. Colls. Bus. Adminstrn. (pres. 1981-82), Acad. Mgmt., Acad. Internat. Bus., Am. Econ. Assn., Eastern Acad. Mgmt. Home: 1 Hudson Harbour Edgewater NY 07020 Office: Pace U New York NY 10038

BONAR, LUCIAN GEORGE, metals company executive; b. Lodz, Poland, June 1, 1934; emigrated to Can., 1941; s. Henry and Janina (Wierska) B.; m. Stephanie Leonard, June 1, 1963; children—Justin Gray, Daphne Leonard. B.A.Sc. in Metall. Engring, U. Toronto, 1958; M.S. in Metallurgy, U. Calif., Berkeley, 1959; Ph.D., Cambridge (Eng.) U., 1962. Mgr. product planning Falconbridge Ltd., Toronto, Ont., 1962-70; pres. Bonar Assos. Ltd., Toronto, 1970-72; sr. v.p. comml., nickel div. Amax Inc., Greenwich, Conn., 1972-80; pres. mineral resources div. Cabot Corp., N.Y.C., 1980-81; v.p. mktg. and sales Falconbridge Ltd., Toronto, 1981—; dir. Falconbridge Internat. Ltd., Hamilton, Bermuda, Falconbridge Japan K.K., Tokyo, Japan, Western Platinum Ltd., Johannesburg, S. Africa, Falconbridge U.S. Inc., Pitts., Falconbridge Europe S.A., Brussels. Author: The Nickel Industry, 1971. Athlone fellow, 1959; Nat. Research Council Can. spl. scholar, 1961. Mem. AIME, Am. Soc. Metals, Metals Soc., Assn. Profl. Engrs. Ont. Clubs: Royal Can. Yacht (Toronto); Metropolitan, Canadian (N.Y.C.); Belle Haven (Greenwich). Home: 96 Glen Rd Toronto ON M4W 2V6 Canada Office: Commerce Ct W Toronto ON Canada

BONAVENTURA, MARIA MIGLIORINI, chemist, educator; b. Somerville, Mass., June 29, 1938; d. Andrew and Maria Civita (Gallinaro) Migliorini; m. Andrew Salvatore Bonaventura, June 9, 1963. B.A. cum laude, Regis Coll., 1960; Ph.D., Tufts U., 1965. Research asst. Tufts U., Medford, Mass., 1960-64, research asso., 1965-66; asst. prof. Suffolk U., Boston, 1965-68, asso. prof., 1968-71, prof., 1971—, chmn. dept. chemistry, 1972—, mem. presdl. search com., 1980; research asso. Bio-Research Inst., Cambridge, Mass., 1968. Contbr. articles to profl. jours. Faculty rep. to trustees Joint Council on Univ. Affairs, Suffolk U., 1973-77, 79-81; convenor President's Commn. on Status of Women, 1974-78, speaker ednl. policy com., 1972-73. Mem. Am. Chem. Soc. (alt. councillor 1976-79, 82—, councillor 1979-82, dir. Northeastern sect. 1976—, chmn. pub. relations sect. 1977-79), New Eng. Assn. Chemistry Tchrs., AAUP (pres. chpt. 1970), Sigma Xi (pres. chpt. 1972-73), Sigma Zeta (sec. chpt. 1970—), Alpha Lambda Delta, Delta Epsilon Sigma. Home: One School St Apt 105 Arlington MA 02174 Office: Suffolk University Beacon Hill Boston MA 02114

BONAWITZ, IRVING MAURICE, educator; b. Nanticoke, Pa., Oct. 17, 1923; s. Maurice I. and Margaret (Carbonovage) B.; m. Barbara H. Anderson, May 19, 1959 (div.); children—Steven C., Douglas I. B.S., Bowling Green (Ohio) State U., 1949; M.B.A., Northwestern U., 1951; D.B.A., Mich. State U., 1964. C.P.A., D.C., Ill., Ohio. Asst. controller Rauland-Borg Corp., Chgo., 1953-55; partner John Seybold & Co. (C.P.A.s), Chgo., 1955; dir. Grad. Sch. Public Acctg., Northeastern U., Boston, 1963-64; chmn. acctg. dept. Bus. Sch., Fla. Atlantic U., Boca Raton, 1964-66; prof., past chmn. acctg. dept. Bus. Sch., SUNY, Albany, 1968—. Served with USAAF, 1943-45; CBI. Mem. Am. Acctg. Assn., Am. Inst. Decision Scis., Am. Inst. C.P.A.s, Fin. Execs. Inst., Inst. Mgmt. Scis., Beta Alpha Psi, Beta Gamma Sigma, Kappa Sigma. Home: 20 Bender Ln Delmar NY 12054 Office: Accounting Dept Bus Sch State U NY Albany NY 12023 *I am grateful to have been born in this country. I am grateful for having been granted an inborn sense of perspective and Long-range viewpoint which have sustained me during the trying periods of my life. I am grateful for the perseverance my parents instilled in me.*

BONAZZI, ELAINE CLAIRE, mezzo-soprano; b. Endicott, N.Y.; d. John Dante and Zina (Rossi) B.; m. Jerome Ashe Carrington, Sept. 21, 1963; 1 step-son, Christopher. B.M. (George Eastman scholar), Eastman Sch. Music. Mem. faculty Peabody Conservatory; vis. prof. voice Eastman Sch. Music, Rochester, N.Y., 1979. Debut, Santa Fe Opera, 1958, Opera Soc. Washington, 1960, N.Y.C. Opera, 1965, Opera Internacional, Mexico City, Mexico, 1966, Mini-Met, 1973, Mini-Met, Europe, with West Berlin Festival opera, 1961, Spoleto (Italy) Festival, 1974, Castel Franco Festival Venetian Music, Venice, Italy, 1975, Berlin Bach Festival, 1976, Netherlands Opera, 1978, Netherlands Opera, Paris; debut, 1979, Spoleto-Charleston Festival, 1981; soloist, with most major Am. orchs., Canadian Broadcasting Corp., NET Opera Theatre, NBC, ABC, CBS TV networks; recs. on, Candide, Columbia, Vanguard, CRI, Folkways, Vox, Grenadilla, and, Pro Arte records. Named 1 of 6 honored alumni 50th Anniversary Year, Eastman Sch. Music, 1971, Trustees Council U. Rochester, 1976; formerly William Matheus Sullivan grantee. Mem. Mu Phi Epsilon. Chosen by Stravinsky, Hindemith, Menotti, Chavez, Rorem, Thomson, Argento, Pasatieri for premieres of their works. Home: 650 West End Av New York NY 10025 Office: care Lew and Benson Mgmt 204 W 10th St New York NY 10014 *In performing great music one tries to be honest as well as inventive-in communicating emotion. And he tries to remain true to the intentions of the composer. It can be a frustrating task requiring infinite patience and infinite care, but what joy for the performer when at last he can touch the heart of the listener*

BOND, ARTHUR CHALMER, retired chemistry educator; b. Salem, W.Va., Feb. 14, 1917; s. Arthur Chalmer and Agnes Lydia (Ashdon) B.; m. Elizabeth M. Dux, Apr. 19, 1973; 1 son by previous marriage, Charles Bradley. B.S., Mich. State U., 1939; M.S., U. Mich., 1940, Ph.D., 1951. Research asst. NDRC, OSRD research projects, U. Chgo., 1941-46; asst. prof. chemistry U. Rochester, N.Y., 1951-57; faculty Rutgers U., New Brunswick, N.J., 1957-83, prof. chemistry, 1967-83. Asst. editor: Jour. Phys. Chemistry, 1951-57. Mem. Am. Chem. Soc. (asst. editor Jour. 1951-57), AAAS, Sigma Xi. Home: 13 Dansfield Dr Talley Hill Wilmington DE 19803

BOND, CALHOUN, lawyer; b. Balt., June 29, 1921; s. Henry Marvin and Lala Belle (Jacobs) B.; m. Jane L. Piper, Apr. 14, 1956; children: Calhoun, James Piper, Louise Cover, Jane Carson. B.A., Washington and Lee U., 1943; LL.B., U. Md., 1949. Bar: Md. 1949. Partner firm Cable, McDaniel, Bowie & Bond, Balt., 1962—. Mem. Md. Bd. Pub. Welfare, 1959-71, Md. Constl. Conv. Commn., 1965-67; mem. Balt. Bd. Fire Commrs., 1972-79, pres., 1976-79; chmn. bd. dirs. Lafayette Square Community Center, 1967-68; trustee Episcopal Ministry for Aging, 1976—, Balt. City Retirement System, 1976-79. Served to comdr. USNR, 1943-46, 50-52. Fellow Md. Bar Found.; mem. Am., Md., Balt. bar assns., Am. Judicature Soc. (dir. 1980-83), Jud. Conf. 4th Circuit, Navy League. Democrat. Episcopalian. Clubs: Maryland, Elkridge. Home: 103 Castlewood Rd Baltimore MD 21210 Office: 915 Blaustein Bldg Baltimore MD 21201

BOND, CHARLES EUGENE, aeronautical engineering educator, renewable energy specialist; b. Royston, Ga., Feb. 1, 1930; s. June Turner and Irene (Nelson) B.; m. Frances Monroe Dixon, Sept. 12, 1952 (div. 1969); children: Turner Laura, Irene, Cynthia, Nelson; m. Carol Ann Vandenberg Unzicker, Apr. 4, 1971; 1 child, Kyle; 1 stepson, Timothy Unzicker. B.S. in Physics, Ga. Inst. Tech., 1951; M.S. in Aero. Engring., U. Mich., 1956; Ph.D. in Aero. and Astronautical Engring., U. Mich., 1964. Project engr. ARO, Inc. Arnold Engring. Devel. Ctr., Tullahoma, Tenn., 1951-54; research asst. U. Mich., Ann Arbor, 1954-56, 58, research engr., 1961-64; project engr. Jet Propulsion Lab., Calif. Inst. Tech., Pasadena, 1956-57; sr. scientist, group leader hyperthermal wind tunnel group AVCO Research and Advanced Devel. Div., Wilmington, Mass., 1959-61; asst. prof. U. Ill., Urbana, 1964-66, assoc. prof., 1966-71, prof. aero. and astronautical engring., 1971—; tech. advisor U.S. Dept. Energy, Chgo., 1978-79; mem. Ill. Solar Resources Adv. Panel, 1978-79; speaker on renewable energy resources. Actor profl. theatre prodns., Ill., summer 1967-72. Pres. Champaign-Urbana Community Theatre, 1971. Robert J. Woods fellow U. Mich., 1957-58, 58-59; Douglas aircraft fellow U. Mich., 1955-56; NSF fellow Princeton Summer Inst., 1964; recipient course devel. Solar Energy Research Inst., Golden, Colo., 1979, tchr. of yr. Aero. Engring. Dept. U. Ill., 1980. Mem. ASME, Am. Solar Energy Soc., ASHRAE, Am. Wind Energy Assn., North Central Sociol. Assn., Actors' Equity, Sigma Xi, Phi Kappa Phi. Methodist. Home: 210 Bliss Dr Urbana IL 61801 Office: U Ill 104 S Mathews St Urbana IL 61801

BOND, CHRISTOPHER SAMUEL, gov. Mo.; b. St. Louis, Mar. 6, 1939; s. Arthur D. and Elizabeth (Green) B.; m. Carolyn Reid, May 13, 1967. B.A. with honors, Princeton U., 1960; LL.B., U. Va., 1963. Bar: Mo. bar 1963, U.S. Supreme Ct. bar 1967. Law clk. to chief judge U.S. Ct. of Appeals, 5th Dist., Atlanta, 1963-64; asso. firm Covington & Burling, Washington, 1965-67; practice law, Mexico, Mo., 1968, asst. atty. gen., chief counsel consumer protection div., State of Mo., 1969-70, auditor, 1971-73, gov. of, Mo., 1973-77, 81—; pres. Gt. Plains Legal Found., Kansas City, Mo., 1978-81; Chmn. Republican Govs. Assn.; chmn. Midwestern Govs. Assn.; exec. com. Nat. Govs. Conf., chmn. com. on econ. and community devel., 1981—. Republican. Presbyterian. Address: Office of Gov State Capitol Jefferson City MO 65101

BOND, CORNELIUS COMBS, JR., investment advisor; b. Balt., Sept. 21, 1933; s. Cornelius Combs and Pauline Woodruff (Sanford) B.; m. Johann Hodges, June 12, 1956; children: Margaret J. Simon, Cornelius Combs III, Katherine K. B.S. in E.E, Princeton U., 1956; postgrad., Johns Hopkins U., 1960. Research analyst T. Rowe Price Assos., Balt., 1960-68, v.p., 1968-82, dir., 1972-82, chmn. fin. com., 1979-82; dir., chmn. adv. com. T. Rowe Price Growth Stock Fund, 1974-79, pres., 1976-79; pres., chmn. bd. TRP Ventures, Inc.; gen. ptnr. New Enterprise Assocs.; dir. Charles Center Properties, Inc. Bd. dirs. Historic Annapolis; asso. trustee U. Pa. Served to capt. USAF, 1957-64. Mem. Balt. Soc. Security Analysts. Episcopalian. Clubs: Nantucket Yacht, Maryland, Bachelors Cotillion; Union (N.Y.C.). Home: 3 Shipwright Harbor Annapolis MD 20401 Office: 235 Montgomery St Suite 1025 San Francisco CA 94104

BOND, ELAINE R., data processing executive; b. Boston, Nov. 1, 1935; d. Frank O. and Rosalie (Salviati) Galante; m. William C. Bond, Sept. 27, 1958. B.S. magna cum laude in Math, Tufts U., 1957. With IBM Corp., 1957-81, dir. exec. resources, 1972-73, dir. programming, 1973-75; dir. Sterling Forest Info. Center, 1975-78, group dir. info. systems, 1978-81; sr. v.p., dir. corp. systems Chase Manhattan Bank, N.Y.C., 1981—. Mem. IEEE. Office: 1 Chase Manhattan Plaza New York NY 10081

BOND, FLOYD ALDEN, economist, educator; b. Farmington, Mich., Aug. 20, 1913; s. Isaac and Ada C. (Wolfe) B.; m. Jean E. Marrow, June 29, 1939; children—Richard Alden, Robert Lowell. A.B. cum laude with honors in Econs, U. Mich., 1938, A.M., 1940, Ph.D., 1942. Faculty dept. econs. U. Mich., Ann Arbor, 1938-46, faculty Horace H. Rackham Grad. Sch., 1942-46, dean, prof. bus. econs. Grad. Sch. Bus. Adminstrn., 1960-78, dean emeritus, Donald C. Cook Disting. prof. bus. econs., 1979—; asso. prof. econs. Carleton Coll., 1946-48, acting chmn. dept. econs., spring 1948; prof. econs. on Stedman-Sumner Found.; chmn. dept. econs. Pomona Coll., 1948-60, Disting. prof., 1955-60; dir. Social Sci. Research Center, 1951-55, chmn. Social Sci. div., 1951-52; prof. econs. Claremont Grad. Sch., 1948-60; Dir., mem. exec. com. Clark Equipment Co.; dir. Nat. Bank Jackson, Mich., Asso. Corp. N.Am., Hayes-Albion Corp., Mass. Mut. Life Ins. Co., Mass. Mut. Mgmt. Realty Investors Trust, U. Hawaii Conf. on Econ. Edn., 1953, Calif. Conf. on Econ. Edn., 1951, 54, 56, Nat. Pilot Program of Residential Confs. on Liberal Arts for Bus. Execs., 1956-60; vis. prof. U. Wis., 1955, U. B.C., 1958; dir. bus.-edn. div. Com. for Econ. Devel., 1959-60; cons. So. Calif. Research Council, 1952-60; trustee Joint Council on Econ. Edn., 1960-70, Calif. Council Econ. Edn. (vice chmn. 1953-60); exec. sec. Nat. Task Force Econ. Edn., 1961; cons. GAO, 1968-78; vis. scholar UCLA, 1979-80. Author: Public Regulation in Action, 1948, (with others) Our Needy Aged, 1954, Preparation for Business Leadership: Views of Top Executives, 1964, Management Succession, 1971, also articles in profl. jours. Elector to Hall Fame for Gt. Americans, 1976—; Fed. Res. Banking fellow, 1950; Ford Found. faculty fellow, 1954-55. Mem. Western Econ. Assn. (sec.-treas. 1951-52, v.p. 1953-54, pres. 1956-57), So. Calif. Econ. Assn. (trustee 1956-60), Midwest Econ. Assn. (v.p. 1947-48), Am. Econ. Assn), AAUP (pres. Asso. Colls. chpt. 1953-54), Am. Assn. Collegiate Schs. Bus. (sec.-treas. 1966-67, v.p. 1967-68, pres. 1968-69), Econ. Club of Detroit (chmn. program com. 1968—), Sphinx (hon.), Katholepistemiad, Phi Beta Kappa (pres. Gamma chpt. of Calif. 1950-51), Phi Eta Sigma, Phi Kappa Phi, Beta Gamma Sigma. Home: 2533 Londonderry Rd Ann Arbor MI 48104

BOND, HORATIO LOCKERBY, consulting engineer; b. Barnstable, Mass., Nov. 30, 1900; s. Horatio Simmons and Ella Jessup (Lockerby) B.; m. Dorothy Anderson Gere, Sept. 21, 1925. S.B., M.I.T., 1923. Asst. econs. M.I.T., 1923-24; engr. Nat. Fire Protection Assn., 1924-39, chief engr., 1939-69; cons. fire protection engr., 1969—; Mem. corp. M.I.T., 1954-59. Editor and author technical books and articles. Fellow Soc. Fire Protection Engrs.; mem. Internat. Assn. Chiefs Police, Internat. Assn. Fire Chiefs (hon.), Nat. Acad. Scis. (com. on fire research of NRC 1956-65), Am. Water Works Assn., Am. Soc. Public Adminstrn., Nat. Fire Protection Assn. (hon.), Fire Protection Assn. Britain, Inst. Fire Engrs. Britain (hon.), Engring. Socs. of New Eng. (New Eng. award 1982), Alumni Assn. M.I.T. (pres. 1953-54). Clubs: Hyannisport (Mass.); Masons. Address: PO Box 393 Hyannis Port MA 02647

BOND, JULIAN, legislator, civil rights leader; b. Nashville, Jan. 14, 1940; s. Horace Mann and Julia Agnes (Washington) B.; m. Alice Louise Clopton, July 28, 1961; children—Phyllis Jane, Horace Mann, Michael, Jeffrey, Julia. B.A., Morehouse Coll., 1971; LL.D. (hon.), Dalhousie U., 1969, U. Bridgeport, 1969, Wesleyan U., Conn., 1969, U. Oreg., 1969, Syracuse U., 1970, Eastern Mich. U., 1971, Tuskegee Inst., 1971, Howard U., 1971, Morgan State U., 1971, Wilberforce U., 1971, D.C.L., Lincoln U., 1970. A founder Com. Appeal for Human Rights, 1960, exec. sec., 1961; a founder Student Nonviolent Coordinating Com., 1960, communications dir., 1961-66; reporter, feature writer Atlanta Inquirer, 1960-61, mng. editor, 1963; mem. Ga. Ho. of Reps., from Fulton County, 1965-75, Ga. senate, 1975—. So. Corr. Reporting Racial Equality Wars. bd. dirs. So. Conf. Edn. Fund, Robert F. Kennedy Meml. Fund, So. Regional Council, Highlander Research and Edn. Center, Nat. Sharecroppers Fund (pres.), So. Elections Fund, Delta Ministry project Nat. Council Chs., Voter Edn. Project, New Democratic Coalition; pres. So. Poverty Law Center. Mem. NAACP (nat. dir., pres. Atlanta br.). Barred from house because of Vietnam statements, 1966; U.S. Supreme Ct. ruled his Constl. rights were violated, 1966. Office: 361 Westview Dr SW Atlanta GA 30310 *Most noticeable in my lifetime has been the success of citizens' movements: for civil rights, for peace in Vietnam and demonstrating the strength of our democracy.*

BOND, LEWIS HONYMAN, banker; b. Ashport, Tenn., July 31, 1921; s. Lewis H. and Ruth (Bowman) B.; m. Le Kathrin Ozbirn, June 7, 1947; children—Kathrin, Susan Lee, Jane Ann. B.S. in Petroleum Engring, U. Okla., 1947. Petroleum engr. Stanolind Oil & Gas Co., 1947-52; petroleum engr. Ft. Worth Nat. Bank, 1952-53, asst. v.p., petroleum engr., 1953-54, v.p., petroleum engr., 1954-59, pres., dir., 1959-72; chmn. bd., chief exec. officer Ft. Worth Nat. Bank, also Ft. Worth Nat. Corp., 1972-74, Tex. Am. Bancshares Inc., 1974—; dir., mem. exec. com. State Res. Life Ins. Co., Millers Ins. Group, Ft. Worth; class A dir. Fed. Res. Bank, 11th dist.; mem. adv. council (11th Fed. Dist.), 1972-74. Former trustee Austin Coll., Ft. Worth Country Day Sch.; bd. dirs. N. Tex. Commn., pres., 1975; bd. dirs. Tex. Christian U. Research Found., Southwestern Expn. and Fat Stock Show; trustee Saint Joseph Hosp.; mem. devel. bd. U. Tex. at Arlington. Mem. Ft. Worth C. of C. (past pres., bd. dirs.), Assn. Res. City Bankers (dir. 1975-78, com. on public affairs), Am. Bankers Assn., Tex. Bankers Assn. (past v.p., mem. legislative com.), Tex. Research League (dir., mem. adv. com., treas. 1973-74, vice chmn. 1975-76, chmn. 1976—), Newcomen Soc. (Ft. Worth com.), Pi Kappa Alpha, Tau Beta Pi, Sigma Tau. Presbyn. (elder). Clubs: Ft. Worth, Exchange (past pres.), Shady Oaks, Century II, Rivercrest Country; City Mid-day, University (N.Y.C.). Home: 429 Rivercrest Dr Fort Worth TX 76107 Office: PO Box 2050 Fort Worth TX 76101

BOND, M. E., economist, univ. ofcl.; b. Bloomfield, Iowa, Sept. 11, 1939; s. M.E. and Marne E. B.; m. Carole Lynne Randall, Nov. 18, 1961. B.B.A., U. Iowa, 1961, M.A., 1965, Ph.D., 1967. Vis. asso. prof. econs. James Wilson dept. econs. U. Va., Charlottesville, 1974; prof.

econs., dir. Bur. Bus. and Econ. Research, Ariz. State U., Tempe, 1976-79; dean Fogelman Coll. Bus. and Econs., Memphis State U., 1979—; ednl. cons. Am. Coll., Bryn Mawr, Pa., 1973—. Contbr. monographs, articles, revs. to profl. publs. Bd. regents Mid-South Sch. Banking, 1979. Recipient Ariz. Gov.'s Merit award, 1977. Mem. Fin. Execs. Inst., Am. Econ. Assn., Ariz. Econ. Roundtable, Trourism and Travel Research Assn. (dir. 1981—), Beta Gamma Sigma, Alpha Kappa Psi, Lambda Alpha. Clubs: Econ. of Memphis (life), Univ., Rotary. Office: Fogelman Coll Bus and Econs Memphis State U Memphis TN 38152

BOND, NILES WOODBRIDGE, former foreign service officer, cultural institute executive; b. Newton, Mass., Feb. 25, 1916; s. George Wood and Clara Mehitabel (Bonney) B.; m. Julia Rice Folsom, June 25, 1940; children: Ellen Dudley, Nancy Kenneth. A.B., U. N.C., 1937; A.M., Fletcher Sch. Law and Diplomacy, Medford, Mass., 1938. U.S. fgn. service officer, 1939-68, vice consul, Havana, Cuba, 1939-40, Yokohama, Japan, 1940-41, 3d sec., vice consul, Madrid, Spain, 1942-45, 2d sec., 1945-46; adviser to U.S. delegation to 4th session Econ. and Social Council, 1947; 2d sec., vice consul, Bern, Switzerland, 1947, 1st sec. and consul, 1947; asst. chief div. N.E. Asian affairs Dept. State, 1947-49, officer in charge Korean affairs, 1949-50; adviser to U.S. delegation to 4th session UN Gen. Assembly, 1949; 1st sec. Office of U.S. Polit. Adviser to Supreme Comdr. Allied Powers, Tokyo, Japan, 1950; acting chmn. Allied Council for Japan, 1952; counselor embassy, Tokyo, 1952, Seoul, Korea, 1953-54, Rome, Italy, 1956-58; dir. Office UN Polit. and Security Affairs, Dept. State, 1954-56; counselor of embassy, vis. lectr. Bologna Center, Johns Hopkins, 1957-58; research fellow Center for Internat. Affairs, Harvard, 1958-59; minister-counselor embassy, Rio de Janeiro, Brazil, 1959-63; coordinator interdeptl. seminar Dept. State, 1963; minister, consul gen., São Paulo, Brazil, 1964-68; sec. bd. trustees Corcoran Gallery Art, Washington, 1970—; exec. dir. Project Orbis, 1972; adviser São Paulo Bienal, 1969; dir. internat. exhbns. com. Am. Fedn. Art, 1976-77; pres., bd. dirs. Brazilian-Am. Cultural Inst., 1976—; mem. ct. system study com. D.C. Bar, 1979—, exec. dir. fee arbitration bd., 1981—. Author: poetry Arcanum, 1965, Elegos, 1967. Decorated commendatore Al Merito della Republica Italiana; grand officer Order So. Cross, Brazil). Club: University (Washington). Interned in Japan upon outbreak of war, repatriated on S.S. Gripsholm, Aug. 1942. Home: 2440 Virginia Ave NW Washington DC 20037

BOND, RICHARD GUY, educator, civil engr.; b. Beecher Falls, Vt., Dec. 9, 1916; s. Richard Henry and Annie (Bassett) B.; m. Betty Telford Wells, Sept. 29, 1953. B.S. in Civil Engring, U. N.H., 1938; M.S. in San. Engring, U. Iowa, 1940; M.P.H., U. Minn., 1948. Registered profl. engr., Minn., Iowa.; Diplomate Am. Acad. Environmental Engrs. Pub. health engr. Iowa Dept. Health, 1940-47; vis. lectr. U. Minn. Sch. Pub. Health, 1943-45, 47-48; asst. prof. civil engring. Cornell U., 1947-49; faculty U. Minn., Mpls., 1949-79, prof., 1958-79, prof. emeritus, 1980—, dir. environ. health and safety, 1949-62, dir. environ. health div., 1962-73; Cons. in field, 1958—; cons. Office Surgeon Gen. Army, 1962-74, U.S. Bur. Prisons, 1976—; chmn. planetary quarantine adv. com. Am. Inst. Biol. Scis., 1966-75; lectr. seminar community health workers from overseas Central Council Health Edn., Britain, 1964; mem. 3d Nat. Conf. Pub. Health Tng., 1967; health planning adv. council Minn. Planning Agy., 1967-72; campus safety assn. Nat. Safety Council, 1955-62; mem. council pub. health cons. Nat. Sanitation Found., 1970-78; mem. life scis. com. NASA, 1971-74; mem. U.S. Nat. Com. on Vital Health Statistics, 1972-74; mem. health care adv. com. Minn. Dept. Corrections, 1974-79. Co-editor: Environmental Health and Safety in Health Care Facilities, 1973. Recipient Outstanding Achievement award U. N.H. Coll. Tech., 1973; WHO travel fellow, S.E. Asia, 1960. Fellow Am. Pub. Health Assn. (gov. council 1962-65, 69-74, chmn. hosp. facilities com. 1955-65), ASCE, Royal Soc. Health Britain (hon.); mem. AAAS, Pub. Health Insps. Assn. Britain (hon.), Am. Coll. Health Assn. (gov. council, exec. bd. 1958-64, Ruth E. Boynton award 1968, Hitchcock award 1977), Health Physics Soc., Nat., Minn. socs. profl. engrs., Sigma Xi, Alpha Tau Omega. Episcopalian. Club: Campus (U. Minn.). Home: Grand Marais MN 55604

BOND, RICHARD NORMAN, political activist; b. N.Y.C., May 30, 1950; s. Harry H. and Mary T. (Rooney) B.; m. Valerie Mueller; children: Michael, Matthew. B.A. in English and Philosophy, Fordham U., 1972. Press sec. Congressman S. William Green of N.Y. (Republican), 1978; caucus campaign mgr. George Bush for Pres., 1979; campaign mgr. Senator Charles McMathias of Md. (Rep.), 1980; dep. chief of staff to Vice-Pres. U.S., 1981-82; dep. chmn./dir. polit. ops. Rep. Nat. Com., Washington, 1982—. Office: Rep Nat Com 310 1st St SE Washington DC 20003

BOND, RICHARD RANDOLPH, univ. pres.; b. Lost Creek, W.Va., Dec. 1, 1927; s. Harley Donovan and Marcella (Randolph) B.; m. Reva Stearns, Apr. 20, 1946; children—H. David, Philip S., Josette Bond Schaffer, Michael R. B.S., Salem Coll., 1948, LH.D. (hon.), 1978; M.S., W.Va. U., 1949; Ph.D. (NSF fellow 1952-53), U. Wis., 1955. Asst. prof. biology Milton (Wis.) Coll., 1949-51; asso. prof. biology Salem Coll., 1955-58, dean men, 1957-58; vis. investigator R.B. Jackson Lab., summer 1958; Mich. fellow Coll. Adminstrn., U. Mich., 1958-59; dean faculty Elmira (N.Y.) Coll., 1959-63, asso. prof. biology, 1959-65; prof. acad. adminstrn. Cornell U., Ithaca, N.Y., 1963-66; coll. curriculum specialist Cornell Team to U. Liberia, acting dean Coll. Liberal Arts, 1963-64, chief of party Cornell Project Team, 1964-66; v.p. acad. affairs, dean faculty, prof. zoology Ill. State U., 1966-71; pres. U. No. Colo., 1971—; founder Nat. Student Exchange. Contbr. articles to profl. jours. Trustee Salem Coll. Served with AUS, 1946-47. Recipient Outstanding Young Man of Am. award, 1965. Fellow AAAS; mem. Ecol. Soc. Am., Am. Ornithol. Union, Assn. Higher Edn., Sigma Xi.

BOND, ROBERT MCGEHEE, air force officer; b. Trenton, Tenn., Dec. 16, 1929; s. Robert U. and Dorothy (McGehee) B.; m. Betty Renick, Aug. 14, 1954; children—Susan Hurry, Michael, Pamela Lunger, Stephen. Student, Marion (Ala.) Mil. Inst., U. Miss., Air Command and Staff Coll., 1966. Enlisted in U.S. Air Force, 1951, commd., through grades to lt. gen.; vice comdr., 1972-73; dep. dir. Gen. Purpose Forces Directorate, Office of Dept. Chief of Staff Research and Devel., Hdqrs. U.S. Air Force, 1973-78; comdr. Armament Devel. and Test Center, Eglin AFB, Fla., 1978-81; vice comdr. Air Force Systems Command, Andrews AFB, 1981—. Decorated Meritorious Service medal, Silver Star, Air medal with 13 oak leaf clusters. Home: 1508 Arkansas Rd Andrews AFB MD 20335 Office: AFSC/CV Andrews AFB MD 20335

BOND, THOMAS ALDEN, university president; b. St. Louis, Mar. 23, 1938; s. Alden R. and Jean Elizabeth (Langen) B.; m. Judy Bess Borchardt, Sept. 2, 1961; children: Thomas A., Jr., Amy Elizabeth. Student, Washington U., 1956-58; A.B., U. Mo., 1961; M.S., U. Okla., 1963, Ph.D. (Humble Oil Co. fellow), 1966. Instr. U. Okla., Norman, 1964-65; geologist Okla. Geol. Survey, Norman, 1965-66; asst. prof. geology, acting chmn. dept. Ga. So. Coll., Statesboro, 1966-69, asso. prof., asst. dean Sch. Arts and Scis., 1969-70; asst. dean Coll. Liberal Arts, Idaho State U., Pocatello, 1970-73, chmn. dept. geology, dir. summer session, 1973-74, dean Coll. Liberal Arts, prof., 1974-76; v.p. for acad. affairs Midwestern State U., Wichita Falls, Tex., 1976-78; provost, v.p. acad. affairs Eastern Ill. U., 1978-80; pres. Clarion U. of Pa., 1980—. Contbr. articles to profl. jours. Chmn. United campaign Idaho State U., 1972; Alt. del. Idaho Democratic Conv., 1972. Fellow Okla. Acad. Sci.; mem. AAAS, Am. Assn. Petroleum Geologists, Soc. Econ. Paleontologists and Mineralogists, Geol. Soc. Am., Am. Assn. Stratigraphic Palynologists, Am. Assn. Quaternary Environment, Southeastern Geol. Soc., Palynological Soc. India, Ga. Geol. Soc., Ga. Acad. Sci., Sigma Xi, Sigma Gamma Epsilon. Home: 840 Wood St Clarion PA 16214

BOND, THOMAS *See* **BURNAM, TOM**

BOND, VICTORIA, conductor, composer; b. Los Angeles, May 6, 1950; d. Philip and Jane (Courtl) B.; m. Stephan Peskin, Mar. 31, 1974. B.Mus. Arts, U. So. Calif., 1968; M.Mus. Arts, Juilliard Sch., 1975, D.Mus. Arts, 1977. Guest condr., Cabrillo Music Festival, Calif., 1974, White Mountains Music Festival, N.H., 1975, Aspen (Colo.) Music Festival, 1976, Shenandoah Music Festival, W.Va., 1977, Colo. Philharm., 1978, Houston Symphony, 1979, Buffalo Philharm., Pitts. Symphony, 1980, Anchorage Symphony, NW Chamber Orch., Seattle, Ark. Symphony, 1981, Hudson Valley Philharm., N.Y., Newton Symphony, Boston, 1982, Hartford Symphony, RTE Symphony, Dublin, Ireland, 1983; music dir., New Amsterdam Symphony Orch., N.Y.C., 1978-80, Pitts. Youth Symphony Orch., Empire State Youth Orch., 1982-83, Southeastern Music Ctr., 1983, Bel Canto Opera Co., 1983-84; Exxon/Arts Endowment condr., Pitts. Symphony, 1978-80; recs. include Twentieth Century Cello (Recipient Victor Herbert Conducting award Juilliard Sch. 1977), Two American Contemporaries; commd. by, Jacob's Pillow Dance Festival, 1979, Am. Ballet Theater, 1981. Mem. ASCAP (awards 1977-84), Am. Symphony Orch. League, Musicians Union, Mu Phi Epsilon. *I believe that it is possible to know our capabilities only to the extent that we challenge ourselves. In learning to overcome obstacles, we learn about our own potential strength and determination.*

BOND, WILLIAM HENRY, librarian, educator; b. York, Pa., Aug. 14, 1915; s. Walter Loucks and Ethel (Bossert) B.; m. Helen Elizabeth Lynch, Dec. 6, 1943; children: Nancy Barbara, Sally Lynch. A.B., Haverford Coll., 1937; M.A., Harvard, 1938, Ph.D., 1941. Research fellow Folger Shakespeare Library, 1941-42; asst. to librarian Houghton Library, Harvard, Cambridge, Mass., 1946-48, curator manuscripts, 1948-64, librarian, 1965-82; lectr. bibliography Harvard, 1964-67, prof., 1967—; asst. keeper manuscripts Brit. Mus., 1952-53; Sandars reader in bibliography Cambridge (Eng.) U., 1981-82. Editor: (Christopher Smart) Jubilate Agno, 1954, Supplement to Census of Medieval and Renaissance Manuscripts in the United States, 1962, The Houghton Library, 1942-67, 1967, Records of a Bibliographer, 1967, 18th Century Studies in Honor of Donald F. Hyde, 1970. Trustee Emerson Meml. Assn., 1964—, Historic Deerfield (Mass.) Inc., 1965—, Concord (Mass.) Free Pub. Library, 1966-71. Served to lt. USNR, 1943-46. Guggenheim fellow, 1982-83. Mem. Bibliog. Soc. Am. (pres. 1974-75), Bibliog. Soc. London, hon. sec. for Am.), Grolier Club, Club of Odd Volumes, Am. Antiquarian Soc., Mass. Hist. Soc., Colonial Soc. Mass. (pres. 1982—), The Johnsonians, Phi Beta Kappa. Club: Century Assn. Home: 109 The Valley Rd Concord MA 01742 Office: Houghton Library Cambridge MA 02138

BONDI, AMEDEO, microbiologist; b. Springfield, Mass., Dec. 13, 1912; s. Amedeo and Amelia (Monteverd) B.; m. Virginia Carstens, Apr. 4, 1939; children: Peter, John, Barbara, Edward. B.S., U. Conn., 1935; M.S., U. Mass., 1937; Ph.D., U. Pa., 1942. Instr., asst. prof. Temple U. Sch. Medicine, Phila., 1942-47; prof., chmn. dept. microbiology Hahnemann U., Phila., 1947-79, dean grad. sch., 1979-84. Editor: The Clinical Laboratory as Aid in Chemotherapy of Infectious Disease, 1977. Recipient Becton-Dickinson clin. microbiology award, 1980. Fellow Am. Bd. Microbiology; mem. AAAS, Am. Public Health Assn., Am. Soc. Microbiology, N.Y. Acad. Sci., Am. Assn. Immunology, Am. Soc. Tropical Disease and Hygiene. Republican. Roman Catholic. Office: Hahnemann U Broad and Vine Sts Philadelphia PA 19102

BONDI, JOSEPH CHARLES, JR., educator, consultant; b. Tampa, Fla., Aug. 15, 1936; s. Joseph C. and Virginia B.; m. Patsy L. Hammer, Aug. 6, 1960; children: Pamela, Beth, Bradley. B.S., U. Fla., 1958, M.Ed., 1964, Ed.D., 1968. Tchr., adminstr. Hillsborough County (Fla.) Pub. Schs., 1958-65; instr. U. South Fla., Tampa, 1965-66, asst. prof., 1966-68, assoc. prof., 1968-74, prof. edn., 1974—; ptnr. Wiles, Bondi & Assocs., edn. cons. Author: ten textbooks, including Developing Middle Schools, 1972, Curriculum Planning, 1979, Practical Politics for School Administrators, 1981, The Essential Middle School, 1981. Councilman City of Temple Terrace, Fla., 1970-74, mayor, 1974-78; ruling elder Presbyterian Ch. Served with USNR, 1958-63. Mem. Fla. Assn. Supervision Curriculum and Devel. (pres.), Am. Ednl. Research Assn. Democrat. Office: Coll Edn U South Fla Tampa FL 33620

BONDS, ALFRED BRYAN, JR., college president; b. Monroe County, Ark., Nov. 3, 1913; s. Alfred Bryan Sr. and Nellie Belle (Hasley) B.; m. Georgianna Arnett, Feb. 23, 1939; children: Anna Belle, Alfred Bryan, III, Alexandra Burke, Stephen Arnett. A.B., Henderson State Tchrs. Coll., Arkadelphia, Ark., 1935; M.A., La. State U., 1936, postgrad., 1936-38; Julius Rosenwald fellow, U. N.C., 1940-41; LL.D., Ohio Wesleyan U., Cleve.-Marshall Law Sch., 1956. Asst. to dean Grad. Sch., La. State U, 1936-41; coordinating officer So. Grad. Sch. Survey and Work Conf., Tulane U., 1941-42; chief ednl. surveys br. Nat. Roster Sci. and Specialized Personnel, War Manpower Commn., Washington, 1942-43; chief edn. div. retng. and re-employment adminstrn. U.S. Dept. Labor, 1946; asst. exec. sec. Pres.'s Commn. on Higher Edn., 1946-48; dir. tng. AEC, Washington, 1948-49; Ark. commr. edn., Little Rock, 1949-53; chief U.S. Ednl. Commn., Egypt; co-dir. Egyptian-Am. Joint Commn. for Edn., 1953-55; pres. Baldwin-Wallace Coll., 1956—; Cons. FSA; council advisers U.S. Commn. Edn.; gov.'s adviser Council on Land Utilization; mem. exec. com. Bd. Control for So. Regional Edn.; dir. Ark. Tchrs. Retirement System; mem. Cleve. Com. Higher Edn. Prepared basic plan and survey for, UNESCO publs., Study Abroad, 1948; Editor: Essays on Southern Life and Culture, 1941; Contbr. articles to profl. jours. Bd. dirs. Cuyahoga Co. Library, Lake Erie Jr. Mus., St. Luke's Hosp., Cleve., YMCA, Cleve.; Mem. World Council on Methodism; v.p. Ohio Council Chs.; mem. coordinating council Gen. Conf. Meth. Ch., mem. program council; del. World Meth. Council, London, Eng., 1966, World Family Life Conf., London, 1966; del. to Consultation on Evangelism, World Meth. Council, Frankfurt, 1970; Trustee Lake Erie Opera Assn. Served from ensign to lt. (s.g.) USNR, 1943-46. Decorated officer's cross Order of Merit, West Germany; recipient medal of honor Nat. Assn., League of New Eng. Women; Grindstone award City of Berea, 1972; Distinguished Alumnus award Henderson State U., 1977. Mem. Ohio Coll. Assn. (pres. 1970), Am. Soc. Internat. Law, Am. Polit. Sci. Assn., NEA, Am. Assn. Sch. Adminstrs., Ark. Edn. Assn., Phi Gamma Mu, Omicron Delta Kappa. Methodist. Clubs: Rotarian, Mason (33 deg.), Union, University, Midday. Office: Office of Pres Baldwin-Wallace Coll 275 Eastland Rd Berea OH 44017 *

BONDURANT, BYRON LEE, agricultural engineering educator; b. Lima, Ohio, Nov. 11, 1925; s. Earl Smith and Joy Koneta (Gesler) B.; m. Lovetta May Alexander, Feb. 28, 1944; children: Connie Jane Bondurant Jaycox, Richard Thayne, Cindy Lynn Bondurant Gardino. Student, Case Inst. Tech., 1943-44, Rensselaer Poly. Inst., 1944; B.S. in Agrl. Engring., Ohio State U., 1949; M.S. in Civil Engring., U. Conn., 1953. Registered profl. engr., Maine, Ohio; registered surveyor, Maine. Dist. agrl. engr., western N.Y., N.Y. State Coll. Agr., Cornell U., 1949-50; instr. agrl. engring., extension agrl. engr., dept. agrl. engring. U. Conn., 1950-53; asso. prof. agronomy and agrl. engring., extension agrl. engr. dept. agronomy and agrl. engring. U. Del., 1953-54; prof. agrl. engring., head dept. U. Maine, 1954-64; prof. agrl. engring. Ohio State U., 1964—; also adviser to dean, later dean Coll. Agrl. Engring., Ludhiana, India, 1964-67, 69-71; vis. prof. agrl. engring. U. Nairobi, Kenya, 1974, Fulbright-Hays prof., 1979-80; project mgr. M.U.C.I.A., Mogadiscio, Somalia, 1976-78. Fellow AAAS, Inst. Engrs. (India and Kenya); mem. Indian Soc. Agrl. Engrs. (sr. life, sec.-treas. Ohio and Tri-State sects. 1972-74, vice-chmn. Ohio sect. 1983-84, dir. internat. div. 1980-82, Kishida Internat. award 1983), Am. Soc. Agrl. Engrs. (vice chmn. N. Atlantic sect. 1956-57, chmn. Acadia sect. 1961-62), AAUP, Soc. Internat. Devel. (life), Am. Soc. Engring. Edn. (chmn. agrl. engring. div.), Nat. Soc. Profl. Engrs., Maine Soc. Profl. Engrs. (pres. 1963), Sigma Xi, Sigma Pi Sigma, Tau Beta Pi, Gamma Sigma Delta, Epsilon Sigma Phi, Alpha Epsilon. Home: 265 Franklin St Dublin OH 43017 Office: 2073 Neil Ave Columbus OH 43210 *A person can approach any worthwhile goal in life only by developing and making use of the talents he has been fortunate enough to be endowed with. Hopefully this pursuit will be a rewarding one for him and for those with whom he has contact without destroying those characteristics which make him a unique individual.*

BONDURANT, EMMET JOPLING, II, lawyer; b. Athens, Ga., Mar. 16, 1937; s. John Parnell and Mary Claire (Brannon) B.; m. Kay Glenn Latimer, Sept. 6, 1958; children: Emmet Jopling, III, Katherine Elizabeth, Melissa Eileen, Christopher Scott, Miles Stephen. A.B. cum laude, U. Ga., 1958, LL.B. magna cum laude, 1960; LL.M., Harvard U., 1962. Bar: Ga. 1959. Law clk. to Judge Clement Haynsworth, Jr. U.S. Ct. Appeals, 4th Circuit, 1960-61; asso. Kilpatrick, Cody, Rogers, McClatchey & Regenstein, Atlanta, 1962-68, partner, 1968-77; partner firm Bondurant, Miller, Hishon & Stephenson, Atlanta, 1977—; vis. lectr. in antitrust law U. Ga., spring 1971; pres. Atlanta Legal Aid Soc., 1972-73; vice chmn. Ga. Gov.'s Commn. on Criminal Justice Standards and Goals, 1974. Contbr. articles on antitrust and reapportionment, right to counsel, bankruptcy, and local govt. issues to profl. jours.; co-editor: Antitrust Law Developments, 1974. Mem. Joint Atlanta-Fulton County Citizens Adv. Com. on Consolidation, 1969; chmn. Atlanta Charter Commn., 1971-72; co-chmn. Com. for Sensible Rapid Transit, Atlanta, 1971-72. Named 1 of 5 Outstanding Young Men of 1970 Atlanta Jaycees. Mem. Am. Bar Assn. (exec. com. Atlanta lawyers com. for civil rights), Ga. Bar Assn., Atlanta Bar Assn. (exec. com. 1975-81), State Bar Ga. (chmn. sect. antitrust law 1972-73), Am. Law Inst., Am. Coll. Trial Lawyers, Am. Judicature Soc., Lawyers Club Atlanta (sec. 1971-72), Kappa Alpha Order, Phi Beta Kappa, Phi Delta Phi, Phi Kappa Phi. Methodist. Home: 3630 Cloudland Dr NW Atlanta GA 30327 Office: 2200 First Atlanta Tower Atlanta GA 30383

BONDURANT, JOSEPH EUGENE, electric utility executive; b. Fulton, Ky., Aug. 11, 1929; s. Eugene and Ruby (Chapman) B.; m. Sarah Garner, Sept. 15, 1956; children: Alyson Ann, Tammy Jo. B.S.E.E., Ga. Inst. Tech., 1956. Registered profl. engr., Tex. With Gulf States Utilities Co., Beaumont, Tex., 1957—, exec. v.p., 1981—. Served with USMC, 1948-53. Home: 4910 Gladys Beaumont TX 77706 Office: Gulf States Utilities Co 350 Pine St Beaumont TX 77701

BONDURANT, STUART, physician, ednl. adminstr.; b. Winston-Salem, N.C., Sept. 9, 1929; s. Stuart Osborne B.; m. Margaret Fortescue, Aug. 28, 1954; children—Stuart, Margaret Lynn, Nancy Vance. B.S., Duke U., 1952, M.D., 1953; Sc.D. (hon.), Ind. U., 1980. Intern Duke Hosp., Durham, N.C., 1953-54, resident in internal medicine, 1954-55; resident Peter Bent Brigham Hosp., Boston, 1958-59; asst. prof. medicine Ind. U. Sch. Medicine, Indpls., 1959-61, asso. prof., 1961-66, prof., 1966-67; asso. dir. Ind. U. Cardiovascular Research Center, 1961-67; chief med. br. artificial heart-myocardial infarction program NIH, Bethesda, Md., 1966-67; prof. medicine, chmn. dept., physician in chief Albany Med. Center Hosp., 1967-74; pres., dean Albany (N.Y.) Med. Coll., 1974-79; prof. medicine, dean Sch. Medicine, U. N.C., Chapel Hill., 1979—. Contbr. articles to med. jours. Recipient Disting. Alumnus award Duke U. Sch. Medicine, 1974; Merit award Am. Heart Assn., 1975. Fellow A.C.P. (regent, pres. 1980), Am. Soc. Clin. Investigation (v.p. 1974), Assn. Am. Physicians (treas. 1974), Inst. of Medicine, Assn. Am. Med. Colls. (exec. com. 1977, adminstrv. bd. of council deans). Office: 125 MacNider Bldg #202H U NC Sch Medicine Chapel Hill NC 27514

BONDY, EUGENE L., JR., lawyer; b. N.Y.C., Dec. 14, 1920; s. Eugene L. and Irene (Kramer) B.; m. Anne Lawrence, July 14, 1950; children: Elizabeth, Priscilla, David. A.B., Harvard Coll., 1942; LL.B., Columbia U., 1948. Bar: N.Y. 1948. Asso. atty. firm Sullivan & Cromwell, N.Y.C., 1948-56, Dwight Royall Harris Koegel & Caskey, 1956-57; partner firm Rogers & Wells, N.Y.C., 1957—; dir. Hanover Ins. Co., Worcester, Mass., United Biscuits (Holdings) plc, London. Served to capt. USAAF, 1942-46; ETO. Mem. N.Y. County Lawyers Assn. (com. on securities and exchanges 1976-79), ABA, Assn. Bar City N.Y. (com. on securities regulation 1963-65, com. corp. law 1967-70), Phi Beta Kappa. Home: 908 The Parkway Mamaroneck NY 10543 Office: 200 Park Ave New York NY 10166

BONDY, MARTIN, ins. co. exec.; b. Bklyn., Dec. 2, 1929; s. Oscar Theodore and Shirley Alma B.; m. Frances Jean Accardi; children—Harold, Elise, Jennifer, Barbara, Rachael, Paul. A.B. cum laude, Bklyn. Coll., 1951. Supervising actuary N.Y. State Dept. Ins., 1954-60; asst. v.p., actuary Consol. Mut. Ins. Co., 1960-65; sr. v.p. ins. ops. Crum & Forster Corp., N.Y.C., 1965—. Author papers in field. Fellow Casualty Actuarial Soc. (past dir.); mem. Mensa. Home: 91/2 N Gate Rd Mendham NJ 07945 Office: PO Box 2387 Morristown NJ 07960

BONDY, PHILIP KRAMER, physician, educator; b. N.Y.C., Dec. 15, 1917; s. Eugene Lyons and Irene (Kramer) B.; m. Sarah B. Ernst, Mar. 18, 1949; children: Jonathan L., Jessica, Steven M. A.B., Columbia U., 1938; M.D., Harvard U., 1942; M.A. (hon.), Yale U., 1961. Intern Peter Bent Brigham Hosp., Boston, 1942-43; mem. staff Grady Meml. Hosp., Atlanta, 1943-48, chief resident medicine, 1947-48; mem. faculty Emory U., 1947, 49-52, asst. prof. medicine, 1951-52; Alexander Browne Coxe fellow physiol. chemistry Yale, New Haven, 1948-49, mem. faculty, 1948-49, 52-74, 77—, prof. medicine, 1961-65, C.N.H. Long prof. medicine, 1965-74, chmn. dept. internal medicine, 1965-72, chmn. com. outpatient services, 1960-62; chmn. med. div. Royal Marsden Hosp., 1972-77; Cancer Research Campaign prof. Inst. Cancer Research, London; cons. Ludwig Inst. Cancer Research, Zurich, Switzerland, 1972-77; asso. chief of staff for research West Haven VA Med. Ctr., 1977-83, chief staff, 1983—; Mem. med. vis. com. Brookhaven Nat. Labs., 1969-73, chmn., 1973; mem. program project com. NIH-Nat. Inst. Arthritis and Metabolic Disease, 1964-68, chmn., 1966-68; mem. exptl. biol. sect. breast cancer task force NIH-Nat. Cancer Inst., 1973-76. Editor-in-chief: Jour. Clin. Investigation, 1957-62, Yale Jour. Biology and Medicine, 1978—; editor: Diseases of Metabolism, 6th, 7th, 8th edits, Yearbook of Endocrinology and Metabolism, 1963-64; editorial bd.: Conn. Medicine, 1959-61, Yearbook of Medicine, 1954—, Medicine, 1963—, Merck Manual, 1969—, Clinics in Endocrinology and Metabolism, 1973—; editor: Cancer Topics, 1975-79. Sec. library bd., Woodbridge, Conn., 1960-67. Served to capt. M.C. AUS, 1943-46. Recipient Edward Sutliffe Brainard prize Columbia, 1938; Sigma Xi prize Emory U., 1949;

Research Career award NIH, 1962, 66. Fellow N.Y. Acad. Scis., Royal Coll. Physicians, Royal Soc. Medicine (v.p. sect. oncology 1975-77); mem. Endocrine Soc. (councillor 1964-67, publs. com. 1965-72, chmn. 1968-72), Assn. Am. Physicians, Assn. Physicians Gt. Britain and Ireland, Am. Soc. Clin. Investigation, Am. Fedn. Clin. Research, Soc. Exptl. Biology and Medicine, AAAS (chmn. Sect. N on Med. Sci. 1979), Interurban Clin. Club, Laurentian Hormone Conf., Boylston Soc., Med. Soc. Santiago (hon.), Inst. Cancer Research (London) (hon.), Phi Beta Kappa, Sigma Xi, Alpha Omega Alpha. Home: 9 Chestnut Ln Woodbridge CT 06525 Office: West Haven VA Med Center West Haven CT 06516

BONE, HUGH ALVIN, JR., polit. scientist, educator; b. Sycamore, Ill., Jan. 14, 1909; s. Hugh Alvin and Florence Lydia (Crowder) B.; m. Elizabeth Browning Purdy, June 11, 1938; children—Christopher Hugh, William James. B.A., North Central Coll., Naperville, Ill., 1931; M.A., U. Wis., 1935; Ph.D., Northwestern U., 1937. Teaching asst. Northwestern U., 1935-37; instr., asst. prof. U. Md., 1937-42, Queens Coll., N.Y.C., 1942-48; faculty U. Wash., Seattle, 1948—, prof. polit. sci., 1948—, chmn. dept., 1959-68; Summer vis. prof. Hunter Coll., 1944, Conn. Coll., 1946-48, Columbia, 1952, U. Hawaii, 1962; vis. prof. Stanford, 1949, Simon Fraser U., 1978; research asso. N.Y. State Joint Com. Indsl. and Labor Conditions, 1945-48; dir. Wash. State-No. Idaho Center Edn. in Politics, 1952-70, sec., 1970-73. Author: Smear Politics: Analysis of 1940 Campaign Literature, 1941, Grass Roots Party Leadership, 1952, American Politics and the Party System, 1971, Party Committees and National Politics, 1958, Political Party Management, 1973, The Initiative and Referendum in the United States, 1975; co-author: Washington Politics, 1960, Politics and Voters, 1981, American Government: Democracy and Liberty in Balance, 1976, The People's Right to Know, 1978, Public Policy Making: Washington Style, 1980. Ford fellow, 1954-55. Mem. Am. Polit. Sci. Assn. (exec. council 1950-52), Western Polit. Sci. Assn. (pres. 1961-62), Pacific N.W. Polit. Sci. Assn. (pres. 1959-60), Pi Gamma Mu, Pi Sigma Alpha. Home: 6001 51st St NE Seattle WA 98115

BONE, ROBERT ADAMSON, educator; b. New Haven, Aug. 12, 1924; s. Robert Burns and Isabelle (Adamson) B.; m. Dorothea Darrow, Sept. 2, 1945; children—Debora, Keira. B.A., Yale U., 1945, M.A., 1948, Ph.D., 1955. Instr. english Yale U., 1954-59; asst. prof. UCLA, 1959-64; asso. prof. Columbia Tchrs. Coll., 1965-67, prof. english, 1967—, chmn. dept. langs. and lit., 1974-80; Fulbright lectr. U. Grenoble, France, 1967-68; Sr. fellow Center for Twentieth Century Studies, U. Wis., Milw., 1973; research fellow Nat Endowment for Humanities, 1980-81. Author: The Negro Novel in America, 1958, rev. edit., 1965, Japanese edit., 1972, Richard Wright, 1969, DownHome: Short Fiction by Black Americans, 1885-1935, 1975. Mem. MLA, Am. Studies Assn., AAUP. Democrat. Home: 560 Riverside Dr New York NY 10027 Office: 525 W 120th St New York NY 10027

BONEBRAKE, ROY CONRAD, lawyer; b. Waynesboro, Pa., Dec. 2, 1906; s. Jacob M. and Lillie (Mickley) B.; m. Jean Aument, Dec. 24, 1939. A.B., Gettysburg Coll., 1928; LL.B., Stanford, 1932. Bar: Calif. bar 1932, N.Y. bar 1941. Asso. firm Call & Murphey, Los Angeles, 1932-39; counsel, v.p. Newmont Mining Corp., N.Y.C., 1939-72, also dir.; dir. O'ckiep Copper Co., Ltd., Magma Copper Co., Newmont Oil Co., Tsumeb Corp. Ltd. Mem. Calif., N.Y. bar assns., Phi Beta Kappa. Clubs: Metropolitan, Canadian (N.Y.C.). Home: 30 Sutton Pl New York NY 10022 Office: 200 Park Ave 36th Floor New York NY 10166

BONELLI, ANTHONY EUGENE, univ. adminstr.; b. Detroit, June 17, 1934; s. Anthony Emile and Ruby (Hughey) B.; m. Charlotte Schattel, Dec. 28, 1957; children—Stella Elizabeth, Anthony Eugene, John Christopher. B.Mus., Coll.-Conservatory of Music, U. Cin., 1956, M.Mus., 1958; Ph.D., Eastman Sch., 1970. Instr. piano and theory Del Mar Coll., Corpus Christi, Tex., 1958-60, asst. prof., 1960-63, asso. prof., 1963-65, prof., 1965-69, chmn. music theory dept., 1960-65, dean div. fine arts, chmn. dept. music, 1965-69; mem. faculty Eastman Sch. Music, 1963-64; prof. music, chmn. div. music So. Meth. U., 1969-74; dean Meadows Sch. Arts, 1978—; Thomas James Kelly prof. music, dean Coll.-Conservatory of Music U. Cin., 1974-78. Contbr. articles to profl. jours. Pres. Corpus Christi Arts Council, 1967-69; bd. dirs. Corpus Christi Symphony, 1965-69, Dallas Symphony, 1970-74, 78—, Cin. Symphony Orch., Cin. Ballet Co., Cin. Opera Co., Cin. Chamber Music Soc., KERA, Channel 13, Dallas Opera; mem. NEA Task Force, 1978, Tex. Commn. on Arts, 1980. Mem. Nat. Assn. Schs. Music (nat. sec. 1975-78, exec. com.), Coll. Music Soc., Music Tchrs. Nat. Assn., Music Educators Nat. Conf., Internat. Council Fine Arts Deans (pres. 1978-80), Dallas Civic Music Assn. (pres. elect 1980), Pi Kappa Lambda (pres. 1980—). Episcopalian. Office: Meadows Sch Arts So Meth U Dallas TX 75275

BONER, J. RUSSELL, editor; b. Boulder, Colo., July 25, 1930; s. J. Russell and Lillian (Morris) B.; m. Darryl Anne Alkire, Dec. 22, 1954; children—Allyn, Polly, Andrew Case. B.A., Yale, 1952. Reporter Internat. News Service, Atlanta, 1956-57, bur. mgr., Hartford, Conn., 1957-58; staff reporter U.P.I., Hartford and Buffalo, 1958-59, Wall St. Jour., Chgo., Pitts. and London, 1959-70; editor-in-chief Internat. Mgmt. mag., Maidenhead, Eng., 1970—, pub., 1977-79. Served to 1st lt. USAF, 1952-56. Home: 61 Cadogan Pl London SW 1 England Office: McGraw-Hill House Maidenhead Berkshire England

BONER, WILLIAM H., congressman; b. Nashville, Feb. 14, 1945. B.A., Middle Tenn. State U., 1967; M.A., George Peabody Coll., 1969; grad., YMCA Night Law Sch., 1978. Tchr., coach Trevecca Nazarene Coll., 1969-71; sr. staff asst. Mayor's Office, Nashville, 1971-72; dir. public relations First Am. Nat. Bank, 1972-76; mem., Tenn.; Ho. of Reps., 1970-72, 74-76; mem., Tenn.; State Senate, 1976-78; mem. 96th-97th Congresses from 5th Tenn. Dist. Office: Rm 118 Cannon House Office Bldg Washington DC 20515 *

BONERZ, PETER, actor, director; b. Portsmouth, N.H., Aug. 6, 1938; s. Christopher Andrew and Elfrieda Anne (Kern) B.; m. Rosalind Ditrapani, Dec. 14, 1963; children: Eric, Eli. B.S., Marquette U., 1960. Actor: The Premise, N.Y.C., 1961; actor: The Committee, 1963-68; actor, co-author: film Funnyman, 1967; actor, Story Theater, 1970-71, The Serial, Medium Cool, Catch-22; actor role of pres.: White House Murder Case, 1970; actor: The Goodbye People, Solari Theatre, Beverly Hills, Calif., 1978-79; TV appearances include Hallmark Hall of Fame, 1970; Hollywood TV Theatre, 1971, The Bob Newhart Show, 1972-78; dir.: E.R., 1984, It's Your Move, 1984. Served with AUS, 1961-63.

BONESIO, WOODROW MICHAEL, lawyer; b. Hereford, Tex., Dec. 27, 1943; s. Harold Andre and Elizabeth (Ireland) B.; m. Michael Ann Dougherty; children: Elizabeth, Jo Kristin, William Michael. B.A., Austin Coll., 1966; J.D., U. Houston, 1971. Bar: Tex. 1971, U.S. Dist. Ct. (we. and no. dists.) Tex. 1973, U.S. Ct. Appeals (5th cir.) 1973, U.S. Ct. Appeals (11th cir.) 1981. Law clk. to U.S. dist. Judge Western Dist. Tex., San Antonio, 1971-73; ptnr. Akin, Gump, Strause, Hauer & Feld, Dallas, 1973—; speaker profl. confs. Democratic precinct chmn. Dallas County; mem. Dallas County Dem. Exec. Com., 1982, 83; elder Northminster Presbyterian Ch., 1981. Mem. ABA, Fed. Bar Assn., Am. Judicature Soc., Dallas Bar Assn., Phi Alpha Delta, Order of Barons, U. Houston Law Alumni Assn. (chpt. pres. 1982). Office: Akin Gump Strauss Hauer & Feld 2800 Republic Bank Dallas Bldg Dallas TX 75201

BONET, FRANK JOSEPH, real estate lawyer; b. N.Y.C., Apr. 6, 1937; s. Frank and Alexandra (Roots) B.; m. Mary Ellen Mathews, July 14, 1962; children—Catherine Ann, Frank Joseph, Elizabeth Mary, Jean Marie. B.A. magna cum laude, St. John's U., 1958, LL.B. (asso. editor law rev.), 1961. Bar: Tex. bar. With Horn & Hardart Co., N.Y.C., 1961-72, corporate sec., head corporate legal dept., 1969—; real estate atty. J.C. Penney Co., Inc., 1972-77, Southwest regional real estate atty., Dallas, 1977—, also asst. corp. sec. Contbr. articles profl. jours. Capt. Merrick Democratic Club, 1965-68. Mem. Assn. Bar City N.Y., State Bar Tex. Home: 1909 Deerfield Dr Plano TX 75023 Office: 12700 Park Central Pl Dallas TX 75251

BONEY, LESLIE NORWOOD, JR., architect; b. Wallace, N.C., Jan. 25, 1920; s. Leslie Norwood and Mary Lily (Hussey) B.; m. Lillian Maxwell Bellamy, May 8, 1954; children—Emmett Hargrove Bellamy, Mary Grist Bellamy, Leslie Norwood III. B.S. in Archtl. Engring, N.C. State U., 1940. Partner Leslie N. Boney (Architect), Wilmington, N.C., 1940-41, 45—. Principal works include N.C. Nat. Bank, 1969, New Hanover Meml. Hosp, 1966, Solomon Towers Apts. for Elderly, 1970, Creekwood South Housing Project, 1971, Dormitory, U. N.C., Wilmington, 1971, Coop. Savs. & Loan Assn, 1955, all Wilmington, Rockingham Community Coll, Wentworth, N.C., 1966, Reid Ross High Sch, Fayetteville, N.C., 1968, Lenoir Community Coll, Kinston, N.C., 1968, Waccamaw Bank & Trust Co. Hdqrs. Bldg, Whiteville, N.C., 1969, Duplin Gen. Hosp, Kenansville, N.C., 1971, Residence Hall, Marietta (Ohio) Coll., 1965, Dormitories, N.C. State U. at Raleigh, 1967, U. N.C., Charlotte, 1972, Caldwell Community Coll., Lenoir, N.C., 1974, New Central Library, U. N.C., Chapel Hill, 1977, Adminstrn. bldgs, E.I. Du Pont de Nemours Co., Inc., Brunswick County, Fayetteville, Healing Springs, N.C. and Charleston, S.C. Mem. N.C. Exec. Mansion Fine Arts Com., 1966-74; exec. com. N.C. Gov.'s Adv. Com. Beautification, 1966-72; pub. relations com. N.C. State U., 1965—; mem. City-County Planning and Devel. Commn., 1960-76, vice chmn., 1972-76; N.C. adv. com. U. N.C.-Charlotte New Coll. Arch., 1965—; Trustee Union Theol. Sem., 1948-68, St. Andrews Presbyn. Coll., 1954-70; pres. N.C. State U. Archtl. Found., 1953. Served to maj., C.E. AUS, 1941-45; PTO. Decorated Bronze Star. Fellow A.I.A. (pres. N.C. 1965, pres. Eastern N.C. 1956, jud. bd. 1971-74, chmn. task force state govtl. affairs 1971-72, nat. dir. 1974-76, chancellor Coll. Fellows 1980-81); mem. N.C. Planning Assn. (pres. 1965-66), N.C. State U. Gen. Alumni Assn. (pres. 1957-58), Lower Cape Fear Hist. Soc. (pres. 1960-61), Phi Kappa Phi. Presbyn. (ruling elder, moderator Wilmington Presbytery 1968). Club: Mason. Home: 2305 Gillette Dr Wilmington NC 28403 Office: 120 S 5th St Wilmington NC 28401

BONFANTE, LARISSA, educator; b. Naples, Italy; came to U.S., 1939, naturalized, 1951; d. Giuliano and Vittoria (Dompè) B.; m. Leo Ferrero Raditsa, May 2, 1973; 1 dau., by previous marriage, Alexandra Bonfante-Warren. Student, Radcliffe U., 1950, U. Rome, 1951; B.A., Barnard Coll., 1954; M.A., U. Cin., 1957; Ph.D., Columbia U., 1966. Instr. Rutgers U., 1963; with NYU, 1963—, prof., chmn. dept. classics, 1978—; cons. in field. Author: Etruscan Dress, 1975; translator: Chronology of the Ancient World (E.J. Bickerman), 1968, The Plays of Hrotswitha of Gandersheim, 1979, Out of Etruria, 1981; contbr. articles to profl. jours. Mem. Archaeol. Inst. Am. (exec. com. 1982—), Istituto di Studi Etruschi (fgn.). Office: 25 Waverly Pl New York NY 10003

BONFIELD, ARTHUR EARL, lawyer, educator; b. N.Y.C., May 12, 1936; s. Louis and Rose (Lesser) B.; m. Doris Harfenist, June 10, 1958; 1 child, Lauren. B.A., Bklyn. Coll., 1956; J.D., Yale U., 1960, LL.M., 1961, postgrad. (sr. fellow), 1961-62. Bar: Conn. bar 1961, Iowa bar 1966. Asst. prof. law U. Iowa, 1962-65, asso. prof., 1965-66, prof., 1966-69, Law Sch. Found. prof., 1969-72, John Murray prof., 1972—; summer vis. prof. law U. Mich., 1970, U. Tenn., 1972, U. N.C., 1974, Hofstra U., 1977; cons. Adminstrv. Conf. U.S., 1968-76; gen. counsel spl. com. state adminstrv. procedure act Iowa Gen. Assembly, 1974-75; spl. counsel adminstrv. procedure exec. br. State of Iowa, 1975; chmn. com. constl. law Nat. Conf. Bar Examiners Multi-State Bar Exam, 1977—; reporter 1981 Model State Adminstrv. Procedure Act, Nat. Conf. Commrs. Uniform State Laws, 1979—; cons. Ark. State Constl. Conv., 1980; chmn. Iowa Gov.'s Com. State Pub. Records Law, 1983. Prin. draftsmen: Iowa Civil Rights Act, 1965, Iowa Fair Housing Act, 1967, Iowa Adminstrv. Procedure Act, 1975, Iowa Open Meetings Act, 1978, Iowa Civil Rights Act, 1978; contbr. numerous articles to law jours. Recipient Outstanding Service to Civil Liberties award Iowa Civil Liberties Union, 1974; U. Iowa Hancher-Finkbine Outstanding Faculty Mem. award, 1980; Frederick Klocksiem fellow Aspen Inst. Humanistic Studies, Summer 1978. Mem. Am. Law Inst., ABA (chmn. div. state adminstrv. law, mem. council sect. adminstrv. law 1976-81), Iowa State Bar Assn. (chmn. com. adminstv. law 1971—). Home: 206 Mahaska Dr Iowa City IA 52240 Office: U Iowa Law Sch Iowa City IA 52242

BONFIELD, GORDON BRADLEY, JR., oil and gas company executive; b. Grand Rapids, Mich., May 23, 1926; s. Gordon Bradley and Helen Louise (Gutekunst) B.; m. Ardella Mae Cowan, Aug. 27, 1949; children: Gordon Bradley III, Kenneth S. B.A., Colgate U., 1950; student, Advanced Mgmt. Program, Harvard, 1967. Pres., dir. Packaging Corp. Am. (and predecessor cos.), Evanston, Ill., 1974-81, chmn. bd., chief exec. officer, 1981-82; sr. v.p. Tenneco, Inc., Houston, 1982—; chmn. bd. Tenn. River Pulp & Paper Co.; dir. State Nat. Bank, Evanston.; Bd. dirs., mem. exec. com. Am. Paper Inst., Fourdrinier Kraft Board Group; trustee Inst. Paper Chemistry; pres. Am. Forest Inst., 1976-77; chmn. Forest Industries Council, 1981; mem. Forest Industries Adv. Council. Served with U.S. Army, 1944-46. Club: Skokie Country (Glencoe, Ill.). Office: Tenneco Inc Tenneco Bldg Houston TX 77002 *

BONFIGLIO, MICHAEL, surgeon, educator; b. Milw., Apr. 3, 1917; s. Joseph and Carmella (Monfre) B.; m. Ruth Marie Wells, Mar. 20, 1943; children—Michael, Robert, Joel David, Kathryn Marie. A.B., Columbia U., 1940; M.D., U. Chgo., 1943. Diplomate: Am. Bd. Orthopaedic Surgery (v.p., bd. dirs. 1972-78). Intern U. Chgo. Clinics, 1943-44, asst. resident in surgery, 1944-45, sr. resident orthopedic surgery, 1947-49, instr. orthopaedic surgery, 1949-50; practice medicine specializing in orthopaedic surgery; mem. staff U. Iowa Hosps., 1950—; chief orthopedic service Iowa City VA Hosp., 1977—; asst. prof. dept. orthopaedic surgery U. Iowa Coll. Medicine, 1951-55, assoc. prof., 1956-61, prof., 1961—; vis. prof. U. Fla., U. Tex., San Antonio, U. Chgo., Med. Coll. Wis.; vis. lectr. U. Lund, Sweden, 1971. Asso. editor: Am. Jour. Bone and Joint Surgery; Contbr. articles on orthopaedic surgery to med. jours. Bd. dirs. Coralville Ind. Sch. Dist., 1955-64, Iowa City Bd. Edn., 1964-69. Served to capt., M.C. U.S. Army. Recipient Distinguished Service award U. Chgo., 1972. Fellow A.C.S.; mem. Am. Acad. Orthopaedic Surgeons (mem. com. on pathology 1955-56), Iowa State, Johnson County med. socs., Iowa, Chgo. orthopaedic socs., Orthopaedic Research Soc. (pres. 1965-66), Am. Orthopedic Assn. (v.p. 1981-82, Shands lecture 1983), Royal Coll. Medicine, Midwest Orthopaedic Club, N.Y. Acad. Scis., Sigma Xi. Democrat. Unitarian. Home: 711- 12th Ave Coralville IA 52241 Office: Dept of Orthopaedic Surgery Univ of Iowa Iowa City IA 52242

The opportunity for an excellent public education, and the encouragement by a few of my college and medical school teachers were my good fortune.

BONFORTE, RICHARD JAMES, pediatrician, educator; b. Newark, Feb. 27, 1940; s. James Sebastian and Lillian Viola (Reiss) B.; m. Linda C. Berti, Dec. 29, 1979; 1 dau., Adrianna Marie. A.B. cum laude, Seton Hall U., 1961, M.D., Georgetown U., 1965. Diplomate: Am. Bd. Pediatrics. Intern Mt. Sinai Hosp., N.Y.C., 1965-66; pediatric resident Mt. Sinai Hosp, N.Y.C., 1966-67; chief pediatric resident Mt. Sinai Hosp., N.Y.C., 1967-68, ednl. fellow in pediatrics, 1970-72; dir. ambulatory pediatrics Mt. Sinai Med. Ctr., N.Y.C., 1972-82; dir. pediatric pulmonary and cystic fibrosis ctrs., 1972—; dir. pediatrics Beth Israel Med. Ctr., N.Y.C., 1982—; prof. pediatrics Mt. Sinai Sch. Medicine, 1982—; med. adv. council Cystic Fibrosis Found., 1976-80. Contbr. articles to profl. jours. Served with M.C. U.S. Army, 1968-70. Decorated Army Commendation medal. Fellow Am. Acad. Pediatrics; mem. Am. Thoracic Soc., Am. Coll. Chest Physicians, N.Y. Acad. Sci., N.Y. Acad. Medicine, N.Y. Pediatric Soc., Am. Soc. Microbiology, Alpha Omega Aplha. Roman Catholic. Office: 10 Nathan D Perlman Pl New York NY 10003

BONGIE, LAURENCE LOUIS, educator; b. Turtleford, Sask., Can., Dec. 15, 1929; s. Louis Basil and Madalena (Pellizzari) B.; m. Elizabeth A.E. Bryson, July 14, 1958; 1 son, Christopher. B.A., U. B.C., 1950; Ph.D., U. Paris, 1952. Lectr., U. B.C., 1953-54, instr. II, 1954-56, asst. prof. French, 1956-61, assoc. prof., 1961-66, prof., head dept., 1966—. Author: David Hume, Prophet of the Counter-Revolution, 1965, Diderot's femme savante, 1977; editor: Condillac, Les Monades, 1980; various articles. Humanities Research Council fellow, 1955-56; Can. Council sr. fellow, 1963-64, 75-76; Killam sr. fellow, 1982-83; recipient French medal, 1950. Mem. French, Internat., Am., Can. socs. 18th Century studies. Home: 3746 W 13th Ave Vancouver BC V6R 2S6 Canada

BONGIORNO, JAMES WILLIAM, electronics company executive; b. Westfield, N.Y., Apr. 2, 1943; s. Samuel Salvatore and Marjorie Ruth (Hardenburg) B. Student public schs. Profl. musician, 1961-65; engr. Hadley Labs., Pomona, Calif., 1965-66, Marantz Co., Woodside, N.Y., 1966-67; chief engr. Rectilinear Research Corp., Bklyn., 1967-68; profl. musician, writer Popular Electronics, also Audio mag., 1968-71; dir. engring. Dynaco Inc., Phila., 1972, S.A.E. Inc., Los Angeles, 1973-74; founder, pres. Gt. Am. Sound Co. Inc., Chatsworth, Calif., 1974-77; since pres. Sumo Electric Co. Ltd., West Hollywood, Calif.; ind. electronic cons. Recipient State of Art Design award Stereo Sound mag., Tokyo, 1976, 80. Mem. Audio Engring. Soc., Am. Fedn. Musicians. Republican. Patentee class A audio amplifier. Office: PO Box 4835 Santa Barbara CA 93103 *Aside from the fact that my lifetime goal has always been to design the world's finest amplifier, I also wanted it to be affordable by as many people as possible. I am happy that I have achieved this goal as there are a lot more poor people than rich people.*

BONGIOVANNI, ALFRED MARIUS, physician, educator; b. Phila., Sept. 22, 1921; s. Joseph Nathaniel and Elisa (DiSilvestro) B. B.S., Villanova U., 1940; M.D., U. Pa., 1943. Diplomate: Am. Bd. Pediatrics. Investigator Marine Lab., Woods Hole, Mass., 1939-41; instr. pharmacology Phila. Coll. Pharmacy and Sci., 1947-49; asst. physician Rockefeller Inst., 1949-51; asst. prof. Johns Hopkins Sch. Medicine, Balt., 1950-52; faculty U. Pa. Sch. Medicine, Phila., 1952—, prof. pediatrics, chmn. dept., 1963-72, prof. pediatrics, dir. pediatric endocrine div., 1973—; physician-in-chief Children's Hosp., Phila., 1963-72; prof., chmn. dept. pediatrics Sch. Health Sci., U. Ife, Nigeria, 1974-75; dean Sch. Medicine, Cath. U. P.R., Ponce, 1977-80; prof. pediatrics U. P.R., San Juan, 1978-80, Pa. Hosp., Phila., 1980—; mem. staff Hosp. U. Pa., Pa. Hosp., Children's Seashore House, Atlantic City; pediatric dir. Elwyn Inst.; Mem. sci. adv. bd. St. Jude's Hosp., Memphis; mem. com. research Am. Cancer Soc.; cons. HEW. Editorial staff: Jour. Steroid Biochemistry; Contbr. articles to profl. jours. Chmn. child devel. and mental retardation tng. rev. com. NIH; sci. adv. bd. Child Devel. Group Miss.; trustee South Jersey Med. Research Found. Recipient award League of Children's Hosp., Phila., 1962; Shaffrey medal St. Joseph's Coll., Phila., 1965; Mendel medal Villanova U., 1968. Fellow N.Y. Acad. Scis., A.C.P.; mem. Endocrine Soc. (Ciba award 1956), Endocrine Soc. P.R., Am. Soc. Clin. Investigation, Am. Pediatric Soc., Am. Acad. Pediatrics (Mead Johnson award 1957, drug dosage com.), Pediatric Research Soc., Endocrine Soc. Peru, Pediatric Soc. Guatemala, Assn. Am. Physicians, Royal Soc. Medicine (affiliate), Wilkins Pediatric Endocrine Soc. (pres. 1980—), U.S. Pharmacopoeia, Alpha Omega Alpha (hon.). Roman Catholic. Club: Union League (Phila.). Office: Pa Hosp 8th and Spruce Sts Philadelphia PA 19107

BONHAM, CLIFFORD VERNON, social worker, educator; b. Paradise, Calif., July 11, 1921; s. Leon C. and Mary M. (Horn) B.; m. Vesta H. Williamson, May 4, 1956; children: William Robert Rohde, Jr. (stepson), Larry Dean, Tami Marie. Student, San Francisco State U., 1948-49; B.A., U. Calif., Berkeley, 1951, M.S.W., 1953. Lic. clin. social worker, marriage and family counselor. Parole Agt. Calif. State Dept. Youth Authority, 1953-59, research interviewer, 1959-61, supervising parole agt., 1961-64; field instr. Grad. Sch. Social Work, Calif. State U., Fresno, 1964-67, asso. prof., 1967-74, prof., 1974—, field sequence coordinator, 1973-81; counselor Suicide Prevention Program, Fresno, Calif., 1964-70; cons. Fresno County Domestic Relations, 1967-70; commr. Fresno County Juvenile Justice Commn., 1971-81; social work cons. various hosps., Fresno, 1971—. Bd. dirs. Piedmont Pines Assn., Oakland, Calif., 1960-64. Served with USN, 1940-46. Mem. Nat. Assn. Social Workers, Calif. Probation and Parole Assn. (regional v.p. 1973-74), Acad. Cert. Social Workers (mem. state legislative com. on housing felons 1980). Democrat. Unitarian. Home: 49717 Meadowood Rd Oakhurst CA 93644 Office: 5241 N Maple St Fresno CA 93740

BONHAM, GEORGE WOLFGANG, magazine editor, foundation executive; b. Free City of Danzig, Aug. 12, 1924; U.S., 1938, naturalized, 1943; s. Walter C. and Kate M. (Selbiger) B.; children—Mary Faith, Mark David. B.A., Ohio State U., 1943; M.A., Oxford U., 1947; postgrad., Columbia U., 1948-49, D.H.L. (hon.), 1975, LL.D., 1977. Cultural info. Supreme Comdr. Allied Forces, Tokyo, N.Y.C., 1949-51, West German Govt., N.Y.C., Washington, 1951-53; account exec. public affairs firms Selvage, Lee & Chase and Communication Counsellors, N.Y.C., 1953-62; v.p. for sci. and edn. Howard Chase Assos., N.Y.C., 1963-66; pres. Sci. and Univ. Affairs, public affairs cons. to univs., New Rochelle, N.Y., 1966—; editor-at-large, pub. Change mag., 1969—; exec. dir. Council of Learning, New Rochelle, 1977—; sr. fellow Aspen Inst., N.Y.C., 1981—. Editor: Inside Academe, 1972, On Learning and Change, 1973, Colleges and Money, 1975, The Future of Foundations, 1978, In the Public Interest, 1978, The Communications Revolution and the Education of Americans, 1980; Contbr. articles to nat. mags. Trustee various nonprofit orgns.; chmn. Citizens Com. Internat. Edn.; bd. dirs. Tech. in Edn. Task Force. Served with 44th Div. M.I. AUS, 1943-45. Home: Coventry Ln New Rochelle NY 10805 also Drakes Island ME 04090 Office: 271 North Ave New Rochelle NY 10801

BONHOMME, MICHEL PAUL, shoe company executive; b. Puynormand, Gironde, France, Feb. 8, 1929; came to U.S., 1980; s. Albert and Fernande (Lacroix) B.; m. Paulette Denise Vidal, Mar. 13,

1948; children: Michele Bonhomme Clark, Daniel, Dominique. Student, Puynormand and Neuvic, France. Prodn. devel. advisor Bata Internat., Toronto, Ont., Can., 1963-67; prodn. devel. mgr. Bata - Europe, Hellocourt, France, 1967-68; mktg. mgr. Bat - Europe, Hellocurt, France, 1968-71; dep. co. mgr. Bata - Senegal, Dakar, 1971; pres. Bata - France, Vernon, 1972-75, Bata- Can., Batawa, 1975-80, Bata - U.S.A., Belcamp, Md., 1980—; dir., v.p. C H B Corp., Belcamp, 1980—. Recipient Human Relations award Shoe & Allied Industries, N.Y.C., 1980. Mem. Am. Mgmt. Assn., Harford C. of C. (Md.), Assn. U.S. Army, Riverside Devel. (dir. Belcamp 1980—). Roman Catholic. Clubs: Md. Golf and Country, Harford County Tennis. Home: PO Box 7 Belcamp MD 21017 Office: Bata Shoe Co Inc Pulaski Hwy Belcamp MD 21017

BONHORST, CARL WILLIAM, educator; b. Van Metre, S.D., Dec. 31, 1917; s. Charles Wilhelm and Minnie (Grupe) B.; m. Harriet Emma Witmer, Oct. 12, 1945; 1 dau., Lena Marie. B.S., S.D. State U., 1943; M.S., Pa. State U., 1947, Ph.D., 1949. Research asso. pharmacology U. Va., Charlottesville, 1951-52; asso. biochemist S.D. State U., Brookings, 1952-56; mem. faculty dept. chemistry U. Portland, Oreg., 1949-51, 56—, prof., 1966—, chmn. dept., 1968-73. NSF faculty fellow, 1962-63. Mem. Am. Chem. Soc., Internat. Platform Assn., Sigma Xi, Gamma Sigma Delta. Home: 4506 N Amherst St Portland OR 97203

BONI, JOHN ANTHONY, TV writer, producer; b. Phila., July 3, 1937; s. John Anthony and Duilia (Brandani) B.; m. Rita O'Connor, Sept. 11, 1967 (div. 1980); m. Donna Pode, Aug. 9, 1981; 1 dau., Alexandra Anne. B.S. in Psychology, St. Joseph's Coll., Phila., 1959. Actor, singer, 1958-71; appeared in Broadway shows, also off-Broadway shows; performed with operas; appeared with, Philip Burton Shakespeare Quartet; writer: Cher Show; co-creator, story editor: TV series When Things Were Rotten; Writer: TV spls. Flip Wilson; head writer: series Capt. and Tennille, 1976; co-head writer: America 2-Nite; co-producer: Bad News Bears; pres., Prosciutto Prodns., Ltd.; exec. script cons.: Three's Company; head writer: TV show Thicke of the Night, 1983—; Author: Drink, Drank, Drunk (spl. show on alcoholism), Public Broadcasting System (Christopher award 1974); Contbg. editor: Nat. Lampoon. Served with AUS, 1961-63. Recipient Emmy award for The Electric Company, 1973. Mem. Actors Equity Assn., Screen Actors Guild, AFTRA, Writers Guild (award for Alan King Spl. 1974). Democrat. Address: 7932 Hillside Ave Los Angeles CA 90046

BONI, ROBERT EUGENE, industrial company executive; b. Canton, Ohio, Feb. 18, 1928; s. Frank and Sara B.; m. Janet Virginia Klotz, Aug. 16, 1952; children: Susan, Leslie. B.S. in Metall. Engring, U. Cin., 1951; M.S., Carnegie Inst. Tech., 1954, Ph.D., 1954. Research engr. Armco Inc., Middletown, Ohio, 1956-61, sr. research engr., 1961-68, mgr. applied sci., 1968-70, dir. metall. research, 1970-75, asst. v.p. research and tech., 1976, v.p. research and tech., 1976-78, group v.p. energy and steelmaking, 1980-83, chief exec. officer steel group, 1982—, pres., chief exec. officer, 1983—, also dir.; dir. Res. Mining Co., First Nat. Bank Southwestern Ohio, Cin. Gas & Electric Co. Trustee U. Cin. Found.; bd. dirs. Greater Dayton Pub. TV, Inc. Served with U.S. Army, 1954-56. Recipient Disting. Engring. Alumnus award U. Cin., 1970. Mem. AIME, Indsl. Research Inst., Am. Iron and Steel Inst., Am. Iron and Steel Engrs., ASTM, Welding Research Council. Patentee in field. Home: 2607 Sherman Ave Middletown OH 45042 Office: Armco Inc Middletown OH 45043

BONICA, JOHN JOSEPH, physician; b. Filicudi Messina, Italy, Feb. 16, 1917; came to U.S., 1927, naturalized, 1928; s. Antonino and Angela (Zagame) B.; m. Emma Louise Baldetti, June 7, 1942; children: Angela, Charlotte, Linda, John. Student, LIU, 1934-37; B.S., NYU, 1938; M.D., Marquette U., 1942; D.Med.Scis. (hon.), U. Siena, 1972, D.Sc., Med. Coll. Wis., 1977, FFARCS, Royal Coll. Surgeons Eng., 1973. Diplomate: Am. Bd. Anesthesiology. Intern St. Vincent's Hosp., N.Y.C., 1942-43, resident, 1943-44; practice medicine specializing in anesthesiology; dir. anesthesiology U. Wash. Med. Center, Seattle, 1960-77, Harborview Med. Center, 1960-77; dir. dept. anesthesiology Tacoma Gen. Hosp., 1947-63, Pierce County Hosp., 1947-63; clin. asso. dept. anatomy U. Wash., Seattle, 1948-60, prof., 1960—, chmn. dept. anesthesiology, 1960-77; dir. Pain Clinic, Med. Center and affiliated hosps., 1961-79, Anesthesia Research Center, 1967-77, Pain Center, U. Wash., Seattle, 1979-83; vis. prof. and lectr. various Am., European, Latin Am., Australian, N.Z., Asiatic, Near Eastern, S. African univs.; sr. cons. anesthesiology Madigan Army Hosp., Ft. Lewis, Wash., 1947-77, VA Hosp., Seattle, 1960—; mem. anesthesia tng. com. NIH, 1965-69, chmn. gen. med. research program-project com., 1970-72, chmn. ad hoc com. on acupuncture, 1972-75; cons. ministries of health, Argentina, 1955, Brazil, 1959, Italy, 1954, 60, Sweden, 1969, Ministry Edn. Japan, 1969, Ministry Edn. and Health Venezuela, 1966, 69; mem. adv. com. Com. on Scholarly Communication with People's Republic of China, Nat. Acad. Scis., 1973-74; mem. Am. Med. Mission to People's Republic of China, 1973. Author: Management of Pain, 1953, Il Dolore, 1959, Tratamiento del Dolor, 1959, Clinical Applications of Diagnostic and Therapeutic Blocks, 1959, Manual of Anesthesiology for Medical Students, Interns and Residents, 1947, Anesthesia for Obstetrical Complications, 1965, Principles and Practice of Obstetric Analgesia and Anesthesia, Vol. 1, 1967, Vol. 2, 1969, Regional Anesthesia, 1969, Obstetric Analgesia and Anesthesia, 1972, 2d edit., 1980, Blocks of the Sympathetic Nervous System, 1981; also articles profl. jours.; Editor: (with P. Procacci, C. Pagni) Recent Advances on Pain, Pathophysiology and Clinical Aspects, 1974, Proc. Internat. Symposium on Pain, 1974, Obstetric Analgesia-Anesthesia, Recent Advances and Current Status, 1975, (with D. Albe-Fessard) Proc. First World Congress on Pain, 1976, Advances in Pain Research and Therapy, 1976, (with D. Albe-Fessard, J. Liebeskind) Proc. 2d World Congress on Pain, Vol. 2, 1979, (with V. Ventafridda) Proc. Internat. Symposium on Pain of Advanced Cancer, 1979, Proc. ARNMD-Ann. Meeting, 1978; (with L. Ng) Procs. NIH Conf. of 1979 Pain, Discomfort and Humanitarian Care, 1980; assoc. editor: Survey of Anesthesiology, 1957-72, Current Contents, 1972-78, Am. Jour. Chinese Medicine, 1973-76, Survey of Anesthesiology, 1957-72; editor: Pain, 1975—; fgn. editor: Revista Mexicana de Anestesiologia, 1958-66. Bd. dirs. Tacoma Symphony, 1951-59, Seattle Opera, 1977—. Served from lt. to maj., M.C. AUS, 1944-46. Decorated comdr. Order of Merit, Italy; recipient Silver medal Swedish Med. Soc., 1969; Gold medal for neuroscis. German Neurophysiologic Soc., 1972, U. Palermo, 1954; Disting. Service award Am. Soc. Anesthesiologists, 1973; Disting. Achievement award Modern Medicine, 1975. Fellow Am. Coll. Anesthesiologists, Internat. Coll. Anesthetists, Am. Acad. Anesthesiology, Royal Coll. Surgeons (hon., faculty anaesthetists); mem. AMA, King County, Wash. State med. socs., Am. Soc. Anesthesiologists (2d v.p. 1961, 1st v.p. 1964, pres. 1966), Assn. Univ. Anesthetists (pres. 1969), Internat. Assn. for Study Pain (chmn. orgn. com. 1973-75, pres. 1978-81), AAAS, World Med. Assn., Wash. State Soc. Anesthesiologists (pres. 1952), Internat. Anesthesia Research Soc., N.Y. Acad. Scis., Seattle, Tacoma surg. socs., Assn. des Anesthesiologistes Européens (hon.), Soc. Academic Anesthesia Chairmen, Assn. Am. Med. Colls., Am. Soc. Pharm. and Exptl. Therapy, Royal Coll. Medicine, World Fedn. Socs. Anaesthesiologists (chmn. sci. adv. com. 1968-72, sec.-gen. 1972-80, pres. 1980-84); hon. mem. Cuban Anesthesiology Soc., Mexican Anesthesiology Soc., Italian Anesthesiology Soc. (hon. pres. 1954), Argentinian Anesthesiology Soc. (hon. pres. 1955), Venezuelan Anesthesiology Soc., Colombian Anesthesiology Soc., Brazilian Anesthesiology Soc., Chilean Anesthesiology Soc., Swedish Anesthesiology Soc., Assn. Anaesthetists of Gt. Brit. and Ireland, Assn. Research on Nervous and Mental Diseases (pres. 1978); mem. Alpha Omega Alpha. Home: 4732 E Mercer Way Mercer Island WA 98040 Office: Dept Anesthesiology RN-10 Univ Washington Seattle WA 98195

BONIFACE, ROBERT LEE, electronics company executive; b. San Diego, Nov. 25, 1924; s. Frank L. and Alice M. (Wood) B.; m. Sue Alexander, Jan. 20, 1951; children: Christine McArthur, Craig. A.A. in Bus. Mgmt, Los Angeles City Coll., 1948. With Neely Enterprises, 1942-63, v.p., gen. mgr., 1952-63; gen. mgr. Hewlett-Packard Co., Palo Alto, Calif., 1963-70, v.p. mktg., 1970-74, v.p. corp. adminstrn., 1974-75, exec. v.p., 1975—, also dir.; dir. Vendo Co. Served to capt., inf. AUS, 1943-46; Served to capt., inf. U.S. Army, 1950-52. Decorated Silver Star medal, Bronze Star medal with oak leaf cluster, Purple Heart. Mem. Radio Pioneers, Electronic Reps. Assn. (past pres. So. Calif. chpt.), Horsemen's Quarter Horse Racing Assn. (pres., dir.), NAM (dir.). Home: 276 Atherton Ave Atherton CA 94025 Office: 3000 Hanover St Palo Alto CA 94304

BONIFIELD, WILLIAM C., economist, educator; b. Chgo., Sept. 29, 1934; s. Clarence W. and Evelyn L. B.; m. Donna Wilcoxon, Aug. 11, 1957; children: Cynthia, Jeffrey, Stephen, Susan. B.S., Bradley U., Peoria, Ill., 1958; Ph.D., U. Minn., 1968. Mem. faculty Wabash (Ind.) Coll., 1967-80, prof. econs., 1978-80; manpower specialist Manpower Assistance Project, Inc., Washington, 1969-70; pres. Crawfordsville Electric Light & Power co., Ind., 1975-80; prof. econs., dean Coll. Bus. Butler U., Indpls., 1981-84; v.p. edn. Lilly Endowment, Inc., Indpls., 1984—; pres. Crawfordsville Electric Light & Power Co., Ind., 1975-80; mediator-fact finder Ind. Edn. Employment Relations Bd., 1973—. Author articles in field. Commnr. Montgomery County, Ind., 1973-75. Served with AUS, 1954-56. Recipient 1st ann. award pvt. enterprise edn. Freedoms Found., 1977. Mem. Am. Econ. Assn., Indsl. Relations Research Assn., Ind. Acad. Social Scis. (dir. 1979-80). Office: 2801 N Meridian St Indianapolis IN 46208

BONILLA, CHARLES FRANCIS, chemical and nuclear engineer, emeritus educator; b. Albany, N.Y., July 11, 1909; s. Rodrigo and Lucy E. (Smith) B.; m. Sigrid Isabel Johnson, Oct. 28, 1938 (dec. May 26, 1980); children: Laurence Huguet, Elisabeth Blair. A.B., Cuenca Inst., Spain, 1925, Columbia U., 1928; B.S. in Elec. Engring, Columbia U., 1929, 1932; Ph.D., 1933. Registered profl. engr., N.Y., Md. Tutor chem. engring. CCNY, 1932-37; from asst. prof. to prof. chem. engring. Johns Hopkins, Balt., 1937-49, chmn. dept. chem. engring., 1943-49; prof. chem. engring. Columbia U., N.Y.C., 1948-78, chmn. dept., 1974-77, prof. nuclear engring., 1960-78, emeritus prof. chem. and nuclear engring., 1978—, dir. nuclear engring. program, 1950-60, TRIGA reactor program, 1960—; founder, dir. Liquid Metals Research Lab., 1948—, sr. cons., 1978—; co-founder Nuclear Heat Transfer Research Facility, 1950, dir., 1960-78; cons. Bd. Econ. Warfare, Fgn. Econ. Adminstrn., Washington, 1942-46; mem. U.S. Indsl. Mission to Brazil, 1942, U.S. Tech. Mission to Cuba, 1943, Atoms for Peace Mission to S. Am., 1956; nuclear exchange specialist to Spain, 1956, Nat. Acad. Sci. mission to Chile, 1960; cons. Phillips Petroleum Co., Bartlesville, Okla., 1942-46, U.S. Naval Engring. Expt. Sta., 1946-51, Brookhaven Nat. Lab., 1948-56, Knolls Atomic Power Lab., Schenectady, 1952-55, E.I. du Pont de Nemours & Co. (Engring. Research Lab.), 1955-62, Bettis Atomic Power Lab., 1956-62, Atomic Power Devel. Assos., 1960-68, Gen. Electric Co., 1960-75, 78, Nat. Lead Co., 1961-69, Argonne Nat. Lab., 1956-59, 70—, Kaiser Engrs., 1977-78; v.p. research Chlormetals, Inc., 1964-67; dir. Belfort Instrument Co., Balt., 1956-78, chmn. bd., 1962-72; dir. P.R. Nuclear Center, AEC, 1957-59; mem. ASME coms. K-13, K-7, 1956—, chmn. K-7, 1968-71; co-chmn. Nat. Heat Transfer Conf. (Am. Inst. Chem. Engrs. and ASME), 1983; OAS lectr. U. Mex., 1972; invited speaker on sodium research tech. Internat. Assn. for Hydraulics Research, 1983; Dir. research projects Rubber Res., Air Force, NASA, AEC, Allison div. Gen. Motors, others; hon. mem. AEC of Peru, 1956—; invited speaker on sodium research tech. Internat. Assn. Hydraulics Research, 1983. Editor, co-author: Nuclear Engineering, 1957; Editor: Nuclear Engring. and Design Jour., 1966—; Contbr. articles on indsl. chemistry, chem. and nuclear engring., heat transfer, liquid metals. Recipient Gt. Tchr. award Columbia U., 1977. Fellow Am. Inst. Chem. Engrs. (chmn. heat transfer and energy conversion div. 1979, D.Q. Kern award 1974, R.E. Wilson award nuclear engring. div. 1983); mem. Am. Chem. Soc., Am. Nuclear Soc. (A.H. Compton award 1976), Am. Soc. Engring. Edn. (chmn. Mid Atlantic sect. 1953), Phi Beta Kappa, Sigma Xi, Tau Beta Pi, Phi Lambda Upsilon, Phi Sigma Kappa. Club: Columbia U. Faculty House. Patentee in field. Home: 7 Coppell Dr Tenafly NJ 07670

BONILLA, TONY, league executive, lawyer; b. Calvert, Tex., Mar. 2, 1936. Grad., Del Mar. Coll., 1955; B.A. in Edn., Baylor U., 1958; LL.B., U. Houston, 1960. Bar: Tex. 1960. Mem. firm Bonilla, Read, Bonilla & Berlanga, Inc., and predecessors, Corpus Christi, Tex., 1960—; mem. Tex. Legislature, 1964-66, Tex. Constn. Revision Commn., 1973; pres. League of United Latin Am. Citizens, Washington; bd. dirs. League of United Latin Am. Citizens, Washington, 1972-75; chmn. Nat. Hispanic Leadership Conf., Tex. Bilingual Task Force, Task Force on Pub. Edn. Appeared, Today Show, McNeil-Lehr Report, Nightline. Mem. coordinating bd. Tex. Coll. and Univ. System, 1973-79. Mem. ABA, Tex. Trial Lawyers Assn., Corpus Christi C. of C. (dir. 1973-78). Office: League of United Latin Am Citizens 400 1st St NW Suite 716 Washington DC 20001

BONINI, WILLIAM EMORY, geophysics educator; b. Washington, Aug. 23, 1926; s. John Emory and Thelma (Scrivener) B.; m. Rose Rozich, Dec. 4, 1954; children: John Allen, Nancy Mara, James Prior, Jennifer Adra. B.S. in Engring, Princeton, 1948, M.S., 1949; Ph.D., U. Wis., 1957. Mem. faculty Princeton, 1953—, prof. civil and geol. engring., 1966-70, George J. Magee prof. geophysics and geol. engring., 1970—, chmn. water resources program, 1971-74, chmn. geol. engring. program, 1973—. Author articles in field. Pres. Yellowstone-Bighorn Research Assn., Red Lodge, Mont., 1959-60, 71-73, v.p., 1966-71. Served with USNR, 1945-46. Nat. Acad. Sci. exchange scientist to Yugoslavia, 1974; NSF sr. postdoctoral fellow U. Newcastle upon Tyne, Eng., 1963-64. Fellow Geol. Soc. Am. (sec.-treas. geophysics div. 1981-83); mem. Am. Assn. Petroleum Geologists, Soc. Exploration Geophysicists, European Assn. Exploration Geophysicists, Assn. Engring. Geologists (chmn. N.Y.-Phila. sect. 1971-72), Nat. Assn. Geology Tchrs. (councilor-at-large 1981-83, v.p. 1983-84). Research on gravity anomalies and crustal structure, seismic crustal studies, geophys. exploration engring. and groundwater studies, environmental geology. Home: 74 Robert Rd Princeton NJ 08540

BONIOR, DAVID EDWARD, congressman; b. Detroit, June 6, 1945; s. Edward John and Irene (Gaverluk) B. B.A., U. Iowa, 1967; M.A. in History, Chapman Coll., Calif., 1972. Mem. Mich. Ho. of Reps., 1973-77; mem. 95th-98th congresses from 12th Mich. Dist. Served in USAF, 1968-72. Democrat. Roman Catholic. Office: 1130 Longworth House Office Bldg Washington DC 20515 *

BONJEAN, CHARLES MICHAEL, foundation executive, sociologist, educator; b. Pekin, Ill., Sept. 7, 1936; s. Bruno and Catherine Ann (Dancey) B. B.A., Drake U., Des Moines, 1957; M.A., U. N.C., 1959, Ph.D. in Sociology, 1963. Mem. faculty U. Tex., Austin, 1963—, Hogg prof. sociology, 1974—, chmn. dept., 1972-74; exec. assoc. Hogg Found., 1974-79, v.p., 1979—; sociology editor Chandler Pub. Co., 1967-73, Crowell Pub. Co., 1973-77, Dorsey Press, 1979—; mem. council Inter-Univ. Consortium Polit. and Social Research, 1972-75; steering com. Council Social Sci. Jour. Editors, 1975-81; 2d v.p. Conf. of Southwestern Founds., 1984-85. Co-author: Sociological Measurement, 1967; Co-editor: Blacks in the United States, 1969, Planned Social Intervention, 1969, Community Politics, 1971, Political Attitudes and Public Opinion, 1972, The Idea of Culture in the Social Sciences, 1973, Social Science in America, 1976; editor: Social Sci. Quar., 1966—; cons. editor: Am. Jour. Sociology, 1974-76; Contbr. to profl. jours. Sigma Delta Chi scholar, 1957; recipient Howard Odom award U.N.C., 1963; Teaching Excellence award U. Tex. Students Assn., 1965; Drake U. Alumni Disting. Service award, 1979. Mem. Am. Sociol. Assn. (chmn. community sect. 1976-78, publs. com. 1978-81, chmn. 1979-81, pres. sect. on orgns. 1983-84, chmn. dist. scholarship com. 1982-84), Southwestern Sociol. Assn. (pres. 1972-73), Am. Polit. Sci. Assn., Southwestern Polit. Sci. Assn., Phi Beta Kappa. Home: 16310 Clara Van Trail Austin TX 78734 Office: WCH 310A Univ Tex Austin TX 78712:

BONKER, DON L., congressman; b. Denver, Mar. 7, 1937; m. Carolyn Jo Ekern, 1971. A.A., Clark Coll., Vancouver, Wash., 1962; B.A., Lewis and Clark Coll, 1964; postgrad., Am. U., Washington, 1964-66. Research asst. to Senator Maurine B. Neuberger of Oreg., 1964-66; auditor, Clark County, Wash., 1966-74; mem. 94th-98th Congresses from 3d Wash. Dist., mem. fgn. affairs com., chmn. internat. econ. policy and trade subcom., mem. select com. on aging, chmn. subcom. housing and consumer interest, chmn. House Export Task Force. Office: 434 Cannon House Office Bldg Washington DC 20515

BONN, PAUL VERNE, lawyer, real estate developer; b. N.Y.C., Mar. 11, 1939; s. Milton J. and Dorothy (Bresky) B.; m. Barbara J. Switzer, Feb. 20, 1959; children—Lori Sue, Gregg Evan; m. N. JoAnne Ashinhurst, Sept. 29, 1969 (div. June 1978); children—Wendy Lee, Rachel Lynn, Adam Benjamin; m. Janet F. Ellenson, Apr. 27, 1980. B.A., Cornell U., 1960; J.D., Yale U., 1963. Bar: Ariz. bar 1963. Since practiced in, Phoenix; law clk. Judge James A. Walsh, U.S. Dist. Ct. Ariz., 1963-64; assoc. Brown, Vlassis & Bain, 1964-67, partner, 1967-72; shareholder, officer, dir. Brown & Bain (Profl. Assn.), 1972-80; ptnr. Bonn, Muldoon & Luscher, 1982—. Pres. Greater Alvarado-Los Olivos Neighborhood Assn., 1975-77, chmn. exec. steering com., 1977-81; mem. Phoenix Urban Form Rev. Com., 1975—. Mem. Am., Ariz., Maricopa County bar assns. Home: 56 E Palm Ln Phoenix AZ 85004 Office: 805 N 2d St Phoenix AZ 85004

BONNEFOUS, JEAN-PIERRE, choreographer; b. Bourg-en-Bresse France, Apr. 9, 1943; s. Laurent and Marie-Therese (Noel) B.; m. Patricia McBride, Sept. 8, 1973. Ed., Paris Opera Sch. Tchr. Sch. of Am. Ballet, N.Y.C.; choreographer, 1975—; ballet artist-in-residence Goucher Coll., Towson, MD, 1984—. Danseur etoile, Paris Opera Ballet, 1958-70; prin. dancer, N.Y.C. Ballet, 1970-81; works include Othello, Tricolore, Une Nuit a Lisbonne, Brandenburg Concerto 4, Haydn Concerto, Quadrille. Decorated officier de L'Ordre du Merite, France). Address: 3 W 61st St New York NY 10023 Address: Goucher Coll Dance Dept Towson MD 21204 *

BONNELL, ALLEN THOMAS, coll. pres.; b. Colon, Panama, Apr. 7, 1912; s. Leander P. and Florence Matilda (Wellington) B.; m. Dorothy Peyton Haworth, June 14, 1937; children—Annette Peyton, Thomas Haworth, David Wellington, Daniel Churchill. A.B., Oberlin Coll., 1933, M.A., 1934; Exchange fellow, U. Bonn, 1935-36; Ph.D., U. Ill., 1937; Litt.D. (hon.), Drexel Inst. Tech., 1969. Instr. econs. St. Louis U., 1937-38; asst. prof. econs. U. N.C., 1938-42; relief adminstr. in unoccupied France Am. Friends Service Com., 1940-41, past chmn. fgn. service exec. com., mem. exec. bd., Phila.; with Office Fgn. Relief and Rehab., Dept. State, 1942-43, Bur. Agrl. Econs., Dept. Agr., 1943-44; div. dir. Bur. Supply, UNRRA, 1944-48; v.p. Drexel Inst. Tech., Phila., 1948-65, provost, 1963-65; pres. Community Coll. Phila., 1965—; Pres. bd. Small Bus. Opportunities Corp.; v.p. Met. Phila. Ednl. Radio and TV Corp., W. Phila. Corp.; Past chmn. family div. adv. com., mem. bd. dirs. Phila. Health and Welfare Council; bd. dirs. Nat. Center Higher Edn. Mgmt. Systems, Ednl. Projects, Inc., Nat. Commn. Coop. Edn.; mem. commn., on higher edn. Middle States Assn. Colls. and Secondary Schs.; pres. Pa. Assn. Colls. and Univs. Author: German Control Over International Economic Relations, 1930-40, Industrial Science-Present and Future, (arranged by Bonnell, edited by Ruth C. Christman), 1952. Fellow AAAS (sec. sect. indsl. sci.); mem. Am. Pub. Relations Assn. (mem. bd. Phila. Forge), Am., So. econs. assns. Mem. Soc. of Friends. Home: 11 Single Ln Wallingford PA 19086 Office: 34 S 11th St Philadelphia PA 19107

BONNER, CHARLES WILLIAM, III, community services executive, writer; b. N.Y.C., Feb. 24, 1928; s. Charles William and Priscilla (Kerley) B.; m. Margaret Lawrence, Aug. 21, 1954 (div. 1957); 1 son, Keith Lawrence; m. Theresa Frances Cipriani, July 25, 1959 (div. May 1970); children: Caroline Cipriani, Charles IV, Ian F. van der Laan; m. Jane Baldwin Gillespie, June 6, 1970 (div. 1974). Student, Columbia U., 1952-54. Fin. news staff N.Y. World-Telegram, 1952-55; public relations dir. N.Y. Multiple Sclerosis Soc., 1955-56; sect. dir. Greater N.Y. Fund, 1956-57; v.p. public relations Campbell, Inc., N.Y.C., 1957-71, v.p. public relations, dir. spl. projects Broadcasting div., 1971; exec. v.p. Popular Publs., Inc., 1972-73; pres. Communications Control Corp., N.Y.C., 1973-75; free-lance writer, artist, 1975-77; exec. dir. Voluntary Action Center, 1978-80, Neighbor-to-Neighbor, 1982—; community service vol., 1980—. Bd. dirs. Assn. Help Retarded Children, N.Y.C.; chmn. N.Y. exec. com. Hands Across the Sea. Served with U.S. Army, 1948-52; Far East Command. Recipient Vol. of Yr. United Way, 1982, Meridian House Found., 1982. Mem. Public Relations Soc. Am., Nat. Soc. Fund Raising Dirs., Environ. Writers Assn., Greenwich Power Squadron, Fairfield County Public Relations Assn., St. Nicholas Soc. Episcopalian. Home: 16 Old Wagon Rd Old Greenwich CT 06870 *To achieve any sort of success we must be strongly self-motivated, believe deeply in our ability to accomplish goals (despite, all along, the doubts of anyone), and work extremely hard. Education and culture are mostly self-inflicted and intellect a matter of reading just about everything at hand. Have fun working and be wise enough to acquire engrossing avocations and diversions. Have the wisdom to recognize the things and situations which cannot possibly be changed. Try to love all people even if we cannot like some of them; be brave and above your normal self if need be. Make decisions even if not completely right. Do not fear the untrod path. Be bold.*

BONNER, FRANCIS TRUESDALE, chemist, educator, university dean; b. Salt Lake City, Dec. 18, 1921; s. Walter Daniel and Grace (Gaylord) B.; m. Evelyn Hershkowitz, Jan. 17, 1946; children: Michael David, Joan Alisa, Rachel Pearl. B.A., U. Utah, 1942; M.S., Yale U., 1944, Ph.D., 1945. Chemist Manhattan Project S.A.M. Labs. Columbia U., 1944-46; chemist Clinton Labs., Oak Ridge, 1946-47; scientist Brookhaven Nat. Lab., Upton, N.Y., 1947-48, research collaborator, 1958—; asst. prof. chemistry Bklyn. Coll., 1948-54; Carnegie vis. fellow Harvard, 1954-55; research phys. chemist Arthur D. Little, Inc., Cambridge, Mass., 1955-58; prof. dept. chemistry SUNY-Stony Brook, 1958—, chmn. dept., 1958-70, dean for internat. programs, 1983—; cons. editor Addison-Wesley Pub. Co., Reading, Mass., 1956-77;

Rockefeller Found. adviser on curriculum, instl. devel. Universidad Del Valle, Cali, Colombia, 1961-62, 64, Ford Found. adviser, 1968; Ford Found. adviser to Universidad de Antioquia, Medellin, Colombia, 1962-64; dir. N.Y. Met. Area Center Chem. Edn. Materials Study, 1961-62; mem. com. for chemistry Coll. Entrance Exam. Bd., 1962-63; mem. adv. council on Coll. Chemistry, 1967-70; mem. coll. proficiency exam. com. chemistry N.Y. State Edn. Dept., 1963-64, 66-70; NSF sr. postdoctoral fellow Service des Isotopes Stables, Centre d'Etudes Nucleaires de Saclay, Gif-Sur-Yvette, France, 1964-65; vis. scientist Swiss Fed. Inst. for Water Resources and Water Pollution Control, Swiss Fed. Inst. Tech., Zurich, 1973; Nat. Acad. exchange visitor, Romania, 1975; mem. grants adv. panel Fund for Overseas Grants and Edn., 1968-76; bd. dirs. Research Found. State U. N.Y., 1976—. Author: (with Melba Phillips) Principles of Physical Science, 1957, 2d edit., 1971; Contbr. articles profl. jours. Mem. bd. edn. Central Sch. Dist. 6, Huntington, N.Y., 1968-72. Fellow AAAS; mem. N.Y. Acad. Scis., Am. Chem. Soc., Geochem. Soc., Am. Geophys. Union, AAUP, Sigma Xi. Home: Box 63 Setauket NY 11733 Office: Dept Chemistry State U NY Stony Brook NY 11794

BONNER, JAMES, educator; b. Ansley, Nebr., Sept. 1, 1910; s. Walter Daniel and Grace (Gaylord) B.; m. Ingelore Silberbach, Nov. 10, 1967; children by previous marriage—Joey, James Jose. A.B., U. Utah, 1931; Ph.D., Calif. Inst. Tech., 1934. NRC fellow Univs. Utrecht, Leiden, Zürich, 1934-35; faculty Calif. Inst. Tech., Pasadena, 1935-81, prof. biology, 1946-81; chmn. bd., chief exec. officer Phytogen, Inc., 1981—. Author: Plant Biochemistry, 1950, 3d edit., 1977, Principles of Plant Physiology, 1952, The Next 100 Years, 1957, The Nucleohistones, 1964, The Molecular Biology of Development, 1965, The Next 90 Years, 1967, The Next 80 Years, 1977. Mem. Nat. Acad. Sci. Home: 1914 Edgewood Dr South Pasadena CA 91030

BONNER, JAMES BROWN, public accountant; b. Herrin, Ill., Nov. 16, 1910; s. James and Ollie Francis (Knisell) B.; m. Jennie Lyon, June 22, 1935; children—James L., John G. A.B., U. Mich., 1932, M.B.A., 1933. C.P.A., Mich. Accountant Standard Oil Co. Inc., Grand Rapids, Mich., 1933-38; with Ernst & Ernst (C.P.A.'s), Detroit, 1938-45, Cunningham Drug Stores, Inc., 1945—, sec., treas., 1963-77, dir., 1959—; pvt. practice pub. accounting, Royal Oak, Mich., 1977—; sec., treas. Mich. Mchts. Council, 1967—; bd. dirs. Detroit Retail Mchts. Assn., 1968-77; past dir. Council Profit Sharing Industries. Mem. fin. com. Detroit Symphony Orch. Mem. Am. Soc. Corporate Secs. (past dir.), Am. Inst. C.P.A.'s, Am. Accounting Assn., Nat. Assn. Accountants. Republican. Presbyterian. Clubs: Detroit Athletic, Detroit Rotary. Address: 4019 Parkway Royal Oak MI 46072

BONNER, JOHN THOMAS, JR., trade assn. exec.; b. Canton, Ohio, July 3, 1921; s. John Thomas and Minnie Jane (Hemphill) B.; m. Betty Bolenbaugh, Aug. 14, 1943; 1 son, Brian. B.Sc., Ohio State U., 1943, M.A., 1946, Ph.D., 1954. Pres. Bonner, Inc. (realtors), Columbus, Ohio, 1948-55; with Ohio State U., Columbus, 1946-78, asso. prof. bus. adminstrn., 1957-61, exec. dean, 1961-68, v.p., 1968-78; v.p. edn. Ohio Assn. Realtors, Columbus, 1978—; dir. Columbus Savs. & Loan.; Civilian aide to sec. army, 1973-77; mem. Army adv. panel on ROTC, 1974-76. Author: Real Estate Practice, 1959; Contbr. profl. jours., books. Bd. dirs. Luther Found., Columbus, 1965-68, Salesian Boys Club, Columbus, Am. Playwrights Theater, Columbus Conv. Bur.; chmn. acad. adv. bd. U.S. Naval Acad., 1972-78. Served to capt. AUS, 1943-46. Decorated Purple Heart; recipient Distinguished Pub. Service medal U.S. Navy, 1971; George Washington Honor medal Freedoms Found., 1971; Outstanding Civilian Service medal U.S. Army, 1972; Exceptional Civilian Service medal USAF, 1973; Sec. of Def. Outstanding Public Service medal, 1978. Mem. Nat. Inst. Real Estate Brokers (bd. govs. 1948-51), Soc. Real Estate Appraisers (pres. 1955), Columbus Sales Execs. Club (pres. 1951), Assn. U.S. Army (pres. Central Ohio chpt. 1974-75), Assn. NROTC Colls. (v.p. 1972-78), Navy League (pres. Columbus council 1979), Beta Theta Pi, Alpha Kappa Psi, Delta Sigma Rho, Phi Eta Sigma, Beta Gamma Sigma. Clubs: Rotarian., Columbus Athletic, Columbus. Home: 4344 Ingham Ave Columbus OH 43214 Office: 200 E Town St Columbus OH 43215

BONNER, JOHN TYLER, biology educator; b. N.Y.C., May 12, 1920; s. Paul Hyde and Lilly Marguerite (Stehli) B.; m. Ruth Anna Graham, July 11, 1942; children: Rebecca, Jonathan Graham, Jeremy Tyndall, Andrew Duncan. Grad., Phillips Exeter Acad., 1937; B.Sc., Harvard U., 1941, M.A., 1942, Ph.D. (Jr. fellow 1942, 46-47), 1947; D.Sc. (hon.), Middlebury Coll., 1970. Asst. to asso. prof. Princeton U., 1947-58, prof., 1958—, chmn. dept. biology, 1965-77, 83-84; lectr. embryology Marine Biol. Lab., Woods Hole, Mass., 1951-52; spl. lectr. U. London, 1957; Bklyn. Coll., 1966; trustee Biol. Abstracts, 1958-63; Mem. bd. editors Princeton U. Press, 1965-68, 71, trustee, 1976-82. Author: Morphogenesis, 1952, Cells and Societies, 1955, The Evolution of Development, 1958, The Cellular Slime Molds, 1959, rev. edit. 1967, The Ideas of Biology, 1962, Size and Cycle, 1965, The Scale of Nature, 1969, On Development, 1974, The Evolution of Culture in Animals, 1980, (with T.A. McMahon) On Life and Size, 1983; also scientific papers.; Editor: Growth and Form, 1961, Evolution and Development, 1981; Asso. editor: Am. Scientist, 1961-69; editorial bd.: Am. Naturalist, 1958-60, 66-68, Jour. Gen. Physiology, 1962-69, Growth, 1955—, Differentiation, 1976—. Served from pvt. to 1st lt. USAC, 1942-46; staff aero. med. lab.; Wright Field, Dayton, Ohio. Sheldon traveling fellow, Panama, 1941; Rockefeller traveling fellow, France, 1953; Guggenheim fellow, Scotland, 1958, 71-72; recipient Selman A. Waksman award for contbns. to microbiology Theobold Smith Soc.; NSF sr. postdoctoral fellow, 1963. Fellow Am. Acad. Arts and Scis.; mem. Am. Soc. Naturalists, Soc. Growth and Devel., Mycol. Soc. Am., Am. Philos. Soc., Nat. Acad. Scis., Phi Beta Kappa, Sigma Xi.

BONNER, OSCAR DAVIS, educator; b. Jackson, Miss., May 9, 1917; s. Oscar Davis and Bertha Elizabeth (Basser) B.; m. Vaudie Vee Ball, Aug. 3, 1940; children—Davis Roy, Richard Edward; Timothy George. B.S., Millsaps Coll., 1939; M.S., U. Miss., 1948; Ph.D., U. Kans., 1951. Chemist Miss. Testing Labs., 1940-42, Filtrol Corp., 1946-47; mem. faculty U. S.C., Columbia, 1951—, prof. chemistry, head dept., 1960-70, R.L. Sumwalt prof. chemistry, 1970—. Contbr. numerous articles to profl. publs. Served to lt. comdr. USNR, 1942-46. Fulbright advanced research scholar, Germany, 1957-58; Fulbright lectr.-researcher, Korea, 1983-84. Mem. Am. Chem. Soc., S.C., N.Y. acads. scis., Internat. Soc. for Supramolecular Biology, Sigma Xi, Phi Lambda Upsilon. Home: 408 Crown Point Rd Columbia SC 29209

BONNER, ROBERT WILLIAM, lawyer; b. Vancouver, C., Can., Sept. 10, 1920; s. Benjamin York and Emma Louise (Weir) B.; m. Barbara Newman, June 16, 1942; children: Barbara Carolyn (Mrs. Wood), Robert York, Elizabeth Louise. B.A. in Econs. and Polit. Sci, U. B.C., 1942, LL.B., 1948. Bar: B.C. 1948, created Queen's counsel 1952. With firm Clark Wilson White Clark & Maguire, Vancouver, 1948-52; atty. gen., Province B.C., 1952-68; sr. v.p. adminstrn. MacMillan Bloedel Ltd., 1968-70, exec. v.p. adminstrn., 1970-71, vice chmn., 1971-74, pres., chief exec. officer, 1972-73, chmn. bd., 1973-74; ret., 1974; chmn. B.C. Hydro & Power Authority, 1976—; partner Bonner & Fouks, 1974—; dir. SCOR Reins. Co. Can., Internat. Nickel Co. Can. Ltd., Montreal Trust Co., Terramar Resource Corp. Mem. B.C. Legislature, 1952-69; v.p. Can. Inst. Internat. Affairs; mem. Energy Supplies Allocation Bd.; Bd. dirs. Canadian Council Christians and Jews. Served to maj. Royal Canadian Army, 1942-45; lt. col. Res. (ret.). Mem. Canadian Bar Assn., Law Soc. B.C. (life bencher), Delta Upsilon. Mem. Social Credit Party. Clubs: Mason., Vancouver; Capilano Golf and Country (West Vancouver); Union (Victoria). Home: 5679 Newton Wynd Vancouver BC Canada V6T 1H6 Office: 1055 W Georgia St Vancouver BC Canada

BONNER, STEPHEN BARNES, financial holding corporation executive, lawyer; b. Mpls., Sept. 13, 1946; s. John Farrington and Jane (Stinchfield) B.; m. Kristin Linda Nyen, Aug. 25, 1967; children: Stephen, Ann, Leslie. B.A., Amherst Coll., 1968; J.D., William Mitchell Coll. Law, 1972. Bar: Minn., Ky., Ill. Various positions with law dept. Prudential Life Ins. Co. Am., Minn., N.J., Ill., 1968-82, v.p., counsel, 1980-82; sr. v.p., gen. counsel Capital Holding Corp., Lousiville, 1982—. Chmn. govt. relations com. Met. United Way Ky., Louisville, 1983. Mem. ABA, Minn. Bar Assn., Ky. Bar Assn., Chgo. Bar Assn., Hennepin County Bar Assn. Office: Capital Holding Corp Commonwealth Bldg 4th Ave at Broadway Louisville KY 40201

BONNER, THOMAS NEVILLE, history and higher education educator; b. Rochester, N.Y., May 28, 1923; s. John Neville and Mary (McGowan) B.; children by previous marriage: Phillip Lynn, Diana Joan. A.B., U. Rochester, 1947, M.A., 1948; Ph.D., Northwestern U., 1952; LL.D., U. N.H., 1974, U. Mich., 1979. Acad. dean William Woods Coll., 1951-54; prof. history, chmn. dept. social sci. U. Omaha, 1955-62; Fulbright lectr. U. Mainz, Germany, 1954-55; prof., head history dept. U. of Cin., 1963-68, v.p. acad. affairs, provost, 1967-71; pres. U. N.H., Durham, 1971-74, Union Coll.; chancellor Union U., Schenectady, 1974-78; pres. Wayne State U., Detroit, 1978-82, disting. prof. history and higher edn., 1983—; vis. prof. U. Freiburg, W.Ger., 1982-83. Author: Medicine in Chicago, 1957, The Kansas Doctor, 1959, (with others) The Contemporary World, 1960, Our Recent Past, 1963, American Doctors and German Universities, 1963; Editor, translator: (Jacob Schiel) Journey Through the Rocky Mountains, 1959. Democratic candidate for Congress, 1962; legis. aide to Senator McGovern, 1962-63. Served with Radio Intelligence Corps AUS, 1942-46; ETO. Guggenheim fellow, 1958-59, 64-65. Mem. Am. Hist. Assn., Orgn. Am. Historians, Phi Beta Kappa, Pi Gamma Mu, Phi Alpha Theta. Home: 408 Hillboro Birmingham MI 48010

BONNER, WALTER D(ANIEL), JR., phys. biochemist; b. Salt Lake City, Oct. 22, 1919; s. Walter Daniel and Grace Amber (Gaylord) B.; m. Josephine Annette Silberberg, May 13, 1944; children—Andrew Daniel, Brian Timothy. B.Sc. in Chemistry, U. Utah, 1940; Ph.D. in Biology, Calif. Inst. Tech., 1946; M.A. (hon.), U. Pa., 1971. Research asso. in biology Harvard U., 1946-49; Am. Cancer Soc. and USPHS fellow Molteno Inst., U. Cambridge, Eng., 1949-52; biochemist Smithsonian Instn., Washington, 1952-53; asst. prof. botany Cornell U., 1953-57, asso. prof., 1957-59; prof. phys. biochemistry Johnson Research Found., U. Pa., 1959-75, prof. biochemistry and biophysics Sch. Medicine, 1975—; mem. molecular biology panel NSF, 1960-63, biochem. program dir., 1974-76. Contbr. numerous articles to profl. jours. Guggenheim fellow and Churchill Coll. overseas fellow, 1967-68. Mem. Am. Chem. Soc., Am. Soc. Biol. Chemistry, Am. Soc. Plant Physiology, Biochem. Soc. (London), Biophys. Soc., N.Y. Acad. Sci., Sigma Xi. Office: Dept Biochemistry/Biophysics Sch Medicine U Pa Philadelphia PA 19104

BONNER, WALTER JOSEPH, lawyer; b. N.Y.C., Nov. 18, 1925; s. Walter John and Marie Elizabeth (Guerin) B.; m. Barbara E. Degnan, Dec. 27, 1951; children: Kevin P., Keith M., Barbara A., Susan E. A.B. cum laude, Cath. U. Am., 1951; J.D., Georgetown U., 1955. Bar: U.S. Supreme Ct., D.C., Va. Law clk. to judge U.S. Ct. Appeals D.C. Circuit, 1954-55; judge U.S. Dist. Ct., Washington, 1955-56; asst. U.S. dist. atty. for D.C., 1956-60; partner firm Bonner, O'Connell, & Scheininger, Washington.; Adj. prof. Georgetown U. Law Center, 1957-58, 67—, chmn. bd. advisors legal intern program, 1965—; appt. to Jud. Conf., 1983. Trustee Lawrence E. Dean Meml. Scholarship Fund, Georgetown U. Med. Center. Served with USNR, 1943-46; now capt. JAGC Res. Fellow Am. Coll. Trial Lawyers; mem. Bar Assn. of D.C., Va. State Bar, Va. Trial Lawyers Assn., Fed., Am. bar assns., Res. Officers Assn., Naval Res. Lawyers Assn., Naval Res. Assn., Phi Delta Phi. Roman Catholic. Clubs: Officers and Faculty (U.S. Naval Acad.); Cath. U. Am. Alumni. Home: 9628 Parkwood Dr Bethesda MD 20814 Office: 900 17th St Washington DC 20006

BONNER, WILLIAM NEELY, JR., energy company executive, lawyer; b. Wichita Falls, Tex., June 12, 1923; s. William Neely and Irma (McKibbin) B.; m. Nancy McFarlane, Dec. 15, 1949; children: William Neely, III, Blake McFarlane. Student, Rice U., 1940-42; J.D., U. Tex., 1948. Bar: Tex. 1948, U.S. Supreme Ct. bar 1958. Staff atty. Phillips Petroleum Co., Houston, 1948-52; gen. counsel, sec. Tex. Gas Corp. and New Ulm Corp., Houston, 1952-55; sr. corp. atty. Transco Energy Co., Houston, 1955—; bd. dirs., mem. corp. editorial bd. Tex. Law Rev., Inc., 1950-61. Served with USAF, 1943-45. Decorated D.F.C. with oak leaf cluster, Air medal with 4 oak leaf clusters. Mem. Am. Bar Assn., Tex. Bar Assn., Houston Bar Assn., Fed. Energy Bar Assn., Houston Museum Fine Arts, Phi Delta Phi, Phi Kappa Psi. Republican. Episcopalian. Clubs: Houston Country, Univ., Allegro, Paul Jones. Home: 5000 Longmont Dr 9 Houston TX 77056 Office: 2800 Post Oak Blvd Houston TX 77056

BONNER, ZORA DAVID, petroleum company executive; b. San Antonio, Feb. 23, 1919; m. Dorothy Shaw, Feb. 28, 1942; children: David Calhoun, Julie Ann. B.S. in Chem. Engring., U. Tex., 1941. With Gulf Oil Corp., after 1941, former pres., chief exec. officer, Houston, also dir.; vice chmn. Tesoro Petroleum Corp., 1980—. Active Houston Mus. Natural Sci.; nat. bd. dirs. Jr. Achievement; mem. adv. council Engring. Found., U. Tex., Austin. Served to lt. comdr. USN, 1941-46. Recipient Disting. Grad. award, Disting. Engring. Grad., U. Tex., 1968. Mem. Am. Petroleum Inst. (dir.). Clubs: Petroleum, Giraud, Dominion Country (San Antonio); Ramada (Houston); University. Address: 8700 Tesoro Dr San Antonio TX 78286

BONNET, JUAN AMEDEE, nuclear engineer, environmental research administrator; b. Santurce, P.R., Apr. 22, 1939; s. Juan A. and Josefa L. (Diez) B.; m. Wally Vargas, Dec. 27, 1963; children: Juan, Carlos, Antonio, Luis, Gerardo, Gabriel. B.S. in Chem. Engring, U. Mich., 1960, Ph.D. in Nuclear Engring, 1971; M.S. in Nuclear Tech, U. P.R., 1961. Registered profl. engr., P.R. Safety and analysis engr. P.R. Water Resources Authority, 1962-67, head nuclear engring. dept., 1971-73, head environ. protection, quality assurance and nuclear divs., 1972-75, asst. exec. dir. planning and engring., 1975-77; dir. Center for Energy and Environment Research, U. P.R., San Juan, 1977—; mem. adj. faculty P.R. Technol. U., 1973-77; adhonorem prof. Sch. Medicine, San Juan, 1979—; adj. prof. Engring. Sch. Mayaguez, P.R., 1979-80; asst. prof. Bayamon Technol. U. Coll., 1980—; cons. Energy and Environ. Engring., 1971—; pres. Profl. Engrs., Architects and Surveyors Exam. Bd. P.R., 1979—. Contbr. articles on energy and environ. matters to profl. publs. Bd. dirs. Rincon Fund Raising, P.R. Soc. Mentally Retarded Children, 1967; mem. Caribbean Islands Directorate of UNESCO-U.S. Com. Men and the Biosphere, 1979—; bd. dirs. U. P.R., 1978—, So. Solar Energy Center, 1979-82. Named Outstanding Young Scientist of P.R. Jaycees, 1978, Disting. Engr. Tau Beta Pi, 1978; Sci. award P.R. Mobil Oil, 1981. Mem. Am. Nuclear Soc., P.R. Inst. Chem. Engrs. (pres. 1977-79), Interam. Confedn. Chem. Engrs. (gen. sec. 1976-78), Internat. Solar Energy Assn., Nat. Soc. Profl. Engrs., P.R. Chemist Soc. (editorial bd. 1979—), Pan Am. Union of Assns. Engrs. (energy com. 1972—), Ateneo de P.R., P.R. Acad. Arts and Scis., Internat. Assn. Hydrogen Energy, Assn. Engrs. and Surveyors (dir. 1967-76), Sigma Xi, Phi Eta Mu. Roman Catholic. Home: Calle 1 No H-7 Los Frailes Norte Guaynabo PR 00657 Office: GPO Box 3682 San Juan PR 00936 *In Puerto Rico, public needs are so very great that public service is especially challenging and its spiritual rewards are very gratifying. The opportunity to serve humanity enlarges one's spirit.*

BONNETTE, RICHARD DAVID, advertising agency executive; b. Larchmont, N.Y., Oct. 27, 1935; s. Norman P. and Eleanor M. (Marshall) B.; m. Catherine L. Pinkey, Dec. 27, 1982; children by previous marriage: Elizabeth, Jennifer, David. B.A., Iona Coll., 1958. Brand mgr. Lehn & Fink Products Corp., N.Y.C., 1959-63; account exec. Benton & Bowles Inc., N.Y.C., 1963-69; sr. v.p., sr. mgmt. rep. Batten, Barton, Durstine & Osborn, N.Y.C., 1969—, dir., 1982—. Chmn. Non-Partisan Com. Sch. Bd., Bronxville, N.Y., 1976-77. Served with U.S. Army, 1958-59. Mem. Phi Kappa Psi. Home: 100 W 57th St New York NY 10019 Office: Batten Barton Durstine & Osborn Inc 383 Madison Ave New York NY 10017

BONNEY, GEORGE WILLIAM, judge; b. Midwest, Wyo., Aug. 22, 1923; s. George William and Bertha Anne (Ormsby) B.; m. Kerminette Schweers, Aug. 27, 1949; children—Susan Mary, George William III, Michael Kermit. A.B., U. Wis., 195O, LL.B., 1952. Bar: Calif. bar 1952. Since practiced in, San Jose; partner firm Rankin, Oneal, Luckhardt, Center, Ingram, Bonney, Marlais & Lund, 1967-72; judge Santa Clara Municipal Ct., 1972-80, presiding judge, 1979-80; judge Santa Clara County Superior Ct., 1980—. Dist. chmn. Santa Clara County chpt. Boy Scouts Am., 1967—, mem. exec. bd., 1967—; commr. Parks and Recreation Commn., City of Saratoga, 1970—. Served as pilot USAAF, 1942-46. Mem. Conf. Calif. Judges, Wis. Alumni Assn., Santa Clara County Trial Lawyers Assn. (pres. 1971), Santa Clara County Conf. Municipal Judges (pres. 1977), Sigma Phi Epsilon. Club: San Jose Rotary. Home: 12740 Carniel Ave Saratoga CA 95070 Office: 1675 Lincoln St Santa Clara CA 95050 *A necessary part of the education of our young, often overlooked, is the teaching of the concept that the rule of law is fundamental and essential to a truly free society. No person who fails to recognize his individual responsibility to that concept will ever possess or enjoy freedom.*

BONNEY, HAL JAMES, JR., judge; b. Norfolk, Va., Aug. 27, 1929; s. Hal J. and Mary (Shackelford) B.; m. Marie McBee, July 4, 1963 (div. 1979); children: David James, John Wesley. B.A., U. Richmond, 1951, M.A., 1953; J.D., Coll. William and Mary, 1969. Instr. Norfolk public schs., 1951-61; supt. Douglas MacArthur Acad., 1961-67; practiced law, 1969-71; law clk. U.S. Dist. Ct., 1969; prof. U. Va., 1964-71, Coll. William and Mary, 1969-71; U.S. bankruptcy judge, Norfolk, 1971—. WTAR radio tchr. Wesleymen Bible class, 1962—; Treas. Wesleymen Found., Inc., Billy Graham Crusades, 1974-76. Recipient S.A.R. Good Citizenship medal; U. Richmond Gold medal. Mem. Am. Bar Assn., Nat. Conf. Bankruptcy Judges (pres. 1983), Va. State Bar, Norfolk and Portsmouth Bar Assn., Nat. Film Soc., Am. Film Inst., Phi Alpha Theta, Pi Sigma Alpha, Phi Alpha Delta. Methodist. Clubs: Masons, Shriners. Home: 1357 Windsor Point Rd Norfolk VA 23509 Office: 408 US Court House Norfolk VA 23501 *Throughout a life of considerable adversity but signal joys, I have been touched by the Master, by the grace of God, and this eternal heritage I would but pass on as a legacy to my sons.*

BONNEY, JOHN DENNIS, oil co. exec.; b. Blackpool, Eng., Dec. 22, 1930; s. John P. and Isabel (Evans) B.; m. Ann Auriol Ross, Nov. 12, 1960; 4 children. B.A., Hertford Coll., Oxford U., Eng., 1954, M.A., 1959; LL.M., U. Calif., Berkeley, 1955. Oil adviser, Middle East, 1959-60; fgn. ops. adviser, asst. mgr., then mgr. Standard Oil Co. of Calif., San Francisco, 1960-72, v.p., 1972—. Clubs: World Trade (Commonwealth); (San Francisco); Univ. (N.Y.C.); Oxford and Cambridge (London). Office: 225 Bush St San Francisco CA 94120

BONNEY, SAMUEL ROBERT, lawyer; b. Dallas, Mar. 10, 1943; s. Herbert Staats, Jr. and Anna Margaret (Hudnall) B.; m. Emily Ellen Cox, Dec. 5, 1970 (div. Apr. 1978); children: Samuel Robert, II, Heather Noel, Sarah Emily. B.A., Austin Coll., Sherman, Tex., 1965; J.D., U. Tex., 1968. Bar: Tex. 1968. Since practiced in, Dallas; partner firm Bonney, Wade & Stripling, 1968—; dir. Stewart Oxygen Co., Guaranty Bank Bus. Devel. Bd. Served with AUS, 1969. Mem. Am., Tex., Dallas bar assns. Clubs: Dallas Country., Plaza Athletic. Home: 3838 Turtle Creek Blvd Dallas TX 75219 Office: 1020 Plaza of Americas North Tower LB 352 Dallas TX 75201

BONNEY, WESTON LEONARD, banker; b. Lewiston, Maine, Sept. 9, 1925; s. Leonard W. and Olive (Jones) B.; m. Elaine Gilbert, June 29, 1946; children—Melody Elaine, Merrilee, Michael, Melissa Jane. A.B in Econs, Bates Coll., Lewiston, 195O. With Union Mut. Life Ins. Co., 1950-52, Fed. Res. Bank Boston, 1952-63; corp. services officer First Nat. Bank Boston, 1963-65; with Depositors Corp., Augusta, Maine, 1966-74, pres., 1970-74; also dir.; with Depositors Trust Co., Augusta, 1965-74, pres., sr. adminstrv. officer, 1967-71, pres., chief exec. officer, 1971-74; also dir.; pres., dir. Cape Ann Bank & Trust Co., Gloucester, Mass., 1975-78, Yankee Bancorp., Gloucester, 1975-76, Bank of New Eng., 1976-80, Bay State Nat. Bank, Lawrence, Mass., 1978—; sr. v.p., dir. Bank New Eng. Corp., Boston. Trustee Bates Coll., Lawrence Gen. Hosp., Lawrence Strategy.; bd. mgrs. Lawrence YMCA. Served with USNR, 1943-46. Mem. Greater Lawrence C. of C. (dir.), Mass. Bankers Assn. (research and planning com.). Home: 176 Farrwood Dr Bradford MA 01830 Office: 238 Essex St Lawrence MA 01842

BONNYCASTLE, LAWRENCE CHRISTOPHER, corporate director; b. Russell, Man., Can., Nov. 19, 1907; s. Angus L. and Ellen M. (Boulton) B.; m. Mary F. Andrews, Jan. 20, 1934; children—John Christopher, Michael Kurt, Stephen Rodney. B.A., U. Man., 1929, Oxford U., 1932. Treas. No. Life Assurance Co. of Can., 1938-39; treas. John Labatt, Ltd., 1940-45, v.p., asst. gen. mgr., 1948-49; gen. mgr. Nat. Life Assurance Co. of Can., 1949-52, dir., 1951-77; v.p. mng. dir. Canadian Corporate Mgmt. Co., Ltd., 1952-63, pres., 1963-72, vice chmn., 1972-79, dir., 1979—; dir. Eldorado Nuclear Ltd. Fellow Actuarial Soc. Clubs: Toronto, University (Toronto). Home: 9 Wychwood Park Toronto ON Canada Office: Commerce Ct West Toronto ON Canada

BONNYCASTLE, RICHARD ARTHUR NORTHWOOD, investor and financial consultant; b. Winnipeg, Man., Can., Sept. 26, 1934; s. Richard Henry and Mary Frances (Northwood) B. B. Commerce, U. Man., 1956. Group rep. Gt. West Life Co., Winnipeg, 1956-58; underwriter Richardson Securities Co., Winnipeg, Toronto, Ont., Can., 1963-68; pres. Harlequin Enterprises Ltd., Toronto, 1968-70, chmn. bd., 1968-82; chmn., chief exec. officer Cavendish Investing Ltd., Calgary, 1970—; chmn. Electra Investments (Can.) Ltd.; co-chmn. MacLeod Stedman Inc.; dir. Camel Oil & Gas Ltd., Pagurian Corp. Ltd., Sulpetro Ltd., C&T Energy Resources. Bd. dirs. Jr. Achievement of So. Alta.-Calgary; bd. govs. Trinity Coll. Sch. Mem. Can. Thoroughbred Horse Soc. (pres.), Jockey Club Can. (steward), N.Am. Wildlife Assn. (trustee), Zeta Psi. Clubs: St. Charles Country (Winnipeg); Royal Canadian Yacht (Toronto, Ont.); Ont. Jockey (trustee); Ranchmen's (Calgary); Manitoba (Winnipeg); Toronto Lawn and Tennis. Home: Rural Route 5 Calgary AB T2P 2G6 Canada

Office: 3300 Bow Valley Sq 11 205 5th Ave SW Calgary AB T2P 2V7 Canada

BONNYMAN, GEORGE GORDON, mining company executive; b. Knoxville, Tenn., Oct. 22, 1919; s. Alexander and Frances (Berry) B.; m. Isabel Fouche Ashe, May 20, 1942; children: Isabel Ashe (Mrs. Brooke Herford Stanley), George Gordon, Anne Berry (Mrs. John M. Lippincott), Alexander Ashe, Brian Andrew. B.S., Princeton U., 1941. With Blue Diamond Coal Co., Knoxville, 1945—, asst. gen. mgr., gen. mgr., pres., 1953-70, chmn. bd., 1970-74, pres., chmn., 1974—. Served as capt. F.A. AUS, World War II. Decorated Silver Star, Bronze Star with oak leaf cluster, Purple Heart. Mem. Princeton Engring. Soc., Soc. Mining Engrs., Am. Inst. Mining, Metall. and Petroleum Engrs., Tau Beta Pi Assn. Home: 6633 Sherwood Dr Knoxville TN 37919 Office: Blue Diamond Coal Co PO Box 10008 Knoxville TN 37919

BONO, JACK ALEX, research laboratory executive; b. Cokeburg Junction, Pa., May 10, 1925; s. Dominick and Maria (Tosi) B.; m. Bette Jackson, Feb. 28, 1946; children: Meri Bono McCarthy, Bette, Steve, John. B.S., Northwestern U., 1946. With Underwriters Labs. Inc., 1946—, now pres., Northbrook, Ill. Served with USNR, 1943-46. Fellow Soc. Fire Protection Engrs., ASTM; mem. Nat. Soc. Profl. Engrs. Episcopalian. Club: Union League (Chgo.). Office: 333 Pfingsten Rd Northbrook IL 60062 *

BONO, PHILIP, aerospace engineer; b. Bklyn., Jan. 13, 1921; s. Julius and Marianna (Culcasi) B.; m. Gertrude Camille King, Dec. 15, 1950; children: Richard Philip, Patricia Marianna, Kathryn Camille. B.E., U. So. Calif., 1947; postgrad., 1948-49. Research and systems analyst N.Am. Aviation, Inglewood, Calif., 1947; engring. design specialist Douglas Aircraft Co., Long Beach, Calif., 1948-49; preliminary design engr. Boeing Airplane Co., Seattle, 1950-59; dep. program mgr. Douglas Aircraft Co., Santa Monica, Calif., 1960-62, tech. asst. to dir. advanced launch vehicles and space stas., Huntington Beach, Calif., 1963-65; br. mgr. advanced studies, sr. staff engr. advanced tech. McDonnell Douglas Astronautics Co., Huntington Beach, 1966-73; sr. engr.-scientist Douglas Aircraft Co., Long Beach, 1973-83; engring. specialist Northrop Advanced Systems Div., Pico Rivera, Calif., 1984—; pres. Cal-Pro Photo Accessories, Costa Mesa, 1973—; lectr. seminars, univs. and insts. including Soviet Acad. Scis., 1965. Author: Destination Mars, 1961, (with K. Gatland) Frontiers of Space, 1969; Contbr. articles to profl. jours., chpts. in books. Served with USNR, 1943-46. Recipient Golden Eagle award Council Internat. Nontheatrical Events, 1964, A. T. Colwell merit award Soc. Automotive Engrs., 1968, M.N. Golovine award Brit. Interplanetary Soc., 1969, cert. of recognition NASA, 1983; named engr. of distinction Engrs. Joint Council, 1971, Knight of Mark Twain, 1979. Fellow AAAS, Royal Aero. Soc., Brit. Interplanetary Soc. (editorial adv. bd.), AIAA (asso.); sr. mem. Am. Astronautical Soc.; mem. N.Y. Acad. Scis., Internat. Acad. Astronautics, ASME. Inventor recoverable single-stage space shuttle. Home: 1951 Sanderling Circle Costa Mesa CA 92626 Office: 8900 E Washington Blvd Pico Rivera CA 90660 *Some call it stubbornness, to others it may appear foolhardy, but I prefer to classify it as determination—therein lies the most powerful driving force which a person can possess for infusing others with the conviction of an idea whose time has come.*

BONO, SONNY SALVATORE, singer, composer; b. Detroit, Feb. 16, 1935; m. Donna Rankin; 1 dau., Christy; children: Santo, Jean; m. Cher LaPiere, Oct. 27, 1964 (div.); 1 dau., Chastity. Song writer, later artist and repertoire man for, Speciality Records; singer with, Cher as team Sonny and Cher, 1964-74; star, The Sonny and Cher Show, 1976-77; now soloist night club act; numerous recs., TV, concert and benefit appearances; composer, lyricist, appearance in: Good Times, 1966; films include: Escape to Athena, 1979, Airplane II—The Sequel, 1982; producer film: Chastity, 1969; Composer: A Cowboy's Work is Never Done. Address: care John LaRocca & Assocs 3907 W Alameda Ave Suite 101 Burbank CA 91505 *

BONOMI, JOHN GURNEE, lawyer; b. N.Y.C., Aug. 13, 1923; s. Felix A. and Bessie (Gurnee) B.; m. Patricia Updegraff, Aug. 22, 1953; children: Kathryn, John. B.A., Columbia U., 1947; J.D., Cornell U., 1950; LL.M., N.Y.U., 1957. Bar: N.Y. bar 1952. Asst. dist. atty., N.Y. County, 1953-60; spl. counsel subcom. antitrust and monopoly U.S. Senate, 1960-61; spl. asst. atty. gen. N.Y. State, 1961-62; chief counsel com. grievances Assn. Bar City N.Y., 1963-76; vis. scholar Harvard U. Law Sch., 1976-77; counsel firm Anderson, Russell, Kill & Olick, N.Y.C., 1977-80; practice law, N.Y.C., 1980—; mem. com. grievances and admissions U.S. Circuit Ct. Appeals for Second Circuit, 1983—. Columnist: N.Y. Law Jour; contbr. articles to legal jours. Trustee Village of Tarrytown, N.Y., 1965-67, 68-72; councilman, dep. supr. Town of Greenburgh, N.Y., 1974. Served with USAAF, 1943-45. Mem. ABA (spl. com. on evaluation disciplinary enforcement 1967-70, cons. spl. com. on evaluation ethical standards), N.Y. State Bar Assn. (vice-chmn. com. grievances 1970-71), Am. Law Inst. (spl. com. peer rev. 1978-80), Assn. Bar City N.Y., Inst. Jud. Adminstrn., Nat. Orgn. Bar Counsel (pres. 1970-71, chmn. spl. com. on Watergate discipline 1974-76). Democrat. Club: Harvard (N.Y.C.). Home: 131 Deertrack Ln Irvington NY 10533 Office: 41 E 42d St New York NY 10017

BONOMO, VICTOR A., soft drink company executive; b. N.Y.C., June 16, 1929; m. Sally Dorothy Alberts, Sept. 11, 1948; children: Nancy, Cynthia Bonomo Mueller, Sandra Bonomo Werner. B.S., U. Pa., 1949. Vice pres. Gen. Foods Corp., White Plains, N.Y., 1957-69; pres. United Vinters, Inc., San Francisco, 1969-70, Pepsi-Cola Co., Purchase, N.Y., 1970-77; exec. v.p. PepsiCo. Inc., 1977—, also dir.; dir. Whirlpool Corp. Trustee Manhattanville Coll. Home: 32 Canaan Close New Canaan CT 06840 Office: Pepsico Inc Purchase NY 10577

BONOSARO, CAROL ALESSANDRA, govt. ofcl.; b. New Brunswick, N.J., Feb. 16, 1940; d. Rudolph William and Elizabeth Ann (Betsko) B.; m. Donald D. Kummerfeld, Sept. 8, 1962 (div. Jan. 1970); m. Athanasios Chalkiopoulos, Nov. 21, 1976; 1 dau., Melissa. B.A., Cornell U., 1961; postgrad., George Washington U., 1961-62. Analytical statistician Office Mgmt. and Budget, Exec. Office of Pres., Washington, 1961-66; asst. dir. fed. programs div. U.S. Commn. on Civil Rights, Washington, 1966-68, dir. Office Fed. Programs, 1968-69, dir. tech. assistance div., 1969-71, spl. asst. to staff dir., 1972, dir. women's rights program, 1972-79, asst. staff dir. for program planning and evaluation, 1979-80, asst. staff dir. congressional and public affairs, 1980—. Vice chmn. Nat. Com. on Asian Wives of U.S. Servicemen, 1975—; Pres. Catholics for a Free Choice, 1980—. Mem. Exec. Women in Govt., Sr. Exec. Assn. (dir. 1981—). Democrat. Home: 8608 Fenway Rd Bethesda MD 20817 Office: 1121 Vermont Ave NW Washington DC 20425

BONSAL, DUDLEY BALDWIN, judge; b. Bedford, N.Y., Oct. 6, 1906; s. Stephen and Henrietta Fairfax (Morris) B.; m. Lois Abbott Worrall, May 16, 1931 (dec. Aug. 1981); children: Lois (Mrs. Frederic B. Osler, Jr.), Stephen; m. Lucia Turner Faithfull, Mar. 5, 1983. A.B., Dartmouth Coll., 1927; LL.B., Harvard, 1930. Bar: N.Y. bar 1932. Asso. firm Curtis, Mallet-Prevost, Colt & Mosle, N.Y.C., 1930-38, mem. firm, 1938-42, 45-61; U.S. dist. judge So. dist. N.Y., 1961—; judge Temporary Emergency Ct. Appeals of U.S., 1977—; chief counsel Office Inter-Am. Affairs, Washington, 1942-45; mem. U.S. del. Inter-Am. Conf. on Problems of War and Peace, Mexico City, 1945; legal adviser Fgn. Bondholders Protective Council, Conf. on German Debts, London, 1951, 52; mem. Internat. Commn. of Jurists, Geneva, Switzerland, 1953-73; chmn. spl. com. on fed. loyalty-security program Assn. Bar City N.Y., 1955-57; mem. com. on criminal justice act Jud. Conf. of U.S., 1964-79, chmn., 1974-79. Trustee Inst. Internat. Edn., 1948-64, Sterling and Francine Clark Art Inst., Williamstown, Mass., 1960-73, William Nelson Cromwell Found., Practising Law Inst. Fellow Am. Bar Found. (dir. 1967-75); mem. Am., N.Y. bar assns., Assn. Bar City N.Y. (pres. 1958-60), N.Y.C. Council on Fgn. Relations. Club: Century Assn. (N.Y.C.). Home: St Mary's Church Rd Bedford NY 10506 Office: US Ct House Foley Sq New York NY 10007

BONSALL, JOSEPH SLOAN, JR., singer, mem. vocal group; b. Phila., May 18, 1948; s. Joseph Sloan and Lillie Maude (Collins) B.; m. Barbara Marion Holt, Oct. 24, 1969; 1 dau., Jenifer Lynn. Mem. gospel singing groups, 1966-73; tenor singer, partner Oak Ridge Boys, 1973—; co-owner Silverline-Goldline Music Pub. Cos. (Recipient Grammy award 1970, 74, 76, 77). Dove award (12) Gospel Music Assn.; named Vocal Group of Year Country Music Assn., 1978. Mem. Country Music Assn., AFTRA, Nat. Acad. Rec. Arts and Scis., Acad. Country Music. Office: care Jim Halsey Co Inc 5800 N Skelly Dr Tulsa OK 74135 *

BONSER, CHARLES FRANKLIN, college dean; b. Youngstown, Ohio, Feb. 15, 1933; s. William Harley and Anita (Bromley) B.; m. Nancy A. Gebhardt, July 3, 1955; children: Catherine, Jeffrey, Andrew. B.A., Bowling Green State U., 1954; M.B.A., Ind. U., 1961, D.B.A., 1965. Asst. dir. Bus. Research Sch. Bus. Ind. U., Bloomington, 1960-63; dir. state Tax Policy Bur. Bus. Research Sch. Bus. Ind. U., Bloomington, Ind., 1963-65, assoc. dir., Bloomington, 1965-69; faculty lectr. Bur. Bus. Research, Sch. Bus. Ind. U., Bloomington, 1963-65, asst. prof. bus. adminstrn., 1965-67, asst. prof., 1967-81, prof. bus. adminstrn. and pub. and environ affairs., 1971—; assoc. dean Sch. Bus., Ind. U., 1969-71, spl. asst. to pres., 1971-72; dean Sch. Pub. and Environ. Affairs (Ind. U.), 1972—; bus. econs. editor Irving Cloud Pub. Co., Chgo., 1966—; mem. Panel to select White House Fellows, 1980-81; mem. com. on career entry U.S. CSC, 1976—; gov.'s designee for adminstrn. Fed. Intergovtl. Personnel Act, State of Ind., 1972-82; Ind. rep. Midwest Intergovtl. Personnel Council, 1972—; bd. dirs Nat. Inst. Pub. Mgmt., Washington, 1976—, chmn., 1976—. Co-author: Developing Patterns in Indiana Post High School Education, 12 vols., 1971, Indiana Economic Development Study, 3 vols., 1969-71, Indiana Library Needs and Resources Study, 1968-69, Business Taxation in Indiana, 1966; editor: Ind. Bus. Rev., 1966-69; assoc. editor: Bus. Horizona, 1965-68. Served with USAF, 1961-63. Recipient Sagamore of Wabash award, Gov. Ind., 1965, 74, Spl. citation U.S. CSC, 1974, 78. Mem. Nat. Assn. Schs. Pub. Affairs Adminstrn. (pres. 1976-77, exec. council 1973-78), Am. Soc. Pub. Adminstrn. (exec. council 1975-76, 81-82), Nat. Acad. Pub. Adminstrn., Am. Pub. Works Assn., Ind. Soc. Pub. Adminstrn. (pres. 1975-76), Beta Gamma Sigma, Pi Alpha Alpha (nat. pres. 1980—). Home: 4625 Inverness Woods Bloomington IN 47401 Office: School Pub and Environ Affairs Ind Univ 400 7th St Bloomington IN 47405

BONSIGNORE, JOSEPH JOHN, publishing company executive; b. Bklyn., Dec. 9, 1920; s. James Joseph and Isabel (Johnson) B.; m. Madelyn Anne Kleutsch, Sept. 27, 1945; children: Mark, Judith, Jay, Andrea, Donna, Regina. B.A., Trinity Coll., Hartford, Conn., 1942; M.A. (H.E. Russell fellow 1942-44), U. Chgo., 1945. Mgr. editorial prodn. Time, Inc., Chgo., 1945-69; with Smithsonian Mag., Washington, 1969—, pub., 1981—; cons. on formation new mags. Sec. Ill. Central Commuters Assn., 1951, pres., 1953; Democratic precinct leader Rich Twp., Ill., 1949-69; pres. Rich Twp. Dem. Club, 1965-66; Program chmn. Christian Family Movement, 1963-68, pres. Chgo. unit, 1960-62; pres. Civil Rights Orgn., South Suburban Cook County, 1967-68. Mem. Pi Gamma Mu. Home: 9105 Santayana Dr Fairfax VA 22030 Office: 900 Jefferson Dr Washington DC 20560 *I hope that I can be ever appreciative that I have been able to stretch my capacity to its fullest potential. I wish that I may ever realize that other persons have great potential and that only circumstances have prevented them from stretching their capacities. I am also determined not only to realize that other persons have great potential but to work toward the creation of environments in which those capacities may be extended and in which people may thereby flourish.*

BONTE, FREDERICK JAMES, educator, physician; b. Bethlehem, Pa., Jan. 18, 1922; s. Frederick R. and Harriett (Stoudt) B.; m. Cecile Poetzel; children—Frederick W., Stephen J., John A., Therese A., Suzanne M., Ann E. B.S., Western Res. U., 1942, M.D., 1945. Diplomate: Am. Bd. Radiology (trustee 1969-75), Am. Bd. Nuclear Medicine. Intern Huntington Meml. Hosp., Pasadena, Cal., 1945-46; resident Univ. Hosp., Cleve., 1948-52; practice medicine, specializing in radiology and nuclear medicine, Dallas, 1956—; mem. faculty Western Res. U. Sch. Medicine, 1952-56, asst. prof., 1952-56, chief radiotherapy and nuclear medicine, 1954-56; prof. U. Tex. Southwestern Med. Sch., Dallas, 1956—, chmn. dept. radiology, 1956-73, dean, 1973-80; dir. Nuclear Medicine Research Center, 1980—; Mem. bd. Nat. Council Radiation Protection and Measurements, 1966-71; radiology tng. com. Nat. Insts. Gen. Med. Scis., USPHS, 1966-70, residency rev. com. radiology AMA, 1966-69, adv. and rev. coms. VA, 1972—; Founding trustee Am. Bd. Nuclear Medicine, 1971-73, chmn., 1977-80. Contbr. articles to profl. jours. Served to capt. USAAF, 1946-48. Fellow Am. Coll. Radiology, Am. Coll. Nuclear Physicians; mem. Am. Roentgen Ray Soc. (mem. exec. com), Radiol. Soc. N.Am., Nuclear Med. Soc. (dir.), AMA (del.), Sigma Xi, Alpha Omega Alpha. Research on exptl. nuclear medicine and radiology. Home: 11138 Wonderland Trail Dallas TX 75229 Office: 5323 Harry Hines St Dallas TX 75235

BONTOYAN, WARREN ROBERTS, chemist, laboratory administrator; b. Balt., Aug. 2, 1932; s. Cesario Baron and Dorothy Bertha (Hunter) B.; m. Gladys Frances Daughaday, May 3, 1958; children: Warren Wendel, Suzanne Cheri. B.S., U. Md., 1956. Food and drug insp. FDA, Balt., 1956-58; research chemist U.S. Dept. Agr., Beltsville, Md., 1958-60; head chemist methods devel., tng., standards and quality control lab. EPA, Beltsville, 1960-78, chief chem. and biol. investigation br., 1978—, also dir. labs.; mem. vector and biol. control expert panel WHO.; U.S. rep. to Collaborative Internat. Pesticide Adv. Council; mem. expert panel pesticide chemistry FAO. Editor: EPA Manual of Chem. Analysis of Pesticides and Devices, 1975; Contbr. articles to profl. jours. Fellow Assn. Ofcl. Analytical Chemists (gen. referee pesticide formulation analysis), Am. Inst. Chemists; mem. Am. Chem. Soc., Assn. Am. Pest Control Ofcls., Assn. Ofcl. Analytical Chemists (pres.), Alpha Chi Sigma. Home: 3910 Meeting House Perry Hall MD 21128 Office: Bldg 306 ARC East Beltsville MD 20705 *I have never met a person who was not superior to me in some aspect of his or her character, talent, or ability.*

BOO, BEN, state legislator; b. Mpls., Jan. 21, 1925; s. Benjamin Charles and Henrietta (Mergens) B.; m. Mary Daley, Oct. 12, 1948; children: Chris, Peter, Michael, Mary, Richard, Matthew. Student, U. Minn., 1943, U. Mo., 1944. Adminstrv. asst., Minn., 1950-58; purchasing agt. St. Louis County, Minn., 1958-66; mayor of Duluth, Minn., 1966-75; exec. dir. Western Lake Superior San. Dist., 1975-79; dir. Upper Great Lakes Regional Commn., 1979—; mem. Minn. State Legislature from dist. 8B. Home: 102 E Arrowhead Rd Duluth MN 55803 Office: State Capitol Saint Paul MN 55155

BOOCHEVER, ROBERT, federal judge; b. N.Y.C., Oct. 2, 1917; s. Louis C. and Miriam (Cohen) B.; m. Lois Colleen Maddox, Apr. 22, 1943; children: Barbara K., Linda Lou, Ann Paula, Miriam Deon. A.B., Cornell U., 1939, LL.B., 1941. Bar: N.Y. 1944, Alaska 1947. Asst. U.S. atty., Juneau, 1946-47; partner firm Faulkner, Banfield, Boochever & Doogan, Juneau, 1947-72; asso. justice Alaska Supreme Ct., 1972-75, 78-80, chief justice, 1975-78; judge U.S. Ct. Appeals for 9th Circuit, 1980—; chmn. Alaska Jud. Council, 1975-78; mem. appellate judges seminar N.Y.U. Sch. Law, 1975; mem. Conf. Chief Justices, 1975-79, vice chmn., 1978-79; mem. adv. bd. Nat. Bank of Alaska, 1968-72. Chmn. Juneau chpt. ARC, 1949-51, Juneau Planning Commn., 1956-61; mem. Alaska Devel. Bd., 1949-52, Alaska Jud. Qualification Commn., 1972—; adv. bd. Juneau-Douglas Community Coll. Served to capt. inf. AUS, 1941-45. Named Juneau Man of Year, 1974. Fellow Am. Coll. Trial Attys.; mem. ABA, Alaska Bar Assn. (pres. 1961-62), Juneau Bar Assn. (pres. 1971-72), Am. Judicature Soc. (dir. 1970-74), Am. Law Inst., Juneau C. of C. (pres. 1952, 55), Alaskans United (chmn. 1962). Clubs: Rotary (pres. Juneau 1966-67), Marine Meml., Wash. Athletic, Juneau Racket, Juneau Yacht, San Francisco Yacht. Home: 2950 Douglas Hwy Juneau AK 99801 Office: Court and Office Bldg Pouch U Juneau AK 99811

BOOCOCK, SARANE SPENCE, sociologist; b. Evanston, Ill., May 7, 1935; d. William Kenneth and Barbara (Gilbreath) Spence; 1 son, Paul Morris. B.A., Vassar Coll., 1957; M.A., Rutgers U., 1961; Ph.D., Johns Hopkins U., 1966. Cost analyst Prudential Life Ins. Co., Newark, 1957-58; social caseworker, child welfare analyst N.J. Bd. Child Welfare, New Brunswick, 1958-59; group leader European Traveling Seminar, 1959; instr., research asst. Rutgers U., 1959-62; asso. Center for Study Social Organ. Schs.; research asso. dept. social relations Johns Hopkins U., 1962-68; asst. prof. sociology U. So. Calif., 1968-70, assoc. prof., 1970-73; sociologist Russell Sage Found., N.Y.C., 1973-76; vis. prof. sociology Yale U., 1974-76; prof., chmn. dept. sociology Rutgers U., New Brunswick, 1976—; co-founder Academic Games Assocs., Balt., 1968, also dir.; vis. prof. Hebrew U., Jerusalem, 1973, Yale U.; vis. lectr. U. Stockholm, U. Goteborg, Sweden, 1973. Author: (with Matilda W. Riley) Sociological Research Methods, 2 vols, 1963, An Introduction to the Sociology of Learning, 1972; assoc. editor: Sociology of Edn., 1969—; contbg. author, co-editor: Simulation Games for Learning, 1968; co-founder, editorial bd.: Simulation and Games, 1969-78; editor, 1973-77; contbg. editor: Ednl. Tech, 1967-69; contbg. author, co-editor: Turning Points: Historical and Sociological Essays on the Family, 1978; contbr. articles to profl. jours. Carnegie Corp. grantee, 1965; NASA grantee, 1969; ESSO Edn. Found. grantee, 1972-73; Russell Sage Found. grantee, 1974-75, 75-77; Nat. Inst. Edn. grantee, 1978-79; recipient Dart award, 1970. Mem. Am. Sociol. Assn., Sociol. Research Assn. Office: Dept Sociology Rutgers U New Brunswick NJ 08903

BOODEY, CECIL WEBSTER, JR., educator; b. Yonkers, N.Y., June 10, 1931; s. Cecil Webster and Dorothy (Mitchell) B.; m. Phyllis Ann Stensland, July 9, 1955; children: William Mitchell, John Barton, Pamela D. Ellen. B.A., U. N.H., 1953; postgrad., Princeton U., 1953-54; M.A. Penfield scholar, NYU, 1960. Tng. program Arabian-Am. Oil Co., Dhahran, Saudi Arabia, 1954; with N.Y. Telephone Co., Westchester, 1957-62; instr. polit. sci. Fashion Inst. Tech., N.Y.C., 1964-68, asst. prof., 1968-72, assoc. prof., 1972-80, prof., N.Y.C., 1980—, chmn. dept. social sci., 1971-73. Treas. Richards Boys Club, Yonkers, 1962-63; v.p. Manasquan-Brielle Little League, N.J., 1969; sec. Manasquan Babe Ruth League, 1972—; Democratic municipal chmn., Manasquan, 1970-78; pres. 11th Ward Democratic Club, Yonkers, 1962; bd. dirs. Manasquan Area Human Relations Council, 1973—, Brookdale Community Coll., Lincroft, N.J., 1979—. Served with U.S. Army, 1954-56. Fellow Ford Found., 1953-54. Mem. Am. Polit. Sci. Assn., Assn. Asian Studies, Internat. Studies Assn., Asia Soc., Am. Profs. for Peace in the Middle East, Phi Kappa Phi, Pi Mu Epsilon, Pi Gamma Mu. Methodist. Home: 80 Allen Ave Manasquan NJ 08736 Office: Fashion Inst Tech 227 W 27th St New York NY 10001 *To assist young adults to develop their qualities for critical thinking and to encourage them to participate in extra-curricular activities—these are the goals of my life.*

BOOHER, EDWARD E., former publisher; b. Dayton, Ohio, July 29, 1911; s. Wilfred Elsworth and Cora Maybelle (Middlestader) B.; m. Selena Read Knight, Aug. 5, 1939 (div. 1961); children: David Knight, Carol Read, Bruce Edward; m. Agnes Martin Whitaker, 1961. A.B., Antioch Coll., 1936. Interviewer, sec. N.Y. State Employment Service, N.Y.C., 1935; joined McGraw-Hill Book Co., Inc., 1936, became v.p., 1944, dir., 1951—, exec. v.p., 1954-60, pres., 1960-68, chmn. bd., chief exec. officer, 1968-70; pres. books and edn. services group McGraw-Hill, Inc., 1970-76; dir.; dir. Nat. Enquiry Into the Prodn. and Dissemination of Scholarly Knowledge, Am. Council Learned Socs., 1976-78; publishing cons., 1978—; dir. Holtzbrinck Pub. Group, Scholastic Mags., Inc. Adv. bd.: Partisan Review. Trustee Asia Soc.; trustee Hazen Found. Clubs: Century, Nassau. Office: 34 Wilson Rd Princeton NJ 08540

BOOK, EDWARD R., resort company executive; b. Cleve., May 9, 1931; s. Raymond John and Grace Elizabeth (Bergstresser) B.; m. Inga M. Scheyer, Feb. 14, 1953; children: Sandra Book Liddick, Edward R., Frederick A. B.S. in Hotel Adminstrn, Pa. State U., 1954. Restaurant mgr. Howard D. Johnson Co., Harrisburg, 1950-55; food and beverage mgr., asst. mgr. Hotel Harrisburger, Harrisburg, 1956-60; v.p., gen. mgr. Hotel Bethlehem, Pa., 1960-68; gen. mgr. Hospitality Motor Inn, Cleve., 1968-69, Hotel Hershey, Pa., 1969; mng. dir. Hotel Hershey and Country Club, 1970; dir. hostelry div. HERCO, Inc. (formerly Hershey Estates), 1971, v.p., 1973-74, exec. v.p., asst. to pres., 1974, chmn. bd., pres., 1974-80; chmn. bd., chief exec. officer Hershey Entertainment & Resort Co., 1980—; bd. dirs. Hershey Trust Co. Mem. bd. mgrs. Milton Hershey Sch., M.S. Hershey Found.; chmn. M.S. Hershey Found., 1981—; trustee Pa. State U., vice chmn. bd. trustees, 1982—; trustee Harrisburg Area YMCA; campaign chmn. Tri-County United Way, 1980, pres., 1982-83; mem. exec. bd. Keystone Area council Boy Scouts Am.; elder Derry Presbyn. Ch., Hershey; chmn. adv. com. Milton S. Hershey Med. Center of Pa. State U., 1977-82; mem. Ams. for Competitive Enterprise System, 1977-82. Served to 1st lt. U.S. Army, 1954-56. Named Pa. Travel Man of Year, 1976; recipient order of achievement Lambda Chi Alpha, 1976. Mem. Pa. Travel Industry Adv. Council (chmn. 1972-76), Pa. State Hotel and Restaurant Soc. (pres. 1964), Harrisburg Area C. of C. (pres. 1975-76), Am. Hotel and Motel Assn. (industry adv. council, long range planning com., trustee ednl. inst., resort com.), Nat. Inst. for Food Service Industry (trustee 1979-82), Travel Industry Assn. Am. (chmn. 1981-82), Pa. State U. Alumni Assn. (pres. 1977-79); mem. Pa. State U. fund council). Clubs: Skal, Rotary. Home: 36 Brownstone Dr Hershey PA 17033 Office: 300 Park Blvd Hershey PA 17033

BOOK, JOHN ALPH, paper co. exec.; b. Jefferson County, Ill., Apr. 1, 1915; s. Hollice E. and Ethel (Bumpus) B.; m. Helen Jane Biasella, Dec. 18, 1948; children—James L., John Robert, JoAnne, Janet. B.A. in Edn, So. Ill. U., 1940; J.D., U. Mo. at Kansas City, 1955; LL.M., N.Y. U., 1961. Bar: Mo. bar 1956. Lawyer Dale Beal & Assos., Kansas City, 1956-57; dir. labor relations Chase Bag Co., N.Y.C., 1957-58, v.p. indsl. relations, 1958-60, v.p. mfg., 1960-64, v.p., dir. mfg., 1965-71, exec. v.p., 1971-73, pres., 1973—, also dir.; dir. Arkell Safety Bag Co., Strawberry Hill Press, Western Textile, Inc. Served with AUS, 1945-46. Mem. Am., Mo., Ind., Kansas City bar assns., Kappa Phi Kappa.

Republican. Presbyn. Clubs: Landmark (Stamford, Conn.); Westchester Country (Rye, N.Y.); Cloud (N.Y.C.). Home: 23 Meeting House Rd Greenwich CT 06830 Office: 2 Greenwich Plaza Greenwich CT 06830

BOOKATZ, SAMUEL, painter, sculptor; b. Phila., Oct. 3, 1910; s. Barnett and Ann (Cohen) B.; m. Helen Meyer, Oct. 12, 1963. Student, John Hunting Poly. Inst., 1928-31, Cleve. Mus. Inst. Art, 1931-35, Boston Mus. Sch. Art, 1935-37, Harvard U., 1935-37, London U., car7-38, Grand Chaumiere, Paris, 1938, Collorossi, Paris, 1939, Am. Acad., Rome, 1938-41. Commd. officer U.S. Navy, advanced through grades to comdr., combat artist, ret., 1964. One man shows, group shows; represented: permanent collections Phillips Collection, Washington, Corcoran Gallery Art, Washington, Library of Congress, Washington, Smithsonian Instn., Washington, Norfolk Mus., Va., Cleve. Mus. Art, Am. Acad., Rome; White House artist (under Pres. Rosseveld Adminstrn.); portraits of Franklin D. Rossevelt, 1943, Mrs. Elinor Roosevelt, 1943, Gov. of Pa David L. Lawrence, 1964. Inst. of Allendo fellow Mexico, 1954; Ford grantee, 1962. Home: 9823 Leeberg Pike Vienna VA 22180 Office: 2700 Que St NW Washington DC 20007

BOOKBINDER, HYMAN H(ARRY), organization executive; b. Bklyn., Mar. 9, 1916; s. Louis and Rose (Palger) B.; m. Bertha Losev, Dec. 25, 1938 (dec. 1976); children: Ellen, Amy. B.S.S., CCNY, 1937; postgrad., N.Y. U., New Sch. Social Research. Economist Amalgamated Clothing Workers, 1938-43, 46-50; labor adv. Nat. Prodn. Authority, 1951-53; legis. rep. CIO, 1953-55, AFL-CIO, 1955-60; spl. asst. to sec. commerce, 1961-62; mem. President's Commn. on Status of Women, 1961-63; dir. Eleanor Roosevelt Meml. Found., 1963-64; exec. officer President's Task Force on Poverty, 1964; asst. dir. OEO, also spl. asst. to vice president U.S., 1964-67; Washington rep. Am. Jewish Com., 1967—; mem. President's Commn. on Holocaust, 1979—; bd. dirs. Pax World Peace Fund, 1972—, Am. Immigration and Citizenship Conf., 1950—; Washington chmn. Ad Hoc Coalition for Ratification of Genocide Treaty, 1970—; Chmn. public policy adv. com. Corp. Public Broadcasting, 1972-77. Author: To Promote the General Welfare, 1950, also articles; editor: Washington Letter, 1970—; moderator: Washington Scene radio series, 1971-75. Bd. dirs. Religion and Labor Found., Ctr. for Nat. Policy, Friends of VISTA, Micronesia Inst., Am. Jewish-Israeli Relations Inst. Served with USNR, 1943-45. Recipient Nat. Brotherhood citation NCCJ, 1977. Mem. Nat. Assn. Inter-group Relations Ofcls., Am. Vets. Com. Democrat. Clubs: B'Nai B'rith, Workmen's Circle. Home: 6308 Bannockburn Dr Bethesda MD 20817 Office: 2027 Massachusetts Ave NW Washington DC 20036 *Born into a world that soon exposed me to depression, war, and the Holocaust, I fast acquired an almost compulsive interest in public affairs. It has been my good fortune to be able to combine career development with opportunities to help shape public policy. Government's principal purpose must indeed be to implement the great promise of America—the securing of life, liberty, and the pursuit of happiness. Above all, this has meant for me the lifting of discriminatory barriers to self-fulfillment—race, religion, national origin. The Hebrew sage Rabbi Hillel, has provided the guideline for my life's work: "If I am not for myself, who will be for me? But if I am only for myself, what am I?"*

BOOKBINDER, JACK, artist, educator; b. Odessa, Russia, Jan. 15, 1911; came to U.S., 1922; s. Israel and Rebecca (Biener) B.; m. Bella Braverman, Sept. 16, 1936; children: Michael Richard, Carl Fredric. Student, Pa. Acad. Fine Arts, 1930-34; B.S. in Edn., U. Pa., 1934; M.F.A., Tyler Sch. Art, Temple U., Phila., 1946; D.F.A., Moore Coll. Art, Phila., 1976. Lectr. art history Barnes Found., Merion, Pa., 1937-44; lectr. art edn. U. Pa., 1946-59; lectr. art history Pa. Acad. Fine Arts, 1949-61; lectr. art edn. Pa. State U., summer 1950; dir. art edn. Phila. Pub. Schs., 1959-77; instr. painting and lithography Kutztown State Coll., Pa., summer 1962; juror nat. and local art exhbns. Exhibited one-man shows, Pa. Acad. Fine Arts, Phila., 1948, 52, Phila. Art Alliance, Phila., 1954-64, Woodmere Art Gallery, Phila., 1955, Nessler Art Gallery, N.Y.C., 1961, William Penn Meml. Mus., Harrisburg, 1974, Gross-McLeaf Gallery, Phila., 1976, one-man shows., Long Beach Island Found., N.J., 1980, one-man shows, Marjorie Cahn Gallery, Los Gatos, Calif., 1980, group shows, Rochester Print Club, N.Y., 1948, Royal Acad., London, 1962, Met. Mus. Art, N.Y.C., 1966, Palacio de Bellas Artes, Mexico City, 1968, Artists Equity Exhbn., Tel Aviv, Israel, 1978, U. Del., 1980, Phila. Print Club, Phila. Art Alliance, 1981; represented in permanent collections, Pa. Acad. Fine Arts, Phila. Mus. Art, Library of Congress, Nat. Gallery of Art, Washington, Yale U. Art Gallery, New Britain (Conn.) Inst., Temple U., Kutztown State Coll., Converse Coll., S.C., Mus. Fine Arts, Abilene, Tex., Reading (Pa.) Mus. and Art Gallery, Frye Mus., Seattle, Widener Coll., Chester, Pa., Bradley U., Peoria, Ill., Gulf Coast Art Ctr., San Jose (Calif.) Mus. Art, Lafayette (Ind.) Art Ctr.; author: Invitation to the Arts, 1944; contbr. to: Compton's History of Sculpture, 1957 edit.; producer, performer: TV shows Art and the Artist, Artists U.S.A., 1955-76. Recipient Gen. Alumni award Temple U., 1964, Superachiever award Juvenile Diabetes Found., 1976. Mem. NAD, Am. Watercolor Soc., Nat. Soc. Painters in Casein and Acrylics (v.p.), Allied Artists Am., Audubon Artists, Phila. Art Alliance, Phila. Watercolor Club (v.p.). Home: 323 S Smedley St Philadelphia PA 19103 Studio: 1720 Sansom St Philadelphia PA 19103

BOOKE, SORRELL, actor; b. Buffalo, Jan. 4. Appeared in Off-Broadway and Broadway plays; Broadway debut The Sleeping Prince; appeared in over: 150 television series including Omnibus, Route 66, Soap, What's Happening; regular television appearances on: TV series The Dukes of Hazard, 1979—; film appearances include: Special Delivery, What's Up Doc?, Freaky Friday, The Other Side of Midnight *

BOOKER, EUGENE M., diversified manufacturing company executive. B.A., U. Minn., 1954. Product supt. Booker & Wallestad, 1954-58; pres. Thermotech Plastics, Inc., 1958-70, ITT Thermotech, 1970-77; v.p. ops., pres. Roper Plastics subs. Plant Industries, 1977-79; v.p. corp. planning McQuay-Perfex, Inc., 1979-81, sr. v.p., group exec., 1981-82, exec. v.p., 1982-83, pres., chief operating officer, 1983—, also dir.

BOOKER, HENRY GEORGE, educator, scientist; b. Barking, Essex, Eng., Dec. 14, 1910; came to U.S., 1948, naturalized, 1952; s. Charles Henry and Gertrude Mary (Ratcliffe) B.; m. Adelaide Mary McNish, July 9, 1938; children—John Ratcliffe, Robert William, Mary Adelaide, Alice. Student, Palmer's Sch., Grays, Essex, 1921-30; B.A., Christ's Coll., Cambridge, 1933, Ph.D., 1936; Guggenheim fellow, Cambridge U., 1954-55. Fellow Christ's Coll., 1935-48; sci. officer Ministry Aircraft Prodn., London, 1940-45; lectr. Cambridge U., 1945-48; prof. elec. engring. Cornell U., 1948-65, dir. sch. elec. engring., 1959-63; asso. dir. Center Radio Physics and Space Research, IBM; prof. engring. and applied math., 1962-65; prof. applied physics U. Calif. at San Diego, 1965—. Author: An Approach to Electrical Science, 1959, A Vector Approach to Oscillations, 1965, also sci. papers on radio wave propagation. Jr. intermediate and sr. county scholarships, Essex, Eng., 1920-30; Entrance scholarship Christ's Coll., 1930; Allen scholarship, 1934-35; Smith's prize, 1935; Duddell, Kelvin and instn. premiums Instn. Elec. Engrs., London, 1948-50. Fellow IEEE; mem. Nat. Acad. Scis., Internat. Union Radio Sci. (hon. pres. 1979—), Sigma Xi. Home: 8696 Dunaway Dr La Jolla CA 92037 Office: Dept Electrical Engineering and Computer Sci U Calif at San Diego La Jolla CA 92093

BOOKER, LEWIS THOMAS, lawyer; b. Richmond, Va., Sept. 22, 1929; s. Russell Eubank and Leslie Quarles (Sessoms) B.; m. Nancy Electa Brogden, Sept. 29, 1956; children: Lewis Thomas, Virginia Frances, Claiborne Brogden, John Quarles. B.A., U. Richmond, 1950, LL.D., 1977; J.D., Harvard U., 1953. Bar: Va. 1953, U.S. Ct. Mil. Appeals 1954, U.S. Supreme Ct. 1958, D.C. 1980. Assoc. Hunton & Williams, Richmond, Va., 1956-63, ptnr., 1963—. Commr., chmn. Richmond Redevel. and Housing Authority, 1961-70; vice chmn. Richmond Sch. Bd., 1970-78; trustee U. Richmond, 1972—, rector, 1973-77, 81—, chmn. exec. commn., 1977-81. Served with U.S. Army, 1953-56; to col. USAR, 1975—. Fellow Am. Coll. Trial Lawyers, Am. Bar Found.; mem. ABA, Fed. Bar Assn., Va. Bar Assn., Richmond Bar Assn. Democrat. Baptist. Clubs: Westwood Racquet, Bull & Bear, Harvard of N.Y. Office: 707 E Main St Richmond VA 23219

BOOKER, SUE, producer, dir., writer; b. Jersey City, Mar. 25, 1946; d. Merrel Daniel and Erma Beatrice (Barbour) B. B.S., U. Ill., 1967; M.S. in Journalism, Columbia, 1968. Prodn. asst. Children's TV Workshop, N.Y.C., 1968-69; co-producer, writer, dir. KUON-TV, Lincoln, Nebr., 1969-70; staff producer, writer, reporter KCET-TV, Los Angeles, 1970-73; freelance TV producer, Los Angeles, 1973-74; staff producer KNBC-TV, Los Angeles, 1975—; asso. prof. radio-TV dept. Calif. State U. at Long Beach, 1973—. Author: (with others) Cry At Birth, 1971. Recipient Gold medal and Grand Jury award for best documentary Atlanta Internat. Film Festival, 1971, best documentary award Calif. Asso. Press TV Radio Assn., 1971, Emmy award, Los Angeles, 1973. Mem. Nat. Assn. of Media Women, Dirs. Guild Am. Office: KNBC-TV 3000 W Alameda Burbank CA 91523

BOOKHAMMER, EUGENE DONALD, state govt. ofcl.; b. Lewes, Del., June 14, 1918; s. William and Winifred (Jenkins) B.; m. Catherine Williams, Jan. 31, 1942; children—Joy, Jean. Student, Am. Tech. Soc., 1938. Owner-pres. Bookhammer Lumber Mill, Lewes, 1939-71, Joy Beach Devel. Co., 1955; pres. Rehoboth Bay Dredging Co., Lewes, 1963; mem. Del. Senate, 1962-68; lt. gov., Del., 1969-76; mem. Del. Health Planning Council, 1976—; Dir. Farmers Bank of Del. Life mem. Boy Scouts Am.; del. Republican Nat. Conv., 1952, 56, 60, 80; chmn. Sussex County Rep. Com., 1964-66; Rep. nat. committeeman from Del., 1977—; bd. dirs. Beebe Hosp., chmn. bd. dirs., 1976—; trustee Wilmington Med. Center, 1971—. Served with AUS, 1944-46; ETO. Decorated Purple Heart. Mem. Am. Legion, Del. C. of C., VFW, DAV, 40 and 8, Am. Inst. Banking. Clubs: Mason (32 deg., Shriner), Lion.). Home: RD 2 Lewes DE 19958 Office: Legislative Hall Dover DE 19901

BOOKHOLT, WILLIAM JOHN, lawyer, accountant; b. Paterson, N.J., Aug. 30, 1916; s. James and Bella (Van Haste) B.; m. Marian E. Bell, June 30, 1943; children: Robert G., Barbara G. Diploma acctg. and bus. adminstrn., Pace Coll., 1939; student, Rutgers U., 1938-40, Newark U., 1945; J.D., Woodrow Wilson Coll. Law, Atlanta, 1950; postgrad., U. Ga., 1951-52. Bar: Ga. bar 1950; C.P.A., Ga. Field auditor Equitable Life Assurance Soc. N.Y., 1935-41; with IRS, 1946-72, dist. dir., Atlanta, 1958-59, regional commr., 1959-72; now in practice, Atlanta. Served to capt. AUS, 1941-45. Mem. Ga. Soc. C.P.A.s (Key award 1951, Outstanding Pub. Service award 1956, 72), Ga. Bar Assn. Home: 13 Downshire Ln Decatur GA 30033

BOOKMAN, GEORGE B., public relations consultant; b. N.Y.C., Dec. 22, 1914; s. Arthur and Judith (Wertheim) B.; m. Janet Schrank, Sept. 22, 1944; children: Ellen Jean Bookman Fincke, Charles Arthur. B.A., Haverford Coll, 1936; student, Ecole des Sciences Politiques, Paris, 1934-35; postgrad. internat. studies, Geneva, Switzerland, 1936. Asso. editor U.S. News and World Report, Washington, 1938-40, 45-48; White House reporter Washington Post, 1940-41; with OWI in, Africa, Lebanon, Syria, Egypt, Italy, Austria, 1941-45; Washington corr. Time mag., 1948-58, nat. econ. corr., N.Y.C., 1958-60; bd. editors Fortune mag., 1961-62; dir. pub. info. and press relations N.Y. Stock Exchange, 1962-71, asst. v.p., 1971-73; dir. pub. affairs N.Y. Bot. Garden, Bronx, 1973-74, v.p., 1974-79, public relations cons., 1979—. Mem. N.Y. Financial Writers Assn., Phi Beta Kappa, Soc. Profl. Journalists-Sigma Delta Chi. Clubs: Nat. Press, Cosmos (Washington); Overseas Press (N.Y.C.). Home: Belgo Rd RD 1 Box 74 Lakeville CT 06039

BOOKOUT, JOHN FRANK, JR., oil co. exec.; b. Shreveport, La., Dec. 31, 1922; s. John Frank and Lena (Hagen) B.; m. Mary Carolyn Cook, Dec. 21, 1946; children—Beverly Carolyn, Mary Adair and John Frank III (twins). Student, Iowa Wesleyan Coll., 1943, Centenary Coll., 1946-47; B.Sc., U. Tex., 1949, M.A., 1950; D.Sc. (hon.), Tulane U., 1978. Geologist Shell Oil Co., Tulsa, 1950-59, div. exploration mgr., 1959-61, area exploration mgr., Denver, 1961-63, The Hague, Netherlands, 1963-64, mgr. exploration and prodn. econs. dept., N.Y.C., 1965, v.p. Denver exploration and prodn. area, 1966, v.p. Southeastern exploration and prodn. region, New Orleans, 1967-70; pres., chief exec. officer, dir. Shell Can. Ltd., Toronto, Ont., 1970-74; exec. v.p., dir. Shell Oil Co., Houston, 1974-76, pres., chief exec. officer, dir., 1976—; dir. Irving Trust Co., Safeway Stores, Inc.; Bd. visitors Tulane U. Bd. dirs. Meth. Hosp., Houston; trustee Found. Bus., Politics and Econs.; adv. com. U. Tex., Austin, Houston Regional Minority Purchasing Council; mem. regional adv. bd. Inst. Internat. Edn. Served with USAAF, 1942-46. Decorated Air medal with 3 oak leaf clusters; recipient Disting. Service award Nat. Assn. Secondary Sch. Prins. Mem. Am. Assn. Petroleum Geologists, Nat. Petroleum Council, Houston C. of C. (dir., The Conf. Bd.), Am. Petroleum Inst. (mgmt. com.), 25 Year Club Petroleum Industry (bd. govs. SW dist.), Internat. C. of C. (U.S. Council; trustee), All-Am. Wildcatters Assn., Bus. Roundtable (mem. policy com.), Am. Council on Edn. (bus.-higher edn. forum). Home: PO Box 13614 Houston TX 77019 Office: Shell Oil Co PO Box 2463 Houston TX 77001

BOOKSH, ROBERT WILLIAM, pipe line company executive; b. Plaquemine, La., July 28, 1926; s. James H. and Esther (Drackett) B.; m. Shirley Ann Newport, July 1, 1945 (div. 1975); children: Deborah Ann Smith, Robert W.; m. Juanita Hatcher, Aug. 16, 1975. B.S. in M.E., Southwestern La. Inst., 1948. Asst. div. mgr. Tex.-N.Mex. Pipe Line Co., Midland, Tex., 1957-61, The Tex. Pipe Line Co., Lafayette, La., 1961-67, div. mgr., 1967-80, pres., 1980—; coordinator pipelines Texaco Inc., N.Y.C., 1967-72, asst. gen. mgr., 1972-80; dir. Dixie Pipe Line Co., Explorer Pipe Line Co., Tex.-N.Mex. Pipeline Co., Colonial Pipeline Co., 1970-76. Served with USAAF, 1945. Mem. Am. Petroleum Inst., Assn. Oil Pipe Lines (exec. com. 1981-82). Republican. Clubs: Brae-Burn Country (Houston); Crown Colony Country (Lufkin). Office: The Texas Pipeline Co 9700 Richman Ave Houston TX 77242

BOOKSPAN, MICHAEL LLOYD, musician; b. Bklyn., Sept. 7, 1929; s. Harry and Sarah (Barban) B.; children: Jolie, Adam. B.S., Juilliard Sch. Music, 1953. Xylophone soloist U.S.O. Camp Shows, 1943-46, N.Y.C. Ballet Orch., 1951-53, Little Orch. Soc., N.Y.C., 1951-53; snare drummer Goldman Band, 1953-55; percussionist and timpanist Phila. Orch., 1953—, prin. percussionist, asso. timpanist, 1972—, commd. and premiered Concerto for Solo Percussionist and Orch. (Robert Suderburg), 1979, marimba soloist, 1980; faculty Phila. Coll. Performing Arts, Curtis Inst. Music.; participated in Marboro, Casals, Aspen and Grand Teton festivals; Organizer Phila. Drummers for Peace, 1969. Served with USAAF, 1946-48. Recipient C. Hartman Kuhn award, 1981. Mem. Percussive Arts Soc., SANE, ACLU, Vets. for Peace in Vietnam. Office: Acad Music Broad and Locust Sts Philadelphia PA 19102

BOOLOS, GEORGE STEPHEN, philosophy educator; b. N.Y.C., Sept. 4, 1940; s. Stephen George and Blanche (Salomon) B.; m. Rebecca Gail Dustin Samuels, Dec. 18, 1970; 1 son, Peter. B.A., Princeton U.l, 1961; B. Phil., Oxford U., Eng., 1963; Ph.D., MIT, 1966. Asst. prof. philosophy Columbia U., 1966-69, MIT, 1969-73, assoc. prof., 1973-80, prof., 1980—, chmn. philosophy sect., 1980-82. Author: The Unprovability of Consistency, 1979, (with R.C. Jeffrey) Computability and Logic, 1974; cons. editor: Jour. Symbolic Logic, 1981. Nat. Endowment Humanities fellow, 1984; Fulbright scholar, 1961-63. Mem. Assn. Symbolic Logic, Am. Philos. Assn., Am. Math. Soc. Home: 89 Pleasant St Brookline MA 02146 Office: Dept of Linguistics and Philosophy Massachusetts Institute of Technology Cambridge MA 02146

BOOMER, DONALD JAMES, business executive; b. Montreal, Que., Can., Oct. 25, 1934; s. James N. and Ethel (Armistead) B.; m. Shirley E. Routledge, May 25, 1957; children—Lynn E., David J., Heather A. B.Sc., Sir George Williams U., Montreal, 1957; M.B.A., U. Western Ont., 1964. Mgr. bus. devel. Europe Polysar Ltd., Brussels, 1967-69; gen. mgr. Polysar Plastics Can., 1969-70, gen. mgr. plastics ops. Can. and U.S., 1971-72; partner Woods, Gordon & Co. (mgmt. cons.), Toronto, 1972-74; exec. v.p., gen. mgr. plastics packaging div. Consumers Glass Co. Ltd., Can., Etobicoke, Ont., 1974-81; v.p. corp. affairs Petrosar Ltd., Sarnia, Ont., 1981—. Mem. Bd. Trade Met. Toronto, Chem. Inst. Can., Can. Soc. Chem. Engring., Am. Chem. Soc., Packaging Inst. Office: 464 Christina St S Sarnia ON Canada

BOOMERSHINE, DONALD EUGENE, development official; b. Brookville, Ohio, Oct. 5, 1931; s. Harold Everett and Elsie (Rhoads) B.; m. Marilyn Sullivan, Aug. 29, 1953; children: Jeffrey, Alan. B.S., Bowling Green (Ohio) State U., 1953; grad., Northwestern U. Bank Mktg. Grad. Sch., 1965; standard certificate, Am. Inst. Banking, 1966; postgrad., Rutgers U. Stonier Sch. Banking, 1969-72, U. Okla. Nat. Comml. Lending Sch., 1974. With jr. exec. program Frigidaire div. Gen. Motors Corp., Dayton, 1955-57; sales rep. IBM, Dayton, Birmingham, Ala., 1957-62; bus. devel. rep., asst. cashier Exchange Security Bank, Birmingham, 1963-65; asst. v.p. charge nat. accounts div. Birmingham Trust Nat. Bank, 1965-68, v.p., 1968-71, v.p. charge metro div., 1971-72, head wholesale-retail div. comml. loan dept., 1972-76, v.p. corp. and indsl. devel., 1974-78; v.p., sales mgr. Otey Crisman Mfg. Co., 1978-80; dir. community devel. Met. Devel. Bd., 1980—; Chmn. Bus. Tomorrow Conf., Auburn U., 1975; ednl. chmn. Asso. Industries Ala., 1975-77; pres. Better Bus. Bur., Birmingham, 1982—. Pres. North Central Ala. chpt. Muscular Dystrophy Found., 1964; mem. Birmingham Community Affairs Com., 1972; chmn. major accounts div. capital funds drive YWCA, Birmingham, 1972, trustee, 1972—, mem. fin. com., 1972—; disaster chmn. ARC, 1975; gen. chmn. U.S. World Youth Game, 1973; regional chmn. blood recruitment ARC, Birmingham, 1974, mem. regional adv. council blood com., 1975—; Ala. pub. relations chmn. U.S. Marine Corps, 1971; charter mem. Downtown Action Com., 1966; mem. adv. bd. U. S.Ala., 1976—, Ala. Bd. Edn., 1975-76; bd. dirs., chmn. long-range planning com. Birmingham Childrens Theatre, 1974—; chmn. Am. Cancer Crusade, 1976; bd. dirs. Downtown YMCA, Muscular Dystrophy, Birmingham Zool. Soc.; mem. adv. bd. U. South Ala., 1975—, Ala. State Bd. Edn., 1976—; bd. dirs., 2d v.p., mem. exec. com. Birmingham Better Bus. Bur., 1980—. Served with USMCR, 1953-55; now col. Res. Mem. Am. Inst. Banking, Ala. Bankers Assn., Bank Mktg. Assn. (nat. dir. 1971-75, Ala. chmn. 1968, regional chmn. 1969, internat. devel. council 1970, nat. v.p. devel. 1971), Ala. Indsl. Devel. Council, So. Indsl. Council, World Trade Assn. Ala., Diplomats of Birmingham (founder, chmn. 1973), Marine Corps Res. Officers Assn. (nat. dir. 1974-76, past Ala. area chmn., chmn. toys for tots 1975), Operation Native Sons and Daus. (chmn. 1972), Birmingham C. of C. (life), Sigma Chi. Kiwanian (officer, dir., chmn. devel. Birmingham 1974). Clubs: Vestavia Country, Downtown, Metropolitan, Touchdown (Birmingham) (founder, dir., treas.). Home: 3801 Cromwell Dr Birmingham AL 35243 Office: Better Bus Bur 1214 S 20th St Birmingham AL 35205

BOOMSLITER, PAUL COLGAN, educator; b. Urbana, Ill., Oct. 24, 1915; s. George Paul and Alice (Colgan) B.; m. Patricia A. Flynn Himes, July 19, 1968; children—Paula Elise, Ann Dekker, Sara Ransone, Paul Lon, Mary Elizabeth Himes, Peter Edmund Himes. A.B., W.Va. U., 1935; postgrad., La. State U., 1937; M.A., U. Iowa, 1938; Ph.D., U. Wis., 1942, Northwestern U., 1948. Asst. prof. Goucher Coll., Balt., 1940-46; asst. prof. Cornell U., 1946-48; prof. State U. N.Y., Albany, 1948-79, chmn. speech pathology and audiology, 1969-73; research asso. prof. Albany Med. Coll., 1968-76; profl. dir. Northeastern N.Y. Speech Center, 1958-63, cons., 1963-76; profl. dir. Capital Area Speech Center, 1976—; cons. speech pathology and audiology Albany VA Hosp., 1956-76, Albany Study Center for Learning Disabilities, 1963-76, Albany Child Guidance Center, 1963—, N.Y. State Dept. Mental Hygiene, 1969—. Author: The Referential Search Organ, 1960, The Boomsliter-Creel Test of Tonal Processing, 1965, Language Capacity and Language Learning, 1970; Contbr. articles profl. jours. Served with USAAF, 1942-46. Recipient certificate of clin. competence in speech Am. Speech and Hearing Assn., 1950. Fellow Am. Speech and Hearing Assn., Acoustical Soc. Am.; mem. AAAS, N.Y. State, Capital Area speech and hearing assns., N.Y. Acad. Scis., Modern Lang. Assn., Phi Beta Kappa. Episcopalian. Home: 8 Lawnridge Ave Albany NY 12208 Office: Capital Area Speech Center 525 Washington Ave Albany NY 12206

BOON, JAMES ALEXANDER, anthropology educator; b. Sarasota, Fla., May 16, 1946; s. Frank Crawford and Lucinda Catherine (Rutledge) B.; m. Olivian Russell Boggs, June 16, 1968; children: Catherine Olivia, Jessica Alexis. B.A., Princeton U., 1968; M.A., U. Chgo., 1969, Ph.D., 1973. Vis. mem. Inst. for Advanced Study, Princeton, N.J., 1973-75; asst. prof. Duke U., Durham, N.C., 1975-77; assoc. prof. anthropology Cornell U., Ithaca, N.Y., 1977-80, prof. anthropology and Asian Studies, 1980—; cons. in, Indonesia, Ford Found., Jakarta, 1971; cons. anthropology Wenner Gren Found., N.Y.C. Author: From Symbolism to Structuralism, 1972, The Anthropolgical Romance of Bali, 1977, Other Tribes, Other Scribes, 1982. Postdoctoral grantee Inst. for Advanced Study Princeton, N.J., 1973-74; NIMH grantee, Bali, Indonesia, 1971-72; fieldwork grantee Am. Philosophical Soc., Bali, 1981. Mem. Am. Anthropol. Assn., Asian Studies Assn. Office: Dept Anthropology Cornell U Ithaca NY 14853

BOONE, DEBORAH ANN (DEBBY BOONE), singer; b. Hackensack, N.J., Sept. 22, 1956; d. Charles (Pat) Eugene and Shirley (Foley) B.; m. Gabriel Ferrer, 1979; children: Jordan Alexander, Gabrielle Monserrate and Dustin Boone (twins). Student Calif. schs. Singer with father, Pat Boone, and family group, 1970—; profl. rec. artist, 1977—; numerous appearances on TV talk and variety programs. Recipient Am. Music award (Song of Year), Grammy award (Best New Artist), Grammy award for best inspirational performance, 1980, Nat. Assn. Theatre Owners award (Best New Personality), Dove award, 1980, Dove award for album Surrender,

1984, Country Music award for Best New Country Artist, 1977; named Singing Star of Yr. AGVA, 1978, Working Mother of Yr., 1982. Mem. Ch. on the Way. Address: 205 S Beverly Dr Suite 205 Beverly Hills CA 90210

BOONE, EDGAR JOHN, teacher educator; b. Varnado, La., June 27, 1930; s. John W. and Daisy M. (Holmes) B.; m. Ethel Bower, July 19, 1959; children: John Bower, David Warner. B.S., La. State U., 1951; M.S., U. Wis., 1955, Ph.D. (Kellogg fellow), 1959. County agt., La., 1951-56; extension program analyst La. State U., 1956-58; prof. agrl. edn., head state extension program U. Ariz., 1959-60; prof. extension adminstrn. U. Wis., 1960-63; prof., head, dept. adult and community coll. edn. N.C. State U., 1963—, mem. com. internat. programs, 1968-83; asst. dir. N.C. Agrl. Extension Service, 1963—, extension exec. Devel. Inst., 1983; prof. extension adminstrn., adminstr. grad. program, adult edn. U. P.R., 1971, 76, 80, 81, 83; Cons. AID, Jamaica, 1962, U.S. Office Edn., 1968, Tuskegee Inst., 1969—, So. Assn. Colls. and Schs., 1971, Philippines, Thailand, Malaysia, Sri Lanka, Ghana, 1978; mem. Nat. Com. on Adult Edn. Research, 1963—, chmn. adult and community coll. forum series, 1983, chmn. agrl. leadership symposium, 1983; mem. Nat. Extension Curriculum Com., 1965—, N.C. Coastal Plains Planning and Devel. Commn., 1968—, accreditation commn. N.C. Dept. Community Colls., 1969—, Nat. Commn. Profs. Adult Edn., 1967-83; pres. Nat. Coalition Adult Edn. Orgns., 1974-75; chmn. Commn. Non-traditional Edn., 1974-75, U. Nebr.'s External Com. Non-traditional Edn., 1977, So. Regional Staff Devel. Com., 1982-83; cons. in field. Author: Public Affairs Education in Yuma County, Arizona, 1961, A Programming Guide for University Extension, 1964, Curriculum Development in Adult Basic Education, 1967, A Conceptual Schema of Programming in the Cooperative Extension Service, 1971, Non-Traditional Education, 1975, Decision-Making and Communications Patterns of Disadvantaged Farm Families, 1976, An Evaluation of Youth Lesson Series in Nutrition Education, 1976, Program Perspectives in Adult Education, 1977, Total Education: The Duty of the States, 1977, Serving Personal and Community Needs through Adult Education, 1979, A Historical and Philosophical Perspective on the External Degree, 1980, A Total Approach to Cooperative Extension Programming, 1983, Programming in Adult Education, 1983; also articles; editor: books including Serving Personal and Community Needs Through Adult Education, 1980; also jours. Mem. Bd. Edn., United Meth. Ch. N.C., 1968—; Bd. dirs. Tuskegee Inst. Nat. Resource Devel. Center, Joint Council Econ. Edn. Recipient Gov.'s Citizenship award, 1968; named Tar Heel of Week News and Observer, Raleigh, N.C., 1971; named to Acad. Outstanding Tchrs. N.C. State U., 1971—, Outstanding Tchr. award, 1974, Outstanding Adult Educator award, 1974. Mem. Adult Edn. Assn. U.S. (chmn. nat. resources planning commn. 1967—, sec. 1968-69, v.p. 1970-71, pres. 1972-73, chmn. non-traditional study com. 1974, Meritorious Service award 1972, 73, 74, 75, 78, 80, 81), Assn. Am. Community and Jr. Colls., Rural Sociol. Soc., Phi Kappa Phi (faculty honor award 1972), Gamma Sigma Delta, Epsilon Sigma Phi (Disting. Service award 1983), Phi Delta Kappa. Democrat. Methodist. Home: 4918 Rembert Dr Raleigh NC 27609 *My philosophy of life is predicated on the work ethic, a strong and abiding belief in the worth and dignity of other human beings, a strong faith in and a commitment to God, and a positive, optimistic outlook for the present and future.*

BOONE, GEORGE CLARK, JR., savings and loan executive; b. Dayton Beach, Fla., July 25, 1934; s. George Clark and Betty Jane B.; children—Deanna, David. B.S. in Bus. Adminstrn, U. Fla., 1956; student, Am. Savs. and Loan Inst., Grad. Sch. Savs. and Loan, Ind. U., 1967. C.P.A., Fla. Acct. Potter, Bower & Co. (C.P.A.s), Orlando, C.P.A.s, 1956, 59, Hogle, Vogt & Jenks, C.P.A.s, Daytona Beach, Fla., 1959-60; with Security First Fed. Savs. and Loan Assn., Daytona Beach, 1960—, v.p. and controller, sr. v.p., now pres., dir.; chmn. bd. First Halifax Corp.; chmn. bd., dir. Fla. Informgmt. Services, Inc.; chmn. bd. The Trails, Inc.; dir. Jacksonville br. Fed. Res. Bank of Atlanta. Pres. Civic League of Halifax Area; pres. trustees and friends div. Fla. Library Assn., 1963-64; pres. Volusia County Library Bd., 1961-75, United Fund East Volusia County, 1971-72; trustee, treas. Ormond Beach Meml. Hosp., 1976—; trustee Bethune-Cookman Coll., 1977—. Served with U.S. Army, 1957-58. Named Outstanding Trustee in Fla. Fla. Library Assn., 1967. Mem. Am. Inst. C.P.A.s, Fla. Inst. C.P.A.s, Fla. Savs. and Loan League (dir.), U.S. League Savs. Assns. (dir.), Fla. C. of C. (dir. 1977—), Dayton Beach Area C. of C. (pres. 1977). Clubs: Com. of 100; Kiwanis, Daytona Beach Quarterback (Dayton Beach); Econs. (Orlando). Office: 501 N Grandview Ave Daytona Beach FL 32018 also PO Box 1270 Daytona Beach FL 32015

BOONE, GRAY DAVIS, editor, publisher; b. Houston, Aug. 27, 1938; d. Edwin Theodore and Martha Scholl (O'Brien) Davis; children: Kenneth Scholl, James Buford III, Martha Frances. B.A., U. Ala., 1975. Chmn. World Antiques Market Conf.; dir. S. Central Bell Telephone Co. Editor, pub.: Antique Monthly mag, Tuscaloosa, Ala., 1967—, Horizon mag, Tuscaloosa, 1978—; pub.: weekly syndicated newspaper column Gray Boone on Antiques; Restorer of historic homes; mem. editorial bd.: Nat. Forum. Bd. dirs. Circle Repertory Theatre, N.Y.C., Wolf Trap Found.; mem. devel. council Birmingham So. Coll.; founders bd. Transylvania U., Lexington, Ky.; adv. com. Colonial Williamsburg Forum, 1978-81; mem. Octagon Com., Washington; mem. com. decorative arts Cooper-Heweitt Mus., N.Y.C.; founding pres. Decorative Arts Trust. Recipient Gordon Gray award Nat. Trust Hist. Preservation, 1978, Disting. Service award Ala. Hist. Commn., 1975, Woman of Achievement award, 1979. Fellow Royal Soc. Art; mem. Am. Soc. Mag. Editors, Victorian Soc. in Am., Newcomen Soc. N.Am. Episcopalian. Gray Boone Day proclaimed in Tuscaloosa, Mar. 29, 1979. Home: 905 21st Ave Tuscaloosa AL 35401 Office: 1305 Greensboro Ave Tuscaloosa AL 35401

BOONE, HAROLD THOMAS, lawyer; b. Oak Hill, W. Va., Dec. 14, 1921; s. Thomas thumb and Cora Anna (McGlamety) B.; m. Ferne Miller, July 31, 1948; 1 dau., Cheryl Ann. B.S., W. Va., 1943; J.D., U. Va., 1948. With Md. Casualty Co., Balt., 1948—, v.p., gen. counsel, corp. sec., 1979—, dir., 1979—. Served to 2d lt. USAAF, 1943-46. Mem. Internat. Assn. Ins. Counsel (v.p. 1979-81). Republican. Club: Hunt valley Golf. Home: 551 Piccadilly Rd Towson MD 21204 Office: Md Casualty Co 3910 Keswick Rd Baltimore MD 21203

BOONE, JERRY NEAL, academic administrator, psychologist; b. Corinth, Miss., Feb. 15, 1927; s. Frank B. and Zettie (Nelms) B.; m. Frankie Elizabeth Smith, Aug. 26, 1949; children: Jerrilyn Sue, Mary Elizabeth, Robert Arthur, Rebecca Ann; m. Doris Jean Gray, Dec. 11, 1971; 1 dau., Katia M. B.A., U. Miss., 1949; M.A., U. Fla., 1951; Ph.D., Vanderbilt U., 1961. Spl. edn. cons. Tenn. Dept. Edn., 1949-50; sr. speech therapist Wilkerson Speech Center, Nashville, 1951-52; dir. speech clinic East Tenn. State U., Johnson City, 1952-56; assoc. prof., then prof. psychology Memphis State U., 1962-69, dean Univ. Coll., 1968-69; asst. prof. pediatrics U. Tenn. Coll. Medicine, 1964-66, assoc. prof., 1966-69; pvt. practice clin. psychology, 1961-69; assoc. dir. acad. affairs Tenn. Higher Edn. Commn., Nashville, 1969-72; v.p. for acad. affairs Memphis State U., 1972—; Mem. Tenn. Bd. Examiners Psychology, 1965-69, chmn., 1968—. Home: 2754 Lombardy Memphis TN 38111

BOONE, MICHAEL MAULDIN, lawyer; b. Henderson, Tenn., Jan. 31, 1941; s. Daniel Lacey and La Nelle Ruby (Stovall) B.; m. Marla Hays, Aug. 2, 1969; children—Michael Hays, Maryjane Mauldin. B.B.A., So. Meth. U., 1963, J.D., 1967. Bar: Tex. Assoc. firm Richard D. Haynes, 1967-69; partner firm Haynes & Boone, Dallas, 1969—; chmn. State Bar Com. on Revision Tex. Corp. Law, 1978-80; adj. prof. law So. Meth. U. Sch. Law, 1972-81. Mem. ABA, Dallas Bar Assn., State Bar Tex. (chmn. sect. on corp., banking and bus. law 1983-84), Phi Gamma Delta, Phi Delta Phi. Mem. Ch. of Christ (deacon). Club: City. Home: 3516 University St Dallas TX 75205 Office: 4300 InterFirst Dallas TX 75270

BOONE, OLIVER KIEL, lawyer; b. Wichita Falls, Tex., Apr. 30, 1922; s. Thomas Relyea and Mary Lemma (Kiel) B.; m. Dorothy Florence Fizzell, Mar. 5, 1945; children—Kathleen (Mrs. Ronald Collins), Thomas Kiel, Cynthia (Mrs. Clark R. Irey II). B.A., U. Tex., 1942; J.D., 1947. Bar: Tex. bar 1943. Asst. dist. atty., Dallas County, Dallas, 1947; asso. Leachman, Matthews & Gardere, Dallas, 1948-49; asso., partner firm Kilgore & Kilgore, Dallas, 1950-71; partner Johnson, McElroy, Cravens & Boone, Dallas, 1971-72, Boone, Pickering & Vendig (and predecessor firm), 1973-77. Chmn. bd. dirs. Park Cities, North Dallas YMCA, 1966-67. Served with USNR, 1943-46. Mem. Dallas Bar Assn. (dir. 1969-74, bd. vice-chmn. 1970, chmn. finance com. 1971-74), U. Tex. Law Sch. Alumni Assn. (pres. 1973-75). Methodist (legal officer N. Tex. Conf. 1971-75). Clubs: Northwood, Dallas Petroleum. Home: 4641 Southern Dallas TX 75209 Office: 1550 Fidelity Union Tower Dallas TX 75201

BOONE, PAT (CHARLES EUGENE), singer, actor; b. Jacksonville, Fla., June 1, 1934; s. Archie and Margaret (Prichard) B.; m. Shirley Foley, Nov. 14, 1953; children: Cheryl Lynn, Linda Lee, Deborah Ann, Laura Gene. Student, North Tex. State Tchrs. Coll., David Lipscomb Coll.; grad. magna cum laude, Columbia, 1958. Winner on, Ted Mack TV Show, 1953, Arthur Godfrey Show, 1954; recs., Dot Records, 1955; now recs., Motown Records; owner Lamb & Lion Records; religious rec. co. singer: Arthur Godfrey TV Show, CBS, 1955; motion picture contract, 20th Century Fox, 1957; star: Pat Boone TV Show, ABC, 1957; appeared in: films Bernadine, 1957, April Love, 1957, Mardi gras, 1958, Journey to the Center of the Earth, 1959, All Hands on Deck, 1961, State Fair, 1962, Main Attraction, 1962, Yellow Canary, 1963, Greatest Story Ever Told, 1965, Perils of Pauline, 1967, The Cross and the Switchblade, 1971; numerous TV appearances.; Author: Twixt Twelve and Twenty, 1958, Between You, Me and the Gatepost, 1960, The Real Christmas, 1961, Care and Feeding of Parents, 1967, A New Song, 1971, Joy, 1973, A Miracle a Day Keeps the Devil Away; My Faith, 1976, Pat Boone Devotional Book, 1977, The Honeymoon is Over, 1977, Together: 25 Years With The Boone Family, 1979, Pray To Win: God Wants You to Succeed, 1980. Bd. regents Oral Roberts U.; mem. pres.'s bd. Pepperdine Coll. Selected 3d of Top Ten Box Office Attractions, 1957; named One of Top Ten Record Artists, 1955; Top 15 Namepower Stars, 1959. Office: Internat Creative Mgmt 8899 Beverly Blvd Los Angeles CA 90048

BOORMAN, HOWARD LYON, history educator; b. Chgo., Sept. 11, 1920; s. William Ryland and Verna (Lyon) B.; m. Mary Houghton, Jan. 20, 1972; 1 son by previous marriage—Scott A. B.A., U. Wis., Madison, 1941; postgrad., Yale U., 1946-47. Divisional asst., div. def. materials Dept. of State, Washington, 1942-43; fgn. service officer to, Peking, Hong Kong, 1947-54; research asso. Sch. Internat. Affairs, Columbia U., N.Y.C., 1955-67; prof. history Vanderbilt U., Nashville, 1967—; mem. Nat. Com. U.S.-China Relations, 1966—; vis. scholar Univ. Center of Va., 1963. Gen. editor: Biographical Dictionary of Republican China, 4 vols, 1967-71; contbr. articles to profl. jours. Served to lt. USNR, 1943-46. Recipient Rockefeller Public Service award, 1954-55. Mem. Am. Hist. Assn., So. Hist. Assn., Tenn. Hist. Assn., Am. Polit. Sci. Assn., Assn. Asian Studies, Council Fgn. Relations. Club: Univ. (Nashville). Home: 12 Redbud Dr Nashville TN 37215 Office: Dept History Vanderbilt U Nashville TN 37235

BOORMAN, JOHN, film director, producer, screenwriter; b. Jan. 18, 1933; s. George and Ivy (Chapman) B.; m. Christel Kruse, 1957; 4 children. Broadcaster, critic BBC Radio; film editor ITN London, 1955-58; dir., producer So. TV, 1958-60. Also contbr.: articles to Manchester Guardian and mags, 1950-54; head documentaries, Bristol, BBC-TV; dir.: documentary The Citizens series The Newcomers, 1960-64; films Catch Us If You Can, 1965, Point Blank, 1967, Hell in the Pacific, 1968, Leo the Last, 1969, Deliverance, 1970, Zardoz, 1973, The Heretic, 1976, Excalibur, 1981; founder: TV mag. Day by Day; author: fiction The Legend of Zardoz, 1973. Recipient Best Dir. prize Cannes Festival, 1970. Office: care Edgar Gross Internat Bus Mgmt 1801 Century Park E Suite 1132 Los Angeles CA 90067

BOORSCH, JEAN, educator; b. Anzin, France, Jan. 25, 1906; s. Auguste René and Laure (Renotte) B.; m. Louise Heathwood Totten, Dec. 16, 1933; children—James, Suzanne, Marie-Louise, John Peter. Agrégation-ès Lettres, Sorbonne, Paris, 1929; M.A. (hon.), Yale U., 1953; L.H.D. honoris causa, Middlebury Coll., 1971. Asst. prof. Middlebury (Vt.) Coll., 1929-34; successively asst. prof. to asso. prof. Yale, 1934-53, Street prof. modern langs., 1953—. Author: Etat Présent des Etudes sur Descartes, 1937, Recherches sur la technique dramatique de Corneille, 1943, Méthode orale de Fran cais, 1948, Structure d'esprit de Montaigne, 1955. Decorated chevalier Legion of Honor, France)., Officer des Pahnes Académiques. Mem. Modern Modern Lang. Assn., Assn. Tchrs. French, Société des Professeurs Francais en Amérique. Home: 61 Millbrook Rd Hamden CT 06518 *Life and Love ARE the Message and the Meaning.*

BOORSTIN, DANIEL J., author, government official; b. Atlanta, Oct. 1, 1914; s. Samuel and Dora (Olsan) B.; m. Ruth Carolyn Frankel, Apr. 9, 1941; children: Paul Terry, Jonathan, David West. A.B. summa cum laude, Harvard U., 1934; B.A. with first class honors (Rhodes scholar), Balliol Coll., Oxford U., 1936, B.C.L., 1937; postgrad., Inner Temple, London, 1934-37; J.S.D. (Sterling fellow), Yale U., 1940; Litt.D. (hon.), Cambridge U., 1967; numerous other hon. degrees. Bar: Admitted as barrister-at-law Inner Temple 1937, Mass. bar 1942. Instr., tutor history and lit. Harvard and Radcliffe Coll., 1938-42; lectr. legal history Harvard Law Sch., 1939-42; asst. prof. history Swarthmore Coll., 1942-44; asst. prof. U. Chgo., 1944-49, asso. prof., 1949-56, prof. Am. History, 1956-64, Preston and Sterling Morton Disting. Service prof., 1964-69; Walgreen lectr. Am. instns., 1952; dir. Nat. Mus. History and Tech., Smithsonian Instn., Washington, 1969-73, sr. historian, 1973-75; librarian of congress Library of Congress, 1975—; Fulbright vis. lectr. Am. history U. Rome, Italy, 1950-51, Kyoto U., Japan, 1957; cons. Social Sci. Research Center, U. P.R., 1955; lectr. for U.S. Dept. State in, Turkey, Iran, Nepal, India, Ceylon, 1959-60, Indonesia, Australia, New Zealand, Fiji, 1968, India, Pakistan, Iceland, 1974, Philippines, Thailand, Malaysia, India, Egypt, 1975; 1st incumbent of chair Am. history U. Paris, 1961-62; Pitt prof. Am. history and instns. U. Cambridge, 1964-65; Shelby and Kathryn Cullom Davis lectr. Grad. Inst. Internat. Studies, Geneva, 1973-74; sr. fellow Huntington Library, 1969; mem. Commn. on Critical Choices for Ams., 1973—, Dept. State Indo-Am. Joint Subcommn. Edn. and Culture, 1974-81, Japan-U.S. Friendship Commn., 1978—; Mem. Am. Revolution Bicentennial Commn.; sr. attorney Office Lend Lease Adminstr., ice Asst. Solicitor Gen., Washington.; Fellow Trinity Coll., 1964-65. Author: The Mysterious Science of the Law, 1941, Delaware Cases, 1792-1830 (3 vols.), 1943, The Lost World of Thomas Jefferson, 1948, The Genius of American Politics, 1953, The Americans: The Colonial Experience, 1958 (winner Bancroft award 1959), America and the Image of Europe, 1960, The Image or What Happened to the American Dream, 1962, The Americans: The National Experience, 1965 (Francis Parkman prize 1966), The Landmark History of the American People, 2 vols, 1968, 70, The Decline of Radicalism, 1969, The Sociology of the Absurd, 1970, The Americans: The Democratic Experience, 1973 (Pulitzer prize 1974); (Dexter prize 1974); Author: Democracy and Its Discontents, 1974, The Exploring Spirit, 1976, The Republic of Technology, 1978, (with Brooks M. Kelley) A History of the United States, 1981, The Discoverers, 1983; Editor: An American Primer, 1966, (with Brooks M. Kelley) American Civilization, 1972, Am. history, Ency. Brit, 1951-55; Author articles, book reviews. Trustee Colonial Williamsburg, Kennedy Center, Cafritz Found., Woodrow Wilson Center, Thomas Gilcrease Mus.; bd. visitors U.S. Air Force Acad., 1968-70. Recipient Bowdoin prize Harvard, 1934, Jenkins prize, Younger prize Balliol Coll., 1935, 36. Mem. Colonial Soc. Mass., Orgn. Am. Historians, Am. Acad. Arts and Scis., Am. Philos. Soc., Am. Antiquarian Soc., Am. Studies Assn. (pres. 1969-71), Internat. House Japan, Royal Hist. Soc. (corr. fellow), Phi Beta Kappa. Jewish. Clubs: Nat. Press, Cosmos; Elizabethan (Yale); Reform (London, Eng.). Home: 3541 Ordway St NW Washington DC 20016 Office: Library of Congress Washington DC 20540

BOOSE, ARTHUR JOHN, judge; b. Hudson, Ohio, June 10, 1920; s. Alvin Charles and Minnie (Barnetson) B.; m. Marsha-Glee Jensen, June 12, 1944; children: Lana, Susan (Mrs. Frank Nelson). Student, Iowa State Tchrs. Coll., 1939-41; B.S.C., U. Iowa, 1948; LL.B., U. Tulsa, 1955. Bar: Okla. bar 1955. With Phillips Petroleum Co., Waterloo, Iowa, 1939-42, Bartlesville, Okla., 1948-56; pvt. practice law, 1956-63, county judge, Washington County, Okla., 1963-69, judge dist. ct., 1969-83. Pres. Bartlesville P.T.A. Council, 1965-67, Council Social Agys., 1966-68; active Bartlesville Mental Health Assn. Served as cpl. USAAF, World War II; ETO. Named hon. mem. DeMolay Legion of Honor. Mem. Am., Okla. bar assns., Oklahoma County Judges Assn. (pres. 1967-69), Am. Legion. Clubs: Mason (Shriner), Kiwanian (dir.). Home: 538 E 16th St Bartlesville OK 74003 Office: Courthouse Bartlesville OK 74003 *You get out of life only what you put into it. There is no such word as "free."*

BOOTH, ALBERT JOHN, automotive component manufacturing company executive; b. Chgo., Dec. 6, 1919; s. Albert and Alida (Hageman) B.; m. Doris Eileen Noakes, Feb. 14, 1942; children: Albert, Donald. Student, Ruger's U., 1938-41. Gen. mgr. Stewart Warner, Chgo., 1959-64, mng. dir., Harlow, Eng., 1964-67; v.p. mfg. Condec, Greenwich, Conn., 1967-69; v.p. mgf. Holley Carburetor div. Colt Industries, Warren, Mich., 1969-79, pres., 1979—. Inventor hot-fuel priming device. Republican. Home: 1301 Knollcrest Circle Bloomfield Hills MI 48013 Office: Holley Carburetor Div 11955 Nine Mile Rd Warren MI 48090

BOOTH, ANDREW DONALD, former university president, scientist; b. East Molesey, Eng., Feb. 11, 1918; s. Sidney Joseph and Catherine Jane (Pugh) B.; m. Kathleen Hylda Valerie Britten, July 9, 1950; children: Ian Jeremy MacDonald, Amanda Jane. B.Sc., U. London, 1940, D.Sc., 1951; Ph.D., U. Birmingham, 1944. Indsl. grad. apprentice, 1937-39; mem. Inst. Advanced Study, Princeton, 1947-48; vis. prof. theoretical physics U. Pitts., 1949; lectr., reader, prof., head dept. computer sci. Birkbeck Coll., U. London, 1948-62; prof., head dept. elec. engring. U. Sask., 1962-63, dean engring., 1963-72; pres. Lakehead U., Thunder Bay, Ont., 1972-78; chmn. bd. Autonetics Research Assos., 1978—; prof. autonetics Case Western U., 1963-72; mem. NRC Can.; chmn. bd. Wharf Engring. Labs., U.K., 1955-62; dir. Sask. Power Corp., 1963-64. Author: Automatic Digital Calculators, 3d edit., 1965, Digital Computers in Action, 1965, Numerical Methods, 3d edit., 1966; also articles.; editor: Machine Translation, 1967. Chmn., Conservative Assn., Warwickshire, Eng., 1956-62; mem. TV Adv. Bd. Thunder Bay, 1972—; bd. dirs. Thunder Bay Symphony, 1972—. Served as flight officer RAF, 1940-42. Recipient Centennial medal Can., 1967; Nuffield fellow, 1946-47; Rockefeller fellow, 1947-48. Fellow Inst. Linguists (hon.), Inst. Physics (U.K.), Inst. Electronic and Radio Engrs. (chmn. Can. div.), Royal Soc. Arts; mem. Assn. Colls. and Univs. of Lakeside (chmn. bd.). Clubs: Athenaeum (London); Univ. of Toronto, R.C.M.I. (Toronto). Home: Timberlane 5317 Sooke Rd Rural Route 1 Sooke BC Canada

BOOTH, BEATRICE CROSBY, biological oceanographer; b. Mpls., Aug. 29, 1938; d. George Christian and Beatrice (Goodrich) Crosby; m. Theordore William Booth, Dec. 23, 1960; children: Marguerite Morse, Kristina Wells, George Crosby. B.A., Radcliffe Coll., 1960; M.A.T., Harvard U., 1962; M.S., U. Wash., 1969. Teaching asst. U. Wash., Seattle, 1974, instr., 1975-78, research oceanographer, 1975-80, sr. oceanographer, 1980-83, prin. oceanographer, 1983—; oceanographer NOAA, Seattle, 1978-79. Contbr. articles to profl. jours. NSF grantee, 1978-80, 80-82, 82—. Mem. Am. Soc. Limnology and Oceanography, AAAS, Phycological Soc. Am. Democrat. Home: 5521 17th St Ave NE Seattle WA 98105 Office: Sch Oceanography Univ of Wash Seattle WA 98195

BOOTH, BRIAN GEDDES, lawyer; b. Roseburg, Oreg., May 30, 1936; s. Harris Wythe and Lois M. (Geddes) B.; m. Anne M. Mautz, June 20, 1959; children: Thomas Scott, Jennifer Susan. B.S., U. Oreg., 1958; LL.B., Stanford U., 1962. Bar: Oreg. 1962. Assoc. Davies, Biggs, Strayer, Stoel and Boley, Portland, 1962-68, partner, 1968-74, Tonkon, Torp, Galen, Marmaduke & Booth, Portland, 1974—; corp. sec. Orbanco Fin. Services Corp., 1975—; chmn. Cablesystems Pacific Adv. Com., 1980-82. Pres. bd. dirs. Portland Art Assn., 1976-78; mem. City of Portland Econ. Devel. Adv. Com., 1977-79; bd. visitors Stanford Law Sch.; trustee Reed Coll., 1980—, Oreg. Community Found., 1980—. Served with U.S. Army, 1958-59. Mem. ABA, Oreg. State Bar Assn. (chmn. joint com. with press and broadcasters 1972-74, chmn. securities sect. 1980-81), Oreg. Securities Law Assn. (pres. 1972-74), Phi Beta Kappa, Order of Coif, Phi Delta Theta. Clubs: Arlington, Racquet (pres. 1980-81), Multonomah Athletic.). Office: 1800 Orbanco Bldg 1001 SW 5th Ave Portland OR 97204

BOOTH, DOUGLAS WADE, utility company executive; b. Atlanta, 1924;. B.S.E.E., U. Ala., 1947. With Duke Power Co., Inc., Charlotte, N.C., 1952—, v.p. mktg., 1965-71, sr. v.p. retail ops., 1971-76, exec. v.p., 1976-82, pres., chief operating officer, dir., 1982—. Office: Duke Power Co Inc 422 S Church St Box 33189 Charlotte NC 28242

BOOTH, EDGAR HIRSCH, lawyer; b. Bklyn., June 8, 1926; s. Benjamin H. and Lee (Benzman) B.; m. Joan E. Blumberg, Oct. 7, 1956; children—Charles, Janet. Student, U. Va., 1944, 46-47; B.A., Stanford, 1949; LL.B., Harvard, 1953. Bar: N.Y. State bar 1954. Since practiced in, N.Y.C.; asso. firm Booth, Lipton & Lipton, 1954-65, mem. firm, 1965—; Mem. nat. panel lawyers Am. Arbitration Assn. Mem. Glen Rock Bd. Edn., 1971-77, pres., 1973-74; bd. dirs. S.M. Louis Fund, Inc., N.Y.C. Served with AUS, 1944-46. Mem. Am., N.Y. State bar assns., Assn. Bar City N.Y., N.Y. County Lawyers Assn., Fed. Bar Council, Bankruptcy Lawyers Bar Assn. Home: 25 Belmont Rd Glen Rock NJ 07452 Office: 405 Park Ave New York City NY 10022

BOOTH, GEORGE, cartoonist; b. Cainsville, Mo., June 28, 1926; s. William and Norene B.; m. Dione Booth. Student, Chgo. Acad. Art, 1948-49, Corcoran Sch. Art, Washington, Adelphi U., Sch. Visual Arts,

N.Y.C. Staff cartoonist Leatherneck Mag., USMC, 1946-52; art dir. Bill Communications, N.Y., 1958-64. Cartoons appearing regularly in New Yorker mag, 1970—; Author: Think Good Thoughts About a Pussycat, 1975, Rehearsal's Off, 1976, Pussycats Need Love, Too!, 1981, Omnibooth, 1984; illustrator: Wacky Wednesday, 1974. Address: Box 841 Stony Brook NY 11790

BOOTH, GEORGE GEOFFREY, finance educator; b. Athens, Ohio, Jan. 13, 1942; s. George Warren and Ellen (Cooley) B.; m. Kathryn Milton, July 8, 1961; children: Christopher, Timothy, James. B.B.A., Ohio U., 1964, M.B.A., 1966; Ph.D., U. Mich., 1971. Fin. analyst Ford Co., Saline, Mich., 1966-67; systems analyst Dow Chem., Midland, Mich., 1967; prof., chmn., dir. research U. R.I., Kingston, 1970-81; prof., chmn. fin. dept. Syracuse (N.Y.) U., 1981—; dir. South Providence Credit Union, 1977-78. Contbr. numerous articles to profl. jours.; editor: Fin. Rev., 1973-76; assoc. editor, 1976—; editor: New Eng. Jour. Bus. and Econs., 1974-81; assoc. editor, 1981—. Mem. Am. Econ. Assn., Am. Fin. Assn., Eastern Fin. Assn., So. Fin. Assn., Fin. Mgmt. Assn., New Eng. Bus. and Econ. Assn., Phi Kappa Phi, Beta Gamma Sigma, Alpha Iota Delta. Office: Sch Mgmt Syracuse U Syracuse NY 13210

BOOTH, GORDON DEAN, JR., lawyer; b. Columbus, Ga., June 25, 1929; s. Gordon Dean and Lois Mildred (Bray) B.; m. Katherine Morris Campbell, June 17, 1961; children: Mary Katherine, Abigail Kilgore, Sarah Elizabeth, Margaret Campbell. B.A., Emory U., 1961, J.D., 1964, LL.M, 1973. Bar: Ga. 1964, U.S. Supreme Ct. 1973. Practice law, Atlanta, 1964-80; ptnr. Filpatrick & Cody, Atlanta, 1980—; dir., v.p. Stallion Music, Inc., Nashville. Contbr. articles to profl. jours. Trustee Met. Atlanta Crime Commn., 1977-80, chmn., 1979-80; mem. assembly for arts and scis. Emory Coll., 1971—, chmn., 1983. Mem. Atlanta Bar Assn., ABA, Internat. Bar Assn. (council sec. bus. law 1974—, chmn. aero. law com. 1971—), Am. Soc. Internat. Law Assn. Bar City N.Y., State Bar Ga., Lawyers Club Atlanta, Sigma Chi. Clubs: Capital City, Lawyers, University, Wings (N.Y.C.). Home: 580 Old Harbor Dr Atlanta GA 30328 Office: Kilpatrick & Cody 3100 Equitable Bldg Atlanta GA 30043

BOOTH, HAROLD WAVERLY, insurance executive, lawyer; b. Rochester, N.Y., Aug. 8, 1934; s. Herbert Nixon and Mildred B. (Anderson) B.; m. Flo Rae Spelts, July 4, 1957; children: Rebecca, William, Eva, Harold, Richard. B.S., Cornell U., 1955; J.D., Duke U., 1961. Bar: Nebr. 1961, Ill. 1967, Iowa 1974; C.L.U., chartered fin. counselor. Staff atty. Bankers Life Nebr., Lincoln, 1961-67; pres. First Nat. Bank, Council Bluffs, Iowa, 1970-74; exec. v.p., treas. Blue Cross-Blue Shield Ill., Chgo., 1974-77; pres., chief exec. officer, chmn. Bankers Life Nebr., Lincoln, 1977—; dir. First Nat. Bank, Lincoln. Served to 1st lt. USAF, 1955-58. Fellow Life Mgmt. Inst. (pres. 1982—); mem. Ins. Fedn. Nebr. (past pres.). Home: 2945 Van Dorn Lincoln NE 68502 Office: 5900 O St Lincoln NE 68501

BOOTH, IRVIN STANLEY, retired insurance executive; b. Waycross, Ga., Dec. 9, 1916; s. Irvin Lester and Amy (Bourn) B.; m. Ruby M. McClellan, Dec. 26, 1938; 1 son, Irvin Stanley. Student pub. schs., Manor, Ga.; bus. coll., Manor, Ga. Agt. Met. Life Ins. Co., Waycross, 1939-42; mem. Ga. Maritime Commn., 1942-46; owner turpentine bus., 1946-48; gen. mgr. McClelland Motors, Waycross, 1948-50; staff mgr. Life of Ga., Waycross and Thomasville, Ga., 1950-57; dist. mgr. and ordinary mgr. Security Life of Ga., Macon, 1957-59; exec. v.p., sec., dir. Lincoln Am. Life Ins. Co., Memphis, 1959-82; cons., realtor, 1982—. Bd. dirs. Tenn. Ind. Coll. Fund. Mem. Nat. Assn. Life Underwriters. Democrat. Methodist. Home: 419 Whitefield Ave Saint Simons Island GA 31522

BOOTH, I(SRAEL) MACALLISTER, photog. co. exec.; b. Atlanta, Dec. 7, 1931; s. Charles Victor and Charlotte Ann (Beattie) B.; m. Frances Marie Henry, Sept. 22, 1956; children—David M., Thomas H., Mary E., Charlotte M. B.M.E., Cornell U., 1955, M.B.A., 1958. With Polaroid Corp., Cambridge, Mass., 1958—, v.p., 1976-78, sr. v.p., 1978-80, exec. v.p., 1980—, chief operating officer, 1982—. Served to capt. USAF, 1955-57. Episcopalian. Office: 549 Technology Sq Cambridge MA 02139

BOOTH, JOHN THOMAS, investment banker; b. N.Y.C., Oct. 21, 1929; s. John E. and Katherine (Keeler) B.; m. Anne C. Mott, Feb. 26, 1960; children: Alison McAdam, Miven, Roxanna Norton. Grad., Deerfield Acad., 1947; B.A. cum laude, Amherst Coll., 1951; LL.B., Harvard U., 1957. Bar: N.Y. 1957. Asso. firm Dewey Ballantine Bushby Palmer & Wood, N.Y.C., 1957-61; mem. buying dept. Eastman Dillon, Union Securities & Co., N.Y.C., 1961—, partner, 1963—; exec. v.p., dir. Blyth Eastman Dillon & Co., Inc., 1972-79; chmn. bd. Eastdil Realty, Inc., 1979-81, Am. Health Capital, Inc., 1982—; dir. SCM Corp., Voluntary Health Enterprises, Inc.; advisor McKinsey & Co., Inc., Profitsharing Retirement Plan; Asst. to dir. Harvard Def. Studies Program, 1956-57; counsel N.Y. State Assembly Com. on N.Y.C., 1960, Com. on Judiciary, 1961. Adv. bd. Winant and Clayton Vols., Inc.; trustee Carnegie Hill Neighborhood Conservation Project, Inc.; bd. dirs. N.Y. Soc. Library; vestryman Trinity Ch., N.Y.C.; mem. major gifts com. Capital Program for Amherst Coll. Served from ensign to lt. (j.g.) USNR, 1951-54. Mem. ABA, N.Y. Bar, Newcomen Soc., Pilgrim Soc., Delta Kappa Epsilon, Delta Sigma Rho. Republican. Episcopalian. Clubs: Links, University (N.Y.C.); Litchfield (Conn.) Country. Office: Am Health Capital Inc Chrysler Bldg New York NY 10174

BOOTH, LAURENCE OGDEN, architect; b. Chgo., July 5, 1936; s. Edwin Shaw and Josephine (Ogden) B.; m. Patricia Hansen, Sept. 24, 1960; children: Fenton, Victoria, Adriene, Edwin. B.A., Stanford U., 1958; postgrad., Harvard U. Sch. Design, 1958; B.Arch., M.I.T., 1960. Partner Booth, Nagle & Hartray (and predecessor), Chgo., 1965-80, Booth/Hansen & Assos., 1980—; vis. prof. U. Ill., 1980—; vis. critic Harvard U., 1981. Designs include Arco Gas Sta, 1972, Adamson House, 1975, Mus. Contemporary Art, 1978, Herman Miller Office, 1979, Printing House Row, 1979, 320 N. Michigan Ave., 1982, House of Light, 1983, Helene Curtis Industries, 1984. Bd. dirs. Mus. Contemporary Art, Chgo., Met. Housing and Planning Council, Chgo., Chgo. Theatre Group, Com. Fgn. Relations. Served to 1st lt. U.S. Army, 1960-62. Fellow AIA. Roman Catholic. Clubs: Cliffdwellers, Chgo. Yacht. Home: 553 Fullerton Chicago IL 60614 Office: 555 S Dearborn St Chicago IL

BOOTH, MITCHELL B., lawyer; b. N.Y.C., June 26, 1927; s. Samuel and Rose (Waxman) B.; m. Barbara C. Ribman, July 13, 1952; 1 son, Brian S. A.B., Clark U., 1949; J.D., N.Y. U., 1952. Bar: N.Y. 1952. Since practiced in, N.Y.C.; asso. I. Moldauer, 1952-54; with firm Sol A. Rosenblatt, 1954-67; individual practice, 1967—; minority counsel joint legis. com. unsatisfied judgments N.Y., 1958-59, joint legis. com. preservation restoration hist. sites N.Y., 1960-64; med. malpractice mediator First Jud. Dept. Supreme Ct. State N.Y., 1980—. Dir. Burgos Art Galleries, Ltd., Dorolyat Corp.; Asst. to chmn. Democratic law com., N.Y. County, 1961-65; Admissions rep. N.Y., N.J., Conn. Clark U., 1968-71. Served to lt. USNR, 1945-46, 51, 52. Mem. ABA, N.Y. State Bar Assn., N.Y.C. Bar Assn. (mem. municipal affairs com.). Home: 75 East End Ave New York NY 10028 Office: 1290 Ave of Americas New York NY 10019

BOOTH, PETER BLAKE, naval officer; b. San Diego, June 20, 1934; s. Charles Thomas and Peggy (Maltman) B.; m. Carolyn Rhodes, Mar. 19, 1959; children: Laura Lee, Renee. B.S., U.S. Naval Acad., 1956; M.B.A., Stanford U., 1965. Commd. ensign U.S. Navy, 1956, advanced through grades to rear adm., 1980; comdr. various fighter squadrons (also USS Forrestal), chief naval air tng., Corpus Christi, Tex. Decorated Air medal, Legion of Merit. Mem. Assn. Naval Aviation, Naval Inst. Episcopalian. Office: Chief Naval Air Tng NAS Corpus Christi TX 78419

BOOTH, PHILIP, poet, educator; b. Hanover, N.H., Oct. 8, 1925; s. Edmund Hendershot and Jeanette (Hooke) B.; m. Margaret Tillman, Aug. 3, 1946; children: Margot, Carol, Robin. A.B., Dartmouth Coll., 1948; M.A., Columbia U., 1949; Litt.D. (hon.), Colby Coll., 1968. Instr. Bowdoin Coll., 1949-50; asst. to dir. admissions Dartmouth, 1950-51, instr., 1954; instr. to asst. prof. Wellesley Coll., 1954-61; asso. prof. Syracuse (N.Y.) U., 1961-65, prof., 1966—. Author: Letter from a Distant Land, 1957, The Islanders, 1961, Weathers and Edges, 1966, Beyond Our Fears, 1968, Margins, 1970, Available Light, 1976, Before Sleep, 1980; Editor: The Dark Island, 1960, Syracuse Poems, 1965, 70, 73, Syracuse Stories and Poems, 1977, 83; Contbr. poems and essays to jours. Served with USAAF, 1944-45. Recipient Hokin prize Poetry mag., 1955, Lamont prize Acad. Am. Poets, 1956, Saturday Rev. Poetry award, 1957, Phi Beta Kappa Poet Columbia, 1962, Emily Clark Balch prize Va. Quar. Rev., 1964, award for poetry Nat. Inst. Arts. and Letters, 1967, Guggenheim Meml. fellow, 1958-59, 65; Rockefeller fellow, 1968; Nat. Endowment for Arts fellow, 1980; Theodore Roethke prize Poetry Northwest mag., 1970. Fellow Am. Acad. Poets; Mem. Dennett's Wharf Hist. Soc., Slocum Soc., Amphibicon Assn., Sphinx, Alpha Delta Phi, Phi Beta Kappa. Club: Castine Yacht (Castine, Maine) (past commodore). Home: Main St Castine ME 04421 Office: Dept English Syracuse U Syracuse NY 13210

BOOTH, RICHARD EARL, former fund raising exec.; b. Toledo, June 10, 1919; s. Earl Arthur and Adelen (Bianchi) B.; m. Ruth Eleanor Fisher, June 17, 1944 (dec. July 1973); m. Karen Lewis Ivey, Feb. 23, 1974; stepchildren-Christina Story, Nanette Marie, Camille Rogers, Julianna Lewis. Ph.B., U. Toledo, 1941; postgrad., Ohio State U., 1941-42; D.H.L., Adelphi U., 1978. Asst. to gen. mgr. Rochester (N.Y.) Community and War Chest, 1942-44; dir. indsl. dept. Community Chest Met. Detroit, 1944-49; asst. gen. mgr., campaign dir. United Found., Detroit, 1949-54; exec. dir. St. Louis Community Chest, 1954-55; exec. v.p. United Fund Greater St. Louis, 1955-57; exec. dir. Greater N.Y. Fund, N.Y.C., 1957, United Fund Greater N.Y., 1968-78; chmn. nat. profl. adv. council, manpower adv. com. United Way Am., Inc.; Bd. dirs. Boys' Club New Rochelle, N.Y., Am. Hearing Soc., Washington; pres. Tri-State United Way, 1977-78; ret., 1978. Recipient Distinguished Service award community services com. N.Y.C. Central Labor Council AFL-CIO., 1966; fellow Adelphi U., 1976. Mem. Ohio Soc. N.Y. (trustee), Sigma Phi Epsilon. Republican. Methodist. Club: Stone Ridge Country (Poway, Calif.). Home: 1535 Robyn Rd Escondido CA 92025

BOOTH, ROBERT EDMOND, librarian, educator; b. Bridgeport, Conn., May 21, 1917; m. Ada Margaret Pfohl, Aug. 19, 1944; children: Ellen Caroline, Margaret Anne. A.B., Wayne State U., 1941; B.S. in L.S, Columbia U., 1942, A.M., U. Mich., 1943; Ph.D., Western Res. U., 1960. Jr. asst. Detroit Public Library, 1943-44; editor, bibliographer Univ. Microfilms, Ann Arbor, Mich., 1944-46; reference librarian Peabody Inst. Library, Balt., 1946-47; asso. librarian M.I.T., 1947-56; research asso., instr. Sch. Library Sci., Western Res. U., Cleve., 1956-60; asso. prof. div. library sci. Wayne State U., Detroit, 1960-64, prof., dir., 1964—; cons. to various libraries, govt. agys. and profl. orgns., 1954—; del. to Library Assn. Australia, summers, 1971, 73, 77; vice chmn. Mich. Library Consortium, 1978-79; mem. adv. com. tng. and research Bur. Library and Ednl. Tech., 1971-73. Author: Culturally Disadvantaged, 1967, Index to Poverty, Human Resources and Manpower Information, 1967, Index to Minority Group Employment Information, 1967, (with M. Ricking) Handbook for Task Analysis, 1972, Personnel Utilization in Libraries, 1974. Named Disting. Alumnus U. Mich. Sch. L.S., 1977, Case-Western Res. U. Sch. L.S., 1979. Mem. ALA, Mich. Library Assn. (pres. 1970-71, Mich. Librarian of Yr. 1979-80), Spl. Libraries Assn., Assn. Am. Library Schs., Friends of Detroit Pub. Library (bd. dirs.), Founders Soc. Detroit Inst. Arts, Book Club of Detroit, World Future Soc., Beta Phi Mu, Phi Delta Kappa. Club: Prismatic. Home: 872 Balfour Rd Grosse Point MI 48230 Office: Div Library Science Wayne State U Detroit MI 48202

BOOTH, TAYLOR LOCKWOOD, computer science educator; b. Middletown, Conn., Sept. 22, 1933; s. George Robert and Della (Bell) B.; m. Aline Loyzim, Jan. 1, 1955; children: Laurine, Michael, Shari. B.S., U. Conn., 1955; M.S. (Fortesque fellow 1955-56), 1956; Ph.D., 1962. Systems engr. Westinghouse Electric Corp., Balt., 1956-59; instr. U. Conn., Storrs, 1959-63, asst. prof., 1963-67, asso. prof., 1967-69, prof. computer sci. and elec. engring., 1969—; cons. computer sci. and engring. to various firms, 1962—. Author: Sequential Machines and Automata Theory, 1967, Digital Networks and Computer Systems, 1972, 2nd edit., 1978, Computing: Fundamentals and Applications, 1974. Fellow IEEE; mem. IEEE Computer Soc. (sec. 1981—, v.p. for edn. 1982-83), Assn. Computing Machinery, Am. Soc. Engring. Edn. (Frederick Emmons Terman award 1972), Sigma Xi. Home: 451 Wormwood Hill Rd Mansfield Center CT 06250 Office: U-157 Univ of Conn Storrs CT 06268

BOOTH, THEODORE HARRINGTON, bronze co. exec.; b. Buffalo, Mar. 24, 1904; s. Charles Arthur and Mabel Louise (Morse) B.; m. Carol Spitzmiller, June 25, 1927 (dec. Dec. 1971); children—Carol (Mrs. Carol Fox), Charles H., T. William, Timothy M.; m. Alice H. Agnew, Feb. 10, 1973. Grad., Phillips Acad., 1921; M.E., Cornell, 1925. With Gen. Electric Co., 1927, Buffalo Forge Co., 1927-37; works mgr. Walworth Co., then asst. v.p. mfg., 1952; v.p. Carborundum Co., Niagara Falls, N.Y., 1953-57; pres. Frontier Bronze Corp., Niagara Falls, 1957-75, chmn., 1975—; chmn. Frontier Foundries Inc.; pres. Aluminum Match Plate Corp., Kenmore, N.Y.; dir. Barclay-Westmoreland Trust Co., Greensburg, Pa., 1946-52, Atlas Steel Casting Corp., Buffalo. Pres. local Community Chest, 1949-51; pres. Niagara Ednl. Found. Mem. Alpha Delta Phi. Clubs: Niagara, Buffalo, Royal Canadian Yacht, Youngstown (N.Y.) Yacht (commodore), Lake Yacht Racing Assn. (pres.). Home: Youngstown NY 14174 Office: Frontier Foundries Inc Niagara Falls NY 14304

BOOTH, WALLACE WRAY, industrial distribution company executive; b. Nashville, Sept. 30, 1922; s. Wallace Wray and Josephine Anderson (Engl) B.; m. Donna Cameron Voss, Mar. 22, 1947; children: Ann Conley (Mrs. F. Brian Cox), John England. B.A., U. Chgo., 1943, M.B.A., 1948. Various positions Ford Motor Co., Dearborn, Mich., 1948-59, v.p. fin., treas. dir., Can., Oakville, Ont., 1959-63; mng. dir., chief exec. officer Ford Motor Co. Australia, Melbourne, 1963-67; v.p. corp. staffs, indsl. products Philco-Ford Corp., Phila., 1967-68; sr. v.p. corp. staffs Rockwell Internat. Corp., El Segundo, Calif., 1968-75; pres., chief exec. officer United Brands Co., Boston, 1975-77; also dir.; pres., chief exec. officer Ducommon Inc., Los Angeles, 1977—, chmn. bd., 1978—; dir. 1st Interstate Bank, Rohr Industries, Litton Industries, Inc., Internat. Harvester Co., Chgo. Past pres. United Way, kLos Angeles. Served to 1st lt. USAAF, 1943-46. Club: Calif. (Los Angeles). Office: Ducommon Inc 612 S Flower St Los Angeles CA 90017

BOOTH, WAYNE CLAYSON, English educator, author; b. American Fork, Utah, Feb. 22, 1921; s. Wayne Chipman and Lillian (Clayson) B.; m. Phyllis Barnes, June 19, 1946; children: Katherine, John Richard (dec.), Alison. A.B., Brigham Young U., 1944; M.A., U. Chgo., 1947, Ph.D., 1950; D. Litt. (hon.), Rockford Coll., 1965, St. Ambrose Coll., 1971, U. N.H., 1977, D.H.L., Butler U., 1984. Instr. U. Chgo., 1947-50; asst. prof. Haverford Coll., 1950-53; prof. English, chmn. dept. Earlham Coll., 1953-62; George M. Pullman prof. English U. Chgo., 1962—, dean Coll., 1964-69, Disting. Service prof. dept. English and Com. on Ideas and Methods, 1970—; Beckman lectr. U. Calif., Berkeley, 1979, Sch. Criticism, Irvine, Calif., 1979; Whitney Oates vis. prof. Princeton U., 1984; Vis. cons. (with wife) South African schs. and univs., 1963; cons. Lilly Endowment, Nat. Endowment for Humanities.; Examiner N. Central Assn. Colls. and Univs., 1959-80; nat. adv. council Danforth Found. Assos. Program, 1963-69. Author: The Rhetoric of Fiction, 1961, Now Don't Try To Reason With Me: Essays and Ironies for a Credulous Age, 1970, A Rhetoric of Irony, 1974, Modern Dogma and the Rhetoric of Assent, 1974, Critical Understanding: The Powers and Limits of Pluralism, 1979 (Laing prize 1981); Editor: The Knowledge Most Worth Having, 1967, Harper & Row Reader, 1984; co-editor: Critical Inquiry, Christian Gauss Seminars in Criticism, Princeton, 1974; chmn. bd. publs., U. Chgo. Press, 1974-75, 79-80. Trustee Earlham Coll., 1965-75. Served with inf. AUS, 1944-46. Recipient Christian Gauss prize Phi Beta Kappa, 1962; Disting. Alumni award Brigham Young U., 1975; Quantrell prize for undergrad. teaching U. Chgo., 1971; Ford Faculty fellow, 1952-53; Guggenheim fellow, 1956-57, 69-70; fellow Ind. U. Sch. Letters, summer 1962; Nat. Endowment for Humanities fellow, 1975-76; Phi Beta Kappa vis. scholar, 1977-78; Rockefeller Found. fellow, 1981-82. Fellow Am. Acad. Arts and Scis.; mem. Acad. Lit. Studies, MLA (exec. council 1973-76, pres. 1981-82), AAUP, Nat. Council Tchrs. English (David H. Russell prize 1966, commn. on lit. 1967-70), Coll. Conf. Composition and Communication. Democrat. Mem. Ch. of Jesus Christ of Latter-day Saints. Home: 5411 Greenwood Av Chicago IL 60615

BOOTH, WILLIAM ROLAND, advertising executive; b. Oil City, Pa., Apr. 29, 1942; s. Howard Worthington and Katherine Louise (Jessop) B.; m. Joan Lucille Brazzale, Sept. 7, 1963; children: Douglas William, David Alan. B.Comm. in Mktg., NYU, 1964. Media buyer, account exec. Compton Advt., N.Y.C., 1964-69; account supr. Ted Bates Advt. Inc., N.Y.C., 1969-71, v.p., account dir. Can., Toronto, 1973-78, exec. v.p., 1978-82; v.p., gen. mgr. Stone & Adler/Direct Ltd., Toronto, 1982—; account supr. Bloom Advt., Dallas, 1971-72. Mem. Alpha Delta Sigma (past officer). Office: 110 Eglinton Ave E Toronto ON M4P 2Y1 Canada *

BOOTHBY, WILLARD SANDS, JR., investment banking company executive; b. Phila., Nov. 11, 1921; s. Willard Sands and Mable (Edgar) B.; m. Florence E. Clifford, Jan. 22, 1946; children: Willard Sands III, Richard C., Ann C. (Mrs. Francis D. Moore, Jr.). Grad., Deerfield Acad., 1940; student, Cornell U., 1940-42; B.S. in Mech. Engring, Lehigh U., 1946, Wharton Sch., U. Pa., 1946-48. Trainee, salesman, corporate finance Drexel & Co., Phila., 1946-50; mgr. municipal bond dept. Eastman Dillon Union Securities & Co. (formerly Eastman Dillon & Co.), Phila. office, 1950-54, resident partner, 1954-64, partner in charge br. offices, N.Y.C., 1964-66, asso. mng. partner, 1966-68, chief operating partner, 1968-70, pres., chief exec. partner, 1970-71; pres., chief exec. officer Blyth Eastman Dillon & Co., Inc., 1972-74, chmn., 1974-80, chief exec. officer, 1974-77, also dir., chmn. policy com.; mng. dir. Blyth Eastman Paine Webber Inc., N.Y.C., 1980—; dir. Burlington Industries, Inc., Commonwealth Telephone Co., Commonwealth Telephone Enterprises, Inc., Getty Oil Co., Ga.-Pacific Corp., Sperry Corp.; mem. Lower Manhattan adv. bd. Chem. Bank; former mem. nominating com. N.Y. Stock Exchange. Mem. exec. bd. Greater N.Y. Council Boy Scouts Am.; bd. mgrs. Children's Hosp. of Phila.; bd. dirs. World Affairs Council Phila.; committeeman Republican Party, Phila., 1952-54; Trustee Springside Sch., Pine Manor Coll.; former trustee Episcopal Hosp., Phila. Mem. Securities Industry Assn. (past chmn., dir., mem. governing council, exec. com.), Soc. Fin. Analysts Investment Bankers Assn. Am. (past dir., past chmn. regional commn.). Clubs: Philadelphia, Phila. Cricket, Sunnybrook Golf, Racquet (Phila.); Links, River (N.Y.C.); Augusta (Ga.) Nat. Golf. Office: Blyth Eastman Paine Webber Inc 1221 Ave of Americas New York NY 10020 *

BOOTHBY, WILLIAM MUNGER, scientist, educator; b. Detroit, Apr. 1, 1918; s. Thomas Franklin and Florence (Munger) B.; m. Ruth Robin, June 8, 1947; children—Daniel, Thomas, Mark. A.B., U. Mich., 1941, M.A., 1942, Ph.D., 1949. Mem. faculty Northwestern U., 1948-59; fellow Am.-Swiss Found. for Sci. Exchange, Swiss Fed. Inst. Tech., Zurich, 1950-51; asso. prof. Washington U., St. Louis, 1959-62, prof., 1962—; NSF sr. postdoctoral fellow Inst. for Advanced Study, Princeton, N.J., 1961-62, U. Geneva, Switzerland, 1965-66; professeur associe U. Strasbourg, France, 1971, 77. Author: Introduction to Differentiable Manifolds and Riemannian Geometry; co-editor: Symmetric Spaces; Contbr. articles to profl. jours. Served with USAAF, 1942-46. Mem. Am., London math. Socs., Math. Assn. Am., Soc. Indsl. and Applied Math., Sigma Xi. Home: 6954 Cornell Ave University City MO 63130 Office: Dept Math Washington U St Louis MO 63130

BOOTHE, ARMISTEAD LLOYD, sem. ofcl.; b. Alexandria, Va., Sept. 23, 1907; s. Gardner Lloyd and Eleanor (Carr) B.; m. Elizabeth Ravenel Peells, June 30, 1934; children—Julie (Mrs. Charles S. Perry), Eleanor (Mrs. John M. Smith), Elizabeth (Mrs. Lee F. Davis Jr.). A.B., U. Va., 1928; B.A., Oxford (Eng.) U., 1931, M.A., 1940; L.H.D., Protestant Episcopal Sem. in Va., 1976. Bar: Va. bar 1929. Practiced in, Alexandria, 1931-70; sr. partner firm Boothe, Dudley, Koontz, Blankingship and Stump, Alexandria, Va., 1950-70; dir. United Virginia Bank, First & Citizens Nat. Bank; dir. devel. Va. Theol. Sem., 1970-77, counsel, 1945—, trustee, 1951-70, spl. counsel to dean, 1976—; Spl. asst. atty. gen. U.S., 1934-36; atty. City of Alexandria, 1938-43. Mem. Va. Ho. Dels., 1948-56, Va. Senate, 1956-64; Trustee Colonial Williamsburg Found., 1952-77. Served with USNR, 1943-45. Mem. Lit. Soc. Washington, Raven Soc., S.A.R., Phi Beta Kappa, Beta Theta Pi. Clubs: Cosmos, Commonwealth. Home: 913 Vicar Ln Alexandria VA 21302

BOOTHE, DYAS POWER, JR., financial corporation executive; b. Berkeley, Calif., Dec. 23, 1910; s. Dyas Power and Margaret (Stewart) B.; m. Margaret Kempenich, June 28, 1933 (div. 1966); children: Margaret Joanne (Mrs. Charles E. Turkington), Barry Power; m. Catherine Causey, 1967; 1 dau., Catherine Elizabeth. A.B., Stanford, 1931. Pres. Boothe Fruit Co., Modesto, Calif., 1946-59, Boothe Leasing Corp., San Francisco, 1954-67; chmn., chief exec. officer Boothe Fin. Corp., Armco-Boothe Corp., to 1972, GATX-Boothe Corp., 1967-81, chmn. emeritus; also domestic and fgn. subsidiaries; chmn. bd., dir. Courier Terminal Systems Inc., Phoenix, 1971-78; pres., chief exec. officer, trustee IDS Realty Trust, 1976-80; chmn., chief exec. officer IDS Mortgage Corp., 1976-80; dir. BEI Electronics, Inc., Delta Queen Steamboat Co.; chmn. Vacu Dry Co., Apple Time Co., Internat. Anasazi Inc. Served to comdr. USNR, 1942-46; PTO. Mem. Delta Tau Delta. Clubs: University, Commercial, Bankers (San Francisco);

Meadow (Fairfax, Calif.); Metropolitan (N.Y.C.). Home: 33 San Carlos Ave Sausalito CA 94965 Office: Four Embarcadero Ctr Suite 2860 San Francisco CA 94111

BOOTHE, LEON ESTEL, university administrator; b. Carthage, Mo., Feb. 1, 1938; s. Harold Estel and Merle Jane (Hood) B.; m. Nancy Janes, Aug. 20, 1960; children: Cynthia, Diana and Cheri (twins). B.S. (Curators' scholar), U. Mo.-Columbia, 1960, M.A., 1962; Ph.D. in History, U. Ill., 1966. Tchr. history Valparaiso (Ind.) High Sch., 1960-61; asst. prof. history U. Miss., Oxford, 1965-68, assoc. prof., 1968-70; assoc. prof. history George Mason Coll. (now U. Va.), Fairfax, 1970-73, prof. history, 1973-80, assoc. dean coll., 1970-71, dean, 1971-72, dean Coll. Arts and Scis., 1972-80; provost, v.p. acad. affairs Ill. State U., Normal, 1980-82; pres. No. Ky. U., Highland Heights, 1983—; dir., mem. exec. com. Greater Cin. Consortium Colls. and Univs. Adv. bd. Cin. Council World Affairs; Bd. dirs. Wesley Found., Fairfax County and McLean County chpts. ARC, McLean County Heart Assn., McLean County United Way.; mem. Met. Bd. YMCA No. Ky. NEH postdoctoral fellow, 1967-68; scholar Diplomat Seminars U.S. Dept. State. Mem. Soc. Historians for Am. Fgn. Relations, McLean County Assn. Commerce and Industry, No. Ky. C. of C., Sigma Rho Sigma, Omicron Delta Kappa, Phi Alpha Theta, Phi Delta Kappa. Democrat. Methodist (pres. governing bd.). Lodges: Rotary; Masons. Home: 1 University Dr. Highland Heights KY 41076 Office: office of Pres No Ky Univ Highland Heights KY 41076

BOOTHE, POWER, artist, set designer, educator; b. Dallas, Mar. 12, 1945; s. Tom Wheeler and Shirlee (Barth) B.; m. Sarah Schoentgen, Mar. 22, 1969 (div. 1974); m. 2d Elizabeth Rheem Rectanus, Aug. 17, 1979. B.A., Colo. Coll., Colorado Springs, 1969. Fellow ind. study program Whitney Mus., 1967-68; instr. painting Sch. Visual Arts, N.Y.C., 1979—; guest artist SUNY-Buffalo, 1981, Mt. Royal Sch. Painting, Md. Art Inst., Balt., 1976, 79, U. Iowa, Ames, 1979. Exhibited one-man shows, A.M. Sachs Gallery, N.Y.C., 1973, 74, 76, 77, 81, 82, group shows throughout U.S.; represented in permanent collections including, Solomon R. Guggenheim Mus., N.Y.C., Hirschhorn Mus. and Sculpture Garden, Washington, Chase Manhattan Bank, N.Y. Bank for Savs., Lehman Bros. Kuhn Loeb, Inc., Phillip Morris Corp., Sony Corp., Estee Lauder Corp.; set designer, Bklyn. Acad. Opera House, 1983, Lynn Austin's Music Theater, 1982, Dance Theater Workshop, 1981, 82, Performing Garage, 1978, Guggenheim Mus., 1970, others; also art dir. various films. Recipient Theodoron award Guggenheim Mus., 1971; Nat. Endowment Arts grantee, 1975, 83; N.Y. State Council grantee, 1982. Address: 49 Crosby St New York NY 10012

BOOTHROYD, HERBERT J., insurance company executive; b. Mason City, Iowa, Dec. 23, 1928; s. Herbert L. and Clara (Schmitt) B.; m. Barbara Elizabeth Dunne, Feb. 9, 1961; children: Diane Lea, John Herbert. A.B., U. Mich., 1952, A.M., 1953. Enrolled actuary, 1976. With Mass. Mut. Life Ins. Co., 1953-57; with New Eng. Mut. Life Ins. Co., Boston, 1957—, v.p., 1967-77, sr. v.p. pension ops., 1977-82, exec. v.p. group ops., 1983—; dir. New Eng. Pension and Annuity Co., 1980—, pres., 1981—; dir. New Eng. Variable Life Ins. Co. Contbg. author: Life and Health Insurance Handbook, 1973. Bd. dirs. New Eng. chpt. Am. Diabetes Assn., 1979—. Served with AUS, 1946-47. Fellow Soc. Actuaries; mem. Better Bus. Bur. Eastern Mass (dir. 1980—), Am. Council Life Ins., Am. Acad. Actuaries, Internat. Congress Actuaries, Phi Beta Kappa, Theta Delta Chi. Home: 51 Indian Hill Rd Weston MA 02193 Office: 501 Boylston St Boston MA 02117

BOOTLE, WILLIAM AUGUSTUS, judge; b. Colleton County, S.C., Aug. 19, 1902; s. Philip Lorraine and Laura Lilla (Benton) B.; m. Virginia Childs, Nov. 24, 1928; children: William Augustus, Ann, James C. A.B., Mercer U., 1924, LL.B., 1925, LL.D., 1982. Bar: Ga. 1925. Since practiced in, Macon; U.S. dist. atty. Middle Ga. Dist., 1929-33; mem. firm Carlisle & Bootle, 1933-54; acting dean Law Sch., Mercer U., 1933-37, part-time prof. law, 1926-37; judge U.S. Dist. Ct. for Middle Dist. Ga., Macon, 1954—, sr. judge, 1972—. Trustee Mercer U., 1933-79, chmn. exec. com., 1941-46, 48-53; trustee Walter F. George Sch. Law Found., 1961—, v.p., 1963-65, pres., 1965-66. Recipient Disting. Alumnus award Mercer U., 1971. Mem. Phi Alpha Delta, Phi Delta Theta. Republican. Baptist. Clubs: Masons, Shriners, Civitan (pres. 1936). Office: Federal Bldg and US Courthouse Macon GA 31202

BOOTY, JOHN EVERITT, clergyman, university dean; b. Detroit, May 2, 1925; s. George Thomas and Alma (Gamauf) B.; m. Catherine Louise Smith, June 10, 1950; children: Carol Holland, Geoffrey Rollen, Peter Thomas, Catherine Jane. B.A., Wayne State U., 1952; B.D., Va. Theol. Sem., 1953; M.A., Princeton U., 1957, Ph.D., 1960. Ordained to ministry Episcopal Ch., 1953; curate Christ Episcopal Ch., Dearborn, Mich., 1953-55; asst. prof. ch. history Va. Theol. Sem., 1958-64, assoc. prof., 1964-67; prof. ch. history Episcopal Theol. Sch., Cambridge, Mass., 1967-82; acting dir. Inst. Theol. Research, 1974-76; dean Sch. Theology U. of the South, Sewanee, Tenn., 1982—; Fulbright scholar U. London, Eng., 1957-58; fellow Folger Shakespeare Library, 1964. Author: John Jewel as Apologist of the Church of England, 1963, Yearning to be Free, 1974, Three Anglican Divines on Prayer: Jewel, Andrewes, and Hooker, 1978, The Church in History, 1979, The Spirit of Anglicanism, 1979; author: The Godly Kingdom of Tudor England, 1981, The Servant Church, 1982, What Makes Us Episcopalians, 1982, Anglican Spirituality, 1982, Anglican Moral Choice, 1983, Meditations on Four Quartets, 1983; Editor: The Book of Common Prayer, 1959, John Jewel: The Apology of the Church of England, 1963, 74, The Elizabethan Prayer Book, 1976, The Works of Richard Hooker, Vol. 4, 1981; Contbr. articles to profl. jours. Chmn. Nat. Youth Commn., P.E. Ch., 1948-50. Recipient Am. Philos. Soc. award, 1964; Nat. Endowment for Humanities fellow, 1978-79. Mem. Council of Deans, Council for Devel. Ministry. Home: Harkin's House Clara's Point Rd Sewanee TN 37375 Office: Sch of Theology Univ of the South Sewanee TN 37375

BOOTZIN, RICHARD RONALD, psychologist, educator; b. Milw., Feb. 25, 1940; s. Arnold and Evelyn (Myslis) B.; m. Maris Kay Pittelman, Dec. 27, 1959; children—Deborah Jeanne, Helaine Beth. B.S., U. Wis., 1963; M.S., Purdue U., 1966, Ph.D., 1968. Ward psychologist Palo Alto (Calif.) VA Hosp., 1967-68; mem. faculty Northwestern U., 1968—, prof. psychology, 1978—, chmn. dept., 1980—; vis. asso. prof. Stanford U., 1977-78; prin. investigator various grants, 1971—. Author books, papers, revs. in field; editorial cons. profl. jours. Fellow Am. Psychol. Assn.; mem. Assn. Advancement Behavior Therapy (dir. 1973-77, chmn. publs. bd. 1975-77), Sleep Research Soc. Jewish. Office: Dept Psychology Northwestern Univ Evanston IL 60201

BOOZER, BRENDA LYNN, mezzo soprano; b. Atlanta, Jan. 25, 1948; d. Jack Stewart and Ruth Malcolm (Tate) B.; m. Robert Martin Klein, Apr. 29, 1973. B.A. (scholar), Fla. State U., 1970; postgrad., Juilliard Sch. Music, 1974-77. Appearances include, Spoleto (Italy) Opera Festival, 1978-79, Carmel (Calif.) Bach Festival, 1978, Chgo. Lyric Opera, Miami (Fla.) Opera, 1979, Houston Opera, San Francisco Spring Opera, 1977, Amsterdam (Netherlands) Opera, 1981, Kansas City (Mo.) Opera, 1979, Los Angeles Symphony, Mostly Mozart Festival, N.Y.C., Met. Opera, 1979-82, Falstaff, with Paris Opera, 1982, 83, Florence Opera House, 1982, Hansel and Gretel, with Met. Opera, 1983; guest appearances on TV, 1977—; TV appearances include, Tonight Show, Merv Griffin Show, Mike Douglas Show, 1980, 82, Entertainment Tonight, Today Show, 1983; Covent Garden-Royal Opera House debut in: Falstaff, 1982; Carnegie Hall debut in: Benvenuto Cellini, 1983; guest appearances, CBS Am. Parade, Phila. Orch., Nat. Symphony, St. Louis Symphony, Seattle Symphony, Wolf Trap Opera Festival, others. Finalist Met. Opera Competition, 1977, Liederkranz Competition, 1977. Mem. Am. Guild Mus. Artists, AFTRA. Democrat. Methodist. Address: care Columbia Artists Mgmt Inc 165 W 57th St New York NY 10019

BOOZER, HOWARD RAI, state edn. ofcl.; b. Monterey, Ky., Aug. 14, 1923; s. Claud D. and Harriet Ruth (Foster) B.; m. Frances Aileen Kintner, Aug. 23, 1946; children—Claudia, Margaret, Catherine, Barbara. A.A., Cumberland (Ky.) Coll., 1942; A.B., Howard Coll., 1946; Ph.D., Washington U., St. Louis, 1960; LL.D. (hon.), Baptist Coll. at Charleston, S.C., 1976. Asst. personnel dir. Mall Tool Co., Chgo., 1946-47; tchr. high sch., Webster Groves, Mo., 1949-51; staff asso. Am. Council Edn., Washington, 1954-61; acting dir. Washington Internat. Center, 1957-58; asst. dir. N.C. Bd. Higher Edn., Raleigh, 1961-65, dir., 1965-68; v.p. Regional Edn. Lab., Durham, N.C., 1968-70; dir. Ednl. Devel. Adminstrn. RCA Corp., Cherry Hill, N.J., 1970-73; exec. dir. S.C. Commn. on Higher Edn., Columbia, 1973—; adj. prof. edn. Duke U., 1968-70; mem. review panel for constrn. of nurse tng. facilities USPHS, 1965-69. Trustee Meredith Coll., 1963-66, Wingate Coll., 1967-70; bd. dirs. Learning Inst. N.C., 1965-68; S.C. del. Edn. Commn. of States, 1974-79. Served with USNR, 1943-46, 51-54. Mem. Am. Assn. Higher Edn., Internat. Assn. of Torch Clubs, Newcomen Soc. N. Am., N.C. League Nursing (pres. 1969-70), Nat. League for Nursing (dir. 1973-77), State Higher Edn. Exec. Officers Assn., So. Regional Edn. Bd., Phi Delta Kappa, Kappa Delta Pi. Democrat. Office: 1429 Senate St Columbia SC 29201

BOOZER, ROBERT CHARLES, lawyer; b. Birmingham, Ala., June 18, 1930; s. Herman Wyse and Teressa (Maybin) B.; m. Sidney Cooper Wesley, Oct. 6, 1961; children—Katherine Wyse, Wesley Robert, Margaret Maybin. A.B., Emory U., 1952; J.D., Harvard, 1955; postgrad., Netherlands Inst. Econs., Rotterdam, 1955-56. Bar: Ga. bar 1954. Practice in, Atlanta, 1956—; partner firm Troutman, Sanders, Lockerman & Ashmore (and predecessor firms), 1965—; lectr. law Woodrow Wilson Coll., Atlanta, 1959-61. Pres. Choral Guild Atlanta, 1959-60. Served with USAF, 1951-52. Mem. Am. Arbitration Assn., Phi Beta Kappa, Kappa Alpha, Alpha Kappa Psi, Omicron Delta Kappa. Episcopalian. Clubs: Atlanta City, Lawyers (Atlanta). Home: 899 W Wesley Rd NW Atlanta GA 30327 Office: 1400 Candler Bldg Atlanta GA 30043

BOOZER, YOUNG JACOB, III, oil company executive; b. Birmingham, Ala., Nov. 23, 1948; s. Young J. and Phyllis (Chamberlain) B.; m. Ann Gergory, Nov. 11, 1977; 1 dau., Alexis. B.A., Stanford U., 1971; M.B.A., U. Pa., 1973. Sr. account officer Citibank N.A., N.Y.C., 1973-78; v.p. Crocker Nat. Bank, Los Angeles, 1978-80; v.p. fin. United Refining, Inc., Houston, 1981—; sr. v.p. Coral Petroleum, Inc., Houston, 1980—. Coordinator, vol. Spl. Olympics, Los Angles, Houston, 1979—. Democrat. Episcopalian. Clubs: Stanford U. (N.Y.C.) (pres. 1977-78); Pine Forest Country). Office: Coral Petroleum Inc 908 Town and Country Blvd Houston TX 77024

BORAH, RICHARD THOMAS, ins. co. exec.; b. York, Pa., Oct. 15, 1927; s. Lewis E. and Elizabeth (Mooney) B.; m. Mary Louise Kilkenny, Sept. 9, 1950; children—Gregory, Kathleen, Christopher, Kevin. B.A., Colby Coll., 1950; M.B.A., N.Y. U., 1954. With Mut. Life Ins. Co. of New York, 1950—, pension specialist, Chgo., 1955-57, N.Y.C., 1957—, sr. v.p., 1972-78, exec. v.p., 1978—. Served with USCG, 1945-46. Home: 318 Southdown Rd Lloyd Harbor NY 11743 Office: 1740 Broadway New York NY 10019

BORAH, WOODROW WILSON, educator; b. Utica, Miss., Dec. 22, 1912; s. Hirsh Hill and Fannie (Ichkovich) B.; m. Therese Rae Levy, Sept. 8, 1945; children—Jonathan, Ruth. A.B., UCLA, 1935, M.A., 1936; Ph.D., U. Calif., Berkeley, 1940. Instr. Princeton (N.J.) U., 1941-42; analyst Dept. State and OSS, Washington, 1942-47; faculty U. Calif., Berkeley, 1948—, Abraham D. Shepard prof. history, 1973-80, Abraham D. Shepard prof. history emeritus, 1980—; chmn. Center Latin Am. Studies, 1973-79; Alfonso Caso Meml. vis. prof. Universidad Nacional Autónoma de Mex., 1981-82; hon. pres. VI Conf. Mex.-U.S. Historians, Chgo., 1981. Asso. editor: Western Jour. Speech, 1955-57; editorial bd.: Hispanic Am. Hist. Rev, 1959-64, 72-77; adv. editor, 1978—; adv. editorial bd.: Guide to Hist. Lit. Latin Am, 1963-67; author: New Spain's Century of Depression, 1951, Early Colonial Trade and Navigation between Mexico and Peru, 1954, (with Sherbourne F. Cook) Essays on the History of Population: Mexico and the Caribbean, 3 vols, 1971-79; contbr. articles to profl. jours. Guggenheim fellow, 1951-52, 58-59; Social Sci. Research Council fellow, 1965-66; medalla de acero al merito historico "Cap. Alonso de Leon" of Sociedad Neuvoleonesa de Historia, Geografia y Estadistica, 1972; with S.F. Cook) Sahagun gold medal in anthropology Mexico, 1971; Disting. Service award Conf. Latin Am. History, 1980. Mem. Nat. Conf. Latin Am. History (chmn. 1966-67), Am. Hist. Assn. (pres. Pacific Coast conf. 1977-78), Academia Mexicana de la Historia (corr.), Sociedad Mexicana de Antropologia, Latin Am. Studies Assn. Democrat. Jewish. Home: 451 Vincente Ave Berkeley CA 94707 Office: Dept History U Calif Berkeley CA 94720

BORCHELT, MERLE LLOYD, electric utility company executive; b. Mercedes, Tex., Jan. 4, 1926; s. George Cornelius and Pauline Caroline (Lange) B.; m. Virginia Mae Gullatt, Aug. 3, 1947; children: Lawrence Frederick, Linda Diane, Mark Randall. B.S. in Elec. Engring., La. Tech. U., 1949; postgrad., Westinghouse Advanced Electric Utility Program, 1958, Harvard U. Advanced Mgmt. Program, 1983. Registered profl. engr., Tex. With Central Power & Light Co., Corpus Christi, Tex., 1949—, gen. mgr. fuels-systems planning, 1975-77, v.p., 1977-79, exec. v.p., chief engr., 1979-81, pres., chief exec. officer, 1981—, dir. Chmn. United Way of Coastal Bend, 1982. Served with USN, 1943-45. Mem. IEEE (pres. Corpus Christi chpt.), Edison Electric Inst. (dir.), Tex. Atomic Energy Research Found. (dir.), South Tex. C. of C. (exec. bd. 1980—), South Tex. Found. Econ. Edn., Tex. Assn. Taxpayers, Assn. Electric Cos. Tex. (dir. 1980—). Lutheran. Clubs: Corpus Christi Country, Town, Nueces. Office: Central Power & Light Co 120 N Chaparral St Corpus Christi TX 78401

BORCHERT, JOHN ROBERT, geography educator; b. Chgo., Oct. 24, 1918; s. Ernest J. and Maude (Gorndt) B.; m. Jane Anne Willson, June 10, 1942; children: Dianne, William, Robert, David. A.B., DePauw U., 1941; M.A., U. Wis., 1946, Ph.D., 1949. Instr. geography U. Wis., 1947-49; asst. prof. U. Minn., Mpls., 1949-51, asso. prof., 1951-56, prof., 1956-81, Regent's prof., 1981—; chmn. dept. geography, 1956-61; urban research dir. Upper Midwest econ. study, 1961-64; dir. Center for Urban and Regional Affairs, 1968-77; chmn. earth scis. div. Nat. Acad. Scis.-NRC, 1967-69; mem. corp. Social Sci. Research Council, 1968—. Author publs. on urbanization and resource devel. in U.S., 1961—, frequency and distbn. of drought in Central N. Am., 1949-71. Served to major USAAF, World War II. Fellow Am. Acad. Arts and Scis.; mem. Nat. Acad. Scis., Assn. Am. Geographers (past pres., Honors award 1976), Am. Geog. Soc. (Van Cleef medal 1970). Home: 23239 St Croix Trail N Scandia MN 55073 Office: Dept Geography Univ of Minn Minneapolis MN 55455

BORCOMAN, JAMES WILLMOTT, museum curator; b. Canada, Jan. 17, 1926; s. Constant James and Dorothy Hatton (Willmott) B.; m. Therese Jomphe, Nov. 3, 1956; 1 dau., Sophie. B.A. with honours, U. N.B., 1955, teaching fellow, postgrad. scholar, 1955-56; M.F.A. in History Photography, SUNY, Buffalo, 1971. Edn. officer, then dir. exhbns. and edn. Nat. Gallery Can., 1960-69, curator photography, 1971—; adj. prof. photography U. Ottawa, 1971-75; chmn. history photography seminar, Arles, France, 1977, 80. Author: David Heath: A Dialogue with Solitude, 1980, Charles Nègre, 1976, The Painter as Photographer, 1979, Eugène Atget, 1984; also articles, mus. catalogues. Served with Can. Army and RCAF, 1943-45. Recipient prize disting. achievement photog. history Photog. Hist. Soc. N.Y., 1977, seal City of Arles, 1977. Mem. Soc. Photog. Edn. (dir. 1969-73), Can. Mus. Assn. (council 1967-69). Mem. Ch. of Eng. Office: Nat Gallery Can Ottawa ON K1A 0M8 Canada

BORDA, RICHARD JOSEPH, banker; b. San Francisco, Aug. 16, 1931; s. Joseph Clement and Ethel Cathleen (Donovan) B.; m. Judith Maxwell, Aug. 30, 1953; children: Michelle, Stephen Joseph. A.B., Stanford U., 1953, M.B.A., 1957. With Wells Fargo Bank, San Francisco, 1957-70, mgr., 1963-66, asst. v.p., 1966-67, v.p., 1967-70; asst. sec. Air Force Manpower Res. Affairs, Washington, after 1970; now exec. v.p. adminstrn. Wells Fargo Bank; dir. Nat. Life Ins. Co. Montpelier, Vt., Wells Fargo Realty Advs., Wells Fargo Found., Wells Fargo Bus. Credit. Pres. Air Force Aid Soc., Washington; Bd. dirs. Central City Assn., So. Calif. Bldg. Fund, Hollywood Presbyn. Hosp. Found.; mem. Central City Assn.; chmn. athletic bd. Stanford U.; trustee Scholarships for Children of Am. Mil. Personnel. Served with USMCR, 1953-55. Mem. Los Angeles Area C. of C. (vice chmn.), Marine Corps Res. Officers Assn., Air Force Assn., Phi Gamma Delta. Republican. Episcopalian. Clubs: Masons; Army-Navy (Washington); Univ. (San Francisco); Los Angeles Country, Calif. (Los Angeles). Home: 8050 Mulholland Dr Los Angeles CA 90046 Office: 444 S Flower St Los Angeles CA 90017

BORDALLO, MADELEINE MARY (MRS. RICARDO JEROME BORDALLO), first lady of Guam, member Democratic National Committee; b. Graceville, Minn., May 31, 1933; d. Christian Peter and Mary Evelyn (Roth) Zeien; m. Ricardo Jerome Bordallo, June 20, 1953; 1 dau., Deborah Josephine. Student, St Mary's Coll., South Bend, Ind., 1952; A.A., St. Katherines Coll., St. Paul, 1953, U. Guam, 1968. Presented in voice recital Guam Acad. Music, Agana., 1951, 62; mem. Civic Opera Co., St. Paul, 1952-53; mem. staff KUAM Radio-TV sta., Agana, 1954-63; freelance writer local newspaper, fashion show commentator, coordinator, civic leader, 1963, nat. Dem. committeewoman for Guam, 1964—, 1st lady of Guam, 1975-79, 83-86; senator 16th Guam Legislature, 1981-82; del. Nat. Dem. Conv., 1964, 68, 72; pres. Women's Dem. Party Guam, 1967-69; rep. Presdl. Inauguration, Washington, 1965, 77; del. Dem. Western States Conf., Reno, 1965, Los Angeles, 1967, Phoenix, 1968, conf. sec., 1967-69; del. Dem. Women's Campaign Conf., Wash., 1965. Pres. Guam Women's Club, 1958-59; del Gen. Fedn. Women's Clubs Convs., Miami Beach, Fla., 1961 del Gen. Fedn. Women's Clubs Convs., New Orleans, 1965 del Gen. Fedn. Women's Clubs Convs., Boston, 1968; v.p. Fedn. Asian Women's Assn., 1964-67, pres., 1967-69; pres. Guam Symphony Soc., 1967-73; del. convs., Manila, Philippines, 1959 del. convs., Taipei, Formosa, 1960 del. convs., Hong Kong, 1963 del. convs., Guam, 1964 del. convs., Japan, 1968 del. convs., Taipei, 1973; chmn. Guam Christmas Seal Drive, 1961; bd. dirs. Guam chpt. ARC, 1963, sec., 1963-67; pres. Marianas Assn. For Retarded Children, 1968-69, 73-74; bd. dirs. Guam Theatre Guild, Am. Cancer Soc.; mem. Guam Meml. Hosp. Vols. Assn., 1966—, v.p., 1966-67, pres., 1970-71; chmn. Hosp. Charity Ball, 1966; pres. Women for Service, 1974—, Beauty World Guam Ltd., 1981—; First Lady's Beautification Task Force of Guam, 1983—. Mem. Internat. Platform Assn., Guam Rehab. Assn. (assoc.), Guam Lytica and Bodig Assn. (pres. 1983—). Clubs: Spanish of Guam., Inetnon Famalaoan (pres. 1983-86). Address: PO Box 1458 Agana GU 96910

BORDEN, CRAIG WARREN, physician, educator; b. Springboro, Ohio, Aug. 31, 1915; s. Carl C. and Ethel (Pence) B. A.B., Oberlin Coll., 1937; M.D., Harvard, 1941. Diplomate: Am. Bd. Internal Medicine (sec.-treas. 1967, vice chmn. 1968, 69). Intern Boston City Hosp., 1941-42; fellow medicine U. Cin., 1942-43; resident medicine U. Minn., 1946-47, mem. faculty, 1947-53, asst. prof. medicine, 1950-53; mem. faculty Northwestern U. Sch. Medicine, 1953-77, prof. medicine, 1960-77; chief med. service VA Research Hosp., Chgo., 1954-74; sr. physician VA, 1971-77; sr. staff physician Northwestern Meml. Hosp., Chgo., 1963-77; dir. med. edn. St. Vincent Infirmary, Little Rock, 1977—; prof. medicine U. Ark. Sch. for Med. Scis., Little Rock, 1977—. Contbr. med. jours. Served with USAAF, 1943-46. Recipient Chief Med. Dirs. commendation VA, 1963. Fellow A.C.P.; mem. Am. Heart Assn., Central Soc. Clin. Research, AMA (residency rev. com. internal medicine 1966-71). Home: PO Box 5503 Little Rock AR 72215

BORDEN, GEORGE ASA, educator; b. Elmira Heights, N.Y., June 16, 1932; s. Arthur Leroy and Matilda Catherine (Hartmann) B.; children—Sherie, Cynthia, Curtis. Student, Bible Inst. Los Angeles, 1950-52, N.Mex. State U., 1955-57; B.A. in Math, U. Denver, 1958, M.A., 1959, 1962; Ph.D. in Speech Behavior, Cornell U., 1964. Mathematician Marathon Oil Co., Littleton, Colo., 1959-62; from asst. prof. to prof. Pa. State U., University Park, 1964-75; prof. dept. communication U. Del., Newark, 1975—, chmn. dept., 1975-78; cons. Augmented Human Intellect Project of Rome Air Devel. Center; cons. human communication systems Universidad Estatal a Distancia, Costa Rica; mem. nat. adv. bd. Eric Clearinghouse on Reading and Communication Skills. Author: (with Gregg and Grove) Speech Behavior and Human Interaction, 1969, Introduction to Human Communication Theory, 1971, (with Stone) Human Communication: The Process of Relating, 1976, La Comunicación Humana: El Processo de interrelación., 1982; contbr. articles to profl. jours. Served with U.S. Army, 1952-54. Mem. Am. Psychol. Assn., Internat. Communication Assn., Speech Communication Assn., Assn. Lit. and Linguistic Computing. Home: 1508 N Lincoln St Wilmington DE 19806 Office: Dept Communication U Delaware Newark DE 19711
Books are filled with knowledge, but it appears that there is little learning without experience, little experience without involvement, and little involvement without commitment to our own understanding and growth and the facilitation of this process in others.

BORDEN, HENRY, barrister, solicitor; b. Halifax, N.S., Can., Sept. 25, 1901; s. Henry Clifford and Mabel (Ashmere) Barnstead) B.; m. Jean Creelman MacRae, June 1, 1929; children—Robert, Ann, Perry, Mary Jean, Henry. B.A., McGill U., 1921; postgrad., Dalhousie Law Sch., 1922-24, LL.D., 1968; B.A. (Rhodes scholar), Exeter Coll., Oxford, 1926; LL.D., St. Francis Xavier U., 1960, U. Toronto, 1972; D.C.L., Acadia U., 1960. Bar: bar, Lincoln's Inn, London 1927, N.S 1927, Ont. bar 1927, King's Counsel 1938. With Royal Bank Can., 1921-22; gen. counsel Dept. Munitions and Supply, Ottawa, 1939-42; chmn. Wartime Industries Control Bd., Ottawa; co-ordinator of controls Dept. Munitions and Supply, 1942-43; past lectr. corp. law Osgoode Hall Law Sch.; sr. mem. Borden, Elliot, Kelley & Palmer, 1936-46; chmn. Royal Commn. on Energy, 1957-59; pres. Brascan Ltd.

(formerly Brazilian Traction, Light & Power Co. Ltd.), 1946-63, chmn., 1963-65; hon. dir. Massey Ferguson, Ltd., Can. Trustco Mortgage Co.; dir. emeritus Canadian Imperial Bank Commerce. Co-author: Handbook of Canadian Companies, 1931; Editor: Robert Laird Borden, His Memoirs, 1938, Letters to Limbo, (by Sir Robert L. Borden), 1971. Past pres., now dir., mem. exec. com. Royal Agrl. Winter Fair; chmn., bd. govs. U. Toronto, 1964-68, hon. chmn. bd. govs., 1968-71; hon. trustee Royal Ont. Mus. Decorated comdr. Order St. Michael and St. George, 1943; grand officer Nat. Order So. Cross, Brazil, 1962; Centennial medal, 1967; medal of service Order Can., 1969. Mem. Phi Kappa Pi. Mem. Anglican Ch. Clubs: York, Can. of Toronto (Toronto) (past pres.). Home: Vinegar Hill Rural Route 2 King ON L0G 1K0 Canada Office: PO Box 125 Commerce Ct Postal Station Toronto ON M5L 1E2 Canada

BORDERS, CHARLES EDWARD, electric utility company executive; b. Bloomfield, Ind., Dec. 30, 1925; s. Roy A. and Roberta E. (Yount) B.; m. Margie Lou O'Hearn, Apr. 13, 1947; children: Kathleen Montgomery, Kristine Storie, Brian C. B.S. in E.E., U. Notre Dame, 1947. Jr. geophysicist Carter Oil Co., Rolling Fork, Miss., 1947; with Indpls. Power & Light Co., 1947—, sr. v.p., 1976—; dir. Carmel Bank & Trust, Ind. Chmn. Better Bus. Bur., Indpls., 1981-82; pres. Indpls. Opera Co., 1982-83; chmn. NCCJ, Indpls., 1982—. Mem. Ind. Electric Assn. (chmn. 1981). Clubs: Indpls. Athletic, Columbia, Highland Golf & Country (dir. 1981-83). Home: 6140 Sunset Ln Indianapolis IN 46208 Office: Indianapolis Power & Light Company 25 Monument Circle Indianapolis IN 46206

BORDERS, WILLIAM ALEXANDER, journalist; b. St. Louis, Jan. 11, 1939; s. William Alexis and Kate (Thompson) B.; m. Barbara D. Burkham, June 17, 1967; 1 son, William Borders. B.A., Yale, 1960. Staff N.Y. Times, N.Y.C., 1960—, corr., Nigeria, 1970-72, Can., 1972-75, India, 1975-79, London, 1979-82, dep. fgn. editor, 1982-83, editor Week in Rev., N.Y.C., 1983—. Mem. Fgn. Corrs. Assn. S. Asia (pres. 1976-78). Home: 227 E 57th St New York NY 10036 Office: NY Times 229 W 43d St New York NY 10036

BORDERS, WILLIAM D., bishop; b. Washington, Ind., Oct. 9, 1913. Ed., St. Meinrad Sem., Notre Dame Sem., U. Notre Dame. Ordained priest Roman Catholic Ch., 1940; rector St. Joseph Cathedral, Baton Rouge, 1964-68; consecrated bishop, 1968, bishop of Orlando Fla., 1968-74, archbishop of Balt., 1974—. Home: 320 Cathedral St Baltimore MD 21201

BORDIE, JOHN GEORGE, educator; b. Chgo., Apr. 3, 1931; s. John and Helena Jozefin (Kozubal) B.; m. Cammila May Berkley, Feb. 11, 1956; children: Ruth Claire, Helena Robin, Ralph Leon. B.A., U. Chgo., 1949; Ph.D., U. Tex., 1958. Asst. prof. linguistics and English Georgetown U., 1958-61; coordinator linguistics and literacy Electronic Teaching Labs., Washington, 1961-63; dep. dir. tng. Peace Corps, N. and E. Africa, also S. Asia, 1963-66; mem. faculty U. Tex., Austin, 1966—, prof. linguistics, curriculum and instrn., 1974—; dir. Fgn. Lang. Edn. Center, 1974—; vis. prof. Cornell U., 1965, Karachi U., 1980-81; mem. solar and wind energy adv. com. Tex. Energy and Natural Resources Council, 1979—; Fellow Am. Council Learned Socs., 1954-55, Rockefeller Found., 1956; Fulbright sr. lectr., Pakistan, 1980-81, 82-83. Author: The Teaching of African Languages, 1961, English Structure Drills, 1963, A Dari Course, 1968; Editor: Jour. Linguistic Assn. S.W, 1976-82. Mem. Linguistic Soc. Am., Tchrs. English to Speakers Others Langs., Am. Oriental Soc., AAAS. Home: 14454 Merriltown Rd Round Rock TX 78664 Office: FLEC U Tex Austin TX 78712

BORDIN, EDWARD S., educator, psychologist; b. Phila., Nov. 7, 1913; s. Morris and Jennie (Zarovsky) B.; m. Ruth Birgitta Anderson, June 2O, 1941; children—Martha Christine (Mrs. Steven A. Hillyard), Charlotte Anna (Mrs. Sung P. Lin). B.S.C., Temple U., 1935, M.A., 1937; Ph.D., Ohio State U., 1942. Asst. to co-ordinator, also counselor univ. testing bur. U. Minn., 1939-42, acting dir. bur., 1945-46; personnel technician (War Dept.), 1942-45; asso. prof. psychology Wash. State U., 1946-48, U. Mich., Ann Arbor, 1948-55, prof., 1955—. Author: Psychological Counseling, 1955, 2d edit. 1968, Research Strategies in Psychotherapy, 1974; Editor: Jour. Cons. Psychology, 1959-64. Mem. Am. Psychol. Assn. (pres. div. counseling psychology 1955), AAAS, Soc. for Psychotherapy Research (pres. 979). Spl. research theory psychotherapy. Home: 1000 Aberdeen Dr Ann Arbor MI 48104 *Willingness to take intellectual and emotional risks plus an obstinacy about accepting new ideas until I made them my own.*

BORDOGNA, JOSEPH, educator, engineer; b. Scranton, Pa., Mar. 22, 1933; s. Raymond and Rose (Yesu) B. B.S. in Elec. Engring, U. Pa., 1955, Ph.D., 1964; S.M., MIT, 1960. With RCA Corp., 1958-64; asst. prof. U. Pa., Phila., 1964-68, assoc. prof., 1968-72, prof., 1972—, assoc. dean engring. and applied sci., 1973-80, acting dean, 1980-81, dean, 1981—; dir. Moore Sch. Elec. Engring., 1976—, Alfred Fitler Moore chair, 1979—; master Stouffer Coll. House, 1972-76; Cons. industry, govt., founds. Author: (with H. Ruston) Electric Networks, 1966, (with others) The Man-Made World, 1971. Served with USN, 1955-58. Recipient Lindback award for distinguished teaching U. Pa., 1967; George Westinghouse award Am. Soc. Engring. Edn., 1974; Engr. of Yr. award, Phila., 1984. Fellow IEEE; fellow AAAS; mem. Franklin Inst., Optical Soc. Am., Sigma Xi, Eta Kappa Nu, Tau Beta Pi. Home: 1237 Medford Rd Wynnewood PA 19096

BORDUA, DAVID JOSEPH, sociology educator; b. Springfield, Mass., Sept. 2, 1927; s. Joseph J. and Marie Rose (Star) B.; m. Cecylia Matyszczyk, June 16, 1951; children: Joseph, Jessica. B.A., U. Conn., 1950, M.A., 1952; Ph.D., teaching fellow, Harvard U., 1957. Asst. prof. sociology U. Mich., Ann Arbor, 1955-63; assoc. prof. U. Ill., Urbana, 1964-67, prof., 1967—; cons. PRC/Pub. Mgmt., McLean, Va., 1975-79, Abt Assocs., Cambridge, Mass., 1977-79. Assoc. editor Am. Sociol. Rev., 1965-68; editor: The Police, 1967; contbr. articles to profl. jours. Served with U.S. Army, 1945-47. Ger. fellow Ctr. Advanced Study in Behavioral Scis., 1971-72. Mem. Am. Sociol. Assn. (chmn. criminology sect. 1971-72). Home: 4 Montclair Rd Urbana IL 61801 Office: 702 S Wright St Urbana IL 61801

BORECKY, ISIDORE, bishop; b. Ostrowec, Ukraine, Oct. 1, 1911. Ed., Theol. Acad. Lwiw, 1932-36, Maximillian U., Munich, Germany, 1936-38. Ordained priest Ukrainian Greek Catholic Ch., 1938; missionary in, Sask. and Man., Can., 1938-40, parish priest, Niagara Peninsula, Ont., Can., 1940-48, titular bishop of Amathas, 1948—; 1st exarch Ukrainian Cath. Exarchate of Eastern Can., 1948-56; 1st eparch of Toronto, 1956—. Address: 61 Glen Edyth Dr Toronto ON M4V 2V8 Canada *

BOREHAM, ROLAND STANFORD, JR., electric motor company executive, electrical engineer; b. Los Angeles, Sept. 2, 1924; s. Roland S. and Anita K. (Brown) B.; m. Mary Ann McSpadden, 1948; children: Debra Rhea, Anita Katherine. B.A. in Physics, UCLA, 1947. Partner R.S. Boreham & Co. (mfr.'s rep. for Baldor Electric Co.), Los Angeles, 1948-61; v.p. sales Baldor Electric Co., Ft. Smith, Ark., 1961-70, exec. v.p., 1970, pres., 1975—, chief exec. officer, 1978—, chmn. bd., 1981—. Served to 1st lt. USAAF, 1943-46; PTO. Mem. Am. Bus. Conf. Office: Baldor Electric Co 5711 S 7th St Fort Smith AR 72901

BOREL, ARMAND, mathematics educator; b. Chaux-de-Fonds, Switzerland, May 21, 1923; m. Gabrielle Pittet, May 8, 1952; children: Dominique, Anne-Christine. Master Mathematics, Federal Sch. Tech., Zurich, Switzerland., 1947; Dr. Degree, U. Paris, 1952; Ph.D. (hon.), U. Geneva, 1972. Asst. Federal Sch. Tech., Zurich, 1947-49, prof., 1955-57; attaché de Recherches French Nat. Center Sci. Research, Paris, 1949-50; acting prof. algebra U. Geneva, Switzerland, 1950-52; mem. Inst. Advanced Study, Princeton, 1952-54, prof., 1957—; vis. prof. U. Chgo., 1954-55, M.I.T., 1958, 69, U. Paris, 1964, Yale U., 1978. Recipient Brouwer medal Dutch Math. Soc., 1978. Mem. Acad. Arts and Sci., Finnish Acad. Scis. and Letters (fgn.), French Acad. Scis. (fgn.), Am., Swiss, French math. socs. Home: 106 Battle Rd Circle Princeton NJ 08540

BORELLI, FRANCIS (FRANK) J(OSEPH), manufacturing company executive; b. Bklyn., Sept. 2, 1935; s. Anthony and Ida B.; m. Madlyn Quadrino, June 25, 1960; children: Frank, Richard. B.B.A. with honors, Baruch Coll., 1956. C.P.A., N.Y. With Deloitte Haskins & Sells, 1956-79, ptnr., 1968-79, mng. ptnr. in charge Bergen County, N.J. office, 1976-79; sr. v.p.-adminstr. Airco, Inc., Montvale, N.J., 1980—, also dir.; dir. Hackensack Water Co., Nanuet Nat. Bank, N.Y. Bd. dirs. Nat. Multiple Sclerosis Soc.; trustee Dominican Coll., Blauvelt, N.Y.; mem. fin. com. Good Samaritan Hosp., Suffern, N.Y.; active numerous pub. service orgns. Mem. Fin. Execs. Inst., Am. Inst. C.P.A.s, N.Y. State Soc. C.P.A.s. Office: Airco Inc 85 Chestnut Ridge Rd Montvale NJ 07645

BOREN, ARTHUR RODNEY, sales mgmt. exec.; b. Dayton, Ohio, June 14, 1916; s. Herbert S. and Katharine Maria (Miller) B.; m. Charlotte Polk, Mar. 14, 1942; children—Katharine Elizabeth, A. Rodney. A.B., Kenyon Coll., 1938. With Mead Corp., 1949-61, asst. to v.p., 1951-53, asst. v.p., 1953-57, v.p., 1957-61; with Ga. Kraft Co., 1952-61; asst. to pres., 1956-61; with Fourdrinier, Kraft Bd. Inst., 1961-77, pres., treas. Past bd. dirs. YMCA, ARC; trustee Kenyon Coll., Aviation Hall of Fame, Dayton Mus. Natural History; vestry St. Paul's Epis. Ch. Served to lt. comdr. USNR, 1940-47; maj. to col. Ohio Air N.G. Mem. Eastern Conservation Commn. (past dir.), Delta Tau Delta. Clubs: Canadian, Met., Board Room (N.Y.C.); Moraine Country, Miami Valley Hunt and Polo (Dayton); Pine Valley Country (N.J.). Home: 1401 Runnymede Rd Dayton OH 45419

BOREN, BENJAMIN N., lawyer; b. Dallas, 1909; s. Samuel H. and Ella (Chilton) B.; m. Martha Ruth Moore, Sept. 1, 1931; children—Martha Ann, Benjamin Chilton. Student, Terrill Sch., Dallas; LL.B., U. Tex., 1933. Bar: Tex. bar 1933. Since practiced in, Dallas; mem. firm Locke, Purnell, Boren, Laney & Neely, 1941—. Mem. Am., Dallas bar assns., State Bar Tex., Phi Delta Phi. Home: 4135 Windsor Pkwy Dallas TX 75205 Office: Republic Nat Bank Tower Dallas TX 75201

BOREN, DAVID LYLE, senator; b. Washington, Apr. 21, 1941; s. Lyle H. and Christine (McKeown) B.; m. Molly Shi, Dec. 1977; children: David Daniel, Carrie Christine. B.A. summa cum laude, Yale, 1963; M.A. (Rhodes scholar), Oxford (Eng.) U., 1965; J.D. (Bledsoe Meml. prize as outstanding law grad.), U. Okla., 1968. Bar: Okla. 1968. Asst. to dir. liaison Office Civil and Def. Moblzn., Washington, 1960-62; propaganda analyst Soviet affairs USIA, Washington, 1962-63; mem. Speakers Bur., Am. embassy, London, Eng., 1963-65; mem. residential counseling staff U. Okla., 1965-66; practiced in, Seminole, 1968-74; mem. Okla. Ho. of Reps., 1966-74; gov., Okla., 1975-79; mem. U.S. Senate from Okla., 1979—; Chmn. govt. dept. Okla. Baptist U., 1969-74. Del. Democratic Nat. Conv., 1968, 76. Named U.S. Army ROTC Disting. Mil. Grad.; One of 10 Outstanding Young Men in U.S. U.S. Jaycees, 1967. Mem. Assn. U.S. Rhodes Scholars, Order of Coif, Phi Beta Kappa, Sigma Delta Rho, Phi Delta Phi. Methodist. Club: Yale of Western Okla. Home: 2369 S Queen St Arlington VA 22202 also Seminole OK 74868 Office: 452 Russell Senate Office Bldg Washington DC 20510

BOREN, HOLLIS GRADY, physician; b. Dallas, Feb. 24, 1923; s. Henry Grady and Lyda Virginia (Higgins) B.; m. Lois Wriborg, Dec. 6, 1963; children—Lisa Catherine, Lois Elise. B.A., So. Meth. U., 1943; M.D., Baylor U., 1946. Diplomate: Am. Bd. Internal Medicine. Mem. staff VA Hosp., Houston, 1953-63, chief pulmonary function labs., 1961-62, asso. chief staff, 1961-62, chief med. service, 1961-63; dir., mem. Trudeau Found., Inc., Saranac Lake, N.Y., 1963-66; chief pulmonary disease research VA Hosp., Denver, 1966-69, chief pulmonary disease, Wood, Wis., 1969-71, med. investigator, 1972, Tampa, Fla., 1972-73; faculty U. South Fla. Coll. Medicine, 1972—, prof., 1973-76, asst. dir. med. center, 1973-76, asso. dean coll., 1973-76, acting dean, 1976-77, dean, 1977-80, dir. med. center, 1977-80; asst. chief med. dir. research and devel. VA Central Office, Washington, 1980—. Contbr. numerous articles to profl. jours. Served with USNR, 1943-49. Mem. A.C.P. (Billings bronze medal), Hillsborough County Med. Assn., Fla. Med. Assn., AMA, Am. Thoracic Soc., Alpha Omega Alpha. Office: VA Central Office 17A 810 Vermont Ave NW Washington DC 20420

BOREN, WILLIAM MEREDITH, business executive; b. San Antonio, Oct. 23, 1924; s. Thomas Loyd and Verda (Locke) B.; m. Molly Brasfield Sarver, Dec. 3, 1976; children: Susan, Patricia, Janet, Jenny, Burton, Cliff. Student, Tex. A&M U., 1942-43, Rice U., 1943-44; B.S. in Mech. Engring, Tex. U., 1949. Vice pres., gen. mgr. Rolo Mfg. Co., Houston, 1949-54; mgr. sales engring. Black, Sivalls & Bryson, Houston, Oklahoma City, 1955-64; vice chmn. bd., dir., mem. exec. com. Big Three Industries, Inc., Houston, 1965—; dir. Nowsco Wells Services Ltd., Calgary, Bowen Tool Co., Houston. Trustee SW Research Inst., San Antonio. Served to lt. (j.g.) USN, 1943-46. Mem. Tau Beta Pi, Pi Tau Sigma. Republican. Inventor Challenge Bridge game. Home: 11214 Montebello Ct Houston TX 77024 Office: PO Box 3047 Houston TX 77001

BORENSTEIN, MILTON CONRAD, corporation executive, lawyer; b. Boston, Oct. 21, 1914; s. Isadore Sidney and Eva Beatrice B.; m. Anne Shapiro, June 20, 1937; children: Roberta, Jeffrey. A.B. cum laude, Boston Coll., 1935; J.D., Harvard U., 1938. Bar: Mass. 1938, U.S. Supreme Ct. 1944. Gen. practice law, Boston, 1938-44; with Sweetheart Paper Products Co., Inc., Chelsea, Mass., 1944—, clk., v.p., 1961—, pres., 1961—; with Sweetheart Plastics, Inc., Wilmington, Mass., 1958—, v.p., 1958—; also dir.; v.p. Md. Cup Corp., Owings Mills, 1960-77, exec. v.p., treas., 1977—, also dir.; Bd. dirs. Am. Assos. Hebrew U., 1968, Ben Gurion U., 1975—. Trustee Boston Coll., 1979—, Combined Jewish Philanthropies, Boston, 1969—, N.E. Sinai Hosp., Stoughton, Mass., 1974—; mem. pres.'s council Sarah Lawrence Coll., 1970-79; pres. Congregation Kehillath Israel, Brookline, Mass., 1977-79, hon. pres., 1979—; mem. pres.'s council Brandeis U., 1979—, fellow, 1981—; v.p. Associated Synagogues of Mass., 1980-81. Recipient Community Service award Jewish Theol. Sem. Am., 1970. Mem. Boston Bar Assn. Mass. Bar Assn., Am. Bar Assn., Single Service Inst., Chelsea C. of C. (dir.). Clubs: Harvard of Boston, Harvard Faculty, 100, Masons, Shriners. Home: 273 Eliot Chestnut Hill MA 02167 Office: 191 Williams Chelsea MA 02150

BORESI, ARTHUR PETER, educator, author; b. Toluca, Ill., Aug. 27, 1924; s. John Peter and Eva (Grotti) B.; m. Clara Jean Gordon, Dec. 28, 1946; children—Jennifer Ann Boresi Hill, Annette Boresi Pueschel, Nancy Jean. Student, Kenyon Coll., 1943-44; B.S. in Elec. Engring, U. Ill., 1948, M.S., 1949, Ph.D., 1953. Research engr. N. Am. Aviation, 1950; materials engr. Nat. Bur. Standards, 1951; mem. faculty U. Ill. at Urbana, 1953—, prof. theoretical and applied mechanics and nuclear engring., 1959-79; Disting. vis. prof. Clarkson Coll. Tech., Potsdam, N.Y., 1968-69; NAVSEA research prof. Naval Postgrad. Sch., Monterey, Calif., 1978-79; prof. civil engring. U. Wyo., Laramie, 1979—, head, 1980—; cons. in field. Author: Engineering Mechanics, 1959, Elasticity in Engineering Mechanics, 2d edit, 1974, Advanced Mechanics of Materials, 1978, also articles. Served with USAAF, 1943-44; Served with AUS, 1944-46. Founding mem. Am. Acad. Mechanics (treas.); mem. ASME, ASCE, Am. Soc. Engring. Edn., Engring. Sci. Soc., Sigma Xi. Office: Engring Hall U Wyo Laramie WY 82071

BORETZ, BENJAMIN AARON, composer, music critic, educator; b. N.Y.C., Oct. 3, 1934; s. Abraham and Leah (Yollis) B.; m. Naomi Messinger, Sept. 1, 1954; 1 son, Avron Albert. A.B., Bklyn. Coll., 1954; M.F.A., Brandeis U., 1957, Princeton U., 1960, Ph.D., 1970. Mem. faculty Brandeis U., 1955-57, 62-63, UCLA, 1957-59, N.Y. U., 1964-69; also dir. group computer synthesis; mem. faculty Columbia U., 1969-72, Bard Coll., 1973—; mem. planning com., steering com., faculty Avery Grad. Sch. in Arts, 1981—; vis. prof. Princeton U., 1967-68, 70-71, 72-74, U. Mich., 1973; Fulbright-Hays prof. U. Southampton, Eng., 1971-72; music critic The Nation, 1962-69; editor Perspectives of New Music, 1962-83, emeritus editor, 1983—; editorial bd. Contemporary Music Newsletter; adv. bd. G.P. Dutton Ency. 20th-Century Music; composer-participant Princeton Seminar Advanced Music Studies, 1959; panel participant congress Internat. Musicol. Soc., Salzburg, Austria, 1964, Berkeley, Calif., 1977, Interdisciplinary Festival Philosophy, 1970, Symposium on Philosophy, 1973, others; vis. composer numerous univs. Composer: Violin Concerto, 1956-57, String Quartet, 1958-59, Donne Songs, 1959-60, Group Variations I, 1967, II, 1969-72, Composition for flute and piano, 1969-71, Liebeslied for pianist alone, 1976, My Chart Shines High Where the Blue Milk's Upset, 1977, 79, Language, as a Music, for voice, piano, and tape, 1978, 80, Passage, for Roger Sessions, 1978, Sound States Nos. 1-100: Unscheduled Resonances Formed in Meditation, 1980, Real Time States, Nos. 1-120, 1980, Nos. 121-204, 1981, Authenticity: A Life in the Day; performance-lecture piece, 1981; Languagings, Nos. 1-75, 1981; collaborative sound expressions Formings, 1982-83; numerous recs.; Author: Meta-Variations, 1970, Fantasia, 1980, Mirage, 1980, Letter, 1980, Expressive Content of Musical Thought, 1981; Editor: Perspectives on Schoenberg and Stravinsky, 1968, Perspectives on American Composers, 1971, Perspectives on Contemporary Music Theory, 1972, Perspectives on Performance and Notation, 1974, If I am a musical thinker . . ., 1983; Contbr.: articles to profl. jours. Ency. Twentieth Century Music; Rec. artist: Group Variations II and all Sound States and Languagings. Recipient composition award Fromm Music Found., Aspen, 1956; Ingram-Merrill Found. grantee in music, 1966; Council of Humanities fellow Princeton, 1972-73; fellow MacDowell Colony, 1974; artist in residence Montalvo Center for the Arts, 1975. Mem. Am. Composers Alliance, Am. Soc. U. Composers (sec., mem. exec. com.), Am. Musicol. Soc., N.Y. Music Critics Circle, Internat. Soc. Contemporary Music (exec. bd.). Home: River Rd Barrytown NY 12504 Office: Bard Coll Annandale NY 12504

BORG, BJORN, tennis player; b. Sweden, June 6, 1956; s. Rune and Margaretha B.; m. Mariana Simionescu. Mem. Sweden's Davis Cup Team; joined World Championship Tennis circuit, 1974. Named World Champion of Men's Tennis Internat. Tennis Fedn., 1978. Won Italian Open, 1974, Swedish Open, 1974, French Open, 1974, 75, U.S. Profl. Tennis championship, 1974, 75, 76, Wimbledon championship, 1976, 77, 78, 79, 80, U.S. Nat. Indoor Tennis championship, 1977, World Championship Tennis, 1976, Swedish Open, 1978, French Open, 1978, Can. Open, 1979, Colgate Grand Prix Masters, 1980 *

BORG, CHARLES ARTHUR, diplomat; b. Bklyn., Dec. 4, 1926; s. Charles Arthur and Sarah Marion (Van Cott) B.; m. Sara Cooper, June 11, 1955; children: James, Marion. B.S., U.S. Mil. Acad., 1944-48, Georgetown U., 1955; M.S., George Washington U., 1968. Joined U.S. Fgn. Service, 1955; visa officer, Hamburg, Ger., 1955-57; fgn. affairs officer Dept. State, Washington, 1958-61; polit. and mil. officer, Tokyo, 1961-63; instr. USAF Acad., 1963-65; spl. asst. to sec. state, 1965-67; assigned Nat. War Coll., 1967-68; polit. counselor, Stockholm, 1968-71, polit. adviser, dep. asst. chief mission, Berlin, 1971-74, assigned to sr. seminar in fgn. policy, 1974-75; dep. exec. sec. Dept. State, Washington, 1975-76, exec. sec., 1976-77; dep. chief of mission, Vienna, 1977-79; sr. insp. Dept. State, Washington, 1979-81; dep. chief mission, Helsinki, 1981—. Served with U.S. Army, 1948-54. Mem. Am. Fgn. Service Assn. Address: American Embassy Helsinki APO New York 09664

BORG, DOROTHY, educator, author; b. Elberon, N.J., Sept. 4, 1902; d. Sidney C. and Madeleine (Beer) B.; (divorced). A.M., Ph.D., Columbia. Research asso. Am. Inst. of Pacific Relations, 1939-58, E. Asian Research Center, Harvard, 1960-61; sr. research asso. E. Asian Inst., Columbia, 1962—; lectr. Peking (China) Nat. U., 1947. Author: American Policy and the Chinese Revolution, 1925-28, 1947, The United States and The Far Eastern Crisis, 1933-1938, 1964; Co-editor: Pearl Harbor as History: Japanese-American Relations, 1931-1941, 1973, Uncertain Years: Chinese-American Relations, 1947-1950, 1980. Recipient Bancroft prize, 1965. Mem. Am. Hist. Assn., Assn. Asian Studies, Acad. Polit. Scis., Orgn. Am. Historians, Soc. for Historians of Am. Fgn. Relations. Home: 22 Riverside Dr New York NY 10023

BORG, MALCOLM AUSTIN, newspaper pub. co. exec.; b. N.Y.C., Jan. 28, 1938; s. Donald Gowen and Flora (Austin) B.; m. Sandra Jean Agemian, Sept. 9, 1961; children—John Austin, Jennifer Ann, Stephen Agemian. B.S. in English Lit, Columbia, 1965; postgrad., Harvard Bus. Sch., 1970. With Bergen Evening Record, Hackensack, N.J., 1959—, gen. assignment reporter, 1960-62, adminstrv. asst. to pub., 1963-64, asst. pub., 1965-66, v.p., 1967-68, exec. v.p., 1968-71, pres., chief exec. officer, 1971-78, chmn. bd., chief exec. officer, 1975—; chmn. bd., dir. Toms River Pub. Co., Gateway Communications, Inc., Gremac, Inc. Mem. exec. bd. Bergen council Boy Scouts Am., 1968-74; mem. med. selections com. Regional Kidney Center Holy Name Hosp., 1968-70; mem. N.J. Health Care Adminstrn. Bd., 1972-76, chmn., 1974-76; mem. advisory bd. N.J. Dept. Health, 1972-74; mem. exec. council Harvard Bus. Sch. Assn., 1974-79, pres., 1976-78; trustee Health Facilities Planning Council N.J., 1965-69; bd. dirs. Boys Club Paterson, 1966-69, Wolfeboro Summer Camp Sch., 1970—, Palisades Interstate Park Commn., 1974—; trustee Hackensack Area Community Chest, 1968-71; nursing adv. com. Bergen Community Coll., 1968-70; trustee Three Sch. Devel. Found., 1973-78, Dwight-Englewood Sch., 1976—; bd. mgrs. Bergen Pines County Hosp., 1974-78. Served with AUS, 1956-58. Recipient Torch of Liberty award B'nai B'rith, 1973, Service to Others award N.J. div. Salvation Army, 1977, Communication and Leadership award Toastmasters, 1976. Mem. Am. Soc. Newspaper Editors, N.J. Press Assn., Am. Newspaper Pubs. Assn., Harvard Bus. Sch. Assn. (coordinator greater met. area alumni 1970-74), Alumni Assn. Hill Sch. (pres. 1973-76, mem. exec. com.), Submarine Meml. Assn. (chmn. 1974—), NE Ice Hockey Ofcls. Assn. (trustee 1976—), Sigma Delta Chi. Clubs: Harvard (N.Y.C.); Arcola Country (Paramus, N.J.); Englewood (N.J.) Field; Bath and Tennis (Spring Lake, N.J.); Mid-Ocean (Tuckers Town, Bermuda); Knickerbocker Country (Tenafly, N.J.). Home: 310 Walnut St Englewood NJ 07631 Office: 150 River St Hackensack NJ 07602

BORG, PARKER W., ambassador; b. Mpls., May 25, 1939. A.B., Dartmouth Coll., 1961; M.P.A., Cornell U., 1965. Vol. Peace Corps, Philippines, 1961-63; officer-gen. Fgn. Service, Kuala Lumpur, Malaysia, 1965-67; with CORDS program AID, 1967-70; staff officer, exec. secretariat State Dept., Washington, 1972-74; spl. asst. to dir. gen. Fgn. Service, State Dept., Washington, 1972-74; spl. asst. to sec. state State Dept., Washington, 1974-75, prin. officer, Lumbumbashi, 1976-78; with Council Fgn. Relations, N.Y.C., 1978-79; dir. Office West African Affairs, State Dept., Washington, 1979-81, U.S. ambassador to Mali, Bamako, 1981—. Recipient Superior Honor award Dept. State, 1978. Office: US Embassy-Mali care Dept State Washington DC 20520 *

BORG, SIDNEY FRED, educator, engineer; b. N.Y.C., Oct. 3, 1916; s. Herman Leo and Pauline (Leibman) B.; m. Audrey Iva Elliott, Apr. 4, 1944; children: Nicholas Elliott, Andrew Douglas, Jill Debora, Kenneth Jeremy. B.S. in Civil Engring., Cooper Union Inst. Tech., 1937; M.C.E., Poly. Inst. Bklyn., 1940; E.D., Johns Hopkins U., 1956; M.Eng. (hon.), Stevens Inst. Tech., 1958. Lic. profl. engr. Engr., City of N.Y., U.S. War Dept., Turner Constrn. Co., Gen. Motors Co., 1937-43; with Grumman Aircraft Corp., 1951-52; asst. prof. civil engring. U. Md., 1943-45; asst. and asso. prof. aero. engring. U.S. Naval Postgrad. Sch., 1945-51; asso. prof. civil engring. Stevens Inst. Tech., 1952-56, head dept. civil engring., 1952-77, prof., 1956-68, prof. applied mechanics, 1968—; Fulbright lectr. Royal Danish Tech. U., 1965-66; vis. prof. Technische Hochschule, Stuttgart, Germany, summer 1966, U. Stuttgart, 1981; sci. exchange prof. Polish Acad. Scis.-Nat. Acad. Scis., summer 1968; vis. prof. Air Force Inst. Tech., summer 1969; postdoctoral fellow in biophysics Marine Biol. Lab., Woods Hole, Mass., summer 1971; vis. prof. Technion Israel Inst. Tech., summer 1970; cons. engr. bd. dirs. Kreisler, Borg, Florman Constrn. Co., Scarsdale, N.Y. Author: textbook An Introduction to Matrix-Tensor Methods in Applied Mechanics, 1956, Advanced Structural Analysis, 1959, Fundamentals of Engineering Elasticity, 1962, Matrix Tensor Methods in Continuum Mechanics, 1963, Modern Structural Analysis, 1969, Earthquake Engineering, 1983; editor textbook series.; contbr. articles to profl. jours. Recipient Disting. Alumnus award Poly. Inst. Bklyn., 1957, Disting. Alumni citation Cooper Union, 1972, Best Tchr. award Sigma Chi Epsilon, 1981, 83. Fellow AAAS, N.Y. Acad. Sci., ASCE; mem. Am. Soc. Engring. Edn., Earthquake Engring. Research Inst., Sigma Xi, Tau Beta Pi. Home: 2 9th St Hoboken NJ 07030

BORGATTA, EDGAR F., educator, social psychologist; b. Milan, Italy, Sept. 1, 1924; came to U.S., 1929, naturalized, 1934; s. Edgar A. and Francis (Zinelli) B.; m. Marie Lentini, Oct. 5, 1946; children: Lynn, Kim, Lee. B.A., N.Y. U., 1947, M.A., 1949, Ph.D., 1952. Certified psychologist, N.Y., Vt. Instr. N.Y. U., 1949-51, lectr., prof., 1954-59; lectr., research asso. Harvard, 1951-54; social psychologist, asst. sec. Russell Sage Found., 1954-59; prof. sociology Cornell U., Ithaca, N.Y., 1959-61; Brittingham Research prof. U. Wis., 1961-72, chmn. dept. sociology, 1962-65, chmn. div. social studies, 1965-68; Distinguished prof. sociology Queens Coll., City U. N.Y., 1972-77, prof Grad. Center, 1972-82; dir. Italian Social Sci. Center, Queens Coll., 1972-77; research dir. CUNY Case Center for Gerontol. Studies, 1978-81, dir. data service, 1981-82; prof. sociology, dir. Inst. on Aging, U. Wash., Seattle, 1981—; cons. to bus. and govt., 1953—, Russell Sage Found., 1970-72; cons. editor Rand McNally & Co., 1961-74; chmn. bd. F.E. Peacock Pubs., Inc.; Nat. Inst. Gen. Scis.; spl. research fellow, 1972. Editor: Research on Aging, Sociol. Methodology, Sociol. Methods and Research; co-editor: Handbook of Personality Theory and Research; Contbr. articles to profl. jours. Fellow Am. Psychol. Assn.; mem. Psychometric Soc., Sociol. Research Assn., Am. Sociol. Assn. (v.p. 1983). Home: 5216 21st Ave NE Seattle WA 98105 Office: Dept Sociology U Wash Seattle WA

BORGE, VICTOR, comedian, pianist; b. Copenhagen, Jan. 3, 1909; U.S., 1940, naturalized, 1948; s. Bernhard and Frederikke (Lichtinger) B.; m. Sarabel Sanna Scraper, Mar. 17, 1953; children—Sanna J., Victor Bernhardt, Frederikke; children by previous marriage—Ronald, Janet. Ed., Borgerdydskolen; D.Mus. (hon.), Butler U., 1970, Dana Coll., Blair, Nebr., 1977. On concert stage, 1922-34; studied at, Conservatory of Copenhagen, 1925, music in, Vienna and Berlin, (with Egon Petri and Frederic Lamond), 3 years; appeared in mus. rev., 1934; and combined music ability and humor, creating new vogue of sophisticated mus. satire; wrote and directed own shows; entered motion pictures, 1937; became one of Denmark's foremost performers, writing script, composing mus. scores and playing the lead Scandinavian tour, 1938; while appearing in Sweden, Denmark was invaded and so came to U.S., 1940; guest 54 consecutive weeks on: Kraft Music Hall; headed: other radio programs Lower Basin St. and; soloist with many famed orchs.; guest condr. numerous symphony orchs. including, Amsterdam Concertgebouw, London Philharmonic, N.Y. Philharmonic, Phila. Orch., Nat. Symphony, Cleve. Orch.; one-man show at, Golden Theatre, N.Y.C., 1953, 849 consecutive performances; numerous one-man TV spls., U.S., Gt. Britain; ltd. engagement, Palace Theatre, London, 1957; appeared before, U.S. Congress, UN; toured, Brit. Isles, 1958, N.Z., Australia, Europe, Far East.; Author: (with Robert Sherman) My Favorite Intermissions. Nat. chmn. pub. service com. CARE, 1959, chmn. internat. pub. service com.; nat. chmn. Multiple Sclerosis Soc.; a founder, nat. chmn. Thanks to Scandinavia scholarship fund; established Victor Borge Scholarship Funds at U. Conn. at Storrs, Dana Coll., Blair, Nebr. Awarded many honors; decorated knight 1st class Order St. Olav, Norway; Royal Order Daneborg, Absalom (Denmark); Order of Vasa, Sweden; recipient Brotherhood award, 1957; Wadsworth Internat. award, 1957; TV Father of Year award, 1958; Georg Jensen Silver award; CARE Pub. Service award, 1973; Gold award for best pub. service comml. Internat. Film and TV Festival N.Y., 1973; also honored U.S. Congress. Began study of music age 5. Address: Field Point Park Greenwich CT 06830 also 56 Hill St Christiansted St Croix VI also care Internat Creative Mgmt 40 W 57th St New York NY 10019 *Being the recipient of physical and mental facilities assigned to me before my birth I am convinced that, as custodian, my efforts toward accomplishments consist mainly of a reasonable amount of discipline and devotion to elementary decency. Perhaps part of my good fortune may be credited to my faults, of which the greatest is modesty.*

BORGELT, BURTON C., dental and optical supply manufacturing company executive; b. 1933; m. B.A., U. Toledo. Pres. Litton Dental Products, Litton Industries, 1968-76; with Dentsply Internat., Inc., York, Pa., 1964-67, 76—; gen. sales mgr.-retail Ransom & Randolph, 1964-76; corporate v.p., gen. mgr. L.D. Caulk Co., 1976-79, corporate v.p., 1979-81, pres., 1981—; also dir. L.D. Caulk & Co. Office: Dentsply Internat Inc 500 W College Ave York PA 17404 *

BORGES, WAYNE HOWARD, physician, educator; b. Cleve., Dec. 7, 1919; s. Howard Henry and Helen Addison Proctor (Crockett) B.; m. Margaret Jane Addison, Oct. 29, 1943; children—Kent, Gretchen. A.B., Kenyon Coll., 1941; M.D., Western Res. U., 1944. Intern St. Luke's Hosp., San Francisco, 1944-45; resident Children's Hosp., Boston, 1947-49; instr. in pediatrics Harvard Med. Sch., 1952; asst. prof. pediatrics Western Res. U., Cleve., 1952-58; asso. prof. pediatrics U. Pitts., 1958-63, Northwestern U. Med. Sch., Chgo., 1963-67, prof. pediatrics, 1967—; chief hematology Children's Meml. Hosp., Chgo., 1963-72, med. dir. for edn., 1971—. Contbr. articles in field to med. jours. Served with M.C. USNR, 1945-46, 53-54. Mem. Am. Acad. Pediatrics, Am. Pediatric Soc., Soc. for Pediatric Research, Midwestern Soc. for Pediatric Research, Inst. Medicine Chgo. Home: 5801 S Dorchester Chicago IL 60637 Office: 2300 Children's Plaza Chicago IL 60614

BORGESE, ELISABETH MANN, author, political science educator; b. Munich, Germany, Apr. 24, 1918; emigrated to U.S., 1938, naturalized, 1941; d. Thomas and Katia (Pringheim) Mann; m. Giuseppe Antonio Borgese, Nov. 23, 1939; children: Angelica, Dominica. Diploma, Conservatory of Music, Zurich, 1937. Research assoc., editor Common Cause, U. Chgo., 1945-51; editor Perspective USA (Diogenes Intercultural Publs.), 1952-57; exec. sec. bd. editors Ency. Brit., Chgo., 1964-66; sr. fellow, assoc. Center for Study Democratic Instns., Santa Barbara, Calif., 1965—; Killam sr. fellow Dalhousie U., Halifax, N.S., Can., 1978-79, prof. dept. polit. sci., 1980—; Chmn. planning council Internat. Ocean Inst.; advisor Austrian del. 3d UN Conf. on Law of Sea, 1976-82; mem. Prep. Commn. Jamaica, 1983—. Author: To Whom It May Concern, 1962, Ascent of Woman, 1963, The Language Barrier, 1965, The Ocean Regime, 1968, The Drama of the Oceans, 1976, Seafarm: The Story of Aquaculture, 1980; contbr. short stories, essays to mags. Mem. Acad. Polit. Sci., AAAS, Am. Soc. Internat. Law, World Acad. Arts and Scis. Home: Sambro Head Halifax NS Canada Office: Dept Polit Sci Dalhousie U Halifax NS B3H 4H6 Canada

BORGET, LLOYD GEORGE, architect; b. Winnipeg, Man., Can., May 25, 1913; s. Henry John and Mabel Anne (Duval) B. B.Arch., U. Minn., 1937. Designer Stanley W. Bliss (Architect), Corpus Christi, Tex., 1937-42; designer, job capt. Alden B. Dow Inc., Houston, 1942-46; pvt. practice architecture, Houston, 1946; job capt. Rather, Moore & Assos., Houston, 1947, Staub & Rather (Architects), 1948; chief designer Lloyd & Morgan (Architects), Houston, 1948-49; chief draftsman MacKie and Kamrath (Architects), Houston, 1949-54, asso., 1954-72, partner, 1973—. Contbr. articles in field to profl. jours. Recipient Scarab medal for design U. Minn., 1935, several awards for work in design. Fellow AIA (mem. Houston chpt.); mem. Tex. Soc. Architects, Nat. Council Archtl. Registeration Bds., Minn. Alumni Assn., Smithsonian Instn., Scarab, Sigma Nu. Republican. Roman Catholic. Home: 4519 W Alabama St Houston TX 77027 Office: 2713 Ferndale Pl Houston TX 77098

BORGLUM, JAMES LINCOLN DE LA MOTHE, sculptor, photographer; b. Stamford, Conn., Apr. 9, 1912; s. John Gutzon and Mary (Montgomery) B.; m. Louella Jones, Dec. 16, 1937 (dec. Nov. 1963); children—Anna Mary April, James Gutzon; m. Mrs. Richard Ellsworth, Apr. 9, 1964; children—Richard, Paul, Robert Ellsworth. Student, Lukin Mil. Acad., San Antonio, Tex., 1925-27, Valley (Wyo.) Ranch Sch., 1928-30; studied sculpture under father for, 1929, 31. Apprentice W. Tex. Pub. Utilities Co., Abilene, 1931; with Mt. Rushmore Nat. Meml., Black Hills, S.D., 1932—, charge measurements and enlarging models, 1934-38; apptd. supt. Meml. by Mt. Rushmore Meml. Commn., 1938, apptd. sculptor to complete Meml. following his father's death, 1940, mem. commn., 1960—; apptd. supt. by Nat. Park Service U.S. Dept. Interior, 1942. Tech. adviser in carving worlds largest known sapphires in likeness: Washington, Jefferson, Eisenhower; designed carving for world's largest known ruby; executed statue: Our Lady of Loreto, La Bahia Mission, Goliad, Tex.; bust Pres. Johnson, near Keystone, S.D.; bronze Statue of founder, Gladys Porter Zoo, Brownsville, Tex.; Has exhibited color photography work in salons at, Milw., Rochester, N.Y., N.Y.C.; colored photographs used for covers of This Week and Sat. Eve. Post; Author: My Father's Mountain, 1965; co-author: Borglum's Unfinished Dream, Mt. Rushmore, 1976, Mount Rushmore, The Story Behind the Scenery, 1977. Hon. mem. Lincoln Sesquicentennial Commn., S.D. Bicentennial Commn.; Trustee Mt. Rushmore Nat. Meml. Soc. Black Hills, Rapid City, S.D.; Pres. Whooping Crane council Girl Scouts U.S.; mem. Beeville City Council, 1955-61. Mem. So. Tex. Hereford Assn. Club: Rotary. Home and office: Box 908 La Feria TX 78559 *After thousands of years, there is very little new in art. An artist's only avenue is the quality of his work.*

BORGMAN, JAMES MARK, editorial cartoonist; b. Cin., Feb. 24, 1954; s. James Robert and Florence Marian (Maly) B.; m. Lynn Goodwin, Aug. 20, 1977. B.A., Kenyon Coll., 1976. Editorial cartoonist Cin. Enquirer, 1976—, King Features Syndicate, 1980—; contbr. to Newsweek Broadcasting's Cartoon-A-Torial (animated editorial cartoon feature), 1978-81. Author: collection of editorial cartoons Smorgasborgman, 1982. Recipient Sigma Delta Chi award, 1978; Thomas Nast prize, 1980; 2d prize for editorial cartooning Internat. Salon Cartoons of Montreal, 1981. Mem. Am. Assn. Editorial Cartoonists. Office: 617 Vine St Cincinnati OH 45201

BORGNINE, ERNEST, actor; b. Hamden, Conn., Jan. 24, 1917; s. Charles B. and Anna (Boselli) B.; m. Tove Newman, 1972. Student pub. schs., New Haven. Appeard in: N. Y. stage plays Mrs. McThing; Appeared in: Harvey; actor, Columbia Pictures Corp., Metro-Goldwyn Mayer, 2Oth Century-Fox; motion pictures include The Mob, From Here to Eternity, Bad Day at Black Rock, Demetrius and the Gladiators, Violent Saturday, Marty, Square Jungle, The Catered Affair, The Best Things in Life Are Free, Three Brave Men, Hell Below, Badlanders, Rabbit Trap, Man on a String, Barrabas, Flight of the Phoenix, 1966, The Oscar, 1966, The Dirty Dozen, 1968, The Wild Bunch, 1969, Willard, 1971, The Poseidon Adventure, 1972, The Emperor of the North, 1973, Law and Disorder, 1974, Hustle, 1975, The Devil's Rain, 1975, Shoot, 1976, The Greatest, 1977, Convoy, 1978, Crossed Swords, 1978, The Day the World Ended, 1979, The Black Hole, 1979, The Double Mcguffin, 1979, When Time Ran Out, 1980; also appeared on TV in McHale's Navy; Super Cop; starred in: TV film All Quiet on the Western Front, 1979 (Recipient Oscar for Best Performance of Year 1956). Served with USNR, World War II. Club: Mason. Office: care APA 120 W 57th St New York NY 10019 *

BORGSTROM, GEORG ARNE, educator, scientist, author; b. Gustav Adolf, Sweden, Apr. 5, 1912; came to U.S., 1956, naturalized, 1962; s. Algot and Anna (Littorin) B.; m. Greta Ingrid Stromback; children: Lars, Gerd Borgstrom Linder, Sven. B.S., U. Lund, Sweden, 1932, M.S., 1933, D.Sc., 1939. Asso. prof. plant physiology U. Lund, 1940-43; head Inst. Plant Research and Food Storage, Nynashamn, Sweden, 1941-48, Swedish Inst. Food Preservation Research, Goteborg, 1948-56, prof., 1953-56; prof. food sci. Mich. State U., 1956—, prof. geography, 1966-81, prof. emeritus, 1981—. Author: The Transverse Reactions of Plants, 1939, Japan's World Success in Fishing, 1964, The Hungry Planet, 2d edit., 1972, Principles of Food Science, 2 vols., 1968, 76, Too Many—A Study of Earth's Ecological Limitations, 2d edit., 1970, Harvesting the Earth, 1973, Focal Points—A Food Strategy for the Seventies, 1973, The Food and People Dilemma, 1973; editor: Fish as Food, 4 vols., 1960-64; Editor: Atlantic Ocean Fisheries, 1961. Recipient Internat. Socrates prize, 1968, Disting. Faculty award Mich. State U., 1969; Lit. Merit prize Swedish Authors Found., 1973; P.A. Wahlberg Gold medal, 1974; Internat. award Inst. Food Technologists, 1975. Fellow World Acad. Arts and Scis., Royal Swedish Acads. Scis., Engring. and Agrl. Scis.; mem. 25 sci. and tech. acads. and profl. orgns. Home: 4550 Comanche Dr Okemos MI 48864

BORING, JOHN WAYNE, physicist, educator; b. Reidsville, N.C., Oct. 9, 1929; s. Robert Lee and Eunice Violet (Clapp) B.; m. Ethel Belle Watts, Aug. 17, 1957; children: Rebecca, Pamela, Judith. B.S., U. Ky., 1952, M.S., 1954, Ph.D., 1961. Ordnance engr. U.S. Naval Proving Ground, Dahlgren, Va., 1951-52; devel. engr. AEC, Oak Ridge, 1953; research asst. Los Alamos Sci. Lab., 1955; sr. scientist U. Va., Charlottesville, 1960-67, prof. engring. physics, 1971—, asst. dir. Center for Advanced Studies, 1968-72; vis. prof. U. Aarhus, Denmark, 1974-75; cons. Internat. Commn. on Radiation Units, Ky. Research Found. fellow, 1956; Sesquicentennial assoc. U. Va., 1974-75. Mem. Am. Phys. Soc., Tau Beta Pi, Pi Tau Sigma. Presbyterian. Club: Birdwood. Home: 3510 W Monacan Dr Charlottesville VA 22901 Office: Dept Nuclear Engring and Engring Physics U Va Charlottesville VA 22901

BORIS, RUTHANNA, dance teacher and therapist, choreographer; b. Bklyn., Mar. 17, 1918; d. Joseph Jay and Frances (Weiss) B. Student, Profl. Children's Sch., N.Y.C. Dir. Boris-Hobi Concert Co., 1955—. Prin. dancer, Am. Ballet, N.Y.C., 1934, Ballet Caravan, N.Y.C., 1936; prima ballerina, Met. Opera Co., N.Y.C., 1939, Ballet Russe de Monte Carlo, N.Y.C., 1942; prima ballerina, choreographer-in-residence, Royal Winnipeg Ballet of Can., 1957; dir., 1957—; choreographer, N.Y.C. Ballet, 1951, Joffrey Ballet, N.Y.C., 1966; prof. dance, U. Wash., Seattle, 1965—; adj. prof. psychiatry, U. Wash., 1982; Choreographer: Cirque de Deux, 1946, Quelques Fleurs, 1947, Cakewalk, 1951, Kaleidoscope, 1951, Will O' The Wisp, 1951, Pasticcio, 1955, Wanderling, 1957, Ragtime, 1975, Tape Suite, 1976, Four All, 1980. Mem. advisory bd. Seattle Psychoanalytic Inst., 1975—. Mem. Am. Guild Mus. Artists (award 1964, gov. 1942-64), Am. Dance Therapy Assn. (charter, gov. 1963). Office: MH 2 Harborview Community Mental Health Ctr 2A-31 U Wash Seattle WA 98195 *I have always believed that each one of us has some specific mission to perform. My mission, to clarify myself for my work and my human connections, keeps me very busy, active, curious and productive.*

BORIS, WALTER R., utility company executive; b. Amsterdam, N.Y., 1921; married. Student, St. Lawrence U., 1948; B.S. in Aero. Engring., U. Mich., 1948, J.D., 1950. Bar: N.Y. 1981, Mich. 1981. Title examiner Consumers Power Co., Jackson, Mich., 1950-52, atty. legal dept., 1952-53, exec. staff asst., 1953-56, sec., 1956-68, v.p. fin., 1968-75, exec. v.p., dir., 1975—; dir. Camp Internat., Nat. Bank of Jackson. Office: Consumers Power Co Inc 212 W Michigan Ave Jackson MI 49201

BORK, ROBERT HERON, judge, educator; b. Pitts., Mar. 1, 1927; s. Harry Philip and Elizabeth (Kunkle) B.; m. Claire Davidson, June 15, 1952 (dec. 1980); children: Robert Heron, Charles E., Ellen E.; m. Mary Ellen Pohl, Oct. 30, 1982. B.A., U. Chgo., 1948, J.D., 1953; LL.D. (hon.), Creighton U., 1975, Notre Dame Law Sch., 1982; L.H.D., Wilkes-Barre Coll., 1976. Bar: Ill. 1953, D.C. 1977. Asso. and ptnr. firm Kirkland, Ellis, Hodson, Chaffetz & Masters, Chgo., 1955-62; asso. prof. Yale Law Sch., 1962-65, prof. law, 1965-75, on leave, 1973-75, Chancellor Kent prof. law, 1977-79; Alexander M. Bickel prof. public law, 1979-81; ptnr. Kirkland & Ellis, Washington, 1981-82; judge U.S. Ct. Appeals (D.C. cir.), 1982—; solicitor gen. U.S. Dept. Justice, Washington, 1973-77; acting atty. gen. U.S., 1973-74; resident scholar Am. Enterprise Inst., Washington, 1977, adj. scholar, 1977-82; Mem. Presdl. Task Force on Antitrust, 1968; cons. Cabinet Com. on Edn., 1972. Author: The Antitrust Paradox: A Policy at War with Itself, 1978. Trustee Woodrow Wilson Internat. Center for Scholars., 1973-78. Served with USMCR, 1945-46, 50-52; 945-46, 50-52. Fellow Am. Acad. Arts and Scis. Home: United States Courthouse Washington DC 20001

BORK, WALTER ALBERT, oil co. exec.; b. Chgo., Apr. 21, 1927; s. Walter Albert and Frances B.; m. Claire Connolly, Dec. 6, 1958; 1 son, Richard. B.S. in Petroleum Engring, U. Okla., 1951. Gen. mgr. coporate supply and distbn. Mobil Oil Corp., N.Y.C., 1972-79, v.p., 1977, dir., 1979—. Served with U.S. Army, 1951-53. Republican. Roman Catholic. Office: 150 E 42d St New York NY 10017

BORKLAND, ERNEST WALDERMAR, JR., investment banker; b. Hartford, Conn., June 20, 1905; s. Ernest W. and Alma W. (Ericson) B.; m. Caroline Whidbee Powell, June 22, 1937; 1 dau., Barbara Legh (Mrs. Philip A. Uzielli). B.S., U. Pa., 1929; grad., Wharton Sch. Finance and Commerce, 1929. With Dillon Read & Co., N.Y.C., 1929-31, J&W Seligman & Co., 1931-37; with Tucker, Anthony and R.L. Day, N.Y.C., 1937—, partner, 1949—. Clubs: University, Recess. Home: 345 E 57th St New York City NY 10022 Office: 120 Broadway New York City NY 10005

BORKO, HAROLD, information scientist, psychologist, educator; b. N.Y.C., Feb. 4, 1922; s. George and Hilda (Karpel) B.; m. Hannah Levin, June 22, 1947; children: Hilda, Martin. Student, Coll. City N.Y., 1939-41; B.A., U. Calif. at Los Angeles, 1948; M.A., U. So. Calif., 1949, Ph.D. in Psychology, 1952. System tng. specialist Rand Corp., 1956-57; with System Devel. Corp., Santa Monica, Calif., 1957-68, asso. staff head lang. processing and retrieval staff, 1965-68; instr. psychology U. So. Calif., 1957-65; instr. Sch. Library Service U. Calif. at Los Angeles, 1965-68, prof. Grad. Sch. Library and Info. Sci., 1968—. Author: Computer Applications in the Behavioral Sciences, 1962, Automated Language Processing, 1967, Targets for Research in Library Education, 1973, (with H. Sackman) Computers and the Problems of Society, 1972, (with C. Bernier) Abstracting Concepts and Methods, 1975, Indexing Concepts and Methods, 1978; Asso. U.S. editor: Information Processing and Management, 1963—; editor: Academic Press Library and Information Science series, 1970—; book rev. editor: Jour. Ednl. Data Processing, 1963-75. Served with AUS, 1942-46; to capt., Med. Service Corps AUS, 1950-56. Mem. Am. Soc. for Info. Sci. (pres. 1966), Assn. Computing Machinery, Am. Psychol. Assn., Assn. Am. Library Schs., Am. Soc. Indexers, Phi Beta Kappa, Sigma Xi, Phi Gamma Mu. Home: 11507 National Blvd Los Angeles CA 90064 *It is unrealistic to expect a person to decide, at age twenty or thereabout, on a career to be followed for the rest of one's life. One should try to attain as good and as general an education as is possible and not be afraid to change professions. The world is changing, and we must be prepared to change with it; only then can we seize the opportunities presented.*

BORKOWSKI, FRANCIS THOMAS, university administrator; b. Weirton, W.Va., Mar. 16, 1936; s. Francis Thomas and Felicia Josephine (Pawlowski) B.; m. Kay Kaiser, Aug. 22, 1959; children: Stanley, Anne-Marie, Christian. B.S., Oberlin (Ohio) Coll., 1957; M.Mus., Ind. U., 1959; Ph.D., W.Va. U., 1967. Clarinetist Indpls. Symphony Orch., 1957-59; music dir. Bishop Kenny High Sch., Jacksonville, Fla., 1959-61; dir. bands W.Va. U., 1961-67; asso. prof. music edn. Ohio U., Athens, 1967-69, asst. dir. Sch. Music, 1969-70, asso. dean faculties, 1970-75; prof. music, vice chancellor, dean faculty Ind. U.-Purdue U., Ft. Wayne, 1975-78; v.p. Ft. Wayne Philharmonic Orch., 1976-78; provost U. S.C. System, 1978-83, exec. v.p., 1983—. Author articles. Mem. nat. adv. council John F. Kennedy Ctr., 1978-80; pres. Palmetto State Orch. Assn., 1982; bd. dirs. United Way of Columbia, 1981. Recipient Amicus Poloniae award Poland mag., 1971. Mem. Am. Assn. Higher Edn., Music Educators Nat. Conf. Roman Catholic. Home: 2312 Raven Trail Columbia SC 29169 Office: Osborne Adminstrn Bldg U SC Columbia SC 29208

BORLAND, JOHN NELSON, publishing company executive; b. N.Y.C., Feb. 21, 1929; s. J. Nelson and Leslie (Fuller) B.; m. Isabelle Clarke, Mar. 15, 1953 (div. 1968); children: Susan Madeleine, Tory

Lloyd, Leslie Fuller; m. Virginia A. Stockfish, Nov. 13, 1969. Student pvt. schs., N.Y.C. Reporter UPI, N.Y.C., 1948-50; export sales promotion mgr. Fairbanks Morse & Co., N.Y.C., 1950-53; with Hazard Advt. Co., N.Y.C., 1953-71, exec. v.p., 1966-71, treas., dir., 1967-71; pres. J. Nelson Borland & Co. Inc., N.Y.C., 1971-75; chmn. bd. Kaleidoscope Graphics, Inc., N.Y.C., 1972-75; pres. Muse Pub. Co., N.Y.C., 1975-78, Opus Pub. Co., 1979—. Clubs: N.Y. Yacht, Met. Opera (N.Y.C.). Home: 110 East End Ave New York NY 10028 Office: 200 Park Ave Suite 303E New York NY 10166

BORLAND, KATHRYN KILBY, author; b. Pullman, Mich., Aug. 14, 1916; d. Paul Melbourne and Vinnie (Bensinger) Kilby; m. James Barton Borland, May 16, 1942; children—James Barton, Susan Lee. B.S. in Journalism, Butler U., 1937. Editor North Side Topics, Indpls., 1938-42. Author: (all with Helen Ross Speicher) Southern Yankees, 1960, Allan Pinkerton, 1962, Miles and the Big Black Hat, 1963, Everybody Laughed, 1964, Eugene Field, 1964, Phillis Wheatley, 1968, Harry Houdini, 1969, Clocks from Shadow to Atom, 1969, Good-Bye to Stony Crick, 1975, The Third Tower, 1974, Stranger in the Mirror, 1974, Good-bye, Julie Scott, 1975, To Walk the Night, 1976, These Tigers' Hearts, 1978, Irena, 1979, Pseudonyms: Alice Abbott, Jane Land. Co-recipient award for most distinguished children's book pub. by Ind. author Ind. U., 1969. Mem. P.E.O., Theta Sigma Phi, Kappa Alpha Theta. Home: 1050 S Maish Rd Frankfort IN 46041

BORLAUG, NORMAN ERNEST, agricultural scientist; b. Cresco, Iowa, Mar. 25, 1914; s. Henry O. and Clara (Vaala) B.; m. Margaret G. Gibson, Sept. 24, 1937; children: Norma Jean (Mrs. Richard H. Rhoda), William Gibson. B.S. in Forestry, U. Minn., 1937, M.S. in Plant Pathology, 1940, Ph.D., 1941; Sc.D. (honoris causa), Punjab (India) Agrl. U., 1969, Royal Norwegian Agrl. Coll., 1970, Luther Coll., 1970, Uttar Pradesh Agrl. U., India, 1971, Kanpur U., India, 1970, Mich. State U., 1971, Universidad de la Plata, Argentina, 1971, U. Ariz., 1972, U. Fla., 1973; L.H.D., Gustavus Adolphus Coll., 1971; LL.D. (hon.), N.Mex. State U., 1973, D.Agr., Tufts U., 1982; others. With U.S. Forest Service, 1935-36, 37, 38; instr. U. Minn., 1941; microbiologist E.I. DuPont de Nemours, 1942-44; research scientist in charge wheat improvement Coop. Mexican Agrl. Program, Mexican Ministry Agr.-Rockefeller Found., Mexico, 1944-60; assoc. dir. assigned to Inter-Am. Food Crop Program, Rockefeller Found., 1960-63; dir. wheat research and prodn. program Internat. Maize and Wheat Improvement Center, Mexico City, 1964-79; assoc. dir. Rockefeller Found., 1964—, cons., 1983—; cons., collaborator Instituto Nacional de Investigationes Agricolas, Mexican Ministry Agr., 1960-64; cons. FAO, North Africa and Asia, 1960; ex-officio cons. wheat research and prodn. problems to govts. in, Latin Am., Africa, Asia.; Mem. Citizen's Commn. on Sci., Law and Food Supply, 1973—, Commn. Critical Choices for Am., 1973—, Council Agr. Sci. and Tech., 1973—; dir. Population Crisis Com., 1971; asesor especial Fundacion para Estudios de la Poblacion A.C., Mexico, 1971—; mem. adv. council Renewable Natural Resources Found., 1973—. Recipient Distinguished Service awards Wheat Producers Assns., and state govts. Mexican States of Guanajuato, Queretaro, Sonora, Tlaxcala and Zacatecas, 1954-60; Recognition award Agrl. Inst. Can., 1966, Instituto Nacional de Tecnologia Agropecuaria de Marcos Juarez, Argentina, 1968; Sci. Service award El Colegio de Ingenieros Agronomos de Mexico, 1970; Outstanding Achievement award U. Minn., 1959; E.C. Stakman award, 1961; named Uncle of Paul Bunyan, 1969; recipient Distinguished Citizen award Cresco Centennial Com., 1966; Nat. Distinguished Service award Am. Agrl. Editors Assn., 1967; Genetics and Plant Breeding award Nat. Council Comml. Plant Breeders, 1968; Star of Distinction Govt. of Pakistan, 1968; citation and street named in honor Citizens of Sonora and Rotary Club, 1968; Internat. Agronomy award Am. Soc. Agronomy, 1968; Distinguished Service award Wheat Farmers of Punjab, Haryana and Himachal Pradesh, 1969; Nobel Peace prize, 1970; Diploma de Merito El Instituto Tecnologico y de Estudios Superiores de Monterrey, Mexico, 1971; medalla y Diploma de Merito Antonio Narro Escuela Superior de Agricultura de la U. de Coahuila, Mexico, 1971; Diploma de Merito Escuela Superior de Agricultura Hermanos Escobar, Mexico, 1973; award for service to agr. Am. Farm Bur. Fedn., 1971; Outstanding Agrl. Achievement award World Farm Found., 1971; Medal of Merit Italian Wheat Scientists, 1971; Service award for outstanding contbn. to alleviation of world hunger 8th Latin Am. Food Prodn. Conf., 1972; named to Oreg. State U. Agrl. Hall of Fame, 1981; numerous other honors and awards from govts., ednl. instns., citizens groups. Hon. fellow Indian Soc. Genetics and Plant Breeding; mem. Nat. Acad. Sci., Am. Soc. Agronomy (1st Internat. Service award 1960, 1st hon. life mem.), Am. Assn. Cereal Chemists (hon. life mem., Meritorious Service award 1969), Crop Sci. Soc. Am. (hon. life mem.), Soil Sci. Soc. Am. (hon. life mem.), Sociedad de Agronomia do Rio Grande do Sul Brazil (hon.), India Nat. Sci. Acad. (fgn.), Royal Agrl. Soc. Eng. (hon.), Royal Soc. Edinburgh (hon.), Hungarian Acad. Sci. (hon.), Royal Swedish Acad. Agr. and Forestry (fgn.), Academia Nacional de Agronomia y Veterinaria (Argentina); hon. academician N.I. Vavilov Acad. Agrl. Scis. Lenin Order (USSR.). Address: Centro Internacional de Mejoramiento del Maiz y del Trigo Apartado Postal 6-641 Londres 40 Mexico City 6 Mexico

BORLE, ANDRÉ BERNARD, physiologist; b. La Chaux-de-Fonds, Switzerland, May 27, 1930; came to U.S., 1956, naturalized, 1969; s. Andre Leon and Fernande Alice (Rubeli-Courvoisier) B.; m. Beverly Ann George, Dec. 17, 1966; children—Caroline Juliette, Christian Dominique. M.D., U. Geneva, Switzerland, 1955. Ship surgeon Johnson Line, Stockholm, 1956; intern Mt. Auburn Hosp., Cambridge, Mass., 1956-57; research fellow in biochemistry Harvard U., Boston, 1957-59; asst. in medicine Peter Bent Brigham Hosp., Boston, 1957-59; resident in medicine Clinique Therapeutique Universitaire Hosp. Cantonal, Geneva, Switzerland, 1959-61; instr. dept. radiation biology and biophysics U. Rochester, 1961-63; asst. prof. physiology U. Pitts., 1963-70, asso. prof., 1970-75, prof., 1975—; cons. research program Atomic Energy Project, U. Rochester, 1969; program-project com. Div. Research Grants NIH Arthritis and Metabolic Diseases, 1971, 72; research program atomic energy project U. Rochester, 1972; mem. Arthritis and Metabolic Diseases Program Project Com., 1973-77; vis. prof. Med. Faculty U. Geneva, 1976. Contbr. articles to profl. jours. Bd. dirs. Association Pour La Creation D'une Fondation Pour Recherches Medicales, Geneva, 1967-72. Recipient Lederle Med. Faculty award, 1964-67, Prix Andre Lichtwitz Republique Francaise, 1970. Mem. Endocrine Soc., Am. Physiol. Soc., Biophys. Soc., Assn. Des Medecins Assts. (pres. Geneva sect. 1960-61). Home: 900 Delafield Rd Pittsburgh PA 15215

BORMAN, BURTON, insurance company executive; b. Chgo., June 2, 1928; s. Jack and Frieda (Greenberg) B.; m. Betty Lee Oscherwitz, Jan. 27, 1952; children: Gary, Scott, Amy. B.S., Ohio State U., 1950; postgrad., Wharton Sch. Bus. U. Pa., 1950. Gen. agt. United Ins. Co. Am., Chgo., 1950-58; pres. Pa. Life Co., Santa Monica, Calif., 1958—, also dir.; vice chmn., dir. Pa. Life Ins. Co., Santa Monica, now chmn., co-chief exec. officer; also officer or dir. various subs. Pa. Life Ins. Co. Bd. govs. Cedars-Sinai; bd. dirs. Reiss-Davis Child Study Center; trustee Immaculate Heart Coll. Mem. Zeta Beta Tau. Clubs: Masons, Shriners. Home: 244 Ladera Dr Beverly Hills CA 90210 Office: Pa Life Ins Co 3130 Wilshire Blvd Santa Monica CA 90406 *

BORMAN, FRANK, former astronaut, airlines exec.; b. Gary, Ind., Mar. 14, 1928; s. Edwin Borman; m. Susan Bugbee; children—Fredrick, Edwin. B.S., U.S. Mil. Acad., 1950; M. Aero. Engring, Calif. Inst. Tech., 1957; grad., USAF Aerospace Research Pilots Sch., 1960, Advanced Mgmt. Program, Harvard Bus. Sch., 1970. Commd. 2d lt. USAF, advanced through grades to col., 1965, ret., 1970; assigned various fighter squadrons, U.S. and Philippines, 1951-56; instr. thermodynamics and fluid mechanics U.S. Mil. Acad., 1957-60; instr. USAF Aerospace Research Pilots Sch., 1960-62; astronaut With Manned Spacecraft Center, NASA, until 1970; command pilot on 14 day orbital Gemini 7 flight, Dec. 1965, including rendezvous with Gemini 6; command pilot Apollo 8, 1st lunar orbital mission, Dec. 1968; sr. v.p. for operations Eastern Air Lines, Inc., Miami, Fla., 1970-74, exec. v.p., gen. operations mgr., 1974-75, pres., chief exec. officer, 1975—, chmn. bd., 1976—. Recipient Distinguished Service award NASA, 1965; Collier Trophy. Nat. Aeros. Assn., 1968. Address: Eastern Air Lines Inc Miami International Airport Miami FL 33148

BORMAN, PAUL, supermarket chain executive; b. Detroit, 1932; s. Abraham B.; married. Grad., Mich. State U., 1954. With Borman's Inc., Detroit, 1959—, gen. mgr., 1959-60, v.p., 1960-65, pres., chief exec. officer, dir., 1965—, mem. exec. com. Office: Borman's Inc 18718 Borman Ave Box 446 Detroit MI 48232 *

BORN, BROOKSLEY ELIZABETH, lawyer; b. San Francisco, Aug. 27, 1940; d. Ronald Henry and Mary Ellen (Bortner) B.; m. Alexander Elliot Bennett, Oct. 9, 1982; children: Nicholas Jacob, Ariel Elizabeth. A.B., Stanford U., 1961, J.D., 1964. Bar: Calif. 1965, D.C. 1966. Law clk. U.S. Ct. Appeals, Washington, 1964-65; legal researcher Harvard Law Sch., 1967-68; asso. firm Arnold and Porter, Washington, 1965-67, 68-73, partner, 1974—; lectr. law Columbus Sch. Law, Cath. U. Am., 1972-74; adj. prof. Georgetown U. Law Center, Washington, 1972-73. Pres.: Stanford Law Rev, 1963-64. Bd. visitors Stanford Law Sch., 1977-79; bd. dirs. Nat. Legal Aid and Defenders Assn., 1972-79; chairperson bd. dirs. Nat. Women's Law Ctr., 1981—; trustee Center for Law and Social Policy, Washington, 1977—, Women's Bar Found., 1981—. Mem. Am. Bar Assn. (chairperson sect. individual rights and responsibilities 1977-78, chairperson fed. judiciary com. 1980—), D.C. Bar (sec. 1975-76, bd. govs. 1976-79), Am. Law Inst., Lawyers' Com. for Civil Rights Under Law (trustee 1978—), Order of Coif. Office: 1200 New Hampshire Ave NW Washington DC 20036

BORN, HAROLD JOSEPH, educator, physicist; b. Evansville, Ind., Nov. 22, 1922; s. Harold O. and Marie J. (Gronotte) B.; m. Betty Jean Rasche, Apr. 15, 1950; children—Christopher Paul, David William. Student, Evansville U., 1940-42; B.S., Rose Poly. Inst., 1949; M.S., Ia. State U., 1958, Ph.D., 196O. Design engr. Electronics Research Corp., Evansville, 1949-52; equipment engr. Phillips Petroleum Co., Bartlesville, Okla., 1952-55; research asst. Ames (Iowa) Lab. AEC, 1955-60; physicist Whirlpool Corp., 1960-61; mem. faculty Ill. State U., Normal, 1961—, prof. physics, head dept., 1966—; Mem. Normal Human Relations Commn., 1964-69, chmn., 1967-68. Contbr. articles in field. Mem. Am. Phys. Soc., Am. Assn. Physics Tchrs., Sigma Xi. Roman Catholic. Spl. research low temperature solid state physics. Home: 806 Highpoint Rd Normal IL 61761

BORNE, MORTIMER, artist; b. Rypin, Poland, Dec. 31, 1902; came to U.S., 1916, naturalized, 1921; s. Harry and Lena (Warshaw) B.; m. Rachel Zipes, Feb. 28, 1929. Student schs. U.S. and abroad. Lectr. Sweet Briar Coll., 1945; lectr. art New Sch. Social Research, N.Y.C., 1945-67. Exhibited major graphic exhbns., 1926—, including, Brit. Mus., London, 1980; one-man shows, New Gallery, Jerusalem, 1935, Internat. Coll., Springfield, Mass., 1940, Cedar Rapids (Iowa) Art Assn., Corcoran Gallery of Art, Washington, 1941, Mus. Fine Arts, Montreal, Can., 1942, Grand Central Art Galleries, N.Y.C., 1943, Smithsonian Instn., Washington, 1944, Currier Gallery, Manchester, 1945, Connoisseur Gallery, N.Y.C., 1959, Connoisseur Gallery, Tel-Aviv, 1965, Tappan Zee Art Center, Nyack, N.Y., 1962, 69, Shulamit Gallery, Tel Aviv, 1980, N.Y. Hist. Soc. Mus.; Author: The Visual Bible: Ninety-two Drawings, 1976, Meet Moses: 54 Drawings, 1978, Drypoints, Etchings, Color Drypoints, 88 Reproductions, 1980; also articles on art.; works reproduced various mags., newspapers; represented in permanent collections, Mus. Modern Art, Library of Congress, Nat. Mus., Smithsonian Inst., N.Y. Public Library, Rosenwald Collection, (100 etchings and drypoints) Met. Mus. Art, N.Y.C., U. Judaism, Los Angeles, Brit. Mus., Israel Mus., Jerusalem, Tel Aviv Mus., Boston Public Library, Bklyn. Mus., Phila. Mus. Art, Nat. Gallery Art, Washington, Mus. Fine Arts, Houston, Victoria and Albert Mus., London, Boymans Mus., Rotterdam, Wadsworth Atheneum, N.Y. Hist. Soc., Detroit Inst. Art, San Francisco Mus., Boston Mus. Fine Arts, Fogg Art Mus., Fort Lauderdale Mus., N.Y. Pub. Library, Herbert F. Johnson Mus., Ithaca, N.Y., Family of Peoples (chromatic wood sculpture), Mcpl. Mus., Ramat-gan, Israel. Recipient J. Frederick Talcott prize Soc. Am. Etchers, 1939, Noyes prize for best print Soc. Am. Etchers 28th Ann. Exhbn., 1943. Inventor color drypoint technique using 3 plates, chromatic wood sculpture, convex canvas painting; originator new method for woodcuts and drawings. Address: 107 S Broadway Nyack NY 10960 *Our enlarged visual vocabulary emcompasses all human experience. Abstract concepts require abstract means. To rigidly apply one style or idion to all our thoughts deprives the artist of full expression. I call this freedom of expression—"syncretism."*

BORNEMANN, ALFRED HENRY, economist, educator; b. Queens, N.Y., Nov. 30, 1908; s. Ernest and Carrie (Wolters) B.; m. Bertha Kohl, Aug. 20, 1938; 1 son, Alfred Richard. B.A. cum laude, N.Y. U., 1933, M.A., 1937, Ph.D., 1941; student, U. Goettingen, summer 1929. Accountant Cities Service Co., 1923-33, Am. Water Works & Electric Co., Inc., 1934-40; teaching fellow N.Y. U., 1940-41; instr. Rutgers U., 1941-44; vis. lectr. N.Y. U., 1944-45, Bklyn. Coll., summer 1945; asst. prof. Boston U., 1945-46, L.I. U., 1946-48; asso. prof. Muhlenberg Coll., 1948-50, Fla. State U., 1950-51; prof., head econs. and bus. adminstrn. dept. Norwich U., 1951-58; chmn. dept. mgmt. St. Francis Coll., 1958-60; prof. economics, bus. adminstrn. C.W.Post Coll. of L.I. U., 1960-66; mem. faculty City U. N.Y.-Hunter, Kingsborough, 1967-74, Fairleigh Dickinson U., 1966, 75, City U. N.Y.-Bklyn. Coll., 1977-78, St. Francis Coll., 1978-79; self-employed, 1979—. Author: J. Laurence Laughlin: Chapters in the Career of an Economist, 1940, Fundamentals of Industrial Management, 1963, Essentials of Purchasing, 1974, Fifty Years of Ideology: A Selective Survey of Academic Economics in the United States 1930 to 1980, 1981, 20th Century Letters and History, 1984; Contbr. articles to profl. jours. Mem. Am. Acctg. Assn., Acad. Mgmt., Am. Econ. Assn., Am. Finance Assn., Bus. History Conf., Vt. Hist. Soc., Alpha Kappa Psi (dep. councilor 1953-54, dist. dir. 1954-67, regional dir. 1962, chmn. expansion com. 1956-62, chmn. history com. 1965-68), Omicron Delta Epsilon, Pi Gamma Mu. Home: 151 Engle St Englewood NJ 07631

BORNEMANN, VALMA M., educator. Dean of studies Barnard Coll., N.Y.C. Office: Office of the Dean of Studies Barnard Coll 106 Malbank New York NY 10027

BORNEO, RUDOLPH JOHN, retail exec.; b. Bklyn., Mar. 22, 1941; s. John R. and Ann (Guarino) B.; m. Charlene L. Stosik, June 20, 1964; children—Michael Charles, Cara Denise, Dana Lynne, Corinne Michele. B.S. in Bus. Adminstrn, Monmouth Coll., West Long Branch, N.J., 1964. With Bamberger's, Newark, 1964—, group v.p., dir. No. stores, 1977, sr. v.p., dir. mdsg., 1977—, also dir. Councilman Burough of Eatontown, N.J., 1972-80, pres., 1976-80, police commr., 1976-80. Democrat. Roman Catholic. Home: 3 Sycamore Ln Rumson NJ 07760 Office: 131 Market St Newark NJ 07102

BORNHOLDT, LAURA ANNA, foundation administrator; b. Peoria, Ill., Feb. 11, 1919; d. John and Barbara (Kohl) B. A.B., Smith Coll., 1940, M.A., 1942; Ph.D., Yale U., 1945. Asst. prof. history Smith Coll., Northampton, Mass., 1945-52; internat. relations asso. AAUW, Washington, 1952-57; dean Sarah Lawrence Coll., Bronxville, N.Y., 1957-59; dean women, adj. prof. history U. Pa., Phila., 1959-61; dean coll., prof. history Wellesley (Mass.) Coll., 1961-64; v.p. Danforth Found., St. Louis, 1964-73; sr. program officer Lilly Endowment Inc., Indpls., 1973-76, v.p. for edn., 1976—; Nat. adv. com. on black higher edn. and black colls. and univs. Dept. Edn., 1977-82; mem. Yale U. Council, 1977—; emerita life trustee Coll. of Wooster, Ohio, 1977—; trustee St. Louis U., 1971-75. Editorial bd.: Jour. Higher Edn., 1970-76; adv. bd.: Change Mag., 1980—. Recipient Yale U. Wilbur Cross medal, 1976. Mem. Am. Assn. Higher Edn., Phi Beta Kappa. Home: 5521 Roxbury Terr Indianapolis IN 46226 Office: 2801 N Meridian St Box 88068 Indianapolis IN 46208

BORNSTEIN, ELI, painter, sculptor; b. Milw., Dec. 28, 1922; naturalized, 1972; m. Christine; 2 children. B.S., U. Wis., 1945, M.S., 1954; student, Art Inst. Chgo., U. Chgo., 1943, Academie Montmartre of Fernand Leger, Paris, 1951, Academie Julian, 1952. Tchr. drawing, painting and sculpture Milw. Art Inst., 1943-47; tchr. design U. Wis., 1949; tchr. drawing, painting, sculpture, design and graphics U. Sask., Can., 1950—, prof., 1963—, head art dept., 1963-71. Painted in, France, 1951-52, Italy, 1957; Exhibited widely, 1943—; retrospective exhbn. (works 1943-64), Mendel Art Gallery, Saskatoon, 1965, one man shows, Kazimir Gallery, Chgo., 1965, 67, Saskatoon Pub. Library, 1975, Can. Cultural Center, Paris, 1976, Glenbow-Alta. Inst. Art, Calgary, Mendel Art Gallery, Saskatoon, 1982, York U. Gallery, Toronto, 1983, Confedn. Ctr. Art Gallery, Charlottetown, P.E.I., Beaverbrook Art Gallery, Frederickton, N.B.; represented in numerous pvt. collections; executed marble sculpture now in permanent collection, Walker Art Center, Mpls., 1947, aluminum constrn. for, Sask. Tchrs. Fedn. Bldg., 1956, structurist relief in painted wood and aluminum for, Arts and Scis. Bldg., U. Sask., 1958, structurist relief in enamelled steel for, Internat. Air Terminal, Winnipeg, Man., Can., 1962, four-part constructed relief for, Wascana Pl., Wascana Ctr. Authority, Regina, Sask., 1983; also structurist reliefs exhibited, Mus. Contemporary Art, Chgo., Herron Mus. Art, Indpls., Cranbrook Acad. Art Galleries, Mich., High Mus., Atlanta, Can. House, Cultural Centre Gallery, London, 1983, Can. Cultural Ctr., Paris, Can. Cultural Ctr., Brussels, model version of structurist relief in 5 parts, 1962, now in collection, Nat. Gallery, Ottawa, Ont., others in numerous collections.; Co-editor: periodical Structure, 1958; founder, editor: ann. publ. The Structurist, 1960—; Contbr. articles, principally on Structurist art to various publs. Recipient Allied Arts medal Royal Archtl. Inst. Can., 1968; honorable mention for 3 structurist reliefs 2d Biennial Internat. Art Exhbn., Colombia, S.Am., 1970; Diploma of Nomination with gold medal Accademia Italia delle Arti e del Lavoro, 1980. Address: Rural Route 5 Saskatoon SK S7K 3J8 Canada Office: Box 378 Sub PO6 U Sask Saskatoon SK S7N 0W0 Canada

BORNSTEIN, GEORGE JAY, literary educator; b. St. Louis, Aug. 25, 1941; s. Harry and Celia (Price) B.; m. Jane Elizabeth York, June 22, 1982; 1 son: Benjamin. A.B., Harvard U., 1963; Ph.D., Princeton U., 1966. Asst. prof. Mass. Inst. Tech., 1966-69, Rutgers U., 1969-70; assoc. prof. U. Mich.-Ann Arbor, 1970-75, prof. English, 1975—; cons. various univ presses, scholastic jours., funding agys., 1970—. Author: Yeats and Shelley, 1970, Transformations of Romanticism, 1976, Postromantic Consciousness of Ezra Pound, 1977; editor: Romantic and Modern, 1977, Ezra Pound Among the Poets, 1985; mem. adv. bd.: Yeats: An Annual, 1982—. Cubmaster Wolverine council Boy Scouts Am., 1977-79. Recipient good teaching award Amoco Found.; fellow Am. Council Learned Socs.; NEH fellow, 1983—; fellow Old Dominion Found., 1968. Mem. Modern Lang. Assn. (mem. exec. com. Anglo-Irish 1976-80, mem. exec. com. 20th Century English 1980—), Keats-Shelley Assn., Phi Beta Kappa. Clubs: Racquet (Ann Arbor); Princeton (N.Y.C.). Home: 2020 Vinewood Blvd Ann Arbor MI 48104 Office: Dept English U Mich Ann Arbor MI 48109

BORNSTEIN, LESTER MILTON, medical center administrator; b. Boston, Feb. 19, 1925; s. Harry and Celia (Adlestein) B.; m. Marilyn Goldstein, Aug. 22, 1948; children: Aura Lynne, Michael Scott, Karen Jane. B.S., Boston U., 1948; M.P.H. in Hosp. Adminstrn, Yale U., 1955. Adminstrv. resident Charles S. Wilson Meml. Hosp., Johnson City, N.Y., 1953-54; asst. dir. Barnert Meml. Hosp., Paterson, N.J., 1954-57, Newark Beth Israel Hosp., 1957-68; exec. dir. Newark Beth Israel Med. Center, Newark, 1968—. Served with AUS, 1943-45; ETO; to maj., Korean War, 1950-53. Decorated Bronze Star. Fellow Am. Coll. Hosp. Adminstrs., N.J. Hosp. Assn. (chmn. bd. trustees 1978-79). Home: 6 Ahern Way West Orange NJ 07052 Office: 201 Lyons Ave Newark NJ 07112

BORNSTEIN, MORRIS, educator, economist; b. Detroit, Sept. 4, 1927; m. Reva Rice, Apr. 7, 1962; children—Susan, Jane. A.B., U. Mich., 1947, A.M., 1948, Ph.D., 1952. Economist U.S. Govt., 1951-52, 55-58; mem. faculty U. Mich., Ann Arbor, 1958—, prof. econs., 1964—, dir. Center Russian and E. European Studies, 1966-69; Asso. Harvard U. Russian Research Center, 1962-63; vis. research fellow Hoover Instn., Stanford, 1969-70; cons. in field, 1959—; Mem. joint com. on Eastern Europe Am. Council Learned Socs.-Social Sci. Research Council, 1977-80. Author: Soviet National Accounts for 1955, 1961, The Soviet Economy, 1962, 4th edit., 1974, Comparative Economic Systems, 1965, 4th edit., 1979, Economia di Mercato ed Economia Pianificata, 1973, Sistemas economicos comparados, 1973, Plan and Market, 1973, Economic Planning, East and West, 1975, Chinese transl., 1980, The Soviet Economy: Continuity and Change, 1981, East-West Relations and the Future of Eastern Europe, 1981; also articles. Served with AUS, 1953-55. Ford Found. faculty fellow, 1962-63. Mem. Am. Econ. Assn., Am. Assn. Advancement Slavic Studies, Assn. Comparative Econ. Studies (exec. com. 1965-67, 73-75), Council for European Studies (exec. com. 1973-75). Office: Dept Econs U Mich Ann Arbor MI 48109

BORNSTEIN, PAUL, physician, biochemist; b. Antwerp, Belgium, July 10, 1934; came to U.S., 1947, naturalized, 1952; s. Abraham and Mina (Ginsburg) B. B.A., Cornell U., 1954; M.D., N.Y. U., 1958. Intern in surgery Yale-New Haven Hosp., 1958-59, intern in medicine, 1959-60, asst. resident in medicine, 1960-62; sr. fellow Arthritis Found. Pasteur Inst., Paris, 1962-63; research asso. NIH, Bethesda, Md., 1963-65, research investigator, 1965-67; asst. prof. biochemistry and medicine U. Wash., 1967-69, asso. prof., 1969-73, prof., 1973—, attending physician, 1968—. Contbr. articles to profl. jours.; editorial bd.: Jour. Biol. Chemistry, 1972-78, 80—; asso. editor: Arteriosclerosis and Collagen and Related Research. Served to sr. surgeon USPHS, 1963-67. Recipient Lederle Med. Faculty award USPHS, 1968, Research Career Devel. award NIH, 1969, Macy Faculty Scholar award, 1975. Mem. Am. Soc. Clin. Investigation, Am. Soc. Biol. Chemistry, Western Soc. Clin. Research, Am. Rheumatism Assn., Assn. Am. Physicians. Home: 5404 Seward Park Ave S Seattle WA 98118 Office: Dept Biochemistry SJ-70 U of Wash Sch Medicine Seattle WA 98195

BORNSTEIN, SAM, newspaper editor; b. Boston, Dec. 3, 1913; s. Harry and Anna (Phillips) B.; m. Ruth Novogroski, Jan. 4, 1938; children: Marjorie, Harold. B.S. in Journalism, Boston U., 1935. Reporter, Boston Am., 1936-38; city editor Boston Sunday Advertiser, 1938-42, mng. editor, 1942-71; exec. editor Boston Herald Am., 1972-77; ret., 1977; instr. journalism U. Miami, Coral Gables, Fla., 1977-79, Nova U., Ft. Lauderdale, Fla., 1981, Fla. Atlantic U., Boca Raton, 1982. Mem. Am. Soc. Newspaper Editors, AP Mng. Editors Assn., Boston U. Alumni Assn., Sigma Delta Chi. Home: Flanders 456J Delray Beach FL 33445

BOROFSKY, JONATHAN, artist; b. Boston, 1942. B.F.A., Carnegie-Mellon U., 1964; postgrad., Ecole de fontainbleau, 1964; M.F.A., Yale U., 1966. Instr. Sch. Visual Arts, 1969-77, Calif. Inst. Arts, 1977-80. Exhibitor one-man shows, Paula Cooper Gallery, N.Y.C., 1975, Wardsworth Atheneum, Hartford, Conn., 1976, U. Calif.-Irvine, 1977, 78, Projects Gallery Mus. Modern Art, N.Y.C., 1978, INK Halle fur Internationale Neue Kunst, Zurich, 1979, Hayden Gallery-MIT, Cambridge, Mass., 1980, The Contemporary Art Mus., Houston, 1981, Kunsthalle Basel, Switzerland, Mus. Boymasn-Van Beuningen, Rotterdam, 1982, Erika and Otto Friedrich Gallery, Bern, Kunstmuseum Basel, Switzerland, 1983, Galleria dell'Ariete Grafica, Milan, Italy, group shows, Paula Cooper Gallery, 1969, Seattle Art Mus., 1970, Vancouver Art Gallery, Artists Space, N.Y.C., 1973, Michael Wyman Gallery, Chgo. Ill., 1974, Whitney Mus. Art., N.Y.C., 1975, 79, 81, 82, 83, Venice Biennale, Italy, 1976, Woods Gerry Gallery, R.I. Sch. Design, Providence, 1977, Holly Solomon Gallery, N.Y.C., Art Mus. U. Calif.-Santa Barbara, 1978, Renaissance Soc. U. Chgo., 1979, Phila. Coll. Art, Yale U. Art Gallery, 1981, Sidney Janis Gallery, N.Y.C., Los Angeles County Mus. Art, Milw. Art Mus., 1983, Walker Art Ctr., Mpls., 1982, Mus. Modern Art, N.Y.C., Hayden Gallery-MIT, Hirshborn Mus. and Sculpture Garden Smithsonian Instn., Washington, 1983, Mus. Modern Art, N.Y.C. Office: care Paula Cooper Gallery 155 Wooster St New York N.Y. 10012 *

BOROK, EMANUEL, concertmaster; b. Tashkent, USSR, July 15, 1944; came to U.S., 1974, naturalized, 1979; s. Reuven and Sarra (Hill) B.; m. Zinaida Shekhtman, Feb. 5, 1966; children: Mark, Sarah. Mus.M., Gnesin Sch. Music, Moscow, 1969. Co-concertmaster Moscow Philharmonic, 1971-73; concertmaster Israel Chamber Orch., 1973-74; asst. concertmaster Boston Symphony Orch., 1974—; concertmaster Boston Pops Orch., 1974—; tchr. violin Boston U. Prize winner All Russian Republic violinist contest, 1965, All Soviet Union violinist contest, 1965. Mem. Boston Musicians Assn. Club: Exec. Health. Office: care Boston Symphony Orch Symphony Hall Boston MA 02115 *

BOROS, EUGENE JOSEPH, chemical company executive; b. Decatur, Ill, May 19, 1940; s. Eugene Joseph and Helen Louise B.; m. Nancy Lea Odum, aug. 28, 1960; children: Eric Eugene, Rohonda Lea. B.S. in Chemistry, U. Ill., 1962; Ph.D. in Inorganic Chemistry, Iowa State U., 1966. Asst. prof. Wash. State U., Pullman, 1966-68; sr. chemist, project scientist, group leader, assoc. dir., dir. research and devel. dept. Union Carbide Corp., South Charleston, W.Va. and Research Triangle Park, N.C., 1968—, v.p. research and devel., Research Triangle Park. Contbr. articles to profl. jours.; patentee. Bd. mem. Youth Orch., Charleston, W.Va., 1980-81. Mem. Am. Chem. Soc., Phi Kappa Phi. Presbyterian. Club: Wildwood country (Raleigh). Home: 8501 E Lake Ct Raleigh NC 27612 Office: Union Carbide Corp PO Box 12014 Research Triangle Park NC 27709

BOROS, STEPHEN, JR., professional baseball manager; b. Flint, Mich., Sept. 3, 1936; s. Stephen B.; m. Sharla Boros; children: Sasha Ayn, Stephen. B.A., U. Mich. Player Detroit Tigers, Am. League, 1957-62, Chgo. Cubs, Nat. League, 1963, Cin. Reds, Nat. League, 1964-65; player with various minor league teams, 1965-69; mgr. Walterloo, Iowa, Midwest League, 1970-72, San Jose League, Calif., 1973-74; coach Kansas City Royals, Am. League, 1975-79; mgr. Calgary Flames, Pioneer League, 1980; coach Montreal Expos, Nat. League, 1981-82; mgr. Oakland A's, Am. League, 1983—. Office: Oakland A's Oakland-Alameda County Coliseum Oakland CA 94621 *

BOROVOY, ROGER STUART, lawyer; b. Milw., Apr. 13, 1935; s. Sam and Anne D. (Finkler) B.; m. Brenda Ruth Gordon, June 7, 1959; children: Amy, Richard. B.S., M.I.T., 1956; J.D., Harvard U., 1959. Bar: Calif. 1961. Patent atty. Chevron Research Corp., San Francisco, 1960-62; asso. Lippincott, Ralls & Hendricson, San Francisco, 1962-63; patent counsel Fairchild Camera & Instrument Corp., Mountain View, Calif., 1963-74; v.p., gen. counsel, sec. Intel Corp., Santa Clara, 1974-83; ptnr. Sevin-Rosen Mgmt., 1983—; dir. Spectragraphics Corp. Served with U.S. Army, 1959. Mem. Am., Santa Clara bar assns., IEEE. Clubs: M.I.T. of No. Calif., Los Altos Golf and Country. Office: 3065 Bowers Ave Santa Clara CA 95051

BOROWITZ, ALBERT IRA, lawyer, author; b. Chgo., June 27, 1930; s. David and Anne (Wolkenstein) B.; m. Helen Blanche Osterman, July 29, 1950; children: Peter Leonard, Joan, Andrew Seth. B.A. in Classics (Detur award 1948) summa cum laude, Harvard U., 1951, M.A. in Chinese Regional Studies, 1953, J.D. (Sears prize) magna cum laude, 1956. Bar: Ohio 1957. Asso. firm Hahn, Loeser, Freedheim, Dean & Wellman, Cleve., 1956-62, partner, 1962-83, Jones, Day, Reavis & Pogue, Cleve., 1983—; dir. Bobbie Brooks, Inc. Author: Fiction in Communist China, 1955, Innocence and Arsenic: Studies in Crime and Literature, 1977, The Woman Who Murdered Black Satin: The Bermondsey Horror, 1981, A Gallery of Sinister Perspectives: Ten Crimes and a Scandal, 1982; contbr. articles to profl. jours. Recipient Cleve. arts prize for lit., 1981. Mem. Am. Law Inst., Am. Bar Assn., Ohio State Bar Assn., Bar Assn. Greater Cleve. Clubs: Union, Rowfant, Ct. of Nisi Prius (Cleve.); Harvard N.Y.C. Office: 1700 Union Commerce Bldg Cleveland OH 44115

BOROWITZ, JOSEPH LEO, pharmacologist; b. Columbus, Ohio, Dec. 19, 1932; s. Joseph Peter and Anna Louise (Grundei) B.; m. Judy Lynn McCarron, Sept. 7, 1963; children: Jon Joseph, Peter Joseph, Lynn Anne. B.Sc. in Pharmacy, Ohio State U., 1955; M.S. in Pharmacology, Purdue U., 1957; Ph.D. in Pharmacology (NIH fellow), Northwestern U., 1960. Postdoctoral fellow dept. pharmacology Harvard U. Med. Sch., Boston, 1963-64; instr., then asst. prof. pharmacology Bowman Gray Sch. Medicine, 1964-69; asso. prof. pharmacology and toxicology Sch. Pharmacy and Pharmacal Scis., Purdue U., 1969-74, prof., 1974—, sabbatical leave to Cambridge, Eng., 1976. Contbr. articles to profl. jours. Treas. Tippecanoe County (Ind.) Comprehensive Health Planning Council, 1971-76. Served as capt. USAR, 1960. Recipient award for excellence in teaching Bowman Gray Sch. Medicine, 1969; Henry Heine award for excellence in teaching Purdue U. Coll. Pharmacy, 1983; NIH postdoctoral fellow, 1962-64; NSF grantee, 1965-68; NIH grantee, 1971-74. Mem. Am. Soc. Pharmacology and Exptl. Therapeutics, Soc. Exptl. Biology and Medicine, Sigma Xi, Rho Chi. Roman Catholic. Office: Dept Pharmacology and Toxicology Purdue U West Lafayette IN 47907

BOROWSKY, IRVIN J., publishing company executive; b. Phila., Nov. 23, 1924; children: Scott, Gwen, Ned, Ted. Founder TV Digest (now TV Guide), 1948; founder, pres. North Am. Pub. Co. (pubs. N.Y. Custom House Guide, Yacht Racing/Cruising, Business Forms and Systems, Am. Sch. and Univ., World Wide Printer, Zip Tarket Mktg. various other consumer, bus. and profl. mags.), Phila., 1958—; lectr., seminar leader, writer and editor. Home: Society Hill Towers Philadelphia PA 19106 Office: 401 N Broad St Philadelphia PA 19108

BORRELL, EUGENE ADAM, medical center executive; b. Gueydan, La., Apr. 18, 1927; s. Avery and Edia (Woods) B.; m. Bobbie Jean Blankenship, Oct. 18, 1946; children: Pamela, Penny, Kathy, Chuck. B.A., McNeese State U., 1962. Owner outdoor advt. bus., Lake Charles, La., 1946-62; personnel mgmt. dept. VA Hosp., Dallas, 1962-63; personnel dir. VA Med. Ctr., Shreveport, La., 1963-71; assoc. dir. VA Med. Ctrs., Phoenix and Indpls., 1971-78, dir., Walla Walla, Wash., 1978-81, Fayetteville, Ark., 1978-81, Olin E. Teague VA Ctr., Temple, Tex., 1981—. Council mem. Tex. State Health Coordinating Council, Austin, 1983—; bd. dirs. Cultural Activities Ctr., Temple, 1983—, C. of C. Served with USNR, 1945-46. Mem. Am. Hosp. Assn., Tex. Hosp. Assn., Am. Assn. Med. Colls. Democrat. Am. Baptist. Clubs: Rotary, Masons (master). Home: 2516 Canyon Creek Dr Temple TX 76502 Office: Olin E Teague VA Med Ctr 1901 S 1st St Temple TX 76501

BORRELLE, FRANK J(OHN), assn. exec.; b. Hudson, N.Y., Oct. 14, 1923; s. Frank and Anna (Astore) B.; m. Rose Rita Rucci, Aug. 27, 1949; children—Frank, Robert, William. B.S. in Commerce, Rider Coll., 1950. With Fedn. Socs. Coatings Tech., Phila., 1950—, exec. sec., 1972-73, exec. v.p., 1973—. Served with U.S. Army, 1943-46. Mem. Nat. Assn. Expn Mgrs. (dir.), Am. Soc. Assn. Execs. Home: 118 N Brookfield Rd Cherry Hill NJ 08034 Office: 1315 Walnut St Philadelphia PA 19107

BORROFF, MARIE, educator; b. N.Y.C., Sept. 10, 1923; d. Albert Ramon and Marie (Bergersen) B. Ph.B., U. Chgo., 1943, M.A., 1946; Ph.D., Yale U., 1956. Teaching asst. U. Chgo., 1946-47; instr. dept. English Smith Coll., 1948-51, asst. prof., 1956-59, asso. prof., 1959; vis. asst. prof. English Yale U., 1957-58, vis. asso. prof., 1959-6O, asso. prof. English, 1960-65, prof., 1965-71, William Lampson prof., 1971—; Phi Beta Kappa vis. scholar, 1973-74; fellow Ezra Stiles Coll., Yale. Author: Sir Gawain and the Green Knight; A Stylistic and Metrical Study, 1962, (with J.B. Bessinger, Jr.) Sir Gawain and the Green Knight; A Stylistic and Metrical Study; recorded dialogues read in Middle English, 1965, Sir Gawain and the Green Knight: A New Verse Translation, 1967, Pearl: A New Verse Translation, 1977, Language and the Poet: Verbal Artistry in Frost, Stevens, and Moore, 1979; editor: Wallace Stevens, A Collection of Critical Essays, 1963. Recipient James Billings Fiske poetry prize U. Chgo., 1943; Eunice Tietjens Meml. prize Poetry mag., 1945; Margaret Lee Wiley fellow AAUW, 1955-56; Guggenheim fellow, 1969-70. Fellow Am. Acad. Arts and Scis.; mem. Modern Lang. Assn. Am., Medieval Acad. Am., Phi Beta Kappa. Home: 311 St Ronan St New Haven CT 06511

BORROWMAN, MERLE L., educator; b. Idaho Falls, Idaho, May 12, 1920; s. Lorus P. and Violet (Norton) B.; m. Ellen Louise Young, June 1, 1962; children—Steven, Betty Jo (Mrs. Sherwood Chang), Phyllis, Erik, Alison. B.A., Brigham Young U., 1942; M.A., U. Idaho, 1947; Ed. D., Columbia, 1953. High sch. tchr., prin., Sugar City, Idaho, 1945-52; instr. to asst. prof. Columbia, 1950-54; asst. prof., asso. prof., prof. ednl. policy studies, history U. Wis., Madison, 1954-69, chmn. dept. ednl. policy studies, 1963-67; dean Sch. Edn., U. Calif. at Riverside, 1969-71; prof. U. Calif. at Berkeley, 1971—, dean, 1971-77; cons. editor Scott Foresman Co., 1963—; cons. Ednl. Testing Services, 1966-67. Author: The Liberal and Technical in Teacher Education, 1956, Teacher Education in America, 1964, What Doctrines to Embrace, 1968; Contbr. profl. jours. Pres. Idaho Interscholastic Activities Assn., 1946-47; v.p. Idaho Sch. Adminstrv. Assn., 1947-49. Served to capt. USMCR, 1943-46. Guggenheim fellow, 1967-68. Mem. History of Edn. Soc. (past pres.), Am. Hist. Assn., Orgn. Am. Historians. Home: 1505 Spruce St Berkeley CA 94709

BORSARI, GEORGE ROBERT, JR., lawyer, broadcaster; b. Washington, July 30, 1940; s. George Robert and Sara Totton (Dunning) B.; m. Regis Ann Herron, Oct. 23, 1964; children: George Robert, III, William Grant. B.S., Va. Poly. Inst., 1962; LL.B., George Washington U., 1965. Bar: D.C. 1966. Since practiced in, Washington; partner firm Daly, Joyce and Borsari, 1969—. Councilman Town of Glen Echo, Md., 1969-74, mayor, 1977-81; mem. Montgomery County (Md.) Muncipality Advisory Bd., 1972-74, Montgomery County CATV Task Force, 1973-74, 80—, Cable TV Adv. Com., 1979—; pres. Montgomery County chpt. Md. Mcpl. League. Served to lt. col. JAG USAR. Decorated Army Meritorious Service medal, Army Commendation medal with oak leaf cluster; recipient Presdl. commendation, 1970; St. George award Roman Catholic Archdiocese Washington, 1970; Silver Beaver award Nat. Capital Area council Boy Scouts Am., 1974. Mem. ABA (chmn. cable TV com. sect. sci. and tech.), Am., D.C., Fed. Communications bar assns., Isaac Walton League, Phi Delta Phi. Democrat. Clubs: Nat. Communications, Kenwood Golf and Country. Home: 6107 Princeton Ave Glen Echo MD 20812 Office: 1830 Jefferson Pl NW Washington DC 20036

BORSCH, FREDERICK HOUK, cleryman, church official, educator; b. Chgo., Sept. 13, 1935; s. Reuben A. and Pearl Irene (Houk) B.; m. Barbara Edgeley Sampson, June 25, 1960; children: Benjamin, Matthew, Stuart. A.B., Princeton U., 1957; M.A., Oxford U., 1959; S.T.B., Gen. Theol. Sem., 1960; Ph.D, U. Birmingham, 1966; D.D. hon., Seabury Western Theol. Sem., 1978, S.T.D., Ch. Div. Sch. of Pacific, 1981. Ordained priest Episcopal Ch., 1960; curate Grace Episcopal Ch., Oak Park, Ill., 1960-63; tutor Queen's Coll., Birmingham, Eng., 1963-66; asst. prof. N.T. Seabury Western Theol. Sem., Evanston, Ill., 1966-69, assoc. prof.N.T., 1969-71; prof. N.T. Gen. Theol. Sem., N.Y.C., 1971-72; pres., dean The Ch. Div. Sch. of Pacific, Berkeley, Calif., 1972-81; dean of chapel Princeton U., 1981—; rep. Faith and Order Commn., Nat. Council Chs., 1975-81; mem. exec. council Episcopal Ch., 1981—. Author: The Son of Man in Myth and History, 1967, The Christian and Gnostic Son of Man, 1970, God's Parable, 1976, Introducing the Lessons of the Church Years, 1978, Coming Together in the Spirit, 1980, Power in Weakness, 1983. Keasbey scholar, 1957-59. Mem. Am. Acad. Religion, Soc. Bibl. Lit., Studiorum Novi Testamenti Societas, Phi Beta Kappa. Home: 17 Ivy Ln Princeton NJ 08540 Office: Princeton Univ Murray Dodge Hall Princeton NJ 08544

BORSKI, ROBERT A., congressman; b. Phila., Oct. 20, 1948; s. Robert Anthony and Rita (Savage) B.; m. Barbara Ann Joniec, Nov. 26, 1977; children: Jill Michele, Dorothy Lynn, Jennifer Marie. B.A., U. Balt., 1971. Floor mgr. Raymond James & Assoc., Phila., 1971-77; mem. Pa. Ho. of Reps., 1977-82, 98th Congress from Pa. Democrat. Roman Catholic. Home: 3545 Emerald St Philadelphia PA 19134 Office: Room 314 Cannon House Office Bldg Washington DC 20515

BORSODY, BENJAMIN FRANK, consulting engineer; b. Budapest, Hungary, Feb. 15 1901; came to U.S., 1907, naturalized, 1923; s. Ferenc and Mathilda (Gould) B.; m. Edith Nora Corcoran, Feb. 17, 1924 (dec. 1975); children: Edith Ann Borsody Lindbergh, Frank Joseph, Eleanor Caroline Borsody Battaile, Robert Peter; m. Mary Frances Powell, Dec. 1976. Student, Cooper Union, Princeton; diploma, Tehran U. Various positions Western Union Co., Western Electric cos., RCA, on freight and passenger steamships, 1924-36; engr., mgr. radio system N.Y.C. Fire Dept., 1936-42; chief engr. constrn. overseas radio stas. for AUS and USAAF, 1942-43; research program for radio mfg. corp., 1946-48; engr., negotiator internat. mil. and civil radio frequency allocations Dept. Def., 1948-52; chief engr. worldwide radio air navigational aids and communications constrn. and installation USAF, 1952-57; profl. engr., organizing adviser communications Iranian Nat. Police, Tehran, and INTERPOL, Paris, 1957, Korean Nat. Police, Seoul, 1961; chief adviser to minister communications Republic of Korea, 1962; chief adviser dir. telecommunications Republic of Vietnam, Saigon, 1964-65; partner Borsody & Bairey (cons. engrs.); pres. B&B Engring. Co., Washington. Author govt. manual. Served with U.S. Army, 1918-19; Served with AEF in France; comdr. USNR, 1943-46; PTO. Recipient numerous citations for U.S. govt. work; Gold medal Shah of Iran. Mem. Soc. Am. Mil. Engrs., IEEE (sr.), Vet. Wireless Operators Assn. (recipient DeForest gold medal 1972), Am. Radio Relay League, Nat. Soc. Profl. Engrs. (sr. life mem.), Fla. Engring. Soc. Patentee in field. Home: 8056 Claries Dr Sarasota FL 33580 Office: Box 3746 Washington DC 20007 *1: Not "Who's right," but "What's right!" 2: Nothing is "Uninteresting"; there are only people who are not interested. 3: (Freely cribbed from the Bible) "Whatever thou turnest thy hand to, do it with thy might; for there is no returning from the grave." 4: The human body itself is a machine. Treat yours and others' at least as well as you treat other machines: automobiles, typewriters, etc. 5: Work at what is interesting. If that isn't possible try to be interested in what you have to work at.*

BORSODY, ROBERT PETER, lawyer; b. N.Y.C., Oct. 6, 1937; s. Benjamin F. and Edith Nora (Corcoran) B.; m. Paula Jane Bercutt, Oct. 14, 1973; children: Lisa M., Daniel B., Sarah E., Alexander S. B.E.E., U. Va., 1961, LL.B., 1964; diploma, U. Teheran, Iran, 1959. Bar: N.Y. 1965, D.C. 1978. Asso. firm Sullivan & Cromwell, N.Y.C., 1964-69; dir. Legal Services for Elderly Poor, 1969-71, Community Health Law Project, 1971-73; individual practice law, N.Y.C., 1973-78; partner firm Epstein Becker Borsody & Green, N.Y.C., 1978—; bd. dirs. Health Law Project, Phila., 1971-73; adj. prof. Manhattan Coll., 1978-82; mem. N.Y. State Council Health Care Financing, 1978—; sec. N.Y. Statewide Health Coordinating Council, 1978—; bd. dirs. N.Y. Bus. Group on Health. Bd. dirs. Mental Health Assn. Bronx and Manhattan. Mem. N.Y. State Bar Assn. (chmn. pub. health com.), Assn. Bar N.Y.C., Am. Bar Assn., Am. Assn. Hosp. Attys., Nat. Health Lawyers Assn., Hosp. Fin. Mgmt. Assn. Club: Univ. Home: 4 Acorn Ln Larchmont NY 10538 Office: 250 Park Ave New York NY 10017

BORST, LYLE BENJAMIN, physicist, educator; b. Chgo., Nov. 24, 1912; s. George William and Jean Carothers (Beveridge) B.; m. Barbara Mayer, Aug. 19, 1939; children: John Benjamin, Stephen Lyle, Frances Elizabeth. A.B., U. Ill., 1936, A.M., 1937; Ph.D., U. Chgo., 1941. Instr. U. Chgo., 1940-41, research asso. metall. lab., 1941-43; sr. physicist Clinton Labs., Oak Ridge, 1943-46; (both labs. working on atomic bomb project); asst. prof. dept. chemistry Mass. Inst. Tech., Cambridge, 1946; chmn. dept. reactor sci. and engring. Brookhaven Nat. Lab., 1946-51; prof. physics U. Utah, 1951; chmn. dept. physics Coll. Engring N.Y. U., 1954-61; prof. physics State U. N.Y. at Buffalo, 1961-83, prof. emeritus, 1983—; master Clifford Furnas Coll., 1969-74. Author: Megalithic Software, Part I: England, Part II: Europe and the Near East. Fellow Am. Phys. Soc.; mem. AAAS, ACLU (nat. bd. 1958-62, chmn. Niagara Frontier chpt. 1967-69), Phi Beta Kappa, Tau Beta Pi, Sigma Pi Sigma. Home: 17 Twin Bridge Ln Williamsville NY 14221

BORST, PHILIP WEST, coll. exec.; b. Fullerton, Calif., Feb. 11, 1928; s. Richard Warner and Beatrice Ione (West) B.; m. Marguerite A. Bruns, Mar. 21, 1959; children—David, Kristin, Pamela. A.A., Fullerton Coll., 1947; B.A., Stanford U., 1949, M.A., 1950; postgrad., U. Calif., 1950-54; Ph.D. (Sch. fellow), Claremont Grad. Sch., 1968. Tchr. history Carlmont High Sch., Belmont, Calif., 1954-57; asst. prof. polit. sci. and history Fullerton Coll., 1957-60, asso. prof., 1960-62, prof., 1962-67; asst. to pres., 1967-70, asst. dean instrn., 1970-72, asso. dean instrn., 1972-73, v.p. instrn., 1973-77, pres., 1977—. Mem. Assn. Calif. Community Coll. Adminstrs., Phi Delta Kappa. Democrat. Home: 426 Pinehurst Placentia CA 92670 Office: 321 E Chapman Ave Fullerton CA 92632

BORSTING, JACK RAYMOND, university dean; b. Portland, Oreg., Jan. 31, 1929; s. John S. and Ruth (Nelson) B.; m. Peggy Anne Nygard, Mar. 22, 1953; children: Lynn Carol, Eric, Jeffrey. B.A., Oreg. State U., 1951; M.A., U. Oreg., 1952, Ph.D., 1959. Instr. math. Western Wash. Coll., 1953-54; teaching fellow U. Oreg., 1956-59; mem. faculty Naval Postgrad. Sch., 1959-80, prof. ops. research, chmn. dept., 1964-73, provost, acad. dean, 1974-80; asst. sec. def. (comptroller), Washington, 1980-83; dean Sch. Bus. U. Miami (Fla.), 1983—; vis. prof. U. Colo., summers 1967, 69, 71; vis. disting. prof. Oreg. State U., summer 1968; IBM lectr., 1966-69; dir. Sun Nat. Bank, Storer Communications Inc. Contbr. to profl. jours. Mem. adv. bd. for personnel labs. U.S. Naval Research, 1971-76; mem. adv. bd. unified sci. and math. for elem. schs. Ednl. Devel. Center.; mem. adv. bd. Naval Postgrad. Sch., 1982—. Served with USAF, 1954-56. Recipient Disting. Pub. Service medal Dept. Def., 1980, 82. Mem. Inst. Mgmt. Sci., Inst. Math. Stats., Am. Statis. Soc., Ops. Research Soc. Am. (Kimball medal 1982), Mil. Ops. Research Soc. (bd. dirs. 1965-72, chmn. edn. com. 1968-69, pres. 1970-71), Ops. Research Soc. Am. (dir. vis. lectureship program 1967-70, council mem. 1969-79, sec. 1972-74, pres. 1975-76), Internat. Fedn. Ops. Research Socs. (treas. 1980—), Soc. Indsl. and Applied Math., Sigma Xi, Pi Mu Epsilon, Beta Theta Pi. Episcopalian. Home: 7601 SW 176th St Miami FL 33157 Office: Sch of Business Univ of Miami Coral Gables FL 33124

BORTEN, WILLIAM H., research company executive; b. N.Y.C., Mar. 1, 1935; s. David and Susan B.; m. Judith Sue Becker, Feb. 13, 1957; children: Jeffry, Daniel, Matthew. B.B.A., Adelphi U., Garden City, N.Y., 1957. Controller Avien, Inc., Woodside, N.Y., 1959-63; asst. gen. mgr. Fairchild Industries, Germantown, Md., 1963-71; exec. v.p., treas. Atlantic Research Corp., Alexandria, Va., 1971-80, pres., chief operating officer, 1980—, also dir. Bd. dirs. Jr. Achievement Met. Washington; advisor for bus. and industry State Bd. for Community Colls., Richmond, Va., 1983—; trustee Montgomery County Soc. Crippled Children and Adults., Adelphi U., Garden City, N.Y., 1982—; founder, bd. dirs. Montgomery Village Day Care Ctr., Gaithersburg, Md., 1972—. Mem. Nat. Assn. Accountants. Office: 5390 Cherokee Ave Alexandria VA 22314

BORTIN, MORTIMER M., physician; b. Milw., Mar. 7, 1922; s. Herman and Anne (Anton) B.; m. Barbara Louise Harris, Oct. 6, 1944; children—Mary Ellen, Bruce Harris. Student, U. Wis., 1939-42; M.D., Marquette U., 1945. Intern Mt. Sinai Hosp., Milw., 1945-46; resident Goldwater Meml. Hosp., N.Y.C., 1948-49, Mt. Sinai Hosp., 1949-50, Montefiore Hosp., 1950-51; practice medicine specializing in internal medicine, Milw., 1951—; dir. Winter Research Lab., Mt. Sinai Med. Center, Milw., 1971—; dir. Internat. Bone Marrow Transplant Registry; clin. prof. medicine Med. Coll. Wis. Contbr. sci. articles to med. jours. and books. Served to capt., M.C. AUS, 1942-48. Decorated chevalier Ordre des Coteaux, France; recipient Disting. Achievement award Milw. Acad. Medicine; Disting. Service to Medicine award Milwaukee County Med. Soc. Mem. AAAS, Am. Assn. Immunologists, Internat. Soc. for Exptl. Hematology, Reticuloendothelial Soc., Transplantation Soc., Alpha Omega Alpha. Home: 426 E Juniper Ln Mequon WI 53092 Office: 950 N 12th St Milwaukee WI 53233

BORTNER, DOYLE MCCLEAN, college dean; b. Gettysburg, Pa., Apr. 4, 1915; s. Homer and Mary A. (McClean) B.; m. Alba Pignatiello, Apr. 24, 1943. A.B., Gettysburg Coll., 1936; M.A., Pa. State Coll., 1937; Ed.D., Temple U., 1950. Tchr. social studies Perkiomen Prep. Sch., Pennsburg, Pa., 1938-41; tchr. social studies and English Bernardsville (N.J.) High Sch., 1945-46; instr. secondary edn. Temple U., 1946-48; prof. edn., chmn. dept. edn. and psychology Bates Coll., 1948-52; vis. prof. edn. U. Me., summers 1950-52; prof. edn., chmn. div. edn. and grad. studies Hofstra Coll., 1952-61; dean coll. Jersey City State Coll., 1961-64; asso. dean, prof. edn. Sch. Edn. Coll. City N.Y., 1964-66, dean Sch. Edn., 1966-79, prof. ednl. adminstrn., 1979—; vis. prof. U. P.R., summer 1959, U. Maine, summers 1950-52, 59, N.Y.U., summer 1960. Author: Public Relations for Teachers, 1959, Public Relations for Public Schools, 1972, rev. edit., 1983; also articles profl. publs. Served as capt. AUS, 1941-45. Mem. N.Y. State Collegiate Assn. Devel. Ednl. Adminstrn. (pres. 1960), Nat. Sch. Pub. Relations Assn., Am. Asso. Sch. Adminstrs., Assn. Supervision and Curriculum Devel., Am. Assn. Higher Edn., AAUP, Phi Beta Kappa, Phi Delta Kappa, Kappa Phi Kappa, Phi Sigma Iota, Pi Delta Epsilon, Kappa Delta Pi. Unitarian. Home: 66 Clinton Ave Montclair NJ 07042 Office: Coll City NY New York NY 10031 *Those affected by a major decision should have a major voice in making it.*

BORTOLAZZO, JULIO LAWRENCE, educator; b. Santa Barbara, Calif., Sept. 17, 1915; s. Santo and Vittoria (Raccanello) B.; m. Alyce Corbin, Sept. 11, 1940; children—Richard Alan, Gerald William, Paul Lawrence. B.A., Santa Barbara State Coll, 1936; M.S., U. So. Calif., 1939; Ed.M., Harvard U., 1942, Ed.D., 1949. Tchr. Santa Barbara Jr. High Sch., 1936-41; tchr., counselor San Francisco City Coll., 1946; prin. Ainsworth Elem. Sch., Portland, Oreg., 1946-48, Jefferson High Sch., Portland, 1948-50; Faculty grad. sch. edn. Harvard U., 1948; faculty San Diego State Coll., 1949; extension center U. Oreg., 1949-52; supt. schs., Lake Oswego, Oreg., 1950-52; faculty summer session U. Maine, 1946, U. Wash., 1951, 53; pres. Stockton Coll., 1952-56; supt. San Mateo Jr. Coll. Dist.; also pres. Coll. San Mateo, 1956-68; supt., also pres. San Joaquin Delta Coll., 1968-69, Santa Barbara City Coll., 1969—; exec. dir. Tech. Edn. Centers, S.C., 1971; ednl. cons., lectr.; Cons. to Italian Govt. in Vocat. Edn., 1955; Ford Found. Study of Italian Edn., 1960; ICA ednl. cons. in vocat. tech., Liberia, 1959; mem. Commn. Accreditation of Service Experiences, Am. Council Edn., 1961—, Vocat. Edn. Study Adv. Com., Commn. Acad. Affairs, 1965—; mem. jr. coll. adv. panel Calif. Bd. Edn.; mem. Calif. Postsecondary Edn. Commn., 1974—; cons. higher edn. Colombia, 1966—; dir. Blue Cross So. Calif., 1979; designer Ultracare; exptl. med. policy Blue Cross So. Calif. Pres. Boys and Girls Aid Soc., Portland; chmn., co-covenor Gray Panthers of Santa Barbara County; mem. Calif. Joint Legis. Com., Am. Assn. Ret. Persons and Nat. Ret. Tchrs. Assn.; sr. senator Calif. Sr. Legislature, 1982. Served as lt. USNR, 1942-46. Mem. Am. Legion., NEA, Calif. Jr. Coll. Assn. (pres. 1966-67), Am. Assn. Jr. Colls., Am. Assn. Sch. Adminstrs., Calif. Tchrs. Assn., Phi Kappa Phi, Phi Delta Kappa, Kappa Delta Pi, Sigma Alpha Kappa. Clubs: Mason., Commonwealth of Calif., Kiwanis. Nationally ranked tennis player (singles and doubles) in age 65 group. Address: 46 Barranca Ave 4 Santa Barbara CA 93109

BORTON, HUGH, educator; b. Moorestown, N.J., May 14, 1903; m. Elizabeth Wilbur; children—Anne Carter, Anthony. B.S., Haverford Coll., 1926; M.A., Columbia, 1932; student, Imperial U., Tokyo, 1931-37; Ph.D., Rijksuniversiteit, Leyden, Holland, 1937; research asst., Inst. Pacific Relations, summer 1938; LL.D., Temple U., 1960, U. Pa., 1961, Haverford Coll., 1969. Mem. faculty Columbia, 1937-57; asso. prof. Japanese and asst. dir. East Asian Inst., 1947-50; prof. Japanese and dir. E. Asian Inst., 1950-57; pres. Haverford Coll., Pa., 1957-67; sr. research asso. E. Asian Inst., Columbia, 1967—; on leave for govt. duty, 1942-48; mem. faculty War Dept. Sch. Mil. Govt., Charlottesville, Va., 1942; also in various positions with Dept. of State, including chief Northeast Asian Affairs div. and spl. asst. office of dir. Far Eastern Affairs, 1942-48; Chmn. U.S. delegation, co-chmn. U.S.-Japan Ednl. and Cultural Conf., Japan, 1962-66, Washington, 1963, U.S. del., 1970, 72; Mem. Harvard vis. com. Far Eastern Civilizations; v.p. Japan Soc., Inc.; dir. Am. Friends Service Com.; v.p. Japan Internat. Christian U. Found. Author: Japan Since 1931; Its Political and Social Development; Peasant Uprisings in Japan, 1968, Occupation of Japan, Korea and Mandated Islands, 1945-47, Japan's Modern Century, 1970, America Presurrender Planning for Postwar Japan; Co-author: A Selected List of Books and Articles on Japan; Japan between East and West, 1957; Editor: Japan 1951; Contbr. numerous articles on Japanese history and politics. Decorated 2d Order of Sacred Treasure 1st class, Japan; recipient Japan Found. award, 1980. Fellow Internat. Inst. Arts and Letters (life); mem. Century Assn., Assn. Asian Affairs (mem. com. coll. and world affairs), Am. Hist. Assn., Council on Fgn. Relations, Phi Beta Kappa. Home: Hillsdown RD 1 Box 273A Conway MA 01341 *Having decided to enter a new field of study and set for myself a high standard of intellectual and personal integrity, I was fortunate to have done so when my special knowledge was useful both for the academic world and for our government in determining its postwar policies towards Japan.*

BORTZ, PAUL ISAAC, economic consultant; b. Cin., Apr. 20, 1937; s. Philip and Reva (Breslau) B.; m. Judith Ann Zimba, Dec. 29, 1962; children—Matthew, Ann, Mark. B.S., Purdue U., 1959; M.A., Harvard U., 1961. Sr. engr., program engr. Ford Aerospace and Communications, Newport Beach, Calif., 1961-69; div. head Denver Research Inst., U. Denver, 1969-78; dep. asst. sec. Commerce, Washington, 1978-79; mng. ptnr. Browne, Bortz & Coddington, Denver, 1979—; telecommunications cons. Mem. Nat. Assn. Bus. Economists, IEEE, Phi Eta Sigma, Sigma Gamma Tau, Tau Beta Pi. Club: Met. Denver Exec.

BORUM, RODNEY LEE, printing corporation executive; b. nr. High Point, N.C., Sept. 30, 1929; s. Carl Macy and Etta (Sullivan) B.; m. Helen Marie Rigby, June 27, 1953; children: Richard Harlan, Sarah Elizabeth. Student, U. N.C., 1947-49; B.S., U.S. Naval Acad., 1953. Design-devel. engr. Gen. Electric Co., Syracuse, N.Y., 1956-58, Cape Kennedy, Fla., 1956-58, missile test condr., 1958-60, mgr. ground equipment engr., 1960-61, mgr. eastern test range engring., 1961-65; adminstr. Bus. and Def. Services Adminstrn.-Dept. Commerce, 1966-69; pres. Printing Industries Am., Arlington, Va., 1969—, mem. exec. com., 1969—, dir.; sec. Graphic Arts Show Corp.; dir. Inter-Comprint Ltd., Strangers Cay, Ltd.; mem. governing bd. Comprints Internat. Mem. exec. council Cub Scouts Am., 1965; bd. dirs. Brevard County United Fund (Fla.), 1964—, v.p., 1964-65; bd. dirs. Brevard Beaches Concert Assn., 1965; mem. edn. council bd. dirs. Graphic Arts Tech. Found., Pitts., 1970—; trustee, founder Graphic Arts Edn. and Research Trust Fund, Arlington, Va., 1978—. Served to 1st lt. USAF, 1953-56. Named Boss of Yr. C. of C., 1965; recipient Bausch and Lomb Sci. award, 1947, Am. Legion award, 1952. Mem. U.S. Naval Inst., U.S. Naval Acad. Alumni Assn., Graphic Arts Council N.Am. (bd. dirs. 1977—), Phi Eta Sigma. Methodist. Clubs: Columbia Country, City Tavern. Home: 4008 Glenrose St Kensington MD 20895 Office: 1730 N Lynn St Arlington VA 22209

BORUS, MICHAEL ELIOT, economist, educator; b. Washington, May 12, 1938; s. Joseph and Rosalie (Bierman) B.; m. Judith F. Weinstein, Feb. 19, 1961 (div. Mar. 1981); children: Emily Anne, Amy Ruth, Joseph Nathan. B.A., Trinity Coll., Hartford, Conn., 1959; M.A., Yale U., 1960, Ph.D., 1964. Acting instr. econs. Yale U., 1963-64; faculty mem. Mich. State U., East Lansing, 1964-77, prof. labor and indsl. relations, 1972-77; vis. assoc. prof. econs. Ohio State U., Columbus, 1970-71; prof. labor and human resources, dir. Ctr. for Human Resource Research, 1977-83; dep. dir. Office of Research and Devel., U.S. Dept. Labor, Washington, 1975-76; prof. indsl. relations and human resources Rutgers U., New Brunswick, N.J., 1983—, chmn. dept., 1984—; cons. U.S. Dept. Labor, 1971-80, Jobs for Ams. Grads., Washington, 1981-83, Rockefeller Found., N.Y.C., 1980—. Author: Measuring the Impact of Employment Related Social Programs, 1979, Evaluating the Impact of Health Programs, 1982; editor: Tomorrow's Workers, 1983; contbr. articles to profl. jours. Mem. adv. com. Lansing Tri-County Manpower Consortium, Lansing, 1975; mem.tech. research adv. com. Columbus Urban League, 1979-83; mem. State Job Tng. Coordinating Council, Columbus, Ohio, 1983. Brookings Instn. econs. fellow, 1968. Mem. Indsl. Relations Research Assn. (co-editor Newsletter 1979-83, editor 1984—, nat. exec. bd. 1979—), Nat. Council on Employment Policy (chmn. 1981-83), Am. Econ. Assn., Soc. Govt. Economists, Phi Beta Kappa, Pi Gamma Mu, Beta Sigma Gamma. Jewish. Office: Inst Mgmt and Labor Relations Rutgers U PO Box 231 New Brunswick NJ 08903

BORWEIN, DAVID, educator; b. Kaunas, Lithuania, Mar. 24, 1924; s. Joseph Jacob and Rachel (Landau) B.; m. Bessie Flax, June 30, 1946; children—Jonathan, Peter, Sarah. B.Sc. in Engring, Witwatersrand (South Africa) U., 1945, 1948; Ph.D., University Coll. London, 1950, D.Sc., 1960. Lectr. St. Andrews U., Scotland, 1950-63; vis. prof. U. Western Ont., London, Can., 1963-64, prof., 1964—, head math. dept., 1967—. Contbr. articles to profl. jours. Served with South African Forces, 1945. NSERC grantee, 1966—. Fellow Royal Soc. Edinburgh; mem. London Math. Soc., Am. Math. Soc., Math. Assn. Am., Canadian Math. Soc. (chmn. research com. 1970-73, v.p. 1973-75). Home: 1032 Brough St London ON N6A 3N4 Canada Office: U Western Ont London ON Canada

BOSCH, ALLAN WHITWORTH, coll. adminstr.; b. Lebanon, Ky., Mar. 1, 1923; s. Frederick William Archibald and Vivian Stewart (Whitworth) B.; m. Louise Coats, Aug. 12, 1946; children—Allan Whitworth II, Anne Louise, Stephen Joel, Susan Carol, Jennifer Lynne. Student, S.W. Mo. State Coll., 1940-41, 46, Va. Poly Inst., 1943-44; B.S., Davidson Coll., 1947; M.A., U. Chgo., 1950, Ph. D., 1965. Tchr. Neosha (Mo.) High Sch., 1947-48; from asst. to prof. history Westminister Coll., Salt Lake City, 1952-57, registrar, chmn. dept. history, 1957-61, acad. v.p., dean coll., 1961-65; asst. dean, dir. instl. studies Marietta (Ohio) Coll., 1965-67, dean coll., 1967-76; acad. v.p. Western New Eng. Coll., Springfield, Mass., 1976—. Served with AUS, 1943-45. Decorated Purple Heart, Bronze Star. Mem. Am. Conf. Acad. Deans, Phi Beta Kappa, Omicron Delta Kappa, Beta Theta Pi, Alpha Phi Omega, Phi Mu Alph. Presbyterian. Club: Rotarian. Home: 22 Tinkham Glen Wilbraham MA 01095

BOSCH, GULNAR KHEIRALLAH, Islamicist, art historian; b. Lake Preston, S.D., Oct. 31, 1909; d. George I. and Anna (Griewisch) Kheirallah; m. Gerhard Bosch, Dec. 23, 1932 (div. 1964); 1 child, Jarir (dec.). B.F.A., Art Inst. Chgo., 1929; M.A. in Art History and Archaeology (Carnegie scholar), N.Y.U., 1940; Ph.D. in Oriental Langs. and Lit, U. Chgo., 1952. Carnegie fellow Inst. Art and Archaeology, U. Paris, summer 1939; Am. Council Learned Socs. fellow Princeton Grad. Coll. Islamic Seminars, 1938, 41; research asst. Oriental Inst., U. Chgo., 1943-45, art cons., 1980-81; asst. prof. art Fla. State Coll. for Women, 1940-43; Catherine Comer prof. art history, chmn. dept. art Wesleyan Coll., 1945-57; prof. art history, chmn. dept. fine arts La. State U., 1957-60; prof. art history, head art dept. Fla. State U., 1960-74, prof. emeritus, 1977—; dir. Study Center, Florence, Italy, 1967-68; curator Oriental art Jacksonville (Fla.) Art Mus., 1978—. Author: An Illustrated Bhagavad Purana Manuscript, 1973; co-author: 25 Islamic Bookbindings and Bookmaking, 1981; Contbr. articles to profl. jours., revs., encys. Research grantee La. State U., XXV Internat. Congress Orientalists, Moscow; grantee Fla. State U. To XXVI congress, New Delhi; participant Iranian Conf., Hoover Inst. Stanford U., 1971; NEH; recipient 1st Disting. Service award Southeastern Coll. Art Conf., 1974; Fla. Gov.'s award for outstanding individual contbn. to art, 1978. Mem. Am. Oriental Soc., Nat., Southeastern coll. art assns., La. Coll. Conf. (sec. art sect. 1959), Southeastern Coll. Art Conf. (pres. 1957-58, v.p. 1965-67). Home: 1501 Hilltop Dr Tallahassee FL 32303

BOSCH, JORGE JOSE, manufacturing executive; b. Havana, Cuba, June 8, 1925; came to U.S., 1960, naturalized, 1966; s. Jose M. and Enriqueta (Schueg) B.; m. Yvelise Molina, Sept. 2, 1950; children: Jose Ignacio, Jorge Alejandro. B.Engring., Yale U., 1947. Master brewer, asst. tech. dir. Hatuey Breweries, Santiago de Cuba, 1949-58; v.p. Bacardi Corp., San Juan, P.R., 1958-63, pres., 1963-73, chmn. bd., 1973-76, Fla. Bearings Inc., Miami, Antilles Bearings, Inc., San Juan, 1975—. Decorated knight Order Holy Sepulchre. Mem. Am. Chem. Soc. Office: 200 SE 1st St Suite 905 Miami FL 33131

BOSCHWITZ, RUDY, U.S. senator; b. Berlin, 1930; m. Ellen; children—Gerry, Ken, Dan, Tom. Student, Johns Hopkins U., 1947-49; B.S. in Bus, N.Y. U., 1950, LL.B., 1953. Bar: N.Y. State bar 1954, Wis. bar 1959. Founder, owner, operator Plywood Minnesota (do-it-yourself bldg. materials chain), 1963—; mem. U.S. Senate from Minn., 1979—; Del. Minn. Republican Conv., 1968-78, Republican Nat. Conv., 1972-76. State chmn. Am. Cancer Soc., Minn. Mental Health Assn., Minn. Kidney Found., Lubavitch House, St. Paul. Served with Signal Corps U.S. Army, 1954-55. Office: Senate Office Bldg Washington DC 20510

BOSCO, DOUGLAS H., congressman; b. N.Y.C., July 28, 1946. B.A. in English, Willamette U., 1968, J.D., 1971. Bar: Calif. Practiced law; mem. 98th Congress from 1st Dist. Calif. Bd. dirs. Marin County Housing Authority, Marin County Consumer Protection Agy., Sonoma County Fair; fundraiser hosp. ship S.S. Hope; co-founder No. Calif. Emeritus Coll. for Sr. Citizens; mem. Calif. Wildlife Conservation Bd., Calif. State Assembly, 1978-81; Democratic caucas chmn. Calif. State Assembly, 1981. Office: 408 Cannon House Office Bldg Washington DC 20515 *

BOSCO, PHILIP MICHAEL, actor; b. Jersey City, Sept. 26, 1930; s. Philip Lupo and Margaret Raymond (Thek) B.; m. Nancy Ann Dunkle, Jan. 2, 1957; children: Diane, Philip, Christopher, Jennifer, Lisa, Celia, John. B.A. in drama, Catholic U. Am., 1957. Roles include Brian O'Bannion in: Auntie Mame, City Ctr., N.Y.C., 1958; Angelo in: Measure for Measure, Belvedere Lake Amphitheatre, N.Y.C., 1960; Heracles in: The Rape of the Belt, 1960; Will Dansher in: Donnybrook, 1961; Hawkshaw in: The Ticket-of-Leave Man, 1961; King Henry in: Henry IV Part 1, Shakespeare Festival, Stratford, Conn., 1962; Kent in: King Lear; Rufio in: Antony and Cleopatra; Pistol in: Henry V; Aegeon in: Comedy of Errors, 1963; Benedick in: Much Ado About Nothing; Claudius in: Hamlet, 1964; title role in: Coriolanus, 1965; Lovewit in: The Alchemist, Lincoln Ctr. Repertory Theatre, 1966; Jack in: The East Wind, 1967; appeared in: Galileo, 1967, Saint Joan, 1968, 77, Tiger at the Gates, 1968, Cyrano de Bergerac, 1968, Camino Real, 1970, Operation Sidewinder, 1970, The Playboy of the Western World, 1971, An Enemy of the People, 1971, Antigone, 1971, Mary Stuart, 1971, Narrow Road to the Deep North, 1972, Twelfth Night, 1972, The Crucible, 1972, Enemies, 1972, The Plough and the Stars, 1973, The Merchant of Venice, 1973, A Streetcar Named Desire, 1973, Mrs. Warren's Profession, 1976, Man and Superman, 1978, Whose Life Is It Anyway?, 1979, A Month in the Country, 1979, Major Barbara, 1980, Inadmissable Evidence, 1981, Hedda Gabler, 1982, Ah! Wilderness, 1983, Misalliance, 1983, Come Back, Little Sheba, 1984, Eminent Domain, 1984, Caine Mutiny, 1984; films including Reguiem for a Heavyweight, A lovely Way to Die, The Pope of Greenwich Village, Flanagan, Catholic Boys; TV Shows including The Prisoner of Zenda, The Nurses, O'Brien, Hawk, The Net Play of the Month. Served with U.S. Army, 1951-54. Recipient Critic's Circle award N.Y. Drama Critics, 1960-61, Clarence Derwent award, 1966-67. Mem. Actor's Equity Assn., Screen Actor's Guild, AFTRA. Roman Catholic. Office: Hesseltine Baker Ltd 165 W 46th St New York NY 10036 *Keep working and hang in there.*

BOSE, AMAR GOPAL, electrical engineering educator; b. Phila., Nov, 1929; s. Noni Gopal and Charlotte (Mechlin) B.; m. Prema Sarathy, Aug. 17, 1960; children: Vanu Gopal, Maya. S.B., S.M., MIT, 1952, Sc.D., 1956. Mem. faculty MIT, 1956—, prof. elec. engring., 1966—; Chmn. bd., tech. dir. Bose Corp., Framingham, Mass., 1964—; mng. dir. Bose Germany GmbH; chmn. bd. Bose AG Swiss; dir. Bose BV, Holland, Bose Investments, N.V., Bose Ltd. Bermuda, Bose Products Rotterdam, B.V., Bose U.K. Ltd., Bose Italy Spa. Author: (with Kenneth N. Stevens) Introductory Network Theory, 1965. Fulbright fellow India, 1956-57; recipient Baker Teaching award Mass. Inst. Tech., 1964, Teaching award Am. Soc. Engring. Edn., 1965. Fellow IEEE; mem. Sigma Xi, Tau Beta Pi, Eta Kappa Nu. Patentee in acoustics, nonlinear systems, communications. Home: 17 Deer Run Wayland MA 01778 Office: Bose Corp The Mountain Framingham MA 01701

BOSE, NIRMAL KUMAR, electrical engineering, mathematics educator; b. Calcutta, West Bengal, India, Aug. 19, 1940; came to U.S., 1961; s. Dhruba Kumar and Roma (Guha) B.; m. Chandra Bose, June 8, 1969; children: Meenekshi, Enakshi. B.Tech., Indian Inst. Tech., Kharagpur, West Bengal, 1961; M.S., Cornell U., 1963; Ph.D., Syracuse U., 1967. Asst. prof. U. Pitts., 1967-70, assoc. prof., 1970-76, prof., 1976—; vis. assoc. prof. U. Calif.-Berkeley, 1973-74. Author: Applied Multidimensional Systems Theory, 1982; editor: Multidimensional Systems: Theory and Application, 1979. Fellow IEEE (chmn. circuits and systems tech. com. on edn. 1979—); mem. Sigma Xi. Hindu. Home: 2124 Beulah Rd Pittsburgh PA 15235 Office: U Pitts 348 Benedum Hall Pittsburgh PA 15261 *Development and cultivation of spiritual and intellectual resources to the best of one's ability supported by parental blessings and encouragement provide the foundation on which the edifice of an individual's contributions to science and society is constructed.*

BOSEMAN, GLENN, educator, management consultant; b. Roanoke Rapids, N.C., Sept. 3, 1941; s. Leon and Blanche B.; m. Joan Boseman, Mar. 7, 1980. B.B.A. with honors, Campbell Coll., 1966; M.B.A., East Carolina U., 1968; D.B.A., Kent State U., 1968-72. Teaching fellow dept. mgmt. Kent State U., 1968-71; vis. lectr. Baldwin Wallace Coll., 1970-71; asst. prof. East Carolina U., 1971-75; asst. prof. dept. mgmt. Sch. Bus. Adminstrn., Temple U., Phila., 1975-79, assoc. prof., 1979-80, prof., 1980-81; vis. scholar U. Western Australia, 1978-79; James S. Bingay prof. creative leadership Am. Coll., 1981—. Author: (with R. E. Schellenberger) Policy Formulation and Strategy Management, 1978, rev. edit., 1982, Decision Making in Administration, 1979; Contbr. articles to profl. jours. Mem. Acad. Mgmt., Acad. Internat. Bus., N.E. Am. Inst. Decision Scis.

BOSHEARS, ONVA K., JR., librarian; b. Bloomington, Ind., Aug. 31, 1939; s. Onva K. and Ruth (Hunter) B. A.B., Greenville (Ill.) Coll., 1961; M.S., U. Ill., 1962; postgrad., Asbury Theol. Sem., 1962-65, M.A. in Religion, 1965; Ph.D., U. Mich., 1972. Asst. librarian B.L. Fisher Library, Asbury Theol. Sem., 1962-65, dir., 1967-70; dir. residence halls libraries U. Mich., 1965-67; asst. prof. Coll. Library Sci., U. Ky., Lexington, 1971-75; chmn., mem. faculty dept. library sci. U. So. Miss., Hattiesburg, 1975-76, prof., dean sch., 1976—; cons. various library projects, 1965—; Active Hattiesburg Hist. Soc., 1979—, Friends of Library, 1979—. Author: John Wesley, the Bookman - A study of His Reading Interests in the Eighteenth Century, 1972. Eli Lilly Found. fellow, 1965-66; Sealantic Found. fellow, 1970-71. Mem. ALA, Am. Acad. Religion, Am. Printing History Assn., Am. Theol. Library Assn., Assn. Am. Library Schs., Freedom to Reach Found., Miss. Library Assn., Southeastern Library Assn., Phi Alpha Theta, Pi Kappa Delta, Theta Phi, Beta Phi Mu. Democrat. Episcopalian. Home: 100 S 22d Ave Hattiesburg MS 39401 Office: Sch Library Science U So Miss Box 5146 Hattiesburg MS 39401

BOSHELL, EDWARD OWEN, JR., industrial supply distribution company executive; b. N.Y.C., Apr. 6, 1935; s. Edward and Margie (Iehl) B.; m. Rosalie Chamberlain, June 14, 1958; children: Chris, Alex, Betsey. B.A., Yale U., 1958; M.B.A., Harvard U., 1961. Pres. Continental Bearings, Chgo., 1966-68; with H.M. Byllesby Ltd., Chgo., 1961-66; pres. Ind. Investors, Chgo., 1962—, Columbia Gen., Dallas, 1968—; dir. Banc Tex., Lane Wood. Author: Venture Capital Source, 1962. Bd. dirs. Greenway Parks Assn., 1978—; trustee Hockaday Sch., Dallas, 1982—. Clubs: Bent Tree (Dallas); Rolling Rock (Pitts.). Address: 12700 Park Central Dr Dallas TX 75251

BOSHES, LOUIS D., physician, educator; b. Chgo., Oct. 15, 1908; s. Jacob and Ethel (London) B.; m. Rhea Amber, Jan. 4, 1942; children: Arlene Phyllis (Mrs. Dennis C. Hirschfelder), Judi Myrl. B.S., Northwestern U., 1931, M.D., 1936; H.H.D., 1976. Diplomate: neurology, psychiatry and child neurology Am. Bd. Psychiatry and Neurology. Intern Michael Reese Hosp., Chgo., 1935-36, Cook County Hosp., 1936-37; pvt. practice medicine, specializing in neurology and psychiatry; fellow psychiatry Ill. Neuro-psychiat. Inst., Chgo., 1941-42, 46-47; sr. attending neurologist and psychiatrist, chief neurology clinic Michael Reese Med. Center, 1958-74; prof. dept. neurology, psychiatry Northwestern U. Sch. Medicine, 1955-63; asso. to clin. prof. neurology Abraham Lincoln Sch. Medicine, U. Ill., Chgo., 1970—; attending neurologist Ill. Research and Ednl. Hosps., 1963—, dir. consultation clinic for epilepsy, 1963-78; asso. and attending neurologist, cons. neurology Cook County Hosp., 1947-63; sr. cons. neurology Downey VA Hosp., 1952-60; prof. neurology Cook County Grad. Sch. Medicine, 1970—; Mem. med. adv. com. Cook County chpt. Nat Found., 1947-55, March of Dimes, 1956—; mem. med. adv. com. Epilepsy Assn. Am., 1964—; bd. dirs., med. adv. com. Epilepsy Found. Am., 1964—; ambassador Internat. Bur. Epilepsy, 1969—; mem. profl. adv. com. Nat. Parkinson Found., 1960—, Nat. Myasthenia Gravis Found., 1972—, profl. adv. bd.; United Cerebral Palsy. Author, contbr. to books, med. jours.; Asso. editor: Diseases of the Nervous System, 1962—, New Physician, Internat. Surgery; cons. editor: Current Med. Digest, 1962—; editor: Chgo. Neurol. Soc. Bull., Behavioral Neuropsychiatry; mem. editorial bd.: Excerpta Medica, Internat. Jour. Neurology and Neurosurgery. Served to lt. comdr. M.C. USNR, 1942-46. Fellow A.C.P., Am. Acad. Neurology, Am. Psychiat. Assn., Inst. Medicine Chgo., AMA (cons. Jour.); mem. Pan Am. Med. Assn. (pres. sect. neurology, D. of Humanities 1976), Central Neuropsychiat. Assn. (pres. 1973-74), Ill. Psychiat. Soc. (sec.-treas. 1949-50), Chgo. Neurol. Soc. (pres. 1964—), Michael Reese Hosp. and Med. Center Alumni Assn. (pres. 1961—), Assn. for Research in Nervous and Mental Diseases, Internat. League Against Epilepsy, Am. League Against Epilepsy, Ill. League Against Epilepsy (med. adv. com.), Ill. Med. Soc. (chmn. sect. neurology and psychiatry 1961—),

Chgo. Med. Soc., World Fedn. Neurology, AAAS, Am. Med. Soc. of Vienna (life), Central Assn. Electroence-Phalographers, Sigma Xi, Phi Delta Epsilon, Alpha Omega Alpha. Home: 3150 N Lake Shore Dr Chicago IL 60657 Office: 30 N Michigan Ave Chicago IL 60602

BOSHKOFF, DOUGLASS GEORGE, univ. dean; b. Buffalo, Nov. 11, 1930; s. George John and Helen (Douglass) B.; m. Ruth Joy Osborne, Nov. 9, 1957; children—Katharine Jean, Ellen Elizabeth, Mary Ruth, Susan Emily. A.B., Harvard, 1952, LL.B., 1955. Bar: N.Y. bar 1955, Mich. bar 1960, Ind. bar 1974. Practice in Buffalo, 1955-57; asso. firm Moot, Sprague, Marcy & Gulick; teaching fellow Harvard, 1957-59; asst. prof. Wayne State U., 1959-60, asso. prof., 1960-63; vis. asso. prof. Ind. U., Bloomington, 1962-63, asso. prof., 1963-65, prof., 1965—, asso. dean, 1969-72, acting dean, 1971-72, dean, 1972-76; vis. prof. Boston Coll., 1966-67. Mem. Am., Ind. bar assns. Home: 3333 S Spring Branch Rd Bloomington IN 47401

BOSHKOV, STEFAN HRISTOV, educator, mining engr.; b. Sofia, Bulgaria, Sept. 29, 1918; came to U.S., 1938, naturalized, 1944; s. Hristo and Karla (Lubich) B.; m. Bianca G. Amaducci, Aug 28, 1943; children—Lynn Karla, Stefan Robert. Diploma, Am. Coll., Sofia, Bulgaria, 1938; B.S., Columbia U., 1941, E.M., 1942. Mem. faculty Columbia, 1946—; prof. Henry Krumb Sch. Mines, 1951—, chmn., 1967—, Henry Krumb prof., 1980—; disting. prof., sr. scientist (Fulbright program), Yugoslavia, 1969, guest lectr., Taiwan, China, 1972, 76, OAS, Chile, 1972, USSR, 1974, Poland, 1976, Bulgaria, 1976, Bolivia, 1977, People's Republic of China, 1980, 81; cons. engr., 1950—; mem. internat. organizing com. World Mining Congress, 1962—; chmn. 4th Internat. Conf. Strata Control and Rock Mechanics, N.Y.C.; 1964; mem. adv. com. metal and nonmetallic health and safety standards Dept. Labor, 1978. Mem. editorial bd.: Internat. Jour. Rock Mechanics and Mining Scis, 1964-76. Pres. Benedict Found., 1973—, Harrison (N.Y.) No. 7 Sch. Bd., 1954-63. Served to 1st lt. AUS, 1943-46; CBI. Recipient Boleslaw Krupinski medal State Mining Council Poland, 1980. Mem. AIME (Mineral Industry Edn. award 1980), Am. Arbitration Assn., Sigma Xi. Presbyterian. (trustee 1965-69). Club: Masons. Home: 119 White Plains Ave White Plains NY 10604 Office: Mudd Bldg Columbia Univ New York NY 10027

BOSKEY, BENNETT, lawyer; b. N.Y.C., Aug. 14, 1916; s. Meyer and Janet (Lauterstein) B.; m. Shirley Ecker, July 3, 1940. A.B., Williams Coll., 1935; LL.B., Harvard U., 1939. Bar: N.Y. bar 1940, U.S. Supreme Ct. bar 1943, D.C. bar 1949. Spl. asst. to Atty. Gen. U.S. Dept. Justice, Washington, 1943; advisor on enemy property U.S. Dept. State, Washington, 1946-47; atty. U.S. Atomic Energy Commn., Washington, 1947-49, dep. gen. counsel, 1949-51; partner firm Volpe, Boskey & Lyons (and predecessors), Washington, 1951—; law clk. Judge Learned Hand, 1939-40, Justice Stanley Reed, 1940-41, Chief Justice Harlan F. Stone, 1941-43; dir. Evans-Rosendorf, Inc., Washington, Evans-Rosendorf of Md., Inc.; trustee Analytic Services Inc., Arlington, Va. Chmn. bd. trustees Primary Day Sch., Bethesda, Md., 1969—. Served with U.S. Army, 1943-46. Mem. D.C. Bar, Bar Assn. D.C., Am. Bar Assn., Fed. Bar Assn., Am. Law Inst. (treas. 1975—), Am. Soc. Internat. Law (mem. bd. rev. and devel. 1973—). Office: 918 16th St NW Washington DC 20006

BOSLAUGH, LESLIE, judge; b. Hastings, Nebr., Sept. 4, 1917; s. Paul E. and Ann (Herzog) B.; m. Elizabeth F. Meyer, Aug. 10, 1943; children—Marguerite Ann, Sarah Elizabeth, Paul Robert. B.B.A., U. Nebr., 1939, LL.B., 1941. Bar: Nebr. bar 1941. Mem. staff Nebr. Statute Revision Commn., 1941-43; pvt. practice law, Hastings, 1946-47, asst. atty. gen., Nebr., 1947-48; mem. firm Stiner & Boslaugh, Hastings, 1949-60; judge Nebr. Supreme Ct., Lincoln, 1961—. Served to lt. AUS, 1943-46. Mem. Nebr. Bar Assn., Am. Judicature Soc., Inst. Jud. Adminstrn., Appellate Judges Conf., Order of Coif. Office: Supreme Ct Box 4638 Lincoln NE 68509

BOSLEY, TOM, actor; b. Chgo., Oct. 1, 1927; s. Benjamin and Dora (Heyman) B.; m. Jean Eliot, Mar. 8, 1962 (dec. Apr. 1978); 1 dau., Amy; m. Patricia Carr, Dec. 21, 1980. Ed. high sch., Chgo.; student, De Paul U., 1946, Radio Inst. Chgo., 1947-48; studied with, Lee Strasberg, 1952. Actor: various roles TV programs Alice in Wonderland, 1953, Arsenic and Old Lace, 1962, Focus, 1961, Naked City, The Right Man, The Nurses, Law and Mr. Jones, Route 66, The Perry Como Show, The Dean Martin Show, Joanie Loves Chachi, The Rebels, Death Trap, Castaways on Gilligan's Island; regular actor on: TV shows Wait Til Your Father Gets Home; star: TV series Happy Days, 1974-83; also appeared on: Profiles in Courage, others; appeared in: TV mini-series The Bastard, 1978; narrator: TV series That's Hollywood; voice in: animated cartoon The Stingiest Man in Town; actor numerous theatrical prodns. in stock companies, also off-Broadway prodns., 1952-56; Broadway debut as Fiorello LaGuardia in: Fiorello, 1959 (Pulitzer Prize play); Broadway roles include: musical Nowhere to Go But Up, 1962; play Natural Affection, 1963, A Murderer Among Us, 1964, The Education of H; film roles include Love with a Proper Stranger, 1963, The World of Henry Orient, 1964, Divorce American Style, Secret War of Harry Frigg, Yours, Mine and Ours, To Find A Man, O'Hara's Wife, Mixed Company, Gus; indsl. film Perfectly Normal Day. Served with USNR, World War II. Recipient Antoinette Perry award for 1959-60 season as best actor in featured role of musical; Newspaper Guild of Am. Page One award and ANTA award for distinguished contbn. to theatre, 1960; N.Y. Drama Critics award for performance in Fiorello, 1960; Festival of Leadership award, Chgo.; Humanitarian award Performing Arts Theater of Handicapped, 1981; Tau award Sacred Heart Rehab. Hosp., Milw. Mem. Actors Equity Assn. (governing council 1961-69), AFTRA, Screen Actors Guild. Address: care Burton Moss Agy 113 N San Vicente Blvd Suite 202 Beverly Hills CA 90211 *I try to go through life by not hurting anyone's feelings, by respecting people for what they are and not what I think they should be; by honoring my heritage and the heritage of others; and by trying to smile at adversity, knowing that if I can, life can be softer and more comfortable than the realities really are.* *

BOSNIAK, MORTON ARTHUR, physician, educator; b. N.Y.C., Nov. 13, 1929; s. Meyer and Sadie B.; m. Tommie Heath Hager, Oct. 25, 1977; 1 dau., Lindie. B.S., M.I.T., 1951; M.D., SUNY Downstate Med. Center, 1955. Intern Mt. Sinai Hosp., N.Y.C., 1955-56; resident in radiology N.Y. Hosp., N.Y.C., 1956-57, 59-61; asso. prof. radiology Boston U. Sch. Medicine, 1964-67, Albert Einstein Coll. Medicine, N.Y.C., 1967-69; prof. radiology N.Y. U. Sch. Medicine, 1969—; chief abdominal radiology sect. N.Y. U. Med. Center; cons. radiologist St. Vincent's Hosp. and Med. Center, Manhattan VA Hosp. Author: (with John Evans) The Kidney, 1971, (with J. Evans, S. Siegelman) The Adrenal Retroperitoneum and Lower Urinary Tract, 1976; Editor: (with J. Becker) Urologic Radiology, 1979—; contbr. articles to profl. jours. Served with USAF, 1957-59. Mem. Radiol. Soc. N. Am., Am. Roentgen Ray Soc., Assn. Univ. Radiologists, Soc. Uroradiology (pres. 1975), Soc. Cardiovascular Radiology (pres. 1977), N.Y. Roentgen Soc. (pres. 1980), Soc. Body Computed Tomography. Home: 343 E 30th St New York NY 10016 Office: NY Univ Med Center New York NY

BOSOMWORTH, PETER PALLISER, medical educator; b. Akron, Ohio, May 2, 1930; s. George Palliser and Vera (Siddle) B.; m. Georgia Simester, July 20, 1956; children: Virginia Kay, David Palliser, Andrew Palliser, Jeffrey Palliser. B.S., Kent State U., 1951; M.D., U. Cin., 1955; M.Med. Sci., Ohio State U., 1958. Diplomate: Am. Bd. Anesthesiology (asso. examiner 1965-73). Intern Cin. Gen. Hosp., 1955-56; resident Ohio State U., Columbus, 1956-58, instr. anesthesiology, 1958; chief anesthesia div. U.S. Naval Hosp., Great Lakes, Ill., 1958-60; dir. anesthesia research, asst. dir. anesthesiology Ohio State U., Columbus, 1960-62; prof., chmn. dept. anesthesiology Med. Ctr. U. Ky., Lexington, 1962-70, v.p. for Med. Ctr., 1970-82, chancellor for Med. Ctr., 1982—, assoc. dean clin. affairs, 1968-70, also several coms., bds. Med. Center, 1962—; Mem. Ky. Hill Burton Council, 1970-73; mem. Ky. Comprehensive Health Planning Council, 1971—; dir. Ky. Physicians Mut., Inc. (Blue Shield); bd. dirs. Eastern Ky. Health Systems Agy., 1976—; vice chmn. Health Resources Devel. Corp. of Ky., 1976—; mem. Ky. Cancer Commn., 1978—, Statewide Health Coordinating Council, 1979-82; pres. Health Care Collection Service, 1976—; mem. steering com. State Ctr. Health Scis. Research. Producer movies, TV programs on med. topics, 1959—; contbr. articles to profl. jours. Bd. dirs. E. McDowell Cancer Network, Lexington, 1975—, Lexington Sister Cities Program, 1978, Frontier Nursing Service, 1979—; bd. dirs. Blue Grass council Boy Scouts Am., 1977—, v.p., 1977-79; trustee Hunter Found., 1971-74, St. Elizabeth Hosp., Covington, Ky., 1970-72; chmn. Commn. on Community Services for Older Persons, 1980—. Recipient medal of honor Cheng Kung U., Taiwan, Cheng Kung U., 1976. Fellow Am. Coll. Anesthesiologists (asso. examiners 1967-73), Am. Coll. Clin. Pharmacology and Chemotherapy, Am. Coll. Chest Physicians; mem. Assn. Univ. Anesthetists, Ky. Med. Assn. (recipient Faculty Sci. Achievement award 1969, del. to Am. Soc. Anesthesiologists 1965-70, mem. ho. of dels.), Internat. Anesthesia Research Soc., AMA (cons. council on drugs), Fayette County Med. Soc. (exec. com. 1965—, v.p. 1970, 75, pres. 1980), Am. Assn. Inhalation Therapy (Ky. bd. dirs. 1968-70), Assn. Acad. Health Centers (dir. 1975—, chmn.-elect 1980, chmn. 1981). Home: 3314 Brookhill Circle Lexington KY 40502

BOSS, RICHARD WOODRUFF, management consultant; b. Arnhem, Netherlands, Oct. 31, 1937; came to U.S., 1948, naturalized, 1955; s. P. Johannes and Albertje (Lagro) B. B.A. in Polit. Sci., U. Utah, 1960; M.A. in L.S, U. Wash., 1962. Order librarian, library U. Utah, Salt Lake City, 1962-63; asst. dir. 1963-64, asso. dir., 1964-70, instr. dept. library sci., 1962-70; dir. library U. Tenn., Knoxville, 1970-75; asso. prof. Grad. Sch. Library and Info. Sci., 1972-75; univ. librarian Princeton U., 1975-78; partner, sr. mgmt. cons. Info. Systems Consultants, Inc., Boston, 1978—; vis. lectr. Sch. Library Sci. Western Mich. U., summer 1968; vis. asso. prof. Sch. Library Sci., U. Iowa, summer 1969; library bldg. and equipment cons. affiliated Library Consultants, Inc., Northfield, Ill., 1972—; mem. com. on Nat. Periodicals Center Nat. Commn. on Library and Info. Sci., 1977—; Bd. dirs. Bibliographic Center for Research, Denver, 1969-70; pres. 1970; trustee Princeton U. Library in N.Y., 1975-78. Contbr. articles to profl. publs. Council on Library Resources fellow, 1969-70. Mem. ALA, New Eng. Library Assn., Phi Beta Kappa, Phi Kappa Phi, Beta Phi Mu, Tau Kappa Alpha. Home: 10620 Muirfield Dr Potomac MD 20854 Office: Info Systems Consultants Inc 4801 Montgomery Ln Bethesda MD 20817

BOSSELMAN, FRED PAUL, lawyer; b. Oak Park, Ill., June 14, 1934; s. Fred and Beulah (Chamberlain) B.; m. Kay Wilson, 1956; children: Judith, Carol, Mark. B.A., U. Colo., 1956; J.D., Harvard U., 1959. Bar: Ill. 1959. Assoc. firm Ross & Hardies, Chgo., 1959-67; partner Ross, Hardies, O'Keefe, Babcock & Parsons, 1967-83, Burke, Bosselman, Freivogel, Weaver, Glaves & Ryan, Chgo., 1983—; asso. reporter Am. Law Inst., 1969-75; dir. Met. Housing and Planning Council Chgo., 1971—; commr. Housing Authority Cook County (Ill.), 1973—. Author: (with David Callies) The Quiet Revolution in Land Use Control, 1971, (with David Callies and John Banta) The Taking Issue, 1973, (with Richard Babcock) Exclusionary Zoning, 1974, In the Wake of the Tourist, 1978. Mem. Am. Bar Assn. (chmn. environ. law com. sect. real property, probate and trust law 1974-77), Am. Soc. Planning Ofcls. (dir. 1977-78), Am. Planning Assn. (sec. 1978-79, pres. 1982-83), Urban Land Inst. (dir. Fed. Policy Council 1982—). Home: 2715 Woodbine Ave Evanston IL 60201 Office: 55 W Monroe St Chicago IL 60603

BOSSEN, DAVID AUGUST, electronics company executive; b. Clinton, Iowa, Jan. 9, 1927; s. August and Rose Faye (Nichols) B.; m. Doris Patricia Stephens, Sept. 1, 1950; children: Alison, Amy, Julie, Laura. B.S. in Indsl. Mgmt, M.I.T., 1951. Indsl. engr. Alcoa, Davenport, Iowa, 1951; v.p. Indsl. Nucleonics Co., Columbus, Ohio, 1951-67; pres. Measurex Corp., Cupertino, Calif., 1968—; v.p. Paper Tech. Found., Western Mich. U., 1974—. Bd. dirs. U. Maine Pulp and Paper Found., Bay Area Council. Served with USMC, 1945-46. Mem. Am. Electronics Assn., Paper Industry Mgmt. Assn., TAPPI, Beta Gamma Sigma, Sigma Alpha Epsilon. Clubs: Menlo Circus., Commonwealth of Calif. Patentee in process control. Address: 1 Results Way Cupertino CA 95014

BOSSERMAN, JOSEPH NORWOOD, architecture educator; b. Harrisonburg, Va., July 12, 1925; s. Joseph Astir and Ethel (Wise) B. B.S., U. Va., 1948; M.F.A., Princeton U., 1952. Designer C. W. Wenger, Harrisonburg, 1948-50, Kenneth Franzheim, Houston, 1952-54; acting asst. prof. architecture U. Va., 1954, asst. prof. architecture, 1954-60, asso. prof., 1960-64; asst. dean Sch. Architecture, 1965, acting dean, 1966, prof., 1966, 81—, dean, 1967-81; vis. prof. architecture Kingston Sch. Art, Kingston-upon-Thames, Eng., 1960-61; sr. Fulbright prof. Technische Hochschule, Stuttgart, Germany, 1964-65; Bd. dirs. Va. Found. Archtl. Edn., Inc.; bd. govs. Am. Assn. Archtl. Bibliographers. Served with USAAF, World War II; PTO. Fellow Royal Soc. Arts. (Eng.), AIA; mem. Raven Soc., Alpha Rho Chi, Omicron Delta Kappa. Democrat. Mem. United Ch. of Christ. Clubs: Mason. Clubs: Colonnade, Greencroft (Charlottesville).

BOSSHART, WILLIAM RUDOLPH, utility consultant, electrical engineer; b. Astoria, Oreg., Apr. 16, 1926; s. Rudolph and Margaret (Fleskes) B.; m. ALice Julie Robbins, June 20, 1953; children: Kathleen Mary, Gail Ann, Jay Allen. B.S. in Elec. Engring., Oreg. State U., 1949. Registered profl. engr., Oreg. Relay engr. Bonneville Power Adminstrn., Vancouver, Wash., 1949-52; ops. engr. Bonneville Poer Adminstrn., Vancouver, Wash., 1952-63; system ops. officer Bonneville Power Admintrn., Portland, Oreg., 1963-73; dir. div. system ops. Bonneville Power Adminstrn., Vancouver, Wash., 1973-80; cons., dir. N.W. Power Pool Coordinating group, N.W. Power Pool, Portland, Oreg., 1980—. Served with USAAF, 1944-45. Fellow IEEE (chmn. subcom. 1975-77). Roman Catholic. Lodge: Elks. Home: 6012 NW 15th Ave Bancouver WA 98665 Office: UTility Services Inc 902 NW 15th Ave Vancouver WA 98665

BOSSIDY, LAWRENCE A., electric manufacturing company executive. B.A. in Econs., Colgate U., 1957. Trainee fin. mgmt. Gen. Electric Co., 1957-63, mem. corp. audit staff, 1963-67, audit adminstr., 1967-70; mgr. fin. subs. GECC, 1970-73, mgr. accounts receivable financing, 1973-74, v.p., mgr. leasing and indsl. loans, 1974-75, v.p., gen. mgr. financing dept., 1975-78, v.p., gen. mgr. financing div., 1978-79, exec. v.p., chief operating officer, 1979-81, exec. v.p., sector exec. services and materials sector, 1981—. Office: Gen Electric Co 3135 Easton Turnpike Fairfield CT 06431 *

BOSSIER, ALBERT LOUIS, JR., shipbuilding co. exec.; b. Gramercy, La., Nov. 29, 1932; s. Albert Louis and Alba Marie (Dufresne) B.; m. Jo Ann Decedue, Jan. 11, 1958; children—Albert Louis III, Brian, Donna, Steven. B.S., La. State U., 1954, 1956; J.D., Loyola U., New Orleans, 1971. Registered profl. engr., La. With Avondale Shipyards, Inc., New Orleans, 1957—, elec. supt., 1961-67, gen. plant supt., 1967-69, v.p. prodn. ops., 1969-72, exec. v.p., 1972-78, pres., 1978—; dir. Homeseekers Savs. & Loan Assn., New Orleans. Bd. dirs. Better Bus. Bur. of New Orleans, C. of C. of New Orleans and River Regions. Served as 1st lt. Signal Corps AUS, 1956. Mem. Am., La. bar assns., Am. Welding Soc., Navy League of U.S. (pres. Greater New Orleans council 1981—). Club: Propeller (New Orleans). Home: 17 Chateau Palmer Kenner LA 70062 Office: PO Box 50280 New Orleans LA 70150

BOSSIO, SALVATORE, lawyer; b. Spokane, Wash., Nov. 29, 1928; s. Salvatore N. and Rosa (Costanza) B.; m. Joan S. Smith, Feb. 16, 1957; children: Lora Jo, Deborah, Amy, Stephen, Bruce. B.A., Stanford U., 1951, J.D., 1953. Asso. firm Hassard, Bonnington, Rogers & Huber, San Francisco, 1955-64, partner, 1964—. Served with U.S. Army, 1953-55. Recipient Pres.'s award for outstanding service Assn. Def. Counsel, 1979. Fellow Am. Coll. Trial Lawyers; mem. Am. Bar Assn., Bar Assn. San Francisco, State Bar Calif., Marin County Bar Assn., Am. Bd. Trial Advs., Internat. Assn. Ins. Counsel, Nat. Assn. R.R. Trial Counsel, Calif. Med.-Legal Assn. (chmn. 1978-79), Assn. Def. Counsel (dir. 1979-80), Am. Bd. Profl. Liability Attys. Office: 44 Montgomery St San Francisco CA 94104 *

BOSSY, MICHAEL, hockey player; b. Montreal, Jan. 22, 1957. With Laval Nat. Hockey Club, 1973-77; right wing New York Islanders, Nat. Hockey League, 1977—. Recipient Calder Meml. trophy, Conn Smythe trophy, 1982, Lady Byng trophy, 1983; named Nat. Hockey League Rookie of Yr. Sporting News, 1978. Office: care Nassau Vets Meml Coliseum New York Islanders Uniondale NY 11553 *

BOST, RAYMOND MORRIS, seminary president; b. Maiden, N.C., Aug. 18, 1925; s. Loy Robert and Virginia (Anderson) B.; m. Margaret Martha Vedder, Aug. 16, 1947; children: Timothy Lee, Penelope Ruth, Peter Raymond, Jonathan Otto. A.B., Lenoir Rhyne Coll., Hickory, N.C., 1949; D.D. (hon.), Lenoir-Rhyne Coll., Hickory, N.C., 1976; B.D., Luth. Theol. So. Sem., 1952; M.A., Yale U., 1959, Ph.D., 1963. Ordained to ministry Luth. Ch., 1952; pastor in, Spartanburg, S.C., 1952-53, Raleigh, N.C., 1953-57; prof. ch. history, dir. field work Luth. Theol. So. Sem., 1960-66; acad. dean Lenoir-Rhyne Coll., Hickory, 1966-68, pres., 1968-76, Luth. Theol. Sem. at Phila., 1976—; dir. N.C. Nat. Bank, Hickory, 1973-76; contact minister Nat. Luth. Council, N.C. State U., 1953-57, Yale U., 1957-59; part-time instr. sociology Columbia Coll., 1962-65; mem. Com. to Implement Refugee Act, 1953; mem. bd. theol. edn. Luth. Ch. Am., 1969-70, mem. standing com. on approaches to unity, 1971-72, del. conv., 1970-76, mem. bd. publ., 1976-84, v.p., 1983-84; pres. Ind. Coll. Fund of N.C., 1974-75; Bd. dirs. Luth. Ednl. Conf. N. Am., 1970-73, 78-80, 84—, v.p. commn. on future, 1972-75; trustee Luth. Theol. So. Sem., 1969-76, sec. bd., 1975-76; pres. bd. dirs. Piedmont U. Center N.C., 1972-73; bd. dirs. Am. Furniture Acad. and Hall Fame, 1975-78. Contbr. to: A History of the Lutheran Church in South Carolina, 1971, Essays and Reports of Lutheran Historical Conference, Vol. 6, 1977; contbr. to: Essays and Reports of Lutheran Historical Conference, Vol. 9, 1980; Contbr. to: A Truly Efficient School of Theology, 1981. Served with USMCR, 1943-47. Luth. Brotherhood Sem. Grad. scholar, 1957-58; Martin Luther fellow Nat. Luth. Ednl. Conf., 1959; faculty fellow Am. Assn. Theol. Schs., 1959-60. Mem. So. Hist. Assn., Luth. Hist. Conf., Am. Soc. Ch. History, Orgn. Am. Historians, N.C. Found. Ch. Related Colls. (sec. 1969-71). Club: Yale (Phila. and N.Y.C.). Home: 7333 Germantown Ave Philadelphia PA 19119 Office: Lutheran Theol Sem at Phila 7301 Germantown Ave Philadelphia PA 19119

BOSTIAN, CAREY HOYT, geneticist; b. China Grove, N.C., Mar. 1907; s. William Russell and Nonie (Cress) B.; m. Neita Corriher, June 5, 1929; children—Richard Lee, Lloyd Russell, Karl Eugene. Student, Heidelberg Coll., Tiffin, Ohio, 1924-25; B.S., Catawba Coll., Salisbury, N.C., 1928, D.Sc., 1953; M.S., U. Pitts., 1930, Ph.D., 1933; D.Sc., Wake Forest Coll., 1954; D.H.C., Nat. U. Engring., Lima, Peru, 1957. Teaching fellow zoology U. Pitts., 1928-30; asst. prof. zoology N.C. State U., 1930-36, asso. prof. zoology and poultry genetics, 1936-44, prof., 1944—, asst. dir. instruction Sch. Agr., 1944-48, dir. instruction Sch. Agr. and prof. genetics, 1948-53, chancellor, 1953-59, prof. genetics, 1959-73, emeritus prof., 1973—. Recipient Watauga medal N.C. State U., 1975. Mem. Sigma Xi, Gamma Sigma Delta, Phi Sigma, Phi Kappa Phi, Alpha Zeta. Presbyterian. Home: 111 Carol Woods Chapel Hill NC 27514

BOSTIAN, RICHARD LEE, educator, musician; b. Raleigh, N.C., Jan. 14, 1932; s. Carey Hoyt and Neita (Corriher) B.; m. Barbara Ann Bunai, Sept. 10, 1955; children—Russell James, Holly Ann, Bradley Earl, Mary Ann, Carey Hoyt. B.A., U. N.C., 1954, M.A., 1958, Ph.D., 1961. Asso. prof. music Radford (Va.) Coll., 1961-62, prof., head div. fine arts, 1962-66; prof. music, chmn. dept. Denison U., 1966—, coordinator arts, 1969-72, 77-79; Founder Radford Community Arts Assn., 1963; cons. music curriculum and phys. facilities. Minister of music 1st Presbyn. Ch. Mem. Am. Musicol. Soc., Phi Beta Kappa. Research on music of 18th and 20th centuries. Home: Route 2 161 Dorrence Rd Granville OH 43023

BOSTICK, CHARLES DENT, law educator; b. Gainesville, Ga., Dec. 28, 1931; s. Jared Sullivan and Charlotte Catherine (Dent) B.; m. Susan Oliver, Sept. 8, 1956; children: Susan, Alan. Student, Emory-at-Oxford U., 1948-49; B.A., Mercer U., 1952, J.D., 1958. Bar: Ga. 1957, Tenn. 1974, U.S. Dist. Ct. (no. dist.) Ga. 1958, U.S. Ct. Appeals (5th cir.) 1959. Individual practice law, Gainesville, Ga., 1958-66; asst. prof. law U. Fla., Gainesville, 1966-68, assoc. prof., 1968, Vanderbilt U., Nashville, 1968-71, prof., 1971—, assoc. dean, dir. admissions, 1975-79, acting dean, 1979-80, dean, 1980—. Served to lt. USNR, 1952-55. Mem. Tenn. Bar. Assn. Episcopalian. Office: Vanderbilt U Law Sch Nashville TN 37240

BOSTON, CHARLES D., lawyer; b. Shamrock, Tex., Nov. 12, 1928; s. P.T. and Myrtle B. (Leverett) B.; m. June Wimberly, Sept. 15, 1951; children: Donn Charles, Wimberly Ann. B.S., W. Tex. State U., Canyon, 1949; LL.B., U. Tex.-Austin, 1956. Bar: Tex. Ptnr. Fulbright & Jaworski, Houston, 1956—. Author (law rev. notes) Tex. Law Rev., 1954-55. Bd. dirs. Cystic Fibrosis, Houston, 1975, Free Market Edn. Found., Houston, 1978-83. 2d lt. USAF, 1951-53. Mem. Tex. Bar Assn., ABA, Houston Bar Assn., Tex. Assn. Def. Counsel, Assn. Ins. Attys., Tex. Bar Found., Order of Coif. Republican. Presbyterian. Clubs: Rotary, Racquet, Champions Golf, Athletic (Houston). Home: 314 Knipp Rd Houston TX 77024 Office: Fulbright & Jaworski Bank of the Southwest Bldg Houston TX 77002

BOSTWICK, RANDELL A., retail food company executive; b. Niles, Ohio, Oct. 24, 1922; s. Clifton A. and May (Lloyd) B.; m. Jane Elizabeth Foster, Aug. 28, 1948; children: Suzanne Elizabeth, Anne Bostwick Taubeneck, Randell A. Ed., U. Mich., Westminster Coll. Asst. traffic mgr. A&P, Youngstown, Ohio, 1948-50, asst. to div. traffic mgr., Pitts., 1952-58, div. traffic mgr., 1958-60, dir. ops., 1960-69, asst. to nat. dir. ops. N.Y. hdqrs., 1969-75; pres. subs. Super Market Service Corp., Montvale, N.J., 1975-83, pres., 1981—; corp. v.p. The Gt. A & P Tea Co., 1981—. Served to capt. Med. Service Corps U.S. Army,

1943-46, 50-52. Presbyterian. Home: 39 Dale Dr Summit NJ 07901 Office: 2 Paragon Dr Montvale NJ 07645

BOSTWICK, RICHARD RAYMOND, lawyer; b. Billings, Mont., Mar. 17, 1918; s. Leslie H. and Maude (Worthington) B.; m. Margaret Florence Brooks, Jan. 17, 1944; children: Michael, Patricia, Ed, Dick. Student, U. Colo., 1937-38; A.B., U. Wyo., 1943, J.D., 1947. Bar: Wyo. 1947. Claim atty. Hawkeye Casualty Co., Casper, Wyo., 1948-49; partner Murane & Bostwick, Casper, 1949—; Lectr. U. Wyo. Coll. Law. Contbr. articles profl. jours. Past trustee Casper YMCA; dep. dir. Civil Def., 1954-58; chmn. local SSS, 1952-70; mem. curriculum coordinating com. Natrona Co. Sch. Dist. 2, High Sch. Dist. Served to capt. AUS, 1943-46. Decorated Bronze Star medal; recipient Silver Merit awards Am. Legion. Mem. ABA, Wyo. Bar Assn. (pres. 1964-65), Natrona County Bar Assn. (pres. 1956), Am. Judicature Soc. (exec. com. 1973-75, sec. 1975-77, Herbert Harley award 1983), Internat. Assn. Ins. Counsel, Nat. Conf. Bar Pres. (exec. council 1970-72), Internat. Soc. of Barristers (dir. 1971—, pres. 1975), Am. Legion (dir. 1951-58, post comdr. 1953-54), Wyo. Alumni Assn. (trustee 1955-57), Casper C. of C. (chmn. legistlative com. 1955-57, dir. 1959-62, v.p.). Presbyn. Club: Mason (Shriner, K.T.). Home: 1137 Granada Ave Casper WY 82601 Office: Wyoming Building Casper WY 82601 *I was fortunate enough to select a profession which I find I have liked from the beginning and with which I am still fascinated. This makes it easy to work hard and to maintain a high standard of pride in the profession and to donate and devote time to the upgrading of it over and above daily routine. To be able to work hard, to create a job well done, and to experience satisfaction over and above the mere elements of a livelihood is a goal worthy of effort.*

BOSWELL, MARION LILLARD, aerospace executive, former air force officer; b. Louisville, Oct. 1, 1923; s. Robert Rhodes and Vivian Lily (Snodgrass) B. B.A., William Jewell Coll., 1946; M.A., George Washington U., 1966. Commd. 2d lt. U.S. Army Air Force, 1944, advanced through grades to lt. gen., 1974; aircraft comdr. SAC, 1947-51; aide to Lt. Gen. Atkinson Alaskan Command, 1952-54; dep. comdr. ops. 97th Bomber Wing, 1961-63; at Hdqrs., Washington, 1963-65, Nat. War Coll., 1965-66; dep. comdr. ops. 49th Tactical Fighter Wing, Ger., 1966-68; vice comdr. 366th Tactical Fighter Wing, Danang AFB, South Vietnam, 1968-69; comdr. 4th Tactical Fighter Wing, N.C., 1969-70; legis. liaison Office Sec. Air Force, Washington, 1970-74; asst. vice chief of staff USAF, 1974-76; comdr. Alaskan Air Command, 1976-78; chief of staff PACOM, Hawaii, 1978-79; asst. vice chief of staff and chief U.S. del. mil. staff com. UN, 1979-81; ret., 1981; chmn. bd. Italian Aerospace Industries (U.S.A.) Inc., 1981—. Decorated Legion of Merit with one oak leaf cluster, D.S.M. with three oak leaf clusters, D.F.C. with oak leaf cluster, Air medal with nineteen oak leaf clusters; Vietnamese Gallantry Cross with gold star; French Legion of Honor. Mem. Sigma Nu. Club: Army Navy Country. Home: 6646 Madison McLean Dr McLean VA 22101

BOSWELL, RICHARD JAMES, company executive; b. Chgo., Sept. 4, 1924; s. James R. and Eleanor (Street) B.; m. Joan Wood, Dec. 25, 1951; children: Gregory, Thomas. B.A., UCLA, 1945; post grad., U. Newcastle-Upon-Tyne, Eng., 1945-46. With Josephson Enterprises, 1947-63, exec. v.p., 1952-63; v.p. Hewlett-Packard Co., Palo Alto, Calif., 1963-73, v.p. mfg., 1973; exec. v.p. Hewlett-Packard co., 1974—, also dir. Bd. dirs. Palo Alto Chpt. Am. Cancer Soc.; former mem. nat. council Muscular Dystrophy Assn. With USN, 1943-46. Mem. Electronic Reps. Assn., IEEE, NAM (dir.). Home: Werik Apts 159 Madeira Coral Gables FL 33134

BOSWORTH, DOUGLAS LEROY, farm implement company executive; b. Goldfield, Iowa, Oct. 15, 1939; s. Clifford LeRoy and Clara (Lonning) B.; m. Patricia Lee Knock, May 28, 1961; children: Douglas, Dawn. B.S. in Agrl. Engring, Iowa State U., 1962, M.S., U. Ill., 1964. With Deere & Co., Moline, Ill., 1959—, reliability mgr., 1967-71, div. engr. disk harrows, 1971-76, mgr. mfg. engring., 1976-80, works mgr., 1980—. Active Am. Cancer Soc., Rock Island Unit; v.p. Skills Inc. Mem. Am. Soc. Agrl. Engrs. (chmn. Ill.-Wis. 1973-74, Engring. Achievement Young Designer award 1973, nat. bd. dirs. 1974-76, 79-82, v.p. 1979-82), Sigma Xi, Alpha Epsilon, Gamma Sigma Delta. Lutheran. Clubs: Toastmasters., Rotary. Home: 4432 37th Ave Rock Island IL 61201 Office: 501 3d Ave Moline IL 61265

BOSWORTH, STEPHEN WARREN, government official; b. Grand Rapids, Mich., Dec. 4, 1939; s. Warren Charles and Mina (Phillips) B.; m. Sandra Lee Depuit, Sept. 9, 1961; children—Andrew, Allison. A.B., Dartmouth Coll., 1961. Joined U.S. Fgn. Service; service in, Panama, Colon, Madrid and Paris, dep. asst. sec. state, 1976-79, ambassador to Tunisia, 1979-81, dep. asst. sec. Inter-Am. affairs, 1981-82; chmn. Policy Planning Council, 1983; ambassador, Manilla, Phillipines, 1983—. Recipient Dept. State Disting. Honor award, 1976, Arthur S. Flemming award, 1976. Address: US Embassy APO San Francisco CA 96528 *

BOSWORTH, THOMAS LAWRENCE, architect, educator; b. Oberlin, Ohio, June 15, 1930; s. Edward Franklin and Imogene (Rose) B.; m. Abigail Lumbard, Nov. 6, 1954 (div. Nov. 1974); children: Thomas Edward, Nathaniel David; m. Elaine R. Pedigo, Nov. 23, 1974. B.A., Oberlin Coll., 1952, M.A., 1954; postgrad., Princeton U., 1952-53, Harvard U., 1956-57; M.Arch., Yale U., 1960. Draftsman Gordon McMaster AIA, Cheshire, Conn., summer 1957-58; resident planner Tunnard & Harris Planning Cons., Newport, R.I., summer 1959; designer, field supr. Eero Saarinen & Assocs., Birmingham, Mich., 1960-61, Hamden, Conn., 1961-64; individual practice architecture, Providence, 1964-68; asst. instr. architecture Yale U., 1962-65, vis. lectr., 1965-66; asst. prof. R.I. Sch. Design, 1964-66, asso. prof., head dept., 1966-68; prof. architecture U. Wash., Seattle, 1968—, chmn. dept., 1968-72; chief architecture Peace Corps Tng. Program, Tunisia, Brown U., summers 1965-66; archtl. cons., individual practice, Seattle, 1972—; vis. lectr. Kobe U., Japan, Oct., 1982; Mem. Seattle Model Cities Land Use Rev. Bd., 1969-70, Tech. Com. Site Selection Wash. Multi-Purpose Stadium, 1970; chmn. King County (Wash.) Environ. Devel. Commn., 1970-74; mem. Medina Planning Commn., 1972-74; chmn. King County Policy Devel. Commn., 1974-77; mem. steering adv. com. King County Stadium, 1972-74. Dir. Pilchuck Sch., Seattle, 1977-80, trustee, 1980—. Served with U.S. Army, 1954-56. Winchester traveling fellow, Greece, 1960; asso. fellow Ezra Stiles Coll. Yale U.; mid-career fellow in architecture Am. Acad. in Rome, 1980-81. Fellow AIA; mem. Soc. Archtl. Historians, AAUP, Tau Sigma Delta. Home: 4532 E Laurel Dr NE Seattle WA 98105 Office: Dept Architecture U Wash Seattle WA 98105

BOSWORTH, WILLIAM JOHN, government agency executive; b. Aurora, Ont., Can., Jan. 13, 1917; s. John Edward and Hanna (Hicks) B.; m. Julia McConnell Angrove, Dec. 31, 1941; 1 son, William J. Pres. Can. Dry. Ltd., Kingston, Ont., 1946-68, Rideau Marina Ltd., 1959-83, Willworth Devel. Ltd., 1968-83; v.p. Kingston Cable TV, 1972-81; pres. Cananoque Realty Ltd., Kingston, Ont., 1973-83; chmn. bd., chief exec. officer Liquor Control Bd. of Ont., Toronto, 1976—. Served to lt. comdr. Can. Navy, 1941-45. Club: Kingston Yacht. Home: 33 Ontario St Kingston ON Canada K7L 2Y2 Office: Liquor Control Bd of Ontario 55 Lakeshore St E Toronto ON Canada M5E 1A4

BOTERF, CHESTER ARTHUR (CHECK BOTERF), artist; b. Ft. Scott, Kans., Apr. 27, 1934; s. Chester Arthur and Vivien Aleta (Sorensen) B.; m. Shirley Jane Baker, Sept. 1, 1957; children: Alexandra V., Check Baker. B.A., U. Kans., 1959; M.F.A. (Helen Elsor fellow), Columbia U., 1965. Lectr. art Hunter Coll., N.Y.C., 1965-71; instr. art Bklyn. Mus. Art, summer 1973; vis. assoc. prof. art Rice U., Houston, 1973-75, assoc. prof., 1976—, chmn. dept. art, art history, 1979-83; lectr. art U. Md., College Park, spring 1976. One-man exhbns. include, Tibor de Nagy Gallery, N.Y.C., 1967, 68, 70, John Bernard Myers Gallery, N.Y.C., 1971, 73, 74, Sewall Gallery, Rice U., 1974, Louisiana Gallery, Houston, 1979, group exhbns. include, Graham Gallery, N.Y.C., So. Ill. U., Carbondale, Aldrich Mus., Ridgefield, Conn., Gallery Simonne Stern, New Orleans, Indpls. Mus. Art, Finch Coll., N.Y.C., Des Moines (Iowa) Art Center, Mus. Modern Art, N.Y.C., Tibor DeNagy Gallery, N.Y.C., John Bernard Meyers Gallery, N.Y.C., Louisiana Gallery, Houston; represented in permanent collections, Mus. Modern Art, N.Y.C., Des Moines Art Center, Aldrich Mus., Columbia U., Fordham U., Rockefeller U., AT&T, Chase Manhattan Bank, Mfrs. Hanover Trust, CitiCorp, First City Nat Bank Houston. Served with AUS, 1954-56, 59-63. Mem. Coll. Art Assn., Res. Officers Assn., Tau Beta Pi. Home: 3718 Arnold St Houston TX 77005 Office: Dept Art and Art History Rice U Box 1892 Houston TX 77001

BOTERO, FERNANDO, artist; b. Medellin, Colombia, Apr. 19, 1932. Student, Academia San Fernando, Madrid, 1952, Prado Museum, Madrid, 1952, Univ. Florence, Italy, 1953-54. Numerous one-man shows, including, Marlborough Gallery, N.Y.C., 1982, Hooks-Epstein Gallery, Houston, Hokin Gallery, Chgo., Benjamin Mangel Gallery, Phila., Galeria Quintana, Bogota, Colombia, Thomas gal Gallery, Boston, 1983, Palazzo Grassi, Venice, Italy, Marlborough Gallery, London, Fondation Veranneman, Kruishoutem, Belgium; represented numerous permanent collections, including, Museo Nacional, Bogota, Colombia, Walrat-Richarts Mus., Cologne, Germany, Museo d'Arte Moderna del Vaticano, Rome, Museo de Arte Contemporaneo, Madrid, Hirshhorn Mus. and Sculpture Garden, Washington, Mus. Modern Art, N.Y.C., Solomon R. Guggenheim Mus., N.Y.C., Nat. Mus., Tokyo, Met. Mus. Art, N.Y.C. Decorated Order Andres Bello, Venezuela; recipient Guggenheim Nat. prize for Colombia, 1960. Home: 5 Boulevard Du Palais Paris France 75004

BOTHMER, BERNARD V., Egyptologist, museum curator; b. Charlottenburg, Germany, Oct. 13, 1912; naturalized, 1944; s. Willy and Marie (Freiin von und zu Egloffstein) von B.;, Oct. 18, 1951; children: Yvette Marina, Nicolas B. (dec.). Student, U. Berlin, 1931-32, 32-36, U. Bonn-am-Rhein, 1932. Asst. Egyptian dept. State Mus., Berlin, Germany, 1932-38; staff OWI, N.Y.C., 1942-43, fgn. lang. sect. War Dept., 1943; asst. dept. Egyptian art Mus. Fine Arts, Boston, 1946-53, asst. curator, 1954-56; asst. treas. Am. Research Center in Egypt, Inc., 1950-56, gen. sec., 1953-54, field dir. in, Egypt, 1954-56; asst. curator ancient art Bklyn. Mus., 1956-58, asso. curator, 1958-64, curator ancient art, 1964-72, curator Egyptian and Classical art, 1972-77, chmn. dept. Egyptian and classical art, 1978-82; vice-dir. mus., 1969-70, Keeper of Wilbour Collection, 1974—; adj. prof. fine arts Inst. Fine Arts N.Y. U., 1960-78, prof. fine arts, 1979—; Mem. Commn. for Cultural Affairs of City of N.Y., 1978-81. Served with Intelligence Corps AUS, 1943-46. Fulbright Research fellow, Egypt, 1954-56, 63-64. Mem. Am. Assn. Museums, Archaeol. Inst. Am. (gen. sec. 1952-54), Egypt Exploration Soc., Compagnie de la Toison d'Or (Dijon, France), Am. Research Center Egypt, Coll. Art Assn. Address: Inst of Fine Arts 1 East 78th St New York NY 10021

BOTHMER, DIETRICH FELIX VON, archaeologist, museum curator; b. Eisenach, Thuringia, Oct. 26, 1918; U.S., 1939, naturalized, 1944; s. Wilhelm Friedrich Franz Karl and Marie Julie Auguste Karoline (Freiin von und zu Egloffstein) von B.; m. Joyce de la Bégassière, May 28, 1966; children: Bernard Nicholas, Maria Elizabeth. Student, Friedrich Wilhelms U., Berlin, 1937-38; diploma classical archaeology (Rhodes scholar), Wadham Coll., Oxford, 1939, U. Calif. at Berkeley, 1940, 1940-41, 1941-42; Ph.D. in Classical Archaeology, 1944, U. Chgo., 1942-43. Asst. curator Greek and Roman art Met. Mus. Art, 1946-51, assoc. curator, 1951-59, curator, 1959-73, chmn., 1973—; adj. prof. N.Y. U., 1966—. Book rev. editor: Am. Jour. Archaeology, 1950-57; assoc. editor, 1970-76; Author: Amazons in Greek Art, 1957, Ancient Art from New York Private Collections, 1961, An Inquiry into the Forgery of the Etruscan Terracotta Warriors, 1961, Corpus Vasorum Antiquorum, USA fasc. 12, 1963, Greek Vase Painting: An Introduction, 1972, Corpus Vasorum Antiquorum, USA fasc. 16, 1976, Greek Art of the Aegean Islands, 1979, A Greek and Roman Treasury, 1984. Served as pvt. AUS, 1943-45. Decorated Bronze Star; Guggenheim Meml. Found. fellowship, 1966. Mem. Archaeol. Inst. Am. (benefactor), Soc. Promotion Hellenic Studies, Deutsches Archaeol. Inst., Vereinigung der Freunde Antiker Kunst (Basle, Switzerland), Archaeologische Gesellschaft zu Berlin, Institut de France, Académie des Inscriptions et Belles-Lettres (corr.). Clubs: Piping Rock., Century Assn. Home: 401 Centre Island Rd Oyster Bay NY 11771 Office: Metropolitan Museum Art New York NY 10028

BOTHNER-BY, AKSEL ARNOLD, chemist; b. Mpls., Apr. 29, 1921; s. Aksel Conrad and Merle Marie (von Hagen) Bothner-B.; m. Christine Treuner, Oct. 15, 1949; children—Peter Ole, Anne Sigrun. Student. U. Nanking, China, 1939; B.Chemistry, U. Minn., 1943; M.S., N.Y.U., 1947; Ph.D., Harvard, 1949. Scientist Brookhaven Nat. Lab., 1949-53; fellow Am. Cancer Soc., 1952-53; instr., lectr. Harvard, 1953-58; cons. Retina Found., 1957-58; staff fellow Mellon Inst., 1958-71, dir., 1960-61, mem. adv. com., 1962-71; prof. chemistry Carnegie-Mellon U., 1967-77, chmn. dept., 1967-70; dean Mellon Inst. Sci., 1971-75, Univ. prof., 1977—; Fulbright lectr. U. Munich, Germany, 1962-63; adj. prof. U. Pitts., 1964—; vis. prof. U. Calif. at San Diego, 1976-77; trustee MPC Corp., 1972-80; Bd. dirs. Pa. Jr. Acad. Scis., 1975—. Author papers in field of theoretical organic chemistry. Served with AUS, 1943-45. Recipient Distinguished Achievement award U. Minn., 1975, IR-100 award, 1978. Mem. Am. Chem. Soc., Am. Soc. Biol. Chemists, Biophys. Soc. Home: 6317 Darlington Rd Pittsburgh PA 15217 Office: Mellon Inst 4400 5th Ave Pittsburgh PA 15213

BOTHWELL, DORR, artist; b. San Francisco, May 3, 1902; d. John Stuart and Florence Isabel (Hodgson) B. Student, Calif. Sch. Fine Arts, Rudolph Schaeffer Sch. Design, U. Oreg. Painter Tau, Mau'a, Am. Samoa, 1928-29, France, 1930-31, Eng., 1960-61, W. Africa and N. Africa, 1966-67; instr. Calif. Sch. Fine Arts, San Francisco, 1945-58, Rudolph Schaeffer Sch. Design, 1960-61, Mendocino (Calif.) Art Center, 1962—, San Francisco Art Inst., 1961; Prof. Sonoma State Coll., summer 1964, U. Calif., Mendocino Art Center, summers 1965-71; faculty Ansel Adams Yosemite Workshop, 1964-77, Victor (Colo.) Sch., 1979. Exhibitor, West Coast exhbns., 1927—, 3d biennial Sao Paulo, Brazil, Pitts. Internat., 1952, 55, Art: U.S.A., 1958, Bklyn. Mus., 1976, works in permanent collection, San Diego Gallery Fine Art, Crocker Gallery, Sacramento, San Francisco Mus. Art, Whitney Mus. Am. Art, Bklyn. Mus., Mus. Modern Art, Fogg Mus., Met. Museum, Victoria and Albert Museum, London, Eng., Bibliotheque Nationale, Paris, France, one-man show, De Young Meml. Mus., San Francisco, 1957, 63; Notan: The Principle of Dark-Light Design, 1968, 2d edit., 1976, Danish edit., 1977. Recipient 1st prize, 4th ann. exhbn. San Francisco Soc. Women Artists, 1929; Pres.'s purchase prize, 1941; Leisser-Farnham award 7th ann. exhbn. San Diego Art Guild, 1932; hon. mention 7th ann. exhbn. So. Calif. Artists, 1933; spl. prize 9th ann. exhbn., 1937; Artists Fund prize ann. exhbn. drawings and prints San Francisco Art Assn., 1943; hon. mention 2d spring ann. Calif. Palace Legion of Honor, San Francisco, 1947. Home and studio: Star Route 1 Box 1055 Joshua Tree CA 92252

BOTHWELL, JOHN CHARLES, bishop; b. Toronto, Ont., Can., June 29, 1926; s. William Alexander and Anne (Campbell) B.; m. Joan Cowan, Dec. 29, 1951; children—Michael, Timothy, Nancy, Douglas, Ann. B.A. with honors in Modern History, U. Toronto, 1948; B.D., Trinity Coll., Toronto, 1950, D.D. (hon.), 1972. Ordained priest Anglican Ch., 1952; curate St. James Cathedral, Toronto, 1951-53, Christ Ch. Cathedral, Vancouver, B.C., 1953-56; rector St. Aidan's Ch., Oakville, Ont., 1956-60, St. James' Ch., Dundas, Ont., 1960-65; canon missioner Niagara Diocese, 1965-69; nat. exec. dir. Anglican Ch. Can., 1969-71; co-adjutor bishop, Niagara, 1971-73; bishop Diocese of Niagara, 1973—; mem. nat. exec. com. Anglican Ch. Co-author: Theological Education for the 70's, 1969; contbr. articles in field to various newspapers. Active numerous nat. and ecumenical coms.; Dir., com. chmn. Hamilton (Ont.) Social Planning Council, 1965-69, 71-75, v.p., 1975-77, pres., 1977—; v.p. United Way, 1982, 83; bd. dirs. Hamilton Found., 1982, v.p., 1983. Clubs: Dundas Golf and Country, Hamilton C. of C. Home: 838 Glenwood Ave Burlington ON L7T 2J9 Canada Office: 67 Victoria Ave S Hamilton ON L8N 2S8 Canada

BOTHWELL, LAWRENCE L., historian; b. Greeley, Colo., Oct. 22, 1932; s. John Edgar and Ethel (Burnett) Bothell; m. Janet Bowers, Feb. 3, 1957. A.B., Harvard U., 1954; B.D., Union Theol. Sem., 1959; M.A., Princeton U., 1964, Ph.D., 1967. Instr., asso. librarian Episcopal Theol. Sch., Cambridge, Mass., 1964-66, asst. prof., asso. librarian, 1966-69, asso. prof., dir. library, 1969-74; prof., dir. libraries Episcopal Div. Sch. and Weston Sch. Theology, 1974-75; v.p. Bowers Found., Inc., 1973-82, project officer, 1983—; Dir. spl. projects Roberson Center for Arts and Scis., Binghamton, N.Y., 1979-81; Broome County historian, 1981—. Author: Broome County Heritage: An Illustrated History, 1983. Served with AUS, 1954-56. Mem. Am. Hist. Assn., Nat. Trust for Historic Preservation, Preservation League N.Y. State (dir. 1983—). Home: Nanticoke Rd Box 23 Maine NY 13802

BOTSAI, ELMER EUGENE, architect, university dean; b. St. Louis, Feb. 1, 1928; s. Paul and Ita May (Cole) B.; m. Patricia L. Keegan, Aug. 28, 1955; children: Donald Rolf, Kurt Gregory.; m. Sharon K. Kaiser, Dec. 5, 1981; 1 dau., Kiana Michelle. A.B., U. Calif.-Berkeley, 1954. Draftsman, asst. to architect So. Pacific Co., San Francisco, 1954-57; project architect Anshen & Allen Architects, San Francisco, 1957-63; prin. Botsai, Overstreet & Rosenberg, Architects and Planners, San Francisco, 1963-79, Elmer E. Botsai FAIA, Inc., Honolulu, 1979—; chmn. dept. architecture U. Hawaii at Manoa, 1976-80, dean Sch. Architecture,, 1980—; dir. Nat. Archtl. Accrediting Bd., 1972-73, 79. Author: Architects and Earthquakes: A Primer, 1977. Served with U.S. Army, 1946-48. NSF grantee, 1974-80. Fellow AIA (pres. San Francisco chpt. 1973, nat. pres. 1978), Royal Can. Inst. Architects (hon.), N.Z. Inst. Architects (hon.), Royal Australian Inst. Architects (hon.); mem. La Societed de Arquitectos Mexicano (hon.), Earthquake Engring. Research Inst., Archtl. Secs. Assn. (hon.), Seismol. Soc. Am., Soc. Wood Sci. and Tech., Internat. Conf. Bldg. Ofcls., AAAS, Nat. Fire Protection Assn. Home: 321 Wailupe Circle Honolulu HI 96821 Office: 2560 Campus Rd GA B2 Honolulu HI 96822

BOTSTEIN, LEON, college president; b. Zurich, Switzerland, Dec. 14, 1946; s. Charles and Anne (Wyszewianski) B.; m. Jill Lundquist, 1970; children: Sarah, Abigail.; m. Barbara Haskell, 1982. B.A. (Woodrow Wilson fellow, Danforth Found. fellow, Sloan Found. fellow), U. Chgo., 1967; A.M., Harvard U., 1968. Tutor gen. edn. Harvard U., 1968-69; lectr. history Boston U., 1969; asst. to pres. N.Y.C. Bd. Edn., 1969-70; pres. Franconia (N.H.) Coll., 1970-75, Bard Coll., Annandale-On-Hudson, N.Y., 1975—, Simon's Rock Early Coll., Gt. Barrington, Mass., 1979—; dir. Interferon Scis., Inc.; prin. condr. White Mountain Music and Art Festival, N.H., 1973-75; guest condr. Hudson Valley Philharmon., N.H., 1981—; adj. prof. Union Grad. Sch., Yellow Springs, Ohio, 1973-75; mem. Commn. on Ind. Colls. and Univs., 1979—; mem., past chmn. N.Y. Council Humanities; cons. Nat. Endowment for Humanities. Contbr. articles to publs. Chmn. bd. Harper's Mag. Found., 1983—. Mem. Assn. Episcopal Colls. (chmn. 1982—). Office: Bard Coll Annandale-On-Hudson NY 12504

BOTT, KENNETH ANDREW, banker; b. Jersey City, N.J., June 22, 1924; s. Andrew and Elsie (Reinke) B.; m. Jeanne Donna Reynolds, June 3, 1949; children: Kenneth A., Richard R., Andrew J., Stephen R. B.S., U.S. Naval Acad., 1949. Vice pres. Citibank, N.Y.C., 1954-74; pres. Meadowlands Nat. Bank, N. Bergen, N.J., 1974-75, First Nat. Bank of Toms River, N.J., 1975-78; exec. v.p. Trust Co. of N.J., Jersey City, 1978-80; pres., chief exec. officer Franklin State Bank, Somerset, N.J., 1980—; dir. New Brunswick Devel. Co., 1980—. Served to capt. USMC, 1943-54. Recipient Silver Star medal, Purple Heart. Club: Spring Lake Country.

BOTTEL, HELEN ALFEA, columnist, free-lance writer; b. Beaumont, Calif.; d. Alpheus Russell and Mary Ellen (Alexander) Brigden; m. Robert E. Bottel; children: Robert Dennis, Rodger M., R. Kathryn Bottel Bernhardt, Suzanne V. Bottel Peppers. A.A., Riverside Coll. Calif.; student, Oreg. State U., 1958-59, So. Oreg. Coll., 1959. Editor Illinois Valley News, Cave Junction, Oreg.; writer Grants Pass (Oreg.) Courier, Portland Oregonian, Medford (Oreg.) Mail Tribune, 1952-58; columnist King Features Syndicate, N.Y.C., 1958—. Contbg. editor, columnist, Real World mag., N.Y.C., 1976—; free-lance mag. writer, author, lectr., 1956—; Author: To Teens With Love, 1969, Helen Help Us, 1970, Parents Survival Kit, 1979; weekly columnist: Yomiuri Shimbun, Tokyo, 1982—; contbr. non-fiction to books, nat. mags. Bd. dirs. Illinois Valley Med. Center, 1958-62, Childrens Center, Sacramento, 1969; mem. Grants Pass br. Oreg. Juvenile Adv. Com., 1960-62, Students League Against Narcotics Temptation, 1968-70; charter patron Cosumnes River Coll., Sacramento, 1972—; mem. nat. adv. bd. Nat. Anorexic Aid Soc., 1977—; mem. Sacramento Women's Council, 1979. Recipient Women's Service Cup Riverside Coll.; citation for aid to U.S. servicemen in Vietnam Gov. Ga., 1967; Disting. Merit citation NCCJ, 1970; 1st Pl. award for books Calif. Press Women, 1970; Sacramento Regional Arts Council Lit. Achievement award, 1974. Mem. Am. Soc. Journalists and Authors, Internat. Platform Assn. Presbyterian. Club: Calif. Writers. Home: 2060 56th Ave Sacramento CA 95822 Office: King Features Syndacate 235 E 45th St New York NY 10017 *"Leap before you look." That's for me. My best moments and finest achievements have resulted from spur-of-the-moment impulses on which I've acted before second thoughts or considered judgment could persuade me they were impossible.*

BOTTI, MARIO ROBERT, advertising executive; b. Bklyn., Oct. 22, 1938; s. Ettore and Filomena (Deluccio) B.; m. Frances Ann Simonelli, Aug. 5, 1962; children: Christopher, Michael, Philip. B.A., Pratt Inst., 1966. Asst. art dir. Doyle Dane Bernbach, N.Y.C., 1963; art dir. BBDO, Inc., N.Y.C., 1964-66; v.p., assoc. creative dir. Needham, Harper, Steers, N.Y.C., 1966-76; sr. v.p., creative group head Benton & Bowles, N.Y.C., 1976—; instr. Sch. Visual Arts, N.Y.C., 1977-80. Served with U.S. Army, 1957-59. Recipient award

Cork Film Festival, 1971, Andy award, 1968, Cilo award, 1978, Art Dirs. Gold Key, 1978. Roman Catholic. Office: Benton & Bowles Inc 909 3d Ave New York NY 10022

BOTTIGLIA, WILLIAM FILBERT, humanities educator; b. Bernardsville, N.J., Nov. 23, 1912; s. Vincent Richard and Quintilia (Mastrobattista) B.; m. Mildred MacDonald, Dec. 21, 1943 (dec. Oct. 1966); stepchildren: Martha (Mrs. Milton Morris), Janet. A.B., Princeton U., 1934, A.M., 1935, Ph.D., 1948. Part-time, then full-time instr. modern langs. Princeton U., 1934-42; engaged in industry, 1942-47; gen. mgr. J & S Tool Co., East Orange, N.J., 1946-47; asst. prof. English, St. Lawrence U., 1948; prof. Romance langs. and lits., chmn. dept. Ripon Coll., 1948-56; mem. faculty MIT, 1956—, prof. fgn. lit. and humanities, 1960-74, head dept. fgn. lit. and linguistics, 1964-73, prof. mgmt. and humanities, 1974-78, prof. emeritus and sr. lectr. mgmt. and humanities, 1978—. Author: Voltaire's Candide: Analysis of a Classic, 2d edit., 1964, (with others) Voltaire (Twentieth Century Views), 1968; editor: Reports of N.E. Conf. on the Teaching of Fgn. Langs, 1957, 62, 63. Mem. Société des Palmes Académiques, Dante Soc. Am., Phi Beta Kappa. Home: 34 Mary Chilton Rd Needham MA 02192 Office: MIT Cambridge MA 02139

BOTTIN, ALBERT CARL, savings and loan executive; b. Pekin, Ill., Apr. 21, 1921; s. Dietrich Carl and Emma Mary (Winters) B.; m. Marilyn Myers, Oct. 20, 1951; children: Carolyn Jane, Linda Kay. B.S., U. Ill., 1947. With Firestone Tire & Rubber Co., Peoria, Ill., 1947-51; with Am. Savs. and Loan Assn., Pekin, 1951—, pres., 1969—, also dir.; dir. Bank for Savs. and Loan Assns., Chgo., 1967-82, vice chmn. bd., 1970-72. Treas. Pekin United Fund, 1966-68; bd. dirs. Everett M. Dirksen Congressional Leadership Research Center, 1977—, Pekin Community Concert Assn. Served with U.S. Army, 1942-46. Mem. Am. Savs. and Loan Inst. Greater Peoria (v.p. 1972-73, pres. 1973-74), U.S. Savs. and Loan League, Ill. Savs. and Loan League (personnel and edn. com. 1964-82, chmn. Career Devel. Sch. 1983-84), U.S. C. of C., Ill. C. of C. (edn. com. 1968-82), Pekin C. of C. (dir. 1972-75), Am. Legion, Tau Kappa Epsilon, Phi Mu Alpha, Kappa Delta Pi, Phi Alpha Chi. Presbyterian. Clubs: Masons, Shriners, Rotary (pres. local chpt. 1972-73), Pekin Country (bd. govs. 1968-70). Home: 717 S 7th St Pekin IL 61554 Office: 300 S 4th St Pekin IL 61554

BOTTOM, DALE COYLE, association executive; b. Columbus, Ind., June 25, 1932; s. James Robert and Sarah Lou (Coyle) B.; m. Frances Audrey Wilson, June 6, 1954; children: Jane Ellen, Steven Dale, Sharon Lynn, Carol Ann. B.S., Ball State U., Muncie, Ind., 1954. Admissions counselor Stephens Coll., Columbia, Mo., 1958-61; exec. asst., then staff v.p. Inst. Fin. Edn., Chgo., 1961-67, pres., 1967—; vice chmn., dir. SAF-Systems & Forms Co. Chmn. bd. Barrington (Ill.) United Meth. Ch., 1981. Served as officer USAF, 1955-58; to comdr. USNR, 1967-78. Mem. Fin. Mgrs. Soc. (dir.), Savs. Instns. Mktg. Soc. Am., Navy League, Ind. Soc. Chgo. Republican. Clubs: Chgo. Rotary (past v.p.), Tavern, Plaza, Medinah Country. Home: 126 Carriage Rd Barrington IL 60010 Office: 111 E Wacker Dr Chicago IL 60601

BOTTOMS, JAMES EUGENE, edn. assn. exec.; b. Cumming, Ga., May 25, 1937; s. W. Jay and Florine Eleanor (Hurt) B.; m. Helen Milford, Aug. 6, 1960; children—Gina, Kevin, Andrea. B.A., U. Ga., 1960, M.S., 1962, Ed.D., 1965. Jr. high sch. tchr., Cherokee County, Ga., 1957-58, sch. prin., Forsythe County, Ga., 1958-59, barrow County, Ga., 1960-61; guidance dir. South Ga. Tech.-Vocat. Sch., Americus, 1961-62; state supr. Ga. Dept. Edn., 1962-63, state supr. vocat. guidance, 1964-66, asst. state dir. vocat. edn., 1966-72, dir. ednl. improvement, 1972-77; exec. dir. Am. Vocat. Assn., Arlington, Va., 1977—; bd. dirs. Nat. Assn. for Industry-Edn. Cooperation; condr. workshops, lectr. in field; cons. sch. dists. U.S. Office Edn., Agy. for Instructional TV. Contbr.: monthly editorial column to VocEd, Jour. American Vocational Association; contbr. articles to profl. jours. Recipient leadership award Ga. Assn. Educators. Mem. Am. Vocat. Assn. (outstanding service award), Ga. Vocat. Assn., Am. Futuristic Soc., Am. Personnel and Guidance Assn., Am. Soc. Execs., Phi Delta Kappa, Kappa Delta Pi. Baptist. Office: 2020 N 14th St Arlington VA 22201 *

BOTTOMS, TIMOTHY, actor; b. Santa Barbara, Calif., Aug. 30, 1951. Film debut in: Johnny Got His Gun, 1971; other films include The Last Picture Show, 1971, Love, Pain and the Whole Damned Thing, 1972, The Paper Chase, 1973, White Dawn, 1974, The Crazy World of Julius Vrooder, 1974, Operation Daybreak, 1975, A Small Town in Texas, 1976, Roller Coaster, 1977, The Other Side of the Mountain, pt. II, 1978, Hurricane, 1979, The First Hello, 1979; TV appearances include Look Homeward, Angel, 1972, The Story of David, 1976, The Moneychangers, 1976, Escape, 1979, A Shining Season, 1979, East of Eden, 1980. Office: care Robert Raison Assos 9575 Lime Orchard Rd Beverly Hills CA 90210 *

BOTTORF, RICHARD MOSER, JR., publisher; b. Bellefonte, Pa., Nov. 20, 1934; s. Richard Moser and Anna Mae Lorraine (Murphy) B.; m. Sara Lee Wheeler, July 11, 1959; children—Lori Sue, Jennifer Ann. B.S., Miami U., Oxford, Ohio, 1958; M.B.A., Rochester Inst. Tech., 1973. Staff auditor Peat, Marwick, Mitchell & Co., Cleve., 1958-61; internal auditor Leaseway Transp. Corp., Cleve., 1961-64; gen. mgr. Boyce-Canandaigua, Inc., N.Y., 1964-71; asst. controller, mktg. dir. Gannett Co., Inc., Rochester, N.Y., 1971-76; pres., pub. Burlington (Vt.) Free Press, 1976—; guest lectr. colls., univs. Active United Way, 1975—; bd. dirs. Salvation Army, Rochester, 1974-76 bd. dirs. Salvation Army, Burlington, Vt., 1976—. Mem. Am. Newspaper Pubs. Assn., New Eng. Daily Newspaper Assn. (gov.). Methodist. Clubs: Ethan Allen, Burlington Country, Rotary (Burlington) (dir. 1978—). Home: 29 Wildwood Dr Essex Junction VT 05452 Office: 191 College St Burlington VT 05401 *

BOTTORFF, DENNIS C., banker; b. Clarksville, Ind., Sept. 19, 1944; s. Irvin H. and Lucille H. B.; m. Jean Brewington, Aug. 21, 1964; children: Todd, Chad. B.E., Vanderbilt U., 1966; M.B.A., Northwestern U., 1968. Pres. Commerce Union Bank; Exec. v.p. also Commerce Union Corp., Nashville; instr. Grad. Sch. Banking, Madison, Wis., 1979—. Chmn. bd. Nashville Area United Way; bd. dirs., chmn. memberships campaign Cumberland Valley council Girl Scouts Am., 1976-77; bd. dirs., treas. Samaritans, Inc., 1975—; chmn. fin. com. Nashville Met. Govt.'s Overall Econ. Devel. Program, 1976—; bd. dirs. Children's Hosp., Nashville, Ensworth Sch., Nashville Symphony. Mem. Am. Inst. Banking, Bankers Assn. Fgn. Trade., Nashville C. of C. (bd. dirs., treas. 1982). Presbyterian. Clubs: Belle Meade Country, Cumberland. Home: 2424 Golf Club Ln Nashville TN 37205 Office: Commerce Union Corp One Commerce Pl Nashville TN 37239

BOTTS, GUY WARREN, banker, lawyer; b. Milton, Fla., July 12, 1914; s. Alonzo O'Hara and Margaret (L) B.; m. Edith M. Huddleston, Nov. 4, 1939; children—Edith, William. J.D., U. Fla., 1937; LL.B. (hon.), Jacksonville U., 1967. Bar: Fla. bar 1937. Mem. firm Fleming, Hamilton, Diver & Jones, Jacksonville, 1937-39, 40-42; with law dept. Fla. br. Prudential Ins. Co. Am., Lakeland, Fla., 1939-40; mem. firm Fleming, Scott & Botts (and predecessor), 1942-55, sr. partner, 1955-57, Botts, Mohoney, Chambers & Adams (and predecessor), Jacksonville, 1957-63; gen. counsel, dir. Barnett Nat. Bank of Jacksonville, 1955-63, pres., chief exec. officer, dir., 1963-70, vice chmn., 1970-73, chmn., 1973—; pres., chief exec. officer The Charter Co., 1960-63; chmn., dir. Charter Mortgage & Investment Co., 1960-63; pres. Barnett Banks Fla., Inc. (formerly Barnett Nat. Securities Corp.), 1963-72, chmn. bd., 1973—, Nat. Bankamericard, Inc., 1973-75; dir. Gulf United Corp., Rhodes, Inc., Fla. Pub. Co. Compiled: Brit. Statutes in Force in Florida, 1943; Editor: Banks and banking statutes sect. Fla. Law Practice. Past mem. Fla. Devel. Commn.; commr. Uniform State Laws Fla., 1955-59; Chmn. bd. trustees Jacksonville U.; dir., past pres. Duval County Legal Aid Assn.; bd. dirs. Am. Found., Inc. Recipient Gold Key award U.S. Jr. C. of C., 1946; Ted Arnold award Jacksonville Jr. C. of C., 1963, 78. Mem. Am. Coll. Probate Counsel (past regent), Jr. C. of C. (past pres.), U.S. C. of C., Jacksonville Area C. of C. (past pres.), ABA, Jacksonville Bar Assn. (past pres.), Fla. Bar (gov.), Am. Bankers Assn. (governing council), Fla. Bankers Assn., Assn. Bank Holding Cos. (past pres.), Phi Eta Sigma, Phi Alpha Delta, Alpha Kappa Psi, Delta Tau Delta. Clubs: River, Univ., Rotary, Fla. Yacht, Ponte Vedra, Timuquana Country. Home: 3737 Ortega Blvd Jacksonville FL 32210 Office: 100 Laura St Jacksonville FL 32202

BOTTUM, CURTIS EDWARD, JR., contractor; b. Ann Arbor, Mich., June 29, 1927; s. Curtis Edward and Gladys Elizabeth (Jarvis) B.; m. Olivia Graye Boyd, Aug. 8, 1953; children: Olivia Lynn, Carolyn Lee. Student, Iowa State Coll., 1944-46; B.S., U. Mich., 1948, M.S., 1949. Registered profl. engr., Mich., Ohio, Utah. Field engr. Townsend & Bottum, Inc., Pa. and Ohio, 1949-52, Ohio Dist. mgr., Lorain, 1954-59, v.p., Ann Arbor, 1959-67, pres., 1968—; dir. Nat. Bank & Trust Co., Ann Arbor. Served with USN, 1944-46, 52-54. Mem. Nat. Soc. Profl. Engrs., ASCE, Tau Beta Pi, Phi Kappa Phi. Republican. Congregationalist. Club: Rotary. Home: 1620 Covington Dr Ann Arbor MI 48103 Office: 2245 S State St Ann Arbor MI 48106

BOTWINICK, MICHAEL, museum official; b. N.Y.C., Nov. 14, 1943; s. Joseph and Helen (Shlisky) B.; m. Harriet Maltzer, Aug. 14, 1965; children: Jonathan Seth, Daniel Judah. B.A., Rutgers Coll., 1964; M.A., Columbia U., 1967. Instr. Columbia U., N.Y.C., 1968-69, CCNY, CUNY, 1969; asst. curator medieval art Cloisters Met. Mus. Art, N.Y.C., 1969, asso. curator medieval art Cloisters, 1970, asst. curator-in-chief, 1971-74; asst. dir. art Phila. Mus. Art, 1971-74; dir. Bklyn. Mus., 1974-83, Corcoran Gallery Art, 1983—; pres. Cultural Instns. Group, 1975-76; mem. N.Y.C. Adv. Commn. Cultural Affairs, 1975-76, N.Y.C. Urban Design Council, 1975—; adv. bd. WNET, N.Y.C., 1979-83; Mem. Nat. Conservation Adv. Council., 1979-80. Mem. Assn. Art Mus. Dirs., Am. Assn. Museums, Coll. Art Assn. Office: Corcoran Gallery Art 17th St and New York Ave NW Washington DC 20006

BOUBELIK, HENRY FREDRICK, JR., car rental co. exec.; b. Chgo., Aug. 16, 1936; s. Henry Fredrick and Anna Mabel (Short) B.; m. Jane V. Boubelik, Oct. 27, 1978; children—Debra Ann, Henry Fredrick III, Steven W., Catherine Earle. Student, U. Ill., 1954-55, Trinity U., 1957-59. Asst. mgr. Avis Rent-A-Car, San Antonio, 1957-60; city mgr. Hertz Rent-a-Car, Corpus Christi, Tex., 1960-67; regional mgr. Nat. Car Rental System, Inc., Mpls., 1967-69, corporate v.p., 1969—. Mem. adv. bd. Corpus Christi Bayfront, 1963-66. Served with AUS, 1955-57. Mem. Car and Truck Rental and Leasing Assn. (v.p. 1973, dir. 1974-77), Am. Car Rental Assn. (pres. 1980-81). Club: Civitan (dir., pres.-elect 1963-66). Home: 6617 Cornelia Dr Edina MN 55435 Office: 7700 France Ave S Minneapolis MN 55435

BOUCHARD, ROLAND, business executive; b. Montreal, Que., Can., Sept. 11, 1924; s. Joseph Edmond and Valeda (Duchesne) B.; m. Simonne St. Laurent, Aug. 23, 1947; children: Nicole, Ginette, Johanne, Sylvianne. Grad., Sir George Williams U., 1942, Can. Credit Inst., Montreal, 1952. Clk. Imperial Tobacco Ltd., Montreal, 1942-53, supr., 1953-64, mgr., 1964-67, provincial mgr., 1967-70, regional sales mgr., 1970-80, sec., 1980—. Served as student RCAF, 1944-45. Mem. Inst. Chartered Sec. and Adminstrs. (council 1979-83). Home: 1401 Blvd d'Auteuil Duvernay PQ Canada H7E 3J3 Office: 3810 Saint Antoine St Montreal PQ Canada H4C 1B5

BOUCHER, (CHARLES) GENE, baritone; b. Tagbilaren, Bohol, Philippines, Dec. 6, 1933; s. Archie D. and Inez (Vince) B. B.A., Westminster Coll., Fulton, Mo., 1955; Diplome du chant, Conservatoire de Lille, Nord, France, 1956. Debut Teatro Nuovo, Milan, Italy, 1958; soloist Little Orch. Soc. N.Y., Cin. Symphony Orch., Am. Symphony Orch., Orch. Am., Robert Shaw Chorale, Dessoff Choir, Eastman-Rochester Orch., Am. Opera Soc., Chgo. Symphony Orch., Cleve. Orch., N.Y. Choral Soc., Bethlehem Bach Festival, Pa., Newport (R.I.) Festival; debut Met. Opera Co., 1965; other opera appearances include Cin. Summer Opera, Phila. Lyric/Grand Opera, Washington Opera Soc., Met. Opera Studio; N.Y. premiere Help! Help, The Globolinks, N.Y. City Center, 1969, Pitts. Civic Light Opera, 1982. Recorded world premiere: Howard Hanson's Four Psalms for Baritone and Strings, 1964. Winner Am. Opera Auditions, 1958. Mem. Am. Guild Mus. Artists (bd. govs. 1964—, pres. 1977-82, nat. exec. sec. 1982—). Address: 235 W 76th St New York City NY 10023 Office: 1841 Broadway New York NY

BOUCHER, LOUIS JACK, dentist, university administrator; b. Ashland, Wis., May 24, 1922; s. Louis Napoleon and Clara (Rappatta) B.; m. Mary Lynn Phyllis Elsner, Nov. 5, 1949; children: Lynn Marie, Ellen Lou, Carol Joy, John Charles. Student, Northland Coll., 1945-48, U. Wis., 1948-49; D.D.S., Marquette U., 1953, Ph.D., 1961. Dir. grad. studies and research Marquette U. Sch. Dentistry, 1955-65, U. Ky. Coll. Dentistry, 1965-66; asso. dean Med. Coll., Ga. Sch. Dentistry, 1966-71; dean Sch. Dentistry, Fairleigh Dickinson U., 1971-75; assoc. dean Coll. Medicine and Dentistry, N.J. Sch. Dentistry, Newark, 1976-77; assoc. dean, dir. prosthodontics Sch. Dental Medicine, SUNY, Stony Brook, 1978—; cons. VA hosps., U.S. Army, Ft. Jackson, S.C., also Ft. Gordon, Ga., USAF Aerospace Medicine, Surgeon Gen. USAF, Nat. Inst. Dentistry, USPHS, Am. Dental Assn. Council on Dental Edn. Author: (with A.O. Rahn) Maxillofacial Prosthetics, 1970, A Comprehensive Review of Dentistry, 1979, Occlusal Articulation, 1979, Treatment of Partially Endentulous Patients, 1982. Served with AUS, 1942-45. Recipient Nat. Inst. Dental Research Spl. Research fellowship and Career Devel. award, 1961-65. Mem. Am., Internat. colls. dentists, Am. Bd. Prosthodontics, Am. Acad. Maxillofacial Prosthodontics (pres. 1965), Am. Acad. Plastics Research in Dentistry (pres. 1967), Am. Coll. Prosthodontists (pres. 1971), Fedn. Prosthodontics Orgns. (pres. 1967-68), Am. Equilibration Soc. (pres. 1976), Sigma Xi, Omicron Kappa Upsilon. Home: 7 Cedar Rd Port Jefferson NY 11777 Office: Coll Dental Medicine SUNY Stony Brook NY 11794

BOUCHER, ROBERT NORMAN, JR., publisher; b. Elizabeth, N.J., Nov. 30, 1946; s. Robert Norman and Charlotte Estelle (Kramer) B.; m. Mary Lou Alfano, Aug. 24, 1968; children: Brian Robert, Michael Brandon. B.A., Bucknell U., 1968. Field sales rep. Scott Paper Co., Pitts., 1968-69; mktg. services mgr. Comml. Car Jour., Radnor, Pa., 1969-72, regional mgr., 1972-74; nat. sales mgr. Chilton Book Co., Radnor, 1974-76; pub. Motor Age mag., Radnor, 1976—; pres. Tech. Info. Distbn. Ser., 1981—. Mem. Automotive Warehouse Distbrs. Assn., Bus. and Profl. Advertisers Assn., Am. Bus. Press. Home: 1427 Cider Knoll Way West Chester PA 19380 Office: 638 E Lancaster Ave Frazer PA 19355

BOUDART, MICHEL, chemical engineering educator; b. Belgium, June 18, 1924; came to U.S., 1947, naturalized, 1957; s. Francois and Marguerite (Swolfs) B.; m. Marina D'Haese, Dec. 27, 1948; children: Mark, Baudouin, Iris, Philip. B.S., U. Louvain, Belgium, 1944, M.S., 1947; Ph.D., Princeton U., 1950. Research asso. James Forrestal Research Center, Princeton, 1950-54; mem. faculty Princeton U., 1954-61; prof. chem. engring. U. Calif. - Berkeley, 1961-64; prof. chem. engring. and chemistry Stanford U., 1964-80, William J. Keck prof. chem. engring., 1980—; cons. to industry, 1955—; dir. Catalytica Assos., Inc.; Humble Oil Co. lectr., 1958, Am. Inst. Chem. Engrs. lectr., 1961, Sigma Xi nat. lectr., 1965; chmn. Gordon Research Conf. Catalysis, 1962. Author: Kinetics of Chemical Processes, 1968, (with A. Djéga-Mariadassov) Kinetics of Heterogeneous Catalytic Reactions, 1983; editor: (with J.R. Anderson) Catalysis: Science and Technology, 1981; adv. editorial bd.: Jour. Catalysis, 1964—, Internat. Chem. Engring., 1964—, Advances in Catalysis, 1968—, Catalysis Rev., 1968—, Accounts Chem. Research, 1978—. Belgium-Am. Ednl. Found. fellow, 1948; Procter fellow, 1949; Recipient Curtis-McGraw research award Am. Soc. Engring. Edn., 1962, R.H. Wilhelm award in chem. reaction engring., 1974. Fellow AAAS; mem. Am. Chem. Soc. (Kendall award 1977), Catalysis Soc., Am. Inst. Chem. Engrs., Chem. Soc., Nat. Acad. Sci., Nat. Acad. Engring.; fgn. assoc. Académie Royale de Belgique. Home: 512 Gerona Rd Stanford CA 94305 Office: Dept Chem Engring Stanford Univ Stanford CA 94305

BOUDIN, LEONARD B., lawyer; b. 1912. B.S.S., CCNY; LL.B., St. John's U., Bklyn. Bar: N.Y. 1936, U.S. Supreme Ct.; others. Ptnr. firm Rabinowitz, Boudin, Standard, Krinsley & Lieberman, P.C., N.Y.C.; Am. counsel govts. of Cuba, Greece, Angola and other countries, also central banks of Cuba and Iran; vis. prof. Harvard Law Sch.; lectr. Yale Law Sch., 1974; disting. vis. prof. U. Calif.-Berkeley, 1975, Stanford Law Sch., 1985; gen. counsel Nat. Emergency Civil Liberties Com., 1952—, Bill of Rights Found.; Mem. adv. bd. William O. Douglas Found. Contbr. articles to Harvard Law Rev., other legal jours. Hon. fellow U. Pa. Law Sch.; Mem. Am. Law Inst., Nat. Lawyers Guild, Am. Soc. Internat. Law. Office: 30 E 42d St New York NY 10017

BOUDIN, MICHAEL, lawyer; b. N.Y.C., Nov. 29, 1939; s. Leonard B. and Jean (Roisman) B. B.A., Harvard Coll., 1961, LL.B., 1964. Bar: N.Y. 1964, D.C. 1967. Clk. U.S. Ct. Appeals, 2 d cir., 1964-65, U.S. Sup. Ct., 1965-66; assoc. firm Covington & Burling, Washington, 1966—, ptnr., 1972—; vis. prof. Harvard Law Sch., 1982-83, lectr., 1983-84. Contbr. revs. to law jours. Mem. ABA, Am. Law Inst. Office: Covington & Burling 1201 Pennsylvania Ave NW PO Box 7566 Washington DC 20044

BOUDOULAS, HARISIOS, physician; b. Velvendo-Kozani, Greece, Nov. 3, 1935; married; 2 children. M.D., U. Salonica, Greece, 1959. Resident in medicine Red Cross Hosp., Athens, Greece, 1960-61, First Med. Clinic, U. Salonica, 1962-64, resident in internal medicine, 1964-66, resident in cardiology, 1967-69, lectr., 1969-70; postgrad fellow, instr. div. cardiology Ohio State U. Coll. Medicine, 1970-73, 75, asst. prof. medicine, 1975-78, assoc. prof., 1978-80, dir. cardiac non-invasive lab., 1978-80, prof. medicine, div. cardiology, 1983—, dir. cardiovascular research div., 1983—; prof. medicine div. cardiology Wayne State U., Detroit, 1980-82, chief clin. cardiovascular research, 1980-82, acting dir. div. cardiology, Detroit, 1982; chief cardiovascular diagnostic and tng. center VA Med. Center, Allen Park, Mich., 1980-83; acting chief sect. cardiology Harper-Grace Hosps., Detroit, 1982; co-dir. Overstreet Teaching and Research Labs. Contbr. numerous articles to med. jours. Disting. research investigator Central Ohio Heart chpt. Am. Heart Assn., Columbus, 1983. Fellow A.C.P., Am. Coll. Angiology, Am. Coll. Clin. Pharmacology, Council Clin. Cardiology, Am. Coll. Cardiology; mem. Am. Heart Assn., Greek Heart Assn., Greek Com. Against Hypertension, Central Soc. Clin. Research, Am. Fedn. Clin. Research. Home: 2108 MacKenzie Dr Columbus OH 43220 Office: Ohio State U Div Cardiology 466 W 10th Ave Columbus OH 43210

BOUDREAUX, JOHN, newspaper editor; b. Franklin, La., July 28, 1946; s. Abel John and Dorothy (Bourgeois) B. B.A., La. State U., 1969. Reporter, copy editor Morning Advocate, Baton Rouge, 1969-71; successively reporter, copy editor, asst. city editor Houston Post, 1971-76, city editor, 1976—. Home: 1116 Bering Dr 19 Houston TX 77057 Office: 4747 Southwest Freeway Houston TX 77001

BOUDREAUX, WARREN LOUIS, bishop; b. Berwick, La., Jan. 25, 1918; s. Alphonse Louis and Loretta Marie (Senac) B. Student, St. Joseph's Sem., Benedict, La., 1931-36, Notre Dame Sem., New Orleans, 1937, 42, LL.D., 1963, Grand Sem. de St. Sulpice, Paris, France, 1938-39; J.C.D., Catholic U. Am., 1946; D.D.; hon., Pope John XXIII, 1962. Ordained priest Roman Catholic Ch., 1942; asst. pastor, Crowley, La., 1942-43; vice chancellor Diocese of Lafayette, La., 1946-54, officialis, 1949-54; Vicar gen., 1957-61, aux. bishop., 1962-71; pastor St. Peter's Ch., New Iberia, La., 1954-71; bishop of Beaumont, Tex., 1971-77, bishop of Houma-Thibodaux, La., 1977—; dean New Iberia Deanery, 1954-71; Vice pres. S.W. La. Registry Newspaper, 1957-75; Mem. New Iberia Community Relations Council, 1963-71, U.S. Bishops Liturgical Commn., 1966-70, U.S. Bishop's Louvain Coll. Commn., 1970-76; imem. adv. council U.S. Cath. Conf., 1969-73; chmn. liaison com. Nat. Conf. Cath. Bishops, 1972-75, mem. liturgy commn., 1975—, mem. com. on canon law, 1975-78; state chaplain K.C. State of Tex., 1975-77; nat. moderator Marriage Encounter in U.S.A., 1975-77; mem. La. Cath. Conf., 1977—, La. Interch. Conf., 1977—. Bd. dirs. S.W. Ednl. Devel. Lab., Iberia Paris Youth Home, Consolata Home for Aged, New Iberia.; Pres. Archdiocesan Conf. Chancery Ofcls. Archdiocese New Orleans, 1950-51, bd. dirs., 1952-55. Address: PO Box 9077 Houma LA 70361

BOUEY, GERALD KEITH, bank exec.; b. Axford, Sask., Can., Apr. 2, 1920; s. John Alexander and Inez Amanda B.; m. Anne Margaret Ferguson, Aug. 8, 1945; children—Kathryn, Robert. Hon. B.A., Queen's U., Kingston, Ont., Can., 1948. Bank clk. Royal Bank of Can., Moosomin, Sask., 1936-40; with Bank of Can., Ottawa, Ont., 1948—, sr. dep. gov., 1972-73, gov., 1973—; dir. Export Devel. Corp., Fed. Bus. Devel. Bank, Can. Deposit Ins. Corp. Served with RCAF, 1941-45. Mem. Can. Econs. Assn. Mem. United Ch. Can. Clubs: Can., Royal Ottawa Golf. Office: 234 Wellington St Ottawa ON K1A 0G9 Canada *

BOUGAS, STANLEY JOHN, librarian, educator; b. Norfolk, Va., Dec. 7, 1921; s. John Constantine and Sapho (Zographos) B.; m. Athena Douvarges, July 4, 1948; children: Athena Joanna, Althea June. A.B., N.Y. U., 1950; M.S. in L.S, Columbia U., 1952; J.D., Emory U., 1962. Asst. librarian Assn. Bar City N.Y., 1946-53; asst. reference librarian N.Y. U. Sch. Law Library, N.Y.C., 1953-54; librarian Emory U. Sch. Law, Atlanta, 1954-61, adminstrv. asst. to dean, 1961-62; librarian, assoc. prof. Catholic U. P.R. Sch. Law, Ponce, 1962-65; librarian HEW Law Library, Washington, 1965-66; librarian, assoc. prof. Washington Coll. Law, Am. U., Washington, 1966-69; dir. U.S. Dept. Commerce Library, Washington, 1969—; spl. asst. tech. adviser, assoc. dir. Office Product and Market Devel. Dept. Commerce Nat. Tech. Info. Service, 1982-83; lectr. Inter-Am. U., Ponce extension, 1963-65; adj. lectr. legal lit. Sch. Library and Info. Service, U. Md., 1966-77; adj. lectr. Potomac Sch. Law, 1975-80; lectr. AJ Seminars, 1979—; cons. in field. Served with USAF, 1942-45.

Mem. ALA (pres. Fed. Librarians Roundtable 1973), Fed. Library Assn. (pres. 1974), Spl. Libraries Assn., Am. Assn. Law Libraries, Law Librarians Soc. Washington, Phi Alpha Delta. Democrat. Greek Orthodox. Clubs: Masons, Toastmasters. Home: 2801 Park Center Dr Alexandria VA 22302 Office: 14th St and Constitution Ave Washington DC 20230

BOUGHTON, JERRY DEAN, banker; b. Rayville, La., Nov. 26, 1932; s. Leon Douglas and Eva Mary (Moore) B.; m. Thelma Jane Mckinney, July 4, 1958; children: David, Laura. B.S., La. Tech. U., 1955; cert., Stonier Grad. Sch. Banking, Rutgers U., 1966. Vice pres. First Nat. Bank, Shreveport, Tex., 1975-81, pres., Shreveport, 1981—. Served to lt. USAF, 1955-58; ETO. Mem. La. Bankers Assn. (chmn. com. 1980-82), Am. Inst. Banking (exec. council Washington 1972-76). Democrat. Presbyterian. Club: Shreveport. Home: 551 Lloyd Ln Shreveport LA 71106 Office: First Nat Bank of Shreveport 400 Texas St Shreveport LA 71154

BOUGHTON, WALTER LEROY, theater educator; b. Toledo, Dec. 27, 1918; s. Solon James and Theodora Ferguson (Prince) B.; m. Gerogia Dagmar Aune, June 9, 1950; 3 sons. A.B., Brown U., 1941, M.A., 1949, M.F.A., 1951. Instr. speech and drama English dept. Brown U., Providence, R.I., 1947-49; Fulbright scholar Shakespeare Inst., Straford, Eng., 1951-52; chmn. drama dept. Ripon Coll., Wis., 1953-56; vis. dir. theater U. Calif-Berkeley, 1956-57; chmn. dept. dramatic arts, dir. Kirby Meml. Theater Amherst Coll., Mass., 1957—; dir. Keuka Coll. Summer Theater, 1950-53, Casino Theater, Holyoke, Mass., summer 1960; producer, dir. Weston Playhouse, Vt., 1972—; actor summer stock, 1950—; actor in film supporting role Universal Studios, 1969. Served to capt. USAAF, 1941-46. Mem. Amherst Edn. Assn., chmn. summer theater project (1959-61); mem. Am. Theater Assn., Am. Nat. Theater Assn. Office: Kirby Meml Theater Amherst Coll Amherst MA 01002 Home: 326 Shays St Amherst MA 01002 *

BOUISSAC, PAUL ANTOINE, educator; b. Perigueux, France, Jan. 17, 1934; emigrated to Can., 1962; s. Antoine Louis and Marguerite Marie (Frene) B. Licence-es-Lettres, U. Paris, 1956, D. Linguistics, 1970. Lectr. in French Victoria Coll., U. Toronto, 1962-65, asst. prof., 1965-69, asso. prof., 1969-74, prof., 1974—; vis. prof. State U. N.Y., Buffalo, 1975, U. Fla., 1975. Author: Les Demoiselles, 1970, La Mesure des Gestes, 1973, Circus and Culture, 1976; Editor-in-chief: Recherches Sémiotiques/Semiotic Inquiry. Circus cons. Berliner Festwochen, 1977-78. Served with French Air Force, 1959-61. Can. Council grantee, 1968, 70, 77-78; Wenner-Gren Found. grantee, 1970; Netherlands Inst. for Advanced Studies fellow, 1972-73; Guggenheim Found. fellow, 1973-74. Mem. Modern Lang. Assn., Am. Anthrop. Assn., Am. Folklore Soc., Linguistics Soc. Am., Semiotic Soc. Am., N.Y. Acad. Scis. Office: 73 Queens Park Toronto ON M5S 1K7 Canada *I have always tried to refrain from indulging in all-encompassing and absolute projects—either intellectual or political—which I view as mere verbalism. This principle does not exclude long range planning nor a philosophy of action, but in my opinion, secures the possibility for humor, tolerance and efficiency.*

BOULDING, ELISE MARIE, sociologist, educator; b. Oslo, Norway, July 6, 1920; came to U.S., 1923, naturalized, 1929; d. Joseph and Birgit (Johnsen) Biorn-Hansen; m. Kenneth Boulding; Aug. 31, 1941; children: John Russell, Mark David, Christine Ann, Philip Daniel, William Frederic. B.A., Douglass Coll., 1940; M.S., Iowa State Coll., 1949; Ph.D., U. Mich., 1969. Research asso. Survey Research Inst., U. Mich., 1957-58, Mental Health Research Inst., 1959-60; research devel. sec. Center for Research on Conflict Resolution, 1960-63; prof. sociology, project dir. Inst. Behavioral Sci., U. Colo., Boulder, 1967-78; Montgomery vis. prof. Dartmouth Coll., 1978-79, chmn. dept. sociology, 1979—; mem. program adv. council Human and Social Devel. Program, UN Univ., 1977-80, v.p. governing council, 1980—. Translator: Polak Image of the Future, 1961; author: From a Monastery Kitchen, 1976, (with Nuss, Carson and Greenstein) Handbook of International Data on Women, 1976, The Underside of History: A View of Women Through Time, 1976, Women in Twentieth Century World, 1977, (with Passmore and Gassler) Bibliography on World Conflict and Peace, 1979, (with Burgess and K. Boulding) Social System of Planet Earth, 1980, Children's Rights and the Wheel of Life, 1980, (with Moen, Lilleydahl and Palm) Women and the Social Costs of Economic Development, 1981. Internat. chairperson Womens Internat. League for Peace and Freedom, 1967-70; mem. U.S. Commn. for UNESCo, 1978—; bd. dirs. Inst. for World Order. Recipient Disting. Achievement award Douglass Coll., 1973, Ted Lentz Peace prize, 1977; Danforth fellow, 1965-67; Faculty fellow U. Colo., 1974. Mem. AAAS, AAUP, Am. Sociol. Assn., Internat. Sociol. Assn., Internat. Peace Research Assn., Internat. Studies Assn., Nat. Council Family Relations, World Future Studies Fedn., World Future Soc., Colo. Women's Forum. Quaker. Home: 890 Willowbrook Rd Boulder CO 80302 Office: Dept Sociology Dartmouth Coll Hanover NH 03755

BOULDING, KENNETH EWART, economics educator; b. Liverpool, Eng., Jan. 18, 1910; came to U.S., 1937, naturalized, 1948; s. William Couchman and Elizabeth Ann (Rowe) B.; m. Elise Biorn-Hansen, Aug. 31, 1941; children: Russell, Mark, Christine, Philip, William. Scholar, New Coll., Oxford U., 1928-32; B.A. first class honors, Oxford U., 1931; M.A., 1939; Commonwealth fellow, U. Chgo., 1932-34. Asst. U. Edinburgh, Scotland, 1934-37; instr. Colgate U., 1937-41; economist League of Nations Econ. and Financial Sect., 1941-42; prof. Fisk U., 1942-43; assoc. prof. Iowa State Coll., 1943-46; Angus prof. polit. economy McGill U., 1946-47; prof. Iowa State Coll., 1947-49; prof. econs. U. Mich., 1949-68; research dir. Center for Research in Conflict Resolution, 1964-66; vis. prof. U. Colo., Boulder, 1967-68, prof., 1968-77, disting. prof., 1977-80, disting. prof. emeritus, 1980—; dir. program on gen. social and econ. dynamics Inst. Behavioral Sci., 1967-81, research assoc., dir. program on polit. and econ. change, 1981—; vis. prof. Univ. Coll., West Indies, Kingston, Jamaica, 1959-60, U. Natal, 1970, U. Edinburgh, 1972; Danforth vis. prof. Internat. Christian U., Tokyo, 1963-64; Andrew D. White prof.-at-large Cornell U., 1974-79; disting. vis. Tom Slick prof. world peace L.B. Johnson Sch., U. Tex., Austin, 1976-77; Montgomery vis. prof. Dartmouth Coll., 1978; disting. vis. prof. Sch. Public Adminstrn., Ohio State U., 1981; Downing fellow Melbourne U., (Australia), 1982; Eugene M. Lang vis. prof. social change Swarthmore Coll., 1982-83. Author: Economic Analysis, 1941, 4th rev. edit., 1966, Economics of Peace, 1945, 2d edit., 1972, There Is a Spirit (The Naylor Sonnets), 1945, A Reconstruction of Economics, 1950, The Organizational Revolution, 1953, The Image, 1956, Principles of Economic Policy, 1958, The Skills of the Economist, 1958, Conflict and Defense, 1962, The Meaning of the Twentieth Century, 1964, The Impact of the Social Sciences, 1966, Beyond Economics, 1968, Economics as a Science, 1970, A Primer on Social Dynamics, 1970, The Prospering of Truth (Swarthmore Lecture), 1970, Collected Papers, Vols. 1-5, 1971-75, The Appraisal of Change (in Japanese), 1972, The Economy of Love and Fear, 1973, Sonnets from the Interior Life and Other Autobiographical Verse, 1975, (with Elise Boulding, Guy M. Burgess) The Social System of the Planet Earth, 1977, 80, Stable Peace, 1978, Ecodynamics, 1978, Beasts, Ballads and Bouldingisms, 1980, Evolutionary Economics, 1981, A Preface to Grants Economics, 1981; editor: (with George J. Stigler) Readings in Price Theory, 1952, (with W.A. Spivey) Linear Programming and the Theory of the Firm, 1960, (with Emile Benoit) Disarmament and the Economy, 1963, Peace and the War Industry, 1970, 73, (with Tapan Mukerjee) Economic Imperialism, 1972, (with Martin Pfaff) Redistribution to the Rich and the Poor, 1972, (with Martin and Anita Pfaff) Transfers in an Urbanized Economy, 1973, (with Thomas F. Wilson) Redistribution through the Financial System, 1978, (with H.R. Porter) General Systems Yearbook, Vol. 23, 1979. Recipient John B. Clark medal Am. Econ. Assn., 1949, prize for distinguished scholarship in humanities Am. Council Learned Socs., 1962; Frank E. Seidman Distinguished award in polit. economy, 1976; Rufus Jones award World Acad. Art and Sci., 1979; fellow Center Advanced Study Behavior Scis., Palo Alto, Calif., 1954-55. Fellow Nat. Acad. Scis., Am. Acad. Arts and Scis., Am. Philos. Soc., Brit. Acad. (coor.); mem. Am. Econ. Assn. (pres. 1968), Nat. Acad. Sci. Inst. of Medicine (sr. 1983—), Soc. Gen. Systems Research (pres. 1957-59), Internat. Studies Assn. (v.p. 1969-70, pres. 1974-75), AAAS (v.p., chmn. sect. K 1966-67, pres. 1979, chmn. bd. dirs. 1980), Peace Research Soc. Internat. (pres. 1969-70), Assn. Study Grants Economy (pres. 1969—), Acad. Ind. Scholars (co-pres. 1980—), Brit. Assn. for Advancement of Sci. (pres. sect. on econs. 1982-83). Mem. Soc. of Friends. Home: 890 Willowbrook Rd Boulder CO 80302

BOULET, GILLES, university president; b. Quebec, P.Q., Can., June 5, 1926; s. Georges Alidor and Yvonne (Hamel) B.; m. Florence Lemire, May 15, 1971; children: Laurent, Marie-Claude. L.th. Catholic U. Paris, 1951; L.Ph., 1953; M.A., 1953; D.E.S., 1954. Prof. lit. and history Sem. Ste.-Marie (Shawinigan), Que., 1953-61, Centre d'etudes universitaires de Trois-Rivieres, 1961-66; prof. French Faculty Lit. Laval U., Quebec, 1955-62; aggregate prof. Faculty Arts, 1959; founder, dir. Centre d'etudes universiraires de Trois-Rivieres, 1960-69; rector U. Quebec a Trois-Rivieres, 1969-78; pres. U. Quebec, 1978—; bd. dirs. Centre de relations internationales, Centre internat. recherche et e'etude en mgmt.; v.p. G.A. Boulet Ltee. Author: books on secondary sch. Can. history, nat. affairs. Recipient Duvernay award La Soc. St. Jean Baptiste de Trois-Rivieres, 1978. Mem. Conf. Rectors and Prins. Univs. Que. (pres.), Assn. universitaire interamericaine (pres.), Assn. Univs. and Colls. Can., Assn. Univs. partiellement ou entierement langue francaise, Assn. Commonwealth Univs., Internat. Assn. Univs., Internat. Assn. U. Presidents, Inst. d'aminstrn. publique Can., Centre quebecois de relations internat., Inst. canadien des affairs internat., French C. of C., Can., C. of C. and Industry Met., Quebec, C. of C. Dist. Montreal, Soc. ecrivains de la Mauricie. Roman Catholic. Clubs: Garrison, Cercle Universitaire (Quebec); St. Maurice Hunting and Fishong. Home: 3021 de la Promenande Ste Foy PQ G1W 2J5 Canada Office: 2875 Laurier Blvd Ste Foy PQ G1V 2M3 Canada

BOULET, ROGER HENRI, art gallery director; b. Winnipeg, Man., Can., Feb. 15, 1944; s. Henri Elzear and Jeanne (Bourget) B. B.F.A. with honors, U. Man., 1970. Dir. curator Burnaby Art Gallery, B.C., 1981—. Author: F.M. Bell-Smith, 1978, The Silent Thunder, 1981, The Tranquility and the Turbulence, 1981, The Canadian Earth, 1982. Can. Council grantee, 1970. Office: Burnaby Art Gallery 6344 Gilpin St Burnaby BC Canada V5G 2J3

BOULEZ, PIERRE, composer, conductor; b. Montbrison, nr. Clermont-Ferrand, France, Mar. 26, 1925; s. Leon and Marcelle (Calabre) B. Pupil, Olivier Messiaen at Paris Conservatory,. Apptd. dir. music Jean-Louis Barrault's Theater Co., 1948; now tchr., lectr., condr.; musical adviser, prin. guest condr. Cleve. Symphony Orch., 1970-71; musical dir. N.Y. Philharmonic Orch., 1971-77; dir. I.R.C.A.M., 1976—. Toured, Orient, Europe, North and South Am., (with Barrault), conducting appearances include, Edinburgh Festival, 1965, Bayreuth Festival, 1966, 76-80; Compositions include Sonatina for flute and piano, 1946, Three Piano Sonatas, 1946, 50, 57, Le Soleil des eaux for voice and orchestra, 1948, Structures, 1952, Le Marteau sans maitre, 1955, Deux improvisations sur Mallarme, 1957; performed, Hamburg, 1958, Polyphony, Donaueschingen Festival, 1951, Doubles for orchestra, 1958, Tombeau, (on text of Mallarmé), 1959, Pli selon pli, 1960, Structures II, 1962, Eclat, 1964, Domaines, 1968, Multiples, 1970, Cummings ist der Dichter, 1970, Explosante/Fixe, 1973, Rituel, 1975, Messagesquisse, 1977, Notations, part I, 1980; Répons, 1981; author: musical criticism and analysis, including Penser la Musique d'Aujourd'hui. Address: Postfach 22 Baden-Baden Germany Office: IRCAM 31 rue St Merri 75004 Paris France

BOULGER, FRANCIS WILLIAM, metallurgical engineer; b. Mpls., June 19, 1913; s. Francis J. and Mary (Armstrong) B. Metall. Engr., U. Minn., 1934; M.S. (Battelle fellow), Ohio State U., 1937. With A.P., 1929-34; engr. Minn. Dept. Hwys., 1935-36; metallurgist Republic Steel Corp., Cleve., 1937; research metallurgist Battelle Meml. Inst., Columbus, Ohio, 1938-45, div. chief, 1945-67, sr. tech. adviser, 1967—; cons. USAF; Materials Adv. Bd. OECD. Author: (with others) Forging Materials and Practices, 1968, Tri-Lingual Dictionary of Production Engineering, 1969, Forging Equipment, Materials and Practices, 1973; also numerous articles. Named Man of Yr. Columbus Tech. Council, 1966; Gold medalist Soc. Mfg. Engrs., 1967; recipient Am. Machinist award, 1975. Fellow Am. Soc. Metals, ASME; mem. AIME (Hunt medal 1955), Soc. Mfg. Engrs., Nat. Acad. Engring., Internat. Inst. for Prodn. Research (pres.), Sigma Xi. Roman Catholic. Home: 1816 Harwich Rd Columbus OH 43221 Office: 505 King Ave Columbus OH 43201

BOULLIANNE, GEORGE EMILE, manufacturing company executive; b. Whitestone, N.Y., Jan. 14, 1931; s. George Joseph B. and Catherine Anne (Connolly) Boulliane; m. Lesley Ann Knoll, Aug. 3, 1964; children: William Kerry, Steven Douglas. B.B.A., Hofstra Coll., 1959. Acct. Coppers & Lybrand, N.Y.C., 1959-65; corp. audit staff Litton Industries, Inc., Beverrly Hills, Calif., 1965-66, v.p. treas., Beverly Hills, Calif., 1967—; corp. staff Teledyne, Inc., Hawthorne, Calif., 1965-67. Served with USN, 1951-55. Mem. Am. Inst. C.P.A.s, N.Y. Soc. C.P.A.s. Republican. Roman Catholic. Clubs: Bel-Air Country (Calif.); Jack Kramer (Rolling Hills Estates, Calif.). Home: 4828 Falconrock Pl Rancho Palos Verdes CA 90274 Office: Litton Industries Inc 360 N Crescent Dr Beverly Hills CA 90210

BOULOS, SAMI IBRAHIM, educator; b. Cairo, Egypt, Feb. 27, 1922; came to U.S., 1958, naturalized, 1968; s. Ibrahim and Ester (Ibrahim) B.; m. Jeanne Makari Salib, July 31, 1949; children—Kamal, Fouad, Michael. B.S., U. Cairo, 1941; H.D.Ed., U. Ein-Shams, 1943, M.A., 1957; Ed.D., U. Fla., 1960. Sci. tchr. campus sch. U. Ein Shams, Cairo, 1943-47; tchr. biology, gen. sci. pub. secondary schs., Cairo, 1947-51, tchr. sci. methods, ednl. psychology, tchr. tng. insts., Egypt, 1951-55; sci. and math. cons. State U. of N.Y. Coll. of New Paltz, 1959-62, asso. prof. sci., math., evaluation, 1962-69, prof. sci. edn., chmn. dept. edn., 1969-73, asso. dean edn., 1973-76, acting dean edn., 1976-78; Field reader U.S. Office Edn., 1966-69; pres. Assn. on World U.; sci. cons. pub. sch. systems; speaker before civic and ednl. groups. Author: Biology for the Senior High Schools, 1955; also articles. Recipient Point 4 award AID, 1955-56. Mem. Nat. Sci. Tchrs. Assn., Nat. Assn. Research in Sci., Teaching, Higher Edn. Assn., Kappa Delta Pi, Phi Delta Kappa. Home: B13 Duzine Rd New Paltz NY 12561 *When you belong to a minority group, you have to work extra hard to achieve success. Dedication to an idea or a group of ideas is extremely important. Another component of success also is sincerity. One has to be true to his cause and try to go about accomplishing it, regardless of the consequences. Honesty also is a very important component. Finally, it has been my experience that throughout all my life there was a quiet, deep faith in God. This was the thing that sustained me during the low points of my life and kept my hopes alive.*

BOULT, REYNALD, laywer; b. Hull, Que., Can., Nov. 20, 1916; s. Richard and Alice (Larose) B.; m. Lyone Migneron, Oct. 5, 1940; children: Francine, Marcel, Lucile. B.A., B.Ph., U. Ottawa, 1938, LL.L., 1958. Bar: called to Que. bar 1959, created queen's counsel 1976. Officer Insp. Bd. U.K. and Can., 1940-45; adminstr. European relief campaigns UNRRA, 1945-47; reviser translation debates Office Sec. State Can., 1947-60; solicitor Sec. State Dept., 1960-62; librarian Supreme Ct., Can., 1962-79. Author: A Bibliography of Canadian Law, 1977; contbr. articles to jours. Club: Cercle Universitaire (Ottawa). Home: 330 Metcalfe St Ottawa ON K2P 1S4 Canada

BOULTINGHOUSE, MARION CRAIG BETTINGER, editor; b. New Albany, Ind., Oct. 7, 1930; d. Losson Edward and Marion Craig (Klarer) Bettinger; m. Ray Allen Boultinghouse, Jan. 1, 1973. Student, Hanover Coll., 1948-50; B.S. 4Fla. So. Coll, 1952; M.Ed., U. Louisville, 1960. Tchr. pub. schs., Lakeland, Fla., 1952, New Albany, 1953-55, 58-60, New Haven, 1955-58; editor Am. Edn. Publs., Middletown, Conn., 1960-63, Holt, Rinehart & Winston, N.Y.C., 1963-64, 69-72, Macmillan, Inc., 1964-69, 72-75, editorial dir., v.p. sch. div., 1975-79; pres. Boultinghouse & Boultinghouse Inc., pub. consultants, N.Y.C., 1976—. Author: Follow Me, Everybody, 1968. Office: 153 E 30th St New York NY 10016

BOULWARE, LEMUEL RICKETTS, retired industrial executive; b. Springfield, Ky., June 3, 1895; s. Judson A. and Martha Price (Ricketts) B.; m. Norma Brannock, Dec. 28, 1935. A.B., U. Wis., 1916; L.H.D., Center Coll., 1953; LL.D., Carroll Coll., 1954, Union Coll., 1957; ScD., Clarkson Coll., 1962; D.Edn. in Econs. (hon.), Hillsdale (Mich.) Coll., 1980. Tchr. bus. adminstrn. U. Wis., 1916-17; tchr. Bklyn. night schs., 1919-20; comptroller E. W. Bliss Co., Hastings (Mich.) div., 1919; purchasing agt., factory mgr. H. B. Sherman Mfg. Co., Battle Creek, Mich., 1920-25; gen. sales mgr. Easy Washing Machine Corp., Syracuse, N.Y., 1925-35; v.p., gen. mgr. Carrier Corp., Syracuse, 1936-39, Celotex Corp., Chgo., 1940-42; asst. to chmn. WPB, 1942, dep. comptroller shipbuilding, 1942-43, operations vice chmn., 1943-44; mem. prodn. exec. com. and standardization of shipbuilding design com. of Combined Chiefs of Staff; with Gen. Electric Co. as marketing cons. and in charge affiliated mfg. cos., 1945; v.p., 1945-47, in charge employee, community and union relations, 1947-56, v.p. public and employee relations, 1956-59, v.p. cons. relations services, 1959-61. Author: The Truth about Boularism: Trying To Do Right Voluntarily, 1969, What You Can Do about Inflation, Unemployment, Productivity, Profit and Collective Bargaining, 1972; lectr., writer, cons. Served as capt., inf. U.S. Army, 1917-19. Recipient Medal of Merit for War Service; Distinguished Am. Citizen award Harding Coll., 1963. Baptist. Clubs: Century (Syracuse); Triton (Can.); Santee (S.C.); Blind Brook (Purchase, N.Y.); Round Hill (Greenwich, Conn.); Gulfstream Golf (Fla.); Gulfstream Bath and Tennis. Home: 1045 S Ocean Blvd Delray Beach FL 33444

BOUMA, ROBERT EDWIN, diversified company executive, lawyer; b. Ft. Dodge, Iowa, July 19, 1938; s. Jack and Gladys (Cooper) B.; m. Susan Lawson, Nov. 26, 1963; children: Jimmy, Whitley. B.A., Coe Coll., 1960; J.D., U. Iowa, 1962. Bar: Iowa 1962, N.Y. 1964. Asso. Cravath, Swaine & Moore, N.Y.C., 1962-70; gen. counsel Xerox Data Systems Co., Los Angeles, 1970-73; sr. group counsel Xerox Corp., Rochester, N.Y., 1973-76; asso. gen. counsel Monsanto Co., St. Louis, 1976-78; sr. v.p., gen. counsel Household Fin. Corp., Prospect Heights, Ill., 1978—. Trustee Coe Coll. Served with USN, 1962-63. Mem. Internat. Bar Assn., Fed. Bar Assn., ABA, Chgo. Bar Assn., Am. Soc. Corp. Secs., Am. Judicature Soc., Nat. Lawyers Club. Clubs: Riviera Tennis (Pacific Palisades, Calif.); Winter, Onwentsia (Lake Forest, Ill.). Home: 901 Church Rd Lake Forest IL 60045 Office: 2700 Sanders Rd Prospect Heights IL 60070

BOUMAN, HARRY DAAN, physician; b. Amsterdam, Netherlands, June 27, 1907; came to U.S., 1931, naturalized, 1943; s. Zweitse Pieter and Riemke (Slaterus) B.; m. Elizabeth S. Loeks, June 15, 1940; 1 dau., Jeanne Marie. Candidate deg. in physics U. Amsterdam, 1928, M.D., 1933. Research instr. Oberlin (Ohio) Coll., 1931-32; staff mem. Univ. Eye Clinic, Amsterdam; research asso. physiology U., Amsterdam, 1932-35, 36-39; asst. prof. psychology U. Rochester, 1941-44; asst. prof. phys. medicine Northwestern U., 1944-47; prof. phys. medicine U. Wis., 1947-64; prof., chmn. dept. phys. medicine and rehab. U. Cin. Coll. Medicine, 1965-68; physician VA, 1968-70; dir. phys. medicine rehab. service VA Central Office, Washington, 1971-72, spl. asst. chief med. dir., 1972-73; chief of staff, VA Hosp, Phoenix, 1973-77, chief rehab. medicine, Fresno (Calif.) VA Med. Center, 1977—. Author: papers med. and sci. jours. Editor Am. Jour. Phys. Medicine, 1952—. Stokvis Found. fellow physiology U. Paris, 1928; Rockefeller fellow Univ. Coll., London, Eng., 1935-36; research fellow physiology and orthopedics U. Rochester, 1940-41; orthopedics, 1941-44; research fellow physiology Washington U., 1940; Recipient Gold medal for original research in physiology U. Amsterdam, 1931. Fellow Am. Psychol. Assn., AAAS; mem. Am. Physiol. Soc., The Biophys. Soc., Audio Engring. Soc. Address: PO Box 617 Downtown Station Phoenix AZ 85001

BOUNDS, VERNON LELAND, law educator; b. Salisbury, Md., Oct. 13, 1918; s. Floyd Solan and Lula F. (German) B.; m. Marjorie Belle Sorrell, July 15, 1966; children: Barbara Lee, Michael Frederick. Student, UCLA, 1941; LL.B., U. Va., 1949; postgrad., U. Pa., 1950-51. Bigelow fellow U. Chgo. Law Sch., 1949-50; prof. Inst. Govt., U. N.C., Chapel Hill, 1952-65, William Rand Kenan, Jr. prof. public law and adminstrn., 1973—; chmn. curriculum adminstrn. of criminal justice, program dir. tng. center on delinquency of youth crime 1962-65; commr. N.C. Dept. Correction, 1965-73; chmn. N.C. Commn. on Criminal Laws Relating to Public Morality, 1966-67; mem. adv. com. on corrections U.S. Dept. Justice, 1967-68; pres. Assn. State Correctional Adminstrs., 1968-69; mem. U.S. Adv. Com. on Naval Corrections, 1970-71. Served with USN, 1936-41; Served with USNR, 1941-45; to comdr. USNR, 1951-52. Bicentennial fellow in criminal law and adminstrn. U. Pa., 1950-51. Democrat.

BOUNDY, RAY HAROLD, chemical engineer; b. Brave, Pa., Jan. 10, 1903; s. George W. and Anetta (Cather) B.; m. Geraldine McCurdy, Nov. 27, 1926; children: Richard Ray, Lois Cather. B.S. in Chemistry, Grove City Coll., Pa., 1924, Case Western Res. U., 1926; M.S. in Chem. Engring, Case Western Res. U., 1930; D.Sc. in Chemistry (hon.), Grove City (Pa.) Coll., 1961. With Dow Chem. Co., Midland, Mich., 1926-68, v.p., dir. research, corp. dir., 1951-68, cons. mgmt. of research, 1968—; vol. Internat. Exec. Service Corps., Taiwan and Iran, 1968—. Co-editor: Styrene, Its Polymers and Copolymers, 1951; Contbr. articles to profl. jours. Bd. dirs. Grove City Coll., Saginaw Valley State Coll. Recipient Gold medal Indsl. Research Inst., 1967; Alumni Achievement award Case Western Res. U., 1967, Grove City Coll., 1968. Mem. NAM, Modern Pioneers in Creative Industry, Nat. Acad. Engring., Am. Chem. Soc., Am. Inst. Chem. Engrs. Clubs: Kiwanis, Torch, Midland Country. Patentee in field. Address: 600 S Ocean Blvd Apt 1503 Boca Raton FL 33432

BOUQUARD, MARILYN LLOYD, congresswoman; b. Ft. Smith, Ark., Jan. 3; d. James Edgar and Iva Mae (Higginbotham) Laird; m. Joseph P. Bouquard; children: Nancy Lloyd Smithson, Mari, Mort II, Deborah Lloyd Riley. Grad., Shorter Coll., 1963. Mem. 94th-98th Congresses from 3d Tenn. Dist.; mem. Pub. Works and Transp. Com., Select Com. on Aging, Sci. and Tech. Com. Chmn. United Democrats of Congress. Home: Washington DC 20515 Office: 2334 Rayburn House Office Bldg Washington DC 20515 *

BOURAS, HARRY, artist; b. Rochester, N.Y., Feb. 13, 1931; s. Harry James and Alice (LaPriesse) B.; m. Arlene Marie Aklin, Aug. 18, 1951; 1 dau., Lorraine Ann. B.A., U. Rochester, 1951; postgrad., U. Chgo., 1955-56; M.F.A., U. Ill., 1978. Artist-in-residence U. Chgo., 1962-64, Columbia Coll., Chgo., 1964—; faculty Northwestern U., 1965-67, U. Ill, 1980—. Contbr. articles on art to publs.; weekly radio program Critic's Choice, 1965—; exhibited in numerous one-man shows, in U.S., fgn. countries, 1956—; represented in permanent collections, Mus. Modern Art, N.Y.C., Art Inst. Chgo., Rochester, N.Y., Tokyo, important sculpture works, Chgo., Aspen, Detroit, N.Y., New Delhi, Tokyo.; Bd. dirs. Creative Student Writers Found. Recipient Pauline Palmer award Chgo. Art Inst., 1962, Logan Gold medal for sculpture, 1964; Hokin Found. grantee, 1969; Guggenheim Found. fellow, 1971-72. Club: Arts of Chgo. Office: 600 S Michigan Ave Chicago IL 60605

BOURBEAU, JOSEPH, corporation executive; b. St. Hyacinthe, Que., Can., Feb. 27, 1922; s. George Auguste and Juliette (Senay) B.; m. Therese O'Connor, July 9, 1949; children: Josee, Marc, Monique. B.A., Coll. Ste-Marie, Montreal, 1942; B.S.A., Ecole Poly, Montreal, 1947. Resident engr. Hydro-Que., Montreal, 1947-53, cost and planning engr., 1953-65, dir. system planning, 1965-76, dir. corp. plan, 1976-80, chmn. bd., 1980—; dir. Nouveler, Montreal, Churchill Falls Lab. Corp., St. John's, Nfld., Can., 1981-83, Found. Ingenierie Canadienne, Montreal, 1982-83, Found. Diplomes Poly., 1983. Bd. dirs. Orch. Symphonique de Montreal, 1982-83. Mem. Ordre des Ingenieurs du Que., Inst. Can. des Ingenieurs. Roman Catholic. Club: St. Denis (Montreal). Home: 8480 Saguenay Brossard PQ Canada J4X 1M6 Office: Hydro-Quebec 75 Dorchester Blvd W Montreal PQ Canada H2Z 1A4

BOURDEAU, PAUL TURGEON, insurance company executive; b. Concord, N.H., June 7, 1932; s. Adelard J. and Marie (A.) B.; m. Patricia Shapiro, Sept. 1, 1979; children: Paul, Corinne, Bonnie, Jacqui. B.A., Pa. State U., 1953; M.B.A., U. Hartford, 1970; postgrad., Stanford U., 1980. C.L.U. Gen. mgr. Layman Motor Co., 1956-60; v.p., actuary Travelers Ins. Co., 1960-81; pres. Phoenix Am. Life Ins. Co., Hartford, Conn., 1981—; sr. v.p. Phoenix Am. Life Ins. Co., Hartford; speaker in field. Contbr. in field. Chmn. organizing com. U.S. Figure Skating Championships, 1977, World Figure Skating Championships, 1981. Served with USN, 1953-56. Fellow Soc. Actuaries; mem. Acad. Actuaries, Soc. C.L.U.s, Hartford Actuaries Club, N.Y. Actuaries Club, Phi Beta Kappa. Clubs: Suffield Golf and Tennis, Skating of Hartford (dir.). Home: 52 S Main St Suffield CT 06078 Office: Corp Hdqrs 1 American Row Hartford CT 06115

BOURDEAU, ROBERT CHARLES JOHN, photographer, educator; b. Kingston, Ont., Can., Nov. 14, 1931; s. William James and Irene (Attwood) B.; m. Mary Eardley, Apr. 8, 1961; children: Robert Marc, Sean Patrick. Tchr. photography U. Ottawa, 1980—. Photographer: books Robert Bourdeau, 1980, The Banff Purchase, 1979, Twelve Canadians, 1981, Canada a Year of the Land, 1967. Ont. Arts Council sr. grantee, 1980; Can. Council grantee, 1971. Roman Catholic. Home: 1462 Chomley Crescent Ottawa ON Canada K1G 0V1

BOURDON, DAVID JOSEPH, JR., writer, editor; b. Glendale, Calif., Oct. 15, 1934; s. David Joseph and Marilyn Edythe (Casale) B. B.S., Columbia U., 1961. Asst. editor Life mag., N.Y.C., 1966-71; asso. editor Smithsonian mag., Washington, 1972-74; art critic The Village Voice, N.Y.C., 1964-66, 74-77; asso. features editor Vogue mag., N.Y.C., 1983—; N.Y. corr. Du, Zurich, 1976-79; columnist Vogue, N.Y.C., 1978—. Author: Christo, 1972, Carl Andre Sculpture 1959-77, 1978, Calder, 1980; cons. editor: Christo: Running Fence, 1979; contbr. articles to numerous mags. Home and office: 315 W 23d St Apt 3C New York NY 10011

BOURGAIZE, ROBERT G., economist. Dir. Peoples Nat. Bank, Seattle; pres. Central Bank, N.A., Tacoma, University Place Water Co., University Place Corp., Central Capital Corp. Mem. Nat. Assn. Bus. Economists, English-Speaking Union U.S.A. (nat. dir.), Royal Commonwealth Soc. Office: 3502 Bridgeport Way West University Place WA 98466

BOURGAULT, ROY FRANCIS, educator; b. Worcester, Mass., Feb. 25, 1920; s. Louis Joseph and Evelyn (Richardson) B.; m. Betty Mae Arp, Aug. 9, 1946; children: Robert Louis, Edward Norman, Susan Elizabeth, Richard Douglas. B.S., Worcester Poly. Inst., 1942; M.S., Stevens Inst. Tech., 1953. Registered profl. engr., Mass. Indsl. engr. U.S. Steel Corp., 1942-43, 46-48, metallurgist, 1948-51; research asso. Stevens Inst. Tech., 1952-53; chief metallurgist Warner Hudnut, Inc., Livingston, N.J., 1953-55; mem. faculty Worcester Poly. Inst., 1955—, prof. mech. engring., 1967—; cons. in field, 1955—. Active local Boy Scouts Am., 1957—, council commr., 1977-82; moderator Worcester Assn. Congl. Chs., 1965-66. Served to 1st lt. USAAF, 1943-46. Recipient Silver Beaver award Boy Scouts Am., 1964; Good Citizenship medal S.A.R., 1965. Mem. Am. Soc. Metals (past chpt. chmn. Am. Soc. Engring. Edn, chmn. materials div. 1979-80, Sigma Xi), Pi Tau Sigma. Mem. United Ch. Christ. Address: 9 Einhorn Road Worcester MA 01609

BOURGEOIS, ANDRE MARIE GEORGES, educator; b. Orleans, France, Dec. 1, 1902; came to U.S., 1927, naturalized, 1936; s. Maurice M. and Yvonne (Assire) B.; m. May Hander, July 1, 1940; children—Maxime W., June Katherine Marie. B.A., U. Paris, 1921, LL.B., 1923; certicats etudes superieures, 1930, doctorat, 1945; M.A., U. Tex., 1934. Mem. faculty Rice U., 1928—, prof. French, 1954-72, prof. emeritus, 1972—, acting chmn. dept., 1957-61, Favrot prof. French lit., 1969—, chmn. dept., 1970-72; vis. prof. U. Houston, 1947, 60, U. Tex., 1940, Tulane U., 1939. Author: Ballades Louisianaises, 1938, Practical French Grammar, 1940, Pastels and Sanguines, 1947, Rene Boylesve, le peintre de la Touraine, 1945, Rene Boylesve, et le probleme de l'amour, 1950, La vie de Rene Boylesve, 1958, Rene Boylesve, le Poete, 1967. Asst. dir. Le Petit Theatre Français de Houston, 1933-38; asso. pub. Le Bayou, 1936-61. Served to maj. AUS, 1942-45; ETO. Decorated Bronze Star; Croix de Guerre, 3(France); officer Ouissam Alaouite Cherifien, Corona d'Italia; comdr. Palmes Academiques; recipient Medaille d'Honneur U. Nancy (France). Mem. S. Central Modern Lang. Assn. (hon.), Alliance Française, Chevaliers du Tastevin. Roman Catholic. Home: 2070 Southgate Blvd Houston TX 77030

BOURGEOIS, LOUISE, sculptor; b. Paris, Dec. 25, 1911; U.S., 1938, naturalized, 1953; d. Louis and Josephine (Fauriaux) B.; m. Robert Goldwater, Sept. 12, 1938; children: Michel, Jean-Louis, Alain. Baccalaureat Ecole des Beaux Artis, U. Paris, 1934; postgrad., Ecole du Louvre, 1936, 37, 38, Academie Ranson, (Atelier Bissiere), 1936-37, Academie de la Grand Chaumiere, (Atelier Vlerick), 1937-38, Academie Julian; also with, Fernand Legar, 1938. Docent Louvre, 1937-38; teaching asst. Atelier Yves Brayer, Grande Chaumiere, 1937, 38; tchr. Great Neck (NY) Schs., program, 1960, Bklyn. Coll., 1963-68, Pratt Inst., 1965-67, Goddard Coll., 1970. One-man shows, Norlyst Gallers, 1947, Peridot Gallery, 1949, 50, 53, Allan Frumkin Gallery, Chgo., 1953, White Art Mus., Cornell U., Ithaca, N.Y., 1959, Stable Gallery, 1964, Rose Fried Gallery, Mus. Modern Art, N.Y.C., 1982; exhibited in numerous group shows,, U.S., Europe; represented in collections, Mus. Modern Art, N.Y.C., Whitney Mus, Mus. Modern Art, N.Y.C., R.I. Sch. Design, NYU, also pvt. collections; works reproduced in Contemporary Sculpture (Giedion Welker), 1955, Sculpture of This Century (Michel Seuphor), 1959, Form and Space (Trier), 1961, A Concise History of Modern Sculpture, (Herbert Read), 1964, Modern American Sculpture (Dore Ashton), 1968, History of Modern Art (H.H. Arnason), 1968, What is Modern Sculpture, 1969, Sculpture in Wood (J.C. Rich), 1970, also various mags. Mem. Sculptors Guild, Am. Abstract Artists, Coll. Art Assn., Women's Caucus (Outstanding Achievement award 1980), La Jeune Sculpture, Paris. Address: care Robert Miller Gallery 724 Fifth Ave New York NY 10019 *

BOURGHOLTZER, FRANK, news correspondent; b. N.Y.C., Oct. 26, 1919; s. Crawford Nicholas and Martha Eugenia (Shafer) B.; m. Audrey Ellsworth Evans; children: Stephen Lee, John Evans; m. Shena Fleming Greig McLaren; 1 son, Andrew Christopher. 2A.B., Ind. U., 1940. Reporter Peking (Ind.) Banner, Salem (Ind.) Democrat, Evansville (Ind.) Courier, 1940-41; free lance writer, 1941-44; with Wall St. Jour., 1944-46, NBC News, 1946—; various assignments include NBC News, Paris, White House, Bonn, Vienna, Dept. State, Moscow, Europe, now West Coast corr. Author: fiction The Borovitsky Apartment, 1965; TV spls. include The Kremlin, 1963, The Man Who Walked in Space, 1965, Hungary, Ten Years Later, 1966. Recipient Best TV Reporting from Abroad award Overseas Press Club, 1965. Mem. AFTRA, Nat., Press Club. Home: 1133 Lincoln Blvd Santa Monica CA Office: 3000 W Alameda Ave Burbank CA

BOURGOYNE, ADAM THEODORE, JR., petroleum engineering educator; b. Baton Rouge, July 1, 1944; s. Adam Theodore and Marceline (Navarre) B.; m. Kathryn Daspit, Jan. 22, 1966; children: Darryl, Dwayne, Tammy, Ben, Brad, Tracey. B.S., La. State U., 1966, M.S., 1967, Ph.D., 1969. Registered profl. engr., La. Sr. systems engr. Continental Oil Co., Houston, 1969-70; asst. prof. petroleum engring. La. State U., Baton Rouge, 1970-74, assoc. prof., 1974-79, prof., 1979—, chmn. dept., 1979-83; dir. IADC Blowout Control Sch., Baton Rouge, 1980-83; pres. B & A, Inc., 1982-83; v.p. Coastal Petroleum Assocs., Inc., Baton Rouge, 1980-82. Author: Applied Drilling Engineering, 1983; inventor well control process. Mem. AIME-Soc. Petroleum Engrs. (disting. achievement for petroleum engring. faculty award 1981), Am. Petroleum Inst., Nat. Soc. Petroleum Engrs. (dir.), Tau Beta Pi, Pi Epsilon Tau. Democrat. Roman Catholic. Designer Blowout Prevention Ctr., 1981. Home: 6006 Boone Dr Baton Rouge LA 70808 Office: Dept Petroleum Engring La State Univ Baton Rouge LA 70803

BOURGUIGNON, ERIKA EICHHORN, anthropologist, educator; b. Vienna, Austria, Feb. 18, 1924; d. Leopold H. and Charlotte (Rosenbaum) Eichhorn; m. Paul H. Bourguignon, Sept. 29, 1950. B.A., Queens Coll., 1945; grad. study, U. Conn., 1945; Ph.D., Northwestern U., 1951. Field work Chippewa Indians, Wis., summer 1946; field work, Haiti; anthropology Northwestern U., 1947-48; instr. Ohio State U., 1949-56, asst. prof., 1956-60, asso. prof., 1960-66, prof., 1966—, acting chmn. dept. anthropology, 1971-72, chmn. dept., 1972-76; dir. Cross-Cultural Study of Dissociational States, 1963-68; Bd. dirs. Human Relations Area Files, Inc., 1976-79. Author: Possession, 1976, Psychological Anthropology, 1979, Italian transl., 1983; editor, co-author: Religion, Altered States of Consciousness and Social Change, 1973, A World of Women, 1980; co-author: Diversity and Homogeneity in World Societies, 1973; adv. editor: Behavior Sci. Research, 1976—; asso. editor: Jour. Psychoanalytic Anthropology, 1977—; editorial bd.: (1979) Ethos; author articles. Fellow Am. Anthrop. Assn.; mem. Central State Anthrop. Soc. (treas. 1953-56), Ohio Acad. Sci., World Psychiat. Assn. (transcultural psychiatry sect.), Am. Ethnol. Soc., Current Anthropology (asso.), Soc. for Psychol. Anthropology (nominations com. 1981-82), Sigma Xi. Office: Dept of Anthropology Ohio State U 124 W 17th Ave Columbus OH 43210 *It is more important to enjoy doing what you do, and to be able to do what you want to do, than to be successful. Success, if it comes, is only a by-product, nothing more.*

BOURJAILY, VANCE, novelist; b. Cleve., Sept. 17, 1922; s. Monte Ferris and Barbara (Webb) B.; m. Bettina Yensen, 1946; children—Anna (dec.), Philip, Robin. A.B., Bowdoin Coll. Newspaperman, TV dramatist, playwright, lectr.; prof. U. Ariz., U. Iowa Writers Workshop, 1958-80; co-founder, editor Discovery, 1951-53; cultural mission to S.Am. auspices State Dept., 1959, 73; Disting. vis. prof. Oreg. State U., summer 1968; vis. prof. U. Ariz., 1977-78. Author: The End of My Life, 1947, The Hound of Earth, 1953, The Violated, 1958, Confessions of a Spent Youth, 1960; non-fiction The Unnatural Enemy, 1963; The Man Who Knew Kennedy, 1967, Brill Among the Ruins, 1970 (nominated Nat. Book Award for fiction 1971); author: non-fiction Country Matters, 1973; Now Playing at Canterbury, 1976, A Game Men Play, 1980. Mem. campaign staff Hughes for Senate, 1968. Served with Am. Field Service, 1942-44; Served with AUS, 1944-46. Home: Redbird Farm Route 3 Iowa City IA Office: care Owen Laster William Morris Agy 1350 Ave of Americas New York City NY 10019

BOURKE, ROBERT SAMUEL, neurosurgeon, educator; b. Malden, Mass., Feb. 20, 1935; s. Robert William and Beatrice (Hoberman) B.; m. Marlene Cohen, Feb. 6, 1965; children: Jaron Robert, Andrew Benjamin. A.B. cum laude, Harvard U., 1956; M.D. cum laude (Mosby scholar 1959), Tufts U., 1960. Diplomate Am. Bd. Neurol. Surgery (mem. 1981—). Intern Barnes Hosp., St. Louis, 1960, gen. surg. asst. resident, 1961, asst. resident neurosurgery, 1964-65, resident neurosurgery, 1966, fellow neurosurgery, 1967; research asso. Lab. Neurochemistry, Nat. Inst. Neurol. Diseases and Blindness, NIH, HEW, Bethesda, Md., 1960-64, chief sect. on devel. neurochemistry, 1967-69; isotope physics Oak Ridge Nuclear Inst., 1963; acting chief neurosurg. service Georgetown U., D.C. Gen. Hosp., 1967-69; instr. SUNY, Buffalo, 1969-74; chief dept. neurosurgery Roswell Park Meml. Inst., Buffalo, 1969-74; prof., chmn. div. neurosurgery Albany (N.Y.) Med. Coll., 1974—, acting chmn. dept. surgery, 1980-81; Chmn. neurology A study sect. sci. rev. br. NIH, 1982; mem. bd. sci. counselors Nat. Inst. Neurol. and Communicative Disorders and Stroke, 1980—, chmn. bd. sci. counselors, 1982—; acting surgeon-in-chief Albany Med. Ctr. Hosp., 1980-81. Contbr. articles to profl. publs. Served with USPHS, 1961-64. Mem. AMA, AAAS, Congress Neurol. Surgeons, D.C. Med. Soc., Assn. Research Neurosurgeons, Am. Assn. Neurol. Surgeons, Soc. Neurosci., Soc. Neurol. Surgeons, Soc. Univ. Neurosurgeons, Alpha Omega Alpha, Phi Delta Epsilon. Office: Div Neurosurgery Albany Med Coll Albany NY 12208

BOURKE, VERNON JOSEPH, philosophy educator; b. North Bay, Ont., Can., Feb. 17, 1907; came to U.S., 1931, naturalized, 1944; s. Joseph Walter and Therese (Trudeau) B.; m. Aileen Baechler, Aug. 15, 1932 (dec. 1945); children: Jane (Mrs. Ray Luckhaupt), Thomas, Nancy (Mrs. Vernal G. Beckmann); m. Janet Leahy, June 12, 1947. B.A., U. Toronto, 1928, M.A., 1929, Ph.D., 1937; Litt.D., Bellarmine Coll., Louisville, 1974, U. St. Thomas, Houston, 1981. Lectr. ancient philosophy U. Toronto, 1928-31; instr. philosophy St. Louis U., 1931-46, prof., 1946-75, prof. emeritus, 1975—; dir. Center for Thomistic Studies, U. Houston, 1977-79, research prof., 1979—; Cullen prof. philosophy U. St. Thomas, 1983—; adv. editor Christian Wisdom Series, Macmillan Co., 1952-68. Author: Pocket Aquinas, 1960, Will in Western Thought, 1964, The Essential Augustine, 1966, Ethics in Crisis, 1966, History of Ethics, 1968, (with T. Miethe) Thomistic Bibliography, 1940-1978, 1980; Editor, translator: Summa contra Gentiles (St. Thomas Aquinas), 2 vols, 1975; asso. editor: Am. Jour. Jurisprudence, 1956—, Speculum, 1950-66, The Modern Schoolman, 1948—, Augustinian Studies, 1969—; Contbr. Ency. of Philosophy, 1967. Chmn. Catholic Commn. on Cultural and Intellectual Affairs, 1950; Bd. dirs. Thomistic Inst., St. Louis U. Recipient Gov. Gen. and Cardinal Mercier Gold medals Toronto, 1928, Loyola U. (Chgo.) Gold Key award, 1960, Aquinas medal Am. Cath. Philos. Assn., 1963. Mem. Mediaeval Acad. Am., Am., Am. Cath. (past pres.) philos. assns., World Union Cath. Philos. Socs. (past pres.). Republican. Home: 638 Laven-Del Ln Kirkwood MO 63122 Office: St Louis U 221 N Grand St Louis MO 63103

BOURKE, WILLIAM OLIVER, manufacturing company executive; b. Chgo., Apr. 12, 1927; s. Robert Emmett and Mable Elizabeth (D'Arcy) B.; m. Elizabeth Philbey, Sept. 4, 1970; children: William Oliver, Judith A., Andrew E., Edward A. Student, U. Ill., 1944-45; B.S. in Commerce, DePaul U., 1951. With Ford Motor Co., 1956-80, nat. distbn. mgr., Dearborn, Mich., 1956-62; gen. sales mgr. Ford Can., Dearborn, 1962-65; asst. mng. dir. Ford Australia, Dearborn, 1965-67, mgn. dir., 1967-70; pres. Ford Asia-Pacific and S. Africa, Inc., Dearborn, 1970-72, Ford Asia-Pacific, Inc., 1971-72, Europe, Inc., 1972-73, chmn. bd., 1973-75, exec. v.p. Ford N.Am. Automotive Ops., Dearborn, Mich., 1975-80, dir. Ford N.Am. Automotive Ops.; exec. v.p. Reynolds Metals Co., Richmond, Va., 1981-83, pres., dir., 1983—. Served to 1st lt. MI U.S. Army, 1944-48. Office: Reynolds Metals Co 6601 Broad St Rd Richmond VA 23261

BOURNE, CHARLES PERCY, information scientist, educator; b. San Francisco, Sept. 2, 1931; s. Frank Percy and Edith (Dunlap) B.; m. Elizabeth A. Scheidtmann, Aug. 15, 1953; children—Glen Wade, Holly Ann. B.S. in Elec. Engring, U. Calif. at Berkeley, 1957; M.S. in Indsl. Engring, Stanford, 1963. Sr. research engr. Stanford Research Inst., Menlo Park, Calif., 1957-66; v.p. Information Gen. Corp., Palo Alto, Calif., 1966-70; pres. Charles Bourne & Assos., Menlo Park, 1970—; prof. in residence Sch. Library and Info. Studies; dir. Inst. Library Research, U. Calif. at; Berkeley, 1971-77; dir. product devel. Dialog Info. Services, Inc., Palo Alto, 1977—; research in info. scis. for libraries, schs., acads., including Library of Congress, Nat. Agrl. Library, U.S. Patent Office, Nat. Acad. Sci.; Guest lectr. univs. including U. Calif. at Berkeley, 1963-66; Sarada Ranganathan lectr., Bangalore, India, 1978; cons. corr. Nat. Acad. Sci. com. on sci. and tech. information, 1968-70; mem. adv. bd. Chem. Abstracts, 1965-68, Ency. Library and Information Scis., 1967—, Documentation Abstracts, 1968-69, Ann. Rev. Information Sci. and Tech., 1966; U.S. rep. to a com. of Internat. Fedn. for Documentation, 1966-76; UNESCO cons. to Indonesia and Tanzania; Nat. Acad. Scis. cons. to Ghana, 1976; mem. U.S.-Egyptian Task Force on Tech. Info. Problems, 1976, U.S. del. UNESCO Intergovtl. Conf. Sci. and Tech. Info. for Devel., 1979. Author: Methods of Information Handling, 1963, Technology in Support of Library Science and Information Service, 1980; Contbr. articles profl. jours. Served with USMCR, 1950-51. 1Recipient ann. award merit Am. Documentation Inst., 1965. Mem. Am. Soc. Information Sci. (pres. 1970 A.L.A, dir. information scis. and automation div. 1966-67). Home: 1619 Santa Cruz Ave Menlo Park CA 94025 Office: Dialog 3460 Hillview Ave Palo Alto CA 94304

BOURNE, DOUGLAS JOHNSTON, natural resource company executive; b. Tulsa, Mar. 18, 1923; s. Alva Fountain and Evabel (Johnston) B.; m. Hilda Hess, Feb. 28, 1944; children: Laurie Douglas Bourne Widman, Janalee Bourne McDonald. B.S. in Chem. Engring, U. Okla., 1943; postgrad., Harvard U. Grad. Sch. Bus., 1966. Asst. chemist Sulphur div. Duval Corp., Orchard, Tex., 1946-47, process engr., chief metallurgist, plant supt. Potash div., Carlsbad, N.Mex., 1948-58, dir. research, v.p. research and planning, v.p. mktg. Sulphur div., Tucson, 1959-72, exec. v.p. Sulphur div., Houston, 1972-77, pres., 1977—, also chmn., chief exec. officer; pres. Duval Sales Corp., Houston, 1968-75; group mgmt. v.p. Pennzoil Co., Houston, 1975-77, also dir.; dir. Anderson, Greenwood & Co. Served to lt. (j.g.) USNR, 1943-46. Mem. Sulphur Inst. (dir., past chmn.), Potash and Phosphate Inst. (dir., vice chmn.), Copper Devel. Assn. (dir.), Fertilizer Inst. (dir.), AIME. Clubs: Petroleum, Marco Polo, River Oaks Country, University. Office: 700 Milam PO Box 2967 Houston TX 77001 *

BOURNE, GEOFFREY HOWARD, anatomist, primatologist; b. Perth, Western Australia, Nov. 17, 1909; came to U.S., 1957, naturalized, 1962; s. Walter;; s. Howard and Mary Ann (Mellon) B.; m. Maria Nelly Golarz, Oct. 31, 1964; children by previous marriage: Peter, (Merfyn). B.Sch., U. Western Australia, 1930, B.Sc. with honors, 1931, M.Sc., 1932, D.Sc., 1935; D.Phil., U. Oxford, Eng., 1943. Biologist Australian Inst. Anatomy, Canberra, 1934-35; biochemist Australian Advisory Council on Nutrition, 1936-37; demonstrator in physiology U. Oxford, 1941-47; reader in histology U. London, 1947-57; chmn. anatomy Emory U., 1957-62; dir. Yerkes Regional Primate Research Center, 1962-78; vice chancellor St. Georges U. Sch. Medicine, Grenada, W.I., 1978—; cons. Sch. Aerospace Medicine, 1964—. Author: books, including Starvation in Europe, 1943, Biochemistry and Physiology of Bone, 1956, Structure and Function of Muscle, 1962, Division of Labour in Cells, 1962, Structure and Function of Nervous Tissue, 1969, Ape People, 1970, Primate Odyssey, 1974, The Gentle Giants: The Gorilla Story, 1975; contbr. numerous articles to profl. publs.; editor: Cytology and Cell Physiology, 1941, (with J. F. Danielli) Internat. Rev. Cytology, 1950-66, World Review of Nutrition and Dietetics. Beit Meml. Research fellow, 1939-41; Mackenzie Mackinnon Research fellow, 1941-43. Fellow Royal Coll. Surgeons, Royal Coll. Physicians, Royal Soc. Medicine, Gerontology Soc., Zool. Soc. London, Inst. Biology; Mem. Anat socs. U.S., U. K., gerontol. socs. U.S., U.K., Am. Rocket Soc., Aerospace Med. Assn., Internat. Primatology Soc., Internat. Soc. Cell Biology. Pioneered in devel. of new sci. of histochemistry; demonstrated (with T. R. Shanthaveeroappa) that nerves have protective covering continuous with covering of the brain; 1st to demonstrate vitamin C. in cells, 1933. Home: 849 Lullwater Pkwy Atlanta GA 30307 Office: St Georges Univ Sch Medicine Grenada West Indies

BOURNE, HENRY CLARK, JR., engr., university official; b. Tarboro, N.C., Dec. 31, 1921; s. Henry Clark and Marion (Alston) B.; m. Margaret Barr Thomas, Aug. 15, 1953; children: Katherine Wimberley, Henry Clark III, Thomas Franklin, Margaret Alston. B.S., Mass. Inst. Tech., 1947, M.S., 1948, D.Sc., 1952. Registered profl. engr., Calif., Tex. Asst. prof. Mass. Inst. Tech., 1952-54; asst. prof., then asso. prof. U. Calif. at, Berkeley, 1954-63; prof. elec. engring. Rice U., Houston, 1963-77, chmn. dept., 1963-74; sect. head engring. div. NSF, Washington, 1974-75, div. dir. engring., 1977-79; dep. asst. dir. Directorate Engring. and Applied Sci., 1979-81; v.p. for acad. affairs Ga. Inst. Tech., Atlanta, 1981—; cons. editor Harper & Row, N.Y.C., 1961-67; cons. elec. engring., 1952—. Author tech. papers in field of magnetics. Served to 1st lt. C.E. AUS, 1943-46. Sci. Faculty fellow NSF, 1960-61; hon. research asso. Univ. Coll. London; Eng., 1961. Fellow IEEE, AAAS; mem. Am. Phys. Soc., Am. Soc. Engring. Edn., Sigma Xi, Tau Beta Pi, Eta Kappa Nu, Phi Kappa Phi, Omicron Delta Kappa, Beta Gamma Sigma, Delta Tau Delta. Episcopalian. Home: 3428 Rilman Rd NW Atlanta GA 30327

BOURNE, LYLE EUGENE, JR., psychology educator; b. Boston, Apr. 12, 1932; s. Lyle E. and Blanche (White) B. B.A., Brown U., 1953; M.S., U. Wis., 1955, Ph.D., 1956. Asst. prof. psychology U. Utah, 1956-61, assoc. prof., 1961-63; vis. assoc. prof. U. Calif.-Berkeley, 1961-62, vis. prof., 1968-69; assoc. prof. psychology U. Colo., Boulder, 1963-65, prof., 1965—, chmn. dept. psychology, 1983—, dir. Inst. Cognitive Sci., 1979—; clin. prof. psychiatry U. Kans. Med. Ctr., 1967—; vis. prof. U. Wis., 1966, U. Mont., 1967, U. Calif.-Berkeley, 1968-69, U. Hawaii, 1969; cons. in exptl. psychology, Va., 1965—. Author: Human Conceptual Behavior, 1966, Psychology of Thinking, 1971, Psychology: Its Principles and Meanings, 1973, Psychology: Its Principles and Meanings, rev. edits., 1976, 79, 82, Cognitive Processes, 1979; acad. editor: Basic Concept Series, Learning-Cognition Series, Scott, Foresman Pub. Co., Charles Merrill Co., 1980—; editor: Jour. Exptl. Psychology: Human Learning and Memory, 1975-80; cons. editor: Jour. Clin. Psychology, 1975—. Recipient Research Scientist award NIHM, 1969-74. Mem. Am. Psychol. Assn. (council editors 1975-80, chmn. early awards com. 1978-79), Psychonomic Soc. (governing bd. 1976-81, chmn. 1980-81), Sigma Xi. Home: 785 Northstar Ct Boulder CO 80302

BOURNE, PETER GEOFFREY, physician, educator; b. Oxford, Eng., Aug. 6, 1939; s. Geoffrey Howard and Gwen (Jones) B.; m. Mary Elizabeth King, Nov. 9, 1974. M.D., Emory U., 1962; M.A. in Anthropology, Stanford U., 1969. Fellow dept. psychiatry Med. Sch.; co-dir. Alcoholism Project, Emory U., 1962-63; intern King County Hosp., Seattle, 1963-64; research psychiatrist Walter Reed Army Inst.; Research, Washington, 1964-67; chief neuropsychiat. br. U.S. Army Med. Research Team, Vietnam, 1965-66; cons. S.E. Asia Health Br. (AID), Dept. State, 1966-67; resident dept. psychiatry, Stanford U. Med. Center, Palo Alto, Calif., 1967-69; dir. mental health unit Southside Comprehensive Health Center, Atlanta, 1969-71; founder, dir. Atlanta S.Central Community Mental Health Center, 1970-71; dir. Ga. Office Drug Abuse, 1971-72; spl. adviser for health affairs to Gov. Jimmy Carter of Ga., 1971-73; asst. dir. White House Spl. Action Office for Drug Abuse Prevention, 1972-74; cons. Drug Abuse Council, Washington, 1974-76; pres. Found. for Internat. Resources, 1975-76; Mid-Atlantic coordinator, dep. campaign dir. Jimmy Carter Presdl. Campaign, 1975-76; spl. asst. for health issues to U.S. Pres., Washington, 1976-78; mem. U.S. del. to Exec. Council UNICEF, 1977; asst. sec. gen. UN, N.Y.C., 1979-81; pres. Global Water, 1981—; mem. U.S. Pres. Commn. on White House Fellows; head U.S. delegation UN Devel. Program Governing Council, 1978; emergency room physician Casualty Hosp., Washington, 1966-67, Kaiser Permanente Hosp., Santa Clara, Calif., 1967-69; psychiat. cons. Santa Clara County Hosp., 1968-69, San Mateo County Hosp., 1969; cons. WHO, Geneva, 1972, UN Div. on Narcotic Drugs, 1976; asst. prof. dept. psychiatry Emory U. Med. Sch., 1969-72, asst. prof. dept. preventive medicine and community health, 1969-72; vis. lectr. dept. psychiatry Harvard U. Med. Sch., 1974; v.p. Nat. Coordinating Council on Drug Abuse Edn., 1971-72; prof. psychiatry St. Georges Med. Sch., Grenada, 1979—. Author: Men, Stress and Viet Nam, 1970; Editor: Psychology and Physiology of Stress, 1969, (with R. Fox) Alcoholism: Progress in Research and Treatment, 1973, Addiction, 1974, Acute Drug Abuse Emergencies, 1976, Water Resources: Social and Economic Aspects, 1983; mem. editorial bd.: Psychiatry, 1968—, Am. Jour. Drug Alcohol Abuse, 1973—; Contbr. articles to med. jours. and chpts. to books. Bd. dirs. Save the Children Fedn., Inst. for So. Studies. Served to capt. U.S. Army, 1964-67. Decorated Bronze Star medal, Air medal, Combat Medics badge; recipient William C. Menninger award Central Neuropsychiat. Assn., 1967, Pub. Service award Nat. Assn. State Drug Abuse Program Coordinators, 1974, Assn. Chinese Ams., 1978; named One of Five Outstanding Young Men Atlanta Jr. C. of C., 1971, One of Five Outstanding Young Men in Ga. Ga. Jr. C. of C., 1972. Mem. Med. Assn. Ga., AAAS, Am. Psychiat. Assn. (chmn. Task Force on Drugs and Drug Abuse Edn. 1969—), Ga. Psychiat. Assn., Washington Psychiat. Soc., Royal Soc. Medicine, Am. Med. Soc. on Alcoholism, Am. Anthrop. Assn., World Fedn. for Mental Health., World Health Assn. (nominating com.). Democrat. Home: 2119 Leroy Pl NW Washington DC 20008 Office: Suite 300 2033 M St NW Washington DC 20036 *I have always felt that my training as a physician was only a starting point in using my life to touch, for the better, the lives of as large a number of people as possible, whether formulating national health policy for the President of the United States, or through the United Nations or through the private voluntary agencies. I believe that ultimate gratification can only come from the sense that one has left the world a better place than when one arrived.*

BOURNE, PHILIP WALLEY, architect; b. Boston, Nov. 30, 1907; s. Frank A. and Gertrude (Beals) B.; m. Mary Elliot Nicholson, June 15, 1932; children: Sallie Bourne Harrison, Philip Elliot (dec.), Jonathan F. Student in architecture, M.I.T., 1925-30, Harvard U. Sch. City Planning, 1933-34. Planner housing div. Pub. Works Adminstrn., 1934-37, U.S. Housing Authority, Washington, 1937-46; housing adviser Hawaii Housing Authority, Honolulu, 1938-39; housing cons. Republic of Haiti, 1949; internat. housing cons. Dept. State, 1950-51; dir. planning Mass. State Housing Bd., Boston, 1952-53; practice architecture, Boston, 1953—; propr. The Boston Athenaeum. Recent works include, Peabody Mus., Salem, Mass., Salem Savs. Bank, Concord (Mass.) Library, G.M. Jones Meml. Library, Salem. Chmn. Mass. Art Commn., 1965-77; Trustee Trustees of Reservations, Mass. Commr. Mass. Designer Rev. Bd., 1965-66. Fellow AIA (dir. New Eng. regional council 1967-70, nat. dir. 1967-70); mem. Boston Soc. Architects (pres. 1964-66), Nat. Assn. Housing Ofcls., Am. Guild Organists. Episcopalian. Clubs: Cosmos (Washington); St. Anthony (N.Y.C.); Harvard (Boston); Union Boat, Eastern Yacht. Home: 5 Chestnut St Salem MA 01970 Office: 80 Broad St Boston MA 02110

BOURNE, RUSSELL, publisher; b. Boston, Oct. 10, 1928; s. Standish T. and Sylvia (Russell) B.; m. Miriam Anne Young, Aug. 22, 1953; children: Sarah Perkins, Jonathan, Louise Taber, Andrew Russell. A.B. magna cum laude, Williams Coll., 1950. Reporter Life mag., 1950-53, asst. to editor-in-chief, 1953-56; assoc. editor Archtl. Forum, 1956-59; editor Am. Heritage Jr. Library, 1959-64, Time-Life Books, Great Ages of Man, 1964-69; assoc. chief Nat. Geog. Book Service, 1969-72; partner Bourne-Thompson & Assocs., Washington, 1972-77; sr. editor Smithsonian Exposition Books, Washington, 1977-80; pub. Hearst Gen. Books, N.Y.C., 1980-81; pub., editor Am. Heritage Books, N.Y.C., 1981—. Served with Counter-Intelligence Corps U.S. Army, 1950-52. Home: RD 1 Blue Swamp Rd Litchfield CT 06759 Office: 10 Rockefeller Plaza New York NY 10020

BOURNE, WILLIAM HAMILTON, natural gas pipeline company executive; b. Tulsa, July 20, 1918; s. William Hamilton and Anna (Detweiler) B.; m. Alberta Smitheram, Mar. 23, 1946; children: William C., Richard G. Student, U. Okla., 1938-39; M.S. in Petroleum Engring, Stanford U., 1948. Registered profl. engr., Calif. Stress analyst Lockheed Aircraft Co., Burbank, Calif., 1939-42; with Amerada Petroleum Corp., 1948-72, mgr. joint venture ops., 1970-72; with Miss. River Transmission Corp., St. Louis, 1972—, exec. v.p., 1977-78, pres., 1978—, chmn., 1983—, dir., 1976—; chmn. bd., chief exec. officer MRT Exploration Co., 1976—, dir., 1973—, Esco Exploration Co.; past pres. Natural Gas Men Okla. Served to lt. USNR, 1942-45. Decorated Air medal with 2 oak leaf clusters. Mem. Soc. Petroleum Engrs., Interstate Natural Gas Assn. Am. (dir.), So. Gas Assn. (dir., Phi Beta Kappa, Tau Beta Pi.). Republican. Methodist. Club: Sunset Country (St. Louis). Home: 12827 Huntercreek Rd St Louis MO 63131 Office: 9900 Clayton Rd St Louis MO 63124

BOURNS, MARLAN E., business executive; b. Brighton, Mich., May 28, 1920; s. Frank E. and Bernice (Muir) B.; m. Rosemary R. Miller, July 7, 1947; children: Gordon, Linda, Anita, Denise. B.S., U. Mich., 1944. Research U. Mich., 1944-45; research asst. Calif. Inst. Tech., 1945; research Gen. Tire & Rubber Co., 1945-46; founder Bourns, Inc., Riverside, Calif., 1946—. Joint chmn. Reagan TV Com., 1968. Recipient Silver Beaver award Boy Scouts Am. Mem. World Bus. Council, Young Presidents Orgn., Phi Beta Kappa. Patentee in field.

BOURQUE, PIERRE, horticulturist; b. Montreal, Que., Can., May 29, 1942; s. Benoit and Marcelle (Girard) B.; children: Enrique, Lucia. Ed., Vilvorde, Belgium. Sect. head, chief horticulturist, tech. dir. Floralies Internationales, Montreal, 1980; now dir. Montreal Bot. Gardens and; asst. dir. public work service City of Montreal; tchr. U. Montreal; cons. Sociéte énergie Baie James. Mem. Internat. Plant Propagators, Am. Nurseryman's Assn. Office: 4101 E Sherbrooke St Montreal PQ H1X 2B2 Canada

BOURS, WILLIAM ALSOP, III, retired chemical company executive; b. N.Y.C., July 20, 1918; s. William Alsop, Jr. and Mary (Wadsworth) B.; m. Elizabeth Wigton, June 21, 1941; children: Elizabeth Bours Layton, William Alsop, IV, Mary Anne Bours Nimmo (dec.), Barbara. B.A., Princeton U., 1939, B.S., 1940; M.S., Columbia U., 1941. Jr. chemist Merck & Co., Rahway, N.J., 1940; with E.I. duPont de Nemours & Co., Wilmington, Del., 1941—, asst. gen. mgr. biochems. dept., 1969-75, v.p., gen. mgr. fabrics and finished dept., 1974-77, v.p. fabrics and finishes, 1978-81; chmn. Verlan Ltd., Ins., 1981. Bd. dirs. Del. League Planned Parenthood, Del. Hosp.; pres. bd. trustees Tower Hill Sch., Wilmington; lic. lay reader Episcopal Ch.; former sr. warden Christ Ch. Christiana Hundred, Wilmington; mem. Princeton U. Alumni Council, Princeton Council Univ. Resources; mem. adv. council dept. chemistry Princeton U.; pres. U. Del. Research Found.; bd. mgrs. Franklin Inst., Phila. Mem. Am. Chem. Soc., Am. Inst. Chem. Engrs., Sigma Xi, Phi Lambda Upsilon, Tau Beta Pi. Clubs: Princeton (N.Y.C.); Wilmington, Pine Valley Golf, Wilmington Country, Greenville Country (pres.). Home: The Devon Apt 1214 2401 Pennsylvania Ave Wilmington DE 19806

BOUSH, GEORGE MALLORY, entomologist; b. Norfolk, Va., June 5, 1926; s. George Webb and Eileen (Lindsley) B.; m. Sara May Gibbs, Aug. 4, 1945; children: Carol Love Boush Nelson, David Mallory, George Andrew. B.S., Va. Poly. Inst., 1948; M.S., Ohio State U., 1950, Ph.D. (USPHS fellow), 1955. Asst. entomologist Va. Agr. Expt. Sta., Holland, 1949-50; with Rockefeller Found., Mexico City, 1952-54; asso. prof. U. Ky., 1955-57, Va. Poly. Inst., Holland, 1957-64, U. Wis., Madison, 1964-67, prof. entomology, 1967—, chmn. dept. entomology, 1976-82; cons. Dept. Agr., Oceanic Inst., Hawaii. Contbr. sci. articles to profl. jours. Served with USAF, 1944-45. Smith-Mundt fellow to Iraq, 1960-61; NIH grantee, 1966-77; NSF grantee, 1971-72; Dept. Agr. grantee, 1965-77. Mem. AAAS, Am. Inst. Biol. Scis., Entomol. Soc. Am. (chmn. field crop sect. 1967-68, br. pres. 1982-83), Soc. Invertebrate Pathology, Wis. Acad. Sci., Sigma Xi, Gamma Sigma Delta. Home: 109 Greenlake Pass Madison WI 53705 Office: 237 Russell Labs U Wis Madison WI 53706

BOUSQUET, THOMAS GOURRIER, lawyer; b. Houston, Oct. 18, 1934; s. John A. and Ophelia Ann (Tucker) B.; m. Katherine Lynn Cummings, Aug. 22, 1959 (div. 1970); children: Thomas Gourrier, Robert Brant, Katherine Lynn; m. Duke Ellen Taylor, Nov. 27, 1970 (div. 1973). B.A., U. Tex., 1956, J.D., 1958. Bar: Tex. 1958, U.S. Supreme Ct. 1971; Cert. family law specialist, civil trial specialist Tex. Bd. Legal Specialization. Practiced in, Houston, 1958—; ptnr. Wandel & Bousquet, 1958-70, firm Bousquet & Assocs., Inc., 1970-79; dir. Electronic Data Labs., Inc., Figure World Internat., all Houston, Lea Haller Internat. Inc. Author: Become an Effective Player at Casino Craps, 1973. Mem. Houston Family Law Council. Served to maj. USAF, 1958-64; maj. Res. Fellow Tex. Bar Found.; Mem. Houston Bar Assn. (sec. 1960, v.p. 1961), Lawyers Soc. Houston (pres. 1973), Tex. Assn. Def. Counsel, Gulf Coast Family Law Specialist Assn. (sec. 1975-78, v.p. 1978—), Tex. Assn. Cert. Civil Trial Lawyers (pres. 1979—), Tex. Assn. Cert. Family Lawyers (pres. 1978-79), Am. Acad. Matrimonial Lawyers, Am. Land Devel. Assn., Order Stars and Bars, Magna Charta Barons, SAR (chancellor 1966), Plantagenet Soc., SCV, Order Descs. Colonial Govs., Houston Heritage Soc., Phi Alpha Delta. Clubs: Cadre (pres. 1975-76, 82), Space City Ski, Caribbee Dance, Luau Dance. Home: 4606 Richmond Ave Houston TX 77027 Office: 2500 West Loop S Suite 480 Houston TX 77027

BOUTHILET, KIRBY OTTESON, lawyer; b. Madison, Wis., Nov. 2, 1948; d. Lloyd Leroy and Flora Isabel (Wallace) Otteson; m. Paul M. Bouthilet, Jan. 30, 1971; children: Andrew Lloyd, Alexander John. B.A. with honors, U. Wis., 1971, J.D., 1973. Bar: Wis. 1973. Atty. Ft. Howard Paper Co., Green Bay, Wis., 1973-79, sec., 1974-82, assoc. gen. counsel, 1979-80, gen. counsel, 1980-82; sole practice, Green Bay, 1982—. Mem. Am., Wis., Brown County bar assns., U. Wis. Law Sch. Alumni Assn. (bd. visitors 1980—). Home and Office: 1168 Eliza St Green Bay WI 54301

BOUTILLIER, ROBERT JOHN, accountant; b. Newark, Jan. 1, 1924; s. William and Millicent (Davies) B.; m. Marie C. Humphries, June 24, 1945; children: Robert Allan, Suzanne Marie. B.S., Rutgers U., 1948. C.P.A., N.J. With Peat, Marwick, Mitchell & Co., 1943-82, ptnr., 1955-82, ptnr. charge Newark office, 1960-70, mem. adv. com. and Eastern area, ptnr., 1965-70, ptnr. in charge U.S. ops., 1970-77, vice-chmn., 1977, ret., 1982; lectr. Rutgers U.; dir. Prudential Ins. Co. Am., Howard Savs. Bank, Hyatt Clark Industries, Inc., Rentaland, Inc. Bd. dirs. Newark YM-YWCA.; trustee Rutgers, The State U. Mem. Am. Inst. C.P.A.s, N.J. Soc. C.P.A.s, Newark Jaycees (pres. 1956-57, Outstanding Young Man of Yr. 1957), Newark Assn. Commerce and Industry, Delta Sigma Pi, Beta Gamma Sigma. Republican. Presbyterian. Clubs: Rotary of N.Y., Baltusrol Golf (past pres., gov.), Echo Lake Country, Seaview Country, Ocean Reef. Home and Office: 920 Minisink Way Westfield NJ 07090 Office: 345 Park Ave New York NY 10154 *I feel very strongly that if you are to be successful in business and want to lead a full and rewarding life you must always give a little more of yourself than is expected by others.*

BOUTIN, BERNARD LOUIS, Former banker; b. Belmont, N.H., July 2, 1923; s. Joseph L. and Annie E. (LaFlam) B.; m. Alice M. Boucher, Apr. 2, 1945; children—Edmund, Joseph, Bernadette, Michelle, Marie, Louis, Elizabeth, John, Paul, Suzanne, Bernard II. Student, Cath. U. Am., 1942-43; Ph.B., St. Michael's Coll., Winooski Park, Vt., 1945, LL.D., 1963; H.D., Franklin Pierce Coll., 1969; L.H.D., U. N.H., 1970. Pres., treas. Boutin Ins. Agy., Inc., Laconia, N.H., 1948-63; propr. Boutin Real Estate Co., 1955-63; incorporator Laconia Savs. Bank; adminstr. Gen. Services Adminstrn., Washington, 1961-64; exec. v.p. Nat. Assn. Home Builders, 1964-65; dep. dir. Office Econ. Opportunity, 1965-66; adminstr. Small Bus. Adminstrn., 1966-67; asst. to pres. Sanders Assos., Inc., 1967-69; pres. St. Michael's Coll., Winooski, Vt., 1969-75; exec. v.p. Burlington Savs. Bank, Vt., 1975-76, pres., treas., trustee, 1976-80; ret., 1980; Mem. Com. on Equal Employment Opportunity, President's Com. on Employment Physically Handicapped; mem. Vt. Commn. on Higher Edn. Facilities; chmn. N.H. State Bd. Edn., 1968-69; mem. Nat. Hwy. Safety Adv. Com., 1969-70. Mayor City of Laconia. 1955-59.; Dem. nat committeeman for N.H., 1956-60, Dem. nominee for gov., 1958, 60; Bd. govs. Vt. Med. Center, trustee, treas., 1975-80; alumni bd. govs. Cath. U., 1968-73; bd. dirs. Nat. Council Ind. Colls. and Univs.; mem. Rice High Sch. Bd., 1976-78; finance bd. Trinity Coll., Vt., 1976-78. Mem. Am. Soc. Pub. Adminstrn., Am. Mgmt. Assn. Clubs: K.C. (past state dep.), Elks (past exalted ruler N.H.), Ethan Allen.). Address: 174 Wallis Rd Rye NH 03870

BOUTON, JAMES ALAN, author, sportscaster, former professional baseball player; b. Newark, Mar. 8, 1939; s. George H. and Trudy (Vischer) B.; m. Barbara Heister, 1962; children: Michael, Laurie, David.; m. Paula Kurman, June 27, 1982. Student, Western Mich. U., 1957-59, Fairleigh Dickinson U. Profl. baseball player N.Y. Yankees, 1962-68, Seattle Pilots, 1969, Houston Astros, 1969-70; formerly sportscaster ABC-TV, CBS-TV; played in Minor Leagues and Mexican League, 1977-78; with Atlanta Braves, 1978; ret., 1978; Mem. Am. League All-Star Team, 1963. Appeared: TV series Ball Four; Author: Ball Four, 1970, I'm Glad You Didn't Take It Personally, 1971, Ball Four plus Ball Five-An Update, 1981, Ball Five, 1981; developed shredded bubble gum: Big League Chew. *

BOUVIER, JOHN ANDRE, JR., lawyer, corp. exec., legal and financial cons.; b. nr. Ocala, Fla., May 16, 1903; s. John Andre and Ella (Richardson) B.; m. Helen A. Schaefer, June 6, 1928; children—Helen Elizabeth (Mrs. William Spencer), John Andre III, Thomas Richardson. Student, Davidson Coll., 1922-24; A.B., U. Fla., 1926, LL.B., 1929, J.D., 1969; M.B.A., Northwestern U., 1930; L.H.D. (hon.), Windham Coll., 1977. Bar: Fla. bar 1929. Practiced in, Gainesville, 1929, Miami, 1930—; specialist corp., real estate and probate law, cons. atty.; gen. counsel Patterson & Maloney, Ft. Lauderdale; chmn. exec. com. Permutit Co., 1964-73; chmn. bd. Prosperity Co. div.; vice chmn. bd. Ward Indsl. Corp.; chmn. bd., pres. Pantex Mfg. Corp., Nat. Leasing Inc., Miami; pres. Knaust Bros., Inc., K-B Products Corp., Iron Mountain Atomic Storage Vaults, Inc., West Kingsway, Inc., East Kingsway, Inc., South Kingsway, Inc.; pres., dir. Ace Solar Constrn. Co.; sec. 50th St. Heights, Inc., Knight Manor, Inc., Dade Constrn. Co. (all Miami), Karen Club Apt. Hotel, Ft. Lauderdale. Surf; Author monographs, newspaper articles in field. Dir. Farquhar Machinery Co., Landmark Banking Corp. Fla., Landmark Bank at the Ocean, Syracuse Govtl. Research Bur.; dir., sec. Wilson Garden Apts. Inc. Commr., Dade County council Boy Scouts Am.; chmn. Malecon Com. Dade County; mem. Planning Council Zoning Bd. Miami; chmn. Coxsackie-Athens Area Redevel. Com.; vice chmn. Nat. Parkinson Found.; bd. dirs. Miami Boys Clubs; trustee Windham Coll., Westminster Manor, Gateway Terrace, Boys Clubs. Mem. Internat. Platform Assn., Am. Judicature Soc., Am., Fla., Dade County, Broward County bar assns., Miami C. of C., Sigma Chi. Presbyterian (chmn. bd. trustees). Clubs: Miami Beach Rod and Reel, Riviera Country, Skaneateles Country, Ponte Vedra Country, Tower, Capital Hill, Masons, Shriners, Elks, Rotary. Home: 2756 NE 17th St Fort Lauderdale FL 33305 also Bienvenue Blowing Rock NC 28605 also Box 14 Climax NY 12042 Office: 6888 NW 7th Ave Miami FL 33150 also Box 7254 Fort Lauderdale FL 33338 *Any success I may have attained in life I feel is due to my faith in God and country, fidelity to principles of honesty and integrity, consideration for others, perseverance in my objectives, love of and loyalty to family and friends, all coupled with a deep sense of humility.*

BOUWER, HERMAN, laboratory executive; b. Haarlem, Netherlands, July 11, 1927; came to U.S., 1952, naturalized, 1959; s. Eduard and Trinette (Dusschoten) B.; m. Agnes N. Temminck, Mar. 29, 1952; children: Edward John, Herman (Archie) Gerard, Annette Nancy. B.S., Nat. Agr. U., Wageningen, Netherlands, 1949, M.S., 1952; Ph.D., Cornell U., 1955. Asso. agr. engr. Auburn U., 1955-59; research hydraulic engr. U.S. Water Conservation Lab., Phoenix, 1959-72, dir., 1972—; lectr. groundwater hydrology Ariz. State U.; cons. in field. Author: Groundwater Hydrology, 1978; Contbr. articles in field to profl. jours. OECD fellow, 1964; recipient Superior Service awards U.S. Dept., Agr., 1963, 73. Mem. ASCE (Walter Huber Research prize 1966, Royce J. Tipton award 1984), Am. Soc. Agr. Engrs., Am. Soc. Agronomy, Nat. Water Well Assn., Dutch Inst. Agr. Engrs. Club: Tempe Racquet and Swim. Home: 338 La Diosa St Tempe AZ 85282 Office: 4331 E Broadway St Phoenix AZ 85040

BOUWSMA, WILLIAM JAMES, history educator; b. Ann Arbor, Mich., Nov. 22, 1923; s. Oets Kolk and Gertrude (DeVries) B.; m. Beverly Jean Hancock, July 9, 1944; children: John Roger, Philip Hancock, Paul Joseph, Sarah Elizabeth. A.B., Harvard U., 1943, M.A., 1947, Ph.D., 1950. Instr. to assoc. prof. U. Ill., 1950-56; asso. prof. history U. Calif., 1956-61, prof., 1961-68, chmn. dept., 1966-67, vice chancellor for acad. affairs, 1967-69; prof. history Harvard U., 1969-71; Sather prof. history U. Calif., Berkeley, 1971—, chmn. dept., 1966-67, 81-83, faculty lectr., 1975. Author: Concordia Mundi: Career and Thought of Guillaume Postel, 1957, Venice and the Defense of Renaissance Liberty, 1968, Culture of Renaissance Humanism, 1973. Served with AUS, 1943-46. Fulbright fellow, 1959-60; Guggenheim fellow, 1960; Behavioral Sci. Center fellow, 1963-64; Nat. Humanities Inst. fellow, 1976-77, 83-85. Fellow Am. Acad. Arts and Scis.; mem. Am. Hist. Assn. (pres. 1978), Am. Philos. Soc., Renaissance Soc. Am. (council), Am. Soc. Reformation Research (pres. 1963), Soc. Italian Hist. Studies (pres. 1973-75). Home: 1530 LaLoma Berkeley CA 94708

BOUYOUCOS, JOHN VINTON, research and devel. co. exec.; b. Lansing, Mich., Nov. 9, 1926; s. George John and Delia (Bemis) B.; m. Stella Wright, Sept. 29, 1953; children—Ann Stephanie, Peter Johnson, Hope Nicola. Student, U. Mich., 1944; A.B., Harvard U., 1949, S.M., 1951, Ph.D., 1953, Smaller Co. Mgmt. Program cert., 1976. Asst. dir. Harvard Acoustics Research Lab., Harvard U., 1955-59; mgr. hydroacoustics dept. Gen. Dynamics Electronics Div., Rochester, N.Y., 1959-71; pres., chief scientist Hydroacoustics Inc., Rochester, 1972—. Pres., chmn. bd. Soc. Chamber Music, Rochester, 1977—; bd. dirs., chmn. summer season com. Rochester Philharm. Orch., 1978—. Served with U.S. Navy, 1944-46. Recipient Rochester Patent Law Assn.; Inventors award, 1973. Fellow Acoustical Soc. Am. (v.p. 1970-71), IEEE; mem. Soc. Exploration Geophysicists, Audio Engring. Soc., Inst. Noise Control Engrs. Club: Harvard Bus. Sch. Rochester (dir. 1981). Patentee in field. Home: 320 Inwood Dr Rochester NY 14625 Office: PO Box 23447 Rochester NY 14692

BOUZA, ANTHONY VILA, chief of police; b. El Seijo, Spain, Oct. 4, 1928; s. José Antonio and Encarnación (Vila) B.; m. Erica, May 18, 1957; children—Anthony S., Dominick. B.B.A., Baruch Sch., City U., N.Y., 1965, M.P.A., 1968. Mem. N.Y.C. Police Dept., 1953-79; adj. prof. John Jay Coll. Criminal Justice, 1979-80; chief of police City of Mpls., 1980—; guest lectr. in field. Author: Police Administration, Organization and Performance, 1978, also articles. Served with AUS, 1950-52. Mem. Am. Acad. Profl. Law Enforcement, Beta Gamma Sigma. Address: 3810 Sheridan Ave S Minneapolis MN 55416

BOVA, BENJAMIN WILLIAM, magazine editor, author, lecturer; b. Phila., Nov. 8, 1932; s. Benjamin Pasquale and Giove (Caporiccio) B.; m. Rosa Cucinotta, Nov. 28, 1953 (div.); children: Michael, Regina; m. Barbara Berson, June 28, 1974. B.S., Temple U., 1954. Editor Upper Darby (Pa.) News, 1954-56; tech. editor Project Vanguard, Martin Co., Balt., 1956-58; motion picture script writer Phys. Sci. Study Com., Ednl. Services, Inc., Watertown, Mass., 1958-60; mgr.

mktg. Avco Everett Research Lab., Avco Corp., Everett, Mass., 1960-71; editor Analog Sci. Fiction-Sci. Fact mag. Conde Nast Pub. Co., N.Y.C., 1971-78; fiction editor Omni mag., N.Y.C., 1978-79, exec. editor, 1979-81, v.p., editorial dir., 1981—. Author: sci. fiction The Star Conquerors, 1959, Star Watchman, 1964, The Weathermakers, 1967, Out of the Sun, 1968, The Dueling Machine, 1969, Escape!, 1970, Exiled from Earth, 1971, (with George Lucas) THX 1138, 1971, Flight of Exiles, 1972, As on a Darkling Plain, 1972, When the Sky Burned, 1973, Forward in Time, 1973, Gremlins, Go Home!, 1974, End of Exile, 1975, The Starcrossed, 1975, City of Darkness, 1976, Millennium, 1976, The Multiple Man, 1976, Colony, 1978, Maxwell's Demons, 1978, Kinsman, 1979, Voyagers, 1981, Test of Fire, 1982, The Winds of Altair, 1983; non-fiction The Milky Way Galaxy, 1961, Giants of the Animal World, 1962, Reptiles Since the World Began, 1964, The Uses of Space, 1965, In Quest of Quasars, 1970, Plants, Life and LGM, 1970, The Fourth State of Matter, 1971, The Amazing Laser, 1972, The New Astronomies, 1972, Starflight and Other Improbabilities, 1973, Man Changes the Weather, 1973, Survival Guide for the Suddenly Single, (with Barbara Berson), 1974, The Weather Changes Man, 1974, Workshops in Space, 1974, Through Eyes of Wonder, 1975, Science: Who Needs It?, 1975, Notes to a Science Fiction Writer, 1975, Closeup: New Worlds, (editor with Trudy E. Bell), 1977, The Seeds of Tomorrow, 1977, The High Road, 1981, Vision of the Future, 1982; anthologies include The Many Worlds of SF, 1971, SFWA Hall of Fame, Vol. II, 1973, Analog 9, 1973, The Analog Science Fact Reader, 1974, Analog Annual, 1976, Analog Yearbook, 1978, Best of Analog, 1978, The Best of Omni Science Fiction, 1980, 2, 1981, 3, 1982; contbr. articles and short stories to numerous newspapers, mags. and anthologies. Recipient Hugo Sci. Fiction Achievement award, 1973, 74, 75, 76, 77, 79; E.S. Smith Meml. award for imaginative fiction New Eng. Sci. Fiction Soc., 1974. Fellow Brit. Interplanetary Soc.; mem. Nat. Space Inst. (dir. 1981), AAAS, Sci. Fiction Writers Am., Explorers Club, Amateur Fencer's League Am. Office: 909 Third Ave New York NY 10022

BOVE, JANUAR D., JR., lawyer; b. Wilmington, Del., Aug. 17, 1920; s. Januar D. and Teresa (A.) B.; m. Lillian Briggs, 1949; children: Jeffrey, Nancy, Kathryn. Grad. with honors, U. Del.; J.D., Harvard, 1948. Bar: Del. 1949, U.S. Supreme Ct. 1959. Practiced in, Wilmington, 1949—; partner Connolly, Bove, Lodge & Hutz, 1953—; asst. city solicitor, 1949-50, city solicitor, 1953-57, dep. atty. gen. Del., 1950-53, atty. gen., 1958-62; Bd. dirs. Del. Citizen's Crime Commn., 1962-71, Del. Council on Crime and Justice, 1977-81. Trustee Tatnall Sch., 1962-73; past sec. Republican Com. of Del.; chmn. Crusade for Freedom, Del., 1958. Served from 2d lt. to maj. AUS, World War II. Recipient Good Govt. award Com. of 39, 1962. Mem. Am., Del. bar assns., Nat. Assn. Attys. Gen. (Wyman award 1962), Harvard Law Sch. Assn. (pres. Del. 1962-63), Del. C. of C. (dir. 1967-70), U. Del. Alumni Assn. (treas. 1979-81), Phi Kappa Phi. Club: Harvard (Wilmington). Home: 714 Princeton Rd Westover Hills Wilmington DE 19807 Office: Girard Bank Bldg Wilmington DE 19899

BOVE, JOHN LOUIS, chemistry and environmental engineering educator, researcher; b. N.Y.C., Apr. 15, 1928; s. Frank and Bridget (Randazzo) B.; m. June Althea Burns, Dec. 28, 1957; children: Adele, Catherine. B.A. in Chemistry, Bucknell U., 1949, M.S.A., 1954, Ph.D., Case Western Res. U., 1973. Asst. prof. chemistry Cooper Union, N.Y.C., 1958-67, prof. chemistry and environ. engring., 1970—, dir. environ. program, 1970—; v.p. Cooper Union Research Found., 1974-80; dep. dir. bur. tech. services N.Y.C. Air Resources, 1967-70; dir. Mid-Atlantic Consortium Air Pollution, 1970-76. Contbr. chpts., articles to profl. publs. Served with M.C. U.S. Army, 1950. Recipient Schweinburg Schweinburg Found., 1964; fellow Dow Chem. Co., 1953—; grantee NSF, 1960—;. Republican. Home: 125 Richards Rd Ridgewood NJ 07450 Office: Cooper Union for Advancement Sci and Art 51 Astor Pl New York NY 10003

BOVEE, KENNETH C., veterinary medicine educator; b. Chgo., Sept. 1, 1936; m., 1958; 3 children. B.Sc., Ohio State U., 1958, D.V.M., 1961; M.Med.Sci., U. Pa., 1969. Intern, resident Animal Med. Ctr., N.Y., 1961-64; from asst. prof. to assoc. prof. U. Pa. Sch. Vet. Medicine, Phila., 1967-78, prof. medicine, 1978—, chmn. dept. clin. studies, 1979-84, Corinne and Henry Bower Chair medicine, 1980—. NIH fellow U. Pa. Grad. Sch. Medicine, 1964-67; cons. Smith Kline & French Labs., 1977-78. Mem. Am. Coll. Vet. Internal Medicine, Am. Soc. Nephrology, Internat. Soc. Nephrology, Am. Fedn. Clin. Research. Office: Sch Vet Medicine U Pa Philadelphia PA 19104

BOVERIE, RICHARD THOMAS, air force officer; b. St. Louis, Mar. 20, 1932; s. Edward W. and Virginia (Sullivan) B.; m. Gudrun Wolf, Nov. 21, 1957; 1 dau., Virginia Mary Boverie Hall. B.S., U.S. Naval Acad., 1954; M.S. in Aero. and Astronautical Engring., U. Mich., 1961, U Mich., 1961, George Washington U., 1967; grad., Nat. War Coll., 1971. Commd. 2d lt. USAF, 1954, advanced through grades to maj. gen., 1980; with Office Asst. Sec. Def for Internat. Security Policy, Pentagon, Washington, 1981—. Decorated D.S.M., Legion of Merit, Meritorious Service medal, Commendation medal with oak leaf cluster. Office: Office of Sec Defense Pentagon Washington DC 20301

BOVEY, EDMUND CHARLES, gas company executive; b. Calgary, Alta., Can., Jan. 29, 1916; s. Charles A. and Dorothy (Smith) B.; m. Margaret Snowdon, Jan. 29, 1941; children: Charles Gordon, Myra. Student, Victoria (B.C., Can.) Coll., 1931, U. B.C., 1935. Joined No. Ont. Natural Gas Co. Ltd. (subsequently Norcen Energy Resources Ltd), 1959; v.p. Norcen Energy Resources Ltd., 1960-65; pres., 1965-74, chief exec. officer, chmn. exec. com., 1968-81, chmn. bd., 1974-81; now dir., mem. exec. com. Norcen Energy Resources Ltd., Toronto; dir., mem. exec. com. Abitibi-Price Inc., Can. Packers Inc., Canadian Imperial Bank of Commerce, Hollinger Argus Ltd.; dir. No. & Central Gas Corp. Ltd., Labrador Mining and Exploration Co. Ltd., Hollinger Ltd., Greater Winnipeg Gas Co., Can. Imperial Bank of Commerce, MONY Life Ins. Co. Can., PPG Industries Inc., Pitts., Duplate Can., Can. Packers, PPG Can. Ltd., Griffith Labs. Ltd., Coleman Collieries Ltd., Mercedes-Benz Can. Inc., No. and Central Gas Corp. Ltd.; Chmn. Council for Bus. and Arts in Can. Past pres., also trustee Art Gallery Ont., Canadian Exec. Service Overseas; bd. govs. U. Guelph; mem. internat. council Mus. Modern Art, N.Y.C.; bd. dirs., v.p. Massey Hall; hon. mem. nat. council Boy Scouts Can. Decorated Order of Can. Mem. Can. Gas Assn. (past pres., dir.). Mem. Anglican Ch. (past warden). Clubs: Rosedale Golf, Granite, Mt. Royal, Toronto, York, Empire (Toronto) (life ltd. dirs.); The Links (N.Y.C.); Duquesne (Pitts.). Home: 33 York Ridge Rd Willowdale ON M2P 1R8 Canada Office: Suite 601 PO Box 221 Toronto ON M5L 1E8 Canada

BOVEY, FRANK ALDEN, research chemist; b. Mpls., June 4, 1918; s. John Alden and Margaret Eugenia (Jackson) B.; m. Shirley June Elfman, June 19, 1941 (div. 1980); children: Margaret Bovey Glassman, Peter, Victoria A. B.S., Harvard U., 1940; Ph.D., U. Minn., 1948. With 3M Co., 1942, 48-62, Nat. Synthetic Rubber Corp., Louisville, 1942-45; with Bell Telephone Labs., Murray Hill, N.J., 1962—, head polymer chemistry research dept., 1967—; v.p., dir. Bodel Corp., Mpls.; adj. prof. Stevens Inst. Tech., 1965-67, Rutgers U., 1971—. Author: Effects of Ionizing Radiation on Polymers, 1958, Nuclear Magnetic Resonance, 1969, Polymer Conformation and Configuration, 1969, High Resolution NMR of Macromolecules, 1972, Chain Structure and Conformation of Macromolecules, 1982; also articles.; Asso. editor: Macromolecules, 1968—; editorial bd.: Accounts of Chem. Research, 1968-74, Biopolymers, 1972—. Recipient Outstanding Achievement award U. Minn. Fellow N.Y. Acad. Scis.; mem. Nat. Acad. Scis., Am. Chem. Soc. (Union Carbide award 1958, Minn. award 1962, Witco award polymer chemistry 1969, Nichols medal 1978, Phillips award 1983), Am. Phys. Soc. (High Polymer Physics prize 1974), Am. Soc. Biol. Chemists, Sigma Xi, Phi Lambda Upsilon. Home: 9C Dorado Dr Morristown NJ 07960 Office: AT&T Bell Laboratories Murray Hill NJ 07974

BOW, STEPHEN TYLER, JR., insurance executive; b. Bow, Ky., Oct. 20, 1931; s. Stephen Tyler and Mary L. (King) B.; m. Kathy O'Connor, July, 1982; children: Sandra, Deborah, Carol, Clara. B.A. in Sociology, Berea (Ky.) Coll., 1953; grad. exec. program bus. adminstrn., Columbia U., 1976. C.L.U. With Met. Life Ins. Co., 1953—, v.p. Midwestern head office, Dayton, Ohio, 1976-78, sr. v.p., 1978—, sr. v.p. Western head office, San Francisco, 1983—; dir. Dayton Power & Light Co. Mem. Area Progress Council Dayton; mem. civic adv. council Kettering Med. Center; bd. dirs. Wright State U. Found., Dayton Art Inst., Dayton Philharmonic; trustee Berea Coll.; adv. bd. Ohio U. Center Econ. Edn.; mem. exec. com. Sch. Medicine Wright State U.; chmn. Bob Hipple Meml. Com. Cancer Research; exec. com. Bob Hipple Lab., 1981; chmn. Dayton Area United Negro Coll. Fund drive.; mem. nat. corp. com. United Negro Coll. Fund. Recipient Outstanding Sales Mgmt. award N.Y. Sales Congress, 1972. Mem. Nat. Assn. Life Underwriters, Gen. Agts. and Mgrs. Assn., Calif. Roundtable. Republican. Methodist. Club: San Francisco Bankers. Home: 241 Riviera Dr San Rafael CA 94901 Office: Met Life Ins Co 245 Market St San Francisco CA 94105 *We achieve goals by thinking positively and focusing on objectives not on problems. We achieve economic success by concentrating on serving our fellow man and finding new ways to satisfy his needs. We achieve personal satisfaction by doing more than is expected of us, and exceeding even our own expectations through determination and persistency. We achieve happiness by becoming so interested and absorbed in our work that we forget selfish, petty matters. We achieve a successful life by living each day as if our entire life is to be judged by that day alone.*

BOWDEN, BENJAMIN JOHN, banker; b. Beverly, Mass., June 13, 1932; s. Benjamin Henry and Kathryn Wilson (MacKinnon) B.; (div.)children—Linda K., Benjamin W., Elizabeth D. B.A., Dartmouth Coll., 1954; M.B.A., Tuck Sch., 1955. With First Nat. Bank Boston, 1960—, v.p., then sr. v.p., 1964-80, exec. v.p., 1980—; dir. FNB Fin. Co., FNB Services Co., FNBC Acceptance Corp., Invenchek, Inc. Served to 1st lt. USAF, 1955-57. Office: 100 Federal St Boston MA 02110

BOWDEN, BURNHAM, business exec.; b. Melrose, Mass., Sept. 22, 1900; s. Frederick Prescott and Mary Eunice Lord (Burnham) B.; m. Margaret Loughridge Cornelison, July 24, 1929; children—Mary Alice (Mrs. Robert Lyman), Elizabeth Forsyth (Mrs. Marshall L. Freimer), Burnham, Margaret Loughridge (Mrs. Andrew B. Murray). A.B., Harvard, 1922, M.B.A., 1923. With Lord & Burnham Co., 1923—, v.p., 1927—, Burnham Boiler Corp., 1932, pres., 1933—, Burnham Corp. (consolidation Lord & Burnham Co., Burnham Boiler Corp.), 1933-69, 72, chmn. bd., 1969—; treas. J.C. Turner Lumber Co. (now Turner Corp.), 1933-65, v.p., 1933-69, dir., 1921-81, chmn. bd., 1970-81; mem. Mid-Atlantic adv. bd. Arkwright-Boston Mut. Ins. Co., 1961-76; dir. Felters Co. Republican. Unitarian. Clubs: N.Y. Florists, Harvard Business Sch., Appalachian Mountain, Corinthians, Huguenot Yacht. Home: 7 Bertha Pl Irvington NY 10533 Office: 2 Main St Irvington NY 10533

BOWDEN, HENRY LUMPKIN, lawyer; b. Atlanta, July 23, 1910; s. John and Mattie (Turner) B.; m. Ellen Marian Fleming, June 30, 1937; children—Mary Lamar Fidler, Anne Turner, Henry Lumpkin. B.Ph., Emory U., 1932, LL.B., 1933, LL.D., 1959; LL.D. (hon.), Clark Coll., 1981. Bar: Ga. bar 1933. Since practiced in, Atlanta; asso. firm William E. Arnaud, 1933-39; partner firm Lokey & Bowden, 1939—; city atty. City of Atlanta, 1963-76; dir. 1st Nat. Bank, Atlanta.; Mem. U.S. Regional Loyalty Bd., 1950-52, U.S. Loyalty Rev. Bd., 1952-53. Trustee Emory U.; chmn., 1957-79, Wesleyan Coll., Macon, Ga., Clark Coll., 1959-81. Served from 2d lt. to lt. col. AUS, 1941-46. Recipient Alexander Meiklejohn award AAUP, 1963, Atlanta Shining Light award Sta. WSB and Atlanta Gas Light Co., 1976, award NCCJ, 1982. Fellow Am. Bar Found., Am. Coll. Probate Counsel; mem. Ga. Bar Assn. (pres. 1955-56), ABA, Fed. Bar Assn., Atlanta Bar Assn. (pres. 1947), Inter-Am. Bar Assn., Am. Law Inst., Am. Judicature Soc., Phi Beta Kappa, Phi Delta Theta, Phi Delta Phi, Omicron Delta Kappa. Methodist. Clubs: Capital City, Lawyers, Piedmont Driving (Atlanta); The 10; Homosassa Fishing (Fla.). Home: 2542 Habersham Rd NW Atlanta GA 30305 Office: 2500 Tower Pl 3340 Peachtree Rd NE Atlanta GA 30026

BOWDEN, JESSE EARLE, newspaper editor, author; b. Altha, Fla., Sept. 12, 1928; s. Jesse Walden and Earline (Rackley) B.; m. Mary Louise Clark, Feb. 4, 1951; children: Steven Earle, Randall Clark. B.S. in Journalism and Polit. Sci, Fla. State U., 1951. Reporter, columnist Panama City (Fla.) News-Herald, 1950; sports editor Pensacola (Fla.) News-Jour., 1953-57, news editor, 1957-65, editorial page editor, 1965-66, editorial cartoonist, 1965—, editor-in-chief, 1966—; Charter mem., chmn. Pensacola Hist. Commn.; chmn. Gulf Islands Nat. Seashore Adv. Com., 1973-83; pres. U. West Fla. Found., 1977-79, Pensacola Hist. Soc., 1977-83. Author: Always the Rivers Flow, 1979, Iron Horse in the Pinelands, 1982. Trustee Pensacola Jr. Coll.; bd. dirs. Fla. Hist. Soc. Served to capt. USAF, 1951-53. Recipient Distinguished Citizen award Pensacola Jr. Coll., 1966; nat. award editorial writing Freedoms Found. at Valley Forge, 1967, 68, 69, 70, 72, 74; awards for editorials and cartoons, 1967, 68, 69, 72; DeLuna award Pensacola Founders' Day, 1979; named Pensacola Profl. Bus. Leader of Yr., 1980; recipient Pensacola Kiwanis Civic award, 1982; U. West Fla. Found. fellow, 1982; J. Earle Bowden jr. historian award named in his honor Pensacola Jr. League, 1983. Mem. Am. Soc. Newspaper Editors, Internat. Platform Assn., Nat. Conf. Editorial Writers, Fla. Soc. Newspaper Editors (pres. 1970). Club: Rotary. Established J. Earle Bowden history endowment U. West Fla. Home: 3725 Bonner Rd Pensacola FL 32503 Office: One NewsJour Plaza Pensacola FL 32501

BOWDEN, SALLY ANN, choreographer, teacher, dancer; b. Dallas, Feb. 27, 1943; d. Cloyd MacAnally and Sally Estelle;; d. Cloyd MacAnally and Tate (Bowden). Student, Boston U., 1960-62. Mem. Paul Sanasardo Dance Co., N.Y.C., 1963-67; pvt. tchr., choreographer, N.Y.C., 1968-70; faculty Merce Cunningham Dance Studio, N.Y.C., 1971-76; faculty, co-dir. Constrn. Co. Dance Studio, N.Y.C., 1972-77; choreographer Constrn. Co. Theatre/Dance Assos., N.Y.C., 1972—; artist-in-residence U. Wis., Madison, fall, 1975, N.C. Sch. of Arts, winter, 1978, U. Minn., Duluth, 1979, 1981-82, Kenyon (Ohio) Coll., fall 1980. Choreographer: Three Dances, 1969, Sally Bowden Dances and Talks at the New School, 1972, The Ice Palace, 1973, White River Junction, 1975, The Wonderful World of Modern Dance or The Amazing Story of the Plie, (1976) Wheat, 1976-77, Kite, 1978, Voyages, 1978, Morningdance, 1979, Crescent, 1980. Recipient Creative Artists Public Service award for choreography, 1976-77; Nat. Endowment for the Arts Choreography fellow, 1975. Address: 41 E First St New York NY 10003 *In my dances and in my teaching I want to make people think, to raise questions, open up possibilities, to leave them with open minds. Unfortunately, people quite often would prefer to be provided with easy, pre-fabricated answers.*

BOWDEN, WILLIAM DARSIE, interior designer; b. Palo Alto, Calif., Aug. 11, 1920; s. Edmund Robert and Elisabeth (Darsie) B.; m. Anne Minor Lile, July 29, 1948; children: Darsie Minor, Raleigh Anne, Elsiabeth Lile. B.A., Stanford U., 1942. Jr. exec. Frederick and Nelson Dept. Store, Seattle, 1946-48; exec., interior designer William L. Davis Co., Seattle, 1948—; mem. accreditation bd. visitors Found. for Interior Design Edn. Research. Served to 1st lt. AUS, 1943-46. Fellow Am. Soc. Interior Designers (pres. Wash. chpt. 1966-67, nat. v.p. 1969-71), Art and Antique Dealers League Am. (regional rep.), Furniture History Soc. (London), Phi Beta Kappa (chpt. trustee), Alpha Delta Phi. Republican. Episcopalian. Clubs: University, Wash. Athletic. Home: 2030 Beans Bight Rd NE Bainbridge Island WA 98110 Office: 1300 5th Ave Seattle WA 98101

BOWDEN, WILLIAM LUKENS, educational institute executive; b. Paducah, Ky., Sept. 8, 1922; s. Homer Marvin and Gertrude (Lukens) B.; m. Carol Lorraine Morris, Dec. 22, 1948; children: William Breckenridge, Andrew Scott, Marion Lorraine, Joseph Craig. B.A., Southwestern at Memphis, 1948; M.A., U. Chgo., 1950, Ph.D., 1957; Pd. D. (hon.), Christian Bros. Coll., 1973. Credit reporter Dun & Bradstreet, Birmingham, Ala., 1947; research asst. to dean U. Chgo., Ill., 1948-50; coordinator Richmond Area U. Center, 1950-51; dir. eve. coll. Coll. William and Mary at, Richmond, 1951-52; dir. confs. U. Va., Charlottesville, 1952, dir. Richmond div., 1952-58; asso. dir. So. Regional Edn. Bd., Atlanta, 1958-66; adviser Ford Found., Buenos Aires, Argentina, 1966-67; prof. edn., chmn. dept. adult edn. U. Ga., Athens, 1967-68, also mem. grad. sch. faculty, 1967-68; vice chancellor U. System Ga., 1968-69; pres. Southwestern at, Memphis, 1969-72; exec. dir. So. Growth Policies Bd., 1972-76; mem. staff Duke U., 1972-76; coordinator So. Assn. Colls. and Schs., Atlanta, 1977-78; pres. Cleve. Inst. Electronics, 1978-81; with Jack Eckerd Ednl. Inst., Clearwater, Fla., 1981-84. Mng. editor: The Electron. Served with USNR, 1942-46. Mem. C. of C. U.S. (com. on edn., employment and tng.), Phi Beta Kappa, Omicron Delta Kappa, Pi Kappa Alpha. Presbyterian (deacon 1960-62, ruling elder 1962—). Home: 27 Turnstone Dr Clearwater FL 33519

BOWDEN, WILLIAM P., JR., lawyer; b. East Orange, N.J., Feb. 29, 1944; s. W. Paul and Catherine (Porter) B.; m. Margo Redman, June 8, 1968; children: Jennifer Porter, Peter Chandler. A.B., Williams Coll., 1966; J.D., Columbia U., 1969. Bar: N.Y. Atty., Davis Polk & Wardwell, N.Y.C., 1969-75, 77-80; gen. counsel, sec. Alaska Interstate Co., Houston, 1976-77; v.p., gen. counsel's office Citibank, N.A., N.Y.C., 1980—. Mem. ABA, Assn. Bar City N.Y. Clubs: Rockaway Hunting, Lawrence Beach, University. Home: 110 Riverside Dr New York NY 10024 265 Sage Ave Lawrence NY 11559 Office: 399 Park Ave New York NY 10005

BOWDITCH, FREDERICK WISE, motor vehicle manufacturers association executive; b. Jamaica, L.I., N.Y., Nov. 17, 1921; s. Frederick Tryon and Eleanor (Wise) B.; m. Dorothy Vucic, June 17, 1944; children: Karalyn A., Dierdra E. B.S. in Mech. Engring, U. Ill., 1943; M.S., Purdue U., 1948, Ph.D., 1951. Sr. research engr. fuels and lubricants Gen. Motors Research Labs., 1951-66; staff engr. emission control Gen. Motors Engring. Staff, 1966-68; dir. automotive emission control Gen. Motors Environmental Activities Staff, 1968-73, exec. asst. to v.p. vehicle emission matters, Warren, Mich., 1973-80; v.p. tech. affairs div. Motor Vehicle Mfrs. Assn., 1980—. Served to lt. (j.g.) USNR, 1943-46. Fellow Soc. Automotive Engrs. (vice chmn. automotive and air pollution com. 1971-72, Horning Meml. award 1952); Mem. Air Pollution Control Assn. (dir. 1968-71), Automobile Mfrs. Assn. (past chmn. air quality com.), Engring. Soc. Detroit. Presbyterian (elder 1971-73). Club: Recess. Home: 2777 Orchard Trail Troy MI 48098

BOWDLER, ANTHONY JOHN, physician, educator; b. London, Eng., Oct. 16, 1928; came to U.S., 1967; s. Edward Thomas and Clara (Anthony) B.; m. Eleanor Madeleine Sladen, July 30, 1955; children: Noelle Clare, Jonathan Francis. B.Sc., U. Coll., London, 1949, M.B., B.S., 1952, M.D. (Bilton Pollard fellow), 1963, Ph.D., 1967; postgrad. (Buswell Sr. fellow), U. Rochester, 1962-64. Intern Univ. Coll. Hosp., London, 1952, Hammersmith Hosp., 1953, Brompton Hosp., 1956, Dorking Hosp., Surrey, Eng., 1957; registrar and research fellow U. Coll. Hosp., London, 1958-62; sr. instr. U. Rochester, N.Y., 1962-64; sr. lectr. U. Coll. Hosp. Med. Sch., London, 1964-67; asso. prof. medicine Mich. State U., East Lansing, 1967-70, prof. medicine, 1971-80, Marshall U. Sch. Medicine, Huntington, W.Va., 1980—. Served as surgeon lt. Royal Navy, 1953-55. Fellow Royal Coll. Physicians, A.C.P.; mem. Am. Fedn. Clin. Research, Central Soc. Clin. Research, Am. Soc. Hematology, Am. Soc. Clin. Oncology, Med. Research Soc. London, Brit. Med. Assn. Researcher in internal medicine. Home: Harmony Hills 2 Compton Ct Milton WV 25541 Office: Dept Medicine Marshall U Sch Medicine Huntington WV 25701

BOWDOIN, ROBERT EMANUEL, savings and loan executive, broker; b. Los Angeles, Mar. 4, 1929; s. Alva Sherry and Vivian (Kochinsky) B.; m. Joan Merdith Howell, Apr. 14, 1956; children: Kimberly J., Robert G., Wendy M. B.S., UCLA, 1951, cert. real estate, 1956. Engaged in acctg., 1951-52; real estate appraiser, loan officer, escrow officer Watts Savs. and Loan Assn., Los Angeles, 1954-57; mgr. Fairway Escrow Co., Los Angeles, 1957-62; pres. Bowdoin, Neal, Weathers, Inc., loan corrs., Los Angeles, 1962-66; asst. real estate mgr. Pasadena (Calif.) Redevel. Agy., 1966-68; dep. adminstr. tech. services Community Redevel. Agy., Los Angeles, 1971-73; pres., chief exec. officer Family Savs. and Loan Assn., Los Angeles, 1973—; dir. Systems Planning Corp., Diversified Appraisal Corp., Family Devel. Corp Trustee Pitzer Coll., Claremont, Calif., 1980—. Past mem. vestry bd. St. Marks Episcopal Ch., Altadena, Calif; past bd. dirs. Altadena Library, San, Gabriel Valley United Way. Served with AUS, 1952-54. Mem. Am. Savs. and Loan League (pres. 1981), U.S. Savs. League, Calif. Savs. and Loan League (past dir.). Democrat. Address: 3683 Crenshaw Blvd Los Angeles CA 90016

BOWE, RICHARD EUGENE, machine co. exec.; b. Van Wert, Ohio, Aug. 27, 1921; s. Hugh Horatio and Clara Magdalene (Heiby) B.; m. Virginia Welbourn Cooley, May 17, 1947; children—Richard Welbourn, Michael Ames, Peter Armistead. Student, U. Mich., 1939-40; B.S., U.S. Naval Acad., 1943; M.B.A., Harvard U., 1949. Salesman Buck Glass Co., Balt., 1949-54; with Ellicott Machine Corp., Balt., 1954—, chmn. bd., pres., 1965—; dir. First Nat. Bank Md., Balt.; adv. dir. Liberty Mut. and Arkwright, Boston. Trustee Gilman Sch., 1970-78, Balt. Mus. Art, 1979—. Served with USN, 1940-47. Decorated Bronze Star medal. Home: 1135 Asquith Dr Arnold MD 21012 Office: 1611 Bush St Baltimore MD 21230

BOWEN, ALBERT REEDER, lawyer; b. Logan, Utah, Apr. 13, 1905; s. Albert Ernest and Aletha (Reeder) B.; m. Lucile Ross, Nov. 17, 1934 (dec. 1952); children: Barbara (Mrs. Ted O. Brunker), David Ross, Beverly (Mrs. Michael W. Walker), Albert Ross, Robert K. Bowen; m. Margret Jenson, Mar. 29, 1954; children: Mark J., Julie (Mrs. Curtis D. Elton), Stephen J. A.B., U. Utah, 1930; J.D., Leland Stanford Jr. U., 1932. Bar: Utah bar 1932. Since practiced in, Salt Lake City; partner firm Ray, Quinney & Nebeker (and predecessors), 1945—; Sec., mem. Utah Sch. Study Com., 1963-64; del. Republican Nat.

Conv., 1964; Bd. regents U. Utah, 1951-55. Fellow emeritus Am. Coll. Trial Lawyers; mem. ABA, Utah Bar Assn. Mem. Ch. of Jesus Christ of Latter Day Saints. Clubs: Timpangogas (pres. 1975-76), Bonneville Knife and Fork (dir. 1962-65). Home: 1847 Laird Ave Salt Lake City UT 84108 Office: Deseret Bldg Salt Lake City UT 84111

BOWEN, BARBARA CHERRY, educator; b. Newcastle-upon-Tyne, Eng., May 4, 1937; came to U.S., 1962; d. Harold E. and Hilda Edith (Meech) Cannings; m. Vincetn E. Bowen, Jan. 12, 1963; children: Sarah, Tessa. B.A., Oxford U., M.A., 1958; Doctorat de l'Universite de Paris, 1962. Instr. French U. Ill., Urbana, 1962-63, asst. prof., 1963-66, assoc. prof., 1966-73, prof., 1973—. Author: Les Caracteristiques essentielles de la farce francaise, 1964, The Age of Bluff, 1972, Words and the Man in French Renaissance Literature, 1983. Guggenheim fellow, France, 1974-75; NEH summer seminar, 1980; NEH fellow, Italy, 1981-82; Villa I Tatti fellow, Florence, Italy, 1981-82. Mem. MLA (exec. council 1978-81), Central Renaissance Conf. (orgn. com.), Medieval Assn. Midwest (exec. council). Episcopalian. Home: 2108 Zuppke Urbana IL 61801 Office: Dept Franch Univ Ill 707 S Matthews St Urbana IL 61801

BOWEN, CHARLES CLARK, museum director, former educator, biologist; b. Detroit, Mar. 18, 1917; s. Charles Clark and Geraldine (Jarvis) B.; m. Vada Robinson, Aug. 28, 1947; children: Clark, Gail (Mrs. Marvin Lindmark), Jean (Mrs. Dean Smith), Lecia (Mrs. William Riva) (dec.). Student, U. Mich., 1935-39, B.A, Mich. State U., 1949, M.S., 1951, Ph.D., 1953. NIH postdoctoral fellow Brookhaven Nat. Lab., 1953-55; faculty Iowa State U., Ames, 1955-80, prof., 1962-80, prof. emeritus, 1981—, chmn. grad. program cell biology, 1966-72, asst. dean scis. and humanities, 1967-75; exec. dir. Kokee Natural History Mus., Kauai, Hawaii, 1981—; faculty improvement leave div. cell biology, U. Tex. Med. Br, Galveston, 1975-76. Contbr. articles to profl. jours. Served with USN, World War II; capt. Res. ret. Mem. Bot. Soc. Am., Am. Soc. Cell Biology, Electron Microscope Soc. Am., AAAS, Sierra Club (chmn. Iowa chpt. 1973-75), Sigma Xi, Phi Kappa Phi, Gamma Sigma Delta. Office: Kokee Mus Box NN Kekaha Kauai HI 96752

BOWEN, CHARLES HUGH, JR., lawyer, electronics engineer, retired naval officer; b. Belle Ellen, Ala., Jan. 8, 1923; s. Charles Hugh and Lavada (Lawley) B.; m. Nina Gwen Stevens, July 29, 1945 (div.); children: David Hugh, Charles Hugh III; m. Joan H. Steffens, Mar. 18, 1978. Student, U. Ariz., 1939-40, 46, U. So. Calif., 1946-47; B.S. in Engring. Electronics, Naval Postgrad. Sch., 1953, M.S., 1954; grad., Naval War Coll., 1961; J.D., U. Santa Clara, 1977. Bar: Calif. Commd. ensign U.S. Navy, 1943, advanced through grades to capt., 1965; flight tng., 1942-43, pilot and flight officer, PTO, 1944-45; flight instr. Aviation Tng. Unit 5, 1947-49; radar projects supr. VX-1 Key West, Fla., 1949-51; operations officer Attack Squadron 55, 1954-55; aviation electronics engring. officer, staff Comdr. Naval Air Force Pacific Fleet, 1956-58; assigned spl. studies sect. Spl. Projects Office, Bur. Weapons, 1958-60; student replace air tng. group Attack Squadron 122, 1961; comdg. officer Attack Squadron 115, 1962-63; navigator U.S.S. Kitty Hawk, 1963-64, exec. officer, 1964; tchr. elec. sci. U.S. Naval Acad., also head sci. dept., 1965-67; command U.S.S. Vesuvius, 1967-68; advanced devel. engr. Sylvania Electronics Systems, Mountain View, Calif., 1968-72, mktg. mgr., 1972-74; jud. extern with Justice Calif. Supreme Ct., 1976; individual practice law Campbell, Calif., 1978-81; ptnr. Finch & Bowen, Campbell, Calif., 1981—. Decorated D.F.C. with gold star, Air medal with silver star. Mem. IEEE, Naval Inst., Internat. Platform Assn. Democrat. Home: 5941 Drytown Pl San Jose CA 95120

BOWEN, DAVID LEON, wire service executive; b. San Antonio, Dec. 21, 1926; s. Francis Joseph and Amanda (Haak) B.; m. Rosemary Anne Meely, Nov. 17, 1951; children: Mary Beth, Patricia, David, Margaret. B.J., U. Tex., Austin, 1947, B.S. in Math, 1947; M.A. in Journalism, Marquette U., 1951. Reporter Temple (Tex.) Daily Telegram, 1947-48; newsman Milw. Bur., AP, 1950-51, editor gen. desk, N.Y.C., 1952-54, feature dept. editor, 1955-60, newsfeature supervising editor, 1961-62, gen. exec. in charge traffic dept., 1964-69, dir. communications, 1970-81, v.p., 1972-81; pres. Satellite Data Broadcast Networks, Inc. subs., 1981—. Served with USN, 1944-47. Recipient By-Line award Marquette U. Coll. Journalism, 1972. Introduced electronic editing systems to AP news ops., 1970; managed devel. AP laserphoto facsimile picture recorder, AP electronic darkroom. Office: 50 Rockefeller Plaza New York NY 10020 *The heart of the matter is more elusive than one would expect. What success I have enjoyed stems from a knack for recognizing it quicker than most.*

BOWEN, DAVID REECE, former congressman; b. Houston, Miss., Oct. 21, 1932; s. David Reece and Lera (Pinnix) B. Ed., U. Mo., 1950-52, postgrad., 1964-65; A.B., Harvard U., 1954; M.A., Oxford U., U. Chgo., 1965-66. Asst. prof. polit. sci. and history Miss. Coll., 1958-59; asst. prof. polit. sci. Millsaps Coll., 1959-64; coordinator S.E. region OEO, Washington, 1966-67; staff asso. for edn. U.S. C. of C., Washington, 1967-68; spl. asst. to gov., coordinator Fed.-State programs State of Miss., 1968-72; mem. 93d-97th congresses, mem. coms. on fgn. affairs, agr., chmn. subcom. on cotton, rice and sugar, mem. com. on mcht. marine and fisheries. Served with AUS, 1957-58. Democrat.

BOWEN, DON LESLIE, government educator; b. Spanish Fork, Utah, Apr. 16, 1922; s. Leslie and Hortense (Lieshman) B.; m. Janice Applegate, Dec. 25, 1944; children: Stephen Leslie, Kathryn (Mrs. Dennis A. Zimdars). B.S., Utah State U., 1944; M.S., U. Denver, 1945; Ph.D., Syracuse U., 1949. Instr., asst. prof. dept. govt. U. Okla., 1946-49; dir. research, acting dir. (Okla., Legislative Com.), 1949-51; adminstrv. asst. to Congressman John Jarman, Okla., 1951-53; dir. Bur. Govt. Research; asso. prof. govt. U. Md., 1953-56; asst. dir. edn. and research, asso. dir. Am. Soc. Pub. Adminstrn., Chgo., 1956-62, exec. dir., 1962-70; coll. adviser for pub. service edn. programs Bowie (Md.) State Coll., 1971; prof. mgmt. and policy U. Ariz., Tucson, 1971—, chmn. dept., 1972-73; Vis. prof. Utah State U., summer 1958; lectr. U. Chgo., Dept. Agr. Grad. Sch.; cons. U.S. Gen. Accounting Office, Ford Found., U.S. Office Edn., Md. Dept. Health, Okla. Personnel Bd. Author: Judicial Personnel, 1949, Judicial Organization and Management, 1949, (with R.S. Friedman) Local Government in Maryland, 1955, Arizona County Government, 1980; editor: Public Service Professional Associations and the Public Interest, 1973; Co-editor: Administrative Leadership in Government: Selected Papers, 1959, Program Formulation and Development: The Role of the Government Executive, 1960, Methods and Goals in Public Managements, 1961; Contbr. articles to profl. jours., mags. Mem. Citizens Com. Constl. Revision Okla., 1948; mem. Prince Georges County (Md.) Study Commn., 1966-67; chmn. County Merit System Rev. com., 1968-69; mem. governing bds. Pub. Am. Service, Govtl. Affairs Inst. (exec. com.); exec. council, Nat. Assn. Schs. Pub. Affairs and Adminstrn. Mem. Internat. City Mgmt. Assn., Internat. Personnel Mgmt. Assn., Am. Pub. Health Assn., Western Govt. Research Assn. (exec. com.), Am. Soc. Pub. Adminstrn. (past pres. Md. chpt., past v.p. Wash. chpt.), Nat. Acad. Pub. Adminstrn., Phi Kappa Phi, Pi Sigma Alpha (past nat. pres.), Pi Alpha Alpha (nat. pres. 1977-80). Unitarian. Home: 4702 E Burning Tree Pl Tucson AZ 85718 Office: University of Arizona Tucson AZ 85721

BOWEN, DUDLEY HOLLINGSWORTH, JR., U.S. district judge; b. Augusta, Ga., June 25, 1941; s. Dudley Hollingsworth and Edna (Maury) B.; m. Madeline Martin, Aug. 14, 1963; children: Laura Madeline, Anna Maury. A.B. in Fgn. Langs., U. Ga., 1964, LL.B., 1965. Bar: Ga. 1965. Gen. practice law, Augusta, 1968-72; bankruptcy judge So. Dist. Ga., 1972-75; partner firm Dye, Miller, Bowen & Tucker, Augusta, 1975-79; U.S. dist. judge So. Dist. Ga., 1979—; tchr. seminars; panelist Atlanta Bar Assn., S.C. Bar and Inst. Continuing Legal Edn., 1976-78. Served to 1st lt., inf. U.S. Army, 1966-68. Decorated Commendation medal. Mem. Am. Bar Assn., State Bar Ga. (chmn. bankruptcy law sect. 1977). Presbyterian. Address: PO Box 2106 Augusta GA 30903

BOWEN, GEORGE HAMILTON, JR., astrophysicist, educator; b. Tulsa, June 20, 1925; s. George H. and Dorothy (Huntington) B.; m. Marjorie Evelyn Brown, June 19, 1948; children—Paul Huntington, Margaret Irene, Carol Ann, Dorothy Elizabeth, Kevin Leigh. B.S. with honor, Calif. Inst. Tech., 1949, Ph.D., 1952. Asso. biologist Oak Ridge Nat. Lab., 1952-54; asst. prof. physics Ia. State Coll., 1954-57; asso. prof. physics Iowa State U., 1957-65, prof., 1965—. Served with USNR, 1944-46. Recipient Iowa State U. Outstanding Tchr. award, 1970, Faculty citation Iowa State U. Alumni Assn., 1971. Mem. Am. Astron. Soc., Astron. Soc. Pacific, Am. Assn. Physics Tchrs. (chmn. Iowa sect. 1966-67), AAAS, Sigma Xi, Tau Beta Pi. Home: 1919 Burnett Ave Ames IA 50010 Office: Dept Physics Iowa State U Ames IA 50011

BOWEN, HOWARD ROTHMANN, economist; b. Spokane, Wash., Oct. 27, 1908; s. Henry G. and Josephine (Menig) B.; m. Lois B. Schilling, Aug. 24, 1935; children—Peter Geoffrey, Thomas Gerard. B.A., Wash. State U., 1929, M.A., 1933; Ph.D., U. Iowa, 1935; 20 hon. doctorates. Instr. to asso. prof. econs. U. Iowa, 1935-42; economist U.S. Dept. Commerce, 1942-44; chief economist (Joint Congressional Com. on Internal Revenue Taxation), 1944-45; economist Irving Trust Co., 1945-47; dean (Coll. Commerce and Bus. Adminstrn.); prof. econs. U. Ill., 1947-52, Williams Coll., 1952-55; pres. Grinnell (Iowa) Coll., 1955-64, U. Iowa, Iowa City, 1964-69; now pres. emeritus; prof. econs. and edn. Claremont Grad. Sch., 1969—, chancellor, 1970-75; dir. Bankers Life Co., 1965-81; mem. U.S. Tax Mission to Japan, 1949; econ. cons. Nat. Council Chs., 1949-53; chmn. Gov.'s Commn. Econ. and Social Trends in Iowa, 1958; mem. Fed. Adv. Com. Intergovtl. Relations, 1961-64; chmn. Nat. Commn. Tech., Automation and Econ. Progress, 1964-66. Author: English Grants in Aid, 1939, Iowa Income, 1934, Unemployment Compensation Applied to Iowa, 1936, Toward Social Economy, 1948, Social Responsibilities of the Businessman, 1953, Graduate Education in Economics, 1953, Christian Values and Economic Life, 1954, (with Garth L. Mangum) Automation and Economic Progress, 1966, The Finance of Higher Education, 1968, (with Gordon Douglass) Efficiency in Liberal Education, 1971, Investment in Learning, 1977, The Costs of Higher Education, 1980, The State of the Nation and The Agenda for Higher Education, 1981; also numerous pamphlets and articles. Chief U.S. AID Mission to Thailand, 1961; chmn. Nat. Citizens Com. for Tax Revision and Reform, 1963; mem. Council for Fin. Aid to Edn., 1968-75; Trustee Grinnell Coll., Claremont U. Center, Tchrs. Ins. and Annuity Assn., Coll. Retirement Equities Fund. Social Sci. Research Council fellow for study in Eng., 1937-38; Carnegie Found. for Advancement Teaching fellow, 1980-81; recipient awards for leadership in higher edn. Nat. Council Ind. Colls. and Univs., 1975, N.Y. Assn. Colls. and Univs., 1976, Nat. Assn. Student Personnel Adminstrs., 1981, Council Ind. Colls., 1983, Ness award Assn. Am. Colls., 1983. Mem. Am. Fin. Assn. (pres. 1950), Royal Econ. Soc. (Eng.), Am. Assn. Higher Edn. (pres. 1975—), Am. Econ. Assn., Western Econ. Assn. (pres. 1977), Nat. Acad. Edn., Assn. Study Higher Edn. (pres. 1980), Phi Kappa Phi, Beta Gamma Sigma, Phi Beta Kappa. Home: 916 W Harrison St Claremont CA 91711 Office: Claremont Grad Sch Claremont CA 91711

BOWEN, JAMES RONALD, banker; b. Falls City, Nebr., July 3, 1941; s. Charles Addison and Vera Mae (White) B.; m. Jacquelyn Ann Westhoff, Mar. 3, 1962; children: Bryan Scott, Susan Lyn. B.S. in Bus. Adminstrn., Kans. State Tchrs. Coll., 1964; postgrad. cert., Rutgers U., 1973. Acctg. mgr. Fed. Res. Bank, Kansa City, Mo., 1968-69, asst. v.p., Kansas City, Mo., 1970-74, v.p., 1975-76, sr. v.p., 1977—; chmn. Fed. Res. System Automation Program Directorate, Kansas City, 1981-82. Mem. Kansas City C. of C. Office: Fed Reserve Bank 925 Grand Ave Kansas City MO 64198

BOWEN, J(EAN) DONALD, educator; b. Malad, Idaho, Mar. 19, 1922; s. John David and Lillian (Larson) B.; m. Catherine Holley, May 27, 1948; children: David James, Douglas Ray, Dale Eugene, Christina Lee, Karen Lucy. A.B., Brigham Young U., 1944; M.A., Columbia U., 1949; Ph.D., U. N.Mex., 1952. Instr. Duke U., Durham, N.C., 1952-53; sci. linguist Fgn. Service Inst., Washington, 1953-58; prof. English UCLA, 1958—, co-dir., 1958-63; field dir. (Survey of Lang. Use and Lang. Teaching in Eastern Africa), 1968-70; vis. prof. Am. U. Cairo, 1974-77, Ain Shams U., 1976-77. Author: Patterns of English Pronunciation, 1975, (with others) Adaptation in Language Teaching, 1978, Patterns of Spanish Pronunciation, 1960, The Sounds of English and Spanish, 1965, The Grammatical Structures of English and Spanish, 1965, English Usage, 1983; author, editor: Studies in Southwest Spanish, 1976, Linguistics in Oceania, 1971, Language in Ethiopia, 1976; contbr. articles to profl. jours. Served with U.S. Army, 1943-46. Mem. Linguistic Soc. Am., MLA, TESL. Mormon. Home: 3055 Corda Dr Los Angeles CA 90049 Office: Dept English UCLA Los Angeles CA 90024

BOWEN, JEWELL RAY, chemical engineering educator; b. Duck Hill, Miss., Jan. 9, 1934; s. Hugh and Myrtle Louise (Stevens) B.; m. Priscilla Joan Spooner, Feb. 4, 1956; children: Jewell Ray, Sandra L., Susan E. B.S., MIT, 1956, M.S., 1957; Ph.D., U. Calif.-Berkeley, 1963. Asst. prof. U. Wis., Madison, 1963-67; assoc. prof. U. Wis.-Madison, 1967-70, prof. chem. engring., 1970-81, chmn., 1971-73, 78-81, asso. vice chancellor, 1972-76; prof. chem. engring. U. Wash., Seattle, 1981—, dean, 1981—; cons. in field; adviser NSF, Dept. Def. Contbr. articles to profl. jours.; editor: 7th-9th Internat. Colloquiums on Dynamics of Explosions and Reactive Systems, 1979, 81, 83. NATO-NSF postdoctoral fellow, 1962-63; sr. postdoctoral fellow, 1968; Deutsche Forschungsgemeinschaft prof., 1976-77. Mem. Am. Inst. Chem. Engrs., Am. Phys. Soc., Combustion Inst. Home: 5324 NE 86th St Seattle WA 98115 Office: Coll of Engring FH-10 Univ of Wash Seattle WA 98195

BOWEN, JOHN RICHARD, chemical company executive; b. Passaic, N.J., May 5, 1934; s. Nathan S. and Florence R. (Schubarth) B.; m. Patricia Joanne Meinke, Feb. 4, 1956; children: Kenneth Alan, Teresa Lynn. B.B.A., U. Mich., 1956, M.B.A., 1957. C.P.A. With Price Waterhouse & Co., Detroit, 1958-66; v.p. Corning Internat. Corp., 1966-72; controller U.S. Postal Service, 1972-74; v.p. fin. Morton Thiokol, Inc., Chgo., 1974—. Home: 42 Little Marryat St Cary IL 60013 Office: 110 N Wacker Dr Chicago IL 60606

BOWEN, JOHN SHEETS, advertising executive; b. Chelsea, Mass., Feb. 4, 1927; s. Charles Parnell and Helen (Sheets) B.; m. Catherine Leigh Stander, June 28, 1952; children: Mark Stander, Charles Parnell III, Holly Leigh. B.A., Yale U., 1949. Salesman Procter & Gamble Co., 1949-51, unit mgr., 1952; account exec. McCann-Erickson, Inc., 1952-58; with Benton & Bowles, Inc., 1959—, mgmt. supr., 1964—, sr. v.p., 1965-68, exec. v.p., 1968-71, pres., 1971—, chief exec. officer, 1973—; bd. dirs. Advt. Council. Bd. dirs. United Way of Tri-State, Advt. Ednl. Found. Served with AUS, 1944-46; ETO. Mem. Am. Assn. Advt. Agys. (dir.-at-large 1977—, vice chmn. 1981-82, chmn. 1982-83, vice chmn. ednl. found.), Better Bus. Bur. (bd. dirs.). Episcopalian (sr. arden). Home: 44 Grace Church St Rye NY 10580 Office: 909 3d Ave New York NY 10022

BOWEN, OTIS RAY, former governor Indiana, physician; b. nr. Rochester, Ind., Feb. 26, 1918; s. Vernie and Pearl (Wright) B.; m. Elizabeth A. Steinmann, Feb. 25, 1939 (dec. Jan. 1981); children: Richard H., Judith I. McGrew, Timothy R., Robert O.; m. Rose May Hochstetler, Sept. 26, 1981. A.B. in Chemistry, Ind. U., 1939, M.D., 1942, LL.D. (hon.); LL.D. (hon.), Anderson Coll., 1973, Valparaiso U., 1973, Butler U., 1973, Vincennes U., Tri-State Coll., Calumet Coll., U. Evansville, Ind. U., Ind. State U., Ball State U., U. Notre Dame, Rose-Hulman Inst., St. Joseph Coll., Calumet Campus of Purdue U., Manchester Coll., Hanover Coll., St. Mary's Coll., Bethel Coll., Marian Coll. Intern, Meml. Hosp., South Bend, Ind., 1942-43; practice gen. medicine, Bremen, Ind., 1946-72; past mem. staff Bremen Community Hosp., Parkview Hosp., Plymouth, Ind., St. Joseph's and Meml. Hosp., South Bend, St. Joseph Hosp., Mishawaka, Ind.; clin. prof. family medicine Sch. Medicine, Ind. U., 1976—; coroner Marshall County, Ind., 1952-56; mem. Ind. Ho. of Reps., 1956-58, 60-72, minority leader, 1965-67, speaker of house, 1967-72; vice chmn. legis. council Ind. (Gen. Assembly), 1967-68, chmn., 1970-72, gov. Ind., 1973-81; mem. staff dept. family medicine Long Hosp., Indpls., 1981—; mem. Council State Govts., 1973—, mem. exec. com.; mem. Edn. Commn. States, 1973-81, chmn.-elect, 1976-77, chmn., 1977-78; mem. Midwest Govs. Conf., 1973-81, vice chmn., 1977-78, chmn., 1978; mem. Republican Govs. Conf., 1973-81, chmn., 1978; mem. Nat. Govs. Conf., 1973—, chmn., 1979; past chmn. com. on crime reduction and pub. safety, mem. energy com.; past mem. Pres.'s Commn. Fed. Paperwork, Pres.'s Commn. Sci. and Tech.; mem. Pres.'s Commn. Federalism, 1981—; past chmn. Interstate Mining Commn.; past med. services dir. Marshall County CD; mem. Midwest Govs. Gt. Lakes Caucus; former mem. adv. com. on curricula Vincennes U.; hon. dir. Center for Pub. Service, Anderson Coll.; chmn. Adv. Council Social Security, 1982; chmn. adv. council BACCHUS, 1979—. Contbr. articles to med. jours. Past trustee Ancilla Coll.; trustee Valparaiso U., 1978—; past mem. adv. council United Student Aid Fund; mem. adv. bd. Indpls. chpt. Fellowship Christian Athletes; mem., past chmn. Lutheran Sch. Bd., Bremen; past v.p. congregation, past fin. bd. chmn. St. Paul's Lutheran Ch., Bremen.; bd. govs. Riley Meml. Assn., 1981—; bd. dirs. Greater Indpls. Council Alcoholism, 1982—, Lilly Endowment Found. Served from 1st lt. to capt. M.C., AUS, 1943-46; PTO. Recipient Merit award Ind. Pub. Health Assn., 1971; named Alumni of Year, Ind. U. Med. Sch., 1971; Disting. Service award Future Farmers Am., 1976; Public Service award Ind. Soc. Public Adminstrn. Mem. AMA (Dr. Benjamin Rush award 1973), Ind. Med. Assn. (legis commn. 1958-71, 13th dist. councilor 1965-71), 13th Dist. Med. Assn. (past pres.), Marshall County Med. Assn. (past pres.), Am. Gen. Practice Assn., Ind. Gen. Practice Assn., 13th Dist. Gen. Practice Assn., Farm Bur., Marshall County Tb Soc. (past v.p.), Bremen C. of C., Am. Legion, VFW, Alpha Omega Alpha, Phi Beta Pi, Delta Chi. Lutheran. Club: Kiwanis (past pres.). Home: Bremen IN 46506 Office: Dept Family Medicine Long Hosp 1100 W Michigan St Indianapolis IN 46223

BOWEN, RICHARD L., State education administrator; b. Avoca, Iowa, Aug. 31, 1933; s. Howard L. and Donna (Milburn) B.; m. Connie Smith Bowen, 1976; children: James, Robert; children by previous marriage—Catherine, David, Thomas. B.A., Augustana Coll., 1957; M.A., Harvard, 1959, Ph.D., 1967. Fgn. service officer State Dept., 1959-60; research asst. to U.S. Senator Francis Case, 1960-62; legis. asst. to U.S. Senator Karl Mundt, 1962-65; minority cons. sub-com. exec. reorgn. U.S. Senate, 1966-67; asst. to pres., asso. prof. polit. sci. U. S.D., Vermillion, 1967-69, pres., 1969-76; commr. higher edn. Bd. Regents State S.D., Pierre, from 1976. Served with USN, 1951-54. Recipient Outstanding Alumnus award Augustana Coll., 1970; Woodrow Wilson fellow, 1957; Fulbright scholar, 1957; Congl. Staff fellow, 1965. Office: Office of Commr of Higher Edn Kneip Office Bldg Pierre SD 57501 *

BOWEN, ROBERT STEVENSON, tire and rubber company executive; b. Chgo., Dec. 4, 1937; s. Earl McDonald and Helen T. (Stevenson) B.; m. Jane Carlson, Oct. 13, 1973; children: Thomas, Anne. A.B., North Park Coll., Chgo., 1955; B.S., Northwestern U., 1958; M.B.A., Harvard U., 1961; postgrad., U. Stockholm, (Sweden), 1963-64. Sr. planning mgr. Ford Motor Co., Dearborn, Mich., 1961-72; v.p. mktg. and internat. Zenith Radio Corp., Chgo., 1972-80; pres. sales and mktg. group Firestone Tire and Rubber Co., Brook Park, Ohio, 1980—; chmn. bd. Zenith Time S.A., LeLocle, Switzerland, 1974-78. Trustee Nat. 4-H Council. George F. Baker scholar Harvard Bus. Sch., 1960; Fulbright scholar, 1963-64. Office: Firestone Tire and Rubber Co 6275 Eastland Rd Brook Park OH 44142

BOWEN, STEPHEN FRANCIS, JR., ophthalmic surgeon; b. Worcester, Mass., Jan. 6, 1932; s. Stephen Francis and Margaret Helen (O'Brien) B.; m. Ann Marie Nooney, July 5, 1958; children: Mary Beth, Alisa, Stephen, Margo. A.B. cum laude, Holy Cross Coll., 1952; M.D., Tufts U., 1956; M.Sc., U. Minn., 1962. Intern U. Minn. Hosp., 1956-57; fellow in ophthalmology Mayo Clinic, Rochester, Minn., 1959-62; practice medicine specializing in ophthalmology St. Louis, 1962—; mem. faculty St. Louis U. Med. Sch., 1962—, clin. prof. ophthalmology, 1972—; Cons. question and answer sect. Jour. AMA, 1968—. Contbr. articles to profl. jours. Served to lt. comdr. M.C. USNR, 1957-59. Mem. Mo. Ophthalmol. (pres. 1968-69), Nat. Mayo Eye Alumni Assn. (pres. 1971—), St. Louis Ophthalmol. Soc. (pres. 1976), Mayo Alumni Assn. (dir. 1973-79), Sigma Xi. Roman Catholic. Office: 16 Hampton Village Plaza St Louis MO 63109

BOWEN, STEPHEN GEORGE, advertising company executive; b. Worcester, Mass., Jan. 17, 1944; s. Stephen G. B. and Jeanne (Daugherty Bowen); m. Valerie Close, Mar. 21, 1970; children: Stephen G., Daniel Walter. A.B. in Econs., Coll. of Holy Cross, 1965. Various account mgmt. positions J. Walter Thompson Co., N.Y.C., 1969—, sr. v.p., group account dir., 1980—. Served to capt. USMC, 1965-69; Vietnam. Roman Catholic. Club: Shenorock Shore (Rye, N.Y.). Office: J Walter Thompson 466 Lexington Ave New York NY 10017

BOWEN, WILLIAM AUGUSTUS, banker; b. Greenville, N.C., Jan. 17, 1930; s. Joseph Francis and Dorothy Lee (Simmons) B.; m. Hilda Carolyn Rowlett, June 8, 1952; children: Carolyn, Elizabeth Lee Bowen Jones, William Augustus, Mary Jane. B.S. in Bus. Adminstrn, U. N.C., 1951, grad. exec. program, 1965. With Wachovia Bank & Trust Co., 1955-80, regional v.p., mgr. So. region, Charlotte, N.C., 1970-79; pres., chief operating officer, dir. First Tulsa Bancorp., also First Nat. Bank and Trust Co, Tulsa, 1980—; Bd. dirs. Industries for Tulsa, Downtown Tulsa Unlimited. Trustee Thomas Gilcrease Mus. Assn., Hillcrest Med. Ctr.; exec. com. Tulsa Area United Way; bd. regents Tulsa Jr. Coll.; vice chmn. Okla. Council Sci. and Tech. Served to lt. USNR, 1951-55. Mem. Assn. Res. City Bankers, Am. Petroleum Inst., Am. Bankers Assn., Okla. Bankers Assn., Met. Tulsa C. of C. (bd. dirs.), Newcomen Soc. N.Am., Okla. State C. of C. (bd. dirs.), Phi

Beta Kappa, Beta Gamma Sigma (pres. 1950-51). Clubs: Tulsa, Golf of Okla., So. Hills Country (Tulsa); Castle Pines Golf (Colo.). Home: 7303 S College Pl Tulsa OK 74136 Office: 15 E 5th St Tulsa OK 74103

BOWEN, WILLIAM GORDON, university administrator, economist; b. Cin., Oct. 6, 1933; s. Albert A. and Bernice (Pomert) B.; m. Mary Ellen Maxwell, Aug. 25, 1956; children: David Alan, Karen Lee. B.A., Denison U., 1955; Ph.D., Princeton U., 1958. Mem. faculty Princeton U., 1958—, prof. econs., 1965—, dir. grad. studies, 1964-66, provost, 1967-72, pres., 1972—; dir. NCR Corp.; bd. regents Smithsonian Instn. Author: The Wage-Price Issue; A Theoretical Analysis, 1960, Wage Behavior in the Postwar Period; An Empirical Analysis, 1960, Economic Aspects of Education: Three Essays, 1964, (with W. J. Baumol) Performing Arts: The Economic Dilemma, 1966, (with T.A. Finegan) The Economics of Labor Force Participation, 1969. Mem. Am. Econ. Assn., Indsl. Relations Research Assn., Phi Beta Kappa. Office: 1 Nassau Hall Princeton U Princeton NJ 08544

BOWEN, WILLIAM HARVEY, banker, lawyer; b. Altheimer, Ark., May 6, 1923; s. Robert James and Lois Ruth B.; m. Mary Constance Wanasek, Aug. 3, 1947; children: Cynthia Ruth Bowen Blanchard, William Scott, Mary Patricia. Student, Henderson State Tchrs. Coll., 1941-42; LL.B., U. Ark., 1949; LL.M. in Taxation, NYU, 1950; postgrad., Grad. Sch. Banking, Rutgers U., 1974. Bar: Ark. 1949, U.S. Supreme Ct. 1950. Atty. adviser U.S. Tax Ct., Washington, 1950-52; spl. asst. to atty. gen. trial sect., tax div. Dept. Justice, Washington, 1952-54; ptnr. Smith, Williams, Friday & Bowen, Little Rock, Ark., 1954-71; pres., dir. Comml. Nat. Bank, Little Rock, Ark., 1971-75, pres., dir., chief exec. officer, 1975-81; chmn. 1st Comml. Bank N.A., Little Rock, Ark., 1981—, pres., chief exec. officer, 1984—; staff Stonier Grad. Sch. Banking Rutgers U., New Brunswick, N.J., 1976—, bd. regents, 1977; mem. fed. adv. council Fed. Res. Bank St. Louis, 1984—. Author: (with M. Moore) Arkansas Estate Planners Handbook, 1967. Trustee Ben J. Altheimer Found., Altheimer, Ark., 1973, Philander Smith Coll., Little Rock, 1968-80; chmn. bd. visitor U. Ark., Little Rock, 1979-80; active U. Ark. Med. Scis. Campus Devel. Council, 1976, Parents Club, 1976. Named Little Rock Man of Yr. Ark. Dem., 1963; recipient Sales and Mktg. Exec. Man of Yr. award, 1963, Citizen-Lawyer of Yr. award Ark. Bar Found., 1971, Disting. Alumni award U. Ark., 1976. Mem. Ark. Bankers Assn. (pres. 1982, chnm. legis. com. 1978-79), Am. Bankers Assn. (council 1984—), Assn. Res. City Bankers, Ark. Bar Assn., Pulaski County Bar Assn. Methodist. Lodge: Masons. Home: 2200 Beechwood Little Rock AR 72207 Office: Comml Nat Bank 200 Main St Little Rock AR 72201

BOWEN, WILLIAM J., management consultant; b. N.Y.C. B.S., Fordham U., 1956; M.B.A., N.Y. U., 1963. Trainee Smith Barney & Co., N.Y.C., 1959-61; asst. v.p. investments 1st Nat. City Bank, N.Y.C., 1961-67; instnl. salesman Hayden Stone, Inc., N.Y.C., 1967-69; successively v.p. and Eastern regional sales mgr., st v.p. and instrnl. sales mgr. Shearson Hammill & Co., Inc., N.Y.C., 1969-73; asso. Heidrick & Struggles, Inc., N.Y.C., 1973-77, v.p., 1977-78, sr. v.p., mgr., 1978-81, pres., chief exec. officer, Chgo., 1981-83, vice chmn., 1984—. Office: Heidrick & Struggles Inc 125 S Wacker Dr Chicago IL 60606

BOWEN, W.J., gas company executive; b. Sweetwater, Tex., Mar. 31, 1922; s. Berry and Annah (Robey) B.; m. Annis K. Hilty, June 6, 1945; children: Shelley Ann, Barbara Kay, Berry Dunbar, William Jackson. B.S., U.S. Mil. Acad., 1945. Registered profl. engr., Tex. Petroleum engr. Delhi Oil Corp., Dallas, 1949-57; v.p. Fla. Gas Co., Houston, 1957-60, pres., Winter Park, Fla., 1960-74; pres., chief exec. officer Transco Cos., Inc., Houston, 1974-81, chmn., 1976—; chief exec. officer Transco Energy Co., 1981—; dir. Crown Zellerbach Corp., S.W. Bancshares, Inc. Chmn. Houston Clean City Commn.; chmn. bd. dirs. YMCA, Houston; bd. dirs. Houston Mus. Fine Arts. Served with AUS, 1945-49. Mem. Am. Gas Assn., Houston C. of C. (dir.), Delta Kappa Epsilon. Episcopalian. Office: PO Box 1396 Houston TX 77251

BOWEN, ZEDDIE PAUL, geologist, education adminsitrator; b. Rockmart, Ga., Mar. 29, 1937;, 1978; 3 children. A.B., Johns Hopkins U., 1958; M.A., Harvard U., 1960, Ph.D. in Geology, 1963. From asst. prof. to assoc. prof. geology U. Rochester, 1962-72, prof., 1972-76, chmn. dept. geol. scis., 1974-76; provost Beloit Coll., 1976-81; dean Faculty Arts and Sci. Coll. William and Mary, 1981-83; provost U. Richmond, Va., 1983—. NSF fellow, 1967-68. Mem. Geol. Soc. Am., Paleontology Soc. Office: Office of the Provost Maryland Hall Univ Richmond Richmond VA 23173 *

BOWER, ALLAN MAXWELL, lawyer; b. Oak Park, Ill., May 21, 1936; s. David Robert and Frances Emily (Maxwell) B.; m. Deborah Ann Rottmayer, Dec. 28, 1959. B.A., State U. Iowa, 1962; J.D., U. Miami, Fla., 1968. Bar: Calif. 1969, U.S. Supreme Ct. 1979. Civil trial practice, Los Angeles, 1969—. Contbr. articles to profl. publs. Mem. Am., Los Angeles bar assns., Lawyer-Pilots Bar Assn., Am. Judicature Soc., Calif. Trial Lawyers Assn., Am. Arbitration Assn. (nat. panel arbitrators), Alpha Tau Omega. Republican. Presbyterian. Home: 603 S Bundy Dr Los Angeles CA 90049 Office: 10920 Wilshire Blvd 15th Floor Los Angeles CA 90049

BOWER, BRUCE LESTER, lawyer; b. Chgo., Sept. 16, 1933; s. Mervin Hartman and Josephine (Lester) B.; m. Irene Kitsonas, Oct. 16, 1960; children: Rebecca, Elizabeth, Katherine. B.A., U. Ill., 1955; J.D. with honors, U. Mich., 1960. Bar: Ill. 1960. Assoc. Winston & Strawn, Chgo., 1960-68, ptnr., 1968—. Mem. Pres.'s Commn. on White House Fellowships, 1981—; trustee Episcopal Home for Aged, Chgo., 1978—; mem. Chgo. Crime Commn., 1980—; bd. dirs. Central YMCA Coll., Chgo., 1965-82. Served to 1st lt. inf. U.S. Army, 1955-57. Mem. ABA, Ill. Bar Assn., Chgo. Bar Assn., 7th Circuit Bar Assn. Republican. Episcopalian. Clubs: Glen View (Golf, Ill.); Univ.; Law (Chgo.). Office: Winston & Strawn One 1st National Plaza Chicago IL 60603

BOWER, GLENN NILS, insurance company executive; b. Allentown, Pa., May 7, 1930; s. Paul George and Emily (Tallock) B.; m. Suzanne Louise Griffiths, Oct. 23, 1954; children: Pamela, Elizabeth, Emily, Priscilla. A.B., Brown U., 1952. C.L.U. Group sales trainee Home Life Ins. Co., N.Y.C., 1952, group mgr., 1954-67, v.p., N.Y.C., 1967-81; sr. v.p. Union Central Life Ins. Co., Cin., 1981—. Exec. com. Fulton County Republican Com., Atlanta, 1966-67. Served with U.S. Army, 1952-54. Episcopalian. Clubs: Indian Hill (Ohio); Short Hills (N.J.). Home: 8025 N Clippinger Dr Cincinnati OH 45243 Office: Union Central Life Ins Co PO Box 179 Cincinnati OH 45201

BOWER, MARVIN, management consultant; b. Cin., Aug. 1, 1903; s. William J. and Carlotta (Preston) B.; m. Helen M. McLaughlin, Aug. 17, 1927; children: Peter Huntington, Richard Hamilton, James McKinsey. Ph.B., Brown U., 1925; LL.B., Harvard U., 1928, M.B.A., 1930. Bar: Ohio, Mass. 1928. Lawyer Jones, Day, Reavis & Pogue, Cleve., 1930-33; asso. McKinsey & Co., 1933-35, partner, 1935-50, mng. partner, 1950-56, mng. dir., 1956-67, dir., 1956-74, cons., 1974—; Cons. to USAF, AUS (Bur. Budget), 1941-43. Author: The Will to Manage, 1966; Editor: Development of Executive Leadership, 1949; Contbr. to various mags. Chmn. McKinsey Found. Mgmt. Research, Inc.; trustee bd. edn., Bronxville, 1945-48; Hon. trustee Com. Econ. Devel., Case-Western Res. U.; bd. dirs. Florence V. Burden Found.; chmn. Joint Council on Econ. Edn., 1967-76; Bd. dirs. Assos. of Harvard Bus. Sch., Religion in Am. Life. Fellow Internat. Acad. Mgmt.; Mem. Alpha Tau Omega, Tau Beta Pi. Clubs: Blind Brook (Port Chester, N.Y.); Siwanoy Country (Bronxville, N.Y.); University (N.Y.C.); Country of Fla. (Gulf); Ocean (Ocean Ridge, Fla.). Home: 3 Stoneleigh Plaza Bronxville NY 10708 Office: 55 E 52d St New York NY 10022

BOWER, MARVIN D., insurance company executive; b. Stanford, Ill., July 20, 1924; s. Charles Howard and Marjorie Dale (Garst) B.; m. Mari Morrissey, June 1, 1946 (dec. 1981); children: Stacie (Mrs. John Killian), Jim, Pete, Molly (Mrs. Christopher Miller), Tom, John.; m. Carolyn Paine Newland, Apr. 24, 1983; stepchildren: Linda (Mrs. Bradley Gleason), Lori, Leslie, William, David. Ph.B., Ill. Wesleyan U., 1948. C.L.U. Agt. Northwestern Mut. Life, Bloomington, Ill., 1949-52; with State Farm Life Ins. Co., 1952—, sec. for Can., Toronto, 1955-58; exec. v.p., sec. State Farm Life and Accident Assurance Co., 1961—; also dir.; v.p. health State Farm Mut. Auto Ins. Co., 1968—; exec. v.p. State Farm Life Ins. Co., Bloomington, Ill., 1973—, also dir. Served to capt. AUS, 1943-46. Fellow Life Office Mgmt. Inst.; mem. Phi Gamma Delta. Home: 49 Country Club Pl Bloomington IL 61701 Office: One State Farm Plaza Bloomington IL 61701

BOWER, PAUL GEORGE, lawyer; b. Chgo., Apr. 21, 1933; s. Chester L. and Retha (Dausmann) B.; m. Eireen L. Thurlow, June 23, 1962; children: Stephanie, Julienne, Aimee. B.A., Rice U., 1955; postgrad., Calif. Inst. Tech., 1959-60; LL.B., Stanford U., 1963. Bar: Calif. 1964, U.S. Sureme Ct. 1969. Assoc. Gibson, Dunn & Grutcher, Los Angeles, 1963-67, ptnr., 1970—. Asst. dir. Nat. Adv. Com. Civil Disorder, 1967-68; spl. asst. to dep. atty. gen. U.S. Dept. Justice, 1968-69, consumer counsel, 1969; bd. dirs. Legal Aid Found.; trustee Sierra Club Legal Def. Fund, 1982—. Served with U.S. Army, 1956-59. Mem. ABA, Calif. Bar Assn., Los Angeles County Bar Assn., Beverly Hills Bar Assn., Order of Coif. Democrat. Office: Gibson Dunn & Crutcher 2029 Century Park E Los Angeles CA 90067

BOWER, RICHARD JAMES, clergyman; b. Somerville, N.J., June 9, 1939; s. Oneil A. and Mildred R. (Goss) B.; m. Helen Ann Cheek, Dec. 29, 1962; 1 son, Christopher Scott. Student, Sorbonne, Paris, 1959-60; B.A., Wesleyan U., 1961; M.Div., Drew U., Madison, N.J., 1965; student, Oxford U., Eng., 1983. Ordained to ministry, Congregational Christian Ch., 1965. Minister Community Congl. Ch., Kewaunee, Wis., 1965-67; sr. minister Congl. Ch., Bound Brook, N.J., 1967-78, Congl. Ch. of the Chimes, Sherman Oaks, Calif., 1978—; exec. com., dir. Nat. Assn. Congl. Christians Chs., 1973-77; chmn. Nat. Assn. Congl. Christian Chs., 1976-77, asst. moderator, 1981-82, moderator, 1982-83. Contbr. poetry and articles to periodicals. Organizer, pres. Am. Field Service, Kewaunee, 1966-67; dir. Children's Bur., Los Angeles, 1981—; bd. fellows Hollywood Congl. Ctr., 1979-82. Mem. Cal-West Assn. (dir.). Republican. Club: Bound Brook Rotary (pres. 1975-76). Home: 5737 Allott Ave Van Nuys CA 91401 Office: Congregational Church of the Chimes 14115 Magnolia Blvd Sherman Oaks CA 91423

BOWER, RICHARD STUART, educator, economist; b. N.Y.C., Aug. 1, 1928; s. Jacob and Elsie (Vander Beugle) B.; m. Dorothy Ann Hagberg, June 23, 1953; children—Gari Ellen, Laura Jane, Nancy Lynne. A.B., Kenyon Coll., 1949; M.B.A., Columbia, 1955; Ph.D., Cornell U., 1962. Instr. econs. Kenyon Coll., 1949-50, Alfred U., 1955-57; asst. prof. econs. and bus. Vanderbilt U., 1959-62; prof. bus. econs. Dartmouth, 1962—. Author: Investment and Liquidity: A Case Study of Clay Construction Products, 1965; Contbr. articles to profl. jours. Commr. N.Y. Public Service Commn., Albany, 1979-82. Served with USNR, 1951-55. Mem. Am. Econ. Assn., Am. Finance Assn., Phi Beta Kappa, Beta Gamma Sigma, Phi Kappa Phi. Home: South Esker Hanover NH 03755

BOWER, RODNEY A., labor union official; b. Buffalo, May 5, 1937; s. Bertram L. and Marion H. B.; m. Betty Jo Anderson, 1949; 3 children. Mem. Internat. Fedn. Profl. and Tech. Engrs., Silver Springs, Md., 1950—, pres., 1972—, pres. local 13, 1953-54, exec. sec., 1954-56, 60-68, exec. v.p., 1968-72, pres. gen. electric locals council, 1957-59, sec.-treas., 1955-57, internat. v.p. Atlantic area, 1964-70. Office: Internat Fedn Profl and Tech Engrs 818 Roeder Rd Suite 702 Silver Spring MD 20910 *

BOWER, WILLIAM WALTER, aeronautical engineer; b. Hammond, Ind., Jan. 9, 1945; s. William Walter and Frances Anita (Good) B. B.S. in M.E., Purdue U., 1967, M.S., 1969, Ph.D., 1971. Sr. engr. Propulsion dept. McDonnell Aircraft Co., St. Louis, 1971-74, sr. scientist flight scis. dept. Research Labs., 1974—; grad. instr. mech. engring. Purdue U., 1970-71. Contbr. articles to tech. jours. NDEA Title IV fellow, 1967-70. Assoc. fellow AIAA (Meritorious Tech. Contbn. award St. Louis Sect. 1977); mem. ASME (fluid mechanics com.). Presbyterian. Club: McDonnell Douglas Corp. St. Louis Mgmt. Home: 4575 Whisper Lake Dr Apt 8 Florissant MO 63033 Office: McDonnell Douglas Corp PO Box 516 Saint Louis MO 63166

BOWER, WILLIS HERMAN, psychiatrist, medical adminstrator; b. Galesburg, Ill., Mar. 1, 1916; s. George Stuart and Katharine Wilhelmina (Barkmann) B.; m. Frances Lorraine Taylor, Sept. 26, 1946; children: George Stuart, Theodore Kent, Penelope Wray. A.B., Knox Coll., 1936; M.D., Northwestern U., 1941. Diplomate: Am. Bd. Psychiatry and Neurology. Intern Presbyn. Hosp., Chgo., 1941-42; resident in psychiatry VA Hosp., McKinney, Tex., 1946-48, McLean Hosp., 1948-49; practice medicine specializing in psychiatry, San Francisco, 1950-52; psychiatrist McLean Hosp., Belmont, Mass., 1952-61; supt. Colo. State Hosp., Pueblo, 1961-63; dir. outpatient dept. UCLA Neuropsychiat. Inst., 1963-65; dep. dir. research and tng. Calif. Dept. Mental Hygiene, 1965-67; supt. Ariz. State Hosp., 1967-74; asst. dir. behavioral health Ariz. Dept. Health Services, 1974-75; mgr. admission services San Bernardino County (Calif.) Dept. Mental Health, 1975-76; dir. psychiat. geriatrics services dept. psychiatry Maricopa County Gen. Hosp., Phoenix, 1976-81, assoc. chmn. dept. psychiatry, 1978-81—; instr. psychiatry Harvard Med. Sch., 1956-61; assoc. prof. clin. psychiatry U. Colo. Sch. Medicine, 1961-63; asst. prof. psychiatry in residence UCLA Sch. Medicine, 1961-63; lectr. psychiatry U. Ariz. Med. Sch., 1972-75. Contbr. articles to profl. jours. Served to capt. M.C. AUS, 1942-46. Fellow Am. Psychiat. Assn.; fellow Am. Coll. Psychiatrists. Home: 2811 E Mission Ln Phoenix AZ 85028 Office: Maricopa County Gen Hosp 2601 E Roosevelt Phoenix AZ 85008

BOWERING, GEORGE HARRY, writer; b. Penticton, C., Can., Dec. 1, 1936; s. Ewart Harry and Pearl Patricia (Brinson) B.; m. Angela May Luoma, Dec. 14, 1962; 1 dau., Thea Claire. Student, Victoria Coll., 1953-54; B.A., U. B.C., 1960, M.A., 1963; postgrad., U. Western Ont., 1966-67. Asst. prof. Am. lit. U. Calgary, 1963-66; writer in residence Sir George Williams U., Montreal, Que., 1967-68, asst. prof., 1968-71; prof. Simon Fraser U., Burnaby, B.C., 1972—. Author: Mirror on the Floor, 1967, Autobiology, 1972, Flycatcher and Other Stories, 1974, A Short Sad Book, 1977, Protective Footwear, 1978, Burning Water, 1980, A Place to Die; poetry Rocky Mountain Foot, 1969; Another Mouth, 1979; poetry Touch, 1971, In the Flesh, 1973, The Catch, 1976, Particular Accidents: Selected Poems, 1981, Smoking Mirror. Served with RCAF, 1954-57. Mem. Assn. Can. TV and Radio Artists. Home: 2499 W 37th Ave Vancouver BC V6M 1P4 Canada

BOWERMAN, RICHARD H., lawyer; b. Newark, 1917. B.A., Yale, 1939, LL.B., 1942. Bar: Conn. 1946. Chmn. bd. So. Conn. Gas Co., Bridgeport; former partner, now counsel firm Tyler, Cooper, Grant, Bowerman and Keefe, New Haven. Chmn. bd. Yale-New Haven Hosp., 1975-82. Mem. ABA (chmn. jr. bar sect. Conn. 1946-49, nat. vice-chmn. 1951-52, nat. chmn. 1952-53, sec., treas. 1957-61), New Haven County Bar Assn., State Bar Assn Conn. (pres. 1967). Office: 880 Broad St Bridgeport CT 06609

BOWERS, ELLIOTT TOULMIN, university president; b. Oklahoma City, Aug. 22, 1919; s. Lloyd and Enah (McDonald) B.; m. Frances Marie Handley, May 29, 1940; children—Linda Lu (Mrs. Charles Rushing), Cynthia Ann Vincent. B.S., Sam Houston State U., 1941, M.A., 1942; Ed.D., U. Houston, 1959. Dir. music Huntsville High Sch., 1937-42; mem. faculty Sam Houston State U., 1946—, v.p. univ. affairs and dean of students, 1964-70, acting pres., 1963-64, pres., 1970—; dir. First Nat. Bank, Huntsville, Tex. Mem. Tex. Criminal Justice Council; bd. dirs. Sam Houston Area council Boy Scouts Am., Salvation Army, Am. Cancer Soc.; pres. bd. Wesley Found., 1962-63. Served with USAAF, 1943-46. Mem. Assn. Higher Edn., Huntsville C. of C. (past pres.), SAR, Alpha Phi Omega, Kappa Delta Pi, Phi Mu Alpha. Clubs: K.T., Masons. Home: 1802 16th St Huntsville TX 77340

BOWERS, EMMETT WADSWORTH, former army officer; b. Fulton County, Ga., July 19, 1926; s. Ross Lee and Creola (Watts) B.; m. Sarah Hammack, Sept. 22, 1951; children: George Erwin, Emmett Wadsworth, Joseph Hammack. A.B., Mercer U., 1951; M.B.A., U. Ala., 1956; grad., Command and Gen. Staff Coll., 1963, Indsl. Coll. Armed Forces, 1970. Served with USMC, 1944-46; Commd. lt. U.S. Army, 1951; advanced through grades to maj. gen., 1977; platoon leader 2d Inf. Div., Korea, 1952; bn. ops. officer and battery comdr. 47th Inf. Div., Ft. Rucker, Alabama, 1953; staff officer U.S. Army Europe, Frankfurt and Munick, Ger., 1956-1959, Logistics Command, U.S. Army Communication Zone, Orleans, France, 1963-1965, DA General Staff, Pentagon, Washington, 1965-1967; bn. comdr. 9th Inf. Div., Vietnam, 1967-1968; staff officer Joint Chiefs of Staff, Pentagon, 1970-1973; comdr. 593d Support Group, Ft. Lewis, Wash., 1973-1975, U.S. Army Troop Support Agy., Ft. Lee, Va., 1974-1978, Def. Personnel Support Center, Phila., 1978-81; dep. comdr. Def. Logistics Agy., Washington, 1981-82; ret., 1982; with Roberts & Bowers Inc., Albany, Ga., 1982—. Mem. mil. adv. bd. USO of Phila., 1978-1979; mem. bd. mgrs. Armed Services br. YMCA, Phila., 1978—; mem. Fed. Exec. Bd., Phila., 1978—. Decorated D.S.M., Def. Superior Service medal, Legion of Merit with oak leaf cluster, Bronze Star with oak leaf cluster, Meritorious Service Medal with oak leaf cluster, Air medal, Purple Heart, Army Commendation medal with 2 oak leaf clusters; Republic of Vietnam Cross of Gallantry with Bronze Star. Mem. Assn. U.S. Army, 9th Inf. Div. Assn., Phil. Fed. Bus. Assn. (v.p. 1979). Methodist. Lodge: Kiwanis. Home: 2300 Wallington Dr Albany GA 31707 Office: Roberts & Bowers Inc 1151 Dawson Rd Albany GA 31707

BOWERS, FRANCIS ROBERT, educator; b. N.Y.C., May 4, 1920; s. William Leo and Catherine (Callahan) B. B.A., Cath. U. Am., 1946, Ph.D., 1959; M.A., Fordham U., 1952. Tchr. Ascension Sch., N.Y.C., 1946-48, St. Augustine's High Sch., Bklyn., 1948-51, St. Peter's High Sch., Staten Island, 1951-53; instr. De La Salle Coll., Washington, 1953-59; asso. prof. English and world lit. Manhattan Coll., 1959—, chmn. dept., 1967-70, chmn. grad. English dept., 1961-70, dean arts and scis., 1970-80, provost, 1980—. Author: Characterization in Narrative Poetry of George Crabbe, 1959. Trustee scholarship Cath. U., 1953-58. Finn grantee, 1962; Manhattan Coll. grantee, 1966. Mem. Am. Assn. Higher Edn., Nat. Cath. Edn. Assn., Phi Beta Kappa. Address: Manhattan Coll Bronx NY 10471

BOWERS, JACK LAWTON, electronic company executive; b. Colorado Springs, Colo., Aug. 25, 1920; s. Ernest Elton and Margaret (Lawton) B.; m. Mildred Neel, July 25, 1942; children: Bruce Neel, Steven Scott, Ann Lawton, Robin. B.S.E.E., Carnegie Inst. Tech., 1943. Asst. chief engr. Gen. Dynamics, San Diego and Pomona, Calif., 1946-50, pres. Convair, Electronics and Pomona divs., 1964-73; asst. sec. Dept. Navy, Washington, 1973-76; pres., chief exec. officer Sanders Assocs., Inc., Nashua, N.H., 1976—. Served with Signal Corps USAAF, 1943-46. Decorated Legion of Merit; recipient award Carnegie-Mellon U. Bd. Trustees, Pub. Service award NASA. Office: Sanders Assocs Inc Daniel Webster Hwy S Nashua NH 03060

BOWERS, JOHN WAITE, speech communication educator; b. Alton, Iowa, Nov. 28, 1935; s. George E. and Clara Frances (Wathier) B.; m. Eleanore Frances Fyock, June 2, 1956 (div. 1975); children: John Steven, Jeanne Terese, Julie Michelle. B.S., U. Kans., 1958; M.A., U.Kans., 1959; Ph.D., U. Iowa, 1962. Faculty mem. U. Iowa, Iowa City, 1962—, prof. communication, 1969—, chmn. dept. communication and theatre arts, 1982—. Author: Designing the Communication Experiment, 1970; with Ochs, Rhetoric of Agitation and Control, 1971, with Courtright, Communication Research Methods, 1984; co-editor: Handbook of Rhetorical and Communication Theory, 1984. Mem. Speech Communication Assn. (editor Communication Monographs 1978-80, 1st v.p. 1983, pres. 1984, Robert J. Kibler Meml. award 1979), Speech Communicatio Assn. (Golden Anniversary Monograph award 1980), Central State Speech Assn. (Outstanding Young Tchr. award 1964), AAUP, Internat. Communication Assn., Iowa Communication Assn. Home: 423 7th Ave Iowa City IA 52240 Office: Dept Communication and Theatre Arts U Iowa Iowa City IA 52242

BOWERS, JOHN Z., physician, educator; b. Catonsville, Md., Aug. 27, 1913; s. John Culler and Adelaide (Schuman) B.; children: John C., David W.; m. Akiko Kobayashi, Apr. 17, 1970. B.S., Gettysburg Coll., 1933, Sc.D., 1958; M.D., U. Md., 1938, Sc.D., 1959; L.H.D., Woman's Med. Coll., 1967; Docteur Honoris Causa, Universite d'Aix-Marseille, France. Intern, resident U. Hosp., Balt., 1938-41; dep. dir. AEC, Washington, 1947-50; dean (Coll. Medicine); dir. radiobiology lab., med. cons. AEC, U. Utah, Salt Lake City, 1950-55; prof. medicine U. Wis., 1955, dean, 1955-61; staff mem. Rockefeller Found., cons., 1980—; pres. Macy Found., 1965-80; adj. prof. N.Y. Med. Coll.; vis. prof. U. Philippines, 1962, Kyoto U. Med. Sch., 1962—; cons. Nat. Acad. Scis., 1982—; Bd. dirs., mem. exec. com. Nutrition Found., exec. dir., 1972—; Cons. surgeon gen. USAF, 1960-64; mem. med. adv. com. Chinese U. Hong Kong. Author: Medical Education in Japan, From Chinese Medicine to Western Medicine, 1965, Doctor on Desima, 1970, Medical Schools for the Modern World, 1970, Western Medical Pioneers in Feudal Japan, 1970, Western Medicine in a Chinese Palace, 1972, National Health Services, 1973, An Introduction to American Medicine, 1975; editor: Essays at Bicentennial American Medicine, 1976, Migration of Medical Manpower, 1975, When the Twain Meet: The Rise of Western Medicine in Japan, 1981; Editor: Jour. Med. Edn, 1956-62; also chmn. editorial bd. Trustee East Asia Research Found., 1980—, Giovanni Lorenzini Found., Inc., 1980—; mem. adv. council Am. Trust for Brit. Library. Served as comdr. USNR, 1941-45. Decorated Purple Heart, Legion of Merit Navy; chevalier Legion of Honor, (France).; Order Rising Sun, (Japan); Alan Gregg travel scholar, 1962. Fellow A.C.P.; mem. AMA (council med. edn. 1958-63), Assn. Am. Med. Colls. (v.p. 1952, exec. council 1953-59), Internat. Acad. History Medicine (sec.-treas. 1975), Alpha Omega Alpha (pres. 1968-78). Home: 25 Sutton Pl S New York NY 10021

BOWERS, KLAUS D(IETER), electronics research company executive; b. Stettin, Germany, Dec. 27, 1929; s. Franz A. and Elisabeth (Schneider) B.; m. Roswitha U. Rau, June 15, 1964; children: Pamela, Colin. B.A., Oxford (Eng.) U., 1950, M.A., Ph.D., 1953. Research lectr. in physics Christ Ch., Oxford U., 1952-56; with Bell Telephone Labs., 1956—, researcher, Murray Hill, N.J., 1956-59, mgr. electronics devel., 1959-66, Allentown, Pa., 1966-71, mng. dir., v.p. Sandia Labs., Albuquerque, 1971-75, exec. dir. Pa. Labs., Allentown, 1975-79, v.p., Murray Hill, 1979—. Contbr. sci. articles to profl. jours. Fellow IEEE. Patentee in field. Office: 600 Mountain Ave Murray Hill NJ 07974

BOWERS, MICHAEL JOSEPH, state attorney general; b. Jackson County, Ga., Oct. 7, 1941; s. Carl Ernest and Janie Ruth (Bolton) B.; m. Bette Rose Corley, June 8, 1963; children: Carl Wayne, Bruce Edward, Michelle Lisa. B.S., U.S. Mil. Acad., 1963; M.S., Stanford U., 1965; M.B.A., U. Utah-Wiesbaden, Germany, 1970; J.D., U. Ga., 1974. Bar: Ga. 1974. Sr. asst. atty. gen. State of Ga., Atlanta, 1975-81, atty. gen., 1981—. Served to capt. USAF, 1963-70. Mem. Lawyers Club. Democrat. Methodist. Lodge: Kiwanis. Home: 817 Allgood Rd Stone Mountain GA 30083 Office: State Judicial Bldg Atlanta GA 30334

BOWERS, PATRICIA ELEANOR FRITZ, economist; b. N.Y.C., Mar. 21, 1928; d. Edward and Eleanor (Ring) Fritz. Student scholar, Goucher Coll., 1946-48; B.A., Cornell U., 1950; M.A., NYU, 1953, Ph.D., 1965. Statis. asst. Fed. Res. Bank N.Y., N.Y.C., 1950-53; lectr. Upsala Coll., East Orange, N.J., 1953-59; researcher Fortune mag., N.Y.C., 1959-60; teaching fellow NYU, N.Y.C., 1960-62, instr., 1962-64; mem. faculty Bklyn. Coll., CUNY, 1964—, prof. econs., 1974—. Author: Private Choice and Public Welfare, 1974. Mem. Am. Econ. Assn., Econometric Soc., Met. Econ. Assn. (sec. 1963-68, pres. 1974-75), Am. Statis. Assn. (univs. chmn. ann. forecasting confs. 1970-71, 71-72). Club: Talbot Country (Easton, Md.). Home: 145 E 16th St New York NY 10003 Office: Dept Econs Bklyn Coll CUNY Brooklyn NY 11210

BOWERS, RICHARD CHARLES, educator, university official; b. Mt. Pleasant, Iowa, May 3, 1927; s. Raymond Paul and Marie (Foster) B.; m. Florence I. Olson, June 17, 1950 (div. 1983); children: Lesly Ann, Janet Mary, Robert Paul.; m. Dana W. Birnbaum, Aug. 1983. B.S., U. Mich., 1948; Ph.D., U. Minn., 1953. Instr. U. Minn., 1953-54; mem. faculty Northwestern U., 1954-65, asso. prof. chemistry, 1960-65, dir. chem. labs., 1962-65; prof., dean Coll. Liberal Arts and Scis., No. Ill. U., DeKalb, 1965-69, v.p., provost, 1969-74; pres. U. Mont., Missoula, 1974-81; prof., acad. v.p. U. Maine, Orono, 1981-83, exec. v.p., 1983—; cons.-examiner Commn. Colls. and Univs., North Central Assn. Colls. and Secondary Schs., 1968-74; Bd. regents Loras Coll., 1971-76. Contbr. profl. jours. Served with USNR, 1944-46. Mem. Northwest Assn. Schs. and Colls. (commn. on colls. 1976-81), Am. Council on Edn. (commn. on women in higher edn. 1977-80), Am. Chem. Soc., Sigma Xi. Office: U Maine Orono ME

BOWERS, RICHARD PHILIP, manufacturing company executive; b. Reading, Pa., July 27, 1931; s. Clarence Philip and Lottie Rose (Linkowski) B.; m. Dolores Rita Dombrowski, June 21, 1952; children: Richard Philip, Karen Marie, Lisa Ann, Julie Louise. Student, St. Bonaventure U., 1949-51. Sales trainee Bowers Battery & Spark Plug Co., Reading, 1954-55, sales mgr., 1955-58; v.p. sales Gen. Battery Corp. (merger Bowers Battery & Spark Plug Co.), Reading, 1958-64; exec. v.p., dir. East Pa. Mfg. Co., Lyons Station, Pa., 1964—; pres. Pioneer Auto Parts, Phila.; dir. Miller Export, Hillsdale, N.J. Served with AUS, 1952-54. Mem. Ind. Battery Mfg. Assn. (dir., chmn. mktg. com. 1967-70, v.p., pres.), Battery Council Internat. (mem. merchandising com., product safety and info. com.), Am. Legion. Democrat. Roman Catholic. Clubs: Moselem Springs (Pa.) Golf, Berkshire Country, Seaview Country. Office: East Pa Mfg Co Lyons Station PA 19536

BOWERS, ROY ANDERSON, college dean; b. Racine, Wis., May 11, 1913; s. Sidney and Dagmar (Anderson) B.; m. Harriett Teresa Byer, Aug. 19, 1940; children—Clarke George, Mary Jane. B.S., U. Wis., 1936, Ph.D., 1940. Asst. instr. pharmacy U. Wis., 1937-40; asst. prof. pharmacy U. Toledo, 1940-41, U. Kans., 1941-43, asso. prof., 1943-45; prof. pharmacy U. N.Mex., 1945-51, dean, 1945-51; prof. pharmacy Rutgers U., New Brunswick, N.J., 1951-81, prof. emeritus, 1981—, dean, 1951-78, emeritus, 1978—; pharmacist, res. officer USPHS; mem. Am. Council on Pharm. Edn., 1968-74. Co-author: The Rho Chi Society, 1981; mem. bd. authors: American Pharmacy (Rufus A. Lyman), 1951, 4th edit. (Lyman, Sprowls), 1955, 5th edit. (J.B. Sprowls), 1960. Trustee, pres. Cedar Grove Pub. Library, 1959-72; trustee Hosp. and Health Council Met. N.J., 1965-72, Hosp. Plan N.J., 1969—, United Way of Central N.J., 1981—; pres. bd. dirs. Metuchen-Edison YMCA, 1974-81. Mem. Am. Pharm. Assn. (1st v.p. 1950-51, hon. pres. 1978-79, council mem. 1957-63), Am. Assn. Colls. Pharmacy (pres. 1963-64), N.J., N.Mex. pharm. assns., Am. Inst. History of Pharmacy (exec. sec. 1978—), Sigma Xi, Phi Lambda Upsilon, Rho Chi (nat. sec.-treas. 1945-56, nat. v.p. 1954-56, nat. pres. 1956-58, exec. council 1958-60), Delta Sigma Theta (hon.), Rho Pi Phi (hon.), Alpha Chi Sigma, Kappa Psi, Phi Kappa Phi. Roman Catholic. Club: Metuchen Rotary (pres. 1978-79).

BOWERS, STANLEY JACOB, lawyer; b. Pickaway County, Ohio, Jan. 1, 1912; s. George W. and Clara L. (Brown) B.; m. Ruth M. Allison, Sept. 15, 1934; children—Judith Ann, Mary Jo. Student, Ohio No. U., 1930-32; LL.B., Franklin U., 1939; J.D., Capital U., 1966. Bar: Ohio bar 1940. Auditor, atty. Ohio Dept. Taxation, 1933-53; tax commr., Ohio, 1954-63; mem. firm Caren & Bowers, Columbus, 1963-67; exec. dir. Nat. Tax Assn.-Tax Inst. Am., Columbus, 1967—; tax counsel Ohio Mfrs. Assn., 1965—. Contbr. articles on taxes to profl. jours. Recipient award for outstanding service as tax commr. Tax Exec. Inst., 1963. Mem. Ohio Bar Assn. (chmn. com. on taxation 1964-67), Pickaway County Bar Assn., Columbus Bar Assn., Tax Inst. Am. (pres. 1962), Nat. Tax Assn. (pres. 1958-59), Nat. Assn. Tax Adminstrs. (pres. 1956), Ohio Soc. Pub. Accountants. Clubs: Masons; University (Columbus). Home: 289 E Main St Ashville OH 43103 Office: 21 E State St Columbus OH 43215

BOWERS, WAYNE ALEXANDER, educator; b. Bilbao, Spain, Mar. 1, 1919; came to U.S., 1926; s. Wayne Heyser and Margaret Sturrock (Cameron) B.; m. Maryellen Severinghaus, Feb. 26, 1944; children—John, Margaret, Ruth, Wayne. A.B., Oberlin Coll., 1938; Ph.D., Cornell U., 1943. Instr. Cornell U., 1943-45; physicist Los Alamos Labs., 1944-46; research asso. M.I.T., 1946-47; asso. prof. physics U. N.C., 1947-55, prof., 1955—; vis. prof. M.I.T., 1968-69; vis. scholar Cavendish Lab., U. Cambridge, Eng., 1977-78. Contbr. articles to profl. jours. Faculty fellow NSF, 1963-64. Mem. Am. Phys. Soc., Am. Assn. Physics Tchrs., AAUP, Am. Fedn. Scientists, Phi Beta Kappa, Sigma Xi. Home: 714 E Franklin St Chapel Hill NC 27514

BOWERSOCK, GLEN WARREN, historian; b. Providence, Jan. 12, 1936; s. Donald Curtis and Josephine (Evans) B. A.B., Harvard U., 1957; B.A., Oxford U., Eng., 1959, M.A. and D.Phil., 1962. Lectr. ancient history Oxford U., 1960-62, vis. lectr., 1966; instr. Harvard U., 1962-64, asst. prof., 1964-67, asso. prof. classics, 1967-69, prof. Greek and Latin, 1969-80, chmn. dept. classics, 1972-77, asso. dean faculty arts and scis., 1977-80; prof. hist. studies Inst. Advanced Study, Princeton, N.J., 1980—; cons. Ednl. Services, Inc., 1964, NEH, 1971—; sr. fellow Center for Hellenic Studies, Washington, 1976—; mem. Internat. Colloquium on the Classics in Edn., 1964-66; vis. prof. Australian Nat. U., 1972; syndic Harvard U. Press, 1977-81. Author: Augustus and the Greek World, 1965, Pseudo-Xenophon, Constitution of the Athenians, 1968, Greek Sophists in the Roman Empire, 1969, Julian the Apostate, 1978, Roman Arabia, 1983; editor: Philostratus' Life of Apollonius, 1970, Approaches to the Second Sophistic, 1974, (with J. Clive, S. Graubard) Edward Gibbon and the Decline and Fall of the Roman Empire, 1977. Rhodes scholar, 1957-60. Fellow Am. Acad. Arts and Scis., Am. Numis. Soc. (council); mem. Am. Philol. Assn., Archeol. Inst. Am., Leschetizky Assn. Am., Soc. Promotion Roman and Hellenic Studies, German Archaeol. Inst. (corr.), The Johnsonians, Phi Beta Kappa. Clubs: Knickerbocker, Century (N.Y.C.). Office: Sch Hist Studies Inst Advanced Study Princeton NJ 08540

BOWERSOCK, JUSTIN DEWITT, III, banker; b. Kansas City, Mo., Dec. 27, 1907; s. Justin Dewitt and Frances (Matteson) B.; m. Betty Bruce Van Antwerp, Oct. 25, 1930; children: Justin Dewitt IV (dec.), Chiles V. (dec.), Frances and Caroline (twins). A.B., Harvard, 1929. Asst. cashier Fidelity Nat. Bank, Kansas City, Mo., 1929-33; v.p. Union Nat. Bank, Kansas City, 1933-49; exec. v.p. 1st Am. Bank (NA), Washington, 1949-67, pres., 1967-70, chmn. bd., 1970-75, chmn. exec. com., 1975—; dir., mem. audit com. First Am. Bankshares, Inc., Washington, 1974—; dir. Fed. Services Fin. Corp., Washington, 1957-67, Group Hospitalization, Inc., 1960-70. Mem. exec. council Washington area Boy Scouts Am., from 1960; mem. exec. com. Fed. City Council, from, 1969; com. on banking and monetary policy U.S. C. of C., from 1968; Trustee, v.p. Washington Hosp. Center, from 1962. Served to lt. (j.g.) USNR, 1944-46; PTO. Mem. Am. Bankers Assn. (v.p. D.C. 1957, 62-63, exec. council 1965-68), D.C. Bankers Assn. (pres. 1958-59). Republican. Episcopalian. Clubs: Chevy Chase (Md.); Metropolitan, Alfalfa (Washington). Office: 1st Am Bank NA 15th and H Sts N W Washington DC 20005

BOWERY, THOMAS GLENN, government official; b. Avalon, Pa., Dec. 17, 1921; s. Frank Joseph and Elizabeth May (White) B.; m. Eleanor Jane Campbell, Nov. 10, 1945; children: Deborah Elaine, Glenn Steven. B.Sc., Mich. State U., 1943; M.Sc., Rutgers U., 1948, Ph.D., 1951. Asst. prof. pesticide chemistry U. Fla., Belle Glade, 1951-52; research prof. N.C. State U., Raleigh, 1953-62; extramural ops. officer Office of Dir. of NIH, HEW, Bethesda, Md., 1962-65, asso. dir., 1965-68, dir., 1969-80, dir. biomed. research support program Div. Research Resources, 1981—. Contbr. articles to profl. jours. Pres. Tilden Woods Recreation Assn., Rockville, Md., 1965-66. Served with USNR, 1943-46. Grantee Am. Cyanamid Co., 1958-62, Chemagro Chem. Co., 1959-60, Dow Chem. Co., 1962, Shell Chem. Co., 1957-62, Union Carbide, 1959-60, USPHS, 1959-62, NIH, 1960-62; recipient Equal Employment Opportunity Spl. Achievement award NIH, 1975, Superior Service award USPHS, 1977. Home: 11608 Stonewood Ln Rockville MD 20852 Office: NIH Bldg 31 Room 5B23 9000 Rockville Pike Bethesda MD 20205

BOWES, BETTY MILLER, painter, art consultant; b. Phila, July 30, 1911; d. George Washington and Elizabeth (Dawson) Miller; m. Thomas David Dowes, June 22, 1946 (div. 1981). ED., Moore Coll. Art., Phila., 1932. One-man shows, Phila. Art Alliance, 1954, 60, 65, Woodmere Gallery, 1958-64, group shows; art cons., Sun Oil Co., Radnor, Pa., 1975—; mem. exhbn. com, Woodmere Gallery; Designer tapestry; (paintings reproduced in art books). George W. Elkins European fellow, 1932; Dolphon fellow; recipient numerous awards. Mem. Am. Watercolor Soc., Phila. Art Alliance, Phila. Watercolor Soc. Republican. Roman Catholic. Home: 301 McClenaghan Mill Rd Wynnewood PA 19096

BOWHILL, SIDNEY ALLAN, electrical engineering educator; b. Dover, Kent, Eng., Aug. 6, 1927; came to U.S., 1955, naturalized, 1962; s. Sidney Allan and Violet (Clarke) B.; m. Margaret M. McLaughlin, Aug. 22, 1959; children: Allan J.C., Amanda M. B.A., Cambridge (Eng.) U., 1948, M.A., 1950, Ph.D., 1954. Research engr. Marconi's Wireless Telegraph Co. Ltd., Chelmsford, Essex, Eng., 1953-55; assoc. prof. elec. engring. Pa. State U., University Park, 1955-62; prof. elec. engring. U. Ill., Urbana, 1962—; Pres. Aeronomy Corp., Champaign, Ill., 1969—; Chmn. U.S.A. Commn. 3, Internat. Sci. Radio Union; assoc. editor Radio Sci., 1964-67, editor, 1968-72; vice chmn. Internat. Commn. 3, 1969-72, chmn., 1972-75; vice chmn. U.S.A. Nat. Com., 1985—; mem. working group 4 Inter-Union Com. Space Research, 1966-79, co-chmn. panel interactions neutral and ionized atmospheres, 1966-79, chmn. sci. commn. C, 1979—, mem. panel sci. ballooning, 1979-82; convenor, program chmn. Symposium (9th meeting), Vienna, Austria, 1966, Seattle, 1971, Solar-Terrestrial Physics Symposium, São Paulo, Brazil, 1974, Innsbruck, Austria, 1978; mem. com. data interchange and data centers Nat. Acad. Scis., 1967-82, potential contamination and interference from space expts., 1963—, com. polar research, 1967-70, chmn. panel upper atmospheric phys., 1967-70, com. on solar terrestrial research, 1969-79; mem. panel on Jicamarca Radio Obs., 1969-83, chmn. panel, 1976-78; mem. Inter-Union Sci. Com. on Solar-Terrestrial Physics, 1967—, chmn. working group II, 1968-73, chmn. atmospheric phys. programs com., 1974-80; chmn. steering com. for middle atmosphere program, 1977—; editorial adv. bd. Jour. Atmospheric and Terrestrial Physics, 1965-81. Contbr. numerous articles to profl. jours. Fellow IEEE (procs. bd. cons., procs. editorial bd. 1965-68), AAAS, Am. Geophys. Union, Am. Astron. Soc., Am. Meteorol. Soc.; mem. Am. Soc. Engring. Edn., Nat. Acad. Engring., Sigma Xi, Sigma Tau, Eta Kappa Nu. Club: Cosmos (Washington). Home: 2203 Anderson St Urbana IL 61801

BOWIE, DAVID (DAVID ROBERT JONES), musician, actor; b. London, Eng., Jan. 8, 1947; m. Angela Bowie, 1970 (div.); 1 son, Zowie. Rec. artist, 1968—; motion pictures include The Man Who Fell to Earth, 1976, Just a Gigolo, 1981, Wir Kinder Von Bahnhof, 1981, Cat People, 1982, The Hunger, 1983, Merry Christmas, Mr. Lawrence, 1983, (concert film) Ziggy Stardust, 1983; recs. include Lodger, David Live, Starting Point, Scary Monsters, Bowie, Golden Years, Let's Dance, others; appeared in: play The Elephant Man, 1980. Office: care William Morris Agy 151 El Camino Beverly Hills CA 90212 *

BOWIE, DONALD S., JR., truck manufacturing company executive; b. Long Branch, N.J., 1921. Grad., Rutgers U., 1943; LL.B., Harvard U., 1948. Exec. v.p., sec., gen. counsel Mack Trucks, Inc., Allentown, Pa.; sec., gen. counsel, dir. Mack Fin. Corp.; sec., dir. Mack Fin. (Can.) Ltd., Mack Trucks Western Hemisphere Trade Corp.; dir., sec. Mack Trucks Worldwide Ltd., Mack Can., Inc., Mack Trucks Export Corp.; dir. Mack Trucks Australia Pty. Ltd.; sec., dir. Mack Trucks Overseas Parts Corp., Mack Properties, Inc., Mack Trucks Overseas Co., Mac Americus, Inc. Office: 2100 Mack Blvd Allentown PA 18105

BOWIE, LESTER, trumpeter, composer; b. Frederick, Md., Oct. 11, 1941; m. Fontella Bass. Founding mem. Assn. Advancement Creative Music, Black Artist Group, Art Ensemble Chgo. Trumpet player, led own groups, toured with various groups. Served with U.S. Army. Office: care Rasa Artists 144 W 27th St New York NY 10001 *

BOWIE, NORMAN ERNEST, university official, educator; b. Biddeford, Maine, June 6, 1942; s. Lawrence Walker and Helen Elizabeth (Jacobsen) B.; m. Bonnie Jean Bankert, June 11, 1966 (div. 1980); children: Brian Paul, Peter Mark. A.B., Bates Coll., 1964; Ph.D., U. Rochester, 1968. Mem. faculty Lycoming Coll., Williamsport, Pa., 1968-69; asst. prof. philosophy Hamilton Coll., Clinton, N.Y., 1969-74, asso. prof. philosophy, 1974-75, U. Del., Newark, 1975-80, prof., 1980—, also dir. Ctr. for Study of Values. Author: Towards a New Theory of Distributive Justice, 1971, Business Ethics, 1982, also articles; co-author: The Individual and the Political Order, 1977; co-editor: Ethical Theory and Business, 1979, 2d edit., 1983, Public Policy and Criminal Justice, 1982; editor: Ethical Issues in Government, 1981, Ethical Theory in the Last Quarter of the Twentieth Century, 1983. Mem. N.Y. Council for Humanities, 1974-75. NDEA fellow, 1965-68. Mem. Am. Philos. Assn. (nat. exec. sec. 1972-77), AAUP, Am. Soc. for Value Inquiry (pres. 1980-81), Am. Soc. Polit. and Legal Philosophy, Phi Beta Kappa. Home: 51 Shull Dr Newark DE 19711 Office: Center for Study of Values Univ Delaware Newark DE 19711

BOWKER, ALBERT HOSMER, university dean; b. Winchendon, Mass., Sept. 8, 1919; s. Roy C. and Kathleen (Hosmer) B.; m. Elizabeth Rempfer, June 14, 1942; children: Paul Albert, Nancy Kathleen, Caroline Anne; m. Rosedith Sitgreaves, Sept. 26, 1964. B.S., Mass. Inst. Tech., 1941; Ph.D., Columbia U., 1949; D.H.L., City U. N.Y., 1971; LL.D., Brandeis U.; D.H.L., N.Y. Bd. Regents, 1972. Asst. statistician Mass. Inst. Tech., 1941-43; asst. dir. statis. research group Columbia, 1943-45; asst. prof. statistics Stanford, 1947-50, assoc. prof., 1950-53, exec. head statistics dept., 1948-59, dean grad. div., 1959-63, prof. math. and statistics, 1953-63, dir. applied math. and statistics labs., 1951-63; chancellor City U. N.Y., 1963-71, U. Calif., Berkeley, 1971-80; asst. sec. for postsecondary edn. Dept. Edn., Washington, 1980-81; dean Sch. Pub. Affairs U. Md., 1981-84, exec. v.p. univ., 1984—; mem. com. grad. edn. Am. Assn. Univs.; mem. Sloan Commn. on Govt. and Higher Edn.; mem. exec. com. div. math. Nat. Acad. Scis.-NRC, 1963-65. Author: (with Henry P. Goode) Sampling Inspection by Variables, 1952, (with Gerald J. Lieberman) Handbook of Industrial Statistics, 1955, Engineering Statistics, 1972; also articles profl. jours.; Asso. editor: Jour. Am. Statis. Assn, 1949-52. Mem. Corp. Mass. Inst. Tech., 1967-72; mem. Centennial Commn. Howard U., 1965; bd. dirs. San Francisco Bay Area Council, 1972-77; trustee Bennington Coll., U. Haifa. Fellow Am. Statis. Assn. (pres. 1964), Am. Soc. Quality Control, Inst. Math. Statistics (pres. 1961-62), AAAS; mem. Math. Assn. Am., Biometric Soc., Operations Research Soc. Am., Soc. for Indsl. and Applied Math., Am. Assn. Univs. (com. grad. edn.), Phi Beta Kappa (hon.), Sigma Xi (exec. com. 1963-66). Address: U Md Central Adminstrn Sch Public Affairs Adelphi MD 20783 *

BOWKETT, GERALD EDSON, editorial consultant, writer; b. Sacramento, Sept. 6, 1926; s. Harry Stephen and Jessie (Fairbrother) B.; m. Norma Orel Swain, Jan. 1, 1953; children: Amanda Allyn, Laura Anne. B.A., San Francisco State Coll., 1952; postgrad., Georgetown U., 1954. Radio wire editor UP, Washington, 1956-57; reporter, columnist Anchorage Daily Times, 1957-64; spl. asst., press sec. to Gov. William A. Egan, 1964-66; pub. Alaska Newsletter, 1966-68; Juneau bur. chief Anchorage Daily News, 1967-68; editor S.E. Alaska Empire, Juneau, 1969-71; mgr. news service U. Alaska, 1971-82. Served with USMC, 1944-46; PTO. Cited for outstanding news and feature writing, editorial works Alaska Press Club, 1962, 64, 73, 77, 79. Mem. Alpha Phi Gamma. Home and Office: Box 80666 Fairbanks AK 99708

BOWLAND, JOHN PATTERSON, educator, former university administrator; b. Man., Can., Feb. 10, 1924; s. Herbert John and Gertrude Evelyn (Patterson) B.; m. Helen May Campbell, May 28, 1946; children: Margaret Anne, Dorothy Lynne. B.S.A., U. Man., 1945; M.S., Wash. State U., 1947; Ph.D., U. Wis., 1949. Agrl. supr. Agr. Can. Brandon Research Sta., 1945-46; asst. prof. dept. animal sci. U. Alta., Edmonton, Can., 1949-54, asso. prof., 1954-62, prof., 1962—, dean agr. and forestry, 1975-83. Contbr. articles to profl. jours. Recipient Borden award Nutrition Soc. Can., 1966. Fellow AAAS, Agrl. Inst. Can.; mem. Alta. Inst. Agrologists, Am. Soc. Animal Sci., Can. Soc. Animal Sci., Nutrition Soc. Can., Sigma Xi. Mem. United Ch. of Can. Home: 11243 79th Ave Edmonton AB Canada Office: Dept Animal Sci U Alta Edmonton AB Canada T6G 2R5

BOWLER, DAVID LIVINGSTONE, electrical engineering educator; b. N.Y.C., June 7, 1926; s. Henry R. and Helen G. (McCron) B.; m. Marjorie H. Cressey, June 5, 1955; children: Bruce C., Margaret W. B.S. in Elec. Engring., Bucknell U., 1948, M.S., MIT, 1951; M.A., Princeton U., 1958, Ph.D., 1964. Instr. Bucknell U., lewisburg, Pa., 1948-49, asst. prof., Lewisburg, Pa., 1953-55; engr., tech. writer Hazeltine Corp., Little Neck, N.Y., 1951-53; asst. prof., assoc. prof. Swarthmore Coll., Pa., 1957-73, prof. elec. engring., 1973—; vis. fellow Bartol Research Found., Swarthmore, 1959-64, Queen's U., Belfast, No. Ireland, 1966-67, U. Fla., Gainesville, 1971, U. Pa., Phila., 1979-80. Co-editor: book series Alternate Energy, 1978—. Served with USN, 1944-46. IBM fellow, 1956-57. Mem. IEEE, Am. Solar Energy Soc., Middle Atlantic Solar Energy Assn., Sigma Xi (pres. chpt. 1981-83), Tau Beta Pi. Democrat. Presbyterian. Home: 505 Yale Ave Swarthmore PA 19081 Office: Swarthmore Coll Swarthmore PA 19081

BOWLES, AUBREY RUSSELL, III, lawyer; b. Richmond, Va., Nov. 21, 1933; s. Aubrey Russell and Martha Mary (Hoadly) B.; m. Jane Moseley Southall, Sept. 8, 1956; children: Aubrey Russell, John Moseley Southall, George Hoadly. B.A., U. Va., 1955, LL.B., 1958; cert., Sorbonne, Paris, 1954. Bar: Va. 1958, D.C. 1978. Assoc. Bowles and Bowles (and predecessors), Richmond, 1958—, ptnr., 1962—, mng. ptnr., 1971—, sr. ptnr., 1984—; mem. council Va. State Bar, 1973-77. Trustee Valentine Mus.; mem. Friends of Henry Ford Mus. and Greenfield Village. Mem. ABA, D.C. Bar Assn., Richmond Bar Assn., Va. Bar Assn., Assn. Bar City N.Y., Va. Assn. Def. Attys., Am. Judicature Soc., Va. Trial Lawyers Assn., Nat. Assn. R.R. Trial Counsel, Am. Soc. Hosp. Lawyers, Internat. Assn. Ins. Counsel, Am. Law Inst., World Assn. Lawyers (founding), Jud. Conf. 4th Jud. Circuit, Jamestowne Soc. (past gov.; atty. gen., mem. council), Am. Power Boat Assn. (racing mem.), Union Internat. Motorboating, Antiquarian Soc. Richmond (past pres.; mem.-at-large), Nat. Trust Historic Preservation, Va. Hist. Soc., Founders Soc. Detroit Mus. Art, Soc. of Cin., Phi Alpha Delta, Sigma Nu. Episcopalian. Clubs: Commonwealth, Country of Va. Home: 5504 Matoaka Rd Richmond VA 23226 Office: PO Box 607 Richmond VA 23205

BOWLES, EDWARD LINDLEY, cons. engr., ret. educator; b. Westphalia, Mo., Dec. 9, 1897; s. Samuel Addison and Julia (Johnson) B.; m. Lois Wuerpel, June 17, 1922; childrenEdmund Addison, Frederick Wuerpel. B.S., Washington U., 1920; M.S., Mass. Inst. Tech., 1922; D.Sc., Norwich U., 1945. Registered profl. engr., Mass. Radio editor Boston Evening Transcript, 1921-22; asst. dept. elec. engring. Mass. Inst. Tech., 1920-21, instr., 1921-25, asst. prof. elec. communications, 1925-27, asso. prof., 1927-37, prof., 1937-63, charge communication div. dept. elec. engring., mem. patent com., dir., cons. prof. elec. communications, 1947-52, cons. prof., 1952-63, prof. emeritus, 1963—; Cons. engr., 1923—; also cons. elec. patent matters; charter mem., sec. microwave sect. Nat. Def. Research Council, 1940-42; cons. sec. war, 1942-47; cons. communications and radar USAAF, 1943, operational and organizational problems, 1944; sci. cons. USAF, 1947-51; sci. warfare adviser weapons evaluation group (Office Sec. Def.), 1950-52, cons. sec. army, 1951-52; gen. cons. Raytheon Co.,

Lexington, Mass., 1947-66; pres. Whitin Machine Works, 1965-66; cons., then spl. asst. to pres. Analex Corp., Boston, 1964-67; chmn. bd., pres. Information Transfer Corp., 1968-70; cons., dir. Anderson-Nichols & Co., 1965-68; now adv. dir., past cons. White COnsol. Industries.; Chmn. bd. ad hoc adv. com. on VHF-UHF (TV allocations, Senate Com. Interstate and Fgn. Commerce), 1956-58; mem. panel on patents Commerce Tech. Adv. Bd. Army; mem. Nat. Acad. Sci.-NRC Research Bd. for Nat. Security, 1945. Past trustee, mem. exec. com. Bentley Coll.; past charter trustee Kodaly Musical Tng. Inst.; trustee Newton-Wellesley Hosp., 1981—; life mem. Boston Mus. Fine Arts. Served as 2d lt. F.A. U.S. Army, 1918. Decorated D.S.M., Presdl. Medal of Merit; comdr. Order Brit. Empire (hon.); recipient distinguished alumni citation Washington U., 1955. Fellow IEEE (fellowship award IRE 1947), Am. Phys. Soc., Am. Acad. Arts and Scis. (v.p. 1954-56); mem. AAAS, Soc. Promotion Engring. Edn., Ops. Research Soc., Westphalia Hist. Soc. (charter), Sigma Xi. Clubs: St. Botolph (Boston); Cosmos (Washington). Holder numerous patents. Address: 15 Greylock Rd Wellesley Hills MA 02181

BOWLES, GROVER CLEVELAND, JR., pharmacist, educator; b. Piedmont, Mo., Feb. 15, 1920; s. Grover Clevel and Oca (Newton) B.; m. Mary Lois Van Inwagen, Dec. 23, 1947; children: Rebecca R., Deborah M. Student, S.E. Mo. State Coll., 1938-39; B.S. in Pharmacy, U. Tenn., 1942; D.Sc., Phila. Coll. Pharmacy and Sci., 1968. Intern hosp. pharmacy U. Mich. Hosp., 1946-47; instr. U. Tenn. Coll. Pharmacy, 1947-48; chief pharmacist Strong Meml. Hosp., also U. Rochester Sch. Medicine and Dentistry, 1948-55; asso. adminstr. Meml. Hosp. Assn., Washington, 1955-56; dir. dept. pharmacy Bapt. Meml. Hosp., Memphis, 1956—; prof. U. Tenn. Coll. Pharmacy, 1959—; mem. revision com. U.S. Pharmacopeia, 1960-70; mem. Tenn. Hosp. Licensing Bd., 1961—. Bd. dirs. Memphis unit Am. Cancer Soc., Memphis Vis. Nurse Assn. Served with USNR, 1942-46. Recipient Remington Medal award, 1973, Meritorious Service citation Tenn. Hosp. Assn., 1976, Disting. Service award U. Tenn. Coll. Pharmacy, 1979. Mem. Am. Pharm. Assn. (pres. 1965-66, chmn. bd. trustees 1966-67, treas. 1967-78, Remington Honor medal 1973, Hugo H. Schaffer medal 1979), Am. Soc. Hosp. Pharmacists (pres. 1952, Harvey A. K. Whitney lectr. 1962), Tenn. Soc. Hosp. Pharmacists (pres. 1948), AAAS, Am. Council Pharm. Edn. (pres. 1982—), Phi Delta Chi. Home: 4997 Warwick Ave Memphis TN 38117 Office: 899 Madison Ave Memphis TN 38146

BOWLES, JOHN, executive; b. Monroe, N.C., Nov. 16, 1916; s. Hargrove and Kelly Bess (Moneyhun) B.; m. Norma Louise Landwehr, Oct. 6, 1950; children: Carol Louise, Kelly Louise, John Hargrove, Norma. B.S., U. N.C., 1938; D.B.A., Woodbury Coll., 1963, Wingate Jr. Coll., 1960. With Rexall Drug Co., Los Angeles, 1949-66, v.p., 1953-55, pres., 1955-65, chmn. bd., 1965-66; v.p., dir. Rexall Drug & Chem. Co., 1955-66; chmn. Sunstates, Inc., Beverly Hills, Calif.; dir. A.S. Haight Co. Inc., El Camino Rodeo Corp.; Mem. Pres.'s Com. for Community Relations; mem. nat. sponsoring com. Duke; mem. pharmacy adv. com. Coll. Pacific; founder Free Enterprise Day; pres. Los Amigos del Pueblo de Los Angeles, Los Amigos de Los Charros, Calif. Mus. Sci. and Industry. Trustee Martin Luther Hosp., U. Calif. at Los Angeles Found., Broadcast Found., Padua Inst., Robert Louis Stevenson Sch.; adv. bd. Pepperdine U.; bd. govs. Am. Found. Religion and Psychiatry; bd. regents St. John's Hosp., Orthopaedic Hosp. Council. Served as lt. comdr. USNR, 1941-46. Recipient Horatio Alger award, 1962. Mem. Sales and Marketing Execs. (trustee), Confrerie des Chevaliers du Tastevin (grand officer), Calif. Wine Patrons (pres.), Master of Foxhounds Assn., Beta Theta Pi. Methodist (steward). Clubs: Masons., Los Angeles Country; Kildare Hunt (Ireland); Santa Ynez Hunt; Rancheros Vistadores (Santa Barbara); Bohemian. Home: 401 Robert Ln Beverly Hills CA 90210 Office: 911 Hillcrest Rd Beverly Hills CA 90210

BOWLES, LAWRENCE THOMPSON, surgeon, university dean, educator; b. Mineola, N.Y., Sept. 23, 1931; s. Ray McCune and Lucille Grace (Wickizer) B.; m. Judith E. LeFever, July 10, 1965; children: Julia, Amy, Lauren. A.B., Duke U., 1953, M.D., 1957; M.S. in Surgery, N.Y. U., 1964, Ph.D., 1971. Intern N.Y. U./Bellevue Hosp., N.Y.C., 1957-57, resident in surgery, 1958-62; dir. div. curriculum and instrn. Assn. Am. Med. Colls., Washington, 1970-73; asso. dean curricular and student affairs, asso. prof. surgery George Washington U. Med. Center, Washington, 1973-76, dean acad. affairs, prof. surgery, 1976—; cons. Children's Nat. Med. Center, Washington, VA Hosp., Washington, Martinsburg, W.Va., Nat. Cancer Inst. Pres. Healing Arts Commn., D.C., 1977-79; Prin. investigator various grants.; mem. Nat. Bd. Med. Examiners, 1982—, mem. exec. bd., 1983—; bd. regents. Nat. Library Medicine, 1982—. Founding editor: Curriculum Directory of Assn. of Am. Med. Colleges; mem. editorial bd.: Jour. Med. Edn., 1982—; contbr. articles to profl. publs. Mem. AMA, D.C. Med. Soc., Washington Acad. Medicine, A.C.S. (com. on continuing edn.), Am. Coll. Chest Physicians, Soc. Thoracic Surgeons (council, chmn. govt. relations com.), Am. Assn. Thoracic Surgery, Am. Gerontol. Soc. Office: 2300 Eye St NW Washington DC 20037 *

BOWLES, PAUL, composer, author; b. N.Y.C., Dec. 30, 1910; s. Claude Dietz and Rena (Winnewisser) B.; m. Jane Sydney Auer, Feb. 1938. Studied with, Aaron Copland, N.Y.C., Berlin, 1930-32; with, Virgil Thomson, Paris, 1933-34. Composer: mus. scores for Roots in the Earth, for Soil Conservation Service, U.S. Dept. Agr., Watch on the Rhine, Jacobowsky and the Colonel, The Glass Menagerie, Cyrano de Bergerac, Summer and Smoke, In the Summer House, Yerma, Sweet Bird of Youth, The Milk Train Doesn't Stop Here Any More; ballets Sentimental Colloquy; opera The Wind Remains; Author: (with Driss ben Hamed Charhadi) Their Heads are Green and Their Hands are Blue; novel The Time of Friendship; autobiography Without Stopping, 1972; Things Gone and Things Still Here, Collected Stories, Midnight Mass, Next to Nothing, Points in Time, (transls. of Mohammed Mrabet) Love With a Few Hairs, The Lemon, M'Hashish,The Boy Who Set The Fire, Look and Move On, Harmless Poisons, The Big Mirror, The Beach Café. Guggenheim fellow, 1941; Rockefeller grantee, 1959.

BOWLES, WALTER DONALD, economist, educator; b. Seattle, Dec. 28, 1923; s. Walter Alexander and Minnie Ellen (Martin) B.; m. Vincenza Pompea Galasso, Dec. 22, 1955; children—Ellen Maria, Walter Donald. B.A. in Econs, U. Wash., 1949, M.A., Columbia, 1952; certificate Soviet economy, Russian Inst., 1952, Ph.D., 1958. Editor Research Program on USSR, N.Y.C., 1953-55; fellow Air U., 1955-57; faculty Am. U., Washington, 1957—, prof. econs., chmn. dept., 1962-65, prof. econs., dean, 1965-69, prof. econs., v.p. acad. affairs, 1969-73, prof. econs., 1974—; on leave as prof. econs., sr. fellow Columbia, 1973-74; on leave as economist U.S. AID, 1983—; prof. econs. Graz Center, Austria, summers 1971-73; lectr., dir. seminars in field. Served with AUS, 1943-46. Mem. Am. Econ. Assn., Assn. Study Comparative Econ. Systems, Assn. for Advancement Slavic Studies, Soc. for Internat. Devel., AAUP, Pi Gamma Mu, Omicron Delta Kappa, Phi Kappa Phi, Omicron Delta Epsilon. Home: 6017 Rossmore Dr Bethesda MD 20814

BOWLEY, ALBERT JOHN, university administrator, retired air force officer; b. Ft. Bragg, N.C., Dec. 4, 1921; s. Freeman Wate and Elizabeth (Carpenter) B.; m. Marjorie Rose Marchand, Jan. 10, 1944; children: Robin Mills, Albert John. B.S., U.S. Mil. Acad., 1943; grad., Air Force Flying Sch., 1943, Armed Forces Spl. Weapons Project, 1948, Advanced Flying Sch., 1953, Command and Staff Coll., 1955, Air War Coll., 1959. Commd. 2d lt. U.S. Army, 1943; advanced through grades to maj. gen. USAF, 1969; assigned 306th Bomb Group, ETO, 1944-47, 63d Bomb Squadron, 43d Bomb Group, SAC, 1947-48, operations officer, 1949-51; squadron comdr. 358th Bomb Squadron, 303d Bomb Wing, SAC, 1952-54; chief tng. surveillance br., tng. div. Hdqrs. SAC, 1955-58; dir. operations Hdqrs. 3d. Air Div., SAC, Guam, 1959-61; chief control div. Hdqrs. 15th Air Force, SAC, March AFB, Calif., 1961; dep. dir. operations Hdqrs. 15th Air Force, 1962; dep. exec. to vice chief staff Hdqrs. USAF, 1963, exec. to vice chief staff, 1963-66; comdr. 40th Air Div., Wurtsmith AFB, Mich., 1966-67, 45th Air Div., Loring AFB, Maine, 1967-68; dep. dir. J-5, joint staff, Washington, 1968-70; dep. chief staff Hdqrs. MACV, South Vietnam, 1971-73; ret., 1973; dir. deferred gifts Office Devel., Stetson U., Deland, Fla., 1973—. Decorated D.S.M. with oakleaf cluster, D.F.C., Air medal with 2 oak leaf clusters, Legion of Merit with oak leaf cluster. Mem. Air. Force Assn., Order Daedalians. Clubs: Army-Navy Country (Arlington, Va.) (chmn. bd. gov.'s 1969-70, v.p. 1972—. Home: 150 Lake Winnemissett Dr Deland FL 32720

BOWLING, FRANCIS S., state justice; b. Madison County, Miss., Dec. 16, 1916; m. Edna Boyette; 2 children. B.A., LL.B., U. Miss. Bar: Miss. Individual practice, Jackson, Miss., 1940-74, circuit ct. judge, 1973-77; justice Miss. Supreme Ct., 1977—. Served with U.S. Army, World War II. Mem. Miss. Trial Lawyers Assn. (past pres.), Internat. Soc. Barristers. Democrat. Methodist. Address: Caroll Gartin Justice Bldg Jackson MS 39205 *

BOWLING, JAMES CHANDLER, tobacco company executive; b. Covington, Ky., Mar. 29, 1928; s. Van Dorn and Belinda (Johnson) B.; m. Ann Jones, Oct. 20, 1951; children: Belinda, Nancy, James Jr., Stephanie. B.S., U. Louisville, 1951; LL.D. (hon.), Murray U., 1976, U. Ky., 1981. Various positions from campus rep. to v.p. sales corp. relations Philip Morris, Inc., N.Y.C.; then exec. v.p., group v.p., dir. marketing, now asst. to chmn. bd., sr. v.p., dir.; dir. Miller Brewing Co., Seven Up Co.; bd. dirs., mem. exec. com. Tobacco Inst., Washington. Author: How To Improve Your Personal Relations, 1959. Mem. nat. council Boy Scouts Am., 1961—; justice of peace, Rowayton, Conn., 1960-68; vice-chmn. Clean World Internat.; bd. overseers U. Louisville; former pres., former chmn., former bd. dirs. Keep Am. Beautiful; bd. dirs. Nat. Automatic Merchandising Assn.; trustee Berea Coll., Midway Jr. Coll.; bd. dirs. Ky. Ind. Coll. Found., Nat. Tennis Found. and Hall of Fame, U. Ky. Devel. Council., Lambda Chi Alpha Found. Served with AUS, World War II; PTO. Recipient Kolodny award as outstanding young exec. in tobacco industry, 1963; named U.S. Young Businessman of Year St. John's U., 1967, Outstanding Alumnus U. Louisville, 1970, Kentuckian of Year, 1977; elected to Tobacco Industry Hall of Fame, 1976. Mem. Nat. Assn. Tobacco Distbg. (dir. exec. mgmt. div.), Pub. Relations Soc. Am., Sales Execs. Club N.Y., The Kentuckians (past pres.). Episcopalian. Clubs: Wee Burn Country.; Union League (N.Y.C.). Home: 13 Tokeneke Trail Darien CT 06820 Office: 100 Park Ave New York NY 10017

BOWLING, MELVIN GENE, engineer, retired air force officer; b. Morgan City, Ala., Mar. 2, 1933; s. John Roy and Cora Lee (Stidger) B.; m. Joan Harrison, Oct. 24, 1958; children: John Michael, James Darrol. B.S., U. Ala., 1954; M.B.A., George Washington U., 1965; postgrad., Air Command and Staff Coll., 1965, Nat. War Coll., 1971. Commd. 2d lt. U.S. Air Force, 1954, advanced through grades to maj. gen., 1976; comdr. SAC 68 Bombardment Wing, Seymour-Johnson AFB, N.C. and Anderson AFB, Guam, 1972-73, vice comdr. 17th Air Div., U-Tapao Royal Thai Air Base, Thailand, 1973, chief, strategic negotiations Joint Chiefs of Staff, Washington, 1973-74, comdr. 4th Air Div., Francis E. Warren AFB, Wyo., 1974-75, dep. chief of staff, ops. Air Tng. Command, Randolph AFB, Tex., 1975-76, comdr. USAF Recruiting Service, Randolph AFB, 1976-78, dep. comdr. 6th Allied Tactical Air Force (NATO), Izmir, Turkey, sr. U.S. nat. rep. in Izmir 6th Allied Tactical Air Force (NATO), 1978-80, chief of staff Allied Air Force, So. Europe (NATO), Naples, Italy, from 1980, now with Teledyne Brown Engring., Huntsville, Ala.; mem. Civilian/Mil. Affairs Com., San Antonio, 1976-78, Cheyenne, Wyo., 1974-76. Author: Advantages and Limitations Systems Analysis in Management, 1965, The Role of Tactical Air Forces in U.S. Foreign Policy, 1971. Decorated Silver Star, D.S.M., Legion of Merit, D.F.C., Air medal with 7 oak leaf clusters. Mem. Am. Mgmt. Assn., Air Force Assn., AIAA. Office: Teledyne Brown Engring 300 Sparkman Dr Stop 108 Research Park Huntsville AL 35802 *Successful leadership depends on loyalty, persistence, dedication to principle, integrity, and the many well-known technical factors; however the meaningful contributions I may have made have resulted from trusting God and application of the Golden Rule in dealing with others.*

BOWLING, WALTER SCOTT, JR., bank holding co. exec.; b. New Albany, Ind., Nov. 14, 1945; s. Walter Scott and Lorene (Striegel) B.; m. Frances Besalu, Jan. 15, 1974; 1 dau., Lauren Page. B.S. in Acctg, La. State U., 1967, M.S., 1970. With Arthur Andersen & Co. (C.P.A.'s), New Orleans, 1969-73, First Nat. Bank Louisville, 1973-75; with Am. South Bancorp., Birmingham, 1975—, sr. v.p., 1979—; pres. Alabanc Properties, Inc.; co-founder Southeastern Bank Tax Assn., 1975; counselor New Orleans Jr. Achievement. (C.P.A.), La. Mem. Am. Inst. C.P.A's, Fin. Execs. Inst., Am. Bankers Assn., La. Soc. C.P.A.'s, La. State U. Alumni Assn. Republican. Clubs: Riverchase Country, Birmingham Tip-Off, L. Office: PO Box 11007 Birmingham AL 35288

BOWLING, WILLIAM GLASGOW, educator; b. St. Louis, May 7, 1902; s. William Walter and Mary Susan (Glasgow) B.; m. Violet Whelen, Aug. 3, 1933; 1 son, Townsend Whelen. A.B., Washington U., St. Louis, 1924, A.M., 1925; postgrad., Harvard U., 1930-31. Instr., asst. prof., asso. prof. English, Washington U., 1925-70, prof. emeritus, 1970—, asst. to dean, acting dean, dean Univ. Coll., 1928-42, dean Coll. Liberal Arts, 1942-46, dean of men, 1942-44; civilian adminstr. pre-profl. unit Army Specialized Tng. Program, Washington U., 1943-44, dean admissions, 1946-65, univ. grand marshal, 1960-68, univ. historian, 1965—; part time drama critic St. Louis Times, 1929-30. Contbr. articles to profl. jours. Recipient Washington U. Alumni award for disting. service, 1960. Mem. Am. Assn. Collegiate Registrars and Admissions Officers (hon.; book rev. editor quar. jour. Coll. and Univ. 1955-66), Greater St. Louis Council Tchrs. of English (pres. 1936-39, exec. sec. 1939-41), Washington U. Assn. Lecture Series (exec. sec. 1940-47), St. Louis Audubon Soc. (dir. 1944—, pres. 1950-52), Phi Delta Theta, Omicron Delta Kappa, Phi Delta Kappa. Republican. Episcopalian. Club: University (St. Louis). Address: 7408 Washington Ave Saint Louis MO 63130

BOWLUS, JOHN MAGRUDER, lawyer; b. Poughkeepsie, N.Y., Aug. 7, 1926; s. Benjamin Harrison and Doris Harding (Smith) B.; m. Mary W. McLaughlin, Aug. 31, 1957; 1 dau., Jane Smith. A.B., Allegheny Coll., Meadville, Pa., 1948; M.A., U. Pa., 1949; J.D., U. Chgo., 1953-56. Bar: Ill. 1956. Fgn. affairs analyst Dept. State, 1949-53; practice, Chgo., 1953—; ptnr. Cotton, Watt, Jones, King & Bowlus, 1966-83; commr. atty. registration and disciplinary commn. Ill. Supreme Ct. Served with USNR, 1944-46. Decorated Bronze Star (2).; Recipient citation of honor Chgo. chpt. Artists Equity Assn. Mem. Am., Ill., Chgo. bar assns., Chgo. Council Lawyers, Theta Chi. Republican. Club: Union League (Chgo.). Home: 2317 Central Park Dr Evanston IL 60201 Office: 3410 Three First National Plaza Chicago IL 60602

BOWMAN, ALBERT HALL, educator; b. Evanston, Ill., Jan. 16, 1921; s. Francis Brainerd and Gertrude (Bowman) B.; m. Joyce Adair Duschl, June 5, 1948; children—Victoria Joyce, Elizabeth Ann, Catherine Louise. Grad., South Kent (Conn.) Sch., 1938; A.B., Trinity Coll., Hartford, Conn., 1947; M.A., Columbia, 1948, Ph.D., 1954. Instr. history N.Y. U., 1948-49; fgn. affairs analyst U.S. Govt., 1951-57; prof. history, chmn. div. social scis. Tenn. Wesleyan Coll., Athens, 1957-62; prof. history, dir. libraries U. Chattanooga, 1962-69; prof. history U. Tenn. at Chattanooga, 1969—; Vis. prof. history L.I.U., summer 1962; Fulbright prof. U. Louvain, Belgium, 1967-68. Contbr. profl. and other jours.; Author: The Struggle for Neutrality, 1974 (Gilbert Chinard Hist. award 1975); Editor: The United States and Europe: A Colloquium, 1968. Served to 1st lt. AUS, 1942-46; mem. N.Y.N.G., 1947-50. Decorated Bronze Star medal, Purple Heart. Mem. Am. Hist. Assn., Chattanooga Hist. Assn. (pres. 1973-74), Orgn. Am. Historians, Soc. Historians Am. Fgn. Relations, Soc. Historians of Early Am. Republic, AAUP (pres. chpt. 1960-62, 64, 74-75), UN Assn. U.S. (pres. Chattanooga 1963-64), ACLU, Alpha Delta Phi. Democrat. Episcopalian. Home: 511 James Blvd Signal Mountain TN 37377 Office: U Tenn at Chattanooga Chattanooga TN 37401

BOWMAN, BARBARA HYDE, biologist, geneticist, educator; b. Mineral Wells, Tex., Aug. 5, 1930; d. John Tom and Cleo (Frost) B. B.S., Baylor U., 1951; M.A., U. Tex., 1955, Ph.D., 1959. Bacteriologist Tex. Dept. Health, 1954-55; research assoc. U. Tex., Austin, 1959-63, prof. human genetics, chmn. dept., Galveston, 1967-81; prof. genetics, chmn. dept. cellular and structural biology U. Tex. Health Sci. Center, San Antonio, 1981—; research assoc. Rockefeller Inst., N.Y.C., 1963-65; asst. prof. Rockefeller U., N.Y.C., 1965-67; mem. genetics study sect. NIH, 1970-74; mem. bd. sci. counselors, div. cancer biology and diagnosis (Nat. Cancer Inst.). Editorial bd.: Clin. Genetics, 1970—, Tex. Reports on Biology and Medicine, 1968-71. Mem. Am. Soc. Biol. Chemists, Harvey Soc., Am. Soc. Human Genetics (treas. 1970-76, pres. 1980), Sigma Xi. Research in human inherited diseases and human protein structure. Office: U Tex Health Sci Center San Antonio TX 77550

BOWMAN, BARBARA TAYLOR, educator; b. Chgo., Oct. 30, 1928; d. Robert Rochon and Dorothy Vaugn (Jennings) Taylor; m. James E. Bowman, June 17, 1950; 1 dau., Valerie June. B.A., Sarah Lawrence Coll., 1950; M.A., U. Chgo., 1952. Tchr. U. Chgo. Nursery Sch., 1950-52, Colo. Women's Coll. Nursery Sch., Denver, 1953-55; mem. sci. faculty Nemazee Sch. Nursing, U. Shiraz, Iran, 1955-61; spl. edn. tchr. Chgo. Child Care Soc., 1965-67; mem. faculty Erikson Inst., Chgo., 1967—, now dir. grad. studies; cons. early childhood edn., parent edn. Contbr. articles to profl. jours. Bd. dirs. Ill. Health Edn. Com., 1969-71, Inst. Psychoanalysis, 1970—, Ill. Adv. Council Dept. Children and Family Services, 1974-79, Child Devel. Asso. Consortium, 1979-81, Chgo. Spl. Task Force on Edn., 1980-81. Mem. Ill. Assn. Edn. Young Children, Nat. Assn. Edn. Young Children (pres. 1980-82), Chgo. Assns. Edn. Young Children (pres. 1973-77), Black Child Devel. Assn., Assn. Childhood Edn. Inc., Orgn. Mondiale pour l'Edn. Prescolaire. Research on math. teaching. Home: 4929 S Greenwood Chicago IL 60615 Office: Erikson Inst #2200 200 N Michigan Ave Chicago IL 60601

BOWMAN, CLAUDE CHARLTON, sociologist; b. Harrisburg, Pa., Sept. 13, 1908; s. Claude C. and Jane Given (Sprout) B.; m. Mary S. Carson, June 29, 1929. A.B., Dickinson Coll., 1928; Ph.D., U. Pa., 1937. Instr. chemistry Dickinson Coll., Carlisle, Pa., 1928-29; fellow in sociology U. Kans., Lawrence, 1929-30; instr. sociology Temple U., Phila., 1930-37, asst. prof., 1937-45, prof., 1945-76, prof. emeritus, 1976—, acting dean of men, 1942-44, dean of students, 1944-45; lectr. in field. Author: The College Professor in America, 1938, re-issued, 1977, Humanistic Sociology, 1973; contbr. articles to sociol., psychiat. jours. Bd. dirs. Horizon House, Planned Parenthood Assn. of S.E. Pa., Phila. ACLU, Phila. Ams. Democratic Action. Mem. Am. Sociol. Assn., AAUP (chpt. pres. 1953-54), Internat. Assn. Applied Psychology, Phi Beta Kappa. Clubs: Franklin Inn, Peale (Phila.). Home: 331 Hamilton Rd Merion Station PA 19066 Office: Temple U Philadelphia PA 19122 *I believe in the importance of ideas in human affairs. Democracies suffer when public intelligence is overwhelmed by narrow self-interest and bigotry. I have devoted my life to the advancement of intelligent citizenship.*

BOWMAN, CLEMENT WILLIS, petroleum research executive; b. Toronto, Ont., Can., Jan. 7, 1930; s. Clement Willis and Emily (Stockley) B.; m. Marjorie Elizabeth Greer, Aug. 21, 1954; children: Elizabeth Ann, John Clement. B.A.Sc., U. Toronto, 1952, M.A.Sc., 1958, Ph.D., 1961. Registered profl. engr., Alta. Research engr. Imperial Oil Ltd., Sarnia, Ont., Can., 1960-63; research mgr. Syncrude Can. Ltd., Edmonton, Alta., Can., 1964-69; chem. research mgr. Imperial Oil. Ltd., Sarnia, 1969-72, petroleum research mgr., 1972-75; chmn. Alta. Oil Sands Tech. and Research Authority, Edmonton, 1975—; dir. Alta. Research Council, 1979—. Recipient Meritorious Service medal U. Toronto Alumni Assn., 1977, Queen's 25-Yr. Jubilee medal, 1977. Mem. Can. Soc. Chem. Engring.; fellow Chem. Inst. Can. Office: 10010 106th St 500 Highfield Pl Canada T5J 3L8

BOWMAN, DAVID BARTHOLOMEW, lawyer; b. Lancaster, Pa., Nov. 5, 1928; s. David Bartholomew and Loretta (Ganse) B.; m. Elsa Elizabeth McPhee, Feb. 4, 1955; children: Megan Jane, Matthew David. B.A. magna cum laude, Pomona (Calif.) Coll., 1953; LL.B., Yale U., 1957. Bar: Wash. bar 1957. Asso. firm Ryan, Askren & Matthewson, Seattle, 1957-61; gen. counsel, sec. Alaska Airlines, Inc., 1961-64; counsel, sec. Lockheed Shipbldg. & Constrn. Co., Seattle, 1964—, dir. legal and public affairs, 1981-82; corp. counsel Lockheed Corp., Burbank, Calif., 1982—. Served with USN, 1946-49. Mem. Wash. Bar Assn., Seattle-King County Bar Assn. Office: 2555 N Hollywood Way Burbank CA 91504

BOWMAN, DAVID LEON, teacher educator; b. Mt. Vernon, N.Y., Jan. 20, 1923; s. Leon C. and Margaret (Bengert) B.; m. Olive J. Johnson, July 9, 1943; children—James, Lawrence, Nancy, Carol Ann. B.A., Colgate U., 1942; M.A., Columbia Tchrs. Coll., 1945, Ed.D., 1954. Tchr. math. Hamilton (N.Y.) High Sch., 1942, Somers (N.Y.) High Sch., 1948-50; tchr. math., sci. and edn. Eau Claire (Wis.) State Coll., 1950-51; research asst. Wis. Bd. Regents of State Colls., 1951-54; dean Coll. Edn. U. Wis., Oshkosh, 1954-76, prof. edn., 1976—; also vocalist and pianist; Mem. Nat. Commn. Assn. Student Teaching, 1960-66; mem. Wis. Curriculum Guiding Com., 1958. Author: A Study of Two and Four Year Curricula for the Preparation of Elementary School Teachers at Wisconsin State College, 1954, Research and Curriculum Development in Fox River Valley, 1964, Quantitative and Qualitative Effects of Revised Selection and Training Procedures in the Education of Teachers of the Disadvantaged, 1970, An Attack on High Attrition of University Underachievers, 1971, also numerous articles. Served with AUS, 1943-45. Mem. NEA, Wis. Edn. Assn., Wis. Elementary Sch. Prins. Assn., Northeastern Wis. Edn. Assn., Oshkosh Edn. Assn., Nat. Assn. Tchr. Educators, Assn. Supervision and Curriculum Devel., Kappa Delta Pi, Mu Pi Delta, Phi Delta Kappa. Club: Rotarian. Home: 1517 Pierce Ave Oshkosh WI 54901

BOWMAN, DEAN ORLANDO, economist, educator; b. Chalmers, Ind., Sept. 22, 1909; s. Bruce and Aletha G. (Taylor) B.; m. Fate Thomas, June 8, 1936; 1 dau., Ann Pennington. B.S., Purdue U., 1933, M.S., 1934; Ph.D. (Brookings fellow), U. Mich., 1941. Regional price exec., dep. regional adminstr. O.P.A., 1946; chief fgn. trade sect., Japan-Korea; econ. affairs div. Dept. State, 1947-48; asst. dir. Office of Industry and Commerce, Dept. Commerce, 1948-50; asst. adminstr. policy coordination N.P.A., 1951-53; coordinator long range planning Crown Zellerbach Corp., 1953-60; v.p. long range planning Autonetics div. Rockwell Internat. Corp., Anaheim, Calif., 1960-63, v.p. mgmt. systems and planning, 1963-70; dir. mgmt. programs, prof. bus. econs. U. Mich. Grad. Sch. Bus. Adminstrn., Ann Arbor, 1970-73; dean Sch. Bus., Calif. State U., Long Beach, 1973-77; asst. dean exec. edn. UCLA, 1978-79. Author: Public Control of Labor Relations, 1942; Contbr. articles to publs. Served to 1st lt. OSS AUS, 1943-45. Recipient Gold medal for exceptional service Dept. Commerce, 1953; Distinguished Service award Office Emergency Planning, 1968. Mem. Am., Western econ. assns., Nat. Planning Assn., Nat. Assn. Bus. Economists, Phi Kappa Phi. Home: 862 Glenwood Circle Fullerton CA 92632

BOWMAN, EDWARD HARRY, business science educator; b. Watertown, Mass., Sept. 30, 1925; s. Harry L. and Florence (Foster) B.; m. Ann Semple, Jan. 31, 1948; children: John E., Susan A. B.S., MIT, 1947; M.B.A., U. Pa., 1949; Ph.D., Ohio State U., 1954; M.A. hon., Yale U., 1967. Instr. Ohio State U., 1949-52; dean Coll. Adminstrv. Sci. Ohio State U., 1974-79; prof. MIT, 1952-66, 69-74, 79-83; asst. to pres. Honeywell Computer div., 1963-65; comptroller Yale U., 1966-69; Reginald Jones prof. corp. mgmt., dir. Reginald Jones Ctr. Wharton Sch., U. Pa., Phila., 1983—. Author: (with R.B. Fetter) Analysis for Production and Operations Management, 1957, Analyses of Industrial Operations, 1959. Served with USNR, 1944-46. Mem. Inst. Mgmt. Sci. (past v.p.). Office: U Pa Wharton Sch Philadelphia PA 19174

BOWMAN, GEORGE SHEPARD, JR., ret. marine corps officer, mil. acad. exec.; b. Hammond, La., Dec. 24, 1911; s. George Shepard and Marie (Hall) B.; m. Velma Elizabeth Roth, Nov. 7, 1959; children—Diane (Mrs. James H. Cunningham), Denham Warren. B.S. in Elec. Engring, La. State U., 1936; grad., Nat. War Coll., 1954. Commd. 2d lt. USMC, 1936, designated naval aviator, 1939, advanced through grades to maj. gen., 1965; various assignments, U.S. and Pacific, 1936-52, comdg. officer, Korea, 1953, dep. asst. dir. aviation, 1958-60, asst. chief staff, 1960-63,, comdg. gen., 1964-66, dep. comdr., Atlantic, Norfolk, Va., 1966-68, Vietnam, 1969-70, comdr., Camp Pendleton, Calif., 1970-71, retired, 1972, supr., Harlingen, Tex., 1972—. Decorated D.S.M., Legion of Merit with combat V and 3 stars, D.F.C., Bronze Star medal with combat V, Air medal. Mem. Nat. Sojourners, Heroes of '76, Churchman's Sports Hall of Fame, Ret. Officers Assn. (dir.), Navy League, D.A.V., Nat. Honor Soc., Scabbard and Blade, Delta Kappa Epsilon, Omicron Delta Kappa, Phi Kappa Phi. Episcopalian. Clubs: Mason (Shriner), Elk., Carolina Pines Country (Havelock, N.C.); Harlingen Country. Address: 30 Los Amigos Dr Harlingen TX 78550 *Live by the "Golden Rule". Be honest in everything you do. Live a Christian life and engage in daily prayer. Be patient with people who come to you with their problems, and give them a helping hand. Take the time to gather information about both sides of an issue and have the courage to support the correct side. Have the moral strength to make the tough decision when the time comes.*

BOWMAN, IRVING HENRY, architect, structural engineer; b. Chgo., Apr. 17, 1906; s. Henry William and Mercedes Ellen (Bjork) B.; m. Winifred Woods, June 26, 1937; children: Henry Woods, Ellen Davis. B.S. in Arch., Ill. Inst. Tech., 1928; postgrad., Lake Forest Found. Architecture and Landscape Architecture, 1928. Registered profl. engr., Ill., W.Va.; registered architect, Ill., W.Va., Md., Va. Archtl. designer Holabird & Root Architects, Chgo., 1928-29; ptnr. Bowman Bros. Architects, Chgo., 1929-36; staff architect Union Carbide Corp., Charleston, W.Va., 1936-38; chief designer H. Rus Warne, Architect, Charleston, 1938-40; architect H. K. Ferguson Co., Cleve., 1941; architect, engr. Irving Bowman & Assocs., Charleston, 1946—; work exhibited Mus. Modern Art, N.Y.C., 1931. Pres. Mcpl. Planning Commn., Charleston, 1952-72. Served to lt. comdr. USNR (ret.), 1946. Recipient Hon. Mention W.Va. Soc. Architects, 1978, James L. Montgomery medal W.Va. Soc. Architects, 1983, 1st medal Beaux Arts Inst. Design. Fellow AIA; mem. Nat. Inst. Bldg. Scis., Am. Arbitration Assn., W.Va. Soc. Architects (pres. 1952-54). Home: 1541 Quarrier St Charleston WV 25311 Office: Irving Bowmans & Assocs 910 Quarrier St PO Box 1827 Charleston WV 25327

BOWMAN, JACK LEWIS, pharm. co. exec.; b. Wallace, Kans., Aug. 17, 1932; s. Lonnie E. and Vera Mae (Frazier) B.; m. JoAnn Hoyt, Aug. 9, 1952; children—Daniel L., Pete L. B.E., Western Wash. U., 1954. Dir. music, high sch., Lynden, Wash., 1954-57; with Ciba Geigy Corp., Summit, N.J., 1957-80, exec. v.p., 1977-80; pres. Lederle Labs. div. Am. Cyanamid Inc., Pearl River, N.Y., 1980—; guest lectr. Fairleigh Dickinson U. Mem. Food and Drug Law Inst. (dir.), Pharm. Mfrs. Assn. (vice chmn. mktg. sect.). Home: 59 Morris Ave Morristown NJ 07960 Office: Berden Ave Wayne NJ 07470

BOWMAN, JAMES EDWARD, physician, educator; b. Washington, Feb. 5, 1923; s. James Edward and Dorothy (Peterson) B.; m. Barbara Taylor, June 17, 1950; 1 dau., Valerie June. B.S., Howard U., 1943, M.D., 1946. Intern Freedmen's Hosp., Washington, 1946-47; resident pathology St. Lukes Hosp., Chgo., 1947-50; chmn. dept. pathology Provident Hosp., 1950-53, Shiraz (Iran) Med. Center, Nemazee Hosp., 1955-61; vis. prof., chmn. dept. pathology Faculty of Medicine, U. Shiraz, 1959-61; dir. labs. U. Chgo., 1971—, prof. dept. pathology, medicine, com. on genetics and biol. scis., collegiate div., 1972—, dir., 1973—; cons. pathology, div. hosp. and med. facilities HEW, USPHS, mem., 1968, (Health and Hosps. Governing Commn. Cook County), 1969-72; mem. exec. com. hemalytic anemia study group NHLI, NIH, Bethesda, Md., 1973-75; Sabbatical fellow Center for Advanced Study in Behavioral Scis., Stanford U., 1981-82. Contbr. articles profl. jours. Served to capt. M.C. AUS, 1953-55. Spl. research fellow NIH Galton Lab., Univ. Coll., London, 1961-62. Mem. Coll. Am. Pathologists, Am. Soc. Clin. Pathologists, Am. Soc. Human Genetics, Central Soc. Clin. Research, Am. Soc. Hematology, Am. Assn. Phys. Anthropologists, Acad. Clin. Lab. Physicians and Scientists. Home: 4929 S Greenwood St Chicago IL 60615 Office: 950 E 59th St Chicago IL 60637

BOWMAN, JAMES HENRY, writer; b. Chgo., Dec. 29, 1931; s. Paul Clarke and Kathryn (O'Connell) B.; m. Winifred M. Moore, July 12, 1969; children—Angela Marie, Kathryn Suzanne, Margaret Elizabeth, James Henry, Peter Daniel, Marietta Therese. A.B., Loyola U., Chgo., 1955, M.A., 1960, Ph.L., 1957, Th.L., 1964. Mem. Soc. of Jesus, 1950-68; asso. editor Ave Maria mag., Notre Dame, Ind., 1968; exec. editor Focus Michiana mag., South Bend, Ind., 1968; religion writer Chgo. Daily News, 1968-78; free-lance writer, 1978—; tchr. St. Ignatius High Sch., Chgo., 1957-58, 65-67, Loyola Acad., Wilmette, Ill., 1958-60, Xavier U., Cin., 1967-68. Roman Catholic. Home and Office: 220 N Harvey Oak Park IL 60302 *Beware slogans. The ultimate goal of education is to learn to think for oneself. Ideology is insignificant compared to compassion and good judgment.*

BOWMAN, JAMES KINSEY, publishing company executive; b. Strongsville, Ohio, Nov. 1, 1933; s. Benjamin H. and Margaret A. (Kinsey) B.; m. Judith Ann Lofton, Mar. 27, 1957; children: J. Reed, Eustacia L., Todd K. B.A., Denison U., Granville, Ohio, 1956. With McGraw-Hill Book Co., N.Y.C., 1956—, gen. mgr., v.p. coll. div., 1965-68, group v.p. higher edn., 1968-73, v.p. marketing, 1973-82, sr. v.p. adminstrn., 1982—. Mem. Am. Assn. Pubs. (pres. coll. div. 1971-72), Phi Gamma Delta. Democrat. Presbyterian. Clubs: Slagle Trout (Mich.); Bedford Chowder and Marching (pres. 1976-77); Theodore Gordon Flyfishers (N.Y.C.); Campfire of Am. (N.Y.). Home: Pound Ridge Rd Bedford NY 10506 Office: 1221 Ave of Americas New York NY 10020

BOWMAN, JOHN WICK, clergyman; b. Brownsville, Pa., Aug. 3, 1894; s. Winfield Scott and Maggie Moore (Wick) B.; m. Alma Louise Coles, June 2, 1919; children: John Scott, Margaret Louise, Douglas Coles. A.B. cum laude, Wooster (Ohio) Coll., 1916, D.D., 1951; A.M., Princeton U., 1919; B.D. (fellow in Bibl. theology), Princeton Theol. Sem., 1920; Ph.D., So. Baptist Theol. Sem., Louisville, 1930; postgrad., U. Zurich, 1936; D.D., Waynesburg Coll., 1943, U. St. Andrews, Scotland, 1951. Ordained to ministry Presbyn. Ch. in U.S.A., 1919; evangelistic and ednl. missionary Punjab Mission, India, 1920-36; guest prof. N.T. Western Theol. Sem., Pitts., 1936-37, assoc. prof., 1937-38, Meml. prof. N.T. lit. and exegesis, 1938-44; Robert Dollar prof. N.T. interpretation San Francisco Theol. Sem., 1944-61; assoc. minister United Ch., Sun City, Ariz., 1964-80; Fulbright fellow, lectr. U. St. Andrews, 1949-50; lectr. Union Theol. Sem., N.Y.C., 1955, 64; Fulbright prof. Christianity Internat. Christian U., Tokyo, 1957-58; lectr. So. Bapt. Theol. Sem., 1957, 58, Union Theol. sems., Tokyo and Manila, Silliman U., Dumaguete City, Philippines, 1957, 58; mem. adv. bd. for revision Am. Standard Version Old and New Testament. Author: several books, most recent being The Gospel from the Mount, 1957, General Epistles, 1962, Jesus' Teaching in Its Environment, 1963, Which Jesus?, 1970; novel Rendezvous with India, 1976, Unless I See, 1976; Contbr. to: Tools for Bible Study, 1956, New Peake Commentary, 1961, Interpreters Bible Dictionary, 1963; Contbr. articles to religious publs. Co-winner Abingdon-Cokesbury award for best religious book, 1948. Mem. Soc. Bibl. Lit. and Exegesis (pres. Pacific Coast br. 1947-48), Nat. Assn. Bibl. Instrs., Societas Novi Testamenti Studiorum, Phi Beta Kappa, Chi Alpha. Home: 7550 N 16th St Apt 102-6 Phoenix AZ 85020

BOWMAN, JOHN WILLIAM, manufacturing company executive; b. Great Falls, Mont., Aug. 23, 1904; s. Edward Jay and Elizabeth (Galt) B.; m. Crete Dillon, June 21, 1928 (dec.); children—Crete Bowman Harvey, Jon G., Timothy (dec.), Diana Bowman Neely; m. Beulah Mathew, May 10, 1969. Ph.B., Yale U., 1926. Asst. cashier Daly Bank & Trust Co., Anaconda, Mont., 1926-34; propr. ins., auditing firm, 1934- 35; with Northwestern Steel & Wire Co., Sterling, Ill., 1935—, dir. purchases, 1938-53, v.p., 1953-63, exec. v.p., 1963-80, vice-chmn. bd., 1980—; chmn. bd., dir. Lincolnway Bank, Sterling; dir. emeritus Central Nat. Bank, Sterling. Bd. dirs. Coe Coll., Cedar Rapids, Iowa, Thacher Sch., Menlo, Calif.; adv. bd. Sterling YWCA; treas. Dillon Found. Mem. Ill. C. of C. (past dir.), Alpha Delta Phi. Presbyterian. Clubs: Union League, Univ. (Chgo.); Yale (N.Y.C.); Rock River Country (Rock Falls, Ill.). Home: RFD 3 Hickory Hills Sterling IL 61081 Office: Northwestern Steel & Wire Co Ave B and Wallace St Sterling IL 61081

BOWMAN, JOSEPH SEARLES, oil company executive; b. Miami, Ariz., June 13, 1920; s. Joseph Vernol and Catherine (Searles) B.; m. Virginia Reid, Jan. 9, 1943; children: Catherine, Joan, J. Richard, Thomas. Student, U. Calif., 1937-38; S.B., Mass. Inst. Tech., 1941. Engring. and geol. positions, asst. to pres. Union Sulphur & Oil Corp., 1941-53; mgr. oil and gas dept. Lambert & Co., N.Y., 1953-54; v.p. Colo. Oil & Gas Corp., Denver, 1954-57, exec. v.p., 1957-64; dir.; pres. Colo. Oil Co., Denver, 1964-73; pres., dir. Fluor Oil and Gas Corp., Denver, 1973—; dir. Fin. Indsl. Funds, World of Tech. Fund. Served to lt. USNR, 1942-46. Mem. Am. Inst. Mining, Metall. and Petroleum Engrs., Am. Assn. Petroleum Geologists, Ind. Petroleum Assn. Am., Am. Petroleum Inst. Home: 353 Ivy St Denver CO 80220 Office: 1050 Colo State Bank Bldg Denver CO 80202

BOWMAN, KENNETH JAMES, publisher, educator; b. Albany, N.Y., Jan. 29, 1943; s. Robert Paul and Grace Alice (Beames) B.; m. June Claire Turner, Mar. 21, 1970. B.A., Ithaca Coll., 1967; M.B.A., Seton Hall U., 1981. Editor McGraw Hill Book Co., N.Y.C., 1967-75; editorial dir. Elsevier Sci. Pub., N.Y.C., 1975-81; pub. Macmillan Pub. Co., N.Y.C., 1981—; adj. prof. bus. Seton Hall U., South Orange, N.J., 1981—. Served with U.S. Army, 1963-66; ETO. Mem. Assn. Computing Machinery, IEEE, Ops. Research Soc. Am. Home: 8 Summit St Glen Ridge NJ 07028 Office: Macmillan Pub Co 866 3d Ave New York NY 10022

BOWMAN, LAIRD PRICE, fund raiser; b. Topeka, Jan. 28, 1927; s. Herbert Douglas and Marion Martha (Price) B.; m. Betty Lou Pote, Dec. 29, 1950; children: Bruce Pote, Susan Lynn. B.S., U. Kans., 1950, LL.B., 1952. Bar: Kans. 1952, Mo. 1956. Law clk. chief judge U.S. Dist. Ct. Kans., 1952-53; asso. firm McAnany, Van Cleave & Phillips, Kansas City, Kans., 1953-55; mem. firm Gage Hodges, Park & Kreamer, Kansas City, Mo., 1955-64; with Gas Service Co., Kansas City, Mo., 1964-83, asst. gen. counsel, 1968-70, sec., asst. gen. counsel, 1970-83, v.p., 1978-83, dir., 1979-83; dir. planned giving Kans. U. Endowment Assn., U. Kans., Lawrence, 1983—. Served with USMC, 1945-47. Mem. ABA, Kans. Bar Assn., Mo. Bar Assn., Lawyers Assn. Kansas City, Sigma Chi, Phi Delta Phi. Methodist. Club: University. Home: 5100 W 102d Terr Overland Park KS 66207 Office: Kans U Endowment Assn U Kans Lawrence KS 66045

BOWMAN, PASCO MIDDLETON, II, lawyer, educator; b. Timberville, Va., Dec. 20, 1933; s. Pasco Middleton and Katherine (Lohr) B.; m. Ruth Elaine Bowman, July 12, 1958; children: Ann Katherine, Helen Middleton, Benjamin Garber. B.A., Bridgewater Coll., 1955; J.D. (Root-Tilden scholar), N.Y. U., 1958. Bar: N.Y. 1958, Ga. 1965, Mo. 1980. Asso. firm Cravath, Swaine & Moore, N.Y.C., 1958-61, 62-64; asst. prof. law U. Ga., 1964-65, asso. prof., 1965-69, prof., 1969-70, Wake Forest U., 1970-78, dean, 1970-78; vis. prof. U. Va., 1978-79; prof., dean U. Mo., Kansas City, 1979—. Mng. editor: N.Y. U. Law Rev, 1957-58; Reporter, chief draftsman: Georgia Corporation Code, 1965-68. Served to col. USAR, 1959—. Fulbright scholar London Sch. Econs. and Polit. Sci., 1961-62. Mem. N.Y. Bar, Ga. Bar, Mo. Bar. Home: 11109 Blue River Rd Kansas City MO 64131 Office: U Mo Sch Law 5100 Rockhill Rd Kansas City MO 64110

BOWMAN, RICHARD CARL, defense consultant, retired air force officer; b. Chgo., July 5, 1926; s. Carl Elias and Lucile (Rutan) B.; m. Lois Jean Hassenauer, June 10, 1950; children: Mary Bowman Millikin, Kristin Bowman Spencer, Margaret Bowman Runsdorf, Victoria Bowman Smoke, Richard Carl. B.S., U.S. Mil. Acad., 1949; M.S., Okla. State U., 1954; M.P.A., Harvard U., 1958, Ph.D., 1964. Enlisted in U.S. Army, 1943; commd. 2d lt. USAF, 1949, advanced through grades to maj. gen., 1975; pilot, flight comdr., Korea, 1951; mem. initial staff Air Force Acad., 1955-57, assoc. prof. polit. sci., 1959-63; mem. staff Nat. Security Council, 1964-66, Office Sec. Air Force, 1967-73; dep. def. adviser to Am. ambassador to NATO, 1973-75; dir. European and NATO affairs Office Sec. Def., 1975-81, ret., 1981; v.p. RBI, Inc., internat. def. coop. cons., 1981—. Contbr. to mil. jours. Decorated Def. D.S.M. (2), Air Force D.S.M., Def. Superior Service medal, Legion of Merit (2), D.F.C., Air medal (3), Commendation medal (2); Grand Service Cross with Star, W. Ger.; comdr. Order of St. Olaf (Norway). Mem. Council Fgn. Relations, Air Force Assn., West Point Assn. Grads., Harvard U. Alumni Assn. Roman Catholic. Home: 7824 Midday Ln Alexandria VA 22306

BOWMAN, ROBERT ALLOTT, state official; b. Evanston, Ill., Apr. 12, 1955; s. John Benjamin and Constance (Judkins) B. B.A., Harvard U., 1977; M. in Bus. Adminstrn., The Wharton Sch., U. Pa., 1979. Spl. asst. domestic fin. U.S. Treasury Dept., Washington, 1979-81; assoc. mcpl. fin. Goldman, Sachs & Co., N.Y.C., 1981-83; state treas. State of Mich., Lansing, 1983—. Democrat. Methodist. Home: 161 Rampart Way#301 East Lansing MI 48823 Office: Treasury Dept PO Box 15128 Lansing MI 48901

BOWMAN, ROBERT GIBSON, publishing company executive; b. Mt. Vernon, N.Y., May 28, 1921; s. Milton Strong and Margaret (Gibson) B.; m. Bette Johnson, May 15, 1948; 1 dau., Margaret Bowman Mack. Student, Dartmouth Coll., 1939-40. With C.R. Gibson Co., Norwalk, Conn., 1940-41, 46—, pres., 1954—, chmn. bd., 1975—; dir. S. Norwalk Savs. Bank; trust dir. Union Trust Co.; Past chmn. bd. Conn. Pub. Expenditure Council. Trustee Greater Norwalk Community Fund; chmn. Norwalk YMCA. Served to maj. U.S. Army, 1941-46. Decorated Bronze Star. Mem. Conn. Bus. and Industry Assn. (dir. 1970-73), Greater Norwalk C. of C. (dir.). Club: Wee Burn Country. Home: 18 Driftway Ln Darien CT 06820 Office: 32 Knight St Norwalk CT 06856 *Work with flexibility and dispatch with concern for the sensibilities and dignity of your associates. Do not dwell on past reverses but rather the challenge of the future.*

BOWMAN, VICTOR, business exec.; b. Morrow, Ohio, Mar. 31, 1894; s. Alva C. and Nannie (Hicks) B.; m. Maddah Craven, Jan. 7, 1922. A.B., Twin Valley Coll., 1912; postgrad., in Europe. Spl. fgn. rep. Dennison Mfg. Co., 1914-21, traveling in, Cuba, P.R., other W.I. Islands, Mex., Central Am. countries, Argentina, Brazil, other South Am. countries; operated in, Hawaii, South Sea Islands, Australia, New Zealand, Africa, Dutch East Indies, Malay States, China, Japan, Philippines, France, Spain, other European countries, domestic dist. sales mgr., N.Y.C., 1921, gen. sales mgr. domestic and fgn. sales, Framingham, Mass., 1922-27; organizer 1st internat. sales orgn., gen. sales mgr. Pacific Mills, N.Y.C., 1927-33; gen. field supr. Schenley Distillers Corp., N.Y.C., 1933; gen. sales mgr. Mohawk Carpet Mills, N.Y., 1933, N.Y.C., 1933; dir., v.p. Mohawk Import and Export Co., 1940-42; v.p., dir. Am. Steel Export Co., 1942, 1st v.p., exec. v.p., 1943-53, v.p., dir. domestic and fgn. subsidiaries, 1942—; Mem. Spl. Econ. Mission, Dept. State to, French North Africa, Middle East and Italy, 1944-45. Treas. Fountain House Found., N.Y.C. Served with Mil. Intelligence to observe pro-German activities in Latin America, 1917-18. Mem. Commerce and Industries Assn. N.Y. (fgn. trade com.), N.Y. State C. of C. (com. on fgn. commerce 1949-52, now chmn.), Ohio Soc. N.Y., Am. Legion, Soc. for Advancement Mgmt. (mgr. N.Y. chpt.), Mktg. Execs. Soc. (charter), English-Speaking Union, Taylor Soc., Vet. Corps of Arty., Mil. Soc. War 1812, Order Ky. Cols., Civic Assn. Palm Beach (Fla.), Alpha Chi Sigma. Clubs: Yale, N.Y. Export Managers, Metropolitan (N.Y.C.); Sleepy Hollow Country (Scarborough); Mexico City Country, Circumnavigators; Everglades (Palm Beach, Fla.); Circle Interallie (Paris). Home: 207 Edgemont Dr Allenhurst NJ 07711 also Morrow OH 45152 Office: Morrow OH 45152

BOWMAN, WARD SIMON, JR., educator, economist; b. Everett, Wash., Oct. 29, 1911; s. Ward Simon and Charity E. (Rice) B.; m. Maxine Beal, Feb. 14, 1937; children—Gary W., George T. A.B., U. Wash., 1933; M.A. (hon.), Yale, 1959. Economist Dept. Justice, 1938-46; research asso. U. Chgo. Law Sch., 1946-56; mem. faculty Yale Law Sch., New Haven, 1956—, prof. law and econs., 1959-73, Ford Found. prof. law and econs., 1973-79, prof. emeritus, 1979—. Author: Patent and Antitrust Law: A Legal and Economic Appraisal, 1973; Contbr. articles to profl. jours. Mem. Am. Econ. Assn. Home: 64 N Lake Dr C-1 Hamden CT 06517 Office: Yale Law Sch New Haven CT 06520

BOWMAN, WILLIAM SCOTT, profl. hockey coach; b. Montreal, Que., Can., Sept. 18, 1933; s. John and Jane Thomson (Scott) B.; m. Suella Belle Chitty, Aug. 16, 1969; children—Alicia Jean, David Scott, Stanley Glen, Nancy Elizabeth and Robert Gordon (twins). Student, Sir George Williams Bus. Sch., 1954. Scout exec. Club de Hockey Canadien, Montreal, 1956-66, coach, 1971-79; coach, gen. mgr. St. Louis Blues Hockey Club, 1966-71; coach, gen. mgr., dir. hockey ops. Buffalo Sabres Hockey Club, 1979—. Office: Buffalo Sabres Meml Auditorium Buffalo NY 14202

BOWMER, JIM DEWITT, lawyer; b. Temple, Tex., May 4, 1919; s. DeWitt and Linnie B. (Morgan) B.; m. Daurice Spoonts, Mar. 26, 1961; children: Bonnie Nell Neal, Mary Helen Bowmer Schreiner, IV. B.A. cum laude, Baylor U., Waco, Tex., 1940, LL.B., 1942. Bar: Tex. 1942. County atty., Bell County, Tex., 1946-47; lectr. Baylor U. Law Sch., 1949-50, 56-57; pres. firm Bowmer, Courtney, Burleson, Pemberton & Normand, Temple, 1964—. Contbr. articles to legal jours. Bd. dirs. Nat. Park Found., 1968-69. Served with AUS, 1942-46. Mem. Am. Law Inst., Am. Judicature Soc., Tex. Assn. Def. Counsel, State Bar Tex. (chmn. bd. 1970-71, pres. 1972-73), Bell-Lampasas-Mills Counties Bar Assn. (past pres.), Temple C. of C. (past pres.), Baylor U. Law Alumni Assn. (past pres.), Phi Alpha Delta. Democrat. Baptist. Clubs: Masons, K.P. (past grand chancellor Tex.), Kiwanis.). Home: Bowmer's Ranch Route 2 Killeen TX 76541 Office: First Nat Bank Bldg Temple TX 76501

BOWN, OLIVER HUTCHINS, educator; b. Denver, Aug. 6, 1921; s. Albert G. and Henrietta H. (Punshon) B.; m. Evelyn E. Struble, Dec. 11, 1943; children: J. Michael, Jennifer L. Bown Keogh, Kathleen A. Bown Chitsey, Kimberly A. Bown Pugh. A.B., U. Denver, 1943; M.A., U. Chgo., 1948, Ph.D., 1954. Lic. psychologist, Tex. Counselor Bd. Vocat. Guidance and Placement, U. Chgo., 1946-47, counselor, 1947-49, profl. services coordinator, 1949-51; lectr. dept. ednl. psychology U. Tex., Austin, 1951-59, asso. prof., 1959-66, prof., 1966—, dir. counseling div., 1951-58, coordinator, 1958-60, assoc. dir. Testing and Counseling Center, 1960-65; assoc. dir. Testing and Research Center Personality Research Center; assoc. dir. Research and Devel. Center for Tchr. Edn., 1965-68, co-dir. Research and Devel. Center for Tchr. Edn., 1968-77, dir. Research and Devel. Center for Tchr. Edn., 1977—; mem. nat. adv. and policy council Ednl. Resources Info. Center on Tchr. Edn., Washington, 1968-82. Contbr. articles in field to profl. jours. Mem. med. profl. adv. bd. United Cerebral Palsy of Tex., Inc., 1962-68. Served with U.S. Navy, 1943-46. Mem. Tex. Psychol. Assn. (pres. 1964-65), Am. Personnel and Guidance Assn. (recipient citation for research of outstanding quality 1961), Am. Psychol. Assn., Southwestern Psychol. Assn., Am. Ednl. Research Assn., Nat. Soc. Study Edn. Episcopalian. Home: 4504 Erin Ln Austin TX 78756 Office: Education Annex 3.203 U Tex Austin TX 78712 *Perhaps one of the reasons for whatever success I may have experienced is that success, in itself, has not been a driving force in my life. It is the intrinsic meaning of my work and my primary relationships, in synergistic balance, rather than the extrinsic rewards, which have guided both major decisions and the quality of day-to-day activities. My "success" has been in pursuing my love affair with life and its continually evolving possibilities.*

BOWNE, JAMES DEHART, museum ofcl.; b. Phila., Mar. 5, 1940; s. Ira Ervin and Mary Bradway (Powell) B.; m. Cheryl Jean Thompson, June 15, 1974; 1 dau., Heather Leigh. Student, George Washington U.

and Corcoran Sch. Art, 1962, 63, 66, 67; A.A., Sandhills Community Coll., Southern Pines, N.C., 1968; A.B. in Art History, E. Carolina U., Greenville, N.C., 1970, M.A., U. N.C. at Chapel Hill, 1972. Profl. artist Channel Galleries, Washington, 1963-67; curatorial asst. Ackland Art Center, Chapel Hill, 1971; grad. asst. U. N.C., Chapel Hill, 1971, research fellow, 1972; dir., curator, instr. art Lauren Rogers Library and Mus. Art, Laurel, Miss., 1973-75; dir. Sheldon Swope Art Gallery, Terre Haute, Ind., 1975-78, Everhart Mus. Natural History, Sci. and Art, Scranton, Pa., 1978-81; exec. dir. Greenville County Mus. Art, Greenville, S.C., 1981—; pres. Laurel Arts Council, 1974-75. Contbr.: articles to A Medieval Treasury From Southeastern Collections, 1971; also to newspapers. Bd. dirs. Terre Haute Symphony Assn., 1976-78; mem. museums adv. panel Ind. Arts Commn., 1977-78. Served with U.S. Army, 1958-61. Recipient award Delta Phi Delta Alumni Scholarship Found., E. Carolina U., 1970. Mem. Am. Assn. Museums, Coll. Art Assn., Smithsonian Instn. Nat. Assos., Asso. Councils of Arts, Midwest Art History Soc., Midwest Museums Conf., Northeastern Museums Conf., Assn. Ind. Museums, Nat. Soc. Lit. and Arts, Scranton C. of C., Visitors and Conv. Bur., Delta Phi Delta, Phi Sigma Pi. Republican. Clubs: Rotary Internat., Nat. Exchange. Office: 420 College St Aug Park Scranton PA 18510 *Mistakes and advancing age seem to be two of the best teachers and are, perhaps, the most difficult to accept. It is not so difficult to reach a goal; rather it is more difficult to decide what the goal will be. If one sets a goal that is too high and is unable to attain it, more harm is done than if one had set no goal at all. Life is built on, and progresses from, one goal to the next. Each day of life is one day nearer death. Therefore, it is important that one choose wisely. To truly care about others is one goal that all men should strive to reach. By so doing, the problems that have faced us in the past, that face us in the present, and that will face us in the future, will be lessened. The decision is ours. One's character is one's soul; one's soul-one's philosophy.*

BOWNES, HUGH HENRY, judge; b. N.Y.C., Mar. 10, 1920; s. Hugh Gray and Margaret (Henry) B.; m. Irja C. Martikainen, Dec. 30, 1944; children—Barbara Ann, David and Ernest (twins). B.A., Columbia U., 1941, LL.B., 1948. Bar: N.H. bar 1948. Since practiced in, Laconia; partner firm Nighswander, Lord & Bownes, 1951-66; asso. justice N.H. Superior Ct., 1966-68; U.S. dist. ct. judge, Concord, N.H., 1968-77; circuit judge 1st Circuit Ct. Appeals, 1977—. Mem. Laconia City Council, 1953-57; chmn. Laconia Democratic Com., 1954-57; mayor, Laconia, 1963-65; mem. Dem. Nat. Com. from N.H., 1963-66; Chmn. Laconia chpt. A.R.C., 1951-52; pres. bd. Laconia Hosp. Assn., 1963-64. Served to maj. USMCR, 1941-46. Decorated Silver Star. Mem. ABA, N.H. Bar Assn., Belknap County Bar Assn. (pres. 1965—), Laconia C. of C. (past pres.). Club: Lion (past pres. Laconia). Home: 4 Poor Richard's Dr Concord NH 03301 Office: Federal Courthouse Concord NH 03301

BOWNS, BEVERLY HENRY, nurse, coll. dean; b. Ontario, Calif.; d. Glenn Alby and Irene Beatrice (Rygymyr) Henry; m. James Bowns, Aug. 30, 1974. B.S.N., Columbia U., 1959; M.P.H., U. Minn., 1960; Dr.P.H., Johns Hopkins U., 1968. Indsl. nurse Sausalito (Calif.) Shipyards, 1945; public health nurse, dist. supr., Pocatello, Idaho, 1953; instr., adminstrv. asso. U. Calif. Coll. Nursing, San Francisco, 1960-63; asst. prof. Grad. Program Coll. Nursing, U. Md., Balt., 1968; asso. prof., chmn. community health nursing dept. Coll. Nursing, Vanderbilt U., Nashville, 1969-72; prof., chmn. Coll. Nursing U. Tenn. Center for Health Sci., Memphis, 1972-76; dean Coll. Nursing Rutgers U., Newark, 1977-81; Bd. dirs. Comprehensive Rape Crisis Center, Memphis, 1974-77, Mid-south Home Health Services, 1974-77, Memphis B, 1974-76. Contbr. chpts. to books, articles to profl. jours. Recipient scholarships and grants. Fellow Am. Acad. Nursing; mem. Am. Nurses Assn., Nat. League Nursing, Am. Assn. Colls. Nursing, Am. Public Health Assn., Council Nurse Researchers, Sigma Theta Tau, Pi Lambda Theta. Home: Route 1 Box 172 Califon NJ 07830 Office: Rutgers U Coll Nursing 392 High St Bradlwy Hall Newark NJ 07102

BOWRON, EDGAR PETERS, art museum director; b. Birmingham, Ala., May 27, 1943; s. James Edgar and Dorothe (Peters) Bowron L.; m. Lornagrace Thomas Grenfell, Aug. 20, 1966 (div. 1981); children: James Edgar III, Clara Beatrice, St. John Grenfell. B.A. in English Lit., Colgate U., 1965; M.A. in History of Art, NYU, 1969, Ph.D., 1979. Edn. lectr. Met. Mus. Art, N.Y.C., 1969-70; registrar Mpls. Inst. Arts, 1970-73; curator Renaissance Baroque art Walters Art Gallery, Balt., 1973-78; adminstrv. asst. to dir. and curator Renaissance Baroque art Nelson Gallery-Atkins Mus., Kansas City, Mo., 1978-81; dir. N.C. Mus. Art, Raleigh, 1981—. Author: Pompeo Batoni(1708-87), 1982, Renaissance Bronzes and the Walters Art Gallery, 1978, Pompeo Batoni and His British Patrons, 1982; co-author: The J. Paul Getty Collection, 1972; editor: Selected Writings of Anthony M. Clark: Studies in Eighteenth Roman Painting, 1981, The North Carolina Museum of Art: Introduction to the Collections, 1983; contbr. articles to jours. in field. Fellow Ford Found., 1967-69, Nat. Endowment for Arts, 1975-76; Am. Acad. in Rome fellow grantee, 1979-85. Mem. Am. Assn. Mus. Dirs., Am. Soc. 18th-Century Studies, Coll. Art Assn. Episcopalian. Office: NC Mus Art 2110 Blue Ridge Blvd Raleigh NC 27607

BOWRON, RICHARD ANDERSON, utility exec.; b. Birmingham, Ala., Jan. 18, 1924; s. James Edgar and Mary Elizabeth (Anderson) B.; m. Ruth Wolmesdorf Matthews, Dec 29, 1961; children—Richard Anderson, Mary Anderson, Lee Matthews. B.S., Ala., 1943; M.B.A., U. Pa., 1948. With Ala. Power Co., Birmingham, 1948—, sec., 1963—. Served to 1st lt. AUS, 1943-46, 50-52. Presbyterian. Clubs: Birmingham Exchange, Mountain Brook, The Club. Home: 3629 Springhill Rd Birmingham AL 35223 Office: 600 N 18th St Birmingham AL 35291

BOWS, ALBERT JULIUS, JR., accounting firm executive; b. Chgo., Oct. 5, 1913; s. Albert Julius and Lily (Waldman) B.; m. Helen Johnson, June 22, 1940; children: David, Sally. B.S.C., Northwestern U., 1934, M.B.A., 1935. C.P.A., Ill., Ga. With Arthur Andersen & Co., C.P.A.s, 1935—; partner in charge Arthur Andersen & Co. (Atlanta office), 1959-69, sr. partner, 1971—; dean Grad. Sch. Bus. Adminstrn., Emory U., 1975-79; dir. Ga. Pacific Corp., Spring Mills Inc., Shaw Industries, Inc., Cronus Industries, Inc., Munich Am. Reassurance Co., N.Am. Royalties, Inc. Contbr. articles to profl. jours. Adv. bd., chmn. youth and bequest and endowment coms., chmn. Salvation Army; chmn. Spl. Task Force on Phase II, 1971; mem. So. Growth Policies Bd.; co-treas. Billy Graham Crusade, Atlanta, 1973; chmn., dir. Nat. Alliance Businessmen, 1971-72; chmn. Met. Atlanta Council on Alcohol and Drugs, 1972; trustee Atlanta Arts Alliance, 1974-77; chmn. High Mus. Arts, 1981. Recipient Liberty Bell award Atlanta Bar Assn., 1969, Layman of Yr. award Christian Council Atlanta, 1969, William Booth award Salvation Army, 1971, Distinguished Bus. Mgmt. award Emory U., 1971. Mem. Am. Inst. C.P.A.s (v.p. 1973-74, mem. accounting principles bd. 1972-73, chmn. com. auditing procedure 1962-65, chmn. com. relations with SEC and stock exchange, mem. council from Ga. 1965-66), Ga. Soc. C.P.A.s (past chmn. Atlanta, Pub. Service award 1983), Atlanta C. of C. (chmn., dir., pres. 1968), Atlanta Jr. C. of C. (hon. life). Mem. Christian Ch. (past treas., elder, deacon). Clubs: Peachtree Golf, Capital City (Atlanta). Home: 22 Muscogee Ave NW Atlanta GA 30305

BOWSER, JAMES WILLIAM, editor; b. Indiana, Pa., Jan. 16, 1929; s. Kenneth William and Thelma Byrd (Smith) B.; m. Dorothy Messing, Aug. 7, 1971. Reporter Johnstown (Pa.) Tribune-Democrat, 1947-54; editor Dell Pub. Co. Inc., N.Y.C., 1956-79; editorial dir. Bonomo Publs., Inc., N.Y.C., 1980-81; editorial/publs. cons., 1981—. Author: Doomsday Vendetta, 1968, The Glass Cypher, 1968, Death of the Falcon, 1974, A High Yield in Death, 1976, Starring Elvis, 1977. Bd. dirs., trustee Back Alley Stock Players. Recipient Distinguished Service award Pa. CD Corp, 1945, Johnstown chpt. ASPCA, 1954. Mem. Order DeMolay, Soc. Profl. Journalists, Sigma Delta Chi. Jewish. Club: Deadline. Home and office: Rivercross Roosevelt Island New York NY 10044

BOWSHER, CHARLES ARTHUR, government official; b. Elkhart, Ind., May 30, 1931; s. Matthew A. and Ella M. (West) B.; m. Mary C. Mahoney, Dec. 14, 1963; children: Kathryn M., Stephen C. B.S., U. Ill., 1953; M.B.A., U. Chgo., 1956. C.P.A., Ill. Partner Arthur Andersen & Co. (C.P.A.s), Chgo., 1956-67, 1971-81; comptroller gen. of U.S., 1981—; asst. sec. (Navy financial mgmt.), 1967-71; Chmn. bd. visitors Def. Mgmt. Sch.; trustee, mem. exec. com. Nat. Security Indsl. Assn.; mem. pub. sector adv. com. Met. Washington Bd. Trade; adv. com. to Sec. Health, Edn., Welfare and Commr. Social Security on Medicare Adminstrn. Served with AUS, 1953-55. Recipient Distinguished Pub. Service award U.S. Navy, 1969, Dept. Def., 1971. Mem. Am., D.C. insts. C.P.A.s, Alumni Assn. Grad. Sch. Bus. U. Chgo. (v.p. 1965-67), Pi Kappa Alpha. Clubs: University (Chgo.); Army-Navy, Burning Tree (Washington). Home: 4503 Boxwood Rd Bethesda MD 20816 Office: Office of Comptroller General GAO 441 G St NW Washington DC 20548

BOWYER, CHARLES STUART, astronomer, educator; b. Toledo, Aug. 2, 1934; s Howard Douglas and Elizabeth (McEuen) B.; m. Jane Baker, Feb. 26, 1957; children—William, Robert, Elizabeth. B.A., Miami U., Oxford, Ohio, 1956; Ph.D. in Physics, Cath. U. Am., 1965. Physicist U.S. Naval Research Lab., 1958-67; asst. prof. space scis. Cath. U. Am., 1965-67; mem. faculty U. Calif., Berkeley, 1967—, prof. astronomy, 1975—, Miller research prof., 1978; vis. research prof. Univ. Coll. London, Eng., 1974; lectr., cons. in field. Sr. research fellow Sci. Research Council Eng., 1974. Contbr. articles to profl. jours. Recipient Tech. Achievement award NASA, 1972, Group Achievement award, 1975, Exceptional Sci. Achievement award, 1976; Humboldt Found. sr. scientist award, 1982; Fulbright sr. prof., 1983. Mem. Am. Astron. Soc., Am. Geophys. Union, Internat. Astron. Union, Internat. Acad. Astronautics, Astron. Soc. Pacific. Research in high energy astrophysics and space astronomy. Patentee in field. Office: Dept Astronomy U Calif Berkeley CA 94720

BOX, DWAIN D., former judge; b. Stuart, Okla., Sept. 15, 1916; s. William Autry and Vera (Johnson) B.; m. Doris Louise Nordstrom, July 27, 1946; children: Kenneth Dwain, Dennis Rae. Student, Oklahoma City Law Sch., 1939; LL.B., Cumberland U., 1940. Bar: Okla. 1940. Pvt. practice law, 1940-46, 52-56; judge Ct. Common Pleas, Oklahoma County, 1956-68; asso. dist. ct. judge, 1968-71; judge Ct. Appeals of State of Okla., Oklahoma City, 1971-83, ret. subject to assignment, 1983; Rep. Okla. Legislature, 1947-50. Sec. Oklahoma County Election Bd., 1954-56. Served with AUS, 1940-45, 50-52. Decorated Bronze Star medal with oak leaf cluster. Mem. Okla., Oklahoma County bar assns., Okla. Jud. Conf., Oklahoma City C. of C., Am. Legion. Baptist.

BOX, GEORGE EDWARD PELHAM, statistics educator; b. Gravesend, Eng., Oct. 18, 1919; s. Harry and Helen (Martin) B.; m. Joan Gunnhild Fisher, Dec. 12, 1959; children: Helen Elizabeth, Harry Christopher. B.Sc., U. Coll., U. London, Eng., 1947, Ph.D., 1952, D.Sc., 1961; D.Sc. (hon.), U. Rochester, 1975. Statistician, head statis. techniques research sect. Imperial Chems. Industries, Blackley, Manchester, Eng., 1948-56; dir. statis, techniques research group Princeton, 1957-59; prof. stats. U. Wis., Madison, 1960—, William F. Vilas prof., 1980; vis. research prof. U. N.C., 1952-53; Ford Found. vis. prof. Harvard Bus. Sch., 1965-66, U. Essex, Eng., 1970-71. Author: (with others) Statistical Methods in Research and Production, 1957, Design and Analysis of Industrial Experiments, 1959, Evolutionary Operation: A Statistical Method for Process Improvement, 1969, Time Series, Forecasting and Control, 1970, Bayesian Inference in Statistical Analysis, 1973, Statistics for Experimenters, 1978; Contbr. articles to profl. jours. Served with Brit. Army, 1939-45. Decorated Brit. Empire medal; recipient Profl. Progress award Am. Inst. Chem. Engrs., 1963; Benjamin Smith Reynolds award for teaching excellence, 1972. Fellow Am. Acad. Arts and Scis., Royal Statis. Soc. (Guy medal 1964), Am. Statis. Assn. (Wilks Meml. medal 1972, pres. 1978), Inst. Math. Statistics (pres. 1979), Am. Soc. Quality Control (Shewhart medal 1968), AAAS (past v.p.); mem. Internat. Statistics Inst., Biometrics Soc. Home: 3437 Edgehill Pkwy Madison WI 53705 *Theory and Practice are like man and wife in a happy marriage. Each complements and inspires the other and without interaction between them there can be no new life.*

BOX, JOHN HAROLD, architect, educator; b. Commerce, Tex., Aug. 18, 1929; s. E.O. and Mary Emma (Haynes) B.; m. Dorothy Jean Baldwin, Jan. 19, 1952 (div. Jan. 1971); children: Richard B., Kenneth W., Gregory V.; m. Eden Van Zandt, Apr. 9, 1977. B.Arch., U. Tex., Austin, 1950. Apprentice O'Neil Ford (Architect), San Antonio, 1948; designer Broad & Nelson (architects), Dallas, 1954-56; asso. Harrell & Hamilton (architects), Dallas, 1956-57; ptnr. Pratt, Box, Henderson & Partners (architects), Dallas, 1957-83, Box Archictects, 1983—; prof., 1st dean Sch. Architecture and Environ. Design, U. Tex., Arlington, 1971-76; prof., dean Sch. Architecture, U. Tex.-Austin, 1976—, Moody prof., 1983—; Chmn. design of city task force Goals for Dallas, 1968-70; chmn. Goals Achievement Com., 1970—; chmn. design com. Greater Dallas Planning Council, 1969; v.p. Save Open Space, 1970. Prin. works include: St. Stephen's Meth. Ch, Dallas, 1962, Great Hall of Apparel Mart, Dallas, 1965, Quadrangle Shopping Center, Dallas, 1965, Garden Center, Dallas, 1970; master plan Griffin Sq., Dallas, 1971; Marsh House, Austin, 1982; Co-author: Prairies Yield, 1962, Goals for Dallas Proposals for Design of City, 1970. Bd. dirs. Dallas Chamber Music Soc., 1960-76, Austin Symphony, 1982—; regional dir. Assn. Collegiate Schs. Architecture, 1975—. Served to lt. C.E. Corps USNR, 1955. Co-recipient Enrico Fermi Meml. Archtl. Competition prize, 1957; Grand prize Homes for Better Living Competition, 1959; Tex. Architecture Found. grantee, 1957. Fellow AIA (pres. Dallas 1967, nat. dir. 1975-78); mem. Tex. Soc. Architects (v.p., commr. edn. and research 1971, design awards 1964-66, 68, 70, 71, 82), Phi Kappa Phi, Alpha Rho Chi, Sigma Nu. Home: 2113 Highgrove Terr Austin TX 78703 Office: U of Texas Austin TX 78712

BOX, ROGER ELDEN, naval officer; b. Detroit, Sept. 25, 1934; s. Clarence Andrew and Thelma Lura (Dutschke) B.; m. Sandra Lynne Tift, June 29, 1957 (div. 1970); children: Kolleen Kay Box Hutchison, Kimberly Ann, Leslie Rene Box Torres; m. ruth McKenna Ellison, May 22, 1971; stepchildren: Laura Rene Olson, James Price Olson. B.S., U.S. Naval Acad., 1956; M.B.A., Auburn U., 1970. Commd. ensign U.S. Navy, 1956, advanced through grades to rear adm., comdg. officer U.S.S. Hassayampa, Paearl Harbor, Hawaii, 1979; comdg. officer Aircraft Carrier Ranger comdg. officer Aircraft Carrier Ranger, Pearl Harbor, 1979-80; chief of staff comdr. Naval Air Forces Pacific U.S. Navy, Coronado, Calif., 1979-81, plans and policy officer SHAPE, Mons, Belgium, 1981-83, carrier group comdr., Payport, Fla., 1983—. Decorated Legion of Merit, D.F.C.; Docorated Air Medals (13). Mem. Soc. Exptl. Test Pilots. Home: 547 Ozbourn Mayport FL 32227 Office: Commander Carrier Group 6 FPO New York NY 09501

BOX, THADIS WAYNE, coll. dean; b. Llano, Tex., May 9, 1929; s. Daniel W. and Mary Madelyn (Hasty) B.; m. Virginia Price, July 16, 1954; children—Dennis, Mary, Paul, Emily. B.S., S.W. Tex. State Coll., 1956; M.S., Tex. A. and M. U., 1957, Ph.D., 1959. Rancher, Burnet, Tex., 1946-51, Welder Wildlife Found. fellow, Sinton, Tex., 1956-59; asst. prof. Utah State U., 1959-61, dean, 1970—; from asso. prof. to prof. Tex. Tech. U., 1962-68; dir. Internat. Center Arid and Semi-Arid Land Studies, 1968-70; cons. FAO, UN (also fgn. govts. and pvt. orgns.). Author articles, books. Served with AUS, 1951-53. Recipient E. Harris Harbison award for Distinguished Teaching, 1967; Commonwealth Sci. and Indsl. Research Orgn. fellow, Australia, 1968-69. Mem. Soc. Range Mgmt., Wildlife Soc., Soil Conservation Soc., Sigma Xi. Home: 914 River Heights Blvd Logan UT 84321

BOXELL, EARL FRANCIS, lawyer; b. Marion, Ind., Dec. 3, 1894; s. Charles F. and Ida M. (Christman) B.; m. Mary A. Dotzler, May 27, 1939; children—Earl Francis, Merle A., Charles K., Mary J. A.B., U. Mich., 1921, J.D., 1923. Bar: Ind. bar 1921, Ohio bar 1923. Since practiced in, Toledo; mem. firm Boxell, Bebout, Torbet & Baker, 1943—; Candidate for judge Maumee (Ohio) Mcpl. Ct., 1964. Fellow Am. Bar Found., Ohio Bar Found.; mem. Am. Arbitration Assn. (internat. panel arbitrators), ABA, Ohio Bar Assn., Toledo Bar Assn. (pres. 1960-61), Am. Legion (post comdr. 1940), Phi Alpha Delta, Delta Sigma Rho. Home: 1718 N Cove Blvd Toledo OH 43606 Office: 711 Adams St Toledo OH 43624

BOXER, BARBARA, congresswoman; b. Bklyn., Nov. 11, 1940; d. Ira and Sophie (Silvershein) Levy; m. Stewart Boxer, 1962; children: Doug, Nicole. B.A., Bklyn. Coll., 1962. Stockbroker Merrill Lynch, N.Y.C., 1962-65; journalist, assoc. editor Pacific Sun, 1972-74; congl. aide to rep. 5th Congl. Dist., San Francisco, 1974-76; mem. Marin County Bd. Suprs., San Rafael, Calif., 1976-82, 98th Congress from 6th Dist. Calif., 1983—. Pres. Marin County Bd. Suprs., 1980-81; mem. Bay Area Air Quality Mgmt. Bd., San Francisco, 1977-82, pres., San Francisco, 1979-81; bd. dirs. Golden Gate Bridge Hwy. and Transport Dist., San Francisco, 1978-82; founding mem. Marin Nat. Women's Polit. Caucus, Marin Community Video; pres. Democratic New Mems. Caucus, 1983. Recipient Open Govt. award Common Cause, 1980. Jewish. Office: 1517 Longworth House Office Bldg Washington DC 20515

BOXER, ROBERT WILLIAM, allergist; b. Kansas City, Mo., Feb. 14, 1933; s. Isadore and Minnie (Ginsberg) B.; m. Marsha Jo Levin, Aug. 10, 1966; children: Stephen Ari, Richard Bentley. B.A. in Chemistry, U. Denver, 1953; M.D., Northwestern U., 1956. Diplomate: Am. Bd. Allergy and Immunology. Intern, then resident in internal medicine Cook County Hosp., Chgo., 1956-61; fellow allergy and infectious diseases U. Ill. Research and Ednl. Hosps., 1961-62; asso. dir. USPHS (sponsored teaching program); then instr. medicine U. Ill. Med. Sch., 1962-67; clin. asso. medicine Abraham Lincoln Sch. Medicine, U. Ill., Chgo., 1975—; practice medicine specializing in allergy, Skokie, Ill., 1962—; asso. attending Lutheran Gen. Hosp., Park Ridge, Ill.; cons. Skokie Valley Hosp., Skokie. Author articles in field, chpts. in books. Fellow Am. Acad. Allergy, Am. Coll. Allergists, Am. Assn. Clin. Allergy and Immunology, Am. Assn. Cert. Allergists, Soc. Clin. Ecology, Ill. Soc. Allergy and Clin. Immunology; mem. Am. Acad. Dermatology, AMA, Pan Am. Allergy Soc., Ill. Med. Soc., Chgo. Med. Soc., Alpha Omega Alpha. Jewish. Club: Lake Cook Rod and Gun. Office: 64 Old Orchard Rd Skokie IL 60077

BOXER, RUBIN, research and development company executive; b. N.Y.C., Aug. 6, 1927; s. Max and Lillian (Zatz) B.; m. Pearl Blumstein, Oct. 1, 1949; children: Diana Gail, Robert Keith, Kenneth Roy, Warren Neal. B.E.E., Cooper Union, 1949; M.E.E., Syracuse U., 1954. With U.S. Air Force Research And Devel. Labs., Ohio, N.J., N.Y., 1949-56; dir. systems engring. Servomechanisms Inc., Santa Barbara, Calif., 1957-63; with Gen. Research Corp., Santa Barbara, Calif., 1963—, exec. v.p., 1979—. Co-inventor Z-forms. Served with USN, 1945-46. Recipient Outstanding Service award (2) USAF. Mem. IEEE (newsletter editor), Sigma Xi. Jewish. Home: 564 Ricardo Ave Santa Barbara CA 93109 Office: PO Box 6770 Santa Barbara CA 93111

BOXER, STANLEY ROBERT, painter, sculptor; b. N.Y.C., June 26, 1926; s. Max and Ida (Gordon) B.; m. Joyce Weinstein, Nov. 28, 1952. Student, Bklyn. Coll., Art Students League, 1946-49. Illus.: vol. aquatint etchings Ringofdustinbloom, 1984; One man exhbns. include, Andre Emmerich Gallery, Zurich, Switzerland, 1975, 78, Andre Emmerich Gallery, N.Y.C., 1975-84, Galerie Wentzel, Hamburg, W. Ger., 1975, 78, 80, 82, 83, Tibor de Nagy Gallery, N.Y.C., 1971-75, 80, 82; One man exhbns. include, Hokin Gallery, Bay Harbor Island, Fla., 1981, Hokin Gallery, Chgo., 1982-84, Hokin Gallery, Palm Beach, Fla., 1981, Galerie von Braunbehrens, Munich, W. Ger., 1982, Am. House, Berlin, W. Ger., Gallery One, Toronto, Ont., Can., 1980-83, Downstairs Gallery, Edmonton, Alta., Can., 1981, 83, Gallery Ulysses, Vienna, Austria, 1983, Aronson Gallery, Atlanta, Salander/O'Reily Gallery, N.Y.C., Ivory Kimpton Gallery, San Francisco; Pa. Acad. Fine Arts, Phila., 1976, sculpture, Boston Mus., 1977, Allrich Gallery, San Francisco, 1979, 81, Galerie Regard, Paris, Meredith Long & Co., Houston, 1979, 80, 81, 83, Thomas Segal Gallery, Boston, 1980, 81, 82, Richard Gray Gallery, Chgo., 1980, retrospectives: (paintings), Boston Mus. Fine Arts, 1977, drawings, Mint Mus. Art, 1978, numerous group exhbns.; represented in permanent collections, Guggenheim Mus., N.Y.C., Whitney Mus., N.Y.C., Boston Mus. Fine Arts, Houston Mus. Fine Arts, Mus. Modern Art, N.Y.C., Corcoran Gallery Art, Washington, Albright-Knox Mus., Buffalo, Mint Mus. Art, Charlotte, N.C., Edmonton (Alta., Can.) Art Gallery Mus., others, also numerous pvt. collections; designer, builder sculptural set for, Erick Hawkins Dance Co., 1972. Served with USN, World War II. Guggenheim fellow, 1975. *To become artist, to remain artist, is both idea and goal. All conduct is congruent to that purpose. The development of "conscience" to Art is the principle of the whole!*

BOY, JOHN BUCKNER, sugar company executive; b. Johnson City, Tenn., Mar. 25, 1917; s. David Clark and Elizabeth Kathleen (Jennings) B.; m. Nancy Elizabeth Adams, Jan. 29, 1944; children: Elizabeth Kathleen, John Buckner, Howard Lane. B.S. in Mech. Engring, Ga. Inst. Tech., 1938. With Buckeye Cotton Oil Co., 1938-41; with U.S. Sugar Corp., 1946—, v.p. adminstrn., 1960-61, exec. v.p., 1961-70, pres., 1970—, also dir.; Past pres. Fla. Sugar Cane League, Inc. Mem. Hendry County (Fla.) Bd. Pub. Instrn., 1956-60. Served to lt. comdr. USNR, 1941-46. Mem. Soil and Crop Sci. Soc. Fla., Fla. Farm. Bur., Internat. Soc. Sugar Cane Technologists, Clewiston C. of C., Fla. C. of C. (dir.), Fla. Council 100, Pi Kappa Phi, Tau Beta Phi, Omicron Delta Kappa. Episcopalian (past vestryman). Clubs: Kiwanis (past pres. Clewiston), Clewiston Country.). Home: 102 W Circle Dr Clewiston FL 33440 Office: US Sugar Corp PO Box 1207 Clewiston FL 33440

BOYAN, NORMAN JOHN, educator; b. N.Y.C., Apr. 11, 1922; s. Joseph J. and Emma M. (Pelezare) B.; m. Priscilla M. Simpson, July 10, 1943; children: Stephen J., Craig S., Corydon J. A.B., Bates Coll., Lewiston, Maine, 1943; A.M., Harvard U., 1947, Ed.D., 1951. Instr. U.S. history Dana Hall Sch., Wellesley, Mass., 1946-48; research asso. Lab. Social Relations, Harvard, 1950-52; asst. prin. Mineola (N.Y.)

High Sch., 1952-54; prin. Wheatley Sch., East Williston, N.Y., 1954-59; asso. prof. edn., dir. student teaching and internship U. Wis., 1959-61; asso. prof. edn. Stanford, 1961-67; dir. div. ednl. labs. U.S. Office Edn., 1967-68, asso. commr. for research, 1968-69; prof. edn. Grad. Sch. Edn., U. Calif. at Santa Barbara, 1969—, dean, 1969-80; asso. in edn. Grad. Sch. Edn., Harvard U., 1980-81; vis. prof. Coll. Edn. Pa. State U., summer 1981; vis. mem. Faculty Edn. U. B.C., summer 1983; cons. numerous U.S. sch. systems, U.S. Govt. and Pacific Trust Ters.; dir. Security Equity Life Ins. Co., Binghamton, Equitable Govt. Securities Account, Inc., Equitable Tax-Free Account, Inc. Co-author: Instructional Supervision Training Program, 1978; Editorial bd.: Harvard Edn. Rev, 1948-50, Jour. Secondary Edn, 1963-68, Jour. Edn. Research, 1967-82, Urban Edn, 1967—; cons. editor, contbr.: 5th edit. Ency. Ednl. Research; Contbr. articles to profl. jours. Trustee Nova Inst., Carl and Lily Pforzheimer Found., Inc.; trustee emeritus Wesleyan U. Served with USAAF, 1943-46. Recipient Shankland award for advanced grad. study in ednl. adminstrn., 1950. Mem. Am. Ednl. Research Assn. (v.p. div. A 1978-80), Am. Assn. Sch. Adminstrs., Nat. Conf. Profs. Ednl. Adminstrn., Phi Beta Kappa, Phi Delta Kappa. Home: 742 Calle de Los Amigos Santa Barbara CA 93105

BOYAR, SIDNEY LEON, corporation consultant; b. Chicago Heights, Ill., Oct. 11, 1913; s. Jacob Leon and Molly (Cohen) B.; m. Selma Ruth Stone, June 30, 1940; children: Janet Lee Boyar Moses, Arthur Kurt, Dorann Lynn Boyar Schaffner. B.S.M.E., Purdue U., 1935. With Sears, Roebuck & Co., 1934-77, nat. mdse. mgr., 1952-65, v.p. affiliated factory relations, 1965-77, also dir.; corp. cons., Chgo., 1977—; dir. Armstrong Rubber Co., Whirlpool Corp., Inglis Ltd. Recipient Distinguished Alumni award Purdue U., 1967. Mem. Sigma Alpha Mu. Jewish (trustee temple). Home: 3150 N Lake Shore Dr Chicago IL 60657 Office: Suite 7656 Sears Tower 233 S Wacker Dr Chicago IL 60606 *I've always lived by the theory "The harder you work, the luckier you get!"*

BOYARSKY, BENJAMIN WILLIAM, journalist; b. Berkeley, Calif., Oct. 21, 1934; s. Herman and Naomi (Heimy) B.; m. Nancy Elaine Belling, July 21, 1956; children: Robin Ann, Jennifer Lynn. A.B., U. Calif. at Berkeley, 1956. Copy boy, reporter Oakland (Calif.) Tribune, 1953-60; reporter, editor AP, San Francisco, 1960, Sacramento, 1960-70; polit. writer Los Angeles Times, 1970-75, nat. polit. writer, Washington, 1975-76, writer met. staff, 1976-78, chief city-county bur., 1978—. Author: The Rise of Ronald Reagan: Backroom Politics, 1974, (with wife) Ronald Reagan: His Life and Rise to the Presidency, 1981. Office: Los Angeles Times Los Angeles CA

BOYATT, THOMAS DAVID, Former U.S. ambassador; b. Cin., Mar. 4, 1933; s. Lynn Craig Haven and Florine (Cloar) B.; m. Maxine Lorraine Shearwood, Dec. 30, 1971; children: Thomas Benton, Christopher Lynn, Jessica Allyn. B.A., Princeton U., 1955; M.A., Fletcher Sch. Law and Diplomacy, 1956. Vice consul Dept. State, Antofagasta, Chile, 1960-62; 2d sec. Am. Embassy, Luxembourg, 1964-66; 1st sec., Nicosia, Cyprus, 1967-70, dir., Washington, 1970-74, assigned, 1974-75; dep. chief mission, minister counselor Am. Embassy, Santiago, Chile, 1976-78; U.S. ambassador to Upper Volta, Africa, Ouagadougou, 1978-80; U.S. ambassador to Colombia, Bogota, 1980-84; v.p. bus. govt. Latin Am. Sears World Trade Inc., Washington, 1984—; U.S. ambassador to Upper Volta, Bogotá, 1980—; with Dept. Treasury, 1962-64. Served to 1st lt. SAC USAF, 1956-59. Recipient Meritorious Honor award Dept. State, 1969, William R. Rivkin award Am. Fgn. Service, 1970, Christian A. Herter award, 1976. Mem. Am. Fgn. Service Assn. (vice chmn. 1970-73, chmn. 1973, pres. 1974—). Office: Sears World Trade Inc 450 Fifth St NW Washington DC 20001

BOYCE, CARROLL WILSON, editor, transportation consultant; b. Montclair, N.J., Dec. 20, 1923; s. Benjamin Knowlton and Gladys (Wilson) B.; m. Jean Corrin Compton, June 15, 1946; children: David Compton, Barbara Ann (dec. 1953), Linda Corrin, Wilson Keith. B.S. in Bus. and Engring. Adminstrn., MIT, 1946. Editorial asst. to mng. editor Factory mag., 1946-58; editor-in-chief Fleet Owner mag., McGraw-Hill, Inc., N.Y.C., 1959-69, 73-77, emeritus, 1977—; dir. truck div. Motor Vehicle Mfrs. Assn., Washington, 1969-73; editor-in-chief Trucks 26-Plus mag., McGraw-Hill, Inc., N.Y.C., 1977-79; pres. Transp. Forecasts & Planning, Inc., 1979-82, Abney Graphics, Inc., North Ft. Myers, Fla., 1981; asso. pub. Milner Assos., North Ft. Myers, 1981; cons. to adminstr. Def. Prodn. Adminstrn., Washington, 1951; vis. lectr. MIT, 1950-51; chmn. motor transp. conf. Nat. Safety Council, 1969-70, chmn. pub. info. conf., 1973-74, bd. dirs., 1963-79, hon. life mem., 1979—. Author: How to Plan Pensions, 1950, Materials Handling Casebook, 1951; contbr. numerous articles to periodicals. Recipient Pub. Service to Safety award Nat. Safety Council, 1963, 64, 65; Jesse H. Neal award for outstanding bus. journalism, 1957, 65, 67; Golden Knight award Internat. Assn. State and Provincial Safety Coordinators, 1965; Uniroyal Hwy. Safety Journalism award, 1975. Mem. Am. Bus. Press (chmn. editorial div. 1967-68), Soc. Automotive Engrs., ASME, Regular Common Carrier Conf. (maintenance com. 1975-79), Eastern Bus Maintenance Men's Conf., Philatelic Found., Royal, Am., Gt. Britain philatelic socs., Soc. Philatelic Americans, Brit. Philatelic Fedn., Nat. Press Club, Met. Ft. Myers C. of C. (com. on area devel. 1980-82). Presbyterian. Club: Collectors (N.Y.C.). Home: 677 Miles Standish Ln North Fort Myers FL 33903

BOYCE, CHARLES ALLEN, lawyer, petroleum company executive; b. Fairmont, W.Va., July 9, 1929; s. Arthur A. and Hattie W. B.; m. Janet Breeze, Apr. 24, 1976; children: Kimberly, Tamara, Jill, C. Gregg. B.S., W.Va. U., 1951; postgrad., U. Tex., 1953-54; J.D., Ohio State U., 1956. Bar: Ohio bar 1956, Pa. bar 1970. Trial lawyer IRS, Phila., 1956-57, Pitts., 1957-64; tax counsel Marathon Oil Co., Findlay, Ohio, 1964-69, Gulf Oil Corp., Pitts., 1969-75, asst. gen. counsel, 1975, corp. sec., asso. gen. counsel, 1976—. Served with USAF, 1951-53. Mem. ABA, Allegheny County Bar Assn., Am. Soc. Corp. Secs., Am. Petroleum Inst. Office: 439 Seventh Ave Pittsburgh PA 15219

BOYCE, DAVID EDWARD, Regional science educator, transportation consultant; b. Newark, Ohio, June 24, 1938; s. Francis Henry and Martha Ann (Neutzel) B.; m. Gale Lynn Strauss, Dec. 30, 1961; children: Lynn, Susan, Michael, Anna, Gregory. B.S. in Civil Engring., Northwestern U., 1961; M. City Planning, U. Pa., 1963, Ph.D., 1965. Registered profl. engr., Ohio. Research economist Battelle Meml. Inst., Columbus, Ohio, 1964-66; asst. prof. U. Pa., Phila., 1966-70, assoc. prof., 1970-74, prof., Phila., 1974-77; prof. transp. and regional sci. U. Ill., Urbana, 1977—; sr. vis. fellow Brit. Sci. Research Council, Leeds, 1972-73. Co-author: Metropolitan Plan Making, 1970, Optimal Subset Selection, 1974; co-editor Jour. Environment and Planning, 1979—. Mem. Regional Sci. Assn. (sec. Phila. 1969-78, internat. conf. coordinator Urbana 1978—), ASCE, Ops. Research Soc. Am. (transp. sci. council 1978-80). Home: Rural Route 1 Box 136 Sadorus IL 61872 Office: Dept Civil Engring U ILL 208 N Romine St Urbana IL 61801

BOYCE, DONALD NELSON, diversified industry exec.; b. Buffalo, May 4, 1938; s. Nelson W. and Mary A. (Gillis) B.; m. Jeris Jane Smith, Sept. 22, 1956; children—Mark D., Tammy J., Timothy R., Daniel E. B.S., Rochester Inst. Tech., 1967, postgrad., 1969-71. Accountant Sylvania Electric Products Co., Buffalo and Batavia, N.Y., 1956-59; accountant, systems mgr., controller Constrn. Equipment div. Eaton Corp., Batavia, 1959-69; controller Strippit div. Houdaille Industries, Inc., Akron, N.Y., 1969-72; treas. Houdaille Industries, Inc., Fort Lauderdale, Fla., 1972-79, v.p. fin. and adminstrn., dir., 1979—; also dir. subs.; dir. P.T. Components, Inc.; mem. adv. bd. Marine Bank-Western, Batavia, 1967-69. Mem. bd. edn. Oakfield-Ala. Central Sch., 1970-77. Mem. Machinery and Allied Products Inst. (fin. council), Am. Mgmt. Assn. Methodist. Clubs: Masons, Fort Lauderdale Tower, Coral Springs Country. Home: 3111 NW 114th Terr Coral Springs FL 33065 Office: One Financial Plaza Fort Lauderdale FL 33394

BOYCE, EARNEST, civil and sanitary engineer; b. Winterset, Iowa, July 11, 1892; s. Marcus James and Grace (Smith) B.; m. Elsie Jane Green, Sept. 21, 1919; 1 son, James Earnest. B.S., Iowa State Coll., 1917, C.E., 1930; M.S.E., Harvard U., 1932. Diplomate: Am. Acad. San. Engrs. Mem. staff sch. engring. U. Kans., 1920-41; dir. div. sanitation, chief engr. Kans. State Bd. Health, 1924-41; chief sanitation facilities sect., san. engring. div. USPHS, Washington, 1941-44; prof. municipal and san. engring., coll. engring., prof. pub. health engring., sch. pub. health U. Mich., 1944-61, chmn. dept. civil engring., 1947-61; cons. san. and pub. health engr., 1961—; Mem. Pub. Health Planning Team, Germany, July-Aug. 1951; mem. WHO vis. team, Indonesia, Apr.-May 1953; san. engring. cons. WHO, Western Pacific region, 1958—, ICA, India and Pakistan, 1960; cons. for Pan Am. Health Orgn. in Latin Am., and WHO, Geneva, 1962-67. Contbr. to tech. jours. Served to capt. U.S. Army, World War I; AEF. Recipient Charles Alvin Emerson medal Water Pollution Control Fedn., 1957; Marston gold medal Iowa State U. Coll. Engring., 1977. Fellow ASCE (hon. mem.); mem. Water Pollution Control Fedn. (Gordon M. Fair award 1976, hon., past pres.), Am. Pub. Health Assn. (v.p. 1961-62), Am. Water Works Assn. (life), Am. Soc. Engring. Edn. (life), Engring. Soc. Detroit (pres. 1956), Am. Pub. Works Assn., Mich. Engring. Soc. (hon.), Sigma Xi, Phi Kappa Phi, Delta Omega, Tau Beta Pi, Chi Epsilon. Presbyterian. Club: Rotary (Paul Harris fellow). Specialist in san. and pub. health engring. Home: 1601 Granger Ave Ann Arbor MI 48104

BOYCE, EDWARD WAYNE, JR., lawyer; b. Tuckerman, Ark., June 20, 1926; s. Edward Wayne and Sylla Jo (Harvey) B.; m. Phyllis Elayne Williams, Oct. 29, 1951; children: Elayne Boyce Zellmer, Edward Wayne III. Student, The Citadel, Charleston, S.C., 1943-44; A.B., U. Ark., 1950, LL.B. (later J.D.), 1951. Bar: Ark. 1951, U.S. Supreme Ct. 1960. Assoc. firm Pickens & Pickens, Newport, Ark., 1951-53; individual practice law, Tuckerman, Ark., 1954-59; pros. atty. 3d Jud. Circuit of Ark., 1956-60; partner firm Pickens, Boyce, McLarty & Watson, Newport, 1959—; del. Nat. Conf. on Continuing Legal Edn., 1968; dir. Ark. Law Rev., 1980—. Dep. Episcopal Gen. Conv., 1979, 82; pres. standing com. Diocese of Ark., 1983. Served with U.S. Army, 1944-47. Mem. Am. Law Inst., Ark. Bar Assn. (pres. 1978-79), Am. Bar Assn., Ark. Bar Found. (dir. 1970-73). Democrat. Club: Rotary (pres. 1963-64). Office: 209 Walnut St Newport AR 72112

BOYCE, FRANK GORDON, educator; b. Binghamton, N.Y., Apr. 8, 1917; s. Clarence and Ethel (Wilcox) B.; m. Joan A. Sweet, Sept. 5, 1941; children: Frank Gordon, Jonathan (dec.), Johanna. A.B., Colgate U., 1939, A.M., 1948; LL.D., Middlebury Coll., 1962, Cornell Coll., Mt. Vernon, Iowa, 1966; L.H.D., Elmira Coll., 1962. Reporter, feature writer Binghamton Sun, 1939-41; asst. to pres. Colgate U., 1946-50; pres. (Expt. in Internat. Living), Brattleboro, Vt., 1950-74, pres. emeritus, 1974—, sec. gen., 1956-72; exec. dir. Vt. Fedn. Ind. Colls., 1976—; dir. internat. programs Nathaniel Hawthorne Coll., 1976—; internat. counselor Nasson Coll., Springvale, Maine., Green Mountain Coll., 1983—; First dir. div. pvt. and internat. orgns. Peace Corps, 1961; mem. ad hoc com. to advise gov. and legislature on devel. Coll. V.I., 1961; pres. (Council Student Travel), 1951-55; mem. U.S. commn. for UNESCO, 1965-70. Trustee Colgate U., 1963-69, Coll. V.I., 1962-74; bd. dirs. Colgate U. Alumni Corp., 1957-62, pres., 1969-71. Served to lt. USNR, 1941-45. Decorated officer's cross Order Merit Fed. Republic Germany, 1964; Legion de O'Higgins award, Chile, 1968; recipient The Experiment citation, 1970; Order of the Sacred Treasure, Japan, 1972. Mem. Delta Phi Alpha, Alpha Tau Omega. Conglist. Address: Box 146 West Brattleboro VT 05301

BOYCE, GERALD G., artist, educator; b. Embarrass, Wis., Dec. 29, 1925; s. Charles William and Selma (Van Norman) B.; m. Kathryn Davis; 1 son, Charles William II. B.S., Wis. State U.; M.F.A., U. Iowa, 1950; postgrad., Americano Guatemaletco Instituto, Ind. U., U. Ill., Oxford (Eng.) U., 1979, Brit. Mus., Courtauld Inst., London. Prof. art history, chmn. fine arts Ind. Central U., Indpls., 1950—; lectr. art history DePauw U., 1968—; tchr. Fresno State Coll., Wabash Coll., DePauw U., Ind. U.; cons. Ind. Bell Telephone Co., 1967-70, U.S. Post Office Dept., 1972, Smithsonian Instn.; Mem. Gov.'s Commn. on the Arts. Exhibited in group shows, Los Angeles County Mus., San Francisco Mus. Art, Art Inst. Chgo., 1954, Mus. Modern Art, N.Y.C., 1956, Corcoran Gallery Art, Washington, 1971, Mus. Contemporary Crafts, N.Y.C.; represented in permanent collections, Ball State U., DePauw U., Earlham Coll., Evansville Coll., St. John's U., Marquis Inc., Ind. State U., Minot Coll., S.D., Wabash Coll., U. Iowa. Served with USAAF, World War II. Mem. Nat. Coll. Art Conf., Am. Crafts Council (sec. N. Central region 1962-66), Coll. Art Assn., Midwest Coll. Art Assn., AAUP, Nat. Art Adminstrs. Conf. Methodist. Home: Rural Route 1 Box 230 Morgantown IN 46160 Office: Ind Central Univ 1400 E Hanna Ave Indianapolis IN 46227

BOYCE, JOSEPH NELSON, journalist; b. New Orleans, Apr. 18, 1937; s. John and Sadie (Nelson) B.; m. Carol Hill, Dec. 21, 1968; children—Leslie, Nelson, Joel. Student, Roosevelt U., Chgo., 1955-65, John Marshall Law Sch., 1965-67. Mem. Chgo. Police Dept., 1961-66; reporter Chgo. Tribune, 1966-70; corr. Time mag., 1970-73, chief, 1973-79, 1979—; guest lectr. various colls. and univs. Chmn. Marin County Black Leadership Forum, 1974-75; mem. Marin Justice Council, 1977-78. Served with USNR. Recipient Outstanding Black Achiever award Met. YMCA, N.Y.C., 1975; co-recipient Unity In Media award Lincoln U., 1975. Mem. NAACP. Episcopalian. Office: Time Mag 233 Peachtree St NW Atlanta GA 30303

BOYCE, PETER BRADFORD, astronomer; b. N.Y.C., Nov. 30, 1936; s. Burke and Mabel (Zoeckler) B.; m. Mary Elizabeth Saffell, Nov. 6, 1976; children—Kevin Robert, Colin MacDonald. A.B., Harvard U., 1958; M.S., U. Mich., 1962, Ph.D., 1963. Staff astronomer Lowell Obs., Flagstaff, Ariz., 1963-73; program dir. NSF, Washington, 1973-79; Congl. fellow, sci. cons. to Congressman Morris K. Udall, Washington, 1977-78; exec. officer Am. Astron. Soc., Washington, 1979—; Dept. Commerce Sci. and Tech. fellow, 1977-78. Contbr. articles to sci. publs. Mem. Am. Astron. Soc., Internat. Astron. Union, Am. Phys. Soc., Am. Inst. Physics (dir. 1979—, mem. exec. com. 1980-82), AAAS, Optical Soc. Am., Sigma Xi. Home: 5700 Sherier Pl Washington DC 20016 Office: 1816 Jefferson Pl Washington DC 20036

BOYCE, THOMAS JOSEPH, JR., commodities futures exec.; b. Phila., Jan. 15, 1933; s. Thomas J. and Irene G. (Dobrow) B.; m. June H. Reeves, Feb. 4, 1961; 1 son, Kenneth. A.B. in Econs. cum laude, LaSalle Coll., Phila., 1959; M.B.A., Harvard, 1961. Financial analyst Federated Dept. Stores, Inc., Cin., 1961-65; cash mgr., asst. treas. Beatrice Foods Co., Chgo., 1965-72; exec. v.p., vice chmn. bd., dir. Wards Foods, Inc., Wilmette, Ill., 1972-80; pres., chief exec. officer REFCO, Inc., Chgo., 1980—; dir. Chamberlain Mfg. Co. Bd. dirs. Jr. Achievement Chgo., 1965-67, Am. Friends of Austria Soc., 1971-76, Zion (Ill.)-Benton Hosp., 1975-76. Served with USCG, 1952-56. Mem. Harvard Bus. Sch. Assn., Am. Mgmt. Assn. Clubs: Met., Mid-Am. (Chgo.); Macatawa Bay Yacht. Home: 180 E Pearson St Chicago IL 60611 Office: 135 S LaSalle St Suite 2400 Chicago IL 60603

BOYCE, WILLIAM EDWARD, mathematician, educator; b. Tampa, Fla., Dec. 19, 1930; s. Edward G. and Marie (Summers) B.; m. Elsa E. Keitzer, Feb. 19, 1955; children—James E., Carolyn E., Ann C. B.A., Southwestern at Memphis, 1951; M.S., Carnegie Inst. Tech., 1953, Ph.D. in Math, 1955. Research asso. applied math. Brown U., 1955-57; mathematician IBM Corp., 1957; mem. faculty Rensselaer Poly. Inst., Troy, N.Y., 1957—, prof. math., 1963—. Author: (with R.C. DiPrima) Elementary Differential Equations and Boundary Value Problems; also research papers.; editor, Case Studies in Mathematical Modeling, 1981; editorial bd., Stochestic Analysis and Applications, 1982. Mem. Am. Math. Soc., Soc. Indsl. and Applied Math. (asso. editor jour. 1969-75, mng. editor Soc. Indsl. and Applied Math. Rev. 1970-77, mem. council 1975-81, v.p. for publs. 1978-81), Math. Assn. Am., AAAS, Phi Beta Kappa. Home: 215 Brunswick Rd Troy NY 12180

BOYCE, WILLIAM GEORGE, museum dir., educator; b. Fairmont, Minn., July 25, 1921; s. William Irving and Nellie Hazel (Goetz) B.; m. Joan Palmer, July 29, 1949; children—Todd William, Robyn Jo, Timothy Palmer. B.S., U. Minn., 1949, M.Ed., 1952; postgrad., Mills Coll., Oakland, Calif., 1954-55. Clk. 1st Nat. Bank, Fairmont, 1939-41; high sch. and jr. coll. tchr., Worthington, Minn., 1949-57; mem. faculty U. Minn., Duluth, 1957—; prof. art, dir. Tweed Mus. Art, 1969—. Author: David Ericson, 1963, also mus. exhbn. catalogues. Served with USNR, 1941-45. Decorated Naval Commendation medal; Ford Found. grantee, 1954-55. Mem. NEA (life), Am. Assn. Museums, Midwest Museums Conf. (v.p. Minn. chpt. 1967-70), Midwest Art History Soc., Minn. Art Edn. Assn. (pres. 1963-65), Minn. Mus. Educator's Roundtable. Democrat. Episcopalian. Home: 2700 Minnesota Ave Duluth MN 55802 Office: 310 Tweed Mus U Minn Duluth MN 55812

BOYCE, WILLIAM HENRY, physician, educator; b. Ansonville, N.C., Sept. 22, 1918; m. Anna Doris Shore; 4 children. B.S., Davidson (N.C.) Coll., 1940, D.Sc., 1982; M.D., Vanderbilt U., 1944. Diplomate: Am. Bd. Urology (trustee 1980—, residency rev. com. for urology 1980—, sec. 1983). Intern Bowman Gray Sch. Medicine and N.C. Baptist Hosp., Winston-Salem, 1944-45, asst. resident in surgery, 1947; asst. resident in urology James Buchanan Brady Found., N.Y. Hosp.-Cornell U. Med. Center, N.Y.C., 1948-49, U. Va. Hosp., Charlottesville, 1950-51, chief resident, 1951-52; instr. urology Bowman Gray Sch. Medicine, Wake Forest U., Winston-Salem, 1952-56, asst. prof., 1956-58, asso. prof., 1958-60, prof., chmn. urology sect., 1960—; mem. staff N.C. Bapt., Forsyth Meml. hosps., Winston-Salem; mem. subcom. urolithiasis, study sect. research in nephrology and urology NIH, 1975-76. Editorial com.: Urology Digest; editorial cons.: Yearbook of Urology; editorial bd.: Jour. Continuing Edn. in Urology; editorial adv. bd.: Vascular Diagnosis and Therapy, 1980. Mem. adv. council Nat. Inst. Arthritis and Metabolic Diseases, NIH, 1975-76. Recipient CINE Golden Eagle award, 1980. Mem. AMA, Am. Urol. Assn. (pres. 1983, research awards 1950-52, 54, 58, 60, 74, 77-78, Hugh Hampton Young award 1974), Am. Assn. Genitourinary Surgeons (Barringer medal 1981), AAAS, So. Soc. Clin. Research, Soc. Exptl. Biology and Medicine, N.Y. Acad. Scis., N.C. Urol. Assn., N.C. Med. Soc., Clin. Soc. Genitourinary Surgeons, Soc. Univ. Surgeons, Société d'Urologie Internationale, Soc. Univ. Urologists, Am. Surg. Assn., A.C.S. (bd. govs.), Am. Inst. Ultrasound and Medicine, Pan-Pacific Surg. Assn., Alpha Omega Alpha. Home: 3969-B Valley Ct Winston-Salem NC 27106 Office: Bowman Gray Sch Medicine Winston-Salem NC 27103

BOYCE-SMITH, JOHN, III, mfg. co. exec.; b. N.Y.C., July 25, 1912; s. John and Harriet Mather (Illsley) B.-S.; m. Lee Ellis Wootten, Oct. 15, 1937; children—Tempe Lee (Mrs. John Brooks), John Gifford. B.A. in Econs, U. Calif. at Los Angeles, 1934. Asst. mgr. fgn. dept. Chem. Bank & Trust Co., N.Y.C., 1934-47; asst. v.p. corp. finance Bank of Am., Los Angeles, 1948-51; mgr. accounting and finance Hughes Aircraft Co., 1951-55; treas., controller Calavo Growers of Calif., Vernon, 1955-58; v.p. Calif. Bank, Los Angeles, 1958-59; with First Western Bank & Trust Co., Los Angeles, 1959-66, sr. v.p., 1961-63, exec. v.p., 1963-66; v.p., treas. Foremost-McKesson, Inc., 1966-77; chmn. bd. Golden State Ins. Co. Ltd. Served to lt. col., F.A. AUS, World War II; ETO. Decorated Bronze Star medal. Mem. Robert Morris Assos., Theta Delta Chi, Alpha Kappa Psi. Club: Inverness Yacht. Home: 10 Pine Hill Dr Inverness CA 94937 Office: 1 Post St San Francisco CA 94104

BOYD, ALAN STEPHENSON, transportation executive; b. Jacksonville, Fla., July 20, 1922; s. Clarence and Elizabeth (Stephenson) B.; m. Flavil Juanita Townsend, Apr. 3, 1943; 1 son, Mark Townsend. Student, U. Fla., 1939-41; LL.B., U. Va., 1948. Bar: Va. 1947, Fla. 1948. Practiced in, Fla., to 1957; gen. counsel Fla. Turnpike Authority, 1955; mem. Fla. R.R. and Pub. Utilities Commn., 1955-59, chmn., 1957-58; mem. CAB, Washington, 1959-65, chmn., 1961-65; under-sec. commerce for transp., 1965-67; sec. Dept. Transp., 1967-69; pres., chief exec. officer, dir. I.C.G.R.R., 1969-76; pres., chief exec. officer Amtrak, Washington, 1978-82; chmn., pres. Airbus Industries N.Am., 1982—; chmn. Am. High Speed Rail Corp.; dir. Sea Services, Inc. Chmn. bd. trustees Nat. Trust Hist. Preservation, 1980—. Democrat. Home: 2301 Connecticut Ave NW Washington DC 20008

BOYD, CHESTER EUGENE, retail co. exec.; b. Gaylord, Kans., Dec. 4, 1924; s. Roy and Ella Matilda (Mattson) B.; m. Betty Jayne Berg, June 10, 1950; children—Linda, Gary, Ronald, James, Kathy. B.S., U. Nebr., 1949. With S.S. Kresge Co. (K Mart Corp.), 1949—, v.p. auto div., 1968-72, gen. v.p. internat. hdqrs., 1972-78; chmn. bd., chief exec. officer K Mart Enterprises Inc., Troy, Mich., 1978—. Served with AUS, 1943-46. Mem. Am. Legion. Republican. Club: Elks. Office: 3100 W Big Beaver St Troy MI 48084

BOYD, CLARENCE ELMO, surgeon; b. Leesville, La., Nov. 2, 1911; s. Isaac Clarence and Ada Lee (Stakes) B.; m. Emma Kittredge Sims, Aug. 13, 1937; children: Charles Elmo, Marjorie Emily (Mrs. James O. Hudson), Frances Ada (Mrs. Thomas H. Thigpen), James E. B.A., U. Tex., 1932, M.D., 1935. Diplomate: Internat. Bd. Proctology, Am. Bd. Abdominal Surgeons (founder 1959). Intern Charity Hosp., New Orleans, 1935-36; resident North La. Sanitarium, Shreveport, 1936-37; gen. practice medicine, 1937-42, specializing in surgery, Shreveport, 1942—; jr. vis. surgeon Charity Hosp., Shreveport, 1937-42; sr. vis. surgeon Confederate Meml. Hosp., 1942—; 1st v.p. vis. staff, 1943-44, founder, 1942; since sr. mem. C. E. Boyd Clinic Ltd.; founding dir. Doctor's Hosp., Shreveport, 1959, chmn. bd., 1959-80, vis. surgeon, 1937—; clin. asst. prof. surgery La. State U. Postgrad. Sch. Medicine, 1957-67, La. State U. Sch. Medicine, Shreveport, 1967—; Founding dir. Shreveport Bank & Trust Co., 1954, chmn. investment com., 1954-78, chmn. bd., 1961—. Author numerous articles; producer films in field. Bd. dirs. Volunteers Am., 1950-58, chmn. bd., 1955-57; trustee Pub. Affairs Research Council La., 1959-79; mem. nat. adv. bd. We, The People, 1964—; mem. sponsors com. Shreveport United Fund, 1962-66; Guest speaker Dean's lecture La. State Med. Sch., 1955, 57;

founder, chmn. Student Loan Fund, 1942—. Hon. col. Gov. La. staff, 1964. Fellow A.C.S., Internat. Coll. Surgeons, Southeastern Surg. Congress, Am. Soc. Abdominal Surgeons (founder 1959, pres. 1966-67, mem. teaching faculty 1962—, Gold medal 1962); mem. AMA (chmn. surg. sect. 1957, mem. surg. sect. 1969-71, alternate del. gen. surg. council 1972-78, mem. surg. council 1972-78, del. 1978-79, Recognition award 1966-69, 70-72, 73-75, 76-78, 79-81), Assn. Am. Physicians and Surgeons (del. 1960-72, chmn. La. membership com. 1950-72, pres. La. chpt. 1972-73), Surg. Assn. La., Am. Mastology Assn., La. State Med. Soc. (Ho. of Dels. 1945-59, chmn. pub. policy and legis. com. 1954-57, chmn. surg. sect. 1957, councilor 1959-66, 1st v.p. 1967-68, chmn. com. on hosps. 1968-71, vice chmn. socio-econs. 1970-71, first chmn. com. medicine and religion 1964-66), Shreveport Med. Soc. (Gold medal 1956-57, pres. 1956-57, 1st chmn. med. progress 1957-59), Am. Cancer Soc. (bd. dirs. Caddo br. 1952-59, vice chmn. bd. 1957-58), So. Med. Assn. (asst. councilor 1959-68), Pan-Pacific Surg. Assn. Episcopalian (vestryman 1966-69; Gold medal Bible Class 1965). Clubs: Mason (32 deg.), Shriner, Rotarian (pres. South Shreveport Chpt. 1940-41), Rotarian (founder 1942). Spl. research operative cholangiography, hernioplasty with local anesthesia. Home: 401 Delaware St Shreveport LA 71106 Office: 1128 Louisiana Ave Shreveport LA 71101 *My goal is to serve God and my fellow man. I am very human and at times have fallen short of my ideals and goal. Each time I slip, I get up with added experience and a renewed will to face a challenging and an interesting world.*

BOYD, DAVID MILTON, process control executive; b. St. Louis, Jan. 5, 1918; s. David M. and Josephine (Drake) B.; m. Louise VanDeventer, June 11, 1941; children—Gwendolyn Boyd Graybar, David Garrison, Barbara Josephine. B.S. Chem. Engring., U. Colo., 1941, Chem.E., 1950. With Barratt Chem. Co., 1941-42, Blaw Knox Constrn. Co., 1942-43, Eastern States Petroleum Co., 1943-45, Monsanto Chem. Co., 1945-46, Oak Ridge Nat. Labs., 1946-48; mgr. instl. engring. design and service Universal Oil Products Co., Des Plaines, Ill., 1948—. Contbr. articles profl. jours.; Contbg. author: McGraw Hill Handbook of Separation Techniques. Recipient Instrument Soc. Am. Sperry award Chgo. Tech. Socs. Council, 1957, Distinguished Engring. Alumnus award U. Colo., 1970; Honeywell internat. award Inst. Measurement and Control, London, Eng., 1981. Fellow Instrument Soc. Am. (mem. admissions com., mem. recommended practices com., chmn. nat. meeting 1979), ASME; sr. mem. IEEE; mem. Am. Inst. Chem. Engrs., Am. Chem. Soc., Sigma Alpha Epsilon. Presbyn. (elder). Club: Ruth Lake Country (Hinsdale, Ill.). Holder 165 domestic and fgn. patents. Home: 315 Ridge Ave Clarendon Hills IL 60514 Office: 20 UOP Plaza Des Plaines IL 60016

BOYD, DAVID PRESTON, surgeon; b. Paisley, Scotland, July 1, 1914; came to U.S., 1928, naturalized, 1941; s. John and Christina (Johnson) B.; m. Mignon Finch, June 24, 1939; children—David Preston, Lew Finch, John Hamilton. Student, Glasgow U., 1930-32; M.D., McGill U., 1938; Postgrad. work in surgery, Montreal (Que., Can.) Gen. Hosp., 1938-42. Diplomate: Am. Bd. Surgery, Am. Bd. Thoracic Surgery. Practice of surgery, Amsterdam, N.Y., 1942-47; surg. staff Lahey Clinic div. Lahey Found., Boston, 1948—, also chmn. emeritus dept. thoracic surgery.; Lectr. in surgery Harvard. Editorial bd.: Chest, 1966—, Year book of Cancer; Contbr. articles profl. jours. Trustee, mem. exec. com. Pine Manor Jr. Coll.; trustee Boston Med. Library, Lahey Found. Fellow A.C.S., Am. Surg. Assn., Soc. Thoracic Surgeons, Royal Coll. Surgeons Can.; mem. Internat. Cardiovascular Soc., Internat. Soc. Surgery, A.M.A., Am. Assn. for Thoracic Surgery, Am. Thoracic Soc., ew Eng., Boston surg. socs., Am. Heart Assn., Am. Coll. Chest Physicians (pres. 1971-72), Am. Assn. History Medicine, Grad.'s Soc. McGill U., Soc. for Vascular Surgery. Presbyn. (elder). Clubs: The Country (Brookline, Mass.); Wellesley (Boston). Home: 20 Albion Rd Wellesley Hills MA 02181 Office: Lahey Medical Center 41 Mall Rd Burlington MA 01805

BOYD, DAVID WILLIAM, mathematician, educator; b. Toronto, Ont., Can., Sept. 17, 1941; s. Glenn Kelvin and Rachael Cecilia (Garvock) B.; m. Mary Margaret Shields, Sept. 26, 1964; children: Deborah, Paul, Kathryn. B.S., Carleton U., 1963; M.A., Toronto U., 1964, Ph.D., 1966. Asst. prof. U. Alta., 1966-67, Calif. Inst. Tech., 1967-70, assoc. prof., 1970-71; U. B.C., Vancouver, Can., 1971-74, prof. math., Vancouver, 1974—. Recipient E.W.R. Steacie Prize, 1978; I.W. Killam sr. research fellow, 1976-77. Fellow Royal Soc. Can.; mem. Math. Assn. Am., Am. Math. Soc., Can. Math. Soc. Office: Dept Math Univ BC Vancouver Canada V6T 1Y4

BOYD, DOUGLAS PERRY, physicist; b. Elizabeth, N.J., Nov. 25, 1941; s. James L. and Lois (Perry) B.; m. Majorie C. Abel, June 24, 1970. B.S., U. Rochester, 1963; Ph.D., Rutgers U., 1968. Mem. tech. staff Bell Telephone Labs., Murray Hill, N.J., 1968-70; research physicist High Energy Physics Lab., Stanford, Calif., 1970-76; prof. U. Calif. at San Francisco, 1976—; pres. Tech. Tranfer Assos., Woodside, Calif., 1977-81; gen. partner Imatron Assocs., 1981-83; pres., dir. Imatron Inc., 1983—. Contbr. articles to profl. jours. in fields nuclear physics, cryogenic technology, radiologic physics, nuclear instruments. Mem. Am. Phys. Soc., Soc. Photo Optical Engring., Am. Assn. Phys. Medicine. Inventor methods and techniques for fan-beam computerized-tomographic scanning of the body, 1971-74; co-developer superconducting pion generator for clin. radiotherapy using negative pion beams, 1975. Home: 150 Sheridan Way Woodside CA 94062 Office: Dept Radiology U Calif Med Center San Francisco CA 94143

BOYD, DREXELL ALLEN, dentist, educator; b. Marshfield, Mo., Apr. 1, 1910; s. John Barnes and Mable (Allen) B.; m. Jean Bosenger, July 24, 1979. Student, DePauw U., 1928-29; D.D.S., Ind. U., 1934; postgrad. tng., Forsyth Infirmary, Boston, 1935, U. Iowa Hosp., 1936. Faculty Ind. U., Indpls., 1937—, asso. prof. pedodontics, dir. dept., 1937-48, prof. operative dentistry, 1948—; in dentistry practice, Indpls., 1940-48; Vis. prof. dentistry U. Rio de Janeiro, 1961. Fellow Am. Coll. Dentistry; mem. Internat. Assn. Dental Research, Beta Theta Pi, Delta Sigma Delta. Democrat. Club: Mason. Home: 5321 White Marsh Indianapolis IN 46220

BOYD, FRANCIS VIRGIL, accounting educator; b. Livermore, Iowa, Feb. 1, 1922; s. Ernest and Gertrude (Marley) B.; m. Mary Celeste Cranny, Nov. 6, 1943 (dec. Sept. 11, 1981); children: Kevin, Therese.; m. Elizabeth Haynes Mauer, Oct. 8, 1983. B.A., Iowa State Tchrs. Coll., 1943; M.B.A., Northwestern U., 1948, Ph.D., 1956. C.P.A., Ill. Tchr. accounting Northwestern U., 1946-63, asso. dean, 1963-66; dean Sch. Bus., Loyola U., 1966-77, prof. acctg., 1977—; cons., tchr. exec. programs, 1956—; cons.-evaluator North Central Assn. Colls. and Univs. Author: (with others) Quantitative Controls in Business. Bd. dirs. Chgo. Crime Commn.; vice chmn. Bd. dirs. Lake Forest Sch. Mgmt.; mem. faculty adv. bd. Pepsi Cola Mgmt. Inst. Served to lt. (j.g.) USNR, 1943-46. Mem. Am. Inst. C.P.A.'s, Econ. Club Chgo., Am. Accounting Assn., Am. Econ. Assn., Beta Gamma Sigma. Office: 820 N Michigan Ave Chicago IL 60611

BOYD, GEORGE EDWARD, physical chemist; b. Evansville, Ind., Sept. 1, 1911; s. Herbert Henry and Mina (Deusner) B.; m. Valborg Richter, Feb. 20, 1942; 1 dau., Monica (Mrs. John F. Myles). B.S. with honors, U. Chgo., 1933, Ph.D., 1937. With U. Chgo., 1937-48, research instr., instr., asst. prof., asso. prof., chief plutonium process devel., Oak Ridge, 1943-45; prin. chemist (Oak Ridge Nat. Lab.), 1945-47, chief chemist, 1947-51, chief research scientist, 1951-55, asst. lab. dir., 1955-70, sr. research adviser, 1970-73; prof. chemistry U. Ga., 1974-82; Reilly lectr. Notre Dame U., 1954; vis. prof. chemistry Purdue U., 1962; R.A. Welch Found. lectr., 1975; Chmn. com. on awards in chemistry under Fulbright Act Nat. Acad. Scis.-NRC, 1959-63, Am. Nuclear Soc. rep. to div. chemistry and chem. tech., 1966-69. Asso. editor: Jour. Phys. Chemistry, 1950-54; editorial adv. bd.: Analytical Chemistry, 1953-55, Radiochimica Acta, 1963-77; Contbr. numerous tech. papers to profl. lit. Mem. AEC Mission to, Japan, Taiwan, P.I., 1957. Recipient So. Chemist gold medal, 1951, award for nuclear applications in chemistry, 1969, Charles H. Stone award, 1976; all Am. Chem. Soc.; Guggenheim and Fulbright fellow, Leiden, 1952-53. Fellow Am. Nuclear Soc. (chmn. div. isotopes and radiation 1961-62, dir. 1963-66), AAAS; mem. Am. Phys. Soc., Am. Chem. Soc. (chmn. div. colloid and surface chemistry 1952, mem. nat. colloid symposium com. 1958-64, chmn. div. nuclear chemistry and tech. 1966, mem. exec. com. div. phys. chemistry 1973-77), Phi Beta Kappa, Sigma Xi, Gamma Alpha. Office: Dept Chemistry U Ga Athens GA 30601

BOYD, GORDON, retired insurance company executive; b. Maplewood, N.J., Mar. 14, 1918; s. James and H. Estelle (Boyd) B.; m. Betty Bleakney, Apr. 4, 1941; children—Randall Bleakney, Gordon Reed. B.S. in Econs, U. Pa., 1940; M.B.A., N.Y. U., 1949. Mortgage investments exec. James Boyd, Inc., N.Y.C., 1940-42; with financial div. Socony-Vacuum Oil Co., N.Y.C., 1946; with Mut. Benefit Life Ins. Co., Newark, 1946—, treas., 1956-72, v.p., treas., 1972-83, ret., 1983; dir. FMI Fin. Corp. Vice pres. Robert Treat council Boy Scouts Am., 1965—; Trustee, mem. finance com. Overseas Ministries Study Center, Ventnor, N.J., 1960—. Served to lt. USNR, 1942-46. Clubs: Bond (N.J.); Treas.'s (N.Y.C.); Money Marketeers (N.Y. U.); Suburban of U. Pa.; Baltusrol (Springfield, N.J.); Essex (Newark). Home: 34 Dogwood Dr Summit NJ 07901 Office: 520 Broad St Newark NJ 07101

BOYD, HARRY DALTON, lawyer, ins. co. exec.; b. Huntington Park, Calif., June 13, 1923; s. Randall and Thelma L. (Lewis) B.; m. Margaret Jeanine Gmewell, June 13, 1948; children—Leslie Boyd Cotton, Wayne, Lynn Boyd Denby, Evan, Lance. LL.B., U. So. Calif., 1949, LL.M., 1960; Asso. in Mgmt., Ins. Inst. Am., 1972. Bar: Calif. bar 1950. Practice in, Los Angeles, 1950-52; asso. Harvey & Viereck, Los Angeles, 1952-55; asso. gen. counsel, corp. sec. Farmers Ins. Group, Los Angeles, 1955-77; group v.p., gen. counsel Swett & Crawford Group, Los Angeles, 1977—; Mem. Western Ins. Info. Service, Speakers Bur.; mem. Sherman Oaks Property Owners Assn., 1967—, pres., 1969, 72; bd. dirs. FIG Fed. Credit Union, 1958-61, pres., 1960-61. Mem. adv. council Chandler Elementary Sch., 1970-73, Milliken Jr. High Sch., 1973-74. Served with USAAF, 1943-46. Mem. Calif. Ins. Guarantee Assn. (bd. govs.), Los Angeles County Bar Assn. (chmn. exec. com. corporate law depts. sect. 1971-72), Reins. Assn. Am. (legal com. 1979-81), Nat. Assn. Ind. Insurers (chmn. surplus lines com. 1980-81), Calif. Assn. Ins. Cos. (exec. com. 1979-81), Wilshire C. of C. (dir. 1971—, pres. 1975), Am. Arbitration Assn. (arbitrator). Republican. Lutheran (pres. council 1964-65). Home: 13711 Weddington St Van Nuys CA 91401 Office: 4201 Wilshire Blvd Los Angeles CA 90010

BOYD, HOWARD TANEY, lawyer, former gas company executive; b. Woodside, Md., June 5, 1909; s. Howard and Mary Violet (Stewart) B.; m. Lucille Belhumeur, June 15, 1935; children: Dennis Brooke, Sharon Ann Boyd Rodriguez, Deborah Boyd Fitch. Grad., Georgetown Prep. Sch., Garrett Park, Md.; A.B. magna cum laude, Georgetown U., 1932, J.D., 1935, LL.D., 1977. Bar: D.C. 1934, Tex. 1953. Sec. to U.S. atty. gen., 1934; spl. atty. U.S. Dept. Justice, 1935; asst. U.S. atty. for D.C., 1935-39; formerly prof. Nat. Law Sch. (now Nat. Law Center), Washington Coll. Law (now Am. U.), Washington; partner firm Hogan & Hartson, Washington, 1939-52; officer, dir. El Paso Co. (formerly El Paso Natural Gas Co.), 1952-79, chmn. bd., chief exec. officer, 1964-79; partner firm Liddell, Sapp, Zivley & Brown, 1979—; adv. dir. Greyhound Corp.; past dir. Armour and Co., El Paso Co., Tex. Commerce Bank, N.A. Regent emeritus Georgetown U.; bd. dirs. Am. Heart Assn.; past bd. dirs. Houston Symphony Soc.; mem. nat. council Salk Inst.; trustee Center for Internat. Bus., U. So. Calif., U.S.-USSR Trade and Econ. Council; mem. devel. council Sch. Bus. Adminstrn., Tex. A&M U. Research fellow Southwestern Legal Found.; Decorated chevalier Legion of Honor, France; recipient Golden Plate award Am. Acad. Achievement. Mem. Groupe Internat. des Importateurs de Gaz Naturel Liquefie (pres.), Am. Bar Assn., State Bar Tex., Bar Assn. D.C. (dir. 1950), Interstate Natural Gas Assn. (pres. 1967-68), Am. Soc. French Legion of Honor, Knights of Malta. Clubs: Barristers, Burning Tree, Chevy Chase, Columbia Country, Met. (Washington); River Oaks Country, Houston Country, Petroleum, Ramada (Houston); Links (N.Y.C.). Home: 6042 Crab Orchard Houston TX 77057 Office: 2727 Allen Pkwy Houston TX 77019 also 500 Gulf Bldg Houston TX 77002

BOYD, JAMES, consulting geologist; b. Kanowna, West Australia, Dec. 20, 1904; s. Julian and Mary (Innes) Cane;; s. Julian and Mary (Innes) B.; m. Ruth Ragland Brown, Aug. 17, 1932 (dec. 1979); children: James Brown, Harry Bruce, Douglas Cane, Hudson; m. Clemence D. Jandray, 1980. B.S., Calif. Inst. Tech., 1927; M.Sc., Colo. Sch. Mines, 1932, D.Sc., 1934. Instr. geology Colo. Sch. Mines, Golden, 1929-34, asst. prof. mineralogy, 1934-37, asso. prof. econ. geology, 1938-41, dean faculty, 1946-47; asst. to sec. interior chmn. interdeptl. com. (Resources for Marshall Plan), 1947; dir. Bur. Mines, 1947-51, Def. Minerals Adminstrn., 1950-51; exploration mgr. Kennecott Copper Corp., 1951-55, v.p. exploration, 1955-60; pres. Copper Range Co., 1960-70, chmn. bd. dirs., 1970-71; exec. dir. Nat. Commn. on Materials Policy, Washington, 1971-73; pres. Materials Assos., 1974-78; geologist U.S. Geol. Survey, 1933-34; cons. geology, mining and geophysics, 1935-40; pres., gen. mgr. Goldcrest Mining Co., 1939-40; dir. engrs. Joint Council and United Engring.; Trustees, 1969-71; chmn. com. on mineral research NSF, 1952-57; vice chmn. Engrs. Commn. on Air Resources, 1970-71; chmn. sec. interior's adv. com. on non-coal mine safety, 1971-74; exec. dir. Nat. Commn. Materials Policy; chmn. materials com. Office Tech. Assessment, 1974-79; mem. nat. materials adv. bd. NRC, 1975-77, mem. mineral and energy resources bd., 1977-80, mem. mineral resources bd., 1973-75, chmn. com. on surface mining and reclamation, 1978-79; mem. tech. adv. com. Office of Nuclear Waste Isolation, 1979-82; Bd. dirs. Watergate S. Corp., 1972-79, pres., 1976-77. First reader Carmel Christian Sci. Ch., 1983-85. Served from capt. to col. AUS, 1941-46. Decorated Legion of Merit with oak leaf cluster; recipient Distinquished Service medal Colo. Sch. Mines, 1949; Distinguished Alumni award Calif. Inst. Tech., 1967; Hoover medal, 1975. Mem. Mining and Metall. Soc. Am. (pres. 1960-63), Am. Inst. Mining Engrs. (Rand gold medal 1963, pres. 1969), Nat. Acad. Engring., Am. Soc. Econ. Geologists, Geol. Soc. Am., Am. Inst. Profl. Geologists (Parker Meml. medal 1973, v.p. 1965-66), Soc. Exploration Geophysicists, Australasia Inst. Mining and Metallurgy (hon.), Acad. Polit. Sci. Clubs: Cosmos (Washington); Burning Tree. Home and Office: 228 Del Mesa Carmel Carmel CA 93921

BOYD, JAMES BROWN, genetics educator; b. Denver, June 25, 1937; s. James and Ruth Ragland (Brown) B.; m. Susie Fay Staats, Apr. 23, 1960; children: Randall Ragland, Pamela Ann. B.A., Cornell U., 1959; Ph.D., Calif. Inst. Tech., 1965. Postdoctoral fellow Max-Planck Institut for Biologie, Tubingen, W.Ger, 1965-68; asst. prof. dept. genetics U. Calif., Davis, 1969-71, asso. prof., 1971-77, prof., 1977—; mem. genetics study sect. NIH, 1976-77; Alexander von Humboldt U.S. sr. scientist, 1982-83. Served with M.S.C. U.S. Army, 1959-60. Helen Hay Whitney fellow, 1965-68; NATO sr. scientist fellow, 1974; Guggenheim fellow, 1975-76; Sr. Am. von Humboldt prize, 1981-82. Mem. Genetics Soc. Am., Am. Soc. Photobiology, Sierra Club, Sigma Xi. Research in analysis of DNA metabolism in Drosophilia. Home: 1615 Redwood Ln Davis CA 95616 Office: Dept Genetics Univ Calif Davis CA 95616

BOYD, JOHN DOMINIC, English educator; b. N.Y.C., Aug. 4, 1916; s. William Joseph and Dora Agnes (McHugh) B. A.B., Georgetown U., 1940; Ph.L., Woodstock Coll., 1941, S.T.L., 1948; postgrad., Rathfarnham Coll., Dublin, 1948-49; M.A., Fordham U., 1951; Ph.D., Harvard, 1958. Joined Soc. Jesus, 1934; ordained priest Roman Catholic Ch., 1947; instr. English Bellarmine Coll., Plattsburg, N.Y., 1955-60; mem. faculty Fordham U., N.Y.C., 1960—, prof. English, 1971—, chmn. dept., 1971-75, rector Murray-Weigel Hall, 1969-73. Author: The Function of Mimesis and Its Decline, 1968, 2d edit, Christ Is Our Light, 1976, A College Poetics, 1983. Fordham Faculty fellow, 1966-67, 75-76, 80-81; recipient Nat. Endowment Arts prize, 1969. Mem. English Inst., Modern Lang. Assn. Home: Loyola Hall Fordham U New York NY 10458

BOYD, JOSEPH ARTHUR, JR., state justice; b. Hoschton, Ga., Nov. 16, 1916; s. Joseph Arthur and Esther Estelle (Puckett) B.; m. Ann Stripling, June 6, 1938; children: Joanne Louise Boyd Goldman, Betty Jean Boyd Jala, Joseph Robert, James Daniel, Jane Nan. Student, Piedmont Coll., Demorest, Ga., 1936-38, LL.D., 1963, Mercer U., Macon, Ga., 1938-39; J.D., U. Miami, Coral Gables, Fla., 1948; LL.D., Western State U. Coll. Law, San Diego, 1981. Bar: Fla. 1948, D.C. 1973, N.Y. 1982, U.S. Supreme Ct. 1959. Practice law, Hialeah, 1948-68, city atty., 1951-58; mem. Dade County Commn., Miami, Fla., 1958-68, chmn., 1963; vice mayor Dade County, 1967; justice Fla. Supreme Ct., Tallahassee, 1969—, now chief justice; mem. Hialeah Zoning Bd., 1946-48; juror Freedoms Found., Valley Forge, Pa., 1971, 73. Bd. dirs. Bapt. Hosp., Miami, 1962-66, Miami Council Chs., 1960-64. Served with USMCR, 1943-46; PTO. Recipient Nat. Top Hat award Bus. and Profl. Women in U.S. for advancing status of employed women, 1967. Mem. ABA, Fla. Bar Assn., Hialeah-Miami Springs Bar Assn. (pres. 1955), Tallahassee Bar Assn., Hialeah-Miami Springs C. of C. (pres. 1956), Am. Legion (comdr. Fla. 1953-54), VFW, Wig and Robe, Iron Arrow, Phi Alpha Delta, Alpha Kappa Psi. Democrat. Baptist (deacon). Lodges: Mason; Shrine (33°); Lion; Moose; Elk. Office: Supreme Ct Bldg Tallahassee FL 32304

BOYD, JOSEPH AUBREY, communications co. exec.; b. Oscar, Ky., Mar. 25, 1921; s. Joseph Ray and Relda Jane (Myatt) B.; m. Edith A. Atkins, May 13, 1942; children—Joseph Barry, Joel Edd. S.B. in Elec. Engring, U. Ky., 1946, M.S., 1949; Ph.D., U. Mich., 1954. Instr., then asst. prof. elec. engring. U. Ky., 1947-49; mem. faculty U. Mich., 1949-62, prof. elec. engring., 1958-62, asso. dir., then dir., 1958-60, dir., 1960-62; exec. v.p. Radiation Inc., Melbourne, Fla., 1962-63, pres., 1963-72; exec. v.p. electronics Harris Corp., Cleve., 1967-71, exec. v.p. ops., 1971-72, pres., dir., 1972—, chmn., 1978—; Cons. Inst. for Def. Analyses, 1956—, Nat. Security Agy., 1957-62; spl. cons. to (Army Combat Surveillance Agy.), 1958-62; mem., chmn. adv. group electronic warfare Office Dir. Def. Research, Engring., Def. Dept., 1959-61, cons., 1959—. Contbr. articles to profl. jours. Fellow IEEE; mem. Assn. U.S. Army, Armed Forces Communications and Electronics Assn. (pres. 1971, 72), AAAS, Sigma Xi, Eta Kappa Nu, Tau Beta Pi. Baptist. Office: Harris Corp Melbourne FL 32919

BOYD, JOSEPH DON, coll. ofcl.; b. Muncie, Ind., Jan. 22, 1926; s. Joseph Corneluis and Waneta May (Barrett) B.; m. Cynthia Reiley, Dec. 28, 1957; children—Jane Elizabeth, Craig A., Michael J. A.B. (Rector scholar), DePauw U., 1948; M.A., Northwestern U., 1950, Ed.D., 1955. Ednl. asst. First Meth. Ch., Anderson, Ind., 1948-49; residence hall counselor Northwestern U., 1949-50, univ. examiner, instr. edn., guidance lab. asst., 1952-54, dean men, asst. prof. edn., 1955-61; exec. dir. Ill. Scholarship Commn., 1961-80; dir. instnl. relations and research Nat. Coll. Edn., Evanston, Ill., 1981—; residence hall dir., head tennis coach, asst. basketball coach Albion Coll., 1950-52. Mem. Nat. Assn. Adminstrs. State Scholarship Programs, Phi Delta Kappa, Delta Tau Delta, Phi Eta Sigma. Methodist. Club: Rotarian. Home: 1232 Warrington Rd Deerfield IL 60015 Office: 2840 Sheridan Rd Evanston IL 60201

BOYD, LANDIS LEE, agrl. engr., educator; b. Orient, Iowa, Dec. 1, 1923; s. Harold Everett and Edith Elizabeth (Lauer) B.; m. Lila Mae Hummel, Sept. 7, 1946; children—Susan Lee, Barbara Edith, Shirley Rae, Carl Steven, Philip Wayne. B.S. in Agrl. Engring, Iowa State U., 1947, M.S., 1948, Ph.D. in Agrl. Engring. and Engring. Mechanics, 1959. Registered profl. engr., N.Y., Minn. Sr. research fellow Iowa State Coll., 1947-48, 54-55; from asst. prof. to prof. Cornell U., Ithaca, 1948-64, coordinator grad. instrn., 1958-64; engring. design analyst Allis-Chalmers Mfg. Co., Milw., 1962-63; mem. faculty U. Minn. at St. Paul, 1964-78, prof. agrl. enging., head dept., 1964-72, asst. dir., 1972-78; dir. (Coll. Agr. Research Center); asso. dean Coll. Agr., Wash. State U., Pullman, 1978—; vis. scholar (Center Study Higher Edn.); vis. faculty-in-residence, intern Office Vice Pres. for Research, U. Mich., 1968, 1975; Cons. FAO, La Molina, Peru, 1964, 69; part-time cons. in field, 1948—. Supt. farm bldg. project N.Y. State Fair, 1956, 57. Served with USNR, 1943-45. NATO postdoctoral grantee, 1962; recipient Iowa 4-H Alumni Recognition award, 1968; profl. achievement citation in engring. Iowa State U., 1980; Japan Soc. Promotion of Sci. fellow, 1981. Fellow Am. Soc. Agrl. Engrs. (grad. paper award 1949, MBMA award 1969, v.p.-regions 1970-73); mem. Am. Soc. Engring. Edn., AAAS, Sigma Xi, Phi Kappa Phi, Gamma Sigma Delta, Alpha Epsilon, Kappa Sigma. Methodist. Club: Rotarian. Home: SE 520 Spring St Pullman WA 99163 Office: 403 Agr Phase II Coll Agr Research Center Washington State U Pullman WA 99164

BOYD, LIONA MARIA, musician; b. London; d. John Haig and Eileen (Hancock) B. B.Music, U. Toronto, 1972; hon. doctorate U. Toronto, 1981. Pres. Liona Boyd Prodns., Inc., MidContinental Music Publ. Classical guitarist appearing in concert tours throughout, Can., U.S.A., Europe, Japan, C. Am., S.Am., N.Z.; appeared on numerous TV variety shows; Recs. include Guitar Liona Boyd, 1975, The Guitar Artistry of Liona Boyd, 1976, The First Lady Guitar, 1978, Liona Boyd, Andrew Davis, English Chamber Orch, 1979, Spanish Fantasy, 1980, A Guitar for Christmas, 1981, Best of Liona Boyd, 1982, Virtuoso Liona Boyd, 1983, Liona Live in Tokyo, 1984; author: (music book) Liona Boyd, 1981. Recipient Juno award for instrumentalist of year Can. Music Industry, 1978, 82, 83; Vanier award Can., 1979; decorated Order of Can., 1982. Mem. Am. Fedn. Musicians, AFTRA, Guitar Soc. Toronto.

BOYD, LOUIS JEFFERSON, agrl. scientist, educator; b. Lynn Grove, Ky., Mar. 14, 1928; s. Bernice B. and Ethel Belle (Turnbow) B.; m. Rebecca Charlotte Conner, June 12, 1948; children—Beverly Boyd Gallagher, Beda Boyd Smith, Garth, Bettina Boyd Mize. B.S., U. Ky., 1950, M.S., 1951; Ph.D., U. Ill., 1956. Extension specialist U. Ky., Lexington, 1951-53; research asso. U. Ill., Urbana, 1953-56; asso. prof. U. Tenn., Knoxville, 1956-62; prof. Mich. State U., East Lansing, 1963-72; prof., chmn. div. animal sci. U. Ga., Athens, 1972-79, head animal and dairy sci. dept., 1974-79, coordinator sponsored programs, 1979—; researcher Inst. Research Animal Diseases (Agrl. Research Council), Compton, Eng., 1970-71; dir. Coble Dairy Products Coop., Inc., 1976—. Breeding columnist: Hoard's Dairyman mag, 1967-72. Served with AUS, 1946-47. Recipient Outstanding Adviser award Am. Dairy Sci. Assn., 1966, Outstanding Extension Specialist award Mich. State U., 1971; NSF travel grantee, France, 1968. Mem. Soc. Study Reprodn., Am. Soc. Animal Sci. (dir. 1981—), Am. Dairy Sci. Assn. (dir. 1973-76), Soc. Study Fertility, AAAS, Farm House (nat. dir. 1960-64), Dairy Shrine Club, Sigma Xi, Gamma Sigma Delta, Sigma Phi, Phi Zeta. Presbyterian (elder). Club: Optimist (v.p. 1961). Patentee process to improve fertility of animal semen. Home: 106 Saint James Ct Athens GA 30606 Office: Coll Agr U Ga Athens GA 30602

BOYD, MALCOLM, clergyman, author; b. Buffalo, June 8, 1923; s. Melville and Beatrice (Lowrie) B. B.A., U. Ariz., 1944; B.D., Ch. Div. Sch. Pacific, 1954; postgrad., Oxford (Eng.) U., 1955; S.T.M., Union Theol. Sem., N.Y.C., 1956. Vice pres., gen. mgr. Pickford, Rogers & Boyd, 1949-51; ordained to ministry Episcopal Ch., 1955; rector in, Indpls., 1957-59; chaplain Colo. State U., 1959-61, Wayne State U., 1961-65; nat. field rep. Episcopal Soc. Cultural and Racial Unity, 1965-68; resident fellow Calhoun Coll., Yale U., 1968-71, assoc. fellow, 1971—; writer-priest in residence St. Augustine-by-the Sea Episcopal Ch.,, 1982—; lectr. World Council Chs., Switzerland, 1955, 64; columnist Pitts. Courier, 1962-65; resident guest Mishkenot Sha'ananim, Jerusalem, 1974. Host: TV spl. Sex in the Seventies, CBS-TV, Los Angeles, 1975; Author: Crisis in Communication, 1957, Are You Running with Me, Jesus?, 1965, Free to Live, Free to Die, 1967, Book of Days, 1968, Human Like Me, Jesus, 1971, The Lover, 1972, When in the Course of Human Events, 1973, The Runner, 1974, The Alleluia Affair, 1975, Christian, 1975, Am I Running with You, God?, 1977, Take Off the Masks, 1978, Look Back in Joy, 1981; plays Boy, 1961, Study in Color, 1962, The Community, 1964, As I Live and Breathe: Stages of an Autobiography, 1969; others; editor: On the Battle Lines, 1964, The Underground Church, 1968; book reviewer: Los Angeles Times.; contbr.: articles to numerous mags. including Newsday, also newspapers. Active voter registration, Miss., Ala., 1963, 64. Malcolm Boyd Collection and Archives established Boston U., 1973; Recipient Integrity Internat. award, 1978; Union Am. Hebrew Congregations award, 1980. Mem. Nat. Council Chs. (film awards com. 1965), P.E.N. (pres. chpt. 1984-85), Am. Center, Authors Guild, Integrity, Nat. Gay Task Force, Clergy and Laity Concerned (nat. bd.), NAACP, Episc. Peace Fellowship. Address: 1227 4th St Santa Monica CA 90401 *The years have taught me the cost of getting involved in life. It is all a risk. One is on stage in an ever-new set without a script. The floor may give way without warning, the walls abruptly cave in. One may die at the hand of an assassin acting on blind impulse. Security, for which men sell their souls, is one of the few real jests in life. Yet the cost of not getting involved in life is higher; one has merely died prematurely. When one has stripped power of its mystique, its robes and artifices, it becomes vulnerable. When you stand up to power, you stand up to one or more individuals. Look an individual, then, in the eye, Laugh, if you feel like it. This may be rightly received as a much-needed expression of human solidarity.*

BOYD, MICHAEL ALAN, investment banking company executive; b. St. Petersburg, Fla., Aug. 19, 1937; s. Horace Clinton and Celeste Elizabeth (Tarpley) B. A.B., Harvard Coll., 1958; LL.B., Harvard U., 1967; student, The Queen's Coll., Oxford (Eng.), 1958-61. Bar: N.Y. 1968. Assoc. Davis Polk & Wardwell, N.Y.C., 1967-71; sr. v.p. gen. counsel Donaldson, Lufkin & Jenrette, Inc., N.Y.C., 1971—. Served with AUS, 1962-64. Thodes scholar, 1958. Mem. Internat. Bar Assn., ABA, N.Y. State Bar Assn., Civil Affairs Assn. (nat. dirs. 1983). Republican. Club: Wall Street. Home: Penthouse 2, 33 Greenwich Ave New York NY 10014 Office: Donaldson Lufkin & Jenrette Inc 140 Broadway New York NY 10005

BOYD, RICHARD HAYS, educator; b. Columbus, Ohio, Aug. 12, 1929; s. Robert E. and Charlotte (Hays) B.; m. Patricia A. Scheible, Sept. 5, 1951; children—David Hays, Elizabeth King. B.Sc., Ohio State U., 1951; Ph.D., MIT, 1955. Research chemist E. I. DuPont de Nemours Co., Wilmington, Del., 1955-62; prof. chemistry Utah State U., 1962-67, prof. chem. engring., prof. materials sci. and engring, adj. prof. chemistry, 1967—, chmn. materials sci. and engring., 1976-82; cons. phys. chemistry and polymer sci.; Swedish NRC vis. fellow Royal Inst. Tech., Stockholm, 1980. Scoutmaster Great Salt Lake council Boy Scouts Am., 1970-73. Recipient Distinguished Research award U. Utah, 1978. Fellow Am. Phys. Soc.; mem. Am. Chem. Soc., Am. Phys. Soc., Am. Inst. Chem. Engrs., AAUP, Phi Beta Kappa, Sigma Xi, Phi Eta Sigma, Phi Kappa Phi, Sigma Chi. Research and publs. in physical chemistry, polymer sci. Office: Dept Materials Sci and Engring U Utah Salt Lake City UT 84112

BOYD, ROBERT GIDDINGS, JR., symphony orchestra director; b. San Juan, Mar. 16, 1940; s. Robert Giddngs and Laura Jean (Stephenson) B.; m. Amanda Gail Rasmussen, July 28, 1967 (div. 1977); 1 dau., Stephanie Gail; m. Denise Ann Ryll, Dec. 10, 1978; 1 son, Robert Giddings III. B.A. in Sociology, Coll. William and Mary, 1962; postgrad. in bus. mgmt., George Washington U., 1965-67. Lic. in real estate, Ariz. Supr. staff services Bellcomm, Inc., Washington, 1964-67; budget mgr. Goodbody & Co., N.Y.C., 1968-70; bus. mgr. Westminster Sch., Simsbury, Conn., 1970-76; pres., gen. mgr. F & R Enterprises, Inc., Scottsdale, Ariz., 1976-78; mng. dir. San Diego Symphony Assnn., 1982—; pub. speaker San Diego Symphony, 1982—. Served to 1st lt. U.S. Army, 1962-64. Mem. Am. Symphony Orch. League, Am. Mgmt. Assn, Am. Arts Alliance, Combined Arts and Ednl. Council, San Diego Employers Assn. Republican. Office: San Diego Symphony PO Box 3175 San Diego CA 63102

BOYD, ROBERT WRIGHT, JR., publishing and mgmt. cons.; b. N.Y.C., May 1, 1911; s. Robert W. and Elsie G. (Bushong) B.; m. Ruth Simpson, June 20, 1939; children—Nancy (Mrs. Richard Moroso), Robert Wright III, James, Richard, Ruth. A.B., Princeton, 1932. Began as makeup man for Newsweek mag., 1933-38; with Time Inc., 1938-76, asso. editor, 1944-49, sr. editor, 1949-67, editorial prodn. mgr., 1967-71, dir. computer composition, 1971-76; with Moroso Performance Products, Guilford, Conn., 1976—; pres., dir. Roxmor Realty Corp. Presbyn. Home: 14 Lockwood Ave Old Greenwich CT 06870 also Woodland Valley Phoenicia NY 12464 Office: care Moroso Carter Dr Guilford CT 06437

BOYD, SAMUEL MATTHEW, retail stores exec.; b. Uniontown, Pa., Mar. 12, 1908; s. Eli Jacob and Martha (Albright) B.; m. Mary Kathryn Collins, July 26, 1932; children—Vance Eugene, Maureen Ellen (Mrs. James F. O'Hara), Suzanne Martha (Mrs. Allan Byrne). Grad., Inst. Mgmt., Am. U., 1956. Sales mgr. Collins Electric Co., Springfield, Mass., 1929-45; pres. New Eng. Service Center, Inc., Springfield, 1945-59, Boyd & Parker, Inc. (builders and developers), 1948-60, Bailey-Wagner, Inc. (retail furniture-appliance stores), 1933—; lectr. merchandising Mass. U. extension, 1938—, Internat. Coll., Springfield, 1956—. Pres. Greater Springfield Vis. Nurses Assn., 1968-69. Mem. Nat. Appliance and Radio-TV Dealers Assn. (pres. 1962-63). Clubs: Longmeadow (Mass.); Mens (pres. 1956). Home: 134 Regency Park Dr Agawam MA 01001 also 3698 NE 19th Ave Fort Lauderdale FL 33308 Office: 1458 Riverdale St West Springfield MA 01089

BOYD, THOMAS MUNFORD, lawyer, educator; b. Roanoke, Va., Sept. 25, 1899; s. James and Emma (Munford) B.; m. Dorothy Pilkington, Sept. 10, 1929; 1 son, Thomas Munford. B.S., U. Va., 1920, LL.B., 1923. Bar: Va. 1923. Pvt. practice, Charlottesville, 1923-40; judge Juvenile and Domestic Relations Ct. of Charlottesville and Albemarle County, 1925-30; legal staff Nat. Def. Adv. Commn., Office Prodn. Mgmt., War Prodn. Bd., Washington, 1940-43; ptnr. Christian, Barton, Parker & Boyd, Richmond, 1943-48, counsel, 1948-70, Paxson, Marshall & Smith, Charlottesville, 1970-73; partner Paxson, Smith, Boyd, Gilliam and Gouldman (P.C.), Charlottesville, 1973-81, Paxson, Smith, Boyd & Gilliam (P.C.), 1982-84; counsel Wood, Wood & Wood, Charlottesville, 1984—, Pippin & Pippin, Norton, Va., 1979—; lectr. law U. Va., 1946-47, prof. law, 1947-65, Doherty prof. law, 1965-70, prof. emeritus, 1970—; (on leave) chmn. appeals bd. Nat. Prodn. Authority, Washington, 1951-52; adv. counsel Va. Code Commn., 1953-58, cons., 1972-77; pres. Stettinius Fund, Inc., 1947-66; dir., gen. counsel Am. and Fgn. Enterprises, Inc., N.Y.C., 1947—; vis. prof. Washington and Lee U., 1961-62. Author: Burk's Pleading and Practice, 4th edit., 1952, Cases on Virginia Procedure, 1958, rev. edit., 1969; co-author: Virginia Civil Procedure, 1982. Bd. dirs. Va. Soc. for Prevention Blindness, 1968-73; mem. Am. Council of the Blind. Recipient Thomas Jefferson award U. Va., 1957, Raven award, 1961; T. Munford Boyd chair established U. Va. Law Sch., 1977; Disting. Service award Va. Trial Lawyers Assn., 1978. Fellow Am. Bar Found.; mem. ABA (Jour. adv. com. 1962), Va. Bar Assn., Va. State Bar, Am. Judicature Soc., Am. Blind Lawyers Assn., Order of Coif, Phi Beta Kappa, Phi Kappa Psi, Phi Delta Phi. Episcopalian. Clubs: Commonwealth, Redland. Home: 1309 Rugby Rd Charlottesville VA 22903 Office: Wood Wood & Wood 230 Court Sq PO Box 471 Charlottesville VA 22902

BOYD, WILLARD LEE, museum president; b. St. Paul, Mar. 29, 1927; s. Willard Lee and Frances L. (Collins) B.; m. Susan Kuehn, Aug. 28, 1954; children: Elizabeth Kuehn, Willard Lee III, Thomas Henry. B.S.L., U. Minn., 1949, LL.B., 1951; LL.M. (William W. Cook fellow 1951-52), U. Mich., 1952, S.J.D., 1962; LL.D., Coe Coll., 1969, Buena Vista Coll., 1969, Marycrest Coll., 1974, U. Fla., 1976; L.H.D., Cornell Coll., 1974, U. Iowa, 1981; Litt.D., Simpson Coll., 1976. Bar: Minn. 1951, Iowa 1958. Asso. firm Dorsey, Owen, Marquart, Windhorst and West, Mpls., 1952-54; mem. faculty U. Iowa Coll. Law, 1954—, prof., 1961—, asso. dean, 1964, v.p. acad. affairs, dean faculties at univ., 1964-69, pres., 1969-81, pres. emeritus, 1981—; pres. Field Mus. Natural History, Chgo., 1981—; dir. Dial Corp.; U.S. del. to Spl. Commn. on Succession Hague Conf. on Pvt. Internat. Law, 1970-72; mem. Commn. on Instl. Coop., 1964-69, Commn. on Arts and Scis., Nat. Assn. Land-Grant Colls. and Univs., 1969-73, Council of Ten, 1969-81, chmn., 1978-81; mem. adv. com. Office Advancement Pub. Negro Colls., 1971-77. Contbr. to profl. jours. Mem. com. on legal affairs, com. on health policy Commn. on Fine Arts; chmn. Gov.'s Com. Assemblies on Future of Iowa, 1972-78; participant cons. Council Higher Edn. in Am. Republics, 1972, 73; bd. dirs. Center for Research Libraries, Chgo., 1965-67, chmn., 1967-68; bd. commrs. Nat. Commn. Accrediting, 1970-75, pres., 1974; chmn. Iowa Coordinating Council for Post High Sch. Edn., 1976-77; mem. U.S. Senate Commn. on Operation Senate, 1975-76, Nat. Council on Arts, 1976—; bd. dirs. Harry S. Truman Library Inst., 1969-81, Council Postsecondary Accreditation, 1977-81; exec. com. Council Postsecondary Accreditation, 1978-81; co-chmn. NEA Task Force Edn., Tng. and Devel. Profl. Artists and Art Educators, 1977-79; bd. dirs. Cemrel, Inc., 1979—; adv. bd. Met. Opera Assn., 1978—; exec. com. div. baccalaureate and higher degree programs Nat. League Nursing, 1979-81; mem. steering com. Arts, Humanities and Older Ams., 1981—; mem. Nat. Com. on Careers for Older Ams., 1978—. Served with USNR, 1945-46. Recipient Outstanding Achievement award U. Minn., 1972. Mem. Am. Bar Assn. (chmn. com. social, labor and indsl. legislation 1963-65, chmn. 1965-66, sect. internat. and comparative law; council sect. legal edn. and admission to bar 1975—, chmn. 1980-81, com. ednl. policies 1975-78, chmn. 1975-76, co-chmn. 1976-78, mem. ABA-AALS Clin. Edn. Guidelines Project 1977-80, Task Force on Lawyer Competency: The Role of Law Schs. 1978-79), Iowa Bar Assn., Assn. Iowa Coll. Presidents (pres. 1974), Am. Assn. UN, Am. Council Edn. (dir. 1978-81, commn. academic affairs 1975-78, com. on fed. relations 1971-74, panelist), Assn. Am. Univs. (exec. com. 1977—, vice chmn. 1978, chmn. 1979-80, mem. health edn. com. 1977—). Conglist. Office: Field Mus. Natural History Roosevelt Rd. at Lake Shore Dr. Chicago IL 60605

BOYD, WILLIAM BEATY, foundation president; b. Mt. Pleasant, S.C., Feb. 2, 1923; s. Francis Thomas and Eunice (Beaty) B.; m. Louise Philson, June 25, 1945 (div. 1976); children: Marcie, Susan.; m. Karen Johnson Keland, June 26, 1982. A.B., Presbyn. Coll., Clinton, S.C., 1946; M.A., Emory U., 1947; Ph.D., U. Pa., 1954. Faculty Mich. State U., 1953-58; dean of faculty Alma (Mich.) Coll., 1958-65; dir. honors program Coll. Arts and Scis., Ohio State U., 1965-66; vice chancellor student affairs U. Calif., Berkeley, 1966-68; pres. Central Mich. U., Mt. Pleasant, 1968-75, U. Oreg., Eugene, 1975-80, Johnson Found., Racine, Wis., 1980—. Served with USNR, 1943-46, 51-53. Address: Johnson Found Racine WI 53401

BOYD, WILLIAM LEE, museum executive, educator, lawyer; b. St. Paul, Mar. 29, 1927; s. Willard Lee and Frances L. (Collins) B.; m. Susan Kuehn, Aug. 28, 1954; children: Elizabeth Kuehn, Willard Lee, Thomas Henry. B.S.L., U. Minn., 1949, LL.B., 1951; LL.M., U. Mich., 1952, S.J.D., 1962; hon. degree, Coe Coll., Cedar Rapids, Iowa, 1969, Buena Vista Coll., Storm Lake, Iowa, 1969, Marycrest Coll., Davenport, Iowa, 1974, U. Fla., 1976, John Marshall Law Sch., Chgo., 1983; L.H.D., Cornell Coll., Mt. Vernon, Iowa, 1974; Litt.D., Simpson Coll., Indianola, Iowa, 1976, Wartburg Coll., Waverly, Iowa, 1982. Bar: Minn. 1951, Iowa 1958. Assoc. Dorsey & Whitney, Mpls., 1952-54; from instr. to prof. law U. Iowa, Iowa City, 1954-64, assoc. dean Law Sch., 1964, v.p. acad. affairs, 1964-69; pres. Dorsey & Whitney, Mpls., 1969-81, Field Mus. Natural History, Chgo., 1981—; dir. Ctr. Research Libraries, 1965-70, chmn., 1967-68; mem. Nat. Commn. on Accreditation, 1970-74, pres., 1974; del. Hague Conf. on Pvt. Internat. Law, 1970-72. Bd. dirs. Elderhostel, Boston, 1981—, Children's Meml. Hosp., Chgo., 1981—, Northwestern Meml. Hosp., Chgo., 1982—, Ill. Humanities Council, Chgo., 1982—; mem. adv. bd. Chgo. Vol. Legal Service Found., 1982—; mem. Nat. Council on Arts, 1976-82, Met. Opera Assn., 1983—, U.S. Senate Commn., 1975-76; dir. Council on Postsecondary Accreditation, 1977-81, Harry S Truman Inst., 1969-81. Served with USN, 1945-47. William W. Cook fellow, 1951-52; recipient Outstanding Achievement award U. Minn., 1972. Mem. Assn. Am. Univs. (chmn. 1979-80), ABA (chmn. council sect. legal edn. and admission to bar 1980-81), Am. Council on Edn. (dir. 1978-81), Order of Coif. Home: 3800 N Lake Shore Dr Chicago IL 60613 Office: Field Museum of Natural History Roosevelt Rd and Lake Shore Dr Chicago IL 60605

BOYD, WILLIAM RICHARD, airline company executive; b. Newark, May 13, 1916; s. Samuel and Marion (Suchoy) B.; m. Katherine Louise Myer, Apr. 24, 1942. Student, U. N.C., 1933-35. Vice pres., gen. mgr. Nationwide Air Transport Service, Miami, Fla., 1947-49; pres., dir., gen. mgr. Frontier Airmotive, Inc., 1950-51; v.p., asst. pres. Resort Airlines, 1951-52; dir., pres., gen. mgr. All Am. Airways, 1952-53, Riddle Airlines, 1953-55; exec. v.p., gen. mgr., dir. Aerovias Sud Americana, 1955-56; exec. v.p., dir. World Airways, 1956-63; v.p. Continental Air Lines, 1964-68; pres., gen. mgr., dir. Airlift Internat., Inc., Miami, Fla., 1968-70; chief exec. officer, dir. Holiday Airlines, Inc., Los Angeles, 1970-71; v.p. Tracinda Investment Co., 1971—; dir. Metro-Goldwyn-Mayer, Inc., Western Airlines Inc. Served to flying officer RAF, 1940-42; to maj. USAAF, 1942-45. Decorated Air medal, D.F.C., U.S. and Eng.). Home: 272 Lasky Dr Beverly Hills CA 90212 Office: 132 S Rodeo Dr Beverly Hills CA 90212

BOYD, WILLIAM, JR., business advisor, banker; b. Pitts., Mar. 14, 1915; s. William and Catherine (McCutcheon) B.; m. Ann Willets, Nov. 6, 1954; 1 dau., Spencer. B.A., Yale U., 1937; postgrad., U. Pitts., 1946-50. With Gulf Oil Corp., Pitts., 1938-54; cons. to pres. Westinghouse Air Brake Co., Pitts., 1954-56; mgmt. cons. W. Boyd, Jr. & Assocs., Pitts., 1956-58; v.p. Pitts. Nat. Bank, 1958-68, sr. v.p., 1968-80, mgr. internat. div., 1962-71; pres. Wm. Boyd, Jr. & Co., 1980—, Table Point Co., 1975—; Mem. adv. bd. Export-Import Bank U.S., 1970-71. Chmn. trustees Laughlin Children's Center; treas. Sewickley Acad. Served with USNR, 1941-46. Decorated knight Order of Leopold II, Belgium). Mem. Bankers Assn. for Fgn. Trade (pres. 1970-71), World Affairs Council Pitts. (past pres., dir.). Clubs: Allegheny Country, Duquesne (Pitts.); Seawanhaka Corinthian (Oyster Bay, L.I.); Royal Ocean Racing (London, Eng.). Home: Woodland Rd Sewickley PA 15143 Office: One Oliver Plaza Suite 1143 Pittsburgh PA 15222

BOYDEN, ALAN ARTHUR, ret. educator; b. Milw., June 16, 1897; s. Arthur and Carrie (Wheeler) B.; m. Mabel Josephine Gregg, Sept. 15, 1923; children—Alan Arthur, Douglas Gregg, Mabel Maxon (Mrs. Thomas Ralph Davenport), Cornelia Wheeler (Mrs. Richard Thum). A.B., U. Wis., 1921, Ph.D., 1925. With Rutgers U., 1925—, New Brunswick, N.J., 1925—, instr., asst. prof., asso. prof., 1925-44, prof., 1944-62, prof. emeritus, 1962—, acting chmn. dept. zoology, 1947-48, chmn., 1954-59; Fulbright lectr. Queen Mary's Coll. U. London, 1960-61, 67-68; Rose Morgan vis. prof. U. Kans., 1964; Co-founder, chmn. Bur. Biol. Research, 1936-39; founder, dir. Serological Mus., 1948-62, dir. emeritus, 1971—, editor, 1948—. Author: Perspectives in Zoology. Served with U.S. Army, 1918. Recipient Distinguished Service citation Beloit Coll., 1970; Am. Cancer Soc. grantee, 1957-58, 58-59; NSF grantee, 1957-59. Fellow AAAS, N.Y. Acad. Scis., N.Y. Zool. Soc.; mem. Am. Soc. Naturalists, Am. Assn. Immunologists, Classification Soc., Soc. Systematic Zoology, Systematics Assn., Franklin Twp. Hist. Soc., Blackwell Mills Canal House Assn. (treas. 1971—), English Speaking Union (pres. New Brunswick br. 1960-62), Rockingham Assn. Home: Redwood RD 1 Princeton NJ 08540 Office: Rutgers University New Brunswick NJ 08903

BOYDEN, ALLEN MARSTON, surgeon, educator; b. Brookings, S.D., Oct. 31, 1908; s. Frank Edson and Maude Eva (Hegeman) B.; m. Margery French Davis, Sept. 19, 1936; children: Frank Davis, Allen Moore, Bradley Hunt. A.B., U. Oreg., 1929; M.D., U. Mich., 1932, M.S. in Surgery, 1936. Diplomate: Am. Bd. Surgery. Surg. house officer Mass. Gen. Hosp., 1932-34; instr. surgery U. Mich. Med. Sch., 1934-37; practice medicine specializing in surgery, Astoria, Oreg., 1937-42; head dept. gen. surgery Portland (Oreg.) Clinic, 1948-79; clin. instr. U. Oreg. Med. Sch., 1946, clin. assoc. surgery, 1946-51, asst. clin. prof. surgery, 1951-54, assoc. clin. prof. surgery, 1954-66, clin. prof. surgery, 1966—; chief surg. service St. Vincent Hosp., 1955-58, 68-70, chief staff, 1964; mem. exec. com., trustee Oreg. Physicians Service, 1954-66, v.p., 1959. Cons. editor: Surgery Gynecology and Obstetrics, 1966-74. Served from capt. to maj., M.C. U.S. Army, 1942-45. Decorated Bronze Star medal. Fellow AMA, A.C.S. (gov. 1948-63, vice chmn. bd. govs. 1958-59, 2d v.p. 1960-61); mem. Am. Surg. Assn. (2d v.p. 1973-74), Western Surg. Assn. (pres. 1976-77), Pacific Coast Surg. Assn. (pres. 1973-74), North Pacific Surg. Assn., Internat. Surg. Soc., Portland Surg. Soc. (pres. 1958-59), Frederick A. Coller Surg. Soc. (pres. 1955-58), Ore., Multonomah County med. socs., Portland Acad. Medicine (pres. 1965), Soc. Surgery Alimentary Tract, Phi Beta Kappa, Alpha Omega Alpha, Phi Kappa Phi, Nu Sigma Nu, Kappa Sigma. Republican. Unitarian. Clubs: Multnomah Athletic (Portland); Flyfishers of Oreg. Home: 4175 SW Greenleaf Dr Portland OR 97221

BOYDSTON, JO ANN, library science educator; b. Hugo, Okla., July 2, 1924; m. Donald N. Boydston, May 8, 1943. B.A. with high distinction, Okla. State U., 1944, M.A., 1947; Ph.D., Columbia U., 1950. Tchr. high schs., instr. jr. coll., Poteau, Okla., 1944-45; lectr. Spanish Columbia U., 1947-49; asst. prof. Spanish U. Miss., 1950-51, asso. prof. Sch. Edn., supr. student tchrs., 1952-55; asst. dir. tchr. tng. So. Ill. U., Carbondale, 1955-61, asso. dir., 1961-66, dir., 1966—, asso. prof. library affairs-adminstrn., 1969-73, prof., 1973—. Editor: The Early Works of John Dewey, vols. 1-5, 1965-72, The Middle Works, vols. 1-15, 1976-83, The Later Works, vols. 1-5, 1981-84, (with Robert E. Andresen) John Dewey - A Checklist of Translations, 1900-1967, 1969, Guide to the Works of John Dewey, 1970, (with Kathleen Poulos) Checklist of Writings about John Dewey, 1887-1976, 1978, Dewey Newsletter, 1967—, The Poems of John Dewey, 1977; gen. editor: The Collected Works of John Dewey, 1965—; Contbr. articles to edn., bibliog. jours. Mem. John Dewey Soc. (pres. 1970-72), MLA (com. scholarly edits.), Bibliog. Soc. Am., Manuscript Soc., Bibliog. Soc. U. Va., Soc. Textual Scholarship, Philosophy Edn. Soc., Midwest MLA, Midwest Philosophy Edn. Soc., Assn. Documentary Editing (pres. 1984), Am. Philos. Assn., Grolier Club, Mortar Bd., Phi Kappa Phi. Home: 1200 W Sycamore St Carbondale IL 62901

BOYER, BENJAMIN FRANKLIN, legal educator; b. St. Joseph, Mo., Sept. 17, 1904; s. John Sidney and Ruby (Hale) B.; m. Marion L. Lehr, Oct. 20, 1928; 1 dau., Judith Ann (dec.). Student, U. Va., 1922-24; A.B., U. Mo., 1926, J.D., 1928; LL.M., Columbia U., 1941; LL.D., Waynesburg Coll., 1952, Dickinson Sch. Law, Carlisle, Pa., 1959. Bar: Mo. 1928, Pa. 1950. Asst. atty. Mo. State Hwy. Commn., 1928-33; mem. firm Otto & Boyer, Washington, Mo., 1933-37; faculty Sch. Law, U. Kansas City (now U. Mo. at Kansas City), 1937-47, assoc. prof. law, 1937-42, prof. law, 1942-47, asst. to dean, 1938-39, chmn. law faculty, 1939-40, dean, 1940-47; dean, prof. law Temple U. Sch. Law, Phila., 1947-65, prof., 1965-69; prof. law U. Calif. at Hastings Coll. Law, 1969-79; Alternate mem. regional enforcement commn. WSB, 1952; Bd. curators Lincoln U. of Mo., 1939-44; bd. advisers Pa. Tax Inst., 1948-61; Mem. Mo. Supreme Ct. Com. on Civil Procedure, sub-com. on suggestion and plan, 1939-41; chmn. Personnel (Civil Service) Bd. of Kansas City, 1946-47. Editor: (with others) Selected Readings on the Legal Profession, 1962, Materials on Professional Responsibilities of the Legal Profession, 1967. Mem. Health and Welfare Council Phila., 1964-69, Commn. on Standards and Accreditation of Services for the Blind, Nat. Accreditation Council of Agys. Serving the Blind and Visually Handicapped, Pa. Gov.'s Commn. on Labor Legislation, 1953-54; bd. dirs. Legal Aid Soc. Phila., 1954-69, pres., 1960-69; council mem. Phila. Medico-Legal Inst., 1955-69. Commd. 2d lt. Inf. Res. U.S. Army, Feb. 1927; apptd. lt. col., Inf., May 1943; col., 1945; active duty under Res. Commn., 1941-46; instr. Commd. and Gen. Staff Sch. at Ft. Leavenworth, Nov. 1942-Dec. 1945; Kans.; comdt. Phila. O.R.C. Sch., 1950-51. Recipient Arthur von Briesen medal Nat. Legal Aid and Defender Assn., 1968. Mem. Am., Mo., Pa., Kansas City, Phila., San Francisco bar assns., Mo. Bar (sr. counsellor 1978), Nat. Acad. Arbitrators, Am. Arbitration Assn. (vol. panel), Lawyers Assn. Kansas City, Am. Law Inst. (life mem.), Am. Judicature Soc., Phi Beta Kappa Associates, Order of Coif, Phi Delta Phi, Alpha Pi Zeta, Sigma Nu, Phi Beta Kappa. Clubs: Mason (San Francisco) (Shriner); Rockhill Tennis). Home: 221 W

48th St Apt 1108 Kansas City MO 64112 Office: Sch Law U Mo 5100 Rockhill Rd Kansas City MO 64110

BOYER, CALVIN JAMES, librarian; b. Charleston, Ill., Mar. 4, 1939; s. Ernest Zimmerman and Velma Hazel (Childress) B.; m. Roberta Lorraine Davis, July 1, 1957; children—Carmellia Christine, Jeffrey Ernest. B.S. in Edn. Eastern Ill. U., 1961; M.L.S., U. Tex., 1964, Ph.D. (HEA Title II-B fellow 1969-72), 1972. Univ. librarian Midwestern U., Wichita Falls, Tex., 1967-69; asso. prof. Ind. U., Bloomington, 1972-75; univ. librarian U. Miss., 1975-80, U. Calif., Irvine, 1980—; bd. dirs Southeastern Library Network, (SOLINET), Atlanta, 1977-80, treas., 1979-80. Author: The Doctoral Dissertation, 1973; gen. editor: UMI Research Press, 1977—. Mem. ALA. Methodist. Home: Box 4777 Irvine CA 92716 Office: Univ Library PO Box 19557 Irvine CA 92713

BOYER, DAVID CREIGHTON, stockbroker; b. Wilmington, Del., Oct. 1, 1930; s. John Walter and Eva (Hammond) B.; m. Lydia Richards, June 3, 1953; children—Margaret Selfridge, Amy Richards, David Creighton. B.A. magna cum laude, Princeton, 1952. Asst. sec. Wilmington Trust Co., 1956-61; with Laird, Bissell & Meeds, Inc., Wilmington, 1961-73, partner, v.p., 1965-69, exec. v.p., 1969-70, pres., 1970-73; sr. v.p., dir. Dean Witter Reynolds Inc., Wilmington, 1973—. Pres. Active Young Republicans, New Castle County, 1958, Tower Hill Sch. Home and Sch. Assn.; bd. dirs. Child Guidance Center, Opportunity Center, Childrens Home. Served to lt. (j.g.) USNR, 1952-56. Baptist. Clubs: Wilmington, Vicmead Hunt (Wilmington); Cap and Gown (Princeton, N.J.). Home: 5701 Kennett Pike Centerville DE 19807 Office: Dean Witter Reynolds Inc DuPont Bldg Wilmington DE 19899

BOYER, ERNEST LEROY, foundation executive; b. Dayton, Ohio, Sept. 13, 1928; s. Clarence and Ethel (French) B.; m. Kathryn Tyson, Aug. 26, 1950; children: Ernest LeRoy, Beverly, Craig, Stephen. A.B., Greenville Coll., 1950; M.A., U. So. Calif., 1955, Ph.D., 1957, LL.D., 1971; postdoctoral, U. Iowa Hosp., 1959; LL.E., Seattle Pacific U., 1980; Litt.D., Chapman Coll., 1971, U. Md., 1978, Rider Coll., 1979, Western New Eng. Coll., 1979; L.H.D., Dowling Coll., 1971, Pace U., 1972, Fairleigh Dickinson U., 1977, City U. N.Y., 1978, Canisius Coll., 1979, Am. U., 1980; LL.D., U. So. Calif., 1971, Fordham U., 1973, U. Akron, 1973, Roberts Wesleyan Coll., 1973, U. Rochester, 1975, Coll. William and Mary, 1978, Beloit Coll., 1978, Hamilton Coll., 1978, Hope Coll., 1978, Wilmington Coll., 1979, Union Coll., 1979, U. Mo., 1979, Drake U., 1979, Va. Union U., 1980, Temple U., 1980, Earlham Coll., 1980; P.S.D., Greenville Coll., 1971, U. Md. Balt. County, 1980; D.Sc., Alfred U., 1973; D.F.A., Wheeling Coll., 1978; D.Paed., Yeshiva U., 1978, Eastern Mich. U., 1979, Doane Coll., 1980. Mem. faculty Upland (Calif.) Coll., acad. dean, prof. speech pathology, 1956-60; teaching asst. U. So. Calif., 1950-55; asst. prof. speech, dir. forensics Loyola U., Los Angeles, 1955-56; dir. commn. to improve edn. tchrs. Western Coll. Assn., 1960-62; dir. Center Coordinated Edn., U. Calif. at Santa Barbara, 1962-65; exec. dean univ. wide activities SUNY, 1965-68, vice chancellor, 1968-70, chancellor, 1970-77; U.S. commr. of edn., 1977-79; pres. Carnegie Found. for Advancement of Teaching, 1979—; scholar-in-residence Aspen Inst. Humanistic Studies, 1974-76; vis. fellow Battelle Research Center, Seattle, 1969, Wolfson Coll. Cambridge (Eng.) U., 1976; mem. adv. panel Inst. Higher Edn., U. New Eng., Australia, 1980; mem. exec. com. Nat. Adv. Bd. of The Center for the Book, Library of Congress, 1980—; mem. Nat. Commn. Financing of Postsecondary Edn., 1972-73, Commn. on Critical Choices for Ams., 1973-74, Carnegie Council on Policy Studies in Higher Edn., 1974-77, Presdl. Com. on Edn. Women, 1975, Pres.'s Adv. Council on Women's Ednl. Programs, 1975-77, N.Y. State Health Planning Commn., Research Found. State U. N.Y.; chmn. bd. State U. Constrn. Fund; chmn. bd. trustees). Bd. dirs. Arts, Edn. and Ams., Inc., 1980—, Washington Chamber Orch., 1980—, Cities in Schs., Inc., 1980—, Am. Council on Edn., Kennedy Center for Performing Arts, Am. Assn. Higher Edn., Inst. Internat. Edn., Saratoga Performing Arts Center, N.Y., Internat. Council Ednl. Devel., Council Fin. Aid to Edn.; bd. mgrs. Haverford Coll., 1980—; trustee Earlham Coll., Messiah Coll., Tchrs. Ins. and Annuity Assn. Am., Ednl. Testing Service, British Open U. Found., 1980—, Nat. Com. Arts for Handicapped, 1980—. Mem. nat. adv. council Hampshire Coll., 1980—; mem. bd. advisors China Inst. in Am., Inc.; assco. China Council of Asia Soc. Recipient Pres.'s medal Tel Aviv U., 1971; Gov.'s award State of Ohio, 1978; Presdl. fellow Aspen Inst. Humanistic Studies, 1978; Achievement in Life award Ency. Brit., 1978; N.Y. Acad. Public Edn. Ann. award, 1979; award Council Advancement and Support of Edn., 1979; spl. citation PUSH-EXCEL, 1979; named one of Am.'s two outstanding leaders in edn. U.S. News and World Report, 1978. Mem. Internat. Council Ednl. Devel. (dir. 1980—, exec. com. 1980—), Nat. Assn. State Univs. and Land-Grant Colls. (pres. 1974-75), Assn. N.Y. State Colls. and Univs. (pres. 1972-74), Nat. Council Fgn. Lang. and Internat. Studies (dir. 1980—), Rensselaerville Inst. on Man and Sci., Pi Kappa Delta, Alpha Kappa Sigma., Soc. Friends. Clubs: University (N.Y.); Hudson River, Fort Orange (Albany). Home: 7016 Benjamin St McLean VA 22101 Office: Carnegie Found Advancement Teaching Five Ivy Ln Princeton NJ 08540

BOYER, HERBERT WAYNE, biochemist; b. Pitts., July 10, 1936. B.A., St. Vincent Coll., Latrobe, Pa., 1958; Ph.D., U. Pitts., 1963; D.Sc. (hon.), St. Vincent Coll., 1981. Mem. faculty U. Calif., San Francisco, 1966—, prof. biochemistry, 1976—; investigator Howard Hughes Med. Inst., 1976—; co-founder, dir. Genentech, Inc., South San Francisco, Calif. Mem. editorial bd.: Biochemistry. Recipient V.D. Mattai award Roche Inst., 1977; Albert and Mary Lasker award for basic med. research, 1980; USPHS postdoctoral fellow, 1963-66. Mem. Am. Soc. Microbiology, Am. Acad. Arts and Scis. Address: Dept Biochemistry HSE 1504 Univ Calif San Francisco CA 94143 *

BOYER, JAMES LORENZEN, physician, educator; b. N.Y.C., Aug. 28, 1936; s. Ralph R. and Alice M. B.; m. Phoebe Bennet, Feb. 23, 1963; children: Phoebe Christine, Anna Birch. A.B., Haverford (Pa.) Coll., 1958; M.D., Johns Hopkins U., 1962. Diplomate: Am. Bd. Internal Medicine. Med. intern N.Y. Hosp., N.Y.C., 1962-63, resident in medicine, 1963, Yale-New Haven Hosp., 1966; postdoctoral fellow liver study unit Yale U., 1966-68; mem. faculty U. Chgo. Pritzker Sch. Medicine, 1972-78, prof. medicine, 1976-78, dir. liver study unit, 1972-78; prof. medicine, dir. liver study unit, chief div. digestive diseases Yale U. Med. Sch., 1978—; treas., bd. dirs. Am. Liver Found., 1976-80; dep. chmn. Nat. Digestive Disease Adv. Bd., 1981—. Author papers, abstracts in field. Served as lt. comdr. USPHS, 1964-66. Josiah Macey faculty scholar, 1976. Mem. Am. Assn. Study Liver Disease (pres. 1980), Am. Fedn. Clin. Research, A.C.P., Am. Gastroenterol. Assn. (councillor 1983—), Internat. Assn. Study Liver Diseases (v.p. 1982-84), Am. Soc. Clin. Investigation, Assn. Am. Physicians, Central Soc. Clin. Research. Office: 333 Cedar St New Haven CT 06510

BOYER, JOE L., university president. Pres. Miss. Valley State U., Itta Bena, Miss. Office: Miss. Valley State U. Itta Bena MS 38941

BOYER, LESTER LEROY, JR., architectural engineer; b. Hanover, Pa., Apr. 6, 1937; s. Lester Leroy and Ruth Florence (Kessler) B.; m. Patricia Barbara Hayes, Dec. 28, 1958; children: Douglas Lester, Blane Edward, Darla Mae. B.Archtl. Engring., Pa. State U., 1960, M.S. in Archtl. Engring, 1964; Ph.D. in Architecture, U. Calif.-, Berkeley, 1976. Instr. archtl. engring. Pa. State U., 1960-64; research engr. Armstrong Cork Co., Lancaster, Pa., 1964-68; course dir. Nat. Soc. Profl. Engrs., 1964-74; sr. cons. acoustics and noise control Bolt Beranek and Newman Inc., Cambridge, Mass., 1968-70; mem. faculty Okla. State U., Stillwater, 1970—, dir. environ. control program, 1970—, prof. architecture, 1979—; Fulbright scholar U. N.S.W. and U. Queensland, 1982; cons. acoustics, environ. comfort and passive energy design, 1970—; dir. earth-sheltered bldg. research Control Data Corp. and U.S. Dept. Energy, 1979-81; gen. chmn. Internat. Conf. Earth Sheltered Bldgs., Sydney, Australia, 1983. Editor: Building Design for Environmental Hazards, 1973, Earth Sheltered Building Design Innovations, 1980, Earth Shelter Performance and Evaluation, 1981, Earth Shelter Protection, 1983. Mem. Am. Solar Energy Soc. (nat. coordinator passive earth cooling program 1981), Am. Underground Space Assn., Human Factors Soc., Nat. Soc. Profl. Engrs., Am. Soc. Engring. Edn., Acoustical Soc. Am., Illuminating Engring. Soc., ASHRAE. Lutheran. Home: Route 1 Meadowbrook 8 Stillwater OK 74074 Office: Sch Architecture Okla State U Stillwater OK 74078

BOYER, PAUL D., biochemist, educator; b. Provo, Utah, July 31, 1918; s. Dell Delos and Grace (Guymon) B.; m. Lyda Mae Whicker, Aug. 31, 1939; children: Gail Anne (Mrs. Denis Hayes), Marjorie Lynne (Mrs. Lukman Clark), Douglas. B.S., Brigham Young U., 1939; M.S., U. Wis., 1941, Ph.D., 1943; D.Sc. (hon.), U. Stockholm, 1974. Instr., research asso. Stanford, 1943-45; asst. prof. to prof. biochemistry U. Minn., 1946-55, Hill research prof., 1955-63; prof. chemistry U. Calif. at Los Angeles, 1963—, dir. Molecular Biology Inst., 1965—; chmn. biochemistry study sect. USPHS, 1962-67; mem. U.S. Nat. Com. for Biochemistry, 1965-71. Editor: Ann. Rev. of Biochemistry, 1965-70, Biochemical and Biophysical Research Communications, 1968-80, The Enzymes, 1970—; Mem. editorial bd.: Biochemistry, 1969-76, Jour. Biol. Chemistry, 1978-83; Contbr. articles to profl. jours. Recipient Am. Chem. Soc. award in enzyme chemistry, 1955, Tolman award, 1982; Guggenheim fellow, 1955. Fellow Am. Acad. Arts and Sci. (council); mem. Nat. Acad. Sci., Am. Soc. Biol. Chemists (past pres., council mem.), Am. Chem. Soc. (past div. chmn.), Biophys. Soc. Home: 1033 Somera Rd Los Angeles CA 90024

BOYER, PHILIP BOYAJIAN, television station executive; b. Portland, Oreg., Dec. 13, 1940; s. Peter Boyajian and Gladys F. (Niebling) B.; m. Kay I. Kebelbeck, Mar. 17, 1962; children: Tammy, Terri, Thomas. B.A., Sacramento State U., 1968. Prodn. mgr. Sta. KEZI-TV, Eugene, Oreg., 1960-65; program dir. Sta. KCRA-TV, Sacramento, 1965-72, Sta. KNBC, Burbank, Calif., 1972-74; v.p. programming ABC stas., N.Y.C., 1974-77; v.p., gen. mgr. Sta. WLS-TV, Chgo., 1977-79, Sta. WABC-TV, N.Y.C., 1979-81; v.p., gen. mgr. product devel. and planning ABC owned TV stas., 1981—; asso. prof. Sacramento State U., 1970-72. Bd. dirs. Chgo. chpt. Boy Scouts Am., 1977-79, Easter Seals, Chgo., 1977-79. Mem. Nat. Acad. TV Arts and Scis., Nat. Assn. Program Execs. (pres. 1976-77, dir.). Presbyterian. Club: Kiwanis. Office: care ABC-TV 1345 Ave of Americas 28th Floor New York NY 10019

BOYER, RAYMOND FOSTER, physicist; b. Feb. 1910. B.S. in Physics, Case Western Res. U., 1933, M.S., 1935, D.Sc. (hon.), 1955. With Dow Chem. Co., Midland, Mich., 1935—, asst. dir. phys. research lab., 1945-48, dir. phys. research lab., 1948-52, dir. plastics research, 1952-68, asst. dir. corporate research for polymer sci., 1968-72, research fellow, 1972-75; partner Boyer and Boyer, Midland, 1975—; research affiliate Midland Macromolecular Inst., 1975—; Vis. prof. Case Western Res. U., 1974, adj. prof., 1979, Central Mich. U., 1980; guest Russian Acad. Scis., 1972, 78, 80, Polish Acad. Scis., 1973; Past chmn. Gordon Conf. on Polymers. Contbr. numerous articles to profl. jours. Recipient Swinburne award Plastics Inst., London, 1972. Mem. Am. Chem. Soc. (past chmn. high polymer div., Borden award in chemistry of plastics and coatings 1970), Am. Phys. Soc. (past chmn. high polymer div.), Soc. Plastics Engrs. (Internat. award in polymer engring. and sci. 1968), Nat. Acad. Engring. Research on physics and phys. chemistry of high polymers with emphasis on transitions and relaxations in polymers. Patentee in field. Office: 415 W Main St Midland MI 48640

BOYER, ROBERT ALLEN, educator; b. Hummels Wharf, Pa., Aug. 27, 1916; s. H. Alvin and Jennie (Saurers) B.; m. Eleanor Rae Moyer, June 24, 1939; children—Patty Rae (Mrs. William H. Hinkle), Stephen C. A.B. summa cum laude, Susquehanna U., 1938; M.A., Syracuse U., 1940; Ph.D., Lehigh U., 1952; D.Sc. (hon.), Muhlenberg Coll., 1981. Instr. physics Clarkson Coll. Tech., 1940-41; instr. physics, acting dept. head Muhlenberg Coll., 1941-52, prof. physics, head dept., 1952-81, prof. emeritus, 1981—; adj. prof. Cedar Crest Coll., 1981—; vis. prof. summer grad. sch. Conn. Wesleyan U., 1963-72, 75. Recipient Lindback award, 1961. Mem. Am. Assn. Physics Tchrs. (pres. Central Pa. sect. 1956-57), Acoustical Soc. Am., Am. Assn. U. Profs. Lutheran (lay speaker Eastern Pa. Synod 1969-70, v.p. ch. 1958-60, 68, 71-75). Home: 20 Beverly Dr Allentown PA 18104

BOYER, ROBERT ERNST, geologist, educator; b. Palmerton, Pa., Aug. 3, 1929; s. Merritt Ernst and Lizzie Venetta (Reinard) B.; m. Elizabeth Estella Bakos, Sept. 1, 1951; children—Robert M., Janice E., Gary K. B.A., Colgate U., 1951; M.A., Ind. U., 1954; Ph.D., U. Mich., 1959. Instr. geology U. Tex., Austin, 1957-59, asst. prof., 1959-62, asso. prof., 1962-67, prof., 1967—, chmn. dept. geol. scis., 1971-80, dean, 1980—; exec. dir. Natural Scis. Found., 1980—; chmn. exec. com. Geology Found., 1971-80. Author: Activities and Demonstrations for Earth Science, 1970, Geology Fact Book, 1972, Oceanography Fact Book, 1974, The Story of Oceanography, 1975, Solo-Learn in the Earth Sciences, 1975, GEO-Logic, 1976, GEO-VUE, 1978; editor: Tex. Jour. of Sci, 1962-65, Jour. of Geol. Edn, 1965-68. Fellow Geol. Soc. Am., AAAS; mem. Tex. Acad. Sci. (hon. life, pres. 1968), Nat. Assn. Geology Tchrs. (pres. 1974-75), Am. Geol. Inst. (pres. 1983), Am. Assn. Petroleum Geologists, Austin Geol. Soc. (pres. 1975), Gulf Coast Asso. Geol. Soc. (pres. 1977). Home: 7644 Parkview Circle Austin TX 78731

BOYER, VINCENT SAULL, utility executive; b. Phila., Apr. 5, 1918; s. Philip A. and Gertrude (Stone) B.; m. Ethel Wolf, June 6, 1942; children: Ruth Ann, Suzanne, Sandra Jean. B.S. in Mech. Engring., Swarthmore (Pa.) Coll., 1939; M.S., U. Pa., 1944; D.Engring. Tech. (hon.), Spring Garden Coll., 1979. With Phila. Electric Co., 1939—, mgr. nuclear power, 1963-65, gen. supt. sta. operating, 1965-67, mgr. electric ops., 1967-68, v.p. engring. and research, 1968-80, sr. v.p. nuclear power, 1980—; mem. adv. com. Electric Power Research Inst., 1978-80. Author papers in field. Served with USNR, 1944-46. Named Engr. of Year of Delaware Valley, 1979. Fellow ASME (chmn. Phila. 1970-71, James M. Landis medal 1981), Am. Nuclear Soc. (pres. 1976-77, honors and award com.); mem. Nat. Acad. Engring., Franklin Inst., Engrs. Club Phila. (George Washington medalist 1982), Edison Electric Inst., Assn. Edison Illuminating Cos., Atomic Indsl. Forum (chmn. com. on Three Mile Island 2 recovery, mem. policy com. on nuclear regulation), Am. Nat. Standards Inst. Clubs: Union League, Aronimink Golf (Phila). Address: 2301 Market St Philadelphia PA 19101

BOYERS, ROBERT, educator; b. N.Y.C., Nov. 9, 1942; s. Paul and Selma (Busell) B.; m. Madelyn Gray Dolen, Aug. 31, 1963 (div. 1975); children: Lowell, Zachary Meyer; m. Margaret Anne O'Higgins, Dec. 16, 1975; 1 son, Gabriel Levin. B.A., Queens Coll., CUNY, 1963; M.A., NYU, 1965. Instr. New Sch. Social Research, N.Y.C., 1967, Baruch Sch., CUNY, 1967-68; asst. prof. English Skidmore Coll., Saratoga Springs, N.Y., 1969-73; assoc. prof., Saratoga Springs, N.Y., 1973-80; prof. Skidmore Coll., Saratoga Springs, N.Y., 1980—. Editor-in-chief: Salmagundi Mag., 1965—, Bennington Rev., 1978-83; author: Excursions: Selected Literary Essays, 1976, Lionel Trilling: Negative Capability and the Wisdom of Avoidance, 1977, F.R. Leavis: Judgement and the Discipline of Thought, 1978, R.P. Blackmur, Poet-Critic: Towards A View of Poetric Objects, 1980; editor: Robert Lowell: A Portrait of the Artist in His Time, 1970, R.D. Laing and Anti-Psychiatry, 1971, The Legacy of the German Refugee Intellectuals, 1972, Psychological Man: Approaches to an Emergent Social Type, 1975, Contemporary Poetry in America, 1975, The Salmagundi Reader, 1983; asoc. editor Rev. of Existential Psychiatry and Psychology, 1973-78. NEH sr. fellow, 1979-80; Rockeffer Found. grantee Bellagio, Italy, 1980. Democrat. Jewish. Home: 163 Spring St Saratoga Springs NY 12866 Office: Skidmore Coll Saratoga Springs NY 128866

BOYES, JON L., association executive; b. Oakland, Calif., July 5, 1921; s. Gordon McBoyes; m. Nancy Mitchell, Oct. 23, 1970; children: Jan Brooke, Christopher Lynne, Virginia Leigh. B.S., U.S. Naval Acad., 1943; M.A., U. Md., 1960, Ph.D., 1970; M.A., U. Hawaii, 1963; M.S., U.S. Naval Postgrad. Sch. Messenger Am. Trust Co., 1940-41; commd. ensign U.S. Navy, 1943, advanced through grades to vice adm.; destroyer and submarine duty; 1st comdr. underice Arctic ops., also nuclear attack squadron Navy Command and Control System; later dep. dir. gen. NATO; ret.; now pres. Armed Forces Communications and Electronics Assn.; mem. faculty U. Md. Grad. Sch.; dir. Seven Springs Estates, SAMA Corp., SOTAS Corp. Author tech. articles. Decorated D.S.M., Legion of Merit (4), Purple Heart; recipient Gold medal Armed Forces Communications and Electronics Assn., Distinguished Service medal. Mem. Electronic Warfare Assn., NATO Service Club. Republican. Episcopalian. Club: Lions. Home: 11807 Wayland St Oakton VA 22124 *It is my conviction that each of us must do good for our fellowman and for those that follow for what we ourse.ves have received on this earth. Hard work, love of life, sensitivity, belief in God and integrity are my watchwords to accomplish my goals.*

BOYKAN, MARTIN, composer, music educator; b. N.Y.C., Apr. 12, 1931; s. Joseph and Matilda (Caspe) B.; m. Constance Berke, June 23, 1963 (div. 1978); children—Rachel, Deborah. A.B. summa cum laude, Harvard U., 1951; student, U. Zurich, Switzerland, 1951-52; M.Mus., Yale, 1953. Asst. prof. music Brandeis U., Waltham, Mass., 1964-67, asso. prof. music, 1967-76, prof., 1976—. Composer: String Quartets, 1949, 65, Flute Sonata, 1950, Violin Duo, 1951, Flute Quintet, 1953, Psalm, 1958, Prelude for Organ, 1959, Chamber Concerto for 13 instruments, 1971, String Quartet No. 2, 1973, Piano Trio, 1975, Elegy for soprano and 6 instruments, 1979; Mem. editorial bd.: Perspectives of New Music; contbr. articles to profl. jours. Recipient Jeunesses Musicales Prize, 1967, Fromm Found. commn., 1975; Martha Baird Rockefeller grantee. Mem. Am. Music Center, Phi Beta Kappa. Home: 155 Sumner St Newton Center MA 02159 Office: Brandeis Univ Waltham MA 02154

BOYKIN, EDWARD MCCALLUM, management consultant; b. Ft. Worth, July 24, 1913; s. James Edward and Daisy (McCallum) B.; m. Teresa Ibarra, Dec. 24, 1938; children—Noel Edward, Grant McCallum, Craig Alexander. B.S., Carnegie Inst. Tech., 1938; grad. Exec. Program, U. Calif. at Los Angeles, 1957. Elec. maintenance supr. San Jose Sugar Co., Provincia de Santa Clara, Cuba, 1932-34; prodn. control and efficiency engr. Beveridge Paper Co., 1938; asst. to supt. distbn. Tex. Electric Service Co., 1938-40; contract relations rep. Metro-Goldwyn Mayer and Paramount for Western Electric Co., 1946-49; mgr. field engring. Hughes Aircraft Co., Culver City, Cal., 1949-53, dir. field service and support div., 1953-56, v.p., mem. policy bd., 1956-69; mgmt. cons. Pacific Palisades, Cal., 1969—. Served to lt. col. USAAF, 1940-46. Mem. I.E.E.E. (sr.), Sigma Xi, Tau Beta Pi, Phi Kappa Phi, Kappa Sigma. Clubs: Grand Lake (Colo.); Yacht. Address: Pacific Palisades CA 90272

BOYKIN, JOSEPH FLOYD, JR., librarian; b. Pensacola, Fla., Nov. 7, 1940; s. Joseph Floyd and Delree (Bailey) B.; m. Evelyn Louise Larson, Aug. 3, 1963; children: Suzanne Michelle, Pamela Denise. Student, Pensacola Jr. Coll., 1958-60; B.S., Fla. State U., 1962, M.S., 1965. Lic. pvt. pilot. Asst. to librarian U. N.C., Charlotte, 1965-68, acting head librarian, 1968-70; dir. library, 1970-81; dir. libraries Clemson (S.C.) U., 1981—; bd. dirs. Southeastern Library Network, Inc., 1975-78, chmn., 1977-78. Trustee OCLC Online Computer Library Center, Inc., 1980—, OCLC Users Council, 1978-82; pres. OCLC Users Council, 1978-80. Mem. ALA, Southeastern Library Assn. (sec. 1980-82), S.C. Library Assn., Delta Tau Delta. Democrat. Baptist. Home: 200 Kings Way Clemson SC 29631 Office: Univ Library Clemson Univ Clemson SC 29631

BOYKIN, ROBERT HEATH, banker; b. Carlsbad, N.M., Jan. 10, 1926; s. Calvin Clay and Ruby (Heath) B.; m. Camille Inkman, Nov. 26, 1948; 1 son, Robert Heath. B.B.A., U. Tex., 1950, LL.B., 1953; student, Park Coll., 1943-44; spl. courses, La. State U., Tex. A. and M. Coll., Am. Mgmt. Assn. Bar: Tex. bar 1952. Tabulating supr. Tex. Edn. Agy., 1948-52; with Fed. Res. Bank of Dallas, 1953—, asst. counsel, 1959-61, asst. counsel, asst. sec. bd., 1961-65, asst. v.p., asst. sec. bd., 1965-67, asst. v.p., sec. bd., 1967-68, v.p., sec. bd., 1968-70, sr. v.p., sec. bd., 1971-75, sr. v.p., 1976, 1st v.p., 1976-80, pres., 1981—; sec. Conf. Pres.'s of Fed. Res. Banks, 1963-64, chmn., 1980; instr. negotiable instruments Dallas chpt. Am. Inst. Banking, 1959-61. Served as lt. (j.g.) USNR, 1943-47. Mem. Tex. Bar Assn., Tex. Bankers Assn., Delta Tau Delta, Phi Alpha Delta. Methodist. Office: 400 S Akard St Dallas TX 75222

BOYLAN, DAVID RAY, chemical engineer, educator; b. Belleville, Kans., July 22, 1922; s. David Ray and Mabel (Jones) B.; m. Juanita R. Sheridan, Mar. 24, 1944; children: Sharon Rae, Gerald Ray, Elizabeth Anne, Lisa Dianne. B.S. in Chem. Engring, U. Kans., 1943; Ph.D., Iowa State U., 1952. Instr. U. Kans., 1942-43; project engr. Gen. Chem. Co., Camden, N.J., 1943-47; sr. engr. Am. Cyanamid Co., Elizabeth, N.J., 1947; plant mgr. Arlin Chem. Co., Elizabeth, 1947-48; faculty Iowa State U., Ames, 1948—, prof. chem. engring., 1956—, asso. dir., 1959—, dir., 1966—, dean, 1970—. Fellow Am. Inst. Chem. Engrs., Am. Chem. Soc., AAAS; mem. Am. Soc. Engring. Edn., Sigma Xi, Phi Lambda Upsilon, Sigma Tau, Phi Kappa Phi, Tau Beta Pi. Research in transient behavior and flow of fluids through porous media, unsteady state and fertilizer tech., devel. fused- phosphate fertilizer processes, theoretical and exptl. correlation of filtration. Patents and papers in field. Home: 1516 Stafford St Ames IA 50010

BOYLAN, J. RICHARD, banker; b. New Rochelle, N.Y., June 25, 1928; s. James Owen and Ethel (King) B.; m. Hildegarde W. Scheffler, Apr.14, 1956; children: Cynthia Ann, James Richard. B.A., Johns Hopkins U., 1950; exchange student, U. Oslo, Norway, 1947; postgrad., Stonier Sch. Banking, 1961. With Provident Nat. Bank, Phila., 1954—, now vice chmn.; chmn. bd., dir. Provident Instl. Mgmt. Corp.; pres., dir. Provident Nat. Investment Corp.; exec. v.p. Independence Sq. Income Securities, Inc.; mng. dir. Shearson Internat. Dollar Res. Fund; vice chmn., dir. PNC Fin. Corp.; dir. Provident Nat. Fin. Corp., Colonial Penn Group, Inc.; S. Chester Tube Co., Tatnall Corp.; trustee Keystone Ins. Co. Pension Trust; mem.

investment policy com. Gen. Accident Fire & Life Assurance Corp., Ltd. Bd. mgrs., chmn. fin. com. Friends Hosp.; trustee Johns Hopkins U., Widener U.; also mem. coms. on budget and investments. Johns Hopkins U. Mem. Am. Bankers Assn. (chmn. trust div.). Club: Union League (Phila.). Home: 303 S Waterloo Rd Devon PA 19333 Office: 1632 Chestnut St Philadelphia PA 19103

BOYLAN, JOHN FRANCIS, construction and agricultural equipment company executive; b. Portage, Wis., Sept. 22, 1940; s. Peter J. and Frances E. (Mattke) B.; m. Kay E. Haagensen, June 15, 1963; children: John Francis, William R., Michael P. B.B.A., U. Wis., Whitewater, 1962. C.P.A., Wis. Sr. acct. Arthur Young & Co., Milw., 1962-67; with J.I. Case Co., Racine, Wis., 1967—, v.p., gen. mgr. service parts supply div., 1977-79, v.p., gen. mgr. constrn. equipment div., 1979-81, exec. v.p. constrn. equipment worldwide, 1981—; dir. M & I Bank. Mem. Constrn. Industry Mfrs. Assn. (dir. Milw. 1982-84), Am. Road and Transp. Builders Assn. (dir. 1982-84), Internat. Road Fedn. (dir. 1982-84). Office: J I Case Co 700 State St Racine WI 53404

BOYLAN, JOHN PATRICK, record producer, songwriter; b. N.Y.C., Mar. 21, 1941; s. John Wilson and Jean Elizabeth (Curtin) B.; 1 dau., Amy Nicole. B.A., Bard Coll. Staff songwriter Koppelman-Rubin Assos., N.Y.C., 1967-69; ind. record producer, Los Angeles, 1969-76, personal mgr., 1971-73; exec. producer CBS Records, Los Angeles, 1976-80, v.p., 1980—. Composer numerous songs, 1967—; including Look Here Comes the Sun; producer sound-track albums: motion pictures Urban Cowboy, Nightshift, Stroker Ace, Footloose, 1969—; producer various rec. artists. Served with USAF, 1963-64. Recipient 8 Platinum Record awards Rec. Industry Assn. Am., 1976-81; 16 Gold Record awards, 1969-81; 9 Platinum Record awards; also numerous Gold and Platinum awards from fgn. contries. Mem. Nat. Acad. Rec. Arts and Scis., AFTRA, Am. Fedn. Musicians. Office: 1801 Century Park W Los Angeles CA 90067

BOYLAN, MERLE NELSON, librarian; b. Youngstown, Ohio, Feb. 24, 1925; s. Merle Nelson and Alma Joy (Kepple) B. B.A., Youngstown U., 1950; M.L.S., Carnegie-Mellon U., 1956; postgrad., U. Ariz., 1950-51, Ind. U., 1952. Librarian Pub. Health Library U. Calif., Berkeley, 1956-58; sci. librarian U. Ariz., Tucson, 1958-59; engring. librarian Gen. Dynamics/Convair, San Diego, 1959-61, Gen. Dynamics/Astronautics, 1961-62; asso. librarian Lawrence Radiation Lab., U. Calif., Livermore, 1962-64, library mgr., 1964-67; chief librarian NASA Ames Research Center, Moffett Field, Calif., 1968-69; asso. dir. libraries U. Mass., Amherst, 1969-70, dir. libraries, Univ. librarian, 1970-72; dir. libraries U. Tex., Austin, 1973-77, U. Wash., Seattle, 1977—, prof. Sch. Librianship, 1982—; exec. bd. Amigos Bibliographic Council, 1974-77; mem. fin. com., governance com., user's council, computer service council Wash. Library Network, 1978—; del. Gov.'s Conf. Libraries and Info. Services, 1979; sec. Texas State Bd. LIbrary Examiners, 1974-77; mem. bibliographic networking and resource sharing advisory group Southwestern Library Interstate Coop. Endeavor, 1975-77; sec., chmn. exec. bd. Pacific N.W. Bibliographic Center, 1977-83; mem. com. centralzed acquisitions of library materials for internat. studies Center for Research Libraries.; del. OCLC Users Council, 1981—. Sec. bd. trustees Littlefield Fund for So. History, 1974-77. Mem. Am., Wash., Pacific NW library assns., Assn. Coll. and Research Libraries (legis. com. 1977-81), Assn. Research Libraries (bibliographic control com. 1979—), Spl. Libraries Assn., Am. Soc. Info. Sci., Beta Phi Mu. Home: 1354 Bellefield Park Ln Bellevue WA 98004 Office: Suzzallo Library U Wash Seattle WA 98195

BOYLAN, PAUL CHARLES, educator; b. Portage, Wis., Oct. 2, 1939; s. Peter James and Frances Elizabeth (Mattke) B.; children—Aaron, Matthew, Jason. B.Mus., U. Wis., 1961, M.Mus., 1962; Ph.D. in Musicology, U. Mich., 1968. Instr. U. Mich., 1965, asst. prof., 1969-72, asso. prof., 1972-77, prof., 1977—, dir. univ. divs. nat. music camp, 1971-75, dean, 1979—. Pub. research on songs and piano music of Hugo Wolf. Pres. bd. dirs. Gt. Lakes Performing Arts Assn.; mem. devel. com. St. Joseph's Mercy Hosp. Rackham research grantee, 1969; Mich. Council Arts grantee, 1978-79. Mem. Soc. Music Theory, Am. Musicol. Soc., Music Tchrs. Nat. Assn., Am. Soc. Aesthetics, Nat. Assn. Music Execs. State Univs. Democrat. Presbyterian. Home: 1722 Shadford Ann Arbor MI 48104 Office: 2300 Sch Music Univ Michigan Ann Arbor MI 48109

BOYLAN, WILLIAM ALVIN, lawyer; b. Marshalltown, Iowa, Sept. 18, 1924; s. Glen D. and Dorothy I. (Gibson) B.; m. Nancy Dickson, Aug. 5, 1950; children: Ross, Laura. Student, U. Iowa, 1943-44; B.A., Drake U., 1947; LL.B., Harvard U., 1950. Bar: Ill. 1950, N.Y. bar 1952. Since practiced in, N.Y.C.; mem. firm Boylan & Evans (and predecessor firms), 1963—; dir. Tribune Oil Corp. Contbr. articles to profl. jours. Served with USAAF, 1943-46. Mem. Am. Bar Assn., N.Y. State Bar Assn., Assn. Bar City N.Y., Phi Beta Kappa, Sigma Alpha Epsilon. Episcopalian. Club: Harvard. Home: 108 E 82d St New York NY 10028 Office: Boylan & Evans 30 Rockefeller Plaza New York NY 10112

BOYLE, BARBARA DORMAN, motion picture company executive; b. N.Y.C., Aug. 11, 1935; d. William and Edith (Kleiman) Dorman; m. Kevin Boyle, Nov. 26, 1960; children: David Eric, Paul Coleman. B.A., U. Calif., Berkeley, 1957; J.D., UCLA, 1960. Bar: Calif. 1961, N.Y. 1964, U.S. Supreme Ct. bar 1964. Atty. bus. affairs dept, corp. asst. sec. Am. Internat. Pictures, Los Angeles, 1960-65; partner firm Cohen & Boyle, Los Angeles, 1967-74; exec. v.p., gen. counsel, chief operating officer New World Pictures, Los Angeles, 1974-82; sr. v.p. prodn. Orion Pictures Corp., Los Angeles, 1982—; co-chmn. entertainment law symposium adv. com. UCLA Law Sch., 1979-80. Author articles in field. Mem. Acad. Motion Picture Arts and Scis., Women in Film (pres. 1977-78), Women Entertainment Lawyers Assn., Calif. Bar Assn., N.Y. State Bar Assn. Office: 11600 San Vicente St Los Angeles CA 90049

BOYLE, BRUCE JAMES, publisher; b. Mpls., Aug. 31, 1931; s. Lorille James and Norma Elizabeth (Blish) B.; m. Betty Jean Tucker, May 28, 1960; children: Katherine Ann, Julia Caroline, Amy Elizabeth. B.J., U. Mo., 1958. Copywriter Sta. KFRU, Columbia, Mo., 1958; continuity dir. KOMO-TV, Columbia, 1959; advt. salesman Better Homes & Gardens mag., 1960; advt. dir. Successful Farming mag., Des Moines, 1969-73, pub., 1973—, Meredith Pub. Services, 1976—, Meredith Video Pub., 1981—. Served with U.S. Navy, 1951-54. Mem. Nat. Agri-Mktg. Assn. (pres. 1973-74), Farm and Indsl. Equipment Inst., Farm Equipment Mfrs. Assn. (chmn. bd. govs. 1971-72), Agr. Pubs. Assn. (dir. 1979-81), Alpha Delta Sigma. Clubs: Des Moines, Des Moines Golf and Country. Home: 718 55th St Des Moines IA 50312 Office: Meredith Corp 1716 Locust St Des Moines IA 50336

BOYLE, DANIEL EDWARD, JR., real estate and oil investor; b. Pueblo, Colo., Feb. 11, 1931; s. Daniel Edward and Claire M. B.; m. Patricia Ann Bellamah, Jan. 9, 1954; children: Daniel Edward, III, Patricia Elaine Boyle Wilken, Cynthia Kay. B.A. in English, N.Mex. Mil. Inst., Roswell, 1953. With Dale J. Bellamah Corp., Albuquerque, 1956-73, pres., 1970-73, chmn. bd., 1972-73; pres., chmn. bd. Dale Bellamah Corp., 1973-78, Bellamah Corp., 1973-80; chmn. bd. D.B. Holding Co., 1978-81, Bellamah Group, Inc., 1980-81; pvt. investor, 1981—; dir. First Interstate Bank Albuquerque, S.W. Distbg. Co., Oilsearch Corp. Mem. bus. sch. adv. council N.Mex. State U., Las Cruces; chmn. N.Mex. Gov.'s Com. on Goals for Future, 1982; Bd. dirs. Southwest Community Health Services, Albuquerque. Served as officer AUS, 1953-56. Methodist. Clubs: Four Hills Country, Tanoan Country. Home: 1425 Stagecoach Rd SE Albuquerque NM 87123 Office: 6121 Indian School Rd NE Suite 141 Albuquerque NM 87110

BOYLE, FRANCIS J., judge; b. 1927. Grad., Providence Coll.; LL.B., Boston Coll. Bar: bar 1952. Judge U.S. Dist. Ct. for R.I., Providence, 1977—, now chief justice. Mem. Am. Bar Assn. Office: US District Ct US Courthouse Providence RI 02903 *

BOYLE, HARRY JOSEPH, consultant, former Canadian government official; b. St. Augustine, Ont., Can., Oct. 7, 1915; s. William A. and Madeleine (Leddy) B.; m. Marion McCaffery, Jan. 4, 1937; children: Patricia Ann, Michael Harry. Grad., St. Jerome's Coll., Kitchener, Ont.; Litt.D. (hon.), Trent U., 1974, Lady Eaton Coll., Trent U. Freelance writer for London Free Press and Toronto Globe and Mail; Sta. CKNX, Wingham, 1931-41; with Stratford (Ont.) Beacon-Herald, 1941-42; commentator CBC, 1942-68; later supr., radio and TV program dir., exec. TV producer; columnist Toronto Telegram, 1957-68; vice chmn. Canadian Radio-TV Commn., Ottawa, 1968-75, acting chmn., 1975-76, chmn., 1976—; faculty mem. Banff Sch. Fine Arts; vis. fellow Inst. Canadian Studies, Carleton U.; cons. editor on lang. and communications Aldus Books, Ltd., London; asso. Exec. Cons., Ottawa. Author: Mostly in Clover, 1961, Homebrew and Patches, 1963, A Summer Burning, 1964, With a Pinch of Sin, 1966, The Great Canadian Novel, 1972, Memories of a Catholic Boyhood, The Luck of the Irish, 1975, Straws in the Wind, 1969; numerous radio and TV stage plays. Bd. dirs. Donwood Inst., Vanier Inst. Recipient John Drainie award for contbn. to broadcasting, 1970, Stephen Leacock medal for humour, 1964, 76, Cybil award for upholding and promoting pub. interest in broadcasting, 1974, Jack Chisholm award Can. Film-TV Dirs. Assn., 1980, E.S./Velma Rogers award for contbn. to broadcasting, 1983; named to Can. Newspaper Hall of Fame, 1980. Mem. Assn. Canadian TV and Radio Artists, Writers Union of Can. Roman Catholic. Club: Arts and Letters (Toronto). Home: 12 Georgian Ct Toronto ON M4P 2J8 Canada

BOYLE, J. ALLAN, banker; b. Orillia, Ont., Can., May 10, 1916. Student, Orillia Collegiate Inst.; grad. mgmt. tng. course, U. Western Ont. With Toronto Dominion Bank, 1934—, gen. mgr. adminstrn., then dep. chief gen. mgr., 1968-72, exec. v.p., chief gen. mgr., 1972—, pres., 1978-81; dir. Excelsior Life Ins. Co., Westinghouse Can. Inc., Costain Ltd., Jannock Ltd., Echo Bay Mines Ltd., Aetna Casualty Co., Can., Toronto Dominion Bank. Mem. adv. com. Sch. Bus. Adminstrn. U. Western Ont.; bd. govs. York U.; mem. Toronto Redevel. Adv. Council. Served with RCAF, 1940-45. Mem. Canadian Bankers Assn. (past pres.). Clubs: Canadian (past pres. Toronto, N.Y.C.), Toronto, Granite, York, Thornhill Country; Sara Bay Country (Sarasota, Fla.). Address: Toronto Dominion Bank PO Box 1 Toronto Dominion Centre Toronto ON M5K 1A2 Canada

BOYLE, KAY, writer; b. St. Paul, Feb. 19, 1902; d. Howard Peterson and Katherine (Evans) B.; m. Richard Brault, June 24, 1923 (div.); m. Laurence Vail, Apr. 2, 1931 (div.); children—Sharon Walsh, Apple-Joan, Kathe, Clover, Faith Carson, Ian Savin; m. Baron Joseph von Franckenstein (dec. 1963). Student, Ohio Mechanics Inst., 1917-19; Litt.D. (hon.), Columbia, 1971, L.H.D., Skidmore Coll., 1977. Mem. faculty San Francisco State U. Author: poems A Glad Day, 1930, Wedding Day; short stories, 1930, Plagued by the Nightingale; novel, 1931, Year Before Last, 1932, Gentlemen, I Address You Privately, 1933, My Next Bride, 1934, Death of a Man, 1936, The White Horses of Vienna; short stores, 1937, Monday Night; novel, 1938, The Crazy Hunter; short novels, 1940, Primer for Combat, 1942, Avalanche, 1943, American Citizen; poems, 1944, A Frenchman Must Die, 1945, Thirty Stories, 1946; 1939, novel, 1947, His Human Majesty, 1949, The Smoking Mountain, 1951, The Seagull on the Step, 1955, Three Short Novels, 1958, The Youngest Camel, 1959, Generation without Farewell, 1960, Collected Poems, 1962, Breaking the Silence, 1962, Nothing Ever Breaks Except the Heart, 1966, Pinky, the Cat, 1967, The Autobiography of Emanuel Carnevali, 1967, Being Geniuses Together, 1968, Pinky in Persia, 1968, Testament For My Students; poems, 1970, The Long Walk at San Francisco State; essays, 1970, The Underground Woman; novel, 1975, Fifty Stories, 1980; Contbr. short stories to mags. Recipient O. Henry Meml. prize, 1936, 1941; San Francisco Art Commn. award, 1978; Guggenheim fellow, 1934, 61; Nat. Endowment for Arts sr. citizen grantee, 1980. Mem. Am. Acad. Arts and Letters.

BOYLE, MICHAEL JOHN, retail company executive; b. Meridan, Conn., May 16, 1944; s. John Joseph and Grace Irene (Raycraft) B.; m. Nina Christine Ramella, Sept. 24, 1976. Student, Monmouth Coll., 1962-63. Pres. Chess King-Mellville Corp. (N.Y.C.), 1974-76; exec. v.p. Fed. Dept. Store, Bklyn., 1976-79; pres. F&R Lazarus Co., Columbus, Ohio, 1979-80, chmn., chief exec. officer, 1980-82; pres., chief exec. officer Petrie Stores, Secaucus, N.J., 1982-83; exec. v.p. Gen. Mills, N.Y.C., 1983—; dir. Huntington Nat. Bank, Columbus. Bd. dirs. Columbus Mus. Art, 1979-82, Restoration Com. to Restore Ohio Theatre, Columbus, 1979-82. Mem. Inst. Retail Mgmt. NYU (mem. nat. adv. council 1983—), Am. Retail Fedn. (dir. 1983—), Columbus C. of C. (dir. 1979-82). Club: N.Y. Athletic (N.Y.C.). Office: Gen Mills Inc 909 3d Ave New York NY 10022

BOYLE, PATRICIA JEAN, judge. Student, U. Mich., 1955-57; B.A., Wayne State U., 1963, J.D., 1963. Bar: Mich. Practice law with Kenneth Davies, Detroit, 1963; law clk. to U.S. Dist. judge, 1963-64; asst. U.S. atty., Detroit, 1964-68; asst. pros. atty. Wayne County, dir. research, tng. and appeals, Detroit, 1969-74; Recorders Ct. judge City of Detroit, 1976-78; U.S. dist. judge Eastern Dist. Mich., Detroit, 1978-83; justice Mich. Supreme Ct., Detroit, 1983—. Active Women's Rape Crisis Task Force, Vols. of Am. Named Feminist of Year Detroit chpt. NOW, 1978; recipient Outstanding Achievement award Pros. Attys. Assn. Mich., 1978; Spirit of Detroit award Detroit City Council, 1978. Mem. Women Lawyers Assn. Mich., Fed. Bar Assn., Mich. Bar Assn., Detroit Bar Assn., Wayne State U. Law Alumni Assn. (Disting. Alumni award 1979). Office: Mich Supreme Ct 1425 Lafayette Bldg Detroit MI 48226

BOYLE, PETER, actor; b. Phila., 1933; m. Loraine Alterman, Oct. 1977. Ed., LaSalle Coll. Monk in Christian Bros. order, until early 1960's. Actor in Off-Broadway shows, N.Y.C., also Second City group, Chgo., and, TV commls.; appeared in: motion pictures including Joe, 1970, T.R. Baskin, The Candidate, 1972, Steelyard Blues, 1973, Slither, 1973, The Friends of Eddie Coyle, 1973, Kid Blue, 1973, Crazy Joe, 1974, Young Frankenstein, 1974, Taxi Driver, 1976, Swashbuckler, 1976, F.I.S.T, 1978, The Brink's Job, 1978, Hardcore, 1979, In God We Trust, 1980, Where the Buffalo Roam, 1980, Hammett, 1980, Outland, 1981, Yellowbeard, 1983; TV movies Tail Gunner Joe, 1977, From Here to Eternity *

BOYLE, RICHARD GUY, electronics company executive, financial executive; b. Preston, Conn., June 10, 1938; s. Charles and Ruth (Porter) B.; m. Muriel F. Maslak, Oct. 4, 1961; children: Kerry Jeanne, Kimberly Ann, Kyle Guy. B.B.A., Western New Eng. Coll., Springfield, Mass., 1965, M.B.A., 1968; A.M.P., Harvard U., 1982. Fin. planning mgr. Hamilton Standard div. UTC, Windsor Locks, Conn., 1961-70; controller Dunham-Bush subs. Signal Corp., West Hartford, Conn., 1970-76; fin. v.p. Brand-Rex Co., Willimantic, Conn., 1976-79; sr. v.p. Brand-Rex. Co., Williamantic, Conn., 1979-82; exec. v.p. Brand-Rex Co., Willimantic, Conn., 1982—. Served with U.S. Army, 1957-60; Korea. Mem. Fin. Execs. Inst. Club: Harvard Bus. Sch. Home: 197 Stanley Dr Glastonbury CT 06033 Office: Brand-Rex Co 1600 W Main St Willimantic CT 06226

BOYLE, RICHARD JOHN, former museum director, author; b. N.Y.C., June 3, 1932; s. James and Gertrude (Eichhorn) B.; m. Patricia Murray, June 19, 1971; 1 son, Eric; stepchildren: Rick, Cheryl, Barbara. B.A., Adelphi U., Garden City, N.Y., 1954; certificate fine art, Oxford (Eng.) U., 1959; postgrad., Art Students League, N.Y.C., 1964. Profl. painter, 1959-66; curator Internat. Art Found., Newport, R.I., 1962; dir. Middletown (Ohio) Fine Arts Center, 1963-65; curator painting and sculpture Cin. Art Mus., 1965-73; former dir. Pa. Acad. Fine Arts; adviser Nexus Gallery, Artist Coop. Author: American Impressionism, 1974, John Twachtman; co-author: Genius of American Painting, 1973; Art editor: Ency. Am. History, vol. 1, 1973. Mem. exec. com. Phila. Devel. Corp.; trustee Center City Found. Served with U.S. Army, 1954-56. Benjamin Franklin fellow Royal Soc. Arts, 1976. Mem. Am. Assn. Mus., Nat. Trust Historic Preservation, Nat. Soc. Lit. and Art, Dunlop Soc. Club: Franklin Inn (Phila.).

BOYLE, ROBERT PATRICK, lawyer, retired government agency consultant; b. Kansas City, Mo., Nov. 21, 1913; s. Roscoe Virgil and Aletha (Pentecost) B.; m. Katherine Warren, Mar. 16, 1940; children: Elizabeth Ann, Carolyn Warren. B.A., Williams Coll., 1935; LL.B., Harvard U., 1938. Bar: Okla. 1938, D.C. 1940. With CAA, 1938-58, atty., asst. to gen. counsel, asst. gen. counsel, dep. gen. counsel, gen. counsel, 1953-58; sr. assoc. gen. counsel FAA, 1959-63; dep. asst. adminstr. Internat. Aviation Affairs, 1963-68, 70-72; cons. internat. aviation affairs Dept. Transp., 1972-76; Chmn. U.S. delegation legal com. Internat. Civil Aviation Orgn., 1957-60, 62, pres. legal commn., 1962, U.S. rep. council, 1968-69, chmn. tech. com. extraordinary assembly, Montreal, 1970, cons., 1976-80; legal adv. on revision air law Govt. of Saudi Arabia, 1977-80; chmn. U.S. delegation Diplomatic Conf. Pvt. Air Law, Guadalajara, Mexico, 1961, Tokyo, 1963, Guatamala, 1971. Contbr. articles to profl. publs. Chmn. legal div. Pres.'s Air Coordinating Com., 1953-60; chmn. working group on Warsaw Conv., Interagy. Group Internat. Aviation, 1971-75. Served from ensign to lt. USNR, 1943-46. Mem. ABA (chmn. aviation criminal law com. of sect. criminal law 1953-67, mem. standing com. on aero. law 1974-79), Okla. Bar Assn., D.C. Bar Assn., Williams Coll. Alumni Assn. (pres. Washington Chpt. 1960-61), Theta Delta Chi. Clubs: Nat. Aviation, Dacor (Washington); Kenwood Golf and Country. (vice chmn. bd. govs. 1983). Home: 3929 N 36th St Arlington VA 22207

BOYLE, ROBERT WILLIAM, geochemist; b. Chatham Twp., Kent County, Ont., Can., June 3, 1920; s. Robert and Jane (Murray) B.; m. Marguerite Lois Brown, Nov. 3, 1945; children: Heather Ann Boyle Robinson, Daniel Robert. B.A.Sc., U. Toronto, 1949, M.A.Sc., 1950, Ph.D. in Geochemistry, 1952. Geochemist Geol. Survey Can., 1952—, sr. research scientist-geochemist, 1974—; Disting. lectr. Can. Inst. Mining and Metallurgy, 1980-81. Contbr. articles to profl. jours. Served with Can. Army, 1939-45. Recipient Barlow medal Can. Inst. Mining and Metallurgy, 1967, 82; Willet G. Miller medal Royal Soc. Can., 1971; Public Service of Can. merit award, 1971. Fellow Royal Soc. Can., Royal Can. Geog. Soc.; mem. Assn. Expln. Geochemists (pres. 1975-76), Internat. Assn. Genesis of Ore Deposits (v.p.), Geochem. Soc., Soc. Econ. Geologists, Can. Inst. Mining and Metallurgy, Geol. Assn. Can. Anglican. Home: 2024 Neepawa Ave Ottawa ON Canada K2A 3L6 Office: 601 Booth St Ottawa ON Canada K1A 0E8

BOYLE, ROBERT WILLIAM, physician; b. St. Paul, Feb. 11, 1908; s. William Henry and Gertrude May (Ritsch) B.; m. Daphne Jennette Connell, Nov. 26, 1931; children—William Charles, Jeanne Marguerite Boyle Hanks and Georgianna Phyllis Boyle Gunaji (twins). Student, Hamline U., 1924-26; B.P.E., YMCA Coll., Chgo., 1929, M.P.E., 1937; Ph.B., U. Chgo., 1930; M.A., Coll. City Detroit, 1933; Ph.D., U. Minn., 1936; M.D., U. Ark., 1940; Baruch fellow, Mayo Clinic, 1946-47. Diplomate Am. Bd. Phys. Medicine and Rehab. Phys. dir. Eau Claire (Wis.) YMCA, 1930-31; instr. physiology, coach freshman football Coll. City Detroit, 1931-32; teaching fellow physiology U. Minn. Sch. Medicine, 1933-36; asst. prof., later prof., head dept. physiology and pharmacology U. Ark. Sch. Medicine, 1936-44; chief phys. medicine and rehab., later chief profl. services VA Hosp., Ft. Thomas, Ky., 1947-54; prof. phys. medicine and rehab. Med. Coll. Wis., Milw., 1954-78, prof. emeritus, 1978—, chmn. dept. phys. medicine and rehab., 1965-73; dir. dept. phys. medicine and rehab. Milw. County Hosp., 1954-78; chmn. rehab. div. Commn. State Dept. (Wis. Med. Soc.), 1956-59; exec. com. health services (United Community Service), Milw., 1958-60, 62-69; dept. Christian social action Episcopal Diocese Milw., 1960-74; cons. VA Center, Wood, Wis., 1954-78; staff physician Cardiopulmonary Rehab. Center, 1978—; participant Internat. Congress Phys. Medicine and Rehab., Washington, 1960, Paris, 1964, Montreal, Que., Can., 1968, Barcelona, Spain, 1972, Rio de Janeiro, Brazil, 1976, Stockholm, 1980. Contbr. articles to profl. jours., chpt. in book. Served as capt., M.C. AUS, 1944-46. Fellow ACP, Am. Coll. Chest Physicians; mem. Am. Acad. Phys. Medicine and Rehab. (bd. govs. pres. 1961-62, sec. 1967-82), Am. Congress Rehab. Medicine, Assn. Acad. Physiatrists, AAUP, AAAS, AMA (sect. council phys. medicine and rehab. 1976-78, alt. mem. interspltу. adv. bd. 1968-76, 77-80), Pan Am. Med. Assn., Internat. Soc. Rehab. Disabled, Nat. Rehab. Assn., Am. Heart Assn., Am. Rheumatism Assn., Am. Geriatrics Soc., Royal Soc. Health, Wis. Soc. Phys. Medicine and Rehab., Sigma Xi, Phi Beta Pi, Alpha Omicron Alpha. Episcopalian. Home: 8705 Glencoe Circle Wauwatosa WI 53226 Office: 5000 W National St Wood WI 53193

BOYLE, WILLARD STERLING, physicist; b. Amherst, N.S., Can., Aug. 19, 1924; naturalized, 1969; s. Ernest Sterling and Bernice Teresa (Dewar) B.; m. Elizabeth Joyce, June 15, 1946; children—Robert, Cynthia, David, Pamela. B.Sc., McGill U., Montreal, Que., Can., 1947, M.Sc., 1948, Ph.D., 1950. Asst. prof. Royal Mil. Coll., Kingston, Ont., 1951-53; mem. staff Bell Labs., 1953-62, 64-79, exec. dir. semiconductor device devel. div., Allentown, Pa., 1968-75, exec. dir. communications scis. div., 1975-79; sr. partner Atlantic Research Assos., 1980—; dir. space sci. Bellcommunications, 1962-64. Author. Served with Canadian Navy, 1942-45. Recipient Ballantine medal Franklin Inst., Nat. Research Council Can. fellow, 1949. Fellow IEEE (Morris Liebman medal 1974), Am. Phys. Soc.; mem. Nat. Acad. Engring. Patentee in field; co-inventor charge coupled device and 1st continuously pumped ruby laser. Address: Wallace NS B0K 1Y0 Canada

BOYLE, WILLIAM LEO, JR., college president; b. Utica, N.Y., July 23, 1933; s. William Leo and Gladys (Kuney) B. A.B., Colgate U., 1955; postgrad., Cornell U. Law Sch., 1960-61; M.A., Columbia U., 1964, Profl. Diploma in Ednl. Adminstrn., 1967, Ed.D., 1969; LL.D. (hon.), Hawthorne Coll., 1979; postdoctoral, Harvard U., 1979-81; L.H.D. (hon.), Mercy Coll., 1983—. Participant advanced mgmt. program, ednl. adviser Procter & Gamble Co., Cin., 1958-60; legis. aide N.Y. State Senate, Albany, 1961-62; account exec., ednl. cons. Batten, Barton, Durstine & Osborn, N.Y.C., 1962-64; asst. dir. devel., presdl. asst. Wesleyan U., Middletown, Conn., 1964-65; program cons. Council for Fin. Aid to Edn., N.Y.C., 1965-70, asst. v.p., 1970-72, v.p., 1972-75; pres. Keuka Coll., Keuka Park, N.Y., 1975-78, Curry Coll., Milton, Mass., 1978—; also trustee, lectr. polit. sci. ednl. cons. to Pres. Ford Com., Washington, 1976; mem. corp. bd. Hyde Park Savs. Bank, Boston, 1981—. Author: The National Corporate Educational Support Movement, 1954-1966, 1969; Contbr. articles to ednl. and profl. jours. Vice-chmn. nat. bus. and industry com. Colgate U., Hamilton, N.Y., 1974—, mem. nat. council, 1975—, ann. fund exec. com., 1975—; bd. overseers Children's Hosp. Med. Center, Boston, 1979—, Council Colls. and Univs., John F. Kennedy Library, Boston, 1979—; bd. dirs. Pres.'s Steering Com., 1980—; mem. Edn. Commn. of States, 1982—. Served to 1st lt. USAF, 1955-58. Decorated Comdr.'s Citation. Mem. various ednl. and profl. orgns. including Milton (Mass.) Hist. Soc., Assn. Ind. Colls. and Univs. in Mass. (dir. 1978—). Clubs: Eire Soc., Gridiron (Boston); Harvard U. Educator's Round Table (Cambridge, Mass.); Columbia U. (N.Y.C.). Home: 956 Brush Hill Rd Milton MA 02186 Office: Curry Coll Milton MA 02186

BOYLES, HARLAN EDWARD, state official; b. Lincoln County, N.C., May 6, 1929; s. Curtis E. and Kate S. B.; m. Frankie Wilder, May 17, 1952; children—Mrs. G.E. Ferrell, Lynn Boyles Butler, Harlan Edward. Student, U. Ga., 1947-48; B.B.A. in Acctg, U. N.C., 1951. C.P.A., N.C. Corp. tax auditor N.C. Dept. Revenue, 1951-56; exec. sec. N.C. Tax Rev. Bd., 1956-76; treas. State of N.C., 1977—; mem. Council of State; mem. mcpl. securities rulemaking bd. SEC, 1975-77. Mem. adv. com. Raleigh Salvation Army; chmn. Local Govt. Commn., dep. treas. and sec., 1960-76; chmn. State Banking Commn., Tax Rev. Bd.; mem. State Bd. Edn., State Bd. Community Colls., N.C. Capital Bldg Authority, Capital Planning Commn., others. Mem. N.C. Assn. C.P.A.s, Nat. Assn. State Auditors, Comptrollers and Treasurers (pres., exec. dir.), Raleigh C. of C. (dir.), N.C. State Employees Assn. Democrat. Presbyterian (deacon, elder, treas., clk.). Clubs: N.C. Young Dems., Rotary (pres.), Execs. of Raleigh (dir.). Home: 1924 Fairfield Dr Raleigh NC 27608 Office: 325 N Salisbury St Albemarle Bldg Raleigh NC 27611

BOYLES, JAMES KENNETH, banking executive; b. Louisville, Jan. 27, 1916; s. Forrest Lee and Florence (Glenn) B.; m. Hilda Margaret Rose, Sept. 13, 1940; children: Margaret, James Douglas, Kevin. Student, Columbia U., Am. Inst. Banking, Rutgers U. Guaranty trust officer Guarnaty Trust Co., N.Y.C., 1933-37; loan officer Chem. Bank, N.Y.C., 1937-50; exec. v.p. The Nat. State Bank, Elizabeth, N.J., 1950—; dir. The Nat. State Bank, Elizabeth, Worldwide Energy Corp., Denver, Supermarkets Gen. Co., Woodbridge, N.J., Heldor Industries, Inc., Morristown, N.J. Trustee Union Coll., Cranford N.J., 1965—. Served to 1st lt. U.S. Army Infantry, 1942-46; ETO. Mem. Robert Morris Assocs. (pres. 1963). Republican. Episcopalian. Clubs: Echo Lake Country (Westfield, N.J.); Wyantenuck Country (Great Barrington, Mass.). Office: The Nat State Bank 68 Broad St Elizabeth NJ 07207

BOYLL, DAVID LLOYD, broadcasting company executive; b. Terre Haute, Ind., Aug. 17, 1940; s. Lloyd A. and Stella Elizabeth B.; m. Margie R. Coker, Apr. 14, 1962; children: Elizabeth Marie, Kelli Renae. B.S.E., Abilene Christian U., 1964. Announcer Sta. KWKC, Abilene, Tex., 1959-68, program dir., 1964-68; sta. mgr. Sta. KFMN, Abilene, 1968-74, owner, 1974-80, partner, gen. mgr., 1981—. Pres. Abilene Downtown Assn., 1980-81, 82-83; chmn. adv. com. Taylor County Juvenile Bd. Mem. Nat. Assn. Broadcasters. Clubs: Rotary (past pres., dir.), Abilene Advt., Abilene Country. Home: 3949 N 9th St Abilene TX 79603 Office: 542 Butternut Abilene TX 79602

BOYNE, WALTER JAMES, national museum director, author, consultant, pilot; b. East St. Louis, Ill., Feb. 2, 1929; s. Walter William and Emily (Campbell) B.; m. Jeanne Quigley, Dec. 26, 1952; children: Mary Louise, Katherine Elizabeth, William James, Margaret Ann. B.B.A., U. Calif., Berkeley, 1958; M.B.A., U. Pitts., 1963. Commd. 2d lt. USAF, 1952, advanced through grades to col., retired, 1974; asst. curator Nat. Air and Space Mus., Washington, 1974-75, curator, 1975-78, exec. officer, 1978-80, asst. dir., 1980-82, dep. dir., 1982-83, dir., 1983—. Author: Boeing B-52, 1981, Messerschmitt Me-262, 1980, Treasures of Silver Hill, 1982, Flying, 1979, Jet Age, 1979, De Havilland DH-4, 1983, McDonnell Douglas F-4, 1983, Vertical Flight, 1983; contbg. author numerous articles. Recipient Best Fgn. Book award Aero Club de France, 1982, Robert A. Brooks award Smithsonian Instn., 1980. Mem. Nat. Press Club, Daedalians, Am. Aviation Hist. Soc. (nat. advisor), Sons of the Desert. Home: 9134 Continental Dr Alexandria VA 22309 Office: National Air and Space Museum Smithsonian Institution 6th and Independence Ave Washington DC 20560

BOYNTON, ROBERT MERRILL, psychology educator; b. Evanston, Ill., Oct. 28, 1924; s. Merrill Holmes and Eleanor (Matthews) B.; m. Alice Neiley, Apr. 9, 1947; children: Sherry, Michael, Neiley, Geoffrey. Student, Antioch Coll., 1942-43, U. Ill., 1943-45; A.B., Amherst Coll., 1948; Ph.D., Brown U., 1952. Asst. prof. psychology and optics U. Rochester, N.Y., 1952-57, asso. prof., 1957-61, prof., 1961-74, dir. Center for Visual Sci., 1963-71, chmn. dept. psychology, 1971-74; prof. psychology U. Calif., San Diego, 1974—; guest researcher Nat. Phys. Lab., Teddington, Eng., 1960-61; vis. prof. physiology U. Calif. Med. Center, San Francisco, 1969-70. Author: Human Color Vision, 1979; Contbr. articles to profl. jours. Served with USNR, 1943-45. Fellow A.A.A.S., Optical Soc. Am. (dir. at large 1966-69), Am. Psychol. Assn., Nat. Acad. Scis. Home: 376 Bellaire St Del Mar CA 92014

BOYNTON, SANDRA KEITH, illustrator, cartoonist, stationery products executive; b. Orange, N.J., Apr. 3, 1953; d. Robert Whitney and Jeanne Carolyn (Ragsdale) B.; m. James Patrick McEwan, Oct. 28, 1978; 1 dau., Caitlin Boynton McEwan. B.A. in English, Yale U., 1974, postgrad. Sch. Drama, 1976-77; postgrad., U. Calif.-Berkeley Drama Grad. Sch., 1974-75. Designer Recycled Paper Products, Inc., Chgo., 1974—, v.p., 1980—; illustrator greeting cards, 1975—. Cartoonist: Hippos Go Berserk, 1977, If At First, 1979, Gopher Baroque, 1979, The Compleat Turkey, 1980, Chocolate: The Consuming Passion, 1982, Moo, Baa, La La La, 1982, The Going to Bed Book, 1982, But Not the Hippopotamus, 1982, Opposites, 1982, A is for Angry, 1983. Quaker.

BOYSE, EDWARD ARTHUR, research physician; b. London, Aug. 11, 1923; s. Arthur and Dorothy Vera (Mellersh) B.; m. Jeanette Grimwood, May 24, 1951; children—Adrienne, Conrad Stonor, Dominic. M.B., B.S., U. London, 1952, M.D., 1957. Research fellow Guy's Hosp., London, 1957-60; research fellow N.Y. U. Sch. Medicine, 1960-61, adj. prof. dept. pathology, 1971—; mem. Sloan-Kettering Cancer Inst., N.Y.C., 1961—; prof. biology Cornell U. Grad. Sch. Med. Scis., 1969—. Served with Brit. Royal Air Force, 1940-45. Recipient Isaac Adler award Rockefeller and Harvard Univs., 1976; award in tumor immunology Cancer Research Inst., 1975. Fellow Royal Soc.; mem. Nat. Acad. Scis., Am. Acad. Arts and Scis. Home: 345 E 68th St New York NY 10021 Office: 1275 York Ave New York NY 10021

BOYSEN, HARRY, obstetrician, gynecologist; b. Harlan, Iowa, Aug. 21, 1904; s. Hans and Dorothea (Brodersen) B.; m. Patricia Dougherty, May 4, 1940; children—Gerald, Patricia Anne (Mrs. Thomas P. Lennon). B.S., U. Iowa, 1924, M.D., 1928. Diplomate: Am. Bd. Obstetrics and Gynecology. Intern Highland Hosp., Oakland, Calif., 1928-29; resident obstetrics and gynecology Presbyn. Hosp., Chgo., 1930-32, now mem. staff; pvt. practice, 1945—; former clin. prof. obstetrics, gynecology Rush Med. Coll.-Presbyn.-St. Luke's Med. Center; now emeritus; chmn. div. obstetrics and gynecology Presbyn.-St. Luke's Hosp. Served from lt. comdr. to comdr., M.C. USNR, 1942-45. Fellow A.C.S.; mem. A.M.A., Chgo. Gynecol. Soc. (pres. 1963-64), Am. Coll. Obstetrics and Gynecology, Phi Kappa Psi, Nu Sigma Nu. Clubs: Obstetrics and Gynecology Travel, Chicago Golf (Wheaton, Ill.); LaQuinta (Calif.); Country. Home: PO Box 495 La Quinta CA 92253 also 237 E Delaware Pl Chicago IL 60611

BOZEMAN, ADDA BRUEMMER, scholar on international relations, educator, consultant, author; b. Geistershof, Latvia, Dec. 17, 1908; came to U.S., 1936, naturalized, 1941; d. Leon and Anna (von Kahlen) von Bruemmer; m. Virgil Bozeman, Mar. 26, 1937 (div. 1947); 1 dau., Anya Bozeman Taylor; m. Arne Barkhuus, Feb. 8, 1951. Diplomee, Sect. Diplomatique Ecole Libre des Scis. Politiques, Paris, 1934; barrister at law, Middle Temple Inn of Ct., London, 1936; J.D., So. Meth. U., 1937; postgrad., Stanford U., Hoover Inst. With law offices Charles H. Huberich, Berlin, Paris, The Hague and London, 1933-36; assoc. prof. history Augustana Coll., 1943-47; prof. internat. history Sarah Lawrence Coll., Bronxville, N.Y., 1947-77, prof. emeritus, 1977—; vis. prof. Northwestern U., 1945, NYU, 1948, 49; Benedict disting. vis. prof. Carleton Coll., Minn., 1978; Leon lectr. U. Pa., 1978; mem. grad. faculty New Sch. Social Research, 1954, 55, 63; dir. postdoctoral seminars on diplomacy internat. history NEH, 1975, 76, 78, dir. postdoctoral seminars on internat. relations in multicultural world, 1981, 82; curricular cons. in intercultural relations Marlboro Coll., Vt., 1982—; curriculum cons. for postdoctoral seminars in intelligence Consortium for Study of Intelligence, 1978—; also mem. bd. founding dirs. Corsortium for Study of Intelligence; cons. USIA, 1982, 83; mem. faculty seminar study peace Columbia U., 1953—; mem. Inter-Univ. Seminar on Armed Forces and Soc., U.S. Global Strategy Council, Congl. Study on Am.'s Role in Multicultural Internat. Soc.; mem. nat. adv. council on fgn. policy East-West com. Nat. Republican Com., mem. human rights and Africa coms. Author: Regional Conflicts around Geneva, 1948, Politics and Culture in International History, 1960, The Future of Law in a Multicultural World, 1971, Conflict in Africa: Concepts and Realities, 1976, How To Think about Human Rights, 1978; monograph The Roots of American Commitment to the Rights of Man, 1980, The Revelance of Hugo Gratius and De Jure Bell ac Pacis for Our Times, 1980, Foreign Policy and Covert Action, 1981, Human Rights and National Security, 1983, The Future of International Law in the Multicultural World, 1983; mem. editorial bd.: Asian Affairs, Orbis; contbr. articles, revs., essays, book revs. to profl. jours. and encys., chpts. to books. Bd. dirs. Am.-Asian Edn. Exchange, Chinese Culture Ctr.; bd. dirs., mem. exec. council Com. on Present Danger. Research grantee Carnegie Endowment Internat. Peace, 1952, Rockefeller Found., 1960. Mem. Am. Soc. Internat. Law, Am. Polit. Sci. Assn., Internat. Sociol. Assn., Internat. Studies Assn., Internat. Law Assn., Internat. Soc. Comparative Study of Civilizations (dir., exec. council). Home: 24 Beall Circle Bronxville NY 10708

BOZICH, ANTHONY THOMAS, motor freight co. exec.; b. Republic, Pa., July 31, 1924; s. Anthony Thomas and Johanna (Sternal) B.; m. Gloria Fallentine, Apr. 9, 1944; children—Anthony Thomas, III, Craig A., Carol K., Gail F., Greta O., Eric D. Student, Duquesne U., 1942-43; A.M.P., Harvard U., 1972; postgrad., U. Calif. at Berkeley Extension Div., 1954-58. Div. mgr. Pacific Intermountain Express Co., Denver, 1946-65; exec. v.p. ops. IML Freight, Inc., Salt Lake City, 1965-74, pres., 1974-77; pres., prin. Clark Tanklines Co., Salt Lake City. Served with USAAF, 1943-45. Decorated Purple Heart. Mem. Am. Trucking Assn. (v.p., gov., exec. com., mem. found., chmn. taxation and reciprocity com.), Western Hwy. Inst. (intermountain v.p., mem. exec. com.), Nat. Alliance of Businessmen (metro chmn.). Republican. Mormon. Clubs: Bonneville Exchange, Salt Lake Country, Alta. Home: 3608 Brighton Point Dr Salt Lake City UT 84121 Office: 1450 N Beck St Salt Lake UT 84110

BOZONE, BILLIE RAE, librarian; b. Norphlet, Ark., Oct. 7, 1935; d. Guy Samuel and Vera (Jones) B. B.S. in Library Sci, Miss. State Coll. for Women, 1957; M.A., George Peabody Coll. for Tchrs., 1958. Asst. ref. librarian Miss. State U., State College, 1958-61, serials librarian, 1961-63; asst. ref. librarian U. Ill. at Urbana, 1963-65; asst. librarian New Eng. Mut. Life Ins. Co., Boston, 1965-67; sr. ref. librarian U. Mass., Amherst, 1967-68; head circulation dept. Smith Coll., Northampton, Mass., 1968-69, asst. librarian, 1969-71, coll. librarian, 1971—; Bd. dirs. Hampshire Inter-library Center, Amherst, 1971—; mem. exec. com. NELINET, 1977-79; chmn. Five Coll. Librarians Council, 1980-82. Mem. ALA, Assn. Coll. and Research Libraries, Alpha Beta Alpha, Alpha Psi Omega. Home: 30 Long Hill Rd Leverett MA 01054 Office: Smith Coll Library Northampton MA 01063

BOZZONE, R. P., steel company executive. Exec. v.p., gen. mgr. Allegheny Ludlum Steel Corp., Pitts. Office: Allegheny Ludlum Steel Corp Oliver Bldg Pittsburgh PA 15222§

BOZZUTO, MICHAEL ADAM, grocery company executive; b. Waterbury, Conn., Aug. 12, 1956; s. Adam John and Lillian (Brangel) B. B.B.A., Stetson U., 1978. Exec. v.p., treas. Bozzuto's, Inc., Cheshire, Conn., 1978—. Mem. Food Mktg. Inst., New Eng. Wholesale Distbrs. Assn., Nat. Am. Wholesale Grocers Assn., Lambda Chi. Roman Catholic. Office: Bozzutos Inc 275 Schoolhouse Rd Cheshire CT 06410

BRACE, FREDERICK FRANKLIN, JR., lawyer; b. Greenville, Mich., Jan. 24, 1934; s. Frederic F. and Mary (Ranney) B.; m. Janet Kahlenberg, Apr. 12, 1956; children: Frederic F., George, Anthony, Mary. B.A., U. Mich., 1959, J.D., 1959. Bar: Ill. 1959, U.S. Supreme Ct. 1970. Mem. Sidley & Austin, Chgo., 1959-81; ptnr. Brace & O'Donnell, Chgo., 1982—. Contbr. articles to profl. jours. Mem. adv. bd. Salvation Army, Chgo., 1960—; mem. adv bd. Booth Meml. Hosp., Chgo., 1968—. Mem. Chgo. Bar Assn., Order of Coif, Phi Eta Sigma. Clubs: Chgo. Athletic Assn., Law, Legal (Chgo.). Office: Brace & O'Donnell 332 S Michigan Ave Chicago IL 60604

BRACHTENBACH, ROBERT F., state justice; b. Sidney, Nebr., Jan. 28, 1931; s. Henry W. and Elizabeth A. (Morfeld) B.; m. Marilyn; children—Rick, Jeff, Randal, Curtis, David. B.S., U. Wash., 1953, LL.B., 1954. Bar: Wash. bar 1954. Instr. U. Calif. Sch. Law, Berkeley, 1954-55; practiced in, Selah, Wash., 1955-72; justice Wash. Supreme Ct., 1972-81, chief justice, 1981—. Contbr. articles to law revs. Mem. Selah Sch. Bd., 1960-72; mem. Wash. State Ho. of Reps., 1963-67; trustee Eastern Wash. State Coll. Office: Wash Supreme Ct Temple of Justice Olympia WA 98504 *

BRACK, O M, JR., English language educator; b. Houston, Nov. 30, 1938; s. O. M. and Olivia Mae (Rice) B.; m. Christine Yvonne Ferdinand, July 5, 1983. Student, U. Houston, 1956-57; B.A., Baylor U., 1960, M.A., 1961; Ph.D., U. Tex., Austin, 1965. Asst. prof. William Woods Coll., 1964-65; asst. prof. English lit. U. Iowa, Iowa City, 1965-68, assoc. prof., 1968-73, dir. center textual studies, 1967-73; prof. English lit. Ariz. State U., Tempe, 1973—; chmn. 18th Century Short Title Catalogue Com., 1970-73; pres. Arete Publs., Ltd., 1976-81; Albert H. Smith Meml. lectr. bibliography Birmingham (Eng.) Bibliog. Soc., 1983. Author: Bibliography and Textual Criticism, 1969, Samuel Johnson's Early Biographers, 1971, Hoole's Death of Johnson, 1972, Henry Fielding's Pasquin, 1973, A Catalogue of the Leigh Hunt Manuscripts, 1973, The Early Biographies of Samuel Johnson, 1974, American Humor, 1977, Shorter Prose Writings of Samuel Johnson, 1982; textual editor: Works of Tobias Smollett, 1966—; gen. editor: Works of Tolias Smollett, 1973—; editor: English Literature in Transition, 1981-82; mem. editorial com., 1982—; editor: Studies in Eighteenth Century Culture, 1981—; mem. editorial com.: Yale edit. Works of Samuel Johnson, 1977—; editorial cons.: The Literature of England, Scott, Foresman & Co., 1977-79; asst. editor: Eighteenth-Century Bibliography, 1964-73, Books at Iowa, 1966-73; mem. editorial com.: Rocky Mountain Rev. of Lang. and Lit., 1980—. Am. Philos. Soc. grantee, 1967; Phi Kappa Phi. disting. scholar, 1975; Huntington Library fellow, 1978; Am. Council Learned Socs. fellow, 1979-80; fellow Newberry Library, 1982; recipient Grad. Coll. Disting. Research award, 1981-82. Mem. Am. Soc. 18th Century Studies, South Central 18th Century Soc. (pres. 1982-83), MLA, Bibliog. Soc. Am., Bibliog. Soc. U. Va., Bibliog. Soc. (London), Printing Hist. Soc., Am. Printing History Assn. Roman Catholic. Club: The Johnsonians. Office: Dept English Ariz State U Tempe AZ 85281

BRACKEN, CHARLES HERBERT, banker; b. Corry, Pa., June 5, 1921; s. Olin Williams and Vellah (Morgan) B.; m. Barbara E. Barton, June 19, 1948; children: Betsy Louise, Sally Anne, Charles Herbert, Barton William, Douglas Morgan. B.S., U. Pa., 1948; student spl. banking courses. Successively asst. to pres., v.p., exec. v.p. and trust officer, pres., dir. Citizens Nat. Bank, Corry, 1948-64; pres., dir. Marine Bank, Erie, Pa., 1964-74, chmn. bd., chief exec. officer, dir., 1974—; chmn. bd. dirs. Personnel Cons. Services Inc.; dir. Public Communications, Inc., Dudleys, Inc., BD Corp., Meadow Brook Dairy Co., Country Fair Inc., Profl. Computer Assocs., Inc. Treas., dir. Erie Indsl. Devel. Corp., 1965; dir. Greater Erie Indsl. Devel. Corp., 1965—, Erie Conf. Community Devel.; Trustee Hamot Med. Center, 1970-79, corporator, 1980—, pres., 1977-78; sec.-treas., trustee Erie Community Found., 1970—; treas. Erie Episcopal Diocese, 1969—; bd. govs., treas. Erie unit Shriners Hosp. Crippled Children, 1967-79; corporator St. Vincent Health Center, 1965—; adv. bd. Titusville campus U. Pitts., 1967—, Mercyhurst Coll., 1968—, Gannon Coll., 1971—; mem. Econ. Research Inst. of Erie Adv. Bd. Pa. State U., Behrend. Served with USAAF, 1942-46; CBI. Mem. Pa. Bankers Assn. (pres. 1966-67, chmn. group boundary task force), Newcomen Soc. N.Am. (dir.), Sigma Alpha Epsilon. Episcopalian. Clubs: Mason, Shriner, Yacht, Rotary, Univ., Erie, Kahkwa (Erie). Home: 5060 Saybrook Pl Erie PA 16505 Office: 901 State St Erie PA 16512 also PO Box 8480 Erie PA 16553

BRACKEN, EDDIE (EDWARD VINCENT), actor, director, writer, singer, artist; b. N.Y.C., Feb. 7, 1920; s. Joseph L. and Catherine B.; m. Connie Nickerson, Sept. 25, 1939; children. Student, Profl. Children's Sch. for Actors, N.Y.C. Founder Trinity Sq. Co., Providence. Vaudeville, night club singer; stage debut in, Lottery, 1930; plays include Lady Refuses, Iron Men, So Proudly We Hail, Brother Rat, Too Many Girls, Seven Year Itch, What a Life, Shinbond Alley, Teahouse of the August Moon, You Know I Can't Hear You When the Water's Running, The Odd Couple, Never Too Late, Sunshine Boys, Hello Dolly!, 1978; motion picture debut in Life with Henry, 1940; others include Fleet's In, Sweater Girl, Young and Willing, Hail the Conquering Hero, Miracle of Morgan's Creek, Girl from Jones Beach, Two Tickets to Broadway, We're Not Married, About Face, Slight Case of Larceny, How to Make a Man, Women's Barracks, Happy Go Lucky, Star Spangled Rhythm, Summer Stock; actor TV Masquerade Party; other programs; syndicated columnist Crackin' with Bracken, 1963—. Office: care Fred Amsel & Assos 215 S La Cienega Suite 200 Beverly Hills CA 90211 *

BRACKEN, HARRY MCFARLAND, educator; b. Yonkers, N.Y., Mar. 12, 1926; s. Harry S. and Grace M. (McFarl) B.; m. Eva Maria Laufkotter, Dec. 24, 1949 (div.); children—Christopher, Timothy. B.A., Trinity Coll., Hartford, Conn., 1949; M.A., Johns Hopkins, 1954; Ph.D., U. Iowa, 1956. Instr. U. Iowa, Iowa City, 1955-57, asst. prof., 1957-61; asso. prof. U. Minn., Mpls., 1961-63; prof. Ariz. State U., Tempe, 1963-66; prof. philosophy McGill U., Montreal, Que., Can., 1966—; Prof. U. Calif. at San Diego, 1970; vis. prof. Trinity Coll., U. Dublin, Ireland, 1973-73, 79-80; vis. prof. metaphysics Univ. Coll., Nat. U. Ireland, Dublin, 1972-73, 79-80. Author: The Early Reception of Berkeley's Immaterialism: 1710-1733, 1959, 2d edit., 1965, Berkeley, 1974; Editorial cons.: Jour. of the History of Philosophy. Served with USNR, 1943-46; PTO. Recipient Acad. Freedom award Ariz. Civil Liberties Union, 1965; Edn. award J. I. Segal Found. for Jewish Culture, 1972. Mem. Am., Canadian, Irish philos. assns., Can., Am. socs. eighteenth century studies. Office: Dept Philosophy McGill U 1001 Sherbrooke St W Montreal PQ H3A 1G5 Canada

BRACKEN, PEG, author; b. Filer, Idaho, Feb. 25, 1918; d. John Lewis and Ruth (McQuesten) B.; m. Parker Edwards, Mar. 17, 1966; 1 dau., Johanna Kathleen. A.B., Antioch Coll., 1940. Author: The I Hate to Cook Book, 1960, The I Hate to Housekeep Book, 1962, I Try to Behave Myself, 1963, Peg Bracken's Appendix to The I Hate to Cook Book, 1966, I Didn't Come Here to Argue, 1969, But I Wouldn't Have Missed It for the World, 1973, The I Hate to Cook Almanack - A Book of Days, 1976, A Window Over the Sink, 1981. Mem. AFTRA, Screen Actors Guild, Authors Guild, PEN.

BRACKENRIDGE, JOHN BRUCE, physicist; b. Youngstown, Ohio, Apr. 20, 1927; s. John and Azile (Townsend) B.; m. Mary Ann Rossi, June 19, 1954; children—Lynn, Sandy, Rob, Scot. B.S., Muskingum Coll., 1951; Ph.D. in Physics, Brown U., 1959; M.S. in History of Sci, London U., 1974. Asst prof. physics Muskingum Coll., New Concord, Ohio, 1955-59; faculty Lawrence U., Appleton, Wis., 1959—, prof. physics, 1976—; chief reader Advance placement exam. physics Ednl. Testing Service, 1976-80. Contbr. articles to profl. jours.; author: Principles of Physics and Chemistry, 1970. Served with USNR, 1944-45. NEH fellow, 1980-81, 78; NSF grantee, 1968-69, 63-66; Research Corp. grantee, 1957-58, 58-60. Mem. Brit. Soc. History of Sci., History of Sci. Soc., AAUP, Am. Assn. Physics Tchrs., Acoustical Soc. Am. Home: 218 N Union St Appleton WI 54911 Office: Lawrence Univ Appleton WI 54911

BRACKETT, DOUGLAS LANE, trade assn. exec.; b. Lawndale, N.C., July 21, 1938; s. J.B. and Blanche Elizabeth (Lane) B.; m. Patricia Delores Peterson, May 26, 1962; children—Peter, Samuel, Hope. A.A., Brevard Jr. Coll., 1957; B.S., High Point Coll., 1961. Acct. Kavanagh-Smith & Co., Greensboro, N.C., 1961-65; auditor Mann Drug Co., High Point, N.C., 1965-66; dir. services So. Furniture Mfrs. Assn., High Point, 1966-71, sec., 1971-80, v.p., 1980—. Bd. dirs. YMCA, High Point, 1972-75. Served with U.S. Army, 1957-59. Named Man of Yr. YMCA, 1969, 74. Mem. Am. Soc. Assn. Execs. Methodist. Club: Y's Men's (pres. 1968-69, 73-74). Home: 1585 Squire Davis Rd Kernersville NC 27284 Office: PO Box 2436 High Point NC 27261

BRACY, MICHAEL BLAKESLEE, energy company executive.; b. St. Louis, Dec. 13, 1941; s. Webb B. and Jane (Blakeslee) B.; m. Ella Bingham Cox, June 13, 1970. B.S. in Engring. Physics, U.S. Naval Acad., 1963. With Chase Manhattan Bank, N.A., N.Y.C., 1969-77, v.p. public utilities div., 1973-77; with El Paso Co., Houston, 1977—, v.p.,

1979—, 1979, sr. v.p., 1979—, chief fin. officer, 1979—. Served as officer USN, 1963-69. Mem. Fin. Execs. Inst. Clubs: N.Y. Athletic; City Midday (N. Y. C.); Houstonian, University (Houston). Office: PO Box 1492 El Paso TX 79978

BRADBURN, DAVID DENISON, retired air force officer, engineer; b. Hollywood, Calif., May 27, 1925; s. Clarence Earl and Florence Lyle (Easton) B.; m. Bertha Evelyn Stout, Nov. 3, 1956; children: Carol (Mrs. Patrick V. Navagato), Susan (Mrs. John A. Fitzpatrick), David Stout, Robert Easton. B.S., U.S. Mil. Acad., 1946; M.S.E., Purdue U., 1952; M.S. in Internat. Affairs, George Washington U., 1966. Commd. 2d lt. U.S. Army, 1946; advanced through grades to maj. gen. USAF, 1974; pilot, flight comdr., Korea, 1950-51, research and devel. staff officer, Balt., 1952-57, mil. space research project officer, Los Angeles, 1957-65, space program mgr., 1966-71; dir. space systems Office Sec. Air Force, Washington, 1971-73, dir. spl. projects, Los Angeles, 1973-75, vice-comdr. Electronic Systems div., Boston, 1975-76; ret., 1976. Mem. U.S. del.; Joint Chiefs Staff rep. to U.S.-Soviet Anti-Satellite Negotiations, Helsinki, 1978, Bern, Vienna, 1979; Sr. staff scientist TRW Def. Systems Group, 1980—; Chmn. bd. Beach Cities Symphony Assn., 1978—. Decorated D.S.M. (2), Legion of Merit (3), D.F.C., Meritorious Service medal, Air medal (4). Mem. Sigma Xi, Tau Beta Pi, Eta Kappa Nu. Mem. United Ch. of Christ. Pioneer mil. applications space vehicles. Home: 421 2d St Manhattan Beach CA 90266

BRADBURN, NORMAN M., behavioral science educator; b. Lincoln, Ill., July 21, 1933; s. Hubert Benjamin and Mary Celeste (Marshall) B.; m. Wendy McAneny, Dec. 15, 1956; children: Isabel Stuart, Andrew Marshall, Laura Humphreys. B.A., U. Chgo., 1952, Oxford U., Eng., 1955; M.A., Harvard U., 1958; Ph.D. in Social Psychology, Harvard U., 1960. Asst. prof. behavioral sci. U. Chgo., 1960-65, asso. prof., 1965-67, prof., 1967—, chmn. dept. behavioral sci., 1973-79, Tiffany and Margaret Blake Disting. Service prof., 1977—; sr. study dir. Nat. Opinion Research Center, Chgo., 1961—, dir., 1967-71, 79—. Author: (with D. Caplovitz) Reports on Happiness, 1967, The Structure of Psychological Well-Being, 1970, (with S. Sudman, G. Gockel) Side by Side: A Study of Integrated Neighborhoods, 1971, (with S. Sudman) Response Effects in Surveys, 1974, Asking Questions: A Practical Guide to Questionnaire Construction, 1982, (with others) Improving Questionnaire Design and Interview Method, 1979. Alexander von Humboldt scholar U. Cologne (Germany), 1970-71. Fellow Am. Statis. Assn.; mem. Am. Sociol. Assn., Am. Assn. Pub. Opinion Research. Home: 5326 S University Ave Chicago IL 60615

BRADBURY, NORRIS EDWIN, physicist; b. Santa Barbara, Calif., May 30, 1909; s. Edwin Perly and Elvira C. (Norris) B.; m. Lois Platt, Aug. 5, 1933; children—James Norris, John Platt, David Edwin. B.A., Pomona Coll., 1929, D.Sc., 1951; Ph.D., U. Calif., 1932; LL.D., U. N.Mex., 1953; D.Sc., Case Inst. Tech., 1956. NRC fellow in physics M.I.T., 1932-34; asst. prof. physics Stanford U., 1934-37, asso. prof., 1937-42, prof., 1942-50; prof. physics U. Calif., 1951-70; dir. Los Alamos Sci. Lab., 1945-70. Contbr. tech. articles to phys. revs., jours. Served with USNR, 1941-45; capt. Res. Decorated Legion of Merit. Fellow Am. Phys. Soc.; mem. Nat. Acad. Sci. Episcopalian. Home: 1451 47th St Los Alamos NM 87544

BRADBURY, RAY DOUGLAS, author; b. Waukegan, Ill., Aug. 22, 1920; s. Leonard Spaulding and Esther Marie (Moberg) B.; m. Marguerite Susan McClure, Sept. 27, 1947; children: Susan Marguerite, Ramona, Bettina, Alexandra. Student pub. schs. First pub. short story, 1941; 51, stories pub. pulp mags., 1941-45; later stories in Best Am. Short Stories, 1946, 48, 52 and in; O. Henry Prize Stories of, 1947, 48. (Benjamin Franklin award best Am. mag. story 1953); Author: Dark Carnival, 1947, The Martian Chronicles, 1950, also screenplay, 1964; The Illustrated Man, 1951, The Golden Apples of the Sun, 1953, Fahrenheit 451, 1953; play The Meadow, 1947; Screenplay Moby Dick, 1954; juvenile Switch on the Night, 1955; The October Country, 1955, Dandelion Wine, 1957, A Medicine for Melancholy, 1959; screenplay Icarus Montgolfier Wright, 1961; stories R Is for Rocket S is for Space, 1962; novel Something Wicked This Way Comes, 1962; plays The Anthem Sprinters, 1962, The Machineries of Joy, 1963; The World of Ray Bradbury, 1965; stories The Vintage Bradbury, 1965, The Autumn People, 1965; play The Wonderful Ice Cream Suit, 1965; paperback edit. Tomorrow Midnight, 1966; illus. stories Twice Twenty-Two, 1966; radio drama Leviathan '99, 1966; screenplays The Picasso Summer, 1968, The Halloween Tree, 1968; play Any Friend of Nicholas Nickleby's is a Friend of Mine, 1968; stories I Sing The Body Electric, 1969, The Small Assassin, 1973, Mars and the Minds of Man, 1973, Zen and the Art of Writing, 1973; poems When Elephants Last in the Dooryard Bloomed, 1973; play Pillar of Fire, 1975; Long After Midnight, 1976, Where Robot Mice and Robot Men Run Round in Robot Towns, 1977, The Mummies of Guanajuato, 1978, The Stories of Ray Bradbury, 1980, About Norman Corwin, 1980, The Last Circus, 1980; poems The Haunted Computer and the Android Pope, 1981; The Ghosts of Forever, 1981; others.; Prodns. one act plays, Royal Shakespeare Festival Theatre, The Pandemonium Theatre Co., 1963. Mem. Screen Writers Guild, Sci. Fantasy Writers Am., Pacific Art Found. (v.p.), Writers Guild Am. (mem. screen writers bd.). Office: care Bantam Books 666 Fifth Ave New York NY 10103 *

BRADBURY, ROBERT MILTON, JR., architect; b. Houston, Nov. 4, 1924; s. Robert Milton and Florence (Geisendorff) B.; m. Monica Lermont, June 21, 1953; children: Jessica Lermont, Claudia Lermont. B.A., Rice U., 1950, B.S., 1951. With William Lescaze (Architect), N.Y.C., 1951-56; with Rogers, Butler, Burgun & Bradbury, N.Y.C., 1956-74, partner, 1967-74; v.p. URS/Hewitt & Royer, N.Y.C., 1974-75; partner Bradbury, Erfan & King (Architects), N.Y.C., 1975-80; v.p. James Barclay Assos., N.Y.C., 1980-83; ptnr. Bradbury & Sullivan, Piermont, N.Y., 1983—. Works include, S.J. Wood Library, William Hale Harkness Research Bldg., Cornell Med. Coll., Harkness House for Ballet Arts, N.Y. Cell and Virus Bldg., Roswell Park Hosp., Buffalo, Mokattam Devel., Cairo. Pres. Piermont Civic Assn., 1966-67; bd. mgrs. St. Barnabas Hosp., Bronx, 1965-71; trustee N.Y. Infirmary, 1977-79; bd. dirs. Harkness Ballet Found., N.Y.C., 1980—. Served to 2d lt. USAAF, 1943-46. Recipient Alpha Rho Chi Gold medal Rice U., 1950. Mem. AIA, N.Y. Soc. Architects, Am. Hosp. Assn., Am. Assn. Hosp. Planning. Clubs: Union (N.Y.C.); Ausable (Keene Valley, N.Y.). Home: 873 River Rd Piermont NY 10968

BRADEMAS, JOHN, university president, former congressman; b. Mishawaka, Ind., Mar. 2, 1927; s. Stephen J. and Beatrice Cenci (Goble) B.; m. Mary Ellen Briggs, July 9, 1977. B.A. magna cum laude (Vets. nat. scholar), Harvard, 1949; D.Phil. (Rhodes scholar), Oxford (Eng.) U., 1954; LL.D. (hon.), U. Notre Dame, Middlebury Coll., Tufts U., (others); L.H.D., Brandeis U., CCNY, (others). Legislative asst. to U.S. Senator Pat McNamara; adminstrv. asst. U.S. Rep. Thomas L. Ashley, 1955; exec. asst. to presdl. nominee Stevenson, 1955-56; asst. prof. polit. sci. St. Mary's Coll., Notre Dame, Ind., 1957-58; mem. 86th-96th Congresses from 3d Ind. Dist.; chief dep. majority whip 93d-94th Congresses; majority whip 95th-96th Congresses; mem. com. house adminstrn., com. on edn. and labor, joint com. on Library of Congress; pres. NYU, 1981—; chmn. Fed. Res. Bank N.Y.; dir. RCA/NBC, Loew's Corp., Scholastic, Inc., N.Y. Stock Exchange, Rockefeller Found.; Past mem. bd. visitors John F. Kennedy Sch. Govt.; bd. overseers Harvard U.; mem. overseers' com. to visit Grad. Sch. Edn.; trustee, mem. adv. council Coll. Arts and Letters U. Notre Dame; bd. visitors dept. polit. sci. M.I.T.; bd. advs. Dumbarton Oaks Research Library and Collection, Woodrow Wilson Center Internat. Scholars; mem. Central Com. World Council Chs.; past mem. Nat. Hist. Publs. Commn., Nat. Commn. on Financing Post-Secondary Edn.; mem. Nat. Commn. Student Fin. Assistance, Study Nat. Needs Biomed. and Behavioral Research NRC, Nat. Acad. Sci. Com. Relations between Univs. and Govt.; bd. dirs. Am. Council Edn. Served with USNR, 1945-46. Recipient Disting. Service award Inst. Internat. Edn., 1966, NEA, 1968, Tchrs. Coll., Columbia U., 1969; Merit award Nat. Council Sr. Citizens, 1972; Disting. Service award Council of State Adminstrs. of Vocat. Rehab., 1973, Conservation Edn. Assn., 1974; Caritas Soc. award for outstanding contbns. in field of mental retardation, 1975; Gold Key award Am. Congress Rehab. Medicine, 1976; named Humanist of Year Nat. Assn. Humanities Edn., 1978; award for disting. service to arts AAAL, 1978; George Peabody award, 1980. Fellow Am. Acad. Arts and Scis.; mem. Am. Legion, Phi Beta Kappa (Senator). Methodist. Clubs: Masons, Ahepa. Office: NY U Office of Pres 70 Washington Square S New York NY 10003 *

BRADEN, CHARLES HOSEA, physicist, univ. adminstr.; b. Chgo., Mar. 21, 1926; s. Charles Eugene and Rachel Irene (Atchison) B.; m. Sara Caroline McKinley, Sept. 7, 1952; children—Patsy Irene, Jack David. Student, U. Ill., 1943-44; B.S. in Engring, Columbia U., 1946; Ph.D. in Physics, Washington U., St. Louis, 1951. Asst. prof. physics Ga. Inst. Tech., 1951-53, asso. prof., 1953-59, prof., 1959-71, Regents prof. physics, 1971—; asso. dir. Sch. Physics, 1971-80, interim dir., 1980-82; asso. program dir. for physics NSF, Washington, 1959-60. Contbr.: articles to Phys. Rev., Dynamica. Served with USNR, 1943-46. Fellow Am. Phys. Soc. Episcopalian. Research in exptl. nuclear physics, modeling of socio-econ. systems. Office: Sch Physics Ga Inst Tech Atlanta GA 30332

BRADEN, DAVID RICE, architect; b. Dallas, Nov. 10, 1924; s. Lois Odneal and Dorrell Fuller (Rice) B.; m. Sara Deering, Apr. 6, 1946; children: Gail Braden Goodwin, Kimberly Braden Chumlea, Shannon Braden Lancaster. B.Arch., U. Tex., Austin, 1949. Diplomate: registered architect, Tex., Ill., N.C., La. Staff architect George L. Dahl (architects and engrs.), Dallas, 1949-52, Howard R. Meyer (Architect), 1952; Assoc. West Dallas Housing Architects, 1953; prin. Braden & Jones (Architects), Dallas, 1953-73; pres., chmn. bd. Dahl, Braden/PTM, Inc. (architects and planners), Dallas, 1973—; dir. Interfirst Bank, Oak Cliff; mem. faculty Dallas Coll., So. Meth. U., 1962-72; mem. Dallas Urban Design Task Force, Greater Dallas Planning Council. Trustee Goals for Dallas; pres. Dallas Citizens Charter Assn., 1974—. Served with USAAF, 1942-45. Decorated D.F.C., Air medal with 5 oak leaf clusters, Purple Heart; recipient George Washington Honor medal pub. address Freedoms Found. Valley Forge, 1968. Fellow AIA (past pres. Dallas, award residential design Dallas chpt. 1952, award enhancement profession in sch. design 1968); mem. Tex. Soc. Architects (past pres.), Tex. Archtl. Found. (trustee), Tau Sigma Delta. Home: Dallas TXOffice: 1800 N Market St Dallas TX 75202

BRADEN, EMMETT WADE, lawyer; b. Henderson, Tenn., June 12, 1901; s. William B. and Annie B. (McKinney) B. B.A., U. Tenn., 1923; LL.B., Yale, 1925. Bar: Tenn. bar 1925. Practiced in, Memphis, 1925—; asso. firm Wilson, Gates & Armstrong, 1925-32; partner firm Armstrong, McCadden, Allen, Braden & Goodman, 1932-66; counsel Armstrong Allen Braden Goodman McBride & Prewitt, 1966—. Served to capt. U.S. Army, 1942-45. Mem. Am., Tenn., Memphis, Shelby County bar assns., Corbey Ct., Kappa Sigma. Clubs: Yale, Petroleum (Memphis). Home: 99 N Main St Apt 1805 Memphis TN 38103 Office: 19th Floor One Commerce Sq Memphis TN 38103

BRADEN, PARICK O' CONNOR, educator, college president; b. Houston, Feb. 1, 1924; s. Albert Henry and Kathleen Veronica (O'Connor) B. B.S., Rice U., 1944; M.S., U. Tex., Austin, 1954, Ph.D., 1961. Ordained priest Roman Catholic Ch., 1952. Isntr. mech. engring. Rice U., Houston, 1946-47; isntr. math. and physics St. Michael's Coll., Toronto, Ont., Can., 1949-53; prof. physics U. St. Thomas, Houston, 1960-79, pres., 1967-79, St. John Fisher Coll., Rochester, N.Y., 1980—; cons. engr. Inst. for Study and Application Integrated Devel., Niger, 1979-80; vice chmn. Rechester Are Colls., 1981—. Contbr. articles to profl. jours. Trustee Houston Symphony, Soc. Performing Arts, Houston; mem. Com. Ind. Colls. and Univs. N.Y. State. Served with USN, 1944-46. Recipient Distings. Engring. Grad. award U. Tex., Austin, 1980; AEC grantee, 1965; NSF grantee, 1966. Mem. ASME (Am. Assn. Physics Tchrs.), C. of C., Sigma Xi, Pi Tau Sigma, Tau Beta Pi. Roman Catholic. Club: Oak Hill. Home and Office: 3690 East Ave Rochester NY 14618

BRADEN, ROBERT GAYNOR, lawyer; b. Parkersburg, W.Va., Jan. 29, 1914; s. Charles Blaine and Dica (Gaynor) B.; m. Muriel Louise Coultis, Apr. 4, 1941; children—Roberta (Mrs. Fred Powell), Bruce F. A.B., U. Kan., 1935; LL.B., Harvard, 1938. Bar: Tex. bar 1938, Kan. bar 1939. Practiced in, Wichita, 1939—; partner firm Jochems, Sargent & Blaes, 1946—; Pres. Braden Drilling, Inc. Pres. Wichita Guidance Center, 1962-66, Wichita Symphony Soc., 1972-74; pres. Wichita Music Theatre, Inc., 1983—. Served with U.S. Army, 1942-46. Mem. Harvard Law Assn. Kan. (pres. 1960—), Ind. Petroleum Assn. Am. (dir. Kan. 1955-60), Wichita bar assns. (dir. 1958-60). Republican. Methodist. Clubs: Wichita Country (pres. 1968-69), Petroleum (Wichita) (pres. 1975-76). Home: 1515 Willow Rd Wichita KS 67208 Office: Farmers and Bankers Life Bldg Wichita KS 67202

BRADEN, SAMUEL EDWARD, economics educator; b. Hoihow, Hainan, China, June 6, 1914; s. Samuel Ray and Mary (Altman) B.); m. Beth Black, 1937; children: Mary Beth, Stephen, John, David. A.B., U. Okla., 1932; M.A., U. Wis., 1935, Ph.D., 1941; LL.D. hon., Ill. State U., 1976, Ind. U., 1983. Instr. to prof. Ind. U., 1937-67; assoc. dean Coll. Arts and Sci., 1954-59, v.p., 1959-67; pres. Ill. State U., 1967-70; chmn. div. bus. and econs. Ind. U. S.E., 1970-80; mem. exec. com. Council Internat. Ednl. Exchange, N.Y., 1967-83; exec. dir. Ind. Conf. Higher Edn., 1963-67; sr. economist Combined Raw Materials Bd., Washington, 1942-43. Author: (with C.L. Christenson, others) Economics, Principles and Problems, 1946, (with G.A. Steiner, others) Economic Problems of the War; Contbr. articles to ednl. publs. Bd. overseers St. Meinrad Coll. Served to 1st lt. USAAF, 1943-46. Fulbright sr. research fellow U.K., 1949-50. Mem. Am., Midwest econ. assns., Am. Finance Assn., Phi Beta Kappa. Presbyterian (mem. bd. Christian edn.). Home: 1714 Crestview Dr New Albany IN 47150 Office: 4201 Grantline Rd New Albany IN 47150

BRADEN, THOMAS WARDELL, newspaperman; b. Greene, Iowa, Feb. 22, 1918; s. Thomas Wardell and Louise (Garl) B.; m. Joan E. Ridley, Dec. 18, 1948; children: David, Mary, Joan, Susan, Nancy, Elizabeth, Thomas Wardell III, Nicholas R. A.B., Dartmouth Coll., 1940; Litt.D., Franklin Coll. Ind., 1979. Newspaperman; instr. English Dartmouth, 1946, asst. to pres. and asst. prof., 1947-48; exec. sec. Mus. Modern Art, N.Y.C., 1949; dir. Am. Com. on United Europe, 1950; editor, pub. Blade Tribune, Oceanside, Calif., 1954-68; columnist Los Angeles Times Syndicate, 1968—. Author: (with Stewart Alsop) Sub-Rosa, 1946, Eight is Enough, 1975. Mem. Calif. Bd. Edn., 1959-67; past. pres. Trustee Calif. State Coll., 1961-64, Dartmouth. Served with King's Royal Rifle Corps Brit. Army; Africa and; Served with King's Royal Rifle Corps Brit. Army, 1941-44; Italy; trans. to inf. AUS, 1944. Office: care Los Angeles Times Syndicate Times Mirror Sq Los Angeles CA 90053 *

BRADEN, WALDO W., educator; b. Ottumwa, Iowa, Mar. 7, 1911; s. Wilbern C. and Stella (Warder) B.; m. Dana Crane, Aug. 18, 1938; 1 dau., Helen Dana. B.A., Penn Coll., 1932; M.A., U. Iowa, 1938, Ph.D., 1942. Tchr. Fremont (Iowa) High Sch., 1933-35, Mt. Pleasant High Sch., 1935-38; tchr. speech Iowa Wesleyan Coll., 1938-40, dean students, 1942-43, 45-46; asso. prof. speech La. State U., Baton Rouge, 1946-51, prof., 1951-73, Boyd prof., 1973-79, Boyd prof. emeritus, 1979—, chmn., 1958-76; vis. prof. Washington U., summer 1952, Mich. State U., summer 1953, U. Pacific, summer 1965, Calif. State Coll., Fullerton, 1969. Author: (with Gray) Public Speaking, 1951, rev. edit., 1963, (with Brandenburg) Oral Decision-Making, 1955, (with Gehring) Speech Practices, 1958, Public Speaking: Essentials, 1966, (with Thonssen and Baird) Speech Criticism, 1970; Editor: Speech Methods and Resources, 1961, rev. edit., 1972, The Speech Teacher, 1967-69, Oratory in the Old South, 1970, Oratory in the New South, 1979, Representative American Speeches, 1970-80, Oral Tradition in the South, 1983; Contbr. (with Thonssen and Baird) articles to speech and hist. jours. Served with AUS, 1943-45. Mem. Speech Communication Assn. (council 1954—, exec. sec. 1954-57, pres. 1962, Disting. Ser. award 1978), So. Speech Assn. (pres. 1969-70), Pi Kappa Delta, Delta Sigma Rho, Tau Kappa Alpha, Omicron Delta Kappa. Methodist. Home: 535 Ursuline Dr Baton Rouge LA 70808

BRADER, WALTER HOWE, JR., petrochem. co. exec.; b. Beaumont, Tex., Oct. 30, 1927; s. Walter Howe and Mabel (Lee) B.; m. Julia Frances Sifford, Dec. 27, 1944; children—Thomas Glen, Mark. B.A., Rice U., 1950; Ph.D., Ga. Inst. Tech., 1954. Research chemist Standard Oil Co. (Ind.), Whiting, Ind., 1954-59; with Jefferson Chem. Co., 1959—, mgr. comml. devel., Houston, 1970-71, dir. research and devel., Austin, Tex., 1971—. Bd. dirs. Austin Jr. Achievement. Mem. Am. Chem. Soc. (counselor), Sigma Xi. Home: 8803 Crest Ridge Circle Austin TX 78750 Office: PO Box 15730 Austin TX 78761

BRADFIELD, JAMES MCCOMB, emeritus teacher educator; b. Lebanon, Mo., July 31, 1917; s. James McComb and Emma Katherine (Johnson) B.; m. Helen Annette Haynes, Jan. 8, 1943; children—Kathleen (Mrs. Frank Norton, Jr.), Christopher, Susan (Mrs. James A. Fuller), Robin, Polly. A.B., U. Kans., 1938; postgrad., U. Chgo., 1939-40, U. Kansas City, 1940-41; M.A., U. Calif., 1946, Ph.D., 1948. Secondary tchr. Oakland (Calif.) Unified Sch. Dist., 1945-48; prof. edn. Calif. State U. at Sacramento, 1948-80, prof. emeritus, 1980—, chmn. dept. behavioral scis. in edn., 1966-71, 79-80; behavioral measurement and research cons.; producer children's TV series Wondertime KCRA-TV, 1960-62; speaker, writer; dean Stebbins Inst., 1951. Author: Measurement and Evaluation in Education, 1957, Secondary School Teaching, 1962, Pupil Attitude Scales, 1973; play Invainity Fair, 1983. Served with USMCR, 1941-45. Mem. Sigma Nu, Phi Delta Kappa. Democrat. Unitarian. Home: 4649 Hixon Circle Sacramento CA 95841

BRADFORD, A. LEE, lawyer; b. Accomac County, Va., Apr. 23, 1906; s. G.A. and Rachel (Linton) B.; m. Vivienne Louvet, Aug. 10, 1948; 1 dau., Winifred (Mrs. Thomas Morgan Moore). Student, William and Mary Coll., 1923-25; J.D., U. Fla., 1929. Bar: Fla. bar 1929. Practiced in, Miami, Fla., 1929—; chmn. firm Bradford, Williams, McKay, Kimbrell, Hamann & Jennings, 1941—; chmn. rules com. U.S. Dist. Ct., So. Dist. Fla., 1964-65; alt. del. Jud. Conf., 5th Circuit, U.S. Ct. Appeals, 1967-68, 69. Author: (with Paul A. Carlson) Captain of the Ship, 1960, (with Joseph F. Jennings) Products Liability Again, 1962. Mem. Fla. Bar Assn. (continuing legal edn. sect. 1967-68), Dade County Bar Assn., ABA (chmn. trial technique com. 1962-63, aviation com. 1968-69), Internat. Acad. Trial Lawyers (dir. 1959), Internat. Assn. Ins. Counsel (chmn. automobile ins. com., chmn. profl. liability and malpractice com. 1959-60, chmn. open forum 1963-64), Am. Coll. Trial Lawyers, Phi Alpha Delta. Methodist. Clubs: Riviera Country (Coral Gables, Fla.) (pres. 1957-58); Wildcat Cliffs Country (Highlands, N.C.) (pres. 1977-78). Home: 1260 Mendavia Ave Coral Gables FL 33146 Office: 799 Brickell Plaza Miami FL 33131

BRADFORD, ADDISON MORTON, JR., lawyer, corp. exec.; b. Lee County, Ark., Jan. 2, 1918; s. Addison Morton and Olivette (Bonner) B.; m. Peggy Caraway, June 18, 1942; children—Paul Randolph, Patricia Gay, Timothy Caraway. B.A., Ark. State U., 1939; postgrad., So. Meth. U., 1940-41, J.D., 1948. Bar: Tex. bar 1948, U.S. Supreme Ct 1948. Practiced in, Dallas, 1948—; partner firm Bradford & Pritchard, Dallas, 1953-68, Anderson, Henley, Shields, Bradford & Pritchard, 1968-77, Bradford & Pritchard, 1977-80, Addison Bradford Jr. Profl. Corp., 1980—; dir. First City Bank-Farmers Br., R.B. Wilber Co.; v.p., dir. Town & Country Vending Service, Inc.; sec., dir. O.E.M. Industries, Inc., Tex. Sign Supply Co., Tex. Screen Process, Inc.; dir. J.T. Chapman Co.; v.p., dir. Mahard Egg Farm, Inc., Mahard Egg Co., Mahard Pullet Farms, Inc., Mahard Feed Mill, Inc. Served as finance officer, capt. AUS, 1943-46. Mem. Am., Dallas bar assns., State Bar Tex., Am. Judicature Soc., Delta Theta Phi. Democrat. Methodist. Clubs: Mason (32 degree), K.T., Shriner, Rotarian., Lancers, Knife and Fork (Dallas); Brookhaven Country. Home: 16850 Village Ln Dallas TX 75248 Office: 5001 LBJ Freeway Suite 770 Dallas TX 75234

BRADFORD, BARBARA TAYLOR, journalist, author, novelist; b. Leeds, Eng., May 10, 1933; came to U.S., 1964; d. Winston and Freda (Walker) Taylor; m. Robert Bradford, Dec. 24, 1963. Student pvt. schs., Eng. Women's editor Yorkshire (Eng.) Evening Post, 1951-53, reporter, 1949-51; editor Woman's Own, 1953-54; columnist London Evening News, 1955-57; exec. editor London Am., 1959-62; editor Nat. Design Center Mag., 1965-69; syndicated columnist Newsday Spls., L.I., 1968-70; nat. syndicated columnist Chgo. Tribune-N.Y. (News Syndicate), N.Y.C., 1970-75, Los Angeles Times Syndicate, 1975—. Author: Complete Ency. Homemaking Ideas, 1968, A Garland of Children's Verse, 1968, How to be the Perfect Wife, 1969, Easy Steps to Successful Decorating, 1971, Decorating Ideas for Casual Living, 1977, How to Solve Your Decorating Problems, 1976, Making Space Grow, 1979; novel A Woman of Substance, 1979; Luxury Designs for Apartment Living, 1981; novel Voice of the Heart, 1982, Hold the Dream, 1984. Recipient Dorothy Dawe award Am. Furniture Mart, 1970, 71. Mem. Authors Guild, Nat. Home Fashions League, Nat. Soc. Interior Designers (Distinguished Editorial award 1969, Nat. Press award 1971), Am. Soc. Interior Designers. Office: 450 Park Ave New York NY 10022

BRADFORD, CHARLES EDWARD, clergyman; b. Washington, July 12, 1925; s. Robert Lee and Etta Elizabeth B.; m. Ethel Lee McKenzie, May 23, 1948; children: Sharon Louise, Charles Edward, Dwight Lyman. B.A., Oakwood Coll., Huntsville, Ala., 1946; grad., Andrews U., 1958, D.D. (hon.), 1978. Ordained to ministry Seventh-day Adventist Ch.; pastor chs. in, La. and Tex., 1946-51, Mo., 1953-57, N.Y., 1959-61; evangelist, dir. lay activities Central States Conf., Seventh-day Adventist Ch., Kansas City, Mo., 1952-53; dir. lay activities Northeastern Conf., St. Albans, N.Y., 1957-59; pres. Lake Region Conf., Chgo., 1961-70; asso. sec. Gen. Conf., Washington, 1970-79; v.p. N. Am., 1979—; trustee Oakwood Coll., Andrews U., Loma Linda (Calif.) U. Author: also articles. Preaching to the Times. Office: 6840 Eastern Ave NW Washington DC 20012 *

BRADFORD, DAVID FRANTZ, economist; b. Cambridge, Mass., Jan. 8, 1939; s. Mark Waldo and Matilda (Frantz) B.; m. Gunthild Klaerchen Huober, Feb. 20, 1964; children—Theodore Huober, Catherine Louise. B.A. magna cum laude (Nat. Merit scholar 1956-60), Amherst Coll., 1960; M.S. in Applied Math. (Woodrow Wilson fellow 1960-61), Harvard U., 1962, Churchill Coll., Cambridge U., 1963-64; Ph.D. in Econs, Stanford U., 1966. Econ. cons. Office Asst. Sec. of Def., Germany, Eng. and; Washington, 1964-65; acting instr. econs. Stanford U., 1965-66; asst. prof. econs. Princeton U., 1966-71, asso. prof. econs. and public affairs, 1971-75, prof. econs. and public affairs, 1975—; asso. dean Woodrow Wilson Sch., 1974-75, 78-80, acting dean, 1980; dep. asst. sec. for tax policy U.S. Treasury Dept., 1975-76; research asso., dir. research in taxation Nat. Bur. Econ. Research, 1977—. Contbr. articles to profl. jours. Recipient Exceptional Service award U.S. Treasury Dept., 1976; Fulbright fellow, Belgium, 1977. Mem. Am. Econ. Assn., Econometric Soc., Nat. Tax Assn., Phi Beta Kappa. Office: Woodrow Wilson School Princeton U Princeton NJ 08544

BRADFORD, DAVID S., surgeon; b. Charlotte, N.C., Oct. 15, 1936; m. Helen Gray MacKay; children: David Mackay, Jennifer Sutherland, Tyler Speir. B.A., Davidson Coll., 1958; M.D., U. Pa., 1962. Diplomate: Am. Bd. Orthopaedic Surgeons. Intern in surgery Columbia-Presbyn. Med. Center, N.Y.C., 1962-63, resident in gen. surgery, 1965-66; resident in orthopaedic surgery N.Y. Orthopaedic Hosp., Columbia-Presbyn. Med. Center, N.Y.C., 1966-68, jr. Annie C. Kane fellow orthopaedic surgery, 1968-69; research trainee orthopaedics Nat. Inst. Arthritis and Metabolic Diseases, 1969-70; prof. orthopaedic surgery U. Minn. Hosps., Mpls.; prof. orthopaedic surgery Fairview Hosp., Twin Cities Scoliosis Center, Mpls.; mem. cons. staff Children's Health Center, Mpls. Mem. editorial bd.: Minn. Medicine; cons. editorial bd.: Jour. Bone and Joint Surgery; bd. editors: Spine; contbr. articles to profl. jours. Trustee Mpls. Soc. Fine Arts; reviewer grant and fellowship com. Orthopaedic Research and Edn. Found. Mem. Internat. Soc. Orthopaedic Surgery and Traumatology, Am. Acad. Orthopaedic Surgeons (dir.), A.C.S., AMA, Am. Orthopaedic Assn., Am. Spinal Injury Assn., Assn. Bone and Joint Surgeons (treas.), Orthopaedic Research Soc., Scoliosis Research Soc. (dir.), Frank E. Stinchfield Club, Pan-Pacific Surg. Assn., Minn. Orthopaedic Soc., Minn. Med. Soc., Western Trauma Assn., Hennepin County Med. Soc., Twin City Orthopaedic Soc. Office: Box 133 Mayo Meml Bldg 420 Delaware St SE Minneapolis MN 55455 *

BRADFORD, HOWARD, graphic artist, painter; b. Toronto, Ont., Can., July 14, 1919; came to U.S., 1923, naturalized, 1948; s. Robert E. and Emily (Beadle) B.; m. Dorothy Louise Bowman (div. Aug. 1967); children—Brock, Cyndra Lisa, Tal Scot, Heather, Delia Contess; m. Jane Kunkel, Apr. 1970 (div. Dec. 1979); m. Catherine Gerber, Jan. 1980 (div. June 1983); children—Brock, Cyndra Lisa, Tal Scot, Heather, Delia Contess. Student, Chouinard Art Inst., 1947-49, Jepson Art Inst., 1950-52. Instr. graphic arts center Sunset Sch., Carmel, Calif. One-man shows, Landau Gallery, Los Angeles, 1950, Anthes Gallery, Los Angeles, Coast Gallery, Big Sur, Calif., 1960, Carmel Art Assn., 1973, 77, 80, exhibited in group shows nationally and internationally with, Am. Fedn. Arts, USIS, 1950—, Carmel Art Assn., 1973, 80, represented in permanent collections, Dallas Mus. Fine Arts, Los Angeles County Mus., Calif. State Fair, Library of Congress, San Diego Mus., N.Y. Pub. Library, Crocker Art Gallery, Sacramento, New Britain (Conn.) Mus., Boston Mus. Fine Arts, U. Wis., U. Ill., Bradley U., Albert and Victoria Mus., London, Phila. Mus. Fine Arts; gallery dir., Serigraph Ltd. Gallery, Monterey, Calif., 1969-72. Served with AUS, 1942-45; ETO. Guggenheim fellow for creative printmaking, 1960; recipient purchase awards Los Angeles County Mus., 1950, Bradley U., 1951, Nat. Serigraph Soc., 1951, 52, Am. Color Print Soc., 1951, 52, 58, 60, Library of Congress, 1951, 56, 57, U. Ill., 1957, Boston Printmakers, 1958, Western Serigraph Inst., 1948, N.W. Printmakers Soc., 1958, Dallas Print Soc., 1952, painting awards Monterey Peninsula Mus., 1965, 68. Mem. Carmel Art Assn., Am. Color Print Soc. Address: 684 Alice St Monterey CA 93940

BRADFORD, JOHN CARROLL, mag. exec.; b. Terre Haute, Ind., June 27, 1924; s. Carroll L. and Martha Fern (Harden) B. Student, U. Minn., 1943-44; B.A., U. Ill., 1948. Designer, asso. art dir. Marshall Field & Co., Chgo., 1949-59; art dir. Rockmore Advt., N.Y.C., 1960-62, CBS-Columbia Records, 1962-64; v.p., art dir. Family Circle mag., N.Y.C., 1970—; cons. graphic design. Served with Inf. AUS, 1943-45; ETO. Decorated Bronze Star. Mem. Art Dirs. Club N.Y., Soc. Publ. Designers. Home: One Fifth Ave New York City NY 10003 Office: 488 Madison Ave New York City NY 10022

BRADFORD, PETER AMORY, state official; b. N.Y.C., July 21, 1942; s. Amory Howe and Carol (Rothschild) B.; m. Mary Condon, Dec. 16, 1978; children: Arthur, Laura, Emily. B.A., Yale U., 1964, LL.B., 1968; D.Ecology (hon.), Unity Coll., 1981, Unity Coll., 1981. Adviser to Gov. Kenneth Curtis of Maine, 1968-71; commr. Maine Public Utilities Commn., 1971-77, chmn., 1974-75, 82—; mem. NRC, 1977-82; mem. cabinet of Gov. Joseph E. Brennan of Maine, Augusta, 1981—; exec. dir. Gov.'s Task Force Energy (Heavy Industry and the Maine Coast), 1971-72. Author: Fragile Structures, A Story of Oil Refineries, National Security, and the Coast of Maine, 1975. Office: Public Utilities Commn 242 State St Augusta ME 04330

BRADFORD, RICHARD ROARK, writer; b. Chgo., May 1, 1932; s. Roark and Mary Rose (Sciarra) B.; m. Julie Dollard, Sept. 15, 1956 (div.); 1 son, Thomas Conway; m. Lee Head, June 25, 1977. B.A., Tulane U., 1952; D.Litt., N.Mex. State U., 1979. Staff writer, editor N.M. Tourist Bur., 1956-59, New Orleans C. of C., 1959-61, Zia Co., Los Alamos, 1963-65; research analyst N.M. Dept. Devel., 1967-68; screenwriter Universal Pictures, 1968-70. Author: Red Sky at Morning, 1968, So Far from Heaven, 1973. Served with USMC, 1953-56. Mem. Edouard Manet Soc., Sigma Chi. Club: Quien Sabe (Santa Fe). Home: PO Box 1395 Santa Fe NM 87501 Office: care McIntosh and Otis Inc 475 Fifth Ave New York NY 10017

BRADFORD, ROBERT ERNEST, motion picture producer; b. Berlin, May 25, 1927; U.S., 1946, naturalized, 1953; s. Siegfried and Doris (Herzberg) B.; m. Barbara Taylor, Dec. 24, 1963. Student, Marie Curie Coll., Paris, 1937; A.B., U. Geneva, 1945. Prodn. cons. Distbn. Corp. Am., N.Y.C., 1946-53; exec. v.p. Jesse L. Lasky Prodns., Beverly Hills, Calif., 1953—; exec. v.p., dir. Samuel Bronston Prodns., N.Y.C., 1955—; exec. v.p. Franco London Films Internat., Ltd., Montreal; pres. Franco London Film S.A., Paris, Franco London Music, Ltd., London; head feature prodn., exec. producer Hal Roach Studios, Hollywood, Calif., 1959—; dir. Hy-Ford Prodns., Inc., Hy-Ford Europea, Rome, Jack London Prodns.; fgn. corr. Overseas News Agy., 1951—; lectr. internat. affairs and interracial problems, 1950—; press relations cons. Sen. Herbert H. Lehman, 1952-53; cons., dir. Nat. Found. for Good Govt., 1952; cons. Internat. Study Tour Alliance, 1951—. Producer: John Paul Jones, Walter Bros., 1958, The Scavengers, Hal Roach Studios, 1959, If You Remember Me, 1959-60, The Golden Touch, 1959-60, Simon Bolivar, 1965, To Die of Love, 1971, Sweet Deception, 1972, Impossible Object, 1973, Voice of the Heart, 1984. Pub. relations dir one-world award com. Am. Nobel Anniversary Com. Served with French Intelligence, 1940-45. Recipient citation for outstanding work and civic achievements Greater N.Y. Citizens Forum, 1952. Mem. Internat. Inst. Arts and Letters (dir.), Internat. Platform Assn. Office: 450 Park Ave New York NY 10022

BRADFORD, THOMAS E., food broker; b. Sweet Water, Ala.; m. Mary Johnson; children: Thomas E., John M. Ed., Birmingham So. Coll., Harvard Grad. Sch. Bus. Adminstrn. In food brokerage bus., 1939—; chmn. bd. Bradford & Co., Inc., Food Brokers, Birmingham; dir. SouthTrust Bank, Allied Products Co., Mrs. Stratton's Salads, Inc., Sunbelt Sweeteners, Inc. Gen. campaign chmn. United Way, 1968; pres. Birmingham Park and Recreation Bd., 1975-76; mem. State Bd. Corrections, 1973-75; chmn. Eye Found., Inc., 1970-71, currently dir.; founder 1st pres. Met. Devel. Bd., 1971. Served to lt. USN; WW II. Recipient Birmingham's Man of Yr. award, 1965, Disting. Alumni award Birmingham So. Coll., 1966; named to Ala. Acad. of Honor, 1983. Methodist. Clubs: Rotary (pres. 1965-66), The Club, Birmingham Country, Shoal Creek. Office: PO Box 278 Birmingham AL 35201

BRADFORD, WILLIAM EDWARD, oilfield equipment manufacturing company executive; b. Dallas, Jan. 8, 1935; m. JoDeane Browning, Aug. 18, 1955; children: William B., A. Kathleen, Jon E. B.S. in Geology, Centenary Coll., 1958; grad. exec. devel. course, Tex. A&M U., 1975. Salesman Hycalog, Inc., 1958-61; v.p., gen. partner Analytical Logging, Inc., 1961-70; with Dresser Industries, Inc., 1979—, with oilfield products group (now oilfield equipment group), 1972—, pres., Houston, 1979—. Mem. bd. equalization Tomball Sch. Dist. Mem. Soc. Petroleum Engrs., Am. Assn. Petroleum Geologists, Petroleum Equipment Suppliers Assn., AAAS, Assn. Oilwell Drilling Contractors, Internat. Petroleum Assn., Tex. Mid-Continentant Oil and Gas Assn. Republican. Presbyterian. Clubs: Petroleum, University (Houston); Champions Golf, Heritage. Office: Dresser Industries Oilfield Equipment Group 601 Jefferson St Houston TX 77005 *

BRADHAM, GILBERT BOWMAN, surgeon; b. Sumter, S.C., Aug. 5, 1931; s. Riley Augustus and Mabel Amelia (Bowman) B.; m. Mary Jane Wood, Nov. 21, 1959; children—Gilbert Bowman, James Bramblett, Riley Augustus. Student, The Citadel, 1949-52; M.D., Med. U. S.C., 1956. Diplomate: Am. Bd. Surgery. Intern Roper Hosp., Charleston, S.C., 1956-57, Hartford Vascular Research Found. teaching fellow, 1959-60; asst. resident in surgery Med. Coll. Hosp., Charleston, 1957-60, teaching fellow cardiovascular surgery, 1958-59, sr. asst. surg. resident, fellow in oncology, 1960-61, asso. in surgery, 1964-65, coordinator sr. surgery teaching program, 1965-69, dir. ICU, 1966-69, dir. Peripheral Vascular Diagnostic Facility, 1967—, pres. full time clin. profl. staff, dir. pvt. diagnostic clinic Peripheral Vascular Diagnostic Facility, 1973—, med. dir. Peripheral Vascular Diagnostic Facility, 1975-81, v.p. clin. affairs, 1981—, asst. prof. surgery Peripheral Vascular Diagnostic Facility, 1965-68, asso. prof. surgery Peripheral Vascular Diagnostic Facility, 1968-72, prof. surgery Peripheral Vascular Diagnostic Facility, 1972—, acting v.p. acad. affairs Peripheral Vascular Diagnostic Facility, 1975—; grad. research trainee surg. cardiology UCLA Health Scis. Center, 1962-64; practice medicine specializing in surgery, Charleston, 1964—; cons. physiol. research Rand Corp., Santa Monica, Calif., 1962-71; surg. cons. Columbia Gen. Hosp., Spartanburg (S.C.) Gen. Hosp., VA Hosp., Charleston, Charleston Naval Hosp., 1968—. Contbr. numerous articles to profl. jours. Mem. A.C.S., AAAS, Am., S.C. aerospace med. assns., Assn. Am. Med. Colls., Nat. Rehab. Assn., S.C. So. surg. assns., S.C. Heart Assn., Soc. Univ. Surgeons, S.C. Medico-Chirurg. Soc., S.C. Vascular Soc., Soc. Relief of Families of Deceased and Disabled Indigent Mems. of Med. Profession S.C., Southeastern Surg Soc., Soc. Surgery Alimentary Tract, U.S. Bioenergetics Group, Société Internationale de Chirurgie, Sigma Xi, Alpha Kappa Kappa. Home: 2 Sayle Rd Charleston SC 29407 Office: 171 Ashley Ave Charleston SC 29425

BRADLEE, BENJAMIN CROWNINSHIELD, journalist; b. Boston, Aug. 26, 1921; s. Frederick J. and Josephine (deGersdorff) B.; m. Jean Saltonstall, Aug. 8, 1942; 1 son, Benjamin Crowninshield; m. Antoinette Pinchot, July 6, 1956; children: Dominic, Marina; m. Sally Quinn, Oct. 20, 1978; 1 son, Quinn. A.B., Harvard U., 1943. Reporter N.H. Sunday News, Manchester, 1946- 48, Washington Post, 1948-51; press attachè embassy, Paris, France, 1951- 53; European corr. Newsweek mag., Paris, 1953-57, reporter Washington bur., 1957-61, sr. editor, chief bur., 1961-65; mng. editor Washington Post, 1965-68, v.p., exec. editor, 1968—. Author: That Special Grace, 1964, Conversations with Kennedy, 1975. Served to lt. USNR, 1942-45. Home: 3014 N St NW Washington DC 20007 Office: 1150 15th St NW Washington DC 20071

BRADLER, JAMES EDWARD, publishing company executive; b. N.Y.C., Jan. 6, 1935; s. Robert Peter and Margaret Ann (O'Connor) B.; m. Edna Mae Siebold, Sept. 12, 1959; children: Janet, James. B.S., Fairleigh Dickinson U., 1966, M.B.A., 1980. Book club mgr. Prentice-Hall Inc., Englewood Cliffs, N.J., 1965-71, word processing and accounts mgr., 1971-78, asst. v.p. mail orders and ops., 1978-81, v.p. ops.-bus prof., 1981-83, exec. v.p., 1983-84, pres., 1984—; lectr. in field. Editor monograph, Credit and Collection, 1981; contbr. articles to profl. jours. Recipient Pres.'s Team Achievement Prentice-Hall, 1982. Mem. Internat. Consumer Credit Assn. (1st v.p. dist. 2), Direct Mktg. Credit Assn., Fulfillment Mgmt. Assn., Soc. Cert. Consumer Credit Execs. Republican. Roman Catholic. Home: 56 Greenbriar Rd Paramus NJ 07652 Office: Prentice-Hall Inc Route 9W Englewood Cliffs NJ 07632

BRADLEY, BILL, U.S. senator; b. Crystal City, Mo., July 28, 1943; s. Warren W. and Susan (Crowe) B.; m. Ernestine Schlant, Jan. 14, 1974; 1 dau., Theresa Anne. B.A., Princeton U., 1965; M.A. (Rhodes scholar 1965-68), Oxford (Eng.) U., 1968. Player N.Y. Knickerbockers Profl. Basketball Team, 1967-77; U.S. senator from, N.J., 1979—, mem. fin., energy and spl. aging coms. Author: Life on the Run, 1976. Served with USAFR, 1967-78. Democrat. Address: 731 Hart Senate Office Bldg Washington DC 20510

BRADLEY, CHARLES JAMES, JR., corporate executive; b. Worthington, Minn., Sept. 13, 1935; s. Charles James and Bernice Edith (Stone) B.; m. Patricia Ann Peters, Mar., 1968 (div. 1978); children: Julie Ann, Jamie Lynn; m. Sandra Lea Smith, Sept. 18, 1978. A.A., East Los Angeles Jr. Coll., 1955; B.S., UCLA, 1958. Vice-pres. human resources Fluor Corp., Irvine, Calif., 1958—. Office: Flour Corp 3333 Michelson Dr Irvine CA 92730

BRADLEY, DAVID GILBERT, theology educator; b. Portland, Oreg., Sept. 1, 1916; s. Rowland Hill and Edith (Gilbert) B.; m. Gail Soules, Mar. 19, 1940; 1 dau., Katherine Ann Bradley Johnson. A.B., U. So. Calif., 1938; postgrad., Drew Theol. Sem., 1938-39; B.D., Garrett Theol. Sem., 1942; M.A., Northwestern U., 1942; Ph.D., Yale U., 1947, Sch. Oriental and African Studies, U. London, 1955-56. Asst. prof. religion, chaplain Western Md. Coll., 1946-49; mem. faculty dept. religion Duke U., Durham, 1949—, prof., 1970—; vis. prof. Garrett Sem., summer 1960, U. Va., summer 1969, U. N.C., Chapel Hill, 1970; mem. N.C. Conf. United Meth. Ch.; mem. Fulbright-Hays sr. screening com., religion, 1966-68. Author: A Guide to the World's Religions, 1963, Circles of Faith, 1966, The Origins of the Hortatory Materials in the Letters of Paul, 1977; contbr. articles to profl. jours. Pres. Durham Civic Choral Soc., 1959-60; mem. citizens adv. com. Durham Urban Renewal Program, 1965-67; treas. Durham Arts Council, 1968-69; pres. Durham Savoyards Ltd., 1976-77. Gt. Religions Fund fellow, South and East Asia, 1969-70. Mem. Am. Acad. Religion (nat. program chmn. 1958, pres. So. sect. 1964), N.C. Tchrs. Religion (pres. 1961), Am. Soc. Study of Religion (sec. 1966-69, editor newsletter 1973—), Assn. Asian Studies, AAUP (pres. Duke U. chpt. 1971-72), Soc. Internat. Devel. (chpt. sec.-treas. 1983—). Democrat. Office: Box 4735 D S Duke Univ Durham NC 27706

BRADLEY, DAVID RALL, newspaper publisher; b. Toledo, Aug. 4, 1917; s. Henry D. and Alta Katherine (Rall) B.; m. Shirley Wyeth, Dec. 27, 1941; children: Margaret, Natalie, Henry, David Rall. A.B., U. Wis., 1939. Advt. salesman Bridgeport (Conn.) Times-Star, 1939-40, Headley-Reed Co., N.Y.C., 1941, Kelly-Smith Co., Chgo., 1942-43; nat. advt. mgr. News-Press & Gazette, St. Joseph, Mo., 1946, dir., 1947—, sec.-treas., prodn. mgr., 1948-57, pub., 1956-81, pres., 1972-81, chmn. bd., 1972—; dir. Landmark Communications, Norfolk, Va.; pres. St. Joseph Indsl. Devel. Co.; chmn. bd. St. Joseph Cablevision, WSAV-TV, Savannah, Ga.; dir. KAAL-TV, Austin, Minn., Broadcasters Miss., Inc., Jackson; former dir., vice chmn. AP. Mem. Am. Newspaper Pubs. Assn., Newspaper Advt. Bur. (past dir.), Chi Psi. Presbyterian. Clubs: Masons; Country, Benton (St. Joseph). Home: 2916 Frederick Blvd Saint Joseph MO 64506 Office: 9th and Edmond Sts Saint Joseph MO 64502

BRADLEY, ED, news correspondent; b. Pa. B.S. in Edn, Cheyney (Pa.) State Coll., 1964. Radio news reporter Sta. WDAS, Phila., 1963-67, Sta. WCBS, N.Y.C., 1967-71; with CBS Television News, 1971—, stringer, 1971-73, corr., 1973-78, prin. corr., 1978, in Paris, 1971, Saigon, 1972-74, Washington, 1974—, CBS Reports, 1978-81, 60 Minutes, 1981—; anchorman CBS Sunday Night News, 1976—. Anchorman: various documentaries including What's Happening to Cambodia, 1978, The Boat People, 1979, The Boston Goes to China, 1979. Recipient George Polk journalism award, 1980, 5 Emmy award, 1979—. Office: care CBS News 524 W 57th St New York NY 10019

BRADLEY, EDWARD SCULLEY, author, educator; b. Phila., Jan 4, 1897; s. Stephen Edward and Annette Evelyn (Palmer) B.; m. Anna Marguerite Cashner, June 11, 1921; children: Deborah Bradley Oberholtzer, Alison Bradley Wilhelm. A.B., U. Pa., 1919, A.M., 1921, Ph.D., 1925; LL.D., Baylor U., 1950. Instr. English U. Pa., 1919-26, asst. prof., 1926-37, asso. prof., 1937-40, prof., 1940-67, vice provost, 1956-63; mem. grad. dept. Am. civilization, asst. dir. Extension Sch., 1932-44; moderator Phila. Radio Forum Pub. Opinion, 1943-49; Asst. lit. editor Phila. Record, 1930-31; vis. prof. Duke U., summers 1932, 37, 41, Northwestern U., 1938, U. So. Calif., 1940; lectr. lit. Ogontz Sch., 1926-32, Rosemont Coll., 1930-33; lectr. Upton Sch. Drama, Phila., 1930-34; lectr. Am. Lit. Bread Loaf Sch. English, Middlebury, Vt., 1945. Author: George Henry Boker, Poet and Patriot (biography), 1927; biography Henry Charles Lea, 1931; editor: (with John A. Stevenson, q.v.) Walt Whitman's Backward Glances, 1947; Editor: Whitman's Leaves of Grass and Selected Prose, 1949, Traubel's With Walt Whitman in Camden, vol. IV, 1953, The Sonnets of George Henry Boker, 1929, Nydia, A Tragic Play (G.H. Boker), 1929, Glaucus and Other Plays (G.H. Boker), 1940; Gen. editor, contbr.: (with Richmond C. Beatty and E. Hudson Long) to The American Tradition in Literature, 1956, rev. edits. (2 vols.), 1967, 74; Contbr.: English Inst. Annual, The United States, 1865-1900, Collier's Ency, 1948, Chamber's Ency. (London), 1948, Dictionary of Am. Biography; Literary History of the U.S, 1948, Revolt in the Arts: Benjamin Franklin Lectures, 1950, also 3d and 4th edits, A Time of Harvest: American Literature 1910-60, 1962; Editor: Gen. Mag. and Hist. Chronicle, Phila., 1945-56; Mem. adv. editorial bd.: American Literature, 1932-34, 1939-43; cons. editor: (with Robert H. Elias) Letters of Theodore Dreiser, 3 vols, 1959; gen. editor (with Gay W. Allen); contbr.: Collected Writings of Walt Whitman, 14 vols; editor: (with Harold W. Blodgett) Reader's Comprehensive Edition of Leaves of Grass, 1965, Leaves of Grass, A Textual Variorum, 1973, Leaves of Grass, a Critical Edition, 1980; Contbr.: articles to lit. mags., scholarly jours. Leaves of Grass, a Critical Edition. Sometime mem. bd. Germantown Friends Sch., Apprentices' Library, Friends Hosp., both Phila.; trustee Walt Whitman Found., Camden, N.J. Served with USN, 1918-19. Fellow Soc. Am. Studies; mem. AAUP, Modern Lang. Assn. Am. (sec. Am. lit. group 1928-36, chmn. 1937-38), Franklin Inn Club, Athenaeum of Phila., Phi Beta Kappa, Delta Sigma Rho, Alpha Chi Rho. Quaker. Home: Kendal at Longwood Box 75 Kennett Square PA 19348

BRADLEY, EMMETT HUGHES, corp. exec.; b. Hampton, Va., Dec. 8, 1927; s. Alfred Thomas and Bessie Margaret (Patrick) B.; m. Linda Alice Frolen; children—Warren Hughes, Mark Harris, Todd Hamilton. B.S. in Elec. Engring. summa cum laude, Duke, 1949, M.S., Mass. Inst. Tech., 1950. With Melpar, Inc., Falls Church, Va., 1950-62, gen. mgr. spl. products div., 1960-62; v.p., gen. mgr. missile systems div. Atlantic Research Corp., 1962-67, pres., 1967-70; chief operating officer Susquehanna Corp., 1968-72, exec. v.p., 1970-72; also mem. exec. com., dir.; sr. exec. v.p. Pan Am. Sulphur Co., 1970-71; mem. exec. com., 1970-71, bd. dirs., 1969-71; chief exec. officer, pres., mem. exec. com., dir. Airtronics, Inc., Chatsworth, Calif., 1973-81, chief exec. officer, mem. exec. com., 1981—; pres., dir. Powertec, Inc., Chatsworth, Calif., 1976—; dir. Azufrera Panamericana, S.A., Fertilizantes Fosfatados Mexicanos. Author. Mem. exec. bd. Nat. Capital area council Boy Scouts Am., 1967-69; Orange Empire area council Boy Scouts Am., 1965-67; chmn. United Fund Duarte-Bradbury, 1964; Bd. dirs. Orange County Safety Council, 1967; mem. president's adv. council Calif. Bapt. Theol. Sem., 1966-68; now bd. trustees. Mem. Nat. Security Indsl. Assn. (exec. com. 1965-67, v.p. 1968, bd. trustees 1969-72), I.E.E.E., Phi Beta Kappa, Sigma Xi, Tau Beta Pi. Patentee in field. Home: 22267 1/2 Erwin St Woodland Hills CA 91367 Office: Powertec Inc 20550 Nordhoff St Chatsworth CA 91311

BRADLEY, FRANCIS XAVIER, mining co. exec.; b. N.Y.C., Aug. 25, 1915; s. Francis Michael and Estelle Veronica (McQuade) B.; m. Mary Ann Flynn, Sept. 10, 1940; children—Robert S. and Bruce (twins), Patricia Bradley Greene. B.S., U. Ala., 1937; M.A., Columbia U., 1951. Planning specialist Martin Co., Balt., 1959-61, gen. sales mgr., 1961-63; v.p. Martin Marietta Aerospace, Denver, 1963-70; v.p. mktg. and planning Martin Marietta Aluminum, Torrance, Calif., 1970-72, exec. v.p., Washington, 1973, pres., chief operating officer, 1974, pres., chief exec. officer, 1975-80; v.p. Martin Marietta Corp., 1973-80; pres., chief exec. officer Halco Mining Inc., 1980—; dir. Martin Marietta Corp. Served with AUS, 1937-59. Mem. Aluminum Assn., Internat. Primary Aluminum Inst. Clubs: George Town, Army-Navy, Army-Navy Country, Pisces, Duquesne, San Diego Yacht. Home: 2101 Connecticut Ave Washington DC 20008 Office: 520 San Gorgonio St San Diego CA 92106

BRADLEY, GENE ELLIOTT, management executive; b. Omaha, May 8, 1921; s. Paul and Gladys (Elliott) B.; m. Mary Ann Sullivan, July 30, 1949; children: David Gerald, Barbara Ann. B.S. in Bus. Adminstrn. (Regents scholar), U. Nebr., 1943. With Batton, Barton, Durstine & Osborn, San Francisco, 1946-51; with Gen. Electric Co., 1953-69; editor Gen. Electric Forum, 1958-64, mgr. internat. govt. relations, 1965-69; pres. Internat. Mgmt. Assn., 1969-70; chmn. and pres. Internat. Mgmt. and Devel. Inst., Washington, 1970—; White House cons., 1970; spl. asst. to dir. Peace Corps, 1964-65; dir. Atlantic Council of U.S., 1965—, also author, lectr. nat. security and internat. bus. affairs. Author: Building the American-European Market, 1967; Contbr. articles to mags. Trustee Council of Ams. Served with

USAAF, 1943-46, 51-53; lt. col. Res. Recipient Mgmt. award Gen. Electric Co., 1963, Cordiner award, 1963, spl. Freedom Leadership award Freedoms Found., 1964, Honor award, 1961, McKinsey award, 1968. Fellow Internat. Acad. Mgmt.; mem. Internat. Mgmt. Assn. (pres. 1969-70); Mem. Fund Multinat. Mgmt. Edn. (dir.), Internat. Mktg. Inst. (dir.), Washington Inst. Fgn. Affairs, Beta Theta Phi, Beta Gamma Sigma. Clubs: N.Y. Athletic (N.Y.C.); Met., Dacor (Washington). Home: Watergate South 700 New Hampshire Ave NW Washington DC 20037 Office: Watergate Office Bldg Suite 905 2600 Virginia Ave NW Washington DC 20037

BRADLEY, GILBERT FRANCIS, retired banker; b. Miami, Ariz., May 17, 1920; s. Ever and Martha (Piper) B.; m. Marion Bebb, June 21, 1941; children: Larry Paul, Richard Thomas, Steven Ever. Grad., LaSalle Extension U., 1942, U. Wash., 1953; Advanced Mgmt. Program, Harvard U. With Valley Nat. Bank, Ariz., Miami, Globe, Clifton, Nogales and Phoenix, 1937—, pres., Phoenix, 1973-76, chmn. bd., chief exec. officer, 1976-82, ret., 1982, dir., vice chmn. exec. com., 1982—, Valley Nat. Corp., 1982—; mem. adv. council Fed. Res. Bd., Comptroller of the Currency, Denver; instr. Am. Inst. Banking. Mem. Tucson Airport Authority, 1960—; mem. adv. council Ariz. State U. Sch. Bus., pres. dean's adv. council; dean's adv. council U. Ariz., Tucson. Served to capt. USAAF, 1942-45. Decorated D.F.C., Air medal with three oak leaf clusters. Mem. Ariz. Bankers Assn. (pres.), Assn. Res. City Bankers, Ariz. C. of C. (v.p., dir.), Tucson C. of C. (dir.), Better Bus. Bur. (dir.), Tucson Clearing House Assn. (past pres.), Navy League, Air Force Assn., Beta Gamma Sigma. Clubs: Masons, Rotary, Phoenix Country, Ariz. Home: 5340 La Plaza Circle Phoenix AZ 85012 Office: 241 N Central Ave Phoenix AZ 85001

BRADLEY, HAROLD WHITMAN, emeritus history educator, former state legislator; b. Greenwood, R.I., July 9, 1903; s. Harold and Lillian (Whitman) B.; m. Elizabeth Forbes, Aug. 28, 1940; 1 dau., Anne (Mrs. Philip Gronbach); m. Pearle E. Quinn, Dec. 5, 1947; 1 son, David. A.B., Pomona Coll., 1925, A.M., 1926; Ph.D., Stanford U., 1932. Tchr. Burbank High Sch., 1926-27; instr. Santa Barbara State Tchrs. Coll., 1929-30; instr. in history Stanford, 1930-36; asst. prof., 1936-42, assoc. prof., 1942-45; asst. prof. history U. Wash., 1938-39; dean and prof. history Claremont (Calif.) Grad. Sch., 1945-53, prof. history, 1953-54, Vanderbilt U., 1954-72, prof. emeritus, 1972—, chmn. dept., 1954-62; lectr. in history U. Tenn., Nashville, 1973-78; Mem. Tenn. Ho. of Reps., 1964-72; Mem. com. on Am. History in Schs. and Colls., 1943. Author: The American Frontier in Hawaii, 1942, The United States 1492-1877, 1972, The United States Since 1865, 1973; Mem. bd. editors: Pacific Hist. Rev, 1940-54, Miss. Valley Hist. Rev, 1946-49; Contbr. to: Ency. Brit., Collier's Ency. Yearbook. Alternate del. Democratic Nat. Conv., 1952; mem. Charter Revision Commn. Nashville-Davidson County, 1978—. Recipient Albert J. Beveridge Meml. prize Am. Hist. Assn., 1943. Mem. Am., So. hist. assns., Orgn. Am. Historians, Am. Studies Assn. (pres. Ky.-Tenn. chpt. 1956-57, nat. council 1972-75), Phi Beta Kappa. Democrat (mem. Davidson County exec. com. 1960-62). Methodist. Home: 212 Craighead Ave Nashville TN 37205

BRADLEY, HOLBROOK, government official; b. Boothbay Harbor, Maine, Sept. 25, 1916; s. Frederick and Ruth (Fletcher) B.; m. Phoebe Footner, June 6, 1946; children: Elsie (Mrs. Michael Mulcahey), Susan (Mrs. Steven Mork), William H., Phoebe F. Student, Columbia U. Bus. Sch., 1938; B.A., Yale, 1940. Salesman Gen. Electric Sales, Buffalo, 1940-41; reporter, war corr., writer Balt. Sun, Balt. Evening Sun, 1941-46; Washington Bur. corr. Life mag., 1946-48; joined U.S. fgn. service; information officer Office Mil. Govt. Germany, Berlin, Nurenberg, Munich, 1948-51; rep. Asia Found., Ceylon, 1952-55, Indonesia, 1955-57; dir. Southeast Asia, San Francisco, 1957-60; fgn. service officer USIA, Washington, 1961-64, Seoul, Korea, 1964-67, Saigon, Vietnam, 1967-69, Ankara, Turkey, 1969-71, Calcutta, India, 1972-76, Washington, 1976. Decorated Purple Heart.; Recipient Meritorius Honor award USIA, 1968. Mem. Beta Theta Pi. Club: Cruising America. Home: PO Box 875 Stinson Beach CA 94970

BRADLEY, J.F., JR., manufacturing company executive; b. Wagoner, Okla., July 7, 1930; s. Jacob F. and Ilsa (Ellington) B.; m. Mary Joan Oberc, June 7, 1952 (div. 1978); children—Jeffrey F., Michael B., Michelle J.; m. Angela C. Cutrone, Aug. 14, 1981. B.B.A., U. Mich., 1952; M.B.A., U. Detroit, 1959. Fin. analyst Ford Motor Co., 1956-60; v.p. corp. finance TRW Inc., Cleve., 1960-72; exec. v.p. adminstrn. and fin. Scott & Fetzer Co., Lakewood, Ohio, 1972-83, dir., 1971—; pres. Scott & Fetzer Fin. Services Group, 1981—; dir. Perlmuter Printing Co., World Book Fin. Co., Rusco Industries, Inc. Trustee Ohio Coll. Podiatric Medicine. Served to 1st lt. AUS, 1952-56. Mem. Nat. Investor Relations Inst. (past dir.), Fin. Execs. Inst. Clubs: Mason (Shriner, Jester), Union, Cleve. Athletic, Lakeside Yacht. Home: 13908 Edgewater Dr Lakewood OH 44107 Office: 865 Bassett Rd Westlake OH 44145

BRADLEY, JOHN ANDREW, healthcare company executive; b. Hammond, Ind., Aug. 3, 1930; s. Andrew C. and Florence (Wolfe) B.; m. Judith E. Salmi, June 1, 1955; children: John Michael, Kerry Kathleen, Kelly Ann. B.S., Loras Coll., Dubuque, Iowa, 1952; M.H.A., St. Louis U., 1955, Ph.D., 1962. Asst. adminstr. Santa Rosa Med. Center, San Antonio, 1958, Incarnate Word Hosp., St. Louis, 1958-60; research asso. St. Louis U., 1958-60; asso. adminstr. Santa Rosa Med. Center, 1961-67, adminstr., 1967-69; sr. v.p., dir. Western div. Am. Medicorp, Inc., 1969-78; pres. Am. Healthcare Mgmt., Inc., Dallas, 1978—; adj. prof. grad. program Hosp. adminstrn. Trinity U., 1967-69; vis. lectr. Baylor U. Sch. Hosp. Adminstrn., 1962-68; Mem. health services research study sect. Nat. Center Health Services Research and Devel., HEW, 1967-69. Chmn. urban devel. com. San Antonio C. of C., 1967; mem. bd. Econ. Opportunities Devel. Corp., 1966-67; vice chmn. Cath. Youth Orgn. Adv. Bd., Archdiocese San Antonio, 1965-66; mem. Blue Cross Assn. Medicare Provider Appeals Com., 1972; Bd. dirs. Cath. Welfare Bur., 1965-66, Patrician Movement, 1964-66, Guadalupe Community Center, 1964-66, San Antonio Neighborhood Youth Orgn., 1965-66; bd. dirs. Fedn. Am. Hosps., 1971-81, pres., 1976; bd. dirs. United Hosp. Assn. Calif., 1977-79; pres. Pvt. Clinics and Hosps. Assn. Tex., 1973-74. Served with AUS, 1953-57. Fellow Am. Coll. Hosp. Adminstrs.; mem. Am. Hosp. Assn. (chmn. adv. panel on chart accounts for hosps.; council on manpower and edn.), Calif. Hosp. Assn., Tex. Hosp. Assn. (v.p. 1969), United Hosp. Assn. Calif. Home: 5611 Harbor Town Dr Dallas TX 75252 Office: 4455 LBJ Freeway Suite 1200 Dallas TX 75234

BRADLEY, JOHN EDMUND, physician, emeritus educator; b. Balt., Oct. 31, 1906; s. Charles Edward and Mary (Henry) B.; m. Kathryn Davis Strong, Sept. 21, 1933; children—Mark, Marcia. B.S., Loyola Coll., 1928; M.D., Georgetown U., 1932; postgrad. in pediatrics, Harvard, 1933-34. Intern Mercy Hosp., Balt., 1932-33; practice medicine specializing in pediatrics Balt., 1935-47; chmn. med. bd. St. Gabriel's Home, 1957-1966; chief pediatrics Luth. Hosp., 1956-66; instr., asst. prof., then assoc. prof. pediatrics U. Md. Sch. Medicine, 1934-46, prof., head pediatrics, 1948-66, emeritus prof. pediatrics, 1966—; dir. Pediatrics Permanente Found., 1947-48; now hon. cons. Childrens' Health Center, San Diego.; Mem. Md. Bd. Health and Mental Hygiene, 1961-1971; mem. adv. bd. Childhood Study Center Md. Editorial bd.: Current Medical Dialog; Contbr. articles to med. jours. Mem. adv. com. Md. Civil Def., 1941-46; mem. health council Md. Conf. Social Welfare; mem. Maternal Child and Welfare Med. Care Com.; mem. nat. adv. com. SSS.; Bd. dirs. Mental Hygiene Soc. Md.; trustee Hosp. Council. Recipient 6 gold medals for gen. acad. excellence, gold medal for sci. in schs. Fellow Am. Acad. Pediatrics; mem. A.M.A., Am. Pediatric Soc., N.Y. Acad. Scis., A.A.A.S., Assn. Med. Writers, So. Med. Assn., Alpha Omega Alpha. Home: Sintonte and Mirasol Rds Rancho Bernardo San Diego CA 92128

BRADLEY, JOHN PAUL, college provost; b. Glasgow, Scotland, June 18, 1919; s. Michael and Margaret (Donohue) B. L. Ph., St. Peter's Coll., Bearsden, Scotland, 1940; M.A., Oxford (Eng.) U., 1950; Diploma Edn. (V.G.), Glasgow U., 1951. Ordained priest Roman Catholic Ch., 1944; asst. pastor archdiocese of, Glasgow, 1944-46; asst. to Archbishop Fulton Sheen, N.Y.C., 1951-52; acting head dept. philosophy, moderator athletics Belmont (N.C.) Abbey Coll., 1952-56, pres., 1970-78, provost, trustee, 1978—; supervisory editor Grolier, Inc., N.Y.C., Good Will Pubs., N.C., 1956-58; sr. editor J.G. Ferguson Pub. Co. affiliate of Doubleday, Inc., N.Y.C., 1958-65; editor-in-chief Good Will Pubs., Inc., 1965-70, dir., 1979—, chmn. bd., chief exec. officer, 1980—; Treas. Ind. Coll. Fund N.C., 1972—, N.C. Found. Ch. Related Colls.; mem. exec. com. N.C. Assn. Ind. Colls. and Univs., 1972—; Vice pres., bd. dirs. Piedmont U. Center N.C., 1973—; mem. acad. adv. bd. Campion Hall Coll., Oxford U., 1975—. Author: Portrait of Christ for Newlyweds, 1954, Come Unto Me, 1958, Our Christian Heritage, 1967; Compiler: The First Hundred Years, 1976, The Morality of a Union-Free Environment, 1980; editor: The Catholic Layman's Library (10 vols.), 1970; Contbr. articles to numerous publs. Mem. Nat. Catholic Edn. Assn. (chmn. So. Regional Unit 1971-72). Address: Belmont Abbey College Belmont NC 28012 also Good Will Publishers Inc PO Box 269 Gastonia NC 28052

BRADLEY, LEE CARRINGTON, JR., lawyer; b. Charlottesville, Va., Sept. 27, 1897; s. Lee C. and Eleanor (Lyons) B.; m. Mary Allen Northington, Jan. 9, 1924; children—Lee Carrington, Merrill Northington, Mary Earle (Mrs. Murray). Litt.B., Princeton, 1918; LL.B., Harvard, 1921. Bar: Ala. bar 1921. Since practiced in, Birmingham; partner firm Bradley, Arant, Rose & White (and predecessors), 1922—. Mem. Phi Beta Kappa. Episcopalian. Club: Rotarian. Home: 2844 Carlisle Rd Birmingham AL 35213 Office: Park Pl Tower Birmingham AL 35203

BRADLEY, LESTER EUGENE, steel and rubber products manufacturing executive; b. Willamette, Oreg., Feb. 2, 1921; s. Alfred A. and Louise J. (Schwerin) B.; m. Gloria Agnes Planton, Dec. 12, 1942; children: Susan K., David Allen; m. June Stumpp, Mar. 27, 1973. B.B.S., U. Oreg., 1947. Vice pres., gen. mgr. No. Studs Ltd., Lac La Hache, B.C., Can., 1954-66; pres., gen. mgr. Star Studs Inc., Afton, Wyo., 1966-71; exec. v.p. New Idria Inc., San Francisco, 1971-74, pres., chief exec. officer, Walnut Creek, Calif., 1974—; v.p. Buckhorn Inc., Columbus, Ohio. Served with USNR, 1942-45. Decorated Bronze Star. Republican. Methodist. Clubs: Elks, Willamette Valley Country. Home: 1806 Barnes Circle West Linn OR 97068

BRADLEY, MARION ZIMMER, novelist, educator; b. Albany, N.Y., June 3, 1930; d. Leslie Raymond and Evelyn Parkhurst (Conklin) Zimmer; m. Robert Alden Bradley, Oct. 1949; 1 son, David Stephen Robert; m. Walter B. Breen, Feb. 11, 1964; children: Patrick Russell Donald, Moira Dorothy Evelyn. B.A., Hardin Simmons U., 1964; postgrad., U. Calif.-Berkeley, 1965-67. Author: (Darkovar novels) Planet Savers, 1962, The Sword of Aldones, 1962, The Bloody Sun, 1964, The Winds of Darkover, 1970, The World Wreckers, 1971, Darkover Landfall, 1972, The Spell Sword, 1972, The Heritage of Hastur, 1975, The Shattered Chain, 1976, The Forbidden Tower, 1977, Stormqueen, 1978, The Bloody Sun (rewriter), 1979, Two to Conquer, 1980, The Keeper's Price, 1980, Sharra's Exile, 1981, Sword of Chaos, 1982, Hawkmistress, 1982, Thendara House, 1983, City of Sorceresses, 1984, (other sci. fiction, anthologies, gothics, mainstream novels), (mainstream novels) The Catch Trap, 1979, The Mists of Avalon, 1983. Home: PO Box 352 Berkeley CA 94701

BRADLEY, MARVIN R., former government official; b. Lebanon, Ind., Jan. 2, 1914; s. Ira and Ada Fern (Rader) B.; m. Mable Morris, Aug. 18, 1934; children: Steven R., Kathleen F. Student, Purdue U., 1931-32, Walton Sch. Commerce, 1935-41. Bookkeeper, Indpls. Star, 1933-34; with Ind. Farm Bur. Coop. Assn., Inc., Indpls., 1934-77, sec., 1948-77, treas., 1964-77; dir. Farm Credit Adminstrn., 1976-82. Coordinator, Speedway (Ind.) Boy Scouts Am., 1949-50; mem. Speedway Town Bd., 1956-59. Mem. Nat. Soc. Accts. for Coops. (past pres.). Mem. Christian Ch. (trustee, deacon, treas.). Clubs: Masons, Lions (past pres. Speedway). Home: 5735 Elaine St Speedway IN 46224

BRADLEY, MELVIN L., government official; b. Texarakana, Tex., Jan. 6, 1938; s. S.T. and David Ella (Garth) B.; m. Ruth Ann Terry, Mar. 3, 1958; children: Cheryl, Eric, Jacqueline, Tracy. Student, Los Angeles City Coll., 1955, Compton Coll., 1965; B.S., Pepperdine U., 1973. Postal clk. U.S. Post Office, 1956-60; real estate broker, Los Angeles, 1960-63; dep. sheriff Los Angeles County, 1963-70; asst. to Gov. Ronald Reagan, 1970-75; dir. public relations Drew Med. Sch., Los Angeles, 1975-77; asst. to v.p. United Airlines, 1977-81; sr. policy advisor to Pres. U.S., White House, 1981-82, spl. asst. to, 1982—. Republican. Office: The White House Washington DC 20500

BRADLEY, PATRICIA ELLEN, professional golfer; b. Arlington, Mass., Mar. 24, 1951; d. Richard Joseph and Kathleen Maureen (O'Brien) B. Asso.B.S. in Phys. Edn, Miami-Dade North Jr. Coll., 1971; B.S., Fla. Internat. U., 1974. Mem. Sun-Star Japan-U.S. Team Matches, 1975-76, All-Am. Collegiate Team, 1971, U.S.A. Com., 1974, 76, Golf Mag.'s All Am. Team, 1976, 77-78, 79-81; qualified for Colgate Triple Crown Tournament, 1975, 76, 77, 78; staff mem. Dunlop Golf Co.; under contract with Colgate-Palmolive Co. Recipient Most Improved Player award Golf Digest, 1976. Mem. Ladies Profl. Golf Assn. Roman Catholic. N.H. Womens Golf Amateur champion, 1967, 69, Mass. Womens Amateur champion, 1972, New Eng. Amateur champion, 1972, 73, Fla. Collegiate champion, 1970; winner Colgate Far East Tournament, 1975, Girl Talk Classic Tournament, 1976, Bankers Trust Classic Tournament, 1977, Lady Keystone Open, Hoosier Classic, Rail Charity Classic, J.C. Penney Classic, 1978, Balt. Classic, Peter Jackson Classic, 1980, U.S. Women's Open, 1981; runner-up Ladies Profl. Golf Assn. Championship, 1977; Played exhbn. golf match with Pres. Ford, Vail, Colo., 1976; 2d on 1978 money list, 4th on 1980 money list; 3d on 1983 money list; 3d on all time money list.

BRADLEY, RALPH ALLAN, statistics educator; b. Smith Falls, Ont., Can., Nov. 28, 1923; came to U.S., 1950, naturalized, 1958; s. Alva Ogle and Ruby (Minnikin) B.; m. Marion Edith MacRae, Sept. 6, 1946; children: Ralph Allan, Linda Irene. B.A., Queens U., 1944, M.A., 1946; Ph.D., U. N.C., 1949. Asst. prof. McGill U., 1949-50; asso. prof., prof. Va. Poly. Inst., 1950-59; prof. stats. Fla. State U., Tallahassee, 1959—, head dept. stats., 1959-78; research prof. U. Ga., 1982—; vis. prof. Rutgers U., 1954; program specialist Ford Found. and; U. Cairo, 1966-67. Editor: Biometrics, 1957-62; contbr. articles to profl. jours. Served to lt., inf. Can. Army, 1944-45. Recipient Brumbaugh award Am. Soc. Quality Control, 1956, Shelton Horsley Research award Va. Acad. Sci., 1957; R.O. Lawton disting. prof., 1970—. Fellow Inst. Math. Stats. (past council mem.), Am. Statis. Assn. (past dir.; pres. 1981—), AAAS; mem. Biometric Soc. (council), Internat. Statis. Inst., Enar Biometric Soc. (past pres.), Sigma Xi. Home: 325 Hickory Hill Dr Watkinsville GA 30677

BRADLEY, RAYMOND JOSEPH, lawyer; b. Phila., July 16, 1920; s. Michael Joseph and Emily Clotilda (Angiuli) B.; m. Sarah Ann Hill, Nov. 26, 1960; children: Michael J., Andrew W., David T. A.B., U. Pa., 1941, LL.B., 1947. Bar: Pa. 1948, U.S. Supreme Ct. 1957. Law clk. to justice Pa. Supreme Ct., 1948; assoc. Barnes, Dechert, Price, Smith & Clark, Phila., 1948-49; asst. prof. U. Pa. Law Sch., Phila., 1950-52, assoc. prof., 1952-55; ptnr. McBride, von Moschzisker & Bradley, Phila., 1955-62, Wolf, Block, Schorr and Solis-Cohen, 1962—; dep. controller City of Phila., 1950; Trustee Community Legal Services, Phila., 1968; bd. dirs. Defender Assn., Phila., 1949-75. Served with USNR, 1942-46. Mem. Am. Coll. Trial Lawyers, Am. Judicature Soc., Am. Law Inst., Am. Bar Assn., Pa. Bar Assn., Phila. Bar Assn., ACLU (dir. 1951—, past pres. Greater Phila. br.), Order of Coif. Office: 12th Fl Packard Bldg Philadelphia PA 19102

BRADLEY, RICHARD EDWIN, university administrator; b. Omaha, Mar. 9, 1926; s. Louis J. and Betsy (Winterton) B.; m. Doris I. McGowan, June 8, 1946; children—Diane, Karen, David. Student, Creighton U., 1946-48; B.S.D., U. Nebr., 1950, D.D.S., 1952; M.S., State U. Iowa, 1958. Instr. State U. Iowa, 1957-58; asst. prof. Creighton U., 1958-59; asst. prof., chmn. dept. periodontics U. Nebr., 1959-62, asso. prof., 1962-65, prof., 1965-67; asso. dean Coll. Dentistry, 1967-68, dean, 1968-80; pres. Baylor Coll. Dentistry, 1980—; cons. VA, also; VA Hosp., Dallas.; Pres. Am. Assn. Dental Schs., 1977-78; Mem. nat. adv. com. on health professions edn. Dept. Health and Human Resources, 1982—. Contbg. editor to: Orban's Textbook of Periodontics, 1963—; Contbr. to: Clark's Clin., 1980. Served with USNR, 1944-46. Fellow Internat. Coll. Dentists; mem. Am. Dental Assn., Am. Acad. Periodontology, Am. Coll. Dentists, Internat. Assn. Dental Research, Sigma Xi, Omicron Kappa Upsilon. Home: 9211 Clover Valley Dallas TX 75243

BRADLEY, ROBERT FRANKLIN, physician; b. Bridgeport, Conn., Jan. 30, 1920; s. Robert Franklin B. and Grace H. (Bradley); m. Elizabeth Savacool, Sept. 18, 1943; children: Robin Bradley Tritta, Pamela Bradley Roche, David B., Amy A., Susan M. B.S., Yale U., 1941, M.D., 1943. Intern Vanderbilt U. Hosp., 1944; fellow in medicine Lahey Clinic, Boston, 1946-49, Joslin Clinic and New Eng. Deaconess Hosp., 1949-50; physician McCarthy Clinic, Lawrence, Mass., 1949-59, Joslin Clinic, 1950—, New Eng. Deaconess Hosp., 1950—; med. dir. Joslin Clinic-Joslin Diabetes Found. Inc., 1968-77, found. v.p., 1968-77; pres. Joslin Diabetes Ctr. Inc., Boston, 1977—; assoc. clin. prof. medicine Harvard Med. Sch.; sr. assoc. in medicine Brigham and Women's Hosp. Contbr. cpts. to books, articles to profl. jours. Served with MC USNR, 1944-46, 1953. Fellow ACP; mem. Am. Diabetes Assn. (dir. 1966-72), AMA, Am. Soc. Internal Medicine, Mass. Med. Soc., Mass. Soc. Internal Medicine (pres. 1964-66), New Eng. Diabetes Assn. (pres. 1960-61). Office: One Joslin Pl Boston MA 02215

BRADLEY, ROBERT LEE, surgeon; b. Hundred, W.Va., Jan. 7, 1920; s. John Henry and Carrie (Allen) B.; children: Robert L., Nancy L., Jan. A.B., W.Va. U., 1939; M.D., Northwestern U., 1943; Ph.D., U. Ky., 1971. Diplomate: Am. Bd. Surgery. Intern Presbyn. Hosp., Chgo., 1942-43; resident VA Hosp., Milw., 1946-49, Roanoke, Va., 1949-51, chief surg. service, Huntington, W.Va., 1951-69, Lexington, Ky., 1974-75; prof. anatomy-surgery Marshall U., Huntington, 1975—, chmn. dept. surgery, 1981—; assoc. clin. prof. surgery U. Ky., Lexington, 1964-75; spl. asst. to surgeon gen. Dept. Army, 1973-80. Contbr. articles to profl. jours. Served with U.S. Army, 1973-80. Fellow ACS; mem. Central Surg. Assn., Soc. Med. Cons. Armed Forces, AMA, Southeastern Surg. Congress, Soc. for Surgery of Alimentary Tract, others. Home: 6220 Booten Creek Rd Barboursville WV 25701 Office: Dept Surgery Marshall U Sch Medicine Huntington WV 25701

BRADLEY, RONALD CALVIN, investment co. exec.; b. Duluth, Minn., Mar. 17, 1915; s. Ralph Dawson and Celeste (Coleman) B.; m. Margot H. Tude, Dec. 31, 1949; children—Margot, Michele. B.S. with honors, U. Cal. at Berkeley, 1937, M.B.A., Harvard, 1939. With Emporium, San Francisco, 1939-41, U.S. Steel Corp. of Del., Pitts., 1941-42; v.p. Doherty, Clifford, Steers & Shenfield (advt. agy.), N.Y.C., 1946-56; sr. v.p., dir. Ted Bates & Co., N.Y.C., 1956-70; investment analyst, adviser, cons., pres. Bradley Investments, Miami, Fla., 1970—; also asso. Oscar E Dooly Assos., Inc. (investment and comml. realty), Miami. Mem. New World Center Action Com. on Redevel. Downtown Miami. Served from lt. (j.g.) to lt. comdr. USNR, 1942-46. Mem. Phi Beta Kappa. Christian Scientist (1st reader, treas., trustee). Clubs: Harvard (Miami) (dir.); Kiwanis.). Home: 8400 Ponce de Leon Rd Miami FL 33143 Office: Suite 2650 AmeriFirst Federal Bldg Miami FL 33131 *Observation and time's perspective gradually make clearer the fallacy of categorizing our likes and dislikes by race, color, or nationality. All that really concerns us are those qualities of spirit and character which, by the test of experience, we find constructive and good, or destructive and evil. It is self-evident that no race, color, or nationality has a monopoly of either grouping. I try never to envy another's wealth unless I'm also willing to accept his problems along with his money. This cures envy every time.*

BRADLEY, RONALD JAMES, neuroscientist; b. Enniskillen, No. Ireland, Feb. 17, 1943; s. Samuel John and Mary Elizabeth (Irvine) B.; m. Doris Brown, Mar. 5, 1966; children—Nicola, Jason. B.Sc., Queens U., Belfast, No. Ireland, 1964; Ph.D., U. Edinburgh, Scotland, 1967. Mem. faculty Yale U., 1967-69, U. N.Mex., 1969-71; mem. faculty U. Ala., Birmingham, 1972—, prof. psychiatry and neuroscis., 1976—; guest prof. U. Saarlands, W. Ger., 1977-81. Co-editor: Internat. Rev. Neurobiology, 1974—. Recipient A. E. Bennett award Soc. Biol. Psychiatry, 1967. Mem. AAAS, Biophys. Soc., Neuroscis. Soc., Soc. Biol. Psychiatry. Home: 2644 Butte Woods Dr Birmingham AL 35243 Office: Neurosciences Program U Ala University Station Birmingham AL 35294

BRADLEY, STERLING GAYLEN, microbiologist, educator; b. Springfield, Mo., Apr. 2, 1932; s. Benn and Lora (Brown) B.; m. Lois Evelyn Lee, May 13, 1951; children—Don, Evelyn, John, Phillip; m. Judith Bond, July 24, 1974; 1 son, Kevin. B.A., B.S., S.W. Mo. State Coll., 1950; M.S., Northwestern U., 1952; Ph.D. (NSF fellow), 1954, Duke, 1957. Grad. teaching asst. Northwestern U., Evanston, Ill., 1950-51, Abbott research asst., 1951-52, instr. biology, 1954; instr. dept. bacteriology and immunology U. Minn., 1956-57, asst. prof. dept. bacteriology, 1957-59, asso. prof. dept. microbiology, 1959-63, grad. faculty genetics, 1961-68, prof., 1963-68, chmn. genetics faculty group, 1964; chmn. dept. microbiology Va. Commonwealth U., Richmond, 1968-82, prof. dept. pharmacology, 1979—, dean basic scis., 1982—; vis. worker in pharmacology Cambridge (Eng.) U., 1978; Mem. bd. sci. counselors NIH, 1968-72, chmn., 1970-72; mem. Internat. Com. Bacteriol. Systematics, 1966-74, exec. bd., 1970-74; mem. U.S. Pharmacopeial Com. of Revision, 1980—; coordinator project 3 U.S.-USSR Joint Working Group on Microbiology, 1979-82. Mem. editorial bd.: Proc. Soc. Exptl. Biol. Medicine, 1966-72, Conf. on Anti-microbial Agts, 1960; editor: Jour. Bacteriology, 1970-78; contbr. articles to profl. jours. Recipient Charles Porter award, 1983; Eli Lilly postdoctoral fellow U. Wis., 1954-55; NSF postdoctoral fellow dept. genetics, 1955-56; NIH Sr. Fogarty internat. fellow, 1978. Fellow Va. Acad. Sci. (past mem. council sec. 1976-77); mem. Am. Assn.

Immunology, Am. Acad. Microbiology, Am. Soc. Cell Biology, AAAS, AAUP, Am. Soc. Microbiology (past mem. council), Soc. Gen. Microbiology, Soc. Protozoologists, Soc. Indsl. Microbiology (past pres.), Am. Inst. Biol. Sci. (past dir.), Mycol. Soc. Am., Soc. for Exptl. Biology and Medicine (past chmn. Minn. chpt.), Genetics Soc. Am., Torrey Bot. Club (life), N.Y. Acad. Scis. (life), Am. Thoracic Soc., Sigma Xi (pres. chpt. 1975-76). Home: 1324 Brookland Pkwy Richmond VA 23227 Office: Med Coll Va Sta PO Box 110 Richmond VA 23298

BRADLEY, STUART B., lawyer; b. Chgo., Jan. 29, 1907; s. Alexander S. and Laura (Bevans) B.; m. Patricia Goodhue, Mar. 15, 1935; children: Stuart, Barbara, Carolyn, Laura. Student, Wash. State Coll., 1923-25, U. Chgo., 1927-30, Ph.B., J.D. Bar: Ill. 1931. Partner firm Bradley, McMurray, Black & Snyder, and predecessors, Chgo., 1934-84, Deerfield, Ill., 1984—; promoter St. Lawrence Seaway, Calumet-Sag projects; dir. Deerfield Savs. & Loan Assn.; mem. adv. com. on admiralty rules U.S. Supreme Ct., 1960-72. Author articles mags., law revs. Scoutmaster Boy Scouts Am., 1949-52; chmn. planning bd. North Shore Area Council, 1953; trustee Glencoe Pub. Library, 1964-73. Served from capt. to lt. col. U.S. Army, 1943-46. Decorated Bronze Star; recipient citation for pub. service U. Chgo., 1955. Mem. Chgo. Assn. Commerce (chmn. harbors and waterways com. 1948-52), Maritime Law Assn. (exec. com. 1963-66), ABA, Ill. Bar Assn., Chgo. Bar Assn. (chmn. admiralty com. 1958-59), Am. Coll. Trial Lawyers, Phi Delta Phi, Kappa Sigma. Methodist. Clubs: Propeller (pres. Port of Chgo. 1948), Jackson Park Yacht, Law, Legal, Attic, Lit. (Chgo.); Skokie Country (Glencoe). Home: 750 Bluff St Glencoe IL 60022 Office: 747 Deerfield Rd Deerfield IL 60015

BRADLEY, THOMAS (TOM BRADLEY), mayor; b. Calvert, Tex., Dec. 29, 1917; s. Lee and Crenner (Hawkins) B.; m. Ethel Arnold, May 4, 1941; children: Lorraine, Phyllis. Student, UCLA, 1937-40; LL.B., Southwestern U., 1956. Bar: Calif. 1956. Police officer Los Angeles, 1940-61; practiced in, Los Angeles, 1956-73; mem. Los Angeles City Council, 1963-73; mayor of, Los Angeles, 1973—; Founder, dir. Bank of Finance. Nat. Urban Coalition. Pres. Nat. League Cities, 1974, also mem. nat. bd. dirs.; pres. League of Calif. Cities, 1979, So. Calif. Assn. Govts., 1968-69, Nat. Assn. Regional Councils, 1969-71; mem. Nat. Energy Adv. Council, Nat. Commn. on Productivity and Work Quality; mem. advisory bd., vice chmn. transp. com. U.S. Conf. Mayors.; Bd. dirs. Nat. Urban Fellows. Mem. Los Angeles World Affairs Council. Democrat. Methodist. Office: Office of Mayor City Hall Los Angeles CA 90012

BRADLEY, VAN ALLEN, rare book and autograph dealer, ret. journalist; b. Albertville, Ala., Aug. 24, 1913; s. Van A. and Lula (Montgomery) B.; m. Patricia Elaine Thompson, Nov. 5, 1939 (div.); children—Van Allen III, Pamela Star, Susan; m. Sharon Lee Luedke, Dec. 3, 1966 (div.); 1 dau., Gremlyn Angelica. Student, Harding Coll., 1930-32; B.J., U. Mo., 1933. Reporter Nashville Tennessean, 1934-35; reporter, columnist, chief copy desk Omaha Bee-News, 1935-37; copy editor Chgo. Herald Examiner, 1937-38; copy editor, asst. picture editor Chgo. Tribune, 1938-42; copy editor, book columnist, chief copy desk Chgo. Sun (now Sun-Times), 1942-48; lit. editor Chgo. Daily News, 1948-71, editorial writer, 1953-60, ret., 1971; pres. Heritage Book Shop, Inc., Chgo., 1964-72, Van Allen Bradley Inc., Lake Zurich, Ill., 1972-78, Scottsdale, Ariz., 1978—; author syndicated rare book column Gold in Your Attic, 1957-71; lectr., tchr. Northwestern U. Medill Sch. Journalism, 1942-54; platform lectr. books, current lit. Author: Music for the Millions, 1957, Gold in Your Attic, 1958, More Gold in Your Attic, 1961, The New Gold in Your Attic, 1968, The Book Collector's Handbook of Values, 1972, 4th edit., 1982; editor: How To Predict What People Will Buy, 1957. Founder mem. Lincolnwood (Ill.) Little Theatre, Inc., pres., 1957-58; mem. Lincolnwood Bd. Edn., 1950-60, pres., 1953-60; mem. Citizens Com. for Chgo. Pub. Library; poetry and lit. adv. coms. Ill. Arts Council. Recipient award for meritorious service to letters Chgo. Found. for Lit., 1956. Mem. Soc. Midland Authors (dir., pres. 1955-57), Friends Chgo. Pub. Library (dir.), Friends Lit. (adv. council), Friends of Barrington (Ill.) Pub. Library (pres. 1975-77), Chgo. Press Vets. Assn. Democrat. Mem. Ch. of Christ. Club: Tavern (Chgo.). Home: 6201 E Cactus Rd Scottsdale AZ 85254 Office: PO Box 4130 Hopi Sta Scottsdale AZ 85261

BRADLEY, WESLEY HOLMES, physician; b. Chaumont, N.Y., Aug. 7, 1922; s. William Holmes and Margaret Jane (Bartrem) B.; m. Barbara Jean Sawyer, Sept. 23, 1945; children: James, Douglas, William, David. A.B., Syracuse U., 1944, M.D., 1946. Intern Mass. Meml. Hosp., Boston, 1946-47; resident in otolaryngology U. Mich., 1949-53; practice medicine specializing in otolaryngology, Syracuse, N.Y., 1953-75; mem. faculty SUNY Coll. Medicine, 1953-75, clin. prof., 1974-75; dir. communicative disorders program Nat. Inst. Neurol. and Communicative Disorders and Stroke, NIH, Bethesda, Md., 1975-78; med. dir. Commd. Corps UPSHS, 1975-78; prof. otolaryngology Albany (N.Y.) Med. Coll., 1978—; chief otolaryngology VA Med. Center, Albany, 1978—; mem. nat. adv. council Boys Town Nat. Inst. for Communicative Disorders in Children. Bd. editors: Rhinology and Laryngology, 1978—; contbr. articles to profl. jours. Served with USN, 1947-49. Mem. AMA, Am. Acad. Otolaryngology-Head and Neck Surgery (v.p. 1970, exec. v.p. 1979-81, exec. council 1972-76), Am. Laryngological Rhinological and Otological Soc. (v.p. 1982, exec. council 1983—), Otosclerosis Study Group (pres. 1976), Am. Otological Soc. (pres. 1974), ACS, Assn. Research in Otolaryngology, Am. Bd. Otolaryngology (exec. com. 1972, 74, 78), Deafness Research Found. (dir. 1967-75, 78—, exec. com. 1970-75), Am. Council Otolaryngology (asso. exec. dir. 1969-72, exec. com. 1972), Alpha Omega Alpha, Alpha Kappa Kappa, Lambda Chi Alpha. Republican. Methodist. Office: 113 Holland Ave Albany NY 12208 *As I think about my life, these are a few of the feelings which seem to have a recurring consistency: maintaining a sense of awe and respect for the wonders of creation around us; keeping faith in oneself, in others, and in the ongoing pageant of life; and having fun each day while not taking oneself too seriously.*

BRADLEY, WILLIAM ARTHUR, civil engr.; b. Lansing, Mich., Nov. 11, 1921; s. Arthur and Amy F. (Barringer) B.; m. Elizabeth G. Ewing, June 29, 1949; children—David, Nancy, Susan. B.S.C.E., Mich. State U., 1943; M.S., U. Ill., 1947; Ph.D., U. Mich., 1956. Engr. Douglas Aircraft, El Segundo, Calif., 1943-44; engr. G.M. Foster (Bridge Cons.), Lansing, 1945-46; mem. faculty Mich. State U., East Lansing, 1947—, prof. mechanics and civil engring., 1961—; cons. Dow Chem. Corp., 1959-61. Mem. Lansing Orgn. for Schs.; bd. dirs. West Side Neighborhood Assn. Recipient Disting. Faculty award Mich. State U., 1963, Western Elec. Fund award, 1966. Mem. ASCE, Am. Concrete Inst., Internat. Assn. Bridge and Structural Engrs., Am. Soc. Engring. Edn., Sigma Xi, Phi Kappa Phi, Tau Beta Pi, Chi Epsilon. Home: 1919 W Kalamazoo St Lansing MI 48915 Office: Coll Engring Mich State U East Lansing MI 48824

BRADSHAW, CONRAD ALLAN, lawyer; b. Campbell, Mo., Dec. 22, 1922; s. Clarence Andrew and Stella (Cashdollar) B.; m. Margaret Crassous Sanderson, Dec. 31, 1959; children—Dorothy A., Lucy E., Charlotte L. A.B., U. Mich., 1943, J.D., 1948. Bar: Mich. bar 1948. Since practiced in, Grand Rapids; as partner firm Warner, Norcross & Judd. Served to lt. USNR, 1943-46. Mem. Am. Bar Assn., State Bar Mich. (chmn. corp., fin. and bus. law sect. 1976), Grand Rapids Bar Assn. (pres. 1970). Home: 2724 Darby SE Grand Rapids MI 49506 Office: 900 Old Kent Bldg Grand Rapids MI 49503

BRADSHAW, EUGENE BARRY, pump company executive, lawyer; b. Sioux City, Iowa, July 22, 1938; s. Eugene Barry and Dorothy Louise (Leamer) B.; m. Carman Janelle Sivill, June 22, 1961; children: Eugene, Janelle, Michelle, Elizabeth. B.S. in Chem. Engring, S.D. Sch. Mines and Tech., 1959; J.D., John Marshall Law Sch., 1969. Bar: Ill. 1969, N.Y. 1970. Design engr. Goulds Pumps, Inc., Seneca Falls, N.Y., 1962-64, sales engr., Chgo., 1964-69, corporate counsel, 1969-75, sec., corporate counsel, Seneca Falls, 1975—, v.p., 1979—; dir. Oil Dynamics, Inc., Tulsa, 1977—. Pres. Bd. of Edn., Seneca Falls Central Sch. Dist., 1973-77; trustee Citizens Pub. Expenditure Survey of N.Y., Inc., chmn., 1979; trustee Village of Seneca Falls., 1980-82. Mem. Am. Soc. Corporate Secs., Am., N.Y., Seneca County bar assns. Republican. Methodist. Lodges: Rotary; Masons. Home: 86 Cayuga St Seneca Falls NY 13148 Office: 240 Fall St Seneca Falls NY 13148

BRADSHAW, GEORGE BLAIR, savs. and loan assn. exec.; b. Magrath, Alta., Can., Oct. 5, 1918; s. Frederick John and Mildred Amy (Hillier) B.; m. Lillie Anne Young, Aug. 22, 1947; children—Russell, Becky, Jeffrey, Kathy, Dick, Suzanne, Thomas. B.S. in Mech. Engring, U. Utah, 1939. Loan officer Am. Savs. & Loan Assn., Salt Lake City, 1945-47, dir., 1947—, v.p., 1947-60, pres., gen. mgr., 1960-74, vice chmn. bd., 1974-78, Home Savs. & Loan, Salt Lake City. Adv. mem. exec. bd. Salt Lake council Boy Scouts Am., 1970-79. Mem. Pi Kappa Alpha, Theta Tau. Republican. Mem. Ch. of Jesus Christ of Latter-day Saints (bishop; stake high council). Home: 1948 Laurelhurst Dr Salt Lake City UT 84108 *I have confidence that achievement is in direct proportion to work and dedication directed toward a goal and that righteousness will prevail over evil.*

BRADSHAW, LILLIAN MOORE, librarian; b. Hagerstown, Md., Jan. 10, 1915; d. Harry M. and Mabel E. (Kretzer) Moore; m. William Theodore Bradshaw, May 19, 1946. B.A., Western Md. Coll., 1937; B.L.S., Drexel U., 1938, Litt.D. (hon.), 1978. Asst. adult circulation dept. Utica (N.Y.) Pub. Library, 1938-41, asst. head, 1941-43; adult librarian Enoch Pratt Free Library, Balt., 1943-44, asst. coordinator work with young adults, 1944-46; br. librarian Dallas Pub. Library, 1946-47, readers adviser, 1947-52, head dept. circulation, 1952- 55, coordinator work with adults, 1955-58, asst. dir., 1958-62, dir., 1962—; mem. adv. group on libraries Library of Congress, 1976-77. Mem. bd. publs. So. Meth. U., 1970-78; mem. curriculum com. Leadership Dallas, 1978-79, mem. adv. com., 1978-82; mem. Tex. Gov.'s Commn. on Status of Women, 1970-72, Tex. Com. for Humanities, 1980-84, Nat. Reading Council, Washington, 1970-73; conferee and asst. task force leader Goals for Dallas, 1966-69, vice chmn. achievement com. for continuing edn., 1971, chmn., 1972, chmn. citizen info. and participation com., 1976-77, trustee, 1977—, sec., 1977, treas., 1979—, exec. com., 1977—; mem. Com. to Plan the Future Goals for Dallas, 1973-74; mem. adv. bd. Tex. Library Systems Act, 1974-77; del. White House Conf. on Library and Info. Services, 1979; Tex. del. Nat. Commn. on Libraries and Info. Services; mem. ad hoc com. for planning and monitoring White House Conf. follow-up activities, 1980; bd. dirs. Hoblitzelle Found., 1971—; trustee Lamplighter Sch., 1974-81. Named Tex. Librarian of Year, 1961; recipient Disting. Alumnus award Drexel U. Library Sch., 1970, Titche's Arete award for epitome of excellence in chosen field, 1970; Public Adminstr. of Yr. award, 1981; Excellence in Community Service award Dallas Hist. Soc., 1981; citation of honor Dallas chpt. AIA, 1982. Mem. ALA (v.p. adult services div. 1966-67, pres. adult services div. 1967-68, council 1968-69, pres. 1970-71), Tex. Library Assn. (pres. 1964-65, chmn. pub. libraries div. 1955-56, chmn. awards com. 1973-74, 79-80, Disting. Service award 1975), Tex. Soc. Architects (hon. 1982). Clubs: Zonta (pres. Dallas I 1976-77, Service award 1981. Home: 6318 E Lovers Ln Dallas TX 75214 Office: 1515 Young St Dallas TX 75201

BRADSHAW, PAUL LUDWIG, lawyer, state senator, airline executive; b. Jefferson City, Mo., July 17, 1930; s. Jean Paul and Catherine Ann (Brandt) B.; m. Susan Ann Ward; 1 son, Jean Paul. Sr. v.p., gen. counsel, dir. Ozark Air Lines, Inc., St. Louis; minority leader Mo. State Senate, 1977-83; partner firm Neale, Newman Bradshaw & Freeman, St. Louis. Served with USAF, 1954-56. Republican. Congregationalist. Home: 5747 Wildwood Circle Springfield MO 65804 Office: 1 Corporate Centre Springfield MO 65804

BRADSHAW, RICHARD BURNETT, ret. advt. exec.; b. Berkhamstead, Eng., Mar. 4, 1927; s. Sidney Basil and Marjorie (Hewett) B.; m. Jayne McGraw, June 11, 1955; children—David, Brian, Bruce, Dean, Tracey. B.S. in Journalism, U. Ill., 1951. With Foote, Cone & Belding, 1951-78, research analyst, Chgo., 1951-53, account exec., 1953-60; pres. Canadian Co., Toronto, Ont., 1960-68, sr. v.p., dir. parent co., 1968-78, pres. internat. co., Brussels, 1969-72, chmn. bd., Toronto, 1972-78; chmn. Palmetto Mktg. & Mgmt., 1980—; dir. Churchill Steel. Served with Brit. Royal Navy, 1943-46. Home: 90 Gloucester Rd 260 Shipyard Plantation Hilton Head Island SC 29928

BRADSHAW, RICHARD JOHN, investment banker; b. Stockton, Calif., June 10, 1948; s. Richard Earl and Dorothy Ann (Woodruff); m. Kathleen Devine, July 25, 1970; children: Lawrence, Karen. B.S., Calif. Poly. State U., 1970; M.B.A., Stanford U., 1972. Asst. v.p. Bank of America, Los Angeles, 1972-74; treas. Republic Corp., Los Angeles, 1974-77; pres. The Henley Corp., Los Angeles, 1977-82; sr. v.p. Security Pacific Capital Markets, Los Angeles, 1982; dir. Myocure, Inc., VCI, Inc., Cedra Properties, Inc. Mem. Am. Fin. Assn., Stanford Alumni Assn., Stanford Bus. Sch. Alumni Assn., Phi Kappa Phi, Kappa Mu Epsilon. Clubs: Jonathan., Oakmont. Home: 1221 Imperial Dr Glendale CA 91207 Office: 333 S Hope St Los Angeles CA 90071

BRADSHAW, RICHARD ROTHERWOOD, engr.; b. Phila., Sept. 12, 1916; s. Joseph Rotherwood and Rosanna (Jones) B.; m. Audrey Grace Skinn, Oct. 3, 1940; children—Linda M., Barbara A., Vicki. B.S., Calif. Inst. Tech., 1939; M.S., U. So. Calif., 1950. L. Pres. Richard R. Bradshaw, Inc., Van Nuys, Calif., 1946—, pres. br. office, Honolulu. Contbr. articles to tech. jours., Important works include, Disneyworld Hotels, Orlando, Fla., U.S. embassy, Warsaw, Poland, U.S. Exhbn. Bldg., Moscow USSR, Taraara Hotel, Tahiti, Gulf Life Bldg., Jacksonville, Fla., Los Angeles City Airport. Recipient Alfred Lindau award Am. Concrete Inst., 1968, many others for structural design. Mem. Am. Soc. C.E., Internat. Assn. Bridges and Structural Engring., Am. Seismol. Soc., Cons. Engrs. Assn., Internat. Assn. Thin Shells, Am. Concrete Inst., Am. Arbitration Assn. Home: 17300 Ballinger St Northridge CA 91325 Office: Richard R Bradshaw Inc 14606 Victory Blvd Van Nuys CA 91411

BRADSHAW, TERRY, professional football player; b. Shreveport, La., Sept. 2, 1948; m. Jo Jo Starbuck, June 6, 1976. Ed., La. Tech. U. With profl. football team Pitts. Steelers, 1970—. Country and western singer, entertainer. Named Most Valuable Player, Super Bowl XIII, 1978; named to Pro Bowl, 1978, 79. Quarterback in Super Bowl win, 1974, 75, 78, 79. Address: care Pitts Steelers Three Rivers Stadium 300 Stadium Circle Pittsburgh PA 15212 *

BRADSHAW, THORNTON FREDERICK, corp. exec.; b. Washington, Aug. 4, 1917; s. Frederick and Julia V. (See) B.; m. Sally Davis, 1940 (div. 1974); children: Nancy M. (Mrs. Thomas Poor), Priscilla W. (Mrs. Richard Page, Jr.), Jonathan G.; m. Patricia Salter West, May 11, 1974; children: Jeffrey D. West, Nicholas S. West, Andrew P. West, Eric R. West. A.B., Harvard U., 1940, M.B.A., 1942, D.C.S., 1950; LL.D. (hon.), Pepperdine U., 1974, Southampton Coll., 1983, D.Social Sci., Villanova U., 1975. Assoc. prof. Grad. Sch. Bus. Adminstrn., Harvard U., 1942-52; partner Cresap, McCormick & Paget, N.Y.C., 1952-56; v.p., dir. Atlantic Richfield Co. (formerly Atlantic Refining Co.), Los Angeles, 1956-62, exec. v.p., 1962-64, pres., 1964-80, mem. exec. com., 1966-81; also dir.; chmn., chief exec. officer RCA, N.Y.C., 1981—, also dir.; dir. NBC, Champion Internat.; Bd. dirs., chmn. Conf. Bd.; bd. dirs. Center for Edn. in Internat. Mgmt.; Bd. dirs. Aspen Inst. for Humanistic Studies, Am. Petroleum Inst., Los Angeles World Affairs Council. Trustee Conservation Found., Rockefeller Bros. Fund; mem. vis. com. John Fitzgerald Kennedy Sch. Govt.; bd. overseers Harvard U.; mem.-at-large bd. govs. Performing Arts Council Los Angeles. Served to lt. (j.g.) USNR, 1943-45. Office: RCA Rockefeller Plaza New York NY 10020

BRADSHER, CHARLES KILGO, chemist, emeritus educator; b. Petersburg, Va., July 13, 1912; s. Arthur Brown and Elizabeth (Muse) B.; m. Dorothy Tideman, June 6, 1938; children—Thorston, Catherine Dunnagan, Marien. A.B., Duke, 1933; A.M., Harvard, 1935, Ph.D. in Organic Chemistry, 1937. Postdoctoral research fellow U. Ill., 1937-39; faculty Duke, Durham, N.C., 1939—, James B. Duke prof. chemistry, 1965-79, prof. emeritus, 1979—, chmn. dept., 1965-70; NRC research fellow, 1941-42; Fulbright lectr. Leiden (Netherlands) U., 1951-52; NSF sr. postdoctoral fellow Fed. Inst. Tech., Zürich, Switzerland, 1959-60. Author sci. papers. Named Disting. N.C. Chemist N.C. Inst. Chemists, 1980. Mem. Am. Chem. Soc., AAAS, Royal Soc. Chemistry. Home: Route 2 Box 720 Timberlake NC 27583

BRADSHER, HENRY ST. AMANT, journalist, foreign affairs analyst; b. Baton Rouge, May 11, 1931; s. Earl Lockridge and Augusta Ford (St. Amant) B.; m. Monica Jean Pannwitt, July 25, 1963; children: Keith Vinson, Neal Clifton. B.A. with distinction in History, U. Mo., 1952, B.J., 1952. Reporter A.P., Atlanta and Montgomery, Ala., 1955-57, editor, N.Y.C., 1957-59, corr., bur. chief, New Delhi, India, 1959-64, bur. chief, Moscow, 1964-68; Nieman fellow Harvard U., Cambridge, Mass., 1968-69; fgn. corr. Washington Star, Hong Kong, 1969-75, diplomatic corr., Washington, 1975-81; fgn. affairs analyst U.S. Govt., 1982—; guest scholar Woodrow Wilson Internat. Center for Scholars, Washington, 1980-81. Author: Afghanistan and the Soviet Union, 1983. Served with USAF, 1952-55. Recipient George Polk Meml. award for fgn. reporting, 1973. Mem. Phi Beta Kappa. Home: 5130 N 15th St Arlington VA 22205

BRADSTREET, BERNARD FRANCIS, computer company executive; b. Framingham, Mass., Feb. 17, 1945; s. Franklin Hose and Kathryn M. (Carragher) B.; m. Carol M. McKenna, Dec. 27, 1968; children—Joshua Franklin, Barret Francis, Kenley Anne. A.B. (NROTC scholar), Harvard U., 1967, M.B.A., 1974. Asst. v.p. Boston regional office 1st Nat. Bank Chgo., 1974-79; treas. Prime Computer Co., Prime Park, Natick, Mass., 1979—; dir. Family Health Plan Mass., Marc Analysis Inc. Served with USMCR, 1967-72. Mem. Fin. Execs. Inst., Harvard Bus. Club Boston. Club: Harvard (Boston). Home: 40 Bowditch Rd Sudbury MA 01776 Office: Prime Computer Co Prime Park Natick MA 01760

BRADT, HALE VAN DORN, physicist, x-ray astronomer, educator; b. Colfax, Wash., Dec. 7, 1930; s. Wilber Elmore and Norma (Sparlin) B.; m. Dorothy Ann Haughey, July 19, 1958; children—Elizabeth, Dorothy Ann. A.B., Princeton U., 1952; Ph.D. in Physics, M.I.T., 1961. Mem. dept. physics M.I.T., 1961—, prof., 1972—; sci. investigator Small Astronomy Satellite, NASA, 1975-79, High Energy Astronomy Obs., 1977-79. Co-editor: X and Gamma Ray Astronomy, 1973; asso. editor: Astrophys. Jour. Letters, 1974-77. Served with USNR, 1952-54. Recipient Exceptional Sci. achievement medal NASA, 1978. Mem. Am. Astron. Soc. (sec.-treas. high energy astrophysics div. 1973-75, chmn. 1981), Am. Phys. Soc., Sigma Xi. Home: Belmont MA Office: 37-581 MIT Cambridge MA 02139

BRADWAY, JOSEPH FOWLER, JR., banker; b. Atlantic City, Mar. 5, 1942; s. Joseph F. and Miriam K. (Eisele) B.; m. Janis A. Broadbent, July 4, 1981. B.S. in Econs., Villanova U., 1965. Gen. mgr., ptnr. Flexitallic Gasket Co., 1965-70; pres. Guarantee Bank, Atlantic City, N.J., 1970-73, vice chmn. bd., 1970-77, pres., chief exec. officer, chmn. bd., 1976—; mayor City of Atlantic City, 1972-76. Mem. com. N.J. Conf. Mayors, 1972-76; bd. dirs. Miss Am. Pageant, 1971-73. Mem. C. of C. (dir.), League of Municipalities (dir.). Home: 315 N Rumson Ave Margate NJ 08402 Office: 1310 Atlantic Ave Atlantic City NJ 08401

BRADY, BENNETT MANNING, mathematician, government official; b. Orangeburg, S.C., Apr. 11, 1943; d. William Ellis and Elizabeth (Mays) Manning; m. Roscoe Owen Brady, June 10, 1972; children: Roscoe Owen, Randolph Owen. Student, Agnes Scott Coll., 1961-62; A.B., Vassar Coll., 1965; Fulbright fellow, Cambridge U., 1965-66; M.A. NSF fellow, U. Calif.-Berkeley, 1968; postgrad., George Washington U., 1969-72. Sr. mgmt. cons. Ernst & Ernst, Washington, 1968-70; research assoc. Pres.'s Commn. Fed. Stats., Washington, 1970-71; U.S. internat. statis. liason OMB, Washington, 1971-78; spl. asst. to commr. labor stats. Bur. Labor Stats., Washington, 1978-79, dir. Office Program Coordination and Evaluation, 1979—; cons. ops. research USAF, 1967-68; mem. faculty U. Calif.-Berkeley, 1968; mem. U.S. delegation UN Statis. Commn., 1972. Author: (with J.S. Duncan) Statistical Services in Ten Years' Time, 1978, (with E. Robins and K.S. Tippet) Going Places with Children in Washington, 9th edit., 1979; editor: OSD Statis. Notes, 1980—; contbr. articles on statis. devels. and research to profl. jours. NASA fellow, 1964. Mem. Am. Math. Soc., Am. Statis. Assn., Inst. Mgmt. Sci., Ops. Research Soc. Am., Washington Ops. Research Mgmt. Sci. Council, Washington Statis. Soc., Phi Beta Kappa. Presbyterian. Club: Vassar (Washington). Home: 9501 Kingsley Ave Bethesda MD 20814 Office: 441 G St NW Washington DC 20212

BRADY, CARL FRANKLIN, aircraft charter company executive; b. Chelsea, Okla., Oct. 29, 1919; s. Kirty A. and Pauline Ellen (Doty) B.; m. Carol Elizabeth Sprague, Mar. 29, 1941; children: Carl Franklin, Linda Kathryn, James Kenneth. Student, U. Wash., 1940. Co-owner Aero Cafe, Yakima, Wash., 1946-47; pilot Central Aircraft, Yakima, 1947-48; partner Economy Helicopters, Inc., Yakima, 1948-60; pres. ERA Helicopters, Inc., Anchorage, Alaska, 1960—, ERA Aviation Center, Inc., 1977—, Livingston Copters, Inc., 1977—; exec. v.p. Rowan Companies, Inc., Houston, 1973—, also dir.; also dir.; dir. Alaska Pacific Bank, Alaska Pacific Bancorp. Mem. Alaska Ho. of Reps., 1965-66, Alaska Senate, 1967-68; pres. Alaska Crippled Childrens Assn., 1963. Served with USAAF, 1943-46. Mem. Helicopter Assn. Am. (pres. 1953, 57, Larry D. Bell award 1976), Anchorage C. of C. (pres. 1963-64), Alaska Air Carriers Assn., Am. Helicopter Soc., Commonwealth North, Air Force Assn., Navy League. Republican. Methodist. Clubs: Petroleum of Alaska, Elks. Home: 510 L St Anchorage AK 99501 Office: PO Box 762 Anchorage AK 99510

BRADY, DONALD GEORGE, chem. co. exec.; b. Oak Park, Ill., June 16, 1928; s. George Oliver and Audrey (Chapman) B.; m. Suzanne

Louise Schmidt, June 27, 1953; children—Terri, Clark, Donald Paul. B.S., U. Ill., 1953. C.P.A., Ill. Auditor Gauger & Diehl (C.P.A.'s), Decatur, Ill., 1953-62; auditor, dir. accounting, asst. controller Internat. Minerals & Chem. Corp., Libertyville, Ill., 1962-73, 75-81, v.p. auditing, asst. controller, 1981—; controller Continental Ore Corp., N.Y.C., 1973-75. Served with U.S. Army, 1946-48, 51. Mem. Am. Inst. C.P.A.'s, Ill. Soc. C.P.A.'s, Acctg. Research Assn., Inst. Internal Auditors, Kappa Sigma. Presbyn. (deacon). Home: 49 Kings Cross Lincolnshire IL 60015 Office: IMC Gen Office 421 E Hawley Mundelein IL 60060

BRADY, FRANCIS PATRICK, mfg. co. exec.; b. Montreal, Que, Can., Feb. 8, 1923; s. Hugh Frank and Catherine J. (O'Connor) B.; m. Grace Bamford, Dec. 2, 1944; children—Thomas, Timothy. B.C.L, McGill U., Montreal, 1949. Bar: Called to Que. bar 1949, queen's counsel 1968. Pvt. practice, Montreal, 1949-51; with Dominion Textile Inc., Montreal, 1951—, v.p. gen. counsel, 1974—, sr. v.p. corp. services, 1978—; past chmn. Bus. Linguistic Centre; chmn. Can. Textiles Inst. Served with Can. Navy, 1943-45. Mem. Can. Mfg. Assn. (dir.), Bar. Assn. Que. Roman Catholic. Clubs: Royal Montreal Golf, Mt. Stephen, Pointe Claire Yacht. Home: 114 Bathurst Ave Pointe Claire PQ Canada Office: 1950 Sherbrooke St W Montreal PQ Canada

BRADY, FRANK R., author, editor, publisher broadcaster, educator; b. Bklyn., Mar. 15, 1934; s. James Joseph and Beatrice Adele (Mignerey) B.; m. Maxine Kalfus, Mar. 31, 1963; children—(from 1st marriage) Sean, Erin. B.S., SUNY, 1954; M.F.A. with honors, Columbia U., 1976; M.A., N.Y. U., 1980, postgrad., 1980—. Assoc. producer The Secret People WPIX-TV, N.Y.C., 1964; producer, broadcaster The Hip 400 Pacifica network, 1964; editor Playboy mag, Chgo., 1965-70; pub. Avant Garde mag N.Y.C., 1970-71; tchr. drama Reid Internat. Sch., Ibiza, Spain, 1971; account exec. Metromedia Corp., 1971-72; editorial dir. Hammond, Inc., 1976-78; mem. faculty English dept. and Washington Sq. Writing Center N.Y. U., 1978-81; mem. communications faculty St. John's U., 1980—; mem. English faculty Bernard Coll., CCNY, Columbia U., 1980-82. Producer: Study in Black and White, BBC, Reykjavik, Iceland, 1972; broadcaster, ABC-TV Wide World of Sports, 1972, Public Broadcasting Service, Nat. Public Radio, 1972-75; Author: Chess: How to Improve Your Technique, 1973, Profile of a Prodigy, 1973, Hefner, 1974, Onassis, 1977, Favorite Bookstores, 1978, Streisand, 1979, Orson Welles, 1984. Elected Internat. arbiter Fedn. Internationale des Echecs, Skopje, Yugoslavia, 1972. Mem. Authors Guild, Authors League, Am., Marshall Chess Club, U.S. Chess Fedn., P.E.N., Internat. Communications Assn., Nat. Acad. TV Arts and Scis., Am. Soc. Journalists and Authors., Soc. Profl. Journalists. Club: Overseas Press. Address: 175 W 72d St New York NY 10023 *I am constantly confronting my own subjectivity. Can we learn to respond to people and ideas without dredging up stock responses and mnemonic irrelevances that trigger our actions and beliefs? Is it possible to know essential truths without the prejudices of our own psychological and cultural baggage?*

BRADY, HUGH, aeronautical engineering executive; b. Stamford, Conn., Nov. 14, 1924; s. James Alexis and Margaret Elizabeth (Gleason) B.; m. Verna Gertrude Henn, Nov. 23, 1946; children—David, Caryn Brady Cheney, Laurie Brady O'Loughlin, James. B.S. in Elec. Engring, Northeastern U., 1954. Registered profl. engr., Calif. Mem. tech. staff Space Tech. Labs., Redondo Beach, Calif., 1958-63; dir. Apollo program electronics div. Gen. Motors Corp., Milw., 1963-69; mgr. electronics ops. Aerojet Gen. Corp., Azusa, Calif., 1969-71; v.p., gen. mgr. space vehicles div. Def. and Space Systems Group, TRW Inc., Redondo Beach, Calif., 1971-77, v.p., gen. mgr. mfg. div., 1977-82; v.p., gen. mgr. Ops. and Support Group, TRW Inc., 1982—. Served with U.S. Army, 1943-46; Served with USAF, 1951-53. Recipient NASA Pub. Service award for work on Apollo program, 1969. Mem. AIAA, 19th Bombardment Group Assn., Electronic Industry Assn. (mfg. tech. com.), Soc. Mfg. Engrs. Roman Catholic. Home: 3881 Mistral Dr Huntington Beach CA 92649 Office: TRW Inc Bldg El Room 5076 1 Space Park Redondo Beach CA 90278

BRADY, JAMES JOSEPH, educator; b. Oregon City, Oreg., Nov. 24, 1904; s. Edward Aloysius and Mary Elizabeth (Reilly) B.; m. Mary Contratto, Sept. 3, 1932; children—Mary Ann (Mrs. Ronald Rodgers), Margaret (Mrs. Howard Rhodes). A.B., Reed Coll., 1927; M.A., Ind. U., 1928; Ph.D. (Whiting fellow), U. Calif. at Berkeley, 1931. Instr. physics St. Louis U., 1932-34, asst. prof., 1934-37, Ore. State Coll., 1937-39, asso. prof., 1939-42; asso. group leader radiation lab. Mass. Inst. Tech., Cambridge, 1942-46; prof. Oreg. State U., Corvallis, 1946—, acting chmn. dept., 1965-66, 69-71; Sr. physicist Navy Electronics Lab., San Diego, summer, 1961; cons. Boeing Airplane Co., 1947-49, Lawrence Radiation Lab. U. Calif., 1948-71. Contbr. to profl. jours. Recipient Carter award for inspiration teaching Oreg. State U., 1948, spl. citation Ore. Acad. Sci., 1970. Fellow Am. Phys. Soc., AAAS; mem. Am. Assn. Physics Tchrs. (Oreg. historian 1966—), Sigma Xi, Phi Kappa Phi. Club: K.C. Home: 2015 Whiteside Dr Corvallis OR 97333

BRADY, JAMES S., lawyer; b. Grand Rapids, Mich., Sept. 17, 1944; s. George Joseph and Emily Mae (Sherman) B.; m. Catherine Ann Yared, Aug. 6, 1966; children: Monica Rose, Michael George, Paul Samuel. B.S., Western Mich. U., 1966; J.D., U. Notre Dame, 1969. Bar: Mich. 1969. Asso. Roach, Twohey, Maggini & Brady (and predecessors), 1969-77, partner, 1972-77; U.S. atty. Western Dist. Mich., Grand Rapids, 1977-81; mem. firm Miller, Johnson, Snell & Cummiskey, 1981—; mem. teaching faculty Nat. Inst. Trial Advocacy, 1979-80, Inst. Continuing Legal Edn., 1980; adj. prof. Cooley Law Sch., Lansing, Mich. Pres. Grand Rapids Jaycees, 1975-76; legal counsel Mich. Jaycees, 1976-77; pres. Villa Elizabeth Adv. Bd., 1977-79; bd. dirs. Legal Aid and Defender Soc., 1970-77; mem. planning council Grand Rapids United Way, 1976-80, chmn. standing com., 1975-77; mem. adv. com. Kent County Sheriff's Dept., 1975-77; bd. dirs. Cath. Social Services. Recipient Disting. Service award Grand Rapids Jaycees, 1978. Mem. ABA, Fed. Bar Assn. (pres.-elect Western Mich. chpt.), Mich. Bar Assn., Grand Rapids Bar Assn. (dir. 1973-74, found. com.), State Bar Mich. (criminal jurisprudence com., spl. com. law and media), Am. Trial Lawyers Assn. Roman Catholic. Clubs: Peninsular, Blythefield, Grand Rapids Press. Home: 1700 Fisk SE Grand Rapids MI 49506 Office: 800 Calder Plaza Bldg Grand Rapids MI 49503

BRADY, JAMES WINSTON, writer, TV commentator; b. N.Y.C., Nov. 15, 1928; s. James Thomas and Marguerite Claire (Winston) B.; m. Florence Kelly, Apr. 12, 1953; children: Fiona, Susan. B.A., Manhattan Coll., 1950. Pub. Women's Wear Daily, N.Y.C., 1964-71; editor, pub. Harper's Bazaar, N.Y.C., 1971-72; editor N.Y. mag., N.Y.C., 1977; syndicated columnist N.Y. Post, N.Y.C., 1980-83; news commentator Sta. WCBS-TV, N.Y.C., 1981; editor-at-large Advt. Age, N.Y.C., 1983—. Author: Superchic, 1974, Paris One, 1976, Nielsen's Children, 1978, The Press Lord, 1981, Holy Wars, 1983. Served to 1st lt. USMC, 1951-52. Recipient Emmy award N.Y. TV Acad., 1975. Democrat. Roman Catholic. Club: University (N.Y.C.). Home: PO Box 1584 East Hampton NY 11937 Office: Advertising Age 220 E 42d St New York NY 10017

BRADY, JANE FRANCES, hospital administrator, nun; b. White Plains, N.Y., Nov. 14, 1935; d. Joseph Andrew and Helen Louise (Mooney) B. B.S. summa cum laude, Coll. St. Elizabeth, 1957; M.S., Columbia U., 1969; M.B.A., Seton Hall U., 1965. Joined Sisters of Charity of St. Elizabeth, 1958; adminstr. St. Joseph's Hosp. and Med. Center, Paterson, N.J., 1972-76, exec. dir., 1976-82, pres., 1982—. Trustee St. Joseph's Hosp. and Med. Center, N.J. Hosp. Assn., Center for Health Affairs, Bergen-Passaic Health Systems Agy., Cath. Family and Community Services.; mem. social services secretariat Diocese of Paterson (N.J.). Fellow Am. Coll. Hosp. Adminstrs.; mem. Am. Hosp. Assn., Am. Assn. Hosp. Planning, Cath. Health Assn. U.S., Alumni Assn. Coll. St. Elizabeth, Alumni Assn. Seton Hall Sch. Bus., Alumni Assn. Columbia Sch. Pub. Health and Adminstrv. Medicine, Kappa Gamma Pi. Address: St Joseph's Hosp and Med Center 703 Main St Paterson NJ 07503

BRADY, JOHN JOSEPH, JR., government official; b. Connellsville, Pa., Aug. 17, 1923; s. John Joseph and Rose M. (Bailey) B.; m. Bonnie J. Pegg, Feb. 10, 1951; 1 son, John Joseph. B.S., St. Vincent Coll., 1948; M.A., U. Notre Dame, 1959; Ph.D., London Sch. Econs., 1967. Enlisted man U.S. Army, 1942-45, Commd. 2d lt., 1945, advanced through grades to lt. col., 1965, ret., 1967; staff cons. Com. on Fgn. Affairs, U.S. Ho. of Reps., Washington, 1967-76, chief of staff, 1976—. Decorated Bronze Star medal, Purple Heart, Army Commendation medal. Home: 5616 19th St N Arlington VA 22205 Office: Room 2170 Rayburn House Office Bldg Washington DC 20515

BRADY, JOHN PAUL, psychiatrist; b. Boston, June 23, 1928; s. James Henry and Evelyn Louise (Rice) B.; m. Christeen Nelson, Mar. 19, 1963; children—James Palmer, Pamela Eros, June Pamela, David Duncan. A.B., Boston U., 1951, M.D., 1955; M.A. (hon.), U. Pa., 1967. Rotating intern Gorgas Hosp., Panama, 1955-56; resident in psychiatry Inst. of Living, Hartford, 1956-59; research psychiatrist Ind. U. Med. Sch., Indpls., 1959-63; mem. faculty U. Pa. Med. Sch., Phila., 1963—, prof. psychiatry, 1968—, Kenneth Appel prof., chmn. dept., 1974—; co-founder, asso. editor Behavior Therapy, 1970—. Author: An Introduction to the Science of Human Behavior, 1963, Classics of American Psychiatry, 1975, Psychiatry: Areas of Promise and Achievement, 1977; co-editor: Controversy in Psychiatry, 1978, Behavioral Medicine; Theory and Practice, 1979, Psychiatry at the Crossroads, 1980, also articles. Recipient Research Scientist award NIMH, 1963-74; Strecker award Inst. of Pa. Hosp., 1972. Fellow Am. Psychiat. Assn., Indian Psychiat. Soc.; mem. Assn. Advancement Behavior Therapy (past pres.), Soc. Biol. Psychiatry (pres. 1979-80), Psychiat. Research Soc. (program chmn. 1973), Soc. Behavioral Medicine (dir. 1980-81), Soc. Interam. de Psicologia, Am. Psychosomatic Soc. Office: Univ Pa Hosp Philadelphia PA 19104

BRADY, JOSEPH JOHN, association executive; b. Ossining, N.Y., Sept. 23, 1926; s. William and Kathryn Mary (Bell) B.; m. Barbara Kenney, Mar. 31, 1951; 1 son, Joseph John. B.S., N.Y. U., 1949; grad. student, John Jay Grad. Center, Coll. City N.Y., 1968-69. Asst. v.p. econ. research Nat. Indsl. Conf. Bd., N.Y.C., 1952-63; v.p., gen. mgr. Benziger Bros., Inc. (ch. and sch. supply), N.Y.C., 1963-67; pres. Hosp. Bur., Inc., Pleasantville, N.Y., 1967-77, ACME, Inc., Assn. Mgmt. Cons. Firms, N.Y.C., 1977—; mem. Westchester adv. bd. Chem. Bank, 1973-77. Commr. Westchester County Pky. Police, 1967-74; mem. Westchester Crime Control Planning Bd., 1968-74; exec. bd. Washington Irving council Boy Scouts Am., 1969-74; mem. Future Bus. Leaders Am.; adv. bd. N.Y. State Dept. Edn., 1974-77; Mem. devel. bd. Westchester Med. Center, 1973-74; mem. Bd. Edn., Ossining, N.Y., 1958-60. Served as officer USAF, 1951-52. Mem. Alpha Delta Sigma. Republican. Roman Catholic. Club: N.Y. Yacht. Home: 209C Lindstrom Rd Schooner Cove Stamford CT 06902 Office: 230 Park Ave New York NY 10169

BRADY, JOSEPH VINCENT, behavioral biologist, educator; b. N.Y.C., Mar. 28, 1922; s. James J. and Mary F. (Michaelson) B.; children: Barbara Ann, Michael Joseph, Kathleen Theresa, Nancy Marie, Joanne Cecelia. B.S., Fordham U., 1943; Ph.D., U. Chgo., 1951. Dep. dir. div. neuropsychiatry Walter Reed Inst. Research, 1951-71; prof. psychology U. Md., 1955-69; prof. behavioral biology Johns Hopkins Sch. Medicine, Balt., 1967—, prof. neurosci., 1982—; Cons. Pres.'s Sci. Adv. Com., Merck Inst. for Therapeutic Research; asso. chmn. Nat. Commn. for Protection Human Subjects of Biomed. and Behavioral Research, 1974-79. Contbr. articles to profl. jours. Served from 2d lt. to col. M.C. U.S. Army. Fellow A.A.A.S., Am. Psychol. Assn. (div. pres.), Am. Coll. Neuropsycho-pharmacology; mem. Eastern Psychol. Assn. (pres.). Home: 1690 N Harbor Ct Annapolis MD 21401 Office: Johns Hopkins U Sch Medicine Baltimore MD 21205

BRADY, LUTHER W., JR., physician; b. Rocky Mount, N.C., Oct. 20, 1925; s. Luther W. and Gladys B. A.A., George Washington U., 1944, A.B., 1946, M.D., 1948. Diplomate: Am. Bd. Radiology (treas. 1980-82, v.p. 1982—). Intern Jefferson Med. Coll. Hosp., Phila., 1948-50, resident in radiology, 1954-55; resident radiology Hosp. U. Pa., Phila., 1955-56; fellow Nat. Cancer Inst., 1953-57, 1957-59; practice medicine, specializing in radiation therapy and oncology, Phila.; asst. instr. radiology Jefferson Med. Coll. Hosp., 1954-55, U. Pa., Phila., 1955, instr., 1956-57, asso. radiology, 1957-59; asst. prof. radiology Coll. of Physicians and Surgeons, Columbia U., N.Y.C., summer, 1959; asso. prof. radiology Hahnemann Med. Coll. and Hosp., Phila., 1959-62, prof., 1963—, chmn. dept. radiation therapy, 1970—; asst. prof. radiology Harvard Med. Sch., Boston, 1962-63; mem. med. radiation adv. com. Bur. Radiation Health, HEW, 1971-74; cons. radiation therapy various hosps.; mem. U.S. del. to Interam. Congress Radiology, 1975, Internat. Congress on Radiology, 1981; sec. gen. Internat. Congress Radiology, 1985; med. adv. radiation therapy, dir. Pa. Blue Shield, Camp Hill. Author: Tumors of the Nervous System, 1975, Cancer of the Lung, Clinical Applications of the Electron Beam; editor: others Cancer Clin. Trials (Am. Jour. Clin. Oncology); editorial bd.: Cancer; asso. editor: Am. Jour. Roentgenology; sr. editor: Internat. Jour. Radiol. Oncology, Assn. Gynecologic Oncology; contbr. articles on radiation therapy to profl. jours. Bd. dirs. Assn. Artists Equity of Phila., Welcome House, 1974—, Settlement Music Sch., 1973—, Phila. Art Alliance, 1977—; trustee Phila. Mus. Art, also mem. oriental art com., 1974—, chmn. exec. com., 1968-72, mem. print, contemporary art and Indian art coms., 1974—. Served to lt. M.C. USN, 1950-54. Recipient Grubbe award Chgo. Radiol. Soc., 1977. Fellow Am. Coll. Radiology (chmn. commn. radiation therapy 1975-81, bd. chancellors 1975-81); mem. Radiol. Soc. N.Am. (bd. dirs. 1977—, chmn. bd. dirs. 1982-83, chmn. refresher course com. com. 1971-75, lectr. 1979), Pa. Radiol. Soc. (dir. 1970-77, councilor to Am. Coll. Radiology 1971-77), Am. Radium Soc. (pres. 1976-77, dir., Janeway lectr. 1980), Am. Cancer Soc. (pres. Phila. div. 1976-78, dir. 1968—, exec. com. 1976-78, mem. breast cancer task force 1974—), Am. Soc. Therapeutic Radiologists (pres. 1971-72), Assn. U. Radiologists, Am. Roentgen Ray Soc., Am. Assn. for Cancer Research, Radiation Research Soc., Am. Fedn. Clin. Oncologic Soc. (exec. com.), Am. Soc. Clin. Oncology, Phila. Roentgen Ray Soc. (pres. 1976-77, mem. exec. com. 1976-78), Am. Fedn. Clin. Research, Coll. Physicians Phila., James Ewing Soc., Assn. Pendergrass Fellows, Philadelphia County Med. Soc., AMA, Med. Soc. State Pa., Internat. Skeletal Soc., Council Acad. Socs., Soc. Chairmen Acad. Radiation Oncology Programs (pres. 1977), Soc. Chairmen Acad. Radiology Depts. (pres. 1974-75), Gynecologic Oncology Group (exec. com. 1971—, assoc. chmn. 1971—), Radiation Therapy Oncology Group (chmn. 1980—), Internat. Club Radiotherapists, Nat. Cancer Inst. (bd. sci. counselors, com. for radiation therapists studies 1971—, chmn. cancer clin. trails com.), Smith-Reed-Russell Soc., Alpha Omega Alpha, Phi Lambda Kappa. Clubs: Merion Cricket, Racquet of Phila., Union League of Phila. Office: 230 N Broad St Philadelphia PA 19102

BRADY, LYNN ROBERT, pharmacognosist, educator; b. Shelton, Nebr., Nov. 15, 1933; s. Connie E. and Laura M. (Vohland) B.; m. Geraldine Ann Walcott, June 23, 1957. B.S., U. Nebr., 1955, M.S., 1957; Ph.D., U. Wash., 1959. Asst. prof. pharmacognosy U. Wash., 1959-63, asso. prof., 1963-67, prof., 1967—, chmn. dept., 1972-80, asst. dean, 1982—; Chmn. conf. Tchrs. Am. Assn. Colls. Pharmacy, 1966-67. Author: (with others) Pharmacognosy, 6th edit., 1970, 7th edit., 1976, 8th edit., 1981. Fellow Acad. Pharm. Scis. (chmn. sect. pharmacognosy and natural products 1969-70); mem. Am. Pharm. Assn., Am. Soc. Pharmacognosy (pres. 1970-71), Sigma Xi, Rho Chi, Kappa Psi. Research in fungal constituents, alkaloid biosynthesis, chemataxonomy. Home: 5815 NE 57th St Seattle WA 98105

BRADY, SISTER MARY WILLIAM, educator; b. Fall River, Mass., Mar. 4, 1906; d. John James and Gladys Marie (Davol) B. B.A., Coll. St. Catherine, 1931; M.A., U. Minn., 1941; Ph.D., U. Chgo., 1947. Faculty dept. English Coll. St. Catherine, St. Paul, 1937-55, pres., 1955-61, prof., to, 1976, prof. emeritus, 1976—; archivist and rare book curator 1976; Pres. Minn. Pvt. Coll. Council, 1957-58; exec. com. Coll. Fund Assn.; mem. bd. studies Sisters of St. Joseph. Mem. A.A.U.W., Assn. Am. Colls., Assn. Minn. Colls., N.E.A., Nat. Catholic Edn. Assn., Phi Beta Kappa, Delta Phi Lambda, Pi Delta Phi. Address: 2004 Randolph St Saint Paul MN 55105

BRADY, NICHOLAS FREDERICK, investment banker; b. N.Y.C., Apr. 11, 1930; s. James C. and Eliot (Chace) B.; m. Katherine Douglas, Sept. 5, 1952; children: Nicholas Frederick, Christopher D., Anthony N., Katherine C. B.A., Yale U., 1952; M.B.A., Harvard U., 1954. With Dillon, Read & Co., Inc., N.Y.C., 1954-82, pres., after 1971, mng. dir.; dir.; chmn. Purolator, Inc.; appointee to U.S. Senate from N.J. to fill unexpired term of Harrison Williams, 1982, resigned, Dec. 1982; dir. Bessemer Securities Corp., Doubleday & Co., Ga. Internat. Corp., Wolverne World Wide Inc., ASA Ltd., Media Gen. Inc., NCR Corp. Trustee assoc. Boys' Club Newark.; Reagan appointee MX missile devel. options panel, Central Am. Study Commn., 1983. Clubs: Bond, Lunch (bd. govs.), Links (N.Y.C.)). Office: Dillon Read & Co 535 Madison Ave New York NY 10022 *

BRADY, NYLE C., government official; b. Manassa, Colo., Oct. 25, 1920; s. C. Frank and Sarah D. (Rasmussen) B.; m. Martha Cornum, Oct. 11, 1936; children: Robert N., Donald R., Dorothy L., Carol A. B.S., Brigham Young U., 1941, 1979; Ph.D., N.C. State Coll., 1947. Asst. prof. N.C. State Coll., 1947; asst. prof. Cornell U., Ithaca, N.Y., 1947-49, assoc. prof., 1949-52, prof., 1952—, head dept. agronomy, 1955-63; dir. research N.Y. State Coll. Agr., Cornell Agr. Expt. Sta., 1965-73; assoc. dean N.Y. State Colls. Agr., 1970-73; dir. Internat. Rice Research Inst., Philippines, 1973-81; sr. asst. adminstr. AID, Washington, 1981—; dir. sci. and edn. Dept. Agr., 1963-65; vis. prof. U. Philippines, 1953-55; chmn. agr. bd. Nat. Acad. Sci., 1968-71. Author: (with T.L. Lyon and H.O. Buckman) The Nature and Properties of Soils, 1952, (with Buckman) The Nature and Properties of Soils, 1960, 69, The Nature and Properties of Soils, 1974; editor: Advances in Agronomy, 1967. Recipient Prof. of Merit award Cornell U. Coll. Agr., 1953; James E. Talmage award Brigham Young U., 1966; Alumni Disting. Service award, 1972. Fellow AAAS (v.p. 1966), Am. Soc. Agronomy; mem. Soil Sci. Soc. Am. (editor-in-chief Proc. 1959-62, pres. 1964), Internat. Soil Sci. Soc., Soil Conservation Soc. Am., N.Y. Acad. Scis., AAUP, Sigma Xi. Mormon.

BRADY, PHILLIP DONLEY, government official; b. Pasadena, Calif., May 20, 1951; s. Donley Lawrence and Evelyn Mary (Doweiler) B.; m. Kathleen Louise Ryan, Mar. 7, 1982. B.A. cum laude, U. Notre Dame, 1973, J.D., Loyola U., 1976. Bar: Calif. 1976, U.S. Ct. Appeals (D.C. cir.) 1978, U.S. Supreme Ct. 1980. Assoc. atty. Spray, Goul & Bowers, Los Angeles, 1976-78; dep. atty. gen. Calif. Dept. Justice, Los Angeles, 1978-79; legis. counsel Congressman Lungren, Washington, 1979-81; western regional dir. U.S. ACTION Agy., San Francisco, 1981-82; dir. Congl. and pub. affairs Immigration and Naturalization Service, U.S. Dept. of Justice, Washington, 1982-83, assoc. dep. atty. gen., 1983—. Loyola U. Law Sch. scholar, 1974, 75. Mem. ABA, Fed. Bar Assn. (dir. Capitol Hill chpt. 1979-81), Los Angeles County Bar Assn., Notre Dame Club Los Angeles (dir. 1980-81). Republican. Roman Catholic. Home: 3234 S Stafford St Arlington VA 22206 Office: Dept of Justice 10th & Constitution Ave NW Washington DC 20530

BRADY, RAYMOND JOHN, broadcast journalist; b. Phila.; s. Raymond John and Meta (Martin) B.; m. Mary Clark Wilson, Jan. 28, 1955; stepchildren: David Wilson, Mary Beth (Mrs. Roger Dowdeswell). B.S., Fordham Coll., 1948. Reporter Long Branch (N.J.) Daily Record, 1950-53; writer Am. Tel. & Tel. Corp., 1953-54; asso. editor Forbes mag., 1954-55, asst. mng. editor, 1956-61; asso. editor Barrons Weekly, 1955-56; editor Dun's Rev., 1961-75; bus. commentator Sta. WCBS, N.Y.C., 1972-76, CBS radio network, 1975-79; bus., fin. commentator CBS TV Morning News, 1978—; commentator CBS Evening News, 1978—; lectr. bus. and finance at univs. Author articles. Served with USNR, 1943-45. Mem. N.Y. Financial Writers Assn. (bd. govs.), Am. Soc. Mag. Editors. Clubs: Nat. Press (Washington); Overseas Press (N.Y.C.); Monmouth County Hunt (gov.). Office: CBS News 524 W 57th St New York NY 10019 *

BRADY, RODNEY HOWARD, college president, business executive, former government official; b. Sandy, Utah, Jan. 31, 1933; s. Kenneth A. and Jessie (Madsen) B.; m. Carolyn Ann Hansen, Oct. 25, 1960; children: Howard Riley, Bruce Ryan, Brooks Alan. B.S. in Accounting with high honors; M.B.A. with high honors, U. Utah, 1957; D.Bus. Adminstrn., Harvard U., 1966; postgrad., UCLA, 1969-70. Missionary Ch. Jesus Christ of Latter-day Saints, Great Britain, 1953-55; teaching assoc. Harvard U. Bus. Sch., Cambridge, Mass., 1957-59; v.p. Mgmt. Systems Corp., Cambridge, 1962-65, Center Exec. Devel., 1963-64, v.p., dir., Boston, 1964-65; v.p. Tamerand Reef Corp., Christiansted, St. Croix, V.I., 1963-65; v.p., dir. Am. Inst. Execs., N.Y.C., 1963-65; v.p., mem. exec. com. aircraft div. Hughes Tool Co., Culver City, Calif., 1966-70; asst. sec. adminstrn. and mgmt. Dept. HEW, Washington, 1970-72, chmn. subcabinet exec. officers group, 1971-72; exec. v.p., chmn. exec. com., dir. Bergen Brunswig Corp., Los Angeles, 1972-78; chmn. bd. Uni-mgrs. Internat., Los Angeles, 1974-78; pres. Weber State Coll., Ogden, Utah, 1978—; dir. Bergen Brunswig Corp., Western Mortgage Loan Corp., Flying J Oil Co., Inc.; mem. No. Utah bd. 1st Security Bank Corp.; bd. advisors Mountain Bell Telephone; chmn. Nat. Adv. Com. on Accreditation and Instl. Eligibility; cons. Dept. Def., Dept. State, Dept. Commerce, HEW, NASA, Govt. of Can., Govt. of India (and indsl. firms), 1962—. Author: An Approach to Equipment Replacement Analysis, 1957, Survey of Management Planning and Control Systems, 1962, The Impact of Computers on Top Management Decision Making in the Aerospace and Defense Industry, 1966, (with others) How To Structure Incentive Contracts—A Programmed Text, 1965, My Missionary Years in Great Britain, 1976, An Exciting Start Along an Upward Path, 1978; contbr. articles to profl. jours. Mem. exec. com. nat. exec. bd. Boy Scouts Am., 1977—; Chmn. nat. Cub Scout commn. Boy Scouts Am., 1977-81, pres. Western region, 1981-83; mem. adv. com. program for health systems mgmt. Harvard U.; mem. adv. council U. Utah, 1971—; mem.

adv. com. Brigham Young U. Bus. Sch., 1972—; mem. dean's round table UCLA Grad. Sch. Mgmt., 1973-78; trustee Ettie Lee Homes for Boys, 1973-79; mem. governing bd. McKay Dee Hosp., Ogden, Utah, 1979—; bd. dirs. Utah Endowment for Humanities, 1978-80. Served to 1st lt. USAF, 1959-62. Recipient Silver Antelope award Boy Scouts Am., 1976, Silver Beaver award Boy Scouts Am., 1979, Silver Buffalo award, 1982. Mem. Am. Mgmt. Assn. (award 1969), Am. Def. Preparedness Assn., Nat. Indsl. Security Assn., U.S. Army Assn., Air Force Assn., Am. Helicopter Soc., Los Angeles C. of C. (tax structure com. 1969-70), Ogden C. of C. (dir. 1978), Utah Supply Distbrs. (dir. 1983—), SAR, Sons of Utah Pioneers, Phi Kappa Phi, Tau Kappa Alpha, Beta Gamma Sigma. Mormon (pres. Los Angeles stake). Clubs: Los Angeles Country (Los Angeles); Ogden Country, Rotary; Harvard (Cambridge, Mass.); Alta (Salt Lake City). Office: Weber State Coll Ogden UT 84408

BRADY, ROSCOE O., physician; b. Phila., Oct. 11, 1923; s. Roscoe O. and Martha (Roberts) B.; m. Bennett Carden Manning, 1972; 2 sons. Student, Pa. State U., 1941-43; M.D., Harvard, 1947; postgrad., U. Pa., 1948-49. NRC fellow U. Pa., 1948-50, USPHS spl. fellow, 1950-52; sect. chief Nat. Inst. Neurol. Diseases and Blindness, NIH, 1954-67, acting lab. chief neurochemistry, Bethesda, Md., 1967; chief developmental and metabolic neurology br. Nat. Inst. Neurol. and Communicative Disorders and Stroke, 1972—; professorial lectr. George Washington Sch. Medicine, 1963—; faculty Georgetown U. Sch. Medicine, 1967—. Author: (with Donald B. Tower) Neurochemistry of Nucleotides and Amino Acids, 1960, Basic Neurosciences, 1975, also numerous articles. Mem. Am. Soc. Biol. Chemists, Am. Chem. Soc., Am. Acad. Neurology, Am. Acad. Mental Retardation, Soc. Exptl. Biology and Medicine, Am. Soc. Clin. Investigation, Nat. Acad. Sci. First demonstration of enzyme system for fatty acid synthesis; biosynthesis of myelin sheath lipids, nature of metabolic defects in Gaucher's disease, Niemann-Pick disease, Fabry's diseases and Tay-Sachs disease; diagnostic tests for Gaucher's Niemann-Pick, Fabry's diseases; control and therapy of lipid storage diseases; metabolism of sphingolipids in neoplastic diseases. Home: 9501 Kingsley Ave Bethesda MD 20814 Office: NIH 9000 Rockville Pike Bethesda MD 20205

BRADY, SCOTT (GERARD KENNETH TIERNEY), actor; b. Bklyn., Sept. 13, 1924; s. Lawrence Hugh and Mary Alice (Crowley) T.; m. Lisa Tirony, Dec. 24, 1967; children—Timothy Eamon Charles Francis, Terence Michael Anthony Vincent. Ed., Roosevelt High Sch., Yonkers, N.Y., 1939-42, Bliss-Hayden Drama Sch., Beverly Hills. Films include In This Corner, 1947, Born to Fight, Canon City, He Walked by Night, Port of New York, Undertow, Kansas Raider, Undercover, Girl, Model and the Marriage, Broker, Bronco Buster, Montana Belle, Untamed Frontier, Yankee Buccaneer, Bloodhounds of Broadway, Perilous Journey, El Alamein, White Fire, Johnny Guitar, Law vs. Billy the Kid, Gentlemen Marry Brunettes, Vanishing American, They Were So Young, Terror at Midnight, Mohawk, Maverick Queen, Fort Utah, Arizona Bushwackers, Dollars, The Loners, Wicked, Wicked, The China Syndrome, 1979, Gremlins, 1983. Served with USNR, 1942-45. Mem. Acad. Motion Picture Arts and Scis. Roman Catholic. Club: N.Y. Athletic. Address: care James McHugh Agy 8150 Beverly Blvd Suite 206 Los Angeles CA 90048

BRADY, WALTER RICHARD, airlines executive; b. N.Y.C., Sept. 18, 1923; s. Walter Edmund and Marion Rose (Roach) B.; m. Eileen Marie Horak, Jan. 22, 1944; children: Walter Gregory, Kristi Mel. Student, Norwich U. Eastern Air lines, Inc., 1946—; service to capt. Eastern Air Lines, Inc., N.Y.C., 1946-57, check airman, 1961-74, dir. flight standards, Miami, Fla., 1974-76; dir. flight standards and test Eastern Airl Lines, Inc., Miami, Fla., 1976-77; dir. flying ops. Eastern Air lines, Inc., Miami, Fla., 1977-81; v.p. flying ops. and safety Eastern Air Lines, Inc., Miami, Fla., 1981—. Author, editor aviation articles. Served to capt. USAAF, 1942-46. Decorated Air medal. Mem. Internat. Air Transport Assn. (flight ops. adv. com. 1977-78), Air Transport Assn. (com. chmn. 1980). Republican. Roman Catholic. Home: 6454 Miami Lakes Dr E Miami lakes Fl 33014 Office: Eastern Air Lines Inc International Airport Miami FL 33148

BRADY, WILLIAM PATRICK, investment adviser; b. Phila., Dec. 4, 1942; s. Patrick Charles and Ellen Marie (Davitt) B.; m. Kathleen Gardner, May 22, 1965; children: Michael, Mark, Brian. B.S., St. Joseph's Coll., Phila., 1964. C.P.A., Pa. With Arthur Young & Co., 1964-67; controller (Del. Group), Phila., 1967-70, fin. v.p., treas., 1970—; dir. Delaware Mgmt. Co. Mem. Am. Inst. C.P.A.s, Pa. Inst. C.P.A.s. Home: 1529 Wyndham Ln East Goshen PA 19380 Office: 10 Penn Center Plaza Philadelphia PA 19103

BRADY, WRAY GRAYSON, educator, mathematician; b. Benton Harbor, Mich., July 20, 1918; s. Wray Grayson and Mildred (Sauters) B.; m. Emilie Peterson, Apr. 30, 1943; children—Susan, Wray Gordon. B.A., Washington and Jefferson Coll., 1940, M.A., 1942; Ph.D., U. Pitts., 1953. Prof., chmn. dept. math. Washington and Jefferson Coll., 1951-65, U. Bridgeport, Conn., 1965-69; dean (Grad. Sch.); dir. research Slippery Rock State Coll., 1969-72, prof. math., 1972—; prof. NSF Summer Inst., U. Ariz., 1963-67; cons. Bettis Plant, AEC, 1955-60. Co-author: Calculus, 1960, Analytic Geometry, 1961. Served with USNR, 1943-46. Fellow AAAS; mem. Am. Math. Soc., Math. Assn. Am., AAUP. Democrat. Presbyterian. 1290 Bestwick Rd Mercer PA 16137 Office: Slippery Rock State Coll Slippery Rock PA 16057

BRAEN, BERNARD BENJAMIN, psychology educator; b. Boston, Oct. 11, 1928; s. Simon Peter and Ethel (Davis) B.; children: Philip, Eric, Benson. B.A., U. Maine, 1949; M.A., Boston U., 1950; Ph.D., Syracuse U., 1955. Lic. psychologist, N.Y., diplomate: clin. psychology Am. Bd. Examiners Profl. Psychology, 1962. Chief clin. psychologist Onondaga County Child Guidance Ctr., Syracuse, N.Y., 1956-60; clin. practice clin. psychology, Syracuse, 1960-64; assoc. prof. psychology SUNY Upstate Med. Ctr., Syracuse, 1964-69, prof., 1969, Syracuse U., 1969—, dir. grad. program in clin. psychology, dir. psychology clinic, 1969-83; exec. dir. Nat. Alliance Concerned with School Age Parents, Syracuse, 1971-74, dir. research and publs., 1974-76. Contbr. articles to profl. publs., 1959-75; editor: Jour. Sch. Health, 1977. Recipient Disting. Service award Nat. Alliance Concerned with Sch. Age Parents, 1976. Fellow Am. Orthopsychiat. Assn.; mem. Am. Psychol. Assn., Sigma Xi. Office: Syracuse U Psychology Dept 430 Huntington Hall Syracuse NY 13210

BRAFFORD, WILLIAM CHARLES, chemical company executive; b. Pike County, Ky., Aug. 7, 1932; s. William Charles and Minnie (Tacket) B.; m. Katherine Jane Prather, Nov. 13, 1954; children—William Charles III, David A. J.D., U. Ky., 1957; LL.M. (fellow), U. Ill., 1958. Bar: Ky. bar 1957, Ga. bar 1965, Tax Ct. bar U.S 1965, Ct. Claims bar 1965, Ohio bar 1966, U.S. Ct. Appeals bar 1966, U.S. Supreme Ct. bar 1970, Pa. bar 1973. Trial atty. NLRB, Washington and Cin., 1958-60; atty. Louisville & Nashville R.R. Co., Louisville, 1960-63, So. Bell Telephone Co., Atlanta, 1963-65; asst. gen. counsel NCR Corp., Dayton, Ohio, 1965-72; v.p., sec., gen. counsel Betz Labs., Inc., Trevose, Pa., 1972—; dir. Betz Process Chems., Inc., Betz, Ltd. U.K., Betz Paper Chem. Inc., Betz Energy Chems., Inc., Betz S.A. France, B.L. Chems., Inc., Betz GmbH, Germany, Betz Entec, Inc., Betz Ges. GmbH, Austria, Betz NV Belgium, Betz Sud S.p.A., Italy. Served as 1st lt. C.I.C. AUS, 1954-56. Mem. Am. Soc. Corp. Secs., Nat. Assn. Corp. Dirs., Mid-Atlantic Legal Found. Republican. Presbyterian. Office: 4636 Somerton Rd Trevose PA 19047

BRAGDON, CLIFFORD RICHARDSON, city planning educator, university administrator; b. St. Louis, June 30, 1940; s. Dudley Acton and Ruth (Butler) B.; m. Sarah Vaughn, Aug. 21, 1965; children: Katherine, Rachel, Elizabeth. B.A., Westminster Coll., 1962; M.S., Mich. State U., 1965; Ph.D., U. Pa., 1970. Urban planner West Philadelphia Community Mental Health Consortium, U. Pa., 1967-69; environ. specialist, acting chief bio-acoustics div. U.S. Environ. Hygiene Agy., Edgewood, Md., 1969-72; prof. dept. city planning Ga. Inst. Tech., Atlanta, 1972—, asst. dean, dir. extension, 1980—, dir. continuing edn., 1982—; clin. prof. Coll. Medicine, Emory U., Atlanta, 1979—; pres. C.R. Bragdon & Assos. (environ. planning.); Cons. to office noise abatement U.S. EPA, 1972; cons. Ga. Dept. Human Resources and House Health and Ecology Com., 1973—; cons. constrn. research lab. U.S. Army C.E., 1973—; cons. Senate Labor, Trade and Tourism Com., 1977—. Author: Noise Pollution: The Unquiet Crisis, 1972, Noise Pollution: A Guide to Information Sources, 1979, General Aviation Airport Noise and Land Use Planning, vols. 1-3, 1980, Municipal Noise Legislation, 1980; Contbr.: chpt. to Environ. Health, 1979, Politics of Neglect, 1974; Contbg. editor: Sound and Vibration, 1974—. Trustee DAK's & Assocs.; Pres. Carriage Hill Civic Assn., 1977-78; mem. Atlanta Urban Design Commn.; chmn. DeKalb County Rapid Transit Sta. Planning Task Force, 1976—; assoc. vestry St. Luke's Ch., 1982—; bd. dirs. Nat. U. of the Air, 1983—. Served to capt. U.S. Army, 1969-72. Mem. Nat. Acad. Sci., Am. Indsl. Hygiene Assn. (pres. Ga. chpt. 1973-74), Am. Nat. Standards Inst., Am. Planning Assn. (pres. Ga. chpt. 1979—), Am. Soc. Planning Ofcls., Underground Space Assn., Acoustical Soc. Am., Assn. Energy Engrs. (dir.), Archtl. Acoustics Soc. (dir.), Nat. Trust Hist. Preservation, Urban Land Inst., World Future Soc., Ga. Council Mil. Educators, Sigma Xi, Omicron Delta Kappa, Kappa Alpha Order. Home: 4270 Autumn Hill Dr Stone Mountain GA 30083 Office: Coll Architecture Ga Inst Tech Atlanta GA 30322

BRAGDON, PAUL ERROL, college president; b. Portland, Maine, Apr. 19, 1927; s. Errol Freemont and Edith Lillian (Somerville) B.; m. Nancy Ellen Horton, Aug. 14, 1954; children: David Lincoln, Susan Horton, Peter Jefferson. B.A. magna cum laude, Amherst Coll., 1950, D.H.L., 1980; J.D., Yale U., 1953. Bar: N.Y. State bar 1954. With firm Dewey, Ballantine, Bushby, Palmer & Wood, N.Y.C., 1953-58, Javits, Trubin, Sillcocks, Edelman & Purcell, 1961-64; counsel Tchrs. Ins. and Annuity Assn. Coll. Retirement Equities Fund, N.Y.C., 1958-61; asst. to mayor, N.Y.C., 1964-65, exec. sec. to mayor, 1965; exec. asst. to pres. City Council, N.Y.C., 1966-67; v.p. N.Y. U., 1967-71; pres. Reed Coll., 1971—; dir. Pres.'s Task Force on Priorities in Higher Edn., 1969-70, N.Y. State Commn. on Powers of Local Govt., 1970-71; mem. commn. on fed. relations Am. Council on Edn., 1972-74, 78—; dir. Tektronix, Inc., Evans Products Co. Mem. Oreg. Environ. Quality Commn., 1973-74; chmn. Oreg. Select Com. on Conflict of Interest Legis., 1973-74; trustee Amherst Coll., 1972-78. Served with USMCR, 1945-46. Mem. N.W. Assn. Schs. and Colls. (com. on colls. 1974-81), Nat. Assn. Ind. Colls. and Univs. (vice chmn.), ABA, Phi Beta Kappa, Beta Theta Pi. Clubs: Century, Univ. (N.Y.C.); City, Univ. (Portland, Oreg.).

BRAGER, GEORGE, educator. Dean Sch. Social Work, Columbia U., N.Y.C. Office: Office of the Dean Columbia U Sch Social Work Broadway & 116th St. New York NY 10027

BRAGG, DAVID GORDON, physician, educator; b. Portland, Oreg., May 1, 1933; s. George Tully and Edith (Lee) B.; m. Marcia Robertson, Aug. 19, 1955; children: Eric Allan, Daniel Robert, James Tully, Anne Elizabeth. A.B. in History, Stanford U., 1955; M.D., U. Oreg., 1959. Intern Phila. Gen. Hosp., 1959-60; resident in radiology Columbia-Presbyn. Med. Center, Coll. Physicians and Surgeons, N.Y.C., 1962-64, chief resident, 1964-65, instr., 1965-66; asst. prof. Cornell U. Med. Coll., N.Y.C., 1966-70, assoc. prof., 1970; chmn. diagnostic radiology Meml. Sloan-Kettering Cancer Center, N.Y.C., 1967-70; prof., chmn. dept. radiology U. Utah Med. Center at Salt Lake City, 1970—; cons. Salt Lake City VA Hosp., Meml. Sloan-Kettering Cancer Soc., 1970—. Editor-in-chief: Yearbook of Diagnostic Radiology; mem. editorial bd.: Biology and Physics, Radiolog, Cancer, Investigative Radiology; Contbr.: chpts. and numerous articles to tech. lit. Bd. dirs. Bergen County (N.J.) dist. Girl Scouts U.S.A., 1968-69. Served with U.S. Army, 1960-62. Fellow mem. Am. Coll. Radiology; mem. Assn. U. Radiologists (pres. 1980-81), Soc. Chmn. Acad. Radiology Depts. (pres. 1979-80), N.Y. Acad. Sci., Am. Gastroenterol. Soc., AMA, Am. Gastroent. Soc., Radiol. Soc. N.Am., Roentgen Ray Soc., James Ewing Soc. Home: 4403 Cove Crest Dr Salt Lake City UT 84124

BRAGG, GEORGE ALBERT, advertising executive; b. Marion, Ind., Apr. 16, 1942; s. Theodore S. and Ruth B. (Watkins) B.; m. Penelope Susan Skells, Jan. 27, 1968; children: Michael, David, Emily. B.S. in End., Ind. U., 1964. Prodn. asst. VPI, Inc., N.Y.C., 1967; producer Compton Advt., N.Y.C., 1967-69, head TV prodn., 1981—; sr. producer Doyle, Dane, Bernbach Advt., N.Y.C., 1969-72; assoc. dir. prodn. BBDO, N.Y.C., 1972-81. Producer TV comml., GE Corporate, 1974 (Clio award 1975), (Gillette Right Guard), 1977, 79 (Clio award 1978, 80). 1st lt. U.S. Army, 1964-66. Presbyterian. Home: 69 Club Rd Stamford CT 06905 Office: 625 Madison Ave New York NY 10022

BRAGG, GEORGE LEE, computer company executive; b. Ada, Okla., Aug. 24, 1932; s. George Lee and Delza E. (Thompson) B.; m. Mary Ann Elizabeth Underwood, Jan. 30, 1958; children: Daniel L., David E., James S., Julie A. B.S. in Bus. Adminstrn., Pepperdine U., 1954; postgrad., Free U. Berlin, W. Ger., 1957-58, U. So. Calif., 1965, UCLA, 1968. Exec. dir. corp. devel. N.Am Aviation, Rockwell, El Segundo, Calif., 1959-71; founder, pres. Dawson & Bragg, Inc., Los Angeles, 1971-73; dir. bus. devel. Collins Radio Co., Dallas, 1973-74; v.p. corp. devel. Memorex Corp., Santa Clara, Calif., 1974-81; pres., chief exec. officer Telex Computer Products, Inc., Tulsa, 1981—, dir., 1983—; dir. Plasma Graphics, Inc., Warren, N.J. Bd. advisors Literacy and Evangelism Internat., Tulsa, 1983—; mem. Growth Industry Task Force, Tulsa C. of C., 1983—; bd. dirs. Pvt. Industry Tng. Council, Tulsa, 1983—. Served with U.S. Army, 1955-56. Mem. Computer and Communications Industry Assn. (exec com.). Republican. Presbyterian. Office: Telex Computer Products Inc 6422 E 41st St Tulsa OK 74135

BRAGG, JAMES HAROLD, manufacturing company executive; b. LaPlata, Mo., Oct. 2, 1921; s. Othy Cecil and Mary Jane (Hall) B.; m. Roberta Larraine Bowen, Dec. 5, 1943; children: Jane, Janet, Joan. B.S.M.E., U. Mo.-Columbia, 1943; postgrad., MIT, 1967. Chief engr., supt. phys. plant U. Mo.-Columbia, 1946-48; factory engr. to v.p. mfg. Lennox Industries, Marshalltown, Iowa, 1948-77; chmn., chief exec. officer Winnebago Industries, Forest City, Iowa, 1977-79; pres. the HONCo., Muscatine, Iowa, 1979—; dir. Iowa Nat. Heritage, Des Moines, 1979—, The Vernon Co., 1983—, Comml. State Bank, Marshalltown, 1967—. Contbr. articles to profl. jours. Chmn. Water and Power Bd., Muscatine, Iowa, 1979—; trustee, pres. YMCA Bd. and Bldg. Com., Marshalltown, 1964-70, 79-82; bd. dirs. U. Mo. Devel. Fund, 1979—; mem. Gov.'s Edn. Adv. Com., Des Moines, 1969; bd. dirs., pres. Community Sch. Dist., Marshalltown, 1961-67. Served with U.S. Army, 1943-46; ETO. Decorated Purple Heart; recipient Disting. Corp. Leadership award MIT, 1979, Honor Award Disting. Service in Engrng. U. Mo., 1979, Disting. Faculty Alumni award, U. Mo., 1978; named Mgmt. Man of the Year Nat. Mgmt. Assn., 1968. Mem. Nat. Office ProductsAssn. (exec. com.), Iowa Mfrs. Assn. (pres. 1970-71), Nat. Mgmt. Assn. (Silver Knight award 1968), Soc. Advancement of Mgmt. Republican. Mem. Christian Ch. Club: Optimist (charter pres.). Lodges: Rotary (dir.); Masons; Shriners. Home: 1230 Glenwood St Muscatine IA 52761

BRAGG, JEFFREY STEVEN, government official; b. Northampton, Mass., Jan. 21, 1949; s. Fred G. and Barbara (Norwood) B.; m. Patricia L. Starke (div. 1979); m. Gail L. Redderson, Oct. 24, 1981. B.A., Ohio State U., 1971. Staff asst. Ohio Ho. of Reps., Columbus, 1969-70, clk.-liaison, 1971-72; state youth dir. Ohio Com. to Re-elect the Pres., Columbus, 1972; legis. affairs dir. Nationwide Ins. Co., Ohio, 1973-76; with govt. and comml. relations dept. Ohio Med. Indemnity Mut. Co., Worthington, 1976-81; adminstr. Fed. Ins. Adminstrn., Washington, 1981—; exec. bd. dirs. Conf. Ins. Legislators, Ohio, 1980-81; bd. dirs. Ohio Med. Profl. Liability Underwriting Assn., 1980-81; mem. adv. com. to rev. Title 39 Ohio Code, 1976-77. Bd. dirs. Columbus Theatre Ballet Assn., 1979; mem. Licking County Regional Planning Com., Columbus, 1978; trustee Beechwood Trails Community Civic Assn., Columbus, 1975. Mem. Columbus Area C. of C. (govt. affairs com. 1980). Republican. Office: Fed Emergency Mgmt Agy Fed Ins Adminstrn 500 C St SW Washington DC 24072

BRAGG, ROBERT HENRY, physicist; b. Jacksonville, Fla., Aug. 11, 1919; s. Robert Henry and Lilly Camille (McFarland) B.; m. Violette Mattie McDonald, June 14, 1947; children: Robert Henry, Pamela. B.S., Ill. Inst. Tech., 1949, M.S., 1951, Ph.D., 1960. Asso. physicist research lab. Portland Cement Assn., Skokie, Ill., 1951-56; sr. physicist physics div. Armour Research Found., Ill. Inst. Tech., Chgo., 1956-61; sr. mem., mgr. phys. metallurgy dept. Lockheed Palo Alto Research Lab., Calif., 1961-69; prof. materials sci. U. Calif., Berkeley, 1969—, chmn. dept. materials sci. and mineral engrng., 1978-81; faculty sr. scientist Lawrence Berkeley Lab., 1969—; dir. Applied Space Products; cons. IBM, NIH., NSF. Contbr. articles to profl. jours. Pres. Palo Alto NAACP, 1967-68. Served with U.S. Army, 1943-46. Decorated Bronze star (2); Recipient Disting. award No. Calif. sect. Am. Inst. Mining and Metall. Engrs., 1970. Mem. Am. Phys. Soc., Am. Ceramics Soc. (chmn. No. Calif. sect. 1980), AIME (chmn. No. Calif. sect. 1970), Am. Carbon Soc., Am. Soc. Metals, AAUP, No. Calif. Council Black Profl. Engrs., Sigma Xi, Tau Beta Pi, Sigma Pi Sigma., Am. Crystallography Assn. Democrat. Home: 2 Admiral Dr 373 Emeryville CA 94608 Office: Dept Materials Sci and Mineral Engring Univ of Calif Berkeley CA 94720

BRAHAM, RANDOLPH LEWIS, political science educator; b. Bucharest, Romania, Dec. 20, 1922; came to U.S., 1948, naturalized, 1953; s. Louis and Esther (Katz) Abraham; m. Elizabeth Sommer, Dec. 15, 1954; children: Steven, Robert. B.A., CCNY, 1948, M.S., 1949; Ph.D., New Sch. for Social Research, 1952. Research assoc. YIVO-Inst. for Jewish Research, N.Y.C., 1954-59; faculty CCNY, N.Y.C., 1959—, prof. polit. sci., 1971—, chmn. dept. polit. sci., 1971-81; dir. Jack P. Eisner Inst. for Holocaust Studies, Grad. Center/City U., N.Y., 1980—; faculty Fairleigh Dickinson U., Hofstra U., Hunter Coll., 1956-59. Author: The Politics of Genocide, 2 vols, 1981, The Hungarian Labor Service System, 1977, Hungarian Jewish Studies, 3 vols, 1966-73, Soviet Government and Politics, 1965, Human Rights, 1979; writer, editor, contbr. to books in field. Mem. Am. Polit. Sci. Assn., Am. Assn. for Advancement of Slavic Studies. Democrat. Home: 114-07 Union Turnpike Forest Hills NY 11375 Office: Dept Political Sci CCNY CUNY New York NY 10031

BRAHMS, THOMAS WALTER, engineering institute official; b. Brookline, Mass., Mar. 12, 1945; s. Samuel David and Barbara Ann (Robinson) B.; m. Virginia Wahlen, Dec. 30, 1966; children—Theodore S., Anna Elisabeth. B.S. in Civil Engring, Northeastern U., 1971. Transp. planner Boston Redevel. Authority, 1965-69; sr. traffic engr. aide, traffic and parking dept. Town of Brookline, 1970-71; project engr. (traffic) Tippetts, Abbett, McCarthy & Stratton, Brookline, 1971-73; dir. tech. affairs Inst. Transp. Engrs., Arlington, Va., 1973-76, exec. dir., 1976—; mini-bus officer Reston Commuter Bus, Inc., Va., 1973-76, 77, v.p., 1976-77, 78-79, pres., 1979; v.p. Ward Six Civic Assn., West Somerville, Mass., 1972-73; bd. dirs. Reston Internal Bus System, 1977. Pres. Fairway Cluster Assn., Reston, 1973-75; coach Reston Soccer Assn., 1975-76; mem. Reston Homeowners Assn. Archtl. Bd. Rev., 1977; rep. Transp. Research Bd., 1976—; mem. Theodore M. Matson Meml. Fund, 1974—; trustee Transp. Mus., Boston, 1981—. Mem. Council of Engring. and Sci. Soc. Execs., ASCE (asso.), Am. Soc. Assn. Execs., Rd. Gang. Office: Inst Transp Engrs Suite 410 525 School St SW Washington DC 20024

BRAIBANTI, RALPH JOHN, political scientist, educator; b. Danbury, Conn., June 29, 1920; s. Daniel Vincent and Jane Helena B.; m. Lucy Kauffman, Feb. 19, 1943; children—Claire, Ralph Lynn. B.S., Western Conn. State U., 1941; A.M., Syracuse U., 1947, Ph.D., 1949. Asst. prof. polit. sci. Kenyon Coll., 1949-52, asso. prof., 1952-53; asst. dir. Am. Polit. Sci. Assn., Washington, 1950-51; cons. Govtl. Affairs Inst., 1950-51; asso. prof. polit. sci. Duke U., Durham, N.C., 1953-58, prof., 1958-68, James B. Duke prof. polit. sci., 1968—; dir. Islamic and Arabian devel. studies, 1977—; cons. AID, 1958-59, Ford Found., 1972, UN, 1974, Govt. Saudi Arabia, 1974—, UNESCO, 1977, Islamic Secretariat, 1980; adviser on adminstrv. reform Pakistan, Malaysia, S. Africa, Lebanon, Morocco. Author: Research on the Bureaucracy of Pakistan, 1966; co-author, editor: Political and Administrative Development, 1969, Pakistan: The Long View, 1976, Asian Bureaucratic Systems Emergent from the British Imperial Tradition, 1966, Tradition, Values and Socio-Economic Development, 1961, Administration and Economic Development in India, 1963; gen. editor 7 vol. series on comparative adminstrn., 1968-73. Served to capt. U.S. Army, 1942-47. Recipient citation outstanding prof. Duke Student Assn., 1972; Alumni award disting. undergrad. teaching, 1979; Ford Found. fellow, 1955-56; Social Sci. Research Council fellow, 1955-56. Mem. Internat. Studies Assn.-South (pres.), Am. Inst. Pakistan Studies (founding pres.), Internat. Cultural Soc. Korea (hon.). Republican. Episcopalian. Home: 3805 Darby Rd Durham NC 27707 Office: Duke Univ 2114 Campus Dr Durham NC 27706 *The encouragement of a profound understanding of seemingly divergent cultural systems is of critical importance. This must embrace helping newly-developed political systems appreciate their own cultural values. Only the strength of such pride can withstand the dynamic interventionism which characterizes the relations of transitorily dominant superpowers and weak, newer political entities.*

BRAIDWOOD, ROBERT J., archeologist, educator; b. Detroit, July 29, 1907; s. Walter J. and Rhea (Nimmo) B.; m. Linda Schreiber, 1937; children: Gretel, Douglas. A.B., U. Mich., 1932, A.M., 1933; Ph.D., U. Chgo., 1942; Sc.D., U. Ind., 1971; Docteur (hon.), U. Paris, 1975. Archeol. field work, Iraq, Syria, Iran, Turkey, Ill., N.Mex., 1930—; faculty Oriental Inst., U. Chgo., 1933—, prof. Old World prehistory, 1954-76, prof. emeritus, 1976—; faculty U. Chgo., 1940—, prof. dept. anthropology, 1954-76, now emeritus. Archeol. Inst. Am. medalist, 1971. Fellow Am. Acad. Arts and Scis., Nat. Acad. Scis., Am. Philos. Soc., Soc. Antiquaries (London) (hon.); mem. Am. Anthrop. Assn. (exec. bd. 1962-64, disting. lectr. 1971), Internat. Union Pre-and-Protohistoric Scis. (former U.S. del. permanent council), Conf. Asian

Archaeology-New Delhi (found. mem.); corr. mem. Deutsche Archaologische Institut, Göteborgs Kungl. Vetenskaps och Vitterhets Samhalle, Instituto Italiano di Preistoria e Protostoria, Jysk Arkaeologist Selskab, Österreichsche Akademie der Wissenschaft. Office: Oriental Inst U Chgo Chicago IL 60637

BRAIN, GEORGE BERNARD, univ. dean; b. Thorp, Wash., Apr. 25, 1920; s. George and Alice Pearl (Ellison) B.; m. Harriet Gardinier, Sept. 28, 1940; children—George Calvin, Marylou. B.A., Central Wash. State U., Ellensburg, 1946, M.A., 1949; Ed.D., Columbia Tchrs. Coll., 1957; postgrad., U. Wash., Wash. State U., Harvard, U. Colo., Stanford. Tchr. math. and sci. Yakima (Wash.) secondary schs., 1946-49; instr. Central Wash. State Coll., 1949-50; elementary sch. prin., Ellensburg, 1950-51, successively elementary sch. prin., asst. supt. schs., supt. schs., Bellevue, Wash., 1951-59; vis. prof. Central Wash. State Coll., 1953, Wash. State U., 1959, U. Md., 1964; supt. schs., Balt., 1960-65, dean; also dir. summer schs. Wash. State U., Pullman, 1965—; lectr. Columbia, U. Conn., Harvard, U. Ga., U. Del., Johns Hopkins, Morgan U., U. Okla., Towson State U., Stanford, Wash. U.; Chmn. Fulbright Group Western European Seminar Comparative Edn., 1959; chmn. ednl. policies commn. N.E.A.; ednl. cons. (Office Edn.), 1962—; cons. Ednl. Testing Service, Princeton, N.J., 1964-67; dir. Intext Pub. Inc., Scranton, Pa., Worldbook-Childcraft (Scott-Fetzer); Bd. dirs. Md. Acad. Sci., 1960-65, Nat. Edn. Found., Field Enterprises Ednl. Corp., 1970—, Pacific Am. Inst., 1977—. Mem. editorial adv. bd.: Scholastics Publs, 1963—, Am. Sch. and Univ, 1960-64, Education, USA, 1964-71; mem. editorial bd.: World Book, 1966—, Jour. Tchr. Edn, 1966—. Served with USNR, 1941- 42; Served with USMCR, 1942-46; maj. Res. Recipient Distinguished Service award Wash. State Jr. Assn. Commerce, 1956; named Man of Year Met. Civic Assn. Balt., 1962; Distinguished Service award in edn. NCCJ, 1963; Fulbright scholar, 1959. Life mem. Am. Assn. Sch. Adminstrs. (exec. com. 1964-66, pres. 1965), N.E.A.; hon. life mem. Wash. State Assn. Sch. Adminstrs. (pres. 1959), Md. Assn. Sch. Adminstrs., Nat. Congress P.T.A.; mem. Wash. Edn. Assn. (pres. dept. adminstrn. and supervision 1957), A.A.A.S. (exec. com. commn. elementary and secondary sci. 1963-66), Assn. Supervision and Curriculum Devel., Univ. Council Ednl. Adminstrn., Nat. Joint Council Econ. Edn. (exec. com. 1963—), Nat. Conf. Profs. Ednl. Adminstrn., AAUP, Internat. Platform Assn., Nat. Council for Edn. in Health Professions, Nat. Acad. Sch. Execs., Nat. Council Fgn. Study League, Exec. Hall Fame, Phi Delta Kappa, Kappa Delta Pi. Presbyn. Club: Rotarian (dir. Balt. 1964-65). Home: 640 SE Spring St Pullman WA 99163

BRAINARD, ALEXANDER NASH, consumer products co. exec.; b. Pitts., Jan. 8, 1927; s. Ira F. and Antoinette (Harrison) B.; m. Suzanne Alderman, Sept. 20, 1952 (div. 1976); children—Stephen, Jeffrey, Laurinda, Leslie; m. Joan M. Serravezza, July 1, 1978. B.S., Syracuse U., 1951. Pres. Inst. Food Service div. Gen. Foods Corp., White Plains, N.Y., 1967-69, pres., White Plains, 1969-71, Consol. Cigar Corp., N.Y.C., 1971—; cons. product group Gulf & Western, N.Y.C., 1971—. Dir. Family Services Westchester, 1969-71. Served with USN, 1944-46. Mem. Psi Upsilon Soc. Clubs: Am. Yacht (trustee 1971-74), Dads Club Rye High Sch. (dir. 1969-73). Home: 70 Waters Edge Rye NY 10580 Office: Consolidated Cigar Corp Gulf & Western 1 Gulf and Western Plaza New York NY 10023

BRAINARD, ALFRED PAUL, foreign service officer; b. N.Y.C.; s. Alfred and Jennie (Heil) B. B.A., U. Conn., 1953, M.A., 1954; Ph.D., U. Washington, 1960. Polit. counselor Am. Embassy, Warsaw, Poland, 1975-77; dep. dir. CU-EE Dept. State, Washington, 1977-78; acting dir. 10 PMS, Washington, 1978-81; alt. rep. UN Gen. Assemblies Com. on Info. and Polit. Coms., N.Y.C., 1979, 81; sr. alt. dir. Dept. State Poland Working Group, Washington, 1981-82; asst. prof. U. Md., Gonn, Germany, 1975; panelist RAnd Workshop Center for Strategic and Internat. Studies, Washington, 1980; participant Lucca Conf. on Eastern Europe, Italy, 1977. Contbr. articles to polit. jours. Named Disting. Lectr. U. Conn., Storrs, 1978; recipient Superior Honor Dept. State, 1973, 80. Mem. Polish Inst. Arts and Scis. of U.S.A., Janusz Korczak Internat. Lit. Competition (awards com. 1980, 81). Office: Am Consulate Gen Zollikerstrasse 141 Zurich Switzerland 8008

BRAINARD, EDWARD AXDAL, ednl. adminstr.; b. St. Cloud, Minn, Apr. 25, 1931; s. Dudley Shattuck and Merl Virginia (Anderson) B.; m. Muriel Sandra Swanson, Feb. 13, 1954; children—Ann F., Thomas E. B.S., St. Cloud State U., 1953; M.A., U. No. Colo, 1957, Ed.D., 1961. Tchr. Billings (Mont.) Jr. High Sch., 1955-57; prin. Lakewood (Colo.) Jr. High Sch., 1958-62; asst. prof. Kans. State U, Manhattan, 1962-63; dir. research Jefferson County Sch. Dist., Lakewood, Colo., 1963-66; dir. ednl. grants div. Charles F. Kettering Found., Dayton, Ohio, 1966-67; pres. CFK Ltd., Engelwood, Colo., 1967-74; dir. leadership devel. Colo. Dept. Edn., Denver, 1974-76; prof. U. No. Colo., Greeley, 1976-81; asst. supt. Aurora (Colo.) Public Schs., 1981—. Co-author: How School Adminstrators Make Things Happen; Contbr. articles to profl. jours. Chmn. citizens adv. com. Red Rocks Campus, Community Coll., Denver, 1971-73. Served with U.S. Army, 1953-55. Mem. NEA, Am. Assn. Sch. Adminstrs., Nat. Assn. Secondary Sch. Prins., Colo. N. Central Assn. (chmn. 1976-81), Phi Delta Kappa. Home: 2527 S Allison St Denver CO 80227 Office: Aurora Public Schools Aurora CO 80011

BRAINARD, PAUL HENRY, musicologist, educator; b. Binghamton, N.Y., Apr. 18, 1928; s. George E. and Frances (Weinhauer) B.; m. Margaret Bent, Jan. 4, 1981. B.A., U. Rochester, 1949, M.A., 1951; postgrad., Heidelberg (Germany) U., 1954; Ph.D., Goettingen (Germany) U., 1960. Research asst. Deutsches Musikgeschichtliches Archiv, Kassel, Germany, 1960; instr. music Ohio State U., 1960-61; faculty Brandeis U., Waltham, Mass., 1961—, prof. music, 1974-81, chmn., 1965-68, chmn. dept. music, 1969-72, 75-77; prof. music Princeton (N.J.) U., 1981—; spl. research music history. Author: Le sonate per violino di Giuseppe Tartini, 1975; Editor: Neue Bach-Ausgabe, Vols. II/7, 1977, II/8, 1979, I/16, 1981, Cantatas, Easter and Ascension Oratorios; Contbr. articles to profl. jours. Served with AUS, 1951-53. Mem. Am., Internat. musicol. socs., Gesellschaft fuer Musikforschung, Phi Beta Kappa. Home: 25 Mercer St Princeton NJ 08540 Office: Dept Music Princeton U Princeton NJ 08544

BRAINARD, WILLIAM CRITTENDEN, economist, educator, university official; b. Jersey City, July 2, 1935; s. William E. and Eleanor (Holston) B.; m. Ellen Rawlings, Oct. 18, 1958; children: David, Michael, Daniel. B.A., Oberlin Coll., 1957; M.A., Yale U., 1959, Ph.D., 1963. Asst. prof. econs. Yale U., 1962-66, asso. prof., 1966-69, prof., 1969—, provost, 1981—; research asso. Brookings Instn., 1965-66; dir. Cowles Found., New Haven, 1971-73, 76-81. Editor: Brookings Papers on Econ. Activity, 1980—; contbr. articles to profl. jours. Fellow Econometric Soc.; mem. Am. Econ. Assn. Home: 35 Hillhouse Ave New Haven CT 06511 Office: Dept Econs Yale U New Haven CT 06520

BRAINERD, CHARLES J(ON), experimental psychologist, applied mathematician, educator; b. Lansing, Mich., July 30, 1944; emigrated to Can., 1971; s. Charles Donald and Geraldine Elaine (Leffler) B.; m. Susan Haske, Jan. 18, 1964; 1 dau., Tereasa Gail. B.S., Mich. State U., 1966, M.A., 1968, Ph.D., 1970. Asst. prof. psychology U. Alta., Edmonton, Can., 1971-73, assoc. prof., 1973-76, H.M. Tory prof. social sci., 1983—; prof. U. Western Ont., London, 1976-83; vis. prof. U. Minn., Mpls., 1980-81. Author: Piaget's Theory of Intelligence, 1978, Origins of the Number Concept, 1979; editor: Alternatives to Piaget, 1978, Recent Advances in Cognitive-Developmental Theory, 1983, Springer-Verlag Series in Cognitive Development, 1979—; assoc. editor: Behavioral and Brain Scis., 1980—. Fellow Am. Psychol. Assn., Can. Psychol. Assn.; mem. Psychonomic Soc., Soc. for Research in Child Devel. (assoc. editor Child Devel. 1977-80). Republican. Office: U Alta Dept Psychology Edmonto AB Canada T6G 2E9

BRAINERD, JOHN G., elec. engr., educator; b. Phila., Aug. 7, 1904; s. John Austin and Mabel (Grist) B.; m. Carol Paxson, Sept. 6, 1930. B.S., U. Pa., 1925, Sc.D., 1934; certificate, Mass. Inst. Tech., 1941, 54. Reporter The N.Am., Phila., 1922-25; faculty Moore Sch. Elec. Engring., U. Pa., Phila., 1925—, prof., 1954—, Univ. prof., 1970—, also dir., 1954-70; chmn. div. phys. scis. U. Pa. Grad. Sch., 1942-48; engr., acting state dir. PWA, 1935-37; cons. engr. govt. agencies; project supr. ENIAC Project (large-scale digital gen. purpose electronic computer, completed), 1946; Mem. sci. adv. com. Nat. Bur. Standards, 1959-65; mem. U.S. nat. com., com. experts Internat. Electrotech. Commn.; chmn. sci. and arts com. Franklin Inst., 1979—; mem. engring. coll. accreditation com., regional chmn. ECPD; public speaker on energy and world food supply, 1974—. Co-author: Ultra High Frequency Techniques, 1942; book reviewer: Tech. and Culture, 1969—; contbr. articles to profl. jours. Recipient numerous profl. awards. Fellow AAAS, IEEE (chmn. nat. com. for elec. engring. films, chmn. awards, com., dir., Founders Gold medal), Royal Soc. Arts, Fellows in Am. Studies; mem. Soc. for History Tech. (pres. 1974-76, treas. 1976—), Engrs. Joint Council, AAUP, Jovians (pres.), Am. Standards Assn. (standards council 1949-51), Sigma Xi, Tau Beta Pi. Club: Faculty (Phila.). Home: Crosslands Apt 227 Kennett Sq PA 19348 Office: 200 S 33d St Philadelphia PA 19104

BRAISLIN, GORDON STUART, banker; b. Bklyn., Jan. 13, 1901; s. William C. and Alice (Cameron) B.; m. Esther Elizabeth Hamm, July 26, 1935; children: Elizabeth Cameron, Alice Stevenson, Gordon Stuart, William Stevenson. A.B., Cornell U., 1923. With Prudence Co., Inc., N.Y.C., 1924-30; pres. Realty Assos. Mgmt., Inc., N.Y.C., 1931-38; founder Gordon S. Braislin, Inc., 1938; (merged into Braislin, Porter & Baldwin, Inc., N.Y.C., Bklyn. and Westchester County, N.Y. 1942), pres., 1942-49, 1949-65; trustee Dime Savs. Bank N.Y., 1946-76, chmn. trustees, chief exec. officer, 1965-74, vice chmn., 1975-76, mem. adv. council, 1976—; dir. Savs. Bank Trust Co., 1969-75; trustee Savs. Bank Life Ins. Fund, 1968-76, chmn., 1973-75. Trustee Bodman Found.; bd. dirs., finance com. Am. Bible Soc.; trustee Bklyn. Inst. Arts and Scis., 1966-75; pres. N.Y. Eye and Ear Infirmary, 1961-77; trustee Roosevelt Hosp., 1961-77; bd. dirs. Bklyn. Eye and Ear Hosp., 1956-61, Community Blood Council Greater N.Y., 1963-76, Downtown Bklyn. Devel. Assn., 1965-75; mem. operating com. Interch. Center, 1959-72; bd. mgrs. dept. missions Episcopal Diocese N.Y., 1956-60. Recipient Gold medal, 1973; Citizen's award Med. Soc. N.Y. County, 1975. Mem. Savs. Banks Assn. N.Y. State (dir. 1965-75), Phi Beta Kappa. Clubs: University, St. Nicholas Soc. (N.Y.C.); Brooklyn; Quaker Hill Country (Pawling, N.Y.). Home: 230 E 48th St New York NY 10017 Office: 589 Fifth Ave New York NY 10017

BRAISTED, PAUL JUDSON, ret. found. exec.; b. Antrim, N.H., Aug. 25, 1903; s. Rev. William E. and Belle (Porter) B.; m. Ruth Evelyn Wilder, May 2, 1927; children—Paul W., Donald A., Richard R. Ph.B., Brown U., 1925, LL.D., 1960; M.A., N.Y. U., 1927; Ph.D., Columbia U., 1935; L.H.D., Lawrence Coll., 1955; D.Litt., Carleton Coll., 1970. Prof., chaplain Judson Coll., Rangoon, Burma, 1930-33; master Mt. Hermon Sch., 1935-37; exec. dir. Student Vol. Movement, 1938-39; field rep., program dir. Edward Hazen Found., Inc., 1940-49, pres., 1949-70, pres. emeritus, 1970—; Mem. internat. div. exec. com. YMCA; mem. internat. div. exec. com. Am. Friends Service Com.; trustee Internat. Film Found.; mem. adv. council Center for Study of World Religions, Harvard U.; Asso. fellow Davenport Coll. of Yale.; Mem. Council Fgn. Relations, Yale-China Assn. Author: Indian Nationalism and the Christian Colleges, 1937, Toward a New Humanism, 1975; Co-editor: Reconstituting the Human Community, 1972; editor: Cultural Affairs and Foreign Relations, rev. edit, 1968. Mem. Soc. of Friends. Club: Cosmos (Washington). Home: 26 Colonial Dr North Haven CT 06473

BRAITHWAITE, J. LORNE, real estate executive; b. Dewberry, Alta., Can., July 16, 1941; s. Joseph and Olga (Prill) B.; m. Josie Bey, Feb. 13, 1962; children: Todd, Jodi, Troy, Travis. B.Comm., U. Alta., 1963; M.B.A., U. Western Ont., 1969. With T. Eaton Co., Calgary, Alta., 1963-67, 71-74, group sales and mdse. mgr., Edmonton, Alta., 1971-74; sales mgr., then v.p. and gen. mgr. South Park Industries Assoc. Cos., Atco Industries, Calgary, 1969-71; with Oxford Devel. Group, 1974-78, v.p. devel., 1976-78; pres. Cambridge Leaseholds Ltd., Toronto, 1978—, part owner, 1980—; pres. and/or officer numerous affiliated cos. Mem. Young Pres. Orgn. Clubs: Ontario, Cambridge. Home: 58 Julia St Thornhill ON L3T 4R9 Canada Office: 390 Bay St Suite 400 Toronto ON M5H 2Y2 Canada

BRAKELEY, GEORGE ARCHIBALD, JR., fund-raising counsel; b. Washington, Apr. 18, 1916; s. George Archibald and Lillian (Fay) B.; m. Roxana Byerly, Sept. 7, 1946; children: George Archibald III, Deborah Fay Buri, Joan Keller, Linda Smith Terry. B.A., U. Pa., 1938. Vice pres., dir. John Price Jones Co., Inc. (fund-raising counsel), N.Y.C., 1938-50; pres., treas. John Price Jones Co. (Can.), Ltd., Montreal, 1950-53, 1953, chmn., chief exec. officer, 1953-61; chmn. G.A. Brakeley & Co., Inc., Los Angeles, 1956—, chmn., treas., N.Y.C., 1957-71, FR Computer Communications, Inc., 1973—; chmn., chief exec. officer Brakeley, John Price Jones Inc., 1972—; Vice-chmn. Center for Study of Presidency. Author: Tested Ways to Successful Fund Raising. Served to capt. C.E. AUS, World War II. Episcopalian. Clubs: Univ. (N.Y.C., Chgo., Washington); Sky, Anglers (N.Y.C.); Montreal Racket, Wee Burn Golf (Darien, Conn.); Capital City (Atlanta); Mill Reef (Antigua). Home: 1 Pilgrim Rd Darien CT 06820 Office: 1600 Summer St Stamford CT 06905

BRAKEMAN, LOUIS FREEMAN, college provost; b. Kalamazoo, Nov. 9, 1932; s. Louis Freeman and Ruth Adelaide (Parsons) B.; m. Lorrie Mallett, Aug. 16, 1953; children: David, Mark, Peter, Paul, Amy. B.A., Kalamazoo Coll., 1954; M.A., Fletcher Sch. Diplomacy, Tufts U., 1955, Ph.D., 1963. Lectr. history Brown U., 1958-59; asst. prof. polit. sci. Carroll Coll., Waukesha, Wis., 1959-62; mem. faculty Denison U., Granville, Ohio, 1962—, prof. polit. sci., 1968—, chmn. dept., 1965-70, dean, 1970-73, provost, 1973—; vis. scholar center for Study of Higher Edn. U. Mich., 1980; Dir. Regional Council Center for Internat. Students, summers 1966-68; chmn. regional selection com. Danforth Found. Assos. Program, 1971-73; Mem. Common Cause, 1972—; chmn. bd. dirs. Council for Intercultural Studies and Programs, 1975—. Co-author: Research Problems in American Politics, 1969; Contbr. articles to profl. jours. Fulbright scholar, India, 1957-58; Danforth grad. fellow, 1954-57. Mem. Am. Polit. Sci. Assn., AAUP, Soc. Values in Higher Edn., Omicron Delta Kappa. Presbyn. (elder). Home: 108 Chapin Pl Granville OH 43023

BRAKER, WILLIAM PAUL, ichthyologist; b. Chgo., Nov. 3, 1926; s. William Paul and Minnie (Wassermann) B.; m. Patricia Reese, Sept. 2, 1950. B.S., Northwestern U., 1950; M.S., George Washington U., 1953; student, U. Chgo., 1954-58. Mem. staff John G. Shedd Aquarium, Chgo., 1953—, dir., 1964—; asst. sec. Shedd Aquarium Soc., 1960-65, sec., 1965—. Served with AUS, 1950-52. Mem. Am. Fisheries Soc., Am. Soc. Icthyologists and Herpetologists, Am. Assn. Zool. Parks and Aquariums. Office: 1200 S Lake Shore Dr Chicago IL 60605

BRAKHAGE, JAMES STANLEY, filmmaker, educator; b. Kansas City, Mo., Jan. 14, 1933; s. Ludwig and Clara (Dubberstein) B.; m. Mary Jane Collom, Dec. 28, 1957; children: Myrrena, Crystal, Neowyn, Bearthm, Rarc. Ph.D., San Francisco Art Inst., 1981. Lectr. Sch. Art Inst. Chgo., 1969-81; prof. U. Colo., Boulder, 1981; mem. filmmakers Coop., N.Y.C.; MEM. Canyon Cinema Coop., San Francisco; mem. London Filmmakers Coop. Films Interim, 1952, Anticipation of the Night, 1958, The Dead, 1960, Blue Moses, 1962, Dog Star Man, 1964, Songs in 8mm, 1964-69, The Weir Falcon Saga, 1970, The Machine of Eden, 1970, Angels', 1971, Foxfire Childwatch, 1971, Eye Myth, 1972, The Riddle of Lumen, 1972, The Women, 1973, Aquarien, 1974, Sol, 1974, Flight, 1974, Hymn to Her, 1974, Short Films, 1975, 76, Sincerity, reel 3, 1978, Duplicity, 1978, Burial Path, 1978, Creation, 1979, Salome, 1980, the Arabic series, 1-19/1981, Unconscious London Strata, 1982, Tortured Dust, Reels 2, 2 & 3, 1983, Hell Spit Flexion, 1983; author: Metaphors on Vision, 1963, A Moving Picture Giving and Taking Book, 1971, The Brakhage Lectures, 1972, Seen, 1975, Film Biographies, 1977, Brakhage Scrapbook, 1982. Recipient Brussels Worlds Fair Protest award, 1958; Avon Found. grantee, 1965-69; Rockefeller fellow, 1967-69; Recipient Brandies citation, 1973, Colo. Gov.'s Award for Arts and humanities, 1974, Jimmy Ryan Morris Meml. Found. award, 1979, Telluride Film Festival medallion, 1981; Nat.l Ednowment of Arts grantee, 1974, 75, 77, 80, 83; Guggenheim fellow, 1978. Democrat. Home: Box 170 Rollingsville CO 80474 Office: Film Studies Colo Univ 120 Hunter St Boulder CO 80302

BRAKKE, MYRON KENDALL, research chemist; b. Fillmore County, Minn., Oct. 23, 1921; s. John T. and Hulda Christina (Marburger) B.; m. Betty-Jean Einbecker, Aug. 16, 1947; children—Kenneth Allen, Thomas Warren, Joan Patricia, Karen Elizabeth. B.S., U. Minn., 1943, Ph.D., 1947. Research asso. Bklyn. Bot. Garden, 1947-52; research asso. U. Ill., 1952-55; research chemist U.S. Dept. Agr., Lincoln, Nebr., 1955—; prof. plant pathology U. Nebr., Lincoln, 1955—. Editor: Virology, 1960-66; Contbr. articles to profl. jours. Fellow AAAS, Am. Phytopath. Soc.; mem. Am. Chem. Soc., Electron Microscope Soc., Nat. Acad. Scis., Am. Soc. Microbiology, Sigma Xi, Phi Lambda Upsilon, Gamma Sigma Delta, Alpha Zeta. Office: Room 406 Plant Science Bldg 8-K U Nebr Lincoln NE 68583

BRALEY, J. WARREN, farmer, coop. exec.; b. New Bedford, Mass., Nov. 25, 1912; s. J. Warren and Elsie Gilbert (Dowley) B.; m. Myrtle Erikson, July 30, 1941; children—Jeffrey Warren, Alexis Jane. A.B., Dartmouth Coll., 1933. Owner, operator dairy farm, Chatham, N.Y., 1950—; dir. Agway, Inc., 1965—, Yankee Milk, 1971-80, H. B. Hood Co., 1980—; cons. agr., 1972—. Town justice, Town of Austerlitz, 1956-60, mem. town council, 1979—, county supr., Columbia County (N.Y.), 1960-65, chmn. county planning, 1964-65; bd. dirs. Columbia County Extension Service, 1970-79, pres., 1978-79. Republican. Elder St. Peter's Presbyterian Ch., Spencertown, N.Y. Clubs: 50 of Columbia County (pres. 1978-79), Spencertown Fire Co.).

BRALLIAR, MAX BURTON, air force officer, surgeon; b. Nashville, May 15, 1927; s. Floyd Burton and Mertie Winifred (Boynton) B.; m. Audrey E. Batson, May 4, 1951; children: F. Burton, Robert B., Briggs B. B.S., Madison (Tenn.) Coll., 1950; M.D., Loma Linda (Calif.) U., 1951. Diplomate: Am. Bd. Colon and Rectal Surgery. Commd. 1st lt. U.S. Air Force, 1950, advanced through grades to lt. gen.; intern Nashville Gen. Hosp., 1950-51; fellow Alton Ochsner Med. Found., 1953-57; surgeon SAC, Offutt AFB, Nebr., 1975-80; command surgeon U.S. Air Force Europe, Rangstein, W. Ger., 1980-82; surgeon gen. Dept. Air Force, Bolling AFB, 1982—. Decorated Disting. Service medal, Legion of Merit, Meritorious Service medal, Air Force Commendation medal with 2 oak leaf clusters, Air medal, Vietnamese Cross of Valor. Fellow A.C.S., Soc. Air Force Clin. Surgeons, Am. Soc. Colon and Rectal Surgeons; mem. Alton Ochsner Surg. Soc. Office: Surgeon Gen Bldg 5681 Bolling AFB Washington DC 20332 *

BRAM, STEPHEN BENNETT, utility company executive; b. N.Y.C., Dec. 9, 1942; s. Vincent and Helen (Shattls) B.; m. Constance Joy Lieberman, Mar. 21, 1964; children: Jeffrey, Neal. B.S. in Elec. Engring., MIT, 1963; M.B.A., NYU, 1966. Adj. assoc. prof. Grad. Sch. Bus. Adminstrn. Pace U., N.Y.C., 1967-80; asst. v.p. system ops. Consol. Edison Co. of N.Y., Inc., N.Y.C., 1978-79, v.p. system and transmission ops., 1979-82, v.p. fossil power, 1982—. Mem. IEEE. Office: Consol Edison Co of NY Inc 4 Irving Pl New York NY 10003

BRAMBLE, JAMES HENRY, educator; b. Annapolis, Md., Dec. 1, 1930; s. Charles Clinton and Edith (Rinker) B.; m. Margaret H., June 25, 1977; children—Margot, Tamara, Mary, James. A.B., Brown U., 1953; M.A., U. Md., 1955, Ph.D., 1958. Mathematician Gen. Electric Co., Cin., 1957-59, Naval Ordnance Lab., White Oak, Md., 1959-60; asst. prof., asso. prof., prof. U. Md., 1960-68; prof. Cornell U., Ithaca, N.Y., 1968—; dir. Center Applied Math., 1974-80; cons. Brookhaven Nat. Lab., 1976—; vis. prof. Chalmers Inst. Tech., Göteborg, Sweden, 1970, 72, 73, 76, U. Rome, 1966-67, Ecole Poly., Paris, 1978, Lausanne, Switzerland, 1979, U. Paris, 1981; lectr. in field. Chmn. editorial bd.: Mathematics of Computation, 1975—; Contbr. articles profl. jours. Mem. Am. Math. Soc. (council), Soc. Indsl. and Applied Math. Address: 220 Berkshire Rd Ithaca NY 14850

BRAMLETT, CHARLES ALLAN, textile executive; b. Dalton, Ga., July 28, 1932; s. Lloyd Edward and Tiles Belle (Stephenson) B.; m. Mary Jane Mitchell, Dec. 25, 1949 (div. 1982); children: Charles Allan, Renda Jane, Elizabeth Adellia, Andrew Wright. Student, pub. schs., Dalton, Ga.; grad., Dale Carnegie Course, 1972. Shipping mgr. E.T. Barwick Mills, Dalton, Ga., 1950-56; asst. plant mgr. Cabin Crafts, Dalton, 1956-62; v.p. mfg. E & B Carpet Mills, Dalton, 1962-68; exec. v.p. Galaxy Carpet Mills, Chatsworth, Ga., 1968—, dir., Chatsworth, 1968—. Contbr. author: I've Had A Millionaire's Fund, 1982. City councilman City of Dalton, 1970-71, mayor, 1972-76; bd. dirs. Ga. Mcpl. Assn., Atlanta, 1972-76. U. Tenn. football scholar, 1950; named Man of Yr. Daily Citizen News, Dalton, 1973. Democrat. Methodist. Clubs: Dalton Golf and Country, Nat. Redbone Hound Assn., Dalton Quarterback, Murray County Wildlife Improvement, Am. Redbone Houns Assn., Nat. English Coon Houng Assn. Home: 101 S Tibbs Rd Dalton GA 30705 Office: Galaxy Carpet Mills Inc PO Box 800 Chatsworth GA 30705

BRAMLETT, CHRISTOPHER LEWIS, educator; b. Canton, N.C., Aug. 31, 1938; s. Martin Vaughn and Annie Mae (Best) B.; m. Patricia Ann Starnes, Aug. 26, 1960; children—Susan, Lewis, John. B.S., Wake Forest Coll., 1960, M.A., 1964; Ph.D., U. Va., 1967. Asst. dean arts and scis. U. Ala., 1970-73, asso. dean, 1973-76, asst. v.p. research, 1976-77; v.p. acad. affairs E. Tenn. State U., 1977-81, v.p. research and grad. studies, 1981—. Pres., dir. Bibb Pickens Mental Health Center. Mem. Am. Assn. Univ. Adminstrs. (pres. Ala. chpt.). Club: Rotary. Address: Box 1175 Albemarle NC 28001

BRAMMER, FOREST EVERT, electrical engineering educator; b. Mabscott, W.Va., July 21, 1913; s. Evert C. and V. Susan (Lilly) B.; m.

Evelyn G. Klitzing, Mar. 7, 1942; children: Robert, Mary, William, Susan. A.B., Concord Coll., 1933; B.S., N.C. State U., 1933; postgrad., U. N.C., 1936-37, Johns Hopkins, 1947-48; Ph.D., Case Inst. Tech., 1951. High sch. tchr., Beaver, W.Va., 1933-36; geophys. engr. Schlumberger Well Surveying Corp., Tex., Ill., Mich., 1937-42; research Johns Hopkins Applied Physics Lab., 1946-48; faculty Case Inst. Tech., 1948-60; prof. elec. engring. Wayne State U., Detroit, 1960-82, prof. emeritus, 1982—, chmn. dept., 1960-70; cons. Goodyear Aircraft Corp., 1954-58; Republic Steel Corp., 1958—. Served to capt. Signal Corps AUS, 1942-46. Mem. I.E.E.E., Am. Soc. Engring. Edn., Sigma Xi, Tau Beta Pi, Eta Kappa Nu. Home: 1312 Devonshire St Grosse Pointe MI 48230 Office: 5050 Anthony Wayne Dr Detroit MI 48202

BRAMMER, LAWRENCE MARTIN, psychology educator; b. Crookston, Minn., Aug. 20, 1922; s. Martin G. and Edna L. (Thiesen) B.; m. Marian S. Sjolin, Feb. 11, 1945; children: Karin Marie, Kristen Lenore. B.S., St. Cloud State U., 1943; M.A., Stanford U., 1948, Ph.D., 1950. Diplomate: Am. Bd. Prof. Psychology. Psychologist Stanford U. Counseling and Testing Ctr., 1948-75; assoc. dean students Sacramento State Coll., 1950-64; prof. psychology U. Wash., Seattle, 1964—. Author: Therapeutic Psychology, 4th edit.,, 1982, Helping Relationship, 2d edit., 1979. Served to lt. M.C. AUS, 1944-46. Fulbright fellow, 1961-62. Fellow Am. Psychol. Assn.; mem. Am. Personnel and Guidance Assn., Assn. Humanistic Psychology. Democrat. Lutheran. Club: Queen City Yacht. Home: 7714 56th Pl NE Seattle WA 98115 Office: U Wash Miller DQ 12 Seattle WA 98195

BRAMS, STEVEN JOHN, political scientist, educator, game theorist; b. Concord, N.H., Nov. 28, 1940; s. Nathan and Isabelle (Tryman) B.; m. Eva Floderer, Nov. 13, 1971; children: Julie Claire, Michael Jason. B.S., MIT, 1962; Ph.D., Northwestern U., 1966. Research assoc. Inst. Def. Analyses, Arlington, Va., 1965-67; asst. prof. polit. sci. Syracuse U., 1967-69; asst. prof. NYU, 1969-73, assoc. prof., 1973-76, prof., 1976—; vis. prof. U. Rochester, U. Pa., U. Mich., Yale U., U. Calif.-Irvine, Inst. Advanced Studies, Vienna; cons. in field. Author: Game Theory and Politics, 1975, Paradoxes in Politics: An Introduction to the Nonobvious in Political Science, 1976, The Presidential Election Game, 1978, Biblical Game: A Strategic Analysis of Stories in the Old Testament, 1980, (with Peter C. Fishburn) Approval Voting, 1983, Superior Beings: If They Exist, How Would We Know, 1983; co-author: Applied Game Theory, 1979, Modules in Applied Mathematics: Political and Related Models, 1983; mem. editorial bd.: Am. Polit. Sci. Rev., 1978-82, Jour. Politics, 1968-73, 78-82, Math. Social Scis., 1980-83, Theory and Decision, 1982-83; mem. manuscript rev. com.: Behavioral Sci., 1972-83. NSF grantee, 1968-70, 70-71, 74-75, 80-83; Social Sci. Research Council grantee, 1968; Social Sci. Research Council fellow, 1964-65. Mem. AAAS, Am. Polit. Sci. Assn., Internat. Studies Assn., Pub. Choice Soc., Policy Studies Orgn., Internat. Peace Sci. Sco. Democrat. Jewish. Home: 4 Washington Sq Village Apt 2N New York NY 10012

BRAMSON, DAVID JAY, merchant; b. Chgo., Nov. 1, 1937; s. Leo and Ann (Travis) B.; m. Suzan Beth Sloan, Feb. 7, 1963 (div. Jan. 1974); children: Nancy Lynne, Jeffrey Michael, Max J.; m. Tina Nitzkin, May 27, 1977. Student, U. Colo., 1959. Pres. Bramson, Inc., Chgo., 1961—; partner 715 Farms, Ltd., Fla., 1961—, Gold-Dobrow-Bramson, 1963—, Harrison & Bramson, 1963—; owner, mgr. Bramson Enterprizes, Fla., 1963—; mng. partner Chgo. Yogurt Co., 1977—; owner, mgr. Bramson Software, Oak Park, Ill., 1974-76, Bramson Adult Food, Chgo., 1979—. Chmn. women's wear trade div. Combined Jewish Appeal, 1965-66, Chgo. Heart Assn., 1966. Mem. Zeta Beta Tau. Clubs: Standard, East Bank (Chgo.). Home and office: 429 W Briar Chicago IL 60657 *Be sensitive to, in touch with, deal with NOW... Tomorrow will be different than anything you can predict today.*

BRAMSON, LEON, social scientist, educator; b. Chgo., Dec. 6, 1930; s. William and Sophie (Dudowitz) B.; m. Mary Elizabeth Hamlin, Mar. 12, 1960 (div. 1982); children: Rachel, Ruth. A.B., U. Chgo., 1950, M.A., 1953; Ph.D., Harvard, 1959. Instr. social relations Harvard, 1959-61, asst. prof., 1961-65; assoc. prof., chmn. dept. sociology and anthropology Swarthmore Coll., 1965-77, prof. sociology, 1971-78; program officer Exxon Edn. Found., N.Y.C., 1978-80; coordinator social analysis, corp. planning dept. Exxon Corp., N.Y.C., 1980-82; asst. dir. div. gen. programs NEH, Washington, 1982—; vis. prof. sociology U. Calif. at San Diego, 1972; cons. Peace Corps Agy., 1965; ednl. cons. Trustee Nat. Service Secretariat, 1967-74, Coll. Retirement Equities Fund, 1978—, Good Hope Sch., Frederiksted, St. Croix, U.S. V.I.; policyholder-elected trustee Tchrs. Ins. and Annuity Assn., N.Y.C., 1973-78. Author: The Political Context of Sociology, 1961; Asso. editor: Am. Sociol. Rev, 1967-69; editor: Robert MacIver: On Community, Society and Power, 1970, (with G. W. Goethals) War: Studies from Psychology, Sociology, Anthropology, 1964. Served with AUS, 1953-55. Fulbright scholar, Netherlands, 1957-58. Fellow Am. Sociol. Assn., Am. Anthrop. Assn. Home: 2501 K St Apt 62 Washington DC 20037 Office: Nat Endowment Humanities 1100 Pennsylvania Ave NW Washington DC 20506

BRAMSON, ROBERT SHERMAN, lawyer; b. N.Y.C., Nov. 11, 1938; s. Oscar David and Gertrude (May) B.; m. Diane Sue Kimmel, Dec. 23, 1941; children: Jonathan, Jennifer, James, Julia. B.M.E., Rensselaer Poly. Inst., 1959; J.D., Georgetown U., 1963; postgrad., U. Chgo. Sch. Bus., 1963-64. Bar: Ill. 1963, Pa. 1968, N.Y. 1984. Patient examiner U.S. Patent Office, Washington, 1959-60; patent agt. Stevens, Davis, Miller & Mosher, Washington, 1960-63; atty. Abbott Labs., North Chicago, Ill., 1963-66, Scott Paper Co., Phila., 1966-68; ptnr. Schnader, Harrison, Segal & Lewis, Phila., 1968; adj. prof. Rutgers U. Law Sch., Camden, N.J. Mem. ABA, Am. Patient Law Assn., Phila. Patient Law Assn., Phila. Bar Assn. Club: Racquet (Phila.). Home: 727 S Latches Ln Merion PA 19066 Office: Schnader Harrison Segal & Lewis 1600 Market St Suite 3600 Philadelphia PA 19103

BRAMSON, THOMAS RICHARD, industrial publishing company executive; b. Detroit, Mar. 3, 1927; s. Roy Theodore and Ruth Elizabeth (Gillespie) B.; m. Judith Lee Swats, Nov. 30, 1964; children: Elizabeth, Michael, Heidi, Katherine, Tom, Christian. B.A., Mich. State U., 1951. Pres. Bramson Pub. Co., Troy, Mich., 1953—; Bd. dirs. Am. Bus. Press, 1967-73, chmn., 1981-82; bd. dirs. Center for Mktg. Communications, 1969-73, Bus. Publ. Audits, 1969-72. Served with AUS, 1944-47, 51-53. Mem. Psi Upsilon. Home: 1592 Redding Rd Birmingham MI 48009 Office: Box 101 Bloomfield Hills MI 48013

BRAMWELL, HENRY, judge; b. Bklyn., Sept. 3, 1919; s. Henry Hall and Florence Elva (MacDonald) B.; m. Ishbel W. Brown, Jan. 29, 1966. LL.B., Bklyn. Law Sch., 1948, LL.D. (hon.), 1979. Bar: N.Y. bar 1948. Asst. U.S. atty., Bklyn., 1953-61; asso. counsel N.Y. State Rent Commn., 1961-63; judge Civil Ct., N.Y.C., Bklyn., 1966, 69—; asst. adminstrv. judge, Kings County, Bklyn., 1974—; judge U.S. Dist. Ct., Bklyn., 1975—; Mem. Community Mayors N.Y. State; trustee Bklyn. Law Sch., 1978—. Served with AUS, 1941-45. Mem. Am., N.Y. State, Bklyn. (trustee 1968-74), Nat. (life) bar assns., Am. Judicature Assn. Home: 101 Clark St Brooklyn NY 11201 Office: US Courthouse 225 Cadman Plaza East Brooklyn NY 11201

BRANAGAN, JAMES JOSEPH, lawyer, electronics and distribution company executive; b. Johnstown, Pa., Mar. 5, 1943; s. James Francis and Caroline Bertha (Schreier) B.; m. Barbara Jeanne Miller, June 19, 1965; children: Sean Patrick, Erin MacKay, David Michael. B.A. in English Lit. with honors magna cum laude (Woodrow Wilson fellow), Kenyon Coll., Gambier, Ohio, 1965; LL.B. cum laude, Columbia U., 1968. Bar: Ohio 1968. Asso. firm Jones, Day, Reavis & Pogue, Cleve., 1968-72; with Leaseway Transp. Corp., Cleve., 1972-81, gen. counsel, 1975-80, sec., 1979-81, v.p. corp. affairs, 1980-81, also officer, dir.; v.p. Premier Indsl. Corp., Cleve., 1981-82; sr. counsel TRW Inc., 1982—. Mem. Am. Soc. Corp. Secs., Am. Bar Assn., Ohio Bar Assn., Cleve. Bar Assn. Office: 4415 Euclid Ave Cleveland OH 44122

BRANAHL, ERWIN FRED, aerospace co. exec.; b. St. Louis, Mar. 8, 1922; s. Erwin Edward and Mildred Wilhelmina (Kelle) B.; m. Adeline Elizabeth Sweeney, Apr. 15, 1944; children—Sandra Beatrice Branahl Cooper, James Erwin. B.S.C.E., Washington U., St. Louis, 1943, M.S. in Applied Mechanics, 1951. Registered profl. engr., Mo. Stress analyst Curtiss-Wright Corp., 1943-44; with McDonnell Douglas Astronautics Co., St. Louis, 1946—, mgr. space and missile engring. programs, 1961-68, v.p. engring., 1968-74, v.p., gen. mgr., 1974—; v.p., dir. McDonnell Douglas Corp.; dir. Vitek Systems, Inc. Served to lt. (j.g.) USNR, 1945-46. Fellow AIAA (asso.). Lutheran. Home: 14 Lake Pembroke St Saint Louis MO 63135 Office: PO Box 516 Saint Louis MO 63166 *

BRANCATO, LEO J., manufacturing company executive; b. N.Y.C., Oct. 27, 1922; s. Leo and Josephine (Abbruscato) B. B.S. in Mech. Engring, Cooper Union, 1950; M.S., Columbia U., 1952. Registered profl. engr., Conn. Design engr. Ermold Co., N.Y.C., 1946-51; with Heli-Coil Corp., Danbury, Conn., 1952-70, exec. v.p., 1963-70, pres., 1970; v.p., dir. Mite-Corp., merger co. including Heli-Coil Co., Danbury, 1970-74; pres. Mite-Corp., 1974—; incorporator Union Savs. Bank, Danbury. Trustee Danbury Hosp., 1961—; chmn. Housatonic Regional Mental Health Council, 1965-68; commr. conservation, Danbury, 1974-79; mem. bd. visitors U. Conn. Sch. Bus. Adminstrn., 1977—. Served to lt., C.E., AUS, 1943-46. Fellow ASME; mem. N.Y. Acad. Scis., Tau Beta Pi. Clubs: Princeton (N.Y.C.); Ridgewood Country (Danbury). Patentee in field of fastener tech. Office: Shelter Rock Ln Danbury CT 06810

BRANCH, BEN SHIRLEY, finance educator; b. Atlanta, Apr. 18, 1943; s. Ben Shirley and Elizabeth Hilman (Harris) B.; m. Patricia Lawrie Kuohn, June 9, 1969; children: Kelly Joseph Dapprich, Benjamin Robert. B.A., Emory U., 1965; M.A., U. Tex., 1967; Ph.D., U. Mich., 1970. Asst. prof. econs. Datmouth Coll., 1970-75; from asst. prof. to prof. fin. U. Mass. Sch. Bus., Amherst, 1976—; staff research Strategic Planning Inst., 1976—. Author: Fundamentals of Investing, 1976. Brookings Instn. fellow, 1969-70; Strategic Planning Inst. grantee, 1976; Chgo. Bd. Trade grantee; Ctr. for Study of Future Markets grantee; N.E. Utilities grantee. Mem. Am. Econ. Assn., Fin. Mgmt. Assn., Am. Fin. Assn., Eastern Fin. Assn., So. Fin. Assn. Home: 239 Aubinwood Amherst MA 01002 Office: U Mass Amherst MA 01003

BRANCH, CHARLES HENRY HARDIN, physician; b. Hopkinsville, Ky., Feb. 14, 1908; s. Charles Henry Hardin and Elisabeth Collins (Reed) B.; m. Erma Smith, Dec. 11, 1937; children—Robert Hardin, Alan Henry. A.B., U. Fla., 1928; M.D., Tulane U., 1935. Intern So. Pacific Hosp., San Francisco, 1935-36; prof., head dept. psychiatry U. Utah Coll. Medicine, 1948-70; emeritus clin. prof. U. So. Calif., 1971—; dir. Am. Bd. Psychiatry and Neurology, sec.-treas., 1961, pres., 1962; mem. nat. adv. mental health council NIMH, 1957-61, spl. cons., 1961—; nat. cons. psychiatry to surgeon gen. USAF, 1959-62; cons. psychiatry and neurology consultants br. Office Surgeon Gen., Dept. Army, 1962—; profl. adv. bd. Internat. Com. against Mental Illness. Editorial bd.: Am. Jour. Forensic Psychiatry. Fellow A.C.P., Am. Geriatrics Soc., Am. Psychiat. Assn. (council, sec., pres. 1962-63), Royal Soc. Medicine; mem. N.Y. Acad. Scis., Nat. Assn. Mental Health (profl. adv. bd., dirs., pres. research found. 1965-69), AAAS, Pan Am., Calif. med. assns., Santa Barbara County Med. Soc., Intermountain Psychiat. Assn., Nat. Acad. Religion and Mental Health, Sigma Xi. Office: 527 San Ysidro Rd Santa Barbara CA 93108

BRANCH, CHARLES WILLIAM, college executive; b. Gaffney, S.C., Dec. 22, 1930; s. Amos Oren and Velma Louise B.; m. Barbara Jean Collins, July 8, 1951; children: Teresa Elaine Branch Matthews, Vicki Jean Branch Stewart. A.A., Spartanburg Jr. Coll., 1951; A.B., Wofford Coll., 1953; M.Ed., U. S.C., 1958; Ed.D., U. Ala., 1971. Dean Midlands Tech. Coll., Columbia, S.C., 1963-71; dir. career edn. Columbia City Schs., 1971-72; asst. exec. sec. Commn. on Colls., So. Assn. Colls., Atlanta, 1972-74; pres. Chattanooga State Tech. Community Coll., 1974—. Bd. dirs. Chattanooga C. of C., Salvation Army, Chattanooga; bd. dirs. Cherokee council Boy Scouts Am.; mem. Chattanooga Econ. Devel. Council. Mem. Phi Delta Kappa, Kappa Delta Pi. Baptist. Club: Kiwanis (dir.). Home: 906 Crown Point Rd E Signal Mountain TN 37377 Office: 4501 Amnicola Hwy Chattanooga TN 37406

BRANCH, CLIFFORD (CLIFF BRANCH), football player; b. Houston, Aug. 1, 1948. Student, Wharton County Jr. Coll., U. Colo. Wide receiver Oakland Raiders (now Los Angeles Raiders), 1972—. Played in Pro Bowl, 1974, 75, 76, 77; played in NFL postseason championship games 1976, 80. Office: care Los Angeles Raiders 332 Center St El Segundo CA 90245 *

BRANCH, JAMES ELLIOTT, architect, educator; b. Martinsville, Ind., July 6, 1906; s. Emmett Forest and Katherine (Bain) B.; m. Mary Eloise Kennedy, Feb. 2, 1928; children—Mary Patricia (Mrs. Robert L. Bundy), James Elliott. B.S. in Archtl. Engring, U. Ill., 1929, M.S., 1933. Registered profl. engr., Ill.; registered architect, Fla. Draftsman, architect Ulen & Co., Lebanon, Ind., 1929-31; instr., then asso. prof. architecture U. Ill., 1931-41, 46-50; prof., chmn. dept. architecture and archtl. engring. U. Miami, Fla., 1950-72, prof. emeritus, 1972—; pvt. practice, 1930—. Served to col., arty. AUS, 1941-46; now ret. Res. Decorated Bronze Star. Mem. A.I.A., Am. Soc. Engring. Edn., Assn. Collegiate Schs. Architecture, Fla. Planning and Zoning Assn., Assn. U.S. Army, Ret. Officers Assn., Gargoyle, Scarab, Iron Arrow, Beta Theta Pi, Tau Beta Pi, Sigma Tau., Kiwanian. Clubs: Century (Coral Gables); Coral Reef Yacht (Coconut Grove, Fla.); University of Miami Faculty; Committee of One Hundred (Miami Beach, Fla.). Home: 19990 Sawgrass Ln 4202 Boca Raton FL 33434

BRANCH, JOSEPH, state justice; b. Enfield, N.C., July 5, 1915; s. James C. and Laura (Applewhite) B.; m. Frances Jane Kitchen, Dec. 7, 1946; children: Jane Branch, James C. LL.B., Wake Forest U., Winston-Salem, N.C., 1938, LL.D. hon., 1983, Campbell U., 1981. Bar: N.C. 1937. Individual practice law, Enfield, 1938-45; ptnr. Dunn and Johnson, Enfield, 1945-66; assoc. justice Supreme Ct. N.C., 1966—, chief justice, 1979—; dir. Enfield Savs. and Loan Assn., Peoples Bank and Trust Co., Enfield; atty., dir. Halifax Mut. Fire Ins. Co.; Mem. N.C. Gen. Assembly, 1947-53; legis. counsel to govs., N.C., 1957, 65. Chmn. Halifax County Democratic Party, 1957-63; del. Dem. Nat. Conv., 1956; trustee Wake Forest U., 1966-68, 71-73, 75-77, 79-80, chmn., 1970-71; trustee Wesleyan Coll., Rocky Mount, N.C.; deacon Enfield Bapt. Ch. Served with U.S. Army, 1943-45. Recipient Alumni Service award Wake Forest U. Sch. Law, 1971; Distinguished Service citation Wake Forest U., 1974; Carroll Wayland Weathers Disting. Alumnus award, 1980. Mem. N.C., Wake County, Halifax County bar assns., N.C State Bar. Lodge: Enfield Lions (past pres.). Office: PO Box 1841 Raleigh NC 27602

BRANCH, ROBERT LEE, Ednl.coll. adminstr.; b. Portsmouth, Ohio, Dec. 20, 1924; s. Clyde C. and Ethel C. (Oliver) B.; m. Dorothy Lee Niquette, Apr. 20, 1946; children: Barbara Lee, Theresa Ann. B.S., La. State U., 1949; M.P.H., U. Mich., 1951; Ed. D., U. Cal. at Berkeley, 1967. Commd. 2d lt. USAAF, 1945; advanced through grades to lt. col. USAF, 1967; mem. (B-29 crew), 1943-46; health educator La. Dept. Health, 1946-52; officer flight, edn. and tng. USAF, 1952-69; prof. aerospace studies, chmn. dept. San Francisco State Coll., 1964-68; staff officer Directorate Personnel Planning, Pentagon, 1968-69; ednl. cons. Westinghouse Learning Corp., 1969-70; supt. Sacramento County Office Edn., 1970—; Pres., dir. Oliver Perry Edn. Center, Fair Oaks, Cal. Decorated Air medal, Meritorious Service medal. Mem. Royal Soc. Pub. Health (Eng.), Delta Chi (pres. 1948), Phi Delta Kappa, Delta Omega. Clubs: Lion., Rancho Cordova (Cal.) (pres. 1959). Home: 8863 Bluff Lane Fair Oaks CA 95628 Office: 9738 Lincoln Village Dr Sacramento CA 95827

BRANCH, WILLIAM BLACKWELL, playwright, producer; b. New Haven, Sept. 11, 1927; s. James Matthew and Iola (Douglas) B.; m. Marie Louise Foster, Aug. 19, 1956 (div.); 1 dau., Rochelle Ellen. B.S., Northwestern U., 1949; M.F.A., Columbia U., 1958; ABC fellow, Yale U., 1965-66. Vis. scholar and lectr. numerous univs.; vis. prof. U. Md., Baltimore County, 1979-82. Actor appearing in: Anna Lucasta, 1945; playwright for theatre, TV and motion pictures, 1951—; asso. in film, Columbia Sch. of Arts, 1968-69; staff writer-producer, Channel 13, Ednl. TV, N.Y.C., 1962-64; co-author: The Jackie Robinson Column in, N.Y. Post and syndication, 1958-60; screenwriter for, Universal Studios, 1968-69; producer, NBC News, 1972-73; pres., William Branch Assos., 1973—; (nominated for Emmy award for documentary 1969, recipient Robert E. Sherwood award for Light in the Southern Sky 1958, Blue Ribbon award for Still a Brother: Inside the Negro Middle Class, Am. Film Festival 1969); Author: Fifty Steps Toward Freedom, 1959; works include (theatre) A Medal for Willie, 1951, In Splendid Error, 1954, A Wreath for Udomo, 1960, To Follow the Phoenix, 1960, Baccalaureate, 1975; TV Light in the Southern Sky, 1958; TV documentary Still a Brother: Inside the Negro Middle Class, 1968; documentary TV series Afro American Perspectives, 1974—; screen Together for Days, 1971; exec. producer: Black Perspective on the News, Pub. Broadcasting System, 1978-79. Bd. dirs. Am. Soc. African Culture, 1963-70; bd. dirs. Nat. Citizens Com. for Broadcasting, 1969-71; mem. nat. adv. bd. Ctr. for Book, Library of Congress, 1979—. Served with AUS, 1951-53. John Guggenheim fellow, 1959-60; recipient Hannah B. Del Vecchio award Columbia, 1958. Address: 53 Cortlandt Ave New Rochelle NY 10801

BRAND, CHARLES MACY, educator; b. Stanford, Calif., Apr. 7, 1932; s. Carl F. and Nan (Surface) B.; m. Mary Joan Shorrock, Aug. 7, 1954; children: Catharine, Stephen. B.A., Stanford U., 1953; M.A., Harvard U., 1954, Ph.D., 1961. Asst. prof. history San Francisco State Coll., 1962-64; asst. prof. Bryn Mawr Coll., Pa., 1964-69, assoc. prof., 1969-75, prof. history, 1975—, chmn. dept. history, 1978-81. Author: Byzantium Confronts the West, 1180-1204, 1968; editor: Icon and Minaret, 1969; translator: Deeds of John and Manuel Comnenus by J. Kinnamos, 1976. Served with U.S. Army, 1955-57. Dumbarton Oaks Center for Byzantine Studies fellow, 1961; Fulbright research fellow, 1968; Gennadius fellow, 1968; Guggenheim fellow, 1972. Mem. U.S. Nat. Com. for Byzantine Studies (1961), Medieval Acad. Am., Am. Hist. Assn., Byzantine Studies Conf. (governing bd.). Home: 508 W Montgomery Ave Haverford PA 19041 Office: Dept History Bryn Mawr Coll Bryn Mawr PA 19010

BRAND, DONALD DILWORTH, educator; b. Chiclayo, Peru, Mar. 6, 1905; s. Willis C. and Martha Susan (Dilworth) B.; m. Joy Morenci Erickson, Sept. 16, 1932; children—Donald Dilworth, Joy Beverly (Mrs. William J. Doughty). A.B., U. Calif., 1929; traveling fellow, 1930-31, Ph.D., 1933. Teaching fellow U. Calif., 1931-33, instr., 1934, lectr. geography, 1934; asst. prof. U. N.Mex., 1934-35, asso. prof., 1935-39, prof. anthrop. geography, 1939-47, head dept. anthropology, 1935-43, 46-47; cultural geographer Smithsonian Inst. Mexico, 1944-46; prof. geography U. Mich., 1947-49, U. Tex., Austin, 1949-75, emeritus, 1975—; organized dept. geography, 1949, chmn. dept. geography, 1949-60. Author: Quiroga, A Mexican Municipio, 1951, Coastal Study of Southwest Mexico, 2 vols, 1957, 58, Coalcoman and Motines del Oro-An Ex-distrito of Michoacán Mexico, 1960, Mexico, Land of Sunshine and Shadow, 1966; monographs; contbr. chpts. to books, tech. articles to profl. jours. and encys. Fellow AAAS, Am. Anthrop. Assn., Explorers Club; mem. Assn. Am. Geographers, Soc. History Discoveries, Latin-Am. Studies Assn., Soc. for Am. Archeology, Soc. Mexicana de Antropologia, Current Anthropology (asso.), Phi Beta Kappa, Sigma Xi, Phi Kappa Phi. Home: 2217 S Lakeshore Blvd Austin TX 78741

BRAND, EDWARD CABELL, shoe company executive; b. Salem, Va., Apr. 11, 1923; s. William F. and Ruth (Cabell) B.; m. Shirley Hurt, June 20, 1964; children: John, Richie, Liza, Caroline, Sylvia, Edward C., Miriam, Marshall. Grad., Va. Mil. Inst., 1944. Econ. analyst econ. div. Mil. Govt., Berlin, 1947-49; with Stuart McGuire Co., Salem, Va., 1949—, sales mgr., v.p., 1949-62, pres., 1962—, chmn. bd., 1973—; pres. Brand Edmonds Assocs. Advt., 1959-66, chmn. bd., 1962—; dir. First Va. Bank in Roanoke Valley, First Va. Banks, Inc.; former instr. bus. adminstrn. and sales mgmt. Roanoke Coll. Former mem. Bus. Leadership Adv. Council.; past bd. dirs. Roanoke Council of Community Services; founder, pres. Total Action Against Poverty, Roanoke Valley, 1965—; former trustee Council on Religion and Internat. Affairs; bd. dirs. Woodlands Conf.; trustee Ethics Resource Ctr.; advisor Inst. Socioeconomic Studies. Served from pvt. to capt. AUS, 1942-46; ETO. Named Businessman in U.S. who has done most to help low income people Vista, 1980. Mem. Am. Mgmt. Assn. (pres.'s assn.), Chief Execs. Forum, Direct Selling Assn. (dir., past chmn.), U.S. C. of C., Conf. Bd. (exec. council), World Bus. Council (past dir.), Newcomen Soc. N.Am., Roanoke Valley Hist. Soc., Archeol. Soc. Va. Clubs: Roanoke Touchdown (past pres.), Valley Torch (past pres.), Roanoke Sales Execs. (past dir.), Roanoke Country, Hunting Hills Country. Home: 701 N Main St Salem VA 24153 Office: Stuart McGuire Co Inc PO Box 551 Salem VA 24156 *In addition to trying to do the best job I could—whether in school, business, public service, or in my family—I have felt a continuing need to improve our system and society. This has led to extensive study, travels, and a variety of extra-curricular activities. Today I have great confidence in the future of the United States and the world, but even more confidence in the need for dramatic changes in our value systems.*

BRAND, GEORGE EDWARD, JR., lawyer; b. Detroit, Oct. 25, 1918; s. George Edward and Elsie Bertie (Jones) B.; m. Patricia Jean Gould, June 7, 1947; children—Martha Christine, Carol Elsie, George Edward. B.A., Dartmouth Coll., 1941; postgrad., U. Minn., Harvard U., 1941; J.D., U. Mich., 1948. Bar: Mich. bar 1948, U.S. Supreme Ct. bar 1958. Mem. firm George E. Brand, Detroit, 1948-63, Butzel, Long, Gust, Klein & Van Zile, 1963—, ptnr., dir., pres., 1974—. Served with USNR, 1942-46. Fellow Am. Bar Found., Am. Coll. Trial Lawyers; mem. ABA, Am. Judicature Soc., Detroit Bar Assn., VFW. Clubs: Detroit, Renaissance. Home: 1233 Kensington Rd Grosse Pointe Park MI 48230 Office: 1881 1st Nat Bldg Detroit MI 48226

BRAND, GERHARD KARLFRIEDRICH, physician, microbiologist, educator; b. Luebeck, Germany, June 10, 1922; came to U.S., 1957, naturalized, 1964; s. Johannes and Kaethe e6(Hoefer) B.; m. Inge Hoellein, Aug. 19, 1949; children—Juliane, Bettina. Grad., Kathareineum High Sch. and Coll., Germany, 1940; student, U. Hamburg and Kiel, Germany, 1942-49, M.D., 1949, diploma tropical medicine, 1954; P.D. in Pub. Health and Microbiology, U. West Berlin, 1956. Resident internal medicine Med. Clinic Luebeck, 1949-52; asso. prof. Tropical Inst., Hamburg, 1952-55, Free U., West Berlin, 1955-57; prof. dept. microbiology U. Minn., Mpls., 1957—; Vis. prof. U. Merida, Venezuela, 1960; prof., dir. Inst. Microbiology, U. Duesseldorf, Germany, 1966-67. Author: (with Inge Brand) monographs Evolution of Cell Cultures, 1962, (with L.C. McLaren) Virus Tropism, 1964, Bacteriology of Otolaryngological Infections, 1973, 2d edit., 1980, Foreign Body Tumorigenesis, 3d edit, 1980, Schistosomiasis-Cancer, 1979, Asbestos-Cancer, 1980; Contbr.: articles on cancer research, cell immunology, virology to sci. jours. Asbestos-Cancer. Recipient Distinguished Teaching awards U. Minn. Med. Sch., 1968, 71, 74, 75; Research grantee USPHS, Am. Cancer Soc., 1957—. Mem. Am. Assn. Immunologists, Soc. Exptl. Biology and Medicine, Tissue Culture Assn., Internat. Soc. Differentiation, others. Home: 3117 W Owasso Blvd Saint Paul MN 55112 Office: Dept Microbiology U Minn Minneapolis MN 55455 *Confidence of others in me has set my standards of conduct and performance, demanding a constant effort to measure up.*

BRAND, IRVING RUBIN, lawyer; b. Mpls., Dec. 23, 1918; s. Harry R. and Ruth (Rubin) B.; m. Ruth Miller, Dec. 20, 1953; children: Judith D., Johanna M., Jonathan M., Jethra E., Joshua L. B.S., U. Minn., 1941, J.D., 1943. Bar: Minn. 1943, also Ill., U.S. Supreme Ct. U.S. Practiced in, Mpls., 1947-51, 66—; law clk. to judge U.S. Ct. Appeals 8th Circuit, 1943-44; asso. atty. U.S. Dept. Justice, Washington, 1944-45; asso. firm Swiren, Heineman & Antonow, Chgo., 1945-47, Karlins, Grossman, Karlins & Brand, 1949-51; judge Municipal Ct. Mpls., 1951-55, Dist. Ct., 4th Judicial Dist. Minn., 1955-66; partner firm Maslon, Edelman, Borman, & Brand, 1966—; professorial lectr. Sch. Dentistry, U. Minn., 1947-78; instr. Law Sch., 1953-66, adj. prof., 1966—; mem. adv. com. on rules of civil procedure and appellate practice Minn. Supreme Ct., 1965-70, mem. adv. com. on rules of Evidence, 1974-77. Mem. adv. com. B'nai B'rith Hillel Found. U. Minn., 1951—, pres., 1952-57; asso. mem. bd. govs. Hebrew U., 1976-79; mem. B'nai B'rith Nat. Hillel Commn., 1967-72; chmn. Israel Bonds, Mpls., 1970-74; Past pres. Twin Cities chpt. Am. Friends of Hebrew U.; past bd. dirs. Jewish Family and Children's Service Mpls., Mpls. Fedn. Jewish Service; bd. govs. Mt. Sinai Hosp. Assn. Mem. Am., Fed., Minn., Hennepin County bar assns., Am. Judicature Soc., Am. Law Inst., Minn. Dist. Judges Assn. (past com. chmn.), Law Alumni Assn. U. Minn. (past dir.). Office: 1800 Midwest Plaza Minneapolis MN 55402

BRAND, JOHN CHARLES, educator; b. Durban, South Africa, May 5, 1921; emigrated to Can., 1969, naturalized, 1975; s. Andrew Nevill and Helen Mabel B.; m. Evelyn Grace Meek, Sept. 8, 1943; 1 son, David Andrew. B.Sc., U. London, 1941, M.Sc., 1943, Ph.D., 1947, D.Sc., 1956. Lectr. chemistry U. Glasgow, Scotland, 1947-56, sr. lectr., 1957-64; prof. Vanderbilt U., 1964-69, U. Western Ont., 1969—. Author: Applications of Spectroscopy, 1965, Molecular Structure, 1976; Contbr. articles to profl. jours. Recipient Herzberg award Spectroscopy Soc. Can., 1982. Fellow Royal Soc. Can.; mem. Can. Inst. Chemistry, Can. Assn. Physicists, Chem. Soc. Home: 1518 Western Rd London ON N6G 1H4 Canada Office: U Western Ontario London ON N6A 5B7 Canada

BRAND, JOSEPH LYON, lawyer; b. Urbana, Ohio, Aug. 11, 1936; s. Vance and Katherine (Lyon) B.; m. Jacqueline Ransford Graham; children: Katherine Elizabeth, Stephanie Lyon, Joseph Howard. A.B., U. Mich., 1958; M.A., Ohio State U., 1959; J.D. with honors, George Washington U., 1963. Bar: Ohio and D.C. 1963. Ptnr. firm Patton, Boggs & Blow (and predecessor), 1967—; professorial lectr. George Washington U. Nat. Law Center, 1983—. Mem. George Washington Law Assn. (past v.p.), Washington Inst. Fgn. Affairs, ABA (chmn. com. on banking and fin. sect. internat. law 1971-72), D.C. Bar Assn., Am. Soc. Internat. Law, Southwestern Legal Found., Order of Coif (chpt. pres. 1970-71). Clubs: Metropolitan, 1925 F Street, Lincoln Mall Polo (Washington). Home: Great Falls VA 22066 Office: 2550 M St NW Washington DC 20037

BRAND, LEONARD, physician, educator; b. Bklyn., Dec. 21, 1923; s. Samuel and Sarah (Berrin) B.; m. Helen Frances Thomashow, Mar. 11, 1951; children: Dana Aron, Jennifer Susan, Stefanie Alice. Student, Bklyn. Coll., 1940-42, U. N.H., 1943-44; B.S., Yale U., 1946; M.D., Columbia U., 1949. Diplomate: Am. Bd. Anesthesiology. Intern L.I. Coll. Hosp., 1949-50; resident physician Leo N. Levi Meml. Hosp., Hot Springs, Ark., 1950-51; resident in anesthesiology Presbyterian Hosp., N.Y.C., 1953-55, asst. in anesthesiology, 1955-57, asst. attending in anesthesiology, 1957-66, assoc. attending in anesthesiology, 1966-72, attending anesthesiologist, 1972—; co-dir. Pain Treatment Service, Dept. Anesthesiology Columbia-Presbyn. Med. Ctr.; instr. anesthesiology Columbia U., 1955-57, assoc., 1957-59, asst. prof., 1959-66, assoc. prof. in clin. anesthesiology, 1966-72, prof., 1972—; vis. prof. Glostrup Hosp., Copenhagen, Denmark, 1966, Radcliffe Infirmary, Oxford, Eng., 1974; cons. VA Hosp., East Orange, N.J. Mem. editorial adv. bd.: Anesthesiology Review, 1975—; Contbr. articles in field to profl. jours. Trustee Englewood Cliffs (N.J.) Sch. Bd., 1961-66, pres., 1964-66. Served with U.S. Army, 1942-46, 51-53. Recipient Carnegie Hero medal, 1952. Fellow Am. Coll. Anesthesiologists, Am. Scandinavian Found.; mem. N.Y. County Med. Soc., N.Y. State Med. Soc., N.Y. State Soc. Anesthesiologists, Am. Soc. Anesthesiologists, Am. Soc. Pharmacology and Exptl. Therapeutics, Found. Thanatology, Am. Pain Soc. Office: 622 W 168th St New York NY 10032

BRAND, NEVILLE, actor; b. Kewanee, Ill., Aug. 13, 1921. Ed. high sch. Appeared in: films D.O.A, 1949, Halls of Montezuma, 1951, Stalag 17, 1953, Riot in Cell Block Seven, 1954, Mohawk, 1955, The Tin Star, 1957, Cry Terror, 1958, Five Gates to Hell, 1959, The Scarface Mob, 1960, Huckleberry Finn, 1960, Birdman of Alcatraz, 1962, That Darn Cat, 1965, The Desperados, 1968, Scalawag, 1973, Cahill, U.S. Marshall, 1973, The Deadly Trackers, 1973, Psychic Killer, 1973, The Ninth Configuration, 1980, Without Warning, 1980; others; appeared on: TV in Laredo, 1965, The Captain and the Kings, The Seekers. Served with AUS, 1938-48. Address: care Internat Creative Mgmt 8899 Beverly Blvd Los Angeles CA 90048 *

BRAND, OSCAR, folksinger, author, educator; b. Winnipeg, Man., Can., Feb. 7, 1920; s. Isidore and Beatrice (Shulman) B.; m. Karen Lynn Grossman, June 14, 1970; children: Jeannie, Eric, James, Jordan. B.A., Bklyn. Coll., 1942. Pres. Harlequin Prodns., Inc., Gypsy Hill Music, Inc.; trustee Newport Festival Corp.; Mem. faculty Hofstra U., New Sch., 1970—; Music adviser nat. bd. YWCA; mem. adv. bd. Sesame Street, Pres.'s Com. on Nutrition.; cons Bill Moyers, PBS-TV, 1983; Curator Songwriters Hall of Fame. Host: HEW program World of Folkmusic, 1962—, N.Y.C.; AM-FM Folksong Festival, 1945—, NET-TV, Oscar Brand's American Odyssey, 1970—; star: show Let's Sing Out, CTV Network, Can., 1962-68, The First Look, NBC-TV, N.Y.C., 1965-68, Brand New Scene, CTV Network, Can., 1966; host: Voices in the Wind, NPR Network, 1974—; composer, lyricist: Joyful Noise, 1966, KAPLAN, 1967; composer: songs for film The Fox; composer, author: How to Steal an Election, 1968, Bridge of Hope, for Lit. Conf., 1969; composer: In White America, 1965, Celebrate, for N.Y. Presbytery, 1970; music dir.: TV series Nat. Geog. Bicentennial, 1974; writer-dir.: Sing, America, Sing, Kennedy Center, 1975; (Recipient Venice, Edinburgh, Valley Forge, Golden Reel, Cannes Festival awards for documentary and ednl. films 1946, Peabody, Scholastic, Freedoms Found., Edison, Emmy nominations awards for radio and TV 1962); Author: Singing Holidays, 1957, Bawdy Songs, 1960, Folksongs for Fun, 1961, Ballad Mongers, 1963, Songs of '76, 1972, When I First Came to This Land, 1975, Party Songs, 1983. Served with M.C. AUS, 1942-45. Mem. N.Y. Folklore Soc. Office: One Times Sq New York NY 10036 *I need more time.*

BRAND, PAUL WILSON, physician, govt. agy. ofcl.; b. India, July 17, 1914; s. Jesse Mann and Evelyn Constance (Harris) B.; m. Margaret Elizabeth Berry, May 29, 1943; children—Christopher W., Jean M., Constance M., Estelle F., Patricia N., Pauline F. Student, Univ. Coll. Sch., London, 1943; M.B., B.S., London U.; LL.D., Wheaton Coll., 1971. Intern Univ. Coll. Hosp., 1943-45, resident, 1944-45, Hosp. for Sick Children, London, 1945-46; tchr. orthopaedic surgery Christian Med. Coll., Vellore, India, 1946-64, prof. surgery, 1954-64; also past pres.; chief rehab. br. USPHS Hosp., Carville, La., 1966—; clin. prof. surgery La. State U. Med. Sch., 1966—, clin. prof. orthopaedic surgery, 1977—; spl. research to correct deformity in leprosy, 1947—; Hunterian prof. reconstructive surgery in leprosy Royal Coll. Surgeons, 1952, 62. Decorated comdr. Order Brit. Empire; recipient Lasker Award for disting. services field rehab., 1960, Founder's medal Nat. Rehab. Assn., 1967, Merit medal (gold) Swedish Red Cross, 1974. Fellow Royal Coll. Surgeons (Eng.), Royal Soc. Medicine, Brit. Orthopaedic Assn., A.C.S. (hon. fellow), Southeastern Surg. Congress, Am. Surg. Assn. (corr. mem.), Am. Soc. Plastic and Reconstructive Surgery, Am. Soc. Surgery Hand. Address: USPHS Hosp Carville LA 70721

BRAND, ROBERT, theatrical lighting designer; b. Stanford, Calif., Apr. 9, 1934; s. Carl F. and Nan Alwilda (Surface) B.; m. Joan Fisher, Dec. 6, 1959; children—Elanor Arwen, David F. Student, Stanford U., 1951-55. Lighting designer for major opera cos. in, U.S., including, Balt. Opera, 1966-80, Conn. Opera Assn., 1973-80, Opera Co. of Phila., 1967-81, San Francisco Opera Co., 1972-75, Houston Grand Opera, 1977-77, Miami Opera Co., Florentine Opera Co., San Antonio Symphony, Opera Group Boston, Nat. Opera Chile; lighting designer for off-Broadway prodns., indsl. shows; lighting cons. architects for, Coca Cola Co. Theatre, Armstrong Cork Co. Theatre, Lyric Theatre, Balt.; lighting designer, Ashland Shakespearean Festival, 1965-67. Mem. United Scenic Artists, Actors Equity Assn. Address: 505 West End Ave New York NY 10024

BRAND, STEWART, editor/publisher; b. Rockford, Ill., Dec. 14, 1938. B.S. in Biology, Stanford, 1960. Formerly with Merry Pranksters; founder Am. Needs Indians; Spl. cons. to Edmund G. Brown, Jr. (gov. of Calif.), 1976-78. Editor/pub.: The Last Whole Earth Catalog, 1968-71 (Nat. Book award), Whole Earth Epilog, 1974, The Next Whole Earth Catalog, 1980-81, The Co-Evolution Quar, 1974—; editor-in-chief: Whole Earth Software Catalog, 1983—, Whole Earth Software Rev., 1983—; Author: Two Cybernetic Frontiers, 1974. Founder Uniommon Courtesy, Sch. of Compassionate Skills, 1982. Fellow Lindisfarne Assn. Address: Box 428 Sausalito CA 94966 *Life rides. Death drives.*

BRAND, VANCE DEVOE, astronaut; b. Longmont, Colo., May 9, 1931; s. Rudolph William and Donna (DeVoe) B.; m. Joan Virginia Weninger, July 25, 1953; children: Susan Nancy, Stephanie, Patrick Richard, Kevin Stephen; m. Beverly Ann Whitnel, Nov. 3, 1979; 1 son, Erik Ryan. B.S. in Bus., U. Colo., 1953, 1960; M.B.A., UCLA, 1964; grad., U.S. Naval Test Pilot Sch., Patuxent River, Md., 1963. With Lockheed-Calif. Co., Burbank, 1960-66, flight test engr., 1961-62, traveling engr. rep., 1962-63, engring. test pilot, 1963-66; astronaut NASA Johnson Space Ctr., Houston, 1966—, command module pilot Apollo-Soyuz mission, 1975, comdr. STS-5 Mission,, 1982, comdr. STS 41-B Mission,, 1984. Served with USMCR, 1953-57. Recipient Disting. Service medal NASA; Exceptional Service medal NASA.; 2 Space medals NASA. Fellow Am. Astron. Soc.; assoc. fellow AIAA, Soc. Exptl. Test Pilots. Office: Code CB Lyndon B Johnson Space Center Houston TX 77058

BRAND, WILLIAM CALVERT, government official; b. Brown County, Ind., Feb. 14, 1918; s. Jesse S. and Calcie I. (Carmichael) B.; m. Betty Leona Ballard, Jan. 14, 1939; children: D. Calvert, Joan Carole, John Scott, Jesse Robert. Student, Ill. State U., 1936-37, Purdue U., 1939, Washington U., St. Louis, 1940, Ind. U., 1960-61. Dunlap & Co., Columbus, Ind., 1938-65, exec. v.p., Columbus, 1965; owner Batesville Lumber Co., Ind., 1965-67; co-owner, pres. chmn. bd., dir. Brands, Inc., Columbus, 1967—; dep. asst. sec. policy and budget Dept. HUD, Washington, 1981-82, gen. dep. asst. sec. for housing, 1982—; dir. ILBSA, Indpls.; cons. (in field). Mem. Columbus City Council, 1955, Ind. Ho. of Reps., 1966-70; adminstrv. asst. to gov. State of Ind., 1960, state budget dir., 1972. Served with U.S. Army, 1945-47. Named Dealer of Decade NLBMDA, 1963; recipient Disting. Service award Jaycees, 1953, Community Service award Columbus C. of C., 1961, others. Mem. Ind. Lumber Bldg Supply Assn. (pres. 1965-66), Nat. Lumber Bldg. Material Dealers Assn. (pres. 1979-80, chmn. bd. 1980-81, exec. com. 1976-80), Am. Legion. Republican. Presbyterian. Clubs: Harrison Lake Country (Columbus); Columbia (Indpls); Indpls. Press. Lodges: Elks; Masons. Home: 906 Franklin St Columbus IN 47201 Office: Dept HUD 451 7th St SW Washington DC 20410

BRANDAUER, FREDERICK PAUL, language educator; b. N.Y.C., Dec. 14, 1933; s. Frederick William and Grace Angeline (Martin) B.; children—Rebekah Susan, Frederick Jonathan. B.A., Lebanon Valley Coll., 1955; M.Div., United Theol. Sem., 1958; M.A., U. Pitts., 1965; Ph.D., Stanford U., 1973. Missionary United Meth. Ch., Hong Kong, 1959-69; acting dir. (Christian Study Center), Hong Kong, 1967-69; lectr. Chinese, Stanford (Calif.) U., 1972-73; asst. prof. Chinese U. Wash., Seattle, 1973-78, asso. prof. Chinese, chmn. dept. Asian lang. and lit., 1978—. Author: (with M. Berkowitz and J. Reed) Folk Religion in an Urban Setting, 1969, Tung Yueh, 1978; contbr.: articles to profl. jours. Tung Yueh. NDEA Title IV fellow, 1969-71; NDFL Title VI fellow, 1971-72; ACLS Chinese Civilization grantee, 1976-77; Alexander von Humboldt fellow U. Munich, 1977-78. Mem. Assn. Asian Studies, Am. Oriental Soc., Soc. Study of Chinese Religions. Roman Catholic. Address: U Wash DO 21 Seattle WA 98195

BRANDBORG, LLOYD LEON, physician, educator; b. Wheatland, Wyo., Oct. 16, 1924; m. Donna Marie Fagerstrom, Jan. 28, 1950; children—Terry Allan, Scott Lee. A.B., U. Calif., 1950; M.D., U. Chgo., 1955. Diplomate: in internal medicine and gastroenterology Am. Bd. Internal Medicine. Postgrad. tng. in internal medicine and gastroenterology U. Wash., 1955-61; chief of gastroenterology VA Hosp., San Francisco, 1961—; clin. instr. medicine U. Calif. at San Francisco, 1961-64, asst. clin. prof., 1964-68, asst. prof. in residence, 1968-69, clin. prof., 1969—, lectr. in pathology, 1969—; Cons. gastroenterology USPHS Hosp., Letterman Gen. Hosp., San Francisco, David Grant Air Force Med. Center, Travis AFB, Calif. Editorial bd.: Gastroenterology; Contbr. articles to profl jours. Served with USAAF, 1943-45. Decorated Air medal. Fellow A.C.P.; mem. Am. Fedn. for Clin. Research, A.M.A., Am. Gastroent. Assn., Western Soc. for Clin. Research, AAAS, Wilderness Soc. Home: 259 Dellbrook Ave San Francisco CA 94131 Office: 4150 Clement St San Francisco CA 94121

BRANDBORG, STEWART MONROE, conservationist, government official; b. Lewiston, Idaho, Feb. 2, 1925; s. Guy Mathew and Edna (Stevenson) B.; m. Anna Vee Mather, Aug. 8, 1949; children: Becky Glyde, Daniel Mathew, Betsy Edna, Anna Lisa, Fern Jennifer. B.S. in Wildlife Tech, U. Mont., 1948; M.S. in Forestry, U. Idaho, 1951. With U.S. Forest Service in, Idaho, Mont. and Oreg., 1942-46; research life history and ecology mountain goat in Mont. Mont. Fish and Game Dept., 1947-48; research fellow Idaho Coop. Wildlife Research Unit, 1949-50; research and mgmt. investigations mountain goat, elk, other big game species Idaho Dept. Fish and Game, 1950-53; asst. conservation dir. Nat. Wildlife Fedn., 1954-60; dir. spl. projects, asso. exec. dir. Wilderness Soc., 1960-63, exec. dir., 1964-76; pres. Citizens Action Center, 1976; spl. asst. to asst. sec. for fish and wildlife and parks Dept. Interior, 1977; spl. asst. to dir. Nat. Park Service, 1977-81; environ. cons., 1981—; co-chmn. Urban Environ. Conf., 1972-74; bd. dirs. Urban Environmental Conf., 1972—; nat. coordinator Regional Environ. Leadership Conf. Series, 1982—. Mem. Wildlife Soc. Club: Cosmos. Home: 14401 Turkey Foot Rd Gaithersburg MD 20760

BRANDENBURG, JOHN NELSON, army officer; b. Enid, Okla., Apr. 29, 1929; s. Roy McClellen and Mabel Illinois (Medlen) B.; m. Beverly A. Haynes Green, Sept. 1, 1973; children: Peggy J. Brandenburg Alford, Kirk R., Kimberly Ann Green, Beverly Paige Green. B.S. in Forestry, Okla. State U., 1951; M.S. in Internat. Relations, George Washington U., 1968. Commd. 2d lt. U.S. Army, 1951, advanced through grades to lt. gen., comdr. 123d Aviation Bn., 23d Inf. Div., then 2d Bn., 21st Inf., 196th Inf. Brigade, 1968-69; chief Service Schs. br. Schs. and Edn. Div. Office Dep. Chief of Staff for Personnel, 1969-70; asst. sec. gen. staff Office Army Chief of Staff, 1970-71; dep. chief of staff for ops. Mil. Dist. Washington, Ft. Lesley J. McNair, 1971-72; comdr. Task Force Garry Owen, 1st Cav. Div. U.S. Army, Vietnam, 1972; chief of staff 3d Regional Assistance Command U.S. Mil. Assistance Command, Vietnam, 1972; chief Plans and Ops. Div. 3d U.S. Army, 1973-74; asst. dep. chief of staff for ops. U.S. Army Forces Command, 1974; asst. div. comdr. 101st Airborne Div. (U.S. Army), Ft. Campbell, Ky., 1974-75; chief of staff XVIII Airborne Corps and Ft. Bragg, 1975-76, 1st U.S. Army, 1976; dep. comdg. gen. 1st U.S Army, 1976-78; comdr. Army Readiness Region III, Ft. George G Meade, Md., 1976-78; comdg. gen. 101st Airborne Div. and Ft. Campbell, Ky., 1978; now comdg. gen. I Corps, Ft. Lewis, Wash. Decorated Silver Star medal with oak leaf cluster, Legion of Merit with 2 oak leaf clusters, D.F.C., Bronze Star medal with oak leaf cluster, Air medal with 14 Oakleaf Clusters, Purple Heart, Combat Inf. badge with star. Office: Ft. Lewis WA 98433

BRANDENBURG, RICHARD GEORGE, university dean, management educator; b. Oak Park, Ill., Feb. 21, 1935; s. George Arthur and Florence (Ream) B.; m. Maxine Toby Newman, Dec. 21, 1957; children—Suzanne Linda, Cynthia Anne. B.Mech. Engring., Cornell U., 1958, M.B.A., 1960, Ph.D., 1964. Asst. to dean Grad. Sch. Indsl. Adminstrn., Carnegie Inst. Tech., Pitts., 1962-64, asst. dean, asst. prof. indsl. adminstrn., 1964-67; acting dean, asso. prof. indsl. adminstrn. Grad. Sch. Indsl. Adminstrn., Carnegie-Mellon U., Pitts., 1967-68; dean, prof. mgmt. Sch. Mgmt., SUNY, Buffalo, 1968-76; adj. prof. mgmt.; v.p. mfg. and engring. The Carborundum Co., Niagara Falls, N.Y., 1976-80; dean, prof. mgmt. Coll. Bus. Adminstrn., Grad. Sch. Bus. and Public Mgmt., U. Denver, 1980—; bd. dirs. mem. long-range planning, accreditation research coms. Am. Assembly Collegiate Schs. Bus.; mem. policy com. regents external degree in bus. adminstrn. N.Y. State Dept. Edn., 1975-80; Mem. mfg. council Machinery and Allied Products Inst., Am. Mgmt. Assn., 1976-80; trustee arts devel. services, Buffalo, 1973-76; bd. dirs., mem. council, mem. exec. seminar adv. com. Niagara Inst.; trustee N.Y. Council for Humanities, 1977-80; vice chmn. Advs. Com. on Mgmt. and Budget for Erie County; bd. regents Canisius Coll., Buffalo, 1974-80; dir. HMO Colo., Mentor Corp, United Bank of Monaco, Denver. Author: (with H.I. Ansoff, Fred E. Portner, R. Radosevich) Acquisition Behavior of U.S. Manufacturing Firms, 1946-65, 1971, Japanese edit., 1972; mem. editorial bd.: Calif. Mgmt. Rev, 1967-76, Jour. Gen. Mgmt, 1970; editor mfg. sect.: AMA Mgmt. Handbook, 1983; contbr. articles to profl. jours. Bd. dirs., v.p. Child and Adolescent Psychiat. Clinic, Buffalo, 1974-80; mem. community affairs steering com. Denver C. of C.; bd. dirs. Colo. Humanities Program. Recipient McKinsey award, 1969. Mem. Am. Mgmt. Assn. (president's council 1980—), Ops. Research Soc. Am., AAAS, Inst. Mgmt. Scis. (steering com., econ. devel. council 1980—), Phi Kappa Tau, Beta Gamma Sigma, Phi Kappa Phi, Pi Tau Sigma, Tau Beta Pi, Delta Sigma Pi (hon.). Home: 5777 S Galena St Englewood CO 80111 Office: Coll Bus Adminstrn Grad Sch Bus and Public Adminstrn U Denver Denver CO 80208

BRANDENSTEIN, DANIEL CHARLES, astronaut, naval officer; b. Watertown, Wis., Jan. 17, 1943; s. Walter C. and Agnes (Holzworth) B.; m. Jane A. Wade, Jan. 2, 1966; 1 dau., Adelle. B.S., U. Wis.-River Falls, 1965; postgrad., U.S. Naval Text Pilot Sch., Patuxent River, Md., 1971. Commd. officer U.S. Navy, 1965, advanced through grades to capt.; student aviator U.S. Navy, NASA, Pensacola, Fla., 1965-67, avaitor, Whidbey Island, Wash., 1967-71, test pilot, Patuxent River, Md., 1971-74, aviator, Whidbey Island, Wash., 1974-78; astronaut NASA Johnson Space Ctr., Houston, 1978—. Recipient 26 medals and award USN, 1968-71, Disting. Alumnus award U. Wis., 1982, Space Flight medal NASA, 1982. Mem. Soc. Exptl. Text Pilots, AIAA, U.S. Naval Inst. Office: NASA Lyndon B Johnson Space Ctr Houston TX 77058

BRANDES, RAYMOND STEWART, history educator, university dean; b. San Diego, Jan. 2, 1924; s. Theodore C. and Mary (Peters) B.; m. Irma Dolores Montijo, Jan. 28, 1961; children: Elena María, Elisa Ann, Laura Raquel, Claudia Reneé, Ramón Antonio, Marta Denise, Paula Nicole. B.A., U. Ariz., 1959, Ph.D., 1965. Asst. prof. history U. San Diego, 1966-67, assoc. prof., 1967-71, prof., 1971—, chmn. dept., 1967-73, grad. dean, 1973—; dir. several grants related to hist. preservation and hist. site archaeology in San Diego area. Author: Diario of Miguel Costansó, 1969, Troopers West: Military and Indian Affairs on the American Frontier, 1970, San Diego: An Illustrated History, 1982; editor: Brand Book 1, San Diego Corral of Westerners, 1970, Masterplanner for Old Town State Historical Park, 1973-74, Old Town San Diego, 1821-1974, 1976. Mem. Gaslamp Quarter Project Area Com., 1977—, chmn., 1980; v.p. San Diego Sci. Found., 1978—. Served with U.S. Army, 1943-46. NDEA grantee, 1961-64; CETA grantee, 1978, 79; named Outstanding Prof. Social Sci. U. San Diego, 1968, 69. Mem. Western History Assn., Mexican-Am. Educators, Soc. Profl. Archaeologists. Democrat. Roman Catholic. Home: 2725 Barnson Pl San Diego CA 92103 Office: Founders Hall Alcalá Park San Diego CA 92110

BRANDIMORE, STANLEY ALBERT, holding company executive, lawyer; b. Highland Park, Mich., Aug. 20, 1927; s. Albert James B. and Genevieve (McCormick) Weideman; m. E. Kennedy Greene, Dec. 27, 1952; children: Vanessa Brandimore Lund, Darrell Stanley. B.B.A. in Acctg., U. Miami, Fla., 1954, J.D., 1957. Bar: Fla. 1957, U.S. Supreme

Ct. 1968. Instr., lectr. acctg. U. Miami, 1954-57; atty. Fla. Pub. Service Com., Tallahassee, 1957-59, Fla. Power Corp., St. Petersburg, 1959-63, asst. gen. counsel, 1963-68, v.p., gen. counsel, 1968-75, sr. v.p., gen. counsel, 1975-83; exec. v.p., gen. counsel Fla. Progress Corp., St. Petersburg, 1983—. Served with USN, 1945-48, 50-52. Mem. St. Petersburg Bar Assn. (treas. 1964-65), Fla. Bar Assn., ABA, St. Petersburg C. of C. Democrat. Clubs: Suncoasters; Tiger Bay (St. Petersburg); Treasure Island Tennis and Yacht (Fla.). Home: 8338 36th Ave N Saint Petersburg FL 33710 Office: Fla Progress Corp 270 1st Ave S PO Box 33042 St Petersburg FL 33733 *My personal standard of conduct has always been premised on this precise list of priorities: God, country, family, business.*

BRANDIN, ALF ELVIN, mining and shipping company executive; b. Newton, Kans., July 1, 1912; s. Oscar E. and Agnes (Larsen) B.; m. Marie Eck, June 15, 1936 (dec. 1980); children: Alf R., Jon, Erik, Mark.; m. Pamela J. Brandin, Jan. 28, 1983. A.B., Stanford U., 1936. With Standard Accident of Detroit, 1936-42; bus. mgr. Stanford (Calif.) U., 1946-52, bus. mgr., exec. officer for land devel., 1952-59, v.p. for bus. affairs, 1959-70; sr. v.p. Utah Internat. Inc., San Francisco, 1970—; also dir., mem. exec. com.; pres. Richardson-Brandin; dir. Saga Corp., Hershey Oil Co. Bd. govs. San Francisco Bay Area Council; trustee Reclamation Dist. 2087, Alameda, Calif.; bd. overseers Hoover Instn. on War, Revolution and Peace, Stanford. Served as comdr. USNR, 1942-46. Mem. Zeta Psi. Clubs: Elk., Stanford Golf, Bohemian, Pauma Valley Country, Silverado Country; Bankers (San Francisco); Royal Lahaina, San Francisco Golf. Mem. VIII Olympic Winter Games Organizing Com., 1960. Home: 668 Salvatierra St Stanford CA 94305 Office: 550 California St San Francisco CA 94104

BRANDIN, DONALD NELSON, bank holding company executive; b. N.Y.C., Dec. 28, 1921; s. Nils F. and Dorothy May (Mead) B.; m. Mary Elliott Keyes, Jan. 1, 1982; children: Robert N., Patricia A., Douglas M.; 1 stepdau., Elizabeth E. White. A.B., Princeton U., 1944. With Bankers Trust Co., N.Y.C., 1946-56; with Boatmen's Nat. Bank, St. Louis, 1956—, chmn. exec. com., 1968-70, pres., chief operating officer, 1971-72, chmn. bd., pres., chief exec. officer, 1973-78, chmn. bd., chief exec. officer, 1978—; also dir.; exec. v.p. Boatmen's Bancshares, Inc., St. Louis, 1969-72, chmn. bd., chief exec. officer, 1973—, also dir.; dir. Boatmen's Bank & Trust Co., Kansas City, Mo., Boatmen's Nat. Bank of Springfield, Mo. Mortgage and Investment Co., Petrolite Corp., Wm. S. Barnickel & Co., Sigma-Aldrich Corp., Laclede Ave. Real Estate, Inc., Laclede Gas Co., all St. Louis, Boatmen's Life Ins. Co., Phoenix., Boatmen's Bank of Cape Girardeau, (Mo.); Bd. dirs. Arts and Edn. Council Greater St. Louis, St. Louis Symphony Soc., Washington U. Served to capt. AUS, 1943-46. Mem. Assn. Bank Holding Companies, Assn. Res. City Bankers, Am., Mo. bankers assns., Bank Adminstrn. Inst., Robert Morris Assos. Clubs: Blind Brook (Purchase, N.Y.); St. Louis, Old Warson Country, Bogey, Stadium (St. Louis); Metropolitan (Chgo.); Garden of Gods (Colorado Springs, Colo.); Kansas City (Mo.). Office: 100 N Broadway PO Box 236 Saint Louis MO 63166

BRANDIS, ROYALL, economist, educator; b. Richmond, Va., Mar. 8, 1920; s. Roland Buford and Ruby Inez (Parsley) B.; m. Mary Lorraine Arnold, Oct. 18, 1941; children—Mary Elizabeth, Margaret Royall. A.B., U. Richmond, 1940; M.A., Duke U., 1947, Ph.D., 1952. War regulations analyst E.I. du Pont de Nemours and Co., Wilmington, Del., 1941-43; fgn. trade economist Nat. Cotton Council, Washington, 1947-49; instr. economics Duke U., 1949-52; asst. prof. U. Ill., 1952-56, asso. prof., 1956-61, prof., 1961—. Author: Economics: Principles and Policy, 1959, 63, Economia: Principios y Politica, 1962, Principles of Economics, 1968, 72, Principios de Economia, 1972, Current Economic Problems, 1972. Served with U.S. Navy, 1943-46. Mem. Am. Econ. Assn., History of Econs. Soc. (pres. 1979-80), Midwest Econs. Assn. (pres. 1975-76), So. Econ. Assn. Presbyterian. Office: Dept Econs U Ill Commerce West University of Illinois 1206 6th St Champaign IL 61820

BRANDNER, J. WILLIAM, publishing company executive, insurance company executive; b. S.I., N.Y., Apr. 1, 1937; s. J. Kenneth and Mary D. (Monaghan) B.; m. Margaret Lawrence, Sept. 26, 1959; children: John William, Robert, Kathleen, Peggy Ann, Jill. B.B.A., Manhattan Coll., 1958. C.P.A., N.Y., N.J. Audit mgr. Arthur Andersen & Co., N.Y.C. and Newark, 1958-71; asst. controller Harcourt Brace Jovanovich, Inc., N.Y.C., 1971-73, controller, 1973-78, v.p., 1976-80, treas., 1978—, sr. v.p., chief fin. officer, 1980—; chmn., chief exec. officer, sr. v.p., treas. HBJ Ins., Orlando, Fla., 1982—. Vice-pres. Maher Ave. Neighborhood Assn., 1979—. Mem. Fin. Execs. Inst., Am. Inst. C.P.A.s, N.Y. State Soc. C.P.A.s. Republican. Roman Catholic. Club: Milbrook Country (Greenwich, Conn.). Home: 9119 Laytham Ct Orlando FL Office: 757 3d Ave New York NY 10017 HBJ Bldg Orlando FL 32887

BRANDO, MARLON, JR., actor; b. Omaha, Apr. 3, 1924; s. Marlon and Dorothy Pennebaker (Myers) B.; m. Anna Kashfi, 1957 (div. 1959); 1 son, Christian; m. Movita (div.); 1 child. Student, Shattuck Mil. Acad., 1939-41. Actor: N.Y. plays, including Streetcar Named Desire; motion pictures include On the Waterfront (Acad. award for best actor 1954), Guys and Dolls, Teahouse of the August Moon, Sayonara, The Young Lions, Fugitive Kind, Mutiny on the Bounty, The Ugly American, Bedtime Story, The Chase, Appaloosa, A Countess from Hong Kong, Reflections in A Golden Eye, Candy, The Godfather, (Acad. award for best actor 1972), Last Tango in Paris, Missouri Breaks, Superman, 1978, Apocalypse Now, 1979, The Formula, 1980; dir., actor: TV appearance in Roots: The Next Generations, 1979. Office: care Screen Actors Guild 7950 W Sunset Blvd Hollywood CA 90046 *

BRANDON, BRUMSIC, JR., cartoonist; b. Washington, Apr. 10, 1927; s. Brumsic and Pearl (Brooks) B.; m. Rita Broughton, Sept. 30, 1950; children: Linda, Brumsic, III, Barbara. Student, N.Y. U. Illustrator O'Brien Assos., Washington, 1952-55, RCA, Alexandria, Va., 1955-57; participant bd. of co-op. edn. Scholars in Residence, 1975, White House Conf. Children, 1970; chalk talk artist Nassau County (N.Y.) Library System. Freelance cartoonist, 1945—; now with, Los Angeles Times Syndicate; designer animator, Bray Studios Inc., N.Y.C., 1957-70; cartoonist: Luther comic strip, 1969—; TV performer as Mr. BB on Joya's Fun Sch, 1970—; polit. cartoonist: Black Media, N.Y.C., 1976—; cartoonist: The Crisis NAACP Publ, 1981—; Author, cartoonist: Luther From Inner City, 1969, Luther Tells It As It Is, 1970, Right On, Luther, 1970, Luther Raps, 1971, Outta Sight, Luther, 1971, Luther's Got Class, 1976. Advisory bd. Afro Am. Bicentennial Corp., 1975-76. Served with AUS, 1950-52. Mem. AFTRA. Office: care Los Angeles Times Syndicate Times Mirror Sq Los Angeles CA 90053

BRANDON, CLEMENT EDWIN, paper technology educator; b. Oct. 3, 1915; s. David Clement and Mary (Van Tilburgh) B.; m. Marian Steingass, June 25, 1939; children: Ralph Edwin, William Lee. A.B., Defiance Coll., 1936; M.S., SUNY, 1942. Chemist Aetna Paper Co., Dayton, Ohio, 1937-40; chief chemist Howard Paper Mills, Dayton, 1941—, tech. dir., until 1958; prof. dept. paper tech. Miami U., Oxford, Ohio, 1958—, chmn. dept., 1961-81. Recipient alumni achievement award Defiance Coll. Fellow Am. Inst. Chemists, TAPPI (chmn. testing div. 1958-61, mem. testing adv. bd. 1961—, past chmn. various coms., Silver medal testing div.); mem. ASTM (chmn. com. D-6 on paper 1970-72, chmn. precision and sampling com. 1975—), Internat. Standards Orgn. (mem., past chmn. U.S. adv. com. tech. com. 6 on paper), Am. Nat. Standards Inst. (mem. com. P-3 on paper), Paper Industry Mgmt. Assn., Graphic Arts Tech. Found., Am. Soc. Quality Control, Sigma Xi. Home: 121 Oakhill Dr Oxford OH 45056 Office: Miami U Oxford OH 45056

BRANDON, DONALD WAYNE, educator, author, essayist; b. Portland, Ore., May 14, 1926; s. Elmer Irving and Edna Louise (Plog) B.; m. Rosemary Vollmar, June 9, 1948; children—Elisabeth, Margaret, Catherine, Jennifer. Student, Reed Coll., 1946-48; A.B., U. Calif. at Berkeley, 1949, M.A., 1950, Ph.D., 1954. Staff writer Portland Oregonian, 1946-48; instr. U. San Francisco, 1953-55; intelligence analyst CIA, Washington, 1955-56; cultural officer Am. embassy, Bonn, W. Germany, 1956-58; faculty U. San Francisco, 1958—, prof. polit. sci., 1966—. Author: American Foreign Policy-Beyond Utopianism and Realism, 1966, A Politica Externa Americana, 1966; contbr. chpts. to books, articles, essays and reviews to nat. jours. Served with AUS, 1944-46; ETO. Decorated Combat Inf. Badge. Mem. Am. Polit. Sci. Assn., Am. Council on Germany, World Affairs Council No. Calif., U.S. Tennis Assn. Home: 524 Moraga St San Francisco CA 94122

BRANDON, EDWARD BERMETZ, banker; b. Davenport, Iowa, Sept. 15, 1931; s. William McKinley and Mary Elizabeth (Bermetz) B.; m. Phyllis Anne Probeck, Aug. 7, 1954; children: William M., Robert P., Beverly A., Beth A., Edward M. B.S., Northwestern U., 1953; M.B.A., Wharton Sch. Banking & Fin., 1956. Mgmt. trainee Nat. City Bank, Cleve., 1956-61, asst. cashier, 1961-64, asst. v.p., 1964-67, v.p., 1967-77, v.p., mgr. met. div., 1977, sr. v.p., 1977-78, sr. v.p., corp. banking head, 1978-79, exec. v.p. corp. banking group, 1979-82, vice chmn., 1982—; dir. Standard Products Co., Austin Powder Co., Erico Products, Inc. Mem. Greater Cleve. Growth Assn.; mem. Cuyahoga County Republican Com., 1958-80; dir. Regional Council on Alcoholism, 1979-81; chmn. corp. gifts United Way, 1980, 81, vice-chmn. corp. gifts, 1979. Served to lt. USN, 1953-55. Mem. Am. Bankers Assn., Ohio Bankers Assn., Assn. Res. City Bankers. Republican. Methodist. Clubs: Union (Cleve.); Shaker Heights (Ohio); Country. Office: 1900 E 9th St Cleveland OH 44114

BRANDON, INMAN, lawyer; b. Atlanta, May 14, 1906; s. Morris and Harriet Frances (Inman) B.; m. Louise Courts Glancy, Nov. 14, 1932 (dec. Mar. 21, 1982); children: Louise (Mrs. Robert Castle), Shane, Christopher Inman.; m. Ruth Woltz Alford, Dec. 14, 1983. B.A. magna cum laude, U. Ga., 1927; LL.B., Yale U., 1930. Bar: Ga. 1930. Since practiced in, Atlanta; partner firm Hansell & Post (and predecessors), 1946—. Co-chmn. Atlanta Community Chest drive, 1956, chmn. budget com., 1957, pres., 1958; chmn. Atlanta United Appeals, Community Chest-A.R.C., 1959; pres., dir. Family Service Soc. Atlanta, 1960-61, hon. dir., 1963—; co-chmn. joint Tech.-Ga. Devel. Fund drive, 1957-58; Co-finance chmn. Ga. Central Republican Com., 1958-62, hon. finance chmn., 1963; Trustee, sec. bd. U. Ga. Found., 1957-61, chmn. trustees, 1961-70, trustee emeritus, 1977—. Served to lt. comdr. USNR, 1942-45; PTO. Recipient Distinguished Alumni award U. Ga., 1961. Mem. Am., Fed., Ga., Atlanta bar assns., Lawyers Club Atlanta, Nat. Lawyers Club, Am. Judicature Soc., Sphinx (hon. mem. U. Ga.), Phi Beta Kappa, Phi Kappa Phi, Phi Delta Phi., Lion (charter pres. Buckhead club 1941-42). Clubs: Commerce, Piedmont Driving, River Bend Gun (pres. 1965-66), Capital City (Atlanta) (dir. 1961-63); Fla. Yacht, River (Jacksonville, Fla.); University Yacht (Lake Lanier, Ga.); ZENAX, The Nine O'Clocks. Home: 3488 Knollwood Dr NW Atlanta GA 30305 Office: First Nat Bank Tower Atlanta GA 30303

BRANDON, LIANE, filmmaker, educator; b. Newark, July 7, 1939; d. Philip and Nita (Poster) B. Student, St. Lawrence U., 1957-59, U. Edinburgh, Scotland, 1959-60; exchange student, U. Moscow, summer 1960; A.B., Boston U., 1962, M.Ed., 1967. Ski instr., Mt. Tremblant, Que., Can., 1960-62; actress Children's Theatre, Cambridge, Mass., 1960-62; film project dir., coordinator media studies dept. English Quincy pub. schs., Mass., 1964-73; assoc. prof. film prodn. and media studies Sch. Edn. U. Mass., Amherst, 1973—; co-founder, mem. New Day Films, 1971—; media cons. N.Y. State Dept. Edn., 1968; film cons. Mass. Gov.'s Commn. on Status of Women, 1974; media cons. Mass. Dept. Edn., 1970-74; coordinator Mass. Young Filmmakers Festival, 1974-75; cons. Mass. Artists Found., 1975, 82; judge New Eng. Film Festival, 1980; trustee Theaterworks, 1981—; bd. dirs. Boston Film-Video Found., 1983—; guest lectr. various confs. on edn. and fil, colls. and art schs. in U.S. Exhibited film, Mus. Modern Art, Whitney Mus. Am. Art, Chgo. Art Inst., Nast. Film Theatre, London, Internat. Women's Film Festivals, Paris, N.Y., John F. Kennedy Ctr. Performing Arts, Washington; Films TV; contbr. articles on film prodn. to profl. jours.; dir., producer: film Anything You Want to Be, 1971 (The Ribbon, Am. Film Festival award), Betty Tells Her Story, 1972 (Internat. Festival of Women's Films award 1974), Once Upon a Choice, 1980 (Silver medal Houston Internat. Film Festival). Recipient Blue ribbon Am. Film Festival, 1972, Creative Artist award AAUW, 1975; Boston Coll. Film grantee, 1971-72; U. Mass. grantee, 1974; Mass. Found. for Humanities and Pub. Policy grantee, 1975. Mem. New Eng. Screen Edn. Assn. (v.p. 1971-72), Assn. Ind. Video and Filmmakers. Office: Sch Edn U Mass Amherst MA 01003

BRANDON, OSCAR HENRY, newspaper editor; b. Mar. 9, 1916; s. Oscar and Ida B. Student, univs. Lausanne (Switzerland), Prague (Czechoslovakia), London Eng.; D.Litt. (hon.), Williams Coll. With Sunday Times of London, 1939-83, war corr., Africa and Europe, then Paris corr., 1945-46; roving diplomatic corr., 1946-49, Washington corr., 1949-83, assoc. editor, 1963-83; syndicated columnist Washington Star.; Adviser UN Conf. Freedom Information, 1948. Author: As We Are, 1961, In the Red, 1966, Conversations with Henry Brandon, 1966, The Anatomy of Error—The Secret History of the War in Vietnam, 1969, The Retreat of American Power, 1973. Recipient journalistic awards U. Calif. at Los Angeles, 1957, Lincoln U., Jefferson City, Mo., 1962; Hannen Swaffer award Odham Press, London, 1964, 67; named to Hall of Fame Washington Profl. Journalists Soc., 1983. Mem. Overseas Writers, Fgn. Press Assn. Club: Nat. Press (Washington). Address: 814 Nat Press Bldg Washington DC 20045

BRANDOW, FLOYD E., lawyer; b. Roxbury, N.Y., Aug. 26, 1925; s. Floyd E. and Rose (O'Hara) B.; m. Florence Brandow, Sept. 1, 1951; children: John, Susan, Peter. B.A., Rutgers U., 1951; LL.M., U. Pa., 1954. Bar: N.Y. Mem. legal staff firm Milbank, Tweed, Hadley & McCloy, N.Y.C., 1951-63, ptnr., 1963—. Office: Milbank Tweed Hadley & McCloy 1 Chase Manhattan Plaza New York NY 10005

BRANDOW, GEORGE EVERETT, civil engr.; b. Crookston, Minn., Oct. 27, 1913; s. Harry William and Laura (Ramstad) B.; m. Anita Dunn, July 1, 1938; children—Peter Dunn, Gregg Everett. Student, U. Calif. at Los Angeles, 1931-34; B.S. in Civil Engring, U. So. Calif., 1936. Structural chief engr. Union Oil Co. Calif., 1943-45; cons. structural engr. Brandow & Johnston, Los Angeles, 1945—. Spl. events chmn. Heart Fund Los Angeles, 1966; mem. City Council San Marino, Calif.; trustee U. So. Calif., 1969—; pres. Los Angeles Music Center Operating Co., 1972-80; bd. overseers Huntington Library, Art Gallery and Bot. Gardens. Named Los Angeles Engr. of Year, 1971. Mem. ASCE (hon., pres. Los Angeles sect. 1956—, nat. dir. 1969), Am. Inst. Cons. Engrs. (pres. 1969), U. So. Calif. Alumni Assn. (pres. engring. alumni 1948-49, chmn. ann. giving 1967-68, pres. 1970-71). Clubs: Jonathan, California (Los Angeles). Home: 1490 Virginia Rd San Marino CA 91108 Office: 1660 W 3d St Los Angeles CA 90005

BRANDS, ALLEN JEAN, cons., former govt. ofcl.; b. Kansas City, Mo., Sept. 19, 1914; s. William Green and Pansy Jeanne (Allen) B.; m. Alvira Bernice Moe, Nov. 27, 1971; 1 son, Allen Jean. B.S. in Pharmacy cum laude, U. So. Calif., 1941; D.Sc. (hon.), Phila. Coll. Pharmacy, 1974. Community pharmacy practice Owl Drug Co., San Francisco, 1941-42, 46-50; commd. lt. USPHS, 1950, advanced through grades to asst. surgeon gen., 1980; chief pharmacy br. Indian Health Service, Washington, 1953-81; chmn. pharmacy career devel. com. USPHS, 1966-81, chief pharmacist officer, 1967-81; cons., 1981—; Harvey A.K. Whitney lectr., 1978; mem. pub. health com. Nat. Assn. Retarded Children, 1969-71; chmn. com. pharmacy services standards Accrediation Council Mental Retardation Residential Facilities, Joint Commn. Accrediation Hosps., 1971, Accrediation Council Payshiat. Facilities, 1971; cons. com. govt. affairs Am. Assn. Colls. Pharmacy, 1971-81; del. U.S. Pharmacopeial Conv., 1970, 75, 80. Served to 1st lt. USMC, 1943-46. Recipient Commendation medal USPHS, 1963, Outstanding Ser. award, 1981; Alumni Merit award U. So. Calif., 1979; named Outstanding Alumnus U. So. Calif. Coll. Pharmacy, 1967. Fellow Am. Coll. Clin. Pharmacology (bd. regents); mem. Am. Pharm. Assn., Am. Soc. Hosp. Pharmacists, Fedn. Internat. Pharmacists, Assn. Mil. Surgeons U.S. (Andrew Craigie award 1973), Commd. Officers Assn. USPHS (chmn. exec. com. 1974), Skull and Dagger, Rho Chi (past chpt. pres.), Phi Kappa Phi. Home: 3024 Tilden St NW Washington DC 20008

BRANDSTATTER, ARTHUR FRANK, govt. ofcl.; b. McKees Rocks, Pa., Dec. 27, 1914; s. Frank and Marie B. (Banyai) B.; m. Mary Elizabeth Walsh, Nov. 12, 1938; children—Arthur Frank, John Frederick, Robert Walsh, Thomas Michael, James Patrick. B.S., Mich. State U., 1938, M.A., 1950. Police officer Detroit Police Dept., 1938-41; chief of police East Lansing (Mich.) Police Dept., 1946-47; dir. public safety Mich. State U., 1947-60, dir., 1946-76, Fed. Law Enforcement Tng. Center, Glynco, Ga., 1976—; mem. Gov.'s Spl. Com. on Traffic Safety, 1964; del. 5th UN Congress on Prevention of Crime, 1975. Author: (with L.A. Radelet) Police and Community Relations: A Sourcebook, 1968, (with Allen A. Hyman) Fundamentals of Law Enforcement, 1971. Served to brig. gen. U.S. Army Res. Recipient Founders award Acad. Criminal Justice Scis., 1977; Enforcement award Assn. Fed. Investigators, 1977; U.S. Legion of Merit award, 1969. Fellow AAAS; mem. Ams. for Effective Law Enforcement (dir.), Acad. Criminal Justice Sci. (dir.), Internat. Assn. Chiefs of Police, Res. Officers Assn. Roman Catholic. Home: 122 St Andrews Dr Simons Island GA 31522 Office: Federal Law Enforcement Training Center Glynco GA 31524

BRANDT, EDWARD NEWMAN, JR., physician, educator; b. Oklahoma City, July 3, 1933; s. Edward Newman and Myrtle (Brazil) B.; m. Patricia Ann Lawson, Aug. 29, 1953; children-Patrick James, Edward Newman III, Rex Carlin. B.S., U. Okla., 1954, M.D., 1960, Ph.D., 1963; M.S., Okla. State U., 1955. Intern Oklahoma City VA Hosp., 1960-61; resident U. Okla. Hosps., 1961; from instr. to prof. preventive medicine and pub. health U. Okla. Med. Center, Oklahoma City, 1961-70, asst. to v.p., prof., chmn. dept. biostatistics, 1967-68, asso. dean, asso. dir., 1968-70; dean Grad. Sch., prof. preventive medicine and community health U. Tex. Med. Br., Galveston, 1970-72, acting dean, 1972-74, asso. dean clin. affairs, 1972-73, prof. preventive medicine and community health, 1972—, acting dean medicine, 1973-74, prof. family medicine, 1973—, dean medicine, 1974-76, exec. dean, 1976-77; vice chancellor health affairs U. Tex. System, Austin, 1977-81; asst. sec. health U.S. Dept. Health and Human Services, 1981—; Mem. Spl. Rev. Com. for Coop. Fed.-State-Local Health Statistics System; chmn. So. Council Med. Deans, 1976; mem. primate center review com. NIH, 1975-79, chmn., 1978-79, mem. research career devel. award com., 1968-72. Editor, contbr.: Proc. of Conf. at U. Okla. Med. Center, 1968; editor: Continuing Education for the Family Physician, 1974-77. Recipient Superior Performance award VA Hosp. Oklahoma City, 1961; Lloyd M. Southwick Meml. award for med. writing, 1974, 75; Spl. Appreciation award Tex. Acad. Family Physicians, 1974; Leone award for adminstrv. excellence, 1976; Outstanding Alumni Service award U. Okla. Coll. Medicine, 1977; Disting. Service award U. Tex. Med. Br., 1977; 19th Ann. Stoneburner lectr. Med. Coll. Va., 1966. Mem. AAAS, Am. Fedn. for Clin. Research, Assn. Am. Med. Colls., AMA (chmn. sect. on med. schs. 1979-81, chmn. com. accreditation continuing med. edn. 1979-81), Tex. Med. Assn., Am., Tex. acads. family physicians, Philos. Soc. Tex., Sigma Xi, Phi Eta Sigma, Alpha Epsilon Delta, Phi Kappa Phi, Phi Sigma, Pi Mu Epsilon, Alpha Omega Alpha. Home: 3401 Spanish Oak Dr Austin TX 78731

BRANDT, FREDERICK WILLIAM, lawyer; b. Chgo., Apr. 11, 1933; s. Frederick William and Helen Lucille (Merriman) B.; m. Judith Anne Buckner, Aug. 15, 1964; children: Wayne Martin, Keith Gordon. Student, Pomona Coll., 1951; B.A. in Econs, Stanford U., 1955; postgrad. in law, Stanford U., 1959; LL.B., Southwestern U., 1964. Bar: Calif. 1964. Dep. county counsel, Los Angeles County, 1964-66; partner Jarrett & Brandt, Los Angeles, 1966-79, Hiestand & Brandt, 1980—. Co-author: Judicial Arbitration in California, 1983. Coach Pasadena S.W. Little League, 1973-77. Served as lt. USAF, 1955-58; Europe.; capt. USAFR. Mem. State Bar Calif., Los Angeles County Bar Assn., Am. Bd. Trial Advocates. Home: 770 Oak Knoll Circle Pasadena CA 91106 Office: 315 W 9th St Los Angeles CA 90015

BRANDT, GIL, professional football team executive. V.p. for personnel devel. Dallas Cowboys, NFL. Office: care Dallas Cowboys 6116 North Central Expressway Dallas TX 75206

BRANDT, HARRY, mechanical engineering educator; b. Amsterdam, Netherlands, Nov. 14, 1925; came to U.S., 1946, naturalized, 1962; s. Friedrich H. and Henny (Rous) B.; m. Muriel Ruth Harman, Jan. 24, 1953; children: Joyce Estelle, Marilyn Audrey, Robert Alan. B.S., U. Calif.-Berkeley, 1949, M.S., 1950; Ph.D., U. Cal. at Berkeley, 1954. Supervising research engr. Chevron Research Co., La Habra, 1954-64; lectr. UCLA, 1962-64; prof. U. Calif. at Davis, 1964—, chmn. dept. mech. engring., 1969-74; dir. Adaptive Technols. Inc., Sacramento, Calif., 1981-83; cons. Lawrence Livermore Nat. Lab., 1969—, State of Calif., 1970—, State of Alaska, 1972. Mem. ASME, Am. Welding Soc., Am. Inst. Aero. and Astronautics, Sigma Xi, Tau Beta Pi. Presbyn. Home: 3309 Middle Golf Dr Box 2533 El Macero CA 95618 Office: Dept Mech Engring U Cal Davis CA 95616

BRANDT, KARL GARET, biochemist; b. Galveston, Tex., Oct. 15, 1938; s. Preston Laroy and Agnes Virginia (Graff) B.; m. Nancy Elizabeth Yeats, Jan. 2, 1965; children: Wendy Elizabeth, Derek Yeats. B.A., Rice U., 1960; Ph.D., M.I.T., 1964. NSF postdoctoral fellow U. Pa., Phila., 1964-65; NIH postdoctoral fellow Cornell U., Ithaca, N.Y., 1965-66; asst. prof. dept. biochemistry Purdue U., West Lafayette, Ind., 1966-69, assoc. prof., 1969-75, prof., 1975—, asst. dean Grad. Sch., 1981—. Mem. Am. Soc. Biol. Chemists, Am. Chem. Soc., AAAS, Alpha Chi Sigma. Office: Dept Biochemistry Purdue U West Lafayette IN 47907

BRANDT, REXFORD ELSON, artist; b. San Diego, Sept. 12, 1914; s. Alfred O. and Ellen D. (Woodward) B.; m. Joan Malloch Irving, June 22, 1938; children: Joan Dale, Shelley Nora. A.B., U. Calif., 1936; postgrad., Stanford, 1938. Dir. Riverside Jr. Coll. Art Center, 1937-41; chief designer South Coast Co. (shipbuilders), 1941-44; head Rex Brandt Assos., Corona del Mar, Calif., 1944-52; now head Brandt Painting Workshops. Author: Watercolor with Rex Brandt, 1949, Watercolor Technique in Fifteen Lessons, 1954, Watercolor Landscape in Fifteen Lessons, 1953, Composition of Landscape Painting, 1959, Watercolor Landscape, 1963, The Artists Sketchbook and Its Uses, 1966, San Diego, Land of the Sundown Sea, 1969, The Winning Ways of Watercolor, 1973, (with Jerome K. Muller) "Rex Brandt,", 1972, West Coast Portfolio, 1977, Seeing with a Painter's Eye, 1981; also articles.; numerous one man shows include, San Diego Fine Arts Gallery, Los Angeles County Mus., Faulkner Gallery Art, Crocker Gallery Art, Sacramento, Calif., Palace Legion of Honor, Santa Barbara Art Mus., numerous colls. and univs., numerous group exhbns. include, Am. Water Color Soc., N.Y.C., Phila. Acad. Fine Arts, Golden Gate Internat. Expn., N.Y. Water Color Soc., Calif. Centennial Exhbns., others, invitational exhibits include, Corcoran Biennial, Nat. Water Color Survey, Nat. Gallery Art, Riverside Mus., Calif. State Fair, John Herron Art Inst., Scripps Gallery, Pasadena Art Inst., others; represented in permanent collections, San Diego Fine Arts Gallery, Crocker Gallery Art, U.S. Treasury Dept., N.A.D., West Tex Mus., Los Angeles County Mus. Art, Walker Art Mus., San Francisco Mus. Art, Reading Mus., Grinnell Coll., Chico State Coll., Am. Airlines, Philco Corp., Chaffey Art Assn., Ford Motor Co., U.S. Maritime Service, others. Recipient numerous awards, 1934—, including; Brugger award Calif. Water Color Soc., 1952; 1st prize, 1970; prize Laguna Beach Festival Arts, 1952; 1st award; James D. Phelan awards de Young Mus., San Francisco, 1953; Adolph and Clara Obrig prize in watercolor N.A.D., 1961; Lena Newcastle Meml. award Am. Watercolor Soc.; Saportas award, 1968; Bronze medal, 1970; Morse medal N.A.D., 1968, 70; certificate of merit, 1977. Fellow Royal Soc. Arts; mem. N.A.D. (academician), Am. Watercolor Soc., Calif. Watercolor Soc. (past pres.). Home: 405 Goldenrod Ave Corona del Mar CA 92625 Office: 407 Goldenrod Ave Corona del Mar CA 92625 *We are sensate creatures and I think that most of our innermost dreams and hopes, and most of the semantic core in us, the idea exchanges, go back to the earth experiences we share. I suspect that most of abstract art, if there is such a thing, is recognized by the body as part of the kinetic experience it has gone through. I'm not sophisticated enough to live in a world of complete abstraction. Few people are, it appears. And so, it comes back to this peculiar sense of phenomena. It comes back to an atavistic sense of nature—to the smell of the earth and the splash of the sea. And I hope these things are never lost to us.*

BRANDT, RICHARD BOOKER, former philosophy educator; b. Wilmington, Ohio, Oct. 17, 1910; s. Henry and Clara Belle (Guyatt) B.; m. Mary Elizabeth Harris, June 19, 1937 (div. Oct. 1968); children—Richard Charles and Karen Elizabeth. A.B., Denison U., 1930, L.H.D. (hon.), 1977; B.A., Cambridge U., 1933; Burney student; Stanton student, Trinity Coll., Cambridge, 1933-35; student, Tuebingen U., Germany, 1934-35; Ph.D., Yale, 1936. Mem. faculty Swarthmore (Pa.) Coll., 1937-64, successively instr., asst. prof., asso. prof., 1937-52, prof., 1952-64, chmn. dept. philosophy and religion, McDowell prof., 1957-64; prof., chmn. dept. philosophy U. Mich., Ann Arbor, 1964-77, Sellars Collegiate prof., 1978-81; assoc. Center for Philosophy and Public Affairs, U. Md., 1980-81; vis. prof. Fla. State U., 1982, Georgetown U. Law Ctr., 1982-83. Author: The Philosophy of Schleiermacher, 1941, Hopi Ethics: A Theoretical Analysis, 1954, Ethical Theory, 1959, Value and Obligation, 1961, A Theory of the Good and the Right, 1979; also articles in profl. publs. Guggenheim fellow, 1944-45; fellow Center for Advanced Study in Behavioral Scis., 1969-70; sr. fellow Nat. Endowment for Humanities, 1971-72; John Locke lectr. Oxford U., 1973-74. Mem. Am. Philos. Assn. (exec. com. Eastern div. 1951-54, v.p. 1965, pres. Western div. 1969-70), Am. Soc. Polit. and Legal Philosophy (pres. 1965-66), Soc. for Philosophy and Psychology (pres. 1979), Am. Acad. Arts and Scis., AAUP, Phi Beta Kappa. Office: Dept Philosophy U Mich Ann Arbor MI 48109

BRANDT, RICHARD MARTIN, university dean, educator; b. Cleve., Sept. 13, 1922; s. Arthur J. and Lucile (Martin) B.; m. Mattice Fritz, Feb. 14, 1947; children: Mattice (Mrs. M. Ranney), Richard Martin, William F., Mark A., Lucile L. B. Mech. Engring., U. Va., 1943; M.A., U. Mich., 1949; D.Ed. (Found. fellow), U. Md., 1954. Indsl. engr., Detroit, 1946-47, tchr. elementary sch., Willow Run, Mich., 1948-49; instr. of edn. U. Del., Newark, 1950-52; instr. edn. U. Md., College Park, 1953-54, asst. prof., 1954-57, asso. prof., 1957-65, Sch. Edn., U. Va., Charlottesville, 1965-68, prof., 1968—, chmn., 1968-74, dean, 1974—. Author: Studying Behavior in Natural Settings, 1972, Public Education Under Scrutiny; co-editor: Observational Methods in the Classroom; contbr. articles on edn. to profl. publs. Served to lt. (j.g.) USNR, 1943-46. Mem. Am. Ednl. Research Assn., Assn. Colls. and Schs. Edn. in State Univ. and Land Grant Colls. (pres. 1982-83), Assn. for Supervision and Curriculum Devel., Va. Assn. Colls. for Tchr. Edn. (pres. 1980,81), Phi Delta Kappa, Kappa Delta Pi. Home: Route 1 Box 619 Crozet VA 22932 Office: School of Education Univ of Virginia Charlottesville VA

BRANDT, RICHARD PAUL, communications and entertainment company executive; b. N.Y.C., Dec. 6, 1927; s. Harry and Helen (Satenstein) B.; m. Helen H. Kogel, May 31, 1975; children: Claudia, David, Matthew, Thomas; 1 stepdau., Jennifer. B.S. with high honors, Yale U., 1948. With Trans-Lux Theatres Corp., 1950-54, v.p., 1952-54; with Trans-Lux Corp., 1954—, v.p., 1959-62, pres., 1962-80, chmn. bd., 1974—; also chief exec. officer, dir.; dir. Am. Book-Stratford Press, Inc., 1962—, mem. exec. com., 1969—; dir. Brandt Theatres, Presdl. Realty Corp.; Founding gov. Ind. Film Importers & Distbrs. Am., 1959-63, bd. dirs., 1959-69; v.p., mem. exec. com. Theatre Owners Am., 1962-65; mem. bill of rights com. Council Motion Picture Orgns., 1963-65; bd. dirs. Film Soc. Lincoln Center, 1968-71; Mem. N.Y. State Bus. Adv. Com. on Mgmt. Improvement, 1966-70; Chmn. bd. Univ. Settlement Soc., 1964-66, hon. pres., bd. dirs., 1966-77; dir. Am. Theatre Wing, 1970—, United Neighborhood Houses, 1968-73; bd. dirs., treas. Settlement House Employment Devel., 1969-72; trustee, mem. exec. com. Am. Film Inst., 1971—, vice chmn., 1980-83, chmn. bd., 1983—; trustee Mus. Holography, 1979-82. Mem. Nat. Assn. Theatre Owners (dir. 1957-78, exec. com. 1965-78), Phi Beta Kappa, Sigma Xi. Clubs: Yale, Landmark. Office: 110 Richards Ave Norwalk CT 06430

BRANDT, WARREN, artist; b. Greensboro, N.C., Feb. 26, 1918; s. Leon Joseph and Jessie (Wooding) B.; m. Carolyn Coker, 1943 (div. 1959); 1 dau., Isabella; m. Grace L. Borgenicht, Dec. 27, 1960. Student, Pratt Inst., 1935-37; B.F.A., Washington U., St. Louis, 1948; M.F.A., U. N.C., 1953. Head dept. art Salem Coll., 1949-50; instr. art Pratt Inst., 1950-52, Guilford Coll., Greensboro, 1952-56; prof., chmn. dept. art U. Miss., 1957-59, So. Ill. U., 1959-61; dir. N.Y. Studio Sch., 1967—. Exhibited one-man shows, Nonagon Gallery, N.Y.C., 1959, New Gallery, Provinceton, Mass., 1960, Mich. State U., Oakland, 1961, Am. Gallery, N.Y.C., Stuttman Gallery, Provincetown, 1962, Grippi Gallery, N.Y.C., 1963, 64, Obelisk Gallery, Washington, 1963, Sachs Gallery, N.Y.C., 1966, 67, 68, 70, 72, 74, U. N.C., 1967, Eyraud-Barnes Galleries, Los Angeles, Reed Coll., Portland, Oreg., Eastern Ill. U., 1968, David Barnett Galleries, Milw., 1969, 74, 78, Mercury Gallery, London, 1969, Allentown (Pa.) Art Mus., Agra Gallery, Washington, 1969, 70, Fontana Gallery, Narberth, Pa., 1970, 74, 79, Benson Gallery, Bridgehampton, N.Y., 1976, Beaumont (Tex.) Mus., Hooks Epstein Gallery, Houston, 1977, Collector's Gallery, N.C. Mus. Art, Raleigh, 1977, Vick Klaus & Rosen Gallery, Phila.; exhibited in group shows, Met. Mus. Watercolor Exhbn., 1952, Am. Fedn. Arts, Bklyn. Mus. Ann. Print Exhbn., 1949, Pratt Inst., 1970; represented in permanent collections, Met. Mus. Art, Chrysler Mus., Mich. State U., Oakland Mus., So. Ill. U., Rochester Art Mus., N.Mex. State Mus., N.Y. U., U. N.C., Michener Found., U. Mo., Kansas City, Carnegie Mellon Inst., Pitts.; Author: Painting with Oils, 1971. Served to 1st lt. USAAF, 1940-46. Mem. Artists Club. Home: 870 United Nations Plaza New York NY 10017 Studio: 1475 3d Ave New York NY 10028 and Fischbach Gallery 29 W 57th St New York NY 10022

BRANDT, WARREN WILLIAM, chemist, university president; b. Lansing, Mich., July 11, 1923; s. Warren Fisher and Esther Antell (Mortimer) B.; m. Esther Mae Cass, Mar. 18, 1944; children: Richard Warren, Sherry Ann. B.S., Mich. State U., 1944, postgrad., 1946; Ph.D., U. Ill., 1949. Teaching asst. Mich. State U., 1943-44, 46-47; teaching asst. U. Ill., 1947-48, univ. fellow, 1948-49; instr. Purdue U., 1949-50, asst. prof., 1950-55, asso. prof., 1955-61; head dept. chemistry Kan. State U., Manhattan, 1961-63, asso. dean, 1962-63; dean Grad. Sch., Va. Poly. Inst., Blacksburg, 1963-65, v.p., 1963-68, exec. v.p., 1968-69; pres. Va. Commonwealth U., Richmond, 1969-74, So. Ill. U. at Carbondale, 1974-79; v.p. gen. adminstrn. U. Md. System, Adelphi, 1979-83, spl. asst. to pres., 1983—. Guggenheim fellow Oxford U., 1958. Mem. Am. Chem. Soc. (past sec.-treas., chmn. div. analytical chemistry), AAAS, Phi Lambda Upsilon (nat. treas.), Alpha Chi Sigma, Phi Kappa Phi, Omicron Delta Kappa. Home: 2871 Hambleton Rd Riva MD 21140

BRANDZEL, SOL, lawyer, labor union official; b. Poland, June 5, 1913; U.S., 1920; s. Benny and Sophie (Grossman) B.; m. Ruth Cohen, Mar. 2, 1941; children: Merle, Joel, Lisa. J.D., DePaul U., 1938. Bar: Ill. 1938. With Amalgamated Clothing and Textile Workers Union, Chgo., 1950—, internat. v.p., asst. gen. sec.-treas., 1966-78; co-mgr. Chgo. and Central states joint bd., 1972-78; mem. exec. bd. Chgo. Fedn. Labor., AFL-CIO, 1972—; dir. Amalgamated Trust and Savs. Bank, Chgo., Amalgamated Bank of N.Y., Amalgamated Cotton Garment and Allied Industries Fund, 1964-79; chmn. Amalgamated Social Benefits Assn., 1973-79, now trustee; chmn. Amalgamated Life and Health Inc. Soc., 1972-79, now trustee; pres. Amalgamated Centre, 1972-79, now dir.; labor rep. Ill. Unemployment Compensation Bd., 1956-60; v.p. Labor Coalition on Pub. Utilities, 1976—. Bd. dirs., treas. Sidney Hillman Found., N.Y., 1962-78, Jewish Bur. Employment Problems, 1955-60, Israel Histradrut Campaign, 1973—, Music for Westchester Symphony Orch., 1966-72, South East Commn., 1974—, Schwab Rehab. Hosp., 1976—; nat. v.p. Am. Jewish Congress; bd. dirs., v.p. Jewish Manpower Council, 1970—; nat. bd. dirs. Nat. Trade Union Council of Histradrut, 1966-72; chmn. Jewish Labor Com., 1973-76, dir.; mem. Ill. Council of Sr. Citizens Orgns.; mem. adv. bd. TRUST, Inc. (To Reshape Urban Systems Together), 1979—; chmn. Ill. Com. on Health Security, 1974—; commr. Chgo. Health Systems Agy., 1978—, chmn. project rev. com., 1978—; mem., past pres. Chgo. Bd. Edn.; trustee Cook County Community Coll. Dist. 508, 1977—; commr. Chgo. Pub. Bldg. Commn., 1983-84. Served to maj. Q.M.C. U.S. Army. Mem. Chgo. Jewish Hist. Soc. (dir. 1977—). Office: Amalgamated Clothing and Textile Workers Union 333 S Ashland Blvd Chicago IL 60607

BRANEGAN, JAMES AUGUSTUS, III, journalist; b. Phila., June 6, 1950; s. James Augustus, Jr. and Emmeline Elizabeth (McBurney) B. B.A., Cornell U., 1972; M.S. in Journalism, Northwestern U., 1973. Reporter Chgo. Today, 1973-74, Chgo. Tribune, 1974-81; with Time, Inc., 1981—, now energy and environment corr., Washington. Co-recipient Pulitzer prize for spl. local reporting, 1976. Home: 2129 Florida Ave NW Washington DC 20008 Office: 888 16th St NW Washington DC *

BRANGES, LOUIS DE, mathematician, educator; b. Paris, Aug. 21, 1932; s. Louis and Diane (McDonald) deB.; m. Tatiana Jakimow, Dec. 17, 1980. B.S., MIT, 1953; Ph.D., Cornell U., 1957. Asst. prof. Lafayette Coll., 1958-59; vis. mem. Inst. Advanced Study, Princeton, N.J., 1959-60; lectr. Bryn Mawr Coll., 1960-61; mem. Courant Inst., NYU, 1961-62; asso. prof. Purdue U., 1962-63, prof., 1963—. Author: Square Summable Power Series, 1984, Espaces Hilbertiens de Fonctions Entieres, 1973. Served to lt. AUS, 1957-58. Alfred P. Sloan Found. fellow, 1963-66; Guggenheim Found. fellow, 1967-68. Mem. Am. Math. Soc. Episcopalian. Home: 331 Hollowood Dr West Lafayette IN 47906 Office: 800 Math Sci Bldg Purdue U West Lafayette IN 47907

BRANN, LESTER WILLIAM, JR., assn. exec.; b. Madison, Wis., Mar. 24, 1925; s. Lester William and Esther (Jacobsen) B.; m. Lois Winter, Sept. 4, 1948; children—Lester William III, Thomas Edwin. Student, Los Angeles City Coll., 1944; J.D., U. Wis., 1950. Bar: Wis. bar 1950. Practiced in, Racine, 1950-57; with Milw. Assn. Commerce, 1957-67, exec. v.p., dir., 1960-67, Credit Bur. Milw., Inc., 1960-67; exec. v.p. Ill. C. of C., 1967-70, pres., 1970—. Alderman, Racine, 1953-55; Pres. Found. Ill. State Chamber, 1971—. Served with AUS, 1943-46. Decorated Purple Heart. Mem. Am., Wis. bar assns., Am. C. of C. Execs. (dir. 1967-71, v.p. 1971-73, chmn. elect 1973-74, chmn. 1974-75), Wis. Alumni Assn., Wis. Law Alumni Assn., Kappa Sigma, Phi Alpha Delta. Clubs: Union League, Economic, Executives, Tower (Chgo.). Home: 337 Forest Rd Hinsdale IL 60521 Office: 20 N Wacker Dr Chicago IL 60606

BRANN, WILLIAM PAUL, univ. adminstr.; b. Swifton, Ark., Apr. 21, 1916; s. Ben S. and Ara A. (Jones) B. B.A., Ark. State U., 1938; postgrad., Tulane U., 1939; M.A., U. Va., 1942, Ph.D. (Gen. Edn. Bd. fellow), 1946; LL.D. (hon.), U. Ala., 1978. Asso. prof. econs. U. Ark., Fayetteville, 1942-44; prof. econs., dir. Bur. Bus. Research, 1945-54; dir. Indsl. Research and Extension Center, Little Rock, 1955-57, Miss. Indsl. Research Center, Jackson, 1958-59; cons. in econs., 1950-65; asst. to v.p. health affairs U. Ala. Med. Center, Birmingham, 1962-64, v.p. for fiscal affairs, 1965-73; v.p., adminstrv. officer, bd. trustees U. Ala., 1974-76, v.p. for adminstrn., 1976—; dir. Participating Annuity Life Ins. Co., Little Rock; v.p. 1st Ark. Capital Credit Bank, Little Rock, 1961-62. Mem. Com. on S.W. Economy Pres.'s Council of Econ. Advisers, 1951—. Mem. Am., So. econ. assns., Pi Gamma Mu, Phi Theta Kappa, Omicron Delta Epsilon. Clubs: Relay House, The Club (Birmingham). Home: 826 Ocean Blvd Atlantic Beach FL 32233

BRANNAN, CHARLES FRANKLIN, lawyer; b. Denver, Aug. 23, 1903; s. John and Ella Louise (Street) B.; m. Eda Seltzer, June 29, 1932. LL.B., U. Denver, 1929, J.D., 1976. Bar: Colo. bar 1929. Regional dir. Resettlement Adminstrn. and Farm Sect. Adminstrn., Denver, 1934-44; asst. sec. U.S. Dept. Agr., Washington, 1944-48, sec., 1948-53; gen. counsel, sec. Nat. Farmers Union Ins. Cos., Denver, 1953—; dir. Central Bank of Denver. Commr., Denver Water Bd. Mem. Denver Bar Assn., Colo. Bar Assn., Am. Bar Assn., Inter-Am. Bar Assn., Am. Judicature Soc., Phi Beta Kappa, Phi Alpha Delta, Sigma Alpha Epsilon. Democrat. Mormon. Clubs: Denver Athletic, Masons. Home: 3131 E Alameda Ave Denver CO 80209 Office: 12025 E 45th Ave Denver CO 80239

BRANNAN, EULIE ROSS, academy president; b. Norwood, Ohio, Sept. 6, 1928; s. Olin Hiram and Bernice Cleo (Beall) B.; m. Ruby Merle Moore, Dec. 16, 1945 (dec.); children: Stephen Earl, Deborah Brannan Watkins, Rebecca, Julie Ross Brannan Noonan; m. Willie Metta Strong, Mar. 7, 1981. A.A., Ala. Christian Coll., 1947; B.A., Huntingdon Coll., 1949; M.S., Auburn U., 1953, Ed.D., 1960; postgrad., Harding Grad. Sch., 1960-63, Oxford (Eng.) U., 1981. Tchr. high sch., Montgomery, Ala., 1949-51; guidance counselor Montgomery Bible High Sch., 1951-53; prin. Ala. Christian High Sch., Montgomery, 1953-55; prof. Ala. Christian Coll., Montgomery, 1953-55, asst. to pres., 1955-56, acad. dean, 1956-69, acad. v.p., 1969-73, pres., 1973-81; field dir. Nat. Edn. Program, Huntsville, Ala., 1981-82; pres. Jefferson Christian Acad., Birmingham, Ala., 1982—. Mem. Ala. Jr. Coll. Assn. (past pres.), Phi Delta Kappa. Mem. Ch. of Christ. Office: 3609 Montclair Rd Birmingham AL 35213

BRANNEN, BARRY, lawyer; b. Tuscon, Feb. 14, 1902; s. Phillip Cornelius and Elizabeth (Barry) B. A.B., U. Cal. at Berkeley, 1922; LL.B., Harvard, 1925. Bar: Cal. bar 1925. Practiced in, Los Angeles, 1930-55, Beverly Hills, 1955-75, Santa Monica, 1975—. Author articles. Served with USNR, 1942-46. Decorated Legion of Merit, Purple Heart; Sovereign Order White Eagle, Yugoslavia; medal of merit V.F.W.; recipient Meritorious Pub. Service citation U.S. Navy (2). Mem. Navy League U.S. (v.p. 1956, dir. 1955, adv. council 1956—). Office: 1020 Palisades Beach Rd Santa Monica CA 90403

BRANNON, CLIFTON WOODROW, evangelist, lawyer; b. Fitzgerald, Ga., Apr. 14, 1912; s. George Wesley and Beulah (Green) B.; m. Ola Ruth Hall, Feb. 16, 1935; children—Beverly Mae, Madlyn Sue, Clifton Woodrow. Student, Ga. Sch. Tech., 1929-30; J.D., Woodrow Wilson Coll. Law Atlanta, 1932; LL.D., Burton Coll. and Sem., 1953. Bar: Ga. bar 1932, Tex. bar 1946, U.S. Supreme Ct. bar 1946. Atty. Home Owners Corp., 1933-35; trial atty. Sinclair Refining Co., 1936-40; gen. counsel, sec. R.G. LeTourneau, Inc., LeTourneau Co. Ga., LeTourneau Co. Miss., Vicksburg, Tex.; Casualty Ins. Co., radio stas. KLTI, WLET, LeTourneau Tech. Inst. Tex., 1946-49; gen. counsel, dir. Winona Lake (Ind.) Christian Assembly, Inc., 1940-49; pres. Whosoever Heareth, Inc.; evangelist So. Bapt. Ch., 1949—, Word for World Pubs., Inc.; pub. Soul Winner's New American Standard New Testament, 1972; v.p., dir. All India Prayer Fellowship, Inc., 1973—; pres. Clift Brannon Evangel. Assn., 1974—; Bd. dirs. Word for World Crusade, Universal Concern Found.; Past pres. Tex. Bapt. Brotherhood Conv.; v.p. So. Baptist Conv., 1973. Editor: Soul Winner's New Testament, 1959, Soul Winner's Living Bible New Testament, 1973; notes, helps and references New Am. Standard New Testament, 1974; Editor notes, helps and references The Guide to God New Testament, 1974; editor: Edicion Para Evangelismo Personal de Nuero Testamento. Mem. Am., Tex., Ga. bar assns. Democrat. Clubs: Mason (32 deg., Shriner), Kiwanian.). Home: 701 Coleman Dr Longview TX 75601 Office: 701 1/2 Coleman Dr Longview TX 75601 *To be fervent in spirit, diligent in business, faithful to your appointments, loyal to your friends and dedicated to God and family assures peace of mind, provisions of needs, and productivity of a life of fruitfulness.*

BRANNON, H(EZZIE) RAYMOND, JR., oil co. scientist; b. Midland, Ala., Jan. 23, 1926; s. Hezzie Raymond and Cora Mae B.; m. Rita Alice Newville, Oct. 19, 1957; 1 dau., Sarah Elaine. B. Engring. Physics, Auburn (Ala.) U., 1950, M.S., 1951. Research asso. Auburn Research Found., 1951-52; engr. Exxon Prodn. Research Co., Houston, 1952—, research scientist, 1973—. Contbr. articles to profl. jours. Served with USNR, 1943-46. Mem. Am. Phys. Soc., Soc. Petroleum Engrs. of AIME (Disting. Lectr. 1976-77), Soc. Exploration Geophysicists, NRC (marine bd.), Nat. Acad. Engring., Sigma Xi, Phi Kappa Phi, Tau Beta Pi, Sigma Pi Sigma. Republican. Patentee in field. Home: 5807 Queensloch St Houston TX 77096 Office: PO Box 2189 Houston TX 77001

BRANSBY, ERIC JAMES, muralist, educator; b. Auburn, N.Y., Oct. 25, 1916; s. Charles Carson and Lillian Holland (Dowsett) B.; m. Mary Antoinette Hemmie, Nov. 23, 1941; 1 dau., Fredericka Jo. Profl. cert., Kansas City Art Inst., 1938-42; B.A., Colo. Coll., 1947, M.A., 1949; M.F.A., Yale U., 1952. Instr. U. Ill., Urbana, 1950-52; asst. prof. art Western Ill. U., Macomb, 1963-65; assoc. prof. art U. Mo., Kansas City, 1965-70, prof., 1970—; authority on history and theory of mural painting. One-man shows include, Okla. Art Center, Oklahoma City, 1973, U. Mo., Kansas City, 1971, 77, Denver U., 1966, Brigham Young U., Colorado Springs (Colo.) Fine Arts Center, 1968, U. Mo., Columbia, 1979, nat. and internat. group shows, murals include, Mech. Engring. Bldg., U. Ill., 1953, U.S. Command and Gen. Staff Sch., 1955, NORAD Hdqrs., Colorado Springs, 1956, Brigham Young U., 1958, Mcpl. Bldg., Liberty, Mo., 1982 (Nat. Mural Competition award), Luth. Ch., Mo. Synod, Internat. Ctr., St. Louis, 1983 (Nat. Mural Competition award), planetarium, USAF Acad., Colorado Springs, 1961-70, Western Ill. U., Macomb, 1965, Rockhurst Coll., Kansas City, 1968, F.D. Roosevelt Meml. Competition, 1961, HUD Nat. Community Art Competition, 1974, U. Mo., Kansas City, 1973-75, Mcpl. Bldg., Sedalia, Mo., 1977, Kans. State Capitol Nat. Mural Competition, 1978; represented in permanent collections. Served with inf. AUS, 1942-45. Edwin Austin Abbey Found. mural painting fellow, 1952; grantee, applied and theoretical studies in mural painting field, U.S., Mex., Italy.; Recipient Veatch award U. Mo., 1977. Mem. Nat. Soc. Mural Painters, AAUP, Coll. Art Assn., Phi Kappa Phi. Home: 401 E 54th St Kansas City MO 64110 Office: Dept Art Univ of Missouri Kansas City MO 64110 *At the center of my personal direction in art is the belief that it belongs in the public environment, performing a socio-cultural function. Corollary to this is the belief that a great number of the highest achievements in art are represented by those works attaining a complex but successful synthesis with architecture.*

BRANSCOM, WILLIAM JAMES, bank holding co. exec.; b. Roanoke, Va., Nov. 29, 1926; s. George Alexander and Georgia Douglas (Firestone) B.; m. Jean Larson, Mar. 24, 1951; children—Dorothy Diane Branscom Forbes, Georgia Kay, Joel Robert, William Eric. B.A. in Econs, Roanoke Coll., 1950; M.B.A. in Fin, Wharton Sch., U. Pa., 1952; cert. comml. banking, Stonier Grad. Sch. Banking, 1963. With First Nat. Exchange Bank, Roanoke, 1954-73, 1sr. v.p. investment div., 1964-73; sr. v.p. fin. group Dominion Bankshares Corp., Roanoke, 1973, sr. v.p., treas., 1973—; instr. Va. Bankers Sch. Bank Mgmt.; chmn. Roanoke Valley Savs. Bond Com. Mem. Botetourt County Planning Commn.; trustee Evergreen Burial Park; bd. dirs. Va. Fuel Conversion Authority; bd. dirs., treas. Greater Roanoke Valley Devel. Found.; deacon Fincastle United Presbyn. Ch. Served with USNR, 1945-46; Served with AUS, 1952-54. Mem. Am. Inst. Banking, Mcpl. Fin. Officers Assn., Richmond Soc. Fin. Analysis, Bond Club, Botetourt County C. of C. Clubs: Botetourt Country, Jefferson. Home: Route 1 Box 145 Fincastle VA 24090 Office: Dominion Bankshares Corp PO Box 13327 Roanoke VA 24040

BRANSCOMB, ANNE WELLS (MRS. LEWIS MCADORY BRANSCOMB), lawyer, communications consultant; b. Staesboro, Ga., Nov. 22, 1928; d. Guy Herbert and Ruby Mae (Hammond) Wells; m. Lewis McAdory Branscomb, Oct. 13, 1951; children: Harvie Hammond, Katharine Capers. B.A., Ga. State Coll. Women, 1949, U. N.C., 1949; postgrad., London Sch. Econs., 1950; M.A., Harvard U., 1951; J.D. with honors, George Washington, 1962. Bar: D.C. 1962, Colo. 1963, N.Y. 1973, U.S. Supreme Ct. 1972. Research assoc. Pierson, Ball and Dowd, Washington, 1962; law clk. to Dist. Ct. Judge,

Denver, 1962-63; sole practice law, Boulder, 1966-69; assoc. Arnold and Porter, Washington, 1969-72; communications counsel Telepromter Corp., N.Y.C., 1973; v.p. Kalba-Bowen Assocs. Inc., communication cons., Cambridge, Mass., 1974-77, chmn. bd., 1977-80; sr. assocs. dir. Kalba-Bowen Assocs. Inc., communicatioin cons., Cambridge, Mass., 1980-82; pres. Moneyscan Inc., 1981—; trustee Pacific Telecommunications Council, 1981-83; cons. FCC, NSF, Carnegie Corp., MIT, Mass. Cable TV Commn., Rockefeller Bros. Fund, Aspen Inst.; mem. tech. adv. bd. Dept. Commerce, 1977-81, chmn. working group on devel. human resources for innovation; WARC adv. com. Dept. State, 1978-79; mem. Carnegie Corp. Task Force on Pub. Broadcasting, 1976-77; mem. overseers, vis. com. Harvard U. Office of Info. Tech., 1977-83; vis. scholar Yale U. Law, 1981-82; mem. Nat. Acad. Scis. evaluation panel for Nat. Bur. Scis., Inst. Computer Sci. and Tech., 1977-80; cons. Sci. Info. activities task force NSF, 1977; mem. Telecommunications Policy Research Conf., 1976. Contbr. articles to profl. jours.; mem. editorial bd.: Info. Soc.; editor: Toward a Law of Global Networks; contbg. editor: Jour. Communications, 1980—. Pub. relations dir. Montgomery County chpt. LWV, 1954-57; mass media chmn. AAUW, Chevy Chase, Md., 1959-62; del. Nat. Conf. Crime, 1967; co-chmn. Coordinating Com. for Low Income Housing for Boulder, 1966-68; bd. dirs. Help for Boulder Inc., 1968-69; housing commr. Boulder Pub. Housing Authority, 1969-70; bd. dirs. Nat. Pub. Radio, 1975-78; mem. program steering com. Aspen Inst. Program on Sci., Tech. and Humanism, 1975-77; trustee EDUCOM, Interuniv. Communications Council Inc., 1975-78; mem. nat. com. Advocates for Arts, 1976-78; Colo. chmn. Democratic Women's Conf., 1966; pres. Dem. Women of Boulder, 1963-64; vice chmn. Colo. Dem. State Central Com., 1967-69, chmn. computer policy com.; del., mem. permanent orgn. com. Dem. Nat. Conv., 1968, hearing officer credentials com., 1972; dir. spl. orgn. services Colo. Citizens for Humphrey-Muskie, 1968; mem. vice chmn.'s adv. com. Dem. Nat. Com., 1972; spl. asst. to nat. campaign McGovern-Shriver campaign, 1972; mem. staff policy planning com. Carter Campaign, 1976; trustee, exec. com. Rensselaer Poly. Inst., 1980—; adv. bd. UCLA Communications Law Program, 1980—; trustee Fund for Peace, 1984—; adv. bd. Consumer Interest Research Inst., 1982—. Recipient Alumni Achievement award Ga. Coll., 1980, Rotary Found. fellowship, 1950-51. Mem. ABA (chmn. communications com. sci. and tech. sect. 1980-82, chmn. communications law div. 1982—, mem. council sci. and tech. sect. 1981—), N.Y. Bar Assn., Colo. Bar Assn., D.C. Bar Assn., Computer Law Assn. (dir. 1981—), Fed. Communications Bar Assn. (seminar com. 1975), Am. Polit. Sci. Assn., Internat. Communications Assn., Intenat. Inst. Communications, Soc. Preservation of First Wives and First Husbands (nat. pres. 1981—), ALA (commun. on freedom and equality of access to info. 1983—), Order of Coif, Valkyries, Phi Beta Kappa, Alpha Psi Omega, Chi Delta Phi, Pi Gamma Mu. Home: 5 Hidden Oak Ln Armonk NY 10504 Office: PO Box 172 Armonk NY 10504 *As a Rotary Foundation Fellow I was often asked to speak on the topic "A Woman's Choice: Kitchen or Career, but I never saw a conflict. Those with careers must spend some time in the kitchen and local, national, and international affairs are a mere extension of hearth and home. Thus I have always followed my father's admonition to live my life in such a way that I would leave the world a better place than I found it.*

BRANSCOMB, HARVIE, JR., lawyer; b. Dallas, Mar. 24, 1922; s. Bennett Harvie and Margaret (Vaughan) B.; m. Mary Josephine Goodearle, Dec. 28, 1951; children: Mary Margaret, Bennett Hill, Richard Lee. A.B., Duke U., 1943; LL.B., Yale U., 1948. Bar: Tex. 1948, D.C. 1980, CPA, Tex. Partner firm Matthews & Branscomb, Attys.-at-Law, Corpus Christi, Tex., 1948—; dir. Merc. Bank, San Antonio, Bank of Corpus Christi; trustee, mem. exec. com. Southwestern Legal Found.; pres., trustee Chapman Cox Found.; bd. dirs. Corpus Christi Indsl. Found. Contbr. articles to profl. jours. Mem. exec. com. Yale Law Sch. Assn. Served with USNR, 1943-46. Fellow Am. Coll. Tax Counsel; Mem. Am. Bar Assn. (chmn. tax sect. 1979-80), State Bar Tex. (chmn. sect. taxation 1961-62), Am. Law Inst., Phi Beta Kappa, Phi Beta Phi. Episcopalian. Home: 4777 Ocean Dr Corpus Christi TX 78412 Office: 1700 First City Bank Tower Corpus Christi TX 78477

BRANSCOMB, LEWIS CAPERS, JR., librarian, educator; b. Birmingham, Ala., Aug. 5, 1911; s. Lewis Capers and Minnie Vaughn (McGehee) B.; m. Marjorie Berry Stafford, Jan. 15, 1938; children—Lewis Capers III, Ralph Stafford, Carol Jean, Lawrence McGehee. Student, Birmingham-So. Coll., 1929-30; A.B., Duke, 1933, U. Mich., 1939, A.M., 1941; postgrad., U. Ga., 1940; Ph.D., U. Chgo., 1954. Clk. Young & Vann Supply Co., Birmingham, 1933-38; order librarian U. Ga., 1939-41; librarian Mercer U., 1941-42; librarian, prof. library sci. U. S.C., 1942-44; asst. dir. pub. service depts., asso. prof. library sci. U. Ill., 1944-48; asso. dir. libraries, prof. library adminstrn., 1948-52; dir. libraries, prof. library adminstrn. Ohio State U., Columbus, 1952-71, prof. Thurber studies, 1971-81, prof. emeritus, 1981—; Mem. Ohio Commn. to Abolish Capital Punishment, 1960-69; Bd. dirs. Center for Research Libraries, 1953-64, exec. com., 1954-56, chmn. bd., 1961-62, mem. council, 1965-71; chmn. bd. trustees Ohio Coll. Library Center, 1968-70, vice chmn., 1970-72; chmn. adv. council on Library Services and Constrn. Act, Ohio, 1967-70; cons. Punjab Agrl. U., India, 1967, Mansfield (Ohio) Pub. Library, 1977. Editor: The Case for Faculty Status for Academic Librarians, 1970; Contbr. articles to profl. jours. Mem. AAUP (sec.-treas. U. Ill. 1947-48, Ohio State U, sec.-treas. U. Ill. 1948-52, pres. 1953-54, nat. council 1952-55, co-author History of the Ohio Conf. 1949-74, chmn. com. E 1979—, mem. exec. com. 1981—), ALA (chmn. nominating com. 1954-55), Assn. Coll. and Research Libraries (dir. 1953-55, v.p. 1957-58, pres. 1958-59), Ohio (chmn. coll. and univ. sect. 1952-53, chmn. library adminstrn. sect. 1969-70, chmn. local conf. com. 1970, chmn. awards and honors com. 1974-75, chmn. notable Ohio librarians com. 1978-79, award of merit 1971), Franklin County library assns., Acad. Library Assn. Ohio, ACLU (exec. com. Central Ohio chpt. 1958-60, 64-66), Common Cause, Thurber Circle, Friends of Ohio State U. Libraries, Beta Phi Mu (exec. council 1955-58), Sigma Alpha Epsilon. Democrat. Clubs: Torch (dir. 1958-59, 72-74, pres. 1971-72); Faculty (Columbus); Crichton. Home: 3790 Overdale Dr Columbus OH 43220 Office: Main Library Ohio State Univ Columbus OH 43210

BRANSCOMB, LEWIS MCADORY, physicist; b. Asheville, N.C., Aug. 17, 1926; s. Bennett Harvie and Margaret (Vaughan) B.; m. Margaret Anne Wells, Oct. 13, 1951; children—Harvie Hammond, Katharine Capers. A.B. summa cum laude, Duke U., 1945, D.Sc. (hon.); M.S., Harvard U., 1947, Ph.D., 1949; D.Sc. (hon.), Poly. Inst. N.Y., Clarkson Coll., Rochester U., U. Colo., Western Mich. U., Lycoming Coll., L.H.D., Pace U. Instr. physics Harvard U., 1950-51; lectr. physics U. Md., 1952-54; vis. staff mem. Univ. Coll., London, 1957-58; chief atomic physics sect. Nat. Bur. Standards, Washington, 1954-60, chief atomic physics div., 1960-62; chmn. Joint Inst. Lab. Astrophysics, U. Colo., 1962-65, 68-69; chief lab. astrophysics div. Nat. Bur. Standards, Boulder, Colo., 1962-69; prof. physics U. Colo., 1962-69; dir. Nat. Bur. Standards, 1969-72; chief scientist, v.p. IBM Corp., Armonk, N.Y., 1972—; chmn. commn. atomic and molecular physics and spectroscopy Internat. Union Pure and Applied Physics, 1972-75; mem. JASON div. Inst. Def. Analyses, 1962-69; chmn. gen. com. Internat. Conf. Physics of Electron and Atomic Collisions, 1969-71; U.S. rep. to CODATA com. Internat. Council Sci. Unions, 1970-73; mem.-at-large Def. Sci. Bd., 1969-72; mem. high level policy group sci. and tech. info. Orgn. Econ. Coop. and Devel., 1968-70; mem. Pres.'s Sci. Adv. Com., 1965-68, chmn. panel space sci. and tech., 1967-68; mem. Nat. Sci. Bd., 1978—, chmn., 1980—; mem. Pres.'s Nat. Productivity Adv. Com., 1981-82; mem. standing com. controlled thermonuclear research AEC, 1966-68; mem. adv. com. on sci. and fgn. affairs Dept. State, 1973-74; mem. U.S.-USSR Joint Commn. on Sci. and Tech., 1977-80; chmn. Com. on Scholarly Communications with the People's Republic of China, 1977-80; dir. Gen. Foods Corp., Mobil Corp.; Mem. pres.'s bd. visitors U. Okla., 1968-70; mem. astronomy and applied physics vis. coms. Harvard bd. overseers, 1969—; mem. physics vis. com. M.I.T., 1974-79; mem. Pres.'s Com. Nat. Medal Scis., 1970-72; Bd. dirs. Am. Nat. Standards Inst., 1969-72; trustee Carnegie Instn., 1973—, Poly. Inst. N.Y., 1974-78, Vanderbilt U., 1980—. Editor: Rev. Modern Physics, 1968-73. Served to lt. (j.g.) USNR, 1945-46. USPHS fellow, 1948-49; Jr. fellow Harvard Soc. Fellows, 1949-51; recipient Rockefeller Pub. Service award, 1957-58, Gold medal exceptional service Dept. Commerce, 1961, Arthur Flemming award D.C. Jr. C. of C., 1962, Samuel Wesley Stratton award Dept. Commerce, 1966, Career Service award Nat. Civil Service League, 1968, Proctor prize Research Soc. Am., 1972. Fellow Am. Phys. Soc. (chmn. div. electron physics 1961-68, pres. 1979), AAAS (dir. 1969-73), Am. Acad. Arts and Scis.; mem. Nat. Acad. Scis. (council 1972-75), Nat. Acad. Engring., Washington Acad. Scis. (Outstanding Sci. Achievement award 1959), Nat. Acad. Public Adminstrn., Internat. Astron. Union, Am. Geophys. Union, Am. Astron. Soc., Internat. Union Geodesy and Geophysics, Am. Philos. Soc., Phi Beta Kappa, Sigma Xi. Club: American Yacht (Rye, N.Y.). Office: Old Orchard Rd Armonk NY 10504

BRANSDORFER, STEPHEN CHRISTIE, lawyer; b. Lansing, Mich., Sept. 18, 1929; s. Henry and Sadie (Kohane) B.; m. Peggy Ruth Deisig, May 24, 1952; children: Mark, David, Amy, Jill. A.B. with honors, Mich. State U., 1951; J.D. with distinction, U. Mich., 1956; LL.M., Georgetown U., 1958. Bar: Mich. 1956, U.S. Supreme Ct. 1959. Trial atty. Dept. Justice, Washington, 1956-58; atty., editor Office of Public Info., Office of Atty. Gen., 1958-59; spl. asst. U.S. Atty. for D.C., 1958-59; assoc. firm Miller, Johnson, Snell & Cummiskey, Grand Rapids, Mich., 1959-63, partner, 1963—; pres. State Bar of Mich., 1974-75, commr., 1968-75; chmn. Mich. Civil Service Commn., 1977-78, mem., 1975-78. Asst. editor: U. Mich. Law Rev, 1956. Pres. Grand Rapids Child Guidance Clinic, 1969-71; chmn. Kent County Coms., Griffin for Senator, 1972, Lenore Romney for Senator, 1966; mem. council legal advisers Republican Nat. Com., 1981—; Rep. candidate for atty. gen., Mich., 1978; trustee Mich. State Bar Found.; mem. Mich. Jud. Coordinating Com., 1981—. Served with U.S. Army, 1951-53. Fellow Am. Bar Found.; mem. 6th Cir. Jud. Conf. (life), Am. Bar Assn., Grand Rapids Bar Assn., Fed. Bar Assn., Phi Kappa Phi. Presbyterian. Clubs: Rotary, Grand Rapids Athletic, Cascade Hills Country. Home: 7250 Bradfield Rd SE Ada MI 49301 Office: 800 Calder Plaza Bldg Grand Rapids MI 49503 *Life is a series of challenges. If you recognize that fact and give your best effort, you need not worry about the results.*

BRANSON, BRANLEY ALLAN, educator; b. San Angelo, Tex., Feb. 11, 1929; s. Branley Allan and Era Elizabeth (Rogers) B.; m. Mary Louise Lewis, June 3, 1964; 1 son, Rogers McGowan. A.A., Northeastern Okla. A. and M. Coll., 1954; B.S., Okla. State U., 1956, M.S., 1957, Ph.D., 1960. Asst. prof. biology Kan. State Coll., Pittsburg, 1960-64; prof. biology Eastern Ky. U., Richmond, 1964—. Contbr. articles to mags. Recipient Sci. award Okla. A. and M. Coll., 1953. Fellow Okla. Acad. Sci., AAAS; mem. Southwestern Assn. Naturalists (bd. govs. 1965—), Am. Malacological Union, Soc. for Study Evolution, Kan. Acad. Sci., Ky. Acad. Sci. (editor transactions), Soc. Systematic Zoologists, Am. Soc. Zoologists, Am. Soc. Ichthyologists and Herpetologists, Sigma Xi, Phi Theta Kappa, Phi Kappa Phi. Research and numerous publs. on description several species unknown animals; described structural workings lateral-line system in various fishes; olfactory system, geog. distbn. fishes and mollusks. Home: Route 10 Deacon Hills Richmond KY 40475 Office: Eastern Ky U Richmond KY 40475 *I've had a long-term love affair with the nature of things, and the fervor doesn't seem to be lessening any with the passage of time. And strongly supported by the very real love affair with my wife and son, I've simply had the best of conditions for being creative.*

BRANSON, DAN EARLE, civil engineer, educator; b. Dallas, Nov. 13, 1928; s. Norm E. and Josephine (Hansen) B.; m. Fredine McBryde, Jan. 29, 1955; children: Kathy Sue, Timothy Earle. Student, Spring Hill Coll., 1946-48; B.C.E., Auburn U., 1954, M.C.E., 1956; Ph.D., U. Fla., 1960. Registered profl. engr., Ia. Instr., asst. prof. Auburn U., 1955-57, asso. prof., 1962-63; instr. U. Fla., 1959-60; asso. prof. U. Ala., 1960-62; prof. structural engring. U. Ia., Iowa City, 1963—; Stress analysis cons. Hayes Internat. Corp., Birmingham, Ala., 1961-65; cons. structural engr., 1964—; lectr. U.S., abroad.; mem. Iowa State Bd. Engring. Examiners. Author: Deformation of Concrete Structures, 1977, Deflexiones de Estructuras de Concreto Reforzado y Presforzado, 1978, Diseno de Vigas de Concreto Presforzado, 1981; Co-author: Handbook of Composite Construction Engineering, 1978, Canadian Metric Design Handbook, 1978, Concrete Engineering, 2d edit., 1983; Contbr. articles to profl. jours. Served to 1st lt. AUS, 1950-53. Fellow Am. Concrete Inst. (com. chmn. 1962-71); mem. Am. Soc. C.E., Internat. Assn. Bridge and Structural Engrs., Am. Soc. Engring. Edn., Prestressed Concrete Inst. (Korn award 1971), Sigma Xi, Chi Epsilon, Tau Beta Pi, Phi Kappa Phi. Home: 1104 Tower Ct Iowa City IA 52240

BRANSON, HERMAN RUSSELL, physicist, university president; b. Pocahontas, Va., Aug. 14, 1914; s. Harry C. and Gertrude (Brown) B.; m. Corolynne M. Gray, Sept. 4, 1939; children: Corolynne G., Herman E. Student, U. Pitts., 1932-34; B.S., Va. State Coll., 1936, Sc.D., 1967; Ph.D., U. Cin., 1939, Sc.D., 1967; Sc.D., Lincoln U., Pa., 1969; L.H.D., Brandeis U., 1972, Shaw Coll., Detroit, 1978; LL.D., Western Mich. U., 1973. Instr. Dillard U., New Orleans, 1939-41; faculty Howard U., 1941-68, prof. physics, 1942-68, head dept., 1955-68; pres. Central State U., 1968-70, Lincoln U., 1970—; mem. Inst. Medicine Nat. Acad. Scis., 1975, Nat. Sea Grant Coll. Program, 1980—; mem. energy research adv. bd. U.S. Dept. Energy, 1981—. Mem. Bicentennial Commn. Pa., 1975; Trustee Carver Found., Woodrow Wilson Nat. Fellowship Found., 1975—; bd. dirs. Nat. Med. Fellowships, Inst. for Services to Edn., 1973—, Am. Found. for Negro Affairs, 1973—; mem. corp. M.I.T., 1979—; mem. Middle Atlantic Consortium for Energy Research, 1980—. Sr. fellow NRC, 1948-49; fellow NSF, 1962-63. Mem. Am. Assn. State Colls. and Univs., Commn. Coll. Physics, Biophysics Soc. (council), Am. Phys. Soc., AAAS (council 1971—), Am. Assn. Physics Tchrs., Pa. Assn. Colls. and Univs. (govt. relations com. 1979—), Middle States Assn. Colls. and Secondary Schs. (com. on higher edn. 1970-76), Nat. Assn. for Equal Opportunity in Edn. (pres. 1970-73, dir.), Sigma Xi. Office: Lincoln U Lincoln University PA 19352

BRANSTAD, TERRY EDWARD, governor Iowa, lawyer; b. Leland, Iowa, Nov. 17, 1946; s. Edward Arnold and Rita (Garl) B.; m. Christine Ann Johnson, June 17, 1972; children: Eric, Allison. B.A., U. Iowa, 1969; J.D., Drake U., 1974. Bar: Iowa. Sr. partner firm Branstad-Schwarm, Lake Mills, Iowa, until 1982; farmer, Lake Mills; mem. Iowa Ho. of Reps., 1972-78; lt. gov. Iowa, from 1979, now gov. Iowa; Bd. dirs. Am. Legion of Iowa Found. Served in U.S. Army, 1969. Mem. Am. Legion, Farm Bur., Lake Mills C. of C., Am. Bar Assn., Iowa Bar Assn., Winnebago County Bar Assn., Jaycees. Republican. Roman Catholic. Club: Lions. Office: Office Gov Statehouse Des Moines IA 50319 *

BRANT, AUSTIN EDWARD, JR., cons. engr.; b. Rockaway Beach, N.Y., Nov. 26, 1929; s. Austin Edward and Anna (Shaughnessy) B.; m. Jeanne Fox, Oct. 27, 1951; children—Claire, Jeanne, Joan, Thomas. B.C.E., Manhattan Coll., Riverdale, N.Y., 1951; M.S., Columbia U., 1958. With Tippetts-Abbett-McCarthy-Stratton, N.Y.C., 1951—, asso. partner, 1966-68, partner, 1968—; mem. maritime transp. research bd. Nat. Acad. Scis., 1977-81, mem. panel future port requirements, 1973. Author papers in field. Fellow ASCE (exec. com. waterway, port, coastal and ocean div. 1972—), Inst. Transp. Engrs.; asso. mem. Ops. Research Soc. Am.; mem. Chi Epsilon. Home: 78 Stratford Rd West Hempstead NY 11552 Office: TAMS 655 3d Ave New York NY 10017

BRANT, HENRY, composer; b. Montreal, Que., Can., Sept. 15, 1913; s. Saul and Bertha (Dreyfuss) B.; children—Piri, Joquin, Linus. Student, Juilliard Sch. Music, N.Y.C., 1930-34. Mem. faculty Juilliard Sch. Music, 1947-55; dept. music Columbia U., 1943-53; mem. faculty Bennington (Vt.) Coll., 1957-80. Composer, condr. documentary films, U.S. Govt., OWI, State Dept., Dept. Agr., 1940-47; composer, condr. various radio network program series for, NBC, CBS, ABC, 1942-46; large ensemble works include Angels & Devils, 1931, Signs and Alarms, 1953, Antiphony 1, 1953, Millenium 2, 1954, Encephalograms 2, 1954, Ceremony, 1954, Galaxy 2, 1954, December, 1954; spatial opera Grand Universal Circus, 1956, Hieroglyphics, 1957, The Children's Hour, 1958, Mythical Beasts, 1958, Atlantis, 1960, Concerto with Lights, 1961, Barricades, 1961, Headhunt, 1962, Voyage 4; total antiphony, in 83 parts, 1963, Odyssey-Why Not?, 1965, Kingdom Come, 1970, Crossroads, 1971, Immortal Combat, 1972, American Requiem, 1973, Prevailing Winds, 1974, Solomon's Gardens, 1974, Homage to Ives, 1975, A Plan of the Air, 1975, Spatial Piano Concerto, 1976, Antiphonal Responses, 1977, Trinity of Spheres, 1978, Orbits; 80 trombones, 1979, The Secret Calendar, 1980, The Glass Pyramid, 1980, others, recs., Columbia, Desto, CRI, New World, Nonesuch records. Recipient Prix Italia, 1955, Alice M. Ditson award, 1962, 1964; Guggenheim fellow, 1946, 55; Inst. Arts and Letters grant, 1955; Copley grantee, 1960; Huber grantee, 1960; Dollard grantee, 1966; Thorne fellow, 1972; N.Y. State Council for Arts grantee, 1974; Nat. Endowment for Arts grantee, 1976. Mem. Am. Acad.-Inst. Arts and Letters (life). Pioneer in devel. spatial-antiphonal music *Undoubtedly, the answer to the riddle of existence must be: perpetual discovery.*

BRANTLEY, LEE REED, chemistry educator; b. Herrin, Ill., Sept. 23, 1906; s. Homer L. and Blanche R. (Reed) B.; m. Audrey Ryan, June 25, 1930 (dec. 1983). A.B., UCLA, 1927; M.S., Calif. Inst. Tech., 1929, Ph.D., 1930. Registered profl. engr., Calif. Instr. physics and chemistry Occidental Coll., Los Angeles, 1930-36, asst. prof. chemistry, 1936-40, asso. prof., 1940-42, prof., 1942-67, head dept. chemistry, 1940-62; research fellow physics Calif. Inst. Tech., 1936-42; research asst., cons. chemistry Nat. Def. Research Council Contract, 1942-44; vis. prof. Lehigh U., 1958-59; prof. chemistry U. Hawaii, Honolulu, 1962-63, vis. prof. chemistry, 1965-66; research prof. edn. Curriculum Research and Devel. Group, emeritus prof., 1972—; phys. sci. dir. Foundl. Approaches in Sci. Teaching, 1966-72, cons., 1972—; pres. A and R Research Assos., 1977—; dir. contract Office Naval Research on Principles of Adhesion, 1949-58, Q.M. Research and Devel. Environmental Protection, 1953-58; dir. Corn Industries Research Found. Adhesion Contract, 1957-59; cons. on protective coatings Nat. Bur. Standards, 1951-53; writer Commn. on Sci. Edn., AAAS. Contbr. articles to profl. publs. Mem., past chmn. environ. health adv. com. Am. Lung Assn. Hawaii; past chmn. air com. Oahu chpt. Conservation Council of Hawaii.; Served as sr. gas officer Glendale (Calif.) Citizens Def. Corps, 1943-45. Recipient Petroleum Research award for advanced study Am. Chem. Soc., 1958-59; John R. Kuebler Man of Yr. award, 1973. Fellow AAAS; mem. Pacific S.W. Assn. Chemistry Tchrs. (past pres.), Calif. Acad. Sci., Am. Chem. Soc. (pres. So. Calif. sect. 1947-48, Hawaiian sect. 1949-50, councilor), Electrochem. Soc., Nat. Ret. Tchrs. Assn., Hawaii Acad. Sci., Sigma Xi, Alpha Chi Sigma (pres. 1958-60), Kappa Sigma. Club: Rotarian. Home: 1025 Wilder Ave Honolulu HI 96822 *I have always tried to offer more than my job required and to treat my disappointments as challenges to more than compensate for each setback.*

BRANTLEY, OLIVER WILEY, lawyer; b. Troy, Ala., Oct. 30, 1915; s. James T. and Julia (Wiley) B.; m. Betty Jane Gaston, Jan. 20, 1936; children— Michael Wiley, Elizabeth Ayers (Mrs. William M. Greshan), Grace Lamar (Mrs. William C. Anderson), Oliver Wiley (dec.). LL.B., U. Ala., 1939. Bar: Ala. bar 1939. Since practiced in, Troy., solicitor, Pike County, 1947-74; Mem. Jud. Commn. Ala., 1972—, chmn., 1973-74, Ala. Jud. Inquiry Commn., 1974-75; mem. bd. commrs. Ala. State Bar, 1952-79. Trustee Ala. State Bar Found., 1961-79; Bd. dirs. U. Ala. Law Sch. Found., 1966—, pres., 1973-74. Served to lt. (j.g.) USNR, 1943-46. Fellow Am. Coll. Probate Counsel, Am. Coll. Trial Lawyers; mem. Am., Ala., Pike County bar assns., Nat. Assn. R.R. Trial Counsel, Delta Kappa Epsilon, Phi Delta Phi, Farrah Order Jurisprudence, Farrah Law Soc. (chmn. 1972-73). Episcopalian. Home: 216 Flavia Circle Troy AL 36081 Office: 220 S Oak St Troy AL 36081

BRANTON, WILEY AUSTIN, lawyer; b. Pine Bluff, Ark., Dec. 13, 1923; s. Leo Andrew and Pauline (Wiley) B.; m. Lucille McKee, Feb. 1, 1948; children: Richard, Toni Cheryl, Wylene Anita, Wiley Austin, Beverly Lucille, Debra Elaine. B.S., U. Ark.-Pine Bluff, 1950, J.D., 1953. Bar: Ark. 1952, U.S. Supreme Ct 1956, Ga. 1962, D.C. 1967, other fed. cts. Practiced in, Pine Bluff, 1952-62; dir. voter edn. project So. Regional Council, 1962-65; spl. asst. to atty. gen. of U.S., 1965-67; exec. dir. United Planning Orgn., 1967-69, Council United Civil Rights Leadership, 1963-65; dir. community and social action Alliance for Labor Action, 1969-71; partner firm Dolphin, Branton, Stafford & Webber (Attys.), 1971-77; of counsel Walker, Kaplan & Mays, Little Rock, 1971-78; dean Sch. Law, Hovard U., Washington, 1978-83; counsel Sidley & Austin, Washington, 1983—; dir. Columbia First Fed. Savs. and Loan Assn.; Bd. dirs. Consol. Ry. Corp. Bd. dirs. Africare, Lawyers Com. for Civil Rights under law, Winthrop Rockefeller Found., NAACP Legal Def. and Edn. Fund. Served with AUS, 1943-46. Named one of 100 most important young men or women in U.S. Life mag., 1962; one of America's 100 most influential Negroes Ebony mag., 1963; recipient numerous awards for participation civil rights litigation, including; Henry W. Edgerton award ACLU, 1977. Fellow Am. Bar Found.; Mem. ABA, Nat. Bar Assn. (C. Francis Stafford award 1958), D.C. Bar Assn., Washington Bar Assn. (Charles Hamilton Houston medallion 1978), Fed. Bar Assn., NAACP, Nat. Urban League, Omega Psi Phi, Sigma Pi Phi, Phi Alpha Delta. Club: Mason. Home: 1611 Tamarack St NW Washington DC 20012 Office: 1722 I St NW Washington DC 20006

BRANTON, WILLIAM COLEMAN, lawyer; b. Greenville, Miss., June 30, 1914; s. William Coleman and Marybelle (Crittenden) B.; m. Mary Shaw, Apr. 12, 1947; children—Leslie, Page. B.S. cum laude, Davidson Coll., 1936; J.D., U. Miss., 1939. Bar: Miss. 1939, Mo. 1946. Practiced in, Greenville, Miss., 1939-40, Kansas City, Mo., 1946-65; sr. v.p. City Nat. Bank & Trust Co., Kansas City, Mo., 1965-70; chmn. bd. Plaza Bank & Trust Co., Plaza Bancshares, Inc., Kansas City, 1970-79; of counsel firm Slagle & Bernard, Kansas City, 1979—; vice chmn. Traders Bank of Kansas City, 1980-82; civilian aide Sec. of Army, 1979-81. Bd. dirs., mem. exec. com. Mo.-Ark. Flood Control

Assn.; mem. Civic Council Kansas City; hon. fellow Harry S. Truman Library Inst.; Bd. govs. Nelson Mus. Art; founding trustee Mo. Repertory Theater, Inc., pres., 1978-81; trustee Parker B. Francis Found., Kansas City Mus. Sci. and Industry, Midwest Research Inst., U. Kansas City, P.B. Francis III Found., Kansas City Assn. Trusts and Founds., 1978-81; founding trustee Greater Kansas City Community Found., Clearinghouse for Midcontinent Founds.; pres. Clearinghouse for Midcontinent Founds., 1976-79; hon. trustee, past pres. Barstow Sch., Kansas City, Mo.; bd. dirs. Starlight Theatre Assn., Kansas City, Liberty Meml. Assn., Kansas City, St. Luke's Hosp., Kansas City; chmn. U. Kansas City, 1976-78; bd. visitors Davidson Coll., 1980—. Served to col. AUS, 1936-66; PTO. Decorated Legion of Merit, Bronze Star with cluster and combat V, Air medal, Army Commendation medal. Mem. Am., Mo., Kansas City bar assns., Lawyers Assn. Kansas City, Kansas City C. of C. (dir.), Assn. U.S. Army (pres. Leavenworth chpt. 1973), N.G. Assn. Mo. (pres. 1954), Mil. Order World Wars (comdr. 1964), Blue Key, Phi Beta Kappa, Phi Gamma Delta, Phi Delta Phi, Omicron Delta Kappa. Episcopalian. Clubs: Kansas City Country, Univ., Mercury (Kansas City, Mo.). Home: 610 W 57th Terr Kansas City MO 64113 Office: 127 W 10th St Suite 500 Kansas City MO 64105

BRANYAN, ROBERT LESTER, university administrator; b. Phila., Jan. 15, 1930; s. Lester Spencer and Martha Augusta (Border) B.; m. Helen Louise Baird, June 9, 1956; children: Jane Baird, George Robert. B.A., Wis. State U., 1955; M.A., U. Iowa, 1957; Ph.D., Okla. U., 1961. Grad. teaching asst. U. Okla., 1957-59; from instr. to prof. history U. Mo., Kansas City, 1959-75, chmn. dept., 1964-73; dean Sch. Grad. Studies, Central Mich. U., Mt. Pleasant, 1976-83; dir. acad. affairs Pa. State U., Schuylkill, 1983—; mem. region 6 Archives Adv. Council, 1970-74; cons. in field. Author: Taming the Mighty Missouri, 1974; co-author: The Eisenhower Administration, 1953-61, A Documentary History, 1971; Co-editor: Urban Crisis in Modern America, 1971. Served with AUS, 1951-53. Danforth Assoc. Mem. Orgn. Am. Historians, Soc. for Historians of Am. Fgn. Relations, Am. Assn. Univ. Adminstrs., Assn. Acad. Affairs Adminstrs., Phi Alpha Theta, Sigma Iota Epsilon. Democrat. Episcopalian. Office: Adminstrn Bldg Pa State U Schuylkill Haven PA 17972

BRASFIELD, EVANS BOOKER, lawyer; b. Richmond, Va., Sept. 21, 1932; s. George Frederick and Minna (Booker) B.; children: Evans Booker, John McDonald, Elizabeth Lee; m. Anne Dobbins Heilig, June 28, 1980; stepchildren: J. Randall Heilig, Mollie A. Heilig. B.A., U. Va., 1954, LL.B., 1959. Bar: Va. 1959. Since practiced in, Richmond; partner firm Hunton & Williams, 1965—; gen. counsel Va. Electric & Power Co., Richmond, 1976—; mem. Richmond adv. bd. F&M Nat. Bank; chmn. Va. Register Commn., 1974—; lectr. Ga. Inst. Tech., 1968-75. Pres. Children's Home Soc. Va., 1972-73, bd. dirs., 1965—; chmn. Central Va. Ednl. TV Corp., 1978—, bd. dirs., 1965—; bd. dirs. Richmond Community Action Program, 1974-76, Richmond Area Community Council, 1973-75, Big Bros. Richmond, 1970-75; vestryman St. Paul's Episcopal Ch., Richmond, 1972-75. Served with USNR, 1954-56. Fellow Am. Bar Found.; Mem. ABA, Va. Bar Assn. (exec. com. 1981—, chmn. exec. com. 1983—), Richmond Bar Assn., Fed. Energy Bar Assn., Va. State Bar, Phi Beta Kappa (v.p. Richmond chpt. 1981-82, pres. Richmond chpt. 1982-83). Clubs: Country of Va., Bull and Bear (Richmond); Rappahannock River Yacht (Irvington, Va.); Knickerbocker, Commonwealth (N.Y.C.). Home: 9 Maxwell Rd Richmond VA 23226 Office: 707 E Main St Richmond VA 23212

BRASHARES, WILLIAM CHARLES, lawyer; b. Charlotte, N.C., June 7, 1939; s. Creighton Ambrose and Merry Ann (Dennis) B.; children—William Creighton, Ann Easton, Justin Samuel, Benjamin Easton. B.A., U. Va., 1961; J.D., U. Mich., 1964. Bar: D.C. bar 1964, Calif. bar 1976. Practiced in, Washington, 1964—; partner firm Cladouhos & Brashares, 1969—. Mem. D.C. Bar Assn., Calif. Bar Assn. Home: 5200 Chamberlin Ave Chevy Chase MD 20015 Office: 1750 New York Ave NW Washington DC 20006

BRASKET, CURT JUSTIN, systems analyst; b. Tracy, Minn., Dec. 7, 1932; s. Curt John and Mary Ann (Jenniges) B.; m. Rita Ann Bronk, July 20, 1963; children: Monica, Barbara, Rebecca. Student, U. Minn., 1950-51; B.A. in Math, St. John's U., Collegeville, Minn., 1954. Systems analyst UNIVAC, St. Paul, 1957—. Served with AUS, 1955-57. Mem. U.S. Chess Fedn. (life master, life mem.), Internat. Chess Fedn. (master 1983—). Roman Catholic. Chess master, 1953—; U.S. Jr. Champion, 1952; 16 times Minn. Champion, 4 times North Central Champion. Home: 220 Spring Valley Dr Bloomington MN 55420 Office: Univac Park Eagan MN

BRASSARD, GERALD MAURICE, association executive, chiropractor; b. Manchester, N.H., Apr. 15, 1922; s. George Napolean and Yvonnne (Dubois) B.; m. May Claire Wurtele, Sept. 27, 1941; children: Richard, Geroge, Raymond Maurice. Dr. Chriopractic, Palmer Chiropractic Coll., Davenport, Iowa, 1949; postgrad., Internat. Coll. chiropractics, 1965, Am. Coll. Chiropractics, 1980.. Dir. Parker Chiropractic Clinic, Beaumont, Tex., 1949-53; owner, dir. Brassard Chiropractic Clinic, Beaumont, Tex., 1953-80; dir. govtl. affairs Am. Chiropractice Assn., Des Moines, Iowa, 1971-80, exec. v.p., Arlington, Va., 1980—; dir. Golden Triangle Savs. & Loan, Bridge City, Tex., 1974-79; chmn. bd. First Tex. Bank, Vidor, 1974-80. Mem. Beaumont City Council, 1960-64; mayor pro-tem City of Beaumont, 1962; mem. Tex. Democratic Exec. Com., Austin, 1974-78. Served with USN, 1944-46; PTO. Recipient resolution Tex. Ho. of Reps., Austin, 1963, 69, testimonrial dinner and scroll Citizens, Community and C. of C., Beaumont, 1969; honoree Dr. G. M. Brassard Dav Beaumont Mayor and City Council, 1969; fellow Internat. Coll. Chiropractics, 1965, Am. Coll. Chiropractics, 1980. Mem. Am. Chiropractic Assn. (pres. 1970-71), Tex. Chiropractic Assn. (pres. 1953-55, Outstanding Chiropractor 1965, legis. rep. 1952-71), Savine Chiropractic Soc. (pres. 1952-53), Am. Legion (vice comdr. Beaumont 1950, Disting. Service award 1962). Lodges: Kiwanis; Elks; K.C. Home: 3009 Federal Hill Dr Falls Church VA 22044 Office: American Chriopractic Assn 1916 Wilson Blvd Arlington VA 22201

BRASTED, ROBERT CROCKER, chemistry educator; b. Lisbon, N.D., Aug. 26, 1915; s. Alva Jennings and Ada (Crocker) B.; m. Corinne Beaudry Mense, Oct. 17, 1942; children: Mary Frances, Barclay Mense, Donald More, Robert Crocker. B.S., George Washington U., 1938, M.A., 1939; Ph.D., U. Ill., 1942. Asst. in instrn. George Washington U., 1935-39, U. Ill., 1939-42; phys. research chemist Celanese Corp., Cumberland, Md., 1942-43; asst. prof. U. Hawaii, 1943-47; prof. chemistry, dir. gen. chemistry program U. Minn., Mpls., 1947—; Operations research chemist Johns Hopkins, 1949; guest prof. Poona U., India, U. Heidelberg, 1961, U. Costa Rica, 1961, Jadavpur U., India, 1964; guest prof., lectr. Taiwan Nat. U., 1970; guest prof., Fulbright lectr. Stuttgart U., 1971; guest prof. Calif. State Coll., Bakersfield, 1972, U. Tokyo, 1977, U. Natal, South Africa. Author: (with Sneed and Maynard) General College Chemistry, 1955, (with others) The Chemistry of Coordination Compounds, 1958, Comprehensive Inorganic Chemistry, 8 vols, 1953-62, (with Conroy and Tobias) Laboratory Operations, 3d edit., 1977, (with E. Fluck) Allgemeine und Anorganische Chemie, 1973, rev., 1981; co-author: A Guide to Chemical Education in the U.S. for Foreign Students, 1981; contbr. articles to profl. jours. Sanders fellow, 1939; Fulbright fellow, 1961, 71; NSF fellow, 1961; recipient Distinguished Tchr. award Inst. Tech., U. Minn., 1969, Morse award Council on Liberal Edn. of U. Minn., 1970, medal for teaching excellence Mfg. Chemists Assn., 1971, Distinguished Alumni award George Washington U., 1975, George Taylor award in Edn. U. Minn., 1975, 79; vis. scholar award Japan Soc. Promotion of Sci., 1977. Fellow AAAS; mem. Am. Chem. Soc. (chmn. Minn. sect. 1962, chmn. div. chem. edn. 1965, com. on edn. 1968—, com. on nominations and elections 1971—, council policy com. 1981, chmn. gen. chemistry exams. com. 1973—, award in chem. edn. 1973, internat. activities com. 1975, bd. council com. on publs. 1979—, Coll. Tchr. award Minn. sect. 1979, Minn. award 1980, James Flack Norris Northeastern sect. award 1980, Carol and Harry Mosher award Santa Clara Valley sect. 1981), Minn. Acad. Sci., Sigma Xi, Omicron Delta Kappa, Phi Lambda Upsilon, Alpha Chi Sigma. Home: 1488 Branston St Saint Paul MN 55108 Office: Dept Chemistry U Minn Inst Tech 207 Pleasant St SE Minneapolis MN 55455 *To serve my profession of Chemistry with dedication and enthusiasm as a teacher; to provide avenues of improvement of the environment in which we live by instruction of our youth; and to work with all peoples in harmony and with humility.*

BRASUNAS, ANTON DE SALES, metall. engr.; b. Elizabeth, N.J., Mar. 11, 1919; s. Anthony J. and Stefana (Zekus) B.; m. Ellen Lydia Wirth, Nov. 16, 1946; children—James Anton, Kay Ellen, Anne Elizabeth. B.S., Antioch Coll., Yellow Springs, Ohio, 1943; M.S., Ohio State U., 1946; Sc.D., M.I.T., 1950. Registered profl. engr., Ohio, Mo. Research engr. Battelle Meml. Inst., Columbus, Ohio, 1943-46; research metallurgist Oak Ridge Nat. Lab., 1950-53; asso. prof. metallurgy U. Tenn., Knoxville, 1953-55; dir. edn. Am. Soc. Metals, Cleve., 1955-64; mem. faculty U. Mo., Rolla, St. Louis, 1964-79, assoc. dean engr., prof. metall. engring., 1964—; cons. in field. Author, editor in field. Recipient Alumni award U. Mo., Rolla, 1971. Fellow Am. Soc. Metals; mem. Nat. Assn. Corrosion Engrs., Am. Nat. Metric Council, St. Louis Engrs. Club, Alpha Sigma Mu (pres. 1968-69). Home: 8030 Daytona St Saint Louis MO 63105 Office: U Mo 8001 Natural Bridge Rd Saint Louis MO 63121

BRASWELL, LOUIS ERSKINE, lawyer; b. Selma, Ala., Mar. 11, 1937; s. Erskine McKinley and Leota (Grubb) B.; m. Mary Hazen, June 23, 1962; children—Margaret, Anne, Helen. A.B., Birmingham So. Coll., 1959; J.D., Harvard U., 1962. Bar: Ala. bar 1962. Asso. firm Hand, Arendall, Bedsole, Greaves & Johnston, Mobile, Ala., 1963-68, partner, 1968—. Bd. dirs. Children's Dental Clinic, Mobile; pres. Friends of Mobile Public Library; bd. dirs. Jr. Achievement of Mobile; pres. YMCA Rockies Alumni Assn., 1978—; bd. dirs. Kidney Found. South Ala. Served with U.S. Army, 1962-63. Mem. Am. Law Inst., Am. Bar Assn., Ala. Bar Assn. Presbyterian. Clubs: Athelstan, Bienville, Mirror Lake Racquet. Home: 3 Ashley Dr Mobile AL 36608 Office: PO Box 123 Mobile AL 36601

BRASWELL, ROBERT NEIL, scientist, engr., govt. ofcl.; b. Boaz, Ala., July 23, 1932; s. Homer Winston and Irene (Wright) B.; m. Wynona Monette Chambers, Apr. 17, 1954; children—John Robert, Jefferson Monroe. B.S., U. Ala., 1957, M.S., 1959; Ph.D., Okla. State U., 1964. U.S. Steel Research fellow, 1957-59; engr. Hughes Aircraft Co., El Segundo, Cal., 1958; mgr. systems engring. Teledyne-Brown Engring., Huntsville, Ala. and; Cape Canaveral, Fla., 1959-64; resident dir. Genesys; prof. indsl. and systems engring. U. Fla., Daytona Beach, 1964-66, chmn. dept., Gainesville, 1965-72; scientist, engr. U.S. Air Force Systems Command, 1972—. Contbr. articles to profl. jours. Served with USAF, 1950-53. Recipient edn. award Rotary, Daytona Beach, 1967; named Outstanding Indsl. Engr., Region 4 Am. Inst. Indsl. Engrs., 1967, One of 5 Outstanding Young Men of Fla. Fla. Jr. C. of C., 1967, Alumnus of Year Snead State Coll., Boaz, 1968. Fellow Am. Inst. Aeros. and Astronautics (asso.), Soc. Logistics Engrs.; mem. Nat. Soc. Profl. Engrs., Am. Inst. Indsl. Engrs. (nat. dir. programs 1964-66, regional v.p. 1968—), Fla. Engring. Soc., Am. Def. Preparedness Assn. (pres.), Am. Soc. Engring. Edn., Operations Research Soc. Am., Inst. Mgmt. Sci., Sigma Xi, Tau Beta Pi, Omicron Delta Kappa, Sigma Tau, Alpha Pi Mu, Pi Mu Epsilon, Chi Alpha Phi, Phi Theta Kappa, Epsilon Lambda Chi. Democrat. Baptist. Club: Rotarian (past pres.). Home: 804 Tarpon Dr Fort Walton Beach FL 32548

BRASWELL, STEPHEN R., insurance company executive; b. Manila, Philippines, Feb. 24, 1940; s. L. Render and Elizabeth W. B.; m. Ernestine Dunlap; children: Elisabeth Dunlap, Wylly Willingham, Catherine Spalding. B.S., Duke U., 1962. With Prudential Ins. Co. Am., 1963—, pres. Southwestern ops., Houston, 1980—. Past pres. Jacksonville (Fla.) and Houston Mental Health Assn.; bd. dirs. YMCA Greater Houston Area., Houston Ballet Found., Interferon Found. Republican. Episcopalian. Club: Forum (Houston) (bd. govs.). Home: 2601 S Wildwind Circle The Woodlands TX 77380 Office: PO Box 2075 Houston TX 77001

BRATHOVDE, JAMES ROBERT, coll adminstr.; b. Glasgow, Mont., June 8, 1926; s. Arnold Morgan and Ebbie Rozella (Hevener) B.; m. Bonnie Dee Cornwell, Oct. 28, 1949; children—James Edgar, Robert Dean, Linė Tonna. B.A., Eastern Wash. Coll., 1950, 1950; M.S., U. Wash., 1955, Ph.D. (Army Ordnance Research fellow), 1956. Tchr. pub. schs., Spokane, 1950-51; asso. prof. chemistry, chmn. dept. Whitworth Coll., Spokane, 1956-60; research scientist Sandia Corp., Albuquerque, 1960-63; program dir. undergrad. sci. edn. NSF, Washington, 163-64; dir. computer center, prof. chemistry State U. N.Y. at Binghamton, 1964-67; chmn. chemistry dept. No. Ariz. U., Flagstaff, 1967-70, dean, 1970-72, prof. environmental sci. and chemistry, 1972—; Pres. Brathovde Lands, Inc., Elk, Wash., 1967—, JRB Enterprises, Inc., Elk, 1967—; dir. Wash. State Sci. Talent Search, 1959-60; pres. Human Growth, Inc., N.Y.C., 1964-70. Bd. dirs. Human Growth Found., 1970—. Served to 1st lt. USMCP, 1944-46, 51-52. NSF Research grantee, 1958-60; Research Corp. grantee, 1957. Mem. Am. Chem. Soc., Am. Crystallographic Assn., A.A.A.S., Am. Assn. Physics Tchrs., Assn. Computer Machinery, Sigma Xi. Lutheran. Home: 519 N James St Flagstaff AZ 86001

BRATT, BENGT ERIK, system engr.; b. Willstad, Sweden, May 18, 1922; came to U.S., 1956, naturalized, 1962; s. Victor A. and Elsa (Modeen) B.; m. Gerlinde Froehner, Nov. 10, 1966; 1 son, Stephen Mark. M.E., Tech. Coll. Gothenburg, Sweden, 1946; B.S. in Bus. Adminstrn. and Econs, Malmo (Sweden) Coll., 1950; postgrad., U. Stockholm, 1955, U. San Diego, 1960; M.S. in Systems Engring, West Coast U., 1966, West Coast U., 1970; D.Sc., Western Colo. U., 1977. Registered profl. engr., Calif., Colo., also France. Marine engr. Kockums Shipbldg. Corp., Malmo, 1947-51; project engr. De Laval Steam Turbine Co., Stockholm, 1951-55; thermodynamics engr. Convair div. Gen. Cynamics Corp., San Diego, 1956-60; sr. scientist Research Inst. Nat. Def., Stockholm, 1961; sr. systems engr. Northrop Space Labs., Hawthorne, Calif., 1962-63; sr. research scientist Lockheed Research Center, Burbank, Calif., 1963-67; engr. long range planning Met. Water Dist. So. Calif., Los Angeles, 1967—; lectr. Calif. State U., Los Angeles; mem. adv. bd. Western Colo. U., Town Hall Calif. Contbr. articles in thermodynamics, space propulsion and systems engring. to profl. jours. Fellow AAAS, ASCE; mem. Ops. Research Soc. Am., Coll. Planning, Inst. Mgmt. Scis., Svenska Teknolog- foreningen (Sweden), West Coast U. Alumni Assn. (pres. 1972). Research contbns. to system efficiency and systems optimization non-mil. applications. Home: 1942 Lemoyne St Los Angeles CA 90026 Office: Met Water Dist So Calif Los Angeles CA 90054

BRATT, FLOYD CLARENCE, retired physician; b. Clarence Center, N.Y., Nov. 19, 1903; s. Clarence Almon and Agnes Ruth (Eshelman) B.; m. Arline Swift Downey, Oct. 12, 1929 (dec. Aug. 1969); 1 dau., Marilyn (Mrs. R. Bruce Kirkwood). B.S., Denison U., 1924; M.D., U. Buffalo, 1928. Intern Buffalo City Hosp., 1928-29; family practice of medicine, Hamburg, N.Y., 1929-31, Rochester, N.Y., 1931-81; med. staff Highland Hosp., Park Ave. Hosp., Rochester.; Mem. Pres. Eisenhower's People-to-People Com. on Health Professions which sponsored Project HOPE; rep. meeting of World Med. Assn., Copenhagen, 1958; cons., mem. orgn. com. Internat. Conf. on Gen. Practice, Montreal, Que., Can., 1964. Contbr. articles to profl. publs. Bd. dirs. Am. Acad. Family Physicians Found., Nat. Health Council, 1961-64. Recipient citation for outstanding achievements and services Denison U., 1962. Mem. Am. Acad. Family Physicians (pres. 1961, v.p., chmn. bd. 1959, mem. congress of dels., past dir., past mem. exec. com.; chmn. com. on internat. affairs 1962-63, rep. to planning conf. gen. practice orgns. 1964), N.Y. State (pres. 1952), Rochester acads. family physicians, A.M.A., World, Pan Am. med. assns., Med. Soc. State N.Y. (chmn. subcom. gen. practice of council com. on pub. health and edn. 1950-59, past sec., chmn. gen. practice sect.; mem. council com. on legislation, Presdl. citation for outstanding community service 1963), Monroe County Med. Soc., Rochester Acad. Medicine, Am. Geriatrics Assn., Rochester Path. Soc., Am. Med. Soc. of Vienna (life), Brit. Coll. Gen. Practice (corr. asso.), Nu Sigma Nu. Methodist (trustee emeritus local ch.; trustee Genesee conf.). Clubs: Mason (Shriner), Kiwanian (past lt. gov. N.Y. dist., past pres. Rochester club), Century of Rochester.). Home: 40 Ambassador Dr Rochester NY 14610

BRATTON, HOWARD CALVIN, judge; b. Clovis, N.Mex., Feb. 4, 1922; s. Sam Gilbert and Vivian (Rogers) B. B.A., U. N.Mex., 1941, LL.D., 1971; LL.B., Yale U., 1947. Bar: N.Mex. 1948. Law clk. U.S. Circuit Ct. Appeals, 1948; mem. firm Grantham & Bratton, Albuquerque, 1949-52; spl. asst. U.S. atty. charge litigation OPS, 1951-52; asso., then partner firm Hervy, Dow & Hinkle, Roswell, N.Mex., 1952-64; judge U.S. Dist. Ct. N.Mex., 1964—, chief judge, 1978—; chmn. N.Mex. Jr. Bar Assn., 1952; pres. Chaves County (N.Mex.) Bar Assn., 1962; chmn. pub. lands com. N.Mex. Oil and Gas Assn., 1961-64, Interstate Oil Compact Commn., 1963-64; Mem. N.Mex. Commn. Higher Edn., 1962-64, Jud. Conf. of U.S. Com. on operation of jury system, 1966-72, 79—. Bd. regents U. N.Mex., 1958-68, pres., 1963-64; bd. dirs. Fed. Jud. Ctr., 1983—. Served to capt. AUS, 1942-45. Mem. Trial Judges Assn. 10th Circuit (pres. 1976-78), Nat. Conf. Fed. Trial Judges (exec. com. 1977-79), Sigma Chi. Home: 1117 Salamanca NW Albuquerque NM 87107 Office: PO Box 38 Albuquerque NM 87103

BRATTON, JAMES HENRY, JR., lawyer; b. Pulaski, Tenn., Oct. 9, 1931; s. James Henry and Mabel (Shelley) B.; m. Alleen Sharp Davis, Oct. 15, 1960; children: Susan Shelley, James Henry III, Margaret Alleen. A.B., U. South, 1952; B.A., Oxford (Eng.) U., 1954, M.A., 1978; LL.B., Yale U., 1956. Bar: Tenn. 1956, Ga. 1957. With antitrust div. Dept. Justice, summer 1955; since practiced in, Atlanta; partner firm Gambrell & Russell; vis. lectr. U. Ga. Law Sch., 1967; adj. prof. law Emory U., 1984. Contbr. articles to profl. jours. Mem. Gov.'s Citizens Adv. Council on Environ. Affairs, 1970—; Bd. dirs. Christian Council Met. Atlanta, Protestant Welfare and Social Services, Chs. Home for Bus. Girls.; trustee U. of the South, 1984—. Mem. ABA (standing com. on aero. law 1962—, chmn. 1977—), Ga. Bar Assn. (founding chmn. environ. law sect. 1970-73), Fed. Bar Assn., Atlanta Bar Assn., Lawyers Club Atlanta, Old Warhorse Lawyers Club, Am. Acad. Polit. and Social Scis., Am. Judicature Soc., Am. Law Inst., Yale Law Alumni Assn. (exec. com. 1976—), Phi Beta Kappa, Phi Delta Phi, Pi Gamma Mu, Gridiron. Democrat. Methodist. Home: 63 N Muscogee Ave NW Atlanta GA 30305 Office: First Nat Bank Tower Atlanta GA 30383

BRATTON, JOSEPH KEY, army officer; b. St. Paul, Apr. 4, 1926; s. John Smith and Maude Katherine (Keys) B.; m. Louise Skelly, Sept. 30, 1950; children: Joseph Key, John, Mary, Anne, James. B.A., U.S. Mil. Acad., 1948; M.S. in Nuclear Engring., MIT, 1959. Commd. 2d lt., C.E. U.S. Army, 1948, advanced through grades to lt. gen., 1980, sec. to U.S. Joint Chiefs of Staff, 1970-72, dir. nuclear activities SHAPE, Belgium, 1972-75; dir. Div. Mil. Application Dept. Energy, Washington, 1975-79; chief of engrs. C.E. U.S. Army, 1980—. Decorated D.S.M., Legion of Merit with 2 oak leaf clusters. Mem. Soc. Am. Mil. Engrs. Roman Catholic. Club: Army Navy Country. Home: Quarters 4 Fort McNair Washington DC 20024 Office: Chief Engrs 20 Massachusetts Ave Washington DC 20314

BRATTSTROM, BAYARD HOLMES, biology educator; b. Chgo., July 3, 1929; s. Wilber LeRoy and Violet (Holmes) B.; m. Cecile D. Funk, June 15, 1952 (div. May 1975); children: Theodore Allen, David Arthur.; m. Martha Isaacs Marsh, July 8, 1982. B.S., San Diego State Coll., 1951; M.A., UCLA, 1953, Ph.D., 1959. Dir. edn. Natural History Mus., San Diego, 1949-51, asst. curator herpetology, 1949-51; asso. zoology U. Calif. at Los Angeles, 1954-56; research fellow paleoecology Calif. Inst. Tech., Pasadena, 1955; instr. biology Adelphi U., Garden City, N.Y., 1956-60; asst. prof. Calif. State U., Fullerton, 1960-61, asso. prof., 1961-66, prof., 1966—; asso. prof. zoology U. Calif. at Los Angeles, summers 1962-63; hon. research asso. herpetology, vertebrate paleontology Los Angeles County Mus., Los Angeles, 1961—; pres. Fullerton Youth Mus. and Natural Sci. Center, 1962-64, dir., 1962-66. Author: poetry The Talon Digs Deeply into My Heart, 1974; Contbr. chpts. to books. Research grantee Am. Philos. Soc., Mex., 1958, Am. Philos. Soc., Panama, 1959; NSF, 1964-66; NSF Sr. Postdoctoral fellow Monash U., Australia, 1966-67; recipient Distinguished Teaching award Calif. State U., Fullerton, 1968. Fellow A.A.A.S. (mem. council 1965—), Herpetological League; mem. Am. Soc. Ichthyologists and Herpetologists (bd. govs. 1962-66, v.p. western div. 1965), Orange County Zool. Soc. (mem. bd. 1962-65, pres. 1962-64), So. Calif. Acad. Sci. (dir. 1964-67), Ecol. Soc. Am., Soc. for Study Evolution, Soc. Systematic Zoology, San Diego Soc. Natural History, Soc. Vertebrate Paleontology, Am. Soc. Mammalogists, Cooper, Am. ornithol. socs., Am. Soc. Zoologists, Sigma Xi. Research and publs. in osteology, paleontology, systematics, behavior, ecology, physiology especially temperature regulation, zoogeography of vertebrates especially amphibians and reptiles, repopulation of volcanic islands, social behavior. Office: Dept Biology Calif State U Fullerton CA 92634 *My life and research has been based on an insatiable curiosity about the natural world, especially as seen in the evolutionary adaptations of animals to their environment and their interactions with each other.*

BRAUDE, ABRAHAM ISAAC, physician, educator; b. Chgo., June 15, 1917; s. Benjamin and Lillian (Schiff) B.; m. Gita Siegel, Jan. 5, 1942; children: Claire, Kathryn. B.S., U. Chgo., 1937; M.D., Rush Med. Coll., 1940; Ph.D., U. Minn., 1950. Diplomate: Am. Bd. Internal Medicine. Intern Michael Reese Hosp., Chgo., 1940-41; resident in internal medicine U. Minn., 1945-48, instr. internal medicine, 1948-50; asst. prof. medicine U. Mich. Med. Sch., 1950-53; hosp. bacteriologist Univ. Hosp. (U. Mich.), 1950-53; asso. prof., then prof. medicine, also dir. microbiology Southwestern Med. Sch., U. Tex., Dallas, 1953-57; prof. medicine, also chief infectious diseases U. Pitts. Med. Sch., 1957-69; prof. medicine and pathology, chief div. infectious diseases, dir. microbiology U. Calif. Med. Sch., San Diego, 1969—; chmn. bacteriology mycology study sect. NIH, 1969-71; mem. Anglo-Am. Amoeba Commn. to India, 1982; mem. exam. com. on microbiology Nat. Bd. Med. Examiners, 1974-78; vis. scientist London Sch. Hygiene and Tropical Medicine, 1981-82. Author: Antimicrobial Drug Therapy, 1976; editor: International Textbook of Medicine, 1981, Microbiology and Infectious Diseases, vol. II, 1981. Served to capt. M.C., AUS, 1941-45. Recipient Kaiser Teaching award, 1973, Maxwell Finland award, 1981; grantee NIH, 1951—; Macy Faculty scholar, 1981-82. Mem. Am. Soc. Clin. Investigation, Am. Assn. Physicians, Am. Assn. Immunologists, Infectious Disease Soc. Am. (pres.), ACP, Am. Soc. Microbiology. Home: 1723 Castellana Rd La Jolla CA 92037 Office: Univ Hosp San Diego CA 92103

BRAUDY, LEO BEAL, educator, author; b. Phila., June 11, 1941; s. Edward and Zelda (Smith) B.; m. Dorothy McGahee, Dec. 24, 1974. B.A., Swarthmore Coll., 1963; M.A., Yale U., 1964, Ph.D., 1967. Instr. English Yale U., New Haven, 1966-68; asst. prof. Columbia U., N.Y.C., 1968-70, asso. prof., 1970-73, prof., 1973-76; prof. English Johns Hopkins U., Balt., 1977-83; prof. English, chmn. U. So. Calif., Los Angeles, 1983—. Author: Narrative Form in History and Fiction: Hume, Fielding, and Gibbon, 1970, Jean Renoir: The World of His Films, 1972, The World in a Frame: What We See in Films, 1976; editor: Norman Mailer: A Collection of Critical Essays, 1972, Focus on Truffaut's Shoot the Piano Player, 1972, (with Morris Dickstein) Great Film Directors: A Critical Anthology, 1978; mem. editorial bd.: ELH, 1976, PMLA, 1979, Quar. Rev. of Film Studies, 1976, Raritan Rev, 1979, Prose Studies, 1979. Guggenheim fellow, 1971-72; Am. Council Learned Socs. grantee, 1971; NEH, 1978, 79. Mem. MLA, Am. Soc. for Eighteenth-Century Studies. Office: Dept English U So Calif Los Angeles CA 90089

BRAUER, FRED GÜNTHER, mathematics educator; b. Königsberg, Germany, Feb. 3, 1932; came to U.S., 1960; s. Richard D. and Ilse (Karger) B.; m. Esther Luterman, June 22, 1958; children: David, Deborah, Michael. B.A., U. Toronto, 1952; S.M., Mass. Inst. Tech., 1953, Ph.D., 1956. Instr. U. Chgo., 1956-58; lectr., then asst. prof. U. B.C., 1958-60; mem. faculty U. Wis., Madison, 1960—, prof. math., 1966—. Author: (with J.A. Nohel) Ordinary Differential Equations: A First Course, 1967, 2d edit., 1973, Elementary Differential Equations; Principles, Problems, Solutions, 1968, Problems and and Solutions in Ordinary Differential Equations, 1968, Qualitative Theory of Ordinary Differential Equations, 1969, (with J.A. Nohel and H. Schneider) Linear Mathematics, 1970. Mem. Am. Math. Soc. (asso. editor Proc. 1971-74), Math. Assn. Am., Canadian Math. Congress, Soc. Indsl. and Applied Math., Sigma Xi. Home: 5113 Coney Weston Pl Madison WI 53711

BRAUER, JERALD CARL, ch. historian, educator; b. Fond du Lac, Wis., Sept. 16, 1921; s. Carl L. and Anna Mae (Linde) B.; m. Muriel I. Nelson, Mar. 18, 1945; children—Christopher, Marian, Thomas. A.B., Carthage Coll., 1943, LL.D., 1957; B.D., Northwestern Luth. Theol. Sem., 1945; Ph.D., U. Chgo., 1948; D.D., Miami U., Oxford, Ohio, 1956; S.T.D., Ripon Coll., 1961; L.H.D., Gettysburg Coll., 1963. Ordained to ministry United Lutheran Ch. Am., 1951; instr. ch. history and history Christian thought Union Theol. Sem., N.Y.C., 1948-50; asst. prof. history of Christianity, federated theol. faculty U. Chgo., 1950-54, asso. prof., 1954-59, dean federated theol. faculty, 1955-60, dean div. sch., 1960-70, prof. history of Christianity, 1959—, Naomi Shenstone Donnelley prof. history of Christianity, 1969—; fellow Center for Policy Studies; cons. N.Y. Edn. Dept., 1969—; vis. lectr. U. Frankfurt, 1971, U. Tokyo, 1966; Mem. bd. theol. edn. Luth. Ch. in Am., pres. bd., 1962-68; ofcl. delegated observer World Council Chs. 3d, 4th sessions Vatican Council II; mem. bd. Council on Religion and Internat. Affairs, chmn., 1979—; bd. dirs. Internat. House, chmn., 1973—; bd. dirs. Rockefeller Bros. Theol. Fellowship Program, 1956-70; trustee Augustana Coll., 1964-66, Carthage Coll., 1958-62; Vis. fellow Center Study Democratic Instns., Santa Barbara, Calif., 1972, 74. Author: Protestantism in America, 1953, Basic Question for the Christian Scholar, 1954, (with J. Pelikan) The Lutheran Reformation, 1955; Editor: (Paul Tillich) The Future of Religions, 1966, My Travel Diary, 1936, (Paul Tillich) My Travel Diary, 1970, Westminster Dictionary of Church History, 1971; gen. editor: Essays in Divinity, 7 vols, 1967—; editor vols. 2 and 5: Religion in the American Revolution, 1976. Nat. Endowment for Humanities sr. fellow, 1977-78. Mem. Am. Soc. Ch. History (pres. 1960), Renaissance Soc. Am., Midwest Conf. Brit. Hist. Studies. Home: 5620 S Blackstone Ave Chicago IL 60637

BRAUER, KINLEY JULES, educator; b. Jersey City, Apr. 16, 1935; s. Sigmund and Dora (Kinley) B.; m. Barbara Sue Stein, Aug. 20, 1961; children—Emily Sophia, Peter Benjamin. B.A., U. Rochester, 1957; M.A., U. Calif., Berkeley, 1958, Ph.D., 1963. Instr. Stanford (Calif.) U., 1960-63; asst. prof. U. Nev., Reno, 1963-65, U. Minn., Mpls., 1965-67, asso. prof., 1967-75, prof. history, 1975—. Bd. editors: Diplomatic History, 1977-80; contbr. articles to profl. jours.; contbr. to: Dictionary of Am. Biography, 1951-55, Ency. of So. History, 1979, World Biography, 1973, Ency. Americana, 1973. Recipient McKnight Found. Humanities award, 1965; U. Calif. Grad. Sch. grantee, 1960; Stanford U. Grad. Sch. grantee, 1962; U. Nev. Desert Research Inst. grantee, 1963; U. Minn. Council of Liberal Edn. grantee, 1967; Office of Internat. Programs grantee, 1968, 73, 75; Nat. Endowment for Humanities sr. research fellow, 1976-77; Deutscher Akademischer Austauschdienst scholar, 1981. Mem. Am. Hist. Assn., Orgn. Am. Historians, Soc. Historians of Am. Fgn. Relations. Office: Dept History U Minn Minneapolis MN 55419

BRAUER, RALPH WERNER, educator, physiologist; b. Berlin, Germany, June 18, 1921; came to U.S., 1937, naturalized, 1941; s. Frederick and A. M. (Doering) B. A.B. in Chemistry, Columbia, 1940; M.S. in Biochemistry, U. Rochester, 1941, Ph.D., 1943. Research chemist Distillation Products, Inc., 1943-44; instr. pharmacology Harvard Med. Sch., 1944-47; asst. prof. pharmacology and biochemistry, acting head pharmacology dept. La. State U. Sch. Medicine, 1947-51; head metabolism sect. U.S. Naval Research and Devel. Lab., 1951-52, head pharmacology br., 1952-64, prin. investigator biol. and med. sci. div., chmn. oceanography planning com., 1964-66; dir. Wrightsville Marine Bio-Med. Lab., Wilmington, N.C., 1966-71; prof. physiology and pharmacology Duke, 1966-71; prof. marine physiology, head dept. marine bio-med. research U. N.C. at Wilmington, 1971-73; dir. Inst. for Marine Biomed. Research, 1973—; vis. prof. physiology U. N.C. at Chapel Hill, 1968—; chief radiol. def. for La., 1950-51; chmn. research com. San Mateo (Calif.) Heart Assn., 1959-65; Mary Scott Newbold lectr. Phila. Coll. Physicians, 1961; Chmn. Gov.'s N.C. Marine Sci. Council, 1974-75. Editor: Liver Function, 1958, Barobiology, 1973; mem. editorial bd.: Jour. Applied Physiology, 1960-66, 79—; author numerous articles in field. Recipient Stover/Link award Undersea Biomed. Soc., 1981. Mem. Soc. Exptl. Biology and Medicine (chmn. Pacific Coast sect. 1959-66), N.Y. Acad. Scis., Am. Physiol. Soc., Am. Soc. Pharmacology and Exptl. Therapeutics, A.A.A.S., Radiation Research Soc., Am. Soc. Study Liver Diseases, Am. Soc. Phys. Anthropology, Marine Tech. Soc., Aerospace Med. Assn., Soc. for Underwater Medicine, Soc. Neuroscis. Home: Route 3 Box 327A Wilmington NC 28401

BRAULT, GERARD JOSEPH, foreign language educator; b. Chicopee Falls, Mass., Nov. 7, 1929; s. Philias J. and Aline E. (Rémillard) B.; m. Jeanne Lambert Pepin, Jan. 23, 1954; children: Francis Gerard, Anne Marie, Suzanne Eveline. A.B., Assumption Coll., Worcester, Mass., 1950, D. Litt., 1976; A.M. cum laude, Laval U., 1952; Ph.D., U. Pa., 1958. Teaching fellow U. Pa., 1954-56, assoC. prof. Romance langs., 1961-65, vice dean Grad. Sch., 1962-65; instr. French Bowdoin Coll., 1957-59; asst. prof. (French, Bowdoin Coll.), 1959-61; prof. French, Pa. State U., University Park, 1965—, head dept. French, 1965-70; fellow Inst. Arts and Humanistic Studies, 1976—; dir. NDEA Summer Insts., Bowdoin Coll., 1961, 62, Assumption Coll., 1964; Fulbright fellow, Strasbourg, France, 1956-57, Fulbright research scholar and Guggenheim fellow, Strasbourg, 1968-69. Author: Celestine: A Critical Edition of the First French Translation (1527) of the Spanish Classic La Celestina, 1963, Cours de langue française destiné aux jeunes Franco-Américains, 1963, rev. edits., 1965, 69, Early Blazon, 1972, Eight Thirteenth-Century Rolls of Arms in French and Anglo-Norman Blazon, 1973 (prix Paul Adam-Even), The Song of Roland: An Analytical Edition (named outstanding book Choice 1979); 2 vols., 1978; mem. editorial bd.: French Forum, 1975—, Purdue U. Monographs, 1978—; contbr. articles to profl. jours. Mem. Catholic Commn. on Intellectual and Cultural Affairs, also, Comité de Vie Franco-Américaine, Société Historique Franco-Américaine. Served with CIC U.S. Army, 1951-53. Decorated Palmes académiques French Ministry Edn., 1965, officer, 1975; officer; Ordre National du Mérite, 1980; recipient Faculty Scholar medal Pa. State U., 1981. Fellow Soc. Antiquaries of London, Heraldry Soc. London, Medieval Acad. Am. (adv. bd. Speculum 1972-75), Académie Internationale d' Héraldique; mem. Société Rencesvals pour l'étude des épopées romanes (v.p. 1973—, pres. Am.-Canadian br. 1970-73, editorial bd. Olifant 1975—), Am. Assn. Tchrs. French, Assn. for Can. Studies in U.S., Middle Atlantic Conf. Canadian Studies (pres. 1981-83), Internat. Arthurian Soc., Modern Lang. Assn. Home: 705 Westerly Pkwy State College PA 16801 Office: Burrowes Bldg Pa State U University Park PA 16802

BRAULT, MICHEL, film dir.; b. Montreal, Que., Can., June 25, 1928; s. Paul Henri and Celine (March) B.; m. Marie-Marthe Tardif, 1952; children—Nathalie, Anouk, Sylvain. B.A., Coll. St. Jean, Que., 1950. Cinematographer: Chronique d'Un Eté, 1960, Mon Oncle Antoine, 1970, Kamouraska, 1972, Mourir à Tue-Tete, 1978, Les Bons débarras, 1979, Threshold, 1980; dir.: Pour La Suite du Monde, 1963, Entre la Mer et l'Eau Douce, 1967, Les Ordres, 1974. Recipient prix de la Mise en Scene, Cannes, 1975. Address: 1168 Richelieu Beloeil PQ J3G 4R3 Canada

BRAUMAN, JOHN I., chemist, educator; b. Pitts., Sept. 7, 1937; s. Milton and Freda E. (Schlitt) B.; m. Sharon Lea Kruse, Aug. 22, 1964; 1 dau., Kate Andrea. B.S., Mass. Inst. Tech., 1959; Ph.D. (NSF fellow), U. Calif., Berkeley, 1963. NSF postdoctoral fellow U. Calif., Los Angeles, 1962-63; asst. prof. chemistry Stanford (Calif.) U., 1963-69, asso. prof., 1969-72, prof., 1972-80, J.G. Jackson-C.J. Wood prof. chemistry, 1980—, chmn. dept., 1979—; cons. in phys. organic chemistry; adv. panel chemistry div. NSF, 1974-78; adv. panel NASA, AEC, ERDA, Research Corp., Office Chemistry and Chem. Tech., NRC. Mem. editorial adv. bd.: Jour. Am. Chem. Soc, 1976—, Jour. Organic Chemistry, 1974-78, Nouveau Jour. de Chimie, 1977—, Chem. Revs, 1978-80, Chem. Physics Letters, 1978-80. Alfred P. Sloan fellow, 1968-70; Guggenheim fellow, 1978-79. Fellow AAAS; mem. Nat. Acad. Scis., Am. Acad. Arts Scis., Am. Chem. Soc. (award in pure chemistry 1973, Harrison Howe award 1976, exec. com. phys. chemistry div.), Brit. Chem. Soc., Sigma Xi, Phi Lambda Upsilon. Home: 849 Tolman Dr Stanford CA 94305 Office: Dept Chemistry Stanford U Stanford CA 94305

BRAUN, ARMIN CHARLES JOHN, educator; b. Milw., Sept. 5, 1911; s. Adolph and Ella (Schreiber) B. B.S., U. Wis., 1934, Ph.D., 1938; predoctoral study European sci. labs., 1936-37. With Rockefeller U., N.Y.C., 1938—, successively fellow, asst., asso., asso. mem., asso. prof., 1938-59, mem. and prof., 1959—, head dept. plant biology, 1955—; mem. sci. panel biology and medicine NSF, 1958-61; mem. sci. adv. bd. Inst. Cancer Research Phila., 1959-65; sci. adv. panel Brookhaven Nat. Lab., 1960-64; mem. adv. com. Aspen Biol. Inst., 1965-68. Author numerous sci. papers, books. Served to capt. AUS, 1943-46. Recipient Newcomb Cleveland award AAAS, 1949, Charles Leopold Mayer prize French Acad. Scis., 1982; Jenkinson Meml. lectr. Oxford U., 1978. Fellow Am. Bot. Soc. (hon.), Am. Phytopath. Soc. (hon.); mem. Am. Acad. Arts and Scis., Nat. Acad. Scis., Harvey Soc. (hon.), Internat. Soc. Developmental Biologists, AAAS, Soc. Developmental Biology, Sigma Xi, Phi Sigma, Alpha Zeta, Delta Theta Sigma. Home: 347 Ridgeview Rd Princeton NJ 08540 Office: Rockefeller U 66th St and York Ave New York NY 10021

BRAUN, CHARLES LOUIS, chemistry educator, researcher; b. Webster, S.D., June 4, 1937; s. Louis Fred and Myrene Clarise (Strand) B.; m. Kathleen Louise Brickel, Aug. 10, 1958; children: Sarah Kathryn, David Charles. B.S., S.D. Sch. Mines and Tech., Rapid City, 1959; Ph.D., U. Minn., 1963; M.A. (hon.), Dartmouth Coll., 1978. Instr. chemistry Dartmouth Coll., 1965-66, asst. prof., 1966-71, assoc. prof., 1971-77, prof., 1977—, chmn. dept., 1982—; vis. prof. U. Stuttgart, 1969-70, Cornell U., 1980-81; cons. Eastman Kodak Co., Rochester, N.Y., 1979—; co-chmn. Gordon Research Conf. on Photoconductivity, 1982. Contbr. articles to profl. jours. Served to 1st lt. U.S. Army, 1963-65. Grantee NSF, 1966-79, Petroleum Research Found., 1981—, Dept. Energy, 1983—. Mem. Am. Chem. Soc., Am. Phys. Soc. Home: 3 Hawk Pine Rd Norwich VT 05055 Office: Dept Chemistry Dartmouth Coll Hanover NH 03755

BRAUN, DANIEL CARL, physician; b. San Diego, July 2, 1905; s. Daniel Jacob and Frida (Lorch) B.; m. Hazel Winfield Beckley, Aug. 10, 1929. Student, Carnegie Inst. Tech., 1923-31; B.S., U. Pitts., 1933, M.D., 1937; postgrad., L.I. Coll. Medicine, 1942, Columbia, 1945. Diplomate: Am. Bd. Preventive Medicine. Intern Mercy Hosp., Pitts., 1937-38; practice medicine specializing in occupational medicine, Pitts., 1938—; med. dir. Pitts. Coal Co., 1944-50, cons. occupational medicine, 1950-52; med. dir. Indsl. Hygiene Found., Pitts., 1952-58, Homestead dist. works U.S. Steel Corp., Munhall, Pa., 1958-61; asst. med. dir. U.S. Steel Corp., 1961-70; mgr. occupational medicine services Indsl. Health Found., 1970-72, pres., 1972—; lectr. indsl. hygiene U. Pitts. Sch. Medicine, 1948—; lectr. occupational medicine Grad. Sch. Pub. Health U. Pitts., 1950—. Contbr. articles to profl. jours. Mem. Mayor Pitts. Com. Reorgn. Pitts. Dept. Health, 1948-50, President's Com. Employment Handicapped, 1958—; mem. SSS appeal bd. Western Fed. Jud. Dist. Pa., 1962-68; active, Allegheny council Boy Scouts Am.; Bd. dirs. St. Clair Meml. Hosp.; trustee Indsl. Health Found. Am. Fellow Am. Coll. Chest Physicians, Am. Acad. Occupational medicine (chmn. standards com. 1967-70), Am. Occupational Med. Assn. (dir. 1950-52), Am. Coll. Preventive Medicine, Am. Inst. Chemists; mem. AMA (recognition award 1976), Pa., Allegheny County med. socs., Alpha Omega Alpha. Clubs: Mason., University (Pitts.). Home: 7555 Penn Bridge Ct Pittsburgh PA 15221 Office: 34 Penn Circle W Pittsburgh PA 15206 *Any success I may have achieved during my lifetime must be attributed to the basic, but nowadays often ridiculed, willingness to do more than was required, to do it conscientiously and honestly, and to the best of my ability.*

BRAUN, EDWARD JOSEPH, private investor; b. Oklahoma City, May 4, 1919; s. Sylvester and Dorothea Elizabeth (Vondran) B.; m. Julia G. McGovern, Sept. 29, 1942; children—Susan Roberts, Beverly Kanaly, Louise Vandaveer, Janie Saltzman. Student Cath. schs., Oklahoma City. With T.G.&Y. Stores Co., Oklahoma City, 1939-78, exec. v.p., 1969-72, pres., chief exec. officer, 1972-78, chmn. bd., 1978; pvt. investor, 1978—; dir. Liberty Nat. Corp., Liberty Nat. Bank & Trust Co., both Oklahoma City. Bd. dirs. local Jr. Achievement, Salvation Army, United Way.; commr. Oklahoma City Housing Authority. Served to capt. AUS, 1941-45. Decorated Legion of Merit; Italian Medal of Honor. Roman Catholic. Club: Twin Hills Golf and Country (Oklahoma City). Home: 4904 NW 33d St Oklahoma City OK 73122

BRAUN, GEORGE AUGUST, biochemist, pharmaceutical company executive; b. Phila., Dec. 11, 1925; s. Charles Edward and Edna (Strehle) B.; m. Patricia Heilmann, Apr. 19, 1952; children: George, Mary, Mark, Janet. B.S., St. Joseph's Coll., Phila., 1951; Ph.D. in Biochemistry, U. Pa., Phila., 1960. Research asso. Grad. Sch. Medicine, U. Pa., Phila., 1955-60, instr. biochemistry, 1960-61, asso. in biochemistry, 1961-62, vis. lectr., 1963-66; sr. research scientist Squibb Inst. Med. Research, New Brunswick, N.J., 1962-63; asst. dir. biol. research, head biochemistry sect. McNeil Labs., Ft. Washington, Pa., 1963-68, dir. biochem. research, 1968-71, exec. dir. research, 1971-72; v.p. research and devel. Ortho Pharm. Corp., Raritan, N.J., 1972-80; also dir.; v.p. tech. affairs Johnson & Johnson Internat., New Brunswick, N.J., 1980—; guest lectr. Phila. Coll. Pharmacy Sci.; finance chmn. 3d Internat. Symposium Drugs Affecting Lipid Metabolism, 1971; industry liaison FDA Panel Rev. Over the Counter Drugs, 1973; temporary cons. Ford Found. Contbr. numerous articles to profl. publs. Served with USN, 1943-46; capt. Res. (ret.). Mem. N.Y. Acad. Scis., Am. Chem. Soc., Am. Fertility Soc., Pharm. Mfrs. Assn. (chmn. research and devel. sect. 1978-79, mem. sci. adv. com. 1978—), Internat. Family Planning Research Assn., AAAS, Sigma Xi. Home: PO Box 401 Pocono Pines PA 18350 Office: Johnson & Johnson Internat One Johnson & Johnson Plaza New Brunswick NJ 08903

BRAUN, JEROME IRWIN, lawyer; b. St. Joseph, Mo., Dec. 16, 1929; s. Martin H. and Bess (Donsker) B.; m. Enne Weissman, Mar. 11, 1957; children: Aaron Hugh, Susan Lori, Daniel Victor. A.B. with distinction, Stanford U., 1951, LL.B., 1953. Asso. firm Long & Levit, San Francisco, 1957-58; asso. Law Offices of Jefferson Peyser, 1958-62; founding partner Elke, Farella & Braun (now Farella, Braun & Martel), San Francisco, 1962—; instr. law San Francisco Law Sch., 1958-69. Pres. Jewish Welfare Fedn. of San Francisco, Marin County and Peninsula, 1979-80; past pres. San Francisco Jewish Community Centers. Served to 1st lt. Judge Adv. Gen. Corps U.S. Army, 1953-57. Mem. Calif. Acad. Appellate Lawyers, Am. Judicature Soc., Am. Coll. Trial Lawyers, Am. Bar Assn., State Bar Calif. (chmn. com. adminstrn. justice 1977), Bar Assn. San Francisco. *

BRAUN, LUDWIG, computer science educator; b. Bklyn., May 14, 1926; s. Ludwig and Wetie (Schmidt) B.; m. Eva Margaret Taylor, Sept. 7, 1947; children: Barbara Ann, Edith Elizabeth, Anne Catherine, John Ludwig. B.E.E., Poly. Inst. Bklyn., 1950, M.E.E., 1955, D.E.E., 1959. Elec. engr. Allied Control Co., N.Y.C., 1950-51; head electronics dept. Anton Electronics Labs., Inc., Bklyn., 1951-55; instr. elec. engring. Poly. Inst. Bklyn., 1955-59, asst. prof., 1959-62, asso. prof., 1962-66, prof. elec. and system engring., 1966-72; prof. engring. SUNY-Stony Brook, 1972-79, dir. bioengring. program, 1976-79, dir. lab., 1979-82, prof. computer sci., 1982—, dir. Acad. Computing Lab., 1982; dir. Nat. Inst. Microcomputer Based Learning; lectr., med. scientist Downstate Med Center, 1970—; cons. Vertol div. Boeing Co., Gen. Electric Co., Ford Found., NSF, Nat. Inst. Edn., IBM. Author: (with E. Mishkin) Adaptive Control Systems, 1961; contbg. author: Signals and Systems in Electrical Engineering, 1962, Perry's Chemical Engineering Handbook, 1962, System Engineering Handbook, 1965, Computer Techniques in Biomedicine and Medicine, 1973; Mem. editorial bd.: T.H.E. Jour. Served with AUS, 1944-46. Mem. IEEE, Sigma Xi, Tau Beta Pi, Eta Kappa Nu. Home: 11 Parsons Dr Dix Hills NY 11746 Office: Old Westbury NY 11568

BRAUN, MATITIAHU, violinist, violist; b. Jerusalem, Israel, Mar. 22, 1940; s. Ze'ev Itzhak and Sarah (Datz) B.; m. Melanie Washburn Moseley.; children: David, Elyssa. Grad., Israeli Acad. Music, Tel Aviv, 1961; postgrad., Juilliard Sch. Music, 1962-66. Mem., N.Y. Philharm., 1969—; prin. violist, Dallas Symphony Orch., 1978-79; solo violinist and violist, Philharmonia Virtuosi of N.Y., 1975-78. Office: Avery Fisher Hall Lincoln Center New York NY *I am very lucky to be part of a profession I dearly love.*

BRAUN, RICHARD LANE, lawyer, university administrator; b. Los Angeles, Oct. 18, 1917; s. Joseph George and Vera Louise (Lane) B.; m. Elizabeth H., Dec. 30, 1964; children from previous marriage: Susan, Richard L., Jeffrey. B.A., Stanford U., 1941; J.D., Georgetown U., 1951, LL.M., 1953. Bar: D.C. 1951, Calif. 1961, Va. 1963, Mich. 1969, Ohio 1974, N.C. 1982. Commd. 2d lt., pilot U.S. Marine Corps, 1942, advanced through grades to lt. col., 973; ret., 1961; prof. Georgetown U. Law Sch., 1961-64; practice law, Springfield, Va., 1963-65; dep. U.S. asst. atty. gen. Dept. Justice, 1965-68; dir. govt. relations and info. Automobile Mfrs. Assn., 1968-70; prof., dean U. Detroit Law Sch., 1970-74; dean U. Dayton Law Sch., 1974-80; prof. Campbell U. Law Sch., 1980—; Trustee Aviation Hall of Fame; mem. N.C. Commn. on Criminal Law, 1981; reporter N.C. Superior Ct. Judges Pattern Instrns. to Jury Com. Contbr. articles to profl. jours. Decorated D.F.C. (6), Bronze Star, Air medals (22). Mem. Am. Bar Assn., Ohio Bar Assn. (chmn. spl. com. law related edn. 1976-80), Dayton Bar Assn., N.C. Bar Assn., Dayton Public Def. Assn. (vice chmn. 1974-77), Am. Law Inst. Methodist. Home: 242 Lakeview Dr Sanford NC 27330 Office: Campbell U Law Sch Bules Creek NC *I've never had an easy job, but believe that faith, persistence, patience and courage make it possible to handle most problems; and don't forget some fun along the way.*

BRAUN, THEODORE E.D., educator; b. Bklyn., Apr. 18, 1933; s. Leopold and Genevieve (Gersitz) B.; m. Anne Wildman, Sept. 4, 1965; 1 dau., Jeanne Rebecca. B.A., St. John's U., N.Y.C., 1955; M.A., U. Calif.-Berkeley, 1961, Ph.D., 1965. Tchr. Bishop Loughlin High Sch., Bklyn., 1954-55, Lycee Emile-Loubet, Valence, France, 1955-56; mem. faculty U. Wis.-Milw., 1964-70; prof. French and comparative lit. U. Del., Newark, 1970—. Author: Un Ennemi de Voltaire, 1972, (with Paul Barrette) First French, 1964, 1970, Second French, 1968, (with G. Culley) Aeschylus, Voltaire and Le Franc de Pomignan's Promethee, 1976, (with V. Baker) Teaching the 18th Century, 1979; numerous articles and revs. Fulbright grantee, 1955-56; grantee Frank L. Weil Inst. Advanced Study, 1981-82; NEH grantee, 1974. Mem. AAUP, MLA, Alliance Francaise, Am. Assn. Tchrs. of French, Am. Soc. 18th Century Studies, East Central Soc. for 18th Century Studies, Am. Comparative Lit. Assn. Office: Langs and Lit Dept Univ Del Newark DE 19711 *By attempting to focus on the postive aspects of students' performances and colleagues' achievements, I have fought the temptation to negative criticism which is so strong in my profession. I believe that this attitude has in itturn contributed towards making me a better person and towards improving the quality of my teaching and research.*

BRAUN, WALTER GUSTAV, educator; b. Springfield, Mass., June 23, 1917; s. Gustav Franz and Alma Emma (Voigt) B.; m. Gloria Jean McCurdy, June 20, 1948; children—Karen Jean, Kenneth Walter. B.Chem. Engring., Cooper Union, 1942; M.S., Pa. State U., 1948, Ph.D., 1955. Jr. chemist Tide Water Asso. Oil Co., Bayonne, N.J., 1936-42; research asst. Pa. State U., 1943-47, instr., 1947-56, asso. prof., 1956-64, prof., 1964—, asst. dean engring., 1970-74, asso. dean engring., 1974-80; ret., 1980. Editor: Technical Data Book - Petroleum

Refining, rev. edit, 1971. Fellow Am. Inst. Chemists; mem. Am. Chem. Soc., Am. Inst. Chem. Engrs., Am. Soc. Engring. Edn., Sigma Xi, Phi Lambda Upsilon, Alpha Chi Sigma. Patentee, publs. in field. Home: 199 Twigs Ln State College PA 16801

BRAUN, WILLIAM JOSEPH, insurance company executive; b. Belleville, Ill., May 21, 1925; s. Walter Charles and Florence (Lauer) B.; m. Elizabeth Ann Braun, July 7, 1951; children: Brian William, Roger Edward, Christopher Burnes, Thomas Barrett, Maura Tracey. B.S. in Mktg, U. Ill., 1949; grad., Inst. Life Ins. Mktg., So. Methodist U., 1950. C.L.U.; chartered fin. cons. Life underwriter Mass. Mut. Life Ins. Co., Decatur, Ill., 1949—; pres. Am. Soc. C.L.U.'s, 1976-77; bd. dirs. Am. Coll. C.L.U.'s, Bryn Mawr, Pa., 1975-78. Bd. dirs. Boys Club of Decatur. Served with USNR, 1943-46. Decorated Navy Air medal. Life mem. Million Dollar Round Table; mem. Assn. Advanced Life Underwriting, Nat. Assn. Life Underwriters., Nat. Assn. Estate Planning Councils (dir.). Roman Catholic. Clubs: Decatur, Decatur Racquet, K.C. Home: 141 Hightide St Decatur IL 62521 Office: PO Box 1446 Decatur IL 62525

BRAUN, ZEV, motion picture producer; b. Chgo., Oct. 19, 1928; s. Julius and Charlotte (Brandau) B.; m. Joan Marie Wilkes, June 23, 1951 (div. July 1970); children: Benjamin, Jonathan, Jeremy; m. MayLing Cheng, Mar. 22, 1972; 1 dau., Sue-Ling. Student, Roosevelt U., Chgo., 1948, Marquette U., 1950, U. Chgo., 1964. Supt., later v.p. sales and dir. Braun-Hobar, Milw., 1951-55; v.p. sales, dir. W. Braun Co., Chgo., 1955-63; pres. div. Braun Internat., Inc. (exports), 1964-65. Producer: film Goldstein, 1964 (U.S. rep. Cannes Film Festival, also recipient Prix de La Nouvelle Critique); exec. producer: Madron, 1970; co-producer: The Pedestrian, 1972-73 (Golden Globe award); pres.: Zev Braun Prodns., 1971; producer: Wanted: Babysitter, 1974-75, The Little Girl Who Lives Down the Lane, 1975 (Best Horror Film, Acad. Sci-Fi, Fantasy and Horror Films), Freedom Road, 1978, The Fiendish Plot of Dr. Fu Manchu, 1979-80; exec. producer: Angela, 1976. Bd. dirs. Little City Found., Palatine, Ill., 1962-63; v.p., dir. Gastro-Intestinal Research Found., U. Chgo., 1964-65; v.p. City of Hope, 1970—; gen. chmn. Ann. Salute to Med. Research, 1969; chmn. UCLA Kidney Inst., 1980. Jewish. Home: 97 W Fremont Pl Los Angeles CA 90005 Office: 291 S La Cienega 33 Penthouse Beverly Hills CA 90211

BRAUNSCHWEIGER, CHRISTIAN CARL, educator; b. Wellsville, N.Y., Oct. 18, 1926; s. Christian and Katherine (Schlenker) B.; m. H. Patricia Kearns, Aug.22, 1953; children—Michael, Susan, Kathleen, Steven, Mary Pat. B.A., Alfred U., 1950; M.S., U. Wis.-Madison, 1951, Ph.D., 1955. Draftsman Air Preheater Corp., Wellsville, N.Y., 1946-50; teaching asst. U. Wis.-Madison, 1950-55; instr. Purdue U., 1955-57; asst., then asso. prof. U. Del., Newark, 1957-67; prof. math. Marquette U., Milw., 1967—, chmn. dept., 1970-73; cons. DuPont Co. Reviewer, Academic Press, John Wiley and Sons, McGraw Hill Pubs.; contbr. articles to profl. jours; revs. in Zentralblatt, 1955—. Served with USNR, 1944-46. Recipient research grants NSF, Office Naval Research, U. Del. Research Found., Marquette Com. Research; NSF Sci. Faculty fellowship, Heidelberg, Germany, 1964-65; Wis. Alumni Research Found. fellowship, 1950-52. Mem. AAUP, Del. Acad. Sci., Am. Math. Soc., Math. Assn. Am., Wis. Acad. Letters and Sci., Pi Mu Epsilon, Pi Delta Mu, Alpha Mu Theta, Sigma Xi. Home: 12505 Centa Ln Elm Grove WI 53122

BRAUNSTEIN, DONALD W., publisher; b. N.Y.C., Dec. 24, 1936; s. Solomon and Ethel (Tackel) B.; m. Robert Braunstein, July 5, 1959; children: Brandy, Douglas. B. Chem. Engring., Poly. Inst. Bklyn., 1957; M.B.A., NYU, 1967. Chem. engr. Allied Chem. Corp., Buffalo, 1957-68; sr. v.p. Doubleday Book Clubs, N.Y.C., 1968-77; exec. v.p. Dell Pub. Co., N.Y.C., 1977-80; pres., publisher Putnam Pub. Group, Children's Books, N.Y.C., 1980—. Office: Putnam Pub Group 51 Madison Ave New York NY 11746

BRAUNSTEIN, PHILLIP, educator, radiologist; b. Carlsbad, Czechoslovakia, Feb. 22, 1930; came to U.S., 1967; s. Judah and Adele (Kleinman) B.; m. Norma Cohen, Mar. 27, 1955; 1 son, Danny. B.Sc., Univ. Coll. London, 1951; M.D., Durham U., 1957. Diplomate: Am. Bd. Radiology, Royal Coll. Physicians and Surgeons of Can., Am. Bd. Nuclear Medicine. Intern Royal Victoria Infirmary, Newcastle, Eng., 1957-58; resident U. Toronto, 1965-69, Michael Reese Hosp., Chgo., 1965-69; instr. radiology N.Y. Med. Coll., N.Y.C., 1970-73, assoc. prof., 1973-77, prof., 1973-77, dir. nuclear medicine, 1971-80; dir. nuclear medicine, prof. radiology U. Calif. Med. Sch., Irvine, 1980—; cons. VA Hosp., N.Y.C., 1972-80, Naval Med. Ctr., San Diego, 1981, VA Hosp., Long Beach, Calif., 1982—, Pres.'s Commn. Study of Ethical Problems in Medicine, 1980-81. Contbr. articles to profl. jours.; co-inventor new radiopharmaceutical, 1982. Served to capt. Brit. Army, 1958-60. NIH grantee, 1973. Mem. Soc. Nuclear Medicine (acad. council), Am. Coll. Radiology. Jewish. Office: U Calif at Irvine Med Ctr 101 City Dr Orange CA 92668

BRAUNSTEIN, RUBIN, educator; b. N.Y.C., May 6, 1922; s. Benjamin and Beatrice (Brunman) B.; m. Jacqueline Berkowitz, Oct. 2, 1948; children—Mark Benjamin, David Phillip. B.S., N.Y. U., 1948; M.S., Syracuse U., 1951, Ph.D., 1954. Research asso. molecular beams Columbia U., 1952-53; mem. research staff solid state physics RCA Labs., Princeton, N.J., 1953-64; asso. prof. physics U. Cal. at Los Angeles, 1964, prof., 1964—; cons. Radio Corp. Am. Labs., 1964—. Served with AUS, 1943-45. Sci. Research Council fellow Oxford, 1974-75. Fellow Am. Phys. Soc.; mem. A.A.A.S. Research, publications patentee molecular beams; microwave spectroscopy; solid state physics; quantum electronics. Home: 1107 Vista Grande Dr Pacific Palisades CA 90272 Office: Dept Physics U Cal at Los Angeles Los Angeles CA 90024

BRAUTIGAN, RICHARD, author; b. 1935. Author: A Confederate General from Big Sur, 1965, Trout Fishing in America, 1967, The Pill Versus the Springhill Mine Disaster, 1968, In Watermelon Sugar, 1969, Rommel Drives on Deep into Egypt, 1970, The Abortion: An Historical Romance, 1971, Revenge of the Lawn, 1971, The Hawkline Monster-A Gothic Western, 1974, Willard and His Bowling Trophies: A Perverse Mystery, 1975, Sombrero Fallout: A Japanese Novel, 1976, Dreaming of Babylon: A Private Eye Novel 1942, 1977, June 30th, June 30th, 1978, The Tokyo-Montana Express, 1980 *

BRAVERMAN, CHARLES DELL, film producer, director; b. Los Angeles, Mar. 3, 1944; s. Herbert and Charlotte (Braverman); m. Pamela Goodman, Nov. 19, 1978. B.A. in Cinema, U. So. Calif., 1967. Free-lance cameraman, 1962-70; resident filmmaker: Smothers Bros. Comedy Hour, TV show, Hollywood, Calif., 1968-69; pres., producer, dir., Braverman Prodns., Los Angeles, 1969—; producer, dir.: films, including Breathe a Sigh of Relief, 1973 (Emmy award for Best Documentary), The Television Newsman, 1976 (Emmy award for Best Documentary), American Time Capsule, 1968. Served with USAFR, 1968. Mem. Dirs. Guild Am., Acad. Motion Picture Arts and Scis., Acad. TV Arts and Scis. Developed technique of kinestasis, animating of stills and graphics to form film montage, as in Am. Time Capsule. Office: care Internat Creative Mgmt 8899 Beverly Blvd Los Angeles CA 90048 *

BRAVERMAN, IRWIN M., educator, dermatologist; b. Boston, Apr. 17, 1929; s. Morris and Molly (Singer) B.; m. muriel S. Freedman, June 5, 1955; children: Paula, David, Michael. A.B., Harvard U., 1951; M.D., Yale U., 1955. Diplomate: Am. Bd. Med. Examiners, Am. Bd. Dermatology, Am. Bd. Pathology. Practice medicine specializing in dermatology New Haven; asst. prof. dermatology Yale U., New Haven, 1962-68, assoc. prof., 1968-73, prof., 1973—. Author: Skin Signs of Systemic Disease, 1970, 2d edit., 1980; contbr. articles to profl. jours. Capt. U.S. Army, 1956-58. Recipient Mr. and Mrs. J.N. Taub Internat. Meml. award for research in psoriasis Baylor Med. Coll., 1980. Mem. New Eng. Dermatologic Soc., Am. Dermatol. Assn., Am. Acad. Dermatology (dir. 1980-83), Soc. Investigative Dermatology (dir. 1982—), Am. Fedn. Clin. Research, AMA. Office: Yale U Med Sch 333 Cedar St New Haven CT 06510

BRAVERMAN, ROBERT JAY, diversified company executive; b. N.Y.C., Mar. 4, 1933; s. Arthur and Ruth Edith (Beck) B.; m. Alice Glantz, Dec. 24, 1954; 1 son, John; m. Claire Hurney, Dec. 31, 1964; children: Sam, Amy. A.B. magna cum laude, Columbia U., 1954; postgrad., Harvard U. Sch. Law, 1956-57, Sch. Bus., 1963. With Harbridge House, Inc. (Mgmt. Cons.), Cambridge, Mass., 1957-66; with ITT, N.Y.C., 1966—, now sr. v.p., chmn., chief exec. officer communications and info. services. Served with U.S. Army, 1954-56. Mem. Phi Beta Kappa. Home: 235 W 76th St New York NY 10023 Office: 100 Plaza Dr Secaucus NJ

BRAWLEY, PAUL HOLM, editor; b. Granite City, Ill., Sept. 27, 1942; s. Paul Virgil and Lucille Melba (Holm) B. B.A. in English, So. Ill. U., 1965; M.S. in L.S, Simmons Coll., Boston, 1968. Recs. librarian Boston Pub. Library, 1965-66, audio-visual librarian, 1966-68; nonprint revs. editor The Booklist (A.L.A.), Chgo., 1969-73, editor-in-chief, art dir., 1973—; Guest lectr. library sci. Kent State U., L.I. U., Dalhousie U., Halifax, N.S., Syracuse U., U. Wash., Seattle. Active Hunger Project. Mem. ALA, Sigma Pi, Phi Eta Sigma.

BRAWNER, LEE BASIL, librarian; b. Seguin, Tex., May 1, 1935; s. Lee Basil and Thelma (Davenport) B.; m. Nancy Jayne Wallis, Dec. 6, 1958; children: Betsy Lynn, Allen Lee. Student, Tex. A. and M. U., 1953-55; B.A., North Tex. State U., 1957; M.A., George Peabody Coll. Tchrs., 1960. Head popular library and circulation dept. Dallas Pub. Library, 1958-60, head Lakewood br., 1961-62, chief br. services, 1964-67; dir. Waco (Tex.) Pub. Library, 1962-64; asst. state librarian Tex. State Library, 1967-71; dir. Met. Library System, Oklahoma City, 1971—; adj. prof. Grad. Sch. Library Sci., Tex. Women's U.; trustee AMIGOS Bibliog. Council, v.p., 1980-81; Chmn. Okla. Humanities Com., 1977-78; adv. bd. Okla. Literacy Council, 1976—. Contbr. articles to profl. jours. Served with AUS, 1957-58. Mem. ALA (council 1978—, intellectual freedom com. 1979—), Okla. Library Assn. (chmn. library devel. 1982-83), Southwestern Library Assn. (pres. 1971-72), Assn. Specialized and Coop. Agys. (dir. 1977—), Freedom to Read Found. (trustee 1982—), ACLU, Okla. C. of C., Sigma Phi Epsilon. Office: Met Library System 131 Dean A McGee Oklahoma City OK 73102

BRAXTON, ANTHONY, composer; b. Chgo., June 4, 1945. Student, Chgo. Sch. Music, Chgo. Music Coll., Roosevelt U. Played clarinet with, Assn. for Advancement of Creative Music; then with, Art Ensemble of Chgo., in Europe, 1969; mem. jazz group, Circle, 1970-71; now leads own groups, U.S. and Europe; appeared as duo with guitarist, Derek Bailey in, London; soloist, Carnegie Hall, 1972, Chateau Le Rault, France, 1973, Burton Auditorium, Toronto, Ont., 1974; (with Joseph Jarman) albums include Together Alone, (with Derek Bailey) Duo 1 and Duo 2, (with Circle) Circle 1 and 2; solo Five Pieces, 1975, New York Fall, 1974, Creative Orchestra Music, 1976, Alto Sax Improv, 1979, 3 Compositions with Abrams Jenkins, 1980. Winner Record of Yr. award Downbeat Mag., 1976; named Clarinetist of Yr.; winner Downbeat Jazz Critics Poll, 1979. Office: care Rasa Artists 144 W 27th St New York NY 10001 *

BRAY, ARTHUR PHILIP, corporation executive; b. San Francisco, Sept. 23, 1933; s. Arthur T. and Anna F. (Nevin) B.; m. Grace McCarthy, June 16, 1956; children: Bernard, Peter, Erin, Eileen, Mary, Florence. A.A., San Francisco City Coll., 1953; B.S.M.E. with highest honors, U. Calif., Berkeley, 1955. With Gen. Electric Co., 1955—, v.p., gen. mgr. nuclear power systems div., San Jose, Calif., 1978—; dir. Gen. Electric Tech. Services Co.; Mem. dean's adv. council Sch. Engring., San Jose State U. Co-author: Nuclear Power and the Public, 1970. Bd. regents Bellarmine Coll. Prep., San Jose., U. Santa Clara. Recipient Ernest O. Lawrence Meml. award U.S. Dept. Energy, 1977. Mem. Nat. Acad. Engring., Am. Nuclear Soc., Atomic Indsl. Forum, ASME, Phi Beta Kappa, Tau Beta Pi, Pi Tau Sigma. Republican. Roman Catholic. Patentee in field. Office: 175 Curtner Ave San Jose CA 95125

BRAY, CHARLES WILLIAM, III, ambassador; b. N.Y.C., Oct. 24, 1933; s. Charles William and Katherine (Owsley) B.; children—Charles W., David C., Katherine M. A.B., Princeton U., 1955; postgrad., Universite de Bordeaux, France, 1955-56, U. Md., 1966-67. With Dept. State, 1958-77, dep. asst. sec. for inter-Am. affairs, 1976-77; dep. dir. Internat. Communication Agy., Washington, 1977-81; Am. ambassador to Senegal, 1981—; adj. lectr. U. Georgetown. Served with U.S. Army, 1956-58. Fulbright fellow, 1955-56; Presdl. fellow, 1966-67. Mem. Council on Fgn. Relations. Club: Cosmos. Office: Dakar Dept State Washington DC 20520

BRAY, DAVID MAURICE, hospital and medical school administrator; b. Abilene, Tex., Feb. 21, 1941; s. Andrew Maurice and Mauress Laneyl (Brown) B.; m. Louise Hardin, Aug. 22, 1964; children: Louisa, Andrew. B.A., So. Meth. U., 1963; postgrad., Oxford (Eng.) U., 1963-64, U. Md., 1964-66. With Office Mgmt. and Budget, Exec. office of Pres., Washington, 1965-76, asst. chief econ. affairs internat. programs div., 1969-73, dep. asso. dir. for econs. and govt., 1973-76; spl. asst. for econ. affairs to dir. CIA, Washington, 1973; asso. v.p. bus. and fin. Med. Center, U. Chgo., 1976-78, asso. v.p. adminstrn. and exec. dir. hosps. and clinics, 1978-82; dean for fin. and adminstrn. Harvard Med. Sch., 1982—. Mem. Am. Econs. Assn., Am. Assn. Med. Colls., Council Teaching Hosps., Am. Hosp. Assn., Ill. Hosp. Assn. Methodist. Home: 25 Shady Brook Ln Belmont MA 02178 Office: 25 Shattuck St Boston MA 02115

BRAY, ERCELL G., mortgage banker; b. Lovelady, Tex., Apr. 5, 1917; s. Alec G. and Lillian (Thomas) B.; m. Mary F. Bray, Dec. 31, 1938; children: Larry, Patricia, Alex, Elizabeth. B.S., Sam Houston State U., 1935. Clk. Fed. Land Bank, Houston, 1937-41; acct. Houston Oil Field Material, 1941-42, Todd Houston Shipyard, 1942-45; exec. v.p. Lomas & Nettleton Co., Houston, 1945—. Served with U.S. Army, 1945. Home: 1074 Bethlehem St Houston TX 77018 Office: Lomas and Nettleton Co 201 Main St Houston TX 77002

BRAY, OSCAR S., cons. engr.; b. Dover, N.J., Dec. 21, 1905; s. Oscar S. and Bertha (Janner) B.; m. Helen L. Shanley, Jan. 11, 1933; children—Helen Margaret (Mrs. William Allen Jeffers Jr.), Mary Elizabeth (Mrs. Edward Peters Womack). B.C.E., U. Cin., 1932. Surveyman D.L. & W. RR, Hoboken, N.J., 1923-27; constrn. supt. Nat. Park Service, Cold Spring, N.Y., 1934-35, field engr., Boston and Salem, Mass., 1936-38, engr., Washington, 1939-40; structural engr., asst. chief structural engr., project mgr. Jackson & Moreland, Boston, 1941-58; pres., chief engr. Jackson & Moreland Internat., Inc., 1959-68, Bray, Backenstoss, Inc. Ltd., Lynnfield, Mass., 1969-71; v.p. Camp Dresser & McKee Internat. Inc., Boston, 1972-76, cons., 1977—, sr. cons., 1980—; lectr. Northeastern U.; guest lectr. U. Ill. Mem. Lynnfield Planning Bd., 1968—, chmn., 1970; mem. Lynnfield Bd. Appeals, 1977-80. Served with AUS, 1933. Fellow ASCE (dir. 1964-66, pres. 1971-72), Am. Cons. Engrs. Council; mem. United Engr. Trustees Bd. (pres. 1980-81), Tau Beta Pi, Chi Epsilon, Sigma Alpha Epsilon. Republican. Presbyn. Home: 18 Lakeview Dr Lynnfield MA 01940 *I was fortunate to inherit from my parents, not material wealth but a sound body and a healthy, inquisitive and active mind, and from my mother, particularly, I acquired a set of values that have been useful to me all of my life.*

BRAY, PHILIP JAMES, physicist; b. Kansas City, Mo., Aug. 25, 1925; s. Harry James and Ruth (Moerdyke) B.; children—Carolyn, Philip James, Katherine. Sc.B. in Physics, Brown U., 1948; A.M., Harvard U., 1949, Ph.D., 1953. Asst. prof. physics Rensselaer Poly. Inst., 1952-55; asso. prof. physics Brown U., Providence, 1955-58, prof., 1958—, chmn. dept., 1963-68; vis. prof. dept. glass tech. U. Sheffield, Eng., 1961-62, 68-69; vis. prof. dept. chemistry U. Exeter, Eng., 1975-76. Asso. editor: Revs. Modern Physics, 1963-65; editorial bd.: Jour. Non-Crystalline Solids, 1968-71; Jour. Nonmetals, 1971-77, Jour. Biol. Physics, 1973-77. NSF fellow, 1961-62; Guggenheim fellow, 1968-69. Fellow Am. Phys. Soc. (chmn. New Eng. sect. 1965-67), Soc. Glass Tech., Korean Phys. Soc., Am. Acad. Arts and Scis., AAAS, Sigma Xi (nat. lectr. 1969-70), Am. Ceramic Soc. (George W. Morey award for outstanding contributions to glass sci. and tech. 1970); mem. Internat. Soc. Magnetic Resonance, AAUP (pres. Brown chpt. 1973-75), N.Y. Acad. Scis., Am. Assn. Physics Tchrs., Groupement Ampere, Assn. Koreans of R.I. (hon.). Congregationalist. Home: 133 Power St Providence RI 02906 Office: Dept Physics Brown U Providence RI 02912

BRAY, PIERCE, telephone company executive; b. Chgo., Jan. 16, 1924; s. Harold A. and Margaret (Maclennan) B.; m. Maud Dorothy Minto, May 14, 1955; children—Margaret Dorothy, William Harold, Andrew Pierce. B.A., U. Chgo., 1948, M.B.A., 1949. Fin. analyst Ford Motor Co., Dearborn, Mich., 1949-55; cons. Booz, Allen & Hamilton, Chgo. and Manila, Phillipines, 1955-58; mgr. pricing, then corp. controller Cummins Engine Co., Columbus, Ind., 1958-66; v.p. fin. Weatherhead Co., Cleve., 1966-67; v.p. Mid-Continent Telephone Corp., Hudson, Ohio, 1967-70, treas., 1967-77, v.p. fin., 1970-81, exec. v.p. fin., 1981-83, exec. v.p., chief fin. officer, 1983—, dir., 1976—, chmn. various subs.; dir. Cardinal Fund, 1969—; trustee Cardinal Govt. Securities Trust, 1980—; instr. fin. and econs. U. Detroit, 1952-54; chmn. investor relations com. U.S. Ind. Telephone Assn., 1974—; chmn. exec. com. Inst. Public Utilities, 1981—. Mem. alumni council U. Chgo. Sch. Bus., 1967; Trustee Beech Brook Children's Home, Pepper Pike, Ohio, 1972—, treas., 1976-79, pres., 1979-81. Served with AUS, 1943-46. Mem. Fin. Execs. Inst., Cleve. Treasurers Club, Delta Upsilon. Presbyterian. Clubs: Union, Midday (Cleve.); Downtown Athletic (N.Y.C.); Walloon Yacht (chmn. bd. 1980-81, commodore 1981—), Walloon Lake Country.). Home: 31173 Northwood Dr Pepper Pike OH 44124 Office: 100 Executive Pkwy Hudson OH 44236

BRAY, R(OBERT) BRUCE, music educator; b. LaGrande, Oreg., July 24, 1924; s. Ernest C. and Leta M. (Haight) B.; m. Donna Marie Siegman, July 2, 1949 (div. 1980); children: Stephen Louis, Ruth Elizabeth, Katherine Ernestine, Anne-Marie. B.A., U. Oreg., 1949, M.Mus., 1955; cert., U. Strasbourg, (France), 1951; postgrad., U. Wash., 1960-61. Music tchr. Harold McCune Jr. High Sch., Pendleton, Oreg., 1951-54; dir. choral music Albany (Oreg.) Union High Sch., 1954-56; music supr. Ashland (Oreg.) Public Schs., 1956-57; asst. prof. music Central Wash. U., Ellensburg, 1957-60; prof. music U. Idaho, Moscow, 1961-68, sec. faculty, editor acad. publs., 1968—. Editor: Oreg. Music Educator, 1954-57, Wash. Music Educator, 1957-60, U. Idaho Music, 1961-68, Idaho Music Notes, 1963-68, U. Idaho Register, 1974—; editorial bd.: Music Educators Jour, 1968-70. Served with USNR, 1942-46. Mem. Music Educators Nat. Conf. (bd. dirs., pres. N.W. div. 1963-65, nat. exec. com. 1964-66), AAUP, Phi Mu Alpha Sinfonia. Democrat. Episcopalian. Home: 208 Henley Ave Apt 3 Moscow ID 83843 *As it turned out, it was my respect for, and consequent facility in, the English language that opened the most important doors.*

BRAYBROOKE, DAVID, philosophy educator; b. Hackettstown, N.J., Oct. 18, 1924; s. Walter Leonard and Netta Rose (Foyle) B.; m. Alice Boyd Noble, Dec. 31, 1948 (div. 1981); children: Nicholas, Geoffrey, Elizabeth Page. Student, Hobart Coll., 1941-43, New Sch. Social Research, 1942, Downing Coll., Cambridge, 1945, Columbia U., 1946; B.A., Harvard U., 1948; M.A., Cornell U., 1951, Ph.D., 1953; postgrad. (Am. Council Learned Socs. fellow), New Coll., Oxford, 1952-53, 1959-60. Instr. history and lit. Hobart and William Smith Colls., Geneva, N.Y., 1948-50; teaching fellow econs. Cornell U., Ithaca, N.Y., 1950-52; instr. philosophy U. Mich., Ann Arbor, 1953-54, Bowdoin Coll., Brunswick, Maine, 1954-56; asst. prof. philosophy Yale U., New Haven, 1956-63; asso. prof. philosophy and politics Dalhousie U., Halifax, N.S., Can., 1963-65, prof., 1965—; dean liberal arts Bridgeport (Conn.) Engring. Inst., 1961-63; vis. prof. philosophy U. Pitts., 1965, 66, U. Toronto, Can., 1966-67, Bowling Green State U. (Ohio), 1982; vis. prof. polit. sci. Hill Found., U. Minn., Mpls., 1971, U. Calif., Irvine, 1980, U. Chgo., 1984; mem. Council Philos. Studies, 1974-79. Author: (with C.E. Lindblom) A Strategy of Decision: Policy Evaluation as a Social Process, 1963, Three Tests for Democracy: Personal Rights; Human Welfare; Collective Preference, 1968, Traffic Congestion Goes Through the Issue-Machine, 1974, Ethics in the World of Business, 1983; contbr. articles to profl. jours.; editor: Philosophical Problems of the Social Sciences, 1965; monograph series Philosophy in Canada, 1973-78; cons. editor: Philos. Studies, 1972-76; editorial bd.: Am. Polit. Sci. Rev., 1970-72; monograph series Ethics, 1979—; Dialogue, 1974-78, 81—. Mem. nat. acad. adv. panel Can. Council, Ottawa, 1968-71; Chmn. Town Democratic Com., Guilford, Conn., 1961-62. Served with AUS, 1943-46. Guggenheim fellow, 1962-63; Social Scis. and Humanities Research Council Can. fellow, 1978-79. Fellow Royal Soc. Can.; mem. Can. Philos. Assn. (pres. 1971-72), Can. Assn. Univ. Tchrs. (v.p. 1974-75, pres. 1975-76), Can. Polit. Sci. Assn., Am. Polit. Sci. Assn. (v.p. 1981-82), Am. Philos. Assn. (exec. com. Eastern div. 1976-79), Am. Soc. Polit. and Legal Philosophy, Friends of the Lake Dist. (life), Can. Peace Research and Edn. Assn., Amnesty Internat., Phi Beta Kappa. Home: 6045 Fraser St Halifax NS B3H 1R7 Canada

BRAYER, MENACHEM MENDEL, psychologist; b. Poland, Mar. 9, 1922; s. Joseph Rabbi and Mollie (Morgenstern) B.; m. Mimi Friedman Boyan, June 18, 1952; children: Yigal Israel, Nehama, Nahum Dov. M.H.L., Yeshiva U., 1949, D.H.L., 1950, Ph.D. in Clin. Psychology, 1958; diploma in psychoanalysis, N.Y. Soc. Psychoanalysis, 1962. Staff psychologist Yeshiva U., N.Y.C., 1959-62, cons. psychologist, 1959—, chmn. Hebrew dept., 1950-55; assoc. prof. Yeshiva Coll. and Grad. Sch. Edn., 1960-66; prof. edn. and Bibl. lit., chmn. dept. Jewish edn. Ferrauf Grad. Sch., 1970-79, Stone-Sapirstein prof. Jewish edn., 1979—; asst. prof. Bible Stern Coll., 1955-60; Cons. to Mayor of N.Y. Com. on Drug Abuse; v.p. Mesivta Tiferet Israel of Rushin, Jerusalem. Author works in field. Jewish Meml. Found. fellow; Am. Found. Jewish Culture fellow. Mem. Am. Psychol. Assn., N.Y. State Psychol. Assn., N.Y. Soc. Psychoanalytic Study, Hebrew Acad. Jewish Learning, Hebrew Pen Club. *

BRAYMAN, HAROLD, public relations consultant; b. Middleburgh, N.Y., Mar. 10, 1900; s. Channing and Minnie C. (Feeck) B.; m. Martha Witherspoon Wood, Jan. 25, 1930; children: Harold Halliday, Walter Witherspoon. A.B., Cornell U., 1920; LL.D. (hon.), Gettysburg Coll., 1965. Tchr. English and history Ft. Lee (N.J.) High Sch., 1920-22; reporter Albany (N.Y.) Evening Jour., 1922-24; asst. legislative corr. N.Y. Evening Post, 1924-26, corr., 1926-1928, Washington corr., 1928-33, Phila. Evening Ledger; writer syndicated column Daily Mirror of Washington, 1934-40; Washington corr. Houston Chronicle and other newspapers, 1940-42; spl. corr. in, London, 1925, covered all nat. convs. and nat. polit. campaigns, 1928-40; asst. dir., public relations dept. E.I. du Pont de Nemours & Co., 1942-44, dir., 1944-65; corporate exec. in residence Am. U., 1968; Dir. Continental Am. Life Ins. Co.; Bd. visitors sch. pub. relations and communications Boston U., chmn., 1961-71. Editor: Pub. Relations Jour, 1956; author: Corporate Management in a World of Politics, 1967, Developing a Philosophy for Business Action, 1969, (with A.O.H. Grier) A History of the Lincoln Club of Delaware, 1970, The President Speaks Off-the-Record, 1976. Bd. dirs. Greater Wilmington Devel. Council, Cornell U. Council; chmn. Cornell U. Council, 1961-63; mem. Cornell Centennial planning com., also chmn. adv. council grad. sch. bus. and pub. adminstrn., 1960-65; Trustee emeritus Gettysburg Coll.; Trustee Found. for Pub. Relations Research and Edn., 1956-62, Wilmington Med. Center.; Mem. sponsoring com. Pub. Relations Seminar, 1952-61. Recipient citation Pub. Relations Soc. Am., 1963; Golden Plate award Am. Acad. Achievement, 1965. Mem. U.S. C. of C. (com. on taxation 1954-60, com. on govt. ops. and expenditures 1964-66), Am. Acad. Achievement (v.p. 1966-74), Mfg. Chemists Assn. (pub. relations adv. com. 1951-56, chmn. 1951-53). Clubs: Rotarian., University (N.Y.C.); Gridiron (pres. 1941), Nat. Press (pres. 1938), Overseas Writers (Washington); Wilmington, Wilmington Country (dir. 1952-64), Greenville Country (Wilmington, Del.)). Accompanied Alfred E. Smith through 1928 campaign and F.D. Roosevelt through 1932 campaign for N.Y. Evening Post, Phila. Public Ledger and Phila. Evening Ledger. Home: Greenville PO Box 3831 Wilmington DE 19807 Office: 11728 Montchanin Bldg Wilmington DE 19801

BRAZAITIS, THOMAS JOSEPH, journalist; b. Cleve., Aug. 8, 1940; s. Joseph R. and Regina G. (Greicius) B.; m. Sheila J. Loftus, Nov. 27, 1965; children: Mark Thomas, Sarah Jean. B.S., John Carroll U., Cleve., 1962. Mng. editor newspapers Collinwood Pub. Corp., Cleve., 1964-71; reporter, then Washington corr. Cleve. Plain Dealer, 1971-79, Washington bur. chief, 1979—. Served to 1st lt. USAR, 1962-64. Mem. Sigma Delta Chi. Office: 930 Nat Press Bldg Washington DC 20045

BRAZEAU, JACQUES, sociologist; b. Riguad, Que., Can., Sept. 5, 1923; s. Denis and Isabelle (St. Denis) B.; m. Alma De Chantal, Dec. 27, 1951; 1 dau., Francine. B.A, McGill U., Montreal, Que., 1949, M.A., 1951; Ph.D., U. Chgo., 1961. Officer Def. Sci. Service, Def. Research Bd., Toronto, Ont., Can., 1953-60; asst. prof. sociology U. Montreal, 1960-61, assoc. prof., 1961-68, prof., 1968—, chmn. dept. sociology, 1965-67; dir. Survey Research Ctr., 1969-75; vice-dean grad. studies U. Montreal, 1972-79; dean grad. studies Survey Research Ctr., 1979—; cons. to Can. and Que. govts. UNESCO. Served with Royal Can. Air Force, 1942-46. Fellow Royal Soc. Can.; mem. Can. Assn. Anthropology and Sociology, Internat. Sociol. Assn., Assn. Internationale des Sociologies de langue francaise. Research, publs. on sociolinguistice, ethnic relations, professions. Office: Dept Sociology U Montreal 2900 Boul Edouard Montpetit Montreal PQ Canada H3C 3J7

BRAZELL, JAMES ERVIN, lawyer, oil co. exec.; b. Cromwell, Okla., Sept. 11, 1926; s. John Edward and Eva May (Black) B.; m. Peggy Lee Carson, Feb. 9, 1951; children—James, Mary Margaret, April Kay. B.S. in Mech. Engring, Okla. State U., 1950; J.D., U. Tulsa, 1959. Bar: Okla. bar 1959, U.S. Supreme Ct. bar 1976. With Texaco Inc., various locations, 1950—; exec. v.p. Texaco Can. Inc., Toronto, Ont., Can., 1978-80, staff dir. exploration and producting exec. com., White Plains, N.Y., 1980—; also dir. Served with USAF, 1945. Mem. Am. PetrPetroleum Inst., Soc. Petroleum Engrs., Okla. Bar Assn., Canadian Geographic Soc. Club: Granite (Toronto). Home: 114 Greenwich Hills Dr Greenwich CT 06830 Office: 2000 Westchester Ave White Plains NY 10650

BRAZELL, KAREN WOODARD, educator; b. Buffalo, Apr. 25, 1938; d. Charles Cary and Josephine Mary (Bordonaro) Woodard; m. James Reid Brazell, Aug. 27, 1961 (div. 1978); children—Katherine Ann, Stephen Reid. Student, Coll. Wooster, 1956-58, Internat. Christian U., Tokyo, Japan, 1958-60; B.A., U. Mich., 1961, M.A., 1962; Ph.D., Columbia, 1969. Asst. prof. Japanese lit. Princeton, 1969-74; asso. prof. Cornell U., Ithaca, N.Y., 1974-79, prof., 1979—, chmn. dept. Asian studies, 1977-82. Author: Confessions of Lady Nijo, 1973, Noh as Performance, 1977, Dance in the Noh Theater, 1981; assoc. editor: Jour. Japanese Studies, 1978—; contbr. articles and book revs. to profl. jours. Trustee Cornell U., 1979-83. Recipient Nat. Book award, 1974; Fulbright-Hayes fellow, 1972-73; Nat. Endowment Humanities fellow, summer 1974; Japan Found. fellow, 1978; Cornell U. Soc. Humanities fellow, 1976-77. Mem. Assn. Asian Studies, Assn. Tchrs. of Japanese (exec. com. 1981-83), Phi Beta Kappa (senator at large 1976-82, trustee found. 1977-82). Home: 311 Root St Ithaca NY 14850

BRAZELTON, WILLIAM THOMAS, engring, educator; b. Danville, Ill., Jan. 22, 1921; s. Edwin Thomas and Gertrude Ann (Carson) B.; m. Marilyn Dorothy Brown, Sept. 23, 1943; children—William Thomas, Nancy Ann. Student, Ill. Inst. Tech., 1939-41; B.S. in Chem. Engring, Northwestern U., 1943, M.S., 1948, Ph.D., 1952. Chem. engr. Central Process Corp., 1942-43; instr. chem. engring. Northwestern U., 1947-51, asst. prof., 1951-53, asso. prof., 1953-63, prof., 1963—, chmn. dept., 1955-56, asst. dean, 1960-61, asso. dean, 1961—; Engring. and ednl. cons., 1949—. Mem. Prospect Heights (Ill.) Bd. Edn., 1957-61. Mem. Am. Inst. Chem. Engrs. (chmn. Chgo. sect. 1966-67), Am. Chem. Soc., Am. Soc. Engring. Edn. (chmn. Ill.-Ind. sect. 1963-64, 73-74), Soc. for History of Tech., Soc. for Indsl. Archeology, Sigma Xi, Tau Beta Pi, Phi Lambda Epsilon, Alpha Chi Sigma, Triangle. Home: 10 E Willow Rd Prospect Heights IL 60070 Office: Technol Inst Northwestern U Evanston IL 60201

BRAZIER, DON ROLAND, railroad executive; b. Pittsburg, Kans., Mar. 30, 1921; s. Hosie O. and Lola Frances (Tow) B.; m. June Darla Harr, Nov. 8, 1941. B.C.S., Benjamin Franklin U., Washington, 1950, M.C.S., 1951. Civilian budget officer Ordnance Corps, Dept. Army, 1940-43, 46-54; asst. sec. def., 1954-67; comptroller Def. Supply Agt., 1967; dep. asst. sec. Army, 1967-68; prin. dep. asst. sec. def.-comptroller, 1968-74; treas. AMTRAK, 1974-75, v.p. fin., treas., 1975-82, group v.p. fin. and adminstrn., 1982—; dir. Washington Union Terminal; pres., dir. Chgo. Union Sta. Served with USAAF, 1943-46. Decorated Meritorious Service medal; recipient Def. Disting. Civilian Service award, 1971, 73, 74. Club: Myrtlewood Country (Myrtle Beach, S.C.). Office: 400 N Capitol St Washington DC 20001

BRAZIER, DONN PAUL, retired museum official; b. Dawson, Minn., Oct. 4, 1917; s. William A. and Bessie (Brown) B.; m. Betty Marion Deppiesse, July 2, 1942; children: Terry Edward, Michael Allan, Liza Lisette, Barry Brooks, Brett Lynn. B.S., U. Wis., 1940; postgrad., Marquette U., 1940-41. Ednl. curator Milw. Pub. Mus., 1946-57; TV tchr. pub. schs., Milw., 1957-58; ednl. supr. Mus. Sci. and Natural History, St. Louis, 1959-61; dir., 1961-83, dir. emeritus, 1983—. Served with USAAF, 1941-46. Recipient Disting. Alumnus award U. Wis. at Milw., 1967. Mem. Acad. Sci. St. Louis. Home: 1455 Fawn Valley St St Louis MO 63131

BRAZIER, ROBERT G., Student, Stanford U. With Airbone Aircraft Service Inc., 1953-63; v.p. ops. Pacific Air Freight Inc., 1963-68; sr. v.p. ops. Airbone Freight Corp., Seattle, 1968-73, exec. v.p., chief operating officer, 1973-78, pres., chief operating officer, dir., 1978—. Office: Airborne Freight Corp 190 Queen Anne N Seattle WA 98111 *

BRAZILLER, GEORGE, publisher. Pres. George Braziller Inc., N.Y.C. Office: George Braziller Inc One Park Ave New York NY 10016§

BRAZNELL, STUART DONIHOO, merchandising company executive; b. St. Louis, Jan. 2, 1942; s. Geroge Stuart and Bernice Jane (Donihoo) B.; m. Virginia Anne Flanery, Feb. 15, 1963; children: Julie Anne, Kathryn Virginia. Student, U. Mo., 1960-63. Vice pres. Braznell Co., St. Louis, 1963-72, Constrn. Assocs., 1972-74; asst. v.p. distbn. Mass. Merchandisers, Inc., Harrison, Ark., 1974-75, v.p. ops., Harrison, 1975-77, exec. v.p. ops., 1977-80, exec. v.p. sales and mktg., 1980-81, pres., 1982, exec. v.p. ops., 1983—. Mem. Nat. Assn. Service Merchandisers. Home: Delmar Route Harrison AR 72601 Office: Mass Merchandisers Inc PO Box 790 Harrison AR 72601

BREADY, RICHARD LAWRENCE, manufacturing company executive; b. Brookline, Mass., July 7, 1944; s. John Norbert and Catherine Rosalie B.; m. Loretta Lipman, July 16, 1971; 1 son, Barrett Wynn. B.A. in Econs, St. Anselm's Coll., Manchester, N.H., 1965; M.S. in Acctg, Northeastern U., Boston, 1966. C.P.A., Mass. With Arthur Andersen & Co. (C.P.A.'s), Boston, 1966-74, audit mgr., 1969-74; ind. cons., 1974-75; pres. Nortek, Inc. (multi-industry indsl. and consumer products mfg.), Cranston, R.I., 1975—. Mem. fin. com. New Eng. Conservatory of Music.; mem. U. R.I. Found.; mem. bus. adv. council, investment com. U. R.I. Served with USAR, 1966-67. Mem. Am. Inst. C.P.A.'s, Am. Mgmt. Assn., NAM. Home: 57 Valley Brook Dr East Greenwich RI 02818 Office: 815 Reservoir Ave Cranton RI 02910

BREAK, GEORGE FARRINGTON, economist, educator; b. London, Ont., Can., June 10, 1920; came to U.S., 1945, naturalized, 1951; s. Thomas Howard and Florence (Farrington) B.; m. Helen Dean Schnacke, July 31, 1948. B. Commerce, U. Toronto, 1942; Ph.D., U. Calif., Berkeley, 1951; Litt.D. (hon.), Hamilton Coll., 1974. Instr. Pomona Coll., Claremont, Calif., 1949-51; faculty U. Calif. at Berkeley, 1951—, prof. econs., 1963—, chmn. dept., 1969-73; cons. to govt., 1963—. Author: Intergovernmental Fiscal Relations in the United States, 1967, The Economic Impact of Federal Loan Insurance, 1961, (with E.R. Rolph) Public Finance, 1961, Federal Lending and Economic Stability, 1965, Agenda for Local Tax Reform, 1970, (with A.S. Blinder, R.M. Solow, P.O. Steiner, Dick Netzer) The Economics of Public Finance, 1974, (with J.A. Pechman) Federal Tax Reform: The Impossible Dream?, 1975, Financing Government in a Federal System, 1980. Served with RCAF, 1942-45. Home: 1844 Yosemite Rd Berkeley CA 94707

BREAKSTONE, ROBERT ALBERT, consumer products company executive; b. N.Y.C., Feb. 20, 1938; s. Morris and Minnie E. (Guon) B.; m. Eileen Fogel, Nov. 5, 1966; children: Warren, Ronald, David. B.S. in Math, CCNY, 1960; M.B.A. in Fin, CUNY, 1964. Systems mgr. IBM, N.Y.C., 1960-64; dir. mgmt. systems Continental Copper & Steel Industries, Inc., N.Y.C., 1964-68; v.p., treas. Systems Audits, Inc., N.Y.C., 1968-70; v.p., group exec. Chase Manhattan Bank, N.Y.C., 1970-74; pres. Health-Tex Inc. subs. Chesebrough-Pond's, Inc., Greenwich, Conn., 1974—; adj. asst. prof. Pace U., 1964-71, N.Y. U.; speaker in field. Bd. dirs. Stamford (Conn.) Mus. and Nature Center. Mem. Soc. Mgmt. Info. Systems, N.Am. Soc. Corporate Planning, Am. Apparel Mfrs. Assn. (dir.), Mu Gamma Tau (pres.). Home: 95 Lynam Rd Stamford CT 06903 Office: 33 Benedict Pl Greenwich CT 06830

BREAM, JULIAN, classical guitarist; b. London, Eng., July 15, 1933; s. Henry G. B. Ed., Royal Coll. Music. First recital, 1946, London debut, 1950, U.S. debut, 1958; formed, Julian Bream Consort, 1960; concerts in, Continental Europe, tours in, Japan, Australia, frequent radio, TV appearances; rec. artist for, RCA Victor, including; Malcolm Arnold's Guitar Concerto written for Bream. Served with Brit. Army, 1952-55. Decorated Order Brit. Empire. Research in Elizabethan lute music. Address: care Harold Shaw Concerts Inc 1995 Broadway New York NY 10023 *

BREAUX, JOHN B., congressman; b. Crowley, La., Mar. 1, 1944; s. Ezra H., Jr. and Katherine (Berlinger) B.; m. Lois Gail Daigle, Aug. 1, 1964; children: John B., William Lloyd, Elizabeth Andre, Julia Agnes. B.A. in Polit. Sci, U. Southwestern La., 1964; J.D., La. State U., 1967. Bar: La. 1967. Partner Brown, McKernan, Ingram & Breaux, 1967-68; legislative asst. to Congressman Edwin W. Edwards, 1968-69, dist. asst., 1969-72; mem. 92d-98th Congresses from 7th Dist. La.; mem. subcom. outer continental shelf, com. pub. works and transp. Mcht. Marine and fisheries com.; chmn. subcom. on fisheries and wildlife conservation and environ., mem. House Dem. Policy and Steering Com.; mem. Forum on Regulation, U.S. del. World Food Conf. Hon. chmn. La. March of Dimes. Recipient Am. Legion award; Moot Ct. finalist La. State U., 1966; Neptune award Am. Oceanic Orgn., 1980. Mem. La., Acadia Parish bar assns., Internat. Rice Festival Assn. (dir.), Crowley Jr. C. of C., La. Jr. C. of C., Pi Lambda Beta, Phi Alpha Delta, Lambda Chi Alpha. Democrat. Office: 2113 Rayburn Office Bldg Washington DC 20515

BREAZEALE, MACK ALFRED, physics educator; b. Leona Mines, Va., Aug. 15, 1930; s. Carl Samuel and Maude Ella (Moore) B.; m. Joanne Morton O'Dell, Oct. 4, 1952; children: Jennifer Lee, David Mark, William Carl. B.A., Berea Coll., 1953; M.S., U. Mo. at Rolla, 1954; Ph.D., Mich. State U., 1957. Asst. research prof. Mich. State U., 1957-62; assoc. prof. U. Tenn., 1962-67, prof. physics and astronomy, 1967—; cons. solid state div. Oak Ridge Nat. Lab., 1962-71; cons. Naval Research Labs., 1971—; prin. investigator contracts Office Naval Research, AEC, 1963—; Guest Inst. Basic Tech. Problems, Warsaw, Poland, 1972; vis. prof. Tech. U. of Denmark, 1977; guest U. Paris, 1977; mem. program com. Internat. Symposium on Nonlinear Acoustics, 1975, 76, 78, 81, 84. Contbr. articles to profl jours. Fulbright research fellow Tech. U., Stuttgart, Germany, 1958-59; NATO research grantee, 1978-81. Fellow Acoustical Soc. Am. (assoc. editor Nonlinear Acoustics 1977—), Inst. Acoustics (Gt. Brit.); mem. Am. Phys. Soc., IEEE (sr.), AAUP, Sigma Xi, Phi Kappa Phi, Sigma Pi Sigma. Home: 110 Greenbrier Dr Knoxville TN 37919 *Scientific progress ultimately depends upon absolute integrity and honesty. A scientist therefore must pursue Truth in such a manner that the path between himself and his goal can never be totally obstructed by any other human being.*

BREBBIA, JOHN HENRY, financial corporation executive, lawyer; b. Boston, Feb. 16, 1932; s. Joseph Dante and Gertrude (Hogan) B.; m. Patricia Mary Burke, Jan. 9, 1965. A.B., Stonehill Coll., 1953; LL.B., Boston Coll., 1956. Bar: Mass. 1957, D.C. 1965. Pvt. practice, Boston, 1960-61; trial atty. Bur. Restraint of Trade, FTC, 1961-64; assoc. firm Davies, Richberg. Tydings, Landa & Duff, Washington, 1965-67; partner firm Alston & Bird, Washington and Atlanta, 1967-83; mng. partner Washington office Alston, Miller & Gaines, 1971-76; dir., v.p., gen. counsel First Western Financial Corp., Las Vegas, 1966-67, 69-83, pres., dir., 1967-69, 83—; dir. First Western Savs. & Loan Assn., Las Vegas, 1966—, vice chmn., 1983—; Mem. atomic safety and licensing bd. panel Nuclear Regulatory Commn., 1972-82. Mem. campaign staff Senator Robert F. Kennedy, 1964, Hulmphrey-Muskie, 1968, Muskie Election Com., 1971-72, Carter-Mondale, 1976; counsel for Inaugural Com., 1976; nat. chmn. Lawyers for Carter-Mondale, 1979-80; mem. Pres.'s Commn. on White House Fellowship, 1977-81. Served to capt. AUS, 1957-60. Mem. Am., Fed. bar assns., Bar Assn. D.C. (chmn. antitrust law com. 1972-74, 80-82). Home: 3176 Montecito Drive Las Vegas NV 89120 Office: First Western Sq 2700 W Sarah Ave Las Vegas NV 89102

BRECHER, EDWARD MORITZ, author; b. Mpls., July 20, 1911; s. Hans and Rhodessa (Roston) B.; m. Ruth Ernestine Cook Stilson, Dec. 27, 1941 (dec. 1966); children—William Earl, John Samuel, Jeremy Hans. Student, U. Wis. Exptl. Coll., 1928-30; B.A. with highest honors, Swarthmore Coll., 1932; M.A., U. Minn., 1934; postgrad., Brown U., 1934-35. Writer Compton's Pictured Ency., Chgo., 1936-37; research supr. U.S. Senate Com. on Interstate Commerce, 1938-41; research supr., asst. to chmn. FCC, Washington, 1941-46; asso. editor Consumer Reports, N.Y.C., 1947-51; editor Tech. Assistance Adminstrn., UN, 1951-52; free lance writer, 1952—; Lectr. on sex research and illicit drugs various colls. and med. schs., 1969—; mem. ad hoc com. Treatment and Prevention of Drug Addiction and Drug Abuse, Washington, 1970; cons. to Ford Found., 1975-77. Author: (with Ruth E. Brecher) Medical and Hospital Benefit Plans, 1961, (with Ruth E. Brecher and others) Consumers Union Report on Smoking and the Public Interest, 1963, (with Ruth E. Brecher) An Analysis of Human Sexual Response, 1966, The Rays: A History of Radiology in the U.S. and Canada, 1968, The Sex Researchers, expanded edit, 1979, Licit and Illicit Drugs, 1972, Methadone Treatment Manual, 1973, Health Care in Correctional Institutions, 1975, Treatment Programs for Sex Offenders, 1977, Love, Sex, and Aging: A Consumers Union Report, 1982; Appeared in: lead role Ripple of Time, 1974, Les Amies, 1978. Justice of the Peace Town of Cornwall, Conn., 1966—, bd. finance, 1963-74, bd. assessors, 1974-78. Recipient George Polk Meml. award, Robert T. Morse Meml. award Am. Psychiat. Assn., 1971, Ellie award Am. Soc. Mag. Editors, 1975, Albert Lasker Meml. award Lasker Found., 1963. Fellow Soc. Sci. Study of Sex (dir.); mem. Authors Guild, Nat. Assn. Sci. Writers, Am. Soc. Journalists and Authors. Address: Yelping Hill West Cornwall CT 06796

BRECHER, GERHARD ADOLF, physician, educator; b. Goldap, Germany, June 14, 1909; came to U.S., 1948, naturalized, 1955; s. Otto Ernst and Hedwig (Wulst) B.; m. Eleanor Baker, Apr. 23, 1941; children—Armin G., M. Herbert, Elisabeth E. Student, U. Hamburg, 1928-29, Ph.D., 1932; M.A., Duke, 1930; postgrad., U. Prague, 1932-34, U. Berlin, 1934-35; M.D., U. Kiel, 1937. Instr. physiology U. Kiel, 1937-38; intern U. Cal. Hosp., San Francisco, 1938-41; asst. resident Orange Meml. Hosp., Orlando, Fla., 1939-40; resident Brewster Hosp., Jacksonville, Fla., 1940-41; sr. instr. physiology U. Prague, 1941-45; asst. prof. Western Res. U., 1948-54, asso. prof., 1954-55; prof., dir. Inst. Research in Vision, Ohio State U., Columbus, 1955-57; prof. physiology Emory U., Atlanta, 1957-66, chmn. dept., 1957-66, chief clin. physiology, dept. internal medicine, 1966; med. cons. Gen. Electric Co., Cleve., 1954—, Tuskegee Inst. Sch. Vet. Medicine, 1963-67; distinguished prof. U. Okla. Med. Center, Oklahoma City, from 1967, now emeritus. Author: Venous Return, 1956, (with P.M. Galletti) Heart Lung Bypass, 1962; Contbr. numerous articles to sci. publs. Fellow Am. Coll. Cardiology; mem. Am. Physiol. Soc., Assn. for Research in Ophthalmology, Am. Heart Assn., Am. Soc. physiology (distinguished mem. circulation group), Am. Illuminating Soc. Home: 7708 Rumsey Rd Oklahoma City OK 73132

BRECHER, IRVING, economics educator; b. Montreal, Wue., Can., Feb. 1, 1923; m. Toba brecher, May 11, 1944; children: Richard, Thomas, Ronald, Teresa. B.A., McGill U., 1943; M.A., Harvard U., 1947, Ph.D., 1951; LL.B., Yale U., 1953. Asst. prof. econs., lectr. law Northwestern U., Evanston, Ill., 1953-55; prof. econs. McGill U., Montreal, 1948-50, 55—, chmn. dept., 1981—, dir. Centre for Developing Area Studies, 1963-71; joint dir. Pakistan Inst. Devel. Econs., Karachi, 1960-61; bd. govs. Internat. Devel. Research Centre, Ottawa, 1970-73; vice chmn. Econ. Council Can., Ottawa, 1972-74. Author: Monetary and Fiscal Thought and Policy in Canada, 1919-1939, 1957; co-author: Canada-United States Economic Relations, 1957, Foreign Aid and Industrail Development in Pakistan, 1972. Pilot, officer RCAF, 1943-45. Recipient Queen's Silver Jubilee medal, 1978; Leave fellow Can. Council, 1971-72. Mem. Am. Econ. Assn., Can. Asian Studies Assn., Can. Econs. Assn., Can. Inst. Internat. Affairs. Home: 1343 Dumfried Rd Montreal PQ Canada o3P 2R2 Office: Dept Econs McGill Univ 855 Sherbrooke St W Montreal PQ Canada H3A 2T7

BRECHER, KENNETH, astrophysicist; b. N.Y.C., Dec. 7, 1943; s. Irving and Edythe (Grossman) B.; m. Aviva Schwartz, Aug. 18, 1965; children: Karen, Daniel. B.S., MIT, 1964, Ph.D., 1969. Research physicist U. Calif., San Diego, 1969-72; asst. prof. physics MIT, Cambridge, 1972-77; assoc. prof. U. Calif., San Diego, 1977-79; assoc. prof. astronomy and physics Boston U., 1979-81, prof., 1981—. Author, editor: (with G. Setti) High Energy Astrophysics and Its Relations to Elementary Particle Physics, 1974, (with M. Feirtag) Astronomy of the Ancient, 1979; contbr. numerous articles to profl. jours. Guggenheim fellow, 1979-80. Mem. Am. Aston. Soc., Internat. Astron. Union, Am. Phys. Soc., Sigma Xi. Home: 35 Madison St Belmont MA 02178 Office: Boston U Astronomy Dept 725 Commonwealth Ave Boston MA 02215

BRECHER, MICHAEL, political science educator; b. Montreal, Que., Can., Mar. 14, 1925; s. Nathan and Gisela (Hopmeyer) B.; m. Eva Danon, Dec. 7, 1950; children: Leora, Diana, Seegla. B.A., McGill U., 1946; M.A., Yale U., 1948, Ph.D., 1953. Mem. faculty McGill U., Montreal, 1952—, prof. polit. sci., 1963—; vis. prof. U. Chgo., 1963; vis. prof. internat. relations Hebrew U. Jerusalem, 1970-75, U. Calif., Berkeley, 1979, Stanford U., 1980. Contbr. articles in field to profl. jours.; author: The Struggle for Kashmir, 1953, Nehru: A Political Biography, 1959, The New States of Asia, 1963, Succession in India, 1966, India and World Politics, 1968, Political Leadership in India, 1969, The Foreign Policy System of Israel, 1972, Decisions in Israel's Foreign Policy, 1975, Studies in Crisis Behavior, 1979, Decisions in Crisis, 1980. Recipient Watumull prize Am. Hist. Assn., 1960; Nuffield fellow, 1955-56; Rockefeller fellow, 1964-65; Guggenheim fellow, 1965-66; Can. Council and Soc. Sci. and Humanities Research Council of Can. research grantee, 1960, 65, 68, 69-70, 75-76, 80-85; Killam awards Can. Council, 1970-74, 76-79; Woodrow Wilson Found. award Am. Polit. Sci. Assn., 1973. Fellow Royal Soc. Can.; mem. Internat. Studies Assn., Internat., Am., Can., Israeli polit. sci. assns. Jewish. Home: 5 Dubnov St Jerusalem Israel Office: 855 Sherbrooke St W Montreal PQ H3A 2T7 Canada

BRECHNER, BERL MARTIN, editor, writer, photographer; b. Washington, Nov. 28, 1946; s. Joseph Louis and Marion B.; m. Katherine Durham, Sept. 4, 1977. B.A. in Journalism, George

Washington U., 1968. Reporter Montgomery County Sentinel, Rockville, Md., 1968-69; freelance writer, photographer, Washington, 1971-73; sr. editor Aircraft Owners and Pilots Assn. Pilot mag., 1973-78, exec. asst. to pres., 1978; exec. editor Flying mag., N.Y.C., 1978—; dir. Mid-Fla. TV Corp., Orlando. Mem. Ossining (N.Y.) Zoning Bd. of Appeals, 1980-83; mem. Westchester County Airport Adv. Bd., 1981—. Served with U.S. Army, 1969-71. Mem. Aircraft Owners and Pilots Assn., Aviation-Space Writers Assn. (nat. photojournalism awards 1982, 83), Sigma Delta Chi. Jewish. Office: Flying Mag 1 Park Ave New York NY 10016

BRECHT, WARREN FREDERICK, utility executive; b. Detroit, May 21, 1932; s. August F. and Margaret (Roos) B.; m. Barbara Boone, July 31, 1983; children: Amy E., Stephen F., David C., Peter J. B.A., DePauw U., 1954; postgrad., U. Mich., 1955; M.B.A., Harvard U., 1959. Systems analyst W.R. Grace & Co., Cambridge, Mass., 1959-61; v.p., treas. Mgmt. Systems Corp., Cambridge, 1961-65; partner in charge adminstrn. Peat, Marwick, Livingston & Co., Boston, 1965-69; prin. in charge profl. practice, mgmt. cons. dept. Peat, Marwick, Mitchell & Co., N.Y.C., 1969-71; dep. asst. sec. for mgmt. and budget U.S. Dept. Interior, Washington, 1971-72; asst. sec. for adminstrn. U.S. Dept. Treasury, 1972-77; v.p. acctg. and mgmt. info. systems Northeast Utilities, Hartford, Conn., 1977—; mem. panel deregulation govt. mgmt. Nat. Acad. Pub. Adminstrn., 1982—. Trustee, Conn. Pub. Expenditure Council, 1978—. Served with USAF, 1955-57. Recipient Outstanding Young Man award Lexington (Mass.) Jaycees, 1968; Exceptional Service award Dept. Treasury, 1976; Alumni citation DePauw U., 1976; Rector Scholar Achievement award DePauw U., 1979. Mem. Phi Beta Kappa. Home: 29 Stevens Pl Rocky Hill CT 06067 Office: Northeast Utilities PO Box 270 Hartford CT 06101

BRECK, ALLEN DU PONT, historian, educator; b. Denver, May 21, 1914; s. Chesney Yales and Isabelle Estelle (Lee) B.; m. Alice Rose Wolfe, Sept. 7, 1944 (dec. June 1973); 1 dau., Anne Rose Breck Peterson; m. Salome Ripley Hansen, Dec. 19, 1974. B.A., U. Denver, 1936, L.H.D. (hon.), 1973; M.A., U. Colo., 1939, Ph.D., 1950; D.Litt. (hon.), Regis Coll., 1974. Tchr. public schs., Denver, 1936-42; prof. history U. Denver, 1946—; Danforth lectr., 1949-61; mem. commn. on coll. student Am. Council on Edn., 1958-61; Mem. Colo. Commn. on Ednl. Standards, 1962-65; v.p. Colo. Commn. on Social Studies, 1964-68; regional program chmn. Danforth Found., 1960-63. Author: A Centennial History of the Jews of Colorado, 1960, Johannis Wyclyf Tractatus de Trinitate, 1962, Episcopal Church in Colorado, 1860-1963, 1963, William Gray Evans, Western Business Executive, 1964, John Evans of Denver, 1971, Episcopal Church in Colorado, 1960-78, 1978, Johannis Wyclyf, Tractatus de Tempore, 1981, (with Salome J. Breck) The Episcopal Church in Colorado since 1963, 1981; editor: (with Wolfgang Yourgrau) Internat. Colloquium I: Physical Science, History, Philosophy, 1968, II: Biological Science, History, Natural Philosophy, 1971, III: Cosmology, History Theology, 1975, The West in America series, 1960—, Colorado Ethnic History series, 1977—; contbr. articles to profl. jours. Served with field arty. U.S. Army, 1942-46. Danforth asso., 1946—. Fellow Royal Hist. Soc. Gt. Britain; mem. Am. Hist. Assn., Medieval Acad. Am., Rocky Mountain Renaissance and Medieval Assn. (pres. 1968—), Far Western Slavic Conv., Western Social Sci. Assn., Western History Assn., Phi Beta Kappa, Lambda Chi Alpha, Phi Alpha Theta, Omicron Delta Kappa. Republican. Episcopalian. Home: 2060 S Saint Paul St Denver CO 80210 Office Dept History U Denver Denver CO 80208 *I have great curiosity about all sorts of history throughout the world, so I am led to develop new courses in which students and I look at human activity as colleagues, rather than as task master and pupils. I see all history as contemporary, equidistant from me as observer, almost as a participant in those glorious or shameful activities which show what man is and what he can do.*

BRECK, HOWARD ROLLAND, geophysicist; b. Kenton, Ohio, Nov. 5, 1912; s. Rolland Franklin and Helen Dunn (Snodgrass) B.; m. Martha Ann Forker, Aug. 7, 1942; 1 son, Robert Rolland. A.B. in Geology, U. Mo., 1934. Geophysicist Seismograph Service Corp., Tulsa, 1937-61, asst. v.p., mgr. acoustic well-logging div., 1954-59; exec. dir. Soc. Exploration Geophysicists, Tulsa, 1962-79, exec. dir. emeritus, 1979—; cons. in assn. mgmt.; mem. exec. com. Offshore Tech. Conf., 1979-82, chmn. awards com., 1981-82. Contbr. articles on acoustic well-logging and synthetic seimograms to profl. jours., 1954-60; gen. mgr.: Geophysicsmag, 1962-78. Mem. Soc. Exploration Geophysicists (hon.), Geophys. Soc. Tulsa (hon. life), Am. Soc. Assn. Execs., Phi Gamma Delta. Home and Office: 9023 S Delaware Ave Apt 604 Tulsa OK 74137

BRECKENRIDGE, ADAM CARLYLE, political science educator; b. Turney, Mo., July 10, 1916; s. Adam Carlisle and Mabel Ruth (Sheldon) B.; m. Marion S. Nickerson, Apr. 13, 1963; 1 step-son, Thomas S. Nickerson. A.B., N.W. Mo. State Coll., 1936; M.A., U. Mo., 1938; Ph.D., Princeton, 1942. Instr. Christian Coll., Columbia, Mo., 1940; instr. to asso. prof. polit. sci. U. Nebr., Lincoln, 1946-55, chmn. dept., 1953-55, prof. polit. sci., 1955—, dean faculties, 1955-66, vice chancellor, 1962-68, acting dir. libraries, 1973-74, acting vice chancellor acad. affairs, 1974-75, vice chancellor acad. affairs, 1975-77, interim chancellor, 1975-76; Vis. prof. Pa. State U., summers 1948, 49. Author: One House for Two, 1957, The Right to Privacy, 1970, Congress Against the Court, 1970, The Executive Privilege, 1974, Electing the President, 1982; Editor: (with L.W. Lancaster) Readings in American State Government, 1950. Mem. City-County Planning Commn., Lincoln, 1965-71. Served from ensign to lt. comdr. USNR, 1942-46, 50-52; capt. Res. Mem. Am. Polit. Sci. Assn., Nebr. Hist. Soc., Pi Sigma Alpha (nat. exec. council 1960-64). Home: 1545 E Manor Dr Lincoln NE 68506

BRECKENRIDGE, BRUCE MCLAIN, physician, educator; b. Bklyn., Iowa, Nov. 7, 1926; s. Robert William and Mildred Elizabeth (McLain) B.; m. Mary Alice Barber, June 18, 1949; children: Lee, Janet, Ellen. B.S., Iowa State U., 1947; M.S., U. Rochester, 1949, Ph.D., 1952, M.D., 1956. Intern Barnes Hosp., St. Louis, 1956-57; fellow dept. pharmacology Washington U., St. Louis, 1957-59, instr., 1959-61, asst. prof., 1961-67, asso. prof., 1967; prof., chmn. dept. pharmacology U. Medicine and Dentistry of N.J.-Rutgers Med. Sch., Piscataway, 1967—, adj. prof. medicine, 1979—; mem. pharmacology A study sect. NIH, 1968-72; mem. test com. Nat. Bd. Med. Examiners, 1976-79; mem. N.J. Drug Utilization Rev. Council, 1977-80; vis. scientist Inst. de Biologie Physicochimique, Paris, 1964-65. Mem. editorial bd.: Molecular Pharmacology, 1968—; adv. bd.: Advances in Cyclic Nucleotide Research, 1972—. Served with USNR, 1945-46. Markle scholar, 1959-64. Mem. Am. Soc. Pharmacology and Exptl. Therapeutics, Am. Soc. Biol. Chemists, Sigma Xi, Alpha Omega Alpha. Office: PO Box 101 Piscataway NJ 08854

BRECKER, MANFRED, retail company executive; b. Dresden, Germany, Mar. 21, 1927; came to U.S., 1938, naturalized, 1944; s. Max and Rosa (Kaufman) B.; m. Anne Sparago, Sept. 24, 1950; children: Marcie, Barry, Jeffrey. B.S. in retailing, NYU, 1949. With S.E. Nichols, Inc., N.Y.C., 1949—, v.p. mass retailing div., 1960-72, pres., 1972—, also dir. Chmn. United Jewish Appeal, 1974. Served with A.C. USNR, 1944-46. Named Retailer of Yr. Brands Names Found., 1970; recipient Cert. of Distinction Brand Names Found., 1969, award Advt. Club, N.Y.C., 1970, Prime Minister's medal, Israel, 1976. Mem. Nat. Mass Retailing Inst. (dir.), Am. Retail Fedn., C. of C. U.S. (labor com.), Mass Retailers (gov. affairs com.), Prime Minister's Club Israel. Clubs: Fresh Meadow Country (dir.), Emerald Hills Country). Office: S E Nichols Inc 500 8th Ave New York NY 10018

BRECKINRIDGE, CHARLES EDWARD, JR., pharmacy practice educator; b. Louisville, June 21, 1923; s. Charles Edward and Elizabeth Clark (Kendall) B.; m. Doris Jean Smith, June 25, 1955; children: Charles Edward, Debbie Jean, Richard Glenn. B.S. with distinction, U. Ky., 1953; M.S., Purdue U., 1959, Ph.D. (NIH fellow), 1960. Instr. U. Ky., Lexington, 1954-57; instr. Purdue U., Lafayette, Ind., 1957-59, prof., 1964; sr. health physicist Oak Ridge Nat. Lab., 1960-63; sr. scientist Hanford Labs., Richland, Wash., 1963; prof. environ. health scis. Sch. Pharmacy, U. Ark. Med. Center, Little Rock, 1965-75, chmn. dept., 1965-75, dir. radiol. health tng. program, 1965-75, prof. clin. pharmacy, chmn. dept. clin. pharmacy, 1975-76, prof. pharmaceutics, 1976-83, prof. pharmacy practice, 1983—, chmn. dept. nuclear pharmacy, 1976-78. Asst. editor: Nuclear Safety, 1962-63; contbr. articles to profl. jours. Mem. AAAS, Am. Assn. Colls. Pharmacy, Am. Pharm. Assn., Ark. Pharm. Assn., Pulaski County Pharm. Assn., Sigma Xi, Rho Chi, Phi Delta Chi. Home: Route 9 Box 80 Benton AR 72015

BRECKINRIDGE, JAMES BERNARD, research physicist; b. Cleve., May 27, 1939; s. Albert Coles and Catherine Rose (Wengler) B.; m. Ann Marie Yoder, July 24, 1965; children: Douglass E., John Brian. B.S. in Physics, Case Inst. Tech., 1961; M.S. in Optical Sci, U. Ariz., 1970, Ph.D., 1976. Research asst. Lick Obs., Mt. Hamilton, Calif., 1961-64; electron tube engr. Rauland Corp., Chgo., 1967; research asst. Kitt Peak Nat. Obs., Tucson, full time, 1964-66, 68, 75-76, part time, 1969-74; mem. tech. staff Jet Propulsion Lab., Calif. Inst. Tech., 1976—; also co-investigator NASA Spacelab 3; author, lectr. Scoutmaster Boy Scouts Am. Mem. Am. Astron. Soc., IEEE, Internat. Astron. Union, Optical Soc. Am., Astron. Soc. of Pacific. Research in remote optical and infrared sensing instrumentation, interferometry, solar spectroscopy, image intensifiers and image analysis. Home: 4565 Viro Rd La Canada CA 91011 Office: JPL Caltech 4800 Oak Grove Dr Pasadena CA 91103

BREDER, W. DONALD, manufacturing company executive; b. Egg Harbor City, N.J., Sept. 18, 1929; s. Wallace Herman and Lillian (Smith) B.; m. Marjorie Cherry Breder Ruttle, May 21, 1955; children: Gary W., David W., Tobias D. Linda M., Bruce A., Susan L. B.S. in E.E., Drexel U., M.B.A. With ITE Imperial Corp., Phila, 1973-74, gen. mgr. switchgear div., Chalfont, Pa., 1975-76; pres. div. sales Gould Brown Boveri, Spring House, Pa., 1977-81; v.p., gen. mgr. Brown Boveri Electric Inc., Columbia, S.C., 1981-82, pres., Spring House, Pa., 1982—; dir. Ruttle-Shaw & Wetherill, Inc., Phila. Pres. Sch. Dirs., Upper Dublin Twp., Pa., 1977. Mem. IEEE. Republican. Methodist. Clubs: Union League of Phila., Greater Wildwood Yacht, Mfrs. Golf. and Country. Lodge: Masons. Officer: Brown Boveri Electric Inc Norristown Rd Spring House PA 19477

BREE, GERMAINE, educator; b. France, Oct. 2, 1907; came to U.S., 1936, naturalized, 1952; d. Walter and Lois Marguerite (Andrault) B. Licence, U. Paris, 1930, Diplome d'Etudes Supérieures, 1931, Agregation, 1932; postgrad., Bryn Mawr Coll., 1931-32; D.Litt., Smith Coll., 1960, Mt. Holyoke Coll., 1963, Allegheny Coll., 1963, Duke U., 1964, Colby Coll., 1964, Oberlin Coll., 1966, Dickinson U., 1968, Rutgers U., 1969, Wake Forest U., 1970, Brown U., 1971, U. Mass., 1976, Kalamazoo Coll., 1977, Washington U., 1978, U. of the South, 1979, Boston Coll., 1979, U. Wis.-Madison, 1981; L.H.D., Wilson Coll., 1960; LL.D., Middlebury Coll., 1965, U. Mich., 1971, Davis-Elkins Coll., 1972, U. Wis. at Milw., 1973, N.Y. U., 1975,. Tchr., Algeria, 1932-36; from lectr. to prof. Bryn Mawr Coll., 1936-53; faculty French summer sch. Middlebury Coll., 1937, 40, 41, 46; chmn. dept. French Washington Sq. Coll., 1953-60; head Romance lang. dept., grad. sch. arts and sci. N.Y. U., 1954-58, head dept. Romance langs. and Russian, 1958-60; Vilas prof. U. Wis. Inst. for Research in Humanities, Madison, 1960-73; Kenan prof. Wake Forest U., 1973—; Disting. vis. prof. Ohio State U., 1981; Whitney Oates vis. prof. Princeton U., 1983; mem. panel translation Nat. Endowment Humanities, 1978-79; cons. lang. depts. Conn. Coll., 1979; Mem. Am. Council Learned Socs. Adv. Bd. Author: (with Margaret Gustin) An Age of Fiction, (with Micheline Dufau) Voix d'aujourd'hui, 1964, The World of Marcel Proust, 1966, (with Al Kroff) Twentieth Century French Drama, 1969, (with G. Bernauer) Defeat and Beyond, An Anthology of French Wartime Writing (1940-1945), 1970, Camus and Sartre: Crisis and Commitment, 1972, Women Writers in France, 1973, Littérature Française, Vol. 16, XX Siecle c.2, 1920-1970, 1978, others; contbr. articles to profl. publs.; book revs. to New Republic. Served with French Army, 1943-45. Decorated Bronze Star medal; chevalier Legion of Honor, France). Mem. MLA (pres. 1975), Am. Assn. Tchrs. French, Société des Professeurs Français, AAUP, P.E.N., Am. Philos. Soc., Alliance Française, Nat. Council Humanities, Am. Acad. Arts and Sci. Home: 2135 Royall Dr Winston-Salem NC 27106 *It is, I think, one of the tasks of the teacher to try to keep a sense of continuity and proportion in the area of his (her) specialization. In the area of the literature and arts currently developing, students and teachers establish a somewhat different relationship, where a rich exchange and mutual enrichment are possible.*

BREED, ALLEN FORBES, correctional administrator; b. Wisconsin Rapids, Wis., Oct. 1, 1920; s. Noel Jerub and May Belle (Forbes) B.; m. Virginia Mae Plaskett, June 24, 1945; children: Marla, Eleanor, Carol. B.A. cum laude, U. Pacific, 1942. With Dept. Youth Authority, State of Calif., 1945-76, supt. correctional schs., 1947-65, chief div. instns., 1965-67; chmn. Youth Authority Bd., State of Calif., 1967-76; dir. Dept. Youth Authority, State of Calif., 1967-76; vis. fellow Dept. Justice, 1976-77; spl. master U.S. Dist. Ct., R.I., 1977-78; dir. Nat. Inst. Corrections, Dept. Justice, Washington, 1978-83; chmn. bd. Nat. Council Crime and Delinquency, Washington, 1983—; chmn. Task Force on Corrections and; mem. Joint Commn. on Juvenile Justice Standards, Am. Bar Assn. and; Inst. Judicial Adminstrn.; mem. nat. adv. com. on Juvenile Justice and Delinquency Prevention; mem. U.S. del. UN Congress on Prevention of Crime and Treatment of Offenders, Caracas, Venezuela, 1980. Contbr. articles to profl. jours., newspapers, mags. Served to maj. USMC, 1942-45. Decorated Purple Heart. Mem. Nat. Assn. State Juvenile Delinquency Program Adminstrs. (past pres.), Interstate Compact on Probation and Parole (past pres.), Am. Correctional Assn., Am. Arbitration Assn., Nat. Council Crime and Delinquency, Calif. Probation, Parole and Correctional Assn. Episcopalian. Home: Box 698 San Andreas CA 95249 Office: 320 1st St NW Washington DC 20534

BREED, FRANCES, association executive; b. N.Y.C., Feb. 21, 1981; d. Henry Eltinge and Ethel (Burns) B.; 1 dau., Ann. Artist's diploma, Juilliard Sch. Music, 1936; A.B. cum laude, Barnard Coll., 1940; postgrad., Berkshire Music Ctr., 1940, Ind. U. Grad. Sch. Bus. Adminstrn., 1965, New Sch. Social Research, 1966, Brookings Inst., 1968, Columbia U. Grad. Sch. Bus., 1969. Dir. adminstrn. Planned Parenthood-World Population, N.Y.C., 1960-66; assoc. dir. community services Sex Info. and Edn. Council U.S., N.Y.C., 1966-69; exec. Harold L. Oram, Inc., N.Y.C., 1969-70; dir. devel. and pub. relations Nat. Audubon Soc., N.Y.C., 1971-77, v.p., 1977—; mgr. population program, 1979—; rep. UN Conf. on Human Environment, Stockholm, 1972, Nat. Council Philanthropy, 1974-75, Internat. Conf. Family Planning, Indonesia, 1981, UN Expert Working Group, Geneva, 1983. Mem. Nat. Inst. Social Scis., Nat. Soc. Fund Raising Execs. (dir. N.Y.C. chpt.), Conf. UN Reps. of UN Assn. U.S. (exec. com. 1982), Council Non-Govt. Orgns. Office: 950 3d Ave New York NY 10022

BREED, NATHANIEL PRESTON, trustee; b. Lynn, Mass., Apr. 24, 1908; s. Nathaniel Pope and Effie Watson (Thomson) B.; m. Elaine Silsby Cammett, Nov. 14, 1936; children: Nathaniel Preston, Elizabeth Pope. A.B., Harvard U., 1929, M.B.A. magna cum laude, 1932; postgrad., N.Y. U., 1934-35. Treas. Provident Instn. for Savs., Boston, 1949-56; sr. v.p. State St. Bank and Trust Co., Boston, 1956-73; cons. State St. Boston Corp., 1973—; dir. Rose Run Co.; trustee Lomas & Nettleton Mortgage Investors, Dallas. Bd. dirs. Grimes-King Found. Recipient Joint Army-Navy certificate of appreciation, 1947, Distinguished Community Service award Brandeis U., 1972. Mem. Greater Boston Real Estate Bd. (hon. life). Home: 25 Somerset St Belmont MA 02178 Office: 225 Franklin St Boston MA 02110

BREED, WILLIAM B., JR., investment corporation executive; b. 1933; m. A.B., Harvard U., 1955, M.B.A., 1960. With Donaldson, Lufkin & Kenrette Inc., 1960-70; v.p. parent co. Securities Corp., 1974-76; cons. Burg Budget, N.Y.C., 1971-72; chmn. Van Bergen & Co., Inc., 1972-74; v.p. Madison Fund., Inc., Wilmington, Del., 1976-82, 1982, pres., 1982—; also dir. Office: Madison Fund Inc 919 Market St Wilmington DE 19801 *

BREEDEN, EDWARD LEBBAEUS, JR., lawyer, former state senator; b. Norfolk, Va., Jan. 28, 1905; s. Edward L. and Cora Lee (McCloud) B.; m. Willie Holland, Sept. 8, 1928 (dec.); m. Virginia Hurt Sneed, Apr. 16, 1966. Student, Hampden-Sydney Coll., LL.D. (hon.), 1973, George Washington U. Law Sch. Bar: Va. 1927. Mem. Va. State Ho. of Dels., 1936-44, Va. Senate, 1944-72; pres., chmn. bd. 1st Va. Bank of Tidewater; dir. Va. Port Authority, 1st Va. Life Ins. Co., 1st Va. Banks Inc., Arlington Mortgage Co.; Pres. Hunter Found.; Bd. dirs. Med. Center Hosps., Norfolk.; Mem. Va. Adv. Legislative Council, 1944, chmn., 1946; mem. Va. Gov.'s Adv. Bd. on Budget, 1968-72. Mem. Am., Va., Norfolk-Portsmouth bar assns., Kappa Sigma. Presbyn. (elder). Clubs: Virginia, Norfolk Yacht and Country, Princess Anne Country, Harbor (Norfolk); Commonwealth (Richmond). Home: 923 Graydon Ave Norfolk VA 23507 Office: First Va Bank Tower Norfolk VA 23510

BREEDLOVE, HOWELL ADAMS, JR., steel company executive; b. Monroe, Ga., June 25, 1935; s. Howell Adams and Annise Bell (Parker) B.; m. Ann Forsyth Merkle, Sept. 3, 1955; children—Mark Howell, Alan Merkle, William Parker, Ann Marie, John Adams, Mary Helen. Student, Oglethorpe U., 1953-55; B.B.A., Emory U., 1957; grad., Sr. Exec. Program, M.I.T., 1976. Trainee in fin. mgmt. Gen. Electric Co., Schenectady, 1957-59; various fin. positions Monsanto Co., Pensacola, Fla., N.Y.C., Hartford, Conn., St. Louis, 1959-68, controller packaging div., 1968-71; controller Monsanto Comml. Products Co., St. Louis, 1971-73, Copperweld Corp., Pitts., 1973-74, v.p., 1974-75, dir., 1974—, v.p. fin. and adminstrn., 1975, sr. v.p. fin. and adminstrn., 1975, exec. v.p., 1975-81, pres., 1981—; dir. Equimark Corp./Equibank, Pitts., 1980—. Mem. fin. com. Heart Fund, Pensacola, Fla., 1959-62; mem. fin. com. S.W. Pa. council Girl Scouts U.S.A., 1973-75; bd. dirs. YMCA of Pitts., 1979—, chmn., 1982—. Mem. Am. Iron and Steel Inst., Steel Service Center Inst., Financial Execs. Inst. Roman Catholic. Clubs: St. Clair Country, Oakmont Country, Duquesne, Rolling Rock. Home: 2015 Blairmont Dr Upper Saint Clair PA 15241 Office: Two Oliver Plaza Pittsburgh PA 15222

BREEDLOVE, WILLIAM DAVIS, banking executive; b. Jacksonville, Tex., Jan. 7, 1940; s. William Clay and Mittie Lee (Wilson) B.; m. Margaret Coleen Johnson, June 17, 1961; children: William Davis, Thomas Ashley, Margaret Coleen. B.B.A. in Fin, U. Tex., 1962. With First Nat. Bank, Dallas, 1962—, sr. v.p., 1970-75, exec. v.p., 1975-79, vice chmn. bd., chief credit officer, 1979-80, chmn. bd., chief exec. officer, 1980—; dir. Tex. Oil & Gas Corp. Inc. Bd. dirs. Dallas chpt. Am. Heart Assn., 1981—. Mem. Am. Bankers Assn. (exec. com., govt. relations com.), Robert Morris Assos., Central Bus. Dist. Assn., Aardvark Soc., Young Presidents Orgn., Assn. Res. City Bankers, Dallas Assembly, Salesmanship Club. Republican. Presbyterian. Office: PO Box 83709 Dallas TX 75283

BREEN, F. GLENN, banker; b. Chgo., Nov. 14, 1912; s. Frank J. and Ella C. (Burke) B.; m. Dorothy I. Otto, Mar. 20, 1937; children—Barbara Jean, F. Glenn, Jr. Ph.B., U. Chgo., 1935. Vice pres., mgr. Standard Fire Ins. Co. of N.J. (merger with Reliance Ins. Co. 1962), Trenton, 1943-51, pres., 1951-62; v.p. Reliance Ins. Co., 1962-68; pres. Trenton Sav. Fund Soc., 1968—, also bd. mgrs. Bd. dirs. Bucks County Contributorship. Home: Evergreen Rd Morrisville PA 19067 Office: 123 E State St Trenton NJ 08608

BREEN, JAMES LANGHORNE, obstetrician, gynecologist; b. Chgo., Sept. 5, 1926; s. John J. and Lucrece Breen Hudgins (Bilisoly) B.; m. Doris Johnson, Dec. 1, 1951; children: Michael, Nash, Anne, Laura, Barbara, Beth. Diploma, Balt. City Coll., 1945; B.S., Johns Hopkins U., 1946; M.D., Northwestern U., 1952. Diplomate: Am. Bd. Obstetrics and Gynecology. Intern Walter Reed Army Hosp., Washington, 1953, resident obstetrics and gynecology, 1954-58, asst. chief, 1957-58, Second Gen. Hosp., Landstuhl, Germany, 1958-60, acting chief, 1959-60; attending, assoc. prof. obstetrics and gynecology N. J. Coll. Medicine and Dentistry, Newark, 1969-75; clin. prof. obstetrics and gynecology Jefferson Med. Coll., Phila., 1975; chmn. dept. obstetrics and gynecology Newark City Hosp., 1963-69, St. Barnabas Med. Center, Livingston, N.J., 1969—. Served with M.C. U.S. Army, 1952-61. Fellow Am. Coll. Obstetricians and Gynecologists (sect. and dist. chmn. Dist. III 1971-73, v.p. 1981-82, pres. 1983-84), A.C.S., Internat. Acad. Pathology, Internat. Coll. Surgeons (regent 1965, chmn. dist. III 1977-80), Soc. Colposcopists and Colpomicroscopists (founding fellow 1965), Armed Forces Instn. Pathology, Acad. Medicine N.J., N.Y. Obstet. Soc., N.J. Obstet. and Gynecol. Soc., N.J. Soc. Surgeons; mem. Am. Soc. Cytology, Vienna Med. Soc. (life), Assn. Mil. Surgeons of U.S., AMA (Meritorious Service award 1966), N.Y. Acad. Scis., Essex County Med. Assn., Assn. Med. Writers, Assn. Profs. Obstetricians and Gynecologists, N.J. Hosp. Assn., Internat. Soc. Cybernetic Medicine, Am. Soc. Clin. Pathologists (asso.), Internat. Soc. for Study Vulvar Disease. Club: Mid-Eastern Travel (N.Y.C.). Home: 9 Kermit Rd Maplewood NJ 07040 Office: Old Short Hills Rd Livingston NJ 07039

BREEN, JOHN EDWARD, civil engineer, educator; b. Buffalo, May 1, 1932; s. Timothy J. and Alice C. (Keenan) B.; m. Marian T. Killian, June 20, 1953; children: Mary L., Michael T., Dennis P., Sheila A., Sean E., Kerry T., Christopher D. B.C.E., Marquette U., Milw., 1953; M.S. in Civil Engring, U. Mo., 1957; Ph.D., U. Tex., Austin, 1962. Registered profl. engr., Tex., Mo. Structural designer Harnischfeger Corp., Milw., 1952-53; asst. prof. U. Mo., Columbia, 1957-59; mem. faculty U. Tex., Austin, 1959—, prof. civil engring., 1969—, J.J. McKetta prof. engring., 1977-81, Carol Cockrell Curran chair in engring., 1981—; dir. P.M. Ferguson Structural Engring. Lab., Balcones Research Center, 1967—; cons. in field. Contbr. articles to profl. jours. Served to lt. USNR, 1953-56. Recipient Teaching Excellence award Gen. Dynamics Corp., 1971, U. Tex. Student Assn., 1963, Standard Oil Found. Ind., 1968. Fellow Am. Concrete Inst. (bd. direction 1974-77, Wason medal 1972, 83, Raymond C. Reese Research medal 1972, 79, Kelly medal 1981, Raymond Davis lectr.

1978); mem. Nat. Acad. Engring., ASCE, Sigma Xi, Chi Epsilon, Tau Beta Pi. Democrat. Roman Catholic. Club: Austin Yacht (commodore 1977). Home: 8603 Azalea Trail Austin TX 78759 Office: Dept Civil Engring Univ Texas Austin TX 78712

BREEN, JOHN FRANCIS, banker; b. Memphis, Feb. 6, 1929; s. John Francis and Eleanor (Cousins) B.; m. Gloria Fransioli, Nov. 27, 1957 (div. 1970); children—John Francis III, Lynne, James; m. Barbara G. Steenberg, 1971. B.S. cum laude, Memphis State U., 1957, M.A., 1961; postgrad., La. State U., 1961. With Memphis br. Fed. Res. Bank of St. Louis, 1957-62, asst. cashier, 1959-62, cashier, 1962-65, v.p., mgr., 1965—; mem. faculty evening div. Memphis State U., 1959-60. Served with inf. AUS, 1948-49, 53-55. Recipient Frank K. Houston award Tenn. Bankers Assn., 1958. Mem. Sigma Phi Epsilon. Roman Catholic. Club: Rotarian. Home: 2003 Clapboard Hill Rd Little Rock AR 72207 Office: 325 W Capitol Ave Little Rock AR 72203

BREEN, JOHN GERALD, manufacturing company executive; b. Cleve., July 21, 1934; s. Hugh Gerald and Margaret Cecelia (Bonner) B.; m. Mary Jane Brubach, Apr. 12, 1958; children: Kathleen Anne, John Patrick, James Phillip, David Hugh, Anne Margaret. B.S., John Carroll U., 1956; M.B.A., Case Western Res. U., 1961. With Clevite Corp., Cleve., 1957-73, gen. mgr. foil div., 1969-73, gen. mgr. engine parts div., 1973-74; group v.p. indsl. group Gould Inc., Rolling Meadows, Ill., 1974-77, exec. v.p., 1977-79; pres., chief exec. officer Sherwin Williams Co., Cleve., 1979-80, chmn. bd., pres., chief exec. officer, 1980—; dir. Parker Hannifin Corp., Cleve., Nat. City Bank, Republic Steel Corp. Served with U.S. Army, 1956-57. Clubs: Pepper Pike, Union, Cleve. Skating. Home: 2727 Cranlyn Rd Shaker Heights OH 44122 Office: Sherwin Williams Co 101 Prospect Ave NW Cleveland OH 44115

BREEN, TIMOTHY HALL, history and American culture educator; b. Cin., Sept. 5, 1942; s. George E. and Mary B.; m. Susan C., Apr. 5, 1963; children: Sarah, Bant. B.A., Yale U., 1964, M.A., 1966, Ph.D., 1968. Asst. prof. history and Am. culture Yale U., 1968-70; assoc. prof. Northwestern U., 1970-75, prof. history and Am. culture, 1975—, dir., 1975-78. Author: Character and Good Ruler, 1970, Shaping Southern Society, 1975, Puritans and Adventurers, 1980, Myne Own Ground, 1980, America: Past and Present, 1983. Awardee Guggenheim Found., 1975, Inst. Advanced Study, 1980, Nat. Humanities Center, 1983; Am. Council Learned Socs. fellow, 1971. Assoc. Newberry Library; mem. Inst. Early Am. History. Office: History Dept Northwestern U Evanston IL 60201

BREER, ROBERT, artist; b. Detroit, Sept. 30, 1926; s. Carl and Barbara (Zeder) B.; m. Frances Foote; children: Sophia, Julia, Emily, Harriet. B.A., Stanford U., 1949. Prof. art Cooper Union, 1971—; dir. Filmmakers Coop., N.Y.C. Design collaborator: Pepsico/Expts. in Art and Tech. Pavilion at Expo '70, Osaka.; One-man shows, Am. Students and Artists Center, Paris, 1956, Galleria Bonino, N.Y.C., 1965, 66, 70, Hammarskjold Plaza, N.Y.C., N.Y.C., 1973, Whitney Mus., N.Y.C., 1977, 80, group shows include, Mus. Modern Art, N.Y.C., 1968-69, Musée Nationale d'Art Moderne, Paris, 1977; represented in permanent collections, Mus. Modern Art, N.Y.C., Modern Mus., Stockholm, Anthology Film Archives, N.Y.C., Modern Art Mus., Krefeld, Germany, Centre Beaubourg, Paris. Served with U.S. Army, 1945-47. Recipient award Creative Film Found., 1957, 60, Oberhausen Film Festival, 1968, 74, N.Y. State Council, 1975, Am. Film Inst., 1977; Guggenheim fellow, 1978; Nat. Endowment for Arts grantee, 1975-76, 81-82. Address: The Cooper Union Cooper Sq New York NY 10003

BREESE, CHARLES REAGAN, civil engineering educator; b. Lewiston, Utah, Oct. 7, 1917; s. Charles L. and Alta L. (Whitt) B.; m. Dorothy L. Edholm, Nov. 26, 1958; children by previous marriage: Charles Reagan, Cheryl Breese Wells. B.S. in Mech. Engring, U. Nev., 1948, M.S. in Civil Engring, 1956. Mem. faculty U. Nev., Reno, 1948-51, 55—, prof. civil engring., 1967—, dean Coll. Engring., 1971-82; prin. civil engr., City of Reno, 1951-55, cons. in field. Author articles mineral aggregate degredation, freeze-thaw behavior of mineral aggregates in Portland cement concretes. Served to lt. comdr., aviator USNR, 1940-45. Mem. ASCE, Am. Soc. Testing and Materials, Am. Concrete Inst., Am. Soc. Engring. Edn., Assn. Asphalt Paving Technologists, Sigma Xi, Tau Beta Pi, Phi Kappa Phi. Club: Masons. Home: 2205 Arcane Ave Reno NV 89503 Office: Coll Engring Univ Nev Reno NV 89557

BREESE, GERALD WILLIAM, sociology educator; b. Horseheads, N.Y., June 4, 1912; s. Bert Minard and Leona (Goodrich) B.; m. Alice Janette Bailey, July 4, 1937 (dec. Feb. 1972); children: Adele Embree, James Bert, Dana Sue Bailey, Brinda Sue Bailey; m. Alice Dodge Osborn Brown, Oct. 18, 1980. A.B., Ohio Wesleyan U., 1935; B.D., Yale U., 1938; Ph.D. (Marshall Field fellow), U. Chgo., 1947. Asst. prof. sociology, dean of men Pacific U., Forest Grove, Oreg., 1938-41; research planner Chgo. Plan Commn., 1942; instr. urban sociology Shrivenham Am. U., Eng., 1945, U. Chgo., 1947; sec. com. on housing research Social Sci. Research Council, 1947-49; asst. prof. sociology Princeton U., 1949-51, asso. prof., 1951-59, prof., 1959-77, prof. emeritus, 1977—; dir. bur. urban research, 1950-66; Fulbright prof. Am. U., Cairo, 1954-55; coordinator Ford Found., Delhi Regional Master Plan Cons. Team, New Delhi, 1957-58; vis. lectr. U. Natal, South Africa, summer 1963; vis. fellow Inst. Advanced Studies, Australian Nat. U., 1966; Mem. N.J. Resources Com., 1950-57. Author: Daytime Population of Central Business District of Chicago, 1949, Industrial Land Use in Burlington County, N.J, 1951, An Approach to Urban Planning, 1953, Regional Analysis Trenton-Camden Area, 1954, Industrial Site Selection, 1954, Accelerated Urban Growth in a Metropolitan Fringe Area, 1954, Urbanization in Old and New Countries, 1964, Urbanization in Newly Developing Countries, 1966, Impact of Large Installations on Nearby Areas, 1966, rev., 1968; Editor, contbr.: The City in Newly Developing Countries, 1969; editor: Urban Southeast Asia, 1973, Urban and Regional Planning in the Delhi-New Delhi Area, 1974. Served with AUS, 1942-45. Recipient Demobilization award Social Sci. Research Council, 1946-47. Mem. Am. Inst. Planners, Am., Eastern sociol. socs., Population Assn. Am., Phi Beta Kappa. Home: 65 Cleveland Ln Princeton NJ 08540

BREESE, MELVIN WILSON, physician; b. Miller, S.D., July 13, 1914; s. Orville V. and Ruth (Wilson) B.; m. Elizabeth J. Beaty, Oct. 31, 1937; children—Shelby L. (Mrs. Thomas Ballen), Mark W., Sheila L. (Mrs. K.D. Esch), Craig E. B.S., Oreg. State U., 1936; M.D., U. Oreg., 1943. Intern Emanuel Hosp., Portland, Oreg., 1943-44; resident U. Oreg. Sch. Hosp., 1944-47; practice medicine, specializing in obstetrics and gynecology, Portland, 1947—; clin. prof. obstetrics and gynecology U. Oreg. Med. Sch., 1947—. Served to capt., M.C. U.S. Army, 1953-54, 65-66. Mem. AMA (council med. edn.), Oreg. Med. Assn. (council med. edn., past pres.), Multnomah County Med. Soc. (past pres.), Am. Coll. Obstetrics and Gynecology, Pacific Coast Obstet. and Gynecol. Soc. (past pres.), Pacific N.W. Obstet. and Gynecol. Soc., Oreg. Obstet. and Gynecol. Soc., Portland Obstet. and Gyncol. Soc. Address: 1133 SW Market St Portland OR 97201

BREESKIN, BARNETT, orchestra conductor; b. N.Y.C., Feb. 20, 1914; s. Saul and Sadye (Koonin) B.; m. Annette Lager, June 6, 1962. Stjdent, L.I. U., 1931-32, Bklyn. City Coll., 1932-34. Pvt. instr., Washington and, Md., 1945-55. Mem. violin sect., Nat. Orch., Washington, 1939-45; condr., mgr., Miami Beach (Fla.) Symphony Orch., 1955—, lifetime contract, 1977—. Chmn. Miami-Beach Social Service Adv. Bd.; Mem. Cultural Execs. Council Dade County, Fla. Office: 1150 NE 191st St North Miami Beach FL 33179

BREFFEILH, LOUIS ANDREW, ophthalmologist, educator; b. Shreveport, La., Sept. 14, 1913; s. John Hypolite and Louise Claire (DeRichi(Marmouget) B.; m. Marianna Franklin, Aug. 13, 1949; children—George Richard, Andrew Louis. Student, Loyola U. South, New Orleans, 1932-34; M.B., La. State U., 1938, M.D., 1939. Diplomate: Am. Bd. Ophthalmology, Am. Acad. Ophthalmology and Otolaryngology, A.C.S., Internat. Coll. Surgeons. Intern Shreveport Charity Hosp., 1938-39; practice medicine specializing in ophthalmology, Shreveport, 1950—; staff Confederate Meml. Med. Center, 1950—, pres., 1966-67; staff Schumpert Meml. Hosp., 1950—, pres., 1971-72; clin. instr. dept. ophthalmology Sch. Medicine La. State U. New Orleans, 1946-50, asst. clin. prof., 1950-51, clin. prof., Shreveport, 1951-64, head dept., prof., 1970—; sr. cons. USAF, 1950—, VA Hosp., 1950—. Contbr. articles to profl. jours. Pres. Breffeilh and Texada Med. Found., 1971—. Served to maj. M.C. AUS, 1941-46; now lt. col. USAFR. Mem. Am., So. med. assns., Pan Am. Ophthal. Soc., La., Miss., Ophthal. and Otol. Soc., Shreveport Med. Soc. (v.p. 1969-70). Club: Shreveport Yacht. Home: 439 Springlake Dr Shreveport LA 71106 Office: PO Box 33932 Dept Ophthalmology Shreveport LA 71130

BREGA, CHARLES FRANKLIN, lawyer; b. Callaway, Nebr., Feb. 5, 1933; s. Richard E. and Bessie (King) B.; m. Betty Jean Witherspoon, Sept. 17, 1960; children: Kerry E., Charles D., Angie G. B.A., The Citadel, 1954; LL.M., U. Colo., 1960. Bar: Colo. 1960. Assoc. firm Hindry & Meyer, Denver, 1960-62, partner, 1962-75, dir., 1975; dir. firm Roath & Brega, Denver, 1975—; lectr. in field; guest prof. U. Colo., U. Denver, U. Nev. (numerous states and), Can. Trustee Pres.'s Leadership Class, U. Colo., 1977—. Served with USAF, 1954-57. Mem. Colo. Trial Lawyers Assn. (pres. 1972-73), Am. Trial Lawyers Assn. (gov. 1972-79), ABA. Episcopalian. Clubs: Cherry Hills Country, Denver Athletic. Home: 4501 S Vine Way Englewood CO 80110 Office: 1873 S Bellaire St No 1100 Denver CO 80222

BREGER, WILLIAM N., educator, architect; b. N.Y.C., Aug. 1, 1922; s. S.A. and B. (Kalvar) B. B.Arch., Harvard, 1945, M.Arch., 1945; M.A. in Philosophy, N.Y. U., 1954. Asst. to Walter Gropius, Cambridge, Mass., 1944-46; tchr. N.Y. Sch. Interior Design, 1945—; prof. architecture, former chmn. dept. archtl. design Pratt Inst., 1946-69; lectr. Columbia Sch. Pub. Health and Hosp. Adminstrn., 1964-78; practice architecture with S. Salzman, 1947-55; architect Breger Ter Jesen Assos., 1955—; vis. Disting. prof. architecture Pratt Inst., 1983-84. Exhibited, Mus. Modern Art, 1952, 79, Chgo. Art Inst., 1954, Gold Medal Exhbn. Archtl. League, 1960, Bklyn. Mus., 1955; Mem. editorial bd.: Ency. Philosophy, 1967. Trustee, dir. N.Y. Sch. Interior Design, 1960—. Served with AUS, 1942-43. Recipient Langford Warren prize, 1944, 3d prize Jefferson Nat. Meml. Competition (with C. Hornbostel and G. Lewis), St. Louis, 1947; Prix de Rome Alternate, 1947; 3d prize N.Y. Pub. Housing Award, 1950; with S. Salzman) Good Design award Mus. Modern Art, 1952; 1st prize House and Garden mag., 1950, Carson Pirie Scott Chicago Loop design, 1954; hon. mention hosp. design Rubberoid Competition, 1958; 1st prize Allegheny Sq. competition (with J. Terjesen and W. Winter), Pitts., 1964; hon. mention Fremont Civic Center Master Plan, 1966; AIA award, 1968; Queens C. of C. award; Bard award City Club of N.Y., 1977; N.Y. State Assn. Architects award, 1978, 80; Archi design award L.I. chpt. AIA, 1979. Fellow AIA. Home: 193 W 10th St New York NY 10014 Office: 21 West St New York NY 10006

BREGGIN, PETER ROGER, psychiatrist, author; b. Bklyn., May 11, 1936; s. Morris Louis and Jean (Weinstein) B.; m. Sally Ann Friedman, 1959 (div. 1971); m. Phyllis Jean Lundy, Oct. 13, 1972; children: Linda Karen, Sharon Jane, Benjamin Jay. B.A. with honors, Harvard U., 1958; M.D., Case Western Res. U., 1962. Diplomate: Nat. Bd. Med. Examiners. Intern State U. N.Y., Upstate Med. Center, Syracuse, 1962-63, resident in psychiatry, 1964-66; psychiat. resident Mass. Mental Health Center, Boston, 1963-64; teaching fellow Harvard Med. Sch., Boston, 1963-64; full-time NIMH cons. in bldg. and staffing mental health centers, Charlottesville, Va., 1966-67, full-time NIMH cons. in edn., Chevy Chase, Md., 1967-68, pvt. practice medicine, specializing in psychiatry, Washington and, Bethesda, Md., 1968—; staff Psychiat. Inst. Washington, 1968—; faculty Washington Sch. Psychiatry, 1968-72; cons. Antioch-Putney Grad. Sch. Edn., 1968-70, U. Md. Grad. Sch. Edn., 1968-70; dir. Project to Examine Psychiat. Technology, Washington Sch. Psychiatry, 1971-72; field faculty Humanistic Psychology Inst., 1975-78; exec. dir., founder Center for Study of Psychiatry, Washington, 1972—; Mem. fellowship adv. com. Center for Libertarian Studies; mem. adv. bd. Task Force on Health, Nat. Taxpayers Union. Author: (with C. Umbarger, J. Dalsimer, A. Morrison and P. Breggin) College Students in a Mental Hospital, 1962; author: The Crazy from the Sane, 1971, After the Good War: A Love Story, 1972, Electroshock: Its Brain-Disabling Effects, 1979, The Psychology of Freedom: Liberty and Love as a Way of Life, 1980; internat. com. contbrs.: Spirali: Mensile Internatazionale di Cultura; Author: Psychiatric Drugs: Hazards to the Brain, 1983; contbg. editor: Libertarian Rev; contbr. articles to profl. jours. Mem. adv. bd. Libertarian Internat.; mem. adv. bd. San Diego Humanist Fellowship. Served to lt. comdr. USPHS, 1966-68. Mem. Am. Psychiat. Assn., Am. Assn. Abolition of Involuntary Mental Hospitalization, Am. Humanist Assn., Libertarian Health Assn. (founding mem.). Libertarian Party. Address: 4628 Chestnut St Bethesda MD 20814 *I have tried to make liberty and love the twin principles of my work and my life. Sometimes I have betrayed one and sometimes the other, and each time I have regretted it. Liberty provides the context within which love for self and others can most easily and fully grow, and liberty and love together provide the nourishment for a happy, rational and creative life.*

BREGMAN, BENJAMIN BERNARD, mfg. co. exec.; b. Boston, May 13, 1909; s. Harry and Esther (Brodsky) B.; m. Irene Faller, July 22, 1934; children—Sheila (Mrs. Charles Morgo), Cydnye (Mrs. Josef Sieghart), Harry. A.B., Tufts U., 1931. Gen. mgr. Macht Shoe Corp., N.Y.C., 1934-37; gen. mgr. Consol. Slipper Corp., Malone, N.Y., 1937-39; pres. Trustitich Slipper Corp., 1939-69, Trustitch Footwear, Bombay Slipper cos., 1969—, Little Falls Slipper, 1979—, Stitching Inc., Manchester, N.H., 1975—; chmn. bd. Wolverine World Wide Inc., Rockford, Mich., 1975-80, chmn. bd. emeritus, 1980—; chmn. adv. bd. Marine Midland, Malone. Pres. Franklin County Tb Assn., 1952-58; pres. Alice Hyde Hosp.; Bd. dirs. Boy Scouts Am., 1945-55, Soc. Prevention Cruelty to Animals, 1955-64; trustee, vice-chmn. Paul Smiths Coll. Jewish (pres. temple 1942-52, 74-75). Clubs: Mason, Elk, Rotarian. Home: 75 Elm St Malone NY 12953 Office: 123 Catherine St Malone NY 12953 *Constantly pursue excellence and in the process step on no toes, but exert every effort to enhance life for your neighbor.*

BREGMAN, JACOB ISRAEL, corporate executive; b. Hartford, Conn., Sept. 17, 1923; s. Aaron and Jennie (Katzoff) B.; m. Mona Madan, June 27, 1948; children: Janet, Marcia, Barbara. B.S., Providence Coll., 1943; M.S., Poly. Inst. Bklyn., 1948, Ph.D., 1951. Research chemist Fels & Co., 1947-48; head phys. chem. labs. Nalco Chem. Co., Chgo., 1950-59; supr. phys. chemistry research sect. Armour Research Found., Chgo., 1959-63; asst. dir. chemistry research Ill. Inst. Tech. Research Inst., Chgo., 1963-65, dir. chem. scis., 1965-67; dep. asst. sec. U.S. Dept. Interior, 1967-69; pres. Wapora Inc., 1969-82; v.p. Dynamac Corp., 1983-84; pres. Bregman and Co., 1984—; Chmn. N.E. Ill. Met. Area Air Pollution Control Bd., 1962-63; chmn. Ill. Air Pollution Control Bd., 1963-67; chmn. adv. bd. on saline water conversion NATO Parliamentarians Conf., 1963; chmn. Water Resources Research Council, 1964-67. Author: Corrosion Inhibitors, 1963, Surface Effects in Detection, 1965, The Pollution Paradox, 1966, Handbook of Water Resources and Pollution Control, 1976; contbr. articles to profl. jours. Mem. plan commn., Park Forest, Ill., 1956-58, trustee, 1958-62; Mem. Md. Democratic State Central Com., 1974-78; treas. Montgomery Dem. Central Com., 1974-76; del. Dem. Conv., 1976. Served with AUS, 1943-46; ETO. Fellow Am. Inst. Chemists; mem. Am. Chem. Soc., Sigma Xi, Phi Lambda Upsilon. Home: 5630 Old Chester Rd Bethesda MD 20814 Office: 911 Silver Spring Ave Silver Spring MD 20910

BREGMAN, MARTIN, film producer; b. N.Y.C.; s. Leon and Ida (Granowski) B.; children: Michael Scott, Christopher Neill. Student, Ind. U., NYU. Owner Martin Bregman Prodns., Inc.; chmn. Mayor N.Y.C. Office Motion Pictures and TV. Film producer; producer: Serpico, 1974, Dog Day Afternoon, 1975, The Next Man, 1977, The Seduction of Joe Tynan, 1979, S H E, 1980, Simon, 1980, The Four Seasons, 1980, Venom, 1982, Scarface, 1983. Office: Martin Bregman Prodns Inc 641 Lexington Ave New York NY 10022

BREHM, ALVIN, composer, educator, double-bassist, conductor; b. N.Y.C., Feb. 8, 1925; s. Samuel and Yetta (Smith) B.; m. Alison Steneck, June 4, 1977; children: Jon Alexander, Marco Eric. B.S., Columbia U., 1950, M.A., 1950; diploma, Julliard Inst., 1943. Mem. faculty Manhattan Sch. Music, 1969-75, Queens Coll., 1972-75; artist-in-residence SUNY-Stony Brook, 1968-75; prof. music SUNY-Purchase, 1974—, dean Sch. Music, 1982—; double-bassist Lincoln Ctr. Chamber Music Soc., 1970—. Composer: Consort and Dialogues, 1974, Violin Concertino, 1976, Concerto for Piano and Orch., 1978, Metamorphy, 1979, Tre Canzoni, 1981, others. Bd. dirs. N.Y. State Arts Council, chmn. music panel, 1982-83; bd. dirs. Am. Music Ctr. Served with airborne div. U.S. Army, 1943-46. Grantee Naumburg Found., 1977, Nat. Endowment for Arts, 1976, 80, N.Y. State Council on Arts, 1972; mem. numerous commns. Mem. ASCAP (awards 1974, 77, 78), Group for Contemporary Music. Jewish. Home: 302 W 86th St New York NY 10024 Office: State Univ New York Purchase NY 10577 *I have often been asked to describe the style and technical components of my work, and I find that I am unable to do so, at least in the sense that such characteristics together provide a common demoninator to all of my work. It seems, rather, that each piece creates its own parameters, with its own technique and shape. If there is an underlying voice, it is the commitment to lyricism as the most integral force in the musical art.*

BREHM, WILLIAM KEITH, consulting company executive; b. Dearborn, Mich., Mar. 29, 1929; s. Walter E. and Lucille (Hankinson) B.; m. Delores Soderquist, June 28, 1952; children: Eric William, Lisa Karen. B.S. with honors in Math, U. Mich., 1950, M.S., 1952. Asst. sec. army Dept. Army, Washington, 1968-70; v.p. corporate devel. Dart Industries, Inc., Los Angeles, 1970-73; asst. sec. def. Dept. Def., Washington, 1973-77; exec. v.p. Computer Network Corp., Washington, 1977-80; chmn. bd. Systems Research and Applications Corp., Arlington, Va., 1980—. Bd. visitors Nat. Def. U.; trustee Fuller Theol. Sem.; bd. dirs. Washington chpt. ARC. Recipient Disting. Civilian Service award Dept. Army, Disting. Pub. Service award Dept. Def. Mem. Ops. Research Soc. Am. Home: 4061 Ridgeview Circle Arlington VA 22207 Office: 2425 Wilson Blvd Arlington VA 22201

BREIBART, JACK, journalist; b. Charleston, S.C., Sept. 6, 1931; s. Sam and Ida (Goldberg) B.; m. Paula Gwile Rowland, May 20, 1962; children: Craig, Leslie. B.S., Coll. Charleston, 1953; postgrad., U. N.C., 1957-58. Sports reporter Charleston News and Courier, 1955-56, Raleigh News and Observer, N.C., 1956-60; sports reporter, then asst. news editor Miami News, 1960-66; from feature editor to mng. editor Cocoa Today, Fla., 1966-69; mem. staff San Francisco Chronicle, 1969—, news editor, 1977—. Jewish. Hoe: 315 Clipper St San Francisco CA 94114 Office: The Chronicle Pub Co 901 Mission St San Francisco CA 94102

BREIDEGAM, DELIGHT EDGAR, battery company executive; b. Fleetwood, Pa., Oct. 3, 1926; s. DeLight Daniel and Helen Mamie (Fenstermacher) B.; m. Helen Merkel, Feb. 28, 1948; children: Daniel, Sally. Attended, Gettysburg Coll., 1944-45. Pres. East Penn Mfg. Co., Inc., Lyon Sta., Pa.; dir. Battery Council Internat. Mem. Kutztown Area Sch. Authority; trustee, treas. Moravian Coll. Served with USAAF. Mem. Kutztown Jaycees, Ind. Battery Mfrs.' Assn., Reading-Berks C. of C. Lutheran. Clubs: Moselem Springs Golf, Fox Fire Golf and Country, Saucon Valley Country, Huguenot Lodge, Shriners. Office: East Penn Mfg Co Inc Deka Rd Lyon Station PA 19536

BREIDENBACH, FRANCIS ANTHONY, lawyer; b. Oakes, N.D., May 12, 1930; s. Theodore Michael and Elizabeth Ann (Ackerman) B.; m. Carol Ann Erenfeld, June 15, 1955; children: Francis Anthony, Kelly Ann, Andrew T. Ph.B., U. N.D., 1952, J.D., 1957. Bar: N.D. 1957, Calif. 1965, diplomate: Am. Bd. Trial Advocates. Asst. atty. gen., State of N.D., 1957-60, practiced in, Bismarck, 1960-63; asso. firm Welsh & Cummins, Los Angeles, 1963-65; partner firm Breidenbach, Swainston, Yokaitis & Crispo (formerly Cummins, White & Breidenbach), 1965—. Served with AUS, 1948-49, 52-53. Mem. Am., N.D., Los Angeles County bar assns., State Bar Calif., Assn. So. Calif. Def. Counsel (pres. 1976-77), Fedn. Ins. Counsel, Assn. Trial Lawyers Am., Nat. Assn. Def. Counsel in Criminal Cases (dir. 1962-64), Bus. Trial Lawyers Assn. Office: 888 W 6th St Los Angeles CA 90017

BREIGHNER, BARTON LEO, financial services executive; b. Gettysburg, Pa., June 11, 1935; s. P.R. and M. Olive (Peters) B.; m. Karen Gerber Breighner; children—Todd, Tammy. B.A. in History, U. Md., 1960; A.M.P., Harvard U., 1982. Tchr. history, coach Annapolis (Md.) High Sch., 1960-62; with World Book-Childcraft Internat. Inc., 1962—, v.p., then sr. v.p., Chgo., 1972-78, exec. v.p., dir. U.S. and Can. sales, 1978-82; founder, pres. Fin. Evaluations, Des Plaines, Ill., 1982—; speaker, cons. in field. Served with USAF, 1954-58. Home: 2400 N Lakeview Ave Chicago IL 60614 Office: O'Hare Office Ctr 3158 River Rd Des Plaines IL 60018

BREIHAN, ERWIN ROBERT, consulting engineering company executive; b. nr. St. Louis, Oct. 31, 1918; s. Arthur George and Genevieve Louise (Wolz) B.; m. Antoinette V. Corcoran, Nov. 24, 1945; children: John Robert, Patricia Anne, Steve Michael. B.S. in Civil Engring, Washington U., St. Louis, 1940, postgrad., 1940-41. Registered profl. engr., Mo., Ill., Ark., Ohio, W. Va. Structural engr. St. Louis Ordnance Plant, 1941-42; with Horner & Shifrin, Inc., St. Louis, 1940—, exec. v.p., 1971-73, pres., chief exec. officer, 1973—. Chmn. Tomahawk dist. Boy Scouts Am., 1978; dir. Transp. and Devel. Council of Mo., 1979-82. Served to capt. USNR, 1942-71. Recipient Washington U. Engring. Alumnus Achievement award, 1979; named Engr. of Yr., St. Louis Mo. Soc. Profl. Engrs., 1980. Fellow ASCE (chmn. profl. activities com. 1983), Cons. Engrs. Council Mo.; mem. AIAA, Am. Assn. Airport Execs., Am. Def. Preparedness Assn., Am. Soc. Mil. Engrs., Am. Water Works Assn., Nat. Soc. Profl. Engrs. (dir. 1981-83), Mo. Soc. Profl. Engrs., ASTM, Cons. Engrs. Council Mo.

(pres. 1977), Am. Road and Transp. Builders Am., Am. Public Works Assn., Soc. Automotive Engrs., Engring. Alumni Assn. Washington U. (pres. 1970), Century Club Engring. (pres. 1969), Mil. Order World Wars (pres. 1976), Mo. Soc. Profl. Engrs. (pres. 1982-83), Engrs. Club of St. Louis (hon. mem., award of merit 1971, Achievement Award medal 1982). Clubs: Washington U., Mo. Athletic. Home: 12945 Star Hill Saint Louis MO 63128 Office: 5200 Oakland Ave Saint Louis MO 63110

BREIMYER, HAROLD FREDERICK, agricultural economist; b. Ft. Recovery, Ohio, Apr. 13, 1914; s. Fred Christian and Ella Anna Margaret (Schulz) B.; m. Rachel Eudora Styles, Dec. 13, 1941; 1 son, Frederick Styles. B.S., Ohio State U., 1934, M.S., 1935; Ph.D., Am. U., 1960. Staff economist Agrl. Adjustment Adminstrn., 1936-39, Bur. Agrl. Econs., 1939-53, Agrl. Mktg. Service, 1954-59, 61-66, Council Econ. Advisers, 1959-61; mem. faculty U. Mo., Columbia, 1966—, prof. agrl. econs., since 1966, extension economist, 1968—. Author: Individual Freedom and the Economic Organization of Agriculture, 1965, Economics of the Product Markets of Agriculture, 1976, Farm Policy: 13 Essays, 1977. Mem. Montgomery County (Md.) Bd. Edn., 1959-62, pres., 1961; pres. Columbia Council Chs., 1974-76. Served with USNR, 1942-45. Recipient Superior Service award Dept. Agr., 1954, 59, Centennial award Coll. Agr. and Home Econs., Ohio State U., 1970, Faculty-Alumni award U. Mo., 1975, Thomas Jefferson award, 1983. Fellow Am. Agrl. Econs. Assn. (pres. 1969); mem. Am. Econ. Assn., Am. Mktg. Assn., Internat. Assn. Agrl. Economists. Democrat. Methodist. Club: Lions. Home: 1616 Princeton Dr Columbia MO 65201 Office: 214 Mumford Hall Univ Mo Columbia MO 65211 *A farm boy reared on Horatio Alger who later adopted Santayana (Last Puritan) and Henry Adams (Education) finds himself molded. Whether success as the world views it is thereby accounted for is moot; that outlook and character are influenced is beyond doubt.*

BREINES, SIMON, architect; b. Bklyn., Apr. 4, 1906; s. Louis and Anna (Backrack) B.; m. Nettie Weissman, 1935; children: Paul, Joseph. B.Arch., Pratt Inst., 1941. Partner Pomerance & Breines, N.Y.C.; adviser Gen. Services Adminstrn.; Bd. dirs. Fine Arts Fedn. of N.Y., N.Y. Landmarks Conservancy.; Mem. Citizens Union, Community Service Soc., Parks Assn., all N.Y.C.; architect mem. Art Commn. City N.Y., 1971—. Architect for: pub. bldgs. including Grand Concourse Pub. Library, Bronx, N.Y.C., Lexington Sch. for Deaf, Rose F. Kennedy Research Center, New Campus, State U. N.Y. at Brockport, New Coll. Dentistry, N.Y. U. Cons. Housing Assistance Adminstrn; Author: Architecture and Furniture of Alvar Aalto, 1942, (with John Dean) The Book of Houses, 1946, (with William Dean) The Pedestrian Revolution: Streets Without Cars, 1976; Contbr.: chpt. to USSR: A Concise Handbook, 1947, Small Urban Spaces, 1969. Arnold W. Brunner scholar N.Y. chpt. AIA, 1947, 66; Recipient Bard award City Club N.Y., 1967. Fellow AIA (honor award 1967). Home: 8 Horseguard Ln Scarsdale NY 10583 *When I was an archtl. student, I was taught, "Make no little plans; they have no magic to stir men's souls". Actually, this persuasive dictum has served society poorly. The combination of vast, over-weening projects and the technology to carry them out quickly hastened the pollution of our environment and the disintegration of our central cities. I have learned that large-scale, "instant" projects leave little room for adjustment for errors or experience. What architecture and planning need, in the future, are a more deliberate pace and a more human scale.*

BREININ, GOODWIN M., physician; b. N.Y.C., Dec. 10, 1918; s. Louis and Mary (Mirsky) B.; m. Rose-Helen Kopelman, June 22, 1947; children: Bartley James, Constance. B.S., U. Fla., 1939; A.M., Emory U., 1940, M.D., 1943. Diplomate: Am. Bd. Ophthalmology (dir., vice chmn., cons.). Intern U.S. Marine Hosp., Stapleton, N.Y., 1944; resident ophthalmology N.Y. U.-Bellevue Med. Center, 1947-51, sr. Heed fellow ophthalmology, 1954, Daniel B. Kirby prof. research ophthalmology, 1958, Daniel B. Kirby prof., chmn. dept. ophthalmology, 1959—, chmn. med. bd., 1975-77; dir. eye service Bellevue and U. Hosps., N.Y.C., 1959—; chmn. vision research tng. com. Nat. Insts. Neurol. Diseases and Blindness, 1963-64; chief cons. Manhattan VA Hosp.; cons. Manhattan Eye, Ear and Throat, USPHS, Stapleton, French, St. Vincent's, Beth Israel hosps., N.Y. Eye and Ear Infirmary, Lenox Hills Hosp., St. Clare's Hosp.; surg. gen. USPHS; chmn. Nat. Res. Rev. Com., 1976-77; vis. prof., cons. Hailie Selassie I Univ. Found., 1972; lectr. Mem. various adv. coms. relating to field, mem. med. adv. bd. Nat. Council to Combat Blindness; pres. Council for U.S./USSR Health Exchange, 1977; mem. Am. com. Internat. Agy. for Prevention of Blindness, 1980—. Author: The Electrophysiology of Extraocular Muscle, 1962; Mem. editorial bd.: Investigative Ophthalmology, Archives of Ophthalmology; Contbr. articles to profl. jours. Served as capt., M.C. AUS, 1944-46. Recipient Knapp Medal for contbn. ophthalmology A.M.A., 1957; Edward Lorenzo Holmes lectr. citation and award for contbns. to med. sci. Inst. Medicine Chgo., 1959; Gifford lectr. and award Chgo. Ophthal. Soc., 1970; Heed Ophthalmic Found. award, 1968; Wright lectr. U. Toronto, 1972; Lloyd lectr. Bklyn. Opthal. Soc., 1971; May lectr. N.Y. Acad. Medicine, 1974. Fellow Am. Acad. Ophthalmology and Otolaryngology (v.p. 1979), A.C.S., N.Y. Acad. Medicine (sec. sect. ophthalmology 1962-63, chmn. sect. 1967-68); mem. AMA (sec. sect. on ophthalmology 1966-69, chmn. 1970-71), Research Ophthalmology, Am. Ophthal. Soc., N.Y. Ophthal. Soc. (pres. 1980), Harvey Soc., AAAS, Am. Commn. for Optics and Visual Physiology (chmn. 1970—), Am. Orthoptic Council, Assn. Univ. Profs. Ophthalmology, Pan. Am. Assn. Ophthalmology, Sigma Xi, Alpha Omega Alpha. Clubs: Cosmos (Washington); Grolier, Century Assn. (N.Y.C.). Home: 912 Fifth Ave New York NY 10021 Office: 550 1st Ave New York NY 10016

BREININ, RAYMOND, painter, sculptor; b. Vitebsk, Russia, Nov. 30, 1910. Student, Chgo. Acad. Fine Arts, Uri Penn Vitebsk Acad. Fine Arts. Instr. art Minn., Breinin Sch. Art, Chgo.; instr. painting and drawing Art Students League, NAD, N.Y.C. Represented in permanent collections, Met. Mus. Art, Mus. Modern Art, Bklyn. Mus., Art Inst. Chgo., Phillips Meml. Gallery, Washington, Boston Mus. Fine Arts, Fogg Mus. Art, San Francisco Mus. Art, San Diego Fine Arts Soc., Newark Mus. Art, Cranbrook Acad. Art, Williams Coll., John Herron Art Inst., U. Ill., Am. Acad. Arts and Letters, U.S. State Dept., Ency. Brit., Capehart Coll., Eli Lilly Co., Nat. Gallery, Scotland, Munson Williams Proctor Inst., Pa. Acad. Fine Arts; designer: costumes, settings Ballet Theatre's Undertow; executed murals, Winnetka (Ill.) High Sch., State Hosp., Elgin, Ill., U.S. Postal Service, Wilmette, Ill., Pump Room in Ambassador East Hotel, Chgo.; Artist-in-residence, So. Ill. U. Recipient awards Art Inst. Chgo. (7), Met. Mus. Art, Pa. Acad. Fine Arts (2), U. Ill. Eccles. Art Guild, others. Mem. NAD. Home: 121 Inwood Rd Scarsdale NY 10583 *It may not be a universally accepted direction, but I believe in art based on the world of ideas, spirit and life extracted from my experiences. How well I project my ideas and how skillfully I execute them is, of course, for others to judge. I believe an artist must be faithful to his own inner-directed vision and to resist the blandishments of fashion and the marketplace. I lament the current view of art as an investment and the parallel decline in the ability of people to look at art with their own eyes and minds and to interact with it in a personal way.*

BREISACH, ERNST, history educator. Prof. history Western Mich. U., Kalamazoo. Author: Introduction to Modern Existentialism, 1962, Caterina Sforza, 1967, Renaissance Europe, 1300-1517, 1973, Historiography: Ancient, Medieval, Modern, 1983. Office: Dept of History Western Mich Univ Kalamazoo MI 49008

BREITBARTH, S. ROBERT, manufacturing company executive; b. Newark, N.J., July 15, 1925; s. Jacob and Rose (Brandman) B.; m. Laurel Patricia Stroh, Oct. 30, 1949; children: Meredith Jane, Jill Gretchen. B.E.E., Cornell U., 1949. Vice pres. Gen. Cable Corp., Greenwich, Conn., 1966-77, exec. v.p., 1976-78; pres. Gen. Cable Internat., Inc., 1978—, also dir.; v.p. GK Technologies, Inc., 1979-82; pres. Gen. Cable Export Corp., Greenwich; dir. Cables de Comunicaciones S.A., Spain, Gen. Cable Ceat, S.A., Plásmica S.A., Saenger S.A., Roque S.A., Ceat Gen. de Colombia, Electrofinance Ltd., Grand Cayman Islands, Indústria Venezolana de Cables Eléctricos S.A., Phillips Cables Ltd., Can. Treas. Stony Point Assn., Westport, Conn., 1973-75, pres., 1975-76. Served with USAAF, 1944-46. Tower Fellow U. Bridgeport. Mem. Council of Americas (mem. adv. bd.), U.S. Investment in Spain Com. (chmn. 1977-80), Spain-U.S. C. of C., Wire Assn., IEEE, Cornell Soc. Engrs., Center for Inter-Am. Relations. Home: 2 Stony Point Westport CT 06880 Office: GK Technologies Inc 500 W Putnam Ave Greenwich CT 06830

BREITEL, CHARLES D., lawyer, former judge; b. N.Y.C., Dec. 12, 1908; s. Herman L. and Regina D. (Zuckerberg) B.; m. Jeanne S. Hollander, Apr. 9, 1927; children: Eleanor Breitel Alter, Sharon H. (dec.), Vivian H. A.B., U. Mich., 1929; LL.B., Columbia U., 1932, LL.D., 1978; LL.D., L.I. U., 1953, Yeshiva U., 1974, N.Y. Law Sch., 1975, Columbia U., 1978, Siena Coll., 1980; L.H.D. (hon.), Hebrew Union, 1979. Bar: N.Y. 1933. Assoc. Moers & Rosenschein, 1933, Engelhard, Pollak, Pitcher, Stern & Clarke, 1934-35; dep. asst. dist. atty., staff Thomas E. Dewey, 1935-37; dep. asst. dist. atty. for spl. rackets investigations, 1938-41; chief Indictment Bur., 1941; asso. with Dewey pvt. law practice, 1942; counsel to Gov. Dewey, 1943-50; apptd. justice State Supreme Ct., 1950; assoc. justice Appellate Div., First Dept., 1952-66; judge Ct. Appeals State N.Y., 1967-73, chief judge, 1974-78; of counsel Proskauer Rose Goetz & Mendelsohn, N.Y.C., 1978—; adj. prof. Columbia Sch. Law, 1963-69; also mem. bd. visitors. Mem. Pres.'s Commn. on Law Enforcement and Adminstrn. of Justice, 1965-67; mem. Fed. Commn. on Internat. Rules Jud. Procedure, 1958-66, N.Y. State Post War Pub. Works Planning Commn., 1943-45, Joint Legis. Com. on Interstate Cooperation (adminstr.), 1946, Gov's Com. on State Ednl. Program, 1945-47, Commn. Mcpl. Revenues and Reduction of Taxes, 1945-46; mem. adminstrv. tribunal Inter-Am. Devel. Bank, 1982—; mem. jud. panel Ctr. Pub. Resources, 1982—. Mem. exec. com. N.Y. chpt. Am. Jewish Com., also mem. nat. bd. govs.; chmn. 20th Century Fund Task Force, 1979. Fellow Am. Soc. Arts and Scis., Am. Bar Found. (hon.); mem. Am. Law Inst. (council, exec. com.), Inst. Jud. Adminstrn., Assn. Bar City N.Y. (past v.p.), N.Y. County Lawyers Assn. (dir.), ABA, N.Y. State Bar Assn. Club: Century (N.Y.C.). Lodge: B'nai B'rith. Home: 146 Central Park W New York NY 10023 Office: 300 Park Ave New York NY 10022

BREITENBECK, JOSEPH M., bishop; b. Detroit, Aug. 3, 1914; s. Matthew J. and Mary A. (Quinlan) B. Student, U. Detroit, 1932-35; B.A., Sacred Heart Sem., Detroit, 1938; postgrad., Gregorian U., Rome, Italy, 1938-40; S.T.L., Catholic U., Washington; J.C.L., Lateran U., Rome, 1949. Ordained priest Roman Catholic Ch., 1942; asst. at St. Margaret Mary Parish, Detroit, 1942-44; sec. to Cardinal Mooney, 1944-58, Cardinal Dearden, 1959; pastor, Assumption Grotto, 1959-67, consecrated bishop, 1965, bishop of, Grand Rapids, Mich., 1969—; Episcopal adviser Nat. Cath. Laymens Retreat Conf. Mem. Nat. Conf. Cath. Bishops (com. chmn.). Office: 265 Sheldon Ave SE Grand Rapids MI 49502 *

BREITENECKER, RUDIGER, pathologist; b. Vienna, Austria, 1929; came to U.S., 1654, naturalized, 1969; s. Leopold and Irma B.; m. Robin Jacques, 1963; children: Rudiger, Richard C., Roland. M.D., U. Vienna, 1954. Intern E.W. Sparrow Hosp., Lansing, Mich., 1955-56; resident in pathology Clevel. Met. Gen. Hosp., 1957-59; mem. teaching staff Western Res. U., 1958-59, Duke U., 1960-61; asst. med. examiner State of Md., Balt., 1962-67; asst. prof. forensic pathology U. Md., 1962—; prof. justice adminstrn. U. Louisville, 1978—; lectr. Johns Hopkins Sch. Medicine, 1979—; pathologist Greater Balt. Med. Ctr., 1967—, assoc. dir. pathology lab., 1970—; cons. legal medicine to fed. govt. Contbr. research publs. on forensic pathology. Fellow Am. Soc. Clin. Pathologists; mem. Am. Acad. Forensic Sci., Nat. Assn. Med. Examiners, Coll. Am. Pathologists, AMA, Am. Med. Soc. Office: Greater Balt Med Ctr Baltimore MD 21204

BREITENFELD, FREDERICK, JR., public broadcasting executive, educator; b. N.Y.C., Sept. 26, 1931; s. Frederick and Dorothy (Falk) B.; m. Mary Ellen Fitzgerald, Dec. 27, 1954; children: Ann Clark, Kathleen Ellen. B.S. in Engring., Tufts U., 1953, M.Ed., 1954; M.S. in Radio-TV, Syracuse U., 1960, Ph.D., 1963; L.H.D. (hon.), U. Md., 1976, Salisbury State Coll., 1982. Tchr. physics and chemistry pub. high sch., North Creek, N.Y., 1958-59; program adminstr. Univ. Coll., Syracuse U., 1960-61; asst. dean Syracuse U., 1961-63; resident cons. in communications U.S. Air Force, Cape Kennedy, Fla., 1963-64; research project dir. Nat. Assn. Ednl. Broadcasters, Washington, 1964-65, assoc. dir. ednl. TV stas. div., 1965-66; exec. dir. Md. Center for Pub. Broadcasting, Owings Mills, Md., 1966—; chmn. Eastern Ednl. TV Network, 1974-76; vice chmn. bd. mgrs. Pub. Broadcasting Service, 1973; cons., lectr. in field; assoc. prof. ednl. tech. Cath. U. Am., 1967-72; prof. Am. U., 1972-74; guest prof. Syracuse U., 1976; vis. prof. Johns Hopkins U., 1978—; chmn. bd. Nat. Univ. Consortium for Telecommunications in Teaching. Bd. dirs. Happy Hills Convalescent Home for Children, Balt., 1967-72. Served as pilot USNR, 1954-58. Recipient Alumni award Radio TV Dept. Syracuse U., 1967; Andrew White medal Loyola U., Balt., 1979; Lord Baltimore medal St. Mary's Coll., 1980. Home: 506 Gatewood Bensalem PA 19020 Office: 150 N 6th St Independence Mall Philadelphia PA 19106 *To live is both to care and to laugh.*

BREITENSTEIN, JEAN SALA, judge; b. Keokuk, Iowa, July 18, 1900; s. George J. and Ida M. (Sala) B.; m. Helen Collamore Thomas, July 8, 1925; children—Eleanore Thomas (Mrs. George M. Wilfley), Peter Frederick. A.B., U. Colo., 1922, LL.B., 1924, LL.D., 1965; LL.D., U. Denver, 1960. Bar: Colo. bar 1924. Asst. atty. gen., Colo., 1925-29, asst. U.S. dist atty., 1930-33, practice law, Denver, 1933-54, atty. State Colo. on interstate water matters, 1940-54, U.S. dist. judge, Colo., 1954-57; U.S. circuit judge 10th Circuit, Denver, 1957-70, sr. circuit judge, 1970—. Mem. Am., Colo., Denver bar assns., Order of Coif, Phi Beta Kappa. Republican. Episcopalian. Clubs: Mason (33 deg.), Law, Denver Country, Denver (Denver); University. Home: 1201 Williams St Denver CO 80218 Office: US Ct House Denver CO 80294

BREITKREUZ, GEORGE WILLIAM, publishing company executive; b. West New York, N.J., Feb. 22, 1928; s. Henry B.; m. Viola Kinkel, 1950; children: Thomas, Linda, Steven, Kenneth. B.B.A., Pace U., 1950. Auditor Ernst & Ernst (C.P.A.s), N.Y.C., 1951-54; v.p., treas. Am. Heritage Pub. Co., N.Y.C., 1955-70; v.p. fin. Daniel Starch & Staff, Mamaroneck, N.Y., 1970; v.p. fin., treas. Elba Systems Corp., Denver, 1970-73; exec. v.p. fin. and corp. services Houghton Mifflin Co., Boston, 1973—; trustee Home Savs. Bank, Boston. Served with AUS, 1946-47. Mem. Fin. Execs. Inst. Baptist. Home: 52 Fairoaks Ln Cohasset MA 02025 Office: 1 Beacon St Boston MA 02107

BREITROSE, HENRY S., educator; b. Bklyn., July 22, 1936; s. Charles and Ruth (Leib) B.; m. Prudence Elaine Martin, Oct. 11, 1968; children—Charles Daniel, Rebecca Marjorie. B.S., U. Wis., 1958; M.A., Northwestern U., 1959; Ph.D., Stanford U., 1966. Writer Internat. Film Bur., 1958; mgr. Midwest office Contemporary Films, 1959; mem. faculty Stanford U., 1959—, prof. communication, 1975—, chmn. dept.; vis. prof. London Sch. Econs., 1976-77; mem. public media panel Nat. Endowment Arts, 1974—; ednl. adv. com. Am. Film Inst., 1974. Author articles, chpts. in books. Grantee Rockefeller Found., 1965-66; Lilly Endowment, 1976-77; fellow Stanford U., 1972-74. Mem. Univ. Film Assn., Broadcast Educators Assn., Internat. Communication Assn., Internat. Inst. Communications. Home: 897 Tolman Dr Stanford CA 94305 Office: Dept Communication Stanford Univ Stanford CA 94305

BREITWIESER, CHARLES JOHN, engr., educator; b. Colorado Springs, Colo., Sept. 23, 1910; s. Joseph Valentine and Ruth (Fowler) B.; m. Irene Louise Kellman, May 29, 1943; children—Diane Louise, Janice Lynn. B.S. in E.E, U. N.D., 1930, D.Sc. (hon.), 1949; student, Chgo. Central Sta. Inst., 1930- 31; M.S., Calif. Inst. Tech., 1933. Instr. engring. and math. U. N.D., 1931; elec. engr. Pub. Service No. Ill., 1930-31; engr. United Sound Products Corp., Los Angeles, 1933-34; cons. engr. and mfg. comml. research, Pasadena, Calif., 1934-37; formed C.J. Breitwieser & Co., 1935, 1937; sec.- treas. Conducto-Therm. Corp., Los Angeles, 1939; cons. engr. DeForest Labs.; and chief engr. DeForest Research; with Consol.-Vultee Aircraft Mfg. Co., chief engring. labs. and electronics, 1940-50; v.p. engring., gen. mgr. research and devel. div. Lear, Inc., Santa Monica, Calif., 1954-57; v.p., gen. mgr. Learcal div. Lear, Inc., 1955-57; pres. Metrolog Corp. (subs. Air Logistics Corp.), 1958-60; v.p. engring. and customer relations Air Logistics Corp., 1958-60; pres., chmn. bd. Dominion Devel. Corp., 1960-76; faculty Calif. Pacific U. Sch. Bus. Adminstrn., 1976—; exec. v.p., gen. mgr. Cubic Corp., San Diego, 1961-73, also dir.; dir. Swan Electronics Corp., U.S. Elevator Corp.; dir. engring. P.R. Mallory & Co., Indpls., 1950-54; cons. engr. Los Angeles Police and Fire depts., 1932- 35; Cons. to Research and Devel. Bd. Author papers in field. Fellow Inst. Radio Engrs.; mem. Am. Inst. E.E. (mem. com. on electronics), AAAS, American Physics Soc., Nat. Aircraft Standards Com., Sigma Xi, Phi Delta Gamma. Patentee. Home: 2738 Caminito Prado La Jolla CA 92037 *To maintain a conscious positive attitude and positive courses of action with goals just beyond that of immediate practical achievement.*

BREMBECK, WINSTON LAMONT, educator; b. Urbana, Ind., Sept. 28, 1912; s. Paul John and Hulda (Speicher) B.; m. Neva Gloyd, June 20, 1940. B.A. magna cum laude, Manchester Coll., N. Manchester, Ind., 1936; M.A., U. Wis., 1938, Ph.D., 1947. Instr. Westmar Coll., LeMars, Iowa, 1936-39; tutor Bklyn. Coll., 1939-42; mem. faculty U. Wis., 1947—, prof. communication and pub. address, 1960—; cons. in communications and persuasion to business, profl. and religious groups, 1947—. Author: (with W.S. Howell) Persuasion a Means of Social Control, 1952, Persuasion a Means of Social Influence, 1976, also articles. Served with AUS, 1943-46. Recipient A.T. Weaver Outstanding Tchr. award Wis. Speech Assn., 1970. Mem. Speech Assn. Am. (exec. com. 1966-68), Central States Speech Assn. (pres. 1965-66), Wis. Speech Assn. (pres. 1949-50), Delta Sigma Rho, Tau Kappa Alpha, Phi Kappa Phi. Republican. Methodist. Home: 3206 Leyton Lane Madison WI 53713

BREMENT, MARSHALL, ambassador; b. N.Y.C., Jan. 10, 1932; s. Isidore and Haya (Glauberman) B.; m. Joan Bernstein, May 2, 1953; children: Diana, Mark, Gabriel; m. Pamela Sanders, June 7, 1973. B.A., NYU, 1952; M.A., U. Md., 1955; Nat. Inst. Pub. Affairs fellow, Stanford, 1966-67. Joined U.S. Fgn. Service, 1956; staff asst. State Dept., asst. sec., Far East, 1956-57; assigned Chinese lang. tng., 1958-60; consul polit. sect. Am. Consulate Gen., Hong Kong, 1960-63; Russian lang. tng., 1963-64; polit. sect. Am. embassy, Moscow, 1964-66, chief polit. sect., Singapore, 1967-70, counselor pub. affairs, Djakarta, 1970-73, minister-counselor pub. affairs, Saigon, 1973-74, counselor polit. affairs, Moscow, 1974-76, Madrid, 1977-79; staff mem. Nat. Security Council, White House, 1979-80; dep. permanent rep. U.S. Mission to UN, 1981—; U.S. ambassador to Iceland, 1981—. Served with USAF, 1952-54. Fellow Nat. Inst. Pub. Affairs; mem. Am. Fgn. Service Assn., Phi Kappa Phi. Address: US Embassy Laufasvegur 21 Reykjavik Iceland

BREMERMANN, HERBERT JOHN, JR., insurance executive; b. New Orleans, Dec. 9, 1922; s. Herbert John and Hilda Marie (Lemarie) B.; m. Mary Gibson Parlour, Feb. 14, 1950; children: Eve P., Herbert John, III. A.B., Tulane U., New Orleans, 1944, LL.B., 1949. Spl. agt. FBI, 1949-53; with Black, Rogers & Co., 1953-56, Md. Casualty Co., 1956-82; successively resident v.p., v.p. casualty div.; v.p. mktg. div. Md. Casualty Co., 1973-75, exec. v.p., 1975-76, pres., chief exec. officer, Balt., 1976—, chmn. bd., 1979—; vice chmn. bd., dir. Am. Gen. Corp., Houston, 1982—; chmn. bd. Life & Casualty Ins. Co. Tenn, 1982—, Nat. Life & Accident Ins. Co., 1982—; sr. chmn. Am. Gen. Corp., Nashville; chmn., chief exec. officer Gulf Life Ins. Co.; dir. Md. Nat. Corp., 3d Nat. Bank, 3d Nat. Corp., Nashville. Mem. pres.'s council Tulane U.; bd. dirs. Assn. Ind. Colls. in Md. Served to capt. USMC, 1943-46. Named Oustanding Alumnus Tulane U. Sch. Law, 1977. Mem. Ins. Info. Inst. (dir.), Am. Ins. Assn. (dir.), Nashville C. of C. (dir.). Clubs: Balt. Country (Balt.); Belle Meade Country; Center, Balt. City, Md. (Balt.); Cumberland, Nashville City (Nashville). Home: 3704-Q Estes Rd Nashville TN 37215 Office: Nat Life & Accident Ins Co Am Gen Ctr Nashville TN 37250

BREMNER, JOHN BURTON, journalist; b. Brisbane, Australia, Dec. 28, 1920; came to U.S., 1950, naturalized, 1960; s. Norman Frederick and Pauline Marcia (Lucas) B.; m. Mary Ann McCue, Dec. 23, 1968. S.T.B., Propaganda Fide U., Rome, 1941; M.S., Columbia U., 1952; Ph.D., U. Iowa, 1965. Ordained priest Roman Catholic Ch., 1943-68; nat. sec. Pontifical Mission Aid Socs., Australia, 1945-48; editor Cath. Missions, Holy Child, Apostolatus, Australia, 1945-48; insp. schs. Brisbane (Australia) Archdiocese, 1948-49; asso. editor Fla. Cath., 1953-54; polit. columnist Los Angeles Tidings, 1954-56; asso. prof. English, asst. to pres. U. San Diego, 1957-61; asst. prof. journalism U. Iowa, 1965-68; asso. prof. U. Kans., Lawrence, 1969-72, prof., 1972—, Oscar S. Stauffer prof. journalism, 1976—; newspaper cons., 1973—. Author: HTK - A Study in News Headlines, 1975, Words on Words - A Dictionary for Writers and Others Who Care About Words, 1980. Pulitzer traveling fellow, 1952-53; recipient Amoco Disting. Teaching award, HOPE award U. Kans., 1971; Gannett Found. grantee for nat. editing seminars, 1980-81, 83-84. Mem. Sigma Delta Chi, Kappa Tau Alpha. Republican. Home: 2614 Orchard Ln Lawrence KS 66044 Office: Sch Journalism Univ Kansas Lawrence KS 66045

BREMNER, JOHN MCCOLL, agronomy and biochemistry educator; b. Dumbarton, Scotland, Jan. 18, 1922; came to U.S., 1959; s. Archibald Donaldson and Sarah Kennedy (McColl) B.; m. Eleanor Mary Williams, Sept. 30, 1950; children: Stuart, Carol. B.S., Glasgow U., 1944; Ph.D., U. London, 1948, Sc.D., 1959. With chemistry dept. Rothamsted Exptl. Sta., Harpenden, Eng., 1945-59; assoc. prof. Iowa State U., Ames, 1959-61, prof. agronomy and biochemistry, 1961—, C.F. Curtiss Disting. prof. agriculture, prof. agronomy, biochemistry, 1975—; tech. expert Internat. Atomic Energy Agy., Austria, 1964-65, Yugoslavia, 1964-65. Recipient Alexander Von Humboldt award

Alexander Von Humboldt Found., W.Germany, 1982, Bouyoucos Soil Sci. Disting. Career award Am. Soc. Agronomy, 1982, Soil Sci. Achievement award, 1967, Outstanding Research award First Miss. Corp., 1979; Rockefeller fellow, 1957; Guggenheim fellow, 1968; recipient Gov.'s Sci. medal State of Iowa, 1983. Fellow Am. Soc. Agronomy, AAAS, Soil Sci. Soc. Am.; mem. Brit. Soc. Soil Sci., Internat. Soil Sci. Soc., Phi Kappa Phi, Sigma Xi, Gamma Sigma Delta. Home: 2028 Pinehurst Dr Ames IA 50010 Office: Iowa State U Dept Agronomy Ames IA 50011

BREMS, HANS JULIUS, economist, educator; b. Viborg, Denmark, Oct. 16, 1915; s. Holger and Andrea (Golditz) B.; m. Ulla Constance Simoni, May 20, 1944; children: Lisa, Marianne, Karen Joyce. Cand. polit., U. Copenhagen, 1941, dr.polit., 1950; Hedersdoktor (hon.), Svenska Handelshögskolan, Helsinki, Finland, 1970. Asst. prof. U. Copenhagen, 1943-51; lectr. U. Calif., Berkeley, 1951-54; mem. faculty U. Ill., Champaign-Urbana, 1954—, prof., 1955—; vis. prof. UCLA, 1953, U. Mich., 1957, U. Calif., Berkeley, 1959, Harvard U., 1960, U. Kiel, (W.Ger.), 1961, U. Colo., 1963, U. Göttingen, (W.Ger.), 1964, U. Hamburg, 1967, U. Uppsala, (Sweden), 1968, U. Stockholm, 1980, U. Zurich, 1983, others. Author: Product Equilibrium under Monopolistic Competition, 1951, Output, Employment, Capital, and Growth, 1959, 2d edit., 1973, Quantitative Economic Theory, 1968, Labor, Capital, and Growth, 1973, A Wage Earners' Investment Fund—Forms and Economic Effects, 1975, Inflation, Interest, and Growth—A Synthesis, 1980, Dynamische Makrotheorie—Inflation, Zins und Wachstum, 1980, Fiscal Theory—Governments, Inflation and Growth, 1983; contbr.: articles to profl. jours. and Ency. Americana. Rockefeller fellow, 1946-47; Fulbright prof., 1961, 64. Mem. Am. Econ. Assn., Royal Econ. Soc., Can. Econs. Assn., Danish Acad. Scis. and Letters (fgn.). Home: 1103 S Douglas Ave Urbana IL 61801 Office: Box 99 Commerce West 1206 S 6th St Champaign IL 61820

BRENDEL, ALFRED, concert pianist; b. b., Wiesenberg, Austria, Jan. 5, 1931; s. Albert and Ida (Wieltschnig) B.; m. Iris Heymann-Gonzala, 1960 (div. 1972); m. Irene Semler, 1975; 1 son, 2 daus. Studied piano under Sofija Dezelic, Zagreb, Yugoslavia, Graz, Austria, Lucerne, Switerland, Basel, Switzerland, Salzburg, Austria; studied composition under A. Michl, Graz; studied harmony under Franjo Dugan, Zagreb; D.Mus. hon., U. London, 1978, D.Litt., Sussex U., 1981. First piano recital, 1948, concert tours through, Europe, Latin Am., N. Am., 1963—, Australia, 1963, 66, 69, 76, appeared at many music festivals including, Salzburg, 1960—, also appeared at festivals of, Vienna, Edinburg, Aldeburgh, Athens, Granada, P.R., has performed with most of major orchs. of, Europe and U.S., also others; recorded: complete piano works of Beethoven, Schubert's piano works of 1822-28; contbr. essays on music to profl. jours. Recipient Premio Citta de Bolzano Concorso Busoni, 1949, Grand Prix du Disque, 1965, Edison prize, 1974, Grand Prix des Disquaires de France, 1975, Deutscher Schallplattenpreis, 1976, 77, Wiener Flotenuhr, 1976, Gramaphone award, 1978, Japanese Grand Prix, 1978, Franz Liszt prize, 1980. Mem. Royal Acad. Music (hon.). Office: care Colbert Artists Mgmt Inc 111 W 57th St New York NY 10019 *

BRENDLINGER, LEROY R., college president; b. Frederick, Pa., Dec. 14, 1918; s. Claude R. and Elsie May B.; m. Virginia Steltz, Dec. 28, 1941; children: Dawn, Brian, Craig. B.S., West Chester State Coll., 1946; M.S., U. Pa., 1949; Ed.D., Temple U., 1959. Former tchr., East Greenville, Pa.; Ordnance Officer Candidate Sch., Aberdeen, Md.; former prin. Pottsgrove (Pa.) Schs.; former asst. supt. Montgomery (Pa.) Schs.; now pres. Montgomery County Community Coll. Past pres. Montgomery County (Pa.) Health and Welfare Council; bd. dirs. Montgomery Hosp., Lutheran Children and Family Service. Served with U.S. Army, 1942-46; ETO. Mem. Am. Assn. Jr. and Community Colls. (past pres. Pa. Commn. Community Colls.). Club: Brookside Country (sec. bd. govs.). Office: 340 De Kalb Blue Bell PA 19422

BRENDON, RUPERT TIMOTHY RUNDLE, advertising agency executive; b. Bristol, Eng., Mar. 7, 1943; s. George Henry and Sydney Frances (Cook) B.; m. Georgia Marquerite Brock, July 17, 1964 (div. Sept. 1979); 1 dau., Sophia Frances Rundle; m. Marion Edith Bras, Oct. 15, 1982. Print prodn.-traffic Erwin Wasey, London, 1961-62; account exec. Spottiswoode, London, 1963-65, McCann-Erickson, 1965-67; dir. Norman Craig & Kummel, Toronto, P.R., London, 1968-73; v.p. Leo Burnett, Toronto, Ont., Can., 1973-78; pres., chief exec. officer Benton & Bowles, Toronto, 1978—. Cons. fund raiser Grenville Christian Coll., Brockville, Ont., 1983; chmn. Hemophilia Found. Can., Toronto, 1982—. Recipient Cert. of Service Ont. div. Can. Cancer Soc., 1982. Mem. Inst. Canadian Advt., Broadcast Execs. Soc., Profl. Mktg. Research Soc., Proprietary Assns. Can., Can. Fragrance and Toiletry Assn. Clubs: Cricket (Toronto); Canadian (N.Y.C.). Office: Benton & Bowles Can Ltd 1235 Bay St Toronto ON Canada M5R 3K4

BRENEMAN, DAVID WORTHY, college president; b. Albuquerque, Oct. 24, 1940; s. Clement David and Muriel Ruth B.; m. Judith Dodge, June 10, 1962; children: Erica, Carleton. B.A., U. Colo., 1963; Ph.D., U. Calif.-Berkeley, 1970. Asst. prof. econs. Amherst Coll., 1970-72; staff dir. Nat. Acad. Sci., 1972-75; sr. fellow Brookings Instn., 1975-83; pres. Kalamazoo Coll., 1983—; professorial lectr. econs. George Washington U., 1979-82. Author: Public Policy and Private Higher Education, 1978, Financing Community Colleges, 1981; exec. editor: Change Mag., 1980—. Trustee Woodrow Wilson Nat. Fellowship Found., 1980—, W.E. Upjohn Inst., 1983—; dir. Nat. Ctr. for Higher Edn. Mgmt. Systems, 1980—. Woodrow Wilson fellow, 1963; Danforth fellow, 1963; NDEA fellow, 1967; recipient Buchanan prize U. Calif.-Berkeley, 1970. Mem. Am. Econ. Assn., Am. Assn Higher Edn. (bd. dirs 1982—). Democrat. Clubs: Park, Kalamazoo Country. Home: 136 Thompson St Kalamazoo MI 49007 Office: Kalamazoo College 1200 Academy St Kalamazoo MI 49007

BRENGEL, FRED L., business executive; b. Hicksville, N.Y., 1923; m. B.S. in Mech. Engring., Stevens Inst. Tech., 1944. With Johnson Controls Inc. (formerly Johnson Service Co.), Milw., 1948—, v.p. sales, 1965-67, pres., chief exec. officer, 1967—; also dir.; dir. First Wis. Co., Heil Col., Sta-Rite Industries, Inc., Twin Disk, Inc. Served to lt. USN, 1943-46. Office: Johnson Controls Inc 507 E Michigan St Box 423 Milwaukee WI 53201 *

BRENNAN, BERNARD FRANCIS, retail chain store executive; b. Chgo., 1938; married. B.A., Coll. St. Thomas, 1964. With Sears, Roebuck & Co., 1964-76, Sav-A-Stop, Inc., 1976—, group v.p.-service mdse. group, 1976-78, pres., chief operating officer, 1978-79, pres., chief exec. officer, 1979-82; exec. v.p. Montgomery Ward & Co., Inc., Chgo., 1982—. Served with U.S. Army, 1958-60, 62. Office: Montgomery Ward & Co Inc Montgomery Ward Plaza Chicago IL 60671 *

BRENNAN, CHARLES MARTIN, III, electronics company executive; b. New Haven, Jan. 30, 1942; s. Charles Martin and Margaret Mary (Gleeson) B.; m. Mary Day Ely, June 22, 1966; children: Elizabeth Martin, Cynthia Herrick. B.A., Yale U., 1964; M.B.A., Columbia U., 1969. Gen. mgr. New Haven Malleable Iron co., 1966-68; fin. analyst Scovill Mfg. co., 1970-71; treas. Cerro Corp., N.Y.C., 1971-74; fin. dir. Imperial Trans Europe N.V., London, 1976, mng. dir., 1977-79; treas. Gould Inc., Chgo., 1974-76, v.p. Latin Am., Sao Paulo, 1979-80, sr. v.p., chief fin. officer, Chgo., 1980—; dir. Victoria Stas. Inc. Chmn. spl. gifts Am. Cancersoc., Chgo, 1980. Mem. Machinery and Allied Products Inst. (fin council 1980-82). Republican. Episcopalian. Clubs: Onwentsia (Lake Forest, Ill.); Casino, Racquet, Econ. (Chgo.). Home: 320 N Mayflower Rd Lake Forest IL 60045 Office: Gould Inc 10 Gould Ctr Rolling Meadows IL 60008

BRENNAN, DONALD P., investment company executive; b. N.Y.C., Dec. 31, 1940; s. Patrick James and Mary B.; m. Patricia A. Callahan, Sept. 22, 1962; children: Eileen, Donald, Maureen, Patrick, Jonathan, Erin. B.S. in Marine Sci, Maritime Coll., 1961; M.B.A. in Mgmt. Sci, CUNY, 1966; postgrad. in ops. research, Baruch Sch., 1967-70. Sr. planning analyst Corning Glass Work, N.Y., 1966-67; with Internat. Paper Co., 1967-82, exec. v.p. planning and adminstrn., N.Y.C., 1977, exec. v.p. paper and packaging bus., 1977-82, vice-chmn., 1980-82; vice-chmn., dir. Can. Internat. Paper Co., 1980-82; adviser, then mng. dir. Morgan Stanley & Co., 1982—; chmn., dir. Bodcaw Co.; Trustee Mary Baldwin Coll.; mem. Pres.'s Commn. on Exec. Exchange, 1977—, Ireland-U.S. Council Commerce and Industry; mem. dean's adv. council Purdue U. Served with USN, 1961-66. Mem. Beta Gamma Sigma (dir.'s table). Home: Foxmount Hoagland's Ln Old Brookville NY 11545 Office: Morgan Stanley & Co 1251 Ave of Americas New York NY 10020 *

BRENNAN, EDWARD A., retail executive; b. Chgo., Jan. 16, 1934; s. Edward and Margaret (Bourget) B.; m. Lois Lyon, June 11, 1955; children: Edward J., Cynthia Walls, Sharon Gardella, Donald A., John L., Linda. B.A., Marquette U., Milw., 1955. With Sears, Roebuck & Co., 1956—, exec. v.p. So. terr., Atlanta, 1978-80, pres., chief operating officer for merchandising, 1980-81, chmn. bd., chief exec. officer Sears mdse. group, 1981—; dir. Sears, Roebuck & Co., Sears-Roebuck Found. Trustee Atlanta U., Marquette U., De Paul U.; mem. bus. adv. council Chgo. Urban League, 1980—. Mem. Nat. Retail Mchts. Assn. (dir.), Am. Retail Fedn. (dir.), Chgo. Econ. Club. Clubs: Chicago, Metropolitan. Address: Sears Merchandise Group Sears Tower Chicago IL 60684

BRENNAN, EILEEN REGINA, actress; b. Los Angeles, Sept. 3, 1935; d. John Gerald and Jeanne (Menehan) B.; m. David John Lampson, Dec. 28, 1969 (div. 1975); children: Samuel John, Patrick Oliver. Student, Am. Acad. Dramatic Arts, 1955-56. Appeared off-Broadway: Little Mary Sunshine (Theatre World award 1960, Obie award 1960, Newspaper Guild award 1960); appeared on Broadway: Hello, Dolly, 1964-66; appeared in nat. co.: The Miracle Worker, 1961-62; films Divorce American Style, 1967, The Last Picture Show, 1971, The Sting, 1974, Murder By Death, 1976, The Cheap Detective, 1978, FM, 1978, Private Benjamin, 1980, also TV series, 1980-81 (Emmy award as best supporting actress 1981). Mem. Actors Equity, Screen Actors Guild, AFTRA. Roman Catholic. Salt Spring Island BC Canada Office: care Creative Artists Agy Inc 1888 Century Park E Suite 1400 Los Angeles CA 90067 *

BRENNAN, FRANCIS PATRICK, banker; b. Somerville, Mass., Jan. 9, 1917; s. John Joseph and Bridget (Sullivan) B.; m. Mary J. Gilhooly, July 23, 1949; children: Mary Ann, Eileen, John, Thomas. A.B. cum laude, Boston Coll., 1939; postgrad., Bentley Coll. Accounting and Finance, 1941. Loan officer Reconstrn. Finance Corp., Boston, 1941-42, 46-53; chmn. Mass. Bus. Devel. Corp., Boston, 1954-61; chmn., chief exec. officer Union Warren Savs. Bank, Boston, 1961—; dir., chmn. audit com. Boston Co. Funds, Inc.; trustee Mass. THRIFTPAC, Am. Express Funds; corporator Mt. McKinley Nat. Bank, Fairbanks, Alaska; dir., exec. and fin. coms., chmn. salary com. Boston Mut. Life Ins. Co. Former trustee vice chmn. exec. com., chmn. fin. com. Stonehill Coll.; bd. dirs. Greater Boston C. of C., Jobs For Mass.; bd. overseers, mem. finance com. Sidney Farber Cancer Inst., Boston. Served to 2d lt. AUS, 1942-45; ETO. Decorated Bronze Star medal. Mem. Savs. Banks Assn. Mass. (pres. 1972-73, dir., mem. com. on corp. structure), Nat. Council Savs. Instns. (com. liaison with fed. agys.), Mortgage Bankers Assn. Am. (Washington com.). Clubs: Algonquin, Clover, Federal (Boston) (pres.); Winchester Country, Boston Madison Square Garden. Home: 36 Central St Winchester MA 01890 Office: 133 Federal St Boston MA 02110

BRENNAN, FRANCIS W., winery exec.; b. Newark, Nov. 18, 1919; s. William J. and B. Agnes (McDermott) B.; m. Betty Kirkwood, Feb. 19, 1944; children—Judith, Francis K., Robert. A.B., Princeton, 1940; LL.B., Harvard, 1947. Bar: N.J. bar 1947, Cal. bar 1973. Asso. firm Pitney, Hardin & Ward, Newark, 1947-53; gen. counsel Cal. Oil Co., Perth Amboy, N.J., 1953-54; v.p. legal, sec. P. Ballantine & Sons, Newark, 1954-71; v.p., sec., gen. counsel Rheingold Breweries, Inc., Bklyn., 1971-72; v.p., counsel E & J Gallo Winery, Modesto, Cal., 1972—; sec. Boston Celtics Basketball Club, 1968-69. Commr. Essex County (N.J.) Park Commn., 1958-73, pres., 1963-65, 70-71; Pres., chmn. trustees Boys Clubs Newark, 1966-69. Served to capt. USAAF, World War II. Mem. Am., Essex County, Stanislaus County bar assns., State Bar Cal. Home: 1812 Camden Dr Modesto CA 95355 Office: 600 Yosemite Blvd Modesto CA 95350

BRENNAN, JAMES G., physicist; b. Hazelton, Pa., Aug. 30, 1927; s. Thomas H. and Helen (Gallagher) B.; m. Anne Searls, July 28, 1951; children—Thomas, Sean, Kathleen, James, Theodore. B.S., U. Scranton, 1948; M.S., Ph.D., U. Wis. Mem. Faculty Cath. U., 1952—, prof. physics, chmn. dept., asso. dean grad. studies Arts & Scis., 1975-77; cons. Naval Ordnance Lab., 1955; liaison scientist Office Naval Research, London, 1965-66; Faculty rep. Cath. U. bd. trustees, 1968-72. Author articles theoretical nuclear physics, atomic physics. Mem. Am. Phys. Soc., Washington Philos. Soc. Roman Catholic. Club: Cosmos (Washington). Home: 8910 Sudbury Rd Silver Spring MD 20901 Office: Keane Physics Bldg Michigan Ave NE Washington DC 20064

BRENNAN, JAMES THOMAS, radiologist; b. St. Louis, Jan. 12, 1916; s. James Thomas and Ellen Loretta (Hayes) B.; children by previous marriage—Martha Ellen, James Thomas; m. Elizabeth Bast Gagné, Aug. 23, 1975; stepchildren—William Roderick, Philip Bast, Elizabeth Lower. B.A. in Philosophy, U. Ill., 1939; M.D., U. Minn., 1943. Diplomate: Am. Bd. Radiology. Commd. 1st lt., M.C. AUS, 1943; advanced through grades to col. U.S. Army, 1959; intern St. Mary's Group Hosps., St. Louis, 1943; engaged in radiation hazard control and radiobiology research Los Alamos Labs., 1948-52; chief biophysics dept. Walter Reed Army Inst. Research, 1952-54; resident radiology Walter Reed Army Hosp., 1954-57; cons. radiol. def. to chief surgeon U.S. Army, Europe, 1957-60; chief radiation therapy Walter Reed Gen. Hosp., 1960-61; dir. Armed Forces Radiobiology Research Inst., 1961-66; ret., 1966; vis. lectr. radiology U. Pa. Med. Sch., Phila., 1966-67, Matthew J. Wilson prof. research radiology, 1967-79; pres. Med. Consultation Corp., Phila., 1979—; cons. in field, 1965—. Decorated Bronze Star, Legion of Merit. Mem. Radiol. Soc. N.Am., AMA, AAUP, AAAS. Home: 9120 Germantown Ave Philadelphia PA 19118

BRENNAN, JOHN ALBERT, building materials company executive; b. Yonkers, N.Y., Apr. 4, 1931; s. Roland J. and Margaret (Smith) B.; m. Maureen McCoy, Feb. 8, 1958; children: Mary, Eileen, Nancy, Bernadette, Terence. B.B.A., Pace U., N.Y.C., 1958. Asst. treas. Hercules, Inc., N.Y.C., 1955-66; credit mgr. Am. Can Co., N.Y.C., 1966-70; asst. gen. mgr. credit Borden, Inc., N.Y.C., 1970-72; sr. v.p. GAF Corp., N.Y.C., 1972—. Served with USAR, 1950-53. Mem. N.Y. Credit and Mgt. Assn. (1st v.p. 1970-74), Asphalt Roofing Mfgrs. Assn. (dir. 1980-83). Republican. Roman Catholic. Club: New York Athletic. Home: 307 Bellevue Ave Yonkers NY 10702 Office: GAF Corp. 140 W 51st St New York NY 10020

BRENNAN, JOHN EDWARD, industrialist; b. N.Y.C., July 12. 1928; s. Michael J. and Catherine T. (Mallon) B.; m. Carol Claire Kissell, Oct. 27, 1956; children: Susan Lynn, Nancy Carol, Pamela Ann, Karen Claire. B.E.E., Manhattan Coll., 1952; M.B.A., NYU, 1955. Registered prof. engr., N.Y. Application engr. Westinghouse Electric, N.Y.C., 1952-55; asst. v.p. atomic power Babcock & Wilcox, N.Y.C., 1955-60; asst. to pres. Garlock Inc., Palmyra, N.Y., 1960-64, mgr., 1964-66, v.p. mech. power, Rochester, N.Y., 1966-76, sr. v.p., Rochester, 1976—; pres. Garlock Spl. Products Div., 1976—; dir. Garlock Bearings, Inc., Garlock GmbH, Garlock Singapore Pte. Served with U.S. Army, 1946-48. Mem. Soc. Plastics Industries, Nat. Fluid Power Assn., IEEE, Am. Nuclear Soc. (N.Y. sec. chmn. 1959-60). Roman Catholic. Home: 44 Little Spring Run Fairport NY 14450 Office: Garlock Special Products Div 1250 Midtown Tower Rochester NY 14604

BRENNAN, JOHN MERRITT, banker; b. Gary, Ind., Aug. 27, 1935; s. John A. and Mary (Merritt) B.; m. Dorothy J. Howland, June 17, 1961; children—David, Judith, James, Daniel. B.B.A., U. Notre Dame, 1957; M.B.A., Ind. U., 1960. Vice-pres. First Nat. Bank Chgo., 1960-70; chmn. exec. com. Boatmen's Nat. Bank, St. Louis, 1970—. Home: 9840 Copper Hill Rd Saint Louis MO 63124 Office: Box 236 Saint Louis MO 63166

BRENNAN, JOSEPH BENJAMIN, lawyer; b. Savannah, Ga., Aug. 17, 1903; s. Patrick and Margaret (Dowling) B.; m. Catherine Ginn, May 30, 1931; children—Helen Ginn (Mrs. William E. Gilbert), John Charles. A.B., Georgetown U., 1925; LL.B., Harvard, 1928. Bar: Ga. bar 1928, D.C. bar 1937. Practiced in, Atlanta, 1928—, Washington, 1937—; asso. firm Sutherland & Tuttle, 1928-33; partner firm Sutherland, Asbill & Brennan (and predecessors), Atlanta, 1933—. Hon. bd. dirs. Atlanta chpt. A.R.C. Mem. Am., Ga., Atlanta bar assns., Georgetown U. Alumni Assn. (John Carroll award 1956, pres. 1954-56). Democrat. Roman Catholic. Clubs: Piedmont Driving, Atlanta Athletic, Lawyers, Commerce (Atlanta); University (Washington); Oglethorpe (Savannah). Home: 2507 Dellwood Dr NW Atlanta GA 30305 Office: First Nat Bank Tower Atlanta GA 30303

BRENNAN, JOSEPH CANTWELL, banker; b. Roslyn, N.Y., Sept. 26, 1910; s. Joseph P. and Evangeline (Walsh) B.; m. Anne C. Patterson, Sept. 7, 1935; 1 dau., Constance C. Student, LaSalle Mil. Acad., 1929; Ph.B., Georgetown U., 1933. With Mfrs. Trust Co., 1933-45, asst. sec., 1940-45; asst. treas. Bankers Trust Co., 1946-49, asst. v.p., 1949-51, v.p., 1951-52; v.p., asst. to pres. Emigrant Savs. Bank, N.Y.C., 1953-56, pres., 1957-67, chmn. bd., 1967-78, chmn. exec. com., 1979—, also trustee; dir. St. Joseph's Union, S.I., Patterson Fuel Oil Co., Floral Park, N.Y., Diamond Internat. Corp.; mem. Project Fin. Agy. of N.Y. State. Mem. Cardinals Com. of the Laity; dir. Cath. Youth Orgn., N.Y.C.; bd. dirs. United Hosp. Fund N.Y.; chmn. bd. dirs. N.Y.C. Community Preservation Corp. Served as lt. comdr. USNR, 1942-46. Decorated Bronze Star medal; recipient Nat. Brotherhood award NCCJ, 1969; Gold medal Cath. Youth Orgn., 1974; Good Scout award Boy Scouts Am., 1975; Knight of Malta. Mem. Friendly Sons of St. Patrick (treas.). Clubs: Union League, Creek. Home: 200 E 66th St New York NY 10021 Office: 5 E 42d St New York NY 10017

BRENNAN, JOSEPH EDWARD, gov. Maine, lawyer; b. Portland, Maine, Nov. 2, 1934; s. John J. and Katherine (Mulkerin) B.; m. children—Joseph E., Tara E. B.S., Boston Coll., 1958; LL.B., U. Maine, 1963. Bar: Maine bar 1963. Pvt. practice, Portland, 1963-70, county atty., Cumberland County, 1971-72; partner firm Brennan and Brennan, Portland, 1972-74; atty. gen., State of Maine, 1975-79, gov., 1979—; mem. Maine Ho. of Reps., 1965-70, asst. minority leader, 1967-70; mem. Maine Senate, 1973-74, also minority leader. Served with AUS, 1953-55. Mem. Nat. Govs. Assn. (internat. trade and fgn. relations com., chmn. legal affairs com., mem. community and econ. devel. com., transp., commerce and tech. com.). Roman Catholic. Home: 104 Frances St Portland ME 04102 Office: State House Augusta ME 04333

BRENNAN, JOSEPH GERARD, educator; b. Boston, Nov. 2, 1910; s. Joseph and Nora (Sheridan) B.; m. Mary Jean McLeod, June 7, 1938; children—Peter, Colin, Mario, Ainslie, Nicholas, Patrick. A.B., Boston Coll., 1933; A.M., Harvard, 1935; Ph.D., Columbia, 1942. Instr., then asso. prof. philosophy Coll. New Rochelle, N.Y., 1937-47; faculty Barnard Coll., Columbia U., 1947—, prof. philosophy, 1962-76, emeritus, 1976, chmn. dept., 1953-65; lectr. Hofstra U., 1949—; vis. lectr. Sarah Lawrence Coll., 1965-66; prof. Naval War Coll., Newport, R.I., 1978—. Author: Thomas Mann's World, 1942, The Meaning of Philosophy, 1953, A Handbook of Logic, 1957, Three Philosophical Novelists, 1964, Ethics and Morals, 1973, The Education of a Prejudiced Man, 1977. Founding trustee Levittown (N.Y.) Pub. Library, 1950-54; dir., trustee Boston Coll., 1969-73; trustee Bethpage (N.Y.) Pub. Library, 1956-80. Served to lt. USNR, 1943-46; comdr. Res.; ret. Mem. Am. Philos. Assn., Am. Comparative Lit. Soc., Phi Beta Kappa. Home: Box 987 Little Compton RI 02837 Office: US Naval War Coll Newport RI 02840

BRENNAN, LAWRENCE EDWARD, electronics engineer; b. Oak Park, Ill., Jan. 29, 1927; s. Lawrence John and Lillian Irene (Day) B.; m. Mary Ellen Green, Sept. 11, 1947; children: Kathleen, Marianne, Treresa, James. B.S. in Elec. Engring., U. Ill, 1948; Ph.D. Elec. Engring., U. Ill., 1951. Mem. tech. staff Rand Corp., Santa Monica, Calif., 1951-57; chief scientist Tech. Service Corp., Santa Monica, 1967-80; v.p. Adaptive Sensors, Inc., Santa Monica, 1980—. Served with USN, 1944-46. Fellow IEEE. Home: 4965 Escobedo Dr. Woodland Hills CA 91364 Office: Adaptive Sensors Inc 216 Pico Blvd Santa Monica CA 90405

BRENNAN, LEO JOSEPH, JR., foundation executive; b. Hancock, Mich., Jan. 24, 1930; s. Leo Joseph and Jane (Larmer) B.; m. Barbara Ann Couzens, July 10, 1958; children: Moira, Leo Joseph, Margaret, Kevin. B.A., U. Notre Dame, 1951, M.A., 1952; cert, Fgn. Service Sch., Georgetown U., 1953. Legis. analyst Ford Motor Co., Dearborn, Mich., 1956-62, mgr. contbns., 1967-75; staff assoc. Ford Motor Co. Found., Dearborn, 1962-67; assoc. dir. Ford Motor Co. found., Dearborn, 1975-79; exec. dir. Ford Motor Co. Found., Dearborn, 1980—; trustee Council Mich. founds., 1980—; pres. Nat. Council of Philanthropy, N.Y., 1976-77; mem. Confs. Bd. Contbns. Council, 1980—; mem. bus. adv. com. Ind. Colls. Am., 1982—. Chmn. S.E. Mich. chpt. ARC, 1981-83; bd. advisors Close-Up Found., Washington, 1979-83; adv. com. Better Bus. Bur. Philanthropic Com., Washington, 1980-83; mem. evaluation com. United Found., Detroit, 1976-83; mem. Detroit Zool. Soc., Founders Soc. Detroit Inst. Art, Mich. Hist. Soc. Served to 1st lt. USAF, 1953-56. Republican. Roman Catholic. Club: Otsego Ski. Home: 3622 Darch Dr Birmingham MI 48010 Office: Ford Motor Co Found American Rd Dearborn MI 48121

BRENNAN, MICHAEL JOSEPH, university administrator; b. Chgo., Aug. 29, 1928; s. Michael J. and Nora (McHugh) B.; m. Isabel Bernice Thomas, Dec. 4, 1954; children: Mark Etienne, Moira Sioban, Keelin Marta. B.S., DePaul U., 1952; M.A., U. Chgo., 1954, Ph.D., 1956. Mem. faculty Brown U., 1956-74, prof. econs., 1964-74, dean, 1966-74; prof. econs., acad. v.p. Wesleyan U., 1974—; Cons. Nat. Endowment on Humanities, 1970-71, U.S. Office of Edn., 1968-70; exec. sec. Howard Found., 1968-74; pres. New Eng. Conf. Grad. Edn., 1973. Author: Preface to Econometrics, 1960, Theory of Economic Statics, 1965, Patterns of Market Behavior, 1965, The Economics of Age, 1967, Economics, Analysis of Principles and Policy, 1970. Bd. dirs. Providence Child Guidance Clinic, Grad. Record Exam. Bd., 1969-72; adv. bd. Danforth Found., 1971-75; trustee Lincoln Sch., 1968-72, mem. exec. com., 1970-72; governing bd. Essex Marine Lab., 1975-79. Served with U.S. Army, 1946-48. Danforth Teaching fellow, 1957; Ford Found. Faculty Research prof., 1960. Mem. Am. Econ. Assn., Econometric Soc., Assn. Grad. Schs. (sec-treas. 1969-74), Council Grad. Schs. Club: University (Providence). Home: 127 Grand St Middletown CT 06457

BRENNAN, PATRICK BRIAN, manufacturing company executive; b. Brainard, Minn., Apr. 22, 1938; s. Joseph William and Esther Ruth (Lambrecht) B.; m. Brigitte Giesela Biernoth, Oct. 18, 1963; children: Richard, Tanya, Shawn. B.S. in Bus. Adminstrn., Ariz. State U., 1960. Vice pres., treas Nat. Semicondr. Corp., Santa Clara, Calif., 1970—. Served with U.S. Army, 1961-64. Republican. Office: Nat Semiconductor Corp 2900 Semiconductor Dr Santa Clara CA 95051

BRENNAN, PETER JOHN, business executive, writer; b. Dublin, Ireland, July 30, 1931; came to U.S., 1939, naturalized, 1957; s. Joseph Desmond and Ethna Mary (McDonald) B.; m. Joan Tristram Hiller, May 15, 1954 (dec.); children: Phillip Alexander (dec.), Joan-Sarane Desmond Brennan Saunders, Peter Nicholas; m. Jilda Fimi Kicak, Oct. 27, 1973. B.Chem. Engring., Catholic U. Am., 1953. Chem. engr., 1953-59; editor McGraw-Hill Corp., N.Y.C., 1959-67; editor-in-chief Engineer, 1967-70; founder, editor Industria Quimica, Morristown, N.J., 1970; editor, pub. UN Indsl. Devel. Orgn., Vienna, Austria, 1971-73; editor-in-chief Instruments & Control Systems, Radnor, Pa., 1973-75; ptnr. Brennan & Garson, N.Y.C., 1983—; cons. to UN, U.S. Govt., Overseas Pvt. Investment Corp., N.Y.C., Washington, Vienna, Ankara, Turkey and India, 1975—. Author 2 books; contbr. articles to profl. jours. Recipient Editorial Achievement award Am. Bus. Press, 1976. Mem. N.Y. Bus. Press Editors Assn. (founder, incorporator), N.Y. Fin. Writers Assn., World Trade Writers Assn. Democrat. Roman Catholic. Office: 485 Fifth Ave New York NY 10017

BRENNAN, ROBERT J., shipping company executive; married. B.B.A., Loyola U., 1950. With Lykes Bros. Steamship Co. Inc., New Orleans, 1942—, various traffic mgr. positions various divs. UK, Mediterranean, asst. tonnage controller, 1964-66, tonnage controller, asst. v.p., 1966-70, v.p. traffic, 1970-74, sr. v.p., 1974-76, exec. v.p., 1976—. Office: Lykes Bros Steamship Co Inc 300 Poydras St Lykes Ctr PO Box 53068 New Orleans LA 70153 *

BRENNAN, TERRENCE DRAKE, banker; b. Des Moines, Oct. 2, 1938; s. Richard Melvin and Margery (Drake) B.; m. Kathryn McCormick, Aug. 29, 1959; children: Kelly B., Ann B. B.B.A., U. Iowa, 1961, M.B.A., 1962. Credit analyst Nat. Bank of Detroit, 1962-64; asst. cashier, asst. v.p. comml. loans St. Joseph Valley Bank (now Midwest Commerce Banking Co.), Elkhart, Ind., 1964-66, v.p. lending, 1966-67, sr. v.p. lending and mktg., 1967-68, exec. v.p., dir., 1968-73, pres., 1973—. Bd. dirs. Elkhart Gen. Hosp., 1972—, Samaritan Health and Living Ctr., 1979—; chmn. Elkhart Gen. Hosp., 1979—; chmn. fund drive Jr. Achievement, 1977. Named Outstanding Young Man Elkhart Jaycees, 1974. Mem. Young President's Orgn., Sigma Chi. Clubs: Elcona Country (dir. 1968-70), Old Capitol). Office: Midwest Commerce Banking Co PO Box 1686 Elkhart IN 46516

BRENNAN, THOMAS EMMETT, law school president; b. Detroit, May 27, 1929; s. Joseph Terence and Jeannette Frances (Sullivan) B.; m. Pauline Mary Weinberger, Apr. 28, 1951; children: Thomas Emmett, Margaret Ann and John Seamus (twins), William Joseph, Marybeth, Ellen Mary. LL.B., U. Detroit, 1952; LL.D., Thomas M. Cooley Law Sch., 1976. Bar: Mich. 1953. Asso. firm Kenny, Radom, Rockwell & Mountain, Detroit, 1952-53; partner firm Waldron, Brennan & Maher, Detroit, 1953-61; judge Detroit Ct. Common Pleas, 1962-63, Wayne County Circuit Ct., 1963-66; justice Mich. Supreme Ct., 1967-73, chief justice, 1969-70; adj. prof. polit. sci. U. Detroit, 1970-72; pres., acting dean Thomas M. Cooley Law Sch., Lansing, 1972-73, dean, 1974-78, pres., 1978—, chmn. bd., 1980-81, also dir.; Mem. Mich. Commn. Law Enforcement and Criminal Justice, 1969-70. Contbr. articles to legal publs. Trustee Marygrove Coll., Detroit, 1968-70. Mem. Am., Detroit, Ingham County bar assns., State Bar Mich. (bd. commrs. 1979—), Delta Theta Phi. Roman Cath. Clubs: K.C., Walnut Hills Country (E. Lansing). Home: 6151 Park Lake Rd East Lansing MI 48823 Office: 217 S Capitol Ave Lansing MI 48933

BRENNAN, WILLIAM JOSEPH, mfg. co. exec.; b. Buffalo, Feb. 11, 1928; s. Laurence J. and Mary Julia (Scherer) B.; m. Rita Jeanne Brooks, Dec. 27, 1947; 1 dau., Susan. B.A., Bryant and Stratton Coll., 1949. With Fedders Corp., 1949—, asst. controller corp., 1962-64, dir. distbn. brs., 1965-67, v.p., dir. sales, 1967-74, v.p., dir. adminstrn., 1974-77; pres. Fedders Fin. Corp., 1977-78, group v.p. diversified products, 1978-80, v.p. fin., chief fin. officer, 1980, exec. v.p., chief fin. officer, dir., 1980—. Served with AUS, 1946-47. Republican. Roman Catholic. Home: 4 Pompano St Rumson NJ 07760 Office: Fedders Corp Hwy 206 Peapack NJ 07977

BRENNAN, WILLIAM JOSEPH, JR., justice U.S. Supreme Ct.; b. Newark, Apr. 25, 1906; s. William J. and Agnes (McDermott) B.; m. Marjorie Leonard, May 5, 1928; children—William Joseph, Hugh Leonard, Nancy. B.S., U. Pa., 1928; LL.B., Harvard, 1931; also LL.D.; LL.D., U. Notre Dame, 1968. Bar: N.J. bar 1931. Practiced, Newark, 1931-49; mem. firm Pitney, Hardin, Ward & Brennan; superior ct. judge, 1949-50, appellate div. judge, 1950-52; justice Supreme Ct. N.J., 1952-56; asso. justice U.S. Supreme Ct., 1956—. Served to col. with gen. staff corps AUS, World War II. Decorated Legion of Merit. Address: Supreme Ct US Washington DC 20543 *

BRENNAN, WILLIAM ROBERT, JR., banker; b. N.Y.C., Mar. 8, 1921; s. William R. and Margeret (Healy) B.; children: William, John Paul, Ellen, Christopher, Vincent, Timothy, Andrew. B.B.A., Manhattan Coll., 1943; J.D., Fordham U., 1948. Bar: N.Y. 1948, U.S. Dist. Ct. (so. and eastern dist. N.Y.) 1949-52, U.S. Ct. Appeals (2d circuit N.Y.) 1952. Ptnr. Hanrahan & Brennan, N.Y.C., 1948-55; dep. supt., counsel N.Y. State Banking Dept., 1955-59, acting supt. banks, 1959; justice N.Y. State Supreme Ct., N.Y.C., 1960-68; ptnr. Reavis & McGrath, N.Y.C., 1968-70; chmn. bd., chief exec. officer Apple Bank for Savings, N.Y.C., 1970—. Served with U.S. Army, 1942-45; ETO. Mem. N.Y. Bar Assn., Nassau County Bar Assn. Clubs: Garden City Country, Sky. Home: 51 Fairway Dr Manhasset NY 11030 Office: Apple Bank for Savings 205 E 42d St New York NY 10017

BRENNEN, STEPHEN ALFRED, internat. bus. cons.; b. N.Y.C., July 7, 1932; s. Theodore and Margaret (Pembroke) B.; m. Yolanda Alicia Romero, Sept. 28, 1957; children—Stephen Robert, Richard Patrick. A.B. cum laude, U. Americas, Mexico City, 1956; M.B.A., U. Chgo., 1959. Supr. Montgomery Ward, Chgo., 1956; credit mgr. Aldens, Chgo., 1956-59; gen. mgr. Purina de Guatemala, 1964-66; pres. Purina Colombiana, Bogotá, 1967-69, Living Marine Resources, Inc., San Diego, 1969-70; mng. dir. Central and S. Am. Ralston Purina, Caracas, Venezuela and; Coral Gables, Fla., 1970-74; pres. Van Camp Seafood Co., San Diego, 1974-79; chmn. P.S.C. Corp., Buena Park, Calif., 1979-81; pres. Inter-Am. Cons. Group, San Diego, 1981—. Author: Successfully Yours. Mem. adv. bd. Mexican-Am. Found. Served with USAF. Mem. Am. Soc. Profl. Cons. Republican. Roman Catholic. Club: U. Chgo. in San Diego (pres.-elect). Office: 7924 Ivanhoe St Suite 6 La Jolla CA 92037

BRENNER, BARRY MORTON, physician; b. Bklyn., Oct. 4, 1937; s. Louis and Sally (Lamm) B.; m. Jane P. Deutsch, June 12, 1960; children: Robert, Jennifer. B.S., L.I. U.; M.D., U. Pitts.; M.A., Harvard U. Asst. prof. medicine U. Calif., San Francisco, 1969-72, asso. prof. medicine and physiology, 1972-75, prof. medicine, 1975-76; Samuel A. Levine prof. medicine Harvard U. Med. Sch., Boston; with Peter Bent Brigham Hosp., Boston, 1976—; dir. renal div. Brigham and Women's Hosp., Boston, 1979—; cons. NIH. Contbr. numerous articles to various publs. Recipient research award NIH. Mem. Am. Physiol. Soc., Am. Soc. Clin. Investigation, Assn. Am. Physicians, Western Assn. Physicians, Am. Soc. Nephrology, Am. Soc. Clin. Investigation (councillor, v.p.), Salt and Water Club, Interurban Clin. Club, Alpha Omega Alpha, Phi Sigma. Office: 75 Frances St Boston MA 02115 *

BRENNER, DAEG SCOTT, university dean, chemistry educator; b. Reading, Pa., Aug. 9, 1939; s. Scott Francis and Helen Esther (Drumm) B.; m. Susan Dorothy Woodruff, June 30, 1973; children: Bethia May, Scott Harold, Jennifer Lynn. B.S. in Chemistry, Rensselaer Poly. Inst., 1960; Ph.D., M.I.T., 1964. With Niels Bohr Inst., Copenhagen, 1964-65, Brookhaven Nat. Lab., Upton, N.Y., 1965-67; faculty Clark U., Worcester, Mass., 1967—, prof. chemistry, 1979—, dean research, 1983—; cons. Lawrence Livermore Nat. Lab., 1973—. NIH predoctoral fellow, 1962-63; NSF predoctoral fellow, 1963-64; NATO postdoctoral fellow, 1964-65; Dept. of Energy research grantee, 1968—. Mem. Am. Chem. Soc., Am. Phys. Soc., Sigma Xi, Phi Lambda Upsilon, Sigma Pi Sigma. Office: 950 Main St Worcester MA 01610

BRENNER, DANIEL LEON, lawyer; b. Kansas City, Mo., Sept. 9, 1904; s. Adolph and Tillie (Brenner) B. A.B., U. Mo., 1925; J.D., U. Mich., 1927. Bar: Mo. 1926. With Borders & Borders, 1927; mem. Roach, Brenner & Wimmell, Kansas City, 1947-51; sr. mem. Brenner, Van Valkenburgh & Wimmell, 1951-59; now Brenner, Lockwood & Peterson; judge Circuit Ct. Jackson County, Mo., 1943-44. Contbr. articles to legal jours. Mem. nat. council Am. Jewish Distbn. Com.; nat. panel Am. Arbitration Assn., 1964—; nat. commr. B'nai B'rith Hillel Founds.; pres. Kansas City Jewish Welfare Fedn. and Council.; Trustee U. Mo. Hillel Found. (charter), Leo N. Levi Meml. Hosp., Bellefarie, Rockhurst Coll.; bd. dirs., v.p., counsel Heart of Am. United Way Greater Kansas City; bd. dirs., counsel United Way; bd. dirs., v.p. Heart of Am. United campaign; bd. dirs. NCCJ, Jewish Vocat. Service Bur.; trustee, mem. investment adv. com. Rockhurst Coll. Endowment Fund, 1969—; pres., bd. curators U. Mo.; chmn., trustee Employees Retirement System, Kansas City, 1973—; bd. curators U. Mo., 1977—; bd. visitors U. Mich. Law Sch. Recipient Brotherhood citation NCCJ, 1956, citation State of Israel, 1961, Non-alumni Achievement award U. Mo. Sch. Law, 1982; named Man of Yr. Jewish Theol. Sem. Am., 1967. Mem. Legion of Honor Order de Molay, ABA, Kansas City Bar Assn., Mo. Bar, Am. Judicature Soc., Native Sons of Kansas City, Order of Coif.; mem. B'nai B'rith (dist. pres. grand lodge 1950-51, v.p. supreme lodge). Jewish (bd. dirs. synagogue). Clubs: Mason; Oakwood Country (Kansas City). Home: 333 Meyer St W Apt 713 Kansas City MO 64113 Office: 915 Traders Bank Bldg 1125 Grand Ave Kansas City MO 64106

BRENNER, DAVID, comedian; b. Phila., 1945. Grad., Temple U. Producer, WBBM-TV, Chgo., WRCV, Phila., KYW-TV, Phila., WNEW-TV, N.Y.C., PBL-TV, N.Y.C.; producer, writer, dir. TV documentaries, N.Y.C., numerous nightclub appearances; TV appearances include Hollywood Squares; also guest host: Tonight Show; author: Soft Pretzels with Mustard, 1983. Served with U.S. Army. Named Las Vegas Entertainer of Year, 1977; AGVA Artist Comedian of Year, 1976. Office: ICM 40 W 57th St New York NY 10019 *

BRENNER, EDWARD JOHN, lawyer; b. Wisconsin Rapids, Wis., June 26, 1923; s. Edward Charles and Lillian (Hephner) B.; m. Jane Segrest, June 1, 1951; children: Beverly, Douglas, Carolyn, Mary. B.S. in Chem. Engring, U. Wis., 1947, M.S., 1948, J.D., 1950. Bar: Wis. bar 1950, D.C. bar 1970, Va. bar 1971. Chem. engr. Esso Standard Oil Co., 1950-53; with Esso Research and Engring. Co., 1953-64, asst. dir. legal div., 1960-64; U.S. commr. patents, 1964-69; v.p., asst. to pres. Gen. Instrument Corp., 1969-70; pvt. practice patent law, Arlington, Va., 1970—. Served with U.S. Army, 1944-46. Mem. Am., Wis., Va. bar assns., Bar Assn. D.C., Am., N.J. patent law assns., Am. Chem. Soc. Home: 586 Bal Harbor Blvd Punta Gorda FL 33950 Office: 586 Bal Harbor Blvd Punta Gorda FL 33950

BRENNER, EGON, university official; b. Vienna, Austria, July 1, 1925; s. Aaron and Margarethe (Adler) B.; m. Rhoda Greenberg, Dec. 24, 1950; children: Dorothy, Claudia. B.E.E., CCNY, 1944; M.E.E., Poly. Inst. Bklyn., 1949, D.E.E., 1955. Mem. faculty CCNY, 1946-81, prof. elec. engring., 1966-81, dean engring., 1971-73, acting provost, 1973-74, provost, v.p. acad. affairs, 1974-76; acting vice chancellor for acad. affairs CUNY, 1976-77, dep. chancellor, 1978-81; exec. v.p. Yeshiva U., 1981—; vis. prof. Tex. Tech. U., summer 1965, U. Okla., 1966. Author: (with M. Javid) Analysis of Electric Circuits, 1959, 2d rev. edit., 1967, Analysis, Transmission and Filtering of Signals, 1963. Served with AUS, 1944-46. Decorated Bronze Star. Fellow IEEE; mem. Am. Soc. Engring. Edn., AAAS, Sigma Xi, Eta Kappa Nu, Tau Beta Pi. Office: Office of Exec Vice Pres Yeshiva U 500 W 185th St New York NY 10033

BRENNER, ERMA, author; b. N.Y.C., Dec. 1, 1911; d. Robert and Amy (Schoenbrunn) Brandt; m. Charles Brenner, Sept. 8, 1935; children: Elsa Brenner Cohen, Lucy (Mrs. Barrie Biven). Student, Harvard, 1931-34; studied with, Eduard Steuermann, 1954-61. Dir., owner Camp Sherbo, Bridgeton, Maine, 1933-40; tchr. nursery sch. Children's Center, Roxbury, Mass., 1942-44, Colonial Heights Nursery Sch., Yonkers, N.Y., 1946-48; owner, developer Scenichrome, 1946-48; mem. staff White Plains (N.Y.) Day Care Center, 1976-77; coordinator play center dept. child psychiatry, mem. staff therapeutic nursery Albert Einstein Med. Coll., 1977—; cons. to staff children's day hosp. N.Y. Hosp. Westchester Div., 1980-81. Author: A New Baby! A New Life!, 1973. Recipient Christophers award, 1973. Home: 30 Rugby Ln Scarsdale NY 10583 Office: 35 E 85th St New York NY 10028

BRENNER, FRANK, judge; b. N.Y.C., Oct. 26, 1927; s. Jack and Betty (Teifer) B.; children: Jay Marlow, Matthew Adam, Amy Rebecca, Diane Rachel. B.A. cum laude, Lehigh U., 1948; J.D., Harvard U., 1951. Bar: N.Y. State 1951, U.S. Supreme Ct. 1955, U.S. Tax Ct. 1975. Asst. dist. atty., N.Y. County, 1951-55, practice law, N.Y.C., 1955-83; judge N.Y.C. Criminal Ct., 1983—. Contbr. articles to legal jours. Served with USNR, 1945-46. Recipient commendation Brit. Royal Commn. on Capital Punishment, 1950. Fellow Am. Acad. Matrimonial Lawyers; mem. Am. Bar Assn. (litigation sect. com. on trial complex bus. crimes 1977—, criminal justice sect. com. on def. function and services 1979—, RICO subcom. of com. on white collar crime 1982—), N.Y. State Bar Assn. (ho. dels. 1978—, conf. bar leaders 1978—), Assn. Bar City N.Y. (spl. com. on legal aid inquiry 1971-72, com. on penology 1972-77, com. on profl. discipline 1982—), N.Y. County Lawyers Assn. (chmn. com. criminal law 1952-70, 80—, spl. com. on matrimonial law 1975—, sec. spl. com. on selection and tenure of judges 1975-77, dir. 1977—, mem. com. public hearings in public interest 1979-80, spl. com. to rev. jud. discipline 1979-80), N.Y. State Dist. Attys. Assn. Club: Harvard (N.Y.C.). Home: 470 Park Ave New York NY 10022 Office: Office of Ct Adminstrn 80 Centre St New York NY 10013

BRENNER, HOWARD M., chemical engineer; b. N.Y.C., Mar. 16, 1929; s. Max and Margaret (Wechsler) B.; children: Leslie, Joyce, Suzanne. B.Ch.E., Pratt Inst., 1950; M.Ch.E., NYU, 1954, Eng.Sc.D., 1957. Instr. chem. engring. NYU, 1955-57, asst. prof. chem. engring., 1957-61, assoc. prof., 1961-65, prof., 1965-66, Carnegie-Mellon U., 1966-77; prof., chmn. dept. chem. engring.U. Rochester, N.Y., 1977—; sr. vis. fellow Sci. Research Council Gt. Britain, 1974; Fairchild Disting. scholar Calif. Inst. Tech., 1975-76. Author: (with J. Happel) Low Reynolds Number Hydrodynamics, 1965, 2d edit., 1973, Russian edit., 1976; contbr. articles to profl. jours.; assoc. editor: Internat. Jour. Multiphase Flow, 1973—. Named to 11th Ann. Honor Scroll Indsl. Engring. Chemistry div. Am. Chem. Soc., 1961. Mem. Am. Inst. Chem. Engrs. (Alpha Chi Sigma 1976), Am. Inst. Civil Engrs., Soc. Rheology, AAAS, Soc. Nat. Philosophy, Am. Acad. Mechanics, Am. Chem. Soc. Home: 155 Danforth Crescent Rochester NY 14618 Office: Drexel Burnham Lambert Inc 60 Broad St New York NY 10004

BRENNER, JOSEPH DONALD, manufacturing company executive; b. Carlisle, Pa., Mar. 1, 1917; s. Clyde E. and Pearl T. (Hastings) B.; m. Jane B. Wimett, June 24, 1944; children: Margaret E. (Mrs. Richard Bushey), Joseph Donald, Nancy E., Katherine H. Ph.B., Dickinson Coll., 1939; M.B.A., Harvard, 1941. Mfg. mgr. AMP, Inc., Harrisburg, Pa., 1947-50, chief engr., asst. div. mgr., 1950-55, div. mgr. automatic machine div., 1955-58; operations mgr., 1958-61, v.p. mfg. divs., 1961-67, corporate v.p. mfg., 1967-71, v.p. ops., 1971, pres., 1971-81, chief exec. officer, 1972-82, chmn. bd., 1981-82, chmn. exec. com., 1982—; dir. AMP, Farmers Trust Co., Carlisle, United Telephone Co. Pa., United Telecommunications Inc. Bd. dirs. Carlisle Hosp. Served to lt. USNR, 1944-46. Mem. Machinery Allied Products Inst. (exec. com.), Phi Kappa Sigma. Presbyn. Home: 1051 Trindle Rd Carlisle PA 17013 Office: Eisenhower Blvd Box 3608 Harrisburg PA 17105

BRENNER, RONALD JOHN, pharmaceutical industry executive; b. Bethlehem, Pa., June 9, 1933; s. Sam Ralph and Frieda V. E. (Buck) B.; m. Sally Gaskill, Oct. 24, 1964; children: Carol, Nancy, Kathy, Richard. B.S. in Pharmacy, U. Cin., 1955; M.S. in Pharm. Chemistry (U. Fla. Grad. Council fellow), 1957; Ph.D. in Pharm. Chemistry (S. B. Penick Meml. fellow), 1959. Pharm. chemist McNeil Labs., Fort Washington, Pa., 1958-62, group leader, 1962-64, mgr. New Products Div., 1964-66, dir. devel. research, 1966-67, exec. dir. New Products Div., 1967-70, exec. v.p., 1974-78, pres., 1978-79; asst. to vice chmn. Johnson & Johnson Internat., New Brunswick, N.J., 1970-71, v.p., 1971-74, co. group chmn., 1978-82; v.p., corp. external research Johnson & Johnson, New Brunswick, N.J., 1982—; Trustee Phila. Coll. Pharmacy and Sci., 1976—; mem. N.J. Gov.'s Commn. on Sci. and Tech., Task Force on Acad.-Indsl. Innovation; mem. adv. bd. Scripps Clinic and Research Found. Mem. Am. Pharm. Assn., AAAS, Acad. Pharm. Scis., Soc. Clem. Industry. Office: Johnson & Johnson One Johnson & Johnson Plaza New Brunswick NJ 08933-7006

BRENNER, THEODORE ENGELBERT, trade association executive; b. N.Y.C., Apr. 18, 1930; s. Engelbert F.J. and Julie M. (Kierschner) B.; m. Maria T. Finn, Sept. 12, 1953; children—John Finn, Elisabeth Ann, Christopher. B.C.E., Manhattan Coll., 1951; M.S., Johns Hopkins, 1954. Registered profl. engr., Pa., N.J.; Diplomate Am. Acad. Environ. Engrs. Mgr. waste treatment dept. Permutit div. Sybron Corp., Paramus, N.J., 1959-62; prin. Hydroscience, Inc., Ft. Lee, N.J., 1963; with Soap and Detergent Assn., N.Y.C., 1963—, v.p., tech. dir., 1970, v.p., dir. govt. affairs, 1971, pres., 1972—; Exec. dir. Joint Industry Govt. Task Force Eutrophication, 1968-70; mem. Dept. Interior Water Resources Sci., Info. Center Adv. Group, 1969-70; mem. spl. adv. com. N.Y. Temp. State Commn. on Water Resources Planning, 1964-67. Contbr.: chpt. to Advances in Environmental Sciences, Vol. II, 1969; articles to profl. jours. Mem. Rumson Bd. Edn., 1968-74, 1st v.p., 1973-74; mem. Rumson-Fair Haven Regional Bd. Edn., 1974-77, v.p., 1976-77. Served to capt. USAF, 1952-59; lt. col. Res. ret. Fellow Am. Pub. Health Assn.; mem. ASCE, Am. Inst. Chem. Engrs., Am. Soc. Assn. Execs. Clubs: Union League (N.Y.C.); Seabright (N.J.) Beach. Home: 5 Tyson Ln Rumson NJ 07760 Office: 475 Park Ave S New York NY 10016

BRENNER, WILLIAM EDWARD, obstetrician-gynecologist; b. Dayton, Ohio, Nov. 6, 1936; s. Norman Edward and Olive Virginia (Lewis) B.; m. Beverly Ann Tucci, Dec. 21, 1957; children—William, Beverly, Brian. A.B., Adelbert Coll., Western Res. U., 1958, M.D., 1962. Diplomate: Am. Bd. Ob-Gyn. Intern Univ. Hosp. Cleve., 1962-63, resident in ob-gyn, 1965-69; instr. in ob-gyn Western Res. U., 1965-69; instr. U. N.C., 1969-70, asst. prof. ob-gyn, 1970-72, asso. prof., 1972-76, prof., 1976-81, Upjohn Disting. prof., 1977-81; prof., chmn. ob-gyn dept. U. Nev., Reno, 1981-82; pres. Triangle Women's Health Center, 1982—; v.p. Chapel Hill Surg. Center, 1982—; cons. in field; mem. nat. med. com. Planned Parenthood; mem. med. adv. com. Internat. Fertility Research Program; fellow Carolina Population Center, 1977—; mem. staff N.C. Meml. Hosp.; mem. Ednl. Materials Project Appraisal Panel, 1977—; bd. dirs. Fields Found. Ltd., 1978-80; chmn. FDA Ob-Gyn Device Classification Panel and Adv. Com., 1979—. Contbr. articles to profl. publs.; editorial adv. bd.: Jour. Reproductive Medicine, 1974—; editorial bd.: Internat. Jour. Ob-Gyn, 1977—; jour. reviewer. Served to lt. USNR, 1963-65. Mem. Am. Assn. Maternal-Neonatal Health (dir. 1978—), Am. Fertility Soc., Am. Coll. Obstetricians and Gynecologists, Robert A. Ross Ob-Gyn Soc., Durham-Orange County Med. Soc., Med. Soc. State N.C., AAUP, A.C.S., AAAS, Piedmont Ob-Gyn Soc., Soc. Gynecol. Investigation, Am. Coll. Clin. Pharmacology, South Atlantic Assn. Obstetricians and Gynecologists, N.C. Ob-Gyn Soc. (exec. com. 1977-80, program chmn. 1978-80), So. Perinatal Assn., Assn. Planned Parenthood Physicians, Hamann Soc., Sigma Xi, Phi Delta Epsilon, Beta Beta Beta, Alpha Omega Alpha, Phi Rho Sigma. Lutheran. Office: 109 Conner D Chapel Hill NC 27514

BRENNER, WILLIAM GEORGE, ins. co. exec.; b. Cin., June 24, 1939; s. William Charles and Catherine Molly (Genau) B.; m. Mary Carol Reinshagen, June 27, 1959; children—Jennifer, Cathleen, William, Steven. A.A. cum laude, U. Cin., 1969. With Union Central Life Ins. Co., Cin., 1958—, mgr. cash div., 1967-74, dir. mortgage loan servicing, 1974-75, asst. treas., 1975-79, asso. treas., 1979-80, treas., 1980—. Pres. North College Hill Baseball Assn., 1976-77. Mem. Am. Assn. Petroleum Landmen, Rocky Mountain Oil and Gas Assn., N.D. Landman's Assn. Roman Catholic. Home: 6949 Rob Vern Dr North College Hill OH 45239 Office: PO Box 179 Cincinnati OH 45201

BRENT, ANDREW JACKSON, lawyer; b. Richmond, Va., Nov. 25, 1918; s. Andrew Jackson and Gussie Millhiser (Reinhardt) B.; m. Virginia Armistead McGuire, Nov. 1, 1941; children: Virginia Armistead (Mrs. Roger P. Hailes), Roberta Harper (Mrs. Leon A. Peek), Elizabeth Marshall McGuire (Mrs. Peter F. Nostrand), Andrew Mason, Maria Meade (Mrs. W. Brady James). LL.B., U. Va., 1941. Bar: Va. 1940. Practice in, Richmond, 1946—; ptnr. Christian, Barton, Epps, Brent & Chappell, 1949—; v.p., gen. counsel, dir. Security Fed. Savs. & Loan Assn.; gen. counsel, sec., dir. Media Gen., Inc.; past chmn., dir. Central Va. Ednl. TV Corp.; sec., dir. Garden State Paper Co., Inc., Garfield, N.J., Richmond Newspapers, Inc., Southeast Media, Inc., Beacon Press, Inc., Piedmont Pub. Co., Inc., Winston-Salem, N.C., Tribune Co., Tampa, Fla., WFLA Inc., Tampa; dir. Cliggott Pub. Co., Greenwich, Conn., Productora Nacional de Papel Destintado S.A. de C.V., Mexico City. Past pres., dir. Richmond Area Community Council, 1963-66; gen. counsel, sec. Richmond Met. Authority; past chmn. Va. Pub. Telecommunications Council; past sec., visitor Virginia Commonwealth Univ.; Past pres., bd. dirs. Richmond Eye Hosp.; trustee Va. Law Found., Richmond Meml. Hosp. Found.; trustee, past pres. Collegiate Schs.; trustee Va. Commonwealth U.; past chmn., trustee Mary Baldwin Coll. Served to lt. comdr. USNR, 1941-46. Recipient Annual Good Govt. award Richmond First Club, 1965, Disting. Service award Va. State C. of C., 1981. Fellow ABA; Mem. Va., Richmond bar assns., Am. Judicature Soc., S.A.R., Richmond C. of C. (past pres., dir.), Omicron Delta Kappa, Phi Alpha Delta, Phi Kappa Psi, Pi Delta Epsilon. Democrat. Episcopalian (warden, vestryman). Clubs: Commonwealth (past pres., gov.), Country of Virginia, Downtown (past pres., dir.). Home: Highland Rd Richmond VA 23229 Office: 12th Floor Mut Bldg Richmond VA 23219

BRENT, JOLEENE ADALIE, artist; b. Dallas, Nov. 27, 1920; d. Joseph Herman and Bertha B. (Raphiel) Margules; m. Allan Rudolph Brent, Dec. 19, 1941; 1 dau., Joanna Raphiel Brent Leake. Student, U. Tex., 1937-38; B.Ed., UCLA, 1941; postgrad., La. State U., 1948-49. Art tchr., supr. Calif. Public Sch. System, 1941-43; art tchr. St. Joseph Acad., 1952-64; also instr. La. State U., 1950-52; dir. La. Arts and Sci. Center, 1962-79; instr. Sch. Landscape Architecture, La. State U., Baton Rouge, 1980-84; cons. gifted and talented program La. Dept. Edn., 1978-83; adv. council Artist-in-Residence Program, 1977-83. Works include: leaded and stained glass windows, Convent Chapel, Sisters of St. Joseph, St. Joseph Cathedral Sacristy, Cath. Life Center, Bishop's Chapel, La. State Univ. Law Center, Woman's Club House, St. Paul Luth. Ch., Blackwater United Meth. Ch., murals, St. Aloysius Convent, Cath. Life Center, St. Joseph Prep. Sch., St. Alphonsus Ch., Am. Bank, Eglise Assumption. Co-chmn. Plaza Com., 1970—; pres. Bicentennial Commn., 1976. Decorated Orden del Mérito Civil Govt. of Spain. Mem. Baton Rouge Gallery (bd. dirs.), Stained Glass Assn. Am., Delta Kappa Gamma., Delta Epsilon. Clubs: Baton Rouge Country, City, Network. Home: 3930 Floyd Dr Baton Rouge LA 70808

BRENT, PAUL LESLIE, educator; b. Douglass, Okla., July 3, 1916; s. Paul Leslie and Ruth (McKee) B.; m. Aledo Render, May 29, 1938; children: Carolyn J., Paul Richard; m. Josephine R. Montilepre, July 15, 1979. B.S., Central State U., 1938; M.Ed., U. Okla., 1949, Ed.D., 1959. Tchr. math. and sci. public schs., Adair, Okla., 1938-40; prin. Alden Public Schs., Carnegie, Okla., 1940-43, supt., 1950-58; tchr. public schs., Cooperton, Okla., 1946-47, prin. high sch., public schs., Washita, Okla., 1947-48, supt., 1948-50; asst. prof. Calif. State U., Long Beach, 1959-63, assoc. prof. edn., 1963-72, asst. to chmn. div. edn., 1961-67, prof. instructional media, 1972—; Mem. Baptist Edn. Study Task, 1966-67; trustee Calif. Bapt. Coll., 1969-74. Served with USNR, 1943- 46. Mem. Calif. Faculty Assn. (pres. elect), NEA, Calif. Media and Library Educators Assn., Am. Assn. Sch. Adminstrs., Congress of Faculty Assns., Phi Delta Kappa, Kappa Delta Pi, Phi Kappa Phi. Democrat. Baptist. Home: 11112 Bos Pl Cerritos CA 90701 Office: 1250 Bellflower Blvd Long Beach CA 90840

BRENT, ROBERT LEONARD, physician, educator; b. Rochester, N.Y., Oct. 6, 1927; s. Charles and Rose (Katz) B.; m. Lillian H. Hoffman, Aug. 21, 1949; children: David A., James R., Lawrence H., Deborah A. A.B., U. Rochester, 1948, M.D. with honors, 1953, Ph.D., 1955. Fellow Nat. Found., Strong Meml. Hosp., 1953-54; intern pediatrics Mass. Gen. Hosp., Boston, 1954-55; chief radiation biology Walter Reed Army Inst. Research, 1955-57; faculty Jefferson Med. Coll., 1955—, prof. radiology, 1962—, also prof. pediatrics, chmn. dept. and dir.; Chmn. med. adv. bd. Nat. Found.; Chmn. med. adv. bd., mem. fertility and maternal health com. FDA.; mem. human embryology study sect. NIH, 1970-74. Editor in chief: Teratology, 1976—. Served with U.S. Army, 1955-57. Travelling fellow Royal Soc. Medicine, 1971-72; vis. fellow FitzWilliam Coll., Cambridge, 1971-72; Recipient Richie meml. prize U. Rochester Med. Sch., 1953; Lindback Found. award for distinguished teaching, 1968; Lady Davis scholar Hadassah Med. Ctr., Jerusalem, 1983-84. Mem. Teratology Soc. (pres. 1967-68), AAAS, Radiation Research Soc., Am. Soc. Exptl. Pathology, Soc. Pediatric Research, Am. Pediatrics Soc., Am. Acad. Pediatrics, Soc. Exptl. Biology and Medicine, Phila. Coll. Physicians, Phila. Pediatric Soc., Am. Assn. Immunology, Soc. Developmental Biology, Congenital Malformations Assn. Japan, European Teratology Soc., Sigma Xi, Alpha Omega Alpha. Office: 920 Chancellor St Philadelphia PA 19107

BRENT, WALTER RUDOLF, non-ferrous metals co. exec.; b. N.Y.C., Aug. 2, 1919; s. Rudolf Emil and Katherine (Mossbacher) B.; m. Dolores M. Germaine, Feb. 15, 1953; children—Alison, Wayne, Andrew. B.B.A., Coll. City N.Y., 1942. C.P.A., N.J. Sr. accountant Scovell Wellington & Co., N.Y.C., 1946-49; asst. treas. Bacardi Imports, N.Y.C., 1950-51; controller Standard Electronics Corp., Newark, 1952-57; sec., asst. treas. Revere Copper and Brass Inc., N.Y.C., 1958—; dir. Multimetals Ltd. Served with U.S. Army, 1942-46. Mem. Am. Inst. C.P.A.'s, Nat. Assn. Accountants, Am. Soc. Corp. Secs. Republican. Presbyterian. Home: 18 Loewen Ct Rye NY 10580 Office: 605 3d Ave New York NY 10158

BRENTLINGER, PAUL SMITH, manufacturing company executive; b. Dayton, Ohio, Apr. 3, 1927; s. Arthur and Welthy (Smith) B.; m. Marilyn E. Hunt, June 23, 1951; children: Paula, David, Sara. B.A., U. Mich., 1950, M.B.A., 1951. Mgr. indsl. devel. Harris Corp., Cleve., 1951-68, v.p. corp. devel., 1969-74, v.p. fin., Melbourne, Fla., 1975-82, sr. v.p. fin., Melbourne, 1982—; dir. Matra-Harris Semicondrs., Inc., Nantes, France, 1979—. Mem. Machinery and Allied Products Inst. (mem. fin. council), Fin. Execs. Inst., Phi Beta Kappa. Clubs: Union (Cleve.); Eau Gallie Yacht (Indian Harbour Beach, Fla.). Home: 1517 S Miramar Ave Indialantic FL 32903 Office: Harris Corp 1025 W NASA Blvd Melbourne FL 32919

BRENTLINGER, WILLIAM BROCK, college dean; b. Flora, Ill., Aug. 21, 1926; s. Arthur Kenneth and Frances (Maxwell) B.; m. Barbara Jean Weir, Dec. 29, 1946; children: Gregory, Gary, Rebecca Anne, Garth, Barbara Sue, Geoffrey. Student, Washington U., 1946-47; A.B., Greenville Coll., 1950; M.A., Ind. State U., 1951; Ph.D., U. Ill., 1959. Instr. speech Greenville Coll., 1951-59, chmn. dept., 1959-62, dean of coll., 1962-69; dean Coll. Fine Arts of Lamar U., Beaumont, Tex., 1969—; cons. higher edn. Served with USNR, 1944-46. Recipient tchr. study award Danforth Found., 1957. Mem. Internat. Council Fine Arts Deans, Speech Communication Assn. Am., Tex. Speech Assn., Tex. Assn. Coll. Tchrs., Tex. Council Arts in Edn. (pres.), Phi Kappa Phi. Baptist. Club: Rotary (Beaumont). Home: 6530 Salem Circle Beaumont TX 77706 *I have always attempted to treat people as subjects, not objects, as fellow creatures of God, and thus to be worked with not worked upon.*

BRESCHI, KAREN LEE, artist, image consultant; b. Oakland, Calif., Oct. 29, 1941; d. Leo John and Delores F. (Swenson) B. B.F.A. with distinction, Calif. Coll. Arts and Crafts, Oakland, 1963; M.A., San Francisco State U., 1965; postgrad., San Fancisco Art Inst., 1966-69; postgrad. in psychology, Calif. Inst. Intergral Studies, 1979-84. Mem. faculty San Francisco Art Inst., 1970-75, San Francisco State U., 1974-81; vis. artist U. Mont., Missoula, 1979, Calif. Coll. Arts and Crafts, Oakland, 1980, U. Calif., Davis, 1981-82, Banff Ctr. Sch. Fine Art, Alta., Can.; prin. Karen Breschi-Image Cons., San Francisco, 1981-83. Exhibited group shows, U. Calgary, 1973, Whitney Mus., N.Y.C., 1974, Everson Mus., Syracuse, N.Y., 1979, Smithsonian Inst., Washington, 1980. Mem. Am. Fedn. Tchrs., Am. Soc. Tng. and Devel., Am. Psychol. Assn., Assn. for Humanistic Psychology. Democrat. Unitarian. Office: care Braustein Gallery 254 Sutter St San Francisco CA 94102

BRESEE, PAUL KIRK, accountant, broadcasting company executive; b. Etna, Ill., July 1, 1901; s. Byrd Elma and Bertha (Kirchgraber) B.; m. Dorothy F. Weber, July 20, 1969; children: Joanne, Jeanne, Paula, Marvin. B.S., Coll. Agriculture, U. Ill., 1923. Cert. tax cons., Calif. Partner Bresee Bros. Cleaners, Champaign, Ill., 1925-40; v.p. System Fin. Co., Champaign, 1934-67; pres. Continental Loan Co., Champaign, 1938-67; partner Byrd Realty Co., Champaign, 1938—; pres. Bresee-Warner, Inc., Champaign, 1926—; chmn. bd. Arrowhead Lanes, Inc., Champaign, 1926—, Kickapoo Broadcasting Co., 1969—; pres. Univ. Fed. Savs. and Loan Assn., Champaign, 1927-77; aux. bd., 1979—, Bloomington Fed. Savs. and Loan Assn., 1977—. Mem. Nat. Soc. SAR, C. of C., Alpha Gamma Rho (grand treas. 1948-68), Phi Kappa Psi, Alpha Kappa Psi, Alpha Gamma Rho (grand pres. 1968). Republican. Presbyterian. Club: Quarterback. Inventor parachute opening device, cardboard concrete mixer, door bumper, others. Home: 1212 Waverly Dr Champaign IL 61820 Office: 602 E Green St Champaign IL 61820

BRESIN, MILLARD, architect; b. Bklyn., Mar. 14, 1925; s. Charles and Gussie (Roffwarg) B.; m. Florence Becker, June 19, 1948; children—Howard, Michael, Barry. B.Arch. magna cum laude, Cath. U. Am., 1949. Chief draftsman C. M. Spindler Assos., Bklyn., 1949-55, partner, 1956; partner firm Haus & Bresin, Queens, N.Y., 1956-64; owner, architect Millard Bresin, Queens, N.Y., 1964—. Mem. Queens Community Planning Bd., 1968—. Served with U.S. Army, World War II. Decorated Silver Star. Mem. AIA (pres. Queens 1967-68), N.Y. State Assn. Architects (dir. 1969-70), Architects' Council N.Y.C. (sec. 1971-72, pres. 1975-76), N.Y. Soc. Architects. Club: K.P. Home: 3421 Oceanside Rd Oceanside NY 11572 Office: 507 Rockaway Ave Valley Stream NY 11580

BRESLER, MARTIN I., lawyer; b. Blkyn., Feb. 25, 1931; s. Eli and Sylvia (Hinitz) B.; m. Shirley Bauer, Apr. 27, 1960; children: Laura E., Ellen. Student, NYU, 1948-49; B.B.A. CUM LAUDE, CCNY, 1952; J.D., Harvard U., 1955. Bar: N.Y. 1956. Assoc. firm Ungar & Liben, N.Y.C., 1957-59, firm Colenbock & Barrell, 1959-66; gen. counsel Caldor, Inc., Norwalk, Conn., 1966-67; ptnr. firm Stein & Rosen, N.Y.C., 1967-71, firm Krause, Hirsch & Gross, 1970-80, firm Stroock & Stroock & Lavan, 1980—. Pres. Lexington Democratic Club, N.Y.C., 1965-66; v.p., dir. Fedn. Employment and Guidance Service, N.Y.C., 1976—; chmn. Joint Task Force on Exec. Suite Am. Jewish Com., 1981, bd. dirs. N.Y. chpt., 1982—; trustee Sam and Esther Miskoff park East Cultural Ctr., 1976. Served with U.S. Army, 1955-57. Mem. Assn. Bar City N.Y., Beta Gamma Sigma, Phi Sigma Delta. Jewish. Home: 910 Park Ave New York NY 10021 Office: Stroock & Stroock & Lavan 7 Hanover Sq New York NY 10006

BRESLIN, JIMMY, newspaperman, author; b. Jamaica, N.Y., Oct. 17, 1929; s. James Earl and Frances (Curtin) B.; m. Rosemary Dattolico, Dec. 26, 1954 (dec. June 1981); children: James and Kevin (twins), Rosemary, Patrick, Kelly, Christopher.; m. Ronnie Myers Eldridge, Sept. 12, 1982; stepchildren: Daniel, Emily, Lucy Eldridge. Student, L.I. U., 1947-50. Syndicated columnist N.Y. Herald-Tribune, Paris Tribune, N.Y. Daily News, others; TV commentator WNBC-TV. Author: Can't Anybody Here Play This Game?, 1963, The Gang That Couldn't Shoot Straight, 1969, World Without End, Amen, 1973, How The Good Guys Finally Won, 1975, Forsaking All Others, 1982, Table Money, 1983; co-author: Forty-Four Caliber, 1978. N.Y.C. Candidate for pres. City Council, N.Y.C., 1969; del. Democratic Nat. Conv., 1972, 76. Recipient award for nat. reporting Sigma Delta Chi, 1964, Meyer Berger award for local reporting, 1964, N.Y. Reporters Assn. award reporting, 1964. Mem. Screen Actors Guild, AFTRA, Writers Guild Am. Office: care NY Daily News 220 E 42d St New York NY 10017 *

BRESLIN, MICHAEL EDWARD, advertising agency executive; b. N.Y.C., Apr. 27, 1937; s. John and Catherine (Malley) B.; m. Catherine Regina Cleary, May 30, 1959; children: Catherine Mary, John Joseph, Patricia Mary, Mary Kay. B.B.A., Pace U., 1960; J.D., Fordham U., 1964. Communications cons. N.Y. Telephone Co., N.Y.C., 1955-60; atty., coordinator labor relations and adminstrn. NBC, N.Y.C. and Chgo., 1960-67; sr. v.p., gen. counsel Leo Burnett Co. Inc., Chgo., 1979—; mem. ad hoc legal com. Assn. of Nat. Advertisers, Proprietary Assn. Served with U.S. Army, 1959, 60-61. Mem. Am. Assn. Advt. Agys. (vice chmn. legal subcom.). Republican. Roman Catholic. Clubs: Chgo. Athletic Assn., Executive of Chgo. (dir.), Plaza (dir.). Home: 395 Westwood Dr Barrington IL 60010 Office: Leo Burnett Co Inc Prudential Plaza Chicago IL 60601

BRESLOW, LESTER, physician, educator; b. Bismarck, N.D., Mar. 17, 1915; s. Joseph and Mayme (Danziger) B.; children: Norman, Jack, Stephen; m. Devra J.R. Miller, 1967. B.A., U. Minn., 1935, M.D., 1938, M.P.H., 1941. Diplomate: Am. Bd. Preventive Medicine and Public Health. Intern USPHS Hosp., Stapleton, N.Y., 1938-40; dist. health officer Minn. Dept. Health, 1941-43; chief bur. chronic diseases Calif. Dept. Public Health, Berkeley, 1946-60, chief div. preventive medicine, 1960-65, dir. dept., 1965-68; lectr. U. Calif. Sch. Public Health, Berkeley, 1950-68, prof. public health, 1968—, chmn. dept. preventive medicine and social medicine, 1969-72; dean Sch. Pub. Health, UCLA, 1972-80; dir. study Pres.'s Commn. Health Needs of Nation, 1952; cons. Nat. Cancer Inst., 1981—. Author med. publs.; editor: Ann. Rev. Pub. Health, 1979—; editorial cons.: Jour. Preventive Medicine. Served to capt. U.S. Army, 1943-45. Decorated Bronze Star; recipient Lasker award; Sedgwick medal Am. Pub. Health Assn.; Outstanding Achievement award U. Minn. Fellow Am. Coll. Preventive Medicine (Disting. service award 1976), ACP; fellow AAAS; mem. Am. Heart Assn. (fellow epidemiology sect.), Am. Public Health Assn. (past pres.), Public Health Cancer Assn. (past pres.), Am. Epidemiol. Soc., Internat. Epidemiol. Assn. (past pres.), Am. Cancer Soc. (nat. dir., Calif. dir., chmn. adv. com. on research etiology), Assn. Schs. Public Health (pres. 1973-74), Inst. Medicine, Nat. Acad. Scis. (council 1978-80, chmn. bd. health promotion and disease prevention 1981—). Home: 10926 Verano Rd Los Angeles CA 90024

BRESLOW, RONALD CHARLES, chemist, educator; b. Rahway, N.J., Mar. 14, 1931; s. Alexander E. and Gladys (Fellows) B.; m. Esther Greenberg, Sept. 7, 1955; children: Stephanie, Karen. A.B. summa cum laude, Harvard, 1952, M.A., 1953, Ph.D., 1955. NRC fellow Cambridge (Eng.) U., 1955-56; mem. faculty Columbia, 1956—, prof. chemistry, 1962-66, S.L. Mitchell prof., 1966—; cons. to industry, 1958—; Mem. medicinal chemistry panel NIH, 1964—; mem. adv. panel on chemistry NSF, 1971—. Editor: Benjamin, Inc, 1962—; Author: Organic Reaction Mechanisms, 1965, 2d edit., 1969; also articles.; Mem. editorial bd.: Organic Syntheses, 1964—, Jour. Organic Chemistry, 1969—, Jour. Bio-organic Chemistry, 1972—, Tetrahedron, 1975—, Tetrahedron Letters, 1975—. Recipient Fresenius award Phi Lambda Upsilon, 1966; Mark Van Doren award Columbia, 1969; Roussel prize, 1978; Centenary lectr. London Chem. Soc., 1972. Fellow Am. Acad. Arts and Scis.; mem. Am. Philos. Soc., Nat. Acad. Scis. (chmn. chemistry div. 1974-77), Am. Chem. Soc. (Pure Chemistry award 1966, Baeheland medal 1969, chmn. div. organic chemistry 1970, Harrison Howe award 1974, Remsen award 1977, J. F. Norris award 1980), Phi Beta Kappa (first marshall 1952). Home: 275 Broad Ave Englewood NJ 07631 Office: Dept Chemistry Columbia Univ New York NY 10027

BRESNAHAN, JAMES FRANCIS, medical ethics educator; b. Springfield, Mass., Dec. 28, 1926; s. James Francis and Margaret Anna (Riley) B. A.B., Coll. Holy Cross, 1947; M.A., Weston Coll, 1953, S.T.L., 1960; J.D., Harvard U., 1954, LL.M., 1955; Ph.D., Yale U., 1972. Bar: Mass sup. ct. 1955. Joined S.J., Roman Catholic Ch., 1949; tchr. Cheverus High Sch., Portland, Maine, 1955-56; asst. prof. religious studies Fairfield U., 1962-66, 69-70; vis. prof. ethics Weston Coll., 1971-72; assoc. prof. religious studies Regis Coll., 1972-74; prof. ethics Jesuit Sch. Theology in Chgo., 1975-81; vis. lectr. in med. ethics Northwestern U. Med. Sch., Chgo., 1978-80; vis. lectr. in legal ethics Northwestern U. Law Sch., 1979; co-dir. ethics program, lectr. ethics Northwestern U. Med. Sch., 1980—. Contr. articles to profl. jours. Mem. com. to draft code for profl. conduct Canon Law Soc. Am., 1978-79. Fellow Soc. Values in Higher Edn.; mem. AAUP (v.p. chpt. 1973-74), Soc. Christian Ethics (convenor ethics and law task force 1979-80, dir. 1981—), Council on Religion and Law, Ill. Coalition Against Death Penalty, Soc. Health and Human Values, Am. Soc. Law and Medicine. Home: Jesuit House 5554 Woodlawn Ave Chicago IL 60637 Office: Ward 4-334 Northwestern Univ Med Sch 303 E Chicago Ave Chicago IL 60611

BRESSLER, BERNARD, lawyer; b. N.Y.C., Jan. 23, 1928; s. Morris and Masha (Roitman) B.; m. Teresa Stern, June 25, 1950; children: Lisa, Jeanette. B.A., Rutgers U., 1949; LL.B. summa cum laude, Harvard U., 1952. Bar: N.Y. 1953, N.J. 1977. Atty. firm Greenman, Shea, Sandomire & Zimet, N.Y.C., 1952-60; ptnr. Bressler, Director & Rothenberg, N.Y.C., 1960—, Bressler, Director & Ross, Morristown, N.J., 1981—; sec., dir. Plenum Pub. Corp., Tad's Enterprises, Inc., Sonomed Tech., Inc.; sec. Electro-Catheter Ctr. Devel. Corp., Microenergy, Inc., Telebyte Tech. Inc. Author: (with others) Tax Annotations Nichols Ency. Forms, 1954-59; Editor: (with B. Meislin) New York Lawyers Manual, 1954, Harvard Law Rev., vol. 65. Campaign dir. Summit (N.J.) United Jewish Appeal, 1957-60; chmn. Summit Democrat Club, 1957; trustee Summit Civic Found., 1958-65; chmn. Summit Area United Negro Coll. Fund, 1979. Served with USNR, 1945-46. Jewish (v.p. temple). Home: 101 Kent Pl Blvd Summit NJ 07901 Office: 90 Broad St New York NY 10004

BRESSLER, BERNARD, psychiatrist, educator; b. Milan, Mich., May 22, 1917; s. Sam and Rose (Grossman) B. A.B., Washington U., 1938, M.D., 1942; grad., Chgo. Psychoanalytic Inst., 1951. Intern St. Louis City Hosp., 1942-43; resident in psychiatry St. Louis City Sanitarium, 1943, Michael Reese Hosp., Chgo., 1943-45; practice medicine specializing in psychiatry, Chgo., 1946-53; mem. faculty Duke U. Med. Ctr., Durham, N.C., 1955—, prof. psychiatry, 1962—; asst. dir. U. N.C.-Duke Psychoanalytic Inst., tng. analyst. Served with U.A. Army, 1953-55. Fellow Am. Psychiat. Assn. (life); mem. AMA, Am. Psychoanalytic Assn., Psychosomatic Soc., Pan-Am. Med. Assn. Episcopalian. Home: 100 Berkshire Rd Richmond VA 23221 Office: 3600 Floyd Ave Richmond VA 23221

BRESSLER, CHARLES, tenor; b. Kingston, Pa., Apr. 1, 1926; s. Herbert Clair and Verna (Snyder) B. Grad., Juilliard Sch. Music, 1950, postgrad. diploma, 1951. Faculty Mannes Coll. Music, 1966—, N.C. Sch. Arts, 1978—, Manhattan Sch. Music, 1978—, Bklyn. Coll. Conservatory of Music. Mem., N.Y. Pro Musica, 1950-63; soloist with orchs. including, N.Y. Philharmonic, Chgo., Boston, San Francisco, Oakland, Mpls., Cin. symphonies, ann. tours of, Europe; rec. artist, Decca, Columbia, Cambridge, Project 3, Nonesuch; appeared with, Santa Fe Opera, Washington Opera Soc.; (Recipient Best Male Singer award for role in The Play of Daniel, Nat. Festival of Paris 1960). Served with USNR, 1944-46, 51-52. Office: care Melvin Kaplan Inc 1860 Broadway New York NY 10023 *

BRESSLER, MARVIN, educator; b. N.Y.C., Apr. 10, 1923; s. George and Clara (Kitzis) B.; m. Nancy Rosner, Feb. 1, 1944; children—Jan Darcy, Amy Gwen. B.S., Temple U., 1947; A.M. in Sociology, U. Pa., 1948, Ph.D., 1952. Asst. prof. sociology U. Pa., 1953-57; asso. prof. sociology N.Y. U., 1957-60, prof., chmn. dept. ednl. sociology, 1961-63; prof. sociology Princeton, 1963—, chmn. dept. sociology, 1970—, chmn. com. on future of coll., 1970-72. Author: (with R. D. Lambert) Indian Students on American Campus, 1956, Tax-Supported Medical Institutional Care for the Needy and Medically Needy, 1957, Report on the Commission on the Future of the College, 1973. Home: 123 Maclean Circle Princeton NJ 08540 Office: Dept Sociology Green Hall Princeton U Princeton NJ 08540

BRESSLER, RICHARD MAIN, railroad executive; b. Wayne, Nebr., Oct. 8, 1930; s. John T. and Helen (Main) B.; m. Dianne G. Pearson, Apr. 17, 1981; children: Kristin M., Alan L. B.A., Dartmouth Coll., 1952. With Gen. Electric Co., 1952-68; v.p., treas. Am. Airlines Inc., 1968-72, sr. v.p., 1972-73; v.p. finance Atlantic Richfield Co., Los Angeles, 1973-75, sr. v.p. fin., 1975-77; pres. Arco Chem. Co., 1977-78, exec. v.p., 1978-80; pres., chief exec. officer, dir. Burlington No., Inc., St. Paul, 1980—, chmn., 1982—; dir. Baker Internat., El Paso Co., Seafirst Corp., Honeywell Inc., Gen. Mills, Inc.; trustee Penn Mut. Life Ins. Co. Office: 999 3d Ave Seattle WA 98104

BREST, PAUL, educator; b. Jacksonville, Fla., Aug. 9, 1940; s. Alexander and Mia (Deutsch) B.; m. Iris Lang, June 17, 1962; children: Hilary, Jeremy. A.B., Swarthmore Coll., 1962; J.D., Harvard U., 1965; LL.D., Northeastern U., 1980. Bar: N.Y. 1966. Law clk. to judge U.S. Ct. Appeals (1st cir.), Boston, 1965-66; atty. NAACP Legal Def. Fund, Jackson, Miss., 1966-68; law clk. Justice John Harlan, U.S. Supreme Ct., 1968-69; prof. law Stanford U., 1969—, now Kenneth and Harle Montgomery Prof. clin. legal edn. Author: Processes of Constitutional Decisionmaking, 1965. Mem. Am. Acad. Arts and Scis. Home: 814 Tolman Dr Stanford CA 94305 Office: Stanford Law Sch Stanford CA 94305

BRETH, JAMES RAYMOND, scrap metals company executive; b. Scranton, Pa., 1929. B.S., M.S., U. Ala., 1955. With David J. Joseph Co., Cin., 1956—, v.p., sec., 1974-76, v.p., 1976-77, exec. v.p., 1977-78, pres., 1978—, then chief operating officer, chief exec. officer, 1980—, also dir.; dir. SHV North Am. Corp. Office: David J Joseph Co Box 1078 Cincinnati OH 45201

BRETHEN, ROBERT HERSCHELL, building components manufacturing executive; b. Rochester, N.Y., June 29, 1926; s. Milton R. and Ethyl H. (Herschell) B.; m. Joan Peet, Sept. 6, 1952; children: Karen E., David M. B.S., Syracuse U., 1949. Regional sales mgr. Delco Appliance div. Gen. Motors Corp., Rochester, 1949-62; v.p., gen. mgr. Kitchen Machine div. Toledo Scale Corp., Rochester, 1963-68; group v.p. Fuqua Industries, Atlanta, 1968-71, Nat. Service Industries, 1971-73; pres., chief operating officer, dir. Philips Industries, Inc., Dayton, Ohio, 1973—; dir. Hobart Bros. Mfg. Co., Sure Care Inc. Bd. dirs. Miami Valley Hosp., Jr. Achievement of Dayton and Miami Valley, Planned Parenthood Assn. Miami Valley, Inc. Mem. Dayton C. of C. (solicitations rev. com.), LWV (adv. bd. greater Dayton area), Sigma Phi Epsilon. Republican. Home: 333 Oakwood Ave Dayton OH 45409 Office: 4801 Springfield St PO Box 943 Dayton OH 45401 *I am conscious of the fact that I must contribute to and draw strength from the full utilization of the resources of lives that are tangent to mine, whatever my radius. While it is true that "no man is an island," it is also true that every man is a wave.*

BRETHERICK, JOHN H., JR, holding company executive. Attended, Temple U. With Phoenix Assurance co., Ltd. (prior to 1968), Continetnal Corp., 1968—; asst. v.p. personal lines ins., then v.p. Continental Corp., 1968-75, sr. v.p., tehn exec. v.p., 1975; now with Fidelity & Casualty Co. N.Y., now exc. v.p., dir.; exec. v.p. Continental Ins. Cos.; chmn. exec. com. Ins. Services Office; dir. Ins. Info. Inst. Office: Fidelity & Causualty Co NY 80 Maiden LN New York NY 10038 *

BRETON, ALBERT A., economist, educator; b. Montmartre, Sask., Can., June 12, 1929; s. Alberic T. and Jeanne (Nadeau) B.; m. Margot Fournier, Sept. 6, 1958; children: Catherine, Natalie, Francoise, Robert. B.A., U. Man., Can., 1951; Ph.D. in Econs., Columbia U., 1965. Asst. prof. U. Montreal, 1957-65; dir. research Social Research Group, Montreal, 1956-65; vis. asso. prof. Carleton U., Ottawa, Can., 1964-65; lectr. econs., reader in econs. London Sch. Econs., 1966-69; vis. prof. Can. studies Harvard U., 1969-70; vis. prof. U. Catholique de Louvain, Belgium, 1968-69; prof. econs. U. Toronto, 1970—. Author books in field; contbr. articles to profl. jours. Vice-chmn., Fed. Cultural Policy Rev. Com.; mem. Royal Commn. Econ. Union and Devel. Prospects for Can. Can. Social Sci. Research council grantee, 1955-56; Can. Council grantee, 1959-60. Fellow Royal Soc. Can.; Mem. Can. Econ. Policy Com. Office: Inst Policy Analysis U Toronto Toronto ON M5S 1A1 Canada

BRETT, GEORGE HOWARD, professional baseball player; b. Moundsville, W.Va., May 15, 1953; s. Jack Francis and Ethel (Hansen) B. Student, El Camino Jr. Coll., Torrance, Calif. Third baseman Kansas City (Mo.) Royals Profl. Baseball Team, 1974—. Named Am. League batting champion, 1976, Am. League Most Valuable Player, 1980. Mem. Am. League All Star Team, 1976, 77, 78, 79, 81, 82, 83. Address: care Kansas City Royals PO Box 1969 Kansas City MO 64141 *

BRETT, THOMAS RUTHERFORD, judge; b. Oklahoma City, Oct. 2, 1931; s. John A. and Norma (Dougherty) B.; m. Mary Jean James, Aug. 26, 1952; children: Laura Elizabeth Brett Tribble, James Ford, Susan Marie Brett Crump, Maricarolyn. B.B.A., U. Okla., 1952, LL.B., 1957, J.D., 1971. Bar: Okla. 1957. Asst. county atty., Tulsa, 1957; mem. firm Hudson, Hudson, Wheaton, Kyle & Brett, Tulsa, 1958-59, Jomes, Givens, Brett, Gotcher, Doyle & Bogan, 1969-79; U.S. dist. judge No. Dist. Okla., Tulsa, 1979—. Bd. regents U. Okla., 1971-78; mem. adv. bd. Salvation Army; trustee Okla. Bar Found. Served to col. JAG USAR, 1953-81. Fellow Am. Coll. Trial Lawyers, Am. Bar Found.; mem. Am. Bar Assn., Okla. Bar Assn., Tulsa County Bar Assn., Am. Judicature Soc., U. Okla. Coll. Law Alumni Assn. (dir.), Phi Alpha Delta, Order Coif. Democrat. Office: 333 W 4th St Rm 4-508 Tulsa OK 74103

BRETTELL, RICHARD ROBSON, museum curator; b. Rochester, N.Y., Jan. 17, 1949; s. Herbert Robson and Ellen Louise (Sackett) B.; m. Carol Bieler, June 9, 1973. B.A., Yale U., 1971, M.A., 1973, Ph.D., 1977. Asst. prof., acad. program dir. art history U. Tex., Austin, 1976-80; curator European painting and sculpture Art Inst. Chgo., 1980—. Author: Historic Denver, The Architects, 1856-1893, 1974; co-author: The Drawings of Camille Pissarro, 1980, Painters and Peasants in the Nineteenth Century, 1983, Paper and Light: The Calotype 1839-1865. Fellow Nat. Endowment Humanities, 1980, Whiting Found., 1974, Carnegie Found., 1972, Samuel H. Kress Found., 1974, U. Tex. Research Inst., 1978-79. Mem. Coll. Art Assn., Soc. Archtl. Historians, Historic Denver, Elizabethan Soc., Phelps Assn. Democrat. Office: Art Inst Michigan Ave Chicago IL 60603

BRETTHOLLE, FRANK MARSH, multinational company executive; b. Carnegie, Pa., May 4, 1917; s. Frank William and Sarah Ann Atkinson (Marsh) B.; m. Thelma Elaine Evans, Nov. 4, 1950; children: Frank Evans, Sarah Ann. A.B., Westminster Coll., 1939; M.B.A., U. Chgo., 1942. Asst. prof. Westminster Coll., 1942-46; controller H.J. Heinz Co., Pitts., 1959-66, v.p., controller, 1966-73, sr. v.p. fin., treas., 1973—; dir. H.J. Heinz Co., Starkist Foods, Inc., Ore-Ida Foods, Inc., Canners Exchange Ins. Co.; mem. adv. bd. Liberty Mut. Ins. Co. Trustee U. Mont. Found.; trustee, mem. exec. com. Westminster Coll. Mem. Fin. Execs. Inst. Clubs: Duquesne, University, Chartiers Country. Lodge: Masons. Office: H J Heinz Co 1062 Progress St Pittsburgh PA 15230

BRETTON, HENRY L, political scientist, educator; b. Berlin, May 18, 1916; m. Marian More, Sept. 8, 1951; children: Elizabeth, Alexander. B.A. with honors, Yale U., 1947, M.A., 1948; Ph.D., U. Mich., 1951. Escort-interpreter Govtl. Affairs Inst., Washington, 1950-51; liaison officer USIA and; dir. Amerika-Institut, Innsbruck, Austria, 1956-57; Distinguished prof. State U. N.Y., Brockport, 1969—; Fulbright lectr. Faculty Law, U. Innsbruck, 1956-57; vis. prof. polit. sci. U. Ghana, Legon, 1964-65; vis. prof. polit. sci., head dept. U.E. Africa, Nairobi, Kenya, 1965-66; cons. and researcher USIS, Nigeria and; Washington, 1963-64; adv. council on Africa U.S. Dept. State, 1962-69; chmn. State U. N.Y. Univ. Awards Com., 1978-83. Author: (with J. K. Pollock and James H. Meisel) Germany Under Occupation, 1949, Stresemann and the Revision of Versailles, 1953, (with others) German Democracy at Work, 1955, Power and Stability in Nigeria: The Politics of Decolonization, 1962, The Rise and Fall of Kwame Nkrumah: A Study of Personal Rule in Africa, 1967, Power and Politics in Africa, 1973, The Power of Money: A Political-Economic Analysis, 1980; editorial bd.: Pan-African Jour, 1968-70; contbr. to books, articles and revs. to profl. publs. Pres. Ann Arbor (Mich.) Community Center, 1962-64; elder 1st Presbyterian Ch., Ann Arbor, 1963-64. Served to 1st lt. M.I., OSS U.S. Army, 1943-45. Decorated Bronze Star; Rockefeller Found. grantee, 1964-66, 68-70. Mem. Am. Polit. Sci. Assn., N.E. Polit. Sci. Assn., African Studies Assn. Field research in Germany, Ghana, Nigeria, Senegal and Ivory Coast, E. Africa. Home: 131 Sherwood St Brockport NY 11420 Office: Dept Polit Sci State U Coll at Brockport Brockport NY 14420

BRETTSCHNEIDER, BERTRAM DONALD, educator; b. Bklyn., May 7, 1924; s. Joseph and Fannie (Cohn) B.; m. Rita Roberta Fischman, June 25, 1950; children—Jane Ann, Joseph Michael. B.A., Tulane U., 1947, M.A., 1948; M.A., Columbia U., 1951; Ph.D., N.Y. U., 1956. Grad. asst. psychology Tulane U., 1947-48; instr. philosophy Ft. Trumbull br. U. Conn., 1949-50; elementary sch. tchr., Valley Stream, N.Y., 1951-54; mem. faculty Hofstra U., 1954—, asso. prof. philosophy edn., 1954-59, asso. dean coll., 1959-63, prof. philosophy, 1963—, chmn. dept. philosophy, 1974—; fellow in philosophy New Coll. of Hosfra U., 1967—; vis. asso. prof. edn. N.Y. U., 1959-62; vis. prof. humanities Manhattan Sch. Music, 1973-74; vis. prof. philosophy Webb Inst. Naval Architecture, 1979—, Soc. Am. Philosophy, 1978-80. Author: The Philosophy of Samuel Alexander: Idealism in Space, Time and Deity, 1963, (with Charles J. Calitri) The Goliath Head, 1972. Bd. dirs. Assn. of Artist-run Galleries, 1975—. Served with AUS, 1943-46. Mem. Am. Soc. Aesthetics, Soc. Phenomenology and Existential Philosophy, Middle Atlantic States Philosophy of Edn. Soc. (exec. com. 1959-61), Eastern Deans Assn., Philosophy Edn. Soc., Am. Philos. Assn., Coll. Art Assn. Home: 2 Crosby Pl Huntington NY 11743 Office: New College of Hofstra Univ Hempstead NY 11550

BRETZFELDER, DEBORAH MAY, museum exhibit designer; b. Hazelton, Pa., Sept. 21, 1932; d. Joseph and Rose (Smulyan) Hirsh; m. Robert Bretzfelder, Dec. 24, 1955; children: Karl, Marc. Student, Syracuse U., 1950-53. Textile colorist, designer Cohn-Hall-Marx, N.Y.C., 1954-55; fashion coordinator Hecht's Dept. Store, Washington, 1956; free lance artist, Washington, 1956-58; exhibits technician Smithsonian Instn., Washington, 1958-59, supr. exhibits prodn., 1959-63, exhibits specialist Nat. Mus. Am. History, 1963-75, visual info. specialist, project mgmt. officer, 1975—, acting chief of design, 1983—; cons. various firms, orgns., mus. personnel, instr. mus. programs. Mem. violin sect. George Washington U. Orch. Mem. Am. Assn. Mus., Internat. Com. Mus., Nat. Soc. Hist. Preservation, Tau Sigma Delta. Jewish. Club: Potomac Appalachian Trail. Home: 2748 Woodley Pl NW Washington DC 20008 Office: Smithsonian Nat Mus Am History 14th and Constitution NW Room 4210 Washington DC 20560

BREUL, FRANK RENNELL, educator; b. Bridgeport, Conn., May 10, 1916; s. Alvin C. and Mildred (Rennell) B.; m. Gertrude L. Kirsten, June 7, 1947; 1 dau., Nancy. A.B., Amherst Coll., 1938; A.M., U. Chgo., 1941; Ph.D., McGill U., 1951. Lectr. McGill U., 1949-51; asso. prof. social welfare U. Wash., 1951-56; mem. faculty U. Chgo., 1956—, prof. social welfare, 1960—, asso. dean, 1966-70. Editor: Social Service Rev, 1973—. Served to maj., F.A. AUS, 1941-46. Decorated Bronze Star medal. Mem. Nat. Assn. Social Work, Nat. Conf. Social Welfare. Episcopalian. Home: 5807 S Dorchester Ave Chicago IL 60637

BREUNINGER, TYRONE, musician; b. Red Hill, Pa., Jan. 9, 1939; s. Linford B.; children—Galen Robert, Lorin James, Michele Louise. B.S. in Music Edn, W. Chester State Coll., 1961; M.Mus. in Trombone, Temple U., 1966. Instr. instrumental music Folcroft (Pa.) Borough Sch. Dist., 1961-64; instr. lower brass instruments W. Chester State Coll., 1964—; instr. trombone Temple U., Phila., 1975—; co-first trombonist Phila. Symphony Orch., 1967—; instr. trombone New Sch. Music, Phila., 1969—, Phila. Coll. Performing Arts, 1972—. Mem. Phi Mu Sinfonia. Home: 6 Barrys Pl Clementon NJ 08021 Office: care Phila Symphony Orch 1420 Locust St Philadelphia PA 19102

BREVERMAN, HARVEY, artist; b. Pitts., Jan. 7, 1934; s. Theodore and Sarah (Haffner) B.; m. Deborah Dobkin, June 26, 1960. B.F.A., Carnegie Inst. Tech., 1956; M.F.A., Ohio U., 1960. Tchr. Carnegie Inst. Tech., summer 1959; tchr. drawing Ohio U., Athens, 1960-61, Ill. State U., Normal, summer 1969, Falmouth (Eng.) Art Sch., 1969; prof. art State U. N.Y., Buffalo, 1961—. Resident painter, State Acad. Fine Arts, Amsterdam, 1965-66; vis. painter, Kalamazoo Inst. Art, summer 1972, 73; vis. artist, Oxford U., 1974, 77; One man shows, Albright-Knox Art Gallery, Buffalo, 1967, U. Oreg., U. Ill., 1970, Canton (Ohio) Art Inst., 1971, Middlebury Coll., 1973, FAR Gallery, N.Y.C., 1974, 79, Gadatsy Gallery, Toronto, 1975, 76, 79, 80, Kalamazoo Inst. Art, 1976, Hackley Art Mus., Muskegon, Mich., 1977, Grand Rapids (Mich.) Art Mus., Gadatsy Gallery, Toronto, 1978, U. Mich., Nardin Galleries, N.Y.C., 1980, U. N.H., 1981, Art Gallery of Hamilton (Ont., Can.), group exhbns. include, Corcoran Biennial, Washington, 1963, Bklyn. Mus., 1964, Assn. Am. Artists, N.Y.C., 1965, Rijksakademie, Amsterdam, 1968, Boston Mus. Fine Arts, NAD, Pa. Acad. Fine Arts Biennial, 1969, 2d and 3d Brit. Internat. Biennal, Bradford, Eng., 1970 72, FAR Gallery, 1972-74, Whitechapel Gallery, London, 1973, Pushkin Mus., Moscow, 1972, 2d Norwegian Internat. Biennial, 1974, Mus. Modern Art, Oxford, Eng., Honolulu Acad. Fine Arts, 1975, 8th Internat. Art Fair, Basel, Switzerland, 1977, Auslands Institut, Dortmund, W. Ger., Arte Fiere '78, Bologna, 1978, Art Gallery Ont., Toronto, 1979, Am. Acad. and Inst. Arts and Letters, N.Y.C., 1980, NYU, N.Y.C., Jewish Mus., N.Y.C., 1982, Queens Mus., N.Y.C., 1983, also traveling exhibits in, U.S., Europe, Central Am., paintings for, U.S. embassies, 1976; rep. permanent collections, Mus. Modern Art, N.Y.C., Whitney Mus., Albright-Knox Art Gallery, Phila. Mus., Butler Inst. Art, Youngstown, Ohio, Nat. Collection Fine Arts, Washington, Library of Congress, Israel Mus., Jerusalem, Bradford City Art Mus., St. Catharines Dist. Arts Council, Ont., Can., Victoria and Albert Mus., London, Cleve. Mus., Balt. Mus. Art. Served with AUS, 1956-58; Korea. Grantee Louis Comfort Tiffany Found., 1962, Netherlands Govt., 1965, N.Y. Council Arts, 1972; fellow Nat. Endowment Arts, 1974-75, 80-81; recipient numerous awards and prizes, 1961—. Address: 76 Smallwood Dr Snyder NY 14226

BREVIG, PER ANDREAS, musician; b. Berg by Halden, Norway, Sept. 7, 1936; s. Knut and Aslaug (Maarud) B.; m. Berit Lillian Johannessen, June 27, 1959; children—Kjetil, Berit Elizabeth, Ingrid Lillian, Per-Christian. Mus.B., Juilliard Sch., 1968, Mus.M., 1969, D.Mus. Arts, 1971; studied trombone under, Palmer Traulsen, Copenhagen, 1958. Mem. trombone and chamber music faculties Juilliard Sch., 1966—; faculty Aspen Music Festival, 1970—. Conducting in, Holland and Sweden, 1962-64; with, Leopold Stokowski, 1966-67; Author: Problems of Notations and Execution; Numerous premiers, solo performances, recordings, master classes, Europe, U.S., Japan; mem., Bergen (Norway) Symphony Orch., 1957-65; 1st trombone, Am. Symphony Orch., 1965-68; prin. trombone, Met. Opera Orch., 1968—. Served with Norwegian Army. Recipient prize XIV Internat. Music Competition, Prague, Czechoslovakia, 1962, Henry B. Cabot award Boston Symphony Orch., 1966; S. Koussevitzky fellow Tanglewood Music Festival. Office: Juilliard Sch Lincoln Center Plaza New York NY 10023

BREVIK, J. ALBERT, communications consultant; b. Seattle, Aug. 1, 1920; s. Anton Christian and Olga Elise (Setter) B.; m. Norma Jacquelin Ringman, June 26, 1953; children: Jay Christian, Jon Henry. B.A., U. Wash., 1947, M.A., 1951. Guidance counselor music dept. U. Wash., Seattle, 1947-52, entertainment dir. athletic dept., 1947-52; vocal music educator Clover Park High Sch., Tacoma, Wash., 1952-54; television coordinator Pierce County Schs., Tacoma, 1954-59; dir. television edn., gen. mgr. KPEC-TV, Clover Park Schs., Tacoma, 1959-72, dir. communications, 1972—; mgr. KPEC-TV, KPEC-FM, 1960-76; also in charge publs. and pub. relations dept., film prodn. unit, new media prodn. and services; gen. mgr. Sta. KCPQ-TV, Tacoma, 1976-80; communications cons., 1980—; pres. Avcom Pacific, communications cons., 1981—; asso. faculty dept. edn. U. Puget Sound, 1955-69; dir. Intermarket Corp., Norwegian Male Chorus, Seattle, 1946-48, Clarion Chorus, 1947-52; free-lance radio musician, Seattle, 1938-52; entertainment dir. BC Lions (profl. football club), Vancouver, Can., 1954-55; ednl. TV cons., B.C., Can., 1960-61; v.p. Wash. Ednl. Network, 1978. Mem. Fir Tree, Phi Mu Alpha Synfonia, Phi Delta Kappa. Lutheran (v.p., dir. 1959-69). Clubs: Kiwanian (Tacoma) (pres. 1963, dir. 1955-71); Tacoma Yacht, Day Island Yacht, Fircrest Golf (Tacoma). Home and Office: 1920 Day Island Blvd W Tacoma WA 98466

BREW, JOHN OTIS, archeologist, educator; b. Malden, Mass., Mar. 28, 1906; s. Michael Parker and Edith (Fryer) B.; m. Evelyn Ruth Nimmo, June 11, 1939; children—Alan Parker, Lindsay Edward. A.B. in Fine Arts, Dartmouth Coll., 1928; student, Harvard Grad. Sch. Arts and Scis., 1928-31; Ph.D., Harvard U., 1941; LL.D. in Internat. Relations, U. Liberia, 1970. Fellow archeology U. Chgo. Expdn., 1930; with Harvard U. Peabody Mus., 1930—, asst. to dir., 1930-47, dir., 1948-67, sci. dir. 1931, dir., 1931-33, asst. to dir., 1934, dir., field seasons 1935-39, mem. staff, 1937—, asst. curator, 1941-45, curator, 1945-48, dir., 1948-67, engaged archeol. reconnaissance for mus., N.Mex. and Ariz., 1946-47, Peabody prof. Am. archeology and ethnology, 1949-72, emeritus, 1972—; mem. bd. syndics Harvard U. Press; vis. prof. So. Meth. U., 1972-76; vis. lectr. U. Calgary, Alta., Can., fall 1977; archaeol. cons. TVA.; Chmn. UNESCO comm. for Monuments (artistic and historic sites and archaeol. excavations); mem. adv. bd. Nat. Parks Service, 1952-58, Nat. Park Service Adv. Council, 1958—; bd. dirs. Human Relations Area Files, chmn. bd., 1954-57; chmn. U.S. Nat. Com. for Preservation of Monuments of Nubia; mem. internat. centre com. Adv. Council Historic Preservation, 1966—. Contbr. articles to jours. and papers of, Peabody Mus. Trustee Fruitlands and the Wayside Museums, Donations for Edn. in Liberia, 1958—; trustee Plimouth Plantation, Inc. Recipient Viking Fund medal for anthropology, 1947, Conservation Service award Dept. Interior; decorated grand comdr. Star of Africa. Fellow Am. Acad. Arts and Scis.; mem. Soc. Am. Archaeology (council 1944-46, pres. 1949-50), Internat. Inst. for Conservation Mus. Objects, Internat. African Inst. (exec. council), Mass. Archaeol. Soc. (exec. council 1941-44, trustee 1949-52), Tree Ring Soc., Soc. Applied Archaeology, Am. Assn. Museums (council 1956-60), Colonial Soc. Mass., Acad. Am. Francisco Hist. (corr. mem.), S.W. Mus. (hon.), Los Angeles, No. Ariz. Soc. Hist. Sci. and Art, Am. Antiquarian Soc., Mass. Hist. Soc., German Archeol. Inst., Soc. Antiquaries London, Prehistoric Soc. (U.K.), Am. Anthrop. Assn. (pres. 1951). Clubs: Harvard Faculty (pres. 1951-55), Odd Volumes (pres. 1964-69); Cosmos (Washington)). Address: Peabody Mus Archaeology and Ethnology Harvard U Cambridge MA 02138

BREW, WILLIAM DANIEL, railroad executive; b. Shelley, Idaho, Mar. 18, 1923; s. Daniel Gratten and Lila Eleanor (Kiholm) B.; m. Alma Aurelia Barman, Sept. 1, 1948; children: Caroline, William Daniel, II, Elaine, Debra, Paul. B.S., U. Utah, 1950; M.B.A., Golden Gate U., 1982. With Western Pacific R.R. Co., San Francisco, 1950—, asst. sec.-asst. treas., 1969-73, sec., 1974-82, sec.-treas., 1982—, dir. taxes, 1973—. Precinct worker Republican Party. Served with USAAF, 1943-46. Decorated Air medal. Mem. Am. Soc. Corp. Secs., Nat. Assn. Ry. Tax Commrs., R.R. Income Tax Adminstrs. Conf., Tax Execs. Inst. Mormon. Home: 1610 Honfleur Dr Sunnyvale CA 94087 Office: 526 Mission St San Francisco CA 94105

BREWER, ALBERT PRESTON, lawyer, former gov. of Ala.; b. Bethel Springs, Tenn., Oct. 26, 1928; s. Dan A. and Clara (Yarber) B.; m. Martha Farmer, Jan. 31, 1951; children—Rebecca Ann, Beverly Alison. A.B., U. Ala., 1952, LL.B., 1952; LL.D., L.H.D., Jacksonville State U., Samford U. Bar: Ala. bar 1952. Mem. Ala. Ho. of Reps., 1955-66, speaker, 1963-66; lt. gov. of, Ala., 1966-68, gov., 1968-71; Mem. exec. com. Nat. Gov.'s Conf.; vice chmn. So. Gov.'s Conf.; chmn. Appalachian Regional Commn., 1970. Mem. Ala. Democratic Exec. Com., 1964—. Named Outstanding Young Man of Decatur Decatur Jr. C. of C., 1963, One of Four outstanding Young Men of Ala. Ala. Jr. C. of C., 1963, Outstanding Mem. Ala. Ho. of Reps., 1963. Charter mem. Ala. Acad. Honor.; Mem. Am., Ala. bar assns., Am. Legion, Phi Alpha Delta, Delta Sigma Phi. Baptist. Club: Mason (Shriner). Home: Route 4 Box 184 Decatur AL 35603 Office: Decatur AL

BREWER, CAREY, coll. pres.; b. Lynchburg, Va., July 8, 1927; s. James Allen and Esther Goode (Leftwich) B.; m. Betty Ann Brighton, Sept. 3, 1949; children—Mary Elizabeth, Robert Allen, Ruth Ann, Catherine Lee. B.A., Lynchburg Coll., 1949; student, Am. U., 1951; M.P.A., Harvard U., 1952, Ph.D., 1956. Analyst with legislative reference service Library of Congress, 1949-56; sr. def. specialist mil. ops. subcom. Ho. of Reps., 1956-60; mem. staff joint com. atomic energy U.S. Congress, 1960-61; various positions Office Emergency Planning, Exec. Office of Pres., 1961-64; pres. Lynchburg Coll., 1964—; lectr. Am. U., 1954-56; Mem. bd. higher edn., also mem. gen. bd., ch. fin. council Christian Ch. (Disciples of Christ); mem. Pres.'s Civil Def. Adv. Council, 1970-72; Bd. dirs. Nat. Lab. for Higher Edn.; pres. Va. Found. Ind. Colls., 1978-80. Author: Civil Defense in the United States, 1951, Implications of a National Service Program, 1952, Science and Defense, 1956, also numerous articles. Served with USNR, 1945-46. Littauer fellow Harvard, 1951-53. Mem. Council Ind. Colls. Va. (pres. 1972-74), Greater Lynchburg C. of C. (past pres.). Mem. Christian Ch. (elder). Office: Office of Pres Lynchburg Coll Lynchburg VA 24501

BREWER, CHARLES MOULTON, lawyer; b. Washington, June 9, 1931; s. Charles M. and Monemia (Moulton) B.; m. Lavon Brown, June 14, 1958; children: Charles Robert, Lisa Ann, John Brian. B.A., U. Md., 1953; J.D., George Washington U., 1957. Bar: Ariz. 1959; Airline transp. pilot. Since practiced in, Phoenix; law clk. to Chief Justice Ariz. Supreme Ct. Levi S. Udall, 1958-59; pvt. practice, 1959—; pres. Charles M. Brewer Ltd.; guest lectr. Stanford U. Law Sch., Ariz. State U. Law Sch. Contbr. articles to profl. jours. Bd. visitors Ariz. State U. Law Sch. Served to capt. USAF, 1954-56. Mem. Am., Ariz., Maricopa County bar assns., Am. Judicature Soc., Am., Calif. trial lawyers assns., Am. Bd. Trial Advs. Office: 1400 First Interstate Bank Plaza Phoenix AZ 85003

BREWER, CHARLES ROBINSON, United States attorney; b. Holly Springs, N.C., Oct. 23, 1948; s. Harold Lee and Clara Belle (Robinson) B.; m. Susan Elaine Guest, June 20, 1971; children: Emily Marie, Sarah Elizabeth, Melissa Anne. B.A., Wake Forest U., 1971, J.D., 1974. Bar: N.C. 1974. Country atty. Caldwell County, Lenoir, N.C., 1980-81; U.S. atty. Dept. Justice, Asheville, N.C., 1981—. Mem. exec. com. Caldwell County Republican Party, Lenoir, 1976-81, pres., Lenoir, 1976-78; mem. Caldwell County Young Reps. Mary Reynolds Babcock Found. grantee, 1975; recipient Am. Jurisprudence award Lawyers Co-Op Pub. Co., 1976. Mem. N.C. Bar Assn. Republican. Baptist. Home: 83 Gracelyn Rd Asheville NC 28804 Office: PO Box 132 Post and Otis St Asheville NC 28802

BREWER, EDWARD EUGENE, tire and rubber company executive; b. Findlay, Ohio, July 19, 1925; s. William B. and Edna (Hurrel) B.; m. Joyce K. Josephsen, Feb. 7, 1948; children: Stephen, Rebecca, Mary, Sara, Debra. B.S. in Mech. Engring., Purdue U., 1949. With Cooper Tire & Rubber Co., Findlay, 1949-56, v.p., 1956-70, exec. v.p., 1970-77, pres., chmn. bd., 1977-82, chmn. bd., chief exec. officer, 1982—. Home:

857 S Main St Findlay OH 45840 Office: Cooper Tire & Rubber Co Lima and Western Aves Findlay OH 45840

BREWER, GARRY DWIGHT, educator, social scientist; b. San Francisco, Oct. 2, 1941; s. Dwight C. and Querida M. (Colson) B.; m. Saundra Neville Tonsager, Dec. 3, 1962 (div. Apr. 1976); children: Gabrielle Anne, Gregory David; m. Shelley Lane Marshall, May, 1976; 1 son, Matthew Douglas. Student, U.S. Naval Acad., 1959-61; A.B. in Econs, U. Calif., Berkeley, 1963; M.S. in Pub. Adminstrn, Calif. State U., San Diego, 1966; M.Ph. in Polit. Sci. (Kent fellow), Yale, 1968, Ph.D., 1970. Research fellow Advanced Research Projects Agy., Dept. Def., Washington, 1967; cons. Rand Corp., Santa Monica, Calif., 1969-70, mem. staff social sci. dept., 1970-72, mem. sr. staff, 1972-74; lectr. in pub. adminstrn. U. So. Calif., Los Angeles, 1972-74; mem. faculty Rand Grand. Inst. Policy Analysis, Santa Monica, 1972-75; asso. prof. Sch. Orgn. and Mgmt., Yale U., 1974-78, prof., 1978—; Cons. Russell Sage Found., 1975-76, Ford Found., 1972—, Datum Bonn, 1972—; cons. Children's Research Inst. Calif., Sacramento, 1974—, Solar Energy Research Inst., 1978—, FAO, Rome, 1978—, Com. for Econ. Devel., 1979, Sci. Applications Inc., 1979. Dir. research, asso. producer: TV documentary What Do We Do Now?, 1976 (co-recipient Ciné Golden Eagle); Author: (with R.D. Brunner) Organized Complexity: Empirical Theories of Political Development, 1971, Politicians, Bureaucrats and the Consultant, 1973, Political Development and Change, (with R.D. Brunner), 1975, Handicapped Children; Strategies for Improving Services, (with J.S. Kakalik), 1979, (with Martin Shubik) The War Game, 1979; co-author: The Foundations of Policy Analysis, 1983, The Energy Decade in Retrospect, 1983; Editor: Policy Scis. jour, 1974-76; book rev. editor, 1976-79; editorial bd., 1976—, Simulation & Games, 1972-76; editor, 1976-79; editorial bd.: Public Policy jour, 1973-81, Transfer jour, 1975—, Policy and Politics jour, 1977-81, Policy Studies Ann. Rev, 1977—, Jour. Conflict Resolutions, 1981—. Served to lt. USNR, 1963-66; Vietnam. Fellow Center for Advanced Study in Behavioral Scis., Stanford, Calif., 1974-75. Mem. Soc. for Values in Higher Edn., Am. Polit. Sci. Assn., Assn. Asian Studies. Office: Sch Orgn and Mgmt Yale U New Haven CT 06520

BREWER, GERALD BERNIE, cotton oil co. exec.; b. Fresno, Calif., Nov. 12, 1929; s. Bernie and Emma (Schafer) B.; m. Lyla Tilston, Dec. 23, 1951; children—Barbara Brewer Johnson, Nancy, William S. B.A., U. So. Calif., 1951. With Producers Cotton Oil Co., Fresno, 1953—, sales mgr., 1958-61, dir. sales, oil mill ops., 1961-62, v.p., dir. sales, 1962-69, exec. v.p., 1969-72, pres., chief exec. officer, 1972—; v.p. Bangor Punta Corp., Greenwich, Conn., 1973-80, sr. v.p., 1980—, also dir.; Mem. chancellor's assos. Calif. State Univs. and Colls., 1974—. Served to lt. USAF, 1951-52. Mem. Calif. C. of C. (dir. 1972-76), Fresno County and City C. of C. (pres. 1972-73). Republican. Clubs: Commonwealth, Sunnyside Country, Downtown, Pres.'s Calif. State U., Fresno. Home: 1465 W Morris Ave Fresno CA 93711 Office: Producers Cotton Oil Co 2907 S Maple Ave Fresno CA 93725

BREWER, JOHN CHARLES, journalist; b. Cin., Oct. 24, 1947; s. Harry Marion and Barbara Ann (Burrier) B.; m. Adeline Laude, Dec. 22, 1973; children: Andrew John, Jeffrey Joseph. B.S., Calif. State Poly. U., Pomona, 1970. Newsman, photographer Daily Report, Ontario, Calif., 1967-69; newsman AP, Los Angeles, 1969-74, news editor, 1974-75, asst. chief bur., Seattle, 1975-76, chief of bur., 1976-82, Los Angeles, 1982—. Mem. Alliance Personal Computer Owners, Sigma Delta Chi. Republican. Roman Catholic. Clubs: Northwest Steelheaders-Trout Unlimited, Nat. Steelhead Trout Assn. Home: 124 N Starflower St Brea CA 92621 Office: 1111 S Hill St Room 263 Los Angeles CA 90015 *I enjoy very much being an executive of the world's largest news-gathering company. Nothing can compare with it. As for finding time for everything—the news and photo reports, our relations with newspapers and broadcasters, my family, my personnel, problems—I am reminded of a woman who had eleven children. She was asked how she had time to take care of all of them. She replied that when she had one child it took 100 percent of her time, and eleven could not take more. I think there's an analogy in this.*

BREWER, JOHN ISAAC, physician, educator; b. Milford, Ill., Oct. 3, 1903; s. John H. and Edna (Ishler) B.; m. Ruth Russell, June 2, 1928; 1 son, John Vernon. Student, Bradley U., 1921-24, D.Sc., 1976; S.B., U. Chgo., 1925, Ph.D., 1935; M.D., Rush Med. Coll., 1928. Diplomate: Am. Bd. Obstetrics and Gynecology (dir.). Intern St. Luke's Hosp., Chgo., 1928-29, resident gynecology and obstetrics, 1929-30; pvt. practice splty., Chgo., 1930—; Instr. Northwestern U. Med. Sch., 1930-36, asst. prof., 1938-42, asso. prof., 1942-47, prof. gynecology and obstetrics, 1948—, chmn. dept., 1972-74, emeritus, 1974—; chief dept. gynecology and obstetrics Passavant Hosp., Chgo. Author: Gynecology, 1950, Textbook of Gynecology, 1953, 1958, 1961, 67; Editor in chief: Am. Jour. Obstetrics and Gynecology; Contbr. sci. publs. Served as lt. col., med. dept. U.S. Army Air Forces, 1942-45. Decorated Legion of Merit. Fellow A.C.S. (regent), Royal Coll. Obstetricians and Gynecologists, Am. Coll. Obstetricians and Gynecologists (pres. 1959-60), Am. Gynecology Soc. (pres. 1964-65); mem. Am. Assn. Obstetricians and Gynecologists (pres. 1968-69), Am. Assn. Anatomists, AMA, Central Assn. Obstetricians and Gynecologists (pres.), Chgo. Gynecol. Soc. (pres.), Chgo. Path. Soc., Chgo. Med. Soc., Ill. Med. Soc. (chmn. Joint Commn. Accreditation Hosps. 1957-74), Alpha Delta Phi, Sigma Xi, Nu Sigma Nu. Club: Flossmoor Country. Home: 860 Lake Shore Dr Chicago IL 60611 Office: 333 E Superior St Chicago IL 60611

BREWER, JOHN WITHROW, political science educator; b. Boston, Mar. 26, 1904; s. Daniel Chauncey and Genevieve (Withrow) B.; m. Thelma Lillian Martin, Aug. 22, 1943. A.B. maxima cum laude, Princeton U., 1926, M.A., 1930, Ph.D., 1932; student, Harvard Law Sch., 1926-28. Instr. polit. sci. George Washington U., Washington, 1933-34, assoc. prof. internat. law, 1939-46, prof., 1946-73, prof. emeritus internat. law and polit. sci., 1973—, head dept. polit. sci., 1946-63; prof. dept. history Harvard U., Cambridge, Mass.; instr. Dartmouth Coll., 1934-35; asst. prof. polit. sci. Conn. State Coll., 1935-38, assoc. prof., 1938-39; vis. prof. U. So. Calif., 1950—. Served with U.S. Army, 1942-46. Decorated Legion of Merit. Mem. Phi Beta Kappa. Home: Springbrook Farm Mill Rd Harvard MA 01451 Office: Dept History Harvard U. Cambridge MA 02138

BREWER, MELVIN DUANE, educational consultant; b. Rochester, Pa., Mar. 6, 1913; s. Percy McPherson and Ida Viola (Noss) B.; m. Lila Margaret Scott, Nov. 28, 1940; children: Melvin Duane (dec.), Barbara Jo (Mrs. John T. Davis), Margaret Scott (Mrs. Robert Brower). Student, Geneva Coll., Beaver Falls, Pa., 1931-32; A.B., Washington and Jefferson Coll., 1937. Served successively as alumni sec. dean freshmen, dir. admissions Washington and Jefferson Coll., 1937-44, asst. to pres., 1946-48; mem. staff Marts & Lundy, Inc., N.Y.C., 1948—, v.p., sec., 1961-69, exec. v.p., treas., 1969-71, pres., 1971—, chmn., 1974-78, sr. cons., 1978—; Trustee Washington and Jefferson Coll. (life). Contbr. articles ednl. adminstrn., fund raising. Bd. dirs. Nat. Soc. Prevention Blindness. Served to lt. (s.g.) USNR, 1944-46. Mem. Am. Assn. Fund Raising Counsel, Phi Kappa Psi. Republican. Presbyterian. Home: 15 Woodhaven Dr Simsbury CT 06070 Office: 1200 Wall St W Lyndhurst NJ 07071

BREWER, OLIVER GORDON, JR., corporate executive; b. Winston-Salem, N.C., Dec. 8, 1936; s. Oliver Gordon and Lula Irene (Masencup) B.; m. Gail Olt, Aug. 29, 1959; children: Nancy Lynne, Oliver Gordon III. B.A., Guilford Coll., 1960; postgrad., Dartmouth Coll. With Phila. Nat. Bank, 1963-70, regional v.p., 1969-70; treas. Alco Standard Corp., Valley Forge, Pa., 1970—, v.p., 1973—; dir. Corp. Ins. and Reins Ltd., Bermuda. Trustee J. Wood Platt Caddie Scholarship Trust. Mem. Pa. Golf Assn. (pres. 1975-76, past exec. com.), U.S. Golfers Assn. (mid amateur com.), Pa. Soc. Clubs: Huntingdon Valley (Pa.) Country (pres., bd. govs.), Pine Valley (N.J.) Golf.). Home: 3645 Holt Ln Huntingdon Valley PA 19006 Office: Alco Standard Corp Valley Forge PA 19482

BREWER, RICHARD GEORGE, physicist; b. Los Angeles, Dec. 8, 1928; s. Louis Ludwig and Elise B.; m. Lillian Magidow, Sept. 23, 1954; children: Laurence R., Emily S., Catherine. B.S., Calif. Inst. Tech., Pasadena, 1951; Ph.D., U. Calif., Berkeley, 1958. Instr. Harvard U., 1958-60; asst. prof. UCLA, 1960-63; mem. research staff IBM Corp. Research Lab., San Jose, Calif., 1963-73, IBM fellow, 1973—; cons. prof. applied physics Stanford U., 1977—; adj. prof. Nat. Inst. Optics, Florence, Italy, 1977—; vis. prof. M.I.T., 1968-69, U. Tokyo, spring 1975, U. Calif., Santa Cruz, fall 1976; mem. Calif. Scientist of Year Awards Jury, 1980, 81; mem. com. atomic and molecular physics Nat. Acad. Scis.-NRC, 1974-77; mem. rev. panel for Nat. Bur. Standards, 1981—; mem. com. on recommendations U.S. Army Basic Sci. Research, 1982-85; rev. com. San Francisco Laser Center, 1980-83, AEC-Lawrence Berkeley Lab., 1974. Asso. editor: Optics Letters, 1977-80, Jour. Optical Soc. Am, 1980—. Served with AUS, 1955-57. Recipient Albert A. Michelson Gold medal Franklin Inst., 1979. Fellow Am Phys. Soc. (Joint Council Quantum Electronics 1982-83, O.E. Buckley prize com. 1982), Optical Soc. Am. (chmn. optical physics tech. council 1978-80, com. on fellows and hon. mems. 1981, W.F. Meggers award com. 1981); mem. Nat. Acad. Scis. Office: IBM Research Lab 5600 Cottle Rd San Jose CA 95193

BREWER, RONALD JUNIOR, ins. co. exec.; b. Celina, Ohio, Aug. 24, 1931; s. Ronald Gerald and Jessie (Krugh) B.; m. Virginia Ruth Linn, June 13, 1954; children—Cynthia Dawn, Scott Alan, Elizabeth Ann. B.S. in Bus. Adminstrn, Miami U., Oxford, Ohio, 1957. Asst. treas. Celina Ins. Group, 1959-65; auditor Arthur Andersen & Co., C.P.A.'s, Chgo., 1957-59; with Am. Mut. Liability Ins. Co., Wakefield, Mass., 1965—, sec., 1971-75, sr. v.p., 1974-75, pres., dir., 1975—; dir., officer Am. Mut. Ins. Co. Boston, Am. Policyholders Ins. Co., AM Life Ins. Co., A M Inc., Am. Mut. Corp., all Wakefield. Served with AUS, 1949-53. Club: Masons. Address: Am Mutual Liability Ins Co Wakefield MA 01880

BREWER, SHELBY TEMPLETON, government official; b. Little Rock, Feb. 19, 1937; s. Donald and Ray (Templeton) B.; m. Marie Anesten, Dec. 29, 1966; children: Jens, Sara. B.A. in Humanities, Columbia U., 1959, B.S. in Mech. Engring., 1960; M.S. in Nuclear Engring., M.I.T., 1966, Ph.D., 1970. Dir. and chief project engr. Organic Reactor Project, MIT, 1974-68; also research assoc., fast reactor test facility; cons. engr. Stone & Webster, 1968-71; mgr. civilian nuclear power programs AEC, 1971-75; chief planning and assessment LMFBR program ERDA, 1975-77; dir. plans and evaluation Office Nuclear Energy, U.S. Dept. Energy, Washington, 1977-81, asst. sec. nuclear energy, 1981—. Contbr. articles to profl. jours. Mem. Am. Nuclear Soc., AAAS, Sigma Xi. Office: Dept Energy Forrestal Bldg 1000 Independence Ave SW Washington DC 20585 *

BREWER, THOMAS BOWMAN, university administrator; b. Fort Worth, July 22, 1932; s. Earl Johnson and Maurine (Bowman) B.; m. Betty Jean Walling, Aug. 4, 1951; children: Diane, Thomas Bowman. B.A., U. Tex., 1954, M.A., 1957; Ph.D., U. Pa., 1962. Instr. St. Stephens Episcopal Sch., Austin, Tex., 1955-56, S.W. Tex. State Coll., San Marcos, 1956-57; from instr. to asso. prof. N. Tex. State U., Denton, 1959-66; asst. prof. U. Ky., 1966-67; asso. prof. Iowa State U., 1967-68; prof. history, chmn. dept. U. Toledo, 1968-71; dean Tex. Christian U. Coll. Arts and Scis., Fort Worth, 1971-72, vice chancellor, dean univ., 1972-78; chancellor E. Carolina U., Greenville, N.C., 1978-82; v.p. acad. affairs Ga. State U., Atlanta, 1982—. Editor: Views of American Economic Growth, 2 vols, 1966, The Robber Barons, 1969; gen. editor: Railroads of America Series. Mem. Econ. History Assn., Bus. History Assn., Am. Assn. Higher Edn. Address: Georgia State U Office of Vice-Pres Acad Affairs Atlanta GA 30303

BREWER, WILLIAM AUGUSTUS, III, environmental, mining and civil engineer; b. Oakland, Calif., May 27, 1930; s. William Augustus and Sarah Mattine (Christensen) B.; children by previous marriage: Ellen, William, Kristin, Carol, James. B.A., U. Calif., Berkeley, 1954, M.A., 1955, Ph.D., 1965; grad., Program for Mgmt. Devel., Harvard U., 1967. Registered profl. geologist, Calif. Sr. geologist Anaconda Co., Chile, 1955-60; asso. in engring. U. Calif., Berkeley, 1960-63; div. chief CIA, Washington, 1963-67; mgr. prelimary design IBM Fed. Systems Co., Gaithersburg, Md., 1968-70; internat. cons., San Francisco, 1970-73; dir. Wash. State Energy Policy Council, also energy cons. to gov. Wash., Olympia, 1973-75; prof. environ. and civil engring., dir. Energy Research Center, U. Wash., Seattle, 1975-79; pres. Brewer-No. Corp., 1979—. Author: Northwest Energy Policy, 1977, also numerous other publs. on energy, geology, engring., sports. Served with USMC, 1950-52. NDEA fellow, 1960-63; Congressional intern U.S. Ho. of Reps., 1977. Mem. Am. Inst. Mining, Metall. and Petroleum Engrs., Am. Soc. Photogrammetry, Harvard U. Bus. Sch. Alumni Assn., Theta Tau. Republican. Unitarian. Home: 12218 9th Ave NW Seattle WA 98177

BREWER, WILLIAM DODD, former ambassador, educator; b. Middletown, Conn., Apr. 4, 1922; s. Arnold and Cornelia (Dodd) B.; m. Alice Van Ess, Jan. 22, 1949; children: John, Daniel, Priscilla. B.A. with honors, Williams Coll., 1944; M.A., Fletcher Sch. Law and Diplomacy, Tufts U., 1947. Staff OWI, 1944, Am. Field Service, 1944-45; instr. Williams Coll., 1946, Bowdoin Coll., 1947; with U.S. Fgn. Service, 1947-78, assigned, Beirut, Lebanon, 1947-49, Jidda, Saudia Arabia, 1949-51, Damascus, Syria, 1952- 55, Kuwait, Persian Gulf, 1955-57; staff Office Near Eastern Affairs, Dept. State, 1957-58; officer charge UAR-Sudan affairs, 1958-61; detailed to Dept. State Sr. Seminar in Fgn. Policy, 1961-62; dep. chief mission, Kabul, Afghanistan, 1962-65; mem. policy planning council Dept. State, 1965-66; country dir. Arabian Peninsula states, 1966-70; ambassador to Mauritius, Port Louis, 1970-73, ambassador to Democratic Republic of Sudan, Khartoum, 1973-77; diplomat-in-residence U. Mass. and 4 asso. colls., 1977-78; Chevalier prof. diplomacy and world affairs Occidental Coll., Los Angeles, 1978—. Recipient Arthur S. Flemming award, 1959. Mem. Theta Delta Chi. Episcopalian (vestryman). Home: 1274 La Loma Rd Pasadena CA 91105 Office: Occidental Coll 1600 Campus Rd Los Angeles CA 90041

BREWER, WILMA DENELL, educator; b. Riley, Kans., Oct. 18, 1915; d. Benjamin Clarence and Rosetta (James) B. B.S., Kans. State U., 1935; M.S., Wash. State U., 1939; Ph.D., Mich. State U., 1950. Instr. Simpson Coll., Indianola, Iowa, 1939-40; from instr. to asst. prof. U. N.H., Durham, 1940-43; faculty Mich. State U., E. Lansing, 1943-57, prof., 1954-57; prof. nutrition Iowa State U., Ames, 1957-81, prof. emeritus, 1981—, dept. head, 1961-77. Mem. Am. Inst. Nutrition, Am. Dietetic Assn., Am. Home Econs. Assn., Am. Chem. Soc., AAAS. Methodist. Home: 777 Cragmont Ave Berkeley CA 94708

BREWSTER, CARROLL WORCESTER, coll. pres.; b. N.Y.C., Mar. 26, 1936; s. Carroll Harwood and Blandina (Worcester) B.; m. Ursula Mary Orange, Mar. 9, 1968; children—Abraham Carroll, Ursula Constant, Blandina Worcester. B.A., Yale, 1957, LL.B., 1961; postgrad., Kings Coll., Cambridge U., 1957-58. Bar: Conn. bar 1962. Law clk. to Chief Judge U.S. Dist. Ct., Dist. Conn., 1961-62; legal asst. to Hon. Mohamed Ahmed Abu Rannat, Chief Justice of Sudan, Khartoum, 1962-65; asso. Tyler, Cooper, Grant, Bowerman & Keefe, New Haven, 1965-69, also U.S. commr., 1966-69; lectr. Yale Law Sch., 1967-69; dean of coll. Dartmouth Coll., 1969-75; pres. Hollins Coll., Va., 1975-81; Trustee Phillips Exeter Acad., 1970-80. Editor of: Sudan Law Jour. and Reports, 1961-65. Mem. Am., Conn. bar assns., Phi Delta Phi.

BREWSTER, FRANCIS ANTHONY, lawyer; b. Foochow, China, Jan. 28, 1929; s. Francis Thoburn and Eva (Melby) B.; m. Susan Brewster, Apr. 6, 1974; 1 dau., Melissa Leigh; children by previous marriage—Sara, Julia, Anne, Ellen, Rebecca. B.S., U. Wis., 1950, LL.B., 1955. Bar: Wis. bar 1955. Corporate counsel Scott Paper Co., Phila., 1955-56, labor counsel, 1957, div. personnel mgr., 1958-60; corp. counsel RCA, Camden, N.J., 1961; pvt. practice law, Madison, Wis., 1961—; shareholder, past pres. and dir. law firm Murphy, Stolper, Brewster & Desmond (S.C.), Madison, 1966—; dir. Nat. Guardian Life Ins. Co., Stephan & Brady, Inc.; lectr. labor law Law Sch., U. Wis.; Law, ins. and bus. Sch. Commerce, U. Wis. Contbr. articles to profl. jours. Chmn. personnel bd. City of Madison, 1970-75; bd. dirs. Capitol div. A.R.C., 1965-74, chmn. div., 1973; bd. dirs. Madison Symphony Inc., 1968-75, gen. counsel, 1975—; bd. dirs., gen. counsel Four Lakes council Boy Scouts Am., 1980—; bd. visitors U. Wis. System, 1972—, pres., 1976-78; pres. bd. visitors U. Wis.-Madison, 1978-80. Served to capt. USMC, 1950-53; Korea. Recipient Certificate of Merit U. Mich.-Wayne State U., 1959; named Outstanding Madisonian, 1969, Wis. Man of Distinction, 1972. Mem. ABA, Dane County Bar Assn. (past sec. and program chmn.), State Bar of Wis., Wis. Bar Found. (dir. 1981—), Interfraternity Alumni Council U. Wis. (pres. 1968—), Delta Upsilon (pres. Wis. 1965-72). Republican. Presbyn. (elder). Club: Kiwanian (Madison) (pres. 1969). Home: 825 Charing Cross Rd Madison WI 53704 Office: 150 E Gilman St PO Box 2038 Madison WI 53701

BREWSTER, JAMES HENRY, educator; b. Ft. Collins, Colo., Aug. 21, 1922; s. Oswald Cammann and Elizabeth (Booraem) B.; m. Christine Barbara Germain, Jan. 23, 1954; children—Christine Carolyn, Mary Elizabeth, Barbara Anne. A.B., Cornell U., 1942; Ph.D., U. Ill., 1948. Chemist Atlantic Refining Co., Phila., 1942-43; postdoctoral fellow U. Chgo., 1948-49; instr. Purdue U., 1949-50, asst. prof., 1950-55, asso. prof., 1955-60, prof., 1960—. Served with Am. Field Service, 1943-45. Mem. Am. Chem. Soc., Chem. Soc. (London, Eng.), AAAS, AAUP, Phi Beta Kappa, Sigma Xi, Phi Lambda Upsilon. Democrat. Unitarian. Research mechanism reductions; stereochemistry rearrangements; epoxide ring opening; relation optical rotation and constitution; absolute configurations cycloalkylidenes and spiranes; inclusion compounds; molecular orbitals saturated systems. Home: 334 Hollowood Dr West Lafayette IN 47906 Office: Dept Chemistry Purdue U Lafayette IN 47907

BREWSTER, JOSEF LELAND, II, lawyer; b. Rockford, Ill, Sept. 6, 1928; s. J. Leland and Helen (Alexander) B.; m. Hazeleen Pace, Sept. 1, 1956; children: Lee Carol, David Pace, Stephen Josef. B.S. in Commerce, U. Ky., 1950, LL.B., 1957. Bar: Ky. 1957. Assoc. Kyte, Conlan, Wulsin & Vogeler, Cin., 1957-62, ptnr., 1962-78, Frost & Jacobs, 1978—; adj. prof. Salmon P. Chase Sch. Law No. Ky. U., 1983—. Mem. council Indian Hill Village, Ohio, 1973—, mayor, 1979—; trustee Bethesda Hosp., Cin., 1966—, vice chmn., Cin., 1982—; trustee Hillsdale-Lotspeick Seven Hills Schs., Cin., 1966-67, pres., Cin., 1968-71. Served to 1st lt. U.S. Army, 1951-53. Mem. ABA, Ohio Bar Assn., Ky. Bar Assn., Cin. Bar Assn. Republican. Presbyterian. Clubs: Commonwealth, Camargo, University (dir. 1980). Home: 5155 Ivy Farm Rd Cincinnati OH 45243 Office: Frost & Jacobs 2500 Central Trust Ctr Cincinnati OH 45202

BREWSTER, KINGMAN, lawyer; b. Longmeadow, Mass., June 17, 1919; s. Kingman and Florence (Besse) B.; m. Mary Louise Phillips, Nov. 30, 1942; children: Constance, Kingman III, Deborah, Alden, Riley. A.B., Yale U., 1941; LL.B., Harvard U., 1948. Chmn., Yale Daily News, 1940-41; spl. asst. to coordinator Inter-Am. affairs, 1941; research asso. dept. econs. MIT, 1949-50; asst. prof. law Harvard U., 1950-53, prof. law, 1953-60; prof., provost Yale U., 1961-63, pres., 1963-77; ambassador to U.K., 1977-81; counsel Winthrop, Stirup, Putnam & Roberts, N.Y.C., 1981-83, resident ptnr. in charge London office, 1984—; chmn. English-Speaking Union of U.S., 1981—; asst. gen. counsel Office U.S. Spl. Rep. in Europe, 1948-49; cons. Pres.'s Materials Policy Commn., 1951, Mut. Security Agy., 1952; mem. Pres.'s Commn. on Law Enforcement and Adminstrn. Justice, 1965-67, Pres.'s Commn. on Selective Service, 1966-67; chmn. Nat. Policy Panel UN, 1968; Former mem. corp. Belmont Hill Sch.; pres. bd. dirs. Buckingham Soc.; mem. internat. bd. United World Colls.; past bd. dirs. Ednl. TV and Radio Center; adv. com. on higher edn. HEW; bd. dirs. Salzburg Seminar in Am. Studies, Common Cause; cons. NEH; mem. policy rev. bd. Pub. Agenda Found.; mem. corp., trustee Carnegie Endowment Internat. Peace; mem. internat. adv. council Population Inst. Author: Anti-trust and American Business Abroad, 1959, rev. edit. (with Atwood), 1981, (with M. Katz) Law of International Transactions and Relations, 1960. Served as lt., aviator USNR, 1942-46. Fellow Am. Bar Found.; mem. Mass. Bar, N.Y. Bar, Am. Philos. Soc., Am. Council Learned Socs. (past dir.), Am. Council Edn., Am. Acad. Arts and Scis., Council Fgn. Relations. Clubs: Met. (Washington); Athanaeum (London); Tavern (Boston); Yacht (New Haven); Century Assn. (N.Y.C.). Home: 7 Fairholt St London SW7 England Office: One College Hill London EC4-R-2RA England

BREWSTER, ROBERT CHARLES, diplomat, consultant; b. Beatrice, Nebr., May 31, 1921; s. Charles Lee and Lillian Aseneth (French) B.; m. Mary Virginia Blackman, Feb. 22, 1951. Student, Grinnell Coll., 1939-41; A.B., U. Wash., 1943, U. Mexico, summer 1946, George Washington U., summer 1947, Columbia U., 1946-48. Fgn. affairs analyst State Dept., 1948-49; fgn. service officer, 1949—; 3d sec. Am. embassy, Mamagua, Nicaragua, 1949-51, 2d sec., 1951-52; vice consul Am. consulate gen., Stuttgart, Germany, 1952-55; policy briefing officer ICA, 1956-57; staff asst. to under sec. of state for econ. affairs, 1958, spl. asst., 1959, spl. asst. to under sec. of state, 1959-60; assigned Nat. War Coll., 1960-61; fgn. service insp., 1961-63; counselor Am. embassy, Asuncion, 1964-66; dep. exec. dir. Bur. European Affairs, Dept. State, Washington, 1966-67, exec. dir., 1967-69, dep. exec. sec., 1969-71, dep. dir. gen. fgn. service, dir. personnel, 1971-73; U.S. ambassador to Ecuador, 1973-76; coordinator for Law of the Sea, Dept. State, 1976, dep. asst. sec. state for spl. activities, Washington, 1976, dep. asst. sec. state for oceans and internat. environ. and sci. affairs, 1977-78, dep. insp. gen., 1978-79, insp. gen., 1979-81. Served to lt. (j.g.) USNR, 1943. Mem. Nat. War Coll. Alumni Assn. (pres. 1981-83). Club: Cosmos (Washington). Home: 2528 Queen Anne's Ln NW Washington DC 20037 Office: Dept State Washington DC 20520

BREWSTER, ROBERT GENE, concert singer, educator; b. Pinson, Ala., July 7, 1938; s. Hubert and Chrisella (Ayers) B. B. Mus., Wheaton Coll., 1958; M.M., Ind. U., 1961; Ph.D., Washington U., St. Louis, 1967; Konzertreife Diploma, Stuttgart Musikhochschule, 1970; diplom., Mozarteum Salzburg, 1969. Tchr. music and French Westfield

(Ala.) High Sch., 1959-60; chmn. dept. music Miles Coll., Birmingham, Ala., 1960-62; chmn. area fine arts Jackson (Miss.) Coll., 1962-63; chmn. dept. music Dillard U., New Orleans, 1974; chmn. dept. voice U. Miami, Coral Gables, Fla., 1974—; guest lectr. Stanford U. in, Germany, Beutelsbach, 1968-70; dozent fur gesang Berliner Kirchenmusikschule, 1970-72. Concert tours throughout, Europe, Asia and, The Ams.; Recs. include I See the Stars, 1961. Seely Mudd fellow, 1964-66; Fulbright fellow, 1966-68; Deutsche Akademische Austausch Dienst award, 1968-70. Mem. Nat. Assn. Tchrs. Singing, Coll. Music Soc., AAUP, Nat. Assn. Schs. Music, Phi Mu Alpha. Home: 3305 Alhambra Circle Coral Gables FL 33134 Office: U Miami Sch Music Coral Gables FL 33124

BREWSTER, SEWARD BLANCHARD, lawyer; b. Newton, Mass., Nov. 6, 1927; s. William Russell and Leona M. (Wright) B.; m. Carol V. Whitham, June 11, 1955; children: Benjamin S., Seth W., William T. Grad., Kimball Union Acad., 1944; A.B., Dartmouth Coll., 1950; J.D., Harvard U., 1955. Bar: Mass. 1956, Maine 1962. Instr. Deerfield Acad., 1950-52; asso. Mirick, O'Connell, DeMallie & Lougee, Worcester, Mass., 1955-61; asst. gen. counsel Central Maine Power Co., Augusta, 1961-68, gen. counsel, sec., clk., 1968—; sec., clk. Maine Yankee Atomic Power Co., Maine Elec. Power Co., Inc., Kennebec Water Power Co. Contact person Maine chpt. Lawyers Alliance for Nuclear Arms Control; co-chmn. Maine Freeze Campaign. Served with AUS, 1946-47. Mem. Am., Me., Kennebec County bar assns. Home: Pond Rd Manchester ME 04351 Office: Edison Dr Augusta ME 04336

BREWSTER, TOWNSEND TYLER, writer, critic, editor; b. Glen Cove, N.Y., July 23, 1924; s. Townsend and Sara Frances (Tyler) B. B.A., Queens Coll., 1947; M.A., Columbia U., 1962. Koussevitzky Found. scholar Berkshire Music Festival, 1947; translator adaptort NBC TV Opra, N.Y.C., 1950-51; questionnaire processor Alfred Politz Research, Inc., N.Y.C., 1953-58; copywriter Hicks & Greist, N.Y.C., 1958-62; librarian Lennen & Newell, N.Y.C, 1962-67; lectr. theatre dept. CCNY, 1969-73; editor Harlem Cultural Rev., N.Y.C., 1973—. Theatre critic for: Denver Quar., Showbus., Amsterdam News, Players, Big Red, Routes; librettist: opers The Tower, 1957; playwright, translator: Please Don't Cry and Say No, 1972; playwright: Black High, 1977, Arthur Ashe and I, 1979; radio appearances on shows on black theatre, Danmarks Radio, Copenhagen, 1972. Recipient Louise Bogan Meml. prize in poetry N.Y. Poetry Forum, N.Y.C., 1975, Jonathan Swift award for satire Commonwealth U., 1979; Nat. Theatre Conf. Playwrights' fellow, 1947; William Morris Playwriting scholar Am. Theatre Wing, 1955; Nat. Endowment for Arts librettists' grantee, 1977. Mem. Dramatists Guild, Outer Critics Circle, Harlen Cultural Council (dir.), Internat. Brecht Soc., Maple Leaf Soc. Home: 171-29 103 Rd Jamaica NY 11433 Office: Harlen Cultural Council 1 W 125 St New York NY 10027 *While I was at the American Theatre Wing, Helen Menken designated me an American Giraudoux; a startling sobriquet; I prefer Anouilh. But should a Black writer be in any wise like conservatives Giraudoux or Anouilh? The persona of my poem, "Black is Beautiful." is a white scholar coping with the title phrase as heard from his cleaning woman. He cites Corneille's belief that Andromeda could not have been Black, or a Greek's aesthetic sense could not have found her beautiful. Corneille is one of my favorite writers; I have translated Le Menteur. How do I reconcile his work with the man?*

BREWSTER, WILLIAM HAFNER, chemical company executive; b. Chgo., Sept. 27, 1922; s. George Ordway and Katherine Irene (Hennessey) B.; m. Nancy Lally, June 9, 1945; children: William, Timothy, George, Nancy Jo, Mary Anne, Constance, Barbara. Student, DePaul U., Chgo., 1945-47; LL.B., Kent Coll. Law, Chgo., 1949. Bar: Ill. 1950, D.C. 1958. Vice-pres. employee relations Am. Can Co., Greenwich, Conn., 1967-75, Am. Can. Co., Washington, 1975-77; govt. liaison, v.p. adminstrn., corp. sec. M & T Chems., Inc., Woodbridge, N.J., 1977—; dir. Gerhardt Assocs., Tampa, Fla. Mem. adv. bd. visitors Mary Baldwin Coll., Staunton, Va., 1970-74, Sacred Heart U., Fairfield, Conn., 1973-75; dir. Urban League, Union County, N.J., 1977—; bd. dirs. Rahway Hosp., N.J., 1982-83. Served with USMC, 1942-45. Recipient disting. service award Gen. Services Adminstrn., Washington, 1965. Mem. Chem. Mfrs. Assn., Bus. Round Table (mem. labor relations com. 1964-67). Roman Catholic. Clubs: Colonia Country (N.J.) (dir. 1977—); Carrollwood Country (Tampa); Bent Tree Country (Sarasota, Fla.). Office: M&T Chemicals Inc 1 Woodbridge Ctr Woodbridge NJ 07090

BREYER, NORMAN NATHAN, metallurgical engineering educator, consultant; b. Detroit, June 21, 1921; s. Max and Fannie (Landesman) B.; m. Dorothy Atlas, Feb. 10, 1952; children: Matthew, Richard, Marjorie. B.S., Mich. Tech. U., Houghton, 1943; M.S., U. Mich., 1948; Ph.D., Ill. Inst. Tech., 1963. Aero. research scientist NACA, Cleve., 1948; chief armor sect. Detroit Tank Arsenal, Warren, Mich., 1948-52; dir. research cast steels and irons Nat. Roll & Foundry, Avonmore, Pa., 1952-54; metallurgist-in-charge armor Continental Foundry & Machine div. Blaw-Knox Co., East Chicago, Ind., 1955-57; mgr. tech. projects LaSalle Steel Co., Hammond, Ind., 1957-64; assoc. prof. metall. engring. Ill. Inst. Tech., Chgo., 1964-69, prof., 1969—, chmn. dept., 1969—. Capt. U.S. Army, 1943-46; ETO. Mem. AIME, Am. Soc. Metals. Home: 1615 Robin Hood Pl Highland Park IL 60035 Office: Dept Metallurgical and Materials Engring Ill Inst Technology 10 W 33d St Chicago IL 60616

BREYER, STEPHEN GERALD, lawyer, educator, judge; b. San Francisco, Aug. 15, 1938; s. Irving G. and Anne R. B.; m. Joanna Hare, Sept. 4, 1967; children: Chloe, Nell, Michael. A.B., Stanford U., 1959; B.A. (Marshall scholar), Oxford U., 1961; LL.B., Harvard U., 1964; LL.D. (hon.), U. Rochester, 1983. Bar: Calif. 1966, D.C. 1966, Mass. 1971. Law clk. Justice Goldberg, U.S. Supreme Ct., 1964-65; spl. asst. to asst. atty. gen. U.S. Dept. Justice, 1965-67; asst. prof. law Harvard U., 1967-70, prof., 1970-81, lectr., 1981—, prof. govt. J.F. Kennedy Sch., 1978-81; asst. spl. prosecutor Watergate Spl. Prosecution Force, 1973; spl. counsel U.S. Senate Judiciary Com., 1974-75, chief counsel, 1979-81; judge U.S. Ct. of Appeals for 1st Circuit, 1981—; vis. lectr. Coll. Law, Sydney, Australia, 1975, Salzburg (Austria) Seminar, 1978; Jud. Conf. rep. to Adminstrv. Conf. U.S. Author: (with Paul MacAvoy) The Federal Power Commission and the Regulation of Energy, 1974, (with Richard Stewart) Adminstrative Law and Regulatory Policy, 1979, Regulation and its Reform, 1982; Contbr. articles to profl. jours. Trustee U. Mass., 1974-81; bd. overseers Dana Farber Cancer Inst., Boston, 1977—. Mem. Am. Bar Found., Am. Bar Assn., Am. Law Inst., Am. Acad. Arts and Scis., Council on Fgn. Relations. Home: 12 Dunstable Rd Cambridge MA 02138 Office: US Ct of Appeals US Courthouse and Post Office Bldg Boston MA 02109

BREYFOGLE, PETER NICHOLAS, management consultant; b. Barcelona, Spain, Sept. 24, 1935; s. Robert J. and Elsie (McLaughlin) B.; m. Josephine King, Dec. 11, 1965; 1 son, Nicholas. B.A. in Engring, Cambridge U., 1957; M.B.A., Harvard U., 1959. Various positions from budget analyst, comptroller to exec. v.p. Europe with Massey Ferguson, 1959-78; sr. v.p. finance Dome Petroleum Ltd., Calgary, Alta., Can., 1978-82; mgmt. cons., Toronto, Ont., Can., 1982—. Office: One Highland Gardens Toronto ON Canada M4W 2A1

BREZZO, STEVEN LOUIS, museum director; b. Woodbury, N.J., June 18, 1949; s. Louis and Ella Marie (Savage) B.; m. Dagmar Grimm, Aug. 10, 1975. B.A., Clarion State Coll., 1969; M.F.A., U. Conn., 1973. Chief curator La Jolla Mus. Contemporary Art, Calif., 1974-76; asst. dir. San Diego Mus. Art, 1976-78, dir., 1978—. Mem. Am. Assn. Mus. (del. to China 1981, to Italian mus. study trip 1982), La Jolla Library Assn. (pres. 1980). Club: University (San Diego). Lodge: Rotary. Office: San Diego Mus Art PO Box 2107 Balboa Park San Diego CA 92112

BRIA, GEORGE EMIL, former newspaperman; b. Rome, Mar. 2, 1916; U.S., 1922, naturalized, 1928; s. Louis E. and Cesarina (Travaglini) B.; m. Mary Ormsbee Whitton, Dec. 5, 1938; children: Judith Bria Storey, John W. B.A., Amherst Coll., 1938; M.A., Middlebury Coll., 1938. Reporter Waterbury (Conn.) Democrat, 1939-40, Hartford (Conn.) Courant, 1940-42; with AP, 1942—, corr., Rome and Berlin, 1944-50, editor broadcast news and fgn. news, N.Y.C., 1950-72; chief corr. UN, 1972-74, supervising editor fgn. news, N.Y.C., 1974-81. Trustee, sec. Hiram Halle Meml. Library, Pound Ridge, N.Y., 1982—. Mem. UN Corrs. Assn. Club: Pound Ridge Tennis (pres. 1977-78). Home: Fancher Rd Pound Ridge NY 10576

BRIAN, HARRY FINDLEY, publishing and advt. co. exec.; b. Lancaster, Pa., Mar. 29, 1914; s. Harry Zellers and Emma Moriah (Findley) B.; m. Margaret Paxson, Aug. 17, 1940; children—Bonnie, Penny, Terry. B.S., Ursinus Coll., 1935; student, U.S. Coast Guard Acad., 1943. Copywriter M.T. Garvin Co., Lancaster, Pa., 1935-36; copywriter Foltz-Wessinger, Inc., Lancaster, 1937-40; v.p. J.G. Kuester, York, Pa., 1940-42; copywriter Vansant Dugdale Co., Inc., Advt., Balt., 1942-43, copychief, 1948, v.p., 1949, creative dir., 1956-64, sr. v.p., 1964-67, pres., chief exec. officer, 1967-74, chmn., chief exec. officer, 1974-76; v.p. Kirkley Press, Inc., Towson, Md., 1976-80; chmn. Bridgman Assos. (advt.), Annapolis, Md., 1976-80; pres. Exec. Pub. Group, Towson, Md., 1980—; prof. advt. Johns Hopkins, 1950-71. Served as lt. (j.g.) USCGR, 1943-46. Mem. Am. Assn. Advt. Agys. (dir. 1970-72), Balt. Assn. Commerce. Methodist. Club: Towson. Home: Box 13 Riderwood MD 21139

BRIAN, PIERRE LEONCE THIBAUT, chem. engr.; b. New Orleans, July 8, 1930; s. Alexis Morgan and Evelyn (Thibaut) B.; m. Geraldine Lou Earl, Aug. 23, 1952; children—Evelyn Ann, Richard Earl, James Edward. B.S. in Chem. Engring, La. State U., 1951, Sc.D., M.I.T., 1956. Asst. prof. chem. engring. M.I.T., 1955-62, asso. prof., 1962-66, prof., 1966-72; v.p. engring. Air Products and Chems., Inc., Allentown, Pa., 1972—, also dir. Author: Staged Cascades in Chemical Processing, 1972; Contbr. articles in field to profl. jours. Mem. Am. Inst. Chem. Engrs. (recipient profl. progress award in chem. engring. 1973), Nat. Acad. Engring., Am. Chem. Soc. Patentee in field. Home: 3981 Lilac Rd Allentown PA 18103 Office: PO Box 538 Allentown PA 18105

BRIANT, CLYDE LEONARD, metallurgist, researcher; b. Texarkana, Ark., May 31, 1948; s. Clyde Leonard and Bonnie Barbara (Green) B.; m. Jacqueline Louise Duffy, July 16, 1977; 1 son, Paul. B.A., Hendrix Coll., Conway, Ark., 1971; B.S., Columbia U., 1971, M.S., 1973, Eng. Sc.D., 1974. Postdoctoral fellow U. Pa., Phila., 1974-76; staff metallurgist Gen. Electric Co., Schenectady, 1976—. Editor: Embrittlement of Engineering Alloys, 1983; contbr. numerous articles to tech. jours. Recipient Alfred Noble prize, 1980. Mem. AIME (Robert Lansing Hardy gold medal Metall. Soc. 1977, Rossiter W. Raymond 1979), Am. Soc. Metals, ASME, IEEE. Democrat. Methodist. Home: 1493 Wyoming Ave Schenectady NY 12308 Office: Gen Electric Co PO Box 8 Met 269 Kl Schenectady NY 12301

BRICCETTI, THOMAS BERNARD, orchestra conductor; b. Mt. Kisco, N.Y., Jan. 14, 1936; s. Thomas Bernard and Joan Therese (Filardi) B.; m. Billie Lee Mommer, July 10, 1978; children: Katherine Anne, David Clark. Student, Dr. Jean Dansereau, 1948-60, Dr. Richard Lert, 1963-64, U. Rochester Eastman Sch. Music, 1953-54, Columbia Grad. Sch. Fine Arts, 1954-55. Pianist, composer, 1955-62; mus. dir. Pinellas County Youth Symphony, Fla., 1962-68, St. Petersburg (Fla.) Philharmonic Orch., 1963-68, St. Petersburg Civic Opera Co., 1964-68; asso. condr. Indpls. Symphony Orch., 1968-78; mus. dir. Ft. Wayne (Ind.) Philharmonic Orch., 1970-78, U. Circle Orch., Cleve. Inst. Music, 1972-75, Omaha Symphony Orch., 1975—, Nebr. Sinfonia, 1977—, Festival 1000 Oaks, 1978—; internat. guest condr., 1972—; prin. guest condr. Nat. Orch. Luxembourg, 1977. Nat. Endowment for Arts commn. to compose Violin Concerto, 1967; 18 pub. compositions. Recipient Prix de Rome for mus. composition Italian Govt., 1958-59; Ford Found. fellow, 1961-62; YADDO grantee, 1963; named Outstanding Young Man Fla. Jr. C. of C., 1967-68, Profl. Artist of Year Indpls., 1970. Mem. A.S.C.A.P., Phi Mu Alpha Sinfonia. Office: Omaha Symphony Orch 310 Aquila Ct Omaha NE 68102 *

BRICE, ASHBEL GREEN, ret. publishing co. exec.; b. York, S.C., July 21, 1915; s. John Steele and Claudia Wilkie (Moore) B. A.B., Columbia U., 1936, M.A., 1937; postgrad., Duke U., 1937-39. Instr. dept. English Duke, Durham, N.C., 1939-45, North Tex. State Tchrs. Coll., 1940, Coll. City N.Y., summers 1937-42; joined Duke U. Press, 1945, asst. editor, 1945-47, editor, asso. dir., 1947-51, dir., editor, 1951-81. Mem. Assn. Am. U. Presses (dir. 1965-66). Democrat. Presbyterian. Home: 813 Vickers Ave Durham NC 27701

BRICE, BILL EUGENE, lawyer; b. Sherman, Tex., Sept. 3, 1930; s. James Ernest and Thelma Venice (Darby) B.; m. Sally Bright Sutton, Nov. 19, 1955; children—Bill Eugene, Julie, Carol, Susan. Student, U. Tex., Austin, 1947-50; LL.B. cum laude, So. Meth. U., 1954. Bar: Tex. bar. Asso. firm Thompson, Knight, Wright & Simmons, Dallas, 1954-56; mng. partner, then pres. firm Geary, Brice, Barron & Stahl, 1956-75; pres. firm Brice & Barron, Dallas, 1975—; chief exec. officer Modern Am. Corp., 1965-66, mem. exec. com., dir., 1965-71; chmn. bd. Carterfone Communications Corp., 1976-78; chmn. bd., chief exec. officer Cable & Wireless N.Am., Inc., 1978—. Contbr.: articles to So. Meth. U. Law Jour. Pres. Dallas Youth Council for Better Govt., 1950-51, Greater Dallas Council of Youth Orgn., 1952-53; chmn. Greater Dallas Council Citizens for Neighborhood Schs., 1972; mem. exec. com., dir. Tex. Council on Econ. Edn., 1973-74; mem. exec. com. Nat. Democratic Fin. Council, 1977—. Mem. State Bar Tex., Dallas Bar Assn., Am. Bar Assn. (nat. pres. div. law students 1953-54, chmn. subcom. on state and local cts. 1970-72). Club: Bent Tree Country. Home: 5251 Rayine Dr Dallas TX 75229 Office: 2001 Bryan Tower Dallas TX 75201

BRICE, JAMES JOHN, accounting firm executive; b. Chgo., Oct. 24, 1925; s. John Patrick and Margaret R. (Stookey) B.; m. Rosemary E. Freemuth, June 19, 1948; children: Susan, John, Kimberley, Pamela, Tracey. Student, U. Ill., 1946-48; B.S., Northwestern U., 1950. Accountant Standard Oil of Ind., 1950-51; staff acct., mgr. Arthur Andersen & Co., C.P.A.s, Chgo., 1951-60, partner, 1960-68, partner in charge, Los Angeles, 1968-72, vice chmn., 1972-74, co-chmn., mng. partner, Chgo., 1974-79, sr. partner, 1980—. Dir., pres. Mental Health Assn. Chgo., 1963-68; mem. Businessmen for Loyola U., 1963-67; bd. dirs. Arlington Heights (Ill.) United Fund, 1963-67, United Way, Los Angeles, 1970-72; dir., chmn. Reading is Fundamental, Chgo., 1972—; dir., treas., pres. United Charities, 1975—; trustee, chmn. Adler Planetarium, 1975—; prin. Chgo. United, 1973—; trustee Provident Hosp., 1975—; dir., v.p. Chgo. Crime Commn., 1974—; dir., chmn. Constl. Rights Found., Chgo. Project, 1974—; dir. nat. bd. Inroads, Inc., 1975—; mem. adv. bd. Urban Gateways, 1975—, pres., bd. dirs., 1978; mem. Com. for Econ. Devel., Chgo., 1977—; chmn. Pvt. Industry Council, 1980. Served with USAF, 1944-46. Mem. Am. Inst. C.P.A.'s, Ill., Calif. socs. C.P.A.'s. Clubs: Chgo., Comml., Mid-Am. (Chgo.); Carlton, Mid-Day, Los Angeles, Barrington Hills Country, Butler Nat. Golf, Old Elm. Home: 30 Steeplechase Rd Barrington IL 60010 Office: Arthur Andersen & Co 33 W Monroe St Chicago IL 60603 *

BRICE, WILLIAM JULES, artist; b. N.Y.C., Apr. 23, 1921; s. Jules and Fanny (Brice) Arndstein; m. Shirley Ann Bardeen, Aug. 23, 1942; 1 son, John. Student, Art Students League, N.Y.C., 1939-40, Choinard Art Inst., Los Angeles, 1937-39, 40-42. Instr. art Jedson Art Inst., Los Angeles, 1948-52; asst. prof. art UCLA, 1953-58, asso. prof., 1958-64, prof., 1964—. One-man shows, Santa Barbara (Calif.) Mus. Art, 1947, 58, 67, The Downtown Gallery, N.Y.C., 1948, Frank Perls Gallery, Los Angeles, 1955, 56, 60, 62, Alan Gallery, N.Y.C., 1955, 56, 61, 64, Felix Landau Gallery, Los Angeles, 1966, 68, San Francisco Mus. Art, 1967, Charlie Campbell Gallery, San Francisco, 1976, Nicholas Wilder Gallery, Los Angeles, 1978, Robert Miller Gallery, N.Y.C., 1980, group shows, Whitney Mus. Nat. Exhbn., N.Y.C., 1948-50, 55, 56, 63, 64, Met. Mus. Art, N.Y.C., 1952, Art Inst. Chgo., 1952, 55, 56, Musée National d'Art Moderne, Paris, 1954, Mus. Modern Art, N.Y.C., 1955-57, 69; represented in permanent collections, Met. Mus. Art, Whitney Mus. Am. Art, Mus. Modern Art, Art Inst. Chgo., Los Angeles County Mus. Art, Santa Barbara Mus. Art, San Diego Mus. Art, Hirshhorn Collection, Washington. Served with AC U.S. Army, 1942-43. Office: UCLA 405 Hilgard Ave Los Angeles CA 90024

BRICHFORD, MAYNARD JAY, archivist; b. Madison, Ohio, Aug. 6, 1926; s. Merton Jay and Evelyn Louise (Graves) B.; m. Jane Adair Hamilton, Sept. 15, 1951; children—Charles Hamilton, Ann Adair Brichford Martin, Matthew Jay, Sarah Lourena. B.A., Hiram Coll., 1950; M.S., U. Wis., 1951. Asst. archivist State Hist. Soc. Wis., 1952-56; methods and procedures analyst Ill. State Archives, 1956-59; records and space mgmt. supr. Dept. Adminstrn. State of Wis., Madison, 1959-63; archivist U. Ill., Urbana, 1963—, asso. prof., 1963-70, prof., 1970—. Contbr. articles in field. Served with U.S. Navy, 1944-46. Council on Library Resources grantee, 1966-69, 70-71; Nat. Endowment for the Humanities grantee, 1976-79. Fellow Soc. Am. Archivists (pres. 1979-80); mem. Ill. Archives Adv. Bd. (chmn. 1979—). Republican. Methodist. Home: 409 Eliot Dr Urbana IL 61801 Office: 19 Library 1408 W Gregory Dr Urbana IL 61801

BRICHTA, IRA, advertising agency executive; b. Chgo., Dec. 12, 1925; s. Jacob Morris and Beck (Friedman) B.; m. Vivian Gollin, Apr. 11, 1948; children: Carol Marcie, William Joseph. Student, Roosevelt U., 1946-48, Inst. Design, 1949. Marketing mgr. Philco Corp., Chgo., Phila., 1948-58; regional dir. McCann Erickson Co., N.Y.C., 1958-60; pres., chief exec. officer Baker and Brichta Advt., Inc., Chgo., 1960-82; exec. v.p. Stern Walters/Earle Ludgin, Inc., Chgo., 1982—; chmn. bd. Wilk & Brichta, Inc. Co-author: The Promise and the Product: 200 Years of Advertising Posters, 1979. Served with AUS, 1943-46. Decorated Bronze Star medal. Mem. Internat. Food Service Mfrs. Assn., Food Service Marketing Assn. Jewish. Clubs: Green Acres Country (Northbrook, Ill.); Eastlakes Country (Palm Beach Gardens, Fla.). Home: 1 E Schiller St Chicago IL 60610 also 122 Lakeshore Dr North Palm Beach FL 33408 Office: 150 E Huron St Chicago IL 60611

BRICK, DONALD BERNARD, consulting company executive; b. Bklyn., Oct. 1, 1927; s. Maxwell B. and Edna (Newman) B.; m. Phyllis Madeline Hahn, Oct. 19, 1952; children: James Laurence, Susan Carol, Howard Andrew. Student, Newark Coll. Engring., 1945-46; A.B. cum laude, Harvard U., 1950, S.M., 1951, Ph.D., 1954. Registered profl. engr., Mass.; registered real estate broker, Mass. Teaching fellow research-asst. fellow Harvard U., 1950-55; sr. scientist, sci. dir. GTE Sylvania, Waltham, Mass., 1955-65; tech. mgmt. cons., Lexington, Mass., 1954-55, 65-75; founder, pres., chmn., tech. dir. Info. Research Assoc.-Infoton Inc., Burlington, Mass., 1965-71; tech. dir., dep. for devel. plans Elec. Systems div. U.S. Air Force, Bedford, Mass., 1975-83; pres. Brick Cons., Lexington, 1983—; v.p. Aetna Telecommunications Cons., Centerville, Mass., 1983—; dir. Softel Inc., Manchester, Mass., Am. Brain Corp., Lexington; cons. in field. Contbr. articles to profl. jours.; patentee in field. V.p., bd. dirs. Temple Emunah, Lexington, 1970; assoc. campaign chmn. Combined Jewish Philanthropies of Greater Boston, 1974-78, trustee, 1975-78, mem. exec. bd., 1980—, chmn. cash collections, 1982—. Served with U.S. Army, 1946-47. Fellow IEEE (chmn. 1969-70); mem. AAAS, N.Y. Acad. Sci., Harvard Soc. Engrs. and Physicists, Armed Forces Communications and Electronics Assn., AIAA, Sigma Xi. Home: 4 Blueberry Ln Lexington MA 02173 *Not compromising ideals or moral standards for easy gain. Striving to produce quality work that I am proud of.*

BRICKEL, JAMES RUSSELL, air force officer; b. N.Y.C., Sept. 18, 1930; s. William Henry and Eileen (Russell) B.; m. Mary Macomb Guilmette, May 20, 1977; children—James Russell, Mary B., William R., Lisa, Andrew. B.S. in Elec. Engring, U.S. Naval Acad., 1952; M.S. in Aero. Engring, U. Mich., 1959, U. Mich., 1959. Commd. 2d lt. U.S. Air Force, 1952, advanced through grades to lt. gen., 1981; F-86 fighter pilot, 1953-57; nuclear weapons systems engr. Kirtland AFB, N.Mex., 1959-62; astron. engr., sect. head NASA Johnson Space Center, Houston, 1962-66; RF-101 pilot and squadron comdr., Thailand, 1966-67; staff officer Dept. Air Force, Washington, 1967-69; staff dep. Exec. Office of Pres., Washington, 1970; wing comdr., Alaska, 1972, dep. asst. to sec. def., Washington, 1973-75; comdt. Air Force ROTC, Ala., 1975-77; asst. dep. chief staff research, devel. and acquisition Hdqrs. U.S. Air Force, Washington, 1978-81; dep. CINC REDCOM, MacDill AFB, Fla., 1981—; Bd. dirs. Combined Fed. Campaign, Montgomery, Ala., 1976, 77. Decorated Air Force Cross, D.S.M. with oak leaf cluster, Silver Star, Legion of Merit with oak leaf cluster, D.F.C.; recipient cert. of appreciation United Way, 1977. Mem. Air Force Assn. (citation for leadership 1977), U.S. Naval Acad. Alumni Assn. Mem. United Ch. of Christ. Home: 405 Staff Loop MacDill AFB FL 33608 Office: Dep CINC REDCOM MacDill AFB FL 33608

BRICKELL, EDWARD ERNEST, JR., supt. schs.; b. Norfolk, Va., June 22, 1926; s. Edward Ernest and Rosa Willie (Babb) B.; m. Nancy Dunn Brickell; children—Dennis Sean, Heidi Josette, Todd Beatty. B.A., Coll. of William and Mary, 1950, advanced cert. sch. adminstrn., 1970, Ed.D., 1973; M.A., U. Chgo., 1952. Tchr., coach, prin. South Norfolk (Va.) Pub. Schs., 1951-61, supt. schs., 1961-62, Franklin (Va.) Pub. Schs., 1962-65; asst. to pres. Coll. of William and Mary, 1965-66; dir. secondary edn., asst. supt. schs. Virginia Beach (Va.) City pub. schs., 1966-68, supt. schs., 1968—; Prof. Nat. Acad. Sch. Execs.; chmn. Tidewater Supts., 1972-77; mem. State Supts. Adv. Council.; Mem. Drug Focus Com. of Virginia Beach, 1970—. Bd. dirs. Big Bros. Virginia Beach, Gen. Hosp. of Virginia Beach, United Community Fund; former chmn. bd. trustees Tidewater Community Coll.; Trustee Bayside Hosp.; rector, bd. visitors Coll. William and Mary. Served with USAAF, 1944-46. Recipient First Citizen award South Norfolk, 1958, Service to Scouting award, 1969; named Va. Ednl. Adminstr. of Year, 1973. Mem. N.E.A. (life), Nat., Va. assns. sch. adminstrs., Va. Assn. Sch. Execs., Va. Congress Parents and Tchrs. (life), Quill and Scroll, Phi Beta Kappa, Phi Delta Kappa (award for contbn. to edn. 1970), Kappa Delta Pi, Phi Kappa Phi. Methodist. Club: Rotarian.

Home: 129 67th St Virginia Beach VA 23451 Office: Princess Anne Station PO Box 6038 Virginia Beach VA 23456

BRICKEN, GORDON L., acoustical engineer, mayor; b. Louisville, Nov. 1, 1936; m. Maureen Mulligan, 1963; children: Barbara, Mary, Patricia, Victoria. B.E.E., Loyola U., Los Angeles, 1960; M.S., UCLA, 1961; cert. urban planning, U. Calif., Irvine. Mem. tech. staff Hughes Aircraft Corp., Fullerton, Calif.; acoustical engr. Northrop Corp.; pres. Bricken, Inc., Santa Ana, Calif.; Mem. Santa Ana Planning Commn., 1963-73, Santa Ana Redevel. Commn., 1973-75; mem. City Council Santa Ana, 1975-81, now mayor. Clubs: Rotary, Elks (Santa Ana). Home: 2424 N Oakmont Santa Ana CA 92706 Office: 1621 E 17th St Santa Ana CA 92701

BRICKER, DONALD LEE, surgeon; b. Denver, Jan. 7, 1935; s. J.F. and Marjorie Ellen (Mahon) B.; m. Evelyn Lucy Borst, Aug. 31, 1958 (div.); children—Donald Lee, II, Alex, Adam.; m. Sammie Lou Mavar, June 5, 1981. B.S., Colo. State U., 1956; M.D., Cornell U., 1959. Diplomate: Am. Bd. Surgery, Am. Bd. Thoracic Surgery. Intern, then resident in surgery N.Y. Hosp., N.Y.C., 1959-61; resident in surgery, then resident in thoracic surgery Baylor U. Affiliated Hosp., Houston, 1961-68; practice medicine specializing in thoracic surgery, Houston, 1968-70, Lubbock, Tex., 1970—; chief of staff St. Mary of Plains Hosp., 1979-80, now dir. hemodynamics lab.; mem. staff St. Luke's Hosp., Tex. Inst. Rehab. and Research, Bellaire Gen., Methodist, Ben Taub Gen. and W. Tex. hosps.; from instr. to asst. prof. surgery Baylor U. Coll. Medicine, Houston, 1961-70; active chief surgery Ben Taub Gen. Hosp., 1968-70; clin. prof. surgery, dir. div. cardiovascular surgery Tex. Tech. U. Med. Sch., Lubbock, 1972-79; pres. Heart Inst. Southwest, 1971. Contbr. numerous articles in field to med. jours. Served to capt. MC USAF, 1965-67; maj. Res., 1968-70. Fellow ACS, Am. Coll. Chest Physicians, Am. Coll. Cardiology, Am. Assn. Thoracic Surgery, Am. Assn. Surgery Trauma, Tex. Surg. Soc.; mem. So. Thoracic Surgery Assn. (President's award for best sci. paper 1973), Soc. Thoracic Surgeons, Tex. Med. Assn., Houston Surg. Soc., Lubbock County Med Soc., Internat. Cardiovascular Surg. Soc., Denton A. Cooley Cardiovascular Surg. Soc. Republican. Methodist. Office: 3420 22d Pl Lubbock TX 79413 *America remains the land of opportunity, a land where those of humble origin can still, through hard work, diligence and the willingness to accept responsibility, gain great rewards, the most important of these being the privilege to serve.*

BRICKER, NEAL S., physician, educator; b. Denver, Apr. 18, 1927; s. Eli D. and Rose (Quiat) B.; m. Miriam Thalenberg, June 24, 1951 (dec. 1974); children—Dale, Cary, Susan; m. Ruth T. Baker, Dec. 28, 1980. B.A., U. Colo., 1946, M.D., 1949. Diplomate: Am. Bd. Internal Medicine (chmn. nephrology test com. 1973-76, gov. 1972-79). Intern, resident Bellevue Hosp., N.Y.C., 1949-52; sr. asst. resident Peter Bent Brigham Hosp., Boston, 1954-55, asso. dir. cardio-renal lab., 1955-56; instr. Harvard, 1955-56; fellow Howard Hughes Med. Inst., 1955-56; asst. prof. Washington U., 1956-62, asso. prof., 1962-65, prof., 1965-72, dir. renal div., 1956-72; Mem. sci. adv. bd. Nat. Kidney Found., 1962-69, chmn. research and fellowship grants com., 1964-65, mem. exec. com., 1968-71; prof. medicine, chmn. dept. Albert Einstein Coll. Medicine, 1972-76; prof. medicine U. Miami, Fla., 1976-78, vice chmn. dept., 1976-78; prof. medicine UCLA, 1978—, also dir. program in kidney diseases; cons. NIH, 1964-68, chmn. gen. medicine study sect., 1966-68, chmn. renal disease and urology tng. grants com., 1969-71; vis. investigator Inst. Biol. Chemistry, Copenhagen, 1960-61; investigator Mt. Desert Island Biol. Labs., 1962-66. Asso. editor: Jour. Lab. and Clin. Medicine, 1961-67, Kidney Internat, 1972; editorial com.: Jour. Clin. Investigation, 1964-68, Physiol. Revs, 1970-76, Am. Heart Assn. Publs. Com, 1974-79, Calcified Tissue Internat, 1978—, Proc. Soc. Exptl. Biology and Medicine, 1978—; editor: Supplements, Circulation and Circulation Research, 1974-79; Contbr. articles to profl. jours., chpts. to books. Served with USNR, 1944-45; Served with U.S. Army, 1952-54. Recipient Gold-Headed Cane award U. Colo., 1949, Silver and Gold Alumni award, 1975; USPHS Research Career award, 1964-72; Skylab Achievement award NASA, 1974; Pub. Service award, 1975. Fellow A.C.P.; mem. Am. Fedn. for Clin. Research, Central Soc. Clin. Research (council 1970-73), Assn. Am. Physicians, Am. Soc. for Clin. Investigation (pres. 1972-73, chmn. com. nat. med. policy 1973-77), Internat. Soc. Nephrology (exec. com. 1966—, v.p. 1966-69, treas. 1969—), Internat. Congress Nephrology (pres. 1981-84), Am. Soc. Nephrology (past pres.), Am. Physiol. Soc., Soc. for Exptl. Biology and Medicine, Western Soc. Clin. Research, So. Soc. Clin. Investigation, Nat. Acad. Scis. (com. on space biology and medicine, ad hoc panel on renal and metabolic effects space flight 1971-72, mem. drug efficacy com. 1966-68, com. space biology, chmn. medicine space sci. bd. 1972—, com. chmn. 1978—, chmn. com. renal and metabolic effects space flight 1972-74, chmn. study com. on life scis. 1976—, mem. space sci. bd. 1977—), Inst. of Medicine of Nat. Acad. Scis., Sigma Xi, Alpha Omega Alpha. Home: 12330 Montana Ave Brentwood CA 90049 Office: West Med Campus UCLA Sch Medicine 1000 Veteran Ave Room 31-75 Los Angeles CA 90024

BRICKER, SEYMOUR MURRAY, lawyer; b. N.Y.C., May 19, 1924; s. Harry and May (Glick) B.; m. Darlene M. Mohilef, July 29, 1951; children: Andrea Helene, Phillip Alan, Julie Ellen. Student, U. Okla., 1943-44; A.B., U. Calif., Los Angeles, 1947; LL.B., U. So. Calif., 1950. Bar: Calif. 1951. Practice in Beverly Hills, 1956—; atty. Calif. Judicial Council, 1951-52; with legal dept. Universal Pictures, 1952-56; partner Cohen & Bricker, 1956-68, Kaplan, Livingston, Goodwin, Berkowitz & Selvin, 1968-81, Mitchell, Silberberg & Knupp, 1982—; exec. v.p. Ed Friendly Prodns. Inc.; pres. Friendly/Bricker Prodns. Served with inf. AUS, 1943-46. Fellow Am. Bar Assn. Found., mem. (mem. council patent, trademark and copyright sect., past chmn. copyright div.; chmn. forum com. on entertainment and sports industries), Los Angeles Copyright Soc. (past pres.), Copyright Soc. U.S. (trustee), Order of Coif. Home: 524 Loring Ave Los Angeles CA 90024 Office: 450 N Roxbury Beverly Hills CA 90210

BRICKER, VICTORIA REIFLER, educator; b. Hong Kong, June 15, 1940; U.S., 1947, naturalized, 1953; d. Ewrin and Henrietta (Brown) Reifler; m. Harvey Miller Bricker, Dec. 27, 1964. A.B., Stanford U., 1962; A.M., Harvard U., 1963, Ph.D., 1968. Vis. lectr. anthropology Tulane U., 1969-70, asst. prof., 1970-73, assoc. prof., 1973-78, prof., 1978—. Author: Ritual Humor in Highland Chiapas, 1973, The Indian Christ, The Indian King: The Historical Substrate of Mays Myth and Ritual, 1981; book rev. editor: Am. Anthropologist, 1971-73; editor: Am. Ethnologist, 1973-76; gen. editor: Supplement to Handbook of Middle American Indians, 1977—. Guggenheim fellow, 1982; Wenner-Gren Found. Anthropol. Research grantee, 1971; Social Sci. Research Council grantee, 1972. Fellow Am. Anthrop. Assn. (exec. bd. 1980-83); mem. Am. Soc. Ethnohistory, Linguistic Soc. Am., Seminario de Cultura Maya, Societe des Americanistes, N.Y. Acad. Sci. Office: Dept Anthropology Tulane Univ New Orleans LA 70118

BRICKER, WILLIAM, corp. exec.; b. Detroit, 1932. B.S. in Agriculture, Mich. State U., 1953, M.A. in Horticulture, 1954. Br. mgr. Calif. Chem. Ortho div., 1954-57; gen. sales mgr. Chemagro, 1957-66; exec. v.p. Velsicol Corp., 1966-69; with Diamond Shamrock Corp., Cleve., 1969—; dir. v.p., gen. mgr. Diamond Shamrock Chem. Co., 1969—, pres., 1972—; corp. v.p. Diamond Shamrock Corp., 1972-73, corp. exec. v.p., 1973-74, corp. exec. v.p., chief operating officer, 1974-75, pres., chief operating officer, 1975-76, pres., chief exec. officer, 1976-80, chmn., chief exec. officer, 1980—, also dir.; dir. AMF Corp., First Internat. Bancshares, Norfolk & Western R.R.; Chmn. Am. Indsl. Health Council. Bd. govs., mem. adv. com. Dallas Symphony Assn.; bd. dirs. Am. Petroleum Inst., ARC. Office: Diamond Shamrock Corp World Hdqrs 717 N Harwood Dallas TX 75201

BRICKER, WILLIAM RUDOLPH, orgn. exec.; b. Reading, Pa., May 5, 1923; s. William Theodore and Elsie Elizabeth (Weber) B.; m. Eleanor Schubert, June 9, 1945; children—Cynthia Anne (Mrs. Mark Hilgendorf), William Randall, Suzanne Lee. B.S., Millersville (Pa.) Coll., 1947; M.A. (Hayden grad. fellow), N.Y. U., 1948; D.H.L., George Williams Coll., 1980. Exec. dir. Boys' Clubs Am., 1948-72; nat. dir., 1972—; Chmn. Nat. Collaboration for Youth, 1975; mem. Pres.'s Nat. Adv. Com. Juvenile Justice and Delinquency Prevention, 1975; mem. adv. bd. Nat. Inst. Juvenile Justice, 1975; bd. dirs. Congressional Award; trustee Nat. Commn. for Coop. Edn. Served to comdr. USNR, 1942-45, 50-70. Home: 79 Huntington Ave Scarsdale NY 10583 Office: 771 1st Ave New York NY 10017

BRICKFIELD, CYRIL FRANCIS, lawyer; b. Bklyn., Jan. 30, 1919; m. Ann Jacobsen, Aug. 4, 1951; children: Anne, Edmund Cyril. M.S., LL.M., S.J.D., George Washington U.; LL.B., Fordham U. Bar: N.Y. 1949, D.C. 1952. With firm Brickfield & Brickfield, Bklyn., 1949; law clk. to chief judge N.Y. Ct. Appeals, 1949-51; counsel judiciary com. U.S. Ho. of Reps., 1951-61; gen. counsel VA, 1961-63, chief benefits dir., 1963-65, dep. adminstr., 1965-67; exec. dir. NRTA/AARP, 1967-69, 77—; pvt. practice law, 1969-75; partner Miller, Singer, Michaelson, Brickfield & Raives, 1975-77; Del. U.S. Internat. Treaty Convs. on Patents, Trademarks, Copywrights, 1958-61; pres. Nat. Sr. Citizens Law Center, U. So. Calif., 1977-79; mem. adv. council White House Conf. on Aging, 1981; pres. Corp. for Older Americans, 1981—; chmn. Leadership Conf. of Aging Orgns., 1980, 83; U.S. del. UN World Assembly on Aging, 1982. Author govt. reports. Trustee Suburban Hosp., Bethesda, Md. Served to maj., pilot USAAF, World War II; ETO. Decorated Air medal with 9 oak leaf clusters. Mem. ABA, Fed. Bar Assn. (pres. 1968, chmn. gen. counsels com., jud. selection com., pres. D.C. chpt.; del. Am. Bar Assn.), Bklyn. Bar Assn., Delta Theta Phi., K.C. Club: Bethesda Country (pres. 1967, 69). Home: 17 Savannah Ct Bethesda MD 20034

BRICKHOUSE, JOHN B. (JACK BRICKHOUSE), radio, TV sports manager; b. Peoria, Ill., Jan. 24, 1916; s. John William and Daisy (James) B.; m. Nelda Teach, Aug. 7, 1939 (div. Dec. 1978); 1 dau., Jean; m. Patricia Ettelson, Mar. 22, 1980. Student, Bradley U., Peoria. Comml., sports announcer Sta. WMBD, Peoria, 1934-40; with WGN, Chgo., 1940-43, 44—; v.p., mgr. sports WGN and WGN TV, 1948—, WGN Continental Broadcasting Co., 1970—; free lance, comml. announcer, Chgo., 1945, sports announcer, 1947, N.Y. Giants baseball announcer, N.Y.C., 1946. Writer for: others Ency. Brit. Yearbook; pub.: Jack Brickhouse's Major League Baseball Record Book, 21 edits. Bd. dirs. Chgo. Boys Clubs, Western Golf Assn., Chgo., Northwestern Meml. Hosp.; trustee Bradley U., Peoria, Ill. Served as pvt. USMCR, 1943-44. Recipient numerous Emmy awards, bronze medallions for World Series coverage Look mag., 1954, 59; Man of Year award City of Hope, 1966; Communications award Lincoln Acad., 1968; named Best Sports Announcer Am. Coll. Radio Arts and Scis.; Nat. Sportscasters and Sportswriters award as outstanding sportscaster of year in Ill. (5 times); Acor award Am. Coll. Radio Arts; Nat. Sportswriters and Broadcasters awards, Nat. Sportcasters and Sportswriters Hall of Fame, 1983, Baseball Hall of Fame, 1983, Chgo. Press Club Journalism Hall of Fame, 1982, Chgo. Cubs Hall of Fame, 1983, Greater Peoria Sports Hall of Fame, 1982; many others. Mem. Acad. Television Arts and Scis. (past pres., gov. Chgo. chpt.). Broadcaster radio and/or TV play-by-play World Series, All Star Baseball Game, All Star Football game, East-West Shrine game, Rose Bowl, Sugar Bowl, Am. Bowl, Orange bowl, Chgo. Cubs, Chgo. White Sox games, Golden Gloves, Louis-Charles and Walcott-Charles fight, Rep. and Dem. nat. convs., Roosevelt Inauguration (1945), Chicago Bears football games, Chgo. Bulls basketball games, Inaugural Ball, Papal audience. Office: WGN Continental Broadcasting Co 2501 W Bradley Pl Chicago IL 60618

BRICKLEY, JAMES ALFRED, banker; b. Chgo., Sept. 20, 1938; s. Brooks Franklin and Phyllis Marie (Dougal) B.; m. Marjorie Ann Colegrove, June 9, 1962; children: Janice Ann, Douglas James. Student, Wabash Coll., 1956-58; B.A. in Econs, U. Mich., 1961; postgrad., Northwestern U., 1963. Mcpl. bond trader, underwriter, money market specialist Harris Trust & Savs. Bank, Chgo., 1961-65; mcpl. bond trader Eastman Dillon Union Securities & Co., Chgo., 1965-66, instl. sales rep., Cleve., 1966-67; mcpl. bond specialist, bond dept. mgr. Nat. City Bank, Cleve., 1967-73; exec. v.p., portfolio mgr. First Nat. Bank, Dallas, 1973—. Chmn. fiscal affairs liaison com. Dallas Citizens Council; bd. dirs. Dallas Orthopaedic Found.; dist. dir., chmn. clubs council U. Mich. Mem. Asset/Liability Mgrs. Assn., Dealer Bank Assn., Public Securities Assn., Kappa Sigma Alumni. Clubs: Northwood, Dallas Petroleum (Dallas); U. Mich. Alumni. Address: PO Box 83754 1401 Elm Dallas TX 75283

BRICKLEY, RICHARD AGAR, surgeon; b. Bluffton, Ind., Aug. 15, 1925; s. Harry Dwight and Ina (Agar) B.; m. Suzanne Slusser, Nov. 28, 1964; children—Dinah M., Sarah Jane, Richard Agar II, Laura Jean, Andrew John. Student, Ind. U., 1943-44; B.S., B.M., Northwestern U., 1947, M.D., 1948. Diplomate: Am. Bd. Surgery. Intern Cook County Hosp., Chgo., 1947-49, surg. resident, 1955-56; gen. practice, Bluffton, 1949-50; surg. preceptorship with Drs. Gatch and Owen, Indpls., 1950-51, 54; pvt. practice medicine, specializing in surgery, Indpls., 1957—; chmn. gen. surgery div. Meth. Hosp., Indpls., 1962-66, Winona Meml. Hosp., 1971-73, chief of med. staff, 1974-75, bd. dirs., 1977—. Served with M.C. USAF, 1951-53. Fellow A.C.S.; mem. Am., Ind., Aerospace med. assns., Marion County Med. Soc. (chmn. bd. dirs. 1976-77), Beta Theta Pi, Nu Sigma Nu. Home: 4530 Crooked Creek Ridge Dr Indianapolis IN 46208 Office: 3266 N Meridian St Indianapolis IN 46208

BRICKLIN, MARK HARRIS, magazine editor; b. Phila., Apr. 13, 1939; s. Arthur Benjamin and Rose (Gaurd) B.; m. Alice Goddard Terry, Apr. 26, 1963 (div.); children: Deirdre, Brendon. B.A., Temple U., 1960, postgrad., 1961-62; postgrad., Boston U., 1960-61. Teaching fellow English Boston U., 1960-61; city editor Phila. Tribune, 1962-71; freelance writer, photographer, 1962-71; with Rodale Press, Emmaus, Pa., 1971—, v.p., 1975—; exec. editor Prevention mag., 1974—; founding editor, editorial dir. Spring mag., 1982—; journalism preceptor Pwky. Exptl. program Phila. Sch. Dist.; cons. book pub. Author: The Practical Encyclopedia of Natural Healing, 1976, Lose Weight Naturally, 1979, Natural Healing Cookbook, 1981, Rodale's Encyclopedia of Natural Home Remedies, 1982. Home: 2347 Union St Allentown PA 18104 Office: Prevention Organic Park Emmaus PA 18049

BRICKLIN, PATRICIA ELLEN, educator, psychologist; b. Los Animas, Colo., Feb. 28, 1932; d. Gregor M. and Cecilia Agnes (Crompton) McIntosh; m. Barry Bricklin, Sept. 8, 1957; children: Brian, Scott, Carol, Alisa. B.S., St. Joseph Coll., 1948; postgrad., Johns Hopkins U., 1948-51; M.Ed., Temple U., 1954, Ph.D., 1963; LL.D., St. Joseph Coll., 1972. Tchr. Matthews Sch., Balt., Fort Washington, Pa., 1948-53; clinician, reading clinic, dept. psychology Temple U., 1953-55, lectr. in psychology, 1955-63, supr., diagnostic div. reading clinic, 1955-60; cons. learning disability clinic Jefferson Med. Coll., Phila., 1961-65; sch. psychologist Bucks County pub. schs., 1964-65; clin. asso. dept. psychiatry Hahnemann Med. Coll. and Hosp., Phila., 1967-70, clin. asso. prof. dept. mental health scis., 1969-78, clin. prof., 1978—; lectr. Johns Hopkins U., Balt., 1978—; parent counselor Parkway Day Sch., Bala Cynwyd, Pa., 1966-70, asso. dir., 1970-74, cons., profl. adv. bd., Phila., 1974-80; vice-chmn. Pa. Bd. Psychologist Examiners, 1973-80, mem., 1981—, chmn., 1982—; Bd. dirs. Hill Top Prep. Sch., Rosemont, 1977—, chmn., 1982—; mem. adv. bd. est. Author: (with B. Bricklin) Bright Child-Poor Grades: The Psychology of Underachievement, 1967, Strong Family-Strong Child, 1970, Conquering The Four Natural Enemies of Marriage, 1977. Mem. Acad. Clin. Edn., Internat. Reading Assn. (pres. disabled reader group), Soc. Personality Assessment (past pres. Phila. chpt.), Am. Psychol. Assn. (council of reps. 1977-80, 82—, bd. profl. affairs 1981-83, chmn. bd. 1983, mem. fin. com. 1983—), Pa. Psychol. Assn. (sec.-treas., pres. clin. div. 1970-72, pres. 1975-76, chmn. profl. affairs bd. 1979—), Phila. Soc. Clin. Psychologists (pres. 1973-74). Home and office: 470 General Washington Rd Wayne PA 19087

BRICKMAN, MARSHALL, screenwriter, director; b. Rio de Janeiro, Brazil; m. Nina Feinberg; 1 dau., Jessica. Ed., U. Wis. Musician Tarriers, 1962; writer Candid Camera TV Show, 1966, The Tonight Show TV show, 1966-70; producer The Dick Cavett Show, 1970-72. Collaborator: (with Woody Allen) on screenplays Sleepers, 1973, Annie Hall, 1977 (Acad. award 1977), Manhattan, 1979; author, dir.: Simon, 1980, Lovesick, 1983; rec.: (with Eric Weissberg) album New Dimensions in Banjo and Bluegrass, 1963; contbr. articles to, New Yorker mag. Officer: c/o ICM 40 W 57th St New York NY 10019 *

BRICKMAN, MORRIE, newspaper cartoonist; b. Chgo., July 24, 1917; s. Samuel David and Rose (Wilson) B.; m. Shirley Kronenthal, Oct. 13, 1945; children—Harriet Esther, Paul Martin. Student, Art Inst. Chgo., 1934, Am. Acad. Art, 1935. Author: Do it Yourself, 1955, Don't Do It Yourself, 1957, This Little Pigeon Went to Market, 1965; Syndicated cartoon Do It Yourself, 1954-59, Blue Chips, 1960-67, The Small Society, 1966—. Served with AUS, World War II. Mem. Nat. Cartoonist Soc., Newspaper Comics Council. Club: Chicago Press. Address: care King Feature Syndicate 235 E 45th St New York NY 10017 *

BRICKMAN, WILLIAM WOLFGANG, teacher educator emeritus; b. N.Y.C., June 30, 1913; s. David Shalom and Chaya Sarah (Shaber) B.; m. Sylvia Schnitzer, Feb. 26, 1958; children—Joy (Mrs. Gary Poupko), Chaim M., Sara V. (Mrs. Schlomo Soudry). B.A., City U. N.Y., 1934, M.S. in Edn, 1935; Ph.D., N.Y. U., 1938; M.A. (hon.), U. Pa., 1972. Instr. edn. N.Y. U., 1940-42, 46-48, lectr. in edn., 1948-50, asst. prof., 1950-51, asso. prof., 1951-57, prof., 1957-62; prof. ednl. history and comparative edn. U. Pa., Phila., 1962-81, prof. emeritus, 1981—; dean Touro Coll., N.Y.C., 1977-79; vis. prof. univs. in, U.S., South Africa, Germany and, Israel.; Pres.'s research fellow in history Brown U., 1950-51. Author: Two Millenia of International Relations in Higher Education, 1975, Education Historiography: Tradition, Theory and Technique, 1983; with others Two Millenia of International Relations in Higher Education; co-author: The Changing Soviet School, 1960, Conflict and Change on Campus, 1970, A Bibliography of American Educational History, 1975; others; Editor: Intellect (formerly School and Society), 1953-76, Western European Education, 1979—; Contbr. articles to encys., yearbooks, jours. Mem. Comparative and Internat. Edn. Soc. (pres.). Home: 15 Jade Ln Cherry Hill NJ 08002 Office: Grad Sch Edn U Pa Philadelphia PA 19104

BRICO, ANTONIA, conductor; b. June 26, 1902. B.A., U. Calif., 1923; grad., Berlin (Germany) State Acad. Music, Master Sch. of Conducting, 1929; pupil, Dr. Karl Muck and Sigismond Stojowski, 1925-30; Doc.Mus. (hon.), Mills Coll., 1933. Founder Bach Soc. of Denver; lectr., guest condr.; tchr. conducting classes and piano, operatic coach. Began as concert pianist, 1919; music coach, Bayreuth Wagner Festival, 1929; condr., Berlin Philharm. Orch., 1930, Los Angeles Symphony Orch., Hollywood Bowl, San Francisco Symphony Orch. and in Berkeley (Calif.) Greek Theater, Hamburg Philharm. Orch., also orchs. in, Riga, Latvia and Warsaw, Poland, 1931, Musicians' Symphony Orch. at Met. Opera House, N.Y.C., summer concerts, White Plains, N.Y., 1933, Detroit and Buffalo Symphony orchs., N.Y. Civic Orch., 1934, Nat. Symphony Orch., Washington, 1935, Brico Symphony Orch., N.Y., Fed. Orch. Concerts, N.Y. World's Fair, 1939; organizer, 1935 and; condr., N.Y. Women's Symphony Orch.; conducted in, Finland, Sept. 1946, spl. Sibelius concert, Helsinki, Dec. 8, 1946, London Philharm. Orch., Royal Albert Hall, 1946, piano and conducting tour, Yugoslavia, 1946, N.Y. Philharmonic, Lewisohn Stadium, 1938; organizer, condr., Brico Symphony Orch., 1939; condr. in, Finland, Vienna, Salzburg, Mozarteum Orch., Frankfurt-am-Main, Boise Symphony Orch., 1956-58, Boise (Idaho) Civic Symphony, 1957—, Boulder (Colo.) Philharm. Orch., also, Denver Community Symphony, Greater Denver Opera Assn.; permanent condr., Brico Symphony, Denver. Office: care Brico Symphony Denver CO *

BRIDEGAM, WILLIS EDWARD, JR., librarian; b. Pottstown, Pa., Oct. 15, 1935; s. Willis Edward and M. Emma (Eberhart) B.; m. Mary Elizabeth Hospador, Dec. 21, 1957; children—Martha Ann. B.Mus., Eastman Sch. Music, 1957; M.S., Syracuse (N.Y.) U., 1963. Med. librarian U. Rochester (N.Y.) Sch. Medicine, 1966-69, asso. dir. univ. libraries, 1969-72; dir. libraries State U. N.Y., Binghamton, 1972-75; librarian Amherst (Mass.) Coll., 1975—. Served with AUS, 1957. Mem. ALA, Assn. Coll. and Research Libraries. Mem. United Ch. Christ. Club: Grolier (N.Y.C.). Home: 52 High Point Dr Amherst MA 01002 Office: Amherst Coll Library Amherst MA 01002

BRIDENBAUGH, WILLIAM, mfg. co. exec.; b. Upland, Calif., Apr. 26, 1932; m. Gail T. L. Howard. B.A., Westminster Coll.; M.B.A., Stanford U. Sales rep. corrugated container div. Boise Cascade Corp., Idaho, 1958—, successively plant mgr., dist. mgr., region mgr., gen. mgr., group v.p., 1972-74, sr. v.p., 1974—. County chmn. Am. Cancer Soc., 1973-74; bd. dirs. Golf for Charity, 1974, Iran-Idaho Synergistic, Office of Gov., 1976, Idaho Council Econ. Edn., 1977—, Boise State U. Found.; pres. Jr. Achievement SW Idaho, Inc., 1976-80; asst. chmn. United Way, 1981. Served with U.S. Army, 1953-55. Mem. Fibre Box Assn., Envelope Mfrs. Assn., Fourdrinier Kraft Bd. Inst. Home: 117 N Walnut St Boise ID 83702 Office: 1 Jefferson Sq Boise ID 83728

BRIDGE, CHARLES SOMMERS, electronics company executive; b. Camden, N.J., Aug. 27, 1925; s. Charles M. and Romayne (Sommers) B.; m. Helen I. Andersen, Sept. 8, 1946; children: Michael C., Nancy C., Alan R. B.S. in Engring. Physics, Lafayette Coll., Eaton Pa., 1950. Engr. Eastman Kodak Co., Rochester, N.Y., 1950-55; sr. engr. N.Am. Aviation, Downey, Calif., 1955-59; v.p. Litton Industries, Beverly Hills, Calif., 1959—; dir. Syntech Internat., Dallas. Served with U.S. Army, 1943-46. Mem. AIAA, Inst. Navigation. Republican. Home: 9749 Calvin Ave Northridge CA 91324 Office: Litton Industries 360 N Crescent Dr Beverly Hills CA 90210

BRIDGES, ALBERT PEYTON, research and development company executive; b. Henderson, Tenn., June 15, 1925; s. Thomas W. and Allie (Horn) B.; m. Joyce Fowler, June 14, 1949; children: Melinda, Margot, John. B.S., U. of South, 1947; M.S., Vanderbilt U., 1950, Ph.D., 1951.

Registered profl. engr., Colo. Staff mem. Sandia Corp., Albuquerque, 1951-55; project engr. Aerophysics Devel. Corp., Santa Barbara, Calif., 1955-57; staff mem. Kaman Scis. Corp., Colorado Springs, Colo., 1957—, pres., 1972—; bus. adv. council U. Colo., Colorado Springs, 1976—, chancellor's adv. council, 1979—; mem. Gov. Colo. Energy Task Force, 1980; adv. tech. study panel inexhaustible energy resources study Dept. Energy, 1977. Served with USNR, 1943-46. Mem. Am. Electronics Assn. (dir., chmn. Colo. council 1975-76), IEEE, Am. Phys. Soc., Am. Assn. Physics Tchrs., Am. Astron. Soc., Am Philatelic Soc., Colorado Springs C. of C. (dir. 1977-80), N. End Comml. Assn. (dir. 1979-83). Office: 1500 Garden of Gods Rd Colorado Springs CO 80907

BRIDGES, B. RIED, lawyer; b. Kansas City, Mo., Oct. 20, 1927; s. Brady R. and Mary H. (Nieuwenhuis) B.; m. Lou George, Feb. 9, 1955; 1 son, Ried George. B.A., U. So. Calif., 1951, LL.B., 1954. Bar: Calif. bar 1954, diplomate: Am. Bd. Trial Advocates. Asso. firm Overton, Lyman & Prince, Los Angeles, 1956-58, partner, 1958-62, Bonne, Jones & Bridges, Los Angeles, 1962-74, Bonne, Jones, Bridges, Mueller & O'Keefe, 1974—. Served with U.S. Army, 1954-56. Fellow Am. Coll. Trial Lawyers, Internat. Acad. Trial Lawyers; mem. Los Angeles County Bar Assn., State of Calif. Bar Assn., Am. Bar Assn. Republican. Clubs: Univ. (Los Angeles); California Yacht; Balboa of Mazatlan (Sinaloa, Mex.). Home: 4460 Wilshire Blvd #406 Los Angeles CA 90010 Office: 600 S Commonwealth 17th Floor Los Angeles CA 90005

BRIDGES, BEAU (LLOYD VERNET III BRIDGES), actor; b. Los Angeles, Dec. 9, 1941; s. Lloyd Vernet and Dorothy (Simpson) B.; m. Juli Bridges; 1 son, Casey. Attended, U. Calif. at Los Angeles. Film appearances include The Incident, For Love of Ivy, 1968, Gaily, Gaily, 1969, The Landlord, 1970, Adam's Woman, The Christian Licorice Store, 1971, Hammersmith is Out, 1972, Child's Play, 1972, Your Three Minutes Are Up, 1973, Lovin' Molly, The Other Side of the Mountain, 1975, Swashbuckler, 1976, Two-Minute Warning, 1976, Greased Lightning, 1977, Norma Rae, 1979, The Fifth Musketeer, 1979, The Runner Stumbles, 1979, Honky Tonk Freeway, 1980, Night Crossing, 1982, Love Child, 1982, Heart Like a Wheel, 1983, The Hotel New Hampshire, 1984; TV appearances include The Man Without a Country, 1973, The Whirlwind, 1974, The Four Feathers, 1978, United States, 1980. Office: care Creative Artists Agy Inc 1888 Century Park E Suite 1400 Los Angeles CA 90067 *

BRIDGES, JAMES, film writer-director; b. Little Rock, Feb. 3; s. Doy and Celestine (McKeen) B. Student, Ark. Tchrs. Coll., U. S.C. Actor: 7 feature films, including Johnny Trouble, 1957; 7 feature films, including TV shows Faces, 1964; TV writer: 18 Alfred Hitchcock Shows (Mystery Writers award for Unlocked Window); writer TV pilot: The Paper Chase, 1978; 14 feature films, including Appaloosa, 1966, Colossus: The Forbin Project, 1968, Limbo, 1972; writer/dir.: feature films The Baby Maker, 1970, The Paper Chase (Best Screenplay/Picture/Dir., Atlanta Film Festival, Best Screenplay, Acad. and nomination 1973), September 30, 1955, 1978, The China Syndrome (Best Writer, Am. Movie award, Best Writer/Dir., Christopher award, Best Screenplay, Japanese Acad. award, Best Screenplay, Acad. award nomination, Best Writer/Dir./Picture, Golden Globe nomination, Best Drama, Wrts. Guild award 1979), Urban Cowboy, 1980. Mem. Writers Guild, Dirs. Guild, Screen Actors Guild, AFTRA. Office: care Steven Roth Creative Artists Agy 1888 Century Park E Los Angeles CA 90067

BRIDGES, LLOYD, actor; b. San Leandro, Calif.; s. Lloyd and Harriet (Brown) B.; m. Dorothy Bridges; children: Beau, Jeff, Lucinda. Student, UCLA. Appeared in stock cos., coll. dramatic prodns., motion pictures, Broadway; motion pictures Rocketship XM, 1950, Walk in the Sun, Home of the Brave, White Tower, Plymouth Adventure, 1952, High Noon, 1952, The Rainmaker, 1958, The Goddess, 1959, Happy Ending, Silent Night, Holy Night, The Fifth Musketeer, 1979, Airplane, 1980, Airplane II, 1983; TV series San Francisco Internat, NBC, Joe Forrester; TV mini-series Roots, 1977, East of Eden, 1981; TV film Disaster on the Coastliner, 1979, Moviola: This Year's Blonde, 1980. Office: care Creative Artists 1888 Century Park E Suite 1400 Los Angeles CA 90067 *

BRIDGES, ROBERT LYSLE, lawyer; b. Altus, Ark., May 12, 1909; s. Joseph Manning and Jeffa Alice (Morrison) B.; m. Alice Marian Rodenberger, June 10, 1930; children: David Manning, James Robert, Linda Lee. A.B., U. Calif., 1930, LL.B., 1933. Bar: Calif. 1933, U.S. Supreme Ct 11938. Practiced in, San Francisco, 1933—; assoc. firm Thelen & Marrin, 1933-39, partner firm, 1939—; firm name Thelen, Marrin, Johnson & Bridges, 1941—; pres., dir. Enging. Mgmt. Inc., San Francisco; emeritus dir. Wells Fargo Bank. Trustee, chmn. exec. com. U. Calif. Berkeley Found.; trustee, chmn. fin. com. John Muir Meml. Hosp.; trustee, mem. exec. com. World Affairs Council. Mem. Am., Calif., San Francisco bar assns. Republican. Clubs: Links (N.Y.C.); Commonwealth of Calif., World Trade, Pacific Union, Stock Exchange (San Francisco); Claremont Country (Oakland); California (Los Angeles). Home: 3972 Happy Valley Rd Lafayette CA 94549 Office: 2 Embarcadero Center San Francisco CA 94111

BRIDGES, WILLIAM BRUCE, research electrical engineer, educator; b. Inglewood, Calif., Nov. 29, 1934; s. Newman K. and Doris L. (Brown) B.; m. Carol Ann French, Aug. 24, 1957; children: Ann Marjorie, Bruce Kendall, Michael Alan. B.E.E., U. Calif. at Berkeley, 1956, M.E.E. (Gen. Electric Rice fellow), 1957, Ph.D. in Elec. Engring. (NSF fellow), 1962. Asso. elec. engring. U. Calif., Berkeley, 1957-59, grad. research engr., 1959-61; mem. tech. staff Hughes Research Labs. div. Hughes Aircraft Co., Malibu, Calif., 1960-77, sr. scientist, 1968-77, mgr. laser dept., 1969-70; prof. elec. engring. and applied physics Calif. Inst. Tech., Pasadena, 1977—, Carl F. Braun prof. engring., 1983—, exec. officer elec. engring., 1978-81; lectr. elec. engring. U. So. Calif., Los Angeles, 1962-64; Sherman Fairchild Distinguished scholar Calif. Inst. Tech., 1974-75; chmn. Conf. on Laser Engring. and Applications, Washington, 1971. Author: (with C.K. Birdsall) Electron Dynamics of Diode Regions, 1966; contbr. articles on gas lasers, optical systems and microwave tube to profl. jours.; asso. editor: IEEE Jour. Quantum Electronics, 1977-82, Jour. Optical Soc. Am, 1978-83. Active Boy Scouts Am., 1968-82; bd. dirs. Ventura County Campfire Girls, 1973-76. Recipient L.A. Hyland Patent award, 1969. Fellow IEEE (chmn. Los Angeles chpt. Quantum Electronics and Applications Soc. 1979-81), Optical Soc. Am. (chmn. lasers and electro-optics tech. group 1974-75, bd. dirs. 1982—); mem. Nat. Acad. Engring., Nat. Acad. Scis., Am. Radio Relay League, Phi Beta Kappa, Sigma Xi, Tau Beta Pi, Eta Kappa Nu (One of Outstanding Young Elec. Engrs. for 1966). Lutheran. Inventor noble gas ion laser, patentee in field. Home: 413 W Walnut St Pasadena CA 91001 Office: Calif Inst Tech 128-95 Pasadena CA 91125

BRIDGES, WILLIAM FRANK, physician, educator; b. Asheville, N.C., July 26, 1932; s. John Dixon and Ruth (Norberg) B.; m. Judith Ann Ware, Nov. 27, 1974; 1 dau., Jana; children from previous marriage: Jeffrey, David, Daniel. B.A., U. of the South, 1954; M.D., Washington U., St. Louis, 1959, fellow in preventive medicine, 1963-65. Intern Barnes Hosp., Washington U., St. Louis, 1959-60, resident, 1962-63; assoc. prof. medicine U. Miami, Fla., 1968; prof., dir. neurosci. program U. Ala. - Birmingham, 1970-72, spl. asst. v.p. health affairs, 1976, chmn., prof. dept. pub. health, 1976-81, dean, prof., 1981—; staff mem. Nat. Acad. Scis., Washington, 1974; mem. governing bd. Nat. Council Internat. Health, Washington, 1981—. Contbr. articles to profl. jours. Recipient Mosby Book award Washington U., 1959. Mem. Assn. Schs. Pub. Health (pres., exec. com.), Am. Pub. Health Assn., Am. Men and Women of Sci., Am. Inst. Nutrition, Am. Soc. Biol. Chemistry, Phi Beta Kappa. Democrat. Home: 2221 22nd Ave S Birmingham AL 35294

BRIDGEWATER, BERNARD ADOLPHUS, JR., business executive; b. Tulsa, Mar. 13, 1934; s. Bernard Adolphus and Mary Alethea (Burton) B.; m. Barbara Paton, July 2, 1960; children—Barrie, Elizabeth, Bonnie. A.B., Westminster Coll., Fulton, Mo., 1955; LL.B., U. Okla., 1958; M.B.A., Harvard, 1964. Bar: Okla. bar 1958, U.S. Supreme Ct. bar 1958, U.S. Ct. of Claims bar 1958. Asst. county atty., Tulsa, 1962; asso. McKinsey & Co., mgmt. cons., Chgo., 1964-68, prin., 1968-72, dir., 1972-73, 75; asso. dir. nat. security and internat. affairs Office Mgmt. and Budget, Exec. Office Pres., Washington, 1973-74; exec. v.p. Baxter Travenol Labs., Inc., Chgo. and Deerfield, Ill., 1975-79; now dir.; pres. Brown Group, Inc., Clayton, Mo., 1979—, chief exec. officer, 1982—; dir. FMC Corp., Chgo., Celanese Corp., N.Y.C., Centerre Bancorp., St. Louis, Centerre Nat. Bank; cons. Office Mgmt. and Budget, 1973, 75. Author: (with others) Better Management of Business Giving, 1965. Trustee Rush-Presbyn.-St. Luke's Med. Center, 1974—, Washington U., St. Louis, 1983—. Served to lt. USNR, 1958-62. Recipient Rayonier Found. award Harvard, 1963; George F. Baker scholar, 1964. Mem. Beta Theta Pi, Omicron Delta Kappa, Phi Alpha Delta. Clubs: Chgo., Econ. (Chgo.); River (N.Y.C.); St. Louis Country, Log Cabin (St. Louis); Indian Hill Country (Winnetka, Ill.). Home: 35 Overhills Dr Ladue MO 63124 Office: 8400 Maryland Ave Clayton MO

BRIDGEWATER, HERBERT JEREMIAH, JR., radio host; b. Atlanta, July 3, 1942; s. Herbert Bridgewater and Mary Sallie (Clark) Bridgewater-H. B.A., Clark Coll., Atlanta, 1968; postgrad., Atlanta U.; L.H.D., Faith Coll., 1978; LL.D., Heed U., 1978. Tchr. bus. edn. and English Atlanta Pub. Sch. System, 1964-67; relocation and family services cons. Atlanta Housing Authority, 1967-70; columnist, writer Atlanta Daily World newspaper, 1968—, Lovely Atlanta; consumer protection specialist FTC, Atlanta, 1970-83; pres. Bridgewater's Personnel Service, 1971—; assoc. prof. bus. edn. and mass communication Clark Coll.; host radio program Enlightenment (WGKA-AM), 1975-79; host pub. affairs program Confrontation WZGC FM and WIGO AM, 1975-79, WYZE AM, 1979—; TV talk show host Bridging the Gap. Mem. Epilepsy Found. Am., Nat. Urban League, Big Bros. Council of Atlanta, Met. Boys Clubs of Atlanta, YMCA, NAACP; active So. Christian Leadership Conf., Ga. and nationwide civil rights movements; bd. dirs. Atlanta Dance Theater, Ralph C. Robinson Atlanta Boys Club, Proposition Theater Co., Am. Cancer Soc., Just-Us Theatre Task Force. Recipient Pres.'s award Clark Coll. United Negro Coll. Fund, 1960, 61, Best Citizens award Delta Sigma Theta, 1962, Humanitarian award Future Soc. Orgn., 1975, award Atlanta Dance Theatre, 1978-79, also; Met. Atlanta Boys Club; FTC Superior service medal, 1978; Bronner Bros. Nat. Beauticians Conv. Excellence in Communication award, 1978; named One of Most Outstanding Young Men in Am. Nat. Jr. C. of C., 1969, One of Most Eligible Bachelors in Am., 1970, One of 1,000 Successful Black Americans, 1973; both Ebony Mag.; One of 10 Outstanding Young People of Atlanta, 1977-78; One of 20 Most Progressive Young People in Atlanta, 1977; Herbert Bridgewater Day proclaimed in his honor, Atlanta. Mem. Atlanta Jr. C. of C., Young Men on the Go, Clark Coll. Alumni Assn., Clark Coll. Assn., Heritage Valley Community Civic Orgn., Hungry Club Forum, Internat. Assn. for African Heritage and Black Identity (founding). Baptist (founder, chmn. bd. jr. deacons). Home: 3569 Rolling Green Ridge SW Atlanta GA 30331 Office: 1718 Peachtree St NE Suite 1000 Atlanta GA 30309 *Any success which I may have achieved is attributed to my deeply rooted religious rearing which impels me to put God first in all my undertaking. Applying myself to the task with diligence, being prayful in all my endeavors, and having a mother who is not only my backbone, but who has also stood steadfastly by my side, are the essential factors which I deam vital in my life's achievement.*

BRIDGFORTH, RICHARD BASKERVILLE, JR., tobacco company executive; b. Kenbridge, Va., Jan. 3, 1925; s. Richard Baskerville and Elizabeth (Cunningham) B.; m. Nancy Dickinson, June 12, 1948; children: Richard Baskerville, III, Andrew Dickinson, Robert Manson, Nancy Hatton, John Cunningham. Student, Va. Mil. Inst., 1942-43, Cornell U., 1943-44, U. Va., 1946-48. Vice pres. Internat. Planters Corp., 1949-56; also dir.; pres. G.R. Garrett Co., 1958-61; v.p. Dibrell Bros., Inc., Danville, Va., from 1961, later pres., now chmn. bd., chief exec. officer, also dir.; dir. Bank Va. Co., Richmond.; Chmn. Nat. Tobacco and Textile Museum, Danville. Trustee, mem. exec. com. Meml. Hosp., Danville; trustee Averett Coll., Colgate Darden Grad. Sch. Bus., U. Va., Charlottesville. Served with USMC. Mem. Tobacco Assn. U.S. (gov.). Presbyterian. Clubs: Commonwealth (Richmond); Danville Golf. Office: 512 Bridge St Danville VA 24541 *

BRIDGMAN, THOMAS FRANCIS, lawyer; b. Chgo., Dec. 30, 1933; s. Thomas Joseph and Angeline (Gorman) B.; m. Patricia A. McCormick, May 16, 1959; children: Thomas, Kathleen Ann, Ann Marie, Jane T., Molly. B.S. cum laude, John Carroll U., 1955, J.D., Loyola U., Chgo., 1958. Bar: Ill. 1958, U.S. Dist. Ct. 1959. Assoc. McCarthy & Levin, Chgo., 1958, Baker & McKenzie, 1958-62, ptnr., 1962—. Trustee John Carroll U., 1982—. Recipient Medal of Excellence Loyola U., 1978. Fellow Am. Coll. Trial Lawyers, Internat. Acad. Trial Lawyers (past pres.). Democrat. Roman Catholic. Clubs: Union League; Beverly Country (Chgo.) (pres. 1983). Office: Baker & McKenzie 130 E Randolph Dr Chicago IL 60601

BRIDSTON, KEITH RICHARD, clergyman; b. Grand Forks, N.D., Feb. 20, 1924; s. Joseph Benjamin and Anna Sofie (Pederson) B.; m. Elizabeth Onstad, Dec. 20, 1945. B.A., Yale U., 1944, B.D., 1947; Ph.D. in Div., Scotland, 1949. Ordained to ministry Lutheran Ch., 1954; grad. sec. Dwight Hall, Yale U., 1944-46; internat. sec. Student Christian Movement Gt. Brit. and Ireland, 1946-48; mem. exec. staff World's Student Christian Movement, Geneva, 1949-52; prof. theology Higher Theol. Coll., Djakarta, Indonesia and Nommensen U., P. Siantar, Sumatra, Indonesia, 1952-57; exec. sec. Commn. on Faith and Order, World Council Chs., Geneva, 1957-61, exec. dir. U.S. Conf., N.Y.C., 1978-82, theol. cons., Geneva, 1982—; dir. study on pre-seminary edn. Lilly Endowment Inc., Mpls., 1961-63; prof. systematic theology Pacific Luth. Sem. and Grad. Theol. Union, Berkely, Calif., 1963-78; Harvard U. Corp. research fellow Div. Sch. and Grad. Sch. Bus. Adminstrn., Harvard U., Cambridge, Mass., 1971-73; dir. Case-Study Inst. (Cambridge), 1971-74; v.p. First Fed. Savs. & Loan Assn., Grand Forks, 1978-82. Author: books, latest being Pre-Seminary Education, 1966; Church Politics, 1969; editor: Orthodoxy, 1960, Old and New in the Church, 1961, One Lord-One Baptism, 1961; contbr. articles to Ency. Brit., Weltkirchenlexikon, Westminster Dictionary of Chruch History; mem. editorial bd.: Ecumenical Press Service, Geneva, 1949-52; mng. editor: Luth. Quar., 1973-78. Yale regional scholar, 1941; Princeton Club N.Y. scholar, 1943; Assn. Am. Theol. Schs. fellow, 1969-70. Club: Elizabethan (Yale U.). Home: 370 Riverside Dr Apt 14-A New York NY 10025 Office: World Council Chs Gen Secretariat 150 route de Ferney 1211 Geneva Switzerland 20

BRIDWELL, BOB S., energy equipment mfg. co. exec.; b. Oklahoma City, Dec. 28, 1940; s. Cecil Clinton and Gladys Izella (Tucker) B.; m. Patricia Gayle Whitmer, June 19, 1964; 1 dau., Melissa Anne. B.S., Calif. State U., Long Beach, 1966, M.B.A., 1968. Dept. chief Western Electric Co., Los Angeles, 1966-68; v.p. Kanasi-Sonnichsen & Co., Long Beach, 1968; also dir.; v.p., treas. Am. Funding Corp., Beverly Hills, Calif., 1968-71; also dir.; sr. v.p., treas., chief fin. officer CRS Group, Inc., Houston, 1971-78; v.p., fin., chief fin. officer Harte-Hanks, Communications, Inc., San Antonio, 1978-80; pres., chief exec. officer, dir. Tescorp., Inc., San Antonio, 1980—. Mem. Fin. Execs. Inst. (officer and dir. Houston chpt.). Republican. Episcopalian. Clubs: Retama Polo, Plaza, Petroleum (San Antonio); Univ., Houston (Houston). Office: 2211 NE 410 Loop San Antonio TX 78217

BRIDWELL, ROBERT KENNEDY, propane marketing and oil and gas company executive; b. Abilene, Tex., May 7, 1943; s. Robert Kennedy and Vivian (Craighead) B.; m. Catherine Gamewell Davis, Sept. 16, 1967; children: Cory Rardin, Christopher Craighead, Emily Herrick. B.A., Westminster Coll., Mo., 1965; J.D., Duke U., 1971; Exec. Program in Bus. Adminstrn., Columbia U., 1980. Bar: N.C. 1971. Asso. firm Thigpen & Hines, P.A., Charlotte, N.C., 1971-74, v.p., 1974; asso. counsel Suburban Propane Gas Corp., Whippany, N.J., 1974-77, v.p., counsel, Morristown, N.J., 1977-82, sr. v.p. corp. planning and devel., 1982—; dir. Dimension Bank of Morristown; Sec. Mid-Atlantic Legal Found., Phila. Served to capt. U.S. Army, 1966-68. Decorated Army Commendation medal. Mem. Am. Bar Assn., N.C. State Bar Assn., Am. Judicature Soc., Phi Delta Theta. Republican. Home: 25 Tingley Rd PO Box 184 Brookside NJ 07926 Office: 334 Madison Ave PO Box CN1915 Morristown NJ 07960

BRIEANT, CHARLES LA MONTE, JR., judge; b. Ossining, N.Y., Mar. 13, 1923; s. Charles La Monte and Marjorie (Hall) B.; m. Virginia Elizabeth Warfield, Sept. 10, 1948; children: Cynthia W. (Mrs. Dale T. Hendricks), Charles La Monte III, Victoria E., Julia W. B.A., Columbia U., 1947, LL.B., 1949. Bar: N.Y. 1949. Mem. firm Bleakley, Platt, Schmidt & Fritz, White Plains, 1949-71; water commr., Village of Ossining, 1948-51, town justice, 1952-58, town supr., 1960-63, village atty., Briarcliff Manor, N.Y., also spl. asst. dist. atty., Westchester County, 1958-59; asst. counsel N.Y. State Joint Legis. Com. Fire Ins., 1968; U.S. dist. judge So. Dist. N.Y., N.Y.C., 1971—. Mem. Westchester County Republican Com., 1957-71; mem. Westchester County Legislature from 2d Dist., 1970-71. Served with AUS, World War II. Episcopalian (past vestryman). Club: S.A.R. Office: US Dist Ct US Courthouse Foley Sq New York NY 10007 *

BRIEF, HENRY, assn. exec.; b. Bklyn., Feb. 18, 1924; s. Jacob and Clara (Tannenbaum) B.; m. Rosalie Menchin, Apr. 16, 1950; children—Andrew S., Judith M. B.B.A., Coll. City N.Y., 1948. Feature writer Overseas News Agy., 1948-50; news editor radio sta. WEOK, Poughkeepsie, N.Y., 1951-52; radio-TV-high fidelity editor Home Furnishings Daily, 1952-60; exec. dir. Rec. Industry Assn. Am., Inc., N.Y.C., 1960-79; exec. v.p. Internat. Tape/Disc Assn., N.Y.C., 1979—. Home: Bellmore NY 11710 Office: 10 Columbus Circle New York NY 10019

BRIEGER, GERT HENRY, medical historian, educator; b. Hamburg, Germany, Jan. 5, 1932; came to U.S., 1938, naturalized, 1943; s. Carl Helmuth and Ylse (Fuchs) B.; m. Katharine Crenshaw, July 2, 1955; children: Heidi E., William N., Benjamin C. A.B., U. Calif., Berkeley, 1953; M.D., UCLA, 1957; M.P.H., Harvard U., 1962; Ph.D., Johns Hopkins U., 1968. Intern UCLA Med. Center, 1957-58; asst. prof. history of medicine Johns Hopkins U. Sch. Medicine, Balt., 1966-70; assoc. prof. community health scis., assoc. prof. history Duke U., Durham, N.C., 1970-75; prof. history of health scis., chmn. dept. U. Calif., San Francisco, 1975-84; William H. Welch prof., dir. Inst. History of Medicine Johns Hopkins U., Balt., 1984—. Soc. Editor: Medical America in the Nineteenth Century, 1972, Theory and Practice in American Medicine, 1976. Served to capt. U.S. Army, 1958-61. Mem. AAAS, Am. Hist. Assn., Am. Assn. History of Medicine (pres. 1980-82), History of Sci. Home: 1211 Grizzly Peak Blvd Berkeley CA 94708 Office: 1900 E Monument St Baltimore MD 21205

BRIER, JACK HAROLD, state official; b. Kansas City, Mo., June 25, 1946; s. Marshall W. and M. Pearl (Munden) B. Student, U. Kans., 1964-67, 77—; B.B.A., Washburn U., 1970. Dep. asst. sec. of state for legis. matters, State of Kans., Topeka, 1969-70, asst. sec. of state, 1970-78, sec. of state, 1978—. Nat. v.p. Muscular Dystrophy Assn.; trustee Kans. Jaycees Found.; bd. advisers Close Up Kans. Named Outstanding Young Topekan, 1979, Outstanding Young Kansan, 1979. Mem. Nat. Assn. Secs. of State (pres.), Counci of State Govts. (exec. com.), Kans. State Hist. Soc. (dir., nominations com.), Shawnee County Hist. Soc., Am. Council Young Polit. Leaders (council); mem. Fraternal Order Police (assoc.); Mem. Blue Key (hon.), Sagamore Nat. Honor Frat. (hon.), Kans. Jaycees (trustee Kans. Jaycees Found.), Topeka Jaycees., Washburn U. Alumni Assn. (dir.). Republican. Home: 1256 Western Ave Topeka KS 66604 Office: Office of Sec State 2d Floor Capitol Topeka KS 66612

BRIER, WARREN JUDSON, journalism educator; b. Seattle, Apr. 25, 1931; s. Howard Maxwell and Grace (Kjelstad) B.; m. Genie Kurack, Sept. 6, 1953 (div. 1976); children: Lynn Diane, Karin Lee; m. Ruthann Crippen Stuart, Mar. 18, 1978 (dec. 1981). B.A., U. Wash., 1953; M.S., Columbia, 1954; Ph.D., U. Iowa, 1957. Copyreader Seattle Times, 1953; reporter Seattle Post-Intelligencer, 1956-57; newsman A.P., Seattle, Los Angeles, N.Y. and Helena, Mont., summers 1959, 61-64, 66, 70; copy editor Anchorage Times, Summer 1983; asst. prof. Calif. State U., San Diego, 1959-60, U. So. Calif., 1960-62; asso. prof. U. Mont., 1962-67, prof., 1967—, dean, 1968-82. Author: The Frightful Punishment, 1969, (with Howard C. Heyn) Writing for Newspapers and News Services, 1969; Co-editor: A Century of Montana Journalism, 1971; also contbr. jours. Served to 1st lt. USAF, 1957-59. Mem. Assn. for Edn. in Journalism, Sigma Delta Chi, Beta Theta Pi, Kappa Tau Alpha. Home: 3711 Bellecrest Dr Missoula MT 59801

BRIERLEY, GERALD P., physiological chemistry educator; b. Ogallala, Nebr., Aug. 14, 1931; s. Phillip and Myrtle (Shireman) B.; m. Miriam Grove, Apr. 17, 1971; children: David, Steven, Glenn, Lynn. B.S., U. Med.-Coll. Park, 1953, Ph.D., 1961. Asst. prof. U. Wis., Madison, 1962-64; faculty mem. Ohio State U., Columbus, 1964—, prof. physiol. chemistry, 1969—, chmn. dept., 1981—. Capt. USAF, 1953-56. USPHS grantee to study ion transport by heart mitochondra, 1965—; USPHS grantee to study pathology mitchondria in ischemia, 1977—. Mem. Am. Soc. Biol. Chemistry, Biophys. Soc., Am. Heart Assn. Office: Dept Physiol Chemistry Graves Hall Ohio State U Columbus OH 43210

BRIERLEY, JOHN E.C., university dean, legal educator; b. Montreal, Que., Can., Mar. 5, 1936. B.A., Bishop's U., Lennoxville, Que., 1956; B.C.L., McGill U., 1959; Docteur de l'Universite de Paris, 1964. Teaching fellow Faculty of Law, McGill U., Montreal, 1960-61, asst.

prof., 1964-68, asso. prof., 1968-73, prof., 1973—, Sir William Macdonald prof. law, 1980—, dean faculty law, 1974-84; vis. prof. U. Montreal, 1967-68, U. Toronto, 1971-72; occasional lectr. McGill Mental Hygiene Inst., McGill Sch. Social Work, 1969-73; vis. occasional lectr. Dalhousie U., 1970-73; Cons. Royal Commn. on Status of Women in Can., 1970; mem. Canadian Delegation of Experts, UNIDROIT, Rome, 1971, Conseil des affairs sociales et de la famille, Ministerial Council to minister Social Affairs, Que., 1971-73; pres. Sous-comite sur les Politiques et programmes familiaux, 1971-73; mem. Commn. des Biens culturels de Que., ministerial council to minister Cultural Affairs, Que., 1972; cons., secretaire-rapporteur various coms. Civil Code Revision Office, Que., 1967—; chmn. Com. Can. Law Deans, 1981—. Mem. Canadian, Que. bar assns., Assn. des professeurs de droit de Que., Assn. Canadian Law Tchrs., John Howard Soc. Que. (dir. 1965-67), Canadian Soc. for Legal History (exec. com. 1972—), Inter-Am. Comml. Arbitration Commn. (exec. com. 1972—). Office: 3644 Peel St Montreal PQ Canada

BRIGGS, DICK DOWLING, JR., physician; b. Electric Mills, Miss., Jan. 28, 1934; s. Dick Dowling and Anita (Carnathan) B.; m. Susan Hunt Davis, June 20, 1959; children: Adrienne Davis, Dick Dowling III, Daniel Roth. B.S. in Chemistry, U. South, Sewanee, Tenn., 1956; M.D., Washington U., St. Louis, 1960. Diplomate: Am. Bd. Internal Medicine (pulmonary diseases). Intern, then resident in internal medicine U. Ala. Hosp., Birmingham, 1960-62, 64-65, chief resident, 1965-66; mem. faculty U. Ala. Med. Sch., Birmingham, 1965—, prof. medicine, 1972—; dir. pulmonary div., dept. medicine, 1971—, vice chmn. dept. medicine, 1981—; dir. med. edn. pulmonary lab., also respiratory therapy Carraway Methodist Med. Center, Birmingham, 1968-71; cons. Birmingham VA Hosp; chmn. claims com. U. Ala. Birmingham Liability Ins. Trust. Author numerous papers in field. Served to capt. M.C. USAF, 1962-64. Baker scholar, 1952-56; Daforth scholar, 1956-60; grantee Nat. Heart, Lung and Blood Inst., 1972-77. Fellow ACP, Am. Coll. Chest Physicians (pres. elect 1983-84); mem. Am. Soc. Internal Medicine, Am. Thoracic Soc., AMA, Assn. Am. Med. Colls., So. Med. Assn., Med. Assn. Ala., Jefferson County Med. Soc., Soc. Medica de Santiago (hon.), Phi Beta Kappa. Episcopalian. Clubs: Mt. Brook Swim and Tennis, The Club, Relay House, Ala. Tennis Assn. (pres. 1967-69). Office: Pulmonary Div Univ Ala Med Sch University Station Birmingham AL 35294

BRIGGS, EDWARD SAMUEL, naval officer; b. St. Paul, Oct. 4, 1926; s. Charles William and Lois Ione (Johnson) B.; m. Nanette Parks, June 7, 1949; 1 son, Jeffrey Charles. B.S., U.S. Naval Acad., 1949. Commd. ensign U.S. Navy, 1949, advanced through grades to vice adm., 1980; asst. chief staff plans chief of staff U.S. 7th Fleet, 1972-73; fleet ops. officer, asst. chief staff ops. U.S. Pacific Fleet, Makalapa, Hawaii, 1973-75; comdr. Crusier-Destroyer Group 3, San Diego, 1975-77, Navy Recruiting Command, Arlington, Va., 1977-79, Naval Logistics Command, U.S. Pacific Fleet, Naval Base, Pearl Harbor, Hawaii, 1979-80; dep. comdr.-in-chief U.S. Pacific Fleet, Pearl Harbor, 1980-82; comdr. Naval Surface Force U.S. Atlantic Fleet, 1982—. Decorated Bronze Star with combat device and one star, Air medal (2), Navy Commedation medal with combat device and 2 stars, Legion of Merit with combat device with 4 stars; Vietnamese Navy Gallantry medal. Mem. U.S. Naval Acad. Alumni Assn., Naval Inst. Home: Qtrs A Nav Amphibase Norfolk VA 23521 Office: Comdr Naval Surface Force US Atlantic Fleet Norfolk VA 23511 *Dedication to our nation and devotion to its ideals are the duties of all. Service to country in all walks of life through patriotism and loyalty will ensure the defense of our precious liberties.*

BRIGGS, EVERETT ELLIS, ambassador; b. Habana, Cuba, Apr. 6, 1934; s. Ellis Ormsbee and Lucy (Barnard) B.; m. Sally Soast, Sept. 9, 1955; children: Everett B., Catherine Briggs Gieszler, Allen T., Lucy H., Church E. A.B., Dartmouth Coll., 1956; M.S., George Washington U., 1972. Fgn. service officer Dept. State, Washington, 1956; consul grn. U.S. Consulate Gen., Luanda, Angola, 1972-74; dep. chief mission U.S. Embassy, Asuncion, Paraguay, 1974-78, Bogota, Colombia, 1978-79; dir. Mexican Affairs Dept. State, Washington, 1979-81, dep. asst. sec. state for inter-Am. affairs, 1981-82; ambassador U.S. Embassy, Panama, 1982—. Mem. Sr. Fgn. Service Officers Assn. Republican. Universalist. Club: Met. (Washington). Home: Kaiowaza Topsfield ME 04490 Office: Am Embassy APO Miami FL 34002

BRIGGS, F. NORMAN, educator; b. Oakland, Calif., Sept. 12; (married), 1950; 1 child. A.B., U. Calif., 1947, M.A., 1948, Ph.D., 1953. Radiologist biology U.S. Naval Radiol. Def. Lab., 1948-49; instr. pharmacology Sch. Dental Medicine, 1952-55, asso. pharmacology, 1956-58; asst. prof. physiology Tufts U. Sch. Medicine, 1958-61, asso. prof., 1961; prof. U. Pitts. Sch. Medicine, 1961-71; prof., chmn. dept. physiology Med. Coll. Va., 1971—. Sect. editor: Am. Jour. Physiology, also Jou. Applied Physiology, 1970—; Contbr. articles to tech. jours. Recipient Pub. Health Service Research Career award Nat. Heart Inst., 1964-71; USPHS Research fellow Max-Planck Institut fur Medezinische Forschung, Heidelberg, Germany, 1955-56. Mem. Am. Physiol. Soc., Cardiac Muscle Soc., Biophys. Soc., Am. Heart Assn., Am. Physiol. Soc. (mem. nat. edn. com. 1971—, editorial bd.). Office: 1101 E Marshall Richmond VA 23298

BRIGGS, FRED(ERICK) JOHN, television news correspondent; b. Chgo., May 31, 1932; s. Finney and Leona Fay B.; m. Dorothy Wagner, May 20, 1961; 1 son, Lowell Frederick. Student, U. Louisville, 1954-57. Reporter and newscaster WSB-TV, Atlanta, 1960-66; corr. NBC News, Cleve., 1966-70, Chgo., 1970-74, San Francisco, 1974-75, Berlin, 1975-79, Chgo., 1979-83, Boston, 1983—. (Nominated for Emmy award 1969). Served in U.S. Army, 1950-52. Recipient Radio & TV News Dirs. award, 1965, Ohio State award, 1965. Mem. Sigma Delta Chi. Methodist. Office: One Gateway Center Newton MA 02158 *

BRIGGS, GARRETT, geologist, university dean; b. Dallas, Dec. 31, 1934; s. Albert Sidney and Margaret Campbell (Garrett) B.; m. Susan Lynn Walters; children: Doug, Jim, Paul, Molly. B.S. in Geology, So. Meth. U., 1958, M.S., 1959, Ph.D., U. Wis., Madison, 1962. Geologist Chevron Oil Co., New Orleans, 1962-65; asst. prof. geology Tulane U., 1965-68; asst. prof. U. Tenn., 1968-69, asso. prof., 1969-74, prof., 1974-81, interim head dept. geology, 1972-74, head dept., 1974-81, asso. dean research and adminstrn., 1977-81; dean Sch. Phys. and Math. Scis. N.C. State U., Raleigh, 1981—; cons. in field. Contbr. articles on sedimentology to profl. publs. ERDA grantee, 1975-77. Fellow Geol. Soc. Am.; mem. Soc. Econ. Paleontologists and Mineralogists, Am. Assn. Petroleum Geologists. Office: Sch Phys and Math Scis NC State U Raleigh NC 27650

BRIGGS, HAROLD MELVIN, corp. exec.; b. Shelbyville, Mich., Apr. 6, 1904; s. Wallace E. and Eva M. (Dowell) B.; m. Helen J. Fadden, Mar. 26, 1949; 1 dau., Helen J. B.S., U.S. Naval Acad., 1927; M.E., U.S. Naval Postgrad. Sch., 1936; student, Harvard Advanced Mgmt. Program, 1948. Registered profl. engr., D.C. Commd. ensign USN, 1927, advanced through grades to rear adm., 1955; naval aide White House, 1940- 41; prodn. officer Bur. Ordnance, 1941-43; exec. U.S.S. St. Louis, 1943-44; staff comdr.-in-chief Atlantic Fleet, 1944-46; comdr. U.S.S. Pocono, 1946-48; comptroller Naval Gun Factory, 1949-51; staff comdr. Naval Forces Far East, sec. UN mil. armistice negotiating group, 1951-52; comdr. Destroyer Squdn. 12, 1952-53; chief of staff comdr. Amphibious Force Atlantic Fleet, 1953-55; dep. comdt. Navy) Armed Forces Staff Coll., 1955-57; comdr. Middle East Force, 1957-58; dir. Pan Am. affairs Naval Missions and Adv. Groups div. Office Chief Naval Operations, Washington, 1958-61; pres., chief exec. Washington Technol. Assos., Inc., 1961—; Mem. sci. bur., indsl. council Washington Bd. Trade. Decorated Silver Star medal, Legion of Merit with 3 gold stars, Bronze Star medal with oak leaf cluster; Order Eulchi, Korea; Order Naval Merit, Brazil; Cross Naval Merit, Peru; Order Abdon Calderon, Ecuador; Order San Carlos, Order of Almirante Padilla, Colombia; Grand Order Naval Merit, Venezuela; Spl. Order Naval Merit, Mexico; Distinguished Service medal, Chile). Mem. Am. Soc. Naval Engrs., Am. Ordnance Assn., Mil. Order Carabao, Naval Acad. Alumni Assn., Harvard Grad. Sch. Bus. Adminstrn. Assn., Navy League U.S., Nat Rocket Club, Advanced Mgmt. Assn. N.Y., Am. Mgmt. Assn., Rockville, Montgomery County chambers commerce. Clubs: Rotarian., Army and Navy (Washington). Home: 4721 Tilden St Washington DC 20016 Office: 979 Rollins Ave Rockville MD 20852

BRIGGS, HERBERT SPENCER, lawyer; b. N.Y.C., Feb. 9, 1910; s. Arthur Vanderbilt and Frances (Cleary) B.; m. Constance Ulmer Twiname, Dec. 30, 1973; children by previous marriage: Natasha, Thomas, Edward George. A.B., Coll. City N.Y., 1929; J.D., Fordham U., 1973. Bar: N.Y. 1975. Personnel research N.Y. and Queens Electric Light and Power Co., 1929-34, job and wage analyst-in-charge, 1934-42; personnel research Consol. Edison Co. N.Y., Inc., 1946-47; sr. research specialist employee remuneration The Conf. Bd., Inc., N.Y.C., 1947-52, asst. sec., 1953, sec., 1953-73; since practiced in, Stormville. Author: Wage Payment Systems, 1948, Evaluating Managerial Positions, 1951. Served to lt. col. USAAF, 1942-46. Mem. Am., N.Y. State bar assns., Delta Sigma Phi. Republican. Episcopalian. Home and office: Rural Route 2 Stormville NY 12582

BRIGGS, JOHN DEQUEDVILLE, III, lawyer; b. Concord, Mass., May 9, 1943; s. John DeQuedville and Delia (Ingelhart) B.; m. Mary McReynolds, Jan. 1, 1972. B.A., Harvard U., 1965; J.D., Georgetown U., 1972. Bar: D.C. bar 1973. Exec. editor Law and Policy in Internat. Bus., Washington, 1971-72; law clk. to Judge Frank J. Murray, U.S. Dist.Ct., Boston, 1972-73; partner firm Howrey & Simon, Washington, 1973—. Served with USN, 1966-69; Vietnam. Decorated Navy Commendation medal. Mem. Am. Bar Assn. (sects. antitrust, internat. and bus. litigation law, chmn. editorial bd. Antitrust Law Devels.), D.C. Bar Assn., Bar Assn. D.C. Clubs: Met., Univ. (Washington); Harvard. Home: 2101 Connecticut Ave NW Washington DC 20008 Office: 1730 Pennsylvania Ave NW Washington DC 20006

BRIGGS, JOHN GURNEY, JR., music critic and editor; b. High Point, N.C., Feb. 17, 1916; s. John Gurney and Hazel Irene (Harmon) B.; m. Elizabeth Balée Westmoreland, Dec. 23, 1938; children—Robert Ragan, Mary Curtis. Student, U. N.C., 1932-35; grad., Curtis Inst. Music, 1938. Music editor, NBC, 1938-40; music critic: N.Y. Post, 1940-49; editor: Etude music mag, 1949-52; music critic: N.Y. Times, 1952-60; sr. writer, Smith, Kline & French Labs., Phila., 1961-70; writer: Camden (N.J.) Courier-Post, 1970—; program annotator, Phila. Orch., 1963—; Author: The Collector's Tchaikovsky, 1959, Leonard Bernstein: The Man, His Work and His World, 1961, The Collector's Beethoven, 1962, Requiem for a Yellow Brick Brewery, 1969; Contbr. articles and short stories to mags. Served with AUS, 1943-46. Mem. Athenaeum of Phila., Phila. Art Alliance, Pa. Hort. Soc. Episcopalian. Home: Cooper River Plaza Pennsauken NJ 08109 Office: Courier-Post Camden NJ 08101

BRIGGS, JONATHAN SCOTT, magazine publisher, marketing executive; b. N.Y.C., Mar. 21, 1950; s. William Bradford and Elizabeth (Buffington) B.; m. Mayke Beckmann, Feb. 12, 1978; children: Jonathan, Marlena, Julia. B.A., Williams Coll., 1972. Export product mgr. Marker Skibindungen, Garmisch-P, W. Ger., 1972-75; dir. advt. Ziff-Davis Pub. Co., N.Y.C., 1975-79, pub., 1979-82, v.p. mktg., 1982—. Republican. Club: Union League. Office: Ziff-Davis Pub Co One Park Ave New York NY 10016

BRIGGS, KENNETH ARTHUR, journalist; b. Gardner, Mass., Apr. 8, 1941; s. Clayton Walter and Dora Adele (Havumaki) B.; 1 son, Matthew Thomas. A.B., Bowdoin Coll., 1963; B.D., Yale, 1967. Ordained to ministry Methodist Ch., 1967; asst. pastor United Methodist Ch., Hempstead, N.Y., 1967-69. Religion writer: Newsday, Garden City, N.Y., 1970-74; religion editor: N.Y. Times, 1974—; Co-author: Getting Married The Way You Want, 1973. Mem. Religion Newswriters Assn. (Supple Meml. award 1972), Alpha Delta Phi. Office: NY Times 229 W 43d St New York NY 10036

BRIGGS, MORTON WINFIELD, Romance language educator; b. Millbrook, N.Y., Mar. 11, 1915; s. Anthony Joseph and Verlina (Reardon) B.; m. Kathryn Minor Ivey, June 26, 1941; children: Christopher Reardon, Anthony Kirk, Katherine Minor. Diplôme d'Etudes Françaises, U. Paris (France), 1936; B.A., Cornell U., Ithaca, N.Y., 1937; M.A., Harvard, 1938, Ph.D. in Romance Langs, 1944. Asst. d'anglais Lycée Descartes, Tours, France, 1937-38; teaching fellow French, tutor Romance langs. Harvard U., 1940-43; faculty Wesleyan U., Middletown, Conn., 1943—, prof. Romance langs., 1956—, sec. faculty, 1958—, acting chmn. and chmn. master arts in teaching program, 1964-66, 68-69, 71-72, chmn. ednl. studies program, 1973—, dir. Honors Coll., 1966—, acting dir. grad. liberal studies program, 1980-81, dir. Wesleyan program in Paris, 1979, 82, 83; dir. Sweet Briar Coll. Jr. Year in France, 1962-63, 72-73; chmn. Fgn. Lang. Adv. Com. Conn., 1963-71. Author: Condensed Spanish Grammar, 1959; co-editor: Petrucci Collection Early Songs, 1962; mng. editor: French Rev, 1968-72; advt. mgr., 1949-72. Pres. bd. Middletown United Fund, 1966; bd. dirs. Middlesex chpt. ARC, 1961—, chmn., 1965-67, chmn. blood program, 1973—. Mem. Am. Assn. Tchrs. French (nat. exec. council 1949-72), Modern Lang. Assn., AAUP, Nord de Paris (hon.), Phi Beta Kappa., Phi Kappa Phi. Episcopalian (vestryman 1952-55, 64-67, 80-82, warden 1968-72). Clubs: Rotarian (dir. 1967—, treas. 1973—), Rotarian (chmn. ednl. awards com. 1980—), Rotarian (Paul Harris fellow 1981). Home: 145 Mount Vernon St Middletown CT 06457

BRIGGS, PAUL WARREN, supt. schs.; b. Mayville, Mich., Nov. 23, 1912; s. Arthur Eugene and Lydia (Miller) B.; m. Arvilla Moran, June 18, 1933; children—Betty Ann (Mrs. Loren Smith), James A. A.B., Western Mich. U., 1934; M.A., Mich. State U., 1943; postgrad., Columbia U., 1956; Ed.D., Baldwin-Wallace Coll., 1964, Central State U., 1965, Cleve. State U., 1966; L.H.D., Case Inst. Tech., 1966; LL.D., Allegheny Coll., 1969; D.P.A., Albion Coll., 1973. Tchr., prin. Brown City (Mich.) High Sch., 1934-40; tchr. Bay City (Mich.) Central High Sch., 1940-42, vice prin., 1942-43, prin., 1943-53; supt. schs., Bay City, 1953-57, Parma Pub. Schs., 1957-64, Cleve. Pub. Schs., 1964-78; ret., 1978; mem. summer sch. staff Mich. State U., 1947-50; lectr. edn. U. Mich., 1952, Columbia U., 1965, Ohio State U., 1963; adj. prof. Cleve. State U.; lectr. U. Ill., 1974, Bowling Green State U., 1975—; vis. lectr. Coll. Edn., Ariz. State U., 1981; faculty Nat. Acad. Sch. Execs., 1970—; vis. lectr. Coll. Edn., Ariz. State U., 1978—; Adv. bd. Edn., 1954-58. Bd. mgrs. Cleve. Met. YMCA, 1964—; mem. exec. bd. Greater Cleve. council Boy Scouts Am., 1960—; bd. overseers Case Western Res. U., 1970—; mem. exec. com. Nat. Urban Coalition; hon. life mem. Nat. PTA; mem. Council Great City Schs., Edn. Commn. of States; mem. exec. com. Ohio Ednl. TV Network Commn.; bd. dirs. Greater Cleve. Growth Assn.; mem. Ohio Rehab. Services Commn., 1970-73. Recipient Ann. Brotherhood award NCCJ, 1974; award Am. Vocat. Assn., 1974. Mem. Nat. Edn. Assn. (Ohio Edn. Assn.), Am., Ohio assns. schs. adminstrs., Mich. High Sch. Athletic Assn. (exec. com. 1949-53). Clubs: Rotary (past pres. Bay City), Masons (33 deg.), Shriners.). Home: 514 E Freemont Dr Tempe AZ 85282 Office: 1380 E 6th St Cleveland OH 44114

BRIGGS, PAUL W(ELLINGTON), utility company executive; b. Fairport, N.Y., Nov. 9, 1922; s. C. LeRoy and Erma B.; m. Beatrice Schroeder, Oct. 14, 1950; children: David, Peter, Thomas. A.S. in Acctg. and Fin, Bentley Coll., 1942. With Rochester Gas and Electric Corp., N.Y., 1945—, sr. v.p. fin. and gen. services, 1973-74, pres., 1974-80, chmn. bd., chief exec. officer, 1980—, also dir.; dir. Security Trust Co., Security N.Y. State Corp., Rochester Hosp. Service Corp.; Blue Cross. Bd. dirs., vice chmn. United Way Greater Rochester, 1979; trustee, pres. Eastman Dental Center, Rochester, 1982; bd. dirs. Rochester Philharm. Orch., Inc.; bd. overseers Strong Meml. Hosp., Rochester. Served in AC U.S. Army, 1943-45. Mem. Am. Gas Assn., Edison Electric Inst. Lutheran. Clubs: Country, University, Genesee Valley (Rochester). Home: 55 Whitestone Ln Rochester NY 14618 Office: 89 East Ave Rochester NY 14649

BRIGGS, PHILIP, ins. co. exec.; b. Paris, Feb. 28, 1928; s. Robert E. and Madeleine (Boell) B. (parents Am. citizens); m. Jean M. Sloan, July 9, 1949; children—Karen, Heather, Peter. A.B., Middlebury Coll., 1948. With Met. Life Ins. Co., N.Y.C., 1948—, v.p., gen. mgr., 1971-73, sr. v.p., 1973-77, exec. v.p., 1977—. Served with AUS, 1946-48, 50-51. Fellow Soc. Actuaries, Can. Inst. Actuaries. Clubs: Stanwich Golf (Greenwich, Conn.); Sky (N.Y.C.). Home: 520 Stanwich Rd Greenwich CT 06830 Office: 1 Madison Ave New York NY 10010

BRIGGS, ROBERT PETER, banker; b. Monroe, Mich., Apr. 3, 1903; s. Robert Douglas and Rose (Pierce) B.; m. Maxine Corliss, Dec. 22, 1925; children—Ruth Terrilyn, Peter Alan. A.B., U. Mich., 1925, M.B.A., 1928, LL.D., 1969; LL.D., Western Mich. U., 1965. C.P.A., Mich. Faculty bus. adminstrn. Kans. Wesleyan U., 1925-27; instr. econs. U. Mich., 1927-35, asst. prof. econs. and accounting, 1935-40, asso. prof., 1940-44, prof. accounting, v.p., 1945-51; v.p., dir. Consumer Power Co., Jackson, Mich., 1951-52, exec. v.p., dir., 1952-68, dir., 1951-75; asst. to pres. Standard Steel Spring Co., 1944-45; jr. accountant, sr. accountant, partner Paton & Ross, F.E. Ross & Co. & Briggs & Icerman, Ann Arbor, Mich., 1927-45; dir., dep. chmn., chmn. Fed. Res. Bank of Chgo., 1956-64; dir. Fed. Home Loan Bank, Indpls., 1975-79; mem. Mich. Job Devel. Authority, 1977—; Commr. Mich. Financial Instns. Bur., Lansing, 1968-73, cons., 1973-74; Pres. Conf. State Bank Suprs., 1972-73. Bd. regents U. Mich., 1964-68. Chief gen. office div. Detroit Ordnance Dist. War Dept., 1941-44. Mem. Mich. C. of C. (past pres.), Mich. Assn. C.P.A.'s, U. Mich. Alumni Assn. (nat. pres. 1979-81). Presbyterian. Home: Box 758 Elk Rapids MI 49629

BRIGGS, RODNEY ARTHUR, association executive, agronomist; b. Madison, Wis., Mar. 18, 1923; s. George McSpadden and Mary Etta (McNelly) B.; m. Helen Kathleen Ryall, June 1, 1944; children: Carolyn, Kathleen, David, Andrew, Amy. Student, Oshkosh (Wis.) State Coll., 1941-42; B.S. in Agronomy, U. Wis., 1948; Ph.D. in Field Crops, Rutgers U., 1953. Extension asso. farm crops Rutgers U., New Brunswick, N.J., 1949-50, 52-53; mem. faculty U. Minn., 1953-73; supt. W. Central Sch. and Expt. Sta., Morris, Minn., 1959-60; prof. agronomy, dean U. Minn., administrv. head, provost, 1960-69, sec. bd. regents, 1971-72, exec. asst. to pres., 1971-73; on leave of absence Ford Found. as asso. dir., dir. research Internat. Inst. Tropical Agr., Ibadan, Nigeria, 1969-71; pres. Eastern Oreg. State Coll., La Grande, 1973-83; exec. v.p. Am. Soc. Agronomy/Crop Sci. Soc. Am./Soil Sci. Soc. Am., Madison, Wis., 1982—; chmn. Nat. Silage Evaluation Com., 1957; sec. Minn. Corp Improvement Assn., 1954-57; columnist crops and soils Minn. Farmer mag., 1954-59; judge grain and forage Minn. State Fair, 1954-61; mem. ednl. mission to Taiwan Am. Assn. State Colls. and Univs., 1978, state rep., 1974-76, spl. task force of pres.'s on intercollegiate athletics, 1976—, nat. com. on agr., renewable resources and rural devel., 1978—, nat. sec.-treas., 1980-81; mem. com. on govt. relations Am. Council Edn. Com., 1981; mem. Gov.'s Commn. on Fgn. Lang. and Internat. Studies, State Oreg., 1980—; Mem. Gov.'s Commn. Law Enforcement, 1967-69; adv. com. State Planning Agy., 1968-69, Minn. Interinstnl. TV, 1967-69. Bd. dirs. Rural Banking Sch., 1967-69, Channel 10 ETV, Appleton, Minn., Grande Ronde Hosp., 1980—; chmn. policy adv. com. Oreg. Dept. Environ. Quality, 1979—. Served with inf. AUS, 1942-46, 50-52. Recipient Staff award U. Minn., 1959, Spl. award U. Minn. at Morris, 1961; commendation Soil Conservation Soc. Am., 1965; Rodney A. Briggs Library named in his honor U. Minn., Morris, 1974. Mem. AAAS, Am. Soc. Agronomy, Crop Sci. Soc. Am., Soil Conservation Soc. Am., Am. Inst. Biol. Scis. (dir. 1982—), ACLU, Sigma Xi, Alpha Gamma Rho. Republican. Congregationalist. Home: 1109 Gilbert Rd Madison WI 53711 Office: Am Soc Agronomy 677 S Segoe Rd Madison WI 53711

BRIGGS, SHIRLEY ANN, organization executive; b. Iowa City, May 12, 1918; d. John E. and Nellie (Upham) B. B.A. with highest distinction, U. Iowa, 1939, M.A., 1940. Instr. art N.D. State Coll., Fargo, 1941-43; illustrator Glenn L. Martin Co., Balt., 1943-45; info. specialist U.S. Fish and Wildlife Service, Washington, 1945-47; chief graphics sect. Bur. Reclamation, 1948-54; sec. Rachel Carson Council, Inc., Washington, 1966—, exec. dir., 1970—; instr. Grad. Sch., U.S. Dept. Agr., 1962—; mem. pesticide policy adv. com. EPA, 1975-77; exec. com. Natural Resources Council Am., 1977-79, 80—, sec., 1981—; mem. adv. panel on monitoring environ. contaminants Office of Tech. Assessment, U.S. Congress, 1978-79. Painter habitat group backgrounds, Smithsonian Instn., 1954-55, diorama prodn., Nat. Park Service, 1956-57; editor: Atlantic Naturalist, 1947-69; Illustrator: The Pronghorn Antelope, 1948, The Wonders of Seeds, 1956, Insects and Plants, 1963; editor, illustrator: The Trumpeter Swan, 1960, Landscaping for Birds, 1973; also spl. assignment writing, illustrating. Mem. Audubon Naturalist Soc. Central Atlantic States (v.p. publs. 1956-69, Paul Bartsch award 1972, hon. v.p. 1975—), AAUW, Soc. Occupational and Environ. Health, Am. Ornithol. Union, Wilson Ornithol. Soc., AAAS, Phi Beta Kappa, Pi Beta Phi. Presbyterian. Home: 7605 Honeywell Ln Bethesda MD 20814

BRIGGS, VERNON MASON, JR., educator; b. Washington, June 29, 1937; s. Vernon Mason and Anne Maria (Cox) B.; m. Martijna Antonia Aarts, Dec. 29, 1971; children: Vernon Mason III, Kees Kanen. B.S., U. Md., 1959; M.A., Mich. State U., 1960, Ph.D., 1965. Asst. instr. econs. Mich. State U., 1960-64; asst. prof. U. Tex., Austin, 1964-68, asso. prof., 1968-74, prof. econs., 1974-78; prof. indsl. and labor relations Cornell U., Ithaca, N.Y., 1978—; research dir. Com. on Adminstrn. Tng. Programs, HEW, 1967-68; mem. Nat. Council Employment Policy, 1977—; Bd. dirs. Corp. Public and Pvt. Ventures, 1978—. Author: (with Ray Marshall) The Negro and Apprenticeship, 1967, The Chicano and Rural Poverty, 1973, (with Walter Fogel and Fred Schmidt) The Chicano Worker, 1977, (with John Adams, Brian Rungeling and Lewis Smith) Employment, Income and Welfare in the Rural South, 1977, (with Ray Marshall and Allan King) Labor Economics: Wages Employment and Trade Unionism, 1980, (with Felician Foltman) Apprenticeship Research: Emerging Findings and Future Trends, 1981. Recipient Jean Holloway Teaching Excellence award, 1974. Mem. Phi Sigma Kappa, Delta Sigma Pi, Omicron Delta Kappa, Omicron Delta Epsilon. Roman Catholic. Home: 332 Winthrop St Ithaca NY 14850

BRIGGS, W. BRADFORD, publisher; b. Jamestown, R.I., Aug. 5, 1921; s. Benjamin Franklin and Dorothy (Green) B.; m. Elizabeth Buffinton, May 28, 1949; children: Jonathan Scott, Peter Leland, Barry Durfee. A.B. cum laude, Bowdoin Coll., 1943. Printing accounts exec. McCall Corp., N.Y.C., 1949-52, publisher, 1952-57; asst. to pres. Ziff-Davis Pub. Co., N.Y.C., 1957-59, exec. v.p., 1959-74, vice chmn., 1974—; also dir.; chmn. Yachting Pub. Corp., 1977—; sr. v.p. Ziff Corp., 1981—; dir. Advt. Council, 1977—; dir. Aviation Simulation Tech., Inc., Bedford, Mass. Pres. U.S. Ski Ednl. Found., also U.S. Ski Team, Inc., 1974-75, hon. chmn. bd., 1976—; active Am. Cancer Soc., 1965-70; gen. chmn. Cancer Care, Inc., 1981. Served with USNR, 1942-45. Mem. Mag. Pub. Assn. (dir. 1972, vice chmn. 1973-81); Bowdoin Coll. Alumni Assn. (council 1965-69), Psi Upsilon. Clubs: Union League (N.Y.C.); New Canaan (Conn.) Country; Pine Valley Country (Clementon, N.J.). Home: 251 White Oak Shade Rd New Canaan CT 06840 Office: 1 Park Ave New York NY 10016

BRIGGS, WALLACE NEAL, educator; b. Meridian, Miss., Mar. 1, 1915; s. Wallace R. and Mary (Neal) B.; m. Olive Terrill, June 24, 1942. A.B., U. Ky., 1937, M.A., 1945; student, Yale, 1953-54, Sorbonne, 1939-40. Tchr. Univ. Sch., Lexington, Ky., 1940-43; dir. Guignol Theatre, U. Ky., Lexington, 1943—, prof. theatre arts, 1962—, chmn. dept., 1966; pres. Lexington Children's Theatre, 1970-71; Bd. dirs. Ky. Living Arts Center, 1970—. Dir.: The Stephen Foster Story, Bardstown, Ky., 1964; actor, dir., Shakertown Theatre, Pleasant Hill, Ky., 1972-74; dir.: Shakespeare in the Park, Louisville, 1973; artistic dir., Lexington Musical Theatre, 1974-75; Author articles. Served with AUS, 1942-43. Recipient Outstanding Tchr. award U. Ky., 1968, Great Tchr. award, 1971; Outstanding Prof. U.S. award, 1975. Mem. Nat. Soc. Arts and Letters (co-chmn. drama div. 1978-79), Am. Ednl. Theatre Assn., Internat. Theatre Edn. Assn., Southeastern Theatre Assn., Ky. Theatre Assn. (v.p. 1968), Ky. Speech Assn., Omicron Delta Kappa, Phi Delta Kappa, Phi Kappa Tau. Home: 3013 Windermere Rd Lexington KY 40502 *After forty years of teaching I am still attempting to reach students with truth, fill them with some amount of sweet reason, and always hoping that they have learned to think. They will prove to what degree I have been successful.*

BRIGGS, WILLIAM EGBERT, mathematics educator; b. Sioux City, Iowa, Mar. 26, 1925; s. Egbert Estabrook and Berenice (Reynolds) B.; m. Muriel Mae Lambert, Aug. 29, 1947; children: William L., Roger P., Barbara E., Lindsey A. B.A., Morningside Coll., 1948, D.Sc., 1968; M.A., U. Colo., 1949, Ph.D., 1953. Asst. instr. Morningside Coll., 1947; math. tchr. Elwood (Iowa) High Sch., 1948, Baseline Jr. High Sch., Boulder, Colo, 1954-55; research assoc. U. Colo., 1953-54, faculty, 1955—, prof. math., 1964—, acting dean, 1963-64, dean, 1964-80, acad. dean semester at sea, fall 1980; NSF faculty fellow, hon. research asso. Univ. Coll., London, Eng., 1961-62; mem. Region XIII Selection com. Woodrow Wilson Found. Fellowship Program; bd. dirs. Edn. Projects Inc., 1966—; chmn. math. adv. com. Colo. Dept. Edn., 1964-66; mem. commn. on arts and scis. Nat. Assn. State Univs. and Land Grant Colls., 1970-73, 75-78; dir. Council Colls. Arts and Scis., 1969-73, 74-77, pres.-elect, 1975, pres., 1976. Author: (with others) Analytic Geometry, 1963; also articles. Bd. dirs. Colo. Congregational Conf., 1953-56, Colo. Conf. United Ch. Christ, 1963-68, Boulder Council Chs. and Synagogues, 1981-84; Pres.-elect Boulder Council Chs. and Synagogues, 1981, pres., 1982. Served to 1st lt. AUS, 1943-46. Recipient Stearns award Associated Alumni U. Colo.; U. Colo. medal. Mem. Math. Assn. Am. (gov. 1963-66), Am. Math. Soc., AAUP, London Math. Soc., Sigma Xi. Home: 1440 Sierra Dr Boulder CO 80302

BRIGGS, WINSLOW RUSSELL, plant physiologist; b. St. Paul, Apr. 29, 1928; s. John DeQuedville and Marjorie (Winslow) B.; m. Ann Morrill, June 30, 1955; children: Caroline, Lucia, Marion. B.A., Harvard U., 1951, M.A., 1952, Ph.D., 1956. Instr. biol. scis. Stanford (Calif.) U., 1955-57, asst. prof., 1957-62, asso. prof., 1962-66, prof., 1966-67; prof. biology Harvard U., 1967-73; dir. dept. plant biology Carnegie Instn. of Washington, Stanford, 1973—. Author: (with others) Life on Earth, 1973; Asso. editor: Annual Review of Plant Physiology, 1961-72; editor, 1972—; Contbr. articles on plant growth and devel. and photbiology to profl. jours. John Simon Guggenheim fellow, 1973-74. Fellow AAAS; mem. Am. Soc. Plant Physiologists (pres. 1975-76), Calif. Bot. Soc. (pres. 1976-77), Nat. Acad. Scis., Am. Acad. Arts and Scis., Am. Inst. Biol. Scis. (pres. 1980-81), Am. Soc. Photbiology, Bot. Soc. Am., Nature Conservancy, Sigma Xi. Home: 480 Hale St Palo Alto CA 94301 Office: Dept of Plant Biology Carnegie Institution of Washington 290 Panama St Stanford CA 94305 *With gifted students, remarkable things are possible.*

BRIGHAM, E. ORAN, communications equipment co. exec.; b. Stamford, Tex., Sept. 13, 1940; s. Elbert Oran and Evelyn Marie (Hargrove) B.; m. Evangeline Rushing, June 12, 1965; 1 dau., Cami. B.S. in E.E, U. Tex., 1963, M.S., 1964, Ph.D. (Ford Found. fellow), 1967; M.S. in Engring. Mgmt, George Washington U., 1971. Supr. info. scis. LTV Electrosystems, Inc., Greenville, Tex., 1967-69, div. tech. coordinator, 1971-73; with Nat. Security Agy., Ft. Meade, Md., 1969-71; asst. dir. signal intelligence systems office Asst. Sect. Def., Washington, 1973-75, dir. reconaissance and surveillance, 1975-76; v.p. engr. Melpar div. E-Systems, Inc., Falls Church, Va., 1976-80, v.p., gen. mgr., St. Petersburg, Fla., 1980-82; chmn. bd., pres. Avantek, Inc, Santa Clara, Calif., 1982—. Author: Fast Fourier Transform, 1974; contbr. articles in field. Mem. IEE, Assn. U.S. Army, Am. Def. Preparedness Assn., Tau Beta Pi, Eta Kappa Nu, Phi Eta Sigma. Club: Assn. Old Crows. Office: PO Box 12248 Saint Petersburg FL 33733

BRIGHAM, SAMUEL TOWNSEND JACK, III, lawyer; b. Honolulu, Oct. 8, 1939; s. Samuel Townsend Jack, Jr. and Betty Elizabeth (McNeil) B.; m. Judith Catherine Johnson, Sept. 3, 1960; children: Robert Jack, Bradley Lund, Lori Ann, Lisa Katherine. B.S. in Bus. magna cum laude, Menlo Coll., 1963; J.D., U. Utah, 1966. Bar: Calif. 1967. Asso. firm Petty, Andrews, Olsen & Tufts, San Francisco, 1966-67; accounting mgr. Western sales region Hewlett-Packard Co., North Hollywood, Calif., 1967-68; atty. Hewlett-Packard Co., Palo Alto, Calif., 1968-70, asst. gen. counsel, 1971-73, gen. atty., asst. sec., 1974-75, sec., gen. counsel, 1975-82; lectr. law Menlo Coll.; speaker profl. assn. seminars. Bd. dirs. Palo Alto Area YMCA, 1974-81, pres., 1978; bd. govs. Santa Clara County region NCCJ. Served with USMC, 1957-59. Mem. Am. Bar Assn., Calif. Bar Assn., Peninsula Assn. Gen. Counsel, MAPI Law Council, Am. Corp. Counsel Assn. (bd. dirs.), Am. Soc. Corp. Secs. (pres. No. Calif. Chpt. 1983—). Home: 920 Oxford Dr Los Altos CA 94022 Office: 3000 Hanover St Palo Alto CA 94304

BRIGHAM, THOMAS MYRON, educator; b. Rochester, N.Y., Feb. 4, 1924; s. Charles Dana and Beatrice (McNaught) B.; m. Aimee Eugenia Doucette, May 13, 1944; children—Pamela Susan Brigham Schramm, Peter Eugene, Timothy James, Corinne Anne Brigham King. A.B., San Francisco State U., 1948; M.S.W., U. Calif. at Berkeley, 1950. Boys' work dir. community program Central YMCA, San Francisco, 1947-50; group program dir. Internat. Inst. San Francisco, 1950-53; faculty Calif. State U., Fresno, 1953—, prof. social work, chmn. dept., 1964—, dir. div. social work, 1965, dean, 1968-71, continuing edn. dir., 1974—; UN adviser, Philippines, 1971-73, cons., 1973—; faculty Calif. Sch. Profl. Psychology, 1974—; cons. Mental Health Tng. Center Central Calif., 1976—; cons. in field, 1955—, UN adviser, Indonesia, 1961-62. Author papers in field. Vice foreman Fresno County Grand Jury, 1963-64; Bd. dirs. Kings View, 1979. Served with AUS, 1943-46. Licentiate mem. Royal Soc. Health (Eng.); mem. Council Social Work Edn., Nat. Assn. Social Workers, AAUP, Internat. Soc. Community Devel. Home: 4838 E Brown Ave Fresno CA 93703

BRIGHT, GERALD, manufacturing company executive; b. Detroit, Geb. 17, 1923; s. Harry B. and Jessie (Vidaver) Breight; m. Carceline Douger, Dec. 28, 1952; children: Russell, Ethan. A.B., U. Mich., 1947, LL.B., 1950. Bar: Mich. 1950. Law clk. presiding justice Mich. Supreme Ct., Lansing, 1950-51; assoc. Travis & Warren, Detroit, 1951-52, Bizer & Sommers, 1952-60; ptnr. Derderian, Guidot & Bright, Detroit, 1960-66; gen. counsel Masco Corp., Taylor, Mich., 1966—, v.p., gen. counsel, 1970—, sec., 1983—. Mem. state central com. Republican Party, Lansing, Mich., 1953-55. Served with USAAF, 1943-46. Mem. Detroit Bar Assn., Mich. State Bar Assn., ABA. Jewish. Office: masco Corp 21001 Van Born Rd Taylor MI 48180

BRIGHT, HAROLD FREDERICK, university provost; b. Smethport, Pa., Aug. 6, 1913; s. Stanley and Florence K. (Dunn) B.; m. Elizabeth Korhumel, Mar. 23, 1938; children: Stanley Joseph, Beverly Ann (Mrs. Leonard R. Kaply). A.B., Lake Forest Coll., 1937; M.S., U. Rochester, 1944; Ph.D., U. Tex., 1952. Chmn. dept. math. San Angelo (Tex.) Coll., 1941-43, registrar, dir. guidance, 1945-49; asst. prof. math. Denison U., 1943-44, U. Rochester, 1944-45; asso. dir. research Am. Assn. Jr. Colls., 1949-52; specialist ops. research and synthesis Gen. Electric Co., 1957-58; dep. dir. Human Resources Office George Washington U., Washington, 1952-56, chmn. dept. statistics, 1958-64, dir. Computer Center, 1963-65, asso. dean faculties, 1964-66, v.p. acad. affairs, 1966-84, provost, 1969-84, prof. emeritus stats., v.p. acad. affairs emeritus, 1984—; cons. in field, 1956—. Mem. AAAS, Am. Soc. Quality Control, Am. Statis. Assn., Am. Psychol. Assn., Inst. Math. Statistics, Math. Assn. Am., Royal Statis. Soc., Assn. Instl. Research, Sigma Xi, Sigma Pi Sigma. Republican. Episcopalian. Club: Cosmos (Washington). Home: 314 Branch Circle SE Vienna VA 22180 Office: George Washington Univ Washington DC 20052

BRIGHT, HARVEY R., oil producer; b. Muskogee, Okla., Oct. 6, 1920; s. Christopher R. and Rebecca E. (Van Ness) B.; m. Mary Frances Smith, May 27, 1943 (dec. Apr. 1971); children—Carol (Mrs. James B. Reeder), Margaret (Mrs. Jerry R. Petty), Christopher R., Clay Van Ness; m. Peggy Braselton, Dec. 15, 1972. B.S., Tex. A. and M. U., 1943. Partner Bright & Co. (oil producers), Dallas; chmn. bd. E. Tex. Motor Freight Lines, Inc., So. Trust & Mortgage Co., Trinity Savs. and Loan Assn.; dir. Dallas Market Center Co., Republic Nat. Bank, Reynolds Penland Co., Southwestern Pub. Service Co., Republic of Tex. Corp., Mass. Mut. Life Ins. Co. Bd. dirs. Dallas Citizens Council; chmn. bd. Children's Med. Center, Dallas. Served with AUS, World War II. Home: 4500 Lakeside Dr Dallas TX 75205 Office: 2355 Stemmons Bldg Dallas TX 75207

BRIGHT, JOHN WILLIS, landscape architect, rancher; b. Norfolk, Va., Nov. 14, 1932; s. John Willis and Miriam Gayle (Winder) B.; m. Beverly Ruth Edwards, Sept. 12, 1953; children—Melanie, John, Eric. Student, Maryville Coll., 1949-51; B.S., SUNY Coll. Environ. Scis. and Forestry, 1955; postgrad., George Washington U., 1968. Landscape architect N.A. Rotunno, Syracuse, N.Y., 1954-55; with Nat. Park Service, 1958—, chief planning div., Washington, 1966-69, chief planning and design office, 1969-71; asst. mgr. Denver Service Center, 1971—; owner, operator ranch, Salida and Evergreen, Colo., 1976—; cons. U.S. and Honduras Nat. Parks, Coll. African Wildlife Mgmt., Tanzania; lectr. at univs. Contbr. articles to profl. jours.; author, editor profl. booklets. Treas., bd. dirs. Hiwan Hills Improvement Assn., Evergreen, 1976-79. Recipient unit citation Dept. Interior, 1966, 68, 71, Meritorious Service award, 1971. Fellow Am. Soc. Landscape Architects; mem. Council Landscape Archtl. Bds. (cert.). Democrat. Methodist. Home: 3911 S Juniper Circle Evergreen CO 80439 Office: Nat Park Service PO Box 25287 Denver CO 80225

BRIGHT, MARGARET, sociologist; b. Bentonville, Ark., Nov. 19, 1918; d. William Ray and Edna May (Woolwine) B.; m. Herman Binder, 1983. A.B., U. Calif.-, Berkeley, 1941; M.A., U. Mo.-, Columbia, 1944; Ph.D., U. Wis.-, Madison, 1950. Lectr. rural sociology U. Mo., 1944-47; asst. project dir. U. P.R., 1950-51; acting assoc. prof. Cornell U., 1951-52; social affairs officer population br. UN, N.Y.C., 1952-54; research assoc. Bur. Applied Social Research Columbia U., N.Y.C., 1954-57; sociologist-demographer UN Tech. Assistance, Bombay, India, 1957-59; asst. prof. chronic diseases Johns Hopkins U., Balt., 1959-63, assoc. prof., 1963-68; dir. research Center for Urban Affairs, 1968-72, assoc. prof. behavioral scis., 1968-70, prof., 1970—; mem. U.S. Mission Coop. Health and Sanitation to, Brazil, 1960; cons. in field. Author: Cooperativas de Consumo de Puerto Rico: Análisis Socio-Económico, 1957; co-author: Graduates of American Schools of Public Health, 1976; contbr. articles to profl. jours. Mem. Balt. Mayor's Task Force on Polit. Redistricting, 1971; mem. Rockefeller Commn. on Population and the Am. Future, 1970-72. Mem. Am. Sociol. Assn., Population Assn. Am., Am. Pub. Health Assn., Internat. Union for Sci. Study Population. Democrat. Home: 4213 Eastview Rd Baltimore MD 21218 Office: 615 N Wolfe St Baltimore MD 21205

BRIGHT, MYRON H., judge; b. Eveleth, Minn., Mar. 5, 1919; s. Morris and Lena A. (Levine) B.; m. Frances Louise Reisler, Dec. 26, 1947; children: Dinah Ann, Joshua Robert. B.S.L., U. Minn., 1941, J.D., 1947. Bar: N.D. and Minn. Asso. firm Wattam, Vogel, Vogel & Bright, Fargo, N.D., 1947-48, partner, 1949-68; judge 8th U.S. Circuit Ct. Appeals, Fargo, 1968—; prof. law St. Louis U., 1985—. Served to capt. AUS, 1942-46; CBI. Mem. Am., N.D. bar assns., Jud. Conf. U.S. (com. on adminstrn. of probation system 1977-83). Office: Federal Bldg US Post Office PO Box 2707 Fargo ND 58108

BRIGHT, SIMEON MILLER, government official; b. Keyser, W.Va., Sept. 11, 1925; s. Simeon Miller and Agnes Virginia (Bane) B.; m. Lorna Mae Stewart, June 10, 1950; children: Sheryl McCarty Bright McWhorter, Simeon Miller, Scott Randolph. A.A., Potomac State Coll., 1946; B.A., W.Va. U., 1949, M.A., 1950. With Dept. of Army, 1951-62, with ordnance tng. command, 1958-62; with Post Office Dept., Washington, 1962-69, spl. asst. to postmaster gen., 1965-69; pres. Bright Assos., Keyser, 1970—, Sim Bright Real Estate, 1971-77; mem. Postal Rate Commn., Washington, 1977—; instr. history U. Md., 1952-62, 69-70, Potomac State Coll., 1973-76. Spl. asst. to conv. mgr. Democratic Nat. Conv., Miami Beach, 1972. Served with USAAF, 1944-45, 51. Mem. Nat. Assn. Regulatory Utility Commrs. (exec. com.), Nat. Assn. Postmasters U.S. (hon.), VFW, Am. Legion. Methodist. Clubs: Lions (past pres.), Masons, Moose, Touchdown (Washington). Home: 1390 Ludwick St Keyser WV 26726 Office: 2000 L St NW Washington DC 20268

BRIGHT, WILLARD MEAD, manufacturing company executive; b. N.Y.C., Mar. 26, 1914; s. William Van Horn and Bernice Hartwell (Reynolds) B.; m. Martha Norris Land, May 15, 1944 (dec.); 1 son, Willard Mead; m. Virginia L. Jones, Mar. 14, 1981. B.S., U. Toledo, 1936, M.S., 1937; postgrad., U. Pitts., 1937-38; A.M., Harvard U., 1941, Ph.D., 1942. Research chemist Kendall Co., Boston, Chgo., 1942-52, asst. lab. dir., 1944-48; lab. dir. (Theodore Clark Lab. div.), Cambridge, Mass., 1948-52; asst. research dir. Lever Bros. Co., 1952-54, research dir., 1954-60, v.p. research and devel., 1960-64, dir., 1962-64; chmn. bd. W. H. Norris Lumber Co., Houston, 1957-64; treas. Border Lumber Co., Weslaco, Tex., 1957-64; v.p., dir. R.J. Reynolds Tobacco Co., 1964-68; sr. v.p., pres. profl. products group, dir. Warner-Lambert Pharm. Co., 1968-70; pres., chief exec. officer (Theodore Clark Lab. div.), Boston, 1970-73; pres., dir. Curtiss-Wright Corp., 1974, Boehringer Mannheim Corp., 1975-81, pres., dir., chief exec. officer, 1979-81; chmn. ZMI Corp., 1982—; dir. 1st Nat. Boston Corp., 1st Nat. Bank Boston, City Stores Co., Furman Lumber Co., Bio-Dynamics, Inc., Liberty Mut. Ins. Co.; Mem. adv. com. on patents U.S. Dept. Commerce, 1966-69; bd. visitors dept. chemistry Boston U. Recipient Gold T award U. Toledo, 1960. Mem. N.A.M. (chmn. sci. tech. com., dir. 1970-73), Am. Chem. Soc., AAAS, N.Y. Acad. Scis., Assn. Research Dirs., Indsl. Research Inst. (dir. 1963-69, pres. 1967-68), Dirs. Indsl. Research, Corn Refiners Assn. (trustee 1965-68), Am. Found. for Pharm. Edn., Nat. Planning Assn., Sigma Xi, Phi Kappa Phi. Clubs: University, Chemists (N.Y.C.); Somerset, Harvard (Boston); The Country (Brookline, Mass.); Forsyth Country (Winston-Salem, N.C.); Comml. (Boston). Home: 172 Beacon St Boston MA 02116 Office: 30 Federal St Boston MA 02110

BRIGHT, WILLIAM OLIVER, linguistics educator; b. Oxnard, Calif., Aug. 13, 1928; s. Oliver Edward and Ethel (Ruggles) B.; m. Elizabeth Halloran, Feb. 2, 1952; 1 dau., Susannah; m. Jane Orstan, June 16, 1962; m. Marcia Andersen, Dec. 24, 1964; m. Debra Levy, Sept. 20, 1975. A.B. in Linguistics, U. Calif.-Berkeley, 1949, Ph.D., 1955. Jr. linguistics scholar Deccan Coll., Poona, India, 1955-57; linguist State Dept., Washington, 1957-58; asst. prof. speech U. Calif. at Berkeley, 1958-59; mem. faculty UCLA, 1959—, assoc. prof. anthropology, 1962-66, prof. linguistics and anthropology, 1966—. Author: The Karok Language, 1957, An Outline of Colloquial Kannada, 1958, Variation and Change in Language, 1976; Editor: Studies in Californian Linguistics, 1964, Sociolinguistics, 1966, Language; jour., Linguistic Soc. Am., 1966—; editorial dir.: Malki Mus. Press, 1977—. Served with AUS, 1952-54. Mem. Linguistic Soc. Am., Linguistic Soc. India. Home: 2275 N Beverly Glen Pl Los Angeles CA 90077 Office: Dept Linguistics U Calif Los Angeles CA 90024

BRIGHTBILL, LORENZO OTIS, III, bank holding company executive; b. Fairmont, W.Va., June 20, 1936; s. Lorenzo Otis; m. Ruth Conley, Aug. 5, 1961; children: Mark Conley, Ann Marie, Amy Patricia, Cynthia. B.S. in Indsl. Mgmt, W.Va. U., 1960; diploma, Southwestern Grad. Sch. Banking, 1971; grad., Advanced Mgmt. Program, Harvard U., 1975. From asst. cashier to v.p. Ft. Worth Nat. Bank, 1965-73; v.p., liaison officer Tex. Am. Bancshares Co., Ft. Worth, 1973-75, pres., 1980—; also dir.; pres. Tex. Am. Bank. Dallas, 1976-80. Mem. exec. bd. Longhorn council Boy Scouts Am. Mem. Am. Inst. Banking. Roman Catholic. Clubs: River Crest Country, Ft. Worth, Century II, Exchange, Rotary. Home: 6116 Merrymount Rd Fort Worth TX 67107 Office: PO Box 2050 Fort Worth TX 76101

BRIGHTMAN, ROBERT LLOYD, importer, textile co. exec.; b. Rockville Center, N.Y., July 17, 1920; s. Harold Warren and Florence (Pennington) B.; m. Marion Altreuter, Oct. 31, 1942; children—Richard Warren, Shelley Anne, Susan Boyd. Grad. cum laude, Montclair Acad., 1936, Phillips Exeter Acad., 1937; B.A., Princeton, 1941. With A. Johnson & Co., Inc., N.Y.C., 1946-48; with Johaneson, Wales & Sparre, Inc., N.Y.C., 1948-67, v.p., 1952-64, pres., 1964-67; v.p. Grangesberg Am. Corp., N.Y.C., 1967-68; pres. R.L. Brightman Co., Upper Montclair, N.J., 1967—; dir. purchases West Point-Pepperell, N.Y.C., 1968-76, corporate v.p., 1976—; Mem. Nat. Council Am. Importers, Inc., 1954-69, dir., 1956-69, v.p., 1959-61, pres., 1961-63, sr. councillor, 1963-69; mem. nat. panel arbitrators Am. Arbitration Assn., 1958—. Served with USNR, 1942-46. Home: 118 Cooper Ave Upper Montclair NJ 07043 Office: 1221 Ave of Americas New York City NY 10020

BRIGHTMIRE, PAUL WILLIAM, judge; b. Washington, Mo., June 12, 1924; s. Quinton Claude and Alvena Matilda (Wehr) B.; m. Lorene E. Edwards, Nov. 7, 1952; children: Deborah Sue, William Paul, Jon Edward, Christina Ann, Thomas Christopher. B.A., U. Tulsa, 1949, J.D., 1951. Bar: Okla. 1951, U.S. Supreme Ct. Mem. firm Rogers & Brightmire, 1954-57, Brightmire & Asso., Tulsa, 1957-70; judge Okla. Ct. Appeals, Div. 2, Tulsa, 1971—, presiding judge, 1971-75; spl. justice Supreme Ct. Okla.; vis. prof. med. jurisprudence Okla. Coll. Osteo. Medicine and Surgery, 1975-82. Founding editor: Tulsa Lawyer, 1962-64; editor in chief: Advocate, 1967-70. Served to 2d lt. USNR, USAR, 1943-46, 51. Fellow Internat. Acad. Law and Sci.; mem. Am. Trial Lawyers Assn., Okla. Trial Lawyers Assn. (pres. 1967, Outstanding Service award 1968), Okla. Bar Assn. (Outstanding Service award 1969), Tulsa County Bar Assn. (Outstanding Service award 1965, exec. com. 1962-64), Kappa Sigma, Phi Beta Gamma, Pi Kappa Delta. Episcopalian. Club: Masons (32 deg., Shriner). Home: 4041 S Birmingham St Tulsa OK 74105 Office: 601 State Bldg 4th and Houston Sts Tulsa OK 74127

BRIGHTON, CARL THEODORE, orthopedic surgery educator;; b. Pana, Ill., Aug. 20, 1931; s. Louis Frederick and Helen (Frinke) B.; m. Ruth Louise Krentz, July 27, 1954; children: David Carl, Susan Ruth, Andrew Paul, Joel Theodore. B.A., Valparaiso U., 1953; M.D., U. Pa., 1957; Ph.D., U. Ill., 1969. Diplomate: Am. Bd. Orthopedic Surgery. Intern U.S. Naval Hosp., Phila., 1957-58, resident orthopedics, 1958-61; resident in orthopedics U. Pa., Phila., 1961-62; staff orthopedist U.S. Naval Hosp., Phila., 1962-63, Naval Hosp., Great Lakes, Ill., 1963-66, USS Sanctuary, South China Sea, 1966-67, resigned, 1967; asst. prof. orthopedic surgery U. Pa. Med. Sch., Phila., 1968-70, dir. orthopedic research, 1968—, assoc. prof., 1970-73, prof., 1973—, chmn. dept. orthopedic surgery, 1977—, Paul B. Magnuson prof. bone and joint surgery, 1977—; attending staff VA Hosp., Phila., 1968—; cons. orthopedic surgery U.S. Naval Hosp., Phila., 1968-78. Commd. lt. (j.g.) U.S. Navy, 1957; advanced through grades to lt. comdr., 1962. Recipient Kappa Delta award for outstanding research, 1974; spl. postdoctoral fellow NIH, 1967-68; Career devel. research award, 1971-76. Fellow A.C.S., Am. Acad. Orthopedic Surgeons; mem. Am. Orthopedic Assn., Orthopedic Research Soc. (pres. 1977), Orthopedic Forum, Canadian Orthopedic Research Soc. (hon.). Lutheran. Pioneered use of electricity in treating nonunion fractures. Home: 14 Flintshire Rd Malvern PA 19355 Office: Two Silverstein 34th and Spruce Sts Philadelphia PA 19104

BRIGHTON, GERALD DAVID, dialog234; b. Weldon, Ill., May 14, 1920; s. William Henry and Geneva (Ennis) B.; m. Lois Helen Robbins, June 7, 1949; children: Anne, William, Joan, Jeffrey. B.S., U. Ill., 1941, M.S., 1947, Ph.D., 1953. C.P.A., Ill. Instr. accountancy U. Ill., Urbana, 1947-53, prof., 1954—, dir. undergrad. acctg. program, 1978—; staff acct. Touche, Niven, Bailey & Smart, Chgo., 1953-54; cons. G.D. Brighton, C.P.A., Urbana, 1954—; vis. prof. U. Tex.-Austin, 1973; program specialist Dept. HUD, Washington, 1979; vice chmn. U. Ill. Athletic Assn., Urbana, 1982—. Contbr. articles to profl. jours. Alderman City of Urbana, 1967-69; officer, bd. dirs. U. Ill. YMCA, Champaign, 1959-81; treas. John Gwinn for Congress, Urbana, 1982-83, Green Meadows council Girl Scouts U.S.A., Urbana, 1981-83. Served to maj. U.S. Army, 1941-46. AACSB Faculty fellow, 1978-79; recipient Bronze Tablet for high honors U. Ill., 1941. Mem. Am. Inst. C.P.A.'s, Am. Acctg. Assn., Assn. Govt. Accts., Mcpl. Fin. Officers Assn., Nat. Tax Assn., Tax. Inst. Am. Democrat. Methodist. Home: 609 W Green St Urbana IL 61801 Office: 1206 S

6th st Champaign IL 61820 *Happiness comes very indirectly. "Seek and ye shall find." That is at best a half truth. If we to rely on direct rewards for our happiness we are in trouble. At best, the string of treats will be irregular. The key is to widen one's circle. Try to rejoice in the good fortunes of your colleagues. Somtimes, jealousy gets in the way. What is the greatest satisfaction I have had from teaching? It is the occasional glimpses that I see that former students are doing well.*

BRIGHTON, JOHN AUSTIN, mechanical engineer, educator; b. Gosport, Ind., July 9, 1934; s. John William and Esther Pauline B.; m. Charlotte L. McCarty, Mar. 20, 1953; children: Jill, Kurt, Eric. B.S., Purdue U., 1959, M.S., 1960, Ph.D., 1963. Draftsman Switzer Corp., Indpls., 1952-56; instr. Purdue U., 1960-63; asst. prof. mech. engring. Carnegie-Mellon U., 1963-65; asst. prof. Pa. State U., 1965-67, asso. prof., 1967-70, prof., 1970-77, Mich. State U., 1977-82, chmn. dept. mech. engring., 1977-82; dir. Sch. Mech. Engring. Ga. Inst. Tech., 1982—; Chmn. Community Sponsors Inc., State College, Pa., 1976-77; chmn. Pre-Trial Alts. Program for First Offenders, State College, 1976-77; bd. dirs. Impression 5. Author: (with Hughes) Fluid Dynamics, 1966. NSF grantee, 1975-77; NIH grantee, 1974-78. Mem. ASME (Engr. of Yr. award for Central Pa. 1977, tech. editor Jour. Biomech. Engring. 1976-79), Am. Soc. Engring. Edn., Am. Soc. Artificial Internal Organs. Home: 525 Kenbrook Dr Atlanta GA 30327 Office: Ga Inst Tech Atlanta GA 30332

BRIGUET, LOUIS JOSEPH, savs. and loan exec.; b. St. Paul, Mar. 6, 1915; s. A. Peter and Amelia (Gay) B.; m. Alvene M. Vannelli, Nov. 25, 1942; children—A. Peter II, Dennis L., Richard J., Kathleen M. Student parochial and pub. schs., St. Paul. Bus. systems salesman Remington-Rand Co., 1937-38; asst. mgr. Commerce Acceptance Co., 1938-41; br. and dist. mgr. U-CIT Credit Corp., 1945-49; gen. mgr. Danielson Enterprises, South St. Paul, Minn., 1949-56; exec. v.p., sec. United Fed. Savs., South St. Paul, 1956-66, pres., 1966—; pres., dir. Gopher Mining & Refining Co., Bismarck, N.D., 1958—. Mem. adv. com. South St. Paul United Fund, 1963-66, pres., 1961-62; mem. exec. bd. Indianhead council Boy Scouts Am.; Trustee St. Paul chpt. A.R.C., Minn. Community Research Council, Automobile Workers Health and Welfare Fund. Served to capt. AUS, 1941- 45. Recipient Community Service award United Fund South St. Paul, 1962. Mem. U.S. Savs. and Loan League, Minn. Savs. and Loan League, Twin City Savs. and Loan League (pres. 1963), Nat. Real Estate Bd., Soc. Residential Appraisers, South St. Paul C. of C. (pres. 1964, Community Service award 1964). Republican. Roman Catholic (trustee). Club: Kiwanian (past treas., dir. S. St. Paul). Home: 1539 Lone Oak Rd Eagan MN 55121 Office: 1151 Southview Blvd South St Paul MN 55075

BRILL, EMIL E., lawyer; b. St. Louis, Sept. 28, 1896; s. Emil and Anna (Schaal) B.; m. Nell Katherine Keiser, June 15, 1920; children—Harold E., Betty Ann. J.D., St. Louis U., 1922; LL.M., City Coll. of Law and Finance, 1923. Bar: Mo. bar 1921. Accountant, asst. auditor and in agy. dept. Internat. Life Ins. Co., St. Louis, 1912-23, asst. gen. counsel, 1927-28; practiced in, St. Louis, 1923-27, 61—; asst. v.p. Mo. State Life Ins. Co., 1928-33, Gen. Am. Life Ins. Co., 1933-34, v.p. group dept., 1934-36, v.p., 1936-56, sr. v.p., 1956-61; travel lectr.; former mem. group and statuary disability ins. com. Bur. Accident and Health Underwriters; former mem. joint group ins. com. Am. Life Conv. and Life Ins. Am.; former chmn. Mo. com. Health Ins. Council. Chmn. com. White House Conf. on Aging, 1961; adv. com. employment older worker Jewish Employment and Vocational Service; chmn. Tree of Lights campaign Salvation Army, life mem., vice-chmn. adv. bd., vice-chmn. exec. com., chmn. bequest and endowment com.; mem. pastoral com. adminstrv. bd., charge local ch. advt. and pub. relations Methodist Ch.; past trustee Gerontol. Research Found. Recipient William Booth award, also numerous De Witt awards Salvation Army. Mem. St. Louis Bar Assn., Mo. Bar, Sales and Mktg. Execs. Assn. Met. St. Louis (past pres.), Tau Kappa Epsilon. Clubs: Masons, Kiwanis (past pres. local chpt., lt. gov. dist.; Man of Year award; Churchman of Year award 1979), Mo. Athletic, Contemporary. Home: 9049 Saranac Dr Richmond Heights MO 63117

BRILL, HENRY, psychiatrist, educator; b. Bridgeport, Conn., Oct. 6, 1906; s. August Michael and Gussie (Kissel) B.; m. Wenonah Beale, Apr. 17, 1948; children: Michael Henry, Jean Malcolm; 1 dau. by previous marriage, Helen Elizabeth (Mrs. Charles Broxmeyer). B.A., Yale U., 1928, M.D., 1932. Intern, resident Pilgrim State Hosp., West Brentwood, N.Y., 932-38, clin. dir. hosp., 1942-50, dir., 1958-74; from instr. to clin. prof. Albany (N.Y.) Med. Coll., 1952-54; professorial lectr. State U. Med. Center at Syracuse; lectr. history psychiatry Columbia Med. Sch., 1957—; dir. Craig Colony, Sonyea, N.Y., 1950-52; clin. prof. psychiatry Downstate Med. Center at Stonybrook, 1973—; from asst. to 1st dep. commr. N.Y. State Dept. Mental Hygiene, 1952-64, regional dir., L.I., 1974-76, cons., 1976—; adminstr. N.Y. State Mental Hygiene Research Program, 1952-64; charge narcotic treatment program, N.Y. State, 1958-64; vice chmn. N.Y. State Narcotic Addiction Control Commn., 1966-68; chmn. com. clin. drug. evaluation NIMH, 1960-65; com. drug dependence NRC, 1959-73; mem. expert panel drug dependence WHO, 1968—; chmn. com. hallicinogenic drugs FDA-NIMH, 1960-70; mem. com. sedatives, stimulating and hallucinogenic drugs FDA, 1969-78; chmn. methadone evaluation com. Columbia Sch. Pub. Health, 1966-73; chmn. Narcotic Addiction Control Commn. Suffolk County, N.Y., 1968-73; FDA Methadone Com.; mem. Nat. Commn. on Marijuana and Drug Abuse, 1971-73; pres. Research Found. Mental Hygiene, Inc., 1976-78; chmn. N.Y. State Drug Abuse Adv. Com., 1980—. Fellow Am. Psychiat. Assn. (life, council 1964-68, chmn. com. nomenclature and statistics 1960-73); mem. AMA (chmn. com. drug dependence and alcoholism 1962-72), Am. Coll. Neuropsychopharmacology (pres. 1969), Internat. Coll. Psychopharmacology, Eastern Psychiat. Research Assn., Am. Psychopath. Assn. (pres. 1972). Home: Box 27 Islip NY 11751

BRILL, NORMAN QUINTUS, physician; b. N.Y.C., Aug. 2, 1911; s. Louis and Ella (Applebaum) B.; m. Doris R. Corcoran, Jan. 21, 1937 (dec. 1968); children—James C., Peter L., Mary C.; m. Alice F. Jennings, May 2, 1970. B.S., Coll. City N.Y., 1930; M.D., N.Y. U., 1934. Practice medicine, specializing in neurology and psychiatry, N.Y.C., 1939-41; pvt. practice, cons. Walter Reed Gen. Hosp., 1946-53; prof., chmn. dept. neurology Georgetown U. Med. Sch., 1946-49; chief research br. neurology and psychiatry div. VA central office, 1946-49; prof. psychiatry U. Calif. Med. Sch., Los Angeles, 1953-79, prof. emeritus, 1979—, chmn. dept., 1953-67; med. supt. Neuropsychiat. Inst., U. Calif. Med. Center, 1953-67; sr. cons. psychiatry Brentwood VA Hosp., Los Angeles, 1953-79, med. educator, 1979—; cons. VA, 1966-70, U.S. Navy Neuropsychiat. Research Unit, 1966-70; cons. in psychiatry USAF, 1962-78; Bd. regents Nat. Library Medicine, 1961-65. Author: Psychiatry in Medicine, 1962, (with other) Treatment of Psychiatric Outpatients, 1967; Contbg. author: Comprehensive Textbook of Psychiatry, 1967, Neuropsychiatry in World War II, I. Zone of Interior, 1966; Chmn. adv. editorial bd.: History of Neuropsychiatry, Med. Dept. U.S. Army, in World War II, 1967; mem. adv. bd.: Internat. Jour. Social Psychiatry; Contbg. author: Readings in Law and Psychiatry, 1968, Compensation for Psychiatric Disorders, 1971, Man for Man, 1971, also numerous articles. Served from capt. to lt. col. M.C. AUS, 1941-46. Decorated Legion of Merit; recipient William C. Porter award Assn. Mil. Surgeons U.S., 1972. Fellow Am. Psychiat. Assn. (com. med. edn., council professions and assns. 1967-75), Soc. Med. Cons. Armed Forces (com. psychiatry), Internat., Am. psychoanalytic assns., Am. Coll. Psychiatrists; mem. AMA (former mem. mental health council), Assn. Mil. Surgeons U.S., Internat., Am. assns. social psychiatry, Am. Coll. Psychoanalysts (pres. 1981—), AAUP, Soc. USAF Psychiatrists, Alpha Omega Alpha. Home: 6911 Oakwood Ave Los Angeles CA 90036

BRILLIANT, RICHARD, art history educator; b. Boston, Nov. 20, 1929; s. Frank and Pauline (Apt) B.; m. Eleanor Luria, June 24, 1951; children: Stephanie, Livia, Franca, Myron. B.A. magna cum laude, Yale U., 1951, Ph.D., 1960; LL.B., Harvard U., 1954. Bar: Mass. bar. From asst. prof. to prof., chmn. dept. art history U. Pa., 1962-70; prof. Columbia U., 1970—; vis. Mellon prof. fine arts U. Pitts., 1971; vis. Lincei prof. Universitá di Pisa, Italy, 1974, 80. Author: Gesture and Rank in Roman Art, 1963, Arch of Septimius Severus in the Roman Forum, 1967, The Arts of the Ancient Greeks, 1973, Roman Art, 1974, Pompeii: A.D. 79, 1979, Visual Narratives, 1983. Fulbright grantee, Rome, Italy, 1957-59; fellow Am. Acad. in Rome, 1960-62; Guggenheim fellow, 1967-68; NEH sr. fellow, 1972-73. Mem. Mass. Bar Assn., Archaeol. Inst. Am., Coll. Art Assn., Am. Numis. Soc., Roman Soc., Hellenic Soc., German Archaeol. Inst. (corr.), Phi Beta Kappa. Democrat. Home: 10 Wayside Ln Scarsdale NY 10583 Office: Dept Art History Columbia New York NY 10027

BRILLINGER, DAVID ROSS, statistician; b. Toronto, Oct. 27, 1937; s. Austin Carlyle and Winnifred Elsie (Simpson) B.; m. Lorie Silber, Dec. 17, 1960; children: Jef Austin, Matthew David. B.A., U. Toronto, 1959; M.A., Princeton U., 1960, Ph.D., 1961. Lectr. math Princeton U. and; mem. tech. staff Bell Labs., 1962-64; lectr. stats. London Sch. Econs., 1964-66, reader, 1966-69; prof. stats. U. Calif., Berkeley, 1970—, chmn. dept., 1979-81. Author: Time Series: Data Analysis and Theory, 1975. Woodrow Wilson fellow, 1959; Bell Telephone Labs. fellow, 1960; Social Sci. Research Council postdoctoral fellow, 1961; Miller prof., 1973; Guggenheim fellow, 1975-76, 82-83. Fellow Am. Statis. Assn., Inst. Math. Stats., AAAS; mem. Internat. Statis. Inst., Inst. Math. Stats., Royal Statis. Soc., Can. Statis. Soc., Seismol. Soc. Am., Bernoulli Soc. Office: Dept Stats U Calif Berkeley CA 94720

BRILOFF, ABRAHAM JACOB, accountant, educator; b. N.Y.C., July 19, 1917; s. Benjamin and Anna (Kaplan) B.; m. Edith A. Moss, Dec. 22, 1940; children: Leonore, Alice. B.B.A., CCNY, 1937, M.S. in Edn., 1941; Ph.D., NYU, 1965; L.H.D. (hon.), SUNY-Binghamton, 1984. C.P.A., N.Y. Tchr. N.Y.C. Pub. Schs., 1937-44; ptnr. Apfel & Englander, C.P.A.s, N.Y.C., 1944-51; propr. Abraham J. Briloff, C.P.A., N.Y.C., 1983—; ptnr. A.J. and L.A. Briloff, N.Y.C., 1983—; mem. faculty Baruch Coll., CUNY, 1966—, prof. accountancy, 1966—, Emanuel Saxe disting. prof. accountancy, 1976—; cons. to govt. Author: Effectiveness of Accounting Communication, 1967, Unaccountable Accounting, 1972, More Debits than Credits, 1976, The Truth About Corporate Accounting, 1981, La Zème Colonne, 1982; contbr.: articles to profl. jours. Recipient disting. service award Baruch Coll. Alumni Assn., 1982, award Fin. Analysts Fedn., 1969, 1970; named disting. alumnus CCNY, 1968, 73, 74. Mem. Am. Inst. C.P.A.s, Am. Acctg. Assn., N.Y. State Soc. C.P.A.s. Democrat. Jewish. Home: 99 Grace Ave Great Neck NY 11021 Office: 17 Lexington Ave New York NY 10010

BRIM, ORVILLE GILBERT, JR., foundation administrator, author; b. Elmira, N.Y., Apr. 7, 1923; s. Orville G(ilbert) and Helen (Whittier) B.; m. Kathleen J. Vigneron, May 30, 1944; children: John G., Scott W., Margaret L., Sarah M. B.A., Yale U., 1947, M.A., 1949, Ph.D. in Sociology, 1951. Instr. sociology U. Wis., 1952-53, asst. prof., 1953-55; sociologist Russell Sage Found., N.Y.C., 1955-64, asst. sec., 1959-64, pres., 1964-72, trustee, 1964-72, cons., 1972-74; pres. Found. for Child Devel., 1974—; chmn. bd. dirs. Automation Engring. Lab., 1959-67; dir. Consumer Behavior, Inc., 1957-61; chmn. environ. panel U.S. Office Edn., 1962-64; mem. drug research bd. Nat. Acad. Scis., 1964-66, adv. com. on child devel., 1971—; mem. mental health tng. com. NIMH, 1959-62; chmn. commn. social scis. NSF, 1968-69; nat. adv. food and drug council HEW, 1967-69; chmn. com. on work and personality in middle years Social Sci. Research Council, 1972-79; vice chmn. Am. Insts. for Research, 1971—; trustee Found. for Child Devel., 1972—, Center for Creative Leadership, 1972-78, Mental Health Law Project, 1973-77, William T. Grant Found., 1975—, Greenwich Hosp., 1972-77. Author: Sociology and the Field of Education, 1958, Education for Child Rearing, 1959, Personality and Decision Processes, 1962, Intelligence, Perspectives, 1965, 66, Socialization after Childhood: Two Essays, 1966, American Beliefs and Attitudes Toward Intelligence, 1969, The Dying Patient, 1970, Learning to Be Parents, 1980; editor: Lifespan Development and Behavior, Vol. 2-6, 1979-83, Constancy and Change in Human Development, 1980; cons. editor: Child Devel., 1958-61, Sociology of Edn., 1963-69, Sociometry, 1959-62; mem. publ. com.: The Public Interest, 1967-75. Served as 1st lt. USAAF, 1943-46. Recipient Wilbur Lucius Cross medal Yale Grad. Sch. Assn., 1975; Kurt Lewin Meml. award Soc. Psychol. Study Social Issues, 1979. Fellow Am. Sociol. Assn., Am. Psychol. Assn., Am. Acad. Arts and Scis., AAAS, Am. Orthopsychiat. Assn. (pres. 1974-75), Eastern Sociol. Soc. (pres. 1971-72); mem. Inst. Medicine of Nat. Acad. Scis., Soc. Research Child Devel., Authors Guild. Club: Century. Home: 164 E 72 St 7A New York NY 10021

BRIMBLE, ALAN, convention bureau executive; b. Langwith, Eng., June 5, 1930; came to U.S., 1967; s. Arthur George and May (Emery) B. B.A. with honors, St. Edmund Hall, Oxford (Eng.) U., 1952, M.A., 1958; fellow, Chartered Inst. Secs. Asst. sec. Crompton Parkinson Ltd., London, 1960-62; music and arts programmes organizer BBC-TV, 1962-67; sec., controller St. Louis Art Mus., 1969-79; dir. adminstrn. Conv. and Visitors Bur. Greater Kansas City, Mo., 1979—. Mem. citizens com. Met. St. Louis Zoo-Mus. Dist., 1970-71; bd. dirs. Internat. Inst., St. Louis, 1970-73, Kansas City Arts Council, 1980—. Served with RAF, 1948-49. Mem. Am. Soc. Assn. Execs., Am. Mgmt. Assn. Home: 800 W Meyer Blvd Kansas City MO 64113 Office: Conv and Visitors Bur Kansas City MO 64105

BRIMELOW, PETER, journalist; b. Warrington, Eng., Oct. 13, 1947; s. Frank Sanderson and Bessie (Knox) B.; m. Margaret Alice Lows, Sept. 20, 1980. B.A. with honors, U. Sussex, Eng., 1970; M.B.A., Stanford U., 1972. Security analyst Richardson Securities of Can., Winnipeg, 1972-73; asst. editor Financial Post, Toronto, 1973-76; bus. editor Maclean's Mag., Toronto, 1976-78; columnist, contbg. editor Fin. Post, 1978-80; assoc. editor Fortune Mag., 1983—; guest editorial bd. Wall St. Jour., 1978; econ. counsel to Senator Orrin Hatch of Utah, 1979-80; asso. editor, Washington columnist Barron's, 1981—. Recipient Fulbright award, 1970; Nat. Bus. Writing award Royal Bank of Canada/Toronto Press Club, 1977; Nat. Bur. Writing citation, 1977, 78. Episcopalian. Office: Fortune Mag Time-Life Bldg Rockefeller Center New York NY 10020

BRIMMER, ANDREW FELTON, economic and financial consultant; b. Newellton, La., Sept. 13, 1926; s. Andrew and Vellar (Davis) B.; m. Doris Millicent Scott, July 18, 1953; 1 dau., Esther Diane. B.A., U. Wash., 1950, M.A., 1951; postgrad. (Fulbright fellow), U. Bombay, India, 1951-52; Ph.D., Harvard U., 1957; LL.D., Nebr. Wesleyan U., 1968, Marquette U., 1968, L.I. U., 1969, Oberlin Coll., 1969, Tufts U., 1970, Colgate U., 1970, Atlanta U., 1970, Middlebury Coll., 1971, U. Notre Dame, 1971, Bishop Coll., 1971, Upsala Coll., 1972, U. Md., 1976, U. Mich., 1979, U. So. Calif., 1980, Washington U., 1982; D.Soc.Sc., Boston Coll., 1971, Temple U., 1974; D.C.L., U. Miami, 1971; D.H.L., DePaul U., 1975. Economist Fed. Res. Bank, N.Y.C., 1955-58; asst. prof. Mich. State U., 1958-61, Wharton Sch. Finance and Commerce, U. Pa., 1961-66; dep. asst. sec. Dept. Commerce, Washington, 1963-65, asst. sec. for econ. affairs, 1965-66; mem. Fed. Res. Bd., 1966-74; Thomas Henry Carroll Ford Found. vis. prof. Grad. Sch. Bus. Adminstrn. Harvard, 1974-76; pres. Brimmer & Co., Inc., Washington, 1976—; bd. govs., vice chmn. Commodity Exchange, Inc.; dir. Bank of Am., Am. Security Bank, Internat. Harvester Co., UAL-United Air Lines, Du Pont Co., Gannett Co., Inc.; mem. Fed. Res. Central Banking Mission to Sudan, 1957; cons. SEC, 1962-63; mem. Trilateral Commn. Author: Survey of Mutual Funds Investors, 1963, Life Insurance Companies in Capital Market, 1962, Economic Development: International and African Perspectives, 1976; Contbr. articles to profl. jours. Chmn. bd. trustees Tuskegee Inst., Com. for Econ. Devel.; mem. vis. com. NYU; co-chmn. Interracial Council for Bus. Opportunity. Served with AUS, 1945-46. Named Govt. Man of Year Nat. Bus. League, 1963; recipient Arthur S. Flemming award, 1966; Russworm award, 1966; Capital Press Club award, 1966; Golden Plate award Am. Acad. Achievement, 1967; Alumnus Summa Laude Dignatus U. Wash. Alumni Assn., 1972; Nat. Honoree Beta Gamma Sigma, 1971; Horatio Alger award, 1974; Equal Opportunity award Nat. Urban League, 1974; One Hundred Black Men and N.Y. Urban Coalition award, 1975. Fellow Am. Acad. Arts and Scis., Nat. Assn. Bus. Economists; mem. Am. Econ. Assn. (Richard T. Ely lectr. 1982), Am. Fin. Assn., Assn. for Study Afro-Am. Life and History (pres. 1970-73), Nat. Economists Club, Council on Fgn. Relations, Am. Statis. Assn. Office: Brimmer & Co Inc 2519 Connecticut Ave NW Washington DC 20008

BRIMMER, CLARENCE ADDISON, judge; b. Rawlins, Wyo., July 11, 1922; s. Clarence Addison and Geraldine (Zingsheim) B.; m. Emily O. Docken, Aug. 2, 1953; children: Geraldine Ann, Philip Andrew, Andrew Howard, Elizabeth Ann. B.A., U. Mich., 1944, J.D., 1947. Bar: Wyo. 1948. Practice in, Rawlins, 1948-71, municipal judge, 1948-54, U.S. commr., magistrate, 1963-71, atty. gen. Wyo., Cheyenne, 1971-74, U.S. atty., 1975, chief U.S. dist. judge Wyo. Dist., Cheyenne, 1975—. Sec. Rawlins Bd. Pub. Utilities, 1954-66, Gov.'s Com. on Wyo. Water, 1963-65; del. Rep. Nat. Conv., 1956; chmn. Wyo. Rep. Platform Com., 1966; sec. Wyo. Rep. Com., 1966, chmn., 1967-71; Rep. gubernatorial candidate, 1974; Trustee Rocky Mountain Mineral Law Found., 1963-75. Episcopalian. Clubs: Masons, Shriners. Home: 1420 W 6th Ave Cheyenne WY 82001 Office: 2308 Federal Bldg Cheyenne WY 82001

BRIMS, JOHN SINCLAIR, foreign service officer; b. Shanghai, China, Dec. 17, 1933; came to naturalized Am. citizen; s. George John and Olga Antonie (Sandbo) B.; m. Dorothy Jeanne O'Connor, May 30, 1959 (div. Jan. 1971); children: Douglas George, Elise Nevin, Kathryn Sinclair; m. Elizabeth Jane Ralston, May 5, 1971; 1 son, David Arthur Graham. A.B., Trinity Coll., Hartford, Conn., 1956; LL.B., Columbia U., 1960. Joined U.S. Fgn. Service, 1962, consul gen., Lahore, Pakistan, 1980-83; dep. chief of mission Am. Embassy, U.S. Fgn. Service, Accra, Ghana, 1983—. Home: 2227 Maricopa Dr Los Angeles CA 90065 Office: US Dept State Accra Washington DC 20520

BRIN, MYRON, biochemist; b. N.Y.C., July 1, 1923; s. Philip and Frances (Kraut) B.; m. Phyllis Bletcher, June 4, 1944; children—Kenneth Philip, Steven Charles, Mitchell Francis. B.S. in Meteorology, N.Y. U., 1945, Cornell U., 1947, M.S., 1948; Ph.D., Harvard U., 1951. Diplomate: Am. Bd. Human Nutrition. Sr. scientist Cancer Research Inst., New Eng. Deaconess Hosp.; instr. biochemistry Tufts Med. Sch., Boston, 1951-53; research fellow Thorndike Lab.; instr. biochemistry Harvard Med. Sch., Boston, 1953-56; chief biologist Food and Drug Research Lab., Inc., Maspeth, N.Y., 1956-58; asso. prof. biochemistry and medicine SUNY, Syracuse, 1958-68; prof. nutrition U. Calif., Davis, 1968-69; dir. clin. nutrition Hoffman-LaRoche, Inc., Nutley, N.J., 1969—; adj. prof. nutrition Cornell U., Columbia; pres. Food and Nutrition Council Met. N.Y., 1976-77. Mem. editorial bd.: Am. Jour. Clin. Nutrition, 1975-77; Contbr. articles to profl. jours. Chmn. Explorer Post in med. sci. Boy Scouts Am., Syracuse, 1964-67. Served with USAAF, 1943-45; ETO. Recipient Cert. of Merit N.Y. State Civil Service Commn., 1965; Research fellow NIH, 1967-68; research grantee NIH, Nat. Vitamin Found., 1958-68. Mem. Am. Inst. Nutrition, Am. Soc. Clin. Nutrition, AAAS, Royal Soc. Medicine (London), Soc. Exptl. Biology, Am. Soc. Biol. Chemists, Am. Inst. Chemists, Am. Chem. Soc., N.Y. Acad. Scis. (A. Cressy Morrison award in natural sci. 1962), Am. Public Health Assn. Home: 30 Wellington Rd Livingston NJ 07039 Office: Hoffman-LaRoche Inc Nutley NJ 07110

BRIN, ROYAL HENRY, JR., lawyer; b. Dallas, Oct. 9, 1919. B.A., U. Tex., 1941, J.D., 1941; postgrad. fellow, Harvard U., 1941-42. Bar: Tex. bar 1941. Atty. OPA, Washington, 1942; asso. firm Strasburger & Price, Dallas, 1946-56, partner, 1956—. Editor-in-chief: Tex. Law Rev, 1940-41; Contbr. articles to profl. jours. Fellow Am. Bar Found.; mem. Am. Bar Assn., State Bar Tex., Tex. Assn. Def. Counsel (pres. 1981-82), Dallas Bar Assn., Dallas Assn. Def. Counsel, Def. Research Inst., Internat. Brotherhood Magicians (pres. 1969-70), Phi Beta Kappa, Phi Eta Sigma. Home: 6506 Lupton Dr Dallas TX 75225 Office: 1200 1 Main Pl Dallas TX 75250

BRINBERG, HERBERT RAPHAEL, publishing company executive; b. N.Y.C., Jan. 27, 1926; s. Henry and Anna (Stambler) B.; m. Blanche Leiman, July 15, 1945; children: Amy Lynn, Todd Michael. A.B., Cornell U., 1947; M.S., Columbia U., 1948; Ph.D., NYU, 1955. Research economist Conf. Bd., 1948-50; cons. economist Boni Watkins, 1951-54; asst. dir. research Licensed Beverage Industries, 1954-55; mgr. econ. research and planning Canco div. Am. Can Co., 1956-61, dir. comml. research, 1961-66, v.p. planning, 1966-71, v.p. info. tech., 1971-78; pres., chief exec. officer Aspen Systems, Rockville, Md., 1978-82, Panel Pubs., Inc., Greenvale, NY, 1982—. Served with USAAF, 1944-45. Mem. Info. Industry Assn. (past chmn.), Associated Info Mgrs. (bd. dirs.). Clubs: Cornell (N.Y.C.); Westchester Country. Office: 330 Madison Ave New York NY 10017

BRINCH HANSEN, PER, computer scientist, consultant; b. Copenhagen, Nov. 13, 1938; s. Jrgen and Elsebeth (Ring) Brinch H.; m. Milena Marija Hrastar, Mar. 27, 1965; children: Mette, Thomas. M.S.E.E., Tech. U. Denmark, 1963, Dr.Techn., 1978. Systems programmer Regnecentralen, Copenhagen, 1963-67, head software devel., 1967-70; research assoc. Carnegie-Mellon U., Pitts., 1970-72; assoc. prof. computer sci. Calif. Inst. Tech., Pasadena, 1972-76; prof. U. So. Calif., Los Angeles, 1976—; cons. Henry Salvatori prof. computer sci., 1982—, cons. Author: RC 4000 Computer and Software, 1969, The Programming Languages: Concurrent Pascal, 1975, Edison, 1981, Operating System Principles, 1973, The Architecture of Concurrent Programs, 1977, Programming a Personal Computer, 1983, also articles. Mem. ACM, IEEE, Internat. Working Group Programming Methodology. Home: 1351 Pleasant Ridge Altadena CA 91001 Office: U So Calif Los Angeles CA 90089

BRINCKERHOFF, SIDNEY BURR, historian; b. N.Y.C., Sept. 27, 1933; s. William Weeks and Marguerite (Hall) B.; children—William, Laura. B.A., Princeton U., 1956; postgrad., U. Ariz., 1963-65. Pres.

Ariz. Publicity Assos., 1959-62; mus. curator Ariz. Hist. Soc., Tucson, 1962-64, asst. dir. for mus., 1964-68, dir., 1968-80, exec. dir., 1980—; chmn. Ariz. Hist. Adv. Commn., 1969-71, State Landmarks Com., 1979—; mem. Ariz. Bicentennial Commn., Ariz. Hist. Records Adv. Commn., 1976—; cons. Ariz. Edn. Dept. Author: Lancers for the King, 1965, Spanish Military Weapons on Colonial America, 1972, Life on the American Nile, 1976; editor: (with Richard C McCormick) Arizona: Its Resources and Prospects, 1967. Chmn. Historic Preservation Task Force, Tucson Tommorrow, 1980; mem. adv. bd. Primavera Sch., 1972-78; bd. govs. Co. of Military Historians, 1976-79. Served with U.S. Army, 1956-59. Mem. Assn. State and Local History, Western History Assn., Am. Assn. Museums, Ariz.-Sonora Desert Mus., Council Abandoned Military Posts, Adobe Corral, The Westerners. Clubs: Old Pueblo, Tucson Racquet. Office: 949 E 2d St Tucson AZ 85718

BRINDEL, JILL RACHUY, cellist; b. Chgo., Jan. 17, 1950; d. Bernard A. and June (Rachuy) B.; m. William Louis Klingelhoffer, July 30, 1972; children: Sarah Brindel, Louis Brindel. Student, Ind. U., 1968-70; B.M. (Tanglewood scholar), Roosevelt U., 1974. Asst. prin. cellist Chgo. Lyric Opera, 1974-76; mem. Chgo. Grant Park Orch., 1974-78; prin. cellist Chgo. Contemporary Chamber Players, 1974-77, Chgo. performances Joffrey Balley, Am. Ballet Theater, N.Y.C. Ballet and Internat. Ballet Festival, 1975-79; mem. Houston Symphony, 1979-80; prin. cellist Joffrey Ballet, San Francisco, 1981; cellist San Francisco Symphony, 1981—; appeared on 5 nationally broadcast chamber concerts Chamber Music Sundaes, 1982; recitalist Chgo. Muscical Coll., ann. 1972-75, 78, North Shore Music Ctr., 1971, Houston, 1978, 79, Old First Series, San Francisco, 1982, 83. Recipient prizes Union Civic League, 1978, William C. Byrd competition, 1976, Chgo. Musical Coll. Concerto competition, 1972, 73, Dumas String award, 1972, Evansville competition, 1972, Crescendo Music Club, 1972, Farwell award, 1972. Mem. Am. Fedn. Musicians. Office: Davies Symphony Hall Van Ness and Hayes Sts San Francisco CA 94102

BRINDLE, JOHN ARTHUR, insurance company executive; b. Manchester, Eng., Dec. 22, 1922; s. Arthur George and Gertrude Ellen (Campbell) B.; m. Muriel Jones, Oct. 30, 1948 (dec.); children: Michael John, Richard David Henry, Helen, Grace Penelope; m. Kathleen Billyard Hawkins, July 9, 1977. Cert., No. U. Sch. Rep. Manchester br. Sun Life Assurance Co., Eng., 1947-53, asst. mgr. Southampton br., 1953, mgr. Manchester central br., 1953-55, asst. mgr. agys., London, 1955-59, mgr. agys., 1959-71, asst. gen. mgr. and mgr. agys., 1971-72, gen. mgr. for Gt. Brit. and Ireland, 1973-75, sr. v.p., gen. mgr. for Gt. Brit. and Ireland, 1975-79, sr. v.p. mktg., Toronto, Ont., Can., 1979, exec. v.p., 1980, pres., dir., 1984—; chief exec. officer, dir. Sun Life Can. Benefit Mgmt. Ltd.; chmn., dir. Suncan Equity Services Co., Sun Life Can. Investment Mgmt. Ltd.; pres., dir. Sun Benefit Services Inc., Sun Growth Variable Annuity Fund Inc.; dir. Sun Life Assurance Co. Can. (U.K.) Ltd., Sun Life Assurance Co. Can. (U.S.), Mass. Fin. Services Co. Served with Royal Tank Reft., 1942-47; Middle East, ETO. Clubs: East India Sports & Pub Schs., Inst. Dirs., Ends of Earth (London); Can. (London, Eng.); Chislehurst Golf (Eng.); Granite (Toronto). Home: 110 Bloor St W Toronto ON Canada M5S 2W7 Office: Sun Life Assurance Co Can 150 King St W Toronto ON Canada M5W 2C9

BRINEGAR, GEORGE KENNETH, agricultural economics educator; b. Bloomfield, Iowa, Jan. 5, 1918; s. George H. and Cora O. (Clouse) B.; m. Joan Barlow, Oct. 23, 1948; children: George, Charles, John, Willard. B.S., Ill. State U., 1940; postgrad., London Sch. Econs., 1945; M.S., U. Chgo., 1948, Ph.D., 1953. Prof. agrl. econs. U. Conn., 1948-60; prof. U. Ill., 1960—, asst. dir., 1963-66, assoc. dean, 1968—, dir., 1968-69, 1968-83; vis. prof. U. Sydney, Australia; cons. in field. Assoc. editor: Jour. of Farm Economics, 1955-58; contbr. in field. Mem. Sch. Bd., Mansfield, Conn., 1957-60. Served with U.S. Army, 1942-46. Mem. Am. Farm Econ. Assn., Am. Econ. Assn., Assn. U.S. Univ. Dirs. Internat. Agrl. Programs, Pi Gamma Mu, Kappa Phi Kappa, Omicron Delta Gamma, Gamma Sigma Delta, Pi Kappa Delta. Home: 1507 Maplecrest Dr Champaign IL 61820 Office: 352 Momford Hall 1301 W Gregory Dr Urbana IL 61801

BRINGHAM, WILLIAM TALBERT, fraternal organization executive; b. Normal, Ill., Dec. 16, 1924; s. Russell Wilson and Sarah E. (Talbert) B.; m. Ruth Irene Jaeger, Jan. 10, 1947; 1 son, William Talbert. Ph.B., Ill. Wesleyan U., 1948; J.D., Vanderbilt U., 1951; grad. trust devel. sch., Northwestern U. Sch. Commerce, 1953. Spl. agt. FBI, 1951-52; exec. sec. Sigma Chi frat., Wilmette, Ill., 1954—; exec. dir. Sigma Chi Found., 1956—, also sec.; sec. bd. grand trustees Sigma Chi; exec. v.p., sec., exec. com., sec. grand council Sigma Chi Corp.; bd. dirs. Nat. Interfrat. Found., Found. ASAE. Author: booklet on alumni chpts. Sigma Chi; chmn. editorial com.: Visitation Manuel for College Fraternities. Del. Ill. Republican Conv.; committeeman Northfield Twp. Rep. Com.; del. Sch. Bd. Caucus; past chmn. Police Commn., Wilmette.; mem. corp. Kendall Coll.; past trustee, City of Wilmette. Served with USNR, 1942-46. Recipient Significant Sig and Order of Constantine awards Sigma Chi, 1975. Mem. Am. Personnel and Guidance Assn., Am. Soc. Assn. Execs. (Key award 1973, mem. awards com.; dir. Found.), Chgo. Soc. Assn. Execs. (v.p.), Wilmette Hist. Soc., Evanston Hist. Soc., Travelers Protective Assn., Am. Legion, Frat. Execs. Assn. (pres., exec. com.), Evanston C. of C. (past dir.), Chgo. Soc. Assn. Execs. (dir.), SAR, Phi Delta Phi. Clubs: Masons (33 deg.), Shriners, KT, Kiwanis (past pres.), Royal Order of Scotland; Univ. (Evanston) (pres.); Westmoreland Country (Wilmette, Ill.)). Address: 4020 Bunker Ln Wilmette IL 60091

BRINGS, LAWRENCE MARTIN, publisher; b. St. Paul, Sept. 29, 1897; s. Lee Brings and Bertha (Haugen) B.; m. Ethel Mattson, Aug. 26, 1921 (dec.); 1 son, Keith; m. Nettie A. Johnson, Jan. 9, 1961. A.B., Gustavus Adolphus Coll., 1920, A.M., 1925. High sch. tchr., 1920- 21; head dept. speech No. State Tchrs. Coll., Aberdeen, S.D., 1921- 23; instr. speech U. Minn., 1923-26; pres., dir. dept. oratory Mpls. Sch. Music, Oratory and Dramatic Art, 1923-25; prof. speech Luther Theol. Sem., St. Paul, 1923-46, Northwestern Theol. Sem., Mpls., 1925-49; founder, pres. Northwestern Coll. Speech Arts, Mpls., 1926-51, Northwestern Press, 1926—, T.S. Denison & Co., 1944—, Brings Press, 1951-77, Denison Yearbook Co., 1952-76; dir. Graphic Arts Cons. Service, 1977—; lectr., dramatic reader. Compiler, editor: numerous books, most recent being Minnesota Heritage, 1960, One-Act Dramas and Contest Plays, 1962, Rehearsal-less Skits and Plays, 1964, Gay Nineties Melodramas, 1963, Golden Book of Christmas Plays, 1963, What God Hath Wrought, 1969. Pres. Minn. Protestant Found., Central Luth. Ch. Found.; pres. Golden Valley Coll. Found.; regent emeritus Golden Valley Luth. Coll., Count Folke Bernadotte Meml. Found. Served in U.S. Army, World War I. Mem. USCG League, Internat. Platform Assn., Nat. Assn. Tchrs. Speech, Nat. Thespian Dramatic Soc. (hon.), Am. Legion, Phi Kappa Delta, Phi Beta (hon.). Republican. Lutheran. Clubs: Mason (32 deg., Shriner), Rotary, Mpls. Auto, Minnetonka Country. Home: 4350 Brookside Ct Minneapolis MN 55436 also 961 Antigua Ave Bay Indies Park Venice FL 33595 Office: 9601 Newton Ave S Minneapolis MN 54431

BRINK, DAVID RYRIE, lawyer; b. Mpls., July 28, 1919; s. Raymond Woodard and Carol Sybil (Ryrie) B.; m. Lucile Adams, June 22, 1974; children: Anne Carol, Mary Brink Maguire, David Owen, Sarah Jane. B.A., U. Minn., 1940, B.S.L., 1941, J.D. with honors, 1941; LL.D., Capital U., 1981, Suffolk U., 1981, Mitchell Coll. Law, 1982. Bar: Minn. 1947, U.S. Dist. Ct. Minn. 1947, U.S. Tax Ct. 1967, U.S. Supreme Ct. 1980, U.S. Ct. Appeals (D.C. Cir.) 1982. Assoc. firm Dorsey & Whitney, Mpls., 1947-53, partner, 1953—, head Washington office, 1982—; trustee Lawyer's Com. Civil Rights Under Law, 1978-81; bd. dirs. Nat. Legal Aid and Defender Assn., 1978-80; bd. visitors U. Minn. Law Sch., 1978-81. Bd. editors: U. Minn. Law Rev, 1941-42; contbr. numerous articles on probate, estate taxation and personal income taxation to law jours. Served to lt. comdr. USNR, 1943-46. Recipient Outstanding Achievement award U. Minn., 1982. Fellow Am. Coll. Probate Counsel (regent, exec. com.); mem. Am. Bar Assn. (gov. 1974-77, 80-83, pres. 1981-82), Fund for Public Edn. of Am. Bar Assn. (pres. 1981-82), Am. Bar Found. (state chmn. 1977-80, gov. 1980-83), Am. Bar Retirement Assn. (pres. 1976-77), Am. Judicature Soc., Nat. Conf. Bar Presidents, Inst. Jud. Adminstrn., Am. Arbitration Assn. (trustee 1981—), Minn. Bar Assn. (pres. 1978-79), Internat. Mgmt. and Devel. Inst., Hennepin County Bar Assn. (pres. 1967-68), Nat. Legal Aid and Defender Assn. Club: Minneapolis. Home: 2301 Connecticut Ave NW Washington DC 20008 Office: 1800 M St NW Washington DC 20036

BRINK, JOHN WILLIAM, company executive; b. Chgo., July 14, 1945; s. M.W. and Alice L. (Nelson) B.; m. Cynthia Hollowell, 1981; children: Bethany, Peter. B.B.A., U. Wis., 1967; M.B.A., W. Tex. State U., 1970. Comml. lending officer Huntington Nat. Bank of Columbus, Ohio, 1970-72; asst. treas. Peabody Internat., Galion, Ohio, 1972-75; v.p., treas. Avis, Inc., N.Y.C., 1975-82, Savin Corp., Valhalla, N.Y., 1983—; faculty Franklin U. Gen. Evening Coll., Columbus, 1971-75. Served with AUS, 1968-70. Mem. Am. Mgmt. Assn. (fin. div. council 1978—). Clubs: Union League, Cherry Valley Country. Office: Savin Corp Valhalla NY 10595

BRINK, MARION FRANCIS, association executive; b. Golden Eagle, Ill., Nov. 20, 1932; s. Anton Frank and Agnes Gertrude B. B.S., U. Ill., 1955, M.S., 1958; Ph.D., U. Mo., 1961. Research biologist U.S. Naval Radiol. Def. Lab., San Francisco, 1961-62; assoc. dir. div. nutrition research Nat. Dairy Council, Chgo., 1962-65, dir. div. nutrition research, 1965-70, pres., Rosemont, Ill., 1970—; vice chmn. human nutrition adv. com. U.S. Dept. Agr., 1980-81. Contbr. articles to prof. jours. Recipient citation of merit U. Mo. Alumni Assn. Mem. AAAS, Am. Dairy Sci. Assn., Am. Inst. Nutrition, Am. Soc. Assn. Execs., Am. Soc. Clin. Nutrition, Animal Nutrition Research Council, Dairy Assn. Execs. Conf., Dairy Shrine Club, Dairy Soc. Internat., Nutrition Soc., Nutrition Today Soc., Chgo. Nutrition Assn., Sigma Xi, Alpha Tau Alpha, Gamma Sigma Delta. Office: 6300 N River Rd Rosemont IL 60018

BRINK, ROYAL ALEXANDER, educator; b. Woodstock, Ont., Can., Sept. 16, 1897; came to U.S., 1920, naturalized, 1933; s. Royal Wilson and Elizabeth Ann (Cuthbert) B.; m. Edith Margaret Whitelaw, Dec. 27, 1922 (dec. May 1962); children: Andrew Whitelaw, Margaret Alexandra; m. Joyce Hickling, Oct. 19, 1963. B.S.A., Ont. Agrl. Coll., 1919; M.S., U. Ill., 1921; D.Sc., Harvard, 1923; postgrad. (NRC fellow), Institut für Vererbungsforschung, Berlin, U. Birmingham, 1925-26, Calif. Inst. Tech., 1938-39. Chemist Western Can. Flour Mills, Winnipeg, Man., Can., 1919-20; Emerson fellow in biology Harvard, 1921-22; asst. prof. of genetics U. Wis., 1922-27, assoc. prof., 1929-31, prof., 1931-68, emeritus prof. genetics, 1968—, chmn. dept., 1939-51. Editor: Heritage from Mendel, 1967; mng. editor: Genetics, 1952-56; Contbr. numerous research papers to biol. jours. Haight Travelling fellow U. Wis., 1960-61; NSF Sr. Postdoctorate fellow, 1966-67. Fellow AAAS; mem. Am. Genetics Assn., Genetics Soc. Am. (pres. 1957), Bot. Soc. Am., Am. Acad. Arts and Scis., Am. Soc. Naturalists (pres. 1963), Nat. Acad. Scis., Wis. Acad. of Scis., Arts and Letters, Sigma Xi (pres. Wis. chpt. 1940-41), Phi Sigma, Phi Eta. Club: University. Home: 4237 Manitou Way Madison WI 53711

BRINK, WILLIAM JOSEPH, JR., ret. editor; b. Indpls., Feb. 29, 1916; s. William Joseph and Emma Elizabeth (Schell) B.; m. Jenny Lou Dwyer, May 24, 1947; children—Timothy, John, William Allen, Robert. B.A., Ind. U., 1940. With U.P.I., Detroit, Chgo., 1945-55, night mgr., Chgo., 1950-55; writer nat. affairs, gen. editor Newsweek mag., N.Y.C., 1956-63, sr. editor, 1963-69; asst. mng. editor N.Y. Daily News, 1969-74, mng. editor, 1974-81, v.p., 1976-81; Pres. N.Y. News Charities, Inc., 1977-80. Author: (with Louis Harris) The Negro Revolution in America, 1962, Black and White, 1966. Served with USAF, 1942-45; MTO. Decorated Air medal with oak leaf cluster. Mem. Am. Soc. Newspaper Editors, Sigma Delta Chi. Home: 11 Birchwood Ln Westport CT 06880

BRINK, WILLIAM P., clergyman; b. Chgo., Sept. 21, 1916; s. Paul W. and Cora (Wagenaar) B.; m. Alta Mae Ibershof, July 25, 1941; children: Paul W., Esther Jean (Mrs. Cornelius A. Leugs), John H., Daniel Jay, Stephen Robert. B.A., Calvin Coll., 1938; B.Th., Calvin Sem., 1941. Ordained to ministry Christian Ref. Ch., 1941; pastor Goshen (Ind.) Christian Ref. Ch., 1941-44, Archer Ave. Christian Ref. Ch., Chgo., 1944-48, Creston Christian Ref. Ch., Grand Rapids, Mich., 1948-53, Bethany Christian Ref. Ch., Holland, Mich., 1953-64, 2d Christian Ref. Ch., Fremont, Mich., 1964-70; stated clk. Christian Ref. Ch., 1970-83; Pres. Young Calvinist Fedn. N. Am., 1958-70, Gen. Synod Christian Reformed Ch., 1966, 69. Author: Learning Doctrine from the Bible, 1965; co-author: Manual of Christian Reformed Church Government, 1979; editor: Acts of Synod, Christian Reformed Church, 1971-82, Yearbook Christian Ref. Ch, 1971-82. Address: 5305 Queensbury Dr SE Grand Rapids MI 49508

BRINKER, JOHN HENRY, JR., industrial equipment company executive; b. Cleve., May 31, 1914; s. John Henry and Marion (Crawford) B.; m. Virginia Grosvenor Bryant, Feb. 10, 1940; children—Ann Grosvenor, Lynn Crawford, John Henry. A.B., U. Rochester, 1936; M.B.A. with high distinction, Harvard U., 1947. Sales engr. Pfaulder Co., Rochester, N.Y., 1937-42; gen. sales mgr., dir. mktg. A.O. Smith Corp., Milw., 1947-55, gen. mgr., 1955-59, v.p. corp., 1957, v.p. mktg., Chgo., 1965-71; pres., dir. A.O. Smith Corp. Tex., Houston, 1971-72; pres. A.O. Smith-Harvestore Products, Inc., Arlington Heights, Ill., 1972-77, chmn. bd., 1977—; exec. v.p., dir. J.I. Case Co., Racine, Wis., 1959-60; exec. v.p. Cherry Burrell Corp., 1960-64; pres. Glascote Products, Inc., Cleve., 1964-65; dir. Howard-Harvestore Ltd., Harleston, Eng., First Bank & Trust Co., Arlington Heights, Ill. Chmn. fund appeal St. Mary's Hosp., 1956; Trustee U. Rochester. Served from ensign to lt. comdr. USNR, 1942-46. Mem. Ill. C. of C. (dir.). Presbyterian. (elder). Clubs: Chicago; Ramada (Houston). Home: 170 April Waters W Montgomery TX 77356

BRINKER, NORMAN EUGENE, restaurant company executive; b. Denver, June 3, 1931; s. Eugene Chatsworth and Katheryn Bess (Payne) B.; m. Maureen Connolly, June 11, 1955 (dec.); children: Cynthia Ann, Brenda Lee, Christina Magrit, Mark Norman. B.A., San Diego State Coll., 1957. Gen. ops. mgr. Foodmaker Co., 1957-63; chmn. bd., chief exec. officer Steak and Ale Restaurants of Am., Inc., Dallas, 1965-83, Chili's, Inc., 1983—; with Pillsbury Co., from 1976, exec. v.p., until 1983, also dir.; pres. Pillsbury Restaurant Group, until 1983; chmn. Burger King Corp., 1982-83; dir. Burger Kings, Inc, 1st Nat. Bank in Dallas. Bd. dirs. Dallas Civic Opera, Dallas Symphony Orch., Mus. Fine Arts, Dallas Assembly; trustee Children's Med. Center, Dallas; mem. adv. council St. Paul's Hosp.; mem. Mayors Blue Ribbon panel on unemployment, Dallas Community Relations Commn. Served with USNR, 1950-54. Named Entrepreneur of Year So. Meth. U., 1974; recipient Disting. Bus. Leadership award U. Tex., Arlington, 1979; named Humanitarian of Year, 1979. Mem. Texx Restaurant Assn., Young Pres. Orgn., Dallas C. of C. (dir.). Republican. Home: 5910 Westgrove Dallas TX 75248 Office: PO Box 222102 Dallas TX 75222 *

BRINKER, WADE OBERLIN, veterinarian, emeritus educator; b. Fulton, Ohio, Oct. 11, 1912; s. Frank Leroy and Elma (Oberlin) B.; m. Eleanor Bayles, May 29, 1939; children: Gerald, Judith, Jack. D.V.M., Kans. State Coll., 1939; M.S., Mich. State U., 1947. With Coll. Vet. Medicine, Mich. State U., East Lansing, 1939—, prof., head dept. surgery and medicine, 1957-67, prof. dept. small animal surgery and medicine, 1967-76, prof. emeritus, 1976—. Author: (with others) Canine Surgery, 1952, rev., 1965, 74, Small Animal Orthopedics and Fracture Treatment, 1983, Manual of Internal Fixation in Small Animals, 1983. Served from 1st lt. to capt., Vet. Corps AUS, 1941-46. Recipient Distinguished Service award, 1959, Centennial award for distinguished service Kans. State U., 1963; Distinguished Faculty award Mich. State U., 1969. Mem. AVMA (award 1959), Mich. Vet. Med. Assn. (pres. 1954-55), Conf. Research Workers N. Am., Vet. Orthopedic Soc. (pres. 1974-76), Am. Coll. Vet. Surgeons (pres. 1968-69), Sigma Xi, Phi Kappa Phi, Phi Zeta. Home: 734 W Grand River Okemos MI 48864

BRINKERHOFF, DERICKSEN MORGAN, art history educator; b. Phila., Oct. 4, 1921; s. Robert Joris and Marion (Butler) B.; m. Mary Dean Weston, Dec. 20, 1946; children: Derick W., Elizabeth, Jonathan D., Caroline. A.B., Williams Coll., 1943; M.A., Yale U., 1947; postgrad., U. Zurich, Switzerland, 1948-49; Ph.D., Harvard U., 1958. Teaching fellow Harvard U., 1949-50; instr. Brown U., 1952-55; asso. prof., head history dept. R.I. Sch. Design, 1955-59, chmn. div. liberal arts, 1956-59; asso. prof. Pa. State U., 1961-62, Tyler Sch. Art, Temple U., Phila., 1962-1965; chmn. dept. art U. Calif. at Riverside, 1965-71, 80—, prof., 1967—. Author monographs on classical and early medieval art; contbr. articles to profl. jours. Trustee Riverside Art Assn., 1968-72. Served with AUS, World War II. Recipient U. Calif. Humanities Inst. award, 1971-72; Summer fellow Belgian Am. Ednl. Found., 1959; sr. fellow classical studies Am. Acad. in Rome, 1959-61; Am. Philos. Soc. grantee, 1960-61. Mem. Am. Numis. Soc. (500 prize seminar 1952), Archaeol. Inst. Am., Art Historians So. Calif. (pres. 1982-83), Coll. Art Assn. Am., Internat. Assn. Classical Archaeology. Home: 4985 Chicago Ave Riverside CA 92507

BRINKERHOFF, JAMES DONALD, manufacturing company executive; b. Merced, Calif., Apr. 22, 1930; s. Joris M. and Margaret (Duncan) B.; m. Patricia O'Keeffe, Jan. 7, 1978; children: J. Vance, Scott R., Lynn Ann. B.S., U. Calif.-Berkeley, 1955, M.B.A., 1955; A.M.P., Harvard U., 1976. Econ. analyst Standard Oil Co. of Calif., San Francisco, 1956-62; mgr. land resources planning Kern County Land Co. subs. Tenneco, San Francisco, 1962-69; fin. v.p. U.S. Natural Resources, Menlo Park, Calif., 1969-72; spl. asst. to chmn. ACF Industries, Inc., N.Y.C., 1972; asst.gen. mgr.leasing ops. div. Shippers Car Line, St. Louis, 1972-73, v.p., gen. mgr. div., 1973-76, sr. v.p. corp., N.Y.C., 1976-83, pres., dir., 1983—. Served with USN, 1948, 51-52. Mem. Nat. Freight Transp. Assn., Am. Petroleum Inst., Soc. Petroleum Engrs. Republican. Club: Sky (N.Y.C.). Office: ACF Industries Inc 750 3d Ave New York NY 10017

BRINKERHOFF, PHILIP RICHARD, financial institution executive; b. Wilmington, N.C., Apr. 2, 1943; s. James Marcus and Billie Lou (Benson) B.; m. Janice Swenson, June 11, 1968; children: Kimberly, Adam, Jennica, Allison, Mark. Student, U. So. Calif., 1960-61, San Fernando Valley State Coll., 1961-62; B.S., Brigham Young U., 1966; J.D., Harvard U., 1969. Bar: Ariz. 1970, U.S. Supreme Ct. 1977. Asso. firm Streich, Lang, Weeks, Cardon and French, Phoenix, 1969-73; v.p., gen. counsel Fed. Home Loan Mortgage Corp., Washington, 1973-75, exec. v.p., chief adminstrv. officer, 1975-77, pres., chief exec. officer, 1977-82; pres., chief operating officer 1st Charter Fin. Corp., Beverly Hills, Calif., 1982—, pres., chief exec. officer, 1982—; dir., mem. exec. com. AMMINET, Inc., 1974-78. Mem. Phi Kappa Phi. Mormon. Home: 745 25th Stn Ct Santa Monica CA 90402 Office: First Charter Financial Corp 9465 Wilshire Blvd Beverly Hills CA 90212 *One of the guiding principles of my life has been a substantial commitment to the establishment of priorities which regulate the use of my time and energy. This has helped me achieve what I believe to be an appropriate and desirable balance among the three major time consumptive elements of my life-my family, church and professional career. It has also assisted me in allocating blocks of time for physical and mental development. I believe that without this setting of priorities and striving for balance, any of these activities could overwhelm the others, to the great detriment of my personal and family goals.*

BRINKHOUS, KENNETH MERLE, pathologist, emeritus educator; b. Clayton County, Iowa, May 29, 1908; s. William and Ida (Voss) B.; m. Frances E. Benton, Sept. 5, 1936; children: William Kenneth, John Robert. Student, U.S. Mil. Acad., 1925; A.B., State U. Iowa, 1929, M.D., 1932; D.Sc., U. Chgo., 1967. Asst. in pathology State U. Iowa, 1932-33, instr., 1933-35, asso. in pathology, 1935-37, asst. prof., 1937-45, asso. prof., 1945-46; prof. pathology U. N.C., Chapel Hill, 1946-61, alumni distinguished prof., 1961-80, emeritus, 1980—; Mem. Nat. Adv. Heart and Lung Council, 1969-74; chmn. med. adv. council Nat. Hemophilia Found., 1954-73; sec. gen. Internat. Com. Hemostasis and Thrombosis, 1966-78. Bd. editors: Perspectives in Biol. Medicine, 1968—; editor: Archives Pathology and Lab. Medicine, 1974—, Yearbook Pathology Clin. Pathology, 1980—. Served from capt. to lt. col. M.C. U.S. Army, 1941-46; col. Med. Res. Corps, 1946—. Co-recipient Ward Burdick award Am. Soc. Clin. Pathologists, 1941; recipient same, 1963, O. Max Gardner award, 1961; N.C. award, 1969; Internat. Heart Research award, 1969; Murray Thelin award Nat. Hemophilia Found., 1972; Distinguished Achievement award Modern Medicine, 1973; H.P. Smith lectr., 1974. Mem. Nat. Acad. Scis. Inst. of Medicine, Am. Acad. Arts and Scis., Assn. Am. Physicians, Internat. Soc. Thrombosis and Haemostasis (pres. 1971), Am. Assn. Pathologists and Bacteriologists (sec., treas. 1968-71, pres. 1973), Am. Soc. Exptl. Pathology (pres. 1965-66), Fedn. Am. Socs. Exptl. Biology (pres. 1966-67), Univs. Asso. Research and Edn. Pathology (pres. 1964-68). Home: 524 Dogwood Dr Chapel Hill NC 27514

BRINKLEY, DAVID, news commentator; b. Wilmington, N.C., July 10, 1920; s. William Graham and Mary (West) B.; m. Ann Fischer, Oct. 11, 1946; children: Alan, Joel, John; m. Susan Adolph, June 10, 1972. Reporter Wilmington (N.C.) Star-News, 1938-41; reporter, bur. mgr. United Press Assns., various So. cities, 1941-43; news writer, broadcaster radio and TV NBC, Washington, 1943—, Washington corr., 1951-81; anchorman ABC This Week, 1981—. Recipient duPont award, Peabody award, Sch. Bell award, other journalism awards. Club: Cosmos (Washington). Office: ABC News 1717 DeSales St NW Washington DC 20036

BRINKLEY, JACK THOMAS, former congressman; b. Faceville, Ga., Dec. 22, 1930; s. Lonnie Elester and Pauline (Spearman) B.; m. Alma Lois Kite, May 29, 1955; children: Jack Thomas, Fred Alen II. Student, Young Harris Coll., 1947-49, Okla. A. and M. Coll., 1952; LL.B. cum laude, U. Ga., 1959. Bar: Ga. 1958, D.C. 1973. Sch. tchr., Ga., 1949-51; asso. firm Young, Hollis & Moseley, Columbus, Ga., 1959-61; partner firm Coffin & Brinkley, Columbus, 1961-66; sr. ptnr. Brinkley and Dugan, 1983—; mem. Ga. Ho. of Reps., 1965-66, 90th-

97th congresses from 3d dist. Ga. Fund raising chmn. Muscogee-Chattahoochee chpt. Nat. Found., 1966, Ga. vol. chmn., 1968; mem. adv. com. to bd. dirs. Met. Columbus Urban League; adv. bd. nat. No Greater Love Com. MIA, 1971; mem. nat. adv. bd. Young Ams. for Freedom; hon. com. Citizens for Decency through Law. Served to 1st lt. USAF, 1951-56. Mem. Ga. Bar Assn., Columbus Bar Assn., D.C. Bar Assn., Younger Lawyers Club of Columbus (pres. 1963-64), Am. Legion, Blue Key, Gideons, Civitan. Democrat. Baptist. Club: Mason.

BRINKLEY, JOEL GRAHAM, editor, journalist; b. Washington, July 22, 1952; s. David McClure and Ann B. A.B., U. N.C., 1975. Reporter AP, 1975, Richmond (Va.) News Leader, 1975-78, Louisville Courier-Jour., 1978-83, editor, 1983—; freelance writer for mags., 1976—. Recipient (Investigative Reporters and Editors grand prize for newspaper reporting 1982, Nat. Clarion award for human rights reporting 1982, Nat. Headliner award for pub. service reporting 1983, William S. Miller award for enterprise reporting 1983). Recipient Pulitzer prize internat. reporting, 1980; 2d prize Scripps-Howard Found.; Roy W. Howard award for pub. service reporting, 1981, 82; grand prize Nat. Consumer Reporting Awards Nat. Press Club, 1981, 83; named Nat. Citizen of Yr. Nat. Assn. Social Workers, 1981. Home: 1334 Cherokee Rd Louisville KY 40204 Office: Courier-Jour 525 W Broadway Louisville KY 40202

BRINKLEY, JOSEPH WILLARD, association executive; b. Portsmouth, Va., May 8, 1926; s. Joseph C. and Iola (Rountree) B.; m. Virginia Wren Northcott, Aug. 14, 1955. A.B., Coll. William and Mary, 1950; student, U. Wis., 1945; M.P.A., NYU, 1972. Asst. to treas. Colonial Williamsburg Found., Williamsburg, Va., 1952-61; dir. Exile Political Affairs Free Europe Com., N.Y.C., 1961-63; broadcast analysis Radio Free Europe, Munich, Germany, 1963-67; v.p. Radio Free Europe Fund, N.Y.C., 1966-67, Am. Farm Sch., Greece, 1967-70; sec.-treas. Alfred P. Sloan Found., N.Y.C., 1970-71; comptroller The Asia Soc., N.Y.C., 1971-74; asso. exec. dir. The Light House, N.Y. Assn. for the Blind, 1974-78; dep. gen. dir. Community Service Soc., N.Y.C., 1978-83; fin. devel. cons., 1970—. Treas. UN Observor, 1978—; bd. dirs., sec.-treas. Am. Friends of Brit. Aldeborough Festival; bd. dirs., treas. Early Music Found., 1982—. Served with USNR, 1944-46. Recipient Jaycees Disting. Service award, 1957. Fellow Met. Opera Guild; mem. Soc. Internat. Devel., Acad. Polit. Sci., Fgn. Service Assn., N.Y. Oratorio Soc. (trustee, mem. exec. com. 1970—, pres. 1973), Nat. Student Nurses Assn. (trustee), N.Y. Soc. Assn. Execs. (dir., treas. 1979). Republican. Clubs: Kiwanis (v.p. 1959-60), Masons, University. Home: 300 E 40th St New York NY 10016 also 707 Powell St Williamsburg VA 23185

BRINKLEY, WILLIAM CLARK, author; b. Custer, Okla., Sept. 10, 1917; s. Daniel Squire and Ruth (Clark) B. Student, William Jewell Coll., 1936-37; B.A., U. Okla., 1940; spl. student, Yale Drama Sch., 1961-62. Reporter Daily Oklahoman, Oklahoma City, 1940-41, Washington Post, 1941-42, 49-51; successively corr., asst. editor, staff writer Life mag., 1951-58. Author: Quicksand, 1948, The Deliverance of Sister Cecilia, 1954, Don't Go Near the Water, 1956, The Fun House, 1961, The Two Susans, 1962, The Ninety and Nine, 1966, Breakpoint, 1978, Peeper, 1981. Served to lt. USNR, 1942-46. Mem. Phi Beta Kappa. Club: Nat. Press (Washington). Address: 500 Wichita St No 79 McAllen TX 78501

BRINKMAN, FRED JOHN, educational consultant; b. Warrenville, Ill., Sept. 13, 1917; s. Fred William and Grace Mae (Stafford) B.; m. Ruth Anderson, June 11, 1946; children: Carol Ann, Robert John. B.V.E., Calif. State U., Los Angeles, 1954, M.A., 1956; Ed.D., UCLA, 1970. Tchr. Frank Wiggins Trade Sch., 1948-49; instr. Los Angeles Trade-Tech. Coll., 1949-55, coordinator, 1955-60, asst. dean, 1960-66, dean, 1966-69, pres., 1969-76; asst. to chancellor Los Angeles Community Coll. Dist., 1976-79; Mem. City Econ. Devel. Bd., Los Angeles, 1969-77; mem. indsl. edn. adv. com. Calif. State U., Los Angeles, 1970-77. Served with USN, 1939-45. Recipient Outstanding Educator award chpt. 27 Soc. Mfg. Engrs., 1974. Mem. Am. Vocat. Assn. (mem. policy com., com. on postsecondary edn.), Calif. Vocat. Assn., Am. Tech. Edn. Assn., Rio Hondo Power Squadron, Assn. Los Angeles/Long Beach Harbor Yacht Clubs (staff commodore), Phi Delta Kappa, Epsilon Pi Tau. Club: Cabrillo Beach Yacht (staff commodore). Home: PO Box 1490 Downey CA 90240

BRINKMAN, GABRIEL, former college president; b. Indpls., Dec. 3, 1924; s. John Henry and Mary Frances (Bartsch) B. Student, Our Lady of Angels Sem., 1943-47, St. Joseph Sem., 1947-51; Ph.D. in Sociology, Cath. U. Am., 1957. Instr. ethics Our Lady of Angels Sem., Cleve., 1955-57; mem. faculty dept. sociology Quincy (Ill.) Coll., 1957-63, prof., 1970-77, pres. coll., 1963-70, 77-83. Author: Social Thought of John de Luga, 1957. Roman Catholic. Office: Quincy Coll Quincy IL 62301

BRINKMAN, JOHN ANTHONY, historian, educator; b. Chgo., July 4, 1934; s. Adam John and Alice (Davies) B.; m. Monique E. Geschier, Mar. 24, 1970; 1 son, Charles E. A.B., Loyola U., Chgo., 1956, M.A., 1958; Ph.D., U. Chgo., 1962. Research asso. Oriental Inst., U. Chgo., 1963, dir. inst., 1972-81, asst. prof. Assyriology and ancient history, 1964-66, asso. prof., 1966-70, prof., 1970—, chmn. dept., 1969-72; ann. prof. Am. Schs. Oriental Research, Baghdad, 1968-69; chmn. Baghdad Schs. Com., 1970—, mem. exec. com., 1973-75, 82—, chmn. exec. com., 1973-75, trustee, 1975—. Author: Political History of Post-Kassite Babylonia, 1968, Materials and Studies for Kassite History, Vol. I, 1976; editorial bd.: Chgo. Assyrian Dictionary, 1977—; mem. staff, 1963—; editor-in-charge Babylonian sect.: Royal Inscriptions of Mesopotamia, 1979—; contbr. numerous articles to profl. jours. Fellow Am. Research Inst., in Turkey, 1971; sr. fellow Nat. Endowment Humanities, 1973-74; Guggenheim fellow, 1984-85. Fellow Am. Council Learned Socs.; mem. Am. Oriental Soc. (pres. Middle West br. 1971-72), Brit. Inst. Persian Studies, Brit. Sch. Archaeology in Iraq, Deutsche Orient Gesellschaft, Brit. Inst. Archaeology at Ankara, Am. Council Learned Socs. fellow. Roman Catholic. Home: 5535 S University Ave Chicago IL 60637 Office: 1155 E 58th St Chicago IL 60637

BRINKMAN, PAUL DEL(BERT), university dean, journalism educator; b. Olpe, Kans., Feb. 10, 1937; s. Paul Theodore and Delphine Barbara (Brown) B.; m. Evelyn Marie Lange, Aug. 5, 1961; children: Scott Michael, Susan Lynn. B.S., Emporia State Coll., 1958; M.A. in Journalism (Newspaper Fund fellow), Ind. U., 1963; Ph.D. in Mass Communications (Scripps-Howard fellow), Ind. U., 1971. Editor, reporter Emporia Gazette, Emporia, Kans., 1954-59; instr. journalism Leavenworth (Kans.) High Sch., 1959-62; lectr. Ind. U., Bloomington, 1962-65, 68-70; asst. prof. Kans. State U., Manhattan, 1965-68; prof., dean Sch. Journalism, U. Kans., Lawrence, 1970—. Bd. dirs. William Allen White Found., 1974; chmn. Big Eight Athletic Conf., 1980-81; faculty rep. Nat. Collegiate Athletic Assn., 1978—. Mem. Am. Assn. Schs. and Depts. Journalism (pres. 1977-78), Inland Daily Press Assn. (chmn. edn. com. 1980-83), Assn. Edn. Journalism (chmn. publs. com. 1974-75, pres. 1980-81), Soc. Profl. Journalists, Lawrence C. of C., Sigma Delta Chi, Kappa Tau Alpha. Home: 2553 Missouri St Lawrence KS 66044 Office: 200 Flint Hall U Kans Lawrence KS 66045

BRINKMAN, RICHARD GENE, oil company executive; b. LaPorte, Ind., Aug. 4, 1927; s. Wilbert Carl and Ruth (Reeder) M.; m. Audrey A. Benson, Aug. 13, 1955; 1 dau., Lisa B. Student, Valparaiso U., 1947; B.S., U. Ind., 1951, postgrad., 1953; postgrad., U. N.Mex., 1951. With Texaco, Inc., N.Y.C., 1956—, asst. comptroller financial reporting, 1963-67, asst. comptroller internat., 1967, asst. comptroller adminstrn., 1968-69, staff coordinator strategic planning, 1969-70, treas., 1971-77, v.p. fin. and econs., 1977—; mem. adv. bd. Mfrs. Hanover Trust Co.; dir. Heddington Ins. Ltd., Heddington Brokers Ltd. Past dir. parents council St. Mary's Coll., Notre Dame, Ind.; bd. govs. White Plains (N.Y.) Hosp. Med. Center. Served with AUS, 1945-47; Served with USAAF, 1951-53. Mem. Am. Petroleum Inst. Office: 2000 Westchester Ave White Plains NY 10650

BRINKMANN, THOMAS HENRY, assn. exec.; b. Indpls., June 30, 1929; s. Frank Fred August and Ruth Edwards (Bates) B.; m. Nancy Evans, Oct. 24, 1952; children—Beth Ruth, James Livingston, John Evans. B.S. in Mech. Engring, Northwestern U., 1952. Asst. prof. Northwestern U., 1955-58; exec. sec., gen. mgr. Marking Device Assn., Evanston, Ill., 1958—. Alderman, City of Evanston, 1969-77; bd. dirs. Evanston Mental Health Bd., 1974-77, Evanston Hist. Soc., 1972-76. Served with U.S. Army, 1953-55. Mem. Am. Soc. Assn. Execs. Republican. Club: Evanston IL

BRINLEY, F(LOYD J(OHN), JR., government administrator, physician; b. Battle Creek, Mich., May 19, 1930; s. Floyd John and Neta Fay (Johnson) B.; m. Marlene Schoen, June 12, 1955; children: Floyd John III, Deborah Anne, William Schoen. A.B., Oberlin Coll., 1951; M.D., U. Mich., 1955; Ph.D., Johns Hopkins U., 1961. Diplomate: Nat. Bd. Med. Examiners. Intern Los Angeles County Gen. Hosp., 1955-56; asst. prof. physiology Johns Hopkins U., Balt., 1961-65, assoc. prof., 1965-76; prof. U. Md., Balt, 1976-79; commd. sr. asst. surgeon USPHS, 1979, med. dir., 1979; dir. Neurol. Disorders Program Nat. Inst. Neurol. and Communicative Disorders and Stroke, 1979-82, dir. Convulsive, Developmental and Neuromuscular Disorders Program, 1982—. Mem. Biophys. Soc., Soc. Neurosci., Am. Neurol. Soc., Am. Acad. Neurology, Am. Physiol. Soc., Am. Biochem. Soc. Home: 11106 Youngtree Ct Columbia MD 21044 Office: NIH Room 812 Fed Bldg Bethesda MD 20205

BRINNER, WILLIAM MICHAEL, educator; b. Alameda, Calif., Oct. 6, 1924; s. Fred and Sadie (Weiser) B.; m. Lisa Johanna Kraus, Sept. 23, 1951; children: Benjamin Elon, Leyla Anat, Rafael Jonathan. B.A., U. Calif. at Berkeley, 1948, M.A., 1950, Ph.D., 1956. Faculty U. Calif. at Berkeley, 1956—, prof. Near Eastern studies, 1964—, chmn. dept., 1965-70, 83—, dir., 1965-70, 72-73, 75-77, dir. Cairo Center Arabic Study Abroad, 1967-70, dir. Jerusalem Study Center, 1973-75; lectr. Harvard, spring 1961; mem. exec. com. Am. Research Center Egypt, 1968-70, Am. Inst. Iranian Studies, 1968-70; mem. joint com. Near and Middle East, Am. Council Learned Socs.-Social Sci. Research Council, 1966-70, chmn., 1969-70; cons. U.S. Office Edn., 1965-68, Com. Internat. Exchange of Persons, 1971-73, Nat. Endowment for Humanities, 1978-82; panelist World Press, Nat. Ednl. TV, 1967-73, 76-77. Author: Advanced Arabic Readers, vol. I and II, 1961-62, Chronicle of Damascus 1389-1397, 2 vols, 1963, Sutro Library Hebraica: A Handlist, 1967, Readings in Modern Arabic Literature, 1972, R. Nissim's Elegant Composition Concerning Relief After Adversity, 1979 (Jewish Book Council award); editorial bd.: Internat. Jour. Middle East Studies, 1968-78; chmn. editorial bd.: Middle East Rev, 1977—. Research fellow Harvard U. Center Middle Eastern Studies, fall 1960; grantee Near Eastern studies Am. Council Learned Socs.-Social Sci. Research Council, 1961-62; Guggenheim fellow, 1965-66; Fulbright-Hays Faculty research award, 1970-71; Nat. Endowment for Humanities grantee, 1977-80. Mem. Medieval Acad. Am., Am. Oriental Soc. (dir. 1967-70, v.p. 1975, pres. 1976), Middle East Studies Assn. (dir. 1967-68, pres. 1970), Am. Assn. Tchrs. Arabic (chmn. 1967-68). Home: 753 Santa Barbara Rd Berkeley CA 94707

BRINNIN, JOHN MALCOLM, author; b. Halifax, N.S., Can., Sept. 13, 1916; s. John Thomas and Frances (Malcolm) B. B.A., U. Mich., 1941; postgrad., Harvard U., 1941-42. Dir., Poetry Center, N.Y.C., 1949-56; prof. English emeritus Boston U. Author: poetry The Garden is Political, 1942, The Lincoln Lyrics, 1942, No Arch, No Triumph, 1945, The Sorrows of Cold Stone, 1951, Skin Diving in the Virgins, 1970; biography Dylan Thomas in America, 1955, The Third Rose: Gertrude Stein and Her World, 1959; juvenile Arthur, The Dolphin Who Didn't See Venice; criticism William Carlos Williams; The Selected Poems of John Malcolm Brinnin, 1965; autobiography Sextet: T.S. Eliot, Truman Capote & Others; editor: (with Kimon Friar) Modern Poetry: American and British, 1951, A Casebook on Dylan Thomas, 1960, The Poems of Emily Dickinson, 1960, Selected Operas and Plays of Gertrude Stein, 1970, The Sway of the Grand Saloon: A Social History of the North Atlantic, 1971, Beau Voyage: Life Aboard the Last Great Ships. Recipient Gold medal for disting. service to poetry Poetry Soc. Am., 1955. Mem. Nat. Inst. Arts and Letters. Home: King Caesar Rd Duxbury MA 02332

BRINSFIELD, SHIRLEY D., diversified manufacturing company executive; b. Seattle, 1922. B.A., U. Wash., 1949; J.D., Columbia U., 1952. Bar: N.Y. Practiced in N.Y.C., 1952-60; spl. asst. to chmn. and pres. Curtiss-Wright Corp., 1960-63, gen. counsel, 1961-63, gen. mgr. electronics div., 1963-65, adminstrv. v.p., 1965-67, exec. v.p., 1967-68; with Dorr-Oliver, Inc., 1968-81, pres., 1969-71, chief exec. officer, 1969-81, vice chmn., 1971-81; chmn. bd., pres., chief exec. officer Cenco, Inc., 1975-81; pres., chief exec. officer Amerace Corp., N.Y.C., 1982—, also dir. Served with USAAF, 1942-45. Office: Amerace Corp 555 Fifth Ave New York NY 10017 *

BRINSLEY, JOHN HARRINGTON, lawyer; b. N.Y.C., Dec. 29, 1933; s. George C. and Charlotte S. B.; m. Louise Cummings, Nov. 6, 1965; children—John Harrington, Christopher C. B.A., Cornell U., 1958, LL.B., 1960. Bar: Calif. bar 1961, U.S. Supreme Ct. bar 1970. With firm Adams, Duque & Hazeltine, Los Angeles, 1961—, partner, 1966—; mem. vis. faculty Calif. Inst. Trial Advocacy; clin. lectr. law U. So. Calif. Law Center; adv. bd. Jr. League Los Angeles; lawyers adv. com. Constl. Rights Found.; bd. dirs., exec. com. Legal Aid Found. Los Angeles. Bd. dirs., exec. com. Los Angeles chpt. ARC. Served with USN, 1951-54. Fellow Am. Bar Assn., Am. Coll. Trial Lawyers; mem. Assn. Bus. Trial Lawyers (pres. 1976-77, gov. 1975-78), Los Angeles County Bar Assn. (pres. 1979-80). Clubs: Univ. (Los Angeles); Chancery. Office: 523 W 6th St Los Angeles CA 90014

BRINSMADE, LYON LOUIS, lawyer; b. Mexico City, Feb. 24, 1924; s. Robert Bruce and Helen (Steenbock) B. (parents Am. citizens); m. Susannah Tucker, June 9, 1956 (div. 1978); children: Christine Fairchild, Louisa Calvert; m. Carolyn Hartman Lister, Sept. 22, 1979. Student, U. Wis., 1940-43; B.S., Mich. Coll. Mining and Tech., 1944; J.D., Harvard U., 1950. Bar: Tex. 1951. Assoc. Butler, Binion, Rice, Cook & Knapp, Houston, 1950-58, ptnr. in charge internat. dept., 1958-83, Porter & Clements, 1983—. Bd. dirs. Houston br. English-Speaking Union of U.S., 1972-75. Served with AUS, 1946-47. Mem. ABA (chmn. com. internat. investment and devel. of sect. internat. law 1970-76, council 1972-76, 81-82, vice chmn. 1976-79, chmn.-elect 1979-80, chmn. 1980-81, co-chmn. com. Mex. 1982—), Internat. Bar Assn., Inter-Am. Bar Assn. (co-chmn. sect. oil and gas laws, com. natural resources 1973-76), Houston Bar Assn., State Bar Tex. (chmn. internat. law com. 1970-74, mem. council sect. internat. law 1975-78), Am. Soc. Internat. Law, Houston World Trade assn. (sec., dir. 1967-70), Houston World Trade Assn. (chmn. legis. com.), Houston C. of C. (chmn. legis. subcom. internat. bus. com. 1970-72), Houston Com. on Fgn. Relations, SAR, Allegro of Houston, Sigma Alpha Epsilon. Episcopalian. Clubs: Houston, Houston Athletic; Harvard (Houston). Home: 1700 Main St The Beaconsfield Houston TX 77002 Office: 3500 Republic Bank Ctr Houston TX 77002

BRINSON, GAY CRESWELL, JR., lawyer; b. Kingsville, Tex., June 13, 1925; s. Gay Creswell and Lelia (Wendelkin) B.; children from former marriage: Thomas Wade, Mary Kaye; m. Bette Lee Butler, June 17, 1979. Student, U. Ill.-Chgo., 1947-48; B.S., U. Houston, 1953, J.D., 1957. Bar: Tex. 1956, U.S. Dist. Ct. (so. dist.) Tex. 1957, U.S. Dist. Ct. (ea. dist.) Tex. 1959, U.S. Dist. Ct. (we. dist.) Tex. 1965, U.S. Ct. Appeals (5th cir.) 1962, U.S. Supreme Ct. 1974, diplomate: Am. Bd. Trial Advocates. Spl. agt. FBI, Washington and Salt Lake City, 1957-59; trial atty. Liberty Mut. Ins. Co., Houston, 1959-62; assoc. Horace Brown, Houston, 1962-64, Vinson & Elkins, 1964-67, ptnr., 1967—; lectr. U. Houston Coll. Law, 1964-65, Tex. Coll. Trial Advocacy, Houston, 1978-83; prosecutor Harris County Grievance Com.-State Bar Tex., Houston, 1965-70. Served with AUS, 1943-46; ETO. Fellow Tex Bar Found.; mem. Am. Bd. Trial Advocates (Houston chpt. pres. 1982-83), Tex. Assn. Def. Counsel, Fedn. Ins. Counsel, Nat. Assn. R.R. Trial Counsel, Phi Delta Phi. Clubs: Houston Center, Beaumont (Tex.). Home: 2938 San Felipe Rd Houston TX 77019 Office: Vinson & Elkins 2935 First City Tower Houston TX 77002

BRINTON, EDGAR HARRY, library adminstr.; b. Kansas City, Mo., July 5, 1916; s. Edgar Parrish and Juanita Irene (Swarner) B.; m. Jane Oliver Dallimore, Apr. 23, 1944 (dec. Aug. 16, 1967); 1 son, William David; m. Ann Furlong Marron, June 12, 1971. A.B., U. Denver, 1938; M.S., Columbia, 1957. Govt. documents librarian Okla. A. and M. Coll., Stillwater, 1938-39; librarian Topeka High Sch., 1939-40; catalog librarian, mgr. traveling libraries Mo. Library Commn., Jefferson City, 1940-41; chief order dept. Kansas City (Mo.) Pub. Library, 1941-47, chief extension dept., 1957-59, acting librarian, 1947-50, adminstrv. asst., 1950-57; dir. Jacksonville (Fla.) Pub. Library, 1959—; lectr. pub. library adminstrn. U. North Fla., 1975—; cons. in field. Trustee Jacksonville Episcopal High Sch., 1966-71. Mem. Mo. Library Assn. (pres. 1957-58), Fla. Library Assn. (pres. 1964-65), Southeastern Library Assn., ALA. Club: University. Home: 1721 Dogwood Pl Jacksonville FL 32210 Office: Jacksonville Pub Library System 122 N Ocean St Jacksonville FL 32202

BRINTON, SAMUEL JERVIS, JR., banker; b. Ardmore, Pa., Aug. 15, 1923; s. Samuel Jervis and Edith V. (Ketcham) B.; m. Helen Marguerite Baker, Aug. 12, 1943; children: Samuel Jervis III, Patricia Carr, James Christopher. B.A., Williams Coll., 1948; M.B.A., NYU, 1953; grad., Stonier Grad. Sch. Banking and Trusts, 1959. With Midlantic Nat. Bank (formerly Nat. Newark & Essex Bank), sr. trust officer, 1964—, sr. v.p., 1969-73, exec. v.p., 1973—; pres. Fla. Coast Midlantic Trust Co., N.A.; trustee Blue Shield of N.J. Pres. Newark Jr. C. of C., 1952-53, Upper N.J. chpt. Nat. Multiple Sclerosis Soc., 1961-63; past pres., bd. dirs. Morristown Area YMCA; bd. dirs. United Way Morris County, vice chmn., 1975; trustee Boys' Clubs Newark, 1961—, Fannie E. Rippel Found., 1967—; v.p., trustee Kessler Inst., 1967—; v.p., treas. Marcus L. Ward Home, 1968—; trustee Morris Mus. Arts and Scis.; treas., trustee Community Found. of N.J.; trustee, pres. Colonial Symphony Soc.; bd. govs. N.J. State Opera; bd. mgrs. Mt. Pleasant Cemetery, Newark. Served with AUS, 1943-46. Mem. Williams Alumni Assn. (pres. No. N.J. chpt. 1961-63), Delta Upsilon. Republican. Clubs: Morris County Golf (Convent, N.J.); Essex (Newark) (gov.); Morristown, Yacht of Stone Harbor (N.J.). Home: 33 Harter Rd Morris Township NJ 07960 Office: 499 Thornall St Edison NJ 08818

BRION, CHRISTOPHER EDWARD, chemist, educator; b. U.K., May 5, 1937; emigrated to Can., 1961, naturalized, 1971; s. Joseph Richard and Bessie May (Carter) B.; m. Elizabeth Mary Rogers, Apr. 15, 1961; children—Cathy, Peter, Susan. B.Sc., U. Bristol, Eng., 1958, Ph.D., 1961. Asst. prof. chemistry U. B.C., Can., Vancouver, 1964-69, asso. prof., 1969-77, prof., 1977—. Contbr. numerous articles to profl. jours. Recipient Noranda award Chem. Inst. Can., 1977, Herzberg award Spectroscopy Soc. Can., 1983; NRC Can. sr. fellow, 1969-70; John Simon Guggenheim Meml. fellow, 1978-79. Mem. Christian Ch. Home: 4097 W 15th Ave Vancouver BC V6R 3A2 Canada Office: Dept Chemistry U BC Vancouver BC V6T 1W5 Canada *The greatest influence in my life has been the decision to become a Christian and follow Jesus Christ.*

BRIONI-MARQUIS, SAVINI GAETANO, high fashion design executive; b. Terni, Italy, Sept. 10, 1909; s. Godfredo and Viclinda (Mazzola) Brioni-M.; m. Eleonora Palombi, Apr. 20, 1940; 1 dau., Gigliola (Mrs. Ettore Perrone). Ed., Tech. Instn., Rome, Italy. Founder Brioni Menswear, Rome, 1944, now chmn. Served with Armed Forces, 1931-32. Recipient numerous recognitions and awards. Club: Lion. Office: 79 via Barberini Rome 00186 Italy

BRISCOE, KEITH G., college president; b. Adams, Wis., Oct. 16, 1933; m. Carmen Irene Schweinler, Aug 15, 1956; 1 dau., Susan Ann. B.S., Wis. State U., La Crosse, 1960; M.Ed., U. N.H., 1968; postgrad., Case Western Res. U., Iowa State U., Okla. State U.; LL.D. (hon.), Coll. Idaho, 1977; L.H.D., Buena Vista Coll., 1979. Asst. dir. Coll. Union, Wis. State U., Stevens Point, 1960-62, U. N.H., 1962-64; dir. Coll. Union; dir. student activities, asst. prof. student life Baldwin Wallace Coll., Berea, Ohio, 1964-70; v.p. Coll. Steubenville, Ohio, 1970-74; pres. Buena Vista Coll., Storm Lake, Iowa, 1974—; higher edn. cons. Cuyahoga Community Coll., Coll. Wooster; v.p., treas. Ednl. Task, Inc., Berea, 1967-69; mem. nat. adv. bd. Coll. Transition Program, Berea, 1967-69; bd. dirs., chmn. Council Ind. Colls., 1981-83; mem. exec. com., bd. dirs., vice chmn. Presbyn. Coll. Union, 1981—; bd. dirs. mem. exec. com. us. Iowa Coll. Found.; bd. dirs. Coll. and Univ. Partnership Program, Am. Council on Edn., mem. coordinating council, 1981; co-chmn. Sino-Am. Inst. Higher Edn., Republic of China, 1981; bd. dirs., officer Coll. of Mid-Am.; past chmn. exec. com. Assn. Ind. Colls. and Univs.; past chmn. Iowa Coll. Pres.'s. Author: Directory of College Unions, 1963, An Annotated Bibliography of the College Union, 1967, A Study of Alternatives to Financing Private Higher Education, 1973; contbr. articles to profl. jours. Served with U.S. Army, 1956-58. Mem. Assn. Coll. and Univ. Concert Mgrs. (trustee), UN Assn., Nat. Meth. Found., Phi Kappa Epsilon, Phi Delta Kappa. Republican. Methodist. Clubs: Masons, Des Moines, Order of Arch, Rotary. Address: Office of Pres Buena Vista Coll Storm Lake IA 50588

BRISCOE, RALPH OWEN, corporation executive; b. Trenton, Mich., Nov. 15, 1927; children: Ralph, Donald, Stephen, Linda, Lisa. B.A., Kenyon Coll., 1950; M.B.A., Harvard, 1952. Fin. staff Ford Motor Co., 1953-56, Curtiss-Wright Corp., 1956-57; with CBS, Inc., N.Y.C., 1958-73, controller, 1963-65, v.p. finance, 1965-69, group pres., 1969-73; pres., chief exec. officer Republic Corp., Los Angeles, 1973—. Served with USAF, 1952-53. Office: 1900 Ave of Stars Los Angeles CA 90067

BRISCOE, WILLIAM ALEXANDER, physician, physiology educator; b. London, May 26, 1918; s. Henry Vincent and Rebecca Kirkwood (Stevenson) B.; m. Anne Briscoe, Aug. 20, 1955. B.A., Oxford U., 1939, M.A., 1940, B.M., B.Ch., 1942, D.M., 1950. Intern, resident, resident med. officer Royal Postgrad. Med. Sch., London, 1947-51; fellow chest service Columbia U. Div., Bellevue Hosp., N.Y.C., 1951; fellow dept. physiology U. Pa., Phila., 1952; mem. pneumoconiosis research unit, Cardiff, Wales, 1953-55; asst. prof. physiology U. Pa., 1955-56; asst. prof. medicine Columbia U., N.Y.C., 1956-61, asso. prof., 1961-68; prof. medicine Cornell U. Med. Coll., N.Y.C., 1971—, clin. prof. physiology, 1975—; cons. in pulmonary medicine Burke Rehab. Ctr.; mem. med. adv. bd. Will Rogers Inst. Author: (with others) The Lung: Clinical Physiology, 1955, 2d edit., 1961. Trustee Stony Wold-Herbert Fund. Served to capt. M.C. Brit. Army, 1943-46. Fellow Royal Coll. Physicians, A.C.P.; mem. Am. Physiol. Soc., Am. Thoracic Soc., Am. Soc. Clin. Investigation, Assn. Am. Physicians, Undersea Med. Soc., N.Y. Lung Club (pres. 1971—). Home: 2 Peter Cooper Rd New York NY 10010 Office: 1300 York Ave New York NY 10021

BRISLEY, CHESTER LAVOYEN, industrial engineer; b. Albion, Pa., Apr. 3, 1914; s. Voyen Francis and Nina May (Dearborn) B.; m. Eva Scott, June 19, 1932. Student, Gen. Motors Inst., 1936-39; B.S., Youngstown State U., 1946; M.S., Wayne State U., 1954, Ph.D., 1957. Indsl. engr. Packard Elec. div. Gen. Motors, Warren, Ohio, 1935-41; supr. indsl. engring. N.Am. Aviation, Dallas, 1942-45; mgr. indsl. engring. Wolverine Tube div. Calumet & Hecla, Inc., Detroit, 1946-58; asst. to dir. ops. Chance Vought Aircraft, Dallas, 1958-59; cons. A.T. Kearney, Chgo., 1960; mgr. indsl. engring. Allis Chalmers, Inc., Milw., 1961-62; mgr. mgmt. services Touche Ross C.P.A., N.Y.C., 1963-64; prof. dept. engring. U. Wis., Milw., 1964—, asso. chmn. dept. engring., 1964—. Contbr. articles to profl. jours. Methods Time Measurement Assn. fellow, 1978. Fellow Inst. Indsl. Engrs. (past pres. Detroit and Milw. chpts., v.p. Region XI, exec. v.p. chpt. ops. 1983-85), Soc. Advancement Mgmt. (past pres. Detroit chpt.); mem. Methods Time Measurement Assn. (v.p. 1979-80), Nat. Soc. Profl. Engrs., Wis. Soc. Profl. Engrs. (pres. 1978-79), Engrs. and Scientists Milw. (pres. 1974-75), Milw. Council Engring. and Sci. Socs. (pres. 1975-76), Am. Soc. Engring. Edn. (chmn. continuing engring. studies div. 1972-73). Home: 1700 Highland Dr Elm Grove WI 53122 Office: 929 N 6th St Milwaukee WI 53203

BRISSEY, RUBEN MARION, container company executive; b. Auburn, W.Va., July 12, 1923; s. Reuben Marion and Draxie (Meathrell) B.; m. Helen Catherine McMicken, July 10, 1945; children: Catherine Ann, Gregory Marion. B.S., Salem Coll., 1943; M.S., W.Va. U., 1948, Ph.D., 1950. With Gen. Elec. Co., 1950-73, lab. mgr., Phila., 1961-66, strategic planning mgr., 1966-73; dir. research and devel. Lavino div. Internat. Minerals and Chems., Plymouth Meeting, Pa., 1973-74; mgr. research and devel. Nat. Can Corp., Chgo., 1974-76, v.p. research and devel., 1976—. Mem. Am. Chem. Soc., IEEE, AAAS. Presbyterian. Home: 3410 Hickory Trail Downers Grove IL 60515 Office: 1000 E Northwest Hwy DesPlaines IL 60016

BRISSON, FREDERICK, theatrical producer; b. Copenhagen, Mar. 17, 1913; s. Carl Brisson; m. Rosalind Russell (dec. Nov. 1976); m. Arlette Janssen, May 1978. Student, Rossall Coll., Fleetwood, Eng. Assoc. producer Gaumont-British, Eng.; talent agy. rep. Brit. and Am. talent, Eng.; jr. ptnr. Vincent Agy., Hollywood. Producer motion pictures in, Eng.; Two Hearts in Three-Quarter Time, Prince of Arcadia, Moonlight Sonata; motion pictures in Hollywood; producer: 22 Broadway plays including Mixed Couples, Coco, Pajama Game, Under the Yum Yum Tree; films including Mrs. Pollifax-Spy. Trustee Los Angeles Internat. Film Expn. (FILMEX); founder, co-chmn. Rosalind Russell Med. Research Center for Arthritis, U. Calif., San Francisco. Spl. cons. to sec. of war, World War II; also lt. col. AAF; chief office radio propaganda. Decorated U.S. Legion of Merit; King Christian X medal, Denmark; recipient N.Y. Drama Critics award for Five Finger Exercise. Clubs: St. James's (London); Eldorado Country (Indian Wells, Calif.); Racquet and Tennis (N.Y.C.). Office: Brisson Prodns Inc 745 Fifth Ave New York NY 10151

BRISTOL, NORMAN, lawyer, former food co. exec.; b. Bronx, N.Y., June 14, 1924; s. Lawrence and Bell (Allchin) B.; m. Doreen Kingan, Mar. 28, 1953; children—Charles L., Norman, Alexander, Barnaby. Grad., Phillips Exeter Acad., 1939-41; A.B., Yale, 1944; student, Columbia Law Sch., 1947-49. Bar: N.Y. bar 1950, Mich. bar 1954. With firm Root, Ballantine, Harlan, Bushby & Palmer, N.Y.C., 1949-53; with Kellogg Co., Battle Creek, Mich., 1954-78, asst. gen. counsel, 1958-64, sec., 1960-78, gen. counsel, 1964-78, sr. v.p., 1968-75, exec. v.p., 1975-78; with firm Howard & Howard, Kalamazoo, 1979—; dir. 1st Am. Bank Corp. Mem. Gull Lake Community Schs. Bd. Edn., 1963-70, pres., 1965-67. Served to lt. (j.g.) USNR, 1943-46. Mem. Am. Bar Assn., State Bar Mich., Kalamazoo Bar Assn. Home: 2962 Sylvan Dr Hickory Corners MI 49060 Office: 407 Kalamazoo Bldg Kalamazoo MI 49007

BRISTOL, REXFORD ALLYN, automation company executive, bank executive; b. Naugatuck, Conn., June 25, 1903; s. Bennet B. and Gertrude (Rexford) B.; m. Margaret E. Chickering, Sept. 15, 1926; children: Betsy B., Margaret A. and Barbara A. (twins). B.A., Amherst Coll., 1924; S.B., Mass. Inst. Tech., 1926; D.C.S., Suffolk U., 1951; LL.D., Curry Coll., 1976. Engaged in mfg., 1926-30, engring., 1930-40, engring. and sales, 1940—; with Foxboro Co., Mass., 1926—, treas., 1943-57, exec. v.p., 1958-62, pres., 1962—, chmn. bd., 1968-71, chmn. exec. com., 1971—; pres. Foxboro Nat. Bank, 1945-63, v.p., 1963—; also dir.; dir. emeritus Arkwright Boston Ins. Co., New Eng. Mchts. Bank, Robertson Factories, Inc., Taunton, Mass.; dir. Sentry Co., Foxboro.; Mem. Mass. Adv. Council on Vocat. and Tech. Edn. Trustee emeritus Suffolk U.; trustee Stadium Realty Trust, Shaeffer Stadium, Foxboro, 1971—; chmn. bd. Mass. Taxpayers Found., 1966-69; past pres., trustee Retina Found., Dean Jr. Coll.; mem. corp. Northeastern U., Mus. Sci. Wentworth Inst., Boston. Recipient Silver Beaver award Boy Scouts Am., award Sci. Apparatus Mfrs. Assn., 1977. Mem. Elec. Mfrs. Club, Instrument Soc. Am. (hon.), Mass. Taxpayers Fedn. (past chmn.), Norfolk Trout Club (pres. 1978-80), Chi Psi. Clubs: Algonquin, University (Boston). Home: 19 Water St Foxboro MA 02035 Office: Foxboro Co Foxboro MA 02035

BRISTOL, RICHARD FREDRICK, veterinary medicine educator; b. Pontiac, Mich., Mar. 5, 1925; s. Glenand H. and Agnes Geraldine (Canuss) B. D.V.M., Mich. State U., 1951; M.S. in Pathology, Iowa State U., 1966. Gen. practice vet. medicine, Montfort, Wis., 1951-62, Merrill, Wis., 1970-74; asst.prof. Iowa State U., Ames, 1962-64, assoc. prof., 1966-68, prof., 1968-70; vis. lectr. U. Wis.-Platteville, 1958-62; prof. vet. sci. dept. U. Wis., Madison, 1974-81, prof. Sch. Vet. Medicine, 1981—, now assoc. dean clin. affairs. Recipient Pioneer Patron award U.-Wis.-Platteville, 1962, Disting. Teaching award Iowa State U., 1966, Cardinal Key, 1967. Mem. AVMA, Am. Assn. Bovine Practitioners, Am. Assn. Vet. Clinicians, U.S. Animal Health Assn., Wis. Vet. Med. Assn. (pres. 1974, Wis. Vet. of Yr. award 1958). Home: 1103 Wexford Waunakee Wi 53597 Office: Sch Vet Medicine Univ Wis 2015 Linden Dr W Madison WI 53506

BRISTOW, DAVID IAN, lawyer; b. Toronto, Ont., Can., May 19, 1931; s. Horace George and Elizabeth (Bourne) B.; m. Suzanne Snow, Sept. 9, 1959; children: Timothy Charles, Julie Anne, Lori Anne. B.A., U. Toronto, 1953; LL.B., Osgoode Hall, Toronto, 1957. Bar: Ont. 1957, apptd. Queen's counsel 1969. Since practiced in, Toronto; mem. firm Shibley Righton McCutcheon, 1969-74, Bristow Cataland Moldaver and Gilgan, 1974—; tchr. Osgoode Hall Law Sch., 1967-74; Dir. Ajax Engring. Ltd., Marley Canadian Ltd. Co-author: Mechanics Liens in Canada, 1962. Bd. dirs. McInnis Undersea Found. Mem. Advocates Soc., Country of York Bar Assn., Canadian Bar Assn., Am. Assn. Trial Lawyers, Phi Delta Phi. Club: Lawyers (Toronto). Home: 88 Blythwood Rd Toronto ON M4N 1A4 Canada Office: 130 Adelaide St W Suite 2714 Toronto ON M5H 3P5 Canada

BRISTOW, EUGENE KERR, drama educator; b. Birmingham, Ala., Feb. 12, 1927; s. Eugene B. and Hope (Kerr) B.; m. Norma L. Jones, June 17, 1950; children: Pamela Ruth, Michael Eugene, Carol Jean, Mary Katherine. A.B., Ind. U., 1950, M.A., 1952; Ph.D., U. Iowa, 1956. Tchr. New Albany (Ind.) High Sch., 1950-51, Reitz High Sch., Evansville, Ind., 1952-54; asst. prof. MacMurray Coll., 1956-57; instr. Ind. U., 1957-60, asst. prof. speech and theatre, 1960-68, asso. prof., 1968-71, asso. prof. theatre drama, 1971-79, prof., 1979—, grad. sch. fellow, 1951-52; asso. prof. theatre and drama Russian East European Inst. of Ind. U., 1972-79, prof., 1979—; research fellow State U. Iowa, 1955-56; vis. asso. prof. U. Calif., Santa Barbara, 1968-69. Author: Five Plays of Alexander Ostrovsky, 1969, Anton Chekhov—s Plays, 1977; contbr. articles profl. jours. and author several pamphlets; news editor: Ednl. Theatre Jour, 1960-63. Served with USAAF, 1945-46. Recipient Citation for Outstanding Contbn. to Dem. Processes Mayor of Bloomington, Ind., 1959; named Outstanding Young Speech Tchr. Central States Speech Assn., 1957. Mem. AAUP, MLA, Theatre Library Assn. Home: 604 Staats Dr Bloomington IN 47401

BRISTOW, LONNIE ROBERT, physician; b. N.Y.C., Apr. 6, 1930; s. Lonnie Harris and Vivian (Wines) B.; m. Margaret Jeter, June 1, 1957 (div. Aug. 1961); children: Mark, Mark; m. Marilyn Hingslage, Oct. 18, 1961; children: Robert, Elizabeth. B.S., CCNY, 1953; M.D., NYU, 1957. Diplomate: Am. Bd. Internal Medicine. Intern San Francisco City and County Hosp., 1957-58; resident VA Hosp., San Francisco, 1959-60, Francis Delafield Hosp., N.Y.C., 1960, VA Hosp., Bronx, N.Y., 1961; practice medicine specializing in internal medicine, San Pablo, Calif., 1964—; mem. staffs Brookside Hosp., San Pablo, Doctor's Hosp., Pinole, Calif.; cons. Calif. Dept. Health, Sacramento, 1976-77, chmn. sickle cell com., 1976-79, mem. genetic disease com., 1977-79; mem. admissions com. U. Calif.-Berkeley, 1972-75; mem. Nat. Council Health Care Tech., Washington, 1980; mem. physician discussion group Health Care Financing Adminstrn., Washington, 1983. Recipient ann. award of excellence Calif. Med. Polit. Action Com., 1977. Fellow ACP; mem. Nat. Acad. Scis., Parker Health Meml., Federated Council Internal Medicine (trustee 1976-83, pres. 1981-82), AMA (council med. service 1976-85), Nat. Med. Assn. Home: 5 Woodmont Ct Berkeley CA 94708 Office: 2023 Vale Rd San Pablo CA 94806

BRISTOW, ROBERT O'NEIL, author, educator; b. St. Louis, Nov. 17, 1926; s. Jesse Reuben and Helen Marjorie (Utley) B.; children by previous marriage—Cynthia Lynn, Margery Jan Wu, Gregory Scott, Kelly Robert. B.A. in Journalism, U. Okla., 1951, M.A., 1965. Asst. advt. mgr. Altus (Okla.) Times Democrat, 1951-53; free-lance writer Altus, 1951-60; prof. English Winthrop Coll., Rock Hill, S.C., 1960—. Author: Time for Glory, 1968, Night Season, 1970, A Faraway Drummer, 1973, Laughter in Darkness, 1974. Served with USNR, 1944-45. Recipient award for lit. excellence U. Okla., 1969, award for novel Friends of Am. Writers, 1974. Mem. Alpha Tau Omega. Home: 321 Aiken Ave Rock Hill SC 29730

BRITAIN, RADIE, composer; b. Amarillo, Tex., Mar. 17, 1908; d. Edgar Charles and Katie (Ford) B.; m. Ted Morton; 1 dau., Lerae. Student, U. Chgo., 1920-21; B.Mus., Am. Conservatory, Chgo., 1924; D.Mus., Mus. Arts Conservatory, 1928,. Composer orchestral, piano and vocal music, debut as composer, Munich, Germany, 1925; represented by string quartet at White House.; catalogue compositions in UCLA Music Library. Awarded numerous nat. prizes for orchestral and vocal compositions; Internat. prize Heroic Poem for Orchestra., Juilliard Publ. prize, 1945; first Nat. prize for We Believe, and for Suite for Strings; award merit Nat. League Am. Pen Women, 1957; Internat. award for Nisan for chorus and orch. Delta Omicron; Achievement award ASCAP; citation Nat. Soc. Arts and Letters; citation of achievement Nat. Band Assn., 1972. Mem. Tex. Composers Guild (life), ASCAP, League of Am. Penwomen (nat. music editor mag.); hon. mem. Gamma chpt. S.A.I., Tex. Fedn. Music Clubs, Los Angeles Woman's Press Club; life hon. mem. Tex. Music Tchrs. Assn. Clubs: Etude (life hon. mem.), Schubert (Los Angeles); Philharmonic (Amarillo, Tex.). Home: 1945 N Curson St Hollywood CA 90046

BRITO, DAGOBERT LLANOS, economist, educator; b. Mex., Apr. 6, 1941; came to U.S., 1945, naturalized, 1958; s. John L. and Guadalupe G. (Llanos) B.; m. Patricia Ann Kendrick, June 29, 1968. B.A., Rice U., 1967, M.A., 1970, Ph.D., 1970. Asst. prof. econs. U. Wis., Madison, 1970-72; asso. prof. econs. and polit. sci. Ohio State U., Columbus, 1972-75, prof., 1976-79; dir. Murphy Inst. Polit. Economy; chmn., prof. econs. Tulane U., New Orleans, 1979—; cons. Dept. State, Dept. Def. Author: A Dynamic Model of the Armaments Race, 1972, Strategic Nuclear Weapons and the Allocation of International Rights, 1977; editor: Strategies for Managing Nuclear Proliferation, 1983. Served with U.S. Army, 1963-66. NSF grantee, 1972, 74, 77, 78, 81; Mershon Center grantee, 1973, 78. Mem. Am. Econ. Assn., Econometric Soc., Public Choice Soc. Home: 839 Webster St New Orleans LA 70118 Office: Dept Econs Tulane U New Orleans LA 70118

BRITT, CHARLES ROBIN, Congressman; b. San Antonio, June 29, 1942; s. James Marion and Marie (Dobbs) B.; m. Susan Thomas, Apr. 13, 1968; children: Elizabeth, Robin, David. B.A., U. N.C., 1963, J.D., 1973; LL.M., NYU, 1975. Ptnr. Smith, Moore, Smith, Schell & Hunter, Greensboro, N.C., 1973-82; mem. 98th Congress from N.C.; past pres., chmn. Bd. of Lawyers, N.C. Chmn. Guilford County Democratic Party, 1979-81; del. Dem. Nat. Conv., 1980; co-chmn. Prayer for Congress, 1978; pres. Guilford County Young Dems., 1977. Recipient Millard S. Breckenridge NYU, 1975. Mem. Congl. Caucas of Women's Issues. Methodist. Home: 600 N Elan Ave Greensboro NC 27408 Office: Rm 327 Cannon House Office Bldg Washington DC 20515

BRITT, DONALD ALLEN, food company executive; b. Madison, Wis., June 14, 1934; s. William C. and Eleanor (Harmining) B.; m. Ruth L. Schmidt, Nov. 11, 1956; children: Thomas, Cathie, Suzanne, Jennifer. B.A., U. Wis., 1956. Adminstrv. services mgr. Arthur Andersen & Co., Milw., 1959-67; dir. systems and computing Joseph Schlitz Brewing Co., Milw., 1968-69, controller, 1970-77, v.p. fin., 1977-82, Basic Am. Foods, San Francisco, 1983—. Served with USAF, 1956-59. Mem. Am. Inst. C.P.A.s, Wis. Soc. C.P.A.s. Home: 20 Robbins Pl Alamo CA 94507 Office: 555 California Suite 4600 San Francisco CA 94104 *Love/Fun/and Work/In that order.*

BRITT, HENRY MIDDLETON, retired judge; b. Olmsted, Ill., June 9, 1919; s. Henry Middleton and Sarah Theodosia (Roach) B.; m. Barbara Jean Holmes, Oct. 29, 1942; children: Nancy Marsh, Sarah Barbara, Melissa Middleton. A.B., U. Ill., 1941, J.D., 1947. Bar: Ill. 1947, Ark. 1948, U.S. Supreme Ct. 1954. Pvt. practice law, Hot Springs, Ark., 1948-67; asst. U.S. atty. Western Dist. Ark., 1953-58; circuit judge 18th Jud. Circuit Ark., Hot Springs, 1967-83; mem. exec. com. Ark. Jud. Council, 1973; mem. Ark.-Fed. Jud. Council, 1973—, pres., 1982-83; fellow Nat. Coll. State Trial Judges, 1971, Nat. Coll. Advocacy, Harvard U., 1974; faculty adviser Nat. Coll. State Judiciary, 1973, Nat. Coll. Dist. Attys., U. Houston, 1976, Am. Acad. Jud. Edn., U. Va., 1976; mem. Midwestern Tng. Conf. Organized Crime and Law Enforcement at U. Notre Dame, 1972, Ark. Coll. Juvenile Justice, 1972; mem. exec. com. Ark. Commn. Crime and Law Enforcement, 1968-71; mem. central planning council Ark. Crime Commn. Republican candidate for Gov. of Ark., 1960; gen. counsel Rep. Party of Ark., 1962-64; permanent mem. Ark. State Rep. Com.; alt. del. Rep. Nat. Conv., 1968; mem. Garland County Bd. Election, 1962-64; chmn. Garland County Rep. Com., 1962-64; bd. dirs. United Fund, 1951-52. Served to capt. JAGC AUS, 1941-46. Recipient Service to Mankind award Sertoma Club, 1973. Mem. ABA (ex-officio mem. ho. dels., exec. council 1982-83, award of merit 1983), Ill. Bar Assn., Ark. Bar Assn. (future of judiciary study group), Garland County Bar Assn. (pres. 1961-62), Am. Legion, VFW, U.S. Navy League (pres. Hot Springs council 1966-68, state pres. 1968-70), Hot Springs Jr. C. of C. (life, pres. 1951-52), Delta Phi, Phi Alpha Delta, Am. Judicature Soc., Am. Judges Assn., Hot Springs C. of C. Presbyterian (elder, deacon, trustee). Clubs: Masons (32 deg.), Shriners, Elks, Kiwanis (pres. 1969-70). Home: 126 Trivista Hot Springs AR 71901 Office: 824 Central Ave Hot Springs AR 71901

BRITT, JOHN ROY, savings and loan executive; b. Los Angeles, Oct. 9, 1937; s. Roy Arthur and Virginia Alice (Vaughn) B.; children: Jeffrey John, Belinda Lynn, Gregory Scott. B.A., Claremont Men's Coll., 1959; grad., Pacific Coast Banking Sch., U. Wash., 1973, Managerial Policy Inst., U. So. Calif., 1978. With Security Pacific Nat. Bank, 1959-83, regional v.p., Los Angeles, 1972-74, sr. v.p., 1974-83, adminstr. Mid City-Eastern div., 1978-83; instr. Essentials of Banking Sch., U. Notre Dame, 1979. Bd. dirs. Friends of the Claremont Colls.; mem. pres.'s adv. council Claremont McKenna Coll.; chmn. bd. dirs., mem. exec. com. Commuter Transp. Services, Inc., Los Angeles; v.p., treas., bd. dirs. So. Calif. Job Creation Corp.; mem. adv. council Orthopaedic Hosp., Los Angeles. Served to capt. USAR, 1959-67. Mem. Newcomen Soc., Robert Morris Assos., Claremont McKenna Coll. Alumni Assn. (pres. 1968-69), Los Angeles C. of C. Republican. Methodist. Clubs: Lakeside Golf, Los Angeles Racquet., Los Angeles Athletic.

BRITT, W. EARL, judge; b. McDonald, N.C., Dec. 7, 1932; s. Dudley H. and Martha Mae (Hall) B.; m. Judith Moore, Apr. 17, 1976; children: Clifford P., Mark E., Elizabeth C. Student, Campbell Jr. Coll., 1952; B.S., Wake Forest U., 1956, J.D., 1958. Bar: N.C. 1958. Practiced law, Fairmont, N.C., 1959-72, Lumberton, N.C., 1972-80; judge U.S. Dist. Ct. Eastern Dist. N.C., 1980—. Trustee Southeastern Community Coll., 1965-70, Southeastern Gen. Hosp., Lumberton, 1965-69, Pembroke State U., 1967-72; bd. govs. U. N.C. Served with U.S. Army, 1953-55. Mem. Am. Bar Assn., N.C. Bar Assn. Baptist. Office: US Dist Ct PO Box 27504 Raleigh NC 27611

BRITTAIN, ALFRED, III, banker; b. Evanston, Ill., July 22, 1922; s. Alfred, Jr. and Sibyl (Collins) B.; m. Beatrice Memhard, Dec. 18, 1948; children: Stephen M., Linda C. B.A., Yale, 1945. With Bankers Trust Co., N.Y.C., 1947—, chmn., 1975—; also dir., mem. exec. com.; chmn., dir., mem. exec. com. Bankers Trust N.Y. Corp.; dir. Philip Morris Inc., Collins & Aikman Corp., Royal Group Inc., Fed. Res. Bank N.Y.; mem. listed co. adv. com. N.Y. Stock Exchange. Trustee Com. Econ. Devel.; bd. dirs. N.Y. Chamber Commerce and Industry., N.Y.C. Partnership Inc.; mem. Bus. Com. for the Arts Inc., N.Y.C.; pres. N.Y.C. Clearing House Assn. Home: 505 Indian Field Rd Greenwich CT 06830 Office: 280 Park Ave New York NY 10017

BRITTAIN, JOHN OLIVER, materials science educator; b. Pitts., Feb. 15, 1920; s. Joseph and Mabel (Morgan) B.; m. Lois Miller, Apr. 20, 1945; children: Douglas, John Oliver, Susan, Lisa. B.S., Pa. State U., 1943, Ph.D., 1951. Research asst. Research Labs., Aluminum Co. of Am., New Kensington, Pa., 1943-44; instr. metallurgy Pa. State U., 1947-48; prin. metallurgist Battelle Meml. Inst., Columbus, Ohio, 1950-51; research asso. sci. staff Columbia, 1951- 55; prof. materials sci. dept. Northwestern U., 1955—, chmn. materials sci. dept., 1968-73, dir., 1976-79; materials cons. Johnson Service Co., Milw., 1964-66, Universal Oil Products Co., Des Plaines, 1968-78, Amphenol Corp., 1968, USAF Materials Lab., 1968, Speed Fam Corp., 1974—; mem. Accreditation Bd. Engring. and Tech., Inc., 1973—. Served to 1st lt. AUS, 1944-46. Recipient Ralph A. Teetor Ednl. award, 1977; Internat. Nickel Co. fellow, 1949-50. Fellow Am. Soc. Metals (chmn. Chgo. No. chpt. 1976-77); mem. Am. Inst. Mining and Metall. Engrs., Am. Phys. Soc., AAUP, Sigma Xi, Tau Beta Pi, Alpha Chi Sigma, Alpha Sigma Mu (nat. pres. 1975-76). Home: 950 Whigam Rd Riverwoods IL 60015

BRITTAIN, JOHN SHERRARD, III, lawyer; b. St. Joseph, Mo., May 18, 1922; s. John S. and Vella Griffith (Schmidt) B.; m. Anne Brewster, Aug. 22, 1957; 1 son, John Sherrard. B.A., Yale U., 1943; LL.B., Columbia U., 1949. Bar: N.Y. 1950, Pa. 1961. Assoc. Breed, Abbott & Morgan, N.Y.C., 1949-58, ptnr., 1958-61, Morgan, Lewis & Bockius, Phila., 1961—; dir. Lease Financing Corp., Radnor, Pa., 1963—. Served to capt. F.A. AUS, 1943-46; ETO. Mem. ABA, Pa. Bar Assn., Phila. Bar Assn. Clubs: Philadelphia, Union League; Gulph Mills Golf (King of Prussia, Pa.). Home: 7360 Huron Ln Philadelphia PA 19119 Office: Morgan Lewis & Bockius 2000 One Logan Sq Philadelphia PA 19103

BRITTAIN, PERRY GEORGE, electric utility company executive; b. Center, Tex., Mar. 10, 1925; s. Zack B. and Donnie (Matthews) B.; m. Martha Nelle Black, Dec. 30, 1945; children: Jennifer Margaret, Martha Katharine. B.S., U. Tex., 1949. Registered profl. engr., Tex. With Dallas Power & Light Co., 1949-72, v.p. engring., purchasing, 1968-72; exec. v.p. Tex. Utilities Services Inc., 1972-73, pres., 1973-81, chmn. bd., chief exec., 1981-83; exec. v.p. Tex. Utilities Co., 1974-81, pres., 1981-83, chmn. bd., chief exec., 1983—; pres. Tex. Utilities Generating Co., 1974-81, chmn. bd., chief exec., 1981—; pres. Tex. Utilities Fuel Co., 1974-81, chmn. bd., chief exec., 1981—, Tex. Utilities Mining Co., 1984—; chmn. bd. Basic Resources Inc., 1983—, Chaco Energy Co., 1983—; dir. Edison Electric Inst. Trustee Tech. Edn. Research Center, 1978—; bd. dirs. Center for Occupational Research and Devel., 1980—, Southwestern Med. Found., Met. Dallas YMCA; mem. Dallas Citizens Council. Served with USAAF, 1943-46. Recipient Disting. Grad. award U. Tex. Coll. Engring., 1976. Mem. IEEE, Tex. Soc. Profl. Engrs. (Engr. of Year award 1977). Office: Tex Utilities Co 2001 Bryan Tower Dallas TX 75201

BRITTAIN, WILLIAM BRUCE, Can. govt. ofcl.; b. Truro, N.S., Can., Feb. 10, 1922; s. William Harold and Mary (McDonald) B.; m. Catherine Ewing Wood, June 22, 1946; children—William Harold Bruce, Elizabeth Ewing, Catherine Bonney. B.Sc., McGill U., 1949. Agrl. work, Can., 1949-54; chief adminstrn. dic. Sci. Ser. Health and Welfare Can., 1954-68; dir. gen. Adminstrn. Bicultural Program Sr. Exec., Quebec, Que., 1967-68; acting asst. sec. mgmt. improvement br. Treasury Bd. Can., 1968-69; dep. minister Veterans' Affairs Can., 1975—. Govt. rep. spl. com. rev. personnel mgmt. and merit prin. Pub. Ser. Can. Served with RCAF, World War II. Decorated D.F.C. Mem. Fed. Inst. Mgmt., Am. Mfgmt. Assn., Inst. Pub. Adminstrn. Can. (past pres.). Home: 10 Chinook Ottawa ON K2H 7E1 Canada Office: 284 Wellington Ottawa ON K1A 0P4 Canada

BRITTEN, GERALD HALLBECK, government official; b. N.Y.C., May 22, 1930; s. William Forster and Carin Anne B.; m. Joan

Willmarth, Feb. 15, 1952; children: Robin, Michael, Daniel, Tracy, Thomas. Student, Northwestern U., 1948-51, Wayne State U., 1960; B.A., U. Nebr., 1964; M.A., Georgetown U., 1969. Commd. 2d lt. U.S. Army, 1951, advanced through grades to lt. col., 1967; asst. for Pacific affairs Office Asst. Sec. for Internat. Security Affairs, Dept. Def., 1968-70, ret., 1971; dir. planning systems Office Program Systems Office Asst. Sec. for Planning and Evaluation, HEW, Washington, 1971-75, acting dept. asst. sec. for program systems, 1975-77, dep. asst. sec. program systems, 1977—. Chmn. pack troop com. Cub Scouts and Boy Scouts Am., 1960-70; pres. Homeowners Assn., 1978. Decorated Legion of Merit with oak leaf cluster, Bronze Star, Dept. Def. Meritorious Service medal, Commendation medal with oak leaf cluster; recipient Disting. Service award HEW, 1975, Sec.'s Spl. citation, 1974, Presdl. Meritorious Rank award, 1982. Episcopalian. Home: 9705 Waterfront Dr Manassas VA 22110 Office: HHS Planning and Eval 200 Independence Ave SW Washington DC 20201

BRITTENHAM, RAYMOND LEE, investment company executive; b. Moscow, Russia, Feb. 8, 1916; s. Edward Arthur and Marietta (Wemple) B.; m. Mary Ann Stanard, Nov. 3, 1956; children—Edward C., Carol. A.B., Principia Coll., Elsah, Ill., 1936; postgrad., Kaiser Wilhelm U., Berlin, Germany, 1937; LL.B., Harvard, 1940. Bar: Ill. 1940, N.Y. 1946. Assoc. firm Pope & Ballard, Chgo., 1940-42, Mitchell Carroll, N.Y.C., 1947-56; v.p., gen. counsel ITT (and subs.), 1962-68, sr. v.p. law, counsel, 1968-80, dir., 1965-80; with Lazard Freres & Co., N.Y.C., 1980—; pres. Spanish Inst., 1980-82, vice chmn., 1982—; sec. U.S. sect. Internat. Fiscal Assn., 1950-57; bd. dirs. Nat. Fgn. Trade Council, 1961-80. Served to maj. AUS, 1942-46. Decorated Bronze Star medal; Croix de Guerre, France and Belgium; chevalier Ordre de Leopold, Belgium). Mem. ABA, Council Fgn. Relations. Club: University (N.Y.C.). Home: 925 Park Ave New York NY 10028 Office: 1 Rockefeller Plaza New York NY 10020

BRITTON, ALLEN PERDUE, music educator; b. Elgin, Ill., May 25, 1914; s. Walter Allen and Mary (Perdue) B.; m. Veronica Fern Wallace, Aug. 30, 1938. B.Sc., U. Ill., 1937, M.A., 1939; Ph.D., U. Mich., 1950. Tchr. music and English Griffith (Ind.) Pub. Schs., 1938-41; instr. music and English Eastern Ill. U., 1941-43; prof. music U. Mich., Ann Arbor, 1949—, asso. dean, 1960-69, dean, 1969-79, dean emeritus, 1979—; Bd. dirs. Mus. Youth Internat., 1965—, U. (Mich.) Mus. Soc., 1972—; cons. Youth for Understanding, 1967; mem. overseas tours screening com. U.S.O., 1962-74; arts and humanities panel U.S. Office Edn., 1964-70. Editor: Jour. Research Music Edn, 1953-72, Am. Music, 1980—; gen. editor: textbook series Foundations of Music Education, 1964—; Author numerous revs., articles. Trustee Interlochen Center for Arts, 1972—. Served with AUS, 1943-46. Mem. Am. Musicol. Soc. (council 1964-66), Am. Studies Assn., Internat. Folk Music Council, Music Educators Nat. Conf. (pres. 1960-62), Internat. Soc. Music Edn., Phi Mu Alpha (dir. 1962-67), Phi Eta Sigma, Phi Kappa Phi, Pi Kappa Lambda, Phi Delta Kappa, Alpha Tau Omega. Home: 1475 Warrington Dr Ann Arbor MI 48103

BRITTON, ERWIN ADELBERT, clergyman, college administrator; b. Huron, Ohio, Feb. 19, 1915; s. John Chester and Lydia Emeline (Jones) B.; m. Carolyn Anne Herron, Sept. 1, 1941; children: Margaret (Mrs. Fred C. Kolloff), Elizabeth (Mrs. Richard R. Quick), Constance. A.B., Oberlin Coll., 1936; B.D., Grad. Sch. Theology, Oberlin, 1939; D.D., Piedmont Coll., 1961; S.T.D., Olivet Coll., 1978. Ordained to ministry Congregational Ch., 1939; pastor Community Ch., Avon Lake, Ohio, 1937-41, First Congl. Ch., Wayne, Mich., 1941-64, Detroit, 1964-75, Union Congl. Ch., Mackinac Island, Mich., 1982—; exec. sec. Nat. Assn. Congl. Christian Chs., 1975-81; Chmn. Congl. Found. for Theol. Studies, 1970-72; dir. Conf. on Crime and Religious Leadership; mem. adv. com. religious and urban studies Wayne State U. Chmn. Met. Agy. for Retarded Children, Wayne County Mental Health Soc., 1969; Trustee Olivet Coll. Named Young Man of Year Jr. C. of C., 1950, Outstanding Religious Leader of Mich. Religious Heritage Am. Mem. Detroit Pastors Union (pres. 1970), Nat. Assn. Congl. Christian Chs. (moderator 1972-73), Internat. Congl. Fellowship (program com.). Office: Olivet Coll Olivet WI 49076

BRITTON, WILLARD P., newspaper publishing company executive; b. Mitchell, S.D., May 28, 1923; s. Clarence B. and Bessie (Price) B.; m. Dorothy Lorraine Hanlon, Apr. 27, 1946; children: Leslie Diane, Linda Gail. B.A., U. Wash., 1949. Staff accountant Haskins & Sells, Seattle, 1949-55; controller, treas. Northwest Publs., Inc., St. Paul, 1955-71; comptroller Ridder Publs., Inc., Los Angeles, 1971—; treas. Knight-Ridder Newspapers, Inc., Miami, Fla., 1976—, controller, 1978—, v.p., 1983—. Treas. March of Dimes, 1957-58. Mem. Inst. Newspaper Controllers and Finance Officers (dir. 1958-59), Tax Execs. Inst., Financial Execs. Inst., Phi Beta Kappa, Alpha Kappa Psi. Home: 385 NE 91st St Miami Shores FL 33138 Office: 1 Hearld Plaza Miami FL 33101:

BRIXEY, JOHN CLARK, educator; b. Mounds, Okla., June 28, 1904; s. Albin Monroe and Ethel Lillian (Buchanan) B.; m. Dorothea B. Morrison, Dec. 26, 1926; children—John Clark, Dorothy Jane (Mrs. George W. Ingels); m. Neoma Jo Durkee, Aug. 18, 1979. B.A., U. Okla., 1924, M.A., 1925; Ph.D., U. Chgo., 1936. Mem. faculty U. Okla., 1925—, prof. math., 1947-74, emeritus, 1974—; cons. prof. biostatistics and epidemiology U. Okla. Med. Center, 1960-74, adj. prof. emeritus, 1974—. Author: (with R.V. Andree) Modern Trigonometry, 1955, Fundamentals of College Mathematics, rev. edit, 1961. Recipient award excellence teaching U. Okla., 1956. Mem. Am. Math. Soc., Math. Assn. Am. (bd. govs. 1951-52, sec. Okla.-Ark. sect. 1939-51), Phi Beta Kappa, Sigma Xi. Democrat. Mem. Disciples of Christ Ch. (past elder). Home: 927 S Pickard St Norman OK 73069

BRIZGYS, VINCENTAS, bishop; b. Plynia, Lithuania, Nov. 10, 1903; came to U.S., 1952, naturalized, 1959; s. Mathew and Mary (Vikelis) B. Student, Priests Sem., Gizai, Lithuania, 1921-27; Dr. Philosophy and Canon Law, Gregorian U., Rome, 1935. Ordained priest Roman Catholic Ch., 1927; parish priest, Lithuania, 1927-30; mem. faculty Priests' Sem., 1936-40; rector Interdiocesan Priest's Sem., Kaunas, Lithuania, 1940-41; dean, prof. Theol. Faculty, State's U., Kaunas, 1941-44; bishop, Kaunas, 1940—; Cons. Commn. for Bishop and Adminstrs. Diocese Preparing Vatican II Ecumenic Council, 1960-61. Mem. AAAS, Pax Romana. Club: K.C. *Having everything from God I gave it back to God serving the people, following the principles I believed. To those who are leading the society, I wish to remember, that injustice, wrong and evil will never be transformed into justice, right and blessing by the erroneus opinion of the day.* *

BRIZZOLARA, CHARLES ANTHONY, lawyer; b. Chgo., Nov. 20, 1929; s. Ralph D. and Florence H. (Hurley) B.; m. Audree Doyle, Aug. 24, 1968. B.A., Lake Forest (Ill.) Coll., 1951; J.D., Chgo.-Kent Coll. Law, 1957. Bar: Ill. 1959. Practiced, Chgo., 1959-67; with Walter E. Heller & Co., also Walter E. Heller Internat. Corp. (now Amerifin Corp.), Chgo., 1967—; v.p., sec., gen. counsel Walter E. Heller & Co., also Walter E. Heller Internat. Corp., 1974-80, sr. v.p., 1980—; v.p. Chgo. Bears Football Club, Inc., 1975—; dir. Abacus Real Estate Fin. Co., Walter E. Heller & Co. S.E., Heller Factoring (Hong Kong) Ltd., Factoring Serfin, S.A., Chandler Leasing Corp., 1975-80; lectr. seminars Am. Mgmt. Assn. Editor: Chgo.-Kent Law Rev., 1956. Bd. advs. Catholic Charities Archdiocese of Chgo., 1978—; bd. dirs. Ill. Inst. Tech. Chgo. Kent Alumni Assn. Served with AUS, 1952-54. Mem. Internat., Am., Ill. bar assns., World Assn. Lawyers, Am. Soc. Corp. Secs., Am. Arbitration Assn., Am. Judicature Soc. Roman Catholic. Home: 253 E Delaware Pl Chicago IL 60611 Office: 105 W Adams St Chicago IL 60603

BROACH, WILSON JAMES, chemist; b. Atkins, Ark., Aug. 14, 1915; s. William James and Margaret Victoria (Pettit) B.; m. Billie Elena Godbey, Aug. 22, 1942; children—Mary Ellena, James Riley, Robert William, Victoria. B.A., Henderson State Coll., 1937; M.S., U. Ark., 1948, Ph.D., 1953. Tchr. sci. high schs., Ark., 1937-41; chemist DuPont Co., 1941-43; instr. Little Rock Jr. Coll., 1946-48, U. Ark., 1948-52; asst. prof. So. State Ark. U., 1952-54, N.W. La. State Coll., 1954-57; head dept. chemistry Little Rock U., 1957-69, prof., 1960-69, U. Ark., 1969—, chmn. phys. sci. div., 1969-74, dean, 1974-81. Served with USNR, 1943-46. Mem. Am. Chem. Soc., AAAS, Ark. Deans Assn., Ark. Acad. Scis., Sigma Xi. Methodist. Home: 5511 Stonewall Rd Little Rock AR 72207 Office: Univ of Ark Little Rock AR 72204

BROAD, ELI, insurance company executive; b. N.Y.C., June 6, 1933; s. Leon and Rebecca (Jacobson) B.; m. Edythe Lois Lawson, Dec. 19, 1954; children—Jeffrey Alan, Gary Steven. B.A. cum laude in Bus. Adminstrn, Mich. State U., 1954. Acct., 1954-56; asst. prof. Detroit Inst. Tech., 1956-57; co-founder Kaufman & Broad, Inc., Los Angeles, 1957, pres., chmn., 1957-72, part-time chmn., 1973-75, chmn., 1976—, Sun Life Ins. Co. Am., Balt., 1976-79, dir., 1979—; chmn. Sun Life Group Am., Atlanta, 1978—; dir. Fed. Nat. Mortgage Assn., 1984—; past dir. Verex Corp.; real estate adv. bd. Citibank, N.Y.C. Dir. devel. bd. Mich. State U., 1969-72; mem. Nat. Indsl. Pollution Control Council, 1970-73; co-founder Council Housing Producers; chmn. Los Angeles Mayor's Housing Policy Com., 1974-75; del. Democratic Nat. Conv., 1968; pres. Calif. Non-Partisan Voter Registration Found., 1971; bd. dirs. Nat. Energy Found., 1979—, NCCJ, YMCA, Los Angeles United Way, Haifa U.; bd. dirs., trustee Windward Sch.; mem. acquisition com. Los Angeles County Mus. Art, 1979-81; exec. com. Internat. Forum for Los Angeles World Affairs Council; exec. com., bd. fellows Claremont Colls.; adv. bd. Inst. Internat. Edn.; chmn. founding bd. trustees Mus. Contemporary Art, Los Angeles, 1980—; vis. com. U. Calif. at Los Angeles Grad. Sch. Mgmt.; trustee City of Hope, Calif. State Univs. and Colls., Pitzer Coll., 1979—; chmn. bd. trustees Pitzer Coll., 1972-79. Recipient Man of Year award City of Hope, 1965; Golden Plate award Am. Acad. Achievement, 1971; Humanitarian award NCCJ, 1977; Housing Man of Yr. Nat. Housing Conf., 1979. Mem. Beta Alpha Psi. Clubs: Regency, Hillcrest Country (Los Angeles). Home: One Oakmont Dr Los Angeles CA 90049 Office: 11601 Wilshire Blvd Los Angeles CA 90025

BROAD, MORRIS N., savings and loan executive; b. Burlington, Vt., Apr. 11, 1935; s. Shepard and Ruth (Kugel) B. B.B.A., U. Miami, 1956. Pres. Am. Savs. and Loan Assn. of Fla., Miami Beach, 1965—. Trustee U. Fla. Found.; mem. founders council Fla. Internat. U.; mem. citizens bd. and law and econ. council U. Miami; mem. adv. bd. and planning com. St. Francis Hosp.; dir. Dade Safety Council; trustee So. Fla. Council Boy Scouts Am.; founder, trustee Mt. Sinai Med. Center of Greater Miami; mem. adv. council Barry Coll.; trustee Nova U. Served with U.S. Army, 1951-58. Recipient Humanitarian award B'nai B'rith. Office: Am Savs and Loan Assn 17801 N 2d Ave Miami Beach FL 33139 *

BROADBENT, JOHN EDWARD, Canadian Member of Parliament; b. Oshawa, Ont., Can., Mar. 21, 1936; s. Percy Edward and Mary Anastasia (Welsh) B.; m. Lucille Allen, Oct. 19, 1971; children: Paul, Christine. B.A. in Philosophy with honors, U. Toronto, 1959, M.A. in Philosophy of Law, 1961, Ph.D., 1964. Mem. faculty polit. sci. York U., Toronto, 1965-68; mem. Parliament, 1968—, apptd. to Privy Council, 1982—; Parliamentary leader New Democratic Party, 1974-75; leader New Dem. Party Can., 1975; v.p. Socialist Internat., 1976—. Author: The Liberal Rip-Off, 1970. Served as officer RCAF, 1955-58. Office: House of Commons Ottawa ON Canada K1A 0A6

BROADBENT, ROBERT R., retail co. exec.; b. Lisbon, Ohio, May 25, 1921; s. Raymond and Ruth Edna (Schoonover) B.; m. Mary; 1 son, William Stuart. B.S., U. Akron, Ohio, 1946. Personal asst. to Cyrus S. Eaton, Cleve., 1946-49; various positions in retailing, 1949-58; exec. v.p., dir. Higbee Co., Cleve., 1958-73, pres., vice chmn. bd., 1979—; also dir.; chmn. bd., chief exec. officer Gimbel's, N.Y.C., 1973-76; pres., chief exec. officer Liberty House-Mainland, San Francisco, 1976-79; dir. Frederick Atkins, Inc., N.Y.C., 1976—; mem. Retail Mfrs. Adv. Bd., Williamsburg, Va., 1965-73. Bd. dirs. 34th St.-Midtown Assn., N.Y.C., 1973-76, Ave. Americas Assn., N.Y.C., 1973-76, Herald-Greeley Sq. Devel. Council, N.Y.C., 1973-76, San Francisco Spring Opera Theater, 1977—; v.p. Davis Cup and Wightman Cup com. Northeasten Ohio Tennis Assn., Cleve., 1959-73; v.p., trustee Cleve. Mental Health Assn., 1968-73, Cleve. Play House, 1969-73; trustee, exec. com. Glen Oak Girl's Sch., Cleve., 1971-73; pres. PEERS, suicide center, Cleve., 1972; vice chmn. region IV Central Ski Assn., Cleve., 1968-73. Served with USAAF, 1943-45; ETO. Decorated D.F.C., Air medal with 4 oak leaf clusters. Clubs: Claremont Country (Oakland, Calif.); San Francisco Tennis; Cleve. Racquet, Cleve. Country, Union (Cleve.); Union League (N.Y.C.). Address: 13515 Shaker Blvd Shaker Heights OH 44120

BROADBENT, THOMAS RAY, surgeon; b. Heber, Utah, Aug. 4, 1921; s. Charles N. and Sarah Jane (Wood) B.; m. Edith Stovall, June 3, 1950; children—Kenneth Ray, Stephanie, Catherine, Lisa Anne. B.A., Brigham Young U., 1943; M.D., Duke, 1946. Diplomate: Am. Bd. Surgery, Am. Bd. Plastic Surgery (examiner, vice chmn. 1972-73). Intern Duke U. Hosp., 1947, gen. surgery residency, 1948-50, plastic surgery residency, 1950-52; instr. surgery Duke, 1951-52; asso. clin. prof. U. Utah Sch. Medicine, 1955; active staff Primary Children's Hosp., Salt Lake City, W.H. Groves Latter-Day Saints Hosp., also dir. residency program, dept. plastic surgery, 1957—, pres., 1974-75; trainee Nat. Cancer Inst., 1950-52; B. K. Rank traveling prof. Royal Australasian Coll. Surgeons, 1982; sec. gen. 3d Internat. Congress Plastic Surgery, 1963. Served to 1st lt. AUS, World War II. Recipient prize on original research Found. Am. Soc. Plastic and Reconstructive Surgery, 1958; Distinguished Service award Brigham Young U., 1969. Fellow ACS, Internat. Coll. Surgeons (vice regent 1959-60); mem. AMA, Utah Med. Assn., Calif. Soc. Plastic Surgery, Am. Soc. Plastic and Reconstructive Surgery (gen. sec. 1958-63, pres. 1968-69, asso. editor jour. 1964-70, travelling prof. Ednl. Found. 1979-80), Internat. Confedn. Plastic Surgeons (exec. com. 1964-75), Am. Assn. Plastic Surgery, Plastic Surgery Research Council (chmn. 1957), Am. Soc. Aesthetic Plastic Surgery, Salt Lake Surg. Soc. (pres. 1968-69), Alpha Omega Alpha. Mormon. Home: 2635 St Mary's Way Salt Lake City UT 48108 Office: 324 10th Ave Suite 206 Salt Lake City UT 84103

BROADBENT, THOMAS VALENTINE, publisher; b. Provo, Utah, May 7, 1935; s. Thomas Lowell and Wilma (Valentine) B.; m. Alison Badger, Apr. 6, 1956; children—Thomas Louis, Hilary Anne. B.A., U. Utah, 1959. Successively engring. writer, publs. engr., sr. publs. engr. Sperry Utah div. Sperry-Rand Corp., Salt Lake City, 1959-63; successively salesman, sales mgr., gen. mgr. Harcourt Brace Jovanovich, Inc., Chgo., 1963-71; dir. coll. dept. St. Martin's Press, Inc., N.Y.C., 1971—. Woodrow Wilson fellow, 1957-58; Fulbright scholar, 1957. Home: Nightingale Rd Katonah NY 10536 Office: St Martin's Press 175 Fifth Ave New York City NY 10010

BROADHEAD, JAMES LOWELL, business executive; b. New Rochelle, N.Y., Nov. 28, 1935; s. Clarence James and Mabel Roseader (Bowser) B.; m. Sharon Ann Rulon, May 6, 1967; children: Jeffrey Thorton, Kristen Ann, Carolyn Mary, Catherine Lee. B.M.E., Cornell U., 1958; LL.B., Columbia U., 1963. Bar: N.Y. 1963. Mech. engr. sales dept. Ingersoll-Rand Co., 1958-59; asso. Debevoise, Plimpton, Lyons & Gates, N.Y.C., 1963-68; asst. sec. St. Joe Minerals Corp., N.Y.C., 1968-70, sec., 1970-77, gen. counsel, 1973-74, v.p. devel., 1976-77, exec. v.p., 1980-81, pres., 1981-82, also dir.; chmn., chief exec. officer Energy Research Corp., Danbury, Conn., 1973-74; v.p. St. Joe Petroleum Co., N.Y.C., 1974-76; pres. St. Joe Zinc Co., Pitts., 1977-80; exec. v.p., dir. U.S. Industries, 1983; sr. v.p. GTE Corp., N.Y.C., 1984—; dir. Pittston Co., Goldome Bank. Editor: Columbia Law Rev., 1963. Served with U.S. Army, 1960-61. Clubs: Union League, Middlesex. Home: 57 Allwood Rd Darien CT 06820 Office: One Stamford Forum Stamford CT 06904

BROADHURST, JEROME ANTHONY, lawyer; b. Cleve., Feb. 4, 1945; s. William and Estelle (Bozak) B.; m. Annette Lou Wilt, Sept. 3, 1966; children: Stephanie, Jerome, Elizabeth. B.S. B.A., U. Akron, 1967, J.D., 1971. Bar: Ohio 1973. Fin. analyst B.F. Goodrich Co., Akron, Ohio, 1971-73, corp. counsel, 1973-77; securities counsel Weatherhead Co., Cleve., 1977; asst. counsel Gen. Tire & Rubber Co., Akron, 1978-80; sec. Holiday Inns, Inc., Memphis, 1982—; sr. atty. HJoliday Inns, Inc., Memphis, 1980—. Comments editor Akron Law Rev., 1970-71. Mem. ABA, Am. Soc. Corp. Secs. Republican. Roman Catholic. Office: 3742 Lamar Ave Memphis TN 38195

BROADMAN, ARTHUR R., corp. exec.; b. 1915. Engring. degree, Yale. With Tenneco Chems., Inc. (and predecessor), 1940-75, v.p., 1953-67, sr. v.p., 1967-75; also dir.; dir. subsidiary Tenneco Mfg. Co.; v.p. Tenneco Inc., 1968-75, Amerada Hess Corp., N.Y.C., 1975—. Address: Amerada Hess Corp 1185 Ave of Americas New York City NY 10036

BROADWATER, JAMES E., publisher; b. Tacoma, Nov. 5, 1945; s. Robert L. and June J. B.; m. Diane K. Plummer, Apr. 22, 1967; children: James Tegan, Kelly Diane, Robert Charles, Krista Dawn. B.S. in Journalism, U. Fla., 1967. Account mgr. Young & Rubicam, Inc., Detroit, Kansas City, Kans., N.Y.C. and Houston, 1968-73; asso. pub. Tex. Monthly Mag., Austin, 1973-78; pres., pub. Saturday Rev. Mag., N.Y.C., 1978-80; regional pub. dir. Baker Publs., Houston, 1980-82; pres. HBC, Inc., Houston, 1982—; seminar instr. N.Y. U. Mem. Mag. Pubs. Assn., Am. Mgmt. Assn., Direct Mail Mktg. Assn., Lambda Chi Alpha. Methodist. Home: 15903 River Roads Dr Houston TX 77079 *All things are possible through Christ. Success requires that one deal in results and not succumb to the desire to rationalize excuses. Unless a man is given more than he can possibly do, he will never do all that he can.*

BROBECK, JOHN RAYMOND, physiology educator; b. Steamboat Springs, Colo., Apr. 12, 1914; s. James Alexander and Ella (Johnson) B.; m. Dorothy Winifred Kellogg, Aug. 24, 1940; children: Stephen James, Priscilla Kimball, Elizabeth Martha, John Thomas. B.S., Wheaton Coll., 1936, LL.D., 1960; M.S., Northwestern U., 1937, Ph.D., 1939; M.D., Yale U., 1943. Instr. physiology Yale, 1943-45, asst. prof., 1945-48, asso. prof. physiology, 1948-52; prof. physiology, chmn. dept. U. Pa., Phila., 1952-70, Herbert C. Rorer prof. med. scis., 1970-82, prof. emeritus, 1982—. Editor: Yale Jour. Biology and Medicine, 1949-52; chmn. editorial bd.: Physiol. Revs, 1963-72. Fellow Am. Acad. Arts and Scis.; mem. Am. Physiol. Soc. (pres. 1971-72), Am. Inst. Nutrition, Nat. Acad. Scis., Am. Soc. Clin. Investigation, Halsted Soc., Phila. Coll. Physicians, Sigma Xi, Alpha Omega Alpha. Home: 224 Vassar Ave Swarthmore PA 19081 Office: U Pa G/3 Philadelphia PA 19104

BROBECK, STEPHEN JAMES, consumer advocate; b. New Haven, Sept. 15, 1944; s. John Raymond and Dorothy Winifred (Kellogg) B.; m. Susan Cheney Williams, May 9, 1971. B.A., Wheaton Coll., 1966; Ph.D., U. Pa., 1972. Asst. prof. Am. studies Case Western Res. U., Cleve., 1970-79; exec. dir. Consumer Fedn. Am., Washington, 1980—; reader U.S. Office Consumer Edn., 1978, 79. Author: (with Naphtali Hoffman) The Cleveland Bank Book: A Survey of Banking Services in Cuyahoga County, 1976, (with Anne Averyt) The Product Safety Book, 1983; contbr. articles to profl. jours. Bd. dirs. Joint Council Econ. Edn., 1981—, Consumer Energy Council Am., 1982—, Citizens for Tax Justice, 1980—, Pub. Voice for Food and Health Policy, 1983—, Nat. Coalition for Consumer Edn., 1981—, Telecommunications Consumer Coalition, 1980—, Citizens for A More Responsive Philanthropy, 1980—, Consumer Fedn. Am., 1976-79, Cleve. Consumer Action, 1976-80. NDEA fellow, 1966-69; U. Pa. fellow, 1969-70; recipient Carl F. Wittke Disting. Teaching award Case Western Res. U., 1979. Mem. Am. Council Consumer Interests. Home: 4700 Connecticut Ave Washington DC 20008 Office: 1314 14th St Washington DC 20005

BROCCOLI, ALBERT ROMOLO, motion picture producer; b. N.Y.C., Apr. 5, 1909; s. Giovanni and Cristina (Vence) B.; m. Dana Natol Wilson, June 21, 1959; children: Michael Wilson, Anthony, Christina, Barbara. Student pub. schs., N.Y.C. Asst. dir. 20th Century Fox, 1941-42; RKO under Howard Hughes, 1947-48; theatrical agt. Charles Feldman, 1948-51; producer Warwick Films, 1951-60, Eon Prodns., Inc., 1960—. Producer: Red Beret, 1952, Hell Below Zero, 1953, Black Knight, 1954, Prize of Gold, 1955, Cockleshell Heroes, 1956, Safari, 1956, April in Portugal, 1956, Fire Down Below, 1956, Odongo, 1956, Pickup Alley, 1957, Arrivederci Roma, 1957, Interpol, 1957, How to Murder a Rich Uncle, 1957, High Flight, 1958, No Time to Die, 1958, The Man Inside, 1958, Killers of Kilimanjaro, 1958, Bandit of Zhobe, 1958, In The Nick, 1959, Jazz Boat, 1960, Let's Get Married, 1960, The Trials of Oscar Wilde, 1960, Idol on Parade, 1960, Johnny Nobody, 1961, Call Me Bwana, 1963, Chitty Chitty Bang Bang, 1967 (Family Film award So. Calif. Motion Picture Council 1968); James Bond films Dr. No, 1962, From Russia With Love, 1963 (Screen Producers Guild certificate of nomination as best picture 1964), Goldfinger, 1963 (Screen Producers Guild cert. of nomination as best picture 1964), Thunderball, 1964 (Mkkin Kogyo Tsushin cert. of award 1966), You Only Live Twice, 1966 (Mkkin Kogyo Tsushin cert. of award 1967), On Her Majesty's Secret Service, 1969, Diamonds Are Forever, 1971, Live and Let Die, 1972, The Man With the Golden Gun, 1974, The Spy Who Loved Me, 1977, Moonraker, 1979, For Your Eyes Only, 1981, Octopussy, 1983. Bd. Dirs. Boys Club of Queens, Inc., 1968. Served to lt. (j.g.) USN, 1942-47; PTO. Decorated grand officer Order of Crown, Italy, Order St. Constantine, Italy; recipient Man of Year award, Irving G. Thalberg Meml. award 54th ann. Acad. Awards, 1982. Mem. Producers Guild, Am. Film Inst. Roman Catholic. Club: Metropolitan (N.Y.C.). Office: care GS Davis 1801 Century Park E Suite 1850 Los Angeles CA 90067

BROCE, THOMAS EDWARD, foundation and educational consultant; b. Fort Meade, Md., Oct. 27, 1935; s. Thomas Louis and Arlene Derma (Seifert) B.; m. Barbara Lynn Barnes, Nov. 25, 1960; children: Ashley Beth, Thomas Allan, David Edward. B.A., Baylor U., 1957; M.A., U. N.C., Chapel Hill, 1965; Ph.D., U. Okla., 1970. Reporter Waco (Tex.) Tribune-Herald, 1953-57; dir. pub. relations and devel. Little Rock U., 1959-61; dir. devel. Duke U., Durham, N.C., 1961-67; v.p. So. Meth. U., 1967-69; exec. asst. to pres. U. Okla., Norman, 1969-73; pres. chmn. bd. Phillips U., Enid, Okla., 1973-78;

pres. The Kerr Found., Oklahoma City, 1979-83; dir. Am. Exchange Bank, Norman; cons. Wofford Coll., Spartanburg, S.C., 1972-75, Rice U., 1974, U. South Fla., 1976-78, Westmont Coll., 1977—, Ark. Coll., 1978-80, Coker Coll., 1978-80, Okla. Med. Research Found., 1978-80, Central Meth. Coll., 1979—, Ursuline Acad., 1980—, Southwestern Coll., 1981—, Wesley Theol. Sem., 1981—, Milw. Sch. Engring., 1981—, Austin Coll., 1982—. Author: Directory of Oklahoma Foundations, 1974, Fund Raising: The Guide to Raising Money from Private Sources, 1979; contbg. author: Handbook Higher Education Adminstration, 1970. Bd. dirs. Inst. Resource Devel., 1972—; bd. visitors Baylor U.; bd. advisors Regis. Coll.; trustee Fellowship of Christian Athletes, Found. for Research on Nature of Man, Okla. Med. Research Found., Cross Acad., Rocky Mountain Heart Research Inst. Served with USAF, 1957-59. Mem. Nat. Soc. Fund Raising Execs. (dir.), Sigma Delta Chi, Phi Delta Kappa. Clubs: Rotarian., Men's Dinner, Petroleum (Oklahoma City). Home: 128 Kings Rd Evergreen CO 80439 Office: PO Box 1652 Evergreen CO 80439 Office: PO Box 8031 Norman OK 73070

BROCHES, ARON, lawyer, arbitrator; b. Amsterdam, Netherlands, Mar. 22, 1914; s. Abraham and Chaja (Person) B.; m. Catherina J. Pothast, May 2, 1939 (dec. Sept. 1982); children: Ida Alexandra, Paul Elias. LL.M., U. Amsterdam, 1936, LL.D., 1939; J.D., Fordham U., 1942. Legal adviser Netherlands embassy, also Netherlands Econ. Mission, Washington and N.Y.C., 1942-46; with World Bank, 1946-79, gen. counsel, 1959-79, v.p., 1972-79; mem. Pres.'s Council, 1965-79; sec. gen. Internat. Centre for Settlement Investment Disputes, 1967-80, mem. panel arbitrators, 1980—; mem. Panel Internat. Arbitrators, London, Am. Arbitration Assn.; mem. Asian-African Legal Consultative Com., Kuala Lampur and Cairo; sec. Netherlands del. UN Monetary and Fin. Conf., Bretton Woods, N.H., 1944; sec., legal adviser Netherlands del. inaugural meeting bd. govs. IMF and IBRD, Savannah, Ga., 1946; chief Internat. Bank gen. survey mission to, Nigeria, 1953-54; mem. Internat. Council for Comml. Arbitration, 1971—. Writer and lectr. on legal aspects of econ. devel. Trustee Internat. Legal Ctr., 1970-77. Decorated comdr. Order Orange Nassau. Clubs: Society De Witte (The Hague); Cosmos (Washington). Home: 2600 Tilden Pl NW Washington DC 20008 Office: 1919 Pennsylvania Ave NW Washington DC 20006

BROCHU, ANDRE, writer, educator; b. St. Eustache, Que., Can., Mar. 3, 1942; s. Edouard and Jeanne (Lacroix) B.; m. Celine Cadieux, June 24, 1964; children—Hugo, Xavier. B.A., Coll. St. Marie, 1960; M.A., U. Montreal, 1961; doctorat de 3e cycle en lettres modernes, U. Vincennes, Paris, 1971. Prof. lit. U. Montreal, 1963—. Author: Adeodat I, 1973, Hugo: Amour/Crime/Revolution, 1974, L'Instance critique, 1974, (with Gilles Marcotte) La Littérature et le reste, 1980. Home: 53 ave Wicksteed Mont-Royal PQ H3P 1P9 Canada Office: U Montreal cp 6128 Montreal PQ J7R 3C3 Canada

BROCK, ALICE MAY, restaurateur, author; b. 1941. Formerly tchr. in, Stockbridge, Mass.; propr. Alice's Restaurant, Stockbridge, 1966-67, 72-76, Alice's at Avaloch, Lenox, Mass., 1976—. Author: Alice's Restaurant Cookbook, 1969, My Life as a Restaurant, 1975. Address: 69 Commercial St Provincetown MA 02657

BROCK, CHARLES LAWRENCE, lawyer, business executive; b. Ottumwa, Iowa, Mar. 7, 1943; s. Charles Harlan and Betty Arlene (Ream) B.; m. Mary Jane Hipp, June 17, 1978; 1 son, William Walker. B.A. with highest distinction, Northwestern U., 1964; J.D., Harvard U., 1967; postgrad. (Rotary Found. fellow), U. Delhi (India) and India Law Inst., 1967-68; grad., Advanced Mgmt. Program, Harvard U., 1979. Bar: N.Y. State bar 1968. Asso. firm Sullivan & Cromwell, N.Y.C., 1969-74; v.p., corp. sec., gen. counsel Scholastic Mags., Inc. (now Scholastic, Inc.), N.Y.C., 1974-80, interim chief fin. and ops. officer, 1975-76, pub. internat. div., 1976-80; pres. Scholastic Tab Publs. Ltd., Can., 1976-80, Ashton-Scholastic Pty. Ltd., Australia, 1976-80, N.Z., 1976-80; chmn. Scholastic Publs. Ltd., U.K., 1976-80; sr. v.p., mgt. dir. Compton Communications, 1980-82; mgr. subsidieries Compton Advertising, 1980-82; counsel Drinker, Biddle & Reath, N.Y.C., Phila., Washington, 1982—. Anniversary gift chmn. Harvard Law Sch. Fund, 1967-68, vice chmn., 1975-77; council Nat. Harvard Law Sch. Assn.; trustee Harvard Law Sch. Assn. N.Y.C.; trustee, treas. Family Dynamics, 1981—; deacon Brick Presbyterian Ch., N.Y.C., 1973-76. Mem. Am. Bar Assn., N.Y. State Bar Assn., N.Y. County Lawyers Assn., Assn. Bar City N.Y., Assn. Am. Pubs., Harvard Law Sch. Assn., Phi Beta Kappa, Kappa Sigma. Clubs: Union, Harvard, N.Y. Yacht, Metropolitan, Down Town (N.Y.C.); Piping Rock (Locust Valley, N.Y.); Maidstone (East Hampton, N.Y.). Home: 840 Park Ave New York NY 10021 Office: 645 Madison Ave New York NY 10022

BROCK, DAN WILLETS, philosophy educator; b. Mineola, N.Y., Dec. 5, 1937; s. Dan S. and Ruth (Willets) B.; m. Jane Curtis, Oct. 7, 1960 (div. 1969); 1 son, Darrell C; m. Delia Ephron, Aug. 16, 1969 (div. 1976); m. Charlene S. Stephens, Jan. 29, 1977; children: David S., Katharine V. B.A. in Econs., Cornell U., 1960; Ph.D. in Philosphy, Columbia U., 1970; M.A. (hon.), Brown U., 1976. Preceptor Columbia U., N.Y.C., 1966-69; asst. prof. philosophy Brown U., Providence, 1969-75, assoc. prof., prof., chmn. philosophy, 1975—; vis. assoc. prof. philosophy U. Mich., Ann Arbor, 1976; staff philosopher Pres's. Commn. for Study of Ethical Problems in Medicine and Biomed. and Behavioral Research, Washington, 1981-82; cons. Pres's Commn. for Study of Ethical Problems in Medicine and Biomed. and Behavioral Research, Washingtn. Editor: Philosphy: An Introduction, 1970; contbr. articles to profl. publs.; bd. editors Philosophy and Phenomenological Research, Applied Philosophy. Served with U.S. Army, 1960. Mem. Am. Philos. Assn., Am. Soc. for Polit. and Legal Philosophy, R.I. Philos. Soc., Soc. for Bus. Ethics, Inst. for Soc., Ethics and Life Scis. Home: 28 Eames St Providence RI 02906 Office: Brown U 54 College St Providence RI 02912

BROCK, DAVID ALLEN, justice New Hampshire Supreme Court; b. Stoneham, Mass., July 6, 1936; s. Herbert and Margaret B.; m. Sandra Ford, 1960; 6 children. A.B., Dartmouth Coll., 1958; LL.B., U. Mich., 1963; postgrad., Nat. Jud. Coll., Reno, 1977. Bar: N.H. 1963. Assoc. Devine, Millimet, McDonough, Stahl & Branch, Manchester, N.H., 1963-69; U.S. atty. N.H., 1969-72; ptnr. Perkins, Douglas and Brock, Concord, N.H., 1972-74, Perkins & Brock, 1974-76; spl. counsel to Gov.l Exec. Council N.H., 1974-76, legal counsel to Gov. N.H., 1976; assoc. justice N.H. Superior Ct., 1976-78, N.H. Supreme Ct., 1978—; chmn. State of N.H. Legal Services Adv. Commn., 1977-79; chmn. dist. ct. reform subcom. Gov.'s commn. for Ct. System Improvement, 1974-75; mem. Select Commn. on Unified Ct. System, 1980—; chmn. N.H. Supreme Ct. Com. on Jud. Conduct, 1981—. Del. N.H. Constl. Conv., 1974; Republican candidate for U.S. Senate, 1972; vice chmn. N.H. Rep. State Com., 1968-69; chmn. Manchester Rep. Com., 1967-69; bd. dirs. Manchester Community Guidance Ctr., 1966-72, pres.l, 1969-72; mem. Gov.'s Commn. for Handicapped, 1978-79. Mem. N.H. Bar Assn. (chmn. constl. revision com. 1976-77), ABA (edn. appellate judges conf. 1981—, appellate advocacy com. 1982), N.H. Jud. Conf. Office: New Hampshire Supreme Ct Supreme Ct Bldg Concord NH 03301

BROCK, HARRY B., JR., banker; b. Ft. Payne, Ala., Mar. 31, 1926; s. Harry B. and Cornelia (Macfarlane) B.; m. Jane Hollock, Oct. 22, 1949; children—Stanley M., Barrett, Harry B. III. B.S., U. Ala., 1949; grad., Sch. Financial Pub. Relations, Northwestern U., 1957; grad. certificate, Am. Inst. Banking, 1964. Exec. v.p. Exchange Security Bank, Birmingham, Ala., 1955-64; pres. Central Bank & Trust Co., Birmingham, 1964-72; chmn., treas., chief exec. officer, dir. Central Bancshares of the South, Inc., Birmingham, Central Bank of South; dir. Daniel Found. of Ala., Marathon Equipment Co. Chmn. bd., past pres. Jr. Achievement Jefferson County; mem. pres.' council U. Ala. and U. Ala.-Birmingham; mem. exec. bd. Birmingham Area council Boy Scouts Am.; trustee Gorgas Scholarship Found.; trustee, mem. exec. com. Samford U., So. Research Inst. Served with USNR, 1944-46. Named Ala.'s Outstanding Young Banker, 1957. Mem. Young President's Orgn., Chief Execs. Forum. Baptist. Clubs: Birmingham Country, Birmingham, Shoal Creek Country. Home: Yamasee Shoal Creek AL 35094 Office: Central Bancshares of South Inc 701 S 20th St Birmingham AL 35223

BROCK, HORACE RHEA, accounting educator, university dean; b. Leggett, Tex., Aug. 26, 1927; s. Hobby B. and Winona (Epperson) B.; m. Frances Euline Williams, May 24, 1955; children: Alan Howard, Mary Ann, Charles. B.S., Sam Houston State U., 1946, B.B.A., 1951, M.A., 1951; Ph.D., U. Tex., 1954. Prof. U. Ark., 1954-55; disting. prof. North Tex. State U., 1955—, chmn. dept. accounting, 1966-74, dean Coll. Bus. Adminstrn., 1983—; adviser AID, Istanbul, Turkey, 1967-69; cons. taxation and financial reporting. Author: Introduction to Taxation, 1972, 7th edit., 1981, Cost Accounting, 1970, 3d edit., 1978, Accounting Concepts, 1974, 3d edit., 1980, Intermediate and Advanced Accounting, 1966, Accounting for Oil and Gas Producers, 1960, (Accounting for Oil and Gas Producing Cos.), 1982. Served with USAF, 1946-49. Mem. Am. Inst. C.P.A.s, Tex. Soc. C.P.A.s, Beta Gamma Sigma. Home: 1900 Westridge St Denton TX 76201

BROCK, JAMES DANIEL, retired airline executive, consultant; b. Montgomery County, Ala., Feb. 19, 1916; s. Alexander Franklin and Rebecca Bookhart (Lamar) B.; m. Alice Ferguson Jones, Jan. 8, 1948; children: James Daniel, Alice Timoxena, Franklin Laurens. Student, Tulane U., 1936-37. Vice pres. TACA Internat. Airlines and TACA Corp., 1953-59, Frontier Airlines, 1959-62; v.p. internat. Nat. Airlines, Miami, Fla., 1962-80, dir., 1974-80; v.p. Pan Am World Airways, 1980-81; dir. Citizens Fed. Savs. and Loan, Miami. Hon. consul Guatemala in, Denver, 1960-62; Mem. Tourist Adv. Council State of Fla.; Bd. dirs. Lighthouse for Blind, Miami., pres., Miami., 1981-82. Served to capt. USAAF, 1941-45. Mem. Caribbean Air Transp. Assn. (pres. 1956-59), Am. Soc. Travel Agts., Nat. Orgn. Travel Orgns. (dir.), Air Traffic Conf. Am. (pres. 1970), Discover Am. Travel Orgns. (dir.), Greater Miami C. of C. (bd. govs.), Phi Delta Theta. Methodist. Clubs: Riviera Country, Miami; Biscayne Bay Yacht (Miami). Home: 4107 Santa Maria Coral Gables FL 33146

BROCK, JAMES ROBERT, mfg. co. exec.; b. Annapolis, Md., July 8, 1944; s. James P. and Dorothy G. (Rogers) B.; m. Patricia Lee Halich, Sept. 11, 1965; children—Kimberly Ann, Stephen James. B.S., U. Balt., 1967. Credit rep. Montgomery Ward & Co., Balt., 1965-67; with Goodyear Tire & Rubber Co., 1967-79, dist. credit mgr., N. Brunswick, N.J. and Boston, 1971-79; treas. Motor Wheel Corp., Lansing, Mich., 1979—. Mem. Nat. Assn. Credit Mgmt., ABCD Credit Assn. Democrat. Roman Catholic. Home: 1220 Sandhill Dr DeWitt MI 48820 Office: 1600 N Larch St Lansing MI 48909

BROCK, JAMES SIDNEY, lawyer; b. Newbury, Vt., Sept. 2, 1913; s. Frank Nelson and Louise (Johnson) B.; m. Gladys H. Linton, Sept. 14, 1940; children: Linda L. Brock Scoggins, Richard L., Elizabeth A. Brock Duncan. B.S., Middlebury Coll., 1935; LL.B., Bklyn. Law Sch., 1942. Bar: N.Y. 1942, Vt. 1947. Practiced law, N.Y.C., 1942-47, Montpelier, Vt., 1947—; claims adjuster Liberty Mut. Ins. Co., 1935-42; asso. LeBoeuf & Lamb, 1942-46; pvt. practice, Montpelier, 1947-50; atty. Nat. Life Ins. Co., 1950-56, asst. counsel, 1956-63, gen. counsel, 1963—, v.p., 1968-70, sr. v.p., 1970-73, exec. v.p. corp. relations, 1973-74, exec. v.p., 1974-78; chmn., pres. Sentinel Group Funds, Inc., 1976-78; dir. Nat. Life Ins. Co. Bd. dirs. Champlain Coll., Central Vt. Med. Center, Inc.; trustee Wood Art Gallery; chmn. Vt. Human Services Bd., 1977-81; mem. Jud. Responsibility Bd. Mem. Assn. Life Ins. Counsel, ABA, Vt. Bar Assn. (pres. 1975). Republican. Congregationalist. Home: 9 Jordan St Montpelier VT 05602 Office: Cheney & Brock 114 Main St Montpelier VT 05602

BROCK, JOHN EDGAR, banker; b. St. Louis, Sept. 14, 1946; s. Earl Elwood and Betty Jo (McNally) Brock S. B.S.B.A., Drake U. C.P.A. Sr. Acct. Alexander Grant and Co., St. Louis, 1968-73; controller Landmark Central, St. Louis, 1973; v.p. and treas. Landmark Bancshares, St. Louis, 1973-78, sr. v.p. and chief fin. officer, 1978-79, exec. v.p., 1979-80, pres., St. Louis, 1980—; dir. Sterling Textile, St. Louis, Nat. Environ., New Orleans, Chemfix Techs., The Daniele Hotel Corp., St. Louis. Served with Mo. N.G., 1968-74. Mem. St. Louis chpt. Young Pres's Orgn., Am. Inst. C.P.A.s, Mo. Soc. C.P.A.s, Fin. Execs. Inst. Club: Clayton (St. Louis). Home: 132a Nor Central Saint Louis MO 63105 Office: Landmark Bancshares Corp 10 S Brentwood Saint Louis MO 63105

BROCK, KARENA DIANE, ballerina; b. Los Angeles, Sept. 21, 1942; d. Orville DeLoss and Sallie Alice (Anderson) B. Grad., Barstow sch., Kansas City, Mo. Tchr. master classes Radford (Va.) Coll., U. Louisville, U. Tampa; staff tchr. Bklyn. Coll.; mem. faculty SUNY-Purchase; guest tchr. Walnut Hill Sch., Boston, Savannah Ballet, Cleve. Ballet. Dancer, David Lichine Concert Group, Los Angeles, 1959-61, Netherlands Nat. Ballet Co., Amsterdam, 1962; mem. corps, Am. Ballet Theatre, N.Y.C., 1963-68; soloist, 1968-73; prin. ballerina, 1973-79; artistic dir., prima ballerina, choreographer, Savannah (Ga.) Ballet Co., 1979—; guest artist, Miami (Fla.) Civic Ballet, Macon (Ga.) Civic Ballet, Tampa (Fla.) Civic Ballet, U. Ill. Ballet Co., Champaign, San Jose (Calif.) Civic Ballet, Ballet de San Juan, P.R., Gala Ballet, Amarillo (Tex.) Civic Ballet, Maywood Ballet Co., Phila., U. Wis., Milw. Civic Ballet, Stars of Am. Ballet, various TV shows, White House, 1966, 69. Mem. AFTRA, AGVA, Am. Guild Mus. Artists. Home: 20 Hanging Moss Rd Savannah GA 31410 Office: 2212 Lincoln St Savannah GA 31406

BROCK, MITCHELL, lawyer; b. Wyncote, Pa., Nov. 10, 1927; s. John W. and Mildred A. (Mitchell) B.; m. Gioia Connell, June 21, 1952; children: Felicity, Marina, Mitchell Hovey, Laura. A.B., Princeton U., 1950; LL.B., U. Pa., 1953. Assoc. firm Sullivan & Cromwell, N.Y.C., 1953-59; ptnr. Sullivan & Cormwell, N.Y.C., 1960—, Sullivan & Cromwell, Paris, 1965-68. Bd. dirs. Frost Valley YMCA, Oliverea, N.Y., 1980—, Am. Found. Blind, 1967—; trustee Helen Keller Internat., N.Y.C., 1970—. Served with USN, 1945-46. Mem. Council on Fgn. Relations, ABA, N.Y. Bar Assn., Asssn. Bar City N.Y., Union Internat. des Avocats. Republican. Episcopalian. Clubs: Anglers, Down Town Assn., River, Princeton, Ivy. Home: 120 East End Ave New York NY 10028 Office: 250 Park Ave New York NY 10177

BROCK, PAUL WARRINGTON, lawyer; b. Mobile, Ala., Feb. 23, 1928; s. Glen Porter and Esther (Goodwin) B.; m. Grace Leigh Blasingame, Sept. 4, 1948 (dec. June 1960); children—Paul W., Bette Leigh, Valerie Grace; m. Louise Morris Shearer, July 6, 1962; children—Louise Shearer, Richard Goodwin. Student, Ala. Poly. Inst., 1944; B.S., U. Ala., 1948, J.D., 1950. Bar: Ala. bar 1950. Practiced in, Mobile, 1953—; mem. firm Hand, Arendall & Bedsole, 1953-56, Hand, Arendall, Bedsole, Greaves & Johnston, 1956—; faculty continuing legal edn. program Ala. Bar Assn. Served to 2d lt. USAF, 1952-53. Recipient Nat. Balfour award Sigma Chi, 1946-47. Mem. Am., Ala., Mobile bar assns., Am. Coll. Trial Lawyers, Internat. Assn. Ins. Counsel, Ala. Def. Lawyers Assn. (past pres.), Def. Research Inst. (past pres.), Fedn. Ins. Counsel, Am. Coll. Mortgage Attys., Nat. Assn. R.R. Trial Counsel, Omicron Delta Kappa, Beta Gamma Sigma. Republican. Episcopalian. Home: 30 Hillwood Rd Mobile AL 36608 Office: PO Box 123 Mobile AL 36601

BROCK, RAY LEONARD, JR., state justice; b. McDonald, Tenn., Sept. 21, 1922; s. Ray Leonard and Ila Venore (Bailey) B.; m. Juanita Addabelle Barker, Sept. 18, 1944; children—Ila Raye, Elaine Rose, Karen Denise. Student, U. Tenn., 1940-43, U. Colo., 1945-46; LL.B., Duke U., 1948. Bar: Tenn. bar 1948. Practiced in, Chattanooga, 1948-63; judge Chancery Ct. of Tenn., 1963-74; justice Supreme Ct. Tenn., 1974—. Served with U.S. Army, 1943-44. Mem. Tenn., Chattanooga bar assns., Am. Judicature Soc., Tenn. Trial Lawyers Assn. Democrat. Mem. United Ch. Christ. Club: Big Orange. Office: 300 Supreme Ct Bldg Nashville TN 37219 *

BROCK, ROBERT LEE, hotel and restaurant executive; b. Pawnee Rock, Kans., Dec. 27, 1924; s. Eddie Ray and Vivian Orpha (Crawford) B.; m. Carol Rae Grigg, June 3, 1978; children: Robert Lee, Edward, Alan, Steven, Darin, Scott, Staci. A.B., U. Kans., 1950, LL.B., 1951; J.D. (hon.), Washburn U., 1979. Bar: Kans. bar 1952. Atty. firm Stinson, Mag, Thomson, McEvers & Fizzell, Kansas City, Mo., 1951-52; individual practice law, Topeka, 1952-58; chmn. bd., chief exec. officer Brock Hotel Corp., Topeka, 1956—. Chmn. Kans. Democratic State Com., 1974-75; Dem. chmn. 2d Congl. Dist. Kans., 1966-74; pres. Kans. Young Dem. Clubs, 1955-61. Served with USNR, 1943-46. Named Kansan of Yr. Native Sons and Daus. of Kans., 1973; recipient Disting. Service citation U. Kans., 1977, Fred Ellsworth Medallion, 1980; named Businessman of Yr. Topeka Capital-Jour., 1980. Mem. Internat. Assn. Holiday Inns, Am. Hotel and Motel Assn., Kans. Hotel and Motel Assn. Methodist. Club: Tower (Dallas). Home: 4260 Bordeaux Dallas TX 75205 Office: 4441 W Airport Freeway Irving TX 75062

BROCK, STANLEY E., life insurance company executive; b. Winnipeg, Man., Can., Sept. 9, 1912; s. William R. and Ann (Williams) B.; m. Gertrude Blondeau, Sept. 21, 1942; children: Donald W., Alan E., Joyann. B.A. with honours, U. Man., 1936. With Equitable Life Assurance Co., Waterloo, Ont., 1933-40; with Indsl. Life Ins. Co., Quebec, 1940—, exec. v.p., then pres., 1958-77, vice chmn. bd., pres. exec. com. of bd., 1977-82, also dir.; dir. Levesque Beaubien Inc. Pres. Jeffrey Hale's Hosp. Centre, Quebec; life gov. Jeffery Hale's Hosp. Corp. Decorated Order of Can. Fellow Soc. Actuaries; mem. Canadian Inst. Actuaries, Que. C. of C. (gov.). Clubs: Rotary, Garrison (Quebec). Home: 1080 Thornhill Park Sillery PQ G1S 3N7 Canada Office: 1122 Saint Louis Rd Suite 202 Sillery PQ G1S 1E5 Canada

BROCK, THOMAS DALE, microbiology educator; b. Cleve., Sept. 10, 1926; s. Thomas Carter and Helen Sophia (Ringwald) B.; m. Mary Louise Louden, Sept. 13, 1952 (div. Feb. 1971); m. Katherine Serat Middleton, Feb. 20, 1971; children: Emily Katherine, Brian Thomas. B.S., Ohio State U., 1949, M.S., 1950, Ph.D., 1952. Research microbiologist Upjohn Co., Kalamazoo, 1952-57; asst. prof. Western Res. U., Cleve., 1957-59, Ind. U., Bloomington, 1960-62, assoc. prof., 1961-64, prof., 1964-71; E.B. Fred prof. natural scis. U. Wis., Madison, 1971—, chmn. dept. bacteriology, 1979-82. Author: Milestones in Microbiology, 1961, Principles of Microbial Ecology, 1966, Thermophilic Microorganisms, 1978, Biology of Microorganisms, 1970, Biology of Microorganisms, 2d edit., 1974, Biology of Microorganisms, 3d edit., 1979, Biology of Microoprganism, 4th edit., 1984. Recipient Research Career Devel. NIH, 1962-68, 71-72, 78-79; Found. for Microbiology lectr. Fellow AAAS; mem. Am. Soc. for Microbiology (chmn. gen. div. 1970-71, Fisher 1984). Club: Town and Gown (Madison). Home: 1227 Dartmouth Rd Madison WI 53705 Office: Dept Bacteriology U Wis 1550 Linden Rd Madison WI 53706 *I have always operated on the principle of fairness, hard work and honesty. If I have made a mistake, I have willingly admitted it, to myself and others. No one succeeds alone, but through the aid and good offices of others. Although personal comfort is one measure of achievement, effective contribution to the growing body of world knowledge is the most satisfying accomplishment.*

BROCK, VENTRESS NOLAN, college administrator; b. Rochester, Tex., Aug. 12, 1924; s. Robert Lawrence and Lamiza Pearl (Brown) B.; m. Mary June Posey, June 22, 1952; children: Roderick Mark, Lisa Junanne. B.A. magna cum laude, Hardin-Simmons U., 1949; M.Ed., U. Tex., 1957; Ed.D., Tex. Tech U., 1970. Tchr. Sweetwater (Tex.) High Sch., 1949-64, dir. publs., 1949-64, vice prin., 1954-64; prin. Snyder (Tex.) High Sch., 1964-69; dean, exec. v.p. Western Tex. Coll., Snyder, 1970—; Guest lectr. Columbia U., N.Y.C., 1964; guest expert-lectr. U. Mo., 1957; lectr. U. Tex., 1961. Contbr. articles to profl. jours. Vice pres. United Way, Snyder, 1963-64; pres. Scurry County Concert Assn., Snyder, 1974—; pres., trustee Scurry County div. Am. Heart Assn., 1981—; chmn. Snyder Bicentennial, 1975—. Served with Signal Corps AUS, 1943-46. Decorated Bronze Star medal; recipient Gold Key award Columbia U., 1963; named Outstanding Young Man in Sweetwater, 1956, Outstanding Journalism Tchr. in Tex., 1964. Mem. Tex. Assn. Jr. Coll. Instructional Adminstrs. (sec.-treas. 1980-81, pres. 1983-84), Tex. Jr. Coll. Tchrs. Assn., Phi Delta Kappa. Democrat. Baptist (deacon). Clubs: Gold Coats (pres. 1984), Rotary (pres. 1963-64), Rotary (dir. 1963-65). Home: 2907 Denison Ave Snyder TX 79549 *My life-long interest has been education: learning for myself and teaching. I find deep satisfaction in motivating students, family, friends and associates to more fully use God-given talents and abilities. I enjoy working behind the scenes in the role of teacher and advisor. The hours I have put into my work have not seemed as important as the work I have put into my hours. Perhaps Proverbs 3:5-6 could be called a compass or guiding light for me and a summary of my basic philosophy: "Trust in the Lord with all thine heart; and lean not unto thine own understanding. In all thy ways acknowledge Him, and He shall direct thy paths."*

BROCKENBROUGH, HENRY WATKINS, banker; b. Richmond, Va., Aug. 28, 1923; s. Benjamin Willard and Kathleen Reading (Watkins) B.; m. Mary Lane Williams, Oct. 30, 1948; children: Henry Watkins, Rebecca Lane, John Reading, Willson Williams. B.A. cum laude, Hampden-Sydney Coll., 1944; LL.B., U. Va., 1948; grad., Stonier Grad. Sch. Banking, Rutgers U., 1957. Bar: Va. 1949. With United Va. Bank, Richmond, 1948—, v.p., trust officer, 1963-67, sr. v.p., trust officer, 1967—; Past pres. Estate Planning Council, Richmond. Chmn. bd. dir. Tuckahoe YMCA, 1975. Served to lt. (j.g.) USNR, 1943-46. Mem. Va. Bankers Assn. (chmn. trust com. 1970-71), Richmond, Va. chambers commerce, Va. State Bar, Lambda Chi Alpha, Delta Theta Phi. Presbyn. Club: Richmond Downtown. Home: 802 Horsepen Rd Richmond VA 23229 Office: 919 E Main St Richmond VA 23219

BROCKERT, RICHARD CLAUDE, union official; b. Madison, Wis., Dec. 26, 1937; s. Claude O. and Geneva A. (Smith) B.; m. Esther S. Skipper, Sept. 22, 1973; 1 son, Patrick. With United Telegraph Workers, Washington, 1962-71, internat. v.p., Rockville, Md., 1971-79, internat. pres., 1979—. Served with USN, 1955-58. Roman Catholic.

Home: 11717 Flints Grove Ln Gaithersburg MD 20878 Office: United Telegraph Workers 701 E Gude Dr Rockville MD 20850

BROCKETT, OSCAR GROSS, educator; b. Hartsville, Tenn., Mar. 18, 1923; s. Oscar Hill and Minnie Dee (Gross) B.; m. Lenyth Spenker, Sept. 4, 1951; 1 dau., Francesca Lane. B.A., Peabody Coll., 1947; M.A., Stanford U., 1949, Ph.D., 1953. Instr. English U. Ky., 1949-50; asst. instr. drama Stanford U., 1950-52; asst. prof. drama Stetson U., DeLand, Fla., 1952-56; asst., then asso. prof. U. Iowa, 1956-63; prof., then distinguished prof. Ind. U., 1963-78; Ashbel Smith prof. drama U. Tex., Austin, 1978-80, dean, 1978-80; DeMille prof. drama U. So. Calif., Los Angeles, 1980-81; Waggener prof. fine arts U. Tex., Austin, 1981—. Contbr. numerous articles to profl jours. Served with USNR, 1943-46. Guggenheim fellow, 1970-71; recipient Fulbright award, 1963-64; Medallion of Honor Theta Alpha Phi, 1977; Am. Coll. Theatre Festival Gold Medallion, 1978. Fellow Am. Theatre Assn. (past pres., Merit award 1979); mem. Am. Soc. Theatre Research, MLA, Nat. Theatre Conf., Speech Communications Assn. Democrat. Episcopalian. Home: 1800 Lavaca #208 Austin TX 78701 Office: U Tex Austin TX 78712

BROCKHAUS, WILLIAM LEE, management consultant, corporate executive, writer, entrepreneur; b. Jan. 22, 1943; s. Herold A. and Leona M. (Stutzke) B. B.S. cum laude in Bus. Adminstrn, U. Mo., 1966, M.B.A. in Fin, 1967; D.Bus.Adminstrn. (fellow), Ind. U., 1970; honor grad. research and devel. mgmt. program, Inst. Tech. Cons. div. mgmt. services Ernst & Ernst, 1967; teaching, research asst. Ind. U., 1968-69; adj. prof. indsl. mgmt. Trinity U., 1970-71; prof. Grad. Sch. Bus., U. So. Calif., 1971-76; prin. Profl. Mgmt. Counsel, 1971-73; cons. to mgmt. Brockhaus, Carlisle & Assos., Los Angeles, 1973-76; chmn. bd., chief exec. officer Edward Hyman Co., Culver City, Calif., 1976-78, BC&A Enterprises, Inc., San Diego, 1978—; speaker in field. Contributing author: Encyclopedia of Professional Management; mem. editorial bd.: Jour. Applied Mgmt, 1977—; contbr. articles to profl. jours. Recipient Am. Legion award, 1969, Delta Sigma Pi award, 1966, Kawneer Co. scholar, 1966, Ford Found. fellow, 1969, U. So. Calif. grantee, 1971-73. Mem. Acad. Mgmt., Am. Fin. Assn., Am. Psychol. Assn., Am. Mgmt. Assn., Soc. Advancement Mgmt., Am. Soc. Tng. and Devel., AAAS, Soc. Entrepreneurship Research, Nat. Council Small Bus. Mgmt. Devel., Newcomen Soc. N.Am., Scabbard and Blade, Sigma Iota Epsilon, Beta Gamma Sigma. Extensive psychol., behavioral sci. research. Office: 11650 Iberia Pl Suite K San Diego CA 92128

BROCKHOUSE, BERTRAM NEVILLE, physicist; b. Lethbridge, Alta., Can., July 15, 1918; s. Israel Bertram and Mable Emily (Neville) B.; m. Doris Isobel Mary Miller, May 22, 1948; children: Ann, Gordon, Ian, James, Alice Elizabeth, Charles. B.A., U. B.C., 1947; M.A., U. Toronto, 1948, Ph.D., 1950; D.Sc., U. Waterloo, 1969. Research officer Atomic Energy of Can., Ltd., Chalk River, Ont., 1950-60, br. head, neutron physics, 1960-62; prof. physics McMaster U., Hamilton, Ont., 1962—, chmn. dept. physics, 1967-70. Contbr. sci. articles to profl. jours. Served with Royal Canadian Navy Vol. Res., 1939-45. Recipient Centennial medal of Can., 1967, Queen's Jubilee medal, 1977, Order of Can., 1982, Duddell medal and prize Inst. Physics and Phys. Soc., 1963; Guggenheim fellow, 1970-71; NRC of Can. grantee, 1962-78. Mem. Royal Soc. Can. (Tory medal), Royal Soc. London, Canadian Assn. Physicists (medal), Am. Phys. Soc. (Buckley prize), Philosophy of Sci. Assn. Roman Catholic. Home: PO Box 7338 Ancaster ON Canada L9G 3N6 Office: McMaster U Inst Materials Research Hamilton ON L8S 4M1 Canada

BROCKIE, DONALD PETER, chemicals, pharmaceuticals, plastics mfg. co. exec.; b. Rupert, Idaho, Nov. 17, 1931; s. Robert and Helen Abigail (Ellsworth) B.; m. Dora DalSoglio, Aug. 30, 1952; children—Karla Sue, Anita, Maria Louise. Student, U. Utah, 1950-52; B.A., So. Meth. U., 1956, LL.B., 1956. Bar: Tex. bar 1956. Rep. labor relations Gen. Dynamics, Ft. Worth, 1956-63, labor relations adminstr., 1963-68, exempt personnel mgr., Quincy, Mass., 1968-69; personnel dir. ICI America, Inc., Stamford, Conn., 1969-71, v.p. personnel, 1971-72, asst. dir. personnel, Wilmington, Del., 1972-78, corp. sec., 1978—. Chmn. corp. services com. Stamford Area Commerce and Industry Assn., 1972; chmn. indsl. services com. Walnut St. YMCA, Wilmington, 1976-78; chmn. indsl. relations adv. com. Mfg. Chemists Assn., 1977-78. Mem. Am. Soc. Corp. Secs. Republican. Home: 117 Falcon Ln Wilmington DE 19808 Office: ICI Americas Inc Wilmington DE 19897

BROCKINGTON, DONALD LESLIE, anthropologist, archaeologist, educator; b. Weslaco, Tex., Apr. 28, 1929; s. Buford Maurice and M. Juanita (Young) B.; m. Lolita Gutierrez, Dec. 19, 1955; children: Laura Alicia, John Carlos, Peter Daniel. B.A., U. N.Mex., 1954; student, U. Calif.-Berkeley, 1953; M.A., Mexico City Coll., 1956-57; Ph.D., U. Wis., 1965. Instr., adminstrv. asst. Mexico City Coll., 1956-57; asst. prof. San Diego State Coll., 1963-67; assoc. prof. anthropology to prof. U. N.C., Chapel Hill, 1967—, chmn. dept. anthropology, 1980—; dir. hwy. archaeology Wis. State Hist. Soc., Madison, 1960-62; manuscript evaluator various pub. cos., 1969—; cons., advisor Nat. Geog. Soc., Washington, 1974—, Museum Archaeology, Cochambamba, Bolivia, 1982. Served with U.S. Army, 1951-53. Fellow Mexico City Coll., 1956-57, U. Wis., 1959-63, 65, Bobbs-Merrill, NSF, 1963, 68, 70, U. N.C., 1968, 71, 74, 76. Fellow Am. Anthrop Assn., Soc. Am. Archaeology; mem. AAAS. Home: 808 Tinkerbell Rd Chapel Hill NC 27514 Office: Dept Anthropology U NC Chapel Hill NC 27514

BROCKMAN, MICHAEL STEPHEN, broadcasting company executive; b. Bklyn., Nov. 19, 1938; s. Gustave and Sonya (Schechter) B.; m. Wendy Kaltman, Nov. 26, 1965; children: Laura, David. B.S., Ithaca Coll., 1963. With ABC-TV, 1963-77, mgr. daytime programming, N.Y.C., 1970-72, dir., 1972-74; dir. daytime programming ABC Entertainment, N.Y.C., 1974, v.p., 1974-77, v.p. tape prodn. and ops., 1977; v.p. daytime and children's programs NBC-TV, Burbank, Calif., 1977-80; v.p. programs Lorimar Prodns., Culver City, Calif., 1980-82; v.p. daytime and children's programs CBS Entertainment, Los Angeles, 1982—. Mem. Nat. Acad. TV Arts and Scis., Acad. TV Arts and Scis., Alpha Epsilon Rho. Home: 22455 Dardenne St Woodland Hills CA 91364 Office: 78 Beverly Blvd Los Angeles CA 90036

BROCKWAY, DAVID HUNT, lawyer; b. Paterson, N.J., Dec. 18, 1943; s. George Pond and Lucille (Hunt) B.; m. Marilyn Bofshever, July 29, 1979. A.B., Cornell U., 1968; J.D., Harvard U., 1971. Bar: N.Y. 1972. Assoc. firm Donovan Leisure Newton & Irvine, N.Y.C., 1971-76; chief staff Joint Com. on Taxation, Washington, 1983—. Served with U.S. Army, 1963-66. Home: 133 E St SE Washington DC 20003 Office: Joint Com on Taxation Longworth House Office Bldg Washington DC 20515

BROCKWAY, DUNCAN, librarian, clergyman; b. Manchester, N.H., July 23, 1932; s. Walter Priest and Eleanor (Duncan) B.; m. Lois Simpson, Jan. 19, 1957 (div. 1974); children: Peter, Andrew, Ellen, Catherine; m. Ruth Pensiero, Sept. 6, 1975 (dec. Sept. 1981). B.A., St. John's Coll., Annapolis, Md., 1953; student, Harvard Div. Sch., 1953-55; B.D., Princeton Theol. Sch., 1956; M.A. in L.S, Rutgers U., 1960. Ordained to ministry Presbyn. Ch., 1956; pastor in, Windham, N.H., 1956-58; order librarian Speer Library, Princeton Theol. Sem., 1958-62; pastor in, Frenchtown, N.J., 1962-65; with Case Meml. Library, Hartford Sem. Found., 1965-76, librarian, 1967-76; pastor Colebrook (Conn.) Congregational Ch., 1971-77; dir. library services Sch. Theology, Dubuque, Iowa, 1977—, U. Dubuque, 1981—. Stated clk. Presbytery Conn. Valley, 1973-77; sec. W. Hartland Fire Dept., 1966-72; mem. Hartland Bd. Edn., 1970-71. Mem. ALA, Iowa Library Assn., Am. Theol. Library Assns. Democrat. Home: 2245 Bennett St Dubuque IA 52001 Office: 2050 University Dubuque IA 52001

BROCKWAY, GEORGE POND, publisher; b. Portland, Maine, Oct. 11, 1915; s. Walter B. and Elizabeth E. (Priest) B.; m. Lucile M. Hunt, Sept. 2, 1939; children: Susan, David, Nancy, Carol, Sally, Douglas, Laura, Andrew. A.B., Williams Coll., 1936, Litt.D., 1982; postgrad., Yale U., 1937. With McGraw-Hill Book Co., 1937-42, W.W. Norton and Co., Inc., N.Y.C., 1942—, editor, 1949-84, pres., 1958-76, chmn., 1976-84; dir. Yale Press., pres., 1982—; columnist The New Leader, 1981—. Author: (with Lucile H. Brockway) Greece, a Classical Tour with Extras, 1966; contbg. author: What Happens in Book Publishing, 1957. Served with AUS, 1944-46. Mem. Soc. Am. Historians (hon.), Phi Beta Kappa. Clubs: Publishers Lunch, Century Assn. Home: 63 Brevoort Rd Chappaqua NY 10514

BROCKWAY, MERRILL LAMONTE, TV producer, director; b. New Carlisle, Ind., Feb. 28, 1923; s. Howard Robert and Melissa Mildred (Bennett) B. Student, Ind. U., 1941-43; B.A., Columbia U., 1948, M.A. in Musicology, 1951. Concert pianist, 1951-53; producer, dir. areas of the arts on film and video tape CBS Television, N.Y.C. and Phila., 1953—; exec. producer, dir. Camera Three, 1968-75; series producer Dance in Am., 1975-80; exec. producer programming for CBS Cable, 1980-82. Served to sgt. C.E. AUS, 1943-45. Decorated Bronze Star; 2 awards Ohio State U.; Christopher award; Am. Festival award; Emmy award for Dance in Am., 1979; award Dirs. Guild Am., 1978; Golden Hugo. Mem. Dirs. Guild Am., Writers Guild Am. Home: 276 Riverside Dr New York NY 10025

BROCKWAY, RICHARD CRANE, ins. orgn. exec.; b. Rochester, N.Y., Feb. 18, 1908; s. Guy H. and Anna (Crane) B.; m. Constance Delinni, Apr. 16, 1934; children—Carla (Mrs. Charles M. Rodstrom), Joanna C. (Mrs. Gerald S. Paonessa). B.S. in Econs, Wharton Sch., U. Pa., 1931. With WPA, 1935-37; with div. employment N.Y. State Dept. Labor, 1938-58, asst. exec. dir., 1948-54, exec. dir., 1954-58; with War Manpower Commn., N.Y.C., 1941-46; exec. dir. Mass. Hosp. Service, Inc. (Blue Cross), Boston, 1959-65; pres. Nat. Health and Welfare Retirement Assn., Inc., N.Y.C., 1966-72, vice chmn., 1972—; Cons. U.S. Dept. Labor.; Mem. Nat. Commn. Community Health Services Task Force on Financing; mem. adv. bd. Booth Meml. Hosp., Boston; mem. council on Blue Cross and finance Am. Hosp. Assn.; bd. govs., chmn. exec. com. Blue Cross Assn., Chgo.; research on unemployment ins. N.Y. State Legislature. Mem. Am. Hosp. Assn., Am. Pub. Health Assn., Nat. Assembly for Social Planning and Welfare (council), Nat. Health Forum (chmn. program planning 1973), Nat. Acad. Pub. Adminstrn. (co-chmn. medicare panel 1970-73), Nat. Health Council (dir., v.p. 1975—). Club: Union (Boston). Home: 41 Corchaug Ave Port Washington NY 11050 Office: 666 Fifth Ave S New York NY 10019

BROCKWAY, WILLIAM ROBERT, architect; b. Marshall, Ill., Sept. 24, 1924; s. Erdice Roark and Dolly Varden (Ritchey) B.; m. Patricia Lee Norman, June 5, 1948; children: Nancy Ann, William Robert. B.Arch., Tulane U., 1951. Draftsman firms in, San Francisco and Baton Rouge, 1951-55; assoc. Robert Cummings, Architect, New Orleans, 1955-56, Bodman, Murrell & Webb, Baton Rouge, 1956-59, 61-64; designer A. Hays Town, Inc., Baton Rouge, 1959-61; propr. William R. Brockway.; Fellow AIA, Architect, Baton Rouge, 1964—; spl. design instr. La. State U., 1964-65; commr. Capitol Region Planning Commn., 1975—, vice-chmn., 1978-79; chmn. La. Architects Selection Bd., 1975; mem. La. Bd. Archtl. Examiners, 1978-82, chmn., 1980—. Author: Historic Landmarks in the Capitol Region, 1973; also articles, newspaper column. Bd. dirs. Capitol Area United Givers Fund, 1969-71; bd. dirs. Found. Hist. La., 1973-75, Friends of the Cabildo, 1982—; mem. project rev. com. Mid-La. Health Services Agy., 1977-78; mem. La State Fire Marshal Bd. Rev., 1981—. Served with AUS, 1943-46; ETO. Decorated Bronze Star.; Fellow La. State U. Mus. Natural Sci., 1981—. Fellow AIA (pres. Baton Rouge 1961, Traveling fellow 1950, Sch. medal 1951); mem. La. Architects Assn. (sec. 1962, dir. 1961-62, 65-66, 76-77), So. Conf. Archtl. Registration Bds. (dir. 1982—), Nat. Rifle Assn., Nat. Muzzle Loading Rifle Assn., La. Wildfowl Carvers and Collectors Guild. Home: 8734 Forest Hill Dr Baton Rouge LA 70809 Office: 1680 Lobdell Ave Baton Rouge LA 70806

BROCKWELL, CHARLES WILBUR, JR., history educator; b. Greenwood, S.C., Nov. 24, 1937; s. Charles Wilbur and Amelia (Wideman) B.; m. Mary Ann Spears, Mar. 25, 1959; children: Cynthia Lynn, Stephen Madison. A.B., Wofford Coll., 1959; S.T.B., Harvard Div. Sch., 1962; Ph.D., Duke U., 1971. Ordained to ministry Methodist Ch., 1963; pastor Trinity United Meth. Ch., Aiken, S.C., 1962-64, Walnut Grove United Meth. Ch., Roebuck, S.C., 1964-66; asst. to minister Trinity Ave. Presbyn. Ch., Durham, N.C., 1966-69; instr. history U. Louisville, 1969-71, asst. prof., chmn. dept., 1971-74, assoc. prof., 1977—, coordinator Coll. Honors Program, 1982—; Mem. Joint Commn. Luth. World Fedn. and World Meth. Council, 1977—; mem. commn. archives and history United Meth. Ch., 1979—; pres. Southeastern Jurisdiction Hist. Soc., United Meth. Ch., 1978—. Contbr. articles to profl. jours., also book. Nat. Meth. scholar, 1957-59; Rockefeller Bros. Theol. fellow, 1959-60; F.C. Slater scholar, 1960-62; Duke U. scholar, 1968-69; Humphrey Centenary scholar, 1976. Mem. Am. Hist. Assn., Am. Soc. Ch. History, Medieval Acad. Am., Phi Beta Kappa, Pi Gamma Mu. Democrat. Home: 3907 Ashridge Dr Louisville KY 40222

BROD, STANFORD, graphic designer, educator; b. Cin., Sept. 29, 1932; s. Morris and Rebecca (Mitman) B.; children—Deborah, Daniel, Michael. B.S in Design, U. Cin., 1955. Graphic designer Rhodes Studio, Cin., 1955-62; tchr. exptl. typography Art Acad. Cin., 1960-75; graphic designer Lipson Assos. Inc., Cin., 1962—; prof. graphic design U. Cin., 1962—. Exhbns. include, Mus. Modern Art, N.Y.C., 1966, Urban Walls, Cin., 1972, City Banners, Sao Paulo, Brazil, 1975, ITC Center, N.Y.C., 1981, Tel Aviv Mus. (Israel), 1982, Internat. Art Exhbn., Dusseldorf, W. Ger. Recipient Communications Arts awards, 1959, 64, 66, 70, 73, 76, Creativity on Paper awards, 1960-67, Internat. Typographic awards, 1965, 70, N.Y. Type Dirs. Club award, 1968, Typographic Composition Assn. awards, 1970-76. Office: 2349 Victory Pkwy Cincinnati OH 45206 *The more I design and paint the more I am sensitive to the movement of my pen and brush, and am able to transmit the image of the subject in my head by way of my arm into my hand, and so to my work. I have become aware that pressure demands counter-pressure, and the difference between order and chaos. This points out the importance of the smallest detail, and that order is the basis of all creative work.*

BRODE, MARVIN JAY, lawyer, former state legislator; b. Memphis, Aug. 26, 1931; s. Howard M. and Erniece J. (Jacob) B.; m. Freda Cohn, June 24, 1965; children—William Howard, Robert Mark, Laura Mary. B.A., Vanderbilt U., 1953, LL.B., 1954; postgrad. law, U. Chgo., 1954, Harvard U., 1962. Bar: Tenn. bar 1955. Since practiced in, Memphis; asso. Brode and Fisher, 1958-65, Brode & Dunlap, 1965-70, Brode & Smith, 1970-72, Brode & Sugg, 1973—; spl. judge City Ct. Memphis, 1957-63; asst. city atty., City of Memphis, 1965-68; mem. Pres.'s Nat. Traffic Adv. Com., 1963-64. Co-editor: Memphis Municipal Code. Mem. Tenn. Art Commn., 1965-72, Mayor's Community Action Com., 1965; hon. col. on staff Tenn. Gov., 1967—; del. So. Regional Edn. Conf., 1964, 65, 66; mem. Tenn. Ho. of Reps., 1962-65, Shelby County Democratic Exec. Com., 1966—; hon. dep. sheriff, Shelby County, 1978—; bd. dirs. West Tenn. chpt. Arthritis and Rheumatism Found., Memphis and Shelby County Multiple Sclerosis Soc., 1978—, West Tenn. Multiple Sclerosis Soc., 1978—. Mem. Am., Tenn., Shelby County, Memphis bar assns., Memphis Arts Council, Phi Alpha Delta. Jewish (dir. temple brotherhood). Clubs: Masons (32 deg.), Shriners.). Home: 4841 Walnut Grove Rd Memphis TN 38111 Office: Suite 3116 100 N Main St Memphis TN 38103

BRODEN, EDWIN RAUCH, retired business executive, foundation executive; b. Cleve., July 20, 1904; s. Edwin Herbert and Helen (Rauch) B.; m. Estelle Frances Gill, Oct. 18, 1935 (div.); children: Gretchen (Mrs. George L. Bartholomew), Ronald Edwin; m. Helen Lee Trumpy, Apr. 16, 1966. Grad., Carnegie Inst. Tech., 1926, postgrad., 1933-36. Indsl. engr., cons. United Natural Gas Co., Oil City, Pa., 1931-36; asst. chief engr. Blaw-Knox Co., Pitts., 1936-41, asst. div. mgr., 1941-44, div. mgr., 1944-47; v.p. in charge operations Carborundum Co., Niagara Falls., N.Y., 1947-51, exec. v.p., 1951-55, SKF Industries, Inc., Phila., 1955-56, pres., 1956-68, chmn. bd., 1957-70; owner Delta Lok Co., Phila., B & R Constrn. Co. Chmn. Am. Heritage Found., Am. Council Co-ordinated Action; bd. dirs., past pres. Jr. Achievement Del. Valley; chmn. bd. Spring Garden Coll.; life trustee Carnegie Mellon U.; chmn. Am. Swedish Hist. Found. Mem. Am. Soc. Corp. Execs., Mfrs. Assn. Delaware Valley (dir., past pres.), Am. Ordnance Assn., ASTM, Am. Welding Soc., ASME, Anti-Friction Bearing Mfrs. Assn. (past pres.), Engrng. Soc. Western Pa., Soc. Automotive Engrs., Sigma Nu. Presbyn. Clubs: Annapolis Yacht, Lafayetta, Union League (Phila.); Duquesne (Pitts.); Engineers, Philadelphia Country (Phila.); N.Y. Yacht. Home and Office: 799 Harrison Rd Ithan PA 19085

BRODER, AARON J., lawyer; b. N.Y.C., May 21, 1924. B.S. cum laude, CCNY, 1945; LL.B., N.Y. U., 1949. Bar: N.Y. Bar 1949. Practice in, N.Y.C., 1949—; partner firm F. Lee Bailey & Aaron J. Broder, 1970—; mem. legal adv. com. N.Y.C. Community Coll., 1973; lectr. in field. Author: Trial Handbook for New York Lawyers, 1973, Dealing with Damages in Personal Injury and Wrongful Death Trials; Columnist: N.Y. Law Jour, 1971—, also numerous articles, chpts. in books.; Editor: Trial Lawyers Quar., 6 vols. Mem. Am. Bar Assn., Am. Trial Lawyers Assn. (gov. 1974, mem. faculty, aviation law com., editor-in-chief quar. 1964-67), Internat. Acad. Law and Sci., N.Y. State Trial Lawyers Assn. (pres. 1965-67), N.Y. State Bar Assn., Assn. Bar City N.Y., Bronx County Bar Assn., Nassau County Bar Assn. Home: 11 Beech Ln Kings Point NY 11204 Office: 350 Fifth Ave New York NY 10001

BRODER, DAVID SALZER, journalist, author; b. Chicago Heights, Ill., Sept. 11, 1929; s. Albert I. and Nina M. (Salzer) B.; m. Ann Creighton Collar, June 8, 1951; children: George, Joshua, Matthew, Michael. B.A., U. Chgo., 1947, M.A., 1951; Litt.D., Denison U., 1975; LL.D. (hon.), Wabash Coll., 1977, Kenyon Coll., 1980, Cleve. State U., 1981, Wittenberg Coll., 1982. Reporter Pantagraph, Bloomington, Ill., 1953-55, Congressional Quar., Washington, 1955-60, Washington Star, 1960-65, N.Y. Times, Washington bur., 1965-66; reporter Washington Post, 1966-75, asso. editor, 1975—; syndicated columnist. Author: (with Stephen Hess) The Republican Establishment, 1967, The Party's Over: The Failure of Politics in America, 1972, Changing of the Guard: Power and Leadership in America, 1980; contbr. articles on public affairs to mags. and books. Former mem. U. Chgo. Alumni cabinet. Served with AUS, 1951-53. Recipient Pulitzer prize in journalism, 1973; fellow Inst. Politics, John F. Kennedy Sch. of Govt., Harvard, 1969-70; Poynter fellow Yale and Ind. univs., 1973. Fellow Inst. Policy Scis. and Pub. Affairs of Duke, Sigma Delta Chi; mem. Am. Polit. Sci. Assn. (adv. bd. Congressional Fellows Program 1964—), Am. Soc. Public Adminstrn. Home: 4024 N 27th St Arlington VA 22207 Office: 1150 15th St NW Washington DC 20071

BRODER, PATRICIA JANIS, art historian, author, lecturer; b. N.Y.C., Nov. 22, 1935; d. Milton W. and Rheba (Mantell) Janis; m. Stanley H. Broder, Jan. 22, 1959; children: Clifford James, Peter Howard, Helen Anna. Student, Smith Coll., 1953-54; B.A., Barnard Coll., Columbia U., 1957; postgrad., Rutgers U., 1962-64. Stock brokerage trainee A.M. Kidder & Co., N.Y.C., 1958; registered rep. Thomson & McKinnon, N.Y.C., 1959-61; ind. registered investment advisor, 1962-64. Art cons.; art investment advisor; writer on art history: books include Bronzes of the American West (Hebert Adam Meml. medal Nat. Sculpture Soc. 1975), 1974 (Gold medal Nat. Acad. Western Art 1975), Great Paintings of the Old American West, American Indian Painting and Sculpture, Taos: A Painter's Dream (Western Heritage Wrangler award, Border Regional Library Assn. award 1980), Hopi Painting: The World of the Hopis, Dean Cornwell: Dean of Illustrators. Recipient Western Heritage Wranglers award for best article on Am. West, 1975. Mem. Western History Assn., AAUW. Home: 488 Long Hill Dr Short Hills NJ 07078

BRODERICK, CARLFRED BARTHOLOMEW, sociology educator; b. Salt Lake City, Apr. 7, 1932; s. Frederick Anthony and Napina (Bartholomew) B.; m. Kathleen Adelle State, July 3, 1952; children: Katherine, Carlfred Bartholomew, Victor, Wendi, Jenifer, Frank, Beverly, Benjamin. A.B. magna cum laude, Harvard, 1953; Ph.D., Cornell U., 1956; postgrad., U. Minn., 1966-67. Asso. prof. family devel. U. Ga., 1956-60; asso. prof. family relations Pa. State U., 1960-69, prof., 1969-71; prof. sociology, dir. marriage and family therapy program U. So. Calif., Los Angeles, 1971—. Author: Sexuelle Entwickland in Kindheit und Jungend, 1970, Couples: How to Confront Problems and Maintain Loving Relationships, 1979, Marriage and the Family, 1979, Marriage and the Family, 2d edit., 1983, The Therapeutic Triangle, 1983; editor: (with Jessie Bernard) The Individual, Sex and Society, 1969, A Decade of Research and Action on the Family, 1971, Jour. Marriage and The Family, 1970-75; Contbr. articles to profl. jours. Pres. Cerritos (Calif.) stake Ch. Jesus Christ Latter-day Saints., 1976-82. Fellow Am. Assn. Marriage and Family Therapists, So. Calif. Assn. Marriage and Family Therapists (pres. 1974), Nat. Council Family Relations (pres. 1976), Assn. Mormon Counselors and Psychotherapists (pres. 1982). Home: 18902 Alfred Ave Cerritos CA 90701 Office: Dept Sociology Univ Southern Calif University Park Los Angeles CA 90089

BRODERICK, EDWIN B., religious organization executive; b. Bronx, N.Y.C., Jan. 16, 1917; s. Patrick J. and Margaret M. (O'Donnell) B. A.B., St. Joseph's Coll., Yonkers, N.Y., 1938; Ph.D. in English, Fordham U., 1951; L.H.D., L.I.U., 1968, Cath. U. Am., 1982; LL.D., Siena Coll., 1969. Ordained priest Roman Catholic Ch., 1942; tchr. Cardinal Hayes High Sch., 1943-47; asst. pastor St. Patrick's Cathedral, N.Y.C., 1947; dir. radio-TV Archdiocese, N.Y., 1951-54; sec. to Cardinal Spellman, 1954-64; pres. St. Joseph's Sem. and Coll., Yonkers, 1964-68; consecrated bishop, 1967, bishop of, Albany, N.Y., 1969-76; exec. dir. Cath. Relief Services, N.Y.C., 1976—; conclavist Papal election, 1958; trustee Key Trust Co., Albany. Theol.; cons. to Danforth Found.; Chmn. N.Y. State Cath. Bishops' Liaison with N.Y. State Cath. Colls.; chmn. N.Y. State Cath. Conf., 1968-76; mem. U.S.

Bishops' Com. on Edn.; mem. adminstrv. bd. U.S. Cath. Conf., 1972—; U.S. rep. Cor Unum. Author: Your Child and Television, 1954, Your Place in Television, 1953. Mem. McKay Commn. to investigate Attica Riot, 1971; mem. adv. com. Yale Div. Sch., 1978—, Hoffstra U. Sch. Law, 1983; pres. Interfaith Hunger Appeal, 1978-80; chmn. Horn of Africa Ecumenical Coalition, 1980—. Recipient LaSalle medal Manhattan Coll., 1971; decorated grand knight Grand Cross Holy Sepulchre. Mem. MLA, Met. Opera Club, Equestrian Order Knights Malta. Club: Friars. Home: 900 Park Ave New York NY 10021 Office: 1011 1st Ave New York NY 10150

BRODERICK, FRANCIS LYONS, historian, educator; b. N.Y.C., Sept. 13, 1922; s. Joseph Aloysius and Mary (Lyons) B.; m. Barbara Baldridge, June 12, 1950; children: Thomas, Joseph, James, Ann. Grad., Phillips Acad., Andover, Mass., 1939; A.B. with high honors, Princeton U., 1943; M.A. in History, Harvard U., 1947; Ph.D. in History Am. Civilization, Harvard, 1955. Instr. history Princeton, 1945-46, State U. Ia., 1948-50, Phillips Exeter Acad., 1951-63; dir. Peace Corps, Ghana, 1964-66; dean Lawrence and Downer Colls.; also Gordon R. Clapp prof. Am. studies Lawrence U., Appleton, Wis., 1966-68; chancellor U. Mass., Boston, 1968-72, Commonwealth prof., 1972—. Author: W.E.B. DuBois: Negro Leader in a Time of Crisis, 1959, Right Reverend New Dealer: John A Ryan, 1963, The Origins of the Constitution, 1964, (with August Meier) Negro Protest Thought in the Twentieth Century, 1966, Reconstruction and the American Negro, 1969; Editor: (John Tracy Ellis) The Life of James Cardinal Gibbons, 1963 (Nat. Cath. Book award 1964). Nat. bd. cons. Nat. Endowment for Humanities.; trustee St. Anselm Coll., Merrimack Coll. Served to 1st lt. USAAF, 1943-45. Woodrow Wilson fellow, 1945-46. Mem. Am. Cath. Hist. Assn. (pres. 1968). Home: Bunker Hill Ave Stratham NH 03885

BRODERICK, JOHN CARUTHERS, librarian, educator; b. Memphis, Tenn., Sept. 6, 1926; s. John Patrick and Myrtle Vaughn (Newson) B.; m. Kathryn Price Lynch, Sept. 10, 1949; children: Kathryn Price, John Caruthers, Jr. A.B., Southwestern U., Memphis, 1948; M.A., U. N.C., 1949, Ph.D., 1953. Instr. English U. Tex., Austin, 1952-57; asst. prof. Wake Forest (N.C.) U., 1957-58, asso. prof., 1958-63, prof., 1963-65; with Library of Congress, Washington, 1964—, specialist, 1964-65, asst. chief, 1965-74, chief, manuscript div., 1975-79, asst. librarian for research services, 1979—; adj. prof. English George Washington U., 1964—; vis. prof. U. Va., 1959, U. N.C., 1968. Compiler: Whitman The Poet, 1961; editor: The Journal of Henry David Thoreau, 1981—; contbr. to profl. jours. Adv. com. U.S. Senate Hist. Office, 1974-78; mem. Nat. Hist. Publs. and Records Commn., 1978-82. Served with U.S. Army, 1945-46. Danforth Found. grantee, 1960; Am. Council Learned Socs. grantee, 1962-63; Council on Library Resources fellow, 1971. Mem. Bibliog. Soc. Am., MLA, Am. Antiquarian Soc., South Atlantic MLA, Sigma Alpha Epsilon, Omicron Delta Kappa. Club: Cosmos (Washington). Home: 8005 Inspection House Rd Rockville MD 20854 Office: Library of Congress Washington DC 20540

BRODERICK, RAYMOND JOSEPH, judge; b. Phila, May 29, 1914; s. Patrick Joseph and Catharine (Haines) B.; m. Marjorie Beacom, Oct. 2, 1945; children—Patrick J., Timothy B., Tara M., Deidre C., Brian X. A.B. magna cum laude, U. Notre Dame, 1935; J.D., U. Pa., 1938; L.H.D., Pa. Coll. Podiatric Medicine, 1968; LL.D. (hon.), Phila. Coll. Osteo. Medicine, 1969, Allentown Coll. St. Frances De Sales, 1977. Bar: Pa. bar. Civilian agt. U.S. Naval Intelligence, 1941-42; practiced in, Phila., 1945-62; sr. partner firm Broderick, Schubert & FitzPatrick, Phila., 1962-71; lt. gov., State of Pa., 1966-71; judge U.S. Dist. Ct. for Eastern Dist. Pa., Phila., 1971—; chmn. Adminstrv. Task Force for Constl. Revision, 1966; mem. Prep. Com. Pa. Constl. Conv., 1967, pres., 1967-68. Chmn. lawyers div. Cath. Charities, Phila.; mem. Phila. Republican Policy Com.; bd. mgrs. Youth Study Center, Phila. Served with USNR, 1942-45. Mem. Am., Pa., Phila. bar assns., Notre Dame Law Assn., Friendly Sons St. Patrick. Clubs: Socialegal, Constl., Overbrook Farms. Home: 6408 Church Rd Philadelphia PA 19151 Office: US Courthouse 601 Market St Philadelphia PA 19106

BRODERICK, VINCENT LYONS, judge; b. N.Y.C., Apr. 26, 1920; s. Joseph A. and Mary Rose (Lyons) B.; m. Sally Brine, Apr. 15, 1950; children: Kathleen, Vincent, Mary, Ellen, Joan, Justin. A.B., Princeton U., 1941; LL.B., Harvard U., 1948. Bar: N.Y. 1948. With firm Barrett, Smith, Schapiro, Simon & Armstrong, N.Y.C., 1948-54; dep. commr. charge legal matters N.Y.C. Police Dept., 1954-56; gen. counsel Nat. Assn. Investment Cos., N.Y.C., 1956-61; chief asst. U.S. atty. So. Dist. N.Y., 1961-62, 62-65, U.S. atty., 1962; police commr., N.Y.C., 1965-66; mem. firm Phillips, Nizer, Benjamin, Krim & Ballon, 1966-71, Forsyth, Decker, Murray & Broderick, 1971-76; judge U.S. Dist. Ct. So. Dist. N.Y., N.Y.C., 1976—. Mem. Assn. Bar City N.Y. Home: 1424 Park Ln Pelham Manor NY 10803 Office: US Courthouse Foley Sq New York NY 10007

BRODERSEN, ARTHUR JAMES, elec. engr.; b. Fresno, Calif., Aug. 31, 1939; s. Arthur James and Edith Elizabeth (McAllister) B.; m. Rebecca Ray Turton, Feb. 6, 1965; children—Arthur James, Kristina. B.S., U. Calif., Berkeley, 1961, M.S., 1963, Ph.D., 1966. Asst. prof. elec. engring. U. Fla., 1966-69, asso. prof., 1969-74, prof., 1974; prof. elec. engring. Vanderbilt U., Nashville, 1974—, chmn. dept. elec. and biomed. engring., 1974-81, asso. dean, 1979—. Contbr. articles to profl. jours. Mem. IEEE (sr.; chmn. Nashville 1978-79), Eta Kappa Nu, Tau Beta Pi. Democrat. Home: 6722 Duquaine Ct Nashville TN 37205 Office: PO Box 1628 Station B Vanderbilt U Nashville TN 37235

BRODERSON, MORRIS, artist; b. Los Angeles, Nov. 4, 1928; s. and Charlotte Ankrum. Student, U. So. Calif., 1943-47. Exhibited one-man shows, M.H. DeYoung Mus., San Francisco, 1961, Carnegie Inst. Internat., 1966, San Diego Mus., 1969, Hirshhorn Mus. and Sculpture Garden, Washington, 1974, U. Ariz. Mus., 1975, San Diego Mus. Art, 1982, Ankrum Gallery, 1983; exhibited group shows, NAD, 1978, travelling show, West' 83 Art and Law, Carnegie/Meilon U., represented in permanent collections, Whitney Mus. Am. Art, N.Y.C., Mus. Fine Arts, Houston, Hirshhorn Mus. and Sculpture Garden, San Francisco Mus. Art, San Diego Mus. Art, others. Recipient award New Talent U.S.A. Art in Am., 1960, Excellence in Art award Art Dirs. Club, Phila., 1963, Gt. Ideas of Western Man award Container Corp. Am., 1963. Address: c/o Ankrum Gallery 657 N La Cienega Blvd Los Angeles CA 90069

BRODEUR, ALPHONSE TONER, industrialist; b. Montreal, Que., Can., Feb. 20, 1902; s. Alphonse and Nellie (Toner) B.; m. Nora Hope, June 14, 1928 (dec. 1979); children: Michael T.H., Alphonse William, James, Christopher John; m. 2d Marguerite Rathbun, June 12, 1981. Chmn. Cassidy's Ltd., Lorlea Steels Ltd., Galord Regethermique Can. Ltee, Modern Kitchen Equip. Ltd., Cody Food Equip. Ltd., Continental Mfrs. Ltd., Reudorb Inc., Deurcol Inc., A.B.C.-Cassidy Inc., Imbrex-Cassidy Ltd., Packer Floor Coverings Ltd., Terminal Sheet Metal Works Ltd., Vancouver, B.C., Can., 1973—. Gov. Montreal Children's Hosp., 1953—; past pres., dir. Que. Assn. Retarded Children; bd. hon. govs. Can. Assn. Mentally Retarded, 1950—; dir. Canadian Council Internat. C. of C. Served with Royal Militia, 1925-47. Mem. Canadian Importers Assn. (past pres.), Hotel and Restaurant Suppliers Assn. (past pres.). Clubs: Royal Montreal Golf, Royal Montreal Curling, Royal St. Lawrence Yacht, Mt. Royal, Montreal Badminton and Squash. Home: 60 Summit Crescent Westmount PQ Canada H3Y 1L6 Office: 2555 Matte Blvd Brossard PQ Canada J4Z 3M1

BRODEUR, ARMAND EDWARD, pediatric radiologist; b. Penacook, N.H., Jan. 8, 1922; s. Felix and Patronyne Antoinette (Lavoie) B.; m. Gloria Marie Thompson, June 4, 1947; children: Armand Paul, Garrett Michael, Mark Stephen, Mariette Therese, Michelle Bernadette, Paul Francis. M.D., St. Louis U., 1947, M.Rd., 1952; LL.D. (hon.), Anselm's Coll., 1974. Intern St. Louis U. Hosps., 1947-48, resident in radiology, 1949-52; pvt. practice medicine specializing in pediatric radiology, St. Louis, 1954-56; radiologist-in-chief Cardinal Glennon Meml. Hosp. for Children, St. Louis, 1956—; instr. St. Louis U. Sch. Medicine, 1952-60, sr. instr., 1960-62, asst. prof., 1962-65, asso. prof., 1965-70, prof. radiology, 1970—, chmn. dept. radiology, 1975-78, vice-chmn. dept., 1978—, prof. pediatrics, 1979—, prof. juvenile law, 1979—; lectr. and cons. in field. Radio show host: Doctor to Doctor, Sta. KMOX, St. Louis; Author: Radiologic Diagnosis in Infants and Children, 1965, Radiology of the Pediatric Elbow, 1980, Radiologic Pathology for Allied Health Professions, 1980; author monographs; contbr. articles to profl. jours., numerous teaching tapes. Dir. Mark Twain Bank.; Bd. dirs. ARC, Tb Soc. Served with U.S. Army, 1942-46; Served with USPHS, 1952-54. Recipient Pillar of Univ. award St. Louis U., 1973. Fellow Am. Coll. Radiology, Am. Acad. Pediatrics; Mem. AMA (Bronze medal), Soc. Pediatric Radiology, Radiol. Soc. N.Am., Sigma Xi, Alpha Omega Alpha, Alpha Sigma Nu, Rho Kappa Sigma. Roman Catholic. Home: 400 Bambury Way Saint Louis MO 63131 Office: 1465 S Grand St Saint Louis MO 63104 *Success is being pleased with what you see in the mirror—every day. It should not be measured by the size of your home or bank account. What you see in the mirror is all that you can take with you. It is measured by what you do for people!*

BRODHEAD, DAVID CRAWMER, lawyer; b. Midison, Wis., Sept. 16, 1934; s. Richard Jacob and Irma (Crawmer) B.; m. Nancie Christensen, Aug. 17, 1963; children: Compton, Peter, Christoffer. B.S., U. Wis., 1956, LL.D., 1959. Bar: N.Y. 1960, Wis. 1959, D.C. 1979. Asoc. firm Paul, Weiss, Rifkind, Wharton & Garrison, N.Y.C., 1959-68; ptnr. Paul, Weiss, Rifkind, Whaton & Garrison, N.Y.C., 1969—; dir. Centennial Industries, Inc., N.Y.C. Editor-in-chief: Wis. Law Rev, 1958-59. Trustee Collegiate Sch., N.Y.C., 1978—; vestryman Christ and St. Stephen's Episcopal Ch., 1972-82. Mem. N.Y. State Bar, Assn. Bar City N.Y., Wis. Bar. Assn., Westside C. of C. of City of N.Y. (dir. 1970—), Order of Coif, Delta Theta Phi. Clubs: Washington (Conn.); Marco Polo (N.Y.C.).

BRODHEAD, GEORGE MILTON, lawyer; b. Phila., May 23, 1904; s. George M. and Clara (Chaplain) B.; m. Pauline W. Hand, Sept. 13, 1934; children: Anne Foster (Mrs. Lewis), Richard Chaplain. A.B., Wesleyan U., Middletown, Conn., 1926; LL.B., U. Pa., 1930. Bar: Pa. 1930. Tchr. Choate Sch., 1926-27; since practiced in, Phila.; asso. Rawle & Henderson, 1930-43, partner, 1943—; dir. Mchts. Warehouse Co. Bd. dirs. Barra Found., Claneil Found., Stephen Watchorn Found.; past dir. Germantown Boys Club. Mem. SR (pres. Pa. soc. 1971-73), Mil. Order Loyal Legion, Soc. War 1812 (past v.p.), Colonial Soc. Pa. (past councillor), Am., Pa., Phila. bar assns., Soc. Sons St. George, Soc. Colonial Wars, Holland Soc. of N.Y., Penn Club, Phi Beta Kappa, Psi Upsilon, Phi Delta Phi. Presbyn. Clubs: Phila. Cricket, Union League (pres. 1969-70), Lawyers (Phila.) (pres. 1967-68). Home: 201 W Evergreen Ave Philadelphia PA 19118 Office: 211 S Broad St Philadelphia PA 19107

BRODHEAD, WILLIAM MCNULTY, lawyer, former congressman; b. Cleve., Sept. 12, 1941; s. William McNulty and Agnes Marie (Franz) B.; m. Kathleen Garlock, Jan. 16, 1965; children: Michael, Paul. A.B., Wayne State U., 1965; J.D., U. Mich., 1967. Bar: Mich. 1968. Tchr., Detroit, 1964-66, practiced in, 1968, atty., City of Detroit, 1969-70; mem. Mich. Ho. Reps., 1971-74, chmn. com. city govt., 1973-74; mem. 94th-97th Congresses from 17th Dist.; now mem. firm Plunkett, Cooney, Rutt, Watters, Stanczyk & Pedersen. Mem. Wayne County Democratic Com., 1971—; membership chmn. Mich. Dem. Party, 1973-74, mem. fin. com., 1973-74. Home: 14320 Glastonbury St Detroit MI 48223 Office: 900 Marquette Bldg Detroit MI 40226 *

BRODIE, BERNARD BERYL, pharmacologist, educator; b. Liverpool, Eng., Aug. 7, 1909; s. Samuel and Esther (Ginsburg) B.; m. Anne Lois Smith, Aug. 30, 1950. B.S., McGill U., 1931; Ph.D., N.Y.U., 1935; D.Sc. (hon.), U. Paris, France, 1963, Phila. Coll. Pharmacy and Sci., 1965, U. Barcelona, 1967, N.Y. Med. Coll., 1970, U. Louvain, Belgium, 1971, M.D., Karolinska Inst., 1968, U. Cagliari, Italy, 1973. Asst. prof. pharmacology N.Y.U. Med. Sch., 1943-47, asso. prof. biochemistry, 1947-50; chief lab. chem. pharmacology Nat. Heart Inst., 1950-70, ret., 1970; sr. cons. Hoffmann-LaRoche Inc., 1971—; vis. prof. pharmacology Pa. State U. Coll. Medicine, 1975—; Vis. prof. George Washington U. Med. Sch., 1950-65; prof. pharmacology U. Ariz. Med. Center, Tucson, 1972-75, 82—; cons. Nat. Heart and Lung Inst., NIH, Bethesda, Md., 1971—; Carl Wilhelm Scheele lectr. Royal Pharm. Inst., Stockholm, 1967; Paul Lamson lectr. Vanderbilt U., 1971; Rosemary Cass Meml. lectr. U. Dundee, Scotland, 1971. Author: Metabolic Factors Controlling Duration of Drug Action, 1963, Drug Enzyme Interactions, 1964, Concepts in Biochemical Pharmacology, vols. I and II, 1972, Bioavialability of Drugs, 1973; Founder, chmn. editorial bd.: Life Sciences, Internat. Jour. Neuropharmacology; editor, co-founder: Pharmacology; Contbr. numerous articles to profl. jours. Served with Canadian Army, 1926-28. Recipient Distinguished Service award Dept. Health, Edn. and Welfare, 1958; Shionogi Commemoration lectr., Japan, 1962; Karl Beyer award, 1962; Julius Sturmer Meml. lectr., 1962; Torald Sollmann award Am. Pharmacology Soc., 1963; Distinguished Achievement award Modern Medicine med. jour., 1964; Albert Lasker award for basic med. research, 1967; Nat. Medal of Sci., 1968; Claude Bernard prof. U. Montreal, 1969; Schmiede-Plakette German Pharmacol. Soc., 1969; Oscar B. Hunter Meml. award Am. Pharm. Soc., 1970; Research Achievement award for stimulation research Acad. Pharm. Scis., 1972; Intrascis. medalist, 1972; medal for research U. Turku, Finland). Mem. Nat. Acad. Scis., Inst. Medicine, Internat. Pharm. Soc., Am. Coll. Neuropsychopharmacology (pres. 1965), Am. Soc. Biol. Chemists, Am. Soc. Pharmacology and Exptl. Therapeutics, Harvey Soc., N.Y., Washington acads. scis., Royal Soc. Medicine. Home: 2231 E Mabel St Tucson AZ 85719

BRODIE, DONALD GIBBS, investment company executive; b. N.Y.C., Oct. 24, 1938; s. Bruce James and Laurene Elizabeth (Rolf) B.; m. Gail Robison, Aug. 26, 1966; children: Lesley Thompson, Alexandra Paget, Ian Rolf. B.S., U. Pa., 1960; postgrad., U. Lausanne, Switzerland, 1962-63; M.B.A., NYU, 1969. With Discount Corp. NY, N.Y.C., 1963—, v.p., asst. sec., 1970-72, v.p., sec., 1972-78, sr. v.p., sec., 1978-81, exec. v.p., dir., N.Y.C., 1981—; dir. Discount Corp. N.Y. Advisers, Discount Corp. N.Y. Futures, Discount Corp. N.Y. (Can.) Ltd., Discount Corp. N.Y. (London) Ltd., 58 Pine St. Corp., DCNY Corp. Trustee, treas. Buckley Country Day Sch., Roslyn, N.Y. Served with USNR, 1960-62. Clubs: University, Downtown Assn. Office: Discount Corp NY 58 Pine St New York NY 10005

BRODIE, HARLOW KEITH HAMMOND, university chancellor; b. Stamford, Conn., Aug. 24, 1939; s. Lawrence Sheldon and Elizabeth White (Hammond) B.; m. Brenda Ann Barrowclough, Jan. 26, 1967; children: Melissa Verduin, Cameron Keith, Tyler Hammond, Bryson Barrowclough. A.B., Princeton U., 1961; M.D., Columbia U., 1965. Diplomate: Am. Bd. Psychiatry and Neurology. Intern Ochsner Found. Hosp., New Orleans, 1965-66; resident in psychiatry Columbia-Presbyn. Med. Center, N.Y.C., 1966-68; clin. assoc. intramural research program NIMH, 1968-70; asst. prof. psychiatry, dir. gen. clin. research center Stanford U. Med. Sch., 1970-74; prof. psychiatry, chmn. dept. Duke U. Med. Sch., 1974-82, prof. law, adj. prof. psychology, 1981—; psychiatrist-in-chief Duke U. Med. Center, 1974-82; chancellor Duke U., 1982—. Co-author: The Importance of Mental Health Services to General Health Care, 1979, Modern Clinical Psychiatry, 1981; co-editor: American Handbook of Psychiatry, vols. 6 and 7, 1975, 81, Controversy in Psychiatry, 1978; asso. editor: Am. Jour. Psychiatry, 1973-81. Chmn. Durham Area Mental Health, Mental Retardation and Substance Abuse Bd., 1981-82; Vice pres., trustee Durham Acad., 1979—. Recipient Psychopharmacology research award Am. Psychol. Assn., 1970, Strecker award Inst. of Pa. Hosp., 1980. Mem. Am. Psychiat. Assn. (sec. 1977-81, pres. 1982-83), Am. Coll. Psychiatrists (chmn. publs. com. 1980—), Inst. Medicine, So. Psychiat. Assn., Royal Coll. Psychiatrists, Soc. Biol. Psychiatry (A.E. Bennet research award 1970), Am. Psychosomatic Soc., Soc. Neurosci. Home: 63 Beverly Dr Durham NC 27707 Office: 215 Allen Bldg Duke U Durham NC 27706

BRODIE, JOHN RILEY, TV sportscaster, former professional football player; b. San Francisco, Aug. 14, 1935; m. Susan; 5 children. B.A., Stanford U., 1957. Quarterback San Francisco 49ers, 1957-73; football commentator NBC Sports, 1974—; also commentator PGA tour events.; Played in Pro Bowl, 1965, 70. Named to Sporting News Western Conf. All-Star team, 1965, Sporting News NFC All-Star team, 1970, Sporting News NFC Player of Yr., 1970. Office: care NBC Sports Press Dept 30 Rockefeller Plaza New York NY 10020 *

BRODIE, MICHAEL LOUIS, lawyer; b. Phila., Nov. 26, 1944; s. Stanley M. and Ethel (Kurta) B.; m. Ricki R. Gottenberg, Aug. 20, 1967; children: Jill Amy, Matthew Jason. B.S., Temple U., 1967, J.D., 1971. Bar: Pa., U.S. Dist. Ct. (ea. dist.) Pa., U.S. Circut. Ct. Appeals (3d cir.), U.S. Supreme Ct. U.S. Tchr. math. Phila. Public Schs., 1967-71; assoc. Matkoff & Shengold, Phila., 1971-72; counsel Publicker Industries Inc., Phila., 1972-78, Greenwich, Conn., 1978-81; also pvt. practice law; mem. Bd. Common Pleas Arbitrators, Phila.; arbitrator Am. Arbitration Assn.; pvt. arbitrations. Bd. dirs., legal counsel Ohev Shalom of Bucks County, Pa., 1978. Recipient cert. achievement Profl. Program Equal Employment Opportunity Laws. Mem. Phila. Bar Assn., ABA (gen. practice and corp., banking and bus. law sects.), Comml. Law League Am. Jewish. Home: 15 Midbrook Ln Old Greenwich CT 06870

BRODIE, NORMAN, life insurance company executive; b. Sask., Can., Mar. 10, 1920; came to U.S., 1923, naturalized, 1943; s. Louis and Annie L. (Harris) B.; m. Florence Wagner, Sept. 8, 1946; children: Pamela Eve Weinman, Terry Jean Brodie Ruben. B.S., CCNY, 1941. With Equitable Life Assurance Soc. U.S., N.Y.C., 1941-77, v.p., 1969-77, dep. controller, 1969, controller, 1970-75, actuary, 1975-77; v.p. Home Life Ins. Co., N.Y.C., 1977—, controller, 1977-81, actuary, 1981—. Served with AUS, 1943-45. Fellow Soc. Actuaries; mem. Am. Acad. Actuaries, City Coll. Alumni Assn. (bd. dirs. 1971-76). Jewish. Club: Bonnie Briar Country. Home: 81 Robert Dr New Rochelle NY 10804 Office: Home Life Ins Co 253 Broadway New York NY 10007

BRODINE, CHARLES EDWARD, physician; b. Sioux City, Iowa, May 10, 1925; s. Ivar and Dorothy B.; m. Lois Bliss, June 26, 1949; children: Stephanie Kay, Jennifer Leah, Charles Edward. B.S., Iowa State U., Ames, 1948, research fellow malaria project, 1948-49; M.D., Washington U., St. Louis, 1953. Intern St. Louis County Hosp., 1953-54, resident in internal medicine, 1954-55, U.S. Naval Hosp., Oakland, Calif., 1957-59; fellow in hematology, clin. instr. medicine U. Cin. and Cin. Gen. Hosp., 1955-57; head hematology service U.S. Naval Hosp., Oakland, 1959-61, Bethesda, Md., 1961-62, cons. in hematology, 1962-73; head div. of research hematology Naval Med. Research Inst., Bethesda, 1962-66, chmn. dept. clin. investigation, 1966-70, exec. officer, 1970-73; program mgr. Navy frozen blood and trauma research program research div. Bur. Medicine and Surgery U.S. Dept. Navy, Washington, 1962-71, dir. research div., 1973-74; spl. asst. med. research and devel. to Surgeon Gen. U.S. Navy, 1974-77; comdg. officer Naval Med. Research and Devel. Command, Nat. Naval Med. Center, Bethesda, 1974-77; asst. med. dir. environ. health and preventive medicine Office Med. Services Dept. State, Washington, 1977—; mem. Agt. Orange Working Group, 1982—; exec. com. Nat. Council Internat. Health, 1982—; Bd. dirs. Gorgas Meml. Inst. Tropical and Preventive Medicine, 1973—; mem. Bur. Medicine and Surgery Policy Council, 1974-77; med. adviser ARC, 1975-79; adv. com. Nat. Sickle Cell Disease, NIH, 1974-77; mem. com. on biomed. research U.S.-Egypt Joint Working Group, 1975-77; mem. White House Working Group on Internat. Health, 1977; clin. asso. prof. dept. medicine Georgetown U., Washington, 1971—; Dept. State mem. Nat. Council for Internat. Health, 1978—. Contbr. articles in field to med. jours. Exec. com. Gorgas Meml. Inst., 1978—. Decorated Legion of Merit for blood research project, 1968; recipient Meritorious Service medal for work at Naval Med. Research Inst. U.S. Dept. Navy, 1973; Robert Dexter Conrad award for outstanding sci. achievement Sec. of Navy, 1977. Mem. Assn. Mil. Surgeons (sustaining membership award 1967), Soc. for Cryobiology (editorial bd. 1964-66), Soc. Fed. Med. Agys., AMA, Western Soc. Clin. Investigation, Soc. Med. Cons. Armed Forces. Home: 9213 Friars Rd Bethesda MD 20034 Office: Office Med Services Dept State Washington DC 20520

BRODKEY, DONALD, state supreme court judge; b. Sioux City, Iowa, Jan. 17, 1910; s. Harry Aaron and Fannie Pearl (Gilinsky) B.; m. Gertrude R. Rothkop, May 30, 1943; children: Bruce Harrison, Amy Catherine, Frank Donald. Student, U. S.D., 1928; B.A., U. Iowa, 1931, J.D., 1933. Bar: Iowa and Nebr. 1933. Individual practice law, 1933-41, 47-56; chief price atty. Omaha Office, O.P.A., 1942-46; mcpl. judge, City of Omaha, 1957-60, presiding judge, 1960; dist. judge 4th Jud. Dist. Nebr., 1960-74, presiding judge, 1966; judge Nebr. Supreme Ct., Lincoln, 1974-82; adv. com. Revision Nebr. Penal Code, 1972-73. Past trustee Goodwill Industries; past bd. dirs., trustee Omaha Home for Boys; active Boy Scouts Am., Cub Scouts; past trustee Temple Israel. Kellogg Found. fellow to Nat. Coll. State Trial Judges, 1964. Mem. Inst. Jud. Adminstrn., Am., Nebr. bar assns., Iowa Alumni Assn., Order of Coif, Order of Artus, Phi Beta Kappa. Democrat. Clubs: B'nai B'rith, Eagles, Masons (33 deg.), Shriners.). Home: 1301 J St Apt 905 Lincoln NE 68508 Office: Room 2222 State Capitol Bldg Lincoln NE 68509

BRODKEY, ROBERT STANLEY, educator; b. Los Angeles, Sept. 14, 1928; s. Harold R. and Clara (Goldman) B.; m. Martha Mahr, Dec. 22, 1958 (div. Nov. 1971); 1 son, Philip Arthur; m. Carolyn Patch, Dec. 6, 1975. A.A., San Francisco City Coll., 1948; B.Chemistry with highest honors, U. Calif.-Berkeley, 1950; M.S. in Chem. Engring, U. Calif.-Berkeley, 1950; Ph.D. in Chem. Engring. (Gulf Oil fellow), U. Wis., 1952. Research chem. engr. Esso Research & Engring. Co., Linden, N.J., 1952-56; research chem. engr. Esso Standard Oil Co., Bayway, N.J., 1956-57; asst. prof. chem. engring. Ohio State U., Columbus, 1957-60, asso. prof., 1960-64, prof., 1964—; cons. Union Carbide Chem. Co., Charleston, W.Va., 1964-75; Inst. Paper Chemistry, Appleton, Wis., 1978-79, Internat. Paper Co., 1980—; expository lectr. GAMM Conf., 1975; vis. prof. Japan Soc. Promotion Sci., 1978.

Author: The Phenomena of Fluid Motions, 1967; Editor: Turbulence in Mixing Operations, 1975; Contbr. articles to profl. jours. Recipient Outstanding Paper of yr. award Canadian Jour. Chem. Engring., 1970; NATO sr. fellow in sci. Max Planck Institut für Strömungsforschung, Göttingen, West Germany, 1972; Alexander Von Humboldt Found. sr. U.S. scientist award, 1975, 83; sr. research award Coll. Engring. Ohio State U., 1983. Fellow Am. Inst. Chemists; mem. Am. Inst. Chem. Engrs., Am. Chem. Soc., N.Y. Acad. Scis., Soc. Engring. Sci., Soc. Rheology, Sigma Xi, Phi Lambda Upsilon, Alpha Gamma Sigma. Patentee in field. Home: Ohio State U 140 W 19th Ave Columbus OH 43210

BRODKIN, ALAN KEITH, investment company executive; b. Kansas City, Mo., Aug. 4, 1935; s. Harry and Betty (Junsberg) B.; m. Judith Ann Lieberman, Nov. 25, 1962; children—Adam Kyle, Paul Laurence, Heather Rebecca. B.A., U. Mo., 1957; M.A., U. Tex., 1960. Portfolio mgr. New Eng. Life Ins., Boston, 1968-70; investment officer Mass. Fin. Services, Inc., Boston, 1970-74, v.p., 1974-76, ptnr., 1976—, mng. ptnr., 1978-82, sr. exec. v.p., 1982—; trustee Provident Bank of Savs.; pres. Mass. Fin. Bond Fund, Inc.; pres., mng. trustee Mass. Fin. High Income Trust; mng. trustee Mass. Fin. Internat. Trust, Mass. Cash Mgmt. Trust, Mass.; Managed Mcpl. Bond Fund., Mass.; Tax-Free Mgmt. Trust. Incorporator Mass. Gen. Hosp., Lewis Country Day Sch. Mem. Boston Security Analysts Soc., Fin. Analysts Fedn., Phi Beta Kappa. Club: Boston Ecom. Office: Mass Fin Services 200 Berkeley St Boston MA 02116

BRODL, RAYMOND FRANK, lumber company executive; b. Cicero, Ill., June 1, 1924; s. Edward C. and Lillian (Cerny) B.; m. Ethel Jean Johnson, Aug. 15, 1953; children: Mark Raymond, Pamela Jean, Susan Marie. Student, Norwich U., Northfield, Vt., 1943, Ill. Coll., 1946-48; J.D., Loyola U., Chgo., 1951. Bar: Ill. 1951. Atty. law office Joseph A. Ricker, Chgo., 1951-58, Brunswick Corp., 1958-62; sec., gen. atty. Edward Hines Lumber Co., Chgo., 1962—. Democratic canidate for local jud. office, 1953, 57. Served with AUS, 1943-46. Mem. Am., Ill., Chgo. bar assns., Am. Soc. Corporate Secs. Home: 366 W Lance Dr Des Plaines IL 60016 Office: 200 S Michigan Ave Chicago IL 60604:

BRODMAN, ESTELLE, educator, librarian; b. N.Y.C., June 1, 1914; d. Henry and Nettie (Sameth) B. A.B., Cornell U., 1935; B.S., Columbia U., 1936, M.S., 1943, Ph.D., 1954; post-doctoral study, U. Calif., Los Angeles, 1959, U. N.Mex., 1960; D.Sc. (hon.), U. Ill., 1975. Asst. librarian Cornell U. Sch. Nursing Library, N.Y.C., 1936-37; asst. med. librarian Columbia Libraries, N.Y.C., 1937-49; asst. librarian for reference services Nat. Library Medicine, Washington, 1949-61; librarian, asso. prof. med. history Washington U. Sch. Medicine, St. Louis, 1961-64, librarian, prof. med. history, 1964-81; documentation expert UN Tech. Assistance program UN, Central Family Planning Inst., New Delhi, 1967-68, WHO, 1970, ECAFE, Bangkok, 1973, AID, 1975, UNFPA, 1976; Mem. Pres.'s Commn. Libraries, 1968-70, Mo. Gov.'s Adv. Commn. Libraries, 1977-78; study sect. NIH, 1971-75, chmn., 1973-75; instr. Columbia U., 1946-52, Cath. U. Am., 1957; vis. prof. Keio U., Tokyo, 1962, U. Mo., 1971, 73, Washington U. Med. Sch., 1964-70. Author: Development of Medical Bibliography, 1954, Bibliographical Lists for Medical Libraries, 1950; Editor: Bull. Med. Library Assn, 1947-47. Mem. ALA, Med. Library Assn. (spl. award 1957, Noyes award 1971, Gottlieb award 1977, pres. 1964-65), Spl. Libraries Assn. (dir. 1949-52, John Cotton Dana award 1981), Bibliog. Soc. Am., Am. Assn. History Medicine. Home: 19-09 Meadow Lake Hightstown NJ 08520 *The transmission of scientific, especially medical, information from research worker to research worker, and from them to the deliverer of medical care and to the laymen who make decisions about these matters, in the past few decades has been an exciting and mind-expanding enterprise. The development of such tools as the computer, and the social diversity of those needing the information for daily use have completely changed scientific librarianship from a passive to an active operation. Transfer versus storage are the keywords. I have just been lucky to be involved in this field at so interesting and purposeful a time.*

BRODSKY, HAROLD MARTIN, manufacturing company executive; b. Lawrence, Mass., Oct. 20, 1923; s. Sam and Belle (Belford) B.; m. Judith Brodsky, July 4, 1948; children: Mark W., Sharon K. Richman. B.S., MIT, 1947. Vice pres. mfg. Fafnir Bearing div. Textron, New Britain, Conn., 1967-74, v.p. ops., 1974-79, exec. v.p., 1979-83, pres., 1983—; dir. Burritt Mut. Bank, New Britain, Art Press, Inc. Trustee New Britain Boys Club, 1981; bd. dirs. New Britain YMCA, 1977. Served with AUS, 1944-46. Mem. New Britain C. of C. (dir. 1981). Home: 178 Barbour Rd New Britain CT 06053 Office: Fafnir Bearing Div Textron 37 Booth St New Britain CT 60650

BRODSKY, IOSIF ALEXANDROVICH, poet; b. Leningrad, USSR, May 24, 1940; came to expelled from Russia, and came to U.S., 1972; s. Alexander I. and Maria (Volpert) B. Student, Russian secondary schs., until 1956; D.Litt. (hon.), Yale U., 1978. Began writing poetry, 1955; poet-in-residence U. Mich., Ann Arbor, 1972-73, 74-79; vis. prof. Smith Coll., Amherst Coll., Queens Coll., Hampshire Coll.; fellow N.Y. Inst. Humanities, NYU; assoc. Russian Inst., Columbia U., N.Y.C. Works include: poetry in Russian and English A Christmas Ballad, 1962, Elegy for John Donne, 1963, Isaac and Abraham, 1963, Verses on the Death of T.S. Eliot, 1965, Song Without Music, 1969, Selected Poems, 1973, A Part of Speech, 1980; essays Less than One, 1981. John D. and Catherine T. MacArthur Found. fellow, 1981. Mem. AAAL. Jewish. Sentenced to 5 yrs. hard labor by Soviet Govt., 1964, commuted 1965. Office: Dept Slavic Lang U Mich Ann Arbor MI 48109 *

BRODSKY, IRWIN ABEL, stock broker; b. N.Y.C., Aug. 12, 1910; s. Morris and Gertrude (Graber) B.; m. Helen B. Kamen, Oct. 19, 1941; children—William, Tina Brodsky Bellet, Howard. Student, Coll. City N.Y., 1934, St. John U., 1937. With J&W Seligman & Co., 1929-60; partner Model, Roland & Co., Inc., 1961-65, dir., v.p., sec., 1965-74; dir., cons. Shields, Model, Roland, Inc., N.Y.C., 1974—; cons. Bache Halsey Stuart Shields Inc., 1974-77, 1st v.p., 1977—; pres., dir. Bache Shields Internat. Corp., Bache Shields Securities Corp.; arbitrator N.Y.C. Small Claims Night Ct., 1959—. Author: Stock Transfer Taxes Practically Applied. Home: 316 Redmont Rd West Hempstead NY 11552 Office: 100 Gold St New York NY 10038

BRODSKY, JACK GERARD, film company advertising, publicity and promotion executive; b. N.Y.C., July 3, 1932; s. Aaron and Shirley (Palatnick) B.; m. Dorothy Chaika, Nov. 26, 1958; children: Richard, Peter. Grad., Shipman Sch. Journalism, 1951. Mem. staff N.Y. Times, 1951-56; v.p. advt.-publicity Filmways Inc., N.Y.C., 1962-64; v.p. Rastar Prodns., Columbia Pictures, N.Y.C., 1967-69; v.p. advt. and publicity Columbia Pictures, Burbank, Calif., 1976-79; ind. motion picture producer, 1969-76; exec. v.p. prodn. Big Stick Prodns., Burbank, 1979-83; exec. v.p. advt., publicity, promotion 20th Century-Fox Film Corp., Beverly Hills, Calif., 1983—. Producer: motion pictures Little Murders, 1971, Summer Wishes, Winter Dreams, 1973; exec. producer: Everything You Always Wanted To Know About Sex, 1973; co-author: The Cleopatra Papers, 1963. Served to cpl. U.S. Army, 1952-54; ETO. Office: 20th Century-Fox Film Corp PO Box 900 Beverly Hills CA 90213

BRODSKY, JUDITH KAPSTEIN, artist, educator; b. Providence, July 14, 1933; d. Israel James and Stella (Cohen) Kapstein; m. David Joel Brodsky, June 7, 1953; children: Frances Martha, John Bernard. B.A., Radcliffe Coll., 1954; M.F.A., Tyler Sch. Art, Temple U., 1967. Lectr. art history Tyler Sch. Art, Temple U., 1966-71; asst. prof. printmaking Beaver Coll., 1972-77, assoc. prof., acting chmn. art dept., 1977-78; assoc. prof. art, chmn. art dept. Rutgers U., Newark, 1978-81, assoc. dean, 1981—, acting assoc. provost, 1982; owner Castle Howard Press; partner Queenston Press. Exhibited in one-person shows, including, Brown U., 1973, U. Pa., 1975, N.J. State Mus., Douglass Coll., 1978, Asso. Am. Artists, Phila., 1979, group shows; exhbns. organized: Contemporary Issues: Works on Paper by Women Artists, 1977, Printed by Women, 1983; represented in permanent collections, Library of Congress, Fogg Mus., N.J. State Mus., Newark Mus., Rockefeller U., Newark Public Library, Princeton U., Tufts U., Boston Printmakers, Temple U., others. Pres. Women's Caucus for Art, 1976-78; founder Coalition Women's Art Orgns., 1978; bd. dirs. N.J. Printmaking Council, Feminist Art Inst. Recipient Lindback Found. award for disting. teaching, 1974; stella C. Drabkin Meml. award Am. Color Print Soc., 1977. Mem. Phila. Print Club (dir.), Washington Printmakers, Calif. Printmakers, Soc. Am. Graphic Artists. Home: 59 Castle Howard Ct Princeton NJ 08540 Office: Dean's Office Hill Hall Rutgers U Newark NJ 07102

BRODSKY, ROBERT FOX, aerospace engineer; b. Phila., May 16, 1925; s. Samuel H. and Sylvia (Fox) B.; m. Patricia Wess, Jan. 24, 1959; children: Bette W., Robert D., David V., Jeffrey M. B.M.E., Cornell U., 1947; M.Aero. Engring., N.Y. U., 1948, D.Sc. in Engring, 1950; M.S. in Math, U. N.Mex., 1957. Registered profl. engr., Calif., Iowa. Instr. N.Y. U., 1948-50; supr. theoretical aerodynamics Sandia Corp., Albuquerque, 1950-56; chief aerodynamics Convair/Pomona, 1956-59; with Aerojet-Gen. Corp., 1959-71; chief engr. Space-Gen., El Monte, Calif., 1963-67, corp. mgr. European ops., Paris, 1969-70, mgr. systems test Aerojet Electrosystems Co., 1970-71; prof., head dept. aerospace engring. Iowa State U., Ames, 1971-80; on faculty improvement leave with space and communications group Hughes Aircraft Co., 1978-79; sr. systems engr. TRW Space Systems, Redondo Beach, Calif., 1980-83; dir. tech. planning TRW Space and Tech. Group, Redondo Beach, Calif., 1983—; cons. in field. Served with USN, 1944-46. Recipient Ednl. Achievement award AIAA/Am. Soc. Engring. Edn. Aerospace Div., 1978; NSF/NATO sr. fellow in sci., 1973. Fellow Inst. Advancement Engring.; mem. Am. Astronautical Soc., Nat. Soc. Profl. Engrs., AIAA (ednl. activities com. 1972—, spacecraft systems tech. com. 1978-82, editorial adv. bd. A&A 1977-81), Am. Soc. Engring. Edn. (chmn. aerospace div., chmn. tech. assessment com.), Am. Soc. Aerospace Edn. (v.p. 1979-80, Univ. Educator of Yr. 1979), Sigma Xi. Lodge: Rotary. Inventor space lifeboat. Home: 401 2d St Hermosa Beach CA 90254 Office: TRW One Space Park R5 2281 Redondo Beach CA 90278

BRODSKY, SAMUEL, lawyer; b. Kansas City, Mo., June 12, 1912; s. Abraham and Anne (Brodsky) B.; m. Margery J. Bach, Oct. 17, 1944; children: Joan E., Alice E. B.A., U. Tulsa, 1933; LL.B., Harvard U., 1936. Bar: N.Y. 1937. Since practiced in, N.Y.C.; law clk. to Fed. Circuit Ct. Judge Julian W. Mack, 1936-37; asst. U.S. atty. So. Dist. N.Y., 1937-43, 46, charge civil div., 1942-43, 46; partner firm Aranow, Brodsky, Bohlinger, Einhorn & Alter, 1947-79, Botein, Hays, Sklar & Herzberg, 1979—; lectr. taxation NYU Law Sch., 1953, 56-64, also; Inst. on Fed. Taxation, NYU, Practicing Law Inst. Contbr. articles to profl. jours. Served to lt. USNR, 1943-46. Mem. ABA, Fed. Bar Assn., N.Y. State Bar Assn. (past chmn. tax sect.), Assn. Bar City N.Y., N.Y. County Lawyers Assn., Harvard Law Sch. Assn. N.Y. Jewish (past pres., trustee synagogue). Home: 1155 Park Ave New York NY 10128 Office: 200 Park Ave New York NY 10166

BRODSKY, WILLIAM JAY, futures exchange exec.; b. N.Y.C., Jan. 29, 1944; s. Irwin A. and Helen B. (Kamen) B.; m. Joan Breier, Dec. 17, 1966; children: Michael, Stephen, Jonathan. A.B., Syracuse U., 1965, J.D., 1968. Bar: N.Y. 1969. Asst. v.p. Model Roland & Co. Inc., N.Y.C., 1968-74; exec. v.p. Am. Stock Exchange, N.Y.C., 1974-82; chief operating officer Chgo. Merc. Exchange, 1982—; former dir. Options Clearing Corp.; former lectr. N.Y. Inst. Fin. Bd. visitors Syracuse U. Coll. Law. Mem. Am. Bar Assn. Office: 30 S Wacker Dr Chicago IL 60606

BRODY, ALEXANDER, advertising executive; b. Budapest, Hungary, Jan. 28, 1933; s. John and Lilly (Pollatschek) B.; m. Patrice Yonemitsu Beatty. B.A., Princeton U., 1953. With Young & Rubicam, Inc., 1953—, v.p., mgr., Frankfurt, W.Ger., 1965-70, sr. v.p., head European ops., 1967-70, internat. pres., Brussels and N.Y.C., 1970-82; pres., chief exec. officer Dentsu Young & Rubicam, N.Y.C., 1983—; dir. Beatrice Foods Co. Mem. Internat. Advt. Assn. (dir.). Clubs: Racquet and Tennis (N.Y.C.); Ivy. Home: Le Petit Chateau 1111 Echichens Switzerland Office: care Dentsu Young & Rubicam Internat 1114 Ave of the Americas New York NY 10036

BRODY, ALFRED WALTER, pulmonologist; b. N.Y.C., Feb. 20, 1920; s. Hyman and Sophia (Naidich) B.; m. Shirley Bloom, Dec. 17, 1943; children: Betty Ann, Carolyn Gale, Frances Linda, Robert Seymour. B.A., Columbia U., 1940, M.A., 1941; M.D., L.I. Coll. Medicine, 1943; D.Sc., U. Pa., 1954. Fellow, instr. physiology and pharmacology U. Pa., Phila., 1951-54; asst. prof. dept. physiology Creighton U., Omaha, 1954-56, assoc. prof., 1956-59, prof., 1959-62, assoc. prof. dept. medicine, 1959-62, prof., 1962—; dir. chest sect. and pulmonary function lab. St. Joseph's Hosp., Creighton Med. Center, Omaha, 1958-78, Douglas County Hosp., 1974-78; cons. in field. Contbr. articles to med. jours. Vice pres. Nebr. Tuberculosis Assn., 1958-59, pres., 1959-60. Served with M.C. AUS, 1945-51. NIH grantee, 1954-81; Am. Heart Assn. grantee, 1959-69; Am. Tuberculosis Assn. grantee, 1954-72. Fellow Am. Pharmacol. Assn., Am. Lung Soc.; mem. AAAS, Am. Physiol. Soc., AMA, N.Y. Acad. Sci., Am. Heart Assn., Omaha Research Soc. (sec.). Jewish. Club: B'nai B'rith. Office: 2500 California St Omaha NE 68178

BRODY, ARTHUR, industrial executive; b. Newark, June 30, 1920; s. Samuel A. and Ruth (Marder) B.; m. Sophie Mark, Mar. 5, 1944; children: Janice, Donald. Student, Columbia U., 1939-42. Organizer, operator Library Service, 1940-42; exec. buyer L. Bamberger & Co., Newark, 1942-43; chmn. Bro-Dart Industries, Williamsport, Pa., 1946—, BDI Investment Corp., San Diego; Past mem. adv. panel study on libraries and industry Nat. Adv. Com. on Libraries; past pres. Friends of N.J. Libraries. Past trustee Newark Symphony Hall.; trustee Ctr. for Book, Library of Congress, Los Angeles County Library Found., Friends of Library USA. Served with AUS, 1943-46. Mem. ALA, NEA. Clubs: Masons, Shriners. Patentee in field. Home: 18767 Lunada Point San Diego CA 92128 Office: 10983 Via Frontera San Diego CA 92127

BRODY, BERNARD B., physician, educator; b. N.Y.C., June 24, 1922; s. Abraham and Sarah (Berman) B.; m. Ruth M. Miller, Jan. 15, 1954; children: Sarah, Rachel. B.S., U. Wis., 1943; M.D., U. Rochester, 1951. Diplomate: Am. Bd. Internal Medicine, Nat. Bd. Med. Examiners. Research chemist U. Chgo. and Monsanto, Dayton, Ohio, 1943-47; resident U. Rochester, 1947-56; pvt. practice internal medicine, Rochester, 1956-67; dir. clin. labs. Genesee Hosp., Rochester, 1967-81, sr. v.p. med. affairs, 1975—; clin. prof. pathology and medicine U. Rochester, 1981—; cons. Eastman Kodak Co., 1971—, Robert Wood Johnson Found., 1975-80; cons., dir. EDMAC Assocs., Inc., 1976—; trustee Gannett Found., 1980—. Bd. dirs. Genesee Valley Med. Care, Rochester, 1962-68; chmn. med. adv. bd. St. Ann's Home, 1964-67; corp. mem. United Way, Rochester, 1980—; mem. Citizens Com. Human Relations, Rochester, 1980—. Served to 1st lt. U.S. Army, 1953-55. Mem. AMA, ACP, Am. Soc. Internal Medicine, N.Y. Acad. Scis., Acad. Clin. Lab. Physicians and Scientists, Am. Assn. Clin. Chemistry, Sigma Xi, Alpha Omega Alpha. Home: 12 Huntington brook Rochester NY 14625 Office: The Genesee Hosp 224 Alexander St Rochester NY 14607

BRODY, CLARK LOUIS, clarinetist; b. Three Rivers, Mich., June 9, 1914; s. Clark L. and Margaret E. (York) B.; m. Florence Chaikin, Feb. 19, 1946; 1 son, Robert David. B.A., Mich. State Coll., 1934; Mus.B., U. Rochester, 1936, 1937. Solo clarinetist CBS Symphony Orch., 1941-51, also; Columbia, RCA Victor rec. orchs.; prof. clarinet Northwestern U., 1978—. Soloist chamber music groups including, New Friends of Music, Gordon Quartet, Paganini Quartet; with, Budapest String Quartet, Library of Congress, 1952, Juilliard Quartet, 1966; solo clarinetist, Chgo. Symphony Orch., 1951-78. Home: 1621 Colfax St Evanston IL 60201

BRODY, ELAINE, musicologist; b. N.Y.C., Apr. 21, 1923; d. S. Lawrence and Helen (Golding) B.; m. David Silverberg, July 4, 1966; 1 dau. by previous marriage, Sue Shapiro. Student, Vassar Coll., 1940-41; A.B. with honors in Russian History, N.Y. U., 1944; Ph.D. in Musicology, N.Y. U., 1964, A.M., Columbia U., 1960. Grad. asst., teaching fellow Washington Square Coll., N.Y. U., 1961-63, instr., 1963-65, asst. prof., 1965-67, assoc. prof., 1967-70, prof. music history, 1970—; chmn. dept. music Univ. Coll., N.Y. U., 1965-73; instr. Sunrise Semester CBS-TV, 1975; lectr. 92d St. Y, 1977, also; N.Y. U. Med. Sch., Cosmopolitan Club, Leo Baeck Inst.; ednl. com. Met. Opera Guild, 1977—; music cons. N.Y. U. Press; organizer symposium Paris 1900/New York Today, 1980. Author: Music in Opera, 1970, (with R.A. Fowkes) The German Lied and Its Poetry, 1971, (with Claire Brook) The Music Guide to Great Britain, 1975, The Music Guide to Austria and Germany, 1975, The Music Guide to Belgium, Holland, Switzerland, 1977, The Music Guide to Italy, 1978, The Music Guide to France, Spain and Portugal, 1984, The French Revival: French Music From 1870-1925, 1983; editor series 10 books on performance-practice; Everywhere a Stranger: The Correspondence of Ernest Bloch and Romain Rolland, 1984; contbr. numerous articles, revs. to profl. publs. William Randolph Hearst Found. grantee, 1972-77; N.Y. U. Challenge grantee Humanities Council, 1978. Mem. Internat. Musicological Soc., Am. Musicological Soc. (chmn. Greater N.Y.C. chpt. 1974-76, nat. council) musicological socs.), Music Library Assn., Internat. Music Library Assn., Consortium Comparativists, Phi Beta Kappa (sec. Beta chpt. 1963-71). Home: 35 E 84th St New York NY 10028

BRODY, EUGENE B, psychiatrist, educator; b. Columbia, Mo., June 17, 1921; s. Samuel and Sophie B.; m. Marian Holen, Sept. 23, 1944; children: Julie Anne Brody d'Autremont, James Clarke, John Holen. A.B., M.A., U. Mo., 1941; M.D., Harvard, 1944; grad., N.Y. Psychoanalytic Inst., 1957. Resident Yale Med. Sch., 1944-46, 48-49, from instr. to asso. prof., 1949-57; prof. psychiatry U. Md. Sch. Medicine, Balt., 1957-76; chmn. dept., also dir. Inst. Psychiatry and Human Behavior, 1959-76, prof. psychiatry and human behavior, 1976—; vis. prof. U. Brazil, 1968, U. W.I., Kingston, Jamaica, 1972, 73; fellow Center for Advanced Studies in Behavioral Scis., Stanford, 1975-76, U. Otago (N.Z.), 1981; mem. adv. bd. Inst. Social Psychiatry, U. San Marcos, 1968-70; mem. nat. profl. adv. bd. psychiatry, psychology, neurology service VA, 1963-67; cons. WHO (Pan Am. Health Orgn. and Geneva, Switzerland), 1965—; program dir. Interam. Mental Health Studies Program, 1967-69; mem. exec. bd. World Fedn. Mental Health, 1969—, adminstrv. mem., 1972-74, mem.-at-large, 1979—, pres., 1981—; mem. epidemiol. studies rev. com. NIMH, 1975-79, cons. clin. infant devel. program, 1979-81, hosp. rev. com., 1979—. Author: The Lost Ones, Social Forces and Mental Illness in Rio de Janeiro, 1973, Sex, Contraception and Motherhood in Jamaica, 1981; Editor: (with F.C. Redlich) Psychotherapy with Schizophrenics, 1952, (with R. Monroe and G. Klee) Psychiatric Epidemiology and Mental Health Planning, 1967, Minority Group Adolescents in the United States, 1968, Behavior in New Environments, 1970; cons. editor: Jour. Nervous and Mental Disease, 1959-67; editor in chief: Jour. Nervous and Mental Diseases, 1967—; adv. editor: Tice Med. Ency., 1967-80, Harper & Row Med. Ency., 1980—; Editorial bd.: Psychiatry Digest, 1967-71, Mental Hygiene, 1968-70, Social Psychiatry, 1970-81; Contbr. numerous articles to profl. jours. Chmn. adv. bd. Balt. chpt. Internat. Students Council, ARC, 1964-67; bd. dirs. Md. Partners of Alliance for Progress, 1965-66, Nat. Assn. Mental Health, 1964-66; mem. profl. adv. bd. Nat. Assn. Mental Health, 1967-71. Served to capt. M.C. AUS, 1946-48. Fellow Am. Psychiat. Assn. (life; chmn. com. transcultural psychiatry 1966-68, rep. interam. council 1965-71, trustee 1968-71, chmn. task force family planning 1973-75), Am. Coll. Psychiatrists (charter), Am. Coll. Psychoanalysts (charter); mem. Assn. Behavioral Sci. and Med. Edn. (pres. 1981), Am., Internat. psychoanalytic assns., Internat. Coll. Pediatrics (senate 1978—), Internat. Assn. Psychosomatic Ob-Gyn (exec. bd. 1977—), Peruvian Psychiat. Assn. (hon.), Peruvian Assn. Psychiatry, Neurology and Neurosurgery (hon.). Club: Cosmos (Washington). Home: 70 Olmsted Green Baltimore MD 21210 Office: 645 W Redwood St Baltimore MD 21201

BRODY, HAROLD, educator; b. Cleve., May 15, 1923; s. Julius and Esther (Barowitz) B.; m. Anne Pertz, Mar. 24, 1951; children—David Andrew, Evan Barrett. Student, L.I. U., 1941-43; B.S., Western Res. U., 1947; Ph.D., U. Minn., 1953; M.D., U. Buffalo, 1961. Instr. anatomy U. Minn., Mpls., 1949-50; asst. prof. U. N.D., Grand Forks, 1950-54, U. Buffalo, 1954-59, assoc. prof., 1959-63, prof., 1963—, asst. dean, 1968-69, assoc. dean, 1969-70, Buswell research fellow, 1970—, chmn. dept. anat. scis., 1971—; acting dir. Center for Study of Aging, SUNY, Buffalo, 1977-80; vis. prof. neurophthalmology St. Mary's Hosp., Rochester, N.Y., 1965-75; mem. com. research and demonstration White House Conf. on Aging, 1971; mem. biology council Canisius Coll., Buffalo, 1969-73; mem. sci. bd. Buffalo Otological Found., 1968; mem. nat. adv. council Nat. Inst. on Aging, NIH, 1975-79. Abstractor: Excerpta Medica Sect. Gerontology and Geriatrics, 1959—; sci. referee: Science, 1956—, Jour. Morphology, 1958—, Jour. Gerontology, 1957-73; assoc. editor, 1973-75; editor-in-chief, 1975-80; editor: Neurobiology of Aging, 1981—; editorial bd.: Gerontology and Geriatrics Edn, 1980—. Trustee Erie County Meals on Wheels, Legal Services for the Elderly. Served with M.C. AUS, 1943-46. NSF Travel award, 1957; Fulbright sr. research scholar, 1963; recipient Robt. W. Kleemeier Research award in gerontology, 1978. Mem. Roswell Park Med. Club (pres. 1978-79), Am. Assn. Anatomists, Am. Assn. Anatomy Chairmen, Am. Aging Assn. (trustee 1970-77), AAAS, Gerontol. Soc. Am. (exec. com. 1961-63, 68-71, pres. 1974-75), Buffalo Neuropsychiat. Soc. (pres. 1967-68), Alpha Omega Alpha. Research on effects of aging on human central nervous system. Home: 144 Capen Blvd Eggertsville NY 14226 Office: Dept Anat Scis U NY Buffalo NY 14214

BRODY, HOWARD, physics educator; b. Newark, July 11, 1932; s. Edward and Charlotte (Huffman) B.; m. Lois Chase, June 30, 1954; children: Lisa, Victoria, Deirdre. S.B., MIT, 1954; M.S., Calif. Inst. Tech., 1956, Ph.D., 1959. Faculty mem. U. Pa., Phila., 1959, now prof. physics. Fellow Am. Phys. Soc.; mem. Am. Assn. Physics Tchrs.,

AAAS. Home: 220 W Rittenhouse Sq Philadelphia PA 19103 Office: Dept Physics U Pa 209 S 33d St Philadelphia PA 19104

BRODY, JACOB ALLAN, epidemiologist; b. Bklyn., May 5, 1931; s. Simon and Rosella (Midell) B.; m. Ann Thomas, Sept. 6, 1969; children: Thomas, Eva. B.A. cum laude, Williams Coll., 1952; M.D., SUNY, (Downstate Coll. Medicine), 1956. Diplomate: Am. Bd. Preventive Medicine. Intern Roosevelt Hosp., N.Y. U., 1956-57; commd. med. officer USPHS Communicable Disease Center, Atlanta, 1957-59; med. officer in epidemiology and virology Nat. Inst. Allergy and Infectious Diseases NIH, Panama, 1960-61; chief epidemiology sect. Arctic Health Research Center, Anchorage, Alaska, 1962-64; chief epidemiology br. Nat. Inst. Neurol. Diseases and Stroke NIH, Bethesda, Md., 1965-75; epidemiology br. Nat. Inst. Alcohol Abuse and Alcoholism, Alcohol, Drug Abuse and Mental Health Adminstrn., Rockville, Md., 1976-77; asso. dir. epidemiology, demography, biometry program Nat. Inst. on Aging NIH, Bethesda, 1977—; exchange scientist, USSR, 1962; research coordinator Atomic Bomb Casualty Commn., Hiroshima, Japan, 1974; sr. asso. dept. epidemiology Johns Hopkins U. Sch. Hygiene and Public Health; mem. Nat. Multiple Sclerosis Soc.; med. advisory bd. and advisory com. on research on etiology, diagnosis, natural history, prevention and therapy, 1966; dir. sci. advisory com. Muscular Dystrophy Assn. Am., Inc., 1971; vice chairperson blue ribbon study commn. on alcoholism and aging Nat. Council on Alcoholism, 1980. Contbr. numerous articles in field to profl. jours.; editor: Current Topics in Microbiology and Immunology, volume 40; mem. editorial bd.: Jour. Clin. and Exptl. Gerontology, 1979—, Preventive Medicine, 1982—. Recipient Disting. Service medal, 1981, Kolker award for service in geriatric medicine Levindale Hebrew Center, Balt., 1980; Best Book on Med. Subject for Physicians Am. Med. Writers Assn., 1977. Mem. Am. Epidemiol. Soc. (pres. 1980-81), Am. Public Health Assn., World Fedn. Neurology, Am. Soc. Tropical Medicine and Hygiene, Am. Acad. Neurology, Soc. for Epidemiologic Research, Research Soc. on Alcoholism, Undersea Med. Soc., Gerontol. Soc. Am. Jewish. Home: 11046 Seven Hill Ln Potomac MD 20854 Office: 7550 Wisconsin Ave Room 612 Fed Bldg Bethesda MD 20205

BRODY, JACOB JEROME, museum director; b. Bklyn., Apr. 24, 1929; s. Aladar and Esther (Kraiman) B.; m. Jean Lindsey, Feb. 13, 1956; children: Jefferson, Jonathan, Allison. Cert. fine arts, Cooper Union, 1950; B.A., U. N.Mex., 1956, M.A., 1964, Ph.D., 1970. Curator of art Everhart Mus., Scranton, Pa., 1957-58; curator collections Isaac Delgado Mus. Art, New Orleans, 1958-60; Mus. Internat. Folk Art, Santa Fe, 1960-61; curator Maxwell Mus., U. N.Mex., Albuquerque, 1962-72, dir., 1972—; univ. prof. art and anthropology, 1964—; mem. adv. bd. Ghost Ranch Mus., N.Mex. Mus. Natural History; mem. fine arts bd., City of Albuquerque, vice chmn., 1970-74; mem. Gov. N.Mex. Task Force Paleontol. Resources, 1978-79. Author: Indian Painters and White Patrons, 1971, Mimbres Painted Pottery, 1977. Recipient Tom L. Popejoy Dissertation award U. N.Mex., 1970, Conservation award N.Mex. Hist. Commn., 1979; Non-Fiction award Border-Regional Library Assn., 1972; Art Book award, 1979; resident scholar Sch. Am. Research, 1980-81. Mem. Am. Assn. Museums, Soc. Am. Archaeology, Mountain Plains Mus. Conf., Council Mus. Anthropology, N.Mex. Mus. Assn., N.Mex. Cactus and Succulent Soc. Office: Maxwell Museum Univ New Mexico Albuquerque NM 87131

BRODY, JACQUELINE, editor; b. Utica, N.Y., Jan. 23, 1932; d. Jack and Mary (Childress) Galloway; m. Eugene D. Brody, Apr. 5, 1959; children—Jessica, Leslie. A.B., Vassar Coll., 1953; postgrad., London Sch. Econs., 1953-56. Asso. editor Crowell Collier Macmillan, N.Y.C., 1963-67; writer Council on Fgn. Relations, N.Y.C., 1968-69; mng. editor Print Collector's Newsletter, N.Y.C., 1971-72, editor, 1972—. Office: 16 E 82 St New York NY 10028

BRODY, JANE ELLEN, journalist; b. Bklyn., May 19, 1941; d. Sidney and Lillian (Kellner) B.; m. Richard Engquist, Oct. 2, 1966; children: Lee Erik and Lorin Michael Engquist (twins). B.S., N.Y. State Coll. Agr., Cornell U., 1962; M.S. in Journalism, U. Wis., 1963. Reporter Mpls. Tribune, 1963-65; sci. writer, personal health columnist N.Y. Times, N.Y.C., 1965—; mem. adv. council N.Y. State Coll. Agr., Cornell U., 1971-77. Author: (with Richard Engquist) Secrets of Good Health, 1970, (with Arthur Holleb) You Can Fight Cancer and Win, 1977, Jane Brody's Nutrition Book, 1981, Jane Brody's The New York Times Guide to Personal Health, 1982. Recipient numerous writing awards, including: Howard Blakeslee award Am. Heart Assn., 1971; Sci. Writers' award ADA, 1978; J.C. Penney-U. Mo. Journalism award, 1978; Lifeline award Am. Health Found., 1978. Jewish. Office: 229 W 43d St New York NY 10036

BRODY, KENNETH DAVID, investment banker; b. Phila., June 30, 1943; s. Herbert and Esther (Forman) Brody S.; m. Judy E. Donahue, Feb. 5, 1964 (div. Feb. 1974); m. Helen M. Tandler, Apr. 6, 1974 (div. Oct. 1978). B.S.E.E. with high honors, U. Md., 1964; M.B.A. with high distinction, Harvard U., 1971. Foreman and staff asst. Chesapeake & Potomac Telephone Co., Washington, 1964-66; with Goldman, Sachs & Co., N.Y.C., 1971—, ptnr., 1978—; dir. Telerate, Inc., N.Y.C. Bd. dirs. Alvin Ailey Am. Dance Theater, N.Y.C., 1981—. Served to capt. U.S. Army, 1966-69. Baker scholar, 1970; Ger. Loeb Rhoades fellow, 1971. Mem. Tau Beta Pi, Eta Kappa Nu, Omicron Delta Kappa, Alpha Tau Omega. Republican. Unitarian. Club: Harvard (N.Y.C.). Office: Goldman Sachs & Co 85 Broad St New York NY 10004

BRODY, MARTIN, food service company executive; b. Newark, Aug. 8, 1921; s. Leo and Renee (Kransdorf) B.; m. Florence Gropper, Nov. 22, 1946; children: Marc, Renee. B.A., Mich. State U., 1943. Pres. Indsl. Feeding Co., Newark, 1951-61; pres., dir. A.M. Capital Corp., N.Y.C., 1961-71; chmn. bd., dir. Waldorf System Inc., Boston, 1963-66, Restaurant Assos., Inc., N.Y.C., 1964-66; chmn. bd. Restaurant Assocs. Industries Inc., 1966—; dir. Jaclyn Inc., Shearson Daily Div. Inc., Anchor Nat. Life Ins. Co. Trustee Child Care and Guidance Assn. Essex County, Opportunity Workshop Essex County; bd. dirs. N.J. Transit Corp. Served to capt. AUS, 1943-45. Clubs: Yale, Orange Lawn Tennis; Greenbrook Country (North Caldwell, N.J.). Home: 30 Kean Rd Short Hills NJ 07078 Office: 1540 Broadway New York NY 10036

BRODY, SAMUEL MANDELL, architect; b. Plainfield, N.J., Aug. 9, 1926; s. Joseph Edward and Mary Eleanor (Greenberg) B.; m. Sally Rich Rosenthal, June 9, 1954; children: Elizabeth, David, Daniel. B.A., Dartmouth Coll., 1947; M.Arch., Harvard U., 1950. Partner Davis, Brody & Wisniewski, N.Y.C., 1952-66, Davis, Brody & Assos., 1966—; adj. prof. Cooper Union Sch. Architecture, 1962—; vis. prof. Davenport chair Yale U. Sch. Architecture, 1974; vis. prof. U. Pa., 1976; vis. lectr. Harvard U., N.Y. State U., Buffalo, Ball State U., Yale U., R.I. Sch. Design, Walker Art Center. Prin. works include Riverbend Houses, 1966, East Midtown Plaza, 1968, U.S. Pavilion, Osaka, 1970, Waterside, 1974, Hampshire Coll. Athletic/Recreation Center, 1975, L.I. U. Bklyn. Center, 1960-70; Prin. works include: Time Inc. Conf. Ctr., 1983, Brown U. Geology/Chemistry Ctr., 1983. Served with USN, 1943-45. Recipient Arnold W. Brunner prize Nat. Inst. Arts and Letters, 1975; Louis Sullivan award, 1977. Fellow AIA (Archtl. Firm award 1975, medal of honor N.Y. chpt.). Jewish. Clubs: Rembrandt (Brooklyn Heights, N.Y.); Century Assn. (N.Y.C.). Home: 266 Henry St Brooklyn NY 11201 Office: 100 E 42d St New York NY

BRODY, SAUL NATHANIEL, English educator; b. N.Y.C., Mar. 6, 1938; s. Irving Bernard and Ethel (Spiegel) B.; m. Frohma-Esther Besner, Jan. 24, 1960; children: Audrey Rachel, Ruth Elizabeth. B.A., Columbia U., 1959, M.A., 1960, Ph.D., 1968. Lectr. Hunter Coll., N.Y.C., 1962-65, City Coll., 1965-68, asst. prof., 1968-73, asso. prof., 1974-78, prof. English, 1979—, dept. chmn., 1979—; Co-prin. investigator Mellon Found. grant, 1978. Author: The Disease of the Soul: Leprosy in Medieval Literature, 1974; contbr. articles to scholarly publs. Mem. Internat. Arthurian Soc., Internat. Courtly Lit. Soc., Medieval Acad. Am., Univ. Seminar in Medieval Studies (Columbia U.). Office: Dept of English City College New York NY 10031

BRODY, STUART STEVEN, jewelry designer and manufacturer; b. Phila.; s. Abraham Eli and Ellena Alexandrovna (Koleshskaya) B. Grad., Curtis Inst. Music, Phila. Co-founder Cadoro Jewels, N.Y.C., 1954; pres. Cadoro Corp., N.Y.C., 1960—; lectr. Israeli design schs., cons. to jewelry industry, 1972. Actor: Broadway debut in Feather's in a Gale; played leads: in touring cos. of ANTA's Hippolytus; appeared in 1000 radio shows and stock prodns.; designs represented in permanent collections, N.Y. Mus. Modern Art, Costume Inst. Met. Mus. Art. Bd. dirs. Spectrum Theatre; founding bd. dirs. Hemingway Fund; bd. dirs. Meml. Sloan-Kettering Cancer Center, 1978. Recipient Fashion award Glamour Mag., 1956, 57, Coty Fashion Critics award, 1970. Mem. Council Fashion Designers of Am. Office: 389 Fifth Ave New York NY 10016 *

BRODY, THEODORE MEYER, educator, pharmacologist; b. Newark, May 10, 1920; s. Samuel and Lena (Hammer) B.; m. Ethel Vivian Drelich, Sept. 7, 1947; children—Steven Lewis, Debra Jane, Laura Kate, Elizabeth. B.S., Rutgers U., 1943; M.S., U. Ill., 1949, Ph.D., 1952. Mem. faculty U. Mich. Med. Sch., Ann Arbor, 1952-66; prof. pharmacology, chmn. dept. Coll. Medicine, Mich. State U., East Lansing, 1966—; cons. NIH, 1969-73, NIDA, 1975—, Internat. Soc. Heart Research, 1973—; mem. sci. adv. com. Pharm. Mfrs. Assn. Found., 1973—; U.S. rep. Internat. Union Pharmacology, 1973-76; mem. bd. Fedn. Am. Socs. for Exptl. Biology, 1973-76; mem. Com. Sci. Soc. Presidents; NSF Distinguished scholar lectr. U. Hawaii, 1974. Mem. editorial bd.: Jour. Pharmacology and Exptl. Therapeutics, 1965—; specific field editor, 1981; editorial bd.: Research Communications in Chem. Pathology and Pharmacology, Molecular Pharmacology, 1972—, Revs. in Pure and Applied Pharmacol. Sci, 1980—. Served with AUS, 1943-46. Mem. Soc. Pharmacology and Exptl. Therapeutics (John Jacob Abel award 1955, chmn. Abel award com. 1966, mem. council 1969-72, sec.-treas. 1970, pres. elect 1973, pres. 1974), Internat. Soc. Biochem. Pharmacology, Am. Coll. Clin. Pharmacology, Assn. Med. Sch. Pharmacologists, Soc. Toxicology, Am. Soc. Pharmacology and Exptl. Therapeutics (pres. 1974-75, awards com. 1977, chmn. 1978), Soc. Neurosci., Japanese Pharmacology Soc., AAUP, Sigma Xi, Rho Chi, Phi Kappa Phi. Home: 842 Longfellow Dr East Lansing MI 48823 Office: Dept of Pharmacology and Toxicology Mich State Univ East Lansing MI 48824

BROECKER, HOWARD WILLIAM, lawyer; b. Chgo., May 16, 1940; s. Wallace Charles and Edith May (Smith) B.; m. Candace Balfour, Aug. 19, 1961; children: Peter Jon, Christopher Curtis, Anne Llewellyn. Student, N. Central Coll., Naperville, Ill., Wheaton (Ill.) Coll., 1959-63; J.D., Chgo.-Kent-Ill. Inst. Tech., 1966. Bar: Ill. 1966. Since practiced in Chgo.; partner Ehrlich, Bundesen, Broecker, Hoffenberg & Seraphin P.C., 1970-80; prin. Howard W. Broecker, 1980—; lectr. Ill. Inst. Continuing Legal Edn., 1970—, Am. Savs. and Loan Inst., 1971-72. Bd. dirs. Fox Valley chpt. ARC; officer, bd. dirs. Sunny Ridge Home Children, Wheaton; pres. Men's Found. of Community Hosp., Geneva, Ill., 1978—. Mem. ABA, Ill. Bar Assn. (assembly 1977—), Chgo. Bar Assn., Kane County Bar Assn., Am. Acad. Matrimonial Lawyers (Ill. gov. 1978—), Chgo. Council Lawyers, Chgo.-Kent-IIT Alumni Assn. (pres. 1975-77, chmn. partnership program 1980-81). Home: 41 W 391 Farview Elburn IL 60119 Office: 69 W Washington St Chicago IL 60602 also 427 S 4th St Geneva IL 60134

BROEG, BOB (ROBERT WILLIAM BROEG), sports editor; b. St. Louis, Mar. 18, 1918; s. Robert Michael and Alice (Wiley) B.; m. Dorothy Carr, June 19, 1943 (dec.); m. Lynette A. Emmenegger, July 23, 1977. B.J., U. Mo., 1941. With A.P., Columbia, Mo., 1939-40, Jefferson City, Mo., 1941, Boston, 1941-42; reporter St. Louis Star-Times, 1942; staff sports dept. St. Louis Post-Dispatch, 1945—, sports editor, 1958—, asst. to pub., 1977—. Author: Don't Bring That Up, 1946, Stan Musial: The Man's Own Story, 1964, Super Stars of Baseball, 1971, Ol' Mizzou, a Story of Missouri Football, 1974, We Saw Stars, 1976, The Man Stan... Musial, Now and Then, 1977, Football Greats, 1977, The Pilot Light and the Gas House Gang, 1980, And the Redbirds, 1981, My Baseball Scrapbook, 1983; also numerous articles. Bd. dirs. Vets. Com. Baseball Hall of Fame, 1972, Honors Ct., Nat. Football Found., 1975. Served with USMCR, 1942-45. Recipient Nat. Sportscasters, Sportswriters awards, Mo., 1962-65, 67; Journalism medal U. Mo., 1971; Faculty-Alumni award U. Mo., 1969; elected to Mo. Sports Hall of Fame, 1978, Hall of Fame Writing award, 1980. Mem. Baseball Writers Assn. Am. (pres. 1958), Kappa Tau Alpha, Sigma Delta Chi, Sigma Phi Epsilon, Omicron Delta Kappa. Home: 60 Frontenac Estates Saint Louis MO 63131 Office: Pulitzer Pub Co Saint Louis MO 63101 *As a newspaperman, I seek as an epitaph only: "He was fair." Hopefully "fair" as in "just," not as in "mediocre".*

BROEHL, WAYNE GOTTLIEB, JR., educator; b. Peoria, Ill., Aug. 11, 1922; s. Wayne G. and Dimple (Rush) B.; m. Jean Kirby, Aug. 4, 1944; children—David Robert, James Richard, Michael Kirby. B.S., U. Ill., 1946; M.B.A., U. Chgo., 1950; D.Sc. in Bus. Adminstrn, Ind. U., 1954; M.A. (hon.), Dartmouth, 1958. Staff labor relations dept. Western Electric Co., 1946-48; asst. prof., asst. dean Coll. Commerce, Bradley U., 1948-51; faculty lectr. Sch. Bus., Ind. U., 1951-54; prof. bus. Amos Tuck Sch. Bus., Dartmouth, 1954—; vis. prof. bus. history U. Coll., Dublin, Ireland, 1960-61; vis. prof. U. Buenos Aires, 1962. Author: Trucks, Trouble and Triumph, 1954, Precision Valley, 1959, The Molly Maguires, 1964, The International Basic Economy Corporation, 1968, The Village Entrepreneur, 1978; co-author: Administering the Going Concern, 1962, Business Research and Report Writing, 1965, Hospital Policy; Process and Action, 1966. Mem. Am. Econ. Assn., Am. Hist. Assn., Econ. History Assn., Acad. Mgmt., Beta Gamma Sigma, Beta Theta Pi. Home: 302 Brook Hollow Hanover NH 03755

BROEKEMA, ANDREW J., university dean; b. Grand Rapids, Mich., Apr. 21, 1931; s. Andrew E. and Helen Henrietta (Nietering) B.; m. Margaret Treiber, Aug. 22, 1953; 1 dau., Anne Margaret. Student, Calvin Coll., 1949-52; Mus.B., U. Mich., 1953, Mus.M., 1954, postgrad., 1956-57; Ph.D., U. Tex. at Austin, 1962. Instr. music U. Tex. at, Austin, 1957-62; asst. prof. music, asst. dir. Sch. Music Ohio State U., Columbus, 1962-65; prof. music, chmn. dept. Eastern Ky. U., Richmond, 1965-68, Ariz. State U., Tempe, 1968-76; dean Coll. Arts, Ohio State U., Columbus, 1976—. Author: The Music Listener, 1978; Editor: Ariz. Music News, 1970-72. Mem. community arts panel com. Ohio Arts Council, 1978-80; trustee Columbus Symphony, 1977-83, Am. Playwrights Theatre, Columbus Mus. Arts, 1978—, Columbus Coll. Art and Design, 1978-82, Columbus Cultural Arts Center, 1978—, Greater Columbus Arts Council, 1978—; pres. Greater Columbus Arts Council; treas. Ohio Alliance for Arts Edn., 1979—, Spl. Audiences, Inc., 1979—. Served with Signal Corps AUS, 1954-56. Mem. Music Tchrs. Nat. Assn., Arts Commn. (chmn.), Nat. Assn. State Univs. and Land Grant Colls., Nat. Assn. Schs. Music (mem. undergrad. curriculum commn.); mem. Internat. Council Fine Arts Deans (exec. com. 1978-80, pres.); Mem. Phi Delta Kappa, Phi Kappa Phi, Pi Kappa Lambda, Phi Mu Alpha Sinfonia. Presbyn. (elder). Club: Columbus Torch (pres. 1980-81). Home: 3048 Leeds Rd Columbus OH 43221

BROEN, WILLIAM ERNEST, JR., psychology educator; b. Marshall, Minn., Aug. 2, 1931; s. William Ernest and Verna Mignon (Skaug) B.; m. Carol Holland Stein, Dec. 28, 1957; children: Karen Simons, Linda Carolyn. B.A., U. Minn., 1952, M.A., 1954, Ph.D., 1956. Asst. prof. psychology U. Kans., Lawrence, 1956-58; mem. faculty UCLA, 1958—; assoc. prof. U. Calif. at Los Angeles, 1964-67; prof. UCLA, 1967—; cons. VA, 1962—; vis. lectr. U. Wis., 1963, U. Mass., 1965-66; vis. prof. U. Konstanz, West Germany, 1973; chmn. bd. admissions and relations with schs. U. Calif., 1977-81, mem. acad. council, 1980-81. Author: Schizophrenia: Research and Theory, 1968; contbg. author: Progress in Experimental Personality Research, 1967, Abnormal Psychology and Modern Life, 1972, Contemporary Issues in Cognitive Psychology, 1973, Internat. Ency. Psychiatry, Psychoanalysis, Psychology and Neurology, 1977, Personality Inventory for Children, 1977, Contributions to the Psychopathology of Schizophrenia, 1977; Cons. editor: Psychol. Bull, 1966-69, Jour. Abnormal Psychology, 1973-76; Contbr. numerous articles to profl. jours. Bd. dirs. Articulation Council Calif., 1980-82. Recipient research grants Nat. Assn. Mental Health, NIMH. Fellow Am. Psychol. Assn.; mem. Sigma Xi, Psi Chi. Home: 25134 Malibu Rd Malibu CA 90265 Office: Dept Psychology U Calif Los Angeles CA 90024

BROERSMA, SYBRAND, educator; b. Harlingen, Netherlands, Sept. 20, 1919; came to U.S., 1947, naturalized, 1957; s. Jacob and Johanna (Zwanenburg) B. Candidaats in Physics, Leiden U., 1939, Doctoraal, 1941; D.Sc. cum laude in Physics, Delft Inst. Tech., 1947. Research asso. Columbia, 1947; instr. U. Toronto, 1948; prof. physics U. Indonesia, Bandung, 1949-51; asst. prof. physics Northwestern U., 1952-58; prof. physics U. Okla., 1959—; adj. prof. materials research U. Tex. at Dallas, 1967-70. Author: Magnetic Measurements on Organic Compounds, 1947, Elementary Physics Laboratory Manual, 1963; collector of native arts. Internat. exchange fellow Northwestern U., 1947; NSF grantee, 1956-68. Mem. Am., Netherlands, European phys. socs., AAUP, Sigma Xi. Research in magnetism and hydrodynamics. Home: 2115 Martingale Dr Norman OK 73069

BROGAN, HOWARD OAKLEY, English educator; s. Jesse and Anne (Braga) B.; m. Isabel Brower, Apr. 2, 1938; children: Patrick Alan, Jesse William, Pamela Ann. B.A., Grinnell Coll., 1936; M.A., U. Iowa, 1938, Ph.D., Yale, 1941. Grad. asst. U. Iowa, 1936-37; instr. Ill. Coll., Jacksonville, 1937-39; asst. prof. The Citadel, Charleston, S.C., 1942-44; lectr. Princeton, 1944-46; asso. prof. Franklin and Marshall Coll., 1946-47, Syracuse U., 1947-53; prof. English Bowling Green State U., 1953-62, chmn. dept., 1955-62; Commonwealth prof. U. Mass., Amherst, 1962—, head dept. English, 1962-67. Author poems, 1 book and articles in scholarly jours. Sterling research fellow Yale, 1941-42; Carnegie intern gen. edn., 1952-53. Mem. AAUP (past chpt. pres.), Coll. English Assn. (past pres.), Internat. Assn. Univ. Profs. English, Byron Soc., Mass. Tchrs. Assn., Mass. Soc. Profs. (past pres.), NEA (chmn. com. recommending new higher edn. sect.), MLA (various offices), Phi Beta Kappa. (past pres. 2 chpts.). Home: 10 Dana St Amherst MA 01002

BROGAN, JOHN ANDREW, III, foreign service officer; b. Jersey City, Mar. 5, 1924; s. John Andrew, Jr. and Marie Jeannette (Ferris) B.; m. Edith Maria Josefa Eyermann, Oct. 25, 1952; 1 dau., Jeannette Marie. Student, Biarritz Am. U., France, 1945; B.S., Georgetown U., 1948. Fgn. rep. King Features Syndicate in, Mexico, Colombia, Argentina, France, Sweden, 1948-50; fgn. service officer, 1951—; spl. asst. to U.S. High Commr., Austria, 1951-52, Germany, 1952; press officer High Commn., Germany, 1952-54; vice consul Am. Consulate, Edinburgh, 1954-56; asst. French desk officer Dept. State, 1957-60; 2d sec. Am. embassy, Buenos Aires, Argentina, 1960-64, 1st sec., 1965; information officer, allied press spokesman U.S. Mission, Berlin, 1965-68; sr. watch officer Dept. State, 1968; dir. Ops. Center, 1969, sr. mem. bd. examiners, 1970-71; consul gen. Am. Consulate Gen., Hamburg, Germany, 1972-76; adv. on polit. and security affairs 32d spl. session UN Gen. Assembly, 1977-78; sr. examiner Dept. State, 1979—. Served with USAAF, 1942-46; ETO. Decorated knight Sovereign Mil. Order of Malta.; Hon. citizen, Quito, Ecuador, 1949. Mem. Am. Fgn. Service Assn. Roman Catholic. Clubs: Hamburg Golf; Metropolitan, Ret. Diplomate and Consular Officers (Washington); Williams (N.Y.C.). Home: 2801 New Mexico Ave NW Washington DC 20007 Office: care Dept State Washington DC 20520

BROGDON, BYRON GILLIAM, physician, educator; b. Fort Smith, Ark., Jan. 22, 1929; s. Paul Preston and Lela Florence (Gilliam) B.; m. Barbara Walkow Schreiber, June 23, 1978; 1 son, David Pope; stepchildren: William and Diane Schreiber. B.S., U. Ark., 1951, B.S.M., 1951, M.D., 1952. Intern Univ. Hosp., Little Rock, 1952-53, resident, 1953-55; resident in radiology N.C. Bapt. Hosp., Winston-Salem, 1955-56; asst. prof. radiology U. Fla., 1960-63; asso. prof. radiology and radiol. scis., radiologist in chief dir. of diagnostic radiology Johns Hopkins U. and Hosp., 1963-67; prof., chmn. dept. radiology U. N.Mex., 1967-77; prof. radiology U. South Ala., Mobile, 1978—, asst. dean continuing med. edn., 1981—. Author: Opinions, Comments and Reflections on Radiology, 1983; Contbr. articles to med. jours. Served to maj. USAF, 1953-60. Recipient Disting. Alumnus award U. Ark., 1978. Mem. Am. Coll. Radiology (pres. 1978-79), Am. Roentgen Ray Soc. (2d v.p. 1979-80), So. Radiol. Conf. (pres. 1967-68), Radiol. Soc. N. Am., Soc. Pediatric Radiology, Assn. Univ. Radiologists (pres. 1973-74), Soc. Chmn. Acad. Radiol. Depts. (sec.-treas. 1969-70), AMA (Physician-Speaker award 1979), Sigma Xi, Alpha Omega Alpha, Sigma Chi. Club: Bienville. Office: Dept Radiology U South Ala Med Center 2451 Fillingim St Mobile AL 36617 *For the physician-scientist-educator, the mere transference of knowledge or the acquisition of new data is not enough. He must participate fully in the affairs of the larger community and has a duty to help others to think about, or form an opinion on issues they otherwise might not have considered.*

BROIDE, MACE IRWIN, mem. Congressional staff; b. Burlington, Vt., May 21, 1924; s. Abraham A. and Ida (Rosenberg) B.; m. Gloria Leah Goldsholl, Dec. 24, 1943; children: Cheryl Ruth Broide Light, Beverly Elaine Broide Frye, Sandra Pat Broide McNees. A.B. (Ernie Pyle scholar 1946), Ind. U., 1947. Polit. editor Evansville (Ind.) Press, 1947-58; senatorial adminstrv. asst., 1959-68; co-owner DeHart and Broide, Inc., public affairs cons., Washington, 1968-78; exec. dir. com. on budget U.S. Ho. of Reps., 1978—; mem. congressional adv. council Internat. Mgmt. and Devel. Inst.; dir. JRB Sound Studios, Bethesda, Md.; lectr. in field. Co-author: Inside the New Frontier, 1963; contbr. articles to newspapers, mags. Sec. Nat. Democratic Senatorial Campaign Com., 1961-62; past bd. dirs. Jewish Community Council Evansville; past pres. B'nai B'rith lodge. Served with AUS, 1943-46. Decorated Silver Star, Bronze Star. Mem. Assn. Adminstrv. Assts. U.S. Senate (past pres.), Congressional Staff Club, Sigma Delta Chi. Democrat. Clubs: Nat. Democratic, 116, Inc. (Washington) (dir.).

Home: 2029 Connecticut Ave NW Apt 53 Washington DC 20008 Office: 222 House Annex 1 Washington DC 20515

BROIDO, ARNOLD PEACE, music publishing company executive; b. N.Y.C., Apr. 8, 1920; s. Samuel S. and Ruth (Lewis) B.; m. Lucille Janet Tarshes, Mar. 5, 1944; children: Jeffrey, Laurence, Thomas. B.S. magna cum laude, Ithaca Coll., 1941; M.A., Columbia U., 1954. Tchr. instrumental music East Jr. High Sch., Binghamton, N.Y., 1941-42; editor, prodn. mgr. Boosey & Hawkes Inc. (music pub.), 1945-55; v.p., gen. mgr. Century Music & Mercury Music Corp., 1955-57; edn. dir. Edward B. Marks Music Corp., 1957-62; dir. publs. and sales Frank Music Corp., 1962-69; v.p. Boston Music Co., 1968-69; pres. Theodore Presser Co., 1969—; also dir.; chmn. Elkan-Vogel Inc., 1970—; Pres. Music Industry Council, 1966-68, v.p., 1969-70. Co-author: Music Dictionary, 1956, Invitation to the Piano, 1959; Asso. editor: Univ. Soc. Ency. of Piano Music; Contbr. articles to profl. jours. Mem. Nassau County (N.Y.) Democratic Com., 1952-63; Bd. dirs. N.Y. Citizens Com. for Pub. Schs., 1963-68, Music Educators Nat. Conf., 1966-68, Am. Music Center, 1968-72, 78-83, Am. Music Conf., 1979-80, Nat. Music Council, 1979—; trustee ASCAP Found., 1976—, Bd. Edn. Union Free Sch. Dist. 21, Rockville Centre, N.Y., 1963-69; sec., dist. clk. Bd. Edn. Union Free Sch. Dist. 21, 1966-67, v.p., dist. clk., 1967-69. Served with USCGR, 1942-45. Mem. ASCAP (dir. 1972-79; 80—, bd. rev. 1980-82), Nat. Music Pubs. Assn. (dir. 1980—), Music Pubs. Assn. U.S. (pres. 1972-74, 80-82, dir. 1980-82, 83—), Internat. Pubs. Assn. (v.p. sect. music 1972-78), Internat. Confedn. Music Pubs. (v.p. 1978—), Internat. Fedn. Serious Music Pubs. (v.p. 1978—), Music Industry Mfrs. Assn. (dir. 1980-82), Phi Mu Alpha Sinfonia. Home: 908 Wootton Rd Bryn Mawr PA 19010 Office: Presser Pl Bryn Mawr PA 19010

BROITMAN, SELWYN ARTHUR, microbiologist, educator; b. Boston, Aug. 30, 1931; s. Julius Z. and Sara (Sallus) B.; m. Barbara Merle Schwartz, June 13, 1953; children: Caryn Beth, Jeffrey Z. B.S., U. Mass., 1952, M.S., 1953; Ph.D., Mich. State U., 1956. Dir. Biotech. Assocs., 1959-62; research instr. dept. pathology Boston U. Sch. Medicine, 1963-64, asst. prof. dept. microbiology, 1965-69, assoc. prof. dept. microbiology, 1969-75, prof., 1975—, asst. dean med. sch. admissions; asso. prof. nutritional scis. Henry Goldman Sch. Grad. Dentistry Boston U., 1974—; assoc. medicine dept. medicine Harvard Med. Sch., 1969-74; research assoc. Mallory Inst. Pathology, Boston City Hosp., Gastro Intestinal Research Lab., 1956-71; assoc. in medicine Thorndike Meml. Lab., 1969-74. Contbr.: articles to profl. jours. Founding mem. Digestive Disease Found. Served with AUS, 1952-66. Recipient Outstanding Teaching award Boston U. Sch. Medicine 1st Yr. Class, 1976. Mem. AAAS, Soc. Exptl. Pathology, Am. Inst. Nutrition, Fedn. for Clin. Research, Am. Soc. Microbiology, Soc. Applied Bacteriology, Soc. Exptl. Biology and Medicine, Nutrition Today Soc. (founding), Am. Gastroent. Assn., Boston Gastroent. Soc., Am. Acad. Scis. (com. diet, nutrition and cancer 1980—), N.Y. Acad. Scis., Boston Bug Club (pres. 1976), Sigma Xi. Office: 80 E Concord St Boston MA 02118 *When problems cannot be resolved by the minds of this generation, the solutions must be sought in the minds of the next. The challenge is to find these young people, encourage them, and wherever possible, remove all obstacles to their learning.*

BROKAW, CHARLES JACOB, educator, cellular biologist; b. Camden, N.J., Sept. 12, 1934; s. Charles Alfred and Doris Evelyn (Moses) B.; m. Darlene Smith, July 29, 1955; children—Bryce, Tanya. B.S., Calif. Inst. Tech., 1955; Ph.D., King's Coll., Cambridge (Eng.) U., 1958. Research asso. Oak Ridge Nat. Lab., 1958-59; asst. prof. zoology U. Minn., 1959-61; mem. faculty Calif. Inst. Tech., 1961—, prof. biology, 1968—, exec. officer div. biology, 1976-80, asso. chmn. div. biology, 1980—. Contbr. articles to profl. jours. Guggenheim fellow, 1970-71. Mem. Biophys. Soc., Am. Soc. Cell Biology, Soc. Exptl. Biology. Home: 940 Oriole Dr Laguna Beach CA 92651 Office: Biology Div Calif Inst Tech Pasadena CA 91125

BROKAW, HAROLD LEE, broadcast executive; b. Evansville, Ind., Dec. 26, 1925; s. Floyd Embre and Lillian Vivian (Painter) B.; m. Thelma Irene Jordan, Sept. 21, 1946; children: Randolph Jordan, Jennifer Lee. Student, Ind. State Tchrs. Coll., 1943-44, Central Tech. Inst., 1946-48. Engring. technician, chief engr. Sta. WOWO, Ft. Wayne, Ind., 1948-64; engring. mgr. Sta. WINS, N.Y.C., 1964-66, Sta. WIND, Chgo., 1966-69; cons. Westinghouse Broadcasting, Stas. KYW, Phila., KDKA, Pitts., CKEY, Toronto, KFWB, Los Angeles, 1962-69; v.p., gen. mgr., part-owner Sta. WMRO, Aurora, Ill., 1969—, Sta. WAUR, Aurora, 1973—; dir., sec., treas. Stevens Broadcasting Corp., 1969—, Stevens Communications Corp., 1969—. Bd. dirs., pres. Fox River Valley Symphony Orch. Assn., 1969-79, Kane County Heart Assn., 1970-78; chmn. Aurora Civic Center Authority and Redevel. Commn., 1973-77; bd. dirs., v.p. Greater Aurora C. of C., 1974-79; mem. Kane County Zoning Bd. Appeals, 1979—, now chmn.; bd. dirs. Kane County Cancer Soc., 1981—; mem. governing bd. Copely Meml. Hosp., 1980; bd. dirs. Copley Meml. Hosp., 1981—; advisor Fox Valley United Arts Bd., 1979—. Served with USNR, 1944-46. Mem. Nat. Assn. Broadcasters, Ill. Broadcasters Assn., Inst. Radio Engrs., IEEE, Audio Engring. Soc., Soc. Broadcast Engrs. Republican. Presbyterian. Clubs: Lions, Union League. Office: PO Box 2010 Aurora IL 60507

BROKAW, NORMAN ROBERT, artists' management company executive; b. N.Y.C., Apr. 21, 1927; s. Isadore David and Marie (Hyde) B.; children—David M., Sanford Jay, Joel S., Barbara M., Wendy E. Student pvt. schs., Los Angeles. With William Morris Agency, Inc., Beverly Hills, Calif., 1943—, sr. agt. and co. exec., 1951-74, v.p. world-wide ops., 1974-80, exec. v.p., dir., 1980—. Pres. Betty Ford Cancer Center, Cedars-Sinai Med. Center, Los Angeles, 1978—; bd. dirs. Cedars-Sinai Med. Center, Los Angeles; industry chmn. United Jewish Welfare Fund, 1975. Served with U.S. Army, World War II. Mem. Acad. Motion Picture Arts and Scis. (dir.), Acad. TV Arts and Scis. Club: Hillcrest Country (Los Angeles). Clients include former Pres. and Mrs. Gerald R. Ford. Home: 530 Vick Pl Beverly Hills CA 90210 Office: 151 El Camino Beverly Hills CA 90212

BROKAW, R. MIRIAM, publishing company editor; b. Kobe, Japan, June 15, 1917; came to U.S., 1930; d. Harvey and Olivia (Forster) B. B.A., Wilson Coll., 1937, Litt D., 1966. Proofreader Westminster Press, Phila., 1937-44; freelance editor Prentice-Hall, N.Y.C., 1944-45; proofreader Princeton U. Press, N.J., 1945-48, editor, then mng. editor, 1948-65, assoc. dir., editor, 1966—; English edit. advisor U. Tokyo Press, 1965-66. Mem. Am. Hist. Assn., Assn. Am. Univ. Presses (pres. 1975-76), Internat. Assn. Scholarly Pubs. (sec.-gen. 1967-70). Democrat. Home: 4674 Province Line Rd Princeton NJ 08540 Office: Princeton Univ Press 41 William St Princeton NJ 08540

BROKAW, THOMAS JOHN, journalist; b. Webster, S.D., Feb. 6, 1940; s. Anthony Orville and Eugenia (Conley) B.; m. Meredith Lynn Auld, Aug. 17, 1962; children—Jennifer Jean, Andrea Brooks, Sarah Auld. B.A. in Polit. Sci, U. S.D., 1962. Morning news editor Sta. KMTV, Omaha, 1962-65; 11:00 news editor, anchorman Sta. WSB-TV, Atlanta, 1965-66; reporter, corr., anchorman Sta. KNBC-TV, Los Angeles, 1966-73; White House corr. NBC, Washington, 1973-76; anchorman Sat. Night News, N.Y.C., 1973-76; host Today show, N.Y.C., 1976-82; co-anchor NBC Nightly News, 1982—; adv. com. Reporters Com. for Freedom of Press. Mem. AFTRA (dir. 1968-72), Sierra Club, Sigma Delta Chi. Office: 30 Rockefeller Plaza New York NY 10020 *

BROLIN, JAMES, actor; b. Los Angeles, July 18. Student, UCLA. Regular in: TV series The Monroes, 1964-65, Marcus Welby M.D, 1969-76, Hotel, 1983; TV movies Marcus Welby M.D, 1969, Short Walk to Daylight, 1972, Trapped, 1973, Steel Cowboy, 1978; film appearances include Take Her, She's Mine, 1963, Goodbye, Charlie, 1964, Von Ryan's Express, 1965, Morituri, 1965, Our Man Flint, 1966, The Boston Strangler, 1968, Skyjacked, 1972, Westworld, 1973, Gable and Lombard, 1976, The Car, 1977, Capricorn I, 1978, Night of the Juggler, 1978, Amityville Horror, 1978, The Gringos, 1980 (Named Most Promising Actor of 1970 by Fame and Photoplay mags., winner Emmy award.). Office: care Internat Creative Mgmt 8899 Beverly Blvd Los Angeles CA 90048 *

BROM, LIBOR, educator; b. Ostrava, Czechoslovakia, Dec. 17, 1923; came to U.S., 1958, naturalized, 1964; s. Ladislav and Bozena (Bromova) B.; m. Gloria S. Mena, Aug. 31, 1961; 1 son, Rafael Brom. Ing., Czech Inst. Tech., 1948; J.U.C., Charles U. Prague, 1951; postgrad., San Francisco State Coll.; M.A., U. Colo., 1962, Ph.D., 1970. Vice pres. Brom, Inc., Ostrava, Czechoslovakia, 1942-48; economist Slovak Magnesite Works, Prague, Czechoslovakia, 1948-49; economist, chief planner, Vodostavba, Navika, Prague, 1951-56; tchr. Jefferson County Schs., Colo., 1958-67; prof., coordinator Russian area studies program U. Denver, 1967—; journalist, mem. editorial staff Demi Hlasatel-Daily Herald, Chgo., 1978—; Pres. Colo. Nationalities Council, 1970-72; comptroller Exec. Bd. Nat. Heritage Groups Council, 1970-72; mem. adv. bd. Nat. Security Council, 1980—; acad. bank participant Heritage Found. Author: Ivan Bunin's Proteges, Leonid Zurov, 1973, in Czech, In the Windstorms of Anger, 1976, On Restoring the Moral Order, 1980, Time and Duty, 1981, Teacher of Nations and Our Times, 1983, On the Way of Light, 1983; translator: Problems of Geography, 1955. V.p. Colo. Citizenship Day, 1968-69, Comenius World Council, 1976—, World Representation of Czechoslovak Exiles, 1976—; acting gen. sec. Czechoslovak Republican Movement. Recipient Americanism medal D.A.R., 1969, Distinguished Service award Am. by Choice, 1968; named Tchr. with Superlative Performance Modern Lang. Assn., 1961, Outstanding Faculty mem. Omicron Delta Kappa, 1972. Mem. Econ. Inst. Research and Edn., Am. Assn. Tchrs. Slavic and Eastern European Langs. (v.p. 1973-75), Am. Assn. Advancement Slavic Studies, Intercollegiate Studies Inst., Western Social Sci. Assn., Comenius World Council (v.p.), Rocky Mountain Assn. Slavic Studies (sec. treas. 1975-78, 1978-81, pres. 1982-83), Czechoslovak Nat. Council of Am., Czechoslovak Christian Democratic Movement in Exile (central com. 1970-79), Dobro Slovo (hon.), Aleksandr Solzhenitsyn Soc., Shavano Inst. Nat. Leadership, Nat. Republican Nationalities Council (co-chmn. human rights com. 1979-81), Lincoln Ednl. Found. Republican. Roman Catholic. Home: 39 Hillside Dr Wheat Ridge CO 80215 Office: Univ Denver Denver CO 80208 *While I lived amidst the adversities that plagued Europe, I had a dream of a mighty country with fantastic resources in which God had placed all the different races, nationalities, interests and opportunities with one purpose only—to show the world how to live. My dream was America. Now, as an American, I regard it as my duty to make my dream WORK.*

BROMAN, KEITH LEROY, finance educator; b. Randolph, Wis., July 13, 1922; s. Oscar Rudolph and H. Marie (Carlson) B.; m. Ruth Jane DuBois, Oct. 27, 1944; children: Rebecca Ann, Lisa Marie. Student, Ind. U., 1940-43, Berea Coll., 1944; M.B.A., Harvard U., 1947; Ph.D., U. Nebr., 1955. With Sears Roebuck & Co., South Bend, Ind., 1940-42, Bendix Corp., South Bend, 1942-43; instr. acctg. Ohio U., 1947-51; instr. bus. orgn. and mgmt. U. Neb., 1951-54, asso. prof., 1955-65, prof. finance, 1966—, chmn. dept., 1968-78; asst. prof. acctg. U. Wis., Madison, 1954-55. Served to comdr. Supply Corps USNR, 1943-46. Ford Found. fellow, 1959; Savs. and Loan League grantee, 1963; Council on Investments grantee, 1966; AT&T grantee, 1968; Recipient Disting. Teaching award U. Nebr., 1979. Mem. Am. Finance Assn., Am. Accounting Assn., Am. Legion, Coll. Football Assn. (sec. faculty reps. com. 1978-82), Beta Gamma Sigma, Delta Sigma Pi. Republican. Presbyterian (chmn. ch. bd. trustees 1981—). Home: 3540 Calvert St Lincoln NE 68506 Office: CBA 114 U Nebr Lincoln NE 68588

BROMBERG, ALAN ROBERT, lawyer, educator, writer; b. Dallas, Nov. 24, 1928; s. Alfred L. and Juanita (Kramer) B.; m. Anne Ruggles, July 26, 1959. A.B., Harvard U., 1949; J.D., Yale U., 1952. Bar: Tex. 1952. Assoc. firm Carrington, Gowan, Johnson, Bromberg and Leeds, Dallas, 1952-56; atty. and cons, 1956-76; of counsel firm Jenkens & Gilchrist, 1976—; asst. prof. law So. Meth. U., 1956-58, assoc. prof., 1958-62, prof., 1962—, mem. presdl. search group, 1971-72; faculty adviser Southwestern Law Jour., 1958-65; sr. fellow Yale U. Law Faculty, 1966-67; vis. prof. Stanford U., 1972-73; mem. adv. bd. U. Calif. Securities Regulation Inst., 1973-78, 79—; counsel Internat. Data Systems, Inc., 1961-65, sec., dir., 1963-65; mem. Tex. Legis. Council Bus. and Commerce Code Adv. Com., 1966-67. Author: Supplementary Materials on Texas Corporations, 3d edit, 1971, Partnership Primer-Problems and Planning, 1961, Materials on Corporate Securities and Finance—A Growing Company's Search for Funds, 2d edit, 1965, Securities Fraud and Commodities Fraud, Vols. 1-5, 1967-83, Crane and Bromberg on Partnership, 1968; mem. ednl. publs. adv. bd., Matthew Bender & Co., 1977—; chmn., 1981—; contbr. articles and revs. to law and bar jours.; adv. editor: Rev. Securities Regulation, 1969—, Securities Regulation Law Jour, 1973—, Jour. Corp. Law, 1976—. Sec., bd. dirs. Community Arts Fund, 1963-73; gen. atty. Dallas Mus. Contemporary Arts, 1956-63; bd. dirs. Dallas Theater Center, 1955-73, sec., 1957-66, fin. com., 1957-65, mem. exec. com., 1957-70, 79—, life, 1973—, v.p., trustee endowment fund, 1974—. Served as cpl. U.S. Army, 1952-54. Mem. Am. Bar Assn. (coms. commodities, partnerships, fed. regulation securities), Dallas Bar Assn. (chmn. com. uniform partnership act 1959-61, library com. 1981—), State Bar Tex. (chmn. sect. corp. banking and bus. law 1967-68, vice-chmn. 1965-67, com. corp. law revision 1957—, chmn. com. securities and investment banking 1965-69, mem. com. partnership 1957—, chmn. 1979-81), Am. Law Inst., Southwestern Legal Found. (co-chmn. securities com. 1982—), AAUP (exec. com. chpt. 1962-63, chmn. acad. freedom and tenure com. 1968-70, 71-72). Office: So Meth U Law Sch Dallas TX 75275 also 2200 First Nat Bank Bldg Dallas TX 75202

BROMBERG, HENRI LOUIE, JR., lawyer; b. Dallas, Jan. 15, 1911; s. Henri Louie and Felice (Fechenbach) B.; m. Janice Mayer, Apr. 12, 1936; 1 son, Henri Louie III. A.B., U. Tex., Austin, 1932; J.D., Northwestern U., 1935. Bar: Tex. 1935, U.S. Supreme Ct. 1950. Since practiced in, Dallas; partner Johnson, Bromberg & Leeds (and predecessor firm), 1935—; vice-chmn. bd., dir. Northpark Nat. Corp., 1980—, Northpark Nat. Bank of Dallas. Nat. vice chmn. Joint Def. Appeal Nat. Council, 1957-58; mem. nat. bd. NCCJ, 1959-62, co-chmn. Dallas chpt., 1960-68; chmn. Dallas chpt. Am. Jewish Com., 1951, dir., 1951—; mem. Gov.'s Com. for White House Conf. on Children and Youth, 1960; del. White House Conf. on Internat. Cooperation, 1965; bd. dirs. West Dallas Social Center, 1953-58, pres., 1955; bd. dirs. Jewish Welfare Fedn. Dallas, 1947-61, pres., 1956-58; bd. dirs. Tex. Psychiat. Found., 1955-62, v.p., 1959-62; sec., bd. dirs. Urban League Greater Dallas, 1967-74, adv. dir., 1974—; sec., bd. dirs. Dallas Grand Opera Assn., 1946—; bd. dirs. Dallas County Assn. for Blind, 1952-60, Council Social Agys. Dallas, 1958-65, Dallas County Community Action Com., 1965-70, Council Jewish Fedns. and Welfare Funds, 1958-60, Tex. United Community Services, 1972-74, Dallas County Community Coll. Dist. Found., 1974—; bd. visitors Law Sch., So. Methodist U., 1965-71, non-trustee mem. Law Sch. com. of bd. trustees, 1975—; trustee Dallas Symphony Assn., 1976—, bd. govs., 1983—; bd. govs. Hebrew Union Coll.-Jewish Inst. Religion, 1968-75, mem. exec. com., 1970-75; vice chmn. Nat. Cabinet Reform Jewish Appeal, 1970. Served to lt. col. USAAF, 1942-46. Recipient Brotherhood award NCCJ, 1970; Recipient (with wife) Human Relations award Am. Jewish Com., 1970. Mem. Am. Judicature Soc., Archeol. Inst. Am., Dallas Art Assn., Am., Tex., Dallas bar assns., Confrerie Des Chevaliers Du Tastevin. Jewish (past pres., dir. temple 1950—). Clubs: Columbian (past pres., dir.), Dallas (dir. 1981—), City (Dallas)). Home: 4842 Brookview Dr Dallas TX 75220 Office: 4400 Republic Nat Bank Tower Dallas TX 75201

BROMBERG, JOHN EDWARD, lawyer; b. Dallas, May 9, 1946; s. Edward S. and Mildred J. (Rosenberg) B.; m. Susan Kay Harkness, Aug. 21, 1971; children—Spencer Harkness, Whitney Payne, Kemp Howitt, Campbell Wynne. B.A., Columbia U., 1968; J.D., U. Tex., 1972. Bar: Tex. Partner firm Johnson, Bromberg & Leeds, Dallas. Past pres. Preston Hollow Park Assn., pre-sch. playground, Dallas. Mem. Am. Contract Bridge League (past pres. Dallas unit). Home: 6214 Desco Dr Dallas TX 75225 Office: 4400 Republic Nat Bank Tower Dallas TX 75201

BROMBERG, MYRON JAMES, lawyer; b. Paterson, N.J., Nov. 5, 1934; s. Abraham and Elsie (Baker) B.; m. Patricia Meyer, Sept. 6, 1980; children—Kenneth Karl, Eric Edward, Bruce Abraham. B.A., Yale U., 1956; LL.B., Columbia U., 1959. Bar: N.J. bar 1960, N.Y. bar 1981. Law asst. to dist. atty., N.Y. County, 1958; law asst. U.S. atty. So. Dist. N.Y., 1958-59; asso. mem. firm Ralph Porzio, Morristown, N.J., 1960-61; partner firm Porzio, Bromberg & Newman, Morristown, 1961-77, 80—, Porzio & Bromberg, 1977-80; atty. Morris County Bd. Elections, 1963-64; town atty., Town of Morristown, 1965-67; lectr. trial practice Rutgers Inst. Continuing Legal Edn., 1965—. Chmn. fund and membership Morristown chpt. ARC, 1965; chmn. retail div. Community Chest Morris County, 1963; chmn. Keep Morristown Beautiful Com., 1963; mem. Morris Twp. Com., 1970-72; committeeman Morris County Democratic Com., 1962-63, 72-77; lay trustee Delbarton Sch., Morristown, 1972-75; trustee Morris Mus., 1973-79. Fellow Am. Coll. Trial Lawyers, Am. Bar Found.; mem. ABA, N.J. Bar Assn. (named outstanding young lawyer 1970, chmn. joint conf. com. with N.J. Med. Soc. 1970-72), Morris County Bar Assn., Am. Judicature Soc., Trial Attys. N.J. (pres. 1976-77), Internat. Soc. Barristers, Internat. Assn. Ins. Counsel, Phillips Acad. Alumni Assn. N.Y.C., Chi Phi, Phi Delta Phi. Jewish. Clubs: Nat. Lawyers (Washington); Yale (N.Y.C. and Central N.J.). Home: Blue Mill Rd Morristown NJ 07960 Office: 163 Madison Ave Morristown NJ 07960

BROMBERG, ROBERT SHELDON, lawyer; b. Bklyn., May 3, 1935; s. Jack and Bertha (Toskey) B.; m. Barbara W. Schwartz, Apr. 1, 1978; children: Jason, David. A.B., Columbia U., 1956, LL.B., 1959; LL.M. in Taxation, N.Y. U., 1966. Bar: N.Y. 1960, D.C. 1972, Ohio 1972, U.S. Ct. Claims 1976, U.S. Supreme Ct 1975. Practiced law, N.Y.C., 1960-66; atty. exempt orgns. br. IRS, Washington, 1966-70, Office Chief Counsel, 1970-72; partner firm Baker, Hostetler & Patterson, Cleve., 1972-79; prin. Robert S. Bromberg, L.P.A., Cleve., 1979-81, Paxton & Seasongood, Cin., 1981—; lectr. tax and health law confs. Author: Tax Planning for Hospitals and Health Care Organizations, 2 vols, 1979; contbr. articles to profl. jours.; cons. editor: Prentice Hall Tax Exempt Organizations Service, 1973—. Recipient award (5) Dept. Treasury, 1966-72, citation Am. Assn. Homes for Aged, 1973. Mem. Am. Bar Assn., Nat. Health Lawyers Assn. (program chmn. Ann. Tax Inst. 1975-83, dir. 1978—), Am. Soc. Hosp. Attys. Home: 691 Riesling Knoll Cincinnati OH 45226 Office: Paxton & Seasongood 1700 Central Trust Tower 5 W 4th St Cincinnati OH 45202

BROMBERG, WALTER, psychiatrist; b. N.Y.C., Dec. 16, 1900; s. George and Anna (Scholtz) B.; m. Ilyana Fatow, Dec. 29, 1927; children: Joan Lisa, David Hannon; m. Esther Boyd, Mar. 11, 1942; 1 son, Mark Boyd. B.S., U. Cin., 1925; M.D., L.I. Med. Coll., 1926. Diplomate: Am. Bd. Psychiatry and Neurology, Am. Bd. Forensic Psychiatry (pres. 1983-84). Intern, resident neurology Mt. Sinai Hosp., 1926-28; asst. physician Manhattan State Hosp., 1928-30; jr., then sr. psychiatrist Bellevue Psychiat. Hosp., 1930-41; psychiatrist-in-charge Psychiat. Clinic, Ct. of Gen. Sessions, 1935-41; asso. psychiatrist Beth Israel Hosp., 1932—; asst. prof. clin. psychiatry N.Y. U. Med. Coll., 1936-41; mem. Group for Advancement Psychiatry, 1947-51; lectr. in criminal psychiatry U. Calif., 1949; clin. dir. Mendocino State Hosp., Talmage, Calif., 1950-51; adj. prof. legal medicine McGeorge Sch. Law, U. of Pacific, 1970—; neuropsychiat. cons. Calif. Dept. Health, 1970—; bd. dirs. Am. Bd. Forensic Psychiatry, 1976. Author: The Mind of Man, 4 edits, 1937-75, Crime and the Mind, 1975, also monographs in medico-legal field. Served to comdr. M.C. USN, 1942-46. Recipient Distinguished Service award Am. Acad. Psychiatry and Law, 1973. Life fellow Am. Psychiat. Assn. (Manfred S. Guttmacher award 1981); mem. Med. Soc. Sacramento County.; Mem. B'nai B'rith. Office: 3353 Cottage Way Sacramento CA 95825

BROMBERGER, SYLVAIN, educator, philosopher; b. Antwerp, Belgium, July 7, 1924; s. Jacques and Esther (Helman) B.; m. Nancy Alice Lilienthal, Aug. 7, 1949; children—Allen Richard, Daniel Martin. A.B., Columbia, 1948; Ph.D., Harvard, 1961. Instr. Princeton, 1954-57, lectr., 1957-60; asso. prof. U. Chgo., 1961-66; mem. faculty Mass. Inst. Tech., 1966—, prof. philosophy, 1967—, chmn. philosophy program, 1976-80. Mem. adv. bd.: Philos. Forum; cons. editor: Metaphilosophy. Served with AUS, 1943-46. Santayana fellow Harvard, 1957-58; recipient Quantrell prize U. Chgo., 1964. Mem. Am. Philos. Assn., AAUP. Home: 146 Beaumont Ave Newtonville MA 02160 Office: Mass Inst Tech Cambridge MA 02139

BROMBERT, VICTOR HENRI, literature educator, author; b. Nov. 11, 1923; U.S., 1941, naturalized, 1943; s. Jacques and Vera B.; m. Beth Anne Archer, June 18, 1950; children: Lauren Nora, Marc Alexis. B.A., Yale U., 1948, M.A., 1949, Ph.D., 1953; postgrad., U. Rome, 1950-51; H.H.D. (hon.), U. Chgo., 1981. Faculty Yale U., New Haven, 1951-75, asso. prof., 1958-61, prof., 1961-75, Benjamin F. Barge prof. Romance lits., 1969-75, chmn. dept. Romance langs. and lit., 1964-73; Henry Putnam Univ. prof. Romance and comparative lit. Princeton U., 1975—; summer prof. Middlebury Coll., 1951-53, Institut d'Etudes Françaises, Avignon, 1962, 64, 73, U. Colo., 1965; Christian Gauss Seminar in criticism Princeton U., 1964; vis. prof. Scuola Normale Superiore, Pisa, Italy, 1972, U. Calif., 1978, Johns Hopkins U., 1979, Columbia U., 1980, N.Y. U., 1980, 81; lectr. Alliance Française, humanities U. Kans., 1966; mem. Fulbright screening com., 1965; dir. fellowships in residence Nat. Endowment for Humanities, Princeton U., 1975-76, dir. summer seminar, 1979, 82; adv. com. for humanities Library of Congress, 1976; mem. Yale U. Council, 1977—; mem. ednl. adv. bd. Guggenheim Found., 1982—. Author: The Criticism of T.S. Eliot, 1949, Stendhal et la Voie Oblique, 1954, The Intellectual Hero, 1961, The Novels of Flaubert, 1966, Stendhal; Fiction and the Themes of Freedom, 1968, Flaubert par lui-même, 1971, La Prison romantique, 1976, The Romantic Prison: The French Tradition, 1978; editor: Stendhal: A Collection of Critical Essays, 1962, Balzac's La Peau de Chagrin, 1962, The Hero in

Literature, 1969; contbg. author: The World of Lawrence Durrell, 1962, Ideas in the Drama, 1964, Instants Premiers, 1973, Romanticism, 1973, Literary Criticism, 1974, Die Romanische Novelle, 1977, The Author in His Work, 1978, Essais sur Flaubert, 1979, Writers and Politics, 1983; contbr. articles to periodicals. Served with M.I. AUS, 1943-45. Decorated officier Ordre des Palmes Académiques; recipient Harry Levin prize in comparative lit., 1978; Howard T. Behrman award for disting. achievement in humanities, 1979; Am. Council Learned Socs. grantee, 1966; Fulbright fellow, 1950-51; Guggenheim fellow, 1954-55, 70; sr. fellow Nat. Endowment for Humanities, 1973-74; Rockefeller Found. resident fellow, Bellagio, Italy, 1975. Fellow Am. Acad. Arts and Scis.; mem. MLA (editorial adv. com. 1979-83), Am. Assn. Tchrs. French, Am. Comparative Lit. Assn., Société des Etudes Françaises, Société des Etudes Romantiques, Acad. Lit. Studies (pres. 1983), Société d'Histoire Littéraire de la France, Società Universitaria per gli Studi di Lingua e Letteratura Francese, Phi Beta Kappa. Clubs: Elizabethan (pres. 1968-70), Yale.). Home: 187 Library Pl Princeton NJ 08540 Office: 245 E Pyne Princeton U Princeton NJ 08540

BROME, ROBERT HARRISON, lawyer; b. Basin, Wyo., June 28, 1911; s. Charles L. and Margaret (Kennedy) B.; m. Mary E. Reed, Aug. 28, 1937; children: Thomas R., Robert H. A.B., Whitman Coll., 1933, LL.D., 1970; LL.B., Columbia U., 1936. Bar: N.Y. 1936, Wyo. 1946. Asst. counsel, asst. sec. Fed. Res. Bank of N.Y., 1936-46, 48-50; resident counsel Bankers Trust Co., N.Y.C., 1950-62, sec., 1955-66, gen. counsel, 1962-66, sr. v.p., gen. counsel, 1966-68, sr. v.p., 1968-74; v.p., sec. Bankers Internat. Corp., 1962-70, also dir.; sec., gen. counsel BT N.Y. Corp., 1966-68, sr. v.p., 1968-75, exec. v.p., 1975-77; chmn., chief exec. officer, dir. Bankers Trust Co. of Hudson Valley, 1975-77, dir., 1975-78; counsel firm Eaton & Van Winkle, N.Y.C., 1978—; dir. BT Capital, N.Y.C., Crossville (Tenn.) Rubber Co. Bd. overseers Whitman Coll.; adv. council Columbia U. Grad. Sch. Bus., 1976-78. Mem. Am. Bar Assn., Am. Bankers Assn., Phi Beta Kappa. Clubs: Tuxedo, University (N.Y.C.); Blackmeadow (Chester, N.Y.); DeBruce Fly Fishing (N.Y.). Home: 7 Schuyler Rd Allendale NJ 07401 Office: 600 3d Ave New York NY 10016

BROMERY, RANDOLPH WILSON, geologist, educator; b. Cumberland, Md., Jan. 18, 1926; s. Lawrence Randolph and Edith (Edmondson) B.; m. Cecile Trescott, June 8, 1947; children: Keith, Carol, Dennis, David, Christopher. Student, U. Mich., 1945-46; B.S., Howard U., 1956; M.S., Am. U., 1962; Ph.D., Johns Hopkins U., 1968; Sc.D. (hon.), Frostburg State Coll., Ed.D., Western New Eng. Coll.; LL.D., U. Hokkaido, 1976; L.H.D. (hon.), U. Mass., 1979. Geophysicist U.S. Geol. Survey, 1948-68, cons., 1968-72; prof., lectr. Howard U., Washington, 1961-65; asso. prof. geology, dep. chmn. dept. U. Mass., 1967-68, prof. geology, chmn. dept., 1969-70, prof. geology, vice-chancellor, 1970-71, prof. geology, chancellor, 1972-77, exec. v.p., 1977-79, Commonwealth prof., 1979—; pres. Resources Cons. Assos.; dir. Singer Co., Exxon Corp., New Eng. Telephone Co., Northwestern Mut. Life Ins. Co.; geophys. cons. Kennecott Copper Corp.; Mem. corp. Woods Hole Oceanographic Instn. Contbr. numerous articles to sci. and profl. jours. Trustee Babson Coll., Talladega Coll., Hampshire Coll., Boston Mus. Sci.; mem. Com. Collegiate Edn. Black Students, 1967-72, pres., 1968-72; mem. human devel. com. Cath. Archdiocese, Springfield, 1971—; vice-chmn. New Coalition for Econ. and Social Change; mem. adv. council NASA; mem. Nat. Acad. Engrs. Com. Minorities in Engring; mem. advisory com. John F. Kennedy Library; mem. bd. overseers vis. com. dept. geol. scis. Harvard U., 1975-79. Served with USAAF, 1943-44. Named hon. pres. Soodo Women's U., Seoul, Korea; Gillman fellow Johns Hopkins, 1964-65. Fellow AAAS, Geol. Soc. Am.; mem. Am. Geophys. Union, Soc. Exploration Geophysicists, N.Y. Acad. Scis., Explorers Club, Council Fgn. Relations, Sigma Xi, Phi Kappa Phi, Phi Eta Sigma. Club: Cosmos. Office: Dept Geology U Mass Amherst MA 01003 *

BROMLEY, DANIEL WOOD, agricultural economics educator, consultant; b. Phoenix, Mar. 27, 1940; s. Frank Wood and Anice (Frankenberg) B.; m. Barbara J. Fashbaugh, Mar. 16, 1963 (div. 1976); children: Kirk, Christopher, Elizabeth; m. Joyce Elizabeth Stover, Aug. 27, 1976; 1 son, Reed. B.S., Utah State U., 1963; M.S., Oreg. State U., 1967, Ph.D., 1969. Asst. prof. dept. agrl. econs. U. Wis.-Madison, 1969-72, assoc. prof., 1972-76, prof., 1976—, chmn. dept. agrl. econs., 1981—; vis. scholar U.S. Dept. Interior, Washington, 1973, AID, 1974; dir. Univ. Bookstroe, Madison, 1983—; cons. AID, World Bank, Ford Found. Author: (with R.C. Buse) applied Economics, 1974, (with A. Sfeir-Younis) Decision Making in Developing Countries, 1976; contrib. articles to profl. jours. Mem. Am. Agrl. Econs. Assn., Am. Econ. Assn., Assn. Environ. and Resource Econs. (bd. dirs. 1980—). Democrat. Office: U Wis 427 Lorch St Madison WI 53706

BROMLEY, DAVID ALLAN, educator, physicist; b. Westmeath, Ont., Can., May 4, 1926; s. Milton Escort and Susan Anne (Anderson) B.; m. Patricia Jane Brassor, Aug. 30, 1949; children—David John, Karen Lynn. B.Sc. in Engring. Physics, Queen's U., Kingston, Ont., 1948, M.Sc. in Physics, 1950; Ph.D. in Nuclear Physics, U. Rochester, 1952; M.A. (hon.), Yale U., 1961, Dr. Nat. Phil., U. Frankfurt, 1978; Docteur (Physique) (hon.), U. Strasbourg, 1980; D.Sc. (hon.), Queen's U., 1981, D.Sci., U. Notre Dame, 1982, U. Witwatersrand, 1982, Litt.D., U. Bridgeport, 1981, Dott., U. Padua, 1983. Operating engr. Hydro Electric Power Commn. Ont., 1947-48; research officer Nat. Research Council Can., 1948; instr., then asst. prof. physics U. Rochester, 1952-55; sr. research officer, sect. head Atomic Energy Can. Ltd., 1955-60; asso. prof. physics, asso. dir. heavy ion accelerator lab. Yale, 1960-61, prof. physics, dir., 1961—, chmn. physics dept., 1970-77, Henry Ford II prof., 1972—; dir. United Nuclear Corp., NE Bancorp Inc., Union Trust Co., United Illuminating Corp., Gen. Ionex Co.; cons. Brookhaven, Argonne, Berkley and Oak Ridge Nat. Labs., Bell Telephone Labs., IBM, G.T.E.; Mem. panel nuclear physics Nat. Acad. Scis., 1964, chmn. com. on nuclear sci., 1966-74, chmn. physics survey, 1969-74; mem.-at-large, mem. exec. com. div. phys. scis. NRC, 1970-74, mem. exec. com., assembly phys. and math. scis., 1974-78; chmn. Office Phys. Scis., 1975-78; mem. U.S. nat. com. Internat. Union Pure and Applied Physics, 1969—, chmn., 1975—, v.p., 1975-81, pres.-elect, 1981—; mem. naval sci. bd. NRC, 1974-78; mem. high energy physics adv. panel ERDA, 1974-78; mem. nuclear sci. adv. panel NSF and Dept. Energy, 1980—; mem. Council Fgn. Relations, 1983—; Mem. White House Sci. Council, 1982—; chmn. Sr. Sci. Panel on Indo-U.S. Coop. in Sci. and Tech., 1982—, Dept. of Energy INSF Panel on Electron Accelerator Facilities, 1983. Editor: Physics in Perspective, 5 vols, 1972, Large Electrostatic Accelerators, 1974, Nuclear Detectors, 1978, Heavy Ion Science, 4 vols, 1981; co-editor: Procs. Kingston Internat. Conf. on Nuclear Structure, 1960, Facets of Physics, 1970, Nuclear Science in China, 1979; asso. editor: Annals of Physics, 1968—, Am. Scientist, 1969-81, Il Nuovo Cimento, 1970—, Nuclear Instruments and Methods, 1974—, Science, Technology and the Humanities, 1978—, Jour. Physics, 1978—, Nuclear Science Applications, 1978—, Technology in Soc, 1981—; cons. editor: McGraw Hill Series in Fundamentals of Physics, 1967—, McGraw Hill Ency. Sci. and Tech. Bd. dirs. Oak Ridge Asso. Univs., 1977-80, U. Bridgeport, 1981—. Recipient medal Gov. Gen. Can., 1948; NRC fellow, 1952; fellow Branford Coll., 1961—; Guggenheim fellow, 1977-78; Humboldt fellow, 1978; Benjamin Franklin fellow Royal Soc. Arts, London, 1979. Fellow Am. Phys. Soc. (mem. council 1967-71), Am. Acad. Arts and Scis., AAAS (chmn. physics sect. 1977-78, pres.-elect 1980, pres. 1981—, chmn. bd. 1982—); mem. Can. Assn. Physicists, European Phys. Soc., Conn. Acad. Arts and Scis., Conn. Acad. Sci. and Engring. (council 1976-78), Sigma Xi (pres. Yale 1962-63). Home: 35 Tokeneke Dr Hamden CT 06518 Office: Wright Nuclear Structure Lab Yale U 272 Witney Ave New Haven CT 06520

BROMLEY, JAMES DUNCAN, company executive; b. Webbwood, Ont., Can., July 12, 1922; s. James Larmour and Bertrude Ada (McPhee) B.; m. Mary Isabelle Jacklin, Sept. 9, 1950; children: David, Susan, John. B.A. in Sci., U. Toronto, 1946. Cert. civil engr. Laborer Can. Pacific Ltd., St. John, N.B., 1940-46, engr., Toronto, Sudbury, Ont., 1946-59, supt., Schreiber, Ont., 1965-68, gen. mgr., Toronto, 1970-72, Vancouver, B.C., 1972-77, v.p., Vancouver, 1977—; bd. govs. Employers Council, B.C., 1978—; dir. Can. Forestry Assn., 1978—, Pacific Forestry Products, 1977—; dir., exec. com. WESTAC, Vancouver, 1979—. Mem. Assn. Profl. Engrs., St. Johns Ambulance, Assn. R.R. Supts. Clubs: Vancouver, Capilano Golf and Country. Lodge: Masons. Home: 647 Andover Pl West Vancouver BC Canada V7S 1Y6 Office: Canadian Pacific Ltd 200 Granville St Cancouver BC Canada V6C 2R3

BROMS, NELSON, insurance executive; b. N.Y.C., Apr. 15, 1919; s. Solomon and Sophia B.; m. Pearl Tasch, Nov. 1, 1964; children: Stuart, Mitchell, Todd, Jane, Sandy. Student, CCNY, 1938-40. Chmn. bd., chief exec. officer Nelson Broms Co., Inc., 1956—, Mergers & Acquisitons Corp., 1957—; chmn. bd. Equitable Life Holding Corp., N.Y.C., 1978; mem. council Hofstra U., Hempstead, N.Y., 1965, established Nelson Broms chair in pvt. enterprise, 1967; dir. Boothe Fin. Corp. (also subsidiaries); Equitable Life Assurance Soc. U.S. Bd. dirs. Spoleto Festival U.S., 1980—, Ethics Resource Center/Am. Viewpoint, 1976-78. Served as officer AUS, 1940-45, 50-52. Decorated Bronze Star. Home: 57 Bank St New Canaan CT 06840 Office: 1285 Ave Americas New York NY 10019

BROMSEN, MAURY AUSTIN, bibliographer, historian, antiquarian bookseller; b. N.Y.C., Apr. 25, 1919; s. Herman and Rose (Eisenberg) B. B.S., CCNY, 1939; M.A., U. Calif.-Berkeley, 1941; Carnegie Endowment for Internat. Peace and U.S. Govt. exchange fellow, U. Chile, 1942; M.A. (Harvard Woodbury Lowery Travelling fellow, also Social Sci. Research Council fellow 1946-48), Harvard U., 1945; doctoral postgrad. in history, Harvard U., 1945-50. Vis. lectr. Am. history Cath. U., Santiago, Chile, 1942; instr. history CCNY, 1943-44; founding editor Inter-Am. Rev. Bibliography, 1950-54, adv. editor, U.S. rep., 1956—; founder, dir. Maury A. Bromsen Assos., Inc. (rare book, manuscript and fine art dealers), Boston, 1954—, pres., treas., 1963—; hon. curator Latin Am. collections Boston Pub. Library, 1977—; vis. prof. U. Chile, Santiago, 1947; editor, sect. chief dept. cultural affairs Pan. Am. Union, Washington, 1950-53; exec. sec. Medina Centennial Celebration, Washington, 1952; mem. adv. council univ. libraries U. Notre Dame, 1981. Author: Simón Bolivar: A Bicentennial Tribute, 1983; Editor: Humanist of the Americas: an Appraisal, 1960, Spanish transl., 1969; Research and publs. in history and bibliography of Ams.; Established Medina and Harrisse rare book collections, U. Fla. Library, 1958, 63. Endowed Archibald Bromsen Meml. scholarship, CCNY, 1964, Bromsen lectureship in Humanistic Bibliography, Boston Pub. Library, 1970, Maury A. Bromsen Latin Am. Acquisitions Fund, Boston Pub. Library, 1976. Named knight comdr. Orden al Mérito Bernardo O'Higgins, Chile). Mem. Antiquarian Booksellers Assn. Am., Am. Hist. Assn., ALA, Bibliog. Soc. Am., Manuscript Soc. (charter), Conf. on Latin Am. History, Academia Nacional de la Historia, Buenos Aires (corr.), Latin Am. Studies Assn., Sociedad de Historia Argentina (corr.), Pan Am. Soc. New Eng. (patron), Bibliog. Soc. (London), Bibliog. Soc. U. Va., Boston Athenaeum, Harvard Library Assn., Boston U. Library Assn., Iowa Library Assn., Bell (Minn.) Library Assn., Ky. Library Assn., Miami Library Assn., Clements (Mich.) Library Assn., Yale Library Asso., Am. Hist. Soc., Jewish Hist. Soc., Va. Hist. Soc., Fla. Hist. Soc., Mo. Hist. Soc., N.Y. Hist. Soc., Sociedad Chilena de Historia y Geografía, Filson Club (life), Phi Beta Kappa. Clubs: Harvard, Boston Athenaeum (Boston). Address: 770 Boylston St Boston MA 02199 *The true bibliographer ought to be more than an inventory maker and describer of the physical qualities of books and other printed material. This is but a minimal qualification of the craftsman. He ought rather to know something about the ideas to which a work relates and in what manner it supplements the known history of its field. Thereby he will make a contribution to humanism and this should be the prime motivator of the scholarly bookman worthy of the name bibliographer.*

BRON, KLAUS MICHAEL, physician; b. Ger., Feb. 7, 1929; came to U.S., 1935, naturalized, 1943; s. Wladimir and Babett B.; m. Lois Diamond, Mar. 20, 1966; children—Kerry A., William H. A.B., Columbia U., 1951; M.D., N.Y. U., 1955. Diplomate: Am. Bd. Radiology. Intern, then resident in radiology Phila. Gen. Hosp., 1955-57, 59-61; instr. radiology Stanford U. Med. Sch., 1961-62; NIH fellow Lund (Sweden) U. Faculty Medicine, 1962-63; mem. faculty U. Pitts. Med. Sch., 1964—, dir. vascular radiology, prof. radiology, 1971—. Author articles in field.; Cons. editor: Cardiovascular Radiology. Served with M.C. USAF, 1957-59. Fellow Am. Coll. Radiology; mem. Assn. U. Radiologists, Radiol. Soc. N.Am., AMA, Pa. Med. Soc., Pa. Roentgen Soc. (dir. 1976-79), Pitts. Roentgen Soc. (pres. 1980-81), Pa. Radiol. Soc., Allegheny County Med. Soc. Office: Dept Radiology Presbyn Univ Hosp Pittsburgh PA 15261

BRON, ROBERT PHILIP, performing arts administrator; b. Oak Park, Ill., Aug. 6, 1942; s. Govert Harry and Eleanore R. (Bassey) B. B.S., Ill. State U., 1966; M.M., No. Ill. U., 1970. Gen. mgr. Krannert Center, Urbana, Ill., 1969-71; chief of prodn. Cin. Symphony-Ballet, 1971; mgr. concert hall John F. Kennedy Center, Washington, 1971-73; gen. mgr. Erie (Pa.) Philharmonic, 1972; asst. to pres. Allied Arts Corp., Chgo., 1973-76; exec. dir. Okla. Symphony Orch., Oklahoma City, 1975; founder, prin. Robert P. Bron, Mgmt. (theatrical press agt., mgr. booking house), Chgo., 1978. Co. mgr.: prodn. The Compliments of Cole, 1977, Same Time, Next Year, 1978, Dracula, 1978-79, The Club, 1980, The Buried Child, 1980; nat. tour of Evita, 1980-81; co-mgr.: Nicholas Nickleby, 1982-83. Bd. dirs. Inst. Christian Studies, Chgo., 1977. Mem. Assn. Theatrical Press Agts. and Mgrs., Am. Symphony Orch. League, Opportunity Resources for the Arts, Assn. Coll., Univ. and Community Arts Adminstrs., Phi Mu Alpha. Republican. Episcopalian. Club: Moose. Home: 7424 W Harrison St Forest Park IL 60130

BRON, WALTER ERNEST, physics educator; b. Berlin, Jan. 17, 1930; U.S., 1939, naturalized, 1946; s. Arthur and Edith (Seidel) B.; m. Ann Elisabeth Berend, June 1, 1952; children: Karen Susanne, Michelle Elise. B.M.E., N.Y. U., 1952; M.S., Columbia, 1953, Ph.D., 1958. Research asso. IBM Watson Lab., Yorktown Heights, N.Y., 1957-58, research physicist, 1958-66; asso. prof. physics Ind. U., Bloomington, 1966-69, prof., 1969—; lectr. George Washington U., 1955-56, Columbia, 1957, adj. lectr., 1964; vis. prof. Physikalisches Institut der Technischen Hochschule, Stuttgart, Germany, 1966-67; vis. scientist Max Planck Inst. for Solid State Research, Stuttgart, Germany, 1973-74, 81-82, 83. Contbr. articles sci. jours. Mem. Bloomington Environ. Quality and Conservation Commn., 1972-81, chmn., 1974-76. Served with AUS, 1954-56. Gen. Electric fellow, 1952-53; W. Campbell fellow, 1953-54, 56-57; Guggenheim fellow, 1966-67; sr. Scientist award Alexander von Humboldt Found., 1973. Fellow Am. Phys. Soc.; mem. AAAS, Sassafras Audubon Soc. (pres. 1976-78), Sigma Xi, Tau Beta Pi, Pi Tau Sigma. Patentee in field. Home: 701 S Jordan St Bloomington IN 47401

BRONARS, EDWARD JOSEPH, organization executive, retired marine corps officer; b. Chgo., Apr. 12, 1927; s. Joseph Charles and Mary Barbara (Krawczyk) B.; m. Dorothea Rosa Bates, June 5, 1950; children: Barbara Annette, Bruce Edward. B.S., U.S. Naval Acad., 1950; M.S., George Washington U., 1969; grad., Nat. War Coll., 1969. Commd. 2d lt. U.S. Marine Corps, 1950, advanced through grades to lt. gen., 1979; comdg. officer 3d Bn., 7th Marines, Vietnam, 1967, plans officer, analyst G-2 div. Hdqrs. Marine Corps, 1967-68, plans officer joint planning group Hdqrs. Marine Corps, 1969-71, comdg. officer 1st Marine Regiment, 1971-72, asst. chief of staff, G-3 1st Marine Div., 1972-73, chief surface operations and plans div., asst. chief of staff, J-3 U.S. Support Activities Group, Thailand, 1973-74, comdg. gen. Landing Force Tng. Command, Atlantic, 1974-75; dep. chief of staff for requirements and programs Hdqrs. U.S. Marine Corps, Washington, 1975-78; comdg. gen. 2d Marine Div., Camp Lejeune, N.C., 1978-79; dep. chief of staff for manpower Hdqrs. USMC, Washington, 1979-82; ret., 1982; pres. Navy Relief Soc., Washington, 1982—. 2d v.p. Navy Mut. Aid Assn. Served in USNR, 1944-46. Decorated Disting. Service medal; Decorated Silver Star medal, Legion of Merit with Combat V and gold star, Bronze Star with combat V and Gold star, Air medal, Navy Commendation medal with Combat V. Mem. Marine Corps Assn., U.S. Naval Inst. (2d v.p.), Marine Corps Aviation Assn., U.S. Naval Acad. Alumni Assn. Roman Catholic. Home: 3354 Rose Ln Falls Church VA 22042 Office: Navy Relief Society 801 N Randolph St Arlington VA 22203

BRONDYKE, KENNETH JAMES, metallurgical engineer; b. Sault Sainte Marie, Mich., June 16, 1922; m. Lois Rose Wiese, Oct. 19, 1946; children: Karen Ann Brondyke McLemore, Donald Scott. B.S. in Metall. Engring., U. Mich., 1948. With Alcoa Co., Alcoa Center, Pa., 1948-84, asst. dir. research, 1970-73, asst. dir. metal processing, 1973-74, asso. dir., prodn., 1974-78; dir. Alcoa Labs., 1978-84; mem. adv. bd. Materials Processing Center, MIT; mem. adv. council dept. materials sci. and engring. U. Pa. Bd. dirs. Citizens Gen. Hosp., New Kensington, Pa. Served with U.S. Army, 1944-46. Am. Soc. Metals fellow, 1971. Mem. AIME, Am. Inst. Mining, Metall. and Petroleum Engrs., Indsl. Research Inst. (rep.), Sci. Research Soc. Am., Dirs. Indsl. Research, Sigma Xi. Clubs: Duquesne, Oakmont Country. Home: 727 14th St Oakmont PA 15139 Office: Alcoa Labs Alcoa Tech Center Alcoa Center PA 15069

BRONER, HERBERT JORDAN, home furnishings company executive; b. Chelsea, Mass., Jan. 10, 1928; s. Irving and Rose L. (Pliner) B.; m. Janice I. Broner, Sept. 6, 1951; children: Lisa F., Karen R., Frank A. A.B., Middlebury Coll., 1949; postgrad., George Washington U. Furniture buyer Hecht Co., Washington, 1948-53; exec. v.p. Rowe Furniture Co., Salem, Va., 1954-67; also dir.; dir. mktg. Mohasco Corp., Amsterdam, N.Y., 1968-71; pres. Unagusta Corp., Waynesville, N.C., 1971-72; also dir.; pres. Cort Furniture Rental Corp.; group v.p. rental ops. Mohasco, 1972-80, exec. v.p., 1980, pres., chief operating officer, 1980-83, pres., chief exec. officer, 1983—, dir., 1980—; dir. Welbilt Corp., N.Y.C., 1971-72. Mem. Niskayuna (N.Y.) Conservation Adv. Council. Served with USNR, 1948-56. Recipient Brotherhood award Furniture div. NCCJ, 1982. Mem. Furniture Rental Assn. Am. (dir.), Nat. Assn. Furniture Mfrs. (dir. 1983—), Am. Mgmt. Assn., Delta Upsilon. Office: 57 Lyon St Amsterdam NY 12010

BRONER, ROBERT, artist; b. Detroit, Mar. 10, 1922; s. Abraham and Ida (Opperman) B.; m. Esther Masserman, Jan. 18, 1948; children: Sari, Adam, Jeremy, Nahama. B.F.A., Wayne State U., 1945, M.A., 1946; student, UCLA, 1946-47; pupil of, Stuart Davis, 1949-50, S.W. Hayter, 1949-51. Prof. dept. art and art history Wayne State U., 1965—. Contbr. art criticism to newspapers and art jours.; one man exhbns. include, Wellons Gallery, N.Y.C., 1955, Phila. Art Alliance, 1956, Werbe and Garelick Detroit Galleries, 1953, 57, 61, Mich. State U., 1957, Drake Gallery, Carmel, Calif., Feingarten Gallery, Los Angeles, 1961, Ohio State U. Galleries, 1969, The J.L. Hudson Gallery, 1971, Bertha Urdang Gallery, N.Y.C., 1973, Arnold Klein Gallery, Detroit, Delson-Richter Gallery, Tel Aviv, 1975, Design Corner Gallery, Cleve., 1976, Troy (Mich.) Art Gallery, 1977, Manhattanville Coll., Purchase, N.Y., J.L. Hudson Gallery, Detroit, numerous group exhbns., U.S. and abroad, 1951—; represented in permanent colls., Art Inst. Chgo., Bklyn. Mus., Cin. Mus., Detroit Inst. Arts, Boston Pub. Library, Met. Mus. Art, Guggenheim Mus., Los Angeles County Mus., Fogg Mus., Harvard, Mus. Modern Art, N.Y.C., Nat. Gallery, Washington, N.Y. Pub. Library, Phila. Mus., Smithsonian Inst., Walker Art Center, Bibliothèque Nationale Paris, Israel Nat. Mus. Art, Jerusalem, Pa. Acad. Fine Arts, also pvt. collections. Recipient Print Purchase prize Bklyn. Mus., 1964, Purchase prize Soc. Am. Graphic Artists, 1969, Detroit Inst. award, 1961,66. Mem. Mich. Assn. Printmakers (pres. 1958), Drawing and Print Club Detroit Inst. Arts (bd. dirs.), Soc. Am. Graphic Artists (pres. 1980), Nat. Print Council (pres. 1979—), Phila. Print Club. Office: Troy Art Gallery 755 W Big Beaver Troy MI 48084 *

BRONFENBRENNER, MARTIN, economist, educator, Japan specialist; b. Pitts., Dec. 2, 1914; s. Jacques Jacob and Martha (Ornstein) B.; m. Teruko Okuaki, Nov. 13, 1951; children—Kenneth, June. A.B., Washington U., St. Louis, 1934; Ph.D., U. Chgo., 1939; postgrad., Northwestern U. Law Sch. Asst. U. Chgo., 1937-38; faculty Central YMCA Coll., Chgo., 1938-40; economist U.S. Treasury, 1940-41; financial economist Fed. Res. Bank, Chgo., 1941-42, 46-47; asso. prof. U. Wis., 1947-54, prof., 1954-57; prof. econs. Mich. State U., 1957-58, U. Minn., Mpls., 1958-62, Grad. Sch. Indsl. Adminstrn., Carnegie-Mellon U., Pitts., 1962-71, chmn. dept. econs., 1966-71; Kenan prof. econs., lectr. Japanese history, acting dir. Asian/Pacific Studies Inst., Duke U., Durham, N.C., 1971—; fiscal economist SCAP, Tokyo, 1949-50; economist UN Econ. Commn. for Asia and Far East, Bangkok, Thailand, 1952; vis. fellow Center for Study Behavioral Scis., Stanford, 1966-67, Inst. Devel. Studies, Sussex, Eng., 1978, Fed. Res. Bank, San Francisco, 1979, Center S.E. Asian Studies, Kyoto U., Japan, 1980; Fulbright lectr., Japan, 1962-63. Author: Academic Encounter, 1961, Income Distribution Theory, 1971, Tomioka Stories, 1975; Editor: Is the Business Cycle Obsolete?, 1969, Macroeconomic Alternatives, 1979; Contbr. numerous articles to profl. jours. Served as officer USNR, 1943-46. Mem. Am. Econ. Assn. (v.p. 1975), So. Econ. Assn. (v.p. 1976-77, pres. 1978-79), Hist. Pol. Econ. (pres. 1982), AAUP, Assn. Asian Studies, Phi Beta Kappa. Home: 2915 Friendship Rd Durham NC 27705 *My life is like an old Harold Lloyd movie; a naive and stupid hero makes every asinine blunder and dumb decision in the book. But somehow things work out not too badly at the last minute, for reasons which even hindsight seldom clarifies.*

BRONFMAN, CHARLES ROSNER, distillery executive; b. Montreal, Que., Can., June 27, 1931; s. Samuel and Saidye (Rosner) B.; m. Andrea Morrison, 1982; children: Stephen Rosner, Ellen Jane. Student, McGill U., 1948-51. With The Seagram Co., Ltd., 1951—, v.p., dir., 1958-71, exec. v.p., 1971-75; pres. Seagram Co. Ltd., 1975-79, dep. chmn., 1979—, chmn. exec. com., 1975—; chmn. bd. Montreal Baseball Club Ltd.; hon. chmn., dir. Super-Sol Ltd., Israel; dir. Bank of Montreal, Can., E.I. duPont de Nemours & Co., Power Corp. Can. Chmn. bd. United Israel Appeal Can.; past pres. Allied Jewish

Community Services, Montreal; life gov. Jewish Gen. Hosp.; bd. govs. Jewish Agy. for Israel; hon. chmn. Can.-Israel Securities Ltd. (State of Israel Bonds Can.); bd. dirs. Can. Council Christians and Jews. Clubs: Montefiore, Mt. Royal, Saint-Denis, Elm Ridge Golf and Country (Montreal); Palm Beach Country. Office: 1430 Peel St Montreal PQ H3A 1S9 Canada

BRONFMAN, EDGAR MILES, distillery executive; b. Montreal, Que., Can., June 20, 1929; s. Samuel and Saidye (Rosner) B. Student, Williams Coll., 1946-49; B.A., McGill U., 1951. Chmn. adminstrv. com. Joseph E. Seagram & Sons, Inc., 1955-57, pres., 1957-71; chmn., chief exec. officer; pres. Distillers Corp.-Seagrams Ltd., Montreal, 1971-75; now chmn., chief exec. officer Seagram Co. Ltd.; chmn., dir. Clevepak Corp., Gulfstream Land and Devel. Corp.; dir. Am. Technion Soc., Internat. Exec. Service Corps; hon. trustee Bank N.Y. Bd. dirs. Citizens Com. for N.Y.C., Interracial Council for Bus. Opportunity; mem. Am. com. Weizmann Inst. Sci.; exec. bd. govs. N.Y. councils Boy Scouts Am.; trustee Mt. Sinai Hosp., Sch. Medicine and Med. Center, Salk Inst. Biol. Studies; trustee, pres. Samuel Bronfman Found.; founding mem. Rockefeller U. Council; pres. World Jewish Congress; mem. exec. com. Am. Jewish Congress, Am. Jewish Com.; mem. nat. commn. Anti-Defamation League, B'nai B'rith. Mem. Center for Inter-Am. Relations, Council Fgn. Relations, Hundred Year Assn. N.Y., United Jewish Appeal, Fedn. Jewish Philanthropies, Com. for Econ. Devel., Nat. Urban League, Fgn. Policy Assn., Bus. Com. for Arts, Inc. Office: Seagram Co Ltd 1430 Peel St Montreal PQ Canada H3A 1S9 *

BRONFMAN, PETER FREDERICK, investment banker; b. Montreal, Que., Can., Oct. 2, 1929; s. Allan and Lucy (Bilsky) B.; children: Linda, Bruce, Brenda. Student, Lawrenceville Sch., 1948; B.A., Yale U., 1952. Chmn. Edper Investments Ltd., Montreal. Offices: Montreal PQ Canada also Brascan Ltd Commerce St W Toronto ON Canada

BRONK, WILLIAM, writer, retail businessman; b. Ft. Edward, N.Y., Feb. 17, 1918; s. William H. and Ethel Elizabeth (Funston) B. A.B., Dartmouth Coll., 1938. Author: collected poems Life Supports, 1981; collected essays Vectors and Smoothable Curves, 1983. Served to 1st lt. AUS, 1941-45. Home: 57 Pearl St Hudson Falls NY 12839

BRONNER, EDWIN BLAINE, history educator; b. Yorba Linda, Calif., Sept. 2, 1920; s. Blaine Garretson and Nellie Elizabeth (Garretson) B.; m. Marian Phillips Taylor, Mar. 9, 1946; children: Margaret G., Judith S. Sylvia T., Virginia H. A.B., Whittier Coll., 1941; M.A., Haverford Coll., 1947; Ph.D., U. Pa., 1952; D. Pedagogy, Susquehanna U., 1974. Faculty Temple U., 1947-62, assoc. prof. history, 1959-62; prof. history, curator Quaker Collection Haverford (Pa.) Coll., 1962—, librarian, 1969—. Author: Thomas Earle as a Reformer, 1948, William Penn's Holy Experiment, 1962, The Other Branch, 1975; Editor: Sharing Our Quaker Faith, 1959, American Quakers Today, 1966, An English View of American Quakerism, 1970; contbg. author: Friends in the Delaware Valley, 1981, Philadelphia, a 300 Year History, 1982, The Intellect and the Spirit: a History of Haverford College, 1983; mem. adv. bd.: Am. Jour. Legal History, 1957-77; Contbr. articles to profl. jours. Mem. Montgomery County (Pa.) Assistance, 1961-64; with Am. Friends Service Com., 1943-46, chmn. internat. centers com., 1961-65, bd. dirs., 1967-73; chmn. Am. sect. Friends World Com. Consultation, 1968-73, Friends World Com. Consultation, London, 1974-80; chmn. planning com. 4th Friends World Conf., 1965-67. Mem. Pa. Hist. Assn., Orgn. Am. Historians, Hist. Soc. Pa., Friends Hist. Assn. (bd. dirs., pres. 1970-72, 74-77), Friends Hist. Soc. (Eng., pres. 1970). Club: Franklin Inn. Home: 4 College Ln Haverford PA 19041

BRONNER, FELIX, physiologist, biophysicist, educator; b. Vienna, Austria, Nov. 7, 1921; came to U.S., 1937, naturalized, 1943; s. Maurice and Lotte (Vogler) B.; m. Leah Horowitz, Oct. 12, 1947; children—Deborah Rachel, Ethan Samuel. B.S., U. Calif. at Berkeley and Davis, 1941; Ph.D. (Quaker Oats fellow 1950-52), Mass. Inst. Tech., 1952; student, Kans. State Coll., 1938, U. Minn., 1943, U. Va., 1946. Research asso. Mass. Inst. Tech., 1952-54; vis. investigator Rockefeller Inst. Med. Research, N.Y.C., 1954-56, asst., 1956; dir. lab. mineral metabolism Hosp. for Spl. Surgery, N.Y.C., 1957-63; asst. prof. Cornell U. Med. Coll., 1961-63; asso. prof. physiology U. Louisville Sch. Medicine, 1963-69; prof. oral biology U. Conn., 1969—; vis. scientist Weizmann Inst., Israel, 1965, 76, Pasteur Inst., Paris, 1977; Cons. USPHS, 1965-68, 70-71, U.S. Dept. Agr., 1978-79; guest scientist INSERM, France, 1972; vis. prof. Tel Aviv U. Sch. Medicine, Israel, 1976. Editor biology, Acad. Press, (with A. Kleinzeller) Current Topics in Membranes and Transport, (with C.L. Comar) Mineral Metabolism—An Advanced Treatise, (with J. Coburn) Disorders of Mineral Metabolism, (with M. Peterlik) Calcium and Phosphate Transport Across Biomembranes; editorial bd.: Am. Jour. Clin. Nutrition, 1968-76; Contbr. numerous articles to profl. jours. Pres. Bur. Jewish Edn., Louisville, 1968-69. Served with AUS, 1942-46. Recipient Andre Lichwitz prize, 1974; research fellow Helen Hay Whitney Found., 1954-55, Arthritis and Rheumatism Found., 1954-56. Fellow AAAS; mem. Am. Physiol. Soc., Biophys. Soc., Harvey Soc., Soc. Exptl. Biology and Medicine, Am. Inst. Nutrition, Orthopedic Research Soc., Am. Fedn. Clin. Research, Am. Soc. Clin. Nutrition, Am. Soc. Bone and Mineral Research. Home: 33 Ferncliff Dr West Hartford CT 06117 Office: Dept Oral Biology U Conn Health Center Farmington CT 06032

BRONSKI, EUGENE WILLIAM, corporate executive; b. Detroit, Apr. 12, 1936; s. Eugene and Frances Mary (Maehler) B.; children: Donna, Karen, Michael. B.A., Wayne State U., 1958, J.D., 1961. Bar: Mich. 1962. Staff atty. Detroit Edison Co., 1963-68; gen. counsel Greyhound Food Mgmt., Inc., Detroit, 1968-74, v.p. indsl. relations, 1974-76, v.p., corp. counsel, 1976-81; sr. v.p. adminstrn. The Greyhound Corp., Phoenix, 1981—; mem. panel arbitrators Am. Arbitration Assn., 1972—; dir. Foodservice & Lodging Inst., Washington, 1975—, treas., 1978-80, pres., 1980—; dir. Restaura, S.A., Restauration Roger Lorent, S.A., Southcoast Systems. Mem. Nat. Restaurant Assn. (action com.), State Bar Mich. Address: 1933 Greyhound Tower Phoenix AZ 85077

BRONSON, CHARLES (CHARLES BUCHINSKY), actor; b. Ehrenfeld, Pa.; m. Harriet Tendler (div.); 2 children; m. Jill Ireland, 1969; 2 stepchildren; 1 dau., Zuleika. Appeared in: films You're in the Navy Now, 1951, Red Skies of Montana, 1952, Pat and Mike, 1952, House of Wax, 1953, Drumbeat, 1954, Jubal, 1956, Machine Gun Kelly, 1958, The Magnificent Seven, 1960, The Great Escape, 1963, The Battle of the Bulge, 1965, The Sandpiper, 1965, This Property is Condemned, 1966, The Dirty Dozen, 1967, Adieu, L'Ami, Once Upon a Time in the West, 1969, Rider in the Rain, 1970, You Can't Win Them All, 1970, Someone Behind the Door, 1971, Chato's Land, 1971, Red Sun, 1972, The Valachi Papers, 1972, The Mechanic, 1972, Death Wish, 1974, Breakout, 1975, Mr. Majestyk, Hard Times, Breakheart Pass, 1976, St. Ives, 1976, Chino, 1976, From Noon Till Three, 1976, Telefon, 1977, Love and Bullets, 1979, Cabo Blanco, 1979, Borderline, 1980; TV appearances include Redigo, Man With a Camera, The Travels of Jamie McPheeters, Twilight Zone, The Big Valley, The FBI, Raid on Entebbe, The Line-Up, The Legend of Jesse James. Served with AUS, 1943-46. Office: care Paul Kohner-Michael Levy Agy 9169 Sunset Blvd Los Angeles CA 90069 *

BRONSON, MARTY, designer, producer; b. N.Y.C., Oct. 30, 1937; s. William and Anne Lee (Fisher) B.; m. Phyllis Ann Lockwood, June 17, 1970; children: Michael, Donald. Cert., Sch. Visual Arts, N.Y.C., 1957. Display dir. Bloomingdales, 1959-63; designer New Vison Displays, N.Y.C., 1963-65; owner, designer Studio G, N.Y.C., 1970-76; gallery dir. Fashion Inst. Tech., N.Y.C., 1976—; pres. Gallery Assocs. of N.Y. State, 1976-78; producer, dir. Coty Am. Fashion Critics Awards, N.Y.C., 1978, 79, 82, Harveys Tribute to the Black Designer, 1978, 79, 80, 81, 83, numerous fashion shows for Am. and French designers, 1979—; designer maj. fashion and textile exhbns. Home: The Poor House Stony Point NY 10980 Office: Fashion Inst Tech 277 W 27th St New York NY 10001 *I hope that my presence will be recognized in many of my works because of the amount of passion I have spent in them and all the love with which I have infused them.*

BRONSON, OSWALD PERRY, educator, adminstr., clergyman; b. Sanford, Fla., July 19, 1927; s. Uriah Perry and Flora (Hollingshed) B.; m. Helen Carolyn Williams, June 8, 1952; children—Josephine Suzette, Flora Helen, Oswald Perry. B.S., Bethune-Cookman Coll., 1950; B.D., Gammon Theol. Sem., 1959; Ph.D., Northwestern U., 1965. Ordained to ministry Meth. Ch., 1957; pastor in Fla., Ga. and Rock River Conf., Chgo., 1950-66; v.p. Interdenominational Theol. Center, Atlanta, 1966-68, pres., 1968-75, Bethune-Cookman Coll., 1975—; dir. Fla. Bank and Trust Co.; Past trustee Carrie Steel Pitts Home, Atlanta; past pres. and chmn. bd. edn. Ga. Conf., Central Jurisdiction, United Meth. Ch.; now mem. bd. ministry DeLand dist., also Fla. Ann. Conf., mem., univ. senate, chmn. div. ministry, mem.-at-large bd. global ministries. Bd. dirs. United Meth. Com. on Relief; mem. Volusia County (Fla.) Sch. Bd., Fla. Gov.'s Adv. Council on Productivity; mem. exec. com. So. Regional Edn. Bd.; mem. adv. com. Fla. Sickle Cell Found., Inc.; past mem. council presidents Atlanta U. Center; past mem. Fla. Bd. Ind. Colls. and Univs.; trustee Hinton Rural Life Center; bd. dirs. Inst. of Black World, Wesley Community Center, Atlanta, Martin Luther King Center Social Change, Work Oriented Rehab. Center, Inc., Fund Theol. Edn.; mem. nat. selection com. Rockefeller Doctoral Fellowships in Religion; bd. dirs. Am. Nat. Red Cross, United Way, Nat. Assn. Equal Opportunity in Higher Edn., United Negro Coll. Fund; also mem. fund raising strategy adv. com. Ga. Pastors' Sch. Crusade scholar, 1957-64. Mem. Ga. Assn. Pastoral Care (past vice-chmn., bd. govs.), Am. Assn. Theol. Schs. (v.p. 1968-70), Ministerial Assn. of Halifax Area, Religious Edn. Assn. (past pres., past chmn. bd. dirs.), Mid-Atlantic Assn. Profs. Religious Edn., Fla. Assn. Colls. and Univs. (dir.), Atlanta Theol. Assn. (past vice chmn.), AAUP, Daytona Beach area C. of C., NAACP, Theta Phi (dir. internat. soc.), Alpha Kappa Mu, Phi Delta Kappa, Sigma Pi Phi, Alpha Phi Alpha. Clubs: Rotary, Daytona Beach area Execs., Daytona Beach Quarterback. Office: Bethune-Cookman Coll 640 2d Ave Daytona Beach FL 32015

BRONSTEIN, AARON JACOB, lawyer; b. Balt., May 6, 1905; s. Max S. and Rose (Lebow) B.; m. Gertrud Nagels, July 5, 1930 (dec. May 1942); m. Jeanette F. Lyons, Apr. 23, 1944; 1 dau., Judith R. (Mrs. Arnold D. Rubin). A.B., Harvard, 1925, LL.B., 1928. Bar: Mass. bar 1928, U.S. Supreme Ct. bar 1928. Practice in, Boston, 1928—; ptnr. firm Schneider, Bronstein, Wolbarsht & Deutsch, 1944-69, Brown, Rudnick, Freed & Gesmer, 1969—; Sec. Am. Biltrite, Inc., Wellesley, Mass., 1954—, dir., 1959—. Pres. New Eng. div. Am. Jewish Congress, 1955-59, Jewish Community Fedn. Greater Lynn, Mass., 1962-67, Jewish Community Council Boston, 1959-61, New Eng. Zionist Region, 1949-51; mem. Nat. Council Joint Distbn. Council, 1954—; hon. pres. Hillel Acad. North Shore, Inc. Mem. Am., Mass., Boston bar assns. Clubs: New Century (Boston); Harvard Varsity, Harvard Glee Club Found. Home: 28 Atlantic Ave Swampscott MA 01907 Office: One Federal St Boston MA 02110

BRONSTEIN, ARTHUR J., linguistics educator; b. Balt., Mar. 15, 1914; s. Gershon and Bessie B.; m. Elsa Metzer, May 15, 1941; children: Nancy Ellen, Abbot Alan. B.A., CCNY, 1934; M.A., Columbia U., 1936; Ph.D., NYU, 1949. Prof. Queens Coll., N.Y.C., 1938-67; Fulbright prof. U. Tel Aviv, (Israel), 1967-68, U. Trondheim, (Norway), 1979; prof. Lehman Coll. and Grad. Sch., CUNY, 1968—, exec. officer Ph.D. program in linguistics, 1981—; cons. in field. Author: Pronunciation of American English, 1960, Essays in Honor of C.M. Wise, 1970, Biographical Dictionary of the Phonetic Sciences, 1977. Served with Signal Corps and JAGC USAA, 1942-46. Fellow Am. Speech and Hearing Assn., Inst. Phonetic Scis., N.Y. Acad. Sci.; mem. Linguistics Soc. Am., MLA, Am. Assn. Phonetic Scis., Phi Beta Kappa. Office: 33 W 42d St New York NY 10036

BRONSTEIN, GERALD MORTON, holding company executive; b. N.Y.C., Jan. 16, 1927; s. Jay and Dorothy (Meyers) B.; m. Carolyn Falitz, July 12, 1953; children: Nancy, John, William, Robert. B.S., UCLA, 1947. C.P.A., Calif. Accountant firm Rashba, Pokart & Greene (C.P.A.s), Los Angeles and San Francisco, 1947-52; partner firm Bronley Bldg. Co., Los Angeles, 1952-67; partner United Continental Devel. Corp., Los Angeles, 1967-69; pres. Bomaine Corp., Los Angeles, 1969—. Served with USNR, 1945-46. Home: 7102 Crest Rd Rancho Palos Verde CA 90274 Office: 2716 Ocean Park Blvd Santa Monica CA 90405

BRONSTEIN, PETER ELI, lawyer; b. N.Y.C., Oct. 27, 1943; s. Eli H. and Madeline (Brill) B.; m. Jean Goldfrank, Dec. 19, 1970; children: Charles Peter, James Eli, Frederick Lionel. A.B. cum laude, Harvard U., 1965; J.D., U. Va., 1968. Bar: N.Y. 1968, Va. 1968. Since practiced in, N.Y.C.; partner firm Bronstein, Van Veen & Bronstein, 1970—. Contbr. articles to legal jours. Bd. dirs. Jewish Found. Edn. Women. Fellow Am. Acad. Matrimonial Lawyers; mem. ABA, Va. Bar Assn., N.Y. State Bar Assn. (chmn. family law sect. 1974-76, ho. dels. 1975-77), Westchester County Bar Assn), Assn. Bar City N.Y. (matrimonial law com.). Clubs: Harmonie, Harvard, Century Country (N.Y.C.). Address: 400 Madison Ave New York NY 10017

BRONSTON, CHARLES BENJAMIN, information service executive; b. Plainfield, N.J., July 13, 1924; s. Harry Edgar and Yetta (Cohen) B.; m. Judith Margaretten, Dec. 20, 1949; children: Beth Bronston Grinker, Jan, Deborah Bronston Gorban, Susan, Ruth. A.B., Harvard U., 1948; student, Rutgers U. Sch. Bus., 1964-65. Vice pres. Bronston Hat Co., Plainfield, 1948-58, 63-65; sec. Service Poly-Pak Inc., N.Y.C., 1958-63; pres. Byer-Rolnick Casual Headwear Co., Plainfield, 1965-67; dist. dir. R.J. Carroll Assos., Inc., 1967-69; personnel mgr. Quindar Electronics, Inc., Springfield, N.J., 1970-75; v.p. FIND/SVP div. Info. Clearing House, Inc., N.Y.C., 1976—; adj. faculty Rutgers U. Grad. Sch. Library and Info. Studies, 1978—. Trustee Temple Emanuel. Served with USAAF, 1943-46. Home: 15 N Wickom Dr Westfield NJ 07090 Office: 500 Fifth Ave New York NY 10110

BRONTE, LOUISA *See* **ROBERTS, JANET LOUISE**

BRONZINO, JOSEPH DANIEL, electrical engineer; b. Bklyn., Sept. 29, 1937; s. Joseph Rocco and Antoinette (Saporito) B.; m. Barbara Louise McGrath, Dec. 2, 1961; children: Michael J., Melissa J., Marcella J. B.S.E.E., Worcester Poly. Inst., 1959, Ph.D. in Elec. Engring, 1968; M.S.E.E., U.S. Naval Postgrad. Sch., 1961. Registered profl. engr., Conn. Instr. elec. engring. U. N.H., 1964-66, asst. prof. elec. engring., 1966-67; NSF faculty fellow Worcester Found. for Exptl. Biology, Shrewsbury, Mass., 1967-68, mem. cooperating staff, 1968—; asso. prof. engring. Trinity Coll., 1968-75, prof., 1975—, Vernon Roosa prof. applied sci., 1977—, chmn. dept. engring., 1981—; dir. biomed. engring. program Hartford (Conn.) Grad. Center, 1969—; clin. asso. dept. surgery U. Conn. Health Center, Farmington, 1971-77; research asso. Inst. for Living, Hartford, 1968—; reviewer NSF; panelist NSF Research Initiation Grants; lectr., speaker in field. Author: Technology For Patient Care, 1977; contbr. articles to profl. publs. Mem. Simsbury (Conn.) Planning Commn., 1977—. Served to 1st lt. Signal Corps U.S. Army, 1961-63. Mem. IEEE (sr.; regional dir. group engring. in medicine and biology 1973-78, v.p. tech. activities 1982—), Am. Soc. Engring. Edn. (exec. com. div. biomed. engring. 1973—, vice chmn. career devel. 1974-76, vice chmn. profl. devel. 1976-77, divisional newsletter editor 1977-79, chmn.-elect div. 1979—), AAAS, Biol. Psychiatry, Neurosci Soc. Republican. Roman Catholic. Club: Rotary (Simsbury) (pres. club 1975). Home: 6 Wyngate Simsbury CT 06070 Office: Trinity Coll Dept Engring Hartford CT 06106

BROOK, ADRIAN GIBBS, educator; b. Toronto, Ont., Canada, May 21, 1924; s. Frank Adrian and Beatrice Maud (Wellington) B.; m. Margaret Ellen Dunn, Dec. 18, 1954; children—Michael A., Katherine M., David L. B.A., U. Toronto, 1947, Ph.D., 1950. Lectr. chemistry U. Sask., 1950-51; research fellow Imperial Coll., London, 1951-52, Iowa State Coll., 1952-53; lectr. chemistry U. Toronto, 1953-56, asst. prof., 1956-60, asso. prof., 1960-62, prof., 1962—, chmn. dept. chemistry, 1969-74; vis. prof. U. Sussex, 1974-75. Contbr. articles in field to profl. jours. Nuffield Overseas fellow, 1951. Fellow Royal Soc. Can., Chem. Inst. Can.; mem. Am. Chem. Soc. (recipient Frederic Stanley Kipping award 1973). Home: 79 Glenview Ave Toronto ON M4R 1P7 Canada Office: Dept Chemistry U Toronto 80 Saint George St Toronto ON M5S 1A1 Canada

BROOK, HERBERT CECIL, lawyer; b. Stronghurst, Ill., Feb. 11, 1910; s. John C. and Maud (Simonson) B.; m. Jane C. Lord, Oct. 17, 1942; children—John L., David M., Susan J. A.B., Northwestern U., 1932; J.D., U. Chgo., 1936. Bar: Ill. bar 1936. Since practiced in, Chgo.; partner Lord, Bissell & Brook (and predecessors), 1948-78, counsel, 1978—; Ill. atty.-in-fact for underwriters Lloyd's of London, 1961-75. Contbr. articles to profl. jours. Life regent Northwestern U., 1970—; pres. Village of Hinsdale, Ill., 1969-73. Served as ensign USNR, 1941-42; to capt. USMCR, 1943-45; PTO. Mem. Am., Ill., Chgo. bar assns., Law Club Chgo., Order of Coif, Phi Beta Kappa. Home: 135 S Park St Hinsdale IL 60521 Office: 115 S LaSalle St Chicago IL 60603

BROOK, ROBERT HENRY, physician, educator, health services researcher; b. N.Y.C., July 3, 1943; s. Benjamin and Elizabeth (Berg) B.; m. Susan Jean Weiss, June 26, 1966 (div. 1980); children: Rebecca, Daniel; m. Jacqueline Barbara Kosecoff Plaut, Jan. 17, 1982; 1 dau., Rachel. B.S., U. Ariz., 1964; M.D., Johns Hopkins U., 1968, Sc.D., 1972. Diplomate: Am. Bd. Internal Medicine. Intern Balt. City Hosp., 1968-69, resident in medicine, 1969-72; project officer Nat. Ctr. Health Services Research-HEW, Washington, 1972-74; prof. medicine UCLA, 1974—, dir. clin. scholar program, 1974—, prof. pub. health, 1974—; health services researcher RAND Corp., Santa Monica, Calif., 1974—. Mem. editorial bd.: Medical Care, 1980—, EMS Quar., 1980—; asst. editor: Jour. Community Health, 1978—; contbr. articles to profl. jours. Mem. sci. rev. com. Community Cancer Control, Los Angeles, 1982—; bd. dirs. Ben Gurion U., 1983—. Served as asst. surgeon USPHS, 1972-74. Lita Annenberg Biomed. fellow Inst. Humanistic Studies, Aspen, Colo., 1981. Fellow ACP (mem. health financing com.); mem. Inst. Medicine, Am. Soc. Clin. Investigation, Assn. Health Services Research (dir. 1982—). Democrat. Jewish. Home: 1278 Norman Pl Los Angeles CA 90049 Office: Rand Corp 1700 Main St Santa Monica CA 90406

BROOKE, DAVID STOPFORD, art gallery ofcl.; b. Walton-on-Thames, Eng., Sept. 18, 1931; came to U.S., 1954; s. Somerset Stopford and Marguerite Louise (Thomas) B.; m. Dixie Ann Cortner, June 6, 1959; children—Peter, Nicholas. B.A., Harvard, 1958, A.M., 1963. Asst. to dir. Smith Coll. Mus. Art, Northampton, Mass., 1963-64; chief curator Art Gallery Ont., Toronto, 1965-68; dir. Currier Gallery Art, Manchester, N.H., 1968-77, Sterling and Francine Clark Art Inst., Williamstown, Mass., 1977—. Contbr. articles to profl. publs. Mem. Am. Assn. Art Mus. Dirs. Office: Box 8 225 South St Williamstown MA 01267

BROOKE, DWIGHT, lawyer; b. West Liberty, Iowa, Sept. 12, 1907; s. Robert and Mayme (Ditmars) B.; m. Margaret Lemley, June 6, 1930; children—Elizabeth, Philip. Student, Grinnell Coll., 1925-28; LL.B., State U. Iowa, 1931. Bar: Iowa bar 1931. Since practiced in, Des Moines; mem. firm Kelly, Shuttleworth & McManus, 1931-35, Holliday & Brooke, 1935-37; atty. Bankers Life Co., 1937-38, asst. counsel, 1938-47, gen. counsel, 1947-72, v.p., 1951-72; ret.; counsel Herrick, Langdon, and Langdon, Des Moines, 1972—. Contbr. articles to profl. jours. Served to lt. USNR, 1944-46. Mem. Am., Iowa, Polk County bar assns., Assn. Life Ins. Counsel, Am. Life Conv. (legal sect.), Order of Coif. Clubs: Des Moines, Law. Home: 126 51st St Des Moines IA 50312 Office: 1300 Financial Center Des Moines IA 50307

BROOKE, EDWARD WILLIAM, lawyer, former senator; b. Washington, Oct. 26, 1919; s. Edward W. and Helen (Seldon) B. B.S., Howard U., 1940, LL.D., 1967; LL.B. (editor Law Rev.), Boston U., 1948, LL.M., 1949, LL.D., 1968; LL.D., George Washington U., 1967, Skidmore Coll., 1969, U. Mass., 1971, Amherst Coll., 1972; D.Sc., Lowell Tech. Inst., 1967,. Bar: Mass. bar 1948, D.C. Ct. Appeals 1979, D.C. Dist. Ct. 1982, U.S. Supreme Ct. 1982. Chmn. Boston Finance com., 1961-62; atty. gen. state of, Mass., 1963-66; mem. U.S. Senate from Mass., 1967-79; chmn. Nat. Low-Income Housing Coalition, 1979—; partner O'Connor & Hannan, Washington; of counsel Csaplar & Bok, Boston, E.F. Hutton, N.Y.C.; ltd. partner Bear Stearns & Co., N.Y.C. Chmn. Boston Opera Co. Served as capt. inf. AUS, World War II; ETO. Decorated Bronze Star; recipient Distinguished Service award Amvets, 1952; Charles Evans Hughes award NCCJ, 1967; Spingarn medal from Mass., N.A.A.C.P., 1967. Fellow Am. Bar Assn., Am. Acad. Arts and Scis. Office: O'Connor & Hannan 1919 Pennsylvania Ave NW Washington DC 20006

BROOKE, MICHAEL HOWARD, neurologist; b. Leeds, Eng., Mar. 4, 1938; came to U.S., 1959, naturalized, 1966; s. Vincent Howard and Margaret (Craven) B.; (div.)children: Jennifer, Brenda, Mark. B.A., Cambridge U., 1955; M.B., B.Ch., Guy's Hosp., London, 1955. Intern San Francisco Children's Hosp., 1959-60; resident in neurology U. Calif. Med. Center, San Francisco, 1960-64; clin. and research fellow NIH, 1964-68; asso. prof. neurology U. Colo. Med. Center, 1968-75; prof. neurology Washington U. Med. Sch., St. Louis, 1975—, prof. preventive medicine, 1979—; dir. Jerry Lewis Neuromuscular Research Center, 1975—; med. dir. I.W.J. Rehab. Inst., 1979—; rehabilitationist-in-chief Barnes Hosp., St. Louis, 1979—. Author: A Clinician's View of Neuromuscular Diseases, 1977; co-author: Muscle Biopsy: A Modern Approach, 1973; editorial bd.: Muscle and Nerve. Served with USPHS, 1966-68. Fellow Am. Acad. Neurology; mem. Am. Neurol. Assn., Amateur Radio Club. Office: Dept Neurology Washington Univ Med Sch St Louis MO 63110 *Sometimes, as a physician wrestling with health care, one seems to be more part of the problem than of the solution. Until we develop effective systems to maintain the health of the community with the same enthusiasm that we* *develop expensive technological machinery, we will never cope with disease in this country. I don't know what the answer is, but I do know that waving "good-bye" to the patient from the doorstep of a multi million dollar hospital is not part of it.*

BROOKER, MARVIN ADEL, former educator; b. Bell, Fla., Sept. 8, 1903; s. Hampton B. and Eula (Roberts) B.; m. Eddie Sue Colson, Dec. 29, 1926 (dec. Oct. 1957); children: Marvin Adel, Ralph, Sue; m. Edith B. Hendrix, Aug. 11, 1958. B.S.A., U. Fla., 1926, M.S.A., 1927; Ph.D., Cornell U., Ithaca, N.Y., 1931. Asso. agrl. economist agrl. expt. sta. U. Fla., Gainesville, 1931-34, prof. agrl. econs., 1947-80, asst. dean, 1955-56, dean, 1956-69, head acad. devel. program,, 1969-74; chief statistician FCA, Columbia, S.C., 1934-39, dir. research, New Orleans, 1941-46, comptroller, 1946; v.p., sec. Columbia Bank for Coops., 1939-41; exec. sec. Price Decontrol Bd., Washington, 1946-47. Author numerous articles on agrl. econs. Past mem. bd. govs. Agr. Hall of Fame. Mem. Am. Farm Econ. Assn., Social Sci. Research Council (agrl. fellow 1929-30), Sigma Xi, Alpha Zeta, Phi Kappa Phi, Gamma Sigma Delta, Sigma Phi Epsilon. Mem. Ch. of Christ. Home: 2244 NW 6th Pl Gainesville FL 32603

BROOKER, ROBERT ELTON, corporate executive; b. Cleve., July 18, 1905; s. Robert and Isadora (Roberts) B.; m. Sally Burton Smith, Mar. 13, 1933; children: Robert Elton, Thomas Kimball. B.S., U. So. Calif., 1927, LL.D., 1969; LL.D., Mich. State U., 1973. With So. Calif. Edison Co., 1928-34, Firestone Tire & Rubber Co., 1934-44; v.p., dir. Sears, Roebuck & Co., Chgo., 1944-58; pres., dir. Whirlpool Corp., 1958-61, Montgomery Ward & Co., 1961-66, chmn. bd., chief exec. officer, dir., 1966-70, chmn. exec. com., dir., 1970-75; chmn., chief exec. officer, dir. Marcor Inc., 1968-70, 75—, chmn. exec. com., dir., 1970-75; dir. Chgo. & Northwestern Transp. Co. Chmn. Pres.'s Bus. Council for Consumer Affairs, 1971-73; chmn. Exec. Service Corps. of Chgo.; trustee U. So. Calif., U. Chgo., Ill. Inst. Tech. Recipient Asa V. Call award U. So. Calif., 1964; Henry Laurence Gantt Medal award Am. Mgmt. Assn., 1973. Mem. Sigma Nu, Chi Epsilon, Tau Beta Pi. Clubs: Economic, Chicago, Indian Hill, Old Elm, Commercial, Mountain Lake, Ristigouche Salmon, Adventurers. Home: 1500 Sheridan Rd Wilmette IL 60091 Office: Exec Service Corps 25 E Washington St 8th Floor Chicago IL 60603

BROOKES, CHARLES ERWIN, chemical company executive; b. Orange, N.J., Feb. 27, 1925; s. Charles Edward and Helen (Timberlake) B.; m. Joan Lincoln Barry, July 28, 1951; children: Stephen, Wendy, John. B.E. in Chem. Engring., Yale U., 1949. V.p. Dewey and Almy Chem. div. W.R. Grace & Co., Cambridge, Mass., 1962-67; pres. Davison Chem. div. W.R. Grace & Co., Balt., 1967-77; v.p. W.R. Grace & Co., N.Y.C., 1972-77, sr. v.p., 1978—. Bd. dirs. Chem. Inst. Toxicology, Research Triangle Park, N.C. Served with inf. AUS, 1943-45; ETO. Mem. Am. Inst. Chem. Engrs., Am. Chem. Soc., Sigma Xi, Tau Beta Pi. Clubs: N.Y. Yacht; Gibson Island (Md.) (commodore 1979-80). Home: Cooleys Pond Rd Gibson Island MD 21056 Office: WR Grace & Co 7379 Route 32 Columbia MD 21044

BROOKES, VALENTINE, lawyer; b. Red Bluff, Calif., May 30, 1913; s. Langley and Ethel (Valentine) B.; m. Virginia Stovall Cunningham, Feb. 11, 1939; children—Langley (Mrs. Jerrold B. Brandt), Lawrence Valentine, Alan Cunningham. A.B., U. Calif., Berkeley, 1934, J.D., 1937. Bar: Calif. bar 1937, U.S. Supreme Ct. bar 1942. Asst. franchise tax counsel, State of Calif., 1937-40, dep. atty. gen., Calif., 1940-42; spl. asst. to U.S. atty. gen., asst. to solicitor gen. U.S., 1942-44; partner firm Kent & Brookes, San Francisco, 1944-70, Alvord & Alvord, Washington, 1944-50, Lee, Toomey & Kent, 1950-79, Brookes and Brookes, San Francisco, 1971—; lectr. Hastings Coll. Law, U. Calif., 1941-48, U. Calif. Law Sch., Berkeley, 1948-70. Author: The Continuity of Interest Test in Reorganizations, 1946, The Partnership Under the Income Tax Laws, 1949, The Tax Consequences of Widows Elections in Community Property States, 1951, Corporate Trasactions Involving Its Own Stock, 1954, Litigation Expenses and the Income Tax, 1957. Bd. dirs. Childrens Hosp. Med. Center of N.Calif., 1963-74, v.p., 1968-70; trustee Oakes Found., 1957-70; regent St. Mary's Coll., Calif., 1968—, pres. bd., 1970-72. Fellow Am. Bar Found.; mem. Am. Law Inst., ABA (chmn. com. on statute of limitations 1954-57, council, tax section 1960-63), Calif. Bar Assn. (chmn. com. on taxation 1950-52, 60-61), San Francisco Bar Assn., Soc. Calif. Pioneers (v.p. 1964, 1975—), Phi Kappa Sigma, Phi Delta Phi. Republican. Clubs: Pacific Union, Orinda Country, Bankers, World Trade. Home: 7 Sycamore Rd Orinda CA 94563 Office: 601 California St San Francisco CA 94108 *Always do the best you can, at everything you undertake.*

BROOKHART, JOHN MILLS, physiologist, educator; b. Cleve., Dec. 1, 1913; s. Leslie Shellabarger and Anna Rose (Mills) B.; m. Anna Louise Simon, Aug. 26, 1939; children: Cornelia Mills, Constance Lee, John Howard. B.S., U. Mich., 1935, M.S., 1936, Ph.D., 1939. Instr., asst. prof. physiology Loyola U. Sch. Medicine, 1940-46; asst. prof. physiology U. Ill. Coll. Medicine, 1946; asst. prof. neurology Northwestern U., Med. Sch., 1947-49; asso. prof. physiology U. Oreg. Med. Sch., Portland, 1949-51, prof., chmn. dept. physiology, 1952-79, prof. emeritus, 1979—, acting v.p. acad. affairs, 1979-82; Cons. OSRD, 1945; spl. cons. USPHS, 1951-76; mem. adv. com. on physiology Office Naval Research, 1960-62; bd. sci. counselors USPHS, 1961-65, mem. physiology tng. com., 1963-67, chmn. physiology tng. com., 1966-67; mem. physiology exam. com. Nat. Bd. Med. Examiners, 1959-62, 77-79. Bd. editors: Jour. Neurophysiology, 1960-64; editor-in-chief, 1964-74; bd. editors: Ann. Rev. Physiology, 1958-61. Fulbright scholar, 1956-57. Fellow Am. Acad. Arts and Scis.; mem. Oreg. Neuropsychiat. Soc., Portland Acad. Med., Am. Physiol. Soc. (council 1960, pres. 1965-66), AAAS, Internat. Brain Research Orgn., Academia delle Science dell'Institute di Bologna, Internat. Union Physiol. Scis. (mem. council, treas. 1974-80), Sigma Xi, Alpha Omega Alpha, Delta Phi. Home: 3126 NE 39th Portland OR 97212

BROOKING, GEORGE EDWARD, JR., lawyer, business exec.; b. Ky., July 14, 1925; s. George Edward and Ollie (Clark) B.; m. Ruth Bradlee Dumaine, Sept. 19, 1953; children—Frederic, Jonathan, Elizabeth, Anne. A.B., U. Ky., 1949; LL.B., Harvard, 1952; grad., Advanced Mgmt. Program, 1962. Bar: Fed. bar 1952. Asst. counsel Office Gen. Counsel, Dept. Navy, Washington, 1952-54; asst. European counsel, London, Eng., 1954-56; asso. firm McKinsey & Co., Inc., Washington, 1956-58; with Amoskeag Co., Boston, 1958-70; pres., chmn. exec. com. Fanny Farmer Candy Shops Inc., 1966-70; chmn., dir. Rollins Environmental Services, Inc., Wilmington, Del., 1970-74; sr. v.p., dir., mem. exec. com. Rollins Internat., 1970-74; pres. Kensington Investment Assos., 1974—; dir. Shawmut Corp., Boston, Fed. St. Capital Corp., Christiana Cos., Santa Monica, Calif.; Mem. spl. adv. com. on pub. opinion Dept. State. Clubs: Union League (N.Y.C.); Idle Hour Country (Lexington, Ky.); Country (Brookline, Mass.). Home: 3709 Kennett Pike Wilmington DE 19807

BROOKINS, DOUGLAS GRIDLEY, geochemist, educator; b. Healdsburg, Calif., Sept. 27, 1936; s. Rex McKain and Ellyn Caroline (Hitt) B.; m. Barbara Flashman, Sept. 16, 1961; children: Laura Beth, Rachel Sarah. A.A., Santa Rosa Jr. Coll., 1956; A.B., U. Calif., Berkeley, 1958; Ph.D., M.I.T., 1963. Geologist Bear Creek Co., San Francisco, 1957-59; research asst. M.I.T., Cambridge, 1958-63; physicist Avco Corp., Wilmington, Mass., 1961; asst. prof. geology Kans. State U., Manhattan, 1963-65, asso. prof., 1965-70; prof. geology U. N.Mex., Albuquerque, 1971—, acting chmn., 1972, chmn. dept., 1976-79. Author: Earth Resources, Energy and the Environment, 1980, Geochemical Aspects of Radioactive Waste Disposal, Physical Geology; contbr. 350 articles to profl. jours. Bd. dirs. Jewish Community Council Albuquerque, 1974; trustee Congregation Albert, 1975—, v.p., 1983-84. Named Researcher-Tchr. of Year, 1971. Fellow Geol. Soc. Am., Am. Inst. Chemists, Mineral Soc. Am., Explorers Club; mem. Geochem. Soc., Meteoritical Soc., Am. Geophys. Union, N.Y. Acad. Sci., AAAS, AAUP, Albuquerque Geol. Soc. (pres. 1973), N.Mex. Geol. Soc., N.Mex. Inst. Chemists (councillor 1974-75), Am. Assn. Petroleum Geologists, Soc. Econ. Paleontologists and Mineralogists, Internat. Assn. Geochemistry and Cosmochemistry, Mineral Soc. Am., Soc. Economic Geologists, Soc. Exploration Geochemists, Materials Research Soc., Am. Chem. Soc., Am. Nuclear Soc., Phi Beta Kappa (pres. Alpha Assn. Kans. 1967-68), Sigma Xi.; Mem. B'nai B'rith (fin. sec. 1974-75). Address: Dept Geology Univ NMex Albuquerque NM 87131

BROOKINS, HAMEL HARTFORD, bishop; b. Yazoo, Miss., June 8, 1925; m. Helene Howard; 1 son, Steven Hartford Carey. B.A., Wilberforce U., 1949; B.Div., Payne Theol. Sem., 1950; D.Div. hon., 1957; postgrad., U. Kans., 1952-53; D.Div. hon., Edwards Waters Coll. Ordained to ministry A.M.E. Ch.; consecrated bishop. Pastor St. Paul A.M.E. Ch., Wichita, Kans., First A.M.E. Ch., Los Angeles, 1950-72; bishop 17th Episcopal Dist. A.M.E. Ch., Central Africa, 1972-75, 5th Episcopal Dist., Los Angeles, 1976—, now presiding bishop; ofcl. Tanzanian spokesman and leader North Am. del to 6th Pan African World Congress, Dar es Salaam, Tanzania, 1974; nat. chmn. bd. Operation PUSH; nat. bd. dirs. SCLC; dir. Bank of Fin.; bd. dirs. Didi Hirsch Mental Health Clinic, Council Chs. Builder 100 units housing devel. Organizer interfaith service Hollywood Bowl, Los Angeles; active in liberation movements, Central Africa, 1972-76; chmn. Mayoral Campaign Thomas Bradley, Los Angeles, numerous voter registration campaigns. Recipient numerous commendations, awards, certs. Mem. NAACP (life). Democrat. Club: Prince Hall. Lodge: Masons. Office: African Methodist Episcopal Ch 4908 Creshaw Blvd Los Angeles CA 90008

BROOKS, ALBERT, actor, writer, director; b. Los Angeles, July 22, 1947; s. Harry and Thelma (Leeds) Einstein. Appeared in: films Taxi Driver, 1976, Private Benjamin, 1980, Twilight Zone-The Movie, 1983, Unfaithfully Yours, 1983; dir., writer, actor: Real Life, 1979, Modern Romance, 1980; TV appearances include Gold-Diggers of, 1969, Saturday Night Live; dir., writer: short films for Saturday Night Live; recs. include A Star Is Bought. Office: care Herb Nanas Scotti Bros 2114 Pico Blvd Santa Monica CA 90405 *

BROOKS, BABERT VINCENT, publisher; b. N.Y.C., Sept. 2, 1926; s. Babert Vincent and Florence (Goodwin) B.; m. Audrey Stephenson, Dec. 6, 1952; children—Torrey, Scott, Wendy. A.B. magna cum laude, Dartmouth Coll., 1947, M.B.A., 1949. Security analyst Arnold Bernhard & Co., N.Y.C., 1952-56; cons. Booz, Allen & Hamilton, N.Y.C., 1956-58; v.p. finance Schine Enterprises, N.Y.C., 1958-61; v.p., treas. Murray Corp. Am., N.Y.C., 1961-62; pres. Westport Travel Service Inc., 1963—, Brooks Community Newspapers, 1974—; pub. Westport (Conn.) News, 1964—, Darien (Conn.) News Rev., 1973—, Fairfield (Conn.) Citizen-News, 1973—, Norwalk (Conn.) News, 1978—; sec.-treas. Airspur Corp., N.Y.C., 1969-70; dir., mem. fin. com. County Fed. Savs. & Loan Assn., Westport; dir. R.C. Memhard & Co., Inc., Greenwich, Conn., Memhard Investment Bankers Inc., Stamford, Conn., Winmark Sports, Westport; pres. Brooks, Torrey & Scott Inc., Westport, 1962—. Bd. dirs., treas. Dartmouth in Greenwich, 1972-81. Served with USNR, 1945-47. Mem. Westport C. of C. (dir. 1964—, v.p. 1974, 77, 78), Phi Beta Kappa. Clubs: Riverside (Conn.); Yacht. Home: Jones Park Dr Riverside CT 06878 Office: 136 Main St Westport CT 06880

BROOKS, CHANDLER MCCUSKEY, educator; b. Waverly, W.Va., Dec. 18, 1905; s. Earle Amos and Mary (McCuskey) B.; m. Nelle Irene Graham, June 25, 1932. A.B., Oberlin Coll., 1928; M.A., Princeton U., 1929, Ph.D., 1931; D.Sc. (hon.), Berea Coll., 1970. NRC fellow, teaching fellow Harvard Med. Sch., 1931-33; instr., then asso. prof. physiology Johns Hopkins Med. Sch., 1933-48; prof. physiology and pharmacology, chmn. dept. L.I. Coll. Medicine, 1948-50; prof. physiology, chmn. dept. State U. N.Y. Downstate Med. Center, Bklyn., 1950-72, dir. grad. edn., 1956-66, dean, 1966-72,, acting pres., 1969-71, distinguished prof., 1971—; vis. prof. Tokyo and Kobe (Japan) med. schs., 1961-62, U. Otago, Dunedin, New Zealand, 1975; vis. scholar U. Aberdeen, Scotland, 1973-74; hon. mem. faculty Catholic U., Santiago, Chile.; Mem. study sects. NIH, 1949-69. Author: (with others) Excitability of the Heart, 1955, Humors, Hormones and Neurosecretions, 1962, (with Kiyomi Koizumi) Japanese Physiology, Past and Present, 1965; Editor: (with P.F. Cranefield) The Historical Development of Physiological Thought, 1959, (with others) Cerebrosphinal Fluid and the Regulation of Ventilation, 1965, The Changing World and Man, 1970, (with H.H. Liu) The Sinoatrial Pacemaker of the Heart, 1972, (with K.K. Koizumi) Integrations of Autonomic Reactions, 1972, Jour. of Autonomic Nervous System, 1978—. Trustee Internat. Fcund., 1972—, chmn. grants com., 1973—. Decorated Order of Rising Sun 3d class, Japan; cited Internat. Physiol. Congress, 1965; Guggenheim fellow, 1946-48; Rockefeller fellow, 1950; China Med. Bd. N.Y. fellow, 1961-62. Mem. Nat. Acad. Scis., Harvey Soc. (pres. 1965), AAAS (council 1950—), N.Y. Heart Assn. (council 1965—), Am. Soc. Pharmacology and Exptl. Therapeutics, Internat. Brain Research Orgn., Nat. Soc. Med. Research, Royal Soc. Medicine, N.Y. Acad. Scis., Soc. Exptl. Biology and Medicine, Soc. Study Internal Secretions, Soc. Study Nervous and Mental Diseases, Am. Coll. Cardiology, Am. Coll. Pharmacology and Chemotherapy, Am. Inst. Biol. Scis., AMA (spl. affiliate), Am. Physiology Soc., Phi Beta Kappa, Sigma Xi, Alpha Omega Alpha; hon. mem. Nat. Acad. Medicine Buenos Aires, Cardiology Soc. Argentina, biol. socs. Montevideo, Uruguay, Inst. Hist. Medicine and Med. Research New Delhi, Alumni Assn., Coll. Medicine Downstate Med. Center. Research, publns. central control autonomic system, function of hypothalamaus, motor cortex function in regulation of posture, activity in heart and nerve cells. Home: 623 2d St Brooklyn NY 11215 *If there is any one secret to success in learning and teaching, I suggest it is to become interested.*

BROOKS, CLAUDE CURRY, chewing gum co. exec.; b. Kansas City, Mo., June 25, 1919; s. Claude Curry and Carrie Estelle (Bridgewater) B.; m. F. Elizabeth Downing, Jan. 9, 1943; children—Barclay Downing, Cathy Dee (Mrs. Michael Dressler), Christy Beth (Mrs. Thomas Snider). B.S., UCLA, 1940. Mgr. Globe (Ariz.) C. of C., 1948-50, Avalon-Catalina Island (Calif.) C. of C., 1950-52; mgr. br. office Arthur Meyerhoff & Assos., Phoenix, 1952-57; asst. to pres. Santa Catalina Island Co., Chgo., 1957-77, pres., mem. exec. com., 1977—, dir., 1971—; asst. sec. Wm. Wrigley, Jr. Co., Chgo., 1963-71, v.p., sec., 1971-74, 1st v.p., sec., 1974—, dir., 1975—. Mem. Planning Com. Kansas City, Mo., 1946; benefactor mem. Santa Catalina Island Conservancy. Served with AUS, 1943-45. Decorated Army Commendation medal. Conglist. Home: 405 N Wabash Ave Chicago IL 60611 Office: 410 N Michigan Ave Chicago IL 60611

BROOKS, DAVID BARRY, resource economist; b. Easton, Mass., Feb. 15, 1934; s. Abraham and Mae (Fox) B.; m. Toby Judith Haftka, Sept. 11, 1955; children: Michael Jan, Naomi Sara. S.B. in Geology, MIT, 1955, M.S., Calif. Inst. Tech., 1956; Ph.D. in Econs., U. Colo., 1963. Geologist U.S. Geol. Survey, 1956-59; research asso. Resources for the Future, Washington, 1961-66; asst. prof. econs. Berea Coll., 1966-67; chief div. mineral econs. Bur. Mines, Dept. Interior, 1967-70; chief Mineral Econs. Research div. Can. Dept. Energy, Mines and Resources, 1970-73; dir. Office Energy Conservation, 1974-77; bd. dirs. Can. Friends of the Earth, pres., 1977-81; prin. Marbek Resource Cons. Ltd., Ottawa, Ont., Canada, 1983—; cons. Nat. Audubon Soc., 1971—, Can. Internat. Devel. Agy., 1983, UN Conf. on Human Environment, 1971-72; mem. study team on non-renewable materials, environ. studies bd. Nat. Acad. Scis., 1972-73; cons. Highlander Research and Edn. Center, New Market, Tenn., 1979; exec. dir. Beaufort Sea Research Coalition; mem. Labrador Resources Adv. Council, 1979, Dept. Indian and No. Affairs, Ottawa, 1979—. Author: Supply and Competition in Minor Metals, 1965, Peaceful Use of Nuclear Explosives: Some Economic Aspects, 1969, Minerals: an Expanding or a Dwindling Resource?, 1973, Zero Energy Growth for Canada, 1981, Life After Oil: A Renewable Energy Policy for Canada, 1983; also monographs on environ. problems of mining and energy conservation; contbr. articles. Chmn. No. Va. chpt. Congress Racial Equality, 1963-65; sec. Fed. Employees for a Democratic Soc. Served with AUS, 1957. Home: 1-202 Flora St Ottawa ON K1R 5R7 Canada Office: 407-2211 Riverside Dr Ottawa ON K1H 7X5 Canada

BROOKS, DAVID WILLIAM, farmer cooperative executive; b. Royston, Ga., Sept. 11, 1901; s. David William and Letty Jane (Tabor) B.; m. Ruth McMurray, Aug. 7, 1930; children: David William, Nancy Ruth. B.S. in Agr, U. Ga., 1922, M.S., 1923; LL.D., Emory U., 1964; D.H.L., Morris Brown Coll., 1978. Tchr. agronomy div. U. Ga., 1922-25; field supr. Ga. Cotton Growers Coop. Assn., 1925-33; gen. mgr. Gold Kist Inc. (formerly named Cotton Producers Assn.), Atlanta, 1933-68, chmn. bd. dirs., 1968-77, chmn. bd. emeritus, chmn. policy com., 1977—; pres. Cotton States Life & Health Ins. Co., 1955-59, chmn. bd., 1959-83, chmn. bd. emeritus, 1983—; pres. Cotton States Mut. Ins. Co., 1947-59, chmn. bd., 1959-83, chmn. bd. emeritus, 1983—; dir. Ga. So. & Fla. Ry. Co., 1963—; Dir. Am. Cotton Coop. Assn., Atlanta, 1940-70; dir. Nat. Council Farmer Coops., Washington, 1938-68, mem. exec. com., 1944-63, pres., 1951-52; mem. cotton adv. com. Dept. Agr., 1947-50; mem. Textiles Industry Adv. Com. of Army-Navy Munitions Bd., 1947-51; industry adv. Internat. Cotton Adv. Com., Washington, 1950; mem. nat. adv. bd. Moblzn. Policy, 1951-52; mem. Nat. Agrl. Adv. Commn., 1953-56, Benson's Cotton Export Adv. Com., 1953-56, chmn., 1953; mem. nat. cotton adv. com. USDA, 1961-63; dir. Found. for Am. Agr., 1960—; mem. Nat. Agrl. Adv. Commn., 1964-65; dir. Agrl. Mission, 1959-67, Coop. Fertilizers Internat., Chgo., 1968-71; mem. Agribus. Industry Adv. Com., Washington, 1968-70, Nat. Adv. Com. Trade Negotiations, 1975—, Presdl. Commn. on World Hunger, 1978—. Trustee Am. Inst. Cooperation, Washington, 1944-69; pres. Ga. Coop. Council, Athens, 1940-47; trustee Reinhardt Coll., Waleska, Ga., Emory U., Atlanta, Wesleyan Coll., Macon, Ga.; chmn. Emory U. Com. of One Hundred, 1958—; bd. govs. Agrl. Hall of Fame, 1958—. Selected Man of Year in Agr. for Ga. Progressive Farmer, 1950, Southwide Man of Year in Agr., 1966; named to Agrl. Hall of Fame U. Ga., 1972; recipient Nat. Coop. Statesmanship award, 1973; Man of Yr. in Ga. award Morris Brown Coll., Atlanta, 1978; named United Meth. Man of Achievement S.E. Jurisdictional Council, United Meth. Ch., 1979; named to Coop. League U.S.A. Hall of Fame, 1979. Mem. N.Y. Cotton Exchange (adv. com. 1948-68), New Orleans Cotton Exchange (adv. com.), Nat. Cotton Council (adv. com., v.p. 1958-69), Farmers Chem. Assn. (chmn. bd. 1960-69, dir. 1969-73), Nat. Council Chs. (governing bd. 1960-72), Nat. Planning Assn. (agrl. com. 1946-63), Alpha Zeta, Phi Kappa Phi. Methodist (steward, bd. mgrs., exec. com. bd. missions). Clubs: Mason, Kiwanian. Home: 2374 Dellwood Dr PO Box 2210 Atlanta GA 30301 *You must have absolute confidence that your goal in life will improve the condition of mankind. You must give complete dedication to the accomplishment of this goal, believing that no personal sacrifice can be considered too great.*

BROOKS, EDWARD HOWARD, retired college administrator; b. Salt Lake City, Mar. 2, 1921; s. Charles Campbell and Margery (Howard) B.; m. Courtaney June Perren, May 18, 1946; children: Merrillee Brooks Way, Robin Anne (Mrs. R. Bruce Pollock). B.A., Stanford U., 1942, M.A., 1947, Ph.D., 1950. Mem. faculty, adminstrn. Stanford, 1949-71; provost Claremont (Calif.) Colls., 1971-79; v.p. Claremont U. Center, 1979-81; sr. v.p. Claremont McKenna Coll., 1981-84. Trustee EDUCOM, 1978-80, Webb Sch. of Calif., 1979—; bd. overseers Hoover Instn., 1972-78; bd. dirs. Student Loan Mktg. Assn., 1973-77. Served with AUS, 1942-45. Clubs: University (Los Angeles); Bohemian (San Francisco). Home: 800 High Point Dr Claremont CA 91711 Office: 321 Bauer Ctr Claremont McKenna Coll Claremont CA 91711

BROOKS, ELBERT DANIEL, ednl. adminstr.; b. Chandler, Ariz., Apr. 4, 1914; s. Ira Delos and Lillian Elizabeth (Stayton) B.; m. Charlotte R. Lee, Feb. 23, 1935; children—James Elbert, Beverly Brooks Goodwin, John Stayton, Bonnie Brooks Thrasher. B.A., No. Ariz. U., 1935; M.A., U. Ariz., 1949; Ed.D., Stanford, 1967. Tchr. high sch., Patagonia, Ariz., 1936-39, tchr., Tucson, 1939-43, 46-53, asst. prin., 1953-55; prin. Pueblo Sch., 1955-64; asst. supt. Tucson Pub. Schs., 1964-68, asso. supt., 1968-70; dir. Met. Nashville Pub. Schs., 1970—; adj. prof. Peabody Coll., 1972-77, U. Tenn., 1973—; mem. Tenn. adv. council tech.-vocat. edn., 1972-79; adv. com. Nat. Rev. Panel on Sch. Desegregation Research. Trustee Joint Council Econ. Edn. Pres., Community Services, Tucson, 1967-68, United Way, Tucson, 1968-69, Peabody Coll.; bd. dirs. WDCN-TV, Nashville, Nashville Symphony Assn., 1972-78, Nashville Children's Theater, Nashville Cumberland Mus., Met. Nashville YMCA; pres. Met. Nashville YMCA, 1979. Served with USNR, 1943-46; PTO. Adminstrv. trainee coop. project in ednl. adminstrn., 1952; John Hay fellow Humanities, 1965. Mem. Ariz. Edn. Assn. (pres. 1952), NEA, Am. Assn. Sch. Adminstrs. (urban fed. policy adv. com. 1978—), Ariz. Assn. Sch. Adminstrs. (pres. 1962), Assn. Supervision and Curriculum Devel., Large City Sch. Supts. Assn., So. Assn. Colls. and Schs. (com. higher edn.), Am. Assn. Colls. Tchr. Edn. (performance based tchr. edn. com. 1974-76), Council Gt. City Schs. (exec. com. 1978—), C. of C. (edn. com.), Phi Delta Kappa. Democrat. Congregationalist. Clubs: U. Nashville, Nashville Kiwanis. Research effect alternative techniques modifying tchr. behavior. Office: 2601 Bransford Ave Nashville TN 37204 *

BROOKS, ERNEST, JR., foundation executive; b. N.Y.C., Dec. 5, 1907; s. Ernest and Jeanne L. (Marion) B.; m. Mary Caroline Schoyer, June 23, 1934; children: Joan (Mrs. John R. McLane III), Peter Preston, Howard Turner, Ernest III. B.A., Yale U., 1930; LL.B., Harvard U., 1933. Bar: N.Y. bar 1934. Assoc. firm Breed, Abbott & Morgan, N.Y.C., 1933-42; officer Old Dominion Found., N.Y.C., 1948-69, trustee, 1951-69, pres., 1956-69; officer Bollingen Found., N.Y.C., 1947-69, trustee, 1948-69, v.p., sec.-treas., 1956-69; cons. Andrew W. Mellon Found., 1969-71; trustee Anne S. Richardson Fund, Nat. Humanities Faculty, 1969-76; bd. dirs. Nat. Audubon Soc., 1957-63, sec., 1959-60, v.p., 1969-80; trustee Conservation Found., 1956—, chmn., 1972—. Trustee New Canaan (Conn.) Country Sch., 1955-64, Putney Sch., 1965-71, Stamford Mus. and Nature Center, 1971-73, Assn. for Protection Adirondacks, 1978-80; bd. govs. Nature Conservancy, 1954-61, 69-73. Served with OSS, 1943-46. Fellow Berkeley Coll., Yale. Mem. Phi Beta Kappa. Clubs: Country (New

Canaan); Century Assn. (N.Y.C.). Home: 152 Marvin Ridge Rd New Canaan CT 06840

BROOKS, EVANS BARTLETT, former graphic arts company executive; b. New Albany, Ind., Jan. 28, 1900; s. William Wilson and Bertha (Evans) B.; m. Margaret Marby, Mar. 6, 1926; children: Marcia Jayne Brooks Browne, Sandra Lee Brooks Jordan. Student bus. adminstrn., Louisville YMCA Extension and Ind. U. Extension. Vice pres. Del. Engraving Co., Muncie, Ind., 1926-30, Ditzel-Brooks Co., Dayton, Ohio, 1931-32; v.p.-sec. Wayne Colorplate Co. Ohio, Dayton, 1932-37, pres., treas., 1937-84; v.p., treas. Brooks Investment Co., Dayton, 1953-84; emeritus chmn. bd. Third Nat. Bank & Trust Co., Dayton. Charter mem. Dayton Area Progress Council, 1961; chmn. Montgomery County Bldg. Commn.; founder, mem. 1st pres. All-Dayton Com., 1945-47; past chmn. Montgomery County chpt. ARC; past pres. Dayton Philharmonic Assn.; mem., past chmn. Bd. Mental Retardation; trustee, exec. com. Air Force Mus.; trustee Dayton and Montgomery County Pub. Library (past pres.); pres. Dayton Art Inst., 1951-53; emeritus trustee U. Dayton. Mem. Am. Photoengravers Assn. (past pres.), Photo-Engravers Research Inst. (dir., past pres.), Dayton Printing Industry Assn. (past pres.), Dayton C. of C. (past pres.), Research and Engring. Council Graphic Arts (dir.), Newcomen Soc. Presbyterian (past pres. Ohio Bd. Home Missions; ch. elder). Clubs: Masons, Rotary (past pres.), Moraine Country, Engineers. Home: 4365 Delco Dell Rd Dayton OH 45429 Office: 40 E 1st St Dayton OH 45401

BROOKS, FRANK CAROTHERS, lawyer; b. Greenville, Tex., Nov. 16, 1912; s. Barry Jenkins and Bess (Carothers) B.; m. Emmy Jane Gulick, Apr. 25, 1942; children—Barry J., Kent F. Student, So. Meth. U., 1930-31, East Tex. State U., 1931-32; B.A., U. Tex. at Austin, LL.B., 1936. Bar: bar. Asso. firm Callaway & Reed, 1936-38, partner, 1938-42; partner firm Callaway, Reed, Kidwell & Brooks, 1942-62; sr. partner firm Brooks & Brooks (and predecessors), Dallas, 1962—. Served with AUS, 1941. Fellow Tex. Bar Found. (life); mem. Am., Tex., Dallas bar assns., Assn. ICC Practitioners, Transp. Club of Dallas, Phi Eta Sigma, Phi Delta Theta. Democrat. Methodist. Club: Dallas Country. Home: 4311 Beverly Dr Dallas TX 75205 Office: 8300 Douglas Ave Suite 800 Dallas TX 75225

BROOKS, FRANK PICKERING, physician, physiologist; b. Portsmouth, N.H., Jan. 2, 1920; s. Frank Edwin and Florence Isabel (Towle) B.; m. Emily Elizabeth Marden, July 5, 1942; children: William Bradley, Sally Elizabeth, Robert Pickering. A.B., Dartmouth Coll., 1941; M.D., U. Pa., 1943, Sc.D. in Medicine, 1951. Intern Hosp. U. Pa., Phila., 1944, resident, 1944-46; USPHS research fellow Jefferson Med. Coll., 1951-52; instr. U. Pa., 1952-53, asst. prof., 1954-60, asso. prof., 1960-70, prof. medicine and physiology, 1970—; sr. lectr. in physiology U. Edinburgh, Scotland, 1955-56; research assoc. VA Center, Los Angeles, 1966-67; mem. Nat. Commn. on Digestive Diseases, 1977-79; mem. council NIADDK, 1983—. Author: The Control of Gastrointestinal Function, 1970, Gastrointestinal Pathophysiology, 2d edit, 1979; editor: Digestive Diseases and Scis., 1982—. Served to lt. (j.g.) USNR, 1946-48. Recipient Research Career Devel. award NIAMDD, 1964-70. Mem. Am. Gastroent. Assn. (pres.-elect 1979-80, pres. 1980-81), Am. Physiol. Soc. (chmn. gastrointestinal sect. 1966), Am. Pancreatic Assn. (pres. 1980-81). Republican. Episcopalian. Club: Union League Phila. Home: 206 Almur Ln Wynnewood PA 19096 *

BROOKS, FREDERICK PHILLIPS, JR., computer science educator; b. Durham, N.C., Apr. 19, 1931; s. Frederick Philips and Octavia Hooker (Broome) B.; m. Nancy Lee Greenwood, June 16, 1956; children: Kenneth Phillips, Roger Greenwood, Barbara Suzanne. B.A., Duke U., 1953; S.M., Harvard U., 1955, Ph.D., 1956. Engr. IBM Corp., Poughkeepsie, N.Y., 1956-59, Yorktown Heights, N.Y., 1959-60, corp. processor devel. system/360 computer, Poughkeepsie, 1960-64, mgr. devel., 1964-65; prof. U. N.C. at Chapel Hill, 1964-75, Kenan prof., 1975—, chmn. dept. computer sci., 1964—; bd. dirs. Triangle Univ. Computation Center, 1966-83, chmn., 1975-77; bd. dirs. N.C. Ednl. Computing Service, 1965—. Author: The Mythical Man-Month-Essays on Software Engineering, 1975, (with K.E. Iverson) Automatic Data Processing, 1963, Automatic Data Processing, System/360 Edition, 1969; Contbr. articles to profl. jours. Chmn. com. Central Carolina Billy Graham Crusade, 1972-73; trustee Durham Acad., pres., 1977-80; mem. corp. Inter-Varsity Christian Fellowship, 1968-77. Recipient McDowell award IEEE Computer Soc., 1970, Computer Pioneer award IEEE Computer Soc., 1982, Man of Year award Data Processing Mgmt. Assn., 1970; NSF grantee; AEC grantee; NIH grantee; Guggenheim fellow, 1975. Fellow IEEE, Am. Acad. Arts and Scis.; mem. Assn. Computing Machinery (council mem.-at-large 1966-70), Nat. Acad. Engring., NRC (computer sci. and tech. bd. 1977-80). Methodist. Inventor (with D.W. Sweeney) Program Interruption System, Alphabetical Read-Out Device. Home: 413 Granville Rd Chapel Hill NC 27514

BROOKS, GENE EDWARD, federal judge; b. Griffin, Ind., June 21, 1931; s. Claude Romelia and Martha Margaret (Crawford) B.; m. Mary Jane Goodman, May 28, 1953; children: Marc, Gregory, Penny. Bar: Ind. bar. Pros. atty., Posey County, Ind., 1959-68; bankruptcy judge So. Dist. Ind., 1968-79, U.S. dist. judge, 1979—; mem. faculty Fed. Jud. Ctr.; pres. Nat. Conf. Bankruptcy Judges. Contbr. articles to legal jours. Served with USMCR, 1953-55. Recipient Disting. Alumni award Ind. State U., Disting. Service cert. Fed. Bar Assn., Outstanding Service award Nat. Conf. Bankruptcy Judges. Mem. Ind. Bar Assn., Posey County Bar Assn., Vanderburgh County Bar Assn., VFW, Am. Legion. Democrat. Episcopalian. Clubs: Elks, Kiwanis. Office: 310 Federal Bldg Evansville IN 47708 *

BROOKS, GWENDOLYN, author; b. Topeka, June 7, 1917; d. David Anderson and Keziah Corinne (Wims) B.; m. Henry L. Blakely, Sept. 17, 1939; children: Henry L., Nora. Grad., Wilson Jr. Coll., Chgo., 1936; L.H.D., Columbia Coll., 1964. Instr. poetry Columbia Coll., Chgo., Northeastern Ill. State Coll.; Mem. Ill. Arts Council. Author: poetry A Street in Bronzeville, 1945, Annie Allen, 1949, Maud Martha; novel, 1953, Bronzeville Boys and Girls; for children, 1956, The Bean Eaters; poetry, 1960, Selected Poems, 1963, In the Mecca, 1968, Riot, 1969, Family Pictures, 1970, Aloneness, 1971, To Disembark, 1981; autobiography Report From Part One, 1972, The Tiger Who Wore White Gloves, 1974, Beckonings, 1975, Primer for Blacks, 1980, Young Poets' Primer, 1981. Named One of 10 Women of Year Mademoiselle mag., 1945; recipient award for creative writing Am. Acad. Arts and Letters, 1946; Guggenheim fellow for creative writing, 1946, 47; Pulitzer prize for poetry, 1950; Anisfield-Wolf award, 1969; named Poet Laureate of Ill., 1969. Mem. Soc. Midland Authors. Home: 7428 S Evans Ave Chicago IL 60619 *To be clean of heart, clear of mind, and claiming of what is right and just.*

BROOKS, HARRY ANGELO, art dealer; b. N.Y.C., Feb. 19, 1913; s. Frederick Williamn and Millicent (Angelo) B.; m. Helen Moffett, Nov. 16, 1963; children: Melissa Millicent, Miranda Elizabeth. B.A., Princeton U., 1935; LL.B., N.Y. Law Sch., 1938. Vice pres. M. Knoedler & Co., N.Y.C., 1946-67; pres. Wildenstein & Co., Inc., N.Y.C., 1968—; mem. adv. bd. Princeton U. Art Mus., 1968—; mem. Joan Whitney Payson Gallery, Westbrook Coll., Portland, Maine, 1978—. Adv. dir. Met. Opera Assn., N.Y.C., 1977—, Joffrey Ballet, N.Y.C., 1965—. Served to lt. col. U.S. Army, 1941-46; ETO. Life fellow Met. Mus. Art. Republican. Episcopalian. Clubs: Racquet and Tennis; Brook (N.Y.C.); Piping Brook (Locust Valley, N.Y.). Home: 78 McCoun's Ln Glen Head NY 11545 Office: Wildenstein & Co Inc 19 E 64th St New York NY 10021

BROOKS, HARRY WILLIAM, JR., retired army officer, corporate executive; b. Indpls., May 17, 1928; s. Harry William and Nora Elaine (Bailey) B.; m. Doris Green, Oct. 8, 1948 (dec. Oct. 1979); children: Harry W. III, Wayne L., Craig E. B.S., U. Omaha, 1962; M.A., U. Okla., 1973. Commd. 2d lt. U.S. Army, 1949, advanced through grades to maj. gen., 1974; student officer Command and Gen. Staff Coll., Fort Leavenworth, Kan., 1965-66; bn. comdr., Ft. Benning, Ga., 1966, Vietnam, 1966-67; staff officer Office of Asst. Chief of Staff, Washington, 1967-69; student officer Army War Coll., Carlisle, Pa., 1969-70; comdr. arty. group, Wertheim, Germany, 1970-72; army dir. of equal opportunity programs Pentagon, Washington, 1972; asst. div. comdr., Korea, 1973, comdg. gen. 25th Inf. div., Hawaii, 1974-76, ret., 1976; v.p. pub. affairs Amfac Inc., Honolulu, 1976-78, sr. v.p., 1978-82, exec. v.p., group chmn. horticulture, 1982—. Hon. chmn. Hawaii Spl. Olympics, 1975; mem. exec. com. Boy Scouts Am., Hawaii, 1974-81; chmn. Hawaii Citizenship Day, 1974. Decorated D.S.M., Legion of Merit with 1 oak leaf cluster, Bronze Star with 1 oak leaf cluster, Air medal with 6 oak leaf clusters, others.; Recipient Freedom award Hawaiian chpt. NAACP, 1975, Top Hat award Pitts. Courier, 1973; named NAACP Meritorious Service award, 1978, Disting. Hoosier State of Ind., 1972. Mem. Hawaii C. of C. (dir. 1977-81). Lodges: Masons (33 deg.); Shriners; Rotary. Home: 14 Antique Forest Ln Belmont CA 94002 Office: Amfac Inc 1601 Bayshore Hwy Suite 323 Burlingame CA 94010

BROOKS, HERBERT PAUL, hockey coach; b. St. Paul, Aug. 5, 1937; s. Herbert David and Pauline (E.) B.;, Sept. 27, 1967; 2 children. B.A., U. Minn., 1962. Head hockey coach U. Minn., 1972-79; coach U.S. Olympic Hockey Team, 1980; hockey coach N.Y. Rangers, Nat. Hockey League, 1981—; pres. Gold Medal, Inc., Minn. Hockey Schs., Inc. Served with U.S. N.G. Named Nat. Hockey League Coach of Yr., 1982. Mem. U.S. Olympians, Am. Hockey Coaches Assn. Club: U. Minn. M. Gold medalist mem. U.S. Olympic hockey teams, 1964, 68; coach Nat. Collegiate Athletic Assn. Champions, 1974, 76, 79. Office: NY Rangers 4 Pennsylvania Plaza New York NY 10001

BROOKS, HERMAN EDGAR, banker; b. Jacksonville, Fla., Dec. 6, 1926; s. Herman E. and Eloise (Drysdale) B.; m. Dorothy Davidson; children—Amy Lynn, Thomas D., John H. B.S. in Bus. Adminstrn, John B. Stetson U., 1950. Vice pres., sec. Atlantic Nat. Bank of Fla.; also v.p., corporate sec. Atlantic Bancorporation, Jacksonville. Served with USN, 1944. Home: 813 Montego Rd E Jacksonville FL 32216 Office: Atlantic Bancorporation Gen Mail Center Jacksonville FL 32231

BROOKS, JACK BASCOM, congressman; b. Crowley, La., Dec. 18, 1922; s. Edward Chachere and Grace Marie (Pipes) B.; m. Charlotte Collins, Dec. 15, 1960; children: Jack Edward, Katherine Inez, Kimberly Grace. A.A., Lamar Jr. Coll., Beaumont, Tex., 1939-41; B.J., U. Tex., 1943, J.D., 1949. Bar: Tex. 1949. Mem. Tex. Legislature, 1946-50, 83-89th congresses for 2d Dist., Tex., 90th-98th congresses from 9th Dist. Tex. Author, Lamar Coll. bill, 1949. Served from pvt. to lst lt. USMCR, 1942-46; col. Res. ret. Mem. Am. Bar Assn., State Bar Tex., Am. Legion, V.F.W., Sigma Delta Chi. Home: 1029 East Dr Beaumont TX 77706 Office: Rayburn House Office Bldg Washington DC 20515 also Fed Building Beaumont TX 77701 and US Post office Bldg Galveston TX 77550

BROOKS, JAMES, artist; b. St. Louis, Oct. 18, 1906; s. William Rodolphus and Abigail (Williamson) B.; m. Mary MacDonald, 1938; m. Charlotte Park, Dec. 22, 1947. Student, So. Meth. U., 1923-25, Art Students League, 1927-31; studied with, Wallace Harrison, 1945. Instr. Pratt Inst., N.Y.C., 1948-55; faculty Columbia U., 1946-48, Queens Coll., N.Y.C., 1966-69, New Coll., 1965-67, U. Pa., Phila., 1971; Andrew Carnegie prof. Cooper Union, N.Y.C.; vis. critic advanced painting Yale U., New Haven, 1955-60; vis. artist New Coll., Sarasota, Fla., 1965-67. One-man shows, Peridot Gallery, N.Y.C., 1950-53, Borgenicht Gallery, N.Y.C., 1954, Stable Gallery, N.Y.C., 1957, 59, Kootz Gallery, N.Y.C., 1961, 63, 64, Phila. Art Alliance, 1966, Martha Jackson Gallery, N.Y.C., 1968, 71, 72, 75, Berenson Gallery, Miami, Fla., 1969, Galleria Lorenzelli, Milan and Bergamo, Italy, 1975, Carone Gallery, Ft. Lauderdale, Fla., 1976, Robinson Gallery, Houston, Lerner-Heller Gallery, N.Y.C., 1978, Grunebaum Gallery, N.Y.C., 1979, 80, 83, Montclair (N.J.) Mus., 1978; exhibited Retrospective Exhbn. at, Whitney Mus., N.Y.C., 1963-64, at Dallas Mus., 1972, Finch Coll. Mus., 1975, Guild Hall Mus., East Hampton, N.Y., Flint (Mich.) Inst. Arts, Grand Rapids (Mich.) Art Mus., Stamford (Conn.) Mus., Cranbrook Acad. Art Mus., Mich., 1975, Portland (Maine) Mus. Art; artist in residence, Am. Acad., Rome, 1963; exhibited, Rose Art Mus., Brandeis U., Walker Art Center, Mpls., UCLA, Balt. Mus., Mus. Modern Art, Washington, 1963, Whitney Mus., Modern, Bklyn., Met., Guggenheim museums, Art Inst. Chgo., Nat. Gallery, Washington, numerous others, also Tokyo, Sao Paulo, Basle, Munich, Milan, London, Berlin, Brussels, Paris, Barcelona, Perth, Australia, 1958; executed murals, Little Falls (N.J.) Post Office, Woodside (L.I.) Library, LaGuardia Airport. Bd. govs. Skowhegan Sch. Art. Recipient prizes Pitts. Internat., 1952, Mobil Oil Hdqrs., Fairfax, Va., Art Inst. Chgo., 1957, 62; Guggenheim fellow, 1967-68; Nat. Endowment for Arts grantee, 1973. Mem. Am. Inst. Arts and Letters. Club: Century (N.Y.C.). Home: 128 Neck Path Springs East Hampton NY 11937 *The artist's function is to initiate, with the tools he knows best, a set of circumstances through which relationships that are important and peculiar to him may generate themselves.*

BROOKS, JAMES ELWOOD, educator; b. Salem, Ind., May 31, 1925; s. Elwood Edwin and Helen Mary (May) B.; m. Eleanore June Nystrom, June 18, 1949; children: Nancy, Kathryn, Carolyn. A.B., DePauw U., 1948; M.S., Northwestern U., 1950; Ph.D., U. Wash., 1954. Research assoc. Ill. Geol. Survey, 1950; geologist Gulf Oil Corp., Salt Lake City, summers 1951-53; instr. geol. scis. So. Meth. U., Dallas, 1952-55, asst. prof., 1955-59, assoc. prof., 1959-62, prof., 1962—, chmn. dept., 1961-70, dean, assoc. provost univ., 1970-72, provost, v.p., 1972-80, pres., 1980-81, Inst. for Study Earth and Man, Dallas, 1981—; cons. geologist firm DeGolyer & MacNaughton, Dallas, 1954-59. Contbr. articles to profl. jours. Trustee Inst. Study Earth and Man, Dallas; bd. dirs. Hockaday Sch., Dallas; exec. bd. Circle Ten council Boy Scouts Am.; mem. So. Meth. U. Bd. Publs.; bd. vistors DePauw U., 1979-83; bd. dirs. Rangaire Corp. Served with USNR, 1943-46. Fellow Geol. Soc. Am., AAAS, Tex. Acad. Sci.; mem. Am. Assn. Petroleum Geologists, Dallas Geol. Soc., Sigma Xi, Sigma Gamma Epsilon, Sigma Phi. Home: 7055 Arboreal Dr Dallas TX 75231 Office: Inst Study Earth and Man Box 274 Dallas TX 75275

BROOKS, JAMES L., screenwriter, producer; b. Bklyn., May 9, 1940; s. Edward M. and Dorothy Helen (Sheinheit) B.; m. Marianne Catherine Morrissey, July 7, 1964 (div.); 1 dau., Amy Lorraine; m. Holly Beth Holmberg, July 23, 1978. Student, N.Y. U., 1958-60. Writer CBS News, N.Y.C., 1964-66; writer-producer documentaries Wolper Prodns., Los Angeles, 1966-67; guest lectr. Stanford Grad. Sch. Communications. Exec. story editor/co-creator: TV series Room 222, 1968-69; exec. producer/co-creator: Mary Tyler Moore Show, 1970-77; writer/producer: Thursday's Game, 1971—, Paul Sand in Friends and Lovers, 1974; co-creator, co-exec. producer: Rhoda show, 1974-75; writer: TV show The New Lorenzo Music Show, 1976; co-exec. producer: TV series Lou Grant, 1977; co-creator, exec. producer: Taxi, 1978-80; exec. producer, co-writer: Cindy, 1978; co-creator, exec. producer: The Associates, 1979; writer, co-producer: film Starting Over; actor: Modern Romance, 1981; co-producer, writer, dir.: Terms of Endearment, 1983 (Acad. awards for best film, best director, best screenplay 1984). Recipient Emmy award for creation of Room 222, 1969, for comedy writing Mary Tyler Moore Show, 1970, 75, also best show, best writing, 1976 for outstanding comedy series Taxi, 1978-79, 79-80, 80-81; TV Critics Circle award for achievement in comedy and in a series, 1976-77; Peabody award for Mary Tyler Moore Show, 1977, Lou Grant Show, 1978; Golden Globe award for Best Comedy Series for Taxi, 1978, 79, 80; Writers Guild Am. award Outstanding script for Cindy, 1978; Humanitas Prize for Taxi episode entitled Blind Date, 1979. Mem. Writers Guild Am., TV Acad. Arts and Scis., Screen Actors Guild. *

BROOKS, JOHN, writer; b. N.Y.C., Dec. 5, 1920; s. John Nixon and Bessie (Lyon) B.; m. Anne Curtis Brown, Mar. 6, 1948 (div. 1952); m. Rae Alexander Everitt, Aug. 15, 1953 (div. 1975); children: Carolyn, John Alexander.; m. Barbara Smith Mahoney, Jan. 29, 1982. A.B., Princeton U., 1942. Contbg. editor Time mag., 1945-47; staff contbr. New Yorker mag., 1949—. Author: The Big Wheel, 1949, A Pride of Lions, 1954, The Man Who Broke Things, 1958, The Seven Fat Years, 1958, The Fate of the Edsel, 1963, The Great Leap, 1966, Business Adventures, 1969, Once in Golconda, 1969, The Go-Go Years, 1973, Telephone, 1976, The Games Players, 1980, Showing Off in America, 1981; also articles and revs.; Editor: The One and the Many, 1962, The Autobiography of American Business, 1974. Trustee N.Y. Pub. Library, 1978—. Served with AUS, 1942-45; ETO. Poynter fellow Yale, 1974-75. Mem. Authors Guild Am. (treas. 1964-71, v.p. 1971-75, pres. 1975-79), P.E.N. (v.p. 1962-66), Soc. Am. Historians (v.p. 1984). Clubs: Coffee House, Century Assn. (N.Y.C.). Home: 41 Barrow St New York NY 10014 Office: New Yorker Mag 25 W 43d St New York NY 10036

BROOKS, JOHN EDWARD, college president; b. Boston, July 13, 1923; s. John Edward and Mildred (McCoy) B. B.S. in Physics, Coll. Holy Cross, 1949; postgrad. in geophysics, Pa. State U., 1949-50; M.A. in Philosophy, Boston Coll., 1954; M.S. in Geophysics, Boston Coll., 1959; S.T.D. in Dogmatic Theology, Gregorian U., Rome, Italy, 1963; H.H.D. (hon.), St. Ambrose Coll., 1976. Joined Soc. of Jesus, 1950; ordained priest Roman Catholic Ch., 1959; instr. mathematics and physics Coll. of Holy Cross, Worcester, Mass., 1954-56, instr. theology, 1963-64, asst. prof., 1964-67, asso. prof. religious studies, 1967—, chmn. dept. theology, 1964-69, v.p., dean coll., 1968-70, pres., trustee, 1970—, sec. com. ednl. policy, 1968-70, chmn., 1970—; Participant bibl. and archeol. consortium Jewish Inst. on Religion, Hebrew Union Coll., 1968; inst. academic deans Am. Council Edn., St. Louis U., 1968; trustee St. Peter's Coll., Jersey City, 1969-75, Canisius Coll., Buffalo, 1974-80; mem. Mass. Postsecondary Edn. Commn., Mass. 1202 Commn., 1974-77; mem. exec. com. New Eng. Colls. Fund, 1974, 78; mem. Mass. Pub./Pvt. Forum; bd. dirs. Worcester Consortium for Higher Edn., chmn., 1976-77; mem. Worcester Downtown Devel. Corp.; bd. visitors Air U., 1978—. Community trustee United Way of Central Mass.; consortium dir. Social Services Corp., Worcester. Served with U.S. Army, 1942-46. Mem. Assn. Jesuit Colls. and Univs. (dir. 1970—), NAACP, Assn. Ind. Colls. and Univs. in Mass. (v.p. 1972-73, chmn. coms., exec. com.), Delta Epsilon Sigma, Alpha Sigma Nu. Clubs: Economic (Worcester) (pres. 1977-78, exec. com. 1978—. Office: College Holy Cross Loyola Hall Worcester MA 01610

BROOKS, JOHN ROBINSON, educator, physician; b. Cambridge, Mass., Nov. 15, 1918; s. Arthur Hendricks and Caroline Elizabeth (Harrington) B.; m. Dorothy Kalbfleisch, Sept. 9, 1944; children: David C., Stephen H., Nancy, Geoffrey R. A.B., Harvard U., 1940, M.D., 1943. Intern Roosevelt Hosp., N.Y.C., 1944; resident Peter Bent Brigham Hosp., Boston, 1951; prof. surgery Harvard Med. Sch., 1970-81, Peter Bent Brigham Hosp., Harvard, 1970-81, pres. med. staff, 1973—; Frank Sawyer prof. surgery Harvard Med. Sch. and Brigham and Women's Hosp., 1981—; chief surgery Harvard Health Services, 1962—. Author: Endocrine Tissue Transplantation, 1960, Surgery of the Pancreas, 1983; Editor: Harvard Med. Alumni Bull, 1956-68; Contbr. articles to profl. jours. Head drs. sect. United Fund, 1969; Trustee Noble and Greenough Sch. Served to capt. AUS, 1946. Mem. ACS (gov. 1974—), Am. Surg. Assn., Soc. Univ. Surgeons, New Eng. Surg. Soc. (pres. 1979), Soc. Surgery Alimentary Tract, Internat. Surg. Soc., Soc. Surg. Oncology. Home: 29 Webster Rd Weston MA 02193 Office: 721 Huntington Ave Boston MA 02115

BROOKS, JOSEPH, producer, composer. Composer music for numerous TV commls.; producer, dir., writer, scorer: film You Light Up My Life, 1977; producer, dir., writer, scorer, and star of: scores for films include If Ever I See You Again; film scores include: Garden of the Finzi-Continis, Marjoe, Jeremy, Lords of Flatbush. Recipient numerous CLIO awards, Acad. award, Grammy award, People's Choice, Am. Music award, Golden Globe award. Office: care Light and Sound Co Inc 41-A E 74th St New York NY 10021

BROOKS, JOSEPH E., retail department stores executive; b. 1928; married. With Federated Dept. Stores, 1955-75; corp. sr. exec. v.p., chmn. Lord & Taylor div. Associated Dry Goods Corp, N.Y.C., 1975—, also dir. Office: Associated Dry Goods Corp 417 Fifth Ave New York NY 10016 *

BROOKS, KEITH, educator; b. Tigerton, Wis., May 14, 1923; s. Oscar Derby and Henrietta (Mierswa) B.; m. Laquata Sue Walters, Dec. 29, 1951; children: Todd Randall, Craig William. B.S., U. Wis., 1949, M.S., 1949; Ph.D., Ohio State U., 1955. Mem. faculty Eastern Ky. State U., Richmond, 1949-53; mem. faculty Ohio State U., Columbus, 1953—, prof. communication, 1968—, chmn. dept., 1968-75; communications cons. Procter & Gamble, Mead World Hdqrs., U.S. Dept. Agr., Ohio Bell Telephone, Eastern R.R. Assn., Shaw U., Raleigh, N.C. Author: (with Bahm and Okey) Literature for Listening, 1968, The Communicative Act of Oral Interpretation, 1967, 2d edit., 1975, The Communicative Arts and Sciences of Speech, 1967, (with Dietrich) Practical Speaking, 1959. Served with USNR, 1945-46. Mem. Speech Communication Assn. (chmn. interpretation div., vice chmn., sec.), Internat. Communication Assn. (co-editor Newsletter 1979—), Central States Speech Assn. (editor Jour. 1958-61), Am. Ednl. Theatre Assn. (dir. 1958-60). Home: 2201 Sandstone Columbus OH 43220 *The most important attribute of all is taking the time to care.*

BROOKS, LORIMER PAGE, patent lawyer; b. Swampscott, Mass., May 11, 1917; s. William Lorimer and Maude (Page) B.; m. Arlene M. Cook, Nov. 9, 1941; children: Lorraine E. Brooks Phillips, Jr., Rosaline P. B.S. in elec. engring. with honors, Northeastern U., 1939; J.D., Fordham U., 1948; postgrad., NYU Law Sch., 1951. Bar: N.Y. 1948, U.S. Supreme Ct. 1971. Patent agt. ITT, 1939-41, patent atty., 1945-50, Ward, Crosby, & Neal, N.Y.C., 1950-54; ptnr. firm Ward, McElhannon, Brooks & Fitzpartrick, N.Y.C., 1954-71, Brooks, Haidt, Haffner & Delahunty, 1971—; rep. Nat. Council Patent Law Assns., 1976-77, chmn. com. past pres.'s, 1977-78. Patentee in field. Vice pres. Drum Fire Inc.; sec. Westchester Park Citizens Assn., 1950-52, pres., 1952-54; dir. Westchester County Cerebral Palsy Assn., 1962-64; mem. Young Men's Republican Club Eastchester, N.Y., 1952-56. Served with AUS, 1941-45. Mem. Westchester County Bar Assn. (ethics com. 1978), N.Y. Patent Law Assn. (bd. govs. 1961-64, 74-78, chmn. subcom. practice and procedure in cts. 1961-62, chmn. com. ethics and grievances 1973-74, 1st v.p. 1974-75, pres. 1975-76), IEEE, Aircraft Owners and Pilots Assn., Fordham Law Alumni Assn., Northeastern U. Alumni Assn., Tau Beta Pi. Clubs: Wings, Sankaty Head Golf and Beach. Home: 6 Hyatt Rd Briarcliff Rd Briarcliff Manor NY 10510 Office: Brooks Haidt Haffner & Delahunty 99 Park Ave New York NY 10016

BROOKS, MAURICE EDWARD, engineering consultant; b. East Windsor, Conn., May 18, 1922; s. Samuel and Anna B.; m. Helen D. Deckel, Feb. 14, 1943; children—Daniel Joseph, Stephanie. B.S.Ch.E., Cooper Union, 1947; postgrad. in chem. engring, Bklyn. Poly. Inst., 1947-48, N.Y. U., 1948-50. With C-E Lummus Co., 1940-80, gen. mgr., Paris, 1954-56, dir. engring., N.Y.C., 1956-58, v.p., Bloomfield, N.J., 1960-72, sr. v.p., 1972-74, exec. v.p., 1974-75, exec. v.p. and chief operating officer, 1975-78, pres., chief exec. officer, 1978-80; pres. Brooks Cons.'s, Inc., 1980—; mem. exec. adv. com. FPC; mem. consultor com.-chem. engring. Manhattan Coll.; mem. adv. council Cooper Union Sch.; mem. indsl. adv. bd. U. Conn. Served with C.E. U.S. Army, 1944-46. Recipient Profl. Achievement citation Cooper Union, 1965, Gano Dunn award, 1976. Mem. Am. Inst. Chem. Engrs. (Steven L. Tyler award 1959), Cooper Union Alumni Assn. (bd. govs. 1966-67). Patentee in field. Office: 24 Shadow Ln Great Neck NY 11021

BROOKS, MEL, director, writer, actor. Author: sketch Of Fathers and Sons in New Faces of 1952, 1952; co-author: All American, 1962; writer for: TV series Your Show of Shows; also Caesar's Hour; co-creator: TV series Get Smart; recordings include 2000 and One Years; motion pictures include; writer, dir.: Producers, 1968, The Twelve Chairs, 1970; co-writer, dir.: Blazing Saddles, 1973, Young Frankenstein, 1974; co-writer dir., star: Silent Movie, 1976; producer, dir., co-writer and star: High Anxiety, 1977; writer, dir., producer, star: History of the World-Part I, 1981; other films include: The Elephant Man, 1980, Frances, 1982, My Favorite Year, 1982. Address: care 20th Century-Fox Studios PO Box 900 Beverly Hills CA 90213

BROOKS, MICHAEL PAUL, university dean; b. Topeka, June 13, 1937; s. Paul Edward and Gladys Leora (Nansen) B.; m. Shirley Birdeen Rhoad, June 8, 1958 (div. Aug. 1983); children: David, Timothy, Susan.; m. Ann DeWitt Watts, Feb. 18, 1984. B.A. magna cum laude, Colgate U., 1959; M. City Planning, Harvard U., 1961; Ph.D., U. N.C., 1970. Dir. research The N.C. Fund, Durham, 1963-66, dir. planning and program devel., 1966-67; lectr. dept. city and regional planning U. N.C., 1967-70, asso. prof., 1970-71; prof. dept. urban and regional planning U. Ill., 1971-78, head dept., 1971-78; dir. Bur. of Urban and Regional Planning Research, 1971-77; dean Coll. Design, Iowa State U., Ames, 1978-84, Sch. Architecture and Design, SUNY-Buffalo, 1984—; cons. in field. Commr. Research Triangle Regional Planning Commn., Chapel Hill, N.C., 1969-71. Editor: Guide to Graduate Education in Urban and Regional Planning, 2d edit., 1976. Mem. Am. Planning Assn. (pres. 1979-80), Am. Inst. Planners, Assn. Collegiate Schs. Planning (pres. 1976-77). Democrat. Office: Sch Architecture and Design SUNY Buffalo NY 14205

BROOKS, NORMAN HERRICK, environmental and civil engineer; b. Worcester, Mass., July 2, 1928; s. Charles Franklin and Eleanor Merritt (Stabler) B.; m. Frederika Nelson, Dec. 22, 1948; children: Diana, Alexander, Laura. A.B. magna cum laude, Harvard U., 1949, M.S. in Civil Engring, 1950; Ph.D. summa cum laude in Civil Engring. and Physics, Calif. Inst. Tech., 1954. With Calif. Inst. Tech., Pasadena, 1953—, prof., 1962—, James Irvine prof., 1976—, dir. environ. quality lab., 1974-84; vis. asso. prof. SEATO Grad. Sch. Engring., Bangkok, 1959-60; vis. prof. M.I.T., 1962-63; vis. environ. scientist Scripps Instn. Oceanography, fall 1971; cons. in hydraulics and ocean pollution control; mem. assembly sci. and tech. advisory com. Calif. State Legislature, 1970-73; mem. environ. studies bd. Nat. Acad. Scis., 1973-76. Co-author: Mixing in Inland and Coastal Waters, 1979; contbr. articles to profl. jours. Chmn. Altadena-Pasadena Human Relations Com.; mem. Altadena Planning Adv. Com. Fellow ASCE (chmn. com. on hydrologic transport processes 1975-76, Huber research prize 1959, Collingwood prize 1959, J.C. Stevens award 1959, Rudolph Hering medal 1957, 62, Hilgard hydraulics prize 1970); mem. Nat. Acad. Engring., Nat. Acad. Scis., Am. Geophys. Union, Internat. Assn. Hydraulic Research, Univ. Council on Water Resources, AAAS, Water Pollution Control Fedn., Sigma Xi. Home: 2521 N Santa Anita Ave Altadena CA 91001 Office: Keck Labs Calif Inst Tech Pasadena CA 91125

BROOKS, PEGGY JONES (MRS. JOHN BENSON BROOKS), editor; b. Orange, N.J., June 19, 1919; d. Thomas Catesby and Louisa R. (Brooke) Jones; m. John Benson Brooks, Apr. 8, 1961. B.A., Vassar Coll., 1940. Account exec. Franklin Spier, Inc., N.Y.C., 1944-47; promotion head Thomas Y. Crowell Co., N.Y.C., 1947-49; advt. mgr. E.P. Dutton & Co., Inc., N.Y.C., 1953-57, editor, 1957-68, exec. editor, 1968-70; sr. editor Coward, McCann & Geoghegan, Inc. (pub. co.), N.Y.C., 1970-76, sec., 1974-76; sr. editor Harcourt Brace Jovanovich, N.Y.C., 1978-80; free-lance editor, N.Y.C., 1980—. Mem. P.E.N. Club: Cosmopolitan (N.Y.C.). Home: 9 Gay St New York NY 10014

BROOKS, PETER (PRESTON), French and comparative literature educator, writer; b. N.Y.C., Apr. 19, 1938; s. Ernest and Mary Caroline (Schoyer) B.; m. Margaret Elisabeth Waters, July 18, 1959; 3 children. B.A., Harvard U., 1959, Ph.D., 1965; postgrad., U. Coll. London, 1959-60, U. Paris, 1962-63; M.A.H., Yale U., 1975. Instr. French Yale U., 1965-67, asst. prof., 1967-72, assoc. prof., 1972-75, prof. French and comparative lit., 1975—, Chester D. Tripp prof. humanities, 1980—, dir. The Lit. Major, 1974-79, dir. Whitney Humanities Ctr., 1980—, chmn. dept. French, 1983—. Author: The Novel of Worldliness, 1969, The Child's Part, 1972, Teh Melodramatic Imagination, 1976; editor: Yale French Studies, 1966—; contbg. editor: Partisen Rev., 1972—. Acad. advisor Marlboro Co., 1975—; regional chmn. Mellon Fellowships in Humanities, 1982—; trustee Hopkins Sch., New Haven, 1983—. Marshall fellow, 1959; Morse fellow, 1967; Guggenheim fellow, 1973; Am. Council Learned Socs. fellow, 1980. Mem. MLA. Democrat. Clubs: Yale (N.Y.C.); Elizabethan (New Haven). Office: Yale Univ Whitney Humanities Ctr 2968 Yale Station New Haven CT 06520

BROOKS, RICHARD, writer, dir.; b. Phila., May 18, 1912. Student, Temple U. Formerly radio writer, narrator, commentator NBC. Now author screenplays for motion pictures.; Author: screen plays Brute Force, Swell Guy, White Savage; author: original screen plays Crossfire, To the Victor; collaborator: screen plays Storm Warning, Key Largo, Mystery Street; dir., author: Elmer Gantry (Acad. award for screen play 1961), The Brothers Karamazov, Cat on a Hot Tin Roof, Sweet Bird of Youth, Deadline, U.S.A., Battle Circus, Last Hunt, Something of Value; dir.: Take the High Ground, Flame and the Flesh, Catered Affair, Looking for Mr. Goodbar, 1977; dir., collaborator: screenplay Last Time I Saw Paris; author: Blackboard Jungle; producer, dir., writer: Lord Jim; dir., writer: The Professionals, In Cold Blood; writer, producer, director: Wrong is Right, 1982; author: novels The Producer, Brick Fox Hole, Boiling Point; also motion pictures The Happy Ending, 1969, Dollars, 1971, Bite the Bullet, 1975. Address: care Directors Guild Am 7950 Sunset Blvd Hollywood CA 90046 *

BROOKS, RICHARD ALBERT EDWARD, educator; b. Karachi, Pakistan, May 14, 1904; s. Septimus Hawkins and Adelaide (Kearns) B.; m. Edith Margaret Hill, Sept. 24, 1926 (dec. Sept. 1966); children—Joan E. Brooks Gindele, Judith Anne Brooks Fitzhugh; m. Harriet Helen Ogsbury, June 30, 1967 (dec. Aug. 1978). Student, Philander Smith Coll., Naini Tal, United Provinces, India, 1920-21; A.B., Wesleyan U., 1926, M.A. (Olin fellow), 1927; Ph.D. (Univ. fellow 1929-30), Yale U., 1936. Instr. English Wesleyan U., 1927-29, F.B. Weeks vis. prof. English, 1952-53; asst. in English Yale U., 1930-32, instr., 1932-33; faculty Vassar Coll., 1933—, successively instr., asst. prof., asso. prof., prof., 1933-69, emeritus, 1969—; faculty fellow, 1939-40, 61-62, Mary Conover Mellon House fellow, 1954-59, chmn. English dept., 1958-60, Henry Noble MacCracken prof. English, 1963—; Instr. Naval Pre-Flight Sch., summer 1944, Biarritz Am. U., 1945-46. Author: Thomas Carlyle's Journey to Germany, Autumn 1858, 1940, The Development of the Historical Mind (in The Reinterpretation of Victorian Literature, reprinted in, Backgrounds to Victorian Literature); Editor: (with H.N. MacCracken) Ben Johnson's Sad Shepherd: Completed by Alan Porter, 1944. Active Am. Friends Service Com., 1955-59; Trustee Poughkeepsie Day Sch., 1944-45, 46-47. Mem. Modern Lang. Assn. Am., AAUP, Phi Beta Kappa. Club: Yale (N.Y.C.). Home: 493-B Heritage Village Southbury CT 06488

BROOKS, RICHARD M., corporation executive; b. 1928; (married). B.S., Yale; M.B.A., U. Calif. at Berkeley; C.L.U. With Mut. of N.Y., to 1957; with Calif. and Hawaiian Sugar Co., 1957-79, sr. v.p. fin. and adminstrn., 1973-79; sr. v.p. fin. Amfac, Inc., San Francisco, 1979—. Past pres. Piedmont council Boy Scouts Am.; trustee Golden Gate council., Coll. Prep. Sch., Oakland. Mem. Oakland Mus. Assn. (past dir., officer). Address: 50 O'Farrell St PO Box 7813 San Francisco CA 94120

BROOKS, ROBERT DALE, educator; b. Topeka, Dec. 5, 1932; s. Arthur A. and Edna Lena (Rouse) B.; m. Alta Rae Fann, June 16, 1961; 1 dau., Allyson Royce. B.A., U. Kans., 1956, M.A., 1963; Ph.D., U. Wis., 1968. News dir. KANU-U. Kans., Lawrence, 1962-65; chief programmer MM Lab.U. Wis., Madison, 1965-68; asst. prof. U. Tex., Austin, 1968-71, assoc. prof., 1971-76, prof., 1976—, TV area head, 1978—; Social Sci. Research assoc. Hogg Found., Austin, 1983; sr. research scientist Ctr. for Communication Research, Austin, 1970-74. Co-dir.: film Information Explosion, 1972 (Gold medal), Work is Child's Play, 1973 (Silver medal), Where There is Love, 1974 (Bronze medal), Six Gun to Sixty One, 1961. Skipper Mariners Westlake Hills Presbyn. Ch., Tex., 1980. Fellow C. of C.; mem. Am. Ednl. Research Assn., Assn. Ednl. Communication and Tech. Home: 1925 Cypress Point W Austin TX 78746 Office: CMA 6 118 U Tex Austin TX 78712

BROOKS, ROBERT WILLIAM, bank executive; b. Bloomfield, N.J., Nov. 1, 1935; s. William George and Marion Agnes (Carter) B.; m. Margaret Caroll Snider, Nov. 11, 1961; children: Robert Scott, Elizabeth Ann. B.S., Lebigh U., 1957. Chemical Bank, N.Y.C., 1957—, exec. v.p., 1983—; chmn. Chem. Bus. Credit Corp., Chemco Internat. Leasing, Inc., 1982—. Served with USAF, 1958-60. Mem. N.Y. Credit and Fin. Mgmt. Assn., Nat. Comml. Fin. Assn. (dir. 1982—). Republican. Roman Catholic. Club: Canoe Brook Country. Office: Chemical Bank 110 E 59th St New York NY 10022

BROOKS, ROGER KAY, ins. co. exec.; b. Clarion, Iowa, Apr. 30, 1937; s. Edgar Sherman and Hazel (Whipple) B.; m. Marcia Rae Ramsay, Nov. 19, 1955; children—Michael, Jeffrey, David. B.A. magna cum laude, U. Iowa, 1959. With Central Life Assurance Co., Des Moines, 1964—, asst. sec., 1964-68, v.p., 1968-70, exec. v.p., 1970-72, pres., 1972—; dir. Iowa-Des Moines Nat. Bank. Fellow Soc. Actuaries; mem. Des Moines C. of C. (dir.), Actuaries Club of Des Moines (past pres.), Phi Beta Kappa. Presbyterian (elder). Home: 215 Tonawanda Dr Des Moines IA 50312 Office: 611 5th St Des Moines IA 50309

BROOKS, ROGER LEON, university president; b. El Dorado, Ark., Apr. 14, 1927; s. Roger Spurgeon and Lumae (Jackson) B.; m. Martha Edwina Withers, Aug. 25, 1950; children:Leslie, Roger, Geoffrey, Stephen, Douglas. B.A., Baylor U., 1949; M.A., U. Ill., 1950; Ph.D., U. Colo., 1959. Instr. English U. Colo., 1955-57, 58-60; prof. Tex. Tech. U., Lubbock, 1960-64, assoc. dean, 1964-67; dean Coll. Arts and Scis., E. Tex. State U., Commerce, 1967-72; pres. Howard Payne U., Brownwood, Tex., 1972-79; v.p. adminstrv. affairs Houston Bapt. U., 1979—; cons. Victorian Studies, 1967, Choice, 1970, Canada Council, 1971. Contbr. articles to profl. jours. Served with USNR, 1945-51; lt. col. USMCR. Recipient research grants U. Colo. at Oxford and Brit. Mus., 1957-58, Tex. Tech. U. at Bibliotheque Nationale, Paris, 1964, Am. Philos Soc. at N.Y. Public Library, 1963, at Brit. Mus., 1980. Mem. Am. Council Learned Socs., C. of C., Phi Kappa Phi, Phi Mu Alpha, Pi Gamma Mu. Club: Rotary. Office: Office Vice Pres Houston Baptist U Houston TX 77074

BROOKS, TERRY, lawyer, author; b. Sterling, Ill., Jan. 8, 1944; s. Dean Oliver and Marjorie Iantha (Gleason) B.; m. Barbara Ann Groth, Apr. 23, 1972; children: Amanda Leigh, Alexander Stephen. A.B., Hamilton Coll., 1966; LL.B., Washington and Lee U., 1969. Bar: bar. Mem. firm Besse, Frye, Arnold & Brooks, Sterling, 1969—. Author: The Sword of Shannara, 1977, The Sword of Shannara: Panamon Creel and Keltset (rec.), 1978, The Elfstones of Shannara, 1982. Mem. Am., Ill., Whiteside County bar assns., Am. Trial Lawyers Assn. Home: 1310 Sinnissippi Rd Sterling IL 61081 Office: Central Nat Bank Bldg Sterling IL 61081

BROOKS, THEODORE WILLIAM, banker; b. Billerica, Mass., June 30, 1918; s. William O. and Mabelle (Baker) B.; m. Patricia Hubbard, Oct. 12, 1946; 1 son, John W. B.A., Williams Coll., 1940. With Chase Manhattan Bank, N.Y.C., 1940-79, sr. v.p., 1965-79; ret., 1979; dir. Raymark Corp., Condec Corp.; cons. Nat. Exec. Service Corps. Served with USNR, 1941-46. Home: PO Box 786-CCNC Pinehurst NC 28374

BROOKS, TONEY, broadcasting executive; b. Tuscaloosa, Ala., July 15, 1943; s. Ralph Stone and Mary London (Pou) B.; m. Mary K. Eppler, June 21, 1969; children—Maxwell M., Mary B., Catherine K. B.B.A., U. Ala., 1965. Mgr. Sta. KLAW, Lawton, Okla., 1971-74; gen. sales mgr. Sta. KBPI, Denver, 1974-79; v.p. KBPI Radio, Denver, 1979-81; pres. Sandusky Newspapers Radio Div., Denver, 1981—. Served with U.S. Army, 1966-69. Decorated Bronze Star. Republican. Episcopalian. Club: Rotary (pres. 1972). Home: 545 S Nelson St Denver CO 80226 Office: 4460 Morrison Rd Denver CO 80219

BROOKS, VERNON BERNARD, scientist, educator; b. Berlin, Germany, May 10, 1923; s. Martin and Margarete (Hahlo) B.; m. Nancy Fraser, June 29, 1950; children—Martin Fraser, Janet Mary, Nora Vivian. B.A., U. Toronto, 1946, Ph.D., 1952; M.Sc., U. Chgo., 1948. Lectr., asst. prof. McGill U., Montreal, Que., Can., 1950-56; asst. prof., asso. prof. Rockefeller Inst., N.Y.C., 1956-64; prof. physiology N.Y. Med. Coll, 1964-71, chmn. dept., 1964-69; prof., chmn. dept. physiology U. Western Ont., London, Can., 1971-76; Vis. fellow Australian Nat. U., Canberra, 1954-55. Co-editor: Exptl. Brain Research, 1980—; editorial bd.: Jour. Motor Studies, 1981—. Mem. Am. Physiol. Soc. (editorial bd. jour. 1962-65, editor sect. neurobiology 1969-71, editor vol. on motor control Handbook of Physiology Series 1977-80), Canadian Physiol. Soc. (asso. editor 1969-73), Soc. Neurosci., Assn. Research Nervous and Mental Diseases, Internat. Brain Research Orgn., Can. Assn. U. Profs., AAAS, Sigma Xi. Unitarian. Spl. research brain mechanisms in motor control. Home: 99 Euclid Ave London ON N6C 1C3 Canada

BROOKSHIER, THOMAS J., television sportscaster; b. Roswell, N.Mex., Dec. 16, 1931; s. Orville Brooks and Dola (Thornton) B.; m. Barbara J. Starrett, June 8, 1953; children: Linda K., Thomas J., Betsy J. B.S., U. Colo., 1953. Defensive back Phila. Eagles, NFL, 1953-61; sportscaster Sta. WCAU-TV, Phila., 1958-77; analyst NFL broadcasts CBS-TV Network, 1977—; sportscaster various events CBS Sports including CBS Sports Spectacular; with trucking firm, Denver, 1957-61; writer weekly sports column Denver Post and Rocky Mountain News, 1957-61; co-host This Is The NFL, NFL Films, Inc., 1970-78; also syndicated series Sports Illustrated, 1976-77; sec.-treas Center City Assos., Phila., 1978—; officer Center City Sports Club, 1978—. Active Union League of Phila., World Affairs Council, Nat. Wildlife Soc. Served to 1st lt. USAF, 1954-56. Named to NFL All-Star Team Sporting News, 1959; named All-Pro, 1959, 60, 61, U. Colo. Hall of Honor, 1973, Pa. Sports Hall of Fame, 1974, Pop Warner Hall of Fame, 1980; recipient Nat. Collegiate Athletic Assn. spl. recognition award, 1972; Bert Bell award, 1976; Sportscaster of Yr. award Nat. Sportscasters and Sportswriters, 1976; Main Line Jr. C. of C. award, 1965; humanitarian award Nat. Cystic Fibrosis Research Found., 1967; appreciation award Nat. Multiple Sclerosis Soc., 1975. Mem. NFL Alumni Assn. Republican. Clubs: Maxwell Football, Pop Warner Little Scholars, Fraternal Order Police. Home and: Home and Office: Gladwyne PA 19035

BROOKSTONE, ARNOLD F., paper packaging company executive; b. Chgo., Apr. 8, 1930; s. Reuben F. and Florence (Kabiller) B.; m. Adrienne Lee Haft, June 12, 1954; 1 dau., Susan Gail. B.S., U. Ill., 1950; postgrad., Northwestern U., 1950-51; J.D., DePaul U., 1952. Bar: Ill. 1953; C.P.A., Ill. Partner Golman, Brookstone & Co. (C.P.A.s), Chgo., 1952-65; with Stone Container Corp., Chgo., 1965—, v.p., controller, 1969-72, v.p., treas., 1972-73, v.p. fin., treas., 1973-77, sr. v.p. fin., treas., 1977-81, sr. v.p., chief fin. and planning officer, gen. mgr. paper bag div., 1982—; v.p., treas., dir. various subsidiaries Stone Container Corp.; v.p., dir. Container Corp., Charter Oaks, Containers, Stone Container Corp., Mo., others, Nat. Packaging Corp., Pomstone Corp., Redstone Corp., Stone Internat., Gulf Container, Tar-Heel Container Corp., S.C. Industries Corp.; v.p. Sierra Pacific Container; dir. Continental Glass Co., Forest Ins. Ltd., Chgo., Transeal Corp., Samson Paper Bag Co., Inc.; dir., chmn. fin. com. Donnelly Mirrors, Inc.; lectr. Fin. Execs. Inst., 1966, Nat. Audio-Visual Inst., 1955-56, Northwestern U. Grad. Sch. Mgmt., 1977. Bd. dirs. Young Men's Jewish Council, Chgo., 1954-58; pres., dir. Child, Inc., Chgo., 1958-65; pres. bd. dirs. Council Jewish Elderly, Chgo., 1979-81. Mem. Am. Inst. C.P.A.s, Ill. Soc. C.P.A.s, Fin. Execs. Inst., Am. Paper Inst. (fin. mgmt. com., steering com.), Tau Epsilon Phi. Jewish. Clubs: Standard, Green Acres Country. Home: 720 C Ballantrae Northbrook IL 60062 Office: 360 N Michigan Ave Chicago IL 60601

BROOM, VERNON HERRIN, state justice; b. Marion County, Miss., Jan. 16, 1924; s. John Calvin and Bertha (Herrin) B.; m. Clemetine Johnson; 2 children. Student, Pearl River Jr. Coll., Poplarville, Miss., 1941-43, Pratt Inst., Bklyn., 1943-44; B.B.A., U. Miss., 1948, LL.B., 1948. Bar: Miss. bar 1948. Practiced law, Columbia, Miss., 1948-70; dist. atty. 1st Jud. Dist. Miss., 1952-64; atty. Columbia Municipal Sch. Dist., 1967-69; judge Circuit Ct., 15th Jud. Dist., 1971-72; asso. justice Miss. Supreme Ct., 1972—. Served with inf. U.S. Army, World War II; ETO. Decorated Bronze Star, Purple Heart. Fellow Miss. Bar Found.; mem. Miss. State Bar Assn. (commr. 1967-68), Marion County C. of C. (pres. 1969-70), Am. Legion, DAV, VFW. Democrat. Baptist. Clubs: Masons, Shriners. Office: Supreme Ct Bldg Jackson MS 39205

BROOM, WILLIAM WESCOTT, newspaper executive; b. Dieterich, Ill., July 12, 1924; s. Albert M. and Wilhelmina (Martens) B.; m. Adeline Birdsall Smith, Mar. 30, 1957; children: William Wescott, Timothy Caleb. B.S. in Journalism, U. Ill., 1948. Mng. editor Momence (Ill.) Progress-Reporter, 1948-49; Washington corr. Ridder Publs. Inc., 1955-65; editor Long Beach (Calif.) Ind. and Press-Telegram, 1965-70; chief Washington bur. Ridder Publs., 1970-77; v.p. pub. affairs Phila. Inquirer & Daily News, 1977—; mem. adv. bd. Calif. State Coll., Long Beach, 1966-70. Bd. dirs. Washington Journalism Center, Old Phila. Devel. Corp., Phila. Hist. Preservation Corp., Phila. Orch. Council. Served with AUS, 1943-46. Clubs: Nat. Press (pres. 1975), Gridiron (Washington); Chevy Chase; Racquet (Phila.). Home: 113 Quaker Ln Villanova PA 19085 Office: 400 N Broad St Philadelphia PA

BROOME, GEORGE CALVIN, III, physicist; b. Hattiesburg, Miss., July 31, 1938; s. George Calvin, Jr. and Ruth (Hudson) B.; m. Margaret Virginia Weeks, May 30, 1962; 1 son, Matthew Calvin. B.S. in Physics, Miss. State U., 1960, M.S., 1962. Mem. staff Langley Research Center, NASA, Hampton, Va., 1962—, mgr. sci. payload studies, advanced space projects, 1967-69, lander sci. instruments mgr. Viking project, 1969-76, Viking project mgr., 1976-78, mgr. earth radiation budget expts. project, 1978—. Recipient Outstanding Leadership medal NASA, 1977. Methodist. Home: 501 Roaring Springs Circle Hampton VA 23663 Office: Langley Research Center MS 158 NASA Hampton VA 23665 *

BROOME, JOHN WILLIAM, architect; b. Middle Haddam, Conn., Mar. 7, 1923; s. Bertram Clinton and Helen Millington (Connery) B.; m. Althea Pratt, May 31, 1980; 1 dau., Sheryl Lynn Broome. B.Arch., U. Oreg., 1951. Archtl. work in, Oslo, Norway, 1951-56; planning technician Vancouver (Wash.) Housing Authority, 1956-58; archtl. designer Edmundson, Kochendoerfer & Kennedy, Portland, Oreg., 1956-58; partner firm Broome, Oringdulph, O'Toole & Rudolf & Assos., Portland, 1958—. Mem. Gov. Oreg. Com. for Livable Oreg., 1967-71; commr. Oreg. Coastal Conservation and Devel. Commn., 1971-75; pres. The Wetlands Conservancy; bd. regents Oreg. Poly. Inst. Served with USMC, 1942-46. Decorated Air medal with 2 gold stars. Fellow AIA (pres. Portland 1966, Oreg. council 1967); mem. Am. Assn. Hosp. Planning, Phi Kappa Psi. Democrat. Club: Portland City. Home: 18815 SW Boones Ferry Rd Tualatin OR 97062 Office: 733 NW 20th St Portland OR 97209

BROOME, OSCAR WHITFIELD, business educator, association executive; b. Monroe, N.C., Feb. 3, 1940; s. Oscar Whitfield and Irma (Hinson) B.; m. Julia Carol Renegar, June 14, 1964; children: Christine Irma, Michael Whitfield. A.B., Duke U., 1962; M.S., U. Ill., 1964, Ph.D., 1971. C.P.A., Va. Instr. U. Ill., Urbana, 1965-67; prof. U. Va., Charlottesville, 1967—; exec. dir. Inst. Chartered Fin. Analysts, Charlottesville, 1978—; faculty fellow Price Waterhouse & Co., N.Y.C., 1964; vis. prof. U. Tex., 1975; exams adminstr. Inst. Chartered Fin. Analysts, 1973-77; vis. prof. Duke U., Durham, N.C., 1977-78. Named Outstanding Educator Va. Soc. C.P.A.'s, 1979. Fellow Fin Analysts Fedn.; mem. Nat. Assn. Accts. (pres. chpt. 1974), Fin. Mgmt. Assn., Am. Inst. C.P.A.'s, C.P.A. Bd. Examiners, Phi Beta Kappa, Phi Kappa Phi, Beta Gamma Sigma. Office: Inst Chartered Fin Analysts 2 Boar's Head Pl Charlottesville VA 22901

BROOME, PAUL WALLACE, engineering research and development executive; b. Oakdale, Pa., Jan. 17, 1932; s. Paul Wallace and Mona Isabel (Lynch) B.; m. Joan Brown, Jan. 17, 1957; children: Ronald W., Virginia K., Paul W., Barbara G. B.S., Carnegie Inst. Tech., 1954, M.S., 1955, Ph.D. (Brown Instrument fellow), 1960. Sr. engr. Gen. Dynamics, San Diego, Calif., 1958-62; sr. staff scientist Pan Am. World Airways, Cocoa Beach, Fla., 1962-64; mgr. applied research Teledyne, Inc., Earth Sci. Div., Alexandria, Va., 1964-69; founder, chief exec. officer dir. ENSCO, Inc., Springfield, Va., 1969—; dir. Comtel Corp., Digital Switch Co. Mem. IEEE, Am. Mgmt. Assn., Sigma Xi; Mem. Eta Kappa Nu. Home: Box 163 Rt 3 Luray VA 22835 Office: 5400 Port Royal Rd Springfield VA 22151

BROOMFIELD, WILLIAM S., congressman; b. Birmingham, Mich., Apr. 28, 1922; s. S.C. and Fern B.; m. Jane Thompson, 1951; children: Susan, Nancy, Barbara. Student, Mich. State U. Mem. 85th to 98th congresses from 19th Dist. Mich.; Prin. del. to Gen. Assembly of UN, 1967-68; dist. del. NATO Parliamentarians Conf., 1960; mem. delegation to Can.-U.S. Interparliamentary Group; Congl. adviser to U.S. delegation to Geneva Disarmament Conf., 1970, 71, 73. Mem. Mich. Ho. of Reps., 1948-54, Mich. Senate, 1954-56. Mem. Am. Legion. Republican. Presbyn. Clubs: Mason, Odd Fellow, Optimist, Lion. Home: 5750 Whethersfield Ln Birmingham MI 48010 Office: 2306 Rayburn House Office Bldg Washington DC 20515 *

BROPHY, DONALD THOMAS, former chemical company executive; b. Louisville, Dec. 21, 1921; s. James Martin and Ernestine Marie (Beal) B.; m. Georgann Travnikar, Aug. 6, 1960; children: Anne Miriam, Donald Thomas, Mary Angela, Margaret Elizabeth, Katharine Jean, Georgeann Christina. B.S.Ch.E., Purdue U., 1942; M.B.A., Harvard U., 1947. With Rohm and Haas, 1947-82, mktg. mgr. chems. div., Phila., 1971-74, gen. mgr. chems. div., 1974-75, corp. bus. dir., 1975-77, group v.p., 1977-82, dir., 1972-82; ret., 1982. Acting chmn. bd. trustees Hahnemann Med. Coll. and Hosp., 1978-79, vice chmn. bd. trustees, 1979-82, chmn. bd. trustees, 1982—; bd. dirs. Diocesan Instl. Services, 1979-81, Nat. Cath. Edn. Assn., 1981—. Served to capt. USAAF, 1943-45. Named Disting. Engring. Alumnus Purdue U., 1979. Home: 10 Cornwall Circle Saint Davids PA 19087 Office: Hahnemann U Broad and Vine Sts Philadelphia PA 19102

BROPHY, JAMES DAVID, JR., humanities educator; b. Mt. Vernon, N.Y., Oct. 5, 1926; s. James David and Mildred (Stall) B.; m. Elizabeth Bergen, Mar. 26, 1951; children: Sheila, David, Katharine, Elizabeth, James Mark. Student, Mass. Inst. Tech., 1944-45; B.A., Amherst Coll., 1949; M.A., Columbia, 1950, Ph.D., 1965; postgrad., U. Dijon, 1950-51. Instr. English Iona Coll., New Rochelle, N.Y., 1951-58, asst. prof., 1958-64, asso. prof., 1964-68, prof., 1968—, chmn. dept., 1968-71, 80-82. Author: Edith Sitwell, 1968, W.H. Auden, 1970; Editor: The Achievement of Galileo, 1962, Modern Irish Literature, 1972, Contemporary Irish Writing, 1983. Served with USNR, 1945-46. Fulbright fellow, France, 1950-51; N.Y. State scholar in internat. studies, 1965; recipient Pro Operis medal Iona Coll., 1971, Bene Merenti award, 1981; Nat. Endowment for Humanities grantee, 1973; Wilton Park asso., 1979. Mem. MLA, English Inst. Home: 35 Crystal St Harrison NY 10528 also Ocean View Dr Southampton NY 11968 Office: Iona Coll New Rochelle NY 10801

BROPHY, JAMES EDWARD, dental association executive; b. St. Louis, Feb. 9, 1921; s. James L. and Emma (Rathmann) B.; m. Delphine E. Wolfe, Oct. 11, 1947. B.A., Washington U., St. Louis, 1946. Exec. sec. Greater St. Louis Dental Soc., 1948-61; exec. dir. Am. Assn. Orthodontists, St. Louis, 1961—, dir. communications, 1968—, editor newsletter, 1964—; cons. to ADA and other health orgns., 1962—; producer dental edn. series Sta. KETC-TV, St. Louis, 1952-55; Mem. bd. control Am. Assn. Orthodontists Found., 1968—; bd. dirs. Mo. Dental Service Corp., 1959-61; trustee Am. Fund for Dental Health, 1979—. Contbr. articles to dental assn. and bus. jours. Recipient Disting. Service scroll Am. Assn. Orthodontists, 1971. Hon. fellow Am. Coll. Dentists; Mem. ADA (hon.); mem. Am. Soc. Assn. Execs., Am. Assn. Dental Editors, Profl. Conv. Mgmt. Assn., Assn. of Dental Exec. Secs. (pres. 1958-59), Southwestern Soc. Orthodontists (hon. mem.), St. Louis Soc. Assn. Execs. (pres. 1968-69, chmn. various coms.). Clubs: Rotary, K.C., Media (St. Louis). Home: 204 Park Rd Webster Groves MO 63119 Office: 460 N Lindbergh Blvd Saint Louis MO 63141

BROPHY, JAMES JOHN, physicist, university official; b. Chgo., June 6, 1926; s. James J. and Ella Helen (Nerad) B.; m. Muriel Ann Johnson, Aug. 26, 1949; children: James J., John R., Thomas C. B.S. in Elec. Engring, Ill. Inst. Tech., 1947, M.S. in Physics, 1949, Ph.D., 1951. Research physicist Armour Research Found. of Ill. Inst. Tech., 1951-53, supr. solid state physics, 1953-56, asst. dir. physics div., 1956-61, dir. tech. devel. of Found., 1961-63, v.p. for tech. devel., 1963-66; acad. v.p. Ill. Inst. Tech., 1967-76; sr. v.p. Inst. Gas Tech., Chgo., 1976-80; v.p. research U. Utah, Salt Lake City, 1980—; trustee Underwriters Labs., Inc. Author: Semiconductor Devices, 1965, Basic Electronics for Scientists, 1966, 4th edit., 1983; co-author: Electronic Processes in Materials, 1963; Co-editor: Organic Semi-conductors; Contbr. articles to profl. jours. Fellow Am. Phys. Soc.; mem. AAAS, Western Soc. Engrs., Sigma Xi. Patentee on semiconductors, magnetic devices. Home: 2592 Elizabeth St Salt Lake City UT 84106 Office: 304 Park U Utah Salt Lake City UT 84112 *I have tried to guard against the presumptuous judgments of the uninformed.*

BROPHY, JERE HALL, manufacturing company executive; b. Schenectady, Mar. 11, 1934; s. Gerald Robert and Helen Dorothy (Hall) B.; m. Joyce Elaine Wright, Aug. 18, 1956; children: Jennifer, Carolyn, Jere. B.S. in Chem. Engring, U. Mich., 1956, 1956, M.S., 1957, Ph.D., 1958. Asst. prof. Mass. Inst. Tech., 1958-63; sect. supr. nickel alloys sect. Paul D. Merica Research Lab., Inco, Inc., Suffern, N.Y., 1963-67, research mgr. non-ferrous group, 1967-72, asst. mgr., 1972-73, mgr., 1973-77, dir. research and devel. and dir., 1978-80; dir. advanced tech. initiation INCO Ltd., N.Y.C., 1980-82; v.p., dir. Materials and Mfg. Tech. Ctr. TRW Inc., Cleve., 1982—. Author: (with J. Wolff) Thermodynamics of Structure; Contbr. tech. articles to profl. jours. Fellow Am. Soc. Metals; mem. Am. Inst. Mining and Metall. Engrs. (dir. IMD div. 1973-76), Am. Mgmt. Assn. (research and devel. council 1975—). Episcopalian. Club: Edgewater Yacht. Home: 31905 Jackson Rd Chagrin Falls OH 44022 Office: TRW Inc 23555 Euclid Ave Cleveland OH 44117

BROPHY, JEREMIAH JOSEPH, stockbroker, former army officer; b. N.Y.C., Mar. 19, 1930; s. John Joseph and Mary Margaret (Moran) B.; m. Jane Guthrie, June 4, 1955; children: John, Sandy, Greg, Elizabeth, Diane, Steven. Student, Manhattan Coll., 1947-48; B.S., U.S. Mil. Acad., 1953; postgrad., Monmouth Coll., 1981. Commd. 2d lt. U.S. Army, 1953; advanced through grades to brig. gen., 1976, advisor 12th Vietnamese Inf. Regiment, comdr. 1st Battalion, 327th Infantry, 101st Airborne div., Vietnam, comdr. U.S. garrison, Aschaffenburg, Germany, comdr. 3d Brigade, 3d Infantry div., 1973-75, comdr. U.S. garrison, Baumholder, Germany, asst. comdr. 8th Infantry div., 1976-78, dep. comdr. Combined Arms Combat and Tng. Devels. Agy., 1978-80; now stockbroker Merrill, Lynch, Pierce, Fenner & Smith, Nashville, Tenn. Decorated Legion of Merit with oak leaf cluster, Bronze Star with oak leaf cluster, Purple Heart, Silver Star. Mem. Assn. U.S. Army, Assn. Grad. U.S. Mil. Acad., West Point Soc. N.Y. Roman Catholic. Home: 302 Sheffield Pl Franklin TN 37064 Office: Merrill Lynch Pierce Fenner & Smith 4th Ave and Church St Nashville TN 37244

BROPHY, JOSEPH THOMAS, insurance company executive; b. N.Y.C., Oct. 25, 1933; s. Joseph R. and Mary (Mitchell) B.; m. Carole A. Johnson, June 8, 1957; children—Thomas J., David W., Patricia J., Maureen A., Kathleen M. B.S. cum laude, Fordham U., 1957. Mathematician Vitro Labs., West Orange, N.J., 1957; dir. mgmt. info. systems Prudential Ins. Co., Newark, 1957-67; v.p. Huggins & Co. (cons. actuaries and mgmt. cons.), Phila., 1967-68; v.p., chief actuary Bankers Nat. Life Ins. Co., 1968-72; sr. v.p. Travelers Corp., Hartford, Conn., 1972—; dir. Engineered Bus. Systems, Security Settlement Corp.; cons. in field, 1967—. Pres. St. Patrick's Pipe Band, Inc. Served with USMCR, 1949-50; Served with AUS, 1952-54. Fellow Soc. Actuaries; mem. Am. Acad. Actuaries, Hartford Actuaries Club, N.Y. Actuaries Club. Club: Hartford. Home: 155 Orchard Rd West Hartford CT 06117 Office: 1 Tower Sq Hartford CT 06115

BROPHY, THEODORE F., telephone company executive; b. N.Y.C., Apr. 4, 1923; s. Frederick H. and Muriel W. (Osborne) B.; m. Sallie M. Showalter, Sept. 16, 1950; children: Stephen F., Anne R. A.B., Yale U., 1944; LL.B., Harvard U., 1949. Bar: N.Y. Assoc. Root, Ballantine, Harlan, Bushby & Palmer, N.Y.C., 1949-55; gen. counsel Lummus Co., 1955-58; counsel Gen. Telephone Co., N.Y.C., 1958-59; v.p., gen. counsel Gen. Telephone & Electronics Corp., 1959-68, exec. v.p., gen. counsel, 1968-72, pres., 1972-76, chmn. bd., chief exec. officer, 1976—, also dir. corp. and various subs.'s; dir. Irving Bank Corp., Irving Trust Co., Reader's Digest Assn., Inc., Procter & Gamble Co.; chmn. listed co. adv. com. N.Y. Stock Exchange. Mem. adv. council Nat. Urban Coalition; mem. Greenwich Hosp. Assn., Smith Coll. Pres.'s Com.; bd. dirs. United Way Tri-State; trustee GTE Found., Ind. Coll. Funds Am.; mem. Brookings council Brookings Instn. Served to lt. (s.g.) USNR, 1944-46. Mem. Am. Bar Assn., Fed. Communications Bar Assn., Conf. Bd., Bus. Council, Bus. Roundtable (co-chmn.; chmn. taxation task force).

BRORBY, MELVIN, advertising agency executive; b. Decorah, Iowa, Sept. 20, 1894; s. Martin J. and Louise (Wimmer) B.; m. Rowena Williams, Jan. 1, 1927; children: Harry, Virginia (Mrs. Wesley Horner). Student, Oxford U., 1919; A.B., U. Wis., 1920, U. Strasbourg, 1920, The Sorbonne, 1920-21, Free Sch. Polit. Scis., Paris, 1921-22. Sr. vice pres. Needham, Harper & Steers, Inc. (formerly known as Needham, Louis & Brorby, Inc.), Chgo., 1925—. Gov., life mem. Art Inst. Chgo.; mem. citizens coms. U. Chgo., U. Ill.; mem. Orchestral Assn.; bd. dirs. Nat. Outdoor Advt. Bur.; Sponsor Nat. Soc. Crippled Children and Adults; mem. Stevenson Com.; trustee, v.p. Johnson Found. Mem. Soc. of Contemporary Am. Art (past pres.), Inst. Internat. Edn. (trustee; mem. midwest adv. com.), Am. Assn. Advt. Agys. (past chmn.), Art Club Chgo., Oxford Soc. (past br. sec.), Chgo. Council Fgn. Relations (dir. past pres.), N.Y. Council Fgn. Relations, Phi Beta Kappa, Phi Gamma Delta, Artus. Clubs: Tavern, Arts, Lake Shore (past pres.), Mid-America (Chgo.); Century (N.Y.C.). Home: 2775 Lake Shore Ave Holland MI 49423 Office: 303 E Wacker Dr Suite 1500 Chicago IL 60601

BROSE, RAYMOND EDWIN, artist; b. Wausau, Wis., Jan. 10, 1921; s. Rudolph Albert and Minnie (Schultz) B.; m. Robin Marilyn Jane Mattocks, July 22, 1954; children—Bonnie, Douglas. Student, Antioch Coll., 1939-42, Escuela de Pintura Y Escultura and Politecnico Instituto, Mexico City, 1949; B.A., U. Hawaii, 1951; M.A., Stanford U., 1952, Ed.D., 1961. Mem. faculty Stanford U., 1953-62, San Jose State U., 1962—, asso. prof. art, 1965-69, prof., 1969—; mem. faculty Universidad Autonoma de Guadalajara, Mexico, 1955. Condr. painting workshops.; One-man shows, Stanford U. Art Gallery, 1952, Montalvo Art Gallery, Saratoga, Calif., 1957, Nev. Art Gallery, Reno, 1961, Desert-S.W. Art Gallery, Palm Desert, Calif., 1963, 64, Nat. Mus. Fine Arts, Caracas, Venezuela, 1964, Monterey Peninsula (Calif.) Mus. Art, 1967, group shows, Honolulu Acad. Arts, 1950, 51, Library of Congress, Washington, Albright Art Mus., Buffalo, Inst. History and Art, Albany, N.Y., 1951, Birmingham (Ala.) Mus. Art, 1954, 56, 62, 64, 65, San Francisco Mus. Art., 1955, Oakland (Calif.) Mus. Art, 1954, 64, 65, Ravinia Art Exhbn., Highland Park, Ill., 1961, Crocker Art Mus., Sacramento, 1961, 64, Palace of Legion of Honor, San Francisco, 1962, 63, Salt Lake City Art Center, 1963, Fukuoka (Japan) Mus., 1964, Frye Mus., Seattle, 1967, Miss. State Coliseum, Jackson, 1968. Served with AUS, 1942-46. Recipient numerous art awards, including Honolulu Acad. Arts, 1950, 51, Library of Congress, 1951, Birmingham Mus. Art, 1956, 62, Calif. State Fair and Expn., Sacramento, 1956, Nat. Exhbn. Small Paintings, Albuquerque, 1962, De Saisset Art Gallery, U. Santa Clara, 1963, 71, Palo Alto (Calif.) Cultural Center, 1973, mural in, San Jose, Calif., 1978. Mem. AAUP, Nat. Hist. Soc., East Bay Artists Assn., Watercolor Soc. Ala., Calif. Hist. Soc., Nat. Wildlife Fedn., Oceanic Soc., Oreg. Archaeol. Soc., Phi Kappa Phi. Home: 850 Richardson Ct Palo Alto CA 94303

BROSHAR, ROBERT CLARE, architect; b. Waterloo, Iowa, May 20, 1931; s. Clare McDanel and Stella Mae (Scott) B.; m. Joyce Elaine Lukes, June 27, 1953; children: Scott, Michael, Matthew, Patrick, Elizabeth. B.Arch., Iowa State U., 1954. Partner Henry & Broshar, 1960-62, Thorson, Brom, Broshar, Snyder (architects), Waterloo, 1963—. Bd. dirs., pres. Blackhawk County YMCA, 1972-75; mem. Gov.'s Com. Employment of Handicapped, 1975-79. Served to 1st lt. AUS, 1954-56. Recipient Disting. Service award Iowa Easter Seal Soc., 1976, Leon Chatelain award Nat. Easter Seal Soc., 1983; recipient Iowa State U. Alumni Achievement award, 1982; named Iowa State U. Parent of Yr., 1980. Fellow AIA (nat. dir. 1975-78, nat. v.p. 1979, 81, chpt. pres. 1972, nat. pres. 1982-83), Royal Architects Inst. Can. (hon.); mem. Delta Upsilon (dir. householding corp. 1970—), Tau Beta Pi, Tau Sigma Delta, Phi Kappa Phi, Knights of St. Patrick. Republican. Presbyterian (trustee). Clubs: Elks, Sunnyside Country. Home: 3131 W 4th St Waterloo IA 50701 Office: 900 Waterloo Bldg Waterloo IA 50701

BROSILOW, COLEMAN BERNARD, educator; b. Phila., Nov. 14, 1934; s. Samuel and Ethel (Stein) B.; m. Rosalie Ziegleman, Feb. 18, 1962; children—Rachelle, Benjamin. B.S., Drexel U., 1957; M.Ch.E., Poly. Inst. N.Y., 1959, Ph.D., 1962. Systems engr. Am. Cyanamid Co., Process Analysis Group, Wayne, N.J., 1962-63; asst. prof. chem. engring. Case Western Res. U., Cleve., 1963-67, asso. prof., 1967-73, prof. chem. engring., 1973—, chmn. dept. chem. engring., 1980—; vis. prof. chem. engring. The Technion, Haifa, Israel, 1971-72; cons. in field. Contbr. articles to profl. jours.; editorial bd.: Am. Inst. Chem. Engrs. Jour, 1980—. Founding mem., pres. bd. trustees Solomon Schecter Day Sch. of Cleve., 1980—. Mem. Am. Inst. Chem. Engrs., Am. Soc. Engring. Edn., Sigma Xi, Tau Beta Pi, Phi Lambda Upsilon. Jewish. Patentee in field. Home: 3115 Berkshire Rd Cleveland Heights OH 44118 Office: Chem Engring Dept A W Smith Bldg Case Western Res Univ Cleveland OH 44106

BROSIN, HENRY WALTER, educator, psychiatrist; b. Blackwood, Va., July 6, 1904; s. Martin and Marie (Danowski) B.; m. Ruth Hatfield, 1949; 1 son, Lloyd Wisdom. A.B., U. Wis., 1927, M.D., 1933; postgrad. (Commonwealth Fund fellow in Psychiatry), U. Colo., 1934-37, Inst. Psychoanalysis, Chgo., 1937-40. Diplomate: Am. Bd. Psychiatry and Neurology (pres. 1961). Rotating intern Cin. Gen. Hosp., 1933-34; fellow Colo. Psychopathic Hosp., Denver, 1934-37; staff div. psychiatry U. Chgo., 1937-41, prof., head div., 1946-50; dir. Western Psychiat. Inst. and Clinics, 1951-69; psychiat. cons. Office Surgeon Gen., Washington, 1944-66; prof., chmn. dept. psychiatry U. Pitts., 1951-69; prof. psychiatry U. Ariz. Coll. Medicine, Tucson, 1970—; Mem. Social Sci. Research Council; fellow Center Advanced Study Behavioral Scis., 1956-66; mem. div. med. scis. Nat. Acad. Sci., NRC, 1958-68, mem. naval med. research com. Asso. edit.: Am. Jour. Psychiatry, 1965-73; Contbr. articles to profl. jours. Served as col. M.C. AUS, 1941-46. Decorated Legion of Merit; recipient Distinguished Service award U. Chgo. Sch. Medicine, 1952; Med. Alumni citation U. Wis., 1962; Col. Wm. S. Porter award Assn. Mil. Surgeons U.S., 1967. Fellow Am. Acad. Arts and Scis., Rorschach Inst., A.C.P., Am. Psychiat. Assn. (councillor 1948-51, pres. 1967-68); mem. AMA, Phila. Psychoanalytic Assn., v.p. (1960-61, Chgo. Psychoanalytic Assns.), AAAS, Am. Psychol. Assn., Am. Coll. Psychiatrists (pres. 1970-71, Bowis award 1975), Am. Soc. Research Psychosomatic Problems (councillor), Assn. Research Nervous and Mental Diseases, Pitts. Neuropsychiat. Soc., Pitts. Psychoanalytic Inst. and Soc., Allegheny County Med. Soc., Group Advancement Psychiatry (pres. 1961-63), Nat. Assn. Mental Health, Soc. Biol. Psychiatry, Royal Psychol. Assn. (hon), Sigma Xi, Alpha Omega Alpha. Club: Cosmos. Home: 240 Sierra Vista Dr Tucson AZ 85719

BROSKI, GERALD STEPHEN, insurance company executive; b. Grand Rapids, Mich., Dec. 23, 1933; s. Floyd Leonard and Margaret Bell (Tolhurst) B.; m. Suzanne Marie Maher, May 3, 1958; children: Michael, Lisa Ann, Kurt. B.A., Mich. State U., 1955. C.P.A., Mich. With Seidman & Seidman (C.P.A.s), Grand Rapids, 1957-63; with Rockford Products Corp., Ill., 1963—, treas., 1967-84, pres., 1980-84; v.p., gen. mgr. Williams-Manny Ins., 1984—; dir. First Nat. Bank & Trust Co. Bd. dirs. St. Anthony Hosp., 1967—, v.p., 1973—; bd. dirs. No. Ill. Blood Bank, 1970, pres., 1973-75; bd. dirs., treas. Rockford Credit Bur., 1970-73; bd. dirs. Vis. Nurses Assn., 1973—, pres., 1975-77; bd. dirs. Community Hosp. Council, 1975, Rockford Boys' Club Assn., 1977, Rockford Med. Edn. Found., 1976; v.p. Rockford Med. Edn. Found., 1977; trustee Rockford Coll., 1980—. Served to 1st lt. U.S. Army, 1955-57. Mem. Am. Inst. C.P.A.s, Nat. Assn. Accountants, Rockford Area C. of C. (v.p., treas., dir.). Clubs: Forest Hills Country (Rockford) (dir. 1974, treas. 1975. Home: 1721 Parkview Rockford IL 61107 Office: 1111 S Alpine Rd Rockford IL 61108

BROSS, IRWIN DUDLEY JACKSON, biostatistician; b. Halloway, Ohio, Nov. 13, 1921; s. Samuel and Mina (Jackson) B.; m. Rida Singer, Aug. 6, 1949; children: Dean, Valerie, Neal. B.A. in Math, UCLA, 1942; M.A. in Exptl. Stats, N.C. State U., 1948, Ph.D., 1949. Research asso. dept. biostatistics Johns Hopkins U., 1949-52; asst. prof. public health and preventive medicine Cornell U., 1952-59; head research, design and analysis Sloan Kettering Inst., 1952-59; dir. biostatistics Roswell Park Meml. Inst., Buffalo, N.Y., 1959-83; pres. Biomed. Metatech., Inc., 1983—; research prof. biostatistics State U. N.Y. at Buffalo, 1961—; asso. dept. epidemiology Johns Hopkins U., 1971—. Author: Design For Decision, 1953, Scientific Strategies in Human Affairs: To Tell The Truth, 1975, Scientific Strategies To Save Your Life, 1981; contbr. numerous articles in field to profl. jours. Served with U.S. Army, 1941-45. Mem. AAAS, Am. Statis. Assn., Biometric Soc., Soc. Epidemiol. Research. Home: 109 Maynard Dr Eggertsville NY 14226 Office: 666 Elm St Buffalo NY 14263

BROSS, JOHN ADAMS, government official; b. Chgo., Jan. 17, 1911; s. Mason and Isabel Foster (Adams) B.; m. Priscilla Prince, June 1936; children: Wendy, John, Justine; m. Joanne Bass, Oct. 28, 1947; 1 son, Peter F. A.B., Harvard U., 1933, LL.B., 1936. Bar: N.Y. 1938. Practiced law, N.Y.C., 1936-42, 46-49; asso. firm Parker & Duryee, N.Y.C., mem. firm, 1941—; asst. gen. counsel U.S. High Commr. to Germany, 1949-51; U.S. govt. cons. fgn. affairs, 1951-57, 60—; adviser, coordinator Am. embassy, Bonn, Germany, 1957-59, dep. to dir. of central intelligence for programs evaluation, 1963-71; Staff mem. task force on nat. mil. establishment Hoover Commn., 1948. Chmn. bd. dirs. Central Atlantic Environment Center, 1971—; trustee Conservation Found. Served from 2d lt. to col. USAAF, 1942-46. Decorated Legion of Merit, Bronze Star medal; Order Brit. Empire; King Christian X Medal of Liberty. Mem. Assn. Bar City N.Y. (chmn. com. state legislation 1946-49), Council on Fgn. Relations N.Y. Clubs: Metropolitan, Harvard (N.Y.C.); Alibi. Home: 4501 Crest Ln McLean VA 22101

BROSS, STEWARD RICHARD, JR., lawyer; b. Lancaster, Pa., Oct. 25, 1922; s. Steward Richard and Katherine Mauk (Hoover) B.; m. Isabel Florence Kenney, May 10, 1943; 1 dau., Donna Isabel Bross Cunneff. Student, McGill U., Montreal, Can., 1940-42; LL.B., Columbia U., 1948. Bar: N.Y. bar 1948. Since practiced in, N.Y.C.; partner firm Cravath, Swaine & Moore, 1958—; adv. com. fgn. direct investment program Office of Sec. Dept. Commerce, 1969; adv. com. regulations Office Fgn. Direct Investment, 1968-70. Served as officer Canadian Navy, 1942-45. Mem. Am., N.Y. State, Internat. bar assns., Assn. Bar City N.Y., Am. Soc. Internat. Law, Union Internat. des Avocats, Pilgrims U.S., Econ. Club N.Y. Clubs: Union, Wall Street, Board Room, Down Town Assn. (N.Y.C.). Home: 215 E 68th St New York NY 10021 also Ashgrove Litchfield Rd Norfolk CT 06058 Office: 1 Chase Manhattan Plaza New York NY 10005

BROSSEAU, IRMA FINN, association executive; b. Boston, Sept. 4, 1930; d. Harry and Alfreda (Zimmerman) Miller; m. George Brosseau, Jan. 14, 1978; children from previous marriage—Hester, Jonathan, Sarah. B.S., Simmons Coll., 1952. Cert. assn. exec. Asst. to prodn. mgr. Houghton Mifflin Pub. Co., Boston, 1952-56; desk editor, women's editor Quincy (Mass.) Patriot Ledger, 1956-58; desk editor, reporter, feature writer, women's editor Anchorage (Alaska) Times, 1958-60, 66-71; desk editor Anchorage News, 1965-66; progam dir. Nat. Fedn. Bus. and Profl. Women's Clubs, Inc., Washington, 1972-77, exec. dir., 1977—; mem. nat. steering com. Nat. Women's Agenda; mem. rev. panel Women's Ednl. Equity Act grants.; workshop leader on women's issues. Public relations dir. Nat. Motorcycle Commuter Assn., 1981—, bd. dirs., 1981-82; bd. advisers Women's Econ. Devel. Council, Ten Outstanding Young Women of Am. Mem. Am. Soc. Assn. Execs., Greater Washington Soc. Assn. Execs. (long-range planning com.), Potomac Bus. and Profl. Women's Club, AAUW. Office: 2012 Massachusetts Ave NW Washington DC 20036

BROSSMAN, WALTER ROBERT, development consultant; b. N.Y.C., Nov. 24, 1920; s. Walter Werner and Mabel Adams (Kelly) B.; m. Susan J. Bertrand, Sept. 23, 1951 (dec. 1958); children: Bruce W., Nancy J.; m. Virginia Kerlin, Nov. 22, 1959; children—Robert Kerlin, Ann Baldwin, Beth Allison. A.B., Allegheny Coll., 1942. Reporter, sports editor Tribune Newspapers, Meadville, Pa., 1942-44; dir. publicity Allegheny Coll., 1946-47; dir. pub. information Cornell U., 1947-56; v.p. Colo. Coll., 1956-69, coordinator devel. activities, 1973, cons., 1969-74, v.p., gen. sec., 1974-82; Cons. to univs. and colls., others. Served in USNR, 1944-46. Mem. Sigma Delta Chi, Phi Sigma Iota, Phi Delta Theta. Mem. United Ch. of Christ (dir. Colo. conf. 1967-70). Club: Broadmoor Golf. Home: 1508 Wood Ave Colorado Springs CO 80907

BROTHERS, JOHN ALFRED, chemical company executive; b. Huntington, W.Va., Nov. 10, 1940; s. John Luther and Genevieve (Monti) B.; m. Paula Sprague Benson, June 21, 1975. B.S., Va. Poly. Inst., 1962, M.S., 1965, Ph.D., 1966; postgrad advanced mgmt. program, Harvard U., 1981. With Internat. Nickel Co., 1962-64; with

Ashland Oil, Inc., Ky., 1966-73, v.p. research and engring., 1971-73; v.p. petrochem. mfg. Ashland Chem. Co., 1974-75, adminstrv. v.p., 1976-80, group v.p., 1980-82, sr. v.p., 1982—; dir. Melamine Chems. Inc., Allemania Chem. Co., Drew Chem. Co., Ashland Export, Inc.; adj. prof. engring. Ohio State U., 1978—, pres. bus. adv. council, 1981—. Active local Boy Scouts Am., Jr. Achievement.; bd. dirs. Ohio Soc. to Prevent Blindness. NSF fellow, 1965-66; named Outstanding Young Man U.S. C. of C., 1972. Mem. Am. Petroleum Inst., Mfg. Chemists Assn., Sigma Xi, Tau Beta Pi, Phi Kappa Phi. Republican. Clubs: Scioto Country, Rolling Rock, Muirfield Country, Columbus Athletic, Mill Reef, Scioto Valley (treas.). Home: 3401 Watergate Ct Columbus OH 43221 Office: PO Box 2219 Columbus OH 43216

BROTHERS, JOYCE DIANE (MRS. MILTON BROTHERS), psychologist; b. N.Y.C.; d. Morris K. and Estelle (Rapoport) Bauer; m. Milton Brothers, July 4, 1949; 1 dau., Lisa Robin. B.S., Cornell U., 1947; M.A., Columbia, 1950, Ph.D., 1953; L.H.D. (hon.), Franklin Pierce Coll. Asst. psychology Columbia, 1948-52; instr. Hunter Coll., 1948-52; research project on leadership UNESCO, 1949. Co-host: TV program Sports Showcase, 1956; appearances: Dr. Joyce Brothers, 1958-63, Consult Dr. Brothers, 1960-66, Ask Dr. Brothers, 1965-75; hostess: TV syndication Living Easy with Dr. Joyce Brothers, 1972-75; columnist, N. Am. Newspaper Alliance, 1961-71, Bell-McClure Syndicate, 1963-71, King Features Syndicate, 1972—, Good Housekeeping mag., 1962—; appearances radio sta., WNBC, 1966-70; radio program Emphasis, 1966-75, Monitor, 1967-75, WMCA, 1970-73, ABC Reports, 1966-67, NBC Radio Network Newsline, 1975—; news analyst, Metro Media-TV, 1975-76; news corr., TVN, Inc., KABC-TV, 1977—, WABC-TV, 1980-82, WLS-TV, NIWS Syndicated News Service, 1982—; spl. feature writer Hearst papers, U.P.I.; Author: How to Get Whatever You Want Out of Life, What Every Woman Should Know About Men, 1982. Co-chmn. sports com. Lighthouse for Blind; door-to-door chmn. Fedn. Jewish Philanthropies, N.Y.C.; mem. fund raising com. Olympic Fund; mem. People-to-People Program. Recipient Mennen Baby Found. award, 1959, Newhouse Newspaper award, 1959, Am. Acad. Achievement award, Am. Parkinson Disease Assn. award, 1971, Sigma Delta Chi Deadline award, 1971, Pres.'s Cabinet award U. Detroit, 1975, Woman of Achievement award Women's City Club Cleve., 1981, award Calif. Home Econs. Assn., 1981, Distributive Edn. Clubs Am., 1981. Mem. Sigma Xi. 64,000 winner TV program $64,000 Question, 1956; winner $70,000 TV program $64,000 Challenge, 1957. Home: 1530 Palisade Ave Fort Lee NJ 07024 Office: NBC 30 Rockefeller Plaza New York NY 10020

BROTHERTON, DAVID LEGGE, film editor; b. Los Angeles, Feb. 29, 1924; s. Howard Prescott and Dorothea Caroline (McEvoy) B.; m. Elyane Louise Vuillermoz, May 3, 1969; children—Candace Charlotte, Melissa Ann. Asst. film editor 20th Century Fox, 1942-52, film editor, 1952-62, United Artists, Metro Goldwyn Mayer, Paramount in, Europe, 1963-68, Paramount, 1969, A.B.C. Pictures Corp., Columbia Picture Corp., 1970, A.B.C. Picture Corp. in, Europe, 1971, Paramount, M.G.M., 20th Century Fox, Am. Film Theatre, United Artists Corp., 1972-77; film editor and supervising film editor. Co-editor: The Living Swamp, 1955, Three Brave Men, 1957, Peyton Place, 1957, The Diary of Anne Frank, 1959, Return to Peyton Place, State Fair, 1962, Empire; TV series, 1963, The Sandpiper, 1965, On a Clear Day You Can See Forever, 1970; film editor: Cabaret, 1972 (Acad. award Motion Picture Arts and Scis. Acad. and award Am. Cinema Editors 1972), Save the Tiger, 1973, Westworld, 1973, Bank Shot, 1974, The Man in the Glass Booth, 1975, Silver Streak, 1976, Coma, 1978, The Great Train Robbery, 1979, Winter Kills, 1979, Big Red One, 1979, Caddy Shack, 1980, The Formula, 1980, Cannery Row, 1981. Mem. Acad. Motion Picture Arts and Scis., Am. Cinema Editors. *

BROTJE, ROBERT JOHN, JR., manufacturing executive; b. Toledo, Apr. 18, 1920; s. Robert John and Martha (Wolf) B.; m. Eileen Marie Wernert, June 6, 1942; children: Susan Lizabeth, Bradford John, Julie Louise. B.B.A., U. Toledo, 1942. C.P.A., Ohio. With Konopak & Dalton (C.P.A.s), Toledo, 1946-57; tax mgr. Champion Spark Plug Co., Toledo, 1957-64, controller, 1964-71, v.p., treas., 1971-78, exec. v.p., dir. fin., 1978-82, exec. v.p., chief fin. officer, 1982-84, exec. v.p., chief operating officer, 1984—, chmn. exec. com., dir., 1971—. Served to lt. (j.g.) USNR, 1943-45. Mem. Am. Inst. C.P.A.s, Ohio Soc. C.P.A.s, Fin. Execs. Inst. Home: 4246 Tejon Rd Toledo OH 43623 Office: 900 Upton Ave Toledo OH 43661

BROTMAN, STANLEY SEYMOUR, judge; b. Vineland, N.J., July 27, 1924; s. Herman Nathaniel and Fanny (Melletz) B.; m. Suzanne M. Simon, Sept. 9, 1951; children: Richard A., Alison B. B.A., Yale U., 1947; LL.B., Harvard U., 1950. Bar: N.J. Sole practitioner, Vineland, 1952-57; partner firm Shapiro, Brotman, Eisenstat & Capizola, Vineland, 1957-75; judge U.S. Dist. Ct. for Dist. of N.J., Camden, 1975—; mem. N.J. Bd. Bar Examiners, 1970-74. Chmn. editorial bd.: N.J. State Bar Jour, 1969-74; contbr. articles to profl. jours. Trustee Newcomb Hosp., Vineland, 1953-68. Served with U.S. Army, 1943-45, 51-52. Winner Ames competition Harvard Law Sch., 1950. Fellow Am. Bar Found.; mem. ABA (ho. of dels. 1975-80, 83—), N.J. State Bar Assn. (pres. 1974-75), Cumberland County Bar Assn. (pres. 1969-70), Harvard Law Sch. Assn. N.J. (pres. 1974-75), Am. Arbitration Assn. (nat. panel), Yale Alumni Assn., Am. Legion, Jewish War Vets. Jewish. Clubs: Yale (Phila.); Harvard of N.J., B'nai B'rith, Masons, Shriners. Home: 2432 Buttonwood Dr Vineland NJ 08360 Office: 230 US Courthouse 4th and Market Sts Camden NJ 08101

BROTT, ALEXANDER, educator, musician; b. Montreal, Que., Can., Mar. 14, 1915; s. Sam and Annie (Fixman) B.; m. Lotta Goetzel, Mar. 27, 1943; children—Boris, Denis. Laureat, Quebec Acad. Music, 1932; Licentiate, McGill U., 1935, Mus.D. (hon.), 1980; postgrad. diploma, Juilliard Sch., 1939; Mus.D. (hon.), U. Chgo., 1960, LL.D., Queen's U., 1973. Prof. music McGill U., 1939—, pvt. tchr. violin, composition, conducting, 1939—; founder, 1939; since permanent condr. McGill Chamber Orch.; mus. dir. Kingston Symphony Orch., 1963-81, mus. dir. and condr. emeritus, 1981—. Concertmaster, asst. condr., Montreal Symphony, 1945-63; mus. dir., Montreal Pops Orch., 1966; condr. TV and radio, CBC, 1948—; composer-condr., BBC, London, 1956, European tour, summers 1948—; Composer: commd. Spheres in Orbit, Montreal Symphony Orch., Three Astral Visions, Lapitsky Found., Royal Tribute, CBC, also numerous symphonic works, chamber works, works for solo instruments. Decorated medal Order of Can.; recipient Elizabeth Sprague Cooledge award composition, 1938, Loeb Meml. award performance, Lord Strathcona award, 1939, CAPAC Composition award, 1943, Olympic medal for composition, 1948, Gold medal Arnold Bax Soc., 1961, 1st prize Pan Am. Condrs. Competition, 1957; Can. Music Council medal, 1976; Queen's Anniversary Silver Jubilee medal, 1978; others. Fellow Royal Soc. Arts; hon. life mem. Musicians Guild; mem. Internat. Soc. Contemporary Music. Home: 5459 Earncliffe St Montreal PQ H3X 2P8 Canada

BROTT, DENIS, cellist; b. Montreal, Dec. 9, 1950; m. Julie Ann Stephanie Shoshana Fraser. Grad., Conservatory P.Q., Montreal; Artist Diploma, Ind. U.; student, Piatigorsky's Master Class, Sch. Performing Arts, U. So. Calif. Now prof. cello N.C. Sch. Arts. Debut, Carnegie Recital Hall, N.Y.C., 1968; concert cellist, U.S., Can., Europe. Recipient top prize 22d Internat. Cello Competition, Munich. Mem. Violoncello Soc. Office: care Affiliate Artists Inc Nat Office 155 W 68th St New York NY 10023 *

BROTT, LOTTE, musician, univ. orch. exec., educator; b. Mannheim, Germany, Aug. 11, 1922; emigrated to Can., 1939, naturalized, 1943; d. Walter and Else (Fuld) Goetzel; m. Alexander Brott, Apr. 11, 1943; children—Boris, Denis. Student, Conservatoire Neufchatel, Switzerland, 1934-36; Diploma with distinction, Conservatorium of Music, Zurich, Switzerland, 1939. Mgr., mgr. pub. relations McGill Chamber Orch., 1950—, prof. cello, 1940—. Cellist, Montreal (Que., Can.) Symphony Orch., 1941—; cellist, McGill String Quartet McGill U., Montreal, 1940-50; first cellist, McGill Chamber Orch., 1950—; Numerous solo recitals over radio, TV; cellist, Pops Concerts Maurice Richard Arena, Montreal, 1963—. Home: 5459 Earnscliffe Ave Montreal PQ H3X 2P8 Canada

BROTT, WALTER HOWARD, cardiac surgeon, educator, retired army officer; b. Alamosa, Colo., Sept. 5, 1933; s. Walter Hugo and Viola Helen (Roscher) B.; m. Marie Helen Kuzniewski; children: Cheryl Marie, Michelle Marie, Kevin Walter. B.A., Yale U., 1955; M.D., U. Kans., 1959. Diplomate: Am. Bd. Surgery, Am. Bd. Thoracic Surgery. Commd. 1st. lt. U.S. Army, 1959, advanced through grades to col., 1974; intern Walter Reed Army Med. Ctr., Washington, 1959; resident in gen. surgery William Beaumont Gen. Hosp., El Paso, Tex., 1960-64; resident in thoracic surgery Fitzsimmons Army Med. Ctr., Denver, 1967-69; comdr. 3d Surg. Hosp., Vietnam, 1969, 18th Surg. Hosp., 1970; asst. chief thoracic and cardiovascular surgery Walter Reed Army Med. Ctr., 1971-76, chief cardiothoracic surgery, 1977-84; ret. U.S. Army, 1984; chief surg. cons. Surgeon Gen. Army, Washington, 1976-77; prof. surgery Uniformed Services U. Health Scis., 1976-84; assoc. clin. prof. surgery U. Tenn., Knoxville, 1984—; mem. joint rev. com. Council for Perfusion Edn. and Accreditation, 1981—. Contbr. articles to profl. jours.; chmn.: NATO editorial bd. Emergency War Surgery Handbook, 1977—. Decorated Legion of Merit with oak leaf cluster, Bronze Star (U.S.), Cross of Gallantry (Vietnam); recipient Cert. of Achievement Surgeon Gen. U.S., 1978. Fellow ACS (grad. edn. com. 1977-78); mem. Soc. Thoracic Surgeons, Washington Med. Soc., Thoracic and Cardiovascular Surgeons, Thoracic Surgery Program Dirs. Assn., Am. Assn. Thoracic Surgeons, Assn. Med. Cons. to Armed Forces, AMA (cons. panel council allied health edn. accreditation 1981—), Assn. Mil. Surgeons, Internat. Soc. Heart Transplant Surgery, Alpha Omega Alpha. Lutheran. Clubs: Yale (Washington); Marine Meml. Office: Dept Surgery U Tenn Meml Hosp Knoxville TN 37920 *Using those opportunities to better the life of one's fellow man not only gives gratification in itself but enhances the person spiritually and occasionally materially by God's rewards.*

BROTTER, RALPH, lawyer, real estate developer; b. N.Y.C., June 13, 1932; s. Isadore and Sarah (Weiss) B.; m. May Lorraine Fleischer, Nov. 17, 1956 (div. 1982); children: Elizabeth, Joshua, Amos. B.A., Bklyn Coll., 1954. Bar: N.Y. Ptnr. firm Douglaston Assocs., N.Y.C., 1958-67, propr., Gt. Neck, N.Y., 1967—; ptnr. firm Kershaw & Co., Gt. Neck, 1970—. Vice pres. Theatre in the Park, Queens, N.Y., 1980-81; pres. Queens Mus., 1980-81, chmn. bd., 1982-83. Served with U.S. Army, 1953-55. Mem. Nassau County Bar Assn. Republican. Jewish. Club: B'nai B'rith.

BROTZEN, FRANZ RICHARD, materials science educator; b. Berlin, July 4, 1915; U.S., 1941; s. Georg and Lena (Paculy) B.; m. Frances Burke Ridgeway, Jan. 31, 1950; children: Franz Ridgeway, Julie Ridgeway. B.S. in Metall. Engring., Case Inst. Tech., 1950, M.S., 1953, Ph.D., 1954. Salesman a Quimica Bayer Ltda., Rio de Janeiro, Brazil, 1934-41; mfrs. rep. R.G. Le Tourneau, Inc., Longview, Tex., 1947-48; sr. research assoc. Case Inst. Tech., Cleve., 1951-54; mem. faculty Rice U., Houston, 1954—, prof. materials sci., 1959—, dean engring., 1962-66, master Brown Coll., 1977-82; vis. prof. Max Planck Inst., Stuttgart, W.Ger., 1960-61, 73-74, Fed. Poly. Inst., Zurich, Switzerland, 1966-67, U. Lausanne, (Switzerland), 1981. Author papers in field. Chmn. Houston Contemporary Arts Assn., 1964-65. Served to 1st lt. AUS, 1942-46. Recipient Sr. Scientist award W. German Govt., 1973-74; Guggenheim fellow, 1960-61. Fellow Am. Soc. Metals (chmn. Houston chpt. 1980-81); mem. AIME, Am. Phys. Soc., Soc. Engring. Sci., Sigma Xi, Tau Beta Pi. Home: 2701 H Bellefontaine Houston TX 77025 Office: Materials Sci Dept Rice U PO Box 1892 Houston TX 77251

BROTZMAN, DONALD GLENN, government official, lawyer; b. Logan County, Colo., June 28, 1922; s. Harry and Priscilla Ruth (Kittle) B.; m. Louise Love Reed, Apr. 9, 1944; children: Kathleen Love, Donald Glenn. B.B.S., J.D., U. Colo., 1949. Bar: Colo. 1949. Since practiced in, Boulder; mem. Colo. Ho. of Reps., 1950-52, Colo. Senate, 1952-56; U.S. atty. Dist. Colo., 1959-61; mem. 88th, 90th-93d congresses from 2d Dist. Colo., mem. ways and means com.; asst. sec. army for manpower and res. affairs, Washington, 1975—; Mem. Colo. Crime Commn., 1952-56; Colo. mem. Commn. Uniform State Laws, 1954—. Colo. chmn. Easter Seal and Colo. Highlander Boys Club drives, 1958, Youth in Govt. program, YMCA, 1958-62; Republican candidate for gov. of Colo., 1956; chmn. Indsl. Energy Users Forum, Washington; pres. Washington Indsl. Round Table. Served to lst lt., inf. AUS, 1942-46; PTO. Selected by Colo. press as Outstanding Freshman Mem. of House, 1951; as Outstanding Freshman Senator, 1953; recipient Distinguished Service award Colo. Jaycees, 1954; named to U. Colo. Hall of Fame, 1976. Mem. Am., Fed., Colo., Boulder County bar assns., Rubber Mfrs. Assn. (pres.), Natural Rubber Shippers Assn. (pres.), Tire Industry Safety Council (chmn.), Am. Legion, V.F.W., Res. Officers Assn., Boulder C. of C., Beta Theta Pi, Phi Delta Phi (past magister). Methodist (trustee). Clubs: Masons, Elks, Rotary (Boulder) (dir.). Home: 705 Swan Creek Rd Fort Washington MD 20744 Office: 1901 Pennsylvania Ave Washington DC 20006

BROUGH, GEORGE, pianist; b. Boston, Lincolnshire, Eng., Feb. 25, 1918; m. Simone Desilets, Dec. 19, 1973. Student, Keble Coll., Oxford, Eng., 1937-40, Royal Coll. Music, London, Eng., 1937-40; Mus.D., Oxford U., 1943. Accompanist, asst. condr., Canadian Opera Co., 1955—; accompanist for, Toronto Mendelssohn Choir, 1960—, Banff Summer Sch. Fine Arts, 1965—; harpsichordist, Toronto Chamber Players, 1969—; opera coach, accompanist, Faculty of Music, U. Toronto, 1972—; accompanist for, Canadian Broadcasting Corp. and, in concerts throughout, Can., 1946—; Recordings with, Toronto Mendelssohn Choir and, Festival Singers of Can. Home: Apt 401 4N Sherbourne St Toronto ON Canada Office: Faculty Music Edward Johnson Bldg Queens Park Toronto ON Canada

BROUGH, KENNETH JAMES, retired educator, librarian; b. Scotch Grove, Iowa, Aug. 22, 1906; s. Rev. R.A. and Sarah (Metcalf) B.; m. Ruth Bloomer, May 22, 1933. A.B., Grinnell Coll., 1927; A.M., U. Colo., 1931; B.L.S., Columbia, 1942; Ph.D., Stanford, 1949. Tchr. Portales (N.Mex.) High Sch., 1927-34; librarian, dir. instrn. Eastern N.Mex. U., 1934-43; asst. reference librarian Stanford, 1946-49; prof. bibliography, librarian San Francisco State Coll., 1949-72; Mem. N.Mex. Library Planning Com., 1940-42, N.Mex. Library Commn., 1946. Author: Scholar's Workshop, 1953; Contbr. articles to profl. jours. Served with 54th A.A.A. replacement tng. bn. U.S. Army, 1943-46. Mem. ALA, NEA, N.Mex. Library Assn. (pres. 1935-36), Calif. Library Assn., Phi Beta Kappa., Phi Delta Kappa. Presbyn. Club: Mason. Home: 2364 S Court Palo Alto CA 94301

BROUGHTON, CARL L(OUIS), business executive; b. Marietta, Ohio, June 22, 1910; s. John H. and Josephine B. (Barnhart) B.; m. Elizabeth Sugden, Aug. 23, 1936; children—Ruth, Mary George W. Student, Ohio State U. Sch. Bus. Adminstrn., 1929-30; LL.D. (hon.), Marietta Coll., 1975. Co-founder, pres. Broughton Foods Co., Marietta, 1933-75, chmn. bd., 1975—, Peoples Bank & Trust Co., Marietta, 1977—; past mem. exec. com., dir. Marmac Corp., Parkersburg, W.Va. Trustee Marietta Coll., 1950-66, chmn. bd., 1966-70; trustee Marietta Meml. Hosp., 1946-77, chmn. bd., 1977-78; mem. adv. bd. Ohio Agrl. Research and Devel. Center, Agrl. Coll., Ohio State U. Served to lt. USNR, 1943-46. Recipient Outstanding Citizens award Marietta Jaycees, 1965, award of merit Ohio State U. Dept. Dairy Tech., 1969. Mem. W.Va. Dairy Products Assn. (pres. 1958-59, dir., award for 45 years service to dairy industry 1978), Ohio C. of C. (dir.), Marietta Area C. of C. (pres. 1955, dir. 1953-63), Ohio Thoroughbred Breeders Assn. (pres. 1969-70). Republican. Congregationalist. Clubs: Rotary (Marietta) (pres. 1948-49); Masons, Elks. Office: PO Box 656 Marietta OH 45750

BROUGHTON, DONALD BEDDOES, chemical engineer; b. Rugby, Eng., Apr. 20, 1917; came to U.S., 1924, naturalized, 1934; s. Walter and Emily (Beddoes) B.; m. Natalie Waitt, Feb. 20, 1943. Asst. prof. chem. engring. M.I.T., 1943-49; with process div. UOP, Inc., Des Plaines, Ill., 1949—, asso. tech. dir., 1979—. Recipient Alpha Chi Sigma award for chem. engring. research Am. Inst. Chem. Engrs., 1967. Fellow Nat. Acad. Engring., Am. Inst. Chem. Engrs.; mem. Am. Chem. Soc. (Rohm & Haas award in Separation Sci. and Tech. 1983), Am. Petroleum Inst. Home: 1639 Hinman Ave Evanston IL 60201 Office: 20 UOP Plaza Des Plaines IL 60016

BROUGHTON, PHILLIP CHARLES, lawyer; b. Findlay, Ohio, Sept. 21, 1930; s. Harold C. and Marian (Pierson) B.; m. Mary M. Lancaster, Sept. 7, 1957; children: Margaret Arndt, Phillip Charles, Anne Pierson, Elizabeth Lancaster. B.A., Bowling Green U., 1953; LL.B., U. Mich., 1957; LL.M., N.Y. U., 1962. Bar: N.Y. 1957. Practiced in, N.Y.C., 1957—; mem. firm Thacher, Proffitt and Wood, 1957—; dir. Moore & White Co., Phila., Firestone McCrann Corp., McLean, Va., Nigerian Diversified Investments, Ltd., Lagos, Potomac Trade Internat., Inc., Washington, Catoctin Stud, Inc., Waterford, Va. Mem. Bernards Twp. (N.J.) Planning Bd., 1966-75, chmn., 1970-73; trustee Kent Pl. Sch., Summit, N.J.; bd. dirs. Midgard Found., N.Y.C., Catoctin Creek Found. Served to lt. USMCR, 1953-55. Mem. Am., N.Y. State bar assns., Assn. Bar City N.Y. Republican. Presbyterian (elder, trustee). Clubs: Downtown (N.Y.C.); Morristown Field. Home: Childs Rd Basking Ridge NJ 07920 Office: 40 Wall St New York NY 10005

BROUILLET, FRANK B., educational administrator; b. Puyallup, Wash., May 18, 1928; s. Vern and Doris B.; m. Margé Sarsten, June 8, 1955; children: Marc, Blair. B.A. in Econs, U. Puget Sound, 1951, B.Ed., 1953; M.A., U. Wash., 1958, Ed.D., 1968; fellow econs., U. Mont., 1952. Tchr., coach Puyallup Jr.-Sr. High Sch., 1955; mem. Wash. Ho. of Reps. from 25th Dist., 1956-72, chmn. edn. com., 1959-63, chmn. Democratic caucus, 1965-69, chmn. joint house/senate com. edn., 1961-71; tchr., counselor Wilson High Sch., Tacoma, 1959-63; instr., counselor, adminstr. U. Wash., Seattle, 1963-67; asst. to pres. Highline Community Coll., Midway, Wash., 1967-72; supt. pub. instruction State of Wash., Olympia, 1972—; commnr. Interstate Compact for Edn.; vice chmn. Wash. Spl. Levy Study Commn.; mem. Nat. Legis. Leaders Conf., Wash. Council Higher Edn. Contbr. articles to profl. jours. Past mem. bd. dirs. Wash. Credit Union League.; mem. Nat. Com. on U.S.-China Relations. Served with AUS, 1953-55. Mem. Council Chief State Sch. Officers, Wash., Wash. State Capitol hist. assns., Am. Heritage Assn. (past dir.), PTA, Edn. Commn. of the States, Wash. Tchrs. Retirement System. Home: 619 7th Ave SW Puyallup WA 98371 Office: Old Capitol Bldg Olympia WA 98504

BROUN, E. C., JR., petroleum industry tool manufacturing company executive. Exec v.p. Hughes Tool Co., Houston. Office: Hughes Tool Co 6500 Tex Commerce Tower Houston TX 77002§

BROUN, ELIZABETH, art historian, museum curator; b. Kansas City, Mo., Dec. 15, 1946; d. Augustine Hughes and Roberta Catherine (Hayden) Gibson; m. Ronald Broun, June 5, 1968; 1 dau., Katherine. B.A., U. Kans., 1968, Ph.D., 1976; cert. advanced study, U. Bordeaux, Frances, 1967. Curator prints and drawings Spencer Mus. Art, Lawrence, Kans., 1976-83; asst. prof. U. Kans., Lawrence, 1978-83; asst. dir. chief curator Nat. Mus. Am. Art, Washington, 1983—. Author: exhbn. catalogues Prints of Zorn, 1979, Prints and Drawings of Pat Steir, 1983; co-author: Benton's Bentons, 1980, Engravings of Marcantonio Raimondi, 1981. Woodrow Wilson fellow, 1968-69; Ford. Found. fellow, 1970-72. Mem. Phi Beta Kappa. Home: 7702 Marbury Rd Bethesda MD 20817 Office: Nat Mus Am Art 8th and G Sts NW Washington DC 20560

BROUN, HEYWOOD HALE, author, broadcaster, actor; b. N.Y.C., Mar. 10, 1918; s. Heywood Campbell and Ruth (Hale) B.; m. Jane Lloyd-Jones, 1949; 1 son, Heywood Orren. B.A., Swarthmore Coll., 1940; studied acting with, Joseph Leon, 1955-56. Sports writer, reporter, columnist N.Y. PM, N.Y. Star, 1940; independent sports and news corr. CBS News; syndicated book show host Sta. WOR-TV, N.Y.C. Author: A Studied Madness, A Tumultuous Merriment, Whose Little Boy Are You?; stage debut I Remember Mama, 1949; Broadway stage debut Love Me Long, 1949; stage appearances include Xmas in Las Vegas; film appearances include For Pete's Sake; television debut Phil Silver's Arrow Television Theatre, 1949; appeared on: television series The Doctors; television appearances include U.S. Steel Hour. Office: care CBS News 555 W 57th St New York NY 10019

BROUN, KENNETH STANLEY, legal educator, university dean; b. Chgo., July 26, 1939; s. Fred G. and Helene (Smith) B.; m. Marjorie Enid Shagam, Jan. 29, 1961; children: Jonathan, Daniel. B.S., U. Ill., 1960, J.D., 1963. Bar: N.C. 1976, Ill. 1963. Assoc. prof. to prof. U. N.C. Law Sch., Chapel Hill, 1969—; dir. Nat. Inst. Trial Advocacy, Chapel Hill, 1976-79; dean Sch. of Law Nat. Inst. U.N.C., Chapel Hill, 1979—. Author: (with I. Seckinger) Materials in Trial Advocacy, 1977, (with R. Meisenholder) Problems in Evidence, 1973, 2d edit. 1981, (with Cleary et al) Handbook on Evidence, 1972. Recipient award for teaching excellence U. N.C., 1978; fellow Internat. Soc. Barristers, 1978. Mem. Nat. Inst. Trial Advocacy (trustee), N.C. Bar Assn., ABA, Order of Coif. Home: 414 Whitehead Cir Chapel Hill NC 27514 Office: Univ NC Ridge Rd Chapel Hill NC 27514

BROUS, PHILIP, retail specialty store chain executive; b. N.Y.C., Oct. 16, 1930; s. Leonard and Harriet (Baron) B.; m. Barbara Biber, Feb. 22, 1962; children—Leonard, Elizabeth, Nancy. B.A., N.Y. U., 1949; M.S., Columbia U., 1950, M.B.A., 1951; postgrad., London Sch. Econs., U. London, 1952. With Bloomingdales, N.Y.C., 1953-70; sportswear buyer, later div. mdse. mgr.; with Miller-Wohl Co., Secaucus, N.J., 1970—, exec. v.p., 1974-76, pres., chief operating officer, 1976—, also dir., mem. exec. com. Pres. Temple B'nai Jeshurun, Short Hills, N.J., 1982—; trustee Jewish Community Found. of Met. N.J., YM-YWHA of Met. N.J. Served to capt. USAF, 1951-58. Office: 915 Secaucus Rd Secaucus NJ 07094

BROUSE, ROBERT CORNELIUS, lawyer; b. Akron, Ohio, June 19, 1913; s. Edwin Walter and Helen (Fouts) B.; m. Martha Ake, July 9, 1938; children: Susannah (Mrs. John L. Feudner III), Martha (Mrs. Jerome J. Joondeph). A.B., Princeton, 1935; J.D., U. Mich., 1938. Bar: Ohio 1938. With Brouse & McDowell (and predecessor firms), Akron, 1938—, partner, 1949-78, of counsel, 1978—, pres., 1970-76; chmn. bd. Permanent Fed. Savs. and Loan Assn., Akron, 1963—; dir. Summit Nat. Life Ins. Co., 1962—. Trustee Western Res. Acad., Hudson, Ohio, 1941—, pres., 1966-72; trustee Childrens Hosp. of Akron, 1941—, pres. bd., 1950-51; trustee Akron Community Trust, 1966—, pres., 1972-73; trustee Akron Childrens Hosp. Found., 1972—, pres., 1972-83. Served to lt. USNR, 1942-46. Mem. Am., Ohio, Akron bar assns., SAR, Phi Delta Phi (pres. Kent chpt. 1938). Republican. Clubs: Akron City (pres. 1963), Portage Country (pres. 1981), Mayflower (Akron); Little (Delray Beach, Fla.). Home: 520 Ridgecrest Rd Akron OH 44303 also 2103 S Ocean Blvd Delray Beach FL 33444 Office: First Nat Tower Akron OH 44308

BROUSSARD, ALLEN E., justice state supreme court; b. Lake Charles, La., Apr. 13, 1929; m. Odessa Broussard; children: Eric, Craig, Keith. A.B. in Polit. Sci., U. Calif.-Berkeley, 1950, J.D., 1953. Bar: Calif. 1954. Sole practice, San Francisco and Oakland, Calif., 1954-56; research atty. for presiding justice Dist. Ct. Appeals 1st Appellate Dist., 1st Div., 1953-54; sole practice, 1956-59; assoc. Wilson, Metoyer & Sweeney, 1959-61; mem. firm Metoyer, Sweeney & Broussard, 1961-64; judge Oakland-Piedmont dist. Mcpl. Ct., 1964-75, Alameda County Superior Ct., Oakland, 1975-81; justice Calif. Supreme Ct., San Francisco, 1981—; mem. faculty Golden Gate Coll., San Francisco, 1971, U. San Francisco, 1972, Calif. Coll. Trial Judges, 1969-72, 74; advisor to exec. com. Jud. Council Calif.; v.p. governing com. Ctr. Jud. Edn. and Research; mem. council judges Nat. Council Crime and Delinquency. Vice pres. East Bay Big Bros. Am.; bd. dirs. Alameda County Community Found.; bd. dirs., past chmn. Oakland Men of Tomorrow, Black Bus. and Profl. Men's Service Orgn. Served with U.S. Army, 1954-56. Arthur Newhouse, Arthur Gold Tashiera scholar. Mem. Conf. Calif. Judges (exec. bd. 1970-71, pres. 1972-73), Nat. Bar Assn. (exec. bd. jud. council), Alameda County Bar Assn. (v.p.), Alameda County Criminal Cts. Bar Assn., Boalt Hall Alumni Assn. (past dir.), State Bar Calif., Phi Alpha Delta. Club: Charles Houston Law. Office: Calif Supreme Ct 350 McAllister San Francisco CA 94102 *

BROUSSARD, JOSEPH OTTO, III, architect; b. Abbeville, La., Jan. 3, 1938; s. Joseph Otto and Dorothy (Kennon) B.; m. Sidney Prejean, Dec. 17, 1960; children: Kent, Kelly, Russ. B.Arch., U. Southwestern La., 1963. Architect firm Tolson & Hamilton, Opelousas, La., 1963-65; architect, prin., owner Laudun & Broussard, Franklin, La., 1965-69; architect Hamilton, Meyer & Assos., Opelousas, La., 1969-81, Corne, Sellers, & Assos, Architects and Engrs., Lafayette, La., 1981-82; ptnr. Corne, Sellers, Broussard & Assocs., Architects and Engrs., Lafayette, La., 1983—; Mem. Acadiana project rev. com. Mid-La. Health Systems Agy. Inc., 1977-79. Mem. Am. Forestry Assn., Constrn. Specifications Inst. (cert. constrn. specifier), Nat. Fire Protection Assn., La. Inst. Building Scis., Theta Xi, Blue Key. Clubs: Indian Hills Country (dir. 1972-73, pres. 1973), Indian Hills Country (dir. 1982-83). Home: 2151 Woodland Dr Opelousas LA 70570 Office: 304 LaRue France Suite 203 Lafayette LA 70508

BROUSSARD, THOMAS ROLLINS, lawyer; b. Houston, May 30, 1943; s. Charles Hugh and Ethel (Rollins) B.; m. Mollie Brewster, Jan. 13, 1968. B.S. cum laude in Econs, U. Pa., 1964, J.D., Harvard U., 1967. Bar: N.Y. 1968, Calif. 1973. Tax atty. Esso Standard Eastern, Inc., N.Y.C., 1967-70; gen. tax counsel Atlantic Richfield Co., N.Y.C., Los Angeles, 1970-74; v.p. corporate affairs, sec., gen. counsel Technicolor, Inc., Los Angeles, 1974-80; mem. firm Nelson & Broussard, Los Angeles, 1980-81; pres. Broussard and Lipscomb, P.C., Los Angeles, 1981—. Mem. Am., Calif., Los Angeles County bar assns., Am. Soc. Corporate Secs., Assn. Bar City N.Y., Beverly Hills Bar Assn. Republican. Office: 2029 Century Park E Suite 2180 Los Angeles CA 90067

BROUTMAN, LAWRENCE JAY, materials engineering educator; b. Chgo., Feb. 9, 1938; s. Carl and Mildred (Glasser) B.; m. Rochelle Nancy Jaffe, Jan. 29, 1961; children: James Hale, Marcy Ann. B.S. in Civil Engring, Mass. Inst. Tech., 1959, M.S. in Materials Engring. and Sci, 1961, Sc.D. (Owens Corning Fiberglas fellow), 1963. Sr. research engr. Ill. Inst. Tech. Research Inst., Chgo., 1963-66, asso. prof. mechanics, 1966-70, prof. materials engring., 1970—; pres. L.J. Broutman & Assocs.; cons. Air Force Materials Lab., Wright-Patterson AFB, Dayton, Ohio, Harry Diamond Labs., Washington, HUD, also numerous indsl. firms. Editor: (with R.H. Krock) Modern Composite Materials, 1967, Treatise on Composite Materials, 1974, (with B. Agarwal) Analysis and Performance of Fiber Compositions, 1980; mem. editorial bd.: Internat. Jour. Polymeric Materials, 1974—, Polymer Engineering and Science, 1975—; Contbr. articles to profl. jours. Grantee Army Mechanics and Materials Research Center, Watertown, Mass., 1966, Army Research Office, Durham, N.C., 1974, Air Force Office Sci. Research, Washington, 1970, AEC, 1977, NSF, 1975. Mem. Soc. Plastics Engrs. (dir. Chgo., Best Paper awards 1964, 69, 73), Soc. Rheology of Am. Phys. Soc., ASTM, Soc. for Exptl. Stress Analysis, Am. Chem. Soc., Am. Inst. Physics, Am. Ceramic Soc., Internat. Soc. Plastics Engrs. (pres. 1977—), Sigma Xi, Chi Epsilon. Jewish. Office: 10 W 33d St Chicago IL 60616

BROUWER, ARIE RAYMOND, religious organization executive; b. Inwood, Iowa, July 14, 1935; s. Arie and Gertie (Brands) B.; m. Harriet Korver, Aug. 16, 1955; children: Milton, Charla, Steven, Patricia. A.A., Northwestern Jr. Coll., Orange City, Iowa, 1954; B.A., Hope Coll., 1956, D.D. (hon.), 1983; B.D., Western Theol. Sem., Holland, Mich., 1959; D.D., Central Coll., Pella, Iowa, 1978. Ordained to ministry Reformed Church in America, 1959; pastor chs., Mich., 1959-63, N.J., 1963-68; sec. for program Ref. Ch. in Am., N.Y.C., 1968-70, exec. sec., 1970-77, gen. sec., 1977-83; dep. gen. sec. World Council Chs., Geneva, 1983—; First chmn. Bd. Theol. Edn., Ref. Ch., 1967-68; v.p. Bd. World Missions, 1967-68; mem. Theol. Commn., 1967-68; mem. gen. bd. Nat. Council Chs., 1969-72, gov. bd., 1973-83; bd. dirs. Bread for the World, 1973-82, v.p., 1976-82; mem. central com. World Council Chs., 1979-83. Contbg. editor: Ch. Herald, 1967-68. Office: World Council Churches 150 route de Ferney 1211 Geneva 20 Switzerland

BROW, B.R., coal company executive; b. 1932. B.S., U. Ariz., 1958. Sr. v.p. Conoco, Inc., 1975-77, pres. coal and minerals ops., 1982—; with Consolidation Coal Co., Pitts., 1977—, exec. v.p., then pres. and chief operating officer, chief exec. officer, 1982—, dir. Office: Consolidation Coal Co 1800 Washington Rd Pittsburgh PA 15241 *

BROWDE, ANATOLE, electonics company executive; b. Berlin, June 10, 1925; U.S., 1940, naturalized, 1946; s. Alexander and Rebecca (Braude) Kutisker; m. Jacqueline Rousseau, Mar. 10, 1973; children: David, Elizabeth, Richard. B.E.E., Cornell U., 1948; postgrad., Northwestern U., Columbia U. Engr. Capehart-Farnsworth Corp., Ft. Wayne, Ind., 1948-51, Arma Corp., Bklyn., 1951-53; project engr. BOMARC, Westinghouse Electric Co., Balt., 1953-55; asso. dir. missile dept. Avco Corp., Cin., 1955-59; with McDonnell Douglas Corp., 1959—, v.p. engring. and mktg., 1979-81; v.p., gen. mgr. info. systems div. McDonnell Douglas Electronics Co., St. Charles, Mo., 1981-82, v.p. Microelectronics Ctr., 1982—. Chmn. secondary schs. com. Cornell U., 1968—, mem. univ. council, 1971-77, 79—; trustee First Unitarian Ch., St. Louis, 1977-80, chmn., 1979-80. Mem. Am. Def. Preparedness Assn., Nat. Def. Transp. Assn., Assn. Old Crows. Republican. Unitarian. Clubs: Forest Hills Golf and Country, Cornell (St. Louis). Developed Mercury, Gemini Spacecraft electronics, 1961-68, airborne collision avoidance system, 1968-72. Home: 15354 Country Ridge Dr Chesterfield MO 63017 Office: PO Box 426 St Charles MO 63301

BROWDER, FELIX EARL, mathematician, educator; b. Moscow, July 31, 1927; s. Earl and Raissa (Berkmann) B.; m. Eva Tislowitz, Oct. 5, 1949; children: Thomas, William. S.B., Mass. Inst. Tech., 1946; Ph.D., Princeton U., 1948. C.L.E. Moore instr. math. Mass. Inst. Tech., 1948-51, vis. assoc. prof., 1961-62, vis. prof., 1977-78; instr. math. Boston U., 1951-53; asst. prof. Brandeis U., 1955-56; from asst. prof. to prof. math. Yale U., 1956-63; prof. math. U. Chgo., 1963-72, Louis Block prof. math., 1972-82, Max Mason Disting. Service prof. math., 1982—, chmn. dept., 1972-77, 80—; vis. mem. Inst. Advanced Study, Princeton U., 1953-54, 63-64; vis. prof. Instituto de Matematica Pura e Aplicada, Rio de Janeiro, 1960, Princeton U., 1968; Fairchild disting. visitor Calif. Inst. Tech., 1967, 78; sr. research fellow U. Sussex, Eng., 1970, 76; vis. prof. U. Paris, 1973, 75, 78. Served with AUS, 1953-55. Guggenheim fellow, 1953-54, 66-67; Sloan Found. fellow, 1959-63; NSF sr. postdoctoral fellow, 1957-58. Fellow Am. Acad. Arts and Scis.; mem. Nat. Acad. Scis., Am. Math. Soc. (editor bull. 1959-68, 78-83, council mem. 1959-72, 78-83, mng. editor 1964-68, 80, exec. com. council 1979-80), Math. Assn. Am., AAAS (chmn. sect. A 1983), Sigma Xi. Home: 5505 S Kimbark Ave Chicago IL 60637

BROWDER, OLIN LORRAINE, JR., legal educator; b. Urbana, Ill., Dec. 19, 1913; s. Olin Lorraine and Nellie (Taylor) B.; m. Edna Olive Forsythe, Sept. 9, 1939; children: Ann (Mrs. William Sorensen), Catherine (Mrs. Randall Morris), John. A.B., U. Ill., 1935, LL.B., 1937; S.J.D., U. Mich., 1941. Bar: Ill. 1939. Practiced in Chgo., 1938-39; asst. prof. bus. law U. Ala., 1939-41; asst. prof. law U. Tenn., 1941-42; mem. legal dept. TVA, 1942-43; spl. agt. FBI, 1943-45; prof. law U. Okla., 1946-53, U. Mich., Ann Arbor, 1953-81, James V. Campbell prof. law, 1979—. Author: (with others) American Law of Property, 1953, (with L.W. Waggoner) Family Property Transactions, 1965, 3d edit., 1980, (with R. A. Cunningham and Allan F. Smith) Basic Property Law, 1966, 4th edit., 1984, (with L. W. Waggoner and R. V. Wellman) Palmer's Cases on Trusts and Succession, 4th edit., 1983. Mem. Am. Bar Assn., Order of Coif, Phi Beta Kappa, Beta Theta Phi, Phi Alpha Delta, Phi Kappa Phi. Home: 1520 Edinborough Rd Ann Arbor MI 48104

BROWDER, ROBERT PAUL, historian, educator; b. Spokane, Wash., Jan. 25, 1921; s. Paul McCroskey and Helen Elizabeth (Hungate) B.; m. Rosemary Meininger, June 1, 1946 (div. 1970); children: Kathleen Hale Heberlein, Ann Elizabeth, Judith Lee. A.B. with distinction (Gamble scholar), Stanford U., 1942, M.A., 1947; M.A. (Austin fellow, Rockefeller fellow Slavic studies 1947-50), Harvard U., 1949, Ph.D., 1951. Instr. history Stanford U., 1951, vis. asst. prof., 1954-55; faculty U. Colo., 1951-65, prof. history, 1960-65, chmn. dept., 1960-63, acting dean, 1962-64, dir. Center for Slavic and East European Studies, 1964-65; prof., head dept. history Kans. State U., 1965-69; prof. U. Ariz., Tucson, 1969—, head dept. history, 1969-78; research asso. Hoover Instn. War, Revolution and Peace, 1956-59; sr. asso. mem. St. Anthony's Coll., Oxford, 1973; vis. scholar Churchill Coll., Cambridge, Eng., 1976. Author: The Origins of Soviet-American Diplomacy, 1953, 2d edit., 1966, (with others) Russian Thought and Politics, 1957, (with A.F. Kerensky) The Russian Provisional Government 1917, 3 vols, 1961, (with others) Soviet Foreign Policy and World Communism, 1965; intro. to V.D. Nabokov and the Russian Provisional Government, 1917, 1976; also articles.; Co-editor: (with others) Arizona's Heritage: Today and Tomorrow, 1972. Served to lt. USNR, 1942-46. Humanities Fund grantee, 1955; Am. Philos. Soc. grantee, 1955, 71, 73; Rockefeller Found. grantee, 1977; Eleanor Roosevelt Inst. grantee, 1979; U. Ariz. Found. grantee, 1981. Mem. Am. Hist. Assn., Am. Assn. Advancement Slavic Studies, Conf. Slavic and East European Studies, Western Slavic Assn., Rocky Mountain Social Sci. Assn. Office: Dept of History Univ Ariz Tucson AZ 85721

BROWDER, WILLIAM, mathematician, educator; b. N.Y.C., Jan. 6, 1934; s. Earl and Raissa (Berkmann) B.; m. Nancy O'Brien, Jan. 30, 1960; children: Julia, Risa, Daniel. B.S., MIT, 1954; Ph.D., Princeton U., 1958. Instr. U. Rochester, 1957-58; from instr. to assoc. prof. math. Cornell U., 1958-63; prof. math. Princeton U., 1964—, chmn. dept., 1971-73; vis. fellow Math. Inst. and Magdalen Coll., Oxford U. (Eng.), 1978-79; chmn. office Math. Scis. NAS-NRC, 1978—. Guggenheim fellow, 1974-75. Mem. Am. Math. Soc. (v.p. 1977-78), Nat. Acad. Scis. Office: Fine Hall 16 Washington Rd Princeton NJ 08544

BROWDER, WILLIAM BAYARD, corporation executive, lawyer; b. Urbana, Ill., Sept. 6, 1916; s. Olin Lorraine and Nellie Sheldon (Taylor) B.; m. Mary Bain Lehmann, Sept. 6, 1942; children: David Sheldon, Wendy Elisabeth, Amy Spence. A.B., U. Ill., 1938, J.D., 1941; LL.D., MacMurray Coll., Jacksonville, Ill., 1979. Bar: Ill. 1941. Atty. I.C.R.R., 1941-47, Union Tank Car Co., Chgo., 1948—, sec., 1952-77, dir., 1954-81, gen. counsel, 1956-79, v.p., 1965-74, sr. v.p., 1974-81; v.p., dir. Trans Union Corp., 1969-81, gen. counsel, 1969-79, sr. v.p., 1974-79, sr. v.p. law, 1979-81; v.p., dir. Ecodyne Corp., 1972-81; dir. Procor, Ltd., 1952-81. Mem. Citizens Com. To Study Police-Community Relations in Chgo., 1966-67; chmn. Com. To Study Financing Community Colls. in Ill., 1974-75; pres. Chgo. Crime Commn., 1965-67; mem. adv. bd. U. Ill. Law Forum, 1963-66; mem. adv. com. U. Ill. Coll. Commerce and Bus. Adminstrn., Champaign-Urbana, 1969-73; mem. Ill. Racing Bd., 1973-74, Ill. Bd. Higher Edn., 1975—; chmn. Ill. Bd. Higher Edn., 1979—; pres. Wilmette United Fund, 1962; trustee YMCA-U. Ill., 1966—, chmn., 1967-79; bd. dirs. Mid Am. chpt. ARC, 1963-65, Wilmette Pub. Library, 1964-67, Northwestern Meml. Hosp., 1970-75; mem. U. Ill. Found., 1969—, bd. dirs., 1973-79, mem. pres.'s council, 1974—; mem. Ill. Gov.'s Task Force on Pvt. Sector Initiatives, 1983—, Ill. Gov.'s Commn. on Sci. and Tech., 1983—; bd. dirs., chmn. organized crime com. Chgo. Crime Commn. Mem. Am., Ill. bar assns., U. Ill. Law Alumni Assn. (pres. 1968-71), Chgo. Law Club, Order of Coif, Phi Beta Kappa, Phi Eta Sigma, Beta Theta Pi, Phi Alpha Delta. Methodist (trustee Wesley Found., U. Ill. 1963-68, 74-78; ch. pres., trustee). Clubs: Union League (Chgo.) (dir. 1974-76); Westmoreland Country (Wilmette, Ill.) (sec., dir. 1979). Home: 1442 Lake Ave Wilmette IL 60091

BROWDY, ALVIN, lawyer; b. Kansas City, Mo., Sept. 19, 1917; s. Harry and Rosa Leah (Levin) B.; m. Letty Lowen, Mar. 15, 1942; children—Roger L., Wendy Ellen, Craig L. B.S. in Chem. Engring, U. Ill., 1937; J.D., Georgetown U., 1948. Bar: D.C. bar 1948. Since practiced in, Washington; partner firm Browdy & Neimark, 1969—. Mem. adv. bd.: Patent, Trademark and Copyright Jour, 1972—. Mem. exec. com. Jewish Community Council Greater Washington, 1962-74, sec., 1969; bd. dirs. Ohr Kodesh Congregation, Chevy Chase, Md., 1952-73, pres., 1960-62; bd. dirs. Bd. Jewish Edn. Greater Washington, 1962—, pres., 1970-73; bd. dirs. Men's Ort, 1974—, United Jewish Appeal, 1978—. Served with USNR, World War II, Korean War. Mem. Am. Patent Law Assn. (chmn. com. meetings and programs 1973-75), Am., D.C. bar assns. Home: 3313 Brooklawn Terr Chevy Chase MD 20015 Office: 419 7th St NW Washington DC 20004

BROWER, DAVID ROSS, conservationist; b. Berkeley, Calif., July 1, 1912; s. Ross J. and Mary Grace (Barlow) B.; m. Anne Hus, May 1, 1943; children: Kenneth David, Robert Irish, Barbara Anne, John Stewart. Student, U. Calif., 1930-31; D.Sc., Hobart and William Smith Colls., 1967; D.H.L., Claremont Colls. Grad. Sch., 1971, Starr King Sch. for Ministry, 1971, U. Md., 1973; Ph.D. in Ecology, U. San Francisco, 1973, Colo. Coll., 1977. Editor U. Calif. Press, 1941-52; exec. dir. Sierra Club, 1952-69, hon. v.p., 1971—; dir. John Muir Inst. Environ. Studies, 1969-71, v.p., 1968-72; founder, pres. Friends of the Earth, 1969-79, chmn., 1979—; founder, pres. Friends of the Earth Found., 1972-79, chmn., 1979—; pres. Friends of the Earth Internat., 1973—; prin. activist in conservation campaigns: saving Dinosaur Nat. Monument, 1952-56; initiating Nat. Outdoor Recreation Resources Rev., 1956-58; Wilderness Act, 1952-64, North Cascades Nat. Park, 1955-68, Redwood Nat. Park, 1963-68; saving Grand Canyon from dams, 1952-68, opposing nuclear proliferation, 1969—, conservation lectr., U.S., 1939—, Finland, 1971, Sweden, 1972, Kenya, 1972, 74, Italy, 1972, 74, 79, N.Z., 1974, Japan, 1976, 78; founder Trustees for Conservation, 1954, sec., 1960-61, 64-65; past v.p., trustee; founder Sierra Club Found., 1960; bd. dirs. Citizens Com. Natural Resources, 1955-78; mem. Natural Resources Council Am., chmn., 1955-57; bd. dirs. North Cascades Conservation Council, 1957—, Rachel Carson Trust for Living Environment, 1966-72, cons. expert, 1973—; founder, steering com. League Conservation Voters, 1969—; founder Les Amis de la Terre, 1970; guarantor Friends of the Earth U.K., 1970—; chmn. Earth Island Ltd., London, 1971-74; mem. bd. Environ. Liaison Center, Nairobi, 1975—. Initiator, designer, gen. editor: Sierra Club Exhibit Format Series, 20 vols, 1960-68, Friends of the Earth series The Earth's Wild Places, 10 vols, 1970-79, Celebrating the Earth series, 1972-73; numerous other films and books including Only a Little Planet, 1972; Song of the Earth Spirit, 1973, Of All Things Most Yielding, 1973, Guale: The Golden Coast of Georgia, 1974, Micronesia: Island Wilderness, 1975, Headlands, 1976, At Home in the Wild: New England: White Mountains, 1978, Wake of the World, 1979; contbr. articles to nat. mags., profl. publs., others; contbr. to U.S. Army mountain manuals, instruction, 1943-45. Mem. bd. Spirit of Stockholm Found., 1977—. Served as 1st lt. with 10th Mountain div. Inf. AUS, 1943-45; maj. Inf.-Res. ret. Decorated Bronze Star; recipient awards Calif. Conservation Council, 1953, Nat. Parks Assn., 1956, Carey-Thomas award, 1964, Paul Bartsch award Audubon Naturalist Soc. of Central Atlantic States, 1967. Mem. Nat. Parks Assn. (hon.), The Mountaineers (hon.), Appalachian Mountain Club (hon.), Sierra Club (editorial bd. 1935-69, dir. 1941-43, 46-53, John Muir award 1977). 1st ascent, Shiprock, N.Mex., 1939; many first ascents, Sierra Nevada, 1933-41. Office: Friends of Earth Found 1045 Sansome St San Francisco CA 94111 *It is true that some major resources of wildlife and wilderness, and all they mean to people, are still intact thanks to conservation battles I have shared. For this I can only be grateful—for the help, and the hope that future battles for these irreplaceable things will be as successful. They will be if enough people realize that this generation is not required to race through all the resources it can find, if humanity comprehends that this is the only earth, and there is no spare.* *

BROWER, LINCOLN PIERSON, biologist; b. Summit, N.J., Sept. 10, 1931; s. Bailey and Helen Romer (Pierson) B.; children: Andrew, Tamsin. A.B., Princeton U., 1953; Ph.D., Yale U., 1957; M.A. (hon.), Amherst Coll., 1968. Mem. faculty Amherst (Mass.) Coll., 1958-80, prof. biology, 1968-80, Stone prof., 1976-80; disting. prof. zoology U. Fla., Gainesville, 1980—; research asso. tropical research N.Y. Zool. Soc., 1962-66; adv. panel environ. biology NSF, 1968-71; researcher div. environ. studies and dept. environ. toxicology U. Calif., Davis, 1973-74; mem. bd. Conn. River Ecology Action Corp., 1971; George J. Spencer Meml. lectr. U. B.C., 1973; safari in Kenya and Tanzania, 1975. Author numerous papers and 5 documentary films in field. Fulbright scholar, 1957-58; NIH spl. fellow, 1963; grantee NSF, 1959—. Fellow AAAS, Linnean Soc. London; mem. Soc. Study Evolution (pres. 1979), Lepidopterists Soc. (v.p. 1970, pres. 1981), Am. Inst. Biol. Scis., Am. Sci. Film Assn., Am. Soc. Naturalists (v.p. 1983-84), Am. Soc. Zoologists, Animal Behavior Soc., Assn. Tropical Biology, Cambridge Entomol. Club, Ecol. Soc. Am., Royal Entomol. Soc., Wilderness Soc., Explorers Club, Sigma Xi. Home: 114 Covered Bridge Apt 1810 NW 23d Blvd Gainesville FL 32605 Office: Dept Zoology U Fla Gainesville FL 32611

BROWER, ROBERT HOPKINS, Japanese literature educator; b. Cambridge, Mass., Mar. 23, 1923; s. John Willis and Marjorie White (Hopkins) B.; m. Sally M. Shy, 1977. B.A., Harvard U., 1944; M.A., U. Mich., 1947, Ph.D. (Horace H. Rackham fellow), 1952. Instr. English U. Mich., Ann Arbor, 1947-48, teaching fellow in Japanese, 1948-51, prof. Japanese lit., 1966—, chmn. dept. Far Eastern lang. and lit., 1971-81; instr. Japanese U. Minn., 1951-54; asst. prof., asso. prof., prof. Stanford, 1954-66; dir. Inter-Univ. Center for Japanese Lang. Studies, Tokyo, 1963-64. Author: A Bibliography of Japanese Dialects, 1950, Japanese Court Poetry, 1961, Fujiwara Teika's Superior Poems of Our Time, 1967, Dictionary of Oriental Literatures, 1974, Fujiwara Teika's Hundred-Poem Sequence of the Shoji Era, 1978; contbr. articles to profl. jours. Life mem. ACLU, Common Cause. Served to capt. AUS, 1942-46. Decorated Bronze Star; Fulbright Sr. Research fellow, Japan, 1962-63; Nat. Endowment for Humanities Sr. Research fellow, 1970-71; several research fellowships from Rockefeller Found., Stanford, U. Mich.; sr. research fellow Japan Found., 1981-82. Mem. Assn. Asian Studies, Am. Oriental Soc., Assn. Tchrs. Japanese (pres. 1971-74), Phi Beta Kappa, Phi Kappa Phi, Lambda Alpha Psi, Sierra Club. Home: 722 Greenhills Dr Ann Arbor MI 48105

BROWN, A. SUE, former hospital administrator; b. Meridian, Miss., June 28, 1946; d. Silas and Macie (Burge) B. B.S., Bloomfield Coll., 1968; M.S.W., Rutgers U., 1969; cert. mgmt. by objectives, U. Pa., 1979; cert. exec. program in health policy and mgmt., Harvard U., 1980. Dir. health Urban League-Essex Co., Newark, 1969-73; health planner Coll. Medicine and Dentistry, Newark, 1973-75; acting asst. dir., then. dir. Newart Comprehensive Health Service Plan, 1973-75; acting exec. dir. Martland Hosp.-Coll. Medicine and Dentistry, Newark, 1975-77, Coll. Univ. Hosp., U. Med. and Dentistry N.J., 1977-83; Robert Wood Johnson health policy fellow Inst. Medicine, Nat. Acad. Scis., Office Congressman Richard Gephardt, Washington, 1983—; lectr. N.J. Med. Sch., Newark, 1979—; mem. acute care com. Regional Health Planning Council, 1980-82; mem. adv. com. Commn. Pub. Gen. Hosps., 1977; mem. N.J. Comprehensive Health Planning Council; mem. adv. com. Region II Health Services Mental Health Adminstrn.-Comprehensive Health Planning, 1972-74. Recipient Citizenship award Bloomfield Coll., 1968, Community Service award Nat. Council Negro Women, 1978, Leadership in Health Services award Leaguers, 1978; named Woman of Achievement Essex County Coll., 1979; scholar Scholarship, Edn. and Def. Fund, 1964-69. Mem. Assn. Am. Med. Colls. (del.), Am. Coll. Hosp. Adminstrs. (nominee), Am. Pub. Health Assn., Nat. Assn. Pub. Gen. Hosps. (founding mem.), Assn. for Children of N.J., NAACP, Nat. Council Negro Women, 100 Women for Integrity in Govt. Baptist. Home: 4261 Nash St NE Washington DC 20019 Office: Inst Medicine Nat Acad Scis 2101 Constitution Ave NE Washington DC 20418

BROWN, ADRIAN WORLEY, manufacturing company executive; b. Orlando, Fla., Feb. 4, 1928; s. James Adrian and Madoline (Worley) B.; m. Mary Lou Morris; children: Adrian W., Nancy, Betsy. A.B., U. Fla., 1950, LL.B., 1955. Bar: Fla. 1955. V.p. Brown & Brown, Inc., Daytona Beach, Fla., 1955-61; chmn. Fla. Indsl. Commn., 1961-64; with Rock-Tenn Co., Norcross, Ga., 1964—, pres., chief exec. officer, 1967—, chmn., chief exec. officer, 1978—. Mem. Fla. Bar Assn., Ga. Bus. and Industry Assn. (chmn., mem. exec. com.), U.S. Indsl. Council (v.p., mem. exec. com.), Paperboard Packaging Council (dir., mem. exec. com., mem. sr. adv. council), Order of Coif, Phi Delta Phi, Phi Delta Theta. Methodist. Office: Rock Tenn Co 504 Thrasher St. Norcross GA 30071

BROWN, ALBERT JOSEPH, JR., banker; b. Cohoes, N.Y., Dec. 18, 1934; s. Albert Joseph and Pauline (Kopcza) B.; m. Susan E. Gladding, Feb. 7, 1959; 9 children. B.A., Manhattan Coll., 1957; grad., Stonier Grad. Sch. Banking, 1970. With Key Banks, Inc., Albany, N.Y., 1958—, exec. v.p., 1982—; pres. Key Bank of Southeastern N.Y., 1977-82. Author: The Efective Branch Manager, 1970, Branch Manger's Workbook, 1975. Served with U.S. Army, 1957-58. Home: 19 Clover Field Loundonville NY 12211 Office: Key Banks Inc 60 State St Albany NY 12207

BROWN, ANDREAS LE, book store and art gallery exec., publisher, editor, author; b. Coronado, Calif., Apr. 29, 1933; s. Harvey Clair and Helene Celeste (Kimball) B. A.B., Calif. State U., San Diego, 1955; postgrad., Stanford, 1955-57. Mem. faculty Calif. State U., 1960-63; staff research fellow Humanities Research Center, U. Tex., 1963-65; appraiser rare books, 1965-67; owner, pres. Gotham Book Mart & Gallery Inc., N.Y.C., 1967—. Served with AUS, 1958-59. Mem. Manuscript Soc., Antiquarian Booksellers Assn. Am., Am. Booksellers Assn., Sigma Chi. Club: Grolier (N.Y.). Specialist in modern rare books. Address: 41 W 47th St New York NY 10036

BROWN, ANN CATHERINE, investment company executive; b. St. Louis, Aug. 12, 1935; d. George Hay and Catherine Doratha (Smith) B. B.A., Northwestern U., 1956; M.B.A., U. Mich., 1958. Copywriter Fred Gardner Advt. Co., N.Y.C., 1959-61, Batten, Barton, Durstine & Osborn, 1961-63, Ogilvy & Mather Co., 1963-64; copy group head Benton & Bowles Co., N.Y.C., 1964-66; pvt. investor, 1966-69; with Baker, Weeks & Co., Inc., N.Y.C., 1969-76, v.p., 1973-76; exec. v.p., dir. Melhado, Flynn & Assocs., Inc., N.Y.C., 1976-83; chmn. A.C. Brown & Assocs. Inc., N.Y.C., 1983—. Columnist: Forbes mag. Mem. devel. adv bd. Sch. Bus. Adminstrn., U. Mich., 1980—; mem. council Grad. Sch. Bus., U. Chgo., 1981—. Mem. Kappa Alpha Theta. Republican. Episcopalian. Club: Cosmopolitan. Home: Sea Island GA 31561 Office: Suite 1432 250 W 57th St New York NY 10107

BROWN, ANTHONY P., lawyer; b. San Francisco, Oct. 7, 1926; s. Hillyer and Emily Longfellow (Burns) B.; m. Marilyn J. Brown, May 26, 1967; children: Diane, Peter H., Henry P., Sameul C., Susan. A.B., Harvard U., 1949; LL.B., Stanford U., 1952. Bar: Calif. 1952. Assoc. firm Pillsbury, Madison & Sutro, San Francisco, 1952-63, ptnr., 1963—. Served with USN, 1944-46. Fellow Am. Coll. Trial Lawyers; mem. Am. Bar. Found. Home: 1096 Whitwell Rd Hillsborough CA 94010 Office: Pillsbury Madison & Sutro 225 Bush St San Francisco CA 94104

BROWN, ARNOLD LANEHART, JR., pathologist, educator, univ. dean; b. Wooster, Ohio, Jan. 26, 1926; s. Arnold Lanehart and Wilda (Woods) B.; m. Betty Jane Simpson, Oct. 2, 1949; children—Arnold III, Anthony, Allen, Fletcher, Lisa. Student, U. Richmond, 1943-45; M.D., Med. Coll. Va., 1949. Diplomate: Am. Bd. Pathology. Intern Presbyn.-St. Luke's Hosp., Chgo., 1949-50, resident, 1950-51, 53-56, asst. attending pathologist, 1957-59; practice medicine specializing in pathology, Rochester, Minn., 1959-78; cons. exptl. pathology, anatomy Mayo Clinic, Rochester, 1959-78, also prof., chmn. dept., 1968-78; prof. pathology U. Wis. Med. Sch., Madison, 1978—, dean, 1978—; mem. nat. cancer adv. council NIH, 1971-72; nat. cancer advisory bd. NIH, HEW, 1972-74; chmn. clearing house on environ. carcinogens Nat. Cancer Inst., 1976-80, chmn. com. to study carcinogenicity of cyclamate, 1975-76; mem. Nat. Com. on Heart Disease, Cancer and Stroke, 1975-79; mem. com. on safe drinking water NRC, 1976-77; mem. award assembly Gen. Motors Cancer Research Found., 1978—; co-chmn. panel on geochemistry of fibrous materials related to health risks Nat. Acad. Scis.-NRC, 1978—. Contbr. articles to profl. jours. Served with USNR, 1943-45, 51-53. Nat. Heart Inst. postdoctoral fellow, 1956-59. Mem. Am. Soc. Exptl. Pathology, Internat. Acad. Pathology, Am. Assn. Pathologists and Bacteriologists, Am. Gastroent. Assn., Electron Microscope Soc. Am., AMA. Home: 1705 Camelot Dr Madison WI 53705 Office: 610 N Walnut St Madison WI 53706

BROWN, ARTHUR, microbiology educator; b. N.Y.C., Feb. 12, 1922; s. Samuel S. and Ida (Hoffman) B.; m. Elaine Belaief, Dec. 24, 1947; children: Karen A., Kenneth M., Stephen S., David P. B.A., Bklyn. Coll., 1943; postgrad., U. Ky., 1946-47; Ph.D. (fellow), U. Chgo., 1950, U. Geneva, Switzerland, 1964. Diplomate: Am. Bd. Microbiology. Research assoc. U. Chgo., 1951; instr. microbiology SUNY, 1951-55; br. chief virology lab., Ft. Detrick, Frederick, Md., 1955-69; head dept. microbiology, prof. U. Tenn., 1969—, disting. service prof., 1983—; vis. prof. Georgetown U., 1967-68, George Washington U., 1957-69, U. Md., 1957-59; mem. tng. grants com. NIH, 1969-73; cons. virus cancer program Nat. Cancer Inst., 1970-74; exptl. viral study sect. NIH, 1979-83. Contbr. articles to profl. jours. Bd. dirs. YMCA, Frederick, Md., 1959-61. Served to 1st lt. USAAF, 1943-46. Macebearer U. Tenn., 1975; Chancelor's scholar, 1979. Fellow Am. Acad. Microbiology; mem. Am. Soc. Microbiology, Soc. Exptl. Biology and Medicine, Am. Assn. Immunologists, Infectious Disease Soc. Am., Am. Assn. Cancer Research, AAAS. Jewish (dir. synagogue, pres. congregation). Club: Masons. Home: 7012 Sheffield Dr Knoxville TN 37919

BROWN, ARTHUR EDMON, JR., army officer; b. Manila, Nov. 21, 1929; s. Arthur Edmon and Grace E. M. (Montgomery) B.; m. Jerry Deane Cook, June 6, 1953; children: Marian Brown Shope, Nan Brown Irick, Arthur Edmon III. B.S., U.S. Mil. Acad., 1953; M.Public and Internat. Affairs, U. Pitts., 1965. Commd. 2d lt. U.S. Army, advanced through grades to lt. gen.; mem. faculty U.S. Army War Coll., 1970-73; comdr. 1st Brigade, 1st Infantry Div., Fort Riley, Kans., 1973-75; mem. gen. staff Dept. Army, Washington, 1975-78; asst. div. comdr. 25th Infantry Div., Hawaii, 1978-80; dep. supt. U.S. Mil. Acad., West Point, 1980-81; comdr. U.S. Army Readiness and Moblzn., Region IV, Fort Gillem, Ga., 1981-83; dir. army staff Dept. Army, Washington, 1983—. Decorated Legion of Merit with 3 oak leaf clusters, Silver Star, Bronze Star with 2 oak leaf clusters. Mem. Assn. U.S. Army. Episcopalian. Club: Lions. Home: 17 Lee Ave Fort Myer VA 22211 Office: Army Staff Dept Army Washington DC 20310

BROWN, ARTHUR THOMAS, architect; b. Tarkio, Mo., May 6, 1900; s. John Vallance and Ada (Moore) B.; m. Margaret Caroline Munn, Dec. 23, 1927; children—Gordon Vallance, Arthur Thomas. B.S., Tarkio Coll., 1923; B.Arch., Ohio State U., 1927; scholar, Lake Forest Found. Architecture and Landscape Architecture, 1927. Draftsman Office David Adler, Chgo., 1928-32; with Century of Progress Expn., Chgo., 1932-34, Richard A. Morse, Tucson, 1936-39, partner, 1939-42; pvt. practice architecture, Tucson, 1942-70; partner Gordon V. Brown, 1970—; Dir. Tucson Fine Arts Assn., 1948-52. Contbr. to archtl. books and mags. Recipient mention for Rosenberg House, Progressive Architecture awards, 1946, award of merit A.I.A., 1949, Western Mountain Dist. awards for Winsor House, Ariz. Biltmore Motor Hotel, 1st Christian Ch., 1953, 54; Smith Meml. Chapel exhibited Pan Am. Congress of Architects, Lima, Peru, 1947; Alumni citation Tarkio Coll., 1958; Disting. Alumnus award Ohio State U., 1960; Disting. Citizen award U. Ariz. Alumni Assn., 1977. Fellow A.I.A. (mem. nat. com. on sch. bldgs. 1948-50, pres. Ariz. chpt. 1946); mem. Palette and Brush Club, So. Ariz. Watercolor Guild, Tucson Gem and Mineral Soc. Presbyn. Club: Rotarian. Patentee prefabricated cylinder house, method of producing a shell roof structure, open wall door frame. Home: 740 N Country Club Rd Tucson AZ 85716 Office: 726 N Country Club Rd Tucson AZ 85716

BROWN, ARTHUR WAYNE, college dean; b. Sheshequin, Pa., Apr. 20, 1917; s. Arthur L. and Helen E. (Laclair) B.; m. Dorothy C. Johnston, Sept. 17, 1938; children—Anne (Mrs. Allan Root), Margaret (Mrs. Frank O'Neill), Michael, Patricia (Mrs. Eugene Crabbe), Thomas, Arthur, Mary, Deborah. A.B., U. Scranton, 1937; M.A., Cornell U., 1938; Ph.D., Syracuse U., 1950. Prof. English Utica Coll. of Syracuse U., 1955-63; prof. English, chmn. dept., dir. Inst. Humanities, Adelphi U., 1963-65, pres., 1965-67; dean faculties, dean Grad. Sch., Fordham U., 1967-68, v.p. for acad. affairs, 1968-69; pres. Marygrove Coll., Detroit, 1969-72; dean Sch. Liberal Arts and Scis., Baruch Coll., City U. N.Y., 1972-77, Coll. Arts and Scis. U. Miami, Coral Gables, Fla., 1977—; Westchester dir. 1st Nat. City Bank. Author: Always Young for Liberty, 1956, William Ellery Channing, 1960, Margaret Fuller, 1964; Co-editor: series Great American Thinkers, 1964-73, World Leaders, 1973—. Sec. Catholic Commn. on Intellectual and Cultural Affairs, 1970—; exec. com. Mich. Colls. Found.; bd. dirs. Catholic Charities, Utica, 1960-62, United Fund, L.I., Fla. Endowment for Humanities; chmn. bd. dirs. St. Elizabeth Sch. Nursing, Utica, 1961-62; trustee Molloy Coll., L.I., 1969-73; bd. govs. St. Paul's Sch., Garden City, 1968-69, 73-74; v.p. Council on Edn. for Public Health, 1979—. Am. Council Learned Socs. grantee, 1961-62. Mem. AAUP, Modern Lang. Assn., Newcomen Soc. N.Am., Phi Beta Kappa. Office: U Miami Coll Arts and Scis Coral Gables FL 33124

BROWN, ARVIN BRAGIN, theatre director; b. Los Angeles, May 24, 1940; s. Herman S. and Annette R. (Edelman) B.; m. Joyce Ebert, Nov. 2, 1969. B.A., Stanford U., 1961; cert. in drama, U. Bristol, (Eng.), 1962; M.A., Harvard U., 1963; postgrad., Yale U., 1963-65; Ph.D. hon., U. New Haven, 1976, U. Bridgeport, 1978. Dir. Childrens Theatre, Long Wharf Theatre, New Haven, 1965-67, artistic dir., 1967—; assoc. dir. Williamstown Theatre Festival, Mass., 1969; lectr. in directing Salzburg Seminar, 1972; del. Internat. Theatre Conf., Bulgaria, Hungary, 1979; guest lectr. New Play Centre, Vancouver, 1980, U. Ill., Urbana, 1980, 82. Tv dir.: The Widowing of Mrs. Holroyd, 1974, Forget-Me-Not Lane, 1974, Ah' Wilderness, 1974, Amahl and the Night Vistors, 1977, Close Ties, 1982; dir.: play Long Day's Journey into Night, 1971, The National Health, 1974, Watch on the Rhine, 1979, American Buffalo, 1981, A view From the Bridge, 1983. Recipient Vernon Rice award for best off-Broadway dir., 1970-71, Variety Critics' Poll award, 1970-71, Antoinette Perry award nomination for best Broadway dir., 1974-75; selected one of 50 faces for America's Furure Time Mag., 1979; recipient Conn. Arts Award Conn. Commn. on Arts, 1983. Mem. Theatre Communications Group (co-dir. 1972-76), Nat. Endowment for the Arts (theatre adv. panel), Internat. Theatre Inst., Soc. Stage Dirs. and Choreographers, Dirs. Guild. Home: 11 Good Hill Rd Weston CT 06883 Office: Long Wharf Theatre 222 Sargent Dr New Haven CT 06511

BROWN, AUBREY NEBLETT, JR., clergyman, editor; b. Hillsboro, Tex., May 6, 1908; s. Aubrey Neblett and Virginia Rose (Sims) B.; m. Sarah Dumond Hill, Oct. 4, 1932; children—Aubrey Neblett III, Zaida English (Mrs. Douglas Robb Paden), Julia Haywood (Mrs. Edward Townsend Diehl), Virginia Sims (Mrs. Rod Edison Ashworth), Eleanor Berkeley (Mrs. Milton Byrum Bigger), William Hill, Ernest Thompson, Katherine Purdie. A.B., Davidson Coll., 1929; B.D., Union Theol. Sem., Va., 1932; Litt.D., Southwestern at Memphis, 1950; D.D., Maryville Coll., 1961; Litt.D., Davidson Coll., 1979. Ordained to ministry Presbyn. Ch. U.S., 1932; pastor Presbyn. chs., Ronceverte, W.Va., 1932-38, Montgomery, W.Va., 1938-43; editor Presbyn. Outlook, Richmond, Va., 1943-78, Going-to-Coll. Handbook, 1946-78; interim pastor All Souls Presbyn. Ch., Richmond, 1963-64, 73-74; coordinator Richmond Area Presbyns., 1979—; moderator Synod of W.Va., Presbyn. Ch. U.S., 1946. Pres. Richmond Area Council Human Relations, 1957-59, Va. Council Human Relations, 1963-65; chmn. Va. Adv. Com. to U.S. Commn. on Civil Rights, 1966-67; pres. Richmond Area chpt. UN Assn. U.S.A., 1967-69, N.Am. area council World Alliance Ref. Chs., 1960-73; del. 20th Gen. Council World Alliance Ref. Chs., Nairobi, Kenya, 1970. Recipient Editorial citation Assn. Ch. Press, 1952, Torch of Liberty award Va. B'nai B'rith, 1966. Democrat. Club: Torch (pres. Richmond chpt. 1951-52). Home: 3213 Brook Rd Richmond VA 23227 Office: 1205 Palmyra Ave Richmond VA 23227

BROWN, B. MAHLON, III, lawyer; b. Las Vegas, Nev., Aug. 8, 1939; s. B. Mahlon and Lucille (Cummings) B.; m. LaVerne Mae Zantello, Sept. 16, 1961; children: Bert M., Bryce Malina, Paige Morgana. Student, U. Nev., Las Vegas, also Reno; B.A., George Washington U., 1965; J.D., Howard U., 1969. Bar: Nev. Exec. dir. Clark County Legal Services, Las Vegas, 1970-73; with firm Brown & Deaner, Las Vegas, 1973-74; justice of the peace, Las Vegas Twp., 1974—; U.S. atty. Dist. of Nev., Las Vegas, 1977-81; sole practice, Las Vegas, 1983—; Past bd. dirs. Operation Life, Clark County Legal Services Program. Past mem. adv. bd. Emergency Sch. Aid Act, Econ. Opportunity Bd. of Clark County; past v.p. Nike House; past mem. So. Nev. Drug Abuse Council, FOCUS. Recipient Good Fellow award City of Hope, 1975. Mem. ACLU (past pres. Nev.). Democrat. Home: 2221 De Osma Las Vegas NV 89102 Office: 704 S 4th St Las Vegas NV 89101

BROWN, BAILEY, U.S. judge; b. Memphis, 1917; s. Joshua Goodlett and Lillian (Pearcy) B.; m. Doris Frances Lawhorn., Dec. 24, 1964; 1 son, Bailey. A.B., U. Mich., 1939; LL.B., Harvard, 1942. Bar: Tenn. bar. Partner firm Burch, Porter, Johnson & Brown, Memphis; judge U.S. Dist. Ct. for Western Tenn., Memphis; chief judge; judge U.S. Ct. Appeals for 6th Circuit, 1979—; mem. Jud. Conf. Com. on Ct. Adminstrn.; guest lectr. Southwestern U., Memphis. Pres. Memphis Symphony, 1958-60, Memphis Pub. Affairs Forum, 1955. Served to lt. USNR, 1942-46. Episcopalian (vestryman). Office: 2670 Union Extended Memphis TN 38112

BROWN, BENJAMIN ANDREW, journalist; b. Red House, W.Va., Apr. 30, 1933; s. Albert Miller and Mary Agnes (Donegan) B.; m. Joanne Gretchen Harder, May 22, 1956; children: Benjamin Andrew, Gretchen, Mark, Betsy. B.S. in Journalism, Fla. State U., 1955. Sportswriter Charleston (W.Va.) Daily Mail, 1955-57; with AP, 1957—, gen. exec., N.Y.C., 1976-78, 82—, chief bur., Los Angeles, 1978-82; bd. dirs. Last Chance Press Club, Helena, Mont., 1969; v.p. Minn. Press Club, 1975. Mem. Sigma Delta Chi. Office: Associated Press 50 Rockefeller Plaza New York NY 10020

BROWN, BENNETT ALEXANDER, banker; b. Kingsrgee, S.C.; m. Mary Alice Rustin, Nov. 30, 1957; children—Charlotte, Bennett, Leila, Katherine. B.S., Presbyn. Coll., Clinton, S.C., 1950, La. State U. Sch. Banking, 1960; grad., Advanced Mgmt. Program, Harvard U., 1965. With Chem. Bank, N.Y.C., 1950, Fed. Res. Bank Atlanta, 1953-55; with Citizens & So. Bank, Atlanta, 1955—, chmn., chief exec. officer, 1979—, also dir.; dir. Citizens & So. Ga. Corp., Piggly Wiggly So., Inc., Vidalia, Ga., Graniteville Co., S.C.; adv. bd. Ga. So. and Fla. R.R. Co. Served with U.S. Army, 1951-53. Mem. Internat. Monetary Conf., Assn. Bank Holding Cos., Assn. Res. City Bankers, Atlanta C. of C. Presbyterian. Clubs: Capital City, Commerce (dir.). Address: Citizens and So Nat Bank 35 Broad St Atlanta GA 30399

BROWN, BILL RONDOL, university dean; b. Hamlin, Tex., Aug. 28, 1942; s. Harold and Lorena (Reynolds) B.; m. Evelynn Grayce, June 6, 1964; children: Christopher Rondol, Gregory Wayne. B.A., North Tex. State U., 1964, M.S., 1965; Ph.D., Tex. Christian U., 1967. Asst. research prof. Tex. Christian U., 1968-69; asst. prof. U. Louisville, 1969-70, assoc. prof., 1970-74, dir. analytical studies, 1974-78, dir. systems sci., 1978-80; dean Grad. Sch. U. No. Colo., Greeley. Contbr. articles to profl. jours. Mem. info. data systems task force Ky. Council Pub. Higher Edn., Frankfort, 1974-78; mem. Task Force Delta, Dept. Def., Ft. Monroe, Va., 1978-80; sponsor research bd. Colo. Commn. on Higher Edn., Denver, 1981—; bd. dirs. Am. Cancer Soc., 1982—; instr. Eldora Handicapped Ski Program, 1981—. Recipient various grants, 1969-80. Mem. AAAS, Psychonomic Soc., Soc. Gen. System Research, N.Y. Acad. Sci., Sigma Xi. Lutheran. Home: 1700 Montview Blvd Greeley Co 80631 Office: Univ No Colo Grad Sch Greeley CO 80639

BROWN, BILLYE JEAN, college dean; b. Damascus, Ark., Oct. 29, 1925; d. William A. and Dora (Megee) B. B.S.N.Ed., U. Tex. Med. Br., Galveston, 1953; M.S.N.Ed., St. Louis U., 1958; Ed.D., Baylor U., 1975. Asst. prof. U. Tex. Med. Br. Sch. Nursing, 1958-60; assoc. prof. U. Tex. Nursing Sch., Austin, 1960-67, assoc. dean, prof., 1968-72, dean, prof., 1972—; mem. Nat. Adv. Council Nurse Tng., 1982—. Nat. League for Nursing fellow, 1957-58; recipient Alumni Merit award St. Louis U., 1981. Mem. Am. Assn. Univ. Adminstrs., Am. Assn. for Higher Edn., Tex. League for Nursing, Tex. Nurses Assn. (Nurse of Yr. 1980), Am. Nurses Assn., Am. Assn. Colls. Nursing (pres. 1982-84). Office: 1700 Red River Austin TX 78701

BROWN, BRITT, ret. publishing co. exec.; b. Long Beach, Calif., Apr. 23, 1927; s. Harry Britton and Victoria (Eaton) B.; m. Anne Louise McCarthy, June 19, 1948; children—Cathy Lynn, Cynthia Ann, Britt Murdock, Bruce McCarthy. Student, U. So. Calif., 1944-46; B.A., U. Kans., 1947. Classified advt. salesman Wichita (Kans.) Eagle (now Wichita Eagle & Beacon Pub. Co.), 1947-50, classified mgr., 1952-55, advt. dir., 1956-62, v.p., sec., 1963-71, formerly pres., from 1971, chmn., 1973-79. Served with USMCR, 1944-46, 50-51. Mem. Sigma Delta Chi, Kappa Alpha.

BROWN, BUTLER MALLOY, painter; b. Vienna, Ga., Dec. 17, 1937; s. Bunk David and Mary Magdalene (Cross) B.; m. Frances Laverne Thompson, Aug. 26, 1959; children: Anthony Allen, Julie Renee. Grad., Famous Artists Sch., 1972. Civilian computer programmer, Robins AFB, Ga., 1956-72, part-time painter, 1968-72, full-time painter, 1973—. One-man exhbns. include, Ann Tutt Gallery, Macon, Ga., 1971, 72, 78-83, Macon Mus. of Arts and Sci., 1973, Hermitage, Richmond, Va., 1975, River North, Macon, Women's Nat. Democratic Club, Washington, 1978, group exhbns. include, Columbus Sq. Art Show, Ga., 1971, Virginia Beach Boardwalk Show, Va., Gardens Art Festival, Callaway Gardens, Ga., 1971-72, Macon Winter Arts Festival, Macon Mus. of Arts and Sci., 1973, Warner Robins Art Festival, Ga., 1972-75, Lenox Sq. Art Show, Atlanta, 12th Ann. Shrimp Boat Race Art Show, Fernandina Beach, Fla., 1975 (second place), Miss. Arts Festival, Jackson, 1976, Callanwold Estates, Ga. Artists Show, Atlanta, 1976-83, Middle Ga. Coll., Cochran, 1982, The Garrett-Fuller House, Dublin, Ga., Savannah Coll. Art and Design, 1983, Gertrude Herbert Inst. Art, Augusta, Ga., The State Capitol, Atlanta, Ga.; designed book jacket, The History of Robins Air Force Base, 1982; rep. permanent and pvt. collections including, The White House, Minister of Culture, Peoples Republic of China, Gov. and Mrs. Joe Frank Harris (2d place 1972). Mem. Pulaski County (Ga.) Bd. Edn., 1975—. Honorable mention Macon Winter Arts Festival, Ga., 1971; second place Macon Winter Arts Festival, Ga., 1972; Flag of Honor Virginia Beach Boardwalk, 1971; Purchase awd. Chattahoochee Valley Art Assn., 1972; ofcl. artist Ga. Semiquincentenary Celebration, 1983. Address: Route 3 Hawkinsville GA 31036

BROWN, BYRON WILLIAM, JR., biostatistician, educator; b. Chgo., Apr. 21, 1930; s. Byron William and Ruth (Munson) B.; m. Janet Louise Hyde, July 30, 1949; children: Byron William III, Eric Paul, Alan Thomas, Nancy Ellen, Mark Andrew, Lisa Anne. B.A. in Math, U. Minn., 1952, M.S. in Statistics, 1955, Ph.D. in Biostatistics, 1959. Asst. prof. biostatistics La. State U. Med. Sch., New Orleans, 1956-57; lectr., asst. prof., assoc. prof. biostatistics Sch. Pub. Health, U. Minn., 1957-65, prof., head biostatistics, 1965-68, Stanford, 1968—; cons. govt. and industry. Co-author: Statistics: A Biomedical Introduction; Contbr. articles to profl. jours., books, encys. Served with USAF, 1949. Fellow Am. Statis. Assn. (sect. pres., asso. editor Jour.), Am. Heart Assn., AAAS; mem. Biometrics Soc. (pres. Western N.Am. region 1978), Inst. Math. Statistics, Phi Beta Kappa, Sigma Xi. Democrat. Lutheran. Home: 981 Cottrell Way Stanford CA 94305

BROWN, CAMERON, insurance company consultant; b. Chgo., Sept. 29, 1914; s. George Frederic and Irene (Larmon) B.; m. Dorothea Fruechtenicht, May 10, 1947 (div. Feb. 1965); children: Reid L., Deborah Sue; m. Jean McGrew, Dec. 22, 1965; 1 dau., Sophia Lyn. A.B., U. Ill., 1937; grad., Indsl. Coll. Armed Forces, 1941. Vice pres. R. B. Jones & Sons, Inc., 1938-41; dir. Geo. F. Brown & Sons, Inc., Chgo., 1947-79, v.p., 1947-50, exec. v.p., 1950-53, pres., 1953-64, chmn., chief exec. officer, 1964-76; dir. Interstate Nat. Corp., 1968-79, pres., 1968-74, chmn., 1970-76; dir. Nat. Student Mktg. Corp., 1970-79, pres., 1970-72, chmn., 1970-75; dir. Interstate Fire & Casualty Co., 1952-79, exec. v.p., 1953-56, pres., 1956-74, chmn., 1970-76; dir. Chgo. Ins. Co., 1957-79, pres., 1957-74, chmn., 1970-76; dir. Interstate Reins. Corp., 1957-79; pres. Cameron Brown Ltd., 1976—; underwriting mem. Lloyd's of London, 1971—; sec., dir. Ill. Ins. Info. Service, 1967-76. Contbg. author: Property and Liability Handbook, 1965. Pres., Chgo. area Planned Parenthood Assn., 1969-72; trustee U. Chgo. Cancer Research Found.; vis. com. U. Chgo.; governing mem. Shedd Aquarium; bd. dirs. Planned Parenthood Fedn. Am., 1976-79; mem. Exec. Service Corps, Chgo., 1978—, John Evans Club, Northwestern U., U. Ill. Pres.'s Club, U. Ill. Found., U. Chgo. Pres.'s Club.; Fellow Aspen Inst. Humanistic Studies, 1976—. Served from 2d lt. to lt. col. Gen. Staff Corps AUS, 1941-45. Decorated Bronze Star with oak leaf cluster. Mem. Lloyd's Brokers Assn. (chmn. 1959-60), Nat. Assn. Ind. Insurers (bd. govs. 1961-77), Ill. St. Andrews Soc., Internat. Wine and Food Soc. (Chgo.), Surplus Line Brokers Assn. (chmn. 1954), English-Speaking Union (bd. govs.), Confrerie des Chevaliers du Tastevin (officier-comdr.), Commanderie de Bordeaux (Maitre honoraire), Knights of the Vine (master knight), Psi Upsilon. Clubs: Chgo., Attic, Exec. (dir. 1969-73), Exec. (1st v.p. 1970-71), Econ., Mid-Am., Arts, Casino (Chgo.); Army-Navy Country (Washington); Old Elm, Shoreacres, Onwentsia (Lake Forest, Ill.); Pine Valley Golf (Clementon, N.J.); Birnam Wood Golf (Montecito, Calif.); The Valley; Hon. Co. Edinburgh Golfers (Muirfield, Scotland); Royal and Ancient Golf, St. Andrews (Scotland). Home: 600 S Ridge Rd Lake Forest IL 60045 Office: 222 E Wisconsin Ave Lake Forest IL 60045

BROWN, CAROLYN RICE, dancer, choreographer; b. Fitchburg, Mass., Sept. 26, 1927; d. James Parker and Marion (Stevens) Rice. B.A. cum laude (Wheaton scholar), Wheaton Coll., 1950, D.F.A. (hon.), 1974; postgrad., Juilliard Sch. Music, 1952-53; studied dance with, Marion Rice, Margaret Craske, Antony Tudor, Merce Cunningham. Tchr. Merce Cunningham Studio, 1954—, Conn. Coll. Sch. Dance, 1958-61, UCLA, 1963, walker Art Center, Mpls., 1967, U. Colo., 1968, U. Calif., Berkeley, 1971, 74, 77, Mills Coll., 1974, U. Md., 1975, Ballet Théâtre Contemporain, France, 1976; past dean of dance SUNY, Purchase; Bd. dirs. Paper Bag Players, 1965-66, Found. for Performance Arts, 1967—; mem. adv. bd. Jacobs Pillow, 1979. Leading soloist, partner, Merce Cunningham Dance Co., N.Y.C., 1953-73; performances throughout, U.S., Can., Europe, Mex., S.Am., India, Thailand, Japan, Iran; duo tours to, Europe, 1958, 60, world tour, 1964, European tours, 1966, 69, 70, 72, TV performances in, U.S., Europe, Can.; performed in: John Cage's Theatre Piece, 1960, Robert Rauschenberg's Pelican, 1963; choreographer: Balloon, 1965, Car Lot, 1967 (Jersey Jour. award for best choreography 1967-68), West Country, 1970, Zellerbach Maul, 1971, As I Remember It, 1972, Bunkered for a Bogie, 1972, Port de Bras for Referees, 1973, 2d version, 1981, Synergy I, 1973, Synergy II, 1974, House Party, 1973-74, Circles, 1975, Balloon II, 1976, Serious Song, 1977, Child's Play, 1979, Rhosymedre, 1979; filmmaker: Dune Dance, 1975-78; Contbr.: articles to Dance Perspectives. Recipient Dance Mag. award, 1970, 100th Anniversary Distinguished Service award Wheaton Coll., 1970; Nat. Endowment for Arts Fellow, 1973, 75, 76; Creative Arts Pub. Service Program fellow, 1974. Mem. Phi Beta Kappa. Address: 28 Greenwich Ave New York NY 10011 *

BROWN, CARROLL, foreign service officer; b. Selma, Ala., Oct. 5, 1928; s. Jack Crisman and Bessie (Bedsole) B.; m. Elvira Marie DiMiceli, Apr. 2, 1953; children: David, Suzanne. A.B., Columbia U., 1951, M.A., 1953; postgrad., Johns Hopkins U., 1964-65. Joined Fgn. Service, 1957, posts include Yugoslavia, Poland, Washington; counselor embassy, Vienna, Austria, 1968-73; dep. dir. for Eastern European affairs Dept. State, Washington, 1974-76; dep. chief mission Am. embassy, Warsaw, 1976-79; consul gen., Munich, W.Ger., 1981—. Served with USN, 1953-57. Mem. Fgn. Service Assn. Club: Army-Navy. Lodge: Rotary. Office: Koeniginstrasse 5 8000 Munich 22 Federal Republic of Germany

BROWN, CECIL, TV-radio news commentator, educator, lectr.; b. New Brighton, Pa., Sept. 14, 1907; s. Maurice I. and Jennie (Broida) B.; m. Martha Leaine Kohn, July 20, 1938. Student, Western Res. U., 1925-27; B.S., Ohio State U., 1929; Litt. D. (hon.), Union Coll. Sailed as seaman to, S. Am., Russia, West Africa; wrote stories of experience, pub. in Youngstown (Ohio) Vindicator, 1928-29; reporter for United Press, Los Angeles, 1931-32; editor Prescott (Ariz.) Jour.-Miner, 1933; staff Pitts. Press, 1934-36, Newark Ledger, 1936-37; free lance writer, Europe, North Africa, 1937-38; with Internat. News Service, 1938-39; news broadcast for CBS, Rome, 1940-41, Yugoslavia, Cairo, Singapore, 1941-42, Australia, N.Y.C., 1943-58; news commentator over MBS, 1944-57; news commentator ABC, 1957-58; Far East bur. chief NBC, Tokyo, 1958-62, TV-radio news commentator, Los Angeles, 1962-64; dir. news and pub. affairs, commentator Community TV of So. Calif., KCET-28, Los Angeles, 1964-67; TV cons. Ency. Brit., 1967-68; prof. communications and internat. affairs Calif. State Poly. U., Pomona, 1967-80. Author: Suez to Singapore, 1942; Introduction to ltd. edits., Club edit. Carlyle's The French Revolution, 1956; chpt. on Japan in Memo to J.F.K.; Contbr. to mags. Recipient awards for distinguished radio news reporting from abroad during 1941 from Sigma Delta Chi, Overseas Press Club, Nat. Council for Edn. by Radio, Nat. Headliners Club, George Foster Peabody Award, Motion Picture Daily's award, winner World-Telegram poll for outstanding single broadcast of 1942, Alfred I. Dupont award for best TV news commentary, 1965; awards for commentary A.P., 1965, 66; named Distinguished Tchr. Calif. State Poly. U., Pomona, 1973-74, Outstanding Prof., 1979-80. Mem. Overseas Press Club (past pres.), Soc. Profl. Journalists. Expelled from Italy, Apr. 1, 1941, by Italian govt. for continued hostile attitude toward Fascism. Survivor of sinking by Japanese bombers of Prince of Wales and Repulse, South China Sea, Dec. 10, 1941. Home: 10450 Wilshire Blvd Los Angeles CA 90024

BROWN, CHARLES ARTHUR, lawyer; b. Greenwood, Miss., Sept. 30, 1929; s. Charles and Lois (Finch) B.; m. Jennifer Sue Carter, June 2, 1957; children: Chryl Adele, Krista Lynne, Charles Carter. Student, Henderson State Tchrs. Coll., Arkadelphia, Ark., 1947-49; LL.B., U. Ark., 1953. Bar: Ark. 1953. Practice in, Little Rock, 1956—; assoc. Patten & Brown, 1956-60, partner, 1960-72, Patten, Brown & Leslie, 1972—; instr. Ark. Law Sch., 1956-67; spl. instr. bus. law Little Rock U., 1965-67; Asso. legal counsel U.S. Jaycees, 1964-65, mem. exec. com., 1964-66, gen. counsel, 1965-66. Pres. Leawood Property Owners Assn., 1966-68; mem. Little Rock Sch. Bd., 1968-72; mem. sch. bd. Pulaski Acad., 1975-78; mem. Pulaski County Democratic Com., 1972-74, Pulaski County Qurom Ct., 1960-62, 70-72; bd. dirs. Ark. Lighthouse for Blind, 1977—, v.p., 1981, pres., 1983. Served with AUS, 1954-55. Recipient Disting. Service award Little Rock Jaycees, 1966; Boss of Year award Greater Little Rock Jaycees, 1970. Mem. ABA, Ark. Bar Assn. (ho. of dels. 1975-78), Pulaski County Bar Assn., Am. Trial Lawyers Assn., Ark. Trial Lawyers Assn. (pres. 1979-80), Little Rock C. of C. (past dir.). Baptist (adult Sunday sch. tchr.). Clubs: Masons, Shriners. Home: 7713 Leawood Blvd Little Rock AR 72205 Office: One Union Plaza Little Rock AR 72201 *Service to God and man is the best goal of life. Service to man is doing more for man than man can do for you. Service to God additionally requires more-faith; but man's service to man cannot be ultimate without God.*

BROWN, CHARLES CARTER, consulting engineer; b. Natchitoches, La., Oct. 22, 1912; s. Cyrus Jay and Berenice Marie (Carter) B.; m. Sylvia Ernestine Gass, Nov. 30, 1934; children: Barbara Anne, Carter Gass, Sylvia Ellen Brown Swinger. B.S. in Civil Engring., La. State U., 1934. Observer, U.S. Coast and Geodetic Survey, Pensacola, Fla., 1934-35; hydraulics engr. Soil Conservation Service, Franklinton, La., 1935-41; from design engr. to state dir. pub. works La. Dept. Pub. Works, Baton Rouge, 1941-48; partner Brown & Butler (cons. engrs.), Baton Rouge, 1948-70, owner, 1970-82; ret., 1982. Served to lt. USNR, 1944-46. Fellow ASCE (past pres. La.), Am. Cons. Engrs. Council (past v.p., dir.); mem. Cons. Engrs. Council La. (past pres., Service awards, A.E. Wilder Meml. award), La. Engring. Soc. Republican. Roman Catholic. Club: City (Baton Rouge). Home: 1682 Carl Ave Baton Rouge LA 70808

BROWN, CHARLES DANIEL, chemical corporation executive; b. Mineral Springs, Ark., Oct. 31, 1927; s. Leonidas Carlton and Willie Pearl (Graves) B.; m. Marjorie Ann Fischer, June 1, 1951; children: Brant Carlton, Karyn Danette, Christopher Daniel. B.S. in Civil Engring., U. Ark, 1951. With E.I. DuPont de Nemours & Co., Inc., Wilmington, Del., 1951—, v.p. engring. dept., 1982—. Task force chmn. constrn. industry cost effectiveness project: books Report on Problems of United States Construction Industry, 1978-81 (Engring. News Record-Constrn. Industry Man of Year award 1982). Served with AUS, 1946-47; PTO. Mem. Bus. Roundtable (chmn. constrn. com. N.Y.C. 1981-83), Theta Tau. Methodist. Clubs: Kennett Square Country (Pa.); Wilmington Country; DuPont Country (Wilmington). Home: 5407 Crestline Dr Wilmington DE 19808 Office: E I DuPont de Nemours & Co Inc 1007 Market St Wilmington DE 19898

BROWN, CHARLES EARL, lawyer; b. Columbus, Ohio, June 6, 1919; s. Anderson and Ruth (Keeran) B.; m. Mary Elizabeth Hiett, May 23, 1959; children: Douglas Charles, Rebecca Ruth. A.B., Ohio Wesleyan U., 1941; J.D., U. Mich., 1949. Bar: Ohio 1949. Since practiced in Toledo, pvt. practice, 1949-50; asso. Zachman, Boxell, Bebout & Torbet, 1950-53; partner Brown, Baker, Schlageter & Craig (and predecessors), 1953—; chmn. bd., dir. Maumee Fabrics Co.; dir. Riker Mfg., Inc., Toledo Truck Tubes, Inc.; chmn. steering and exec. coms. Auto Trim Wholesalers div. Automotive Service Industry Assn., 1960-68. Republican county chmn. policy com., 1968-74, mem. exec. com., 1968-74, 76—. Served to capt. AUS, 1941-46; col. Res. ret. Decorated Bronze Star; recipient John J. Pershing award U.S. Army Command and Gen. Staff Coll., 1963. Fellow Am. Bar Found. (state chmn.), Ohio State Bar Found., Am. Coll. Probate Counsel; mem. ABA, Ohio Bar Assn. (bd. govs. real property sect. 1953-76, council of dels. 1973-84, exec. com. 1984), Toledo Bar Assn. (past mem. exec. com.), Toledo Area C. of C. (past trustee, com. chmn.), Res. Officers Assn., Assn. U.S. Army, Phi Beta Kappa. Congregationalist (past chmn. trustees). Club: Masons (32 deg.). Home: 3758 Brookside Rd Toledo OH 43606 Office: First Fed Plaza 711 Adams St Toledo OH 43624

BROWN, CHARLES FREEMAN, lawyer; b. Boston, Mar. 7, 1914; s. Arthur Harrison and Nellie Abigail (Kenney) B.; m. Caroline Gotzian Tighe, Nov. 12, 1949 (dec. Jan. 1951); m. Pamela Judith Wedd, Nov. 29, 1952; children—Penelope Susan, Nicholas Wedd. A.B., Harvard U., 1936, LL.B., 1941. Bar: Mass. bar 1941. Asso. atty. Sherburne, Powers & Needham, Boston, 1941-43; asst. gen. counsel, gen. counsel OSRD, Washington, 1943-47; counsel Research and Devel. Bd. and mil. liaison com.; mem. Govt. Patents Bd., Office Sec. Def.; counsel Def. Prodn. Bd., NATO; dep. asst. sec. gen. for prodn. and logistics NATO detailed from Office Sec. Def., Washington, London, Paris, 1947-53; asst. to pres. Hydrofoil Corp., Annapolis, Md., 1953-54; asso. gen. counsel CIA, Washington, 1954-60; v.p., treas. Sci. Engring. Inst., Waltham, Mass., 1960-66; dep. gen. counsel NSF, Washington, 1966-73, gen. counsel, 1973-76, chmn. interim compliance panel, 1970-71; cons., 1976—. Trustee Belmont (Mass.) Day Sch., 1963-66; bd. dirs. Hillcrest Children's Center, Washington, 1978—, pres., 1980—; pres. Cleveland Park Book Club, 1979—. Recipient Disting. Service award NSF. Mem. Fed. Bar Assn. Clubs: Cosmos (Washington); West River Sailing (Galesville, Md.). Home and Office: 3500 Macomb St NW Washington DC 20016

BROWN, CHARLES LEE, telephone company executive; b. Richmond, Va., Aug. 23, 1921; s. Charles Lee and Mary (McNamara) B.; m. Ann Lee Saunders, July 25, 1959; 1 son, Charles A. B.S. in Elec. Engring, U. Va., 1943. With AT&T (and affiliates), 1946—; v.p., gen. mgr. Ill. Bell Telephone Co., 1963-65, v.p. ops., dir., 1965-69, pres., dir., 1969-74; exec. v.p., chief fin. officer AT&T, N.Y.C., 1974-76, vice chmn. bd., chief fin. officer, 1976-77, pres., 1977-79, chmn. bd., 1979—; dir. E.I. du Pont de Nemours Co., Chem. Bank and Chem. N.Y., Gen. Foods Corp. Trustee Presbyn. Hosp., Colonial Williamsburg Found., Inst. Advanced Study. Served with USNR, 1943-46. Mem. Bus. Council, Bus. Roundtable, Ctr. Innovative Tech. of Va., Delta Upsilon, Theta Tau, Omicron Delta Kappa. Presbyterian. Clubs: River, Links, Met. (N.Y.C.); Pine Valley Golf. Office: 550 Madison Ave Room 3400 New York NY 10022

BROWN, CHARLES STUART, state supreme court justice; b. Freedom, Wyo., June 30, 1918; s. Charles William and Julia Teola (Rainey) B.; m. Jane Hurst, Aug. 6, 1941; children: Ann (Mrs. Paul Christensen), Julia (Mrs. Dan Gibson), James Stuart, Colleen (Mrs. Rick Perkins), Patricia (Mrs. Richard Mills), Robert William, Helen (Mrs. Timothy Curry), Virginia. B.S., Utah State U., 1943; J.D., U. Utah, 1950. Bar: Wyo. 1950, Utah 1950. Prin. Freedom Elem. Sch., 1946-47; individual practice law, Kemmerer, Wyo., 1950-59, pros. atty., Lincoln County, 1959-65; judge 3d Jud. Dist. Wyo. Dist. Ct., Kemmerer, 1965-81; asso. justice Wyo. State Supreme Ct., Cheyenne, 1981—; asso. solicitor Dept. Interior, Washington, 1961-62. Author: Wyoming Ranch and Farm Law, 1959. Served to col. AUS, 1942-46. Office: Supreme Ct Bldg Cheyenne WY 82001

BROWN, CLAUDE P., transport company executive; b. Lithia Springs, Ga., July 12, 1917; s. James A. and Lula M. B.; m. Mary L. Stroud, Dec., 1941 (dec. Feb. 1981); children: Bruce, Jim (dec.), Sue, Bill; m. Grace Holman, Nov. 1982. Student, pubs. schs., Ga. Chmn. bd. Brown Transport Corp., Atlanta, 1946—, Tri Tractor, Cumming, Ga., 1980—. Bd. dirs. Old Time Gospel Hour, Lynchburg, Va., 1980—, Campus Crusade for Christ, San Bernardino, Calif., 1980—. Republican. Clubs: Capital City; Commerce (Atlanta); Lost Tree (North Palm Beach, Fla.). Office: Brown Transport Corp 352 University Ave SW Atlanta GA 30310

BROWN, CLIFFORD F., state supreme ct. justice; b. Bronson Twp., Ohio, Jan. 21, 1916; s. Ignatius A. B.; m. Katherine Brown; adopted children—Charles, Margaret (Mrs. David Kramb), Sheila, Ann (Mrs. Leonard Playko, Jr.). A.B. magna cum laude, U. Notre Dame, 1936, LL.B. cum laude, 1938. Bar: Ohio bar 1938, Mich. bar 1938. Practice law, Norwalk, Ohio, 1938-64; judge Huron County Ct., 1958-65, Ohio Ct. Appeals, 1965-81; asso. justice Ohio State Supreme Ct., Columbus, 1981—. Served with U.S. Army, World War II. Mem. Am. Bar Assn., Ohio State Bar Assn., Lucas County Bar Assn., Toledo Bar Assn. Democrat. Clubs: Kiwanis, Torch, Eagles, Athletic. Office: Ohio State Supreme Ct 30 E Broad St Columbus OH 43215 *

BROWN, COLIN W(EGAND), diversified company executive, lawyer; b. Port Jefferson, N.Y., Mar. 26, 1949; s. Keirn C. and Jane (Schuhl) B.; m. Cynthia Porter, Aug. 21, 1971; 1 dau., Courtney. B.A., Williams Coll., 1971; J.D., Duke U., 1974. Bar: N.Y. 1975, N.C. 1983. Assoc. Simpson Thacher & Bartlett, N.Y.C., 1974-81; sr. v.p.-gen. counsel Cannon Mills Co., Kannapolis, N.C., 1981-82; v.p., gen. counsel Fuqua Industries, Inc., Atlanta, 1982—. Mem. ABA, Am. Corp. Counsel Assn. Home: 400 King Rd NW Atlanta GA 30342 Office: Fugua Industries Inc 3800 First Atlanta Tower Atlanta GA 30383

BROWN, DALE DUWARD, basketball coach; b. Minot, N.D., Oct. 31, 1935; m. Vonnie Ness; 1 dau., Robyn. B.S., Minot State U., 1957; M.S., Oreg. State U., 1964. Asst. coach Utah State U., Logan, 1966-71, Wash. State U., Pullman, 1971-72; head basketball coach La. State U., Baton Rouge, 1972—. Recipient Rupp Cup; named Nat. Coach of Yr. Chevrolet and Sporting News, 1981, Dist. Coach of Yr. Nat. Assn. Basketball Coaches, Kodak and La. Coach of Yr., SEC Coach of Yr., Coach of Yr. Southeastern Conf., 1978-79. Office: Basketball Office La State U Assembly Ctr. Baton Rouge LA 70893 *Any success that I have obtained is probably due to the fact I have a huge FQ – Failure Quotient. My friend, Bob Richards, once told me, "It's not your IQ in life that counts but your FQ," which simply means your ability to bounce back from failure. Some call it preserverence.*

BROWN, DALE WEAVER, clergyman, theology educator; b. Wichita, Kans., Jan. 12, 1926; s. Harlow J. and Cora Elisa (Weaver) B.; m. Lois D. Kauffman, Aug. 17, 1947; children: Deanna Gae, Dennis Dale, Kevin Ken. A.B., McPherson Coll., 1946; B.D., Bethany Bible Sem., 1949; postgrad., Drake U., 1954-56, Northwestern U. and Garrett Bibl. Inst., 1956-58, Ph.D., 1962. Ordained to ministry Ch. of Brethren, 1946; pastor Stover Meml. Ch. of Brethren, Des Moines, 1949-56; dir. religious life, asst. prof. philosophy and religion McPherson Coll., 1958-62; assoc. prof. Christian theology Bethany Theol. Sem., Oak Brook, Ill., 1962-70, prof. Christian theology, 1970—; Del. standing com. Ch. of Brethren, 1954; moderator Middle Iowa Dist., 1952-53, mem. dist. and regional bds., gen. bd., 1960-62, moderator-elect ann. conf., 1970-71, moderator, 1971-72. Author: In Christ Jesus: The Significance of Jesus as the Christ, 1965, Four Words for World, 1968, So Send I You, 1969, Brethren and Pacifism, 1970, The Christian Revolutionary, 1971, Flamed by the Spirit, 1978, Understanding Pietism, 1978, Bevea College: Spiritual and Intellectual Roots, 1982. Mem. Fellowship Reconciliation, Am. Theol. Soc., Soc. Ch. History. Home: 18W709 22d St Lombard IL 60148 Office: Bethany Theol Sem Oak Brook IL 60521

BROWN, DALLAS COVERDALE, JR., army officer; b. New Orleans, Aug. 21, 1932; s. Dallas Coverdale and Rita Sydney (Taylor) B.; m. Joyce Regina Bush, July 26, 1955; children—Dallas Coverdale, III, Leonard, Jan, Karen, Barbara. B.A. in History and Polit. Sci. (Disting. Mil. Grad. 1954), W.Va. State Coll., 1954; M.A. in Govt, Ind. U., 1967; grad., Command and Gen. Staff Coll., 1968, Naval War Coll., 1974. Commd. 2d lt. U.S. Army, 1954, advanced through grades to brig. gen., 1978; service in, Korea, W. Ger. and, Vietnam, dep. chief staff intelligence, 1978-79, dep. vice dir. fgn. intelligence, 1979-80, dep. comdr., Carlisle Barracks, Pa., 1980—. Mem. exec. bd. Keystone Area council Boy Scouts Am., 1980-81. Decorated Def. Superior Service medal, Meritorious Service medal (2), Joint Service Commendation medal, Army Commendation medal, Master Parachutist badge; named Alumnus of Yr. W.Va. State Coll., 1978. Mem. Assn. U.S. Army, Nat. Eagle Scout Assn., W.Va. State Coll. Alumni Assn., Alpha Phi Alpha. Roman Catholic. Club: Rocks. Home: Quarters 2 Carlisle Barracks PA 17013 Office: US Army War Coll Carlisle Barracks PA 17013

BROWN, DANIEL H., university administrator; b. Wisconsin Rapids, Wis., Jan. 14, 1928; s. Wayne Kennon and Josephine (Ibinger) B.; m. Ruth M. Spiering, June 26, 1948; children: Diane, Suzanne, Thomas, Ellen. Student, U. Ill., 1945-46, U. Wis.-LaCrosse, 1947-48; B.S., U. Wis.-Eau Claire, 1950; M.S., U. Wis.-Superior, 1958; Ed.D., U. Kans., 1962. Tchr. Superior Bd. Edn., Wis., 1950-58; prin. elem. sch. Platteville Bd. Edn., Wis., 1958-60; instr. U. Kans., 1960-62; prof. U. Wis., River Falls, 1962-71, dean Coll. Edn., 1971—. Served with U.S. Army, 1945-47. Mem. NEA, Phi Beta Kappa. Roman Catholic. Lodges: Lions; Moose. Office: Coll Edn Univ Wis 410 S 3d St River Falls WI 54022

BROWN, DANIEL HERBERT, manufacturing company executive; b. N.Y.C., Feb. 22, 1933; s. Harry and Celia (Weiner) B.; m. Myrna Serotick, June 15, 1958; children: Ian, Jennifer, Eric. A.B., CCNY, 1955; J.D., Fordham U., 1960. Bar: N.Y. 1961. Mem. firm Brumbaugh, Free Graves & Donohue, N.Y.C., 1960-68; with Rheem Mfg. Co., N.Y.C., 1968—, v.p., sec., gen. counsel, dir., 1973—; dir. Land Holdings, Ltd., Rheem P.R., Inc., Rheem Textile Systems, Inc.; legal adv. counsel Mid-Atlantic Legal Found., 1983—. Served to 1st lt. AUS, 1955-57. Mem. N.Y. Patent Law Assn. (gov. 1971-74, com. profl. ethics 1979—), Assn. Bar City N.Y. (mem. legal assistance com. 1967-71, profl. responsibility com. 1969-73), Gas Appliance Mfrs. Assn. (chmn. task force on consumer legislation 1975—, mem. legis. com. 1974—), Am. Bar Assn. (sect. antitrust law, mem. corp. law depts. 1976—), Assn. Bar City N.Y. (com. corp. law depts. 1978—). Home: 21 The Fenway Roslyn Estates NY 11576 Office: 59 Maiden Ln New York NY 10038

BROWN, DAVID, motion picture producer, writer; b. N.Y.C., July 28, 1916; s. Edward Fisher and Lillian (Baren) B.; m. Liberty LeGacy, Apr. 15, 1940 (div. 1951); 1 son, Bruce LeGacy; m. Wayne Clark, May 25, 1951 (div. 1957); m. Helen Gurley, Sept. 25, 1959. A.B., Stanford U., 1936; M.S., Columbia U., 1937. Apprentice San Francisco News, also Wall St. Jour., 1936; night editor, asst. drama critic Fairchild Publs., 1937-39; editorial dir. Milk Research Council, 1939-40; asso. editor Street & Smith Publs., 1940-43; assoc. editor, exec. editor, editor-in-chief Liberty mag., 1943-49; editorial dir. Nat. Edn. Campaign, A.M.A., 1949; assoc. editor, mng. editor Cosmopolitan mag., 1949-52; mng. editor, story editor, head scenario dept. 20th Century-Fox Film Corp. Studios, Beverly Hills, Calif., 1952-56, mem. studio exec. com., 1956-60, producer, 1960-62; also exec. story editor, head scenario dept.; editorial v.p. New Am. Library World Lit., Inc., 1963-64; v.p., dir. story operation 20th Century Fox Film Corp., 1964-69, exec. v.p. creative operations, 1969-70, dir., 1968-70; exec. v.p. creative operations, dir. Warner Bros., 1971-72; partner Zanuck/Brown Co., 1972—. Author: stories and articles pub. others; Editor: I Can Tell It Now, 1964, How I Got That Story, 1967; Contbr. to: Journalists in Action, 1963; films include The Sugarland Express; Final judge best short story pub. in mags. (ann. Benjamin Franklin Mag. awards 1955-58). Trustee com. on film Mus. Modern Art, N.Y.C. Served as 1st lt., M.I. AUS, World War II. Mem. Acad. Motion Picture Arts and Scis., Producers Guild Am., Am. Film Inst. (vice-chmn., trustee, mem. exec. com.). Clubs: Players, Dutch Treat, Century Assn., Overseas Press (N.Y.C.); Nat. Press (Washington). Home: One W 81st St New York NY 10024 Office: 200 W 57th St New York NY 10019 *Success, after all, is no more and no less than doing well what one wants to do most-regardless of where such an endeavor places one in the hierarchy of society.*

BROWN, DAVID, retired corporation executive; b. New Rochelle, N.Y., Apr. 25, 1917; s. Allan R. and Mary C. (Robinson) B.; m. Jeannine Brisebois, Jan. 28, 1956; children: Wendy Mottmann, Christopher C. B.A., Swarthmore Coll., 1938; M.S., M.I.T., 1939. Engr. Standard Oil Calif., 1940, Thompson Weinman, 1941, M.W. Kellogg Co., 1942-44, Shell Devel. Co., 1946-52; with Halcon Internat., Inc., N.Y.C., 1952-81, dir. process devel., 1952-54, vice chmn., 1979-81; cons. Manhattan Coll., U. Calif., Berkeley, Stanford U. Served with USNR, 1944-46. Recipient award Am. Inst. Chem. Engrs., 1977. Mem. Nat. Acad. Engring., Am. Chem. Soc., Am. Inst. Chem. Engrs. Republican. Clubs: Greenwich (Conn.) Country; Union League (N.Y.C.); Ocean Reef. Home: 003 Andros Rd Ocean Reef Club Key Largo FL 33037

BROWN, DAVID FAIN, financial executive; b. N.Y.C., Feb. 19, 1941; s. William Heren and Fain (Goodson) B.; m. Nancy Verity, Oct. 24, 1982. B.A. in Econs., Rutgers U., 1964, LL.B., 1966. Assoc. Cravath, Swaine & Moore, N.Y.C., 1966-72; v.p., gen. counsel City Investing Co., N.Y.C., 1972—. Mem. N.Y.C. Bar Assn., N.Y. State Bar Assn. Republican. Club: Knickerbocker. Home: PO Box 128 Mastic Beach Suffolk NY 11951 Office: City Investing Co 59 Maiden Ln New York NY 10038

BROWN, DAVID GRANT, university president; b. Chgo., Feb. 19, 1936; s. Wendell J. and Margaret (James) B.; m. Eleanor Rosene, Aug. 16, 1958; children: Alison, Dirksen. A.B., Denison U., 1958; M.A., Princeton U., 1960, Ph.D., 1961. Research asst. Indsl. Relations Center, Princeton, summers 1959-60; asst. prof., assoc. prof. econs., dir. academic labor market study, gen. coll. adviser U. N.C., 1961-66; faculty St. Augustines Coll., N.C. Coll., 1961-66; Am. Council on Edn. intern in academics adminstrn. U. Minn., 1966-67; provost, v.p. academic affairs Drake U., 1967-70; exec. v.p., provost Miami U., Oxford, Ohio, 1970-82; pres. Transylvania U., Lexington, Ky., 1982-83; spl. cons. Assn. Governing Bds. Study on Strengthening Coll. Presidency, 1983-84; chancellor U.N.C.-Asheville, 1984—; dir.

Leadership Vitality Project, 1978-79. Author: The Market for College Teachers, 1965, The Mobile Professors, 1967, Leadership Vitality Workbook, 1979; contbr. articles to profl. jours. U. N.C. Research Council grantee, 1961-63; recipient Tanner teaching award, 1965; Dept. Labor grantee, 1964; NSF grantee, 1965; U.S. Office Edn. grantee, 1965; Harold Dodds fellow, 1960-61. Mem. Nat. Assn. State Univs. and Land Grant Colls. (chmn. council academic affairs 1975, mem. exec. com. 1978-80), Am. Council on Edn. (chmn. council of chief acad. officers 1979-80), Am. Assn. Higher Edn. (chmn. 1981-82), Ohio Provosts (chmn. 1971, 78), Ohio Com. Univ. Autonomy (chmn. 1977), Assn. Am. Colls. (Commn. on Nat. Affairs), Higher Edn. Colloquium (chmn. 1984—), Blue Key, Phi Beta Kappa, Phi Kappa Phi, Beta Gamma Sigma, Phi Delta Kappa, Omicron Delta Kappa. Home: 62 Macon Ave Asheville NC 28814

BROWN, DAVID SPRINGER, educator; b. Bangor, Maine, Dec. 27, 1915; s. Lyle Lincoln and Myra Jane (Springer) B.; m. Evelyn Lovett, May 1, 1943 (dec. 1967); children: David Springer, Christopher, Robert, Adele; m. Anne Elizon, 1968. A.B., U. Maine, 1936; Ph.D., Syracuse U., 1955. Newspaper reporter Bangor Daily News, 1931-36; teaching asst. Syracuse U., 1937-40; with Dept. Agr., 1940, 42, N.Y. State Dept. Edn., 1941, CAA, 1946-48; Air Coordinating Com., 1948-50, ECA, 1950-52; exec. sec. pub. adv. bd. Mut. Security Agy., 1952-53; asst. exec. dir. Com. Nat. Trade Policy, 1953-54; asso. prof. pub. adminstrn. George Washington U., Washington, 1954-57, prof., 1957-69, prof. mgmt., 1969—, chmn. dept. pub. adminstrn., 1972-76; pres. Leadership Resources, 1970-75; dir. USAF adv. mgmt. program, 1954-61; vis. prof. Royal Coll. Sci. and Tech., Glasgow, Scotland, 1958. Author: Federal Contributions To Management, 1971, Managing the Large Organization, 1982; and articles, monographs. Sec. U.S. delegation Internat. Civil Aviation Orgn., Montreal, Que., Can., 1950; mem. U.S. delegation Internat. Inst. Adminstrv. Scis., Brussels, Belgium, 1958; adv. com. tng. Internal Revenue Service, 1959-60; dep. chief U. So. Cal. Party in Pub. Adminstrn., Lahore, Pakistan, 1961-62. Mem. Am. Soc. for Pub. Adminstrn., Soc. Personnel Adminstrn., AAUP, Acad. Mgmt. Home: 2804 O St NW Washington DC 20007 Office: George Washington U Washington DC 20052 *My own experience, as well as the history of people everywhere, is one of learning few things of value easily or quickly.*

BROWN, DEE ALEXANDER, author; b. La., 1908; s. Daniel Alexander and Lulu (Cranford) B.; m. Sara B. Stroud, Aug. 1, 1934; children—James Mitchell, Linda. B.S., George Washington U., 1937; M.S., U. Ill., 1951. Librarian Dept. Agr., Washington, 1934-42, Aberdeen Proving Ground, Md., 1945-48; agrl. librarian U. Ill. at Urbana, 1948-72, prof., 1962-75. Author: Wave High the Banner, 1942, Grierson's Raid, 1954, Yellowhorse, 1956, Cavalry Scout, 1957, The Gentle Tamers: Women of the Old Wild West, 1958, The Bold Cavaliers, 1959, They Went Thataway, 1960, (with M.F. Schmitt) Fighting Indians of the West, 1948, Trail Driving Days, 1952, The Settler's West, 1955, Fort Phil Kearny, 1962, The Galvanized Yankees, 1963, Showdown at Little Big Horn, 1964, The Girl from Fort Wicked, 1964, The Year of the Century, 1966, Bury My Heart at Wounded Knee, 1971, The Westerners, 1974, Hear That Lonesome Whistle Blow, 1977, Tepee Tales, 1979, Creek Mary's Blood, 1980, The American Spa, 1982, Killdeer Mountain, 1983; editor: Agricultural History, 1956-58, Pawnee, Blackfoot and Cheyenne, 1961. Served with AUS, 1942-45. Mem. Authors Guild, Soc. Am. Historians, Western Writers Am., Beta Phi Mu. Home: 7 Overlook Dr Little Rock AR 72207

BROWN, DEMING BRONSON, educator; b. Seattle, Jan. 26, 1919; s. Kirk Charles and Lois (Bronson) B.; m. Glenora Washington, June 18, 1941; children: Kate Deming, Sarah Fuller. A.B., U. Wash., Seattle, 1940, M.A., 1942; postgrad., Cornell U., 1945-46; Ph.D. (Rockefeller fellow 1946-48), Columbia U., 1951. Instr., then asst. prof. Russian lang. and lit. Northwestern U., Evanston, Ill., 1948-57; mem. faculty U. Mich., Ann Arbor, 1957—, prof. Slavic lang. and lit., 1959—, chmn. dept. Slavic lang. and lit., 1957-61, dir. Center Russian and E. European Studies, 1978-80; mem. joint com. Slavic studies Am. Council Learned Socs.-Social Sci. Research Council, 1960-64. Author: Soviet Attitudes Toward American Writing, 1962, Soviet Russian Literature Since Stalin, 1978, A Guide to Soviet Russian Translations of American Literature, 1917-47, 1954. Served with AUS, 1943-45. Research fellow Am. Council Learned Socs.-Social Sci. Research Council, 1964; Fulbright-Hays fellow, 1969. Mem. Am. Assn. Slavic Studies (exec. council 1961-63), MLA, Am. Assn. Tchrs. Slavic and E. European Langs. Home: 602 Oswego St Ann Arbor MI 48014 Office: Dept Slavic Langs and Lits U Mich Ann Arbor MI 48109

BROWN, DENNIS EDWARD, journalism educator; b. Marshalltown, Iowa, Feb. 4, 1933; s. Theodore Thomas and Pauline Evangeline (Bootjer) B.; m. Maureen Ann Cavanaugh, Sept. 7, 1963; children: Katherine Ann, Douglas Edward, Laura Elizabeth. A.B. magna cum laude, Harvard U., 1955; postgrad. (Rockefeller Theol. fellow), Union Theol. Sem., 1955-56; M.A., U. Iowa, 1961; Ph.D. (U.S. Steel Found. fellow), U. Mo., 1970. Reporter Des Moines Register, 1959-60; editor-writer Office Public Info., U. Iowa, Iowa City, 1960-65; assoc. dir. Office Public Info., U. Mo., Columbia, 1966-67; asst. dir. Freedom of Info. Center, 1967-68; mem. faculty dept. journalism and mass communications San Jose State U., 1968—, prof. journalism, 1971—, chmn. dept., 1970—. Editorial bd.: Harvard Crimson, 1954-55; Contbr. articles to profl. jours. Served to 2d lt. U.S. Army, 1957-58. Mem. Am. Soc. Journalism Sch. Adminstrs., Am. Assn. Schs. and Depts. Journalism, Assn. Schs. Journalism and Mass Communications, Assn. Edn. Journalism, Sigma Delta Chi, Kappa Tau Alpha. Home: 7008 Elmsdale Dr San Jose CA 95120

BROWN, DENNISON ROBERT, mathematician; b. New Orleans, May 17, 1934; s. Elihu Thomson and Floy Clements (Edwards) B.; m. Janet Madden, June 9, 1956; children—Robert Leslie, Alan Madden. B.S., Duke U., 1955; M.S., La. State U., 1960, Ph.D., 1963. Instr. math. La. State U., New Orleans, 1958-61, Baton Rouge, 1962-63; asst. prof., then assoc. prof. U. Tenn., Knoxville, 1963-67; mem. faculty U. Houston, 1967—, prof. math., 1970—, deptl. dir. grad. studies, 1969-72; vis. lectr. Math. Assn. Am., 1965-72, cons., 1972—. Editor: Semigroup Forum, 1970—; Contbr. profl. jours. Mgr. local Little League, 1964-80. Served to lt. USNR, 1955-58. NSF grantee, 1965-69; sr. investigator NASA Contract, 1972-79. Mem. Am. Math. Soc., Math. Assn. Am., Sigma Xi, Kappa Sigma. Methodist. Home: 8411 Langdon Ln Houston TX 77036 Office: Dept Math Univ Houston Houston TX 77004

BROWN, DONALD, lawyer; b. Phila., Aug. 22, 1932; s. Paul and Sarah (Magil) B.; m. Bernice Katz, May 15, 1960; children: Harold Mordechai, Louis Joseph, Seth Michael. B.A., Antioch Coll., 1954; J.D., Yale U., 1957. Bar: Pa. 1958. Assoc. mem. firm Fox, Rothschild, O'Brien & Frankel, Phila., 1958-62, ptnr., 1963—, mng. ptnr., 1979—; dir. Porkland Industries, Inc., Ezra W. Martin Co. Bd. dirs. Am. Technion Soc., Phila. Served with AUS, 1957-58. Mem. Am. Arbitration Assn. (nat. bd. 1966-67), ABA (sect. draftsman com. supplement atty. gen.'s report on antitrust laws), Pa. Bar Assn., Phila. Bar Assn., Am. Judicature Soc. Clubs: Radnor Country, Yale, B'nai B'rith. Home: 523 Howe Rd Merion PA 19066 Office: 2000 Market St 10th Floor Philadelphia PA 19103

BROWN, DONALD ARTHUR, lawyer; b. Washington, Feb. 1, 1929; s. Louis S. and Rose (Kliban) B.; m. Ann Winkelman, July 13, 1959; children: Cathy, Laura. B.A. in Econs., George Washington U., 1949, LL.B. (Case Club oral argument competition winner), 1952, LL.M., 1958. Bar: D.C. 1952. Sr. partner Brown, Gildenhorn & Jacobs (and predecessor), Washington, 1955—; mem. faculty Practising Law Inst.; guest lectr. Am. U., Nat. Assn. Real Estate Counselors, Nat. Assn. Real Estate Investors; pres., sec. JBG Constrn., Inc.; partner JBG Assos.; v.p., treas. JBG Properties, Inc.; trustee, gen. counsel Nat. Bank Rosslyn, Arlington, Va.; Mem. minority enterprises com. SBA; finance com. Housing Devel. Corp.; mem. Model Cities Com. D.C. Co-author: Understanding Real Estate Investments, 1967; Contbr. articles to profl. jours. Exec. bd. Forest Hills Citizens Assn.; bd. dirs. D.C. Jr. C. of C.; mem. Friends Kennedy Center, Friends Corcoran Gallery, Big Bros. Orgn. D.C.; bd. dirs. Washington Area Tennis Patrons Found., 1964—, pres., 1973-75; trustee Woodley House, psychiat. half-way house, Washington, 1973—, pres. bd. dirs., 1975—; trustee U. D.C., Sidwell Friends Sch.; mem. art adv. com. D.C. Conv. Ctr. Served as officer USNR, 1952-55. Mem. Am., Fed., D.C. bar assns., Washington Bd. Realtors (chmn. lawyer-realtor liaison com. 1972, chmn. investment property com. 1970). Jewish (bd. mgrs. congregation 1962, treas. 1965). Club: Georgetown (Washington). Home: 3005 Audubon Terr NW Washington DC 20008 Office: 1220 19th St NW Washington DC 20036

BROWN, DONALD DAVID, biology educator; b. Cin., Dec. 30, 1931; s. Albert Louis and Louise (Rauh) B.; m. Linda Jane Weil, July 2, 1957; children: Deborah Lin, Christopher Charles, Sharon Elizabeth. M.S., U. Chgo., 1956, M.D., 1956, D.Sc. (hon.), 1976, U. Md., 1983. Staff mem. dept. embryology Carnegie Instn. of Washington, Balt., 1963-76, dir., 1976—; prof. dept. biology Johns Hopkins U., 1968—. Served with USPHS, 1957-59. Recipient U.S. Steel Found. award for molecular biology, 1973; V.D. Mattia award Roche Inst., 1975; Boris Pregel award for biology N.Y. Acad. Scis., 1976; Ross G. Harrison award Internat. Soc. Developmental Biology, 1981; Bertner Found. award, 1982. Fellow Am. Acad. Arts and Scis., AAAS; mem. Nat. Acad. Scis., Soc. Developmental Biology (pres. 1975), Am. Soc. Biol. Chemists, Am. Soc. Cell Biology, Am. Philos. Soc. Home: 5721 Oakshire Rd Baltimore MD 21209 Office: Carnegie Instn of Washington 115 W University Pkwy Baltimore MD 21210

BROWN, DONALD ROBERT, psychology educator; b. Albany, N.Y., Mar. 5, 1925; s. J. Edward and Natile (Roseberg) B.; m. June Gole, Aug. 14, 1945; children: Peter Douglas, Thomas Matthew, Jacob Noah. A.B., Harvard U., 1948; M.A., U. Calif.-Berkeley, 1951, Ph.D., 1951. Mem. faculty Bryn Mawr Coll., 1951—, prof. psychology, 1963—; sr. research cons. Mellon Found., Vassar Coll., 1953-63; part-time vis. prof. Swarthmore Coll., U. Pa., also U. Calif., Berkeley, 1953-63; fellow Center Advanced Study Behavioral Scis., 1960-61; prof. psychology, sr. research scientist Center Research Learning and Teaching, U. Mich., 1964—; cons. Peace Corps, 1965-71; hon. research fellow Univ. Coll., London, 1970-71; Fulbright sr. research fellow Max Planck Inst., Berlin, 1982; Netherlands Basic Sci. fellow, Leyden, 1983. Author articles, chpts. in books; editor: Changing Role and Status of Soviet Women, 1967. Served with AUS, 1943-46; ETO. Fellow Am. Psychol. Assn.; mem. Soc. Psychol. Study of Social Issues, AAAS, AAUP, Sigma Xi, Psi Chi. Home: 2511 Hawthorn Ann Arbor MI 48104

BROWN, DOROTHY LAVINIA, physician; b. Phila., Jan. 7, 1919; foster parents Samuel and Lola Redmon; 1 adopted dau., Lola Denise. B.A., Bennett Coll., Greensboro, N.C., 1941; M.D., Meharry Med. Coll., Nashville, 1948. Intern Harlem Hosp., N.Y.C., 1948-49; surg. resident Hubbard Hosp., Nashville, 1949-54; now clin. prof. surgery Meharry Med. Coll.; chief surgery Riverside Hosp.; attending surgeon Hubbard, Met.-Gen., Nashville hosps. Mem. Tenn. Youth Guidance Commn., Tenn. Consumer Protection Com.; Past mem. Tenn. Ho. of Reps.; mem. So. Regional Edn. Bd., 1967—; Trustee Bennett Coll. Fellow A.C.S.; mem. AMA, AAUP, Nat. Council Negro Women, Nashville Acad. Medicine, R.F. Boyd Med. Soc., Nat. Med. Assn., Assn. Am. Med. Colls., Negro Bus. and Profl. Women's Clubs, NAACP (life), Internat. Platform Assn., Delta Sigma Theta, Kappa Delta Pi. Home: 3109 Centennial Blvd Nashville TN 37209 Office: 3109 John A Merritt Blvd Nashville TN 37209

BROWN, DOUGLASS VINCENT, educator; b. Wilkes Barre, Pa., May 16, 1904; s. George Henry and Frederica (Beinert) B.; m. Mary A. Nuss, Dec. 2, 1933; children—Deborah, Constance. A.B., Harvard, 1925, A.M., 1926, Ph.D., 1932. Instr., tutor econ. Harvard, 1927-33; as. prof. med. econ. Harvard Med. Sch., 1933-38; asst. prof., asso. prof. and prof. indsl. relations Mass. Inst. Tech., Cambridge, 1938-46, Alfred P. Sloan prof. indsl. mgmt, 1946—; Various positions with adv. commn. to Council of Nat. Def. and OPM, 1940-41; staff mem. Harriman-Beaverbrook Mission to Russia, 1941; cons. to War Dept., 1942-43; pub. mem. Nat. War Labor Bd., Region I, 1943-45. Author: (with others) Economics of the Recovery Program, 1934, Industrial Wage Rates, Labor Costs and Price Policies, Temporary National Economic Committee, Monograph 5, 1940. Fellow Am. Acad. Arts and Sci.; mem. Indsl. Relations Research Assn., Nat. Acad. Arbitrators. Home: 46 Griggs Rd Brookline MA 02146 Office: Mass Institute of Technology Cambridge MA 02139

BROWN, DUDLEY EARL, JR., VA administrator, former naval officer; b. Berryville, Va., Apr. 10, 1928; s. Dudley Earl and Rosa Lee (Costello) B.; m. Lelia Adrienne Motley, June 22, 1953; children—Lelia Brown Farr, David, Kevin. B.A., Washington and Lee U., 1949; M.D., Med. Coll. Va., 1953. Diplomate: Am. Bd. Psychiatry and Neurology. Commd. lt. (j.g.) M.C. U.S. Navy, 1953, advanced through grades to rear adm., 1974; intern Naval Hosp., Portsmouth, Va., 1953-54, resident in neuropsychiatry, Bethesda, Md., 1957-60; service in, Vietnam; comdg. officer Nat. Naval Med. Center, Bethesda, 1975-76, Naval Regional Med. Center, San Diego, 1976-78; fleet surgeon U.S. Pacific Fleet and staff surgeon, comdr.-in-chief U.S. Forces, Pacific, Pearl Harbor, Hawaii, 1978-80; ret., 1980; dep. asst. chief med. dir. for profl. services VA Central Office, Washington, 1980-82; assoc. dep. chief med. dir. VA, Washington, 1982—; prof. clin. psychiatry Uniformed Services U. Health Scis., Bethesda, Md.; asst. prof. clin. psychiatry U. Pa. Med. Sch., 1967-70. Contbr. to med. jours. Decorated Legion of Merit, Meritorious Service medal, Navy Commendation medal. Fellow A.C.P., Am. Psychiat. Assn., Am. Coll. Psychiatrists; mem. Washington Psychiat. Soc., Assn. Mil. Surgeons U.S., Soc. Med. Cons. to Armed Forces, Phi Gamma Delta, Alpha Epsilon Delta. Presbyterian. Home: 2415 Black Cap Ln Reston VA 22091 Office: VA Central Office 810 Vermont Ave NW Washington DC 20420

BROWN, D.V., food broker and import company executive. Pres. Bromar Inc., Sausalito, Calif. Office: Bromar Inc. 2658 Bridgeway Sausalito CA 94565

BROWN, EARL KENT, historian, clergyman; b. Kent, Ohio, July 26, 1925; s. Earl Royal and Bernice Blanche (Howard) B. B.A., Columbia U., 1948; S.T.B., Boston U., 1953, Ph.D. (Howard fellow 1953-54, United Methodist Ch. Dempster fellow 1954-55), 1956. Asst. prof. history Baldwin Wallace Coll., 1956-63, asso. prof., 1963; asso. prof. church history Boston U., 1963-70, prof., 1970—; ordained to ministry United Meth. Ch., 1957; vis. prof. Case Western Res. U., 1961, Union Theol. Sem., Manila, 1970, United Theol. Coll., Bangalore, India, 1978, U. Manchester, Eng., 1979; mem. United Meth. Ch. Commn. on Archives and History, 1965—. Author: Women of Mr. Wesley's Methodism, 1983; Contbr. articles to acad. jours., religious periodicals. Fulbright fellow, 1962. Mem. Am. Soc. Ch. History, Am. Hist. Assn., Am. Catholic Hist. Assn., Am. Acad. Religion. Office: 580 Commonwealth Ave Suite 10 Boston MA 02215

BROWN, EARLE, composer, conductor; b. Lunenburg, Mass., Dec. 26, 1926; s. Earle Appleton and Grace (Freeman) B.; m. Carolyn Rice, June 28, 1950. Student, Northeastern U., 1944-45; grad., Schillinger Sch. Music, Boston, 1950; pvt. student of, Roslyn B. Henning and Kenneth McKillop; Mus.D. (hon.), Peabody Conservatory, 1970. Tchr. Schillinger System Mus. Composition, Denver, 1950-52; asso. Project Music Magnetic Tape, N.Y.C., 1952-54; faculty Conservatory of City Cologne, Germany, 1966; guest prof. composition conservatories of Rotterdam, 1974, Basel, 1975, Calif. Inst. Arts, Los Angeles, 1974-83, U. Calif., Berkeley, 1976; vis. prof. Yale U., 1980-81. Dir.: Contemporary Sound Series for, Time-Mainstream Records, Inc., 1960, W. Alton Jones chair composition, Peabody Conservatory, 1968-70, 71-72; composer in residence, Artists Program, West Berlin, 1970-71; 1970-71, Tanglewood and Aspen Festivals, summer 1975; condr. own works at, N.Y. Philharmonic, 1964, Rome Radio Orch., 1962, Domaine Mus., Paris, 1963, Internat. Chamber Ensemble, Darmstadt, Germany, 1964, Munich (Germany) Radio Orch., 1963, Cologne (Germany) Radio Orch., Contemporary Chamber Ensemble, N.Y.C., works performed in, Paris, Venice, Zagreb, Cologne, Munich, Hamburg, Prague, Rome, Helsinki, The Hague, Vienna, Bremen, Buenos Aires, Tokyo, Stockholm, Madrid, Berlin, throughout U.S.; Composer: Perspectives, 1952, Folio and Four Systems, 1952-54, Indices, 1954, Pentathis, 1958, Available Forms I and II, 1961-62, Times Five, 1963, From Here, 1963, Calder Piece, 1963-66, String Quartet, 1965, Corroboree, 1964, Nine Rarebits, 1965, Modules I and II, 1966, Syntagm III, 1970, Centering, 1973, Cross Sections and Color Fields, 1975, Windsor Jambs, 1976-79, also others. Served with USAAF, 1945-47. Recipient commns. from Domaine Mus., 1958, City of Darmstadt, 1961, Rome Radio Orch., 1962, Found. Performance Arts, 1963; Radio Diffusion Française, 1963; Bremen Radio, 1964; Sudwestfunk, Baden- Baden, 1964; Donaueschingen, Germany, 1965; Koussevitzky Found., 1972; N.Y. State Council for Arts, 1974; Guggenheim fellow, 1965; Nat. Endowment for Arts grantee, 1974, award Nat. Inst. Arts and Letters, 1972, creative awards Brandeis U., 1977. Mem. Broadcast Music Inc. Address: care ICI 799 Broadway New York NY 10003

BROWN, EDGAR CARY, economics educator; b. Bakersfield, Calif., Apr. 14, 1916; s. Verne Brainard and Ruth (Cary) B.; m. Tomlin Edwards, May 28, 1937 (div.); children: Rebecca, Gretchen; m. Margaret Durham, June 6, 1969; children: Elizabeth, Robert. B.S., U. Calif., Berkeley, 1937; Ph.D., Harvard U., 1948. Teaching fellow U. Calif. at Berkeley, 1937-39; economist U.S. WPB, 1940-41; teaching fellow Harvard U., 1941-42; economist U.S. Treasury Dept., 1942-47; prof. econs. Mass. Inst. Tech., 1947-, head dept., 1965-83; vis. prof. econs. Yale U., 1953-54, U. Chgo., 1963-64; cons. economist U.S. Treasury; also cons. Brookings Instn., N.Y. State Regents. Author: Financing Defense, 1951, Depreciation Adjustments for Price Changes, 1952, Stabilization Policies, 1963, Studies in Economic Stabilization, 1967, Paul Samuelson and Modern Economic Theory, 1983; acting editor: Nat. Tax Jour, 1958-59; asso. editor: Jour. Pub. Econs, 1972-81. Guggenheim fellow, 1957; Ford Found. Faculty Research fellow, 1956-57. Mem. Nat. Tax Assn., Am. Econ. Assn., Am. Acad. Arts and Scis., Phi Beta Kappa, Beta Gamma Sigma. Home: 163 Valley Rd Concord MA 01742 Office: E52-373A 50 Memorial Dr Cambridge MA 02139

BROWN, EDGAR HENRY, JR., mathematician, educator; b. Chgo., Dec. 27, 1926; s. Edgar Henry and Viola (Offen) B.; m. Gail Hamilton, June 13, 1954; children: Jessica, Nicholas. B.S., U. Wis., 1949; M.S., Wash. State U., 1951; Ph.D., Mass. Inst. Tech., 1954. Instr. Washington U., St. Louis, 1954-55, U. Chgo., 1955-57; Office Naval Res. fellow Brown U., 1957-58; faculty Brandeis U., 1958—, prof. math., 1963—. Served with USNR, 1944-46. NSF fellow, 1962-63; Guggenheim fellow, 1965-66; Brit. Sci. Research Council fellow, 1973-74, 82-83. Mem. Am. Math. Soc., Am. Acad. Arts and Sci. Home: 32 Fisher Ave Newton MA 02161 Office: Math Dept Brandeis Univ Waltham MA 02154

BROWN, EDMUND GERALD (PAT BROWN), lawyer, former governor California; b. San Francisco, Apr. 21, 1905; s. Edmund Joseph and Ida (Schuckman) B.; m. Bernice Layne, Oct. 30, 1930; children: Barbara Brown Casey, Cynthia Brown Kelly, Edmund Gerald, Kathleen Brown Rice. LL.B., San Francisco Law Sch., 1927; LL.D., U. San Francisco, 1959, U. San Diego, 1961, U. Santa Clara, 1961; D.C.L., Calif. Coll. Medicine, Los Angeles, 1964. Bar: Calif. bar 1927. Practiced in, San Francisco, 1927-43; dist. atty. City and County San Francisco, 1943-47, 47-50; atty. gen., Calif., 1951-58, gov. of Calif., 1959-66; head Nat. Commn. Reform Fed. Criminal Laws; sr. partner firm Ball, Hunt, Hart, Brown & Baerwitz. Mem. Franklin Delano Roosevelt Meml. Commn.; del. Democratic Nat. Conv., 1940, 44, 48, 52, 56, 60, 64; mem. Golden Gate Bridge and Hwy. Dist.; chmn. San Francisco Coordinating Council, 1947. Fellow Am. Coll. Trial Lawyers; mem. Dist. Attys. Assn. Calif. (pres. 1950-51), Western Assn. Attys. Gen. (past pres.), Nat. Assn. Attys. Gen. (exec. bd.), Am., Beverly Hills bar assns., State Bar Calif. Democrat. Roman Catholic. Clubs: Native Sons Golden West, Bel-Aire Country, Olympic, La Quinta Country. Address: Ball Hunt Hart & Brown 450 N Roxbury Dr Beverly Hills CA 90210

BROWN, EDMUND GERALD, JR., former gov. of Calif.; b. San Francisco, Apr. 7, 1938; s. Edmund Gerald and Bernice (Layne) B. B.A., U. Calif., Berkeley, 1961; J.D., Yale U., 1964. Bar: Calif. 1965. Research atty. Calif. Supreme Ct., 1964-65; atty. Tuttle & Taylor, Los Angeles, 1966-69; sec. state, Calif., 1970-74, gov. of Calif., 1975-83. Trustee Los Angeles Community Colls., 1969. Office: Nat Commn Indsl Innovation 1125 W 6thSt Los Angeles CA 90017

BROWN, EDWARD JAMES, educator; b. Chgo., July 12, 1909; s. Edward James and Marie (O'Neill) B.; m. Catherine Stillman Cossum, Oct. 7, 1941; 1 dau., Meredith Ann. A.B., U. Chgo., 1933, A.M., 1946; Ph.D., Columbia U., 1950. From instr. Russian to prof. Brown U., 1947-65, chmn. dept. Slavic langs., 1960-65; prof. Russian, chmn. dept. Slavic langs. and lits. Ind. U., Bloomington, 1965-69; prof. Slavic langs. Stanford, 1969—; Mem. Am. Com. Slavists, 1958; del. IV Internat. Congress Slavists, 1958; cons. Fgn. Area Fellowship Program, 1964-66; cons. grants Am. Council Learned Socs., 1964-71; mem. Joint Com. Slavic Studies, 1964-65, 67-71; exec. com. Inter-Univ. Com. Travel Grants, 1965-67. Author: The Proletarian Episode in Russian Literature, 1953, reissued, 1971, Russian Literature Since the Revolution, 1963, rev., 1969, 3d rev. edit., 1982, Stankevich and His Moscow Circle, 1966, Major Soviet Writers: Essays in Criticism, 1973, Mayakovsky: A Poet in the Revolution, 1973. Served with USAAF, 1943-45. Rockefeller fellow, 1946; Am. Council Learned Socs. fellow, 1946-47; Howard fellow, 1955-56; exchange prof. to USSR Am. Council Learned Socs.-Acad. Scis. Program, fall 1963; sr. fellow Russian Inst., Columbia U., 1969, vis. prof., 1981; vis. prof. Harvard U., 1982. Mem. MLA, Am. Assn. Tchrs. Slavic and Eastern European Langs. (pres. 1966), Am. Assn. Advancement Slavic Studies (pres. 1967-70), Phi Beta Kappa. Home: 801 Tolman Dr Stanford CA 94305

BROWN, EDWARD MAURICE, lawyer, business exec.; b. Watertown, N.Y., Aug. 22, 1909; s. Ernest E. and Eunice (Lewis) B.; m. Anne Amos, Oct. 2, 1937; children—Edward Dustin, Ernest Amos. A.B. magna cum laude, Miami U., 1931, LL.D., 1972; J.D., Harvard, 1934. Bar: Ohio bar 1934, U.S. Supreme Ct 1941, N.Y. bar 1948. Asso. firm Nichols, Wood, Marx & Ginter, 1934-47; asst. to pres. McCall Corp., N.Y.C., 1947-49, v.p., asst. sec., 1949-51, v.p., sec., 1951-57, dir., 1953-57; treas. Sperry Gyroscope Co. div. Sperry Rand Corp., 1958-59, v.p., treas., 1959-60, v.p., adminstr., 1960-65; v.p. Sperry Group, 1965-68; asst. treas. Sperry Rand Corp., 1958-68; group exec. of Teledyne, Inc., 1968-80; chmn. bd. Teledyne Can. Ltd., 1971-81. Trustee Village of Pelham Manor, N.Y., 1961-65, village mayor, 1965-67; Bd. govs., trustee Human Resources Center; chmn. Abilities, Inc. Served as lt. comdr. USNR, 1942-45. Member Am. Bar Assn., Phi Beta Kappa, Phi Eta Sigma, Phi Sigma, Beta Theta Pi. Republican. Episcopalian. Home: 165 Shadowy Hills Oxford OH 45056 Office: Box 372 Pelham NY 10803

BROWN, EDWARD MCLAIN, JR., lawyer; b. Balt., Apr. 26, 1929; s. Edward McLain and Rita Virginia (House) B.; m. Patsy Sue Millikan, Jan. 28, 1956; children: Carol Lorraine, Ruth Virginia, David William. Student, U. Pa., 1946-47; B.B.A., U. Tex., 1958, LL.B., 1960. Bar: Tex. 1960, U.S. Supreme Ct. 1965. Assoc. firms Karl Cayton, Lamesa, Tex., 1960-62, Lyne, Blanchette, Smith & Shelton, Dallas, 1962-65; partner firms Brown, Elliott & Brown, Dallas, 1965-70, Brown & Moore, 1970-75, Brown, Moore & Lee, 1975-79, Brown & Walker, 1980-81; sole practice, Dallas, 1981—; sec., dir. Fas-Pak Inc., Pat Jetton Inc., Ranchmen's Mfg. Co., Inc.; pres. dir. Courtland Devel. Co., Inc.; sec., dir. Woodcraft Constrn. Co. Inc., Phalanx Corp. Mem. charter com. Farmers Br., Dallas, 1967-70, chmn., 1969-70, mem. library bd., 1964-68, chmn. library bd., 1967-68, mem. indsl. devel. com., 1971. Served with USAF, 1950-56. Mem. Dallas Bar Assn., State Bar Tex., Tex. Trial Lawyers Assn., Farmers Br.-Carrollton Lawyers Assn. (pres. 1973). Republican. Episcopalian (sr. warden 1967). Clubs: Rotary, Lions. Home: 3212 Rolling Knoll Pl Dallas TX 75234 Office: 2711 Valley View Ln Dallas TX 75234

BROWN, EDWARD RANDOLPH, lawyer; b. Cleve., Sept. 17, 1933; s. Percy Whiting and Helen Campbell (Hurd) B.; m. Sally Reed, Sept. 9, 1961; children: Rosalind Whiting, Jocelyn Gayden. B.A., Harvard U., 1955; LL.B., Case Western Res. U., 1962. Bar: Ohio State bar 1962. Reporter Mpls. Tribune, 1958-59, Lorain Journal, Ohio, 1959; asso. firm Squire Sander & Dempsey, Cleve., 1963-67; staff atty. Cleve. Legal Aid Defenders Office, 1963-67; asso. firm Arter & Hadden, Cleve., 1967-75, partner, 1975—; lectr. law Case Western Res. U., 1965-66; Pres. Legal Aid Soc. of Cleve., Inc., 1976-79. Served with U.S. Army, 1955-58. Mem. Am. Law Inst., Am. Bar Assn., Ohio State Bar Assn., Cleve. Bar Assn. Democrat. Office: 1100 Huntington Bldg Cleveland OH 45115

BROWN, EDWIN GARTH, social worker, educator; b. Bingham Canyon, Utah, June 30, 1931; s. Harold King and Emma (Featherstone) B.; m. Carma Jeanne Johnson, June 6, 1958; children—Laura, Michael, Melanie, Rosanne, Benjamin, Angela. B.S. in Sociology, Brigham Young U., Provo, Utah, 1953; M.S.W. (NIMH scholar 1958-59), U. Utah, 1959; Ph.D. in Social Service Adminstrn. (NIMH scholar 1964), U. Chgo., 1970. Resident in mental health Menninger Found., Topeka, 1959-60, social case worker, 1960-63; asso. prof. social work U. Chgo., 1964-71; mem. faculty U. Utah, 1972—, prof. social work, 1974—; dean Grad. Sch. Social Work, 1976-79, dir. bus. and industry splty., 1978—; vis. prof. Brigham Young U., Hawaii, 1979-80; commr. Salt Lake County Housing Authority, 1974—; cons. in field. Author: The New Partnership: Human Service, Business and Industry, 1981; mem. editorial: Bd. Social Work. Recipient Outstanding Teaching award U. Utah Grad. Sch. Social Work, 1972-79. Mem. Nat. Assn. Social Workers (chmn. public assistance com. Chgo. chpt. 1965-69), Nat. Acad. Cert. Social Workers, Internat. Conf. Schs. Social Work. Mormon. Office: Grad Sch Social Work U Utah Salt Lake City UT 84112 *A belief in the basic worth and goodness of people has always been a source of optimism and hope for me. The capacity for growth throughout life has given me the firm conviction that opportunity is essential for all. A belief in God gives me purpose and personal strength in times of adversity. My parents taught me the value of hard work and caring.*

BROWN, EDWIN LEWIS, JR., lawyer; b. Parker, S.D., Mar. 15, 1903; s. Edwin Lewis and Lucy Elizabeth (Lowenberg) B.; m. Faye Hulbert, May 8, 1926; children—Betty Lou Brown Trainer, Lewis Charles. J.D., U. Nebr., 1926. Bar: Nebr. bar 1926, Ill. bar 1933, U.S. Supreme Ct. bar 1960. Practiced in, Chgo., 1933—; partner firm Brown, Cook, Hanson, 1950—; Mem. Nat. Conf. Lawyers and Collection Agys., 1964-74. Mem. wills and bequests com. Shriners Crippled Children's Hosp., Chgo. Named Time mag.-NADRA Man of Year, 1974. Mem. ABA, Ill. Bar Assn. (sr. counsellor 1976), Chgo. Bar Assn., Am. Judicature Soc., Comml. Law League Am. (pres. 1963-64), Comml. Law Found. (treas. 1969-74), Nat. Conf. Bar Presidents, Phi Alpha Delta. Republican. Presbyterian. Clubs: Masons (32 deg.), K.T., Shriners; Union League (Chgo.); Westmoreland Country (Wilmette, Ill.). Home: 2617 Hurd Ave Evanston IL 60201 Office: 135 S LaSalle St Chicago IL 60603 also 2114 Central St Evanston IL 60201

BROWN, EDWIN WILSON, JR., physician, educator; b. Youngstown, Ohio, Mar. 6, 1926; s. Edwin Wilson and Doris (McClellan) B.; m. Patricia Ann Currier, Aug. 9, 1952; children: Edwin Wilson, John Currier, Wende Patricia. Student, Carnegie Inst. Tech., 1943, Houghton Coll., 1946-47, Amherst Coll., 1943-44; M.D., Harvard U., 1953; M.P.H. (Nat. Found. fellow), Harvard U., 1957. Research fellow U. Buffalo, 1953-54; intern E. J. Meyer Meml. Hosp., Buffalo, 1954-55; resident pub. health Va. Dept. Health, 1955-56; tchr. medicine, specializing in preventive medicine, Boston, 1958-61, Hyderabad, India, 1961-63; asso. med. dir. People-to-People Health Found., Washington, 1965-66; dir. internat. activities Ind. U.; also dir. div. internat. affairs Ind. U.-Purdue U., Indpls., 1966-74, assoc. dean student services, dir. internat. services, 1979—; assoc. prof. Ind. U. Sch. Medicine, 1966—; med. dir. Ind. Dept. Correction, 1974-76; sr. med. edn. advisor King Faisal U., Dammam, Saudi Arabia, 1977-78; field dir. Harvard Epidemiol. Project, Egedesminde, Greenland, 1956-57; asst. prof. preventive medicine Sch. Medicine Tufts U., 1958-61; dep. chief staff Boston Dispensary, 1961; vis. prof. preventive medicine Osmania Med. Coll., Hyderabad, India, 1961-63; asst. dir. div. internat. med. edn., dir. AAMC-AID project internat. med. edn. Assn. Am. Med. Colls., Evanston, 1963-65; exec. sec. Study Group on Childhood Accidents, Boston, 1959-61; research asso. Sch. Pub. Health, Harvard U., 1959-60; dir. Curtis Pub. Co., Inc.; cons. Boston City Health Dept., 1959-60, WHO, 1973—; chmn. bd. dirs. Med. Assistance Programs, Inc. Contbr. articles to profl. jours. Bd. dirs. Paul Carlson Found., Campus Teams, Iran Found., CARE/MEDICO, Internat. Students Inc. Served with AUS, 1944-46; ETO. Fellow Am. Pub. Health Assn.; mem. Assn. Tchrs. Preventive Medicine, Indian Assn. Advancement Med. Edn., Mass. Med. Soc., Sigma Xi. Club: Rotary Internat. Home: 8153 Oakland Rd Indianapolis IN 46240 Office: Ind U-Purdue U at Indpls 925 W Michigan St Indianapolis IN 46202

BROWN, ELIZABETH ANN, fgn. service officer; b. Portland, Oreg., Aug. 15, 1918; d. Edwin Keith and Grace Viola (Foss) B. A.B., Reed Coll., 1940; postgrad. (teaching fellow), Wash. State Coll., 1940-41; A.M., Columbia, 1943. Exec. asst. to chmn. 12th region WLB, Seattle, 1943-45; internat. affairs officer Dept. State, 1946-56; joined U.S. Fgn. Service, 1956; assigned Office UN Polit. Affairs, Dept. State, 1956-60; 1st sec. Am. embassy, Bonn, Germany, 1960-63; dep. dir. Office UN Polit. Affairs, 1963-65, dir., 1965-69; mem. State Dept. Sr. Seminar in Fgn. Policy, 1969-70; counselor for polit. affairs Am. embassy, Athens, Greece, 1970-75, dep. chief mission, The Hague, Netherlands, 1975-78; sr. insp. Dept. State, 1978-79, cons., 1980—; ret., 1979; adviser U.S. del. UN Gen. Assembly, 1946-50, 53, 55, 57-59, 64-65. Recipient 7th ann. Fed. Woman's award, 1967. Mem. Am. Fgn. Service Assn., Phi Beta Kappa. Home: 4848 Reservoir Rd NW Washington DC 20007 Office: Dept State Washington DC

BROWN, ELLIS L., chemical company executive; b. Duncan, Okla., 1915. Grad., Okla. U., 1939. Ind. oil producer, 1946-66; with Petrolite Corp., St. Louis, 1966—, chmn., chief exec. officer, 1981—. Office: Petrolite Corp 100 N Broadway St St Louis MO 63102 *

BROWN, ELSA CLARA LUSEBRINK, college dean; b. Bridgeport, Conn., Sept. 21, 1920; d. Herman Joseph and Elsa Anna (Wendler) Lusebrink; m. Herbert A. Brown, Oct. 11, 1958; 1 dau., Martha Ann. Assoc. Sci., Jr. Coll. Conn., 1939; diploma, Bridgeport Hosp. Sch. Nursing, 1942; B.S. in Nursing Edn, Tchrs. Coll., Columbia U., 1945, M.S., 1951; Ph.D., U. Toledo, 1980; D.Sc. (hon.), U. Bridgeport, 1980. Assoc. exec. dir. Bridgeport (Conn.) Hosp. Sch. Nursing, 1942-53; dir. Sch. Nursing and Nursing Services, Danbury (Conn.) Hosp., 1953-57, asst. adminstr., 1957-61; assoc. prof. nursing U. Bridgeport, 1961-65, prof., 1966-70; dean Jr. Coll. Conn., Bridgeport, 1970—, prof. nursing, 1970—; dean Sch. Allied Health, Med. Coll. Ohio at Toledo; accreditor and cons. nursing programs, 1952-80. Recipient Alumni award U. Bridgeport, 1954, Disting. Alumni award U. Bridgeport, 1980. Mem. Am. Assn. Community and Jr. Colls., Am. Assn. Allied Health Profls., Am. Nurses Assn., Ohio Nurses Assn., Ohio League for Nursing, Nat. League for Nursing (pres. 1981-83), Internat. Congress Nurses. Home: 2703 Densmore Dr Toledo OH 43606 Office: Med Coll Ohio Caller 10008 Toledo OH 43699

BROWN, ELVIN J., lawyer; b. Larned, Kans., Apr. 4, 1922; s. Elvin Gilbert and Ruth Ida (Horning) B.; m. Doris Elaine Huxman, Dec. 2, 1944; children: Rhonda (Mrs. Daniel W. Bjork), Carla, Randall, Douglas. Student, McPherson Coll., 1941-43, 46-47; J.D., U. Okla., 1950. Bar: Okla. 1950. Asst. county atty. Cleveland County, Norman, Okla., 1951-55, state trial judge, 1955-79; pres. Okla. Jud. Conf., 1975. Author: New Developments in Civil Law, 1973. Mem. exec. com. Last Frontier council Boy Scouts Am., 1973—; mem. adv. bd., sec. Salvation Army. Served with USN, 1942-46. Recipient Silver Beaver award. Mem. Norman C. of C. (dir.), Delta Theta Phi. Mem. Christian Ch. Clubs: Mason, Shriner, Lion (past dist. gov.). Home: 1115 W Brooks St Norman OK 73069 Office: 117 E Main St Norman OK 73069

BROWN, EMERSON LEE, textbook publisher; b. Hemple, Mo., Dec. 28, 1901; s. Aubrey S. and Della (Holmes) B.; m. Marguerite Bangs, June 6, 1926; children: Emerson Lee, Robert Tindall. A.B., Baker U., 1924; M.A., U. Kans., 1929; postgrad., Sch. Bus. Columbia, 1956. Instr. history Marion (Kans.) High Sch., 1924-26, prin., 1926-30; field rep. Harcourt, Brace & Co., 1930-38, social studies editor, 1938-52; gen. mgr. sch. dept. McGraw-Hill Book Co., N.Y.C., 1952-63, editorial dir., 1963-67, v.p., dir., 1954-67; sr. v.p. BCMA Assos., 1967-81; v.p. Moseley Assos., 1981—; Del. UNESCO internat. seminar on improvement textbooks, Brussels, Belgium, 1950; mem. Govt. Adv. Com. on Nat. Book Programs, 1964-66; Pres. Am. Textbook Pubs. Inst., 1964-65; Bd. dirs. CEMREL, Inc., St. Louis, 1972-81. Mem. Nat. Council Social Studies, Phi Delta Kappa. Democrat. Congregationalist. Home: 13 Sachem Rd Greenwich CT 06830 Office: Moseley Assos Inc 485 Fifth Ave Room 400 New York NY 10017

BROWN, EPHRAIM TAYLOR, JR., lawyer; b. Birmingham, Ala., Aug. 31, 1920; s. Ephraim Taylor and Lida (Otts) B.; m. Clara DeBardeleben Ebaugh, Oct. 21, 1949; children—Ephraim Taylor III, Clara DeBardeleben, Lida Otts. A.B., Princeton, 1941; LL.B., Cornell U., 1943. Bar: Ala. bar 1943. Since practiced in, Birmingham; asso. Cabaniss, Johnston, Gardner, Dumas & O'Neal, 1943-52, partner, 1952—; Chmn. spl. com. on Revision Probate Laws Ala., 1967; chmn. bd. bar examiners Ala. State Bar, 1967-79. Bd. dirs. Childrens Fresh Air Farm. Fellow Am. Coll. Probate Counsel; mem. ABA, Ala. Bar Assn. (pres.), Birmingham Bar Assn., Ala. Law Inst. (mem. counsel), Sigma Alpha Epsilon. Presbyn. (trustee, elder, deacon). Club: Birmingham Country. Home: 3105 Sterling Rd Birmingham AL 35213 Office: 1900 First Nat-Southern Natural Bldg Birmingham AL 35203

BROWN, ERIC REEDER, immunologist, educator; b. Cortland, N.Y., Mar. 16, 1925; s. Harold McDaniel and Helen (Seitz) B.; m. Chloe Cassandra Ledbetter, May 11, 1961; children—Carl F., Christopher H.A., Amy Elizabeth French; children by previous marriage—Eric Reeder II, Christine Virginia, Dianne Mary, Daniel K. B.A., Syracuse U., 1949, M.S., 1951; Ph.D. (Nat. Cancer Inst. Fellow), U. Kan., 1957; D.Sc., Quincy Coll., 1966. Instr. U. Ill. Med. Sch., 1957-58; asst. prof. U. Ala., 1958-60, U. Minn. Sch. Medicine, 1960-61; sr. research asso. Hektoen Inst., Chgo., 1961-67; assoc. prof. Northwestern U. Med. Sch., 1964-68; chmn. dept. microbiology Chgo. Med. Sch., 1967-82; cons. Newport Pharms., Inc., Strategic Med. Research Corp., U. Ill.; med. adviser to Ill. dir. SSS; dir. Lake Bluff Labs., Inc., Chesterton, Ind.; reviewer grants NSF, 1978—, Am. Cancer Soc. fellow, 1960-63, Leukemia Soc. scholar, 1965—; mem. med. adv. bd. Leukemia Research Found. Co-author: Cancer Dissemination and Therapy, 1961; author: Textbook of Micromolecular Biology, 1974, Immunobiological Characteristics of Leukemia, 1975, Sailing Made Easy, 1978; contbr. articles to profl. jours. Served with USCGR, 1942-46; served to col. USAF, 1951-55; col. Res. Fellow Am. Inst. Chemists, Am. Acad. Microbiology, Chgo. Inst. Medicine; mem. Royal Soc. Medicine, Histochem. Soc., Internat. Soc. Lymphology, AAUP, Am. Mus. Natural History, Med. Mycol. Soc. of Ams., Soc. Exptl. Biology and Medicine, Res. Officers Assn., Phi Beta Kappa, Sigma Xi, Psi Chi, Phi Sigma. Research on virus etiology of cancer and leukemia. Home: PO Box 335 7704 Camellia Chicago IL 60097 Office: Chicago Med Sch 3333 Greenbay Rd North Chicago IL 60064 *

BROWN, ERNEST JOSEPH, lawyer; b. Lake Providence, La., May 30, 1906; s. John Ernest and Pearl (Fisher) B. A.B., Princeton, 1927; LL.B., Harvard, 1931. Bar: N.Y. bar 1934. Practiced in, Buffalo, 1934-41; prof. law U. Buffalo Law Sch., 1937-42; prof. Harvard Law Sch., 1946-71, Langdell prof. law emeritus, 1971—; with tax div. U.S. Dept. Justice, Washington, 1970—; mem. legal staff A.A.A., 1933, WPB, 1942; hearing commr. N.P.A., 1952. Editor: (with Freund, Sutherland and Howe) Constitutional Law, Cases and Other Problems. Served to capt. AUS, 1942-45; CBI. Recipient Disting. Service award Dept. Justice, 1981. Fellow Am. Acad. Arts and Scis.; mem. Am., N.Y. bar assns. Home: 4201 S 31st St Arlington VA 22206 Office: Tax Div US Dept of Justice Washington DC

BROWN, ESTHER LUCILE, author, lecturer; b. Manchester, N.H.; d. Charles Wesley and Nellie (Morse) B. B.A. with spl. honors, U. N.H., 1920; Ph.D. in Social Anthropology, Yale, 1929; LL.D., Skidmore Coll., 1950. Asst. prof. social sci. U. N.H., 1926-29; research assoc. Russell Sage Found., N.Y.C., 1930-45, dir. dept. studies in profession, 1945-48, exec. program planning and direction, 1948-63; writer, lectr., cons.; Vis. prof. U. Wis. at Madison, 1970; Cons. for WHO, 1952-53. Author: The Professional Engineer, 1935, Social Work as a Profession, 4th edit, 1942, Nursing as a Profession, 2d edit, 1940, Physicians and Medical Care, 1934, Lawyers and the Promotion of Justice, 1938, Lawyers, Law Schools and the Public Service, 1948, Nursing for the Future (translated into Swedish, Portuguese, Japanese), 6th edit, 1953, (with Milton Greenblatt and Richard H. York) From Custodial to Therapeutic Patient Care in Mental Hospitals, 1955, Newer Dimensions of Patient Care; Part I, The Use of Physical and Social Environment of the Hospital for Therapeutic Purposes, 1961, Part II, Improving Staff Motivation and Competence in the General Hospital, 1962, Part III, Patients as People, 1964, Newer Dimensions of Patient Care, vol. 1 (translated into Japanese), 1965, Nursing Reconsidered: A Study of Change, Part 1 (translated into Japanese), 1970, Part II, 1971; also numerous articles. Social Sci. Research Council fellow in, France, 1929-30. Hon. life mem. Nat. League for Nursing; mem. Am. Sociol. Assn., Soc. Applied Anthropology. Address: 1400 Geary Blvd San Francisco CA 94109

BROWN, EVERETT AUSTIN, interior color and design cons.; b. Remmington, Ind., Apr. 3, 1913; s. Luther and Zoe Lee (Blackwell) B.; m. Martha Isabel Wilson, Jan. 11, 1934; children—Marcia, Zoe Lee. Ed. pub. schs., Ind. With home furnishing sects. Marshall Field & Co., Chgo., 1934-37, interior design sect., 1939-44; with Stower's Furniture Co., Houston, 1937-39; color and design coordinator Grand Rapids Furniture Makers Guild, Mich., 1944-50; propr. Everett Brown Assos., N.Y.C. and San Francisco, 1950-67; pres. Everett Brown Assos., Inc., N.Y.C., 1967—; Bd. advisers Pavilion Am. Interiors; also design com. House Good Taste, N.Y. World's Fair, 1964; color and design cons. to various cos. Com. mem. Industry Found. Recipient Product Design award Resources Council, 1976. Fellow Am. Inst. Interior Designers (nat. bd. 1955-57, chmn. nat. bd. 1963-66, bd. govs. No. Calif. chpt. 1954-61, 66, chmn. internat. design awards com. 1963-66, gov. N.Y. chpt. 1967—, dir. N.Y. Met. chpt. 1980-81), Am. Soc. Interior Designers (nat. indsl. relations com. 1976-77, Designer of Distinction award 1980), Color Assn. U.S. (chmn. homefurnishings adv. com.). Home: 15 W 55th St New York NY 10019 Office: 225 E 57th St New York NY 10022

BROWN, FIELDING, physics educator, physicist; b. Berlin, N.H., Jan. 2, 1924; s. William Robinson and Hildreth (Smith) B.; m. Eleanor Reier, Oct. 26, 1944; children: Angela, Elizabeth, Marcia, Lucinda. B.A., Williams Coll., Williamstown, Mass., 1947, M.A., 1949; Ph.D., Princeton U., 1953. Research physicist Sprague Electric Co., North Adams, Mass., 1952-59; mem. faculty Williams Coll., Williamstown, Mass., 1959—, prof. physics, 1967—, Charles L. MacMillan prof., 1977—; dir. Bronfman Sci. Ctr., Williamstown, Mass., 1965-67; vis. prof. Grad. Sch. Physics U. Tokyo, 1965-66; vis. scientist Frances Bitter Nat. Magnet Lab. MIT, 1968-76, Research Lab. of Electronics, 1976—, Lincoln Lab., 1961-62; cons. solid state physics Arthur D. Little, Inc., Cambridge, Mass., 1959-61; cons. infrared physics MIT, 1974—. Served to 1st lt. AUS, 1943-46. Research grantee NSF, 1960-78, U.S. Army, 1962-65, USAF, 1966-71, Dept. Energy, 1978. Mem Am. Phys. Soc.; mem. Kappa Alpha. Home: 179 Park St Williamstown MA 01267 Office: Dept Physics Williams Coll Williamstown MA 01267

BROWN, FIRMAN HEWITT, JR., educator, theatrical dir.; b. Bradenton, Fla., Sept. 27, 1926; s. Firman Hewitt and Eunice (DeVane) B.; m. Margery Arlene Hunter, Mar. 21, 1953; children—Sarah Hunter, Blakely DeVane. Student, U. Fla., 1944; B.A. in Journalism, U. Mont., 1949, M.A., 1953; postgrad., Columbia, 1954; Ph.D. in Speech, U. Wis., 1963. Reporter Havre (Mont.) Daily News, 1950-51; dir. pub. service, instr. No. Mont. Coll., Havre, 1951-54; vis. lectr. U. Mont., 1956-57, prof., chmn. dept. drama, 1957-69; prof., chmn. dept. drama-speech Ithaca (N.Y.) Coll., 1969-79; prof., chmn. dept. theatre arts and speech communication, dir. Annie Russell Theatre, Rollins Coll., Winter Park, Fla., 1979-81; prof., chmn. dept. theatre Ohio State U., Columbus, 1981—; guest lectr., 1961—; Mem. Mont. Arts Council, 1967-69, Nat. Theatre Conf., 1965—; bd. dirs. Rocky Mountain Theater Conf., 1967-69, Fla. Theatre Conf., 1979-81. Producer-dir.-owner, Bigfork (Mont.) Summer Playhouse, 1960-67; founder, dir., Mont. Repertory Theatre Co., Missoula, 1967-69; co-founder, dir., Ithaca Summer Repertory Theatre, 1970-79, Rollins Repertory Theatre, 1980-81; columnist: On Stage, Sunday Missoulian, 1965-68. Served with USNR, 1944-46. Recipient 1st Arts Mgmt. Career Service award for outstanding contbn. to theatre over past decade, 1969. Mem. Am. Theatre Assn., Am. Soc. Theatre Research, Mont. Inst. Arts (certificate of merit 1966). Democrat. Spl. research Mont. Theatre history. Home: 372 W 5th Ave Columbus OH 43201

BROWN, FRANCIS CABELL, JR., lawyer; b. Washington, Jan. 6, 1936; s. Francis Cabell and Helen Montrose (Howes) B.; m. Nancy Adeline Leitzow, June 18, 1960; children—Caroline Montrose, Francis Cabell III, James Herman Loughborough, Jennifer Nancy. B.A., Princeton, 1958; LL.B., Harvard, 1961. Bar: N.Y. bar 1962, D.C. bar 1964. Asso. firm White & Case, N.Y.C., 1961-64, 67, Paris, 1964-65, Brussels, 1966; spl. asst. to asst. atty. gen. U.S. Dept. Justice, Washington, 1968; practice law, N.Y.C., 1969—. Bd. regents (emeritus) Georgetown U.; trustee Female Acad. of Sacred Heart of N.Y. Mem. Soc. Mayflower Descs. Clubs: Union League, University (N.Y.C.); Travellers (Paris). Home: 520 E 86th St New York NY 10028 Office: 200 Park Ave Suite 2616 New York NY 10166

BROWN, FRANCIS ROBERT, educator; b. Fairbury, Ill., Dec. 19, 1914; s. Edwin Henry and Annie L. (Besgrove) B.; m. Helen Elizabeth Tucker, Aug. 22, 1940; children—Robert Alan, David Lee, Bruce William, Mark Leslie. B.E., Ill. State U., 1937; M.A., Columbia U., 1940; Ed.D., U. Ill., 1954. Tchr., head dept. math. Centennial Jr. High Sch., Decatur, Ill., 1937-41; tchr. Decatur High Sch., 1941-42; civilian instr., adminstr. USAAF, Chanute Field, Ill., 1943-44; asst. prof. math. Millikin U., Decatur, Ill., 1946-49; prof. math. Ill. State U., Normal, 1949-77, prof. emeritus, 1977—, dir. div. univ. extension and field services, 1958-73, asst. dir. summer session, 1968-77, dir. div. continuing edn. and pub. service, 1973-77; State math. cons. Office of Supt. of Pub. Instrn., Springfield, Ill., 1960-63; cons. Homer Consol. Sch. System, Lockport, Ill., 1971-73; mem. evaluation teams Nat. Council for Accreditation for Tchr. Edn., 1967-77, chmn., 1976, 77; chmn. alumni outstanding achievement awards com. Ill. State U., 1979—. Author: Numbers and Operations, 1963, New Dimensions in Mathematics-Grades 1-6, 1970, Mathematics Course/Grade 7, 1973, Mathematics Course 2, Grade 8, 1973; Mem. editorial com.: Ill. Quar, 1965-77; mem. editorial rev. com.: Math. Tchr.-Nat. Council for Tchrs. Math, 1964—. Mem. Ill. Law Enforcement Commn., 1970—, chmn., 1977-78; cons., chmn. Citizens Study Com. for Developing Bldg. Codes, Normal, 1973-74; mem. advisory bd. Salvation Army, 1976—, chmn., 1979-81; mem. Normal Planning Commn., 1979—; co-founder State of Ill. Arson Prevention Com., 1974, dir., 1974-78; mem. regional adv. com. Sr. Olympics, 1981—. Served with USAAF, 1944-46. Recipient Max Beberman award Ill. Council Tchrs. Math., 1974; Friends of Sport award Ill. State U., 1977. Mem. Nat. Council Tchrs. Math. (coordinator Onarga community devel. 1966-69), Math. Assn. Am., Nat. Univ. Extension Assn., Assn. Field Sers. for Tchr. Edn.

(pres. 1964-65), Assn. Orgns. Tchr. Edn. (chmn. 1969-70), Am. Assn. Colls. for Tchr. Edn. (exec. bd. 1969-70), NEA, Ill. Council Tchrs. Math. (pres. 1961-62), Ill. Adult Edn. Assn. (pres. 1962-63), Adult Edn. Assn. U.S.A. (dir. 1963-66), Phi Delta Kappa, Kappa Phi Kappa, Phi Kappa Phi, Kappa Mu Epsilon, Kappa Delta Pi. Mem. Christian Ch. (elder 1943—). Club: Kiwanis (dir. 1973-75). Home: 601 Normal Ave Normal IL 61761 *The continual establishment of reasonable goals provides necessary stimulation and motivation. To live in such a world of change one must have a solid foundation as a support. This has been provided by family, church, co-workers and friends. A strong sense of personal responsibility is the glue that holds everything together and furnishes the necessary rapport to work successfully with others.*

BROWN, FRANK, university dean, educator; b. Gallian, Ala., May 1, 1935; s. Tom and Ora L. (Lomax) B.; m. Joan Drake, July 6, 1963; children: Frank G., Monica J. B.S., Ala. State U., 1957; M.S., Oreg. State U., 1962; M.A., U. Calif.-Berkeley, 1969, Ph.D., 1970. Asst. to prin., tchr. U.S. Jones High Sch., Demopolis, Ala., 1960-61; sci. tchr. Oakland Pub. Schs. (Calif.), 1962-68; assoc. dir. N.Y. Com. on Edn., N.Y.C., 1970-72; dir. Urban Inst. CCNY, 1971-72; prof., coll. master SUNY, Buffalo, 1972-77; dean, prof. ednl. adminstrn. U. N.C., Chapel Hill, 1983—; project dir. Ford Found., N.Y.C., 1973-76, Spencer Found., Buffalo, 1976-78, Nat. Inst. Edn., 1977-79, NSF, Washington, 1979-80. Author: (with others) Fleischmann Commn. Report, 1973, Minority Enrollment in U.S. Institutions of Higher Education, 1977; editor: Emergent Leadership, 1976-80; guest editor: Edn. and Urban Soc., 1978. Grad. fellow Washington U., St. Louis, 1958, Oreg. State U., 1961, U. Calif.-Berkeley, 1968; fellow Rockefeller Found., 1979. Mem. Am. Ednl. Research Assn. (div. A sec. 1980-82), Nat. Orgn. Legal Problems of Edn. (editorial bd. 1979-80), Assn. Social and Behavioral Scientists, Afro-Am. Hist. Assn. N.Y., Phi Delta Kappa. Democrat. Baptist. Office: U NC 101 Peabody Hall 037A Chapel Hill NC 27514

BROWN, FRED ELMORE, investment executive; b. Muskogee, Okla., July 20, 1913; s. Fred E. and Alice (Washington) B.; m. Margaret Ann Gillham, Nov. 15, 1941 (dec.); 1 son, Frederick Elmore; m. Enid Sillcox Darlington, Dec. 22, 1977. B.S., U. Okla., 1934; M.B.A., Harvard U., 1936. Sr. partner J. & W. Seligman & Co. Inc., 1955-81, chmn., chief exec. officer; chmn. Seligman Securities Inc.; chmn., chief exec. officer Tri-Continental Corp., Seligman Capital Fund, Inc., Seligman Cash Mgmt. Fund, Inc., Seligman Common Stock Fund, Inc., Seligman Communications and Info. Fund, Inc., Seligman Growth Fund, Inc., Seligman Income Fund, Inc., Liberty Cash Mgmt. Fund, Inc., Union Data Service Center, Inc.; dir. J.&W. Seligman & Co. Mktg., Inc.; vice chmn. Assn. Publicly Traded Investment Funds.; Mem. N.Y. Stock Exchange. Trustee Morristown (N.J.) Meml. Hosp., Trudeau Inst.; mem. adv. com. Center for Study Fin. Instns., Law Sch., U. Pa., Coll. Bus. Adminstrn., U. Okla. Served from 2d lt. to lt. col. OQMG AUS, 1942-46. Decorated Legion of Merit.; recipient Disting. Service citation U. Okla., 1982; inducted Okla. Hall of Fame, 1982. Mem. N.Y. Soc. Security Analysts, Beta Theta Pi, Delta Sigma Pi, Beta Gamma Sigma. Episcopalian. Clubs: Downtown Assn., Lake Placid, Somerset Hills Country. Endowed Fred E. Brown chair in fin. Coll. Bus. Adminstrn., U. Okla. Home: Van Beuren Rd Morristown NJ 07960 Office: One Bankers Trust Plaza New York NY 10006

BROWN, FREDERIC JOSEPH, army officer; b. Fort Sill, Okla., July 18, 1934; s. Frederic Joseph and Kathryn (Richardson) B.; m. Harriette Anne Upham, July 7, 1956; children: Kathryn, Harriette, Judith. B.S., U.S. Military Acad., 1956; M.A., Grad. Inst. Internat. Studies, U. Geneva, Switzerland, 1963, Ph.D., 1967. Commd. officer U.S. Army, advanced through grades to maj. gen.; comdr. 1st squadron 4th cavalry, Vietnam, 1969-70; mem. staff Nat. Security Council, 1972-73; comdr. 1st brigade 2d Armored Div., Ft. Hood, Tex., 1975-76; comdr. U.S. Army Tng. Center Armor, Ft. Knox, Ky., 1977-78; asst. div. comdr. 8th Inf. Div., Baumholder, W. Ger., 1978-81; dep. chief of staff tng. U.S. Army Tng. and Doctrine Command, Ft. Monroe, Va., 1981—; comdg. gen. U.S. Army Armor Ctr., Ft. Knox, Ky.; asst. prof. dept. social scis. U.S. Mil. Acad., West Point, N.Y. Author: Chemical Warfare - A Study in Restraints, 1968; co-author: The United States Army in Transition, 1973. Decorated Silver Star, Legion of Merit.; Olmstead scholar, 1961-63. Mem. Council Fgn. Relations, Internat. Inst. Strategic Studies. Episcopalian. Home: Qtrs 1 Fort Knox KY 40121 Office: Fort Knox KY 40121

BROWN, FREDERICK CALVIN, physicist, educator; b. Seattle, July 6, 1924; s. Fred Charles and Rose (Mueller) B.; m. Joan Schauble, Aug. 9, 1952; children—Susan, Gail, Derek. B.S., Harvard U., 1945, M.S., 1947, Ph.D., 1950. Physicist Systems Research Lab., Harvard (NDRC), 1945-46; staff physicist Naval Research Lab., Washington, 1950; physicist Applied Physics Lab., U. Wash., 1950-51; asst. prof. Reed Coll., Portland, Oreg., 1951-55, U. Ill., Urbana, 1955-58, assoc. prof., 1958-61, prof., 1961—; assoc. Center for Advanced Study, 1969-70; prin. scientist, area mgr. Xerox Palo Alto Research Center, 1973-74; cons. prof., applied physics dept. Stanford, 1973-74. Author: The Physics of Solids-Ionic Crystals, Lattice Vibrations and Imperfections, 1967; Contbr. articles profl. jours. Recipient Alexander von Humboldt sr. scientist award U. Kiel, 1978; NSF sr. postdoctoral fellow Clarendon Lab., Oxford, 1964-65. Fellow Am. Phys. Soc. Innovator use of synchrotron radiation for spectroscopy. Home: 31 Ashley Ln Champaign IL 61820 Office: Dept Physics U Ill Urbana IL 61801

BROWN, FREDERICK ISAAC, JR., steel fabricating co. exec.; b. Little Rock, Jan. 26, 1923; s. Frederick Isaac and Josephine (Miller) B.; m. Mary Patricia Saer, Apr. 15, 1950; children—Frederick Isaac, Robert Saer, Thomas McQueen, Mary Patricia, Carolyn Louise. B.S., U. Ariz., 1944, M.I.T., 1949. With AFCO Steel Co., and affiliates, 1949—; pres. Ark. Foundry Co., Little Rock, 1962—; sec.-treas. AFCO Metals Co., 1963—. Bd. dirs. Little Rock Boys Club, 1960—, pres., 1968-69; chmn. Little Rock Port Authority, 1965—; pres. Associated Industries Ark., 1970-71, chmn., 1971; bd. dirs. Pulaski County chpt. ARC, 1972—. Served with USNR, 1943-46. Mem. NAM (dir. 1962-64, 79—). Roman Catholic. Clubs: Country of Little Rock; Boston (New Orleans). Office: PO Box 231 Little Rock AR 72203

BROWN, GAIL NILE, accounting firm executive; b. Weiser, Idaho, Sept. 21, 1918; s. Nile Little and Marvella (Olsen) B.; m. Evelyn Snyder, Dec. 5, 1941; children: Gary Lee, Christopher J. B.S., Brigham Young U., Provo, Utah, 1942. C.P.A., N.Y., Calif. Sec. to pres. Brigham Young U., 1940-42; with Wayne Mayhew & Co., C.P.A.s, Modesto, Calif. and; Rochester, N.Y., 1946-54; with Touche Ross & Co., C.P.A.s, 1954—, sr. partner, San Francisco, 1979—; industry nat. dir. agribus., 1970—. Co-editor: Accounting and Taxation for Cooperatives. Chmn. fin. com. Assn. C. of C., 1967. Served to lt. USNR, 1942-46. Mem. Nat. Soc. Accts. for Coops. (pres. 1965), Am. Inst. C.P.A.s, N.Y. Soc. C.P.A.s (past pres. Rochester chpt.), Calif. Soc. C.P.A.s, Nat. Council Farmer Coops. (past chmn. com.), Am. Legion (past county treas.). Republican. Mormon. Clubs: Orinda Country, San Francisco Comml. Office: Touche Ross & Co Alcoa Bldg 1 Maritime Plaza San Francisco CA 94111

BROWN, GENE MONTE, educator, biochemist; b. Pioneer, Mo., Jan. 21, 1926; s. John Arthur and Leah (Hart) B.; m. Shirley Lewis, June 14, 1954; children: James Lewis, Lindsey Arthur, Holly Ann. Student, Coll. Idaho, 1943-44; B.S., Colo. A&M Coll., 1949; M.S. (Wis. Alumni Research Found. fellow), U. Wis., 1950, Ph.D., 1953. Research scientist U. Tex., Austin, 1951-54; instr. dept. biology MIT, 1954-56, asst. prof., 1956-61, asso. prof., 1961-67, prof., 1967—, exec. officer dept. biology, 1967-72, asso. head dept., 1972-77, head dept., 1977—; cons. NSF, 1964-67; mem. panel NSF Grad. Fellowship Program, 1968-72, chmn. biochemistry sect., 1970-72. Editorial bd.: Jour. Biol. Chemistry, 1969-74, 82—. Served with USAAF, 1944-45. Mem. Am. Soc. Biol. Chemists, Am. Chem. Soc., Am. Acad. Arts and Scis., Sigma Xi, Phi Kappa Phi. Office: 77 Massachusetts Av Cambridge MA 02139

BROWN, GEORGE EDWARD, JR., Congressman; b. Holtville, Calif., Mar. 6, 1920; s. George Edward and Bird Alma (Kilgore) B.; m. Rowena Somerindyke. B.A., UCLA, 1946; grad. fellow, Fund Adult Edn., 1954. Mgmt. cons., Calif., 1957-61; v.p. Monarch Savs. & Loan Assn., Los Angeles, 1960-68; mem. Calif. Assembly from 45th Dist., 1959-62, 88th-91st congresses from 29th Dist. Calif., 93d Congress from 38th Dist. Calif., 94th-97th Congresses from 36th Dist. Calif., Standing Com. on Agr.; apptd. to Office of Tech. Assessment; candidate U.S. Senate, 1970; coll. lectr., radio commentator, 1971. Mem. Calif. Gov.'s Adv. Com. on Housing Problems, 1961-62; Mayor Los Angeles Labor-Mgmt. Com., 1961-62; Councilman, Monterey Park, Calif., 1954-58, mayor, 1955-56. Served to 2d lt., inf. AUS, World War II. Mem. Am. Legion, Colton C. of C., Urban League, Internat. Brotherhood Elec. Workers, AFL-CIO, Friends Com. Legislation, Ams. for Dem. Action. Democrat. Methodist. Quaker. Lodge: Kiwanis. Home: Colton CA 92324 Office: 2256 Rayburn House Office Bldg Washington DC 20515 *

BROWN, GEORGE HAROLD, radio engineer; b. North Milwaukee, Wis., Oct. 14, 1908; s. James Clifford and Ida Louise (Siegert) B.; m. Julia Elizabeth Ward, Dec. 26, 1932; children: James Ward and George H. (twins). B.S., U. Wis., 1930, M.S., 1931, Ph.D., 1933, E.E., 1942; Dr.Eng. (hon.), U. R.I., 1968. With RCA, 1933-37, 38-73, successively research engr., Camden, Princeton, N.J., dir. Systems Research Lab., chief engr. Comml. Electronic Products div., Camden, chief engr. indsl. electronic products, 1933-59, v.p. engring., 1959-61, v.p. research and engring., 1961-65, exec. v.p. research and engring., 1965-68, exec. v.p. patents and licensing, 1968-72; dir. Trane Co., 1967-79, cons. engr., 1937—; dir. RCA Global Communications, 1962-71, RCA, 1965-72, RCA Internat., Ltd., 1968-72; Shoenberg Meml. lectr. Royal Instn., 1972; Marconi Centenary lectr. AAAS, 1974. Author: (with R.A. Bierwirth and C.N. Hoyler) Radio Frequency Heating, 1947, And Part of Which I Was, 1982; contbr. articles to sci. jours. Exec. bd. George Washington council Boy Scouts Am.; bd. govs. Hamilton Hosp. Recipient Silver Beaver and Silver Antelope awards Boy Scouts Am.; citation Internat. TV Symposium, Montreux, Switzerland, 1965; DeForest Audion award, 1968; David Sarnoff award for outstanding achievements in radio and TV U. Ariz., 1980. Fellow IEEE (Edison medal 1967, Centennial medal 1984), AAAS, Royal TV Soc.; mem. Nat. Acad. Engring., Am. Mgmt. Assn., Sigma Xi, Tau Beta Pi, Eta Kappa Nu (eminent mem.). Clubs: Nassau, Springdale. Patentee in field. Home: 117 Hunt Dr Princeton NJ 08540

BROWN, GEORGE HAY, association executive; b. Denver, Feb. 4, 1910; s. Orville G. and Clara Amsden (Topping) B.; m. Catherine Smith, June 11, 1932 (dec. May 1962); 1 dau., Ann. A.B., Oberlin Coll., 1929; M.B.A., Harvard, 1931; Ph.D., U. Chgo., 1945. Divisional sales mgr. Mallinckrodt Chem. Works, St. Louis, 1931-38; instr. mktg. U. Chgo., 1938-41, asst. prof., 1941-42, asso. prof., 1942-44, prof., 1945-54, dir. bus. problems bur., 1942-46, dir. devel. for social sci., bus. and social service adminstrn., 1947-49; mgr. mktg. research Ford. div. Ford Motor Co., 1954-60, dir. mktg. research, mktg. staff, 1960-69; dir. U.S. Census Bur., 1969-73; sec. Conf. Bd., N.Y.C., 1973-81, sr. research fellow, 1981-83; vis. prof. Sch. Bus., North Fla. U., 1981—; mem. exec. com. nat. marketing adv. com. U.S. Dept Commerce, 1964-69; head U.S. del. UN Conf. Asian Statisticians, Manila, 1972; cons. Oak Ridge Nat. Lab., 1973-78, U.S. Gen. Accounting Office, 1974-82, U.S. News and World Report, 1974-79, Western Union Co., 1978—. Author: The International Economic Position of New Zealand, Journal of Business Monograph, 1946, (with Jeuck and Peterson) Readings in Marketing and Price Policy, 1951; Editor: Marketing Series, Henry Holt & Co., 1950-55; Contbr. articles to econ. jours. Trustee Found. for Research on Human Behavior, Ann Arbor, 1962-69, Mktg. Sci. Inst., Phila., 1963-69, Advt. Research Found., N.Y., 1967-69; bd. dirs. Fed. Statis. Users Conf., Washington, 1976-79, Campaign Communications Inst. Am., Inc., N.Y.C., 1981—; Bd. govs. subcom. ARC, 1977—; gen. chmn. ARC of Greater N.Y. Community Appeal, 1976-77; trustee Fifth Avenue Presbyn. Ch., 1977-80, dir. long-range planning com., 1980-82; bd. dirs. Hosp. Chaplaincy, Inc., N.Y.C., 1981—. Fellow Am. Psychol. Assn., Am. Statis. Assn. (dir. 1973-75); mem. Am. Econ. Assn., Am. Mktg. Assn. (nat. pres. 1951-52), Mktg. Research Council N.Y. (dir. 1980-81), Assn. Univ. Bus. and Econ. Research (life), Internat. Statis. Inst., Delta Sigma Pi, Beta Gamma Sigma. Club: River (N.Y.C.). Home: 870 United Nations Plaza New York NY 10017 Office: Coll Bus U North Fla 4567 Saint Johns Bluff Rd S Jacksonville FL 32216

BROWN, GEORGE LESLIE, former lieutenant governor of Colorado, manufacturing company executive; b. Lawrence, Kans., July 1, 1926; s. George L. and Harriett Alberta (Watson) B.; m. Modeen; children: Gail Brown Chandler, Laura Nicole, Kim Doreen, Cynthia Renee, Ronnie, Carol, Angela, Sharolyn, Nyra. B.S. in Journalism, U. Kans., 1950; postgrad., U. Colo., 1950-51; A.M.P., Harvard Bus. Sch., 1980. Mem. writing staff Denver Post, 1950-65; asst. exec. dir. Denver Housing Authority, 1965-69; exec. dir. Met. Denver Urban Coalition, 1969-75; lt. gov. Colo., Denver, 1974-79; v.p. Grumman Corp., N.Y., 1979—; coordinator Colo. Jud./Heritage Constrn. Project, Colo. Reorgn. Plan; chmn. Colo. Sch. Budget Rev. Bd.; mem. exec. com. Nat. Conf. Lt. Govs. Mem. Colo. Ho. of Reps., 1955, Colo. Senate, 1956-74; vice chmn. Nat. Statewide Democratic Elected Ofcls.; mem.-at-large Dem. Nat. Com.; chmn. Dem. Nat. Com. Black Caucus. Served with USAAF, 1944-46. Recipient Adam Clayton Powell award for polit. achievement, 1975, Opportunities Industrialization Center Nat. Govt. award, 1975; George Brown Urban Journalism scholarship established at U. Kans. William Allen White Sch. Journalism, 1976. Mem. Kappa Alpha Psi. Office: Grumman Corp 1111 Stewart Ave Bethpage NY 11714 *

BROWN, GEORGE WALLACE, hydrologist; b. Warrensburg, Mo., Jan. 31, 1939; s. George Wallace and Fern Elizabeth (Dierking) B.; m. Joan Lee Isham, Sept. 12, 1964; children: Christen, Ann. B.S., Colo. State U., 1960, M.S., 1962; PhD., Oreg. State U., Corvallis, 1967. Research hydrologist U.S. Forest Service, 1964; mem. faculty Oreg. State U., 1966—, prof. forest hydrology, 1975—, chmn. dept. forest engring., 1973—; cons. to govt. and industry. Author: Forestry and Water Quality, 2d edit, 1983; editorial bd.: Jour. Forestry. Served with USAR, 1962-64. Mem. Am. Geophys. Union, Soc. Am. Foresters, Sigma Xi. Office: Dept Forest Engring Oregon State Univ Corvallis OR 97331

BROWN, GILES TYLER, educator, lecturer; b. Marshall, Mich., Apr. 21, 1916; s. A. Watson and Ettroile (Kent) B.; m. Crysta Beth Cosner, Nov. 21, 1951. A.B., San Diego State Coll., 1937; M.A., U. Calif.-Berkeley, 1941; Ph.D., Claremont Grad. Sch., 1948; post-doctoral seminar, U. Edinburgh, Scotland, 1949. Tchr., counselor, Binet intelligence tester San Diego City Schs., 1937-46; dir. social sci. project, chmn. social sci. div. Orange Coast Coll., Newport Beach, Calif., 1948-60; prof. history, chmn. social sci. div. Calif. State U., Fullerton, 1961-66, also chmn. history dept., dean grad. studies, 1967-83, asso. v.p. acad. programs, 1979-83; pub. lectr. nat., internat. affairs, 1951—; also cons. gerontology; participant Wilton Park Conf., Eng., 1976; mem. joint grad. bd. Calif. Postsecondary Edn. Commn., 1978; moderator Behind the Headlines Forum, Orange Coast Coll.; lectr. Laguna Hills Leisure World Forum; past chmn. Hist. Landmarks Com. Orange County. Author: Ships That Sail No More, 1966; Contbr. to: Help in Troubled Times, 1962; contbr. articles, book reviews to profl. jours. Trustee, past pres. and chmn. bd. World Affairs Council Orange County; past pres. U. Calif. Irvine Friends Library; nat. bd. dirs., nat. pres. Travelers Century Club; mem. grad. fellowship adv. com., State of Calif., 1980; bd. dirs. Pacific Symphony Orch. Served from ensign to lt. USNR, 1942-46. Recipient Pacific History award Pacific Coast br. Am. Hist. Assn., 1950; named Outstanding Prof. Calif. State U., 1966, Hon. Citizen of Orange County, 1969. Mem. AAAS, Am. Hist. Assn., Internat. Platform Assn. (past western pres.), Western Assn. Grad. Schs. (exec. com. 1981-83), SAR, Phi Beta Kappa, Phi Delta Kappa, Phi Alpha Theta, Kappa Delta Pi. Baptist. Clubs: Explorers, Masons. Home: 413 Catalina Dr Newport Beach CA 92663

BROWN, GLENN HALSTEAD, chemist, educator; b. Logan, Ohio, Sept. 10, 1915; s. James E. and Nancy J. (Mohler) B.; m. Jessie Adcock, May 27, 1943; children—Larry H., Nancy K., Donald S., Barbara J. B.S., Ohio U., 1939; M.S., Ohio State U., 1941; Ph.D., Iowa State U., 1951; D.Sc. (hon.), Bowling Green State U., 1972. Asst. prof. U. Miss., 1941-46, 49-50; instr. Iowa State U., 1946-49; asst. prof. U. Vt., 1950-52; asso. prof. U. Cin., 1952-60; with Kent (Ohio) State U., 1960—, prof. chemistry, head dept., 1960-65; dir. Liquid Crystal Inst., 1965—, dean for research, 1963-69, Regents prof. chemistry, 1968—; Bikerman lectr., 1981. Author: (with F.A. Anderson) Fundamentals of Chemistry, 1944, (with Wollett and Fogelsong) Laboratory Manual for Organic Chemistry, 1944, Record Book for Quantitative Analysis, 1954, (with E. M. Sallee) Quantitative Chemistry, 1963, (with others) Liquid Crystals, 1967, Review of the Structure and Properties of Liquid Crystals, 1970, (with J.J. Wolken) Liquid Crystals and Biological Structures; contbr. articles to sci. jours.; editor: Liquid Crystals 2, Parts I and II, 1969, Photochromism, 1971, Liquid Crystals 3, parts I and II, 1972, Advances in Liquid Crystals, vol. I, 1975, vol. II, 1976, vol. III, 1978, vol. IV, 1979; editor-in-chief: Jour. Molecular Crystals and Liquid Crystals, 1968—. Recipient Morley award in chemistry, 1977; Pres.'s award Kent State U., 1980; 8th Internat. Liquid Crystal Conf. dedicated in his hon., Tokyo, 1980. Fellow Ohio Acad. Sci. (pres. 1960, Distinguished Service award 1966); mem. Am. Chem. Soc. (chmn. Akron sect. 1965, nat. councilor Akron sect., chmn. regional meeting planning com. 1968, Distinguished Service award Akron sect. 1971), Am. Inst. Chemists (chmn. Ohio 1969-71), Am. Crystallographic Assn., AAAS, N.Y. Acad. Scis., Sigma Xi (nat. lectureship 1970), Alpha Chi Sigma, Phi Lambda Upsilon, Omicron Delta Kappa. Methodist. Spl. research X-ray structural studies liquids, concentrated salt solutions, photochromism, liquid crystals. Home: 470 Harvey Ave Kent OH 44240

BROWN, H. W(ILLIAM), railroad company executive; b. Bryn Mawr, Pa., July 29, 1938; s. Howard W. and Viola (Vercoe) B.; m. Constance Forster, Mar. 7, 1964; children: Bradley J., Diana. B.S. in B.A., Bucknell U., 1960. C.P.A., Pa. Audit mgr. Price Waterhouse & Co., Phila., 1962-68; controller, ops. mgr. Bioren & Co., Phila., 1968-70; controller Ins. Co. N. Am., Phila., 1970-72; sr. v.p., chief officer Investment Annuity, Inc., Valley Forge, Pa., 1972-78; v.p., treas. Consol. Rail Corp., Phila., 1978—; dir. Can. So. Rwy. Co., 1980—, Fruit Growers Express, 1980—, Pa. Truck Lines, 1980—, Niagara River Bridge Co., 1981—. Served with U.S. Army, 1960-62. Mem. Fin. Execs. Inst., Am. Inst. C.P.A.s, Pa. Soc. C.P.A.s, Am. Assn. Railroads (vise chmn. Treasury div.). Home: 4137 Jackson Dr Lafayette Hill PA 19444 Office: Consolidated Rail Corp room 1334 6 Penn Center Plaza Philadelphia PA 19104

BROWN, HANK, congressman; b. Denver, Feb. 12, 1940; s. Harry W. and Anna M. (Hanks) B.; m. Nana Morrison, Aug. 27, 1967; children: Harry, Christy, Lori. B.S., U. Colo., 1961; J.D., 1969. Bar: Colo. 1969. Tax acct. Arthur Andersen, 1967-68; asst. pres. Monfort of Colo., Inc., Greeley, 1969-70, corp. counsel, 1970-71; v.p. Monfort Food Distbg., 1971-72, v.p. corp. devel., 1973-75, v.p. internat. ops., 1975-78, v.p. lamb div., 1978-80; mem. 97th-98th Congresses from Colo. 4th dist., Colo. State Senate, 1972-76, asst. majority leader, 1974-76. Served with U.S. Navy, 1962-66. Decorated Air Medal. Mem. Colo. Bar Assn. Republican. Congregationalist. Office: US House of Reps 1510 Longworth Bldg Washington DC 20515

BROWN, HAROLD, scientist, educator, corporate director, consultant, secretary defense; b. N.Y.C., Sept., 19, 1927; s. A.H. and Gertrude (Cohen) B.; m. Colene Dunning McDowell, Oct. 29, 1953; children: Deborah Ruth, Ellen Dunning. A.B., Columbia U., 1945, A.M., 1946, Ph.D. in Physics (Lydig fellow 1948-49), 1949; D.Eng., Stevens Inst. Tech., 1964; LL.D., L.I. U., 1966, Gettysburg Coll., 1967, Occidental Coll., 1980, U. Calif., 1969; Sc.D., U. Rochester, 1975, Brown U., 1977, U. of the Pacific, San Francisco, 1978, U. S.C., 1979, U. S.C. Research scientist Columbia U., 1945-50, lectr. physics, 1947-48, Stevens Inst. Tech., 1949-50; research scientist Radiation Lab., U. Calif. at Berkeley, 1950-52, lectr. physics, 1951-52; various positions from group leader to dir. Radiation Lab. at Livermore, 1952-61; dir. def. research and engring. Dept. Def., 1961-65; sec. of air force, 1965-69; pres. Calif. Inst. Tech., Pasadena, 1969-77; sec. Def., Washington, 1977-81; Disting. vis. prof. nat. security Sch. Advanced Internat. Studies, Johns Hopkins U., Washington, 1981—; cons., 1981—; dir. AMAX, CBS, IBM, Hoover Universal; mem. Polaris Steering Com., 1956-58; cons., mem. Air Force Sci. Adv. Bd., 1956-61, Pres.'s Sci. Adv. Com., 1958-61; sr. sci. adviser Conf. Discontinuance Nuclear Tests, 1958-59; U.S. del. SALT, Helsinki, Vienna and; Geneva, 1969-77; chmn. Tech. Assessment Adv. Council to U.S. Congress, 1974-77; mem. exec. com. Trilateral Commn., 1973-76. Decorated Medal of Freedom; named One of 10 Outstanding Young Men U.S. Jaycees, 1961; recipient Medal of Excellence Columbia U., 1963; Joseph C. Wilson award in internat. affairs, 1976; award for disting. contbns. to higher edn. Stony Brook Found., 1979. Mem. Nat. Acad. Engring., Am. Phys. Soc., Am. Acad. Arts and Scis., Nat. Acad. Scis., Council on Fgn. Relations, N.Y.C. (dir. 1983—), Phi Beta Kappa, Sigma Xi. Clubs: Bohemian (San Francisco); California (Los Angeles); Athenaeum (London). Office: Johns Hopkins U Sch Advanced Internat Studies 1740 Massachusetts Ave NW Washington DC 20036

BROWN, HARRISON SCOTT, chemist, educator; b. Sheridan, Wyo., Sept. 26, 1917; s. Harrison H. and Agatha (Scott) B.; m. Rudd Owen, Nov. 11, 1949; 1 son, Eric Scott; m. Theresa Tellez, 1975. B.S., U. Calif., 1938, LL.D., 1970; Ph.D., Johns Hopkins U., 1941; LL.D., U. Alta., 1961; Sc.D., Rutgers U., 1964, Amherst Coll., 1966, Cambridge U., 1969. Instr. chemistry Johns Hopkins U., 1941-42; asst. dir. chemistry Clinton Labs., Oak Ridge, 1943-46; research asso. plutonium project U. Chgo., 1942-43; asst. prof. Inst. Nuclear Studies, 1946-48, asso. prof., 1948-51; prof. geochemistry Calif. Inst. Tech., 1951-77, prof. sci. and govt., 1967-77; dir. Resource Systems Inst., East-West Center, Honolulu, 1977—. Author: Must Destruction Be Our Destiny?, 1946, The Challenge of Man's Future, 1954, The Next Hundred Years, 1957, The Cassiopeia Affair, 1968, The Human Future

Revisited, 1978, Learning How To Live in a Technological Society (Ishizaka lectures, Japan), 1979. Recipient Lasker Found. award, 1958, N.Y. Acad. Scis. award, 1978. Mem. Nat. Acad. Scis. (fgn. sec. 1962-74, chmn. world food and nutrition study 1975-77), Internat. Council Sci. Unions (pres. 1974-76), Am. Chem. Soc. (award in pure chemistry 1952), Geol. Soc. Am., AAAS (ann. award 1947), Am. Geophys. Union, Phi Beta Kappa, Sigma Xi. Home: 965 Prospect St Honolulu HI 96822 Office: East-West Center Honolulu HI 96848

BROWN, HARRY LEONARD, publisher; b. Mansfield, Ohio, Mar. 27, 1927; s. Harry Leonard and Agnes Elizabeth (Greene) B.; m. Patricia Jennings, Feb. 10, 1951; children—Stacie, Thomas, Meredith, Robert. B.A., Brown U., 1949. With McGraw-Hill, Inc., advt. sales, 1952-56, asst. regional mgr., Detroit, 1957-59, asso. regional mgr., Phila., 1960-64, regional mgr., Dallas, 1965-68; pub. Postgrad. Medicine mag., Mpls., 1968-75; creator, pub. The Physician and Sportsmedicine mag., Mpls., 1973-75; pub. Med. World News, N.Y.C., 1976-78, v.p. med. publs., 1979, group v.p., 1979—. Served with USNR, 1945-46; to 1st lt. USMCR, 1950-52; Korea. Mem. Pharm. Mfrs. Assn., Nat. Wholesale Druggists Assn., Pharm. Advt. Club, Midwest Pharm. Advt. Club, Am. Bus. Press, Assn. Ind. Clin. Publs., Phi Delta Theta. Republican. Presbyterian. Club: Brown of N.Y. Home: 23 E Lyon Farm Dr Greenwich CT 06830 Office: 1221 Ave of Americas New York NY 10020

BROWN, HARRY S., publisher, banker, restaurateur, land developer; b. Pitts., Mar. 12, 1933; s. Harry S. and Florence (Archer) E.; m. Nancy Jane May, June 21, 1958; children: Bonnie Jane, Charles Lawrence, Sallie Anne. B.S. in Finance, Pa. State U., 1958; M.B.A., U. Pitts., 1964. With Pitts. Nat. Bank, 1958-65, asst. cashier, 1963-65; with Hygrade Food Products Corp., Detroit, 1965-69, asst. treas., 1965-67, v.p., treas., 1967-69; treas. Rand McNally & Co., Chgo., 1969-73, v.p. fin., 1973-76; pres., chief exec. officer, dir. Chgo. Bank of Commerce, 1976-78; pres., dir. HSB, Inc., 1978—, Dos Amigos, Inc., 1980—; partner Whitefish Enterprises, 1980—; developer Sun Crest Properties, 1980—; pres. Pioneer Pies Restaurants and Bakeries; dir. Rand McNally Coll. Pub. Co., Hubbard/McNally Co., Impresora y Editora de Mexico (SA. de C.V.), Lion Mountain, Inc. Author: chpt. in The Bankers Handbook. Mem. adv. com. Coll. Bus., U. Ill.; bd. dirs., treas. Chgo. Platform Tennis Charities; bd. dirs. Chgo. Better Bus. Bur. Served with USN, 1951-54. Mem. Fin. Execs. Inst., Am. Platform Tennis Assn. (v.p.), Alpha Sigma Phi, Delta Sigma Pi, Beta Gamma Sigma. Clubs: Mid-Am. (Chgo.); Glen View (Ill.). Home: 1840 Lion Mountain Dr Whitefish MT 59937 Office: Box 1630 Whitefish MT 59937 *You never get a second chance to make a good first impression!!*

BROWN, HELEN GURLEY, author, editor; b. Green Forest, Ark., Feb. 18, 1922; d. Ira M. and Cleo (Sisco) Gurley; m. David Brown, Sept. 25, 1959. Student, Tex. State Coll. for Women, 1939-41, Woodbury Coll., 1942. Exec. sec. Music Corp. Am., 1942-45, William Morris Agy., 1945-47; copywriter Foote, Cone & Belding (advt. agy.), Los Angeles, 1948-58; advt. writer, account exec. Kenyon & Eckhardt (advt. agy.), Hollywood, Calif., 1958-62; editor-in-chief Cosmopolitan mag., 1965—; editorial dir. Cosmopolitan internat. edits. Author: Sex and the Single Girl, 1962, Sex and the Office, 1965, Outrageous Opinions, 1966, Helen Gurley Brown's Single Girl's Cook Book, 1969, Sex and the New Single Girl, 1970, Having It All, 1982. Recipient Francis Holmes Achievement award for outstanding work in advt., 1956-59; Distinguished Achievement award U. So. Calif. Sch. Journalism, 1971; Spl. award for editorial leadership Am. Newspaper Woman's Club, Washington, 1972; Disting. Achievement award in Journalism Stanford U., 1977; named 1 of 25 most influential women in U.S. World Almanac, 1976-81. Mem. Authors League Am., Am. Soc. Mag. Editors, AFTRA, Eta Upsilon Gamma. Office: Cosmopolitan 224 W 57th St New York NY 10019

BROWN, HERBERT CHARLES, chemistry educator; b. London, May 22, 1912; U.S., 1914; s. Charles and Pearl (Gorinstein) B.; m. Sarah Baylen, Feb. 6, 1937; 1 son, Charles Allan. A.S., Wright Jr. Coll., Chgo., 1935; B.S., U. Chgo., 1936, Ph.D., 1938, D.Sc., 1968, hon. doctorates, 1968; hon. doctorates, Wayne State U., 1980, Lebanon Valley Coll., 1980, L.I. U., 1980, Hebrew U. Jerusalem, 1980, Pontificia Universidad de Chile, 1980, Purdue U., 1980, U. Wales, 1981. Asst. chemistry U. Chgo., 1936-38; Eli Lilly post-doctorate research fellow, 1938-39, instr., 1939-43; asst. prof. chemistry Wayne U., 1943- 46, asso. prof., 1946-47; prof. inorganic chemistry Purdue U., 1947-59, Richard B. Wetherill prof. chemistry, 1959, Richard B. Wetherill research prof., 1960-78, emeritus, 1978—; vis. prof. U. Calif. at Los Angeles, 1951, Ohio State U., 1952, U. Mexico, 1954, U. Calif. at Berkeley, 1957, U. Colo., 1958, U. Heidelberg, 1963, State U. N.Y. at Stonybrook, 1966, U. Calif. at Santa Barbara, 1967, Hebrew U., Jerusalem, 1969, U. Wales, Swansea, 1973, U. Cape Town, S. Africa, 1974, U. Calif., San Diego, 1979; Harrison Howe lectr., 1953, Friend E. Clark lectr., 1953, Freud-McCormack lectr., 1954, Centenary lectr., Eng., 1955, Thomas W. Talley lectr., 1956, Falk-Plaut lectr., 1957, Julius Stieglitz lectr., 1958, Max Tishler lectr., 1958, Kekule-Couper Centenary lectr., 1958, E. C. Franklin lectr., 1960, Ira Remsen lectr., 1961, Edgar Fahs Smith lectr., 1962, Seydel-Wooley lectr., 1966, Baker lectr., 1969, Benjamin Rush lectr., 1971, Chem. Soc. lectr., Australia, 1972, Armes lectr., 1973, Henry Gilman lectr., 1975, others; chem. cons. to indsl. corps. Author: Hydroboration, 1962, Boranes in Organic Chemistry, 1972, Organic Synthesis via Boranes, 1975, The Nonclassical Ion Problem, 1977; Contbr. articles to chem. jours. Bd. govs. Hebrew U., 1969—. Served as co-dir. war research projects U. Chgo. for U.S. Army, Nat. Def. Research Com., Manhattan Project, 1940-43. Recipient Purdue Sigma Xi research award, 1951; Nichols medal, 1959; award Am. Chem. Soc., 1960; S.O.C.M.A. medal, 1960; H.N. McCoy award, 1965; Linus Pauling medal, 1968; Nat. Medal of Sci., 1969; Roger Adams medal, 1971; Charles Frederick Chandler medal, 1973; Chem. Pioneer award, 1975; C.U.N.Y. medal for sci. achievement, 1976; Elliott Cresson medal, 1978; C.K. Ingold medal, 1978; Nobel prize for chemistry, 1979; Priestley medal, 1981; Perkin medal, 1982; others. Fellow Royal Soc. Chemistry (hon.), AAAS, Indian Nat. Sci. Acad. (fgn.); mem. Am. Acad. Arts and Scis., Nat. Acad. Scis., Chem. Soc. Japan (hon.), Pharm. Soc. Japan (hon.), Am. Chem. Soc. (chmn. Purdue sect. 1955-56), Ind. Acad. Sci., Phi Beta Kappa, Sigma Xi, Alpha Chi Sigma, Phi Lambda Upsilon (hon.). Research in phys., organic, inorganic chemistry relating chem. behavior to molecular structure; selective reductions; hydroboration; chemistry of organoboranes. Awarded patents (with others) on preparation of borohydrides, diborane, hydroboration; synthesis of aliphatic derivatives. Home: 1840 Garden St West Lafayette IN 47906

BROWN, HERBERT JOSEPH, banker; b. Oakland, Calif., Jan. 27, 1914; s. Harry Lewis and Yetta (Jacobson) B.; m. Beatrice Brenner, June 4, 1939; 1 son, Richard David. Student, San Francisco State Coll., 1932-33, Pacific Coast Banking Sch., 1961-64. With Levi Strauss & Co., 1930-32, 36, Bank of Am., 1936-46; with First Nat. Bank Nev., Reno, 1946—, v.p., 1967—. Pres. Better Bus. Bur. No. Nev., 1966, bd. dirs., 1964-70, hon. bd. dirs., 1970—; Bd. dirs. Community Welfare Reno, 1951—, pres., 1969-80, 80—; treas. Vis. Homemaker and Home Aide Service Washoe County, 1962-68, pres., 1969-70, bd. dirs., 1962-72; treas. United Jewish Appeal Reno, 1955-77; bd. dirs. Washoe County chpt. Nev. Heart Assn., 1973-83; chmn. Washoe County chpt. Nat. Conf. Christians and Jews, 1975—, nat. bd. dirs., 1980—; mem. nat. council Am. Jewish Joint Distbn. Com.; Bd. dirs. Nat. Jewish Welfare Bd. Served as glider pilot, flight officer AUS, 1942-45. Mem. Am. Inst. Banking (past pres. Sierra Nev. chpt.), Nev. Soaring Assn. (sec.-treas. 1974—). Jewish (pres. congregation Temple Emanuel, 1952-54, 68-71, 73-74, bd. dirs., 1952—, treas. 1954-68). Clubs: Lion (treas. Reno 1966-67, dir. 1976-80. Home: 1200 W 12th St Reno NV 89503 Office: PO Box 11007 Reno NV 89520

BROWN, HERMIONE KOPP, lawyer; b. Syracuse, N.Y., Sept. 29, 1915; d. Harold H. and Frances (Burger) Kopp; m. Louis M. Brown, May 30, 1937; children—Lawrence D., Marshall J., Harold A. A.B., Wellesley Coll., 1934; LL.B., U. So. Calif., 1947. Bar: Calif. bar 1947. Story analyst 20th Century-Fox Film Corp., 1935-36, 36-42; since practiced in, Los Angeles; partner firm Gang, Tyre & Brown, Inc., 1952-80, prin., 1980—; lectr. copyright and entertainment law U. So. Calif. Law Sch., 1974-77. Contbr. to profl. publs. Mem. Am., Los Angeles bar assns., Los Angeles Copyright Soc. (pres. 1979-80), Phi Beta Kappa, Order of Coif. Office: 6400 Sunset Bldg Los Angeles CA 90028

BROWN, HOWARD C., horticulture educator, consultant; b. Holmes Park, Mo., Mar. 16, 1921; s. Howard Clarence and Ethel (Crawford) B.; m. Elizabeth I. Thompson, June 6, 1941; children: Howard C. III, Barbara Jeanne. B.S., Calif. Poly. State U., 1943; M.S., Ohio State U., 1954, Ph.D., 1963. Asst. prof. ornamental horticulture Calif. Poly. State U., San Luis Obispo, 1946-51, assoc. prof., 1952-58, prof., 1959-76, head dept. ornamental horticulture, 1954-76, dean Sch. Agr., 1976-81, prof., 1981—; cons. horticulture, 1954—; horticulture specialist Bur. Agrl. Edn. Calif., 1964-65; trustee Saratoga (Calif.) Hort. Found., 1973-76; mem. Calif. Bd. Food and Agr., 1979-83. Editor, contbg. author: Nursery Management, 1964; editor: Nursery Practices, 1965; contbr.: numerous articles to Internat. Plant Propagators Soc. publs. Chmn. Arbor Day, landscape chmn. Obispo Beautiful Assn., San Luis Obispo; mem. San Luis Obispo Tree Adv. Com.; merit badge counselor Santa Lucia council boy Scouts Am. Served to staff sgt. AC U.S. Army, 1943-46; PTO. Recipient Outstanding Educator award Calif. Assn. Nurserymen, Sacramento, 1966, Research and Edn. award Soc. Am. Florists, Washington, 1974, L.C. Chadwick teaching award Am. Assn. Nurserymen, Washingtono, 1977. Mem. Am. Univ. Agr. Adminstrs. (v.p. 1977-79), Am. Assn. Univ. Agr. Adminstrs. (exec. v.p. 1979-80), Am. Inst. Floral Designers (hon.), Sigma Xi, Alpha Zeta, Gamma Sigma Delta. Home: 276 Graves Ave San Luis Obispo CA 93401 Office: Dept Ornamental Horticulture Calif Poly State U San Luis Obispo CA 93407

BROWN, HOWARD JAMES, clergyman; b. St. Louis, Aug. 6, 1907; s. John C. and Mary (O'Hara) B.; m. Helen Janney, June 18, 1931; children—Jacelyn (Mrs. Robert Dininny), Patricia (Mrs. Kenneth Kropp), H. James. B.A., Ohio Wesleyan U., 1929; D.D., 1952; B.D., Garret Theol. Sem., 1932. Ordained to ministry Methodist Ch., 1932; minister in, Ft. Wayne, Ind., 1934-41, Goshen, Ind., 1941-43, Richmond, Ind., .1941-49, Ch. of Savior, Cleveland Heights, Ohio, 1949-72; Dean Ind. Sch. of Prophets, 1947-48, Ohio Area Meth. Pastor's Sch., 1956-61, Coll. Preachers Ohio East Area, 1965-72; pres. Cleve. Council Chs., 1960-62; sec. gen. Commn. Pub. Relations and Meth. Information, 1964—; del. World Meth. Conf., 1951, 61. Trustee Ohio Wesleyan U., 1958—. Mem. Phi Kappa Tau, Omicron Delta Kappa, Theta Alpha Phi. Clubs: Mason (33 deg.), Rotarian.). Home: Epworth Forest North Webster IN 46555

BROWN, HUBERT JUDE, professional basketball coach; b. Hazelton, Pa., Sept. 25, 1933; s. Charles Joseph and Anna Marie (Breslin) B.; m. Claire Manning, Aug. 27, 1960; children: Mary Katherine, Virginia Anne, Julie Margaret, Brendan John. B.S. in Econs., Niagara U., Niagara Falls, N.Y., 1955, M.Ed., 1959. Athletic dir., coach basketball and baseball St. Mary's High Sch., Little Falls, N.Y., 1955-56; coach basketball, baseball and football Cranford High Sch., (N.J.), 1959-64, Fair Lawn High Sch., 1964-67; asst. basketball coach Coll. William and Mary, Williamsburg, Va., 1967-68, Duke U., 1969-72; asst. coach Milw. Bucks, Prof. Basketball Team, 1972-74; head coach Ky. Cols., profl. basketball team, Louisville, 1974-76, Atlanta Hawks, profl. basketball team, 1976-81; commentator NBA games USA Cable TV Network, 1981-82; head coach N.Y. Knickerbockers, profl. basketball team, 1982—. Served with AUS, 1956-58. Winner Am. Basketball Assn. Championship, 1975; named NBA Coach of Yr. News Media, 1978, CBS-TV, 1979. Mem. Nat. Basketball Coaches Assn., Nat. Volley Ball Assn. Roman Catholic. Office: New York Knickerbockers Madison Square Garden Four Penn Plaza New York NY 10001 *

BROWN, JACK ERNEST, information scientist; b. Edmonton, Alta., Can., Mar. 1, 1914; s. Ernest William and Maud Alice (Jarman) B.; m. Estelle A. Coles, Dec. 26, 1944; children: Keith, Frances. B.A., U. Alta., 1938; B.L.S., McGill U., 1939; M.A.; ALA fellow, U. Chgo., 1940; LL.D. (hon.), U. Waterloo, 1965, McMaster U., 1978. Reference librarian Edmonton (Alta., Can.) Pub. Library, 1940-42; library asst. N.Y. Pub. Library, N.Y.C., 1942-45, first asst. sci. and tech. div., 1947-52; asst. librarian Brown U., Providence, 1946-47; dir. Nat. Sci. Library, Ottawa, Ont., Can., 1957-74, Can. Inst. Sci. and Tech. Info., Ottawa, 1974-77; prof. McGill U. Grad. Sch. Library Sci., 1978-82; sci. info. cons., 1982—; v.p. Internat. Fedn. Documentation, 1964-68; mem. adv. council Pahlavi Nat. Library, Iran, 1974—. Contbr. articles to library jours. Mem. ALA, Can. Library Assn. (Outstanding Service award 1979), Spl. Libraries Assn., Can. Assn. Info. Sci., Assn. Library and Info. Services (award for Spl. Librarianship in Can. 1979). Anglican. Home: 417 Meadow Dr Ottawa ON K1K 0M3 Canada

BROWN, JACK HAROLD UPTON, university official, educator, biomedical engineer; b. Nixon, Tex., Nov. 16, 1918; s. Gilmer W. and Thelma (Patton) B.; m. Jessie Carolyn Schulz, Apr. 14, 1943. B.S., S.W. Tex. State U., 1939; postgrad., U. Tex., 1939-41; Ph.D., Rutgers U., 1948. Lectr. physics Southwest Tex. State U., San Marcos, 1943-44; instr. phys. chemistry Rutgers U., New Brunswick, N.J., 1944-45, research asso., 1944-48; lectr. U. Pitts., 1948-50; head biol. scis. Mellon Inst., Pitts., 1948-50; asst. prof. physiology U. N.C., Chapel Hill, 1950-52; scientist Oak Ridge Inst. Nuclear Studies, 1952; asso. prof. physiology Emory U. Med. Sch., Atlanta, 1952-58, prof., 1959-60, acting chmn. dept. physiology, 1958-60; lectr. physiology George Washington U. and Georgetown U. med. schs., Washington, 1960-65; exec. sec. biomed. engring. and physiology tng. coms. Nat. Inst. Gen. Med. Scis., NIH, Bethesda, Md., 1960-62; chief spl. research br. div. research facilities and resources NIH, 1962-63, acting chief gen. clin. research centers br., 1963-64, asst. dir. ops. div. research facilities and resources, 1964-65; acting program dir. pharmacology/toxicology program Nat. Inst. Gen. Med. Scis., NIH, 1966-70, asst. dir. ops., 1965-66, asso. dir. sci. programs, 1967-70, acting dir., 1970; spl. asst. to adminstr. Health Services and Mental Health Adminstrn., USPHS, Rockville, Md., 1971-72, asso. dep. adminstr. for devel., 1972-73; spl. asst. to adminstr. Health Resources Adminstrn., 1973-78; coordinator Southwest Research Consortium, San Antonio, 1974-78; prof. physiology U. Tex. Med. Sch., San Antonio, 1974-78; prof. environ. scis. U. Tex. at San Antonio, 1974-78; adj. prof. health services adminstrn. Trinity U., 1975-78; asso. provost research and advanced edn., also prof. biology U. Houston, 1978—; adj. prof. U. Tex. Sch. Public Health, 1978—; adj. prof. public adminstrn. Tex. Women's U., 1978—; Fulbright lectr. U. Rangoon, 1950; cons. health systems WHO, Oak Ridge Inst. Nuclear Studies, VA, Lockheed Aircraft Co., Drexel Inst. Tech., NASA, Vassar Coll.; Mem. adv. bd. Center for Cancer Therapy, San Antonio, 1974—; bd. dirs. S. Tex. Health Edn. Center. Author: Physiology of Man in Space, 1963, (with A.B. Barker) Basic Endocrinology, 1966, 2d edit., 1970, (with J.F. Dickson) Future Goals of Engineering in Biology and Medicine, 1968, Advances in Biomedical Engineering, vol. II, 1972, vols. III, IV, 1973, vol. V, 1974, vol. VI, 1976, Vol. VII, 1978, (with J.E. Jacobs and L.E. Stark) Biomedical Engineering, 1972, (with D.E. Gann) Engineering Principles in Physiology, vols. I, II, 1973, The Health Care Dilemma, 1977, Integration and Control of Biol. Processes, 1978, Politics and Health Care, 1978, Telecommunications in Health Care, 1981, Management in Health Care Systems, 1983; editor: (with Ferguson) Blood and Body Functions, 1966, Life Into Space, (Wunder), 1968; contbr. numerous articles on biomed. engring. to sci. jours. Served with USNR, 1941. Recipient spl. team award NASA, 1978; Gerard Swope fellow Gen. Electric Co., 1946-48; Fulbright grantee, 1950; NIH grantee, 1950-60; Cancer Soc. grantee, 1958; Damon Runyon Cancer award grantee, 1959; Dept. Energy grantee, 1980-81. Fellow AAAS, Nat. Acad. Engring., IEEE (mem. joint com. engring. in medicine and biology 1966—); mem. Am. Chem. Soc. (sr.), Biomed. Engring. Soc. (pres. 1969-70, dir. 1968-69), Inst. Radio Engrs. (nat. sec. profl. group biomed. engring. 1962-64), N.Y. Acad. Scis., Endocrine Soc., Am. Physiol. Soc. (com. mem. 1959-63), Soc. for Exptl. Biology and Medicine, Sigma Xi (research award 1961, pres. Alamo chpt. 1977-78), Council Biology Editors, Soc. Research Adminstrn., Pi Kappa Delta, Phi Lambda Upsilon, Alpha Chi. Club: Cosmos. Inventor capsule manometer, respirator for small animals and basal metabolic apparatus for small animals, dust sampler, apparatus for partitioning human lung volumes. Home: 2908 Whisper View San Antonio TX 78230 Office: U Houston 4800 Calhoun St Houston TX 77004

BROWN, JACK LEONDUS, sewer pipe co. exec.; b. Huntington, W.Va., Sept 16, 1913; s. Wyatt Thornton and Lillian Vivian (Williams) B.; m. Lillian Louise Matchett, Jan. 5, 1935; children—Marjorie Brown Sheldon, Sally Brown Good, Jack Leondus. Ed. pub. schs. With Am. Vitrified Products Co., 1935-66, v.p., 1959-63, pres., 1963-66; gen. mgr. Superior Concrete Pipe Corp., Cleve., 1966—. Trustee Ohio Turnpike Commn. Mem. Ohio Contractors Assn. (dir.), Clay Sewer Pipe Assn. (v.p.), Nat. Clay Pipe Inst. (dir.), Am. Concrete Pipe Assn. (past dir.), Ohio Contractors Assn. (dir.), Bluecoats Inc. Baptist. Club: Acacia Country (Lyndhurst, Ohio). Home: 13415 Shaker Blvd Apt 8F3 Cleveland OH 44120 *I would say devotion of thought, a sincere dedication, plus understanding the needs of people in my employ have created a successful and harmonious operation for all.*

BROWN, JACK WYMAN, architect; b. Detroit, Oct. 17, 1922; s. Ernest E. and Mary Morse (Jones) B.; m. Joan M. Graham, Oct. 4, 1971; 1 dau., Elizabeth. B.S., U. Mich., 1945. Designer Odell, Hewlett & Luckenbach, Inc., Birmingham, Mich., 1952-57; pres. Brown & Deyo & Assocs. Architects, Inc., Bloomfield Hills, Mich., 1957—; part-time instr. design Lawrence Inst. Tech., 1959. Mem. Mayor Detroit Task Force, 1969-70. Served with USNR, 1943-46. Co-recipient 1st prize nat. competition design Nat. Cowboy Hall Fame, 1967; recipient Institutions mag. award, 1980. Mem. AIA (chmn. working coms.), Am. Soc. Ch. Architecture (dir. 1960-64, 72—), Mich. Soc. Architects (design award St. Regis Ch. 1969, Fox Hills Elem. Sch. 1970, Andor Office Bldg. 1972), Mich. Soc. Planning Ofcls. Home: 5980 Braemoor Birmingham MI 48010 Office: 4190 Telegraph Rd Bloomfield Hills MI 48013

BROWN, JACOB A., agriculture educator, university dean; b. Swift Current, Sask., Can., July 12, 1926; s. Abraham Jacob and Anna (Remple) B.; m. Elizabeth Hildebrandt, Aug. 17, 1953; children: Debra, Myron, Gerald, Myrna. B.S.A., U. Sask., 1951; M.Sc., N.D. State U., 1953; Doctoral candidate, U. Minn., 1964. Dir. farm mgmt. div. Sask. Dept. Agr., 1957-62, dir. econs. and stats. br., 1962-67; prof. agrl. econs. U. Sask., Saskatoon, 1967-74, dean Coll. Agr., 1974—. Chmn. Sask. Fram Ownership Bd., 1974—, Sask. Crop. Ins. Bd., 1962-74; mem. Sask. Land Bank Commn., 1972-83. Agrl. Inst. Can. fellow, 1980; recipient Recognition award City of Saskatoon, 1982. Fellow Agrl. Inst. Can.; mem. Am. Agrl. Econs. Assn., Can. Agrl. Econs. Assn., Internat. Agrl. Econs. Assn., Internat. Right of Way Assn., Gamma Sigma Delta, Phi Kappa Phi. Home: Box 338 Sub PO 6 Saskatoon SK Canada S7N 0W0 Office: U Sask Coll Agr Saskatoon SK Canada S7N 0W0

BROWN, JAMES, singer, broadcasting executive; b. Pulaski, Tenn., June 17, 1928. Pres. J.B. Broadcasting, Ltd., 1968—, James Brown Network, 1968—; chmn. James Brown Enterprises, James Brown Prodns. Leader musical group, Famous Flames, from 1956; now solo performer, rec. artist with, King, Smash Records; recordings include Original Disco Man, Please, Please, Please, Hot on the One, Poppa's Got a Brand New Bag; U.S. tours include performances at, Apollo, N.Y.C., Howard U., Washington. Recipient 44 Gold Record awards; recipient Grammy award, 1965. Address: care Network Talent Internat Box 82 Suite 342A 98 Cuttermill Rd Great Neck NY 11021 *

BROWN, JAMES ANDREW, naval architect; b. Columbia, Tenn., Aug. 19, 1914; s. Charles Allen and Martha (Crawford) B.; m. Frances Adelaide Jones, June 7, 1941; children: James Andrew, Martha Janet; m. Mary Julia Hargroves Greene, Feb. 16, 1973. B.S., U.S. Naval Acad., 1936; M.S., Mass. Inst. Tech., 1941. Registered profl. engr., Va. Commd. ensign U.S. Navy, 1936, advanced through grades to rear adm., 1963; jr. officer in U.S.S. W.Va., 1936-38; asst. hull supt. charge new constrn. Boston Naval Shipyard, 1942-45; mem. staff Comdr. Service Force Pacific, 1945-47; with Bur. Ships, Dept. Navy, 1947-50, project officer destroyer types, 1950- 51, head hull design, 1955-59, asst. chief design, shipbldg. and fleet maintenance, 1963-65; prof. naval architecture Mass. Inst. Tech., 1951-54; comdg. officer ship repair facility, Subic Bay, P.I., 1954-55; planning officer N.Y. Naval Shipyard, 1959, prodn. officer, 1959-61; supr. shipbldg. U.S. Navy, Camden, N.J., 1961-63; comdr. Norfolk Naval Shipyard; also supr. shipbldg. 5th Naval Dist., Portsmouth, Va., 1965-70; ret., 1970; prodn. mgr. J.L. Smith Constrn. Co., Portsmouth, 1970-77; pres. CDI Marine of Va., 1978—; mgr. Hampton (Va.) Office, 1980-81; Sr. engr. QED Systems Inc., 1981—. Pres. Tidewater Fed. Exec. Agy., 1968; exec. bd. Inter Agy. Bd. Examiners Civil Service for Va., 1968-70; commr. Tidewater Transp. Dist. Commn., 1978—; mem. Supplemental Fire and Police Retirement Bd., City of Portsmouth, 1978—, chmn., 1980—; bd. dirs. Portsmouth Community Action, 1969-70, 78-79; Mem. Panel Spl. Advisers Auditor Gen. U.S.A., 1972; mem. Citizen Adv. Com. for Transit Devel. Study, Southeastern Va. Planning Dist. Commn.; bd. dirs. Portsmouth United Fund, 1965-77. Decorated Legion of Merit; recipient Commendation medal Sec. of Navy. Mem. Soc. Naval Engrs. (council 1959), Naval Inst., Naval Architects and Marine Engrs. (council 1968-69, chmn. Chesapeake sect. 1959, chmn. Hampton Roads sect. 1969—, v.p. 1969-70), Am. Philatelic Soc., World Affairs Council Greater Hampton Roads (v.p. 1969-70, pres. 1971, 72), English Speaking Union, Portsmouth Hist. Soc. (hon., dir. 1977-78), Portsmouth C. of C. (dir., chmn. urban affairs com., v.p. for urban affairs 1972-73, chmn. com. hwys. and mass transit 1974-75, 76-78, bd. dirs. 1971-73, 79—), Navy League, Sigma Xi. Clubs: Portsmouth Execs. (dir. 1975-76, 78-79, mem. Ship structure com. 1963-65), Portsmouth Execs. (chmn. subcom. 1955-59). Home: 3800 Pine Rd Portsmouth VA 23703

BROWN, JAMES BARROW, bishop; b. El Dorado, Ark., Sept. 26, 1932; s. John Alexander and Ella May (Langham) B.; m. Mary Joanna Strausser, Oct. 3, 1970; 2 daus., Clare Elizabeth, Mary Laura. B.S., La.

State U., 1954; B.D., Austin Presbyn. Sem., Austin, Tex., 1957; D.D., U. of South, Sewanee, Tenn., 1976. Ordained priest Episcopal Ch., 1965; teaching fellow Princeton Theol. Sem., 1962-64; curate chs. in, La., 1965-70, archdeacon of, 1971-76, bishop of, 1976—. Served as chaplain AUS, 1957-59. Alumni fellow Austin Presbyn. Sem., 1957; recipient Sam Bailey Hicks prize, 1957. Mem. La. Clergy Assn., Phi Delta Theta. Club: Rotary. Address: 1623 Seventh Street New Orleans LA 70115 *

BROWN, JAMES BRIGGS, business forms company executive; b. Sterling, Ill., Oct. 10, 1922; s. Lloyd H. and Marguerite (Briggs) B.; m. Lois Dorothy Brenner, June 13, 1946; children—Bradford James, Todd Wells. B.A., Carleton Coll., 1943; J.D., Northwestern U., 1949. Bar: Ill. bar 1949. Atty. Pabst Brewing Co., Chgo., 1949-51; atty., asst. sec. Miehle-Printing Press & Mfg. Co., 1951-57; asst. sec. Miehle-Goss-Dester, Inc., Chgo., 1957-62, sec., counsel, 1962-70, UARCO, Inc., Barrington, Ill., 1970—, v.p., 1972—. Served to lt. comdr. USNR, 1943-46, 52-53. Mem. Am., Chgo. bar assns., Phi Delta Phi. Clubs: Legal, Economic, Tavern (Chgo.). Home: 355 Birch St Winnetka IL 60093 Office: West County Line Rd Barrington IL 60010

BROWN, JAMES E., banker; b. St. Louis, 1919. Sr. v.p. Mercantile Trust Co., St. Louis, 1954-70; pres., dir. Mercantile Bancorp., St. Louis, 1970—, also dir. Pres., bd. dirs. Downtown St. Louis, Inc., 1975-77; bd. dirs. Deaconess Hosp., 1975—, Easter Seal Soc., 1981; chmn. Better Bus. Bur., 1970-72. Served with AUS, 1941-45. Mem. Assn. Bank Holding Cos. Office: Mercantile Bancorporation Inc Mercantile Tower St Louis MO 63101

BROWN, JAMES EDWARD (JIM ED BROWN), singer; b. Sparkman, Ark., Apr. 1, 1934; s. Floyd and Birdie Lea (Tuberville) B. Attended, Ark. A&M Coll., 1952-53, Ark. Tchrs. Coll., 1953-54. Appeared as: regular mem. Barnyard Frolic, Sta.-KLRA, Little Rock; featured on: Louisiana Hayride, Sta.-KWKH, Shreveport, La., 1954-55; on: Ozark Jubilee, ABC-TV, 1955-56; regular mem.: Grand Ole Opry, Sta.-WSM, Nashville, 1964—; group mem.: The Browns, 1954-67; including tours of, U.S., Europe and Japan; solo act debut The Browns, Atlanta, 1968; rec. artist, Fabor, 1954-56, RCA, 1956—, currently rec. with, Helen Cornelius; co-host: TV series Nashville on the Road, 1975-76; other TV appearances include Country Night of the Stars II. Served with U.S. Army. Recipient award Country Music Assn., 1977. Office: care Top Billing Inc PO Box 121077 Nashville TN 37212 *

BROWN, JAMES H., JR., state official; b. May 6, 1940. B.A., U. N.C.; J.D., Tulane U. Bar: La. 1966. Practiced law, 1966—; mem. La. State Senate, 1972-80; sec. of state State of La., 1980—. Del. La. Constl. Conv., 1973. Democrat. Presbyterian. Office: Office Sec of State PO Box 44125 Baton Rouge LA 70804 *

BROWN, JAMES HAMILTON, railroad executive; b. St. Louis, Nov. 27, 1926; s. William Floyd and Lucy Morris (Gentry) B.; m. Eleanor Habs, June 4, 1948 (div. 1975); m. Lois Miller, Aug. 27, 1977; children: Linda Brown Urben, James, Clare Brown Stewart, Thomas, John Simons, Daniel. B.S. in Civil Engring., U. Mo-Columbia, 1948; A.M.P., Harvard U., 1964. Registered profl. engr., Mo., Tex. With St. Louis-Santa Fe Railway Co., various locations, 1948-80, v.p. ops., 1980; pres. ry., 1981-82; regional v.p., gen. mgr. Burlington No. R.R., Ft. Worth, 1983—; dir. Port Term Ry., Houston, Houston Belt Ry. Co., Tex., Am. Bank Corp. Bd. dirs. Springfiedl Sch. Bd., Mo., 1969-71; pres. Ozarks council Boy Scouts Am., 1969-72; mem.adv. bd. U. Mo. Coll. Engring., 1968—; trustee Sch. of Ozarks, Pt. Lookout, Mo., 1968—. Served with Air Corps. U.S. Army, 1944-45. Named Young Engr. Yr. State of Mo., 1961. Mem. Mo. C. of C. (dir. 1974-80), Am. Ry. Engr. Assn. (dir 1961-66), Roadmasters and Maintenance of Way Assn. Am. (dir., pres. 1958-66). Clubs: Ft. Worth; Rivercrest Country (Ft. Worth). Home: 6154 High Woods Ct Fort Worth TX 76112 Office: Burlington No Railroad PO Box 943 Fort Worth TX 76101

BROWN, JAMES HARVEY, neuroscientist, government research administrator; b. Yankton, S.D., Sept. 9, 1936; s. Robert Heath and Hildegarde (Grover) B.; m. Betty Jean Pruitt, Aug. 29, 1959; children: Christopher Heath, Karen Elizabeth, Kimberly Frances. B.A., Wesleyan U., 1957; M.S., Purdue U., 1959; Ph.D. (DuPont fellow), U. Va., 1962. Research scientist U.S. Army Med. Research Lab., Ft. Knox, Ky., 1962-66, head vesibular br., 1966-68; asso. program dir. for psychobiology NSF, Washington, 1968-71, program dir. for neurobiology, 1971-76, dep. dir. div. behavioral and neural scis., 1976-77, 79-82, dep. asst. dir., biol., behavioral and social scis. directorate, 1977-79, div. dir., div. physiology, cellular and molecular biology, 1982—; adj. prof. U. Ky., Louisville U., 1962-68, George Washington U., 1970—; v.p. NSF Employees Assn., 1970. Contbr. articles to profl. jours. Active Little League, Potomac, Md. Served to capt. U.S. Army, 1960-65. Mem. Sigma Xi, Phi Sigma, Sigma Chi. Home: 8803 Quiet Stream Ct Potomac MD 20854 Office: 1800 G St NW Washington DC 20550

BROWN, JAMES ISAAC, rhetoric educator; b. Tarkio, Mo., Dec. 15, 1908; s. John Vallance and Ada (Moore) B.; m. Ruth Bernice Sam, Sept. 19, 1942; children: Katherine Ada, Susan Phyllis. B.A., Tarkio Coll., 1930, D.H.L. (hon.), 1976; M.A., U. Chgo., 1933; Ph.D., U. Colo., 1949. Instr. English Monmouth Coll., 1933-34; faculty U. Minn., 1934—, successively instr., asst. prof., assoc. prof., 1934-54, prof. rhetoric, 1954—, acting chief rhetoric, 1947-48; Vis. lectr. U. Colo., summers 1950, 52, 54, U. Utah, summer 1955; staff mem. Effective Communication in Industry Course, summer 1954, 55; instituted Reading Efficiency Program in Industry, summers 1957, 58; conf. leader Mgmt. Clinic, Hot Springs, Va., 1956; communications cons. Minn. Mining & Mfg. and Caterpillar Tractor Cos., 1964. Author: Efficient Reading, 1952, (with G. Robert Carlsen) Brown-Carlsen Listening Comprehension Test, 1954, Lex-o-Gram, 1954, (with Eugene S. Wright) Minnesota Efficient Reading Tachistolide Series, Minnesota Clerical Training Tachistoslide Series and Minnesota Timing Series, 1955, Revision of Nelson Denny Reading Test, 1960, (with Rachel Salisbury) Building a Better Vocabulary, 1959, Explorations in College Reading, 1959, Exercise Manual for Explorations in College Reading, 1959, Efficient Reading, rev. edit., 1962, 6th edit., 1983, (with George Sanderlin) Effective Writing and Reading, 1962, Pyramid, 1963, Programmed Vocabulary (TV edit., coll. edit. and high sch. edn.), 1964, 2d edit., 1971, Guide to Effective Reading, 1966, (with O.M. Haugh) College English Placement Test, 1969, Accelerad System, 1970, also the visual-linguistic basic reading series, 1966—, (with O.M. Haugh) Efficient Reading, Revised Form A, 1971, Forms C and D, Nelson-Denny Reading Test, 1973; Forms E and F, Nelson-Denny Reading Test, 1981; (with O.M. Haugh) also the visual-linguistic basic reading series Reading Power, 1975, alt. edit., 1978, 2d edit., 1983, Efficient Reading, Revised Form B, 1976, (with Thomas E. Pearsall) Better Spelling, 2d edit, 1978; mem. adv. bd., cons. ednl. edit., Reader's Digest, 1957—; courses ednl. TV Success thru Better Spelling; tapes Putting Words to Work, for U.S. Dept. Edn. Served with AUS, 1943-45; ETO. Recipient Tarkio Coll. Student Assn. Hall of Fame Award, 1965; Certificate of Merit in recognition outstanding ind. study course Efficient Reading Nat. Extension Assn., 1972; award of merit Gamma Sigma Delta, 1977. Mem. Internat. Platform Assn., Nat. Council Tchrs. English, Nat. Soc. Study Communication (exec. sec. 1951, chmn. com. on reading comprehension 1951-63, pres.), Internat. Reading Assn., Conf. Coll. Composition and Communication, Speech Assn. Am., AAUP, Am. Council Edn., Phi Delta Kappa. Methodist (pres. bd. trustees 1960, 72-73, lay leader 1961-63). Home: 1395 Solar Heights Dr Prescott AZ 86301 *Tolstoy comes very close to expressing my feelings, when he says: "The man whose only goal is his own happiness is bad; he whose goal is the good opinion of others is weak; he whose goal is the happiness of others is good; he whose goal is God, is great."*

BROWN, JAMES JOSEPH, desk manufacturing company executive; b. N.Y.C., Apr. 4, 1928; s. Peter J. and Mary (O'Neil) B.; m. Mary E. McKeon, Dec. 30, 1961; children: Patricia, James, Carolyn, Denise, Erin. B.S., Fordham U., 1952. C.P.A., N.Y. Acct. Touche, Ross, Bailey & Smart (C.P.A.s), N.Y.C., 1952-54; sr. acct. Price Waterhouse & Co. (C.P.A.s), Caracas, Venezuela and N.Y.C., 1954-63; mgr. internal audit Litton Industries, 1963-65; sr. v.p., dir. Kidde, Inc., 1965-72; chmn. bd. Am. Desk Mfg. Co., 1982—. Bd. dirs. Irish U.S. Council for Commerce and Industry. Served with AUS, 1946-48. Named Alumni Man of Year Fordham U. Coll. Bus. Adminstrn., 1971. Mem. Am. Inst. C.P.A.s, N.Y. State Soc. C.P.A.s. Clubs: Treasurers of N.Y., Ridgewood Country, N.Y. Athletic. Home: 441 Weymouth Dr Wyckoff NJ 07481 Office: 33 Sicomac Rd North Haledon NJ 07508

BROWN, JAMES M., finance company executive; b. Jamaica, N.Y., 1932. B.A., U. Notre Dame, 1954; LL.B., Fordham U., 1960; M.A., NYU, 1961. Bar: N.Y. 1960. Law clk. Mackin Speer Harin & McKernan, 1956-57; cert. pub. acct., 1957-62; dir. fin. Financeamerica Corp., Allentown, Pa., 1971-74, pres., chief exec. officer, dir., 1974—. Address: Financeamerica Corp 1105 Hamilton St Allentown PA 18101 *

BROWN, JAMES MONROE, III, museum administrator; b. Bklyn., Oct. 7, 1917; s. James Monroe and Helen (Adriance) B.; m. Alice De Wolf Doggett, Nov. 16, 1946; children: Barbara Allison, Amy, Elizabeth. B.A., Amherst Coll., 1939, M.A. (hon.), 1954, Harvard, 1946. Asst. to dir. Inst. Contemporary Art, Boston, 1941, asst. dir., 1946-48; asst. to dir. Dumbarton Oaks Research Library and Collection, Washington, 1946; dir. William A. Farnsworth Art Mus., Rockland, Maine, 1948-51, Corning Glass Center, N.Y., 1951-63; dir. div. pub. affairs Corning Glass Works, 1956-59, dir. mgmt. devel., 1959-61; pres. Corning Glass Works Found., 1961-63; dir. Oakland (Calif.) Mus., 1963-68, Norton Simon, Inc. Mus. Art, Fullerton, Calif., 1968-69, Va. Mus. Fine Arts, Richmond, 1969-76, Soc. of Four Arts, Palm Beach, Fla., 1978—; Trustee Internat. Exhbns. Found.; trustee Merrimack Valley (Mass.) Textile Mus. Served with USNR, 1942-45. Mem. Am. Assn. Museums (pres. 1970-72, exec. com.), Assn. Art Mus. Dirs., Internat. Council Museums, Am. Fedn. Arts. Clubs: Harvard, Grolier, Explorers (N.Y.C.); Bath and Tennis (Palm Beach, Fla.). Address: Soc of Four Arts Palm Beach FL 33480

BROWN, JAMES STEPHEN, mental health administrator; b. Memphis, Oct. 14, 1925; s. James S. and Josie (Postal) B.; m. Terry Kimbrough, June 1, 1956; children: Caroline K., James Stephen. B.A., U. Miss., 1949; M.S., M.D., U. Tenn., 1954; postgrad., Kennedy Sch. Govt., Harvard U., 1980. Diplomate: Am. Bd. Pediatrics. Pvt. practice pediatrics, Memphis, 1959-68; asso. prof. pediatrics U. Tenn. Center for Health Scis., from 1973; commr. Tenn. Dept. Mental Health and Mental Retardation, Nashville, 1979—. Contbr. chpts. to textbooks, articles to profl. jours. Served with M.C. U.S. Army, 1943-46; ETO. Fellow Am. Acad. Pediatrics, mem. various profl. socs. Republican. Episcopalian. Office: 3d Floor JK Polk Bldg DMH/MR Nashville TN 37219

BROWN, JAMES WARD, mathematician, educator; b. Phila., Jan. 15, 1934; s. George Harold and Julia Elizabeth (Ward) B.; m. Jacqueline Read, Sept. 3, 1957; children: Scott Cameron, Gordon Elliot. Grad., Lawrenceville Sch., 1951; A.B., Harvard U., 1955; M.A., U. Mich., 1958, Ph.D. (Inst. Sci and Tech. predoctoral fellow), 1964. Asst. prof. math. U. Mich.-Dearborn, 1964-66, asso. prof., 1968-71, prof., 1971—, acting chmn. dept., 1974; asst. prof. Oberlin Coll., 1966-68; editorial cons. Math. Rev., 1970—; Dir. NSF Grant, 1969. Author: (with R.V. Churchill) Complex Variables and Applications, 4th edit, 1984, Internat. Student edit., 1974, Japanese edit., 1975, Spanish edit., 1978, Fourier Series and Boundary Value Problems, 3d edit, 1978, internat. student edit., 1978; Japanese edit., 1980; contbr. articles to U.S., fgn. sci. jours. Recipient Disting. Faculty award U. Mich.-Dearborn, 1976, Mich. Assn. Governing Bds. Colls. and Univs., 1983. Mem. Am. Math. Soc., Math. Assn. Am., Research Club of U. Mich., Sigma Xi. Home: 1710 Morton Ave Ann Arbor MI 48104 Office: 4901 Evergreen Rd Dearborn MI 48128

BROWN, JAMES WILSON, educator; b. Hanford, Wash., Sept. 18, 1913; s. Harrison and Sophia Estelle (Tuttle) B.; m. Winifred Louise Weersing, Dec. 31, 1940 (dec. Mar. 1977); children: Martha Lee, Pamela Jean, Gregory James; m. Shirley Marie Stromme Norman, Nov. 5, 1977. Student, U. Wash., 1931-32; B.A., Central Wash. Coll., 1935; M.A., U. Chgo., Ph.D., 1947. Marine radio operator, 1930-31; Gen. Edn. Bd. fellow motion picture project Am. Council Edn., 1940; state supr. teaching materials Va. Dept. Edn., Richmond, 1941-42, 1945-46; asst. prof. edn. Syracuse U., 1947-48; supr. Univ. Film Center, U. Wash., 1948-53; info. specialist U.S. Dept. State OSR, Paris, 1951-52; prof. edn., dean grad. studies and research San Jose State U., 1953-78, prof. instnl. tech., 1972-78; Former mem. adv. panels Far West Regional Lab. for Research and Devel., also Stanford U. Center for Research and Devel. in Teaching; asso. dir. ERIC Clearinghouse on Info. Resources, Stanford, 1974-76. Author: Virginia Plan for Audio-Visual Education, 1947, New Media in Public Libraries, 1976; co-author: New Media in Higher Education, 1963, Going to College in California, 1965, New Media and College Teaching, 1968, Administering Educational Media, 1972, AV Instruction, Technology, Media and Methods, 1977, 83, College Teaching: A Systematic Approach, 1971; editor: Educational Media Yearbook, 1973-83. Served to lt. comdr. USNR, 1942-45; ETO. Mem. NEA (v.p. 1950-51, pres. dept. audio-visual instrn. 1952-53), Western Assn. Grad. Schs. (chmn. 1963-64), Phi Delta Kappa, Phi Kappa Phi. Home: 8413 Chenin Blanc Ln San Jose CA 95135

BROWN, JASON WALTER, neurologist, educator, researcher; b. N.Y.C., Apr. 14, 1938; s. Samuel Robert and Sylvia (Brown) B.; m. Jo-Ann Marie Gelardi, Sept. 21, 1967; children: Jonathan Schilder, Jovana Millay. B.A., U. Calif.-Berkeley, 1959; M.D., U.S.C., 1963. Intern St. Elizabeth's Hosp., Washington, 1963-64; resident in neurology UCLA, 1964-67; practice medicine specializing in neurology, N.Y.C., 1970—; instr. Boston U. Med. Sch., 1969-70; asst. clin. prof. Columbia-Presbyn. Hosp., N.Y.C., 1970-75; vis. asst. prof. neurology Albert Einstein Coll. Medicine, N.Y.C., 1972-75; vis. assoc. prof. Rockefeller U., N.Y.C., 1978-79; clin. assoc. prof. neurology NYU, 1975-79, clin. prof., 1979—. Author: Aphasia, Apraxia and Agnosia, 1972, Mind, Brain and Consciousness, 1977; editor: Jargonaphasia, 1982; English Translation of Aphasie by Arnold Pick Aphasia, 1973; contbr. numerous articles on neurology to med. jours.; mem.editorial bd.: Psycholinguistika; mem.: Jour. Communication Disorders, Brain and Language, Jour. Nervous and Mental Disease, Advances in Neurolinguistics. Grantee NIH; fellow Alexander von Humboldt Found., 1979—, World Rehab. Fund, 1982, Founds. Fund for Research in Psychiatry, 1974-75. Mem. Acad. Aphasia. Jewish. Office: Dept Neurology NYU Med Ctr 550 1st Ave New York NY 10016 Also: 360 E 72d St New York NY 10021

BROWN, JEAN WILLIAM, advertising and public relations agency executive; b. San Antonio, June 29, 1928; s. Frank William and Gladys (Irvine) B.; m. Kathleen Budine Gordon Peckinpaugh, Nov. 1, 1980; children: Blake Conner, Borden Matthew. B.J., U. Tex., 1949. Copywriter Wilkinson, Schiwetz & Tips, Inc. (merged with McCann Erickson, Inc. 1954), 1950-54; account exec. Foote, Cone & Belding, 1955, Rives, Dyke and Co., Inc. (merged with Young & Rubicam, Inc. 1975), Houston, 1956-60, v.p., 1960-67, dir., 1961—, pres., 1967—, chief exec. officer, 1970—; chmn. Rives, Smith, Baldwin & Carlberg, 1978—; founder, pres. Jean William Brown Inc., Houston, 1979—. Served with USAF, 1951-53. Mem. Houston C. of C., Alpha Delta Sigma. Clubs: Houston, Lakeside Country. Address: 1420 Nantucket Houston TX 77057

BROWN, JERRAM LEFEVRE, biologist; b. Glen Ridge, N.J., July 19, 1930; s. Bailey LeFevre and Marion Alice (Appelbee) B.; m. Esther Reava Rosenbloom, Sept. 13, 1953; children: Jeffrey Jerram, Karen Beth, Sheryl Diane. A.B., Cornell U., 1952, M.S., 1954; Ph.D. in Zoology, U. Calif., Berkeley, 1960. Postdoctoral fellow U. Zurich, Switzerland, 1960-62; mem. faculty dept. biol. sci. U. Rochester, 1962-78, prof., 1972-78; prof. biol. sci. SUNY, Albany, 1978—. Author: The Evolution of Behavior, 1975; editor: Animal Behavior series SUNY Press; Contbr. articles to profl. jours.; Mem. editorial bd.: Behavioral Ecology, Sociobiology. Served with U.S. Army, 1954-56. Fellow Animal Behavior Soc., Am. Ornithologists Union; Mem. Soc. for the Study of Evolution, Am. Ecol. Soc., Cooper Ornithol. Soc., Wilson Ornithol. Soc., AAAS. Home: Overlook Ln RD 1 Box 428 East Berne NY 12059 Office: Dept Biol Sci SUNY Albany NY 12222 *"Study nature, not books." This motto of Louis Agassiz has reminded me throughout my life to distrust books, dogmas, and ideolgies and to seek the truth from my own observations of the world. Especially untrustworthy are the ideologies that spread violence over the world—whether in the name of a god or for "social justice."*

BROWN, JERRY GLENN, manufacturing company executive; b. Birch Tree, Mo., Aug. 19, 1933; s. Glenn Oliver and Alma Pearl (Brown) B.; m. Shirleen Wolfe, Oct. 16, 1953; 1 dau., Theresa Ann. B.S., S.W. Mo. State U., Springfield, 1953; postgrad., St. Louis U., 1956-58. With McDonnell Douglas Corp., St. Louis, 1956—, v.p., 1972—, treas., 1975—; dir. Microdata Corp, McDonnell Douglas Fin. Corp. Pres. Delmar Baptist Ch. Endowment Fund; trustee Mo. Baptist Hosp. Served with AUS, 1954-56. Home: 13325 Crossland St Louis MO 63131 Office: PO Box 516 St Louis MO 63166

BROWN, JIM, former profl. football player, film actor; b. St. Simon's Island, Ga., Feb. 17, 1936; s. Swinton and Theresa B.; m. Sue Jones, 1958; children—Kim and Kevin (twins), Jim. Grad., Syracuse U. Fullback for Cleve. Brown Profl. Football Team, 1957-65. Now film actor: appeared in Rio Conchos, 1964, The Dirty Dozen, 1967, Ice Station Zebra, 1969, The Split, 1968, Riot, 1969, 100 Rifles, 1969, Kenner, 1971, Slaughter, 1972, Slaughter's Big Rip-off, 1973, I Escaped from Devil's Island, 1973, The Slams, 1973, Three the Hard Way, 1974, Take a Hard Ride, 1975, Adios Amigo, 1976, Gus, 1976, I Will, I Will... For Now, 1976, Fingers, 1977, Superbug, The Wild One, 1977, One Down, Two to Go, 1982, others. Founder Black Economic Union. Recipient numerous Nat. Football League awards including Player of Year, 1958, 63; Hickock Belt as Profl. Athlete of Yr., 1964; named to every all-star team, 1963. Holder rushing mark and greatest distance gained in one season. Address: care Phil Gersh Agy 232 N Canon Dr Beverly Hills CA 90210 *

BROWN, JIM ED *See* **BROWN, JAMES EDWARD**

BROWN, JOE BLACKBURN, lawyer; b. Louisville, Dec. 9, 1940; s. Knox and Miriam (Blackburn) B.; m. Marilyn McGowen, Aug. 10, 1963; children: Jennifer Knox, Michael McGowen. B.A., Vanderbilt U., 1962, J.D., 1965. Bar: Ky. 1965, Tenn. 1972, U.S. Supreme Ct. 1979. Asst. U.S. atty. Dept. Justice, Nashville, 1971-73, 1st asst. U.S. atty., 1974-81, U.S. atty., 1981—; instr. math. and bus. law Augusta (Ga.) Coll., 1966-69. Contbr. articles to legal jours. Bd. dirs. Mid Cumberland Durg Abuse Council, Nashville, 1977—; asst. scoutmaster Boy Scouts Am., Nashville; mem. vestry St. David's Episcopal Ch., Nashville. Served to maj. U.S. Army, 1965-71. Recipient Owens prize in math. Vanderbilt U., 1962. Mem. Nashville Bar Assn., Fed. Bar Assn. (treas. 1978), Ky. Bar Assn., Order of Coif, Phi Beta Kappa. Republican. Home: 858 Rodney Dr Nashville TN 37205 Office: US Atty Room 879 US Courthouse Nashville TN 37205

BROWN, JOE ROBERT, ret. physician, educator; b. Mt. Pleasant, Iowa, Nov. 24, 1911; s. James Smith and Olive (Smith) B.; m. Rebecca Frisbee, Aug. 14, 1937; children—Hugh Frisbee, Carolyn Emily, Stephen Robert. B.A., U. Iowa, 1933, M.D., 1937; M.S. in Neurology and Psychiatry (fellow), Mayo Grad. Sch., U. Minn., 1943. Diplomate: Am. Bd. Neurology. Intern Presbyn. Hosp., Chgo., 1937-38; faculty Mayo Grad. Sch., U. Minn., Rochester, 1949-76, asso. prof. neurology, 1949-63, prof., 1963-76, prof. emeritus, 1976—, dir. neurologic edn., 1966-76; clin. asst. prof. U. Minn., 1946-48, clin. asso. prof., 1948-49; chief neurology service VA Hosp.; also asst. chief neurology U. Minn. Hosps., Mpls., 1946-49; cons. Mayo Clinic, Rochester, 1949-53, head sect. neurology, 1953-66, sr. cons., 1966-76, emeritus staff, 1976—; clin. prof. neuroscis. U. Calif., San Diego, 1978—; cons. VA, 1949—; from mem. to chmn. neurol. sci. research tng. com. Nat. Inst. Neurologic Diseases and Blindness, 1957-61; mem. com. perinatal research collaborative program NIH, 1965-66; mem. med. adv. bd. Nat. Multiple Sclerosis Soc., 1959—, chmn., 1971—; mem. med. adv. bd. Ability Bldg. Center Rochester, 1954-60. Editorial bd.: Neurology, 1957—. Pres. Minn. Council Liberal Chs., 1956-58; mem. Rochester Art Center Bd., 1959-65, Rochester Com. for Mpls. Symphony, 1954-58. Served from capt. to maj. M.C. AUS, 1943-46; PTO. Mem. Am. Acad. Neurology (v.p. 1967-68, pres. 1971-73, trustee), Am. Neurol. Assn., Assn. for Research in Nervous and Mental Disease, Central Neuropsychiat. Assn. (pres. 1966-67), AMA, Minn. Soc. Neurol. Scis., Assn. U. Profs. Neurology, Acad. Aphasia (chmn. 1968-69). Unitarian-Universalist (pres. 1953, 66, trustee). Research and publs. speech and lang. disorders. Home: 1784 Alta Vista Dr Vista CA 92083

BROWN, JOHN C., medical educator, business executive; b. Bishop Aukland, Eng., Oct. 27, 1938; s. Thomas and Eliza (Canvin) B.; m. Anne J., Apr. 10, 1963; children: Stephanie Anne, Michael Thomas, Suzanne Jane. B.Sc. with honors, Kings Coll, Durham U., Newcastle Upon Tyne, Eng., 1961; Ph.D., U. Newcastle Upon Tyne, Eng., 1964, D.Sc., 1977. Vis. scientist U. Wash., Seattle, 1964-65; asst. prof. U. B.C., Vancouver, Can., 1965-69, assoc. prof., 1969-72, prof., 1972—;; vis. prof. U. Gottingen, W.Ger., 1974-75; dir. Quadra Logic Tech. Inc., Vancouver, B.C., Can., 1981—; pres. Albiol Tech. Ltd., Vancouver, B.C., Can., 1982—; mem. Med. Research Council Granting Body, 1980—, BCHCRF Granting Body, 1980-83. Author: Gastric Inhibitoru Polypeptide, 1982; research, numerous publs. in field, 1966-83. Recipient Bernardo Houssay award Venezualan Physiology Soc., 1978, Moses Barron award Twin Cities Diabest Assn., 1979, Gold medal Sci. Council B.C., 1983. Fellow Royal Soc. Can. (McLaughlin Gold medal 1982); mem. Endocrinology Soc. (Ernst Oppenheimer award 1979), Physiology Soc., Can. Physiology Soc., B.C. Diabetes Assn. Office: Dept Physiology U BC 2075 Westbrook Mall Vancouver BC Canada V6T 1W5

BROWN, JOHN CALLAWAY, banker; b. Bedford, Va., June 2, 1928; s. John Callaway and Margaret McKay (McCutchen) B.; m. Julia Agnes Foster, Apr. 15, 1949; 1 dau., Anne Callaway. Diploma, Stonier Grad. Sch. Banking, Rutgers U., 1965. Cashier Bank of Big Island, Va., 1955-58, First Nat. Bank, Gate City, Va., 1958-61; with Raleigh County Nat. Bank, Beckley, W.Va., 1961—, pres., 1972—, Gulf Nat. Bank, Sophia, W.Va., 1975—. Served with AUS, 1946-48. Clubs: Glade Springs Country, Black Knight Country. Home: 704 Woodlawn Ave Beckley WV 25801 Office: Box 1269 Beckley WV 25801

BROWN, JOHN CARTER, art museum director; b. Providence, Oct. 8, 1934; s. John Nicholas and Anne (Kinsolving) B.; m. Pamela Braga, 1976; 1 son, John Carter IV. A.B. summa cum laude, Harvard U., 1956, M.B.A., 1958; postgrad., Munich (Germany) U., 1958; with, Bernard Berenson in, Florence, Italy, 1958-59; mus. tng. course, Ecole du Louvre, Paris, 1959, Netherlands Inst. Art History, 1960; M.A., Inst. Fine Arts, N.Y. U., 1962; LL.D. (hon.), Brown U., 1970, L.H.D., Mt. St. Mary's Coll., 1974, Georgetown U., 1975, George Washington U., 1978, D.F.A., Roger Williams Coll., 1978, D.P.S., Bowling Green Coll., 1979. Asst. to dir. Nat. Gallery Art, Washington, 1961-63, asst. dir., 1964-68, dep. dir., 1968-69, dir., 1969—; chmn. U.S. Commn. of Fine Arts; mem. Fed. Council on Arts and Humanities, Nat. Portrait Gallery Commn. Author-dir.: film The American Vision, 1965. Trustee N.Y. U. Inst. Fine Arts, John F. Kennedy Center for Performing Arts, Nat. Trust for Historic Preservation, Am. Acad. in Rome, Corning Mus. Glass, Nat. Geog. Soc.; trustee Am. Fedn. Arts, also chmn. exhbn. com., 1966—; mem. overseers com. art museums Harvard U.; treas. White House Hist. Assn.; trustee Mus. Computer Network; mem. Com. for Preservation of White House. Recipient Gold medal of honor Nat. Arts Soc., 1972; comdr. Ordre des Arts et des Lettres, France; Légion d'Honneur; comdr. Order Republic of Egypt; knight Order of St. Olav, Norway; others. Mem. AIA (hon.), Phi Beta Kappa. Episcopalian. Clubs: N.Y. Yacht, Cruising Am., Century, Knickerbocker (N.Y.C.); 1925 F St. (Washington). Office: Nat Gallery of Art Washington DC 20565

BROWN, JOHN EDWARD, college president; b. Lawrence, Kans., May 28, 1939; s. Frank Louis and Ruth Mildred B.; m. Nancy Lee Varney, Sept. 6, 1961; children: Hadley Lee, Jennifer Lynn. B.A., U. Kans., 1961; M.A., Stanford U., 1962, Ph.D. in History, 1966. Instr. dept history Stanford U., 1965-67; asst. prof. history Lewis and Clark Coll., Portland, Oreg., 1967-71, assoc. prof., 1972-81, prof., 1981-82, dean of faculty, v.p. acad. affairs, 1972-82, provost, 1979-82; pres. Coe Coll., 1982—, prof. history, 1982—; chmn. Oreg. Com. for Humanities; cons. Danforth Found., HEW. Summerfield scholar, 1958-61; Woodrow Wilson fellow, 1961-62; Woodrow Wilson dissertation fellow, 1964-65. Mem. Oreg. Hist. Soc., Phi Beta Kappa, Phi Alpha Theta, Pi Sigma Alpha. Clubs: University (Portland); Cedar Rapids Country. Lodge: Rotary. Office: Coe Coll Cedar Rapids IA 52402

BROWN, JOHN ELWARD, JR., univ. chancellor; b. Siloam Springs, Ark.; s. John Elward and Juanita (Arrington) B.; m. Ella Caroline Trahin, Nov. 23, 1941; children—Karen Jean, John Elward III, Melinda Suzanne. B.S., John Brown U., 1943; LL.D., Biola Bible Coll., 1952, Tex. Wesleyan Coll., 1954. Vice pres. John Brown U., 1946-48, pres., 1948-79, chancellor, 1979—; pres., mem. bd. radio sta. KUOA, Siloam Springs, Ark., KOME, Tulsa, KGER, Long Beach, Cal. Mem. Northwest Ark. council Boy Scouts Am.; Pres. Brown Mil. Acad., San Diego, Brown Sch. for Girls, Glendora, Calif., So. Calif. Mil. Acad., Long Beach. Mem. Siloam Springs C. of C. (pres.). Clubs: Mason (K.T., 32 deg.), Rotarian.). Address: John Brown University Siloam Springs AR 72761 *

BROWN, JOHN JOSEPH, newspaper executive; b. N.Y.C., Nov. 20, 1943; s. John Joseph and Stella (Keudis) B.; m. Susan Noel Seelinger, Mar. 4, 1967. B.S., U. Tex.-El Paso, 1965. Prodn. mgr. Phila. Newspapers, Inc., 1974-76; circulation dir. Phila. Newspaperrs, Inc., 1976-78; v.p. Phila. Newspapers, Inc., 1978-80, sr. v.p., 1980—; pres. Vu, Text Info., Phila., 1983—. Exploring dir. Boy Scouts Am., 1981-83. Served to lt. (j.g.) USCG, 1967-70. Recipient Silver Beaver award Boy Scouts Am., 1983, Disting. award Pa. Press Assn., 1978. Lutheran. Home: 1217 Foxglove Ln West Chester PA 19880 Office: Phila Newspapers Inc 400 N Broad St Philadelphia PA 19101

BROWN, JOHN LOTT, university president; b. Phila., Dec. 3, 1924; s. John Lott and Carolyn Emma (Francis) B.; m. Catharine Hertfelder, June 11, 1948; children: Patricia Carolyn, Judith Elliott, Anderson Graham, Barbara Smith. B.S. in Elec. Engring, Worcester (Mass.) Poly. Inst., 1945; M.A., Temple U., 1949; Ph.D., Columbia U., 1952. Personnel tng. and personnel mgr. Olney foundry Link-Belt Co., Phila., 1948-50; tech. dir. air force contract, dept. psychology Columbia U., 1952-54; head psychology div., aviation med. lab. Naval Air Devel. Center, Johnsville, Pa., 1954-59; dir. grad. tng. program physiology, 1962-65; asst., then asso. prof. physiology U. Pa. Med. Sch., 1955-65; prof. physiology and psychology Kans. State U., 1965-69; dean Grad. Sch., 1965-66, v.p. acad. affairs, 1966-69; prof. optics and psychology, dir. center visual sci. U. Rochester, N.Y., 1969-78; pres., prof. psychology, physiology and opthalmology U. South Fla., Tampa, 1978—; chmn. com. vision NRC-Nat. Acad. Scis., 1965-70; chmn. vision research program com. Nat. Eye Inst., 1975-78; trustee Worcester Poly. Inst., 1970-83, mem. alumni council, 1975-76; trustee Illuminating Engring. Research Inst., 1974-79; mem. U.S. nat. com. Internat. Commn. Optics, 1977; dir. Pioneer Fed. Savs. and Loan Assn., Fla. Author chpts. in books, also monographs, articles; cons. editor: Perception and Psychophysics, 1972—; editorial adv. bd.: Vision Research, 1971-77. Bd. dirs. Public Broadcasting Service, 1980-83, Mid-Am. Inst. Profl. Devel., 1980—; Bd. dirs. Fla. Gulf Symphony, 1979-81, Tampa Gen. Hosp. Found., 1980-81; mem. Fla. Council 100, 1978—, Tampa Performing Arts Hall Corp. Bd., 1980—; chmn. Tampa Bay Area Research and Devel. Authority, 1979—, Tampa Bay Area Fgn. Affairs Com., 1979—. Served with USNR, 1943-46. Recipient Research Career Devel. award NIH, 1961-62, Robert Goddard award Worcester Poly. Inst., 1969; sr. fellow USPHS, 1959-61; grantee NIH, NSF, Office Naval Research, Nat. Eye Inst., NIMH, NASA. Fellow Optical Soc. Am. (exec. council Rochester chpt. 1975-76, asso. editor jour. 1972-77), Am. Psychol. Assn., AAAS; mem. Assn Research Vision and Ophthalmology (pres. 1978), Soc. Neurosci., Psychonomic Soc., Sigma Xi, Psi Chi, Phi Eta Sigma, Phi Kappa Phi, Omicron Delta Kappa, Phi Gamma Delta. Quaker. Home: 1405 Julie Lagoon Lutz FL 33549 Office: 4202 Fowler Ave Tampa FL 33620

BROWN, JOHN MARSHALL, psychologist, educator; b. Manasquan, N.J., Aug. 27, 1924; s. John Marshall Jr. and Ella Beatrice (VanSickle) B.; m. Harriet Cox, Jan. 29, 1949; children: Wayne Marshall, Jeffrey Paul, Lynn Cheryl. B.S., Pa. State U., 1947, Ph.D., 1951. Grad. asst. Pa. State U., 1947-50; asso. Psychol. Corp., N.Y.C., 1947-50; asst. then asso. prof. Bucknell U., 1950-54; faculty Lafayette Coll., Easton, Pa., 1954—, prof., 1960—, head dept. psychology, 1958-81; vis. prof. U. Hawaii, 1972, summer 1974, 81; psychol. cons., 1950—. Editor, maj. author: Applied Psychology, 1966. Mem. Easton Area Joint Sch. Bd., 1959-70, Forks Twp. Sch. Bd., 1959-70; mem. bd. Northampton County Prison, 1960-78, chmn., 1966-77, sec., 1978; mem. Northampton County Mental Health/Mental Retardation Bd., 1967-71, chmn., 1970-71; chmn. Pa. Bd. Psychologist Examiners, 1972-80. Served with USAAF, 1943-45. Fellow Am. Psychol. Assn., Eastern Psychol. Assn., Pa. Psychol. Assn. (pres. 1966- 67, bd. exams. for cert. of psychologists 1967-71, Disting. Service award 1981), AAAS; mem. Am. Assn. State Psychology Bds. (exec. bd. 1977-80, Roger C. Smith award 1983), Lehigh Valley Psychol. Assn. (past pres., Disting. Service award), Psi Chi, Pi Gamma Mu, Alpha Chi Rho. Presbyterian (deacon 1956-69). Home: 401 Dogwood Terr Easton PA 18042 *Most of the really important contributions in my life have been accomplished without apparent attempts to produce, but after much general preparation. Good background work followed by incubation time produces results without conscious striving for goals.*

BROWN, JOHN O., bank exec.; b. Kansas City, Mo., Jan. 15, 1934; s. O.L. and Harriett M. (Baker) B.; m. Peggy, Sept. 16, 1955; children—Anne, J. David, Carol, J. Alan. B.S. in Bus. Adminstrn, U. Kans., 1955. Vice chmn. Commerce Bank of Kansas City, Mo.; dir. Commerce Bank of Kansas City, Key Industries, Inc.; Vice chmn. Greater Kansas City chpt. ARC. Mem. Robert Morris Assos. Presbyterian. Club: University. Home: 4809 W 81st Prairie Village KS 66208 Office: 922 Walnut Kansas City MO 64106

BROWN, JOHN PATRICK, newspaper executive; b. N.Y.C., Oct. 14, 1925; s. Patrick and Emma A. (McCarrick) B.; m. Caroline T. Hopkins, Oct. 17, 1959; children: John Patrick, Anne S. B.B.A., St. John's U., Jamaica, N.Y., 1949; M.B.A., N.Y.U., 1960. C.P.A., N.Y. Accountant Arthur Young & Co., C.P.A.s, N.Y.C., 1950-58; asst. treas. Paramount Pictures Corp., 1962-65; controller, treas. Washington Star, 1966-76; v.p. fin., treas. Bergen Evening Record Corp., N.J., 1976-82; fin. fin. and adminstrn. Washington Times, 1982—. Bd. dirs., treas. Ridgewood-Glen Rock council Boy Scouts Am. Served with AUS, 1944-46. Mem. Fin. Execs. Inst., Inst. Newspaper Controllers and Fin. Officers, Am. Inst. C.P.A.s. Roman Catholic. Club: Metropolitan (Washington). Home: 4230 Embassy Park Dr NW Washington DC 20016 Office: 3600 New York Ave NE Washington DC 20002

BROWN, JOHN ROBERT, judge; b. Funk, Nebr., Dec. 10, 1909; s. E. E. and Elvira (Carney) B.; m. Mary Lou Murray, May 30, 1936 (dec. 1977); 1 son, John R.; m. Vera Smith Riley, Sept. 14, 1979. A.B., U. Nebr., 1930, LL.D., 1965; J.D., U. Mich., 1932, LL.D., 1959. Bar: Tex. 1932. Practiced in, Houston and, Galveston; mem. Royston & Rayzor, 1932-55; judge 5th Circuit U.S. Ct. Appeals, 1955—, chief judge, 1967-80. Chmn. Harris County Republican Com., 1953-55. Served from lt. to maj. Transp. Corps USAAF, 1942-46. Mem. Am., Tex., Houston bar assns., Am. Judicature Soc., Am. Law Inst., Maritime Law Assn. U.S., Assn. ICC Practitioners, Order of Coif, Phi Delta Phi, Sigma Chi. Presbyn. (elder). Clubs: Houston, Houston Country; Boston (New Orleans). Office: 11501 US Courthouse Houston TX 77002 *

BROWN, JOHN WILLIAM, former government official; b. Athens, Ohio, Dec. 28, 1913; s. James A. and Daisy (Foster) B.; m. Violet A. Helman; 1 dau., Rosalie Brown Angelus. Grad. high sch.; LL.D., Ashland Coll., 1975. With Ohio Hwy. Patrol, 1941; mayor City of Medina, Ohio, 1950-53; lt. gov. State of Ohio, 1953-57, 62-75, gov., 1957, lake lands adminstr., 1975-81; state dir. Farmers Home Adminstrn., U.S. Dept. Agr., 1981-83; mem. Ohio Ho. of Reps., 1959-60, Ohio Senate, 1961-62; exec. dir. John W. Brown Center for Current Govt. Studies, Ashland (Ohio) Coll.; chmn. Ohio Commn. on Interstate Coop., 1965-72; co-founder Nat. Conf. Lt. Govs., 1962, chmn., 1966-67; dep. comdr.-in-chief Ohio Naval and Mil. Forces, 1969-75; commodore Ohio Naval Militia, 1978. Mem. Medina Vol. Fire Dept., 1953—. Served with USCGR, World War II; comdr. Res. ret. Mem. Am. Legion (life), VFW (life), Amvets (life), Ohio Gun Collectors Assn., Res. Officers Assn., Pi Kappa Alpha. Clubs: Masons (33 deg.), Shriners, Columbus Athletic. Home: 401 Baxter St Medina OH 44256

BROWN, JOHN Y., former governor; 3 children; m. Phyllis George, Mar. 1979; 1 son, Lincoln Tyler. Grad. law sch., U. Ky., 1960. Pres. Ky. Fried Chicken, 1971, chmn. bd., 1971-74; owner Ollie's Trolley, Inc., Louisville; gov. Ky., 1980-84; former owner Boston Celtics, profl. basketball. Bd. govs. Nat. Basketball Assn.; Chmn. Ky. Gov.'s Econ. Devel. Com.; Nat. chmn. Democratic Nat. Telethon, 1972-73; nat. chmn. Nat. Young Leadership Council; chmn. Nat. Govs. Assn. Task Force on Small Bus., 1980. Recipient Spl. Service to Am. award Lions Am. Bowl, 1974; award Am. Acad. of Achievement, 1980; others. Address: 413 Dutchman's Ln Louisville KY 40207

BROWN, JONATHAN, educator, art historian; b. Springfield, Mass., July 15, 1939; s. Leonard Melvin and Jeanette (Levy) B.; m. Sandra Backer, July 22, 1966; children: Claire, Michael, Daniel. A.B., Dartmouth Coll., 1960; M.F.A., Princeton U., 1963, Ph.D., 1964; M.A., Oxford U., 1981. Mem. faculty Princeton, 1965-73, asso. prof. art and archaeology, 1971-73; asso. prof. art N.Y. U., 1973-75, prof., 1976—; dir. Inst. Fine Arts, 1973-78; Slade prof. fine arts Oxford (Eng.) U., 1981—; vis. mem. Inst. Advanced Study, Princeton, N.J., 1978-79; adv. com. dept. European paintings Met. Mus. Art, 1974-79; adv. bd. Master Drawings jour. Author: Prints and Drawings by Jusepe de Ribera, 1973, Zurbaran, 1973, Murillo and His Drawings, 1976, Images and Ideas in Seventeenth Century Spanish Painting, 1978, A Palace for a King: The Buen Retiro and the Court of Philip IV, 1980; (with J.H. Elliott) also articles on Spanish art., (with others) El Greco of Toledo, 1982; Co-editor: Sources and Documents in the History of Art: Italy and Spain 1600-1750, 1970. Fulbright fellow, 1964-65; Am. Council Learned Socs. fellow, 1968-69; Nat. Endowment Humanities fellow, 1978-79; Guggenheim fellow, 1980-81. Mem. Coll. Art Assn. Am. (Arthur Kingsley Porter prize 1971), Hispanic Soc. Am. (corr.). Home: 71 Battle Rd Princeton NJ 08540 Office: 1 E 78th St New York NY 10021

BROWN, JOSEPH, sculptor, lectr.; b. Phila., Mar. 20, 1909; s. Max and Lena (Novak) B.; m. Gwyneth Noreen King, Aug. 19, 1939. Student, Temple U., 1927-31, B.S. (hon.), D.F.A., 1980; D.F.A. (hon.), Western Md. Coll., 1978. Profl. boxer, 1929-30; sculpture studio asst. to Dr. R. Tait McKenzie, 1931-38; boxing coach Princeton U., 1937-62, instr., resident sculptor, 1939-45, asst. prof., resident sculptor, 1945-48, asso. prof., 1948-62, prof., 1962-77, prof. emeritus, 1977—; Mem. Phila. Art Commn. Exhibited in one-man shows at, Nat. Acad. Arts and Letters, 1948, Yale U., 1952, 56, 60, Johns Hopkins U., 1965, U. Va., 1957, Bucknell U., 1958, Colgate U., Princeton U., 1938-66, Springfield Coll., 1964, U. Bridgeport, 1957, NEA, Washington, 1964, Sessler Gallery, Phila., 1963, Braverman Gallery, N.Y.C., 1969, Lehigh U., 1950, Olympic Games, Mexico City, 1968, Mangel Gallery, Phila., 1975, group shows at, Nat. Acad. Design, 1933-78, Pa. Acad. Fine Arts, 1932-42, Chgo. Art Inst., 1940, Archtl. League of New York, 1933, 35, Phila. Art Alliance, Phila. Mus., 1949, N.J. Art Mus., N.J. Pavilion, Worlds Fair, N.Y.C., 1965, Can. Olympic House, Expo '67; represented in permanent collections at, N.J. Art Mus., Pa. Acad. Fine Arts, Kennedy Meml. Library, Madison Sq. Garden, Nat. Acad. Design, also numerous univs., important works include two heroic bronze statues, White Athletic Center, Johns Hopkins U., heroic stone carving, St. Barnabus Ch., Phila., AAU swimming monument, Yale U., heroic bronze, McGonigle Hall, Temple U., four 16 foot bronze statues, Vets. Stadium, Phila.; Contbr. articles to profl. jours. Trustee Pop Warner Little Scholars, Service to Youth award, 1973. Recipient Barnett prize Nat. Acad. Design, 1944, 1st medals for sculpture Montclair Art Mus., 1940, DeVinci Soc., Phila., 1951, Creative award Am. Acad. Phys. Edn., 1968; asso. academician Nat. Acad. Design; elected to Cultural Hall of Fame South Phila. High Sch., 1957; Athletic Hall of Fame Temple U., 1975. Fellow Nat. Sculpture Soc.; mem. Nat. Assn. for Sport and Phys. Edn., Nat. Sport Hall of Fame, Order of Owl, Temple U. Club: Franklin Inn. Office: RD 1 Box 122A Princeton NJ 08540 *As a teacher of art I have tried to make the point that while we are each unique, we remain more alike than different from each other and that art is not something that is done by a few people for a few people; nor is it something that is conceived and born in a studio so it can die on a wall or a pedestal. As an artist I've tried to shape my material so that others will know what I've seen and felt. My deepest concern is that they know what I mean.*

BROWN, JOSEPH A., lawyer, business executive; b. Worcester, Mass., Sept. 18, 1926; s. Joseph A. and Anna G. (Moynihan) B.; m. Joan E. Auchter, June 11, 1949; children: Margaret, Jeanne, Joseph, Theresa, Timothy, Michael, Richard. B.S., Franklin and Marshall Coll., 1948; J.D., Georgetown U., 1951. Bar: D.C. 1951, Pa. 1974. Atty. Workmen's Compensation Appeals Bd., U.S. Dept. Labor, 1951-53; patent atty. B.E. Shlesinger, Washington and Rochester, N.Y., 1953-55, Sperry New Holland div. Sperry Corp., New Holland, Pa., 1955-64, patent counsel, 1964-67, gen. counsel, asst. sec., 1967-75, v.p., gen. counsel, govt. relations, 1976—. Chmn. Eastern dist. Lancaster County council Boy Scouts Am., 1965-66; bd. dirs. 1965; div. chmn. United Way, 1979. Served with USNR, 1944-46. Mem. Am., Pa. bar assns., Am. Patent Law Assn., Lancaster C. of C. (dir. 1979-82). Roman Catholic. Home: 1360 Hunter Dr Lancaster PA 17601 Office: Sperry Corp New Holland PA 17557

BROWN, J(OSEPH) GORDON, university administrator; b. Terre Haute, Ind., Aug. 25, 1927; s. Joseph H. and Helen (Gordon) B.; m. Patsy Ralston Myers; children: Sheridan Lynn Brown Hume, Karen Sue DeBord, Michael Gordon. Student, U. Ky., 1946-47; B.S., East Tenn. State U., 1950; M.S., U. Tenn., 1957. Prin. Bassel Sch., Alcoa, Tenn., 1950-51, Springbrook Sch., Alcoa, 1951-57; dean men, dir. student activities Emory and Henry Coll., Emory, Va., 1957-60, dean men, asso. prof. edn., 1960-64; dean men Va. Poly. Inst. and State U., Blacksburg, 1964-68, dean for student services, 1968-77, dean for student programs and services, 1977-79, dir. univ. student devel. services, 1979-82, asst. dir. placement services/alumni, 1982—. Pres. Blacksburg Community Fedn.; Bd. dirs. Blacksburg United Fund; mem. alumni bd. dirs. East Tenn. State U., 1977-83, v.p., 1979-80, pres., 1981-82. Served with USNR, 1945-46. Mem. Nat. Assn. Student Personnel Adminstrs. (commns. on profl. relations and fin. aids; Region III Va. state dir., Region III Disting. Service citation 1975, 77), Va. Assn. Student Personnel Adminstrs. (past pres., Disting. Service citation 1979), So. Assn. Colls. and Schs., Phi Delta Kappa, Phi Eta Sigma, Pi Delta Epsilon, Omicron Delta Kappa. Methodist. Club: Rotary (past pres.). Home: 2703 Chelsea Ct Blacksburg VA 24060

BROWN, JOSIAH, educator, physician; b. Centerfield, Utah, Dec. 19, 1923; s. Nathan and Sophie (Lederman) B.; m. Pearl Holen, Oct. 21, 1944; children—Jeffrey Josiah, Celia Lynn, Todd Evan. A.B., U. Calif. at Los Angeles, 1944, M.D., 1947. Intern San Francisco City and County Hosp., 1947- 48; jr. resident Mallory Inst. Pathology, Boston City Hosp., 1948-49; resident medicine Cin. Gen. Hosp., 1949-51; mem. faculty U. Calif. Sch. Medicine at, Los Angeles, 1956—, prof., chief div. endocrinology, 1966—, chmn. ednl. policy and curriculum com., 1968-70. Author: (with C.M. Pearson) Clinical Uses of Adrenal Steroids, 1962. Served with USPHS, 1951-53. Hon. fellow Courtauld Inst. Biochemistry, Middlesex Hosp. Med. Sch., 1964-65. Mem. Am. Soc. Clin. Investigation, A.A.A.S., Endocrine Soc., Diabetes Assn. So. Cal. Home: 10640 Somma Way Los Angeles CA 90024

BROWN, JUDITH OLANS, lawyer, educator; b. Boston, May 29, 1941; d. Sidney and Evelyn R. (Lefkovitz) Olans; m. James K. Brown, Oct. 5, 1969. A.B. magna cum laude with distinction, Mt. Holyoke Coll., 1962; LL.B. cum laude, Boston Coll., 1965. Bar: Mass. 1965. Law clk. Supreme Jud. Ct., 1965-66; assoc. Foley, Hoag and Eliot, Boston, 1966-69; chief counsel Mass. Dept. Community Affairs, Boston, 1969-70; atty. adv. Office of Regional Counsel, HUD, Boston, 1970, asst. regional counsel, Boston, 1971, assoc. regional counsel, 1971-72; instr. Boston U. Law Sch., 1971, Northeastern U. Sch. Law, Boston, 1972, assoc. prof., 1972-75, prof., 1975—; corporator Arlington Five Cents Savs. Bank, 1974—. Contbr. articles to legal jours.; article and book rev. editor: Boston Coll. Indsl. and Comml. Law Rev., 1964-65. Mem. steering com. Lawyers com. for Civil Rights under Law; bd. dirs. Big Brother Assn. Boston. Loeb fellow, 1972-73. Mem. Order of Coif, Phi Beta Kappa. Home: 336 North Ave Weston MA 02193 Office: 400 Huntington Ave Boston MA 02115

BROWN, JUNE, journalist; b. Detroit, July 19, 1923; d. Simpson and Vela (Wilkerson) Malone; m. Warren C. Garner, June 28, 1961; 1 dau., Sylvia G. Mustonen. Student, Wayne State U., 1941. Columnist, classified advt. mgr. Mich. Chronicle, Detroit, 1945-74; columnist Detroit News, 1974—. Author: June Brown's Guide to Let's Read, 1981. Bd. dirs. Scholarship Fund for Children, 1982—. Recipient Best Column awards Detroit Press Club, 1971, 72, Nat. Newspaper Assn., 1968, 69. Methodist. Home: PO Box D Holly MI 48442 Office: Detroit News Assn 615 W Lafayette St Detroit MI 48231

BROWN, JUNE GIBBS, government official; b. Cleve., Oct. 5, 1933; s. Thomas D. Gibbs and Lorna M. (Gibbs); m. Ray L. Brown, Jan. 1, 1975; children: Ellen, Sheryl, Linds, Victor, Gregory, Carol. B.B.A. summa cum laude, Cleve. State U., 1971, M.B.A., 1972; postgrad., Cleve. Marshall Law Sch., 1973-74; J.D., U. Denver, 1978; postgrad. Advanced Mgmt. Program, Harvard U., 1973. Real estate broker, officer mgr. N.E. Realty, Cleve., 1963-68; staff acct. Frank T. Cicirelli, C.P.A., Cleve, 1970-71; asst. to comptroller S.M. Hexter Co., Cleve., 1971; grad. teaching fellow Cleve. State U., 1971-72; dir. internal audit Navy Fin. Ctr., Cleve., 1972-75; mgr. fin. systems design burs. Dept. Interior, Denver, 1975-79; insp. gen., Washington, 1979-81, NASA, Washington, 1981—. Recipient award Am. Soc. Women Accts., 1969, 70, 71, Raulston award Cleve. State U., 1971, Pres's award, 1971, Outstanding Achievement award U.S. Navy, 1973, Career Service award Chgo. region Fed. Exec. Bd., 1974, Outstanding Contbn. to Fin. Mgmt. award, 1977, Fin. Mgmt. Improvement award Join Fin. Mgmt. Improvement Program, 1980, Outstanding Service award Nat. Assn. Minority C.P.A. Firms, 1980; named Meritorious Exec. Presdl. rank, 1983, Woman of Yr. Bur. Land Mgmt., Dept. Interior, 1975. Mem. Assn. Govt. Accts. (nat. exec. com. 1977-80, 82-84, vice chmn. nat. ethics com. 1978-80, chmn. fin. mgmt. standards bd. 1981-82, Service award 1973, 76, Outstanding Achievement award 1979), Am. Inst. C.P.A.s, Am. Accts. Assn., Assn. Fed. Investigators, Beta Alpha Psi. Office: Office Insp Gen NASA 400 Maryland Ave SW Washington DC 20546

BROWN, KEITH, musician, educator; b. Colorado Springs, Colo., Oct. 21, 1933; s. Kenneth Vernon and Audrey Lucille (Nelson) B.; m. Leslee Joanne Scullin, June 13, 1954; children: Robert Vernon, Lise Joanne, Kristin Patricia. B.Mus., U. So. Calif., 1957; M.Mus., Manhattan Sch. Music, 1964. Trombonist Indpls. Symphony Orch., 1957-58, N.Y. Brass Quintet, 1958-59; asso. 1st trombonist Phila. Orch., 1959-62; 1st trombonist Met. Opera Orch., 1962-65; dir. instrumental activities, prof. music, condr. univ. orch. Temple U., Phila., 1965-71; prof. music, condr. Univ. Orchs. and contemporary chamber ensemble Ind. U., Bloomington, 1971—; mem. faculty, solo trombonist Aspen Festival, 1957-69; chmn. brass dept., condr. Music

Acad. of West, 1978-82. Participant, Marlboro Festival, 1970-73; prin. trombonist, Casals Festival, San Juan, P.R., 1958-80; condr., music dir., Bloomington Symphony Orch., 1975-81; regular guest condr., Orquesta Sinfonica Venezuela; coach, adv., guest condr, Orquesta Nacional Juvenil Simón Bolívar, Caracas, 1979—, performances with, Chamber Music Soc. of Lincoln Center, 1969—; tchr. master classes, lectr., recitalist (1st western trombonist), conservatories in, Beijing and Shanghai, China, 1982; author 10 vols. orchestral studies for trombone and tuba, numerous edits. of solos, brass ensembles, study materials, 1960—. Served with U.S. Army, 1953-56. Recipient spl. award Asociacion Musical, Caracas, Venezuela, 1979, Alumni award U. So. Calif. Sch. Music, 1957. Mem. Internat. Trombone Assn., Phi Mu Alpha Sinfonia, Pi Kappa Lambda, Kappa Kappa Psi (hon.). Methodist. Club: Rotary. Home: 2114 Georgetown Rd Bloomington IN 47401 Office: Sch Music Indiana Univ Bloomington IN 47405

BROWN, KEITH LAPHAM, U.S. ambassador to Lesotho, investor; b. Sterling, Ill., June 18, 1925; s. Lloyd Heman and Marguerite (Briggs) B.; m. Carol Louise Liebmann, Oct. 1, 1949; children: Susan, Briggs (dec.), Linda, Benjamin. Student, U. Ill., 1943-44, Northwestern U., 1946-47; LL.B., U. Tex., 1949. Bar: Tex., Okla., Colo. Assoc. Lang, Byrd, Cross & Ladon, San Antonio, 1949-55; v.p., gen. counsel Caulkins Oil Co., Oklahoma City, 1955-70, Denver, 1955-70; pres. Brown Investment Corp., Denver, 1970—; U.S. ambassador to Kingdom of Lesotho, 1982—; founder, developer Vail Assocs., Colo., 1962; developer Colo. State Bank Bldg., Denver, 1971. Trustee Soil Sci. Found. of U. Denver, 1981—; mem. Council Fgn. Relations, Denver, 1981—; dir. Nat. Western Stock Show, Boys Club, Denver, 1980—; trustee, past pres. Colo. Acad., 1975-80; past pres. Mile-Hi Club, Denver, 1981; nat. committeeman Republican Party, 1975-82. Mem. Tex. Bar Assn., Okla. Bar Assn., Colo. Bar Assn. Presbyterian. Clubs: Denver Country; Univ. (Denver). Home: Am Embassy PO Box 333 Maseru Lesotho 100 Office: Brown Investment Corp 1600 Broadway Denver CO 80202

BROWN, KENNETH JAMES, labor union executive; b. Toronto, Ont., Can., 1925; came to U.S., 1960; s. Arthur W. and Evelyn (Ball) B.; 3 daus. Lithographer in, Can., 1942; pres. Toronto local union Lithographers Internat. Union, 1954-60, mem. internat. council, 1955-60, pres. union, 1960-66; pres. Lithographers and Photo Engravers Internat. Union, 1964-72, Graphic Arts Internat. Union, 1972-83, also chmn. supplemental retirement and disability fund, Graphic Communications Internat. Union, 1983—. Address: 1900 L St NW Washington DC 20036

BROWN, KENNETH LEE, diplomat; b. Seminole, Okla., Dec. 6, 1936; s. Roy Lee and Juanita (Martin) B.; m. Claudia Lee McCue, Sept. 14, 1957 (div. July 1981); children: Kai Devin, Craig Evan; m. 2d Bonnie Heather Lea, Sept. 12, 1981. B.A., Pomona Coll., 1959; M.A., Yale U., 1960, NYU, 1975. Fgn. service officer Dept. State, Algiers, Kinshasa, N.Y.C. and Washington, 1961-72; polit. and press officer Am. Embassy, Brussells, 1972-77; assoc. spokesman Dept. State, Washington, 1977-79, dep. dir. UN polit. affairs, 1979-80, dir. Central Africa, 1980-81; ambassador People's Rep. of the Congo, Brazzaville, 1982—. Served as 2d lt. U.S. Army, 1960-61. Recipient Superior Honor award Dept. State, 1979; Penfield fellow NYU, 1968; jr. fellow Ctr. Internat. Studies, NYU, 1967; Woodrow Wilson fellow, 1959. Mem. Am. Fgn. Service Assn., Sr. Fgn. Service Assn., Phi Beta Kappa, Nu Alpha Phi. Address: American Embassy BP 1015 Brazzaville People's Republic of the Congo

BROWN, KENNETH RAY, banker; b. Cherokee, Okla., July 6, 1936; s. Tom Melton and Mary Elizabeth (Foster) B.; m. Elizabeth Kay Callahan, Oct. 17, 1964; children—Kathryn Sue, Elizabeth Ann, Angela Kay. B.B.A., U. Okla., 1957. Vice pres., then sr. v.p., sr. investment officer Liberty Nat. Bank & Trust Co., Oklahoma City, 1965-79, exec. v.p., 1979—. Mem. Inst. Chartered Fin. Analysts, Okla. Soc. Fin. Analysts, Econ. Club Okla. Presbyterian. Office: PO Box 25848 Oklahoma City OK 73125

BROWN, KENNETH TAYLOR, physiologist; b. Purcellville, Va., Apr. 7, 1922; s. Ralph Birdsall and Gertrude Janney (Birdsall) B.; m. Virginia Williams Stern, June 30, 1948; children—Stephen Kenneth, Laurence Bunting. Student, U. Cin., 1940-41, Miami U., Oxford, Ohio, 1941-43; B.A., Swarthmore Coll., 1947; M.S., U. Chgo., 1949, Ph.D., 1951. Research psychologist Aero-Med. Lab., Wright Air. Devel. Center, Dayton, Ohio, 1950-54; research asso. Brown U., 1954-55; mem. faculty Wilmer Inst., Johns Hopkins Sch. Medicine, Balt., 1955-58, Sch. Medicine U. Calif. at San Francisco, 1958—, prof. physiology, 1966—; mem. Nat. Adv. Eye Council. Served to 1st lt. AC AUS, 1943-45. Decorated Air medal with 8 oak leaf clusters.; NSF fellow, 1954-55; USPHS Spl. Research fellow, 1957-58; Commonwealth Fund fellow, 1964-65; Faculty Research lectr. U. Calif. San Francisco, 1969-70. Fellow AAAS; mem. Am. Physiol. Soc., Assn. Research in Vision and Ophthalmology, Soc. Neurosci. Research in retinal neurophysiology; devel. of microelectrode techniques for neurophysiology. Home: 1459 Willard St San Francisco CA 94117

BROWN, KENT LOUIS, surgeon; b. Westfield, N.Y., 1916; m. Elizabeth Myers; children: Karen (Mrs. Lyman Johnson), Kent Louis, David, Garry. M.D., U. Buffalo, 1942. Diplomate: Am. Bd. Surgery. Rotating intern St. Luke's Hosp., Cleve., 1942-43, asst. resident surgery, 1946-49, chief resident surgeon, 1949-50; now mem. active staff; active staff, past pres. staff St. Vincent Charity Hosp.; courtesy staff Hillcrest Hosp., Westfield (N.Y.) Meml. Hosp., Euclid Gen. Hosp., Cleve.; asst. clin. prof. Case-Western Res. U. Med. Sch. Author: Medical Problems and the Law, The Medical Witness; Editor: The Cleve. Physician, 1970—, Medicine in Cleveland and Cuyahoga County: 1810-1976; author monographs; contbr. articles to profl. jours. Past trustee Cleve. Med. Library; pres. bd. trustees Cleve. Med. Library Assn., 1972; past pres. City of Cleve. Safety Dept. Served as lt., M.C. USNR, 1943-46. Fellow A.C.S. (trauma com.); mem. AMA, Am. Assn. Surgery of Trauma, Am. Arbitration Assn., Cleve. Acad. Medicine (dir.). Clubs: Kiwanian (past pres.), Aesculapian Soc. Cleve. (past pres.), Innominatum Soc., Pasteur, Medical Arts, Union. Home and Office: 148 S Portage St Westfield NY 14787

BROWN, KENT LOUIS, JR., magazine editor; b. Cleve., Nov. 23, 1943; s. Kent L. and Elizabeth (Myers) B.; m. Margaret Frances Beale, June 17, 1967; children: Maj Turi, Boyd Benjamin, George Kent. Student, U. Hawaii, 1963-65; B.A. in English, Hobart Coll., 1967; postgrad., SUNY-Oswego, 1969; M.S. in Engring. Edn., Syracuse U., 1971. Cert. tchr., N.Y. State. Mgmt. trainee Agway, Inc., Phelps, N.Y., 1967-68; vegetale grower, Clyde, N.Y., 1968-71; tchr. Lyons Central Sch., N.Y., 1969-71; asst. editor Highlights for Children, Honesdale, Pa., 1971-76, mng. editor, 1976-78, editor, 1978—, dir., 1976—; chmn. bd. Serendipity Ctr., Inc., Honesdale, 1971-72. Mem. Coop. Extension Assn., Wayne County, Pa., 1979-81. Served with U.S. Army, 1963-65. Recipient Craftsmanship award Printing Industries of Am., 1979. Mem. Am. Soc. Mag. Editors, Wayne County Farmers Assn., Ednl. Press Assn. Am. (regional rep.). Republican. Club: Honesdale Country (dir. 1981-82). Home: Boyd Mills Rd Milanville PA 18443 Office: Highlights for Children 803 Church St Honesdale PA 18431

BROWN, LAURIE MARK, physicist, educator; b. Bklyn., Apr. 10, 1923; s. William and Elvira (Fleischman) B.; m. Judith Kobrin, Dec. 27, 1942 (dec. May 1963); children: Joanna Lisa, Julie Elena; m. Brigitte Dziumbla-Winzeler, June 6, 1969; children: Judith, Jean. A.B., Cornell U., 1943, Ph.D., 1951. Mem. faculty physics Northwestern U., Evanston, Ill., 1950—, prof., 1961—; Mem. Inst. for Advanced Study (NSF fellow), Princeton, 1952-53; cons. Argonne Nat. Lab., 1960-70; vis. prof., Vienna, 1966, Rome, 1967, São Paulo, 1972-73. Contbr. articles profl. jours. Fulbright research scholar, Italy, 1958-60. Fellow Am. Phys. Soc., AAAS. Home: 724 Noyes St Evanston IL 60201

BROWN, LAWRENCE HARVEY, basketball coach; b. Bklyn., Sept. 14, 1940. Student, U. N.C., 1959-63. Amateur basketball player Akron Goodyears, (Ohio), 1963-65; asst. basketball coach U. N.C., Chapel Hill, 1965-67; player, New Orleans Am. Basketball Assn., 1967-68, Oakland, 1968-69, Washington, 1969-70, Va. Squires-Denver Nuggets, 1970-71, Denver Nuggets, 1971-73; coach Carolina Cougars (Am. Basketball Assn.), 1972-74; coach Denver Nuggets Nat. Basketball Assn., 1974-79; coach basketball UCLA, 1979-81; coach N.J. Nets Nat. Basketball Assn., 1981-83; coach basketball U. Kans., Lawrence, 1983—; mem. ABA All-Star Team, 1968-70; led ABA in assists, 1968-70, coached team to NCAA Basketball Finals, 1980; mem. U.S. Olympic Team, 1964, ABA Championship Team, 1969. Named Most Valuable Player ABA All-Star Game, 1968, ABA Coach of the Yr., 1973, 75. Office: Allen Fieldhouse Univ of Kans Lawrence KS 66045 *

BROWN, LEE PATRICK, city official; b. Wewoka, Okla., Oct. 4, 1937; s. Andrew and Zelma B.; m. Yvonne C. Streets, July 14, 1958; children: Patrick, Torri, Robyn, Jenna. B.S. in Criminology, Fresno State U., 1961; M.S. in Sociology, San Jose State U., 1964, U. Calif., Berkeley, 1968, D.Criminology, 1970; D.Pub. Affairs (hon.), Fla. Internat. U., 1982. Mem. San Jose Police Dept., 1960-68; prof., dir. dept. adminstrn. of justice Portland (Oreg.) State U., 1968-72; prof. pub. adminstrn., dir. criminal justice programs, asso. dir. Inst. Urban Affairs and Research, Howard U., Washington, 1972-75; sheriff, dir. pub. safety Multnomah County, Oreg., 1975-77; dir. Multnomah County Dept. Justice Services, 1977-78; pub. safety commr., Atlanta, 1978-82, chief of police, Houston, 1982—; adj. prof. Tex. So. U., 1982—, U. Houston, 1982—; cons. Law Enforcement Assistance Adminstrn. and; Community Relations Service, Dept. Justice; chmn. edn., tng. and manpower devel. task force Nat. Adv. Commn. on Criminal Justice Standards and Goals; mem. Nat. Adv. Commn. on Higher Edn. for Police; chmn. Nat. Minority Adv. Council on Criminal Justice, Nat. Com. on Accreditation of Police Agys.; mem. Nat. Adv. Com. on Juvenile Justice Assessment Center Program; U.S. rep. as nat. corr. UN Program on Prevention Crime and Treatment of Offenders. Co-author: The Police and Society: An Environment for Collaboration and Confrontation; Contbr. articles to profl. jours. Past chmn. Oreg. Black Caucus; mem. adv. council Nat. Neighborhood Foot Patrol Ctr.; active NAACP, Atlanta Urban League; Oreg. adv. com. for United Negro Coll. Fund, Albena Voter Registration and Edn. Com., Portland, Portland Human Relations Commn.; bd. dirs. Martin Luther King Jr. Scholarship Fund of Oreg. Recipient Danforth Asso. award, 1972, Disting. Service award Multnomah County Div. Pub. Safety, 1976, Outstanding Law Enforcement award Nat. Black Police Assn., 1982, Disting. Alumnus award Fresno State U., 1983. Mem. Internat. Assn. Chiefs Police, Internat. Assn. Fire Chiefs, Nat. Orgn. Black Law Enforcement Execs., Am. Corrections Assn., Nat. Assn. Blacks in Criminal Justice, Police Exec. Research Forum, Nat. Acad. Pub. Adminstrn., Tex. Police Chiefs Assn., Atlanta Jaycees (life), Alpha Phi Alpha. Democrat. *Many others have sacrificed for me to succeed. Therefore, I have dedicated my life to attempting to make life better for others. Also, I make decisions based on what is right, moral, ethical, legal, just and in the best interest of the community. This principle has served me well.*

BROWN, LEON, architect, educator; b. Blackville, S.C., Sept. 25, 1907; s. Isador and Sadie (Cohen) B.; m. Marguerite Kahn, Aug. 30, 1944; 1 son, Warren Lee. Student, Cornell U., 1924-25; B.S. in Architecture, Ga. Inst. Tech., 1929; M.Arch., U. Pa., 1933. Designer-draftsman R. B. Okie, Phila., 1929-31; jr. partner Thalheimer & Weitz, Phila., 1934-42; propr. Leon Brown (architect), Washington, 1946-50; partner Brown & Wright (architects), Washington, 1950-68, 71-81, Brown, Wright & Mano (architects), 1968-71; prof. architecture Howard U., Washington, 1947-72; Mem. Washington Bldg. Congress, 1958-76; chmn. D.C. Bd. Appeals and Rev., Licenses and Insp., 1956-60; mem. bd. Washington Planning and Housing Assn., 1958-70; mem. urban renewal planning com. Washington Urban League, 1960-65; nat. panel arbitrators Am. Arbitration Assn., 1959—; sec. D.C. Bd. Registration Architects, 1964-67, pres., 1967-69. Author: (with others) R. Brognard Okie, Architect of Philadelphia, 1955; also articles. Treas. D.C. Com. Job Opportunities, 1956-60; co-chmn. D.C. NCCJ, 1966-72, bd. govs., 1967, bd. Wash. chpt., 1968; pres. Forest Hills Citizens Assn., 1965-68; Mem. com. planning and housing Democratic Central Com., 1963-64; Bd. dirs. N.W. Settlement House, 1952-73. Served to capt., C.E. AUS, 1942-46. Recipient Meritorious Pub. Service award Mil. Dist. Washington, 1946. Fellow AIA (pres. Washington met. chpt. 1956-58, Coll. Fellows); mem. Zeta Beta Tau. Jewish. Club: Cosmos (Washington). Home and Office: 4158 Linnean Ave NW Washington DC 20008

BROWN, LEON CARL, educator; b. Mayfield, Ky., Apr. 22, 1928; s. Leon Carl and Gwendolyn (Travis) B.; m. Anne Winchester Stokes, Aug. 29, 1953; children: Elizabeth Boone, Joseph Winchester, Jefferson Travis. B.A., Vanderbilt U., 1950; postgrad., U. Va., 1950-51, London Sch. Econs., 1951-52; Ph.D., Harvard, 1962. U.S. fgn. service officer, Beirut, Lebanon, 1954-55, Khartoum, Sudan, 1956-58; asst. prof. Middle Eastern studies Harvard, 1962-66; asso. prof. Near Eastern history and civilization Princeton, 1966-70, prof., 1970—, chmn. dept. Near Eastern studies, 1969-73, dir. program Near Eastern studies, 1969-73, 80—. Author: (with C.A. Micaud and C.H. Moore) Tunisia: the Politics of Modernization, 1964, The Tunisia of Ahmad Bey, 1974; Editor: State and Society in Independent North Africa, 1966, From Madina to Metropolis: Heritage and Change in the Near Eastern City, 1973, (with Norman Itzkowitz) Psychological Dimensions of Near Eastern Studies, 1977; Translator with commentary: The Surest Path: the Political Treatise of a 19th Century Muslim Statesman, 1967. Served with USAAF, 1945-46. Mem. Middle East Studies Assn. (pres. 1975-76). Home: 191 Hartley Ave Princeton NJ 08540

BROWN, LEONARD CARLTON, educator; b. Mineral Springs, Ark., Mar. 26, 1915; s. Leonidas C. and Willie (Graves) B.; m. Hazel Elizabeth Weatherly, Aug. 27, 1938; 1 dau., Jo Carol. A.B., Henderson State Coll., Ark., 1937; M.A., Fla. State U., 1952; Ph.D., Ohio State U., 1955. Research asso. Ohio State U., 1955-57, asst. prof., 1957-59, asso. prof., 1959-64, prof. physics, 1964—. Served with USAAF, 1943-46. Mem. Am. Phys. Soc., Am. Assn. Physics Tchrs., Sigma Xi, Sigma Pi Sigma. Home: 2170 Lane Rd Columbus OH 43220

BROWN, LES (LESTER LOUIS), journalist; b. Indiana Harbor, Ind., Dec. 20, 1928; s. Irving H. and Helen (Feigenbaum) B.; m. Jean Rosalie Slaymaker, June 12, 1959; children: Jessica, Joshua, Rebecca. B.A. in English, Roosevelt U., Chgo., 1950. Entertainment industry reporter, reviewer theatrical events Chgo. bur. Variety, 1953-55; asso. editor Downbeat mag., 1955; co-founder, operator folk music cabaret The Gate of Horn, Chgo., 1956; bur. mgr. Chgo. Variety, 1957-65; editor radio-TV dept., N.Y.C., 1965-73, asst. mng. editor, 1973; radio-TV corr. N.Y. Times, 1973-80; editor-in-chief Channels of Communications mag., 1980—;; cons. Revson Found., 1978; lectr. creative writing and entertainment industries Columbia Coll., Chgo., 1959-62; lectr. communications Hunter Coll., N.Y.C., 1973-75, New Sch., 1977—; Poynter fellow in modern journalism Yale U., 1977, lectr., 1978—; asso. fellow Morse Coll., 1978—; Presdl. fellow Aspen Inst., 1978; mem. bd. Humanitas Prize, 1980—, Peabody Awards, 1983—; dir. Banff Am. Author: lyrics Abilene, 1956, Television: The Business Behind The Box, 1971, Electric Media, 1973, New York Times Encyclopedia of Television, 1977, Keeping Your Eye on Television, 1979; Les Brown's Encyclopedia of Television, 1982, Fast Forward: The New Television and American Society, 1983; also articles. Mem. Film-TV adv. bd. N.Y. State Council on Arts, 1975; pres. Media Commentary Council Inc. Served with AUS, 1951-53. Home: 131 N Chatsworth Ave Larchmont NY 10538 Office: 304 W 58th St New York NY 10019

BROWN, LESTER RUSSELL, association executive; b. Bridgeton, N.J., Mar. 28, 1934; s. Calvin C. and Delia (Smith) B.; m. Shirley Ann Woolington, June 12, 1960 (div.); children: Brian, Brenda. B.S. in Agrl. Sci, Rutgers U., 1955; M.A. in Agrl. Econs., U. Md., 1959; M.P.A., Harvard U., 1962; hon. degrees from numerous instns. including, Dickinson Coll., U. Md., Franklin Coll., Williams Coll., Rutgers U., Glassboro State Coll. With Dept. of Agr., 1959-69, adminstr. internat. agr. devel. service, 1966-69; sr. fellow Overseas Devel. Council, 1969-74; pres. Worldwatch Inst., Washington, 1974—; Faculty mem. Salzburg Seminar in Am. Studies, summer 1971, 74; guest scholar Aspen Inst., summers 1972-74; project dir. State of the World, 1981. Author: Man, Land and Food, 1963, Increasing World Food Output, 1965, Seeds of Change, 1970, World Without Borders, 1972, In the Human Interest, 1974, (with Erik Eckholm) By Bread Alone, 1974 (Christopher award), The Twenty-Ninth Day, 1978 (Ecologia Firenze award), Building a Sustainable Society, 1981; numerous others, also articles. Mem. U.S. com. for UNICEF; mem. Planning Commn. for New Directions; bd. dirs. Overseas Devel. Council. Recipient Superior Service award Dept. Agr., 1965; Arthur S. Flemming award, 1965; named one of 10 outstanding young men in Am. U.S. Jr. C. of C., 1966. Mem. Am. Farm Econs. Assn., Soc. Internat. Devel., Internat. Assn. Agrl. Economists, Am. Acad. Arts and Scis. (working group on year 2000), Am. Econs. Assn., Council of Fgn. Relations, Zero Population Growth, Common Cause, World Future Soc., Amateur Athletics Union. Club: Cosmos. Office: 1776 Massachusetts Ave NW Washington DC 20036

BROWN, LEWIS ARNOLD, banker; b. Chattanooga, Feb. 28, 1931; s. Edward Emerson and Dorothy (Gregory) B.; m. Sidney Sherman Walsh, June 17, 1953; children: Lewis Arnold, Chaille Emerson, Houghton Gregory, Anthony Atwood. B.S., U. N.C., 1953; postgrad. banking, Northwestern U., 1959-60, Rutgers U., 1961-63; grad. Advanced Mgmt. Program, Harvard, 1974. With Tex. Commerce Bank Nat. Assn., Houston, 1955—, asst. v.p., 1960-62, v.p., 1962-70, sr. v.p., trust officer, 1970-78; pres., dir. Union Bank of Houston, 1978-83. Bd. dirs., sec. Alley Theatre, 1971, pres., 1972-73; bd. dirs. Houston Estate and Financial Forum; bd. mgrs. Downtown YMCA, 1961-66; trustee Mus. Fine Arts, 1976-78; bd. dirs. Miller Theatre, 1978—. Served to 1st lt. USMCR, 1953-55. Episcopalian. Clubs: Houston Country (dir. 1975-77), Tejas, Houston. Home: 5440 Sugar Hill Houston TX 77056 Office: PO Box 2728 Houston TX 77001

BROWN, LORENE B(YRON), library educator, educational administrator; b. Plant City, Fla., Nov. 9, 1933; d. Benjamin and Sallie (Barton) Byron; m. Paul L. Brown, Aug. 1, 1974. B.S., Fort Valley State Coll., 1955; M.S.L.S., Atlanta U., 1956; Ph.D., U. Wis., 1974. Cataloguer N.C. Central U., Durham, 1956-58, Gibbs Jr. Coll., St. Petersburg, Fla., 1958-60, Fort Valley State Coll., Ga., 1960-65, Norfolk State U., Va., 1965-70; assoc. prof., dean Atlanta U., 1970—; dir. Info. Retrieval Workshops, Atlanta, 1976-78; evaluator Coop. Coll. Library Ctr., Atlanta, 1979-82; cons. United Bd. Coll. Devel., Atlanta, 1976-79. Mem. Friends of Library, Atlanta, 1982. Recipient Rachel Schenk award Library Sch. U. Wis., Madison, 1971; So. Fellowship Found. fellow, Atlanta, 1972-74. Mem. ALA, Am. Soc. for Info. Sci., Assn. Library and Info. Sci. Edn., Ga. Library Assn., Met Atlanta Library Assn. Democrat. Baptist. Home: 855 Flamingo Dr SW Atlanta GA 30311 Office: Atlanta U 223 Chestnut St SW Atlanta GA 30314

BROWN, LOUIS M., lawyer; b. Los Angeles, Sept. 5, 1909; s. Emil and Anna B.; m. Hermione Kopp, 1937; children: Lawrence David, Marshall Joseph, Harold Arthur. A.B. cum laude, U. So. Calif., 1930; J.D., Harvard, 1933; LL.D., Manhattan Coll., Riverdale, N.Y., 1977. Bar: Calif. bar 1933, U.S. Supreme Ct. bar 1944. Practiced in, Los Angeles, 1933-35; with Emil Brown & Co., Dura Steel Products Co., both Los Angeles, 1936-41; counsel RFC, Washington, 1942-44; partner firm Pacht, Warne, Ross and Bernhard, Los Angeles, also; Beverly Hills, Calif., 1944-47; partner firm Irell & Manella, Los Angeles, 1947-69, counsel, 1969-72; Lectr. in law Southwestern U. Law Sch., Los Angeles, 1939-41, U. Calif. at Los Angeles, 1944-46; lectr. in law U. So. Calif., 1950-51, lectr., adj. prof. law, 1960-74, prof. law, 1974-80, prof. emeritus, 1980—, acad. dir. program for legal paraprofls., 1970-77; mem. planning com. Tax Inst., 1948-69; vis. prof. law Loyola-Marymount Law Sch., Los Angeles, 1977—; Disting. vis. prof. Whittier Coll. Sch. Law, 1980—; mem. nat. panel arbitrators Am. Arbitration Assn., 1956-63. Author: Preventive Law, 1950, How to Negotiate a Successful Contract, 1955, also case books, articles profl. jours.; co-Author: Planning by Lawyers: Materials on a Non-Adversarial Legal Process, 1978; Editor: Major Tax Problems, 3 vols, 1948-51; Mem. Am. Community Symphony Orch., European Tour, 1968. Mem. com. Jewish Personnel Relations Bur., Community Relations Com., 1950-60; founder, adminstr. Emil Brown Fund Preventive Law Prize Awards, 1963—, Client Counseling Competition, 1968-73; cons. Client Counseling Competition, 1973—; pres. Friends of Beverly Hills Pub. Library, 1960. Recipient Merit award U. So. Calif. Gen. Alumni Assn., 1979. Fellow Am. Bar Found., Soc. for Values in Higher Edn.; mem. ABA (chmn. standing com. legal assistance for servicemen 1969-72, mem. accreditation com. sect. legal edn. and admissions to bar 1978-81), Beverly Hills Bar Assn. (pres. 1961, Disting. Service award 1981), Los Angeles County Bar Assn. (chmn. prepaid legal services com. 1970-71), San Francisco Bar Assn., State Bar Calif., Am. Judicature Soc., Am. Bus. Law Assn., Internat. Assn. Jewish Laywers and Jurists, Town Hall Los Angeles, Order of Coif. Jewish. Clubs: Mason (mem.), B'nai B'rith., Harvard Southern Calif. An issue of So. Calif. Law Rev. pub. in his honor, 1975. Home: 606 N Palm Dr Beverly Hills CA 90210 Office: 1901 Ave of Stars Suite 850 Los Angeles CA 90067 *The obvious is too often overlooked. Find it. Identify it. Explore it. There is much that lies hidden in the fundamentals and complexities of the obvious.*

BROWN, LOWELL SEVERT, physicist, educator; b. Visalia, Calif., Feb. 15, 1934; s. Volney Clifford and Anna Marie Evelyn (Jacobson) B.; m. Shirley Isabel Mitchell, June 23, 1956; 1 son, Stephen Clifford. A.B., U. Calif., Berkeley, 1956; Ph.D. (NSF predoctoral fellow 1956-61), Harvard U., 1961; postgrad., U. Rome, 1961-62, Imperial Coll., London, 1962-63. From research asso. to asso. prof. physics Yale U., 1963-68; mem. faculty U. Wash., Seattle, 1968—, prof. physics, 1970—; vis. prof. Imperial Coll., London, 1971-72; summer vis. scientist Brookhaven Nat. Lab., 1965-68, Lawrence Berkeley Lab., 1966, Stanford Accelerator Ctr., 1967, CERN, Geneva, 1979; mem. Inst. Advanced study, Princeton, N.J., 1979-80; cons. Los Alamos Sci. Lab.; trustee Aspen Ctr. for Physics, 1982—. Editorial bd.: Phys. Rev.,

1978-81; contbr. articles to profl. publs. Postdoctoral fellow NSF, 1961-63; sr. post-doctoral fellow, 1971-72; Guggenheim fellow, 1979-80. Fellow Am. Phys. Soc. (exec. com. div. particles and fields 1982—); mem. AAAS, Phi Beta Kappa, Sigma Xi. Home: 1157 Federal Ave E Seattle WA 98102 Office: Physics Dept Univ Wash Seattle WA 98195

BROWN, MARCIA, author, artist, photographer; b. Rochester, N.Y., July 13, 1918; s. Clarence Edward and Adelaide Elizabeth (Zimber) B. Student, Woodstock Sch. Painting, summers 1938, 39; student painting, New Sch. Social Research, Art Students League; B.A., N.Y. State Coll. Tchrs., 1940. Tchr. English, dramatics Cornwall (N.Y.) High Sch., 1940-43; library asst. N.Y. Pub. Library, 1943-49; tchr. puppetry extra-mural dept. U. Coll. West Indies, Jamaica, B.W.I., 1953. Illustrator: The Trail of Courage (Virginia Watson), 1948, The Steadfast Tin Soldier (Hans Christian Andersen), 1953, Anansi (Philip Sherlock), 1954, The Three Billy Goats Gruff (Asbjornsen and Moe), 1957, Peter Piper's Alphabet, 1959, The Wild Swans (Hans Christian Andersen), 1963, Giselle, 1970, The Snow Queen (Hans Christian Andersen), 1972, Shadow (Blaise Cendrars), 1982; author, illustrator: The Little Carousel, 1946, Stone Soup, 1947, Henry Fisherman, 1949, Dick Whittington and His Cat (retold), 1950, Skipper John's Cook, 1951, The Flying Carpet (retold), 1956, Felice, 1958, Tamarindo, 1960, Once a Mouse (retold), 1961 (Caldecott award), Backbone of the King, 1966, The Neighbors, 1967, The Bun (retold), 1972, All Butterflies, 1974 (Boston Globe Honor Book, Horn Book), The Blue Jackal (retold), 1977, Walk Through Your Eyes, 1979, Touch Will Tell, 1979, Listen to a Shape, 1979; translator. illustrator: Puss in Boots, 1952, Cinderella (Charles Perrault), 1954 (Caldecott award), How, Hippo!, 1969 (honor book Book World Spring Book Festival); author, photographer: film strip The Crystal Cavern, 1974; woodcut prints exhibited, Bklyn. Mus., Peridot Gallery, Hacker Gallery, Library Congress, Carnegie Inst., Phila. Print Club, prints in permanent collection, Library of Congress, N.Y. Pub. Library, pvt. collections; writer, illustrator picture books for children. Recipient Disting. Service to Children's Lit. award U. So. Miss., 1972; Regina medal Cath. Library Assn., 1977; Disting. Alumnus medal SUNY, 1969; U.S. nominee Andersen award illustration, 1966, 75; Life fellow Internat. Inst. Arts and Letters, 1961. Mem. Authors Guild, Print Council of Am., Art Students League. Office: care Franklin Watts 387 Park Ave New York NY 10016

BROWN, MELVIN F., corporate executive; b. Carlinville, Ill., June 4, 1935; s. Ben and Selma (Frommel) B.; m. Jacqueline Sue Hirsch, Sept. 2, 1962 (dec.); children: Benjamin Andrew, Mark Steven. A.B., Washington U., 1957, J.D., 1961. Bar: Mo. bar 1961. Pvt. practice, St. Louis, 1961-62; asst. to gen. counsel Union Elec. Co., St. Louis, 1962-65; sec., atty. ITT Aetna Corp., St. Louis, 1965-72, v.p., gen. counsel, 1972; also dir.; corp. sec., gen. counsel ITT Financial Corp., 1974-77, exec. v.p., 1977—; now also pres. ITT Diversified Credit Corp., also dir.; Dir. Civic Employment Corp., 1970—; mem. Interracial Conf. Bus. Opportunities, 1969—. Mem. Mo. Commn. Democratic Party Constn. By-laws and Party Structure, 1969-70, Mo. Dem. Platform Com., 1966, 68; mem. Bd. Adjustment City of Clayton, Mo., 1974—; Chmn. St. Louis chpt. Am. Jewish Com., 1968—. Served to capt. AUS, 1957-64; mem. Res. Hon. col. Mo. Gov.'s staff. Mem. Bar Assn. Met. St. Louis (pres. young lawyers sect. 1965-66), Mo. Bar Assn. Office: ITT Diversified Credit Corp 8251 Maryland Ave Clayton MO 63105

BROWN, MICHAEL ARTHUR, lawyer; b. San Angelo, Tex., Oct. 15, 1938; s. Edwin Michael and Sadie Beatrice (Johnson) B.; m. Teresa Anne Boyd, Feb. 24, 1979; children—Michael Paul, Michele Louise. B.B.A., St. Marys U., San Antonio, 1959, LL.B., 1961; LL.M., Georgetown U., 1970. Bar: Tex. 1962, D.C. 1974. Commd. 2d lt. U.S. Army, 1961, advanced through grades to maj., 1967; ret., 1969; dep. asst. gen. counsel Dept. Commerce, Washington, 1969-73; gen. counsel U.S. Consumer Product Safety Commn., Washington, 1973-77, exec. dir., 1977-79; dep. gen. counsel U.S. EPA, Washington, 1982, enforcement counsel, 1982-83. Author: (with others) Consumer Product Safety Law, 1975. Decorated Meritorious Service medal; recipient Gold medal for disting. service U.S. Consumer Product Safety Commn., 1978. Mem. Fed. Bar Assn., Tex. Bar Assn., D.C. Bar Assn. Home: 3129 9th St N Arlington VA 22201 Office: 401 M St SW Washington DC 20460

BROWN, MICHAEL STUART, geneticist; b. N.Y.C., Apr. 13, 1941; s. Harvey and Evelyn (Katz) B.; m. Alice Lapin, June 21, 1964; children: Elizabeth Jane, Sara Ellen. B.A., U. Pa., 1962, M.D., 1966. Intern, then resident in medicine Mass. Gen. Hosp., Boston, 1966-68; served with USPHS, 1968-70; clin. assoc. NIH, 1968-71; asst. prof. U. Tex. Southwestern Med. Sch., Dallas, 1971-74; Paul J. Thomas prof. genetics, dir. Center Genetic Diseases, 1977—. Recipient Pfizer award Am. Chem. Soc., 1976, Passano award Passano Found., 1978, Lounsbery award U.S. Nat. Acad. Scis., 1979; Lita Annenberg Hazen award, 1982. Mem. Nat. Acad. Scis., Am. Soc. Clin. Investigation, Assn. Am. Physicians, Harvey Soc. Home: 5719 Redwood Ln Dallas TX 75209 Office: 5323 Harry Hines Blvd Dallas TX 75235

BROWN, MILTON PEERS, business administration educator; b. Yonkers, N.Y., Jan. 19, 1919; s. George Edwin and Linda Miriam (Schneider) B.; m. Joan Hawley, Aug. 25, 1945; children—Susan, Janet, Pamela. S.B. cum laude, Harvard U., 1940, M.B.A., 1942. Mem. faculty Harvard U. Bus. Sch., 1942—, prof. bus. adminstrn., 1958—, Lincoln Filene prof. retailing, 1963—; mgmt. cons., 1950—; dir. Allied Stores Corp., Collins & Aikman Co., both N.Y.C., Dunkin Donuts, Randolph, Mass., Savogran Co., Norwood, Hollingsworth and Vose, Walpole, Mass., C.R. Bard Inc., Blue Bell Inc., Greensboro, N.C., High Voltage Engring. Co., Burlington, Mass.; Mem. adv. com. Navy Resale System Office.; Pres., bd. dirs. Harvard Coop. Soc. Author: Operating Results of Multi-Unit Department Stores, 1961, Problems in Marketing, 3d edit, 1968; co-author: Strategy Problems in Mass Retailing and Wholesaling. Mem. Nat. Retail Mchts. Assn. (dir.). Home: PO Box 687 Weston MA 02193 Office: Morgan Hall Harvard Business Sch Soldiers Field Boston MA 02163

BROWN, MILTON WOLF, art historian, educator; b. Newark, July 3, 1911; s. Samuel and Celia (Harriton) B.; m. Blanche R. Levine, July 15, 1938. B.A., N.Y.U., 1932, M.A., 1935; Ph.D., Inst. Fine Arts, 1949; postgrad., Courtauld Inst., summer 1934, U. Brussels, summer 1937, Harvard, 1938-39. Instr. art dept. Bklyn. Coll., 1946-49, asst. prof., 1949-56, asso. prof., 1956-60, prof., 1960-70, chmn. dept. art, 1964—; exec. officer doctoral program in art history City U. N.Y., 1971-79, resident prof., 1979—; Chmn. adv. bd. Archives Am. Art, 1967—; mem. council Smithsonian Instn. Author: Painting of the French Revolution, 1937, American Painting from the Armory Show to the Depression, 1955, The Story of the Armory Show, 1963, American Art to 1900, 1977; co-author: American Art, 1978; Contbg. editor: Ency. Painting, 1955. Served with AUS, 1943-46; ETO. Decorated Bronze Star medal. Mem. Coll. Art Assn. Am. Home: 15 W 70th St New York NY 10023 Office: Grad Center City U NY 33 W 42d St New York NY 10036

BROWN, MORGAN CORNELIUS, III, manufacturing executive; b. Jamestown, N.Y., Feb. 4, 1948; s. Morgan Cornelius and Anne Lee (Boles) B.; m. Margaret Danita Hair, Dec. 17, 1977; children: Morgan Cornelius, Benjamin Thomas, Stephanie Leanne. A.B., Syracuse U., 1970; J.D., Harvard U., 1973. Bar: N.Y. 1975. Assoc. Davis Polk & Wardwell, N.Y.C., 1973-77; sr. atty., asst. sec. Bangor Punta Corp., Greenwich, Conn., 1977-79, sec., 1979-82, v.p., sec., 1982—; asst. v.p., asst. sec. Piper Aircraft Corp., Greenwich, 1977-79, sec., 1979—. Mem. ABA, Am. Soc. Corp. Secs., Westchester-Fairfield County Corp. Counsel Assn. Home: 80 Lawrence Hill Rd Stamford CT 06903 Office: Bangor Punta Corp One Greenwich Plaza Greenwich CT 06830

BROWN, MYRTLE IRENE, nursing educator; b. East Peoria, Ill., Feb. 1, 1915; d. Clifford Richard and Sarah (Scoville) B. B.A., Eureka Coll., 1939; B.S., U. Minn., 1942, M.S., 1947; Ph.D., N.Y. U., 1961. Instr. supr. pediatric nursing Mont. State Coll., Great Falls, 1939-41; instr., supr. pediatric nursing U. Minn., 1942-46, instr. advanced pediatric nursing, 1947-49; nursing cons. maternal and child health team WHO, India, 1949-50; public health staff nurse Wayne County Health Dept., Eloise, Mich., 1950-52; asst. prof. maternal and child health Johns Hopkins, Balt., 1952-55; instr., then asso. prof. introductory epidemiology, sr. clin. nursing maternal and children's nursing N.Y. U., 1955-61; research cons. Am. Nurses' Found. N.Y.C., 1961-64; asso. prof. community health and med. practice U. Mo. Sch. Medicine, Columbia, 1964-67; asso. prof. Sch. Nursing, 1964-67; dean, prof. Sch. Nursing, Duke, 1967-70; prof., asso. dean grad. studies Coll. Nursing, U. S.C., Columbia, 1970-80; mem. S.C. Bd. Examiners for Nursing Home Adminstrs.; instr. health maintenance to employees of various govt. agys. Bd. dirs. Episcopal Housing Corp., Columbia; chmn. Episcopal Bishop's Task Force of Upper S.C. for Ministry for the Aged. Fellow Am. Acad. Nursing; mem. Trained Nurse Assn. India (life), Am. Sociol. Assn., Am. Public Health Assn., Am., S.C. nurses assns., Nat., N.C. leagues nursing, Kappa Delta Pi, Alpha Kappa Delta, Sigma Theta Tau. Home: 5400 Lake Shore Dr Columbia SC 29206

BROWN, NANCY ANN, librarian; b. London, Ontario, Can.; d. Wilbur Franklin and Kathaleen Mary (Grogan) B. B.S., Carelton U., 1957; B.L.S., McGill U., 1964; M.L.S., U. Toronto, 1968, M.B.A., 1979. Asst. librarian Meteorol. Library Library, Can. Dept. Transport, Toronto, Ont., 1964-66; physics librarian U. Toronto, 1966-69; math, physics librarian Queen's U., Kingston, Ont., 1969-71; head sci. div. U. Guelph, Ont., 1971-79; univ. librarian, dir. libraries U. Saskatchewan, Saskatoon, 1979—. Mem. Canadian Library Assn. Home: PO Box 84 Saskatoon SK S7K 3K1 Canada Office: Library Administration Univ of Saskatchewan Saskatoon SK S7N 0W0 Canada

BROWN, NORMAN, educator; b. Lynn, Mass., Feb. 7, 1921; s. David and Ruth T. B.; m. Doris J. Gordon, 1943 (dec.); m. Miriam E. Jones, Oct. 24, 1970; children—Fredric, Hollis, Norman, Regina, Jonathan, Edmund. B.S., M.I.T., 1942; M.S., Stanford U., 1950; Ph.D., U. Calif., Berkeley, 1952. Metallurgist Naval Torpedo Sta., Newport, R.I., 1942-43; ballsitician Aberdeen Proving Grounds, Md., 1946-48; asst. prof. dept. material sci. and engring. U. Pa., Phila., 1952-55, asso. prof., 1955-61, prof., 1961—. Pres. Haverford Grange Estate, 1976-80; chmn. Twp. Environ. Commn. Served with USAAF, 1943-44; Served with U.S. Army, 1944-48. Guggenheim fellow, 1958-59; NIH fellow, 1966-67. Mem. Am. Soc. Metals, Am. Phys. Soc., Am. Chem. Soc., Soc. Rheology. Quaker. Home: 727 Panmure Rd Haverford PA 19041 Office: Dept Material Sci U of Pa Philadelphia PA 19104

BROWN, OSCAR, JR., writer, entertainer; b. Chgo., Oct. 10, 1926; s. Oscar Cicero and Helen Clark (Lawrence) B.; m. Irene Hebert, Dec. 26, 1948 (div. Nov. 1953); children—David, Donna; m. Maxine Fleming, Jan. 15, 1954; children—Joan, Iantha, Oscar, Margaret. Student pub. schs., Chgo. Writer book, music and lyrics, Kicks & Co., Chgo., 1961; appeared in: Village Vanguard, 1961, Apollo Theater, Carnegie Hall, 1962, Blue Angel, 1962, Hungry I, 1962, Crescendo, 1962, Berns, Stockholm, 1963, Waldorf Astoria, Cool Elephant, London, Eng., 1965, one-man shows, Prince Charles Theater, London, 1963, Music Box Theater, Los Angeles, 1964, Gramercy Arts Theater, N.Y.C., 1965; producer, dir.: Joy '66, at, Happy Medium Theater, Summer in the City, at, Harper Theater, In de Beginin', 1977, Alley Theater; resident composer: Am. Folk Theater; Composer: Brown Baby, 1960, Work Song, 1960, Dat Dere, 1960, The Snake, 1963, Muffled Drums, 1965. Mem. Author's League Am. *

BROWN, PAT *See* **BROWN, EDMUND GERALD**

BROWN, PAUL, football exec.; b. Norwalk, Ohio, July 9, 1908. Ed., Ohio State U., Miami U., Ohio. Coach Severn (Md.) Prep. Sch., 1930-32; coach football and basketball Massillon (Ohio) High Sch., 1932-41; coach Ohio State U., Columbus, 1941-43, Great Lakes Coll., 1944-45; coach profl. football team Cleve. Browns, 1946-62, Cin. Bengals, 1968-76, v.p., gen. mgr., 1976—. Office: care Cincinnati Bengals 200 Riverfront Stadium Cincinnati OH 45202 *

BROWN, PAUL A., physician, business executive; b. Boston, Apr. 1, 1938; s. Morton G. and Helen C. (Appleton) B.; m. Cynthia R. Shrier, June 4, 1961; children: Richard, Mark. A.B., Harvard U., 1960; M.D., Tufts U., Boston, 1964. Intern Tufts New Eng. Med. Ctr., Boston, 1964-65; resident in pathology Columbia Presbyn. Hosp., N.Y.C., 1965-69; chmn., chief exec. officer Metpath Inc., Teterboro, N.J., 1970-83, chmn., 1983—; chmn., chief exec. officer Kinetix Inc., Saddle River, N.J., 1983—, Scientific Advances Corp., Teaneck, N.J., 1982—; lectr. pathology Columbia U., 1981—. Trustee Tufts U., 1980—; bd. dirs. New Eng. Med. Ctr. Hosps., Boston, 1982—; mem. vis. com. Tufts U. Sch. Medicine, 1981—. Served with U.S. Navy, 1969-70. Home: 174 Elmsley Ct Ridgewood NJ 07450

BROWN, PAUL BRADLEY, architect; b. Lake City, Minn., Apr. 20, 1912; s. Clark William and Belle (Patton) B.; m. Betty V. Padou, Dec. 29, 1945; children: Barry, Bennett, Bradley. A.B., Oberlin Coll., 1933; B.Arch., U. Mich., 1936. Draftsman Hugh Keyes (Architet), Detroit, 1936-37; designer I.M. Lewis (Architect), Detroit, 1937-39, Harley Ellington Assos. Inc., 1939-48, project architect, 1948-55, prin., 1955-70; exec. partner Harley Ellington Pierce Yee & Assos., 1970-82. Pres. Birmingham (Mich.) Planning Commn., 1956-58; pres. Forum for Detroit Area Met. Goals, 1962-67. Served with USNR, 1943-45. Fellow AIA (pres. Detroit chpt. 1961-63), Engring. Soc. Detroit; mem. Mich. Soc. Architects (dir. 1964-65). Home: 4586 Paper Birch Ln Traverse City MI 49684

BROWN, PAUL W., lawyer, retired state supreme court justice; b. Cleve., Jan. 14, 1915; s. William and Mary (Foster) B.; m. Helen Page; children: Susan, Julie, Barbara, Mary, Jeffrey, Molly, Daniel. A.B., Ohio State U., 1937, J.D., 1939. Bar: Ohio 1939, U.S. Supreme Ct. 1939. Practiced in, Youngstown, Ohio, 1939-40, 46-60; faculty, asst. to pres. Youngstown U.; judge 7th Dis. Appeals of Ohio, 1960-64, Ohio Supreme Ct., Columbus, 1964-69; atty. gen. state of Ohio, Columbus, 1969-71; assoc. justice Supreme Ct. Ohio, 1973-81; ptnr. Thompson, Hine and Flory,, Columbus and Cleve., 1983—. Del. Republican Nat. Conv., 1948. Served with AUS, 1941-45. Decorated Purple Heart, Silver Star. Mem. Ohio, Mahoning County bar assns., ABA (Council of dels.), Inst. Jud. Adminstrn., Am. Legion, DAV, 1st Armored Div. Assn., Mil. Order Purple Heart. Club: Masons. Home: 2396 Wimbledon Rd Columbus OH 43220 Office: Thompson Hine & Flory 100 E Broad St Columbus OH 43215 Office: Nat City Bank Bldg Cleveland OH 44114 Office: 1920 N St Washington DC

BROWN, PETER CAMPBELL, lawyer; b. Aug. 12, 1913; s. Peter P. and Ellen (Campbell) B.; m. Joan Gallagher, June 8, 1943; children: Peter Campbell, Patricia, Thomas, Michael, Robert. A.B., Fordham Coll., 1935, LL.B., 1938; LL.D., St. Bonaventure U., New York, 1951. Bar: N.Y. 1938. Practiced in, Bklyn., 1938-41; asst. U.S. atty. for Eastern Dist. of N.Y., Bklyn., 1946; 1st. asst. criminal div. Dept. of Justice, 1947-48; exec. asst. to atty. gen. U.S., 1948, spl. asst. to atty. gen., 1949-50, mem. subversive activities control bd. (under the Internal Security Act of 1950), 1950-53, chmn., 1952-53, commr. investigation, N.Y.C., 1954-55; corp. counsel City of N.Y., 1955-58; mem. Manning, Hollinger & Shea, 1958-65; ptnr. Brown, Carlino & Emmanuel, 1965-72; counsel Winer, Neuburger & Sive, 1972-78; sole practice, N.Y.C., 1978—; dir. Thomas Pub. Co., Fedn. Bank & Trust Co. Bd. dirs. St. Mary's Coll., South Bend, Ind. Served to maj. AUS, 1942-45; ETO. Decorated 6 Battle Stars on European African Middle Eastern ribbon, Fourragere of Belgium for Battle of Ardennes (The Bulge); named Knight Holy Sepulchre Knight Malta. Fellow Am. Coll. Trial Lawyers, Bar Supreme Ct. U.S., Fed. Dist. Cts., U.S. Ct. Appeals, Am., N.Y. State bar assns., V.F.W., Legion, Catholic Lawyers Guild, Assn. Bar City of N.Y., St. Patrick Soc. Bklyn. (past pres., dir.), Friendly Sons St. Patrick City N.Y., Fordham Coll. Alumni Assn. (past pres.). Democrat. Roman Catholic. Clubs: Lawyers, Montauk (Bklyn.); Manhattan, New York Athletic, Pinnacle (N.Y.C.); Army-Navy (Washington); Pelham Country; Westchester Country (Rye, N.Y.). Home: 275 N Ridge St Town of Rye Rye Brook NY 10573 Office: 90 Park Ave New York NY 10016

BROWN, PETER GILBERT, philosopher; b. New Haven, Jan. 15, 1940; s. C. Victor and Margaret Elizabeth (Tullock) B.; m. Judith Ann Ball; children: David, Ethan. B.A., Haverford Coll., 1961; M.A., Columbia U., 1964, Ph.D., 1969. Tutor St. John's Coll., Annapolis, Md., 1965-70; vis. asst. prof. philosophy U. Md., College Park, 1969-70; asst. v.p. for research Urban Inst., Washington, 1970-73; affiliate asso. prof. U. Wash., Seattle, 1973-74; vis. fellow Battelle Seattle Research Center, 1973-74; fellow Acad. Contemporary Problems, Washington, 1974-76; dir. Center Philosophy and Public Policy, U. Md., 1976-81; asso. dean Sch. Public Affairs, U. Md., 1980—. Contbr. articles to profl. jours.; author/editor books and monographs. Fellow Inst. Soc. Ethics and Life Scis.; mem. Assn. for Pub. Policy and Mgmt. Home: 3708 35th St NW Washington DC 20016 Office: Sch Public Affairs U Md College Park MD 20742 *Over the past decade I have endeavored to broaden and deepen our ideas about policy-oriented research. We need to examine our basic moral concepts as they apply to public policy without examining these concepts and the obligations they imply we are without standards to judge the legitimacy of our policies and the means to determine the ideals to which we should aspire as a nation and as individuals.*

BROWN, PETER MEGARGEE, lawyer; b. Cleve., Mar. 15, 1922; s. George Estabrook and Miriam (Megargee) B.; m. Alexandra Green Johns, May 18, 1974; children: Peter, Blair Tillyer, Andree, Nathaniel; stepchildren—Alexandra, Brooke Stoddard. B.A., Yale U., 1944, J.D., 1948. Bar: N.Y. State 1949. Spl. asst. atty. gen. State N.Y. and asst. counsel N.Y. State Crime Commn., 1951-53; asst. U.S. atty. So. Dist. N.Y., 1953-55, spl. asst., 1956; partner firm Cadwalader, Wickersham & Taft, N.Y.C., 1959-82, Brown & Seymour, 1983—; mem. Mayor's Com. on Judiciary, 1965-72, vice chmn., 1972-74. Mem. N.Y. County Republican Com., 1958—; pres. Riot Relief Fund; bd. dirs., sec. Episcopal Ch. Found.; bd. dirs. Yale Alumni Fund, 1979—. Served in AUS, 1943-46. Decorated knight Order St. John of Hosp. of Jerusalem. Fellow Am. Coll. Trial Lawyers, Am., N.Y. State bar founds.; mem. World Assn. Lawyers (founding), Am. Judicature Soc., Soc. Colonial Wars, Internat., Am., N.Y. State, N.Y. County bar assns., Assn. Bar City N.Y., Fed. Bar Council (pres. 1961-62, chmn. bd. 1962-64, chm. judiciary com. 1960—), St. Nicholas Soc. (past pres.), Delta Kappa Epsilon, Phi Delta Phi (magister Waite Inn 1947, pres. province I 1950-55). Episcopalian (vestryman, sr. warden 1961-77). Clubs: Down Town Assn., Union (N.Y.C.); Mill Reef (Antigua); Coral Beach (Bermuda). Home: 1125 Park Ave New York NY 10028 Office: 100 Park Ave New York NY 10017

BROWN, QUINCALEE, association executive; b. Wichita, Kans., Nov. 9, 1939; d. Quincy Lee and Lorene (York) B.; m. James Parson Simsarian, June 24, 1978. B.A., Wichita State U., 1961; M.A., U. Pitts., 1963; Ph.D., U. Kans., 1975. Asst. prof. speech communications, dir. debate Wichita State U., 1963-69, Ottawa U., 1970-73; adminstrv. asst. Montgomery County (Md.) Commn. for Women, 1973-74, exec. dir., 1975-80; mgr. fed. women's program Govt. Printing Office, Washington, 1974-75; exec. dir. AAUW, Washington, 1980—. Contbr. articles to profl. jours. Recipient award for contbn. to public service Women for Equality, Montgomery County Govt., 1975, Outstanding Contbn. to Sex Equity, 1979, Career Achievement award Profl. Fraternity Assn., 1981. Mem. Speech Communications Assn., AAUW, Kappa & Delta Epsilon (hon.), Zeta Phi Eta (Outstanding Service award 1975). Office: 2401 Virginia Ave Washington DC 20037 *

BROWN, R. HARPER, packaging company executive; b. Oak Park, Ill., Apr. 22, 1923; s. Arthur E. and Edith (Watters) B.; m. Anne Richardson, Oct. 8, 1949; children: Carol, Margaret, Nancy, Linda. A.B., Brown U., 1945; M.B.A., Harvard, 1947. With Container Corp. Am., 1947-80, v.p., 1965-67, sr. v.p., 1967-72, exec. v.p., 1972-74, pres., 1974-80, vice chmn. bd., 1977-80; also dir.; pres., chief exec. officer, dir. Meyercord Co., Carol Stream, Ill., 1980—; dir. Matthey Print Corp. Trustee Brown U. Served to lt. (j.g.) USNR, World War II. Mem. Ill. St. Andrews Soc., Ill. Mfrs. Assn. (dir.), Alpha Delta Phi. Clubs: University, Economic (Chgo.); Exmoor Country (Highland Park, Ill.). Home: 965 Castlegate Ct Lake Forest IL 60045 Office: Meyercord Co Carol Stream IL 60187

BROWN, RALPH MANNING, JR., insurance company executive; b. Elizabeth, N.J., July 1, 1915; s. Ralph Manning and Anna Alethea (Rankin) B.; m. Margrette Burnham, Oct. 6, 1950; children: Anne Alethea Brown Durney, Ralph Manning. Grad., Gilman Sch., 1932; A.B., Princeton U., 1936. With Gen. Motors Acceptance Corp., 1936-51; asst. v.p. N.Y. Life Ins. Co., N.Y.C., 1951-53, v.p., 1953-55, v.p. in charge real estate and mortgage loan dept., 1955-62, exec. v.p., 1962-69, pres., chief adminstrv. officer, 1969-72, chmn. bd., chief exec. officer, 1972-81, now dir.; dir. La. Land & Exploration Co., Asso. Dry Goods Corp., Avon Products, Inc., J.P. Morgan & Co., Inc., Union Camp Corp., Union Carbide Corp. Trustee Princeton. Clubs: University, Links (N.Y.C.); Pretty Brook Tennis (Princeton). Home: 50 Westcott Rd Princeton NJ 08540 Office: 51 Madison Ave New York NY 10010

BROWN, RALPH SAWYER, JR., bus. exec., lawyer; b. Cohasset, Mass., July 21, 1931; s. Ralph Sawyer and Rosemary (Wyman) B.; m. Elizabeth Atkinson Rash, June 12, 1953; children—Lucy Victoria Phillips, Alexander Sawyer Batson. B.A., Swarthmore Coll., 1954; LL.B., Harvard, 1957. Bar: Mass. bar 1957, N.Y. State bar 1963. Asso. Hutchins & Wheeler, Boston, 1957-62, Carter, Ledyard & Milburn, N.Y.C., 1962-68; partner Janklow & Traum, N.Y.C., 1968-71; sec., asst. gen. counsel Indian Head, Inc., N.Y.C., 1971-76, v.p., treas., 1976-79; v.p., gen. counsel, sec. Esquire, Inc., 1979—. Bd. mgrs. West Side YMCA, N.Y.C. Mem. Phi Beta Kappa. Home: 390 West End Ave New York NY 10024 Office: 488 Madison Ave New York NY 10022

BROWN, RAY KENT, biochemist, physician; b. Columbus, Ohio, Apr. 7, 1924; s. Ray Stemen and Grace (Nunemaker) B.; m. Gertrude Lydia Harris, Jan. 25, 1947; children—Kimberly, Kitene, Kevin. B.A.,

Ohio State U., 1944, M.D., 1947, M.S., 1948; Ph.D., Harvard U., 1951. Intern Boston City Hosp., 1947-48; sr. asst. surgeon USPHS, Bethesda, Md., 1951-53; asst. dir. div. labs. and research N.Y. State Dept. Health, Albany, 1953-59, asso. dir. div., 1959-63; asst. prof. biochemistry Albany Med. Coll., 1954-56, asso. prof., 1956-61, prof., 1961-63; prof., chmn. dept. biochemistry Wayne State U. Sch. Medicine, 1963—. Mem. Highland Twp. (Mich.) Planning Commn., 1968—. Served with U.S. Army, 1943-45; Served with USPHS, 1951-53. Mem. Am. Soc. Biol. Chemistry (Travel award 1958, 61, 64), Am. Assn. Immunologists, Biochem. Soc. Gt. Britain, Am. Chem. Soc. Home: 3820 Middle Rd Milford MI 48042 Office: 540 E Canfield St Detroit MI 48201

BROWN, RAY WILLIAM, lawyer, chemical company executive; b. Corning, N.Y., Apr. 19, 1929; s. Robert W. and Emma (Park) B.; m. Margaret Jeanne Holden, Apr. 25, 1953; children: Robert W., Margaret. A.B., Princeton U., 1951; J.D., Cornell U., 1957. Bar: N.Y. 1957, Pa. 1968. Assoc. Chadbourne, Parke, Whiteside & Wolff, N.Y.C., 1957-64; ptnr. Saperston, Wiltse, Duke, Day & Wilson, Buffalo, 1964-67; counsel Blaw-Knox Co., Pitts., 1967-69; asst. gen. counsel Westinghouse Electric Corp., Pitts., 1969-75; gen. counsel Mobay Chem. Corp., Pitts., 1975—, v.p., 1978—, sec., 1975—. Chmn Mt. Lebanon (Pa.) Zoning Hearing Bd., 1976-83; elder Southminster United Presbyn. Ch., Pitts., 1974-82. Served with USN, 1951-54. Mem. ABA, N.Y. State Bar Assn., Allegheny County Bar Assn. Clubs: Chartiers Country; Princeton (N.Y.C.); Duquesne (Pitts.). Home: 1380 Terrace Dr Pittsburgh PA 15228 Office: Mobay Chem Corp Penn-Lincoln Pkwy W Pittsburgh PA 15205

BROWN, RAYMOND LLOYD, lawyer; b. Clarksdale, Miss., July 7, 1936; s. Russell Lloyd and Sallie Agnes (Hayes) B.; m. Carolyn Morris Shoemaker, June 22, 1958; children—Lynne Allison, Raymond Lloyd, Beverly Hayes. B.B.A., U. Miss., 1958, J.D., 1962. Profl. football player Balt. Colts, 1958-60; law clk. to Justice Tom C. Clark U.S. Supreme Ct., 1962-63; with firm Megehee, Brown, Williams & Mestayer (and predecessors), Pascagoula, Miss., 1962— now partner. Pres. Pascagoula Jaycees, 1964; nat. bd. dirs. U.S. Jaycees, 1965; bd. dirs. Pascagoula Salvation Army, 1975—; mem. exec. com. Jackson County Republican Com., 1968—, chmn., 1972-76. Mem. Miss. N.G. Recipient Disting. Service award City of Pascagoula, 1964. Fellow Am. Coll. Trial Lawyers, Am. Bar Assn., Miss. Bar Assn. (pres. 1978-79); mem. Miss. Def. Lawyers Assn. (pres. 1975-76). Methodist. Club: Pascagoula Rotary (past pres.). Office: 3112 Canty St PO Box 787 Pascagoula MS 39567 *

BROWN, RICHARD HOLBROOK, library administrator, historian; b. Boston, Sept. 25, 1927; s. Joseph Richard and Sylvia (Cook) B. B.A., Yale U., 1949, M.A., 1952, Ph.D., 1955. Instr. history U. Mass., Amherst, 1955-59, asst. prof., 1959-62; assoc. prof. history No. Ill. U., De Kalb, 1962-64; dir. The Amherst Project, Amherst and Chgo., 1964-72; dir. research and edn. Newberry Library, Chgo., 1972-83, acad. v.p., 1983—; mem. Ill. Humanities Council., 1980—, chmn., 1982-83; cons. Nat. Endowment Humanities, 1977—; nat. adv. bd. Ctr. Study of So. Culture, U. Miss., 1979—; vis. prof. history and edn. Northwestern U., Evanston, Ill., 1971—. Author: The Hero and the People, 1964, The Missouri Compromise: Political Statesmanship or Unwise Evasion?, 1964; gen. editor: Amherst Project Units in American History, 25 vols., 1964-75. Recipient George Washington Eggleston prize Yale U., 1955; Andrew Mellon post doctoral fellow, 1960-61. Mem. Social Sci. Edn. Consortium (Pres. 1975-77), Orgn. Am. Historians, Am. Hist. Assn. Democrat. Roman Catholic. Home: 880 Lake Shore Dr Apt 16E Chicago IL 60611 Office: The Newberry Library 60 W Walton St Chicago IL 60610

BROWN, RICHARD L., lawyer, association executive; b. N.Y.C., Nov. 9, 1944; s. S. Robert and Frances S. B.; children: Jesselyn Alicia, Justin Alexander, Jeremy Brandon. B.A., Emory U., 1966; J.D., NYU, 1969. Bar: N.Y. 1969, D.C. 1973, U.S. Ct. Appeals (D.C. cir.) 1974, U.S. Ct. of Claims 1980, U.S. Supreme Ct. 1980. Atty., advisor FCC, Washington, 1969-72; assoc. firm Farrow, Cahill, Kaswell & Schildhaus, Washington, 1972-75; sr. ptnr. Brown & Finn, Chartered, Washington, 1975—; gen. counsel Community Antenna TV Assn., 1972-75; pres. Alaskan Cable Network, Inc., Fairbanks, 1980—; v.p., gen. counsel Soc. for Pvt. and Comml. Earth Stas. Author: Low Power TV Handbook, 1981, licensing manual for land mobile radio-TV, 1980. Mem. ABA, Fed. Communications Bar Assn. Office: Brown & Finn 1920 N St NW Suite 510 Washington DC 20036

BROWN, RICHARD LEE, lawyer; b. Ft. Worth, Dec. 7, 1925; s. Marvin H. and Janie (McIntosh) B.; m. Elizabeth McPherson, Nov. 19, 1949; children: Beverly Elizabeth, Leigh Ann. Student, Rice U., 1942-43; LL.B., U. Tex., 1949; LL.M., George Washington U., 1954. Bar: Tex. 1949. Practice law, Ft. Worth, 1956-81, asst. dist. atty., Tarrant County, 1949- 50; spl. atty. Chief Counsel's Office, IRS, Washington, 1953-56; partner Friedman & Brown, 1956-60, Stone, Parker, Snakard & Brown, 1961-66, Law, Snakard, Brown & Gambill, 1967-81, 83—; judge Ct. Appeals Tex. 2d Dist., 1981-83; dir. Riverside State Bank, Ft. Worth, 1967-81, Tex. Security Bancshares, Inc. Former mem. bd. commrs. Pub. Housing Authority Ft. Worth, chmn., 1976-77; Chmn. bd., chmn. competition Van Cliburn Internat. Piano Competition, 1966-69. Served with AUS, 1944-46; Served with U.S. Army, 1950-53. Decorated Bronze Star medal. Fellow Tex. Bar Found. (life); mem. ABA, Tex. Bar Assn., Ft. Worth-Tarrant County Bar Assn. (pres. 1977-78). Office: Texas American Bank Bldg Fort Worth TX 76102

BROWN, RICHARD P., lawyer; b. Phila., Dec. 21, 1920; s. Richard P. and Edith (Gillette) B.; m. Virginia M. Curtin Hanavan, Nov. 12, 1965. A.B., Princeton U., 1942; LL.B., U. Pa., 1948. Bar: Pa. 1949, U.S. Supreme Ct. 1957. Assoc. Morgan, Lewis & Bockius, Phila., 1948-56, ptnr., 1956—; dir. Fidelcor Inc., Fidelity Bank, Phila. Pres. Phila. Council for Internat. Visitors, 1966-67; chmn. World Affairs Council, Phila., 1968-70; mem. council Fgn. Relations, N.Y.C., 1975—; bd. dirs. Internat. Peace Acad., N.Y.C., 1977—, Greater Phila. Partnership, 1968—; bd. overseers U. Pa. Law Sch., 1969—, William Penn Charter Sch., Phila., 1969—; trustee U. Pa., 1979—; bd. mgrs. U. Pa. Mus., 1967-82, St. Christopher's Hosp. for Children, Phila., 1977-80; vice chmn. United Hosp., 1980—; trustee Eisenhower Exchange Fellowships, 1982—. Fellow Am. Coll. Trial Lawyers, Am. Bar Found.; mem. ABA (chmn. sect. internat. law 1975-76), Internat. Bar Assn., Inter-Am. Bar Assn., Phila. Bar Assn., Am. Soc. Internat. Law, Internat. Law Assn. (Am. br.), Order of Coif. Home: 8800 Towanda St Philadelphia PA 19118 Office: Morgan Lewis & Bockius 2100 Fidelity Bldg 123 S Broad St Philadelphia PA 19109

BROWN, RITA MAE, author; b. Hanover, Pa., Nov. 28, 1944. B.A., NYU, 1968; Ph.D., Inst. Policy Studies, 1976. Lectr. Fed. City Coll., 1970-71; mem. faculty Goddard Coll., 1973—; mem. lit. panel Nat. Endowment Arts, 1978-81; Hemingway judge for 1st fiction PEN Internat., 1983. Author: The Hand that Cradles the Rock, 1971, Rubyfruit Jungle, 1973, Songs to a Handsome Woman, 1973, A Plain Brown Rapper, 1976, Six of One, 1978, Southern Discomfort, 1982, Sudden Death, 1983; TV shows I Love Liberty, ABC-TV, 1982. Recipient award Writers Guild Am., 1982. Office: care Julian Bach Lit Agy 747 3d Ave New York NY 10017

BROWN, ROBERT ALAN, construction materials company executive; b. Mt. Vernon, Ill., July 20, 1930; s. Herbert E. and Opal (Clayborn) B.; m. Norma Jean Falz, June 16, 1953; children: Carla, Todd, Scott, David. B.B.A., U. Minn., 1953; postgrad., Harvard U. Bus. Sch., 1971. With Firestone Tire & Rubber Co., 1953-73, plant mgr., Albany, Ga., 1967-73, asst. to v.p., Akron, Ohio, 1973; dir. mfg. Firestone Internat. Co., Akron, 1973-75; exec. v.p. Firestone Can. Ltd., Hamilton, Ont., Can., 1975-78; pres. Carlisle Tire & Rubber Co., Pa., 1978-82, Carlisle Syntec Systems (Pa.), 1982. Served with U.S. Navy, 1948-49. Presbyterian. Home: 1312 Kiner Blvd Carlisle PA 17013 Office: 1285 Ritner Hwy Carlisle PA 17013

BROWN, ROBERT CURTIS, city official; b. Peabody, Kans., Oct. 27, 1920; s. Orville Curtis and Rena Margaret (Runyon) B.; m. Helen Robinson Hale, Aug. 24, 1944; children: Dennis, Carol, Steven. Student public schs., Topeka. Laborer Internat. Harvester, Topeka, Kans., 1939-41, truck salesman, br. mgr., Topeka and Lubbock, Tex., 1945-54; ter. mgr. White Motor Co., Dallas, 1954-56; v.p. to chmn. bd. Wichita (Kans.) White Truck Sales, 1956-78; v.p. Wichita Truck Lease & Fin., 1956-78; pres. Jaybo Leasing, Wichita, 1956-78; city commr., Wichita, 1979-81, 82-83, 83—, mayor, 1981-82. Bd. govs. Kans. League Municipalities. Served with USN, 1941-45; PTO. Mem. Kans. Motor Carriers Assn. (hon., dir., corp. sec.), Kans. League Municipalities, VFW, Am. Legion. Republican. Methodist. Clubs: Masons, Shriners, Lions. Home: 3915 N Charles St Wichita KS 67204 Office: City Hall 455 N Main St Wichita KS 67202

BROWN, ROBERT DELFORD, artist; b. Portland, Colo., Oct. 25, 1930; s. Robert Delford and Faye (Kelly) B.; m. Harriett Rhett Gurney, Mar. 21, 1963. B.A., UCLA, 1952, M.A., 1958. One-man shows Drawings, N.Y.C., 1959-70, Bob Brown and His Friends (photography), 1965-69, Wall Hangings, 1973, Ceramics, 1973, Tinted Photographs, 1973, The Great Building Crackup, 1967; retrospective exhbn., 1958-81, Phyllis Kind Gallery, N.Y.C.; other exhibits Originale, Judson Hall, N.Y.C., 1964, Meat Show, N.Y.C., 1964; Author: Hanging, 1967, First Class Portraits, 1973, Ulysses, An Altered Plagiarism, 1975. Address: 251 W 13th St New York NY 10011 *I want the image to assume primary importance in all my work. Dazzling technique and established procedures are so often used not to enlighten but to obfuscate one's vacuity. The artist's responsibility is to tell the truth as he sees it, not to enhance his own self importance as an expert, thereby perverting his responsibility as a moral force in society.*

BROWN, ROBERT G., business executive, engineer; b. 1923; married. B.S. in Mech. and Indsl. Engring., U. Mich., 1948; M.S. in Auto Engring., Chrysler Inst., 1950. With Chrysler Corp., 1948-53, project engr., 1951-53; with Eaton Corp., 1953-82, mgr. labs., Detroit, 1953-60, asso. dir. engring. and research center, 1960-65, gen. mgr. center, 1965-68, corp. v.p. research and devel., 1968-70, v.p. engring. and research, 1970-74, exec. v.p.-corp. devel., 1974-79, exec. v.p. engring. and corp. devel., 1979-82; vice-chmn., dir. Donn, Inc., 1982—, vice chmn., dir., Westlake, Ohio, 1982—; dir. S-P Mfg. Co., Soc. Nat. Bank of Cleve., Society Corp. Bd. dirs. Boy Scouts Am., Gt. Lakes Shakespeare Festival '81. Mem. Soc. Automotive Engrs., Cleve. Engring. Soc., Nat. Planning Assn., Blue Coats Inc.

BROWN, ROBERT GROVER, engineering educator; b. Shenandoah, Iowa, Apr. 25, 1926; s. Grover Whitney and Irene (Frink) B. B.S., Iowa State Coll., 1948, M.S., 1951, Ph.D., 1956. Instr. Iowa State Coll., Ames, 1948-51, 53-55, asst. prof., 1955-56, assoc. prof., 1956-59, prof., 1959-76, Disting. prof., 1976—; research engr. N. Am. Aviation, Downey, Calif., 1951-53; cons. various aerospace engring. firms., 1956—. Author: (with R.A. Sharpe, W.L. Hughes) Lines, Waves and Antennas, 1961, (with J.W. Nilssm) Linear Systems Analysis, 1962, Random Signal Analysis and Kalman Filtering, 1983. Mem. IEEE, Inst. Navigation (Burka award 1978), Am. Soc. Engring. Edn. Home: Route 1 Skycrest Dr Ames IA 50010 Office: Iowa State U Ames IA 50011

BROWN, ROBERT HALL, JR., textile company executive; b. Boston, Nov. 12, 1931; s. Robert Hall and Laura (Aitken) B.; m. Joyce Hemenway, June 26, 1954; 1 dau., Elesse Throwbridge. B.S.M.E., MIT, 1954. With Belding Heminway Co., N.Y.C., 1954—, div. mgr., 1965-72, v.p., 1972-77, exec. v.p., 1977-79, pres., chief operating officer, 1979—, also dir. Trustee Convent of the Sacred Heart, 1978—. Served with U.S. Army, 1954-56. Mem. The Thread Inst. (dir. 1973—), Sigma Xi, Tau Beta Pi, Pi Tau Sigma. Home: Upland Dr Greenwich CT 06830 Office: Belding Heminway Co 1430 Broadway New York NY 10018 *

BROWN, ROBERT HAROLD, educator, geographer; b. Rochester, N.Y., Sept. 16, 1921; s. Harold Cecil and Marion (Johnson) B.; m. Helene Adeline Zukey, Sept. 1, 1945; children: Suzanne Odette, Kurtis Johnson. B.S., U. Minn., 1948, M.A., 1949; Ph.D., U. Chgo., 1957. Mem. faculty St. Cloud (Minn.) State Coll., 1949-64; prof. geography dept. U. Wyo., 1964—. Author: Political Areal Functional Organization, 1957, (with Phillip Tideman) Atlas of Minnesota Occupancy, 3d edit, 1969, Wyoming Occupance Atlas, 1970, Wyoming: A Geography, 1980. Served to 1st lt. AUS, 1939-45; with USAF, 1951-52. Mem. Assn. Am. Geographers. Home: 1250 Frontera Dr Laramie WY 82070

BROWN, ROBERT HORATIO, ret. orthopedic surgeon; b. Dedham, Mass., Aug. 30, 1917; s. Walter Horatio and Harriet (Crocker) B.; m. Virginia Fales Lane, Dec. 26, 1943; children—Edith Persis, Robert Horatio, Betsy. B.S., Tufts U., 1940; M.D., Harvard, 1943. Diplomate: Am. Bd. Orthopedic Surgery. Intern, surg. resident Mass. Gen. Hosp., 1944-45; surg. resident Cushing VA Hosp., 1946-47; orthopedic resident USN, Duke, 1952-56; commd. lt. (j.g.) USN, 1945; ret., 1946; commd. lt. USN, 1950, advanced through grades to capt., 1959; chief orthopedic service U.S. Naval Hosp., Nat. Naval Med. Center, Bethesda, Md., 1964-70; gen. practice medicine, Sharon, Mass., 1947-50; course dir. orthopedic pathology Armed Forces Inst. Pathology, 1963-64; asst. clin. prof. orthopaedic surgery George Washington U. Sch. Medicine, 1968-70; courtesy staff Eastern Maine Med. Center, 1970—; cons. rehab. service, 1971—; Navy liaison mem. musculoskeletal com. NRC, 1965-70; surg. study group B. NIH, 1968-70. Fellow A.C.S.; mem. AMA, Mass. Med. Soc., Am. Acad. Orthopedic Surgeons, Soc. Med. Cons. to Armed Forces, Maine Med. Assn., Phi Beta Kappa. Home: 23 Stoneybrook Rd Hampden ME 04444

BROWN, ROBERT JOSEPH, govt. ofcl.; b. Seattle, Sept. 10, 1929; s. George Robert and Eileen (Bagley) B.; m. Iolene Cecilia Gau, June 24, 1950; children—Mary, Joseph, Timothy, Patrick, Barbara, Susan, Thomas, Brenda. A.A., U. Minn., 1951. Personnel officer State of Minn., St. Paul, 1955-62, dep. commr. conservation, 1962-64, commr. employment security, 1964-66; asst. manpower adminstr. U.S. Dept. Labor, Washington, 1966-69; asso. manpower adminstr. and dir. U.S. Tng. and Employment Service, 1969-72; asso. adminstr. Manpower Adminstrn. and dir. U.S. Employment Service, 1972-74; Denver regional adminstr. Employment and Tng. Adminstrn., 1974-77, under sec., 1977-79; mem. Nat. Mediation Bd., Washington, 1979—, chmn., 1981—. Roman Catholic. Office: Nat Mediation Bd 1425 K St NW Washington DC 20572

BROWN, ROBERT LAWRENCE, news correspondent; b. Tulsa, June 29, 1944; s. Frank Eugene and Mary Lois (Knie) B.; m. Nancy A. Gillota, Oct. 1982; 1 son, Kevin Eliot. Student, Carnegie Inst. Tech., 1962-63; B.S. in Journalism, U. Tulsa, 1968. News reporter Radio Sta. KRMG, Tulsa, 1960-61, Radio Sta. KAKC, 1961-62, KOTV-TV, 1964-68, 70-73; news anchorman KHOU-TV, Houston, 1973-75; news anchorman, producer WFAA-TV, Dallas, 1975-77; news corr. ABC-TV Network, N.Y.C., 1977—; now corr. 20/20 News Mag.; tchr. journalism and cinematography U. Tulsa, 1972, 73. (Emmy awards Nat. Acad. TV Arts and Scis. 1980, 82); Author: China and the World, 1973, U.S. History, Vol. V, 1973; Columnist: TV Guide Newswatch, 1977. Served with U.S. Army, 1968-70. Decorated Army Commendation medal; recipient Disting. Service award U. Tulsa, Coll. Arts and Scis., 1980. Mem. Am. Film Inst., AFTRA, Nat. Acad. TV Arts and Scis. Episcopalian. Office: ABC News 7 W 66th St New York NY 10023 *Time spent on the road is a search for lost corners hidden by franchise signs and the intransigent sentinels of American identity.*

BROWN, ROBERT LEE, physician, educator; b. Franklin, Pa., Feb. 26, 1908; s. Robert E. and Amy (Lee) B.; m. Alice Johnston, Sept. 26, 1940; children—David W., Jean A., Anne K. A.B., U. Mich., 1929; M.D., Harvard, 1933. Diplomate: Am. Bd. Surgery. Clin. fellow, resident surgeon Meml. Hosp., N.Y.C., 1935-38; instr. surgery U. Rochester Sch. Medicine, 1939-42, asso. surgery, 1947-52, Emory U. Sch. Medicine, Atlanta, 1952-54, asst. prof., 1954-57, asso. prof., 1957-66, prof., 1966-76, prof. emeritus, 1976—; dir. Robert Winship Clinic, Emory U., 1958-66, Emory U. Clinic, 1966-76; med. dir. Ga. Cancer Mgmt. Network, 1976-80; oncology cons. State of Ga. Dept. Human Resources, 1977—; med. dir. Wesley Homes, 1977—. Fellow A.C.S.; mem. AMA, Am. Cancer Soc. (exec. bd. Ga., nat. dir.), Am. Radium Soc., Soc. Surg. Oncology, Ga. Med. Assn., Med. Assn. Atlanta. Presbyterian. Home: 321 Robin Hood Rd NE Atlanta GA 30309

BROWN, ROBERT LYLE, foreign affairs consultant; b. Dayton, Ohio, July 21, 1920; s. Joseph Sebastian and Elsie Lenore (Miller) B.; m. Marion Jean Jenkin, Nov. 14, 1947; 1 son, Garry Lyle. A.B., Syracuse U., 1943; postgrad., Northwestern U., 1950-51, George Washington U., 1963-65. With Evered, Inc., Camden, N.J., 1943-44; officer-in-charge consulate, Noumea, 1944-48, vice consul, chief econ. sect., consulate gen., Casablanca, 1948-50, vice consul, chief econ. sect., Kobe, Osaka, 1951-54, consul, 2d sec., chief econ. sect., asst. comml. attache embassy, Brussels, 1954-58; alt. U.S. observer Customs Coop. Council, 1954, chief loan coordination br. econ. devel. div., 1959-62; dep. U.S. rep. Tripartite Gold Commn., Belgium; adviser U.S. dels. com. trade, com. industry and natural resources UN Econ. Commn. Asia and Far East, 18th Session, Bangkok; adviser U.S. del. Econ. Commn. Asia and Far East, Tokyo, 1962; assigned Sr. Seminar in Fgn. Policy, 1962; in charge European personnel ops., 1963-65; counselor econ. affairs Am. embassy, Taipei, Taiwan, 1965-68, also acting AID rep.; dep. exec. sec. to sec. State, 1968-71; dep. dir. Office Personnel Dept. State, 1972-75; minister-counselor, polit. adviser to Supreme Allied Comdr. Europe, 1975-79; sr. insp. Fgn. Service, 1979-80; insp. gen. Fgn. Service, Dept. of State, 1981-83; assoc. Office of Gen. Alexander Haig Hudson Inst., 1983—; cons. Betac Corp., Washington, Mgmt. Logistics Internat.; adviser U.S. del. 24th Gen. Assembly UN, 1969; spl. asst. to sec. State for UN 25th Anniversary, 1970; observer N. Atlantic Assembly, 1976-79, Western European Union, 1979; mem. Pres.'s Council on Integrity and Efficiency, 1981. Coordinator Dept. State United Givers Fund campaign, 1960; bd. dirs. Internat. Sch., Brussels, Fulbright Com., Republic of China, 1965-68. Served with USNR, 1943. Mem. U.S., Washington fgn. service assns., Delta Sigma Rho. Address: 3021 N Peary St Arlington VA 22207

BROWN, ROBERT MCAFEE, clergyman, educator; b. Carthage, Ill., May 28, 1920; s. George William and Ruth Myrtle (McAfee) B.; m. Sydney Thomson Brown, June 21, 1944; children: Peter Thomson, Mark McAfee, Alison McAfee, Thomas Seabury. B.A., Amherst Coll., 1943, D.D., 1958; M. Div., Union Theol. Sem., N.Y.C., 1945; Ph.D., Columbia, 1951; postgrad., Mansfield Coll., Oxford (Eng.) U., 1949-50, St. Mary's Coll., 1959, St. Andrews (Scotland) U., 1959-60; Litt.D., U. San Francisco, 1964; L.H.D., Lewis and Clark Coll., 1964, St. Louis U., 1966, Hebrew Union Coll., 1982; LL.D., U. Notre Dame, 1965, Loyola U., 1963, Boston Coll., 1965, St. Mary's Coll., 1968; D.D., Hamilton Coll., 1968, Pacific Sch. Religion, 1967, Kalamazoo Coll., 1980. Ordained to ministry Presbyn. Ch., 1944; asst. chaplain Amherst Coll., 1946-48; prof. religion, chmn. dept. Macalester Coll., St. Paul, 1951-53; faculty Union Theol. Sem., N.Y.C., 1953-62, prof. ecumenics and world Christianity, 1976-79; prof. religion Stanford U., 1962-76; prof. theology and ethics Pacific Sch. Religion, Berkeley, 1979—. Author: P.T. Forsyth: Prophet for Today, 1952, The Bible Speaks to You, 1955, The Significance of the Church, 1956, (with Gustave Weigel) An American Dialogue, 1960, The Spirit of Protestantism, 1961, Observer in Rome: A Protestant Report on the Vatican Council, 1964, The Collected Writings of St. Hereticus, 1964, The Ecumenical Revolution, 1967, Vietnam: Crisis of Conscience, 1967, The Pseudonyms of God, 1972, Religion and Violence, 1973, Frontiers for the Church Today, 1973, Is Faith Obsolete?, 1974, Theology in a New Key: Responding to Liberation Themes, 1978, The Hereticus Papers, 1979, Creative Dislocation—The Movement of Grace, 1980, Gustavo Gutierrez, 1980, Making Peace in the Global Village, 1981, Elie Wiesel: Messenger to all Humanity, 1983; gen. editor: The Layman's Theological Library, 12 volumes, 1956-58; Translator: (deDietrich): God's Unfolding Purpose, 1960; (Casalis), Portrait of Karl Barth, 1963; (Dumas), Dietrich Bonhoeffer: Theologian of Reality, 1971; Editor: (with David Scott) The Challenge to Reunion, 1963; Contbr. books; mem. editorial bd. various mags. and jours. Served as chaplain USNR, 1945-46. Mem. Am. Theol. Soc., Soc. Theol. Discussion, Phi Beta Kappa. Home: 2090 Columbia Ave Palo Alto CA 94306

BROWN, ROBERT MINGE, lawyer; b. Mobile, Oct. 16, 1911; s. Collier Harrison Minge, Jr. and Madie (Diggett) B.; m. Gloria Frances Gillingham, May 29, 1935; children: Douglas Minge, Harrison Minge. A.B., Stanford U., 1931; B.C.L. (Rhodes scholar), Oriel Coll., Oxford (Eng.) U., 1934. Bar: Calif. bar 1935. Since practiced in, San Francisco; ptnr. firm McCutchen, Doyle, Brown & Enersen (and predecessors), 1946—; Chmn. bd. Calif. Water Service Co., 1961-81. Dir. San Jose Water Works, Hewlett-Packard Co., Greyhound Corp.; Trustee Stanford U., pres., 1971-76. Served with USNR, 1942-46. Fellow Am. Acad. Arts and Scis.; mem. Am., Calif., San Francisco bar assns., Phi Beta Kappa. Clubs: Bohemian, Pacific-Union (San Francisco); Burlingame (Calif.) Country. Home: 943 Hayne Rd Hillsborough CA 94010 Office: 3 Embarcadero Center San Francisco CA 94111

BROWN, ROBERT TAYLOR, oil company executive; b. Brantford, Ont., Can. B.A. in Bus. Adminstrn. with honors, U. Western Ont., 1948. Coordinator advt. and merchandising Gulf Can., Toronto, 1966-67, dir. corp. advt., 1967-71, v.p. mktg., 1971-75, v.p. planning and control, 1975-77; v.p. corp. planning Gulf Oil Corp., Pitts., 1977-81; pres. Gulf Can. Products Co., Toronto, 1981—; dir. Inter-provincial Pipeline. Clubs: Granite, National (Toronto). Office: Gulf Can Products Co 800 Bay St Toronto ON Canada M5S 1Y8

BROWN, ROBERT UTTING, editor; b. Yonkers, N.Y., Oct. 20, 1912; s. James Wright and Sarah A. (Wilson) B.; m. Susan C. Steele, May 21, 1938; children: Robin (Mrs. Richard M. Woods), Elizabeth

(Mrs. W.I. Phillips, Jr.). B.A., Dartmouth Coll., 1934; student, Empire State Sch. Printing, Ithaca, N.Y., 1935. Reporter Trenton (N.J.) Times, 1935; reporter United Press, Phila., 1935; reporter, apprentice editorial writer Auburn (N.Y.) Citizen-Advertiser, 1935-36; reporter Editor & Pub., N.Y.C., 1936-39, news editor, 1939-47, mng. editor, 1942-43, exec. editor, 1943-44, editor, 1944—, dir., sec., 1940—, v.p., editor, 1947-52, pres., 1952—, pub., 1958—. Mem. Inter-Am. Press Assn. (chmn. exec. com. 1963-69, pres. 1976-77), Am. Soc. Newspaper Editors, Sigma Delta Chi (pres. 1953-54). Presbyterian. Clubs: Nat. Press (Washington); N.Y. Athletic, Union League, Dutch Treat, Bohemian (N.Y.C.). Office: Editor & Publisher 575 Lexington Ave New York NY 10022 *

BROWN, ROBERT WALLACE, mathematics educator; b. Portland, Oreg., May 20, 1925; s. Bert and Stella (Conway) B.; m. Doris Arrilda Burroughs, Sept. 4, 1948; children: Robert Wallace, Janice Dianne. B.S., Pacific U., 1950; M.S., Oreg. State U., 1952, Ph.D., 1958. Mathematician, Nat. Bur. Standards, Corona, Calif., 1952-54; Mathematician Boeing Co., Seattle, 1958-66; vis. asso. prof. Oreg. State U., Corvallis, 1966-67; prof. math. U. Alaska, Fairbanks, 1967-82, head dept., 1967-77, 79-82; vis. prof. math. Lewis and Clark Coll., Portland, Oreg., 1982—. Contbg. author: Error in Digital Computation, 1965. Served with USNR, 1942-45. Mem. Math. Assn. Am., Am. Math Soc., AAAS, Sigma Xi, Pi Mu Epsilon, Sigma Pi Sigma. Home: 20755 SW Prindle Rd Tualatin OR 97062 Office: LC Box 114 Lewis and Clark College Portland OR 97219

BROWN, ROBERT WALLACE, banker; b. Los Angeles, Feb. 27, 1925; s. Atlas M. and Gladys (Brewster) B.; m. Jacqueline Dee, Jan. 18, 1947; children: David, Christopher. B.S. in Finance, U. So. Calif., 1948. Examiner FDIC, 1948-51; comml. loan officer Wells Fargo Bank, 1951-56; v.p. United Calif. Bank, Los Angeles, 1956-61; pres. Robert W. Brown & Assocs., Los Angeles, 1961-63, Bank of Los Angeles, 1963-66; exec. v.p. First Western Bank (became Lloyds Bank Calif. 1974), Los Angeles, 1966-72, pres., chief adminstrv. officer, dir., mem. exec. com., 1974—; exec. v.p., mem. exec. com. Union Bank, 1972-74; dir. Farmers Group, Inc. Mem. Am., Calif. bankers assns., Assn. Res. City Bankers, Los Angeles C. of C. Clubs: California (Los Angeles); Oakmont Country (Glendale). Office: 612 S Flower St Los Angeles CA 90017 *

BROWN, ROBERT WAYNE, physician; b. Atwood, Kans., June 27, 1923; s. Paul D. and Florence (Sawer) B.; m. Julia L. Potochnick, Dec. 15, 1945; children—Sandra S., Craig. B.A., U. Colo., 1949; M.D., Kans. U., 1955. Intern Kans. U. Med. Center, 1955-56, resident, 1956-59; practice medicine specializing in internal medicine, Kansas City, Kans., 1959—; mem. faculty Kans. U., 1959-61; chief med. service Kansas City (Kans.) VA Hosp., 1961-64, cons., 1964—; asst. prof. endocrinology and metabolism Kans. U. Med. Center, 1965-68, prof. internal medicine, 1969—; dir. Kans. Regional Med. Program, Kansas City, 1968-76, Salina Health Edn. Found.; program dir. Salina Family Practice Residency Program, 1977—; cons. USAF. Served to 1st lt. USAAF, 1943-46. Fellow A.C.P.; mem. Am. Pub. Health Assn., Am. Fedn. Clin. Research, Phi Beta Pi, Alpha Omega Alpha. Home: 910 Marymount Rd Salina KS 67401 Office: PO Box 1747 Salina KS 67401

BROWN, ROBERT WELLS, marketing counsel; b. Newton, Mass., Aug. 9, 1921; s. John Franklin and Gladys Brigham (Lobdell) B.; m. Louise Blair Stewart, Feb. 2, 1944; children—Stewart Jason, Margaret Wells, John Franklin III. B.A. in Internat. Relations, Yale, 1944. With Compton Advt., Inc., N.Y.C., 1958-74, sr. v.p. mgmt., 1969-74; prin. Wells Brown Assos. (bus. counselling and tax analysis for small bus.), Dorset, Vt., 1974—. Served with USNR, World War II. Decorated Purple Heart. Mem. St. Andrew's Soc., Alpha Sigma Phi. Republican. Presbyterian. Home and office: RFD 1 Dorset VT 05251

BROWN, (ROBERT) WENDELL, lawyer; b. Mpls., Feb. 26, 1902; s. Robert and Jane Amanda (Anderson) B.; m. Barbara Ann Fisher, Oct. 20, 1934; children: Barbara Ann (Mrs. Neil Maurice Travis), Mary Alice (Mrs. Alfred Lee Fletcher). A.B., U. Hawaii, 1924; J.D., U. Mich., 1926. Bar: Mich. 1926, Supreme Ct. Mich 1934, U.S. Supreme Ct 1934, 6th U.S. Circuit Ct. of Appeals 1952, U.S. Dist. Ct (ea. dist.) Mich. 1927, U.S. Dist. Ct. (we. dist.) Mich. 1931, U.S. Bd. Immigration Appeals 1944, U.S. Tax Ct 1973. Lawyer firm Routier, Nichols & Fildew, Detroit, 1926, Nichols & Fildew, 1927-28, Frank C. Sibley, 1929, Ferguson & Ferguson, 1929-31; asst. atty. gen., Mich., 1931-32; with legal dept. Union Guardian Trust Co., Detroit, 1933-34; sole practice law, Detroit, 1934-81, Farmington Hills, Mich., 1981—; Legal adviser Wayne County (Mich.) Graft Grand Jury, 1939-40; asst. pros. atty. civil matters Wayne County, 1940; spl. asst. city atty. to investigate Police Dept., Highland Park, Mich., 1951-52. Chmn. citizens com. to form Oakland County (Mich.) Community Coll., 1962-63; Pres. Farmington (Mich.) Sch. Bd., 1952-56; chmn. Oakland County Republican County Conv., 1952; trustee Farmington Twp., Oakland County, 1957-61; pres. Oakland County Lincoln Rep. Club, 1958; Treas., bd. dirs. Friends of Detroit Library, 1943-44; bd. dirs. Farmington Friends of Library, Inc., 1952-58, pres., 1956-57; Hon. mem. Farmington Hist. Soc., 1966, St. Anthonys Guild, Franciscan Friars, 1975. Mem. Am. Bar Assn., Detroit Bar Assn. (dir. 1939-49, treas. 1942-44, sec. 1944-46, 2d v.p. 1947-48, 1st v.p. 1947-48, pres. 1948-49, chmn. or mem. various coms. 1935-52, 77-82), State Bar Mich. (chmn. or mem. various coms. 1935-52, 77-80), Oakland County Bar Assn. Presbyn. (elder). Home: 29921 Ardmore St Farmington Hills MI 48018 Office: Quakertown Plaza 32969 Hamilton Ct Suite 115 Farmington Hills MI 48018

BROWN, ROGER OSCAR, securities firm exec.; b. Chgo., Dec. 22, 1925; s. Isidore and Gladys (Jordan) B.; m. Barbara E. Russell, May 16, 1953; children—Jeffrey R., Owen S., Andrew W., Henry G., Vanessa J. Grad., Phillips Exeter Acad., 1943; B.S., Yale, 1946; M.B.A., Harvard, 1949. With A.G. Becker & Co., Chgo., 1949—, sr. v.p., dir., 1969-73; with The Harris Group Inc., 1974-76; pres. Harris Assos. Inc., 1976—; dir. United Communications Corp., Kenosha News, Attleboro (Mass.) Sun-Chronicle. Mem. alumni council Phillips Exeter Acad., Exeter, N.H.; mem. citizens com. U. Chgo.; mem. Assos. Northwestern U.; bd. dirs. I & G Charitable Found.; pres., bd. dirs. Thresholds. Served with USNR, 1943-46. Jewish. Clubs: Standard, Mid-Day, Bond of Chicago, Northmoor Country. Home: 1261 Clavey Rd Highland Park IL 60035 Office: 120 S LaSalle St Chicago IL 60603

BROWN, ROGER WILLIAM, psychologist, educator; b. Detroit, Apr. 14, 1925; s. Frank Herbert and Muriel Louise (Graham) B. A.B., U. Mich., 1948, Ph.D., 1952; M.A. (hon.), Harvard, 1962, D. Univ., U. York, Eng.; D.Sc., Bucknell U., 1980; D.Sci., Northwestern U., 1983. Asst. prof. psychology Harvard, Cambridge, Mass., 1952-57, prof. social psychology, 1962—, John Lindsley prof. psychology in memory William James, 1974—, chmn. dept. social relations, 1967-70; asso. prof. psychology Mass. Inst. Tech., Cambridge, 1957-61, prof. social psychology, 1961-62; Chmn. behavioral scis. study sect. NIH, 1961-63. Author: Words and Things, 1958, (with others) New Directions in Psychology, 1962, The Acquisition of Language, 1964, Social Psychology, 1965, Psycholinguistics, 1970, A First Language, 1973, (with R. Herrnstein) Psychology, 1975. Recipient Distinguished Research award Nat. Council Tchrs. English, 1974. Mem. Am. (Distinguished Sci. Contbn. award 1971, G. Stanley Hall award), New Eng. Psychol. Assn. (pres. 1965-66), Eastern Psychol. Assn. (pres. 1971-72), Linguistic Soc. Am., Am. Acad. Arts and Scis., Nat. Acad. Scis. Home: 100 Memorial Dr Cambridge MA 02142

BROWN, RONALD, banker; b. Brownwood, Tex., Jan. 18, 1933; s. Steve Edward and Sarah Helen (Davenport) B.; m. Elizabeth Rorah; children: James Edward, David Martin. B.A., Baylor U., 1954; grad., Southwestern Grad. Sch. Banking, 1966. With Republic Nat. Bank of Dallas, 1959-75, sr. v.p., gen. mgr., London, Eng., 1970-75; pres. Houston Nat. Bank, 1975—, chmn. bd., chief exec. officer, 1976—; mng. dir. Republic Bank Corp., 1982—; dir. Asso. Credit Services, Inc. Bd. dirs. St. Joseph Hosp. Found., Houston Grand Opera Assn., Alley Theatre. Served with USNR, 1956-69. Mem. Assn. Res. City Bankers, Am. Inst. Bankers, Am. Bankers Assn., Houston Clearing House Assn. (dir.), Japan-Tex. Assn., Houston C. of C. (dir.). Methodist. Clubs: River Oaks Country, Univ. (Houston); Wentworth Golf, Virginia Water (Surrey, Eng.); Royal and Ancient Golf (Scotland). Office: 1010 Milam St PO Box 299001 Houston TX 77299

BROWN, ROSCOE CONKLING, JR., coll. pres.; b. Washington, Mar. 9, 1922; s. Roscoe Conkling and Vivian Jeanette (Kemp) B.; children—Doris Brown Bodine, Diane Brown Ransom, Dennis, Donald. B.S. with Highest Praise, Springfield Coll., 1943; M.A., N.Y. U., 1949, Ph.D., 1951. Social investigator N.Y.C. Dept. Welfare, 1946; instr. phys. edn. W.Va. State Coll., Institute, 1946-48; research asst. N.Y. U., 1949-51, instr. edn., 1951-53, asst. prof., 1953-56, asso. prof., 1956-60, prof., 1960-69; dir. Inst. Afro-Am. Affairs, 1969-77; pres. Bronx Community Coll., 1977—; cons. USPHS, U.S. Office Edn., N.Y. State Dept. Edn., Ednl. Testing Service, Nat. YMCA, Boys' Clubs Am. (Emmy award for Black Arts 1973); Author: (with H. Ploski) Negro Almanac, 1967, Classical Studies in Physical Activity, 1968, New Perspectives of Man in Action, 1969, The Black Experience, 1972, Black Culture Quiz, 1971, 73, 78; contbr.: articles to profl. jours. Black Culture Quiz. Former chmn. examining bd. Manhattan and Bronx Surface Transit Operating Authority, N.Y.C.; bd. dirs. Am. Jour. Nursing, Boys' Clubs Am., Negro Ensemble Co., Sickle Cell Center for Research, Inc.; chmn. bd. dirs. Sports Found., N.Y.C.; chmn. N.Y.C. Employment and Tng. Council; bd. advs. WNET-PBS; v.p., bd. dirs. One Hundred Black Men. Served with USAAF, 1943-45. Decorated D.F.C., Air medal with 8 oak leaf clusters.; Rosenwald fellow, 1948; recipient Honor award Eastern Dist. A.A.H.P.E.R., 1971, Distinguished Alumnus award Springfield Coll., 1973; Rev. Martin Luther King, Jr. award JFK Library for Minorities, 1974; Nat. Honor award AAHPER, 1975; Distinguished Alumnus award N.Y. U. Sch. Edn., 1975. Mem. Am. Edn. Research Assn., AAHPER, AAUP (pres. N.Y. U. chpt. 1967-69), Ednl. Research Assn. N.Y. (pres. 1968-69), AAAS, N.Y. State Black Studies Conf. (pres. 1976—), N.A.A.C.P. Home: 20 Commerce St New York NY 10014 Office: Bronx Community Coll 181st St at University Ave Bronx NY 10453

BROWN, ROWINE HAYES, physician; b. Harvey, Ill., Feb. 15, 1913; d. Robert and Nancy Detrich (Steel) Hayes; m. William Lee Brown, Jr., June 12, 1943 (dec. July 1952). Grad., Thornton Jr. Coll., 1931; student, Stanford U., 1931-32; B.S., M.D., U. Ill., 1938, D.Sc. (hon.), 1975; J.D., Chgo. Kent Coll. Law, 1961. Intern Ill. Research and Ednl. Hosp., Chgo., 1938-39; resident Children's Meml. Hosp., Chgo., 1940-43; asst. med. supt. Mcpl. Contagious Disease Hosp., Chgo., 1944-49, Cook County Hosp., 1950-65, asso. dir. pediatrics, 1965-73, acting dir. pediatrics, 1973, med. dir., 1973—; clin. prof. pediatrics U. Ill., from 1973; now emeritus clin. prof.; adj. prof. law Chgo. Kent Coll. Law, 1972—; Med. dir., sec. bd. Chgo. Foundling Home. Contbr. articles to profl. jours. Bd. dirs. Women's Share Pub. Service, Paxton Arms Corp., Met. YWCA of Chgo. Mem. A.M.A., Chgo. Med. Soc., Chgo. Pediatric Soc., Ill., Chgo. bar assns., Women's Bar Assn. Ill. (pres. 1975—), Am. Acad. Pediatrics, Am. Coll. Law and Medicine, U. Ill. Alumni Assn. (dir. 1979—), Chgo. Kent Coll. Law Alumni Assn. (1st v.p. bd. dir., pres. 1979—), 600 Club Presbyn.-St. Lukes Hosp. Home: 1700 E 56th St Chicago IL 60637 Office: 1835 W Harrison St Chicago IL 60612

BROWN, ROWLAND CHAUNCEY WIDRIG, information systems executive; b. Detroit, Oct. 11, 1923; s. Rowland Chauncey and Rhea (Widrig) B.; m. Kathleen Heather Sayre, May 18, 1946; children: Stephanie Anne, Geoffrey Rowland Sayre, Kathleen Heather. B.S. cum laude, Harvard U., 1947, LL.B., 1950; sr. mgmt., Sloan Sch., MIT, 1969. Bar: D.C. 1951. Counsel Econ. Stablzn. Agy., 1950-52; staff counsel SBA, 1954; counsel Machinery and Allied Products Inst., Washington, 1955-59; with Dorr Oliver, Stanford, Conn., 1959-70, pres., 1968-70; pres., chief exec. officer Buckeye Internat., Inc., Columbus, Ohio, 1970-80, OCLC, Columbus, 1980—; dir. Midland Mut. Life Ins., Matryx Corp. Bd. dirs. Citizens' Council for Ohio Schs.; chmn. Columbus Assn. Performing Arts, Ctr. Pub. Edn., Columbus Urban League, Columbus Area Leadership Lab., Women's Center; bd. dirs. Ohio Dominican Coll. Served to maj. USMCR, 1942-46, 51-53. Decorated Air medal (3), Purple Heart; Korean Republic citation. Mem. Am., Fed., Inter-Am. bar assns., Columbus C. of C. (trustee). Clubs: Harvard (N.Y.C. and Central Ohio); Columbus, Rotary, Sciota Country, Hoover Yacht, Torch (Columbus). Home: 2711 Edington Rd Upper Arlington OH 43221 Office: 6725 Frantz Rd Dublin OH 43017

BROWN, SAMUEL JESSEE, oilfield service co. exec.; b. Bartlesville, Okla., Oct. 3, 1917; s. Homer Daniel and Emma Almeta (Ratley) B.; m. Martha Lou Gillis, June 1, 1942; 1 dau., Martha Gail. B.S., U. Tulsa, 1946; M.B.A., Stanford U., 1958; postgrad., U. Tex. Vice pres. Cornell's of Calif., 1948-51; former asso. prof. U. Tex., U. Tulsa; v.p. Helmerich & Payne Drilling Inc., 1955-73; sr. v.p. Tesoro Land & Marine Co., 1973-76; pres. N.L. Acme Tool Co., 1976-80, Sunstone Corp., Conroe, Tex., 1980—; dir. Mid Am. Life Ins. Co., 1956-58, IADC Corp., 1956-73; asso. partner Springfield Cons., 1954-55. Served as officer USAAF, 1941-45. Decorated D.S.C., Silver Star, D.F.C. (2), Air medal (22); Croix de Guerre with palm, France). Mem. Assn. Oilwell Service Contractors, Petroleum Equipment Suppliers Assn., Internat. Assn. Drilling Contractors, Am. Petroleum Inst., Air Force Aces Assn., Combat Pilots Assn. Republican. Methodist. Clubs: Petroleum (Tulsa); Dallas Petroleum, Oakhills Country, River Plantation Country. *

BROWN, SAMUEL PRESTON, consulting engineer, industrial consultant; b. Orange, N.J., May 16, 1913; s. Samuel Percy and Elizabeth (Sloan) B.; m. Helen Marie Cook, Oct. 27, 1934 (dec. Nov. 1976); children: Donald Kendrick, Joan Catherine; m. Harriet Runcie Hartz, Feb. 20, 1977 (dec. Apr. 1978); m. Natalie Earl Humphrey, Jan. 7, 1979; children—Donald Kendrick, Joan Catherine. B.S., Mass. Inst. Tech., 1935. Cons. engr. Research Corp., N.Y.C., 1936-38; sales engr. Delehanty Inst. and Def. Mfg. Co., N.Y.C., 1938-41; with Coverdale & Colpitts (cons. engrs.), N.Y.C., 1945-75, partner, 1952-75; chmn. bd. Coverdale & Colpitts, Inc., 1970-75; dir., mem. exec. com. Bklyn. Union Gas Co.; dir. Catawba Newsprint Co., S.C. Sr. mem. The Conf. Bd. Served to maj. USAAF, 1942-45. Decorated Legion of Merit. Fellow Am. Cons. Engrs. Coucil; mem. ASME, Theta Delta Chi. Clubs: Burnt Store Golf (Punta Gorda, Fla.); Pocono Manor (Pa.); Canoe Brook Country (Summit, N.J.). Home: 601 Shreve St PO Box 77 Punta Gorda FL 33951 *Do not send your children to religious services, but take them with you on a regular basis. Then show your children, and your social and business contemporaries, an example of uncompromising honesty, fairness and observance of the Golden Rule. This simple formula gives one the power to conquer adversity and be truly content.*

BROWN, SEYMOUR R., lawyer; b. Cleve., Oct. 24, 1924; s. Leonard and Ella (Rubinstein) B.; m. Madeline Kusevich, July 8, 1956; children: Frederic M., Thomas R., Barbara L. N. B.A., Case-Western Res. U., 1948; J.D., Cleve. State U., 1953. Bar: Ohio 1953. Partner firm Brown & Assocs., Cleve.; pres. Carnegie Fin. Corp., Cleve., 1961—; dir. numerous small Ohio cos.; spl. counsel to atty. gen. State of Ohio, 1963-70. Editor, pub.: Gt. Lakes Architecture, 1955-59. Chmn. CSC, University Heights, Ohio; mem. exec. com. Cuyahoga County Republican Orgn., 1966—. Served with AUS, 1943-45. Decorated Purple Heart, Bronze Star. Mem. Am. Bar Assn., Am. Arbitration Assn., Zeta Beta Tau (nat. dir., nat. pres. 1978-80). Club: Mason. Home: 3718 Meadowbrook Blvd University Heights OH 44118 Office: 1501 Euclid Ave Cleveland OH 44115 *Dedication to family, community, profession, and friends, and a willingness to be of help and assistance in the lives of others motivates me, and has contributed to whatever success I have attained in business, professional, and community life. I believe that way to lead is to participate actively in any undertaking together with others involved. If anything I am an activist, moving as vigorously as I am able to accomplish a result.*

BROWN, SEYMOUR WILLIAM, consulting engineer; b. N.Y.C., Nov. 1, 1914; s. Davis and Fannie (Buckler) B.; m. Ruth Bushell, Dec. 6, 1941; 1 dau., Barbara Diane. B.M.E., Coll. City N.Y., 1937. Registered profl. engr., N.Y., N.J., Pa., Conn. Chief engr., then acting mgr. marine dept. Carrier Corp., 1937-55; prin., partner S.W. Brown & Assos. (cons. engrs.), N.Y.C., 1955—; pres., dir. Draftech Corp., N.Y.C., 1967-69, Michael Baker, Jr. N.Y., Inc., 1971-79, chmn. bd., 1980-82; pres. Seymour W. Brown & Assocs., 1982—. Contbr. profl. publs. Adv. council Nat. Energy Found., 1976—; Mem. Community Planning Bd. 14, Riverdale, N.Y., 1964-68, Community Planning Bd. 6, N.Y.C., 1969-71; bd. dirs. City Coll. Fund of City Coll. N.Y., 1967—; dean's adv. council U. Miami. Served with U.S. Army Res., 1935-42. Recipient 125th Anniversary award City Coll. N.Y., 1973. Fellow Am. Soc. Heating, Refrigerating and Air Conditioning Engrs. (past pres. N.Y. chpt., Distinguished Service award 1963), Am. Con. Engrs. Council (award engring. excellence 1967), N.Y. Acad. Scis., Am. Soc. Mil. Engrs. (post pres. 1976-77); mem. Assn. Energy Engrs., Am. Soc. Naval Engrs., Soc. Naval Architects and Marine Engrs., Nat., N.Y. State socs. profl. engrs., N.Y. Bldg. Congress (bd. govs., chmn. ad hoc com. energy 1976), Engrs. Joint Council, ASME, Internat. Dist. Heating Assn., Newcomen Soc. N.Am., Engring. and Architecture Alumni Assn. City Coll. N.Y. (pres. 1967-69), Alumni Assn. City Coll. N.Y. (dir. 1965—, Service medal 1969, Career Achievement award 1980). Clubs: Alpine (N.J.) Country, 100 (pres. 1975-77). Patentee in field. Home: 420 E 51st St New York NY 10022 Office: 866 UN Plaza New York NY 10017

BROWN, SEYOM, international relations educator, government consultant; b. Hightstown, N.J., May 28, 1933; s. Benjamin I. and Sarah E. (Sokolow) B.; m. Martha Jane Morelock, Jan. 16, 1976; children: Matthew, Jeremiah; m. Rose Samuels, Feb. 10, 1963 (dec. Aug. 1974); children: Lisa, Steven, Elliot, Nell, Benjamin. B.A., U. So. Calif., 1955, M.A., 1957; Ph.D., U. Chgo., 1963. Social scientist Rand Corp., Santa Monica, Calif., 1962-69; sr. fellow Brookings Instn., Washington, 1969-76; program dir. Carnegie Endowment, Washington, 1976-78; vis. prof. Harvard U., summers 1979-83; acting dir. Univ. Consortium for Research on N. Am., Harvard U., 1983-84; cons. Dept. Def., Dept. State, Washington, 1967-68. Author: New Forces in World Politics, 1974, The Crises of Power, 1979, The Faces of Power, 1983. Mem. Internat. Studies Assn. (Harold and Margaret Sprout award 1980), Council on Fgn. Relations. Office: Dept Politics Brandeis U. Waltham MA 02254

BROWN, SHERROD CAMPBELL, state official; b. Manfield, Ohio, Nov. 9, 1952; s. Charles G. and Emily (Campbell) B.; m. Larke Ummel, Aug. 25, 1979; children: Emily, Elizabeth. B.A., Yale U., 1974; M.A. in Edn., Ohio State U., 1979, Ohio State U., 1981. Mem. Ohio Ho. of Reps., Mansfield, 1975-82; Sec. of State State of Ohio, Columbus, 1983—; instr. Ohio State U., Mansfield, 1978-79; sec. Commrs. Sinking fund, Columbus, 1983—. Mem. State Democratic Exec. Com., Columbus, 1976-83, Ohio Pub. Facility Commn., Columbus, 1983—, United Way Allocation Com., Columbus, 1983—. Recipient Pro Deo et Patria Boy Scouts Am., 1966, Friend of Edn. award, 1978. Mem. Nat. Assn. Secs. State. Democrat. Lutheran. Office: State of Ohio 30 E Broad St Columbus OH 43215

BROWN, SPENCER HUNTER, historian; b. Knoxville, Tenn., June 10, 1928; s. John Orville and Edith Frances (Hunter) B.; m. Doris Lucille Craig, Aug. 4, 1951; 1 dau., Rebecca Lee. B.A. in Teaching Social Studies magna cum laude, U. Ill., 1954, M.A. in History; fellow, 1955; Ph.D. in History (African Studies fellow), Northwestern U., 1964. Tchr., chmn. social scis. dept. Carl Sandburg High Sch., Orland Park, Ill., 1955-59; mem. faculty Western Ill. U., Macomb, 1962—, prof. history, 1971—, chmn. dept., 1976—. Gen. editor: Jour. Developing Areas, 1965-76; bus. mgr., 1976—. Served with USNR, 1945-47. Ford Found. fellow, 1961-62. Mem. African Studies Assn., Am. Hist. Assn. AAUP, Phi Beta Kappa. Home: Box 47 Tennessee IL 62374 Office: Dept of History Western Illinois University Macomb IL 61455

BROWN, STEPHEN IRA, educator; b. Bklyn., July 14, 1938; s. Milton Frank and Ruth (Mittman) B.; m. Eileen Thaler, June 12, 1960; children: Jordan David, Sharon Jean. A.B., Columbia Coll., 1960; M.A. in Teaching (Sloan fellow 1960-61), Harvard U., 1961, Ed.D., 1967. Instr. math. and edn. Simmons Coll., Boston, 1962-65; asst. prof. edn. Harvard U., 1966-72; vis. prof. Hebrew U., Jerusalem, 1970-71; asso. prof. Syracuse (N.Y.) U., 1972-73; mem. faculty SUNY, Buffalo, 1973—, prof. math. edn., 1979—, prof. philosophy of edn., 1982—; vis. prof. U. Ga., Athens, 1979-80; participant ethics workshops Coll. Jewish Studies, Buffalo, 1974-76. Author: Some Prime Comparisons, 1978; co-author: The Art of Problem Posing, 1983; editor: Creative Problem Solving, 1978; mem. rev. bd.: Ednl. Theory; contbr. articles to profl. jours.; mem. editorial bd.: For Learning of Mathematics. Mem. adv. council Inst. Jewish Life, 1973-75. Grantee Dewey Found., 1977, NSF, 1981-84. Fellow Philosophy Edn. Soc.; mem. John Dewey Soc. (dir. 1976-78), Math. Assn. Am., Nat. Council Tchrs. Math., Phi Beta Kappa, Phi Delta Kappa. Home: 86 Sherbrooke Dr Williamsville NY 14221 Office: Faculty Edn Studies SUNY Buffalo Amherst NY 14260 *I attribute a large part of my success to lack of clarity and specificity with regard to goals, to ambiguity and vagueness with regard to principles, to a sense of humor which provides distance between a taken for granted reality and my personal world, and to a general disinclination to analyze what accounts for my success.*

BROWN, STERLING WADE, clergyman, educator; b. Cookville, Tex., Dec. 28, 1907; s. Charles A. and Pludie (Bready) B.; m. Mary Jeanne Murray, Sept. 8, 1938; children—Charlene Ann, Vicki Sue. A.B., Tex. Christian U., 1930, B.D., 1932; Ph.D., U. Chgo., 1936; LL.D., Eureka Coll., 1965, Tex. Christian U., 1966. Ordained to ministry Disciples of Christ Ch., 1928; prof. religion U. Okla., 1936-40; chmn. dept. religion Drake U., 1940-43; dir. Vassar Intergroup Workshop, Poughkeepsie, N.Y., 1945-46; field supr. Nat. Conf. Christians and Jews, St. Louis, Chgo., 1943-45, asst. to pres., N.Y.C., 1945-47, gen. dir., 1949-53, exec. v.p., 1953-65, pres., 1965-73, pres.

emeritus, spl. cons. to pres., 1973—; adj. prof. human relations U. Okla., 1973—. Author: Changing Functions of Disciple Colleges, 1936, Developing Christian Personality, 1944, Primer on Intergroup Relations, 1946. Mem. staff Mil. Govt., 1947-49; Germany. Mem. Alpha Tau Omega. Democrat. Home: 1508 Sunset Dr Norman OK 73069 Office: 1508 Sunset Dr Norman OK 73069

BROWN, STUART MACDONALD, JR., coll. ofcl.; b. Concord, N.C., Mar. 14, 1916; s. Stuart MacDonald and Maud (Reynolds) B.; m. Catherine Hemphill, June 21, 1941; children—James, Deborah, Margaret, Peter. B.S., Cornell U., 1937, Ph.D., 1942. Instr. zoology Mass. State Coll., spring 1938; asst. philosophy Cornell U., Ithaca, N.Y., 1940-42, instr., 1942-43, spring 1946, asst. prof., 1946-49, asso. prof., 1949-56, prof., 1956-70, chmn. dept., 1953-63; dean Coll. Arts and Scis., 1964-69, v.p. for acad. affairs, 1968-70; prof. philosophy, v.p. for acad. affairs U. Hawaii, Honolulu, 1970-73; prof. philosophy, exec. dir. humanities, sci., tech. program Cornell U., 1974-75, asso. dir. sci., tech. and society program, 1974-81, prof. emeritus, 1981—; Chmn. bd. dirs. Center for Research Libraries, 1973-74. Mng. editor: The Philos. Rev, 1950-54, 59-61. Served with AUS, 1943-46. Rockefeller post-war fellow in philosophy, 1947-48; Guggenheim fellow, 1957. Mem. Am. Philos. Assn., Am. Soc. Polit. and Legal Philosophy, Acad. Polit. Sci. Home: 515 Lower Creek Rd Ithaca NY 14850

BROWN, SY, retail exec., mgmt. cons.; b. Hoboken, N.J., Mar. 4, 1921; s. Robert and Anna (Rose) B.; m. Thelma Venin, June 22, 1948; children—Sherry Brown Riello, Diane, Robert. Grad. high sch. Successively store mgr., field supr., gen. mgr., v.p. ops., pres. mens and boys div., sr. v.p., dir. Unishops, Inc., Jersey City; corporate officer, v.p. Hartfield Zody's, Inc., N.Y.C.; corporate v.p. ops. Vornado, Inc., Garfield, N.J.; dir. ops. and merchandising men and boys div. Great Eastern Discount Dept. Stores div. Daylin, Inc.; now pres., chief exec. officer Stanley & Brown Assos. Inc., Livingston, N.J.; pres., chief exec. officer Gaylen & Brown Assos., Inc., Livingston; exec. v.p. Kent Eastern Corp., Hackensack, N.J. Bd. dirs. Daniel and Budd Kessler Found. Jewish. Clubs: B'nai B'rith, Mens (South Orange, N.J.)

BROWN, TEMPLE NIX, metals company executive; b. Hot Springs, Ark., Oct. 30, 1930; s. James Frank and Susie Jane (Nix) B.; m. Barbara Sue McNabb, Apr. 10, 1955; children: Donna Sue Helfand, Carol Lynne Pickworth. B.S.E.E., U. Ark., 1953. Registered profl. engr., Ark., Ala., N.Y. Project engr. Reynolds Metals Co., Malvern, Ark., 1956-67, plant engr., Arkadelphia, Ark., 1967-70, plant supt., Sheffield, Ala., 1970-74, plant mgr., Massena, N.Y., 1974-78, Sheffield, Ala., 1978-80, v.p., Richmond, Va., 1980—; pres. Reynolds Pipeline Co., Richmond, 1982—, Reynolds Energy Resources Corp., 1982—. Bd. dirs. Jr. Achievement, Sheffield, Ala., 1978-80; chmn. bd. N.W. Ala. Health Care, Florence, Ala., 1978-80; bd. dirs. YMCA, Florence, 1978-80. Recipient Cert. of Recognition Nat. Secs. Assn., 1973; named Boss of the Yr. Nat. Secs. Assn., 1973, Nat. Secs. Assn., 1978; recipient Cert. of Recognition Nat. Secs. Assn., 1977. Mem. Assoc. Industries of Ala. (dir. 1978-80), Tennessee Riverr Valley Assn. (dir. 1978-80), Ala. Soc. Profl. Engrs., AIME, Ala. C. of C. (dir. 1978-80), Muscle Shoals C. of C. Club: Rotary. Home: 10814 Brewington Rd Richmond VA 23233 Office: 6601 W Broad St Richmond VA 23261

BROWN, TERENCE MICHAEL, college president; b. Charleston, W.Va., Nov. 16, 1941; s. Charles Wilkerson and Pauline Marie (Pell) B.; m. Janet Elizabeth Hart, May 21, 1966; children: Elizabeth Michelle, Terence Michael, Cara Susan. B.S., Lamar U., 1963; M.A. in English, Stephen F. Austin State U., 1965, Ph.D., So. Ill. U., 1975. Instr. English So. Ill. U., Carbondale, 1966-72, asst. dean, asst. prof., 1972-77; Am. Council on Edn. fellow U. Ark., Fayetteville, 1977-78; v.p. acad. affairs Ark. State U., Jonesboro, 1978-82; pres. No. State Coll., Aberdeen, S.D., 1982—; cons. Mus. Sci. and Industry, Little Rock, 1982, Ark. Electric Cooperative, 1979-82; sec. S.D. Council of Presidents, Pierre, 1983. Editor: New Directions in Post-Secondary Education, 1974; author poetry; contbr. articles on English and Am. lit to profl. jours. Mem. Am. Council on Edn., Am. Assn. State Colls. and Univs. (S.D. reps.), Pi Gamma Mu, Phi Kappa Phi, Beta Gamma Sigma. Lodges: Rotary (Aberdeen); Masons. Home: 1302 N Jay St Aberdeen SD 57401 Office: Office of Pres No State Coll Aberdeen SD 57401

BROWN, THEODORE LAWRENCE, educator, chemist; b. Green Bay, Wis., Oct. 15, 1928; s. Lawrence A. and Martha E. (Kedinger) B.; m. Audrey Catherine Brockman, Jan. 6, 1951; children: Mary Margaret, Karen Anne, Jennifer Gerarda, Philip Matthew, Andrew Lawrence. B.S. in Chemistry, Ill. Inst. Tech., 1950; Ph.D., Mich. State U., 1956. Faculty U. Ill., Urbana, 1956—, prof. chemistry, 1965—; vice chancellor for research, dean Grad. Coll., 1980—; vis. scientist Internat. Meteorol. Inst., Stockholm, 1972; Boomer lectr. U. Alta. (Can.), Edmonton, 1975; Firth vis. prof. U. Sheffield (Eng.), 1977; Bd. dirs. Champaign County Opportunities Industrialization Center, 1970-79, chmn., 1975-78; bd. govs. Argonne Nat. Lab., 1982—. Author: (with R.S. Drago) Experiments in General Chemistry, 3d edit., 1970, General Chemistry, 2d edit., 1968, Energy and the Environment, 1971, (with H.E. LeMay) Chemistry: The Central Science, 1977, 2d edit., 1981; asso. editor: Inorganic Chemistry, 1969-78; editorial adv. bd.: Jour. Organometal Chemistry; contbr. articles to profl. publs. Served with USN, 1950-53. Sloan research fellow, 1962-66; NSF sr. postdoctoral fellow, 1964-65; Guggenheim fellow, 1979. Fellow Chem. Soc. (London); mem. Am. Chem. Soc. (award in inorganic chemistry 1972), AAAS, Sigma Xi, Alpha Chi Sigma. Home: 309 Yankee Ridge Ln Urbana IL 61801 Office: 107 Coble Hall 801 S Wright St Champaign IL 61820

BROWN, THEODORE MOREY, art history educator; b. Winthrop, Mass., Nov. 11, 1925; s. Isydor and Nettie (Schwartz) B.; m. Barbara M. Rome, May 29, 1951; children: Lisa N., David O. B.Arch., M.I.T., 1953; M.A., Harvard U., 1956; Ph.D., U. Utrecht, The Netherlands, 1958. Asst. prof. history of art U. Louisville, 1958-62, asso. prof., 1962-67; prof. history art Cornell U., 1967—; cons. in field. Author: The Work of G.T. Rietveld, Architect, 1958, Margaret Bourke-White Photojournalist, 1972. Served with USN, 1943-46. Mem. Coll. Art Assn., Soc. Archtl. Historians, Am. Studies Assn. Home: 92 Ithaca Rd Ithaca NY 14850 Office: Department of History of Art Cornell University Ithaca NY 14850 *I have tried to cultivate my intellect and my senses as integrated instruments to help me understand something of the human condition. And as a teacher, I tried to help others discover where, what, and who we are. On the way, I had hoped to achieve the serenity which I imagine comes with a sense of being at home in the world. I failed.*

BROWN, THOMAS ANDREW, research administrator; b. Iowa City, Iowa, July 24, 1932; s. Charles Valentine and Mary Clementine (Proestler) B.; m. Louise Grafton Baggott, Aug. 31, 1957; children: James, Mary, Catherine. B.A., State U. Iowa, 1953, Oxford U., 1955; M.A., Harvard U., 1958, Ph.D., 1962. With Rand Corp., 1962-74, asso. head info. sci., 1966-74; asst. v.p. Sci. Applications, Inc., Los Angeles, 1974-77; dep. asst. Sec. of Def. program analysis and evaluation Dept. Def., Washington, 1977-81; partner Booz, Allen & Hamilton, Bethesda, Md., 1981-83; dir. strategic studies Rand Corp., Washington, 1983—. Served with USAF, 1955-57. Rhodes scholar, 1953-55; NSF fellow, 1957-61. Home: 1405 Layman St McLean VA 22101 Office: 2100 M St NW Washington DC 20037

BROWN, THOMAS FRANCIS, III, naval officer; b. Scranton, Pa., Oct. 23, 1932; s. Thomas and Marian Constance (Thomson) B.; m. Martha C. Bramer, June 15, 1957; children: Thomas F., Stephanie M., Deidre L., Donald E. B.A. in English, Mt. St. Mary's Coll., 1954; M.A. in Polit. Sci., U. Calif.-Berkeley, 1963; student, Nat. War Coll., 1973-74. Commd. U.S. Navy, 1955; advanced through grades to rear admiral; combdg. officer Attack Squadron Thirty Seven, USN, Jacksonville, Fla., 1971-72; comdr. Caloosahatchee, USN, Norfolk, Va., 1975-77, USS Midway, USN, Yokoshuka, Japan, 1978-79, Mil. Enlistment Processing Command, USN, Fort Sheridan, Ill., 1979-80, Carrier Wing Nineteen, USN, Lemoore, Calif., 1972-73, Carrier Group One, USN, San Deigo, 1980-82, Battle Force 7th Fleet, USN, Republic of Philippines, 1982—. Decorated Silver Star, Def. Superior Service medal, Legion of Merit (3), D.F.C. (4). Republican. Roman Catholic. Home: 935 Grandview St Scranton PA 18509

BROWN, THOMAS GARRETT, bakery company executive; b. Knoxville, Tenn., May 22, 1950; s. T.G. Brown III and Barbara Thomas (Henslee) B.; m. Sandra Marie Hale, Dec. 12, 1981. Grad. in bus. adminstrv. mgmt., Pompano Beach Sch. Bus., Fla. Co-mgr. warehouses Kern's Bakery, Knoxville, 1968-74, asst. printshop, 1975-81, v.p., dir. sales, 1981-82, v.p., dir., dir. sercurity, 1983—. Speaker before County Commn. Crestwood Hills subdiv. Mem. Am. Legion. Republican. Methodist. Clubs: Cherokee Country, Men's Cotillion (Knoxville). Lodge: Eagles. Office: Kerns and Assoc Bakeries 2100 Chapman Hwy Knoxville TN 37901

BROWN, THOMAS PAUL, oil co. exec.; b. Miles City, Mont., Aug. 5, 1927; s. Thomas Ambrose and Eleanor Ann (Boyce) B.; m. Virginia Sue Sayers, June 2, 1961; children—Dana, Tina, Nelson, Paul, Susan, Diane, David. With mktg. dept. Carter Oil Co., 1946-53; v.p. Modern Oil Co., 1953-55, N.W. Oil & Refining Co., 1955-58; Berry Refining Co., 1958-64; v.p. Pana Refining Co., 1964-68; cons. Tosco Corp., 1968-70; pres. Tosco Petro Co., 1970-73; v.p. Tosco Corp., 1973-78, exec. v.p., Los Angeles, 1978-80; also dir.; founder, pres., chmn. bd. Synthetic Crude Devel. Co., Santa Barbara, Calif., 1980—. Served with AC USAR. Republican. Roman Catholic. Clubs: California, Johnathon, Los Angeles Athletic, Los Angeles Petroleum, Billings Petroleum. Home: 4235 Cresta Ave Santa Barbara CA 93110 Office: 3892 State St Suite 110 Santa Barbara CA 93105

BROWN, THOMAS PHILIP, III, lawyer; b. Washington, Dec. 18, 1931; s. Raymond T. and Beatrice (Cullen) B.; m. Alicia A. Sexton, July 28, 1955; children: Thomas, Mark, Alicia, Maria, Beatrice. B.S., Georgetown U., 1953, LL.B., 1956. Bar: D.C., Md. Practice law, Washington and Bethesda, Md., 1958—; mem. adv. bd. Nat. Bank of Washington. Author books and articles on legal malpractice. Pres. Cath. Youth Orgn. of Washington, 1972. Served to lt. USMCR, 1955-58. Mem. Bar Assn. D.C. (past sec., dir.), Am. Bar Assn. (council sect. on econs. law practice), D.C. Bar. Clubs: Barristers (treas., exec. com. 1976), University, Columbia Country. Home: 5430 Wickford Dr Rockville MD 20852 Office: 4803 St Elmo Ave Bethesda MD 20814

BROWN, TRAVIS WALTER, oil field drilling equipment company executive; b. Oklahoma city, June 18, 1934; s. H. Travis and Irene (Robison) B.; m. Marilynn Davis, June 1, 1957; children: Deborah Sue, Travis Carson, Thomas Walter, Darla Lynn. B.B.A., Okla. U., 1956; J.D., Oklahoma city U., 1962. Bar: Okla. 1956. Pres. Geolograph Co. and related cos., Oklahoma City, 1948-79; ptnr. Robinwood Farms, Oklahoma City, 1968; pres. Geolograph-Pioneer div. Geosource, Inc., Oklahoma City, 1979—; chmn. bd. Robinwood's Poor Boy Feed co., Edmond, Okla., 1980—; owner S.W. Am. Pub. Co., Edmond, Okla., 1982—; pres. XIT Robinwood Pub. Co. (pub. Horse Digest), Leesburg, Va. Author: Sub Surface Geology, 1976, Freeze Branding of Cattle, Horses and Mules, 1982; contbr. articles to profl. jours. Served to lt. (j.g.) USN, 1956-57. Recipient Wall St. Jour. award, 1956, Disting. Service award Cosmopolitan Internat. Civic Club, 1964, 67; named to Am. Cattle Breeders Hall of Fame, 1979. Mem. Internat. Assn. Oilwell Drilling Contractors (surface equipment co-chmn.), Am. Soc. Petroleum Engrs., Can. Inst. Mining and Metallurgy, Am. Mining Congress, Can. Diamond Drilling Assn., Ind. Petroleum Assn. Nomads (v.p. 1984), Palomino Horse Breeders Am. (nat. pres. 1981-82, Hall of Fame 1982), Internat. Brangus Breeders (promotion com.), Am. Quarter Horse Assn., Am. Horse Shows Assn. (Palomino com.), Indian Nations Brangus Breeders Assn., ABA, Golden Saddlebred Assn., Okla. Bar Assn. (Disting. Service award 1964), Okla. Petroleum Assn., Okla. Palomino Horse Breeders Assn. (pres. 1979-80), Okla. Brangus Breeders Assn. (pres. 1982-83), Okla. Horse Council (pres. 1983-84), Western Okla. Brangus Breeders (sec.-treas. 1982-84), Okla. Beef Inc. (dir.), Okla. County Cattleman's Assn. (pres. 1974-75), Okla. Quarter Horse Assn., Okla. County Beef Com., Okla. Poultry Fedn., Okla. County Bar Assn. Republican. Methodist. Club: Petroleum (Oklahoma City). Home: Route 1 Box 154 Oklahoma City OK 73131 Office: Geolograph-Pioneer Geosource PO Box 25246 Oklahoma City OK 73125

BROWN, TRISHA, dancer; b. Aberdeen, Wash. B.A. in Dance, Mills Coll., Calif.; Ph.D. in Fine Arts, Oberlin Coll. Lectr. Mills Coll., Calif., Reed Coll., Oreg., NYU; conductor, workshops, seminars, throughout the world; founder, pres. Trisha Brown Dance Co., New York, NY, 1970—; founding mem. Judson Dance Theatre. Dancer worldwide; choreographer: Man Walking Down the Side of a Building, 1969, Accumulation, 1971, Locus, 1975; visual presentations Glacial Decoy, 1979, Set and Reset, 1983, Opal Loop, 1980, Son of Gone Fishin', 1981; featured TV show, WNET-PBS, New York City, Dance in America, WGBH-PBS, Boston, Dancing on the Edge, WGBH-PBS, Boston, Making Dances, WGBH-PBS, Boston; artists: drawings Venice Biennale, Toulon Museum; drawings, group exhibition Numerals: Mathematical Concepts in Contemporary Art, Drawings: The Pluralist Decade, New Notes for New Dance, Art and Dance, Images From the Modern Dialogue. Guggenheim fellow; fellow Nat. Endowment Arts, Creative Artists Service Program; grantee New York State Council on the Arts; recipient Creative Arts award medal Brandeis U. Home and Office: Trisha Brown Co 541 Broadway New York NY 10012

BROWN, TROY ANDERSON, JR., elec. distbg. co. exec.; b. Tampa, Fla., July 7, 1934; s. Troy Anderson and Valerie Aldona (Mohler) B.; m. Jean Thompson, Aug. 22, 1962; children—Troy Anderson, III, George Albert, Douglas Alan. A.B., Harvard U., 1956; J.D., U. N.C., 1959. Bar: Fla. bar 1959. With Raybro Electric Supplies Inc., Tampa, 1960—, exec. v.p., 1964-74, pres., 1974—; also dir.; dir. Exchange Bank & Trust, Tampa. Mem. exec. com. Tampa Com. 100, 1975, U. S.Fla. Found., 1974-75; chmn. bd. fellow U. Tampa, 1978; bd. dirs., vice chmn. Tampa Museum, 1977-79; bd. dirs. Tampa YMCA, 1977-79, Tampa Marine Inst., 1976-77. Served with USAFR, 1959. Mem. Nat. Assn. Elec. Distbrs., Fla. Bar, Young Pres. Orgn., Greater Tampa C. of C. (gov. 1968-74), Exchange Club Tampa (pres. 1970), Presidents Round Table Tampa (pres. 1971), Tampa Mchts. Assn. (dir. 1980). Episcopalian. Clubs: Ye Mystic Krewe Gasparilla, Tampa Yacht and Country, Palma Ceia Golf and Country, Merry Makers, Shriners, Jesters, University. Home: 2901 Villa Rosa St Tampa FL 33611 Office: 907 Ellamae St Tampa FL 33602

BROWN, VICTOR LEE, clergyman; b. Cardston, Alta., Can., July 31, 1914; s. Gerald S. and Maggie (Lee) B.; m. Lois A. Kjar, Nov. 13, 1936; children: Victor Lee, Gerald E., Joanne K., Patricia L., Stephen M. Student, Latter-Day Saints Bus. Coll., U. Utah; spl. studies, U. Calif. at Berkeley. With United Air Lines, 1940-61, successively supr., reservations mgr., Washington, Chgo., chief payload control, Denver, mgr. space control, 1956-60, asst. to dir. reservations, Chgo., 1960-61; dir. Beneficial Life Ins. Co.; 2d counselor presiding bishopric Ch. of Jesus Christ of Latter-day Saints, 1961-72, presiding bishop, 1972—; pres., chmn. bd. Deseret Mut. Benefits Assn., to 1978; mem. Deseret Mgmt. Corp., Deseret News Pub. Co.; pres. Hotel Utah Co., until 1982, chmn. bd., 1982—; vice chmn. Deseret Trust Co.; dir. Western Air Lines, O.C. Tanner Jewelry Co. Mem. Utah Bicentennial Commn., chmn. festival com., 1975-77; mem. gen. welfare services com. Ch. of Jesus Christ of Latter-day Saints, mem. bd. edn.; trustee Coll. Bus. Brigham Young U.; mem. Utah Symphony Bd. Mem. Beta Gamma Sigma. Home: 1653 Orchard Dr Salt Lake City UT 84106 Office: 50 E North Temple St Salt Lake City UT 84150

BROWN, W. PERRY, personnel executive; b. Hamilton, Ohio, Sept. 21, 1930; s. Wilbur Lewis and Lenora (Blackburn) B.; m. Marjorie Ann Rogers, June 20, 1953; children: Scott, Allison, Matthew. A.B., Miami U., Oxford, Ohio, 1952. Dir. indsl. relations Gardner div. Diamond Internat. Corp., Middletown, Ohio, 1952-61; asst. v.p. adminstrn. Hudson Pulp and Paper Corp., Palatka, Fla., 1961-72; exec. dir. personnel and indsl. relations Merck & Co. Inc., Rahway, N.J., 1972-78; v.p. personnel Am. Cyanamid Co., Wayne, N.J., 1978—. Served with U.S. Army, 1954-56. Mem. Miami U. Alumni Assn. (exec. council 1979-82, pres. 1981-82), Putnam County C. of C. (pres. 1967), Fla. State C. of C. (bd. dirs. 1968). Republican. Presbyterian. Clubs: Canoe Brook Country (Summit, N.J.); Palatka Country (pres. 1969-70). Office: Am Cyanamid Co One Cyanamic Plaza Wayne NJ 07470

BROWN, WALSTON SHEPARD, lawyer; b. Darien, Conn., Jan. 20, 1908; s. Clarence Shepard and Alma Mary (Mitchell) B.; m. Ellen F. Regan, August 13, 1955. A.B., Leland Stanford, 1930; student, L'Ecole Libre des Science Politiques, Paris, 1931-32; LL.B., Harvard, 1935. Bar: D.C. bar 1936. Atty. various govt. depts., 1935-40; asst. gen. counsel U.S. Maritime Commn., also mem. various adv. coms. on drafting and adminstrn. mem. various adv. coms. on drafting, reconversion and contract termination legislation, 1940-45; practiced in, N.Y.C., 1945—; ptnr. firm Willkie Farr & Gallagher (and predecessors.). Mem. Newcomen Soc. N. Am., Am. Bar Assn., S.R., Phi Beta Kappa. Unitarian. Clubs: Univ., River (N.Y.C.); Tuxedo, Travelers (Paris). Home: Mountain Farm Rd Tuxedo Park Orange County NY Office: 153 E 53d St New York NY 10022

BROWN, WALTER HAROLD, JR., lawyer; b. Johnson City, Tenn., May 20, 1910; s. Walter H. and Constance (Malone) B.; m. Phyllis Elizabeth Barnard, June 6, 1935; children—Walter Barnard, Phyllis Deborah (Mrs. George J. Pillorgé). B.A., Birmingham-So. Coll., 1931; LL.B., Columbia, 1934. Bar: N.Y. 1935, U.S. Supreme Ct. Assoc. firm Willkie, Farr & Gallagher (and predecessors), 1934-43, ptnr., 1943-80, counsel, 1980—; gen. counsel Seaboard Coast Line R.R. Co., 1965-70; spl. counsel to maj. life ins. cos. in pvt. placement investments; co-counsel Penn Central Trustees, 1978; reorgn. mgr. Mo. Pacific R.R. Co., 1956, Instl. Investors Penn Central Group, 1970-78, Erie Group, 1973-80. Trustee Finch Jr. Coll., 1943-53. Fellow Am. Bar Found. (life); mem. Am., N.Y. State bar assns., Sigma Alpha Epsilon, Omicron Delta Kappa. Clubs: University (N.Y.C.); Port Washington (N.Y.); Yacht. Home: 100 Ivy Way Port Washington NY 11050 Office: 153 E 53d St New York NY 10022

BROWN, WENDELL JAMES, assn. ofcl.; b. Des Moines, Aug. 7, 1913; s. Velora O. and Mamie (Durham) B.; m. Vivian Rose Young, Jan. 18, 1935; children—Wendell J., Beverly Marie, Loren Dennis. Ed. pub. schs., Iowa. Partner Master Tire & Supply Co., 1935-48, Master Sales Co., 1948—; v.p., dir. Graymills Corp. Nat. v.p. United Cerebral Palsy Assn., 1955-59, pres., 1960-64; vice chmn. United Cerebral Palsy Research Found.; vice chmn. bd. Coll. Osteo. Medicine and Surgery, Des Moines. Recipient citation plaques United Cerebral Palsy Assn. Baptist. Clubs: Mason (Shriner), Kiwanian., Des Moines Golf and Country. Address: 2300 Ashworth Rd West Des Moines IA 50265

BROWN, WESLEY ERNEST, U.S. judge; b. Hutchinson, Kans., June 22, 1907; s. Morrison H.H. and Julia (Wesley) B.; m. Mary A. Miller, Nov. 30, 1934; children: Wesley Miller, Loy B. (Mrs. John K. Wiley). Student, Kans. U., 1925-28; LL.B., Kansas City Law Sch., 1933. Bar: Kans. 1933, Mo. 1933. Practiced in, Hutchinson, 1933-58, county atty., Reno County, Kans., 1935-39; referee in bankruptcy U.S. Dist. Ct. Kans., 1958-62, judge, 1962-79, sr. judge, 1979—; chief judge, 1971-77; appointee Temporary Emergency Ct. of Appeals of U.S., 1980—; Dir. Nat. Assn. Referees in Bankruptcy, 1959-62; mem. bankruptcy div. Jud. Conf., 1963-70; mem. Jud. Conf., U.S., 1976-79. Served with USNR, 1944-46. Mem. ABA, Kans. Bar Assn. (exec. council 1950-62, pres. 1964-65), Reno County Bar Assn. (pres. 1947), Wichita Bar Assn., S.W. Bar Kan., Delta Theta Phi. Office: 423 US Courthouse 401 N Market St Wichita KS 67202

BROWN, WILLARD A., JR., real estate executive; b. Evanston, Ill., Sept. 11, 1931; s. Willard A. and Elaine (Grannis) B.; m. Margaret E. Drew, May 7, 1960; children: Suzanne, Stacy, Peter. B.S., Western Mich. U., 1953. With Arthur Rubloff & Co., Chgo., 1955—, pres., 1980—, chief exec. officer, 1980—; also dir.; dir. Ryan Ins. Group. Mem. Chgo. exec. council Boy Scouts Am., 1980—; mem. revolving loan com. City of Chgo., 1981—. Served with USAF, 1953-55. Mem. Urban Land Inst., Nat. Assn. Realtors, Soc. Indsl. Realtors. Republican. Clubs: Mid Day, Union League, Barrington Hills Country. Office: 69 W Washington St Chicago IL 60602 *

BROWN, WILLIAM BURBRIDGE, state supreme ct. justice; b. Chillicothe, Ohio, Sept. 10, 1912; s. Henry Renick and Mabel R. (Downs) B.; m. Jayne Stone, Aug. 18, 1943; children—Susan Brown Eshbaugh, Henry Renick. A.B., Williams Coll., 1934; LL.B., Harvard U., 1937. Bar: Ohio bar 1938, Hawaii bar 1945. Law clk. firm Ritter & Daugherty, Toledo, 1937-39; mem. firm Simpson & Brown, Chillicothe, 1939-42; price atty. Hawaii OPA, Washington, 1942-43, Honolulu, 1943-44, chief atty., 1944-45; practiced law in, Honolulu, 1945-46, Chillicothe, 1955-57, 67-72; Judge Ct. Tax Appeals of Terr., Hawaii, 1946-47, 2d Circuit Ct. of Terr., 1951-55, Chillicothe Municipal Ct., 1957-61; treas. State of Hawaii, 1947-51; judge Ohio Ct. Appeals, 4th Dist., 1961-67, presiding judge, 1965-67; asso. justice Ohio Supreme Ct., 1973—. Vestryman St. Paul's Episcopal Ch., Chillicothe, 1957-61. Mem. ABA, Ohio Bar Assn., Hawaii Bar Assn., Ross County Bar Assn. (Pres. 1966), Am. Judicature Soc., Inst. Jud. Adminstrn., Lincoln's Inn Soc. (treas. 1936-37), Delta Kappa Epsilon. Clubs: Rotary, Masons, Shriners, Columbus Athletic, Chillicothe Country; Pacific (Honolulu); Univ. (Toledo); (Washington). Office: Ohio Supreme Ct Columbus OH 43215

BROWN, WILLIAM CLIFFORD, publishing company executive; b. Ottumwa, Iowa, Nov. 12, 1911; s. Walter Mahlin and Zella Audrey (Mathews) B.; m. Eunice Mary Farley, May 20, 1936; children: Lawrence W., Cheryl (Mrs. Mark Falb). Grad. high sch.; LL.D., Bowling Green State U., 1970. Dist. sales mgr. John S. Swift Co., Inc., St. Louis, 1934-44; founder, chmn. William Brown Co., Pubs., Dubuque, Iowa, 1944—; Chmn. Dubuque Bank & Trust Co., 1968-82; chmn. exec. com. Life Investors, Inc., Cedar Rapids, Iowa, 1967-82; chmn. Heartland Bancorp., 1982—. Bd. dirs. U. Dubuque, 1969—. Mem. Dubuque Shooting Soc. Clubs: Masons, Shriners, Elks,

Dubuque Golf and Country; Vero Beach Golf and Country, Riomar Bay Yacht (Vero Beach, Fla.). Home: 1495 Treasure Cove Ln Vero Beach FL 32963 Office: 2460 Kerper Blvd Dubuque IA 52001

BROWN, WILLIAM ERNEST, dentist; b. Benton Harbor, Mich., Aug. 29, 1922; s. William Ernest and Gertrude (Eliot) B.; m. T.N. McDonald, Oct. 21, 1944 (dec. July 1969); children: Judith M. Brown Smith, Wendy E. Brown Kerschbaum, Terrence N.; m. E.M. Tyree, Sept. 11, 1970. D.D.S., U. Mich., 1945, M.S., 1947. Practice pedodontic dentistry, Ann Arbor, Mich., 1947-62; part-time tchr. U. Mich., 1947-62; asst., then asso. prof. dentistry, asso. dir. W.K. Kellogg Found. Inst. Grad. and Postgrad. Dentistry, 1962-69; dean Coll. Dentistry, U. Okla., Oklahoma City, 1969—, acting provost Health Scis. Ctr., 1973-75. Author: Oral Health, Dentistry and the American Public, 1974, Dental Education in the United States, 1976. Mem. City of Ann Arbor Human Relations Commn., 1960-66, chmn., 1965-66. Recipient Gies Editorial award, 1965, 67. Mem. ADA, Am. Assn. Dental Schs. (pres.-elect 1983-84), Am. Acad. Pedodontics, Am. Soc. Dentistry for Children. Club: Rotary. Home: 24 S Easy St Edmond OK 73034 Office: Coll Dentistry U Okla PO Box 26901 Oklahoma City OK 73190

BROWN, WILLIAM F(ERDINAND), writer, artist; b. Jersey City, Apr. 16, 1928; s. Douglas and Dorothy (Ferrett) B.; m. Christina Tippit, Oct. 3, 1981; children by previous marriage—Debra Susan, William Todd. A.B. cum laude in Psychology, Princeton, 1950. Staff writer: Look mag, 1951-52; talent agt., MCA, 1953-54; agy. TV producer, Batten, Barton, Durstine and Osborn, 1954-62; freelance writer, artist, 1962—; asso. producer: Silents Please, 1959-60; sketch and lyric writer: Julius Monk revues, 1960-69; writer: Max Liebman Spls, 1960-61, Jackie Gleason Show, 1962; sketch and lyric writer: That Was The Week That Was, 1964-65; author: The Girl in the Freudian Slip, 1967; sketch writer: New Faces of 1968, 1968; book writer: How To Steal an Election, 1968, The Wiz, 1975, A Broadway Musical, 1978; contbr. to: Love, American Style; co-author, co-artist: comic strip Boomer, syndicated by United Features, 1972-81; writer for cabarets, night club acts, indsl. shows, 1962—; Author; illustrator: Tiger, Tiger, 1950, Beat Beat Beat, 1959, The Girl in the Freudian Slip, 1959, The Abominable Showmen, 1960, The World Is my Yo-Yo, 1963; also illustrator other books.; Contbr. articles, fiction and, cartoons to popular mags. Trustee Princeton Tiger, 1950—. Served to 1st lt. AUS, 1952-53. Mem. Nat. Cartoonists Soc., Newspaper Comics Council, A.S.C.A.P., Writers Guild Am. East, Dramatists Guild, Artists and Writers, Phi Beta Kappa. Club: Round Hill (Greenwich, Conn.). Home: 164 Newtown Turnpike Westport CT 06880 *Living would be so easy if it all took place on a practice range.*

BROWN, WILLIAM HOLMES, government official; b. Huntington, W.Va., Sept. 3, 1929; s. William Holmes and Katherine Louise (Tillette) B.; m. Jean Elizabeth Smith, June, 24, 1971; 1 dau., Sara Holmes. B.S., Swarthmore (Pa.) Coll., 1951; J.D., U. Chgo., 1954. Bar: W.Va. 1957, D.C. 1960, U.S. Supreme Ct 1967. Asst. parliamentarian U.S. Ho. Reps., 1958-74, parliamentarian, 1974—. Editor: House Rules and Manual, 1975—. Served to lt. comdr. USNR, 1954-57. Quaker. Home: Oakland Green Lincoln VA 22078 Office: Speaker's Rooms US Capitol Washington DC 20515:

BROWN, WILLIAM L., banker; b. Hendersonville, N.C., Feb. 1, 1922; s. William W. and Sarah (Maxwell) B.; m. Helen Presbrey, June 1947; children: Kathryn H., Richard P., Steven J., Melissa M. Student, Mars Hill Coll., Newberry Coll.; M.B.A., Harvard, 1947. With First Nat. Bank Boston, 1949—, now chmn., dir.; dir. Stone & Webster, Inc., N.Y.C., Standex Internat. Corp., Salem, N.H., Gen. Cinema Corp., Boston, Liberty Mut. Ins. Co., Liberty Mut. Fire Ins. Co., Boston. Trustee Children's Hosp. Med. Center, Boston, Boston Coll.; trustee, mem. corp. Mus. of Sci.; bd. dirs. Jobs for Mass., Inc. Served to lt. USNR, World War II. Office: 100 Federal St Boston MA 02110

BROWN, WILLIAM LACY, genetic supply company executive; b. Arbovale, W.Va., July 16, 1913; s. Tilden L. and Mamie Hudson (Orndoff) B.; m. Alice Hevener Hannah, Aug. 17, 1941; children: Alicia Anne, William Tilden. B.A., Bridgewater Coll., Va., 1936; M.S., Washington U., St. Louis, 1939, Ph.D., 1941. Cytogeneticist Dept. Agr., Washington, 1941-42; dir. maize breeding Rogers Bros. Co., Olivia, Minn., 1942-45; with Pioneer Hi-Bred Internat., Inc., 1945—, v.p., dir. corp. research, Des Moines, 1965-75, pres., 1975-79, chief exec. officer, 1975-81, chmn., dir., 1979—; dir. Am. Farmland Trust, Winrock Internat, Pioneer de Centroamerica, S.A., Pishrow Seed Co., Iowa-Des Moines Nat. Bank; extra-mural prof. botany Washington U., 1957-65; mem. Gov. Iowa Sci. Adv. Council, 1977—. Author papers maize cytogenetics, evolution, germplasm conservation. Bd. regents Nat. Colonial Farm. Trustee Accokeek Found., Washington, Bridgewater (Va.) Coll. Fulbright advanced research scholar Imperial Coll. Tropical Agr., Trinidad, 1952-53; Univ. fellow Drake U., 1981—. Fellow Am. Soc. Agronomy, Iowa Acad. Sci. (dir.); mem. AAAS, Nat. Acad. Scis. (trustee), Am., Can. genetics socs., Am. Genetics Assn., Am. Inst. Biol. Scis., Bot. Soc. Am., Soc. Econ. Botany (Disting. Econ. Botanist award 1980), Phi Beta Kappa, Sigma Xi. Quaker. Clubs: Hyperion Field, Des Moines. Home: 6980 NW Beaver Dr Johnston IA 50131 Office: 6800 Pioneer Pkwy Johnston IA 50131

BROWN, WILLIAM LEE LYONS, JR., distilling company executive; b. Louisville, Aug. 22, 1936; s. William Lee Lyons and Sara (Shallenberger) B.; m. Alice Cary Farmer, June 13, 1959; children—William Lee Lyons III, Alice Cary, Stuart Randolph. B.A., U. Va., 1958; B.S., Am. Grad. Sch. Internat. Mgmt., 1960. Sales rep. Ariz., Brown-Forman Distillers Corp., Phoenix, 1960-61, v.p., Louisville, 1965-68, sr. v.p., 1968-72, exec. v.p., 1972-76, pres., chief exec. officer, 1976—; asst. v.p. Jos. Garneau Co. import div. Brown-Forman, N.Y.C., 1961-62, dir., Paris, France, 1962-65, Brown-Forman Distillers Corp., First Ky. Nat. Corp. Louisville, 1st Nat. Bank, Louisville, Diamond Shamrock Corp., Dallas. Bd. dirs. Ky. Center for Arts Endowment Fund, Louisville, Shakertown, Inc., Pleasant Hill, Ky.; pres., bd. govs. J.B. Speed Art Mus., Louisville; mem. Nat. Republican Senatorial Trust Com. Served to 1st lt. U.S. Army, 1958-59. Decorated chevalier de L'Ordre du Merite Agricole, France; hon. consul France. Mem. Soc. Sons Colonial Wars. Republican. Episcopalian. Clubs: Travellers (Paris); Fishers Island (N.Y.) Country; River Valley, Wynn Stay, Pendennis, Louisville Country (Louisville); University (N.Y.C.). Home: Fincastle Prospect KY 40059 also Fishers Island NY 06390 Office: 850 Dixie Hwy Louisville KY 40210

BROWN, WILLIAM MILTON, electrical engineer; b. Wheeling, W.Va., Feb. 14, 1932; s. John David and Marjorie Jennie (Walter) B.; m. Norma Jean Hulett, Aug. 24, 1963; children: Cherryl Lynn, Mark William, Jennifer Christine. B.S. in Elec. Engring, W.Va. U., 1952; M.S., Johns Hopkins U., 1955, D.Engring., 1957. Registered profl. engr. Asst. instr. physics, W.Va. U., 1950-52; engr. Air Arm div. Westinghouse Electric Corp., Balt., 1952-54; project supr. countermeasures group radiation lab. Johns Hopkins U., Balt., 1954-57; also part-time lectr.; mem. tech. staff Inst. Def. Analysis, Weapons Systems Evaluation Group, The Pentagon, 1957-58; mem. faculty U. Mich., Ann Arbor, 1958—, prof. elec. engring., 1963-73, adj. prof., 1975—, head radar and optics lab., 1960-68; pres. Environ. Research Inst. Mich., 1972—; cons. in field. Author: Analysis of Time-Invariant Systems, 1963, Random Processes; co-author: Communications and Radar, 1969; Asso. editor: Trans. Aerospace and Electronic Systems, 1965-74; editor-in-chief, 1974—; Contbr. articles to profl. jours. Recipient Rufus A. West prize W.Va. U., 1952. Mich. Fellow IEEE; mem. Aerospace and Electronic Systems Soc. (gov. 1978-82). Club: Rotary. Home: 525 Huntington Dr Ann Arbor MI 48104 Office: PO Box 8618 3300 Plymouth Rd Ann Arbor MI 48107

BROWN, WILLIAM PAUL, investment banker; b. Detroit, Oct. 23, 1919; s. Paul Joseph and Adele (LaFerte) B.; m. dau., Barbara (Mrs. Boyd Kenyon Knowles). A.B., U. Detroit, 1941. Vice pres. Baker, Simonds & Co., Detroit, 1945-64; instl. sales mgr. E.F. Hutton & Co., Inc., Detroit, 1964—; Treas. Detroit Stock Exchange, 1964. Served to lt. (s.g.) USNR, 1941-45; PTO. Decorated Bronze Star medal. Mem. Investment Bankers Assn. Am. (gov. 1969—, chmn. Mich. group, 1967), Bond Club Detroit, Security Traders Assn. Detroit (pres. 1955). Clubs: Country of Detroit, University of Detroit (pres. 1973 bd. govs.). Home: 1300 Lafayette St E Apt 2012 Detroit MI 48207 Office: 600 Renaissance Center Suite 1800 Detroit MI 48243

BROWN, WILLIAM RANDALL, geology educator; b. Staunton, Va., Oct. 31, 1913; s. Thornton Lee and Ellen (Greer) B.; m. Elizabeth Blessing Whitmore, Aug. 20, 1942; children—Elizabeth Dudley, Denison Greer, Elaine Daingerfield. B.S. with final honors, U. Va., 1938, M.A., 1939; Ph.D., Cornell U., 1942. Geologist Va. Geol. Survey, Charlottesville, 1942-45; mem. faculty dept. geology U. Ky., 1945—, assoc. prof., 1947-50, prof., 1950—; geologist U.S. Geol. Survey, 1965-76; rep. Am. Geol. Inst. to Internat. Field. Inst., Japan, 1967. Contbr. articles to profl. jours. Fellow Geol. Soc. Am. (chmn. S.E. sect. 1970-71), A.A.A.S.; mem. Am. Assn. Petroleum Geologists, Soc. Econ. Paleontologists and Mineralogists, Sigma Xi. Home: 253 Shady Ln Lexington KY 40503 Office: Dept Geology U Ky Lexington KY 40506

BROWN, WILLIAM ROBERT, association executive; b. Delaware, Ohio, Jan. 19, 1926; s. Omar Lloyd and Olive Ida (Johnson) B.; m. Dorothy Judd Curtis, Dec. 30, 1950; children—Darmae Judd, Ann Barlett Brown Nutt. B.A., Ohio Wesleyan U., 1948; M.A.; research scholar, Ohio State U., 1949. Asst. Inst. Practical Politics, Ohio Wesleyan U., 1947-48; research dir. Mo. State C. of C., 1950-64; govtl. research dir. Del. State Chamber, 1964-65; assoc. research dir. Council of State Chambers of Commerce, Washington, 1965-78, pres., 1979—. Editor: State Tax Report, 1969-81, Jud. Report, 1969-81, Property Tax Report, 1979, State UC Report, 1983—. Mem. adv. com. State and Local Tax Inst., Georgetown U. Law Center.; Precinct chmn. Republican Party, 1968-70. Mem. Nat. Tax Assn., Govtl. Research Assn., Phi Beta Kappa, Pi Sigma Alpha, Kappa Delta Pi, Sigma Chi. Republican. Methodist. Club: Capitol Hill. Home: Keyes Ferry Acres Box 602 Harpers Ferry WV 25425 Office: 122 C St NW Washington DC 20001

BROWN, W(ILLIAM) THACHER, financial executive; b. Orange, N.J., Dec. 9, 1947; s. John A. and Helen (Thacher) B.; m. Lloyd Hall, Aug. 29, 1970; children: Quincyl, Lee. B.S.E., Princeton U., 1969; M.B.A., U. Pa., 1972. Cert. fin. analyst. Statistician Smith Barney, N.Y.C., 1969-70; mgr. investment adv. dept. Drexel Burnham Lambert, Phila., 1970—. Bd. dirs., sec. Agnes Irwin Sch., Rosemont, 1981—; planning commr. Tredyffrin Twp., Berwyn, 1978—. Mem. Fin. Analysts Phila., Cert. Fin. Analysts. Clubs: Corinthian Yacht (dir.), Union League, Racquet. Office: 1500 Walnut St Philadelphia PA 19102

BROWN, WILLIE LEWIS, JR., state legislator, lawyer; b. Mineola, Tex., Mar. 20, 1934; s. Willie Lewis and Minnie (Boyd) B.; children: Susan, Robin, Michael. B.A., San Francisco State Coll., 1955; LL.D., Hastings Coll. Law, 1958; postgrad. fellow, Crown Coll., 1970, U. Calif.-Santa Cruz, 1970. Bar: Calif. 1959. Mem. Calif. State Assembley, Sacramento, 1965—, speaker of the Assembley, 1980—, chmn. Ways and Means Com., 1971-74; chmn. revenue and taxation com., 1976-79; Democratic Whip Calif. State Assembley, 1969-70, majority floor leader, 1979-80, chmn. legis. black caucus, 1980, chmn. govtl. efficiency and economy com., 1968—. Mem. U. Calif. bd. regents, 1972; co-chmn. Calif. del. to Nat. Black Polit. Conv., 1972, Calif. del. to Nat. Dem. Conv., 1980. Mem. State Legis. Leaders Found. (dir.), Nat. Conf. State Legislatures, NAACP, Black Am. Polit. Assn. Calif. (co-founder, past chmn.), Calif. Bar Assn., Alpha Phi Alpha, Phi Alpha Delta. Democrat. Methodist. Address: Calif Assembley Office of Speaker State Capitol Sacramento CA 95714

BROWN, WILSON GORDON, physician, educator; b. Bosworth, Mo., Jan. 18, 1914; s. Arthur Grannison and Clemma (Frock) B.; m. Anne Buckalew, Oct. 25, 1940; 1 son, Gordon Alan. A.B., William Jewell Coll., 1935; M.D., Washington U., St. Louis, 1939. Diplomate: Am. Bd. Clin. Pathology, Am. Bd. Anatomic Pathology. Intern pathology Barnes Hosp., St. Louis, 1939-40; resident in pathology St. Louis City Hosp., 1940-41; instr. pathology Washington U., 1945-51; clin. assoc. prof. Baylor U. Coll. Medicine, Houston, 1951—; clin. prof. U. Tex. Med. Sch. at Houston, 1972—; Pathologist, dir. labs. Hermann Hosp., Houston, 1951-71; dir. labs. Twelve Oaks Hosp., Houston, 1965—, Polly Ryon Hosp., Richmond, Tex., 1954—, Park Plaza Hosp., Houston, 1975—; partner Brown & Assocs. Med. Labs., Houston, 1954—; Mem. adv. bd. Living Bank, Houston, 1968—; founding mem. Mus. Med. Sci., Houston, 1969—, trustee, 1969—, pres. bd. trustees, 1974-75; Bd. dirs. Ewing Center Inc., Am. Cancer Soc. Harris County (Tex.) Br., 1952, pres, 1967-68. Contbr. articles to med. publs. Served to maj. M.C. AUS, 1942-46; ETO, MTO. Decorated Bronze Star medal. Mem. Am., Tex. med. assns., Harris County Med. Soc., Coll. Am. Pathologists, Am. Soc. Clin. Pathology, Houston, Tex. socs. pathologists, Sigma Xi, Beta Beta Beta, Theta Chi Delta, Aeons, Phi Gamma Delta. Clubs: Warwick, Forum (Houston). Home: 3518 Westridge St Houston TX 77025 Office: 220 Park Plaza Profl Bldg Houston TX 77004

BROWN, WILSON M., JR., banker; b. 1926; married. A.B., Princeton U., 1948; postgrad., Rutgers U., 1960. Vice pres. comml. lending First & Mchts. Nat. Bank, Richmond, Va., 1948-62; sr. v.p. N.C. Nat. Bank, 1963-72; pres., chief exec. officer S.E. Nat. Bank Pa., 1971-78; pres. Central Nat. Bank Cleve., 1978-83, chmn. bd., pres., chief exec. officer, 1983—; pres., chief exec. officer, chmn. bd. Centran Corp., 1978—. Fellow Am. Soc. Adolescent Psychiatry. Office: Central Nat Bank Cleve E 9th & Superior Ave Cleveland OH 44114 *

BROWN, WOOD, III, lawyer; b. New Orleans, Jan. 13, 1936; s. Wood and Martha Hyland B.; m. Sandra Anne Brown, July 30, 1960; children—Carolyn, Charles, Martha, Claiborne. B.A., Tulane U., 1958, LL.B., 1961. Bar: La. 1961, U.S. Supreme Ct. 1980. Asso. firm Montgomery, Barnett, Brown & Read, New Orleans, 1961-66, partner firm, 1966—; mem. adj. faculty Tulane U. Law Sch. Editor: La. Bar Jour, 1971-73. Mem. New Orleans Civil Service Commn., 1977-83, chmn., 1981-83; bd. dirs. YMCA Greater New Orleans, Protestant Home for Aged. Served with U.S. Army, 1958-59. Recipient Monte Lemann award La. Civil Service League, 1981. Fellow Am. Coll. Trial Lawyers; mem. La. State Bar Assn. (ho. of dels. 1964-70, 73—, sec.-treas. 1971-73, com. bar admissions 1974-78, com. on profl. responsibility 1975—), New Orleans Bar Assn., Am. Bar Assn., Am. Law Inst., Am. Judicature Soc., Internat. Assn. Def. Counsel, Def. Research Inst., La. Assn. Def. Counsel. Democrat. Presbyterian. Clubs: Boston, Stratford. Home: 2129 Palmer Ave New Orleans LA 70118 Office: 1800 First Nat Bank of Commerce Bldg New Orleans LA 70112

BROWNE, ALAN KINGSTON, bank consultant; b. Alameda, Calif., Nov. 12, 1909; s. Ralph Stuart and Etta E. (Bouve) B.; m. Elisabeth Leone Henrotte, Feb. 7, 1942. Student, U. Calif., 1929. With Bankamerica Co. (formerly securities div. Nat. Bank Italy Co.), 1929-41; successively clk., mgr. mcpl. bond dept., asst. v.p.; with Bank of Am. Nat. Trust & Savs. Assn., 1941-71, asst. cashier, 1941-42, asst., v.p., mgr. mcpl. bond dept., 1946-52, v.p., 1952-65, sr. v.p., 1965-71, head investments, 1964-71; cons., 1971-72; sr. v.p., dir. Drexel Firestone Inc., N.Y.C., 1972-73; dir. Drexel Burnham & Co., Inc., 1973; cons., 1974—; past pres., dir. San Francisco Stadium, Inc., Candlestick Park. Contbr. articles to profl. jours. Mem. San Francisco Mus. Art, The Museum Soc.; past chmn. bd., past pres. Friends of San Francisco Pub. Library; chmn. adv. bd. on financing San Francisco Bay Area Rapid Transit Dist.; chmn. San Francisco Bay Area Rapid Transit Commn.; bd. dirs. Adminstrv. Bldg. Corp., Calif. Alumni Berkeley Found., Golden Rain Found., Rossmoor and Walnut Creek, Calif.; past mem. Presdl. Adv. Com. Fed. Debt Mgmt. Served from pvt. to maj. AUS, 1942-46. Recipient Disting. Citizens award Nat. Mcpl. League, 1964. Mem. San Francisco C. of C. (past pres.; chmn. sr. council), Mcpl. Forum N.Y., Mcpl. Fin. Forum Washington, San Francisco Mcpl. Forum, Air Force Assn., Assn. U.S. Army, Calif. Alumni Assn., Calif. Geneal. Soc., Calif. Hist. Soc., Friends Bancroft Library, Investment Bankers Assn. Am. (now Securities Industry Assn.) (past gov., v.p. mcpl. div.), SAR, Navy League, Mechanics Inst., Phi Kappa Sigma. Clubs: Bond (past pres.; named outstanding investment banker of yr. 1958), Olympic, Merchants Exchange, Commonwealth, Stock Exchange, Municipal Bond (San Francisco); Faculty (Berkeley); Rotary. Home: 1113 Singingwood Ct 6 Walnut Creek CA 94595

BROWNE, ALLAN ROLAND, lawyer; b. El Paso, Tex., Nov. 18, 1900; s. Cecil W. and Anne (Welsh) B.; m. Blanche Longan, June 27, 1925; children: Virginia Browne Mount, Carol Harrington Haney; m. Phoebe Mosman Harrington, July 5, 1958. A.B., Harvard U., 1922; J.D., U. Mo., Kansas City, 1925; grad., Command and Gen. Staff Coll., Ft. Leavenworth, Kans. Bar: Mo. 1923, Hawaii 1956, Kans. 1962, U.S. Supreme Ct., Ct. Appeals, Dist. Ct. 1962. Practice law, Kansas City, Mo., 1923-42, 56—; served from capt. to col. U.S. Army, 1942-56; acting judge adv. gen. for Pacific Ocean area, 1945-46, judge adv. 8th Army, Japan, 1946-49; presiding officer Bd. Review, Washington, 1949-53; judge adv. U.S. Army Pacific, 1953-56; ret., 1956; of counsel Ennis, Browne & Jensen. Mem. ABA, Kansas City Bar Assn. (pres. 1962-63, chmn. grievance com., fee disputes com.), Mo. Assn. Trial Attys. (v.p. 1970, pres. 1973), Mo. Bar, Alumni Assn. Sch. Law U. Mo. at Kansas City (pres. 1967, v.p. alumni bd. 1973), Delta Theta Phi, Alpha Sigma Phi. Presbyterian. Home: 6545 Overbrook Rd Shawnee Mission KS 66208 Office: Traders Bank Bldg Kansas City MO 64106

BROWNE, CHARLES IDOL, radiochemist; b. Atlanta, Feb. 8, 1922; s. Charles Idol and Lillian Aurelia (Thweatt) B.; m. Nancy Elizabeth Brown, Aug. 9, 1942; 1 son, Carter T. A.B., Drew U., 1941; M.A., U. Tex., 1942; M.S., Calif. Inst. Tech., 1948; Ph.D., U. Calif.-Berkeley, 1952. With Los Alamos Sci. Lab., 1955—, assoc. div. leader, 1965-72, div. leader, 1972-74, assoc. dir., 1974—; sci. advisor AEC, 1965-74. Served with USAF, 1943-55. Fellow Am. Phys. Soc., Am. Inst. Chemists; mem. Sigma Xi. Republican. Home: 428 Estante Way Los Alamos NM 87544 Office: PO Box 1663 Los Alamos NM 87545

BROWNE, CLEMENT GEORGE, mgmt. cons., broker; b. Vienna, Austria, Feb. 17, 1930; emigrated to U.S., 1940, naturalized, 1946; s. Herman H. and M. Steffy (Herrmann) B.; m. Gisela Helene Pluskat, Mar. 22, 1954; children—Bruce Clement, Eric Clement (dec.), Cordelia Gisela. B.A., Syracuse U., 1951; M.S., Columbia, 1955. With Procter & Gamble Co., Cin., 1955-62, asst. brand mgr., 1960-62; with Andrew Jergens Co., Cin., 1962-68, mktg. dir., Europe, 1965-68; exec. v.p., dir. Andrew Jergens Co. Ltd., 1968-71; owner C.G. Browne & Assos. (mktg. services firm), Toronto, Ont., Can., 1971—; spl. rep. to Can. for industry, trade and tourism of State of Ga., 1973-80; former cons. Toronto-Dominion Bank; cons. various firms; broker and importer. Served to 1st lt. USAF, 1951-53. Office: Box 353 Sta P Toronto ON M5S 2S8 Canada

BROWNE, CORNELIUS PAYNE, physics educator; b. Madison, Wis., Oct. 30, 1923; s. Frederick Lincoln and Vera (Payne) B.; m. Cynthia Cochrane, July 6, 1957; children: Margaret, Cornelius. B.A., U. Wis., 1946, Ph.D., 1951. Research asso. MIT, Cambridge, 1951-56; prof. physics U. Notre Dame (Ind.), 1956—; cons. Argonne Nat. Lab., 1961-66, Los Alamos Nat. Lab., 1963-66; vis. prof. U. Tex. at Austin, 1972, U. Wis., summers 1959-61; program officer for nuclear physics NSF, 1980-81. Contbr. articles profl. jours. Served with USNR, 1944-45. Fellow Am. Phys. Soc. (div. nuclear physics program com. 1972-73, nominating com. 1973-74); mem. Am. Assn. Physics Tchrs., Sigma Xi (pres. chpt. 1969-70), Phi Beta Kappa, Theta Delta Chi. Episcopalian (chpt. mem. 1968-70, 74). Club: Eagle Lake (Mich.) Yacht (dir. 1968-70, 73-76, commodore 1974-75). Research in nuclear reactions and excitation levels Browne-Buechner broad-range magnetic spectrograph. Home: 1606 E Washington Ave South Bend IN 46617 Office: Physics Dept U Notre Dame Notre Dame IN 46556

BROWNE, DIK, cartoonist; b. N.Y.C., Aug. 11, 1917; m. Joan Kelly; children—Bob, Chris, Sally. Studied at, Cooper Union. Formerly with, N.Y. Jour., Newsweek, firm Johnstone & Cushing; collaborator (with Mort Walker); on comic strip Hi And Lois, 1954—; creator, cartoonist: Hagar the Horrible, 1973—; Recipient (Banshees Silver Lady award, Elzie Segar award.); Author: (with Mort Walker) Land of Lost Things, 1973, Hagar the Horrible, 1973, Wit and Wisdom of Hagar the Horrible. Served with AUS, World War II. Mem. Nat. Cartoonists Soc. (2 Reuben awards). Home: King Features 235 E 45th St New York NY 10017

BROWNE, EDWARD MANNING, army officer; b. N.Y.C., July 13, 1930; s. Elbert and Kathryn (Doman) B.; m. Mary Lynne Howell, Nov. 11, 1950; children—Michael, Karen, Patrick, Lauren. B.S. summa cum laude, St. Benedict's Coll., 1968; M.S., Auburn U., 1972, Fla. Inst. Tech., 1973. Commd. 2d lt. Transp. Corps U.S. Army, 1950, advanced through grades to maj. gen.; service in, Korea, Vietnam and Ger.; project mgr. light observation helicopter systems and quiet aircraft systems; mgr. advanced scout helicopter program, until 1976; program mgr. advanced attack helicopter U.S. Army Devel. and Readiness Command, St. Louis, 1976—. Decorated Bronze Star, Legion of Merit, Air medal with four oak leaf clusters, others; recipient award for program mgmt. Sec. Army. Mem. Assn. U.S. Army, Army Aviation Assn., Am. Helicopter Soc., Am. Def. Preparedness Assn. Roman Catholic. Address: Advanced Attack Helicopter Program 4300 Goodfellow Blvd USA DARCOM Saint Louis MO 63166

BROWNE, FRANCIS CEDRIC, judge; b. Cleve., Jan. 22, 1915; s. William Henry and Anna Loretta (Ginley) B.; m. Elizabeth Ann Cullen, July 3, 1937; children—Richard C., James F., Barbara Ann Browne Elliott, Martha Louise Browne Schwartz, David F. Student, Ohio State U., 1935; A.B., U. Akron, 1936; J.D., Cleve. State U., 1942; postgrad., George Washington U., 1942, 50. Bar: D.C., Md. bars. Patent lawyer, Washington, 1945-75; partner firm Browne, Beveridge, DeGrandi & Kline (and predecessors); patent solicitor Indsl. Rayon Corp., Cleve., 1938-41; trial judge U.S. Ct. of Claims, 1975-80, sr. trial judge, 1981-82, sr. judge, 1982—. Served as patent atty. USAF, 1945; col. Judge Adv. Gen. Dept., USAF res. ret. Mem. Am., Fed., D.C., bar assns., Am. Patent Law Assn., Thomas More Soc. (treas. 1961-72), Delta Theta Phi, Phi Delta Theta (pres. Washington alumni 1962-63), Omicron Delta Kappa, Pi Kappa Delta. Clubs: K.C. (4th deg.), Nat. Lawyers (gov. 1959-80), Nat. Lawyers (sec. 1959-75), Kenwood Golf and Country, Cosmos (Washington). Home: 4601 N Park Ave Apt 319 Chevy Chase MD 20815 4601 N Park Ave Apt 803 Chevy Chase MD 20815

BROWNE, GERALD MICHAEL, educator; b. Detroit, Dec. 13, 1943; s. Walter Whitney and Marjorie Marie (Eckard) B.; m. Alma Lorraine Colk, May 31, 1975. A.B., U. Mich., 1966, M.A., 1967, Ph.D., 1968. Hon. research asst., U. Coll. London, 1968, instr., Harvard U., 1968-69, lectr., 1969-70, asst. prof., 1970-73; jr. fellow Center Hellenic Studies, Washington, 1973-74; asst. prof. U. Ill., Urbana, 1974-75, asso. prof., 1975-80, prof. classics and linguistics, 1980—. Author: Documentary Papyri from the Michigan Collection, 1970, Michigan Papyri, 1975, The Papyri of the Sortes Astrampsychi, 1974, Michigan Coptic Texts, 1978, Griffith's Old Nubian Lectionary, 1982, Sortes Astrampsychi, 1983, Chrysostomus Nubianus, 1983. Woodrow Wilson fellow, 1965-66; NDEA Title IV fellow, 1966-68. Mem. Internat. Assn. Coptic Studies, Am. Soc. Papyrologists (editor bull.), Soc. Nubian Studies (council), Am. Philological Assn. Home: 909 Sunnycrest Dr Urbana IL 61801 Office: 4072 FLB 707 S Mathews Urbana IL 61801

BROWNE, HARRY L., lawyer; b. South Bend, Ind., July 27, 1911; s. Alex and Lena (Godfried) B.; m. Helen Lieberman, Apr. 16, 1942; 1 son, Douglas F. B.S., Ind. U., 1934, J.D., 1936; postgrad. labor law, Columbus U., Washington, 1939. Bar: Ind. bar 1936, Mo. bar 1948, U.S. Supreme Ct. bar 1948. Pvt. practice, South Bend, 1936-38; atty. NLRB, 1938-49, regional atty. 6th region, 1948-49; practiced in, Kansas City, Mo., 1949—; mem. firm Spencer, Fane, Britt & Browne, 1951—; Past chmn. Kansas City Personnel Appeal Bd.; bd. dirs. Starlight Theatre Assn., Kansas City, Mo., Menorah Hosp., Kansas City, Planned Parenthood, Greater Kansas City Sports Commn., Heart of Am. United Way Campaign, Kansas City Amateur Sports Hall of Champions; bd. govs., trustee Kansas City Philharmonic Assn.; hon. trustee Rockhurst Coll., Kansas City U., Truman Med. Ctr., Kansas City Conservatory; hon. fellow Truman Library Inst. Contbr. articles to profl. jours. Served to lt. USNR, 1942-45; PTO. Mem. ABA (co-chmn. com. on relations between lawyers and agys. and depts. in field labor Law 1965-72, mem. com. on practice and procedure under Nat. Labor Relations Act), Kansas City Bar Assn. (chmn. labor com. 1960-63), Mo. Bar (chmn. labor com. 1957-61), Am. Judicature Soc., Lawyers Assn. Kansas City (bd. dirs.), Kansas City C. of C., Nat. Retail Mchts. Assn., Am. Retail Fedn., Indsl. Relations Research Assn., Downtown, Inc., Rotarian (past dir., sec.-treas., pres. 1970-71 Kansas City). Home: 1220 W 69th Terr Kansas City MO 64113 Office: Power & Light Bldg 106 W 14th St Kansas City MO 64105

BROWNE, H(ERBERT) MONROE, ambassador; b. Long Beach, Calif., May 9, 1917; s. Allen Walter and Ruth Ann B.; m. Mary Frances Ashby, Aug. 19, 1939; children—Elizabeth Ann Denny, Richard Allen, David Ashby. A.B., UCLA, 1939; postgrad., U. Calif., Berkeley, 1940-41. Owner Browne Cattle Co., 1950-81; owner Hartman Concrete Materials, 1950-70, McCoy Truck Co., 1950-65, Wheatland Land and Cattle Co., 1950-70; pres. Inst. for Contemporary Studies, San Francisco, 1975-81; U.S. ambassador to N.Z., Wellington, 1981—; Mem. Calif. OSHA Commn., 1971-74; mem. Reagan Exec.-Adv. Campaign Com., Com., 1980-81; chmn. Pres. Reagan's Small Bus. Task Force, 1980, mem. transition team, 1980-81. Served to lt. USNR, 1942-45. Mem. Am. Nat. Cattlemen's Assn., U.S. C. of C., Calif. C. of C., Calif. Farm Bur. Republican. Clubs: Pacific-Union (San Francisco); Sutler (Sacramento); Stockdale Golf and Country (Bakersfield, Calif.); Masons. Home: 99 Ludlam Crescent Lower Hutt New Zealand Office: Am Embassy Private Bag Wellington New Zealand

BROWNE, JACKSON, singer, songwriter; b. Calif.; s. Clyde Browne. Back-up guitarist for singer, Nico; songs recorded by, The Nitty Gritty Dirt Band, Tom Rush, Linda Ronstadt; own albums include Jackson Browne, 1972, For Everyman, 1973, Late for the Sky, 1974, The Pretender, 1976, Running on Empty, 1977, Hold Out, 1980, Lawyers in Love, 1983; songs include Rock Me on the Water, Song for Adam, These Days. Office: care Peter Golden & Assos 1952 Crossroads of the World Hollywood CA 90028 *

BROWNE, JOHN ROBINSON, banker; b. Ft. Worth, Aug. 29, 1914; s. Virgil and Maimee Lee (Robinson) B.; m. Elizabeth Anne Hargett, Sept. 1, 1945; children—John Robinson, Ann Browne (Mrs. John M. Dunker); stepchildren—Bob Allen Street, David H. Street. A.B., Okla. U., 1938, J.D., 1939; postgrad., Harvard Grad. Sch. Bus. Adminstrn., 1939-40; grad., Stonier Grad. Sch. Banking, Rutgers U., 1965. Bar: Okla. bar 1939. With Liberty Nat. Bank & Trust Co., Oklahoma City, 1945-46, 60-71, sr. v.p., 1960-71; gen. mgr. Coca-Cola Bottling Co., Colorado Springs and Pueblo, Colo., 1946-59; mgr. credit dept. Bank of Mid-Am., Oklahoma City, 1959-60; pres., chmn. bd., chief exec. officer Security Nat. Bank, Cairo, Ill., 1959-62; chief exec. officer Union Bank & Trust Co. (formerly May Ave. Bank and Trust Co.), Oklahoma City, 1971—. Pres. Community Chest, Colorado Springs.; Trustee Deaconess Hosp. Served from 2d lt. to lt. col., F.A. AUS, 1940-45. Mem. Okla. Bar Assn. Presbyterian (elder, trustee). Clubs: Petroleum, Oklahoma City Golf and Country (Oklahoma City); Garden of the Gods (Colorado Springs, Colo.). Home: 1506 Drury Ln Oklahoma City OK 73116 Office: 4921 N May Ave Oklahoma City OK 73112

BROWNE, KINGSBURY, lawyer; b. Brookline, Mass., Nov. 18, 1922; s. Kingsbury and Sophie (Acheson) B.; m. Annette Wright Upson, June 11, 1949; children—Annette, Kingsbury, Mark, Christopher, Juliet, Gabriella. A.B. cum laude, Harvard U., 1944, LL.B., 1950. Bar: Mass. 1950. Law clk. Judge of U.S. Tax Ct., Washington, 1950-53; partner Hill & Barlow, Boston, 1965—; faculty Northeastern U., Law Sch., Boston, 1955, Suffolk Law Sch., 1956, Boston U. Grad. Tax Program, 1957; tax cons. nat. and regional environ. orgns.; dir. Guilford Industries, Maine, 1960-82, Sugarloaf Mountain Corp., 1965-78, Boston & Worcester Corp., Mass., 1970-79; mem. corp. Brookline Savs. Bank, 1966—; fellow Lincoln Inst. of Land Policy; vis. scholar Harvard Law Sch., 1980; Chmn. Brookline Council for Planning and Renewal, 1954-56; mem. Selectmen's Com. for Study of Legal Services, 1974-75; corporator Boston Hosp. Women, 1973-78; Mem. Corp. Winsor Sch., 1963—, exec. com., 1967-70; trustee Skowhegan Sch. Sculpture and Painting, 1966—, Plimouth Plantation, 1978—; mem. vis. com. Sch. Visual Arts, Boston U., 1975-80, Peabody Mus. Archaeology and Ethnology Harvard U., 1976—. Contbr. articles to profl. jours. Former bd dirs. Mus. Sch. Boston Mus. Fine Arts, Miramichi Salmon Assn., N.B., Can., 1968-79. Served to capt. USAAF, 1943-46. Mem. Am., Mass., Boston bar assns., Am. Law Inst., Am. Bar Found. Home: 61 Walnut Pl Brookline MA 02146 Office: 225 Franklin St Boston MA 02110

BROWNE, LESLIE, dancer, actress; b. N.Y.C., June 29, 1957; d. Kelly and Isabel (Mirrow) Brown. Grad., Profl. Children's Sch., N.Y.C. Mem. corps de ballet, N.Y.C. Ballet, 1974-76; soloist, Am. Ballet Theatre, 1976—; appearances: in films Turning Point, Nijinsky. Recipient Dance Edn. of Am. award. Mem. Acad. Motion Picture Arts and Scis. Address: Am Ballet Theatre 890 Broadway New York NY 10003

BROWNE, MALCOLM WILDE, journalist; b. N.Y.C., Apr. 17, 1931; s. Douglas Granzow and Dorothy Rutledge (Wilde) B.; m. Huynh thi Le Lieu, July 18, 1966. Student, Swarthmore Coll., 1948-50, N.Y.U., 1950-52. Cons. chemist, tech. writer, 1952-56; newsman, copy editor Middletown (N.Y.) Daily Record, 1958-60; with Balt. bur. A.P., 1960-61, chief corr. for, Viet Nam, 1961-65; Saigon corr. ABC, 1965-66; freelance writer and corr., N.Y.C., 1966-68; corr. New York Times in, Buenos Aires, 1968-71, in S. Asia, 1971-73, in Eastern Europe, 1973-77, sci. corr., 1977-81; sr. editor Discover mag., 1981—. Author: The New Face of War, 1965, also numerous articles. Served with AUS, 1956-58. Recipient First prize World Press Photo award, The Hague, 1963, Pulitzer prize fgn. corr., 1964, Overseas Press Club award, 1964, Sigma Delta Chi award, 1964, Louis M. Lyons award, 1964, Nat. Headliners Club award, 1964; A.P. Mng. Editors award, 1964; Edward R. Murrow Meml. fellow Council on Fgn. Relations, 1966-67. Address: 36 E 36th St New York NY 10016

BROWNE, MICHAEL DENNIS, poet, educator; b. Walton-on-Thames, Eng., May 28, 1940; came to U.S., 1965, naturalized, 1978; s. Edgar Dennis and Winifred Margaret (Denne) B.; m. Lisa Furlong McLean, July 18, 1981. B.A. with 1st class honors, Hull (Eng.) U., 1962; M.A. with honors, U. Iowa, 1967. Vis. lectr. creative writing U. Iowa, 1967-68; adj. asst. prof. Sch. Arts, Columbia U., fall 1968; mem. lit. div. Bennington (Vt.) Coll., 1969-71; mem. faculty U. Minn., Mpls., 1971—, asso. prof. English, 1975-83, prof., 1983—. Author: The Wife of Winter, 1970, The Sun Fetcher, 1978, Sun Exercises, 1976; libretti How The Stars Were Made, 1968, The Wife of Winter, 1969, The Sea Journey, 1970, Non Songs, 1974, (with Stephen Paulus) Canticles, 1977; Fountain of my Friends, 1977, Mad Book, Shadow Book, 1977, North Shore, 1978, A Village Singer, 1979, All My Pretty Ones, 1981; also poems for magazines, included in anthologies. Nat. Endowment Arts poetry fellow, 1977; librettist fellow, 1978; Bush Found. fellow, 1981. Home: 1040 16th Ave SE Minneapolis MN 55414 Office: 207 Lind Hall Univ Minn Minneapolis MN 55455

BROWNE, MILLARD CHILD, former newspaper editor; b. Sprague, Wash., Feb. 7, 1915; s. Clarence Swain and Irma Josephine (Child) B.; m. Jane Sweet, Aug. 25, 1939; children: Katherine Anne (Mrs. Samuel Kunkle), Millard Warren, Jeffrey Child, Barbara Jane (Mrs. S. Terry Atlas). A.B., Stanford U., 1936, M.A., 1939; postgrad. (Nieman fellow), Harvard U., 1942-43. Reporter, Columnist, editorial writer Calif. newspapers Santa Paula Chronicle, Santa Ana Jour., Sacramento Union, 1936-42; asso. editor Sacramento Union, 1943-44; editorial writer Buffalo Evening News, 1944-80, chief editorial writer, 1953-66, editorial page editor, 1966-80; sr. mem. Wolfson Coll., Cambridge (Eng.) U., 1980-81. Recipient Freedoms Found. citation for editorial writing, 1953, 54, 55, 57, 69. Mem. Nat. Conf. Editorial Writers (pres. 1962-63), Am. Soc. Newspaper Editors, Internat. Press Inst., World Press Freedom Com., Soc. Profl. Journalists/Sigma Delta Chi, Sigma Alpha Epsilon. Unitarian. Home: 2140 Santa Cruz Ave Apt D 301 Menlo Park CA 94025

BROWNE, M(ILLARD) WARREN, chem. corp. exec.; b. Sacramento, May 22, 1944; s. Millard Child and Velma Jane (Sweet) B.; m. Mary Suzanne Pandjiris, Jan. 12, 1980. A.B. magna cum laude, Princeton U., 1966; J.D., Columbia U., 1970. Bar: N.Y. bar 1971. Chemist CIA, Washington, 1966-67; atty. White & Case, N.Y.C., 1970-73; staff atty. Celanese Corp., N.Y.C., 1973-77; sec., gen. counsel Philip A. Hunt Chem. Corp., Palisades Park, N.J., 1978—. Home: 930 Fifth Ave New York NY 10021 Office: Philip A Hunt Chem Corp Roosevelt Pl Palisades Park NJ 07650

BROWNE, MORGAN TREW, editor; b. Chestertown, Md., Nov. 22, 1919; s. Morgan and Mary Groome (Trew) B.; m. Ann Elizabeth Riley, Feb. 14, 1949; children—Elizabeth, Morgan. Student, Balt. City Coll., 1934-37, Johns Hopkins, 1937-40. Mgr. Sci. Book Club, Religious Book Club, 1945-46; mng. editor Tide mag., 1946-49, 49-53, editor, 1953-50; exec. v.p., also gen. mgr.; pres., editorial dir. Bill Communications.; Dir. periodicals N.A.M., 1949-51. Home: 42 Prides Crossing New Canaan CT 06840 Office: 633 3d Ave New York City NY 10017

BROWNE, RACHEL, dancer, choreographer; b. Phila., Nov. 6, 1934; emigrated to Can., 1956, naturalized, 1961; d. Israel and Eva (Minkoff) B.; m. Donald Browne, July 18, 1953 (div.); children: Ruth Miriam, Annette. Student, Martha Graham Sch. Contemporary Dance, N.Y.C., 1965-77, Am. Ballet Theatre Sch., N.Y.C., 1953-55, Benjamin Harkarvy, N.Y.C., 1951-57, Merce Cunningham Sch., N.Y.C., 1974-76, Jose Limon Sch., N.Y.C., 1974-77, Robert Joffrey, N.Y.C., 1953-55. Founder, artistic dir., choreographer, tchr., dancer Winnipeg's Contemporary Dancers, 1964—; guest tchr. in modern dance techniques at confs., univs., schs. throughout Can.; on jury Can. Council Modern Dance awards, 1975, Chalmers Choregraphic awards, 1977. Dancer, N.Y. Dance-Drama Co., N.Y.C., 1955-57; solo dancer, Royal Winnipeg (Man., Can.) Ballet, 1958-63; Recent choreography includes The Woman I Am, 1975, Interiors, 1976, Just About Us, 1977, The Other, 1979. Named Woman of Year Man. YMCA, 1977; Can. Council Arts grantee, 1967, 69, 1971. Mem. Dance in Can. Assn., Am. Assn. Danee Cos., Actor's Equity, Voice of Women, Assn. Canadian TV and Radio Artists. Home: 166 Cathedral Ave Winnipeg MN Canada R2W 0W5 *

BROWNE, ROBERT SPAN, economist; b. Chgo., Aug. 17, 1924; s. William Henri and Julia Louise (Barksdale) B.; m. Huoi Nguyen, Apr. 6, 1956; children: Hoa Nguyen, Mai Julia, Ngo Alexi, Marshall Xuan. B.A. in Econs, U. Ill., 1944; M.B.A., U. Chgo., 1947; postgrad. in econs., CUNY. Economist U.S. Govt. Fgn. Aid Program, Cambodia and Vietnam, 1955-61; project dir. Phelps-Stokes Fund, N.Y.C., 1963-65; asst. prof. econs. Fairleigh Dickinson U., Teaneck, N.J., 1965-71; dir. Black Econ. Research Center, N.Y.C., 1969-80; exec. dir. African Devel. Fund, 1980-82; sr. research fellow Howard U., 1982—; mem. adv. com. Congl. Budget Office, 1976—, Office Tech. Assessment, 1976—. Author: (with others) The Social Scene, 1972; Editor: Rev. Black Polit. Economy, 1970-71. Del. Nat. Democratic Conv., 1968, Black Polit. Conv., Gary, Ind., 1972; Pres., bd. dirs. 21st Century Found.; bd. dirs. Emergency Land Fund, Nat. Rural Center. Served with USAAF, 1944-46. Mem. Am. Econ. Assn., Club of Rome (U.S. chpt.), Council Fgn. Relations. Home: 214 Tryon Ave Teaneck NJ 07666 Office: 112 W 120th St New York NY 10027

BROWNE, ROSCOE LEE, actor, director, writer; b. Woodbury, N.J. Ed., Lincoln U.; postgrad., Middlebury (Vt.) Coll. Columbia. Nat. sales rep. Schenley Import Corp., 1952-56; instr. French and lit. Lincoln U., to 1952. Performed with, N.Y. Shakespeare Festival, 7 seasons; performed various Shakespearian roles for, Canadian Broadcasting Co., Toronto; guest artist, Spolato Festival Two Worlds; reader classics and modern poetry in univs. throughout U.S.; (with Anthony Zerbe in) ann. tour Behind The Broken Words; appeared in: Broadway plays The Ballad of the Sad Cafe, 1963, The Cool World, 1960, General Seeger, 1962, Tiger, Tiger Burning Bright!, 1962, The Connection, 1962, Black Like Me, 1964, The Old Glory, 1964-65, My One and Only, 1983; actor, dir.: A Hand is On The Gate, 1966, The Blacks, 1961, Aria de Capo, 1958; motion pictures include The Comedians, 1967, Uptight, 1968, The Liberation of L.B. Jones, 1970, The Cowboys, 1972, The World's Greatest Athlete, 1973, Superfly, 1972, TNT, 1973, Topaz, 1969, Uptown Saturday Night, Logan's Run, 1976, Twilight's Last Gleaming, 1977; also TV film The Big Ripoff, 1975; also TV series Soap, 1977—; other TV appearances., (recipient Obie award for best actor in Benito Cereno 1964-65, Los Angeles Drama Critics award for best actor in Dream on Monkey Mountain 1971); Author poems, short stories. Trustee Millay Colony Arts, N.Y., Los Angeles Free Pub. Theatre, KPFK, Pacifica Radio, Los Angeles. Track champion (1000 yard indoors) Amateur Athletic Union, 1949, 51; twice named All-American. Address: care Georgia Gilly 8721 Sunset Blvd Los Angeles CA 90069

BROWNE, SECOR DELAHAY, educator, consultant; b. Chgo., July 22, 1916; s. Aldis Jerome and Elizabeth (Cunningham) B.; m. Mary Denise Giles, Aug. 23, 1945; children: Patrick R., Giles C.; m. Constance Ely Haden, Sept. 6, 1970; stepchildren: Dana M., Sabra I., Russell L., C. Keller, Chesley E., Kinard E. A.B., Harvard U., 1938. Engr. draftsman Kroeschell Engring. Co., Chgo., 1938-39; engr. salesman Barber-Colman Co., Rockford, Ill., 1939-42, mgr. aircraft prodn., 1946-51; with Clifford Mfg. Co., Waltham, Mass., 1951-55; pres., chmn. bd. Browne & Shaw Co., 1955-69, Browne & Shaw Research Corp., 1963-68; asso. prof. Mass. Inst. Tech., 1958-69; v.p. Bolt, Beranek and Newman, Inc., Cambridge, Mass., 1968-69; asst. sec. for research and tech. Dept. Transp., 1969; chmn. CAB, 1971-73; prof. Mass. Inst. Tech., 1973-75; cons. Secor D. Browne Assos. Inc., 1973—. Author articles. Mem. Lincoln (Mass.) Republican Town Com., 1962-68; chmn. Flight Safety Found. Served to maj. USAAF, 1942-46. Decorated Bronze Star. Fellow Royal Aero. Soc., Royal Soc. Arts, AIAA (asso.); mem. Soc. Automotive Engrs., Royal Commonwealth Soc. Clubs: Harvard, Wings (N.Y.C.); Metropolitan, Nat. Aviation (Washington); Atheneum, American (London). Home: PO Box 217 Charlestown RI 02813 also 4000 Massachusetts Ave NW Apt 1122 Washington DC 20016 Office: 2101 L St NW Suite 207 Washington DC 20037

BROWNE, STANHOPE STRYKER, lawyer; b. Colorado Springs, Colo., July 22, 1931; s. Samuel Stanhope Stryker and FlorenceJeanette (Reynolds) B.; m. Elizabeth Whitney Sturges, Sept. 12, 1964; children: Katrina C., Whitney R. A.B., Princeton U., 1953; LL.B., Harvard U., 1956. Bar: Pa. 1957, D.C. 1972. Assoc. Dechert Price & Rhoads, Phila., 1956-65, ptnr., 1965—, resident ptnr., Brussels, Belgium, 1972-76; lectr. internat. bus. law. Contbr. articles to profl. jours. Chmn. Penn's Landing Corp., Phila., 1981—; vice chmn. World Affairs Council, Phila., 1978—; sec. Independence Hall Assn., Phila., 1978—; mem. exec. com. Old Phila. Devel. Corp., 1968-72, 77—; mem. Phila. Dist. Export Council U.S. Dept. Commerce, 1983—; vice pres. Pa. Prison Soc., 1962-69; pres. Greater Phila. Council of Chs., 1966-67; chmn. Democrats Abroad, Belgium, 1975-76, Pa. Internat. Trade Conf., 1977-79; mem. adv. commn. Independence Nat. Hist. Park, Phila., 1969-72; bd. dirs. Greater Phila. Movement, 1970-71. Recipient Pub. Service and Polit. Courage award Southeastern Pa. chpt. Ams. for Democratic Action, 1965. Mem. ABA (vice chmn. com. on fgn. investment in U.S. 1981—), Phila. Bar Assn., Pa. Bar Assn., Phi Beta Kappa. Democrat. Episcopalian. Clubs: Philadelphia; Racquet (Phila.); Brook (N.Y.C.). Home: 306 S 2d St Philadelphia PA 19106 Office: Dechert Price & Rhoads 3400 Centre SquareWest 1500 Market St Philadelphia PA 19102

BROWNE, WALTER SHAWN, chess player, journalist; b. Sydney, Australia, Jan. 10, 1949; s. Walter Francis and Hilda Louis (Leahy) B.; m. Raquel Emilse Facal, Mar. 9, 1973; 1 stepson, Marcello Facal. Grad. high sch. Chess player, 1957—, U.S. Jr. Champion, 1966, U.S. Open Champion, 1971, 72, Nat. Open Champion, 1972, 73, 84, U.S. Champion, 1974, 75, 76, 77, 78, 80, 81, 82, 83, Pan-Am. Champion, 1974, Internat. German champion, 1975, mem. U.S. Olympic Team, 1974, 78, 82, 84; columnist Chess Life & Rev., Berkeley, Calif., 1973—; lectr. in field. Publisher: Strongest International Chess Tourneys, 1978—. Named Internat. Master Fedn. Internat. des Eshecs, 1969, Internat. Grandmaster, 1969; 1st place, Rejkavik, Iceland, 1978; 1st pl., Wijk Am. Zee, Holland, 1980, Indonesia, 1982. Performer simultaneous chess exhbns., including record of 29-0 in 45 minutes, Adelaide, Australia, 1971. Played 106 competitors, including a computer, for world record score and time of 7 hours, 20 minutes, 1973. Address: 8 Parnassus Rd Berkeley CA 94708

BROWNE, WILLIAM RITNER, lawyer; b. Springfield, Ohio, Nov. 23, 1914; s. John Franklin and Etta Blanche (Bitner) B.; m. Dorothy Ruth Gilbert, Aug. 31, 1939; children: Franklin G., Dale Ann Browne Compton. A.B., Wittenberg U., 1935, LL.D. (hon.), 1970; postgrad., U. Bordeaux, 1935-36; LL.B. cum laude, Harvard U., 1939. Bar: Ohio 1939, U.S. Dist. Ct. (so. dist.) Ohio 1941, U.S. Ct. Appeals (6th cir.) 1950, U.S. Supreme Ct. 1970. Assoc. Donovan, Leisure, Newton & Lumbard, N.Y.C., 1939-40; assoc. Corry, Durfey & Martin, Springfield, Ohio, 1940-48; ptnr. Corry, Durfey, Martin & Browne and successors, Springfield, Ohio, 1948—; dir. Ohio Bar Title Ins. Co. Contbr. (articles to legal jours.). Bd. dirs. Wittenberg U., 1955—; pres. Greater Springfield & Clark Assn., Ohio, 1948-49; vice chmn. Clark County Republican Central and Exec. coms., Ohio, 1948-52; mem. Springfield City Bd. Edn., Ohio, 1950-53; mem. exec. com. United Appeals Clark County, Ohio, 1956-62. Served to capt. OSS Signal Corps, U.S. Army, 1942-46. Decorated Bronze Star, Croix de Guerre with palm, medaille de Reconnaissance Francaise. Fellow Am. Coll. Trail Lawyers, Am. Bar Found., Am. Coll. Probate Counsel, Ohio Bar Found. (pres. 1979, Fellows award 1976); mem. ABA (del. 1971-76), Ohio Bar Assn. (pres. 1969-70, medal 1973), Springfield Bar Assn. (pres. 1967), Springfield C. of C. (pres. 1961-62). Episcopalian. Clubs: Zanesfield Rond and Gun, Springfield Country. Lodges: Rotary; Masons. Office: Martin Browne Hull & Harper 203 First Nat Bank Bldg Springfield OH 45501

BROWNELL, DAVID WHEATON, editor; b. Fall River, Mass., Feb. 17, 1941; s. Frank Wheaton and Mary Katherine (Coughlin) B.; m. Mary Elizabeth Chute, Sept. 24, 1966. Student, Coll. Gen. Edn., Boston U., 1959-61; B.S. in Visual Design, Durfee Coll., Fall River, 1964. Chief copywriter Goldsmith-Tregar Advt. Co., Providence, 1969-71; editor Old Cars (newspaper, Krause Publs.), Iola, Wis., 1971-77, Cars & Parts, 1977-78, Spl.-Interest Autos, 1978—. Bd. dirs. Nat. Motor Racing Mus.; mem. selection com. Automotive Orgn. Team Hall of Fame, 1977, 78, 79, 80. Served with USCGR, 1965. Mem. Antique Automobile Club of Am., Vet. Motor Car Club of Am. (pres. chpt. 1958, 66), Brooklands Soc., Milestone Car Soc. (hon. life), Soc. Automotive Historians (dir., pres. 1981), Internat. Motor Press Assn., Internat. Soc. Appraisers, Guild Motoring Writers, Vintage Sports Car Club Am. Home: White Creek Rd North Bennington VT 05257 Office: Box 196 Bennington VT 05201

BROWNELL, GORDON LEE, physicist; b. Duncan, Okla., Apr. 8, 1922; s. Roscoe David and Mabel (Gourley) B.; (div.)children—Wendy L., Peter G., David L., James K. B.S., Bucknell U., Lewisburg, Pa., 1944; Ph.D., Mass. Inst. Tech., 1950. Mem. faculty Mass. Inst. Tech., 1950—, prof., 1970—; dir. Physics Research Lab. Mass. Gen. Hosp., Boston, 1950—; trustee Retina Found.; bd. dirs. Boston Biomed. Found., Neuroresearch Fund. Served to lt. (j.g.) USNR, 1944-46. Fellow Am. Phys. Soc., Am. Nuclear Soc.; mem. Am. Assn. Physicists in Medicine, Soc. Nuclear Medicine (Paul C. Aebersold award 1975), European Soc. Nuclear Medicine (de Hevesy medal

1979). Clubs: Union Boat (Boston); Cambridge (Mass.); Tennis. Home: 100 Memorial Dr Apt 8-2B Cambridge MA 02142 Office: Physics Research Lab Mass Gen Hosp Boston MA 02114

BROWNELL, HERBERT, former atty. gen. of U.S., lawyer; b. Peru, Nebr., Feb. 20, 1904; s. Herbert and May A. (Miller) B.; m. Doris A. McCarter, June 16, 1934; children—Joan, Ann, Thomas McCarter, James Barker. A.B., U. Nebr., 1924; LL.D.; L.B., Sch. Law, Yale, 1927. Bar: N.Y. bar 1927. With Root, Clark, Buckner & Ballantine, 1927-29, Lord, Day & Lord, 1929-53, 57-77, of counsel, 1977—; atty. gen. of U.S., 1953-57. Mem. Am. Judicature Soc., Am., N.Y. State bar assns., Assn. Bar City New York, Pilgrims Soc., Order of Coif, Phi Beta Kappa, Sigma Delta Chi, Delta Upsilon. Republican. Methodist. Clubs: Century Assn., Links, Recess (N.Y.C.). Office: 25 Broadway New York NY 10004

BROWNELL, JAMES GARLAND, editor; b. Valparaiso, Ind., July 29, 1933; s. Walter Ezra and Floy Gladys (Binyon) B. B.A. in Polit. Sci, Ind. U., 1955; diploma, Internat. Grad. Sch. for English Speaking Students, U. Stockholm, Sweden, 1956; postgrad., Valparaiso U. Law Sch., 1959-60. With Scholastic Mags., Inc., N.Y.C., 1961—; asst. to asso. editor Sr. Scholastic, 1961-64; mng. editor World Week mag., 1964-66, Sr. Scholastic, 1966-68; editor Jr. Scholastic, 1968-75; asso. editorial dir. Jr.-Sr. Scholastic, 1975-77, editorial dir., 1977—. Served to 1st lt. AUS, 1957-59. Home: Upper Kent Hollow Rd RFD 1 Kent CT 06757 Office: 50 W 44th St New York NY 10036

BROWNELL, JOHN ARNOLD, university administrator; b. Whittier, Calif., Sept. 26, 1924; s. Benjamin E. and Anna (Arnold) B.; m. Rena Topping, Feb. 28, 1946; children: Ann Elizabeth, William Alan, Robert Benjamin. B.A., Whitter Coll., 1947, M.A., 1948; Ed.D., Stanford, 1952. Tchr. Punahou Sch., Honolulu, 1948-50; tchr.-counsellor Whittier High Sch., 1951-54; asst. prof. Calif. State Coll. at Long Beach, 1954-58; asso. prof. Claremont (Calif.) Grad. Sch., 1958-65, prof., 1965-66; vis. prof. Internat. Christian U., Tokyo, 1964-65; prof. edn., researcher, asso. dir. Hawaii Curriculum Center, U. Hawaii, 1966-68; dep. chancellor acad. affairs East-West Center, 1968-75, v.p. for acad. affairs and ops., 1975-79, research assoc., 1979-82; vice chancellor acad. affairs U. Alaska, Anchorage, 1982—; Chmn. com. Coop. English in Japan, 1967-74; bd. dirs. Nat. Council Tchrs. English, 1960-64; mem. Hawaii Adv. Council Title III, Elementary Secondary Edn. Act, 1968-75, chmn., 1970-75; adv. council (Title IV), 1975-76; mem. exec. com. Nat. Assn. State Adv. Council Chairmen, 1974-75; cons. curriculum theory and design IBM Corp., 1963-64; project dir. feasibility study Pacific region ednl. lab. U.S. Office Edn., 1966—; v.p. Pacific States Student Presidents Assn., 1947-48; mem. chmn. Hawaii State Ednl. Needs Assessment Rev. Bd., 1972-74. Author: (with A.R. King) The Curriculum and the Disciplines of Knowledge, 1966, Japan's Second Language, 1967; also articles. Bd. dirs. Orange Coast YMCA, 1957-58; chmn. bd. Christian edn. Bay Shore Community Ch., 1957-58; moderator Claremont Congl. Ch., 1960-62, mem. exec. com., 1962-64. Phi Delta Kappa grantee, 1967-68; Harold Benjamin fellow Kappa Delta Pi, 1964-65. Mem. Am. Ednl. Research Assn., Nat. Council Research English, Internat. House (Tokyo), Japan Assn. Coll. English Tchrs. (hon.), Inst. Mgmt. Sci., Soc. Gen. Systems Research, U.S. Assn. for Club of Rome, Phi Delta Kappa. Home: 6917 Gemini Dr Anchorage AK 99504

BROWNING, CARROLL WELLES, ophthalmologist; b. Springfield, Ill., Sept. 2, 1916; s. Cornelius Alfred and Mabel (Welles) B.; children—Ronald, Elizabeth, Katherine. B.S., U. Ill., 1940, M.D., 1943. Basic sci. fellow in ophthalmology U. Ill. Med. Sch., 1946-47, Northwestern U. Med. Sch., 1947; resident, instr. ophthalmology Ill. Eye and Ear Infirmary, 1948-50, chief resident, instr. eye surgery, 1950; mem. faculty U. Tex. Southwestern Med. Sch., Dallas, 1950—, prof. ophthalmology, 1953—, chmn. dept., 1953-63; practice medicine specializing in ophthalmology, Dallas; chief dept. ophthalmology Parkland City-County Hosp., Dallas, 1953-63; former chmn. eye dept. Meth. Hosp. of Dallas; adminstr. Oak Cliff Eye Center, Dallas, 1968—. Contbr. articles to med. jours. Founder Dallas Eye Bank, 1955. Served to capt. M.C. AUS, 1944-46. Fellow A.C.S.; mem. Am. Acad. Ophthalmology (instr. ophthalmic plastic surgery 1966-71), AMA, Nat. Found. Ophthalmic Research, Assn., Assn. Ophthalmology, Am. Intraocular Lens Soc., Am. Soc. Contemporary Opthalmology, Am. Keratorefractive Surg. Soc., Am. Soc. Ophthalmic Plastic Surgery, Tex. Med. Assn., Tex. Soc. Ophthalmology, Tex. Soc. Prevention Blindness, Dallas Med. Soc., Dallas Acad. Ophthalmology. Baptist. Home: 4242 Shorecrest St Dallas TX 75209 Office: Oak Cliff Eye Center 836 N Zang Blvd Dallas TX 75208 *My clearest experiential insight is that my greatest gratification in living comes not from my achievements but rather from my love and compassion for others.*

BROWNING, CHARLES BENTON, agricultural educator, university dean; b. Houston, Sept. 16, 1931; s. Earl William and Emma (Summerlin) B.; m. Magda Luest, Jan. 14, 1956; children: Susan Elaine Browning Kreps, Charles Benton, Steven Randolph, Karen Diane, Heidi Charlene, Gary Thomas. B.S. in Animal Sci., Tex. Tech., 1955; M.S. in Dairy Sci., Kans. State U., 1956; Ph.D. in Animal Nutrition, Kans. State U., 1958. Asst. prof. Miss. State U., State Coll., 1958-60, assoc. prof., 1960-61, prof., 1961-66, U. Fla., Gainsville, 1961-66, dean resident instrn., 1969-79; dean and dir. div. agr. Okla. State U., Stillwater, 1979—; mem. numerous state agrl. coms.; head team to rev. agrl. problems and programs of Jamaica for AID, 1978; mem. USDA, SEA Joint Council on Food and Agrl. Scis., 1977; cons. Dept. State Internat. Communication Agy., Venezuela, 1978; del. 6th Working Conf. of Reps., Paris, 1978. Div. chmn., countrywide chmn., pres. United Way, 1971-78; committeeman, com. chmn., instnl. rep. Boy Scouts of Am., 1969-78; pres. Williams Middle Sch. PTA, 1970-71. Named Outstanding Prof. Alpha Zeta, 1966; recipient Z.W. Craine Research award Nat. Silo Assn., 1967. Mem. Am. Dairy Sci. Assn., Am. Soc. Animal Sci., Am. Grassland Council, AAAS, Sigma Xi, Phi Kappa Phi, Omicron Delta Kappa, Gamma Sigma Delta, Alpha Zeta. Episcopalian. Home: 1002 West Will Rogers Stillwater OK 74074 Office: Okla State U 139 Agrl Hall Stillwater OK 74078

BROWNING, CHAUNCEY H., state ofcl.; b. Charleston, W.Va., Nov. 21, 1934; s. Chauncey H. and Evelyn (Mahone) B.; m. Patricia Ann Lewis; children—Chauncey Hoyt, III, Charles Preston, Steven Thomas. A.B., W.Va. U., 1956, LL.B., 1958. Law clk. U.S. Dist. Ct. for So. Dist. W.Va., 1958; practice law, Charleston, 1958-62; atty.-in-charge Legal Aid Soc. Kanawha and Putnam Counties, W.Va., 1959-60; commr. pub. instns. State of W.Va., 1962-68, atty. gen., 1968—; mem. Nat. Commn. Rev. Antitrust Laws and Procedures; pres. Nat. Assn. Attys. Gen., 1978-79; del. to exec. com. Council of State Govts., 1979—, permanent mem. exec. com. Editor: W.Va. Law Quar. Recipient Outstanding Public Servant award W.Va. State Bar Assn.-W.Va. Trial Lawyers Assn., 1978. Mem. Am., W.Va., Kanawha County bar assns., W.Va. State Bar, W.Va. Trial Lawyers Assn., Order of Coif, Phi Delta Phi, Kappa Sigma. Office: Capitol Bldg Charleston WV 25305

BROWNING, DANIEL DWIGHT, chemist, manufacturing executive; b. New Albany, Miss., Mar. 24, 1921; s. James Virgil and Eppie (Maddox) B.; m. Harriet Nimick McKnight, Nov. 28, 1946 (dec. Nov. 1965); children: Daniel, Paul, David; m. Nancy Ann Carlson, Feb. 25, 1967; children: Nancy, Thomas. B.S., Miss. Coll., 1941; postgrad., U. Pitts., 1941-44, 46-49. Chemist E.I. DuPont de Nemours & Co., Memphis, 1941; research fellow Mellon Inst., Pitts., 1942-44, 46-50; research chemist Armstrong World Industries, Lancaster, Pa., 1950-58, mgr. floor products research, 1958-62, gen. mgr. bldg. products research, 1962-68, asst. dir. research, 1968-76, v.p., dir. bus. info. services, 1976-81, v.p., dir. research, 1981—. Patentee in field. Pres. Lancaster City Sch. Bd., 1964-65. Served to comdr. USN, 1944-46; PTO. Mem. Am. Chem. Soc., Lancaster C. of C. (dir. 1973-76). Republican. Clubs: Hamilton, Lancaster Country; Tucquan (Lancaster). Home: 25 Eshelman Rd Lancaster PA 17601

BROWNING, DAVID STUART, lawyer; b. Amarillo, Tex., June 6, 1939; s. Stuart W. and Pauline (Rogers) B.; m. Judith Helen Jackson, July 31, 1958; 1 son, Mark. B.A., U. Tex., 1960, J.D., 1962; M.A., Johns Hopkins U., 1964. Bar: D.C. bar 1963, Tex. bar 1964, N.Y. bar 1970. Atty. firm Fulbright & Jaworski, Houston, 1964-70; asst. counsel Schlumberger Ltd., N.Y.C., 1970-75, sec., gen. counsel, 1976—. Contbr. articles to legal jours. Mem. Am., N.Y. State, Tex., Houston bar assns., Assn. Bar City N.Y., Am. Soc. Internat. Law, Southwestern Legal Found. (adv. bd.), Am. Soc. Corporate Secs. Office: Schlumberger Ltd 277 Park Ave New York NY 10172

BROWNING, DON, religion educator; b. Trenton, Mo., Jan. 13, 1934; s. Robert W. and Nelle J. (Trotter) B.; m. Carol Kohl, Sept. 27, 1958; children: Elizabeth Dell, and Christopher Robert. A.B., Central Methodist Coll., 1956; B.D., U. Chgo. Div. Sch., 1959, M.A., 1962, Ph.D., 1964. Asst. prof. Grad. Sem. Phillips U., Enid, Okla., 1963-65; instr. religion and personality U. Chgo. Div. Sch., 1965-66, asst. prof., 1967-68, assoc. prof., 1968-77, prof., 1977-80, Alexander Campbell prof., 1980—. Author: Atonement and Psychotherapy, 1966, Generative Man, 1973, The Moral Context of Pastoral Care, 1976, Pluralism and Personality, 1980, Practical Theology, 1983; editor: Religious Ethics and Pastoral Care, 1983. Nat. Book award finalist, 1974; Guggenheim fellow, 1975-76. Mem. Am. Acad. Religion, Soc. Sci. Study Religion., Assn. Christian Ethics. Office: Univ Chicago 1025 E 58th St Chicago IL 60637

BROWNING, EDMOND LEE, bishop; b. Corpus Christi, Tex., Mar. 11; s. Edmond Lucian and Cora Mae (Lee) B.; m. Patricia Sparks, Sept. 10, 1953; children: Robert Mark, Patricia Paige, Philip Myles, Peter Sparks, John Charles. B.A., U. of South, 1952, B.D., 1954, D.D., 1970. Ordained priest Episcopal Ch., 1954, named bishop, 1968; curate Ch. of the Good Shepherd, Corpus Christi, 1954-56; rector Redeemer Ch., Eagle Pass, Tex., 1956-59, All Souls Ch., Okinawa, 1959-63, St. Matthews Ch., 1965-67; archdeacon Okinawa Episcopal Ch., 1965-67, 1st missionary bishop of Okinawa, 1968-71; bishop of convocation Episcopal Chs. in Europe, 1971-74; exec. Nat. and World Mission Exec. Council, N.Y.C., 1974-76, 82—; bishop of, Hawaii, 1976—; Bd. dirs. Anglican Center, Rome, 1971-74, St. Stephens Sch., 1971-74; mem. Anglican Consultative Council, 1983—. Named hon. canon St. Michaels Cathedral, Kobe, Japan. Address: Queen Emma Sq Honolulu HI 96813

BROWNING, GEORGE MOORE, JR., air force officer; b. Kansas City, Mo., Nov. 22, 1928; m. Gerrie Lawson, Feb. 14, 1958; children: George Moore III, William F., Thomas J., Stephen M. B.S., UCLA, 1952; M.S., George Washington U., 1971; grad., Naval War Coll., 1971. Commd. lt. U.S. Air Force, 1952, advanced through grades to lt. gen., 1981; chief combat ops. div. 432d Tactical Reconnaissance Wing, Udorn AFB, Thailand, 1969, squadron ops. officer 13th Tactical Fighter Squadron, 1969, asst. dep. commdr. ops., 1969-70; student officer U.S. Naval War Coll., Newport, R.I., 1970-71; asst. for Congressional matters, dep. chief of staff comptroller Hdqrs. Air Force, 1971-73; wing vice comdr. 86th Tactical Fighter Wing, Ramstein Air Base, Germany, 1973-75; comdr. 26th Tactical Reconnaissance Wing, Zweibrucken Air Base, Germany, 1974-76; insp. gen. U.S. Air Force in Europe, Ramstein Air Base, Germany, 1976-78, asst. dep. comdr. for ops. and intelligence, 1978-79; dir. budget Air Force Comptroller Office, Hdqrs. U.S. Air Force, Washington, 1979-81; comptroller of Air Force, 1981—. Mem. bd. commrs. U.S. Soldiers and Airmen's Home, 1981—; chmn. bd. dirs. Army and Air Force Exchange Service, 1982; trustee Air Force Aid Soc., 1981—. Decorated Legion of Merit with one oak leaf cluster, D.F.C., Air medal with one silver and two bronze oak leaf clusters, Air Force Commendation medal with one oak leaf cluster, Army Commendation medal; Republic of Vietnam Gallentry Cross with device. Mem. Am. Soc. Mil. Comptrollers, Beta Theta Pi. Presbyterian. Home: 30 Westover Dr Bolling AFB DC 20336 Office: AF/AC Pentagon Room 4E128 Washington DC 20330 *Our nation remains free because dedicated citizens provided for and served in a strong military. A glorious history of personal sacrifices characterizes this dedication. Is is my firm belief that more sacrifices will be necessary for many years to come if this nation, with its high ideals, is to survive.*

BROWNING, GRAYSON DOUGLAS, educator; b. Seminole, Okla., Mar. 7, 1929; s. Grayson Douglas and Dorothea (Cook) B.; m. Becky Beck, July 15, 1972; children by previous marriage—Tony Louis, Luke Matthew, Lauren Beth. B.A., U. Tex., Austin, 1954, M.A., 1955, Ph.D., 1958. Instr., asst. prof., asso. prof., prof. U. Miami, Coral Gables, Fla., 1958-69; vis. instr. U. Tex., Austin, summer 1963, vis. prof., 1969-71, prof. philosophy, 1971—, chmn. dept. philosophy, 1972-76. Author: Act and Agent, 1964, Poems and Visions, 1965; Editor: Philosophers of Process, 1965; Contbr. articles to profl. jours. Served with USAF, 1948-52. Mem. Am. Philos. Assn., Southwestern Philos. Assn. (pres. 1976-77, Fla. Philos. Assn., pres. 1967), So. Soc. for Philosophy and Psychology (pres. 1972-73). Home: 185 Faubion Dr Georgetown TX 78626

BROWNING, HENRY PRENTICE, banker; b. Montclair, N.J., Apr. 23, 1911; s. Henry P. and Ida Stewart (Bartow) B.; m. Nancy Jane Littell, Oct. 7, 1939; children—Penny (Mrs. Russell Fortune III), Nancy (Mrs. Walter Afield), Henry Prentice Jr. Grad., Amherst Coll., 1933, Rutgers U. Sch. Banking, 1949. With Winthrop, Mitchell & Co., Chgo., 1933-34; financial cons. E.M. Stark, Chgo., 1934-40; asst. cashier Continental Ill. Nat. Bank & Trust Co., Chgo., 1944, 2d v.p., 1946; v.p. Worcester County Trust Co., Mass., 1948-56; exec. v.p. Am. Fletcher Nat. Bank & Trust Co., Indpls., 1956-57, pres., chief exec. officer, dir., 1957-69; vice chmn. Nat. Bank N.Am., N.Y.C., 1969-70; pres., chief exec. officer Exchange Bancorp., Inc., Tampa, Fla., 1970-71; dir. Palm State Bank, Palm Harbor, Fla., Arvin Industries, Inc., Columbus, Ind.; Former trustee U. Tampa. Served as lt. USNR, 1944-46. Episcopalian. Clubs: Sky (N.Y.C.); Tampa Yacht and Country, Bradenton Country. Home: 632 Emerald Ln Holmes Beach FL 33510

BROWNING, IBEN, biophysicist, inventor; b. Vanderbilt, Tex., Jan. 9, 1918; s. Bede and Lugilla (McCormick) B.; m. Florence A. Pinto, July 30, 1945; 1 dau., Evelyn. B.S., S.W. Tex. State Tchrs. Coll., 1937; M.A., U. Tex., 1947, Ph.D. in Physiology, Genetics and Bacteriology, 1948. Tutor in physiology U. Tex., Austin, 1937-38, technician, 1938-39, instr. biology, 1946-47; pres. Tex. Cedar Products Co., 1940-41; Nat. Research fellow in biophysics U. Pa., Phila., 1948-49; asst. biologist M.D. Anderson Hosp., Houston, 1949-52, asst. prof., 1950-52; devel. physicist Am. Optical Co., 1952-54; supr. optics div. Bell Aircraft Corp., 1954-57; staff mem., scientist Sandia Lab., Albuquerque, 1957-60; prin. investigator Panoramic Research Co., Palo Alto, Calif., 1960-64; exec. dir. Thomas Bede Found., Los Altos, Calif. and Albuquerque, 1963—; pres. Sydnor-Barent Scanner Corp., Albuquerque, 1971—; cons. in field to numerous bus. and fin. instns. and research orgns. Author: (with N. Winkless) Climate and the Affairs of Men, 1975, Robots on Your Doorstep, 1978, The Browning Newsletter, 1977—; holder numerous U.S. and fgn. patents. Served with USAAF, 1941-45. Mem. AAAS, Soc. Zoology, Genetics Soc., Sigma Xi. Researcher and inventor in field of optical engring., info. theory, brain physiology, enzymes, climatology, and others. Home and Office: PO Drawer 130 Sandia Park NM 87047 *Life is so brief that personal opinions are too transient to be worth anything to Mankind. Data, and objective interpretations, are the only contributions with lasting value. Physical achievements, and ideas which constitute tools with which Man can achieve his goals, are significant.*

BROWNING, JAMES ALEXANDER, inventor, engring. co. exec.; b. Great Neck, N.Y., Feb. 24, 1922; s. James Herbert and Willa Bullett (Alexander) B.; m. Marian Lucille Barkdull, June 16, 1949; children—William A., Joel B., James H. A.B., Dartmouth, 1944; M.E. in Engring, Stanford, 1949. Faculty Thayer Sch., Dartmouth, 1949-66; prof. mech. engring., 1960-62, adj. prof. engring., 1962-66; chmn. bd. Thermal Dynamics Corp., Lebanon, N.H., 1958- 68; pres. Browning Engring. Corp., Hanover, N.H., 1960—; cons. high temperature research and applications, 1951—; Overseer Thayer Sch., 1978—. Mem. ASME, Am. Rocket Soc., Am. Welding Soc., Phi Beta Kappa, Sigma Alpha Epsilon. Inventor miniature rocket devices for indsl. use, also plasmaarc apparatus; developer spl. apparatus used to pierce first holes through 1,400 foot Ross ice shelf in Antarctica; patentee. Home: PO Box 6 Hanover NH 03755

BROWNING, JAMES FRANKLIN, professional society executive; b. Tonawanda, N.Y., Feb. 19, 1923; s. Charles Oscar and Gertrude (Keller) B. Student, La. State U., 1943, U. Buffalo, 1948-49; pvt. study music, 1942—. Regional dir. Civic Concert Services, N.Y. C., 1954-57; asst. mgr. Pitts. Symphony Orch., 1957-59; adminstr. Met. Opera Nat. Council, N.Y.C., 1959-62; spl. rep. to chmn. John F. Kennedy Center Performing Arts, 1962-63; gen. mgr. Am. Music Center, N.Y.C., 1963-72; exec. sec. Nat. Music Council, N.Y.C., 1965-72, Nat. Assn. Tchrs. Singing, 1973—; Tech. cons. N.Y. State Council of Arts, 1963—; sec. Pioneer Editions, N.Y.C., 1965-67; mem. exec. com. Nat. Council Arts and Govt., N.Y.C., 1964-73; treas. Arlington (Va.) Opera Theatre, 1962-63; bd. dirs. U.S. Inst. Theatre Tech., 1960-62; U.S. rep. Internat. Music Council Congress, Rotterdam, Holland, 1966, Internat. Rostrum Composers, Paris, 1966; adv. bd. Musicians Club Fla., 1969—. Contbr. to publs. in field.; editor: Music Today Newsletter, 1963-72, Nat. Council Music Bull., 1965-72; mem. adv. council: Music Jour., 1964—. Bd. dirs. Symphony of New World, 1973-76. Served with USAAF, 1943-46. Life mem. NAACP; mem. Contemporary Music Soc. (dir. 1968—); life hon. profl. mem. Phi Mu Alpha. Home: 114 W 70th St New York NY 10023 Office: 35 W 4th St New York NY 10003

BROWNING, JAMES ROBERT, U.S. judge; b. Great Falls, Mont., Oct. 1, 1918; s. Nicholas Henry and Minnie Sally (Foley) B.; m. Marie Rose Chapell, Aug. 14, 1941. LL.B. with honors, Mont. State U., 1941; LL.D. (hon.), U. Mont., 1978. Bar: Mont. bar 1941, D.C. bar 1950, U.S. Supreme Ct. bar 1952. Spl. atty. antitrust div. Dept. Justice, 1941-46, chief, 1948-49, asst. chief gen. litigation sect. antitrust div., 1949-51, 1st asst. civil div., 1951-52; exec. asst. to atty. gen. U.S., 1952-53, chief, 1953; pvt. practice, Washington, 1953-58; lectr. N.Y.U. Sch. Law, 1953, Georgetown U. Law Center, 1957-58; clk. Supreme Ct. U.S., 1958-61; judge U.S. Ct. Appeals 9th Circuit, 1961—, chief judge, 1976—. Mem. Am. Law Inst., Am., Mont., Fed. bar assns., Inst. Jud. Adminstrn., Am. Judicature Soc., Am. Soc. Legal History (adv. bd. jour.). Office: US Court of Appeals and Post Office Bldg San Francisco CA 94101

BROWNING, JOHN, pianist; b. Denver, May 23, 1933; s. John and Esther (Green) B. Student, Occidental Coll., D.Mus. (hon.), 1975, Juilliard Sch. Music; D.Mus. (hon.), Ithaca Coll., Lee Pattison, Calif., Rosina Lhevinne, N.Y.C. Debut, Denver, 1943, debut, N.Y. Philharmonic Orch. at Carnegie Hall, 1956; appearances with numerous orchs., U.S., Europe, Mexico, Russia, Eng.; recitalist; pianist: for world premiere performance Samuel Barber's First Piano Concerto with Boston Symphony Orch; pianist with, Cleve. Orch. on Dept. State tour to USSR, 1965; rep., Am. govt. World's Fair, Brussels, 1968; instr. master classes, Northwestern U., 1975—; rec. artist. Served with U.S. Army. Recipient Jr. award KFI-Hollywood Bowl Young Artists Competition, 1945, Steinway Centennial award Nat. Fedn. Music Clubs, 1954, Edgar M. Leventritt award, 1955, Queen Elizabeth Internat. Concours award, 1956. Mem. Pi Kappa Lambda. Office: Columbia Artist Mgmt 165 W 57th St New York NY 10019

BROWNING, LAURENCE LEWRIGHT, JR., electric company executive; b. Maysville, Ky., May 13, 1929; s. Laurance LeWright and Dorothy (Nulton) B.; m.; children: Virginia Louise, Kathryn Nulton, Dorothy Winslow. Grad., Phillips Exeter Acad., 1947; B.M.E., Cornell U., 1952. Salesman Browning Mfg. Co., Pitts., 1954-56, mfg. engr., 1956-58, sec., 1958-61, v.p., 1961-67, exec. v.p., 1967-69, dir., 1964-69; group v.p. Emerson Electric Co., St. Louis, 1970-72, exec. v.p., chief adminstrv. officer, 1972—. Patentee adjustable tightener. Curator Transylvania U., 1972-74; chmn. Opera Theatre of St. Louis, 1978—; trustee Emma Willard Sch., 1972-76, Episcopal Theol. Sem. in Ky., 1977, St. Louis Art Mus., 1977, St. Louis Children's Hosp., 1977—; bd. dirs. Arts and Edn. Council St. Louis, 1978—, Inroads, 1977—; exec. com. St. Louis Symphony Soc. Served to lt. USAF, 1952-54. Mem. NAM (bd. dirs. 1968-71). Office: Emerson Electric Co 8000 W Florissant Ave St. Louis MO 63136

BROWNING, NORMA LEE (MRS. RUSSELL JOYNER OGG), journalist; b. Spickard, Mo., Nov. 24, 1914; d. Howard R. and Grace (Kennedy) B.; m. Russell Joyner Ogg, June 12, 1938. A.B., B.J., U. Mo., 1937; M.A. in English, Radcliffe Coll., 1938. Reporter Los Angeles Herald-Express, 1942-43; with Chgo. Tribune, from 1944, Hollywood columnist, 1966-75; Vis. lectr. creative writing, editorial cons., mem. nat. adv. bd. Interlochen Arts Acad., Northwood Inst. Author: City Girl in the Country, 1955, Joe Maddy of Interlochen, 1963, (with W. Clement Stone) The Other Side of the Mind, 1965, The Psychic World of Peter Hurkos, 1970, (with Louella Dirksen) The Honorable Mr. Marigold, 1972, (with Ann Miller) Miller's High Life, 1972, Peter Hurkos: I Have Many Lives, 1976, Omarr: Astrology and the Man, 1977, (with George Masters) The Masters Way to Beauty, 1977, (with Russell Ogg) He Saw A Hummingbird, 1978, (with Florence Lowell) Be A Guest At Your Own Party, 1980, Face-Lifts: Everything You Always Wanted to Know, 1981, (with Edith Head) Edith Head's Hollywood, 1982; Contbr. articles to nat. mags. Recipient E.S. Beck award Chgo Tribune. Mem. Theta Sigma Phi, Kappa Tau Alpha. Address: 226 Morongo Rd Palm Springs CA 92262

BROWNING, RALPH LESLIE, cement co. exec.; b. Buffalo, Apr. 18, 1915; s. Leslie E. and Bertha L. (Rea) B.; m. Nancy B. Crane, Sept. 6, 1940; children—Peter Crane, Richard Leslie, Pamela (Mrs. David Durrant). A.B., Colgate U., 1937. With Lehigh Portland Cement Co., Allentown, Pa., 1937—, asst. v.p., 1951-52, v.p., asst. gen. sales mgr., 1952-55, v.p. of sales, 1955-59, exec. v.p., 1959—; also dir.; dir. Mchts. Nat. Bank, Allentown, Lehigh Realty Co., Allentown. Served as lt. (j.g.) Supply Corps USNR, 1944-46. Mem. Kappa Delta Rho. Republican. Episcopalian. Clubs: Lehigh Country, Livingston, Allentown; Ponte Vedra (Fla.); Saucon Valley Country (Bethlehem,

Pa.); University, Tavern (Chgo.); University (Jacksonville, Fla.). Home: Saucon Valley Rd RD 4 Bethlehem PA 18015 Office: 718 Hamilton St Allentown PA 18105

BROWNING, ROBERT MARCELLUS, emeritus foreign language educator, editor, translator; b. Centerville, Kans., Apr. 1, 1911; s. Marcellus Alonzo and Olive Allytte (Sutton) B.; m. Helene Marie Ulmer, Sept. 8, 1940. A.B., William Jewell Coll., Liberty, Mo., 1937; Ph.D., Princeton U., 1948. Instr. modern langs. Princeton U., 1939-41, 46-49; Instr. German Wake Forest Coll., 1941-43; Mem. faculty Hamilton Coll., Clinton, N.Y., 1949—; Marjorie and Robert W. McEwen prof. German Clinton Coll., 1973-79, prof. emeritus, 1979—; vis. prof. U. Colo., 1962-63, Ind. U., summer 1964, State U. N.Y. at Buffalo, summer 1967, U. Pitts., 1968, Dartmouth Coll., spring 1969; O'Connor vis. prof. Colgate U., 1976-77. Author: Literary History of German Baroque, 1971, German Poetry in the Age of the Enlightenment, 1978, Deutsche Lyrik des Barock, 1980; also textbooks, articles, revs.; Book rev. editor: German Quar, 1963-65; editor, 1965-67; cons. editor: McGraw-Hill Series German Lit, 1966—; editor, translator: Continuum Pub. Co., N.Y.C., 1981—; translator: Suhrkame/Insel, Boston, 1982-83. Served with AUS, 1944-46. Sr. fellow Nat. Endowment Humanities, 1974-75. Mem. Modern Lang. Assn. Am. (del. 1971-74), Am. Assn. Tchrs. German, Am. Lessing Soc. Home: 9 Griffin Rd Clinton NY 13323

BROWNING, ROBERT MASTERS, management consultant; b. Stratford, N.J., June 30, 1912; s. M. Corbit and Florence I. (Masters) B.; m. Margaret Helms, June 12, 1937 (dec. Aug. 1979); children: Deborah Browning LeVeen, Elizabeth Browning Thiel, Lucy Browning Wallace, Margaret; m. Jeanne Smith Borie, Feb. 23, 1980; stepchildren: Virginia Borie Bonneau, Martha Borie Wood, Lisa Stuart Borie. B.A., Swarthmore Coll., 1934; LL.D. (hon.), Lebanon Valley Coll., 1965. With Gen. Electric Co., 1934-45; with Booz, Allen & Hamilton, Inc., 1945-70, partner, 1948-61, v.p., 1962-70; dir., mem. exec. com. Standard Pressed Steel Co., 1965-72; Mem. Pomfret (Vt.) Planning Com., 1971-79, chmn., 1972-79; mem. Two Rivers Regional Planning and Devel. Commn., Vt., 1971-80, chmn., 1973-80; mem. corp. Mary Hitchcock Hosp.; bd. mgrs. Swarthmore Coll., 1958-71, 72-74, chmn. bd. mgrs., 1966-71; bd. dirs., chmn. Upper Valley Youth Services, Inc., 1977—; trustee Ottauquechee Regional Land Trust, 1983—; hon. trustee Germantown Hosp. Mem. Delta Upsilon., Soc. Friends. Club: Woodstock (Vt.) Country. Home: Birch Knolls RD 2 South Royalton VT 05068

BROWNING, RODERICK HANSON, banker; b. Salt Lake City, Oct. 9, 1925; s. Frank M. and Eugenia H. B.; m. Mary Wadsworth, Mar. 7, 1956; children—Patricia Ann, Jonathan Wadsworth, Frank Wadsworth, Anthony Stuart, Carolyn Rae. A.B., Stanford U., 1948. Vice pres. Bank of Utah, Ogden, 1954-59, chmn. bd., pres., 1959—, Bank of Brigham City, Utah, 1973—; chmn. bd. Bank No. Utah, Clearfield, 1971—; dir. Salt Lake City br. Fed. Res. Bank San Francisco, 1969-74; Bd. dirs., treas. Ogden Indsl. Devel. Corp., Weber County (Utah) Indsl. Devel. Bur.; adv. bd. St. Benedicts Hosp.; bd. dirs. Weber State Coll., Ogden; former pres. United Fund No. Utah. Served with U.S. Army, 1948-53. Mem. Am. Bankers Assn., Utah Bankers Assn. (former mem. exec. com.), Am. Legion. Clubs: Rotary (Ogden); Weber, Alta, Ogden Golf and Country. Office: Box 231 Ogden UT 84402

BROWNING, VAL ALLEN, sporting goods exec.; b. Ogden, Utah, Aug. 20, 1895; s. John Moses and Rachel Teressa (Child) B.; m. Ann Chaffin, Aug. 9, 1924; children—John Val, Carol (Mrs. Edmund W. Dumke), Bruce W., Judith Ann (Mrs. Leon L. Jones). Student, Cornell U., 1914-17; D.Sc., Weber State Coll., Ogden, 1967. With Browning (name formerly Browning Arms Co.), Ogden, 1927—, pres., 1935-62, hon. chmn. bd., 1949—; also dir.; dir. First Security Corp. Served with U.S. Army, World War I. Decorated chevalier de l'Ordre de Leopold, officier l'Ordre de Leopold II, Officier Order of Leopold I, Belgium; named hon. citizen of Herstal, Belgium). Home: 1515 Beverly Dr Ogden UT 84403 Office: RFD 1 Morgan UT 84050

BROWNING, WARREN WEBSTER, lawyer; b. Marion, Ill., May 26, 1927; s. John Roy and Bertha Joan (Raum) B.; m. Caroline Agnes Thrasher, June 2, 1951; children: Laura Browning Johnson, Warren Webster. B.A., Stanford U., 1949; J.D., Northwestern U., Chgo., 1952. Bar: Ill. 1952. Atty. U.S Renegotiation Bd., Chgo., 1952-53; ptnr. Browning & Parkin, Chgo., 1953-57, Browning & Browning, 1957-72; v.p., sec., gen. counsel Elgin Nat. Industries Inc., Chgo., 1972—. Served with U.S. Army, 1945-46. Mem. Chgo. Bar Assn., Ill. State Bar Assn. Home: 699 Bluff Rd Lake Bluff IL 60044 Office: Elgin Nat Industries Inc 120 S Riverside Plaza Chicago IL 60606

BROWNING, WILLIAM EARLE STRAIN, banker; b. N.Y.C., July 7, 1932; s. Samuel Pearce and Dorothea (Strain) B.; m. Amy Marie Connelly, Aug. 15, 1964; children: William E.S. Jr., John Christian, Andrew Hamilton, Alexander Connelly. A.B., Princeton U., 1953; J.D., Harvard U., 1960. Bar: N.Y. 1962. Assoc. Sullivan & Cromwell, N.Y.C., 1960-67; v.p., dir. Drexel Firestone, Inc., N.Y.C., 1967-72; 1st v.p. Bache Halsey Stuart Shields, N.Y.C., 1972-78; sr. v.p. Bankers Trust Co., N.Y.C., 1978—. Served to lt. (j.g.) USNR, 1954-57. Republican. Club: Down Town Assn. (N.Y.C.). Home: 136 Rosebrook Rd New Caanan CT 06840 Office: Bankers Trust Co 280 Park Ave New York NY 10017

BROWNLEE, DONALD EUGENE, II, astronomer, educator; b. Las Vegas, Nev., Dec. 21, 1943; s. Donald Eugene and Geraldine Florence (Stephen) B.; m. Paula Szkody. B.S. in Elec. Engring, U. Calif., Berkeley, 1965; Ph.D. in Astronomy, U. Wash., 1970. Research assoc. U. Wash., 1970-77, asso. prof. astronomy, 1977—; asso. geochemistry Calif. Inst. Tech., Pasadena, 1977—; cons. NASA, 1976—. Author papers in field, chpts. in books. Grantee NASA, 1975. Mem. Internat. Astron. Union, Am. Astron. Assn., AAAS, Meteoritical Soc., Com. Space Research Dust. Home: 3118A Portage Bay Pl E Seattle WA 98102 Office: Dept Astronomy Univ Wash Seattle WA 98195

BROWNLEE, OSWALD HARVEY, economist, educator; b. Moccasin, Mont., Apr. 14, 1917; s. William and Sarah (Fyffe) B.; m. Lela McDonald, June 11, 1939; children—Barbara, Richard. B.S., Mont. State Coll., 1938; M.A., U. Wis., 1939; Ph.D., Iowa State U., 1945. Prof. econs. Iowa State Coll., 1943-47, Carnegie Inst. Tech., 1947-48, U. Chgo., 1948-50; prof. econs. faculty U. Minn., 1950—; dep. asst. sec. Treasury, 1973-74; economist ICA mission to Chile, 1956-57; vis. prof. econs. Cath. U. Chile, 1967-69; vis. scholar Office Comptroller of Currency, 1965; cons. in field, 1947—. Author: (with J.A. Buttrick) Consumer and Social Choice, 1968, (with Robert I. Chien) Issues in Pharmaceutical Economics, 1979, Taxing the Income from U.S. Corporation Investment Abroad, 1980; also articles. Farm Found. fellow, 1941-42; Ford faculty fellow, 1958. Mem. Am. Econ. Assn., Econometric Soc., Phi Kappa Phi. Home: 1943 East River Rd Minneapolis MN 55414

BROWNLEE, PAULA PIMLOTT, college president, chemistry educator; b. London, June 23, 1934; U.S., 1959; d. John Richard and Alice A. (Ajamian) Pimlott; m. Thomas H. Brownlee, Feb. 10, 1961; children: Kenneth Gainsford, Elizabeth Ann, Clare Louise. B.A. with honors, Somerville Coll., Oxford (Eng.) U., 1957; D.Phil. in Organic Chemistry, Oxford (Eng.) U., 1959; Postdoctoral fellow, U. Rochester, N.Y., 1959-61. Research chemist Am. Cyanamid Co., Stamford, Conn., 1961-62; lectr. U. Bridgeport, Conn., 1968-70; asst. prof. Rutgers Coll., Rutgers U., 1970-73; asso. prof. chemistry Douglass Coll., 1975-76, asso. dean, then acting dean coll., 1972-76; dean faculty, prof. chemistry Union Coll., Schenectady, N.Y., 1976-81; pres., prof. chemistry Hollins (Va.) Coll., 1981—; dir. Colonial Am. Bank; bd. dirs. Roanoke Valley Sci. Mus., Va. Sci. Mus., Roanoke Symphony. Author articles, lab. manual. Fellow Chem. Soc. London; mem. Am. Chem. Soc., Am. Women in Sci., Am. Assn. Higher Edn. (chair). Office: Office of Pres Hollins College Hollins College VA 24020 *

BROWNLEE, RICHARD SMITH, historian; b. Brookfield, Mo., Mar. 12, 1918; s. Ellis Crance and Mary Margaret (Shore); m. Alice Lucille Rowley, Oct. 31, 1942; children: Richard Smith, III, Margaret Ann. A.B., U. Mo., Columbia, 1939, B.J., 1940, M.A. in History, 1950, Ph.D., 1955. Asst. prof. history extension div. U. Mo., Columbia, 1950-60, asst. dir. adult edn., 1950-60; sec., dir. State Hist. Soc. Mo., Columbia, 1960—; mem. Mo. Records Commn., 1967—, Civil War Centennial Commn., 1961-65, Historic Sites Adv. Commn., 1961-81, State Capitol Restoration Commn., 1967, Am. Revolution Bicentennial Commn., 1976-78, Nat. Hist. Publs. and Records Commn., 1978—; cultural dir. Mo. Pavilion, N.Y. World's Fair, 1962. Author: Gray Ghosts of the Confederacy, 1959; editor: Missouri Hist. Rev, 1960—, A Catalogue of Specialized Libraries of Missouri, 1962; co-editor: Messages and Proclamations of Governors James T. Blair and John M. Dalton, 1961-64. Served with AUS, 1941-42; to capt. USAAF, 1942-45. Mem. Am. Hist. Assn., Mississippi Valley Hist. Soc., So. Hist. Assn., Mo. Press Assn., Mo. Mus. Assocs. (founding mem.), Acad. Mo. Squires, Friends of U. Mo. State Hist. Soc. Libraries, Am. Legion, Phi Beta Kappa, Kappa Tau Alpha, Sigma Nu. Presbyterian. Club: Mo. Country. Home: 100 Bingham Rd Columbia MO 65201 Office: State Hist Soc Mo 1020 Lowry St Columbia MO 65201

BROWNLEE, ROBERT CALVIN, pediatrician, educator; b. Due West, S.C., Mar. 13, 1922; s. Robert Calvin and Eleanor Louise (Pressly) B.; m. Judith Frances Irby; children: Eleanor Koets, Susan, Katherine, Jonathon, Robert Calvin. A.B., Erskine Coll., 1943; M.D., Vanderbilt U., 1945. Diplomate: Am. Bd. Pediatrics (pres. 1975), Am. Bd. Family Practice. Intern Vanderbilt U. Hosp., Nashville, 1945-46, resident, 1948-49, U. Va., Charlottesville, 1949-50; chief resident Vanderbilt U., 1950-51; practice medicine, specializing in pediatrics Christie Pediatric Group, Greenville, S.C., 1951-70; dir. pediatrics Greenville Hosp. System, 1970-75; asso. exec. sec. Am. Bd. Pediatrics, Chapel Hill, N.C., 1976, exec. sec., 1977—; clin. prof. pediatrics U. Pa., 1976-78; prof. pediatrics Med. U. S.C., 1971-75; clin. prof. pediatrics U. N.C., 1978—. Contbr. articles to med. jours. Served with AUS, 1943-45; with M.C. USAF, 1946-48, 53. Mem. Am. Acad. Pediatrics, AMA, Ambulatory Pediatric Assn., So. Soc. Pediatric Research. Presbyterian. Clubs: Greenville Country, Chapel Hill Country. Home: 2533 Booker Creek Rd Chapel Hill NC 27514 Office: 111 Silver Cedar Ct Chapel Hill NC 27514

BROWNLEE, THOMAS MARSHALL, energy management company executive; b. Omaha, Oct. 11, 1926; s. John Templeton and Reed (Marshall) B.; m. Olive Ann Gettman, Sept. 13, 1950; children: Linda Sue, Thomas John, Curtis Marshall, Reed Ann. B.S. in Bus. Adminstrn, U. Nebr., 1950. Asst. mgr. Daytona Beach (Fla.) C. of C., 1950, Tampa (Fla.) C. of C., 1952-53; exec. mgr. Tallahassee C. of C., 1953- 58; exec. v.p. Greater Columbia (S.C.) C. of C., 1959-63, Winston-Salem (N.C.) C. of C., 1963-64, Orlando Area (Fla.) C. of C., 1964-78; pres. Brownlee Energy Mgmt. Co., Orlando, 1978—; Mem. energy policy com. Orange County (Fla.) Schs.; mem. Fla. Energy Action Com.; mem. energy com. Nat. League Cities. Contbr. articles to profl. jours. Bd. dirs. Loch Haven Art Mus., Chamber Inst., U. Ga.; mem. Orlando City Council.; pres. Christian Service Ctrs. Daily Bread. Served with USNR, 1944-46; as 1st lt. AUS, 1951-52. Mem. Fla. Energy mgmt. Assn. (pres.), Illuminating Engring. Soc. (pres. elect Central Fla. chpt.), Am. C. of C. Execs. Assn. (pres. 1966, Mem., v.p., treas. So. Assn.), S.C. C. of C. Execs. Assn., Fla. C. of C. Execs Assn. (pres. 1971), Better Bus. Bur. Central Fla. (chmn.), Phi Delta Theta. Presbyterian (deacon). Clubs: Rotarian., Country of Orlando, University, Citrus. Office: 1101 W Princeton St Orlando FL 32804

BROWNLEY, FLOYD IRVING, JR., cons., former ednl. adminstr.; b. Atlanta, Jan. 1, 1918; s. Floyd Irving and Ruth (Ballentine) B.; m. Martine Newlin Watson, July 23, 1943; children—Tina, Karen. B.S., Wofford Coll., 1939; M.S., Va. Poly. Inst., 1942; Ph.D., Fla. State U., 1951; D.Sc., Wofford Coll., 1966. Chemist Hercules Powder Co., Radford, Va., 1946; instr. Clemson (S.C.) U., 1941, asst. prof. chemistry, 1947-52, asso. prof., 1952-53, prof., head dept. chemistry and geology, 1953-66, dean grad. sch., 1966-73, dir. univ. research, 1967-69; vice chancellor U. Tenn., Chattanooga, 1969-73; provost Winthrop Coll., Rock Hill, S.C., 1973-79; with Delphian Consultants, 1979—; Sr. postdoctoral fellow in Europe Organization European Econ. Coop., 1962. Served from ensign to lt. (j.g.) USNR, 1942-46. Mem. Am. Chem. Soc., Am. Water Works Assn., A.A.A.S., Alpha Chi Sigma, Pi Kappa Phi, Phi Kappa Phi. Clubs: Kiwanis (pres. 1958-59), Rotary (pres. 1977-78). Home: 556 Ascot Ridge Dr Rock Hill SC 29730 Office: Box 3542 Rock Hill SC 29730

BROWNMILLER, SUSAN, author, feminist activist; b. Bklyn., Feb. 15, 1935. Student, Cornell U., 1952-55, Jefferson Sch. Social Sci. Reporter NBC-TV, Phila., 1965; network newswriter ABC-TV, N.Y.C., 1965-67; former researcher Newsweek mag.; former staff writer Village Voice. Freelance writer mags. newspapers; author: books including Shirley Chilsholm, 1970, Against Our Will: Men, Women and Rape, 1975. Founder Women Against Pornography. Office: care Simon and Schuster 1230 Ave of Americas New York NY 10020

BROWNRIGG, WALTER GRANT, designer, consultant; b. Boston, Oct. 26, 1940; s. Philip Parker and Mary Jane (Grant) B.; (div.)children—Elizabeth Grant, Christopher Hertel. A.B. in History cum laude, Princeton U., 1962; M.B.A., Columbia U., 1964. Asst. plant mgr. Berwick Weaving, Inc., Pa., 1964-72; asst. to v.p. Frank & Stessel, Inc., N.Y.C., 1972-73; sr. asso. Drake Sheahan/Stewart Dougall, Inc., N.Y.C., 1973-76; exec. dir. Greater Hartford (Conn.) Arts Council, 1976-79; dir. Am. Council Arts, N.Y.C., 1979-83; cons., greeting card designer, N.Y.C., 1983—; speaker, cons. in field. Author: Effective Corporate Fundraising, Corporate Fundraising: A Practical Plan of Action. Mem. Beta Gamma Sigma. Roman Catholic. Clubs: Princeton (N.Y.C.); University (Hartford). Home: 317 W 99th St New York NY 10025

BROWNSON, JACQUES CALMON, architect; b. Aurora, Ill., Aug. 3, 1923; s. Clyde Arthur and Iva Kline (Felter) B.; m. Doris L. Curry, 1946; children—Joel C., Lorre J., Daniel J. B.S. in Architecture, Ill. Inst. Tech., 1948, M.S., 1954. Instr., asst. prof. architecture Ill. Inst. Tech., 1949-59; prof. architecture, chmn. dept. U. Mich., 1966-68; chief design C.F. Murphy Assos., Chgo., 1959-61; project architect, chief designer Chgo. Civic Center Architects, 1961-68; mng. architect Pub. Bldg. Commn. Chgo.; dir. planning and devel. Auraria Center for Higher Edn., Denver; dir. Capital Constrn., Denver; now dir. state bldg. div. State of Colo. Prin. works include Chgo. Civic Center. Recipient award for Geneva House Archtl. Record mag., 1956; Design award for steel framed factory Progressive Architecture mag., 1957. Mem. AIA. Home: 659 Josephine Denver CO 80206 Office: State Services Bldg 1525 Sherman St Denver CO 80203

BROWNSON, ROBERT HENRY, anatomy educator; b. Evanston, Ill., Mar. 14, 1925; s. Walter Converse and Martha Virginia (White) B.; m. Carol Ann Priestaf, June 15, 1957; children: Michael R., Patrick S., Barbara L., Timothy T. B.S., John Carroll U., 1948; M.S., George Washington U., 1950, Ph.D., 1953. Instr. anatomy U. So. Calif. Med. Sch., 1952-54; asst. prof. anatomy Med. Coll. Va., 1954-62, assoc. prof., 1962-66, prof., 1966-68, chmn. dept., 1967-68; vis. prof. postdoctoral NIH fellow Donner Lab., Lawrence Radiation Lab., U. Calif. at Berkeley, 1964-66; prof. human anatomy U. Calif. Sch. Medicine—Davis, 1968-78; vice chmn. dept. human anatomy U. Calif. Sch. Medicine-Davis, 1968-70, 71-75; acting chmn. dept. human anatomy U. Calif. Sch. Medicine—Davis, 1970-71; prof. Eastern Va. Med. Sch., Norfolk, 1978—, chmn. dept. anatomy, 1978-83; vis. prof. dept. anatomy U. Helsinki, Finland, 1975. Author articles and nat. audiovisuals in field. Active Boy Scouts Am. Served as hosp. corpsman USNR, 1943-46; capt. Med. Services Corp Res. ret. Mem. Am. Assn. Anatomists, Am. Assn. Neuropathologists, Am. Acad. Neurology, Radiation Research Soc., Electron Microscopy Soc. Am., Soc. Neuroscis., World Fedn. Neurology, Am. Physiol. Soc., Sigma Xi, Phi Chi. Home: 816 N Villier Ct Virginia Beach VA 23452 Office: Dept Anatomy Eastern Va Med Sch 700 Olney Rd PO Box 1980 Norfolk VA 23501

BROWNSTEIN, BARBARA LAVIN, educational administrator, geneticist; b. Phila., Sept. 8, 1931; d. Edward A. and Rose (Silverstein) Lavin; m. Melvin Brownstein, June 1949 (div. 1955); children: Judith Brownstein Kaufmann, Dena. Asst. editor Biol. Abstracts, Phila., 1957-58; research fellow dept. microbial genetics Karolinska Inst., Stockholm, 1962-64; assoc. Wistar Inst., Phila., 1964-68; asoc. prof. molecular biology, dept. biology Temple U., Phila., 1968-74, chmn. dept., 1978-81, provost, 1983—; vis. scientist dept. tumor cell biology Imperial Cancer Research Fund Labs., London, 1973-74; mem. Cancer Scientist Tng. Program, Temple U., com. instl. grants, Am. Cancer Soc.; cons. Cancer Info. Dissemination Analysis Ctr., Franklin Inst., Saunders Pubs., Holt, Rinehart, Wadsworth pubs. Recipient Liberal Arts Alumni award for excellence in teaching Temple U., 1980, Outstanding Faculty Woman award Temple U., 1980. Mem. AAAS, Am. Soc. Cell Biology, N.Y. Acad. Sci., Assn. Woem in Sci. (Temple U. rep.). Home: 201 Pennsylvania Ave Philadelphia PA 19130 Office: Office of Provost Temple U Philadelphia PA 19122

BROWNSTEIN, MARTIN HERBERT, dermatopathologist, educator; b. N.Y.C., Aug. 20, 1935; s. Samuel C. and Florence (Sturm) B.; m. Ann Lehman, June 23, 1964; children: Sara Leah, Michael Ari. A.B., Harvard U., 1956; M.D., Albert Einstein Coll. Medicine, 1961. Intern Lenox Hill Hosp., N.Y.C., 1961-62; resident in internal medicine VA Hosps., N.Y.C., 1962-65; resident in dermatology NYU, N.Y.C., 1965-66; practice medicine specializing in dermatopathology, N.Y.C., 1970-72, Gt. Neck, N.Y., 1972—; Osborne fellow Armed Forces Inst. Pathology, Washington, 1968-69; mem. staff N.Y. Med. Coll.-Met. Hosp. Center, N.Y.C.; asst. clin. prof. dermatology N.Y. Med. Coll., N.Y.C., 1970-73, clin. assoc. prof. dermatology, 1973-78, clin. prof. dermatology, 1978—, clin. asst. prof. pathology, 1971—. Contbr. articles to profl. jours. Served with M.C. U.S. Army, 1966-68. Recipient Pres.'s award Union Orthodox Jewish Congregations of Am., 1983. Mem. Am. Soc. Dermatopathology (pres.-elect 1982-83), Soc. Investigative Dermatology, N.Y. State Soc. Dermatology, Am. Acad. Dermatology (chmn. com. on pathology 1980-82), Internat. Soc. Tropical Dermatology, Med. Soc. N.Y. State, Med. Soc. N.Y. County, AMA, A.C.P., Dermatol. Soc. Greater N.Y. (pres. 1978-79), N.Y. Acad. Medicine. Home: 2 Jordan Dr Great Neck NY 11021 Office: 185 Great Neck Rd Great Neck NY 11021 *One path to accomplishment is hard work, close personal attention to details, and careful organization and preparation.*

BROWNSTEIN, PHILIP NATHAN, lawyer; b. Ober, Ind., Feb. 14, 1917; s. Max and Anna (Katz) B.; m. Esther Savelle, Sept. 4, 1938; 1 son, Michael. Student, George Washington U., 1937-38; LL.B., Columbus U. (now Cath. U.), Washington, 1940, LL.M., 1941. Bar: D.C. bar 1940. With FHA, 1935-44, commr., 1963-66; with VA, 1946-63, dir. loan guaranty service, 1956-61, chief benefits dir., 1961-63; asst. sec. mortgage credit HUD, 1966-69; partner firm Brownstein Zeidman & Schomer; commr. Fed. Housing Adminstrn., 1963-69; mem. Pres.'s Task Force on Low Income Housing, 1970, Sec.'s Task Force on Role of Fed. Housing Adminstrn., 1977-78, HUD Task Force on Center for Housing Mgmt., 1980, Pres.'s Adv. Com. on Housing, 1980; Bd. dirs. Fed. Nat. Mortgage Assn., 1963-69, 70-72; vice chmn. Nat. Housing Conf., 1969—; bd. dirs. Nat. Commn. against Discrimination in Housing, 1972—. Served with USMCR, 1944-46. Recipient Exceptional Service award, VA, 1960, Top Performer in Housing award, House and Home, 1964; Career Service award Nat. Civil Service League, 1967; Isaac Shallcross award U.S. League Savs. Assns., 1982. Home: 550 N St SW Washington DC 20024 Office: 1025 Connecticut Ave NW Washington DC 20036

BROWNSTONE, PAUL LOTAN, educator; b. N.Y.C., Jan. 21, 1923; s. Harry and Mollie B.; m. Enid Barbara Klein, Nov. 6, 1955; children: Hugh M., Susan L., Karen A. B.A., Bklyn. Coll., 1947; M.A., U. Denver, 1948; Ph.D., Pa. State U., 1960. Mem. faculty dept. speech and theatre Bklyn. Coll., 1953-69, asst. prof., 1960-69; prof., chmn. dept. speech and theatre, dir. humanities div. L.I.U.-Bklyn. Center, 1969-74, sr. prof. humanities, 1974—, chmn. dept. speech communication, 1979—; assigned to C.W. Post Component Campus, Nassau County, 1974-76; cons. leadership tng. center U. Calif. at Berkeley, 1960. Contbr. articles to profl. jours. Patron Nat. Soc. Study Communication, 1964—. Postdoctoral grantee in ednl. tech. Cornell U., summer 1967. Mem. Speech Assn. Am. (del. legis. assembly 1966-68), Speech Assn. Eastern States (pres. 1970-71, program chmn. conv. 1977), N.Y. State Speech Assn., Lawrence Assn. (gov. 1975-80), AAUP. Home: 23 Washington Ave Lawrence NY 11559 Office: LIU Bklyn Center Richard L Conolly Coll Dept Speech Communication Brooklyn NY 11201

BROYHILL, JAMES THOMAS, congressman; b. Lenoir, N.C., Aug. 19, 1927; m. Louise Robbins; children—Marilyn Broyhill Beach, Ed, Phil. B.S. in Bus. Adminstrn, U. N.C., 1950; LL.D. (hon.), Catawba Coll., Salisbury, N.C., 1966. Formerly exec. Broyhill Furniture Industries, Lenoir; mem. 88th-98th Congresses from 9th and 10th N.C. Dists., ranking minority mem. energy and commerce com.; vice chmn. Congl. Textile Caucus; dean N.C. Congl. delegation. Trustee Wake Forest U., 1970-74; vice chmn. bd. advs. Lees-McRae Coll., Banner Elk, N.C.; mem. devel. bd. Lenoir-Rhyne Coll., Hickory, N.C. Republican. Baptist. Clubs: Masons, Shriners. Office: 2340 Rayburn House Office Bldg Washington DC 20515

BROYHILL, PAUL H., furniture manufacturing company executive; b. 1924; m. B.A., U. N.C., 1947. With Broyhill Furniture Industries, Inc., Lenoir, N.C., 1947—, salesman, 1947-50, v.p. sales and merchandising, 1950-60, pres., 1960-76, chmn. bd., 1976—; v.p. Interco Inc. Office: Broyhill Furniture Industries Inc Broyhill Park Lenoir NC 28633 *

BROYLES, WILLIAM DODSON, JR., editor; b. Houston, Oct. 8, 1944; s. William Dodson and Elizabeth (Bills) B.; m. Sybil Ann Newman, Aug. 15, 1973; children: William David, Susannah. B.A. in History, Rice U., 1966, Oxford U., 1968, M.A., 1971. Tchr. philosophy U.S. Naval Acad., 1970-71; asst. supt. Houston Public Schs., 1971-72. Editor: Tex. Monthly, Austin, 1972-81; editor-in-chief, 1981—, Calif. mag, 1981—, Newsweek Mag., 1982—. Served with USMCR, 1969-71. Decorated Bronze Star. Mem. Tex. Inst. Letters (bd. councillors, v.p.). Office: Newsweek Mag 444 Madison Ave New York NY 10022

BROZEK, JOSEF, scientist, psychology educator; b. Melnik, Bohemia, Aug. 14, 1913; came to U.S., 1939, naturalized, 1945; s. Josef Francis and Filomena (Sourek) B.; m. Eunice Magnuson, Mar. 23, 1945; children: Josef, Margaret, Peter. Ph.D., Charles U., Prague, Czechoslovakia, 1937. Asst. dept. philosophy Charles U., 1936-37; psychotechnologist Bata Shoe Co., Zlin, Czechoslovkia, 1937-39; jr. psychologist lab. physiol. hygiene Sch. Pub. Health, U. Minn., 1941-43, assoc. scientist, 1943-44, asst. prof., 1944-49, assoc. prof., 1949-56, prof., 1956-59; prof. psychology, chmn. dept. Lehigh U., Bethlehem, Pa., 1959-63, research prof., 1963-79, adj. prof. psychology, 1982—; resident coordinator UN Univ. World Hunger Program, M.I.T., 1980-81; dir. Summer Inst. Hist. Psychology, U. N.H., 1968; bd. dirs. Lehigh U., 1971; Adviser nutrition WHO, 1964-68, 73; mem. U.S. Malnutrition Panel, U.S.-Japan Coop. Med. Sci. Program, 1973-78; mem. com. on nutrition, brain devel and behavior Food and Nutrition Bd., NRC, 1974-79, chmn., 1980. Co-author: The Biology of Human Starvation, 1950; Editor, contbr.: Symposium on Nutrition and Behavior, 1957, Body Measurements and Human Nutrition, 1956, Performance Capacity A Symposium, 1961, Techniques for Measuring Body Composition, 1961, Soviet Studies on Nutrition and Higher Nervous Activity, 1962, Body Composition, 1963, Human Body Composition, 1965, The Biology of Human Variation, 1966, Physical Growth and Body Composition, 1970, Origins of Psychometry, 1970, Psychology in the USSR, 1972, R.I. Watson's Selected Papers on the History of Psychology, 1977, Behavioral Effects of Energy and Protein Deficits, 1979, Historiography of Modern Psychology, 1980, Explorations in the History of Psychology in the United States, 1983; adv. editor: Slavic lits. Contemporary Psychology, 1960-79; mem. editorial bd.: Jour. of History of Behavioral Scis, 1976—, Revista de Historia de la Psicología, 1980—, Storia e Critica della Psicologia, 1980—, Archiv für Psychologie, 1980—. Sr. Fulbright research fellow U Würzburg, Ger., 1979-80. Mem. AAAS, Am. Psychol. Assn., History of Sci. Soc., Pavlovian Soc., Deutsche Gesellschaft für Psychologie. Home: 265 E Market St Bethlehem PA 18105

BROZEN, YALE, economist, educator; b. Kansas City, Mo., July 6, 1917; s. Oscar and Sarah (Sholtz) B.; m. Lee Parsons, Apr. 26, 1962; children—Yale II, Reed. Ph.D., 1941. Asst. prof. social sci. U. Fla., 1940-41; asst. prof. econs. Ill. Inst. Tech., 1941-44, assoc. prof., 1944-46; asso. prof. econs. U. Minn., 1946-47, vis. prof. econs., 1948; prof. econs. Northwestern U., Evanston, Ill., 1947-57; dir. Research Transp. Center, 1957-59; prof. econs. U. Chgo., 1957—, dir. research mgmt. program, 1959-67, dir. applied econ. program, 1960—; adj. scholar Am. Ent. Inst., 1972—; Cons. State Dept., 1956-63; vis. prof. econs. São Paulo, Brazil, 1954, Rikkyo U., Tokyo, 1964, U. Va., 1965, Grad. Inst. Internat. Studies, 1969; research assoc. Social Sci. Research Council, 1949; cons. pub. utility econs. Cook County State's Atty's Office, 1950; dir. econ. tng. Am. Tel. & Tel. Co., 1951; cons. President's Materials Policy Commn., 1951, Anti-Trust Div., Dept. Justice, 1952, NSF, 1954-55, N.A.M., 1954-55, Loewi & Co., 1969; Dir. Univ. Nat. Bank, West Burton Place Corp., Carus Corp. Author: Workbook for Economics, 1946, Textbook for Economics, Vol. I, 1948, Advertising and Society, 1974, The Competitive Economy, 1975, Concentration, Mergers, and Public Policy, 1982, Mergers in Perspectives, 1982. Civilian tng. adminstr. Signal Corps U.S. Army, 1942-43. Mem. Am. Econ. Assn., Mont Pelerin Soc., Phi Beta Kappa, Delta Sigma Pi. Clubs: Quadrangle, Technology (Chgo.). Address: U Chgo 1101 E 58th St Chicago IL 60637

BRUBAKER, CARL H., JR., educator; b. Passaic, N.J., July 13, 1925; s. Carl H. and Lillian (Rochow) B.; m. Mary Ellen Fiske, June 26, 1949; 1 son, Peter. B.S., Franklin and Marshall Coll., 1949; Ph.D., Mass. Inst. Tech., 1952. Asst. prof. Mich. State U., 1952-58, asso. prof., 1958-61, prof., 1961—; research asso. Mass. Inst. Tech., 1952, summer 1955, Argonne Nat. Lab., summer 1957; Smith-Mundt-Fulbright lectr. radiochemistry U. Chile, 1958. Asst. editor: Jour. American Chem. Soc, 1964-69; asso. editor, 1969-70, 73—; bd. editors, 1970-73. Served with AUS, 1943-46. Mem. Am. Chem. Soc. (council 1971-74), Royal Soc. Chemistry, AAAS, Sigma Xi, Phi Beta Kappa. Research on electron transfer in transition element organometallic compounds and their use as reagents and in molecular nitrogen fixation and organic reaction catalysis. Home: 4466 Tacoma Blvd PO Box 128 Okemos MI 48864 Office: Dept Chemistry Mich State U East Lansing MI 48824

BRUBAKER, CHARLES EDWARD, clergyman; b. Birmingham, Ala., Dec. 22, 1917; s. Lauren E. and Nora (Drake) B.; m. Doris Jane King, Sept. 14, 1946; children: Wendy, Scott, Lynn, Laurie. B.A., Maryville (Tenn.) Coll., 1938, D.D., 1956; M.Div., Princeton U., 1941; postgrad., Union Theol. Sem., N.Y.C., 1941-43, 46-48; spl. study, Mansfield Coll., Oxford (Eng.) U., 1976; D.D., Missouri Valley Coll., 1980. Ordained to ministry Presbyn. Ch., 1941; asst. pastor, New Rochelle, N.Y., 1941-43; pastor Central Presbyn. Ch.; also dir. Westminster Found., Fayetteville, Ark., 1948-53; pastor Tabernacle Presbyn. Ch., Phila.; also dir. Westminster Found., Phila., 1953-60; pastor First Presbyn. Ch., Englewood, N.J., 1960-69, Wichita, Kans., 1969-79; synod exec. Synods of Mid-Am., United Presbyn. Ch. and Presbyn. Ch. U.S., 1979—; Brit. Am. exchange minister, summer 1963; chmn. dept. chaplains and service personnel United Presbyn. Ch., 1963-69; chmn. Gen. Commn. Chaplains and Armed Forces Personnel, 1969-71, Gen. Assembly Spl. Com. Membership Trends, 1974-76; moderator Presbytery So. Kans., 1977; Trustee Princeton Theol. Sem., 1960-63, Maryville Coll., 1958-82. Bd. dirs. Wichita Symphony, 1974-79. Served as chaplain USNR, 1943-46; PTO. Decorated Bronze Star. Mem. Theta Alpha Phi, Pi Kappa Tau. Address: 6400 Glenwood Suite 111 Overland Park KS 66202

BRUBAKER, CHARLES WILLIAM, architect; b. South Bend, Ind., Sept. 28, 1926; s. Ralph and Mary (Holderman) B.; m. Elizabeth Allen Rogers, June 25, 1955; children: William Rogers, Elizabeth Allen, Robert Andrew. Student, Purdue U., 1945; B.Arch., U. Tex., 1950. Architect, designer, partner Perkins & Will, Chgo., 1950-69, exec. v.p., Chgo., Washington and N.Y.C., 1970—; Pres. Council of Edni. Facilities Planners; bd. govs. Met. Housing and Planning Council. Prin. works include Richland Coll., Dallas, First Nat. Bank Chgo. Served with USNR, 1945-46. Fellow AIA; mem. Chgo. Assn. Commerce and Industry, Phi Gamma Delta. Clubs: Chicago Yacht, Mid-Day (Chgo.); Cosmos (Washington). Home: 82 Essex Rd Winnetka IL 60093 Office: 2 N LaSalle St Chicago IL 60602

BRUBAKER, LAUREN EDGAR, educator, clergyman; b. Birmingham, Ala., Oct. 8, 1914; s. Lauren Edgar and Nora (Drake) B.; m. Leonte Saye, June 6, 1944; children: Lauren Eugene, Edward Saye. A.B., Birmingham So. Coll., 1935; M.Div., Princeton Theol. Sem., 1938, postdoctoral, 1946-47; S.T.M., Union Theol. Sem., N.Y., 1943, Th.D., 1944. Ordained to ministry Presbyn. Ch., 1938; asst. pastor in, Parkersburg, W.Va., 1938-41; grad. instr. Union Theol. Sem., 1941-43; grad. asst. Princeton Theol. Sem., 1946-47; prof. philosophy and religion, chaplain Parsons Coll., Fairfield, Iowa, 1947-49; asso. prof. U. S.C. at Columbia, 1949-58, prof., 1958-79; Disting. prof. U. S.C., 1979-80, Disting. prof. emeritus, 1980—, chmn. dept. religion, 1949-80, chaplain, 1949—; adj. prof. Luth. Theol. So. Sem. Contbr. articles to profl. jours. Dir. S.C. Council Human Relations, 1966-69; exec. committeeman Columbia and Richland County Democratic party, 1950-60. Served to maj. AUS, 1943-46. Mem. Inst. Religion (dir. 1960-63), S.C. Acad. Religion (founder 1968, pres. 1968), Am. Acad. Religion (pres. 1960), Presbyn. Edn. Assn. South, Columbia Ministers Assn. (pres. 1972), AAUP (past officer), Nat. Assn. Coll. and Univ. Pastors, Soc. Bibl. Lit. (past officer), Omicron Delta Kappa (faculty adviser 1968-71), Pi Gamma Mu, Phi Kappa Phi, Tau Kappa Alpha. Clubs: Executive of Columbia (pres. 1960-61), Kiwanis). Research teaching religion in accredited colls. and univs. Home: 9 Churchill Circle Columbia SC 29206

BRUBAKER, ROBERT STEWART, speech communication educator; b. Paris, Ill., Mar. 8, 1924; s. A. Allen and Luella (Graham) B.; m. Caryl Morse, Jan. 29, 1949; children: Leslie, Kevin. B.A., U. Ill., 1948, A.M., 1950, Ph.D., 1952. Asst. prof. speech communication Pa. State U., University Park, Pa., 1952-56, assoc. prof., University Park, 1956-66, prof., 1966—, head dept. speech communication, 1975—; staff engr. HRB-Singer, State College, Pa., 1956-70. Co-author: Oral Communication in the Classroom, 1970; co-editor: Speech Pathology, 1966; assoc. editor Jour. Communication Disorders, 1967—; bd. editor Jour. Psycholinguistic Research, 1970—. Served with U.S. Army, 1942-46. U. Ill. Grad. Sch. fellow, 1951-52; Am. Speech and Hearing Assn. travel grantee, Italy, 1962. Mem. Central Pa. Acoustical Soc. (pres. 1974-75), Assn. for Communication Adminstrn., Acoustical Soc. Am., Speech Communication Assn., Am. Speech and Hearing Assn., Am. Assn. Phonetic Scis., Phonetic Soc. Japan. Home: 814 Jackson Circle State College PA 16801 Office: Pa State U. 213 Sparks Bldg University Park PA 16802

BRUBECK, DAVID WARREN, musician; b. Concord, Calif., Dec. 6, 1920; s. Howard and Elizabeth (Ivey) B.; m. Iola Whitlock, Sept. 21, 1942; children: David Darius, Michael, Christopher, Catherine, Daniel, Matthew. B.A., U. Pacific, 1942; Ph.D. (hon.), U. Pacific, Fairfield U., U. Bridgeport; postgrad., Mills Coll., 1946-49; Ph.D. hon., Mills Coll. Mem. adv. com. for Hopkins Center at Dartmouth. Formed trio, 1950; Formed with bookings throughout U.S. in jazz night clubs; formed Dave Brubeck Quartet, 1951, concert tours, U.S. Colls., festivals, etc., 1958—, 3 month tour, Europe and Middle East for U.S. State Dept., many tours, Europe and S. Am., Australia and Japan, European tour as soloist with Cin. Symphony, 1969; affiliated with, Atlantic Record Co.; Columbia Record Co., Decca, Horizon, Concord Jazz, Fantasy Records; Composer: (oratorios) Beloved Son, The Light in the Wilderness; (cantatas) La Fiesta de la Posada, Games of Justice, Truth; (orchestral) They All Sang Yankee Doodle, Elementals; (ballets) Tritonis; (for flute and guitar) Festival Mass to Hope, chorus with soloists; (chorus and orch.) Pauge Lingua; and over 100 jazz compositions. Named Editor's Choice, Metronome mag., 1952; recipient first place in popularity poll, 1953-55; 1st place in critics poll, Downbeat mag., 1953; cover story Time mag., 1954; named one of Calif.'s 5 outstanding young men, 1957; winner jazz polls conducted by Downbeat, Melody Maker, Cashbox, Billboard, Playboy mags., 1962; Duke Ellington fellow Yale U. Fellow Internat. Inst. Arts and Scis; mem. Broadcast Music, Inc., Phi Mu Alpha. Home: 221 Millstone Rd Wilton CT 06897 Office: Derry Music Co 601 Montgomery St San Francisco CA 94111

BRUCCOLI, MATTHEW JOSEPH, educator, publisher; b. N.Y.C., Aug. 21, 1931; s. Joseph M. and Mary (Gervasi) B.; m. Arlyn Shuey Firkins, Oct. 5, 1957; children: Mary Firkins, Joseph Matthew, Josephine Arlyn, Arlyn Barbara. B.A., Yale U., 1953; M.A., U. Va., 1956, Ph.D., 1961. Prof. English U. S.C., Columbia, 1969—, Jefferies prof. English, 1976—; dir. Center for Editions of Am. Authors, 1969-76; pres. Bruccoli Clark Publishers, 1976—. Author: The Composition of Tender Is the Night, 1963, The Last of the Novelists, 1977, The O'Hara Concern, 1975, Scott and Ernest, 1978, Selected Letters of John O'Hara, 1978, Just Representations: A James Gould Cozzens Reader, 1978, Correspondence of F. Scott Fitzgerald, 1980, Some Sort of Epic Grandeur: The Life of F. Scott Fitzgerald, 1981, James Gould Cozzens, 1983; Editor: lit. works of Fitzgerald/Hemingway Annual, 1969-79; series editor Dictionary of Literary Biography, 1978—, Lost Am. Fiction, 1972—, Pittsburgh Series in Bibliography, 1971—. Guggenheim fellow, 1973. Club: Yale, Century (N.Y.C.). Home: 31 Heathwood Circle Columbia SC 29205 Office: Dept English U South Carolina Columbia SC 29208

BRUCE, E(STEL) EDWARD, lawyer; b. Hutchison, Kans., Nov. 23, 1938; s. Kenneth Dean and Josephine (Vigna) B.; m. Marnell Elaine Higley, Aug. 9, 1960; children—Anthony Dean, Caroline Summers. B.A. summa cum laude, Yale U., 1960, LL.B. magna cum laude, 1966. Bar: D.C. bar 1967. Law clk. U.S. Supreme Ct., Washington, 1966-67; asso. firm Covington & Burling, Washington, 1967-73, partner, 1973—; adj. prof. constitutional law Georgetown U. Law Center, 1970-75. Served to lt. (j.g.) USN, 1960-63. Mem. Am. Law Inst., Am. Bar Assn., D.C. Bar, ACLU, Order of Coif, Phi Beta Kappa. Clubs: Met. (Washington); Chevy Chase. Home: 2701 Foxhall Rd Washington DC 20007 Office: Covington & Burling 1201 Pennsylvania Ave NW Washington DC 20044

BRUCE, HARRY JAMES, transportation company executive; b. Newark, July 2, 1931; s. John William and Anna Margaret (Ackerman) B.; m. Vivienne Ruth Jennings, Sept. 10, 1955; children: Robert, Stacy, Bethann. B.S., Kent State U., 1957; M.S., U. Tenn., 1959; cert. Advanced Mgmt. Program, Harvard U., 1979.. Transp. research asst. U.S. Steel Co., Pitts., 1959-64; dir. market devel. Spector Freight Co., Chgo., 1964-67, v.p. mktg., 1967-69; dir. distbn. Joseph Schlitz Brewing Co., Milw., 1969-71, asst. v.p.plant ops., 1971-72; v.p.mktg. Western Pacific R.R., San Francisco, 1972-75; sr. v.p. mktg. Ill. Central Gulf R.R., Chgo., 1975-83, chmn., chief exec. officer, 1983—, also dir.; dir. Affiliate Artists, N.Y.C., 1975—, Far Hills Woodworking Co., Mendham, N.J., 1983. Author: How to Apply Statistics to Physical Distribution, 1967, Distribution and Transportation Handbook, 1971; inventor vari-deck, 1970; mem.editorial bd.: Jours. Bus. Logistics. Pres. Woodley Rd. Assn., Winnetka, Ill., 1982-84; mem.adv. bd. U. Tenn. Served to 1st lt. U.S. Army, 952-55; ETO. Mem. Newcomen Soc., Nat. Council Phys. Distbn., Nat. Freight Transp. Assn., Nat. Def. Transp. Assn. Republican. Presbyterian. Clubs: Glenview (Ill.); Mid-Am. (Chgo.); Metropolitan (N.Y.C.). HOme: 88 Woodley Rd Winnetka IL 60093 Office: Ill Central Gulf RR 233 N Michigan Ave Chicago IL 60601

BRUCE, HARRY WILLIAM, JR., dentist, dental association executive; b. Nashville, Tenn., July 19, 1920; s. Harry W. and Ethel (Scruggs) B.; m. Grace Brooks, June 12, 1944; children: Harry William III, Neal Irvin. B.S., Carson Newman Coll., 1943; D.D.S., U. Tenn., 1946; M.P.H., U. Mich., 1950; L.H.D. (hon.), Loyola U., Chgo., 1970, Des Moines Coll. Osteopathic Medicine and Surgery, 1971, Med. U. of S.C., 1977, LL.D., Creighton U., 1981, Sc.D., Georgetown U., 1981. Practice dentistry specializing in public health, 1946—; dental officer Chattanooga-Hamilton County Health Dept., 1947-48; dental trainee Public Health Service, Atlanta, Ga., 1954-56; regional public health cons., Charlottesville, Va., 1956-61; dental officer USPHS, 1961, asst. surgeon gen., from 1971; assoc. dir. ops. Bur. of Health Manpower, Health Resources Adminstrn., Bethesda, Md., 1973-75; exec. dir. Am. Assn. Dental Schs., Washington, 1975—; Lister Hill lectr. U. Ala., 1980; mem. adv. com. dental radiology Nat. Center for Health Care Tech., 1980-81; mem. nat. adv. com. Hosp. dental program Robert Wood Johnson Found., 1979-82. Contbr. articles to jours. in dentistry. Served with U.S. Army, 1942-44. Recipient Disting. Service award USPHS, 1975, Award of Merit Georgetown U. Sch. Dentistry, 1971, Fairlie Dickinson U., 1971; Named Outstanding Alumnus U. Tenn., 1981. Fellow Am. Public Health Assn., Am. Coll. Dentists; mem. Am. Assn. Dental Schs., Am. Assn. of Public Health Dentists, Am. Dental Assn. (cons. 1975—). Democrat. Baptist. Home: 7726 Greentree Rd Bethesda MD 20034 Office: 1619 Massachusetts Ave Washington DC 20036

BRUCE, IMON ELBA, coll. pres. emeritus; b. Blevins, Ark., Dec. 9, 1910; s. Jewell Joseph and Ada Lee (Wortham) B.; m. Catherine Coles, Dec. 24, 1938; children—Catherine Jane, Carolyn Louise, Elizabeth Ann. B.A., Henderson State Coll., 1932; M.S., La. State U., 1937; D.Ed., Ind. U., 1952. Tchr. math. and sci. Hope (Ark.) High Sch., 1932-33; tchr. math and sci. Fordyce (Ark.) High Sch., 1933-36; supt. schs. Fordyce, 1937-49; teaching fellow math. La. State U., 1936-37; dir. student teaching Ark. State Tchrs. Coll., Conway, 1949-53; supt. schs., Hot Springs, Ark., 1953-59; pres. So. Ark. U., Magnolia, 1959-76, pres. emeritus, 1976—; summer vis. lectr. Ind. U., 1955, U. Ark., 1956, 57, U. N.Mex., 1958. Mem. NEA, Ark. Edn. Assn., Am., Ark. (past pres.) assns. sch. adminstrs., Magnolia C. of C. (past pres.), Phi Delta Kappa. Methodist. Club: Rotarian (past pres.). Home: 912 Lawton Circle Magnolia AR 71753

BRUCE, JACKSON MARTIN, JR., lawyer; b. Milw., Apr. 10, 1931; s. Jackson Martin and Harriet (Edgell) B.; m. Lilias M. Morehouse, June 30, 1954; children: Lilias Stephanie, Andrew Edgell. A.B. magna cum laude, Harvard U., 1953, J.D. cum laude, 1957; M.A. with 1st class honors in Law, Cambridge U., 1955. Bar: Wis. 1957, Fla. 1973. Assoc. Quarles & Brady, Milw., 1957-64, partner, 1964—. Contbr. articles to profl. jours. Sec. St. John's Home of Milw; bd. dirs. Bruner Corp., Living Ch. Found., Inc.; trustee Univ. Sch. Milw., 1973-79. Fellow Am. Coll. Probate Counsel (bd. regents); mem. State Bar of Wis. (chmn. bd. govs. 1979-80), Am. Bar Assn. (mem. council, div. dir., chmn.-elect sect. real property, probate and trust law), Am. Bar Found., Am. Law Inst., Internat. Acad. Estate and Trust Law (exec. council), Nat. Conf. Bar Presidents. Clubs: University (Milw.) (bd. dirs.); Town.). Home: 9008 N Bayside Dr Milwaukee WI 53217 Office: 780 N Water St Milwaukee WI 53202

BRUCE, JAMES DONALD, electrical engineering educator; b. Livingston, Tex., June 28, 1936; s. Vivian Eugene and Edna Lee (St. Clair) B.; m. Eleanor MacLaren, Nov. 25, 1959; children: David MacLaren, Heather MacLaren, Nathaniel MacLaren. B.S. in Elec. Engring, Lamar State Coll., Beaumont, Tex., 1958; S.M. in Elec. Engring, MIT, 1960, Sc.D., 1964. Mem. faculty MIT, 1964—, assoc. dean, 1971-78, acting dean, 1977-78, prof. elec. engring., 1973—, dir. indsl. liaison, 1979-82, dir. info. systems, 1983—; trustee Harvard Coop. Soc., 1974—; cons. to govt. and industry. Trustee Park St. Congregational Ch., Boston, 1977—, Vice chmn. bd. trustees, 1977-80, chmn., 1981-82. Recipient Bullard award M.I.T., 1978; Ford Found. postdoctoral fellow, 1964-65. Sr. mem. IEEE; mem. Am. Soc. Engring. Edn. (Black engring. colls. devel. com.), Eta Kappa Nu, Tau Beta Pi. Home: 12 Woodpark Circle Lexington MA 02173 Office: 77 Massachusetts Ave Room 10-219 Cambridge MA 02139

BRUCE, JAMES EDMUND, utility company executive; b. Boise, Idaho, June 23, 1920; s. James E. and Bessie (Barcus) B.; m. Lois I. Stevens, Aug. 24, 1946; children: James E., IV, Steven, Robert, David. Student, Coll. Idaho, 1938-39; B.A., Portland U., 1941; postgrad., Georgetown U., 1941-42; LL.B., U. Idaho, 1949. Bar: Idaho bar 1948. Asst. atty. gen. State of Idaho, 1948-49; dep. pros. atty. Ada County (Idaho), 1949-51; with Idaho Power Co., Boise, 1951—, v.p., 1968-74, pres., chief operating officer, 1974-76, pres., chief exec. officer, 1976—, also dir.; dir. Albertson's Inc., First Security Corp. Bd. dirs. United Fund, Boise, 1976—; mem. Boise Park Bd., 1958-78; Idaho chmn. U.S. Savs. Bonds, 1968—; trustee Coll. Idaho. Served with U.S. Army, 1942-46. Mem. Boise Execs. Assn., YMCA, Bishop Kelly Found., Am. Bar Assn., Edison Electric Assn. (dir. 1978—), Northwest Electric Light and Power Assn. (pres. 1982), Boise C. of C. Roman Catholic. Clubs: Arid, Crane Creek Country, Rotary, Elks, K.C. Office: 1220 Idaho St Boise ID 83707 *

BRUCE, JOHN IRVIN, university official, government agency administrator; b. Ellicott City, Md., Aug. 1, 1929; s. John Irvin and Mary E. (Simms) B.; m. Alease Sully, Sept. 2, 1967; 1 dau., Shawn Francelia. B.S., Morgan State Coll., 1953; postgrad., Columbia U., 1953-54, NYU, 1953-54, U. Md., 1957-58; M.S., Howard U., 1965, Ph.D., 1968. Jr. chemist Met. Hosp., N.Y.C., 1953-54; research asst. Columbia U., 1954-55; med. research technician Walter Reed Army Inst. Research, Washington, 1955-59, parasitologist, 1959-68, chief composite drug screening unit, Japan, 1968-71, chief schistosomiasis research unit, 1971-73; dean Coll. Pure and Applied Sci. U. Lowell, Mass., 1973-78, now dir. Center for Tropical Diseases, Coll. Pure and Applied Sci.; dep. asst. adminstr. devel. tech. Bur. Devel. Support, AID, Washington, 1978—; chief U.S. del. UNIDO Appropriate Indsl. Tech., Anand, India, 1978; mem. spl. sci. commn. U.S. Army Med. Research and Adv. Panel; cons. Smithsonian Instn. (Mekong River Delta Project, Thailand, U.S. Civil Adminstrn., Ryukyu Islands), 1969-71; Bd. dirs. Gorgas Meml. Inst. Tropical and Preventive Medicine, Inc. Editorial bd.: Jour. Exptl. Parasitology. Recipient Outstanding Performance award Dept. Army, certificate of Achievement 406th Med. Lab. Fellow Royal Soc. Tropical Medicine and Hygiene; mem. Am. Soc. Parasitologists, Wildlife Disease Assn., Japan, Korea sci. socs., Helminthological Soc. Washington (council mem. at large), N.Y. Acad. Sci., Am. Inst. Biol. Sci., Am. Soc. Primatologists, Am. Soc. Tropical Medicine and Hygiene. Home: 8 Rose Glen Dr Andover MA 01810 Office: Ctr Tropical Diseases/Coll Pure and Applied Sci Univ Lowell 450 Aiken St Lowell MA 01854

BRUCE, JOHN MARTIN, automotive co. exec.; b. Vincennes, Ind., Feb. 10, 1930; s. Jesse Frank and Margaret (McCain) B.; m. Barbara Theophelis, July 30, 1972; 1 dau., Johanna. B.S. in Mech. Engring, Purdue U., 1952. With Monsanto Chem. Co., St. Louis, 1952; with Chrysler Corp., Indpls. and Detroit, 1955-80, v.p., gen. mfg. div., 1976-80; pres. Automotive Products div. United Technologies Corp., 1981—. Bd. dirs. Inter City Bus. Improvement Forum, 1975-76; bd. dirs. Jr. Achievement Southeastern Mich., 1978—; mem. Pres.'s Council, Dean Engring Vis. Com. Purdue U. Served to 1st lt. C.E. U.S. Army, 1952-55. Republican. Greek Orthodox. Clubs: Detroit Athletic, Country of Detroit. Home: 136 Moran Rd Grosse Pointe Farms MI 48236 Office: PO Box 1030 Dearborn MI 48121

BRUCE, PETER WAYNE, insurance company executive; b. Rome, N.Y., July 12, 1945; s. G. Wayne and Helen A. (Hibling) B.; m. Joan M. McCabe, Sept. 20, 1969; children: Allison, Steven. B.A., U. Wis., 1967; J.D., U. Chgo., 1970. Bar: Wis. 1970. Atty. Northwestern Mut. Life Ins. Co., Milw., 1970-74, asst. gen. counsel, 1974-80, gen. counsel, sec., 1980—. Bd. dirs. Alverno Coll., Milw., Horizons, Milw., Curative Rehab. Services, Milw. Mem. ABA, Am. Life Ins. Counsel, Am. Council Life Ins., Wis. Bar Assn., Milw. Bar Assn. Lodge: Rotary.

Office: NorthwesternMut Life Ins Co 720 E Wisconsin Ave Milwaukee WI 53202

BRUCE, ROBERT JAMES, university president; b. Aug. 12, 1937; m. Judith Garland; children: Kimberley, Scott. A.B., Colby Coll., 1959; M.A., Boston State Coll., 1964; postgrad., U. Manchester, Eng., 1964-65. Tchr. history Kents Hill Sch., Maine, 1959-60, Brookline High Sch., Mass., 1960-64; lectr. Brit. history Chorley Tchrs. Coll., Eng., 1964-65; lectr. Am. history Queen Anne's Coll., Blackburn, Eng., 1964-65; instr. history Clitheroe Royal Grammar Sch., Eng., 1964-65; devel. officer, dir. ann. giving Colby Coll., Waterville, Maine, 1965-69; dir. devel. Bard Coll., Annandale-on-Hudson, N.Y., 1969-75; v.p. Bard Coll., Annandale-on-Hudson, 1970-75, acting pres., 1974; v.p. univ. relations Clark U., Worcester, Mass., 1975; v.p. devel. Widener U., Chester, Pa., 1975-81, pres., 1981—; bd. dirs. Elwyn Insts., Pa.; dir. Riverfront Corp., Inc., Pa., Quick & Reilly, Inc., N.Y.C.; mem. Commn. on Ind. Colls. and Univs. Bd. dirs. Delaware County Econ. Partnership; trustee West Nottingham Acad., Md. Fulbright grantee, 1964-65. Mem. Council for Advancement and Support of Edn., Am. Assn. Higher Edn., Nat. Assn. Ind. Colls. and Univs., Pa. Assn. Colls. and Univs., Phi Kappa Phi, Alpha Sigma Lambda. Clubs: Union League (Phila.); University, Yale (N.Y.C.); Univ. and Whist (Wilmington). Home: 10 Church Rd PA Wallingford 19086 Office: Widener U 10 Church Rd Chester PA 19013

BRUCE, ROBERT ROCKWELL, lawyer; b. Mt. Kisco, N.Y., Mar. 8, 1944; s. Robert R. and Nona (Burtch) B.; m. Collot Guerard, Aug. 30, 1969; 1 son, Benjamin. B.A. magna cum laude, Harvard U., 1966, J.D., 1970; M.P.A., Kennedy Sch. Govt., 1970. Bar: D.C. bar 1972. Dir. communications planning Public Broadcasting Service, 1970-72; asso. firm Hogan & Hartson, Washington, 1972-77; gen. counsel FCC, Washington, 1977-81; partner firm Leva, Hawes, Symington, Martin & Oppenheimer, Washington, 1981—. Office: 815 Connecticut Ave NW Washington DC 20006

BRUCE, ROBERT VANCE, historian; b. Malden, Mass., Dec. 19, 1923; s. Robert Gilbert and Bernice Irene (May) B. Student, Mass. Inst. Tech., 1941-43; B.S., U. N.H., 1945; M.A., Boston U., 1947, Ph.D., 1953. Instr. U. Bridgeport, Conn., 1947-48; master Lawrence Acad., Groton, Mass., 1948-51; research asst. to Benjamin P. Thomas, Washington, 1953-54; mem. faculty Boston U., 1955—, asso. prof. history, 1960-66, prof., 1966—; vis. prof. U. Wis., Madison, 1962-63. Author: Lincoln and the Tools of War, 2d edit, 1973, 1877: Year of Violence, 2d edit, 1970, Bell: Alexander Graham Bell and the Conquest of Solitude, 1973, Lincoln and the Riddle of Death, 1982; Contbr. articles to profl. jours. Served with AUS, 1943-46. Guggenheim fellow, 1957-58; Henry E. Huntington fellow, 1966. Fellow Soc. Am. Historians; mem. Orgn. Am. Historians, Soc. History of Tech. (adv. council 1975—), Am. Hist. Assn., AAAS, Lincoln Group of Boston (pres. 1969-74). Democrat. Home: Evans Rd RFD Durham NH 03824 Office: 226 Bay State Rd Boston MA 02215

BRUCE, RUFUS ELBRIDGE, JR., physicist; b. New Orleans, Mar. 20, 1926; s. Rufus Elbridge and Lucy (Salles) B.; m. Beverly Francis Bond, Oct. 6, 1951; children: Rebecca, Allison, Lucy, Annadora. B.S., La. State U., 1950; M.S., Okla. State U., Ph.D., 1966. With Liberty Mut. Ins. Co., New Orleans, Jackson, Miss., Shreveport, La., 1950-58, ind. agt., Monroe, La., 1958-60; instr. math. N.E. La. State Coll., Monroe, 1959-60; head dept. math and physics Ark. State U., Jonesboro, 1965-66; asso. prof. physics U. Tex., El Paso, 1966-73; research physicist U.S. Army Atmospheric Scis. Lab., White Sands Missile Range, N.Mex., 1967-69; prof. physics U. Tex., El Paso, 1973—, dir. MSIS program, 1980—, chmn. physics dept., 1983—. Contbr. articles to profl. jours. Chmn. El Paso County Precinct Republican Com., 1972, mem. exec. com., 1972-77; mem. Mayor's Liaison Com., 1977-79; bd. dirs. United Way El Paso, 1976-79, NCCJ, El Paso, 1975—. Served with USN, 1944-46. NASA fellow, 1970; NSF fellow, 1971; recipient grants, awards NASA, U.S. Army, Atmospheric Sci. Lab., 1970—. Fellow AAAS; mem. Soc. Photo Optical Intrumenation Engrs., Sigma Xi, Phi Delta Theta. Home: 4259 Boy Scouts Ln El Paso TX 79922 Office: Dept Physics U Tex El Paso TX 79968

BRUCE, THOMAS ALLEN, educator, physician; b. Mountain Home, Ark., Dec. 22, 1930; s. Rex Floyd and Dora Madeline (Fee) B.; m. Dolores Fay Montgomery, May 28, 1960; children: T.K. Montgomery, Dana Fee. B.S.M., M.D., U. Ark., 1955. Intern Duke Hosp., 1956-57; resident medicine Bellevue Hosp., N.Y.C., 1957, Meml. Center Cancer and Allied Diseases, 1958, Parkland Meml. Hosp., Dallas, 1958-59; cardiopulmonary trainee Southwestern Med. Sch. of U. Tex., 1959-60; cardiac research fellow Hammersmith Hosp. and U. London Postgrad. Med. Sch., London, 1960-61, Harvard Bus. Sch., 1974; instr. to prof. medicine Wayne State U., 1961-68, also asst. dean; prof., head cardiovascular sect. U. Okla. Med. Center, 1968-74; prof. medicine, dean Coll. Medicine, U. Ark. Med. Scis., 1974—; med. dir. Barton Research Inst.; coordinator Sino-Am. Med. Exchange Program; mem. ednl. adv. com. Nat. Fund Med. Edn., 1982—; mem. research support rev. com. NIH, 1983—. Dir. Comml. Nat. Bank.; Mem. Ark. Commn. on Health Cost Containment; active Friends of the Zoo, Partners of the Ams., Ark. Symphony Assn., Ark. Opera Theater, Ark. Art Center, Ark. Chamber Music Soc., Friends of Library. Recipient Ark. Gov.'s Meritorious Achievement award. Fellow A.C.P., Am. Coll. Cardiology, Internat. Coll. Angiology, Council Clin. Cardiology, Council Arteriosclerosis; mem. Assn. Univ. Cardiologists, Assn. Am. Med. Colls. Council Deans (chmn. so. council deans 1977-78, com. on payment physician services in teaching hosps. 1983—), Central Soc. Clin. Research, Am. Fedn. Clin. Research, Ark. Heart Assn., Internat. Soc. Heart Research, Soc. for Human Values in Medicine, Am. Rural Health Assn. (nat. cabinet), Ark. Caduceus Club, Old Statehouse Founders Soc., Ark. Med. Soc., Pulaski County Med. Soc. (exec. com.), Ark. Hist. Assn., Ark. Geneal. Soc. (bd. dirs. 1983—), Pulaski County Hist. Soc., Smithsonian Inst. Assocs., Sigma Xi, Alpha Omega Alpha. Clubs: Rotary, Cosmos (Washington). Bruce Soc. Am. Research and publs. on cardiovascular disease including left ventricular function in cardiac denervation, coronary heart disease, myocardial metabolism relating to phospholipids in graded cardiac ischemia, med. edn. with particular reference to rural health care. Home: 4 Hillandale Robinwood Little Rock AR 72207 Office: 4301 W Markham Little Rock AR 72201

BRUCE, WILLIAM HENRY, JR., consulting engineer; b. Bradford, Eng., June 3, 1908; s. William Henry and Isabella (Lowe) B.; m. Ruth Hope Short, July 27, 1940; children: William Henry, Ruth Marina, Richard David. B.C.E., Northeastern U., 1930. Constrn. engr. various cos., 1930-39; constrn. engr., chief field engr. Parsons, Brinckerhoff, Hall & MacDonald, 1939-54; partner Parsons, Brinckerhoff, Quade & Douglas, N.Y.C., 1954-73; sr. v.p., then pres. Parsons, Brinckerhoff, Quade & Douglas, Inc., N.Y.C., 1954-73, dir., asso. cons., 1973—. Treas., trustee N.J. Citizens Hwy. Com.; bd. dirs. Nat. Council Northeastern U., Boston; mem. corp. Northeastern U. Served with USNR, 1944-46; PTO. Recipient Distinguished Attainment citation Northeastern U., 1973. Fellow Am. Cons. Engrs. Council (past nat. del.); mem. ASCE (life), Nat. Soc. Profl. Engrs., Soc. Am. Mil. Engrs., Cons. Engrs. Council N.J. (past pres.). Methodist. Clubs: Hopewell (N.J.); Country; Bedens Brook (Skillman, N.J.); Seaview Country (Absecon, N.J.); Honeywell Twp. Lions (sec., past pres.), Masons., Shriners. Home: Box 205 Federal City Rd Pennington NJ 08534 Office: 1 Penn Plaza 250 W 34th St New York NY 10019

BRUCE, WILLIAM RANKIN, insurance executive; b. Columbia, S.C., Oct. 18, 1915; s. Charles Joy and Anna (Rankin) B.; m. Jane Parsley Emerson, Jan. 12, 1946; children: William Rankin, Jane Emerson, Charles Joy. B.S. in Commerce, U. S.C., 1937. With Seibels Bruce & Co., Columbia, 1937—, v.p., 1958-66, pres., 1966-82, chmn., 1982—, also dir.; chmn., dir. S.C. Ins. Co.; pres., dir. Consol. Am. Ins. Co., Catawba Ins. Co., Argus Life Ins. Co., Am. Agy. Inc., Louisville, Premium Service Corp., Columbia, Investors Nat. Ins. Co., 1966—, Ky. Ins. Co., Louisville, Seibels, Bruce Policy Mgmt. Systems Ltd., Toronto, S.C. Fed. Savs. and Loan Assn., Columbia, First Service Corp. S.C., Service Mortgage Corp., S.C. Electric & Gas Co.; chmn., dir. Gay and Taylor, Winston-Salem, N.C., Rathbone, King & Seeley; chmn. Am. Star Corp., San Francisco. Served to lt. comdr. USNR, 1941-45. Mem. Nat. Assn. Mng. Gen. Agts. (pres. 1966), Columbia C. of C., Columbia Ball Soc. (pres. 1963). Clubs: Forest Lake (pres. 1967-68), Palmetto, Summit. Home: 4367 Chicora St Columbia SC 29206 Office: 1501 Lady St Columbia SC 29201 also PO Box 1 Columbia SC 29202

BRUCE, WILLIAM ROBERT, physician, educator; b. Hamhung, Korea, May 26, 1929; s. George Findlay and Ellen (Tate) B.; m. Margaret MacFarlane, June 15, 1957; children: Graham Douglas, Lynda Jeanne, Kevin Robert. B.Sc., U. Alta., 1950; Ph.D., U. Sask., 1956; M.D., U. Chgo., 1958. Intern Billings Hosp., Chgo., 1958-59; mem. faculty U. Toronto, Can., 1959, prof. biophysics, 1966—; mem. physics sect. Ont. Cancer Inst., Toronto, 1959-81; dir. Ludwig Inst. for Cancer Research, Toronto, 1981—. Fellow Royal Coll. Physicians (Can.), Royal Soc. Can.; mem. Assn. Cancer Research. Research, publns. on X-ray and gamma ray penetration, control red blood cell prodn., action of anti-cancer agts. on normal and tumor cells, sperm prodn., computers in med. records, origins of human cancer. Home: 4 Marshfield Ct Don Mills ON Canada Office: 9 Earl St Toronto ON M4Y 1M4 Canada

BRUCHEY, STUART WEEMS, educator; b. Washington, Aug. 6, 1917; s. Walter Latrobe and Nellie (Richardson) B.; m. Eleanor Stephens Small, June 16, 1956; children—Stuart Andrew, Samuel Lawrence. A.B., Johns Hopkins, 1943, M.A., 1946, Ph.D., 1955. Instr. Dickinson Coll., 1956-57; asst. prof. Northwestern U., 1957-59, Mich. State U., 1959-60, asso. prof., 1960-64, prof., 1964-67, Columbia, N.Y.C., 1967-68, Allan Nevins prof. Am. econ. history, 1968—; faculty fellow Social Sci. Research Council, 1963-64; fellow Center for Recent Am. History, Johns Hopkins, 1965; mem. Inst. for Advanced Study, Princeton, 1973-74, Council on Research Econ. History, 1966—, Internat. Com. on History of Social Movements and Social Structures.; Mem. adv. bd. Bus. History Rev., 1962-65, 76—. Author: Robert Oliver, Merchant of Baltimore, 1783-1819, 1957, The Roots of American Economic Growth, 1607-1861, 1965, The Colonial Merchant, 1966, Cotton and the Growth of the American Economy, 1967, (with others) The Changing Economic Order, 1968, The Growth of the Modern American Economy, 1975; editor, contbr.: Small Business in American Life, 1980; contbr. sect. to: Ency. Brit, 1963. Guggenheim fellow, 1973-74; fellow Center for Advanced Study in Behavioral Scis., Stanford, 1975-76, Nat. Endowment for Humanities, 1975-76. Mem. Am. Hist. Assn., A.A.U.P., Econ. History Assn. (v.p. 1974-75). Democrat. Home: 460 Riverside Dr New York NY 10027

BRUCK, FERDINAND FREDERICK, architect; b. Breslau, Germany, Jan. 24, 1921; came to U.S., 1937; s. Eberhard Friedrich and Irmgard Adelheid (Jentzsch) B.; m. Phoebe Ann Mason, June 30, 1956. A.B., Harvard, 1941, B.Arch., 1949, M.Arch., 1951. Draftsman Stone & Webster Engring. Corp., Bogner & Richmond, Carl Koch & Assos., The Architects Collaborative, 1946-52, 79—; pvt. practice architecture, Cambridge, Mass., 1953-65; pres. F. Frederick Bruck, Architect & Assos. Inc., 1965—; with The Architects Collaborative, 1979—, asso., 1981—; instr. architecture Harvard Grad. Sch. Design, later asst. prof. architecture, 1953-64. Prin. works include Internat. House, Harvard Sch. Pub. Health, 1961, Christian Edn. Bldg, Bulfinch Office Bldg., Govt. Center, Fire Sta, Newton Edn. Center, 1974; project architect with Architects Collaborative,: Bahrain Embassy, Blue Shield Corp. Hdqrs; architect pvt. residences in, Mass., Conn., Maine, N.H., R.I. Served with M.I. AUS, 1943-46; ETO. Milton B. Medary scholar A.I.A., 1949; Arthur W. Wheelright travelling fellow, 1954-55; recipient Sch. medal, 1949, Merit award, 1964; both A.I.A.; Design award Boston Arts Festival, 1964; award Excellence for House Design Archtl. Record, 1965. Mem. A.I.A., Boston Soc. Architects, Boston Archtl. Center, Inst. Comtemporary Art, Citizens Housing and Planning Assn., Mass. Audubon Soc. Home: 148 Coolidge Hill Cambridge MA 02138 Office: 148 Coolidge Hill Cambridge MA 02138

BRUCK, STEPHEN DESIDERIUS, biochemist; b. Budapest, Hungary, Feb. 4, 1927; naturalized, 1951; s. Laszlo and Renee (Paschkesz) B.; m. Anne Katherine Anderson, Oct. 17, 1970; children—Stephanie, Lewis, Debra. Ed., Faculty of Medicine, U. Budapest, 1945-46; B.S., Boston Coll., 1951; M.A. (Univ. scholar), Johns Hopkins U., 1953, Ph.D., 1955. Research chemist E. I. du Pont de Nemours & Co., Inc., Wilmington, Del., 1955-60; project leader Nat. Bur. Standards, Washington, 1961-62; sr. staff scientist Johns Hopkins U. Applied Physics Lab., Laurel, Md., 1962-66; acting mgr. polymers Watson Research Center, IBM, Yorktown Heights, N.Y., 1966-67; prof. chem. engring. Cath. U., Washington, 1967-69; program dir. for biomaterials Nat. Heart, Lung and Blood Inst., NIH, Bethesda, Md., 1969-78; affiliate prof. chem. engring. Washington U., St. Louis, 1977-79; vis. research prof. biomed. engring. div. biomed. engring. sch. Medicine U. Va., Charlottesville, 1979-80; pres. Medi-Tech, Inc., Bethesda, 1978—. Author: Blood Compatible Synthetic Polymers, 1974, Properties of Biomaterials in the Physiological Environment, 1980, Controlled Drug Delivery, Vols. 1 and 2, 1983; editor: Biomaterials, 1979-82; mem. editorial adv. bd.: Jour. Biomed. Materials Research, 1972-80, Biomaterials, Medical Devices, Artificial Organs-An Internat. Jour, 1972—; sect. editor for: biomaterials Internat. Jour. Artificial Organs, 1978—; contbr. to publs. in field. Research grantee NIH, NSF, Dept. Interior. Fellow AAAS, Am. Inst. Chemists, Royal Soc. Chemistry (U.K.); mem. Am. Chem. Soc., Am. Soc. Artificial Internal Organs, Internat. Soc. Artificial Organs, European Biomaterials Soc., Biomaterials Group Biol. Engring. Soc. (U.K.), N.Y. Acad. Scis., Sigma Xi. Clubs: Johns Hopkins (Balt.); Cosmos (Washington). Home: 1113 Pipestem Pl Rockville MD 20854 Office: 7315 Wisconsin Ave Suite 727 E Bethesda MD 20814

BRUCKER, EDMUND, artist, portrait painter; b. Cleve., Nov. 20, 1912; s. Ludwig and Theresa (Strung) B.; m. Marcelline B. Spencer, Jan. 28, 1939; 1 son, Robert. Diploma in portrait painting, Cleve. Inst. Art, 1934, postgrad., 1934-36. Instr. Cleve. Inst. Art, 1936-38, John Herron Art Sch., Indpls., 1938-67; lectr. painting Herron Sch. Art, Ind. U., Indpls., 1967-68, asso. prof., 1968-73, prof., 1973—. One-man shows, Herron Art Inst., 1947, 63, Hoosier Art Gallery, Indpls., 1953, group shows include, Carnegie Art Inst., Pitts., 1941, Library of Congress, 1945, Met. Mus. Art, N.Y.C., 1952, Ind. State Mus., 1979, represented in permanent collections, Eli Lilly & Co., Indpls., Northwestern U., Ind. U., Purdue U., Cleve. Mus. Art, Dartmouth Coll., Evansville (Ind.) Mus. Arts and Scis., City of Cleve. Warner Collection, Scholl Mfg. Co., Chgo., Phillips Oil Co., Bartlesville, Okla., Weir Cook Internat. Airport, Indpls., numerous others; portrait cover artist Ind. Bus. and Industry Mag, 1960-71. Recipient Milliken award Art Assn., Indpls., 1963; named Sagamore of the Wabash Gov. of Ind., 1965. Mem. Ind. Artists Club, Hoosier Salon Patrons Assn., Indpls. Mus. Art. Club: Riviera. Home: 545 King Dr Indianapolis IN 46260

BRUCKER, ERIC, college dean; b. Cheltenham, Pa., Dec. 7, 1941; s. Walter and Julia B.; m. Sharon Marie Bowerman, Aug. 28, 1965; children: Matthew Eric, Mark Daniel,Jennifer J. B.A., U. Del., 1963; Ph.D., Duke U., 1966. Asst. prof. So. Ill. U.-Carbondale, 1966-70; asst. prof. then assoc. prof. econs. U. Del.-Newark, 1970-73, chmn. dept. econs., 1973-76, dean Coll. Bus. and Econs., 1976—. Chmn. Lenape dist. Boy Scouts Am., 1981; vice chmn. bus. and econs. devel. com. Del. C. of C., 1981—. Ford Found. fellow, 1965-66. Mem. Middle Atlantic Assn. Coll. Bus. Adminstrn. (pres. 1982-83), Am. Econ. Assn., Am. Fin. Assn., So. Econ. Assn., Omicron Delta Kappa, Phi Kappa Phi, Omicron Delta Epsilon. Presbyterian. Home: Box 268 RD 1 Hockessin DE 19707 Office: Univ Del Newark DE 19711

BRUCKER, WILBER MARION, lawyer; b. Saginaw, Mich., Apr. 13, 1926; s. Wilber Marion and Clara (Hantel) B.; m. Doris Ann Shover, June 23, 1951; children: Barbara Ann, Wilber Marion, Paul Bradford. Student, Wayne State U., 1943; A.B., Princeton U., 1949; J.D., U. Mich., 1952. Bar: Mich. 1953. Asso. atty. firm Clark, Klein, Brucker & Waples, Detroit, 1952-58; individual practice, Detroit, 1958-61; partner firm Brucker & Brucker, Detroit, 1961-67, McInally, Rockwell & Brucker, 1968-78, McInally, Brucker, Newcombe, Wilke and DeBoana, 1978—; dir. Bank of Dearborn (Mich.), Mich. Boiler & Engring. Co.; legal counsel Econ. Club Detroit, 1968—; arbitrator Am. Arbitration Assn., 1965-79; Mem. bd. canvassers City Grosse Pointe Farms, Mich., 1972-74; Bd. govs. Wayne State U., Detroit., 1967-78, chmn. bd. govs., 1972. Served with USNR, 1944-46. Mem. Am., Mich., Detroit bar assns., Mason. Clubs: Detroit Athletic, Grosse Pointe Hunt, Renaissance, Indian Village Tennis. Home: 253 Touraine Rd Grosse Pointe Farms MI 48236 Office: 3800 City Nat Bank Bldg Detroit MI 48226

BRUCKMANN, DONALD JOHN, investment banker; b. Montclair, N.J., Jan. 4, 1929; s. William A. and Elizabeth M. (Fullmer) B.; m. Mary Thudium, June 1, 1957. B.A., Lafayette Coll., Easton, Pa., 1950; LL.B., Columbia U., 1955. Bar: N.Y. bar 1955. Asso. firm Simpson, Thacher & Bartlett, N.Y.C., to 1960; sr. v.p., dir. Smith Barney, Harris Upham & Co. (investment bankers), 1963-73, Dean Witter Reynolds Inc., N.Y.C., 1973—; pres., chief exec. officer Dean Witter Reynolds Internat. Inc., 1974—; Chmn. bd. mgrs. N.Y. Bot. Garden, 1976—; trustee, mem. bd. Morningside House, N.Y.C., 1960—; bd. dirs. Pa. Ave. Devel. Corp., Washington, 1973-81, vice chmn., 1973-79; trustee Central Park Conservancy, N.Y.C., 1980; mem. internat. capital markets adv. com. N.Y. Stock Exchange. Co-chmn. adv. com. Columbia U. Research Inst. of Internat. Change. Served to 1st lt. AUS, 1950-52. Mem. Bar Assn. City N.Y., Bond Club N.Y.C. Republican. Presbyterian. Clubs: Knickerbocker (gov.), Down Town Assn. (N.Y.C.); Devon (L.I.); Yacht; Maidstone (L.I.). PO Box 64 Lily Pond Ln East Hampton NY 11937 Office: 130 Liberty St New York NY 10006

BRUCKNER, ANDREW MICHAEL, educator; b. Berlin, Germany, Dec. 17, 1932; s. Ferdin and Bettina (Pollack) B.; m. Judith Brostoff, Jan. 27, 1957; children—Theodore, Michael. B.A., U. Calif. at Los Angeles, 1955, Ph.D., 1959. Mem. faculty U. Calif. at Santa Barbara, 1959—, asst. prof., 1959-64, asso. prof., 1964-68, prof. math., 1968—; acting dean grad. div., 1966-69. Recipient NSF grants, 1962—. Mem. Am. Math. Soc., Math Assn. Am. Home: 910 Mission Canyon Rd Santa Barbara CA 93105

BRUDER, HAROLD JACOB, artist, educator; b. N.Y.C., Aug. 31, 1930; s. Julius and Della (Wlodinger) B.; m. Anet Sirna, July 15, 1979; children from previous marriage—David, Shari. Cert., Cooper Union, 1951. Mem. faculty Kansas City Art Inst., 1963-65, Pratt Inst., 1965-66; prof. art Queens Coll., Flushing, N.Y., 1965—, chmn. art dept., 1982—. Artist-in-residence, Aspen, Colo., 1967; One-man shows include, Robert Isaacson Gallery, N.Y.C., 1962, Forum Gallery, N.Y.C., 1968, 69, 72, 76, 79, Durlacher Bros., N.Y.C., 1964, 1967, William and Mary Coll., 1979, Queens Coll., N.Y.C., 1974, Queens Mus., N.Y.C., 1982, group exhbns. include, Whitney Mus., 1970, Balt. Mus., Butler Inst., 1972, Cleve. Mus., 1974, Phila. Mus., 1976, represented in permanent collections, Hirshhorn Mus., Washington, Sheldon Meml. Gallery, Lincoln, Nebr., N.J. State Mus., Trenton. Mem. Coll. Art Assn. Home: 175 Madison Ave New York NY 10016 Office: Queens Coll Dept Art Flushing NY 11367

BRUDEVOLD, FINN, dentist, educator; b. Gjovik, Norway, June 12, 1910; came to U.S., 1939, naturalized, 1949; s. Peder and Ingrid (Haugom) B.; m. Esther Asher, June 27, 1941; children—Anne, Catherine, Christine. D.D.S., U. Minn., 1940; M.S. in Dental Sci, U. Rochester, 1954; A.M. (hon.), Harvard U., 1958, Doctoral, U. Oslo, Norway, 1965; Dr. Odont. h.c, U. Umea, Sweden, 1969. Instr. dental pathology Tufts Coll. Dental Sch., 1942, instr. clin. dentistry, 1945-46, asst. prof. prosthodontia, 1946-48, asst. prof. clin. dentistry, 1948-49; asst. prof. dental research U. Rochester, 1949-58; dir. dental research Eastman Dental Center, Rochester, 1949-58; prof. Harvard Sch. Dental Medicine, 1958-67; chief chemistry and preventive dentistry Forsyth Dental Center.; Mem. dental study section NIH, 1955-69. Served as capt. Norwegian Army, 1942-45. Recipient H. Trendley Dean award for fluoride research, 1969; Outstanding Achievement award, U. Minn., 1974; award of research European Orgn. for Caries Research, 1983. Mem. Am. Dental Assn., Internat. Assn. Dental Research (pres. 1978-79, recipient award for basic research in oral therapeutics 1966), Swedish Dental Assn. (hon.), Sigma Xi, Omicron Kappa Upsilon. Corr. mem. European Orgn. for Research Fluorine and Dental Caries Prevention, Norwegian Dental Assn. Office: Forsyth Dental Center 140 The Fenway Boston MA 02115

BRUDNER, HARVEY JEROME, scientist; b. N.Y.C., May 29, 1931; s. Joseph and Anna (Fiddelman) B.; m. Helen Gross, Dec. 18, 1963; children: Mae Ann, Terry Joseph, Jay Scott. B.S. in Engring. and Physics, N.Y. U., 1952; M.S., NYU, 1954, Ph.D., 1959; postgrad., U. Md., 1954-56, CCNY, 1958, Columbia U., 1959-61. Electronics engr. Bendix Corp., Teterboro, N.J., 1952; physicist U.S. Naval Ordnance Lab., White Oak, Md., 1953-54; sr. physicist Emerson Research Labs., Washington, 1954-57; prin. physicist Emerson Radio, Jersey City, 1957-61; research assoc. NYU Inst. Math. Scis., N.Y.C., 1957-60; guest scientist Rockefeller Inst. for Med. Research, 7N.Y.C., 1960-61; sr. research assoc. Am. Can Co., Princeton (N.J.) Lab., 1964-67; v.p. research and devel. Westinghouse Learning Corp., N.Y.C., 1967-71, pres., 1971-76; also dir.; mem. adminstrv. com. Westinghouse Electric Corp., Pitts., 1971-76, pres., 1971-76, H.J.B. Enterprises, N.Y.C., 1961—, Med. Devel., Inc., 1962; dir. Ideal Sch. Supply Corp., Ednl. Products, Inc., Document Reading Services, Ltd., Linguaphone Inst. Ltd., Info. Synergy, Inc., Cambridge Learning Connection, Inc.; chmn. new devels. com. Project Aristotle; acting dir. Gottscho Info. Center, Coll. Engring., Rutgers U.; prof. math., physics, dean sci. and tech. N.Y. Inst. Tech., 1962-64; instr. atomic physics N.Y. U., 1953-54; cons. Nat. Inst. Edn., Mass. Inst. Tech., Rutgers U., Worcester Poly. Inst., Poly. Inst. N.Y., Nat. Inst. Community Devel., U.S. Ho. of Reps. Com. on Sci. and Tech.; mem. adv. com. Middlesex County Coll., 1966—, Paterson State Coll., 1975; mem. exec. planning com. tng. adv. sect. Nat. Security Indsl. Assn., 1966; nat. adv. bd. Am. Coll. in

Jerusalem; dir. computers in edn. study Nat. Inst. Edn., 1979; bd. dirs. World Learning and Communications, 1978—. Editorial commentator: Another Opinion, WCBS, N.Y.C., N.Y. Power Authority; Author: College Technical Mathematics, 1967, Semiconductor Physics, 1954, On Fermat's Last Theorem, 1979; columnist Light-On Series: Ednl. Tech. Mag.; columnist Source Data: Datamation Mag.; chmn. editorial adv. bd.: Tech. Horizons in Edn. Jour. Mem. steering com. Project PROCEED, NSF.; Capt. long range planning com. Highland Park (N.J.) Sch. Bd.; trustee Ross Hall Heights Assn., 1966. Fellow IEEE (ednl. adminstrn. com., solar standards com., photovoltaic subcom.), mem., Am. Phys. Soc., Soc. Motion Picture and TV Engrs., Internat. Fedn. Med. Electronics, AAAS, Electronic Industries Assn. (edn. com.), Am. Ednl. Research Assn., Adult Edn. Assn. U.S.A., N.Y. Acad. Scis., Am. Mgmt. Assn. (ednl. adv. com.), Math. Assn. Am., Am. Soc. Tng. and Devel., Council Ams., Am. Judicature Soc., Am. Math. Soc., Am. Soc. Curriculum Devel., Sigma Xi, Sigma Pi Sigma, Tau Beta Pi. Clubs: Chemists (N.Y.C.); N.Y. Univ., Toastmasters. Research in atomic physics, radar, ednl., med., energy, electronic systems, biol. effects of radiation, laser tech., others. Home: 812 Abbott St Highland Park NJ 08904 333 Montgomery St Highland Park NJ 08904 *I have tried: to play a constructive part in permitting others to make a positive contribution to society; to achieve a proper mix of idealism, reason, and faith in my decision making; to apply science and technology for the betterment of humanity.*

BRUDNER, HELEN GROSS, educator; b. N.Y.C.; d. Nathan and Mae (Grichtman) Gross; m. Harvey Jerome Brudner, Dec. 18, 1963; children: Mae Ann, Terry Joseph, Jay Scott. B.S., NYU, 1959, M.A., 1960, Ph.D., 1973. Tchr. N.Y.C. Bd. Edn., 1959-60; instr. Pratt Inst., Bklyn., 1959-61; asst. prof. history N.Y. Inst. Tech., N.Y.C., 1961-63, dir. guidance, 1962-63; assoc. prof. Fairleigh Dickinson U., Rutherford, N.J., 1963-73, prof. history and polit. sic., 1974—, dir. Honors Coll., 1972—, chmn. dept. social sci., 1980—, pres. univ. senate, 1975-78, asst. provost, 1983—; v.p. HJB Enterprises, Highland Park, N.J., 1970—; vice chmn. bd. WLC Inc., Highland Park, 1976—; cons. auto ednl. systems, 1971—. Contbr. articles to profl. jours. Bd. dirs. NSF Women in Politics project, 1981; bd. dirs. Nat. Endowment for the Humanities and Woodrow Wilson Found. project Women in Am. History, Princeton, N.J., 1980; bd. dirs. Fairleigh Dickinson U. Fed. Credit Union. Recipient Woman of Yr. award Am. Businesswomen's Assn., 1980. Mem. Am. Judicature Soc., Am. Hist. Soc., Acad. Polit. Sci. Home: 812 Abbott St Highland Park NJ 08904 Office: Dept Social Sci Fairleigh Dickinson U Rutherford NJ 07070 Office: HJB Enterprises Inc 333 Montgomery St Highland Park NJ 08904

BRUDNEY, VICTOR, legal educator; b. 1917. B.A., CCNY, 1937; LL.B., Columbia U., 1940. Bar: N.Y. 1940, Mass. 1974. Weld prof. Harvard U. Law Sch. Co-author: Cases and Materials in Corporate Finance: New Developments Supplement. Mem. Am. Acad. Arts and Scis. Office: Harvard Univ Sch Law Cambridge MA 02138 *

BRUECKHEIMER, WILLIAM ROGERS, social science educator; b. Gary, Ind., Aug. 19, 1921; s. Albert Gustav and Lucille (Schwartz) B.; m. Mary Ellen Roe, Nov. 7, 1942; children: William Rogers, David Rogers, Suzanne Rogers. Student, Wabash Coll., 1941-42; M.A. in Social Sci., U. Chgo., 1949, U. Mich., 1952, Ph.D., 1953. Instr. geography Fla. State U., 1949-51; teaching fellow, instr. geography U. Mich., 1951-53; asst. prof., then asso. prof. geography So. State Coll., Magnolia, Ark., 1953-55; faculty Western Mich. U., Kalamazoo, 1955-64, prof. geography and geology, head dept., 1958-64; prof., head dept. geography Fla. State U., Tallahassee, 1964-71; dir. London Study Center, 1971-72; dir. interdisciplinary program in social sci. London (Eng.) Study Center, 1979—, prof., 1972—; vis. scholar U. Mich., 1974; Mem. Fla. Gov.'s Resource Use Edn. Com., 1964-71; mem. adv. bd. Tall Timbers Research, Inc.; Fellow in bus. Found. Econ. Edn., summer 1955; Henry L. Beadel fellow Tall Timbers Research Sta., summers 1973-83. Contbr. articles to profl. jours.; sect. editor Atlas of Fla., 1981. Served with AUS, 1942-46; ETO. Fellow Royal Geog. Soc.; mem. Assn. Am. Geographers (chmn. East Lakes div. 1957-58), Mich. Schoolmasters Club (chmn. geography sect. 1958-59), AAUP, Nat. Council Geog. Edn., Nat., Fla. Audubon socs., Fla. Soc. Geographers, Leon County Soc. Geographers and Anthropologists. Club: Exchange. Home: 1210 Waverly Rd Tallahassee FL 32302

BRUECKNER, KEITH ALLAN, theoretical physicist, educator; b. Mpls., Mar. 19, 1924; s. Leo John and Agnes (Holl) B.; children: Jan Keith, Anthony Leo, Leslie. B.A., U. Minn., 1945, M.A., 1947; Ph.D., U. Calif. at Berkeley, 1950; D.Sc. (hon.), Ind. U., 1976. Prof. physics U. Ind., 1951-55; physicist Brookhaven Nat. Lab., N.Y., 1955-56; prof. physics U. Pa., 1956-59, U. Calif. at San Diego, 1959—, chmn. dept. physics, 1959-61, dean, 1963, dean letters and sci., 1963-65, dean grad. studies, 1965; dir. Inst. Pure and Applied Phys. Scis., 1965-69; v.p., dir. research Inst. Def. Analysis, Washington, 1961-62 (on leave); tech. dir. Helliodyne Corp., San Diego, 1968-69 (on leave), KMS Tech. Center, 1969-70; exec. v.p., tech. dir. KMS Fusion, Inc., Ann Arbor, Mich., 1971-74 (on leave). Co-editor: Pure and Applied Physics series. Served with USAAF, 1943-46. Recipient Dannie Heineman prize for math. physics, 1963. Fellow Am. Phys. Soc., Am. Acad. Arts and Scis.; mem. Nat. Acad. Scis. Club: Am. Alpine. Office: Dept Physics U Calif La Jolla CA 92093

BRUEMMER, FRED, writer-photographer; b. Riga, Latvia, June 26, 1929; emigrated to Can., 1951, naturalized, 1956; s. Arist and Dorothea (Wahl) B.; m. Maud van den Berg, Mar. 31, 1962; children: Aurel, Rene. Student W. German schs. Self-employed writer-photographer specializing in arctic and antarctic regions, 1961—; books include The Long Hunt, 1969, Seasons of the Eskimo, 1971, Encounters with Arctic Animals, 1972, The Arctic, 1974, The Life of the Harp Seal, 1977, Children of the North, 1979, Summer at Bear River, 1980. Decorated Order of Can.; Recipient Queen Elizabeth II Silver Jubilee medal, 1978. Mem. Arctic Inst. N.Am., Royal Can. Acad. Art, Travel Journalists Guild. Address: 5170 Cumberland Ave Montreal PQ H4V 2N8 Canada

BRUEN, JOHN DERMOT, army officer; b. Glen Cove, N.Y., Oct. 19, 1930; s. John D. and Kathleen M. (Halferty) B.; m. Ann Theone Lee, June 22, 1957; children: Michael J., Kathleen A., Thomas L., Lisa M. B.S. in Mil. Sci, U. Md., 1959; M.B.A. in Transp. and Public Utilities, U. Pitts., 1963; grad., Naval War Coll. Command and Staff Course, 1966, Army War Coll., 1972. Enlisted in U.S. Army, 1948, commd. 2d lt., 1953, advanced through grades to lt. gen., 1983; service in, Korea, Germany, Azores, Thailand and Vietnam, dir. resources and mgmt. Office Dep. Chief Staff Logistics, 1977-79, comdr. Mil. Traffic Mgmt. Command, Washington, 1979-83, comdr. 21st Support Command, Europe, 1983—. Author numerous articles and papers. Decorated Legion of Merit with two oak leaf clusters, Bronze Star with oak leaf cluster, Meritorious Service medal with oak leaf cluster, Army Commendation medal with oak leaf cluster (2), Def. Disting. Service medal (2); named to U.S. Inf. Hall of Fame, 1979. Mem. Nat. Def. Transp. Assn., Assn. U.S. Army. Roman Catholic. Club: Ft. Belvoir (Va.) Officers. Office: 21st Support Command APO New York NY 09325

BRUENING, RICHARD PATRICK, lawyer; b. Kansas City, Mo., Mar. 17, 1939; s. Arthur Louis, Jr. and Lorraine Elizebeth (Gamble) B.; m. Jane Marie Egender, Aug. 25, 1962; children—Christiana G., Paul R., Erin E. A.B., Rockhurst Coll., 1960; J.D., U. Mo. at Kansas City, 1963. Bar: Mo. bar 1963. Since practiced in, Kansas City; law clk. U.S. Dist. Judge R.M., Duncan, 1963-65; asso. firm Houts, James, McCanse & Larison, 1965-68; gen. atty. Kansas City So. Ry. Co., 1969; asst. gen. counsel Kansas City So. Industries, Inc., 1970-76, gen. counsel, 1976-82, v.p., gen. counsel, 1982—. Bd. dirs. Kansas City Met. chpt. Nat. Found. March of Dimes, 1969-73, treas., 1971; trustee Livestock Mktg. Inst., 1978—. Mem. Am., Mo., Kansas City bar assns., Lawyers Assn. Kansas City, Nat. Assn. R.R. Trial Counsel, Practising Law Inst., Phi Delta Phi, Omicron Delta Kappa. Roman Catholic. Clubs: Kansas City Country, Carriage. Home: 606 W Meyer Blvd Kansas City MO 64113 Office: 301 W 11th St Kansas City MO 64105

BRUENN, HOWARD GERALD, physician; b. Youngtown, Ohio, June 6, 1905; s. Alexander H. and Fanny (Bergstein) B.; m. Dorothy Conner, June 10, 1937; children: Stephen, Nancy Bruenn Clement, James. A.B., Columbia U., 1925, M.S., 1934, D.M.S., 1934; M.D., Johns Hopkins U., 1929. Diplomate: Am. Bd. Internal Medicine, Am. Bd. Cardiovascular Disease. Intern Boston City Hosp., 1929-31; asst. resident Presbyn. Hosp., N.Y.C., 1932-34, chief med. resident, 1934-35, attending physician, 1961—; chief cardiology Bethesda Naval Med. Center and 3d Naval Dist., 1942-46; chief Vanderbilt Cardiac Clinic, N.Y.C., 1946-70; asso. attending physician Vanderbilt Cardiac Clinic, 1946-61; clin. prof. medicine Columbia U., N.Y.C., 1962-70; cons. in medicine Columbia Med. Center, 1970—; physician to Pres. F. Roosevelt, 1945-46. Contbr. articles on cardiology to profl. jours. Served to comdr. USNR, 1942-46. Markle fellow medicine, 1935-37. Fellow Am. Heart Assn., Council of Clin. Cardiology; mem. AMA, Soc. Med. Cons. to Armed Services, N.Y. County Med. Soc., N.Y. Acad. Medicine, N.Y. Acad. Sci., Harvey Soc. Home: 4551 Livingston Ave New York NY 10471

BRUES, ALICE MOSSIE, phys. anthropologist, educator; b. Boston, Oct. 9, 1913; d. Charles Thomas and Beirne (Barrett) B. A.B., Bryn Mawr Coll., 1933; Ph.D., Radcliffe Coll., 1940. Faculty U. Okla. Sch. Medicine, 1946-65, prof., 1960-65; vis. prof. anthropology U. Colo., Boulder, 1965-66, prof., 1966—, chmn. dept. anthropology, 1969-71. Asso. editor: Am. Jour. Phys. Anthropology, 1962-66; Author: People and Races, 1977; contbr. articles to profl. jours. Fellow Am. Anthrop. Assn.; mem. Am. Assn. Phys. Anthropologists (v.p. 1966-68, pres. 1971-73), AAAS, Am. Soc. Human Genetics, Soc. Study Evolution, Am. Acad. Forensic Scis., Soc. Naturalists, Sigma Xi. Home: 4325 Prado Dr Boulder CO 80303

BRUES, AUSTIN MOORE, physician, emeritus educator; b. Milw., Apr. 25, 1906; s. Charles Thomas and Beirne (Barrett) B.; m. Mildred Carter, June 1, 1930; children: Roger Austin, Nancy Carter, Charles Thomas. A.B., Harvard U., 1926, M.D., 1930. Med. resident Collis P. Huntington Meml. Hosp., Boston, 1930-31; responsible investigator OSRD, 1941-44; sr. biologist Metall. Lab., Manhattan Engrs. Dist., Chgo., 1944-46; assoc. prof. medicine U. Chgo., 1945-52, prof., 1952-77, prof. emeritus, 1978—; mem. Inst. Radiobiology and Biophysics, 1945-54; sr. biologist, dir. biol. and med. research Argonne Nat. Lab., AEC, 1946-62, sr. biologist, 1962-71, med. cons., 1971-72, 79—; med. dir. Center for Human Radiobiology, 1972-79; Served as expert to Sec. of War in study of atomic bomb casualties, in Japan, 1946-47; mem. com. on atomic casualties NRC; mem. U.S. del. UN Sci. Com. on Atomic Radiation, 1957—; mem. sci. adv. bd. Armed Forces Inst. Pathology, 1950-60, Internat. Commn. on Radiol. Protection, 1957—; expert cons. WHO, 1962—; mem. research adv. council Am. Cancer Soc., 1969-72. Editor: Low Level Irradiation, 1959, Aging and Levels of Biological Organization, 1965; Contbr. articles to med., sci. jours. Mem. Am. Acad. Arts and Scis.; Mem. AAAS, Am. Assn. for Cancer Research (dir. 1946—, pres. 1954-55), Am. Physiol. Soc., Am. Assn. Anatomists, Am. Clin. and Climatol. Soc., Soc. Cell Biol., Soc. Exptl. Biology and Medicine, Soc. Clin. Investigation, Soc. Epidemiol. Research, Central Soc. for Clin. Research, Radiation Research Soc. (council 1952-60, pres. 1955-56). Clubs: Quadrangle, Literary (Chgo.); Harvard (Boston). Home: 2 Orchard Pl Hinsdale IL 60521 Office: Argonne Nat Lab Argonne IL 60439

BRUESCH, SIMON RULIN, physician, educator; b. Norman, Okla., July 7, 1914; s. Jacob John and Lyda (Matlock) B. A.B., La Verne Coll., 1935, D.Sc., 1967; Ph.D., Northwestern U., 1940, M.D., 1941. Intern Passavant Hosp., Chgo., 1940-41; mem. faculty Tenn. Med. Units, Memphis, 1941—, prof., 1946-63, Goodman prof. anatomy, 1961—. Named La Verne Coll. Alumnus of Year, 1967. Mem. Am. Assn. History Medicine (council 1969-72), Am. Assn. Anatomists, Am. Physiol. Soc., Tenn. Hist. Soc., Sigma Xi, Phi Beta Pi. Research, publs. on structure and function of nervous systems; history of medicine. Home: 1431 Carr Ave Memphis TN 38104 Office: 800 Madison Ave Memphis TN 38163

BRUESCHKE, ERICH EDWARD, physician, researcher, educator; b. nr. Eagle Butte, S.D., July 17, 1933; s. Erich Herman and Eva Johanna (Joens) B.; m. Frances Marie Bryan, Mar. 25, 1967; children: Erich Raymond, Jason Douglas, Tina Marie, Patricia Frances, Susan Eva. B.S. in Elec. Engring, S.D. Sch. Mines and Tech., 1956; postgrad., U. So. Calif., 1960-61; M.D., Temple U., 1965. Diplomate: Am. Bd. Family Practice. Intern Germantown Dispensary and Hosp., Phila., 1965-66; mem. tech. staff Hughes Research and Devel. Labs., Culver City, Calif., 1956-61; practiced gen. medicine, Fullerton, Calif., 1968-69; dir. research Ill. Inst. Tech. Research Inst., Chgo., 1970-76; research asst. prof. Temple U. Sch. Medicine, 1965-69; mem. staff Mercy Hosp. and Med. Center, Chgo., 1970-76; vis. prof. Rush Med. Coll., Chgo., 1974-76, prof., chmn. dept. family practice, 1976—; trustee Anchor HMO, 1976—, v.p. med. and acad. affairs, 1981—; sr. attending Presbyn.-St. Luke's Hosp., Chgo., 1976—; med. dir. Chgo. Bd. of Health West Side Hypertension Center, 1974-78; Bd. dirs. Comprehensive Health Planning Met. Chgo., 1971-74. Assoc. editor: The Female Patient, 1979—; Asso. editor: Primary Cardiology, 1979—; contbr. articles to profl. jours. Served with USAF, 1966-68. Fellow Am. Acad. Family Physicians, Inst. of Medicine of Chgo.; mem. IEEE (chmn. Chgo. sect. Engring. in Medicine and Biology group 1974-75), Am. Fertility Soc., Am. Occupational Med. Assn. (recipient Physician's recognition award 1969, 72, 75), Chgo. Med. Soc., Am. Heart Assn., Assn. for Advancement Med. Instrumentation, N.Y. Acad. Scis., Sigma Xi, Phi Rho Sigma, Eta Kappa Nu. Home: 314 N Lincoln St Hinsdale IL 60521 Office: Rush-Presbyn St Luke's Med Center W Congress Pkwy Chicago IL 60612 *It is important to be courageous and do what you really want to do rather than what is expected or what seems to be currently popular. If life is approached with a spirit of goodwill and one is strong enough to follow one's own desires, then the contribution made and the success achieved can be a credit to humanity and also a source of endless enjoyment. The real secret of life is self-discipline; this allows the tempering of short-term needs with the necessities from long-term planning.*

BRUESTLE, BEAUMONT, educator, writer, actor; b. Phila., Dec. 23, 1905; s. Adolph and Florence (Schrader) B. A.B., U. Pa., 1927, A.M., 1930, Ph.D., 1932. Faculty English dept. U. Pa., 1927-31, Temple U., 1931-45; actor profl. theatre, N.Y.C., 1945-47; faculty dept. speech and English U. Tulsa, 1947-70, chmn. dept., 1953-70. Actor, dir., writer ednl., community and profl. theatre; one-man show Scenes and Songs from the Theatre; active on stage and TV, Los Angeles; lectr. theatre and opera.; Author: poetry Storm Signals, 1931, Things of Earth, 1935; children's play The Wonderful Tang, 1952; mus. comedy The Gusher, 1958, The Name Is Jones, 1959; mus. play Lola, 1963; comedy Love, Art and Anthony Thorndyke, 1963; mus. comedy But Don't Gild Lily, 1968, Young B.F, 1970, (new adapation from Norwegian of Henrik Ibsen) Peer Gynt, 1970, At the Carlton, 1973; drama Nobody Leaves Empty-Handed, 1973, Good Friday, 1865, 1976; children's mus. A Trip to Saturn, 1979; drama And the Survivors Are, 1980. Mem. Broadway Theatre League Tulsa (pres. 1959-65, chmn. bd. 1965—), Internat. Platform Assn., Theta Alpha Phi. Home: 2149 Panorama Terr Los Angeles CA 90039 *Don't adhere to any life practice that you can't change to benefit someone you love.*

BRUGGEMAN, TERRANCE JOHN, business executive; b. Mandan, N.D., Oct. 20, 1946; s. George Edward and Marcella Merle (Gray) B.; m. Nancy Ellen Hohman, June 28, 1969; children: Todd M., Megan P. B.A., U. Notre Dame, 1968; postgrad. bus. adminstrn., U. Chgo., 1968-70. Div. mgr., v.p. Continental Ill. Nat. Bank, Chgo., 1968-77; asst. treas. Gould Inc., Rolling Meadows, Ill., 1977-78, treas., 1978-80, v.p., treas., 1980-81; chmn. Gould Fin. Inc., Rolling Meadows, 1978-81; v.p. fin. and adminstrn. AM Internat., Inc., Chgo., 1981—; dir. Nat. Comml. Fin. Conf., 1979-80. Bd. dirs., v.p. fin. Lincoln Park Zool. Soc., 1972—; bd. dirs. North Shore Youth Health Services, 1979—. Mem. Fin. Execs. Inst., Am. Assn. Equipment Lessors. Clubs: Chicago Athletic, Economics of Chgo., Chicago, Notre Dame. Home: 2707 Hartzell St Evanston IL 60201 Office: AM Internat Suite 1005 Prudential Plaza Chicago IL 60601

BRUGGER, JAMES RAYMOND, former bank public relations exec.; b. Erie, Pa., Dec. 8, 1920; s. Eugene William and Gertrude (Pletz) B.; m. Dorothy Mae Walsh, May 1, 1943; children—Marie Therese (Mrs. James P. Curry), Dorothy Mae (Mrs. Christopher Coyne), James Raymond, Thomas Aquinas. Ph.B., John Carroll U., 1942. Reporter U.P., Cleve., 1942; instr. Gannon Coll., 1946-48; pub. relations officer N.Y.C. R.R. Co., N.Y.C., 1948-54; pub. relations J.P. Morgan & Co., Inc., N.Y.C., 1954-59; mgr. pub. relations Morgan Guaranty Trust Co., N.Y.C., 1959-62, v.p., 1962-71, sr. v.p., 1971-80. Bd. dirs. Scarsdale (N.Y.) Family Counseling Service, 1967-74, pres., 1972-73. Served to capt. AUS, 1942-46. Mem. Soc. Silurians. Home: 12 Pond St Chatham MA 02633

BRUHN, ERIK BELTON EVERS, ballet dancer, producer, director, teacher, actor; b. Copenhagen, Denmark, Oct. 3, 1928; s. Ernst Emil and Ellen Evers B. Student, Royal Danish Theatre, Copenhagen, Royal Danish Ballet Sch. Dancer with Royal Danish Ballet, 1946-61; dancer Am. Ballet Theatre, 1949-58; dir. Royal Swedish Ballet, 1967-71; resident producer Nat. Ballet of Can., Toronto, 1973-76, artistic dir., 1983—. Choreographed: Swan Lake, Nat. Ballet Corp., 1967; choreographer, Am. Ballet Theatre, N.Y.C., 1981—; guest appearances with numerous major ballet cos.; principal roles include those in: Giselle, Swan Lake, Carmen, Les Sylphide, The Sleeping Beauty, Miss Julie, Night Shadow, Spectre de la Rose, A Folk Tale; also classical pas de deux and various abstract ballets; Dr. Coppélius in: Coppélia; Peppo in: Napoli; Choreographed: La Sylphide, Nat. Ballet Can., 1964, 73, Swan Lake, Nat. Ballet Can., 1967, Coppelia, Nat. Ballet Can., 1975, Here We Come, Nat. Ballet Can., 1983; Author: Bournonville and Ballet Technic. Elected to roll of honor Student's Assn. Denmark, 1965; recipient Copenhagen Critics' Threatre Cup, 1962, Nijinsky Prize, 1963, Dancemagazine award, 1968, Diplôme d'honneur, (Canada), 1974, Litteris et Artibus medal King Carl Gustaf of Sweden, 1980, Knight of Dannebrog, 1963. Office: Nat Ballet of Canada 157 King St E Toronto Ont Canada M5C 1G9

BRUHN, JOHN GLYNDON, college dean; b. Norfolk, Nebr., Apr. 27, 1934; s. John Franz and Margaret Constance (Treiber) B. B.A., U. Nebr., 1956, M.A., 1958; Ph.D., Yale, 1961. Research sociologist Grace-New Haven Hosp., 1960-61, U. Edinburgh, Scotland, 1961-62; mem. faculty U. Okla. Med. Center, 1962-72, prof., chmn. dept. human ecology, 1969-72; assoc. dean for community affairs, prof. preventive medicine and community health U. Tex. Med. Br., Galveston, 1972-81, acting dean Sch. Allied Health Scis., 1980-81, spl. asst. to pres. for community affairs, dean Sch. Allied Health Scis., 1981—; prof. preventive medicine and community health U. Tex. Sch. Pub. Health, Houston, 1975—; cons. in field. Bd. dirs. Galveston County Coordinated Community Clinics, Galveston County Orch. Assn., United Way of Galveston, Galveston Heart Assn., Friends of Rosenberg Library. Served with U.S. Army, 1957-58. Commonwealth Fund-Yale fellow, 1958-60; USPHS fellow, 1960-61; Fulbright fellow, 1961-62; Danforth Found. assoc., 1973—; recipient Career Devel. award Nat. Heart Inst., 1968-69, Catherine and Nicholas C. Leone award, 1983. Fellow Am. Sociol. Assn., Am. Pub. Health Assn., Am. Heart Assn., Royal Soc. Health; mem. Am. Psychosomatic Soc., Assn. Am. Med. Colls., Assn. Tchrs. Preventive Medicine, AAAS, Tex. Soc. Allied Health Professions, Am. Soc. Allied Health Professions, AAUP, Tex. Acad. Physician Assts. (dir.), Southwestern Sociol. Assn., N.Y. Acad. Scis., Sigma Xi, Alpha Kappa Delta, Kappa Sigma. Home: 7521 Beluche St Galveston TX 77550 *I feel it is important to take advantage of the many opportunities available and to create new opportunities in whatever setting or geographical area you may be. Then work hard and do the most creditable job you can with your given abilities. Never forget to recognize and help others who may not have the same opportunities. Everyone has a purpose and contribution to make in life.*

BRUHN, SOREN FREDERICK, ins. co. exec.; b. Enumclaw, Wash., May 24, 1928; s. Soren Frederik and Helen Mae (Schumacher) B.; m. Nola Katherine Hansen, Sept. 9, 1951; children—Tracy Lee, Rebecca Helen, Robin Margaret, Amy Katherine. B.A., U. Wash., Seattle, 1952, tchrs. cert., 1953, J.D. (asso. editor law rev. 1958-59), 1959. Bar: Wash. bar 1959. Asst. atty. gen., State of Wash., 1959-61, chief dep. ins. commnr., 1961-67; with Safeco Corp., Seattle, 1967—, asso. gen. counsel, 1972—, gen. counsel, 1974—, v.p., 1979—; dir. Safeco Ins. Co. Am. and affiliates. Chmn. Safeco Polit. Action Com. Served with AUS, 1946-47. Mem. Am. Bar Assn., Nat. Com. Ins. Guaranty Funds, Wash. Bar Assn., Wash. Ins. Council, Seattle-King County Bar Assn. Club: Sand Point Country. Home: 1508 9th Ave W Seattle WA 98119 Office: Safeco Plaza Seattle WA 98185

BRUINS, PAUL FASTENAU, chemical engineer, educator; b. Albert Lea, Minn., Dec. 22, 1905; s. Henry Martin and Lillian (Fastenau) B.; m. Bess L. Collins, Aug. 11, 1946; children: Barbara (Mrs. Robert Henninges), Janna, Ruth (Mrs. Lyle Prince), Lillian (Mrs. Cather Boyd), Cynthia (Mrs. Joseph Lucas); m. Lillian M. Munson, July 16, 1981. B.S., Central Coll., Pella, Iowa, 1926, D.Sc., 1960; M.S., Iowa State U., 1927, Ph.D., 1930; D.Sc. (hon.), Poly. Inst. N.Y., 1978. Instr. Iowa State U., 1927-30; chem. engr. A.O. Smith Corp., 1930-32, Geuder, Paeschke & Frey Co., Milw., 1932-34, Fulton Co., 1934-35; faculty Bklyn. Poly. Inst., 1935—, prof. chem. engring., 1946-74, emeritus, 1974—; Cons. plastics engring. and tech., 1935—. Editor: Unsaturated Polyester Technology, Packaging with Plastics, Thermoforming, Rotational Molding, Polyblends and Composites, Silicone Technology, New Polymeric Materials, Polyurethane Technology, Epoxy Resin Technology, Plastics for Electrical Insulation. Fellow Am. Inst. Chem. Engrs.; mem. Soc. Plastics Engrs. (Outstanding Achievement award 1980, Plastics Educator award 1981, chmn. nat. edn. com. 1966-68), Am. Chem. Soc., Sigma Xi, Phi Lambda Upsilon, Tau Beta Pi, Omega Chi Epsilon, Alpha Chi Sigma. Mem. Community Ch. (chmn. council 1967-69). Home: 708 Harris

Ave Austin TX 78705 Office: 333 Jay St Brooklyn NY 11201 *The joy and satisfaction of: 1. Teaching, molding the lives of thousands of students. 2. Family-children. 3. Contributions to Man's welfare. 4. Church and Sunday school. 5. Instrument flying.*

BRUINSMA, HENRY ALLEN, educator, university dean; b. Prospect Park, N.J., July 29, 1916; s. Henry John and Anna (Wierenga) A.; m. Grace Lois Hekman, June 7, 1939; children: Bruce Henry, James Allen. Mus.B., U. Mich., 1937, Mus. M., 1938, Ph.D., 1949; student, Harvard, 1940, 42, U. Utrecht, 1947-48. Dir. summer opera U. Mich., 1938, 39; asst. prof. music, dir. undergrad. studies Duke, 1938-43; prof. music Calvin Coll., 1946-55; vis. prof. U. Mich., 1953-54; chmn. dept. music Ariz. State U., 1955-56, 64-75; dean Coll. Fine Arts, 1964-75; chmn. dept. music So. Ill. U., 1956-59; dir. Sch. Music, Ohio State U., 1959-64; mem. pres. univ. permanent planning com.; dean Sch. Humanities and Arts, San Jose (Calif.) State U., 1975-80; research scholar Netherlands Inst. for Advanced Study, 1980-82; Nat. Endowment for Humanities sr. research scholar, 1981-82; Specialty Reformation music and drama; lectr. U. for Presidents, 1963; v.p. String Teaching Research & Devel., Inc., 1962—. Composer orchestral and choral compositions; author numerous articles in field. Mem. citizen's adv. com. Grand Rapids (Mich.) pub. schs., 1952-55; nat. chmn. com. ch. music Christian Reformed Ch., 1952-60; Mem. Ariz. Council on Arts and Humanities, Phoenix Arts Council; chmn. Ariz. Alliance Arts Edn., 1973-75; Bd. dirs. Phoenix Symphony Orch., Nat. Alliance for Arts Edn., Kennedy Center, Washington, 1975-77, Calif. Alliance for Arts Edn., 1975-80, Inst. Human Environment, San Francisco, 1977—. Served with AUS, 1943-45. Recipient Distinguished Alumnus award U. Mich., 1968, Grand Rapids Jr. Coll., 1970; Travelling fellow Am. Council Learned Socs., 1947-48. Mem. Nat. Fedn. Music Clubs (chmn. crusade for strings), Music Tchrs. Nat. Assn. (chmn. coll. music com.), Nat. Assn. Schs. Music (chms. liason com.; grad. commn. 1963-68), Coll. Music Assn. (exec. com.), Am. Musicol. Soc., Music Educators Nat. Conf., Ohio Music Tchrs. Assn. (chmn. Central dist. 1962—), Vereeniging voor Nederlandsche Muziekgeschiedenis, Internat. Council Fine Arts Deans, Willamette Writers Club, Phi Kappa Phi, Phi Delta Kappa, Phi Mu Alpha, Pi Kappa Lambda, Phi Sigma Kappa. Club: Rotarian. Home: 21 Condolea Dr Lake Oswego OR 97034

BRUINSMA, THEODORE AUGUST, association executive; b. Paterson, N.J., Aug. 3, 1921; s. Theodore and Ella (Ullman) B.; m. Edith Moog, July 16, 1943; children—Tim Charles, Lynn Ellen, Dayle. B.A., Washington and Lee U., 1941; student, Harvard Bus. Sch., 1943; LL.B., Harvard U., 1948. Bar: N.Y. bar 1949, Ga. bar 1953, U.S. Supreme Ct. bar 1980. Atty. Whitman Ransom & Coulson, N.Y.C., 1948-56; v.p., gen. counsel McCall Corp., N.Y.C., 1956-58; pres. Systematics, Inc., N.Y.C., 1958-61, Lear Jet, Inc., Wichita, Kans., 1966-67; also dir.; pres. Harvest Industries, Inc., Los Angeles, 1969-78; also dir.; exec. v.p. Capital for Tech. Industries, Santa Monica, Calif., 1963-65, Packard Bell Electric, Los Angeles, 1965-66; Councilman, Glen Park, N.J., 1956-60; former dean Law Sch., Loyola U., Los Angeles; pres. Los Angeles C. of C., 1983—; dir. Charter Fin. Corp., Los Angeles, Rank Orgn., Chgo., Logex Inc., Los Angeles. Mem. Citizens Com. on Rapid Transit, Los Angeles, 1969-70; mem. Los Angeles Republican Central Com.; bd. dirs. San Pedro (Calif.) YMCA, 1964-66, Am. Edn. League, 1979—; trustee Boys Scouts Am., San Pedro, 1965-66; bd. dirs. Law Sch., Loyola U.; Calif. chmn. Assembly Rep. Polit. Action Com., 1978; trustee Calif. Rep. Assos.; founder Los Angeles Polit. Affairs Council, 1977; Rep. candidate for U.S. Senate, 1982. Served to lt. comdr. USNR, 1943-46, 50-51; PTO. Recipient award Freedoms Found., 1978. Mem. Am. Arbitration Assn., Harvard Bus. Sch. Assn., Am. Bar. Assn., Los Angeles World Affairs Council, Copyright Soc. U.S.A. (original trustee 1949-56). Clubs: Rotary, Los Angeles Athletic, University (Los Angeles). Office: 1440 W 9th St Los Angeles CA 90015

BRUK, JOHN, foundation administrator; b. Blato, Yugloslavia, Mar. 5, 1930; emigrated to Can., 1951; s. Kuzma and Jelica (Kalogjera) B.; m. Carol Jane Sparling, Dec. 20, 1954; children: Mark, Ian, Bruce, Steven. B.Com., U. B.C., Can., 1957, LL.B., 1958. Lectr. U. Wash., Seattle, 1957-58; articling student Lawrence & Shaw, Vancouver, B.C., 1959-60; ptnr. Nemetz, Austin, Christie & Bruk, Vancouver, B.C., 1960-63, Lawrence & Shaw, 1963-74; pres., chief exec. officer Cyprus Anvil Mining Corp., Vancouver, B.C., 1975-82; chmn. bd., mem. founding com. Asia Pacific Found. Can., Vancouver, B.C., 1983—; dir. Can. Devel. Corp., Toronto, Ont., Can. Devel. Investment Corp., Vancouver. Mem. Can. Bar Assn., Law Soc. B.C. Roman Catholic. Clubs: Capilano Golf and Country, Vancouver (Vancouver). Home: 5662 Cypress St Vancouver BC Canada V6M 3R6 Office: 355 Burrard St 404 Vancouver BC Canada V6C 2G8

BRULE, JOHN D., electrical and computer engineering educator, consultant; b. Hancock, Mich., Mar. 13, 1927; s. Edward J. and Stella (Fish) B.; m. Sally C., Aug. 30, 1947; children: James, Nannette, Mark. B.S.E.E., Mich. Tech. U., 1949; M.S.E.E., Iowa State U., 1950; Ph.D., Syracuse U., 1958. Engr. Bell Aircraft Corp., Buffalo, 1950-56; asst. prof. elec. and computer engring. Syracuse U., N.Y., 1956-61, assoc. prof., 1961-71, prof., 1971—; cons. IBM, 1972—. Pres. Catholic Interracial Council, Syracuse, 1965; bd. dirs. Syracuse Peace Council, 1972. Mem. IEEE. Home: 212 Standish Dr Syracuse NY 13224 Office: Syracuse U 111 Link Hall Syracuse NY 13210

BRUMBACK, CHARLES TIEDTKE, newspaper executive; b. Toledo, Sept. 27, 1928; s. John Sanford and Frances Hannah (Tiedtke) B.; m. Mary Louise Howe, July 7, 1951; children: Charles Tiedtke, Anne V., Wesley W., Ellen P. B.A., Princeton U., 1950; postgrad., U. Toledo, 1953-54. C.P.A., Ohio, Fla. With Arthur Young & Co. (C.P.A.s), 1950-57; bus. mgr., v.p., treas., pres., chief exec. officer, dir. Sentinel Star Co., Orlando, Fla., 1957-81; pres., chief exec. officer Chgo. Tribune Co., 1981—; Pres., dir. Sentinel Star Community Assn. Mem. Orlando Mcpl. Planning Bd., 1958-63; trustee Orlando Public Library, 1958-63; bd. govs. Orange Meml. Hosp., 1960-76; bd. dirs. Orlando Regional Med. Center, 1976-81, chmn. bd. dirs., 1976-78; trustee Robert R. McCormick Charitable Trust, Northwestern U., Northwestern Meml. Hosp. Served to 1st lt. U.S. Army, 1951-53. Decorated Bronze star. Mem. Ohio, Fla. socs., C.P.A.'s, Am. Inst. C.P.A.'s, Fla. Press Assn. (treas. 1969-76, pres. 1980, dir.), Inst. Newspaper Controllers and Fin. Officers, Fla. Council of 100. Clubs: Rotary (hon.), Orlando Country, Princeton of N.Y., Univ., Orlando, Chgo. Office: 435 N Michigan Ave Chicago IL 60611

BRUMBACK, CLARENCE LANDEN, public health physician; b. Denver, Apr. 19, 1914; s. Carl Alvin and Hildur Athelia (Landen) B.; m. Lucile Leslie Gillie, June 17, 1943; children—Richard, Carl. A.B., U. Kans., 1936, M.D., 1943; M.P.H., U. Mich., 1948. Diplomate: Am. Bd. Preventive Medicine. Intern U.S. Marine Hosp., San Francisco, 1943-44; dir. public health, Laclede County, Mo., 1947, AEC, Oak Ridge, 1948-50; dir. Palm Beach County (Fla.) Health Dept., 1950—; clin. prof. U. Miami; adj. prof. Fla. Atlantic U., Boca Raton, Fla. Editorial bd.: Jour. Public Health Policy, 1981—; contbr. articles to med. and public health jours. Bd. dirs. Palm Beach County chpt. A.R.C., Am. Lung Assn. S.E. Fla., Heart Assn. Palm Beach County, Community Mental Health Center Palm Beach County, Palm Beach County unit Am. Cancer Soc., Palm Beach County Mental Health Assn.; pres. YMCA of Palm Beaches, 1970. Served with AUS, 1944-47. Decorated Meritorious Service medal; recipient Meritorious Service award Fla. Public Health Assn., 1968; Merit award State of Fla., 1972; Physician of Yr. award Am. Assn. Public Health Physicians, 1975. Fellow Am. Coll. Preventive Medicine, Am. Public Health Assn., Royal Soc. Health; mem. AMA, Fla. Med. Assn., Palm Beach County Med. Soc. Democrat. Lutheran. Clubs: Rotary, Elks. Home: 7405 S Flagler Dr West Palm Beach FL 33405 Office: 826 Evernia St West Palm Beach FL 33402

BRUMBAUGH, JOHN MAYNARD, lawyer, educator; b. Annapolis, Md., Feb. 9, 1927; s. Heber Byron and Nina Elizabeth (Maynard) B.; m. Alice Austin Soled, 1983. B.A., Swarthmore Coll., 1948; J.D., Harvard U., 1951. Bar: D.C. 1951. Law clk. firm Haight, Deming, Gardner, Poor & Havens, N.Y.C., 1951, 53-55; teaching fellow Harvard U., 1955-56; asst. prof. law U. Md., 1956-59, asso. prof., 1959-63, prof., 1963—. Contbr. articles to profl. jours. Mem. Am. Law Inst., Am., Md. bar assns. Clubs: Hamilton St., Wranglers. Office: 500 W Baltimore St Baltimore MD 21201

BRUMBAUGH, ROBERT SHERRICK, philosophy educator; b. Oregon, Ill., Dec. 2, 1918; s. Aaron John and Marjorie Ruth (Sherrick) B.; m. Ada Zarbell Steele, June 5, 1940; children: Robert Conrad, Susan Christianna, Joanna Pauline. A.B., U. Chgo., 1938, M.A., 1938, Ph.D., 1942. Faculty Bowdoin Coll., 1946-49, Ind. U., 1949-52; faculty Yale, New Haven, 1951—, prof. philosophy, 1961—; Research fellow Am. Sch. Classical Studies, Athens, Greece, 1962-63; Fulbright vis. prof. Hebrew U., Jerusalem, 1967. Author: (with N.P. Stallknecht) The Spirit of Western Philosophy, 1950, Plato's Mathematical Imagination, 1953, The Compass of Philosophy, 1954, Plato on the One, 1960, Plato for the Modern Age, 1961, (with Nathaniel Lawrence) Philosophers on Education, 1963, The Philosophers of Greece, 1964, Ancient Greek Gadgets and Machines, 1966; Co-editor: Plato Manuscripts: A Catalogue of the Plato Microfilm Project, Yale University Libraries, parts I and II, 1962, part III, 1974, (with Nathaniel Lawrence) Philosophic Themes in Modern Education, 1973, The Most Mysterious Manuscript: The Voynich "Roger Bacon" Cipher Manuscript, 1978; Contbr. to jours. and encys. Morse fellow, 1954-55; Guggenheim fellow, 1976-77. Mem. Metaphys. Soc. Am. (councillor 1961-65, pres. 1966), Am. Philos. Assn., Soc. Ancient Greek Philosophy, AAUP (nat. council 1975-78), Phi Beta Kappa. Home: 150 Ridgewood Ave Hamden CT 06517 Office: Saybrook College Yale Univ New Haven CT 06520

BRUMBLAY, RAY ULYSSES, educator, chemist; b. Azusa, Calif., Feb. 8, 1912; s. Joseph E. and Cora (Reed) B.; m. Lolita Dorothy Roska, Aug. 16, 1941; children—Lynn L. (Mrs. Robert D. Falconer), Raymond S., Jean M. (Mrs. Clemence C. Richau), Robert J., Laurie E. A.B., Ind. U., 1934; M.S., U. Wis., 1936, Ph.D., 1938. Instr. Ind. U. Calumet Center, 1938-43; from instr. to prof. chemistry U. Wis.-Milw., 1946-69, chmn. dept., 1957-64; prof. chemistry U. Wis., Marathon County Center, 1969-78, prof. emeritus, 1978—; cons. Bradley Corp., 1950—. Author: Quantitative Analysis, 1960, Qualitative Analysis, 1964, A First Course in Quantitative Analysis, 1970. Served with AUS, 1943-46. Mem. Am. Chem. Soc., Sigma Xi. Conglist. Home: PO Box 133 McNaughton WI 54543

BRUMFIELD, JOHN RICHARD, artist, educator; b. Los Angeles, Apr. 1, 1934; s. Arthur Clifton and Arletta (Austin) B.; m. Elaine Watson, Mar. 18, 1977; 1 son, Noah Austin; stepchildren: Paige Harkey, Noel Harkey. M.A. in Lit, Los Angeles State U., 1960, U. Calif., Berkeley, 1969; M.F.A. in Design, Calif. Inst. Arts, 1974. Public relations editor assembly div. Gen. Motors Corp., 1962-64; free-lance comml. photographer, San Francisco, 1964-69; head photography program Calif. Inst. Arts, 1974-80; chmn. div. photog. studies R.I. Sch. Design, Providence, 1980-81; chmn. photography Calif. Inst. Arts, Valencia, 1981—; vis. artist, vis. lectr. Chgo. Art Inst., San Francisco Art Inst., Yale U., Ryerson Inst., UCLA, Boston U., Los Angeles Center, U. N.Mex., Ariz. Center Photography, N.C. U. Contbr. chpts. to books; contbr.: articles to Afterimage, Obscura, Exposure, other mags; exhbns. include, Santa Barbara Mus., 1979, Camera Work, San Francisco, L A Issue, Los Angeles, Visual Studies Workshop, Rochester, 1980, G. Ray Hawkins, Los Angeles, 1981; represented in permanent collections, Mus. Modern Art, N.Y.C., San Francisco Mus. Modern Art, Los Angeles County Mus., Santa Barbara Mus., Gruenvald Collection, UCLA, Mpls. Ins. Arts. Served with U.S. Army, 1957-59. Nat. Endowment Arts grantee, 1979. Mem. Coll. Art Assn. Office: Calif Inst Arts Valencia CA 91355

BRUMFIELD, RICHARD MANOAH, manufacturing executive; b. Princeton, Ind., Oct. 21, 1909; s. John A. and Myrtle (Smith) B.; m. Martha Boren, Dec. 23, 1935; children: Ann, Alice. B.S., Purdue U., 1931, D.Engring. (hon.), 1979; LL.D., Ind. State U., Evansville, 1977. Engr. Hansen Mfg. Co., Princeton, 1931-33; sec.-treas. Potter & Brumfield Mfg. Co., Princeton, 1933-47, pres., 1947-66, N.Y.C., 1954, group exec. elec. products group, 1959-62; chmn. Potter & Brumfield div., 1966-72; now chmn. Hurst Mfg. Corp.; dir. AMP Inc., Gibson County Bank, Gibson County Perpetual Bldg. & Loan Assn., Hurst Tool & Mfg. Co. Active fund drives.; Trustee Purdue U., 1963-78. Mem. Princeton C. of C., Scabbard and Blade, Lambda Chi Alpha, Pi Tau Sigma. Presbyterian. Clubs: Mason (Shriner), Elk.). Home: Petersburg Rd PO Box B Princeton IN 47670

BRUMLEVE, STANLEY J., physiology educator; b. Teutopolis, Ill., July 3, 1924; children: Marcid, Theresa, Cindy, Michael. B.S., St. Louis U., 1950, M.S., 1955, Ph.D., 1957. Asst. prof. physiology U. N.D. Sch. Medicine, Grand Forks, 1957-64, assoc. prof., 1964-73, prof., 1973—, temporary chmn. dept. physiology, 1965, chmn., 1972—. Fellow Am. Physiol. Soc. Home: Rural Route 1 Belmont Rd Grand Forks ND 58201 Office: U N D Sch Medicine Dept Physiology Grand Forks ND 58201

BRUMLIK, JOEL, neurologist; b. Chgo., Jan. 5, 1933; s. Charles and Esther (Rothschild) B.; m. Stephanie Ann Holmquist, Sept. 5, 1981; children: Marc David, Rachel Vanessa. B.S., Northwestern U., 1953, M.D., 1956, M.S., 1959, Ph.D., 1961. Diplomate: Am. Bd. Neurology. Intern Chgo. Wesley Meml. Hosp., 1956-57; resident in neurology Northwestern U. Med. Sch. hosps., 1957-60; instr., then assoc. prof. neurology; mem. faculty Stritch Sch. Medicine, Loyola U., Maywood, Ill., chmn. dept. neurology, 1970-82, now prof. Author articles, revs. in field. Recipient S. Wier Mitchell award, 1962. Mem. AMA, Am. Neurol. Assn., Am. Assn. Neurologists, Ill. Med. Soc., Chgo. Med. Soc. Jewish. *

BRUMM, GREGG EDWARD, financial executive; b. St. Louis, May 8, 1942; s. Joseph D. and Virginia Leona B.; 1 son, Chase Allen. B.A., Amherst Coll., 1963; M.B.A., Stanford U., 1965. Mgmt. cons. Touche, Ross & Co., St. Louis, 1965-68; investment officer St. Louis Union St. Co., 1965-72; fin. adminstr. D'Arcy-MacManus & Masius, Inc., St. Louis, 1972-75, corp. v.p., treas., 1975-80; pres. Ziegler Fin. Planning, 1980-81; chief fin. officer Advanced Computer Mgmt. Inc., 1981—. Chmn. suburban dist. fund drive Boy Scouts Am., 1976; treas. Girls Home, St. Louis, 1977. Mem. Fin. Execs. Inst., Amherst Coll. Alumni Assn. Lutheran. Clubs: Old Warson Country, Missouri Athletic, Orchard Lake Country. Address: 5335 Brookdale Rd Bloomfield Hills MI 48013

BRUMM, JOSEPH DANIEL, investment banker; b. St. Louis, Aug. 8, 1916; s. Edward and Henrietta (Knehans) B.; m. Virginia Crady, July 13, 1940; children—Gregg Edward, Eric Joseph. Certificate in commerce, St. Louis U., 1939. With Bemis Bros. Bag Co., 1934-41; with Stix, Baer & Fuller Co., St. Louis, 1941-69, sec.-treas., 1957-69, exec. v.p., 1961-69; also dir.; financial v.p., treas., dir. Rich's, Inc., Atlanta, 1969-72; exec. v.p., dir. Zeal Corp., St. Louis, 1972—; exec. v.p., treas., dir. Guarantee Elec. Co., St. Louis, 1975—; mem. adv. bd. Liberty Mut. Ins. Co., Mercantile Bank; dir. DePaul Med. Office Bldg. Bd. dirs. Atlanta chpt. Nat. Found. March of Dimes, Boy Scouts Am., Atlanta, Heart Assn., Atlanta, Salvation Army, St. Louis; chmn. Salvation Army, St. Louis, 1983-84; mem. hosp. assn. bd. Mo. Bapt. Hosp. Mem. Financial Execs. Inst. Clubs: Capital City, Old Warson Country, Mo. Athletic, Strathalbyn Farms. Home: 12679 Spruce Pond Rd Saint Louis MO 63131

BRUMMEL, MARK JOSEPH, magazine editor; b. Chgo., Oct. 28, 1933; s. Anthony William and Mary (Helmreich) B. B.A., Cath. U. Am., 1956, S.T.L., 1961, M.S. in L.S, 1964. Joined Order of Caretians, Roman Cath. Ch., 1952, ordained priest, 1960; librarian, tchr. St. Jude Sem., Momence, Ill., 1961-70; asso. editor U.S. Cath. mag., Chgo., 1971-72, editor, 1972—; dir. Claretian Publs., Chgo., 1972—; Bd. dirs. Eastern Province Claretians, 1973—; pres. bd. dirs. Claretian Med. Center, 1980—; bd. dirs. 8th Day Center, 1980—. Editor: Today mag, 1970-71. Treas. Associated Ch. Press, 1981—. Home: 3200 E 91st St Chicago IL 60617 Office: 221 W Madison St Chicago IL 60606

BRUMMET, RICHARD LEE, educator; b. Ewing, Ill., Mar. 16, 1921; s. George Otto and Iva Talitha (Smith) B.; m. Nellie Eldora Riddle, Aug. 6, 1942; children—Carmen, John. B.E., Ill. State U., 1942; M.S., U. Ill., 1947; Ph.D., U. Mich., 1956. Prof. Cornell U., 1954-55; prof. U. Mich., 1955-69, dir. mgmt. edn., 1966-68; Willard J. Graham distinguished prof. U. N.C., 1970—; cons. Ford Found., Cairo, Egypt, 1963-64; vis. prof. Netherlands Sch. Econs., 1969, U. South Africa, 1974, U. New South Wales, Australia, 1976; cons. in field. Author: Overhead Costing, 1957, Cost Accounting for Small Manufacturers, 1953; 197l, Record Keeping for Small Home Builders, 1952, The Metal Finishing Industry, 1966; Contbr. articles to profl. jours. articles. Served to capt. AUS, 1942-46. Mem. Am. Inst. C.P.A.'s (council 1975-77), Am. Accounting Assn. (treas. 1967-69, pres. 1974-75), Nat. Assn. Accountants (v.p. 1970-71, pres. 1979-80, chmn. 1980-81). Pioneer in social accounting, human resources accounting. Home: 810 Kenmore Chapel Hill NC 27514

BRUMMETT, MARVIN KIGHT, lawyer; b. Claude, Tex., Dec. 7, 1913; s. William Andrew and Mae (Kight) Wilson; m. Fanella Clift, Aug. 17, 1940; children—Marla (Mrs. Marla Cochran), Jay C. B.S., Okla. State U., 1934; LL.B., U. Tex., 1937. Bar: Tex. bar 1937. Asso. Simpson, Dorenfield & Fullingim, Amarillo, Tex., 1937-38; lawyer Halliburton Co., Duncan, Okla., 1938-69, asso. gen. counsel, 1946-69, sec., 1953-69, v.p., 1959- 67, sr. v.p., 1967-69; trustee Halliburton Employees' Benefit Fund, 1949-69, chmn. bd trustees, 1962-69; pres., dir. Life Ins. Co. of S.W., Dallas, 1964-69; dir. Security Nat. Bank and Trust Co., Duncan, J & M Steel Co., Fort Worth, Security Corp., Duncan, Marla Marine Corp., Dallas. Mem. Am., Okla., Dallas bar assns., State Bar Tex., Am. Soc. Corporate Secs. (v.p. 1968-69), Sigma Phi Epsilon. Home: 7216 Glendora Ave PO Box 30245 Dallas TX 75230

BRUN, HERBERT, composer; b. Berlin, 1918; m. Marianne Kortner; children: Michael, Stefan. Student composition with, Stefan Wolpe, Jerusalem Conservatory Music, Columbia U. Mem. faculty U. Ill. Sch. Music, Urbana, 1963—. Composer scores for theatre. Research in computer composition. Address: Sch Music U Ill Urbana IL 61801

BRUNDAGE, HOWARD DENTON, investment counselor; b. Newark, Nov. 9, 1923; s. Edgar Ray and Salome (Denton) B.; m. Nancy Williams, Oct. 20, 1945; children—Louise, Peter, Joanne, Geraldine. B.A., Dartmouth Coll., 1944; postgrad., Harvard U. Bus. Sch., 1944-45. With Morgan Stanley & Co., 1945-50; asst. sec. Hanover Bank, 1950-52; with J.H. Whitney & Co., 1952-58, partner, 1958, 1960-62; v.p., sec., treas. Plymouth Rock Publs., Inc., 1958-60; dir., chmn. N.Y. Herald Tribune, 1958-59; exec. v.p. finance, dir. J. Walter Thompson Co., 1962-74; exec. v.p. Dresdner & Brundage Assos., 1974-77, Conn. Investment Mgmt., Inc., 1978—; dir. Phoenix Assurance Co., London Guarantee & Accident Co., N.Y.C., Smith Barney Equity Fund. Former trustee, treas. Montainside Hosp., Montclair. Home: Ely's Ferry Rd Lyme CT 06371 Office: PO Box 280 Old Lyme CT 06371

BRUNDAGE, JAMES ARTHUR, historian, educator; b. Lincoln, Nebr., Feb. 5, 1929; s. Frank L. and Anna (Morrissey) B.; m. Victoria Claire Conlin, 1979; children: James Arthur, Brigitte, Gregory C., David B., Thomas T., Ann Kristin. B.A., U. Nebr., 1950, M.A., 1951; Ph.D., Fordham U., 1955. Instr. Fordham U., 1953-57; asst. prof. U. Wis. Milw., 1957-60, assoc. prof., 1960-65, prof., 1965—, chmn. dept. history, 1972-76; vis. fellow Clare Hall Cambridge U., 1977-78; Catedratico visitante U. Madrid, 1967-68; postdoctoral research at Cambridge U., Munich U., Innsbruck, Rome, and Madrid. Author: The Chronicle of Henry of Livonia, 1961, The Crusades: A Documentary Survey, 1962, Medieval Canon Law and the Crusader, 1969, Richard Lion Heart: A Biography, 1974; Contbr. articles to profl. jours.; assoc. editor: Jour. Medieval History. Guggenheim fellow, 1964-65; Fulbright grant to Spain, 1967-68; NEH fellow Newberry Library, Chgo., 1983-84. Fellow Royal Hist. Soc.; mem. Am. Hist. Assn., Am. Catholic Hist. Assn. (past mem. exec. council), Mediaeval Acad. Am. (council), AAUP (past chpt. pres.). Democrat. Home: 3496 N Cramer St Milwaukee WI 53211

BRUNDAGE, JOHN DENTON, ins. co. exec.; b. Newark, Mar. 28, 1919; s. Edgar Ray and Salome (Denton) B.; m. Ann Lounsbury, Nov. 29, 1941; children—Elizabeth Ann, Susan, Patricia, John. A.B., Princeton U., 1941. C.L.U. Agy. asst. Bankers Nat. Life Ins. Co., Montclair, N.J., 1945-46, asst. to pres., 1953-54, adminstrv. v.p., 1955-57, exec. v.p., 1957-58, pres., dir., 1958-71; sales promotion mgr. Mut. Benefit Life Ins. Co., Newark, 1946-47, regional supt. agys., 1948-50, dir. agys., 1950-52, agy. mgr., N.Y.C., 1952-53; chmn., dir. Palisades Life Ins. Co., New City, N.Y., 1965-71; chmn., pres., dir. Ga. Internat. Life, Atlanta, 1972-74; pres., dir. Dominion Trust Life, Houston, 1972-74; chmn., chief exec. officer Globe Life Ins. Co., Chgo., 1974-77, 79—, pres., 1977-79, chmn., pres., 1980; dir. Geneva Life, Gt. Equity Life. Chmn. Montclair Urban Coalition, 1969-70; chmn. bd. Am. Heart Assn., 1962-65, chmn., 1980—; bd. govs. Chgo. Heart Assn., 1976—; trustee Sch. of the Ozarks, 1976—. Served from ensign to lt. comdr. USNR, 1940-45. Recipient Gold Heart award Am. Heart Assn., 1965, Citizens award for distinguished community service N.J. Acad. Medicine, 1964. Fellow Life Office Mgmt. Assn.; mem. Nat. Assn. Life Underwriters, Am. Coll. Life Underwriters. Clubs: Princeton (N.Y.C.); Short Hills (N.J.); Indian Hill (Winnetka); Chgo.; Quadrangle (Princeton). Home: 290 White Oak Ln Winnetka IL 60093 Office: 222 N Dearborn St Chicago IL 60601

BRUNDAGE, RUSSELL ARCHIBALD, data processing executive; b. N.Y.C., Feb. 16, 1929; s. Eugene Columbus and Sophia Catherine (Gillies) B.; m. Barbara Jane Nelson, May 18, 1958; children: Russell Archibald, Nelson David, Beth Ellen, Paul Winston. B.A., Washington Sq. Coll., NYU, 1957. With U.S. Fgn. Service, State Dept., 1950-55; applied sci. writer IBM Corp., N.Y.C. and White Plains, N.Y., 1957-60; with Colonial Penn Group, Phila., 1960-61, v.p., 1972-81; pres.

Colonial Penn Group Data Corp., 1970-77; v.p. Nat. Assn. Plans, Inc., 1971-81; v.p. data processing SAI Group, Inc., 1982; pres. SAI Data Services Div., 1983—. Chmn. Lee Magisterial Dist. Republican Com., Fairfax County, Va., 1966. Served with USAF, 1947-50. Mem. Vets. 7th Regt. N.Y. Republican. Presbyn. (ret. elder). Home: 630 Leopard Rd Berwyn PA 19312 Office: 900 Dudley Ave Cherry Hill NJ 08002

BRUNDETT, GEORGE LEE, JR., gas company executive; b. Rockport, Tex., Mar. 17, 1921; s. George Lee and Sarah Thomas (Drake) B.; m. Jonell Brundett, July 25, 1953; children: Barbara Jan, George Lee. B.B.A., U. Tex., 1946, LL.B., 1950. Bar: Tex. 1949. With firm Fischer, Wood, Burney, Corpus Christi, Tex., 1950-64, Coastal States Gas Corp. (now Coastal Corp.), Houston, 1964—; now sr. v.p., gen. counsel, sec., dir. Coastal Corp. Served with USAAF, 1943-46. Mem. Am. Assn. Corp. Secs., ABA, Tex. Bar Assn., Harris County Bar Assn., Neuces County Bar Assn. Presbyterian. Home: 11815 Wink Rd Houston TX 77024 Office: Coastal Tower 9 Greenway Plaza Houston TX 77046

BRUNEAU, CLAUDE, insurance company executive; b. Sept. 7, 1931. B.A., Coll. Sainte-Marie, Montreal, Que., Can., 1951; LL.L., U. Montreal, Que., Can., 1954; M.B.A., U. Western Ont., Can., 1959. Asst. sec.-treas. Chatelaine Hosiery Ltd., Monteal, Que., Can., 1955-57; with investment and stock-brokerage firm, Monteal, Que., Can., 1959-60; spl. asst. to Minister of Justice, Govt. Can., Ottawa, Ont., 1960-62; asst. to dir. planning Molson Breweries Ltd., Montreal, Que., Can., 1962-64; dir. legal dept., asst. sec., legal counsel Steinberg Ltd., Montreal, Que., Can., 1964-67; assoc. dir. Can. Com. Mut. Funds and Investment Contracts, Toronton, Ont., Can., 1967-69; cons. find. services holding subs. Winnipeg Power Corp. Can., Monteal, Que., Can., 1970-71, v.p., 1970-73, pres. computer service subs., Montreal, Que., Can., 1971-77, v.p., 1977-82, sec., gen. counsel, 1980-82; chmn. bd. Montreal United Workshop Assn., 1973-80; exec. v.p. Life Ins. Laurentian Group Corp., 1983—, dir.; chmn. bd. Imperial Life Assurance Co. Can., Toronto, Ont., 1983—, pres., chief exec. officer, 1983—; vice chmn., dir. Imbrook Properties Ltd.; chmn., dir. Impco Properties Ltd.; pres., dir. laurentian Fund Inc.; dir. Brook Securities & Co. Ltd., A. Bruneau Can. Ltd., Can. Film Devel. Corp., Castlemere Properties Ltd., Banque Nationale du Can., Loyal Am. Life Ins. Co., La Maison Cousin Inc.; N. Hollander Inc.; dir. Nat. Bank Leasing Inc. (formerly Laurentide Fin. Corp. Ltd.). Mem. Que. Bar Assn. Club: Mt. Bruno Country. Office: Imperial Life Assurance Co Can 95 St Clair Ave W Toronto ONCanada M4V 1N5

BRUNELL, PHILIP A., physician; b. N.Y.C., Feb. 1, 1931; s. Irving and Rose B.; m. Barbara Abse, Sept. 7, 1951; children—Wayne, Robert, Rhonda. B.S., CCNY, 1950; postgrad., N.Y. U., 1950-51; M.S. in Physiology, U. Ill., 1952; M.D., U. Buffalo, 1957. Diplomate: Am. Bd. Pediatrics. Research asst. physiology U. Ill., 1951-52, teaching asst., 1952-53; intern E.J. Meyer Meml. Hosp., Buffalo, 1957-58; resident in pediatrics Children's Hosp., Buffalo, 1958-60; asst. in pediatrics Cornell U., 1960-61; instr. pediatrics Emory U., 1961-64; asst. prof. pediatrics N.Y. U. Sch. Medicine, 1964-71, asso. prof., 1971-75; prof., chmn. dept. pediatrics U. Tex. Health Sci. Center, San Antonio, 1975-81, prof., head div. infectious diseases dept. pediatrics, 1981—; chief pediatrics Bexar County Hosp. Dist. Teaching Hosps., San Antonio, 1975-81; attending physician Santa Rosa Children's Hosp., San Antonio, 1975-81; cons. Brooke Army Med. Center, Wilford Hall USAF Med. Center, 1977—. Contbr. chpts. to books; contbr. articles to med. jours. Chmn. Internat. Year of Child, San Antonio, 1979-80; bd. dirs. Santa Rosa Children's Hosp. Found. Served with USPHS, 1961-64. USPHS fellow, 1971-72. Fellow Infectious Diseases Soc. Am. (awards com. 1979—); mem. Am. Acad. Pediatrics (chmn. com. pediatric research 1977-78, mem. com. infectious diseases 1978—), Am. Soc. Microbiology, Am. Pediatric Soc., N.Y. Acad. Scis., Soc. Pediatric Research, San Antonio Pediatric Soc., Tex. Pediatrics Soc. (awards com.), Council Tex. Pediatric Dept. Chmn. (chmn. 1978-81), Tex. Med. Assn. (sec. treas. pediatric sect. 1979-80, pres. 1980-81), Bexar County Med. Soc., AMA, Tex. Infectious Disease Soc. Home: 12818 King's Forest Dr San Antonio TX 78230 Office: Dept Pediatrics U Tex Health Sci Center 7703 Floyd Curl Dr San Antonio TX 78284

BRUNER, CHARLOTTE HUGHES, educator; b. Urbana, Ill., May 8, 1917; d. Charles Hughes and Nell Converse (Bomar) Johnston; m. David Kincaid Bruner, July 16, 1939; children: Nell Kincaid Bruner Sedransk, Charles Hughes. B.A., U. Ill., 1938; M.A., Columbia U., 1939. Tchr. French Iowa State U., 1942-44, 55—, prof., 1980—; instr. U. Ill., 1944-45. Writer, dir. radio series, 1974, 79, 80—; contbr. articles to profl. jours. Mem. African Lit. Assn. (vice chmn. 1978-79), African Studies Assn., Am. Tchrs. French, Am. Council Teaching Fgn. Lans., Coll. Lang. Assn., MLA, Phi Beta Kappa, Phi Kappa Phi, Phi Sigma Iota. Home: 4625 Westbend Dr Ames IA 50010 Office: Dept Fgn Langs and Lits Iowa State U Ames IA 50011

BRUNER, EDWARD M., educator; b. N.Y.C., Sept. 28, 1924; s. Milton J. and Bessie (Hinds) B.; m. Elaine C. Hauptman, Mar. 21, 1948; children—Jane R., Dan M. B.A., Ohio State U., 1948, M.A., 1950; Ph.D., U. Chgo., 1954. Instr. dept. anthropology U. Chgo., 1953-54; asst. prof. dept. anthropology Yale U., 1954-60; asso. prof. dept. anthropology U. Ill., Urbana, 1961-65, prof., 1965—, head dept., 1966-76; dir. Doris Duke Am. Indian Oral History Project, 1967-73; Cons. Ford Found., Nat. Assessment Edn. in Indonesia, 1969-70; chmn. test com. in anthropology Ednl. Testing Service, Princeton, N.J., 1967-69; cons. cultural anthropology rev. com. NIMH, 1966; mem. grants com. Social Sci. Research Council, N.Y.C., 1966. Contbr. articles to profl. jours. Center for Advanced Study in Behavioral Sci. fellow, 1960-61; sr. scholar East West Center Inst. Advanced Projects, Honolulu, 1963; research grantee NIMH, NSF, Wenner Gren Found., Ford Found., Social Sci. Research Council. Fellow Am. Anthrop. Assn. (rep. to AAAS 1979—); mem. Royal Anthrop. Soc., Am. Ethnol. Soc. (pres. 1981-82), Soc. Applied Anthropology, Assn. for Asian Studies (mem. Indonesian studies com. 1973—, chmn. 1976-78). Field research Am. Indians, Indonesia. Home: 2022 Cureton Dr Urbana IL 61801

BRUNER, ROBERT B., hospital administrator; b. N.Y.C., Aug. 4, 1933; s. Samuel Wolf and Pauline (Rothstein) B.; m. Janet Bergman, Aug. 26, 1956; children: Steven Wayne, Marc Richard. Student, N.Y. U., 1950-53; B.A. cum laude, L.I. U., 1956; M.S., 1959. Adminstrv. asst., asst. adminstr. Bklyn. Hebrew Home and Hosp. for Aged, 1958-62; asst. adminstr. Montefiore Hosp., Bronx, N.Y., 1962-64, L.I. Jewish Hosp., New Hyde Park, N.Y., 1964-66, adminstr., Queens, 1966-69, Univ. Hosp., SUNY, Stony Brook, 1969-71; exec. dir., pres. Mt. Sinai Hosp., Hartford, Conn., 1971—; trustee State Bank for Savs., Hartford; adj. faculty U. Hartford; asst. prof. SUNY, 1969-71; prof. N.Y. U., 1973-75; preceptor Yale Sch. Public Health.; Mem. Conn. Commn. on Hosps. and Health Care, 1976-81; mem. Nat. Commn. on Certification of Physicians Assts., 1976—, pres., 1981—; chmn. blue ribbon com. New Eng. Hosp. Assembly, 1979—; pres. Combined Hosps. Alcoholism Program, 1977-79; v.p. Capital Area Health Consortium, 1978-79, pres., 1982-84. Named Boss of Yr. Greater Hartford Jaycees, 1977. Fellow Am. Coll. Hosp. Adminstrn., Am. Public Health Assn., Royal Soc. Health, Am. Acad. Med. Adminstrn.; mem. Conn. Hosp. Assn. (trustee, T.S. Hamilton Disting. Service award), Am. Hosp. Assn., Am. Assn. Hosp. Planning, N.Y. Acad. Sci., C. of C. (futures com.), AAAS., Hosp. Execs., Chief Execs. of Jewish Hosps. Club: Tumblebrook Country. Home: 141 Sunny Reach Dr West Hartford CT 06117 Office: 500 Blue Hills Ave Hartford CT 06112

BRUNER, VAN BUREN, JR., architect, planner; b. Washington, May 22; s. Van Buren and Flora Louise (Harris) B.; m. Lillian E. Almond, Aug. 21, 1954; 1 son, Scott Vincent. B.S. in Design, U. Mich., 1954, Drexel U., 1965. Job. capt. Vincetn G. Kling, Architect, Phila., 1959-65; head dept. bldg. constrn. tech. dept. Spring Garden Inst., Phila., 1965—, chmn., prof. dept. architecture, constrn. design and civil engrng. tech. studies, 1979-81; pvt. practice architecture and planning, Haddonfield, N.J., 1966—; mem. N.J. Hotel Multiple Dwelling Health and Safety Bd. Served with USAF, 1954-57. Fellow AIA (past nat. v.p., Whitney Young citation 1975); mem. Full Gospel Businessmen's Fellowship Internat. (pres.). Home and Office: 506 W Park Blvd Haddonfield NJ 08033

BRUNER, WILLIAM WALLACE, banker; b. Orangeburg, S.C., Nov. 6, 1920; s. Robert Raysor and Bessie (Livingston) R.; children—William W., Thomas W., James L. C.P.A., S.C. Accountant J. W. Hunt & Co. (C.P.A.'s), Columbia, S.C., 1945-48; with First Nat. Bank S.C., Columbia, 1948—, sr. v.p., 1961-64, pres., 1964—, also chmn. bd., dir.; pres., dir. First Bankshares Corp. S.C.; dir. Home Security Life Ins. Co., Durham, N.C., Spartan Mills, Spartanburg, S.C., Columbia Coca-Cola Bottling Co. S.C., Atlantic States Bankcard Assn., Raleigh, N.C. Treas. United Fund Columbia, 1958-59, bd. dirs., 1956- 58, chmn. large firms div., 1965, bd. dirs. treas., 1956-57; chmn. chpt. ARC, 1958-60, nat. fund vice chmn., 1960-61; trustee Providence Hosp., Columbia, chmn. fin. com., 1978-79, chmn. bd. trustees, 1980—; trustee Bus. Partnership Found. U. S.C., Columbia, sec.-treas., 1972-73; treas. S.C. Soc. Crippled Children and Adults, 1967-70, v.p., 1970-71, pres., 1971-72; trustee Columbia Museums Art and Sci., 1981—. Served to lt. comdr. USNR, 1941-45. Mem. Am. Inst. C.P.A.'s, S.C. Assn. C.P.A.'s, Columbia C. of C. (treas. 1961, v.p. 1962), Urban League Columbia (dir.), Am. Bankers Assn. (adv. com. on fed. legislation 1966-71, governing council 1972-74, bd. dirs. 1972-73, trustee fund for edn. in econs. 1976-77, chmn. 1977), S.C. Bankers Assn. (v.p. 1967-68, pres. 1970-71), U.S. C. of C. (banking, monetary and fiscal affairs com. 1977-79), Phi Beta Kappa, Beta Gamma Sigma, Sigma Nu. Methodist. Office: 1401 Main St PO Box 111 Columbia SC 29202

BRUNET, BARRIE KIRK, hotel co. exec.; b. Scobey, Mont., Mar. 4, 1925; s. Alfred L. and E. Fay (Richardson) B.; m. Barbara Walker, July 19, 1952; children—Dennis, Douglas, Craig. B.A., U. Wash., 1949. C.P.A., Wash. Auditor, acct., mgr. adminstrv. services Arthur Andersen & Co., Seattle and Los Angeles, 1949-58; studio controller, corporate controller, exec. v.p. Metro-Goldwyn-Mayer, Inc., Los Angeles and N.Y.C., 1958—; pres., chief exec. officer MGM Grand Hotel-Reno, Inc. Served with AUS, 1943-46. Mem. Motion Picture Controllers Assn. (pres. 1964-65), Nat. Assn. Accountants (asso. dir. Los Angeles chpt. 1960), Phi Beta Kappa, Beta Gamma Sigma, Beta Alpha Psi. Methodist. Office: 2500 E 2d St Reno NV 89595

BRUNET, MEADE, ret. mfg. co. exec.; b. Petersburg, Va., June 21, 1894; s. Robert Edward and Sally (Minson) B.; m. Edythe Redman, Oct. 2, 1925; children—Sally (Mrs. K.H. Beyan), Stuart. B.E., Union Coll., 1916; LL.D., 1966. Prodn. clk. Gen. Electric Co., Schenectady, 1915-16, Sperry Gyroscope Co., 1916-17; comml. engr. Gen. Electric, Pub. Utility Dept., 1919-22; with Radio Corp. Am., 1922-66, dist. mgr., Chgo., 1923-25, asst. gen. sales mgr. in charge merchandising, 1925-28; v.p. Radio Victor, 1928-29; sales mgr. R.C.A. radiotron, 1929-32; v.p. mfg. RCA, Washington rep., 1939-45; mgr. engring. products dept. RCA Victor Div., 1945-46; v.p. Radio Corp. Am., 1946-66; mng. dir. RCA Internat. Div., 1946-57; Dir. Nat. Fgn. Trade Council, 1946-67, Pan Am. Soc.; chmn. Bus. Council Internat. Understanding, 1957-60; mem. adv. bd. Internat. and Comparative Law Center; chmn. bd. trustees Union Coll., Schenectady, 1963-69, acting pres., 1966; past trustee U.S. Inter Am. Council, Far East Council; adviser internat. bus. program Rutgers Grad. Sch. Bus. Adminstrn.; gov. Union U., Albany, 1956-69; mem. adv. bd. Internat. Assn. Students in Econs. and Industry. Author: History of the 56th Engineers in First World War. Former mem. bus. and industry adv. com. Orgn. for European Cooperation and Devel.; Past mem. N.J. Republican Finance Com.; Trustee Speedwell Village, Morristown, N.J. Served as 1st lt. 56th Engrs., World War I; mil. combat service with French VIII Army and 1st Am. Army AEF. Decorated Officer Cruzeiro do Sul, Brazil, Order El Merito, Chile). Fellow Radio Club Am.; mem. Internat. C. of C. (exec. com., trustee U.S. council), Arbitration Assn., NAM (chmn. internat. econs. affairs com. 1962-63, dir.), IEEE (life), Acad. Polit. Sci. (life), Conf. Nat. Orgns. (hon.), Sigma Phi, Sigma Xi, Tau Beta Pi. Clubs: University (N.Y.C.); Army and Navy (Washington); Somerset Hills (Bernardsville, N.J.); Farmington Country (Charlottesville, Va.),, Radio Pioneers (life). Home: Millsdale Farm Corey Ln Mendham NJ 07945

BRUNET, MICHEL, historian, educator, concultant; b. Montreal, Que., Can., July 24, 1917; s. Leo and Rose (De Guise) B.; m. Berthe Boyer, May 17, 1945 (dec. 1974); m. Leone Dussault, Dec. 5, 1975. B.A., U. Montreal, 1939, B.Pedagogie, 1941, M.A., 1947; Ph.D., Clark U., 1949. Tchr. Commn. des Ecoles Catholique de Montreal, 1941-49; asst. prof. dept. history U. Montreal, 1949-50, assoc. prof., 1950-59, prof., 1959-83, chmn. dept. history, 1959-67, emeritus prof., 1983—; vis. prof. Sorbonne, Paris, 1972, U. Poitiers, Frances, 1976; sec. Faculty of Letters, U. Montreal, 1961-66, vice-dean, 1966-67; pres. Inst. History of French Am., 1970-72. Author: Histoire du Canada, 1963, Les Canadiens apres la Conquete 1759-1775, 1969 (Gov. Gen. Lit. prize 1969, France-Que. prize 1970); of hist. essays. Sec.gen. Soc. St. John the Baptist, Montreal, 1957-61, v.p., Montreal, 1961-63, recipient Duvernay prize, Montreal, 1969. Mem. Hist. Soc. Can., Hist. Soc. Montreal (recipient medal 1978). Roman Catholic. Home: 1790 Rue Dauphin Laval PQ Canada H7G 1N3 Office: Dept History U Montreal 2900 Blvd Edouard Montipetit Montreal PQ Canada H3C 3J7

BRUNGRABER, ROBERT J., educator; b. Birmingham, Mich., Dec. 20, 1929; s. Louis Rudolph and Beatrice Emogene (Crawford) B.; m. Ruth Ann Rupp, June 13, 1951; children—Robert Lyman, Margaret Ruth. B.S. in Civil Engring. (Regents Alumni scholar), U. Mich., 1951; M.S. (John McMullen scholar), Cornell U., 1956; postgrad., U. Pitts., 1957-58; Ph.D. (Ford Found. fellow), Carnegie Inst. Tech., 1963. Field engr. Porter-Urquhart-Skidmore, Owings & Merrill (cons. engrs.), Casablanca, Morocco, 1951-53; instr. Cornell U., Ithaca, N.Y., 1953-56; research engr. Alcoa Research Labs., New Kensington, Pa., 1956-60; asst. prof. civil engring. Princeton, 1962-66; asso. prof. civil engring. Union Coll., Schenectady, 1966-68; prof. civil engring. Bucknell U., Lewisburg, Pa., 1968—, Presdl. prof., 1979—; founder, pres. Slip-Test Inc. (Structural cons. Borough Hall), Princeton, N.J., 1966; v.p. B.K.L.B. Inc., Cons. Engrs.; Intergovtl. Personnel Act appointee Nat. Bur. Standards, 1974-75; structural cons. English Engring., Williamsport, Pa., 1970—, Sprout-Waldron, Muncy, Pa.. 1973—; dir., treas., mem. nat. exec. com. Nat. Inst. Bldg. Scis., 1976—. Contbr. articles on civil engring. to profl. publs. AAAS Congl. fellow, 1975-76. Mem. ASCE (chmn. com. lightweight alloys of metals structural div. 1969-73), Moles, Sigma Xi, Tau Beta Pi, Chi Epsilon, Phi Kappa Phi, Phi Gamma Delta. Club: Nassau. Extensive research in structural applications of aluminum, particularly welded applications, pile foundations, and rehab. of steel truss bridges; supr. design and constrn. of Stephen J. Potter Meml. Lab., Union Coll., 1967. Home: 409 S 21st St Lewisburg PA 17837 Office: Dana Engineering Bldg Lewisburg PA 17837

BRUNIE, CHARLES HENRY, investment manager; b. N.Y.C., July 17, 1930; s. Charles Henry and Olive (Swanston) B.; m. Jean Isbell Corley, June 23, 1965; stepchildren: William Corley, Jean Corley Yankus, Ellen Corley. B.A., Amherst Coll., 1952; M.B.A., Columbia, 1956. Analyst N.Y. Life Ins. Co., N.Y.C., 1956-60; sr. analyst firm Faulkner, Dawkins & Sullivan, 1960-63; sr. analyst Oppenheimer & Co., N.Y.C., 1963-65, gen. partner, 1965-82, mem. exec. com., sr. partner, 1969-82; chmn. Oppenheimer Capital Corp., 1977—, Manhattan Inst., 1980—. Served with AUS, 1952-54. Mem. N.Y. Soc. Security Analysts, Chartered Financial Analysts, Mont Pelerin Soc., Delta Upsilon. Clubs: Knickerbocker (N.Y.C.); Bronxville Field, Siwanoy Country (Bronxville). Home: 21 Elm Rock Rd Bronxville NY 10708 Office: 1 New York Plaza New York NY 10004

BRUNING, JAMES LEON, university official; b. Bruning, Nebr., Apr. 1, 1938; s. Leon G. and Delma Dorothy (Middendorf) B.; m. E. Marlene Schaff, Aug. 24, 1958; children: Michael, Stephen, Kathleen. B.A., Doane Coll., 1959; M.A., U. Iowa, 1961, Ph.D., 1962. Lic. psychologist, Ohio. Chmn. dept psychology Ohio U., Athens, 1972-76, acting dean arts and scis., 1976-77, assoc. dean, 1977-78, vice provost, 1978-81, provost, 1981—; planning cons. NCHEMS, Boulder, Colo., 1979-80. Author: Computational Handbook of Statistics, 1968, Research in Psychology, 1970; contbr. articles to profl. jours. Grantee Esso., 1963-64, NIMH, 1963-66, EPDA, 1974-75. Mem. Am. Psychol. Assn., Midwestern Psychol. Assn., AAAS, Sigma Xi. Democrat. Lutheran. Home: 86 Melnor Dr Athens OH 45701 Office: Ohio Univ Cutler Hall Athens OH 45701

BRUNINGS, KARL JOHN, chemist, research executive, government official, educator; b. Balt., Dec. 4, 1913; s. Johann Karl and Eleanor Marie (Meyrahl) B.; m. Helen Medcalf; children: Frieda (Mrs. Geoffrey Gardner), Laura (Mrs. Edwin C. Hoffman, Jr.). Student, U. Heidelberg, Germany, 1935-36; Ph.D., Johns Hopkins, 1939; grad., Harvard Bus. Sch. Advanced Mgmt. Program, 1960. Chemist Eastman Kodak Co., 1939-41; research fellow, instr. Johns Hopkins, 1941-44, asso. prof., 1946-48; asst. prof. N.Y. U., 1944-46; dir. chem. research and devel. Chas. Pfizer & Co., Inc., 1948-61, adminstrv. dir. research, 1961-62; pres. Geigy Research div. Geigy Chem. Corp., 1962-68; sr. v.p., dir. medicinal research Geigy Pharms. div. Geigy Chem. Corp., 1968-71; sr. v.p. pharm. research CIBA-Geigy Corp., Ardsley, N.Y., 1971-77; program dir. and cons. Office Tech. Assessment, U.S. Congress, 1977-78; prof. U. Rochester Med. Sch., part time 1979-80, cons. chem. and sci. policy, 1980—; Rennebohm lectr. U. Wis., 1965; chmn. 1st Internat. Pharmacology Meeting, Stockholm, Sweden, 1961; participant seminar series NRC-Dept. Commerce, 1976; I.R.I. advisor Dept. Commerce, 1983—. Contbr. articles to profl. jours. Bd. dirs. Westchester div. Am. Cancer Soc.; adv. council Westchester (N.Y.) Office Aging, 1978-80. Mem. Pharm. Mfrs. Assn. (chmn. subcom. 1965-67), AAAS (chmn. medicinal chem. sect.), Am. Chem. Soc. (corp. asso., dir. N.Y. sect.; mem. subcom. sci. exhibits centennial 1976, chmn. pharm. task force on health, congl. sci. counselor 1981), Indsl. Research Inst. (chmn. tellers com., bd. editors; chmn. bd. editors, adv. editorial bd., chmn. emeritii com. Research Mgmt. 1972—, dir. 1975-78, bd. rep. mid-mgmt. groups com. 1975-76, edn. com. 1976), Soc. Chem. Industry (hon. sec. 1959, exec. com. 1960-63), Assn. Research Dirs., Am. Inst. Chemists, Chamber Music Assn. N.Y. (honor scroll award). Club: Chemists (N.Y.C.). Home and Office: 3 Harcourt Rd Scarsdale NY 10583

BRUNK, HUGH DANIEL, educator; b. Manteca, Calif., Aug. 22, 1919; s. Hugh Dennis and Velma Lee (Benson) B.; m. Elizabeth Jean Young, Oct. 17, 1942; children—Bridget (Mrs. Derald Lee Glidden), Gretchen (Mrs. David Lee Armacost), Heidi (Mrs. David Wayne Wright). A.B., U. Calif. at Berkeley, 1940; M.S., Rice Inst., Houston, 1942, Ph.D., 1944. Instr., then asst. prof. Rice Inst., 1946-51; mathematician Sandia Corp., 1951-52; asso. prof., then prof. math. U. Mo., 1952-61, prof. stats., 1963-69; prof. math. U. Calif., Riverside, 1961-63; prof. stats. Oreg. State U., Corvallis, 1969—. Author: (with R.E. Barlow, D.J. Bartholomew, J.M. Bremner) Statistical Inference Under Order Conditions, 1972; Contbr. articles to profl. jours. Served with USNR, 1944-46. Fellow Inst. Math. Stats., Am. Statis. Assn.; mem. Internat. Statis. Inst., Am. Math. Soc., Math. Assn. Am., Royal Statis Soc., Danish Math. Soc., AAUP, SIAM, Psychometric Soc., Classification Soc., Sigma Xi. Home: Route 1 Box 303F Corvallis OR 97330

BRUNK, MAX EDWIN, emeritus marketing educator; b. Roswell, N.Mex., Sept. 12, 1914; s. Miller Michael and Susan Virginia (Sandy) B.; m. Letta Olga Reck, Mar. 30, 1941; children: Norma Marie Brunk Sullivan, Kathryn Sue Brunk Brennan. Student, Clemson Coll., 1934-35; B.S., U. Fla., 1938; M.S., Cornell U., 1941, Ph.D., 1947. Asst. agrl. economist U. Fla., 1941-44, assoc., 1944-45; assoc. prof. mktg. Cornell U., 1947-51, prof., 1951-82, prof. emeritus, 1983—; pres. Eastern Market Research Service, Inc., Ithaca, N.Y., 1954—; chmn. Beef Task Force for Council of Agrl. Sci. and Tech., Internat. Conf. Beef Producers, 1975—. Author: (with L.B. Darrah) Marketing Agricultural Products, 1954; Contbr. articles in field to profl. jours. Dir. Tompkins County Area Devel. Corp.; Award trustee, bd. govs. Livestock Merchandising Inst., 1979—. Recipient Research award Nat. Apple Inst., 1954, 64, 83, Found. for Floriculture, 1964; award for disting. service to Am. agr. Am. Farm Bur., 1965; Klinck lectr. Agrl. Inst. Can., 1975. Mem. Am. Farm Econs. Assn., Internat. Conf. Agrl. Economists, N.Y. Agrl. Soc. Republican. Presbyterian. Clubs: Cornell of N.Y., Statler, Tower. Home: 1315 Hanshaw Rd Ithaca NY 14850 Office: 307 Warren Hall Cornell University Ithaca NY 14853

BRUNK, WILLIAM EDWARD, astronomer; b. Cleve., Nov. 24, 1928; s. Edgar Rea and Mabel Mowbray (Pearson) B.; 1 dau., Anna Kathryn. B.S., Case Inst. Tech., 1952, M.S., 1954, Ph.D., 1963. Aero. research scientist Lewis Flight Propulsion Lab., NACA, Cleve., 1954-58; aerospace engr. Lewis Research Center, NASA, Cleve., 1958-64; staff scientist for planetary astronomy NASA Hdqrs., Washington, 1964-65, program chief planetary astronomy, 1965-77, discipline scientist planetary astronomy, 1977-82, chief planetary sci. br., 1982—. Fellow AAAS; mem. Am. Astron. Soc., Internat. Astron. Union; Mem. Sigma Xi. Home: 9348 Cherry Hill Rd College Park MD 20740 Office: Code EL-4 NASA Hdqrs Washington DC 20546

BRUNN, FREDERICK ALBERT, perfume and film prodn. co. exec.; b. Jersey City, July 19, 1936; s. Max Joseph and Elizabeth Maria (Mueller) B.; m. Marguerite Kirchmann, Aug. 22, 1959; children—Mark, Laura, Matthew. B.S. in Accounting, Seton Hall U., E. Orange, N.J.; M.B.A. in Fin, Fordham U. Accountant Colgate Palmolive Co., N.Y.C., 1959-61; adminstrv. asst. Lanvin-Charles of the Ritz, N.Y.C., 1961-69; asst. treas. Faberge, Inc., N.Y.C., 1969-72, treas., 1972—. Bd. dirs. Catholic Charities St. Catherine's, Blauvelt. Mem. Fin. Execs. Inst. (chmn. chpt. com.), Treasurer's Group, N.Y.C. Roman Catholic. Club: K.C. Home: River Vale NJ 07675 Office: Fabrege Inc 1345 Ave Americas New York NY 10105

BRUNNER, CLARENCE EUGENE, financial executive; b. Newark, Jan. 9, 1929; s. Clarence Frederick and Helen (Gramens) B. B.S., Rider Coll., Lawrenceville, N.J., 1950. C.P.A., N.J. Accountant Ernst &

Ernst, C.P.A.s, Newark, 1953-60; asst. treas., asst. comptroller N.J. Zinc Co., 1960-70; treas. UV Industries Inc., N.Y.C., 1970-80; dir. Richmond Eureka Mining Co. Served with AUS, 1951-53. Decorated Bronze Star. Mem. Am. Inst. C.P.A.s, N.J. Soc. C.P.A.s. Club: Masons (33 deg.). Home: 10 Biltmore Dr Green Brook NJ 08812 Office: 277 Park Ave 26th Floor New York NY 10022

BRUNNER, ENDRE KOPPERL, physician, hosp. adminstr.; b. Debrecen, Hungary, Dec. 4, 1900; came to U.S., 1920, naturalized, 1928; s. Lajos and Gabrielle (Kopperl) B.; m. Eleanor Carroll, July 10, 1937; children—Endrea, John Stephen. Student, U. Ala. Med. Sch., 1922-23; M.D., N.Y. U., 1926. Diplomate: Am. Bd. Obstetrics and Gynecology. Intern Tuxedo Park Meml., Bellevue hosps., N.Y.C., 1925-28; chief gynecology clin. N.Y. U. Coll. Medicine, 1929-48, instr., asst. prof. obstetrics and gynec., 1930-50; lectr. hygiene Washington Sq. Coll.; pvt. practice gynecology and obstetrics, N.Y.C., 1929-41; clin. dir. Halloran VA Hosp., N.Y.C., 1947-51; chief med. officer VA Center, Me., 1951-52; dir. profl. services VA Hosp., Boston, 1952-54, mgr., Manchester, N.H., 1954-55, Bronx, N.Y.C., 1956-57; adv. bd., vis. lectr. Columbia Sch. Pub. Health and Adminstrv. Medicine, 1956-65; hosp. adminstrn. adviser ICA, U.S. Operations Mission, Asunción, Paraguay, 1958-60; acting dir. Servicio Cooperativo Interamericano de Salud Publica, Paraguay, 1960-61; dir. S.C.I.S.P.; chief health div. U.S. AID, La Paz, Bolivia, 1961-63; pub. health adviser Africa Bur. AID, Dept. State, Washington, 1963-64; chief of staff U.S. VA Hosp., Providence, 1964-65; supt. Rutland Heights Hosp., Commonwealth Mass., 1965-76; dir. pub. health hosps., Commonwealth Mass., 1973; Hon. prof. medicine U. San Andres, La Paz, Bolivia.; Dir. human services and health care programs Worcester Consortium for Higher Edn., 1972-76; trustee Becker Jr. Coll., Worcester/Leicester, Mass., 1980—. Author: Dirección del Hospital Moderno, 1960; Contbr. articles to profl. jours. Served from lt. comdr. to comdr. M.C. USNR, 1941-47. Decorated Bronze Star, Purple Heart, Presdl. Unit citation. Fellow N.Y. Acad. Medicine, Am. Coll. Hosp. Adminstrs.; mem. A.M.A., Mass. Med. Assn., Worcester Dist. Med. Soc., Mass. Hosp. Assn. (Worcester area council), New Eng. Hosp. Assembly, Am., Mass. pub. health assns., Alpha Omega Alpha, Phi Beta Pi. Calvinist. Club: New York University. Address: Route 200 Thompson CT 06277

BRUNNER, JOHN WILSON, foreign language educator; b. Phila., Oct. 5, 1924; s. Harry Leroy and Viola (Batman) B.; m. Ingrid Arvide, July 2, 1953; children: Karin A., Kirstin E., Inge L., Erika E., Bjoern E. B.A., Ursinus Coll., 1949; Ph.D., Columbia U., 1957. Intelligence officer OSS-CIA, China, 1944-47; lectr. German Columbia U., 1950-52, 54-55; prof. German, head fgn. lang. dept. Muhlenberg Coll., 1954, 1955—. Author: The Natur-Geist Polarity in Hermann Hesse, 1968; contbr. articles to jours. Served with AUS, 1943-46. Mem. Am. Assn. Tchrs. German (exec. com. Central Pa. 1970-72), MLA, Linguistic Soc. Am., Am. Oriental Soc. Home: 328 N 26th St Allentown PA 18104

BRUNNER, RICHARD FRANCIS, shipyard executive; b. New Orleans, Sept. 9, 1926; s. Raymond Francis and Eunice (Laux) B.; m. Vivian Elizabeth Mayer, July 25, 1948; children: Dale Ann, Richard G., Scott R. B.S. in Mech. Engring., Tulane U., 1951. With Avondale Shipyards, Inc., New Orleans, 1945—, v.p. contract adminstrn, 1970-72, exec. v.p., 1972-77, sr. v.p., 1977—. Served with USNR, 1944-46. Mem. Soc. Naval Architects and Marine Engrs., Navy League, Tau Beta Pi. Roman Catholic. Office: Avondale Shipyards Inc PO Box 50280 New Orleans LA 70150

BRUNO, HAROLD ROBINSON, JR., journalist; b. Chgo., Oct. 25, 1928; s. Harold R. and Tallulah H. (Kandel) B.; m. Margaret E. Christian, Nov. 12, 1959; children—Harold, Daniel. B.S. in Journalism, U. Ill., 1950. Reporter Advt. Age, Chgo., 1950; sports editor DeKalb (Ill.) Chronicle, 1950-51; reporter City News Bur., Chgo., 1953-54, Chgo. American, 1954-60, Newsweek mag., 1960-63, bur. chief, Chgo., 1963-66, news editor, N.Y.C., 1966-71, chief polit. corr., Washington, 1971-78; polit. dir. ABC News, Washington, 1978—. Columnist: Firehouse mag; Contbr. articles to various publs. Bd. dirs. Nat. Council for Traditional Arts, Chevy Chase Fire Dept.; adv. bd. Presdl. Classroom for Young Ams., Duke U. Center Study Communications Policy; mem. Port Chester (N.Y.) Vol. Fire Dept. Served with U.S. Army, 1951-53. Fulbright scholar, 1956-57. Mem. White House Corrs. Assn., Chgo. Newspaper Reporters Assn., AFTRA, Friendship Fire Assn., U. Ill. Alumni Assn. (dir.), Bethesda-Chevy Chase Rescue Squad Alumni, Sigma Delta Chi, Tau Delta Phi. Jewish. Office: 1717 De Sales St NW Washington DC 20036

BRUNO, VINCENT JOHN, art history educator; b. N.Y.C., Feb. 28, 1926; s. Anthony James and Inez (D'Antoni) B. B.A., Kenyon Coll., 1951; M.A., Columbia U., 1965, Ph.D., 1969; cert. in painting, Academie Julian, Paris, 1949. Cultural affairs officer Fgn. Service, Dept. State and USIA, 1951-55; instr. Wellesley Coll., 1964-65, Bennett Coll., 1958-60; Colgate U., 1957-58; asso. prof. C.W. Post Coll., L.I. U., 1965-66; prof., chmn. dept. art and art history SUNY, Binghamton, 1966-76; prof. art history and archaeology U. Tex., Arlington, 1976—, chmn. dept. art, 1976—; Research Found. of SUNY grantee, Nat. Endowment for Humanities grantee for archaeol. explorations at Cosa, 1969-74; Sam and Ayala Zachs prof. art history Hebrew U., Jerusalem, 1978; archaeol. explorations at Tuscan Archipelago under auspices of Am. Acad. in Rome; dir. Rockland Found. for Arts, Rockland County, N.Y., 1956-57. Author: The Parthenon, 1974, Form and Color in Greek Painting, 1977; contbr. articles to profl. jours. Served with USAAF, 1944-45. Guggenheim Found. fellow, 1978; Am. Council Learned Socs. grantee, 1980; Am. Philos. Soc. grantee, 1982. Mem. Archaeol. Inst. Am., Coll. Art Assn. Office: Box 19089 Dept Art U Tex at Arlington Arlington TX 76019

BRUNS, HENRY GERARD, former railway executive; b. N.Y.C., Mar. 14, 1904; s. August and Anne (Grieme) B.; m. Mildred Scott, June 30, 1956; children: Priscilla Bruns Glander, Elizabeth. Grad., Speyer Sch., N.Y.C., 1918. Sr. partner H.G. Bruns & Co., N.Y.C., 1939-52, T.L. Watson & Co., 1952-69; chmn. bd. Norfolk So. Ry. Co., 1956-77, now dir. Clubs: Downtown Athletic (N.Y.C.); Lake Sunapee Country. Home: PO Box 1114 New London NH 03257

BRUNS, NICOLAUS, JR., fertilizer executive, lawyer; b. N.Y.C., Sept. 27, 1926; s. Nicolaus and Emily Marie (Hawkins) B.; m. Joan-Carol Littleton, Aug. 29, 1959; children: Nicolaus III, Gregory. B.S., U. Miami, Fla., 1947; J.D., Georgetown U., 1949, LL.M., 1952. Bar: D.C. 1950, ILL. 1965, U.S. Supreme Ct. 1965, N.Y. 1980. Spl. asst. U.S. Navy Dept., Washington, 1950-57; sr. trial atty. U.S. Dept. Justice, Washington, 1957-65; sr. atty. Internat. Minerals and Chem. Corp., Skokie, Ill., 1965-70, asst. gen. counsel, 1970-74, gen. counsel ops., 1974-79, v.p., sec., assoc. gen. counsel, Northbrook, Ill., 1979—; adj. prof. Lake Forest Sch. Mgmt., Ill., 1981—, Loyola U., Chicago, 1980-81; antitrust policy counsel U.S. C. of C., Washington, 1981—. Treas. and adminstrv. asst. to v.p. Boy Scouts Am., N.E. Ill. area, 1967, 80; pres. Fund for Perceptually Handicapped, Skokie, Ill., 1976, Concerned Help in Learning Devel., Highland Park, Ill., 1974-75. Served with U.S. Army, 1945-46. Mem. ABA (antitrust and securities com.), Chgo. Bar Assn., Fed. Bar Assn., Am. Soc. Corp. Secs. (v.p. midwest region 1983). Republican. Roman Catholic. Club: Michigan Shores (Wilmette, Ill.). Lodge: KC (Washington council) (council). Home: 1335 Chestnut Ave Wilmette IL 60091 Office: Internat Minerals and Chem Corp 2315 Sanders Rd Northbrook IL 60062

BRUNS, WILLIAM JOHN, JR., business administrator educator; b. Pasadena, Calif., July 13, 1935; s. William John and Carol Jane (Stalder) B.; m. Barbara Jean Dodge, Apr. 12, 1957 (div. 1980); children: Robert William, John Richard, David James, Michael Alan.; m. Sharon Merle McKinnon, July 16, 1982. B.A., U. Redlands, Calif., 1957, D.B.A. (hon.), 1976; M.B.A., Harvard U., 1959; Ph.D., U. Calif. at Berkeley, 1963. Asst. prof. econs., then asst. prof. econs. and indsl. adminstrn. Yale U., 1962-66; asso. prof., then prof. accounting U. Wash., 1966-72; prof. bus. adminstrn. Harvard, 1972—; cons. to industry. Author: Accounting for Decisions: A Business Game, 1966, Accounting and Its Behavioral Implications, 1969, Introduction to Accounting: Economic Measurement for Decisions, 1971, A Primer on Replacement Cost Accounting, 1976, Cases in Management Accounting, 1981; Book rev. editor: Accounting Rev, 1967-69; mem. editorial bd., 1969-72, 76-78; advisory editor: Addison-Wesley Pub. Co; mem. editorial bd.: Accounting, Orgns., and Soc, 1975-79. Mem. Quinnipiac council Boy Scouts Am., 1964-66; Chief Seattle council, 1966-72, Algonquin council, 1972-81. Danforth grad. fellow, 1957-62; Danforth asso., 1967—. Mem. Am. Acctg. Assn., Am. Econ. Assn., Am. Inst. Decision Scis. Home: 46 Garden Rd Wellesley MA 02181 Office: Harvard Bus Sch Soldiers Field Boston MA 02163

BRUNT, HARRY HERMAN, JR., psychiatrist; b. Phila., Jan. 22, 1921; s. Harry Herman and Ann (Zurbrugg) B.; m. Zoe M. Bower, July 2, 1944; children: Marianne Brunt Tallman, Margaret B. Griffin, Jane. B.S. with honors, Va. Poly. Inst., 1942; M.D., U. Pa., 1945. Diplomate: Am. Bd. Psychiatry and Neurology. Intern, Lankenau Hosp., 1946; resident psychiatry Trenton (N.J.) State Hosp., VA Hosp., Coatesville, 1948-52; practice medicine specializing in psychiatry, Trenton, 1952, Princeton, N.J., 1952-54, Hammonton, N.J., 1954-69, Long Branch, N.J., 1969—; acting asst. clin. dir. Trenton State Hosp., 1952; asst. supt. N.J. Neuropsychiat. Inst. Princeton, 1952-54; med. dir. Ancora State Hosp., 1954-69; dir. dept. psychiatry Monmouth Med. Center and Pollak Clinic, Long Branch, 1969-74; pvt. practice, 1974—; assoc. prof. psychiatry Jefferson Med. Coll., 1952-66; instr. psychiatry U. Pa., 1953-65; adj. asso. prof. psychiatry Temple Med. Sch., 1968-70; prof. psychiatry Hahneman Med. Coll., 1970-74; clin. prof. psychiatry Rutgers Med. Sch., New Brunswick, N.J., 1971. Cons. bur. family services Dept. Health, Edn. and Welfare Dept., 1960-68. Served to capt. M.C. AUS, 1946-48. Fellow ACP, Am. Psychiat. Assn. (chmn. future planning com. Assembly Dist. Brs., mem. policy com. area III 1968, recorder 1969, speaker 1971-72, trustee 1972-73, 74—, life fellow), AAAS, Am. Geriatric Soc., Am. Coll. Psychiatrists (founding fellow); mem. AMA, Monmouth County Med. Soc. (exec. com.), N.J. Neuropsychiat. Assn. (past pres.), Med. Soc. N.J. (chmn. council mental health), Alpha Kappa Kappa, Phi Kappa Phi. Club: Haven Beach. Home: 3404 W Hurley Pond Rd Wall NJ 07719 Office: Brinley Rd Hwy 38 Wall NJ 07719 *I have obtained a great deal of satisfaction from helping others throughout my life but little of this would have been possible without my family's backing and sacrifice. The family is still what makes life worth living.*

BRUNTON, PAUL EDWARD, diversified industry executive; b. Decatur, Ind., July 8, 1922; s. John Harrison and Jessie (Holthouse) B.; m. Margaret Alice Rice, July 10, 1945; children—Patricia Ann, David John, Thomas Edward, Mary Josephine, Elizabeth Alice, Daniel William. B.S. in Fin, St. Joseph's Coll., 1944. Staff accountant Haskins & Sells (C.P.A.'s), Chgo. and Mpls., 1946-48; sr. accountant Reinking Kein & Co. (C.P.A.'s), Ft. Wayne, Ind., 1948-53; controller, sec. Ft. Wayne Builders Supply Co., 1953-54; with ITT, 1954-61; controller Farnsworth Electronics, 1954-57, asst. controller, 1958-61, dir. fin. and adminstrn., 1961; with Litton Industries, Inc., 1961-75, v.p. adminstrn., Pascagoula, Miss., 1966, v.p. fin., bus. equipment group, 1967, corp. controller, Beverly Hills, Calif., 1967-70, pres., Milw., 1970-72, v.p. def. and marine group, Los Angeles, 1972-73, v.p. bus. equipment group, 1973-75; sr. v.p. fin., chief fin. officer Rohr Industries, Inc., Chula Vista, Calif., 1976—. Served to lt. (j.g.) USNR, World War II. Mem. Am. Inst. C.P.A.'s, Calif. Soc. C.P.A.'s. Home: 1714 Monterey Ave Coronado CA 92118 Office: Foot of H St Chula Vista CA 92012

BRUSH, ALLEN SHARPE, former financing company executive; b. Bklyn., June 10, 1913; s. W. Elwood and Harriet E. (Hubbs) B.; m. Jean F. Henke, Nov. 1, 1941; children: David A., Donald H., Robert F. A.B., Dartmouth Coll., 1935, M.C.S., 1936. Mem. treas.'s staff Gen. Motors Corp., 1936-50, dir. gen. accounting sect., 1950-55; dir. financing and operations analysis Gen. Motors Acceptance Corp., N.Y.C., 1955-56, treas., 1956-60, v.p., 1960-74, exec. v.p., 1974-78, dir., 1960-78. Served to capt. AUS, 1942-46. Home: South Cove PO Box 1370 New London CT 03257

BRUSH, CAREY WENTWORTH, college administrator, history educator; b. Tisbury, Mass., Sept. 25, 1920; s. Bartlett W.W. and Zelda (Goodwin) B.; m. Margaret Eloise Marks, Apr. 8, 1946; children: Bartlett M., Elizabeth W. B.S., State Tchrs. Coll., Bridgewater, Mass., 1941; M.A., Columbia, 1949, Ph.D., 1961. Tchr. Gallup (N.Mex.) Pub. Schs., 1949-50; instr. State Tchrs. Coll., Oneonta, N.Y., 1951; chmn. social sci. dept. Cortland (N.Y.) Pub. Schs., 1951-57; prof. history, v.p. acad. affairs State U. Coll. at Oneonta, 1958—; Mem. Bd. Edn., Oneonta, 1968-69. Author: In Honor and Good Faith: A History of the State University College at Oneonta, New York, 1965. Served with USAAF, 1942-46. Tchrs. Coll. fellow, 1957-58. Mem. Am. Hist. Assn., Orgn. Am. Historians, Middle States Assn. Colls. and Secondary Schs. (mem. accreditation team), Nat. Council Accreditation Tchr. Edn. (mem. accreditation team). Home: Greystone 20 Fair St Cooperstown NY 13326

BRUSH, CHARLES FRANCIS, anthropologist; b. Cleve., Apr. 3, 1923; s. Charles Francis and Dorothy Adams (Hamilton) B.; m. Ellen Sparry, July 25, 1958; children: Barbara Brush Wright, Karen Alexandra, Charles Francis. B.A., Yale U., 1947, M.A., 1948; Ph.D., Columbia U., 1969. Ind. researcher in anthropology, N.Y.C., 1961—; dir. Brush Wellman Inc. Sec.-treas. Internat. Planned Parenthood Fedn. Western Hemisphere Region, 1968-74; bd. dirs. Brush Found., Cleve., 1969—; chmn. Yale U. Com. for Peabody Museum, 1983; bd. dirs. Sierra Club Found., 1981—. Fellow AAAS, Am. Anthropol. Assn., Am. Geog. Soc. (dir. 1969—), Explorers Club (dir. 1971, pres. 1978-80); mem. Soc. Am. Archeology., Am. Scandinavian Soc. (pres 1983). Clubs: Union, Yale, N.Y. Athletic., Century Assn. Excavated earliest ceramics known in Mexico, 1961, first evidence of deliberate alloying of bronze in Mexico, 1961. Home: 42 Ram Island Rd Shelter Island NY 11964

BRUSH, LUCIEN MUNSON, JR., hydrologist, educator; b. Pitts., Dec. 10, 1929; s. Lucien Munson and Elizabeth Sara (Noyes) B.; m. Grace Somers, Sept. 7, 1953; children: Lucien Noyes, George Somers, John Matthew. B.S. in Engring., Princeton U., 1952; Ph.D., Harvard U., 1956. Hydrologist, U.S. Geol. Survey, Washington, 1956-58; asst. prof., then asso. prof. hydraulics U. Iowa, 1958-63; asso. prof. Princeton U., 1963-69; prof. hydrology Johns Hopkins U., Balt., 1969—, assoc. dean undergrad. and grad. studies, 1982—; cons. to govt. and industry. Author articles in field. Grantee NSF, Office Water Resources. Mem. ASCE, AAAS, Internat. Assn. Hydraulic Research, Internat. Assn. Hydrological Scis., Engring. Soc. Balt., Am. Geophys. Union, Sigma Xi. Clubs: Green Spring Valley Hunt, Johns Hopkins. Home: 109 Elmhurst Rd Baltimore MD 21210 Office: Merryman Hall Johns Hopkins Univ Baltimore MD 21218

BRUSHWOOD, JOHN STUBBS, educator; b. Glenns, Va., Jan. 23, 1920; s. John Benson and Evelyn (Stubbs) B.; m. Carolyn Darrach Norton, May 19, 1945; children: David Benson, Paul Darrach. B.A., Randolph-Macon Coll., 1940, Litt.D. (hon.), 1981; M.A., U. Va., 1942; Ph.D., Columbia, 1950. Instr. Romance langs. Va. Poly. Inst., 1942-44; from instr. to prof. Spanish U. Mo. at Columbia, 1946-67; Roy A. Roberts prof. Latin Am. lit. U. Kans., 1967—; reviewer Latin Am. books Kansas City Star, 1967-79; Fulbright lectr. Colombia, 1974. Author: The Romantic Novel in Mexico, 1954, (with Jose Rojas Garciduenas) Breve historia de la novela mexicana, 1959, Mexico in Its Novel, 1966, Spanish edit., 1974, Enrique Gonzalez Martinez, 1969, Los ricos en la prosa mexicana, 1970, The Spanish American Novel: A Twentieth Century Survey, 1975, Genteel Barbarism: New Readings of Nineteenth-Century Latin American Novels; also articles.; Translator: (with Carolyn Brushwood) The Precipice (by Sergio Galindo), 1969, Don Goyo (by D. Aguilera-Malta), 1981. Fellow Fund Advancement Edn., 1951-52; grantee Am. Philos. Soc., 1957, Am. Council Learned Socs., 1961, Social Sci. Research Council, 1971, Nat. Endowment for Humanities, 1976; scholar-in-residence Bellagio Study and Conf. Center, 1978; Balfour Jeffrey award for research in the humanities and social scis. Mem. MLA (pres. 1962-63, chmn. Spanish 7 1966, Spanish 6, 1972), Inst. Internacional de Literatura Iberomericana, Am. Assn. Tchrs. Spanish and Portuguese, Am. Assn. U. Profs. Home: 2813 Maine Ct Lawrence KS 66044

BRUSILOW, ANSHEL, conductor; b. Phila., Aug. 14, 1928; s. Leon and Dora (Epstein) B.; m. Marilyn Rae Dow, Dec. 23, 1951; children: David, Jennie, Melinda. Grad., Curtis Inst. Music, 1943; artist's diploma, Phila. Mus. Acad., 1947. Concertmaster, asst. condr. New Orleans Symphony, 1954-55; asso. concertmaster Cleve. Orch., 1955-59; concertmaster Phila. Orch., 1959-66; founder, condr. Phila. Chamber Orch., 1961-65, Chamber Symphony Phila., 1966-68; exec. dir., condr. Dallas Symphony Orch., 1970-73; prof. North Tex. State U., 1973-82; dir. orch. activities So. Meth. U., Dallas, 1982—. Host: TV program Portraits in Music, Sta. WRCV, 1961-63. Bd. dirs. Ednl. TV Council; adjudicator Pres. of U.S. Com. for Scholarship Awards, 1979-80. Named Outstanding Young Man of Year Phila. C. of C., 1963. Home: 4545 Laren Ln Dallas TX 75234

BRUSILOW, SAUL, pediatrics educator; b. Bklyn., June 7, 1927; s. Samuel Michael and Marie (Arenson) B.; m. Sallie Evans (dec.); children: William, Susan, Alexander (dec.). A.B., Princeton U., 1950; M.D., Yale U., 1954. Diplomate: Am. Bd. Pediatrics, Am. Bd. Pediatric Nephrology. Asst. resident Johns Hopkins U., Balt., 1956-57, research fellow, 1957-59, instr., 1959-60, asst. prof., 1960-64, assoc. prof., 1964-74, prof., 1974—. Contbr. articles on pediatrics to profl. jours.; patentee in field; author: Inborn Errors of Metabolism. Served with USNR, 1945-46. Grantee NIH, 1959—. Mem. Soc. Pediatric Research, Am. Fedn. Clin. Research, Am. Physiol. Soc., Am. Pediatric Soc. Democrat. Jewish. Home: 4804 Keswick Rd Baltimore MD 21210 Office: Johns Hopkins U. Sch. Medicine 600 N Wolfe St Baltimore MD 21205

BRUSSEL-SMITH, BERNARD, artist; b. N.Y.C., Mar. 1, 1914; s. Raymond and Belle (Epstein) B.-S.; m. Mildred Cornfeld, Sept. 25, 1937; 1 son, Peter. Student, Penn Acad. Fine Arts, 1931-36. Art dir. Geyer Publs., 1939-42; head advt. dept. Chance-Voight Aircraft Co., 1942-44; art dir. Noyes & Sproul, 1944-45; free lance wood engraver, 1945—; instr. Cooper Union, Bklyn. Mus., Phila. Mus. Sch. Art, N.A.D., Coll. City N.Y. Prints included in collections, Library of Congress, Carnegie Inst., N.Y. Pub. Library, U. Ill., Phila. Mus., Smithsonian Instn., Boymans Mus., Rotterdam, Nat. Collection, Bklyn. Mus. Recipient Frank Hartley Anderson award, 1948, Am. Artist Group award, 1948, John Taylor Arms Meml. prize, 1970, Samuel Morse award, 1976, Cannon award, 1981; asso. Nat. Acad., 1952. Clubs: Art Directors, Type Directors, Dutch Treat. Home: 328 Cherry St Bedford Hills NY 10507

BRUST, LEO T., bishop; b. St. Francis, Wis., Jan. 7, 1916. Student, St. Francis Sem., Wis., Canisianum, Austria, Cath. U., Washington. Ordained priest Roman Catholic Ch., 1942; ordained titular bishop of Sueli and aux. bishop, Milw., 1969—. Office: 3501 S Lake Dr Milwaukee WI 53207 *

BRUST, PAUL CHRISTOPHER, architect; b. Milw., July 18, 1905; s. Peter J. and Olga (Greulich) B.; m. Mary McGinn, May 18, 1936 (dec. 1960); children: Barbara, Peter, Charlotte, Daniel, Richard, William, Janet, Marian; m. Ruth Gaunt, Oct. 22, 1962. Student, Marquette U., 1924-25; B.S. in Architecture, U. Notre Dame, 1928; postgrad., Columbia, 1928-29. With Fed. Architect's Office, Treasury Dept., 1933-35, FHA, 1935-36, Office of Peter Brust, 1936-46; partner firm Brust & Brust, Milw., 1946-73, Brust-Zimmermann, Inc., 1973-77; ret., 1978; Chmn. Wis. Bd. Examiners Architects, 1971. Prin. works include hosps., schs., instl. bldgs., comml. projects, also bldgs. for city, county, state and fed. govt. Mem. St. Jude Parish Bd. Edn., 1966-69; chmn. Milw. County Archdiocesan Charity Dr., 1972; Bd. dirs. Cath. Information Center. Milw., 1962—, pres., 1975-79. Recipient Nat. Sch. of Month award for Alexander Hamilton High Sch., Milw. Mem. AIA Wis. Architects Assn., Friends of Art of Milw. Art Center, St. Vincent de Paul Soc., Holy Name Soc. (past pres.), Archdiocesan Council Cath. Men (past pres.), Milw. Assn. Commerce. Clubs: K.C. (past grand knight, 4 deg.); Milwaukee Athletic, Serra (Milw.); Lake Beulah (Wis.) Yacht (past commodore). Home: 429 Horseshoe Ln Mukwonago WI 53149

BRUSTEIN, LAWRENCE, financial executive; b. Liberty, N.Y., Oct. 11, 1936; s. Leo and Rae (Smoller) B.; m. Ellen Gloria Sheppard, June 20, 1965; children: Jacqueline, Michael. B.S., U. Buffalo, 1958. C.P.A. With Irving Handel & Co., C.P.A.s, N.Y.C., 1959-62, Robert Simons & Co., C.P.A.s, 1962-64, E & L Distbrs., Inc., 1964-66, Barney's, N.Y.C., 1966-68; controller Holly Stores div. K-Mart, North Bergen, N.J., 1968-70; v.p., treas. Marcade, Jersey City, 1970—. Exec. v.p. Reform Temple of East Brunswick, 1977—. Mem. Am. Inst. C.P.A.s, N.Y. State Soc. C.P.A.s. Home: 1 Jamestown Ct East Brunswick NJ 08116 Office: 21 Caven Point Ave Jersey City NJ 07305

BRUSTEIN, ROBERT SANFORD, English language educator, theatre director, author; b. N.Y.C., Apr. 21, 1927; s. Max and Blanche (Haft) B.; m. Norma Ofstrock, Mar. 25, 1962 (dec.); children: Phillip Cates (stepson), Daniel Anton. B.A., Amherst Coll., 1948, Litt.D.; postgrad., Yale Drama Sch., 1948-49, U. Nottingham, Eng., 1953-55; M.A., Columbia U., 1950, Ph.D., 1957; Litt.D., Lawrence U.; LL.D., Beloit Coll., 1975; Arts D., Bard Coll., 1981; L.H.D., Emory U., 1983. Instr. English Cornell U., 1955-56; instr. drama Vassar Coll., 1956-57; faculty Columbia, 1957-66, prof. English and comparative lit., 1965-66; prof. English Yale U., New Haven, dean; founder, artistic dir. Yale Repertory Theatre, 1966-79; dir. Loeb Drama Centre; also founder, artistic dir. Am. Repertory Theatre Co.; prof. English Harvard U., 1979—; drama critic New Republic, 1959-67, 78—, contbg. editor, 1959—; guest theatre critic London Observer, 1972-73; contbr. to N.Y. Times, 1972—; panel mem. Nat. Endowment for Arts, 1969-72, 81—. Author: The Theatre of Revolt: Studies in the Modern Drama, 1964, Seasons of Discontent: Dramatic Opinions 1959-65, 1965, The Third Theatre, 1969, Revolution as Theatre: Notes on the New Radical Style, 1971, The Culture Watch, 1975, Critical Moments, 1980, Making Scenes, 1981; Contbr. numerous articles to profl. jours.; Editor: The Plays and Prose of Strindberg, 1964. Trustee Sarah

Lawrence Coll., 1973-77. Served with U.S. Mcht. Marine, 1945-47. Recipient George Jean Nathan award dramatic criticism, 1962, George Polk Meml. award outstanding criticism, 1965, Eliot Morton award, 1984, award in criticism Jersey City Jour., 1967; Fulbright fellow, 1953-55; Guggenheim fellow, 1961-62; Ford Found. fellow, 1964-65. Home: Cambridge MA Office: Loeb Drama Center Cambridge MA 02138

BRUTLAG, RODNEY SHELDON, association executive; b. Perham, Minn., Feb. 18, 1938; s. Herbert H. and Elsie V. (Luhning) B.; m. Teresa Townsend, Nov. 26, 1977; children by previous marriage: Constance, Jacqueline, Craig, Michael, Sheldon, Julienne. B.S. in Distributive Edn, U. Minn., 1961; postgrad., Roosevelt U., Chgo., 1975-76. Tchr., vocat. adminstr., dir. adult edn. Fairmont (Minn.) Public Schs., 1961-64; ednl. dir., asso. dir. Hosp. Fin. Mgmt. Assn., Chgo., 1964-69; v.p. Bank Mktg. Assn., 1969-76; exec. dir. In-Plant Printing Mgmt. Assn., Chgo., 1976-77, Am. Dental Hygienists Assn., 1977-81; exec. v.p., chief staff officer Soc. Real Estate Appraisers, Chgo., 1981—; speaker in field. Chmn. Lombard (Ill.) Drug Abuse Council, 1971-72. Recipient various Jaycee awards. Mem. Am. Soc. Assn. Execs., Assn. Econs. Council, Chgo. Soc. Assn. Execs. (dir.), World Future Soc., Nat. Execs. Club. Republican. Home: 1212 N Lake Shore Dr Chicago IL 60610 Office: 645 N Michigan Ave Chicago IL 60611

BRUTON, HENRY JACKSON, educator, economist; b. Dallas, Aug. 30, 1921; s. Guss and Mary (Clark) B.; m. Mary Frances Barnes, Apr. 21, 1959. A.B., U. Tex., 1943; Ph.D., Harvard, 1952. Prof. econs. Yale, 1952-58; prof. econs. Williams Coll., Williamstown, Mass., 1962—; econ. cons. in Iran, 1958-60, Pakistan, 1960-61, Malaysia, 1970-71, Egypt, 1975-76; vis. prof. econs. U. Bombay, 1961-62, U. Chile, 1965-66. Author: Inflation in a Growing Economy, 1963, Principles of Development Economics, 1965, Productividad en America Latina, 1968; Contbr. articles profl. jours. Served with AUS, 1943-46; ETO. Home: 300 Syndicate Rd Williamstown MA 01267

BRUTON, JAMES DEWITT, JR., former judge; b. Magazine, Ark., Feb. 2, 1908; s. James David and Pattie Lee (Bruton) B.; m. Quintilla Geer, June 11, 1932. J.D., U. Fla., 1931. Bar: Fla. 1931. Practiced law, Plant City, 1931-61, asst. criminal court solicitor, Tampa, 1934-37; elected to Fla. Ho. of Reps., 1935-36; municipal judge, Plant City, 1937-57, corp. and civil lawyer, 1931-61, probate judge, Tampa, 1961-64; circuit judge 13th Jud. Circuit Fla., 1964-75; founder, owner Bruton's Audubon Acres Bird Sanctuary (donated to U. Fla. Law Coll.), Plant City, 1952—; dir. Tampa Abstract and Title Ins. Co., Hillsboro Bank, Plant City, Fla. Bd. dirs. Children's Home, Tampa, 1947-67, Tampa Mental Health Assn., 1962-68, Inter-Profl. Family Council, Inc., Tampa chpt. ARC, 1967-68; bd. dirs., life mem. Tampa Humane Soc.; mem. Fla. State Bd. Law Examiners, 1950-54; chmn. bd. editors Fla. Bar Jour., 1950-52. Recipient Trustee's award U. Fla. Law Coll. Fellow Am. Coll. Probate Counsel (jud. fellow 1961), Am. Bar Found. (life fellow 1961); mem. Fla. Mcpl. Judges Assn. (pres. 1956-57), C. of C. (dir.), Plant City Civic Music Assn. (pres. 1949), Tampa Symphony Soc. (dir. 1952), Jr. C. of C. (pres. 1940), Fla. County Judges Assn. (v.p. 1962), U. Fla. Alumni Assn. (v.p. 1948), ABA (ho. of dels. 1951-58), Fla. Bar Assn. (state chmn. com. on integration, gov. 1949-50, chmn. com. Am. citizenship 1952-53, chmn. com. on co-operation with Am. Bar Assn. 1956-59, chmn. com. on world peace through law 1959-63), Tampa Bar Assn., Fla. Bar (del. to Am. Bar Assn. Conf. on World Peace 1959, chmn. com. on memls. 1962-72), Seldon Soc. London, Am. Judicature Soc. (dir. 1953-58), Audubon Soc. (life), Am. Ornithologists Union (life), Fla. Cattle Assn., Fla. Hist. Soc. (life, dir. 1967-68), East Hillsborough County Hist. Soc. (life patron), SAR, Blue Key, Chi Phi. Democrat. Methodist. Clubs: Elk; Kiwanian (past lt. gov.; bd. dirs. Plant City club), Tampa Executives (pres. 1951-52), Tampa Executives (dir. 1948-55), Tampa Audubon, University (Tampa). Home: 812 Mahoney St Plant City FL 33566 *Any success I have achieved is due to following the policy of hard work and honesty, spending less than I have earned, and having appreciation for and devotion to my parents.*

BRUTON, LEONARD THOMAS, b. London, Sept. 9, 1942; s. Archibald Stanley and Marie Florence B.; m. Avis Makin, Aug. 22, 1964; children: Alexander, Michelle, Nicole, Adrian. B.Sc., U. London, 1964; M. Eng., Carleton U., Ottawa, Ont., Can., 1967; Ph.D., U. Newcastle-Upon-Tyne, Eng., 1970. Registered profl. engr., B.C. Mem. sci. staf circuit design Bell No. Research, Ltd., Ottawa, Ont., Can., 1964-67; lectr. elec. engring. U. Newcastle-Upon-Tyne, Eng., 1967-70; asst. prof., then assoc. prof. and prof. elec. engring. U. Calgary, Alta., Can., 1979-83; dean Faculty Engring., U. Victoria, B.C., Canada, 1983—; cons. signal processing and microelectronics. Author: RC-Active Filters: Theory and Design, 1980. Recipient teaching award Pacific N.W. sect. Am. Soc. Edn., 1977. Fellow IEEE; mem. Assn. Profl. Engrs., Geologists and Geophysicists Alta. Home: 4062 Jason Pl Victoria BC Canada V8N 4T6 Office: Faculty Engring Univ Victory PO Box 1700 Victoria BC Canada V8W 2Y2

BRUTON, PAUL WESLEY, educator; b. Woodland, Calif., Aug. 1, 1903; s. Philip and Nancy (Gilstrap) B.; m. Margaret Perry, Sept. 2, 1931; children—Margaret Jane (Mrs. Duane R. Batista), David, Laura (Mrs. L. Wallace Clausen). A.B., U. Calif., 1929, LL.B., 1929; J.S.D., Yale, 1930; M.A. (hon.), U. Pa., 1971. Bar: Calif. bar 1930, Pa. bar 1943, Supreme Ct. U.S 1935. Sterling fellow law Yale, 1929-30, instr. law, 1930-32; asso. prof. law Duke, 1932-35; atty., office chief counsel Bur. Internal Revenue, Washington, 1935-37; vis. asso. prof. law U. Pa., Phila., 1937-38, asso. prof., 1938-39, prof., 1939—, acting dean, 1951-52, Ferdinand Wakeman Hubbell prof. law, 1964-69, Algernon Sidney Biddle prof. law, 1969-74, emeritus, 1974—; asso. firm Ballard, Spahr, Andrews & Ingersoll, Phila., 1943-44; tax cons. law firm MacCoy, Evans & Lewis, Phila., 1953-62; Vis. prof. Stanford, 1941, 52, U. Tex., 1947, McGill U., 1961; spl. asst., gen. counsel A.A.A., 1934; chief price atty. Phila. region OPA, 1942-43; Chmn. Phila. Tax Rev. Bd., 1953-59; mem. Task Force on Revision Pa. Tax Law. Editor: Cases on Taxation, 1941, 2d edit., 1949, Cases on Federal Taxation, 1950, (with R.J. Bradley, 1953, 55) Cases on Federal Taxation, (with Edward L. Barrett and John Honnold) Cases and Materials on Constitutional Law, 1959, 4th edit., 1973. Mem. Juristic Soc. Phila., Phi Beta Kappa, Pi Sigma Alpha, Delta Sigma Rho, Order of Coif. Democrat. Mem. Soc. of Friends. Clubs: Franklin Inn, Penn Faculty. Home: Foulkeways N-11 Gwynedd PA 19436 Office: 3400 Chestnut St Philadelphia PA 19104

BRUTON, THOMAS BARMORE, air force officer; b. Weslaco, Tex., Aug. 30, 1930; s. Lausane Thomas and Helen Gillis (Gowgill) B.; m. Peggy Ann Rose, June 26, 1965; children: Andrew, Daniel. B.S. in Bus., U. Colo., 1954, J.D., 1954; M.B.A., George Washington U., 1966; M.Polit. Sci., Auburn U., 1971; grad. Air Command and Staff Coll., 1965, 1971. Bar: Colo. 1954, U.S. Dist. Ct. Colo. 1954, U.S. Ct. Mil. Appeals 1955, U.S. Ct. Mil. Appeals 1955. Commd. 2d lt. U.S. Air Force, 1965, maj. gen., 1980; asst. staff judge adv. McGuire AFB, N.J., 1956, Otis AFB, Mass., 1956, Selfridge AFB, Mich., 1956; performed legal duties Wheelus AB, Libya, 1956-57; gen. cts. martial prosecutor Wiesbaden AB, Germany, 1957-59; Gen. cts. martial prosecutor Hdqrs. 17th AF (Romstein AB), Germany, 1959-60; instr., then asst. prof. law Air Force Acad., Colo., 1960-64; with office Staff Judge Adv., Tan Son Nhut AB, Vietnam, 1965-66; mem., then chief litigation div. Office Judge Adv. Gen. Hdqrs., USAF, 1966-70; dep. staff judge adv. Mil. Airlift Command, Scott AFB, Ill., 1971-73; dep. staff judge adv., then staff judge adv. Hdqrs, USAFin Europe, Romstein AB, 1973-77; staff judge adv. Strategic Air Command, Offutt AFB, Nebr., 1978-80; judge adv. gen. Hdqrs. USAF, Washington, 1980—. Decorated Legion of Merit with 2 oak leaf cluster, Bronze Star medal; W Meritorious Service medal; w. Air Force Commendation medal with oak leaf cluster. Office: Dept of Air Force Judge Advocate General The Pentagon Washington DC 20330

BRUTUS, DENNIS VINCENT, educator; b. Harare, Zimbabwe, Nov. 28, 1924; came to U.S., 1971; s. Francis Henry and Margaret Winifred (Bloemetjie) B.; m. May Jaggers, May 14, 1950; children: Jacinta, Marc, Julian, Antony, Justina, Cornelia, Gregory, Paula. B.A. in English with distinction, Ft. Hare U., S. Africa, 1947, Coll. Ed. Diploma, 1946; postgrad. in law, Witwaterstrand U., Johannesburg, S. Africa, 1963-64; L.H.D. (hon.), Worcester State Coll., (Mass.), 1982. Tchr. public high schs., Port Elizabeth, 1948-61, journalist, 1960-61; dir. World Campaign for Release of S. African Polit. Prisoners, London and; mem. staff Internat. Def. and Aid Fund, London, 1966-71; prof. English Northwestern U., Evanston, Ill., 1971—; vis. prof. English U. Denver, 1970; vis. prof. English, and African and Afro-Am. Studies Research Center U. Tex., Austin, 1974-75; vis. prof. African and African-Am. studies Dartmouth Coll., 1983. Author: poetry A Simple Lust, 1972, Strains, 1975, China Poems, 1975, Stubborn Hope, 1978, Salutes and Censures, 1982; contbr. poems to lit. jours.; editorial bd.: Africa Today, 1976—; guest editor: The Gar, 1978. Sec. S. African Sports Assn., 1959—; pres. S. African Non-Racial Olympic Com., 1963—; chmn. Internat. Campaign Against Racism in Sport, 1972—; chmn. adv. bd. ARENA: The Inst. for Study of Sport and Social Analysis, U.S., 1975—; bd. dirs. Black Arts Celebration, Chgo., 1975—; chmn. Internat. Adv. Commn. to End Apartheid Sport, 1975—; mem. steering com. Midwest Coalition for Liberation So. Africa, 1978—; mem. Emergency Com. for World govt., 1978—, Working Com. for Action Against Apartheid, Evanston, 1978—; pres. Third World Energy Inst. Recipient Chancellor's prize U. South Africa, 1947, Mbari award CCF, 1963; Freedom Writer's award Soc. Writers and Editors, 1975; key City of Sumter, S.C., 1979. Fellow Internat. Poetry Soc.; mem. MLA, Internat. Platform Assn., Union of Writers of African People (Ghana) (v.p. 1974—), African Lit. Assn. U.S.A. (founding chmn. 1975—, exec. com. 1979—). Served 18 months in Robben Island Prison, S. Africa, for opposition to apartheid, 1964-65. Home: 624 Clark St Evanston IL 60201 Office: English Dept Northwestern U Evanston IL 60201 *I grew up imbued with a sense of fair play: a desire for justice and sympathy for the underdog. I believe that this has animated my activities—in literature, in academia and in politics. It explains my fight against apartheid, racism and injustice.*

BRUYN, HENRY BICKER, physician; b. Bklyn., Jan. 24, 1918; s. Henry Bicker and Mary Janet (Retter) B.; m. Marion Helen Burkhardt, Sept. 19, 1942; children—Martha Elizabeth, Barbara Jane, Charles DeWitt, Jonathan Henry; m. Harriet Hall Brainerd, Apr. 22, 1973. B.A., Amherst Coll., 1940; M.D., Yale, 1943. Intern pediatrics New Haven Hosp., 1943-44; resident Buffalo Children's Hosp., 1944-45; fellow infectious disease U. Calif. Med. Sch., San Francisco, 1946-47, mem. faculty, 1948—, asso. prof. medicine, pediatrics, 1956-69, clin. prof. medicine, pediatrics, 1969—; chief isolation service San Francisco Gen. Hosp., 1950-59, chief pediatrics, 1954-59; lectr. Sch. Pub. Health U. Calif. at Berkeley, 1960—, dir. student health service, 1959-72; dir. child health and disability prevention, City of San Francisco, 1974—; cons. U.S. Naval Hosp., U.S. Army Hosp., Children's Hosp. East Bay.; Cons. Calif. viral and rickettsial disease lab., City and County San Francisco; mem. med. service com. Alameda County Council Social Planning, 1962-64; med. cons. Morrison Center Rehab., 1954-58, Medic-Alert Found., Elizabeth Kenney Found., San Francisco, 1950-52; med. dir. Drug Abuse Rehab., New Bridge Inc.; pres. Berkeley Med. Instrument Co., 1960-68; Alumni fund chmn. N.Calif. sect. Yale Med. Sch. Co-author: Handbook of Pediatrics, 1st-13th edit, 1979, Handbook of Medical Treatment, 1972, Current Diagnosis and Therapy, 1972, Practice of Pediatrics, 1963, Drinking Among Collegians, 1970, Parents Guide to Child Raising, 1978, Parents Medical Manual, 1978; contbr. articles to profl. jours. Bd. dirs. Alameda County Suicide Prevention, 1962-70, Carmel Valley Manor, 1969—, Goodwill Industries, 1972—, Ronoh Sch., 1966-70, Alameda County Council Alcoholism, 1960-70, Com. Children's TV, 1977—, Jack B. Goldberg Found., 1978—; trustee, mem. ch. council Arlington Community Ch., 1954-72. Served to lt. comdr. M.C. USNR, 1945-46, 53-54. Mem. A.M.A., Royal Soc. Health, Am. Pub. Health Assn., Am. Coll. Health Assn. (pres. 1965-66), Pacific Coast Coll. Health Assn. (pres. 1968-69), Am. Fedn. Clin. Research, Western Soc. Clin. Research, Am. Acad. Pediatrics (chmn. pub. health com. No. Calif. sect. 1962-69), Calif. Fedn. Pediatric Socs., Cal. Acad. Medicine, Order Golden Bear, Delta Tau Delta, Nu Sigma Nu. Home: 432 Woodland Rd Kentfield CA 94904

BRUYNES, CEES, manufacturing company executive; b. Netherlands, Aug. 3, 1932; s. Arie and Petronella (Borst) B.; m. Elly Nagel, Feb. 1, 1963; children: Irene W., Jan Paul. Grad., Chr. Lyceum, Arnhem, Netherlands, 1951. With N.V. Philips' Gloeilampenfabrieken, Netherlands, 1953-71; pres., chief exec. officer Philips Can., 1971-74; exec. v.p. N.Am. Philips Corp., N.Y.C., 1975-78, pres., chief operating officer, 1978—, chief exec. officer, 1981—. Served with Dutch Air Force, 1951-53. Clubs: Union League, Sky, Netherlands (N.Y.C.); Greenwich (Conn.) Country., Lyford Cay. Home: Khakum Woods Greenwich CT 06830 Office: 100 E 42d St New York NY 10017

BRUZDA, FRANCIS JOSEPH, banker; b. Minersville, Pa., May 23, 1935; s. Stanley Joseph and Agnes K. B.; m. Irene Humphreys, June 15, 1963; children: Kimberly Anne, Elizabeth Anne. A.B., Temple U., 1970. With Girard Bank, Phila., 1959-72, exec. v.p., head trust dept., 1975—; dep. dir. Office Bus. Assistance, Dept. Commerce, 1972-73; commr. President's Commn. Exec. Exchange, 1979. Chmn., bd. dirs. Salvation Army Greater Phila.; trustee Bucks County Hist. Soc.; bd. dirs. Phila. Coll. Pediatric Medicine, Old Phila. Devel. Corp. Served with U.S. Army, 1957-59. Roman Catholic. Club: Union League (Phila.). Office: 3 Girard Plaza Philadelphia PA 19101

BRUZELIUS, NILS JOHAN AXEL, journalist; b. Stockholm, Feb. 27, 1947; U.S., 1958; s. Axel Sture and Constance (Brickett) B.; m. Margaret Ann Kuppinger, May 20, 1972. B.A. in History, Amherst Coll., 1968. Reporter, bur. chief Middlesex News, Framingham, Mass., 1968-70; reporter, state house corr. AP, Boston, 1970-73; med./mental health writer Boston Globe, 1973-79, investigative reporter, 1979-81, asst. met. editor, 1981—. Mem. Boston Globe investigative team receiving Disting. Investigative Reporting award Investigative Reporters and Editors Assn., 1979, Disting. Journalism citation Scripps-Howard Found., 1979, Pulitzer prize for spl. local reporting, 1980. Mem. Investigative Reporters and Editors Assn. Clubs: Appalachian Mountain, Cambridge Sports Union. Home: 40 Fountain St West Newton MA 02165 Office: Boston Globe MA 02107

BRYAN, ANTHONY JOHN ADRIAN, corporate executive; b. Saltillo, Mexico, Feb. 24, 1923; came to U.S., 1945, naturalized, 1967; s. Vincent A. and Marjorie I. (Blackett) B.; m. Pamela Zauderer, June 30, 1978; children: Caroline (Mrs. Russell McCandless), Pamela C., Anthony John Adrian. M.B.A., Harvard U., 1947. With Monsanto Co., St. Louis, 1947-73, gen. mgr. internat. div., 1968, corporate v.p., 1969-73, dir., 1971-73, Cameron Iron Works, Inc., Houston, 1966-73, pres., chief exec. officer, 1973-77; chmn., pres. Copperweld Corp., Pitts., 1977-81, chmn., chief exec. officer, 1981—; dir. Chrysler Corp., Detroit, Hamilton Bros. Petroleum, Denver, Fed. Express Corp., Memphis, Imetal, Paris, PNC Fin. Corp., Allegheny Internat., Inc., Pitts. Trustee, bd. dirs. numerous charitable and ednl. instns. Served with RCAF, 1940-45. Decorated D.F.C. Office: Copperweld Corp Two Oliver Plaza Pittsburgh PA 15222

BRYAN, ARTHUR, manufacturing company executive; b. Eng., Mar. 4, 1923; s. William Woodall and Isobel Alan (Tweedie) B.; m. Betty Ratford, 1947; 2 children. Student schs. in, Inst. Mktg., Stoke-on-Trent, Eng. Trainee Barclays Bank; with Josiah Wedgwood & Sons Ltd., 1947—, London mgr., 1953-57, gen. sales mgr., 1959-60; dir., pres. Josiah Wedgwood & Sons Inc of Am., 1960-62; now chmn.; dir. Josiah Wedgwood & Sons Ltd., Barlaston, Eng., Josiah Wedgwood & Sons (Canada) Ltd.; dir. Josiah Wedgwood & Sons (Australia) Pty. Ltd., 1962—, mng. dir., 1963—, chmn., 1968—, Franciscan Ceramics, Inc., 1979—. Chmn. N.Am. adv. group Brit. Overseas Trade Bd., 1977-82. Created Knight St. John Jerusalem, 1972; Lord-Lt. Staffordshire, 1968—. Fellow Royal Soc. Artists, Inst. Mktg., British Inst. Mgmt.; mem. British Ceramic Mfrs. Fedn. (pres. 1970-71). Office: Josiah Wedgwood & Sons Inc 41 Madison Ave New York NY 10010

BRYAN, CLARENCE RUSSELL, coll. pres.; b. Red Oak, Iowa, Apr. 12, 1923; s. Clarence Russell and Alyce Marie (Gates) B.; m. Ardis Froyd, Dec. 26, 1944; children—Curtis R., Sidra Bryan Van Norden. B.S., U.S. Naval Acad., 1944; M.S., M.I.T., 1952. Commd. ensign U.S. Navy, 1944; advanced through grades to vice adm.; design supt. Portsmouth Naval Shipyard, 1963-65; force material officer, dep. comdr. submarine force Atlantic Fleet, 1965-66, asst. chief of staff, 1966-68, fleet maintenance officer, asst. chief of staff maintenance and logistic plans, 1969-72; dep. comdr. for prodn. Naval Ship Systems Command Hdqrs., Washington, 1972-74; dep. comdr. for submarines Naval Sea Systems Command, 1974; dir. ship material readiness div. Office Chief Naval Ops., 1974-76; comdr. Naval Sea Systems Command, Washington, 1976-80; pres. Webb Inst. Naval Architecture and Marine Engring., Glen Cove, N.Y., 1980—; bd. mgrs. Am. Bur. Shipping. Decorated Legion of Merit, D.S.M., others. Mem. Am. Soc. Naval Engrs. (pres. 1979-81), Soc. Naval Architects and Marine Engrs., Sigma Xi. Home: President's House Webb Inst Glen Cove NY 11542 Office: Webb Inst Naval Architecture Glen Cove NY 11542

BRYAN, COLGAN HOBSON, educator; b. Trenton, S.C., Oct. 7, 1909; s. John William and Mary (Hobson) B.; m. Sara Lucille Turbeville, June 18, 1938 (dec. Nov. 17, 1975); 1 son, Colgan Hobson; m. Carol Lindsay Smelley, July 14, 1979. B.S. in Elec. Engring, U. S.C., 1932; M.Ed., Duke U., 1940; M.S. in Aero. Engring, Ga. Inst. Tech., 1948. Registered profl. engr., Ala. Faculty U. Ala., 1942—, prof. aerospace engring., 1948—, chmn. dept., 1952—; research scientist NASA, 1962; on leave with U. Tenn. Space Inst., 1968-69; cons. to industry, 1941—. Mem. Ala. Aero. Commn., 1944-48. Recipient Charles Henry Ratcliff award for excellence in teaching, 1976; Outstanding Faculty award Delta Tau Delta, 1976; George H. Denny Outstanding Faculty award Sigma Chi, 1976. Asso. fellow AIAA (Disting. Service award 1980); mem. ASME, Am. Soc. Engring. Edn., Am. Ordnance Assn., AAUP, Nat., Ala. socs. profl. engrs., NEA, Ala. Edn. Assn., Acacia (life), Pi Tau Chi (faculty adviser). Episcopalian. Clubs: Kiwanian (pres. Tuscaloosa 1966, recipient Service award 1966), Kiwanian (Distinguished Service award 1977). Research projects in theoretical and applied aerodynamics, energy (solar and wind). Home: 171 Woodland Hills Tuscaloosa AL 35405 Office: PO Box 1461 University AL 35486

BRYAN, COURTLANDT DIXON BARNES, author; b. N.Y.C., Apr. 22, 1936; s. Joseph III and Katharine (Barnes) O'Hara; m. Phoebe Miller, Dec. 28, 1961 (div. Sept 1966); children: J. St. George III, Lansing Becket; m. Judith Snyder, Dec. 21, 1967 (div. July 1978); 1 dau., Amanda Barnes. Grad., Berkshire Sch., 1954; B.A. in English, Yale U., 1958. Writer-in-residence Colo. State U., winter 1967; vis. lectr. writers workshop U. Iowa, 1967-69; editor Monocle mag., 1961—; spl. cons. editorial matters Yale U., 1970; vis. prof. U. Wyo., 1975; adj. prof. Columbia U., 1976; fiction dir. Writers Community, N.Y.C., 1977—. Author: P.S. Wilkinson, 1965 (Harper prize novel), The Great Dethriffe, 1970, Friendly Fire, 1976, The National Air and Space Museum, 1979, Beautiful Women; Ugly Scenes, 1983; also short stories, criticism, articles, polit. satire, introductions; represented anthologies; narration: Swedish film The Face of War, 1963. Served with AUS, 1958-60, 61-62. Club: Yale. Home: 719 Podunk Rd Guilford CT 06437 Office: care Brandt & Brandt 1501 Broadway New York NY 10036

BRYAN, DAVID TENNANT, former newspaper executive; b. Richmond, Va., Aug. 3, 1906; s. John Stewart and Anne Eliza (Tennant) B.; m. Mary Harkness Davidson, May 11, 1932; children: Mary Tennant, John Stewart, Florence. Student, U. Va., 1925-28; LL.D., U. Richmond, 1973. Chmn., dir. Media Gen., Inc.; former publisher Richmond Times-Dispatch and; Richmond News Leader, to 1978. Hon. trustee Va. Union U.; overseer Hoover Instn. Mem. Am. Newspaper Pubs. Assn. (pres. 1958-60), Soc. of Cin., Va. Hist. Soc. (pres. 1977-80), Sigma Delta Chi. Clubs: Commonwealth, Country of Va. (Richmond); Farmington Country (Charlottesville); St. Anthony, Union (N.Y.C.); Nat. Press, Alfalfa (Washington); Bohemian (San Francisco). Home: Ampthill Rd Richmond VA 23226 Office: 333 E Grace St Richmond VA 23219

BRYAN, JACK YEAMAN, former diplomat, photographer, author; b. Peoria, Ill., Sept. 24, 1907; s. James Yeaman and Regina (Gibson) B.; m. Margaret Gardner, June 21, 1934; children: Joel Yeaman, Guy Kelsey, Donna Gardner, Kirsten Stuart Winkle-Bryan. Student, U. Chgo., 1925-27; B.A. with high distinction, U. Ariz., 1932, M.A., 1933; postgrad. (fellow philosophy), Duke U., 1933-35; Ph.D., U. Iowa, 1939. Research analyst Fed. Emergency Relief Adminstrn., Washington, 1935-36; from instr. English to prof., head dept. journalism U. Md., 1936-48; pub. relations adviser OCD, 1942-43; dir. pub. relations Welfare Fedn. Cleve., 1943-45; pub. info. officer UNRRA, 1945-46; cultural attaché Am. Embassy, Manila, 1948-51; chief program planning Internat. Exchange Service, State Dept., 1951-53; pub. affairs officer USIS, Bombay, India, 1953-54, Bangalore, India., 1954-55; cultural affairs officer embassy, Cairo, Egypt, 1956, Tehran, Iran, 1956-58, cultural attaché, chief cultural affairs officer embassy, Karachi, Pakistan, 1958-63; personnel officer for Africa USIA, 1964-65; officer in charge Project AIM, U.S. Dept. State, Washington, 1965; officer-in-charge spl. recruitment program Bur. Edn. and Cultural Affairs, 1965-67; chief cultural affairs adviser USIA, 1968; ret., 1968; Lectr. creative photography U. Calif. at Riverside, 1968-80. Author: novel Come to the Bower, 1963; Contbr. short stories, articles, photographs to numerous mags.; Photog. exhibits one man shows, Pakistan, 1961-62, U.S., 1964, 66, Perspectives Eastward on tour U.S., 1968-71. Chmn. publs. bd. U. Md., 1946-48; chmn. bd. dirs. U.S. Ednl. Founds, Philippines, 1949-51 chmn. bd. dirs. U.S. Ednl. Founds, Pakistan, 1958-63; exec. dir. Iran Am. Soc. in Tehran, 1956-58; founder, exec. dir. Pakistan-Am. Cultural Center, 1959-60, 62-63. Recipient ann. prize for best fiction Tex. Inst. Letters, 1964, Summerfield Roberts award, 1964. Mem. Am. Soc. Mag. Photographers, Friends of Photography, Tex. Inst. Letters (best short story award 1974), Tex. Hist. Assn., Am. Mus. Natural History, Am.

Fgn. Service Assn., Nat. Parks and Conservation Assn., Sierra Club, Phi Delta Theta, Delta Sigma Rho, Phi Gamma Mu. Club: Faculty of U. Calif. at Riverside. Home: 3594 Ramona Dr Riverside CA 92506

BRYAN, JAMES EDWARD, editor, writer, cons., adminstr. sci. societies; b. Asbury Park, N.J., Apr. 6, 1906; s. Joseph Harker and Irene (Dobbins) B.; m. Lucile Marvin Elder, Dec. 1, 1928 (div. 1970); m. Helen Arnold Roché, Jan. 15, 1971; children—Faith Elder (Mrs. Hedley V. Tingley), June Harker (Mrs. James Belfie). Ph.B., Wesleyan U., Conn., 1927. Lay mgr. Am. Inst. Homeopathy, N.Y.C., 1929-31; exec. sec. Westchester County (N.Y.) Med. Soc.; mng. editor Westchester Med. Bull., 1933-44; exec. sec. N.Y. County Med. Soc.; also mng. editor N.Y. Medicine, 1944-47; exec. officer Med. Soc. N.J., 1947-50; adminstr. Med.-Surg. Plan N.J., 1950-55; med. adminstrn. cons., 1955—; exec. sec. Nat. Med. Found Eye Care, 1956-63; research asso. administrv. medicine Columbia Sch. Pub. Health and Administrv. Medicine, 1956-63; exec. sec. Am. Fedn. Clin. Research, 1958-70, Am. Med. Writers Assn., 1962-66, Am. Acad. for Cerebral Palsy, 1972-80; exec. dir. Am. Soc. Information Sci., 1964-70, Nat. Investor Relations Inst., 1969-73, Children's Eye Care Found., 1972-80; dir. Washington office Nat. Assn. Blue Shield Plans, 1963-70; Washington rep. Am. Assn. Founds., for Med. Care, 1971-76; pres. Med. Soc. Execs. Assn., 1950; Professorial lectr. George Washington U. Med. Sch., 1969—; lectr. community medicine and internat. health Georgetown U. Sch. Medicine, 1970; Pres. Westchester Tb and Health Assn., 1940-41, Tb and Health Assn. So. Fairfield County, Conn., 1963-64. Author: Public Relations in Medical Practice, 1954, The Role of the Family Physician in America's Developing Medical Care Program, 1968; Contbr. articles to profl. jours. Trustee N.J. Soc. Crippled Children and Adults, 1948-56, v.p., 1955-56. Fellow Am. Med. Writers Assn., AAAS; mem. Nat. Assn. Sci. Writers, Washington Assn. N.J., Am. Soc. for Information Sci. (hon. life), Nat. Investor Relations Inst. (hon. life). Home and office: 1255 New Hampshire Ave NW Washington DC 20036

BRYAN, JAMES LEE, oil field service co. exec.; b. Waco, Tex., Aug. 18, 1936; s. Andrew Walton and Thelma Lee (Clements) B.; m. Joretta Griffin, Nov. 28, 1958; children—Deborah Lee, Catherine Ann, Rebecca Kaye, Cynthia Jean. B.S. in Geology, Baylor U., 1958. Drilling fluids engr. Dresser Industries, La., 1959-61, dist. engr., Utah, 1961-62, dist. mgr., Mont., 1962-65, gen. mgr., Nigeria, 1965-67, mng. dir., Kuwait, 1967-69, area mgr. Middle and Far East, 1969-72, Europe, Africa, 1972-74, v.p. Western ops., 1974-77, exec. v.p., Houston, 1977-79; pres. Magcobar Group, 1980—. Mem. Inst. Mech. Engrs., Am. Petroleum Inst., Soc. Petroleum Engrs., Petroleum Equipment Supply Assn., Nomads, Pi Epsilon Tau. Republican. Baptist. Clubs: Champions, Lochinvar, Houston, Petroleum, Ramada. Office: 601 Jefferson St Houston TX 77002 *

BRYAN, JOHN ALEXANDER, pathologist; b. Louisville, July 21, 1940; s. Henry Werne and Frances Carter (Swope) B.; m. Ann Carol Lindsey, Aug. 23, 1963; children: Rebecca Lindsey, John Alexander, II. B.A., U. Louisville, 1962, M.D., 1966. Diplomate: Am. Bd. Internal Medicine, Am. Bd. Pathology. Intern U. Mich. Med. Center, Ann Arbor, 1966-67, resident internal medicine, 1967-68, 70-71; mem. staff Center Disease Control, Atlanta, 1968-79; chief hepatitis br., dep. dir. viral diseases div. Bur. Epidemiology, 1972-76, dir. viral diseases div., 1976-79; resident dept. pathology and lab. medicine Emory U. Sch. Medicine, 1979—, instr., 1980-82, asst. prof., 1982—; officer USPHS, 1968-79. Fellow Am. Coll. Preventive Medicine, Am. Soc. Clin. Pathology; mem. Internat. Epidemiol. Assn., Am. Pub. Health Assn., AAAS, Soc. Edpidemiologic Research, N.Y. Acad. Scis., Internat. Assn. Pathologists, Am. Soc. Tropical Medicine and Hygiene, Am. Soc. Microbiology. Office: Dept Pathology and Lab Medicine Emory U Sch Medicine 1364 Clifton Rd NE Atlanta GA 30322

BRYAN, JOHN HENRY, JR., food company executive; b. West Point, Miss., 1936. B.A. in Econs. and Bus. Adminstrn, Southwestern at Memphis, 1958. With Consol. Foods Corp., Chgo., 1960—, exec. v.p. ops., 1974-75, pres., chief exec. officer, 1975-76, chmn. bd., chief exec. officer, 1976—, also dir.; dir. Standard Oil Co. (Ind.), First Chgo. Home: 140 Melrose St Kenilworth IL 60043 Office: Consolidated Foods Corp Three First National Plaza Chicago IL 60602 *

BRYAN, JOHN LELAND, educator; b. Washington, Nov. 15, 1926; s. George W. and Buena (Youe) B.; m. Sarah Emily Barton, June 7, 1950; children—Joan Marie, Steven Leland. A.A., Okla. State U., 1950, B.S., 1953, M.S., 1954; D.Ed., Am. U., 1965. Field rep. Grain Dealers Mut. Ins. Co., Indpls., 1950, Jackson, Miss., 1950-52; sr. instr. U. Md., 1954-56, prof., 1956—; fire prevention engr., civil engring. div. U.S. Coast Guard, Washington, summers 1960-64. Author: Fire Detection and Suppression Systems, 1973, 2d edit., 1982, Automatic Sprinkler and Standpipe Systems, 1976. Mem. Am. Soc. for Engring. Edn., Soc. Fire Protection Engrs., Nat. Fire Protection Assn., ASTM, Iota Lambda Sigma, Psi Chi, Kappa Delta Pi, Phi Kappa Phi. Home: 933 Schindler Dr Silver Spring MD 20903 Office: Fire Protection Engring U Md College Park MD 20742

BRYAN, J(OSEPH), III, writer; b. Richmond, Va., Apr. 30, 1904; s. Joseph St. George and Emily Page (Kemp) B.;, 1930 (div. 1954); children—St. George II (dec. 1969), Joan Bryan Gates, Courtlandt D.B.; m. Jacqueline de la Grandière, 1960. Grad., Episcopal High Sch.; A.B., Princeton U., 1927. Reporter and editorial writer Richmond News Leader, also; Chgo. Jour., 1928-31; asso. editor Parade, Cleve., 1931-32; mng. editor Town & Country, 1933-36; asso. editor Sat. Eve. Post, 1937-40; freelance writer, 1940—. Author: (with Philip Reed) Mission Beyond Darkness, 1945, (with Admiral Halsey) Admiral Halsey's Story, 1947, Aircraft Carrier, 1954, The World's Greatest Showman, 1956, The Sword Over the Mantel, 1960, (with Charles J.V. Murphy) The Windsor Story, 1979. Trustee Poe Found. Spl. asst. to sec. USAF, 1952-53; Served as lt. U.S. Field Arty. Res., 1927-37; lt. comdr. USNR, 1942-53; col. USAFR, 1953-62. Recipient Distinguished Pub. Service award USN. Fellow Va. Mus. Fine Arts (trustee 1963-73); mem. Va. Hist. Soc., Soc. Cincinnati, Soc. Colonial Wars. Episcopalian. Clubs: Commonwealth (Richmond); Buck's (London, Eng.); Ivy (Princeton); Princeton (N.Y.C.). Home: Brook Hill Richmond VA 23227

BRYAN, LAWRENCE EDWARD, medical microbiologist, educator; b. Calgary, Alt., Can., June 29, 1937; s. John William and Jessie Evelyn (Riley) B.; m. Eleanor Mary Betts, Dec. 1, 1962; children: Dawn Margaret, Gregory Lawrence. M.D., U. Alta., Edmonton, 1961, Ph.D., 1970. Intern Calgary Gen. Hosp., 1961-62; resident in internal medicine U. Alta. Hosp., 1962-63; pvt. practice medicine, specializing in gen. medicine, Chilliwack, B.C., 1963-66; resident in med. microbiology U. Alta. Hosp., 1966-67; asst. prof. to prof. dept. med. bacteriology U. Alta., 1970-78, prof. dept. pathology, 1978-81, prof., chmn. dept. microbiology and infectious diseases, 1981—; chief microbiology Foothills Hosp., Calgary, 1978—. Author: Bacterial Resistance and Susceptibility to Chemotherapeutic Agents, 1982; editor: Antimicrobial Resistance, 1983. Grantee Med. Research Council, Can. Cystic Fibrosis Found., Nat. Def. Can. Fellow Royal Coll. Physicians Can., Infectious Diseases Soc. Am.; mem. Alliance for Prudent Use of Antibiotics, Alpha Omega Alpha. Office: Dept Microbiology and Infectious Diseases Univ Calgary 3300 Hospital Dr Calgary AB Canada T2N 4B1

BRYAN, LESLIE AULLS, transportation economist; b. Bath, N.Y., Feb. 23, 1900; s. Daniel Beach and Anna (Aulls) B.; m. Gertrude Catherine Gelder, Aug. 22, 1931; children: Leslie A., George G. B.S., Syracuse U., 1923, M.S., 1924, J.D., 1939; Ph.D., Am. U., 1930; Sc.D. (hon.), Southwestern, 1972. Prof. bus. adminstrn. Southwestern Coll., Winfield, Kans., 1924-25; asst. coach of track Syracuse U., 1925-42, dir. athletics, 1934-37; also instr., 1925-28, asst. prof. transp., 1928-31, asso. prof., 1931-39, prof., 1939-45, Franklin prof. transp., 1945-46; also pres. Seneca Flying Sch., Syracuse, N.Y., 1943-46; dir. Inst. Aviation; prof. mgmt. U. Ill., 1946-68, emeritus, 1968—; aviation advisory bd. Norwich U., 1954-59; mem. Pres. Kennedy's Task Force on Aviation Goals, 1961; U. Ill. faculty rep. Intercollegiate Conf. (Big Ten), 1959-68, acting dir. athletics, 1965-66; Dir. aviation State of N.Y., 1945; Pres. Eastern Intercoll. Boxing Assn., 1936-38, N.Y. State Aviation Council, 1944-46, Traffic Club of Syracuse., 1942; Transp. cons. Nat. Resources Planning Bd., 1942-44; aviation cons. New Standard Ency., 1947—; mem. nat. aerospace ednl. adv. com. Civil Air Patrol, 1948-68, chmn., 1965-66; mem. bd. aero. advisers, State of Ill., 1949-69; tech. assistance bd. Link Found., 1953-71; adv. com. FCDA, 1957-60; chmn. Pres. Eisenhower's Gen. Aviation Facilities Planning Group, 1957-58; adv. com. Washington Internat. Airport, 1958-62; cons. FAA, 1959-62; mem. adv. bd. Air Tng. Command, 1964, cons., 1965-69; mem. adv. bd. Ill. State Archives, 1980—. Author: Aerial Transportation, 1925, Industrial Traffic Management, 1929, Principles of Water Transportation, 1939, (with others) Aviation Study Manual, 1949, (with Wilson) Air Transportation, 1949; (with others) rev. Fundamentals of Aviation and Space Technology, 1968; Traffic Management in Industry, 1953, Aulls-Bryan and Allied Families, 1966, Aulls Genealogy, 1974, Thomas Bryan and Some of His Descendants, 1979, Immigrant Ancestors, 1981; also monographs and articles.; Adv. editor: Nat. Air Rev, 1948-50; editorial adviser (aeros.), Holt, Rinehart & Winston, Inc., 1960-64; bd. editors, Air Affairs, 1949-51; cons.: Our Wonderful World, 1954-55; contbr.: World Book Ency, 1952-68, Funk and Wagnalls New Ency, 1947—, Compton's Pictured Ency, 1959—, McGraw Hill Ency. of Sci. and Tech, 1959; cons. editor: Above and Beyond Ency, 1967—, Illustrated Ency. of Aviation and Space, 1970. Bd. dirs. Nat. Found. for Asthmatic Children, 1956-65; Pres. Arrowhead council Boy Scouts Am., 1954-60, mem. at large nat. council, 1960-70, regional exec. bd., 1959-70. Served as lt., inf. and Air Corps U.S. Army, 1917-19; overseas; col. USAF Res.; Res. ret. Awarded Sec. War Commendation, 1946; Arents medal, 1955; Brewer Trophy, 1953; Sigma Delta Chi award, 1955; Air Power award, 1956; Silver Beaver award Boy Scouts Am., 1957; Silver Antelope, 1959; Tissandier diploma Fedn. Aeronautique Internat., 1958; distinguished service award Am. Assn. Airport Execs., 1959; Continental Air Command certificate of recognition, 1960; Nat. Aero. Assn. certificate of recognition, 1966; FAA distinguished pub. service award, 1965; Elder Statesman of Aviation, 1966; Distinguished Alumni award Am. U., 1969; Letterman of Distinction award Syracuse U., 1969; Patriots medal, 1968; Minuteman award S.A.R., 1976; others. Fellow U. Aviation Assn. (pres. 1948-49, Wheatley award 1955); mem. Am. Soc. Traffic and Transp. (bd. examiners 1948-60), Nat. Aerospace Edn. Council (pres. 1952-53, 64-66, dir. 1953-54, 59-64, 66-67), Nat. Aero Assn. (v.p. 1953-56, 60-61, 65-66, dir. 1950- 52, 54-55, 57-59, 62-64), Civil Air Patrol (Distinguished Service medal 1954), Am. Assn. Airport Execs. (v.p. 1953-55, pres. 1955-56, dir. edn. 1952-68, hon. life mem.), Am. Inst. Aeros. and Astronautics, Acad. Mgmt., ICC Practitioners Assn., Aerospace Writers Assn., Soc. of Cincinnati, Nat. Air and Space Mus. (Hall of Honor), Nat. Huguenot Soc. (pres. Ill. 1971-73, Disting. Service medal 1976, pres. gen. 1977-78, hon. pres. gen. 1979—), Newcomen Soc. N.Am., Scabbard and Blade, Am. U. Alumni Assn. (chmn. bd. govs. 1970-71), S.A.R. (genealogist gen. 1973-75, trustee 1975-76, 77—, v.p. gen. 1976-77, pres. Ill. 1974-76), Ill. Geneal. Soc. (pres. 1972-73, Distinguished Leadership award 1974), Soc. War 1812 (asst. adj. gen. 1975—, pres. Ill. 1976-81), Arnold Air Soc., Pershing Rifles, Sigma Alpha Tau, Alpha Eta Rho, Phi Gamma Mu, Zeta Psi, Phi Delta Phi, Phi Kappa Alpha, Alpha Kappa Psi, Phi Kappa Phi, Alpha Phi Omega, Kappa Phi Kappa, Alpha Delta Sigma, Delta Nu Alpha, Tau Omega, Beta Gamma Sigma. Home: 34 Fields East Champaign IL 61821

BRYAN, MONK, bishop; b. Blooming Grove, Tex., July 25, 1914; s. Gid. J. and Era (Monk) B.; m. Corneille Downer, July 22, 1941; children: Lucy (Mrs. Samuel S. Barlow, Jr.), James J., Robert M. B.A., Baylor U., 1935; M.Th., So. Meth. U., 1938; D.D., Central Meth. Coll., Fayette, Mo., 1958; L.H.D. hon., Nebr. Wesleyan U., 1977, Hum.D., Westman Coll., 1982. Ordained to ministry United Methodist Ch., 1939; consecrated bishop, 1976; minister Boyce Circuit, Waxahachie Dist. Central Tex. Conf., 1939-40, St. Luke's Meth. Ch., St. Louis, 1940-47, Centenary Meth. Ch., Bonne Terre, Mo., 1947-49, Meth. Ch., Maryville, Mo., 1949-57, Mo. United Meth. Ch., Columbia, 1957-76; bishop S. Central Jurisdictional Conf., Lincoln, Nebr., 1976—; mem. World Meth. Council, 1953—; participant confs., Lake Junaluska, N.C., 1956, Oslo, 1961, London, 1966, Denver, 1971, Dublin, Ireland, 1976, Honolulu, 1981, exchange minister in Eng., 1953; pres. Mo. Conf. Bd. Edn., 1956-64, Mo. Council Chs., 1966-68; chmn. Mo. East Conf. Bd. Christian Social Concerns, 1968-72; mem. Meth. Gen. Bd., divs. ecumenical and inter-religious concerns and health and welfare Meth. Gen. Bd. Global Ministries, 1972-76. Bd. dirs. Wesley Found., Columbia, 1957-76, Columbia United Fund, 1964-70; trustee So. Meth. U., 1952-68, 76—, St. Paul Sch. Theology, Kansas City, 1968-72, 76—, Mo. Sch. Religion, Columbia, 1957-76, Philander Smith Coll., Little Rock, 1976—, Lydia Patterson Inst., El Paso, 1976—, Mt. Sequoyah Assembly, Fayetteville, Ark., 1976—, Nebr. Wesleyan U., 1976—, Omaha Meth. Hosp., 1976—, Bryan Meml. Hosp., 1976—, Western Nebr. Gen. Hosp., 1976—; adv. council Gt. Rivers council Boy Scouts Am., 1960-76. Recipient Silver Beaver award Boy Scouts Am., 1972. Lodges: Masons (33d deg.); K.T.; Scottish Rite; Rotary. *

BRYAN, PAUL ROBEY, JR., musician, educator; s. Paul Robey and Margaret Winifred (Buck) B.; m. Emily Virginia Schmitt, Aug. 1941; children: Paul John, Elizabeth Virginia. Mus.B., U. Mich., 1941, Mus.M., 1948, Ph.D., 1956. Instr. music theory U. Mich., 1948-51, 54-55, summer 1962; asst. prof. music theory, brass instruments, bands Duke U., Durham, N.C., 1951-58, asso. prof. music theory, brass instruments, bands, 1958-75, prof. musicology, music theory, condr. wind symphony, 1975—; condr., bd. dirs. Triangle Symphony Inc., Durham Civic Choral Soc., 1959-67, Durham Savoyards Ltd., 1961-67, 69, 74-75, 77; condr. Durham Youth Symphony, 1972-79. Editorial bd.: Jour. Band Research; editor: Georg Wagenseil concerto for trombone, Symphonies of Johann Vanhal; contbr. mus. articles to profl. jours. Served with U.S. Army, 1942-46. Mem. Am. Bandmasters Assn., Am. Musicol. Soc., Am. Fedn. Musicians, Coll. Band Dirs. Nat. Assn. (chmn. nat. com. on early European repertoire), Internationale Gessellscaft. Research in 18th Century symphony. Home: 1108 Watts St Durham NC 27701 Office: Box 6695 College Station Durham NC 27708

BRYAN, RICHARD H., governor Nevada; b. Washington, July 16, 1937; married; 3 children. B.A., U. Nev., 1959; LL.B., U. Calif.-San Francisco, 1963. Bar: Nev. 1963, U.S. Supreme Ct. 1967. Dep. dist. atty., Clark County, Nev., 1964-66, public defender, Clark County, 1966-68; counsel Clark County Juvenile Ct., 1968-69; mem. Nev. Assembly, 1969-71, Nev. Senate, 1973-77; atty. gen. State of Nev., 1979-82, gov. Nev., 1982—. Bd. dirs. March of Dimes; former v.p. Nev. Easter Seal Soc.; former pres. Clark County Legal Aid Soc. Served with U.S. Army. Mem. ABA, Clark County Bar Assn., Am. Judicature Soc., Phi Alpha Delta, Phi Alpha Theta. Democrat. Clubs: Masons, Lions, Elks. Office: Office of Gov Capitol Complex Carson City NV 89710

BRYAN, ROBERT ARMISTEAD, educator, univ. ofcl.; b. Lebanon, Pa., Apr. 26, 1926; s. Morris Armistead and Katherine (Maulfair) B.; m. Kathryn Elizabeth Williams, Feb. 3, 1953; children—Lyla, Matthew. B.A., U. Miami, 1950; M.A., U. Ky., 1951, PhD., 1956. Teaching asst. U. Ky. at Lexington, 1950-54, instr., 1956-57; lectr. extension div. U. Calif., Tokyo, Japan, 1955-56; mem. faculty, adminstrn. U. Fla., Gainsville, 1957—, prof. English, 1968—, dean faculties, 1970-71, asso. v.p. academic affairs, 1971-75, v.p. academic affairs, 1975—; Reader Coll. Bd. Exams, Ednl. Testing Service, 1958-61; cons. So. Assn. Schs. and Colls., 1965-73, also chmn. visitation com., 1966-67; cons. HEW, 1977. Bibliographer: Twentieth Century Literature, 1958-61. Served with U.S. Merchant Marine, 1944-47; Served with AUS, 1954-56. Mem. Southeastern Renaissance Conf., S. Atlantic Mod. Lang. Assn., Modern Lang Assn., Sigma Chi. Episcopalian. Home: 704 NW 40th Terr Gainesville FL 32607

BRYAN, ROBERT FESSLER, former investment analyst; b. New Castle, Pa., Jan 19, 1913; s. Harry A. and Nell (Fessler) B.; m. Elaine A. Norwood, Sept. 7, 1940; children: Diane Elaine (Mrs. James M. Lyon), Barbara Norwood (Mrs. Michael C. Bowen); m. Dorothy Darr MacKenzie, Aug. 11, 1961; m. Gertrude B. Bruneau, Feb. 10, 1978. A.B. summa cum laude, Oberlin Coll., 1934; Ph.D., Yale, 1939. Instr. econs. Yale U., 1935-36, 37-39, Princeton U., 1936-37; economist Lionel D. Edie & Co., Inc., N.Y.C., 1939-40, asst. v.p., 1943-45, v.p., 1946-48; price exec., rubber br. OPA, 1941-42; economist Goodyear Aircraft Corp., Akron, Ohio, 1943; with J.H. Whitney & Co., N.Y.C., 1948-50, partner, 1951-59; financial v.p., treas., dir. Whitney Communications Corp., 1959-69; dir. M.L. Ready Assets Trust, Merrill Lynch Capital Fund; partner Whitcom Investment Co., 1967-69. Mem. exec. com. Yale Grad. Sch. Council; trustee Oberlin Coll., 1960-70. Mem. Am. Mgmt. Assn (finance council 1952-55), Phi Beta Kappa. Clubs: Ocean, Gulfstream Golf, St. Andrews (Delray Beach, Fla.); Blind Brook (Purchase, N.Y.); Apawamis (Rye, N.Y.); Mt. Bruno Country (Montreal, Que.); Economic, Board Room (N.Y.C.). Home: 200 N Ocean Blvd Delray Beach FL 33444 also 52 Water's Edge Rye NY 10580

BRYAN, THORNTON EMBRY, JR., family practice physician; b. Frankfort, Ky., Mar. 16, 1927; s. Thornton Embry and Mary Ellen (Stivers) B.; children: Mike, Kathy, David, Leslie, Thornton Embry III. B.S., U. Ky., 1949; M.D., U. Louisville, 1954. Diplomate: Am. Bd. Family Practice. Intern Phila. Gen. Hosp., 1954-55; instr. anatomy U. Louisville, 1950-52; practice family medicine Cadiz Clinic, Ky., 1955-71; asso. prof. dept. family practice U. Iowa, coordinator residency program, dept. family practice, 1971-74; dir. Oakdale Family Practice Office, Iowa, 1971-74; prof., chmn. dept. family medicine U. Tenn. Center Health Scis., Memphis, 1974—; mem. med. bd. City of Memphis Hosp.; active staff St. Francis Hosp.; cons. residency assistance program, chmn. statewide com. family practice planning U. Tenn., 1974—; mem. Council Dept. Chairmen, 1974—; mem. task force on screening for hypertension in rural areas Nat. High Blood Pressure Coordinating Com. of Nat. Heart, Lung and Blood Inst., 1979. Mem. editorial bd.: Seminars in Family Medicine, 1979—; editor: Acad. Mission Family Medicine, Fogarty Procs. 38. Served with USNR, 1945-46. Charter fellow Am. Acad. Family Physicians (pres. Ky. chpt. 1967-68); mem. AMA, Shelby County Med. Soc., Tenn. Med. Assn., Soc. Tchrs. of Family Medicine, Assn. Depts. Family Medicine (bd. dirs.). Office: 66 N Pauline Suite 300 Memphis TN 38105

BRYAN, WILLIAM ROYAL, educator; b. Muncie, Ind., Apr. 16, 1932; s. Frank Cain and Bertha Ellen (Bishop) B.; m. Fanny Elisabeth Bennigsen, Apr. 20, 1979; 1 dau. by previous marriage—Rebecca Gay. B.S., Ball State U., 1954; M.S., U. Wis., 1958, Ph.D., 1961. Tchr. public schs., Cedar Lake, Ind., 1954-55; grad. teaching asst. U. Wis., Madison, 1957-60; sr. economist Fed. Res. Bank of St. Louis, 1960-66; vis. asst. prof. Washington U., St. Louis, 1962-66; prof. fin. U. Ill., 1966—; cons. joint econ. com. U.S. Congress, 1977-79; dir. United of Am. Bank, Chgo. Editor: Illinois Business Rev, 1978—; contbr. articles in field. Served with USAF, 1955-57. Fed. Res. Bank of St. Louis fellow, 1959-60. Mem. Am. Econ. Assn., Western Econ. Assn., Atlantic Econ. Assn., Fin. Mgmt. Assn. Unitarian. Home: 501 W Indiana St Urbana IL 61801 Office: 196 Commerce W 1206 S 6th St Champaign IL 61820

BRYANT, ANITA JANE, entertainer; b. Barnsdall, Okla., Mar. 25, 1940; d. Warren Gene and Lenora (Cate) B.; m. Robert Einar Green, June 25, 1960 (div. Aug. 1980); children: Robert Einar, Gloria Lynn, William Bryant and Barbara Elisabet (twins). Student, Northwestern U., 1959. Owner The Wardrobe, Selma, Ala.; spokeswoman for Coca-Cola Co., 1963-67, State of Fla. Citrus Industry, 1968-80, Friedrich Air Conditioning Co., 1969—. Guest star: Bob Hope's Christmas Tours, 1960-67; sang: Star Spangled Banner for, Democratic and Republican Nat. Convs., 1968, numerous White House performances, 1964-69, numerous Billy Graham Evangelistic Crusades, 1965—; performed at, Orange Bowl and Super Bowl games, 1970-71; TV, rec. artist, author, 1971—; Author: Mine Eyes Have Seen the Glory, 1970, Amazing Grace, 1971, Bless This House, 1972, Fishers of Men, 1973, Light My Candle, 1974, Bless This Food-The Anita Bryant Family Cookbook, 1975, Running the Good Race, 1976, The Anita Bryant Story, 1977, Raising God's Children, At Any Cost; most recent recs. Singing a New Song. Mem. USO Nat. Council, 1961-66; bd. mem. Women's USO of N.Y., 1965—; hon. chmn. Freedoms Found. at Valley Forge, 1969-70, First Found. for One Nation Under God, 1969—; mem. Am. Orchid Soc., 1970—, Friends of Art Soc., 1970—; com. mem. Project Survival, 1970—; film narrator Drugs Are Like That, 1970; hon. chmn. Mental Health Assn. Fla., 1970—; pres. Save Our Children, Inc.; vol. chmn. bd. Performing Arts Ctr., Selma/Dallas County. Recipient USO 25th Ann. Silver Medallion award, 1966, VFW Gold medal and citation award, 1966, Leadership award Freedoms Found. at Valley Forge, 1969, Woman of Year award, 1970; VFW Citizenship Gold medal and citation, 1978; named Number One Most Admired Women in Am. Good Housekeeping poll, 1978-80; named to Gallup Poll Most Admired Women List, 1978; listed on 25 Most Influential Women in Am. List, 1978-79; nominated for Grammy award for best religious recording of How Great Thou Art, 1968; named to Okla. Hall of Fame, 1966; Miss Okla. and runner-up in Miss Am. contest, 1959. Mem. U. Tampa Alumni Assn. (hon.), Fla. Future Bus. Leader of Am. Office: The Wardrobe 219 Lapsley St Selma AL 36701

BRYANT, ARTHUR HERBERT, II, rubber and plastics company executive; b. Washington, June 23, 1942; s. J.C. Herbert and Margret Manning (Couzens) B.; m. Norma Sue Andrews, Oct. 5, 1963; children: Arthur Herbert, James Andrew. Student, Lees McRae Coll., 1960-62, Miami (Fla.) Dade Coll., 1962-63. Vice pres. United Va. Bank, 1963-70, Herbert Bryant, Inc., Alexandria, Va., 1970-75; exec. v.p. O'Sullivan Corp., Winchester, Va., 1975-76, pres., 1976-84, chmn. bd., pres., chief exec. officer, 1984—, also dir.; gen. partner Herbert Bryant Assos.; dir. Gen. Paving Corp., United Va. Bank/Nat. Mem. Va. Mfrs. Assn., Shenandoah Valley Mfrs. Assn. Episcopalian. Clubs: Belle Haven Country, Winchester Country, Loudoun Golf and Country, Middleburg Tennis, Gulf Stream Golf., Gulf Stream Bath and Tennis. Home: Lilliput Farm Middleburg VA 22117 Office: PO Box 603 Winchester VA 22601

BRYANT, BERTHA ESTELLE, retired nurse; b. Va., Jan. 11, 1927; d. E.F. and Julia B. Diploma, Sibley Meml. Hosp., Washington, 1947; B.S., Am. U., 1948; M.A., Tchrs. Coll., Columbia U., 1962. Staff nurse, head nurse NIH, Bethesda, Md., 1954-59; asst. dir. nursing USPHS Alaska Native Hosp., Mt. Edgecumbe, 1959-61; instr. Sch. Nursing, U. Mich., 1962-64; chief div. clin. nursing Bur. Nursing, D.C. Dept. Public Health, Washington, 1964-65; commd. Nurse Corps, USPHS, 1965, nurse dir., 1974—; nurse cons., hosp. facilities services br., div. hosps. and med. facilities Bur. Health Services, HEW, Silver Spring; nurse cons., social analysis br., div. health services research and analysis Nat. Center Health Services Research, Health Resources Adminstrn., HEW, Rockville, Md.; nurse cons. div. extramural research Nat. Center Health Services Research, Office Asst. Sec. Health, HHS, Hyattsville, Md., 1977-81. Contbr. articles to profl. jours. Mem. Am. Nurses Assn., Nat. League Nursing, Am. Public Health Assn., Assn. Mil. Surgeons U.S., Commd. Officers Assn. USPHS. Home: 8004 Westover Rd Bethesda MD 20814

BRYANT, BILLY FINNEY, educator; b. McKenzie, Tenn., Nov. 29, 1922; s. Robert Picard and Ray Ona (Pace) B.; m. Mary Nelle Park, Aug. 28, 1946; children—Robert, David, Elizabeth. B.S., U. S.C., 1945; M.A., Peabody Coll., 1948; Ph.D., Vanderbilt U., 1954. Mem. faculty Vanderbilt U., 1948—, asst. prof. math., 1954-60, asso. prof., 1960-66, prof., 1966—, chmn. dept., 1970-76. Served with USNR, 1942-46. Ford Found. Faculty fellow Princeton, 1955-56; NSF Faculty fellow U. Calif. at Berkeley, 1967-68. Mem. Am. Math. Soc., Math. Assn. Am. (chmn., sec.-treas., gov. Southeastern sect.). Research publs. in topology. Home: 6020 Sherwood Dr Nashville TN 37215

BRYANT, BRITAIN HAMILTON, former state senator, lawyer; b. Louisville, Mar. 21, 1940; s. William Hamilton and Virginia (Throgmorton) B.; m. Peyton Gresham, Apr. 24, 1965; children: Anne Hamilton, Stewart Wells. Student, Centre Coll. Ky., 1958-59; B.S. in Law, U. Louisville, 1962, J.D., 1964, Sch. Law, Washington and Lee U., 1963. Bar: Ky. bar 1965, V.I. bar 1965, U.S. Supreme Ct. bar 1972. Partner firm Bryant and Lenahan, Christiansted, St. Croix, V.I., 1970—; mem. V.I. Senate, 1973-79, v.p., 1975-79; state chmn. Democratic Party, 1980-81. Mem. Law Enforcement Assistance Commn., V.I. Am. Bicentennail Commn.; bd. dirs. St. Croix Chpt. ARC. Mem. V.I. Bar Assn. (sec. 1969-71, v.p. 1972), ABA, St. Croix C. of C. (sec. 1969-72), Am. Trial Lawyers Assn., World Peace Through Law Assn., Am. Law Inst., V.I. Jud. Council (permanet mem. 3d circuit jud. comf.), Beta Theta Pi, Phi Delta Phi. Home: PO Box 3009 Christiansted St Croix VI 00820 Office: 7 King St Christiansted St Croix VI 00820 *You are only here once and no one knows for how long. I believe that every moment should be used to the maximum possible extent, working with, meeting and helping others, which in turn makes life worth living to its fullest extent.*

BRYANT, CECIL FARRIS, lawyer, insurance company executive; b. Ocala, Fla., July 26, 1914; s. Charles Cecil and Lela Margaret (Farris) B.; m. Julia Burnett, Sept. 18, 1940; children: Julie Lovett, Cecilia Ann, Allison Adair. Student, Emory U., 1931-32; B.S., U. Fla., 1935; J.D., Harvard U., 1938; LL.D., Rollins Coll., Fla. State U., Fla. Atlantic U., Fla. So. Coll. Bar: Fla., U.S. Supreme Ct. Auditor Fla. Comptroller's Office, 1939-40; counsel to law Bryant, Miller & Olive, Tallahassee; pres. Voyager Group, Inc., Jacksonville, 1968—; pres., chmn. bd. Voyager Life Ins. Co., Jacksonville, 1965—; mem. Fla. Ho. Reps., 1942, 46-55, speaker of ho., 1953; del. Dem. Nat. Conv., 1952, 60, 68, alt. del., 1964, chmn. Fla. delegation, 1964; gov., State of Fla., 1961-65; dir. Calif. Fed. Savs. & Loan Assn. Fla. div., Ocala, Air Fla. System Inc. Dir. Office of Emergency Planning, 1966-67; mem. Nat. Security Council, 1966-67; chmn. adv. Commn. on Intergovtl. Relations, 1966-69; U.S. rep. NATO, 1967. Served with USN, 1942-46. Named Most Valuable Mem. Fla. Ho. of Reps., 1949, 51, 53, St. Petersburg Times Poll, 1949, 51, 55; recipient Top Mgmt. award Sales and Mktg. Execs. Assn., 1976. Mem. Fla. Bar Assn., Am. Legion, VFW, Fla. Council of 100, Phi Delta Phi, Alpha Kappa Psi, Kappa Delta Pi, Alpha Phi Omega, Alpha Tau Omega. Methodist. Clubs: Rotary, Elks, Masons, Shriners. Office: PO Box 2918 Jacksonville FL 32203

BRYANT, CELIA MAE SMALL, educator; b. Porum, Okla., Aug. 11, 1913; d. George Milton and Elsie (Sigmon) Small; m. William Cullen Bryant III, Oct. 3, 1932 (div. May 1945); children—Ann (Mrs. Robert L. Trent), Mary Carol (Mrs. Robert Fritchof Hansen), Culleen (Mrs. Ronald George Tobin). Mus.B. in Piano, U. Okla., 1947, Mus.M., 1948; pvt. study, Frank Mannheimer. Mem. faculty U. Okla., Norman, 1948—, prof. music, 1967—; vis. prof. Interlochen Center for Arts, 1972-73; mem. Okla. Commn. Tchr. Edn. and Profl. Standards, 1962-63; Mem. U.S. Commn. for UNESCO, 1974-79; leader dels. profl. musicians U.S. Goodwill People-to-People Program, Eastern Europe and USSR, 1974, 75, People's Republic of China, 1981. Appeared as pianist numerous recitals; music adjudicator, clinican; Editor piano pedagogy dept.: Clavier Mag, 1961—; writer: series Music Lesson, 1963—; Contbr. articles to publs. Bd. dirs. Nat. Music Council, 1971-73. Named one of Nine Outstanding Music Educators in Nation Mu Phi Epsilon, 1962; nat. citation Phi Mu Alpha, 1972; Okla. award as outstanding state musician, 1973. Mem. Music Tchrs. Nat. Assn. (nat. v.p. 1965-69, nat. pres. 1969-73), Am. Music Scholarship Assn. (adv. bd. 1972-78), Okla. Music Tchrs. Assn. (pres. 1962-66), U. Okla. Tchr. Edn. Council (chmn. 1958-62), Pi Kappa Lambda (chpt. pres. 1965-67). Club: MacDowell Allied Arts Club (treas., pres. 1962-66). Home: 614 E Okmulgee St Norman OK 73071 *I have always loved my chosen profession and considered my talent in music as a special blessing. A sincere interest and respect for my students, professional colleagues and people in general have brought genuine rewards. No one can ever succeed without the support of others. Efficiency, enthusiasm, and dedication are undoubtedly the three major factors for success, with the perseverance to make yourself do all the things that must be done even when they lack major interest.*

BRYANT, CLIFTON DOW, sociologist, educator; b. Jackson, Miss., Dec. 25, 1932; s. Clifton Edward and Helen (Dow) B.; m. Nancy Ann Arrington, Sept. 13, 1953; m. Patty Maurine Watts, Feb. 1, 1957; children: Melinda Dow, Deborah Carol, Karen Diane, Clifton Dow II. Student, U. Miss., 1950-53, B.A., 1956, M.A., 1957; postgrad., U. N.C., Chapel Hill, 1957-58, La. State U., 1958-60, Ph.D., 1964. Vis. instr. dept. sociology and anthropology Pa. State U., summer, 1958; instr., research asso. dept. sociology and anthropology U. Ga., 1960-63; asst. prof., asso. prof., chmn. dept. sociology and anthropology Millsaps Coll., Jackson, Miss., 1963-67; summer research participant, tng. and tech. project Oak Ridge Asso. Univs., summer 1967; prof., head dept. sociology and anthropology Western Ky. U., Bowling Green, Ky., 1967-72; prof. sociology Va. Poly. Inst. and State U., Blacksburg, 1972—; head dept. Va Poly. Inst. and State U., Blacksburg, 1972-82. Author: Khaki-Collar Crime: Deviant Behavior in Military Context, 1979, Sexual Deviancy and Social Proscription, 1982; editor and contbr.: Deviant Behavior: Occupational and Organizational Bases, 1974, The Social Dimensions of Work, 1972, Sexual Deviancy in Social Context, 1977; co-editor, contbr.: Deviancy and the Family, 1973; compiler: Handbook of Audio-Visual Resources to Accompany Social Problems Today, 1971; editor: Social Problems Today: Dilemmas and Dissensus, 1971; co-editor: Introductory Sociology: Selected Readings for the College Scene, 1970; editor-in-chief: Deviant Behavior: An Interdisciplinary Jour, 1978—; editor: So. Sociologist, 1970-74; mem. editorial bd.: Criminology: An Interdisciplinary Jour, 1978-81; chmn. editorial bd.: Sociological Symposium, 1968-80; asso. editor: Sociol. Forum, 1979-80, Sociol. Spectrum, 1981—; mem. bd. adv. editors: Sociol. Inquiry, 1981—; assoc. editor spl. issue: Marriage and Family Relations, fall 1982; contbr. chpts. to books, articles, book reviews to profl. publs. Served to 1st lt., M.P. U.S. Army, 1953-55. Mem. Am. Sociol. Assn., Am. Soc. Criminology, So. Sociol. Soc. (pres. 1978-79), Mid-South Sociol. Assn. (pres. 1981-82), Rural Sociol. Soc., Inter-Univ. Seminar on Armed Forces and Society, So. Assn. Agr. Scientists (rural sociology sect.), Phi Kappa Phi, Pi Kappa Alpha, Alpha Phi Omega, Alpha Kappa Delta. Presbyterian. Home: 6 East Ridge Dr Blacksburg VA 24060 Office: Dept Sociology Virginia Polytechnic Inst State Univ Blacksburg VA 24061

BRYANT, DAVID ERNEST, editor; b. Appanoose County, Iowa, Feb. 14, 1922; s. David Reo and Bessie Bly (Harl) B.; m. LeVergne C. Bookwalter, June 5, 1965; children—Marilyn K., Virginia L., David W. B.S. in Agrl. Journalism, Iowa State U., 1950. Farm editor Globe-Gazette, Mason City, Iowa, 1950-51; field editor Wallaces Farmer, Des Moines, 1951-57; editor Iowa Rural Electric News, Des Moines, 1957-64; asso. editor mng. editor Today's Farmer, Columbia, Mo., 1964-71, editor, 1971-80, Ag Newsletter Service, Des Moines, 1980—. Served with U.S. Army, 1942-46. Recipient Disting. Service award; Gamma Sigma Delta, 1974. Mem. Am. Agrl. Editors Assn. (pres. 1977), Coop. Editorial Assn. U.S.A. (Klinefelter award 1973), Sigma Delta Chi. Democrat. Methodist. Club: Press. Home: 3920 Adams Ave Des Moines IA 50310 Office: Ag Newsletter Service 801 Park St Des Moines IA 50309

BRYANT, DONALD LOUDON, pharmaceutical company executive; b. N.Y.C., June 25, 1908; s. Mortimer D. and Florence (Loudon) B.; m. Elizabeth Sheetz, 1956 (dec. 1983). B.A., Williams Coll., 1930; grad., Advanced Mgmt. Program, Harvard U., 1962. With Fed. Advt. Agy., N.Y.C., 1931-35, Publ. Corp., 1935-45; with Warner Lambert Pharm. Co., Morris Plains, N.J., 1945-59, with Richard Hudnut div., 1953-55, pres. Ciro Perfumes div., 1957, v.p., asst. to pres., 1956-59; pres., dir. Q-Tips, Inc., L.I., N.Y., 1959-63; with Miles Labs., Inc., Elkhart, Ind., 1963-76, group v.p., dir. consumer products div., mem. exec. and finance coms., 1964-73, sr. v.p., 1972-73, dir., 1964-76. Mem. Proprietary Assn. (exec. com. 1964-73, v.p.), World Fedn. Proprietary Medicine Mfrs. (chmn. 1970-73), Assn. Ex-mems. Squadron A, Elkhart C. of C., Delta Kappa Epsilon. Presbyn. Clubs: Williams (N.Y.C.); Boca Raton, Broken Sound Golf, Harvard Bus. Sch. S. Fla. Home: 875 E Camino Real Boca Raton FL 33432 Office: 1127 Myrtle St Elkhart IN 46514 *I would emphasize to a young person starting business: (1) Finish whatever you start. Don't quit because the going gets rough; (2) Conversely don't become so comfortable and secure in your job as to blind yourself to other possibilities; (3) As you gain in responsibility surround yourself with people you have to hold in check, not people you have to push; and with them school yourself to be a patient listener; (4) Most business decisions can be made in one or more different ways without altering the course of the enterprise. Make these with dispatch. The rare one that might have a profound effect calls for time to study all your options. Once you have made your best judgement don't look back.*

BRYANT, DONALD LOYD, insurance company executive; b. Orchard, Iowa, Jan. 30, 1919; s. Lester E. and Bessie (Farless) B.; m. Eileen Galloway, May 11, 1941; children: Donald Loyd, Hedy E. Bryant Garlock, Brenda K., Becky Bryant Hubert. B.Ed., So. Ill. U., 1940. With War Manpower Commn., Mt. Vernon, Ill., 1940; agt., dist. mgr. Equitable Life Assurance Soc. U.S., Elgin and Carbondale, Ill., 1946-54, agy. mgr., St. Louis, 1954-69, v.p., chief agy. staff ops., N.Y.C., 1969-71, v.p. corp. relations, 1971-72, sr. v.p. corp. relations, 1972-74, exec. v.p., spl. asst. to pres., 1974-78, exec. v.p., 1978-81; dir. Tandy Corp., Roper Corp.; bus exec.-in-residence Tex. Christian U., Ft. Worth, 1980—. Served to lt. USN, 1942-46. Recipient Alumni Achievement award So. Ill. U., 1964. Presbyterian. Clubs: Algonquin Golf (St. Louis); Quail Ridge Golf and Tennis (Boynton Beach, Fla.). Home and Office: 1489 Partridge Pl N Boynton Beach FL 33436 *On each job, behave as though you will be on that job for the remainder of your working life. In this way you avoid mistakes because you'd have to live with those mistakes. You are careful to pick good associates because you will have to live with them forever. You give security to your subordinates, command their loyalty, because they sense you'll be there forever. Ironically you'll then do such a superior job that you'll be promoted over and over while behaving as though you'll be on your job forever.*

BRYANT, DOUGLAS WALLACE, librarian; b. Visalia, Calif., June 20, 1913; s. Albert George and Ethel (Wallace) B.; m. Rene Leilani Kuhn, Apr. 6, 1953; 1 dau., Heather Corbally. Student, U. Munich, Germany, 1932-33; A.B., Stanford, 1935; A.M. in L.S, U. Mich., 1938. Asst. curator printed books William L. Clements Library, U. Mich., 1936-38; sr. reference asst., tech. dept. Detroit Pub. Library, 1938-41; asst. chief Burton Hist. Collection, 1941-42; asst. librarian U. Calif. at Berkeley, 1946-49; attache Am. Embassy, London, 1949-52; adminstrv. asst. librarian Harvard Coll. Library, 1952- 55; asso. dir. Harvard U. Library, 1955-64; univ. librarian Harvard, 1964-72, dir. univ. library, prof. bibliography, 1972-79, prof. bibliography, librarian emeritus, 1979—; trustee, exec. dir. Am. Trust for Brit. Library, 1979—; mem. U.S. nat. commn. for UNESCO, 1953-55; v.p. Internat. Fedn. Library Assns., 1952-58, Internat. Fedn. for Documentation, 1956-58; cons. Ford Found., Ankara, Turkey, 1954, Rockefeller Found., London, 1956; lectr., cons. Japanese univ. libraries, 1963; cons. Inst. Am. Studies, Free U., Berlin, 1964-66, London Sch. Econs., 1965-66; Chmn. bd. dirs. Center Research Libraries, 1969-70. Served to lt. comdr. USNR, World War II; head tech. data br. Bur. Aeros. Navy Dept.; Washington. Fellow Am. Acad. Arts and Scis., Royal Soc. Arts; mem. ALA (chmn. internat. relations com. 1952-55, chmn. coordinating com. on Slavic and East European library resources 1959-61, chmn. Assn. Research Libraries Com. on preservation research library materials 1960-68, pres. 1969-70), Mass. Hist. Soc., Am. Antiquarian Soc. Clubs: Grolier, Harvard (N.Y.); Odd Volumes (Boston). Home: 35 Woodland Rd Lexington MA 02173 Office: PO Box 463 Cambridge MA 02238

BRYANT, EDWARD ALBERT, art gallery director, art educator; b. Lenoir, N.C., July 23, 1928; s. Edmond Henry and Shelton Emmaline (Robbins) B.; m. Tamara Thompson, May 28, 1965; children: Adam Edmond, Mary Emmaline. A.B., U. N.C., 1950, M.A., 1955; postgrad., U. Italiana per Stranieri, Perugia, 1954, U. di Pisa, Italy, 1954-55, U. di Ravenna, Italy, 1955, N.C. State Coll., 1956, Columbia U., 1958. Fellow Bklyn. Mus., 1957-58; European study grant for research contemporary Italian drawings, 1958-59; gen. curator Wadsworth Atheneum, Hartford, Conn., 1959-61; asso. curator Whitney Mus. Am. Art, N.Y.C., 1961-65; dir. U. Ky. Art Gallery, Lexington, 1965-68, Picker Gallery; assoc. prof. Colgate U., 1968-80, prof. art, 1980; acting chmn. dept. fine arts, 1976-77; prof. art, dir. Art Mus., U. N.Mex., Albuquerque, 1980—; cons. Ky. Arts Commn., 1967-68. Author: Painting, 1958, Jack Tworkov, 1964, 32 Drawings by Robert Broderson, 1964, Jason Seley, 1980, Joseph Pennell's New York City, 1980; Co-author: African Sculpture, 1958, Forty Artists Under Forty, (with Lloyd Goodrich), 1962; exhbns. include African sculpture, Bklyn. Mus., 1958, contemporary Italian drawings and collage, Am. Fedn. Arts, 1959; Jack Tworkov Retrospective Exhbn, Whitney Mus., 1964; contemporary Italian drawings and collage A Decade of New Talent, Am. Fedn. Arts, 1964; Graphics, 1968, Larry Zox, Jason Seley, Alex Katz, John Koch, Sidney Tillim, Nell Blaine, Tom Doyle, Leon Golub, Nancy Spero, Victor Burgin, Michael Mazur, Edward Ruscha, ElectrostaticPrints, Folk Art of Central N.Y. State, Viewpoint exhbn. series, Colgate U.; Concepts and Issues exhbn. series, Photography series, Images from N.Mex., Geometric Formalism in Am. Art, U. N.Mex. Pres. Poolville (N.Y.) Vol. Fire Dept., 1972-73, Cub master Boy Scouts Am., Earlville, N.Y., 1975-76; treas. Cub master Boy Scouts Am., 1976-77. Fulbright fellow, 1954-55; spl. research grant Colgate U., 1969-70, 76; Nat. Endowment for the Arts grantee, 1974-75. Mem. Gallery Assn. N.Y. State (treas., dir. 1973-78). Home: 1400 Marron Circle NE Albuquerque NM 87112 Office: Art Museum U NMex Albuquerque NM 87131

BRYANT, EDWARD CLARK, contract research company executive; b. Hat Creek, Wyo., June 28, 1915; s. Alpha Clark and Pearl Amelia (Hunter) B.; m. Virginia May DeGering, June 15, 1941; children: Edward Hunter, Bonnie Jeanne Bryant Kirkpatrick. B.S., U. Wyo., 1938, M.S., 1940; Ph.D. in Stats, Iowa State U., 1955. Jr. statistician, asst. economist ICC, 1940-42; asso. economist WPB, 1942-43; civilian chief statistician Armed Forces Middle Pacific, 1946-47; from asst. prof. to prof. stats., head dept. U. Wyo., 1947-61; vis. prof. math. Ariz. State U., 1961-63; pres. Westat, Inc., Rockville, Md., 1963-78, chmn. bd., 1978—; bd. dirs. Profl. Service Council. Author: Statistical Analysis, rev. edit, 1965; also articles. Mem. Laramie (Wyo.) Planning Commn., 1958-61. Served with AUS, 1943-46. Recipient Disting. Civilian Service award U.S. Army, 1947, Disting. Alumnus award U. Wyo., 1975. Fellow Am. Statis. Assn., AAAS. Republican. Home: 9000 Rouen Ln Potomac MD 20854 Office: 1650 Research Blvd Rockville MD 20850

BRYANT, EDWARD KENDALL, civil engr.; b. Norwood, Mass., Apr. 13, 1902; s. Edward Andem and Alice Elizabeth (Crandell) B.; m. Tamara Herne, Nov. 23, 1966; children—Edward Andem, John Dixon. C.E., Rensselaer Poly. Inst., 1925. Engr. William S. Lozier, Rochester, N.Y., 1924-28; prin. John L. Weber, Inc., Trenton, N.J., 1928-30; owner, operator Edward K. Bryant (Cons. Engr.), Mt. Holly, N.J., 1930-42; project engr. Tippetts Abbett McCarthy Stratton, N.Y.C., 1946-56, partner, 1956-73; owner, operator Edward K. Bryant (Cons. Engr.), Chevy Chase, Md., 1974—. Served from lt. to comdr. Civil Engr. Corps USN, 1942-46. Mem. ASCE, Am. Cons. Engrs. Council, Soc. for Internat. Devel., Am. Arbitration Assn., Soc. Am. Mil. Engrs., Theta Chi. Republican. Episcopalian. Club: Army and Navy (Washington). Home and Office: 4620 N Park Ave Chevy Chase MD 20815

BRYANT, FREDERIC M., III, investment banking firm executive; b. Camden, S.C., June 20, 1932; s. Fred Morse and Inez (Wooten) B.; m. Mary Hering, Aug. 20, 1955; children: Frederic M. IV, Kendal, Mary. B.S., U. Med., 1956. Rep. Alex Brown & Sons, Twoson, Md., 1959-72, sales mgr., Balt., 1972-76, gen. ptnr., 1976—. Chmn. Lung Assn. North Central Md., Towson, 1976-78; bd. dirs. Presbyterian Home, Towson, 1981—. Mem. Bond Club Balt. (pres. 1980-81). Republican. Presbyterian. Clubs: Balt. Country; Merchants, Engrs. (Balt.); Tred Avon Yacht (Oxford, Md.). Office: Alex Brown & Sons 135 E Baltimore St Baltimore MD 21202

BRYANT, GAY, magazine editor, writer; b. Newcastle, Eng., Oct. 5, 1945; came to U.S., 1970; s. Richard King and Catherine (Shiel) B.; m. Charles Childs, Apr. 10, 1982. Student, St. Clare's Coll., Oxford, Eng., 1961-63. Sr. editor Penthouse Mag., N.Y.C., 1968-74; assoc. editor Oui mag., N.Y.C., 1974-75; founding editor New Dawn mag., N.Y.C., 1975-79; exec. editor Working Woman mag., N.Y.C., 1979-81, editor, 1981-84; editor, v.p. Family Circle mag., N.Y.C., 1984—; adj. prof. Sch. Journalism, NYU, 1982—. Author: The Underground Travel Guide, 1973, How I Learned To Like Myself, 1975, The Working Woman Report, 1984. Active NOW. Recipient award Acad. Women Achievers, YMCA, N.Y.C., 1982. Mem. Women's Media Group, Women in Communications, Am. Soc. Mag. Editors. Club: Liberty (N.Y.C.). Home: 34 Horatio St New York NY 10014 Office: Family Circle Mag 488 Madison Ave New York NY 10022

BRYANT, HUBERT HALE, lawyer; b. Tulsa, Jan. 4, 1931; s. Roscoe Conkling and Curlie Beatrice (Marshall) B.; m. Elnora Geraldine Roberson, Oct. 25, 1952; children—Cheryl Denise, Tara Kay. B.A., Fisk U., 1952; LL.B., Howard U., 1956. Bar: Okla. bar 1956, U.S. Dist. Ct. bar for No. Dist. Okla 1956, U.S. Supreme Ct. bar 1980. Individual practice law, Tulsa, 1956-67, 81—; asst. city prosecutor, City of Tulsa, 1961-63, chief city prosecutor, 1963-67, asst. U.S. atty., No. Dist. Okla., 1967-77, U.S. atty., 1977-81. Trustee 1st Baptist Ch., Tulsa, 1970-75; bd. dirs. Tulsa Urban League, 1962-64. Recipient Outstanding Alumni award Howard U. Sch. Law, 1981. Mem. Nat., Okla., Tulsa County bar assns., Sigma Pi Phi, Alpha Theta Boule, Alpha Phi Alpha. Democrat. Clubs: Nat. Set, Masons (named Mason of year local chpt. 1963), Masons (Outstanding Citizen award 1978). Home: 1818 N Boston St Tulsa OK 74106 Office: 1623-A N Peoria St Tulsa OK 74106

BRYANT, JAMES FREDERIC, food company executive; b. Lincoln, Nebr., Feb. 4, 1938; s. James Chilton and Loraine (Fender) B.; m. Linda K. Jurgensen, Mar. 17, 1979; children by previous marriage: James Mark, Jill Rae. B.S. in B.A., U. Nebr., 1960. With Internorth, Omaha, 1960-66; adminstrv. asst. to v.p. prodn. IBP, Inc., Dakota City, Nebr., 1966-69, v.p. prodn., 1976-81, group v.p. human resources, 1981—; v.p. indsl. relations, engrng. and constrn. Spencer Foods, Spencer, Iowa, 1969-76; dir. PBX, IBP, Inc., 1981—. Eagle Scout Boy Scouts Am., 1957. Republican. Lutheran. Lodge: Masons. Home: 655 Shady Lane Dr Sioux City IA 51104 Office: PO Box 515 Hwy 35 Dakota City NE 68731

BRYANT, JOHN HAROLD, electronics company executive; b. Baird, Tex., Apr. 15, 1920; s. John Peden and Cordie Elizabeth (Peek) B.; m. Barbara Alice Everitt, Aug. 14, 1948; children: Linda J., Randal E., Lois B. B.S.E.E., Tex. A&M U., 1942; M.S., U. Ill., 1947, Ph.D., 1949. Div. head, microwave electron tubes IT&T Labs., 1949-55; staff engr., radar systems and microwave components Bendix Corp. Research Labs., Southfield, Mich., 1955-62; founder, pres., chief exec. officer Omni Spectra, Inc., Merrimack, N.H., 1962-75, chmn. bd., 1975-78, dir., 1962-80; cons. Omni Spectra, Inc. subs. Macom, Inc., 1980—. Contbr. articles to profl. jours. Served with AUS, 1942-46. Recipient Disting. Alumnus award U. Ill. Coll. Engring., 1971, honor award for entrepreneurship, 1980. Fellow IEEE; mem. IEEE Microwave Theory and Techniques Soc. (pres. 1970), Sigma Xi, Eta Kappa Nu, Tau Beta Pi. Republican. Presbyterian. Patentee in field. Home: 1505 Sheridan Dr Ann Arbor MI 48104

BRYANT, JOHN WILEY, congressman; b. Lake Jackson, Tex., Feb. 22, 1947; s. Robert Link and Billie Rae (Willey) B.; m. Janet Elizabeth Watts, Dec. 28, 1968; children: Amy, John Wiley, Jordan. B.A., So. Meth. U., 1969; J.D., So. Meth U., 1972. Bar: Tex. 1972. Atty. at law Stanford and Bryant, Dallas, 1972—; chief counsel Tex. senate Subcom. on Consumer Protection, Austin, 1973; adminstrv. asst. Tex. Senate, Austin, Dallas, 1972-73; mem. Tex. Ho. of Reps., 1973-82, 98th Congress from 5th dist. Tex.; mem. exec. com. U.S. Ho. dem. Study Group, 1983. Named Hardest Working Mem. Tex. Capital Press Corps., 1977, Outstanding Legislator Tex. Monthly Mag., 1977, 79,

One of Five Outstanding Young Texans Tex. Jaycees, 1979. Mem. Old Scyene Hist. Soc., Hist. Preservation Soc., Deaf Action Center Dallas (bd. dirs.), Lion's Eye Bank (Dallas) (life). Democrat. Methodist. Lodge: Rotary. Home: 8035 E R L Thornton St Dallas TX 75228 Office: US Ho of Reps 506 Cannon House Office Bldg Washington DC 20515

BRYANT, JOSEPH ALLEN, JR., educator; b. Glasgow, Ky., Nov. 26, 1919; s. Joseph Allen and Florence Morford (Rogers) B.; m. Mary Virginia Woodruff, Dec. 28, 1946; children—Joseph Allen, III, Garnett Woodruff. A.B., Western U., 1940; M.A., Vanderbilt U., 1941; Ph.D., Yale U., 1948. Instr., then asso. prof. English Vanderbilt U., 1948-56; asso. prof. U. South, Sewanne, Tenn., 1956-59, Duke U., 1959-61; prof., chmn. dept. U. N.C., Greensboro, 1961-68, Syracuse (N.Y.) U., 1968-71; prof. English U. Ky., Lexington, 1971—, chmn. dept., 1973-81; Fulbright lectr. U. Nantes, France, 1965-66. Author: Hippolyta's View, 1961, Eudora Welty, 1968, Compassionate Satirist, 1973; editor: Romeo and Juliet, 1964. Served to lt. (j.g.) USNR, 1942-46. Recipient Research award U. Ky., 1973; Ford fellow, 1952-53; Sewanee Rev. fellow, 1958-59. Mem. MLA, Renaissance Soc. Am., Shakespeare Soc. Am., S.Atlantic Modern Lang. Assn. (Book award 1972), So. Humanities Conf., Southeastern Renaissance Conf., Soc. Study So. Lit. Democrat. Episcopalian. Home: 3268 Foxtale Ct Lexington KY 40502 Office: 1377 Patterson Office Tower Univ Ky Lexington KY 40506

BRYANT, KEITH LYNN, JR., university dean, historian; b. Oklahoma City, Nov. 6, 1937; s. Keith Lynn and Elsie L. (Furman) B.; m. Margaret A. Burum, Aug. 14, 1962; children: Jennifer Lynne, Craig Warne. B.S., U. Okla., 1959, M.Ed., 1961; Ph.D., U. Mo., 1965. Asst. prof., asso. prof., prof., asso. dean U. Wis., Milw., 1965-76; prof., head dept. history, dean Coll. Liberal Arts, Tex. A&M U., College Station, 1976—; cons. So. Ry., Nat. Endowment for Humanities. Author: Atchison, Topeka and Santa Fe Railway, 1974, Arthur E. Stilwell, Promoter With a Hunch, 1971, Alfalfa Bill Murray, 1968. Various offices local Rep. Party, Okla. Various offices local Rep. Party, Tex.; chmn. Bush for Pres., Brazos County, 1979-80. Served to 1st lt. U.S. Army, 1959-60. Recipient William H. Kiekhofer award U. Wis., 1968. Mem. Am. Hist. Assn., Orgn. Am. Historians, So. Hist. Assn., Tex. State Hist. Assn., Lexington Group. Presbyterian. Home: 2102 Briar Oaks Bryan TX 77802 Office: College Liberal Arts Texas A&M Univ College Station TX 77843

BRYANT, LESTER R., surgeon; b. Louisville, Sept. 8, 1930; s. L.R. and Pearl B.; children—Leslie Bond, Lance Bryant. B.S. with high distinction, U. Ky., 1951; M.D., U. Cin., 1955, D.Sc. in Surgery, 1962. Diplomate: Am. Bd. Surgery., Am. Bd. Thoracic Surgery. Intern Cin. Gen. Hosp., 1955-56, asst. resident in surgery, 1956-61, chief resident in surgery, 1961-62; fellow in physiology Baylor U. Coll. Medicine, 1961; mem. faculty U. Ky. Coll. Medicine, 1962-73, prof., 1969-73, chief div. cardiothoracic surgery, 1967-73, vice chmn. dept. surgery, 1972-73; prof. surgery, chief sect. thoracic and cardiovascular surgery La. State U., 1973-77; prof., chmn. dept. surgery East Tenn. State U. Coll. Medicine, Johnson City, 1977—; cons. VA Hosp., Johnson City, 1977—; attending staff Med.Center Hosp., Johnson City, 1978—; chmn. Surg. Merit Rev. Bd., VA, 1972-76; mem. anesthetic and life support drugs adv. com. HEW, Public Health Service, FDA, Washington, 1975-80; mem. research com. Tenn. affiliate Am. Heart Assn., 1978-80; vis. prof. U. Hong Kong, 1968. Contbr. articles to med. jours. Fellow A.C.S., Am. Heart Assn.; mem. Am. Assn. Thoracic Surgery, Am. Surg. Assn. Am. Coll. Chest Physicians, Central Surg. Assn., Soc. Thoracic Surgeons, Soc. Surg. Chmn., Soc. Univ. Surgeons, So. Surg. Assn., So. Thoracic Surg. Assn., U. Cin. Grad. Surg. Soc., Phi Beta Kappa, Alpha Omega Alpha, Pi Kappa Epsilon. Home: 906 Woodland Ave Johnson City TN 37601 Office: East Tenn State U Coll Medicine Box 19750A Johnson City TN 37614

BRYANT, MARGARET M., retired educator; b. Trenton, S.C., Dec. 3, 1900; d. John Lee and Harriet (Yonce) B. A.B., Winthrop (S.C.) Coll., 1921, L.H.D., 1968; student, U. Va., 1922; A.M., Columbia, 1925; Ph.D., 1931; Ph.D. Inst. Gen. Semantics, N.Y. U., 1945, Folklore Inst., Ind. U., 1946; Litt.D., Cedar Crest Coll., 1966; L.H.D., Winthrop Coll., 1968; D.H., Francis Marion Coll., 1979; D.Litt., No. Mich. U., 1979. Prin. public and pvt. schs., S.C., Kans., W.Va., N.Y., 1921-25; head English dept. Chowan Coll., N.C., 1925-26; faculty Hunter Coll., 1926-33; instr. to prof. Bklyn. Coll., City U. N.Y., day session 1930-71, evening session 1931-38, departmental rep. English dept., evening session, 1937-40, acting chmn. English dept., 1940-41, chmn., 1941-44, asst. prof. to prof., 1937-71; vis. prof. univs., Vt., Ark., Utah, Colo., New Sch. Social Research, 1947-50; vis. prof. Columbia U., 1952-53, adj. prof., fall 1955-56; vis. prof. univs. Uppsala, Stockholm and Handelshögskolan, 1950-51; vis. prof. Rutgers U., summer 1962; with commn. on English; grad. faculty City U. N.Y., 1962-71; Distinguished prof. Winthrop Coll., summer 1973. Author: English in the Law Courts, 1931, 2d edit., 1962, A Functional English Grammar, 1945, Japanese edit., 1971, Proverbs and How to Collect Them, 1945, Modern English and Its Heritage, 1948, 2d edit., 1962, Introduction to R.H. Thornton's An American Glossary, 2d edit. (3 vols.), 1962, Modern English Syntax, 1976; co-author: Psychology of English, 1940, 2d edit., 1962, English at Work (4 vols.), 1953, The Development of General and English Linguistic Studies in Japan, 1981; Editor: Essays Old and New, 1940, Current American Usage, 1962; co-editor: Prose Pieces, 1941; Contbr. to periodicals. Hon. v.p. Internat. Congress Onomastic Scis., 1981. Recipient gold medal for conspicuous service Columbia, 1941, Mary Mildred Sullivan award Winthrop Coll., 1956. Mem. N.Y. Council Tchrs. English, Coll. Council English in Central Atlantic States (chmn. 1942-44), Modern Lang. Assn., Nat. Council Tchrs. English (dir. 1946-60, exec. com. 1948-50), Am. Dialect Soc. (exec. council 1952-54), Am. Name Soc. (pres. 1958-59, 1st v.p. 1973-74, pres. 1974-75), Internat. Assn. U. Profs. English, Philol. Soc. Eng., Internat. Folk Music Council, Am. (council 1946-60), N.Y. (v.p. 1949-52) folklore socs), Nat. Folk Festival Assn. (cons. 1949-77), Linguistic Soc. Am., Am. Soc. Geolinguistics (exec. council 1975-79, 81—, pres. 1979-80), AAUP, Internat. Linguistic Assn. (pres. 1972-73, exec. council 1973-76, adv. council 1976-82), AAUW (pres. N.Y.C. 1955-59, recipient Founders' Day citation 1962, 66, Woman of Achievement award N.Y.C. br. 1969), Univ. Women's Forum (chmn., pres. 1958-75), Internat. Fedn. U. Women, Virginia Gildersleeve Internat. Fund for U. Women (trustee, dir. 1976-82), N.Y. Coll. English Assn., Modern Humanities Research Assn. (Am. com. 1960-65), Coll. English Assn., English Inst., Internat. Soc. for Gen. Semantics, Medieval Club N.Y. (pres. 1973-75), Friends of Sarah Tucker Schs. (pres. 1960-77), Phi Beta Kappa (v.p. N.Y. assn. 1971-74, pres. 1974-76), Phi Kappa Phi. Home: 205 Clemson Downs Clemson SC 29631 *One must accumulate knowledge in a field in order to go forward.*

BRYANT, MARVIN PIERCE, bacteriologist; b. Boise, Idaho, July 4, 1925; s. Melvin Berry and Emma Louise (Bucklin) B.; m. Margaret Amelia Betebenner, June 30, 1946; children—Margaret Patricia Bryant Smith, Susan Jean Bryant Kruidenier, Katherine Clair Bryant Smith, Robert Marvin, Steven Edward. Diploma, Boise Jr. Coll., 1947; B.S., Wash. State U., 1949, M.S., 1950; postgrad., Cornell U., 1950; Ph.D., U. Md., 1955. Research bacteriologist U.S. Dept. Agr., Beltsville, Md., 1951-62; leader rumen microbiology investigations, 1962-64; asso. prof. bacteriology U. Ill., Urbana, 1964-66, prof. microbiology, 1966—; vis. scientist Inst. for Microbiology, Göttingen, W.Ger., 1976; univ. vis. prof. U. Guelph, Ont., Can., 1978; cons. on anaerobic bacteria and biol. methane formation. Editor: Applied and Environ. Microbiology, 1969-71; editor-in-chief, 1971-80; trustee: Bergey's Manual of Determinative Bacteriology, vice chmn, 1975—. Served with U.S. Air Corps, 1944-45. Recipient Superior Service award Dept. Agr., 1959, Borden award Am. Dairy Sci. Assn., 1978; Paul A. Funk award for research, 1979. Fellow AAAS, Am. Acad. Microbiology; mem. Am. Soc. for Microbiology, Soc. for Gen. Microbiology, Am. Dairy Sci. Assn., Council Biol. Editors, Phi Beta Kappa, Sigma Xi, Phi Kappa Phi. Research on isolation and characterization of anaerobic bacteria of gastro-intestinal tract and methanogenic fermentations and research on their ecology and metabolism. Home: 1003 S Orchard St Urbana IL 61801

BRYANT, MATTHEW CHARLES, advertising executive; b. Westerham, Kent, Eng., Sept. 23, 1947; came to U.S., 1976; s. Hugh Charles and Sylvia (Montgomery) B.; m. Janice Ann Repko, June 4, 1977; 1 son, James Charles. Grad., Ardingly Coll., Sussex, Eng. Media trainee Masuis Wynne William, London, 1968-70, media buyer, 1970-73; media dir. Media Buying Services, Toronto, Ont., Can., 1973-75, v.p., Toronto, 1975-76, pres., N.Y.C., 1977—. Home: 30 Waterside Plaza New York NY 10010 Office: Media Buying Services 104 Fifth Ave New York NY 10011

BRYANT, OSCAR SIMS, JR., investment advisor; b. Jakin, Ga., Aug. 9, 1920; s. Oscar Sims and Enzie (Lay) B.; m. Nancy Lee Stevens, Sept. 1, 1950; children: Oscar Sims III, Melissa Dunbar. Ed., Draughn Sch. Commerce, Atlanta, 1946. Br. mgr. J.J. & Hilliard & Sons, Louisville, 1951-57; v.p., trust officer People's First Nat. Bank, Paducah, Ky., 1957-64; exec. v.p. Liberty Nat. Bank & Trust Co., Louisville, from 1964; also mem. exec. com., sec. bd. dirs.; registered investment adv. Morton H. Sachs & Co. Pres. Four Rivers council Boy Scouts Am., 1962-63; now mem. exec. com. Old Ky. Home council.; Bd. dirs. Gheens Found., Louisville, Ky. Soc. Prevention of Blindness, Recs. for Blind. Served with AUS; 1942-45. Mem. Newcomen Soc. N.Am. Episcopalian. Clubs: Mason (32 deg., Shriner), Lion., Pendennis (Louisville); Owl Creek Country (Anchorage). Home: 12215 Old Henry Rd PO Box 23317 Anchorage KY 40223 Office: 2705 Citizens Plaza Louisville KY 40202

BRYANT, ROBERT GEORGE, chemistry educator; b. Mineola, N.Y., Sept. 13, 1943; s. George E. and Ruth L. (Haak) B.; m. Marcia H. Stroup, July 17, 1965; children—Marc, Ellen, Scott. A.B., Colgate U., 1965; Ph.D., Stanford U., 1969. Asst. prof. U. Minn., Mpls., 1969-72, asso. prof., 1972-78, prof. chemistry, 1978—; vis. assoc. prof. SUNY, Stony Brook, 1973; vis. scientist IBM Watson Labs., 1976; sec. Exptl. NMR Conf. Camille and Henry Dreyfus tchr.-scholar, 1975-79. Contbr. articles to profl. jours. NIH grantee; NSF grantee. Mem. Am. Chem. Soc., Biophys. Soc., AAAS. Home: 9824 Dellridge Rd Bloomington MN 55420 Office: Dept Chemistry U Minn 207 Pleasant St SE Minneapolis MN 55455

BRYANT, RUTH ALYNE, banker; b. Memphis, Jan. 12, 1924; d. James Walter and Leola (Edgar) B. Student, Southwestern Coll., Memphis, 1941-43. Clk. Fed. Res. Bank of St. Louis (Memphis Br.), 1943-47, exec. sec., 1947-68, asst. cashier, 1968-69, asst. v.p., 1969-73, v.p., 1973—; Bd. dirs. Assocs. of St. Louis U. Libraries, 1977—, pres., 1983—; mem. chancellor's council U. Mo., St. Louis, 1979—; Bd. dirs. The Vanderschmidt's Sch., 1980—. Mem. Am. Inst. Banking (nat. women's com. 1962-63, pres. Memphis chpt. 1968-69), Mo. Bankers Assn. (mktg. and pub. relations com. 1974-76), Nat. Assn. Bank Women (editor Woman Banker 1959-62, v.p. so. region 1967-68, v.p. 1969-70, pres. 1970-71, trustee ednl. found. 1974-75), English Speaking Union, Bank Mktg. Assn. (dir. Mo.-Ill. chpt. 1976-79). Home: 4605 Lindell Blvd Saint Louis MO 63108 Office: Fed Res Bank of St Louis 411 Locust St Saint Louis MO 63102

BRYANT, STEVEN KENT, association executive; b. Tulsa, Dec. 28, 1949; s. Colvin Bernard and Francis Bernadene (Pingleton) B.; m. Diane Martin, Feb. 12, 1971; 1 dau., Jacqueline Diane. B.S. in Bus. Adminstrn. with honors (USAF ROTC scholar 1969-71), U. Ark., 1971; M.B.A. in Exec. Mgmt., Rockhurst Coll., 1982. Bus. mgr. Nat. Bd. Respiratory Therapy, 1974-75, exec. dir., 1975—. Editor assn. newsletters, directories. Served as officer USAF, 1971-74. Mem. Am. Soc. Assn. Execs., Mid-Am. Soc. Assn. Execs., Beta Gamma Sigma, Sigma Iota Epsilon. Republican. Office: 11015 W 75th Terr Shawnee Mission KS 66214

BRYANT, THOMAS EDWARD, physician-lawyer; b. Bellamy, Ala., Jan. 17, 1936; s. Howard Edward and Alibel (Nettles) B.; m. Lucie Elizabeth Thrasher, July 9, 1961; children: Thomas Edward, Evelyn Thaxton. A.B., Emory U., 1958, M.D., 1962, J.D., 1967. Bar: Ga. 1967. Intern Grady Meml. Hosp., Atlanta, 1962-63; dir. health affairs OEO, Washington, 1969-71; pres. Nat. Drug Abuse Council, 1971-79; chmn., dir. Pres.'s Commn. Mental Health, 1977-79; vis. lectr. Georgetown U.; chmn. Public Com. on Mental Health, 1978—. Served with USAF, 1963-65. Recipient Exceptional Service award OEO, 1971. Mem. Inst. Medicine, Am. Public Health Assn., Ga. Bar Assn., D.C. Bar Assn. Democrat. Clubs: Cosmos (Washington); Century Assn. (N.Y.C.). Home: 1527 35th St NW Washington DC 20007 Office: 2918 M St NW Washington DC 20007

BRYANT, WILLIAM B., U.S. district judge; b. Wetumpka, Ala., Sept. 18, 1911; s. Benson and Alberta B.; m. Astaire A. Gonzalez, Aug. 25, 1934; children: Astaire, William B. A.B., Howard U., 1932, LL.B., 1936. Asst. U.S. atty. for D.C., 1951-54; partner firm Houston, Bryant & Gardner, 1954-65; U.S. sr. dist. Judge for D.C., 1965—; prof. law Howard U. Sch. Law, 1965—; Sec. D.C. Bd. Edn. Served with AUS, 1943-47. Mem. ABA. Office: US Court House 3d and Constitution Aves Washington DC 20001 *

BRYANT, WILLIAM H., assn. exec.; b. Albany, N.Y., June 21, 1933; s. James W. and Olma A. (Bryant) B.; m. Nancy McClurg, Aug. 26, 1972; children—Dana, Alethea, Jeff. B.S. in Bus. Adminstrn, Akron U., 1960. Trainee Mohawk Tire, Akron, Ohio, 1954; dir. research Tri County Planning Assn., Akron, 1957-63, Ohio Dept. Devel., Columbus, 1963-69; with Greater Cleve. Growth Assn., 1969—, pres., 1980—; Bd. dirs. Conv. and Visitors Bur., 1980—, Cleve. Area Devel. Corp., 1980—. Served with USAF, 1952-56. Mem. U.S. C. of C. (bd. dirs.), Ohio C. of C. Home: 4720 West Point Dr Fairview Park OH 44126 Office: 690 Union Commerce Bldg Cleveland OH 44115

BRYANT, WILLIAM JUNIOR, archaeological foundation executive; b. Springfield, Vt., May 4, 1904; s. William LeRoy and Blanche (Brown) B.; m. Frances Hazelton, May 29, 1926; 1 son, Bruce Hazelton. Grad., Phillips Exeter Acad., 1921; B.A., Dartmouth Coll., 1925. With Bryant Chucking Grinder Co., Springfield, 1925-59, pres., 1946-58; founder William L. Bryant Found. (conducting excavations Fla., Carribean and Spain, also publs. in Am. and Spanish), 1950—, Centro Arqueologico Hispano-Americano de Los Baleares. Author: Flames of Life, 1961, The Magic of Spain, 1967, others, also book revs., articles. Trustee Eaglebrook Sch., Deerfield, Mass., 1946-51, 55-60, Calvin Coolidge Meml. Found., 1964-82; mem. exec. com. Friends of Dartmouth Library, 1953-75, chmn., 1972-74; mem. visitors com. classical dept. Museum Fine Arts, Boston, 1960-77. Mem. Am. Inst. Archaeology, Fla. Anthrop. Soc., Real Sociedad Arqueologica Tarraconense, Am. Forestry Assn., Boston Anthenaeum, Explorers Club, Sigma Alpha Epsilon. Club: Union (Boston). Patentee machine tools and measurement. Home: RFD South Woodstock VT 05071 *My guide words for satisfying living: compassion—passion—humor.*

BRYANT, WINSTON, lieutenant governor of Arkansas; b. Donaldson, Ark., Oct. 3, 1938. B.A., Ouachita Bapt. U., 1960; LL.B., U. Ark., 1963; LL.M. in Adminstrv. Law, George Washington U., 1970. Bar: Ark. bar 1963. Individual practice law, Malvern, Ark., 1964-66, 71-75; atty. Ark. Ins. Commn., 1966; asst. U.S. atty. for Eastern Dist. Ark., 1967; legis. asst. to Senator from Ark., 1968-71; dep. pros. atty. Hot Spring County, Ark., 1971-75; mem. Ark. Ho. of Reps., 1973-76; sec. of state State of Ark., Little Rock, 1976-80, lt. gov., 1981—; instr. polit. sci. Ouachita Bapt. U., 1971-73, Henderson (Ark.) State U., 1973—. Mem. Ark. Youth Services Planning Adv. Council, 1974, Ark. Gov.'s Ad Hoc Com. on Workmen's Compensation, 1975. Served to capt., inf. U.S. Army, 1963-64. Mem. ABA, Ark. Bar Assn. (ho. of dels.), Malvern C. of C. (pres. 1972), Am. Legion, Ark. Farm Bur. Baptist. Office: Office of Lt Gov State Capitol Little Rock AR 72201 *

BRYDON, DONALD JAMES, news service executive; b. Bloomfield, Mo., Aug. 8, 1922; s. Doc Richard and Maud Elizabeth (Walker) B.; m. Helen Merrill, Apr. 14, 1967; 1 stepson, Allan Preston Sachs. B.J., U. Mo., 1946. Reporter, editor UPI, St. Louis, Chgo., Detroit, Milw., Indpls., Dallas, 1947-62, v.p. for Asia, Tokyo, 1962-72, mgr. central div., Chgo., 1972-77, v.p. mktg., N.Y.C., 1977-82, sr. v.p., 1982—. Served to 1st lt. USAAF, 1942-45. Mem. Sigma Delta Chi, Alpha Tau Omega. Democrat. Baptist. Clubs: Overseas Press (bd. dirs. 1964—), Fgn. Corrs. Japan, Marco Polo. Home: 77 Park ave New York NY 10016 Office: UPI 220 E 42d St New York NY 10017

BRYER, BEN F., physician, surgeon, educator; b. Flint, Mich., May 21, 1912; s. Samuel and Leah (Ehrlich) B.; m. Elsa Kastor, Mar. 24, 1942; 1 son, Elliott K. B.S. cum laude, U. Pitts., 1933, M.D., 1937. Intern Montefiore Hosp. Pitts., 1937-38; resident in surgery Phila. Orthopedic Hosp. div. U. Pa. Med. Center, 1938-39, Queens Gen. Hosp. Center, N.Y.C., 1939-41, Mt. Sinai Hosp., 1946-47; grad. study surgery Columbia Coll. Phys. and Surg.-Presbyn. Med. Center, 1948; practice medicine specializing in surgery, N.Y.C., 1949—; sr. clin. surgeon Mt. Sinai Hosp., 1949—; assoc. attending surgeon Elmhurst Gen. Hosp., N.Y.C., 1949—; instr. surgery U. Pa., 1938-39; lectr. surgery Grad. Sch. N.Y. U.-Bellevue Med. Center, 1950-60; asst. clin. prof. surgery N.Y. Med. Coll., 1950-57; dir. surg. tng. N.Y.C. Hosp.; surgeon Gracie Sq. Hosp.; mem. staff Doctors Hosp., Beekman Downtown Hosp.; dir. surgery World Health Medical Dental Center, World Trade Center, N.Y.C., 1976—; surg. cons. Med. and Surg. Specialists Plan, N.Y.C., N.Y. State Workmen's Compensation Bd. Author: (with Robert Kennedy) The Multiple Injury Patient, 1956; Contbr. articles to med. jours. Served to lt. col., M.C. AUS, 1941-45. Recipient Gold Achievement award Am. Soc. Abdominal Surgeons, 1962, Sci. award A.C.S., 1959, Clin. Research award N.Y. State Med. Soc., 1957. Fellow A.C.S. (N.Y.-Bklyn. Com. on trauma), Am. Coll. Gastroenterology, N.Y. Acad. Medicine, N.Y. Acad. Gastroenterology; mem. AMA, Am. Soc. Abdominal Surgeons, Am. Bd. Abdominal Surgeons, Internat. Coll. Abdominal Surgeons, N.Y. Acad. Medicine, N.Y. Acad. Scis., Am. Geriatric Soc., AAAS, Assn. Mil. Surgeons (exec. com., bd. dirs.), U.S., N.Y. County, N.Y. State, Allegheny County, Pa. med. socs., Am. Trauma Soc. (founder), Nat. Found. Ileitis and Colitis, World Congress Gastro-Enterology, Internat. Fedn. Gastroenterology, Digestive Disease Found. (founder), Pi Tau Phi, Phi Delta Epsilon. Club: Mason. Home and Office: 1115 Fifth Ave New York NY 10028

BRYNNER, YUL, actor; b. Sakhalin (Island), Japan, July 11, 1920; came to U.S., 1940; m. Virginia Gilmore, Sept. 6, 1944; 1 son, Rock; m. Doris Kleiner (div.); m. Jacqueline de Croisset. (div.); m. Kathy Lee, 1983. Ed. chiefly in France including at the Sorbonne. Connected with entertainment field since 12 yrs. old.; made debut in circus and on legitimate stage in, Paris; first appeared on U.S. stage, 1941; in Shakespearean role with, Michael Chekhov company; debut on: Broadway stage in Lute Song, 1946; later on tour throughout U.S. in same prodn.; appeared abroad in: Dark Eyes, 1947-48; also as entertainer in Paris night clubs; actor, producer, dir. 1st TV talk show for, NBC, 1948; became TV dir. CBS programs; on legitimate stage in The King and I, 1951-54; star of play, 1952-54; also on tour; in: film prodns. as Ramses in The Ten Commandments, 1955; as the king in: The King and I, 1956; co-star with Ingrid Bergman in: Anastasia, 1956; other films Brothers Karamazov, 1958, Journey, Sound and the Fury, 1959, Solomon and Sheba, 1959, Once More With Feeling, Magnificent Seven, 1960, Cast a Giant Shadow, 1966, Triple Cross, 1967, The Long Duel, 1967, The Double Man, 1968, The Madwoman of Chaillot, 1969, Flight of the Golden Goose, 1969, The Battle of Neretva, 1971, The Light at the Edge of the World, 1971, Fuzz, 1972, Westworld, 1973, Futureworld, 1976; TV series Anna and the King, 1972; toured with prodn. of The King and I, through 1984; Author: Bring Forth the Children, 1960. Served as radio announcer and commentator (in French) OWI, 1942-46. Recipient Donaldson award for best actor, 1951; Nat. Bd. Rev. Motion Pictures award for best performance in The King and I, 1956; Acad. Award in Motion Pictures, 1956; also Tony award; Critics Circle award. Office: care Robert Lantz 888 7th Ave New York NY 10106

BRYSON, ARTHUR EARL, JR., engring. educator; b. Evanston, Ill., Oct. 7, 1925; s. Arthur Earl and Helen Elizabeth (Decker) B.; m. Helen Marie Layton, Aug. 31, 1946; children—Thomas Layton, Stephen Decker, Janet Elizabeth, Susan Mary. Student, Haverford Coll., 1942-44; B.S., Iowa State U., 1946; M.S., Calif. Inst. Tech., 1949, Ph.D. in Aeros, 1951; M.A. (hon.), Harvard., 1956. With Container Corp. Am., 1947-48, United Aircraft Corp., 1948; research asst. aero, Calif. Inst. Tech., 1949-50; mem. tech. staff Hughes Research & Devel. Labs., 1950-53; mem. faculty Harvard, 1953-68, Gordon McKay prof. mech. engring., 1961-68; mem. faculty Stanford, 1968—, chmn. dept. applied mechanics, 1969-71, chmn. dept. aeros. and astronautics, 1971-79, Paul Pigott prof. engring., 1972—; Hunsaker prof. Mass. Inst. Tech., 1965-66; Mem. nat. com. Fluid Mechanics Films, 1961-68. Author: (with Y.C. Ho) Applied Optimal Control, 1969. Served as ensign USNR, 1944-46. Recipient Rufus Oldenberger medal ASME, 1980. Fellow Am. Inst. Aeros. and Astronautics (asso. editor Jour. 1963-65, bd. dirs. 1965-68, Pendray Award 1968, mechanics and control of flight award 1980); mem. Am. Acad. Arts and Scis., Am. Soc. Engring. Edn. (Westinghouse award 1969), Nat. Acad. Engring. (aero. and space engring. bd. 1970-79), Nat. Acad. Scis., Sigma Xi, Tau Beta Pi. Conglist. Home: 761 Mayfield Ave Stanford CA 94305

BRYSON, BRADY OLIVER, lawyer; b. Overton, Nev., Mar. 14, 1915; s. Samuel Oliver and Emma (Brady) B.; m. Mary Elizabeth Brown, Nov. 1, 1938; children: Linda Bryson Lucatorto, David Brady, John Alan, Timothy Sean. A.B., Western Md. Coll., 1935, LL.D., 1973; LL.B., Columbia U., 1938. Bar: D.C. bar 1938, Pa. bar 1942, N.Y. bar 1946, Md. bar 1952. Practice in, Washington, 1943-47, 55-80, N.Y.C., 1948-54, Phila., 1955-80; mem. firm Alvord & Alvord, 1943-47, Chapman, Bryson, Walsh & O'Connell, 1948-54, Morgan, Lewis & Bockius, 1955-80; chmn., chief exec. officer, dir. Remington Rand Corp., Princeton, N.J., to 1981; chmn. Locust Wines, Ltd., Westminster, Md.; wine columnist Evening Sun, Hanover, Pa.; dir. Ind. Publs., Inc., Phila., Devel. Co. Am., Westminster, Md., S.H. Tevis & Son, Inc., Westminster. Trustee Louis L. Stott Found., Reading.

Served to lt. (j.g.) USNR, 1944-46. Mem. Am., N.Y. State, Pa., Phila., D.C. bar assns., Masters of Foxhounds Assn. Am., Green Spring Valley Hounds, Elkridge-Harford Hounds., Howard County Hounds. Clubs: Knickerbocker (N.Y.C.); Birnam Wood Golf (Montecito, Calif.) (founder). Home: Box 868 Westminster MD 21157

BRYSON, GARY SPATH, cable TV executive; b. Longview, Wash., Nov. 8, 1943; s. Roy Griffin and Marguerite Elizabeth (Spath) B.; m. Suzanne D. Grotelueschen, Oct. 18, 1969; children: Kelly Suzanne, Lisa Christine. A.B., Dartmouth Coll., 1966; M.B.A., Tuck Sch., 1967. With Bell & Howell Co., Chgo., 1967-79, pres. consumer group, also consumer and audio-visual group, 1977-79; chmn. bd., chief exec. officer Bell & Howell Mamiya Co., Chgo., 1979-81; sr. v.p. mktg. Am. TV & Communications Corp., subs. Time, Inc., 1981—. Republican. Lutheran. Home: 5246 S Jamaica Way Englewood CO 80111 Office: 160 Inverness Dr W Englewood CO 80112

BRYSON, GEORGE TARRY, JR., department store executive; b. Montreal, Que., Can., May 20, 1929; s. George Tarry and Sophie (Harris) B.; m. Constance Tyson, May 6, 1955 (dec.); children: Elizabeth Ellston, George Tarry, Mary Hamilton.; m. Carol Jones Hudgens, Jan. 1, 1983. B.A., Hampden-Sydney Coll., 1950. With Miller & Rhoads Dept. Store, Richmond, Va., 1950—, v.p., gen. mdse. mgr., now v.p. community relations, leases, restaurants. Mem. Richmond C. of C. (past dir.), Richmond Retail Mchts. Assn. (dir.), Va. Retail Mchts. Assn. (dir.). Republican. Episcopalian. Club: Country of Va. Office: 517 E Broad St Richmond VA 23261 *

BRYSON, REID ALLEN, educator; b. Detroit, June 7, 1920; s. William Riley and Elma (Turner) B.; m. Frances Edith Williamson, June, 13, 1942; children—Anne, William, Robert, Thomas. A.B., Denison U., 1941, D.Sc. (honoris causa), 1971; postgrad., U. Wis., 1941, 46; Ph.D., U. Chgo., 1948. Asst. prof. meteorology and geology U. Wis., 1946-48, asst. prof. meteorology, 1948-50, asso. prof., 1950-56, chmn. dept., 1948-50, 52-54, prof., 1957—; dir. Inst. for Environ. Studies, 1970—; prof. U. Ariz., 1956-57; Mem. various coms. Nat. Acad. Sci.-NRC, 1958—, mem. remote sensing com., 1964-67, mem. com. on mil. geography, 1966-69; mem. (Smithsonian Council), 1976—, sr. cons., 1975—; Trustee Univ. Corp. for Atmospheric Research. Author: Atlas of 500 mb Wind Characteristics for the Northern Hemisphere, 1958, Atlas of Five-Day Normal Sea-Level Pressure Charts for the Northern Hemisphere, 1958, Atlas of 300 mb Wind Characteristics, 1959; Editor: (with F.K. Hare) Climates of North America, 1974, Climates of Hunger, 1977 (Banta medal 1978); Contbr.: articles to profl. jours. Climates of Hunger. Cited by Denison U., 1966. Fellow Am. Meteorol. Soc., Explorers Clubs, Wis. Acad. Scis., Arts and Letters; mem. Wis. Phenological Soc. (past pres.), Soc. Am. Archaeology, Assn. Am. Geographers, Am. Soc. for Limnology and Oceanography, Arts and Letters (pres. 1981), Phi Beta Kappa, Sigma Xi, Phi Kappa Phi (hon.). Application of climatology to archaeol. problems; regional and global climatic modification; climatic changes and world food supply; interdisciplinary environmental studies. Home: 11 Rosewood Circle Madison WI 53711

BRZANA, STANISLAUS JOSEPH, bishop; b. Buffalo, July 1, 1917; s. Frank and Catherine (Mikosz) B. B.A., St. Bonaventure Coll., 1938, M.A., 1946; S.T.D., Gregorian U., Rome, Italy, 1953. Ordained priest Roman Catholic Ch., 1941; Assigned Buffalo Missionary Apostolate, 1941; asst. St. Joseph's Ch., Gowanda, N.Y., 1942, Sts. Peter and Paul, Jamestown, N.Y., 1943, 46; dir. Cath. Information Center, Buffalo; also weekend asst. Transfiguration Ch., 1949, asst., 1953; weekend asst. St. John Kanty Ch., Buffalo, 1950; vice officialis of Tribunal of Diocese of Buffalo; in charge Tribunal Office, 1954-64; weekend asst. Our Lady of Grace Parish, Woodlawn, N.Y., 1956, adminstr., 1957; appt. officialis tribunal Diocese of Buffalo (St. Adalbert's Parish), Buffalo, 1958; adminstr. Resurrection Parish, Cheektowaga, N.Y., 1959; pastor Queen Peace Ch., Buffalo, 1959, 61-68; domestic prelate, 1959-64; aux. bishop Diocese of Buffalo, 1964-68, vicar gen., 1966-68; bishop Diocese of Ogdensburg, N.Y., 1968—; Chmn. Diocesan Commn. on Sacred Liturgy, Music and Art, 1964. Served to 1st lt. Chaplain Corps AUS, 1944-46. Office: Chancery Office 622 Washington St Ogdensburg NY 13669 *

BRZECZEK, RICHARD JOSEPH, lawyer, former superintendent police; b. Chgo., Oct. 8, 1942; s. Raymond Martin and Elizabeth B. (Janczura) B.; m. Elizabeth J. Weszley, Jan. 16, 1965; children: Natalie Ann, Mark Douglas, Kevin Martin, Holly Lynn. B.S., Loyola U., Chgo., 1965; M.P.A., Ill. Inst. Tech., 1968; J.D., John Marshall Law Sch., Chgo., 1972; grad., Nat. Exec. Inst., FBI, 1980. Bar: Ill. 1972, U.S. Supreme Ct. 1976. Mem. Chgo. Police Dept., 1964—, exec. asst., legal counsel to supt., 1973-80, asst. dep. supt., 1979-80, supt., 1980-83; ptnr. firm Levy & Erens, Chgo., 1983; guest lectr. Northwestern U. Traffic Inst., 1975—; adj. instr. Sch. Police Adminstrn., U. Louisville, 1977—; mem. law enforcement adv. bd. City Colls. Chgo., 1976—; of counsel Americans for Effective Law Enforcement, 1979, adv. bd., 1979—, Southwest Police Inst., Southwestern Legal Found., 1980—, Ill. Dangerous Drug Commn., 1980—, Center Research Criminal Justice, U. Ill., Chgo. Circle, 1980—, Inst. Criminal Justice, John Marshall Law Sch., 1980—; commr. Chgo.-Cook County Criminal Justice Commn., 1980—. Adv. bd. Felician Coll., Chgo., 1980—; mem. Archidiocese Chgo. Sch. Bd., 1979—; active local Boy Scouts Am., youth football. Recipient Gavel award John Marshall Law Sch., 1970, Disting. Alumi award, 1980; also numerous citations. Mem. Internat. Assn. Chiefs Police (spl. counsel exec. com. 1980—), Am. Bar Assn. (Silver Key award 1971), Ill. Bar Assn., Chgo. Bar Assn. (chmn. police-lawyer relations com., young lawyers sect. 1975-78), Advocates Soc. (chmn. coms. 1975-80, 3d v.p. 1978-80), Chgo. Assn. Commerce and Industry, Phi Alpha Delta (Outstanding Mem. award Lincoln chpt. 1971). Office: 1121 S State St Chicago IL 60605

BRZEINSKI, JOSEPH EDWARD, educational administrator; b. Denver, Jan. 1, 1926; s. Lad H. and Jennie L. (Schutte) B.; m. Willow Hasse, Sept. 4, 1948; children: John, Judith, Betsy. A.B., U. Denver, 1949, M.A., 1951; Ed.D. (Macmillan fellow), Columbia U., 1956. With Denver Public Schs., 1949—, asst. supt. adminstrv. services, 1973-75, asst. supt. sch. and bus. services, 1975-77, supt., 1977—; mem. research steering com. Great City Schs.; mem. adv. com. research and devel. Colo. Dept. Edn.; project evaluator Nat. Inst. Edn. Contbr. articles in field to profl. jours. Served with U.S. Army, 1944-46. Mem. Am. Assn. Sch. Adminstrs., Assn. Childhood Edn., Assn. Supervision and Curriculum Devel., Internat. Reading Assn. (pres. Denver br. 1962-63), Council Great City Schs. (exec. bd. 1977-81), Rocky Mountain Sch. Study Council (pres. 1980-81), Phi Beta Kappa. Office: 900 Grant St Denver CO 80203

BRZEZINSKI, JOHN CHARLES, brewery executive; b. Bloomfield, N.J., Aug. 24, 1925; s. Martin and Jennie (Kubiatowski) B.; m. Rita Luczynski, June 19, 1947; children: John C., Elise Marie, Bonnie, Denise, Robert. B.S. in Chemistry, Seton Hall U., 1948. With P. Ballantine and Sons, Newark, 1948-71, quality control mgr., 1955-69, tech. dir., 1969-71; v.p. prodn., tech. dir. Lone Star Brewing Co., San Antonio, 1971-75, v.p., gen. mgr., 1975-76, exec. v.p., gen. mgr., 1976-82; exec. v.p. ops. Pabst Brewing Co., Milw., 1982—; dir. Lone Star Brewing Co., 1979—. Mem. exec. com. San Antonio United Way. Served with U.S. Army, 1943-45. Decorated Purple Heart, Bronze Star. Mem. Master Brewers Am., Packaging Inst. (profl. mem.), Am. Soc. Quality Control, Am. Soc. Brewing Chemists, San Antonio C. of C. (dir.). Roman Catholic. Clubs: Rotary, Exchange. Home: 911 17th Ave Grafton WI 53024 Office: Pabst Brewing Co PO Box 766 1000 N Market St Milwaukee WI 53201

BRZEZINSKI, ZBIGNIEW, political science educator, author; b. Warsaw, Poland, Mar. 28, 1928; came to U.S., 1953, naturalized, 1958; s. Tadeusz and Leonia (Roman) B.; m. Emilie Ann Benes, June 11, 1955; children: Ian, Mark, Mika. B.A. with 1st class honors in Econs. and Polit. Sci., McGill U., 1949, M.A. in Polit. Sci., 1950; Ph.D., Harvard U., 1953. Inst. Govt. and research fellow Russian Research Center, Harvard U., 1953-56; asst. prof. govt., research asso. Russian Research Center and Center Internat. Affairs, Harvard U., 1956-60; asso. prof. public law and govt. Columbia U., 1960-62, prof., 1962-77, 81—; dir. Research Inst. Internat. Change (formerly Research Inst. Communist Affairs), 1962-77; mem. faculty Russian Inst., 1960-77; dir. Trilateral Commn., 1973-76; asst. to Pres. U.S. for nat. security affairs, 1977-81; ofcl. Nat. Security Council, 1977-81; cons. internat. affairs Dean, Witter, Reynolds Inc., N.Y.C., 1981—; sr. adv. Georgetown U. Center Strategic and Internat. Studies, 1981—; mem. policy planning council Dept. State, 1966-68; Mem. joint com. contemporary China, Social Sci. Research Council, 1961-62; guest lectr. numerous pvt. and govt. instns., 1953—, participant internat. confs., 1955—. Author: The Permanent Purge-Politics in Soviet Totalitarianism, 1956, The Soviet Bloc—Unity and Conflict, 1960, Ideology and Power in Soviet Politics, 1962, Alternative to Partition, 1965, Between Two Ages, 1970, The Fragile Blossom, 1971; co-author: Totalitarian Dictatorship and Autocracy, 1957, Political Power: USA/USSR, 1964 (German edit. 1966), also numerous articles.; editor, co-author, contbr.: Political Controls in the Soviet Army, 1954; Editor, co-author, contbr.: Africa and the Communist World, 1963, Dilemmas Of Change In Soviet Politics, 1969, Dilemmi Internationazionali In Un-epoca. Teonetronica, 1969; columnist: Newsweek, 1970-72. Mem. hon. steering com. Young Citizens for Johnson, 1964. Guggenheim fellow, 1960; Ford Found. fellow, 1970. Fellow Am. Acad. Arts and Scis.; mem. NAACP, Council Fgn. Relations. Club: Federal City (Washington). Address: Ctr Strategic and Internat Studies Georgetown U 1800 K St NW Washington DC 20006

BRZUSTOWICZ, RICHARD JOHN, neurosurgeon, educator; b. Bklyn., Dec. 19, 1917; s. John B. and Victoria Eleanor (Szutarska) Brzustowicz; m. Alice Lorraine Cinq-Mars, May 30, 1945; children: Richard John, Thaddeux P., Victoria Barbara, John, Teresa, Krystyna, Mary. B.S., CCNY, 1938; M.D., SUNY, 1942; M.S. in Neurol. Surgery, U. Minn., 1951. Diplomate: Am. Bd. Psychiatry and Neurology, Am. Bd. Neurol. Surgery. Intern Bklyn. Hosp., 1942-43, asst. resident in surgery, 1947-48; resident in pathology Kings County Hosp., Bklyn., 1946-47; fellow in neurol. surgery Mayo Found., U. Minn.-Rochester, 1948-51; practice medicine specializing in neurol. surgery, Rochester, N.Y., 1951—; asst. prof. anatomy U. Rochester Sch. Medicine and Dentistry, 1961-68, clin. sr. instr. neurol. surgery, 1962-71, clin. asst. prof., 1971—; chmn. div. neurol. surgery St. Mary's Hosp., Rochester, 1951—, pres. med. adv. bd., 1972-75; cons. in neurosurgery to various hosps., 1951—. Assoc. editor: Bull. Polish Med. Sci. and History, 1963-67; contbr. articles on neurology to med. jours. Served to capt., N.C. U.S. Army, 1943-46. Mem. N.Y. State Med. Soc., Monroe County Med. Soc. (editor bull. 1967-73, 76-79), Am. Assn. Neurol. Surgeons, N.Y. State Neurosurg. Soc., Rochester Acad. Medicine (Paine prize 1952), Am. Acad. Neurology, Assn. Am. Med. Colls., Assn. Am. Physicians and Surgeons, Congress Neurol. Surgeons, Catholic Physicians Guild (pres. 1956-57), Nat. Med. and Dental Assn., Polish Inst. Arts and Scis., Am. Med. Writers Assn., AMA, N.Y. Acad. Scis., Soc. Tech. Communications, AAAS, Am. Heritage Soc., Rochester Civic Music Assn., Polish Med. Alliance, Am. Physicians Art Assn., Alumni Assn. Mayo Found., Sigma Xi. Roman Catholic. Home: 366 Oakdale Dr Rochester NY 14618 Office: Rochester Neurol Group 909 W Main St Rochester NY 14611 *As a young man I treasured diligence and curiosity about life; as a;ysician I have tried to be compassionate and caring; as a father I have firmly believed in the sancitity of the family and shared with my wife the greatest desire to have children honest, hard-working, moral and dedicated citizens of our country which has provided unlimited opportunities.*

BRZUSTOWSKI, THOMAS ANTHONY, ednl. adminstr.; b. Warsaw, Poland, Apr. 4, 1937; s. Jerzy Michal and Helena (Bielicka) B.; m. Louise Marguerite Burke, Apr. 4, 1964; children—John Michael, Marc-Andre, Paul Thomas. B. Applied Sci, U. Toronto, 1958; A.M., Princeton, 1960, Ph.D., 1963. Registered profl. engr., Ont. Asst. prof. mech. engrng. U. Waterloo, Ont., Can., 1962-64, asso. prof., 1964-66, prof., 1966—, chmn. dept. mech. engrng., 1967-70, asso. dean engrng., 1971-74, v.p. acad., 1975—; engrng. asso. environmental control and safety div. Esso Engrng. & Research Co., Florham Park, N.J., 1970-71; also cons.; cons. Energetex Engrng., Exxon Research and Engrng. Co., Canmar Ltd.; Am. Soc. Engrng. Edn.-Ford Found. resident in engrng. practice, 1970-71. Author: Introduction to the Principles of Engineering Thermodynamics, 1969; Contbr. articles to profl. jours. Fellow Engrng. Inst. Can.; mem. ASME, AIAA, Am. Soc. Engrng. Edn., Inst. Energy, Combustion Inst., Can. Soc. Mech. Engrng., Sigma Xi. Home: 23 Sunbridge Crescent Kitchener ON N2K 1T4 Canada Office: Needles Hall U Waterloo Waterloo ON N2L 3G1 Canada

BUA, NICHOLAS JOHN, judge; b. Chgo., Feb. 9, 1925; s. Frank and Lena (Marino) B.; m. Camille F. Scordato, Nov. 20, 1943; 1 dau., Lisa Annette. J.D., DePaul U., 1953. Bar: Ill. 1953. Trial atty., Chgo., 1953-63; judge Village Ct., Melrose Park, Ill., 1963-64; asso. judge Circuit Ct. Cook County, Chgo., 1964-71, circuit judge, 1971-76; justice Appellate Ct. Ill., 1st Dist., 1976-77; judge U.S. Dist. Ct., Chgo., 1977—; Mem. exec. com. Jud. Conf. Ill., also mem. supreme ct. rules com., 1970-77; lectr. DePaul U.; mem. faculty Def. Tactics Seminar, Ill. Def. Counsel Seminar, 1971; Fellow Nat. Coll. State Trial Judges, U. Nev., 1966. Contbr. articles to legal publs. Bd. govs. Gottlieb Meml. Hosp., 1978—; trustee Schwab Rehab. Hosp., 1977—. Served with AUS, World War II. Named Man of Yr. Justinian Soc. Lawyers, 1977; recipient Alumni award DePaul U., 1977. Mem. Am. Justinian Soc. Jurists (pres. 1978). Clubs: Nat. Lawyers, Legal, Union League, Lex Legio DePaul U. (Chgo.). Office: US Courthouse 219 S Dearborn St Chicago IL 60604

BUBB, HARRY GEIPLE, insurance company executive; b. Trinidad, Colo., Dec. 16, 1924; s. Harry H. and Grace Alleine (Geiple) B.;, June 9, 1951; children—Melinda, Howard, Susan, John, Mary. B.A. in Econs, Stanford U., 1946; M.B.A., 1949; grad., Advanced Mgmt. Program, Harvard U., 1973. With Pacific Mut. Life Ins. Co., 1949—, asst. v.p., 1966-68, then v.p., 1968-72, sr. v.p. group ins., 1972-75, pres., 1975—. Bd. dirs. Orange County Bus. Com. for Arts; United Way of Orange County North/South; trustee U.S. Acad. Decathlon; adv. bd. U.S. Olympic Com., Town Hall of Orange County; trustee Calif. Mus. Found., Newport Harbor Art Mus. Served as pilot USNR, World War II. Mem. World Affairs Council Orange County, Health Ins. Assn. Am. (dir.), Los Angeles Area C. of C. (dir.). Clubs: Lincoln of Orange County, Balboa Yacht. Home: 27 Beacon Bay Newport Beach CA 92660 Office: 700 Newport Center Dr Newport Beach CA 92660

BUBB, HENRY AGNEW, savs. and loan assn. exec.; b. Williamsport, Pa., Mar. 26, 1907; s. Harry A. and Marjorie (Wheeler) B.; m. Elizabeth Black, June 26, 1929; 1 dau., Barbara Elizabeth (Mrs. John C. Dicus). Student, U. Kans., 1924-27; D.B.A. in Bus, Washburn U. Chmn. bd. Capitol Fed. Savs. and Loan Assn., Topeka; former chmn. and dir. Mortgage Guaranty Ins. Corp. of Milw.; chmn. emeritus MGIC Investment Corp., Milw.; dir. Columbian Nat. Title Ins. Co., Topeka, Capitol Funds, Inc., Security Benefit Life Ins. Co.; former chmn. Fed. Home Loan Bank of Topeka; former vice chmn. MGIC Indemnity Corp., N.Y.; former dir. MGIC Fin. Corp., MGIC Mortgage Co., Milw.; Past pres. Mid-West Savings and Loan Conf.; past trustee Am. Savs. and Loan Inst.; mem. adv. com. of savs. and loan bus. Treasury Dept.; past mem. task force Fed. Home Loan Bank Bd., Washington. Past sr. mem., chmn. Kans. State Bd. Regents; past chmn. Kans. Edn. Commn.; chmn. Higher Edn. Loan Program.; Former dir. Shawnee County ARC; former chmn. numerous charitable drives, chmn., mem. war loan and victory fund coms.; past vice chmn., mem. Topeka Planning Bd.; past chmn. Topeka Housing and Planning Com.; mem. Fiscal Adv. Bd. Topeka; chmn. United Fund; bd. regents Washburn U.; Nat. chmn. Young Republican Nat. Fedn., 1937-38; del. Rep. Nat. Conv., 1964; nat. chmn. Citizens for Reagan, 1968; former trustee Inst. Fiscal and Polit. Edn., N.Y.C.; trustee U. Kans. Endowment Assn.; bd. dirs., past pres. Downtown Topeka, Inc. Recipient award Treasury Dept., 1946; Wisdom award of honor; Disting. Service citation; Higher Edn. Leadership prize; also Fred Ellsworth medal U. Kans.; Disting. Kansan award Native Sons and Daus., 1974; Bubb Light Circle Washburn U., 1980; others. Disting. fellow Internat. Union Bldg. Socs. and Savs. and Loan Assns.; mem. U.S. Savs. and Loan League (chmn. legis. com. 1954-63, legis. cons., exec. com. 1949-63, pres. 1949-50), Kans. Savs. and Loan League (past pres.), U.S. League Savs. Assns. (sr. adv. group com. on polit. action), Topeka C. of C. (past pres., dir.), Kans. U. Alumni Assn. (past nat. pres.), Newcomen Soc. N. Am., S.A.R., 35th Div. Assn., Sigma Chi (past pres. alumni chpt., named Significant Sig 1977), Alpha Kappa Psi. Episcopalian (past sr. warden). Clubs: Mason (Disting. Service award 1968) (33 deg., Potentate, Shriner, Jester, past dir.), Rotarian., Topeka Country (Topeka) (past pres., past dir.); Cabiri; Garden of the Gods (Colorado Springs, Colo.); Paradise Valley Country (Ariz.). Home: 2323 Mayfair Pl Topeka KS 66611 Office: 700 Kansas Ave Topeka KS 66603 *I have always had a deep feeling for people and have enjoyed good friendships most of all. My goal has always been to reach the top of any organization I joined—but in doing so to be fair, to never compromise principles or the highest standard of conduct, to always be frank and state my position and thoughts, to let people know where I stand, regardless of what it might do or not do to my business. I believe in never going back on a friend or a principle.*

BUBE, RICHARD HOWARD, materials scientist; b. Providence, Aug. 10, 1927; s. Edward Neser and Ella Elvira (Baltteim) B.; m. Betty Jane Meeker, Oct. 9, 1948; children: Mark Timothy, Kenneth Paul, Sharon Elizabeth, Meryl Lee. Sc.B., Brown U., 1946; M.A., Princeton U., 1948, Ph.D., 1950. Mem. sr. research staff RCA Labs., Princeton, N.J., 1948-62; prof. materials sci. and elec. engrng. Stanford U., 1962—, chmn. dept., 1975—; cons. to industry and govt. Author: A Textbook of Christian Doctrine, 1955, Photoconductivity of Solids, 1960, The Encounter Between Christianity and Science, 1968, The Human Quest: A New Look at Science and Christian Faith, 1971, Electronic Properties of Crystalline Solids, 1974, Electrons in Solids, 1981, Fundamentals of Solar Cells, 1983; also articles; editor: Jour. Am. Sci. Affiliation; editorial bd.: Solid State Electronics; asso. editor: Ann. Rev. Materials Sci., Materials Letters. Fellow Am. Phys. Soc., AAAS, Am. Sci. Affiliation; mem. Am. Soc. Engrng. Edn., Internat. Solar Energy Soc., Sigma Xi. Evangelical. Home: 753 Mayfield Ave Stanford CA 94305 Office: Dept Materials Sci and Engring Stanford Univ Stanford CA 94305 *I find no contradiction or conflict between science and Christian faith, but rather a marvelous compatibility that touches all aspects of life.*

BUBLITZ, WALTER JOHN, JR., former educator, consultant; b. Kansas City, Mo., Sept. 26, 1920; s. Walter J. and Mary Louise (Zimmerschied) B.; m. Mary H. Chase, Dec. 18, 1954; children: Philip (dec.), David. B.S., U. Ariz., 1941; Ph.D., Inst. Paper Chemistry, Appleton, Wis., 1949. Indsl. researcher Munising Paper Co., Mich., 1949-52, Kimberly-Clark Corp., Neenah, Wis., 1952-59, Minn. Mining and Mfg. Co., St. Paul, 1959-66; mem. faculty, acad. researcher Oreg. State U., Corvallis, 1966—, asso. prof., 1966-78, prof., 1978-83; ret., 1983, cons. on pulp and paper, 1983. Served to 1st. lt. USAAF, 1942-45. Mem. TAPPI (Fellow award 1980), Can. Pulp and Paper Assn., Sigma Xi, Phi Beta Kappa, Phi Kappa Phi, Phi Lambda Upsilon, Xi Sigma Pi. Methodist. Home and Office: 1430 NW 14th Pl Corvallis OR 97330

BUCCELLO, HENRY LOUIS, advt. exec.; b. Des Moines, Aug. 31, 1920; s. Louis Nicholas and Victoria (Loffredo) B.; m. Mary Elizabeth Callahan, Jan. 7, 1944; children—Thomas James, David Anthony. B.S., U. Iowa, 1943. Account supr. Chas. R. Stuart (advt.), San Francisco, 1946-52; dir. advt. Bank of America, San Francisco, 1952-57; sr. v.p. Guild, Bascom & Bonfigli, Inc., San Francisco also N.Y.C., 1957-65, Dancer, Fitzgerald Sample, N.Y.C., 1965-69; sr. v.p., dir. Compton Advt. Inc., N.Y.C., 1969—; dir. Devel. Assos. Inc. Served with USNR, 1943-46. Mem. Sigma Nu. Club: Aspetuck Valley Country (Weston, Conn.). Home: 8 Placid Lake Ln Westport CT 06880 Office: 625 Madison Ave New York City NY 10022

BUCCINO, GERALD P., financial executive; b. Belleville, N.J., Apr. 22, 1938; s. Charles and Jean (Fiscello) B.; m. Lorraine M. Falivene, Aug. 20, 1960; children: Gerard, Lauren, Jennifer, Christopher. Student, Fordham U., 1958-60; B.S. in Acctg, Seton Hall U., 1963. C.P.A., Ill., N.J. Sr. acct. Haskins & Sells, N.Y.C., 1963-66; acctg. mgr. Becton Dickinson, E. Rutherford, N.J., 1966-68; acquisition dir. Walter Kidde & Co., Clifton, N.J., 1968-70; v.p. fin. Stanray Corp., Chgo., 1970-76; sr. v.p. Interstate United, Chgo., 1976-79; exec. v.p., dir., chmn. fin. com., mem. exec. com. Goldblatt Bros., Inc., Chgo., 1979-81; pres. Buccino & Assos., Inc. (investment banking), 1981—, Am. Hydraulics, Inc.; dir., chmn. fin., audit and exec. coms. Homan Services, joint venture Sears, Roebuck & Co.; dir. Mead Fluid Dynamics, Eng., Jetway Equipment Co., Leverage Layout. Pres. Tee & Green Homeowners Assn., 1974. Served with U.S. Army, 1956-57. Mem. Fin. Execs. Inst., Am. Inst. C.P.A.s, Soc. C.P.A. Ill., N.J. Soc. C.P.A.s, Planning Execs. Inst. Clubs: Glen Oak Country (Glen Ellyn, Ill.); Union League, Execs. (Chgo.). Home: 1394 Shady Ln Wheaton IL 60187 Office: 2 N La Salle St Chicago IL 60602

BUCHALTER, STUART DAVID, retail paint company executive; b. Los Angeles, Aug. 13, 1937; s. Irwin R. and Ethel M. B.; children: Stephanie, Michael, Douglas. B.A., U. Calif., Berkeley, 1959; LL.B., Harvard U., 1962. Bar: Calif. 1963, D.C. 1975. Partner firm Buchalter, Nemer, Fields, Chrystie & Younger, Los Angeles, 1964-80; spl. counsel SEC, 1975; chmn. bd. Standard Brands Paint Co., Torrance, Calif., 1980—; exec. v.p. Constl. Rights Found., 1979; dir. City Nat. Bank, Beverly Hills, Calif., Loriman, Culver City, Calif. Author articles in field. Vice pres. Am. Jewish Com., 1979. Served with USCG, 1962-63. Mem. State Bar Calif., State Bar D.C. Home: Los Angeles CAOffice: 4300 W 190th St Torrance CA 90509

BUCHANAN, CHARLES BRENEMAN, corporation executive; b. Appleton, Wis., Nov. 3, 1931; s. William Eugene and Josephine (Breneman) B.; m. Patricia Schonberg, Aug. 27, 1955 (div. 1970); 1 son, Douglas Clare; m. Charlotte Stark, Mar. 26, 1971; 1 son, Michael David. B.A., Dartmouth Coll.; M.B.A., Harvard U. Asst. to plant mgr. Appleton Wire Works, Wis., 1957-64, v.p. mgr., 1964-69, pres. and chief exec. officer, 1969-73; v.p. Albany Internat., N.Y., 1973-76, v.p. and asst. to pres., 1976-80, v.p. and sec., 1980—, also dir.; chmn. Murry Machinery Inc., Wausau, Wis., 1973—; dir. Fox Valley Corp., Appleton. Trustee Skidmore Coll., 1981, Albany Med. Coll., 1980; mem. Appleton Bd. Den., 1962-66, pres., 1966-69. Lt. Armed Forces, 1953-55. Banker scholar, 1957. Mem. Phi Beta Kappa. Republican. Home: 20 Schuyler HillsRd Loudonville NY 12211 Office: Albany Internat PO Box 1907 Albany NY 12201

BUCHANAN, D(ANIEL) HARVEY, educator; b. New Haven, Sept. 18, 1923; s. James and Kathryn (Dolan) B.; m. Penelope Minturn Draper, Dec. 28, 1949. B.A., Yale, 1945, M.A., 1948, Ph.D., 1953. War relief work in France and Germany with Am. Friends Service Com., 1944-47; with Quaker UN Relief Program, Gaza, Palestine, 1949; mem. faculty Case Inst. Tech., 1952-67, prof. history, head dept. humanities and social studies, 1962-67; asso. dean humanities, head div. interdisciplinary studies Case Western Res. U., 1967-71, dean humanities, fine arts, 1971-72, provost, 1972-77, prof. humanities, art history, 1977—, chmn. art dept., 1978—; Cons. Ohio Arts Council, 1966-68; mem. nat. bd. consultants Nat. Endowment for Humanities. Contbr. articles to profl. jours. Pres. Cleve. Soc. Contemporary Art, 1965—; Bd. dirs. Cleve. Music Sch. Settlement, Univ. Circle Inc.; adv. council Cleve. Mus. Art. Decorated chevalier Ordre des Palmes Academiques.; Fulbright fellow Italian Inst. Hist. Studies, Naples, 1949-51. Mem. Am. Hist. Assn., Ohio Acad. History. Mem. Soc. Friends. Club: Elizabethan (Yale). Home: Battles Rd Gates Mills OH 44040 Office: Mather House Case Western Res U Cleveland OH 44106

BUCHANAN, DONALD DUANE, banker; b. Pueblo, Colo., Oct. 13, 1935; s. Donald Hubbard and Reba (Levine) B.; m. Eleanor Louise Opie, Spet. 8, 1956; children: Scott Alan, Karen Lynn. Student, U. Denver, 1953-57; grad., U. Colo. Grad. Sch. Banking, 1963, Advanced Mgmt. Program, Harvard U., 1979. With United Bank of Denver, 1956-75, v.p., sr. trust officer, 1970, sr. v.p., ops. div. exec., 1970-75; exec. v.p., ops. group exec. N.C. Nat. Bank, Charlotte, 1975-79, exec. v.p., trust group exec., 1979-83; pres. NCNB Nat. Bank Fla., Tampa, 1983—; corp. exec. v.p. NCNB Corp., 1983—; exec. v.p. NCNB Nat. Bank N.C., also dir.; mem. Fed. Res. 5th Dist. Adv. Com., 1978—; instr. Colo. Sch. Banking, U. Colo., 1974-76, Sch. Banking, U. Wis., Madison, 1972-74. Nat. bd. dirs. Campfire Girls Inc., 1973-76; bd. dirs. Denver Zool. Found., 1973-75, Better Bus. Bur., Charlotte, 1978-79; div. chmn. Charlotte United Way, 1978; mem. exec. com. ARC, Charlotte, 1978—; bd. mgrs. The Meth. Home, Charlotte, N.C. Mem. Am. Bankers Assn. (exec. com. div. ops. automation 1974-79, communications council 1977-78, chmn. fed. res. membership/pricing task force 1978-79), N.C. Bankers Assn. (chmn. ops. com.), Bank Adminstrn. Inst., Am. Forestry Assn. (treas., dir.), Charlotte C. of C. Democrat. Methodist. Clubs: Quail Hollow Country, Carmel Country, Charlotte City; Arapahoe (Denver). Office: PO Box 120 Charlotte NC 28255

BUCHANAN, DONALD RICHARD, food company executive; b. Columbus, Ohio, Oct. 20, 1920; m. Leona Mae Beal, May 31, 1941; children: Jack, Judy Buchanan Windtberg, Janet Buchanan Elsberry. B.S., George Washington U., 1946. Cert. data processing. Mgr. IBM Service Bur. Civil Aeros., Washington; mgr. data processing Giant Food, Inc., Washington, 1954-67, dir. data processing, 1967-70, v.p. data processing, 1970-79, sr. v.p. data processing, 1979—; lectr. IBM European exec. classes, Blaricum, Netherlands, 1968, LeHulpe, Belgium, 1976. Served with USN. Mem. Data Processing Mgmt. Assn. (former pres.). Republican. Home: 6620 Michaels Dr Bethesda MD 20013 Office: Giant Food Inc PO Box 1804 Washington DC 20013

BUCHANAN, GEORGE FRANCIS, book wholesaling co. exec.; b. Phila., Sept. 21, 1924; s. Charles Joseph and Mary Veronica (White) B.; m. Patricia Rose Earley, Apr. 3, 1948; children—Geraldine, James, Mary, George, Hugh, Brian, Matthew, Regina, Michael, David. B.S., St. Joseph's U., 1950; M.A., Temple U., 1952. Instr. indsl. psychology St. Joseph's U., 1950-52; with RCA, Cherry Hill, N.J., 1952-68; v.p. distbn. Random House, Inc., Md., 1968-75; exec. v.p. Baker & Taylor Co., N.Y.C., 1975—. Served with U.S. Army, 1943-46. Mem. Systems & Procedures Assn., Am. Mgmt. Assn. Home: 106 Holiday St Mount Laurel NJ 08054 Office: 1515 Broadway New York NY 10036

BUCHANAN, JAMES DAVID, writer, producer; b. Detroit, Dec. 17, 1929; s. Harry Martin and Marjorie Ellen (Hilligoss) B.; m. Elinor Louise Harrison, Nov. 21, 1951; children: Alexandra Elinor, Carrie Elizabeth. B.A., Mich. State U., 1951; postgrad., CCNY, 1953, New Sch. Social Research, 1954, Calif. State U., Northridge, 1961-63. Jazz musician; tchr. elem. grades Los Angeles Sch. System, 1961-63. Author: (novel) Red Dog, The Professional, The Prince of Malta; (with Ron Austin) (movie) Harry in Your Pocket; TV author: The Paper Man, The Death Squad; (with Ron Austin) others; producer: (TV series) Jigsaw John, Q.E.D.; author and producer TV pilots. Active civil rights movement, 1960's. Mem. Writers Guild Am. (dir.), Acad. Motion Picture Arts and Scis., Mystery Writers Am. Democrat. Episcopalian. Home: 21222 Lopez Woodland Hills CA 91364

BUCHANAN, JAMES MCGILL, economist, educator; b. Murfreesboro, Tenn., Oct. 2, 1919; s. James McGill and Lila (Scott) B.; m. Anne Bakke, Oct. 5, 1945. B.S., Middle Tenn. State Coll., 1940; M.A., U. Tenn., 1941; Ph.D., U. Chgo., 1948; Dr.h.c., U. Giessen, 1982. Prof. econs. U. Tenn., 1950-51; prof. econs. Fla. State U., 1951-54, prof., chmn. dept., 1954-56; prof. econs. U. Va., 1956-62, Paul G. McIntyre prof. econs., 1962-68, chmn. dept., 1956-62; prof. econs. U. Calif., Los Angeles, 1968-69; univ. disting. prof. econs. Va. Poly. Inst., 1969-83, dir. Center for Pub. Choice, 1969—; univ. disting. prof. econs. George Mason U., 1983—; Fulbright research scholar, Italy, 1955-56, Ford Faculty research fellow, 1959-60; Fulbright vis. prof. Cambridge U., 1961-62. Author: (with C.L. Allen and M.R. Colberg) Prices, Income and Public Policy, 954, Public Principles of Public Debt, 1958, The Public Finances, 1960, Fiscal Theory and Political Economy, 1960, (with G. Tullock) The Calculus of Consent, 1962, Public Finance in Democratic Process, 1966, The Demand and Supply of Public Goods, 1968, Cost and Choice, 1969, (with N. Devletoglou) Academia in Anarchy, 1970; Editor: (with R. Tollison) Theory of Public Choice, 1972, (with G.F. Thirlby) LSE Essays on Cost, 1973, The Limits of Liberty, 1975, (with R. Wagner) Democracy in Deficit, 1977, Freedom in Constitutional Contract, 1978, What Should Economists Do?, 1979, (with G. Brennan) The Power to Tax, 1980; contbr. articles to profl. jours. Served as lt. USNR, 1941-46. Decorated Bronze Star medal. Fellow Am. Acad. Arts and Scis.; mem. Am. Econ. Assn. (exec. com. 1966-69, v.p. 1971), So. Econ. Assn. (pres. 1963), Western Econ. Assn. (pres. 1983). Home: PO Box G Blacksburg VA 24060

BUCHANAN, JAMES WEDDLE, lawyer; b. Denver, Apr. 30, 1929; s. James Harry and Helen Elaine (Weddle) B.; m. Janet Teichgraeber, June 18, 1952; children—Mark James, Ross Brian, Todd Matthew, Wade Byron. B.A., U. Colo., 1951; LL.B., U. Mich., 1954. Bar: Colo. bar 1954. Asso. firm Tippet, Haskell & Welborn, Denver, 1960-61; partner firm Welborn & Dufford, Denver, 1961-62, Hutchinson & Hutchinson, Boulder, Colo., 1962-66; asso. prof. law U. Colo., 1966-67, asso. dean, 1966-67; partner firm Hutchinson, Black, Hill, Buchanan & Cook, Boulder, 1967—; vis. lectr. trial advocacy U. Colo., 1967-73, 77, 80; mem. grievance com. Colo. Supreme Ct., 1978—. Mem. City of Boulder Library Bd., 1963-67; bd. dirs. Colo. Chautauqua Assn., 1969-78. Served with U.S. Navy, 1955-59. Fellow Internat. Soc. Barristers, Am. Coll. Trial Lawyers; mem. Boulder County Bar Assn. (pres. 1973-74), Colo. Bar Assn., Am. Bar Assn., Colo. Trial Lawyers Assn. (dir. 1970-72), Assn. Trial Lawyers Am., Am. Law Inst., Order Coif. Congregationalist. Office: PO Box 1170 1215 Spruce St Boulder CO 80306

BUCHANAN, JESSE EVERETT, civil engr.; b. nr. Algona, Iowa, Apr. 22, 1904; s. Sophus and Jessie Ann (Samuelson) B.; m. Leah Rachel Tuttle, June 10, 1929; children—Nancy Tuttle, John Austin. B.S., U. Idaho, 1927, M.S., 1929, C.E., 1936, L.H.D., 1951, Sc.D., 1953. Instr. civil engring., testing engr. U. Idaho, Idaho Bur. Hwys., 1927-29, asst. prof., testing engr., 1929-36, dean, dir. engring., prof. civil engring., 1938-42, pres., 1946-54; research engr. Asphalt Inst., 1936-38, pres., 1954-69, cons., 1969—. Mem. Idaho Bd. Engring. Examiners, 1939-48; sec. Automotive Safety Found., Washington, 1956-69; sec., treas. Road Information Program, Inc., Washington, 1970—. Served to lt. col. C.E. AUS, 1942-46; CBI. Decorated Legion of Merit. Mem. Nat., Idaho, Md. socs. profl. engrs., ASCE, Am. Rd. and Transp. Builders Assn., Washington Soc. Engrs. (hon.), Phi Beta Kappa, Sigma Xi, Tau Beta Pi, Sigma Tau. Home: 709 Gilbert Coeur d'Alene ID 83814 Office: Asphalt Inst College Park MD 20740 also TRIP Inc 1899 L St NW Suite 401 Washington DC 20036

BUCHANAN, JOHN DONALD, radiochemist, health physicist; b. Mesa, Ariz., Oct. 1, 1927; s. John Freeborn and Marguerite (Brimhall) B.; m. Donna Marie Smith, Aug. 27, 1955; children—Margaret MacNeil, John Michael, Andrew Tierney, David Brimhall. B.S. in Chemistry, U. Ariz., 1949. Diplomate: Am. Bd. Health Physics, Nat. Cert. Commn. in Chemistry and Chem. Engring. Sr. chemist Tracerlab, Inc., Richmond, Calif., 1950-59; staff asso. Gen. Atomic div. Gen. Dynamics Corp., San Diego, 1959-62; mgr. nuclear applications and measurements Teledyne-Isotopes Co., Palo Alto, Calif., 1962-71; mgr. applied research Internat. Nutronics Inc., Palo Alto, 1971-73; supr. radiol. monitoring programs NUS Corp., Rockville, Md., 1973-75; health physicist, radiochemist U.S. Nuclear Regulatory Commn., Washington, 1975—. Author papers on radiation protection, radioanalytical chemistry, radioactivity measurements, radiosotope applications. Served with USNR, 1945-46. Recipient Meritorious Service award U.S. Nuclear Regulatory Commn., 1981. Fellow Am. Inst. Chemists, AAAS; mem. Health Physics Soc., Am. Nuclear Soc., Am. Chem. Soc., Soc. Environ. Geochemistry and Health, Phi Lambda Upsilon, Phi Delta Theta. Home: 7508 Dew Wood Dr Derwood MD 20855 Office: US Nuclear Regulatory Commn Washington DC 20555:

BUCHANAN, JOHN MACLENNAN, Canadian government official; b. Sydney, N.S., Can., Apr. 22, 1931; s. Murdoch William and Flora Isabel (Campbell) B.; m. Mavis Forsyth, Sept. 1, 1954; children: Murdoch, Travis, Nichola, Natalie, Natasha. B.Sc.; cert. engring., Mt. Allison U., 1954; LL.B., Dalhousie U., Halifax, N.S., 1958; D.Eng. (hon.), N.S. Tech. Coll., 1979; LL.D., St. Mary's U., 1982; D.C.L., Mt. Allison U., 1981. Bar: Called to bar, created queen's counsel 1972. Pvt. practice, Halifax, 1958-71; mem. N.S. Legislature, 1967—; minister public works, then fisheries; premier of N.S., 1978—; leader Progressive Conservative Party in N.S., 1971—; bd. dirs. Legal Aid for N.S. Barristers Assn. Active Boy Scouts Assn. Mem. Can. Bar Assn., N.S. Barristers Assn., Royal Can. Legion. Mem. United Ch. Can. Clubs: Halifax, City, Lions, Shriners, Odd Fellows. Office: Province House Halifax NS B3J 2T3 Canada

BUCHANAN, JOHN ROBERT, physician, educator; b. Newark, Mar. 8, 1928; s. John Hamilton and Elsie (Castles) B.; m. Susan Townsend Carver, Oct. 27, 1962; children: Ross, Allyn. A.B. cum laude, Amherst Coll., 1950; M.D., Cornell U., 1954; student, Inst. Arthritis and Metabolic Diseases, USPHS, 1956-57, 60-61. Diplomate: Am. Bd. Internal Medicine, Nat. Bd. Med. Examiners. Intern, asst. resident physician N.Y. Hosp., N.Y.C., 1954-58, physician to outpatients, 1956-57, 60-62, from asst. to asso. attending physician, 1962-71, attending physician, 1971-76, asso. dir. welfare med. care project, 1961-64; vis. asst. physician Rockefeller Inst. Hosp., N.Y.C., 1960-61; asso. vis. physician Bellevue Hosp., N.Y.C., 1965-68; instr. medicine Cornell U., 1961-63, asst. prof. medicine, 1963-67, asst. dir. comprehensive care and teaching program, 1961-64, asst. to chmn. dept. medicine, 1964-65, asso. dean, 1965-69, dean, 1969-76, clin. asso. prof. medicine, 1967-69, asso. prof., 1969-71, prof., 1971-76; pres. Michael Reese Hosp. and Med. Center, Chgo., 1977-82; prof. medicine Pritzker Sch. Medicine, U. Chgo., 1977-82, asso. dean, 1978-82; gen. dir. Mass. Gen. Hosp., Boston, 1982—; prof. medicine Harvard U. Med. Sch., Boston, 1982—; mem. com. on sci. policy Sloan-Kettering Inst., 1969-76; mem. State of Ill. Med. Determination Bd., 1980—; sr. program cons. prepaid managed health care program Robert Wood Johnson Found., 1982—; mem. adminstrv. bd. Council Teaching Hosps., 1984—. Chmn. nat. adv. council Children's Television Workshop, 1974-75; Bd. dirs. Pub. Health Research Inst. of N.Y.C., 1969-76, Winnifred Masterson Burke Relief Found., 1972-80, 82—; trustee Cornell U., 1970-76, China Med. Bd. of N.Y., Inc., 1970—; vice chmn. China Med. Bd. of N.Y., Inc.; bd. mgrs. Meml. Hosp., 1969-76; mem. adv. com. Edwin L. Crosby and W.K. Kellogg Found. Fellowships, 1979-80; trustee Center for Effective Philanthropy, 1981—. Served as AUS, 1958-60. Fellow A.C.P., Am. Pub. Health Assn.; mem. Harvey Soc., N.J. State, N.Y. County med. socs., N.Y. Acad. (council deans 1969-76, exec. council 1971-76), Assn. Am. Med. Colls. (vice chmn. liaison com. on med. edn. 1982-83, chmn. 1983), Assn. Med. Schs. N.Y. and N.J. (trustee 1970-76, pres. 1972-76), Inst. Medicine-Nat. Acad. Scis., Ill. Hosp. Assn. (chmn. 1979-80), N.Y. Acad. Medicine, Royal Soc. for Promotion Health, Sigma Xi. Office: Mass Gen Hosp Boston MA 02114

BUCHANAN, PATRICK JOSEPH, columnist; b. Washington, Nov. 2, 1938; s. William Baldwin and Catherine E. (Crum) B.; m. Shelley Ann Scarney, May 8, 1971. A.B. in English cum laude, Georgetown U., 1961; M.S. in Journalism, Columbia U., 1962. Editorial writer St. Louis Globe Democrat, 1962-64, asst. editorial editor, 1964-66; exec. asst. to Richard M. Nixon, 1966-69; spl. asst. to Pres. Nixon, 1969-73; cons. to Presidents Nixon and Ford, 1973-74; columnist syndicated N.Y. Times (spl. features), 1975-78, Chgo. Tribune-N.Y. News (Syndicate), 1978—; commentator NBC Radio Network, 1978—. Author: The New Majority, 1973, Conservative Votes, Liberal Victories, 1975. Mem. President's Commn. White House Fellowships, 1969-73; v.p. Am. Council of Young Polit. Leaders, 1974-75, 76-79. Republican. Roman Catholic. Club: University (Washington). Home and office: 1017 Savile Ln McLean VA 22101

BUCHANAN, PETER T., investment banker; b. Orange, N.J., Sept. 12, 1934; s. Percy H. and Ruth C. (Townley) B.; m. Lane Eichhorn, Oct. 20, 1956; children: Richard, Linda. A.B. with honors, Princeton U., 1956. With The 1st Boston Corp., N.Y.C., 1956-57, 60—, v.p., 1967-73, mgr. equity securities dept., 1972-74, exec. v.p., dir. charge trading, sales, ops. and adminstrn., 1974-78, pres., 1978—, chief exec. officer, 1983—, also dir. Trustee Kenyon Coll., Gambier, Ohio, 1981—. Served with USAF, 1957-60. Mem. Security Traders Assn. N.Y., Securities Industry Assn. (governing council, bd. dirs., exec. com., vice chmn. 1981—). Clubs: Bond, Princeton (N.Y.C.); Links, Morris County Golf, Baltusrol Golf. Home: 32 Crescent Rd Madison NJ 07940 Office: First Boston Corp Park Ave Plaza New York NY 10055

BUCHANAN, ROBERT EDGAR, advt. exec.; b. Auburn, Ind., Mar. 17, 1919; s. Verne Edgar and Ida Mary (Hachet) B.; m. Estalee Hazel Haddock, Nov. 22, 1961; children—Heather Hachet and Holly Haddock (twins). B.S., Northwestern U., 1940, M.S., 1941; post grad., U. Ill., 1941-42. Instr. U. Ill., 1941-42; instr., dir. padio pub. relations Northwestern U., 1947-49; broadcast supr. Young & Rubicam (advt.), 1950-56; with J. Walter Thompson, N.Y.C., 1956—, sr. v.p. charge all media, 1972-80, exec. v.p., U.S. media dir., 1980—, also dir. Served with USAAF, 1942-46. Recipient Harrington Meml. award Northwestern U., 1941. Mem. Internat. Radio and TV Soc., Deru, Phi Beta Kappa, Beta Theta Pi, Sigma Delta Chi. Home: 3 Dogwood Ln Darien CT 06820 Office: 466 Lexington Ave New York NY 10017

BUCHANAN, ROBERT FRANCIS, petroleum company executive; b. Calgary, Alta., Can., May 26, 1923; s. John Guy and Evelyn Hope (Hall) B.; children: Christine Hoeppner, Susan Lyons, Robert, William, Deborah. Chartered acctg. student Price Waterhouse & Co., 1946-51; treas., fin. v.p., sr. v.p., pres., dir. Gt. Plains Devel. Co. Can. Ltd., Calgary, 1951-75; fin. v.p. Pacific Petroleums Ltd., Calgary, 1975-79. Served with RCAF, 1942-45. Mem. Ind. Petroleum Assos. Can. (dir.), Conf. Bd. Can. (adv. fin. council), Fin. Execs. Inst. (N.Am. area v.p. 1978-79, dir. 1977-79). Progressive Conservative. Mem. United Ch. of Canada. Clubs: Glencoe, Petroleum, Earl Grey Golf. Home: 1124 39th Ave SW Calgary AB T2T 2K5 Canada

BUCHANAN, WESLEY EVANS, builder, developer; b. Washington, Oct. 6, 1917; s. J. Wesley and Rosalyn (Evans) B.; m. Mary Clifton LaForce, Mar. 12, 1941; children: Robert Evans, Dorothy Elaine Buchanan Fickensher, Hope Louise Buchanan Wilmarth, Jane Adele Buchanan Gurley. B.S., Wharton Sch. of U. Pa., 1940. With W. Evans Buchanan Cos., 1940—, pres., 1960—; v.p., dir. County Fed. Savs. & Loan Assn., Rockville, Md., 1957—; Bd. dirs. Nat. Council Good Cities, 1964-65; mem. housing and urban devel. adv. com. AID, 1964-65; mem. performance concept in bldg. com. Bldg. Research Adv. Bd., Nat. Acad. Scis., 1965; mem. com. vol. home mortgage credit program HHFA, 1963; mem. home improvement adv. com. FHA, 1959-60; pub. mem. Geneva (Switzerland) Conf. Housing, Bldg. and Planning Com. (Econ. Commn. for Europe), 1963; trustee Nat. Housing Center, 1964-65; mem. nat. adv. council Urban America; mem. advisory bd. AID, HUD, 1971; cons. (Project Rehab.). Pres. Montgomery County Boys Baseball Assn., 1956; mem. Pres.'s Nat. Tax Revision Com., 1963; Bd. govs. Nat. Cathedral Sch., 1960-66. Named to Housing Hall of Fame, 1979. Mem. Nat. Assn. Home Builders (pres. 1963), Home Builders Assn. Met. Washington (pres. 1958), real estate bds. D.C., Md. Presbyterian (past vice chmn. bd. trustees). Clubs: Columbia, Country (Chevy Chase, Md.); Touchdown, University (Washington). Home: Box 1000 Cove Creek Club Stevensville MD 21666 Office: 13415 Connecticut Ave Suite 105 Silver Spring MD 20906

BUCHANAN, WILLIAM, political science educator; b. Richmond, Va., Dec. 25, 1918; s. Daniel Littleton and Cora (Briggs) B.; m. Vivian Landrum, Aug. 8, 1946; children: James Landrum, David Briggs, Mary Warrington. A.B., Washington and Lee U., 1941, M.A., 1941; M.A., Princeton U., 1953, Ph.D., 1955. Instr. English Roanoke Coll., 1946-47; asso. dir. Bicentennial of Washington and Lee, 1947-49; asst. prof. govt. Miss. State U., 1952-55; exec. dir. Woodrow Wilson Centennial Commn. Va., 1956; asst. prof. polit. sci. U. So. Cal., 1956-68, asso. prof., 1958-62; vis. research prof. legislative process U. Cal. at Berkeley, 1959-60; prof. polit. sci. U. Tenn., 1962-66; prof., head dept. polit. sci. Washington and Lee U., Lexington, Va., 1966—; Mem. council Interuniv. Consortium Polit. Research, 1964-66. Author: (with Hadley Cantril) How Nations See Each Other, 1953, Legislative Partisanship, The Deviant Case of California, 1963, Understanding Political Variables, 3d edit, 1980, (with Joseph B. Thompson) Analyzing Psychological Data, 1979; mem. editorial bd.: Western Polit. Quar, 1963-64; contbr. articles to profl. jours. Bd. dirs. Clinch-Powell River Valley Assn., 1965-66. Served to lt. comdr. USNR, 1942-46. Mem. Am. Polit. Sci. Assn. (past council), Am. Assn. U. Profs., Phi Beta Kappa, Omicron Delta Kappa. Democrat. Methodist. Home: 618 Ross Rd Lexington VA 24450

BUCHANAN, WILLIAM EUGENE, former wire works corporation executive; b. Appleton, Wis., Jan. 11, 1903; s. Gustavus E. and Josephine (Pond) B.; m. Josephine Breneman, Jan. 3, 1931; children: Charles, William Eugene, Jean, Robert. B.S., Dartmouth, 1924, M.A.; hon., 1962; LL.D., 1977; M.B.A., Harvard U., 1926; M.A. (hon.), Lawrence U., 1959, LL.D., 1978. With Appleton Wire Works, Inc. (merged with Albany Felt Co. (N.Y.), 1969, name now Albany Internat. Corp.), 1926-75, v.p., 1935-38, pres., chief exec. officer, 1938-69, chmn. bd., dir., 1969-75; chmn., dir. Outagamie Corp., Appleton, 1958-83, Fox Valley Corp., 1974—. Trustee Lawrence U., Appleton, 1938-77; trustee Dartmouth Coll., 1961-73. Mem. Sigma Nu. Republican. Conglist. Clubs: Mason, Rotarian., Riverview Country, North Shore Golf, Milwaukee Country; Gulf Stream Golf, Country of Fla. (Delray Beach). Home: 19 Par Club Circle Village of Golf FL 33436 Office: PO Box 727 Appleton WI 54912

BUCHANAN, WILLIAM HOBART, JR., publishing company executive; b. Summit, N.J., July 2, 1937; s. William Hobart and Margaret R. B.; m. Eleanor A. Lincoln, June 18, 1966; children: Diana A., Jessica R. A.B., Princeton U., 1959; LL.B., Harvard U., 1963. Bar: N.Y. 1963. Asso. firm Shearman & Sterling, N.Y.C., 1963-70; v.p., sec., gen. counsel Reuben H. Donnelley Corp., N.Y.C., 1970—; asst. sec., asso. gen. counsel Dun & Bradstreet Corp., N.Y.C., 1976-79, v.p., sec., asso. gen. counsel, 1979—. Served with USMCR, 1959-60. Mem. Am. Soc. Corp. Secs. (pres. N.Y. regional group 1979-80, nat. treas. 1979-83, bd. dirs. 1983—), ABA, N.Y. State Bar Assn., Assn. Bar City N.Y. Republican. Presbyterian. Clubs: Princeton (N.Y.C.); New Canaan Field. Office: 299 Park Ave New York NY 10171

BUCHANAN, WILLIAM WALTER, publisher; b. Kansas City, Mo., Mar. 6, 1927; s. Walter Roy and Eleanor Findley (O'Rear) B.; m. Marilyn Woodbury, Dec. 8, 1951; children: William Scott, Stephen Woodbury, Patricia Lynn. B.S., Georgetown U., 1950. Intelligence officer CIA, 1950-57; mgmt. cons. George Fry & Assos., Chgo., N.Y.C., George Fry & Assos., Teheran, Iran, 1957-58, mgr., 1959-60; gen. mgr. internat. div. DCA Food Industries, N.Y.C., 1960-63; mgr. Washington office R.R. Bowker Co., 1963-67; pres. Carrollton Press Inc., Arlington, Va. and; Irvine, Scotland, 1967—; pres. U.S. Hist. Documents Inst., Inc. (pubs.), Arlington, 1970-81, The Hist. Documents Inst., 1977-81. Editor: Combined Retrospective Index Sets (History, Political Science and Sociology). Trustee Georgetown U. Library Assos. Served with AUS, 1945-46. Mem. A.L.A., Information Industry Assn., Nat. Microfilm Assn., Assn. Am. Publishers, Sigma Chi. Clubs: Nat. Press, Capitol Hill (Washington); Washington Golf and Country (Va.). Home: 3847 N River St Arlington VA 22207 Office: 1611 N Kent St Arlington VA 22209

BUCHEN, JOHN GUSTAVE, judge; b. Sheboygan, Wis., Sept. 3, 1920; s. Gustave William and Elinor (Jung) B.; m. Anne Armstrong, Aug. 9, 1943; children—John Stephen, Laura, Elizabeth, Timothy, James. B.A., U. Wis., 1942, LL.B., 1948. Bar: Wis. bar 1948. Dist. atty., Sheboygan County, 1949-55; partner firm Buchen & Heffernan, Sheboygan, 1955-63; asst. city atty., City of Sheboygan, 1957-63; commr. Family Ct., Sheboygan County, 1959-63; judge Sheboygan County Circuit Ct. (Br. II), 1963—; mem. faculty Wis. Jud. Coll., 1968-78; chmn. Wis. Bd. Criminal Ct. Judges, 1977-78. Served with

USAAC, 1944-48. Mem. Am. Bar Assn. (1st Place Nat. award for outstanding progress in improvement of traffic ct. practices and procedures 1969), State Bar Wis., Am. Law Inst. Home: 422 St Clair Ave Sheboygan WI 53081 Office: 615 N 6th St Sheboygan WI 53081

BUCHEN, PHILIP WILLIAM, lawyer; b. Sheboygan, Wis., Feb. 27, 1916; s. Gustav W. and Elenor (Jung) B.; m. Beatrice Loomis Gold, Feb. 27, 1947; children: Victoria Buchen Johnson, Roderick L. A.B., U. Mich. at Ann Arbor, 1939, J.D., 1941. Bar: Mich. 1941. Pvt. practice law, Grand Rapids, Mich., 1941-74; partner law firm Ford & Buchen, Grand Rapids, 1941-42, Butterfield, Keeney & Amberg, 1943-47, Amberg, Law & Buchen, 1948-61; v.p. Grand Valley State Coll., Allendale, Mich., 1961-67; partner firm Law, Buchen, Weathers, Richardson & Dutcher, Grand Rapids, 1967-74; counsel to Pres. Ford, Washington, 1974-77; partner firm Dewey, Ballantine, Bushby, Palmer & Wood, Washington, 1977—; dir. Communications Satellite Corp., Washington, 1969-74, Old Kent Fin. Corp., Grand Rapids, 1962-74, 77—. Mem. U.S. Commn. on Fine Arts, Washington, 1977-81. Mem. D.C. Bar Assn. Clubs: Kent Country (Grand Rapids); Chevy Chase, University (Washington). Home: 800 25th St NW Washington DC 20037 Office: 1775 Pennsylvania Ave NW Washington DC 20006

BUCHENHOLZ, JANE JACOBS, assn. exec.; b. Bklyn., Oct. 28, 1918; d. Joseph and Sofia (Frucht) Jacobs; m. Bruce Buchenholz, Feb. 22, 1942 (div. 1962); children—Nancy Jan, Susan Jay. A.B. magna cum laude, Hunter Coll., 1942; postgrad. psychology, New Sch. Social Research, 1947-48. Successively tchr. math., control chemist, plant pathologist, 1942-46; remedial reading tchr. Reading Clinic, N.Y. U., 1946-49; spl. tchr. emotionally disturbed children, 1948-49, pianist, accompanist modern dance classes, 1955-61; dir. Nat. Roosevelt Day Dinner Ams. for Democratic Action, 1961-66, nat. sec., 1963-67, mem. nat. bd., nat. exec. com., 1963—; recipient Chpt. Chairmen's award, 1963; dir. devel. New Sch. Social Research, 1968-72, New Lincoln Sch., 1971-72; exec. dir. Sta. WMCA (Call for Action), 1962-64; research cons. voter registration Nat. Council Negro Women, 1964; spl. cons. systems and inventory control Crown Fabrics div. Bangor Punta Industries, 1966-68; gen. distbr. Golden Products, 1972—; asst. to dir. Children's Day Treatment Center and Sch., 1973—; real estate salesman, 1973—; mem. nat. bd. Com. for Sane Nuclear Policy, 1966-68; mem. nat. adv. council Nat. Conf. for New Politics, 1966-67; exec. dir. Broadway For Peace, 1968; mem. nat. council, nat. exec. com. Nat. Emergency Civil Liberties Com., 1969—. Sec.- treas. fgn. policy council N.Y. Democrats, 1966—; alt. del. 19th congressional dist. to Dem. Nat. Conv., 1968; dist. leader 67th Assembly Dist. Dem. Party, N.Y.C., 1971-76. Mem. Phi Beta Kappa, Phi Sigma. Home: 205 West End Ave New York City NY 10023

BUCHER, CHARLES AUGUSTUS, physical education educator; b. Conesus, N.Y., Oct. 2, 1912; s. Grover C. and Elizabeth (Barr) B.; m. Jacqueline N. Dubois, Aug. 24, 1941; children: Diana, Richard, Nancy, Gerald. B.A., Ohio Wesleyan U., 1937; M.A., Columbia, 1941; Ed.D., N.Y. U., 1948; post-grad., Yale, 1948-49. Tchr. pub. schs., N.Y., 1937-41; asso. prof. New Haven State Coll., 1946-50; prof. edn. N.Y. U., 1950-79, dir. Sch. Health, Phys. Edn., Recreation and Dance,; prof. U. Nev., Las Vegas, 1980—; editor Appleton-Century-Crofts, N.Y.C.; Am. specialist U.S. State Dept., 1962; del. Pres. Eisenhower's White House Conf. on Youth Fitness, 1956; cons. Pres.'s Council on Phys. Fitness and Sports, 1972—; chmn. nat. adv. bd. Am. Fitness Club. Author: Methods and Materials in Physical Education and Recreation, 1954, Foundations of Physical Education, rev. edit, 1983, Recreation for Today's Society, 1984, Methods and Materials Secondary School Physical Education, rev. edit, 1983, Physical Education in Modern Elementary School, rev, 1971, College Ahead, rev. edit, 1961, Athletics in Schools and Colleges, 1965, Guiding Your Child toward College, 1967, Physical Education for Life, 1969, Dimensions of Physical Education, 2d edit, 1974, Administration of Health and Physical Education Programs, 1983, Administrative Dimensions of Health and Physical Education Programs, 1971, The Foundations of Health, 1976, Physical Education for Children: Movement Foundations and Experiences, 1979, Physical Education: Change and Challenge, 1981, Health, 1981, Fitness for College and Life, 1985; also numerous articles. Trustee, chmn. scholarship com. Coll. Scholarship Plan, Inc., 1959—. Served to capt. USAAF, 1941-46. Recipient Sch. Bell award, 1960; named One of 10 Ams. who have contributed most to nation's health and fitness Jaycees, 1982. Fellow A.A.H.P.E.R., Am. Coll. Sports Medicine, Am. Sch. Health Assn.; mem. N.E.A. Home: 4239 Pinecrest Circle W Las Vegas NV 89121 Office: U Nev 4505 Maryland Pkwy Las Vegas NV 89154 *Qualities that I feel are important to being a success in life include: hard work; enthusiasm for one's work and endeavors; dedication; keeping in mind long-range goals with continual evaluation and modification of plans where necessary.*

BUCHER, JEFFREY MARTIN, lawyer, banker; b. Los Angeles, Feb. 9, 1933; s. Harold Martin and Afton Marie (Kurtz) B.; m. Ana Maria Boitel, Mar. 29, 1980; children: Stephanie, Kendall, Stacey, Jeffrey, Heidi. A.B., Occidental Coll., Los Angeles, 1954; J.D., Stanford U., 1957. Bar: Calif. 1958, D.C. 1975. With 1st Interstate Bank of Calif., Los Angeles, 1957-72, sr. v.p., 1969-72; bd. govs. FRS, Washington, 1972-76; ptnr. Lillick McHose and Charles, Los Angeles and Washington, 1976—; chmn. bd. Nat. Enterprise Bank, Washington; trustee PNB Mortgage and Realty Investors, Phila., 1978—; mem. adv. bd. task force bank regulation FDIC, 1976-77. Author articles in field. Mem. corp. bd. Children's Hosp. Nat. Med. Center. Served with USAR, 1954-62. Mem. ABA, Am. Soc. Corp. Secs., Calif. Bar Assn., D.C. Bar Assn. Republican. Club: Cosmos (Washington). Home: 1117 Chain Bridge Rd McLean VA 22101 Office: 21 DuPont Circle NW Washington DC 20036

BUCHER, ROBERT MONROE, college dean, surgeon; b. Phila., May 28, 1920; s. Jonas W. and Ellen K. (Drager) B.; m. Elizabeth Ann Matlack, Mar. 23, 1946; children—Elizabeth Ann, Robert David, Barbara Jean. Student, U. Pa., 1941; M.D., Temple U., 1944, M.S. in Surgery, 1950. Diplomate: Am. Bd. Surgery, Am. Bd. Thoracic Surgery. Intern Temple U. Med. Center, 1944-45, resident surgery, 1945-46, 48-50, instr. surgery, 1950-54, asso. surgery, 1954-57, asst. prof. surgery, 1957-60, asso. dean, 1958-59, dean, 1959-69, asso. prof. surgery, 1960-69; dep. dir. Bur. Health Manpower Edn., NIH, Bethesda, Md., 1969-71; dean Coll. Medicine, U. South Ala., Mobile, 1971-74, prof. surgery, 1973—, v.p. for health affairs, 1973-74. Contbr. articles to med. jours. Fellow A.C.S.; mem. A.M.A., Ala., Mobile med. socs., Babcock Surg. Soc., Phi Chi, Alpha Omega Alpha. Republican. Episcopalian. Club: Isle Dauphine. Home: PO Box 309 Dauphin Island AL 36528

BUCHHOLZ, DONALD ALDEN, stock brokerage company executive; b. LaPorte, Tex., Mar. 10, 1929; s. Fred T. and Chrystine (McCombs) B.; m. Ruth Vernon, May 17, 1958; children—Robert, Chrystine Louise. B.B.A., North Tex. U., 1952. C.P.A., Tex. Acct., staff auditor Peat, Marwick & Mitchell, Dallas, 1952-54; asst. sec.-treas., chief acct. ICT Discount Corp., 1954-56; comptroller Eppler-Guerin & Turner, Inc., 1956-59; partner Cheshier-Buchholz (pub. accountants), 1959-60; comptroller, sec. Parker Ford, Inc. (stock brokers), Dallas, 1960-63, also dir., 1962-63; v.p., chief adminstrv. officer, sec. Weber, Hall, Cobb & Caudle, Inc., Dallas, 1963-72; also dir.; ptnr., chief exec. officer Southwest Securities, Inc. (formerly MidSouthwest Securities, Inc.), 1972—; dir. Mercantile N.Bk-Garland, Tex.; Tchr. N.Y. Inst. Finance. Bd. govs. N.Y. Stock Exchange, 1969-71; trustee Garland Ind. Sch. Bd., 1971-74, pres., 1973-74; pres. bd. trustees Dallas County Community Coll. Dist., 1982—; bd. dirs. Garland Meml. Hosp., 1981—, Garland Meml. Hosp. Found., 1981—. Served with USAAF, 1946-49. Mem. Dallas Security Dealers Assn. (sec. 1961), Tex. Stock and Bond Dealers Assn. (treas., dir. 1982—), N.Y. Stock Exchange (allied), Midwest Stock Exchange, Chgo. Bd. Trade. Baptist. Club: Kiwanian (pres. 1968). Home: 3627 Glenbrook Ct Garland TX 75041 Office: Mercantile Bank Bldg Dallas TX 75201

BUCHHOLZ, WERNER, electrical engineer; b. Detmold, Germany, Oct. 24, 1922; came to U.S., 1946, naturalized, 1954; s. Julius and Elsa (Hellwitz) B.; m. Anna Odor, Oct. 23, 1952; children: John (dec.), Sham Rang S. Khalsa. B.A. Sc., U. Toronto, Ont., Can., 1945, M.A.Sc., 1946; Ph.D., Calif. Inst. Tech., 1950. With IBM Devel. Lab., Poughkeepsie, N.Y., 1949—, sr. engr. in central systems arch., 1969—; chmn. IFIP Congress 65, N.Y.C., 1965. Editor, co-author: Planning A Computer System, 1962; editor: IEEE Transactions on Computers, 1952-54. Fellow IEEE (dir. 1969-70); mem. IEEE Computer Soc. Home: 24 Edge Hill Rd Wappingers Falls NY 12590 Office: PO Box 390 Poughkeepsie NY 12602

BUCHI, GEORGE HERMANN, organic chemistry educator, consultant; b. Baden, Switzerland, Aug. 1, 1921; came to U.S., 1948; s. George Jakob and Martha (Muller) B.; m. Anne Westfall Barkman, Aug. 20, 1955. D.Sc., Swiss Fed. Inst. Tech., Zurich, 1947; Ph.D. hon., U. Heidelberg, W. Germany, 1983. Firestone postdoctoral fellow U. Chgo., 1948-51; asst. prof. chemistry MIT, Cambridge, 1951—, assoc. prof., prof., Camilyy Dreyfus prof., 1971—. Fellow Royal Soc. Chemistry; mem. Swiss Chem. Soc. (Fritzsche 1958, award for creative work in organic chemistry 1973), Nat. Acad. Scis., Pharm. Soc. Japan (hon.). Republican. Office: MIT 77 Massachusetts Ave Cambridge MA 02139

BUCHIN, IRVING D., orthodontist, educator; b. N.Y.C., Feb. 17, 1920; s. David and Lillian (Polovick) B.; m. Jean Jacobs, May 18, 1941; children: Peter Jay, John David. D.D.S., N.Y. U., 1943; postgrad., U. Detroit, 1949, Tenple U., 1951. Diplomate: Am. Bd. Orthodontics. Practice dentistry limited to orthodontics, Forest Hills, N.Y., 1946—; chief of orthodontics Jewish Chronic Disease Hosp., 1955-57; orthodontist Jewish Meml. Hosp., 1950; asst. vis. dental surgeon City Hosp., 1946; mem. panel of orthodontists N.Y.C. Dept. Health, 1949—, constituent, mem. adv. bd., 1972—; orthodontist U. Hosp., Boston U., Meml. Hosp. Mass., 1963-68; cons. div. dentistry, dept. surgery Children's Hosp. Phila., 1979—; lectr., clinician in postgrad. edn. ADA (Am. Assn. Orthodontists); instr. Charles H. Tweed Found. Orthodontia Research; vis. asso. prof. orthodontics Boston U. Sch. Medicine; asso. prof. orthodontics U. Pa. (Sch. Dental Medicine), 1967-73, prof., 1974—; guest lectr. Columbia U., Fairleigh Dickinson U., Baylor U., N.Y. U., Howard U., Tufts U., U. So. Calif., U. Toronto, U. Caracas (Venezuela), 1969—; cons., mem. orthodontic peer rev. com. 11th dist. N.Y. State. Constituent editor: Am. Jour. Orthodontics; editor: Eastern Component Angle Soc. Orthodontia, 1964-66; contbr. articles to dental jours., textbooks. Served to capt. Dental Corps AUS, 1943-46. Fellow Am. Coll. Dentists; mem. Eastern Assn. Strang-Tweed Study Groups (sec. 1951-57), Am. Assn. Orthodontists (council on orthodontic edn.), Am. Acad. Dental Medicine, Internat. Assn. Dental Research, Pierre Fauchard Acad., N.Y. Acad. Scis., Fedn. Dentaire Internationale, Charles H. Tweed Found. for Orthodontic Research (dir., pres. Eastern sect. 1972-73), N.E. Soc. Orthodontists (pres. 1977-78, chmn. exam bd. preceptee accreditation, del. Am. Assn. Orthodontists, constituent editor 1972-75, edn. com. 1972—, bd. censors 1979—), Edward H. Angle Soc. Orthodontics (nat. treas. 1970-75, dir. 1981—). Clubs: Muttontown Golf and Country, Univ. Pa. Faculty. Designer Buchin cephalometric template. Office: 107-21 Queens Blvd Forest Hills NY 11375 also 800A Fifth Ave New York NY 10021

BUCHLER, HAROLD ANDREW, lawyer; b. New Orleans, Nov. 29, 1919; s. Conrad and Doretta L. (Vallee) B.; m. Margaret Maloney, Sept. 4, 1946; children: Harold, Colleen, Sheila, Conrad, Celeste. B.A., Loyola U., New Orleans, 1941, J.D., 1947. Bar: La. 1947. Mem. firm McDonald & Buchler, Metairie, La., 1950-70; asst. dist. atty. Jefferson Parish, Gretna, La., 1951-53; mem., ptnr. Buchler & Buchler, Metairie, 1970—; chmn. bd. Nat. Bank of Commerce in Jefferson Parish, Jefferson, La., 1978—. Served with U.S. Army, 1943-46; ETO, PTO. Mem. ABA, La. Bar Assn., Jefferson Bar Assn. (pres. 1960-61), Am. Legion, VFW (comdr.). Democrat. Roman Catholic. Club: Metairie Country. Home: 107 Sena Dr Metairie LA 70005 Office: Buchler and Buchler 3014 Metairie Rd) PO Box 127 Metairie LA 70004

BUCHLER, JUSTUS, philosopher, educator; b. N.Y.C., Mar. 27, 1914; s. Samuel and Ida (Frost) B.; m. Evelyn Urban Shirk, Feb. 20, 1943; 1 dau., Katherine Urban. B.S.S., CCNY, 1934; M.A., Columbia U., 1935, Ph.D., 1939. Lectr. philosophy Columbia U., 1937-42; instr. philosophy Bklyn. Coll., 1938-43; faculty Columbia U., 1942-71, prof. philosophy, 1956-71, Johnsonian prof., 1959-71, chmn. dept. philosophy, 1964-67, chmn. Contemporary Civilization program in coll., 1950-56; distinguished prof. philosophy SUNY, Stony Brook, 1971—. Author: Charles Peirce's Empiricism, 1939, (with J.H. Randall Jr.) Philosophy: An Introduction, 1942, (with others) The Philosophy of Bertrand Russell, 1944, Toward a General Theory of Human Judgment, 1951, 2d rev. edit., 1979, Studies in the Philosophy of Charles Sanders Peirce, 1952, A History of Columbia College on Morningside, 1954, Nature and Judgment, 1955, The Concept of Method, 1961, Metaphysics of Natural Complexes, 1966, The Main of Light: On the Concept of Poetry, 1974; Editor: (with B. Schwartz) The Obiter Scripta of George Santayana, 1936, The Philosophy of Peirce: Selected Writings, 1940, (with Randall and Shirk) Readings in Philosophy, 1946, (with others) Introduction to Contemporary Civilization in the West, 2 vols, 1946, (with Randall and Shirk) Chapters in Western Civilization, 2 vols, 1948. Mem. Am. Philos. Assn., ACLU (vice chmn. nat. acad. freedom com. 1958-64). Home: 3 Homestead Ave Garden City NY 11530 Office: Old Physics Bldg State U NY Stony Brook NY 11790

BUCHMAN, JOEL, lawyer; b. N.Y.C., Apr. 25, 1938; s. Abraham Martin and Ann (Parker) B.; m. Joyce Goldfinger, June 16, 1966; children: Jonathan Lee, Jennifer Lynn. B.A., Cornell U., 1960; J.D., Columbia U., 1963. Bar: N.Y. 1963. Practiced in, N.Y.C., 1963—; assoc. firm Buchman Buchman & O'Brien, N.Y.C., 1963-69; mem. firm Buchman, Buchman & O'Brien, 1969—. Bd. dirs. Greater N.Y. Fund. Mem. Assn. Bar City N.Y., N.Y. State, Am., Fed. bar assns. Clubs: Sky, Princeton (N.Y.C.); Mashomack Fish and Game Preserve (Pine Plains, N.Y.). Home: 140 E 72d St New York NY 10021 also Greenport NY 12534 Office: 10 E 40th St New York NY 10016

BUCHMEYER, JERRY, U.S. district court judge; b. Overton, Tex., Sept. 5, 1933. Student, Kilgore Jr. Coll., 1953; B.A., U. Tex., 1955, LL.B., 1957. Bar: Tex. 1957. Asso. firm Thompson, Knight, Simmons & Bullion, Dallas, 1958-63; partner, 1963-66, sr. partner, from, 1968; now judge U.S. Dist. Ct., No. Dist. Tex., Dallas. Mem. Am. Bar Assn., Dallas Bar Assn. (pres. 1979), State Bar Tex. (chmn. com. 1978-79, dir. 1982-84). Office: Room 15E6 US Courthouse 1100 Commerce St Dallas TX 75242

BUCHSBAUM, RALPH, zoology educator; b. Chickasha, Okla., Jan. 2, 1907; s. Maurice and Mabel (Roberts) B.; m. Mildred Shaffer, June 14, 1933; children: Monte, Vicki (Mrs. John Pearse). B.S., U. Chgo., 1928, Ph.D., 1932. Mem. faculty U. Chgo., 1932-50; prof. zoology U. Pitts., 1950-72; Dir. Inst. for Edn. Research, Palo Alto, Calif., 1962-63; cons. UNESCO; editor Boxwood Press, Pacific Grove, 1956—; assoc. curator of invertebrates Carnegie Mus., Pitts., 1950-72. Author: Animals Without Backbones, (with Lorus Milne) The Lower Animals, (with Mrs. Buchsbaum) Basic Ecology. Served to capt. USAAF, 1942-46. Fulbright prof., Thailand, 1959-60. Mem. Ecol Soc. Am., Am. Soc. Zoology, Biol. Photographers Assn. Unitarian. Home and office: 183 Ocean View Blvd Pacific Grove CA 93950

BUCHSBAUM, SOLOMON JAN, physicist; b. Stryj, Poland, Dec. 4, 1929; came to U.S., 1953, naturalized, 1957; s. Jacob and Berta (Rutherfoer) B.; m. Phyllis N. Isenman, July 3, 1955; children: Rachel Joy, David Joel, Adam Louis. B.S., McGill U., 1952, M.S., 1953; Ph.D., Mass. Inst. Tech., 1957. Mem. tech. staff Bell Labs., Murray Hill, N.J., 1958-61, dept. head, 1961-65, dir., 1965-68; v.p. Sandia Labs., Albuquerque, 1968-71; exec. dir. Bell Labs., 1971-76, v.p., 1976-79, exec. v.p., 1979—; sr. cons. Def. Sci. Bd., chmn., 1972-77; mem. AEC Controlled Thermonuclear Fusion Com., 1965-72, Pres.'s Sci. Adv. Com., 1970-73, Pres.'s Com. on Sci. and Tech., 1975-76; mem. fusion power coordinating com. ERDA, 1972-76; mem. advisory group sci. and tech. NSF, 1976-77; chmn. Energy Research Adv. Bd., 1978—; mem. Naval Research Adv. Com., 1978—; mem. vis. com. M.I.T., 1977—, mem. corp. devel. com., 1980—; cons. (Office Sci. and Tech.), 1976—. Asso. editor: Revs. Modern Physics, 1968-72, Jour. Applied Physics, 1968-70, Physics of Fluids, 1963-64; Co-author: Waves in Plasmas, 1963; contbr. numerous articles to profl. jours. Trustee Argonne Univs. Assn., 1979—. Moyse traveling fellow, 1953-54; IBM fellow, 1954-56; recipient Anne Molson Gold medal and Sec. Def. medal Outstanding Pub. Service, 1977. Fellow Am. Phys. Soc. (chmn. div. plasma physics 1968, mem. council 1973-76), IEEE, Am. Acad. Arts and Scis., AAAS; mem. Nat. Acad. Engring. (exec. com. 1975-76), Nat. Acad. Scis., Cosmos Club. Research in gaseous and solid state plasmas, communications. Patentee in field. Office: Bell Labs Holmdel NJ 07733

BUCHWACH, BUCK AARON, newspaper editor; b. Portland, Oreg., Feb. 21, 1921; s. Morris B. and Lenya (Berez) B.; m. Elinor Stewart Akers, July 4, 1947; children: Brett, Barbara, Bonita, Brian, Bruce; m. Margaret Anne Kehoe, July 13, 1962; children: Brendan, Barron. B.S., U. Oreg., 1942. Reporter Honolulu Advertiser, 1946-50, city editor, 1955-58, mng. editor, 1959-70, exec. editor, 1971—; v.p., dir. Hawaii Newspaper Agy., 1963—; pres. BeeBee Assos., 1950—. Vice pres. HNA Charitable Found.; mem. Hula Bowl Com. Served with AUS, 1942-46. Recipient Communications Father of Yr. award Honolulu C. of C., 1958; award of tribute for distinguished work in cause of statehood Ter. of Hawaii, 1959; Distinguished award Hawaii chpt. World Brotherhood, 1960; nat. award for distinguished reporting Am. Polit. Sci. Assn., 1964; award for humanitarian service Hawaii Variety Club, 1974. Mem. Am. Soc. Newspaper Editors, U. Oreg. Alumni Assn. (pres. Hawaii 1947-57), Honolulu Press Club (dir. 1947, 48, pres. 1949-50, 72-74), Soc. Profl. Journalists (pres. Hawaii chpt. 1983-84), Phi Beta Kappa. Clubs: Variety, Honolulu Press, Pacific. Home: 5627 Halekamani Honolulu HI 96821 Office: Honolulu Advertiser PO Box 3110 Honolulu HI 96802

BUCHWALD, ART, columnist, author; b. Mt. Vernon, N.Y., Oct. 20, 1925; s. Joseph and Helen (Kleinberger) B.; m. Ann McGarry, Oct. 11, 1952; 3 children. Student, U. So. Calif., 1945-48. Syndicated columnist, 550 newspapers throughout world; columnist Los Angeles Times Syndicate. Author: Paris After Dark, 1950, Art Buchwald's Paris, 1954, The Brave Coward, 1957, A Gift From the Boys, 1959, More Caviar, 1958, Un Cadeau Pour Le Patron (Prix de la Bonne Humeur 1958), Don't Forget to Write, 1960, Art Buchwald's Secret List to Paris, 1963, How Much Is That in Dollars?, 1961, Is It Safe to Drink the Water?, 1962, I Chose Capitol Punishment, 1963, And Then I Told the President, 1965, Son of the Great Society, 1966, Have I Ever Lied To You, 1968, The Establishment Is Alive and Well in Washington, 1969, Counting Sheep, 1970, Getting High in Government Circles, 1971, I Never Danced at the White House, 1973, The Bollo Caper, 1974, I Am Not a Crook, 1974, Irving's Delight, 1975, Washington is Leaking, 1976, Down the Seine and Up the Potomac, 1977, The Buchwald Stops Here, 1978, Laid Back in Washington, 1981, While Reagan Slept, 1983. Served as sgt. USMCR, 1942-45. Recipient Pulitzer prize for outstanding commentary, 1982. Club: Anglo-American Press (Paris). Office: 1750 Pennsylvania Ave NW Washington DC 20006

BUCHWALD, ELIAS, public relations executive; b. N.Y.C., Feb. 24, 1924; s. Louis and Sara (Gottfried) B.; Oct. 25, 1952; children: Monita, Lee Ezer, Gena Golda. B. Chem Engring., Sch. Tech. CCNY, 1944. Process engr. Union Carbide, Oak Ridge, 1946-48; acct. exec. Sheldon, Morse, Hutchins & Easton, N.Y.C., 1948-50; sr. assoc. Harold Burson, Pub. Relations, N.Y.C., 1950-52; v.p. Burson-Marsteller, N.Y.C., 1952—75, vice chmn., 1975—; pres. Marsteller Found., N.Y.C., 1980—. Contbr. articles to profl. jours. Served with U.S. Army, 1944-46. Recipient Presdl. Citation Pub. Relations Soc. Am., 1980-82. Mem. Pub. Relations Soc. Am., Am. Inst. Chem. Engrs. Republican. Jewish. Home: 35 Lawrence Ave Lawrence NY 11559 Office: Burson Marsteller 866 3d Ave New York NY 10022

BUCK, ALFRED ANDREAS, physician, epidemiologist; b. Hamburg, Germany, Mar. 9, 1921; came to U.S., 1958, naturalized, 1967; s. Heino C. and Antonie (Schwarz) B.; m. Kay A. Amann, Sept. 21, 1962; children—Suzanne Karen, Alfred Andreas. M.D. in Pharmacology, U. Hamburg, 1945; M.P.H., Johns Hopkins U., 1959, Dr.P.H., 1961. Med. resident Univ. Hosp., Hamburg, 1945-52; physician, cons. Gen. Govt. Hosp., Makassar, Celebes, Indonesia, 1952- 55; head physician Red Cross Hosp., Pusan, Korea, 1955-58; mem. faculty Johns Hopkins U., 1963—, prof. epidemiology and internat. health, 1967—, dir. div. bacteriology and mycology, 1967—, prof. epidemiology and internat. health, chmn. tropical medicine council, 1973-74, also research dir., geog. epidemiology group; cons. AID, Ethiopia, 1962-64, West and Central Africa, 1971; mem. sr. staff WHO, Geneva, 1971-73, chief med. officer div. malaria and other parasitic diseases, 1974-78; chief research coordination, epidemiology and tng. and sec. sci. working group for epidemiology, spl. program research and tng. in tropical diseases; tropical medicine adv. Office of Health, Dept. State, AID, Washington, 1978—; vis. lectr. Harvard U., Boston; vis. prof. U. Hamburg, W. Ger.; adj. prof. Tulane U., New Orleans; sr. asso. Johns Hopkins U., Balt. Author books; contbr. articles in field; asso. editor: Tropenmedizin und Parasitologie. Recipient Meritorious Honor award Dept. State, 1980; Bernhard Nocht medal in tropical medicine, 1981. Fellow Am. Coll. Epidemiology, Am. Public Health Assn.; mem. Epidemiol. Research Assn., AMA, Am. Soc. Tropical Medicine, Internat. Epidemiologic Soc., Am. Epidemiol. Soc., Tropical Medicine Assn. D.C. Lutheran. Home: 1603 East Ave McLean VA 22101

BUCK, CHARLES ABNER, JR., advertising executive; b. Bethlehem, Pa., Sept. 30, 1942; s. Charles Abner and Marie (Taglang) B. B.A., Lehigh U., 1964. Mktg. assoc. Time, Inc., N.Y.C., 1966-67; v.p. personnel Doyle Dane Bernbach, Inc., N.Y.C., 1967-77; v.p. mng. dir. Canter Achenbaum Heekin Exec. Search, N.Y.C., 1978-80; sr. v.p., dir.

adminstrv. services Batten, Barton, Durstine and Osborn, N.Y.C., 1980—. Club: University. Home: 360 E 65th St New York NY 10021 Office: BBDO 383 Madison Ave New York NY 10021

BUCK, ERVIN OSCAR, financial adviser, investor; b. Stamps, Ark., Apr. 20, 1904; s. Thomas Ervin and Willy Maud (Hawley) B.; m. Nina Marie Bohn, Oct. 8, 1941. B.S. in Indsl. Edn, Tex. A. and M. Coll., 1926. Geologist Gulf Oil Corp., 1926-31; dist. engr. Tex. R.R. Commn., 1931-33; chmn. Conroe Operators Assn., 1933-35; cons. geologist and petroleum engr., 1935-41; dir. prodn., dist. 3 Petroleum Adminstrn. War, 1941-43; mgr. Rowan Drilling Co., Ft. Worth, 1943-47; with Tex. Nat. Bank Commerce, Houston, 1948—, sr. v.p., exec. asst. to chmn. bd., 1961-66, adv. dir., 1965-66, vice chmn. bd., dir., 1966-69, adv. dir., tech. adviser petroleum, 1969—; personal, corporate and indsl. investments; mgr. Estate John F. Merrick; dir., mem. exec. com. Coastal States Gas Corp.; dir. First Nat. Bank, Stafford, Tex. Mem. adv. bd. Houston Salvation Army; bd. dirs. St. Joseph Hosp. Found., Houston. Mem. Houston C. of C., Houston Geol. Soc., Am. Assn. Petroleum Geologists. Clubs: Houston, Petroleum (Houston); Sugar Creek Country (Sugar Land, Tex.). Home: 1607 Sugar Creek Blvd Sugar Land TX 77478 Office: Suite 102 14301 Southwest Freeway Sugarland TX 77478

BUCK, GENEVIEVE CAROL, fashion journalist; b. Joliet, Ill., Dec. 18, 1932; d. Leo and Hattie (Boraczewski) Wisniewski; m. Robert Mitchell Buck, Oct. 6, 1962; children—Gregory, Michelle. B.A., Coll. St. Francis, Joliet. Mem. editorial dept. Extension Mag., 1954-56; mem. publs. and pub. relations dept. Am. Inst. Laundering, Joliet, 1956-60; mem. Chgo. Bur., Women's Wear Daily, 1960-64; fashion writer Chgo. Daily News, 1967-71, Chgo. Tribune, 1971-77, fashion editor, 1977—. Recipient Lulu award Men's Fashion Assn. Mem. Fashion Group. Roman Catholic. Office: 435 N Michigan Ave Chicago IL 60611 *

BUCK, JACK, sportscaster; b. Holyoke, Mass.; m. Carol Buck. Grad., Ohio State U. Previously sportscaster baseball games, Columbus, Ohio, Rochester, N.Y.; sportscaster, commentator Sta. KMOX (CBS Radio), St. Louis, 1954—, now sports dir.; announcer St. Louis Baseball Cardinals, 1954—; sportscaster CBS Sports NFL Football, 1970-74, TV, 1978—; sportscaster NBC Sports, 1975-78, CBS Radio Network Monday Night Football broadcasts, 1978—; commentator World Series Game, 1968, 82, Super Bowl Games, 1970, 78—. Campaign chmn. Cystic Fibrosis Found., St. Louis. Served in; World War II. Decorated Purple Heart; recipient Cert. of Excellence Abe Lincoln awards. Office: KMOX Radio Gateway Tower 1 Memorial Dr Saint Louis MO 63102 *

BUCK, JOHN BONNER, biologist; b. Hartford, Conn., Sept. 26, 1912; s. George Sumner and Carrie Elizabeth (Bonner) B.; m. Elisabeth Tennent Mast, Dec. 22, 1939; children—Peter, Susan, Judith, Alan. A.B., Johns Hopkins, 1933, Ph.D., 1936. Asst. zoology Johns Hopkins, 1933-36; NRC fellow Calif. Inst. Tech., 1936-37; research asso. Carnegie Instn., 1937-39; asst. prof. zoology U. Rochester, 1939-45; physiologist NIH, 1945—, chief lab. phys. biology, 1962-74; mem. Johns Hopkins expdns. to Jamaica, 1936, 41, 62; vis. prof. U. Wash., 1951, Calif. Inst. Tech., 1953, Cambridge (Eng.) U., 1963-64, U. Calif., Santa Barbara, 1978; instr. Marine Biol. Lab., Woods Hole, Mass., 1942-44, 57-59, trustee, 1959—; spl. research chromosome structure, insect respiration, firefly physiology. Leader Alpha Helix Expdn. to New Guinea, 1969; Mem. NRC, 1957-59, 71-74. Mem. editorial bd.: Biol. Bull, 1957-60, 65-68, 75-78, Jour. Morphology, 1964-68; contbr. articles in field. Mem. Soc. Gen. Physiologists (sec. 1953-55, pres. 1960), Am. Soc. Zoologists (v.p. 1956). Home: 4505 Saul Rd Kensington MD 20895 Office: Nat Insts Health Bethesda MD 20205

BUCK, LEE ALBERT, retired insurance company executive, evangelist; b. Jonesboro, Ark., July 28, 1923; s. Lee A. and Annie (Ballew) B.; m. Audrey Ruth McMurphy, Feb. 26, 1945; children—Melody Anne, Merrilee Ruth, Bonnie Sue, Lisa Carol. B.A. with honors, U. Mich., 1947, M.A. in Colonial Am. History, 1948; C.L.U., 1960. With N.Y. Life Ins. Co., 1949—, dir. agys., 1962-63, 2d v.p., 1963-64, v.p. agys., 1964-66, regional v.p. charge Southeastern U.S., 1964-67, v.p. mktg., N.Y.C., 1967-74, sr. v.p. group mktg., 1974-78, sr. v.p. mktg., 1978-83; lay evangelist St. Paul's Episcopal Ch., Darien, Conn., 1983—. Past bd. dirs. Greater N.Y. councils Boy Scouts Am.; formerly bd. dirs. Ams. for Indian Opportunity; bd. dirs. Walter Hoving Home; regent C.B.N. U.; former chmn. bd. Life Underwriter Tng. Council; past trustee Barrington (R.I.) Coll.; bd. dirs. Faith Alive; lay evangelist Episcopal Ch. U.S.A.; nat. v.p., chmn. evangelism commn. Brotherhood of St. Andrew. Served to lt. USNR, 1942-46, 50-52. Mem. Nat. Assn. Life Underwriters, Am. Soc. C.L.U.'s, Life Ins. Mktg. and Research Assn. (dir.), Agy. Mgmt. Tng. Council. Episcopalian. Home: 126 Huckleberry Hill Rd New Canaan CT 06840

BUCK, R. CREIGHTON, educator, mathematician; b. Cin., Aug. 30, 1920; s. Robert Jirah and Martha (Creighton) B.; m. Ellen Fedder, Dec. 28, 1944; children: Nancy Elizabeth, Donald Paul. B.A., U. Cin., 1941, M.A., 1942; Ph.D., Harvard, 1947. Mem. Harvard Soc. Fellows, 1942-43, 45-47; asst. prof. Brown U., 1947-50; asso. prof. U. Wis., 1950-54, prof., 1954—, chmn. dept., 1964-66, acting dir. Math. Research Ctr., 1973-75, Hilldale prof., 1980—; Mem. project FOCUS, Inst. Def. Analyses, 1959-60; chmn. Com. Undergrad. Program, 1959-63; mem. panel on grad. record exam. Ednl. Testing Service, 1962-71; mem. U.S. Commn. Math. Instrn., 1963-67; exec. com. div. math. NRC, 1963-65; math. panel Nat. Security Agy. Sci. Adv. Bd., 1962-71; mem. evaluation panel Nat. Bur. Standards, 1974—; mem. nat. adv. council Ednl. Professions Devel., 1970-71, 73-76; vis. prof. Stanford U., 1958-59. Author: Advanced Calculus, 3d edit, 1978, (with R.P. Boas) Polynomial Expansions, 1958, (with A.B. Willcox) Calculus of Several Variables, 1972, (with E.F. Buck) Introductory Differential Equations, 1976; also articles.; Editor: Studies in Modern Analysis, 1962, Modern Analysis Series, 1962-70. Guggenheim fellow, 1958-59. Fellow AAAS (L.R. Ford award 1981); Mem. Am. Math. Soc. (council 1959-63, 64-70, exec. com. 1960-64, editor proc. 1964-67, v.p. 1972-74), Math. Assn. Am. (editor monographs 1957-60, bd. govs. 1960-63, vis. lectr. 1962-63, v.p. 1975-77), Soc. for Indsl. and Applied Math. (trustee 1973-75), Lutheran Acad. Scholarship, Phi Beta Kappa, Sigma Xi. Republican. Home: 3601 Sunset Dr Madison WI 53705

BUCK, ROBERT FOLLETTE, banker, lawyer; b. Superior, Nebr., June 7, 1917; s. Samuel Rea and Faye (Follette) B.; m. Barbara J. Carlson, Apr. 29, 1963; children by previous marriage: Carolyn (Mrs. Robert G. Norman), Vincent Templin. B.A., U. Wash., 1938, LL.B., 1942. Bar: Wash. 1946, D.C. bar 1960. Pres. Orcas Power & Light Co., Eastsound, Wash., 1947-54; regional dir. Small Bus. Adminstrn., Seattle, 1954-59, dep. adminstr., Washington, D.C., 1959-61; v.p. Rainier Nat. Bank, Seattle, 1961-66, sr. v.p., 1966-74, exec. v.p., 1974-82; of counsel Roberts & Shefelman, Seattle; pros. atty. San Juan County, Wash., 1947-54; Pres. Pacific Northwest Trade Assn., 1969-70. Trustee Assn. Wash. Business, 1968—, chmn., 1978-79; v.p. Seattle Municipal League, 1966-67, trustee, 1964-72; trustee Econ. Devel. Council Puget Sound, 1970—, pres., 1975-77, chmn., 1977-79; trustee Wash. State Internat. Trade Fair, 1963—, pres., 1967-69. Served with USNR, 1942-46; PTO. Decorated Bronze Star medal. Mem. Seattle C. of C. (trustee 1965-66, v.p. 1968-69), Am. Bankers Assn. (dir. 1976-78), Wash. Bankers Assn. (dir. 1975-82, pres. 1978-79), Nat. Mcpl. League (regional v.p. 1977—), Phi Gamma Delta, Phi Delta Phi. Clubs: Mason (32), Wash. Athletic, Rainer, Seattle Yacht. (Seattle). Home: 1120 8th Ave Seattle WA 98101 Office: 4100 Seafirst Fifth Ave Plaza 800 Fifth Ave Seattle WA 98104

BUCK, ROBERT TREAT, JR., museum director, educator; b. Fall River, Mass., Feb. 16, 1939; s. Robert Treat and Hazel (Sayward) B.; m. Nicole Challamel, July 2, 1966; children: Thomas, Philip. B.A., Williams Coll., 1961; student, Mus. Tng. Program Met. Mus. Art, 1963-64; M.A., N.Y. U., 1965. Lectr., researcher Toledo Mus. Art, 1964-65; asst. curator, instr. art and archaeology Washington U., St. Louis, 1965-67, dir. art gallery, 1968-70; asst. dir. Albright-Knox Art Gallery, Buffalo, 1970-73, dir., 1973-83, Bklyn. Mus., 1983—; adj. prof. dept. art State U. N.Y. at Buffalo, 1972-80; Mem. N.Y. Council for Humanities, 1976—; mem. art adv. panel IRS, 1978—. Author: Sam Francis: Paintings, 1942-1972, 1972, Diebenkorn: The Ocean Park Paintings, 1976, Sonia Delaunay: A Retrospective, 1980. Mem. Assn. Art Mus. Dirs. (sec.). Office: the brooklyn museum 188 eastern pkwy Brooklyn NY 11238 *

BUCK, THOMAS RANDOLPH, lawyer; b. Washington, Feb. 5, 1930; s. James Charles Francis and Mary Elizabeth (Marshall) B.; m. Alice Armistead James, June 20, 1953; children: Kathryn James, Thomas Randolph, Douglas Marshall, David Andrew; m. Sunny Clark, Sept. 15, 1971; 1 dau., Carey Virginia.; m. Yvonne Brackett, Nov. 27, 1981. B.A. summa cum laude, Am. U., 1951; LL.B., U. Va., 1954. Bar: Va. 1954, Ky. 1964, Fla. 1974. Asst. gen. atty. Seaboard Air Line R.R. Co., 1958-63; sec., gen. counsel Am. Comml. Lines. Inc., Houston, 1963-68; asst. gen. counsel Tex. Gas Transmission Corp., 1968-72; sec., gen. counsel Leadership Housing Inc., 1972—; pres. law firm T. Randolph Buck (P.A.), 1975—; dir. Hanover Bank of Fla., Plantation, Computer Resources Inc., Ft. Lauderdale, Fla., So. Aviation Inc., Opa Locka, Fla. Bd. dirs. Sheridan House for Boys. Served to capt. USMCR, 1954-58. Mem. Assn. ICC Practitioners (nat. v.p., mem. exec. com.), Am., Va., Ky., Fla. bar assns., Maritime Law Assn. U.S., Am. Judicature Soc., Omicron Delta Kappa, Alpha Sigma Phi, Delta Theta Phi. Clubs: Kiwanian., Propeller of U.S. Home: 7061 NW 8th Ct Plantation FL 33317 Office: 8211 W Broward Blvd Fort Lauderdale FL 33324

BUCK, WILLIAM MAJOR, JR., coal co. exec.; b. Phila., June 4, 1931; s. William Major and Mabel Irene (Mattis) B.; m. Jacquelin Rae Machin, June 26, 1959; children—Allyson Paige, Jennifer Leigh. B.A. in Liberal Arts, Wesleyan U., Middletown, Conn., 1953; M.B.A., U. Chgo., 1960. Mgmt. trainee, supr. tng., asst. to labor relations mgr. The Budd Co., Phila. and Gary, Ind., 1953-62; labor relations mgr. Miles Labs., Elkhart, Ind., 1962-64; employee relations mgr. Internat. Minerals & Chem. Co., Bartow, Fla., 1964-66; v.p. employee relations Consumer Products Group, The Singer Co., N.Y.C., 1966-75; v.p. employee relations, officer Berwind Corp., Phila., 1975-78; sr. v.p. human resources Peabody Coal Co., St. Louis, 1978—. Sect. chmn. fund drive United Way Greater St. Louis, 1981; bd. dirs. Jr. Achievement Greater Miss. Valley, 1981. Served with ordnance AUS, 1953-55. Presbyterian. Club: Mo. Athletic. Home: 13648 Van Courtland Dr Des Peres MO 63131 Office: 301 N Memorial Dr Saint Louis MO 63102

BUCKALEW, JAMES KENNETH, radio producer, educator; b. Peru, Ind., Oct. 24, 1933; s. Clarence Homer and Marguerite Lois (Anderson) B.; m. Sally J. Long, Aug. 20, 1977; children—Michael, Thomas, Robert, Brett, Kevin. A.B., Ind. State U., 1958, M.A., 1961; student, U. Hawaii, 1955, 58-60; Ph.D., U. Iowa, 1967. Instr., head radio-TV news U. Iowa, 1963-67; prof. journalism San Diego State U., 1967—; reporter, newscaster Sta. WBOW, Terre Haute, Ind., 1957-58; news editor, anchorman Sta. WTHI-TV, Terre Haute, 1960-63; news dir. Sta. WSUI, Iowa City, Iowa, 1963-67; producer documentaries, reporter Sta. KCBQ, San Diego, 1968—; cons. in field. Contbr. articles to profl. jours. Served with AUS, 1954-56. Nat. Assn. Broadcasters grantee, 1966, 70. Mem. AFTRA (dir. San Diego chpt. 1970-75), Assn. Edn. in Journalism, Internat. Soc. Gen. Semantics, Radio TV News Dirs. Assn. (adv. bd. 1967-68), Nat. Broadcast Editorial Conf., Assn. Profl. Broadcasting Edn., Sigma Delta Chi, Tau Kappa Alpha. Home: 2049 Wind River Rd El Cajon CA 92020 Office: Journalism Dept San Diego State U San Diego CA 92182

BUCKER, WILLIAM EARL, English and American literature educator; b. Loretto, Ky., Oct. 10, 1924; s. William Oscar and Mary (Hiestand) Buckler. A.B., U. Ky., 1944, M.A., 1946; Ph.D., U. Ill., 1949. Asst. prof. English and Am. lit. NYU, N.Y.C., 1953-57, assoc. prof., 1957-59, prof., 1959—, assoc. dean Washington Sq. Coll., 1958-60, dean Washington Sq. Coll., 1960-69, vice chancellor univ., 1969-70. Author: numerous books including Matthew Arnold's Books: Towards a Publishing Dairy, 1958, Prose of the Victorian Period, 1958, The Literature of England, 1966, The Major Victorian Poets, 1973, The Victorian Imagination, 1980, On the Poetry of Matthew Arnold, 1982, The Poetry of Thomas Hardy, 1983, Matthew Arnold Prose, 1983; numerous articles. Am. Philos. Soc. fellow, 1957; Fulbright fellow, 1949-50; Ford Found. fellow, 1951-52. Mem. MLA. Home: 2 Horatio St New York NY 10014 Office: NYU 19 University Pl New York NY 10003

BUCKINGHAM, CHARLES EDWARD, aerospace executive, former air force officer; b. Chgo., Jan. 22, 1924; s. William J. and Mary E. (Sedgwick) B.; m. Gloria J. Doyle, June 6, 1946; children: Peggy E. (Mrs. Robert Barrowclough), James T., Charles Lance, David T., Jon B. Student, Bradley U., Peoria, Ill., 1941-43; B.S., U.S. Mil. Acad., 1946; M.B.A., George Washington U., 1961; grad., Indsl. Coll. Armed Forces, 1967. Commd. 2d lt. USAAF, 1946; advanced through grades to lt. gen. USAF, 1975; chief Program Control Office. Minuteman System Program Office, Los Angeles, later, Norton AFB, Calif., 1961-66, chief aircraft br., materiel programs group to dir. prodn. and programming Office Dep. Chief of Staff, systems and logistics, Hdqrs. USAF, 1967-69, chief aircraft and missile programs div. for asst. Research, Devel. and Acquisition Programming, 1969-70, asst. for requirements, devel. and acquisition programming Office Dep. Chief Staff Research and Devel., Hdqrs. USAF, 1970-72, dep. chief of staff for procurement and prodn. Air Force Logistics Command, Wright-Patterson AFB, Ohio, 1972-74, dep. chief staff for acquisition logistics, Air Force Logistics Command, 1974-75, chief staff, Air Force Logistics Command, 1975; comptroller Hdqrs. USAF Air Force, Washington, 1975-78; now asst. to v.p. and gen. mgr. E. Systems Melpar Div., Falls Church, Va. Decorated D.S.M., Legion of Merit, Air Force Commendation medal with oak leaf cluster, Army Commendation medal; recipient Thomas P. Gerrity award Air Force Assn. Mem. Am. Nat. Metric Council (pres. 1978-81). Home: 10204 Brennanhill Ct Great Falls VA 22066 Office: 7700 Arlington Blvd Falls Church VA 22046

BUCKINGHAM, LINDSEY, musician; b. Oct. 3, 1947; m. Stevie Nicks. Mem. musical group Fleetwood Mac, 1975—. Albums include Fleetwood Mac, 1975, Rumours, 1977, Tusk, 1979, Fleetwood Mac—Live, 1980; solo albums include Law and Order, 1982. Office: care Elektra Asylum Records 665 Fifth Ave New York NY 10022 *

BUCKINGHAM, LISLE MARION, lawyer; b. Monroeville, Ohio, July 20, 1895; s. Jesse and Bretna (Latham) B.; m. Mildred Heter, Oct. 9, 1920 (dec. Sept. 1951); m. Ruth Heter, Feb. 25, 1959. A.B., Western Res. U., 1917, LL.B., 1919. Bar: Ohio bar 1919. And since practiced trial law and served as corp. counsel, Akron; sr. partner firm Buckingham, Doolittle & Burroughs, 1942—; asst. county prosecutor, 1922; gen. counsel Ohio Motor Trucking Assn. Assn. of Motor Carries of Ohio, 1951; dir. 1st Nat. Bank, Roadway Express (many other corps.); Trial counsel for entire rubber industry in hearings at Washington and before War Labor Bd., 1943- 45; chief counsel in Big 4 Negotiations for Firestone, B. F. Goodrich, Goodyear and U.S. Rubber Cos., 1946-47. Trustee Community Chest; chmn. drive, 1933, Y.M.C.A., Peoples Hosp., Summit County Tb Assn.; pres. Akron Community Trusts; trustee U. Akron, pres. devel. found.; gov. Western Res. U., 1947-69; mem. Ohio State Bar Examiners, 1938-43, chmn., 1943. Mem. ABA, Ohio Bar Assn., Akron Bar Assn. (pres. 1931), Akron C. of C. (pres. 1935), Phi Beta Kappa, Delta Upsilon, Order of Coif, Phi Delta Phi, Delta Sigma Rho. Presbyn. (trustee). Clubs: Mason., Rotary (trustee). Home: 474 N Portage Path Akron OH 44303 Office: Cascade Bldg Akron OH 44308

BUCKLAND, CHARLES FRANCIS, forest products company executive; b. N.Y.C., Nov. 3, 1920; s. Charles Richard and Frances (Walsh) B.; m. Doris A. Christensen, June 10, 1950; children: Gary, Deborah. B.S. in Civil Engring., U. Colo., 1948. Vice-pres. sales Jim Walter Corp., Tampa, Fla., 1964-66; v.p. mktg. Abitibi-Price Corp., Troy, Mich., 1966-72, pres., 1972—; group v.p. Abitibi-Price Inc., Troy, 1982—. Maj. USAAF, 1942-46; PTO. Club: Birmingham Country (Mich.) (dir. 1982—). Office: Abitibi-Price Corp 3250 Big Beaver Rd Troy MI 48084

BUCKLAND, MICHAEL KEEBLE, librarian, educator; b. Wantage, Eng., Nov. 23, 1941; came to U.S., 1972; s. Walter Basil and Norah Elaine (Rudd) B.; m. Waltraud Leeb, July 11, 1964; children: Anne Margaret, Anthony Francis. B.A., Oxford U., 1963; postgrad. diploma in librarianship, Sheffield U., 1965, Ph.D., 1972. Grad. trainee Bodleian Library, Oxford, Eng., 1963-64; asst. librarian U. Lancaster (Eng.) Library, 1965-72; asst. dir. for tech. services Purdue U. Libraries, West Lafayette, Ind., 1972-75; dean Sch. Library and Info. Studies, U. Calif., Berkeley, 1976—; v.p. Ind. Coop. Library Services Authority, 1974-75; vis. scholar Western Mich. U., 1979; vis. prof. U. Klagenfurt, Austria, 1980. Author: Book Availability and the Library User, 1975, (with others) The Uses of Gaming in Education for Library Management, 1976; co-author: Reader in Operations Research for Libraries, 1976, Library Services in Theory and Context, 1983. Mem. Library Assn. (London), ALA, Am. Soc. for Info. Sci., Assn. Records Mgrs. and Adminstrs., Assn. Am. Library Schs., Calif. Library Assn. Office: Sch Library and Info Studies U Calif Berkeley CA 94720

BUCKLER, BEATRICE, editor; b. N.Y.C., Nov. 4, 1933; d. S. and Ida (Frost) B.; m. Edgar I. Gotthold, Nov. 20, 1955; 1 dau., Jessica Frost. Research dir. Hill & Knowlton, N.Y.C., 1957-61; asso. service editor Good Housekeeping mag., 1961-63; asso. editor articles Parents' mag., 1966-69; writer-editor Woman's Day, 1963-66; with Family Circle mag., 1969-77, exec. editor, 1970-77; v.p. (1st woman) Family Circle, Inc., N.Y. Times Co., 1973-77; founder, editor-in-chief, pub. Working Woman, 1977; editorial cons., 1977-79; cons. editor Prime Time mag., 1980; co-founder, editor Hers mag., 1981—. Recipient N.Y. Women in Communications award, 1977. Home: 137 E 36th St New York NY 10016 *I had the good fortune to have the support and constant encouragement of my husband.*

BUCKLER, SHELDON A., photog. co. exec.; b. N.Y.C., May 18, 1931; s. Morris H. and Mollie M. (Smith) B.; m. Dorothea J. Chandler, June 30, 1978; children—Julie, Eve, Sarah. B.A., N.Y. U., 1951; Ph.D., Columbia U., 1954. Research asso. U. Md., 1954-56; research group leader Am. Cyanamid Co., Stamford, Conn., 1956-62; mgr. organic unit AMF, Springdale, Conn., 1962-64; with Polaroid Corp., Cambridge, Mass., 1964—, exec. v.p., 1980—. Contbr. articles to profl. jours. Trustee Va. Union U., 1973-75. Served with U.S. Army, 1954-56. Mem. Am. Chem. Soc., Phi Beta Kappa. Patentee. Office: Polaroid Corp 730 Main St Cambridge MA 02139

BUCKLES, ROBERT EDWIN, chemistry educator; b. Fallon, Nev., Aug. 11, 1917; s. Maynard Robert and Llewellah Stemler (Price) B.; m. Rachel Elsie Hurley, Apr. 8, 1944 (dec. Mar. 1977); children: William Robert, Richard John; m. Arlyne Fuller, July 27, 1979. A.A., Lassen Jr. Coll., 1936; B.S., U. Calif.-Berkeley, 1939, M.S., 1940; postgrad., Ill. Inst. Tech., 1940-41; Ph.D., UCLA, 1942. Postdoctoral fellow U. Minn., 1942-43, instr., 1943-45; instr. chemistry U. Iowa, 1945-48, asst. prof., 1948-53, asso. prof., 1953-59, prof., 1959-84, prof. emeritus, 1984—. Author: Laboratory Manual of Organic Chemistry, 1949. Mem. Am. Chem. Soc., AAAS, AAUP, Iowa Acad. Sci., Sigma Xi, Alpha Chi Sigma, Gamma Alpha, Phi Lambda Upsilon. Unitarian. Home: 3113 Cambridge Rd Cameron Park CA 95682 *I am a professor of chemistry. In dealing successfully with all levels of students in this discipline I have found that it is necessary to be hard-nosed but not hard-hearted. One must be hard-nosed because of the demands of the discipline. One must be soft-hearted because of the demands of dealing with human beings.*

BUCKLES, ROBERT HOWARD, investment company executive; b. Champaign, Ill., June 30, 1932; s. Renick Hull and Ethel Maxine (Beach) B.; m. Linda Carol Porter, Dec. 27, 1958; children: Meredith Ann, Christopher John. B.A., Stanford U., 1953; M.B.A., Harvard U., 1957. Security analyst Lehman Corp., N.Y.C., 1957-65, v.p., 1965-69, exec. v.p., 1969-73, pres., 1973—, also dir.; pres. Gas Properties, Inc.; exec. v.p., dir. Lehman Mgmt. Co.; pres., chief fin. officer Rothschild Asset Mgmt. Inc.; mng. dir. Rothschild, Inc.; dir. One William St. Fund.; Bd. dirs. Assn. Publicly Traded Investment Funds. Contbr. to profl. publs. Served with Security Agy. AUS, 1954-56. Mem. N.Y. Soc. Securities Analysts. Home: 420 E 72d St New York NY 10021 Office: 55 Water St New York NY 10041

BUCKLEW, NEIL S., univ. pres.; b. Morgantown, W.Va., Oct. 23, 1940; s. Douglas Earl and Lanah L. (Martin) B.; m. JoAnn M. Krudwig, June 9, 1962; children—Elizabeth, Jennifer, Jeffrey. A.B., U. Mo.; M.S., U. N.C.; Ph.D. (grad. fellow), U. Wis. Dir. personnel Duke U., 1964-66; dir. employee relations U. Wis., 1966-70; prof., v.p. Central Mich. U., Mt. Pleasant, 1970-76; prof., provost Ohio U., Athens, 1976-80; pres. U. Mont., Missoula, 1981—; vis. research fellow Pa. State U.; Arbitrator State of Wis. Author: Academic Collective Bargaining, 1976. Mem. Am. Assn. Higher Edn., Acad. for Academic Personnel Adminstrn. Office: Main Hall Univ Montana Missoula MT 59801

BUCKLEY, CHARLES EDWARD, III, physician, educator; b. Charleston, W.Va., Sept. 2, 1929; s. Charles Edward and Gladys (Kuh) B.; m. Rebecca Anne Hatcher, July 9, 1955; children—Charles Edward, Elizabeth Ann, Rebecca Kathryn, Sarah Margaret. B.S., Va. Poly. Inst., 1950; M.D., Duke U., 1954. Intern Duke U. Med. Center, Durham, N.C., 1954-55, resident in medicine, 1957-60, instr., 1960-63, asso. in medicine, 1963-65, asst. prof. medicine, 1965-68, asso. prof., 1968-77, prof. medicine, 1977—; mem. adv. council to dir. Nat. Inst. Allergy and Infectious Diseases, 1975-79. Contbr. chpts. to books, articles to med. jours. Served with USNR, 1955-57. USPHS career devel. awardee, 1961-68. Mem. Am. Thoracic Soc. (exec. com. 1979-80), N.C. Thoracic Soc. (pres. 1967-69), Southeastern Allergy Assn. (pres. 1972-73), Am. Acad. Allergy, Am. Assn. Immunologists, So. Soc.

Clin. Investigation, A.C.P., Gerontol. Soc., Sigma Xi, Phi Sigma, Tau Kappa Alpha, Alpha Omega Alpha. Republican. Episcopalian. Office: Box 3804 Duke U Med Center Durham NC 27710

BUCKLEY, EMERSON, conductor, music director; b. N.Y.C., Apr. 14, 1916; s. Wendell and Minnie (Buckley) B.; m. Mary Henderson, May 27, 1948; children: Robert Allen, Richard Edward. B.A., Columbia U., 1936; L.H.D., U. Denver, 1959; Mus. D. (hon.), Nova U., 1980. Mem. faculty U. Denver, 1956, Columbia, 1957-58, Manhattan Sch. Music, 1958-70, Temple U., 1970, N.C. Sch. Arts, 1971. Music dir., Columbia Grand Opera, 1936-38, Palm Beach (Fla.) Symphony and Chorus, 1938-41, N.Y.C. Symphony, 1941-42, San Carlo Opera, 1943-45, WOR-MBS, N.Y.C., 1945-54, Marquis de Cuevas Ballet, 1950, Mendelssohn Glee Club, N.Y.C., 1954-63, P.R. Opera Festival, 1954-58, Symphony of the Air, also Empire State Mus. Festival, 1955, Chgo. Opera, 1956, Tagarazuka Dance Theatre, also Greek Theatre, Los Angeles, 1958, Chautauqua Festival, N.Y., 1960; music and artistic dir., Miami (Fla.) Opera Guild, 1950—, Central City (Colo.) Opera, 1956-69; music dir., condr., Ft. Lauderdale Symphony, 1963—; music dir., Seattle Opera, 1964—; condr., N.Y.C. Opera, 1955-78, Duluth (Minn.), New Orleans and Balt. Operas, 1970—, Phila. Lyric Opera, San Francisco Opera, 1975—, Houston, Milw., Tulsa operas, 1976—, Madrid Opera, 1983, Met. Opera of Caracas, Venezuela, 1977-81; Guest appearances with various orchs., including, Toronto (Ont., Can.) Philharmonic, Mpls. Symphony, Miami Symphony, P.R. Symphony, Mex. Symphony, Maracaibo (Venezuela) Symphony, Seoul (Korea) Philharmonic, Phoenix Symphony, Boston Symphony, Montreal Symphony, Houston Symphony, N.J. Symphony, Dallas Symphony, Los Angeles Philharm., Hollywood Bowl, New World Festival; dir.: world premiers of Am. operas including The Ballad of Baby Doe, 1956, Gallantry, 1958, He Who Gets Slapped, 1959, The Crucible, 1961, Gentlemen Be Seated, 1963, Lady from Colorado, 1964, Minutes 'Till Midnight, 1982; recordings for, Deutsche Grammophon, M-G-M, Columbia, Composers Records Inc., London-Polydor, Heliodor; condr. 1st Luciano Pavarotti film for, M-G-M, Yes, Giorgio. Recipient Fox prize Columbia Coll., 1936, Alice M. Ditson Conductor's award, 1964, Colo. Ambassadors Sash, 1965, Gold Chair award Central City Opera, 1965, Am. Patroit award, Fla., 1971, John Jay award for disting. profl. achievement, 1984; chevalier Order Arts and Letters (France), 1970. Mem. Nat. Assn. Am. Composers and Condrs. Club: Mason (Shriner). Office: 1430 N Federal Hwy Fort Lauderdale FL 33304 also *A combination of ideas and ideals of creativity and interpretation, adapted pragmatically to the maelstrom of life surrounding us.*

BUCKLEY, FRANK WILSON, newspaper executive; b. Prentiss, Miss., Oct. 7, 1914; s. Frank Wylie and Otto (Watts) B.; m. Vonnie Verette Crouch, Dec. 22, 1940; children: Charles Ray, Ronald L., Mary Carole. B.A., La. Coll., 1936; LL.B., Vanderbilt U., 1954; M.A., Fla. State U., 1955; Ph.D., So. Ill. U., 1966. Bar: Miss. 1954. Mng. editor Daily News, Mt. Pleasant, Tex., 1936-37; reporter-photographer Daily Town Talk, Alexandria, La., 1937-40; telegraph editor Morning Free Press, Easton, Pa., 1940-41, Mobile Register, 1941; copy editor Buffalo Evening News, 1941-42; editor, pub. Carroll County Democrat, Huntingdon, Tenn., 1945-46; mgr. security brokerage office, Alexandria, 1947-49; grad. asst. journalism Fla. State U., 1949-50; copy editor, editor fin. sect. Nashville Tennessean, 1950-55; prof., head dept. journalism U. So. Miss., 1955-64, assoc. prof. journalism, 1966-67; lectr. journalism So. Ill. U., 1964-65; chmn. dept. journalism Southwest Tex. State U., San Marcos, 1967-73, assoc. prof., 1967-70, prof., 1970-80; Pres. Buckley Newspapers, Inc. (pubs. The News-Bay Springs), Miss., The Reformer, Raleigh, Miss., The Weekly Leader, Pearl, Miss., The Signal, Taylorville, Miss., Impact, Laurel, Miss., Jackson, Miss., The News, Brandon, Miss. Served from ensign to lt. (s.g.), naval aviator USNR, 1943-46; lt. Res., 1945-54. Mem. Miss. Bar Assn. Democrat. Baptist (deacon). Address: 4 Marseilles Brandon MS 39042

BUCKLEY, JAMES LANE, broadcasting executive, lawyer; b. N.Y.C., Mar. 9, 1923; s. William Frank and Aloise Josephine (Steiner) B.; m. Ann Frances Cooley, May 22, 1953; children: Peter P., James W., Priscilla L., William F., David L., Andrew T. B.A., Yale U., 1943, LL.B., 1949. Bar: Conn. 1950, D.C. 1953. Asso. firm Wiggin & Dana, New Haven, 1949-53; v.p. Catawba Corp., N.Y.C., 1953-70; also dir.; mem. U.S. Senate from N.Y. State, 1971-77; bus. cons., dir. (various corps.), 1977-80; undersec. for security assistance U.S. Dept. State, Washington, 1980-82; pres. Radio Free Europe/Radio Liberty, Munich, W.Ger., 1982—. Author: If Men Were Angels, 1975. Served with USNR, 1943-46. Office: RFE/RL Oettingenstrasse 67 8000 Munich 22 West Germany

BUCKLEY, JEROME HAMILTON, English educator; b. Toronto, Ont., Can., Aug. 30, 1917; came to U.S., 1939, naturalized, 1948; s. James Ora and Madeline Isabelle (Morgan) B.; m. Elizabeth Jane Adams, June 19, 1943; children: Nicholas, Victoria, Eleanor. B.A., U. Toronto, 1939; A.M., Harvard U., 1940, Ph.D., 1942. Successively instr., asst. prof., asso. prof., prof. English U. Wis., 1942-54; Guggenheim fellow, 1946-47; vis. asso. prof. Columbia U., 1952-53, prof., 1954-61; prof. English Harvard U., 1961—, Gurney prof., 1975—; summer vis. prof. various univs. Author: William Ernest Henley, 1945, The Victorian Temper, 1951, Tennyson, the Growth of a Poet, 1960, The Triumph of Time, 1966, Season of Youth, 1974, The Turning Key, 1984; Editor: Poems of Tennyson, 1958, Victorian Poets and Prose Writers, 1976, The Pre-Raphaelites, 1968, The Worlds of Victorian Fiction, 1975; Co-editor: Twelve Hundred Years, 1949, Poetry of the Victorian Period, 1965, Masters of British Literature, 1962. Guggenheim fellow, 1963-64; Recipient Christian Gauss award Phi Beta Kappa, 1952. Mem. Internat. Assn. U. Profs. English, Modern Lang. Assn., Tennyson Soc., Acad. Literary Studies, Am. Acad. Arts and Sci. Episcopalian. Home: 191 Common St Belmont MA 02178 Office: Widener Library 245 Harvard U Cambridge MA 02138

BUCKLEY, JOHN BEECHER, lawyer, pharm. mfg. co. exec.; b. N.Y.C., Aug. 31, 1923; s. John B. and Emily (Enstrom) B.; m. Ruth N. Eck, Aug. 15, 1947; children—John B., Beverly P., Alison M., Denis E. B.A., Rutgers U., 1950, LL.B. cum laude, 1950; LL.M., N.Y. U., 1951. Bar: N.Y. bar 1953, Ind. bar 1959. Instr. law N.Y. U., 1951-53; trial atty. and spl. assignments as spl. asst. to Atty. Gen. U.S. Dept. Justice, 1953-57; with Miles Labs., Inc., Elkhart, Ind., 1957—, now exec. v.p., dir.; lectr. Contbr. to law reviews and jours. Served to capt. AC AUS, 1943-46. Mem. Am., Elkhart City bar assns. Home: 51745 Winding Waters Ln N Elkhart IN 46514 Office: 1127 Myrtle St Elkhart IN 46514

BUCKLEY, JOHN LEE, JR., former food company executive; b. Balt., July 7, 1916; s. John Lee and Marie (Freburger) B.; m. Rita M. Scanlan, Sept. 30, 1939; children—Barbara Lee Buckley Kleinhen, Susan Scanlan Buckley Adeszko, Patricia Marie Buckley Christensen, Karen Rita Buckley Cronin. Student, Balt. Poly. Inst., 1930-34; B.S. in Econs, Wharton Sch. U. Pa., 1938. C.P.A., Md. Acct. Consol. Gas & Electric Co. Balt., 1938-41; acct. Ernst & Ernst, Balt., 1941-45, 46-47; controller McCormick & Co., Inc., Balt., 1947-76, v.p., 1969-80, also dir., mem., chmn., 1951-52; dir. Ampacco, Inc., Balt., 1956-79. Treas., mem. exec. com. Cath. Youth Orgn. Retreat House, Balt., 1961—; mem. council Coll. Notre Dame, Balt., 1974-79; Trustee Bon Secours Hosp., Balt., chmn. finance com., 1972—; chmn. bd. Health Care Corp. of Sisters of Bon Secours Inc., 1980-83, Bon Secours Heartlands, 1982—. Served as lt. (j.g.) USNR, 1945-46. Recipient Outstanding Community Service award, 1974. Mem. Fin. Execs. Inst. (pres. Balt. chpt. 1965-66, nat. dir. 1972-75), Golfers' Charitable Assn. (pres. 1981—), Fin. Execs. Inst. (nat. v.p. 1978-79), Am. Inst. Accts., Md. Assn. C.P.A.'s, Md. Acad. Scis. (exec. com., controller 1968-72), Am. Mgmt. Assn., Pa. Alumni Club Balt., Am. Legion (chmn. post scholarship com. 1953-82), Oriole Advs. (pres. 1974-75), Kappa Sigma. Democrat. Roman Catholic (chmn. ch. fin. com. 1968-73, mem. adv. bd. 1968-73). Clubs: Hunt Valley Golf (exec. dir. 1978-83), Balt. Country. (bd. govs. 1983—). Home: 11248 Falls Rd Lutherville MD 21093

BUCKLEY, JOHN WILLIAM, petroleum company executive; b. N.Y.C., June 22, 1920; s. William F. and Aloise (Steiner) B.; m. Ann B. Harding, Nov. 1949 (div. dec); children: Mary, Aloise, John M. B.A., Yale U., 1942. Engaged in exploratory and producing aspects of oil, various fgn. countries; pres., dir. Pantepec Internat., Inc.; dir. Can. So. Petroleum, Ltd. Served from pvt. to 1st lt. AUS, 1942-46; N. Africa, France. Mem. Nat. Rifle Assn. Roman Catholic. Clubs: Camp Fire of America; Racquet and Tennis, Union League (N.Y.C.). Office: Pantepec Internat Inc 37 Lewis St Suite 500 Hartford CT 06103 *

BUCKLEY, JOHN WILMER, accounting educator, author; b. Lepi, Angola, Africa, Aug. 18, 1934; s. Edward Alexander and Lillian E. (Cross) B.; children: Lynette Gyneth, William J., Harold Edward. Student, Helderberg Coll., 1952-54, Walla Walla Coll., 1960-61; M.B.A., U. Wash., 1962; Ph.D. (Ford dissertation fellow 1963-64), U. Wash., 1964. Fiscal/econ. adminstr., Kenya, East Africa, 1954-60; fin. officer, mgr. ops. Pacific Sci. Center, Seattle, 1961-64; prof. acctg. Grad. Sch. Mgmt., UCLA, 1964—, Arthur Young disting. prof. acctg., 1978—, assoc. dean, 1975-77, acting dean, 1977-78; mem. adv. panel to U.S. GAO, 1975—; dir. Bishop Internat., Inc.; founder Malibu Savs. & Loan Assn., Calif. Author: numerous books including Accounting: An Information Systems Approach, 1973; Management Problem-Solving with APL, 1974; twelve books including SEC Accounting, 1979, Regulation and the Accounting Profession, 1980. Dir. Malibu Twp. Council, 1981-82; mem. Mayor Tom Bradley's task force on Africa, 1978—, Arthur Young Profs. Council. Recipient faculty excellence award Calif. Soc. C.P.A.s, 1974, Outstanding Tchr. award Grad. Sch. Mgmt., UCLA, 1973, Grad. Sch. Mgmt. Alumni award, 1973. Mem. Am. Acctg. Assn., Nat. Assn. Accts. Republican (nat. com.). Home: 6324 Zumirez Dr Malibu CA 90265 Office: Grad School Management UCLA Los Angeles CA 90024

BUCKLEY, JOSEPH PAUL, pharmacologist, educator; b. Bridgeport, Conn., Jan. 12, 1924; m. Shirley Elizabeth Jane Shipman, Aug. 16, 1947. B.S., U. Conn., 1949; M.S., Purdue U., 1951, Ph.D., 1952. Registered pharmacist, Conn., Tex. Asst. prof. pharmacology U. Pitts., 1952-55, asso. prof., 1955-58, prof., head dept. pharmacology, 1958-73, asso. dean, 1969-73, dean; dir. Cardiovascular Research U. Houston, 1973—; staff pharmacologist St. John's Gen. Hosp., Pitts., Western Pa. Hosp.; cons. pharmacologist Carter-Wallace Labs., Cranberry, N.J., E.R. Squibb & Sons, Princeton, N.J., VA Hosp., Houston. Contbr. articles profl. jours.; Cons. editor: Jour. Behavioral Pharmacology; asso. editor: Jour. Clin. and Exptl. Hypertension. Served as 2d lt. USAAF, 1943-45. Decorated Air medal with clusters; Am. Found. Pharm. Edn. fellow, 1950-52; recipient award Angiology Research Found., 1965, Am. Pharm. Assn., 1966. Mem. Acad. Pharm. Scis. (chmn. sect. pharmacology and bio-chemistry 1965-67, v.p. 1969-70), Am. Soc. Pharm. and Exptl. Therapeutics, Tex. Pharmacologists Assn. (pres. 1982—), Am. Pharm. Assn. (Pharmacodynamics award 1966), AAAS (sec. sect pharm. scis. 1961-67, chmn. sect., v.p. 1969, 76), N.Y. Acad. Sci., Interam. Soc. Hypertension (dir.), Council High Blood Pressure Research, Phi Kappa Phi, Sigma Xi, Rho Chi, Phi Sigma, Phi Lambda Upsilon, Kappa Psi. Methodist. Home: 13714 Pebble Brook Houston TX 77079 Office: Coll Pharmacy U Houston Houston TX 77004

BUCKLEY, JOSEPH PAUL, III, polygraph specialist; b. Chgo., July 6, 1949; s. Joseph Paul and Helen (Lavelle) B.; m. Patricia Nemeth, June 17, 1972; children: Megan, Michael, Patrick. B.A., Loyola U., Chgo., 1971; M.S. in Detection of Deception, Reid Coll. Detection of Deception, Chgo., 1973. Lic., Ill. Detection of deception examiner John E. Reid & Assocs., Inc., Chgo., 1971—, chief polygraph examiner, 1978-80, dir. Chgo. office, 1980-82, pres. corp., Chgo., Denver, Milw., 1982—; chmn. Ill. Detection of Deception Examiner Com., 1978-82; mem. adv. com. Office of Tech. Assessment, 1983. Contbr. articles to profl. jours. Lobbyist Ill. Polygraph Soc., 1981—. Mem. Am. Polygraph Assn. (v.p. 1979-80, chmn. pub. relations com. 1979-80, awards), Ill. Polygraph Soc. (v.p. 1981, pres. 1982-83), Am. Soc. Indsl. Security (investigations com. 1983—), Spl. Agts. Assn., Nat. Assn. State Dirs. of Law Enforcement, Acad. Security Educators and Trainers. Office: 250 S Wacker Dr Suite 1100 Chicago IL 60606

BUCKLEY, MORTIMER JOSEPH, physician; b. Worcester, Mass., July 1, 1932; s. Mortimer Joseph and Kathleen Josephine (O'Sullivan) B.; m. Marilyn Scully, June 16, 1962; children—Kathleen, Deirdre, Kara, Mortimer. A.B., Coll. Holy Cross, 1954; M.D., Boston U., 1958. Diplomate: Am. Bd. Surgery, Am. Bd. Thoracic Surgery. Intern in surgery Mass. Gen. Hosp., 1958-59, 3d asst. resident in surgery, 1959-60, 2d asst. resident, 1960-62, 1st asst. resident, 1964-65, resident in surgery, 1965-66, asst. in surgery, 1966-67; chief Vascular Clinic, 1967-69, asst. surgeon, 1968-71, asso. in surgery, 1968-69, chief cardiac surg. unit, 1970—, asso. vis. surgeon, 1972-76, vis. surgeon, 1977—; teaching fellow in anatomy Harvard Med. Sch., Boston, 1960-62, teaching fellow in surgery, 1965-66, instr. surgery, 1966-68, asso. in surgery, 1968-69, asst. prof. surgery, 1969-72, asso. prof. surgery, 1972-76, prof. surgery, 1977—; clin. asso. Clinic of Surgery, Nat. Heart Inst., Bethesda, Md., 1962-64. Mem. N.Y. Acad. Sci., AMA, Mass. Med. Soc., Am. Assn. Acad. Surgery, Soc. Univ. Surgeons, A.C.S., Internat. Cardiovascular Soc., Soc. for Vascular Surgery, New Eng., Boston surg. socs., Am. Assn. Thoracic Surgeons (chmn. membership com. 1980—), Soc. Thoracic Surgeons, Am. Heart Assn. (chmn. cardiovascular surg. council 1980—), Mass. Heart Assn., Am. Soc. Artificial Internal Organs, Am. Coll. Cardiology, Am. Surg. Assn., Am. Coll. Chest Physicians. Home: 20 Foxcroft Rd Winchester MA 01890 Office: Mass Gen Hosp Boston MA 02114

BUCKLEY, PAUL DOUGLAS, hotel exec.; b. Boston, Jan. 28, 1942; s. Robert Dennis and Anne Delores (Dubovy) B.; children—Nicole Lynn, Natalie. Student, Bryant & Stratton Coll., 1959-60; B.A., Boston U., 1963; postgrad., Cornell U., 1971-72. Cargo sales mgr. Aer Lingus/Irish Airlines, Boston, 1963-68; sales mgr. Hilton Hotels Corp., Boston, 1968-70, resident mgr., Buffalo, 1970-73, gen. mgr., Northampton, Mass., 1973-75, Ryetown Hilton, Westchester, N.Y., 1975-76; resident mgr. Conrad Hilton, Chgo., 1976-78; gen. mgr. Logan Airport Hilton, Boston, 1978—; dir. Skal Internat., Boston. Mem. Greater Boston Hotel-Motel Assn. (dir. com.). Roman Catholic. Club: Boston Tennis. Home and Office: Logan Airport Hilton 75 Service Rd Boston MA 02128

BUCKLEY, PRISCILLA LANGFORD, magazine editor; b. N.Y.C., Oct. 17, 1921; d. William Frank and Aloise (Steiner) B. B.A., Smith Coll., 1943. Copy girl, sports writer U.P., N.Y.C., 1944, radio rewrite, 1944-47, corr., Paris, France, 1953-56; news editor radio sta. WACA, Camden, S.C., 1947-48; reports officer CIA, Washington, 1951-53; with Nat. Review mag., N.Y.C., 1956—, mng. editor, 1959—. Columnist: One Woman's Voice Syndicate, 1976-80. Clubs: Sharon (Conn.) Country (sec. 1973-77, pres. 1978-80. Home: Great Elm Sharon CT 06069 Office: National Review 150 E 35th St New York NY 10016

BUCKLEY, REBECCA HATCHER, physician; b. Hamlet, N.C., Apr. 1, 1933; d. Martin Armstead and Nora (Langston) Hatcher; m. Charles Edward Buckley, III, July 9, 1955; children—Charles Edward, IV, Elizabeth Ann, Rebecca Kathryn, Sarah Margaret. B.A., Duke U., 1954; M.D., U. N.C., 1958. Intern Duke U. Med. Center, 1958-59, resident, 1959-61, practice medicine, specializing in pediatric allergy and immunology, Durham, N.C., 1961—; dir. Am. Bd. Allergy and Immunology, Phila., 1971-73, chmn. exam. com., 1971-73, co-chmn. exam. com., 1982-84; mem. staffs Duke U. Med. Center; asst. prof. pediatrics Duke U., 1965-68, asst. prof. immunology, 1961-68, asso. prof. pediatrics, 1972-76, asso. prof. immunology, 1972-79, prof. pediatrics, 1976-79, prof. immunology, 1979—, J. Buren Sidbury prof. pediatrics, 1979—, Disting. prof., 1979—. Contbr. numerous articles to med. publs. Recipient Allergic Diseases Academic award Nat. Inst. Allergy and Infectious Diseases, 1974-79. Fellow Am. Acad. Allergy (mem. exec. com. 1975—, pres. 1979-80); mem. Am. Assn. Immunologists, Soc. Pediatric Research, Am. Acad. Pediatrics, Southeastern Allergy Assn. (pres. 1978-79), Am. Pediatric Soc. Republican. Episcopalian. Home: 3621 Westover Rd Durham NC 27707 Office: Box 2898 Duke Med Center Durham NC 27710

BUCKLEY, RICHARD EDWARD, conductor; b. N.Y.C., Sept. 1, 1953; s. Emerson and Mary (Henderson) B. B.M., N.C. Sch. of Arts, 1973; M.Mus., Cath. U. Am., 1974; student, Aspen Sch. of Music, 1974, Mozarteum, Salzburg, Austria, 1977. Asst. condr., chorus master, Opera Soc. Washington, 1973-74; asst. condr., music adminstr., Seattle Opera, 1974-75; mus. asst., Seattle Symphony, 1975-77; asst. condr., Seattle Symphony, 1977-79; assoc. condr., Seattle Symphony, 1979-81; resident condr., Seattle Symphony, 1981-83; prin. concert condr., Seattle Symphony, 1983-84; music dir., Oakland Symphony, Calif., 1983—; guest condr., Ft. Lauderdale Symphony, Oreg. Symphony, Alaska Festival Music, N.Y. Philharmonic, 1978-81, BBC Symphony, Winnipeg Symphony, Nashville Symphony, Oakland Symphony, Pasadena Symphony, Houston Symphony, opera cos., N.Y.C., Seattle, Houston, Miami, Anchorage, Washington, Milw., B.H., Ft. Worth, Balt., Columbus. Bd. visitors U. Puget Sound, 1981-84. Home: 12 Starview Dr Oakland CA 94705 Office: Oakland Symphony 2025 Broadway Oakland CA 94612

BUCKLEY, ROBERT JOSEPH, manufacturing executive; b. N.Y.C., Mar. 16, 1924; s. Thomas William and Catherine Alberta (Nolan) B.; m. Polly Dee, June 18, 1948; children: Robert Joseph, John Nolan, Peter Thomas, Clare Dee, Brian Burke, Mark Charles, Christopher Lawrence, Paul Gerard. B.A. with distinction, Wesleyan U., Middletown, Conn., 1950; J.D., Cornell U., 1953. Bar: N.Y. bar 1954. Asst. plant engr. Nat. Cash Register Co., 1951-52; supr. N.Y. State Law Revision Commn., 1952-53; with Gen. Electric Co., 1953-61, mgr. union relations, Schenectady, 1959-61; with Baldwin-Lima-Hamilton Corp., 1961-68, gen. mgr., 1962-68, v.p. corp., 1962-68; exec. v.p. Ingersoll Milling Machine Co., Rockford, Ill., 1968-70, pres., 1970-71, Allegheny Internat. Inc., Pitts., 1971—, chief exec. officer, 1975—, chmn., 1981—; dir. Mellon Bank, Wilkinson Match, Sword Group Ltd., Tyco Labs., Inc., Bell Telephone of Pa., Liquid Air Corp. Bd. dirs. Pitts. Symphony Soc., Pitts. Ballet Theatre, Pitts. Opera, Duquesne U.; trustee Childrens Hosp. Pitts. Served with inf. AUS, 1942-46. Decorated Purple Heart. Mem. N.Y. State Bar Assn., Pa. Mfrs. Assn., Am. Ordnance Assn., Transp. Assn. Am., Machinery and Allied Products Inst., Newcomen Soc. Knight of Malta, Knight of Holy Sepulchre. Clubs: Duquesne (Pitts.) (dir.); Edgeworth, Allegheny Country; 29, Metropolitan (N.Y.C.); Rolling Rock. Home: RD 1 Scaife Rd Sewickley PA 15143 Office: 2700 Two Oliver Plaza PO Box 456 Pittsburgh PA 15230

BUCKLEY, T. GARRY, state official; b. Albany, N.Y., Sept. 13, 1922; m. Patricia S. Buckley. Student, Brown U. Realtor, Bennington, Vt., 1950—; mem. Vt. Senate, 1955, 57, 69-70, 71-72, 73-74, chmn. judiciary com., 1971-72, 73-74; lt. gov. State of Vt., Montpelier, 1977—; mem. legal com. Sanitas Inc., Bethany, Conn., 1976—. Chmn. Bennington Regional Planning Commn., 1962-63; bd. dirs. Bennington Mus., 1960—. Served with USAAF, 1941-44. Republican. Roman Catholic. Home: 1102 Spyglass Ln South Passage Vero Beach FL 32963 Office: State House Montpelier VT 05602

BUCKLEY, THOMAS HUGH, history educator; b. Elkhart, Ind., Sept. 11, 1932; s. Bernard Leroy and Martha B. (Swoveland) B.; children: Christopher, Kathryn, Elizabeth, Thomas, Barbara. Student, Northwestern U., 1950-53; A.B., Ind. U., 1955, M.A., 1956, Ph.D. (grad. fellow), 1961; postdoctoral fellow, Stanford U., 1968, U. Wis., 1983. From instr. to prof. U. S.D., 1960-69; vis. prof. Ind. U., 1969-71; prof., chmn. dept. U. Tulsa, 1971-81, chmn. humanistic studies, 1975-81, Jay Walker research chair Am. History, 1981—; cons. on overseas edn. to Nat. Edn. Corp. Author: The United States and the Washington Conference, 1921-1922, 1970 (award as best first book by an historian 1971); editor: Research and Roster Guide of Soc. Historians of Am. Fgn. Relations, 1980—; contbr. chpts. in books. Mem. Orgn. Am. Historians, Soc. Historians of Am. Fgn. Relations, Tulsa Com. Fgn. Relations, Phi Alpha Theta, Lambda Chi Alpha. Republican. Methodist. Home: 2315 S Richmond Tulsa OK 74114 Office: Dept of History University of Tulsa Tulsa OK 74104 *Success comes in the race of life not always to the swiftest but to those who keep on running*

BUCKLEY, VIRGINIA LAURA, editor; b. N.Y.C., May 11, 1929; d. Alfred and Josephine Marie (Manetti) Iacuzzi; m. David Patrick Buckley, June 30, 1960; children: Laura Joyce, Brian Thomas. B.A., Wellesley Coll., 1950; M.A., Columbia U., 1952. Tchr. English Bennett Coll., Millbrook, N.Y., 1954-56, Berkeley Inst., Bklyn., 1956-58; copy editor World Pub. Co., N.Y.C., 1959-69; children's book editor Thomas Y. Crowell, N.Y.C., 1971-80; editorial dir. Lodestar Books, E.P. Dutton, Inc., N.Y.C., 1980—. Contbr. articles to profl. jours. Mem. ALA. Office: Lodestar Books EP Dutton Inc 2 Park Ave New York NY 10016

BUCKLEY, WILLIAM ELMHIRST, publisher; b. Rahway, N.J., Oct. 6, 1913; s. John A. and Margaret Elsie (Elmhirst) B.; m. Virginia Smith, Aug. 2, 1941; children: Carolyn E., William E. Student, U. Pa., 1932-34. Jr. exec. Quinn & Boden Co., Inc. (book mfrs.), Rahway, N.J., 1935-42, Doubleday & Co., N.Y.C., 1945-49; with Henry Holt & Co., N.Y.C., 1949-58, v.p., dir., 1951-58; v.p. sales World Pub. Co., Cleve., 1958-60; v.p. book div. McCall Corp., N.Y.C., 1960-62; v.p. Curtis Pub. Co., N.Y.C., 1962-68, dir. book div., 1962-68; asst. to pres. Cowles Communications, Inc., 1968-72; chmn. Cowles Book Co., 1968-72; chmn., pres. Cambridge Book Co. (subsidiaries Cowles Communications Inc.), 1968-72; publishing cons., 1972—. Served to lt. comdr. USNR, 1942-45. Mem. Phi Delta Theta. Clubs: Dutch Treat (N.Y.C.); Soc. Four Arts (Palm Beach, Fla.). Home: 151 Seaview Ave Palm Beach FL 33480

BUCKLEY, WILLIAM FRANK, JR., magazine editor, author; b. N.Y.C., Nov. 24, 1925; s. William Frank and Aloise (Steiner) B.; m. Patricia Taylor, July 6, 1950; 1 son, Christopher T. Student, U.

Mexico, 1943; B.A., Yale U., 1950; L.H.D., Seton Hall U., 1966, Niagara U., 1967, Mt. St. Mary's Coll., 1969; LL.D., St. Peter's Coll., 1969, Syracuse U., 1969, Ursinus Coll., 1969, Lehigh U., 1970, Lafayette Coll., 1972, St. Anselm's Coll., 1973, St. Bonaventure U., 1974, U. Notre Dame, 1978, N.Y. Law Sch., 1981; D.Sc.O., Curry Coll, 1970; Litt.D., St. Vincent Coll., 1971, Fairleigh Dickinson U., 1973, Alfred U., 1974, Coll. William and Mary, 1981, William Jewell Coll., 1982. Assoc. editor Am. Mercury, 1952; editor-in-chief Nat. Rev., N.Y.C., 1955—; syndicated columnist, 1962—; host weekly TV show Firing Line, 1966—; Froman Distinguished prof. Russell Sage Coll., 1973. Author: God and Man at Yale, 1951, (with L. Brent Bozell) McCarthy and His Enemies, 1954, Up from Liberalism, 1959, Rumbles Left and Right, 1963, The Unmaking of a Mayor, 1966, The Jeweler's Eye, 1968, The Governor Listeth, 1970, Cruising Speed, 1971, Inveighing We Will Go, 1972, Four Reforms, 1973, United Nations Journal, 1974, Execution Eve, 1975, Saving the Queen, 1976, Airborne, 1976, Stained Glass, 1978, A Hymnal, 1978, Who's On First, 1980, Marco Polo, If You Can, 1982, Atlantic High, 1982, Overdrive, 1983, The Story of Henri Tod, 1984; editor: The Committee and Its Critics, 1962, Odyssey of a Friend, 1970, American Conservative Thought in the Twentieth Century, 1970; contbr.: Racing at Sea, 1959, The Intellectuals, 1960, What is Conservatism?, 1964, Dialogues in Americanism, 1964, Violence in the Streets, 1968, The Beatles Book, 1968, Spectrum of Catholic Attitudes, 1969, Great Ideas Today Annual, 1970, Essays on Hayek, 1976; also periodicals. Mem. USIA Adv. Commn., 1969-72; pub. mem. U.S. del. to 28th Gen. Assembly UN, 1973. Served to 2d lt., inf. AUS, 1944-46. Recipient Bellarime medal, 1977; Am. Journalism award Friends of Haifa U., 1980; Creative Leadership award NYU, 1981. Fellow Soc. Profl. Journalists, Sigma Delta Chi; mem. Council on Fgn. Relations, Mont Pelerin Soc. Clubs: New York Yacht, Century, Bohemian. Office: 150 E 35th St New York NY 10016

BUCKLIN, DONALD THOMAS, lawyer; b. Providence, July 11, 1938; s. Elmer F. and Anne (Scott) B.; m. Kathryn L. Alfera, Nov. 30, 1963; children: Donald R., Heather Anne. B.S. in Acctg., Providence Coll., 1960; J.D. cum laude, Am. U., 1967. Bar: Va. 1968, D.C. 1968. Supervisory acct. GAO, 1960-67; law clk. to judge U.S. Dist. Ct. D.C., 1967-68; asst. U.S. atty. for D.C. Dept. Justice, Washington, 1968-71; ptnr. Rowley & Scott, Washington, 1971-74, Truitt, Fabrikant, Bucklin & Lenzner, 1974-76, Wald, Harrader & Ross, 1977. Contbg. author: Antitrust Counseling and Litigation Techniques, 1984. Served to 1st lt. USAR, 1960-68. Mem. ABA (com. on sentencing, probation and reintegration of offenders 1975-76, com. corrections and rehab. offenders 1976-77, civil practice and procedures com., litigation sect. com. on liaison with state and local bar assns.), D.C. Bar Assn. (com. on probation 1976-77, co-chmn., treas. Criminal Practice Inst. 1972-73, exec. council young lawyers sect. 1973-75, Young Lawyer of Yr. 1975, litigation sect. steering com.), Phi Delta Phi. Office: Wald Harkrader & Ross 1300 19th St NW Suite 700 Washington DC 20036 *

BUCKMAN, LOUIS CASS, air force officer; b. Shelbina, Mo., Aug. 2, 1932; s. Paul Sylvester and Beryl (Lanham) B.; m. Gloria Byrne Woodell Foy, Aug. 10, 1957; children: Deborah Diane, Bradley Joseph, Blake Louis. B.S., U. Mo., 1954; M.S., George Washington U., 1964; postgrad., Air Command and Staff Coll., 1964, Air War Coll., 1972. Joined U.S. Air Force, 1954, advanced through grades to maj. gen., 1980; dep. dir. for combat readiness Dep. Chief of Staff Plans and Ops., Hdqrs. U.S. Air Force, 1975-78; comdr. 42d Air Div., Blytheville AFB, Ark., 1978, 3d Air div., Andersen AFB, Guam, 1979-80; dep. chief of staff ops. Hdqrs. SAC, Offutt AFB, Nebr., 1980-82; chief Joint U.S. Mil. Aid Group, Greece, 1982—. Decorated D.S.M., Legion of Merit, Bronze Star, Air medal, others. Mem. Order of Daedalians, Air Force Assn. Office: JUSMAGG APO New York NY 09253

BUCKMAN, THOMAS RICHARD, educator, foundation executive; b. Reno, May 3, 1923; s. Thomas Eli and Georgia Christina (Damm) B.; m. Gunhild Margareta Malmkjell, May 1, 1948; children: Anne Christina, Carol Erica. B.A., U. Pacific, 1947; cert., U. Stockholm, 1951; M.A. (fellow Scandinavian studies), U. Minn., 1952; B.L.S. (H.W. Wilson scholar), U. Minn., 1953. Clk., Permit Office for Germany, Allied High Commn., Stockholm, 1949-50; sr. clk. U. Minn. Library, 1952-53; asst. reference librarian Oreg. State U. Library, 1953-54; King Gustav V fellow in Sweden, Am. Scandinavia Found., 1954-55; asst. librarian Modesto (Calif.) Jr. Coll. Library, 1955-56; head acquisitions dept. U. Kans. Library, 1956-60, asso. dir., 1960-61, dir. libraries, 1961-68, lectr. in Scandinavian, 1958-61; prof. bibliography, univ. librarian Northwestern U., Evanston, Ill., 1968-71; pres. Found. Center, N.Y.C., 1971—; dir. internat. relations office ALA, 1966-67. Editor, translator: Modern Theatre: Seven Plays and an Essay (by Pär Lagerkvist), 1966; editor: Bibliography and Natural History, 1966; Editor: University and Research Libraries in Japan and the United States, 1972; contbr. articles to profl. jours. Mem. Gov. Kans. Com. Library Service, 1963-64; mem. Kans. State Library Adv. Commn., 1963-67; mem. master plan com. Ill. Bd. Higher Edn., 1968-69. Served with USNR, 1943-46. Guggenheim fellow, 1964-65. Mem. ALA (chmn. internat. relations adv. com. for liaison with Japanese libraries 1967-71), Kans. Library Assn. (chmn. intellectual freedom com., pres. 1967-68), Assn. Research Libraries (pres. 1971-72), Bibliog. Soc. Am., Soc. Advancement Scandinavian Study (sec.-treas. 1959-69), Am. Soc. Infor. Sci. Office: 888 7th Ave New York NY 10016

BUCKMASTER, JOHN DAVID, mathematics and aeronautical engineering educator; b. Belfast, No. Ireland, Feb. 2, 1941; came to U.S., 1962; s. Frederick Hubert and Peggy B.; m. Annette Helen Winstein, June 5, 1966; children: Simon Ben-David, Rachel Peggy Ann. B.Sc. in Aero. Engring., Imperial Coll., London, 1962; Ph.D. in Applied Math, Cornell U., 1969. Research engr. Cornell Aero. Lab., Buffalo, 1962-65; asst. prof. math. NYU, 1969-72; asst. prof. dept. engring. and applied sci. Yale U., 1972-74; assoc. prof. dept. math and dept. theoretical and applied mechanics U. Ill., Urbana, 1974-78, prof., 1978-82, prof. math. and aero. engring., 1982—. Author: Theory of Laminar Flames, 1982, Lectures in Mathematical Combustion, 1983; Contbr. numerous articles to sci. jours. Mem. Combustion Inst., Am. Phys. Soc., Soc. Indsl. and Applied Math. Club: Illini Gliding. Home: 2014 Boudreau Urbana IL 61801 Office: Univ Ill Urbana IL 61801

BUCKMORE, ALVAH CLARENCE, JR., ballistician; b. Lewiston, Maine, Sept. 11, 1944; s. Alvah Clarence and Mary (Begin) B. Student, Holyoke Community Coll., Nat. Radio Inst., Famous Writers Sch., U. Mass. Cert. firearms instr. Pres. Buckmore Enterprises, Westfield, Mass., 1974—; pioneer in amateur radio satellite comunications; mgmt. cons. firearms industry; instr. Mass. Mil. NCO Acad., 1976; mem. Mass. State Rifle and Pistol Team, 1976. Contbr. Collier's Ency., articles to profl. jours.; patentee in field. Served with U.S. Army, 1974; served with Mass. Army N.G., 1975-78. Recipient Internat. Recognition award, 1979; NSF fellow, 1978—. Mem. AAAS, Am. Def. Preparedness Assn., Nat. Rifle Assn. Address: 18 Tannery Rd Westfield MA 01085 *Since the age of 15 years it has been my consistent objective in life to develop a genuine ability to think, talk and use information properly and, over these years—which include experience of my serving as an illegal POW with no official recognition— I have wavered very little, if at all.*

BUCKNAM, JAMES ROMEO, former newspaper editor, consultant labor-management relations; b. Livermore Falls, Maine, Apr. 26, 1911; s. Howard Lel and Rose Alma (Deschenes) B.; m. Adrienne Meteyer, Aug. 6, 1934 (div. Dec. 1965); children: Beverly Anne Bucknam Marcou, Howard V., James L., Nancy R. Bucknam Weidinger; m. Cecile LeBlanc, Jan. 14, 1967 (dec. Dec. 1975); m. Myrna Nicholas, May 23, 1981. Student, U. N.H., 1930-33. Reporter-editor Berlin (N.H.) Reporter, 1933-43; deskman Manchester (N.H.) Union Leader, 1943-49, night editor, 1949-62, mng. editor, 1962-69, exec. editor, 1969-79, personnel mgr., labor relations dir., 1971-79; cons. labor-mgmt. relations, 1979—. Mem. Gov.'s Traffic Safety Commn., 1963-65; chmn. N.H. Traffic Safety Commn., 1965—; mem. CJIS adv. bd. to N.H. Commn. on Crime and Delinquency, 1972-73; mem. bd. rev. Boy Scouts Am., 1968-70; mem. Joint Hosp. Commn., Manchester, 1969-71; pres., bd. govs., mem. adv. bd. Notre Dame Hosp., 1969-71; trustee Castle Jr. Coll., Windham, N.H., 1971—; moderator Town of Bow, N.H., 1980-83. Served with USMCR, World War II; PTO. Mem. Am. Assn. Automotive Medicine, Internat. Assn. Accident and Traffic Medicine, Am. Legion, VFW, Marine Corps Combat Corrs. Assn., Marine Corps Res. Officers Assn. (pres. Concord chpt.). Clubs: Manchester Country; Bow (N.H.); Community Men's. Home and Office: 34 Albin Rd Bow NH 03301 *Perhaps the most significant contribution to my future came while I was a student at the University of New Hampshire. The late president of U. N.H., Dr. Edward M. Lewis, in discussing with me a problem involving my editorship of the university student newspaper, handed me this quotation: "The mark of an educated man and the measure of an educated man is the extent to which he can withhold his judgment until he knows all the facts." I believe the quote to be from Newton D. Baker, secretary of war under President Woodrow Wilson.*

BUCKNER, ELMER LA MAR, insurance executive; b. Provo, Utah, Apr. 27, 1922; s. Elmer R. and Altis LaVern (Maxfield) B.; m. Melba Hale, Oct. 3, 1945; children: Lynda, Brent, Terry, Kathy, David. B.S., Brigham Young U., 1946. C.L.U. Partner, Buckner-Radmall Ins. Counselors, Ogden, Utah, 1947-62, co. inc., pres., 1962—; mem. Utah Ho. of Reps., 1965-67, Utah Senate, 1967-75, asst. majority leader, 1971-75. Bd. govs. ARC, 1956-62; gen. bd. Young Men's Mut. Improvement Assn., Ch. Jesus Christ of Latter Day Saints, 1957-58; bishop Ogden 55th Ward, 1958-63; 2d counselor Weber Heights Stake presidency, 1963-68; pres. Weber State Coll. Stake, 1968-73, Sacramento mission, 1975-78; mem. young men's gen. bd. Latter Day Saints Ch., 1980, regional rep., 1981—; former dir. Citizens Com. for Hoover Report; mem. Com. on Religion in Am. Life Inc.; former mem. adv. com. FOA; mem. exec. com. Am. Nat. Red. Cross, 1961-62; v.p. Lake Bonneville council Boy Scouts Am., 1968-69, pres., 1970, program chmn. Western region Sect. II, 1973-75, recipient Silver Beaver award, 1967; bd. alumni Brigham Young U., 1959-63, pres., 1961-62; v.p. Ogden Area United Fund, 1962; pres. No. Utah United Fund, 1963; mem. Utah Bd. Regents Higher Edn., 1981—; chmn. Utah Cancer Crusade, 1970; v.p. Utah Cancer Soc., 1971, Utah div. Am. Cancer Soc. Utah; del. Republican Nat. Conv., Chgo., 1960; chmn. Weber County Rep. party, 1960-64; Utah state Rep. elector, 1964. Served as 1st lt. USAAF, World War II; 23 missions. Named Utah Ins. Agt. of Year,, 1973; recipient Silver Antelope award Boy Scouts Am., 1983, Disting. Alumni award Weber State Coll., 1983. Mem. U.S. C. of C. (dir. 1955-56), U.S. Jaycees (pres. 1954-55), Utah Jaycees (pres. 1952-53), Ogden C. of C. (dir. 1980, pres. 1982), Ogden Jaycees (pres. 1950), Jr. Chamber Internat. (treas. 1956), Weber Coll. Alumni Assn. (pres. 1958-59), Sigma Gamma Chi (internat. pres. 1967-69). Club: Kiwanis (pres. Ogden 1967). Home: 1550 Country Hills Dr Ogden UT 84403 Office: 1180 28th St Ogden UT 84403

BUCKNER, JAMES LOWELL, dentist; b. Vicksburg, Miss., July 29, 1934; s. Clarence Eugene and Florice (Williams) B.; m. Gwendolyn T. Peaks, Sept. 12, 1959. Student, Va. State Coll., 1951-53; B.S.D., U. Ill., 1957, D.D.S., 1959. Pvt. practice dentistry, Chgo., 1959—; Dir. Seaway Nat. Bank, Chgo., 1964—; partner State-51st Shopping Center, Chgo., 1962—; chmn. Chgo. Financial Devel. Corp.; v.p. Seaway Communications Inc., 1977—; pres. Trains & Boats & Planes Travel, 1978—; bd. advisers Supreme Life Ins. Co. Bd. dirs. Chgo. Econ. Devel. Corp., 1966-81; pres. Chgo. Urban League, 1973-75; mem. Pres.'s Council Minority Bus. Enterprise, 1972—; pres. The Foodbasket, Inc., 1980—; mem. dental adv. council Ill. Dept. Pub. Aid, 1973—; Mem. bd. City Colls. Chgo., 1971-76; treas. PUSH (People United to Save Humanity) Found.; advisor WTTW ednl. TV sta.; trustee U. Ill. Dental Alumni, 1974-81. Named outstanding young man Chgo. South End Jr. C. of C., 1964, Man of Yr. Chgo. Urban League, 1972. Mem. Chgo., Ill. dental socs., Nat., Am. dental assns., Council Nat. Urban League Presidents (pres. 1975-76), Am. Inst. Banking, Ill. Com. Better Govt. Office: 5050 S State St Chicago IL 60609

BUCKNER, JOHN HUGH, construction company executive, retired air force officer; b. Cleburne, Tex., Jan. 11, 1919; s. John Franklin and Eleanor (Wimberly) B.; m. Ann Sonfield, Apr. 24, 1946; children: John Hugh, Ann Lynn, Robert Chantland. A.S., John Tarleton Coll., 1938; student, Tex. A. and M. Coll., 1938-39; B.S., U.S. Mil. Acad., 1943; M.S., Springfield Coll., 1952. Commd. 2d lt. U.S. Army, 1943; advanced through grades to maj. gen. USAF, 1970; assigned, Europe, 1943-46, 60-64, 1946-53, Korea, 1953-54, 1954-57, 1957-60, 1964-67, Azores, 1967-69, 1969-70, Vietnam, 1970-71, ret., 1971; pres. Buckner Constrn. Co., Jacksonville, Tex., 1971—. Decorated Legion of Merit, D.F.C., Air medal; Croix de Guerre, France; Medal Mil. Merit, Portugal). Mem. Assn. Gen. Contractors Am. (pres. Tex. hwy. heavy br. 1981, dir. 1979-81), Air Force Assn., Order Daedalians, Mil. Order World Wars, Phi Kappa Phi. Club: Rotarian. Home: Emerald Bay 1 Williamsburg Ln Bullard TX 75757 Office: Box 1778 Jacksonville TX 75766

BUCKNER, JOHN KNOWLES, corporate executive; b. Springfield, Mo., Sept. 8, 1936; s. Ernest Godfrey and Mary Helen (Knowles) B.; m. Lorraine Catherine Anderson, Sept. 22, 1962; children: John Knowles, Allison. B.A., Williams Coll., 1958; M.S., Mass. Inst. Tech., 1960; Ph.D., Stanford U., 1965; grad., Advanced Mgmt. Program, Harvard, 1974. Mgr. analysis dept. EG&G Inc., Bedford, Mass., 1966-70; dir. electronic data processing, controller, v.p. financial ops. Eastern Gas & Fuel Assos., Boston, 1970-77; exec. v.p., chief operating officer, dir. Waters Assos., Inc., Milford, Mass., 1970-80; v.p., chief fin. officer Prime Computer, Inc., Natick, Mass., 1980-83; sr. v.p., chief fin. officer EG & G, Inc., Wellesley, Mass., 1983—. Contbr. articles on engring., data analysis and systems to profl. jours. Trustee Boston Mus. Sci. Corp.; mem. Belmont Hill Sch. Corp. AEC spl. fellow nuclear sci. and engring., 1959, 62-65. Mem. Phi Beta Kappa, Sigma Xi, Chi Psi. Club: Maugus. Home: 34 Livermore Rd Wellesley Hills MA 02181 Office: 45 William St Wellesley MA 02181 *My present success, such as it is, has resulted from a willingness and ability to work hard, motivate others, and apply my own training and ideas to the particular task at hand, irrespective of the nature of the field of endeavor. My approach has always been to attain a level of technical and managerial competence necessary to bring about change. Generally, my goal is to make a contribution in as many areas of human conduct as my diligence and native ability will allow.*

BUCKNER, PHILLIP ALFRED, historian, educator; b. Toronto, Ont., Can., June 4, 1942; s. Albert and Mary B.; m. Charmian Henderson-Tate, July 31, 1969 (dec. 1982). B.A., U. Toronto, 1965; Ph.D. in History, U. London, 1969. Mem. faculty U. New Brunswick, Fredericton, Can., 1968—, prof. history, 1980—. Editor: Acadiensis: Jour. of History of Atlantic Region, 1970-81; co-editor: Eastern/Western Perspectives, 1981; contbr.: articles to Dictionary Can. Biography. Woodrow Wilson fellow, 1965; U.K. Commonwealth Scholarship, 1965-68; Can. Council fellow, 1974; Leger fellow, 1981. Mem. Can. Hist. Assn, Atlantic Assn. Historians, Assn. Can. Archivists. Office: Campus House Univ of New Brunswick Fredericton NB E3B 5A3 Canada

BUCKNER, WILLIAM J., professional baseball player; b. Vallejo, Calif., Dec. 14, 1949; d. Leonard Dean and Marie Katharine (Dapper) B.; m. Jody Ann Schenck, Feb. 16, 1980. Student, U. So. Calif., 1968-73, DePaul U., from 1981. With Los Angeles Dodgers, 1968-76; 1st baseman Chgo. Cubs, 1977-84, Boston Red Sox, 1984—; mem. Nat. League All Star team, 1981. Mem. Baseball Players Assn. Republican. Episcopalian. Office: Boston Red Sox Fenway Park Boston MA *

BUCKO, JOHN JOSEPH, investment corporation executive; b. N.Y.C., Mar. 19, 1937; s. John Francis and Sophia Helen (Roog) B.; m. Mary Catharine Doyle, Dec. 29, 1962; children: Kathlene, Christopher, Julie Anne. B.S., NYU, 1961. Controller Reynolds Securities, Inc., N.Y.C., 1970-73, v.p., chief fin. officer, 1973-78; first v.p., dir. internal audit Dean Witter Reynolds Inc., N.Y.C., 1978-79, sr. v.p., controller, 1979—. Mem. Wall St. Tax Assn., Securities Industry Assn. (fin. mgmt. div.). Republican. Roman Catholic. Home: 438 Manchester Way Wickoff NJ 07483 Office: Dean Witter Reynolds Inc Five World Trade Center New York NY 10048

BUCKS, CHARLES ALAN, consultant, former airline executive; b. Lubbock, Tex., Dec. 14, 1927; s. Charles Henry and Nell (Lattimore) B.; m. Joyce Laverne Turner, Aug. 19, 1949; children: Jimmy Charles, David Alan, Robert Doyle, Dawne Alyce. Student, Tex. Technol. Coll., 1947-48, Amarillo Jr. Coll., 1948-49. With Continental Air Lines, Inc., 1948—, gen. sales mgr., 1958-61, v.p. field sales, 1961-65, v.p. sales, Los Angeles, 1965-66, v.p. sales and service, 1966-69, sr. v.p., 1969-75, exec. v.p. mktg., 1975-81, exec. v.p., asst. to pres., 1981-82, also dir.; pres. C. Bucks & Assoc. Inc., 1982—. Pres. One Shot Antelope Hunt, Lander, Wyo., 1968, dir., African First Shotters; pres. Calif. Tourism Council, 1975-77; Trustee Continental Found., Denver, 1970-81; bd. dirs. Mustang Sanctuary Found.; trustee Buckley Schs., Sherman Oaks, Calif., 1977-83. Served with USNR, 1945-46; PTO. Recipient Disting. Alumnus award Tex. Tech. U., 1970. Mem. Conquistadores del Cielo (chmn. bd. dirs., past pres.), So. Calif. Safari Club (bd. dirs.), Nat. Aeros. Assn. (bd. dirs.), Pacific Area Travel Assn. Democrat. Presbyterian. Clubs: Lakeside Country (Hollywood, Calif.); Walden Yacht and Country (Montgomery, Tex.). Office: 330 Washington St Suite 605 Marina del Rey CA 90292

BUCUR, NICHOLAS ANTHONY, JR., lawyer; b. Parma, Ohio, Nov. 4, 1924; s. Nicholas A. and Aurelia (Stefan) B.; m. Jacoba Galo, May 30, 1948; children: Nicholas Anthony III, Philip A., Gregory B. B.S., John Carroll U., 1946; J.D., Cleve.-Marshall Law Sch., (now attached to Cleve. State U.), 1951, LL.M., 1959, D. Juridical Sci., 1964. Bar: Ohio 1951. Since practiced in, Cleve., asst. atty. gen., Ohio, 1961-63; Chmn. Mayor's Adv. Council World Trade, 1971-75; chmn. Ohio World Trade Show, 1974, 75, 76; sec; gen. counsel Ohio World Trade Center Inc., 1976-77; chmn. bd., chief exec. officer Cleve. World Trade Center; mgr. internat. trade City of Cleve., 1976-79; pub. Cleve. Pan Am. Bull.; moderator radio religious programs. Author Ceausescu of Romania, Champion of Peace; also serialized book Group Defamation of Romanians; founder, editor: For the Record; editor: Lilyan and Jack Mandel series. Chmn. Cleve. Sister Cities; mem. exec. com. Nat. Conf. Christians and Jews; leader trade missions to, Israel, Rumania; mem. exec. com. Greater Cleve. Bicentennial Commn.; chmn. bd. Cleve. Transit System, 1971-75; pres. Am. Nationalities Movement of Ohio; founder, chmn. bd. World Survival, Inc.; bd. dirs. United Torch, Downtown Cleve. Corp., Cleve. Civic Ballet, 1979, Cleve. Ethnographic Mus., 1979; founder, pres. Am. Romanian Anti-Defamation League, Inc., 1983; trustee Cuyahoga Community Coll., 1982—; founder, chief exec. officer Cleve. Internat. Programs, Inc., 1983. Recipient Honors for lectures on Jewish history B'nai B'rith, for good citizenship and human relations Am. Legion Dunca Post, Ch. Civic League, and Cath. Interracial Council; Ann. Vets. Day award Joint Vets. Commn. Mem. YMCA. Republican. Romanian Byzantine Catholic. Home: 10206 Clifton Blvd Cleveland OH 44102 Office: Bucur and Kaplow Gordon Sq Arcade 6516 Detroit Ave Suite 248 Cleveland OH 44102 *Being neither wise nor vain enough to outline a way for others to follow I can only share some of my perplexity as to this mysterious universe: how to hold to values in a changing world; to have hope in the midst of pain, to learn more and not be crushed by the weight of the unknown, to return love for hate, to maintain faith, and to grow closer to God, and yet be of this earth; these are perpetual challenges, which, I confess, I have not and cannot meet alone. Family, faith, friends... what is anyone without them.*

BUCY, J. FRED, electronics company executive; b. Tahoka, Tex., July 29, 1928; s. J. Fred and Ethel (Montgomery) B.; m. Odetta Greer, Jan. 25, 1947; children: J. Fred, Roxanne, Diane. B.Physics, Tex. Tech. U., 1951; M.Physics, U. Tex., 1953. With Tex. Instruments, Inc., Dallas, 1953—, corp. v.p., 1963-67, corp. group v.p. components, 1967-72, exec. v.p., 1972-75, exec. v.p., chief operating officer, 1975-76, pres., chief operating officer, 1976—, dir.; rep. dir. TI Japan Ltd., gen. dir. several subsidiaries. Patentee in field. Mem. Tech. Assessment of U.S. Congress, Comptroller Gen.'sPanel, Pres.'s Commn. for Nat. Agenda for 80's; mem. bd. regents Tex. Tech. U., Tex. Tech. U. Sch. Medicine; chmn. Tex. Tech. U. Medicine, 1980-82; mem. vis. com. Russian Research Ctr., Harvard U.; mem. physics vis. com. MIT. Recipient Disting. Engrs. award Tex. Tech. U., 1972. Fellow IEEE; mem. Nat. Acad. Engring., Soc. Exploration Geophysicists, Conf. Bd., Sigma Pi Sigma, Tau Beta Pi. Methodist. Clubs: Cosmos (Washington); Dallas Petroleum; Northwood (Dallas). Office: Tex Instruments Inc 13500 N Central Expressway PO Box 225474 Dallas TX 75265

BUCY, PAUL C., neurological surgeon; b. Hubbard, Iowa, Nov. 13, 1904; s. Isaac and Lillian (Clancy) B.; m. Evelyn Richards, June 12, 1927; children: Paul Craig, James Gordon. B.S., State U. Iowa, 1925, M.S., 1927, M.D., 1927; M.D. (hon.), U. Thessaloniki, 1970; Dr. h.c., U. Utrecht, 1971. Diplomate: Am. Bd. Psychiatry and Neurology, Am. Bd. Neurol. Surgery (dir. 1940-48, sec.-treas. 1943-47, residency rev. com.-AMA 1963-69). Intern Henry Ford Hosp., Detroit, 1927-28; resident, instr. neurosurgery U. Chgo., 1928-30, instr., 1930-33, asst. prof., 1933-38, asso. prof. in charge neurosurgery, 1938-41; prof. neurology and neurol. surgery U. Ill., 1941-54; prof. surgery, med. sch. Northwestern U., 1954-72, in charge neurosurgery, 1964-72, prof. emeritus, 1972—; clin. prof. neurology and neurosurgery Bowman-Gray Med Sch., 1974-83, emeritus, 1983—; traveling fellow to Eng. and Ger., 1930-31; research asst. Yale U., 1933; attending neurologist and neurol. surgeon Ill. Neuropsychiat. Inst. and Research and Ednl. Hosps., U. Ill., 1941-54; attending neurol. surgeon, v.p. bd. trustees Chgo. Meml. Hosp., 1941-54, chief of staff, 1943-54; attending neurol. surgeon charge dept. neurol. surgery Chgo. Wesley Meml. Hosp., 1954-72; editorial bd. Jour. Neuro-Surgery, 1951-61, chmn., 1957-61, dir. pubs., 1959-72; Gorgas lectr. U. Ala., 1944; John Black Johnston lectr. U. Minn., 1949; Commonwealth vis. prof. U. Louisville, 1950; George A. Ball vis. prof. Ind. U., 1953; vis. hon. prof. U. Minas Gerais, Brazil, 1954; Fedor Krause lectr. German Neurosurg. Soc. (recipient Fedor Krause medal), 1961, 62; J.H. Jackson meml. lectr. Montreal Neurol. Inst., 1965; W.P. Van Wagenen lectr. U. Rochester, 1965; vis.

lectr. Free U. Berlin, 1963; vis. prof., lectr. Creigton U., 1966; vis. prof. Med. Coll. Ga., 1966, 80, U. Wis., 1968, Harvard U., 1969, 83, U. Md., 1983; Fulbright vis. prof. U. Utrecht, 1969; Norman Dott Meml. lectr. U. Edinburgh, 1984; adv. council Nat. Inst. Neurol. Disease and Blindness, 1961-65, mem. program projects com., 1965-69, mem. adv. subcom. on stroke and nervous system trauma, 1976-80; chmn. Nat. Com. Research in Neurol. Disorders, 1969-74, chmn. emeritus, 1974—, treas., 1974—; chmn. med. adv. com. Nat. Paraplegic Found. Author: (with P. Bailey and D.N. Buchanon) Intracranial Tumors of Infancy and Childhood, 1939, The Precentral Motor Cortex, 1944, 49, (with R.R. Grinker and A.L. Sahs) Neurology, 1959, Neurosurgical Giants, 1984; also publs. sci. jours.; book sects. on various phases nervous system; editor: Surgical Neurology. Recipient Cert. of Accomplishment, State U. Iowa, 1947; Disting. Service award Med. Alumni. U. Chgo., 1955; Disting. Achievement award Modern Medicine mag.; Speedy award Paralyzed Vets. Am., 1969. Fellow ACS, Am. Surg. Assn.; mem. Am. Neurol. Assn. (v.p. 1954-55, pres. 1971-72, mem. council 1972-77), Soc. Neurol. Surgeons (pres. 1959-60), Am. Assn. Neurol. Surgery (pres. 1951-52, dir. publs. 1959-72), Am. Physiol. Soc., AMA (sec. 1936-39, chmn. sect. nervous and mental disease), Chgo. Neurol. Soc. (pres. 1947-48), Chgo. Path. Soc., Inst. Medicine Chgo., Chgo. Med. Soc. (council 1948- 52), Ill. State Med. Soc., Central Neuropsychiat. Assn., Soc. Exptl. Biology and Medicine, Chgo. Surg. Soc. (v.p. 1955-56), Soc. Biol. Psychiatry, World Fedn. Neuro-Surg. Socs. (pres. 1957-61, hon. pres. 1961—), 2d Internat. Congress Neurol. Surgery (pres. 1957-61), Phi Chi, Delta Sigma Rho, Alpha Omega Alpha, Sigma Xi; hon. mem. various fgn. profl. socs. including Soc. Brit. Neurol. Surgeons. Clubs: Univ., Lit., pres. (Chgo.). Home: PO Box 1457 Tryon NC 28782

BUCY, RICHARD SNOWDEN, aerospace engineering and mathematics educator, consultant; b. Washington, July 20, 1935; s. Edmond Howard and Marie (Glinke) B.; m. Ofelia Teresa Rivva, Aug. 25, 1961; children: Phillip Gustav, Richard Erwin. B.S. in Math., MIT, 1957; Ph.D. in Math. Stats., U. Calif.-Berkeley, 1963. Researcher in math. Research Inst. Advanced Studies, Towson, Md., 1960-61, 63-64; research asst. U. Calif.-Berkeley, 1961-63; asst. prof. math. U. Md., College Park, 1964-65; assoc. prof. aerospace engring. U. Colo., Boulder, 1965-66; prof. aerospace engring. and math. U. So. Calif., Los Angeles, 1966—; professeur associe French Govt., Toulouse, 1973-74, Nice, 1983-84; cons. to industry. Author: Filtering for Stochastic Processes, 1968; contbr. numerous articles to profl. publs. Recipient Humbolt prize Govt. W.Ger., Berlin, 1975-76, grant Air Force Office Sci. Research, 1965-81. Fellow IEEE; mem. Am. Math. Soc. Republican. Home: 1 bis Ave Dr Picaud Cannes France 06400 Office: Aerospace Engring Dept U So Calif Los Angeles CA 90007

BUDALUR, THYAGARAJAN SUBBANARAYAN, educator; b. India, July 14, 1929; came to U.S., 1969, naturalized, 1977; s. Subbanarayan Subbuswamy and Paravatham (Gopalakrishnan) B.; children: Chitra, Poorna, Kartik. M.A., U. Madras, 1951, M.Sc., 1954, Ph.D., 1956. Reader organic chemistry U. Madras, 1960-68; prof. chemistry U. Idaho, Moscow, 1968-74; prof. chemistry, dir. div. earth phys. sci. U. Tex., San Antonio, 1974—; lectr. in field. Author: Mechanisms of Molecular Migrations; Selective Organic Transformations; Editorial bd. chem. jours.; contbr. articles to profl. jours. Recipient Intra Sci. Research award, 1966. Fellow Am. Chem. Soc.; mem. Chem. Soc. London, AAAS, N.Y. Acad. Sci., Am. Inst. Chemists, Sigma Xi, Phi Kappa Phi. Club: Lions. Home: 1914 12711 Interstate San Antonio TX 78230 Office: U Tex FM 1604 San Antonio TX 78285

BUDD, EDWARD HEY, insurance executive; b. Zanesville, Ohio, Apr. 30, 1933; s. Curtis Eugene and Mary (Hey) B.; m. Mary Goodrich, Aug. 24, 1957; children: Elizabeth, David, Susan. B.S. in Physics, Tufts U., Medford, Mass., 1955. With Travelers Ins. Co., Hartford, Conn., 1955—, v.p., then sr. v.p., 1967-76, pres., 1976-83, chief exec. officer, 1981—, chmn. bd., 1983—, also dir.; dir. Cushman Industries.; adv. bd. Hartford Nat. Bank & Trust Co., East Hartford. Corporator Hartford Hosp., St. Francis Hosp.; mem. corp. bd. Am. Sch. for Deaf; corporator, bd. dirs. Inst. of Living. Fellow Casualty Actuarial Soc.; mem. Conn. Bus. and Industry Assn. (dir.), Am. Acad. Actuaries., Am. Ins. Assn. (vice chmn.), Nat. Assn. Casualty and Surety Execs. (v.p.), Property-Casualty Ins. Council (vice chmn.). Episcopalian. Clubs: Hartford, Hartford Golf, New York Athletic. Office: One Tower Sq Hartford CT 06115

BUDD, GENE F., capital equipment and component manufacturing company executive; b. Cleve., Sept. 4, 1938; s. Frank J. and Helen B.; m. Regina M. Golenski, Sept. 6, 1958; children—Darlene, Jaye. B.S., Kent (Ohio) State U., 1960, M.B.A., 1965; grad., Advanced Mgmt. Program, Case Western Res. U., 1979. With Glidden Co., Cleve., 1960-67; asst. mgr. investments Chessie Systems, Inc., Cleve., 1967-69; asst. to treas. AM Internat., Cleve., 1969-72; asst. treas. Cin. Milacron, Inc., 1972-77; treas. Samuel Moore Co., Cleve., 1977-79; v.p. fin., treas. Lamson & Sessions Co., Cleve., 1979—. Served with USAR, 1961-62. Mem. Fin. Execs. Inst., Fin. Analysts Fedn., Cleve. Treasurers Club. Home: 2412 Victoria Pkwy Hudson OH 44236 Office: 2000 Bond Ct/ 1300 E 9th St Cleveland OH 44114

BUDD, JOHN HENRY, physician; b. St. Stephen, N.B., Can., Dec. 6, 1908; came to U.S., 1933, naturalized, 1947; s. Frederick Willis and Alice Gertrude (Henry) B.; m. Irma Helen Jackson, Nov. 4, 1937 (dec. 1982); children: John Henry, Charles Frederick. B.A., Dalhousie U., Halifax, N.S., Can., 1929, M.D., C.M., 1933; LL.D., 1978; A.S., W.Va. No. Community Coll., 1978. Intern Victoria Gen. Hosp., Halifax, 1932-33; intern St. Vincent Charity Hosp., Cleve., 1933-34, resident, 1934-35, hon. cons. staff, 1965—; resident Deaconess Hosp., Cleve., 1935-36, chief of staff, 1968-72, mem. staff, 1937—, emeritus chief of staff, 1979, hon. trustee, 1974; practice medicine specializing in gen. practice, obstetrics and gynecology, Cleve., 1937—; mem. staff Parma Community Gen. Hosp., 1958—, pres. med. staff, 1958-62, hon. med. staff, 1970—. Trustee Blue Cross N.E. Ohio, 1954-77, chief cons. med. affairs, 1979—. Served with M.C. AUS, 1943-45; ETO. Named hon. Ky. col., hon. Ozark Hillbilly, 1978; recipient Headliner award Press Club of Ohio, 1978. Fellow Am. Acad. Family Physicians (charter); mem. Cleve. Acad. Medicine (pres. 1953-54, Honors of Acad. award 1967, Disting. Mem. award 1973), Ohio State Med. Assn. (Disting. Service citation 1974, hon. pres. 1979), AMA (pres. 1977-78), Nat. Med. Vets. Soc., 4th Aux. Surg. Group Assn., Interstate Postgrad. Med. Assn. (pres. 1979-80), New Orleans Jazz Club, Phi Delta Theta, Phi Rho Sigma. Republican. Presbyterian. Clubs: Pasteur, Bklyn. Exchange, Med. Arts (Cleve.). Home: 3417 W 148th St Cleveland OH 44111 Office: 2060 E 9th St Cleveland OH 44115

BUDD, LOUIS JOHN, educator; b. St. Louis, Aug. 26, 1921; s. Vincent and Sophia (Kajszo) Budrewicz; m. Isabelle Amelia Marx, Mar. 3, 1945; children: Catherine Lou, David Harry. B.A., U. Mo., 1941, M.A., 1942; Ph.D., U. Wis., 1949. Instr. U. Mo., Columbia, 1941, 46; asst. prof. U. Ky., Lexington, 1949-52; asst. prof. dept. English Duke U., Durham, N.C., 1952-60, assoc. prof., 1960-66, prof., 1966—, chmn. dept. English, 1973-79; mem. vis. faculty Washington U., St. Louis, summer 1954, Northwestern U., Evanston, Ill., summer 1961; lectr. seminar Kraft div. Internat. Paper Co., summer 1959; Fulbright lectr., India, 1967, 72; vis. lectr. U. Damascus, Syria, 1978; mem. Am. adv. com. Am. Studies Research Centre, Hyderabad, India; chmn. Jay B. Hubbell Center for Am. Lit. Historiography. Author: Mark Twain: Social Philosopher, 1962, Robert Herrick, 1971, Newspaper and Magazine Interviews with Samuel L. Clemens, 1874-1910, 1977, Our Mark Twain: The Making of His Public Personality, 1983; Editor: (Robert Herrick) The Web of Life and Clark's Field, 1970, (with others) Toward a New American Literary History, 1980, Critical Essays on Mark Twain, 1867-1910, 1982; mem. editorial bd.: A Selected Edition of W.D. Howells, South Atlantic Rev, 1978-81, U. Miss. Studies in English, 1979—, South Atlantic Quar, 1980—; mng. editor: Am. Lit, 1979—; Contbr. numerous articles to profl. jours. Served to 2d lt. USAAF, 1942-45. Guggenheim fellow, 1965-66; Am. Philos. Soc. grantee, 1956, 70, 73; Nat. Endowment for Humanities sr. fellow, 1979-80. Mem. Internat. Assn. Univ. Profs. English, MLA, Am. Humor Studies Assn. (pres. 1979), AAUP (pres Duke chpt. 1971-72), Phi Beta Kappa (pres. Duke chpt. 1963-64), Phi Eta Sigma. Home: 2753 McDowell St Durham NC 27705 Office: Dept English Duke U Durham NC 27706

BUDD, RICHARD WADE, communications scientist, educator; b. Henderson, Md., Aug. 24, 1934; s. Bryan William and Dorothea Marie (Fouvy) B.; m. Beverly Ann Knight, Aug. 28, 1955; children: Kimberly, Richard Wade, Janna. B.A., Bowling Green U., 1956; M.A., U. Iowa, 1962, Ph.D., 1964. Reporter, staff writer Dayton (Ohio) Daily News, 1956-57; research assoc., instr., asst. prof., dir. inst. communication studies U. Iowa, Iowa City, 1960-71; prof., disting. prof., assoc. dean (Rutgers Coll.); chmn. dept. human communication Rutgers U., New Brunswick, N.J., 1971-80, dir. Sch. Communication Studies, 1980—; chmn. bd. Newstatements Communications Cons., New Brunswick, 1973—; cons. in field. Author: Introduction to Content Analysis, 1964, Content Analysis of Communication, 1967, Approaches to Human Communication, 1972, Human Communication Handbook Simulations and Games, 1975, Mass Communication: Dialogue and Alternatives, 1976, Beyond Media, 1979, Interdisciplinary Approaches to Communication, 1979; asso. editor: Human Communication Research, 1974—, Communication Quar, 1975—; editorial bd.: Jour. Communication, 1976—, Communication Yearbook, 1977—, Mass Communications Yearbook, 1979—. Mem. Community Arts Council East Brunswick, 1973—; exec. council East Brunswick Youth Baseball Program, 1974; active Boy Scouts Am.; sr. warden Holy Trinity Ch., South River, N.J. Served to lt. USNR, 1957-60. Mem. Internat. Communication Assn. (pres. 1976-77), AAAS, Speech Communication Assn., Am. Assn. Public Opinion Research, Assn. Edn. in Journalism., ALA. Episcopalian. Home: 3 Pilgrim Run East Brunswick NJ 08816 Office: Dept Human Communication Van Dyck Hall Rutgers U New Brunswick NJ 08903

BUDENHOLZER, ROLAND ANTHONY, mechanical engineering educator; b. St. Charles, Mo., Nov. 24, 1912; s. Joseph P. and Mary (Willey) B.; m. Florence C. Christiansen, Nov. 28, 1941; children: Francis Edward, John Christopher, Robert Joseph. B.S. in Mech. Engring, N.Mex. State U., 1935, M.S., Calif. Inst. Tech., 1937, Ph.D., 1939. Grad. asst. Calif. Inst. Tech., 1935-39; research fellow Am. Petroleum Inst., 1939-40; faculty Ill. Inst. Tech., 1940—, prof. mech. engring., 1947—; resident research asso. Argonne Nat. Lab., summer 1961; cons. IIT Research Inst., 1946—; dir. Midwest Power Conf., 1949-52, Am. Power Conf., 1952-78, chmn., 1978—; rep. Am. Power Conf. to World Energy Conf., 1965—; bd. dirs. U.S. nat. com. World Energy Conf., 1972-78, mem. exec. com., 1973-78. Author handbooks; contbr. to encys., profl. jours. Recipient George Westinghouse gold medal Am. Soc. M.E., 1968; award Chgo. Tech. Socs. Council, 1975. Hon. mem. ASME (sec., exec. com. power div. 1967-68, chmn. 1970-71); mem. Am. Nuclear Soc., Am. Soc. Engring. Edn., Nat. Soc. Profl. Engrs., Western Soc. Engrs. (dir. 1969-72), AAUP (pres. Ill. Inst. Tech. chpt. 1963-64), Sigma Xi (pres. Ill. Inst. Tech. chpt. 1948-49), Tau Beta Pi, Pi Tau Sigma, Tau Kappa Epsilon, Triangle. Club: Armour Faculty. Home: 306 Harris Ave Clarendon Hills IL 60514 Office: Ill Inst Tech Chicago IL 60616

BUDGE, HAMER HAROLD, mut. fund co. exec.; b. Pocatello, Idaho, Nov. 21, 1910; m. Jeanne Keithly, Aug. 30, 1941; 1 dau., Kathleen. Student, Coll. of Idaho, 1928-30; A.B., Stanford, 1933; LL.B., U. Idaho, 1936. Bar: Idaho bar 1936. Practiced in, Boise, 1936-42, 46-51, dist. judge, 1961-64; commr. SEC, 1964-69, chmn., 1969-71; chmn. bd., dir. Investors Mut., Inc., Investors Stock Fund, Inc., Investors Selective Fund, Inc., Investors Variable Payment Fund, Inc., IDS New Dimensions Fund, Inc., IDS Progressive Fund, Inc., IDS Growth Fund, Inc., IDS Bond Fund, Inc., IDS Cash Met Fund Inc., Mpls., 1971—. Mem. Idaho Legislature, 1939, 41, 49, majority floor leader; mem. 82d-86th Congresses from 2d Dist. Idaho, mem. rules, appropriations and interior coms.; Bd. dirs. Salvation Army. Served to lt. comdr. USNR, 1942-45. Mem. Am., Idaho bar assns., Sigma Alpha Epsilon. Republican. Mem. Ch. of Jesus Christ of Latter-day Saints. Clubs: Rotarian., Minneapolis, Birnam Wood, Congressional Country, Thunderbird, Burning Tree. Home: 46-790 Amir Dr Palm Desert CA 92260 Office: 1000 Roanoke Bldg Minneapolis MN 55402

BUDIANSKY, BERNARD, educator; b. N.Y.C., Mar. 8, 1925; s. Louis and Rose (Chaplick) B.; m. Nancy Cromer, Dec. 21, 1952; children: Michael, Stephen. B.C.E., CCNY, 1944; Sc.M., Brown U., 1948, Ph.D., 1950. With NACA, Langley Field, Va., 1944-55, head structural mechanics br., 1952- 55; faculty Harvard, 1955—, Gordon McKay prof. structural mechanics, 1961—; vis. prof. Technion, Haifa, Israel, 1976; Mem. research adv. com. on aircraft structures NASA, 1966-71, also adv. com. on space systems and tech., 1978—; mem. U.S. Nat. Com. on Theoretical and Applied Mechanics, 1970-80; mem. materials research council DARPA, 1968—. Bd. editors: Jour. Math. and Physics, 1961-68; cons. editor: Addison-Wesley Pub. Co, 1962-78, North Holland Pub. Co, 1978—; Author tech. reports. Recipient Townsend Harris medal City Coll. N.Y., 1974; Guggenheim fellow Tech. U. Denmark, 1961. Fellow AIAA (asso. editor Jour. 1963-66), ASME; mem. Nat. Acad. Scis., Nat. Acad. Engring., Am. Acad. Arts and Scis., Royal Netherlands Acad. Arts and Scis. (fgn.), Danish Center for Applied Math. and Mechanics (fgn. mem.), ASCE (von Karman medal 1982), Am. Geophys. Union, Sigma Xi, Tau Beta Pi. Home: 11 DeMar Rd Lexington MA 02173 Office: Pierce Hall Harvard Cambridge MA 02138

BUDIG, GENE ARTHUR, university chancellor; b. McCook, Nebr., May 25, 1939; s. Arthur G. and Angela (Schaaf) B.; m. Gretchen VanBloom, Nov. 30, 1963; children: Christopher, Mary Frances, Kathryn Angela. B.S., U. Nebr., 1962, M.Ed., 1963, Ed.D., 1967. Exec. asst. to gov. Nebr., Lincoln, 1964-67; adminstrv. asst. to chancellor, asst. prof. ednl. adminstrn. U. Nebr., Lincoln, 1967-70, asst. vice chancellor acad. affairs, prof. ednl. adminstrn., 1970, asst. v.p., dir. pub. affairs, 1971; v.p., dean univ. Ill. State U., Normal, 1972, pres., 1973-77, W.Va. U., Morgantown, 1977-81; chancellor U. Kans., Lawrence, 1981—. Author: (with Dr. Stanley G. Rives) Academic Quicksand: Expectations of the Administrator, 1973; Editor, contbr.: chpts. Perceptions in Public Higher Education, 1970, Dollars and Sense: Budgeting for Today's Campus, 1972, Higher Education—Surviving the 1980s, 1981; editorial cons.: Phi Delta Kappan, 1976—; Contbr. articles to profl. jours. Mem. Integovernmental Council on Edn., 1980—; trustee William Rockhill Nelson Gallery of Art, Kansas City, Mo.; bd dirs. Truman Library Inst.; bd. dirs. Midwest Research Inst., University Field Staff Internat. Named one of ten outstanding young persons Ill. Jaycees, 1975; one of top 100 leaders in Am. higher edn. Change mag. and Am. Council on Edn., 1979; one of 75 outstanding young men and women educators of Am. Phi Delta Kappa, 1981. Home: 1532 Lilac Ln Lawrence KS 66044

BUDILL, EDWARD JOSEPH, manufacturing company executive; b. Chgo., Apr. 21, 1939; s. Edward Joseph and Anna Louise (Hajek) B.; m. Anne N. Sadler, Dec. 23, 1961; children: Edward McRae, Stephen James. B.S., Purdue U. Prodn. mgr. Harnischfeger Corp., Milw., 1964-69, mktg. mgr., 1969-70, Allis-Chalmers Corp., Milw., 1979-80; pres. Hartman Material Handling Systems, Inc., Victor, N.Y., 1980—; v.p. edn. com. Material Handling Inst., Pitts., 1983—. Lt. USN, 1960-64. Presbyterian. Home: 14 Wandering Trail Pittsford NY 14534 Office: Hartman Material Handling Systems Inc 66 School St Victor NY 14564

BUDINGTON, WILLIAM STONE, librarian; b. Oberlin, Ohio, July 3, 1919; s. Robert Allyn and Mabel (Stone) B. B.A., Williams Coll., 1940, L.H.D., 1975; B.S. in L.S, Columbia, 1941, M.S., 1951; B.S. in Elec. Engring, Va. Poly. Inst., 1946. Reference librarian Norwich U., 1941-42; librarian, engring. and phys. scis. Columbia, 1947-52; asso. librarian John Crerar Library, Chgo., 1952-65, librarian, 1965-69, exec. dir., librarian, 1969—; Mem. U.S.-USSR Spl. Libraries Exchange, 1966; bd, dirs. Center for Research Libraries, 1970-72, chmn., 1972; mem. vis. com. on libraries Mass. Inst. Tech., 1972-77. Served with AUS, 1942-46. Fellow AAAS; mem. ALA, Am. Soc. Info. Sci., Spl. Libraries Assn. (pres. 1964-65), Am. Soc. Engring. Edn., Med. Library Assn., Assn. Research Libraries (dir. 1970-74, pres. 1973, Acad. Research Librarian of Year 1982), Phi Beta Kappa, Tau Beta Pi, Eta Kappa Nu. Clubs: Caxton, Arts. Home: 1350 Lake Shore Dr Chicago IL 60610 Office: 35 W 33d St Chicago IL 60616

BUE, CARL OLAF, JR., judge; b. Chgo., Mar. 27, 1922; s. Carl Olaf and Mabel Port (Shollar) B.; m. Mary Kathryn Waring, Dec. 27, 1948; children—Kathryn Anne, Richard Charles. A.A., U. Chgo., 1942; student, U. Rome, Italy, 1945; Ph.B., Northwestern U., 1951; LL.B., U. Tex., 1954. Bar: Tex. bar 1954. Asso. firm Royston, Rayzor & Cook, Houston, 1954-58, mem. firm, 1958-70; U.S. dist. judge So. Dist. Tex. (Houston div.), 1970—; lectr. various law schs. and admiralty seminars in Tex. and other states. Contbr. articles to profl. jours. Served to capt., Adj. Gen. Dept. AUS, 1942-46; MTO. Recipient Good Citizenship medal Houston chpt. SAR, 1975, Joe R. Greenhill award Tex. Municipal Cts. Assn., 1976-77. Mem. Am., Fed., Tex., Houston bar assns., Maritime Law Assn. of U.S., Am. Judicature Soc., English Speaking Union, Houston Philos. Soc. at Rice U., Alpha Delta Phi, Phi Alpha Delta. Republican. Lutheran. Home: 338 Knipp Rd Houston TX 77024 Office: US Courthouse 515 Rusk Ave Houston TX 77002

BUECHE, WENDELL FRANCIS, manufacturing company executive; b. Flushing, Mich., Nov. 7, 1930; s. Paul D. and Catherine (McGraw) B.; m. Virginia M. Smith, June 14, 1952; children: Denise, Barbara, Daniel, Brian. B.S.M.E., U. Notre Dame, 1952. With Allis-Chalmers Corp., 1952—, dist. mgr., Detroit, 1961-64, sales and mktg. mgr., 1964-69, group exec. v.p., West Allis, Wis., 1973-76, exec. v.p. elec. groups, 1976-77, exec. v.p., chief adminstrv. and fin. officer, 1977-80, chief adminstrv. officer, 1977-80, exec. v.p., head solids process equipment sector and fluids processing group, chief fin. officer, 1980-81, pres., chief operating officer, dir., 1981-83, pres., chief exec. officer, dir., 1984; dir. Fiat-Allis, Siemens-Allis, Svenska Fluid carbon A.B., M&I Marshall Illsley Bank., M&I Corp., Wis. Gas Corp., WICOR, Inc. Mem. The Chgo. Com., 1981—, Greater Milw. Com., 1981—; mem. council Med. Coll. Wis., 1983—. Mem. IEEE, ASME, AIME, Machinery and Allied Products Inst., Nat. Sand and Gravel Assn. (dir.), Nat. Elec. Mfrs. Assn. (gov.). Clubs: Milwaukee Country, Westmoor Country. Office: Allis-Chalmers Corp P O Box 512 Milwaukee WI 53201

BUECHNER, CARL FREDERICK, clergyman, author; b. N.Y.C., July 11, 1926; s. Carl Frederick and Katherine (Kuhn) B.; m. Judith Friedrike Merck, Apr. 7, 1956; children: Katherine, Dinah, Sharman. Grad., Lawrenceville Sch., 1943; A.B., Princeton, 1947; B.D., Union Theol. Sem., 1958. Tchr. English Lawrenceville Sch., 1948-53; tchr. creative writing, summer sessions N.Y.U., 1954-55; chmn. dept. religion Phillips Exeter Acad., 1958-60, sch. minister, 1960-67; ordained to ministry United Presbyn. Ch. U.S.A., 1958; William Belden Noble lectr. Harvard, 1969; Russell lectr. Tufts, 1971; Lyman Beecher lectr. Yale U., 1977; Harris lector Bangor Sem., 1979; Smyth lectr. Columbia Sem., 1981; Trustee Barlow Sch., 1965-71. Author: A Long Day's Dying, 1950, The Seasons' Difference, 1952, The Return of Ansel Gibbs, 1958, The Final Beast, 1965, The Magnificent Defeat, 1966, The Hungering Dark, 1969, The Entrance to Porlock, 1970, The Alphabet of Grace, 1970, Lion Country, 1971 (Nat. Book award nominee), Open Heart, 1972, Wishful Thinking, 1973, Love Feast, 1974, The Faces of Jesus, 1974, Treasure Hunt, 1977, Telling the Truth, 1977, Peculiar Treasures, 1979, The Book of Bebb, 1979, Godric, 1980, The Second Journey, 1982, Now and Then, 1983. Served with AUS, 1944-46. Recipient Irene Glascock Meml. intercollegiate poetry award, 1947; O'Henry prize for story The Tiger, 1955; Richard and Hinda Rosenthal award for the Return of Ansel Gibbs, 1958. Mem. Nat. Council Chs. (com. on lit. 1954-57), Council for Religion in Independent Schs. (regional chmn. 1959-63), Found. for Arts, Religion and Culture, Presbytery No. New Eng., P.E.N., Author's Guild. Club: Century Assn.

BUECHNER, HOWARD ALBERT, physician; b. New Orleans, Feb. 1, 1919; s. Daniel A. and Grace O. (McCrackan) B.; m. Emajean V. Jordan, May 18, 1947. B.S., Tulane U., 1939; M.D., La. State U., 1943. Intern Los Angeles County Gen. Hosp., 1943-44; resident in internal medicine and pulmonary diseases U.S. Army, 1946-47, VA Hosp., New Orleans, 1947-50, chief pulmonary disease sect., 1950-56, chief med. service, 1956-73; clin. prof. medicine Tulane U. Med. Sch., 1956-73; prof. medicine La. State U. Med. Sch., New Orleans, 1973—, chief pulmonary disease sect., 1976—; dir. Tb service Charity Hosp. La., New Orleans, 1976—. Author; editor in field. Served to col., M.C. AUS, 1944-47; Served to col., M.C. USAR, 1960-61. Decorated Bronze Star, Commendation medal, Med. Combat badge. Fellow A.C.P., Am. Coll. Chest Physicians (past gov.); mem. Am. Thoracic Soc., Am. Lung Assn. (past pres. La. chpt., Disting. Service plaque La. chpt. 1969), Phi Beta Kappa., Alpha Omega Alpha. Republican. Baptist. Office: 1542 Tulane Ave New Orleans LA 70112 *My life has been devoted to medicine, primarily as a teacher whose goal has been to impart to his students the true art of medicine and the art of life in terms of integrity, compassion and unselfishness. My rewards have been great, not only in the form of a successful career and many tangible awards from my students, but in the satisfaction that my thoughts and ideas will live on in my books and papers and in the hearts, minds and lives of the legions of young physicians whom I have had the honor to instruct. Thus I have many lives in many places for many years to come.*

BUEDING, ERNEST, educator, biochemist, pharmacologist; b. Frankfurt am Main, Germany, Aug. 19, 1910; came to U.S., 1939, naturalized, 1944; s. Frederick and Katia (Margoulieff) B.; m. Raya Palzeff, Apr. 3, 1940; 1 son, Robert. B.A., Goethe Coll., Frankfurt, 1928; M.D., U. Paris, France, 1936. Fellow Pasteur Inst., Paris, 1933-35; asst. biochemistry U. Istanbul, Turkey, 1936-38; research fellow Coll. Medicine, N.Y.U., 1939-44; asst. prof. pharmacology, then asso. prof. Western Res. U. Med. Sch., 1944-54; prof. pharmacology, chmn. dept. Sch. Medicine, La. State U., 1954-60; prof. pathobiology Sch.

Hygiene and Pub. Health, Johns Hopkins, 1960—, dir., 1969—, prof. pharmacology and exptl. therapeutics, 1966—; vis. Fulbright prof. U. Oxford, Eng., 1959; Guggenheim fellow Oxford, summer 1963; Investigator OSRD, 1941-45; mem. bd. Nat. Vitamin Found., 1949-52; mem. commn. parasitology Armed Forces Epidemiol. Bd., 1953-72; cons. to Surgeon Gen. Dept. Army, 1973—; mem. study sect. tropical medicine and parasitology NIH, 1956-60; mem. panel metabolic biology NSF, 1962-65; cons. WHO, 1961, 63, mem. expert com. schistosomiasis, 1959, 62, expert adv. panel parasitic diseases (bilharziasis), 1963-75; mem. parasitic diseases panel U.S.-Japan Coop. Med. Sci. Program, 1965-71; chmn. U.S. Schistosomiasis del. to, Peoples Republic China, Apr. 1975. Contbr. articles to profl. jours., revs., also chpts. in books.; Mem. editorial bd.: Exptl. Parasitology, 1952-63, Biochem. Pharmacology, 1958-68, Molecular Pharmacol, 1969—, The Johns Hopkins Mag, 1971-73. Founder Cleve. Chamber Music Soc., 1949, pres., 1953-54; founder New Orleans Friends Music, 1955, counselor, 1955-60; pres. Shriver Hall Concert Series, Johns Hopkins, 1965-78. Fellow AAAS; mem. Am. Acad. Arts and Scis., Am. Soc. Biol. Chemists, Am. Soc. Pharmacology and Exptl. Therapeutics (recipient first Theodor Weicker Meml. award 1978), Am. Chem. Soc., Brit. Biochem. Soc., Brit. Pharmacol. Soc. (asso.), Phi Beta Kappa (hon.), Brazilian Soc. Tropical Medicine (hon.). Home: 4001 Roundtop Rd Baltimore MD 21218

BUEHRIG, EDWARD HENRY, educator; b. Minier, Ill., Oct. 4, 1910; s. Edward S. and Emma (Kuhfuss) B.; m. Margaret E. Masters, June 18, 1935; children—Edward M., Robert M. Ph.B., U. Chgo., 1932, M.A., 1934, Ph.D., 1942. Instr. polit. sci. Ind. U., Bloomington, 1934-42, asst. prof., 1942-46, asso. prof., 1946-53, prof., 1953-63, Univ. prof., 1963—, acting chmn. dept., 1966-67; officer Dept. State, 1944-46; faculty Nat. War Coll., 1951; with Brookings Instn., 1952; vis. prof. Am. U., Beirut, 1957-58; Vis. mem. Inst. for Advanced Study, Princeton, N.J., 1948. Author: Woodrow Wilson and the Balance of Power, 1955, The UN and the Palestinian Refugees, 1971; Editor: Wilson's Foreign Policy in Perspective, 1957, Essays in Political Science, 1966; Contbr. articles profl. jours. Recipient Smith-Mundt award, 1957-58, Social Sci. Research Council grant, 1965-66. Mem. Am. Polit. Sci. Assn., Am. Soc. Internat. Law. Home: 1301 Maxwell Ln Bloomington IN 47401

BUELL, EUGENE F(RANKLIN), lawyer; b. Elrama, Pa., Dec. 3, 1916; s. Frank Currey and Altina (Ecklund) B.; m. Elizabeth Ellen Foster, Dec. 28, 1940; children: Ellen E. (dec.), Erik Foster. B.S., St. Vincent's Coll., 1938; grad., Carnegie Inst. Tech., 1938-40, U. Pitts., 1941, Johns Hopkins U., 1942; J.D., Duquesne U., 1944. Bar: D.C. 1949, Canadian Patent Office 1949, U.S. Supreme Ct. 1952. Chemist U.S. Steel Corp., 1938-42; chief chemist Homestead works, 1942-45; with Stebbins, Blenko & Webb, 1945-48; partner firm Blenko, Hoopes, Leonard & Glenn, 1949-52; Blenko, Hoopes, Leonard & Buell, Pitts., 1953-66, Blenko, Leonard & Buell, 1966-72; partner firm Blenko, Buell, Ziesenheim & Beck (P.C.), 1973-79; pres., chmn. Buell, Blenko, Ziesenheim & Beck, P.C., 1979—, Tartan Industries Inc.; treas. Pitts. Performance Products, Inc.; instr. Law Sch. U., Pitts., 1954-59, adj. prof. law, 1959—. Past pres. Richland Com. for Better Govt., Babcock Sch. Dist. Dirs.; chmn. Richland Sch. Authority; mem. Sch. Bd. Richland Twp. Mem. Am. Bar Assn., Am. Patent Law Assn., Engrs. Soc. Western Pa., Pa. Soc., Assn. Bar City N.Y., Licensing Exec. Soc., Am. Arbitration Assn., Interam. Bar Assn., Am. Judicature Soc., Pa. Bar Assn., Allegheny County Bar Assn., Assn. Internationale pour la Protection de la Propriete Industrielle, Order of Coif. Clubs: Duquesne, Elks, Masons, Press, Allegheny, Amen Corner. Home: RD 2 Box 418 Gibsonia PA 15044 Office: 322 Blvd of the Allies Pittsburgh PA 15222

BUELL, HAROLD GEORGE, newspaperman; b. Chgo., Apr. 28, 1931; s. George Clifford and Ethel Lucille (Fisher) B.; m. Angela Barbara Mantell, June 26, 1954; 1 dau., Barbara Kathryn. B.S. in Journalism, Northwestern U., 1953, M.S., 1954. Editor, writer Homewood Review, 1952; writer, photographer UPI, 1953; successively writer and reporter, fgn. corr., picture editor, exec. newsphoto editor, asst. gen. mgr. for newsphotos AP, N.Y.C., 1956—; lectr. on photography; photo contest judge. Author: Young Japan, 1961, Festivals of Japan, 1962, Mainstreets of Southeast Asia, 1963, World of Red China, 1965, Vietnam: Land of Two Dragons, 1968; Picture editor: Triumph and Tragedy, 1968; editor, co-author: The Instant It Happened, 1973; Contbr. articles on photography to periodicals. Served with AUS, 1954-56. Named picture editor of year Nat. Press Photographers Assn., 1972. Mem. Nat. Press Photographers Assn., Sigma Delta Chi. Roman Catholic. Office: care Associated Press 50 Rockefeller Plaza New York NY 10020 *

BUELL, TEMPLE HOYNE, architect, engineer; b. Chgo., Sept. 9, 1895; s. Charles Clinton and Modrea (Hoyne) B.; m. Donna Sherrill Montague, Jan. 14, 1977; children: Callae Mackey (Mrs. E. Atwill Gilman), Temple Hoyne, Beverly Milne (Mrs. John More), Marjorie Daphne (Mrs. Carl Groos), Sidney J. Montague, Jeffrey Clayton Montague. Grad., Lake Forest Acad., 1912; B.S., U. Ill., 1916; M.S., Columbia U., 1917. Registered architect, Colo., N.Mex., Tex., Wyo., Nebr., Utah. Founder, pres. Buell & Co., architects & engrs., Denver, 1923—, Buell Devel. Corp., 1949—; chmn. bd. Kings County Devel. Co. Spl. works include univ. bldgs. secondary and elementary schs., municipal, state and fed. bldgs., shopping centers, others. Chmn. Cherry Hills Planning Commn., 1937—, Arapahoe County Planning Commn., 1939—, Tri-County Planning Commn. and Upper Plate Valley Planning Commn., 1940-42; Trustee Temple Hoyne Buell Found. Served to 1st lt. U.S. Army, 1917-19. Recipient Alumni medal Columbia U., 1932; Alumni Achievement award U. Ill., 1977. Fellow AIA; Mem. Colo. Soc. Engrs., Soc. Mil. Engrs., Nat. Council Archtl. Registration Bds., Chi Psi (pres. 1967—). Clubs: Denver, Country, City, Denver Athletic (Denver); Cherry Hills Country; Metropolitan (N.Y.C.); Camp Fire of Am.; California (Los Angeles). Lodges: Masons (32 deg.); Shriners; K.T.; Jesters; Rotary. Home: 106 S University Blvd Denver CO 80209 Office: Buell Bldg 14th and Stout St Denver CO 80202

BUELL, THOMAS ALLAN, lumber company executive; b. Toronto, Ont., Can., Nov. 14, 1931; s. Allan Foster and Jessie L. (Stayner) B.; m. Phyllis Ann Lee, Aug. 27, 1955; children: Elizabeth, Christopher, Michael, Robert. B.S.C.F. in Forestry, U. Toronto, 1956. Forester Kimberly Clark of Can., 1956-61; mgr. No. Plywoods Co., 1961-64; with Weldwood of Can. Ltd., Vancouver, B.C., 1964—, v.p. mfg., until 1975, pres., chief exec. officer, 1975-79, chmn., pres., chief exec. officer, 1979—; pres. Babine Forest Products Ltd.; vice chmn. Seaboard Lumber Sales Ltd.; dir. Bank of B.C., Goodyear Can. Inc., Lornex Mining Corp. Ltd., Placer Devel. Ltd.; Bd. dirs. Council of Forest Industries of B.C.; chmn. bd. govs. Employers Council B.C. Clubs: Royal Vancouver Yacht, Vancouver. Office: PO Box 2179 Vancouver BC V6B 3V8 Canada

BUELL, VICTOR PAUL, educator, management consultant, author; b. McAlester, Okla., Oct. 18, 1914; s. Victor Paul and Genevieve (Keller) B.; m. Virginia Stevens, May 16, 1942; children: Elizabeth Wilson Buell Barrow, Nancy Trimble Buell Tamms, Victor Paul III. A.B., Pa. State U., 1938; grad., Advanced Mgmt. Program, Harvard U., 1943. Mgr. market research, mgr. ops. Real Silk Hosiery Mills, Inc., Indpls., 1938-51; mktg. cons. McKinsey & Co., N.Y.C., 1952-55; mgr. mktg. div. Hoover Co., North Canton, Ohio, 1955-59; v.p. mktg. Archer Daniels Midland Co., Mpls., 1959-64; corp. v.p. mktg. Am. Standard, Inc., N.Y.C., 1964-70; prof. mktg. Sch. Mgmt., U. Mass., Amherst, 1970-83, prof. emeritus, 1983—; cons. to bus., govt. publs. and assns. Author: Marketing Management in Action, 1966, Changing Practices in Advertising Decision-Making and Control, 1973, Organizing for Marketing/Advertising Success, 1981, Marketing Management: A Strategic Planning Approach, 1984; contbg. author: Effective Marketing Action, 1958, The Marketing Job, 1961, Handbook of Business Administration, 1966, Readings in Marketing Research, 1970, Ency. Profl. Mgmt., 1978, Handbook of Industrial Marketing, 1984; also articles in mags., mktg. jours.; editor-in-chief: Handbook of Modern Marketing, 1970; editorial bd.: Indsl. Mktg.; speaker mgmt., mktg. groups, and seminars. Bd. dirs. Hennepin County United Fund, vice chmn. indsl. campaign; trustee Grad. Sch. Sales Mgmt. and Marketing, Syracuse U. Served from pvt. to maj. Q.M.C., AUS, 1941-45. Recipient award Alpha Kappa Psi, 1975. Mem. Am. Mktg. Assn. (dir. 1957-59, chmn. nat. co. membership com. 1957-58, nat. v.p. 1960-61, pres. 1968-69, chmn. mktg. fund bd., editorial bd. Jour. Mktg.), Home Mfrs. Assn. (dir.), Am. Mgmt. Assn. (mem. nat. planning council), NAM (mktg. com.), Canton Sales Execs. Club (dir. 1956-58, v.p. 1958-59), Sales and Mktg. Execs. Internat., Sales and Mktg. Execs. Western Mass. (dir. 1980—), Assn. Nat. Advertisers (dir.), Beta Gamma Sigma. Congregationalist. Clubs: Faculty (U. Mass.), Hickory Ridge Golf, Rotary. Home: 9 Bridle Path Amherst MA 01002

BUELOW, FREDERICK HENRY, educator; b. Minot, N.D., Mar. 13, 1929; s. Albert Wilhelm Gustav and Frieda Alvina Adele (Hass) B.; m. Selma Lois Ione Eia, July 21, 1954; children—David Frederick, Diane Louise, Darci Jo, Darin Martin. B.S., N.D. Agrl. Coll., 1951; M.S.E., Purdue U., 1952; Ph.D., Mich. State U., 1956. Faculty agrl. engring. Mich. State U., 1956-66, prof., 1965-66; prof., chmn. dept. agrl. engring. U. Wis.-Madison, 1966—. Served to lt. USAF, 1952-54. NSF grantee, 1963, 69, 70. Mem. Am. Soc. Agrl. Engrs. (Jour. Paper award 1957, dir. 1972-74, 77-79), Am. Soc. for Engring. Edn., Sigma Xi, Gamma Sigma Delta. Lutheran. Club: Kiwanis. Home: 6401 Landfall Dr Madison WI 53705

BUELOW, GEORGE JOHN, musicologist, educator; b. Chgo., Mar. 31, 1929; s. George J. and Florence (Cook) B. Mus.B., Chgo. Mus. Coll., 1950, Mus.M., 1951; postgrad., U. Hamburg, Germany, 1953-54; Ph.D., N.Y. U., 1961. Instr. music history Chgo. Conservatory, 1959-61; from asst. prof. to asso. prof. musicology U. Calif., Riverside, 1961-68; prof., chmn. dept. music U. Ky., 1968-69; prof., dir. grad. program in music Rutgers U., New Brunswick, N.J., 1969-77; prof. musicology Ind. U., 1977—; mem. Commn. Mixte Internat. Inventory Musical Sources; co-chmn. Internat. Johann Mattheson Symposium, Wolfenbüttel, W. Ger., 1981. Author: Thorough-bass Accompaniment According to J.D. Heinichen, 1966, Johann Mattheson's Opera, Cleopatra, in Das Erbe deutscher Musik, vol. 69, 1975, (with D. Daviau) The Ariadne auf Naxos by Hofmannsthal and Strauss, 1975; Am. editor: ACTA Musicologica, 1967—; editor: Coll. Music Soc.'s Symposium, 1970-71; mem. exec. com.: The New Grove Dictionary of Music and Musicians, 1971-80; editor: UMI Research Press Studies in Musicology, 1977—; Contbr. articles profl. jours. Fulbright scholar, Germany, 1954-55; Guggenheim fellow, 1967; Rutgers Research Council fellow, 1974-75. Mem. Am., Internat. musicol. socs., Coll. Music Soc., Music Library Assn. Home: 2935 Bankers Dr Bloomington IN 47401 Office: Indiana U Sch Music Bloomington IN 47405

BUEMER, RICHARD EUGENE, engineering, architecture firm executive; b. St. Louis, Feb. 26, 1938; s. Eugene Henry and C. Florence (Braun) B.; m. Judith Louise Rockett, June 25, 1960; children: Kathryn, Karen, Mark. B.S.E.E., Valparaiso U., 1959. Registered profl. engr., Mo., Ill., Ariz., Md., Okla., Ohio, Ga. With Sverdrup & Parcel and Assocs., 1959—, v.p., St. Louis, 1974-78; sr. v.p. Sverdrup & Parcel Assocs., St. Louis, 1979-81; pres. Sverdrup & Parcel Assos., St. Louis, 1982—; dir. Sverdrup Corp., St. Louis, 1979. Bd. dirs. Downtown St. Louis Inc.; div. chmn. United Way St. Louis, 1980; chmn. bd. Lutheran Med. Ctr., St. Louis; trustee St. Louis Luth. High Schs. Recipient Disting. Alumni award Valparaiso U., 1983. Mem. Am. Cons. Engrs. Council (nat. bd. dirs. 1979-82), Am. Nuclear Soc., Assn. Iron and Steel Engrs., Cons. Engrs. Council Mo. (pres. 1980), St. Louis Elec. Bd. (pres. 1983). Lutheran. Clubs: Mo. Athletic, University, Old Warson Country (St. Louis). Office: Sverdrup & Parcel and Assocs Inc 801 N 11th St Saint Louis MO 63101

BUENGER, CLEMENT LAWRENCE, banker; b. Cin., Apr. 27, 1926; s. Clement Lawrence and Estelle (Pelzer) B.; m. Ann McCabe, Apr. 22, 1950. Student, U. Wis., 1943-44; B.S.B.A., Xavier U., Cin., 1950. Acct. Kroger Co., Cin., 1950; exec. v.p. Selective Ins. Co., Cin., 1952-67, Life Ins. Co. Ky., Louisville, 1967-69; pres. Fifth Third Bank, Cin., 1969—, also dir.; dir., pres. Fifth Third Bancorp., parent co. Fifth Third Bank; dir. Hooven & Allison Co., H & A Industries Inc. Trustee St. Xavier High Sch., Cin., Xavier U.; bd. dirs. Boy Scouts Am., ARC; co-chmn. Cin. Bus. Com.; mem. adv. bd. Cin. Council World Affairs. Served with USN, 1943-45. Mem. Assn. Res. City Bankers., Ohio Bankers Assn. (dir.). Republican. Roman Catholic. Clubs: Cin. Country, Bankers, Comml., Queen City. Office: 38 Fountain Sq Plaza Cincinnati OH 45263

BUENO DE MESQUITA, BRUCE JAMES, political science educator; b. N.Y.C., Nov. 24, 1946; s. Abraham Buenio de Mesquita and Clara (Pieniek) Bueno de Mewquita; m. Arlene Carole Bueno de Mesquita, Aug. 11, 1968; children: Erin, Ethan, Gwen. B.A., Queens Coll., 1967; M.A., U. Mich., 1968, Ph.D., 1971. Asst. prof. Mich. State U., East Lansing, 1971-73; asst. prof. to full prof. U. Rochester, 1973—, chmn. dept. polit. sci., 1982—; vis. prof. Yale U., 1979, Cornell U., 1981; bd. dirs. Policon Corp., Ann Arbor, 1983—; cons. Def. Dept., 1982—, Data Resources, inc., 1982—, State Dept., others. Author: The War Trap, 1981, India's Political System, 1979, Strategy, Risk and Personality in Coalition Politics, 1975; contbr. articles to profl. jours. Fgn. polit. adviser John Anderson campaign, 1979-80. Recipient Dag Hammarskjold award City of N.Y., 1966; Guggenheim fellow, 1978; Scaife Family Trusts grantee, 1979—; Hoover Instn. grantee, 1982-83. Fellow Am. Inst. Indian Studies; mem. Am. Polit. Sci. Assn., Internat. Studies Assn. Jewish. Home: 460 Bonnie Brae Ave Rochester NY 14618 Office: Dept Polit Sci Univ Rochester Rochester NY 14627

BUENZ, JOHN BEUCHLER, architect; b. North Platte, Nebr., June 9, 1933; s. Harold Richard and Catherine Louise (Buechler) B.; m. Olga Maries Lindfors, June 19, 1960; children: Theodore, Anne. B.A., Iowa State U., 1957; M.A., Ga. Inst. Tech., 1958. Designer Ero Saarinen & Assocs., 1958, Harry Weese & Assocs., 1960-61, Keck & Keck, 1961-63; designer, pres. Solomon, Cordwell, Buenz & Assocs., Inc., Chgo., 1963—. Mem. Chgo. Com. on Hi-Rise Bldgs., Lincoln Park Conservation Assn., North Michigan Ave. Assn. Fellow AIA. Club: Yacht (Chgo.). Lodge: Rotary Internat. Office: Solomon Cordwell Buenz & Assocs Inc 444 W Grant Pl Chicago Il 60614

BUERGENTHAL, THOMAS, lawyer, educator; b. Lubochna, Czechoslovakia, May 11, 1934; came to U.S., 1951, naturalized, 1957; s. Mundek and Gerda (Silbergleit) B.; children: Robert, John, Alan. B.A., Bethany Coll., 1957; J.D., N.Y. U., 1960; LL.M., Harvard U., 1961, S.J.D., 1968. Bar: N.Y. State 1961, D.C. 1982, U.S. Supreme Ct. 1982. Instr. law U. Pa., 1961-62; asst. prof. SUNY, Buffalo, 1962-64, assoc. prof., 1964-67, prof., 1967-75; vis. prof. U. Tex., Austin, 1975-76, prof., 1976-77, Fulbright and Jaworski prof., 1977-80; judge Inter-Am. Ct. Human Rights, 1979—; dean, prof. law Am. U., Washington, 1980—; asso. reporter, mem. adv. com. Restatement of the Fgn. Relations Law of the U.S.; chmn. human rights com. U.S. Nat. Commn. for UNESCO, 1976-79; U.S. rep. UNESCO Human Rights Working Group, 1977-78; U.S. expert UN Interregional Expert Meeting on Crime Prevention and Control, 1978; mem. adv. bd. Pres. Holocaust Commn., 1978-80; v.p. UNESCO Congress on Teaching of Human Rights, 1978. Author: Law-Making in the International Civil Aviation Organization, 1969, (with L.B. Sohn) International Protection of Human Rights, 1973, (with J.V. Torney) International Human Rights and International Education, 1976, Human Rights, International Law and the Helsinki Accord, 1977, (with R.E. Norris) Human rights: The Inter-Am. System,, 1982; (with Norris and Shelton) Protecting Human Rights in the Americas, 1982; Contbr. articles to profl. jours. Recipient Pro-Humanitas Ring, West-Ost Kulturwerk Fed. Republic of Germany, 1978. Mem. Am. Law Inst., Am. Soc. Internat. Law (v.p. 1980-82), Internat. Law Assn. Democrat. Jewish. Office: American U Coll Law Office of Dean Massachusetts and Nebraska Aves NW Washington DC 20016

BUERGER, DAVID BERNARD, lawyer; b. Phila., Dec. 1, 1909; s. Charles B. and Ada (Fischel) B.; m. Anne M. Fortun, June 30, 1946; 1 son, David C. A.B., U. Pitts., 1928, A.M., 1929; LL.B., Columbia U., 1932, J.D., 1969. Bar: Pa. 1932. Since practiced in, Pitts.; sr. ptnr. Buchanan, Ingersoll, Rodewald, Kyle & Buerger (and predecessors), 1947-83; sole practice, Pitts., 1983—; lectr. taxation and corp. law Com. Continuing Legal Edn., Am. Law Inst., 1951—; pres., Pres., dir. Fourteen Bell Corp. (Jersey City Investment Co.); dir. Don Irwin, Inc., O. Hommel Co., Munroe, Inc., Gestion Milway; sec. Elmhurst Co.; sec., dir. Vantage Broadcasting Co., Heritage Hills Realty, Pitts. Stage, Inc.; Gen. counsel Magee Womens Hosp., Hunt Found., Roy A. Hunt Found., Allegheny Acad., Hampton Civic Assn.; trustee Helen Clay Frick Found., Davis & Elkins Coll. Editor: Columbia Law Rev, 1930-32. Pres. Hampton Civic Assn., 1956-57. Fellow Am. Bar Found.; mem. Am. Law Inst., Am. Arbitration Assn., Am. Judicature Soc., Am. Bar Assn., Sigma Alpha Mu, Omicron Delta Kappa, Delta Sigma Rho. Home: 3000 McCully Rd Allison Park PA 15101 Office: 600 Grant St Rm 5600 Pittsburgh PA 15219

BUERKLE, JACK VINCENT, sociologist, educator; b. West Frankfort, Ill., Aug. 9, 1923; s. Henry Adam and Clemence (Henderson) B.; m. Martha Louise Edwards; children: Stephen Vincent, Melanie Lake. B.A., U. Ill., 1948, M.A., 1949; Ph.D., U. Ia., 1954. Asst. prof. Lake Forest Coll., 1954-55, Yale, 1955-60; mem. faculty Temple U., 1960—, prof. sociology, 1963—, chmn. dept., 1963-71; vis. prof. Der Wirtschaftschochschule, Mannheim, West Germany, 1966-67. Author: Bourbon Street Black, 1973; assoc. editor: Jour. Marriage and the Family, 1982—; Contbr. articles to profl. publs. Served with AUS, 1943-46. Mem. Am. Sociol. Assn., Am. Psychol. Assn., Eastern Sociol. Soc., Institut International de Sociologie, Sigma Xi. Presbyn. (ruling elder). Club: Corinthian Yacht of Cape May (N.J.) (commodore). Home: 526 Revere Rd Merion Station PA 19066 Office: Dept Sociology Temple Univ Philadelphia PA 19122

BUESCHEN, ANTON JOSLYN, physician, educator; b. Toledo, June 7, 1940; s. Robert F. and Mary J. (Joslyn) B.; m. Norma Jean McClanahan, Sept. 5, 1964; children—Anton, Elaine. Student, Va. Mil. Inst., 1958-61; M.D., U. Va., 1965. Diplomate: Am. Bd. Urology. Intern in surgery Vanderbilt U., 1965-66, asst. resident in surgery, 1966-67; resident in urology Ind. U., Indpls., 1969-72; practice medicine specializing in urology, Birmingham, Ala., 1973—; instr. urology Tulane U. Sch. Medicine, 1972-73; asst. prof. div. urology dept. surgery U. Ala., Birmingham, 1973-75, asso. prof., 1975-79, prof., 1979—, dir. div. urology, 1975—; chief urology sect. Children's Hosp., Birmingham, 1978—. Contbr. numerous articles on urology to profl. jours. Served with M.C. U.S. Army, 1967-69. Mem. A.C.S., Am. Urol. Assn., Am. Assn. Clin. Urologists, Soc. Univ. Urologists, Birmingham Urology Club, Jefferson County Med. Soc., Soc. for Pediatric Urology, AMA (Billings Gold medal 1978), AAUP, So. Med. Assn., Med. Assn. Ala. Office: Div Urology Univ Alabama University Station Birmingham AL 35294

BUESCHER, EDWARD LOUIS, virologist; b. Cin., July 24, 1925; s. Edwin B. and Geneva (Summe) B.; m. Elizabeth L. Fincel, June 19, 1947; children: M. Christine, E. Stephen, Michael D., Monica A., Teresa M. B.S., U. Dayton, 1945; M.D., U. Cin., 1948. Diplomate: Am. Bd. Microbiology. Intern Cin. Gen. Hosp., 1948-49; research asso. Children's Hosp. Research Found., Cin., 1948, 49-50; virologist dept. virus and rickettsial diseases Army Med. Dept., Research and Grad. Sch., Washington, 1950-51; chief dept. virus diseases Far East Med. Research Unit, U.S. Army, Tokyo, 1951-54; with Walter Reed Army Inst. Research, Washington, 1954-75, chmn. dept. viral diseases, 1956-67, dir. div. communicable disease and immunology, 1967-70, dep. dir. inst., 1968-70, dir. inst., 1970-75; chmn. D/A Vol. Program Study Group, Office Surgeon Gen. U.S. Army, Washington, 1975-77; dep. chief staff research ops. U.S. Army Med. Research and Devel. Command, Washington, 1977-79; program dir. RSCH Health Hazards, 1979-80; dir. Task Force Antidote Devel., 1980-82, dir. devel. and prodn. mgmt., 1982—; clin. asso. prof. pediatrics Georgetown U., 1963-69, prof., 1969—; mem. commn. on virus infections Armed Forces Epidemiol. Bd., 1965-72. Recipient Gorgas medal Assn. Mil. Surgeons U.S., 1965. Fellow Am. Acad. Microbiology; mem. Am. Soc. Tropical Medicine and Hygiene, Am. Assn. Immunologists, Am. Soc. Microbiology, Am. Fedn. Clin. Research, Am. Epidemiol. Soc., Infectious Disease Soc. Am. Research, numerous publs. on natural history of Japanese encephalitus virus. Co-discoverer Rubella virus; ecology of human respiratory viruses; mil. occupational medicine. Home: 9213 Midwood Rd Silver Spring MD 20910 Office: Hdqrs US Army Med Research and Devel Command Fort Detrick MD *Progress in research and development, much like sailing, depends upon maintaining "steerage way." In research "way" is maintained by continuous flow of new information. When that flow is slowed or interrupted, "steerage way" is lost; without it, change in direction is impossible.*

BUESINGER, RONALD ERNEST, security and commodity brokerage executive; b. Taylorville, Ill., Nov. 22, 1933; s. Ernest Vern and Emma Gene (Newman) B.; m. Jean Ford, Aug. 20, 1955; children: Robert F., Janet L., Judith B., Mary J., Ronald Ernest. B.A. cum laude, Washington U., 1955. Corp. v.p. A.G. Edwards & Sons, Inc., St. Louis, 1959—, dir., 1967—, corporate sec., 1967—, chief of staff, 1967—, mem. exec. com., 1967—; Mem. Chgo. Bd. of Trade, 1968—, Phila.-Balt.-Washington Stock Exchange, 1972—; mem. test adv. com. N.Y. Stock Exchange. Served to capt. USAF, 1955-58. Mem. Securities Industry Assn. (human resources com. 1978—), Am. Soc. Personnel Adminstrn., Indsl. Relations Assn. St. Louis, Nat. Assn. Securities Dealers (chmn. com. on qualifications), Tau Kappa Epsilon. Home: 8029 Davis Dr Clayton MO 63105 Office: 1 N Jefferson St St Louis MO 63103

BUESSELER, JOHN AURE, ophthalmologist; b. Madison, Wis., Sept. 30, 1919; s. John Xavier and Gerda Pernille (Aure) B.; m. Cathryn Anne Hansen, Dec. 26, 1959; 1 son, John McGlone. Ph.B., U. Wis., 1941, M.D., 1944; M.S., U. Mo., 1965. Intern Cleve. City Hosp.,

1944-45; resident U. Pa. Hosp., 1948-51; practice medicine, specializing in ophthalmology, Madison, 1953-59; prof., founding chief ophthalmology U. Mo., Columbia, 1959-66; exec. officer Mo. Crippled Children's Service, 1967-70; exec. dir. Kansas City Gen. Hosp. and Med. Center, 1969-70; v.p. health affairs Tex. Tech U. Complex, Lubbock, 1970-75, founding dean, 1970-73, prof. dept. ophthalmology, 1971—, prof. health orgn. mgmt., 1971—, prof. grad. sch. faculty, 1972-80, chmn. dept. ophthalmology, 1973-75, chmn. dept. health orgn. mgmt., 1972-75; Univ. prof. (distinguished and multidisciplinary) Univ. Complex, 1973—, v.p. health scis., 1972-74; pres. Radiol. Testing Lab., Inc., Madison, 1956-59; dir. House of Vision, Inc., Chgo., 1973-82; v.p. Madison Radiation Center, Inc., 1956-59; cons. NASA; mem. space medicine adv. group on devel. Orbiting Space Lab., Washington, 1963-66; cons. AEC; mem. Asso. Midwestern Univs.-Argonne Nat. Lab. biology com., Argonne, Ill., 1965-69; cons. to pres. Argonne Univs. Assn., Chgo., 1967-68; comdr. 94th Gen. Hosp., U.S. Army Res., Mesquite, Tex., 1973-75; co-founder, incorporator, bd. dirs., past pres. Joint Commn. on Allied Health Personnel in Ophthalmology, Inc.; mem. Residency Rev. Com. for Ophthalmology, 1974-80, chmn., 1978-80; sr. cons. Health Orgn. Mgmt. Systems Internat., 1978—. Contbr. articles to profl. jours. Served to capt. AUS, World War II; ETO; to maj. USAF, Korean Conflict; to col. USAR; Indochina, S. Vietnam. Decorated Air medal; Combat Med. badge; recipient Gold Medallion award for distinguished achievement in ophthalmology Mo. Ophthal. Soc., 1967, Tex. Tech U. Bd. Regents resolution of congratulations, 1973, certificate of citation Tex. Ho. of Reps., 1973. Fellow A.C.S., Am. Acad. Ophthalmology (Distinguished Service in Edn. award 1969); mem. AMA, Tex. Med. Assn., Assn. Mil. Surgeons U.S., Soc. Mil. Ophthalmologists, Mo. Ophthal. Soc. (founder, past sec.-treas., pres., dir.), Acad. Mgmt., Am. Assn. Univ. Adminstrs., AAAS, Soc. U.S. Army Flight Surgeons, Sigma Xi., Alpha Omega Alpha. Home: 3313 23d St Lubbock TX 79410

BUESSEM, NIELS CHRISTIAN, publishing company executive; b. Berlin, Germany, Feb. 5, 1934; s. Wilhelm R. and Gritta (Hennig) B.; m. Janet Evans, June 18, 1960; children: Christopher, William. B.A., Pa. State U., 1958; student, U. Munich, Germany, 1955-56, Sorbonne, Paris, 1956. Editorial dir. Charles E. Merrill (pub.), Columbus, Ohio, 1959-61; exec. editor Harcourt, Brace, Jovanovich, N.Y., 1961-69; pres. Grune & Stratton, Inc., N.Y.C., 1969-73; v.p., gen. mgr. John Wiley & Sons, Inc., N.Y.C., 1973-81; sr. v.p. C.B.S. Profl. Pub., W.B. Saunders Co., Phila., 1981—. Served with USAF, 1961-62. Mem. Internat. Group Sci., Tech. and Med. Pubs., Am. Med. Publ. Assn. (pres.), Am. Mgmt. Assn., Am. Inst. Ultrasound in Medicine, Assn. Ind. Clin. Publs. (dir.), Sigma Nu. Home: 1500 Pine St Philadelphia PA 19102 Office: West Washington Sq Philadelphia PA 19105

BUESSER, FREDERICK GUSTAVUS, JR., lawyer; b. Detroit, Mar. 3, 1916; s. Frederick G. and Lela (Carpenter) B.; m. Betty Ronal, Jan. 2, 1939; children: Frederick Gustavus III, William Ronal, Anne Alexander (Mrs. Edward Reynolds). A.B., U. Mich., 1937, LL.B., 1940. Bar: Mich. 1940. Practiced in, Detroit, 1940-44, 46-48; mem. firm Chase, Goodenough & Buesser, Detroit, 1948-66, Buesser, Buesser, Snyder & Blank, 1966—; columnist The Detroit Lawyer, 1949—; counsel Wayne County Med. Soc. Trustee Detroit Country Day Sch., 1942-70; trustee Mich. Delta Found., 1948—, pres., 1951-53; dir. U. Mich. Alumni Interfrat. Council, 1953-58, pres., 1956-58. Served from pvt. to 1st lt. 770 Mil. Police Bn. AUS, 1944-46. Fellow Am. Bar Found., Am. Coll. Trial Lawyers, Internat. Soc. Barristers, Am. Acad. Matrimonial Lawyers; mem. ABA (state del. for Mich.; past chmn. standing com. on unauthorized practice law, former mem. standing com. nat. conf. groups, chmn. standing com. on fed. judiciary), Mich. Bar Assn., Detroit Bar Assn. (dir. 1953-59, 1st v.p. 1957, pres. 1958-59), Am. Judicature Soc., State Bar Mich. (pres. 1971-72), Nat. Conf. Bar Presidents, 6th Circuit Fed. Jud. Conf. (life), Lambda Sigma, Delta Tau Delta, Phi Delta Phi. Episcopalian (asst. chancellor Mich. diocese, chmn. bishop's com., sr. warden). Clubs: Thomas M. Cooley, Detroit Athletic, Huron River Hunting Fishing, University of Michigan (gov. 1956-60), Detroit (Detroit); Delray Beach Yacht. Home: 2450 Bradway Blvd Birmingham MI 48010 Office: 4190 Telegraph Rd Bloomfield Hills MI 48226

BUETER, ARNOLD GERHARD, govt. ofcl.; b. N.Y.C., July 31, 1917; s. Frederick W. and Johanna (Mertins) B.; m. Mary Eleanor Minzler, Aug. 22, 1945; 1 dau., Christine E. Rudy. B.B.A. cum laude, Coll. City N.Y., 1939; M.B.A., George Washington U., 1965. C.P.A., N.Y. Sr. accountant Seidman & Seidman (C.P.A.'s), N.Y.C., 1939-43; with auditor gen. USAF, 1946-59, dist. dir., Chgo., 1954-59, asso. dir. accounting and fin., Washington, 1959-65, dep. comptroller, 1965-74, prin. dep. to asst. sec. Air Force for fin. mgmt., 1974-80; dir., treas. ACCA Day Care Center, Annandale, Va., 1981—; chmn. panel Air Force Bd. for Correction of Mil. Records, 1969-80; mem. Air Force Contract Adjustment Bd., 1974-80; asso. prof. bus. adminstrn. Univ. Coll., U. Md., 1962—; lectr. acctg. George Mason U., 1980—; cons., 1980—. Served with USAAF, 1943-46. Recipient Disting. service medal Dept. Def., 1980. Mem. Am. Inst. C.P.A.'s, Am. Accounting Assn., Am. Soc. Mil. Comptrollers, Fed. Govt. Accountants Assn. (Meritorious Civilian Service award 1965, Exceptional Civilian Service award 1971, 74, 75, 77), Beta Gamma Sigma. Lutheran (trustee 1966—). Home: 3412 Fiddlers Green Falls Church VA 22044

BUETOW, DENNIS EDWARD, educator; b. Chgo., June 20, 1932; s. Earl Frank and Helen Anna (Roeske) B.; m. Mary Kathleen Carney, 29, 1960; children—Katherine, Thomas, Michael, Ellen. B.A., UCLA, 1954, M.S., 1957, Ph.D., 1959. Biologist NIH, Bethesda, Md., 1959-65; biochemist Balt. City Hosps., 1959-65; asso. prof. physiology U. Ill., Urbana, 1965-70, prof., 1970—; cons. in field. Contbr. articles in field. NIH grantee; NSF grantee; Life Ins. Med. Research Fund grantee. Fellow Gerontological Soc.; mem. Am. Soc. Cell Biology, Am. Physiol. Soc., AAAS, Am. Inst. Biol. Sci., Soc. Protozoologists, Am. Fedn. Aging Research, N.Y. Acad. Sci., Am. Soc. Plant Physiology. Home: 2 Eton Ct Champaign IL 61820 Office: 524 Burrill Hall University of Illinois Urbana IL 61801

BUFF, CONRAD, III, architect; b. Glendale, Calif., Aug. 5, 1926; s. Conrad, II and Mary (Marsh) B.; m. Mary Elizabeth Grider, Sept. 5, 1947; children: Conrad, IV, Christopher Ann. B.Arch., U. So. Calif., 1952. Asst. prof. architecture U. So. Calif., 1952-60; partner firm Buff, Straub & Hensman, Los Angeles, 1952-60, Buff & Hensman, Pasadena, Calif., 1960—. Prin. works include Gov.'s Residence, State of Calif., Sacramento, Paul Anka residence, Carmel, Calif., James Garner residence, Los Angeles, Stanley Marsh III residence, Amarillo, Tex., Dr. Ben Mirman residence, Pasadena, Calif. Served with USNR, 1944-46. Fellow AIA (27 excellence archtl. design awards). Office: 1450 W Colorado Blvd Pasadena CA 91105 *

BUFF, FRANK PAUL, chemist, educator; b. Munich, Germany, Feb. 13, 1924; came to U.S., 1937, naturalized, 1944; s. Heinrich and Johanna Helene (Guggenheimer) B.; m. Iva Mary Moore, Dec. 21, 1956; children—Susan Kathleen, Marjorie Anne. A.B., U. Calif., Berkeley, 1944; Ph.D., Calif. Inst. Tech., 1949. Jr. chemist Shell Devel. Co., Emeryville, Calif., 1946; research fellow Calif. Inst. Tech., Pasadena, 1949-50; prof. chemistry U. Rochester, N.Y., 1950—; vis. prof. Inst. Theoretical Physics, Utrecht, Netherlands, 1959-60; cons. Mobil Research Corp.; summer visitor Bell Telephone Labs., 1962. Contbr.: chpt. to Handbook of Physics, 1960; Bd. editors: Jour. Statis. Physics, 1971—; Contbr. articles profl. jours. Served with AUS, 1944-46. Recipient research grants NSF, Office Saline Water; AEC postdoctoral fellow, 1949-50; NSF sr. postdoctoral fellow, 1959-60. Fellow Am. Phys. Soc., Am. Inst. Chemists, A.A.A.S.; mem. Am. Chem. Soc., AAUP, Phi Beta Kappa, Sigma Xi. Home: 90 Roby Dr Rochester NY 14618

BUFFETT, JIMMY, singer, songwriter; b. Pascagoula, Miss., Dec. 25, 1946; s. James Delaney and Loraine (Peets) B.; m. Jane Slagsvol, Aug. 27, 1977. B.S. in History and Journalism, U. So. Miss., 1969. Free-lance journalist: Inside Sports, Outside mag; Albums include Changes in Latitudes (Platinum Album), Son of a Son of a Sailor, (Platinum Album), You Had To Be There, (Platinum Album), Volcano, (Gold Album), Coconut Telegraph, Somewhere Over China, One Particular Harbour; performed benefit concert for anti-nuclear legislation. Chmn. Save the Manatee Commn., Fla. Mem. Cousteau Soc., Greenpeace Found. (hon. dir.). Democrat. Roman Catholic. Office: 9044 Melrose Ave Los Angeles CA 90069

BUFFETT, WARREN EDWARD, corporate executive; b. Omaha, Aug. 30, 1930; s. Howard Homan and Leila (Stahl) B.; m. Susan Thompson, Apr. 19, 1952; children: Susan, Howard, Peter. Student, U. Pa., 1947-49; B.S., U. Nebr., 1950; M.S., Columbia, 1951. Investment salesman Buffett-Falk & Co., Omaha, 1951-54; security analyst Graham-Newman Corp., N.Y.C., 1954-56; gen. partner Buffett Partnership, Ltd., Omaha, 1956-69; chmn. bd. Berkshire, Hathaway, Inc., Nat. Indemnity Co., Nat. Fire & Marine Ins. Co., Asso. Retail Stores, Inc., See's Candy Shops, Inc., Columbia Ins. Co., Buffalo Evening News; dir. Blue Chip Stamps, Omaha Nat. Corp., Washington Post Co. Bd. govs. Boys Clubs Omaha, 1962—; trustee Grinnell Coll., 1968—, Urban Inst. Home: 5505 Farnam St Omaha NE 68132 Office: 1440 Kiewit Plaza Omaha NE 68131

BUFFINGTON, RALPH MELDRIM, architect; b. White Sulphur, Ga., Feb. 7, 1907; s. Marion Cook and Frances Louvinia (Moss) B. B.S. in Architecture, Ga. Inst. Tech., 1928; scholar pvt. study, Europe, 1929-30; also, Ecole Speciale d'Architecture. Registered profl. architect, Tex., Ga. Practice architecture as Ralph M. Buffington, Houston, 1939-42, 1946-66, 76—; asso. Buffington & McAllister, Houston, 1966-75; cons. Bapt. fgn. mission projects, Hawaii, Hong Kong, Taiwan, Thailand, Philippines, Indonesia, Mexico, Santo Domingo, Barbados, Antigua Barbados, and, Venezuela. Prin. archtl. works include Chinese Bapt. Evangelistic Temple; 8 Houston schs., Taipeh Bapt. Sem, Taiwan, schs.; auditorium, 1st Bapt. Ch., Curitiba, Brazil; Bapt. Theol. Sem., State of Minas Gerais, Belo Horizonte, Brazil; other instns. and residences.; Author: Buffington Family in America, 1965. Served with AUS, 1942-45; PTO. Recipient Outstanding Service commendation Houston C. of C., 1962, also various archtl. awards. Mem. AIA, Tex. Soc. Architects, Nat. Geog. Soc. Nat. Council Archtl. Registration Bds. Democrat. Baptist. Home: Route 1 Box 184 Pendergrass GA 30567 *Man's greatest privilege is the opportunity to work and serve creatively his fellowman—in so doing he serves God.*

BUFFINTON, PHILIP GARDNER, insurance company executive; b. North Adams, Mass., Oct. 18, 1923; s. Arthur H. and Mary (Edwards) B.; m. Rita Gagnier, Oct. 22, 1945; children: Denise Buffinton Adamson, Nancy Buffinton Kurth, Joan Buffinton Sellberg. B.S., Worcester Poly. Inst., 1949. Registered profl. engr., R.I. Fire protection engr. Factory Mut. Ins. Cos., Providence, 1949-54, mgr. Factory Mut. Rating Bur., 1954-61; exec. asst. State Farm Fire & Casualty Co., Bloomington, Ill., 1961, v.p., 1961—, sec., 1975—, chief adminstrv. officer, 1975, dir.; dir. State Farm Gen. Ins. Co., Bloomington, State Farm Lloyd's of Tex. Served to 1st lt. USAAF, 1942-45; ETO. Mem. Casualty Actuarial Soc. (assoc.), Am. Acad. Actuaries, Seismol. Soc. Am., Am. Meteorol. Soc. Republican. Clubs: Bloomington Country; Belleview Biltmore Country (Belleair, Fla.). Home: 210 Imperial Dr Bloomington IL 61701 Office: State Farm Fire& Casualty Co 112 E Washington St Bloomington IL 61701

BUFFKINS, ARCHIE LEE, performing arts adminstr.; b. Memphis, Mar. 30, 1934; s. John and Ada (Stittians) B.; (div.)1 dau., LeRachel Harombe. B.S., Jackson State U., 1956; M.A., Columbia, 1961, Ed.D., 1963; postgrad. research, Harvard, summer 1972, Oxford U., summer 1972, U. Amsterdam, summer 1972, Tel-Aviv U., 1973-74, U. Me., 1970-71, Chgo. Conservatory, summer 1956. Instr. div. band music Ft. Ord (Calif.) Mil. Band Sch., 1957-58; instr., chmn. div. humanities Morristown (Tenn.) Coll., 1958-59; asst. prof., dir. freshman studies, div. fine arts Jackson (Miss.) State U., 1960-61; asso. prof., head dept. music Ky. State U., Frankfort, 1963-66; prof., dir. grad. research in music, dept. music and fine arts Tex. So. U., Houston, 1966-68; prof., chmn. dept. music R.I. Coll., Providence, 1968-70; exec. asst. to chancellor U. Maine Eight-Campus System, Portland, 1970-71; chancellor U. Md., Eastern Shore, Princess Anne, 1971-75, asst. dean grad. studies, 1975-79; pres. Nat. Commn. on Cultural Diversity, Kennedy Center, 1979—; commr. higher edn. Afro-Am. Edn. Assn. in R.I., 1968-71; dir. Conf. on Black Students and Higher Edn. in R.I., R.I. Coll., 1969, Conf. on Higher Edn. and Urban Setting, Boston, 1969; coordinator Conf. on Afro-Am. Studies and High Sch. Curriculum, U. Maine, 1971; chmn. Nat. Black Think Tank, 1976; pres. John F. Kennedy Center Nat. Commn. on Blacks in the Arts; Chief adminstr. Free Urban Edn. Center, Houston, 1966-68; dir. Acad. Tutorial Inst. in Black Community of Houston, 1966-68, Black Fine Arts Festival, 1966; exec. dir. Eastern div. Council on Afro-Am. Studies, Boston, 1968-71; chmn. exptl. curriculum com. Gov.'s Sch. for Gifted in Arts, Providence, 1968, bd. dirs., 1969-70; chmn. ednl. policy com., bd. dirs. Nat. Sch. Vol. Program, Inc., N.Y.C., 1968—; chmn. edn. task force (Portland Model Cities Project), 1970-71; founder, dir. Center for Exptl. Studies in Higher Edn. Adminstrn., Portland, 1970-71; sr. adviser Nat. Accrediting Assn. for Afro-Am. Programs, N.Y.C., 1968-71; mem. U.S. Nat. Adv. Council on Adult Edn., 1944—; chmn. Nat. Task Force on Adult Edn. and Urban Policy, 1977, Nat. Black Music Colloquium and Competition, 1978, Md. Black Congress on Higher Edn.; coordinator Black Higher Edn. Caucus of U. Md. System; chmn. Nat. Task Force on Urban Policy and Adult Edn.; chmn. exec. council Regional Research and Clearinghouse Network on Minorities and Grad. Edn. Producer: Tribute to Historically Black Colls. and Univs, 1980, White House/Kennedy Center Jazz Salute to Lionel Hampton, White House Phase I, Kennedy Center Concert Hall Phase II, 1981; appeared with, Monterey Symphony Orch., Bach Festival Orch., Columbia U. Orch., Riverside Symphony Orch., Waukegan Community Orch., Tchrs. Coll. Concert Wind Ensemble, Ft. Ord Symphonic Concert Band, San Jose Woodwind Ensemble, Memphis String and Woodwind Chamber Ensemble.; co-producer: television series Tell It Like It Is, Community Service Television Project, Houston, 1967; Author: An Intellectual Approach to Musical Understanding, 1965, Philosophical Thoughts of a University Scholar, 1973, Arts Advocacy: The Economic Impact of the Arts in an Age of Austerity, Parts I and II; mem. bd. advisers, bd. dirs.: Urban Concerns mag; contbr. articles to profl. jours.; Composer: The Night Is Dark, 1967, Trio in A Minor, 1967, Mass, 1967, Integrity: Tone Poem for String Orchestra, 1968, Symphony For Tomorrow, 1969, Melodies For A Soprano, 1969, String Quartet No. 2, 1972, Sonata For Violin and Piano, 1972, Suite For Violin and Piano, 1972, Sonatina for Violin and Piano (for Sanford Allen), 1980, others. Bd. dirs. Eastern Shore Heart Assn., Salisbury, Md., R.I. Council on Arts, R.I. Philharmonic Orch., Internat. Econ. Devel. Corp., 1969-70, Afro-Art Center, Inc., 1968-70, Maine Savs. Bank, Center for Experiments in Higher Edn., Houston, 1967-70; trustee Peninsula Gen. Hosp., Salisbury, Portland Symphony Orch.; mem. exec. bd. Afro-Am. Soc., N.Y.C., 1966-70, New Eng. States Coll. Assn. Music Faculties, Plymouth, N.H., 1968-70, Delmarva council Boy Scouts Am., Wilmington, Del.; mem. corp. bd. Edn. Devel. Center, Inc., Newton, Mass., 1970-72, Peoples Savs. Bank & Trust, Providence, 1968-70; mem. exec. bd. Nat. Christian Leadership Conf. for Israel; mem. Nat. Arts Evaluation Panel for Minority Programs; bd. dirs. Afro-Am. Museums Assn., Washington, 1980—; mem. adv. bd. D.C. Youth Chorale Assn., 1981—; mem. nat. task force on anti-Semitic incidents Anti-Defamation League, N.Y.C., 1980—; mem. nat. steering com. Martin Luther King Holiday, Washington, 1980—; mem. planning com. Nat. Black Coll. Day, Washington, 1981—; mem. Com. for a Free World, N.Y.C., 1981—; mem. exec. com. Coalition for Strategic Stability in Middle East, Washington, 1981—. Served with AUS, 1956-58. Recipient Young Classical Musician award Memphis Music Soc., 1952; Black Intellectual Leadership award Houston, 1967; Disting. Alumni award Jackson State U., 1973; Nat. Cultural Recognition award, Tuskegee, Ala., 1981; named to Mid-Eastern Athletic Conf. Hall of Fame, Durham, N.C., 1981. Mem. Md. Assn. for higher Edn. (chmn. panel adminstrv affairs 1973), Middle States Assn. Colls. and Secondary Schs. (evaluation bd. 1972—), Am. Council on Edn., Nat. Assn. State Univs. and Land-Grant Colls., NAACP (exec. bd. Prince George's chpt. 1979—, chmn. edn. com. 1980—). Address: Exec Suite Kennedy Center Washington DC 20566

BUFFUM, WILLIAM BURNSIDE, govt. ofcl.; b. Binghamton, N.Y., Sept. 10, 1921; s. Frederic Francis and Lucy (Davis) B.; m. Alma Emma Bauman, Sept. 25, 1944; children—Karen Buffum Clarkson, Diane Buffum Klieforth, Andrea. B.E., Oneonta State Tchrs. Coll., 1943; M.Litt., U. Pitts., 1949; student, Oxford U., 1946, Harvard U., 1952-53. Instr. U. Pitts., 1946-49; vice-consul U.S. Dept. State, Stuttgart, 1946-49; polit. officer, Bonn, 1953-58; dir. polit. affairs Bur. Internat. Orgn. Affairs, Washington, 1959-67, dep. asst. sec., 1965-67; dep. U.S. rep. to UN, 1967-70; U.S. ambassador to Lebanon, 1970-73, asst. sec. state for internat. orgn. affairs, Washington, 1973—; now under-sec.-gen. for polit. and Gen. Assembly affairs UN. Served with AUS, 1943-46. Mem. Sigma Chi Sigma. Address: United Nations New York NY 10017 *

BUFKIN, ISAAC DAVID, energy diversified company executive; b. Haynesville, La., May 16, 1922; s. Floran E. and Pauline E. B.; m. Lee Elmo Renfrow, Apr. 23, 1944; children: Peggy Bufkin Gerst, David Michael. B.S., La. Tech. U., 1948. Mech. engr. NACA, Langley Field, Va., 1948-49; with Tex. Eastern Transmission Corp., Houston, 1949-79, v.p. gas mktg. and rates, 1968-71, v.p. gas ops., 1971-79; exec. v.p. Tex. Eastern Corp., Houston, 1979, pres., chief operating officer, 1979-80, pres., chief exec. officer, 1980—, chmn. bd., chief exec. officer, 1980—; dir. First City Bancorp. Tex., Inc., Transwestern Pipeline.; Bd. dirs. Conf. Bd., Gas Research Inst., Am. Petroleum Inst.; mem. Nat. Petroleum Council, Interstate Oil Compact Commn. Bd. dirs. Stehlin Found. for Cancer Research, Central Houston, Inc., Rice Ctr., Sam Houston area Boy Scouts Am. Served with USAAF, 1943-46. Mem. La. Engring. Soc., Nat. Soc. Profl. Engrs., Pacific Coast Gas Assn., New Eng. Gas Assn., Soc. Gas Lighting, Gas Men's Roundtable Washington, So. Gas Assn., Interstate Natural Gas Assn. Am. (dir.), Newcomen Soc. N. Am., Houston C. of C. (bd. dirs.). Baptist. Club: Forum (Houston) (dir.). Office: PO Box 2521 Houston TX 77252

BUFMAN, ZEV, producer, theatre chain executive; b. Tel Aviv, Oct. 11, 1930; naturalized, 1963; s. Mordekhai and Haya (Torban) B.; m. Vilma Greul, July 6, 1962; children: Denise, Kurt, Gil. A.A., Los Angeles City Coll., 1953; B.A., Los Angeles State Coll., 1955, M.A., 1956; Ph.D. (hon.), Nova. U., 1981. Owner, operator Zev Bufman Entertainment, Inc. (theatre chain), Miami Beach, Fla., Palm Beach, Fla., Ft. Lauderdale, Fla., New Orleans, Kev Bufman Entertainment, Inc. (theatre chain), Orlando, Fla., St. Petersburg, Fla. Actor theatre, films and TV, 1952-56; theatre dir., 1957-58; producer: Broadway plays Vintage 60, 1960, Marat/Sade, 1966, Your Own Thing, 1968 (Drama Critics Best Musical 1968), Spofford, 1968, Jimmy Shine, 1969, Buck White, 1969, Peter Pan, 1980, Oklahoma, 1980, Brigadoon, 1980, Little Foxes, 1981, Joseph and the Amazing Technicolor Dreamcoat, 1982, Private Lives, 1983, A View From the Bridge, 1983, The Corn is Green, 1983, Peg, 1983, Smile, 1983; co-producer: nat. tour of Nine and Jerry's Girls, 1984—. Served to 1st lt. Israeli Army, 1948-50. Named Man of Yr. Miami Beach C. of C., 1977.

BUFORD, CURTIS DONALD, railroad car leasing company executive; b. Sioux City, Ia., July 6, 1920; s. Charles Homer and Bess (Thomas) B.; m. Barbara Anderson, Apr. 29, 1947; children—Nancy Joanne, Jerome Donald, Roberta Jane, William Warwick, Ruth Elizabeth, John Anderson. B.S., Mass. Inst. Tech., 1942. With N.Y. Central R.R., 1946-59; v.p. operations and maintenance Assn. Am. Railroads, 1959-64; exec. v.p. P. & L.E. R.R., 1964, pres., dir., 1965-69, Trailer Train Co., 1969-82, chmn., 1982—; dir. Alleghany Corp. Served to capt. AUS, 1942-46; PTO, ETO. Mem. Am. Soc. M.E., Newcomen Soc. N.Am., Transp. Assn. Am. (dir.). Clubs: Duquesne (Pitts.); Metropolitan (Washington); Glen View Country (Golf, Ill.); Chicago (Chgo.). Office: 101 N Wacker Dr Chicago IL 60606

BUFORD, EDWIN RUCKER, mfg. co. exec.; b. Dallas, Feb. 19, 1935; s. John Edwin and Georgia Sue (Rucker) B.; m. Virginia Elaine Hampton, Feb. 15, 1958; children—Berrick Rucker, John Blanchard. B.B.A., North Tex. U., 1957; M.B.A., Tex. Christian U., 1963. Cost analyst LTV, Inc., Grand Prairie, Tex., 1957-61; budget supr. Gen. Dynamics Corp., Ft. Worth, 1961-66; comptroller, plant mgr. Baifield Industries, Inc., Carrollton, Tex., 1966-69; asst. corp. controller ATO, Inc., Cleve., 1969; with Temtex Industries Inc., Dallas, 1970—, sr. v.p., 1974-78, pres., 1978—, also dir. Mem. Fin. Execs. Inst., Chief Execs. Round Table. Republican. Methodist. Home: 10 Forest Park Dr Richardson TX 75080 Office: 1601 LBJ Freeway Suite 605 Dallas TX 75248

BUGG, JAMES LUCKIN, JR., univ. pres.; b. Farmville, Va., July 25, 1920; s. James Luckin and Clair (Woodruff) B.; m. Anne Barrington Hunter, June 25, 1956; children—Anne Barrington, James Luckin, III. A.B., Hampden-Sydney Coll., 1941; M.A., U. Va., 1942, Ph.D., 1950. Instr. history U. Mo., Columbia, 1949-50, asst. prof., 1950-54, asso. prof., 1954-60, prof., 1960-63, chmn. dept., 1959-62, dean faculty, 1963-65, chancellor, 1965-69; pres. Old Dominion U., Norfolk, Va., 1969-76, Constance and Colgate Darden Chair prof. in history and edn., 1976—; Mem. Nat. Commn. Coll. work, Episcopal Ch., 1964-69; chmn. dept. coll. work and commn. ministry Diocese of So. Va., 1969-80; chmn. cons. stewardship; mem. region XI selection com. Woodrow Wilson Scholarship Found., 1958-69; mem. adv. council Va. Commn. on Higher Edn., 1969-76; chmn. Tidewater Va. Consortium Higher Edn., 1973-76; mem. adv. com. Eastern Va. Med. Sch., 1969-76; bd. dirs. Central Midwestern Regional Edn. Labs., 1966-69, St. Louis Higher Edn. Coordinating Council, 1963-69, Norfolk Symphony Soc., Com. on Urban Edn., Assn. State Colls. and Univs., 1970-76, Eastern Va. Health Authority, 1976-79. Author articles.; Editor: Jacksonian Democracy: Myth or Reality, 1962. Trustee Va. Episc. Theol. Sem., 1978—. Served with USAAF, 1942-46. Recipient Thomas Jefferson award U. Mo., 1969. Mem. Va., So. hist. assns., State Hist. Soc. Va., Assn. Higher Edn., Orgn. Am. Historians, Am. Acad. Polit. and Social Scis., Raven Soc., Phi Beta Kappa, Omicron Delta Kappa, Pi Sigma

Alpha, Lambda Chi Alpha. Club: Kiwanian. Home: 1102 Rockbridge Ave Norfolk VA 23508

BUGGS, CHARLES WESLEY, microbiologist, educator; b. Brunswick, Ga., Aug. 6, 1906; s. John Wesley and Leonora Vane (Clark) B.; m. Maggie Lee Bennett, Dec. 27, 1927; 1 dau., Margaret Leonora. A.B., Morehouse Coll., Atlanta, 1928; M.S. (Rosenwald scholar 1931-34), U. Minn., 1932; Ph.D. (Shevlin fellow medicine 1933), U. Minn., 1934. Prof. biology, chmn. div. scis. Dillard U., 1935-43, 49-56; from instr. to asso. prof. bacteriology Sch. Medicine, Wayne U., 1943-49; prof. microbiology Sch. Medicine, Howard U., 1956-71, chmn. dept., 1958-70; emeritus prof. microbiology; project dir. Faculty Allied Health Scis. Charles R. Drew Postgrad. Med. Sch., Los Angeles, 1969-72, dean, 1972; interim program dir. Calif. Regional Med. Program, Area IX, 1970-71; vis. prof. microbiology U. Calif. at Los Angeles, 1969-72, U. So. Calif., 1969-76; prof. microbiology Calif. State U., Long Beach, 1973—; spl. research resistance bacteria to antibiotics. Author: Premedical Education for Negroes, 1949. Mem. med. and sci. com. So. Calif. chpt. Arthritis Found., 1971-73; mem. State Alcoholism Adv. Council, 1972-73; bd. dirs. Comprehensive Health Planning Assn. Los Angeles County, 1972-73. Fellow Am. Acad. Microbiology; mem. Am. Soc. Microbiology, Sigma Xi, Alpha Phi Alpha, Sigma Pi Phi; past fellow AAAS, Washington Acad. Scis.; past mem. Am. Assn. Dental Schs., Am. Public Health Assn., Assn. Am. Med. Colls., Assn. Schs. Allied Health Professions, Nat. Assn. Standard Med. Vocabulary, N.Y. Acad. Scis., Soc. Exptl. Biology and Medicine. Home: 5600 Verdun Ave Los Angeles CA 90043

BUGHER, ROBERT DEAN, association executive; b. Lafayette, Ind., Oct. 17, 1925; s. Walter Earl and Lillie Victoria (Feldner) B.; m. Patricia Jean McConnell, Sept. 7, 1945; children: Vickie Leigh, Robert James. Student, Millsaps Coll., 1943, Miami U., Oxford, Ohio, 1944; B.S. in Civil Engring, Purdue U., 1948; M.P.A., U. Mich., 1951. Staff engr. Mich. Municipal League, 1948-53; mgr. Municipal Purchasing Service, 1951-53; sec.-treas. Mich. Municipal Utilities Assn., 1951-53; asst. dir. Am. Pub. Works Assn., 1953-58, exec. dir., 1958—; Lectr. Internat. Seminar on Ekistics, Athens, Greece, 1970; Chmn. nat. adv. council Keep Am. Beautiful, Inc., 1974-75; chmn. Nat. Conf. on Solid Waste Disposal Sites, Washington, 1971; advisor pub. mgmt. program Northwestern U., 1977—; Bd. dirs. Govtl. Affairs Inst., Pub. Adminstrn. Service, Chgo., 1958-73; trustee Nat. Acad. Code Adminstrs.; chmn. Council Internat. Urban Liaison, 1982-83; trustee Nat. Tng. and Devel. Service, Am. Consortium for Internat. Pub. Adminstrn.; adv. com. internat. div. GAO, 1979-80. Editor: pub. works sect. Municipal yearbook, Internat. City Mgmt. Assn., 1953-58; cons. editor, Municipal Pub. Works Adminstrn., 1957. Served to 1st lt. USMCR, 1943-45. Mem. ASCE, Am. Soc. Assn. Execs., Am. Water Works Assn., Am. Soc. Pub. Adminstrn., Am. Road and Transp. Builders Assn., Internat. Union Local Authorities (pres. U.S. sect. 1977—, v.p. 1968-70, 75-77), Internat. Solid Wastes and Pub. Cleansing Assn. (v.p. 1968-70), Internat. Fedn. Mcpl. Engrs. (treas. 1976-79), Sigma Alpha Epsilon. Baptist. Home: 418 Indiana St Park Forest IL 60466 Office: 1313 E 60th St Chicago IL 60637

BUGLIARELLO, GEORGE, university president; b. Trieste, Italy, May 20, 1927; came to U.S., 1951, naturalized, 1964; s. Federico and Spera (Gefter-Wondrich) B.; m. Virginia Upton Harding, 1960; children: Federico David, Nicholas Luigi. Dr. Ing. summa cum laude, U. Padua, Italy, 1951; M.S. in Civil Engring, U. Minn., 1954; Sc.D., Mass. Inst. Tech., 1959. Research engr. U. Padua, 1951; from research asst. to research asso. Mass. Inst. Tech., 1956-59; mem. faculty Carnegie-Mellon U., 1959-69, prof. biotech. and civil engring., 1956-69, chmn. biotechnology program, 1964-69; dean engring. U. Ill. at Chgo. Circle, 1969-73; pres. Poly Inst. N.Y., 1973—; Mem. bd. hydraulic cons. U.S. Waterways Expt. Sta., 1968-74; sci. adv. panel Armed Forces Explosive Safety Bd., 1968-69; biomed. tng. engring. com. NIH, 1966-70; commn. edn. Nat. Acad. Engring., 1970-73, chmn. com. ednl. systems, 1970-73; chmn. bd. sci. and tech. for internat. devel. Nat. Acad. Sci., 1975—; mem. NATO Adv. Com. on Sci. for Stability Program, 1983; dir. Lord Corp. (Comtech Corp.). Co-author: Computer Systems and Water Resources, 1974, The Impact of Noise Pollution, 1976, Technology, The Community and the University, 1976; Author papers in field.; Editor: Bioengineering-An Engineering View, 1967, Women in Engineering, 1972, The History and Philosophy of Technology, 1979; editor-in-chief: Technology in Society. Trustee ANSER, Teagle Found., Greenwall Found.; bd. overseers U. Pa. Coll. Engring.; bd. visitors Duke U. Sch. Engring., 1975—; mem. N.Y. Partnership, Mayor's Commn. Sci. and Tech., 1984. Recipient Alza prize Biomed. Engring. Soc.; NATO sr. fellow Tech. U. Berlin, 1968. Fellow AAAS, Am. Soc. Engring. Edn.; Mem. ASCE (chmn. exec. com. engring. mechanics div. 1971—, chmn. interdivisional task com. civil engring. in medicine and health care delivery 1969—, Huber research prize 1967), Internat. Assn. Hydraulic Research (chmn. task com. computer langs. 1969—), Internat. Soc. Hemorheology (sec. 1966-69). Home: 5 Terrace Dr Port Washington NY 11050 Office: Poly Inst NY 333 Jay St Brooklyn NY 11201

BUGLIOSI, VINCENT T., lawyer; b. Hibbing, Minn., Aug. 18, 1934; s. Vincent and Ida (Valerie) B.; m. Gail Margaret Talluto, July 21, 1956; children: Wendy Suzanna, Vincent John. B.B.A., U. Miami, Fla., 1956; LL.B., UCLA, 1964. Bar: Calif. 1964. Dep. dist. atty., Los Angeles County, 1964-72, pvt. practice law, Beverly Hills, Calif., 1972—; Prof. criminal law Beverly Sch. Law, Los Angeles, 1968-74. Co-author: Helter-Skelter, The True Story of the Manson Murders, 1974, Till Death Us Do Part; a true murder mystery, 1978. Democratic candidate for dist. atty., Los Angeles County, 1972, Calif. atty. gen., 1974. Served to capt. AUS, 1957. Office: 9300 Wilshire Blvd Suite 470 Beverly Hills CA 90212

BUHAGIAR, MARION, editor; b. N.Y.C., Oct. 27, 1932; d. George and Mae (Pietrzak) B.; 1 dau., Alexa Ragozin. B.A. cum laude, Hunter Coll., 1953; postgrad., Mt. Holyoke Coll., 1954. Economist U.S. Dept. Commerce, 1954-57; bus. reporter Time mag., 1957-59; assoc. editor Fortune mag., 1960-73, story devel. editor, 1970-73; text editor Time-Life Books, N.Y.C., 1973-76; v.p., editor Boardroom Reports, N.Y.C., 1977—; exec. editor Bottom Line/Personal, N.Y.C., 1980—. Office: Boardroom Reports 500 Fifth Ave New York NY 10110

BUHLER, AARON, clergyman; b. Plum Coulee, Man., Can., Mar. 19, 1920; came to U.S., 1948, naturalized, 1954; s. Abram and Susan (Braun) B.; m. Dorothy Rhoda Ross, July 25, 1942; children—Donna Ruth (Mrs. Roger Schimke), Douglas Ross, Dwight Aaron. Diploma, Winnipeg Bible Coll., 1942; student, Mennonite Brethren Bible Coll., Winnipeg, 1945-46, Mich. State U., 1953-55. Ordained to ministry Baptist Ch., 1947; pastor in, Alta., Can., 1946-48, N.D., 1948-52, Lansing, Mich., 1952-59, Lodi, Calif., 1959-67, Cleve., 1968-74, Bernal Rd. Bapt. Ch., San Jose, Calif., 1975-80, Harbor Trinity Bapt. Ch., Costa Mesa, Calif., 1981—; moderator N.Am. Bapt. Gen. Conf., 1970-73; keynote speaker N.Am. Bapt. Conf., Wichita, Kans., 1973; Bible tchr. All Conf. Missionary Personnel in Cameroon, Africa, 1971; chmn. counciling and follow-up for Billy Graham Cleve. Crusade, 1972; mem. exec. com. Bapt. World Alliance, 1970-73, mem. steering com., 1981-83; Trustee N.Am. Bapt. Sem. Served with Canadian Army, 1942-45. Mem. Am. Assn. Bible Colls. (hon.), Internat. Platform Assn. Address: 19690 N Hwy 99 #172 Acampo CA 95220

BUHLER, CURT FERDINAND, historian, librarian; b. N.Y.C., July 11, 1905; s. Conrad and Martha (Warburg) B.; m. Alexandra M. London, Nov. 19, 1927 (div. Mar. 1939); 1 son, Conrad Alexander (dec.); m. Frances Lynham, Apr. 28, 1939 (dec. Nov. 1966); m. Lucy Jane Ford, July 10, 1971; 1 step-dau., Lucile Ford Schoettle. A.B., Yale, 1927; Ph.D., Trinity Coll., U. Dublin, 1930, Litt.D., 1947; postgrad., U. Munich, 1931-33; Litt.D. honoris causa, Columbia U., 1980. Staff printed books Pierpont Morgan Library, 1934-48, keeper printed books, 1948-66, research fellow for texts, 1967-73, emeritus, 1973—, hon. fellow, 1974—; Del. Union Académique Internationale, Brussels, 1957—; vis. fellow All Souls Coll., Oxford, 1969; Mem. adv. council U. Notre Dame, 1972—. Author: The Sources of the Court of Sapience, 1932, The Dicts and Sayings of the Philosophers, 1941, The Bible, Manuscripts and Printed Bibles from the Fourth to the Nineteenth Century, 1947, (with Selmer) The Melk Salbenkrämerspiel, 1948, Fifteenth Century Books and the Twentieth Century, 1952, The University and the Press in Fifteenth Century Bologna, 1958, William Caxton and His Critics, 1960, The Fifteenth Century Book, 1960, Neue Kunst und neue Welt, der Buchdruck und Amerika, 1963, The History of Tom Thumbe, 1964, The Epistle of Othea, 1970, Early Books and Manuscripts, Forty Years of Research, 1973, also articles, essays to learned publs. Rosenbach fellow U. Pa., 1947, 58-59; Guggenheim fellow, 1965, 77, 78. Fellow Medieval Acad., Am. Acad. Arts and Scis., Gutenberg Gesellschaft, Brit. Acad. (corr.); mem. Am. Philos. Soc. (com. on library), Bibliog. Soc. Am. (pres. 1952-54), Am. Council Learned Socs. (sec. 1960-74, chmn. 1974—), Early English Text Soc. (council 1971—), Modern Lang. Assn. (exec. council 1956-60), Bibliog. Soc. Eng. (treas. U.S. 1949-64), Renaissance Soc. Am. (pres. 1961-63), Ligue Internationale de la Librarie Ancienne (hon.), Union Academique Internat. (dir. 1968-71), Dante Soc. Am. (com. on hon. mems.), Phi Beta Kappa. Clubs: Century Assn., Grolier (N.Y.C.); Cosmos (Washington); East India (London); Royal Dublin, University (Dublin); Gutenberg Gesellschaft (Mainz). Home: 200 E 66th St New York NY 10021 Office: 33 E 36th St New York NY 10016

BUHLER, JEAN EMIL, naval architect; b. Hazleton, Pa., Oct. 7, 1917; s. Emil and Jeannette Marguerite (Voyer) B.; m. Phyllis Hugh Arthur, May 20, 1955; 1 son, Phillip Arthur. Grad., Hill Sch., 1936; student, Stevens Inst. Tech., 1936-39; B.S., U. Mich., 1941. Prin. naval architect Miami Shipbldg. Corp., 1939-45, 48-60; naval architect Burgess Co., 1945-48; naval architect, hydrofoil designer, test pilot Marine Systems Corp., also N. Am. Hydrofoils, Inc., Miami, N.Y.C. and Chgo., 1960-64; naval architect J.B. Hargrave, Naval Architects, Inc., West Palm Beach, Fla., 1964-74; dir. Link Engring. Lab., Harbor Branch Found., Inc., Ft. Pierce, Fla., 1974-83; marine cons. naval architect in pvt. practice, Vero Beach, Fla., 1983—. Mem. Soc. Naval Architects and Marine Engrs. (v.p. S.E. sect.), Internat. Oceanographic Found., Internat. Hydrofoil Soc., Chi Phi. Club: Biscayne Bay Yacht (Miami, Fla.) (past commodore). Home and Office: 8970 SW 87 Ct Miami FL 33176

BUHNER, JOHN COLIN, political science educator; b. Seymour, Ind., May 18, 1920; s. John H. and Marietta (Sawyer) B.; m. Betty Bevis, Mar. 27, 1942; children: Carol, John Colin, Byron. A.B. magna cum laude, Franklin (Ind.) Coll., 1942; M.A. in Polit. Sci. Ind. U., 1949, Ph.D., 1963. Editorial asst. Commonwealth Life Ins. Co., Louisville, 1945-46; grad. asst. Ind. U., 1946-48, 51-52, asst. dir., instr. govt., 1948-51, dir., instr. govt., 1952-59, instr. govt., 1959-61, dir., instr. govt., 1961-63, dir., asst. dean div. univ. extension, also asst. prof. govt. N.W. campus, 1963-66, dean, asso. prof. govt. N.W. campus, 1966-68; dean, acting chancellor Ind. U. N.W., 1968-69; prof. polit. sci. and health adminstrn. Ind. U.-Purdue U. at Indpls., 1969—, adj. prof. nursing, 1982—, vice chancellor, acad. dean, 1969-77; mem. commn. instns. higher edn. North Central Assn. Colls. and Schs., 1976-80. Contbr. articles in field. Recipient Distinguished Alumnus citation Franklin Coll., 1958; named Outstanding Prof. N.W. Campus Ind. U., 1964; recipient Outstanding Civic Service award I.U. Gents, 1968. Presbyn. (elder). Club: Rotarian. Home: 548 Bryn Mawr Dr Indianapolis IN 46260 Office: Indiana U Purdue U at Indianapolis Indianapolis IN 46205

BUHRMASTER, KENNETH E., banker; b. Scotia, N.Y., June 19, 1915; m. Flower Sheldon; children—Louis H., James R., Lois Ann. Grad., Syracuse U., 1937. Chmn. bd. J.H. Buhrmaster Co., Inc., Schenectady, First Nat. Bank of Scotia. Mem. Scotia-Glenville Sch. Bd., 1948—, pres., 1950-53, 56-61; area dir. N.Y. Sch. Bds. Assn., 1953-61, pres., 1961—; dir. Nat. Sch. Bds. Assn., 1966-68, sec.-treas., 1968, 2d v.p., 1969, 1st v.p., 1970, pres., 1971; chmn. N.Y. Ednl. Conf. Bd., 1963-69; mem. adv. bd. N.Y. Employees Retirement System; mem. N.Y. State Tchrs. Retirement Bd., 1967—, pres., 1968—; chmn. N.Y. State Bankers Assn. Retirement System; mem. N.Y. State Regents Com. on Edn. Leadership; rep. N.Y. State on Edn. Commn. of the States, 1966; mem. council State U. N.Y., Albany, 1968—; v.p. Schenectady Indsl. Devel. Council; mem. Schenectady County Fund Raising Rev. Bd.; mem. adv. bd. U.S. Comptroller Currency, 1975—; Vice pres., bd. dirs., trustee Schenectady YMCA. Recipient Distinguished Service award N.Y. State Sch. Bds. Assn., 1965, Alfred E. Smith award for outstanding service in edn. N.Y. State Tchrs. Assn., 1966. Mem. Am. Bankers Assn. (dir. 1974-75), N.Y. State Bankers Assn. (pres. 1974-75, past chmn. Group Five, mem. Council of Adminstrn.), Schenectady C. of C. (past dir.), Theta Chi, Phi Kappa Alpha. Methodist. Clubs: Rotarian., Mohawk. Address: 809 Charles St Scotia NY 12302

BUHROW, WILLIAM CARL, consumer credit executive; b. Cleve., Jan. 18, 1934; s. Philip John and Edith Rose (Leutz) B.; m. Carole Corinne Craven, Feb. 14, 1959; children: William Carl, David Paul, Peter John, Carole Lynn. Diploma, Phila. Coll. Bible, 1954; B.A., Wheaton (Ill.) Coll., 1956, M.A., 1959. Ordained to ministry Gen. Assn. Regular Bapt. Chs., 1958—; asst. pastor (Hydewood Park Bapt. Ch.), N. Plainfield, N.J., 1959-63; with Continental Fed. Savs. & Loan Assn., Cleve., 1963-81, sr. v.p., 1971-75, pres., chief exec. officer, dir., 1975-81; with IDS/Am. Express, Cleve., 1982-83; gen. credit mgr. Forest City Enterprises, Inc., Cleve., 1983—; pres. Forest City Ins. Agy., Inc., Cleve., 1983; chmn. bd. Security Savs. Mortgage Corp., Citizens Service Corp., New Market Corp., CFS Service Corp., 1975-81; trustee Credit Bur. Cleve., Bldg. Expositions, Inc. Trustee Bapt. Bible Coll. and Sch. Theology, Clarks Summit, Pa.; vice chmn. bd. deacons Cedar Hill Bapt. Ch., Cleveland Heights, Ohio. Mem. Internat. Consumer Credit Assn., Soc. Cert. Consumer Credit Execs., Consumer Credit Assn. of N.E. Ohio, Christian Bus. Men's Com. Internat. Club: Cleve. Rotary. Home: 1044 Linden Ln Lyndhurst OH 44124 Office: 10800 Brookpark Rd Cleveland OH 44130 *The supreme goal of my life is to please and honor the Lord Jesus Christ in all that I say and do. The standards, goals, and ideals outlined in the Bible, God's Holy Word, are the ones which I have adopted for my life. True happiness for me lies in the accomplishment of God's perfect will in my life and that of my family and in introducing others to Christ so they may know Him as their own personal Saviour, too. Herein lies the key to my success as a Christian business man.*

BUHSMER, JOHN HENRY, publisher; b. Wilkes-Barre, Pa., Aug. 4, 1932; s. Charles P. and Dorothy R. B.; m. Maurita Carr, May 31, 1958; children—John Henry, Mary, Patricia, Judith, Dennis, Kathleen, Caroline. B.A., King's Coll., Wilkes-Barre, 1956. Formerly with Ingersoll-Rand Co., N.Y.C., Bethlehem Steel Corp., Pa.; with Independent Publs. Inc., Bryn Mawr, Pa., 1972—, v.p., 1973—. Served with U.S. Army, 1956-58. Address: 945 Haverford Rd Bryn Mawr PA 19010

BUIE, ROBERT FRANK, real estate development company; b. Washington, May 29, 1942; s. Paul Douglas and Mary Margaret (Bullock) B.; dau., Tatia Christina. B.S. in Civil Engring, Va. Poly. Inst., 1964; M.B.A., Harvard U., 1971. Asst. to pres. Avco Community Developers, San Diego, 1971-72, project mgr., 1972-73, dir. mktg. multi-family div., 1973-74, mgr. multi-family div., 1974, v.p., gen. mgr., 1975-79, exec. v.p., 1979—, also dir.; pres., chmn. Buie Corp., A Real Estate Devel. Co.; Vice pres., bd. dirs. Housing Opportunities, Inc., 1980-81. Served with USN, 1965-69. Decorated Air medal. Mem. San Diego Bldg. Contractors Assn. (dir.). Republican. Methodist. Club: Yacht (San Diego). Office: 16770 W Bernardo Dr San Diego CA 92127

BUIRKLE, HAROLD W., diversified company executive; b. Morris Plains, N.J., Sept. 14, 1920; s. George and Anna (Jensen) B.; m. Helen Jane Moorhead, Mar. 5, 1949; children: Richard, James, Robert, Janet, Ruth. B.S. magna cum laude, N.Y.U., 1947. Various positions to gen. mgr. Cal. Tex. Oil Corp., N.Y.C., 1937-67; sr. v.p. Allied Corp., N.Y.C., 1967—. Served with USAAF, 1942-45. Home: 150 Broad Ave Leonia NJ 07605 Office: PO Box 1219 R Morristown NJ 07960

BUITENHUIS, PETER MARTINUS, educator; b. London, Eng., Dec. 8, 1925; s. John A. and Irene (Cotton) B. B.A. with honors, Jesus Coll. Oxford (Eng.) U., 1949, M.A., 1954; Ph.D., Yale, 1955. Instr. U. Okla., Norman, 1949-51; instr. Am. studies Yale, 1954-59; asso. prof. English Victoria Coll. U. Toronto, Ont., Can., 1959-66; vis. prof. U. Calif.-Berkeley, 1966-67; prof. McGill U., Montreal, Que., Can., 1967-75; prof., chmn. dept. English Simon Fraser U., Burnaby, B.C., Can., 1975-82. Author: Hugh MacLennan, 1968, The Grasping Imagination: the American Writings of Henry James, 1970; Editor: Selected Poems of E. J. Pratt, 1968, (with D. Staines) The Canadian Imagination; Contbr. articles to profl. jours., popular press. Served to sub-lt. Royal Navy, 1943-46; Eng. Can. Council fellow, 1962-63; Am. Council Learned Socs. fellow, 1972-73; Social Scis. and Humanities Research Council fellow, 1982-83. Mem. Am. Studies Assn., Brit. Assn. Am. Studies, Can. Assn. Am. Studies (pres. 1968-70), Can. Assn. Univ. Tchrs. Home: 7019 Marine Dr West Vancouver BC V7W 2T4 Canada Office: Dept of English Simon Fraser U Burnaby 2 BC Canada

BUJAKE, JOHN EDWARD, JR., beverage company executive; b. N.Y.C., May 23, 1933; s. John E. and Mary (Muzyka) B.; m. Gail E. Cruise, Aug. 1, 1964; children—John Edward, Laura, Jacquelyn, William. B.S., Manhattan Coll., 1954; M.S., Holy Cross Coll., 1955; Ph.D., Columbia U., 1959; M.B.A., N.Y. U., 1963. Research asso. Lever Bros., Edgewater, N.J., 1959-68; dir. research and devel. Foods div. Coca Cola Co., Houston, 1968-72; dir. foods research and devel. Quaker Oats Co., Barrington, Ill., 1972-77; dir. research and devel. Seven Up Co., St. Louis, 1977-78, v.p. research and devel., 1978—. Editorial bd.: Research Mgmt, 1976-77; contbr. articles to profl. jours. Mem. Indsl. Research Inst., Am. Chem. Soc., Inst. Food Technologists. Home: 24 Twin Springs Ln Ladue MO 63124 Office: Seven Up Co 121 S Meramec Saint Louis MO 63105

BUJOLD, GENEVIEVE, actress; b. Montreal, Que., Can.; d. Firmin and Laurette (Cavanaugh) B.; m. Paul Almond; 1 son, Matthew James. Ed., Montreal Conservatory Drama. Chmn. bd. Gendon Distbn. Co. (Recipient Susanne Bianchetti award for La Guerre est Fini 1966, Best Actress award Carthagenia Film Festival, Golden Globe award for Anne of a Thousand Days, Earle Grey award 1972); Stage roles include A House—A Day, The Barber of Seville, A Midsummer Night's Dream; U.S. stage debut in St. Joan; films include La Guerre est Finie, La Fleur de L'Age, Entre La Mer et L'Eau Douce, Final Assignment, King of Hearts, The Thief, Isabel, Anne of a Thousand Days, The Act of the Heart, Earthquake, Alex and the Gypsey, Kamouraska, Obsession, Swashbuckler, Another Man, Another Chance, Coma, Murder by Decree. *

BUJONES, FERNANDO CALLEIRO, ballet dancer; b. Miami, Fla., Mar. 9, 1955; s. Fernando and Marie (Calleiro) B.; m. Marcia Kibitschek, June 8, 1980; 1 dau., Alejandra Patricia Kubitschek. Grad., Profl. Children's Sch., 1972. Mem. Sch. Am. Ballet, 1967-72; mem. Corps de Ballet, Am. Ballet Theatre, 1972—, soloist, 1973-74, prin. dancer, 1974—, guest prin., 1976; guest tchr. schs.; restaged Jacob's Pillow Festival, 1973; prin. Bujones, Ltd. Recipient Varna Gold medal and tech. achievement award, 1974; Key to City Ft. Worth, 1975; Dance Mag. award, 1982. Mem. Movimento Democratico Brazil. Roman Catholic. *

BUKANTZ, SAMUEL CHARLES, physician, educator; b. N.Y.C., Sept. 12, 1911; s. Barnett and Bertha (Stelson) B.; m. A. Jewell Williams, Apr. 5, 1941; children: Jessica, Dorothy (Mrs. Jonathan Lawrence). B.S., Washington Sq. Coll., N.Y. U., 1930; M.D., N.Y. U. Coll. Medicine, 1934. Intern in pathology Mt. Sinai Hosp., N.Y.C., 1934-35, intern in medicine, 1935-36, house physician, asst. resident, 1936-38; asso. prof. medicine Washington U., St. Louis, 1946-58, fellow in allergy, 1946-47; asso. prof. medicine U. Colo., 1958-63; dir. medicine and research Children's Asthma Research Inst. and Hosp., 1958-63; asso. prof. clin. medicine N.Y. U., 1963-72; prof. medicine U. South Fla., 1972—, head div. allergy and immunology, 1972-82; pvt. practice medicine specializing in allergy and immunology, N.Y.C., 1938-40, 66-72, St. Louis, 1954-58, Tampa, Fla., 1972-82; chief sect. allergy and clin. immunology VA Hosp., Tampa, 1972-82. Editor: Hosp. Practice, 1968—; Contbr. numerous articles on allergy and immunology to profl. jours. Served with AUS, 1941-46. Lucius Littauer and Parmelee fellow in pneumonia research, 1938-41; NIH grantee, 1947-63. Mem. A.C.P., Am. Coll. Chest Physicians, Am. Soc. Clin. Investigation, Central Soc. Clin. Research, Am. Acad. Allergy, Am. Coll. Allergy, Alpha Omega Alpha. Democrat. Jewish religion. Home: 4940 San Rafael St Tampa FL 33609 Office: VA Hosp 13000 N 30th St Tampa FL 33612

BUKER, ROBERT HUTCHINSON, SR., army officer, thoracic surgeon; b. Loi Mwe, Kengtung, Burma, Dec. 6, 1928; came to U.S., 1940; s. Richard S. and Minola (Hutchinson) B.; m. Ethel Hunt, Sept. 25, 1949; children: Robert Hutchinson, Traci, Nina Ruth. A.B., Boston U., 1949; M.S., U. Maine, 1952; M.D., Columbia U., 1956; postgrad., Indsl. Coll. of Armed Forces, 1978-79. Diplomate: Am. Bd. Surgery, Am. Bd. Thoracic Surgeons. Intern Gorgas Hosp, C.Z., 1956-57; gen. surg. residency Gorgas Hosp., C.Z., 1957-60; resident in thoracic surgery Kennedy V.A. Hosp., 1962-64; rsident in thoracic surgery Tenn. Med. Ctr., 1962-64; commd. capt. U.S. Army, 1964, advanced through grades to brig. gen.; chief surg. cons. Pentagon, Washington, 1973-76; comdr. U.S. Army Hosp., Wuerzburg, Germany, 1976-78; dep. chief staff opns. Health Services Command, Fort Sam Houston, Tex., 1979-80; comdr. Gen. Leonard Wood Army Hosp., Ft. Leonard Wood, Mo., 1980-81; combdt. Acad. Health Scis., Ft. Sam Houston, 1981-83; comdg. gen. Brooke Army Med. Center, Ft. Sam Houston, 1983—; clin. prof. surgery Uniform U. Health Scis., Bethesda, Md., 1981—. Fellow A.C.S. (bd. govs. 1973-77), Am. Coll. Chest Physicians; mem. Soc. Thoracic Surgeons, So. thoracic Surg. Assn., Assn. Mil. Surgeons U.S. Baptist. Home: 11 Staff Post Fort Sam Houston TX 78234 Office: Commandant Acad Health Scis Fort Sam Houston TX 78234

BUKETOFF, IGOR, orchestral conductor; b. Hartford, Conn., May 29, 1915; s. Constantin and Millitza (Lebedeff) B.; m. Margaret Elizabeth Smith, Sept. 18, 1941; 1 dau., Barbara Elizabeth. Student, U. Kans., 1931-32; B.S., Juilliard Inst. Mus. Art, 1935, M.S., 1941, Juilliard Grad. Sch., 1939-42; Mus.D. (hon.), Los Angeles Conservatory Music and Art, 1949. Mem. faculty Juilliard Sch., 1935-45, Chautauqua Sch. Music, summers 1941-47, Columbia, 1943-47; asso. prof. music Butler U., 1953-63; vis. prof. U. Houston, 1977-79; founder, chmn. World Music Bank (now Internat. Contemporary Music Exchange), 1959. Condr.: Broadway co. Menotti's operas The Medium, The Telephone, tours Am. and Europe, 1947-48; Ft. Wayne Philharmonic Orch., 1948-66, Young Peoples Concerts, N.Y. Philharmonic Orch., 1948-53; mus. dir., 1950-53; composer choral works; guest condr., Oslo Philharmonic, 1957, Danish State Radio Orch., 1959, Royal Philharmonic, 1968, Lisbon Radio Orch., 1969, Orquestra Sinfonica Nacional, Rio de Janeiro, Brazil, Hague Philharmonic, 1970, Prague Radio Orch., 1972, Prague Symphony, 1971, 73, 75, Kansas City Philharmonic, Chautauqua, Chgo., Denver, Hartford, Houston, Indpls., Juilliard, Minn., San Diego, symphony orchs.; mus. dir., condr., St. Paul Opera Assn., 1968-74; mus. dir., Iceland State Symphony, 1964-65; artistic dir., Tex. Chamber Orch., 1980-81; dir. contemporary composers project, Inst. Internat. Edn., 1967-70; Contbr.: chpt. on Russian Music Music in Middle Ages; Recs. with, Oslo Philharmonic and Iceland Symphony Orch., London Symphony, Royal Philharmonic, New Philharmonia, Vienna State Opera Orch. Bd. dirs. Am. Symphony Orch. League, 1959-62. Alice M. Ditson grantee, 1956, 70, 72; Rockfeller Found. grantee for establishment of World Music Bank, 1959; State Dept. Cultural Exchange grantee to USSR, 1972; Ford Found. grantee for establishment Internat. Contemporary Music Exchange, 1973; recipient Alice M. Ditson Ann. award, 1967. Home: 500 E 85th St New York NY 10028 Office: 58 W 58th St New York NY 10019 also 2128 Willowick Houston TX 77027

BUKOVAC, MARTIN JOHN, horticulturist, educator; b. Johnston City, Ill., Nov. 12, 1929; s. John and Sadie (Fak) B.; m. Judith Ann Kelley, Sept. 5, 1956; 1 dau., Janice Louise. B.S. with honors, Mich. State U., 1951, M.S., 1954, Ph.D., 1957. Asst. prof. horticulture Mich. State U., East Lansing, 1957-61, assoc. prof., 11961-63, prof., 1963; NSF sr postdoctoral fellow Oxford U., U. Bristol, Eng., 1965-66; vis. lectr. Japan Atomic Energy Research Inst., 1958; adviser IAEA, Vienna, Austria, 1961; Nat. Acad. Scis. exchange lectr. Council Acads., Yugoslavia, 1971; vis. scholar Va. Poly. Inst., Blacksburg, 1973; guest lectr. Polish Acad. Scis., 1974; disting vis. prof. N.Mex. State U., 1976; vis. prof. Japan Soc. Promotion Sci., Osaka Prefecture U., 1977; guest lectr. Serbian Sci. Council, Fruit Research Inst., Cacak, Yugoslavia, 1979; vis. prof. U. Guelph, Ont., Can., 1982, Ohio State U., 1982, U. Zagreb, Yugoslavia, 1983; guest researcher Hort. Research Inst., Budapest, Hungary, 1983; mem. agrl. research adv. com. Eli Lilly Co., Indpls., 1971—; cons. Dept. Agr. Contbr. numerous articles to sci. jours.; patentee in field. Pres. Okemos Music Patrons, Mich., 1973-74. Served to 1st lt. U.S. Army, 1951-53. Recipient Joseph Harvey Gourley, 1969, 76, citation for meritorious research Am. Hort. Soc., 1970, Disting. Faculty Mich. State U., 1971, Disting. Service Mich. Hort. Soc., 1974, M.A. Blake award for disting. grad. teaching, 1975. Fellow Am. Soc. Hort. Sci. (Marion Meadows 1975, citation of appreciation 1975, pres. 1974-75), AAAS; mem. Nat. Acad. Scis., Am. Soc. Plant Physiologists, Bot. Soc. Am., Scandinavian Soc. Plant Physiologists, Japanese Soc. Plant Physiologists, Internat. Soc. Hort. Sci., Soc. Exptl. Biology, Sigma Xi (pres. 1978-79, research award Mich. chpt.), Phi Kappa Phi. Club: Mich. State U. Faculty. Home: 4428 Seneca Dr Okemos MI 48864 Office: Dept Horticulture Mich State U East Lansing MI 48824

BUKOWSKI, CHARLES, author; b. Andernach, Ger., Aug. 16, 1920; came to U.S., 1923; (div.)1 dau., Marina Louise. Student, Los Angeles City Coll., 1939-41. Editor: Laugh Literary and Man the Humping Guns, 1970; author (novels): Post Office, 1971, Factotum, 1975, Women, 1978, Ham on Rye, 1982; (short stories) Confessions of a Man Insane Enough to Live with Beasts, 1965, All the Assholes in the World and Mine, 1966, Notes of a Dirty Old Man, 1969, Erections, Ejaculations and General Tales of Ordinary Madness, 1972, South of No North, 1973, You Kissed Lilly, 1978, Hot Water Music, 1983; (poetry) Flower, Fist and Bestial Wail, 1960, Poems and Drawings, 1962, Longshot Pomes for Broke Players, 1962, Run with the Hunted, 1962, It Catches My Heart in Its Hands, 1963, Crucifix in a Deathhand, 1965, Cold Dogs in the Courtyard, 1965, The Genius of the Crowd, 1966, A Terror Street and Agony Way, 1968, Poems Written Before Jumping Out of an 8 Story Window, 1968, The Days Run Away Like Wild Horses Over the Hills, 1969, Fire Station, 1970, Mockingbird Wish Me Luck, 1972, Me and Your Sometimes Love Poems, 1972, While the Music Played, 1973, Burning in Water, Drowning in Flame, 1974, Africa, Paris, Greece, 1975, Scarlet, 1976, Maybe Tomorrow, 1977, We'll Take Them, 1978, Love is a Dog from Hell, 1978, Play the Piano, 1979, Dangling in the Tournefortia, 1981, Horsemeat, 1982; (screenplay) Barfly, 1979; (travel book) Shakespeare Never Did This, 1979; narrator: (documentary film) Poetry in Motion (Ron Mann), 1983; film produced from short stories: Tales of Ordinary Madness (Marco Ferreri), 1982. Nat. Endowment for Arts grantee, 1974. *Don't try.*

BULA, RAYMOND J., agronomist; b. Antigo, Wis., Aug. 3, 1927; s. Stanley and Mary (Klamerus) B.; m. Mary G. Wipperfurth, Aug. 9, 1952; children—R. Gregory, William J., Margaret A., Joseph M., Michael S., Catherine M., Julie C., Carol P. B.S., U. Wis., 1949, M.S., 1950, Ph.D., 1952. Asst. prof. N.Y. State Agr. Exptl. Sta., Geneva, N.Y., 1952-53; agronomist Alaska Agr. Expt. Sta., Palmer, 1953-56; agronomist, prof. Purdue U., West Lafayette, Inc., 1956-79; also area dir. U.S. Dept. Agr., 1974-79; dir. U.S. Dairy Forage Research Center, Madison, Wis., 1979—. Tech. editor: Agronomy Jour, 1980—. Served with AUS, 1945-47. Fellow AAAS, Am. Soc. Agronomy; mem. Crop Sci. Soc. Am., Am. Soc. Plant Physiologists, Sigma Xi. Roman Catholic. Office: US Dairy Forage Research Center U Wis Madison WI 53706

BULBULIAN, ARTHUR H., medical museum director; b. Talas, Turkey, Dec. 20, 1900; came to U.S., 1920, naturalized, 1931; s. Hagop C. and Naomi (Iynejian) B.; m. Wilhelmine M. Wilson, Sept. 9, 1944; children—Naomi, Josephine, Rachel. B.S., Middlebury Coll., 1925, M.S., 1926, D.Sc. (hon.); D.D.S., U. Minn., 1931. Asst. Mus. Natural History, U. Ia., 1927-28; instr. Coll. Dentistry, U. Minn., 1931-32; with Mayo Found., Rochester, Minn., 1933—; asso. prof. med. edn. Mayo Grad. Sch. Medicine; dir. Mayo Found. Mus. of Hygiene and Medicine, 1935—; mem. staff Mayo Clinic, 1935—; clin. prof. maxillofacial prosthetics U. Minn. Sch. Dentistry, 1966—; spl. cons. U. Minn. Hosps., Mpls.; prepared Mayo Found. exhibit Hall of Science, A Century of Progress, Chgo., 1932-33; pres. 1st Internat. Symposium on Facial Prosthetics., Arnhem, Netherlands, 1976. Author: textbook Facial Prosthesis, 1945; co-author: (with Dry, Edwards et al) Atlas on Congenital Anomalies of the Heart and Great Vessels, 1948, Facial Prosthetics Textbook, 1973, (with Dry, Edwards et al) articles on medical mus. techniques and facial prosthetic methods. Mem. Nat. Resources Planning Bd., 1942-44; mem. com. on conservation culture resources. Recipient Billings Gold medal A.M.A., 1955, 58, 64, Am. Acad. of Achievement golden plate award, 1965, Award of Merit Am. Assn. Inhalation Therapy, 1960, Andrew Ackerman award, 1964; Outstanding Achievement award U. Minn., 1972. Fellow Am. Coll. Dentists; mem. Am. Dental Assn., Assn. Med. Illustrators, Am. Acad. Maxillofacial Prosthetics (pres. 1956-58, dir. 1953—, editor jour.), Sigma Xi. Co-inventor (with Lovelace and Boothby), BLB Oxygen Mask for oxygen therapy and high altitude flying; designer A-14 oxygen mask used by USAAF during World War II. Home: 1229 Skyline Rochester MN 55902 Office: Mayo Clinic Rochester MN 55901

BULEN, LAWRENCE KEITH, lawyer; b. Pendleton, Ind., Dec. 31, 1926; s. Lawrence and Ople (Benefiel) B.; children: Leslie, Lisa, Kassee, Kellee. A.B., Ind. U., 1949, J.D., 1952. Bar: Ind. bar 1952. Since practiced in, Indpls.; sr. mem. firm Bulen, Castor & Robinette. Chmn. Marion County Republican Com., 1966-72, 11th Dist. Rep. Com., 1966-74; mem. exec. com. Rep. State Com., 1966-74; mem. Rep. Nat. Com. from Ind., 1968-74, Rep. Nat. Exec. Com., 1968-74; del. Rep. Nat. Conv., 1968, co-chmn. del., 1972, 76, 80; chmn. Ind. Nat. Inaugural Com., 1968, 72; mem. Ind. Legislature, 1960-64; U.S. del. ECOSOC, UN, Geneva, Switzerland, 1970, 73; U.S. observer UN Natural Resources Conf., Nairobi, Kenya, 1972; regional coordinator Reagan for Pres. com., 1976, dep. chmn., 1979-80; asso. dir. presdl. personnel Office Pres. Elect, 1980-81; commr. Internat. Joint Commn. U.S. and Can. Served with USAAF, 1945-46. Recipient Good Govt. award Indpls. Jr. C. of C., 1972. Mem. Am., 7th Circuit, Ind., Indpls. bar assns., Indpls. Laywer Assn. (past pres.), U.S. Trotting Assn., Sigma Nu, Phi Delta Phi. Clubs: Mason (Shriner), Columbia, Capitol Hill. Home: 8323 Rahke Rd Indianapolis IN 46217 Office: 1 Indiana Sq Indianapolis IN 46204

BULGER, ROGER JAMES, university president, physician; b. Bklyn., May 18, 1933; s. William Joseph and Florence Dorothy (Poggi) B.; m. Ruth Ellen Grouse, June 8, 1960; children: Faith Anne, Grace Ellen. A.B., Harvard U., 1955, M.D., 1960; postgrad., Emmanuel Coll., Cambridge (Eng.) U., 1955-56. Intern, resident internal medicine U. Wash. Hosps., 1960-62, 64-65; postgrad. trainee infectious disease and microbiology U. Wash., 1962-63, 65-66; renal and metabolic diseases Boston U., 1963-64; asst. prof., then assoc. prof. medicine U. Wash. Med. Sch., Seattle, 1966-70; med. dir. Univ. Hosp., Seattle, 1967-70; prof. community health scis., asso. dean allied health Duke U. Med. Center, 1970-72; exec. officer Inst. Medicine, Nat. Acad. Scis., 1972-76; prof. internal medicine George Washington U. Sch. Medicine, 1972-76; prof. internal medicine, family and community medicine, dean Med. Sch., chancellor Worcester campus U. Mass., 1976-78; pres. U. Tex. Health Sci. Center, Houston, 1978—; mem. report rev. com. Nat. Acad. Scis.; adv. panel nat. health ins. com., ways and means com. U.S. Ho. Reps., 1975-76. Author: Hippocrates Revisited, 1973, also articles, chpts. in books.; Mem. editorial bds. various jours. Bd. dirs. Georgetown U. Lionel de Jersey Harvard fellow, 1955-56. Fellow A.C.P.; mem. Inst. Medicine, Am. Soc. Microbiology, Infectious Disease Soc. Am., Am. Fedn. Clin. Research, Soc. Tchrs. Preventive Medicine, Am. Soc. Nephrology, Soc. Health and Human Values. Office: Office of Pres U Tex Health Sci Center at Houston PO Box 20036 Houston TX 77225

BULGER, WILLIAM MICHAEL, state senator; b. Boston, Feb. 2, 1934. LL.B., Boston Coll. Bar: Mass. bar. Mem. Mass. Ho. of Reps., 1961-70, Mass. Senate, 1971—; pres. Senate, 1978—. Pres. Boston Coll. Law Sch. Alumni Council. Club: K.C. Address: Office Senate Pres State House Boston MA 02133 *

BULKIN, BERNARD JOSEPH, chemist, university administrator; b. Trenton, Mar. 9, 1942; s. Jacob and Beatrice B.; m. Susan H. Lees, Dec. 31, 1975; children: Anna, Noah, David. B.S., Poly. Inst. Bklyn., 1962; Ph.D., Purdue U., 1966. Research asso. Swiss Fed. Inst. Tech., 1966-67; asst. prof. chemistry Hunter Coll., CUNY, 1967-69, asso. prof., 1970-73, prof., 1974-75, chmn. dept. chemistry, 1972-75; dean arts and scis. Poly. Inst. N.Y., 1975-82, v.p. research and grad. affairs, 1982—, dir. Inst. Imaging Scis., 1982—; bd. dirs. CUNY Research Found.; chmn. vis. com. chemistry dept. U. Ga.; vis. com. Bklyn. Bot. Garden; mem. com. on equal opportunities in sci. and tech. NSF. Contbr. numerous articles to profl. jours. Recipient medal N.Y. Soc. Applied Spectroscopy, 1978, Oscar Foster award Sci. Tchrs. Assn. N.Y., 1979. Mem. Am. Chem. Soc., N.Y. Acad. Scis., Soc. Applied Spectroscopy, Optical Soc. Am., Coblentz Soc. (award 1975). Home: 531 Main St New York NY 10044 Office: 333 Jay St Brooklyn NY 11201

BULKLEY, BERNADINE HEALY, physician, educator; b. N.Y.C., Aug. 2, 1944; d. Michael J. and Violet (McGrath) Healy; 1 dau., Bartlett Anne. A.B. summa cum laude, Vassar Coll., 1965; M.D. cum laude, Harvard U., 1970. Diplomate: Am. Bd. Internal Medicine, Am. Bd. Cardiology. Intern in medicine Johns Hopkins Hosp., Balt., 1970-71, asst. resident in medicine, 1971-72; staff fellow Nat. Heart and Lung Inst.-NIH, Bethesda., Md., 1972-74; fellow cardiovascular div. Johns Hopkins U. Sch. Medicine, Balt., 1974-75, dept. pathology and medicine, 1975-76; practice medicine specializing in cardiology, Balt.; asst. prof. medicine Johns Hopkins U. Sch. Medicine, 1976-77, asst. prof. pathology, 1976-81, assoc. prof. pathology, 1981—, assoc. prof. medicine, 1977-82, prof. medicine, 1982—, asst. dean postdoctoral programs, 1979—; dir. CCU Johns Hopkins Hosp., 1977—, mem. staff, 1976—; cons. Nat. Heart, Lung and Blood Inst.-NIH, 1976—; mem. cardiology adv. com. HEW, 1979-82. Mem. editorial bd.: Cardiovascular Medicine, Circulation, Am. Jour. Cardiology, Am. Jour. Medicine, Jour. Am. Coll. Cardiology, Jour. Med. Edn.; contbr. articles on cardiovascular disease to med. jours. Mem. bd. dirs. Bethesda-Chevy Chase (Md.), YMCA, 1974-75, Stetler Research Fund, 1979-81. Stetler Research fellow, 1976-77. Fellow Am. Coll. Cardiology (state gov.), Am. Heart Assn. (chmn. sci. sessions 1982—), Council on Clin. Cardiology; mem. Am. Fedn. Clin. Research (councilor Eastern sect. 1977—, sec.-treas Eastern sect. 1978-79), Am. Fedn. Clin. research (nat. council 1977—), Am. Fedn. Clin. Research (chmn. pub. policy com., 1982-83, pres.-elect 1982-83, pres. 1983-84), Am. Assn. Med. Colls., Council Acad. Socs. (mem. adminstrv. bd.), Am. Soc. Clin. Investigation, Alpha Omega Alpha, Phi Beta Kappa, ACP. Home: Stevenson MD 21153 Office: 600 N Wolfe St Baltimore MD 21205

BULL, BERGEN IRA, equipment mfg. co. exec.; b. Lansing, Mich., Feb. 28, 1940; s. W. Ira and Thelma (Roof) B.; m. Janet Mary Blachford, Sept. 22, 1961; children—Damon, Lauren. B.A., Mich. State U., 1962; M.A., Middle Tenn. State U., 1965; J.D., Northwestern Sch. Law of Lewis and Clark Coll., 1969. Bar: Oreg. bar 1969. Accountant Hyster Co., Portland, Oreg., 1965-66, mem. credit dept., 1966-67, asst. to sec., 1967-71, asst. sec., 1971-72, sec., 1972-79, v.p., legal officer, sec., 1979—; instr. bus. law Portland State U., 1971-72. Loaned exec. United Fund, 1968; bd. dirs. Associated Oreg. Industries, 1981, Columbia Empire Inc., Jr. Achievement, 1980. Served to lt. USAF, 1963-65. Mem. Am., Multnomah County, Ore. bar assns. Episcopalian. Office: 700 NE Multnomah St Portland OR 97208

BULL, BRIAN STANLEY, physician, educator; b. Watford, Hertfordshire, Eng., Sept. 14, 1937; came to U.S., 1954, naturalized, 1960; s. Stanley and Agnes Mary (Murdoch) B.; m. Maureen Hannah Huse, June 3, 1963; children: Beverly Velda, Beryl Heather. B.S. in Zoology, Walla Walla Coll., 1957; M.D., Loma Linda (Calif.) U., 1961. Diplomate: Am. Bd. Pathology. Intern Yale U., 1961-62, resident in anat. pathology, 1962-63; resident in clin. pathology NIH, Bethesda, Md., 1963-65, fellow in hematology and electron microscopy, 1965-66, staff hematologist, 1966-67; research asst. dept. anatomy Loma Linda U., 1958, dept. microbiology, 1959, asst. prof. pathology, 1968-71, assoc. prof., 1971-73, prof., 1973—, chmn. dept. pathology, 1973—; vis. prof. Institut de Pathologie Cellulaire, Paris, 1972, 74, Royal Postgrad. Med. Sch., London, 1972, U. Wis.-Madison, 1973, U. Ohio, Columbus, 1974, U. Minn., Mpls., 1979, U. Hawaii, 1981, St. Thomas Hosp. and Med. Sch., 1981. Bd. editors: Jour. Clin. and Lab. Haematology, U.K., 1980—, Blood, U.S., Clin. Lab. Automation, U.S., Blood Cells, Paris; contbr. chpts. to books and numerous articles to med. jours. Served with USPHS, 1963-67. Nat. Inst. Arthritis and Metabolic Diseases fellow, 1967-68; recipient Daniel D. Comstock Meml. award Loma Linda U., 1961, Merck Manual award, 1961, Mosby Scholarship Book award, 1961; Ernest B. Cotlove Meml. lectr. Acad. Clin. Lab. Physicians and Scientists, 1972. Fellow Am. Soc. Clin. Pathologists, Am. Soc. Hematology, Coll. Am. Pathologists, N.Y. Acad. Scis.; mem. AMA, Assn. Pathology Chmn., Calif. Soc. Pathologists, San Bernardino County Med. Soc., Acad. Clin. Lab. Physicians and Scientists, Am. Assn. Pathologists, Sigma Xi, Alpha Omega Alpha. Seventh-day Adventist. Patentee in field. Home: 24489 Barton Rd Loma Linda CA 92354 Office: Department of Pathology and Laboratory Medicine Loma Linda University School of Medicine Loma Linda CA 92350

BULL, COLIN BRUCE BRADLEY, educator; b. Birmingham, Eng., June 13, 1928; s. George Ernest and Alice Matilda (Collier) B.; m. Diana Gillian Garrett, June 16, 1956; children—Nicholas, Rebecca, Andrew. B.Sc., Birmingham U., 1948, Ph.D., 1951. Geophysicist later chief scientist Brit. N. Greenland Expdn., 1952-56; sr. lectr. physics Victoria U., Wellington, New Zealand, 1956-61; asso. prof. geology Ohio State U., Columbus, 1962-65; prof., dir. Inst. Polar Studies, 1965-69, chmn. dept. geology, 1969-72, dean, 1972—; Vis. fellow geophysics Australian Nat. U., Canberra, 1960; vis. scholar Cambridge (Eng.) U., 1969; vis. prof. Nat. Inst. Polar Research, Tokyo, Japan, 1983; U.S. rep. working group on glaciology Sci. Com. Antarctic Research, 1974—, sec., 1978—. Contbr. articles to profl. jours. Recipient Polar medal Queen Elizabeth, 1954; U.S. Antarctic Service medal, 1974. Fellow Arctic Inst. N. Am. (bd. govs. 1966-72); Fellow Geol. Soc. Am., Royal Soc. Arts; mem. Internat. Glaciology Soc. (council 1974-78), Am. Geophys. Union, Phi Beta Kappa (hon.). Home: 4187 Olentangy Blvd Columbus OH 43214

BULL, DAVID, fine art conservationist; b. Bristol, Eng., Mar. 5, 1934; came to U.S., 1979; s. Andrew John Michael and Betty (Horler) B.; m. Janette Christine Brewer, July 26, 1955; children: Victoria, Stephen, Matthew, Nicholas, Sebastian. Nat. diploma, city and guilds diploma, West of Eng. Coll. Art, 1955. Restorer of paintings City Art Gallery, Bristol, 1957-60; restorer Nat. Gallery, London, 1960-65; partner David Bull and Robert Shepherd (art restorers), London, 1965-78; head painting conservation J. Paul Getty Mus., Malibu, Calif., 1978-80; dir. Norton Simon Mus., Pasadena, Calif., 1980-81; pres. Fine Art Conservation and Restoration Inc., Los Angeles, 1981—. Fellow Internat. Inst. Conservation; asso. mem. Am. Inst. Conservation. Home: 4936 Vanalden Ave Tarzana CA 91356 Office: 1390 Kelton Ave Suite 305 Los Angeles CA 90024

BULL, HENRIK HELKAND, architect; b. N.Y.C., July 13, 1929; s. Johan and Sonja (Geelmuyden) B.; m. Barbara Alpaugh, June 9, 1956; children: Peter, Nina. B.Arch., Mass. Inst. Tech., 1952. With Mario Corbett, San Francisco, 1954-55, Goetz & Hansen, 1955-56; pvt. practice architecture, 1956-68; partner Bull, Field, Volkmann, Stockwell, San Francisco, 1968—; Vis. lectr. Syracuse U., 1963, U. Calif. Extension, 1964; Mem. adv. com. San Francisco Urban Design Study, 1970-71. Works include restoration, Columbus Tower, San Francisco, Christ Ch. Parish Hall, Sausalito, Calif., Sunset mag. Discovery House, Tahoe Tavern Condominiums, Tahoe City, Snowmass Villas, Aspen, Colo., Northstar Master Plan and bldgs., U. Calif. at Santa Cruz bookstore and gymnasium, McKinley Sch., San Francisco, U. Calif. at Santa Barbara student union addition, Spruce Saddle Restaurant, Beaver Creek, Vail, Colo., 1980. Dir. Golden Gate chpt. Children's Home Soc., 1969; dir. French- Am. Bilingual Sch., 1970-71. Served as 1st lt. USAF, 1952-54. Winner competition for master plan new Alaska capital city, Willow, 1978. Fellow AIA (pres. N. Calif. chpt. 1968). Democrat. Office: 350 Pacific Ave San Francisco CA 94111

BULL, HOWARD IRVING, oil field service company executive; b. Balt., May 31, 1940; s. Howard Irving and Jane (Curlett) B.; m. Dorothy Evelyn Fisher, Mar. 26, 1960 (div. 1973); children: Elisabeth Bowen, Brian Douglas; m. Elaine Carolyn Cunningham, Nov. 23, 1973. B.S.M.E. with honors, Johns Hopkins U., 1964, M.S. in Mgmt. Sci., 1967. Registered profl. engr., Md., 1968. Ops. mgr. space TV systems Westinghouse Def. and Space Ctr., Balt., 1961-73; prodn. planning and control mgr. Black & Decker Mfg. Co., Hampstead, Md., 1973-78, mfg. mgr., Hampstead, 1978-79; v.p. mfg. Reed Tubular Product Co., Houston, 1979-80, pres., 1980-83, Baker Sand Control, 1983—; dir. Reed-Nippon Corp., Tokyo. Club: Petroleum (Houston). Home: 9110 Ashbridge Park Spring TX 77379 Office: Baker Sand Control Division 1010 Rankin Rd Houston TX 77208

BULL, RICHARD SUTTON, JR., paper company executive; b. Chgo., Jan. 21, 1926; s. Richard Sutton and Sara Rozet (Smith) B.; m. Lois Karna Werme, July 19, 1950; children: Lois Karna Bull Bouton, Sara Annette Bull Greene, Richard Sutton, Harry Calvin, Mary Ellen Frantz. Student, Ill. State U., 1944, 46, Columbia U., 1944-45; B.A., Yale U., 1948, J.D., 1951; LL.M. (Food Law Inst. fellow), NYU, 1952. Bar: Ill. 1953, U.S. Supreme Ct. 1963. Instr. econs. Stone Coll., New Haven, 1950-51; atty. Swift & Co., 1952-57; with Bradner Central Co., Chgo., 1957—, pres., 1965-66, pres., chmn. bd., 1966—; sec., treas., dir. Clearview Farms Corp., 1957—; dir. 1st Security Bank of Chgo. Past bd. dirs. Duncan Med. Center, YMCA, 1968—; trustee, bd. dirs. Goodwill Industries, 1975—, vice chmn., 1977-79; mng. dir. Civic and Arts Found., vice chmn., 1978—; mem. Chgo. Crime Commn., 1983—. Served with USNR, 1944-46. Mem. Chgo. Bar Assn., Chgo. Assn. Commerce and Industry (dir. 1973—), Am. Arbitration Assn. (nat. panel arbitrators 1968—). Clubs: Morey's Assn. (New Haven); Paper (dir., past pres.), Yale, Press, Union League, Chgo., Economic, Execs. (Chgo.); Yale, N.Y. U. (N.Y.C.); Ruth Lake Country, Khyble Bay Yacht (past commodore, bd. govs.). Home: 4 Countryside Ct Hinsdale IL 60521 Office: 333 S Desplaines St Chicago IL 60606

BULL, WILLIAM EARNEST, educator; b. Lonedel, Mo., Jan. 17, 1933; s. Claude Everett and Daisy Eugenia (Matheny) B.; m. Margaret Jean Whitaker, June 11, 1955; children—Lawrence Alan, Jeffrey Scott, Gregory Bruce. B.A., So. Ill. U., 1954; M.A., U. Ill., 1955, Ph.D. (Socony Mobil fellow), 1957. Asst. prof. U. Tenn., Knoxville, 1957-61, asso. prof., 1961-70, prof. chemistry, 1970—; Fulbright lectr. Univ. Coll., Dublin, Eire, 1970-71; Cons. Oak Ridge Nat. Lab., 1965-69. Author: (with others) Fundamentals of College Chemistry, 1961, 3d edit., 1972, Laboratory Manual for College Chemistry, 6th edit, 1980. Mem. Am. Chem. Soc. (chmn. E. Tenn. sect. 1966-67), Tenn. Acad. Sci., Am. Assn. U. Profs., A.A.A.S., Sigma Xi. Research and publ. in inorganic chemistry. Home: 5400 Shenandoah Dr Knoxville TN 37919

BULLA, CLYDE ROBERT, writer; b. King City, Mo., Jan. 9, 1914; s. Julian W. and Sarah Ann (Henson) B. Columnist Tri-County News, King City, Mo., 1942-47. Author: 60 books for young people including White Bird, 1966, Shoeshine Girl, 1975, A Lion to Guard Us, 1981.

Recipient Commonwealth Children's Book award Commonwealth Club, Calif., 1970, Christopher award The Christophers, 1972, Sequoyah Book award Okla. Sch. Children, 1978, Charlie May Simon award Ark. Sch. Children, 1976, book award S.C. Sch. Children, 1980. Mem. Intenat. PEN Club (pres. Los Angeles br. 1963-65), Authors Guild.

BULLARD, CLAUDE EARL, newspaper, commercial printing and radio-TV executive; b. Louisville, July 21, 1920; s. George Adolph and Clara Etta (House) B.; m. Mildred Gambert, July 24, 1934; 1 dau., Susan Earle. Student, U. Louisville, 1946-47. Owner, mgr. C.E. Bullard Printing Co., Louisville, 1938-43; journeyman printer Courier-Jour. and Louisville Times, 1946-65, supt. composing room, 1965-68, dir. ops., 1968-72; v.p., dir. Courier-Jours. and Louisville Times; v.p. WHAS Radio/TV, Standard Gravure, Stand Colorprint, Morristown, Tenn., 1972-75, sr. v.p., dir., 1975—. Vice pres. bd. dirs. Bridgehaven, Louisville, 1980-83; chmn. admissions com. Met. United Way, Louisville, 1983-84, mem. agy. relations and allocations com., Louisville, 1983-84; bd. dirs. New Directions, Louisville, 1980—. Served with USN, 1943-46; PTO. Mem. Am. Newspaper Pubs. Assn., Am. Newspaper Personnel Assn., Am. Soc. Tng. Dirs., So. Newspaper Pubs. Assn., Louisville Personnel Assn. Democrat. Clubs: Jefferson, First Tuesday Assocs.; Magicians (Louisville). Home: 3510 Hughes Rd Louisville KY 40207 Office: Courier-Jour and Louisville Times 525 W Broadway Louisville KY 40202

BULLARD, EDGAR JOHN, III, museum director; b. Los Angeles, Sept. 15, 1942; s. Edgar John and Katherine Elizabeth (Dreisbach) B. B.A., UCLA, 1965, M.A., 1968. Asst. to dir., curator spl. projects Nat. Gallery Art, Washington, 1968-73; dir. New Orleans Mus. Art, 1973—; Alternate mem. Citizens Stamp Adv. Com., 1969-71; mem. mus. adv. panel Nat. Endowment for Arts, 1974-77. Author: Edgar Degas, 1971, John Sloan 1871-1951, 1971, Mary Cassatt: Oils and Pastels, 1972, A Panorama of American Painting, 1975. Bd. dirs. New Orleans Jazz and Heritage Found., 1974-78; trustee Ga. Mus. Art, U. Ga., Athens., 1975-80. Named one of 10 outstanding persons Inst. Human Understanding, New Orleans, 1978; Decorated Order of Republic, Egypt; Samuel H. Kress Found. fellow, 1967-68. Mem. Assn. Art Mus. Dirs., Am. Assn. Museums, Coll. Art Assn. Democrat. Episcopalian. Club: Nat. Arts (N.Y.C.). Home: 1805 Milan St New Orleans LA 70115 also Greenlea Reach Rd Deer Isle ME 04627 Office: New Orleans Mus Art PO Box 19123 New Orleans LA 70179

BULLARD, K(ENNEDY) C(ORNELIUS), state official; b. Palatka, Fla., Dec. 9, 1917; s. George Frank and Eva Marie (Mealor) B.; m. Carmen Martha Valdespino, Dec. 14, 1941; children: Patricia Bullard Willis, Timothy Bruce. Student, U. Fla., 1935-37, Bus. U. Tampa, 1938. Accountant Hillsborough County Tax Collector's Office, Tampa, Fla., 1946-52, exec. asst. to tax collector, 1952-68, county tax collector, 1968-75; adj. gen. State of Fla., St. Augustine, Fla., 1975—. Served with U.S. Army, 1940-45; maj. gen. Fla. N.G., 1975—. Decorated Bronze Star, Purple Heart. Mem. Fla. N.G. Officers Assn. (past pres.), Delta Tau Delta. Democrat. Methodist. Office: Office of the Adj Gen State Arsenal Saint Augustine FL 32084

BULLARD, RAY ELVA, JR., psychiatrist, hosp. adminstr.; b. Dallas, Jan. 25, 1927; s. Ray Elva and Beatrice (Taylor) B.; children by previous marriage: Suzanne, Ray Elva. B.S., U. Wash., 1948; M.D., U. Tex. Med. Br., Galveston, 1953, B.A. (Mead Johnson scholar), 1957. Diplomate: Am. Bd. Psychiatry and Neurology. Intern Houston VA Hosp., 1953-54; resident in gen. practice U. Iowa, summer 1954, Nan Travis Meml. Hosp., Jacksonville, Tex., 1954-55; gen. practice medicine, Normangee, Blanco and Austin, Tex., 1955-63; resident in psychiatry VA Hosp., Topeka, 1963-66, chief sect. psychiatry, 1966-71; asso. prof. psychiatry U. Okla., 1971-73; supt. Hollidaysburg (Pa.) State Hosp., 1973-76, Torrance (Pa.) State Hosp., 1976—; guest lectr. Pa. State U., U. Pitts. Served with U.S. Army, 1944-46. Menninger Found. fellow, 1963-66. Mem. Am. Psychiat. Assn., Pa. Psychiat. Assn., AMA (Physician's Recognition award 1982), Pa. Med. Assn., Assn. Med. Supts. Mental Hosps., Pa. State Mental Hosp. Supts. Assn., Assn. Am. Med. Colls. Episcopalian. Club: Masons. Home: PO Box 10 Torrance PA 15779 Office: Torrance State Hosp Torrance PA 15779

BULLARD, TODD HUPP, college president; b. Wheeling, W.Va., May 31, 1931; s. Luther Todd and Virginia (Netting) B.; m. Ella J. Rickey, June 6, 1953; children: Todd Whittam, Katharine Anne, Alice Elizabeth, Janice Louise, James Hupp. Student, Bethany (W.Va.) Coll., 1949-50; B.A., W.Liberty (W.Va.) State Coll., 1953; M.A., W.Va. U., 1956; Ph.D., U. Pitts., 1964. Dir. edn. W.Va. State Penitentiary, Moundsville, 1953; research asst. Bur. Govt. Research, W.Va. U., 1956- 57; asst. dir. W.Va. League Municipalities, 1956-57; asst. prof. polit. sci., dir. Falk program practical politics Bethany Coll., 1959-60; sr. research analyst Bur. Govt. Research, W.Va. U., 1960-61, dir. Parkersburg br., 1961-63; acad. dean Potomac State Coll. of univ., Keyser, 1963-64, pres., 1964-70; provost, v.p. acad. affairs Rochester (N.Y.) Inst. Tech., 1970-80; pres., prof. polit. sci. Bethany (W.Va.) Coll., 1980—; with north central, middle states and so. regional accrediting bodies; participant state studies of higher edn.; dir. health ins. cos. Author: (with E. R. Elkins) Manual of West Virgina Municipal Goverment, 1957, Labor and The Legislature, 1965; Contbr.: articles to profl. jours. Labor and The Legislature. Bd. dirs. Boy Scouts Am., various community orgns. Mem. Am. Polit. Sci. Assn., W.Va. Assn. Coll. and Univ. Pres., Pi Sigma Alpha. Home: Pendleton Heights Bethany College Bethany WV 26032 Office: Cramblet Hall Bethany College Bethany WV 26032

BULLARD, WILLIS CLARE, JR., state legislator; b. Detroit, July 12, 1943; s. Willis C. and Virginia Katherine (Gilmore) B.; m. Ruth Ann Leppala, Dec. 20, 1969; children: Willis C. III, Melissa Ann. A.B., U. Mich., 1965; J.D., Detroit Coll. Law, 1971. Bar: Mich. bar 1971. Practice of law, Detroit, 1971-77, Troy, Mich., 1977-80, supr., Highland Twp., Mich., 1980-82; mem. Mich. Ho. of Reps., 1983—. Bd. dirs. Dunham Lake Property Owners Assn., 1975-78, treas., 1975-76, pres., 1976-78; trustee Highland Twp., 1978-80, mem. zoning bd. appeals, 1979. Mem. Oakland County Bar Assn., State Bar Mich., Oakland County Assn. Twp. Suprs. (sec.-treas. 1981), Michigamua. Clubs: U. Mich. of Greater Detroit, Highland Republican, Highland Men's (sec. 1979), Highland Men's (pres. 1980). Home: 851 Blue Heron Dr Milford MI 48042 Office: State Capitol Lansing MI 48909

BULLEN, RICHARD HATCH, corporation executive; b. Logan, Utah, May 9, 1919; s. Asa and Georgia Vivian (Hatch) B.; m. Annabelle Smith, June 19, 1942 (div. 1965); children: Richard Hatch, Steven Asa, Thomas Kenneth; m. Anne-Marie deLeur, Aug. 16, 1965. B.S., Utah State U., 1941, LL.D., 1965; M.B.A., Harvard, 1943. With IBM Corp., 1946-72, treas., 1961-63, v.p., 1963-64, v.p., group exec., 1964- 67, sr. v.p., mgmt. com., 1967-72; pres. Richard H. Bullen Assocs., Inc., 1972—; dir. Upjohn Co., Enstar Corp. Served to 1st lt. Q.M.C. AUS, 1943-46. Mem. Sigma Chi. Club: Racquet and Tennis (N.Y.C.). Home and Office: 1050 Fifth Ave New York NY 10028

BULLER, ALLAN RAY, food company executive; b. Morse, Sask., Can., Dec. 2, 1917; came to U.S., 1924; s. Jacob H. and Stella G. (Loewen) B.; m. Mildred Walberg, Sept. 6, 1942; children: Calol E., Janice D., Suzanne E., Allan G. B.A., Andrews U., 1941; M.B.A., Ohio State U., 1952. Asst. mgr. Worthington Foods, Ohio, 1946-48, gen. mgr., sec.-treas., 1948-69; exec. v.p. Worthington Food div. Miles Lab., 1970-82; pres. Worthington Foods, Inc., 1982—. Trustee Harding Hosp., 1950—, Andrews U., 1972-76. Served with M.C., AUS, 1941-45. Mem. Am. Mgmt. Assn., Worthington C. of C. (pres. 1960), Worthington Bus. and Profl. Men's Assn. (pres. 1954). Club: Rotary. Office: Worthington Foods Inc. 900 Proprietors Rd Worthington OH 43085

BULLERJAHN, EDUARD HENRI, architect; b. Milw., Mar. 9, 1920; s. Adolph David and Hazel Roselle (te Selle) B.; m. Julianna Sweetser, 1951; children: Stephen R., John te Selle, George S. Student, U. Wis., 1937-39; B. Arch., Mass. Inst. Tech., 1943; diploma, Royal Acad. Fine Arts, Stockholm, Sweden, 1957. Designer Perry Shaw and Hepburn, Boston, 1948, Edward Durrell Stone, N.Y.C., 1951-54; partner Robert Hegardt, N.Y.C., 1954-57; individual practice architecture, Marion, Mass., 1957-61; ptnr. Andrew Hepburn, Boston, 1961-67; ind. practice Bullerjahn Assos., Boston, 1967-70; assoc. with Johan Valentijn N.A., Newport, R.I., 1982—; residential architect, yacht interiors and arrangements with Knud H. Reimers, Stockholm, G. DeVries Lentsch, Jr., Amsterdam, J.B. Hargrave, West Palm Beach; cons. in field. Contbr.: articles to Yachting mag. Mem. Marion Planning Bd., 1960-61; Bd. dirs. Boston Children's Theatre, Cambridge Sch. Ballet. Served to lt. USNR, 1943-46. Fellow Swedish Am. Found., 1946; Recipient King Gustav V Gold Medal Architecture, Stockholm, 1948; Rotch travelling scholar, 1949. Clubs: Royal Swedish Yacht, American Station; Wednesday Evening of 1777, Somerset (Boston); Brit. Officers New Eng.; Mill Reef (Antigua, B.W.I.); Fauquier (Warrenton); Sakonnet Golf, Warren's Point Beach. Address: West Main Rd Little Compton RI 02837

BULLINGTON, JAMES R., ambassador; b. Chattanooga, Oct. 27, 1940. A.B., Auburn U., 1962; M.P.A., Harvard U., 1969; grad., Fgn. Service Inst., 1971. Asst. desk officer Central Treaty Orgn. Affairs, Dept., 1963-65; vice consul, Hue, 1965-66, staff adie to ambassador, Saigon, 1966-67, dep. province sr. adviser, Quang Tri, Vietnam, 1967-68; intelligence analyst Bur. Intelligence and Research, Dept. State, 1969-70; vice consul, Chaing Mai, Thailand, 1971-73; polit. officer Vienam Working Group, Dept. State, 1973-75; consul, Mandalay, Burma, 1975-76, polit. and econ. counselor, Rangoon, 1976-78; dep. chief mission N'Djamena, 1979-80, Cotonou, 1980-82; sr. adviser African affairs U. S. Del. to UN Gen. Assembly, N.Y.C., 1982; U.S. ambassador to Burundi, 1982—. Office: Am Embassy-Bujumbura c/o Dept State Room 4246 Washington DC 20520 *

BULLINS, ED, author; b. Phila., July 2, 1935; s. Edward and Bertha Marie (Queen) B. Ed. bus. sch. and various colls.; Litt.D. (hon.), Columbia Coll., Chgo., 1976. Mellon lectr. for dramatic lit. Amherst (Mass.) Coll., 1977—; writers unit coordinator N.Y. Shakespeare Festival, 1975—. Author: Five Plays, 1968, New Plays From the Black Theatre, 1969, The Duplex, 1971, The Hungered One, 1971, Four Dynamite Plays, 1972, The Theme is Blackness, 1973, The Reluctant Rapist, 1973, The Taking of Miss Janie, 1974 (N.Y. Drama Critics Circle award 1974-75). Served with USN, 1952-55. Recipient Obie award, 1971, 75, Vernon Rice award, 1968; Rockefeller grantee, 1968, 70, 73; Guggenheim fellow, 1971, 76; NEA grantee; CAPS grantee. *

BULLITT, JOHN CHRISTIAN, lawyer, investment company executive; b. Phila., June 6, 1925; s. Orville H. and Susan B. (Ingersoll) B.; m. Lelia M. Wardwell, Nov. 20, 1954 (div.); children: Thomas W., Clarissa W.; m. Judith Ogden Cabot, May 15, 1976; stepchildren: Elizabeth, Edward, Timothy. B.A., Harvard, 1950; LL.B., U. Pa., 1953. Bar: N.Y. 1956. Asso. Shearman & Sterling, N.Y.C., 1953-60; dep. asst. sec. internat. affairs U.S. Treasury, Washington, 1961-62, asst. sec. internat. affairs, 1962-64; U.S. exec. dir. Internat. Bank Reconstrn. and Devel., 1962-65; dir. N.J. Office Econ. Opportunity, 1964-67; asst. adminstr. for East Asia AID, Dept. State, 1967-69; partner Shearman & Sterling, 1969—, partner in charge Hong Kong Office, 1978-81. Bd. dirs. OBOR, Indonesian pub., Manhattan Country Sch. Served with inf. AUS, World War II. Mem. Council Fgn. Relations. Clubs: N.Y. Yacht, Downtown Assn., Recess (N.Y.C.); Fed. City (Washington); Philadelphia; Royal Hong Kong Yacht, Am., Shanghai Frat. Assn., Nautilus (Hong Kong). Home: RD 1 Princeton NJ 08540 Office: 53 Wall St New York NY 10005

BULLITT, JOHN MARSHALL, educator; b. Seattle, July 9, 1921; s. Keith Logan and Dorothy (Terry) B.; m. Sarah Cowles, Aug. 11, 1948 (div.); children: Elizabeth, Margaret, Sarah, John; m. Sandra Merrihue, June 27, 1969; 1 son, David, 1 stepson, Jeffrey Merrihue. A.B., Harvard, 1943, Ph.D., 1950. Mem. faculty English dept. Harvard, 1946—, asso. prof., 1956-62, prof., 1962—; master Quincy House, 1957-66; asso. dir. Peace Corps, Bolivia, 1966-68; pres. Elmasar Inc., 1977—. Author: Jonathan Swift and the Anatomy of Satire, 1953; Editor: Pamela-Shamela, 1980; co-editor: Samuel Johnson, The Idler and the Adventurer, 1963, 18th Century Poetry and Prose, 1973. Served from pvt. to capt., inf. AUS, 1943-46. Mem. Modern Lang. Assn., U.S. Power Squadron (chief chart instr. Pequossette div. 1977-80), Phi Beta Kappa. Clubs: Manchester Yacht, Cambridge Tennis. Home: 28 Ticehurst Ln Marblehead MA 01945

BULLMORE, (JOHN) JEREMY DAVID, advertising executive; b. Nov. 21, 1929; s. Francis Edward and Adeline Gabrielle (Roscow) B.; m. Pamela Audrey Green, Feb. 14, 1958; children: Edward T., Adam B., Amelia M. Student, Oxford U., 1950-52. With J. Walter Thompson Co. Ltd., London, 1954—, dir., 1964—, dep. chmn., 1975-76, chmn., 1976—; dir. J. Walter Thompson Co. (USA). Mem. Nat. Com. Electoral Reform, 1978—. Served with Brit. Army, 1949-50. Mem. Advt. Assn. (chmn. 1981—). Home: 20 Embankment Gardens London England SW3 Office: J WALTER Thompson Co 40 Berkeley Sq London England WI

BULLOCH, JOHN FREDERICK DEVON, orgn. exec.; b. Toronto, Ont., Aug. 24, 1933; s. John Alexander and Belle (Halter) B.; m. Mary Helen McClenegham, Aug. 22, 1955; children—Pete, Martha. M.B.A., Toronto, 1964. Mgr. Imperial Oil Ltd., Toronto, 1956-57; mgr. heavy oil sales Cities Service Oil, Ltd., Toronto, 1957-59; mgr. Baier Fuels, Ltd., Kitchener, Ont., 1959-63; lectr. Ryerson Poly. Inst., Toronto, 1964-70; pres., founder Can. Council Fair Taxation, Toronto, 1970-71; chmn., dir. Can. Centre for Entrepreneurial Studies, Ryerson Poly. Inst., 1972-73; pres. Can. Fedn. Ind. Bus., Don Mills, Ont., 1971—; mem. adv. groups reporting to Prime Minister of Can. and Ont. Premier. Ryerson Poly Inst. fellow, 1981. Mem. Assn. Profl. Engrs. Office: Canadian Fedn of Ind Business 4141 Yonge St Willowdale ON M2P 2A6 Canada

BULLOCK, ELLIS WAY, JR., architect; b. Birmingham, Ala., Sept. 11, 1928; s. Ellis Way and Martha (Alexander) B.; m. Ann Pope, Nov. 28, 1950; children: Ellis Way III, Pope, Keith, Frank. B.Arch., Auburn U., 1954. Registered architect, Fla., Ala., Ga., Miss., S.C., N.C. Apprentice architect Yonge, Look & Morrison, Pensacola, Fla., 1954-58; owner Ellis Bullock Architect, Pensacola, 1958-73; pres. The Bullock Assocs., Pensacola, 1973—; treas. AIA Research Corp., Washington, 1980-81; chmn. Energy in Arch., Washington, 1980-82; mem. faculty adv. com. Auburn U. Sch. Architecture, 1980—; mem. Nat. Architecture Accrediting Bd., Washington, 1982—. Chmn. Pensacola Hist. Commn., 1967, City of Pensacola Archtl. Review Bd., 1968, Pensacola Bldg. Bd. of Appeals, 1970. 1st lt. U.S. Army, 1950-53. Recipient 1st Honor AIA-Navy, 1977, Award of Merit AIA-Navy, 1976, Outstanding Design USAF, 1980; named Profl. of Yr. Pensacola News Jour., 1977. Fellow AIA (dir. 1979-82, v.p. 1981-82); mem. Fla. Assn. AIA (pres. 1977). Clubs: Rotary, St. Andrews Soc. (Pensacola). Home: 2 Hyde Park Rd Pensacola FL 32503 Office: The Bullock Assocs Architects and Planners Inc 1823 N 9th Ave Pensacola FL 32503

BULLOCK, H. RIDGELY, business executive, lawyer; b. N.Y.C., June 6, 1934; s. H.R. and Marian (Batterman) B.; m. Leslie Kitchell deBraux, Sept. 26, 1973; children: James William, Sylvia Marian, David Duncan Ridgely, Ariane deBraux, Sabrina Carpenter, Karena Ridgely. B.A., Colby Coll., 1955; J.D., U. Va., 1967. Bar: Va. 1967, N.Y. 1970. Theatrical producer, N.Y.C., 1955-64; assoc. Mudge Rose Guthrie & Alexander, N.Y.C., 1967-70, ptnr., 1970-75, of counsel, 1979—; sec. UMC Industries, Inc., 1969-70, exec. v.p., 1970, pres., 1970—, chief exec. officer, 1971—, chmn. bd., 1976—, also dir.; chmn. bd. Electro Audio Dynamics, Inc.; chmn. bd., pres. Aveneg, Inc.; dir. Knoedler Modarco (S.A.), CBT Corp., Conn. Bank & Trust Co., Peerless Fabrikkerne (A/S.). Bd. dirs. Nat. Boys' Clubs Am.; chmn. bd. trustee Colby Coll.; trustee Am. Shakespeare Festival Theatre, Stamford Hartman Theatre. Served to capt. USAF, 1956-59. Mem. ABA; mem. N.Y. State Bar Assn., Va. State Assn.; Mem. Assn. Bar City N.Y. Clubs: Piping Rock Country, N.Y. Yacht, Down Town Assn., Greenwich Country, Indian Harbor Yacht, Lyford Cay, Madison Sq. Garden. Office: UMC Industries Inc High Ridge Park PO Box 1090 Stamford CT 06904

BULLOCK, HUGH, investment banker; b. Denver, June 2, 1898; s. Calvin and Alice Katherine (Mallory) B.; m. Marie Leontine Graves, Apr. 5, 1933; children: Florence Eno Bullock Weymouth, Fair Alice Bullock McCormick. B.A., Williams Coll., 1921, LL.D., 1957; LL.D., Hamilton Coll., 1954. Investment banker, 1921—; chmn. bd., chief exec. officer Calvin Bullock, Ltd.; pres., dir. Bullock Fund, Ltd., Canadian Investment Fund, Ltd., Dividend Shares, Inc., Canadian-Fund, Inc.; chmn., dir. Carriers and Gen. Corp., Nation-Wide Securities Co., Monthly Income Shares, Money Shares, Bullock Tax Free Shares. Author: The Story of Investment Companies, 1959. Mem. Marshall Scholarship Regional Com., 1955-58; life trustee, mem. exec. com. Williams Coll., 1961-69; trustee Roosevelt Hosp., 1949-69; hon. trustee St. Lukes Roosevelt Hosp. Center; adv. council Grad. Sch. Bus., Columbia U., 1958; chmn. Westminster Abbey Am. Appeal Com. Served as 2d lt., inf., World War I; lt. col., World War II; Civilian aide to sec. Army, for First Army Area, 1952-53. Decorated knight grand cross Order Brit. Empire; knight of grace Order of St. John of Jerusalem (v.p. Am. soc.); knight comdr. Royal Order George I, Greece; recipient U.S. Army certificate of appreciation, 1953; James C. Rogerson Cup for Service, Loyalty, Achievement Williams Coll., 1961; Exceptional Service award Dept. Air Force, 1961; Disting. Public Service award Dept. Navy, 1972; Disting. Citizens award City of Denver; Benjamin Franklin fellow Royal Soc. Arts. Mem. France-Am. Soc., Mil. Order Fgn. Wars in U.S., Am. Legion, Pilgrims of U.S. (chmn., pres.), St. George's Soc., New Eng. Soc., English-Speaking Union, Fgn. Policy Assn., Acad. Polit. Sci., Investment Bankers Assn. Am. (gov. 1953-55), Am. Mus. Natural History, Assn. Ex-mems. Squadron A (gov. 1945-50), Calvin Bullock Forum (pres.), Council Fgn. Relations, Nat. Inst. Social Scis. (pres. 1950-53), Newcomen Soc., Acad. Am. Poets (dir.), Ends of the Earth, Gargoyle Alumni Assn., Kappa Alpha. Episcopalian. Clubs: Chevy Chase, Met. (Washington); Racquet and Tennis, Recess (gov.), N.Y. Yacht, Bond, Century Assn., River, Williams, Ch., Union (N.Y.C.); West Side Tennis (Forest Hills, N.Y.); Sleepy Hollow Country (Scarborough, N.Y.); Denver Country, Mount Royal (Montreal); Edgartown (Mass.); Yacht (commodore 1966-67), Edgartown Reading Room; White's (London). Home: 1030 Fifth Ave New York NY 10028 Office: 1 Wall St New York NY 10005

BULLOCK, MRS. HUGH (MARIE LEONTINE GRAVES), civic leader; b. Paris, France, June 30, 1911; d. William Leon and Florence Christmas (Eno) Graves; m. Hugh Bullock, Apr. 5, 1933; children—Florence Eno (Fleur) Bullock Weymouth, Fair Alice Seymour (Mrs. Peter H. McCormick). Grad. student, Sorbonne, Paris, also Columbia, 1933-37, Julliard Sch. Music, 1937; mem., Tchrs. Astronomy Course, Hayden Planetarium, 1952-53; L.H.D., Williams Coll., 1975. Founder of Acad. Am. Poets, 1934, pres., 1939—; bd. dirs. Edward MacDowell Assn., 1945-79; bd. dirs., exec. com. Theodore Roosevelt Assn.; ex-officio mem. pres. adv. com. on arts John F. Kennedy Center Performing Arts, 1960; Dir. Calvin Bullock, Ltd. Chmn. belles lettres com. Office Cultural Affairs, City of N.Y., 1964; mem. Citizens Advisory Commn., 1963; Mem. vis. com. dept. astronomy Harvard Coll., 1968-74, 75-81, 82—. Council fellows Pierpont Morgan Library, 1969-73; Recipient King's medal for service in cause of freedom; Distinguished Service award National Inst. Arts and Letters, 1963; Gold medal Nat. Inst. Social Scis., 1961; decorated dame Order St. John of Jerusalem. Mem. Nat. Soc. Colonial Dames, Poetry Soc. Am. (exec. bd. 1938-39), Nat. Inst. Social Sci. (gold medal 1961), Hroswitha Club, Philharm. Symphony Soc, Brit. Astron. Union, English Speaking Union. Episcopalian. Clubs: Colony (N.Y.C.) (bd. govs. 1968-76, mem. com. lit. and art 1966); Colony (N.Y.C.) (chmn. library com. 1973, chmn. sub-com. for hon. visitors 1976—); River (N.Y.C.); Sulgrave (Washington). Address: 1030 Fifth Ave New York NY 10028

BULLOCK, JOHN MCDONELL, banker; b. Cin., June 21, 1932; s. John R. and Marion (McDonell) B.; m. Ann Gibson Vaughan, Dec. 28, 1956; children: Lynn A., John R. II, Amy V. Student, U. Ky., 1950-51; B.A., U. Mich., 1954; J.D., U. Va., 1959. Bar: Ohio 1959. Asso. firm Taft, Stettinius & Hollister, Cin., 1959-67, partner, 1967-69; sr. v.p. First Nat. Bank Cin., 1969—; dir. Clopay Corp., U.S. Precision Lens, Inc., Franchise Developers, Inc. Trustee, pres. Community Chest and Council Cin. Area; trustee, chmn. bd. Coll. Mt. St. Joseph, 1978—; mem. community bd. advisers Paul I. Hoxworth Blood Center, 1980—. Mem. Am., Ohio bankers assns., Delta Tau Delta. Clubs: Queen City, Gyro (Cin.); Ryland Lakes Country (Covington, Ky.). Home: 701 Riesling Knoll Cincinnati OH 45226 Office: PO Box 1118 Cincinnati OH 45201

BULLOCK, KENNETH C., educator; b. Pleasant Grove, Utah, Sept. 8, 1918; s. Irving and Cora M. (Carlson) B.; m. Annie Alena Gardiner, Sept. 8, 1938; children—Kenneth G., Virginia, Mary A., Sherilyn. B.S., Brigham Young U., 1940, M.A., 1942; Ph.D., U. Wis., 1949. Research asst. U. Wis., 1942-43, 48-49; instr. geology Brigham Young U., 1943-48, asst. prof., 1948-52, asso. prof. geology, 1952-57, prof., 1957—, chmn. dept., 1956-62; field geologist U.S. Mining, Smelting & Refining Co., summers 1947-48, Interstate Brick Co., summers 1949-50; geol. engr. Columbia-Geneva Steel Co., summers, 1951-52, Columbia Iron Mining Co., 1953-54, 60, Utah Geol. and Mineral Survey, 1967, U.S. Bur. Mines, 1975. Author: Principles of Optical Mineralogy, 1955, Geology of Lake Mountain, Utah, 1961, Minerals and Mineral Localities of Utah, 1960, Minerals of Utah, 1967, Iron Deposits of Utah, 1971, Fluorite Occurrences of Utah, 1976, Minerals and Mineral Localities of Utah, 1981; co-author: Uranium, Where It Is and How To Find It, 1954. Served from ensign to lt. (j.g.) USNR, 1944-46. Fellow Geol. Soc. Am.; mem. Am. Inst. Mining and Metall. Engrs., Mineral. Soc. Am., Nat. Assn. Geology Tchrs., Utah Acad. Arts, Sci. and Letters, Utah Geol. Assn., Sigma Xi, Sigma Gamma Gamma Epsilon. Home: 1035 N 900 E Provo UT 84604

BULLOCK, MAURICE RANDOLPH, lawyer; b. Colorado City, Tex., Aug. 20, 1913; s. Jesse H. and Georgia (White) B.; m. Wilda

Marie Frost, Nov. 25, 1939; children: Dan Randolph, Sara Virginia. LL.B., U. Tex., 1936. Bar: Tex. 1936. Mem. firm Silliman & Bullock, Ft. Stockton, Tex., 1936-39; Pecos County atty., 1939-43, pvt. practice law, Ft. Stockton, 1946—; partner firm Bullock, Kerr & Scott, Ft. Stockton, 1963-65; now partner firm Bullock, Scott & Neisig, Midland, Tex.; mem. adv. com. Tex. Supreme Ct. Past chmn. State Securities Bd. Tex.; Texas adv. com. to Civil Rights Commn., 1960-62; chmn. bd. executors, exec. com. Permian Basin Petroleum Mus., Library and Hall of Fame; mem. exec. com. Tex. Law Enforcement Found., 1964—; past pres. Midland Symphony Assn., Midland-Odessa Symphony and Chorale, Inc.; Served as chmn. 1958 Tex. Dem. Conv. Served as spl. agt. Security Intelligence Corps AUS, 1943-46. Fellow Am., Tex. bar founds., Am. Coll. Probate Counsel; mem. ABA (house of dels. 1958-62), Trans-Pecos Bar Assn. (pres. 1964-65), Midland County Bar Assn., State Bar Tex. (pres. 1955-56), Southwestern Legal Found. (trustee 1969—, exec. com. 1973—), Tex. Trial Lawyers Assn., Am. Judicature Soc. (past dir.), Permian Basin Petroleum Assn. (past dir.), Ft. Stockton Hist. Soc. (past dir.), Pecos County C. of C. (past pres.), West Tex. C. of C. (past v.p.), Order of Coif. Democrat. Methodist. Lectr. on oil and gas and securities law. Home: 3200 Racquet Club Dr Midland TX 79705 Office: 1st Nat Bank Bldg Midland TX 79701

BULLOCK, ORIN MILES, JR., architect; b. Oakland, Calif., Dec. 26, 1905; s. Orin Miles and Annie Maria (Ford) B.; m. Lucy Meadowcroft Beaman, Apr. 25, 1964; 1 dau., Amanda (Mrs. Joseph J. Scalabrin, Jr.). Spl. student certificate, Harvard Grad. Sch. Architecture, 1927. Draftsman Cram & Ferguson (architects), Boston, 1926-27; constrn. supr. Perry Shaw & Hepburn (architects), Williamsburg, Va., 1929-34; regional architect Nat. Park Service, Richmond, Va., 1934-40; practice architecture, Portsmouth, Va., 1948-51; dir. archtl. research Colonial Williamsburg, Va., 1953-61; profl. practice restoration historic bldgs., Balt., 1967—; faculty U. Md. Sch. Architecture; cons., lectr. historic preservation; prin. investigator NEH grant for preservation tech., 1980; Dir. Historic Annapolis Inc.; Chmn. Nat. Park Service adv. bd. Am. Bldg. Survey, 1967-68. Prin. works include restoration Friends Meeting House, 1699, Newport, R.I., Brooklandwood Mansion, nr. Balt., Tudor Hall, Leonardtown, Md. Bd. dirs. Preservation Md. Antiquities; hon. bd. dirs. Stratford Plantation Va.; archtl. adviser Soc. Preservation Md. Antiquities, Sleepy Hollow Restoration, Tarrytown, N.Y. Served from lt. to comdr. USNR, 1942-47. Recipient Design prize San Francisco Archtl. Club, 1924, Calvert prize for preservation Md. architecture, 1980. Fellow AIA (nat. com. chmn. 1965-66, treas. Va. 1950, sec. Balt. 1964-66); mem. Nat. Trust for Historic Preservation, Assn. Preservation Tech. Club: Mason. Address: 1352 Telegraph Rd Rising Sun MD 21911

BULLOCK, THEODORE HOLMES, biologist, educator; b. Nanking, China, May 16, 1915; s. Amasa Archibald and Ruth (Beckwith) B.; m. Martha Runquist, May 30, 1937; children—Elsie Christine, Stephen Holmes. Student, Pasadena Jr. Coll., 1932-34; A.B., U. Calif. at Berkeley, 1936, Ph.D., 1940; Sterling fellow zoology, Yale, 1940-41, Rockefeller fellow exptl. neurology, 1941-42. Research asso. Yale U. Sch. Medicine, 1942-43, instr. neuroanatomy, 1943-44; instr. Marine Biol. Lab., Woods Hole, Mass., 1944-46, head invertebrate zoology, 1955-57, trustee, 1955-57; asst. prof. anatomy U. Mo., 1944-46; asst. prof. zoology U. Calif. at Los Angeles, 1946, asso. prof., 1948, prof., 1955-66; Brain Research Inst., U. Calif. at Los Angeles, 1960-66; prof. neuroscis. Med. Sch., U. Calif. at San Diego, 1966—; Mem. AEC 2d Resurvey of Bikini Expdn., 1948. Author: (with G.A. Horridge) Structure and Function in the Nervous Systems of Invertebrates, 2 vols, 1965, (with others) Introduction to Nervous Systems, 1977. Fulbright scholar Stazione Zooologica, Naples, 1950-51; fellow Center Advanced Study in Behavioral Scis., Palo Alto, 1959-60. Fellow A.A.A.S.; mem. Am. Soc. Zoologists (chmn. comparative physiology div. 1961, pres. 1965), Soc. Neuroscis. (pres. 1973-74), Am. Physiol. Soc., Soc. Gen. Physiologists, Am. Acad. Arts and Scis., Nat. Acad. Scis., Am. Philos. Soc., Internat. Brain Research Orgn., Phi Beta Kappa, Sigma Xi. Home: 3258 Caminito Ameca La Jolla CA 92037

BULLOCK, WILLIAM CLAPP, JR., banker; b. Bronxville, N.Y., June 28, 1936; s. William and Elizabeth (Van Wagnen) B.; m. Edith Swain, June 21, 1958; children: Wendy, Martha, Sarah, Bill. B.A., Yale U., 1958; postgrad., NYU, 1958-60. Asst. treas., asst. v.p. nat. div. Morgan Guaranty Trust Co., N.Y.C., 1958-69; v.p., sr. loan officer Merrill Trust Co., Bangor, Maine, 1969-71, exec. v.p., 1971-73, pres., 1973-80, pres., chief exec. officer, 1980-82, chmn. bd., pres., 1982—; pres. Merrill Bankshares Co., 1973-80, pres., chief exec. officer, 1980-82, chmn. bd., pres., 1982—; dir. Courier Gazette, Pepsi-Cola Bottling Co., Maine Capital Corp., Bangor Hydro-Electric Co., Eastern Maine Health Care. Bd. dirs. Gov. Longley's Task Force on Indian Land Claims, 1979-80, Assoc. Industries of Maine, 1978-81, New Eng. Council, 1981—. Mem. Maine Bankers Assn. (dir., v.p.), Am. Bankers Assn., Maine C. of C. (former dir.). Clubs: Yale, N.Y. Anglers. Home: RFD 2 PO Box 121 Orrington ME 04474 Office: Merrill Bankshares Co Exchange St Bangor ME 04401

BULLOCK, WILLIAM H., clergyman; b. Maple Lakes, Minn., Apr. 13, 1927; s. Loren W. and Anne C. (Raiche) B. B.A., Notre Dame U., 1948, M.A., 1962; Ed.S., St. Thomas Coll., St. Paul, 1969. Ordained priest Roman Catholic Ch.; ordained bishop Roman Catholic Ch. Assoc. pastor Ch. of St. Stephens, Mpls., 1952-55, Ch. of Our Lady of Grace, Edina, Minn., 1955-56, Ch. of Incarnation, Mpls., 1956-57; instr. St. Thomas Acad., Mendota Heights, Minn., 1957-61, headmaster, 1968-71; pastor Ch. of St. John the Baptist, Excelsior, Minn., 1971-80, Ch. of Our Lady of Perpetual Help, Mpls., 1980—; aux. bishop Archdiocese of St. Paul and Mpls., 1980—, vicar for parishes-deaneries, 1980—, consultor, 1980—; vicar for edn. programs Coll., Seminaries, Catholic Edn. Ctr. and Youth Ctrs.; vicar for ministry to handicapped-charismatic. Contbr. in field. Trustee St. Paul Sem., St. Mary's Jr. Coll. Served with USN, 1944-46. Mem. Minn. Bishops Conf. (sec.), U.S. Bishops-Region VIII, Bishops Com. on Liturgy, Commn. on Continuing Edn. for Priests. Lodges: D.C.; Knights of Holy Sepulchre. Office: Archdiocese of Saint Paul and Minneapolis 226 Summit Ave Saint Paul MN 55102

BULLOUGH, JOHN FRANK, organist, music educator; b. Washington, Oct. 15, 1928; s. John and Mabel Jean (McCalip) B.; m. Dorothy Baines, Apr. 10, 1950; children: John Frank, Lynn Diane, Patricia Ann. A.B., George Washington U., 1954; S.M.M., Union Theol. Sem., 1958. Organist, asst. prof. music Hartford Theol. Sem. Found., Conn., 1958-64; asst. prof. music Fairleigh Dickinson U., Teaneck, N.J., 1964-70, assoc. prof., 1970-74, prof., 1974—, chmn. dept. fine arts, 1974-79; music dir. Hartford Ctr. Ch., 1960-64; organist, choirmaster St. Paul's Episcopal Ch., Englewood, N.J., 1973—. Contbr. articles to profl. jours. V.p. bd. trustees Bergen Philharm. Orch., N.J., 1973—. Mem. Am. Guild Organists (dean Hartford chpt. 1963-64, No. Valley chpt. 1975—), Coll. Music Soc., AAUP. Episcopalian. Home: 488 Fairidge Terr Teaneck NJ 07666 Office: Fairleigh Dickinson U Teaneck NJ 07666

BULMAN, JAMES CORNELIUS, state judge; b. Greenfield, Mass., July 24, 1911; s. James Henry and Mary (Shea) B.; m. Marian B. McLaughlin, Mar. 23, 1935 (dec. 1977); children—Georgia (Mrs. Douglas K. Goss), James Cornelius, Sarah Shea (Mrs. Douglas P. Caraganis). B.S., U. Mass., 1933; LL.B., Fordham U., 1940. Bar: N.Y. bar 1946, R.I. bar 1947. Spl. agt. FBI, 1942-46; trial lawyer firm Boss, Conlan, Keenan, Bulman & Rice, Providence, 1947-64; judge R.I. Superior Ct., 1964—. Mem. ABA, R.I. Bar Assn. (pres. 1963-64), Nat. Conf. Bar Presidents, Inst. Jud. Adminstrn., Nat. Conf. State Trial Judges. Home: 20 Indian Ave Portsmouth RI 02871 Office: Providence County Courthouse Providence RI 02903

BULZACCHELLI, JOHN G., financial executive; b. N.Y.C., July 7, 1939; s. Vito N. and Mary B.; m. Frances R. Rocco, Nov. 30, 1963; children—John F., Robert V. B.S., CUNY, 1962. Staff acct. Haskins & Sells, N.Y.C., 1962-65; treas., controller Grumman Allied Ind., Inc., Garden City, N.Y., 1965-69; controller Wellington Tech. Ind., Inc., Englewood, N.Y., 1969; v.p. fin. Gulf & Western Systems, Inc., N.Y.C., 1970-76; exec. v.p. Kayser-Roth Corp., N.Y.C., 1976-81, Gulf & Western Consumer Products Co., 1981, Gulf & Western Consumer and Indsl. Products Group, 1983—. Bd. dirs. Cotswold Civic Assn., 1968-69. Served with USMC, 1962. Mem. Am. Apparel Mfrs. Assn. Republican. Roman Catholic. Club: Coveleigh (Rye, N.Y.). Home: 33 Medford Ln Scarsdale NY 10583 Office: 640 Fifth Ave New York NY 10019

BUMBERY, JOSEPH LAWRENCE, diversified company executive; b. St. Louis, May 30, 1929; s. John Andrew and Lillian Belle (DeVinney) B. B.S., St. Louis U., 1951. Asst. comptroller Magic Chef, Inc., St. Louis, 1955-57; dir. audits and systems Bemis Corp., St. Louis, 1957-62; asst. comptroller Studebaker Corp., South Bend, Ind., 1962-65; with ITT, N.Y.C., 1965—, v.p., 1979—, asst. comptroller, 1969—. Served to 1st lt. USAF, 1951-53. Decorated Officer Order St. John of Jerusalem (U.K.); St. Louis U. scholar, 1947-51. Episcopalian. Office: 320 Park Ave New York NY 10022

BUMBRY, GRACE, soprano; b. St. Louis, Jan. 4, 1937; d. Benjamin and Melzia (Walker) B. Student, Boston U., 1954-55, Music Acad. West, 1956-59; studied with, Lotte Lehmann, Northwestern U., also; H.H.D. (hon.), St. Louis U., Rust Coll., D. Mus., Rockhurst Coll. Operatic debut, Paris Opera, 1960, concert and operatic appearances in, Europe, Japan, Bayreuth, Germany and U.S.; also command performance, The White House; performed, Met. Opera, N.Y.C., Royal Opera House Covent Garden, London, La Scala Milan, Vienna Stateopera, Teatro Colon Buenos Aires, Chgo. Lyric Opera, Berlin Opera, San Francisco Opera, others., recs. for, Deutsche Grammophon, Angel, London and, RCA. Recipient John Hay Whitney award, 1959, Richard Wagner medal, 1963, awards Nat. Assn. Negro Musicians, Boston U., numerous others; hon. citizen Balt., Los Angeles, Phila., St. Louis. Mem. Zeta Phi Beta, Sigma Alpha Iota. Office: care Columbia Artists Mgmt 165 W 57th St New York NY 10019 *

BUMGARDNER, ALBERT ORIN, architect; b. Springfield, Ill., Jan. 3, 1923; s. Alfred Orin and Florence (Lonas) B. Student, Ill. State U., 1941-43, City Coll. N.Y., 1943-44; B.Arch. summa cum laude, U. Ill., 1949. Pvt. practice architecture, Seattle, 1953-61; partner firm A. O. Bumgardner & Partners, Seattle, 1961-70; prin. The Bumgardner Partnership, Seattle, 1970—; cons. editor Architecture West, 1957-71; vis. lectr. U. Wash., 1961, 67, Mont. State U., 1967; Mem Municipal Art Commn. Seattle, 1965-69; chmn. Design Commn. Seattle, 1969-71; mem. exec. bd. Commn. 2000, Seattle, 1972—. Served with USAAF, 1943-46. Recipient Sunset mag. Design awards, 1965, 69; Seattle chpt. A.I.A. Honor awards for Excellence of Design, 1954, 56, 58, 60, 63, 65, 67, 69, 70, 73, 75, 83. Fellow A.I.A. (pres. Seattle 1962-63); mem. Alpha Rho Chi. Home: 2017 Broadway East Seattle WA 98102 Office: 51 University St Suite 300 Seattle WA 98101

BUMGARNER, JOHN CARSON, SR., mgmt. cons.; b. Tulsa, Feb. 5, 1908; s. Aaron Alvin and Lottie Esther (Turkington) B.; m. Susan Elizabeth Nall, Nov. 6, 1937; children—Betty Sue, John Carson. Student, U. Tulsa, 1925-26; B.S., U. Ill., 1929. C.P.A., Tex. Staff accountant Haskins & Sells (C.P.A.'s), Tulsa, 1929-40; sec.-treas. Lawson Petroleum Co., Tulsa, 1940-42, v.p., 1942-44; sec.-treas. Wood River Oil & Refining Co., Inc., Wichita, Kans., 1944-54; controller Mid-Continent Petroleum Corp., Tulsa, 1954-55, D-X Sunray Oil Co., 1955-58, Sunray DX Oil Co., 1958-68; asst. controller Sun Oil Co. DX Div., 1968-70; mgr. gen. accounting Sun Oil Co., 1970-72; mgmt. cons., 1972—. Mem. Financial Execs. Inst. (past pres. Okla.), Nat. Assn. Accountants (past pres. Wichita), Am. Inst. C.P.A.'s, Am. Petroleum Inst. Presbyn. Club: Tulsa Country. Home: 3714 S Delaware Pl Tulsa OK 74105 Office: 3714 S Delaware Pl Tulsa OK 74105

BUMP, BOARDMAN, investment mgr.; b. Pittsfield, Mass., Dec. 8, 1908; s. Charles Henry and Esther Elizabeth (Boardman) B.; m. Eleanor Myrick, June 28, 1933; children—Carolyn Bump Marsh, Daniel Boardman, Susan Bump Vancura, Jonathan. A.B. magna cum laude, Amherst Coll., 1930; M.B.A., Harvard U., 1932. Asst. purchasing agt. Mt. Holyoke Coll., 1932- 34, comptroller, 1934-51, asst. treas., 1939-42, treas., 1942-73, v.p., 1951-54, trustee, 1955-65, 66-76; partner Morrison & Bump, 1955, Morrison, Bump & Morse, 1956-63, Bump, Morse & Marsh, 1963—; mng. gen. partner Vance, Sanders Exchange Fund, 1976—; hon. dir. Liberty Mut. Ins. Co. Recipient Distinguished Service medal Bd. Trustees Mt. Holyoke Coll., 1976. Mem. Phi Beta Kappa. Club: Harvard of Boston. Home: East Run Farm RFD 3 Box 104 Putney VT 05346 Office: 31 Milk St Boston MA 02109

BUMP, GERALD JACK, executive recruitment consultant; b. Chgo., June 7, 1927; s. Gerald Chism and Margaret Aileen (Raede) B.; m. Jeanne A. Courtney, Sept. 4, 1947; children: Jana Lee, Jerry Lyle, Jamie Lou, Jeffrey Lee. B.S. in Edn., Purdue U., 1949, M.S. in Indsl. Sociology, 1950. With Kimberly Clark Corp., 1950-60, supr. personnel procurement, Neenah, Wis., 1958-60; from mgr. staff employment to regional sales mgr. Trane Co., 1960-69; with Billington, Fox & Ellis, Inc., Chgo., 1969-81, exec. v.p., 1977-80, pres., dir., 1980—; mng. dir. Spencer Stuart & Assocs., Atlanta, 1980—. Bd. govs. Ga. Bus. and Industry Assn., 1971-75; bus. mgr., bd. dirs. LaCrosse (Wis.) Community Theatre, 1964-67; mem. ann. fund com. U. Ga., 1982—. Served with USNR, 1945-46. Mem. Assn. Exec. Recruiting Cons. (v.p., dir. 1977-81), Atlanta C. of C. Republican. Episcopalian. Club: Peachtree World of Tennis. Home: 2470 Stonington Rd Atlanta GA 30338

BUMPASS, LARRY LEE, sociologist, educator; b. Detroit, Feb. 16, 1942; s. Yancy Washington and Emma Lee (Moore) B.; m. Janet Arlene Angles, Aug. 3, 1962; children—Shauna Lynn, Carri Noelle. B.A., Wheaton Coll., 1963; M.A., U. Mich., 1965, Ph.D., 1968. Research asso. Office of Population, Princeton U., 1967-70; mem. faculty dept. sociology U. Wis., Madison, 1970—, prof., 1973—; dir. Center for Demography and Ecology, 1977-80; fellow Econ. Commn. for Europe, UN, Geneva, Switzerland, 1974; chmn. population and social sci. study sect. NIH, 1978-80. Author: The Later Years of Childbearing, 1970, Social Demography, 1978; Editor: Demography, 1978-81. Mem. Population Assn. Am. (bd. dirs. 1973-77, 2d v.p. 1982), Am. Sociol. Assn. (chmn. population sect. 1982), Internat. Union for Sci. Study of Population, AAAS, ACLU. Home: 5821 Barton Rd Madison WI 53711 Office: 3224 Social Sci 1180 Observatory Dr Madison WI 53706

BUMPERS, DALE L., senator, former governor of Arkansas; b. Charleston, Ark., Aug. 12, 1925; s. William Rufus and Lattie (Jones) B.; m. Betty Lou Flanagan, Sept. 4, 1949; children: Dale Brent, William Mark, Margaret Brooke. Student, U. Ark., 1943, 46-48; J.D., Northwestern U., 1951. Bar: Ark. 1952. Pres. Charleston Hardware and Furniture Co., 1951-66; pvt. practice, Charleston, 1952-70; operator Angus cattle farm, 1966-70; gov. of, Ark., 1970-74, U.S. senator, 1975—. Pres. Charleston Sch. Bd., 1969-70. Served with USMC, 1943-46. Mem. Charleston C. of C. (pres.). Methodist. Home: Charleston AR 72933 Office: Room SD-229 Dirksen Senate Office Bldg Washington DC 20510

BUNCE, DONALD FAIRBAIRN MACDOUGAL, II, anatomist, physician; b. Harrisburg, Pa., July 15, 1920; s. Wesley Hibbard and Jean (Fairbairn) B.; m. Lorraine Pelch, May 1, 1954 (dec. Nov. 1975); children: Chip Gregory Alan, Dale Graham Alison; m. Suzanne Brockman, July 13, 1978. B.S., U. Miami, 1951; M.Sc., U. Ill., 1959, Ph.D., 1960; D.O., Coll. Osteo. Medicine and Surgery, 1973. Pres., Bunce Sch. Lab. Technique, Coral Gables, Fla., 1945-48; clin. physiologist Armour Labs., Chgo., 1953-56; dir. research Chgo. Pharmacal Co., 1956-57; instr. anatomy Tulane Sch. Medicine, 1960-62; research prof. physiology Coll. Osteo. Medicine and Surgery, Des Moines, 1962-67, dir. grad. sch., 1962-73, prof. pathology, acting chmn. dept., 1966-68, prof. physiology, chmn. dept., 1967-73; intern, house physician Des Moines Gen. Hosp., 1973-74; gen. practice medicine, Forest City, Iowa, 1974-78, Dubuque, Iowa, 1978-80; clin. assoc. prof. dept. medicine U. Ala. Sch. Medicine, Tuscaloosa, 1982—; chief of staff Forest City Hosp., 1977-78; chief physician Acute Med. Care Unit, Bryce Hosp., Tuscaloosa, Ala., 1980—, vice-chief of staff, 1984—; former mem. staff Mercy, Finley and Xavier hosps., Dubuque; now mem. staff Hale and Druid City hosps., Tuscaloosa; vis. fellow Inst. Exptl. Surgery, Copenhagen, 1962; vis. prof. Karolinska Inst., Stockholm, 1965, Edinburgh, Scotland, 1966, Kennedy Inst. Rheumatology, London, 1969-70; travelling fellow NSF-Internat. Union Physiology; program dir. grad. tng. program in med. scis. NIH; ofcl. del. 4th Internat. Congress Angiology. Editorial bd.: Angéiologie, Paris, 1960—, Jour. Psychiat. Medicine, 1984—; author: Laboratory Guide to Microscopic Anatomy, 1964, The Nervous System in Canine Medicine, 3d edit., 1968, Atlas of Arterial Histology, 1973; also articles. Bd. dirs. Mus. Sci. and Industry, Des Moines, 1971-75. Recipient Billups Meml. Research award La. Heart Assn., 1960. Fellow Am. Coll. Angiology, AAAS, N.Y., Iowa acads sci., Royal Soc. Medicine; mem. AMA, Iowa Med. Soc., Dubuque County Med. Soc., Ala. Med. Assn., Tuscaloosa County Med. Soc., Am. Osteo. Assn., Am. Assn. Anatomists, Anat. Soc. Gt. Britain, So. Soc. Anatomists (exec. sec. 1960-62), Path. Soc. Gt. Britain, Soc. Exptl. Biology and Medicine, Am. Assn. U. Profs., Instn. Nuclear Engrs., L'Union Internationale d'Angéiologie, Société Francais d'Angéiologie et d'Histopathologie, Mensa, Sigma Xi, Sigma Alpha Epsilon. Club: Mason. Research in anatomy and diseases of blood vessels, fetal pathophysiology. Invented Bunce double hemostat used to remove surgically blood vessels and other tissues for study in vitro; patentee in field. Home: 404 Woodland Hills Tuscaloosa AL 35405

BUNCE, STANLEY CHALMERS, educator, chemist; b. Bayonne, N.J., Aug. 21, 1917; s. Arthur Chalmers and Elizabeth (Sticht) B.; m. Lillis Adelle Jackson, Oct. 2, 1943; children: Gale Elizabeth Bunce Schmidt, Judith Preston Bunce Turner, James Arthur. B.S. in Chemistry, Lehigh U., 1938, M.A., 1942; Ph.D. in Chemistry, Rensselaer Poly. Inst., 1951. Secondary sch. tchr. Hershey (Pa.) Indsl. Sch., 1939-41, Bound Brook (N.J.) High Sch., 1941-43; research chemist Johns-Manville Corp., 1943-46; mem. faculty Rensselaer Poly. Inst., Troy, N.Y., 1946—, prof. chemistry, 1958—, asso. chmn. dept., 1972-75. Author: (with others) Principles of Chemistry, 1966, An Approach to Physical Science, 1967; also research publs. Fellow AAAS; mem. Am. Chem. Soc. (chmn. Eastern N.Y. sect. 1961), Chem. Soc. (London), Fedn. Am. Scientists, N.Y. Acad. Scis., Sigma Xi, Phi Lambda Upsilon. Home: Taconic Lake Rd Grafton NY 12082 Office: Dept Chemistry Rensselaer Poly Inst Troy NY 12181

BUNCH, FRANKLIN SWOPE, architect; b. Madison, Ind., Jan. 4, 1913; s. Walker Franklin and Susan Beatrice (Swope) B.; m. Virginia Aurelia Boggs, June 8, 1937; children: Franklin Swope, Dean Boggs. B.S. in Arch, U. Fla., 1934. Draftsman, designer, architect and constrn. supr. various Fla. architects, 1934-41; archtl. engr. U.S. Engrs. Dist. Office, Jacksonville, Fla., 1942-43, Jacksonville Naval Air Sta., 1944-45; partner Kemp, Bunch & Jackson (Architects, Inc.), Jacksonville, 1946-69, sr. v.p., 1970-82; Pres. Fla. Bd. Architecture, 1959-61; mem. com. on exams. Nat. Council Archtl. Registration Bds., 1961-62; pres. bldg. code adv. bd., Jacksonville, 1949-68, mem. examining com., 1949—; chmn. bldg. codes adjustment bd. Jacksonville Consol. Govt.; mem. housing com. Jacksonville Council on Aging, 1962. Projects include S. Central Home Office Prudential Ins. Co. Am., gen. offices Seaboard Coast Line R.R., Fla. State Prison, Starke, Hdqrs. Bldg. State Rd. Dept., Tallahassee. Pres. Little Theatre of Jacksonville, 1952-53. Fellow AIA (emeritus); mem. Fla. Assn. Architects (pres. 1947-48, now emeritus), Jacksonville Jr. C. of C. (chmn. luncheon club 1938), Jacksonville Area C. of C. (chmn. city, county, state affairs com. 1963, chmn. fed. assistance 1949-68), Phi Kappa Tau. Baptist. Club: Riverbend Country (Sugar Land, Tex.). Home: 26 River Creek Way Sugar Land TX 77478

BUNCH, JOHN BLAKE, instructional technology educator; b. Cohocton, Ohio, Sept. 14, 1940; s. Ralph Theodore and Lorena mae (Gentry) B.; m. Elaine Rosann O'Rourke, Dec. 16, 1968; children: Royanne, Lorraine, Kathleen Rose. B.A., U. Ky., 1971; M.A., Ind. U., 1974; Ph.D. in Edn., 1978. Sr. ops. supr. Flying Tiger Line, 1962-69; grad. instr. Ind. U., Bloomington, 1973-77; dir. faculty devel. U. Va., Charlottesville, 1980—, prof. instructional tech., dir. instructional services, 1977—. Contbr. articles to profl. jours. Served with U.S. Army, 1959-62. Mem. Am. Soc. Tng. and Devel. (exec. com. media div.), Assn. Ednl. Communications and tech. (nat. council 1979-80), Va. Higher Edn. Media Assn. (pres.), Va. Folklore Soc. (treas.), Phi Beta Kappa. Home: 2316 Crestmont Ave Charlottesville VA 22903 Office: U Va Ruffner Hall 405 Emmet St Charlottesville VA 22903 *Wisdom is when you arrive at that state of life where you realize that real satisfaction comes from devoting your talents to matters bigger than and beyond your own ego, and when you know that you shouldn't take yourself to seriously.*

BUNCHER, JAMES EDWARD, health care company executive; b. Moline, Ill., Sept. 19, 1936; s. Ralph Frank and Mae Loretta (Eis) B.; m. Mary Alice Dodge, Sept. 3, 1961; 1 son, Douglas James. B.S. in Acctg., U. Ill., 1961, M.Acctg. Sci., 1962. C.P.A. Staff auditor Peat, Marwick, Mitchell & Co., St. Louis, 1962-63; controller, asst. v.p. SCM Corp., Cleve., 1963-72; controller Hosp. Products div. Abbott Labs., North Chicago, Ill., 1972-74; pres., chief operating officer Hosp. Affiliates Internat., Inc., Nashville, 1974-82; chmn., chief exec. officer Republic Health Corp., Dallas, 1982—; pres., chief operating officer INA Healthplan (Dallas), 1979-80, 81-82. Served with USN, 1956-58. Mem. Fedn. Am. Hosps. (dir., v.p., vice-chmn. adminstrv. affairs com., chmn. by-laws subcom.). Methodist. Clubs: Gleneagles Country, University. Office: 14951 Dallas Pkwy Suite 1100 Dallas TX 75240 *

BUNDICK, WILLIAM ROSS, physician; b. Balt., Nov. 22, 1917; s. Percy Ross and Edith Ruth (Smith) B.; m. Katherine Harrison Epps, Apr. 22, 1945; children: Susan Bundick Sukeforth, Karen Lee, Paul

Ross. M.D., U. Md., 1941; postgrad., N.Y.U., 1947-48. Diplomate: Am. Bd. Dermatology. Intern Baroness Erlanger Hosp., Chattanooga, 1941-42; resident Ft. Howard (Md.) VA Hosp., 1946-47; practice medicine specializing in dermatology, 1947—; assoc. dermatologist Mercy Hosp., Balt., 1947-67; assoc. in dermatology U. Md. Sch. Medicine, 1952-58, Johns Hopkins U. Sch. Medicine, 1952-58; asst. dermatologist St. Joseph Hosp., Towson, Md., 1947-69, chief dermatology, 1970—; pvt. practice medicine, Timonium, Md., 1971—. Chess editor: Balt. Sunday Sun, 1963-74; compiler, editor: directory Internat. Assn. Jazz Record Collectors; contbr. articles to med. jours. Served to capt. M.C. AUS, 1942-46. Fellow Am. Acad. Dermatology; mem. AMA, Md. Dermatol. Soc., Med. and Chiurg. Faculty of Md., Md. Chess Assn. (pres. 1964), U.S. Chess Fedn. (dir. 1959-64), Assn. Internationale de la Presse Echiqueene. Club: Towson Chess (pres.) (1959, 65). Lodge: Timonium Rotary (pres. 1961-62). Home: 131 Beech Bark Ln Towson MD 21204 Office: 10 Gerad Ave Timonium MD 21093

BUNDSCHUH, GEORGE AUGUST WILLIAM, insurance company executive; b. Yonkers, N.Y., Sept. 24, 1933; s. George and Anna B.; m. Joanne Detjen; children: Russell, Erica. B.B.A., Pace U., 1955; M.S., Columbia U. Grad. Sch. Bus., 1959. Chartered fin. analyst. With N.Y. Life Ins. Co., N.Y.C., 1959—, sr. v.p., 1979-80, exec. v.p., 1980—. Served with AUS, 1956-58. Mem. Inst. Chartered Fin. Analysts. Office: 51 Madison Ave New York NY 10010

BUNDY, CHARLES ALAN, foundation executive; b. Cheraw, S.C., Jan. 5, 1930; s. Jackson Corbett and Ruby Jones (Hughes) B.; m. Margaret Ellen Jackson, Feb. 27, 1954; children: Charles Alan, Robert Jackson, Dan Hughes. A.B., Wofford Coll., 1951. Mgr. prodn. planning J.P. Stevens & Co., Inc., Rockingham, N.C., 1951-54; mgr. Jesup (Ga.) C. of C., 1954-56, Lancaster (S.C.) C. of C., 1956-61; dist. mgr. U.S. C. of C., Birmingham, Ala., 1961-65; exec. v.p. Macon (Ga.) C. of C., 1965-71, Greg Enterprises, Lancaster, 1971-72; pres. Elliott White Springs Found., Inc. and Frances Ley Springs Found., Inc., Lancaster, 1972—. Chmn., S.C. Dept. Parks, Recreation and Tourism Commn.; trustee Columbia Coll.; chmn. bd. 1st Meth. Ch., 1978, 79. Mem. Council on Founds., S.E. Council Founds (past chmn.), Lancaster County C. of C. (past pres.). Club: Rotary (past pres.). Home: 518 Briarwood Rd Lancaster SC 29720 Office: 206 S White St Lancaster SC 29720

BUNDY, HARVEY HOLLISTER, banker; b. Cambridge, Mass., May 1, 1916; s. Harvey Hollister and Katherine Lawrence (Putnam) B.; m. Edith Southerland Wright, May 29, 1943; children: Harvey Hollister, Harriet Southerland Bundy Burgin, Peter Putnam, Rodman Richards. B.A., Yale U., 1938; M.B.A., Harvard U., 1940. C.P.A., Mass. Accountant Lybrand Ross Bros. & Montgomery (C.P.A.'s), Boston, 1940-41; with Gorton Group, Gloucester, Mass., 1946-78, treas., 1948-78, fin. v.p., 1958-69, exec. v.p., 1969-78; pres., chief exec. officer Bank of New Eng.-North Shore, 1978-84, chmn. bd., 1984—. Mem. Manchester (Mass.) Sch. Com., 1948-54, chmn., 1951-53; agt. Class of '38, Yale Alumni Fund, 1967-71; mem. coms. to visit math. and statistics depts. Harvard Coll., 1970-77; bd. overseers Bates Coll.; trustee Addison Gilbert Hosp., Gloucester. Served to maj. AUS, 1941-46. Mem. Nat. Fisheries Inst. (dir. 1955—, pres. 1961-62, chmn. bd. 1962-63), Am. Inst. Accountants, Mass. Soc. C.P.A.'s. Club: Myopia Hunt. Home: 26 Masconomo St Manchester MA 01944 Office: 154 Main St Gloucester MA 01930

BUNDY, JEAN DAVIS, educator; b. Seattle, Sept. 21, 1924; s. Leo Wesley and Edna (Torgerson) B.; m. Ann Hemenway Becker, Aug. 17, 1957 (div. 1981); children: Christopher Davis, Alison Fairchild, Lisa Lanham, Nicholas Bennett. B.A., Wash. State U., 1950; M.A., U. Wis., 1952, Ph.D., 1957; student, U. Dijon, U. Paris, France, 1953-55; M.A., Colby Coll., 1964. From instr. to asso. prof. U. Tex., 1957-63; prof. French Colby Coll., 1963-69, Dana prof. French lit., 1969—, chmn. dept., 1963-72; Cons. Ednl. Testing Service, Coll. Entrance Exam. Bd. Editor: Three French Comedies, 1965. Served with inf. AUS, 1943-46. Decorated Bronze Star; Fulbright scholar, 1953-55, 67-68. Mem. AAUP, Modern Lang. Assn., Am. Assn. Tchrs. French, Assn. Internat. des Etudes Francaises, Phi Beta Kappa, Phi Kappa Phi, Sigma Kappa Phi. Address: PO Box 159 Unity ME 04988

BUNDY, MCGEORGE, educator, former government official; b. Boston, Mar. 30, 1919; s. Harvey Hollister and Katharine Lawrence (Putnam) B.; m. Mary Buckminster Lothrop, June 10, 1950; children: Stephen, Andrew, William, James. A.B., Yale, 1940. Polit. analyst Council Fgn. Relations, 1948-49; vis. lectr. Harvard, 1949-51, asso. prof. govt., 1951-54, dean faculty arts and scis., 1953-61, prof., 1954-61; spl. asst. to the President for nat. security, 1961-66; pres. Ford Found., 1966-79; prof. history N.Y. U., N.Y.C., 1979—. Author: (with Stimson) On Active Service, 1948, The Strength of Government, 1968; Editor: Pattern of Responsibility, 1952. Mem. Am. Polit. Sci. Assn., Phi Beta Kappa. Office: Dept History 19 University Pl New York NY 10003

BUNDY, WILLIAM PUTNAM, editor; b. Washington, Sept. 24, 1917; s. Harvey Hollister and Katharine Lawrence (Putnam) B.; m. Mary Acheson, Jan. 30, 1943; children—Michael, Carol, Christopher. A.B., Yale, 1939, M.A. (hon.), 1961, Harvard, 1940, LL.B., 1947. Bar: D.C. bar 1947. With firm Covington & Burling, Washington, 1947-51; with CIA, 1951-61; staff dir. President's Commn. Nat. Goals, 1960; dep. asst. sec. def. internat. security affairs, 1961-63, asst. sec. def. internat. security affairs, 1963-64, asst. sec. state for East Asian and Pacific affairs, 1964-69; vis. prof., research asso. Center Internat. Studies, Mass. Inst. Tech., 1969-71; editor Fgn. Affairs, Quar. mag., N.Y.C., 1972—. Trustee Am. Assembly, N.Y. Fellow Yale U. Corp., 1961-80. Mem. Council Fgn. Relations. Democrat. Office: 58 E 68th St New York NY 10021

BUNGE, CHARLES ALBERT, library science educator; b. Kimball, Nebr., Mar. 18, 1936; s. Louis Herman and Leona Hazel (Cromwell) B.; m. Joanne C. VonStoeser, Aug. 20, 1960; children: Lorraine A., Jeffrey C. Stephen L. A.B., U. Mo., 1959; M.S. in Library Sci, U. Ill., 1960, Ph.D., 1967. Reference librarian Daniel Boone Regional Library, Columbia, Mo., 1960-62; Ball State Tchrs. Coll., Muncie, Ind., 1962-64; research asso. Library Research Center, U. Ill., 1964-67; mem. faculty Library Sch., U. Wis., Madison, 1967—, now prof. Author: Professional Education and Reference Efficiency, 1967; columnist: Wilson Library Bull, 1972-81. Mem. ALA (Hudge award 1983), Assn. Am. Library Schs. (pres. 1980-81), Wis. Library Assn. (pres. 1972-73, Librarian of Yr. 1983), Phi Beta Kappa, Beta Phi Mu. Home: 840 Woodrow St Madison WI 53711 Office: Univ Wis Library Sch 600 N Park St Madison WI 53706

BUNGE, MARIO AUGUSTO, physicist, philosopher, educator; b. Buenos Aires, Argentina, Sept. 21, 1919; s. Augusto and Marie (Müser) B.; m. Marta Irene Cavallo, Feb. 5, 1959; children: Eric Russell, Silvia Alice; children by previous marriage: Carlos F., Mario A.J. Doctorate physico-math. scis, U. Nat. de La Plata, 1952. Instr. theoretical physics U. Buenos Aires, 1946-52; prof. theoretical physics univs. Buenos Aires and La Plata, 1956-59; prof. philosophy U. Buenos Aires, 1957-62; vis. prof. philosophy U. Pa., 1960-61, U. Tex., 1963; vis. prof. physics and philosophy Temple U., 1963-64, U. Del., 1964-65; prof. philosophy McGill U., Montreal, Can., 1966—; founder, sec. gen. Universidad Obrera Argentina, 1938-43; founder Asociación Mexicana de Epistemología, 1976; assessor Internat. Union History and Philosophy of Sci., 1969-71. Author: Causality, 1959, Metascientific Queries, 1959, La cinemática del electrón relativista, 1960, Intuition and Science, 1962, The Myth of Simplicity, 1963, Foundations of Physics, 1967, Scientific Research, 2 vols, 1967, Philosophy of Physics, 1973, Sense and Reference, 1974, Interpretation and Truth, 1974, The Furniture of the World, 1977, A World of Systems, 1979, The Mind-Body Problem, 1980, Scientific Materialism, 1981, Economía y filosofía, 1982, Lingüística y filosofía, 1983, Controversias en física, 1983, Exploring the World, 1983, Understanding the World, 1983; editor: Studies in the Foundations, Methodology and Philosophy of Science, 1967—, Library of Exact Philosophy, 1970—, Foundations and Philosophy of Science and Technology, 1980—; editorial bd.: Theory and Decision; contbr. articles to profl. jours. Recipient Principe de Asturias prize, 1982; Fellow Conselho de Pesquisas Físicas, Brazil, 1953, Fundación E. Santamarina, Argentina, 1954, Alexander von Humboldt-Stiftung, 1965-66; Guggenheim fellow, 1972-73. Mem. Acad. Internat. de Philosophie des Sci., Inst. Internat. de Philosophie, Assn. Rioplatense de Lógica y Filosofía Cientifica (pres. 1959-63). Office: 3479 Peel St McGill U Montreal PQ Canada H3A 1W7

BUNGE, WALTER RICHARD, publishing co. exec.; b. Fond du Lac, Wis., June 19, 1911; s. Richard H. and Dorothea (Wagner) B.; m. Gertrude Clara Wendland, June 29, 1932; children—Walter Richard (dec.), Carol W. (Mrs. James D. Newman), Margaret Ruth (Mrs. Richard G. Raabe). M.Accounting, Madison (Wis.) Coll. C.P.A., Wis. Pub. accountant, Milw., 1941-42; mgr. budgets Allis-Chalmers Mfg. Co., 1942-54, Inland Steel Co., 1955-61; dir. financial planning Hughes Aircraft Co., 1961- 62; dir. financial operations Jos. Schlitz Brewing Co., 1962-66, controller, 1966-68; v.p., treas., dir. Zerand Corp., 1968-70; tchr. U. Wis. Grad. Sch., 1955-56; chmn. bd. Northwestern Pub. House, Milw., 1951-56, mgr., 1971—; cons. publishing, 1952—. Author: Managerial Budgeting for Profit Improvement, 1968; Contbr. to: Managerial Budgeting, 1964, Handbook of Modern Accounting. Corp. mem. United Community Service Greater Milw., 1952-65, mem. gen. budget com., chmn. budget com. for property, 1952-56; pres. Wis. Lutheran Synod Found., 1965-70. Fellow Budget Execs. Inst. (pres. 1951-52, Neil Dennen award 1962), Wis. Soc. C.P.A.'s (sec. 1949-51), Beta Alpha Psi (life). Republican. Home: 3158 N 104 St Wauwatosa WI 53222

BUNGER, WILLIAM BOONE, educator, chemist; b. Alta Vista, Kans., Feb. 14, 1917; s. Harry T. and Lila (Beagel) B.; m. Ida Margaret Chitwood, May 29, 1941; 1 dau., Jane Margaret Bunger Winn. B.S., Washburn Coll., 1940; M.S., Kans. State U., 1941, Ph.D., 1949. Chemist Hill Packing Co., Topeka, 1939, Hercules Powder Co., 1941-45; instr. chemistry Kans. State U., 1947-49; asst. prof., then asso. prof. Auburn U., 1949-65; prof. chemistry, chmn. dept. Ind. State U., Terre Haute, 1965-82, prof. and chmn. emeritus, 1982—; vis. prof. Oak Ridge Nat. Lab., 1951, 53, Ala. State Chem. Lab., 1955, Humble Oil and Refining Co., 1957. Author: (with others) Organic Solvents, 3d edit., 1971. Mem. AAAS, Am. Chem. Soc. (chmn. Auburn sect. 1953-54), Ind. Acad. Sci., Sigma Xi, Phi Lambda Upsilon. Home: 1610 Rice Ave Terre Haute IN 47803

BUNIM, MARY-ELLIS, TV producer; b. Northampton, Mass., July 9, 1946; d. Frank Roberts and Roslyn Dena (LaMontagne) Paxton; m. Robert Eric Bunim, Jan. 31, 1971; 1 dau., Juliana. Student, Fordham U., 1970-74. Asso. producer Leo Burnett Co. (advt.), N.Y.C., 1975-76; mem. profl. adv. com. Randolph (Vt.) Vocat. Sch., 1979. Exec. producer: daily TV series Search for Tomorrow, N.Y.C., 1976-81, As the World Turns, 1981—. Mem. Nat. Acad. TV Arts and Scis., Dirs. Guild Am. Home: New York NYOffice: 524 W 57th St New York NY 10019

BUNKER, GEORGE M., mfg. co. exec.; b. Chgo., 1908; (married). B.S., M.I.T., 1937. Vice pres. mfg. Kroger Co., 1942-49; pres. Trailmobile Inc., 1949-52; chmn. Martin Marietta Corp., 1952-77; chmn. bd. Bunker Ramo Corp., 1975—, also dir.; dir. Bulova Watch Co., Nuclear Corp. Am., Fla. Capital Corp., Washington Senators. Office: 900 Commerce Dr Oak Brook IL 60521 *

BUNKER, JOHN BIRKBECK, sugar company executive; b. Yonkers, N.Y., Mar. 28, 1926; s. Ellsworth and Harriet (Butler) B.; m. Emma Cadwalader, Feb. 27, 1954; children: Emma, Jeanie, Harriet, John C., Lambert C. B.A., Yale U., 1950. With Nat. Sugar Refining Co., 1953-62; pres., dir. Gt. Western Sugar Co., Denver, 1966, Holly Sugar Co., Colorado Springs, Colo., 1967—; chmn., 1971-81, chief exec. officer, 1971-81; dir., pres. Calif. and Hawaiian Sugar Co., 1981; dir., mem. exec. com., past chmn. The Sugar Assn., Inc., Washington; dir., mem. exec. com. World Sugar Research Orgn., London. Bd. dirs. Bay Area Council, San Francisco; adv. bd. Leavey Sch. Bus. and Adminstrn., Santa Clara U.; trustee, mem. exec. com. Colo. Coll.; adv. bd. Leavey Sch. Bus. and Adminstrn., Santa Clara U. Served to 1st lt., inf. AUS, 1951-52. Office: One California St Room 2000 San Francisco CA 94111

BUNN, EMORY FREEMAN, advertising agency executive; b. Morristown, N.J., July 7, 1935; s. Howard Stolpp and Helen Whitman (Freeman) B.; m. Anne Allison Overman, Apr. 11, 1959; children: Howard Stolpp II, Andrew Overman, Christopher Freeman, Allison Pennell. B.A., Princeton U., 1957. Research analyst Lennen and Newell, Inc., N.Y.C., 1957-59; acct. mgmt. trainee Dancer-Fitzgerald-Sample, Inc., N.Y.C., 1959-60, asst. acct. exec., 1960-61; acct. exec. Dancer-Fitzgerald-Sample, N.Y.C., 1961-66; acct. supr., v.p. Dancer-Fitzgerald-Sample, Inc., N.Y.C., 1966-76, mgmt. supr., sr. v.p., 1976-80, exec. v.p., mgmt. dir., 1980—. Served with U.S. Army, 1958. Republican. Episcopalian. Clubs: Short Hills (N.J.); Princeton, Union League (N.Y.C.); Minneapolis. Home: 365 Hobart Ave Short Hills NJ 07078 Office: Dancer Fitzgerald Sample Inc 405 Lexington Ave New York NY 10174

BUNN, GEORGE, educator; b. St. Paul, May 26, 1925; s. Charles and Harriet (Foster) B.; m. Fralia S. Hancock, July 9, 1949 (div.); children—Peggy Joan, Peter Wilson, Matthew George; m. Anne Crosby Coolidge, July 30, 1974. B.S. in Elec. Engring, U. Wis., 1946; LL.B., Columbia, 1950. Bar: D.C. bar 1950, Wis. bar 1969, also U.S. Supreme Ct. bar 1956. Atty. Gen. Counsel's Office, AEC, 1950-51; assoc., then partner firm Arnold, Fortas & Porter, Washington, 1951-61; mem. staff preparedness subcom. U.S. Senate, 1957; counsel to President's adviser on disarmament, 1961; gen. counsel U.S. ACDA, 1961-69; vis. prof., prof. Law Sch., U. Wis., Madison, 1969—, dean, 1972-75; Stockton chair internat. law Naval War Coll., Newport, R.I., 1973-74. Mem. U.S. del. 18 Nation Disarmament Conf., 1962-68; dep. chmn. U.S. del., 1966-67; mem. U.S. del. UN Disarmament Commn., 1965; U.S. rep. Western 4 Jurists Group, 1963-66; alt. U.S. rep. with rank of ambassador 18 Nation Disarmament Conf., 1968; Mem. com. on campus tensions Am. Council on Edn., 1969-70; mem. Wis. Jud. Council, 1972-74; chmn. hearing bd. on plutonium recycle Nuclear Regulatory Commn., 1976-77. Served with USNR, 1943-46. Mem. Wis. Bar Assn. Home: 1906 Capital Ave Madison WI 53705

BUNN, RONALD FREEZE, university administrator; b. Jonesboro, Ark., Aug. 1, 1929; s. S. Neal and Velma (Freeze) B.; m. Rita E. Hess, Mar. 29, 1955; children: Robin Gail, Katharine Sue, Lisabeth Joann. B.A., Southwestern at Memphis, 1951; M.A., Duke, 1953, Ph.D., 1956; postgrad., Universität zu Köln, 1954-55; LL.D., Southwestern at Memphis, 1973. Instr. U. Tex., Austin, 1956-59, asst. prof., 1960-64; asso. prof. La. State U., Baton Rouge, 1964-67, U Houston, 1967-69, prof., dean, 1969-74, interim dean arts and scis., 1972-74, asso. dean faculties, 1974-75, acting v.p., dean faculties, 1975-76; v.p. acad. affairs State U. N.Y. at Buffalo, 1976-80; provost U. Mo., Columbia, 1980—; cons. Council of Grad. Sch. Author: Politics and Civil Liberties in Europe, 1967, German Politics and the Spiegel Affair: A Case Study of the Bonn System, 1968; Contbr. articles profl. jours. Bd. dirs. S.W. Center for Urban Research, Houston, chmn. bd., 1975-76. Fulbright research scholar, 1963; NATO sr. fellow in sci., 1973. Mem. So. Polit. Sci. Assn. (past mem. exec. council), Southwestern Polit. Sci. Assn. (past v.p.), Am. Council on Germany, Phi Beta Kappa, Omicron Delta Kappa. Office: Provost 114 Jesse Hall U Mo Columbia MO 65211

BUNN, WILLARD, JR., banker; b. Springfield, Ill., Oct. 27, 1913; s. Willard and Ruth (Regan) B.; children: Ada Octavia Bunn Casper, Willard, Robert H. A.A., Springfield Jr. Coll., 1934; student, U. Wis., 1935. With Springfield Marine Bank, 1935—, pres., 1961-74, chmn. bd., chief exec. officer, 1974—, also dir.; dir. Ill. Bell Telephone Co., Bunn-O-Matic Corp.; v.p., dir. Bunn Capitol Co.; dir. Dickey-John C. Chmn. lay adv. bd. St. John's Hosp., Springfield; vice chmn. Capitol City R.R. Relocation Authority. Mem. Psi Upsilon. Republican. Roman Catholic. Home: 2101 Willemore Ave Springfield IL 62704 Office: East Old State Capitol Plaza Springfield IL 62701

BUNNELLE, ROBERT ELLSWORTH, newspaper publisher; b. Urbana, Ohio, Aug. 21, 1903; s. Elmer Ellsworth and Olivemay (Colbert) B.; m. Margaret Elizabeth Harrison, Oct. 30, 1926 (dec.); m. Frances McKay Peace, Aug. 23, 1962. Student, Wittenberg Coll., 1921-23, Northwestern U., 1924. Reporter Lynchburg (Va.) News, Asheville (N.C.) Times; also mng. editor Bristol (Va.) Bull., 1925-31; with A.P., 1931-54, beginning as editor, Atlanta, successively chief of bur., mng. exec., London, Eng., chief bur., Can., 1931-49, gen. exec., N.Y.C., 1949-54; chmn. bd., pub. Asheville Citizen-Times, 1954-74, pres., 1958-74; dir. Multimedia, Inc. Mem. N.C. Hwy. Commn., 1957-61; pres. Greater Asheville Council, Council, 1962-64; Trustee Meml. Mission Hosp., 1968-69. Mem. N.C. Press Assn. (pres. 1962-63), Am. Corrs. Assn. (pres. London 1943-44), Parliamentary Press Gallery Assn. (dir. 1950-51), Asheville C. of C. (pres. 1967), Phi Kappa Psi. Clubs: Biltmore Forest Country, Mountain City (pres. 1959), Litchfield Country (Pawleys Island, S.C.)). Home: Lower Waverly Plantation PO Box 156 Pawleys Island SC 29585 Office: 14 O'Henry Ave Asheville NC 28801

BUNNETT, JOSEPH FREDERICK, chemist, educator; b. Portland, Oreg., Nov. 26, 1921; s. Joseph and Louise Helen (Boulan) B.; m. Sara Anne Telfer, Aug. 22, 1942; children—Alfred Boulan, David Telfer, Peter Sylvester (dec. Sept. 1972). B.A., Reed Coll., 1942; Ph.D., U. Rochester, 1945. Mem. faculty Reed Coll., 1946-52, U. N.C., 1952-58; mem. faculty Brown U., 1958-66, prof. chemistry, 1959-66, chmn. dept., 1961-64; prof. chemistry U. Calif. at Santa Cruz, 1966—; Erskine vis. fellow U. Canterbury, New Zealand, 1967; vis. prof. U. Wash., 1956, U. Würzburg, Germany, 1974; research fellow Japan Soc. for Promotion of Sci., 1979; Lady Davis vis. prof. Hebrew U., Jerusalem, Israel, 1981. Contbr. articles to profl. jours. Trustee Reed Coll., Societá Chimica Italiana (hon.). Fulbright scholar Univ. Coll., London, Eng., 1949-50; Guggenheim fellow, Fulbright scholar U. Munich, Germany, 1960-61. Fellow AAAS; mem. Am. Acad. Arts and Scis., Am. Chem. Soc. (editor jour. Accounts of Chem. Research), Chem. Soc. (London), Internat. Union Pure and Applied Chemistry (chmn. commn. on phys. organic chemistry 1978—, sec. organic chemistry div. 1981—). Home: 608 Arroyo Seco Santa Cruz CA 95060 Office: U of California Santa Cruz CA 95064

BUNSHAFT, GORDON, architect; b. Buffalo, May 9, 1909; s. David and Yetta (Bunshaft) B.; m. Nina Elizabeth Wayler, Dec. 2, 1943. B.Arch., M.I.T., 1933, M.Arch. (fellow), 1935; D.F.A. (hon.), U. Buffalo, 1962. Chief designer Skidmore, Owings & Merrill, 1937-42, partner, N.Y.C., Chgo., San Francisco and; Portland, Oreg., 1949-79; Vis. com. Sch. Architecture, M.I.T., 1940-42, Harvard U., 1954-60, Yale U., 1959-62; mem. President's Commn. on Fine Arts, 1963-72; former trustee Carnegie Mellon U., Pitts.; trustee, mem. internat. council Mus. Modern Art. Partner charge design: Fifth Ave. br. Mfrs. Trust Co, Lever House-Park Ave., both N.Y.C., Conn. Gen. Life Ins. Co and Emhart Hdqrs., Hartford, H.J. Heinz Co., Ltd, Hayes Park, Middlesex, Eng., Banque Lambert, Brussels, Beinecke Rare Book and Manuscript Library, Yale U., Reynolds Metals Co. Bldg, Richmond, Va., Albright-Knox Art Gallery, Buffalo, Chase Bank, N.Y.C., Lyndon Baines Johnson Library and Sid W. Richardson Hall, U. Tex. at, Austin, Hirshhorn Mus. and Sculpture Garden, Washington, Am. Can Co, Greenwich, Conn., 140 Broadway, N.Y.C., Philip Morris Factory, Richmond, Va., Nat. Comml. Bank, Jeddah, Saudi Arabia, Haj Terminal and Support Complex, Jeddah Internat. Airport. Served As maj. C.E. AUS, 1942-46. Recipient M.I.T. and Rotch travelling fellowships for study Europe and N. Africa, 1935-37; Brunner award Am. Acad. and Inst. Arts and Letters, 1955; Gold medal Am. Acad. and Inst. Arts and Letters, 1984; medal of honor N.Y. chpt. AIA, 1961; Chancellor's medal U. Buffalo, 1969. Academician NAD; Fellow AIA; mem. Am. Acad. and Inst. Arts and Letters, Municipal Art Soc. N.Y., Buffalo Fine Arts Acad. (hon.).

BUNT, JAMES RICHARD, credit corporation executive; b. St. Cloud, Minn., Sept. 24, 1941; s. Eberhard Joseph and Christine Frances (Bromberg) B.; m. Arlene Anita Weisberg, Aug. 12, 1965; children: Gregory, Ashlee. B.A., U. S.D., Vermillion, 1967; M.A., Claremont Grad. Sch., Calif., 1968. Mgmt. trainee Gen. Electric Co., Schenectady, N.Y., 1968-70, corp. auditor, 1970-73, mgr. fin. ops. Nuclear Energy div., San Jose, Calif., 1973-77, cons. fin. planning, Fairfield, Conn., 1977-79; mgr. fin. planning and analysis MABG, Louisville, Ky., 1979-81; v.p., controller Gen. Electric Credit Corp., Stamford, Conn., 1981—; Dir. Trafalgar Credit Corp., Miami, Fla., GECI, N.V., Netherlands Antilles. Coach Am. Youth Soccer Assn., Trumbull, Conn., 1977-79. Fellow NDEA, 1967. Mem. Fin. Execs. Inst., Elfun Soc., Phi Beta Kappa. Republican. Roman Catholic. Club: Quarter Deck (Stamford). Home: 447 Thayer Pond Rd Wilton CT 06897 Office: Gen Electric Credit Corp 260 Long Ridge Rd Stanford CT 06902

BUNTING, ANNE EVELYN (EVE BUNTING), author; b. Maghera, Ireland, Dec. 19, 1928; came to U.S., 1958, naturalized, 1969; d. Sloan Edmund and Mary (Canning) Bolton; m. Edward Davison Bunting, Mar. 26, 1951; children—Christine Ann, Sloan Edward, Glenn Davison. Student, Meth. Coll., Belfast, Ireland, 1935-45, Queen's U., 1945-47. Lectr. U. So. Calif., Pasadena City Coll., Sierra Writing Camp; mem. faculty Orange Coast Community Coll., UCLA, 1978-79. Author: numerous children's books, including Barney the Beard, 1975 (Honor book Chgo. Book Clinic), One More Flight, 1976 (Golden Kite award, Outstanding Sci. Book award), Ghost of Summer, 1977 (Jr. Lit. Guild selection), The Big Cheese, 1977, Winter's Coming, 1977, (with Glenn Bunting) Skateboards, How to Make Them, How to Ride Them, 1977. Mem. PEN, Author's Guild, Soc. Children's Book Writers, Calif. Writers Guild (v.p.), So. Calif. Council on Writing for Children and Young People. Democrat. Home: 1512 Rose Villa St Pasadena CA 91106 *My life divides rather neatly into two parts, Pre-American and American—the first part spent in Ireland, the second in the United States. In the first period I was young, I got married I had babies.*

In the second I'm growing older, I'm still married, my babies have grown, I'm writing books. Writing books is like having babies: after the work and pain comes the joy and fulfillment. Better 50 books and 3 children than the other way around

BUNTING, EVE *See* **BUNTING, ANNE EVELYN**

BUNTING, GEORGE LLOYD, JR., chemical company executive; b. Balt., 1940; (married). B.S., Loyola Coll., Balt., 1962; M.B.A., Columbia U., 1964. Bar: bar. Account exec. SSC & B, 1964-66; with Noxell Corp., 1966—, exec. v.p., 1970-73, pres., chief exec. officer, 1973—, also dir. Address: PO Box 1799 Baltimore MD 21203 *

BUNTING, JAMES WHITNEY, retired college president, economist, consultant; b. Phila., Nov. 23, 1913; s. George Miller Lewis and Helen Elizabeth (Whitney) B.; m. Mildred Eleanor Griscom, Oct. 14, 1939; 1 dau., Helen Whitney Bunting Pickett. B.S., U. Pa., 1934, M.A., 1936, M.B.A., 1937, Ph.D., 1946; postgrad., U. Louisville, 1938-39. Economist Pa. State Planning Bd., Harrisburg, 1934-35; gen. freight agt. Preston Trucking Co., Md., 1935-36; instr. econs., marketing, finance Jr. Coll. Commerce, New Haven, 1937-39, coll. dean, 1949-50; asst. prof. bus. adminstrn. Hanover (Ind.) Coll., 1939-42; also dir. pub. relations; prof. applied econs. Hobart Coll., Geneva, N.Y., 1945-49, assoc. and acting dean, 1946-48, dir. indsl. community program, 1947-48; asst. treas. Market Basket Corp., Geneva, 1948-49; prof. econs., chmn. dept. U. Ga., Atlanta, 1950-51, prof. econs., Athens, 1951-52, dir. bur. bus. research, 1951-52; exec. v.p. Oglethorpe U., 1952, pres., 1953-55; prof. finance N.Y. U., 1957-60; cons. higher edn. and research Gen. Electric Co., 1955-62; dean Coll. Bus. Adminstrn., U. Ga., 1962-68; pres. Ga. Coll., Milledgeville, 1968-81; Cons. Exchange Bank of Milledgeville; consultation utility costs Ga. Pub. Service Commn.; economist WPB, Washington, 1942. Author: Effective Retail Selling, 1953, Ethics for Modern Business Practice, 1953, Higher Education, A Twenty Year Look Ahead, 1957, Your Share in America's Prosperity, 1960; author, editor: Business Leaders in People's Capitalism, 1959; editor: Atlanta Econ. Rev, 1950-51, Ga. Bus, 1951-52; booklet Productivity: Some Thoughts for Business Leaders, 1977; contbg. econs. editor: Elec. South, 1952-70; Contbr. articles to profl. jours. Pres. Citizens Com. for Rye Pub. Schs.; vice chmn. Atlanta Regional Export Expansion Council, 1971-74; chmn. com. on pub. relations Am. Assn. State Colls. and Univs., 1970-75; mem. adv. bd. Concerned Educators Against Forced Unionism. Served as lt. Supply Corps USNR, 1942-45. Recipient medal of honor Freedoms Found., 1954; Am. Eagle award Nat. Council Invest-in-Am., 1976. Life fellow Internat. Inst. Arts and Letters; mem. Nat. Invest in Am. Com. (pres. nat. council, bd. govs., eastern regional chmn., mem. exec. com.), Am. Econ. Assn., Am. Geog. Soc., Am. Marketing Assn., Am. Acad. Polit. and Social Sci., Nat. Sales Execs., So. Econ. Soc., Ga. Bus. and Industry Assn., Gamma Omicron Tau, Delta Sigma Pi, Delta Chi, Beta Gamma Sigma, Phi Kappa Phi, Pi Gamma Mu. Clubs: Milledgeville Country, Rotary. Home: 211 Lakeshore Dr Milledgeville GA 31061

BUNTING, JOHN PEARCE, business executive; b. Toronto, Ont., Can., Sept. 6, 1929; s. Alfred and Harriet (Lee) B.; m. Stephanie Keeley, Sept. 26, 1977; children: Mark Alfred, Elsa Brend, Harriet Elizabeth, Alexandra Keeley. B.Comm., McGill U., 1952. With McLeod, Young Weir & Co., Ltd., Toronto, 1952-55; with Alfred Bunting & Co., Ltd., Toronto, after 1955, pres., 1967-77; mem. Toronto Stock Exchange, 1962-77, bd. govs., 1968-74, vice-chmn., 1972-73, chmn., 1973-74, mem., 1962-77, pres., chief exec. officer, 1977—; dir. Can. Gen.-Tower Ltd.; mem. Bd. Trade Met. Toronto. Bd. govs. Appleby Coll., 1968—; bd. dirs. St. John's Convalescent Hosp., Toronto, 1968—. Mem. Kappa Alpha. Anglican. Clubs: Ticker (pres. 1976-77), Univ. (pres. 1979-80), Toronto Golf (Toronto); Granite, Osler Bluff Ski. *

BUNTON, CLIFFORD ALLEN, chemist, educator; b. Chesterfield, Eng., Jan. 4, 1920; came to U.S., 1963, naturalized, 1978; s. Arthur and Edith (Kirk) B.; m. Ethel Clayton, July 28, 1945; children—Julia Margaret, Claire Jennifer. B.Sc., Univ. Coll., London, 1941, Ph.D., 1945. Successively asst. lectr., lectr., reader Univ. Coll., 1944-63; prof. chemistry U. Calif. at Santa Barbara, 1963—, chmn. dept., 1967-72; Commonwealth Fund fellow U. Columbia, 1948-49; Brit. Council vis. lectr., Chile and Argentina, 1960; vis. prof. U. Calif. at Los Angeles, 1961, U. Toronto, 1962, U. Sao Paolo, Brazil, 1973, U. Lausanne, Switzerland, 1976, 79; Mem. policy com. U. Chile-U. Calif. Coop. Program, chmn. sci. and engring. sub-com., 1969—. Contbr. articles to profl. jours. Mem. Am. Chem. Soc., Chem. Soc. (London); corr. mem. Chilean Acad. Scis. (1974). Home: 935 Cocopah Dr Santa Barbara CA 93110

BUNTON, LUCIUS DESHA, federal judge; b. Del Rio, Tex., Dec. 1, 1924; s. Lucius Desha and Avis Maurine (Fisher) B.; m. Mary Jane Carsey, June 18, 1947; children:Cathryne Avis Bunton Warner, Lucius Desha. Student, U. Chgo., 1943-44; B.A., U. Tex., Austin, 1947, J.D., 1950. Bar: Tex. 1949. Individual practice law, Uvalde, Tex., 1950; asso. firm. H.O. Metcalfe, Marfa, Tex., 1951-54; dist. atty. 83d Jud. Dist. Tex., 1954-59; mem. firm Shafer, Gilliland, Davis, Bunton & McCollum, Odessa, Tex., 1959-79; judge U.S. Dist. Ct. for Western Dist. Tex., Midland, 1979—. Trustee Ector County (Tex.) Ind. Sch. Dist., 1967-76. Served with inf. U.S. Army, 1943-46. Mem. Tex. Bar Found. (charter), Am. Bar Assn., Am. Bar Found., Am. Coll. Probate Counsel, Am. Acad. Matrimonial Lawyers, State Bar Tex. (chmn. 1971-72, v.p. 1973-74, pres.-elect 1979). Baptist. Club: Masons (Marfa).

BUNTS, FRANK EMORY, artist; b. Cleve., Mar. 2, 1932; s. Alexander Taylor and Mary (Corbin) B.; m. Norah Jean Grassle, Aug. 1, 1964. Student, Yale U., 1951-53, 55-57; diploma, Cleve. Inst. Art, 1964; M.A., Case Western Res. U., 1964. Instr. Cleve. Inst. Art, 1963-64, Ark. State U., 1965-67; mem. faculty U. Md., 1967-77, prof., 1973-77, dir. grad. art studio program, 1972-77. Exhibited in one-man shows, Comara Gallery, Los Angeles, 1967, 68, Franz Bader Gallery, Washington, 1969, 73, 75, St. John's Coll., Annapolis, Md., 1972, Deson Zaks Gallery, Chgo., Gallery 118, Mpls., 1974, Nat. Acad. Scis., Washington, 1976, Cath. U. Am., Washington, 1978, Plum Gallery, Washington, 1979, Plum Gallery, Street Exhbn., Red Sq. Moscow, 1982, group shows, San Francisco Mus. Art, Cleve. Mus. Art, Corcoran Gallery Art, Indpls. Mus. Art, Fine Arts Gallery San Diego, Gallery K, Washington, Studio Gallery, Washington, Modern Mus. Art, Rijenka, Yugoslavia, Brooks Meml. Art Gallery, Memphis; represented in collections, Phila. Mus. Art, Cleve. Mus. Art, Aldrich Mus. Contemporary Art, Ridgefield, Conn., Fine Arts Gallery, San Diego, Library of Congress, Corcoran Gallery Art, Washington, Cooperstown Art Assn., N.Y., Works reproduced in jours. Studio: 15 W 24th St New York NY 10010

BUNZL, RUDOLPH HANS, diversified manufacturing company executive; b. Vienna, Austria, July 20, 1922; came to U.S., 1940, naturalized, 1945; s. Robert Max and Nellie Margaret (Burian) B.; m. Rema R. Templeton, Apr. 6, 1947; children: Ann Mary Bunzl Kamoe, Carol Elizabeth Bunzl Showker; m. Esther R. Mendelsohn, Nov. 14, 1970. B.S. in Chem. Engring, Ga. Inst. Tech., 1943. With Shell Chem. Co., Calif., 1943-54; v.p. Am. Filtrona Corp., Richmond, Va., 1954-59, pres., 1959-83, chmn., 1983—. Served with U.S. Army, 1944-46. Mem. Am. Inst. Chem. Engrs. Office: Am Filtrona Corp 8401 Jefferson Davis Hwy Richmond VA 23234

BUONO, VICTOR CHARLES, actor, author; b. San Diego, Feb. 3, 1938; s. Victor Francis and Myrtle Bell (Keller) B. Student, Villanova U., 1956-57. Appeared in 5 seasons of Shakespeare, 5 seasons of contemporary plays, San Diego Jr. Theatre and Old Globe Theatre, Stratford-on-Avon, Eng., 1956-78; numerous stage, motion picture and TV appearances including: movies Whatever Happened to Baby Jane?, 1962, Hush, Hush, Sweet Charlotte, 1965, The Greatest Story Ever Told, The Evil, 1978, The Man with Bogart's Face, 1980; TV Sunset Strip; Author: book It Could Be Verse; performer, author poems, also recs.; lectr., performer, condr. workshops at colls., univs., 1960— (Recipient Atlas award for acting Old Globe Theatre 1956, 57, 60, Los Angeles Critics Circle award 1975, Entertainer of Yr. award San Diego Press Club 1978). Mem. Screen Actors Guild, Actors Equity Assn., AFTRA, Acad. Motion Picture Arts and Scis. Roman Catholic. *

BUOY, ROGER MARTIN, publishing company executive; b. Bristol, Eng., July 1, 1945; came to U.S., 1968; s. Irvine Thomas and Edith (Turner) B.; m. Christine J. Baker, May 20, 1966; children: Julie Anne, Matthew Thomas. Student, Bristol Coll. Commerce, 1961-64. Dir. software HETRA, Melbourne, Fla., 1970-71; mgr. Arthur Young & Co., N.Y.C., 1971-74, ptnr., 1980-81, Arthur Young, Sydney, Australia, 1975-80; exec. v.p. Scholastic Inc., N.Y.C., 1981-83; pres., chief exec. officer Mindscape Inc., Northbrook, Ill., 1983—. Author Computer Performance—A Management Approach, 1976. Mem. Brit. Computer Soc., Inst. Elec. Engrs., Assn. Computing Machinery, MENSA, Inst. Systems Mgmt. Office: Minscape Inc 3444 Dundee Rd Northbrook IL 60662

BURBANK, HOWARD DONALD, clergyman; b. Detroit, Dec. 20, 1918; s. Bester Pierce and Carrie Ella (Woodward) B.; m. Helen Greavu, Mar. 12, 1939; children: MaryAnn Carol Burbank Roberts, Donna Jean Burbank Lindsay. Student, Lansing (Mich.) Bus. Coll., LaSalle Extension U. Ordained to ministry Seventh-day Adventist Ch., 1952; pastor chs. in, Howell and Grand Rapids, Mich., 1939-46; dir. pub. dept. Mich. Conf. Seventh-day Adventists, Lansing, 1946-48, Greater N.Y. conf., N.Y.C., 1949-53; pastor Seventh-day Adventist Tabernacle, Battle Creek, Mich., 1953; dir. laymen's activities and disaster relief Mich. Conf., 1954-61; sec. Tex. Conf. Corp., Ft. Worth, 1961-65, Southwestern Union Conf. Corp., Dallas, 1965-70; dir. publs. Seventh-day Adventist Ch., Europe and North Africa, 1970-73; exec. dir. Seventh-day Adventist World Service, Washington, 1974-80; exec. com. Gen. Conf. Seventh-day Adventists. Author articles in field; producer ch. films. Bd. dirs. CARE, Ch. World Service, Am. Council Vol. Agys. for Fgn. Service, Interch. Med. Assistance Corp.; rep. adv. com. AID. Club: Lions. Home: 19980 Lomo Ranchos Rd Volcano CA 95689 Office: 6840 Eastern Ave NW Washington DC 20012 *Experience has taught Me: 1. To have a complete faith in a Higher Power. 2. God's ownership of all things. 3. Time is a talent more valuable than money. 4. God pays double and triple time for all overtime. 5. By caring for suffering mankind throughout the world a special blessing is awarded every individual. 6. Recognize all people as equal without regard to race, color, religion or national origin for they are all God's creation.*

BURBANK, NELSON STONE, investment banker; b. Winchester, Mass., Sept. 16, 1920; s. Willis H. and Vivian (Casson) B.; m. Rita B. Healey, Feb. 12, 1950; children: Peter N., Nelson Stone, Jane Vivian. Student, Boston U., 1946-47. Registered rep. Vance, Sanders & Co., Inc., Boston, 1946-53; pres. Burbank & Co., Inc., Boston, 1953-82; pres., dir. Colonial Investment Services, Inc., 1983—; dir. Health Ins. Vt., Inc., New Eng. Digital Corp., Norwich, Vt.; trustee, mem. investment com. Massbank for Savs.; Bd. govs. Boston Stock Exchange, 1965-73, vice chmn., 1968-71, chmn., 1971-73. Bd. dirs. Reading (Mass.) chpt. ARC, 1963—, vice chmn., until 1982. Served with AUS, 1942-45. Decorated D.F.C., Air medals. Mem. Nat. Assn. Securities Dealers (gov. 1974-77). Home: 24 Juniper Circle Reading MA 01867 Office: Colonial Investment Services Inc 75 Federal St Boston MA 02110

BURBANK, RONALD E., manufacturing company executive. Grad., U. So. Calif. With Consol. Freightways, Inc., 1966—; v.p., gen. mgr. Consol. Metco Inc. subs., 1966, pres., 1967-73; exec. v.p. subs. Consol. Freightways Corp. Del., 1973-75, pres., chief operating officer, 1975-80, pres. parent co., 1980—. Office: 3240 Hillview Ave Palo Alto CA 94304 *

BURBIDGE, ELEANOR MARGARET PEACHEY, astronomer; b. Davenport, Eng.; d. Stanley John and Marjorie (Stott) Peachey; m. Geoffrey Burbidge, Apr. 2, 1938; 1 dau., Sarah. B.S., Ph.D., U. London; Sc.D. hon., Smith Coll., 1963, U. Sussex, 1970, U. Bristol, 1972, U. Leicester, 1972, City U., 1973, U. Mich., 1978, U. Mass., 1978, William Coll., 1979. Mem. staff U. London Obs., 1948-51; research fellow Yerkes Obs., U. Chgo., 1951-53, Calif. Inst. Tech., Pasadena, 1955-57; Shirley Farr fellow Yerkes Obs., 1957-59, assoc. prof., 1959-62; mem. Enrico Fermi Inst. for Nuclear Studies, 1957-62; prof. astronomy dept. physics U. Calif.-San Diego, 1964—; dir. Royal Greenwich Obs. (Herstmonceaux Castle), Hailsham, Sussex, Eng., 1972-73. Author: (with G. Burbidge) Quasi-Stellar Objects, 1967; editor: Observatory mag., 1948-51; mem. editorial bd.: Astronomy and Astrophysics, 1969—. Recipient with husband Warner prize in Astronomy, 1959; hon. fellow Univ. Coll., London, Girton Coll., Lucy Cavendish Coll., Cambridge. Fellow Royal Soc., Nat. Acad. Scis., Am. Acad. Arts and Scis., Royal Astron. Soc.; mem. Am. Astron. Soc. (v.p. 1972-74, pres. 1976-78), Internat. Astron. Union (pres. commn. 28 1970-73). Office: U Calif-San Diego Dept Physics La Jolla CA 92093 *

BURBIDGE, FREDERICK STEWART, transportation company executive; b. Winnipeg, Man., Can., Sept. 30, 1918; s. Frederick Maxwell and Susan Mary (Stewart) B.; m. Cynthia Adams Bennest, Apr. 27, 1942; children: John Bennest, George Frederick. B.A., U. Man., 1939, LL.B., 1946. With law dept. Canadian Pacific Ltd., Winnipeg, 1947-50, Montreal, 1950-62, asst. v.p. traffic, 1962-66, v.p. rail adminstrn., 1966-67, v.p., exec. asst., 1967-69, v.p. adminstrn., 1969; v.p. mktg. and sales CP Rail, 1969-71, sr. exec. officer, also v.p. parent co., 1971-72, pres., dir., mem. exec. com. parent co., Montreal, Que., Can., 1972—, chmn., chief exec. officer, 1981—; dir., exec. com. Bank of Montreal; dir. Canadian Pacific Enterprises Ltd., Canadian Pacific Steamships Ltd., Amca Internat. Ltd., Canadian Pacific (Bermuda) Ltd., Pan Can. Petroleum Ltd., CP Air, C.I.L., Cominco Ltd., Marathon Realty Co., Ltd., Soo Line R.R. Co., CNCP Telecommunications. Bd. dirs. Royal Victoria Hosp. Found.; Gov.; citizens adv. bd. Salvation Army.; bd. govs. McGill U., Bishop's Coll. Sch., Douglas Hosp., Jr. Achievement Can. Mem. Conf. Bd. Can. (bd. dirs., mem., Sr.), Bus. Council on Nat. Issues. Clubs: St. James's, Mt. Royal. Office: Canadian Pacific Ltd Windsor Sta PO Box 6042 Station A Montreal PQ H3C 3E4 Canada

BURBIDGE, GEOFFREY, astrophysicist, educator; b. Chipping Norton, Oxon, Eng., Sept. 24, 1925; s. Leslie and Eveline B.; m. Margaret Peachey, 1948; 1 dau. B.Sc. with spl. honors in Physics, Bristol U., 1946; Ph.D., U. Coll., London, 1951. Asst. lectr. U. Coll., London, 1950-51; Agassiz fellow Harvard, 1951-52; research fellow U. Chgo., 1952-53, Cavendish Lab., Cambridge, Eng., 1953-55; Carnegie fellow Mt. Wilson and Palomar Obs., Calif. Inst. Tech., 1955-57; asst. prof. dept. astronomy U. Chgo., 1957-58, assoc. prof., 1958-62, U. Calif.-San Diego, La Jolla, 1962-63, prof. physics, 1963-83; dir. Kitt Peak Nat. Obs., Tucson, 1978-84; Phillips vis. prof. Harvard U., 1968; bd. dirs. Associated Univs. Research in Astronomy, 1971-74; trustee Associated Univs., Inc., 1973-82. Author: (with Margaret Burbidge) Quasi-Stellar Objects, 1967; Contbr. articles to sci. jours. Fellow Royal Soc. London, Am. Acad. Arts and Scis., Royal Astron. Soc.; mem. Am. Phys. Soc., Am. Astron. Soc., Internat. Astron. Union, Astron. Soc. of Pacific (pres. 1974-76). Office: Kitt Peak Nat Obs PO Box 26732 Tucson AZ 85726

BURCH, DEAN, lawyer, former govt. ofcl.; b. Enid, Okla., Dec. 20, 1927; s. Bert Alexander and Leola (Atkisson) B.; m. Patricial Meeks, July 7, 1961; children—Shelly, Dean, Dianne. LL.B., U. Ariz., 1953. Bar: Ariz. bar 1953. Asst. atty. gen., Ariz., 1953-54; adminstrv. asst. to Sen. Bary Goldwater, 1955-59; mem. firm. Dunseath, Stubbs & Burch, Tucson, 1959-69, Pierson, Ball & Dowd, 1975—; chmn. FCC, Washington, 1969-74; counselor to Pres. Nixon, 1974, to; Pres. Ford, 1975; Dep. dir. Goldwater for President Com., 1963-64; chmn. Republican Nat. Com., 1964-65; mgr. Goldwater for Senate Campaign, 1968; chief of staff George Bush Vice Presdl. Campaign, 1980; sr. adv. Reagan-Bush Com., 1980. Mem. Ariz. Bd. Regents, 1969-70. Served with AUS, 1946-48. Mem. Blue Key, Phi Delta Theta. Home: 9311 Persimmon Tree Rd Potomac MD 20854 Office: 1000 Ring Bldg Washington DC 20036

BURCH, FRANCIS BOUCHER, lawyer; b. Balt., Nov. 26, 1918; s. Louis Claude and Constance (Boucher) B.; m. Mary Patricia Howe, Apr. 12, 1947; children: Francis Boucher, Catherine Howe Jenkins, Richard Claude, Constance B. McGrain, Edwin Howe, Robert Stuart, Mary Patricia. Ph.B. summa cum laude (scholar 1937-41), Loyola Coll., Balt., 1941; LL.B. (scholar 1941-43), Yale U., 1943; LL.D., U. Balt., 1976. Bar: Md. 1943, U.S. Supreme Ct 1943. Pres. Balt. CSC, 1960-61; mem. Balt. Bd. Estimates, 1961-63, Gov.'s Crime Commn., 1970—; city solicitor, Balt., 1961-63, ins. commr., Md., 1965-66, atty gen., 1966-78; mem. firm Siskind, Burch, Grady & Rosen; instr. bus. law Loyola Coll., Evening Sch., 1945-57; ptnr. Sheraton Fontainebleau Hotel, Ocean City, Md., Family Entertainment Ctrs., Fla., 1981—, Cove Road Joint Venture, Stuart, Fla. Author: On Calling of a Constitutional Convention, 1950. Chmn. bd. Lauderdale '70, Inc., Ft. Lauderdale, Fla., 1964-68; mem. bd. Balt. Credit Union, 1961-63; mem. Pension Study Com. Balt., 1962; chmn. Mayor Balt. Com. Scholarship Program, 1961, Mayor Balt. Com. Mass. Transit, 1961; mem. Standard Salary Bd. Md., 196O-61, Mayor Balt. Com. Conflict of Interest, 1960; chmn. Md. Cancer Crusade, 1967-68, Constl. Prayer Found., 1963-66; pres. Balt. Safety Council, 1963-65, chmn. exec. com., 1965-67, v.p., 1958-62; lay chmn. Papal Volunteers Com. Latin Am., Archdiocese Balt., 1962-65; vice chmn. Alumni div. Loyola Coll. Devel. Program, 1957, chmn. spl. gifts div., 1971; chmn. Md. Cath. Lawyers Retreat, 1957-59; pres. Reciprocity Club Balt., 1956-57, bd. dirs., 1954-59; bd. dirs. Legal Aid Bur. Balt., 1954, Goodwill Industries Balt., 1959-65; trustee Loyola Coll., Balt., 1974-75, Camp Fire Girls Balt., 1960-65; chmn. maj. gifts div. Loyola and Notre Dame Coll. (Balt.) Library Devel. Dr., 1972; vice chmn. devel. drive Loyola Coll., 1981. Served with USCGR, 1944-45. Recipient Pope John XXIII medal, 1965, Spiritum award Cardinal Gibbons High Sch., Balt., 1966; Man of Year award Hibernian Soc. Md., 1967; Pub. Servant award Md. Cath. War Vets., 1967; Humanitarian award Nu Beta Epsilon, 1967; Nat. Jewish Hosp. award, 1969; Alumnus of Year award Loyola Coll., 1970; Andrew White medal for distinguished citizenship Loyola Coll., 1973; Wyman award as outstanding atty. gen., U.S., 1975. Mem. Am., Md., Balt. bar assns., Am. Arbitration Assn. (panel 1954—), Nat. Assn. Attys. Gen. (pres. 1970-71, exec. com. 1969—, Wyman award 1975), Council State Govts. (exec. com. 1971—), So. Md. Soc., Hibernian Soc. Md., St. Thomas More Soc. (pres. Md. 1962-63), St. Georges Soc. Md., Friendly Sons of St. Patrick. Clubs: Paint and Powder (bd. govs. 1957-63), Engrs., Balt. Country (Balt.); Tri-State Anglers (Md.-Del.-Va.); Sawgrass (Ponte Vedro, Fla.). Office: 2E Fayette St Baltimore MD 21202

BURCH, HOBART ALEXANDER, social worker, educator; b. Appleton, Wis., July 29, 1932; s. Hobart Alexander and Margaret Leone (Marshall) B.; m. Genevieve Walters, Aug. 29, 1953 (dec. 1981); children—Juanita, David, Peter, Eric.; m. Gwen Baumann, Apr. 22, 1982. A.B., Princeton U., 1953; M.Div., Union Theol. Sem., N.Y.C., 1956; M.S.S.W., Columbia U., 1956; Ph.D. (NIMH fellow), Brandeis U., Waltham, Mass., 1965. Ordained to ministry United Ch. of Christ, 1956; dir. social service dept. Buffalo Council of Chs., 1958-62; spl. asst. to manpower adminstr. Dept. Labor, 1964-65; asst. to commr. welfare HEW, 1965-67; dep. chief Office Program Liaison, NIMH, 1967-69; gen. sec. div. health and welfare United Ch. Bd. Homeland Ministries, N.Y.C., 1969-74; exec. dir. Nat. Social Welfare Assembly, N.Y.C., 1974-76; prof., dir. Sch. Social Work, U. Nebr., Omaha, 1976—. Recipient Merit award Dept. Labor, 1965. Mem. Nat. Assn. Social Workers, Council Social Work Edn. Democrat. Club: Princeton (N.Y.C.). Home: 3315 Paddock Rd Omaha NE 68124 Office: University of Nebraska Omaha NE 68182 *

BURCH, JOHN THOMAS, JR., lawyer; b. Balt., Feb. 22; s. John T. and Katheryn Estella (Peregoy) B.; m. Linda Anne Shearer, Nov. 1, 1969; children: John Thomas, Richard James. B.A., U. Richmond, 1964, J.D., 1966; LL.M., George Washington U., 1971. Bar: Va. 1966, D.C. 1974, U.S. Supreme Ct. 1969, Mich. 1983. Pvt. practice, Richmond, 1966, Washington, 1974—; pres. firm Burch, Kerns and Klimek, 1977-81, Burch & Assocs., P.C., 1982-83; Burch, Wilhelm & McDonald, P.C., 1983—; pres. firm Burch, Wilhelm and McDonald, P.C.,, 1983—; pres. Internat. Procurement Cons. Ltd., Washington, 1977-81; Republican committeeman, City of Alexandria, Va., 1975-80, a.d.c. to gov., State of Va., 1976—; gen. counsel adv. bd. Vietnam Vets. Found., 1982—; coordinator Nat. Vietnam Vets. Coalition. Served to maj. JAGC, U.S. Army, 1966-74; Vietnam. Decorated Bronze Star, Meritorious Service medal, others. Mem. ABA (sec. public contract law sect. 1976-77), Fed. Bar Assn. (nat. council, dep. sec. 1982-83), Am. Arbitration Assn., Vietnam Vets. Am., Am. Legion, VFW, AMVETS, Spl. Forces Assn., Va. Soc. SAR (pres. 1975-76, Patriots medal 1978, Good Citizenship medal 1970), Sons Confederate Vets., Scabbard and Blade, Phi Alpha Delta, Phi Sigma Alpha. Republican. Episcopalian. Home: 1015 N Pelham St Alexandria VA 22304 Office: 1320 19th St NW Suite 200 Washington DC 20036

BURCH, LUCIUS EDWARD, JR., lawyer; b. Nashville, Jan. 25, 1912; s. Lucius Edward and Sarah (Cooper) B.; m. Elsie Caldwell, Dec. 27, 1935; children: Sarah Polk (Mrs. John F. Gratz, Jr.), Elsie Caldwell Burch Donald, Edith Montague (Mrs. Burch Caywood), Lucia Newell Doggrell. B.A., Vanderbilt U., 1934, LL.B., 1936. Bar: Tenn. 1936. Since practiced in, Memphis; sr. partner firm Burch, Porter & Johnson, 1947—; dir. Nat. Commerce Bancorp., Nat. Bank of Commerce. Author articles. Bd. dirs. Nat. Park Found., Memphis Civic Research Com., 1947-67; mem. Plough Park Devel. Bd.; chmn. Leadership Memphis; founder, charter mem. Memphis Com. Community Relations, 1958-59, pres., 1959; chmn. Tenn. Game and Fish Commn., 1949-55; pres. Tenn. Conservation League, 1955-56; mem. Nat. Council Atlantic Union, 1949—; adv. com. Internat. Movement Atlantic Union, 1961—; mem. devel. council Vanderbilt U. Law Sch., 1968—; Del. Democratic Nat. Conv., 1952; mem. Tenn. Dem. Exec. Com., 1962, 74-81; trustee Edward J. Meeman Found.; bd. govs. Assn. Advancement Aging Research, 1968—; bd. dirs. Memphis Sunshine Home, 1940—. Recipient Cartter-Patten award Tenn.

Conservation League, 1956; certificate of merit Memphis Urban League, 1952. Fellow Am. Coll. Trial Lawyers; mem. ABA, Tenn. Bar Assn. (gov. 1958), Memphis and Shelby County Bar Assn. (dir. 1962-63), Tenn. Acad. Sci. (hon. life), Tenn., West Tenn. hist. socs. Clubs: Memphis Country Memphis Hunt and Polo, Tennessee, Wolf River Soc. (Memphis) (founder, 1st pres.). Home: Whiteacre Farm Collierville TN 38017 Office: 130 N Court Ave Memphis TN 38103

BURCH, LYNDON WALKUP, design engr., inventor; b. Grand Rapids, Mich., Feb. 9, 1899; s. Thomas Walkup and Grace B.; m. Isabella Keys, June 1919 (div. 1926); children—Hadley K., Marilyn K. (Mrs. Harry Kindle); m. Sarah C. Wells, Aug. 17, 1946. Student, Curtiss Sch. Aviation, Buffalo, 1917, U. Calif., 1920. Test engr. Packard Motor Car Co., 1925-30; design engr., sales engr. Wilcolator Co., Newark, 1930-41; tank proof officer, Aberdeen Proving Ground; also project engr. Tank Automotive Center, Detroit, 1942-43; project officer USAAF, Wright Field Equipment Lab., 1943-44, asst. chief personal flight equipment lab., 1944-45; organizer, v.p., sales mgr. Control Products, Inc., Harrison, N.J., 1946-54; engring. and sales cons. metals and controls div. Tex. Instruments, Inc., Attleboro, Mass., 1954-60; pvt. practice, Boston, 1960—. Fellow Acad. Applied Sci.; mem. Soc. Automotive Engrs., Explorers Club. Inventor of automotive and aircraft circuit breaker, aircraft and tank fire detector systems, basic electromechanical sine switch element, thermostat for temperature control indsl., domestic and aircraft devices, new design for elec. contactors for all types of elec. switching; designer switch elements used in Mercury projects, Mariner, Telstar and all Apollo projects for critical control functions. Address: 3 River St Pl Boston MA 02108

BURCH, ROBERT DALE, lawyer; b. Washington, Jan. 30, 1928; s. Dallas Stockwell and Hepsy (Berry) B.; m. Joann D. Hansen, Dec. 9, 1966; children—Berkeley, Robert Brett, Barrett Bradley. Student, Va. Mil. Inst., 1945-46; B.S., U. Calif. at Berkeley, 1950, J.D., 1953. Bar: Calif. bar 1954. Since practiced in, Los Angeles and Beverly Hills; partner firm Gibson, Dunn & Crutcher, 1961—; lectr. U. So. Calif. Inst. Fed. Taxation, 1960, 62, 65, 75; guest lectr. U. Calif. at Los Angeles Law Sch., 1959; lectr. C.E.B. seminars U. Calif. Author: Federal Tax Procedures for General Practitioners; Contbr. profl. jours., textbooks. Bd. dirs. charitable founds. Served with AUS, 1945-47. Mem. Am. Law Inst. (tax adv. group), Beverly Hills Bar Assn., bd. govs., chmn. probate and trust com., Law Trust, Tax and Ins. Council (past czar), Los Angeles World Affairs Council, Beverly Hills C. of C. Home: 1301 Delresto Dr Beverly Hills CA 90210 Office: 2029 Century Park E Los Angeles CA 90067

BURCH, ROBERT JOSEPH, writer; b. Fayette County, Ga., June 26, 1925; s. John Ambrose and Nell (Graham) B. B.S.A., U. Ga., 1949. Author: 18 books for children including Queenie Peavy, 1966. Served with U.S. Army, 1943-45. Winner Children's Book award Child Study Assn. Am., 1966, Jane Addams Award Child Study Assn. Am., 1967. Democrat. Methodist. Home and Office: 2201 Forest Dr Fayetteville GA 30214

BURCH, THADDEUS JOSEPH, JR., physics educator, clergyman; b. Balt., June 4, 1930; s. Thaddeus and Francis Fidelis (Greenwell) B. A.B., Bellarmine Coll., 1954; M.A., Fordham U., 1956, M.S., 1966, Ph.D., 1968; S.T.B., Woodstock Coll., 1960, S.T.L., 1962. Ordained priest, Roman Catholic Ch., 1961. Joined S.J. Roman Catholic Ch., 1948; asst. prof. St. Joseph's Coll., Phila., 1969-72; assoc. prof. Fordham U., N.Y.C., 1972-74; vis. assoc. prof. U. Conn., Storrs, 1974-76; assoc. prof. Marquette U., Milw., 1976-80, chmn. dept. physics, 1977—, prof., chmn. dept. physics, 1980—; univ. del. Argonne (Ill.) Univs. Assn., 1977-82. Contbr. articles on physics to profl. jours. Mem. Am. Phys. Soc., Am. Assn. Physics Tchrs., Sigma Xi. Home: 230 Jefferson St Leonardtown MD 20650 Office: Marquett U Dept Physics Milwaukee WI 53233

BURCH, VORIS REAGAN, lawyer; b. Liberty, Tex., Feb. 10, 1930; s. Voris Reagan and Jessamae (Coffey) B.; m. Claudia Ramsland, Dec. 30, 1978; children: Melissa Burch Lively, Voris Reagan. B.B.A., Tex. A&M U., 1952; J.D., U. Tex.-Austin, 1957. Bar: Tex. 1957. Ptnr. Baker & Botts, Houston, 1957—. Served to 1st lt. USAF, 1952-54. Mem. ABA, State Bar Tex. (chmn. labor law sect. 1972-73), Houston Bar Assn. Republican. Methodist. Home: 5761 Indian Circle Hoston TX 77057 Office: Baker & Botts 3000 One Sell Plaza Houston TX 77002

BURCH, WILLIAM RICHARD, JR., environmental sociologist; b. Portland, Oreg., Mar. 27, 1933; s. William Richard and Edna Maude (Parker) B.; m. Judith Lorraine Hughes, Nov. 7, 1950; children—Laurel Burch Minakan, Steven Richard, Marcel Burch Terry. B.S., U. Oreg., 1955, M.S., 1957; Ph.D., U. Minn., 1964; M.Lit. (hon.), Yale U., 1976. Social sci. analyst U.S. Forest Service, Portland, 1962-64; lectr. sociology Victoria U., Wellington, N.Z., 1964-67; profl. research asso. SUNY Coll. Forestry, Syracuse, 1967-68; mem. faculty Yale U. Sch. Forestry and Environ. Studies/Instn. Social and Policy Studies, 1968—, prof. social ecology, 1976—; fellow Morse Coll., 1968; mem. research coms. Nat. Acad. Scis., 1968—. Author: Daydreams and Nightmares: A Sociological Essay on the American Environment, 1971; co-author: Measuring the Social Impact of Natural Resource Policies, 1983; editor: Long Distance Trails, 1979, also articles, revs., chpts. in books; co-author: The Social Organization of Leisure in Human Society, 1976; co-editor: Social Behavior, Natural Resources and The Environment, 1972. Bd. dirs. Conn. Forest and Park Assn., 1973—, Branford (Conn.) Land Trust, 1977—; mem. research com. Appalachian Mountain Club, 1974—. Grantee U.S. Forest Service, Dept. Energy, Conoco. Mem. Am. Sociol. Assn. (chmn. environ. sociology sect. 1976-78), Rural Sociol. Assn., Sigma Xi, Alpha Kappa Delta. Clubs: Yale (N.Y.C.); Morys Assn. (Yale U.). Home: 98 Linsley Lake Rd North Branford CT 06471 Office: 205 Prospect St New Haven CT 06510

BURCHARD, CHARLES, architect, former college dean; b. N.Y.C., June 27, 1914; s. Carl and Mary (Jahn) B.; m. Helen Schwob, Aug. 7, 1943; children: Linda Sue, Thomas Kirk, Peter. B.Arch., MIT, 1938; M.Arch. (Nelson Robinson fellow 1940-41), Harvard U., 1940. Asst. prof. architecture Harvard U., 1946-53; Fulbright sr. fellow, vis. lectr. Archtl. Assn., Sch. Architecture, London, 1950-51; pvt. practice, Cambridge, Mass., 1946-53; sr. partner A.M. Kinney Assos.-Charles Burchard, Cin., 1953-63; cons. A.M. Kinney Assos., 1964-68; dean Coll. Architecture and Urban Studies, Va. Poly. Inst. and State U., 1964-81, Univ. Disting. prof., 1966—; archtl. and ednl. cons., 1981—; cons. A.M. Kinney Assos., 1964-68, D.C. Redevel. Land Agy., 1966—, Study Profession Landscape Architecture, 1969—; mem. spl. study com. for selection architects and engrs. GSA, 1972-74; cons. Nat. Archtl. Restructuring Study, 1973-74; mem. Nat. Archtl. Accrediting Bd., 1974—; profl. adv. Govt. Relocation Center Competition, Fairfax County, Va., 1979. Works include Agoos residence, East Andover, N.H., 1948; Thompson Cadillac Agy., Cin., 1953, Hilltop and Clovernook elementary schs., Heinold Jr. High Sch., Aiken High Sch, all Cin., 1955-62, Miles Research Lab., Elkhart, Ind., 1961, U.S. Post Office Annex, Cin., 1963, Crosley Tower & Brodie Engring. & Sci. Complex, U. Cin., 1963. Mem. adv. council Princeton Sch. Architecture and Planning, 1974—; mem. alumni council Harvard Grad. Sch. Design, 1972; mem. Commonwealth of Va. Laureate Commn., 1977—; trustee Roanoke Fine Arts Center. Recipient award Progressive Architecture mag., 1954, Am. Assn. Sch. Adminstrs., 1955, 56, 59 60, Sch. Exec. mag., 1955, 56; Honor award Ohio Soc. Architects, 1970; Nat. Joint award for excellence in architecture and edn. AIA-Assn. Collegiate Schs. of Architecture, 1983. Fellow AIA (nat edn. and research com. 1967-69, dir. Va., exec. com.; commr. for edn.; council on licensing and edn. 1969—); mem. Archtl. Assn. (London), Va. Assn. Professions (edn. com.), Assn. Collegiate Schs. Architecture (treas. 1967-69, pres. 1969-71, dir.; life mem.), Tau Sigma Delta, Alpha Rho Chi (nat. pres. 1979-80), Omicron Delta Kappa. Home: 1605 Greenwood Dr Blacksburg VA 24060

BURCHARD, JOHN KENNETH, chem. engr.; b. St. Louis, May 12, 1936; s. Kenneth Reginald and Vernora Emma (Angell) B.; m. Elizabeth Lee Suesserott, Aug. 23, 1958; children—John Christopher, Gregory Charles. B.S., Carnegie Mellon U., 1957, M.S., 1959, Ph.D., 1962. Head systems analysis group United Tech. Center, Sunnyvale, Calif., 1961-68; chief scientist Combustion Power Co., Menlo Park, Calif., 1968-70; lab. dir. EPA, Research Triangle Park, N.C., 1970-80; dir. chem. engring. div. Research Triangle Inst., Research Triangle Park, 1980—; mem. bd. sci. advisors N.C. Energy Inst. Contbr. articles to profl. jours. Served with AUS, 1963-64. Shell Oil fellow, 1958-59; NSF fellow, 1960-61. Mem. Am. Inst. Chem. Engrs., Sigma Xi, Tau Beta Pi. Club: Chapel Hill Country. Office: PO Box 12194 Research Triangle Inst Research Triangle Park NC 27709

BURCHARD, WALDO WADSWORTH, sociologist, educator; b. Satanta, Kans., Nov. 28, 1916; s. Charles and Jennie Grace (Swink) B.; m. Rachael Caroline Ballenger, May 24, 1945; children—Gina Michel, Petrea Celeste, Stuart Gregory, Margot Theresa. A.B., U. Calif. at Berkeley, 1949, M.A., 1951, Ph.D., 1953. Instr. sociology U. Denver, 1952-53, U. Kan., 1953-55; asst. prof. sociology Hollins Coll., 1955-58; asso. prof. No. Ill. U., 1958-61, prof., 1961—, head dept. social scis., 1959-61, head dept. sociology and anthropology, 1961-68. Contbr. articles to profl. jours. Served with USMC, 1942-46. Mem. Am. Sociol. Assn., Midwest Sociol. Soc. (past chmn. publs. com., exofficio dir.), So. Sociol. Soc., North Central Sociol. Soc. (past exec. com.), Soc. Sci. Study Religion, Ill. Sociol. Assn. (hon. past pres.), Religious Research Assn., Assn. Sociology Religion. Home: 907 Sharon Dr DeKalb IL 60115

BURCHELL, HERBERT JOSEPH, manufacturing company executive; b. Brussels, Ont., Can., Oct. 19, 1930; s. Frederick William and Maggie Aileen (Scott) B.; m. Trudy E. McCallum, Sept. 5, 1953; children: Steven L., Sandra A. B.S. in Mining Engring., Queen's U., 1954. V.p. Canadian Industries Ltd., 1975-78; pres., chief exec. officer Jarvis Clark Co., North Bay, Ont., Can., 1977-78, Atlas Powder Co., Dallas, 1978—; dir. subs., Tyler Corp., Strategic Investments, Inc., Nobel Ins. Mem. Can. Inst. Mining and Metallurgy, Profl. Engrs. Ont. and Que., Inst. Makers Explosives. Club: Aerobics Activity Centre. Office: Atlas Powder Co 12700 Park Central Pl Dallas TX 75251

BURCHENAL, JOSEPH HOLLAND, physician; b. Milford, Del., Dec. 21, 1912; s. Caleb E. and Mary E. (Holl) B.; m. Margaret Pembroke Thom, Oct. 15, 1938; m. Joan Barclay Riley, Mar. 20, 1948; children—Mary Holland, Elizabeth Payne, Joan Littlefield, Barbara Fahys, Caleb Wells, David Holland, Joseph Emory Barclay. Student, Princeton U., 1930-33; M.D., U. Pa., 1937. Diplomate: Am. Bd. Internal Medicine. Rotating intern Union Meml. Hosp., Balt., 1937-38; intern pediatrics N.Y. Hosp.; also research pathology Cornell U., 1938-39; asst. resident medicine Boston City Hosp., 1940-42; spl. fellow medicine Meml. Hosp., N.Y.C., 1946-49, asst. attending physician, 1949-52, attending physician, 1952-83, attending physician emeritus, 1983—, chief chemotherapy service, 1952-64, asso. med. dir. for clin. investigation, 1964-66, dir. clin. investigation, 1966—; research fellow medicine Harvard, 1940-42; research fellow Sloan-Kettering Inst., 1946-48, asso., 1948-52, mem., 1952-83, mem. emeritus, 1983—, v.p., 1964-72, field coordinator human cancer, 1973—, head Applied Therapy Lab., 1973—; asst prof. clin. medicine Cornell U., 1949-50, asst. prof. medicine, 1950-51, asso. prof., 1951-52, prof., 1952-55; prof. medicine Cornell U. Med. Coll., 1955-80, emeritus, 1980—; spl. cons. clin. panel Cancer Chemotherapy Nat. Service Center, 1955-64; spl. cons. pub. health service, hematology study sect. NIH, 1955-58; cons. Am. Cancer Soc., 1958-64; chmn. U.S. nat. com. Internat. Union Against Cancer, 1960-63, chmn. chemotherapy panel of research commn., 1962-66; chmn. WHO expert com. on cancer chemotherapy, 1961; mem. WHO expert adv. panel on cancer, 1961—; chmn. chemotherapy adv. com. Nat. Cancer Inst., 1970-71; mem. nat. panel consultants conquest of cancer U.S. Senate Com. Labor and Pub. Welfare, 1970; cons. in oncology Stamford (Conn.), St. Albans (N.Y.) Naval hosps. Asso. editor: Cancer Research, 1969-74; mem. editorial adv. bd.: Cancer. Mem. Rep. Town Meeting, Darien, Conn., 1957—. Served M.C. AUS, 1942-45. Recipient Alfred P. Sloan Cancer Research award, 1963; Albert Lasker award in clin. cancer chemotherapy, 1972; prix Lepold Griffuel, 1970; John Phillips award Phillips Exeter Acad., 1974; David A. Karnofsky meml. award Am. Soc. Clin. Oncology, 1974; Jeffrey A. Gottlieb Meml. award, 1980; others. Mem. Am. Soc. Clin. Investigation, Soc. Exptl. Biology and Medicine, Am. Assn. for Cancer Research (pres. 1965-66), European, Internat., Am. socs. hematology, Am. Soc. Tropical Medicine, Soc. Study Blood, Am. Fedn. Clin. Research, N.Y. Acad. Scis., Harvey Soc., Am. Soc. Pediatric Research (rep. to div. med. scis. NRC 1955-58), AMA, A.C.P., med. socs. County N.Y., State N.Y., Am. Inst. Nutrition, Leukemia Soc. Am. (v.p. med. and sci. affairs 1970-75, chmn. med. and sci. adv. com. 1970-74), James Ewing Soc., Academia Nacional de Medicina de Buenos Aires (corr.), Czechoslovak Med. Soc. (corr.), Brazilian Nat. Acad. Medicine (corr.). Office: Walker Lab 145 Boston Post Rd Rye NY 10580

BURCHFIEL, BURRELL CLARK, geology educator; b. Stockton, Calif., Mar. 21, 1934; s. Beryl Edward and Agnes (Clark) B.; children: Brian Edward, Brook Evans. B.S., Stanford U., 1957, M.S., 1958; Ph.D., Yale U., 1961. Prof. geology Rice U., 1961-76, M.I.T., 1977—. Served with U.S. Army, 1958-59. Fellow Geol. Soc. Am.; mem. Geol. Soc. Australia; Mem. Am. Assn. Petroleum Geologists, Am. Geophys. Union. Home: 8 Eastern Ave Arlington MA 02174 Office: 54-1010 MIT Cambridge MA 02139

BURCHFIELD, HARRY PHINEAS, JR., consultant biochemistry; b. Pitts., Dec. 22, 1915; s. Harry Phineas and Florence Faye (Fearl) B.; m. Eleanor Emerett Storrs, Nov. 29, 1963; children: Sarah Storrs, Benjamin Hyde. A.B., Columbia U., 1938, M.A., 1938, Ph.D., 1956. Chemist, Nat. Oil Products Co., Harrison, N.J., 1938-40; research scientist Uniroyal Corp., Naugatuck, Conn., 1940-50, dir. plantations research dept., Indonesia and Malaysia, 1951-52; asso. dir. Boyce Thompson Inst. Plant Research, Yonkers, N.Y., 1952-61; inst. scientist, mgr. S.W. Research Inst., San Antonio, 1961-65; chief pesticides research lab. USPHS, Perrine, Fla., 1965-67; sci. dir. Gulf South Research Inst., New Iberia, La., 1967-76; adj. prof. chemistry U. Southwestern La., 1967-77; prof. chemistry, head div. molecular biology Med. Research Inst., Fla. Inst. Tech., Melbourne, 1977-81; charter mem. Soc. Univ. Fellows, 1978; prin. scientist Research Assos., 1976—; trustee Gulf Univs. Research Consortium, 1971-76; mem. carcinogenesis panel of secs. HEW Commn. on Pesticides, 1969; mem. nat. tech. adv. com. pesticides EPA, 1971-72, project reviewer research grants, 1972; cons. carcinogensis Nat. Cancer Inst., 1965-67; cons. leprosy Pan Am. Health Orgn., WHO, 1974, EPA, 1976—. Author: (with Eleanor E. Storrs) Biochemical Applications of Gas Chromatography, 1962, (with D.E. Johnson and Eleanor Storrs) Guide to the Analysis of Pesticide Residues, 1965; contbr. chpts. to books, articles to profl. jours. Recipient award Chgo. Rubber Group, 1946; EPA grantee, 1969-76; Nat. Inst. Environ. Health Scis. grantee, 1977—. Mem. Am. Chem. Soc., Soc. Toxicology, Am. Inst. Biol. Scis., AAAS. Episcopalian. Office: 72 Riverview Terr Indialantic FL 32903

BURCHILL, THOMAS FRANCIS, broadcasting executive; b. N.Y.C., Jan. 12, 1942; s. Thomas Francis and Margaret Elizabeth (Flanagan) B.; m. Cathryn Ann Esser, May 16, 1964; children: Thomas, Mark, Melissa. B.A., Holy Cross Coll., 1963; M.B.A., Columbia U., 1980. Vice pres., sales mgr. Edward Petry Co., N.Y.C., 1966-70; sales exec. John Blair Co., N.Y.C., 1970-74; v.p. radio Bolton Burchill Ltd., N.Y.C., 1974-77; pres. sales div. RKO Radio, 1977-79; pres. RKO Radio Network, RKO Gen., Inc., N.Y.C., 1979—; mem. bd. Electronic Media Rating Council. Served to lt. USN, 1963-65. Named Radio Rep. of Yr. Hall Radio, 1976, Radio Exec. of Yr. Gallagher Report, 1982. Mem. Inernat. Radio and TV Soc. and Found. (dir.), Sales and Exec. Club, Museum Broadcasting., Network Radio Assn. (vice chmn.). Roman Catholic. Clubs: Garden Mich. C. of C. (dir.), City Casino, Westhampton Country. Office: 1440 Broadway New York NY 10018

BURCIAGA, JUAN GUERRERO, U.S. dist. judge; b. Roswell, N.Mex., Aug. 17, 1929; s. Melesio Antonio and Juana (Guerrero) B.; m. Carolyn Jacoby, Oct. 28, 1958 (dec.); children—Lisa Anne, Lora Anne, Amy Virginia, Carlos Antonio, Pamela. B.S., U.S. Mil. Acad., 1952; J.D., U. N.Mex., 1963. Bar: N.Mex. bar 1964. Asso., then partner firms in, Albuquerque, 1964-79; U.S. dist. judge Dist. N.Mex., 1979—; lectr. U. N.Mex. Sch. Law, 1970-71. Bd. dirs. Albuquerque YMCA, 1964-74, NCCJ, Albuquerque, 1969-73; urban renewal commnr. City of Albuquerque, 1972-76. Served as officer USAF, 1952-60. Mem. Am. Bar Assn., Am. Judicature Soc. (dir.), Def. Research Inst., Am. Bd. Arbitration, Am. Trial Lawyers Assn., Am. Bd. Trial Advocates, Albuquerque Bar Assn. Democrat. Roman Catholic. Office: US Dist Courthouse 5th and Gold Sts Albuquerque NM 87103

BURCK, ARTHUR ALBERT, corp. merger expert; b. Mpls., June 8, 1913; s. Herman J. and Emma (Wirth) B.; m. Rutilia Poli-Sandri, June 2, 1945; children—Stephan W. (dec.), Adriana, Jeffrey L., Christopher C. B.S., U. Minn., 1935; LL.B., 1937; LL.D., U. Cin., 1969. Bar: N.Y. bar 1938. Asso. Carter, Ledyard & Millburn, N.Y.C., 1937-39, Simons, Schur & Straus, 1953-54; with SEC, 1939-53; head corp. reorgn. dept. Fahnestock & Co., N.Y.C., 1954-56; partner McClellan & Burck (negotiators bus.-mergers, acquisitions), N.Y.C., 1957-58; pres. McClellan & Burck, Inc., N.Y.C., 1958-62; partner Arthur Burck & Co. (planners, negotiators bus. mergers, acquisitions, corporate reorgns.), 1963—; pres. Arthur Burck & Co., Inc., 1968—. Bd. dirs. Fund for the Republic, Center for Study of Democratic Instns., 1974-76, S.I. Acad., 1965-67; chmn. bd. trustees Palm Beach Acad., 1971-72; bd. fellows Tampa (Fla.) U., 1969-74. Served to maj. AUS, 1942-47. Decorated Bronze Star medal; recipient SEC citation, 1952. Club: Richmond Country (S.I.). Home: Villa Pompano 240 El Vedado Way Palm Beach FL 33480 Office: 324 Royal Palm Way Palm Beach FL 33480

BURDAKIN, JOHN HOWARD, railroad executive; b. Milton, Mass., Aug. 11, 1922; s. L. Richard and M. and Gertrude (Rogers) B.; m. Jean Campbell Moulton, Oct. 2, 1948; children: John Howard, David Campbell, Dan Edward. B.C.E., Mass. Inst. Tech., 1947. Mgr. r.r. div. Panama Canal Co., 1960-61; with Pa. R.R., 1947-68, asst. gen. mgr., 1965-68; with Penn Central R.R., 1968-71, v.p., gen. mgr., to, 1971; v.p. ops., exec. v.p., then pres. Grand Trunk Western R.R., 1974—; pres. Central Vt. Ry., 1976—, Duluth, Winnipeg & Pacific R.R., 1976—, Grand Trunk Corp., 1976—; Detroit, Toledo and Ironton R.R., 1980—; dir. Belt Ry. Chgo. Mem. Mich. Job Devel. Authority. Served to 1st lt. C.E. AUS, World War II. Mem. Mich. C. of C. (dir.). Republican. Presbyterian. Clubs: Bloomfield Hills Country, Detroit Athletic, Kitchi Gammi, Masons. Office: 131 W Lafayette Blvd Detroit MI 48226

BURDE, RONALD MARSHALL, neuro-ophthalmologist; b. N.Y.C., Dec. 24, 1938; s. Eli and Helene B.; m. Sharon Della Kaplan, June 20, 1960; children: Howard, Bradley, Jeffrey. S.B., MIT, 1960; M.D., Jefferson Med. Coll., Phila., 1964. Diplomate Am. Bd. Ophthalmology (dir.). Intern Jefferson Med. Coll., 1964-65; resident in ophthalmology Washington U. Med. Center, St. Louis, 1965-68; spl. fellow Nat. Inst. Neurol. Diseases and Blindness, 1968-70; mem. faculty Washington U. Med. Sch., 1970—, prof. ophthalmology, 1974—, prof. neurology, 1975—, prof. neurol. surgery, 1981—; vis. prof. Hebrew U. Med. Sch., Jerusalem, 1977. Editor: Survey of Ophthalmology, 1980—, Jour. Clin. Neuro-ophthalmology, 1981—, also various specialized jours. Bd. dirs. Jewish Community Center, St. Louis, Am. Jewish Com., St. Louis; past pres. Traditional Congregation, Creve Coeur, Mo., 1974-76, bd. dirs., 1970—; past mem. ethnic studies adv. bd. Forest Park Community Coll., St. Louis. Fellow Am. Acad. Ophthalmology (asso. sec. continuing edn. 1980—), A.C.S.; mem. Am. Neurol. Assn., Am. Ophthalmol. Soc., Am. Assn. Neurol. Scis., AMA, Assn. Research in Vision and Ophthalmology, Mo. Med. Assn., St. Louis Met. Med. Soc., St. Louis Ophthal. Soc., Pan Am. Ophthal. Assn., St. Louis Soc. Neurosci., M.I.T. Alumni Assn. (past treas., dir. St. Louis chpt. 1972-73). Home: 1 Spoede Ln Creve Coeur MO 63141 Office: 660 S Euclid Ave Saint Louis MO 63110

BURDEN, CHRIS, artist; b. Boston, Apr. 11, 1946. B.F.A., Pomona Coll., 1969; M.F.A., U. Calif., Irvine, 1971. Vis. artist Fresno (Calif.) State U., 1974. Works in broadcast TV and live performances.; One-person shows, Riko Mizuno Gallery, Los Angeles, 1972, 74, 75, Ronald Feldman Fine Arts, N.Y., 1974, 75, Hansen Fuller Gallery, 1974, Alessandra Castelli Gallery, 1975; represented in permanent collections, Mus. Modern Art, N.Y.C., Long Beach (Calif.) Arts Mus. Recipient New Talent award Los Angeles County Mus. Art, 1973; Nat. Endowment Arts grantee, 1974.

BURDEN, JEAN PRUSSING, poet, author, editor; b. Waukegan, Ill., Sept. 1, 1914; d. Harry Frederick and Miriam (Biddlecom) Prussing; m. David Charles Burden, 1940 (div. 1949). B.A., U. Chgo., 1936. Sec. John Hancock Mutual Life Ins. Co., Chgo., 1937-39, Young & Rubicam, Inc., 1939-41; editor, copywriter Domestic Industries, Inc., Chgo., 1941-45; office mgr. O'Brion Russell & Co., Los Angeles, 1948-55; adminstr. pub. relations Meals for Millions Found., Los Angeles, 1955-65; editor Stanford Research Inst., South Pasadena, Calif., 1965-66; lectr. poetry to numerous colls. and univs., U.S., 1963—; supr. poetry workshop Pasadena City Coll., Calif., 1961-62, 66, U. Calif. at Irvine, 1975; also pvt. poetry workshops. Propr. Jean Burden & Assos., Altadena, Calif., 1966-82. Author: Naked as the Glass, 1963, Journey Toward Poetry, 1966, The Cat You Care For, 1968, The Dog You Care For, 1968, The Bird You Care For, 1970, The Fish You Care For, 1971, A Celebration of Cats, 1974, The Classic Cats, 1975, The Woman's Day Book of Hints for Cat Owners, 1980; Poetry editor: Yankee Mag, 1955—; pet editor: Woman's Day Mag, 1973-82; Contbr. numerous articles to various jours. and mags. MacDowell Colony fellow, 1973, 74, 76; Recipient Silver Anvil award Pub. Relations Soc. of Am., 1969, 1st prize Borestone Mountain Poetry award, 1963. Mem. Poetry Soc. Am., Acad. Am. Poets, Authors Guild. Address: 1129 Beverly Way Altadena CA 91001 *I think that man is* *constantly trying to bring down into the world of time the essences of what he dimly but intuitively feels is timeless. One of the ways in which he tries is through poetry. Without poetry, a certain kind of Reality is speechless. Or to put it a slightly different way, I believe that we inhabit two worlds at once, the world of time and the world of timelessness, and that poetry is a bridge that lets us cross over.*

BURDEN, WILLIAM ARMISTEAD MOALE, financier; b. N.Y.C., Apr. 8, 1906; s. William A. M. and Florence Vanderbilt (Twombly) B.; m. Margaret Livingston Partridge, Feb. 16, 1931; children: William A. M. (dec.), Robert Livingston (dec.), Hamilton Twombly, Ordway Partridge. A.B. cum laude, Harvard U., 1927; D.Sc., Clarkson Coll. Tech., 1953; LL.D., Fairleigh Dickinson U., 1965, Johns Hopkins U., 1970. Analyst aviation securities Brown Bros., Harriman & Co., N.Y.C., 1928-32; charge of aviation research Scudder, Stevens & Clark, N.Y.C., 1932-39; v.p., dir. Nat. Aviation Corp. (aviation investment trust), N.Y.C., 1939-41; v.p. Def. Supplies Corp. subs. RFC, 1941-42; spl. aviation asst. Sec. of Commerce, 1942-43; mem. NACA, 1942-47; asst. sec. Commerce for Air, 1943-47; U.S. del. Civil Aviation Conf., 1944; chmn. U.S. del. interim assembly Provisional Internat. Civil Aviation Orgn., 1946; aviation cons. Smith Barney & Co., Inc., 1947-49; partner William A.M. Burden & Co., 1949—; spl. asst. for R & D to Sec. of Air Force, 1950-52; mem. Nat. Aeros. and Space Council, 1958-59; U.S. ambassador to Belgium, 1959-61; mem. U.S. Citizens Commn. for NATO, 1961-62; dir. emeritus Am. Metal Climax, CBS, Inc.; cons. Aerospace Corp. Author: The Struggle for Airways in Latin America, 1943, Peggy and I, 1982. Trustee, past chmn. Inst. for Def. Analyses; trustee, past pres., chmn. Mus. Modern Art; hon. life gov. Soc. of N.Y. Hosp., 1950—; trustee emeritus Columbia U.; trustee Fgn. Service Edn. Found., French Inst. in U.S.; regent Smithsonian Instn., 1962—; bd. dirs. Atlantic Council U.S., 1961—; bd. govs. Atlantic Inst., 1964—. Decorated comdr. Cruzeiro do Sul, Brazil; comdr.'s cross Order of Merit, Fed. Republic Germany; grand official El Sol del Peru, Peru; grand officer French Legion of Honor; comdr.'s cross Order of Merit, Italy; grand cordon Order of Leopold, Belgium; asso. comdr. (Bro.) Order of St. John. Mem. Council Fgn. Relations (hon. dir.), AIAA, France-Am. Soc. (pres.), Council French-Am. Socs. in N.Y. (chmn.). Clubs: Somerset (Boston); The Brook, Racquet and Tennis, River, Links, Century (N.Y.C.); Metropolitan (Washington); Buck's and White's (London); Jockey (Paris). Address: 630 Fifth Ave New York NY 10020

BURDETT, PHILIP HAWLEY, former firearms company executive; b. Lawrence, Mass., July 30, 1914; s. William Nelson and Myrtle (Hawley) B.; m. Cecelia Kochiss, Aug. 31, 1967; children: Christopher C., Elaine (Mrs. David Rose), R. Lorraine (Mrs. Robert Heath). B.A., Drew U., 1936; M.S. in Chemistry, Syracuse U., 1937; Ph.D., U. N.C., 1939; LL.D., Sacred Heart U., 1979. Chemist Remington Arms Co., Bridgeport, Conn., 1939-42, group leader tech. dept., 1942-46, supr., 1946-55, asst. to dir. research and devel., 1955-58, asst. mgr. govt. sales, 1958-59, dir. marketing, 1964-66, v.p., 1965-74, asst. gen. mgr., 1966-73, pres., 1974-79, also dir., 1973-80; dir. Citytrust, Bridgeport, Conn. Citytrust Bancorp, Bridgeport., Page-Wilson Corp., Progressive Growth and Global Opportunities; trustee Shearson/Am. Express, FMA & Daily Tax-Free Dividend Funds, Am. Telecommunications Trust. Mem. pres.'s adv. council Bridgeport Engring. Inst., 1970—; bd. dirs., treas. Bridgeport United Way; vice chmn., bd. dirs. Bridgeport Hosp.; bd. dirs. Bridgeport Symphony, Conn. Grand Opera, Goodwill Industries Am., Jr. Achievement of Bridgeport; trustee Goodwill Industries Western Conn.; treas. United Health Care, Inc.; vice chmn. bd. trustees Drew U. Mem. Am. Chem. Soc., Wildlife Mgmt. Inst. (dir. 1965-79), Sporting Arms and Ammunition Mfrs. Inst. (exec. com. 1964-79), Am. Def. Preparedness Assn. (adv. service bd. 1960), Bridgeport Area C. of C. (chmn. bd. dirs. 1979-80), Sigma Xi, Tau Kappa Alpha. Club: Brooklawn Country.

BURDETTE, WALTER JAMES, surgeon, educator; b. Hillsboro, Tex., Feb. 5, 1915; s. James S. and Ovazene (Weatherred) B.; m. Kathryn Lynch, Apr. 9, 1947; children: Susan, William J. A.B., Baylor U., 1935; A.M., U. Tex., 1936, Ph.D., 1938; M.D., Yale, 1942. Diplomate: Am. Bd. Surgery, Am. Bd. Thoracic Surgery. Intern Johns Hopkins Hosp., 1942-43; Harvey Cushing fellow surgery Yale, 1943-44; resident staff surgery New Haven Hosp., 1944-46; instr., asst., assoc. prof. surgery La. State U., 1946-55; vis. surgeon Charity Hosp. of La., 1946-55; cons. Touro Infirmary and So. Baptist Hosp., 1952-55, Oak Ridge Inst. Nuclear Studies Hosp., 1953-59; vis. investigator Chester Beatty Inst. Cancer Research, Brompton, and Royal Cancer Hosp., London, 1953, Max Planck Institut Fuer Biochemie, Tuebingen, Germany, summer 1955; prof., chmn. dept. surgery U. Mo., 1955-56; prof. clin. surgery St. Louis U. Sch. Medicine, 1956-57; prof., head dept. surgery U. Utah, 1957-65; dir. lab. clin. biology, surgeon-in-chief Salt Lake Gen. Hosp., 1957-65; chief surg. cons. VA Hosps., Salt Lake City, 1957-65; prof. surgery, assoc. dir. U. Tex-M.D. Anderson Hosp. and Tumor Inst., Houston, 1965-72; prof. surgery U. Tex. Sch. Medicine at Houston, 1971-79; adj. prof. pharmacology U. Houston, 1975—; pres. Nat. Biomed. Found., 1972—; cons. St. Luke's Hosp., 1975—, Park Plaza Hosp., 1976—, Meth. Hosp., 1976—; Gibson lectr. advanced surgery Oxford U., 1966; vis. prof. U. Oxford, spring 1965; ofcl. U. Congo, summer 1968. Editor, author: Etiology, Treatment of Leukemia, 1958, Methodology in Human Genetics, 1962, Methodology in Mammalian Genetics, 1962, Methodology in Basic Genetics, 1963, Primary Hepatoma, 1965, Carcinoma of the Alimentary Tract, 1965, Viruses Inducing Cancer, 1966, Carcinoma of the Colon and Antecedent Epithelium, 1970, Planning and Analysis of Clinical Studies, 1970, Invertebrate Endocrinology and Hormonal Heterophylly, 1974; mem. editorial bd.: Surg. Rounds; contbr. articles to med. and sci. jours. Chmn. genetics study sect., mem. morphology study sect. NIH; cons. Nat. Cancer Inst.; mem. Nat. Adv. Cancer Council, Nat. Adv. Heart Council, Surgeon General's Com. on Smoking and Health; chmn. U.S.A. nat. com. Internat. Union Against Cancer; mem. transplantation com. Nat. Acad. Scis.; chmn. working Cadre on cancer large intestine Nat. Cancer Inst.; elder, deacon Christian Ch. Alpha Epsilon Delta Disting. Alumni award Baylor U., 1983; Rockefeller travel fellow, summer 1957. Fellow A.C.S.; mem. Soc. Surgery Alimentary Tract, Am. Assn. Cancer Research (dir.), Am. Cancer Soc. (chmn. research adv. council, mem. council on analysis and projection), Am. Surg. Assn., Soc. Clin. Surgery (treas.), Soc. U. Surgeons, A.M.A., Soc. Exptl. Biology and Medicine, Genetics Soc. Am., AAAS, Western Soc. Clin. Research, Am. Assn. Thoracic Surgery, Transplantation Soc., N.Y. Acad. Sci., Soc. Am. Naturalists, New Orleans, St. Louis, Salt Lake City, Houston surg. socs., Tex. Med. Soc., Harris County Med. Soc., So. Western surg. assns., So. Thoracic Surg. Soc., Peruvian Cancer Soc. (hon.), Am. Assn. for Cancer Research, Soc. for Surgery Alimentary Tract, Am. Soc. Clin. Oncology, Am. Soc. for Cancer Edn., Tex. Surg. Soc., Assn. Yale Alumni in Medicine (exec. com. 1977), Soc. Internat. de Chirurg, Sigma Xi, Alpha Omega Alpha. Home: 239 Chimney Rock Rd Houston TX 77024 Office: Plaza Med. Center 1200 Binz St Suite 740 Houston TX 77004

BURDGE, JEFFREY J., metal products executive. Student, Youngstown State U. C.P.A., Ohio. Acct. Clark & Collins, C.P.A.s, 1947-53; with Harsco Corp., 1953—; asst. treas. Clark & Collins, C.P.A.s, 1959-69; pres. Heckett Engring. Co. div. Harsco Corp., 1969, exec. v.p., chief operating officer, 1975, pres., chief operating officer, 1976-77, pres., chief exec. officer, 1977-83, chmn. bd., chief exec. officer, 1983—, also dir.; dir. Dauphin Deposit Corp., Dauphin Deposit Bank & Trust Co., AMP Inc., Pamcor Inc., Penn Blue Shield. Bd. dirs. Polyclinic Med. Ctr. of Harrisburg. Served with Brit. Army, 1939-45. Mem. Am. Iron and Steel Inst. (bd. dirs.). Office: Harsco Corp 350 Poplar Church Rd Camp Hill PA 17011

BURDI, ALPHONSE ROCCO, anatomist; b. Chgo., Aug. 28, 1935; s. Alphonse Rocco and Anna (Basilo) B.; m. Sandra Shaw, Mar. 22, 1968; children—Elizabeth Anne, Sarah Lynne. B.S., No. Ill. U., DeKalb, 1957; M.S., U. Ill., 1959, U. Mich., 1961, Ph.D., 1963. Predoctoral fellow physiology U. Ill., 1957-59; NSF summer fellow U. Mich., 1960, NIH trainee, 1960-61, NIH predoctoral research fellow, 1962, mem. faculty, 1962—, prof. anatomy, 1974—; sr. scientist Center for Human Growth and Devel. Editorial bd.: Cleft Palate Jour, 1972—, Am. Jour. Phys. Anthropology, 1971-75, C.C. Thomas Am. Lectr. Series in Anatomy, 971—, Jour. Dental Research, 1977—. Grantee NIH. Mem. Internat., Am. assns. dental research, Am. Cleft Palate Assn., Teratology Soc., Tissue Culture Assn., Am. Assn. Phys. Anthropology, Sigma Xi. Home: 2600 Page Ct Ann Arbor MI 48104 Office: Dept Anatomy Med Sci Bldg 2 Univ Mich Ann Arbor MI 48109

BURDICK, ALLAN BERNARD, geneticist; b. Cin., Aug. 16, 1920; s. Theodore Allan and Rachel C. (Mullen) B.; m. Sally Ann Cummins, Feb. 17, 1943; children—Michael Allan, Nancy Cecilia, Stephen Franklin, Lindy Lou. B.S., Iowa State U., 1945, M.S., 1947; Ph.D., U. Cal., at Berkeley, 1949. Asst. prof. genetics U. Ark., 1949-52; asst. prof. Purdue U., 1952-54, asso. prof., 1954-59, prof. genetics, 1959-63; prof., asso. dean sci. Am. U., Beirut, Lebanon, 1963-66; prof., chmn. biology dept. Adelphi U., Garden City, N.Y., 1966-69; prof., chmn. dept. genetics U. Mo., Columbia, 1969-73, prof. genetics, 1973—; dir., co-founder Tomato Genetics Coop., 1950-62; cons. Pahlavi U., Shiraz, Iran, 1965-66, Jordanian Ministry Edn., 1964-65. Contbr. articles profl. jours. Mem. Com. Edn. Women in Sci., 1962; Bd. dirs. Ecumenical Center, Columbia, Mo., 1970-73. Served to maj. USAAF, 1942-46. Recipient medallion of H.I.M. Shah of Iran, 1966; Guggenheim fellow, 1959-60; Fulbright research scholar Kyoto U., 1959-60. Fellow A.A.A.S.; mem. Genetics Soc. Am., Am. Soc. Naturalists, Am. Soc. for Human Genetics, Soc. Craniofacial Genetics, Birth Defects and Clin. Genetics Soc., Environ. Mutagen, Soc., Sigma Xi, Sigma Phi Epsilon (bd. dirs. Mo. Alpha Corp. 1970-74). Episcopalian (vestryman 1954-62, 71-74, warden 1957, 72-74, lay reader 1951—). Established single gene heterosis for lethal gene, 1959, that minor genes have higher mutation rates than major genes, 1958-59. Home: 3000 Woodkirk Dr Columbia MO 65201

BURDICK, CHARLES LALOR, chemical engineer; b. Denver, Apr. 14, 1892; s. Frank Austin and Anna (Lalor) B.; m. Alison Ward, 1938; children: Lalor, Cynthia. B.S., Drake U., 1911, LL.D. (hon.), 1970; B.S., Mass. Inst. Tech., 1913, M.S., 1914; postgrad., Kaiser Wilhelm Inst., Berlin, and Univ. Coll., London, 1914-16; Ph.D., U. Basel, Switzerland, 1915; D.Sc. (hon.), U. Del., 1955, D.Eng., Widener Coll., 1976. Research asso. in chemistry Mass. Inst. Tech. and Cal. Inst. Tech., 1916-17; metall. engr. Guggenheim Bros., N.Y. and, Chile, 1919-24; v.p. and cons. engr. Anglo-Chilean Consol. Nitrate Corp., 1924-28; with E.I. du Pont de Nemours, 1929-57, in various positions as asst. chem. dir., ammonia dept., spl. asst. to pres., chmn. bds. in, Mexico of; DuPont (S.A., and), Cia. Mexicana de Explosives. Mem. sci. adv. com. Henry Francis du Pont Winterthur Mus.; mem. exec. com. Internat. Planned Parenthood Fedn., 1962-68; Pres. Christiana Found., 1960-73; exec. dir., trustee Lalor Found., Wilmington; founding hon. mem. U. Del. Research Found.; hon. life mem. Del. Acad. Medicine; bd. dirs. Planned Parenthood-World Population, 1961-67. Served to 1st lt. Ordnance div. U.S. Army, 1917-18. Fellow AAAS; mem. N.Y. Acad. Sci. (life), Am. Inst. Chem. Engrs., Am. Chem. Soc., Am. Fertility Soc., Am. Assn. Planned Parenthood Physicians, Soc. Study Social Biology, Am. Inst. Biol. Scis., Soc. for Study Reprodn. (charter), Soc. Study Fertility (Eng.) (Marshall medal 1984), Phi Beta Kappa. Clubs: Wilmington, Greenville Country. Home: 900 Barley Dr Wilmington DE 19807 Office: 3801 Kennett Pike Bldg B-108 Wilmington DE 19807

BURDICK, EUGENE ALLAN, retired judge, lawyer, surrogate judge; b. Williston, N.D., Oct. 15, 1912; s. Usher Lloyd and Emma Cecelia (Robertson) B.; m. May Picard, Feb. 14, 1939; children: William Eugene, Elizabeth Jane Burdick Cantarine. B.A., U. Minn., 1933, J.D., 1935. Bar: N.D. 1935, U.S. Dist. Ct., N.D. Sole practice, Williston, 1935-53; state's atty. Williams County, 1939-45; dist. judge, 1953-78; commr. Uniform State Laws for State of N.D., 1959—; draftsman N.D. Rules of Civil Procedure, 1954-57; mem. Juvenile Ct. Judges Adv. Council for Children and Youth, 1959-67, 68—; draftsman Rules of Ct. for Dist. Cts., 1962-63; pres. Nat. Conf. Commrs. on Uniform State Laws, 1971-73. Pres. James Meml. Library, Williston, 1948-65; mem. exec. com. N.D. Conf. Social Welfare, 1963-67; chmn. Gov.'s Com. on Children and Youth, 1965-71; mem., vice chmn. exec. com. Gov.'s Council Human Resources. Recipient outstanding trustee award ALA, 1956. Mem. ABA, State Bar Assn. N.D., Am. Law Inst., Inst. Jud. Adminstrn., Am. Contract Bridge League, Hon. Order Ky. Cols., Order of Coif, Phi Alpha Delta (hon.), Sigma Nu. Lodges: Kiwanis (past pres. Williston); Elks (hon. life mem.); Williston Toastmasters (hon. mem.). Home: 405 14th St Williston ND 58801

BURDICK, QUENTIN NORTHROP, U.S. senator; b. Munich, N.D., June 19, 1908; s. Usher Lloyd and Emma (Robertson) B.; m. Marietta Janecky, Mar. 18, 1933 (dec. Mar. 1958); children: Jonathan, Jan, Mary, Jennifer, Jessica; m. Jocelyn Birch Peterson; 1 son, Gage; stepchildren: Leslie, Birch. B.A., U. Minn., 1931, LL.B., 1932. Bar: N.D. 1932. Practiced in, Fargo, 1932-58; mem. 86th Congress, N.D. at large; U.S. senator from N.D., 1960—; Candidate for lt. gov., 1942, for gov., 1946, for U.S. sentor, 1956. Mem. Sons of Norway, Sigma Nu. Democrat. Conglist. Clubs: Mason, Elk, Eagle, Moose. Office: 511 Hart Senate Office Bldg Washington DC 20510 *

BURDITT, JOHN FREDERIC, retired manufacturing company executive; b. Newton, Mass., Apr. 4, 1918; s. Frederic McGregor and Florence Lovejoy (Willey) B.; m. Jane Spaulding Nye, Sept. 6, 1947; children—Faraday Nye (Mrs. Manuel de la Camara), Frederic McGregor, John Carver, Timothy Nye, Benjamin Ames. Student, Browne and Nichols Sch., Cambridge, Mass.; B.A., Yale U., 1940. With Chem. Bank & Trust Co., N.Y.C., 1945-48; with ACF Industries, Inc., N.Y.C., 1948-83, chmn., chief exec. officer, 1968-83; dir. ACF Industries, Inc., Gen. Pub. Utilities Corp., Parsippany, N.J., Amstar Corp., N.Y.C., Transway Internat. Corp., Warner-Lambert Co., Morris Plains, N.J., Park City Consol. Mines, Salt Lake City. Trustee Am. Enterprise Inst., Washington, No. Westchester Hosp., Mt. Kisco, N.Y.; bd. dirs. United Fund Greater N.Y. Served to lt. comdr. USNR, 1941-46. Clubs: Board Room (N.Y.C.); Bedford Golf and Tennis (N.Y.). Home: PO Box 503 Bedford Hills NY 10507 Office: 750 3d Ave New York NY 10017

BURFORD, BYRON LESLIE, artist, educator; b. Jackson, Miss., July 12, 1920; s. Byron Leslie Buford and Floy Evelyn (Smith) B.; m. Kathleen Marguerite, Mar. 21, 1944; children: Kathleen Lewis, Kevin Scott, Joanna Kay. B.F.A., U. Iowa-Iowa City, 1942, M.F.A., 1947. Prof. art U. Iowa, Iowa City, 1947—; vis. prof. U. Minn., Mpls., 1959, Calif. Coll. Arts, Oakland, 1962, U. Mass., Amherst, 1967. Exhibited group shows include, Am. Acad. Arts and Letters, 1966,72, one-man shows, Walter Art Ctr., Mpls., 1958, U. Wis., Madison, 1964, George Washington U., Washington, 1968, Des Moines Art Ctr., 1968, 69, 73, U. Iowa Mus. Art, Iowa City, 1962, 72, 76, Waterloo Art Ctr., Iowa, 1981, Davenport Mcpl. Art Gallery, Iowa, group shows include, Walker Art Ctr., 1956, 58, 60, 62, 66, Pa. Acad., Phila., 1966, Venice Biennale, Italy, 1968, Royal Coll. Art, London, 1971, galleries and museums, Dusseldorf and Darmstadt, 1972, Musée des Artes Decoratif, Paris, Circus International, Madison Square Garden, N.Y.C., 1976, Nat. Inst. Arts and Letters, N.Y.C., 1980; represented permanent collections, Davenport Mcpl. Art Gallery, Des Moines Art Ctr., High Mus. Art, Atlanta, Sheldon Meml. Art Gallery, Lincoln, Nebr., San Francisco Mus. Art, Walker Art Ctr., others. Served with A.C. U.S. Army, 1942-46. Recipient award Nat. Inst. Arts & Letters, 1975; Nat. Endowment for Arts grantee, 1973; fellow Rosenwald Found., 1947, Guggenheim Found., 1960. Democrat. Home: 113 S Johnson St Iowa City IA 52240

BURFORD, ROBERT FITZPATRICK, government official, rancher; b. Grand Junction, Colo., Feb. 5, 1923; s. Ellery Eugene and Cleone Elizabeth (Fitzpatrick) B.; m. Judith M. Allen, Mar. 17, 1951; children: Joe, Kelley, Richard, Joyce. E.M., Colo. Sch. Mines, 1944. Mining engr. Permanente Aluminum Corp., Jamaica, 1948-50; owner, operator cattle ranch, Grand Junction, Colo., 1950—; mem. Colo. Ho. of Reps., 1975-81, speaker of house, 1979-81; dir. Bur. Land Mgmt., Dept. Interior, Washington, 1981—; dir. 1st Nat. Bank, Grand Junction. Chmn. Mesa County (Colo.) Republican Com., 1961-69. Served with USMC, 1944-46. Mem. Profl. Engrs. Colo., Colo. Cattlemen's Assn., Colo. Woolgrowers Assn., Western Sope Quarter Horse Assn. Republican. Episcopalian. Club: Masons. Office: Bur Land Mgmt 18th and C Sts NW Washington DC 20240 *

BURG, FREDRIC DAVID, physician, university dean; b. Chgo., May 23, 1940; s. Paul S. and Muriel C. (Buchsbaum) B.; m. Barbara L. Brock, June 3, 1967; children: Benjamin, Bethanny, David, Kathryn, Paul James, Jennifer Margaret. B.A. cum laude, Miami U., 1961; M.D. with distinction, Northwestern U., 1965. Diplomate: Am. Bd. Pediatrics. Intern, resident, chief resident in pediatrics Northwestern U. Med. Sch., Chgo., 1965-68; cons., sr. surgeon Bur. Community Environ. Mgmt., USPHS, 1968-70; dir. evaluation and research Am. Bd. Pediatrics, Chgo. and Phila., 1971-77; asso. dir. Nat. Bd. Med. Examiners, Phila., 1971-78, v.p., dir. dept. grad. and continuing med. evaluation, 1976-80; adj. asso. prof. U. Pa., 1976-80, asso. prof., 1980-82, prof. pediatrics, 1982—, asso. dean for acad. programs, 1980—. Contbr. articles to med. jours.; editorial bd., publs. com. Joint Commn. Accreditation of Hosps., 1983—. Served with USPHS, 1968-70. Fellow Am. Acad. Pediatrics; mem. Ambulatory Pediatrics Assn. (sec.-treas. 1977-80, pres. 1983-84), Assn. Am. Med. Schs., Am. Edn. Research Assn., Phila. Pediatrics Soc. (treas. 1980—). Home: Country Club Rd Phoenixville PA 19460 Office: Suite 100 Medical Edn Bldg U Pa Philadelphia PA 19104

BURG, GEORGE ROSCOE, journalist; b. New Lexington, Ohio, Apr. 1, 1916; s. Roscoe E. and Erie (Kreider) B.; m. Mary Vesta Ford, Oct. 31, 1941; children: George F., Mary Jane Burg Coffyn. B.S. in Journalism, Ohio State U., 1938, 1939. Tchr. Pike Twp. High Sch., Madison County, Ohio, 1939-40; engaged in newspaper work, 1948—; mng. editor Kansas City (Mo.) Star, 1967-75, asso. editor, asst. to pub., 1975-82. Trustee U. Mo., Kansas City; v.p. Kansas City Indsl. Found.; mem. Mayor's Corps of Progress; bd. dirs. Kansas City Corp. for Indsl. Devel., Sci. Pioneers and Shepherd Ctr., Greater Kansas City Area Safety Council., Downtown Council, Downtown Inc. Served with AUS, 1940-48. Mem. Kansas City C. of C., A.P. Mng. Editors Assn., NW Mo. Press Assn., Mid-Am. Press Inst. (dir.), Mil. Order World Wars, Res. Officers Assn., Tau Kappa Epsilon. Methodist. Clubs: Kansas City Press., Kansas City, Homestead. Lodge: Elks. Office: 1729 Grand Ave Kansas City MO 64108

BURGART, HERBERT JOSEPH, art school president; b. St. Marys, Pa., Apr. 27, 1932; s. Herbert Edmund and Bertha (Franzen) B.; children: Herbert Andrew, Nicholas Walter, Sarah Marie, Rachel Helene. A.B., Calif. State U., Long Beach, 1952; M.Ed., Pa. State U., 1957, D.Ed., 1961. Tchr., researcher Calif. Sch. for Blind, Berkeley, 1957-58; chmn. art edn. La. State U., Baton Rouge, 1958-61; chmn. art U. South Fla., Tampa, 1961-62; chmn. art edn. U. Ga., Athens, 1962-65; chmn. arts Peabody Coll., Nashville, 1965-66; dean Sch. Arts, Va. Commonwealth U., Richmond, 1966-76; pres. Moore Coll. Art, Phila., 1976-81, Ringling Sch. Art and Design, Sarasota, Fla., 1981-84; cons. in field. Author: Creative Art: The Child and the School, 1964. Pres. Richmond Civic Ballet, 1972-76, Nat. Exhibits for the Blind, 1979-81; bd. dirs. Phila. Art Alliance, Nat. Council for Arts, Nat. Council for Art Adminstrs., Nat. Assn. Schs. Art. Served to sgt. U.S. Army, 1954-56. Am. Council for Edn. fellow, 1970, 76. Republican.

BURGDOERFER, JERRY J., photographic company executive; b. Connersville, Ind., Nov. 20, 1934; s. Louis M. and Edna (Seele) B.; m. Barbara Jean Hofherr, Aug. 15, 1954; children: Steven, Jerry, Jeffrey, Stuart. B.S., Ind. U., 1957. Indsl. engr. Colgate Palmolive Co., Jeffersonville, Ind., 1958-59, mktg. mgr., N.Y.C., 1959-63, Am. Can Co., Green Bay, Wis., 1953-65, dir. sales, 1966-67, v.p., Greenwich, Conn., 1968-70; pres., dir. Am. Garden Products, Inc., Boston, 1970-71; exec. v.p. Facelle Co. div. Internat. Paper Co., N.Y.C., 1971-73; v.p. worldwide mktg. Hertz Corp., N.Y.C., 1973-77, exec. v.p., dir., from 1977; now pres., chief exec. officer Berkey Photo, Inc., N.Y.C. Served with arty. U.S. Army, 1957-58. Recipient Torch of Liberty-Man of Yr. award B'nai B'rith. Mem. Acad. Alumni Fellows (Ind. U.), Phi Delta Theta. Office: Berkey Photo Inc 1 Water St White Plains NY 10601

BURGE, DAVID RUSSELL, concert pianist, composer, piano educator; b. Evanston, Ill., Mar. 25, 1930; s. Russell David and Sylvia (Swensen) B.; m. Lois Ardel Svard, June 10, 1972; son by previous marriage, Russell David. Mus.B., Northwestern U., 1951, Mus.M., 1952; D.Mus. Arts artists diploma, Eastman Sch. Music, 1956; student, Cherubini Conservatory, Florence, Italy, 1956-57; D.F.A., Bucknell U., 1980. Instr. piano Northwestern U., 1949-52; asso. prof. music, composer-pianist in resident Whitman Coll., 1957-62; dir. MacDowell Hall Concert Series at coll., 1959-62; organist Ch. of Christ Scientist, Walla Walla, 1958-62; asst. prof. music U. Colo., 1962-64, assoc. prof., 1964-68, prof., 1968-75; chmn. piano dept. Eastman Sch. Music, U. Rochester, N.Y., 1975—, Kilbourn prof., 1978-79; artist-in-residence U. Calif., Davis, 1975; guest prof. composition U. Pa., 1977; guest prof. music history U. Gothenberg, Sweden, 1980; guest prof. piano U. Stockholm, Sweden, 1981, Banff Ctr., Can., 1983; mus. dir. Boulder Philharm. Orch., 1965-72; founder, dir. New Music Ensemble; dir. Festival Contemporary Music, U. Colo. Rec. artist, Mercury, Advance, Candide, Nonesuch, CRI Records, Mus. Heritage Soc. Records, Vox Records; Composer: opera Intervals, 1961, Trio; trio for violin, cello, piano, 1962; work for piano Eclipse, 1963; for flute-piano Sources I, 1964; for violin-celeste-piano Sources II, 1965; for piano Eclipse II, 1966; for clarinet-percussion Sources III, 1967; for soprano-piano A Song of Sixpence, 1967; for flute-clarinet-violin-cello-piano-tape Aeolian Music, 1968; for piano Sources IV, 1969; String Quartet, 1969, Twone in Sunshine, an Entertainment for Theater, 1969; for violin-orch. that no one knew, 1969; also songs, anthems.; Contbr. articles to periodicals; regular columnist: Keyboard Mag; music reviewer: Music Library Assn. Notes; first major postamristice concert, Seoul, Korea, 1953, New York debut playing all-modern program, 1961; toured, Korea, 1953-

54, Europe, 1956-57, U.S.A., annually, 1960—, Eastern Europe, 1974, Far East, Australia, N.Z., 1984. Served with AUS, 1952-54; Korea. Decorated by U.S. Army for cultural relations work in Korea, 1954; recipient Alumni Merit award Northwestern U., 1974, Colo. Gov.'s award, 1975, Distinguished Alumni award Eastman Sch. Music, 1975, Deems Taylor award for mus. journalism ASCAP, 1978, 79; Fulbright fellow in, Italy, 1956-57; Faculty Research lectr. U. Colo., 1972. Mem. Internat. Webern Soc. (charter), Am. Soc. Univ. Composers (a founder; nat. chmn. 1970-74), Pi Kappa Lambda. Address: 111 East Ave Apt 633 Rochester NY 14604

BURGE, HENRY CHARLES, architect; b. Peyton, Somerset, Eng., May 28, 1911; came to U.S., 1923, naturalized, 1930; s. Charles Henry and Gladys (Chedgey) B.; m. Doris Greener, Jan. 12, 1932; children: Charles Henry, Evilaura (Mrs. Lawrence Linker-Hus), William Temple. B.Arch., U. So. Cal., 1935. With Clifford A. Truesdell, 1927-32, Samuel Lunden, 1934, Meyer & Holler, 1935-40, Risly & Gould, 1944-45; layout artist Walt Disney Prodns., Burbank, Calif., 1943-44; with Douglas Aircraft Interiors, Los Angeles, 1944, U. So. Calif., 1945-62, acting dean, 1962-63; with Burge-Roach (and successor firm Urban Architects), Irvine, Calif., 1945—, pres., 1969—; dir. Atlantic Savs. & Loan Assn., Los Angeles, Universal Sav. and Loan Assn., Rosemead, Calif.; cons. Calif. Bd. Architecture, Los Angeles Civil Service. Bd. dirs. La Canada Youth House. Recipient nat. better neighborhood award Nat. Assn. Home Builders, 1951; many A.I.A. and A.R.A. awards. Fellow A.I.A., A.R.A.; mem. Pasadena Fine Arts Club, Montebello C. of C. Creator polychromatic stratiform stained glass, 1958-60. Home: 11795 Kitching St Sunnymead CA 92388

BURGE, JAMES DARRELL, personnel executive; b. Hannibal, Mo., June 16, 1934; s. Darrell Raymond and Lorene Mable (Huffman) B.; m. Harriet Ann Drake, Sept. 12, 1958; children: David James, Susan Elizabeth, Mary Kate. A.A., Hannibal-LaGrange Jr. Coll., 1954; B.S. in Bus. Admnstr., U. Mo.-Columbia, 1956; M.S., Ariz. State U., 1965. Dir. human resources Motorola Exec. Inst., Tucson, 1970-72; dir. personnel Motorola Inc. Europe, Geneva, Switzerland, 1972-74; dir. personnel auto and indsl. products Motorola Inc., Franklin Park, Ill., 1974-76, v.p., dir. personnel communication sector, Schaumburg, Ill., 1976-78, v.p., dir. personnel U.S., 1978—; vice chmn. human resources council Electronics Industries Assn. Served with U.S. Army, 1956-58. Mem. Am. Soc. Personnel Adminstrn., Human Resources Mgmt. Assn. Chgo. (dir.), UN Assn. U.S.A. (econ. policy council). Home: 619 S Kennicott St Arlington Heights IL 60005 Office: 1303 E Algonquin Rd Schaumburg IL 60196

BURGE, JOHN WESLEY, JR., electric manufacturing company executive; b. Mobile, Ala., Sept. 11, 1932; s. John Wesley and Mary Jo (Guest) B.; m. Shirley Paulette Roberts, Mar. 29, 1958; children: John, Delene, Eric, Kurt, Karen. Student, Centenary Coll., San Antonio Coll., UCLA. Various engring. and mgmt. positions ITT Gilfillan, 1954-69; pres., gen. mgr. Rantec, Calabasas, Calif., 1969-71, chmn. bd., 1971—; pres., gen. mgr. electronics and space div. Emerson Electric Co., St. Louis, 1971-80, corp. group v.p. govt., def., 1977—; cons. crisis mgmt., fin. planning for execs., 1975—; chmn. bd. Fourdee, 19—. Dir. Progressive Youth Center, Presbyterian Ch., 1975—. Served with USAF, 1950-54. Decorated Grand Cordon of Order Al-Istiqlal, Jordan). Mem. U.S. Navy League, Air Force Assn., Def. Preparedness Assn., Am. Mgmt. Assn., Air Force Communication and Electronics Assn., Internat. Security Assn. Home: 11711 Chanticleer Ct Pensacola FL 32507 Office: Emerson Electric Co 8100 W Florissant St Saint Louis MO 63136

BURGE, WILLIAM LEE, business information executive; b. Atlanta, June 27, 1918; s. William Frederick and Leona (Payne) B.; m. Willette Richey, Feb. 27, 1937; children: Judith (Mrs. Judith Phillips), William Roger. Ed., Ga. State Coll. Bus. Adminstrn., 1937-42; LL.D. (hon.), Mercer U., 1978. With Equifax Inc. (formerly Retail Credit Co.), 1936—, br. mgr., Greensboro, N.C., 1949-51, div. mgr., Pitts., 1951-58, v.p., Atlanta, 1959-65, exec. v.p., 1964-65, pres., 1965—, chief exec. officer, 1967—, chmn. bd., 1976—, chmn., Can.; Dir. First Nat. Bank Atlanta, Nat. Service Industries, Informes de Centrales of Mex. Gen. chmn. United Way, Atlanta, 1961; chmn. United Negro Coll. Fund, 1974-75; regional chmn. Nat. Alliance of Businessmen, 1969-70; chmn. bd. regents Univ. System Ga., 1972-73; mem. coll. accreditation commn. So. Assn. Colls. and Schs.; mem. Commn. Postsecondary Edn.; trustee Atlanta Arts Alliance, YMCA; mem. bd. Central Atlanta Progress; bd. dirs. Atlanta chpt. ARC. Served with AUS, World War II. Named Atlanta's Young Man of Year, 1948, one of Atlanta's Leaders of Tomorrow Time mag., 1952, Alumnus of Yr. Ga. State U., 1968. Mem. Conf. Bd., Atlanta C. of C. (pres. 1966), Nat. C. of C. (panel on privacy), Jr. C. of C. (pres. 1947-48). Club: Kiwanis (pres. 1965). Home: 3659 Northside Dr NW Atlanta GA 30305 Office: 1600 Peachtree St NW Atlanta GA 30309

BURGEE, JOHN HENRY, architect; b. Chgo., Aug. 28, 1933; s. Joseph Zeno and Helen (Dooley) B.; m. Gwendolyn Mary Henson, June 30, 1956; 1 son, John Gerard. B. Arch., U. Notre Dame, 1956, Dr.Engr. (hon.), 1983. Supt. constrn. Holabird & Root & Burgee, Chgo., 1955-56; project mgr. Naess & Murphy, Chgo., 1958-61; adminstr. design, project architect C. F. Murphy Assos., Chgo., 1961-65; assoc. ptnr. C. F. Murphy Assocs., 1965-67, ptnr., 1967; assoc. Philip Johnson (Architects), N.Y.C., 1967-68; ptnr. Johnson/Burgee, N.Y.C., 1968-82; ptnr. with Philip Johnson John Burgee Architects, N.Y.C., 1982—; Chmn. Archtl. Rev. Bd., Bronxville, N.Y., 1974-75; chmn. Bronxville Planning Commn., 1975-77. Works include, I.D.S. Center, Mpls., Niagara Falls Conv. Center, Pennzoil Place, Houston, Crystal Cathedral, Los Angeles, Am. Tel. & Tel. Hdqrs., N.Y.C., PPG Hdqrs., Pitts., Transco Tower, Houston, Republic Bank, Houston, Nat. Center for Performing Arts, Bombay.; Subject of: book Johnson/Burgee Architecture, 1979. Pres. German-Am. Club, Bad Kreuznach, Germany, 1957-58; Chmn. bldg. material sect. Met. Crusade of Mercy, Chgo., 1966-67; pres. Chgo. Nr. North Montessori Sch. Bd., 1962-63, Lawrence Park Hilltop Assn., 1974-75; chmn. architecture com. Statue of Liberty/Ellis Island Centennial Commn.; mem. adv. council Coll. Engring. U. Notre Dame; bd. dirs. Lenox Hill Hosp. Served with AUS, 1956-58. Recipient Reynolds Aluminum prize, 1978, honor award U. Notre Dame, 1981. Fellow AIA; mem. Archtl. League N.Y. (dir.), Inst. Architecture and Urban Studies (chmn., pres.). Clubs: Am. Yacht, Century Assn. Home: 79 E 79th St New York NY 10021 Office: 375 Park Ave New York NY 10022

BURGER, CHESTER, management consultant; b. Bklyn., Jan. 10, 1921; s. Benjamin W. and Terese (Felleman) B.; m. Hannah Kaufman, Jan. 30, 1948; children: Jeffrey Allen, Todd Oliver, Amy Louise; m. Ninki Hart, Jan. 9, 1959 (dec. Jan. 1969); m. Elisabeth Miller Owen, Sept. 2, 1971. B.A., Bklyn. Coll., 1946. With CBS Radio, 1941-42; reporter, visualizer CBS TV News, 1946-48; asst. news editor CBS-TV, 1948-50, news editor, 1950-52, film assignment editor, 1952-53, nat. mgr., 1953; writer-producer Omnibus program for Ford Found., 1954-55; cons. Life mag., 1955; pub. relations dept. Am. Tel. & Tel. Co. and asso. cos., 1955—; pub. relations counsel, asst. to pres. Ruder and Finn, Inc., 1955-57, v.p. plans, 1957-60; pres. Communications Counselors (pub. relations div. Interpublic, Inc.), N.Y.C., 1960-62, Echelons Office Temporaries, Inc. (and asso. cos.), 1963-65, Chester Burger & Co., Inc. (mgmt. cons.), 1964—; cons. Coca-Cola Export Corp., 1964-65; guest lectr. New Sch. for Social Research, 1967, U. Mich. Grad. Sch. Bus. Adminstrn., 1969-72, N.Y. U. Div. Bus. and Mgmt., 1970-76, Dalhousie U., 1970; cons. Am. Bankers Assn., 1973—, Alyeska Pipeline Service Co., 1974; author, lectr. pub. relations role in mgmt. Author: Survival in the Executive Jungle, 1964, Executives Under Fire, 1966, Executive Etiquette, 1969, Walking the Executive Plank (also pub. as Creative Firing), 1972, The Chief Executive, 1978; editor: Inside Public Relations, 1984; Author also articles.; Editor: Mike and Screen Press Directory, 1953, 54, 55; Contbg. editor: Quar. Rev. Pub. Relations (name now Pub. Relations Quar.), 1959—, Popular Photography mag, 1967-68; editor: monthly newsletter Persuasion, 1972-74; editorial adv. bd.: Pub. Relations Jour, 1975-79. Bd. dirs. N.Y. Interracial Council for Bus. Opportunity, 1965-68; sec., mem. exec. com., trustee Nat. Urban League, 1967-76; pub. relations chmn. Young Pres.' Orgn., 1962-63; mem. adv. com. Black Exec. Exchange Program, 1969—; 1st v.p. Nat. Urban League Devel. Found., Inc., 1970-72; bd. dirs. N.Y. Diabetes Assn., 1964-67, Nat. Communications Council for Human Services, 1973-76. Served with AUS, 1942-46. Recipient Distinguished Service citation United Negro Coll. Fund, 1974, award for outstanding service USIA, 1982. Mem. Telephone Pioneers Am. (hon.), Am. Pub. Relations Assn. (dir. N.Y. chpt. 1959-60, Eastern v.p. 1960-61, nat. dir. 1959-60), Pub. Relations Soc. Am. (dir. 1961-63, accredited 1967, John W. Hill award N.Y. chpt. 1980), Am. Arbitration Assn. (nat. panel arbitrators 1972—), Women in Communications. Home: 33 W 67th St New York NY 10023 Office: 171 Madison Ave New York NY 10016

BURGER, EDMUND GANES, architect; b. Yerington, Nev., Mar. 28, 1930; s. Edmund Ganes and Rose Catherine (Kobe) B.; m. Shirley May Pratini, Jan. 21, 1968; 1 dau., Jane Lee. B.M.E., U. Santa Clara, 1951; B.Arch., U. Pa., 1959. Engr. Gen. Electric Co., 1951-52; design engr. U. Calif. Radiation Lab., 1952-57; John Stewardson fellow in architecture, 1959; architect Wurster, Bernardi & Emmons, San Francisco, 1960-63; founder Burger & Coplans, Inc. (Architects), San Francisco, 1964, pres., 1964-79; owner Edmund Burger (Architect), 1979—; guest lectr. U. Calif., Berkeley. Important works include Acorn Housing Project, Oakland, Calif., Crescent Village Housing Project, Suisun City, Calif., Coplans Residence, San Francisco, Betel Housing Project, San Francisco, Grand View Housing Project, San Francisco, Albany (Calif.) Oaks Housing, Grow Homes, San Pablo, Calif., Mariposa Housing, San Francisco. Recipient citation for excellence in community architecture AIA, 1969, award of merit AIA, Homes for Better Living, 1970, 79, 1st Honor award, 1973, 81; Holiday award for a beautiful Am., 1970; Honor award 4th Biennial HUD awards for design excellence, 1970; Bay Area awards for design excellence, 1969, 74, 78; Apts. of Year award Archtl. Record, 1972; Houses of Year award, 1973; Calif. Affordable Housing Competition award, 1981; HUD Building Value into Housing award, 1981. Home: 1331 Oxford St Berkeley CA 94709 Office: PO Box 10193 Berkeley CA 94709

BURGER, HENRY G., anthropologist, educator; b. N.Y.C., June 27, 1923; s. B. William and Terese R. (Felleman) B. B.A. with honors (Pulitzer scholar), Columbia Coll., 1947; M.A., Columbia U., 1965, Ph.D. (State Doctoral fellow), 1967. Indsl. engr. various orgns., 1947-51, Midwest mfrs. rep., 1952-55, social sci. cons., Chgo. and N.Y.C., 1956-67; anthropologist Southwestern Coop. Ednl. Lab., Albuquerque, 1967-69; assoc. prof. anthropology and edn. U. Mo., Kansas City, 1969-73, prof., 1973—, founding mem. univ.wide doctoral faculty, 1974—; lectr. CUNY, 1957-65; Adj. prof. ednl. anthropology U. N.Mex., 1969; anthrop. cons. U.S. VA Hosp., Kansas City, 1971-72. Author: Ethno-Pedagogy, 1968, 2d edit., 1968; compiler, pub.: The Wordtree, a Transitive Cladistic for Solving Physical and Social Problems, 1983; contbr. to anthologies, articles to profl. jours., cassettes to tape libraries. Served to capt. AUS, 1943-46. NSF Instl. grantee, 1970. Fellow Council on Anthropology and Edn. (editorial bd. Quar. 1975-80), Soc. Applied Anthropology, Current Anthropology, AAAS, Internat. Union Anthrop. and Ethnol. Scis., World Acad. Art and Sci., Am. Anthrop. Assn. (life), Royal Anthrop. Inst. Gt. Britain (life); mem. Classification Soc., Soc. Med. Anthropology, Semiotic Soc. Am., Am. Ethnol. Soc., Soc. Gen. Systems Research, Internat. Founds. of Edn. Soc., Soc. Profl. Anthropologists, Am. Soc. for Info. Sci., Dictionary Soc. N.Am., Internat. Social Sci. Council (com. on conceptual and terminological analysis), Phi Beta Kappa. Home: 7306 Brittany St Shawnee Mission KS 66203 Office: U Mo Kansas City MO 64110 *The computer analyzes prose information into tabulation, whence it can be re-formed diversely. Therefore computerization has revolutionized my authorship from textbooks to reference books.*

BURGER, HERBERT FRANCIS, advertising agency executive; b. Ligonier, Pa., Mar. 5, 1930; s. Adolph G. and Elizabeth (Johannsen) B.; m. Jane Coulter, Oct. 1, 1966; children: Matthew F., Jennifer. B.S. in Econs, Thiel Coll., Greenville, Pa., 1952; M.A. in Journalism, Syracuse (N.Y.) U., 1955. C. Mgmt. trainee Joy Mfg. Co., 1955-56; account exec. Ketchum, MacLeod & Grove, Pitts., 1956-58, Marsteller Inc., 1958-65; with Creamer Inc., Pitts., 1965—, pres., 1976—, also dir., mem. exec. com. Served with U.S. Army, 1953-55. Mem. Pitts. Advt. Club (dir.), Pitts. Press Club. Republican. Lutheran. Clubs: Duquesne, Longue Vue Country, University. Home: 300 Field Club Ridge Rd Pittsburgh PA 15238 Office: 4800 US Steel Bldg Pittsburgh PA 15219

BURGER, MARY LOUISE, psychologist, educator; b. Chgo., Nov. 3; d. Robert Stanley and Margaret Agnes (Brennan) Hirsh; m. William Bronson Burger, Mar. 16, 1968. B.A., Mundelein Coll.; M.Ed., Loyola U.; Ed.D., No. Ill. U., 1972. Tchr. Chgo. Bd. Edn., 1954-68; mem. faculty DePaul U., 1960-61, Roosevelt U., 1967-70; cons. psychologist Worthington-Hurst & Assos., Headstart Program, Chgo., 1972-74; prof. dept. early childhood edn. Northeastern Ill. U., 1968—, chmn., 1968-80; chmn. faculty assembly (Coll. Edn.); chmn. subcom. Chgo. region White House Conf. on Children, 1979-81; ednl. dir., owner Childhood Edn. Nursery and Day Care Center, Evanston, Ill.; cons. Chgo Mayor's Office Child Care Services. Editor: bull. and pamphlets Assn. Childhood Edn. Internat, 1975-77. Chmn. bd. dirs. Univ. Community Care Center. Mem. Assn. Childhood Edn. Internat. (pres. Ill. and Chgo. brs., chmn. nominating com. 1980, tchr. edn. com. 1981—, v.p. exec. bd. 1983—), Nat. Assn. Edn. Young Children, Assn. Higher Edn., N.W. Assn. Nursery Schs., AAUP, Phi Delta Kappa, Delta Kappa Gamma. Club: Zonta Internat. Home: Fairfax Village 1 Kittery on Auburn Rolling Meadows IL 60008 Office: Northeastern Illinois University 5500 N St Louis Ave Chicago IL 60025 also Childhood Edn Center 2727 Crawford Evanston IL 60201

BURGER, OTHMAR JOSEPH, univ. dean; b. Jasper, Ind., May 23, 1921; s. August and Katherine (Lechner) B.; m. Elizabeth Ann Evans, Aug. 21, 1943; children: Thomas Glen, Robert Howard, David William. B.S., Purdue U., 1943, M.S., 1947, Ph.D., 1950. Prof. agronomy W.Va. U., 1950-57, asst. dean agr., 1959-68, asst. to provost for instrn., 1968-69; prof. agronomy Iowa State U., 1957-59; dean Sch. Agr. and Home Econs., Calif. State U., Fresno, 1969—, also prof. agronomy. Cubmaster local council Boy Scouts Am., 1956-58; Bd. dirs. United Fund, Morgantown, W.Va., 1953-55. Served with USMCR, World War II; PTO. Decorated Bronze Star, Purple Heart. Fellow Am. Soc. Agronomy; mem. Nat. Assn. Colls. and Tchrs. of Agr. (pres. 1978-79, Disting. Educator award 1982), Gamma Sigma Delta, Phi Lambda Upsilon, Alpha Zeta. Club: Kiwanis. Home: 2689 W San Carlos Ave Fresno CA 93711 Office: Cedar at Shaw Ave Fresno CA 93740

BURGER, ROBERT EUGENE, author, chess expert; b. Yerington, Nev., June 21, 1931; s. Edmund Ganes and Rose Catherine (Kobe) B.; m. Mary Theresa Dunne, June 26, 1954; children: Eileen, Marlene, Robert, Diane, Elisabeth, Joseph, Daniel, John, Clare, Christopher. B.A., U. Calif.-Berkeley, 1953, M.A., 1955. Founder Ad Agy., San Francisco, 1958, pres., 1958-68, writer, 1968—; lectr. Stanford, 1964, U. Calif. at Hayward, 1972, various Calif. state colls., 1973; U.S. chess master, 1965-73; internat. problems judge. Author: Where They Go to Die, 1968, McCarthy, Words to Remember, 1969, Out From Under, 1970, Twilights Believers, 1971, Pietro on Wine, 1972, The Love Contract, 1972, Ego Speak, 1973, The Simplified Guide to Personal Bankruptcy, 1974, The Chess of Bobby Fischer, 1975, Inside Divorce, 1975, Forbidden Cures, 1976, Jogger's Catalog, 1978, The Polish Prince, 1978, The Jug Wine Book, 1979, The Whole Life Diet, 1979, Meganutrition, 1980, The Courage to Believe, 1980, The Ford Reports, 1983. Trustee Mechanics Inst. Library, San Francisco. Fellow Brit. Chess Problem Soc.; mem. U.S. Chess Fedn. (dir.), Author's Guild Am. Office: 478 Jackson Street San Francisco CA 94111

BURGER, WARREN EARL, Chief Justice U.S.; b. St. Paul, Sept. 17, 1907; s. Charles Joseph and Katharine (Schnittger) B.; m. Elvera Stromberg, Nov. 8, 1933; children: Wade Allan, Margaret Mary Elizabeth. Student, U. Minn., 1925-27; LL.B. magna cum laude, St. Paul Coll. Law (now Mitchell Coll. Law), 1931. Bar: Minn. 1931. Ptnr. Faricy, Burger, Moore & Costello (and predecessors firms), 1935-53; faculty Mitchell Coll. Law, 1931-48; asst. atty. gen., U.S., 1953-56; judge U.S. Ct. Appeals, Washington, 1956-69; Chief Justice U.S. Supreme Ct., 1969—; Hon. master bencher Middle Temple, 1969; pres. Bentham Club, U. Coll. London, 1972-73; hon. chmn. Inst. Jud. Adminstrn.; criminal justice project ABA Chancellor. Bd. regents Smithsonian Instn.; ex-officio mem. bd. trustees Nat. Gallery Art, Washington; trustee emeritus Mitchell Coll. Law, Macalester Coll., St. Paul, Mayo Found., Rochester, Minn.; trustee Nat. Geog. Soc. Office: Supreme Ct Bldg Washington DC 20543

BURGESS, ALFRED FRANKLIN, lawyer; b. Greer, S.C., June 1, 1906; s. Franklin and Minnie (Cunningham) B.; m. Mary Wyche, June 25, 1938; children: Mary Wyche Burgess Lesesne, Caroline Burgess Ansbacher, Alfred Franklin, Granville Wyche, Victoria Burgess Pitman. A.B. cum laude, Davidson (N.C.) Coll., 1928, LL.B., U. Va., 1931. Bar: S.C. 1931. Since practiced in, Greenville; partner firm Wyche, Burgess, Freeman & Parham, P.A., 1931—; spl. circuit judge, 1948, 50, 55, 61; spl. hearing officer Dept. Justice, Greenville, 1956—; mem. com. rules of practice U.S. Dist. Cts., 1965; dir. Multimedia, Inc., Builder Marts Am., Inc., Pecan Shoppe of Pasco, Inc., Star Theatres, Inc. Numerous appearances in little theatre prodns. Chmn. Greenville County Democratic Com., 1940-42; del. Dem. Nat. Conv., 1944; bd. dirs. Greenville Community Youth Commn., 1955, Greenville Children's Center, 1954-55, Friends of Bach Choir, 1940-45, Greenville Community Concert Assn., 1960-63, St. Francis Community Hosp., Greenville, 1966, Shriners Hosp., Greenville, 1973-78, Greenville United Fund, 1961-66, The Savoyards, 1979—, Greenville Community Relations Bi-Racial Com., 1964-66, Greenville County Found., 1965-66, Greenville Little Theatre, 1973—, Greenville Met. Arts Council, 1975-76; pres. Greenville Symphony Assn., 1958-59. Mem. Am. Bar Assn., Am. Judicature Soc., Am. Fedn. Ins. Counsel (Law Sci. Acad.), S.C. Bar Assn., Greenville Bar Assn. (pres. 1947). Episcopalian (former vestryman). Clubs: Green Valley Country, Greenville Country, Poinsett, Thirty-Nine. Lodges: Shriners; Rotary (past pres., dist. gov.). Home: 308 W Faris Rd Greenville SC 29605 Office: 44 E Camperdown Way Greenville SC 29601

BURGESS, ANTHONY, author; b. Manchester, Eng., Feb. 25, 1917; s. Joseph and Elizabeth (Wilson) B.; m. Llewela Isherwood Jones, Jan. 23, 1942 (dec. 1968); m. Liliana Macellari, 1968. B.A. with honours, Manchester U., 1940. Lectr., schoolmaster, 1946-54, edn. officer in, Malaya and Borneo, 1954-59, composer, 1933—, play producer, 1947—, jazz pianist, 1941—; vis. fellow Princeton U., 1970-71; Disting. prof. CCNY, 1972-73. Contbr. to: others; Author: The Right to an Answer, 1961, Devil of a State, 1962, The Wanting Seed, 1963, A Clockwork Orange, 1963, Honey for the Bears, 1964, Nothing Like the Sun, 1964, The Long Day Wanes, 1965, Language Made Plain, 1965, Re Joyce, 1965, The Doctor is Sick, 1965, Tremor of Intent, 1966, The Novel Now, 1967, Enderby, 1968, Urgent Copy, 1969, Shakespeare, 1970, MF, 1971, Cyrano de Bergerac-a version for the modern stage, 1971, Oedipus the King, 1972, Napoleon Symphony, 1974, The Clockwork Testament, 1974, Moses, 1976, A Long Trip to Teatime, 1976, Beard's Roman Women, 1976, ABBA ABBA, 1977, Nineteen Eighty-Five, 1978, World, 1978, Hemingway and His Man of Nazareth, 1980, Earthly Powers, 1980, On Going to Bed, 1982, This Man and Music, 1982, The End of the World News, 1982. Served with British Army, 1940-46. Address: 44 Rue Grimaldi Monte Carlo *

BURGESS, CHARLES HARRY, Mining co. exec.; b. Sheridan, Wyo., Apr. 3, 1910; s. James Henry and Mary Helen (Helvey) B.; m. Linda Cannon, May 24, 1934 (div. 1954); children—Walter Pierce, Heather, James Helvey, Pamela, Martha; m. Elisabeth Blessing Halliday, July 1, 1961; stepchildren—Donald A. Halliday, Jr., Barry Halliday. A.B., Harvard, 1931, A.M., 1933, Ph.D., 1936. Instr. geology Harvard, 1934-36; geologist Anaconda Copper Mining Co., 1936-38; mine leasee and cons., 1938-41; analyst Adminstrn. Export Control, Bd. Econ. Warfare; also dep. chief aluminum and magnesium sect. OPA, 1941-42; chief wire, rod and bar sect., aluminum and magnesium div. WPB, 1942-44; geologist Hoover, Curtice and Ruby, N.Y.C., 1944-46, M.A. Hanna Co., 1946-47; dep. dir., then dir. strategic materials div. ECA, 1948-50; treas. United Electric Coal Co., Chgo., 1950-52; dist. geologist Bear Creek Mining Co., Mpls., 1952-56, pres., dir., N.Y.C. and Salt Lake City, 1956-60; v.p. exploration Kennecott Copper Corp., 1960-73, v.p., asst. to pres., 1973-74; pres., dir. B.C. Molybdenum Ltd., 1963-66; formerly pres., dir. Kennecott Exploration, Inc., Kennecott Costa Rica (S.A.), P.T. Kennecott Indonesia; chmn. bd., dir. Kennecott Explorations (Australia) Ltd.; v.p., dir. Kennecott Coal Co.; dir. Kennco (Stikine) Mining Ltd., Stikine Copper Ltd., Kennarctic Exploration Ltd., Kennco Explorations (Western), Ltd., Kennecott Pacific Pty. Ltd., Bear Creek Mining Co., Flambeau Mining Corp., Kennecott Explns. (S.W. Africa) (Pty.) Ltd., Bear Tooth Mining Co., Great Lakes Exploration, Inc., Kennecott Italia S.P.A.; Mem. vis. com., dept. geol. scis. bd. overseers Harvard, 1963-68, 70-71, 72-74, 75-76; nat. com. Center for Earth and Planetary Physics, 1974—; vis. com. Lander Coll. Mem. Am. Inst. Mining Engrs., Am. Geol. Inst. (pres. 1970), Mining and Metall. Soc., Geol. Soc. Am., Soc. Econ. Geologists, Harvard Grad. Soc. for Advanced Study and Research, Phi Beta Kappa. Home: Route 3 Abbeville SC 29620

BURGESS, CHARLES ORVILLE, history educator; b. Portland, Oreg., Jan. 18, 1932; s. Rex Orville and Glendora Almanda (Sundrud) B.; m. Patricia Stewart Anderson, Apr. 22, 1976; children: Donna Claire, Jo Dell, Robert Charles. B.A., U. Oreg., 1957; M.S. (Danforth fellow), U. Wis., 1958, Ph.D., 1962; Nat. Postdoctoral fellow, Harvard U., 1967-68. Asst. prof. U. Calif. at Riverside, 1962-64; asst. prof. history edn. U. Wash., Seattle, 1964-66, assoc. prof., 1966-70, prof., 1970—, chmn., 1971-80; vis. prof. Rutgers U., 1963, 67, U. B.C., Can., 1971; v.p. div. F Am. Ednl. Research Assn., Seattle, 1977-79. Author: (with M.L. Borrowman) What Doctrines to Embrace, 1969; Author: Profile of an American Philanthropist (Nettie Fowler McCormick), 1962; co-editor: (with Charles Strickland) G. Stanley Hall on Natural

Education, 1965. Mem. Wash. com. civil rights ACLU, 1965-67; bd. dirs. Seattle Folklore Soc., 1966—. Served in USAF, 1950-54. Mem. Orgn. Am. Historians, Am. Hist. Assn., History Edn. Soc. (pres. 1971-72), Assocs. for Research on Pvt. Edn. (trustee 1982-83), Phi Beta Kappa. Home: 2111 SW 174th St Seattle WA 98166

BURGESS, DAVID LOWRY, artist; b. Phila., Apr. 27, 1940; s. Eric Turner and Ruth Elizabeth (McNees) B.; m. Janet Lucille Levengood, Mar. 25, 1960; children—Kirsten Deidre, Audrey Veronica, Vashti Gabrielle. Grad. F.A., Pa. Acad., Fine Art and U. Pa., 1961. Lectr. Phila. Coll. Art, 1964-66; arts advisor Edn. Devel. Center, 1966-68; instr. Boston U., 1969; prof. Mass. Coll. Art, 1969—; head grad. fine arts studies; fellow Center for Advanced Visual Studies M.I.T., 1971-78; mem. Nat. Humanities faculty, 1968-80. Author: Fragments, 1967, Looking and Listening, 1969, Memory, Environment, Utopia, 1973; one man exhbns. include, Inst. Contemporary Art, Boston, 1971, Carpenter Center, Harvard U., 1975, M.I.T., 1978, group exhbns. include, Boston Mus. Fine Arts Elements Exhbn., 1971, Multiple Interaction Team, ten cities, 1972-74, CAYAC, Spain and Latin Am., Documenta 6, Kassel, W. Ger., 1977, Documenta 6, Vienna Bienal, 1979, Sky Arts Conf., M.I.T., 1981; represented in permanent collections of, Boston Mus. Fine Arts, Houghton Library, Harvard U., Nat. Collection Fine Arts, Washington. Founding mem., exec. bd. Cambridge Arts Council; mem. adv. bd. Art, Edn. and Americans. Recipient Am. Acad. Arts and Letters, Nat. Inst. Arts and Letters award, 1972; Guggenheim fellow, 1973-74; Nat. Endowment Arts grantee, 1977-78; Rockefeller Found. grantee, 1979-80. Address: 27 Sherman Cambridge MA 02138

BURGESS, HAROLD DEMPSTER, lawyer; b. Dundee, Ill., July 10, 1894; s. John W. and Sadie E. (Dempster) B.; m. Mary Ellen Evans, Sept. 16, 1964. Ed. pub. schs., Beatrice, Nebr.; student, U. Colo., 1913-14, U. Nebr., 1914-17; A.B. in absentia, U. Nebr., 1920, U. Chgo., 1920-21. Bar: Ill. 1921. Since practiced in Chgo.; of counsel Keck, Mahin, Cat. Mem. Am., 7th Circuit, Ill., Chgo. bar assns., Legal Club Chgo., Law Club. Republican. Episcopalian. Clubs: Metropolitan (Chgo.); Edgewood Valley Country (LaGrange). Home: 300 E Claymoor Hinsdale IL 60521 Office: 233 S Wacker Dr 8300 Sears Tower Chicago IL 60606

BURGESS, JAMES HARLAND, physics educator, researcher; b. Portland, Oreg., May 11, 1929; s. Harland F. B. and Marion U. (Burgess); m. Dorothy R. Crosby, June 10, 1951; children: Karen, Donald, Joanne. B.S., Wash. State U., 1949, M.S., 1951; Ph.D., Washington U., St. Louis, 1955. Sr. engr. Sylvania Electric Products, Mountain View, Calif., 1955-56; research assoc. Stanford U., Palo Al to, Calif., 1956-57, asst. prof. physics, Palo Alto, Calif., 1958-62; assoc. prof. Washington U., St. Louis, 1963-73, prof., 1973—; cons. in field, 1956-58. Mem. Am. Phys. Soc., Am. Assn. Physics Tchrs., Phi Beta Kappa, Sigma Xi. Office: Washinton U Lindell and Skinker Blvds St Louis Mo 63130

BURGESS, JOHN FRANK, utility executive, former army officer, management consultant; b. Lanett, Ala., Nov. 18, 1917; s. John Frank and Mary Catherine (Heard) B.; m. Helen Hamby, Aug. 26, 1939; children: Beverly, Barbara, Frank. B.S., Auburn U.; M.A., George Washington U. Commd. 2d lt. U.S. Army, 1941, advanced through grades to col., ret., 1969; v.p. Consol. Edison Co. of N.Y., Inc., N.Y.C., 1969—; pvt. practice mgmt. cons., Melville, N.Y., 1983—. Active bds. various civic and profl. orgns., Queens, N.Y., 1969-83. Decorated Legion of Merit with 2 oak leaf clusters; named Man of Yr. Queens County Bldg and Contractors Assn., 1977. Episcopalian. Home: 24 Woodmont Rd Melville NY 11747 Office: Consolidated Edison Co of NY Inc 4 Irving Pl New York NY 10003

BURGESS, JOHN HERBERT, physician, educator; b. Montreal, Que., Can., May 24, 1933; s. John Frederick and Willa Reta (McGinness) B.; m. Andrea Clouston Rutherford, May 30, 1958; children: Willa, Cynthia, Lynn, John. B.Sc., McGill U., 1954, M.D., C.M., 1958. Med. resident Montreal (Can.) Gen. Hosp., 1958-60, 62-64; Nuffield research fellow U. Birmingham, Eng., 1960-62; McLaughlin research fellow Cardiovascular Inst., San Francisco, 1964-66; asst. prof. medicine McGill U., 1966-69, asso. prof., 1969-75, prof., 1975—; Examiner in internal medicine and cardiology Royal Coll. Physicians and Surgeons Can., 1969—, mem. council, 1981—, chmn. com. on exams., 1981—, chmn. examining bd. for cardiology. Med. Research Council Can. scholar, 1966-71. Fellow Am. Heart Assn., Am. Coll. Cardiology, ACP (gov. 1979-83); mem. Med. Research Soc. Gt. Britain, Am. Physiol. Soc., Canadian Soc. Clin. Investigation, Canadian Cardiovascular Soc., N.Y. Acad. Sci., Alpha Omega Alpha. Home: 639 Murray Hill Montreal PQ Canada H3Y 2W8 Office: Montreal General Hospital Montreal PQ Canada H3G 1A4

BURGESS, JOHN STANLEY, retired research and development executive; b. Milw., May 1, 1918; s. Stanley T. and Margaret M. (Twomey) B.; m. Delma Ruth Frelick, Sept. 11, 1948; children: Leslie, Michael, Robert. B.S., St. Lawrence U., 1940; M.S., U. Notre Dame, 1942; Ph.D., Ohio State U., 1949. Research asst. Gen. Electric Co., 1942-46; asst. prof. St. Lawrence U., 1949-51; engr. Rome (N.Y.) Air Devel. Center, 1951-60, chief scientist, 1960-71, dep. dir. Shape Tech. Center, 1971-76, chief scientist, 1976-80. Contbr. articles to profl. jours. Mem. council for upper div. Coll. Mohawk Valley, N.Y.; pres. Rome Community Concerts, 1959-60; adv. bd. Salvation Army, 1961, 71-76; pres. bd. dirs. Rome United Way, 1966-71, 76—; elder Presbyn Ch.; mem. research and rev. com., State of N.Y. Recipient Exceptional Civil Service award, 1965, 71, 80. Fellow IEEE; mem. Am. Phys. Soc., Phi Beta Kappa, Sigma Xi, Pi Mu Epsilon, Sigma Pi Sigma. Republican. Address: PO Box AB Sylvan Beach NY 13157

BURGESS, JOHN STUART, lawyer, former lt. gov. Vt.; b. N.Y.C., May 10, 1920; s. Frederick Vaughn and Olive Hornbrook (Moore) B.; m. Ronda Helen Prouty, June 28, 1947; children—Frederick Moore, Helen Prouty. B.A., U. Vt., 1947; LL.B., Northeastern U., 1949, J.D., 1972. Bar: Mass. bar 1949, Vt. bar 1950. Practice in, Brattleboro, 1950—; legal counsel OPS, 1951; town atty., Brattleboro, 1953-81; spl. counsel Vt. Hwy. Dept., 1955-58; mem. Vt. Ho. Reps., 1966-70, speaker, 1969-70, chmn. constl. revision commn., 1968-71; lt. gov., Vt., 1971-75; chmn. Vt. Labor Relations Bd., 976-78; dir. Burlington Savs. Bank. Chmn. Vt. Bicentennial Commn., 1973-77; exec. com. Nat. Conf. Lt. Govs., 1972-75; corporator Brattleboro Meml. Hosp.; trustee Mark Hopkins Coll., Vt. Multiple Sclerosis Soc., Rock Point Sch. Served to capt. AUS, 1941-45; to lt. USAF, 1951-53; lt. col. Res.; ret. Decorated D.F.C., Air medal. Mem. Am., Vt., Windham County bar assns., Am. Legion, DAV, VFW, Grange. Republican. Episcopalian. Clubs: Masons, Shriners, Elks. Home: 50 Western Ave Brattleboro VT 05301 Office: 12 Park Pl Brattleboro VT 05301 also 12 Park Pl Brattleboro VT 05301

BURGESS, KENNETH ALEXANDER, chemist; b. Stamford, Conn., June 27, 1918; m. Jean Waldron; children: Kenneth, Ross, Janet, Andrena. A.B., Princeton U., 1939; M.S., Pa. State U., 1941. Chemist Columbian Carbon Co., 1946-51, chief chemist, 1951-56, asst. dir. research, 1956-61, dir. carbon black research, 1961-63, dir. pigments and elastomers research, 1963-69; dir. research Columbian Chems. Div., Cities Service Co., Cranbury, N.J., 1969-71, dir. petrochems. research, 1971-76, dir. research and devel., 1976-79, dir. tech. assessment and planning, 1979—; cons. Columbian Chems. Co., 1981—. Mem. Am. Chem. Soc., Am. Inst. Chemists, Instn. of Rubber Industry, N.Y. Acad. Sci., Phi Lambda Upsilon. Address: 1647 Kensington St Port Charlotte FL 33952

BURGESS, LLOYD ALBERT, constrn. co. exec.; b. Culver, Oreg., Oct. 4, 1917; s. Estell Elmer and Arrista (Ditterline) B.; m. Wanda Marie Gregory, Dec. 18, 1955; children—Gregory Scott, Elizabeth Anne, Jeffrey Lloyd; 1 son by previous marriage, Jason M. B.C.E., Oreg. State U., 1939. Engr. C.E., Portland, Oreg., 1939-40, 41; engr. Douglas Aircraft Co., 1940-41, Tidewater Asso. Oil Co., 1941-42; pres. Burgess Constrn. Co., Fairbanks, Alaska, 1946-69, Spruce Equipment, Inc., Fairbanks, 1955-64, Grove Inc., 1955-64, Alaska Freight Lines, 1959-60, Burgess Internat. Inc., Seattle; chmn. Burgess Intercontinental, Inc., 1969-72, Burgess Overseas Sales Corp.; dir. Alaska Title & Guarantee Co., Canon—Holosonics, Tokyo, Holosonics, Richland, Wash., Earth Resources Co., Dallas, Simasko Prodn. Co., Denver, Pacific Alaska Airlines, Fairbanks. Chmn. Alaska Rep. Fin. Com., 1958-62; del. Rep. Nat. Conv., 1968, mem. nat. platform com., 1968; mem. Nat. Rep. Com. from Alaska, 1964-69. Served to lt. comdr. USNR, 1942-46; PTO. Mem. Asso. Gen. Contractors (pres. Alaska 1960). Clubs: Seattle Golf and Country, Seattle Yacht. Home: 5919 77th Ave SE Mercer Island WA 98040 Office: PO Box 410 Mercer Island WA 98040

BURGESS, ROGER, church official; b. Sioux City, Iowa, Oct. 1927; s. Frederick Earl and Mabel (Irwin) B.; m. Donah Jean Salyer, 1953; 3 sons, 1 dau. B.A., Morningside Coll., Sioux City, 1950, LL.D., 1965; postgrad., Am. U. Grad. Sch. Journalism, 1966. Dir. Morningside Coll. Press Bur., Sioux City, 1948-50; projects sec. Nat. Conf. Methodist Youth, Nashville, also editor youth publs., 1950-53; editor publs., dir. communications Meth. Gen. Bd. Temperance, 1953-56, asso. gen. sec., 1956-60; dir. communications Meth. Gen. Bd. Christian Social Concerns, also editor news mag., 1960-61, asso. gen. sec. with responsibility div. alcohol problems and gen. welfare, 1961-65; exec. v.p. charge creative planning in advt., graphic arts and audio visual Design Center, Inc., 1965-67; nat. exec. dir. Joint Action in Community Service, 1967-68; gen. sec. bd. health and welfare ministeries United Meth. Ch., 1968-72, asso. gen. sec. bd. global ministries, 1972-73; editorial dir. United Meth. Pub. House, 1974-76, v.p. pub. relations, 1976—; Mem. gen. bd. Nat. Council Chs.; sec., bd. dirs. Joint Action in Community Service; pres. council secs. United Meth. Ch. Bd. Contbr. articles to profl. jours. Bd. dirs. Scarritt Coll.; v.p. bd. dirs. United Way of Nashville. Served U.S. Navy, 1945-46; Served USNR, 1946-48. Address: 201 8th Ave S Nashville TN 37202

BURGESS, WILLIAM HENRY, financier; b. Mpls., June 30, 1917; s. Gerald Henry and Louise (Bailey) B.; m. Clara Ethel Woodward, June 21, 1941; children: Sarah Louise Burgess Cadenhead, Molly. B.B.A., U. Minn., 1939; M.B.A., Harvard U., 1941. Indsl. engr. R.R. Donnelly & Sons Co., Chgo., 1941-42; mgmt. engr. Hollister & Evans, Los Angeles, 1946; founder, pres. Electronic Splty. Co., Los Angeles, 1949-66, chmn. bd., 1949-69; founder, chmn. bd., pres. Shavex Corp., Los Angeles, 1949-62; chmn. bd. Continental Controls Corp., 1972-78, Internat. Controls Corp., 1978—; entrepreneur, 1969—; pres., chmn. bd. William H. Burgess Found., 1954—; chmn. bd. Hydro-Jet Corp., 1971-74, Timelapse, Inc., 1976—, RHG Corp., 1976—; dir. Titech, Inc., Early Calif. Industries; cons. Century Indsl. Assos., 1968-70, prin. asso., 1976-77, Profl. Assos., 1976-77; mem. Los Angeles panel arbitrators N.Y. Stock Exchange, 1971—. Mem. council regents Forest Lawn, 1959-65; vice chmn. commerce and industry United Crusade, 1968-70; mem. adv. bd. Pasadena YWCA, 1955-57; bd. dirs. Jr. Achievement So. Calif., 1965-70, adv. council, 1971-75; founding mem. Los Angeles Music Center, 1964; dir. The Founders, 1971-78; v.p., bd. dirs. Calif. Inst. Tech. Assos., 1964-65, 70-78; bd. overseers, vis. com. Harvard U., 1964-70; bd. dirs. Huntington Meml. Tumor Clinic, 958-60; life mem., trustee Pasadena Mus. Modern Art, 1956-74; mem. pres.'s council Calif. Inst. Tech., 1968-71; mem. Pasadena Tournament of Roses Assn., 1971-74; bd. govs. Otis Art Inst., 1967-74; bd. dirs. So. Calif. council Inst. Internat. Edn., 1970-72; founding fellow, bd. dirs. L.S.B. Leakey Found., 1969-79; trustee San Gabriel Valley Found. Boy Scouts Am., 1968-69; mem. Nat. Assn. Eagle Scouts, 1974—; world ambassador Internat. Student Center, UCLA, 1970-73; mem. pres.'s adv. council U. Redlands, 1971-74; mem. Econ. Round Table, 1970-75; mem. curriculum adv. com. U. So. Calif. Bus. Sch., 1972-78; mem. orthopedic council Los Angeles Orthopedic Hosp., 1972-75; mem. vol. adv. com. Calif. Atty. Gen., 1971-78; hon. adv. bd. Internat. Profl. Tennis Assn., 1967-71; life mem. Nat. Edni. Tennis Found.; nat. adv. bd. Am. Security Council, 1971—; bd. dirs. Palm Springs Friends Philharm., 1974-78, Coachella Valley YMCA, 1977-78; trustee Space Age Hall Sci., 1973-76, Palm Springs Desert Mus., 1974-77. Served to lt. USNR, 1941-45. Recipient Rep. Minnesotan award U. Minn., 1939, Bus. Achievement award Harvard Bus. Sch. Club So. Calif., 1963; citation for Distinguished Service DAV, 1963; Outstanding Achievement award U. Minn., 1964. Mem. Nat. Inst. Social Scis. (life), Chief Execs. Forum (dir. 1969-73), Young Pres. Orgn. (nat. dir. 1958-67, internat. pres. 1966), Palm Springs World Affairs Council (dir. 1974—, v.p. 1980), Harvard Bus. Sch. Club So. Calif. (pres., dir. 1955-56, dir. 1970-74), Internat. Mktg. Inst. (adv. council 1959-63), Nat. Rep. Eagles Assn., Los Angeles World Affairs Council (v.p. and dir. 1962—, treas. 1964), Soc. for Improvement of Human Functioning, Metric Soc., Tarrytown One Hundred (founding mem.), U. Minn. Alumni Assn., U.S. Lawn Tennis Assn. (life), Tennis Patrons Assn. So. Calif. (bd. govs. 1966), Pasadena Foothill Tennis Patrons Assn. (hon. bd. mem. 1964-74), Phi Delta Theta Alumni Assn., Phi Delta Theta. Republican. Episcopalian. Clubs: Valley Hunt, Harvard, Calif., Lincoln (Los Angeles); Racquet, Tennis, Eldorado Golf, Vintage Golf (Palm Springs, Calif.); Desert Riders; River (N.Y.C.); Harvard, President's. Address: 550 Palisades Dr Palm Springs CA 92262 *Determine your lifetime goals; list the steps of your plan to accomplish the goals. Decide what on the list you should do today. Do it.*

BURGESS, WILLIAM HOWARD, educator; b. Boston, Mar. 13, 1924; s. William Herbert and Dorothy Elizabeth (Meek) B.; m. Mary Ruth Bond, Nov. 25, 1949; children—Ellen Elizabeth, Ruth Isabel. B.Chem. Engring., Cornell U., 1949, M.F.S., 1950, Ph.D., 1954. Research, teaching asst. Cornell U., 1949-54; mem. faculty U. Toronto, 1954—, prof. chem. engring., 1968—; Dir. Chem. Engring. Research Cons. Ltd. Served with AUS, 1944-46. Mem. Am. Chem. Soc., Sigma Xi, Phi Kappa Phi. Mem. Anglican Ch. Home: 59 Donlea Dr Toronto ON M46 2M3 Canada

BURGGRAF, ODUS ROY, aeronautical engineering educator; b. Ft. Wayne, Ind., Feb. 27, 1929; s. Odus and Grace F. (Windle) B.; m. Helen Catheine Rapp, Aug. 12, 1950; children: Lisa Anne, Donna Lynn, Susan Kay. B.Aero.E., Ohio State U., 1952, M.Sc., 1952; Ph.D., Calif. Inst. Tech., 1955. Aerodynamicist Douglas Aircraft Co., El Segundo, Calif., 1952; asst. prof. USAF Inst. Tech., Dayton, Ohio, 1954-56; engring. specialist Curtiss-Wright Corp., Santa Barbara, Calif., 1956-59; staff scientist Lockheed Research Lab., Palo Alto, Calif., 1960-64; assoc. prof. aero. engring. Ohio State U., Columbus, 1964-66, prof., 1966—; cons. Astro Research Corp., Santa Barbara, 1959-66; spl. lectr Univ. Coll., London, 1978; mem. vis. com. Engrs. Council Profl. Devel., N.Y.C., 1971-76. Contbr. articles to profl. jours. Served to 1st lt. USAF, 1954-56. Guggenheim fellow, 1952-54; Sci. Research Council Gt. Britain grantee, 1972; Nat. Ctr. Atmospheric Research sr. postdoctoral fellow, 1977. Assoc. fellow AIAA (nat. tech. com. fluid dynamics 1978-80); mem. AAUP, Sigma Xi. Home: 1370 Stoneygate Ln Columbus OH 43221 Office: Dept Aero Engring Ohio State U Columbus OH 43210

BURGHART, JAMES HENRY, elec. engr.; b. Erie, Pa., July 18, 1938; s. Chester Albert and Mary Virginia (Burke) B.; m. Judith Ann Hoff, July 8, 1961; children—Jill Kathryn, Mark Alan. B.S. in Elec. Engring, Case Inst. Tech., 1960, M.S. (U.S. Steel Found. fellow 1961-63), 1962, Ph.D., 1965. Asst. prof., then asso. prof. elec. engring. SUNY, Buffalo, 1969-75; prof. elec. engring., chmn. dept. Cleve. State U., 1975—. Served as officer USAF, 1965-68. Mem. IEEE (chmn. Cleve. sect. 1980-81), Am. Soc. Engring. Edn., Sigma Xi, Eta Kappa Nu. Home: 2528 Newbury Dr Cleveland OH 44118 Office: 1983 E 24th St Cleveland OH 44115

BURGIN, E.J., natural gas pipeline company executive; b. White Pine, Tenn., Sept. 27, 1927; s. Martin Lee and Virginia (Bailey) B.; m. Barbara Jean Inman, Dec. 28, 1971; 1 dau., Stacey Jean. B.S.M.E., U. Tenn., 1955; postrad., Stanford U., 1981. Vice pres. So. Ga. Natural Gas Co., Thomasville, 1955-58; gen. supt. ops. Fla. Gas Transmission Co., Winter Park, 1959-73, v.p. ops., 1974-77, v.p. mktg., 1978-81, exec. v.p., 1981—, dir., 1979—. Served to capt. U.S. Army, 1951-59. Mem. Am. Gas. Assn. (award of merit 1975), So. Gas. Assn., Fla. Natural Gas Assn. (dir.). Republican. Club: Rolling Hills Country (pres. 1979-81). Lodge: Masons. Home: 312 Pressview Ave Longwood FL 32750 Office: PO Box 44 Winter Park FL 32789

BURGIN, ROBERT AUGUSTUS, transportation company executive; b. Rolling Fork, Miss., July 20, 1924; s. Robert Augustus and Jane (Sullivan) B.; m. Sara Porter Shofner, Dec. 4, 1948 (dec.); children: Sally Burgin Margolis, Robert Augustus, III, Christopher. B.S., U. Tenn., 1949. With Oak Ridge Inst. Nuclear Studies, 1949-51; br. chief Dept. Def., Washington, 1951-52, Albuquerque, 1953-56; cons. Stanford Research Inst., 1956-57; with TRW Inc., 1958-78; v.p. planning and devel. TRW Electronics, Los Angeles, 1973-78, corp. v.p., group exec., 1965-78; chmn., chief exec. officer Leaseway Transp. Corp., Beachwood, Ohio, 1977-82, pres., 1981—; also dir.; dir. E. F. Johnson Co., Waseca, Minn., CFS Continental, Chgo., Provident Life & Accident Ins. Co., Chattanooga, Storage Tech. Corp., Louisville, Colo., Telenova, Inc., San Jose, Calif., Western Union, N.Y.C. Mem. devel. council U. Tenn.; mem. So. Calif. Olympics Com.; com. mem. Hugh O'Brian Youth Found., Los Angeles; bd. dirs. Greater Cleve. Growth Assn.; trustee Fuller Theol. Sem.; mem. exec. bd. Greater Cleve.; council Boy Scouts Am. Served to capt. USAAF, 1943-45; Served to capt. USAF, 1951-52. Clubs: Desert Horizon Country., Sunrise Country. Office: 3700 Park E Dr Beachwood OH 44122

BURGIO, JANE, state government official; b. Nutley, N.J.; m. John Burgio; children: John E., James. Student, Newark Sch. Fine and Indsl. Arts. Mem. N.J. State Assembly, Trenton, 1973-81; sec. of state State of N.J., Trenton, 1982—. Mem. Essex County Improvement Authority, Trustees for Support of Free Pub. Schs.; trustee devel. com. St. Barnabas Hosp., Livingston, N.J.; trustee Planned Parenthood Essex County; alt. del. Republican Nat. Conv. Recipient Alumni Recognition award Univ. Coll., Rutgers U., Newark; rcipient hist. award N.J. League Hist. Socs.; recipient cert. N.J. Humane Soc., Newark. Mem. Nat. Assn. Secs. of State, Nat. Conf. State Legislature, Bus. and Profl. Women's Assn. of Millburn, N.J. Home: 586 Mountain Ave North Caldwell NJ 07006 Office: New Jersey Dept State State House CN 300 Trenton NJ 08625

BURGOON, NORMAN AARON, JR., surety bond and insurance company executive; b. Balt., Oct. 27, 1916; s. Norman Aaron and Nellie (Ricker) B.; m. Doris Hunter, June 30, 1939; children: Norman Richard, Harvey Ronald, Alan Charles, Michele Doris. Student, Balt. City Coll., 1931-34; J.D., U. Balt., 1939. Bar: Md. bar 1940. With Fidelity & Deposit Co., Md., 1935-79, exec. v.p., 1966-79; also dir., mem. exec. com.; dir. Suburban Bancorp., Suburban Trust Co.; lawyer, gen. counsel Nat. Assn. Surety Bond Producers, 1979—; Past v.p., dir. Bur. Contract Info., Inc.; dir. Med. Mut. Liability Ins. Soc., Md., 1981—. Mem. exec. com., dir., past pres. Commerce and Industry Combined Health Appeal, Balt., 1967-80; mem. finance com. Presbyn. Hosp., Balt., 1955—; Bd. dirs. Greater Balt. Med. Center, 1966—, United Fund, 1974-80; trustee U. Balt., 1971-74. Served with AUS, World War II. Mem. Am. Ins. Assn., Am. Mgmt. Assn., Surety Assn. Am. (chmn. exec. com.), Md. Hist. Soc. Presbyn. (ruling elder). Club: Maryland (Balt.). Home: 304 Wynell Ct Timonium MD 21093 Office: Fidelity Bldg Baltimore MD 21201

BURGOS-CALDERON, RAFAEL, nephrologist, educator; b. Bayamon, P.R., Oct. 31, 1936; s. Marcelino Burgos and Emilia Calderon.; m. Milagros Maldonado; children: Rafael Antonio, Ricardo Rafael, Vismal Rafael, Ariadné. B.S., U. P.R., M.D., 1965. Intern Univ. Hosp., Rio Piedras, P.R., 1965-66, resident in internal medicine, 1966-69, chief resident in medicine, 1969, dir. hemodialysis unit, 1971—, exec. dir. hosp., 1977—, chief nephrology sect., 1980—; exec. dir. P.R. Med. Center, 1979—; clin. fellow in nephrology La. State U., 1969-70; research fellow in nephrology N.C. Meml. Hosp., 1970-71; instr. U. P.R. Sch. Medicine, 1971-73, asst. prof. medicine, 1973-77, asso. prof., 1978—; pres. End State Renal Disease Network 29, P.R. and V.I., 1974—; dir. Preventive Program for 1979 Renal Disease Dept. Health, P.R. Served with U.S. N.G. Mem. P.R. Med. Assn., Am. Soc. Nephrology, Internat. Soc. Nephrology, U. P.R. Sch. Medicine Ex-Alumni Assn. (pres. 1973-74). Roman Catholic. Home: St Number I Urb Los Frailes Norte Guaynabo PR 00657 Office: Univ Hosp PR Med Center Rio Piedras Sta San Juan PR 00921 *We are born to live, We are born to be, We are born to love, We are born to give.*

BURGOYNE, EDWARD EYNON, educator; b. Montpelier, Idaho, Sept. 26, 1918; s. Sidney Eynon and Beatrice (Holmes) B.; m. Mary Ida Ream, June 30, 1950; children—Mary Anne (Mrs. Daniel George Catlin), Elaine (Mrs. Mark A. LeVan), Edward Ream, Bryce William. Student, Idaho State U., 1937-39; B.S., Utah State U., 1941; postgrad., U. Chgo., 1942-43; M.S., U. Wis., 1947, Ph.D., 1949. Research chemist Phillips Petroleum Co., Bartlesville, Okla., 1949-51; asst. prof. Ariz. State U., Tempe, 1951-56, asso. prof., 1956-59, prof. chemistry, 1959—. Author: A Short Course in Organic Chemistry, 1979; Contbr. articles to profl. jours. Served with USAAF, 1942-46; PTO; lt. col. USAF Res; ret.). Fellow AAAS; mem. Am. Chem. Soc., Ariz. Acad. Sci., Sigma Xi. Mem. Ch. of Jesus Christ of Latter-day Saints. Patentee in field. Home: 223 E 15th St Tempe AZ 85281

BURGUIERES, PHILIP JOSEPH, metal products company executive; b. Franklin, La., Sept. 3, 1943; s. Denis P.J. and Emma L. (LeBlanc) B.; m. Cheryl A. Courrege, Aug. 21, 1965; children: Emily Louise, Philip Martial. B.S. in Mech. Engring, U. Southwestern La., 1965; M.B.A., U. Pa., 1970. Adminstrv. asst. Cameron Iron Works, Inc., Houston, 1971, controller European ops., 1972-75, v.p. corp. services, v.p. forged products div. European ops., 1975-79, exec. v.p. ops. European ops., 1979-81, pres., chief operating officer, 1981—; chmn. J.M. Burguieres Co., Ltd., New Orleans; dir. 1st City Nat. Bank, Houston. Served with USN, 1966-69. Mem. ASME, Forging Industry Assn., Petroleum Equipment Suppliers Assn., Nat. Ocean Industries Assn., Tau Beta Pi, Pi Tau Sigma. Republican. Roman Catholic. Office: Cameron Iron Works Inc PO Box 1212 Houston TX 77001

BURGUN, J. ARMAND, architect; b. Rochester, Pa., Nov. 19, 1925; s. Paul John and Wilda (Whitehill) B.; m. Muriel Ann DePowel, Dec. 30, 1944; children: Douglas Armand, Bruce Eric. B.Arch., Columbia U., 1950. Designer Ferrenz & Taylor, architects, N.Y.C., 1950-55; asst. dir. N.Y. State Joint Hosp. Planning Commn., Albany, 1955-60; assoc. Rogers Burgun Shahine & Deschler, architects, N.Y.C., 1960-63, ptnr., 1963—; spl. lectr. Grad. Sch. Med. Adminstrn. N.Y. Med. Coll. Author: Handbook-Hospital Construction, 1958, Institutional Fires, 1977; contbr. articles to profl. jours. Archtl. cons. Hosp. Council Greater N.Y., 1957—, USPHS, VA; mem. Pres.'s Com. Mental Retardation, N.Y. State Bldg. Code Council; trustee N.Y. Sch. for Deaf. Served to lt. comdr. USCG, 1942-44. Decorated Purple Heart. Fellow AIA; mem. N.Y. Soc. Architects, N.Y. State Assn. Architects, Am. Hosp. Assn., Nat. Fire Protection Assn. (dir., chmn. bd.), Internat. Hosp. Fedn., Am. Assn. Hosp. Planning (pres.), N.Y. Bldg. Congress, Res. Officers Assn. Clubs: Winged Foot Country, Union League. Home: 235 Manville Rd Pleasantville NY 10570 Office: Rogers Burgun Shahine & Deschler Inc 521 Fifth Ave New York NY 10175

BURHENNE, HANS JOACHIM, physician, educator; b. Hannover, Ger., Dec. 27, 1925; emigrated to U.S., 1955, naturalized, 1959; s. Adolph and Clara (Ditges) B.; m. Linda Jean Warren, Oct. 20, 1978; children by previous marriage: Mark, Antonia, Yvonne. Matura, Gymnasium, Salzburg, Austria, 1944; M.D. magna cum laude, Maximilian Med. Sch., Munich, 1951. Intern Monmouth Med. Center, Long Branch, N.J.; resident in radiology Peter Bent Brigham Hosp., Boston, 1955-59; instr. Harvard U., 1955-59; chmn. dept. radiology Children's Hosp., San Francisco, 1960-78; clin. prof. radiology U. Calif., San Francisco, 1960-78; prof. radiology U. B.C., 1978—, head dept. radiology, 1978—. Author: (with A.R. Margulis) Alimentary Tract Roentgenology, 3d edit., 1983, Sierra Spring Ski Touring, 1971; Editor: (with A.R. Margulis) Mammography, 1969; mem. editorial bd.: Radiologica Clinica, 1964—, Oncology, 1973-77, Gastrointestinal Radiology, 1976—, (with A.R. Margulis) Western Jour. of Medicine, 1975-79. Chmn. bd. dirs. Cathedral Sch., San Francisco, 1976-77. NIH fellow, 1959; recipient Walter B. Cannon medal, 1982. Fellow Am. Coll. Radiology (counsellor 1973-77), Royal Coll. Physicians Can.; mem. Calif. Radiol. Soc. (pres. 1967-78), Soc. Gastrointestinal Radiologists (pres. 1977). Home: 1063 W 7th Ave Vancouver BC V6H 1B2 Canada Office: 10th Ave and Heather St Vancouver BC V5Z 1M9 Canada *Strive for good judgment, derive it from experience, but admit that valuable experience may be based on poor judgment.*

BURHOE, RALPH WENDELL, theology educator; b. Somerville, Mass., June 21, 1911; s. Winslow Page and Mary Trenaman (Stumbles) B.; m. Frances Bickford, Aug. 4, 1931 (dec. Aug. 1967); children: Winslow Newton, Laura Jean Burhoe Maier, Thomas Allen, Diana May Burhoe Chase; m. Calla Crawford Butler, Apr. 6, 1969. Student, Harvard, 1928-32, Andover Newton Theol. Sch., 1934-36; Sc.D., Meadville Lombard Theol. Sch., Chgo., 1975; L.H.D., Rollins Coll., 1979. Observer, research asst., librarian, asst. to dir. Blue Hill Meteorol.; Obs. Harvard, 1936-47; asst. sec. Am. Meteorol. Soc., Milton, Mass., 1936-47, treas., 1942-47; exec. officer Am. Acad. Arts and Sciences, Boston, 1947-64; research prof. theology and scis. Meadville Theol. Sch., Chgo., 1964-74, emeritus, 1974—, sec., sr. fellow Center for Advanced Study in Religion and Sci., 1972—. Author-editor: (with Hudson Hoagland) Evolution and Man's Progress, 1962; Author, editor: Science and Human Values in the Twenty-first Century, 1971, Toward a Scientific Theology, 1981; Editor: Zygon, Jour. Religion and Sci, 1965-79; founding editor, 1979—; Contbr. to profl. jours. and books. Co-founder, hon. pres. Inst. Religion in an Age of Sci. First Am. recipient Templeton prize for progress in religion, 1980. Fellow World Acad. Art and Sci., Am. Acad. Arts and Scis., AAAS; mem. Am. Acad. Relgion, Am. Theol. Assn., Soc. Sci. Study Religion (treas. 1965-70), Inst. on Theol., Encounter with Sci. and Tech. Office: 1524 E 59th St Chicago IL 60637

BURIGANA, ENUS ANTHONY, insurance company executive; b. Scranton, Pa., June 13, 1928; s. Guerino and Veneranda (Piccotti) B.; m. Geraldine M. Christmas, Aug. 7, 1948; children: Steven Enus, Barbara Ann, Nancy Ann. B.S., Bucknell U., 1950. Acctg. supr. Nationwide Mut. Ins. Co., Harrisburg, Pa., 1951-53, acctg. mgr., White Plains, N.Y., 1953-62, reins. acctg. mgr., Columbus, Ohio, 1962-65, adminstrn. mgr., 1965-68, corp. reins. mgr., 1968-70, v.p. reins., 1970—, v.p. nat. accounts, 1976—; bd. govs. Mut. Atomic Energy Pool, 1979—. Mem. Internat. Coop. Ins. Fedn. (exec. com. 1981—), Internat. Coop. Reins. Bur. (chmn. 1980—), Fgn. Credit Inst. Assn. (dir), U.S. Aviation Ins. Group (policy com. 1981—), Phi Gamma Delta. Republican. Roman Catholic. Club: Brookside Country. Lodge: K.C. Home: 922 Bluff RidgeDr Worthington OH 43085 Office: Nationwide Mut Ins Cos 1 Nationwide Plaza Columbus OH 43215

BURK, CARL JOHN, biological sciences educator; b. Troy, Ohio, Dec. 30, 1935; s. Carl J.B. and Louise H. (Burk); m. Iale Aka, May 6, 1966; children: John Seljuk, Nicholas Murat. A.B., Miami U., Oxford, Ohio, 1957; M.A., U. N.C., 1959, Ph.D., 1961. Instr. U. N.C., 1960-61; mem. faculty Smith Coll., Northampton, Mass., 1961—, prof. biol. scis., 1973—, Gates prof., 1982—. Author: (With M. Holland) Stone Walls and Sugar Maples: An Ecology for Northeasterners, 1979. Mem. Ecol. Soc. Am., Am. Soc. Plant Taxonomists, AAAS, Sigma Xi, Phi Beta Kappa. Episcopalian. Home: 281 Crescent St Northampton MA 01060 Office: Smith Coll Sci Ctr Northampton MA 01060

BURK, DEAN, biochemist; b. Oakland, Calif., Mar. 21, 1904; s. Frederic and Caroline (Frear) B.; m. Mildred Chaundy; children—Diana (Mrs. Richard A. Barker), Wendy (Mrs. Charles Maiorana), Frederic Chaundy. B.S., U. Calif., 1923, Ph.D., 1927; fellow NRC and Internat. Edn. Bd., at U. London (Univ. Coll.), 1927-29, Kaiser Wilhelm Inst. for Biology, 1927-29; fellow NRC and Internat Edn. Bd., Harvard U., 1927-29. Asso. phys. chemist Fixed Nitrogen Research Lab., Dept. Agr., Washington, 1929, chemist, 1937-39; sr. chemist Nat. Cancer Inst., NIH, Bethesda, Md., 1939-48, prin. chemist, 1948-51, head chemist, 1951-58, chief chemist, 1958—; asso. prof. biochemistry Cornell U. Med. Coll., 1939-41; research master grad. faculty George Washington U., 1947—; guest research worker USSR Acad. Scis. (Biochem. Inst.), Moscow, 1935. Author, editor: Cancer, 1945, Approaches to Tumor Chemotherapy, 1947, Cell Chemistry, 1953; Asso. editor: Record Chem. Progress, 1943—, Proc. Soc. Exptl. Biology and Medicine, 1948-53, Enzymologia, 1937—; Contbr. to sci. jours. Pres. Dean Burk Found., Inc. Recipient Domagk prize for cancer research, 1965; Nat. Health Fedn. Humanitarian award, 1971; Wisdom award Honor, 1973; Humanitarian award Cancer Control Soc., 1973; decorated knight comdr. Med. Order Bethlemen; knight Mark Twain. Fellow A.A.A.S. (organizer, chmn. research confs. on cancer 1942-45); mem. Am. Chem. Soc. (Hillebrand award 1952), Am. Soc. Biol. Chemists, Am. Assn. Cancer Research, Am. Soc. Plant Physiologists, Soc. Exptl. Biology and Medicine (chmn. 1949-50, sec.-treas. 1948-49), N.Y., Washington acads. sci., Soc. Gen. Physiology, L.I. Biol. Assn., Harvey Soc., Chem. Soc. Washington, Max Planck Assn. Munich, Inst. for Cell Physiology Berlin, Royal Soc. Medicine London, Nat. Trust Gt. Britain, Dolmetsch Found. Haslemere (fgn.), Max Planck Inst. Biochemistry, Munich, Soc. Cal. Pioneers, Gamma Alpha, Sigma Xi. Clubs: Cosmos (Washington); Commonwealth (Cal.). Home and office: 4719-44 St NW Washington DC 20016

BURK, WILLIAM CHARLES, railroad executive; b. Beaumont, Tex., Aug. 19, 1921; s. John Leonard and Dona (Robinson) B.; m. Mary Irene Meyer, Aug. 19, 1945; children: John Paul, Donald William, Mary Catherine. Student, Central State Coll., Edmond, Okla., 1939-42, Inst. Bus. Econs., U. So. Calif., 1955. Newspaper work in, Okla., before World War II; system photographer A., T. & S.F. Ry., Los Angeles, 1946-47; spl. rep. in, Chgo., 1947-53, spl. rep. public relations, Topeka, 1953-61; mgr. public relations Santa Fe Ry. System, Chgo., 1961-73, v.p. public relations, 1973—. Trustee William Allen White Found. Mem. R.R. Pub. Relations Assn. (past pres.), Pub. Relations Soc. Am., Public Relations Clinic (past pres.), Am. Agrl. Editors Assn. (pres.), Inland Daily Press Assn. (charter assoc.), Sigma Delta Chi, Alpha Tau Omega. Republican. Episcopalian. Clubs: Masons, Shriners, Chgo. Athletic, Chgo. Press, Western Ry., San Diego Press, Kansas City (Mo.) Press (Wilmette); Nat. Press (Washington). Home: 923 Cornell St Wilmette IL 60091 Office: 80 E Jackson Blvd Chicago IL 60604

BURKART, WALTER MARK, manufacturing company executive; b. Ferndale, Mich., Sept. 29, 1921; s. Michael A. and Beatrice (Pominville) B.; m. Mary Jane Hilts, Apr. 22, 1942; children: Michael Robert, Michele Sue. Student, Lawrence Inst. Tech., 1941-43. Supr. Ex-Cello Corp., Detroit, 1940-51, v.p. machine tool div., 1965-69; chief process engr. Wright Aero Co., Detroit, 1951-55; mgr. Machine Tool div. Sheffield Corp. div. Bendix, Dayton, Ohio, 1956-65; chmn. bd. Kingsbury Machine Tool Corp., Keene, N.H., 1969—. Active Boy Scouts Am., 1958—. Served with USNR, 1944-46. Mem. Keene C. of C. (dir. 1971), Bus. and Industry Assn. N.H. (dir. 1980-81), Am. Mgmt. Assn., Soc. Mfg. Engrs., Nat. Machine Tool Builders Assn. Republican. Presbyterian. Office: 80 Laurel St Keene NH 03431 *It has been my managerial philosophy to give people a goal and let them choose which road to take in reaching that goal. This allows people to utilize their strengths while becoming more committed and involved. Through this participation the individual can get a greater sense of personal accomplishment. Rarely will two people go about solving a problem in the same way. While some problems do require a group solution, most simply require a solution and I believe the method is not as important as the result.*

BURKE, ALEXANDER JAMES, JR., publishing company executive; b. N.Y.C., Apr. 24, 1931; s. Alexander James and Josephine Eleanor (McGrath) B.; m. Suzanne Jeanne Gatti, June 25, 1955; children: James, Brian, Christopher, Nancy, Thomas, Matthew, Alexander John. B.A. cum laude, Holy Cross Coll., 1953; M.A., Fordham U., 1956. Prof. English Fordham U., 1953-56, 59-60; editor W.H. Sadlier Co., N.Y.C., 1959-60; mgr. Doubleday Bookstore, Manhasset, N.Y., 1952; with McGraw-Hill Book Co., N.Y.C., 1960—, gen. mgr., 1969-70, v.p., 1970-73, exec. v.p., 1973-74, pres., 1974-82, McGraw-Hill Internat. Book Co., 1982—; dir. McGraw-Hill Ryerson, Ltd.; dirs. Ctr. for the Book, 1978—. Bd. dirs. Audult Edn. Council St. Louis, 1965, Commn. on Radio and TV, Cath. Archdiocese St. Louis, 1968-72. Served with USAF, 1956-59. Mem. Assn. Am. Pubs. (exec. com., dir. 1978—), Book Industry Study Group (exec. com., dir. 1976—), Am. Soc. Curriculum Devel., Nat. Council Tchrs. English, Alpha Sigma Nu. Roman Catholic. Home: 455 Ryder Rd Manhasset NY 11030 Office: McGraw-Hill Internat Book Co 1221 Ave of Americas New York NY 10020

BURKE, AUGUSTIN EMILE, bishop; b. Sluice Point, N.S., Can., Jan. 22, 1922. Ordained priest Roman Catholic Ch., 1950; consecrated bishop of, Yarmouth, N.S., Can., 1968—. Office: PO Box 278 53 Park St Yarmouth NS B5A 4B2 Canada *

BURKE, BERNARD FLOOD, physicist, educator; b. Boston, June 7, 1928; s. Vincent Paul and Clare (Brine) B.; m. Jane Chapin Pann, May 30, 1953; children—Geoffrey Damian, Elizabeth Chapin, Mark Vincent, Matthew Brine. S.B., M.I.T., 1950, Ph.D., 1953. Staff mem. terrestrial magnetism Carnegie Instn. of Washington, 1953-65, chmn. radio astronomy sect., 1962-65; prof. physics Mass. Inst. Tech., 1965—; vis. prof. U. Leiden, Netherlands, 1971-72; trustee N.E. Radio Obs. Corp., 1973—, vice chmn., 1975-82, chmn., 1982—; cons. NSF, NASA. Trustee Associated Univs., Inc., 1972—. Recipient Helen Warner prize Am. Astron. Soc., 1963; Rumford prize Am. Acad. Arts and Scis., 1971. Fellow AAAS; mem. Nat. Acad. Scis., Am. Acad. Arts and Scis., Am. Phys. Soc., Am., Royal astron. socs., Internat. Astron. Union, Internat. Sci. Radio Union. Research on microwave spectroscopy, radio astronomy, galactic structure, antenna design. Home: 10 Bloomfield St Lexington MA 02173 Office: Mass Inst Tech Cambridge MA 02139

BURKE, COLEMAN, lawyer; b. Summit, N.J., Feb. 1, 1914; s. Daniel and Kate (Bundy) B.; m. Mary Poston, Nov. 20, 1937; children: Daniel II, Coleman P., Mary C. A.B., Hamilton Coll., 1934, LL.D., 1982; J.D., Harvard U., 1937; LL.D., Rikkyo U., Tokyo, 1958. Bar: N.Y. 1938, N.J. 1943. Assoc. firm Burke & Burke, N.Y.C., 1937-42, ptnr., 1942-78, counsel, 1978—; partner firm Burke & Peer (and predecessors), Summit, N.J., 1943—; dir. LFE Corp., Summit Bancorp., other corps. Author: Voting Trust Currently Observed, 1940. Chmn. emeritus Hamilton Coll.; chmn. Humane Soc. U.S.; dir. Christian Herald Mag., Bowery Mission, Children's Home; v.p., chmn. exec. com. Am. Bible Soc. Mem. Am., N.Y. State, N.J. bar assns., Assn. Bar City N.Y., Phi Beta Kappa, Chi Psi. Methodist. Clubs: Harvard (N.Y.C.); Short Hills, Baltusrol Golf, Gulf Stream Golf. Home: 45 Stewart Rd Short Hills NJ 07078 Office: 529 Fifth Ave New York NY 10017 also 382 Springfield Ave Summit NJ 07901

BURKE, DANIEL BARNETT, communications corporation executive; b. Albany, N.Y., Feb. 4, 1929; s. J. Frank and Mary (Barnett) B.; m. Harriet Shore, Aug. 31, 1957; children: Steve, James, Sarah, William. A.B., U. Vt., 1950; M.B.A., Harvard, 1955. Various positions product mgmt. and devel. Jell-O div. Gen. Foods Corp., 1955-61; gen. mgr. WTEN-TV, Albany, 1961-64, corporate v.p., 1962; gen. mgr. WJR AM/FM, Detroit, 1964-69, corporate exec. v.p., dir., 1967; pres. pub. div. Capital Cities Broadcasting Corp., N.Y.C., 1969-72, pres., chief operating officer corp., 1972—; dir. Palm Beach Co., Conrail, St. Regis Paper Co., Newspaper Advt. Bur., Cities in Schools, Inc. Past chmn. bd. trustees U. Vt., Med. Mission Sisters, Phila. Served to 1st lt., inf. AUS, 1951-53; Korea. Mem. Phi Delta Theta. Office: 24 E 51st St New York NY 10022

BURKE, DANIEL WILLIAM, college president emeritus, English educator; b. Pitts., Oct. 25, 1926; s. Daniel Joseph and Mary Elizabeth (Stack) B. B.A. in English, Cath. U. Am., 1949, M.A., 1952, Ph.D., 1957; D.H.L. (hon.), Washington and Jefferson Coll., 1974, Litt.D., Haverford Coll., 1976, LL.D., La Salle Coll., 1977. Instr. English W. Phila. Cath. High Sch. for Boys, 1949-51, La Salle Hall, Ammendale, Md., 1951-52; instr. English De La Salle Coll., Washington, 1952-57; asst. prof. La Salle Coll., Phila., 1957-62, asso. prof., 1962-69, prof., 1969—, v.p. acad. affairs, 1960-69, pres., 1969-77, dir. art mus., 1981—. Contbr. verse and criticism to profl. jours. Trustee emeritus Manhattan Coll., U. Bethlehem; bd. dirs. Fels Fund; mem. exec. com. Cath. Comm. on Cultural and Intellectual Affairs. Mem. MLA, Am. Soc. Aesthetics, Phi Beta Kappa. Home and office: LaSalle Coll 20th and Olney Ave Philadelphia PA 19141

BURKE, DONALD ROBERT, insurance company executive; b. New Iberia, La., Aug. 2, 1921; s. Donald Robert and Celeste (Dimitry) B.; m. Jacqueline Theresa LeJeune, Oct. 26, 1946; children: Donald, Stephen, Timothy, Torrence, Kevin, Jack, Mary Margaret. Student, U. Southwestern La. Claims adjuster Am. Gen. Ins. Co., Houston, 1946-50; br. claims mgr. Am. Gen. Inst. Co., Houston, 1950-60; chief claims supr. Am. Gen. Ins. Co., Houston, 1960-70, v.p. claims, 1970-73; v.p., sr. v.p. claims Md. Casualty Co., Balt., 1973—, dir., 1980—; bd. govs. Ins. Crime Prevention Inst., Westport, Conn., 1980-83; adv. bd. C.P.C.U.-Ins. Inst. Am., Malvern, Pa., 1982—; customer conf. com. Gen. Adjustment Bur., Bus. Services Inc., N.Y.C., 1982—. Bd. dirs. Balt. Jr. Achievement, 1982-83. Served to 1st lt. inf. AUS, 1940-45; PTO, ETO. Mem. Claims Exec. Council, Am. Isn. Assn. (vice chmn. claims adminstrn. com. 1981-83), Am. Inst. Assn. (chmn. claims adminstrn. com. 1984—). Democrat. Roman Catholic. Club: Hunt Valley Golf (Balt.). Home: 2455 Springlake Dr Baltimore MD 21093 Office: Md Causalty Co 3910 Keswick Rd Baltimore MD 21211

BURKE, DUVA *See* **BURKE, KENNETH**

BURKE, E. AINSLIE, artist, educator; b. Omaha, Jan. 26, 1922; s. Charles Alvin and Flora (Glanville) B.; m. Barbara Chase, Sept. 26, 1947. Student, Md. Inst. Fine Arts, 1938-41, Johns Hopkins U., 1939-41, Art Students League, N.Y.C., 1945-47. Vis. artist-in-residence Syracuse (N.Y.) U., 1962-63, asso. prof., 1963-65, prof. art, 1965—, chmn. dept. studio art, 1970-80; vis. artist Exeter (N.H.) Acad., 1970; chmn. Woodstock Artists Assn., 1960-62. One-man shows, AAA Galleries, N.Y.C., L.I. U., Polari Gallery, Woodstock, N.Y., Storm King Art Center, Mountainville, N.Y., Philips Exeter Acad., N.Y., Albany (N.Y.) Inst. History and Art, Lehigh (Pa.) U., Gorham State Coll., U. Maine, Deer Isle Artist Assn., Stonington, Maine, 1975-77, 78, 80, Kraushaar Galleries, N.Y.C., 1960, 63, 67, 71, 74, 77, 80, LeMoyne Coll., Syracuse, 1973, Lowe Art Center, Syracuse U., 1974, Manlius (N.Y.) Library, 1975, Oxford Gallery, Rochester, N.Y., 1977, 81, Munson Williams Proctor Mus., Utica, N.Y., 1979, Everson Mus., Syracuse, 1979, 80, U. Maine, Orono, 1980, Cazenovia (N.Y.) Coll., 1981, group shows include, Toledo Mus., Bklyn. Mus., Riverside Mus., N.Y.C., Pa. Acad., Phila., Schneider Gallery, Rome, U. Nebr., Mary Washington Coll., Am. Acad. Arts and Letters, Albany Inst. History and Art, Proctor Mus., Springfield (Mass.) Mus., Columbia (S.C.) Art Mus., Columbus (Ohio) Gallery Art, Corcoran Gallery, Washington, Stamford (Conn.) Mus., Phila. Mus., Marietta (Ohio) Coll., Nat. Acad., N.Y.C., Audubon Artists, N.Y.C., Ill. Wesleyn U., Smithsonian Instn. Traveling Exhn., Va. Mus. Fine Art, Everson Mus., Nat. Arts Club; represented in permanent collections, Columbia U., N.Y.C., Syracuse U., Springfield Mus., Lehigh U., Munson-Williams Proctor Inst., Utica, St. Lawrence U., others. Served in USN, 1942-45. Fulbright fellow, Italy, 1957-58; Creative Artists Public Service grantee, 1976-77; recipient numerous awards NAD, N.Y. Worlds Fair, others. Mem. AAUP, Art Students League, Maine Coast Artists, Audubon Artists, Associated Artists Syracuse, others. Office: Care Kraushaar Galleries 724 Fifth Ave New York NY 10019

BURKE, EDMOND WAYNE, judge; b. Ukiah, Calif., Sept. 7, 1935; s. Wayne P. and Opal K. B.; m. Sharon E. Halverson, Jan. 25, 1977; children: Kathleen R., Jennifer E. A.B., Humboldt State Coll., 1957, M.A., 1958; J.D., U. Calif., 1964. Bar: Calif., Alaska. Individual practice law, Calif. and Alaska, 1965-67, asst. atty. gen., State of Alaska, 1967, asst. dist. atty., Anchorage, Alaska, 1968-69; judge Superior Ct., Alaska, 1970-75; justice Supreme Ct. State of Alaska, Anchorage, 1975—, now chief justice. Mem. Alaska Bar Assn., Am. Judicature Soc. Republican. Presbyterian. Office: 303 K St Anchorage AK 99501 *

BURKE, EDMUND CHARLES, aerospace co. exec.; b. Bridgeport, Conn., June 21, 1921; s. Edmund Charles and Leola (Barber) B.; m. Peggy Williams, Mar. 22, 1947. B.S., U. Mo., 1943; M.S., Case Western Res. U., 1949; Ph.D., Yale U., 1951. Research metallographer Alcoa Cleve. Research Lab., 1943-48; research metallurgist Dow Chem. Co., Midland, Mich., 1951-56; chief metallurgist Hunter Engring. Co., Riverside, Calif., 1956-58; with Lockheed Missiles & Space Co., Sunnyvale, Calif., 1958—; dir. materials scis. Palo Alto (Calif.) research labs., 1965—; cons. in field. Author papers in field. Fellow Am. Soc. Metals; mem. AIME. Republican. Club: Los Altos (Calif.) Golf and Country. Home: 241 Ferne Ave Palo Alto CA 94306 Office: 3251 Hanover St Palo Alto CA 94304

BURKE, JAMES, writer, broadcaster; b. Londonderry, No. Ireland, Dec. 22, 1936; s. John James and Mary Matilda B.; m. Frances Madeline Hamilton, 1967. B.A. with honors, Jesus Coll., Oxford U., 1961, M.A., 1966. Dir. English Sch., Rome, Italy, 1961-66; free-lance broadcaster BBC-TV, London, 1966—; visitor Urbino U. Author: Tomorrow's World, 1970, Tomorrow's World II, Connections, 1979. Served with RAF, 1955-57. Recipient Silver medal Royal TV Soc., 1973, Gold medal for Outstanding Creative Contbn. to TV, 1974. Mem. Royal Instn. (London). Club: Savile (London). Address: Henley House The Terrace Barnes London SW 13 ONP England

BURKE, JAMES JOSEPH, insurance company executive; b. Wilkes-Barre, Pa., July 7, 1928; s. Joseph Hugh and Elizabeth Annette (Conroy) B.; m. Kathleen O. Nauss, Oct. 7, 1950; children: James, Kathleen, Molly, Ann, Patricia, Thomas. B.S., King's Coll., 1950. Vice pres., controller Monroe div. Litton Industries, South Orange, N.J., 1962-67; v.p., treas. Paramount Pictures Corp., N.Y.C., 1967-69; exec. v.p. IU Internat. Corp., Wilmington, Del., 1969-79, Colonial Penn Group Inc., Phila., 1979—; dir. Provident Nat. Corp. Bd. dirs. King's Coll. Opera Co. Phila. Mem. Fin. Execs. Inst. Roman Catholic. Club: Union League. Home: 724 Signal Light Rd Moorestown NJ 08057 Office: Colonial Penn Group Inc 5 Penn Center Plaza Philadelphia PA 19181

BURKE, JOE, professional baseball executive; m. Mary B. Burke; children: Joe, Mary Ann, Jimmy, John, Alice, Bobby, Vincent. Successively ticket mgr., bus. mgr., gen mgr. Louisville Colonels, 1948-60; successively asst. gen. mgr., bus. mgr., treas., v.p. Washington Senators (now Tex. Rangers), 1961-73; v.p. bus. Kansas City Royals, 1973-74, exec. v.p., gen. mgr., 1974-81, pres., 1981—; chmn. com. ondivisional play, mem. com. on expansion, schedule, div. of receipts, player relations Am. League. Named Major League Exec. of Yr. Sporting News, 1976; recipient Mr. Baseball award 7th Ann. Kansas City Baseball Award Dinner, 1978. Office: Kansas City Royals Box 1969 Kansas City MO 64141 *

BURKE, JOHN FRANCIS, surgeon, educator; b. Chgo., July 22, 1922; s. Frank A. and Mary B. B.; m. Agnes Redfearn Goldman, June 24, 1950; children: John Selden, Peter Ashley, Ann Campbell, Andrew Thomas. B.S., U. Ill., 1947; M.D., Harvard U., 1951. Intern Mass. Gen. Hosp., Boston, 1951-52, resident in surgery, 1952-57, vis. surgeon, Boston, 1968—, chief trauma services, 1980; program dir. Burn Trauma Research Center, 1973—; assoc. prof. surgery Harvard Med. Sch., 1969-75, prof. surgery, 1975-76, Helen Andrus Benedict prof. surgery, 1976—; chief of staff Shriners Burns Inst., Boston, 1969-80; vis. prof. dept. nutrition and food sci. M.I.T.; program dir. New Eng. Burn Demonstration Program, 1977-80. Co-editor 6 books in field; contbr. articles to profl. jours. Served with USAAF, 1942-45. Moseley Traveling fellow, 1955. Mem. Am. Burn Assn. (pres. 1982—), Boston Surg. Soc. (v.p. 1980—), N.Y. Acad. Scis., AMA, Am. Thoracic Soc., Mass. Med. Soc., A.C.S., Soc. Univ. Surgeons, Infectious Disease Soc. Am., Am. Surg. Assn., New Eng. Surg. Soc., Am. Assn. Surgery of

Trauma, Surg. Infection Soc. (founding mem., pres. 1983), Internat. Soc. Burn Injuries, Am. Trauma Soc. (founding mem.), Am. Assn. Med. Instrumentation (com. on barriers). Home: 216 Prospect St Belmont MA 02178 Office: Mass Gen Hosp Boston MA 02114

BURKE, JOHN GARRETT, educator; b. Boston, Aug. 12, 1917; s. Edmund Joseph and Catherine Cecelia (Barry) B.; m. Mary Margaret Porter, Oct. 13, 1945; children—Alison (Mrs. John Mitchell Ball), Kevin, Eileen. B.S., Mass. Inst. Tech., 1938; M.A., Stanford U., 1960, Ph.D., 1962. Metallurgist Bethlehem Steel Co., Johnstown, Pa. and; Houston, 1938-41; v.p. Cummins Diesel Engines, Inc., Pitts., 1945-48; pres. Dry Ice Converter Corp., Tulsa, 1949-58; asst. prof. history U. Calif. at, Los Angeles, 1962-67, asso. prof., 1967-71, prof., 1971-81, prof. emeritus, 1981—, dean social scis., 1970-73, dean, 1974-77. Author: Origins of the Science of Crystals, 1966, Atoms, Blacksmiths and Crystals, 1967, The Science of Minerals in the Age of Jefferson, 1978; editor: The New Technology and Human Values, 1966, 1972, Technology and Change, 1980; contbr. articles to profl. jours. Served with AUS, 1941-42; Served with USAAF, 1943-45. Decorated Air medal with one oak leaf cluster.; Recipient Abbott Payson Usher award, 1967; NSF grantee, 1965-68; Nat. Endowment Humanities grantee, 1973, 74, 78; Guggenheim fellow, 1979-80. Fellow AAAS; mem. Am. Hist. Assn., History of Sci. Soc. (treas. 1971-75), Soc. History of Tech. (mem. exec. council 1974-79), Am. Soc. M.E., History and Heritage Commn. Home: 242 Pinecrest Dr Kala Point Port Townsend WA 98368

BURKE, JOHN JAMES, utility exec.; b. Butte, Mont., July 25, 1928; s. John James and Mary C. (Hubber) B.; m. Nancy M. Calvert, July 12, 1952; children—Cheryl Ann, Mary, Kathleen, John James, III, Elisabeth. B.S. in Bus, U. Mont., 1950, J.D., 1952. Bar: Mont. bar 1952, U.S. Supreme Ct. bar 1957. Partner firm Weir, Gough, Booth and Burke, Helena, 1954-60; with Mont. Power Co., Butte, 1960—, exec. asst., counsel, then v.p., 1965-79, exec. v.p., 1979—; pres., dir. Lakeshore Devel. Co., Butte. Dir. Blue Shield Mont.; Mem. U. Mont. Council 50; pres. Butte-Silver Bow Planning Bd., 1966-70. Served as capt. USAF, 1952-54. Mem. Am. Bar Assn., State Bar Mont., Butte-Silver Bow Bar Assn., Butte-Silver Bow C. of C. (v.p. 1965-72). Roman Catholic. Clubs: Montana, Butte Country, Elks, Rotary (sec. Helena 1955-58); 116 (Washington)). Home: 50 Burning Tree Ln Butte MT 59701 Office: 40 E Broadway Butte MT 59701

BURKE, JOHN MILES, specialty chemical corporation executive; b. Glendale, Calif., Nov. 5, 1938; s. Avery John and Dorice Katherine (Davidson) B.; m. Barbara G. Gibbs, Feb. 23, 1963; 1 dau., Elena K. B.A. in Econs., Claremont Men's Coll., 1961; B.S. in Engring., Stanford U., 1961; M.B.A., UCLA, 1965; Ph.D. in Bus. Mgmt., UCLA, 1968. With Litton Industries, 1968-72; gen. mgr. Heim Universal Bearing div. Rockwell Internat., 1972-76; group v.p. auto splty. group W.R. Grace, 1976-78; pres., chief exec. officer Automotive and Consumer Group, Loctite Corp, Cleve., 1978—. Mem. Motor and Equipment Mfrs. Assn. (dir.). Home: 172 Aurora St Hudson OH 44236 Office: Automotive and Consumer Group Loctite Corp 4450 Cranwood Ct Cleveland OH 44128

BURKE, JOHN RICHARD, foreign service officer; b. Madison, Wis., Dec. 7, 1924; s. Patrick J. and Katherine M. (Boyle) B.; m. Amelie Marthe Cecillon. A.B., U. Wis., 1948, M.A., 1950. Teaching fellow U. Wis., 1954-55; spl. asst. to dir. Wis. Hist. Soc., 1954-55; joined U.S. Fgn. Service, 1956; various assignments, 1957-68; dir. Office Viet Nam Affairs, State Dept., 1968-69; assigned Nat. War Coll., 1969-70; dep. chief mission, Port-au-Prince, Haiti, 1970-72; dir. Office Caribbean Affairs, Dept. State, 1972-75; mem. Sr. Seminar in Fgn. Policy, 1975-76; minister-counselor, dep. chief mission Am. Embassy, Bangkok, Thailand, 1976-77; ambassador to, Guyana, 1977-79; dir. Nat. Collection Planning Office, Dept. State, Washington, 1980-82; dep. asst. sec. of state for adminstrn. Dept. State, 1982—. Served to lt. comdr. USNR, 1943-46, 50-53. Recipient Superior Honor award State Dept., 1966, 79. Mem. Chi Phi. Address: A/CDC Room 2811 Dept of State Washington DC 20520

BURKE, JOSEPH C., university president; b. New Albany, Ind., Mar. 20, 1932; s. Dennis F. and Beatrice V. (McDevitt) B.; m. Joan Thompson, Sept. 1, 1956; children—Maura Burke Dykhuis, Colleen Burke. B.A., Bellarmine Coll., Louisville, 1954; M.A., Ind. U., 1958, Ph.D., 1965. Instr. Ohio Wesleyan U., Delaware, 1960-62; asst. prof. to prof. history Duquesne U., Pitts., 1962-70; prof. history Loyola of Montreal, 1970-73, acad. v.p., 1970-73, SUNY Coll.-, Plattsburgh, 1973-74; pres. State U. Coll., 1974—; dir. Northeastern adv. bd. Key Bank, Plattsburgh.; cons. leadership and planning for colls. and univs. Contbr. to: to profl. jours. including Ednl. Record; publs. of Nat. Center Higher Edn. Mgmt. Bd. dirs. Champlain Valley Physicians Hosp. Med. Center.; Trustee Miner Agrl. Inst. Recipient Am. Council Learned Socs. grant, 1969-70; Am. Philos. Soc. fellow, summer 1966; Social Sci. Research fellow and; Am. Bar Found. fellow, 1969-70. Office: State U Coll Plattsburgh NY 12901

BURKE, KELLY HOWARD, former air force officer, consultant; b. Mobile, Ala., June 7, 1929; s. Kelly Howard and Vesta (Trussell) B.; m. Denny Ray Hosey, Dec. 30, 1951; children: Bethany, Patricia, Kelly Howard, III. B.S. in History, Auburn U., 1952; M.S. in Internat. Relations, George Washington U., 1968; postgrad., Naval War Coll., 1967-68, RAF Staff Coll., 1969-71, Indsl. Coll. Armed Forces, 1964-65. Commd. 2d lt. U.S. Air Force, 1953, advanced through grades to lt. gen., 1979; comdr. 379th Bomb Wing, Wurtsmith AFB, Mich., 1973-74, comdr. 2d Bomb Wing, Barksdale AFB, La., 1974-75; dep. chief of staff/plans SAC, 1975-78; dir. operational requirements Hdqrs. U.S. Air Force, Washington, 1978-79, dep. chief of staff/research, devel. and acquisition, 1979-82; ret., 1982; chmn. bd. Stafford, Burke and Hecker, Inc., Alexandria, VA, 1982; dir. Singer Co., Ballistic Shelters Corp., August Systems, Inc.; cons. White House Sci. Office, NRC, Def. Sci. Bd., Sci. Adv. Bd., others. Contbg. editor: Armed Forces Jour., Aerospace America. Decorated D.S.M. with oak leaf cluster, Legion of Merit, D.F.C., Meritorious Service medal, Air medal with oak leaf clusters. Mem. Nat. Space Club (dir.), Nat. Aviation Club (dir.). Episcopalian. Home: 7217 Valon Ct. Alexandria VA 22307 Office: Stafford Burke and Hecker 1006 Cameron St Alexandria VA 22314

BURKE, KENNETH (DUVA BURKE), author; b. Pitts., May 5, 1897; s. James Leslie and Lillyan May (Duva) B.; m. Lily Mary Batterham, May 19, 1919 (div.); children—Jeanne Elspeth, Eleanor Duva, Frances Batterham; m. Elizabeth Batterham, Dec. 18, 1933; children—James Anthony, Kenneth Michael. Ed., Ohio State U., Columbia; D.Litt. (hon.), Bennington Coll., 1966, Rutgers U., 1968, Dartmouth, 1970, L.H.D., Fairfield U., 1970, Rochester U., 1972, Northwestern U., 1972, Ind. State U., 1976, Kenyon Coll., 1979. Research work Laura Spelman Rockefeller Meml., 1926-27; music critic The Dial, 1927-29; editorial work Bur. Social Hygiene, 1928-29; vis. prof. English U. Chgo., 1949-50; music critic of The Nation, 1934-36; lectr. on practice and theory of lit. criticism New Sch. for Social Research, 1937; lectr. psychology of lit. form and on Samuel Taylor Coleridge U.Chgo., 1938; course in theory and practice, lit. criticism Bennington Coll., 1943-61; lit. critic Drew U., 1962, 64; modern lit. critic Pa. State U., 1963; Regents prof. U. Calif. at, Santa Barbara, 1964-65; prof. Central Washington State Coll., 1966; lit. theory Harvard, 1967; lit. critic, Fannie Hurst vis. prof. Washington U., 1970-71; critic Wesleyan U. Center for Humanities, 1972; Andrew W. Mellon vis. prof. English U. Pitts., 1974; seminar in lit. criticism Princeton, 1975; Walker-Ames vis. prof. English U. Wash., 1976; seminar in lit. criticism U. Nev., Reno, 1976; fellow Center for Advanced Study Behavioral Scis., 1957-58. Writer of stories, translations, critical articles, book revs.; Author: The White Oxen and Other Stories, 1924, Counter-Statement, 1931, rev. edit. 1953, 1968; novel Towards a Better Life; a Series of Declamations, or Epistles, 1932, rev. edit., 1966, Permanence and Change Anatomy of Purpose, 1935, rev. edit., 1954, Attitudes Toward History (Vol. I, Acceptance and Rejection: The Curve of History, Vol. II, Analysis of Symbolic Structure), 1937, rev. 1 vol. edit., 1959, Philosophy of Literary Form, Studies in Symbolic Action, 1941, abridged edit., 1957, rev. unabridged edit., 1967, A Grammar of Motives, 1945, new edit., 1969, A Rhetoric of Motives, 1950, new edit., 1969, Book of Moments, Poems, 1915-54, 1955, The Rhetoric of Religion, 1961, new edit., 1970, Perspectives by Incongruity, Terms for Order, 1964, Language as Symbolic Action, 1966, Collected Poems, 1915-1967, 1968; short stories The Complete White Oxen, 1968, Dramatism and Development, 1972; Translator several books.; Contbr. to numerous mags. Recipient Dial award for distinguished service to Am. Letters, 1928; Guggenheim Meml. fellow, 1935; Am. Acad. Arts and Letters and Nat. Inst. Arts and Letters grant, 1946; Rockefeller Found, grant, 1966; Creative Arts award Brandeis U., 1967; Poet of Year award N.J. Assn. Tchrs. English, 1968; award Nat. Endowment for Arts, 1969; Horace Gregory award New Sch. Social Research, 1970; Ingram Merrill Found. award, 1970; gold medal for eminance in belles lettres and criticism Nat. Inst. Arts and Letters, 1975. Hon. fellow MLA; mem. Am. Acad. and Inst. Arts and Letters, Am. Acad. Arts and Scis. (emeritus, award for contbn. to humanities 1977, Nat. Medal for Lit. 1981). Home: RD 2 Box 293 Andover NJ 07821

BURKE, KEVIN CHARLES ANTONY, geologist; b. London, Nov. 13, 1929; U.S., 1973; s. Charles Henry and Kathleen (Daly) B.; m. Angela Marion Phipps, Jan. 23, 1960; children: Nicholas, Matthew, Jane. B.Sc., Univ. Coll., London, 1951, Ph.D., 1953. Lectr. U. Ghana, 1953-56; geologist Brit. Geol. Survey, 1956-61; head geology dept. U. West Indies, Kingston, Jamaica, 1961-65; prof. geology U. Ibadan, Nigeria, 1963-71, SUNY-Albany, 1973-83; prof. U. Houston, 1983—; dir. Lunar and Planetary Inst. NASA, 1983—; vis. prof. U. Toronto, 1971-73, Calif. Inst. Tech., 1976, U. Minn., 1977, U. Calgary, 1979; cons. in field. NSF grantee, 1976—. Fellow Geol. Soc. Am.; mem. Am. Geophys. Union, Nigerian Mining, Geol. and Metall. Soc. Research in plate tectonics. Office: Lunar and Planetary Inst NASA Road 1 Houston TX 77058 *There is much luck in a scientific career. I could not have known when I chose to become a geologist in 1948 that understanding of the problems I studied would be revolutionized by Plate Tectonics in 1965. To make the most of such an opportunity in geology a breadth of experience, both geographically and in different branches of geology, has proved a great asset.*

BURKE, LILLIAN WALKER, judge; b. Thomaston, Ga., Aug. 2, 1917; d. George P. and Ozella (Daviston) Walker; m. Ralph Livingston Burke, July 8, 1948; 1 son, R. Bruce. B.S., Ohio State U., 1947; LL.B., Cleve. State U., 1951, postgrad., 1963-64; grad., Nat. Coll. State Judiciary, U. Nev., 1974. Bar: Ohio bar 1951. Gen. practice law, Cleve., 1952-62, asst. atty. gen., Ohio, 1962-66; mem., vice chmn. Ohio Indsl. Commn., 1966-69; judge Cleve. Mcpl. Ct., 1969—, chief judge, 1981—; guest lectr. Heidelburg Coll., Tiffin, Ohio, 1971; cons. Bur. Higher Edn., HEW, 1972. Pres. Cleve. chpt. Nat. Council Negro Women, 1955-57, recipient certificate of award, 1969; sec. East dist. Family Service Assn., 1959-60; mem. council human relations Cleve. Citizens League, 1959—; mem. Gov.'s Com. on Status of Women, 1966-67; pres. Cleve. chpt. Jack and Jill of Am., Inc., 1960-61; v.p.-at-large Greater Cleve. Safety Council, 1969—; v.p. Downtown Restoration Soc.; pres., woman ward leader 24th Ward Republican Club, 1957-67; mem. Cuyahoga County Central Com., 1958-68; sec. Cuyahoga County Exec. Com., 1962-63; alt. del. Rep. Nat. Conv., Chgo., 1960; bd. dirs., chmn. minority div. Nat. Fedn. Rep. Women, 1966-68; life mem., past bd. dirs. Cleve. chpt. NAACP; bd. dirs. Greater Cleve. Neighborhood Centers Assn., Catholic Youth Counselling Services; trustee Ohio Commn. on Status of Women, Consumers League Ohio; bd. mgmt. Glenville YWCA. Recipient Achievement award Parkwood C.M.E. Ch., Cleve., 1968, Martin Luther King Citizens award, 1969, Outstanding Achievement award Ta-Wa-Si Scholarship Club, Cleve., 1969, Outstanding Service award Morning Star Grand chpt., Cleve., 1970, award of honor Cleve. Bus. League, 1970, Service award St. Paul A.M.E. Ch., Lima, Ohio, 1972, Woman of Achievement award Inner Club Council, Cleve., 1973; named Career Woman of Year Cleve. Women's Career Clubs, 1969. Mem. Am., Nat., Ohio, Cuyahoga County, Cleve. bar assns., Am. Judicature Soc., Bus. and Profl. Women's Club (Erieview chpt.), Phillis Wheatley Assn., Women Lawyers Assn. (hon. adviser), Am. Bridge Assn., Alpha Kappa Alpha. Episcopalian. Clubs: Women's City (Cleve.); Altrusa. Home: 829 East Blvd Cleveland OH 44108 Office: Room 13B Justice Center 1200 Ontario St Cleveland OH 44113

BURKE, LLOYD HUDSON, judge; b. Oakland, Calif., Apr. 1, 1916; s. James H. and Edna L. (Taylor) B.; m. Virginia Joan Kerchum, Apr. 27, 1941; children—Brian Hudson, Bruce Thomas. A.B., St. Mary's Coll., 1937; LL.B., U. Calif., 1940, J.D., 1972; LL.D., St. Mary's Coll. of Calif. Dep. dist. atty., Alameda County, Calif., 1940-53, sr. criminal trial dep., 1950-53, U.S. atty., 1953-58; U.S. dist. judge Northern Dist. Calif., 1958—. Served with U.S. Army, 1942-46; capt. Res., to 1951. Mem. Phi Delta Phi. Office: US Court House 450 Golden Gate Ave San Francisco CA 94102

BURKE, MARY THOMAS, teacher; b. Westport, County Mayo, Ireland, Nov. 28, 1930; d. Thomas T. and Anne T. (McGuire) B. B.A., Belmont (N.C.) Abbey Coll., 1958; M.A., Georgetown U., 1965; Ph.D., U. N.C., Chapel Hill, 1968. Tchr. elem. and jr. high schs., N.C., N.Y., 1952-58; guidance counselor, dir. guidance Our Lady of Mercy and Charlotte (N.C.) Cath. High Sch., 1960-64, tchr., 1958-64; instr. humanities Sacred Heart Coll., Belmont, 1963-65, asso. prof., acad. dean, 1967-69, chmn., asso. prof. edn. dept., 1969-70; asso. prof. human devel. and learning U. N.C., Charlotte, 1970-76, prof., 1976-79, prof., area head support services, 1979-81, chmn. human services dept., 1981—; chmn. State Adv. Council on Pupil Personnel Services, 1972-76. Bd. dirs. Mcklenburg chpt. Am. Cancer Soc. and state div., 1977-83, treas., 1983—; chairperson United Way, U. N.C., Charlotte, 1974; bd. dirs. St. Joseph Hosp., Asheville. Recipient Anti-Defamation award B'nai B'rith Women, 1978, Ray Thompson Human Relations award N.C. Assn. for Non-White Concerns, 1978, WBT Woman of Yr. award, 1979. Mem. N.C. Personnel and Guidance Assn. (exec. com. 1973—, editorial bd. jour. 1975-78, pres. Metrolina chpt. 1973-74, state pres.-elect 1980-81, pres. 1981-82, leadership award 1983), N.C. Guidance Assn. (program com. 1974—), Nat. Cath. Guidance Assn. (state rep. 1974-79), N.C. Assn. Religious and Value Issues (chairperson 1975-78), N.C. Assn. Counselors Educators and Suprs., Am. Personnel and Guidance Assn., Am. Counselor Educators and Suprs. Assn., Assn. Religious Values in Counseling, N.C. Assn. Group Work, N.C. Mental Health Assn., N.C. Sch. Counselors Assn. (Counselor Educator of Yr. award 1975), So. Assn. Counselor Educators and Suprs., Phi Delta Kappa., Delta Kappa Gamma. Office: Human Devel and Learning Dept Univ NC Charlotte NC 28223 *Life is a journey. Each moment is sacred. We need to live in the present and respond to the sacredness of the moment, always being sensitive to the needs of others, particularly those whom we serve. We must use power as a gift and not impose our values on others. The way we live and treat others is much more poignant than anything we may say.*

BURKE, REDMOND A(MBROSE), clergyman, librarian, educator; b. Missouri Valley, Iowa, Aug. 4, 1914; s. James Joseph and Susan Marie (Haffey) B. A.B., U. Ill., 1935, A.M., 1938; B.S. in Library Sci, Cath. U. Am., Washington, 1944; Ph.D., U. Chgo., 1948. Ordained priest Roman Catholic Ch.; assoc. prof. English, asst. librarian Dowling Coll., Des Moines, 1939-44; assoc. prof. library sci. and philosophy Rosary Coll., River Forest, Ill., 1944-51; dir. libraries De Paul U., Chgo., 1948-67; vis. prof. Cath. U. Am., 1962-63, acting dir. univ. press, 1967-70; assoc. prof. library sci. U. Wis.-Oshkosh, 1970-80, prof. library sci., 1980—, coordinator grad. studies, 1983—; Apptd. ednl. cons. on univ. libraries edn. br. U.S. Mil. Govt., in Germany, 1949; vis. prof. U. Ill., summers 1970, 71. Author: Great Books and Christian Democracy, 1948, A Survey of German University and Scholarly Libraries, 1949, German Librarianship From an American Angel, 1952, What is the Index, 1952; assoc. editor: Buecher und Zeitschriften ueber Erziehung and Verwandt Gebiete, 1945-50, 52, Catholic Booklist Annual, 1953-70; editor: Worship on Law Library Problems, 1953, Culture and Communication Through the Ages, 1953; Contbr. articles and revs. to profl. jours. Mem. edn. com. NCCJ, 1949-60; chmn. edn. com. Community Fund of Chgo., 1953-54; bd. dirs. Oshkosh Boys Club, 1980—; treas. Winnebago County Hist. Soc., 1982—. Fellow Royal Soc. Lit.; mem. Manuscript Soc. (dir., chmn. pub. relations com. 1957-65), Chgo. Assn. Law Libraries (pres. 1954-55), Cath. Lang. Tchrs. Assn. (pres. 1947-48), Bibliog. Soc. Ireland, ALA, AAUP, Am. Philos. Assn., Bibliog. socs. Am., London, Gutenberg Gesellschaft, Inst. Graphic Arts, Ill. Library Assn., Medieval Acad. Am., MLA, Ill. Cath. Library Assn. (pres. 1944-45, chmn. sect. 1957-61), Renaissance Soc., Winnebago County Hist. Soc. (treas. 1981—). Clubs: Century Assn., Groller (N.Y.C.); Arts, University (lit. com. 1967—), Caxton (Chgo.); Rotary (dir. 1980—, pres. 1983-84. Lodges: Rotary (dir. 1980—, pres. 1983-84). Collector pages of incunabular and illuminated manuscripts, Am. pvt. press books and fine printing. Home: 200 Merritt Ave Oshkosh WI 54901 Office: U of Wis Oshkosh WI 54901

BURKE, RICHARD FRANCIS XAVIER, computer mfg. co. exec.; b. Phila., Mar. 12, 1940; s. Edward Francis and Agnes Marie (Boylan) B.; m. Halina Monica Spiewak, Nov. 24, 1960; children—Richard Francis Xavier, Patrick Michael, Laura Ann. B.A., Coll. Holy Cross, 1961; B.B.A., U. Md., 1966; M.B.A., Rutgers U., 1969. Staff asst. W.R. Grace & Co., N.Y.C., 1966-68; staff asst. Hatco Group, Fords, N.J., 1969-70; treas. Raritan Valley Farms, Sommerville, N.J., 1968-69; asst. treas. Singer Co., N.Y.C., 1970-78; v.p., treas. Mgmt. Assistance Inc., N.Y.C., 1978—. Served with USN, 1961-66. Home: Mulberry Ln Colts Neck NJ 07722 Office: Mgmt Assistance Inc 560 Lexington Ave New York NY 10022

BURKE, RICHARD KITCHENS, lawyer, educator; b. Helena, Ark., Aug. 21, 1922; s. James Graham and Myrtie May (Kitchens) B.; m. Bonnie Beth Byler, Jan. 21, 1946; children—Charles, Bonnie Louise. Student, U. Va., 1939-40; B.A., U. Ark., 1942, LL.B., 1947; Ph.D. (Ford fellow), Vanderbilt U., 1957. Bar: Ark. bar 1947, Ariz. bar 1959, S.D. bar 1974. Partner firm Burke, Moore & Burke, Helena, 1947-52; asst. prof. polit. sci. U. Ariz., 1957-60; partner firm Robertson, Childers, Burke & Drachman, Tucson, 1960-67; prof. polit. sci. U. Southwestern La., 1967-69; U.S. atty. Dist. Ariz., Dept. Justice, 1969-72, dep. asst. atty. gen. U.S., Washington, 1972-73; prof. law U. S.D. Sch. Law, 1973—, dean, 1974-80; mem. Jud. Council S.D. Mem. Ariz. Republican State Com., 1963-67; Rep. congl. candidate So. Dist. Ariz., 1972; chmn. citizen's adv. com. Amphitheater Sch. Dist., Tucson, 1964-66. Served with USN, 1942-45, 53-54. Decorated Air medal. Mem. Am. Bar Assn., State Bar S.D., State Bar Ariz., Ark. Bar Assn., Am. Judicature Soc. Republican. Mem. Christian Ch. Club: Rotary (Vermillion, S.D.). Home: 1211 Valley View Vermillion SD 57069 Office: U SD Sch Law Vermillion SD 57069

BURKE, ROBERT EUGENE, history educator; b. Chico, Calif., July 22, 1921; s. Ralph Ambrose and Frieda (Rupp) B.; m. Helen Blom, Oct. 31, 1952 (dec. 1976); m. Edith Baras, 1978. A.B., Chico State Coll., 1946; M.A., U. Calif. at Berkeley, 1947, Ph.D., 1950. Dir. Bancroft Library research project, Eng., 1950-51; head manuscript div. Bancroft Library, U. Calif. at, Berkeley, 1951-56; asst. prof. history U. Hawaii, 1956-57; faculty U. Wash., Seattle, 1957—, prof. history, 1965—, chmn. dept., 1962-67; summer vis. prof. Columbia U., 1960, Stanford, 1968, U. Wyo., 1969, U. Oreg., 1971, Yugoslav-Am. Seminar, Novi Sad, 1965. Author: Olson's New Deal for California, 1953, (with J.D. Hicks and G.E. Mowry) The American Nation, 5th edit, 1971, The Federal Union, 5th edit, 1970, A History of American Democracy, 4th edit, 1970, (with Richard Lowitt) The New Era and the New Deal, 1920-1940, 1981; mng. editor: Pacific N.W. Quar.; gen. editor: Americana Library Series. Served with AUS, 1942-45; PTO. Mem. Am., So. hist. assns., Orgn. Am. Historians (exec. bd. 1967-70), Agrl. History Soc. (exec. bd. 1968-71), Western History Assn., Am. Assn. State and Local History (award of merit 1978). Home: 7336 19th Ave NE Seattle WA 98115

BURKE, RONALD G., banking association executive; b. Anderson, Ind., Mar. 16, 1932; s. Gary and Louise (Beckman) B.; m. Constance Burke. B.S., Ball State U.; M.B.A., Northwestern U. With Booz Allen & Hamilton-Booz Allen Applied Research Corp., Chgo., 1964-69; dir. personnel Computer Scis. Corp., Falls Church, Va., 1969-71; dir. personnel planning and devel. Fed. Res. Bd., Washington, 1971-75; dir. Fed. Res. Bank Ops., Fed. Res. Bd., Washington; pres., chief exec. officer Bank Adminstrn. Inst., Rolling Meadows, Ill., 1975—; dir. First Fed. Savs. and Loan, Chgo.; Mem. rev. panel productivity study grant NSF, 1977—. Dir. alumni bd. Northwestern U. Served with USAF, 1955-59. Mem. Chgo. Assn. Commerce and Industry, Nat. Banking Orgns., Beta Gamma Sigma.; mem. Phi Beta Kappa. Methodist. Clubs: Chgo. Exec., Meadow.

BURKE, RONALD RUFUS, oil company executive; b. Homedale, Idaho, Aug. 22, 1930; s. Rufus and Ella (Hoffman) B.; m. Donna Zell Willis, June 6, 1952; children: Frank, Nick, Richard, William, Matthew. B.S. in Geology, U. Wyo. Geophys. party chief Gen. Geophys. Co., 1952-58; geophys. supr. Ohio Oil Co., Benghazi, Libya, 1958-62, Brisbane, Australia, 1962-64; chief geophysicist Marathon Intenat. Oil Co., Findlay, Ohio, 1964-70; exploration mgr. Marathon Internat. Oil Co., Findlay, Ohio, 1970-77, v.p. prodn. exploration U.S. and Can., 1977—. Mem. high council Brisbane, Queensland, Australia Stake Mormon Ch., 1962-64, bishop Finlay, Ohio, Ward of Ft. Wayne, Ind. Stake, 1965-76, mem. Stake Presidency, Ft. Wayne, 1977-79, pres. Toledo, Ohio Stake, 1980—; charter mem. Republican Presdl. Task Force, Findlay, 1982-83; sustaining mem. Rep. Nat. Com., 1982-83; v.p. Put-Han-Sen council Boy Scouts Am., Findlay, 1983. Mem. Soc. Exploration Geophysicists, Am. Assn. Petroleum Geologists, Am. Petroleum Inst. (eexploration affairs com.), Tex. Mid Continent Oil and Gas Assn. Club: Genghazi Golf (Libya) (pres. 1959-60). Home: 461 Westchester Dr Finlay OH 45840 Office: Marathon Oil Co 539 S Main St Findlay OH 45840

BURKE, THOMAS FRANCIS, communication company executive; b. Newton, Mass., Jan. 27, 1929; s. Thomas James and Mary Ann (McFarland) B.; m. Mary E. Sughrue, Nov. 12, 1955; children: Thomas J., Robert F., Maureen E., Daniel R., Paul J., Sheila Rose,

John P. A.B. magna cum laudein Econs., Boston Coll., 1951, M.A. in Econs., 1959; cert. with honors in acctg., Bentley Coll. Acctg. and Fin., 1954. Asst. chief acct. Hollingsworth & Whitney Co., Boston, 1951-54; asst. controller CBS Electronics, Danvers, Mass., 1954-61; asst. comptroller M/A-Com, Inc., Burlington, Mass., 1961-64, comptroller, 1964—, v.p. fin. and treas., 1978—, exec. v.p. adminstrn. and fin., 1982—, also dir., 1983—. Author: periodicals Budgetary Control, 1959, Fin. Planning, 1961. Mem. Town Com. re Revaluation, Stoneham, Mass., 1969, St. Vincent de Paul Soc., Stoneham, 1968; mem. fin. com., Andover, Mass., 1973. Mem. Fin. Execs. Inst., Nat. Assn. Accts., Treasurers Assn. Roman Catholic. Lodge: K.C. Home: 75 Bridle Path North Andover MA 01845 Office: M/A-Com Inc 7 New England Exec Park Burlington MA 01830

BURKE, VINCENT C., JR., lawyer; b. Louisville, Ky., July 29, 1922; s. Vincent and Julia (Burns) B.; m. Celine M. Gallagher, May 4, 1946; children: Louise Burke Whalen, Vincent C., Mary Virginia Burke Chambers, Julia Marie, Thomas Michael, Celine Marie. B.S., Georgetown U., 1943, LL.B., 1950; grad., Sch. Banking, Rutgers U., 1961. Bar: D.C. bar 1951. Dep. clk. U.S. Dist. Ct., Washington, 1947-49; law clk., 1949-51, asst. U.S. atty., Washington, 1951-53, individual practice law, 1953-54; asst. trust officer Riggs Nat. Bank, Washington, 1954-58, trust officer, 1959-63, v.p., trust officer, 1964-66, sr. v.p., 1966-70, exec. v.p., 1971-73, pres., chief adminstrv. officer, dir., 1973-76, chmn. bd., chief exec. officer, dir., 1976-83; dir. Acacia Mutual Life Ins. Co., H St. Bldg. Corp., Riggs Nat. Bank, Potomac Electric Power Co., Chesapeake and Potomac Telephone Co., Cafritz Cos., Fed. Riggs Nat. Corp.; adj. prof. law Georgetown U., 1964-69; mem. Fed. Res. Adv. Council. Bd. dirs. Mcpl. Research Bur.; gen. chmn. Heart Assn. D.C.; mem. adv. bd. Center for Banking Edn. Howard U.; gen. campaign United Givers Fund, 1974; bd. dirs. Fed. City Council, Heroes, Inc., Met. Washington Bd. Trade, D.C. chpt. ARC; trustee George Washington U.; bd. visitors Georgetown U. Sch. Bus. Adminstrn.; gen. chmn. United Negro Coll. Fund, 1978; bd. dirs. Community Found. Greater Washington, Tax Found., Inc., NCCJ; gen. chmn., 1980, Fund Nat. Symphony Orch.; chmn. fund drive Providence Hosp., 1980; trustee Nat. Jewish Hosp. and Research Center, Denver; chmn. Washington Area, Washington-Balt. Regional Assn. Served with USN, 1943-46. Mem. Supreme Ct. Hist. Soc. (exec. com., treas.), Nat. Alliance Businessmen, Navy League, Washington Clearing House. Clubs: Barrister, Alfalfa, Burning Tree Columbia Country, Met., Nat. Lawyers, Rotary (past dir.), Soc. Sons St. Patrick, 1925 F St. Home: 4300 Carriage Ct Kensington MD 20795 Office: Steptoe & Johnson Chartered 1250 Connecticut Ave NW Washington DC 20036

BURKE, WILLIAM HAROLD, financial executive; b. N.Y.C., June 12, 1919; s. Harold Joseph and Elizabeth Elvina (Crotty) B.; m. Margaret P. McNamara, Oct. 28, 1944; children: Michael C., Margaret P., Mary E. B.A., Fordham U., 1939. Treas. Am. Tobacco Co.; Former treas. James B. Beam Distilling Co., Master Lock Co., Wilson Jones Co., Sunshine Biscuits, Inc., Acushnet Co., Swingline Inc., Andrew Jergens Co., MCM Products, Inc., Duffy-Mott Co., Inc.; dep. treas. Am. Brands, Inc., N.Y.C.; dir. Am. Tobacco Co. of the Orient. Mem. Borough council Florham Park, N.J., 1955-60; mem. twp. com., Scotch Plains, N.J., 1966. Served with USN, World War II; Korea. Mem. Corporate Transfer Agts. Assn. Republican. Roman Catholic. Home: 7 Clydesdale Rd Scotch Plains NJ 07076 Office: 245 Park Ave New York NY 10167

BURKE, WILLIAM JAMES, chemist, educator, consultant; b. Lowellville, Ohio, May 24, 1912; s. Sylvester L. and M. Catherine (Saltzman) B.; m. Katharine M. King, June 21, 1940; children: Mary Katharine (Mrs. Frank Noyes), Susan E. (Mrs. Victor Burke), Thomas W.J., D. Kevin. A.B., Ohio U., Athens, 1934; Ph.D., Ohio State U., 1937. Research chemist central chem. dept. E.I. duPont de Nemours & Co., Henry Clay, Del., 1937-46; asso. prof. Ohio U., Athens, 1946-47, U. Utah, 1947-50, dept. head, 1949-62, prof., 1950-62; v.p. Ariz. State U., Tempe, 1962-76, prof. chemistry, 1962—, dean Grad. Coll., 1963-76; cons. U.S. Army, 1956-62, 72-75, Monsanto Co., 1961-70; Mem. ICA team to survey higher edn. in Ethiopia U.S. State Dept., 1959-60; past pres. Western Assn. Grad. Schs; mem. exec. com. Nat. Assn. State Univs. and Land Grant Colls., 1969-71; mem. Grad. Record Exam. Bd., 1972-74; chmn. editorial bd. Grad. Programs and Admissions Manual; generalist cons. Nat. Council Archtl. Registration Bd., 1969-72; mem. Nat. Archtl. Accrediting Bd., 1973-78. Contbr. articles to profl. jours. Past pres., dir. Catholic Charities Salt Lake City. Fellow AAAS; mem. Am. Chem. Soc. (vis. asso. com. on profl. tng. 1959—, councilor for Central Ariz. sect. 1967-70), Am. Rock Art Research Assn., Midwest Conf. on Grad. Study and Research (past chmn.), Phi Beta Kappa, Sigma Xi, Phi Lambda Upsilon, Gamma Alpha, Phi Kappa Phi (pres. Ariz. State U. chpt. 1977-78). Patentee in field. Home: 501 Bishop Dr Tempe AZ 85282

BURKE, WILLIAM TEMPLE, JR., lawyer; b. San Antonio, Oct. 30, 1935; s. William Temple and Adelaide H. (Raba) T.; m. Mary Sue Johnson, June 8, 1957; children: William Patrick, Michael Edmond, Karen Elizabeth. B.B.A., St. Mary's U., San Antonio, J.D., 1961. Bar: Tex. Practice law, Dallas; dir. Phil Ross Realtors, Inc., Saar Personnel Service, Inc. Pres., founder Dallas Assn. KC, 1968-69; v.p., co-founder Dallas KC Credit Union, 1966-69; grand knight, trustee Dallas Council 799 KC, 1964-69; dist. exemplar 4th degree KC, 1968—; pres., dir. Dallas County Small Bus. Devel. Center, 1965-66; v.p. Dallas County Hist. Survey Com., 1966; pres. Dallas Mil. Govt. Assn., 1962-63; pres. men's club St. Patrick's Parish Roman Catholic Ch., 1963, prin. jr. high sch. Christian devel. program, 1970, chmn. scout troop com., 1976-78, chmn. fin. com., 1976-77, mem. bldg. com., 1978—, chmn. bd. consultors, 1978-81; bd. dirs. Dallas County War on Poverty, 1965-66. Served to 1st lt. AUS, 1958-60; capt. Res. ret.; ret.). Recipient Man of Yr. award, 1969-70. Mem. ABA, Tex. Bar Assn., Dallas Bar Assn. (chmn. bankruptcy and comml. law sect. 1977-78), Phi Delta Phi (magister 1960-61), Tau Delta Sigma (pres. 1956). Clubs: Seroco-Empire Toastmasters (past pres.), Dallas Optimist (past v.p., President's award 1968), Exchange, Internat. Order Alhambra. Home: 9751 Larchcrest St Dallas TX 75238 Office: Suite 2000 One Main Pl Dallas TX 75250

BURKE, WYATT WARNER, psychology educator, consultant; b. Dekalb County, Ala., May 12, 1935; s. Alfred Vernard and Ruby Inez (Gilbert) B.; m. Roberta Joann Luchetti, Oct. 5, 1974; children: Donovan Warner, Courtney Robyn, Warner Brian. B.A., Furman U., 1957; M.A., U. Tex.-Austin, 1961, Ph.D., 1963. Diplomate: Am. Bd. Profl. Psychology. Asst. prof. psychology U. Richmond (Va.), 1963-66; dir. NTL Inst., Arlington, Va., 1966-74; sole practice cons. in psychology, Washington, 1974-76; prof., chmn. dept. mgmt. Clark U., Worcester, Mass., 1976-79; prof. psychology and edn. Tchrs. Coll., Columbia U., N.Y.C., 1979—; chmn. Forum Cons. Group, Boston and N.Y.C., 1983—. Author: (with others) Techniques of Organizational Change, 1981, (with M. Plovnick and R. Fry) Organization Development: Cases, Exercises and Readings, 1982, Organization Development: Principles and Practices, 1982; editor: The Cutting Edge: Current Theory and Practice in Organization Development, 1978, Organizational Dynamics Quar., 1979—. Served to 1st lt. U.S. Army, 1958-60. Mem. Am. Psychol. Assn., Acad. Mgmt. (bd. govs. 1981-83, chmn. orgn. devel. div. 1980-81), ASTD. Episcopalian. Clubs: Pelham County (N.Y.); Imperial Yacht (New Rochelle, N.Y.). Home: 235 Pelhamdale Ave Pelham NY 10803 Office: Tchrs Coll Coumbia U PO Box 24 New York NY 10027

BURKE, YVONNE WATSON BRATHWAITE (MRS. WILLIAM A. BURKE), lawyer; b. Los Angeles, Oct. 5, 1932; d. James A. and Lola (Moore) Watson; m. William A. Burke, June 14, 1972; 1 dau., Autumn Roxanne. A.A., U. Calif., 1951; B.A., UCLA, 1953; J.D., U. So. Calif., 1956. Bar: Calif. bar 1956. Mem. Calif. Assembly, 1966-72, chmn. urban devel. and housing com., 1971, 72; mem. 93d Congress from 37th Dist. Calif., 94th-95th Congresses from 28th Dist. Calif., House Appropriations Com.; chmn. Congl. Black Caucus, 1976; now counsel firm Fine, Perzik & Friedman, Los Angeles; Dep. corp. commr., hearing officer Police Commn., 1964-66; atty., staff McCone Commn. (investigation Watts riot), 1965; mem. Los Angeles County Bd. Suprs., 1979-80. Mem. Women's Democratic Forum; vice chmn. 1984 U.S. Olympics Organizing Com., Dem. Charter Commn.; Bd. dirs. or bd. advisers numerous orgns. including U. Calif. at Los Angeles Found., Nat. Athletic Health Inst., United Negro Coll. Fund. Recipient Profl. Achievement award U. Calif. at Los Angeles, 1974; named one of 200 Future Leaders Time mag., 1974; recipient Achievement awards C.M.E. Chs., Nat. Assn. Black Women Attys., Nat. Assn. Negro Bus. and Profl. Women's Clubs; numerous other awards, citations.; Fellow Inst. Politics John F. Kennedy Sch. Govt. Harvard, 1971-72; Chubb fellow Yale, 1972. Office: Fine Perzik & Friedman Suite 1900 10960 Wilshire Blvd Los Angeles CA 90024 *

BURKER, KENNETH NEIL, pharmacy administration educator; b. Spring Valley, Ohio, Mar. 25, 1937; s. Kenneth Clyde and Marjorie Dorothy (Smith) Barker; m. Louise Arlene Ferguson, Aug. 17, 1957; children: Bradford Neil, Linda Louise, Douglas Adams. B.S., U. Fla., 1959, M.S., 1961; Ph.D., U. Miss., 1971. Mgr. sterile products Pharmacy Service, U. Ark. Med. Center-Little Rock, 1961-62, project dir. drug systems research, 1962-66; projects coordinator Sch. Pharmacy, U. Miss., 1966-70; dir. adminstrv. research U.S. Pharmacopeia, 1970-72; assoc. prof. pharmacy adminstrn., assoc. dir. Research Inst. Sch. Pharmacy, N.E. La. U., 1972-75; now alumni prof., head dept. pharmacy care systems Sch. Pharmacy, Auburn U., Ala. Co-inventor unit dose dispensing concept for hosps., 1959. Recipient Harvey A.K. Whitney award, 1981, commendation HEW, 1974. Mem. Am. Pharm. Assn., Acad. Pharm. Scis., Am. Soc. Hosp. Pharmacists (research award 1973), Am. Assn. Colls. Pharmacy, Ala. Pharm. Assn., Ala. Soc. Hosp. Pharmacists, Rho Chi. Presbyterian. Home: 412 Blake St Auburn AL 38630 Office: Auburn Univ Auburn AL 36849

BURKERT, ROBERT RANDALL, artist; b. Racine, Wis., Aug. 20, 1930; s. Clarence George and Margaret Ann (Sorenson) B.; m. Nancy Ekholm, Aug. 29, 1953; children: Claire, Rand. B.S., U. Wis., 1952, M.S., 1955. Instr. art Denison U., 1955-56; prof. drawing, printmaking, painting U. Wis., Milw., 1956—. One man shows include, Bradley Galleries, Milw., 1972, 73, 75, 77, 79, 82, Rubiner Galleries, 1973, 75, 78, 81, 83, others, group shows include, Pratt Graphic Center, 1972, U.S. Cultural Center, Tel Aviv, 1973, Milw. Art Center, 1975; represented in permanent collections, Tate Gallery, London, Boston Mus. Fine Arts, Met. Mus. Art, Fogg Mus.; wall mural Road to the Country, 1972; work reproduced in Artists Proof, 1971; Work reproduced in Compleat Printmaker, 1973, Art of The Print, 1976. Trustee Milw. Art Mus. Recipient numerous awards for graphics; U. Wis. research grantee, 1969, 71, 73, 75, 77; Knapp grantee for ednl. research, 1973; Wis. Arts grantee, 1977; Fromkin grantee, 1980. Mem. Boston Printmakers. Home: 3228 N Marietta Ave Milwaukee WI 53211 Office: Art Dept Sch Fine Arts U Wis-Milw Milwaukee WI 53211

BURKET, GEORGE EDWARD, JR., family physician; b. Kingman, Kans., Dec. 10, 1912; s. George Edward and Jessie May (Talbert) B.; m. Mary Elizabeth Wallace, Nov. 12, 1938; children: George Edward III, Carol Sue, Elizabeth Christine. Student, Wichita State U., 1930-33; M.D., U. Kans., 1937. Diplomate: Am. Bd. Family Practice (pres. 1976-78). Intern Santa Barbara (Calif.) Gen. Hosp., 1937-38, resident, 1938-39; grad. asst. in surgery Mass. Gen. Hosp., Boston, 1956-57; practice medicine, Kingman, 1939-73; preceptor in medicine U. Kans. Med. Sch., 1950-73, asso. prof., 1973-78, clin. prof., 1978—. Contbr. articles to profl. jours. Mem. Kingman Bd. Edn., 1946-58; mem. Kans. State Bd. Health, 1960-66. Mem. Kans. Med. Soc. (pres. 1966-67), Am. Acad. Family Physicians (pres. 1967-68, John Walsh Founders award 1979), inst. Medicine, AMA, Assn. Am. Med. Colls., Soc. Tchrs. Family Medicine, Alpha Omega Alpha. Republican. Episcopalian. Clubs: Masons, Shriners, Garden of Gods (Colorado Springs, Colo.); Wichita Country, Wichita. Home: Spring Lake Route 1 Kingman KS 67068 Office: Rainbow Blvd at 39th St Kansas City KS 66103

BURKET, HARRIET (MRS. FRANCIS B. TAUSSIG), editor; b. Findlay, Ohio; d. John Franklin and Betty (Hoege) B.; m. Maurice C. Reinecke, Sept. 24, 1935 (div. Apr. 1952); 1 dau., Rosalind; m. Francis Brewster Taussig, Oct. 8, 1960 (dec. May 1970). A.B., Vassar Coll., 1931. Asso. editor Arts and Decoration, 1933-35, Creative Design, 1935-37; asso. editor House and Garden, 1937-44, home furnishings mdse. editor, 1952-55, exec. editor, 1955-58, editor-in-chief, 1958-70; partner Editors Inc., 1970—; interior design editor Woman's Home Companion, 1944-52. Editor: House & Garden's Complete Guide to Interior Decorating, 7th edit, 1970, House & Garden's Complete Guide to Creative Entertaining, 1971. Mem. Internat. Fashion Group (bd. govs. 1953-55, v.p. 1958-59), Nat. Home Fashions League, Am. Inst. Interior Designers, Internat. Platform Assn. Clubs: Field (Sarasota, Fla.); Decorators, Cosmopolitan, Vassar, Harvard. Home: 14 Sutton Pl S New York City NY 10022

BURKET, RICHARD EDWARD, agriprocessing executive; b. Sandusky, Ohio, Apr. 25, 1928; s. Firm C. and Marie (Bock) B.; m. Carolyn Anne McMillen, Feb. 22, 1951 (div. 1979); children: Leslie, Buffie, Lynn Murphy Burket. B.A., Oberlin Coll., 1950. Tech. sales mgr. Rhoades Equipment Co., Ft. Wayne, Ind., 1954-55; with Chemurgy div. Central Soya Co., Ft. Wayne, Ind., 1955-69, dir. mktg., Chgo., 1966-69; v.p. protein specialties Archer Daniel Midland Co., Decatur, Ill., 1969-74, v.p., asst. to pres., 1974-80, v.p., asst. to chmn., Decatur, 1980—. Bd. dirs. Decatur Area Arts Council, 1972—, Macon County United Way, 1974-77, Boys Club, Decatur, 1979—, Decatur Metro C. of C., 1982—. Served to 1st lt. U.S. Army, 1974-77. Mem. Sales and Mktg. Execs., Inst. Food Technologists, Am. Mgmt. Assn., Soy Protein Council (chmn. 1974-76). Clubs: Decatur, Decatur Country. Home: Route 1 Box 84A Blue Mound IL 62513 Office: Archer Daniels Midland Co 4666 Faries Pkwy Decatur IL 62525

BURKETT, WILLIAM ANDREW, banker; b. nr. Herman, Nebr., July 1, 1913; s. William H. and Mary (Dill) B.; m. Juliet Ruth Johnson, Oct. 5, 1940; children—Juliet Ann (Mrs. Rodman L. Hooker, Jr.), Katherine C. (Mrs. Jeffrey H. Congdon), William Cleveland. Student, U. Nebr., 1931-32, Creighton U. Law Sch., 1932-33; LL.B., U. Omaha, 1936. Sr. spl. agt., intelligence unit Treasury Dept., 1945-50; exec. v.p. Calif. Employers Assn. Group, Sacramento, 1950-53; dir. Calif. Dept. Employment, 1953-55; supt. banks, chmn. Dept. Investments Calif., 1955-59; dir. Liquidation Yokohama Specie Bank; also Sumitomo Bank, San Francisco, 1955-59; cons. Western Bancorp, San Francisco, 1959-61; chmn. bd., pres. Security Nat. Bank Monterey County, Monterey-Carmel, Calif., 1961-66, Burkett Land Co., Monterey, 1966—; cons. United Calif. Bank, Los Angeles, 1966—; chmn. bd. Securities Properties Corp., Monterey. Author: Mount Rushmore National Memorial's History of America, 1776-1904, 1971. Dir. banking and investments, cabinet gov., Calif., 1953-59; dir. Calif. Emergency Manpower Commn., 1953-55; chmn. Gov. Calif. Com. Refugee Relief, 1953-55; mem. Calif. Securities Commn., 1955-59; mem. financial bd. Pine Manor Jr. Coll., Chestnut Hill, Mass., 1967—; mem Monterey County Hist. Commn.; bd. dirs. Monterey Symphony Assn.; chmn. bd. trustees Nat. Hist. Found.; trustee Monterey Mus. Art, Bishop Kip Sch., Carmel Valley, Calif.; mem. adv. bd. Robert Louis Stevenson Sch., Pebble Beach, Calif., 1971—; candidate for gov. Calif., 1978. Served as officer USCGR, 1943-45. Mem. Am., Calif., Ind. bankers assns., Nat. Assn. Supts. State Banks (pres. 1958-59), Monterey History and Art Assn., Mt. Rushmore Nat. Meml. Soc. (life mem., trustee), Amvets (dept. comdr. Calif. 1947, nat. vice comdr. 1948), Soc. Calif. Pioneers. Episcopalian. Clubs: Monterey Peninsula Golf and Country, Beach and Tennis, Stillwater Yacht (Pebble Beach); Carmel Valley Golf and Tennis; Commonwealth, Rotary (San Francisco); Sutter Lawn (Sacramento). Home: PO Box 726 Pebble Beach CA 93953 Office: Viscaino Rd Pebble Beach CA 93953

BURKHARDT, HANS GUSTAV, artist; b. Basel, Switzerland, Dec. 20, 1904; came to U.S., 1924, naturalized, 1930; s. Gustav and Anna (Schmidt) B.; m. Louise Thile, Mar. 25, 1929 (div. 1938); 1 dau., Elsa Burkhardt Brown; m. Thordis Olga Westhassel, June 18, 1955. Student, Cooper Union, 1924-25, Grand Central Sch. Art, N.Y.C., 1928-29; pvt. student, with Gorky, 1930-37. Asso. prof. art Long Beach State U., 1959; prof. art U. So. Calif., 1959-60; parttime instr. U. Calif. at, Los Angeles, 1960-63, asso. prof., Northridge, 1963-73, Chouinard Art Inst., 1962—; prof. emeritus Calif. State U., Northridge. Collaborator: (with Ray Bradbury) Man Dead? Then God is Slain, prints, 1977; (with William Everson) prints Rattlesnake August, 1978, (with Ray Bradbury) The Kiss, 1983; One-man exhbns. include, Los Angeles County Mus., Oreg. State U., Museo de Bellas Artex, Gualalajara, Mexico, Occidental Coll., Inst. de Allende, San Miguel de Allende, Mexico, Mt. St. Mary Coll., Palos Verdes Community Art Assn., Pasadena Art Mus., Valley Jr. Coll., Van Nuys, Santa Monica Pub. Library, Glendale Pub. Library, Whittier Art Assn., U. So. Calif., Santa Barbara Mus. Art, Palace Legion of Honor, Los Angeles Municipal Art Gallery, La Jolla Art Center, Pierce Coll., Los Angeles, Freie Schule, Basel, Switzerland, San Fernando Valley State Coll., Bay City Jewish Community Center, Laguna Beach Mus. Art, San Diego Art Inst. (forty year retrospective), ACA-American Masters Gallery, Los Angeles, San Diego Fine Arts Gallery, Michael Smith Gallery, Los Angeles, Long Beach Mus. Art (retrospective 1950-72), Calif. State U., Northridge, 1973, 75, Santa Barbara Mus. Art, Pasquale Ianetti, San Francisco, 1977, Palm Springs Desert Mus., 1979, Robert Schoelkopf Gallery, N.Y.C., Alana Gallery, Oslo, Norway, 1978, 80, C.H. Wenger Gallery, Basel, 1981, Jack Rutberg Fine Arts, Los Angeles, 1982, 83, 84, group shows, Los Angeles Inst. Contemporary Art, San Francisco Mus. Art, numerous others; represented in permanent collections, Mus. Modern Art Stockholm, Oakland Mus., Palm Springs Desert Mus., Corcoran Gallery, Washington, Guggenheim Mus., N.Y.C., St. Louis Mus. Art, Tamarin Inst., U. N.Mex., Los County Art Mus., Pasadena Art Mus., Santa Barbara Mus. Art, Long Beach Art Mus., La Jolla Art Mus., San Diego Fine Art Center, Jocelyn Art Center, Lincoln, Nebr., Kunstmuseum, Basel, Switzerland, Ahmanson collection, Hirshhorn Mus. Recipient purchase prize in oil Los Angeles County Mus., 1946, cash awards, 1954, 57; award Terry Art Inst., Miami, Fla., 1951; purchase prize Santa Barbara Mus. Art, 1957; award Calif. Watercolor Soc., 1961; purchase oil Los Angeles All-City Show, 1958,61; purchase watercolor, 1961, Long Beach Mus., Pasadena Art Mus., Los Angeles County Mus., Santa Barbara Mus. Art, La Jolla Art Center, Emily and Joe Lowe Meml.; Outstanding Tchrs. award Calif. State U., Northridge, 1973. Mem. Santa Barbara Mus. Art, Los Angeles Art Assn., Long Beach Art Mus., Kappa Pi, Phi Kappa Phi (hon.). Address: 1914 Jewett Dr Los Angeles CA 90046 *Always to be true to myself. To give to the best of my ability in all my endeavors. To let each person choose his own path and destiny, but to help clarify goals and methods where there is a need. To respect the endeavors of others.*

BURKHARDT, LAWRENCE, III, naval officer; b. Camden, N.J., Nov. 8, 1932; s. Lawrence and Elizabeth Hammell (Bartolett) B.; m. Barbara Jean Horan; children: Laurie Jean, William Alan, Beth Ann. B.S. in Engring, U.S. Naval Acad., 1954. Commd. ensign U.S. Navy, 1954, advanced through grades to rear adm., 1978; div. officer USS Point Cruz, 1954-55; communications officer USS Trigger, 1955-57; navigator USS Nautilus, 1958-61; engr. officer USS Pollack, 1962-64; with Div. Naval Reactors, U.S. AEC, 1964-66; exec. officer USS Benjamin Franklin (Blue), 1967-69; comdg. officer USS Gato, 1969-71; exec. officer USS Long Beach, 1971-73; personnel mgr. submarine nuclear power, 1973-76; comdr. Submarine Squadron Four, 1976-77; chief of staff Submarine Force, Atlantic Fleet, 1977-78; dir. Attack Submarine Div. OPNAV, 1978-80; asst. dep. CNO Submarine Warfare, Washington, 1980-81; comdr. Submarine Group Five, 1981-83; asst. dep. to Chief Naval Ops. for manpower, personnel and tng., Washington, 1983—. Decorated Legion of Merit, Bronze Star, Meritorious Service medal, Navy Commendation medal. Republican. Home: Quarters R Washington Navy Yard Washington DC 20374

BURKHARDT, RICHARD WELLINGTON, historian, educator; b. Newton, Mass., May 18, 1918; s. Edgar and Ruth (Wellington) B.; m. Dorothy Josephine Johnson, June 18, 1941; children: Jon Edgar, Richard W., Claire Elizabeth. A.B., Knox Coll., 1939; A.M., Harvard U., 1940, A.M.T., 1942, Ed.D., 1950. Tchr. Lenox (Mass.) Sch., 1941, Tulsa Central High Sch., 1941-44, Syracuse U., 1945-52; dean Ball State U., Muncie, Ind., 1952-62, v.p., dean of faculty, 1962-78, acting pres., 1978-79, provost, dean faculties, 1979-80, Univ. Disting. Service prof. history, 1980—; v.p. Coop. Ednl. Research Lab., 1966. Author: (with Ann McGuinness) Elementary Social Studies Series, 1954, (with Lawhead and Bell) Introduction to College; Contbr. articles to profl. jours. Mem. Ind. Commn. on Aged and Aging, 1958-66, Ind. Scholarship Commn., 1965-70; nursing rev. com. HEW, 1966-71; mem. Gov.'s Commn. on Med. Edn., 1969; vice chmn. Acad. Affairs Conf. Midwestern Univs., 1971-72, chmn., 1972-73; Vice pres. bd. dirs. Muncie YMCA, 1959-65; bd. dirs. United Fund Delaware County, 1968-71; chmn. evaluation bd. Nat. Commn. on Accreditation Tchr. Edn., 1972-75; chmn. bd. dirs. Ind. Higher Edn. Telecommunications System, 1974-77. Recipient Distinguished Alumni award Knox Coll., 1974. Mem. No. Central Assn. Acad. Deans (pres. 1965), North Central Assn. (chmn. commn. on research and service 1966-68, dir. 1964-75, pres. assn. 1973-74), Ind. Congress Parents and Tchrs. (exec. bd. 1963-66), Phi Beta Kappa, Phi Delta Kappa, Phi Gamma Delta. Episcopalian (vestryman, mem. Indpls. Diocesan Council 1965-66). Lodge: Rotary (pres. 1957-58). Home: 1312 N Woodridge Ave Muncie IN 47304

BURKHART, CHARLES BARCLAY, advertising executive; b. Atchison, Kans., May 18, 1914; s. Charles Bert and Claudene (Barclay) B.; m. Elinor Karr, Apr. 19, 1936; children: Sherry (Mrs. Peter C. John), Janette (Mrs. W. Scott Miller). Grad., Ft. Scott Jr. Coll., 1932. Pres. Stalcup, Inc., Kansas City, Mo., 1945-54, Cream City Outdoor Advt. Co., Milw., 1954-58, Naegele Outdoor Advt. Co., 1958-62, Outdoor Advt. Assn. Am., Chgo., 1962-64; chmn. bd. Burkhart Advt., Inc., South Bend, Ind., 1964—; pres. Barday Corp., 1970—; former mem. advt. com. U.S. Dept. Commerce; past dir. Am. Fedn. Advt., Advt. Council Am., Traffic Audit Bur. N.Y., Nat. Sign Assn.; past chmn. Notre Dame Outdoor Advt. Assn. Am. Found. Mem. at large nat. council Boy Scouts Am.; Chmn. founding bd. govs. Inst. Outdoor Advt.; bd. dirs., exec. com. Central Outdoor Markets. Mem. Outdoor Advt. Assn. Am. (dir., recipient Myles Standish award), Outdoor Advt. Assn. Ind. (dir.), Transit Advt. Assn. (past dir.), Young Presidents Orgn., South Bend-Mishawaka C. of C. (dir.). Clubs: South Bend Country, Summit, University (South Bend); Wisconsin (Milw.); (Chicago Athletic Assn.). Home: 55721 Country Club Rd South Bend IN 46615 Office: 1247 Mishawaka Ave South Bend IN 46615

BURKHART, CRAIG GARRETT, dermatologist; b. Toledo, Ohio, Apr. 15, 1951; s. Garrett Giles B. and Mary Katherine (Egarius) Burkhardt; m. Anna Kristiina Jutila, Apr. 12, 1975; children: Kristiina Maria, Craig Nathaniel, Heidi Rebecca. B.A., U. Pa., 1972; M.D., Med. Coll. Ohio, 1975; M.Sc. Ed., U. Toledo, 1983. Diplomate: Am. Bd. Dermatology. Intern, resident, fellow (U. Mich. Hosps.), 1976-79, Practice medicine, specializing in dermatology;, 1979—. Editor: Jour. Dermatology and Allergy, 1980—; editorial bd.: Jour. Current Adolescent Medicine, 1980—; editorial adv. bd.: Ohio State Med. Jour., 1982—; contbr. articles to profl. jours. Mem. Toledo Zoo, Toledo Mus. Art. Mem. AMA, Acad. Dermatology, Assn. Profs. Dermatology, Ohio State Med. Assn., Mich. Dermatologic Assn., Toledo Acad. Medicine, Med. Coll. Ohio Alumni Assn., Phi Beta Kappa Grad. Assn. Home: 2241 Orchard Rd Toledo OH 43606 Office: 3939 Monroe St Suite 108 Toledo OH 43606

BURKHOLDER, DONALD LYMAN, mathematician, educator; b. Octavia, Nebr., Jan. 19, 1927; s. Elmer and Susie (Rothrock) B.; m. Jean Annette Fox, June 17, 1950; children—Kathleen, Peter, William. B.A., Earlham Coll., 1950; M.S., U. Wis., 1953; Ph.D., U. N.C., 1955. Asst. prof. U. Ill. at Urbana, 1955-60, asso. prof., 1960-64, prof. math., 1964—; prof. Center for Advanced Study, 1978—; sabbatical leaves U. Calif. at Berkeley, 1961-62, Westfield Coll., U. London, 1969-70; vis. prof. Rutgers U., 1972-73; research Stanford U., 1961, Hebrew U., 1969, Mittag-Leffler Inst., Sweden, 1971, 82, U. Paris, 1975. Editor: Annals Math. Statistics, 1964-67. Fellow Inst. Math. Statistics (Wald lectr. 1971, pres. 1975-76); mem. Am. Math. Soc. (editor Trans. 1983—), London Math. Soc. Research in probability theory and its applications to other branches of analysis. Home: 506 W Oregon St Urbana IL 61801

BURKHOLDER, PETER MILLER, physician, educator; b. Cambridge, Mass., May 7, 1933; s. Paul Rufus and Lillian Maud (Miller) B.; m. Barbara Beers, June 3, 1956; children: Kristen Ryner, Lisanne Ryner. B.S., Yale U., 1955; M.D., Cornell U., N.Y.C., 1959. Intern pathology N.Y. Hosp.-Cornell Med. Ctr., 1959-60; NIH trainee in pathology Cornell U., 1960-63, instr., 1963-64, asst. prof., 1964-65, Duke U., 1965-69, asso. prof., 1969-70, U. Wis.-Madison, 1970-72, acting chmn. dept. pathology, 1971-72, prof., 1972-79, chmn. dept. pathology, 1972-74; dir. Kidney Disease Inst., N.Y. State Dept. Health, 1979-80, dep. dir. div. labs. and research, 1980-81, dir. Ctr. Lab. Scis., 1981-82; chief of staff VA Med. Ctr., Ann Arbor, Mich., 1982—; prof. pathology U. Mich., Ann Arbor, 1982—; cons. pathologist Nat. Nephrotic Syndrome Therapeutic Study. Author: Atlas of Human Glomerular Pathology, 1974; contbg. author: Structural Basis of Renal Diseases, 1968, Pathobiology Annual, 1971, Tissue Typing and Transplantation, 1973, Glomerulonephritis Morphology Natural History and Treatment, 1973, Cornell Seminars in Nephrology, 1975; Editorial bd.: Kidney Internat, 1970-76, Lab. Investigation, 1972—; contbr. numerous articles to profl. jours. NIH grantee, 1961-78. Mem. Am. Soc. Exptl. Pathology, Am. Assn. Pathology, Am. Soc. Immunology, Am. Soc. Nephrology, Internat. Acad. Pathology, Internat. Soc. Nephrology, AAAS, N.Y. Acad. Sci., Reticuloendothelial Soc., Pluto Soc. Sigma Xi. Home: 2023 Devonshire Rd Ann Arbor MI Office: VA Medical Center 2023 Devonshire Ann Arbor MI 48105

BURKHOLDER, WENDELL EUGENE, entomologist; b. Octavia, Nebr., June 24, 1928; s. Elmer and Susie (Rothrock) B.; m. Leona Rose Flory, Aug. 18, 1951; children: Paul Charles, Anne Carolyn, Joseph Kern, Stephen James. A.B., McPherson Coll., 1950; M.Sc., U. Nebr., 1956; Ph.D., U. Wis., 1967. Research entomologist U.S. Dept. Agr., 1956—, Madison, Wis., 1965—; asst. prof. U. Wis.-Madison, 1967-70, asso. prof., 1970-75, prof. entomology, 1975—. Mem. editorial bd.: Jour. Chem. Ecology, 1980—; Contbr. chpts. to books, articles to profl. jours. Served with U.S. Army, 1951-53. NSF grantee, 1972-75, 79; Rockefeller Found. grantee, 1974-77; Nat. Inst. Occupational Safety and Health grantee, 1977-79. Mem. Entomol. Soc. Am., Soc. Invertebrate Pathology, AAAS, Wis. Entomol. Soc. (pres. 1980), Wis. Acad. Sci. Arts, and Letters. Patentee in field. Home: 1726 Chadbourne Ave Madison WI 53705 Office: 537 Russell Labs U Wis Madison WI 53706

BURKI, FRED ALBERT, labor union official; b. Chgo., Apr. 8, 1926; s. John and Helen (Kramer) B.; m. Barbara Maday; children—Bill, Ken, Scott, Mark, Laura. Student, Northwestern U., U.Ill. Started as grocery clk., 1947; pres. local 470 United Retail Workers Union, Westchester, Ill., 1951-53, rep., 1953-62, field supr., 1963-65, nat. v.p., 1966-71, nat. exec. dir., 1971-81; internat. v.p. United Food and Comml. Workers Union, AFL-CIO, 1981—; pres. local 881, 1981—; guest lectr. labor edn., advisor U. Ill. Circle Campus, Chgo.; labor edn. adv. U. Ind., 1967—, Loyola U., 1978—; mem. Midwest Com. Labor Study in Europe; labor adv. com. Senator Charles Percy, 1977—. Bd. dirs. Chgo. Regional Blood Bank/Blood Services, Blood Ctr. of No. Ill., 1983—; trustee United Retail Workers Union-Super-Valu Trust Fund.; mem. Ill. Detection of Deception Com., 1982—. Served with AUS, 1943-47; maj. Res. ret. Decorated Bronze Star medal; named Man of Year Combined Counties Police Assn., 1977. Mem. V.F.W. (past officer), Mil. Police Assn., Res. Officers Assn. Office: 9865 W Roosevelt Rd Westchester IL 60153

BURKOFF, JOHN MICHAEL, law educator, lawyer; b. Louisville, Nov. 16, 1948; s. Stanley Thomas and Joyce Ann (Switow) B.; m. Nancy Mammen, Aug. 17, 1969; children: Amy Nicole, David Michael. A.B., U. Mich., 1970, J.D., 1973; LL.M., Harvard U., 1976. Bar: Mich. 1974, Pa. 1979. Law clk. Mich. Supreme Ct., 1973-75; vis. asst. prof. law Wayne State U., Detroit, 1974-75; instr. law Boston U., 1975-76; asst. prof. U. Pitts., 1976-79, assoc. prof., 1979-82, prof., 1982—; counsel Newderlander, Dodge & McCauley, Detroit, 1975-83; cons. counsel Neighborhood Legal Services, Pitts., 1976—, ACLU, 1976—; counsel Titus, Murcus & Shapira, Pitts., 1979, NAACP Legal Def. Fund, N.Y.C., 1979. Author: Criminal Offenses and Defenses in Pennsylvania, 1984. Mem. Instn. Rev. Bd. for Biomed. Research U. Pitts., 1979—; del. Democratic Nat. Conv., N.Y.C., 1980; bd. dirs. House of the Crossroads, Pitts., 1980-81, Persad Ctr., Pitts., 1980-83. Named Hon. Chief Police City of Louisville, 1980; Ford Found. fellow, 1976. Mem. Assn. Am. Law Schs. (chairperson criminal justice sect. 1980, exec. council 1977-82), Soc. Am. Law Tchrs., Am. Judicature Soc., ACLU. Democrat. Jewish. Home: 7526 Graymore Rd Pittsburg PA 15221 Office: U Pitts Law Sch 3900 Forbes Ave Pittsburgh PA 15260

BURKS, ARTHUR WALTER, philosophy educator; b. Duluth, Minn., Oct. 13, 1915; s. Walter Demoree and Cora Belle (Voyles) B.; m. Alice Grace Rowe, Feb. 27, 1943; children—Edward, Nancy, Douglas. A.B. (Rector scholar), DePauw U., 1936, D.Sc., 1973; A.M., U. Mich., 1937, Ph.D. (Univ. fellow, Rackham predoctoral and postdoctoral fellow), 1941. Teaching and research, a prin. designer ENIAC, Moore Sch. Engring., U. Pa., 1941-46; cons. Inst. Advanced Study Digital Computer, 1946-48; cons. digital computers Burroughs Corp., 1948-54; cons. Oak Ridge Computer, Argonne Nat. Lab., 1950-51; asst. prof. philosophy U. Mich., Ann Arbor, 1946-48, asso. prof., 1948-54, prof., 1954—, chmn. dept. communication scis., 1967-71; research assoc. U. Chgo., 1950-51, Harvard, 1955; vis. prof. applied math. U. Ill., 1960; vis. prof. Indian Inst. Tech., Kanpur, India, 1965-66; fellow Center for Advanced Study in Behavioral Scis., Stanford, Calif., 1971-72; Henry Russel lectr. U. Mich., 1978; Pioneer lectr. Digital Computer Mus., 1982; disting. sr. faculty lectr. Coll., Lit., Sci. and Arts, U. Mich., 1982; Gillies lectr. U. Ill., 1983; mem. Soc. Fellows, U. Mich., 1975-80, chmn., 1975-80. Author: Chance, Cause, Reason, 1977; articles in field.; Editor: Collected Papers of Charles Sanders Peirce (vols. 7, 8, 1958, John von Neumann's Theory of Self-Reproducing Automata, 1966, John von Neumann's Essays on Cellular Automata, 1970; Cons. editor: Synthese, 1966—; editor: Jour. Computer and System Scis, 1975—. John Simon Guggenheim Meml. fellow, 1953-54; fellow Am. Council Learned Socs., 1962-63; recipient (with others) Louis E. Levy medal Franklin Inst., Phila., 1956; Distinguished Faculty Achievement award U. Mich., 1970. Mem. Assn. Symbolic Logic (council, exec. com. 1956-58), Am. Philos. Assn. (program, exec. com., v.p. Western div. 1971-72, pres. 1972-73), Assn. Computing Machinery, Philosophy of Sci. Assn. (gov., pres. 1975—), Charles S. Peirce Soc. (pres. 1954-55), Sigma Xi, Phi Beta Kappa, Phi Eta Sigma, Delta Sigma Rho, Phi Kappa Phi, Eta Kappa Nu. Home: 3445 Vintage Valley Rd Ann Arbor MI 48105

BURKS, VERNER IRWIN, Architect; b. Des Arc, Ark., June 16, 1923; s. Verner Irwin and Leta Beatrice (Burton) B. B.Arch., Washington U., St. Louis, 1951. Partner Burks & Landberg Architects, St. Louis, 1955-76; v.p., sec. Burks & Landberg Architects, Inc., St. Louis, 1976-78; propr. Burks Assos., Architects and Planners, St. Louis, 1978—; chmn. Landmarks and Urban Design Comm., City of St. Louis, 1969-77; chmn. condemnation com. St. Louis Bd. Bldg. Appeals, 1962-68; co-chmn. Old Post Office landmark Com., 1963—; 1st v.p. Campbell House Found., 1965-75, hon. dir., 1975—. Jr. warden Christ Ch. Episcopal Cathedral, 1975. Served with C.E. AUS, 1943-46. Decorated Bronze Star; recipient spl. honor award for renovation Christ Ch. Episcopal Cathedral, Guild Religious Architecture, 1970, honor award for St. John's Episcopal Ch., Sullivan, Mo., 1969; designated cathedral architect, 1980. Fellow AIA. Home: 330 N Newstead St Saint Louis MO 63108 Office: 1221 Locust St Saint Louis MO 63103

BURKS, WILLIAM BURGESS, retail executive; b. Saltillo, Miss., Mar. 22, 1927; s. Joseph Lee and Ethel (Burgess) B.; m. Doris Irma Uhl, Aug. 19, 1950; children: Robin, Steven, Alyson. B.S., U. Akron, 1952. C.P.A., Ohio, N.Y. Sr. acct. Arthur Young & Co., Cleve., 1952-54; controller Thomas Phillips Co., Akron, Ohio, 1954-56, M. O'Neil Co., Akron, 1956-64; pres. McCurdy & Co., Rochester, N.Y., 1964—, dir., Midtown Holdings Corp., Rochester. Bd. dirs. Meml. Art Gallery, Rochester, Citizens Tax League, Rochester, Salvation Army, Rochester, N.Y. State Council Retail Mchts. Served in USMC, 1945-49; PTO. Mem. Fin. Execs. Inst. Republican. Clubs: Genesee Valley; Rochester Yacht (Rochester) (treas. 1974-78). Lodge: Rotary. Home: 135 Hillary Ln Penfield NY 14526 Office: McCurdy & Co Midtown Plaza Rochester NY 14645

BURLAND, BRIAN BERKELEY, novelist, poet, playwright, scenarist; b. Paget, Bermuda, Apr. 23, 1931; s. Gordon Hamilton and Alice Croydon (Gosling) B.; m. Edwina Ann Trentham, 1962 (div. 1979); children: Susan, Anne, William, Benjamin. Student, U. Western Ont., Can., 1948-51. Writer in residence So. Sem., Buena Vista, Va., 1973; condr. seminars on novel, London, 1974; read own stories and poems BBC, 1968—. Author: A Fall from Aloft, 1968, A Few Flowers for St. George, 1969, Undertow, 1971, The Sailor and the Fox, 1973, Surprise, 1975, Stephen Decatur, The Devil and the Endymion, 1975, The Flight of the Cavalier, 1979; (children's book) St. Nicholas and the Tub, 1964. Served with Brit. Mcht. Service, 1944. Mem. Authors Guild, Authors League Am., Soc. Authors (London). Club: Chelsea Arts (London). Address: Book Hill Rd Essex CT 06426 *

BURLEIGH, WILLIAM ROBERT, newspaper executive; b. Evansville, Ind., Sept. 6, 1935; s. Joseph Charles and Emma Bertha (Wittgen) B.; m. Catherine Anne Husted, Nov. 28, 1964; children: David William, Catherine Anne, Margaret Walden. B.S., Marquette U., Milw., 1957; LL.D. (hon.), Ind. State U., 1979. From reporter to editor and pres. Evansville Press, 1951-77; editor Cin. Post, 1977-83; v.p., gen. editorial mgr. Scripps-Howard Newspapers, 1984—. Trustee First Amendment Congress, 1979-81; Chmn. Leadership Cin., 1979-81. Served with AUS, 1957-58. Mem. Am. Soc. Newspaper Editors, Sigma Delta Chi, Alpha Sigma Nu. Roman Catholic. Clubs: Queen City, Cincinnati Lit., Cincinnati Country, Cincinnati Commercial. Office: 1100 Central Trust Tower Cincinnati OH 45202

BURLESON, CLAUDE ALFRED, communications company executive; b. Danville, Ill., July 21, 1924; s. Claude Harold and Grace Alma (Carter) B.; m. Norma J. Zitani, Feb. 6, 1946; children: Ronald, Susan, Neil. B.S., Rutgers U., 1950; M.B.A., U. N.Y., 1957. Asst. tax mgr. St. Regis Paper Co., N.Y.C., 1950-55; asst. treas. Merritt-Chapman & Scott, N.Y.C., 1955-61; asst. controller taxes GTE Corp., N.Y.C., 1961-76, v.p. taxes, Stamford, Conn., 1976—; dir. Telect Ins. co.; chmn. The Bus. Roundtable Taxation Coordinating Com., 1979—. Mem. Tax Exec. Inst., Nat. Tax Assn., Tax Inst. Am., Internat. Assn. Assessing Officers, Wash. State Research Council, Stamford Tax Assn. (pres., founder). Club: Stamford Yacht. Office: GTE Corporation One Stamford Forum Stamford CT 06904

BURLESON, IRA LEE, insurance company executive; b. Athens, Ala., June 6, 1920; s. Luther A. and Marie (Witt) B.; m. Anna Kate Givens, Sept. 7, 1948 (dec. 1982). B.S., Florence (Ala.) State Coll., 1940; student, U. Ala., 1941; LL.B., U. Va., 1948. Bar: Ala. 1948. With firm Spain, Gillon, Grooms & Young, Birmingham, 1948-50; with Liberty Nat. Life Ins. Co., Birmingham, 1950—, v.p., 1967-73, sec., gen. counsel, 1967—, sr. v.p., 1973—, also sec. to bd. dirs., dir., now vice-chmn. bd., gen. counsel; sec., dir. Brown Service Funeral Homes Co., Inc., 1960—, Liberty Nat. Fire Ins. Co., 1971—; vice chmn. bd., gen. counsel Torchmark Corp., 1979—; dir. Globe Life Ins. Co., United Am. Ins. Co., Am. Life & Accident Ins. Co. Contbr. legal periodicals. Trustee Birmingham-So. Coll., 1979; bd. dirs. Assoc. Industries Ala., United Funds Inc. Served to comdr. USNR, 1942-46; PTO. Mem. ABA (vice chmn. com. life ins. law), Ala. Bar Assn. (vice chmn. sect. corp. law), Assn. Life Ins. Counsel (pres. 1980), Am. Soc. Corp. Secs., Am. Life Ins. Assn. (chmn. legal sect. 1973), Am. Council Life Ins., U.S. C. of C. (antitrust council), Ala. C. of C. (dir.). Methodist (chmn. ofcl. bd. 1964-66). Clubs: The Club, Creek Country, Country of Birmingham (Birmingham). Lodge: Kiwanis. Home: 3924 Forest Ave Birmingham AL 35213 Office: 301 S 20th St Birmingham AL 35202

BURLESON, PAUL RICHARD (RICK BURLESON), baseball player; b. Lynwood, Calif., Apr. 29, 1951; s. Bill Gene and Jeanne (Rathbun) B.; m. Karen Crofoot, Feb. 1974; children: James Tyler, Richard Chad, Richard Kyle. Student, Cerritos Coll., 1970, 72, Calif. State U., Fullerton, 1975, Whittier Coll., 1975, 76. With Boston Red Sox, 1974-80, Calif. Angels, 1980—; player for Am. League in All Star Game, 1977, 78, 79, 81. Recipient Gold Glove award, 1979, Silver Bat award, 1981; Thomas A. Yawkey Meml. award Boston Red Sox, 1979, 80; 1st ann. Anhauser Busch Team Leader award, 1980; named to All Time Red Sox Dream Team, 1983. Mem. Baseball Players Assn.

BURLEW, JOHN SWALM, scientist; b. Washington, Sept. 10, 1910; s. Ebert Keiser and Marion Kate (Swalm) B.; m. Grace Anne Schaum, June 16, 1934; children: David Schaum, Thomas Ebert. A.B., Bucknell U., 1930, Sc.D., 1955; Ph.D. in Chemistry, Johns Hopkins, 1934; Sc.D., Drexel Inst. Tech., 1956. Sterling Fellow in chemistry Yale, 1934-36; phys. chemist Geophys. Lab., Carnegie Instn. of Washington, 1936-43, 47-52; tech. aide NDRC, 1943-47; tech. dir. Cambridge Corp., 1952-54; asst. dir. Franklin Inst., 1954-55, dir., 1955-56, exec. v.p., 1956-59; dir. research Carrier Corp., 1960-66; dir. Conn. Research Commn., 1966-71; pres. New Directions Inc., Glastonbury, Conn., 1971—. Editor: Algal Culture from Laboratory to Pilot Plant, 1953. Decorated Presdl. Medal for Merit, 1948. Fellow AAAS; mem. Am. Chem. Soc. (chmn. Connecticut Valley sect. 1982, gen. chmn. Northeast regional meeting 1983), Ops. Research Soc. Am., Conn. Acad. Sci. and Engring. (incorporator 1976), Am. Geophys. Union, Phi Beta Kappa, Sigma Xi. (pres. elect Hartford chpt. 1983-84). Home: 93 Russet Rd Glastonbury CT 06033 Office: PO Box 418 Glastonbury CT 06033

BURLIN, ROBERT BRADFORD, educator; b. Cleve., Oct. 7, 1928; s. Leslie Robert and Helen (Svoboda) B.; m. Katrin Ristkok, June 27, 1970. B.A., Yale, 1950, M.A., 1952, Ph.D., 1956. Instr. Yale, 1955-59; asst. prof., asso. prof., prof. Bryn Mawr (Pa.) Coll., 1960—, chmn. dept. English, 1968-75. Author: The Old English Advent, 1968, Chaucerian Fiction, 1977; Editor: Old English Studies in Honour of John C. Pope. Mem. Modern Lang. Assn., Mediaeval Acad. Am. Home: 140 Morris Ave Bryn Mawr PA 19010

BURLING, ROBBINS, educator, anthropologist; b. Mpls., Apr. 18, 1926; s. Fred) Temple and Katherine (White) B.; m. Sibyl Plesaunce Straub, July 29, 1951; children: Stephen, Helen, Adele. B.A., Yale, 1950; Ph.D., Harvard, 1958. Instr. U. Pa., 1957-59, asst. prof., 1959-63; asso. prof. anthropology U. Mich., Ann Arbor, 1963-67, prof. anthropology and linguistics, 1967—, chmn. dept., 1980-83; guest prof. dept. anthropology U. Gothenburg, Sweden, 1979-80. Author: Rengsanggri: Family and Kinship in a Garo Village, 1963, Hill Farms and Padi Fields, 1965, Man's Many Voices, 1970, English in Black and White, 1973, The Passage of Power, 1974, Sounding Right, 1983. Served with USNR, 1944-46. Ford fellow, 1954-56; Fulbright prof. U. Rangoon, Burma, 1959-60; Center for Advanced Studies in the Behavioral Scis. fellow, 1963-64; Guggenheim fellow, 1971-72. Office: Dept Anthropology U Mich Ann Arbor MI 48109

BURLINGAME, EDWARD LIVERMORE, publishing company executive; b. N.Y.C., Jan. 21, 1935; s. Anson and Elizabeth Harlow (Hussy) B.; m. Perdita Remony Plowden, May 18, 1963; children: Remony Elizabeth, Phyllida Anne, Roger Anson. B.A., Harvard U., 1957; A.M.P., Harvard Bus. Sch. Editor MacGibbon & Kee, Ltd., London, 1959-61; sr. editor New Am. Library, N.Y.C., 1961-65; v.p., editor in chief Walker & Co., N.Y.C., 1965-69; sr. v.p., editor-in-chief trade div. J.B. Lippincott Co., Phila. and N.Y.C., 1969-78, dir., 1970-78; v.p., pub. Lippincott & Crowell, N.Y.C., 1979-80; v.p., editorial dir., pub. trade group Harper & Row, Pubs., Inc., N.Y.C., 1980—. Mem. Eastern regional panel Pres.'s Commn. on White House Fellowships, 1982—. Served to lt. (j.g.) USNR, 1957-59. Mem. Am. Assn. Pubs. (copyright com. 1976-77, internat. freedom to publish com. 1977-80, exec. council gen. pub. div. 1981—), P.E.N. (treas., exec. bd. 1970-73). Clubs: Century Assn. (N.Y.C.); University. Home: Todd Rd Katonah NY 10536 Office: 10 E 53d St New York NY 10022

BURLINGAME, JOHN FRANCIS, electrical equipment company executive; b. Somerville, Mass., June 18, 1922; s. John Francis and Irene Mae (Walsh) B.; m. Genevieve Keohane, July 21, 1947; children: Susan M., Janet E., Mary E., Elizabeth A. B.S., Tufts U., 1942. With Gen. Electric Co., 1946—, v.p., gen. mgr. computer systems div., Phoenix, 1969-71, v.p. employee relations, N.Y.C., 1971-73, v.p., group exec. internat. group, 1973-77, sr. v.p., internat. sector exec., Fairfield, Conn., 1977-79, vice chmn., 1979—. Served with USNR, 1943-46. Mem. AAAS, Conf. Bd., Am. Arbitration Assn. (dir. 1973-81), Fgn. Policy Assn. (dir. 1976-80), C. of C. of U.S. (dir. 1980-83), Sigma Pi Sigma. Home: 45 Hancock Ln Darien CT 06820 Office: General Electric Co Fairfield CT 06431

BURMAN, BEN LUCIEN, writer; b. Covington, Ky., Dec. 12, 1895; s. Sam and Minna B.; m. Alice Caddy, Sept. 19, 1927. A.B., Harvard U., 1920. Reporter Boston Herald, 1920; asst. city editor Cin. Times Star, 1921; spl. writer N.Y. Sunday World, 1922-23; staff contbr. NEA Scripps Howard Newspapers, 1927-29; lit. reviewer The Nation, other publs.; regular contbr. Readers Digest; contbr. Saturday Rev. Author: (film version starred Will Rogers) Steamboat Round the Bend, 1933, Blow for a Landing, 1938 (So. Authors prize), Rooster Crows for Day, 1945 (Thomas Jefferson Meml. prize), Everywhere I Roam, 1949, Children of Noah, 1951, High Water at Catfish Bend, 1952, The Four Lives of Mundy Tolliver, 1953, Seven Starts for Catfish Bend, 1956, It's Big Country, 1956, The Street of Laughing Camel, 1959, The Owl Hoots Twice at Catfish Bend: It's Big Continent, 1962, The Generals Wear Cork Hats, 1963, The Sign of the Praying Tiger, 1966, Blow A Wild Bugle for Catfish Bend, 1967, Look Down That Winding River, 1973, High Treason at Catfish Bend, 1977, The Strange Invasion of Catfish Bend, 1980, Thunderbolt at Catfish Bend, 1983. Served with AEF, World War I. Decorated French Legion of Honor, 1946; recipient So. Ill. U. Capt. Donald T. Wright award Congress Water Resources, Gold medal for Disting. Service to Am. Lit. Dutch Treat Club; named hon. citizen New Orleans, 1980, Natchez, Miss., 1980, Louisville, 1981, Biloxi, Miss., 1982, Baton Rouge, 1983, Ambassador of St. Louis, 1980, Ky. Col., 1981, La. Col., 1983; recipient plaque in his honor at Great River Rd. with proclamations by govs. La. and Ky., Port Hudson, La. Mem. Authors League Am., PEN. Clubs: Players, Overseas Press, Silurians; Savile (London); Dutch Treat. First writer to reach Free French in Africa; war corr. Free French, Brit. 8th Army, 1941 initial voyage of Mississippi Queen, St. Louis to St. Paul, Ben Lucien Week, 1980. Office: Wieser & Wieser Penthouse B 80 Madison Ave New York NY 10016

BURMAN, MARSHALL LYLE, lawyer; b. Chgo., July 22, 1929; s. Henry L. and Florence (Rosin) B.; m. Marian Sondheimer, June 28, 1953 (div. July 1966); children: Julie Anne, Jamie Alison. B.S., Northwestern U., 1951; LL.B., Yale, 1954. Bar: Ill. bar 1954. Practice in, Chgo., 1957—; assoc. firm Arvey, Hodes, Costello & Burman, 1957-60, mem., 1961—; dir. Helene Curtis Industries, Inc., TCI, Inc.; Mem. financial investment adv. panel Amtrak, 1970-75. Pres. Young Mens Jewish Council, 1965; chancellor Lincoln Acad. of Ill., 1978—; dir., vice chmn. Ill. Bd. Investment; pres. Water Tower Condominium Assn., 1978—; dirs. Lincoln Park Zool. Soc. Served with AUS, 1954-56. Recipient medallion Boys Clubs Am., 1966. Mem. Ill., Chgo. bar assns., Phi Alpha Delta, Phi Epsilon Pi (pres. 1951). Clubs: Chicago, Standard (dir.), Yale (Chgo.); Harmonie (N.Y.C.). Home: 180 E Pearson Chicago IL 60611 Office: 180 N LaSalle St Chicago IL 60602

BURMASTER, M.R., oil company executive; b. Milw., May 2, 1934. B.B.A., U. Wis., 1956, LL.B., 1959. Bar: Wis. 1956, Ohio 1960, Mo. 1983. Atty. Clark Oil & Refining Corp., Milw. and St. Louis, 1961-70, asst. sec., 1970-73, sec., 1973-75, v.p., gen. counsel, 1975—. Mem.

Milw. Art Ctr. Mem. ABA, Wis. Bar Assn., Ohio Bar Assn., Milw. Bar Assn., Mo. Bar. Office: 7930 Clayton Rd Saint Louis MO 63117

BURMEISTER, EDWIN, educator; b. Chgo., Nov. 30, 1939; s. Edwin Carl and Dorothy (Braithwaite) B. B.A., Cornell U., 1961, M.A., 1962; Ph.D., MIT, 1965. Asst. prof. econs. Wharton Sch., U. Pa., Phila., 1965-68, assoc. prof., 1968-71; vis. prof. econs. Duke U., 1971-72, vis. prof. econs. Fuqua Sch. Bus. and dept. econs., 1981-82; vis. prof. econs. Sch. Gen. Studies and vis. fellow dept. econs. Research Sch. Social Sci. Australian Nat. U., 1974-75; prof. econs. U. Pa., Phila., 1972-76; pro. econs., mem. Ctr. for Advanced Studies U. Va., Charlottesville, 1976-79, Commonwealth prof. econs., 1979—; vis. prof. econs. U. Chgo., 1980; prof. econs. and fin. U. Ill., 1982. Author: (with A. Rodney Dobell) Mathematical Theories of Economic Growth, 1970, Capital Theory and Dynamics, 1980, (others); contbr. articles to profl. jours. Guggenheim fellow, 1974-76; NSF grantee, 1979-81, 83—; FTC contractee, 1979-80; NSF grantee, 1967-78; NSF grad. fellow, 1962-65; NSF summer fellow, summer 1962; hon. Woodrow Wilson fellow, 1961-62. Fellow Econometric Soc. Address: Dept Econs Univ Va 114 Rouss Charlottesville VA 22901

BURNAM, PAUL WAYNE, educator, accountant; b. Abilene, Tex., Jan. 2, 1913; s. Joseph Edward and Opha Carrie (Jobe) B.; m. Anita Maxie Kellow, June 8, 1941; children—Roy Edward and Ray Thomas (twins). B.A. in Math. and Accounting, Hardin-Simmons U., 1934; M.B.A., U. Tex., 1939; Ph.D., U. Ala., 1959; postgrad., La. State U., 1946. C.P.A., La. Grad. asst. U. Tex., 1934-35; head dept. math. Conroe (Tex.) High Sch., 1935-41; mem. faculty U. Southwestern La., 1942—, prof. accounting, 1950—, head dept., 1952—, dean, 1976—; auditor, adviser U. Southwestern La. Found., 1960—; real estate broker in, La., 1966—; Vis. prof. McNeese State Coll., Lake Charles, 1969. Contbr. profl. jours. Chmn. bd. trustees Kellow's Tech. Coll., Houston, 1961—. Served with AUS, 1942-45. Mem. Am. Inst. C.P.A.'s, Am. Accounting Assn., Soc. La. C.P.A.'s (exec. bd. 1961), Beta Gamma Sigma, Beta Alpha Psi, Phi Kappa Phi, Phi Eta Sigma, Theta Xi. Baptist. Home: 188 Ronald Blvd Lafayette LA 70503

BURNAM, TOM (THOMAS BOND), English language educator, author; b. Swan Lake, Mont., Oct. 2, 1913; s. Clarence Miles and Ora Harmer (Bond) B.; m. Phyllis Anderson, Mar. 29, 1940. B.A., U. Idaho, 1936, M.A., 1937; Ph.D., U. Wash., 1949. Instr. Lewis and Clark State Coll., 1938-42; ground sch. supr. CAA, 1942-44; instr. B-29 sch. Boeing Airplane Co., 1944-45; assoc. dept. English U. Wash., Seattle, 1946-49; asst. prof. to prof. English U. No. Colo., 1950-63; prof. Portland (Oreg.) State U., 1963—; vis. Fulbright prof. U. Helsinki, 1961; spl. lectr. U. Caen, France, Leangkollen, Norway, 1961; guest prof. San Jose State U., 1964. Author: The Dictionary of Misinformation, 1975, 77, Encyclopédie des idées reçues, (with Claude Vallette), 1978, More Misinformation, 1980; mem. editorial bd.: Harvest mag, 1974-76; contbr.: articles, stories and poems to Am. Quar, Modern Fiction Studies, Tex. Quar, others. Portland State U. research grantee, 1970. Mem. Modern Lang. Assn., AAUP, AFTRA, Philol. Assn. Pacific Coast, Rocky Mountain Am. Studies Assn. (pres. 1952), Rocky Mountain Modern Lang. Assn. (pres. 1953), Phi Beta Kappa (alumnus mem. U. Idaho). Democrat. Episcopalian. Club: Willamette Valley Country. Home: 2765 SW Park Rd Lake Oswego OR 97034 Office: Dept English Portland State Univ Portland OR 97201

BURNET, GEORGE, JR., educator; b. Ft. Dodge, Iowa, Jan. 30, 1924; s. George and Myrtle Violet (Hutchinson) B.; m. Betty Arlene Riggs, Oct. 8, 1944; children—Kathryn Ann, Betty Jo, Dolores Unalee, Joan Marie, Elaine Kaye, George VI. B.S. in Chem. Engring, Iowa State U., 1948, M.S., 1949, Ph.D., 1951. Registered profl. engr., Iowa. Mem. faculty Iowa State U., 1949-51, 56—, prof. chem. engring., 1958—, head dept., 1961-78, chmn. dept. nuclear engring., 1978-83, coordinator engring. edn. projects office, 1978—, Anson Marston distinguished prof., 1975—; process design engr. Comml. Solvents Corp., 1952-56; successively engr., sr. engr., div. chief Ames Lab., U.S. Dept. Energy, 1956—; Phillips lectr. Okla. State U., 1970; Dir. for planning Iowa State U. Civil Def. Orgn., 1961-69; AID cons. in higher edn. to, India, 1967; mem. pres.'s task force on energy research and devel. U.S. AEC, 1973. Contbr. articles. Active Boy Scouts Am.; Trustee Iowa State U. Alumni Achievement Fund, chmn. bd., 1973-74; mem. Nat. Sci. Bd. Commn. Pre-coll. Edn., 1982-83. Served to lt. col. AUS, 1944-48. Recipient Faculty citation Iowa State U., 1969; Iowa Citizen Chem. Engr. award, 1970. Mem. Am. Inst. Chem. Engrs. (chmn. Terre Haute sect. 1956, chmn. Iowa sect. 1967, nat. rep. to Engrs.' Council for Profl. Devel. 1969—, chmn. nat. com. on chem. engring. tech. 1969-70, Founders award 1981), Am. Soc. Engring. Edn. (hon. mem., chmn. chem. engring. div. 1964, nat. dir. 1972-74, pres. 1976, Lamme medal 1982), Am. Chem. Soc. (chmn. div. fertilizer and soil chemistry 1969), Engrs.' Council for Profl. Devel. (chmn. engring. edn. and accreditation com. 1975-77, dir. 1977-83, exec. com. 1981-83), Am. Assn. Engring. Socs. (chmn. ednl. affairs council 1980-81), Sigma Xi, Tau Beta Pi, Phi Lambda Upsilon, Phi Kappa Phi, Alpha Chi Sigma, Tau Kappa Epsilon, Omega Chi Epsilon (nat. pres. 1970). Methodist (chmn. ofcl. bd., bd. trustees). Club: Cardinal Key. Patentee in field. Home: 4813 Dover Dr Ames IA 50010

BURNETT, ANNE PIPPIN, educator; b. Salt Lake City, Oct. 10, 1925; d. Roy F. and Edith G. (Robertson) Newton; m. Virgil Burnett, 1961; children: Maud, Melissa. B.A., Swarthmore Coll., 1946; M.A., Columbia U., 1947; Ph.D., U. Calif. - Berkeley, 1953. Asst. prof. Vassar Coll., Poughkeepsie, N.Y., 1957-58, U. Chgo., 1961-65, assoc. prof., 1966-70, prof. dept. classical lang. and lit., 1970—. Author: Euripides, Ion, 1970, Catastrophe Survived, 1971, Three Archaic Poets, 1983, The Art of Bacchylides, 1984. Grantee AAUP, Am. Acad. in Rome, Am. Philos. Soc., Am. Council Learned Socs., John Simon Guggenheim Found. Home: 51 Avon St Stratford ON Canada N5A 5N5 Office: Univ Chicago Dept Classical Lang and Lit 5801 Ellis Ave Chicago IL 60637

BURNETT, ARTHUR LOUIS, judge; b. Spotsylvania County, Va., Mar. 15, 1935; s. Robert Louis and Lena Victoria (Bumbry) B.; m. Ann Lloyd, May 14, 1960; children: Darnellena, Arthur Louis, Darryl, Darlisa, Dionne. B.A. summa cum laude, Howard U., 1957; LL.B., NYU, 1958; grad., Fed. Exec. Inst., 1978. Bar: D.C. 1958, U.S. Dist. Ct. Md. 1963, U.S. Supreme Ct. 1964. Atty. Gen.'s Honor Program atty. fraud sect. criminal div. U.S. Dept. Justice, Washington, 1958, atty. to acting dep. chief gen. crimes sect., 1960-65; spl. asst. U.S. atty., Balt. and East St. Louis, Ill., 1961-63; asst. U.S. atty. D.C., 1965-68; legal adviser, gen. counsel D.C. Dept. Met. Police, 1968-69; U.S. magistrate U.S. Dist. Ct., Washington, 1969-75; asst. gen. counsel legal adv. div. U.S. CSC, 1975-78; asso. gen. counsel Office of Personnel Mgmt., 1979-80; U.S. magistrate U.S. Dist. Ct. D.C., 1980—; faculty Jud. Center, 1970—, Nat. Jud. Coll., 1974—; program chmn. ann. meeting Nat. Conf. Spl. Ct. Judges, Washington, 1973, chmn. elect, acting chmn., 1974-75, chmn., 1975—; program chmn. ann. meeting Nat. Council U.S. Magistrates, Williamsburg, Va., 1974, pres., 1983-84; program participant D.C. Circuit Jud. Conf., 1974, U.S. Ct. Claims Jud. Conf., 1979. Served with AUS, 1958-60. Recipient Founders Day award NYU, 1958; Army Commendation medal, 1960; Sustained Superior Performance award U.S. Atty. Gen., 1963; Disting. Service award CSC, 1978; Meritorious Service award U.S. Office of Personnel Mgmt., 1980; Outstanding Disting. Service award Fed. Bar Assn., 1983. Mem. ABA, Washington Bar Assn., Fed. Bar Assn. (Disting. Service award 1978, chmn. fed. litigation sect. 1983-84, chmn. standing com. on U.S. magistrates, dep. chmn. sect. adminstrn. of justice 1983-84), Nat. Bar Assn., Bar Assn. D.C., D.C. Unified Bar, Am. Judicature Soc., Am. Judges Assn., Phi Beta Kappa, Omega Psi Phi. Office: US Dist Ct 3d and Constitution Ave NW Washington DC 20001

BURNETT, CAROL, actress, comedienne, singer; b. San Antonio, Apr. 26, 1936; d. Jody and Louise (Creighton) B.; m. Joseph Hamilton, 1963 (div.); children: Carrie Louise, Jody Ann, Erin Kate. Student, U. Calif. at Los Angeles, 1953-55. Introduced: comedy song I Made a Fool of Myself Over John Foster Dulles, 1957; Broadway debut in Once Upon a Mattress, 1959; regular performer: Garry Moore TV show, 1959-62; appeared several CBS-TV spls., 1962-63; Broadway play Fade Out-Fade In, 1964; play Plaza Suite, 1970; musical play I Do, I Do, 1973, Same Time Next Year, 1977; films Pete 'n' Tillie, 1972, Front Page, 1974, A Wedding, 1977, Health, 1979, Four Seasons, 1981, Chu Chu and the Philly, 1981, Annie, 1982; TV movie Friendly Fire, 1978; club engagements, Harrah's Club, The Sands, Caesar's Palace, MGM Grand; star: Carol Burnett Show, CBS-TV, 1966-77. Recipient outstanding comedienne award Am. Guild Variety Artists, 5 times; Emmy award for outstanding variety performance Acad. TV Arts and Scis., 5 times; TV Guide award for outstanding female performer, 1961, 62, 63; Peabody award, 1963; Golden Globe award for outstanding comedienne of year Fgn. Press Assn., 8 times; Woman of Year award Acad. TV Arts and Scis.; People's Choice award favorite all-around female entertainer, 1975, 76, 77; 1st ann. Nat. TV Critics Circle award for outstanding performance, 1977; San Sebastian Film Festival award for best actress for A Wedding, 1978. Address: care Robinson Luttrell & Assocs 141 El Camino Dr Suite 110 Beverly Hills CA 90212 *

BURNETT, DAVID ALAN, photojournalist; b. Salt Lake City, Sept. 7, 1946; s. Ted and Barbara B. B.A. in Polit. Sci, Colo. Coll., 1968. Contract photographer Time mag., Washington, 1968-69, Miami, Fla., 1969-70; freelance photographer Time & Life, Saigon, Viet Nam, 1970-72; contract photographer Life mag., 1972; freelance photographer Gamma Agy., Paris, France, 1973-75; founding mem. Contact Press Images, N.Y.C., 1976—. Photographs published mags. worldwide.; Producer: film NATO, 1982, Make it Fast, 1982. Winner Robert Capa gold award Overseas Press Club, 1973; Press Photo of Year award World Pressphoto Found., 1980; Best Photo Reporting from Abroad Overseas Press Club, 1980. Mem. Am. Soc. Mag. Photographers, Nat. Press Photographers Assn. (Mag. Photographer of Year 1980). Office: Contact Press Images Suite 10 NC 135 Central Park W New York NY 10023

BURNETT, HENRY, lawyer; b. N.Y.C., Feb. 24, 1927; s. Lucien Dallam and Ruth (Hinkle) B.; m. Florence Stewart, July 19, 1952; children—Marian Starr, Betsy Callaway, Henry Stewart. B.A., U. Va., 1947, LL.B., 1950. Bar: Va. bar 1950, Fla. bar 1951. Ptnr. firm Fowler, White, Burnett, Hurley & Strickroot (and predecessors), Miami, Fla., 1957—, pres. firm, 1977—. Bd. dirs. Dade County Citizens Safety Council, Travelers Aid, United Family and Children's Services. Served with USNR, 1945-46. Fellow Am. Coll. Trial Lawyers; mem. Am., Fla., Dade County bar assns., Fla. Def. Lawyers Assn. (pres. 1967-68), Dade County Def. Bar Assn. (pres. 1966-67), Internat. Assn. Ins. Counsel (exec. com. 1972-74, pres. 1976-77). Episcopalian. Clubs: Riviera Country, Miami, Bankers, Biscayne Bay Yacht. Home: 4720 SW 85th St Miami FL 33143 Office: 25 W Flagler St 5th Floor Miami FL 33130

BURNETT, HOWARD JEROME, coll. pres.; b. Holyoke, Mass., Oct. 14, 1929; s. William and Bridget (Breck) B.; m. Barbara J. Ransohoff, June 12, 1954; children—Lee Ann, Sue Allison, Mark Howard. B.A., Amherst Coll., 1952, Oxford U., 1954; M.A. (Rhodes scholar), Oxford U., 1958; LL.D., Ithaca Coll., 1965; Ph.D., N.Y. U., 1965. Cons. Booz, Allen & Hamilton, 1958; sec. A.L. Ransohoff Co., Inc., N.Y.C., 1958-60; mem. internatl. econs. staff Texaco, Inc., N.Y.C., 1960-62; asst. to pres. Corning (N.Y.) Community Coll., 1962-64; pres. Coll. Center of the Finger Lakes, Corning, 1964-70, Washington and Jefferson Coll., Washington, Pa., 1970—; Dir. Cyclops Corp.; mem. adv. bd. Mellon Bank, Washington. Served to lt. USNR, 1955-58. Mem. Assn. Am. Rhodes Scholars, Pa. Assn. of Colls. and Univs. (exec. com.), Ind. Coll. Funds Am. (exec. com.), Phi Beta Kappa, Delta Kappa Epsilon. Clubs: Duquesne, University, Allegheny (Pitts.). Office: Washington and Jefferson Coll Washington PA 15301

BURNETT, JAMES E., JR., lawyer, government official; b. Sept. 20, 1947; s. James E. B. B.A., J.D., U. Ark. Bar: Ark. Mem. Burnett and Stripling, Clinton, Ark., 1973—; judge Van Buren County Juvenile Ct., Ark., 1973-79; city judge, Damascus, Ark., 1979-81; chmn., mem. Nat. Transp. Safety Bd., Washington, 1981—; spl. assoc. justice Supreme Ct. Ark. Mem. ABA, Ark. Bar Assn., Nat. Conf. Spl. Ct. Judges. Office: Nat Transp Safety Bd Office of Chmn 800 Independence Ave NW Washington DC 20594 *

BURNETT, JOE RAY, educator, college dean; b. Welch, W.Va., May 7, 1928; s. James B. Weaver and Vada Christine (Watson) B.; m. Rita Dee Burnett, Aug. 1980. B.A. in Philosophy, U. Tenn., 1951, M.A., 1953; Ph.D. in Philosophy of Edn, N.Y.U., 1958. Tchr. English Columbia Grammar Sch., N.Y.C., 1954-55; asst. instr. philosophy and sociology N.Y.C. Community Coll., 1955-56; asst. prof. philosophy edn. Kansas City U., 1956-57; instr., then asst. prof. philosophy of edn. N.Y. U., 1957-59; mem. faculty U. Ill. at Urbana, 1959—, prof. philosophy of edn., 1966—, chmn. dept. history and philosophy of edn., 1972-73, dean, 1980—; vis. asso. prof. ad honorem U. P.R., fall 1965; vis. lectr. U. B.C., summers 1969, 70. Co-author: Democracy and Excellence in American Secondary Education, 1964; Mem. adv. bd.: Coop. Research on Dewey Publs, So. Ill. U., 1961—; editorial bd., trustee: Studies in Philosophy and Education, 1962—; asso. editor: Educational Theory, 1962-65, 1970-71; editor, 1971-80. Fellow Am. Philos. Assns., Am. Ednl. Research Assn., Am. Ednl. Studies Assn.; mem. John Dewey Soc. (pres. 1966-68), Philosophy of Edn. Soc. (pres. 1968-69), Midwest Philosophy of Edn. Soc. (pres. 1963-64), AAUP, Soc. Profs. Edn. (pres. 1981-83), Ill. Assn. Deans Pub. Univ. Colls. Edn. (chmn. 1982-83). Home: 702 Hessel Blvd Champaign IL 61820 Office: Coll of Edn Univ Ill Urbana IL 61801

BURNETT, LOWELL JAY, physicist, educator; b. Portland, Oreg., June 15, 1941; s. Jay Duffy and Barbara Montana (Blair) B.; m. Joan Susan Merk, June 17, 1961; children—David Alan, Craig Michael. B.S., Portland State U., 1964; Ph.D. (NSF predoctoral trainee), U. Wyo., 1970. Instr. physics U. Wyo., Laramie, 1970; presdl. fellow chemistry div. Los Alamos (N.Mex.) Sci. Lab., 1971-72; prof. physics San Diego State U., 1972—, chmn. physics dept., 1979—, dir. applied physics research lab., 1981—; cons. energy conservation utilization, environ. monitoring and control, sci. instrumentation design USN; Assoc. Western Univs. faculty fellow, 1973-74; cons. UOP, Inc., Sci. Applications, Inc., IRT Corp., Gillette Corp., Control Data Corp., Los Alamos Sci. Lab., IRT Corp.; mem. internat. adv. panel Electronics, McGraw-Hill. Contbr. articles to profl. jours. Am. Chem. Soc. petroleum research grantee, 1974—. Co-developer membrane for oxygen enrichment of air. Home: 8696 Jackie Dr San Diego CA 92119 *Once, when I was young and trying to hurry through a delicate job, an elderly craftsman brought me up short: "Son," he said, "if you don't have time to do it right, how are you going to find time to do it twice?" These words, and the later realization that most real progress is made by carefully choosing and then completing day-to-day tasks, have guided my career ever since.*

BURNETT, ROBERT A., publisher; b. Joplin, Mo., June 4, 1927; s. Lee Worth and Gladys (Plummer) B.; m. Gloria M. Cowden, Dec. 25, 1948; children: Robert A., Stephen, Gregory, Douglas, David, Penelope. A.B., U. Mo., 1948. Salesman Cowden Motor Co., Guthrie Center, Iowa; then Equitable Life Assurance Soc., Joplin, Mo.; now pres., chief exec. officer Meredith Corp.; dir. Whirlpool Corp., Iowa Des Moines Nat. Bank, Interstate Life Assurance Co., Vernon Co., Dayton Hudson Corp. Past chmn. Discover Am. Travel Orgns.; bd. dirs. Grinnell Coll. Served with AUS, 1945-46. Mem. NAM (dir.), Phi Delta Theta. Congregationalist. Home: 315 37 St Des Moines IA 50312 Office: 1716 Locust St Des Moines IA 50303

BURNETT, THEODORE S., JR., advt. agy. exec.; b. Los Angeles, Oct. 8, 1933; s. Theodore S. and Mary (Engel) B.; m. Susan Rickey Platt, Dec. 17, 1960; children—Theodore S., Cynthia Lynn. B.A. in Econs, Claremont (Calif.) Men's Coll., 1955; M.B.A., Stanford U., 1959. Account exec. Norman, Kraig & Kummel Inc., N.Y.C., 1959-61; account exec., account supr. Benton & Bowles, Inc., N.Y.C., 1961-66; mgr. supr. Erwin Wasey Inc., Los Angeles, 1966-69; gen. mgr. McCann-Erickson Inc., Los Angeles, 1970-73; gen. mgr., sr. v.p. Benton & Bowles, Inc., Los Angeles, 1973-80, sr. v.p., group exec., N.Y.C., 1980—; instr. Inst. Advanced Advt. Studies, U. So. Calif. Trustee Calif. chpt. Nat. Multiple Sclerosis Soc., 1975-80; mem. pres.'s adv. council Claremont Men's Coll., 1968—. Served to 1st lt. U.S. Army, 1956-57. Mem. Am. Assn. Advt. Agencies (chmn. bd. govs. So. Calif. chpt. 1979). Republican. Presbyterian. Clubs: Siwanoy Golf (Bronxville); Annandale Golf (Pasadena, Calif.). Office: 909 3d Ave New York NY 10022

BURNETT, WILLIAM EARLE, JR., insurance company executive; b. Louisville, Feb. 15, 1927; s. William E. and Bessie (Davis) B.; m. Margaret Alberta Erny Crenshaw, Mar. 21, 1975; children: Bruce E., Cindy C., Suzanne L., John A. B.S., U. Louisville, 1949. Treas. Louisville Fire & Marine Ins. Co., 1949-54; asst. sec. - treas. Ky. Ins. Agy., Lexington, 1955-59; sec.-treas. Ky. Central Life Ins. Co., Lexington, 1959-74, exec. v.p., 1975-76, pres., 1976—, mem. exec. and fin. coms., 1961—, dir., 1961—; pres. Ky. Central Life Ins. Co. and Property and Casualty Co. subs.; dir. Central Bank, Lexington, Peoples Comml. Bank, Winchester, Ky., First Nat. Bank, Georgetown, Ky., Ky. Fin. Co., Lexington; sec., dir. Triangle Found. Mem. Lexington Econ. Devel. Commn.; bd. dirs. United Way of Bluegrass; mem. Bluegrass council Boy Scouts Am.; mem. adv. council Coll. Bus. and Econs., U. Ky. Served with U.S. Army, 1945-47. Fellow U. Ky. Mem. Ins. Accts. and Statisticians Assn., Life Officers Mgmt. Assn., Nat. Assn. Life Underwriters, Ky. C. of C., Lexington C. of C., Georgetown Coll. Assocs. Presbyterian. Club: Lafayette. Lodges: Shriners; Masons. Office: Ky Central Life Ins Co Kincaid Towers Lexington KY 40507

BURNEY, CECIL EDWARD, lawyer; b. Riesel, Tex., Oct. 6, 1914; s. Frank Edward and Allye Stacye (Goodman) B.; m. Kara Hunsucker, Jan. 15, 1949 (dec. Feb. 1973); children: Cecil Edward, Kara Lisa, Frank Burleson. B.A., U. Tex., 1936, J.D., 1937; LL.D., U. Corpus Christi, 1975. Bar: Tex. 1938. Since practiced in, Corpus Christi; partner firm Wood & Burney (and predecessors), 1941—; pres. Merc. Nat. Bank, 1955-56; past chmn. bd. 1st Nat. Bank, Ingleside; formerly chmn. bd. First City Bank, Aransas Pass; dir. Parkdale State Bank, Merc. Nat. Bank, Kingsville, Nueces Nat. Bank, Corpus Christi, Cullen-Frost Bankers, Inc., San Antonio; sec. Corpus Christi Broadcasting Co., K-SIX TV Inc.; Spl. asst. atty. gen., Tex., 1956. Mem. exec. bd. Gulf Coast council Boy Scouts Am., 1948-77; chmn. Gov.'s Traffic Safety Com., 1956; past chmn. Corpus Christi Housing Authority, Nueces County Red Cross; past pres. Jr. C. of C. Served to lt. comdr. USNR, 1942-45. Recipient St. Thomas More award St. Mary's U., 1964; Arthur Von Briesen award Nat. Legal Aid and Defender Assn., 1963; Humanitarian award NCCJ, 1981; named Outstanding Alumnus Tex. A & I U., 1978, Jaycees Hall of Fame, 1983. Fellow Am. Bar Found.; mem. State Bar Tex. (pres. 1951-52), Am. Bar Assn. (bd. govs. 1965-68), Am. Judicature Soc. (pres. 1960-62), Nat. Legal Aid Assn. (dir. 1955-65), Nat. Conf. Bar Presidents (chmn. 1955-56), Tex. Hist. Found. (pres. 1970-74), Tex. Hist. Commn. (chmn. 1977-81). Presbyn. Clubs: Rotarian., Town (Corpus Christi); Nueces. Home: 4500 Ocean Dr Corpus Christi TX 78412 Office: 1700 First City Tower II Corpus Christi TX 78403

BURNHAM, BRYSON PAINE, retired lawyer; b. Chgo., Oct. 11, 1917; s. Raymond and Patti (Paine) B.; m. Frances Katherine Burns, Feb. 8, 1941; children: Janice Young, Stephanie Paine. B.A., U. Chgo., 1938, J.D., 1940. Bar: Ill. 1940, Colo. 1983. Assoc., then ptnr. Mayer, Brown & Platt, Chgo., 1940-83. Served to 1st lt. U.S. Army, 1942-46. Home: 315 Highland Hill Dr Durango CO 81301

BURNHAM, CHARLES WILSON, mineralogy educator; b. Detroit, Apr. 6, 1933; s. Charles Hubbard and Anne (Wilson) B.; m. Mary Sue Morgan, June 21, 1958; children—Jeffrey Wentworth, David Wilson. S.B., Mass. Inst. Tech., 1954, Ph.D., 1961; A.M., Harvard, 1966. Postdoctoral fellow Geophys. Lab. Carnegie Instn., Washington, 1961-63, staff scientist, 1963-66; assoc. prof. mineralogy Harvard, 1966-69, prof., 1969—, chmn. dept. geol. scis., 1983-84. Assoc. editor: Am. Mineralogist, 1974-77. Mem. Acton (Mass.) Planning Bd., 1974-78, chmn., 1976-77. Served as 1st lt. USAF, 1955-57. Fellow Mineral. Soc. Am. (councillor 1980—); mem. Am. Crystallographic Assn., AAAS, Am. Geophys. Union, Sigma Xi, Phi Gamma Delta. Episcopalian. Club: Appalachian Mountain (Boston) (pres. 1979-81). Home: 6 Captain Browns Ln Acton MA 01720 Office: 20 Oxford St Cambridge MA 02138

BURNHAM, DAVID BRIGHT, journalist; b. Boston, Jan. 24, 1933; s. Addison Center and Dorothy (Moore) B.; m. Sophy Tayloe Doub, Mar. 12, 1960 (div. 1984); children: Sarah Tayloe, Molly Bright. B.A., Harvard, 1955. Reporter U.P.I., Washington, 1959-61; reporter Newsweek mag., Washington, 1961-63; writer CBS, N.Y.C., 1963-65; asst. dir. President's Commn. Law Enforcement and Adminstrn. of Justice, 1965-67; reporter N.Y. Times, N.Y.C., 1967-80, reporter Washington bur., 1982—; journalist/writer Aspen Inst. Humanistic Studies, 1980-82. Author: The Rise of the Computer State, 1983. Recipient George K. Polk award L.I. U., 1968; Silurians award, 1968; N.Y. Newspaper Guild award, 1968; Gold Typewriter award for investigative reporting N.Y. Reporters Assn., 1972. Clubs: Spee, Hasty Pudding (Cambridge, Mass.). Home: 524 6th St SE Washington DC 20003

BURNHAM, DONALD CLEMENS, manufacturing company executive; b. Athol, Mass., Jan. 28, 1915; s. Charles Richardson and Freda (Clemens) B.; m. Virginia Gobble, May 29, 1937; children: David Charles, Joan (Mrs. Robert Graham), John Carl, William Lawrence, Mary Barbara (Mrs. F. David Throop). B.S. in Mech. Engring, Purdue U., 1936, D.Eng. (hon.), 1959, Ind. Inst. Tech., 1963, Drexel Inst. Tech., 1964, Poly. Inst. Bklyn., 1967. With Gen. Motors Corp., 1936-54, asst. chief engr., 1953-54; with Westinghouse Electric Corp., 1954—, group v.p., 1962-63, pres., chief exec. officer, 1963-68, chmn., chief exec. officer, 1969-75, dir.-officer, 1975-80; adv. bd. Mellon Bank (N.A.). Mem. The Bus. Council; life trustee Carnegie-Mellon U.; trustee Carnegie Inst.; bd. dirs. Am. Wind Symphony

Orch., Logistics Mgmt. Inst.; chmn. bd. dirs. Goodwill Industries of Pitts. Served to maj. AUS, World War II. Recipient Outstanding Achievement in Mgmt. award Am. Inst. Indsl. Engrs., 1964. Mem. ASME, Soc. Mfg. Engr. (Hoover Medal award 1978), Soc. Automotive Engrs., IEEE, Nat. Acad. Engring., Am. Assn. Engring. Socs. (Nat. Engring. award 1981). Club: Duquesne (Pitts.). Home: 615 Osage Rd Pittsburgh PA 15243 Office: Westinghouse Bldg Gateway Center Pittsburgh PA 15222

BURNHAM, JAMES BERNARD, banker; b. N.Y.C., Oct. 22, 1939; s. James and Marcia (Lightner) B.; m. Anne Mullin, Nov. 7, 1964; children: James, Clara, William, Mary. A.B., Princeton U., 1961; Ph.D., Washington U., St. Louis, 1969. Vice pres. Mellon Bank, Pitts., 1971-81; staff dir. Pres. Council of Econ. Advisors, Washington, 1981-82; U.S. exec. dir. The World Bank, Washington, 1982—. Served as intelligence officer USN, 1963-65. Republican. Office: The World Bank 1818 H St NW Washington DC 20433

BURNHAM, JOHN CHYNOWETH, historian, educator; b. Boulder, Colo., July 14, 1929; s. William Allds and Florence (Hasbrouck) B.; m. Marjorie Ann Spencer, Aug. 21, 1957; children: Leonard, Abigail, Peter, Melissa. B.A., Stanford U., 1951, Ph.D., 1958; M.A., U. Wis., 1958. Lectr. Claremont Men's Coll., Calif., 1956-57; mem. faculty Stanford U., 1956, 57-58; postdoctoral fellow Founds. Fund for Research in Psychiatry, New Haven, 1958-61; asst. prof. San Francisco State Coll., 1961-63; mem. faculty Ohio State U., Columbus, 1963—, prof. history, 1969—; sr. Fulbright lectr. U. Melbourne, Australia, 1967, Univs. Tasmania and New Eng., 1973; Tallman vis. prof. history and psychology Bosdoin Coll., Brunswick, Maine, 1982; cons. panelist NEH, 1974—, dir. nat. seminar for professions, 1975, 76, 79; assoc. area advisor Council on Internat. Exchange of Scholars, 1975-78; mem. spl. study sect. NIH, 1978-79. Author: Psychoanalysis and American Medicine 1894-1918, 1967, Jelliffe-American Physician and Psychoanalyst, 1983, (with Buenker and Crunden) Progressivism, 1977; editor: Science in America-Historical Selections, 1971. Mem. Am. Assn. for History of Medicine, Orgn. Am. Historians, Am. Hist. Assn., History of Sci. Soc., Midwest History of Sci. Junto (pres. 1982-83), Cheiron Internat. Soc. for History of Behavioral and Social Scis. (presiding officer 1977-78), Am. Psychol. Assn. (recognition mem.). Home: 4158 Kendale Rd Columbus OH 43220 Office: Dept History Ohio State U 230 W 17th Ave Columbus OH 43210

BURNS, ALLAN P., writer, TV producer; b. Balt., May 18, 1935; s. Donald L. and Pauline D. (Dobbling) B.; m. Joan Irene Bailey, June 11, 1964; children—Eric, Matthew. Student, U. Oreg., 1956. With program story dept. NBC, 1956-58; writer Jay Ward Prodns., 1959-62. Writer, creator: The Munsters show, CBS, 1962; writer: The Smothers Bros. Show, 1964; head writer: He & She program, CBS, 1967-68; story editor: Get Smart program, NBC, 1968-69; writer, producer: Room 222, ABC, 1969-70; creator, exec. producer: The Mary Tyler Moore Show, CBS, 1970-77; creator, producer: The Rhoda Show, 1974-75, Friends and Lovers, 1974-75; co-exec. producer-creator: Lou Grant, 1977-82; writer: screenplays A Little Romance, 1980 (Academy award nominee 1980), Butch and Sundance-The Early Days, 1980, The Mary Tyler Moore Show, 1970-71. Recipient Emmy awards for best comedy writing for He & She, 1968-69, award for best comedy writing for Room 222 Writers Guild Am., 1969, award for best comedy writing for Mary Tyler Moore Show, 1970-71. Mem. Acad. TV Arts and Scis., Acad. Motion Picture Arts and Scis., Friends of the Earth, Common Cause. Office: 4024 Radford Ave Studio City CA 91604

BURNS, ARNOLD IRWIN, lawyer; b. N.Y.C., Apr. 14, 1930; s. Herman Leon and Rose (Lauterstein) B.; m. Felice Bernstein, June 17, 1951; children: Linda Susan, Douglas Todd. A.B., Union Coll., Schenectady, 1950; LL.B., Cornell U., 1953; postgrad., Parker Sch. Internat. Law, 1960. Bar: N.Y. 1953, D.C. 1977. Partner firm Burns Summit Rovins & Feldesman (and predecessors), N.Y.C., 1960—, Burns Summit Rovins & Washington (and predecessor), Washington, 1977—; dir., vice chmn. bd. Cook United, Inc.; counsel N.Y. State Joint Legis. Com. on Ethics, 1964. Note editor: Cornell Law Quar, 1952-53. Counsel, chmn. bd. trustees Union Coll., Schenectady; bd. govs. Union U.; vice chmn., bd. dirs., nat. chmn. Freedoms Found., Valley Forge, Pa.; nat. trustee Boys Clubs Am.; mem. Council Governing Bds.; mem. adv. council Cornell U. Law Sch., Ithaca, N.Y.; mem. Cornell U. Council; nat. chmn. Cornell Law Sch. Fund; mem. adv. council Hofstra Sch. Law; mem. Nat. Rep. Senatorial Com., Rep. Senatorial Inner Circle, U.S. Senatorial Bus. Adv. Bd., Presdl. Task Force. Served to capt. AUS, 1953-57. Mem. Am., Fed., N.Y. State bar assns., Fed. Bar Council, Assn. Bar City N.Y., Cornell Law Assn. (exec. com.), Am. Arbitration Assn. (nat. panel arbitrators), Order of Coif, Phi Kappa Phi, Kappa Nu, Alpha Phi Omega. Republican. Jewish. Clubs: Westhampton Country; Arm and Navy, Internat. (Washington); Atrium, Merchants, Friars. (legal com.), Mohawk Golf). Home: 25 Sutton Pl S New York NY 10022 also 338 Dune Rd Westhampton Beach NY 11978 Office: 445 Park Ave New York NY 10022

BURNS, ARTHUR EDWARD, economist; b. Oakland, Calif., Sept. 3, 1908; s. William Thomas and Anne (Bruns) B.; m. Marcella Eugenie Wyss, Oct. 30, 1933; 1 son, Robert Lee. A.B., U. Calif., 1931, M.A., 1934; Ph.D., George Washington U., 1935. Instr. George Washington U., 1934-35, asst. prof., 1935-37, assoc. prof., 1937-40, adj. prof., 1940-45, prof. econs., 1945-74, prof. emeritus, 1974—; acting dean Sch. Govt., 1946-49, dean, 1949-57, dean, chmn. grad. council, 1957-67; dean Grad. Sch. Arts and Scis., 1967-74; dir. acad. planning Consortium of Univs., Washington, 1974-75; econ. cons. on profit renegotiation, 1972—; Vis. prof. econs. U. Calif., summer 1949, Getulio Vargus Found.; nat. faculty econ. scis. U. Brazil, Rio de Janeiro, 1952; Economist Fed. Emergency Relief Adminstrn., 1934-35; economist, asst. dir. research WPA, 1935-40, adviser, 1941-42; spl. cons. OPA, 1942-43; dep. dir. Office of Materials and Facilities, War Food Adminstrn., 1943-45; cons. White House Office, 1957-60, Renegotiation Bd., 1961-72, U.S.-P.R. Status Commn., 1965-66; vis. lectr. Indsl. Coll. Armed Forces, 1950—; pub. mem. Fgn. Service Selection Bd., Dept. State, 1951; cons. Fgn. Operations Adminstrn., ICA, 1953-57, Operations Research Office, 1951-60, Italian Govt., Rome, 1955. Author: (with Neal and Watson) Modern Economics, 1948, rev. edit. 1953, Arabic edit., 1960, (with D.S. Watson) Government Spending and Economic Expansion, 1940, (with E.A. Williams) Federal Work, Security, and Relief Programs, 1941; Contbr. articles and revs. to profl. jours., govt. publs. Mem. Am. Econ. Assn., Artus, Delta Phi Epsilon (nat. pres. 1948-50). Club: Cosmos.

BURNS, ARTHUR F., ambassador; b. Stanislau, Austria, Apr. 27, 1904; m. Helen Bernstein, Jan. 25, 1930; children: David S., Joseph M. A.B., Columbia U., 1925, A.M., 1925, Ph.D., 1934; LL.D., Lehigh U., 1952; L.H.D., Rutgers U., 1955; LL.D., Brown U., 1956, Dartmouth Coll., 1956, Oberlin Coll., 1956, Wesleyan U., 1958, Swarthmore Coll., 1958, L.I.U., 1960, U. Chgo., 1960, Rikkyo U., Tokyo, 1965, Fordham U., 1969, Columbia U., 1970, NYU, 1970, U. Calif., 1970, The Cath. U., 1973, George Washington U., 1973, Ill. Coll., 1974, Yeshiva U., 1974, U. Akron, 1975, Washington U., 1976, S.C. U., 1977, Carnegie Mellon U., 1977, Notre Dame U., 1977, Gonzaga U., 1977, Ripon Coll., 1978, U. Vt., 1979, Chapman Coll., 1979, Fairleigh Dickinson U., 1979, U. So. Calif., 1979, Hofstra U., 1980, Allegheny Coll., 1980, Xavier U., 1981; Sc.D., U. Pa., 1958, U. Rochester, 1963, Fla. Inst. Tech., 1976, Lake Forest Coll., 1978; other hon. degrees. Asst. stats. Columbia U., 1926, Gilder fellow, 1926-27; instr. econs. Rutgers U., 1927-30, asst. prof., 1930-33, assoc. prof., 1933-43, prof., 1943-44; research assoc. Nat. Bur. Econ. Research, 1930-31, mem. research staff, 1933-69, dir. research staff, 1945-53, chmn., 1967-68; chief statistician Ry. Emergency Bd., 1941-, Columbia U., 1941-42, vis. prof. econs., 1942-44, prof., 1944-58; chmn. Pres. Adv. Bd. on Econ. Growth and Stability, 1953-56, Pres. Council Econ. Advisers, 1953-56, Cabinet Com. Small Bus., 1956; mem. Adv. Council on Social Security Financing, 1957-58; John Bates Clark prof. econs. Columbia U., 1959-69, prof. emeritus, 1969—; mem. Temporary State Commn. on Econ. Expansion, N.Y., 1959-60, Pres. Adv. Com. on Labor-Mgmt. Policy, 1961-66; chmn. Nat. Bur. Econ. Research, 1967-68; mem. Gov.'s Com. on Minimum Wage, N.Y., 1964; vis. prof. econs. Stanford U., 1968; counsellor to Pres. U.S., 1969-70; chmn. bd. govs. Fed. Res. System, 1970-78; alt. gov. IMF, 1973-78; disting. scholar in residence Am. Enterprise Inst., 1978-81; disting. professorial lectr. Georgetown U., Washington, 1978-81; ambassador to Fed. Republic of Germany; bd. dirs. Nat. Bur. Econ. Research, 1945—, hon. chmn., 1969—; Anheuser-Busch disting. guest lectr. St. Louis U., 1980; Kathleen Price Bryan lectr. U. N.C., 1981; Founders' Day lectr. Xavier U., Cin., 1981. Recipient Jefferson award Am. Inst. Pub. Service, 1976, Alexander Hamilton award U.S. Treasury Dept., 1976, Am. Democratic Legacy award Anti-Defamation League, B'nai B'rith, 1978, award Fed. City Club, Washington, 1978, Econ. Club, N.Y.C., 1978, Grand Cross of Order of Merit, W.Ger., 1978, Am. Eagle award Invest-in-Am. Nat. Council, 1978, McMahon Meml. award Fordham U. Club Washington, 1978, award Citizens Budget Commn., N.Y.C., 1978, Frank E. Seidman Disting. award, 1978, George Washington award Am. Hungarian Found., 1978, Gold Medal award Inst. Social Scis., 1978, Francis Boyer award Am. Enterprise Inst. Pub. Policy Research, 1978, medal for disting. achievement Am. Soc. French Legion of Honor, 1978; Per Jacobsson Lectr., Belgrade, Yugoslavia, 1979. Fellow Am. Econ. Assn. (pres. 1959), Am. Statis. Assn., Econometric Soc., Am. Acad. Arts and Scis., Acad. Polit. Sci. (pres. 1962-68, mem., bd. dirs. 1957—), Am. Philos. Soc., Council Fgn. Relations, Pilgrims Soc., Institut de Sci. Economique Appliquee (corr.), Phi Beta Kappa. Clubs: Cosmos, City Tavern (Washington); Century Assn. (N.Y.C.). Office: Office of the Ambassador Am Embassy APO New York NY 19080

BURNS, ARTHUR LEE, architect; b. Indpls., July 5, 1924; s. Charles Raymond and Dorothy Frances (Young) B.; m. Dorothy Maxine Kingsland, Oct. 26, 1946; children—Stephen Robert (dec.), Melody Lee. B.S. in Architecture, U. Cin., 1949. Archtl. draftsman Foster Engring. Co., Ltd., Indpls., 1941-42; archtl. draftsman Albert V. Walters (Architect), Cin., 1946-48; chief draftsman Arend & Arend (Architects), Cin., 1948-49; architect The McGuire & Shook Corp., Indpls., 1949—, v.p., 1964-71, sec.-treas., 1972-73, 80—, pres., 1974-75, exec. v.p., 1976-77, v.p., 1978-79, sec.-treas., 1980-83. Served with USAAF, 1943-46. Fellow AIA (sec. treas. Indpls. chpt. 1965-66, v.p. 1967, pres. 1968, mem. documents bd. 1973—, chmn. 1978-79); mem. Ind., Soc. Architects (dir. 1968-69, v.p. 1971, pres. 1972, Edward D. Pierre Meml. medal 1972), Constrn. Specifications Inst. (Indpls. chpt. v.p. 1966-67, pres. 1967-68). Republican. Methodist. Clubs: Broad Ripple Sertoma Indpls. (v.p. 1973-74, pres. 1974-75), Broad Ripple Sertoma Indpls. (Gold Honor Club pres.). Home: 7130 Wexford Dr Indianapolis IN 46250 Office: 7440 N Shadeland Ave Indianapolis IN 46250

BURNS, BRIAN PATRICK, lawyer; b. Cambridge, Mass., July 12, 1936; s. John Joseph and Alice (Blake) B.; m. Sheila Ann O'Connor, June 23, 1962; children: Sheila Ann, Brian Patrick, Sean Richard, Roderick O'Connor. A.B., Holy Cross Coll., 1957; LL.B., Harvard, 1960. Bar: Mass. 1960, N.Y. 1961, Calif. 1965. Law clk., spl. asst. to regional adminstr. New York Regional Office, SEC, 1958-59; asso. Webster, Sheffield, Fleischmann, Hitchcock & Brookfield, N.Y.C., 1960-64; partner Cullinan, Hancock, Rothert & Burns, San Francisco, 1965-74; sr. partner Cullinan, Burns & Helmer, San Francisco, 1975-78; firm Burns & Whitehead, San Francisco, 1978—; Dir. U.S. Banknote Corp., N.Y.C., from 1967, chmn. exec. and finance coms., from 1973; dir. Coca Cola Bottling Co., N.Y., 1974—, chmn. exec. com., 1979—; dir., mem. exec. com. Kellogg Co., 1979; dir., chmn. ops. review com. Brink's Inc., Chgo., 1976-78; dir., chmn. acquisition com. Pacific Holding Corp., Los Angeles, 1972-78; dir., mem. exec. com. Beverly Wilshire Hotel, Beverly Hills, Calif., Calif., 1967—; dir. Boothe Fin. Corp., San Francisco, 1976—, chmn., chief exec. officer, chmn. exec. com., 1981—; dir., chmn. exec. com. USR Industries, Morristown, N.J., 1979—; dir., chmn. audit com. Rocor Internat., Palo Alto, Calif., 1976—; dir. Edward L. Scarff & Assos., San Francisco; underwriting mem. Lloyds of London, 1978—; lectr. continuing edn. of bar U. Calif., 1969, 74, 76, advanced bus. seminar, 1971; seminar on investment opportunities in wine industry McGraw Hill Coll., N.Y., 1973, Legal Edn. Inst., 1976. Bd. dirs. Boys Club of San Francisco, Am. Irish Found., 1978—; trustee Holy Cross Coll., 1978—. Mem. Am. Bar Assn. (mem. small bus. com. corp. bus. and banking sect. 1972—), State Bar Cal. (vice chmn. com. on corps. 1971-75), Bar Assn. San Francisco (chmn. com. on corp. banking and bus. law 1968-69), Royal Dublin Soc., Newcomen Soc., Mil. and Hospitaller Order St. Lazarus of Jerusalem (comdr. companion). Roman Catholic. Clubs: Bohemian, Burlingame Country, Family, Olympic, Sky, N.Y. Athletic, Les Ambassadeurs (London). Office: Burns & Whitehead 100 Bush St. San Francisco CA 94104 *

BURNS, BUSHROD W., JR., holding company executive; b. Lynchburg, Va., July 26, 1933; s. Bushrod W. and Eunice (Puckette) B.; m. Delores Ann Salajcik, Nov. 14, 1959; children: Brendalyn Kay, Bushrod W. III. B.S. in Acctg., Va. Tech. U., 1955. With Ford Motor Co., Dearborn, Mich., 1955-67; asst. controller Gen. Cable Corp., N.Y.C., 1967-72; controller Wheelabrator Frye, N.Y.C., 1972; staff v.p. RCA, N.Y.C., 1972-77; v.p. ops. Dyson-Kissner-Moran, N.Y.C., 1977—; chmn. bd. Esterline Corp., Darien, Conn., 1978—, Kearney-Nat. Corp., N.Y.C., 1978—, Leader Nat. Corp., Cleve., 1979—; pres., chmn. bd. Raydon Tech. Corp., N.Y.C., 1977—. Served to lt. U.S. Army, 1956. Home: 35 Henry St Scarsdale NY 10583 Office: Dyson-Kissner-Moran 230 Park Ave New York NY 10169

BURNS, CARROLL DEAN, insurance company executive; b. Chattanooga, Dec. 22, 1932; s. William Thomas and Lillis (Gill) B.; m. Jean Baird, Aug. 29, 1954; children: Randy, Lori. B.S., U. Tenn., 1954. C.P.A., Tenn., Ohio. With Provident Life and Accident Ins. Co., Chattanooga, 1957-63, mgr. data processing, 1960-63; with Union Central Life Ins. Co., Cin., 1963-79, exec. v.p., comptroller, 1974-79; also dir.; sr. v.p. Life Ins. Co. Ga., Atlanta, 1979—; chmn. bd. Ga. U.S. Data Services; dir. Union Central Life Assurance Corp., Life Ins. Co. Ga., First of Ga. Ins. Group; Former chmn. Civil Service Bd., Fairfield, Ohio. Trustee Better Bus. Bur. Cin. Served with USAF, 1955-57. Mem. Life Office Mgmt. Assn. (mem. financial controls and reports com.), Fin. Execs. Inst., Am. Council Life Ins. (com. on ann. statements and valuation of assets), Beta Alpha Psi. Baptist. Clubs: Lions, Hamilton City; Bankers (Cin.); Atlanta Country., Georgian. Home: 4830 Dunwoody Junction Dunwoody GA 30338 Office: Life of Georgia Tower Atlanta GA 30308

BURNS, DAN, manufacturing company executive; b. Auburn, Calif., Sept. 10, 1925; s. William and Edith Lynn (Johnston) B.; 1 son, Dan. Dir. materials Menasco Mfg. Co., 1951-56; v.p., gen. mgr. Hufford Corp., 1956-58; pres. Hufford div. Siegler Corp., 1958-61; v.p. Siegler Corp., 1961-62, Lear Siegler, Inc., 1962-64; pres., dir. Electrada Corp., Culver City, Calif., from 1964; now pres., chief exec. officer, dir. Sargent Industries and related cos.; chmn., chief exec. officer Arlington Industries, Inc.; dir. Data Design Corp., Gen. Automotive Corp. Served from pvt. to capt. U.S. Army, 1941-47; prisoner of war; Japan; asst. mil. attache, 1946; China; a.d.c. to Gen. George C. Marshall, 1946-47. Mem. Orgn. Am. States Sports Com. (dir.). Clubs: Los Angeles Country., St. Francis Yacht, Calif., Conquistadores del Cielo, Garden of the Gods. Home: 10851 Chalon Rd Bel Air Los Angeles CA 90024 Office: Sargent Industries 1901 Bldg Suite 1251 Century City Los Angeles CA 90077

BURNS, DAVID MITCHELL, sci. assn. exec.; b. Pineville, Ky., Dec. 1, 1928; s. Judge Mitchell and Mary Louise (Cooke) B.; m. Sandra Lynn Dunlop, June 8, 1955; children—David A.D., Patrick C.C. A.B., Princeton, 1953; student, Sch. Advanced Internat. Studies, Johns Hopkins U., 1957, 60, Howard U., 1957, 60, Fgn. Service Inst., Tangier, Morocco, 1967-69. Advt. trainee Gen. Electric Co., 1953; instr. English U. Kan., 1954-55; asst. cultural affairs officer Am. embassy, Damascus, Syria, 1955-56, Beirut, Lebanon, 1956; dir. Iran-Am. Soc., Isfahan, 1957; information officer Am. consulate general, Salisbury, Fedn. Rhodesia and Nyasaland, 1957-59; pub. affairs officer Am. embassy, Bamako, Mali, 1960-62; cultural affairs officer, Tunis, Tunisia, 1962-63; cultural policy officer Africa, USIA, Agy., 1963-67; pub. affairs officer Am. interests sect. embassy of, Switzerland, Algiers, Algeria, 1969-72; dir. sci. and tech. programs USIA, 1972-77; dir. climate project AAAS, Washington, 1978—. Author: newspaper column Science and the Future, 1981—; contbr. articles to lit. and profl. jours. Served with USAAF, 1946-49. Fulbright grant l'Universite de Lille, Salzburg Seminar in Am. Studies, 1953-54. Mem. Nat. Assn. Sci. Writers. Club: Cosmos (Washington). Home: 1712 19th St NW Washington DC 20009 Office: AAAS 1776 Massachusetts Ave NW Washington DC 20520

BURNS, E(DWARD) BRADFORD, history educator; b. Muscatine, Iowa, Aug. 28, 1932; s. Edward Sylvester and Wanda Adaline (Schwandke) B. B.A., U. Iowa, 1954; M.A., Tulane U., 1954; Ph.D., Columbia U., 1964. Instr. SUNY, Buffalo, 1963-64; asst. prof. history UCLA, 1964-67, prof., 1969—, dean div. honors, 1979-83; assoc. prof., Columbia U., 1967-69. Author: books including The Unwritten Alliance, 1966, A History of Brazil, 1970, Latin America, A Concise Interpretive History, 1977, The Poverty of Progress, 1980. Served with USNR, 1956-59. Decorated Order Rio-Branco, Brazil; recipient Bolton Meml. prize Conf. Latin Am. History, 1967, award for disting. scholarly reporting in non-acad. periodical Latin Am. Studies Assn., 1976, Hubert Herring award, 1979. Mem. Instituto Historico e Geografico Brasileiro (corr.). Home: 2341 Allview Terr Los Angeles CA 90068 Office: Dept History U Calif Los Angeles CA 90024 *

BURNS, SISTER ELIZABETH MARY, hospital administrator; b. Estherville, Iowa, Mar. 3, 1927; d. Bernard Aloysius and Viola Caroline (Brennan) B. Diploma in Nursing, St. Joseph Mercy Sch. Nursing, Sioux City, Iowa, 1952; B.S. in Nursing Edn, Mercy Coll., Detroit, 1957, M.Sc., Wayne State U., 1958; Ed.D., Columbia U., 1969. Joined Sisters of Mercy, Roman Cath. Ch., 1946; nursing supr. Mercy Med. Center, Dubuque, Iowa, 1952-55; supr. orthopedics and urology St. Joseph Mercy Hosp., Sioux City, 1955-56; dir. Sch. Nursing, 1958-63; chairperson dept. nursing Mercy Coll. of Detroit, 1963-73; dir. health services Sisters of Mercy, Province of Detroit, 1973-77; pres., chief exec. officer Marian Health Center, Sioux City, 1977—; dir. Security Nat. Bank. Bd. dirs. Mercy Sch. Nursing of Detroit, 1968-77; mem. exec. com. Greater Detroit Area Hosp. Council, 1973-77; trustee St. Mary Coll., Omaha, 1981—, Briar Cliff Coll., Sioux City, 1981—; chmn. Mercy Health Adv. Council, 1978-80. Mem. Western Iowa League for Nursing (pres. 1960-62), Nat. League Nursing, Sisters of Mercy Shared Services Coordinating Com., Cath. Hosp. Assn. (trustee 1977-80). Home: 2101 Court St Sioux City IA 51104 Office: 801 5th St PO Box 3168 Sioux City IA 51102

BURNS, ELLEN BREE, judge; b. New Haven, Conn., Dec. 13, 1923; d. Vincent Thomas and Mildred Bridget (Bannon) Bree; m. Joseph Patrick Burns, Oct. 8, 1955 (dec.); children: Mary Ellen, Joseph Bree, Kevin James. B.A., Albertus Magnus Coll., 1944, LL.D. (hon.), 1974; LL.B., Yale U., 1947; LL.D. (hon.), U. New Haven, 1981. Bar: Conn. 1947. Dir. legis. legal services, State of Conn., 1949-73; judge Conn. Circuit Ct., 1973-74, Conn. Ct. of Common Pleas, 1974-76, Conn. Superior Ct., 1976-78, U.S. Dist. Ct. Conn., New Haven, 1978—. Trustee Fairfield U., 1978—; Recipient John Carroll of Carrolton award John Barry Council K.C., 1973; Judiciary award Conn. Trial Lawyers Assn., 1978; Cross Pro Ecclesia et Pontifice, 1981. Mem. New Haven County Bar Assn., ABA, Am. Bar Found. Roman Catholic. Office: 141 Church St New Haven CT 06510

BURNS, GEORGE, comedian; b. N.Y.C., Jan. 20, 1896; m. Gracie Allen, Jan. 7, 1926 (dec. Aug. 1964); adopted children: Sandra Jean, Ronald John. Student pub. schs., N.Y.C. Began as dancer vaudeville performer; formed (with Gracie Allen) team, 1923; team toured, U.S. and Europe; making radio debut with, B.B.C.; co-star radio show, 1932-50; screen debut, 1932; films include The Big Broadcast, 1932, 36, 37, International House, 1933, Love in Bloom, 1933, College Humor, 1933, Six of a Kind, 1934, We're Not Dressing, 1934, College Holiday, 1936, A Damsel in Distress, 1937, College Swing, 1938, Many Happy Returns, 1939, Honolulu, 1939, Two Girls and a Sailor, 1944, The Sunshine Boys, 1975, Oh God!, 1977, Sgt. Pepper's Lonely Hearts Club Band, 1978, Just You and Me, Kid, 1979, Two of a Kind, 1979, Oh God! Book Two, 1980; co-star: TV show George Burns and Gracie Allen Show, 1950-58; star: George Burns Show, 1958-59; appeared on: Wendy and Me, 1964-65; numerous TV and personal appearances; producer: Meet Mona McCluskey, NBC, 1965; record albums include I Wish I Was Young Again, 1981, George Burns in Nashville, 1981; Author: I Love Her, That's Why!, 1955, Living It Up, or, They Still Love Me in Altoona, 1976, How to Live to be One Hundred or More, 1983. Recipient Acad. award as Best Supporting Actor, 1976. Address: care Putnam Pub Group 200 Madison Ave New York NY 10016 *

BURNS, GEORGE WASHINGTON, educator; b. Cin., Nov. 20, 1913; s. George Washington and Caroline (Little) B.; m. Hermine McDonald, June 15, 1942; children: George McDonald, Barbara Lynette, Theodore Scott. A.B., U. Cin., 1937; Ph.D., U. Minn., 1941. Teaching fellow botany U. Minn., 1937-41, instr., 1945- 46, faculty, summer sessions, 1948-49; asst. prof. botany Ohio Wesleyan U., 1946-50, asso. prof., 1950-54, prof. botany, 1954—, chmn. dept., 1954-70, acting v.p., dean, 1957-59, acting pres., 1958-59, v.p., dean, 1959-61; vis. prof. Kerala U., India, 1964, U. Bombay, 1965, 66; Cons. State Dept. Edn. Mission to India, AID, summers 1964-67; Head insts. sect. NSF, 1961-62. Author: The Science of Genetics, 1969, 72, 76, 80, 83, The Plant Kingdom, 1974; also articles in tech. jours. Served as lt. USNR, 1942-45. Fellow A.A.A.S., Ohio Acad. Sci. (v.p. 1956-57, sec. 1957-63, pres. 1969-70); mem. Am. Genetic Assn., Am. Soc. Human Genetics, Bot. Soc. Am., Arctic Inst. in N.Am., Sigma Xi. Home: 354 Troy Rd Delaware OH 43015

BURNS, GERALD PHILLIP, educator; b. Winthrop, Mass., Oct. 1, 1918; s. Gerald John and Lillian (Griffin) B.; m. Cecile Gayzik, June 20, 1970; children—Gerald, Michael, James. B.S., Boston U., 1941; M.A., Columbia, 1946, Ed.D., 1948; Ph.D., N.Y. U., 1962. Vice-pres. Reed Coll., 1955-58; pres. Ind. Coll. Funds, N.Y.C., 1958-67; v.p. Johns Hopkins, 1967-69; prof. higher edn. Fla. State U., 1969-73; pres.

Our Lady of the Lake U., San Antonio, 1973-78, prof., 1978—; dir. Tex. State Bank. Author: Administrators in Higher Education, 1962, Trustees in Higher Education, 1965, Faculty in Higher Education, 1973, Principles of Leadership, 1978; contbr. to UNESCO Studies in Postsecondary Edn., Internat. Ency. Higher Edn. Mem. Higher Edn. Colloquium, Chgo., 1959; chmn. Univ. Roundtable.; Trustee S.W. Research Inst.; Vice-chmn. Inst. of the Ams.; chmn. bd. dirs. San Antonio Public Library. Served with USAAF, 1941-46. Fulbright fellow, Latin Am. Mem. Assn. Higher Edn., Public Relations Soc. Am., Am. Inst. Character Edn. (dir.), Phi Epsilon Kappa, Phi Delta Kappa. Clubs: University (N.Y.C.); Argyle (San Antonio). Home: 6915 Callaghan Rd San Antonio TX 78229

BURNS, HUGH ALLAN, lawyer; b. Denver, July 28, 1930; s. O. H. and Mary G. (Gerkin) B.; m. Beverly Mae Faubion, Aug. 29, 1954; children: Laurel Elisabeth, Hugh Allan, Catherine Mary. A.B., Princeton U., 1952; B.A. in Jurisprudence, Hertford Coll., Oxford U., 1954, M.A., 1960; J.D., U. Chgo., 1955. Bar: Colo. bar 1956, U.S. Supreme Ct. bar 1966. Asso. firm Dawson, Nagel, Sherman & Howard, Denver, 1955-61, partner, 1962-80; mem. firm Burns & Figa, P.C., 1980—; instr. law U. Denver, 1960-65. Chmn. Denver Democratic Party, 1968-70; trustee Princeton U., 1969-73. Served with U.S. Army, 1956-58. Rhodes scholar, 1952-54. Fellow Am. Coll. Trial Lawyers; mem. Denver Bar Assn., Colo. Bar Assn., Am. Bar Assn., Am. Law Inst. Unitarian. Home: 615 Garfield St Denver CO 80206 Office: 333 Steele Park 50 S Steel St Denver CO 80209

BURNS, IVAN ALFRED, diversified company executive; b. Leamington Spa, Eng., 1935. B.S., Birmingham U. Conventry Coll. Engring. Tech., 1958. Various positions Deer & Co., U.S.A., Europe, 1960-69; corp. mgr. capital budgets ACF Industries Inc., N.Y.C., 1969-72, exec. dir. internat. ops., 1972-74, v.p. internat. ops., 1974-78, v.p., gen. mgr. W-K-M Group, 1978-81, chief exec. officer, chmn. bd., 1978-81, dir., ACF Bt. Britain Ltd. (subs.), W-K-M (Sinapore) Pvt. Ltd., KK Itabashi, Japan. Office: ACF Industries Inc 750 3d Ave New York NY 10017 *

BURNS, JAMES FRANCIS, financial advisor; b. N.Y.C., Sept. 28, 1922; s. Martin and Ellen (Lavelle) B.; m. Irene M. O'Reilly, Nov. 22, 1951; children: Mary Ellen, Michael, Betty Anne, Maureen. B.B.A. in Acctg., Iona Coll., New Rochelle, N.Y., 1944; M.B.A. in Fin., NYU, 1950. C.P.A., N.Y. Audit mgr. Price Waterhouse & Co., C.P.A.s, N.Y.C., 1944-63; treas., controller United Brands Co., N.Y.C., 1963-74; v.p., chief fin. officer C.D. Mallory & Co., N.Y.C., 1976-79; controller Gen. Host Co., N.Y.C., 1974-76; v.p. fin. Dairylea Coop. Inc., Pearl River, N.Y., 1979-82; fin. tax adv., Tallman, N.Y., 1982—. Vice chmn. bd. lay trustees Iona Coll.; treas., lector St. Aedan Roman Cath. Ch., Pearl River. Mem. Am. Inst. C.P.A.s, N.Y. State Soc. C.P.A.s. Republican. Club: Pearl River Nauraushaun Swim (past pres., dir.). Home: 145 S Nauraushaun Rd Pearl River NY 10965 Office: 321 Route 59 Tallman NY 10982

BURNS, JAMES FRANCIS, JR., bank executive; b. N.Y.C., July 9, 1937; s. James Francis and Sarah (Mulligan) B.; children: Kimberly, Karen, Karla. B.B.A., Loyola U., Los Angeles, 1959. Audit mgr. Arthur Andersen & Co., Los Angeles, 1959-66; controller St. Joseph Hosp., Burbank, Calif., 1966-68; v.p. First Interstate Bank, Los Angeles, 1979-82, v.p., chief fin. officer, 1972-75, sr. v.p., chief fin. officer, 1975-78, exec. v.p., chief fin. officer, 1978, First Interstate Bancorp, 1982—; mem. bus. adv. council Loyola U., Los Angeles, 1981—; chmn. fin. and monetary services com. Seismic Safety Commn. Calif., Sacramento, 1981—. Mem. Am. Inst. C.P.A.s. Republican. Roman Catholic. Office: First Interstate Bancorp 707 Wilshire Blvd Lso Angeles CA 90017

BURNS, JAMES MACGREGOR, political scientist, historian; b. Melrose, Mass., Aug. 3, 1918; s. Robert Arthur and Mildred Curry (Bunce) B.; m. Janet Rose Dismorr Thompson, May 23, 1942; children: David MacGregor, Timothy Stewart, Deborah Edwards, Margaret Rebecca Antonia; m. Joan Simpson Meyers, Sept. 7, 1969. B.A. Williams Coll, 1939; postgrad., Nat. Inst. Pub. Affairs, 1939-40; M.A., Ph.D., Harvard, 1947, London Sch. Econs., 1949. Exec. sec. non ferrous metals commn. NWLB, 1942-43; faculty polit. sci. Williams Coll., Williamstown, Mass., 1941—, prof., 1953—; co-dir. Project 87, interdisciplinary study of constitution during bicentennial era, 1976-87; Mem. staff Hoover Commn., 1948; faculty Salzburg Seminar in Am. Studies, 1954, 61. Author: Guam: Operations of the 77th Infantry Div, 1944, Okinawa: The Last Battle, (with others), 1947, Congress on Trial, 1949, Government by the People, (with Jack W. Peltason and Thomas E. Cronin), 1981, Roosevelt: The Lion and the Fox, 1956, John Kennedy: A Political Profile, 1960, The Deadlock of Democracy: Four Party Politics in America, 1963, Presidential Government: The Crucible of Leadership, 1966, Roosevelt: The Soldier of Freedom, 1970, Uncommon Sense, 1972, Edward Kennedy and the Camelot Legacy, 1976, Leadership, 1978, The Vineyard of Liberty, 1982, The Power to Lead, 1984; Contbr. to periodicals. Mem. Mass. delegation Democratic Nat. Conv., 1952, 56, 60, 64, Dem. Charter Conv., 1974; mem. Mass. Dem. Party Charter Commn., 1977-79, Mass. Dem. Charter Conv., 1979, Berkshire County delegation Mass. state conv., 1954; Dem. candidate for Congress, 1st Dist. Mass., 1958; Former trustee Stockbridge Sch., Woodrow Wilson Internat. Center for Scholars. Served with AUS, 1943-45; combat historian; Guam, Saipan, Okinawa. Recipient Tamiment Inst. award for best biography, 1956; Woodrow Wilson prize, 1957; Pulitzer prize in history, 1971; Nat. Book award, 1971; Francis Parkman prize, 1971; Christopher award, 1983. Mem. Am. Polit. Sci. Assn. (pres. 1975-76), New Eng. Polit. Sci. Assn. (pres. 1960-61), Internat. Soc. Polit. Psychology (pres. 1982-83), Am. Hist. Assn., Am. Philos. Soc., ACLU, Am. Legion, Phi Beta Kappa, Delta Sigma Rho. Home: High Mowing Bee Hill Williamstown MA 01267 Office: Dept Polit Sci Williams Coll Williamstown MA 01267

BURNS, JAMES WILLIAM, power company executive; b. Winnipeg, Man., Can., Dec. 27, 1929; s. Charles William and Helen Gladys (Mackay) B.; m. Barbara Mary Copeland, Aug. 12, 1953; children: James F.C., Martha J., Alan W. B.Comm., U. Man., 1951; M.B.A., Harvard U., 1953. With Great-West Life Assurance Co., 1953—, exec. v.p., 1970, pres., dir., 1971-79, chmn., dir., 1979—; chmn. exec. com. Investors Group, Montreal Trustco Inc.; dir. Bathurst Paper Ltd., Consol.-Bathurst Inc., CB Pak Inc.; pres. Power Corp. Can.; pres., chief exec. officer Power Fin. Corp.; dir. Can. Pacific Ltd., Genstar Ltd., IBM Can. Ltd. Bd. dirs. Council for Bus. and Arts in Can.; trustee N.Am. Wildlife Found.; chmn. Adv. Group on Exec. Compensation in Pub. Service. Hon. lt. col. Queen's Own Cameron Highlanders of Can. Mem. Ducks Unltd. (dir.). Clubs: St. Charles Country, Man. (Winnipeg); Albany (Toronto); Toronto; Mount-Royal, Mount-Bruno Country (Montreal); John's Island (Fla.). Office: 759 Victoria Sq Montreal PQ H2Y 2K4 Canada

BURNS, JOHN JOSEPH, pharmaceutical company executive, pharmacology educator; b. Flushing, N.Y., Oct. 8, 1920; s. Thomas F. and Katherine (Kane) B.; m. Margaret Hitchcock, 1974. B.S., Queens Coll., 1942; M.A., Columbia U., 1948, Ph.D., 1950. With lab. chem. pharmacology Nat. Heart Inst., 1950-60, dep. chief lab., 1957-60; head sec. clin. pharmacology, also adj. asst. prof. biochemistry N.Y. U. research service Goldwater Meml. Hosp., Welfare Island, N.Y., 1950-57; dir. research pharmacodynamics div. Wellcome Research Labs., Burroughs Wellcome & Co. (U.S.A.) Inc., Tuckahoe, N.Y., 1960-66; v.p. for research Hoffmann-LaRoche Inc., Nutley, N.J., 1967—; Vis. prof. pharmacology Albert Einstein Coll. Medicine, 1960-68; adj. prof. pharmacology Cornell U. Med. Coll., 1969—; sr. cons. pharmacology-toxicology programs NIH; chmn. com. problems drug safety Drug Research Bd., 1965-72. Author articles metabolism drugs, vitamins and carbohydrates. Served with AUS, 1944-46. Fellow Am. Inst. Chemists; mem. Inst. Medicine, Nat. Acad. Scis., N.Y. Acad. Scis. (v.p. 1964-65), Am. Soc. Pharmacology and Exptl. Therapeutics (pres. 1972-73), Am. Soc. Biol. Chemists, Am. Inst. Nutrition, Am. Coll. Neuropsychopharmacology, Internat. Union Pharmacology (pres. 1975-78). Home: PO Box 104 Southport CT 06490 Office: Hoffmann-LaRoche Inc Nutley NJ 07110

BURNS, JOHN JOSEPH, aerospace executive, retired air force officer; b. Jersey City, June 28, 1924; s. Walter Joseph and Gertruce Agnes (Leslie) B.; m. Patricia Ann Boyle, Oct. 21, 1945; children: John Joseph, Jeffrey A., Judith P. B.S. in Math., U. Omaha, 1964. Commd. 2d lt. USAAF, 1943; advanced through grades to lt. gen. USAF, 1974; comdr. 522d tactical fighter squadron, Bergstrom AFB, Tex., 1957-59, comdr. 91st and 92d Tactical Fighter Squadrons, Bentwaters, Eng., 1959-62, asst. dir. ops., later dir. ops. 4th Tactical Fighter Wing, Seymour Johnson AFB, N.C., 1962-64, comdr. Detachment 2, Hdqrs. 831st Air Div., Edwards AFB, Calif., 1964-65, asst. dir., dir. requirements Directorate of Ops., Tactical Air Command, Langley AFB, Va., 1965-67, dep. comdr. ops. 8th Tactical Fighter Wing, Ubon Royal Thai AFB, Thailand, 1967, vice comdr. 8th Tactical Fighter Wing, 1967-68, comdr. 4525th Fighter Weapons Wing, Nellis AFB, Nev., 1968-69, comdr. 58th Tactical Fighter Tng. Wing, Luke AFB, Ariz., 1969-70, dep. dir. Gen. Purpose Forces, Directorate Operational Requirements and Devel. Plans, Hdqrs. USAF, 1970-72, dir., 1972-73; comdr. 12th Air Force, Bergstrom AFB, 1973, Air Force Test and Evaluation Center, Kirtland AFB, N.Mex., 1974, U.S. Support Activities Group, 7th Air Force, Nakhon Phanom Royal Thai AFB, 1974-75; dep. comdr. in chief U.S. Forces Korea/UN Command Korea, Seoul, 1975-77, U.S. Readiness Command, MacDill AFB, Fla., 1977-79; ret., 1979; v.p. advanced engring. MacDonnell Aircraft Co., St. Louis, 1979-84, v.p., gen. mgr. advanced tactical fighter and spl. projects, 1984—. Decorated D.S.M. with 2 oak leaf clusters, Silver Star, Legion of Merit with oak leaf cluster, D.F.C. with 2 oak leaf clusters, Bronze Star, Meritorious Service medal with 2 oak leaf clusters, Air medal with 33 oak leaf clusters, Air Force Commendation medal. Mem. Order Daedalians. Home: 19 Seven Oaks Dr Chesterfield MO 63017 Office: MacDonnell Aircraft Co Room 314-Dept 007 PO Box 516 Saint Louis MO 63166

BURNS, JOHN JOSEPH, JR., business executive; b. Cambridge, Mass., June 27, 1931; s. John Joseph and Alice (Blake) B.; m. Barbara Ann Miller, Oct. 18, 1958; children: John J. III, Christine, Gregory, Timothy, Jennifer. B.S. in Fin, Boston Coll., 1953; M.B.A., Harvard U., 1955. Asso. buying dept. and arbitrage dept. Goldman Sachs & Co., N.Y.C., 1957-63; asso. N.Y. Securities, N.Y.C., 1963-67, gen. partner, 1968; v.p. fin., dir. Alleghany Corp., N.Y.C., 1968-77, pres., 1977—, mem. exec. com., 1977—; dir., exec. com. Investors Diversified Services, Inc., Mpls., 1977—; dir. MSL Industries, Lincolnwood, Ill. Served with USN, 1955-57. Roman Catholic. Club: Oyster Harbors. Office: Park Ave Plaza New York NY 10022

BURNS, JOHN LAWRENCE, investments company executive; b. Watertown, Mass., Nov. 16, 1908; s. Michael P. and Ellen (Holihan) B.; m. Beryl M. Spinney, Aug. 29, 1937; children: John Spinney, Lara Burns Cunningham. B.S., Northeastern U., 1930, D.B.A. (hon.), 1957; Sc.D., Harvard U., 1934. Supt. wire div. Republic Steel Corp., 1934-42; vice chmn. exec. com., coordinating partner Booz, Allen & Hamilton, 1942-57; pres. RCA, 1957-62; vice chmn. bd. Cities Service Co., 1965-66, chmn. bd., 1966-68; pres. John L. Burns & Co., N.Y.C., 1968—; chmn. bd. trustees Magnavox Govt. and Indsl. Electronics Co.; dir. State Nat. Bank Conn. Chmn. bd. dirs. Boys' Clubs Am.; mem. corp. Northeastern U. Mem. Com. for Econ. Devel. (hon. trustee). Clubs: Round Hill (Greenwich, Conn.); Preston Mountain (Kent, Conn.); Blind Brook (Portchester, N.Y.); Sky, Econ. (N.Y.C.); Seminole (Palm Beach, Fla.). Home: 81 Doubling Rd Greenwich CT 06830 Office: The News Building 16th Floor 220 East 42nd St New York NY 10017

BURNS, JOHN TOLMAN, cons., former manufacturing company executive; b. Montgomery, Ala., May 16, 1922; s. Loren J. and Harriett (McFerran) B.; m. Patricia Jacques, Sept. 25, 1954; children: Scott, Kent. B.S., U. Louisville, 1943. Asst. hydraulic group engr. Douglas Aircraft Co., 1946-56; dist. sales mgr. aerospace div. Vickers, Inc., Torrance, Calif., 1956-58, gen. sales mgr., 1958-61, marketing mgr., 1961- 62, gen. mgr., 1962-64, v.p., gen. mgr., 1964-68; pres. Vickers div. Sperry Rand Corp., Troy, Mich., 1968-80; cons., 1980—. Served to lt. (j.g.) USNG, 1944-46. Home: 792 W Starlight Heights Dr La Canada CA 91011 Office: 1401 Crooks Rd Troy MI 48084

BURNS, JOSEPH WILLIAM, lawyer; b. N.Y.C., June 5, 1908; s. William E. and Susan (Stearns) B.; m. Marion E. Tucker, May 25, 1934; children: Richard W., Kenneth H., Margaret E. (Mrs. Edward M. Fried). A.B., Columbia U., 1929, J.D., 1932. Bar: N.Y. bar 1933. Practiced in, N.Y.C., 1933—; mem. firm Fulton, Walter & Halley, 1945-58, Austin, Burns, Smith & Walls, 1959-68, Davies, Hardy, Loeb, Austin & Ives, 1968-69, Burns, Van Kirk, Greene & Kafer, 1970-79, Lovejoy, Wasson, Lundgren & Ashton, P.C., 1979-81; prin. Joseph W. Burns P.C., 1981-83; mem. firm Fanelli, Burns & Neville, 1983—; asst. U.S. atty. So. Dist. N.Y., 1934-38; atty. tax div. Dept. Justice, 1938-43; spl. asst. to U.S. Atty. Gen., 1943-45; chief counsel, staff dir. Subcom. on Antitrust and Monopoly, U.S. Senate Com. on Judiciary, 1955-56. Author: A Study of the Antitrust Laws, 1958, Antitrust Dilemma: Why Congress Should Modernize The Antitrust Laws, 1969; Contbr. articles to profl. jours., popular mags. Mem. Am., Internat., N.Y. State, Fed. bar assns., Assn. Bar City N.Y., Internat. C. of C. (mem. U.S. council 1960), Cath. Men's Midtown Luncheon Club (chmn. 1965), Knights of Holy Sepulchre, Knights of Malta, Confrerie Des Chevaliers Du Tastevin. Roman Catholic. Club: Wykagyl Country (New Rochelle, N.Y.). Home: 127 Oxford Rd New Rochelle NY 10804 277 North Ave New Rochelle NY 10801

BURNS, JUNE DUDLEY, chemical company executive; b. Houston, May 18, 1933; s. John Heard and Annie Lee (Peeples) B.; m. Margaret Alice Garrett, May 19, 1962; children: John Arthur, Dan Garrett, William Dudley. B.A., Rice U., 1955, B.S. Ch.E., 1956; P.M.D., Harvard U., 1973. Mgr. mfg. Conoco Chems., Saddle Brook, N.J., 1971-73, asst. gen. mgr., 1973-75; v.p. comml. Conoco, Inc., Houston, 1975-78, v.p., gen. mgr. ops., 1978-79, sr. v.p., 1979-80, exec. v.p. chems., 1980—; v.p., dir. Petroquimica Espanola S.A., Madrid; dir. Condea, Hamburg, Germany, Nissan-Conoco, Tokyo, Nippon Aluminum Alkyls. Mem. Soap and Detergent Assn. (dir.), Soc. Chem. Industry. Republican. Methodist. Clubs: River Oaks, Westlake (Houston) (founding bd. govs. 1982). Office: Conoco Inc 15990 N Barkers Landing Houston TX 77079

BURNS, KENNETH DEAN, air force officer; b. Los Angeles, May 13, 1930; s. Claude Theodore and Phillys May (Barker) B.; m. Dorothy Louise Lyne, June 6, 1954; children: Pamela L., Alison J. B.S., U.S. Naval Acad., 1954; postgrad., Armed Forces Staff Coll., 1965, Royal Air Force Coll. Air Warfare, 1970. Commd. officer USAF; advanced through grades to maj. gen., 1974, fighter pilot instr., 1956-60, ops. staff officer, Korea, Japan, 1961-62, flighter squadron comdr., Vietnam, 1969; comdr. 20th Tactical Fighter Wing, RAF, Upper Heyford, Eng., 1974, USAF Electronic Security Command, Kelly AFB, San Antonio, 1975-78; comdr. Logistics Group, Turkey, 1979-81, comdr. 13th Air Force, Clark Air Base, Philippines, 1981—. Decorated D.S.M., Legion of Merit, Bronze Star, D.F.C. (3), Air Medal (13), others. Mem. Air Force Assn., Assn. Old Crows. Home: 4800 Williamsburg Ln Apt 234 La Mesa CA 92041 Office: PSC 4 Box 17466 APO San Francisco CA 96274

BURNS, KENNETH JONES, JR., lawyer, natural resources company executive; b. Cleve., Oct. 3, 1926; s. Kenneth Jones and Isabel (Nanson) B.; m. Edith Louise Mitten, June 23, 1949; children: Deborah, Kenneth Jones III, Sarah, Elizabeth, Nancy, Andrew. B.S., Northwestern U., 1948, J.D., 1951. Bar: Ill. 1951, Ohio 1972. Asso. Jenner & Block, Chgo., 1951-60, partner, 1961-72; sr. v.p., gen. counsel, sec. Anchor Hocking Corp., Lancaster, Ohio, 1972-79; v.p., gen. counsel Internat. Minerals & Chem. Corp., Northbrook, Ill., 1979—; legal counsel Chgo. Jr. Assn. Commerce and Industry, 1955-58; lectr. Northwestern U. Sch. Law, 1955. Pres. Wilmette Civic Improvement Assn., 1958-62; v.p., dir. Citizens of Greater Chgo., 1961-64; mem. Chgo. Crime Commn.; bd. dirs. Am. Bar Endowment, 1975—, v.p., 1981-83, pres., 1983—. Served with USNR, 1945-46, 51-52. Recipient Key award Chgo. Jr. Assn. Commerce, 1956. Fellow Am. Bar Found. (dir. 1983—); mem. ABA (chmn. jr. bar conf. 1961-62, ho. of dels. 1962-64, 71—, asst. sec. 1967-71, sec., gov. 1971-75), Ill. Bar Assn., Chgo. Bar Assn. (bd. mgrs. 1961-63), Am. Bar Retirement Assn. (bd. dirs. 1982—), Assn. Gen. Counsel, Chgo. Barrister Inn (pres. 1966-67), Legal Club Chgo. (exec. com. 1981—), Law Club Chgo., Order of Coif, Sigma Chi, Phi Delta Phi. Club: Skokie (Ill.) Country. Home: 115 Fuller Ln Winnetka IL 60093 Office: IMC Corp 2315 Sanders Rd Northbrook IL 60062

BURNS, LAWRENCE, lawyer; b. Corning, Ohio, May 3, 1910; s. Lawrence and Anna (Amberge) B.; m. Elinor Bresnahan, Oct. 8, 1935; children: Lawrence (dec.), David William. Student, Aquinas Coll., Columbus, Ohio, 1928; J.D., Ohio State U., 1933. Bar: Ohio 1933. Practice of law, Coshocton, 1933—; atty. Bank-One, Coshocton, Ohio, Conrail, Ohio Power Co.; dir. Bank-One of Dover, Ohio, Novelty Advt. Co., Buckeye Fabric Finishing Co., Auto Supply Co., Muskingum Valley Lumber Co., Coshocton. City solicitor, Coshocton, 1942-44; chmn. Republican County Exec. Com., 1943-62. Trustee Coshocton Found., Ohio Legal Center, Columbus. Served to lt. (s.g.) USNR, 1942-46. Mem. ABA, Ohio Bar Assn. (pres.), Coshocton County Bar Assn., Am. Judicature Soc., Ohio State U. Alumni Assn., C. of C., Internat. Assn. Ins. Counsels, Am. Coll. Probate Counsel. Rotarian. Home: 920 Kensington Rd Coshocton OH 43812 Office: 309 Main St Coshocton OH 43812

BURNS, MARVIN GERALD, lawyer; b. Los Angeles, July 3, 1930; s. Milton and Belle (Cytron) B.; m. Barbara Irene Fisher, Aug. 23, 1953; children: Scott Douglas, Jody Lynn, Bradley Frederick. B.A., U. Ariz., 1951; J.D., Harvard U., 1954. Bar: Calif. bar 1955. Ptnr. Burns & Resnick, Beverly Hills. Served with AUS, 1955-56. Clubs: Sycamore Park Tennis, Braemar Country. Home: 27024 Malibu Cove Colony Malibu CA 90265 Office: 9601 Wilshire Blvd Beverly Hills CA 90210 *I believe that hard work in its time and place; play in its time and place; love, understanding and practice of the golden rule at all times, in all places; a firm belief in truth and honesty and that there is no better land, no better system, no better life than our imperfect, necessary to improve, America, leads to personal fulfillment and a better life for all.*

BURNS, MARY ANN THERESA, college administrator; b. Phila., Jan. 24, 1928; d. John Joseph and Anna Marie (McLean) B. A.B., Rosemont Coll., 1949; A.M., U. Pa., 1950, Ph.D. (Fund for Advancement Edn. fellow 1954-55), 1960. Tchr. Springfield (Pa.) High Sch., 1951-60; faculty U. Wis., Milw., 1960-73, asso. prof., 1964-68, prof., 1968-73; dean Wilson Coll., Chambersburg, Pa., 1973-76, Emmanuel Coll., Boston, 1977-79; v.p. acad. affairs, dean Mary Washington Coll., Fredericksburg, Va., 1979—; vis. lectr. Marquette U., 1965; exec. sec. Eta Sigma Phi. Author: Lingua Latina: Liber Primus, 1964, Lingua Latina Liber Alter, 1965; also articles, revs. Mem. Am. Philol. Assn., Archaeol. Inst. Am., Classical Assn. of Middle West and South, Am. Classical League (pres. 1980—). Address: 101 Wilderness Ln Fredericksburg VA 22401

BURNS, MICHAEL JOSEPH, manufacturing executive; b. Passaic, N.J., Feb. 18, 1943; s. Michael Joseph and Ellen Kathryn (Warman) B.; m. Emma Anne, Dec. 19, 1964; children: Michael, Jeffrey, Tricia, Stephen. B.A. in English, William Paterson Coll., Wayne, N.J., 1964; J.D., Seton Hall U., Newark, 1975. Purchasing analyst Am. Brands Co., 1972-75; div. purchasing mgr. Dutch Boy Paints, NL Industries, 1975-76; v.p. purchasing Dutch Boy, Inc., 1977-78, pres., gen. mgr., 1978-80; pres., chief exec. officer Kroehler Mfg. Co., furniture mfg., Naperville, Ill., 1980—. Served to capt. USMCR, 1964-67. N.J. State scholar; recipient Disting. Alumni award Wm. Paterson Coll. Mem. ABA, Am. Arbitration Assn. Presbyterian. Office: 747 Pratt Blvd Elk Grove Village IL

BURNS, MITCHEL ANTHONY, trucking company executive; b. Mesquite, Nev., Nov. 1, 1942; s. Mitchel and Zella (Pulsipher) B.; m. Joyce Jordan, Nov. 14, 1962; children: Jill, Mike, Shauna. B.S. in Bus. Mgmt, Brigham Young U., 1964; M.B.A. in Finance, U. Calif., Berkeley, 1965. With Mobil Oil Corp., N.Y.C., 1965-74, controller, 1970-72, cost-of-living coordinator, 1973, fin. analysis mgr., 1973-74; pres., chief exec. officer, chief operating officer, exec. v.p., group v.p., treas., dir. corp. planning Ryder System, Inc., Miami, Fla., 1974; also dir.; exec. v.p., chief fin. officer subs. Ryder Truck Rental, Inc., Miami, 1975—. Office: 3600 NW 82d Ave Miami FL 33166

BURNS, NED HAMILTON, civil engineering educator; b. Magnolia, Ark., Nov. 25, 1932; s. Andrew Louis and Ila Mae (Martin) B.; m. Martha Ann Fontaine, June 11, 1955; children: Kathryn Jane, Stephanie Ann, Michael Everett. B.S., U. Tex., 1954, M.S., 1958; Ph.D., U. Ill., 1962. Registered profl. engr., Tex. Instr. U. Tex., Austin, 1957-59, asst. prof., 1962-65, assoc. prof., 1965-70, prof. civil engring., 1970-83, Zarrow Centennial prof. engring., 1983—; research asst. U. Ill., Urbana, 1959-62. Author: (with T. Y. Lin) Design of Prestressed Concrete Structures, 1981 (McGraw Hill Book of Month 1982), S.I. Version—Design of Prestressed Concrete Structures, 1982; contbr. tech. papers, reports on structural engring. to profl. publs. Served with U.S. Army, 1955-57. Recipient Gen. Dynamics Teaching award U. Tex. Coll. Engring., 1965, AMOCO Teaching award, 1983. Mem. Am. Concrete Inst. (bd. dirs. 1983—), Post-Tensioning Inst. (dir. 1975—), ASCE (com. chmn. 1975—), Prestressed Concrete Inst. (com. mem. 1968—), Nat. Soc. Profl. Engrs. (chpt. pres. 1970), Tex. Soc. Profl. Engring. (Young Engr. of Yr. award 1970). Democrat. Baptist. Home: 3917 Rockledge Dr Austin TX 78731 Office: Dept Civil Engring U Tex Austin TX 78712

BURNS, PAUL PATRICK, army officer; b. Alliance, Ohio, Mar. 17, 1933; s. William M. and Helen M. (Henning) B.; m. Ann T. Ewing, June 19, 1954; children: William, Mary Ellen, Kevin, Brian, Colleen. B.S. in Bus. Adminstrn., John Carroll U., 1954; M.B.A., Ind. U., 1966. Commd. 2d lt. U.S. Army, 1951, advanced through grades to maj. gen., 1981; dir. data processing ops. U.S. Army Fin. and Acctg. Ctr.,

Indpls., 1975-76, spl. asst. to comdr., 1976, dep. comdr. automation, 1976-78, dep. comdg. gen., 1978-80, comdg. gen., 1981—; asst. comptoller Army for fin. and acctg. Mem. Assn. U.S. Army, Am. Soc. Mil. Comptrollers, C. of C. Indpls., Sigma Iota Epsilon, Beta Gamma Sigma. Roman Catholic. Lodges: Rotary; Kiwanis. Home: 652 Lawton Loop Port Benjamin Harrison IN 46216 Office: US Army Fin and Acctg Ctr Indianapolis IN 46249

BURNS, RICHARD DEAN, educator; b. Des Moines, June 16, 1929; s. Richard B. and Luella (Everling) B.; m. Frances R. Sullivan, Jan. 14, 1950; 1 son, Richard Dean. B.S. with honors, U. Ill., 1957, M.A., 1958, Ph.D., 1960. Mem. faculty dept. history Calif. State U. at Los Angeles, 1960—, prof., 1970—, chmn. dept., 1969-72; vis. lectr. Los Angeles City Coll., Whittier Coll., U. Minn., Mpls., 1964-65, U. Calif. at Los Angeles, U. So. Calif.; program cons., lectr. Western Center, Nat. Endowment for Humanities, 1973-75. Author: (with W. Fisher) Armament and Disarmament, 1964, (with D. Urquidi) Disarmament in Historical Perspective, 4 vols, 1969, (with E. Bennett) Diplomats in Crisis, 1975; bibliographer, series editor: War/Peace Bibliographies, 1973—; (with M. Leitenberg) including The Vietnam Conflict, 1973, An Arms Control and Disarmament Bibliography, 1977, Guide to American Foreign Relations Since 1770, 1982; contbr. articles to profl. jours. Served with USAF, 1947-56. Named Univ. Outstanding Prof., 1978-79; Social Sci. Research Council fellow, 1959-60; Nat. Endowment for Humanities grantee, 1978-79. Mem. Conf. on Peace Research (nat. council 1970-72), Soc. Historians Am. Fgn. Relations, Phi Kappa Phi, Phi Alpha Theta. Office: Dept History Calif State U Los Angeles CA 90032

BURNS, ROBERT EDWARD, editor, publisher; b. Chgo., May 14, 1919; s. William Joseph and Sara (Foy) B.; m. Brenda Coleman, May 15, 1948; children: Maddy F., Martin J. Student, De Paul U., 1937-39; Ph.B., Loyola U., Chgo., 1941. Pub. relations dir. Cath. Youth Orgn., Chgo., 1943-45, 47-49; exec. dir. No. Ind. region Nat. Conf. Christians and Jews, 1946; exec. editor U.S. Cath. mag.; gen. mgr. Claretian Publs., Chgo., 1949—. Author: The Examined Life, 1980, Catholics on the Cutting Edge, 1983. Chmn. bd. trustees Rosary Coll.; bd. dirs. Thomas More Assn. Home: 616 High Rd Glen Ellyn IL 60137 Office: 221 W Madison St Chicago IL 60606

BURNS, ROBERT IGNATIUS, clergyman, historian, educator; b. San Francisco, Aug. 16, 1921; s. Harry and Viola Marie (Whearty) B. B.A., Gonzaga U., 1945, M.A., 1947, D.Litt., 1968; M.A., Fordham U., 1949; Phil.B., Jesuit Pontifical Faculty, Spokane, Wash., 1946, Phil.Lic., 1947, S.Th.B., 1951, S.Th.Lic., 1953; postgrad., Columbia, 1949, Oxford (Eng.) U., 1956-57; Ph.D. summa cum laude, Johns Hopkins U., 1958; Doc.ès Sc.Hist. double summa cum laude, Fribourg (Switzerland) U., 1961, Marquette U., 1977, Loyola U., Chgo., 1978; hon. doctorates, Boston Coll., 1982, Georgetown U., 1982, U. San Francisco, 1983. Joined S.J.; ordained priest Roman Catholic Ch., 1952; asst. archivist Jesuit and Indian Archives Pacific N.W., Province, Spokane, 1945-47; instr. history dept. U. San Francisco, 1947-48, asst. prof., 1958-62, assoc. prof., 1963-66, prof., 1967-76; sr. prof. dept. history UCLA, 1976—; dir. Inst. Medieval Mediterranean Spain, 1976—; prof. methodology, faculty history Gregorian U., Rome, 1955-56; guest lectr. humanities honors program Stanford, 1960; vis. prof. Coll. of Notre Dame, Belmont, Calif., 1963; James chair Brown U., Providence, 1970; faculty mem. Inst. Advanced Study, Princeton U., 1972; Levi della Vida lectr. UCLA, 1973; vis. prof., Hispanic lectr. U. Calif. at Santa Barbara, 1976; staff UCLA Near Eastern Center, 1979—, UCLA Center Medieval-Renaissance Studies, 1977—. Author: The Jesuits and the Indian Wars of the Northwest, 1966, The, Crusader Kingdom of Valencia: Reconstruction on a Thirteenth-Century Frontier, 1967, Islam Under the Crusaders: Colonial Survival in the Thirteenth-Century Kingdom of Valencia, 1973, Medieval Colonialism: Post-Crusade Exploitation of Islamic Valencia, 1975, Moors and Crusaders in Mediterranean Spain, 1978, Jaume I, els Valencians del segle XIII, 1981; co-author: Islamic Middle East, 1981, Muslims, Christians and Jews in the Crusader Kingdom of Valencia, 1983, Elreino de Valencia en el siglo XIII, 1983; bd. editors: Trends in History, 1979—; editor: Viator, 1980—; Contbr. articles to profl. jours. Trustee Hill Monastic Manuscript Library, 1977-81; mem. adv. bd. Am. Bibliog. Center, 1982—. Recipient Book awards Am. Hist. Assn. Pacific Coast Br., 1968, Am. Assn. State Local History, 1967, Am. Cath. Hist. Assn., 1967, 68, Inst. Mission Studies, 1966, Am. Cath. Press Assn., 1975, Phi Alpha Theta, 1976; Haskins medal Medieval Acad. Am., 1976; Premi de la Critica, 1982; Preme Catalonia, 1982; Guggenheim fellow, 1963-64; Ford Found. and Guggenheim publ. grantee, 1967; Rockefeller travel grantee, 1980; Nat. Endowment Humanities fellow, 1971, 73, 75-83; Am. Council Learned Socs. fellow, 1972; travel grantee, 1975; Robb publ. grantee, 1974; Darrow publ. grantee, 1975; Consejo Superior de Investigaciones Científicas (Spain) travel grantee, 1975, 82; Valencia province and Catalan region publ. grantee, 1981; De Amo grantee, 1983; U.S.-Spain treaty grantee, 1983. Fellow Medieval Acad. Am. (trustee 1975-77, prize com. 1980), Acció Cultural del País Valencià; mem. Am. Cath. Hist. Assn. (pres. 1975, council 1976—), Soc. Spanish Portuguese Hist. Studies (mem. exec. council 1974-77), Am. Hist. Assn. (del. internat. congress Hist. scis. 1975, 80, pres. Pacific Coast br. 1979-80, exec. council 1981—), Medieval Assn. Pacific (mem. exec. council 1975-77), Acad. Research Historians on Medieval Spain (pres. 1976), N.Am. Catalan Soc. (exec. officer 1978—). Address: History Dept Univ Calif Los Angeles CA 90024

BURNS, ROGER GEORGE, mineralogist, educator; b. Wellington, N.Z., Dec. 28, 1937; s. Alexander Parker and Jean Gertrude (Rodgers) B.; m. Virginia Anne Mee, Sept. 7, 1963; children: Kirk George, Jonathan Roger. B.Sc. (Sir George Grey scholar 1958, Emily Lilias Johnson scholar 1959), Victoria U. of Wellington, 1959, M.Sc., 1961; Ph.D. (Sci. fellow), U. Calif., Berkeley, 1965; M.A. in Geology (Brit. Council scholar 1965-66, Natural Environ. Research Council, Eng. fellow 1966), Oxford U., 1968. Demonstrator chemistry dept. Victoria U. of Wellington, 1959-60, sr. lectr. geochemistry, 1967; sci. officer Dept. Sci. and Indsl. Research, Wellington, 1961; research asso. dept. engring. scis. U. Calif., Berkeley, 1965; sr. research visitor, dept. mineralogy and petrology Cambridge U., Eng., 1966; lectr. geochemistry Oxford U., 1968-70; asso. prof. geochemistry MIT, Cambridge, 1970-72, prof. mineralogy and geochemistry, 1972—; vis. prof. Scripps Instn. Oceanography, La Jolla, Calif., 1976; UNESCO prof. Jadavpur U., Calcutta, India, 1981; prin. investigator, lunar sample analysis team Apollo Program, NASA, 1970—, mem. lunar and planetary proposal rev. panel, 1978—; mem. exec. com. Manganese Nodule Project, Seabed Assessment Program, Internat. Decade of Ocean Exploration, NSF, 1974-80; mem. adv. panel DOMES Project, NOAA, 1975; adv. panel Marine Minerals Office, 1976; mem. rev. panel Nat. Scis. and Engring. Research Council Can. Author: Mineralogical Applications of Crystal Field Theory, 1970; Editor: Chem. Geology, 1968—; asso. editor: Geochimica et Cosmochimica Acta, 1978—; Contbr. sci. articles to profl. publs. Fulbright travel grantee U.S. Govt., 1961; Sci. Research fellow Com. for Exhbn. of 1851, London, 1961-63; Pacific scholar English Speaking Union, San Francisco, 1961-63; fellow Wolfson Coll. Oxford U., 1970. Fellow Mineral. Soc. Am. (life; award 1976, councillor 1978—); mem. Mineral. Soc. Gt. Britain; Mem. Am. Geophys. Union, Geochem. Soc., N.Z. Geochem. Group. Presbyterian. Home: 7 Humboldt St Cambridge MA 02140 Office: 54-816 Dept Earth and Planetary Scis MIT Cambridge MA 02139

BURNS, RONALD JAMES, mfg. co. exec.; b. Michigan City, Ind., Apr. 18, 1937; s. Melvin B. and Alice K. (Shindler) B.; m. Sandra Kay Bratton, June 19, 1960; children—Dwight, Rhonda. B.S. in Bus, Ind. U., 1959. Methods analyst Ryerson Steel Co., Chgo., 1960; dir. ops. analysis Asso. Corp., South Bend, Ind., 1960-70; v.p., gen. mgr. Allis-Chalmers Corp., Milw., 1970-80, sector exec., v.p., 1980—. Dir. West Allis State Bank.; Bd. dirs. Meth. Manors, Inc., Elmore Found. Served with U.S. Army N.G., 1959-65. Office: Allis-Chalmers Corp 1126 S 70th St Milwaukee WI 53201

BURNS, THAGRUS ASHER, manufacturing company executive, former life insurance company executive; b. Columbia City, Ind., Feb. 19, 1917; s. Harlow A. and Hazlette (Wise) B.; m. Dorothy Kimble, May 1, 1942; children: Steven L., Gerald A. A.B., Wabash Coll., 1939. With Lincoln Nat. Life Ins. Co., Ft. Wayne, Ind., 1939-80, treas., 1967-80, Lincoln Nat. Life Co., 1967-80, Lincoln Nat. Corp., 1968-80; pres. Burns Mfg. Inc., Ft. Wayne, 1980—; Treas., dir. Lincoln Nat. Life Found. Served to lt. USNR, 1942- 45. Mem. Financial Execs. Inst., Phi Beta Kappa. Inventor automatic feeder for typewriter, inserting machine and clipping catcher for hedge trimmer. Home and Office: 2203-7 Abbey Dr Fort Wayne IN 46815

BURNS, THOMAS WADE, educator; b. Dayton, Ohio, July 29, 1924; s. Samuel Thomas and Ina (Treadway) B.; m. Joan Marie Fletcher, July 26, 1952; children: Thomas F., Margaret F., James L., Richard W. A.A., UCLA, 1943; B.A., U. Utah, 1945, M.D., 1947, M.S. in Pharmacology and Biochemistry, 1948. Intern Boston City Hosp. Harvard Med. Unit, 1948-49; asst. resident teaching fellow Harvard Med. Sch., Boston, 1949-50; clin. research fellow medicine Duke U., Durham, 1950-51; clin. investigator, metabolic research faculty Nav. Hosp., Oakland, Calif., 1951-52, Nav. Research Unit, Cairo, Egypt, 1952-54; research physician metabolic unit Med. Center, U. Calif. at San Francisco, 1955; mem. faculty U. Mo., Columbia, 1955—, asso. prof., 1957-65, prof. medicine, 1965—, also dir. div. endocrinology and metabolism, 1969—, dir., 1974-75; vis. research worker U. Cambridge, Eng., 1965-66. Author: Syllabus for the Endocrine Lecture Series, 1964; Contbr. articles to profl. jours. Bd. dirs. Cosmopolitan-U. Mo. Diabetes Center. Served with USNR, 1943-45, 51-54. Fellow A.C.P. (gov. Mo. region 1975-79, regent 1982—); mem. Am. Diabetes Assn., A.A.A.S., Boone County Med. Soc. (pres. 1962), So. Soc. Clin. Research, Central Soc. Clin. Research, Endocrine Soc., Alpha Omega Alpha. Home: 310 E Brandon Rd Columbia MO 65201

BURNS, WARD, textile company executive; b. New Bedford, Mass., May 31, 1928; s. Frederick Lloyd and Pauline (Ward) B.; m. Cynthia A. Butterworth, Dec. 19, 1964; children: Helen Abby, David Ward, Walton Lloyd. B.A., Amherst Coll., 1950; M.B.A., Harvard U., 1952; spl. student, NYU, 1955-57. C.P.A., N.Y. Mgr. Price Waterhouse & Co. (C.P.A.s), N.Y.C., 1954-62; asso. Laurence S. and David Rockefeller, Brussels, Belgium, 1962-65; with J.P. Stevens & Co., Inc., N.Y.C., 1965—, controller, 1969-78, group v.p., 1978-80, pres., 1980—; also dir., mem. exec. com.; dir. Foote & Davies, Inc., Atlanta, Ruralist Press, Inc.; cons. ARS, Milan, Italy, HVL, Brussels, ARCO, Florence and Milan, 1963-65. Mem. editorial adv. bd.: Jour. Accountancy, 1969-72. Treas., dir. Internat. Sch. Brussels, 1963-65; pres. bd. dirs. Internat. Sch. Brussels Found., N.Y.C., 1965—; pres., bd. dirs. Friends New Cavell Hosp. Inc., N.Y.C., 1972-78. Served as capt. USAF, 1952-53. Mem. Am. Inst. C.P.A.'s, N.Y. State Soc. C.P.A.'s, Financial Execs. Inst., St. Andrews Soc., Phi Alpha Psi, Phi Kappa Psi. Clubs: Univ., Links, Econs. (N.Y.C.); Pilgrims. Home: 19 Angus Ln Greenwich CT 06830 Office: 1185 Ave of Americas New York NY 10036

BURNS, WILLIAM A., museum administrator, author; b. N.Y.C., Oct. 7, 1909; s. William A. and Florence (Willis) B.; m. Adelaide Jordan, Oct. 7, 1955. B.A., Manhattan Coll., 1934; M.A., Columbia U., 1937, Ed.D., 1949. Field dir. Occupational Adjustment Study, 1939-40; with Am. Mus. Natural History, N.Y.C., 1940-62, asso. curator dept. edn., asst. chmn. dept., 1945-51, asst. to dir., membership sec., editor popular publs., 1951-62; dir. Witte Meml. Mus., San Antonio, 1962-70; exec. dir., sec. bd. dirs. San Diego Natural History Mus., 1970-73; dir. Florence (S.C.) Mus., 1975-83, dir. emeritus, 1983—; Mem. adv. bd. Florence Mus., Gay Head Mus., Fairfield County (Conn.) Mus. Art, Sci. and Industry, Nimitz Mus.; mem. cultural adv. com. Hemis Fair '68; mem. Inter-Am. Ednl. Commn., Latin Am. Studies Conf.; mem. environ. ednl. adv. com. HEW; mem. Creative Ednl. Resources Com. Exec. Council, City of San Diego; mem. inter-museums council Balboa Parks Museums; chmn. Cultural Heritage Commn., San Diego County. Author: Enjoying the Arts: Museums; contbr.: Museum Registration Methods; editor: Natural History of the Southwest; Witte Mus. Quar, 1963-70; Co-editor: Illustrated World Geography. Mem. Com. of 100; mem. Irish Writers Conf., Listowel, Eire, Southeastern Mus. Conf., Gov.'s Hist. Commn., Florence Hist. Preservation Com.; bd. dirs. San Antonio ARC, Florence Symphony Orch., Children's Symphony Music Fair, Craft Guild, Weavers' Guild; trustee San Antonio Art League, Florence council Boy Scouts Am. Served to 1st lt. AUS, 1943-46. Mem. Mexican-Am. Art Council, San Antonio Little Theater, Am. Assn. Museums (council), Assn. Sci. Mus. Dirs. (pres.), Internat. Council Museums, Tex. Mus. Conf., Tex. Art Mus. Conf., Tex. Hist. Soc., Bexar County Hist. Soc. (survey commn.), Florence Hist. Soc., Florence Heritage Found., Trinity U. Library Council, Sci. Dirs. Assn., San Antonio Conservation Soc., San Antonio Art Guild, Rocks and Minerals Soc., Nat. Speleological Soc., Chamber Music Soc., Kappa Delta Pi, Gamma Theta Upsilon. Clubs: Rotarian (Paul Harris fellow 1981), Jazz Society, Torch, Alamo, Press, Argyle, Shell, Manuscript, University. Address: 1826 W Sandhurst Dr Florence SC 29501

BURNS, WILLIAM GRADY, lawyer; b. Ashdown, Ark., Apr. 16, 1907; s. William Franklin and Ida (Graham) B.; m. Margaret McDonald, Nov. 28, 1934; children: Margaret Ann, Susan, Catherine, Graham William, David John. Ph.B., U. Chgo., 1929, J.D., 1931. Bar: Ill. 1931. Since practiced in, Chgo.; mem. firm Bell, Boyd & Lloyd (and predecessors), 1943-81. Mem. Joseph Sears Bd. Edn., Kenilworth, 1956-62, pres. bd., 1960; trustee, Village of Kenilworth, 1965-69; chmn., vice chmn. rev. coms. Community Fund Chgo., 1965-70; mem. citizens bd. U. Chgo.; mem. nat. panel Am. Arbitration Assn., 1965-76; bd. dirs., sec., mem. exec. com. Exec. Service Corps Chgo. Mem. Am., Ill., Chgo. bar assns., Law Club Chgo., Legal Club Chgo., U. Chgo. Law Sch. Alumni Assn. (pres., dir. 1970-72), Phi Beta Kappa, Order of Coif, Delta Tau Delta, Phi Delta Phi. Republican. Baptist. Clubs: University, Econ., Comml. (exec. com. 1976-78), Attic (Chgo.) (pres. 1978-80); Kenilworth (pres. 1965-66), Westmoreland Country (Wilmette, Ill.) (sec., dir. 1974-76). Home: 320 Cumberland Ave Kenilworth IL 60043 Office: 3200 Three 1st Nat Plaza 70 W Madison St Chicago IL 60602

BURNSHAW, STANLEY, writer; b. N.Y.C., June 20, 1906; s. Ludwig Behr and Sophia (Kievmann) B.; m. Lydia Powsner; children: Sandra Bonnie, Valerie, Amy, David. B.A., U. Pitts., 1925; M.A., Cornell U., 1933; L.H.D. honoris causa, Hebrew Union Coll.-Jewish Inst. Religion, 1983. Advt. bus., Pitts., 1925-27, N.Y.C., 1928-32; drama critic, co-editor New Masses, N.Y.C., 1933-36; v.p. The Cordon Co., Inc., pubs., N.Y.C., 1936-39; pres., gen. mgr. Dryden Press, Inc., N.Y.C., 1939-58; v.p. Holt, Rinehart & Winston, Inc., N.Y.C., 1958-65, adviser to pres., 1965-68; Regents lectr. U. Calif., winter 1980; Mem. organizing group, then lectr., dir. studies in World lit. Grad. Inst. of Book Publishing, N.Y. U., 1958-62; Bd. judges Nat. Book Award, 1967, 72; awards adv. com. Nat. Book Com., 1967—; Mem. organizing bd. editors, then cons. editor Adult Leadership (mag. supported by Fund for Adult Edn., Ford Found.), 1953-55. Author: The Wheel Age, 1928, André Spire and His Poetry, 1933, The Iron Land, 1936, The Bridge, 1945, The Revolt of the Cats in Paradise, 1945, The Sunless Sea, 1949, Early and Late Testament, 1952, Caged in an Animal's Mind, 1963, The Seamless Web, 1970, In the Terrified Radiance, 1972, Mirages: Travel Notes in the Promised Land, 1977, The Refusers, 1981; Editor: Two New Yorkers, 1934, The Poem Itself, 1960, 2d edit., 1981, Varieties of Literary Experience, 1962, The Modern Hebrew Poem Itself, 1965; Poetry Folio mag., 1926-28; Contbg. editor: Modern Quar, 1932-33, Theatre Workshop, 1935-38; Contbr.: Columbia U. Dictionary Modern European Literature, 1947, Dictionary World Literature; L'Approdo Letteraria, Italy, Delphica Tetradia, Greece, Nouvelle Revue Francaise, N.Y. Times Book Rev, Poetry, Atlantic Monthly, Sewanee Rev, Saturday Rev. Recipient award for lit. Nat. Inst. Arts and Letters, 1971. Mem. Am. Inst. Graphic Arts (dir. 1960-61), Coll. Pubs. Group. Home: Lambert's Cove Martha's Vineyard MA 02568

BURNSIDE, HELEN H., social services administrator; b. Honolulu, Sept. 10, 1925; d. Samuel Steinhauser and Katharine S. Hutchinson; m. son, Curtis Burnside. Diploma in Nursing, Columbia U. Presbyn. Hosp., 1946; B.S., Simmons Coll., Boston, 1948; M.A. in Nursing, Tchrs. Coll., Columbia U., 1954, M.Ed., 1970, Ed.D., 1972. Instr. Ballard Sch. Practical Nursing, N.Y.C., 1948-49; staff nurse, instr. U.S. Navy, 1949-51; tchr. Yorkville Vocat. High Sch., N.Y.C., 1952-54; instr. Henry Ford Community Coll., Dearborn, Mich., 1954-58; chmn. dept. nursing and allied health technologies Dutchess Community Coll., Poughkeepsie, N.Y., 1959-64, Cuyahoga Community Coll., Cleve., 1964-68; program dir. nursing Hostos Community Coll., Bronx, N.Y., 1970-71; asso. provost for health scis. Central Adminstrn., SUNY, Albany, 1972-76; prof., dean Sch. Nursing U. Hawaii, Honolulu, 1976-80; dir. Office of Human Resources, City and County of Honolulu, 1981—. Mem. Gov.'s Adv. Council for Children and Youth, 1981—; mem. budget and allocations com. Aloha United Way, 1981—; pres. bd. dirs. Mott-Smith Laniloa Condominium, 1980—; bd. dirs. Health and Community Services Council of Hawaii, 1982—, Waikiki Health Ctr., 1983-85; vice chmn. Ptnrs. in Health, 1981—; bd. dirs. Kokokahi World Hunger Found., 1983—; mem. policy adv. council Office Community Support. Served with U.S. Navy, 1949-51. Mem. Am. Nurses Assn., Hawaii Nurses Assn., Tchrs. Coll. Columbia U. Nursing Edn. Alumni Assn., Sigma Theta Tau. Home: 1717 Mott-Smith Dr Apt 714 Honolulu HI 96822 Office: Office of Human Resources City and County of Honolulu Honolulu Mcpl Bldg 650 S King St Honolulu HI 96813

BURNSIDE, JOHN WAYNE, medical educator; b. Bryn Mawr, Pa., Jan. 15, 1941; s. Wayne D. and Catherine (Neaman) B.; m. Lynda Deanne Haskins, Mar. 21, 1964; children: Andrew, Matthew, Paul. M.D., U. Ill., 1966. Resident Mass. Gen. Hosp., Boston, 1966-72; instr. Harvard U., Cambridge, Mass., 1969-72; asst. prof. Hershey Med. Ctr., Pa. State U., 1972-74, prof. medicine, 1980—, assoc. provost and dean for health affairs, 1982—. Author: Physical Diagnosis, 1972, Physical Diagnosis, 2d edit., 1978, Health and Human Values, 1982. Bd. dirs. Central Pa. Arthritis Found., 1974-79, Health Systems Agy., Camp Hill, 1978-80, Blue Shield, Camp Hill, 1982—; co-dir. Ctr. for Humanistic Medicine, 1979—; legis. asst. to senator, Washington, 1979, to congressman, 1980. Served with USNR, 1968-74. Recipient Senear award, U. Ill., 1968; Health Policy fellow Robert Wood Johnson Found., 1979-80. Fellow ACP; mem. Am. Soc. Internal Medicine, Soc. Health and Human Values, Dauphin County Med. Soc. (pres. 1982), Alpha Omega Alpha. Republican. Episcopalian. Club: Rotary. Office: Hershey Med Ctr PO Box 850 Hershey PA 17033

BURNSIDE, WALDO HOWARD, department store executive; b. Washington, Nov. 5, 1928; s. Waldo and Eleanor B.; m. Jean Mae Culbert, June 24, 1950; children: Diane Louise, Leslie Ann, Arlene Kay, William Howard. B.S., U. Md., 1949. With Woodward & Lothrop, Washington, 1949-80, divisional mdse. mgr., 1957-65, v.p., gen. mdse. mgr., 1965-74, exec. v.p., 1974-78, pres., 1978-80; also dir.; vice chmn., chief operating officer Carter Hawley Hale Stores, Inc., Los Angeles, 1980-83, pres., chief operating officer, 1983—; dir. Security Pacific Corp. Trustee Md. Ednl. Found.; trustee St. John's Hosp. and Health Ctr. Found.; trustee, past chmn. U. Md. Alumni Internat.; bd. dirs. Ind. Colls. So. Calif. Mem. Los Angeles Area C. of C. (dir.), Automobile Club So. Calif. (dir.), Phi Kappa Phi, Sigma Chi. Episcopalian. Clubs: California, Los Angeles Country; Stock Exchange (Los Angeles); N.Y. Athletic. Office: Carter Hawley Hale Stores Inc 550 S Flower St Los Angeles CA 90071

BURNSKY, PAUL JOHN, labor union official; b. Throop, Pa., Apr. 7, 1921; s. John and Anastasia Dzerneyko B.; m. Marian Ian Smith, 1944; 5 children. Cert. master mechanic, Acad. Aeros., Newark, 1941; student, U. Chgo., 1942, Roosevelt U., 1947. Vice pres. Local Lodge 1487, Internat. Assn. machinists, 1948-50; spl. rep. Local Lodge 1487, Internat. Assn. mechinists, 1950-55, grand lodge rep., 1955-64; adminstrv. asst. to v.p. Local Lodge 1487, Internat. Assn. machinists, 1964-65, adminstrv. asst. to pres., 1965-69; dir. orgn. Internat. Assn. Machinists and Aerospace Workers, Washington, 1970-71; pres. metal trades dept. AFL-CIO, Washington, 1971—. Served with USN, 1944-46. Office: Metal Trades Dept AFL-CIO Bldg Room 503 815 16th St NW Washington DC 20006 *

BURR, ARTHUR ALBERT, educator; b. Manor, Sask., Can., Aug. 23, 1913; came to U.S., 1940, naturalized, 1950; s. Charles A. and Mary (Hay) B.; m. Leslie Dickin, July 1, 1941; children—Janet Leslie, Leonard Charles. B.S., U. Sask., 1938, M.S., 1940; Ph.D., Pa. State U., 1943. Teaching asst. U. Sask., 1938-40, Pa. State U., 1940-43; research physicist Armstrong Cork Co., 1943-46; faculty Rensselaer Polytech. Inst., 1946—, prof., asso. head dept. metall. engring., 1953-55, prof., head dept., 1955-61, acting dean, 1961-62, dean, 1962-74, Rensselaer prof., 1974-78, prof. emeritus, engring. research prof., 1978—. Mem. Am. Soc. Metals (award outstanding ability tchr. metallurgy 1952, Chmn. Eastern N.Y. chpt. 1958), Soc. Nondestructive Testing (chmn. Mohawk Hudson chpt. 1949), Am. Soc. Mining, Metall. and Petroleum Engrs. (chmn. Hudson Mohawk chpt. 1959), Am. Soc. Engring. Edn., Sigma Xi, Sigma Pi Sigma, Phi Lambda Upsilon. Presbyn. (elder). Home: 983 Spring Ave Troy NY 12180

BURR, DAVID ANTHONY, educational administrator; b. Columbus, Kans., Apr. 19, 1925; s. Hugh Henry and Grace Elizabeth (Mitchell) B.; m. Carol Jean Robinson, Nov. 18, 1962; children: Michael James, Kathleen Elizabeth, Thaddeus Mitchell. A.A., Northeastern Agrl. and Mech. Coll., 1948; B.A., U. Okla., 1952; LL.D. hon., Pepperdine U., 1981. Editor Sooner Mag. U. Okla., Norman, 1950-57, asst. to pres., 1957-59, asst. to pres., dir. univ. relations and devel., 1959-68, v.p., dir. univ. community, 1968-71, v.p. devel., 1971-77, v.p. univ. relations and devel., 1977-79, v.p. univ. affairs, 1979—; coordinator, dir. U. Okla. leadership program, 1961; dir. Editorial Projects Edn., Inc. Dir. Okla. Gov.'s Opportunity Program, 1964; mem. Civic Improvement Council, Norman, 1965; deacon 1st Presbyn. Ch., Norman, 1968-69, elder, Norman. Served to lt. U.S. Army, 1944-46. Recipient Sibley award, 1956; named Outstanding Alumnus Northeastern A&M U., 1971, Disting. Service citation U. Okla., 1983. Mem. Council Advancement and Support of Edn., Okla. Higher Edn. Alumni Council, U. Okla.

Assn., Norman C. of C. (dir. 1968-70, 81—), Lambda Chi Alpha. Democrat. Home: 1409 Brookdale St Norman OK 73069 Office: U Okla 900 Asp Ave Norman OK 73019

BURR, DONALD DAVID, business executive; b. N.Y.C., Apr. 20, 1923; m. Anne Marie Scheitlie, June 28, 1975; children by previous marriage: Cynthia Parry, Cory Howell. Account exec. Bache & Co., 1946-47; gen. mgr. LaPlaya Products, Inc., 1948-52; gen. sales mgr. Hazel Bishop, Inc., 1952-54, v.p. mktg., 1954, pres., 1955-57, also dir., Parry Labs., Inc., 1957-61, also dir.; v.p., dir. Am. Motor Scooter Corp., 1960-61; dir. Tracey Enterprises, Inc., 1960-61; v.p. Faberge, Inc., 1961-63, exec. v.p., 1963-64; v.p. Parfum Lorle, Inc., 1961-64, Odell Co., Inc., 1962-64, Yardley of London, Inc., 1964-66, exec. v.p., 1966-68, pres., 1968-69, also dir.; chmn., pres. Burr Corp., 1970-72; chmn. Am. Pharm. Co., Inc., Devon Products Co., Inc., Trylon Products Co. Inc., 1970-72; chmn. bd. Brandwynne Burr Advt., Inc., N.Y.C., 1972-76, Cyncory Investments, 1976—; pres. D.D. Burr Investors Group, 1982—. Trustee Big Bros. Inc. of N.Y., 1974—. Served with USNR, 1942-44; as lt. (j.g.) USCGR, 1944-46. Clubs: New York Athletic; Devon Yacht (Amagansett, L.I.); Maidstone (East Hampton, L.I., N.Y.). Home: PO Box JJ East Hampton NY 11937 Office: 620 Fifth Ave New York NY 10020

BURR, FRANCIS HARDON, lawyer; b. Nahant, Mass., July 14, 1914. A.B. cum laude, Harvard U., 1935, LL.B, 1938, LL.D., 1982. Bar: Mass. 1938. Assoc. Ropes & Gray, Boston, 1938-47, ptnr., 1947—; dir. Am. Airlines, Inc., Corning Glass Works, Equitable Life Assurance Soc., State St. Growth Fund, Fiduciary Trust Co. N.Y., New Eng. Electric System, Raytheon Co., Real Estate Investment Trust Am., State St. Investment Corp.; trustee Union Warren Savs. Bank; mem. com. fin. advisers Comml. Union Corp.; mng. gen. ptnr. State St. Exchange Fund. Chmn. bd. dirs. Mass. Gen. Hosp. Fellow Harvard Coll., 1954-82; sr. fellow Harvard Coll., 1971-82. Fellow Am. Acad. Arts and Scis., Am. Bar Found; mem. ABA, Boston Bar Assn., Am. Law Inst. Office: Ropes & Gray 225 Franklin St Boston MA 02110

BURR, HELEN GUNDERSON (MRS. HORACE BURR), speech pathology educator; b. Iowa City, Dec. 30, 1918; d. George Byron and Grace (Farrell) Gunderson; m. Horace Burr, July 24, 1954; 1 son, David Stanford. B.A., Stanford, 1937; M.A., U. So. Calif., 1940; Ph.D., Columbia, 1949; post-doctoral study, U. So. Calif., summer 1950, U. Mich., summer 1952. Speech pathologist, N.Y.C. and Los Angeles, 1944-50; asst. prof., dir. speech clinic State U. N.Y., 1950-53; asst. prof. U. Va., Charlottesville, 1953-60, asso. prof. speech pathology and audiology, 1961-66, prof., 1966—; dir. Speech and Hearing Center, 1961—, chmn. dept. speech pathology and audiology, 1961-78. Editor: SHAV Jour, 1961—, The Aphasic Adult, 1965. Bd. dirs. Va. Hearing and Speech Found.; profl. adv. bd. Va. Soc. for Crippled Children and Adults; mem. coordinating com. on crippled children's services Va. Council on Health and Med. Care. Fellow Am. Speech and Hearing Assn., N.Y. Acad. Scis., Speech and Hearing Assn. Va. (pres. 1960, Honors of Assn. 1980); mem. Am. Assn. U. Women, English Speaking Union, Albemarle Hist. Assn., Albemarle Art Assn., A.A.A.S., Am. Assn. U. Profs., Linguistic Soc. Am., Speech Assn. Am., Internat. Soc. for Gen. Semantics, Delta Delta Delta, Pi Lambda Theta, Kappa Delta Pi, Delta Kappa Gamma (chpt. pres. 1972-74). Home: Carrsgrove Stribling Ave Charlottesville VA 22903

BURR, JOHN GREEN, chemistry educator; b. Ft. Sill, Okla., Mar. 12, 1918; s. John Green and Ruth Guyer (Oeschlin) B.; m. Irma Therese Garrigan, June 12, 1943; children: John G., Sara Garrigan Burr, Kathleen Burr (Mrs. James Oliver), Maryellen (Mrs. Brian Sax), Elizabeth, Mark C., Matthew E. B.S., MIT, 1940, M.S., 1940; Ph.D., Northwestern U., 1948. Asst. prof. Miami U., Oxford, Ohio, 1947-48; sr. scientist Oak Ridge Nat. Lab., 1948-57, N.Am. Rockwell Corp., Los Angeles, 1957-69; prof. chemistry and radiology U. Okla., 1969—; vis. prof. Hebrew U., Israel, 1975, Max Planck Radiation Inst., Germany, 1975; vis. scientist Cambridge U., 1983-84. Contbr. articles profl. jours.; Past mem. editorial bd.: Radiation Effects. Served with USNR, 1945-46. USPHS Service fellow, 1975; Guggenheim fellow, 1964; USPHS sr. fellow, 1953-54; Eastman fellow Northwestern U., 1946-47. Mem. Am. Chem. Soc. (chmn. Okla. sect. 1975-76), A.A.A.S., Radiation Research Soc. (council for chemistry 1974—), Okla. Acad. Sci., Okla. Inst. Chemists (pres. 1974-75), Am. Photobiology Soc. (charter). Democrat. Roman Catholic. Home: 1101 Woodland Dr Norman OK 73069

BURR, JOHN ROY, philosophy educator; b. Oshkosh, Wis., July 18, 1933; s. Lester John and Dorothy Viola (Hoffman) B.; m. Marjorie Jean Bakirakis, July 4, 1963; children: Michael John, Christopher Scott, Kara Jean. B.A., U. Wis.-Madison, 1955; M.A. (Univ. grantee), Columbia U., 1956, Ph.D., 1959. Adj. faculty Franklin and Marshall Coll., 1959-61; asst. prof. philosophy Hood Coll., 1961-64; faculty dept. philosophy U. Wis.-Oshkosh, 1964—, assoc. prof., 1966-68, prof., 1968—, John McN Rosebush univ. prof., 1984—, chmn. dept., 1966-76, chmn. humanities div., 1966-76, asst. dean letters and sci., 1976-79, mem. faculty senate, 1981—, pres. faculty senate, 1983-84. Editor: Handbook of World Philosophy: Contemporary Developments Since, 1945, 1980, (with Milton Goldinger) Philosophy and Contemporary Issues, 3d rev. edit, 1980, 4th rev. edit., 1984; Contbr. articles to profl. jours. Pres. Oshkosh Community Players, 1968-69, bd. dirs., 1966-69. Ford Found. grantee, 1963-64; Wis. State U. Regents Research grantee, 1971-72. Mem. Am. Philos. Assn., Am. Soc. Aesthetics, Metaphys. Soc. Am., Assn. Asian Studies, AAUP (chpt. pres. 1975-76, 80-82), Wis. Acad. Scis., Arts and Letters. Clubs: Masons, Candlelight (Oshkosh). Home: 2114 Doemel St Oshkosh WI 54901 *All of my activity, whether intellectual or not, is governed by an unyielding sense, not of mere mortality, but of honor: I will not lie and I will not be bought. I realize that such a sense of honor strikes many Americans as puzzling, eccentric, elitist, even immoral. However, I long ago reconciled myself to being a man of honor rather than a team player.*

BURR, RAYMOND, actor; b. New Westminster, C., Can., May 21, 1917. Student, Stanford, U. Calif., Columbia, U. Chungking. Formerly radio actor. Appeared on stage, numerous countries, in, Night Must Fall, Mandarin, Crazy with the Heat, Duke in Darkness; dir., Pasadena Community Playhouse, 1943; star: TV series Perry Mason Show, 1961, 62 (recipient Emmy award as best actor), Ironside, 1967-75, Kingston: Confidential, 1977; appeared: numerous motion pictures, including They Were So Young, 1955, You're Never Too Young, 1955, A Man Alone, 1955, Count Three and Pray, 1955, Please Murder Me, 1956, Godzilla King of the Monsters, 1956, Great Day in the Morning, 1956, Secret of Treasure Mountain, 1956, Cry in the Night, 1956, Criss Cross, 1949, P.J, 1968, Rear Window; others; appeared in: TV movies Kingston: The Power Play, 1976, Mallory: Circumstantial Evidence, 1976, 79 Park Avenue, 1977, Centennial, 1978, Disaster on the Coastliner. Office: care David Shapiro & Assos Inc 9100 Wilshire Blvd East Tower Suite 231 Beverly Hills CA 90210 *

BURR, ROBERT LYNDON, Library dir.; b. Boonville, N.Y., May 9, 1944; s. James Isaac and Virginia Ellen (Davidson) B.; m. Angela Delores Tucci, June 26, 1965; 1 son, Robert Anthony. Student, U. Rochester, 1962-65; A.B., Canisius Coll., 1972; M.S. in L.S, Case-Western Res. U., 1973; Ed.D., Gonzaga U., 1981. Asst. prodn. mgr., purchasing mgr. Carleton Controls Corp., Buffalo, 1966-71; asst. to pres. Audn Corp., Buffalo, 1971-72; circulation services librarian Coll. William and Mary, Williamsburg, Va., 1973-77; dir. libraries Gonzaga U., Spokane, Wash., 1977—, adj. asso. prof. edn., 1979—; library cons. Contbr. articles to profl. jours. Trustee Mus. Native Am. Cultures, 1979—. Served with AUS, 1967-69. Mem. ALA (nat. research award 1974), Nat. Libraries Assn., Wash. Library Assn., Pacific N.W. Library Assn., AAUP, Mensa. Club: Westerners-Spokane Corral. Office: Crosby Library Gonzaga U Spokane WA 99258

BURRELL, CRAIG DONALD, physician; b. Gravesend, Kent, Eng., July 5, 1926; came to U.S., 1960, naturalized, 1968; m. Mary Elizabeth Granger, 1960; children—Catherine, Sarah, Craig, Walter, David. M.B., B.Surgery, U. N.Z., 1951; D.Sc. (hon.), Ricker Coll., 1975, LL.D., Union Coll., 1975. Rotating intern Wellington (N.Z.) Hosp., 1951-52; locum sr. house officer pediatrics Nottingham (Eng.) Children's Hosp., 1953; house physician gen. medicine and endocrinology Hammersmith Hosp. and Royal Postgrad. Med. Sch. Gt. Britain, London, 1954, sr. house officer endocrinology, 1954-56; registrar gen. medicine Royal Infirmary and Welsh Nat. Sch. Medicine, Cardiff, Wales, 1957-60; asst. prof. medicine and medicine in psychiatry Cornell U. Med. Sch., 1960-61; dir. clin. labs. Payne Whitney Psychiat. Clinic, 1960-61; with Sandoz Pharms., Inc., East Hanover, N.J., 1961-72, v.p. med. affairs, 1969-72; v.p., dir. external affairs Sandoz, Inc., East Hanover, 1973—; asst. attending physician Cornell 2d Div., Bellevue Hosp., 1966-68; clin. asso. prof. medicine Coll. Medicine and Dentistry N.J., Newark, 1968—; clin. prof. dept. community and family medicine U. Calif.-San Diego Sch. Medicine, 1982—; participant numerous internat. profl. confs.; mem. tech. com. White House Conf. on Aging, 1980—. Mem. editorial bd.: Internat Jour. of Addictions; editor: Drug Assessment in Ferment, 1976, Primary Health Care in Industrialized Nations, 1978; contbr. articles profl. jours. Vice pres. Sandoz Found.; v.p., trustee Playfair Found., Kessler Inst. for Rehab., West Orange, N.J. Fellow Am. Sch. Health Assn. (hon.), N.Y. Acad. Scis. (pres. elect 1983), Royal Soc. Medicine, Am. Sch. Health Assn. (hon.),); mem. AAAS, Am. Coll. Clin. Pharmacology and Therapeutics, A.M.A., Endocrine Soc., European Soc. for Study Drug Toxicity, Sierra Club, Delaware County (N.Y.), Conservation Assn. Presbyterian (elder). Office: Sandoz Inc East Hanover NJ 07639

BURRELL, DAVID BAKEWELL, educator; b. Akron, Ohio, Mar. 1, 1933; s. Roger Allen and Nancy deLauriel (Bakewell) B. B.A. (Woodrow Wilson fellow, Fulbright fellow), U. Notre Dame, 1954; S.T.L., Gregorian U., Rome, 1960; Ph.D. (Kent fellow), Yale, 1965. Ordained priest Roman Catholic Ch., 1959; asst. prof. philosophy U. Notre Dame, 1965-70, asso. prof., 1970-77, prof., 1977—, chmn. dept. theology, 1971-80; rector Ecumenical Inst. for Theol. Research, Jerusalem, 1980—. Author: Analogy and Philosophical Language, 1973, Exercises in Religious Understanding, 1975, Aquinas: God and Action, 1979. Mem. Am. Philos. Assn., Am. Acad. Religion, Soc. for Values in Higher Edn. Home: Box 402 Notre Dame IN 46556

BURRELL, JOSEPH EARL, chemical manufacturing company executive; b. Aurora, Ill., Sept. 7, 1919; s. Fred W. and Rosa (Greenman) B.; m. Margaret Macatee, Apr. 7, 1942; children: Robert, John, Marcia, Christopher, Jane, Susan. B.S., U. Mich., 1941; postgrad., Harvard U., 1957. Chem. engr. research dept. and chem. div. ops. PPG Industries, Inc., Barberton, Ohio, 1941-52, ops. supt., Natrium, W.Va., 1952-56, asst. to v.p. ops., Pitts., 1956-58, v.p. ops., 1958-66, v.p., gen. mgr. chem. div., 1966-75, pres., 1976—, also dir.; dir. Pitts. Nat. Corp., Pitts. Corning, Duplate Can. Trustee Nat. Safety Council; bd. visitors Sch. Bus., U. Pitts.; bd. dirs. Duquesne U. Mem. Mfg. Chemists Assn., Am. Inst. Chem. Engrs., Am. Chem. Soc., Profl. Engrs. Ohio, Greater Pitts. C. of C. (bd. dirs.). Home: 136 Devonwood Dr Pittsburgh PA 15241 Office: 1 Gateway Center Pittsburgh PA 15222

BURRELL, KENNETH EARL, guitarist, composer; b. Detroit, July 31, 1931; s. William Henry and Elizabeth (Day) B. Mus.B., Wayne State U., 1955. Exec. dir. Guitar Player Prodns., 1974; pres. Jazz Heritage Found., 1975-78; faculty UCLA, 1978-79. Guitarist, Oscar Peterson Trio, 1955, Benny Goodman Orch., 1957-59, Jimmy Smith Trio, 1959; formed, Kenny Burrell Trio, 1960, Kenny Burrell Quartet, 1963; rec. artist 50 records. Recipient Internat. Jazz Critics awards, 1957, 60, 65, 69-73; winner Downbeat Readers Poll, 1968-71, Downbeat Critics Poll, 1968-73, Swing Jour. Poll, 1970-72, 74. Mem. Phi Mu Alpha, Kappa Alpha Psi. Office: care ABC 199S Broadway New York NY 10023 *

BURRELL, SIDNEY ALEXANDER, history educator; b. Choteau, Mont., Feb. 24, 1917; s. Sidney Harris and Frances (Timmis) B.; m. Ann Theresa Gibbons, Sept. 2, 1945; children: John A., Sidney Antony, Andrew J. Student, DePauw U., 1934-35; A.B., U. Chgo., 1938; Ph.D., Columbia, 1953. Mem. faculty seamanship and navigation U.S. Naval Acad., 1945-46; instr. history Columbia, 1948-50, Barnard Coll., 1950-52; mem. research staff Center Research on World Polit. Instns., Princeton, 1952-53; mem. faculty Barnard Coll., 1953-66; prof., chmn. dept. history Boston U., 1966-79. Author: (with others) Political Community in the North Atlantic Area, 1957; Editor: Amiable Renegade: Memoirs of Capt. Peter Drake, 1671-1753, 1960; Editor, compiler: Role of Religion in Modern European History, 1964; Contbr. to: Some Modern Historians of Britain, 1951, The Protestant Ethic and Modernization (S.N. Eisenstadt, ed.), 1968; Contbr. articles profl. jours. Served with USNR, 1942-46; PTO. Recipient Metcalf cup and prize for Disting. Teaching Boston U., 1981; Univ. lectr. Boston U., 1982; Guggenheim fellow, 1961-62. Mem. Am. Hist. Assn., New Eng. Hist. Assn. (pres. 1972-73), Am. Soc. Ch. History, Acad. Polit. Sci., Conf. Brit. Studies, Colonial Soc. Mass., Econ. History Soc. (Gt. Britain), Phi Beta Kappa, Phi Delta Theta. Home: 43 Walker Ln Needham MA 02192 Office: Boston Univ Boston MA 02215

BURRELL, THOMAS JASON, advertising executive; b. Chgo., Mar. 18, 1939; s. Thomas Jason and Evelyn (Kendall) B.; children: Bonita Aldridge, Alexandra, Jason. B.A. in English, Roosevelt U., 1961. Copywriter Wade Advt., Chgo., 1960-64, Leo Burnett Advt., 1964-67; copywriter, supr. Foote Cone & Belding, London, 1967-68; copy supr. Needham Harper & Steers, Chgo., 1968-71; pres., chief exec. officer Burrell Advt. Inc., Chgo., 1971—. Mem. bd. dirs. Chgo. Urban League; prin. Chgo. United. Mem. Am. Assn. Advt. Agys. (govt. relations com.). Office: Burrell Advertising Inc 625 N Michigan Ave Chicago IL 60611

BURRESS, JAMES RUSSELL, organization administrator; b. Hampton, Va., Aug. 22, 1913; s. James Russell and Jennie (Adams) B.; m. Ruth R. Nicholson, July 17, 1942; children: Melvin L., Cynthia K., Margaret J. B.S., N.C. A&T State U., 1937; M.S., Columbia U., 1941; Ed.D., U. No., Colo., 1980. Social worker, vocat. counselor D.C. Rehab. Services, 1942-51; vocat. rehab. adv. specialist Office Vocat. Rehab., U.S. Dept. Health, Edn. and Welfare, Washington, 1951-59; assoc. regional rep. Vocat. Rehab. Adminstrn., Region VIII, Denver, 1959-67; regional commr. Social and Rehab. Service, 1967-76; exec. dir. com. for handicapped People to People Internat., 1976—; Mem. bd. Metro-Denver Fair Housing Center, Inc., 1966-70; chmn. adv. com. Com. Civil Rights and Minority Employment, 1965-71; mem. Denver Fed. Exec. Bd., 1967-75; del. 12th World Conf. Rehab. Disabled, Sydney, Australia, 1972, Internat. Conf. Social Welfare, Niarobi, Kenya, 1974, U.S. del., San Juan, P.R., 1976; mem. social-vocat. commn. World Congress on Disabled, Athens, 1976; U.S. del. 14th World Congress, Rehab. Internat., Winnipeg, Man., Can., 1980; cons. Internat.; Yr. of Disabled Persons, 1980-81. Author reports and publs. in field. Recipient Spl. Service award, 1966, Superior Service award, 1969, Distinguished Service award, 1970, Sec.'s Spl. award, 1976; all HEW; Man of Year award Omega Psi Phi, 1969; Adminstrs. citation Social and Rehab. Service, 1974; Mary Switzer award Nat. Rehab. Assn., 1974; Meritorious Service award, 1976; Service award Pres.'s Com. Employment of Handicapped, 1980. Mem. Nat. Assn. Social Workers, Nat. Rehab. Assn. (pres. 1971-72), Nat. Rehab. Counseling Assn., Am. Pub. Welfare Assn., Am. Soc. Pub. Adminstrn., Am. Acad. Polit. Social Sci., Nat. Conf. for Social Welfare, Nat. Assn. Hearing and Speech Agys. (nat. bd.), Photog. Soc. Am. First Louis P. Ortale Meml. lectr. on placement services 1970 Ann. Conf. Nat. Rehab. Assn., San Diego. Home: 3290 Leyden St Denver CO 80207 Office: 3809 V St SE Suite 101 Washington DC 20020

BURRIDGE, KENELM OSWALD LANCELOT, anthropologist; b. Malta, Oct. 31, 1922; s. William and Jane (Cassar-Torregiani) B.; m. Rosabelle Griffiths, Sept. 1950; 1 son, Julian Langford. Diploma in anthropology, Exeter Coll., Oxford (Eng.) U., 1949, B.A., 1948, B.Litt., 1950, M.A., 1951; Ph.D., Australian Nat. U., 1953. Scholar Australian Nat. U., 1951-54; research fellow U. Malaya, 1954-56; prof. anthropology U. Baghdad, 1956-58; univ. lectr. Pitt Rivers Museum, Oxford U., 1958-68; prof. anthropology U. B.C., Vancouver, 1968—, also head dept. anthropology and sociology. Author: Mambu: A Melanesian Millennium, 1960, New Heaven, New Earth, 1969, Tangu Traditions, 1969, Encountering Aborigines, 1973, Someone, No one, 1979. Served to lt. Brit. Navy, World War II. Fellow Can. Council, 1970, Guggenheim Found., 1972; Killam fellow, 1979-80; SSHRCC fellow, 1979-80. Fellow Royal Soc. Can., Royal Anthrop. Inst. (hon.); mem. Can. Sociol. and Anthrop. Assn., Am. Anthrop. Assn., Chgo. Ethnology Soc. Home: 901-4665 W 10th St Vancouver BC Canada V6R 2J4 Office: Dept Anthropology and Sociology Univ Brit Columbia Vancouver BC Canada V6T 1W5

BURRIDGE, ROBERT ERIC, university administrator; b. Plaster Rock, N.B., Can., Aug. 29, 1931; s. Albert Charles and Bessie Anne (MacInnes) B.; m. Ardeth Elma Ball, May 16, 1953; children: Stephen Robert, Colin Andrew, Lori Anne. B.Sc. (Lord Beaverbrook scholar 1948-53), U. N.B., 1953; M.S. in Elec. Engring, U. Wis., 1962; Ph.D., McGill U., 1969. Registered profl. engr., N.B. Mem. faculty U. N.B., 1955—, prof. elec. engring., 1970—, chmn. dept., 1970-75; dean Faculty Engring., 1976-80, v.p. acad., 1980—, also mem. univ. bd. govs.; cons. in field. Author research papers in field. Athlone fellow, 1953-55; grantee Nat. Research Council Can. Sr. mem. IEEE; mem. Engring. Inst. Can. (Sir George Nelson award 1966), Am. Soc. Engring. Edn. (mem. council), Assn. Profl. Engrs. N.B. (2d v.p. 1982, 1st v.p. 1983). Baptist. Home: 790 Windsor St Fredericton NB E3B 4G5 Canada Office: Univ New Brunswick Fredericton NB E3B 5A3 Canada

BURRINGTON, DAVID EDSON, journalist; b. Rapid City, S.D., Mar. 11, 1931; s. Therlo Edson and Mary Josephine (Nissen) B. Student, S.D. State Sch. Mines and Tech., 1949-50; B.A. in Journalism, U. Minn., 1953; M.A. in Am. Studies, U. Minn., 1959; degre moyen, Faculte des Lettres, U. Paris, 1957; postgrad., UCLA, 1963-64. News reporter Sta. KSTP-TV, Mpls., 1959-61, Sta. WRCV-TV, Phila., 1961-63; news reporter, writer Sta. KNBC, Los Angeles, 1964-66; fgn. corr. NBC News, Saigon, VietNam, 1966-67, news corr., Los Angeles, 1967-69, fgn. corr., Paris, 1969-71, fgn. corr., bur. chief, Tel Aviv, Israel, 1971-74; fgn. corr., Rome, Italy, 1974-77, fgn. corr., bur. chief, Madrid, Spain, 1977-78, fgn. corr., Cairo, Egypt, 1978-79, network corr., Los Angeles, 1979-82, San Francisco, 1982—. Served with U.S. Army, 1954-56. David Sarnoff fellow, 1963-64. Mem. Overseas Press Club. Office: NBC News 1255 Post St Suite 714 San Francisco CA 94109

BURRIS, B. CULLEN, psychiatrist; b. Miss., 1924; married; 2 children. M.D., U. Tenn., 1946. Intern Wesley Meml. Hosp., Chgo., 1946-47, resident internal medicine, 1949, resident neuropsychiatry, 1949-50, mem. staff, 1953-58; resident Johns Hopkins Hosp., 1950; fellow psychiatry Northwestern U. Med. Sch., 1952-53, clin. instr. psychiatry, 1953-58, assoc. prof. psychiatry, 1967-75, Albany (N.Y.) Med. Coll., 1975—; chief psychiat. services VA Med. Center, Albany, 1975-81, chief mental hygiene clinic, 1981—; med. dir. Milw. Sanitarium Found., Wauwatosa, Wis., 1961-67; asso. prof. psychiatry Marquette U. Med. Sch., 1958-67. Served with M.C. USNR, 1950-52. Address: Albany VA Med Center Albany NY 12208

BURRIS, CONRAD TIMOTHY, chemical engineering educator; b. Edmonton, Can., May 17, 1924; came to U.S., 1950, naturalized, 1956; s. James Edward and Mary Elizabeth (Salzl) B. B.Chem. Engring., U. Alta., 1946, M.Chem. Engring., 1948; Ph.D., Cath. U. Am., 1955. Asst. prof. Manhattan Coll., Bronx, N.Y., 1958-61, asso. prof., 1961-63, prof., 1963—, head dept. chem. engring., 1961-71, 83—, dean engring., 1971-80. Mem. Am. Inst. Chem. Engrs., Am. Soc. Engring. Edn., Am. Chem. Soc., Sigma Xi, Tau Beta Pi. Address: Manhattan Coll Bronx NY 10471

BURRIS, ROBERT HARZA, biochemist, educator; b. Brookings, S.D., Apr. 13, 1914; s. Edward T. and Mable C. (Harza) B.; m. Katherine Irene Brusse, Sept. 12, 1945; children: Jean Carol, John Edward, Ellen Louise. B.S., S.D. State Coll., 1936, D.Sc., 1966; M.S., U. Wis., 1938, Ph.D., 1940. NRC fellow Columbia U., 1940-41; faculty U. Wis., Madison, 1941—, prof., 1951—; chmn. biochemistry Coll. Agr., 1958-70, W.H. Peterson prof. biochemistry, 1976—. Recipient Charles Thom award Soc. Indsl. Microbiology, 1977; Nat. Medal of Sci., 1980; Guggenheim fellow Cambridge U., 1954. Mem. Am. Chem. Soc., Am. Soc. Biol. Chemistry, Am. Soc. Plant Physiologists (Stephen Hales award 1968, Charles Reid Barnes award 1977, pres. 1960), Japanese Soc. Plant Physiology, Biochem. Soc., AAAS, Am. Soc. Microbiology, Nat. Acad. Scis., Am. Acad. Arts and Scis., Am. Philos. Soc. Home: 1015 University Bay Dr Madison WI 53705

BURRIS, ROLAND WALLACE, state official; b. Centralia, Ill., Aug. 3, 1937; s. Earl L. and Emma M. (Curry) B.; m. Berlean Miller, Dec. 23, 1961; children: Rolanda Sue, Roland Wallace II. B.A., So. Ill. U., 1959; postgrad., U. Hamburg, 1959-60; J.D., Howard U., 1963. Bar: Ill. 1964. Comptroller of currency, nat. bank examiner Treasury Dept., 1963-64; 2d v.p., comml. banking officer, tax cons. Continental Ill. Nat. Bank & Trust Co., Chgo., 1964-73; dir. Dept. Gen. Services, State of Ill., Chgo., 1973-77; nat. exec. dir. Operation Push, Chgo., 1977-78; comptroller, State of Ill., 1978—; candidate for Dem. nomination U.S. Senate, 1984; Vice chmn. Com. on Ill. Govt., 1969-72; pres. Independent Polit. Orgn., 1967-68; Democratic candidate Ill. Legislature, 1968; mem. 6th ward Independent Voters of Ill., 1965-70; co-chmn. Ill. del. Dem. Nat. Conv., 1980; mem.-at-large Dem. Nat. Com., 1981. Bd. dirs. So. Ill. U. Found. Named One of Ten Outstanding Young Men of Chgo., 1970, 72, 1,000 Successful Black Men of Am., 1973, Blackbook's Outstanding Bus. Man of Year, 1974; recipient Community Service award Operation Push, 1975, Donald L. Scantlebury Meml. award for state leadership, 1982; named to list of 100 Most Influential Black Americans Ebony Mag., 1979, 80, 81, 82, 83, 84. Mem. ABA, Ill. Bar Assn., Cook County Bar Assn. (Pub. Service award 1975), Chgo. Bar Assn. (chmn. subcom.), Nat. Assn. State Auditors, Comptrollers and Treasurers (2d v.p. 1983-84), Am. Inst. Banking, Nat. Bus. League, Cosmopolitan C. of C., Chgo. South End Jaycees (pres. 1967-68, Disting. Service award 1968), NAACP,

Howard U. Law Sch. Alumni Assn. (chmn. bd.). Baptist (trustee). Office: Office of Comptroller 201 State Capitol Springfield IL 62706

BURROUGHS, FRANK S(IDNEY), JR., engineering and construction company executive; b. Los Angeles, July 3, 1925; s. Frank Sidney and Marjorie (Pope) B.; m. Patricia Jane Menzies, Sept. 10, 1949; children: Robert, Claudia, John. B.E., U. S.C., 1945, M.S., 1948. Cert bus. mgmt., tech., UCLA. With C.F. Braun & Co., Alhambra, Calif., 1948—, sr. v.p. and dir., 1981—; vice chmn. and dir. Saudi Braun Co. Ltd., Jaddah, Saudi Arabia, 1982—. Served with USNR, 1943-46. Mem. Am. Chem. Soc., Am. Inst. Chem. Engrs., Tau Beta Pi. Republican. Club: Annandale Golf (Pasadena, Calif.). Office: C F Braun & Co 1000 S Fremont Ave Alhambra CA 91802

BURROUGHS, JOHN ANDREW, JR., U.S. ambassador; b. Washington, July 31, 1936; s. John A. and Yeasavale B.; m. Audrey C. Shields, Feb. 25, 1966. B.A. in Polit. Sci, U. Iowa, 1959; postgrad., George Washington U., 1962. Passport examiner Dept. State, 1960-63; adminstrv. asst. Bur. Econ. Affairs, Washington, 1963-66; employee relations specialist Dept. Navy, Washington, 1970-77; spl. asst. for equal employment to Asst. sec. of Navy, 1970-77; dep. asst. sec. for equal employment opportunity Dept. State, Washington, 1977-81; U.S. ambassador to Malawi, 1981—; Pres., bd. dirs. Ridgecrest Condominium, 1964-70. Mem. Kappa Alpha Psi. Office: US Dept State Lilongwe Malawi Washington DC 20520

BURROUGHS, MARGARET TAYLOR GOSS, museum dir.; b. St. Rose, La., Nov. 1, 1917; d. Alexander and Octavia (Pierre) Taylor; m. Bernard Goss, 1937; 1 dau., Gayle; m. Charles Burroughs, 1949; 1 adopted son, Paul. B.A. in Edn, Art Inst. Chgo., 1946, M.A., 1948; L.H.D. (hon.), Lewis U., 1972. Tchr. art Chgo. Public Schs., 1944-68; prof. humanities Kennedy King Coll., Chgo., 1969-79; exec. dir. Dusable Mus. African Am. History, Chgo., 1961—; mem. Chgo. Council Fine Arts, 1976-80, Nat. Commm. Negro History and Culture, 1981—; founder Nat. Conf. Artists, 1959. Fellow Nat. Endowment Humanities, 1968. Office: Dusable Museum 740 E 56th Pl Chicago IL 60657 *

BURROUGHS, RAYMON, coll. dean; b. Union, Miss., Oct. 11, 1913; s. H.J. and Ethel (Arnold) B.; m. Elizabeth Rives, Apr. 30, 1934; 1 dau., Judith Ray Burroughs Keith. B.A., Bethel Coll., McKenzie, Tenn., 1939, D.D., 1959; M.A., Western Ky. State Coll., Bowling Green, 1946; B.D., Vanderbilt U., 1942. Ordained to ministry Cumberland Presbyn. Ch., 1934; mem. faculty Bethel Coll., 1945—, acad. dean, 1947-77, Distinguished prof., 1977—; Moderator Cumberland Presbyn. Ch., 1967—. Active local Boy Scouts Am. Mem. Reelfoot Regional Library Bd., McKenzie C. of C. Club: Rotary (pres. 1977-78). Home: 215 Magnolia St McKenzie TN 38201

BURROUGHS, WILLIAM SEWARD, writer; b. St. Louis, Feb. 5, 1914; s. Perry Mortimer and Laura (Lee) B.; m. Joan Vollmer, 1945; 1 son, William Seward. A.B., Harvard U., 1936; postgrad. in ethnology and archeology; med. student, U. Vienna. Formerly newspaper reporter, pvt. detective, exterminator, now full-time writer. Author: Junkie: Confessions of an Unredeemed Drug Addict, 1953, re-issued, 1977, Naked Lunch, 1959, The Exterminator, 1960, Minutes to Go, 1961, The Soft Machine, 1961, The Ticket That Exploded, 1962, Dead Fingers Talk, 1963, (with Allen Ginsberg) The Yage Letters, 1963, Nova Express, 1964, (with Daniel Odier) The Job, 1969, Wild Boys, 1971, Exterminator!, 1973, White Subway, 1974, The Last Words of Dutch Schultz, 1975, (with Brion Gysin) The Third Mind, 1978, Ah Pook Is Here, 1979, City of the Red Night, 1981. Served with AUS, World War II. Address: care Peter Matson 30 W 40th St New York NY 10018 *

BURROW, GERARD NOEL, physician, educator; b. Boston, Jan. 9, 1933; s. William and Noelle Elvira (Money) B.; m. Ann Huntington Rademacher, June 22, 1956; children: Peter Noel, Elisabeth Huntington, Sarah Rogers. B.A., Brown U., 1954; M.D., Yale U., 1958. Diplomate: Am. Bd. Internal Medicine. Intern in internal medicine Yale-New Haven Med. Ctr., 1958-59, asst. resident in internal medicine, 1961-63, fellow in endocrinology and metabolism, 1963-65, chief resident, 1965-66; asst. prof. to prof. Yale U. Sch. Medicine, New Haven, 1966-76; prof. dept. medicine U. Toronto, Ont., Can., 1976-81, Sir John and Lady Eaton prof. medicine, 1981—, chmn. dept., 1981—, coordinator endocrine program, 1978-81; physician-in-chief Toronto Gen. Hosp., 1981—; med. examiner Anglican Diocese of Arctic, 1978—; mem. endocrine grants com. Med. Research Council Can., 1980—. Author: The Thyroid Gland in Pregnancy, 1972; co-author: The Endocrine Glands Structure and Function in Disease, 1974; editor: (with Ferris) Medical Complications during Pregnancy, 1975, 82, Perinatal Thyroid Physiology and Disease, 1975, Neonatal Thyroid Screening, 1980; contbr. numerous articles to profl. jours. Bd. dirs. Conn. Ballet, New Haven, 1973-76, Nat. Ballet Of Can., 1983—. Served with USPHS, 1959-61. Recipient career research devel. award USPHS, 1968-73; fellow Calhoun Coll., Yale U., 1972-76. Fellow ACP, Royal Coll. Physicians (Can.); mem. Soc. Clin. Investigation, Assn. Am. Physicians, Am. Thyroid Assn. (dir. 1982—), European Thyroid Assn. Clubs: University, Toronto Cricket, Groton Long Point Yacht. Home: 92 Sherwood Ave Toronto ON Canada M4P 2A7 Office: Dept Medicine Univ Toronto 101 College St Toronto ON Canada M5G 1L7

BURROW, HAROLD, gas company executive; b. Navasota, Tex., Dec. 1, 1914; s. Benjamin Donald and Minnie (Weaver) B.; m. Vassa Woodley; children—Larry W., Harry W., Janice K. Grad., Advanced Mgmt. Program, Harvard U. With Tenneco, Inc., Houston, 1943-66, pres., dir., mem. exec. com., 1960-66; chmn. bd., dir., chief exec. officer Colo. Interstate Gas Co., Colorado Springs, 1974—; vice chmn. bd. Coastal States Gas Corp., Houston, 1974—, also mem. exec. com.; chmn. bd., chief exec. officer, dir. Colo. Interstate Corp., 1982—; Mem. Petroleum Club Houston. Methodist. Club: Ramada (Houston). Office: Colo Interstate Gas Co Colorado Springs CO 80944 *

BURROWS, ABE, playwright, dir.; b. N.Y.C., Dec. 18, 1910; s. Louis and Julia (Salzberg) B.; m. Carin Smith Kinzel, Oct. 2, 1950; children: James Edward, Laurie Ellen (Mrs. Peter Grad). Student, Coll. City N.Y., 1928-29, Sch. of Finance, N.Y. U., 1929, 30, 31. Writer of: This is New York, for CBS, 1938-39, Texaco Star Theatre, CBS, 1939, Rudy Vallee-John Barrymore program, NBC, 1940, Duffy's Tavern, CBS and NBC, 1941-45; writer-producer, Paramount Pictures, 1946; writer: Joan Davis program, CBS, and, Ford Program, 1946; writer and star: Abe Burrows Show, CBS, 1946-47; made personal appearances in theatres and night clubs, 1947-48; writer-performer-producer, CBS, 1949; writer and star of: Breakfast with Burrows, CBS, 1949, Abe Burrows Almanac, CBS-TV, 1950; also in: This is Show Business, CBS-TV and, We Take Your Word, CBS Radio, and TV, 1950; co-author: musical comedy Guys and Dolls, 1950 (Tony award); dir.: musical Two on the Aisle, 1951; co-author, dir.: Three Wishes for Jamie, 1952; author, dir.: Can-Can, 1953, First Impressions, 1959; dir.: play Reclining Figure, 1954, Golden Fleecing, 1959; author, dir.: Say, Darling, 1958; co-author, dir.: How To Succeed in Business without Really Trying, 1961; dir.: musical What Makes Sammy Run?, 1964; author, dir.: Am. version Cactus Flower, 1965; dir.: Broadway play Forty Carats, 1968; Broadway musical Happy Hunting; adapter, dir.: play Four on a Garden, 1972; dir.: Broadway play No Hard Feelings (Recipient Radio Critics award for best comedy show 1947, N.Y. Drama Critics Award as co-author Guys & Dolls 1951, as co-author How To Succeed in Business without Really Trying 1961, Pulitzer prize as co-author How To Succeed in Business without Really Trying 1961, Tony award as co-author and dir. 1961); Composer lyricist and performer, Decca Record Album, Columbia Record album, Abe Burrows Sings?, 1950; Author: song The Girl with the Three Blue Eyes, 1944, Abe Burrow's Song Book, 1955, Solid Gold Cadillac; screenplay, 1956; co-author: Broadway musical comedy Silk Stockings; autobiography Honest, Abe, 1979. Mem. Dramatists Guild (v.p. 1964), ASCAP, AFTRA, Writers Guild Am. West, Dirs. Guild Am., Soc. Stage Dirs. and Choreographers, Explorers Club. Office: William Morris Agency 1350 Ave of Americas New York NY 10102

BURROWS, BENJAMIN, educator, physician; b. N.Y.C., Dec. 16, 1927; s. Samuel and Theresa Helen (Handelsman) B.; m. Nancy Kreiter, June 14, 1949; children—Jan C., Susan K., Lynn A., Steven M. M.D., Johns Hopkins, 1949. Intern Johns Hopkins Hosp., 1949-50; resident King County Hosp., Seattle, 1950-51, U. Chgo., 1953-55, instr. to asso. prof. medicine, 1955-68; prof. internal medicine, head sect. pulmonary diseases U. Ariz. Coll. Medicine, Tucson, 1968—; Cons. Tucson VA Hosp.; dir. div. respiratory scis. Nat. Heart Lung and Blood Inst. Specialized Center Research in Pulmonary Diseases, U. Ariz. Coll. Medicine, 1971—. Mem. editorial bd.: Am. Rev. Respiratory Disease, 1967-71, 74-80, Chest, 1971-76, Annals Internal Medicine, 1973-76, Archives of Environ. Health, 1976—; Contbr. articles to profl. jours., chpts. to books. Served to capt. USAF, 1951-53. Research grantee USPHS, 1958—. Fellow Am. Coll. Chest Physicians (regent dist. 11 1970-75), A.C.P.; mem. Am. Thoracic Soc. (counsilor), Ariz. Thoracic Soc. (pres.), Assn. Am. Physicians, Am. Soc. Clin. Investigation (emeritus), Am. Physiol. Soc. Home: 6840 Table Mountain Rd Tucson AZ 85718 Office: U Ariz Health Scis Center Tucson AZ 85724

BURROWS, DOUGLAS KENNETH, law enforcement officer; b. London, Ont., Can., Oct. 2, 1932; s. Kenneth Maitl and Thelma (Keil) B.; m. Roberta Rose Nisbet, Sept. 11, 1960; children: Shelley, Gentry, Matthew, Jonathan. B.A., U. Toronto. With Ont. Provincial Police, 1955-59; with Mississauga and Peel Regional Police Forces, Brampton, Ont., Can., 1959—; now Peel regional chief of police.; mem. Police Exec. Research Forum, Washington. Served with Royal Canadian Naval Air, 1950-55. Recipient Canadian Bankers award for bravery, Police Officer of the Month award, Ont. medal for bravery, Queen's Jubile medal. Mem. Canadian Assn. Chiefs Police, Ont. Assn. Chiefs Police (past pres.), Internat. Assn. Chiefs Police, Mich.-Ont. Identification Assn. (past pres.). Office: PO Box 7750 7750 Hurontario St Brampton ON Canada L6V 3W6

BURROWS, FRANK FERGUSON, building contractor; b. Salt Lake City, July 21, 1901; s. Frank Edmond and Elsie (Lang) B.; m. Alice Elizabeth Small, June 30, 1927; children: Frank Robert, Nancy Alice, William Douglas. Student, U. Utah, 1918-20; B.S. in Civil Engring, U. Calif. at Berkeley, 1922; A.B., San Francisco Law Sch., 1937. Asst. hydraulic engr. State of Calif., 1922-24; sec., dir. G.W. Williams Co., 1926-72, Am. Homes Co., 1926-72, Am. Homes Devel. Co., 1943-72; v.p., dir., gen. mgr. Williams & Burrows, Inc., now chmn. bd.; dir. Bell Savs. & Loan Assn.; dir. emeritus Beaver Ins. Co. Mayor City of Burlingame, 1943-44, councilman, 1940-44; Chmn. Calif. Council Home Builders, 1947; pres. Peninsula Gen. Contractors Assn., 1946-47. Mem. Asso. Gen. Contractors (nat. dir., pres. central chpt. 1953, nat. pres. 1962), Newcomen Soc., Cons. Constructors Am. Clubs: Engineers (San Francisco); Menlo Country, Commonwealth., Pacific Union. Lodges: Masons; Shriners. Home: 120 Fallenleaf Dr Hillsborough CA 94010 Office: 500 Harbor Blvd Belmont CA 94002

BURROWS, GEORGE SWIGARD, JR., arts consultant; b. Chgo., Nov. 23, 1948; s. George S. and Marjory (Scholotzhauer) B.; m. Candace Jo Stouman, Nov., 1969 (div.); 1 dau., Amanda. Student, U. Calif.-Berkeley, 1967, Franconica Coll., 1968, Harvard U. extension, 1969, Calif. State U.-Humboldt, 1970-73. Editor Porter Sargent Pub., Boston, 1969-75; playwright-in-residence Theatre Arts Corp., 1973-75, pres., producing dir., 1975-76; ind. dance co. booking mgr., 1976-77; grants and program devel. officer,, artistic dir. performing arts Rising Sun Armory for the Arts, Santa Barbara, 1976-78, pres., artistic dir., 1978-80; dir. pub. relations and mktg. Am. Conservatory Theatre, San Francisco, 1980-81; San Francisco press rep. Children of a Lesser God, 1981; cons. for arts, San Francisco, 1981—. Pres. bd. dirs. Maria Benitez Spanish Dance Co., Santa Fe; mem. nat. adv. bd. Mass. Prison Arts Project; mem. fundraising adv. com. Acad. Media and Theatre Arts, San Francisco. Mem. Assn. Theatrical Press Agts. and Mgrs. Clubs: Univ. of Chgo., Onwentsia. Office: 1845 Gough Apt 2 San Francisco CA 94109

BURROWS, SELIG SAUL, industrialist; b. N.Y.C., June 1, 1913; s. Louis A. and Julia (Salzberg) B.; m. Gladys Spatt, Sept. 18, 1938; children: Kenneth, David, Jonathan Lowell, Patricia. Student, Fordham U., 1930-33, N.Y. U. Law Sch., 1933-36. Chmn. bd., chief exec. officer Cellu-Craft, Inc.; dir. Central Industries, Inc., Jersey City; pres. Realty Enterprises of N.J., Inc., Real Estate Indsls., N.Y.C.; partner Burmel Enterprises Co.; dir. Central Industries Inc. Mem. U.S. Assay Commn., 1963; Pres. Burrows Found., Inc.; bd. dirs. Norton Gallery and Sch. Art, West Palm Beach, Fla.; trustee Friends Acad., Whitney Mus. Am. Art, L.I. Jewish Hosp., New Hyde Park, N.Y., North Shore Hosp., Manhasset, N.Y., United Cerebral Palsy N.Y., Nat. Soc. Prevention Blindness; vice chmn. Fedn. Jewish Charities, L.I.; mem. exec. com. United Jewish Appeal. Mem. Confrerie des Chevaliers du Tastevin. Clubs: City Athletic, Sky, Dutch Treat (N.Y.C.); Beaver Dam Winter Sports; Glen Oaks (L.I.); Palm Beach (Fla.) Country., Soc. of the Four Arts. Home: 999 Indian Rd Palm Beach FL 33480 Office: 514 W 49th St New York NY 10019 also 1401 4th Ave New Hyde Park NY 11040

BURROWS, WILLIAM CLAUDE, retired air force officer, airospace exec.; b. Washington, Aug. 13, 1925; s. Paul Edmund and Lynna (Cary) B.; m. Patricia Dawn Huntley, Sept. 6, 1952; children: William Claude, Barry Huntley. Student, Cornell U., 1943-44; B.S., U.S. Mil. Acad., 1948; M.A., Columbia, 1953, Nat. War Coll., 1965-66. Commd. 2d lt. USAAF, 1948; advanced through grades to maj. gen. USAF; polit. sci. instr. (U.S. Mil. Acad.), 1953-56, asst. prof. geography, 1955-56, chief staff, Taipei, Taiwan, 1972-74, dep. dir. plans, mem., Washington, 1974-76, dep. chief staff plans and programs, Colo., 1976-77, vice comdr. in chief, 1977-79, ret., 1979; with systems analysis br. Boeing Aerospace Co., Seattle, 1979—. Active Boy Scouts Am. Decorated D.S.M., Legion of Merit with 2 oak leaf clusters, Bronze Star, Air medal; Order of Cloud and Banner, Republic of China). Mem. Air Force Assn., Order Daedaleans. Home: 6180 93d Ave SE Mercer Island WA 98040 Office: Boeing Aerospace Co PO Box 3999 Seattle WA 98124

BURRUS, CHARLES SIDNEY, electrical engineering educator; b. Abilene, Tex., Oct. 9, 1934; s. Charles Hooker B. and Aleta (Hunter) Hoffman; m. Mary Lee Powell, June 7, 1958; children: Mary Virginia, Charles Stephen. B.A., Rice U., 1957, B.S., 1958, M.S., 1960; Ph.D., Stanford U., 1965. Registered profl. engr., Tex. Lectr. Stanford U., Calif, 1964-65; asst. prof. elec. engring. Rice U., Houston, 1965-70, assoc. prof., 1970-74, prof., 1974—; vis. prof. U. Erlangen, Ger., 1975,79,82; cons. IBM, Tex. Instruments, VA Hosp., 1975—. Author: Algorithms for DSP, 1984; contbr. articles to profl. jours. Served to lt. USN, 1958-62. Fulbright fellow, 1979; recipient Von Humbolt Sr. award, 1975. Fellow IEEE (sr. paper award 1974); mem. Sigma Si, Tau Beta Pi. Democrat. Baptist. Home: 4018 Whitman Houston TX 77027 Office: Rice U Dept Elec Engring Houston TX 77261

BURRUS, JOHN N(EWELL), sociology educator emeritus; b. Gilmer, Tex., Jan. 23, 1920; s. Herman Clifford and Beulah (Blaylack) B. A.B., U. Miss., 1942; M.A., La. State U., 1944, Ph.D., 1950; postgrad., U. Minn., 1945-47, Vanderbilt U., 1947-48. Asst. prof. sociology U. Miss., Oxford, 1943-45; instr. Vanderbilt U., Nashville, 1947-48; research asso. rural sociology La. State U., Baton Rouge, 1949-50; asst. prof. U. Fla., Gainesville, 1950-51, U. So. Miss., Hattiesburg, 1951-52, asso. prof., 1952-57, prof., 1957-70, Disting. Univ. prof. sociology, 1970-83, Disting. Univ. prof. sociology emeritus, 1983—, chmn. dept. sociology, 1951-70, chmn. dept. sociology and anthropology, 1978-80. Author: monographs Differential Mortality in Mississippi, 1951, (with M.B. King and H.A. Pedersen) Mississippi's People, 1955, Mississippi Life Tables, 1950-51, 1954, Composition of Population of the Coastal Counties; (with T.L. Smith) book Social Problems, 1955, (with others) A Legacy of Knowledge: Sociological Contributions of T. Lynn Smith, 1980; contbr. to: History of Mississippi, 2 vols, 1973; Contbr. chpts., articles and revs. to books, profl. jours., Ency. Brit. Bd. dirs. Hattiesburg Area Hist. Soc., 1971-73, S. Central Miss. chpt. A.R.C., 1961-71. Miss.-Ala. Sea Grant Consortium grantee, 1973-74. Mem. So. Sociol. Soc. (mem. exec. com. 1955-58), Rural Sociol. Soc., Population Reference Bur., Sigma Chi, Phi Kappa Phi, Alpha Kappa Delta, Pi Gamma Mu, Omicron Delta Kappa. Club: Kiwanian (dir. Hattiesburg 1975-76). Home: 213 Arlington Loop Hattiesburg MS 39401 Office: PO Box 8389 So Sta U So Miss Hattiesburg MS 39401

BURRUSS, ROBERT CARL, advertising executive; b. Denver, Feb. 12, 1942; s. Robert L. and Jane C. (Bandeline) B.; m. Susan J. Jaros, Aug. 12, 1972; children: Michael Lawrence, Matthew Robert, Sarah Jane. A.B., Princeton U., 1963; M.B.A., Wharton Sch., U. Pa., 1965. Sr. v.p. Grey Advt. Inc., N.Y.C., 1971—. Served with USAFR, 1965-71. Office: Grey Advt 777 3d Ave New York NY 10021

BURSON, HAROLD, public relations executive; b. Memphis, Feb. 15, 1921; s. Maurice and Esther (Bach) B.; m. Bette Ann Foster, Oct. 30, 1947; children: Scott, Mark. B.A., U. Miss., 1940. Corr., reporter Memphis Comml. Appeal, 1938-40; dir. Ole Miss News Bur., Oxford, Miss., 1939-40; dir. pub. relations H.K. Ferguson Co., N.Y.C., 1941-43; chmn. Burson-Marsteller, N.Y.C., 1953—; dir., mem. exec. com. Marsteller, Inc., N.Y.C., Young & Rubicam; officer, dir. Burson-Marsteller subs. in Can., Latin Am., Europe, Australia, Middle East. Bd. dirs., mem. exec. com., chmn. public info. com. Joint Council on Econ. Edn.; bd. dirs., exec. com., v.p. public info. Nat. Safety Council, 1968-76; bd. dirs. Kennedy Center Prodns., Washington, Catalyst Inc.; former trustee World Wildlife Fund, 1979-81, Found. for Public Relations Research and Edn.; trustee Hackley Sch., Tarrytown, N.Y., 1968-76; mem. Fine Arts Commn., 1981—. Served with AUS, World War II. Named Public Relations Profl. of Year Public Relations News, 1977; recipient Gold Anvil award Public Relations Soc. Am., 1980; named to U. Miss. Hall of Fame, 1980. Mem. Am., Internat. public relations assns., N.Y. Soc. Security Analysts, Am. Philatelic Soc., Blue Key, Omicron Delta Kappa. Clubs: Overseas Press, Marco Polo, Pinnacle (N.Y.C.); Mid-Am. (Chgo.); Internat. (Washington); Scarsdale (N.Y.) Golf. Home: 260 Beverly Rd Scarsdale NY 10583 Office: 866 3d Ave New York NY 10022

BURSTEIN, ELIAS, physicist, educator; b. N.Y.C., Sept. 30, 1917; s. Samuel and Sarah (Plotkin) B.; m. Rena Ruth Benson, Sept. 19, 1943; children—Joanna Bliss, Sandra Joy, Miriam Stephanie. A.B., Bklyn. Coll., 1938; A.M., U. Kans., 1941; postgrad., MIT, 1941-43, Cath. U., 1946-48; D. Tech. (hon.), Chalmers U. Tech., Göteborg, Sweden, 1982. Asst. instr. U. Kans., 1939-41; research asst. M.I.T., 1941-43, research asso., 1943-44; project engr. White Research Assos., Boston, 1944-45; physicist Crystal br. U.S. Naval Research Lab., 1945-58, head semiconductor br., 1958; prof. physics U. Pa., Phila., 1958—, Mary Amanda Wood prof. physics, 1982—; Jubilee vis. prof. physics Chalmers U. Tech., Göteborg, 1981. Editor-in-chief: Solid State Communications, 1969—; co-editor: Comments on Solid State Physics, 1971—. Recipient John Price Wetherill medal Franklin Inst., 1979; Guggenheim fellow, 1980. Fellow Am. Phys. Soc., Optical Soc. Am.; mem. Nat. Acad. Scis., AAAS, Sigma Xi. Club: Cosmos (Washington). Patentee in field. Office: Dept Physics U Pa Philadelphia PA 19104

BURSTEIN, ROSE ANNE KORNBLUM, librarian; b. N.Y.C., May 3, 1922; d. M.J.C. and Myrille (Soloman) Kornblum; m. Lucien Burstein, Nov. 15, 1943; children: Barton M., Emily M., Daniel. A.B. with honors, Olivet Coll., 1943; M.A., Yale U., 1949; M.S. with honors, Sch. Library Sci., Columbia U., 1965. Econ. analyst U.S. Dept. State, Washington, 1944-45; reference librarian New Haven Pub. Library, 1947-48; research librarian advt. agys., N.Y.C., 1949-52; library staff Sarah Lawrence Coll., Bronxville, N.Y., 1956—, library dir., 1974—; mem. N.Y. State Librarians' Task Force on Statewide Serials Database, 1979. Editor: Westchester Union List of Serials, 3d edit., 1979. Bd. vistors Pratt Grad. Sch. Library and Info. Sci., Bklyn., 1981—. Mem. ALA, N.Y. Library Assn., Spl. Libraries Assn., N.Y. Met. Reference and Research Library Agy. (trustee, small library com.), Westchester Library Assn. (bd. dirs.), AAUW. Office: Esther Raushenbush Library Sarah Lawrence Coll Glen Washington Rd Bronxville NY 10708

BURSTYN, ELLEN (EDNA RAE GILLOOLY), actress; b. Detroit, Dec. 7, 1932; m. Paul Roberts; m. Neil Burstyn; 1 son, Jefferson. Co-artistic dir. The Actor's Studio, N.Y.C., 1982—. Appeared regularly on: Jackie Gleason TV show, 1956-57; made Broadway debut in: Fair Game, 1957-58; other play appearances include: summer stock John Loves Mary, 1960; Broadway prodn.: Same Time, Next Year, 1975 (Tony award as best actress); Broadway prodn. 84 Charing Cross Road, 1982; film appearances include: Goodbye Charlie under name Ellen McRae, 1964, Tropic of Cancer, Alex in Wonderland, 1971 (named Best Supporting Actress, N.Y. Film Critics, Nat. Soc. Film Critics; Acad. Award nominee for Best Supporting Actress), The King of Marvin Gardens, 1972, The Exorcist, 1973 (Acad. Award nominee for Best Actress), Harry and Tonto, Alice Doesn't Live Here Anymore, 1974 (Acad. Award as Best Actress), Providence, 1977, A Dream of Passion, 1978, Same Time Next Year, 1978 (Acad. award nominee, Golden Globe award), Resurrection, Silence of the North, 1980; appeared in: TV movie Thursday's Game, 1974, The People vs. Jean Harris, 1981 (Emmy nomination); dir.: off-Broadway play Judgement, 1981. Mem. Actors Equity Assn. (pres. 1982—). Office: The Actors Studio Inc 432 W 44th St New York NY 10036 *

BURSTYN, JOAN NETTA, educator; b. Leicester, Eng., Mar. 6, 1929; d. David Edward and Nellie (Wachman) Jacobs; m. Harold L. Burstyn, Aug. 19, 1958; children: Judith, Gail, Daniel. B.A. with honors, U. London, 1950, Cert of Edn., 1952, Acad. Diploma in Edn., 1958, Ph.D., 1968. Teaching fellow edn. Harvard U., Cambridge, Mass., 1959-64; lectr. U. Pitts., 1967; lectr. psychology and edn. Carnegie Mellon U., Pitts., 1967-68, instr., 1968, asst. prof., 1969-74, dir. tchr. edn., 1970-74; assoc. prof., chairperson dept. edn. Douglass Coll., Rutgers U., New Brunswick, N.J., 1974-81, prof. edn., 1981—, dir. women's studies program, 1981—; co-dir. Fund for Improvement of Post-Secondary Edn. Grant, 1983—. Author: Victorian Education and the Ideal of Womanhood, 1980, Song Cycle, 1976; mem. editorial bd.: Issues in Education; contbr. articles to profl. jours.; assoc. editor: Signs, 1974-80; mem. editorial bd., 1980—, History of Edn. Quar., History of Higher Edn. Ann. Mem. adv. bd. nurse-midwifery ednl. program U. Medicine and Dentistry N.J., 1978-83; bd. dirs. Children's Sch. Sci., Woods Hole, Mass., 1977-80; assoc. dir. N.E. Council Women in Devel., 1981-82; mem. joint com. Am. Hist. Assn. and Can. Hist. Assn., 1978-81. Recipient grant-in-aide John F. Kennedy Sch. Govt. and Bunting Inst., 1964-65; Marion Talbot fellow AAUW, 1965-66; recipient Faculty Merit award Rutgers U., 1977, 81; dir. Nat. Endowment for Humanities pilot grant, 1980-82. Fellow AAAS; mem. Am. Hist. Assn., Am. Ednl. Research Assn. (com. on freedom of inquiry and human rights 1984—), History of Edn. Soc. U.S., History of Edn. Soc. Eng., Assn. Study Higher Edn., Am. Ednl. Studies Assn. (chmn. publs. com. 1984—), Conf. Brit. Studies, AAUW. Office: Grad Sch Edn Rutgers Univ New Brunswick NJ 08903

BURT, ALVIN MILLER, III, anatomist, educator; b. Bridgeport, Conn., Aug. 14, 1935; s. Alvin Miller and Esther Louise (Carey) B.; m. Dorothy Hanlin, July 15, 1961; children: Constance Walker, Carolyn Marie. B.A., Amherst Coll., 1957; Ph.D. (USPHS fellow 1960-61), U. Kans., 1962. Asst. prof. anatomy Med. Coll. Va., Richmond, 1962-63; instr. Yale U. Med. Sch., 1963-66; mem. faculty Vanderbilt U. Med. Sch., 1966—, prof. anatomy, 1974—; vis. scientist Agrl. Research Council, Inst. Animal Physiology, Babraham, Cambridge, Eng., 1972-73. Author articles in field, chpts. in books. Mem. vestry Episcopal Ch. of Advent, Brentwood, Tenn., 1977-81, sr. warden, 1979-81, lay reader, chalice bearer, 1975—, tchr. adult classes, mem. diocesan lay ministry com., 1981—. Recipient Research Career Devel. award USPHS, 1968-73. Mem. Am. Assn. Anatomists, AAAS, Am. Soc. Neurochemistry, Internat. Soc. Neurochemistry, Internat. Brain Research Orgn., Soc. Neurosci., Tenn. Outdoor Writers Asn., Southeastern Outdoor Press Assn., Sigma Xi. Clubs: Tenn. Spoonplugging (dir. 1980—, editor newsletter 1980—), Bass Anglers Sportsmens Soc., Profl. Bass Fishermen. Home: 8108 Devens Dr Brentwood TN 37027 Office: Dept Anatomy Vanderbilt U Nashville TN 37232

BURT, ALVIN VICTOR, JR., newspaperman; b. Oglethorpe County, Ga., Sept. 11, 1927; s. Alvin Victor and Mabel (Sorrow) B.; m. Gloria White. B.A. in Edn, U. Fla., 1949. With U.P., 1949-50, Atlanta Jour., 1950-51, Jacksonville (Fla.) Jour., 1951-55; with Miami (Fla.) Herald, 1955-66, Latin Am. editor, 1962-66, assigned, Washington, 1962, editorial writer, 1967-73, coumnist, 1973—; editor Hartwell (Ga.) Sun, 1966-67. Co-author: Papa Doc, 1969; author: Florida A Place in the Sun, 1974, Becalmed in the Mullet Latitudes, 1983. Recipient Ernie Pyle award for newspaper writing, 1961; State award A.P. for feature writing, 1964; citation Fla. Legislature, 1965; Scripps-Howard award for best interviews in nation, 1966; Editorial Writing award Fla. Soc. Newspaper Editors-Fla. Press Assn., 1973; Overseas Press award, 1974; J.C. Penney spl. award U. Mo., 1980. Mem. Sigma Delta Chi. Office: Miami Herald Miami FL 33101

BURT, CHRISTOPHER MURRAY, editor; b. Dunedin, New Zealand, Nov. 24, 1933; s. Melville Ross and Mercia (Arnett) B.; m. Elizabeth Evaschesen, Sept. 5, 1959; children—Katherine, David. Student public schs., Dunedin, New Zealand. Journalism cadet Evening Star, Dunedin, 1951-53; writer Internat. News Service/Internat. News Photos, London, 1954-55; reporter, city editor Times Herald, Moose Jaw, Sask., Can., 1956-60; city editor The Standard, St. Catharines, Ont., Can., 1960-67; copy editor, nat. editor, city editor The Globe and Mail, Toronto, Ont., 1967-79; mng. editor Winnipeg (Man., Can.) Free Press, 1979—. Mem. Can. Mng. Editors Conf. (dir.), Can. Daily Newspaper Pubs. Assn. (chmn. editorial div.). Anglican. Club: Royal Canadian Yacht. Home: 80 Waterloo St Winnipeg MB R3N 0S2 Canada Office: 300 Carlton St Winnipeg MB T3C 3C1 Canada

BURT, CLEON LEROY, diversified company executive, lawyer; b. Central Cove, Idaho, May 23, 1923; s. Charles Andrew and Grace (Godfrey) B.; m. Imogene Troop, Dec. 23, 1949; children: Karen, Glenna. Student, U. Idaho, 1940-43, Midwestern U., 1946-47; J.D., St. Louis U., 1950. Bar: Mo. bar 1950. Practiced in, St. Louis, 1950-51; asst. sec., asst. gen. counsel Mo.-Pacific Corp., St. Louis, 1952-60, gen. atty., 1960-69, v.p., gen. counsel, 1969-82, Mississippi River Transmission Corp., 1972—. Served with USAAF, 1944-46. Mem. Am., Mo., St. Louis, St. Louis County, Fed. Energy bar assns., Alpha Sigma Nu, Phi Alpha Delta, Tau Kappa Epsilon. Home: 605 N Woods Mill Rd Saint Louis MO 63017 Office: Mo Pacific Corp 9900 Clayton Rd Saint Louis MO 63124

BURT, JAMES MELVIN, sugar manufacturing company executive; b. Los Angeles, June 20, 1933; s. Earl Jefferson and Sara Frances (Cook) B.; m. Lynne A. Johnson, June 18, 1954; children: Kathleen, Karen, Peggy, Laurie. B.A., Occidental Coll., Los Angeles, 1955. With Lever Bros. Co., N.Y.C., 1959-65, Heinz Co., Pitts., 1965-69; v.p., dir. consumer products Facelle Co., Oxnard, Calif., 1969-73; v.p., dir. brokerage ops. Bromar Inc., Newport Beach, Calif., 1973-80; sr. v.p. sales and mktg. C & H Sugar Co., San Francisco, 1980—. Served as capt. USMC, 1955-58. Mem. Am. Mgmt. Assn. (mktg. council 1981-82). Republican. Presbyterian. Clubs: Sharon Heights (Menlo Park, Calif.); World Trade (San Francisco). Office: C&H Sugar Co 1 California St San Francisco CA 94111

BURT, JOHN HARRIS, bishop; b. Marquette, Mich., Apr. 11, 1918; s. Bates G. and Emily May (Bailey) B.; m. Martha M. Miller, Feb. 16, 1946; children—Susan, Emily, Sarah, Mary. B.A., Amherst Coll., 1940, D.D. (hon.), 1960; B.A., Va. Theol. Sem., 1943, D.D., 1967; D.D., Youngstown U., 1958, Kenyon Coll., 1967. Boys worker Christodora House, N.Y.C., 1940-41; ordained to ministry Episcopal Ch., 1943; canon (Christ Ch. Cathedral), rector, St. Louis, 1943-44; chaplain to Episc. students U. Mich., 1946-50; rector St. John's Ch., Youngstown, Ohio, 1950-57, All Saints Ch., Pasadena, Calif., 1957-67; bishop coadjutor, Ohio, 1967-68, Episc. bishop of, 1968—; pres. So. Calif. Council Chs., 1962-65; mem. bd. Ch. Soc. Coll. Work, 1964-71; chmn. clergy deployment bd. Episc. Ch., 1971-73. Co-author: World Religions and World Peace, 1969. Pres. Youngstown Coordinating Council, 1954-56, Pasadena Community Council, 1964-66; trustee Pomona Coll., 1963-66, Va. Theol. Sem., 1967-72, Colgate-Rochester Div. Sch., 1968—, Kenyon Coll., 1967—; bd. dirs. United Way Los Angeles, 1964-67, Cleve. Urban Coalition, 1968-70, Ams. for Energy Independence, 1975—; chmn. bd. dirs. St. John's Home for Girls, Painesville, Ohio, 1968—; governing bd. Nat. Council Chs., 1970-81; mem. Com. on Ch. Order, Consultation on Ch. Union, 1980—; chmn. com. on theology Episc. Ch. House Bishops, 1973-80; chmn. Urban Bishops Coalition, 1977—, Faith and Order Commn. Ohio Council Chs., 1970-74; chmn. commn. ecumenical relations Episc. Ch., 1973-79, also chmn. commn. middle judicatories, cons. on ch. union, 1975-79; chmn. com. human affairs and health Epis. Ch.; chmn. Bishops Com. Nat. and Internat. Affairs. Served as chaplain USNR, 1943-46. Recipient Arvona Lynch Human Relations award, Youngstown, 1956; Rissica Human Relations award Jewish War Vets., 1966; Pasadena Community Relations award, 1967; Cleve.'s Simon Bolivar award, 1972; Pitts.'s Thomas Merton award, 1978; Human Rights award Ohio br. ACLU, 1980. Mem. Phi Gamma Delta. Home: 18200 Shelburne Rd Shaker Heights OH 44118 Office: 2230 Euclid Ave Cleveland OH 44115

BURT, ROBERT AMSTERDAM, lawyer, educator; b. Phila., Feb. 3, 1939; s. Samuel Matthew and Esther (Amsterdam) B.; m. Linda Gordon Rose, June 14, 1964; children—Anne Elizabeth, Jessica Ellen. A.B., Princeton U., 1960; B.A. in Jurisprudence, Oxford (Eng.) U., 1962, M.A., 1968; J.D., Yale U., 1964, M.A. (hon.), 1976. Bar: D.C. bar 1966, Mich. bar 1973, U.S. Supreme Ct. bar 1971. Law clk. to chief judge U.S. Ct. Appeals D.C., 1964-65; asst. gen. counsel Office President's Spl. Rep. Trade Negotiations, 1965-66; senatorial legis. asst., 1966-68; asso. prof. law U. Chgo. Law Sch., 1968-70; asso. prof., then prof. law U. Mich. Law Sch., 1970-76; prof. law in psychiatry U. Mich. Med. Sch., 1973-76; prof., then Southmayd prof. law Yale U. Law Sch., 1976—. Bd. dirs. Benhaven Sch. Autistic Persons, New Haven, 1977—. Rockefeller fellow, 1976. Mem. Inst. Medicine. Democrat. Jewish. Home: 66 Dogwood Circle Woodbridge CT 06525 Office: Yale U Law Sch 127 Wall St New Haven CT 06520

BURT, WAYNE VINCENT, oceanographer, educator; b. South Shore, S.D., May 10, 1917; s. John David and Mary Pearle (McDuffee) B.; m. Grace Louise DuBois, Jan. 15, 1941; children: John Alan, Christine Louise, Laurence W., Darcy Jean. B.S. in Math, Pacific Coll., 1939; M.S., UCLA, 1948, Ph.D. in Phys. Oceanography, 1952; D.Sc. (hon.), George Fox Coll., Newberg, Oreg., 1963. Instr. Oreg. high schs., 1939-42; material engr. Kaiser Co., Inc., Wash. State, 1942; instr. math. U. Oreg., 1946; asst. Scripps Instn., 1946-48, assoc. oceanographer, 1948-49; asst. prof. oceanography, research oceanographer Chesapeake Bay Inst., Johns Hopkins, 1949-53, asst. dir., 1953; research oceanographer dept. oceanography U. Wash., 1953-54; assoc. prof. oceanography Oreg. State U., Corvallis, 1954-59, prof., chmn. dept., 1959-67, assoc. dean research, 1967-76, assoc. dean oceanography, 1976-78, 81—, dir. marine sci. center, 1964-72; oceanographer London br. Office Naval Research, U.S. Navy, 1979-80; Mem. sci. expdns. to Eastern tropical Pacific Ocean Scripps Instns. Oceanography, 1955, 58, Can. Hudson expdn., 1970, Brit. Royal Soc. expdns., 1972, 77, 78, German expdn., 1973, Japanese expdn., 1975; rep. XIV Limnology Congress, Vienna, Austria, 1959; rep. to UN Research Vessel Forum, Tokyo, Japan, 1961; rep. UNESCO Intergovtl. Oceanographic Commn., Paris, 1965; mem. Nat. Adv. Com. on Oceans and Atmosphere, 1971-75. Editor: Wiley-Intersci. series Wastes in the Oceans, 1982—; Contbr. articles to profl. jours. Trustee George Fox Coll., 1970-73. Served to lt. USNR, 1942-46; comdr. Res. Recipient Alumni Disting. Prof. award Oreg. State U., 1968, Centennial award, 1968; Gov.'s Scientist award Oreg. Mus. Sci. and Industry, 1969; Man of Year award Willamette Valley Research Council, 1971. Fellow Am. Meteorol. Soc. (council 1969-71, exec. com. 1972); mem. Am. Geophys. Union (pres. oceanography sect. 1964, ocean sci. award 1984), Am. Soc. Limnology and Oceanography (pres. Pacific sect. 1958, editorial bd. 1963-64), Oreg. Acad. Sci., Oreg. Marine Biol. Soc. Club: Cosmos (Washington). Home: 1615 NW Hillcrest Dr Corvallis OR 97330

BURTIS, THEODORE ALFRED, oil company executive; b. Jamaica, N.Y., May 17, 1922; s. Theodore Alfred and Florence Angela (Whalen) B.; m. Billie Joyce King, June 2, 1945; children: Barbara, Theodore, Pamela. B.S., Carnegie Inst. Tech., 1942; M.Sc., Tex. A&M Coll., 1946; D.Sc., Ursinus Coll., 1972, Villanova U., 1981; LL.D., Widener U., 1983. With Magnolia Petroleum Co., 1943-45, Owens-Corning Fiberglass Corp., 1946-47, Houdry Process Corp., Phila., 1947—, pres., 1956-62, chmn., pres.; v.p., dir. Air Products & Chems. Inc., 1962-67; dir. comml. devel. Sun Co. Inc., 1967-68, adminstrv. dir. research and engring., 1969-70, v.p. R & D, 1970-72, v.p. mktg., 1970-72, pres. products group, 1974-75, exec. v.p. dir., 1975—, pres., 1976—, chief exec. officer, 1978—, chmn. bd., 1979—. Fellow Am. Inst. Chem. Engrs. (pres. 1967); mem. Am. Chem. Soc., Kappa Sigma, Tau Beta Pi. Clubs: Union League (Phila.); Philadelphia Country (Gladwyne, Pa.). Office: Sun Oil Co Inc 100 Matsonford Rd Radnor PA 19087

BURTON, A. PAUL, publisher; b. Camden, N.J., June 10, 1909; s. Paul and Beatrice (Eadson);; s. Paul and Beatrice (Burton); m. Mildred S. Leonard, Feb. 1, 1936 (dec. 1967); 1 son, A. Paul (dec.); m. Agnes S. Donahue, June 1968. B.Sc., Rutgers U., 1932; grad., Advanced Mgmt. Program, Harvard, 1951. Dist. mgr. Curtis Pub. Co., 1932-40; with W.B. Saunders Co., Phila., 1940—, v.p. sales, 1950-56, exec. v.p., 1956—, also dir.; dir. Rutgers U. Press, W.B. Saunders Co., Ltd., London, Eng.; Mem. cons. panel internat. uses of textbooks State Dept., 1963-70. Mem. bd. edn., Pitman, N.J., 1938-41, pres., 1940-41; mem. Pitman Borough Council, 1948-50; Trustee Rutgers-The State U., N.J., 1963—; vice chmn. bd. trustees Gloucester County Coll, 1967-70. Served to lt. USNR, 1943-46; PTO. Mem. Med. Exhibitors Assn. (dir. 1948-50, pres. 1950-52), Assn. Am. Med. Schs. World Med. Assn., Mil. Order World Wars. Methodist. (ofcl. bd.). Clubs: Mason., Union League, Downtown (Phila.); Seaview Country (Absecon, N.J.). Home: 11509 Paradise Dr Stone Harbor NJ 08247

BURTON, AL, producer, director, writer; b. Chgo., Apr. 9, 1928; s. D. Chester and Isabelle (Olenick) G.; m. Sally Lou Lewis, Jan. 8, 1956; 1 dau., Jennifer. B.S. cum laude, Northwestern U., 1948. Dir. 42 Products Ltd., Inc. Producer (1949-52) various youth-oriented TV series; producer: Johnny Mercer's Mus. Chairs, 1952-55, Oscar Levant Show, 1955-61; creative producer: Teen-Age Fair, 1962-72; exec. v.p. creative affairs, Norman Lear-Embassy Communications, Inc., 1973-83; exec. producer-cons., Universal TV, 1983—; exec. producer Charles in Charge, CBS-TV, 1984—; creative supr.: Mary Hartman, Mary Hartman; prodn. supr.: One Day At a Time, Facts of Life, Silver Spoons, The Jeffersons, Diff'rent Strokes; composer-lyricist: theme songs for Facts of Life, Diff'rent Strokes, Charles in Charge; cons.: Domestic Life, CBS-TV, 1983-84; (Recipient Emmy award for outstanding comedy series All in the Family 1978-79, honored for Diff'rent Strokes, NCCJ 1979-80). Media cons. Democratic Congl. Com., Calif. Dem. State Com.; trustee Oakwood Sch. Mem. Caucus for Producers, Writers and Dirs., Dirs. Guild Am., Writers Guild Am., AFTRA, Acad. of TV Arts and Scis., Acad. Magical Arts. Home: 2300 Coldwater Canyon Beverly Hills CA 90210 Office: Universal Studio Universal City CA 91608 *I believe that, in order to achieve success, one must make an occupation of his or her hobby.*

BURTON, ARTHUR HENRY, JR., insurance company executive; b. Phila., Jan. 24, 1934; s. Arthur H. and Gertrude May (Williams) B.; m. Gail M. LaBonte, Sept. 6, 1955; children: Bradford, Steven, Robert, John. A.B., Princeton U., 1955. C.L.U. With Prudential Inc. Co. Am., 1968—, assoc. dir. group ins., Newark, 1968-70, dir. group ins., Chgo., 1970-75, v.p. group ins., Mpls., 1975-78, v.p., Newark, 1978-80, Parsippany, N.J., 1980-81, pres. Central Atlantic ops., Ft Washington, Pa., 1981-83, pres. North Central ops., Mpls., 1983—. Trustee United Way SE Pa., Phila., 1982-83; bd. dirs. World Affairs Council, Phila., 1982-83, Chgo. Area Council, 1983—; counties chmn. United Way S.E. Pa., 1982-83. Served to 1st lt. U.S. Army, 1956-57. Mem. Ins. Fedn. Pa. (bd. dirs., chmn. 1981-83), Pa. Economy League (bd. govs. 1981-83). Republican. Episcopalian. Club: Princeton Club of N.Y. Home: 405 Oxford Rd Long Lake MN 55356 Office: Prudential Ins Co Am North Central Home Office Minneapolis MN 55440

BURTON, BENJAMIN THEODORE, govt. ofcl.; b. Wiesbaden, Ger., Aug. 29, 1919; came to U.S., 1938; (married); 2 children. B.S., U. Calif., Berkeley, 1941, M.S., 1943, Ph.D. in Microbiology and Biochemistry, 1947. Research chemist Mills Orchards Corp., 1941-42; outside supr., tech. cons. Rosenberg Bros. & Co., 1942-48; v.p., tech. dir. Pacific States Labs., Inc., 1952-55; staff cons. nutrition H.J. Heinz Co., 1955-60; with Nat. Inst. Arthritis, Diabetes, Digestive and Kidney Diseases, NIH, Bethesda, Md., 1960—, asso. dir. for program planning, chief artificial kidney program, 1965—. Mem. Am. Inst. Nutrition, Internat. Soc. Nephrology, Am. Soc. Nephrology, Am. Soc. Artificial Internal Organs, European Dialysis and Transplant Assn., Am. Soc. Extracorporeal Tech. Office: Nat Inst Arthritis Diabetes Digestive and Kidney Diseases NIH Bethesda MD 20205

BURTON, CHARLES HENNING, lawyer; b. Washington, Nov. 25, 1915; s. Charles Henry and Bessie R. (Harrell) B.; m. Mary Sheppard, Sept. 6, 1941; children: Nancy Leigh Burton Wysling, Susan C. Burton Hawkins, Mary Ellen Burton Will, Charles S. Student, George Washington U., 1937-41; LL.B., Am. U., 1936, LL.M., 1937. Bar: D.C. 1936, Md. 1957. Gen. counsel D.C. Unemployment Compensation Bd., 1938-42; mem. firm MacCracken & O'Rourke, Washington, 1946-50; mem. Law Offices Robert Ash, Washington, 1950-56; gen. partner firm Ash, Bauersfeld & Burton, Washington, 1954—; gen. partner Tingle Nursery, Burton & Hearn, Bauersfeld & Burton, Burton & Mooers; ltd. and gen. partner Fairplay Assos.; ltd. partner Drake Assos., A.W.S. Assos., Highview Assos., S & H Assos., PM Assos.; pres., dir. North Shore Corp., Links, Inc., Affiliated Underwriters; v.p., dir. Modern Pioneers Life Ins. Co.; sec., dir. Alturas Corp., Camden Stamp & Seal Co., Walton Stamp Co., Adams Tchrs. Agy., Cosco Industries, Inc., Hiss Stamp Co., Lang Stamp Works, Oraton Rubber Stamp Co.; dir. Mattos, Inc., Sisk Mailing Service Inc., Forster Mfg. Co., Inc., Jana Label Co., Fries, Beall & Sharp Co., Inc., Montgomery Golf Corp., Dividend/Growth Fund; Gen. counsel Bapt. World Alliance, Washington, 1958—; trustee, gen. counsel Calvary Bapt. Ch., Bapt. Student Union Found., Kendall Mission Fund, Center Union Mission. Served to comdr. USNR, 1942-46. Fellow Am. Bar Found.; mem. Am. Bar Assn. (editor Young Lawyer 1946-48, nat. sec. Jr. Bar 1949, nat. vice-chmn. 1950, nat. chmn. 1951, ho. of dels. 1952-59), Sigma Chi, Sigma Nu Phi. Club: Montgomery County Country. Home: 21600 Davis Mill Rd Germantown MD 20874 Office: 4520 East-West Hwy Suite 505 Bethesda MD 20814

BURTON, CLARK DECKER, banker; b. Bklyn., Feb. 16, 1919; s. John Reginald and Grace (Rhinehardt) B.; m. Eva May Larson, June 22, 1946; children—Jeanne Leslie (Mrs. Julian Lenwood McPhillips), Mark Linne, Craig Kimball, Keith Clark. B.A., Cornell U., 1941; postgrad., Escola Livre de Sociologia e Politica, U. Sao Paulo, Brazil, 1941-42, U. Colo. Law Sch., 1945-46. Trainee First Nat. Bank of, Boston, 1947, mgmt. asst., Rio de Janeiro, Brazil, 1947, sub-accountant to mgr., Sao Paulo, 1948-62, exec. mgr., Rio de Janeiro, 1962-65, v.p., Buenos Aires, Argentina, 1965-70, Boston, 1972-74, sr. v.p., 1974—, dep. head internat. banking, 1980—; exec. v.p. Bank Boston Internat., N.Y.C., 1970-71, also dir.; dir. Bank of Boston Internat., Miami, Fla., Los Angeles, Boston Overseas Financial Corp. Bd. dirs., officer Escola Americana do Rio de Janeiro. Served to capt. AUS, 1942-45. Decorated Ordem de Merito Militar, Brazil). Mem. Am. C. of C. (Sao Paulo, Rio de Janeiro, Buenos Aires; dir.), Am. Soc. Sao Paulo (pres.), Scabbard and Blade, Phi Gamma Delta. Clubs: Halfway House, Rio Clube de Campo Jockey (Sao Paulo, Rio de Janeiro, Buenos Aires); Country, Rio-Sao Paulo Golf, Am. (Rio de Janeiro, Buenos Aires); Met. (N.Y.C.). Home: 111 Bogle St Weston MA 02193 Office: 100 Federal St Boston MA 02105

BURTON, COURTNEY, mining and shipping company executive; b. Cleve., Oct. 29, 1912; s. Courtney and Sarita (Oglebay) B.; m. Marguerite Rankin, Sept. 7, 1933 (dec. Apr. 1976); children: Sarita Ann Burton Limbocker, Marguerite Rankin (Mrs. George M. Humphrey II); m. Margaret Butler Leitch, Dec. 20, 1978. Student, Mich. Coll. Mining and Tech., 1933-34, B.S., 1956. Dir. E.W. Oglebay Co., Cleve., 1934-57, pres., 1947-57; v.p. Ferro Engring. Co., Cleve., 1950-57; pres. Fortuna Lake Mining Co., Cleve., 1950-57; treas., dir. Columbia Transp. Co., Cleve., 1950-57; v.p. Montreal Mining Co., Cleve., 1950-57; pres. North Shore Land Co., Cleve., 1950-57; v.p., dir. Brule Smokeless Coal Co., Cleve., 1950-57; chmn. bd., chmn. exec. com. Oglebay Norton Co., Cleve., 1957—; 1dir. Nat. Bank W.Va., 1951-59, Central Nat. Bank Cleve., 1941-42, Cleve. Trust Co., 1950-76. Dir. Ohio Civilian Def. and Rationing, 1941-42; exec. asst. Office Coordinator Inter-Am. Affairs, 1942-44; mayor Village of Gates Mills, Ohio, 1948-61; mem. Cleve. Met. Park Bd., 1969-74; chmn. Ohio Republican Finance Com., 1954-61, Rep. Nat. Finance Com., 1961-64; former trustee, founder, mem. adminstrv. bd. Nat. Recreation and Park Assn.; bd. dirs. Nat. Park Found.; trustee Bethany Coll.; hon. trustee Univ. Hosp., Cleve., Oglebay Inst., Wheeling, W.Va.; pres. America's Future Trees Found. Served to lt. USNR, 1944-46. Mem. Am. Iron and Steel Inst., Nat. Coal Assn., Cleve. Zool. Soc. (pres. 1968-76). Episcopalian. Clubs: Chagrin Valley Hunt (Gates Mills) (master of hounds 1946-54); Tavern, Union (Cleve.); Rolling Rock (Ligonier, Pa.); Fort Henry, Wheeling Country, Ye Olde Country (Wheeling, W.Va.); Kirtland (Willoughby, Ohio). Office: 1100 Superior Ave Cleveland OH 44114

BURTON, DANNY LEE, congressman; b. Indpls., June 21, 1938; m. Barbara Jean Logan, 1959; children: Danielle Lee, Danny Lee II. Businessman, ins. and real estate firm owner, 1968—; mem. 98th Congress from 6th Dist. Ind. Pres. Vols. of Am., Ind. Christian Benevolent Assn., Com. for Constl. Govt., Family Support Ctr.; mem. Ind. Ho. of Reps., 1967-68, 77-80, Ind. State Senate, 1969-70, 81-82. Served with U.S. Army, 1957-58. Republican. Office: 120 Cannon House Office Bldg Washington DC 20515 *

BURTON, DELMAR LEE, insurance corporation executive; b. Kansas City, Kans., Dec. 25, 1929; s. Delmar Leroy and Helen Elmina (Wood) B.; m. Glenna L. Branstetter, July 22, 1951; children: Deborah, Dan. B.S., U. Mo., 1951. Underwriter Nat. Surety Corp., Kansas City, Mo., 1951-53, Ohio Casualty Co., Hamilton, 1953-55, Employers Reins. Corp., San Francisco, 1956-71, v.p., 1971-78, sr. v.p., 1978-83, exec. v.p., Overland Park, Kans., 1983—; dir. Western Ins. Info. Service, San Francisco, 1978-81. Served to 1st lt. U.S. Army, 1951-53; Korea. Republican. Mem. Ch. of Christ. Clubs: Merchants Exchange; Presidio Golf (San Francisco). Office: Employers Reins Corp 5200 Metcalf St PO Box 2991 Overland Park KS 66201

BURTON, DONALD JOSEPH, educator; b. Balt., July 16, 1934; s. Lawrence Andrew and Dorothy Wilhelmina (Koehler) B.; m. Margaret Anna Billing, June 21, 1958; children—Andrew, Jennifer, David, Julie, Elizabeth. B.S., Loyola Coll., Balt., 1956; Ph.D., Cornell U., 1961; postgrad., Purdue U., 1961-62. Asst. prof. chemistry dept. U. Iowa, Iowa City, 1962-67, asso. prof., 1967-70, prof., 1970—. Mem. Am. Chem. Soc. (chmn. fluorine div. 1978), Chem. Soc. London, Sigma Xi, Alpha Chi Sigma. Home: Rural Route 2 Iowa City IA 52240

BURTON, DWIGHT LOWELL, educator; b. Carson Lake, Minn., Aug. 9, 1922; s. Benjamin Otis and Beryl (Green) B.; m. Claudia Holland, Feb. 15, 1968; children: Barbara Kay, Christine Beryle. B.S., U. Minn., 1943, M.A., 1947, Ph.D., 1951. High sch. tchr. English, Superior, Wis., 1946-47; tchr. English, head dept. U. Minn. High Sch., 1947-52; prof. English edn. Fla. State U., 1952—, chmn. dept. curriculum and instrn. Author: Literature Study in the High Schools, 1958, rev. edit., 70; co-author: Teaching English in Today's High Schools, 1965, rev. edit., 1970, Teaching English Today, 1975; editor: English Jour., 1955-64; cons. editor: Research in the Teaching of English. Served from pvt. to capt. AUS, 1943-46. Decorated Bronze Star; Croix de Guerre (France); recipient Honor award Adolescent

Lit. Assembly, 1981. Mem. Nat. Conf. Research in English, Conf. English Edn. (past chmn.), Nat. Council Tchrs. of English (2d v.p. 1966, Disting. Service award 1970), Phi Delta Kappa, Sigma Tau Delta. Home: 423 Vinnedge Ride Tallahassee FL 32303

BURTON, GARY, musician; b. Anderson, Ind., Jan. 23, 1943; s. Wayne and Bernice B.; m. Catherine Goldwyn, July 12, 1975; 1 dau., Stephanie Clare. Ed., Berklee Coll. Music, Boston Conservatory Music. Vibraphone player, leader jazz group, 1967—; instr. Berklee Coll. Music, 1972-78. Rec. artist, including: Alone At Last, 1972 (Grammy award 1972). Named Jazzman of Yr. Downbeat Mag., 1968; winner Downbeat Mag. Poll, 1968, 79 *

BURTON, GLENN WILLARD, geneticist; b. Clatonia, Nebr., May 5, 1910; s. Joseph Fearn and Nellie (Rittenburg) B.; m. Helen Maurine Jeffryes, Dec. 16, 1934; children: Elizabeth Ann (Mrs. John Edward Fowler), Robert Glenn, Thomas Jeffryes, Joseph William, Richard Bennett. B.Sc., U. Nebr., 1932, D.Sc. (hon.), 1962; M.Sc., Rutgers U., 1933, Ph.D., 1936, D.Sc. (hon.), 1955. With U.S. Dept. Agr. and U. Ga. at Tifton Expt. Sta., 1936—, prin. geneticist, 1952—, chmn. div. agronomy, 1950-64; Univ. Found. prof. U. Ga., 1957. Mem. Tift County Bd. Edn., 1953-58. Recipient 1st ann. agrl. award So. Seedsmen Assn., 1950; Sears-Roebuck research award, 1953, 60; Superior Service award Dept. Agr., 1955; Disting. Service award, 1980; 1st Ford Almanac Crops and Soils Research award, 1962; Pres.'s award for Disting. Fed. Civilian Service, 1981; Nat. Medal of Sci., 1983; named Man of Year in So. Agr. Progressive Farmer, 1954; numerous other awards and citations. Fellow Am. Soc. Agronomy (Stevenson award 1949, John Scott award 1957, v.p. 1961, pres. 1962); mem. Am. Genetic Assn., Am. Soc. Range Mgmt., Nat. Acad. Sci., Sigma Xi, Alpha Zeta, Gamma Sigma Delta. Home: 421 W 10th St Tifton GA 31794

BURTON, JOHN CAMPBELL, university dean, educator, consultant; b. N.Y.C., Sept. 17, 1932; s. James Campbell and Barbara (French) B.; m. Jane Garnjost, Apr. 6, 1957; children: Eve Bradley, Bruce Campbell. B.A., Haverford Coll., 1954; M.B.A., Columbia U., 1956, Ph.D., 1962. C.P.A., N.Y. Staff acct. Arthur Young & Co., N.Y.C., 1956-60; prof. acctg. and fin. Grad. Sch. Bus. Columbia U., N.Y.C., 1962-72, Arthur Young prof. acctg. and fin., 1978—, dean Grad. Sch. Bus., 1982—; chief acct. SEC, Washington, 1972-76; dep. mayor fin. City of N.Y., 1976-77; dir. Scolastic Inc., 1969-72, 77—; dir., chmn. audit com. Commerce Clearing House Inc., 1979—, First Pa. Corp.-First Pa. Bank, 1982—; chmn. bd. dirs. Congdon & Weed, 1982—; mem. U.S. Comptroller Gen. Cons. Panel, 1978—; trustee Fin. Analysts Research Found., 1978—; dir. Accts. for Pub. Internest, 1978—. Editor: Corporate Financial Reporting: Conflicts and Challenges, 1969, Corporate Financial Reporting: Ethical and Other Problems, 1972, (with Russell Palmer and Robert Kay) Handbook of Accounting and Auditing, 1981, The International World of Accounting: Challenges and Opportunities, 1981; author: Accounting for Business Combinations, 1970, (with W.T. Porter) Auditing: A Conceptual Approach, 1971, (with H. Goodman, A. Phillips and M. Vasarhelyi) Illustrations and Analysis of Disclousres of Inflation Accounting Information, 1981; contbr. articles to profl. jours. Pres., trustee Millbrook Sch. (N.Y.), 1958—; trustee ex officio Am. Assembly, 1982—. Recipient Disting. Scholar award Hofstra U., 1975; Ford Found. fellow, 1961-62. Mem. Am. Inst. C.P.A.'s (council 1980-83), Am. Acctg. Assn. (acad. v.p. 1980-82), Am. Fin. Assn., Am. Econ. Assn., Fin. Execs. Inst., Assn. Govtl. Accts. Pres., trustee. Clubs: Metropolitan (N.Y.C.); Lake Sunapee Yacht (Sunapee, N.H.). Home: 130 East End Ave Apt 12A New York NY 10028 Office: Columbia U Columbia Bus Sch 101 Uris Hall New York NY 10027

BURTON, JOHN ROUTH, lawyer; b. Virginia City, Va., Apr. 30, 1917; s. John David and Ida May (Kerley) B.; m. Virginia A. Dewey, Oct. 12, 1942 (dec.); children: Sara Elizabeth, Julie Catherine; m. Elizabeth A. Bumpus, June 12, 1965; 1 dau., Terry Lynn. B.S. in B.A, Roanoke Coll., 1937; LL.B., Case Western Res. U., 1940. Bar: Va. 1939, N.Y. 1940, Ohio 1981. Assoc. firm Reid & Priest, N.Y.C., 1940-48, ptnr., 1949-70; pres., chief exec. officer, dir. Pvt. Export Funding Corp., N.Y.C., 1970-73; assoc. gen. counsel Am. Electric Power System, 1974-81, dep. gen. counsel, 1981—, sec. sub. cos., 1974—; v.p., dir. Am. Electric Power Service Corp., Columbus, Ohio, 1975—, dir. various operating utility subs.; cons. in internat. field, 1950-70. Police justice, Plandome, N.Y., 1959-60. Served with USN, 1942-45. Mem. ABA, Assn. Bar City N.Y., N.Y. State Bar Assn., Va. Bar Assn., Ohio Bar Assn., Inter-Am. Bar Assn., Internat. Bar Assn. Republican. Congregationalist. Clubs: The Recess (N.Y.C.); Brookside Golf and Country, Athletic (Columbus). Home: 3100 Stoney Bridge Ln Columbus OH 43220 Office: 1 Riverside Plaza Columbus OH 43215

BURTON, LEVARDIS ROBERT MARTYN, JR. (LEVAR BURTON), actor; b. Germany; s. Levardis Robert and Erma Christian B. Student, U. So. Calif. Profl. debut in television series Roots, 1977; television films include Almos' A Man, 1977, Billy: Portrait of a Street Kid, 1979, Dummy, 1979, The Hunter, 1980, Guyana Tragedy: The Story of Jim Jones, 1980; film appearances include Looking for Mr. Goodbar, 1977. Office: care The Artists Agy 190 N Canon Dr Beverly Hills CA 90210

BURTON, MALCOLM KING, clergyman, author; b. Mpls., Mar. 28, 1905; s. Charles Emerson and Cora (King) B.; m. Carol Berkemeier, Feb. 24, 1930. Student, Phillips Acad., Andover, Mass., 1919-23; B.A., Carleton Coll., 1927; postgrad., Chgo. Theol. Sem., 1927-29. Ordained to ministry Congl. Ch., 1928; pastor in, Massena, N.Y., 1929-33, Pelham, N.Y., 1933-38, New London, Conn., 1938-52, Pontiac, Mich., 1952-71, asso. pastor, Springfield, Mass., 1973—; Exec. vice chmn., dir. com. on continuation Congl. Christian Chs. in U.S., 1954—; chaplain Police Protective Assn., Massena, 1930-33; moderator Nat. Assn. Congl. Christian Chs., 1968-69, historian, 1973-77. Author: Destiny for Congregationalism, 1953, Constitution for Congregationalism?, 1954, How Church Union Came, 1966, Sermons on Special Days of the Church Year-Vol. I, 1977, Vol. II, 1980, (with A.H. Abbott) Early Merger Pamphlets, 1978, Disorders in the Kingdom, 1978, 2d edit., 1981, Sermons on the Mysteries of Life and Death, 1980, sermons on Controversial Subjects, 1981, Bible Sermons on God, 1981, Bible Sermons With Unique Insights, 1981; also numerous pamphlets, articles.; Editor: (with A.H. Abbott) The Message for Our Day-The Bearing of Science on Religious Faith (C.E. Burton), 1975. Served as chaplain AUS, 1945. Recipient citation Nat. Assn. Congl. Christian Chs., 1964. Mem. Delta Sigma Rho. Club: Conn. Valley Congl. (pres. 1977-79). Home: 1159 River Rd Agawam MA 01001 *To me the need for intellectual integrity in religious beliefs and approach to biblical understanding has been paramount, with full acceptance and use of the historical and critical approach to the Bible. With this goes the recognition that Jesus was, himself, a fully integrated individual and that his method of teaching, with its frequent use of "What think ye?", stressed intellectual integrity and the wholeness of personality.*

BURTON, PHILIP WARD, advertising executive, educator; b. Chgo., May 23, 1910; s. Carl Marshall and Gladys (Mann) B.; m. Ellen Schell Garber, Dec. 21, 1941; children: Elisabeth, Philip Ward and Bruce Garber (twins). A.B. summa cum laude, Stanford U., 1944, A.M., 1945. With advt. dept. Colgate-Palmolive Co., 1929-31; sales promotion adminstr. Bird & Son, Inc., 1932-34; mgr. med. promotion Bell & Howell Co., 1935-37; copy editor Procter & Gamble Co., 1938-41; asst. prof. Syracuse U. Sch. Journalism, 1945-46, prof., head advt. dept., 1949-55, chmn. advt. dept., after 1956; J. Stewart Riley prof. journalism Ind. U., Bloomington, 1976—; asso. prof. journalism and bus. adminstrn. State U. Iowa, 1946, prof., head dept., 1947-49; creative dir. Bruce B. Brewer Advt. Agy., Mpls., 1955-57; dir. marketing and research Barlow Advt. Agy., 1956—; copy chief T.A. Best Co.; dir. Auburn Pub. Co.; book rev. editor Skaneateles (N.Y.) Press; editor Internat. Corr. Schs.; also editor-cons. internat. textbook div.; vis. prof., Riley prof. Sch. Journalism, Ind. U. Author: Advertising Copywriting, 1949, 4th edit., 1978, 5th edit., 1983, Retail Advertising for Small Stores, 1951, Putting Advertising to Work, 1953, Principles of Advertising, 1955, Making Media Work, 1958, Which Ad Pulled Best, rev. edit, 1971, 4th edit., 1981, Advertising Fundamentals, 3d edit, 1980, Account Management for General Learning Corporation, 1976, Casebook of Advertising Management, 1981; contbg. author: Marketing Managers Handbook for Dartnell Corporation, 1976, 2d edit., 1983; also articles in mags. Named Advt. Educator in U.S., 1961. Fellow Am. Acad. Advt. (regional dean); mem. Advt. Fedn. Am. (dir. 1953-57), Nat. Indsl. Advertisers Assn., Alpha Delta Sigma (nat. pres. 1953-57, chmn. nat. council 1957-59, recipient citation for contbns. to frat.), Sigma Delta Chi, Delta Upsilon. Home: 108 E Genesee St Skaneateles NY 13152 Office: Sch Journalism Indiana U Bloomington IN 47401

BURTON, RALPH JOSEPH, internat. devel. cons.; b. Syracuse, N.Y., Nov. 7, 1911; s. Louis and Sarah B.; m. Elaine Becker, June 24, 1934 (div. Nov. 1961); children—Sharone L., Brenda R., Rhoda S.; m. Helena Felton, May 1962. A.B., Syracuse U., 1932; Ph.D., U. Chgo., 1939. With Chgo. City Govt., 1935-40, adminstrv. asst. to corp. counsel, 1938-40; with U.S. Bur. Budget, 1940-56, asst. chief govt. orgn. br., 1947-52, asst. chief internat. div., 1952-56; mem. U.S. Fgn. Service, 1956-68; spl. asst. to asst. sec. state for adminstrn., 1956-58; spl. detail to Pres.'s Adv. Com. on Govt. Orgn., 1957, to Pres.'s Com. to Study U.S. Mil. Assitance Program, 1959; dep. prin. officer U.S. consulate gen., São Paulo, Brazil, 1958-61; officer charge Brazilian affairs Dept. State and Alliance for Progress, 1962-65; dir. AID Mission to Nicaragua, 1965-68; gen. adv. loan adminstrn. Inter Am. Devel. Bank, 1968-71; Cons. to com. pub. adminstrn. Social Sci. Research Council, 1941; cons. gov., P.R., 1948, 54; lectr. polit. sci. Syracuse U., George Washington U., Am. U., 1940-50; cons. Pub. Adminstrn. Mission to Colombia, 1950-51; mem. U.S. delegation Internat. Inst. Adminstrv. Sci., Florence, Italy, 1950; U.S. delegation to NATO, Lisbon, Portugal, 1952. Author: (with Edward B. Strait) The Central Machinery of Government: Its Role and Functioning, 1951. Mem. Am. Fgn. Service Assn. Home: 815 Oak Dr Bradenton FL 33507

BURTON, RICHARD (RICHARD JENKINS), actor; b. Pontrhydfen, South Wales, Nov. 10, 1925; m. Sybil Williams (div. 1963); 2 children; m. Elizabeth Taylor, Mar. 15, 1964 (div.); m. Susan Hunt, 1976 (div. 1983); m. Sally Anne Hay, July 3, 1984. Ed., Exeter and Oxford. Lst stage appearance in: Druid's Rest, Royal Court Theatre, Liverpool, Eng., 1943; later on London stage; Brit. debut in film Last Days of Dolwyn, 1948; on London stage in A Phoenix Too Frequent; N.Y. stage debut Phoenix Too Frequent, 1950; later appeared: Legend for Lovers, 1951; on Broadway in Time Remembered; then musical Camelot, also Equus, 1976; U.S. tour of Camelot, 1980-81; Broadway and U.S. tour of Private Lives, 1983; title role in: Broadway prodn. Hamlet, Old Vic Company, Edinburgh Festival, 1953; continued 1953-54 season with, Old Vic Company; later appeared in: Hollywood film debut in My Cousin Rachel, 1954; other films include Circle of Two; TV roles in Wuthering Heights, 1958, Divorce His, Divorce Hers, Brief Encounter; title role in: TV miniseries Life of Richard Wagner, 1982; appeared as White Knight: TV prodn. Alice in Wonderland, 1983; later appeared in: recs. include A Personal Anthology; (Recipient Golden Globe award 1954, 78; also, 7 acad. awards nominations.); Author: A Christmas Story, 1964, Meeting Mrs. Jenkins, 1965. Served with RAF, 1944-47. Office: care Valerie Douglas 9004 Ashcroft Ave Los Angeles CA 90048

BURTON, ROBERT GENE, publishing executive; b. Pontiac, Mich., Apr. 4, 1938; s. Earl R. and Verna L. B.; m. Paula M. Suwanski, May 26, 1972; children: Robert Gene, Jr., Michael, Joseph. B.S., Murray (Ky.) State U., 1962; M.A., U. Tenn., 1964. From salesman to nat. sales dir. SRA/IBM Corp., Dallas and Chgo., 1967-76; Midwest dir., then dir. Mktg. CBS, Chgo. and N.Y.C., 1976-78, v.p., 1978-79, CBS Pub., N.Y.C., 1978-79, ABC Pub., 1980—; pres. ABC Leisure Mags., N.Y.C., 1981—, ABC Pub. div., 1982—; dir. Newton Falls Paper Mill. Mem. Mag. Pubs. Assn. (dir.), Am. Bus. Press. Republican. Methodist. Home: 96 Ridgecrest Rd Stamford CT 06903 Office: 1330 Ave of Americas New York NY 10019

BURTON, ROBERT WILLIAM, office products executive; b. Seymour, Conn., Aug. 1, 1927; s. Loren Nelson and Christina Marguerite (Duff) B.; m. Virginia Bigelow Kernochan, Nov. 19, 1955; children: Robert Mark, Jeffrey James, Virginia Lee Burton Fowler. B.A., Western Res. U., 1951. Floor dir. WEWS-TV, Cleve., 1951-52; v.p. Spero & Burton, Inc., Cleve., 1952-53; asst. to dir. sales promotion Anaconda-Am. Brass Co., Waterbury, Conn., 1953-58; sales mgr. Times Wire & Cable Co., Wallingford, Conn., 1958-66, v.p. sales, 1966-68, v.p., gen. mgr., 1968-69, pres., 1969-77, Rolodex Corp., Secaucus, N.J., 1977—; Pub. relations A.R.C., Waterbury, 1954-58, United Fund, 1954-58. Bd. dirs. Cheshire Community Theatre, 1959-70; corporator Meriden-Wallingford Hosp., bd. dirs., 1975-77. Served with USNR, 1955-58. Mem. Wholesale Stationers Assn. (dir. 1981—), Nat. Office Products Assn., Meadowlands C. of C. (dir. 1977—), Phi Gamma Delta. Republican. Conglist. Home: 870 Cherokee Ln Franklin Lakes NJ 07417 Office: 245 Secaucus Rd Secaucus NJ 07094

BURTON, ROGER VERNON, psychologist; b. Fresno, Calif., Jan. 18, 1928; s. Vernon Gibson and Eunice Margaret (Bethea) B.; m. Gabrielle Diane Baker, Aug. 18, 1962; children: Maria Christina, Jennifer Susan, Ursula Catherine, Gabrielle Cecilia, Charity Heather. B.Mus., U. So. Calif., 1949, A.B., 1953, M.S., 1955; Ph.D., Harvard U., 1959. Research psychologist NIMH, Bethesda, Md., 1955-74; prof., dir. devel. psychology program SUNY, Buffalo, 1974—; cons. Fisher-Price Co., also various pubs. Author: (with M.R. Yarrow, J.D. Campbell) Child Rearing, 1968, Recollections of Childhood, 1970, (with J.W.M. Whiting) The Absent Father and Cross-Sex Identity, 1961, Generality of Honesty Reconsidered, 1963, Assessment of Moral Training Programs: Where Are We Going?, 1976. Served with U.S. Army, 1950-52. Fellow Am. Psychol. Assn., AAAS, Soc. Research in Child Devel.; mem. Eastern Psychol. Assn., Soc. Cross-Culture Research, Am. Fedn. Musicians (life). Democrat. Home: 174 LeBrun Rd Eggertsville NY 14226 Office: Dept Psychology SUNY Buffalo NY 14226

BURTON, WILLIAM BUTLER, astronomer; b. Richmond, Va., July 13, 1940; s. Joseph Ashby and Denison (Laws) B.; m. Judy Marie Johnson, Mar. 26, 1972; children: Hannah Marie, Benjamin Joseph, Molly Catherine. B.A., Swarthmore Coll., 1962; postgrad. (Fulbright scholar 1962-63, 63-64, Kovalenko scholar 1964), U. Leiden, Netherlands, 1965, Ph.D., 1970. Research asso. Nat. Radio Astromomy Obs., 1971-73, asst. scientist, then scientist, 1973-78; prof. astronomy, chmn. dept. U. Minn., 1978-81; prof. astronomy U. Leiden, 1981—. Mem. Am. Astron. Soc., Internat. Astron. Union, Netherlands Astron. Soc., Sigma Xi. Address: Sterrewacht U Leiden PO Box 9513 Leiden Netherlands

BURTT, EVERETT JOHNSON, econ. cons.; b. Jackson, Mich., Aug. 6, 1914; s. Everett Johnson and Eve Mildred (Meisenhelter) B.; m. Cynthia Webb, June 15, 1940; children—Michael Coburn, Judith. A.B., Berea Coll., 1935; M.A., Duke, 1937, Ph.D., 1950. Instr. econs. U. Me., 1939-41; instr. Denver U., 1941-42; labor market analyst War Manpower Commn., 1942-43; employment analyst U.S. Bur. Labor Statistics, Boston, 1946-47; asst. prof. Boston U., 1947-52, asso. prof., 1952-57, prof. econs., 1957-80, prof. emeritus, 1980—, chmn. dept., 1952-68, chmn. all-univ. dept., 1956-68, acting chmn. dept. econs., 1971-74; asso. dir. Manpower Inst., 1974-75. Author: Labor Markets, Unions and Government Policies, 1963, Plant Relocation and the Core City Worker, 1967, Social Perspectives in the History of Economic Theory, 1972, Labor in the American Economy, 1979; Contbr. profl. periodicals, reports. Mem. Am. Econ. Assn., Indsl. Relations Research Assn. (pres. Boston 1966-67), AAUP, Phi Beta Kappa. Address: 9 Mary Dyer Ln North Easton MA 02356

BURUM, JOHN JAMES, banker; b. Rock Springs, Wyo., Sept. 19, 1934; s. John N. and Ivy Mae (Knox) B.; m. Rose Marie Chaussert, Aug. 19, 1956; children: Brad, Scott. B. Bus Acctg., Idaho State U., 1957; postgrad, U. Wis., 1970; postgrad., Purdue U., Carnegie Inst. Tech., Stanford U., 1983. Comptroller Idaho First Nat Bank, Boise, 1968, cashier, 1968-70, v.p., cashier, 1977-79, sr. v.p., 1977-79, exec. v.p., 1980—; dir. Western Loan Co. Chmn. legis. com. IBA, Boise, 1982-83; bd. dirs. Pacific Coast Banking Sch., U. Wash., 1979-83, Blue Cross of Idaho Health Services, Boise, 1980-83, Coll. Bus. Adv. Council, Idaho State U., 1982—. Served to 1st lt. U.S. Army, 1957-59. Mem. Idaho Bankers Assn., Am. Mgmt. Assn., Bank Adminstrn. Inst. Clubs: Arid, Crane Creek Country. Home: 804 Curling Ln Boise ID 83702 Office: Idaho First Nat Bank 101 S Capitol Blvd Boise ID 83733

BURWELL, DUDLEY SALE, food distribution company executive; b. Ebenezer, Miss., Nov. 21, 1931; s. Clement Lucas B. and Winfree Henry (Burwell); m. Joan Fay Berman, July 26, 1952; children: Lana, Dudley S., Joel B., Gregory Todd, Troy E. Student, Holmes Jr. Coll., 1950, Draughons Bus. Coll., 1951; grad., LaSalle Extension U., 1965. With Lewis Grocer Co., Indianola, Miss., 1954—, v.p., sec., 1972-79, pres., chief exec. officer, 1979—, Sunflower Stores, Inc., 1979—, dir. Bd. dirs. Miss. Econ. Council. Served with USMC, 1952-54. Mem. Am. Inst. C.P.A.s, Miss. Soc. C.P.A.s, Indianola C. of C. (pres. 1976-77). Methodist. Lodge: Rotary. Home: 4 Morningside Dr Indianola MS 38751 Office: Lewis Grocer Co Hwy 49 S Indianola MS 38751

BURWELL, LEWIS CARTER, JR., airline exec.; b. Charlotte, N.C., Apr. 23, 1908; s. Lewis Carter and Saida Stoney (Jones) B.; m. Edith Branson, Nov. 6, 1942; children—Margaret S. (Mrs. Thomas M. Barnhardt III), Lewis Carter III, Henry M., Robert E.L., Edith Lynne. A.B. cum laude, U. South, 1928; C.L.U., Wharton Sch., U. Pa., 1934. Pres. Plans Inc., Charlotte and Houston, 1930-42, chmn., Washington, 1960; pres. Resort Airlines, Pinehurst, N.C. and; Miami, Fla., 1946-51; v.p. Flying Tiger Line, Washington, 1951-57; chmn. bd. Overseas Nat. Airways, Washington, 1957-60, Pinehurst Airlines, 1973—; dir. Airlift Internat., Miami, Wilson-Murrow Cos., Washington, Air Shipping Agys., Ltd., London, Eng. Author: Scrapbook, 1947. Trustee U. South, 1932-35. Served to col. USAAF, 1942-46. Decorated Bronze Star, Air medal with 2 oak leaf clusters, D.F.C. with 2 oak leaf clusters, U.S.; Y'un Hui medal; Grand Star of Honor, Republic of China). Episcopalian. Clubs: Pinehurst Country, Green Valley Country. Home: 106 Collins Creek Greenville SC 29607 Office: Donaldson Air Park Greenville SC 27605 *I have always thought that the first half of your life should be spent in trying to learn all possible from the generation before you, and the second half should be dedicated to teaching by example and instruction these things to the generation that is taking your place.*

BURWELL, ROBERT LEMMON, JR., chemist; b. Balt., May 6, 1912; s. Robert Lemmon and Anne Hume (Lewis) B.; m. Elise Frank, Dec. 23, 1939; children: Mary Elise, Augusta Somervell. A.B., St. John's Coll., Annapolis, Md., 1932; Ph.D. (Procter fellow), Princeton U., 1936. Instr. chemistry Trinity Coll., 1936-39; instr. Northwestern U., 1939-45, asst. prof., 1946, asso. prof., 1946-52, prof., 1952—, Ipatieff prof. chemistry, 1970-80, Ipatieff prof. emeritus, 1980—, chmn. dept. chemistry, 1952-57; Humboldt sr. scientist Tech. U. Munich, 1981; vis. prof. Université Pierre et Marie Curie, Paris, 1982; dir. Internat. Congress Catalysis, 1956-65; chmn. Gordon Research Conf. Catalysis, 1957; sec. Council Internat. Congress Catalysis, 1968-72, v.p., 1972—, pres., 1980—. Served as lt. USNR, 1942-45. Fellow Royal Soc. Chemistry (London); mem. Am. Chem. Soc. (chmn. div. phys. chemistry 1958-59, mem. council policy com. 1969-72, Kendall award in colloid and surface chemistry 1973, Lubrizol award in petroleum chemistry 1983), Catalysis Soc. (dir. 1977-81, pres. 1973-77, First Burwell lectr. 1983), Internat. Union Pure and Applied Chemistry (titular mem. colloid and surface chemistry commn. 1969-77), Sigma Xi. Research in heterogeneous catalysis and surface chemistry. Home: 2759 Girard Ave Evanston IL 60201

BURY, JOHN, theatre designer, consultant; b. Abtrystwyth, Wales, U.K., Jan. 27, 1925; s. Charles Rusely and Emily Frances (Adams) B.; m. Margaret Liela Greenwood, 1947 (div. 1964); 1 son, Christopher Rugely; m. Elizabeth Margaret Duffield, Jan. 1966; children: Adam Charles, Abigail Frances, Matthew John. Student, Univ. Coll., London. Theatre designer, London, 1947—; head of design Royal Shakespeare Theatre, London, 1964-68, Nat. Theatre, 1973—; chmn. Soc. Brit. Theatre Designers, 1966—. Served to lt. Brit. Royal Navy, 1942-45. Comdr. Order Brit. Empir. Fellow Royal Soc. Arts. Home: 14 Woodlands Rd London England SW13 Office: Nat Theatre South Bank London England SE1

BURY, THOMAS LINCOLN, constrn. co. exec.; b. Gowanda, N.Y., Dec. 1, 1942; s. Burt John and Ruth (Lincoln) B.; m. Rene Priemazon, Aug. 29, 1970; children—Matthew Lincoln, Sarah Elizabeth. B.S. in Bus. Adminstrn, Bowling Green (Ohio) State U., 1965; M.B.A., Syracuse U., 1969. Corp. acct. Samsonite Corp., Denver, 1969-70; controller Electronic Processors Inc., Englewood, Colo., 1970-72, Natkin & Co., Englewood, 1972-77, sec.-treas., 1977—, also dir.; sec.-treas. The Johansen Co., South Plainfield, N.J.; dir. Natkin Service Co., Charter Page, Inc., Englewood. Served with U.S. Army Res., 1965-67. Mem. Fin. Execs. Inst. (dir.), Nat. Assn. Accts., Delta Tau Delta. Presbyterian. Club: Mason. Office: PO Box 1258 Englewood CO 80150

BURZYNSKI, NORMAN STEPHEN, editor; b. Pitts., Nov. 21, 1928; s. Ladislaus and Eleanor Marie B.; m. Ann Louise Adams, June 11, 1951; children: Michael Derek, Stephanie Ann, Eric Adams, Karen Ruth, John Kerstan, Joan Lorraine. B.A. in Journalism, U. Pitts., 1953; M.S. in Bus. Adminstrn., George Washington U., 1971; A. Applied Sci. summa cum laude in Aviation Tech.—Airport Mgmt., No. Va. Community Coll., Manassas, 1977, No. Va. Community Coll., Manassas, No. Va. Community Coll., Manassas, 1982. Editor corporate pubs. PPG Industries, Pitts., 1958-72, pub. relations rep., 1972-73; air res. forces liaison officer Office of Info., U.S. Air Force, Washington, 1968-72; chief Office of Info., U.S. Air Force Res., 1973-76; editor The Officer, Res. Officers Assn. U.S., Washington, 1976—. Served to lt. U.S. Army, 1951-52; to col. USAF, 1968-76. Mem. Res.

Officers Assn., Internat. Assn. Communicators, Air Force Assn., Aircraft Owners and Pilots Assn., Aviation and Space Writers Assn. Home: 5900 F Kingsford Rd Springfield VA 22152 Office: One Constitution Ave NE Washington DC 20002

BUSA, PETER, artist; b. Pitts., June 23, 1914; s. Salvatore and Ernestine (Chrispo) B.; m. Jeanne Juhl, June 26, 1943; children—Christopher, Stephen, Paul, Marianne, Nicholas. Student, Carnegie Inst. Tech., 1929-30, Art Students League, N.Y.C., 1934-37; studied with, Raymond Simboli, Sam Rosenberg, Harry Sternberg, Thomas Benton, Hans Hofmann. With WPA Art Project, N.Y., 1935-40; mem. faculty dept. art U. Minn., Mpls., 1961-82, prof., 1963-82, prof. emeritus, 1982—; tchr. Cooper Union, 1945-53, La. State U., 1958-59, SUNY, Buffalo, 1954-57; vis. artist U. Mich., 1960, Kans. State U., 1972. One-man exhbns. include, Bertha Schaefer Gallery, Parrish Mus., 1972, Walker Art Center, 1962-67, U. Minn. Gallery, 1966, Tweed Gallery; represented in permanent collections, Peggy Guggenheim, Walker Art Center, Whitney Mus. Am. Art, Met. Mus., Smithsonian Instn., others. Recipient Ford Found. Purchase award, 1962, Distinguished Tchr. award Coll. Liberal Arts U. Minn., 1975, Guggenheim award, 1976-77. Mem. Coll. Art Assn., Artist Equity Assn. (past pres.), Art Studens League N.Y. (life). Home: 52 A Spring Close Hwy Easthampton NY 11937

BUSBY, DAVID, lawyer; b. Ada, Okla., Jan. 29, 1926; s. Orel and Hope (Threlkeld) B.; m. Mary Beth Baker, June 9, 1962; children by previous marriage—Helen Hope Busby Burleigh, Alison Sears Busby McGeary; children—David, John Orel. Student, Miss. Coll., Duke U., 1944-46; B.A., Yale U., 1948; LL.B., Okla. U., 1951. Bar: Okla. bar 1950, D.C. bar 1959, N.Y. bar 1959, also U.S. Supreme Ct. bar 1959. Assoc. firm Busby, Harrell & Trice, Ada, 1951-53; partner Busby, Standfield, Busby & Deaton, Ada, 1953-55; counsel Subcom. on Automobile Mktg. Practices, Com. on Interstate and Fgn. Commerce, U.S. Senate, Washington, 1955-58, Subcom. Fgn. Commerce, 1958; partner Hays, Busby & Rivkin, N.Y.C., 1958-62, Busby, Rivkin, Sherman, Levy & Rehm, Washington, 1962-77, Busby, Rehm & Leonard, 1977—. Mem. Nat. Motor Vehicle Safety Adv. Council, 1966-68; pres. League Young Democrats of Okla., 1951; city judge, Ada, 1952-53; bd. dirs. Legal Aid Soc., D.C.; mem. bldg. com. Washington Cathedral. Served to ensign USNR, 1944-46. Mem. Fed. Bar Assn., ABA (chmn. standing com. on customs law 1973-76), D.C. Bar Assn., Assn. Customs Bar, Phi Delta Phi. Episcopalian. Clubs: Univ., Nat. Press (Washington); Yale (N.Y.C.). Office: 1629 K St NW Washington DC 20006

BUSBY, EDWARD OLIVER, college administrator; b. Macomb, Ill., June 22, 1926; s. Lynn John and Pauline (Hoebel) B.; m. Lois E. Tehan, June 17, 1950; children—Thomas L., John E., Paula L. B.S., U. Wis., 1950, M.S., 1962, Ph.D., 1971. Resident engr. Wis. Hwy. Commn., 1950-51; asst. engr., City of LaCrosse, Wis., 1951-53; sales engr. Wis. Culvert Co., 1953-59; lectr. civil engring. U. Wis., Madison, 1959-66, dean, Platteville, 1966—; mem. Wis. Examining Bd. for Profl. Engrs., 1981—; v.p. Platteville Area Indsl. Devel. Corp., 1977-80. Contbr. articles in field to profl. jours. Served with U.S. Navy, 1944-46. NSF fellow, 1970-71. Fellow ASCE; mem. Wis. Soc. Profl. Engrs. (pres. 1972-73), Nat. Soc. Profl. Engrs. (nat. dir. 1976-81, vice chmn. engrs. edn. 1971-73). Republican. Home: 825 Stonebridge RdApt 5C Platteville WI 53818 Office: University of Wisconsin Platteville WI 53818

BUSBY, MARJORIE JEAN (MARJEAN BUSBY), journalist; b. Kansas City, Mo., Jan. 31, 1931; d. Vivian Eric and Stella Mae (Lindley) Phillips; m. Robert Jackson Busby, Apr. 11, 1969. B.J., U. Mo., 1952. With Kansas City (Mo.) Star Co. (became div. Capital Cities Communications 1977), 1952—, editor women's news, 1969-73, asso. Sunday editor, People Sect. editor, 1973-77, fashion editor, 1978-81, feature writer, 1981—. Mem. Fashion Group (1st recipient Kansas City appreciation award 1978), Women in Communications, LSV, Mortar Board, Sigma Delta Chi, Kappa Alpha Theta (pres. Alpha Mu chpt. 1951-52). Presbyterian. Clubs: Leawood Country, Belle of Am. Royal Orgn. Home: 9804 Mercier St Kansas City MO 64114 Office: 1729 Grand Ave Kansas City MO 64108

BUSCH, AUGUST A., JR., brewing executive; b. St. Louis, Mar. 28, 1899; s. August A. and Alice (Zisemann) B.; m. Margaret Snyder, Mar. 11, 1981. Ed., Smith Acad.; LL.D. (hon.), St. Louis U., 1969. With Mfrs. Ry. Co., Lafayette South Side Bank & Trust Co.; gen. supt. Anheuser-Busch, Inc., 1924-26, 6th v.p., gen. mgr., 1926-31, 2d v.p., gen. mgr., 1931-34, 1st v.p., gen. mgr., 1934-41, pres., 1946-72, chmn. bd., 1956-77; hon. chmn. bd. Anheuser-Busch Cos., Inc., 1977—, chief exec. officer, 1971-75; pres., chmn. bd., chief exec. officer St. Louis Cardinals, 1953—; chmn. Mfrs. Ry. Co., St. Louis Refrigerator Car Co.; dir. Centerre Trust Co., Gen. Am. Life Ins. Co., Centerre Bank, St. Louis; mem. brewing industry adv. com. WPB, 1942. Chmn. pub. relations com. United Fund St. Louis, 1964—; chmn. bd. Civic Progress, Inc., 13 years, St. Louis U. Devel. Fund drive; bd. dirs. St. Louis Municipal Opera; chmn. St. Louis Bicentennial Celebration Com. Served as col. Ordnance Dept. AUS, 1942-45. Recipient Fleur-de-Lis award St. Louis U., 1960; named Man of Year St. Louis Globe-Democrat, 1961; Man and Boy award nat. bd. Boys' Clubs Am., 1966; Citizen No. 1 award Press Club Met. St. Louis, 1967; Man of Year award So. Calif. Retail Liquor Dealers Assn., 1971; hon. commodore USCG Aux., 1972. Clubs: St. Louis Country, Racquet, Old Warson, Log Cabin, Bridlespur Hunt (St. Louis); Rolling Rock (Ligonier, Pa.). Office: 1 Busch Pl Saint Louis MO 63118

BUSCH, AUGUST ADOLPHUS, III, brewery executive; b. St. Louis, June 16, 1937; s. August Adolphus and Elizabeth (Overton) B.; m. Virginia L. Wiley, Dec. 28, 1974; children: Steven August, Virginia Marie; children by previous marriage: August Adolphus IV, Susan Marie II. Student, U. Ariz., 1957, 58, Siebel Inst. Tech., 1960-61. With Anheuser-Busch, Inc., St. Louis, 1957—, sales mgr., 1962-64, v.p. mktg. ops., 1964-65, v.p., gen. mgr., 1965-74, pres., 1975-79, chief exec. officer, 1975—, chmn. bd., 1977—; chmn., pres. Anheuser Busch Cos., Inc., 1979—, also dir.; v.p. Busch Properties, Inc.; dir. St. Louis Nat. Baseball Club, Mfg. RW Co., Laclede Gas Co., 1st Nat. Bank in St. Louis, Norfolk & Western Ry., 1st Union Bancorp., St. Louis Union Trust Co., Southwestern Bell Telephone Co., Gen. Am. Life Ins. Co.; trustee St. Louis Refrigerator Car Co.; dir., chmn. U.S. Brewers Assn. Mem. advisory bd. St. John Mercy Med. Center; bd. dirs., chmn. Nat. Center for Resource Recovery; trustee Washington U.; bd. dirs. United Way Greater St. Louis, St. Louis Symphony Soc., Jr. Achievement Miss. Valley, Sch. Bus. Adminstrn. Sponsors Coll. William and Mary; bd. overseers Wharton Sch., U. Pa.; mem. exec. bd. Boy Scouts Am. Mem. C. of C. U.S. (dir.). Clubs: St. Louis, Frontenac Racquet, St. Louis Country, Racquet (St. Louis); Noonday, Log Cabin, Stadium. Office: Anheuser-Busch Cos Inc One Busch Pl Saint Louis MO 63118 *

BUSCH, BENJAMIN, lawyer, educator; b. N.Y.C., June 12, 1912; s. S. Henry and Dorothy (Busch) B.; m. Phyllis Toby Schnell, Nov. 8, 1935; children: Frederick Matthew, Eric Edwin. Student, CCNY, 1928-30; LL.B., St. Lawrence U., 1933. Bar: N.Y. 1934. Partner firm Katz & Sommerich, 1946-76; counsel firm Hamburger, Weinschenk, Molnar & Busch, 1976—; Adj. prof. comparative and internat. law N.Y. Law Sch., 1973—. Author: (with Otto C. Sommerich) Foreign Law-A Guide to Pleading and Proof, 1959; also articles. Explorer adviser Boy Scouts Am. Served with AUS, 1944-45. Decorated Bronze Star medal, Purple Heart. Mem. ABA (chmn. sect. internat. law 1972-73, observer to UN 1974-79), N.Y.C. Bar Assn. (mem. internat. law com. 1973-76, fgn. law com. 1978-79), N.Y. State Bar Assn., Am. Judicature Soc., Am. Fgn. Law Assn. (pres. 1969-70), Consular Law Soc., Am. Soc. Internat. Law. Club: Appalachian Mountain (life mem.). Office: 36 W 44th St New York NY 10036

BUSCH, BRITON COOPER, historian; b. Los Angeles, Sept. 5, 1936; s. Niven and Phyllis (Cooper) B.; m. Deborah B. Stone, Aug. 16, 1958; children: Philip Briton, Leslie Cooper. A.B., Stanford U., 1958; M.A., U. Calif. at Berkeley, 1960, Ph.D., 1965. Instr. Colgate U., 1963-65, asst. prof. history, 1965-68, asso. prof. history, 1968-73, prof., 1973-78, William R. Kenan, Jr. prof., 1978—, dept. chmn., 1980—. Author: Britain and the Persian Gulf, 1894-1914, 1967, Britain, India and the Arabs, 1914-1921, 1971, Mudros to Lausanne: Britains Frontier in West Asia, 1918-1923, 1976, Master of Desolation: The Reminiscences of Capt. Joseph J. Fuller, 1980, Hardinge of Penshurst: A Study in The Old Diplomacy, 1980, Alta California, 1840-1842: The Journal and Observations of William Dane Phelps, Master of the Ship Alert, 1983. Woodrow Wilson fellow, 1963; Nat. Endowment for the Humanities fellow, 1967-68; Social Sci. Research Council fellow, 1968-69. Mem. Am. Hist. Assn., Royal Soc. Asian Affairs, Middle East Inst., Middle East Studies Assn., N.Am. Soc. Oceanic History (exec. council 1983—), AAUP. Home: PO Box 154 Hamilton NY 13346 Office: Dept History Colgate U Hamilton NY 13346

BUSCH, COREY, professional baseball team executive. V.p. for adminstrn. San Francisco Giants, Nat. League. Office: care San Francisco Giants Candlestick Park San Francisco CA 94124

BUSCH, HARRIS, medical educator; b. Chgo., May 23, 1923; s. Maurice Ralph and Rose Lillian (Feigenholtz) B.; m. Rose Klora, June 16, 1945; children: Daniel Avery, Laura Anne Busch Smolkin, Gerald Irwin, Fredric Neal. B.S., U. Ill., 1944, M.D. with honors, 1946; M.S., U. Wis., 1950, Ph.D., 1952. Intern Cook County Hosp., Chgo., 1946-47; asst. surgeon, sr. asst. surgeon USPHS, 1947-49; postdoctoral fellow Nat. Cancer Inst., 1950-52; asst. prof. biochemistry, internal medicine Yale U., 1952-55; asso. prof., prof. pharmacology U. Ill., 1955-60; prof. biochemistry, chmn. dept. Baylor U. Coll. Medicine, 1960-62, prof. pharmacology, chmn. dept., 1960—, disting. service prof., 1978—, chmn. student promotions com., 1969—, mem. policy planning com., 1972—, dir. Cancer Research Center; vis. prof. U. Chgo., 1968, 71, Northwestern U., 1968, Ga. Med. Coll., 1971, Washington U., St. Louis, 1972, U. Ala., Birmingham, 1972, Ind. U., Indpls., 1972, U. Nev., Reno, 1978, U. Colo., Denver, 1980; cons. lectr. U. Tenn., U. Tex., San Antonio, 1971; disting. lectr. SUNY, Buffalo, 1977; Centennial lectr. U. Ill. Coll. Medicine, 1981; cons. VA, Meth. hosps., both Houston, Bristol-Myers.; mem. adv. com. cell and devel. biology Am. Cancer Soc., 1978—; cancer chemotherapy study sect. USPHS; mem. Nat. Cancer Planning Com., 1971; mem. bd. sci. counselors to div. cancer treatment Nat. Cancer Inst., 1975. Author: Chemistry of Pancreatic Diseases, 1959, An Introduction to the Biochemistry of the Cancer Cell, 1962, Histones and Other Nuclear Proteins, 1965; co-author: Chemotherapy, 1966, The Nucleolus, 1970; editor: Frontiers in Medical Biochemistry, 1962, The Nucleus of the Cancer Cell, 1963, Jour. Phys. Chemistry and Physics, Methods in Cancer Research, vol. I, 1966, vols. II and III, 1967, vol. IV, 1968, Methods in Cancer Research, vol. V, 1970, vol.VI, 1971, vols. VII-IX, 1973, vol. X, 1973, Methods in Cancer Research, vol. XI, 1975, vols. XII and XIII, 1976, Methods in Cancer Research, vols. XIV, XV, 1978, Molecular Biology of Cancer, 1974, Cell Nucleus, Vols. I-III, 1974, IV-VII, 1978, VIII-IX, 1980; editorial bd.: Jour. Cancer Research and Clin. Oncology, Jour. Biol. Chemistry, Cancer Investigation, New Drugs, Physiol. Chemistry, Phys. Life Scis. Recipient Outstanding Alumnus award for service to edn. and research U. Ill., 1977, Disting. Faculty award Baylor U. Coll. Medicine, 1982; Baldwin scholar oncology Yale U. Sch. Medicine, 1952-55; scholar cancer research Am. Cancer Soc., 1955. Mem. Am. Soc. Biol. Chemists, Am. Assn. Cancer Research (public issues com. 1977), Am. Chem. Soc., Soc. Pharmacology and Exptl. Therapeutics, Soc. Exptl. Biology and Medicine, Sigma Xi, Alpha Omega Alpha. Home: 4966 Dumfries Dr Houston TX 77096

BUSCH, J. WILLIAM, tractor company executive; b. Reading, Pa., Feb. 13, 1923; s. Conrad J. B.; m. Virginia Lynne Busch, July 13, 1944 (dec. 1982); children: Nancy, Ned. B.A. in Econs., Gettysburg Coll., 1948. Chmn. bd., v.p. Caterpillar Tractor Co., Peoria, Ill. Home: 21 ch des Ramiers Collogne-Bellerive Geneva Switzerland Office: Caterpillar Overseas SA 118 rue du Rhone 1204 Geneva Switzerland

BUSCH, NIVEN, author; b. N.Y.C., Apr. 26, 1903; s. Briton Niven and Christine (Fairchild) B.; m. Teresa Wright, May 12, 1942 (div. 1952); m. Carmencita Baker, Mar. 14, 1956 (div. Sept. 1969); children: Peter, Briton, Terence, Mary Kelly, Joseph, Nicholas and Eliza (twins); m. Suzanne de Sanz, Dec. 8, 1973. Grad., Princeton, 1926. Assoc. editor Time mag., 1927, 31; assoc. editor, contbr. New Yorker mag., 1927, 31; motion picture writer with Warner Brothers, 20th Century, Goldwyn, Paramount, Universal studios, 1931-40; Regents' prof. English and fine arts U. Calif. at Irvine, 1970, 71, 75, U. Calif. at San Diego, 1972, U. Calif. at Berkeley, 1977. (Nominated for Acad. Motion Picture Arts and Scis. award for best original screen play In Old Chicago 1937); Author: Twenty-One Americans (originally pub. New Yorker mag.), 1930; novels The Carrington Incident, 1941, Duel in the Sun, 1944, They Dream of Home, 1944, Day of the Conquerors, 1946, The Furies, 1948, The Hate Merchant, 1953, The Actor, 1955, California Street, 1958, The San Franciscans, 1961, The Gentleman from California, 1965, The Takeover, 1977, No Place For a Hero, 1976, Continent's Edge, 1980; original screen-plays Pursued, 1946, The Capture, 1946, Distant Drums, 1951, Man from the Alamo, 1952, The Moonlighter, 1953, The Treasure of Pancho Villa, 1955. Mem. Acad. Motion Picture Arts and Scis., Authors Guild, Writers Guild Am., Assn. Former Intelligence Officers. Clubs: Press (San Francisco); Princeton (N.Y.C.). Home: 2625 Baker St San Francisco CA 94123

BUSCH, NOEL FAIRCHILD, author, editor; b. N.Y.C., Dec. 27, 1906; s. Briton Niven and Christine (Fairchild) B.; m. Mary Smart, June 5, 1950; children: Mary Fairchild, Beatrix Akiko. Student, St. Bernard's Sch., 1917-21, St. George's Sch., 1921-25, Princeton, 1925-27. Asso. editor Time mag., 1927-38; sportswriter N.Y. Daily News, 1928-31; sr. editor Life mag., 1938-42, war corr., 1942-45, sr. writer, 1945-52; rep. The Asia Found., Tokyo, 1952-54, Bangkok, 1954-58, spl. asst. to the pres., 1958-59; staff writer Reader's Digest, 1959-76. Author: My Unconsidered Judgment, 1944, What Manner of Man, a biography of Franklin Delano Roosevelt, 1944, Lost Continent, 1945, Fallen Sun, a Report on Japan, 1948, Briton Hadden a biography of the co-founder of Time, 1949, Thailand: An Introduction to Modern Siam, 1958, Two Minutes to Noon, The Story of the Great Tokyo Earthquake, 1962, T.R.: The Story of Theodore Roosevelt, 1963, The Emperor's Sword, 1969, A Concise History of Japan, 1972, Winter Quarters: George Washington at Valley Forge, 1974; Contbr. articles: Atlantic, Town and Country, Horizon. Mem. Am. Hist. Soc. Clubs: PEN, Princeton, Century Assn., Racquet and Tennis (N.Y.C.); Millbrook Golf and Tennis. Home: South Rd Millbrook NY 12545

BUSCH, RONALD, pub. co. exec. Various positions, including v.p. mktg. and corp. devel. with Bantam Books, 16 years; pres. Ballantine Books, N.Y.C., 1974-78, Pocket Books, 1978—, Mass Market Pub. Group, 1983—. Office: Simon & Schuster 1230 Ave of the Americas New York NY 10020

BUSCHE, EUGENE MARVIN, insurance company executive; b. Decatur, Ind., July 2, 1926; s. Louis Martin and Ruby (Smith) B.; m. Barbara Ann Sherow, Aug. 1, 1954; children: David Alan, Sara Lynn. B.S., Ind. U., 1950. C.L.U. Agt., Am. United Life Ins. Co., Lafayette, Ind., 1950-55; asst. gen. agt. State Mut. Life Assurance Co., Indpls., 1955-56; field supr. Indpls. Life Ins. Co., 1956-63, ednl. dir., 1963-70, adminstrv. v.p., dir., 1970-72, pres., chief exec. officer, 1972—; dir. Ind. Nat. Corp./Ind. Nat. Bank. Bd. dirs. Meth. Hosp. Found.; Bd. dirs. Children's Mus., Landmarks Found. Ind.; bd. govs. United Way Greater Indpls.; vice chmn. Jr. Achievement; chmn. bd. trustees Meth. Hosp.; trustee Arthur Jordan Found., Benjamin Harrison Found.; chmn., bd. dirs. Wesley Med. Care Corp. Served with USNR, 1944-46. Fellow Life Mgmt. Inst.; mem. Indpls. Soc. C.L.U. s, Indpls. Assn. Life Underwriters, Assn. Ind. Life Ins. Cos. (pres.), Delta Tau Delta. United Methodist. Clubs: Rotary, Economic (Indpls.) (dir.). Home: 1320 Lawrence Rd Carmel IN 46032 Office: 2960 N Meridian St Indianapolis IN 46208

BUSCHKE, HERMAN, neurologist; b. Berlin, Oct. 15, 1932; U.S., 1934, naturalized, 1945; s. Franz Julius and Ruth Helen (Minkowski) B.; m. Carol Schneider, June 22, 1957 (div. 1974); children—Thomas, Katherine. B.A., Reed Coll., 1954; M.D., Western Res. U., 1958. Diplomate: Am. Bd. Psychiatry and Neurology. Intern Bronx (N.Y.) Mcpl. Hosp. Center, 1958-59, resident in neurology, 1959-62; asst. instr. neurology Albert Einstein Coll. Medicine, Bronx, N.Y., 1961-62, asso. prof., 1969-74, prof., 1974—, prof. neurosci., 1974—; practice medicine specializing in neurology, Bronx, N.Y., 1969—; staff mem., attending neurologist Hosp. of Albert Einstein Coll. of Medicine; instr. medicine Stanford U., 1962-63, asst. prof., 1963-69. Recipient research scientist devel. award NIMH, 1964-69; named Lena and Joseph Gluck Disting. Scholar in Neurology, 1973. Home: 35 E 85 St New York NY 10028 Office: Saul R Korey Dept Neurology Albert Einstein Coll Medicine 1300 Morris Park Ave Bronx NY 10461

BUSCIGLIO, RICHARD, advt. agy. exec.; b. Newark, Mar. 18, 1935; m. Elizabeth H. Bannerman, Aug. 9, 1958; children—Lauren Ruth, Elizabeth Jane. B.A., Seton Hall U., South Orange, N.J., 1957. Vice pres., dir. TV programming Cunningham & Walsh, Inc., N.Y.C., 1960-79; v.p., asso. dir. network programming BBDO, Inc., N.Y.C., 1979-80; sr. v.p., dir. network programming McCann-Erickson, Inc., N.Y.C., 1980, sr. v.p., dir. broadcasting, U.S.A., 1981—; lectr. TV advt. N.Y. U., Seton Hall U., New Sch., La. State U. Served with U.S. Army, 1957-59. Mem. Nat. Acad. TV Arts and Scis., Internat. Radio and TV Soc., Am. Assn. Advt. Agys. (com. on comml. and network TV practices). Home: 10 Puddingstone Rd Morris Plains NJ 07950 Office: 485 Lexington Ave New York NY 10017

BUSCOMBE, WILLIAM, astronomer; b. Hamilton, Ont., Can., Feb. 12, 1918; s. William Henry, Jr. and Ethel (Minett) B.; m. Katherine Royal Kee, May 30, 1942; children: Dawn Buscombe Richardson, Eve Buscombe Jones, Peter, Andrew, Martin, Lucy Buscombe Talley, Katherine, Timothy. B.A., U. Toronto, 1940, M.A., 1948; Ph.D., Princeton U., 1950. Meteorologist, Canadian Dept. Transp., 1940-45; instr. math. U. Sask., 1945-48; research fellow Hale Obs., 1950-52; astronomer Australian Nat. U., 1952-68; prof. astronomy Northwestern U., 1968—; vis. prof. No. Ill. U., 1970-73. Contbr. numerous articles on sci. research to profl. jours.; compiler catalogs stellar data. Chmn., Parent and Citizen Dist. Council, Canberra, 1956. Home: 1231 Asbury Ave Evanston IL 60202

BUSE, FREDERIC JEROLD, banker; b. N.Y.C., Sept. 12, 1941; s. Frederic Jerold and Renee (Figenwald) B.; children—Christopher, Malcolm. B.S., Columbia U., 1965, postgrad., 1966. With Bankers Trust Co., N.Y.C., 1962-65; with Security Trust Co., Rochester, N.Y., 1966-74, v.p., 1969-74; 1st v.p. parent co. Security N.Y. State Corp., Rochester, 1970-73, 1st exec. v.p., 1973—; dir. Griffley Corp.; chmn. Rochester Health Network, Inc., Western N.Y. Motor Lines, Inc. Past trustee, treas. Harley Sch., Rochester; Trustee, chmn. research com. Ctr. Govtl. Research, Rochester; trustee, chmn. housing com. United Way, Greater Rochester; mem. N.Y. State Adv. Com. Employment and Unemployment Ins.; past dep. vice chmn. Monroe County Democratic Com.; past chmn. fin. com. Rochester Urban League; past trustee Third Presbyterian Ch., Rochester. Mem. N.Y. State Bankers Assn. (mem. govt. relations com.). Home: 274 Avalon Dr Rochester NY 14618 Office: 1 East Ave Rochester NY 14638

BUSEY, GARY, actor, musician; b. Goose Creek, Tex., 1944; m. Judy Helkenberg, 1969; 1 son, Jake. Student, Coffeyville Jr. Coll., Okla. State U. Played drums with, The Rubber Band, 1963-70; played: drums as Teddy Jack Eddy, with Leon Russell, Kris Kristofferson, Willie Nelson; actor, 1972—; made: film debut in The Last American Hero, 1972; films include Straight Time, 1978, Big Wednesday, 1978, Buddy Holly Story, 1978, Carny, 1980, Fooling Around, 1980, Barbarosa, 1982; television films include Blood Sport; appeared in: television series The Texas Wheelers, 1974-75; other television appearances include Saturday Night Live. Office: care Creative Artists Agy. Inc. 1888 Century Park Plaza Suite 1400 Los Angeles CA 90067 *

BUSEY, JAMES BUCHANAN, IV, naval officer; b. Peoria, Ill., Oct. 2, 1932; s. James Buchanan and Louise (Rogers) B.; m. Jean L. Cole, Aug. 14, 1954; children: Angela R., Nancy J., James Buchanan V. Student, U. Ill., 1951; B.S., U.S. Naval Postgrad. Sch., 1965, M.S., 1966. Served as enlisted man U.S. Navy, 1952-54, commd. ensign, 1954, advanced through grades to rear adm., 1979; auditor gen. of the navy Dept. Navy, Falls Church, Va., from 1978; now comdr. light attack wings U.S. Pacific Fleet, Lemoore, Calif. Decorated Navy Cross, Legion of Merit, D.F.C. Mem. Am. Soc. Mil. Comptrollers. Presbyterian. Office: NAS Lemoore CA 93245

BUSH, BARBARA PIERCE, wife of Vice Pres. U.S.; b. Rye, N.Y., June 8, 1925; d. Marvin and Pauline (Robinson) Pierce; m. George Herbert Walker Bush, Jan. 6, 1945; children: George Walker, John Ellis, Neil Mallon, Marvin Pierce, Dorothy Walker. Student, Smith Coll., 1943-44; hon. degrees, Stritch Coll., Milw., 1981, Mt. Vernon Coll., Washington, 1981, Hood Coll., Frederick, Md., 1983. Bd. dirs. Reading is Fundamental, Morehouse Sch. Medicine, Soc. Meml. Sloan-Kettering Cancer Center, Children's Oncology Sers. Met. Washington; hon. mem. bd. dirs. The Washington Home; trustee Kingsbury Center, U.S. Capitol Hist. Soc.; sponsor Laubach Literacy, Inc.; mem. Women's Com. Smithsonian Assos.; nat. hon. chmn. Leukemia Soc. Am.; pres. Ladies of the Senate, 1981. Mem. Tex. Fedn. Republican Women (life). Episcopalian. Clubs: Internat. II, Republican (N.Y.C.); Magic Circle Republican Women's (Houston). Address: The Vice Pres's House Washington DC 20501

BUSH, BEVERLY, assn. exec., artist; b. Kelso, Wash.; d. Edward Lawrence and Gunild Hedvig (Hansen) Stover; m. William Bush, Jan. 8, 1944. B.A., U. Wash.; student, Art Student's League, Nat. Acad. Design. Exec. sec., 1958—. Nat. exhbns. include, Audubon Artists, N.A.D., Nat. Assn. Women Painters, USA 59; rep. pvt. colls. with, Artists Equity Assn., Inc., 1956—. Mem. Zeta Phi Eta. Home: 3521 E Spruce St Seattle WA 98122 Office: 229 Broadway E Seattle WA 98102

BUSH, CHARLES VERNON, cosmetic mfg. co. exec.; b. Tallahassee, Dec. 17, 1939; s. Charles Henry and Marie (Baker) B.; m. Bettina M. Wills, Feb. 8, 1964; children—Charles, Kyra, Bettina. B.S. in Engring, USAF Acad., 1963; M.A. in Internat. Relations, Georgetown U., 1964; M.B.A. in Fin, Harvard U., 1972. Commd. 2d lt. USAF, 1963, advanced through grades to capt., 1970; resigned, 1970; asso. corp. fin. White, Weld & Co., N.Y.C., 1972; asst. treas. Celanese Corp., N.Y.C., 1976; v.p., treas. Max Factor & Co., Hollywood, Calif., 1978-80, v.p., corp. controller, 1980—. Decorated Bronze Star, Joint Services Commendation medal, USAF Commendation medal with Oak leaf cluster. Mem. Fin. Execs. Inst., Harvard U. Bus. Sch. Alumni Assn. (v.p. exec. council), Harvard U. Bus. Sch. Black Alumni Assn. (dir.), Alpha Phi Alpha, Pi Sigma Alpha. Club: Harvard Bus. Sch. So. Calif. (dir.). Office: 222 North Vincent Ave Covina CA 91722

BUSH, DOROTHY VREDENBURGH, sec. Dem. Nat. Com.; b. Baldwyn, Miss., Dec. 8, 1916; d. Will Lee and Lany (Holl) McElroy; m. Peter Vredenburgh, 3d, Dec. 27, 1940 (dec.); m. John W. Bush, Jan. 13, 1962; 1 stepson, Peter (dec.). Student, George Washington U., summer 1935; B.S., Miss. State Coll. for Women, 1937. Sec. to dir. ins. bur. Tenn. Coal, Iron & R.R. Co. (subsidiary U.S. Steel), Birmingham, Ala., 1937-40; Nat. committeewoman Ala. Young Democrats, 1941-50; asst. sec. conv. Young Dems. Am., 1941, v.p., 1943-48; co-chmn. Jackson Day dinners of Ala., 1944; sec. Dem. Nat. Com., 1944; (1st woman to hold this position); acting pres. Young Dems. Am., 1944; sec. Dem. Nat. Convs., 1944, 48, 52, 56, 60, 64, 68, 72, 76, 80. Life mem. Ark. Traveler, Beta Sigma Phi. Baptist. Clubs: Maskers (Miss. State Coll. for Women); Jane Jefferson (life), National Fedn. Business and Profl. Women's.). Home: 106 Moorings Park Dr Naples FL 33942 Office: Democratic Nat Com Washington DC 20036

BUSH, FREDERIC ANDREW, geologist; b. Silver City, N.Mex., Mar. 10, 1904; s. Frederic Andrew and Elizabeth (Argenbright) B.; m. Margaret Devlin, Aug. 4, 1928; 1 dau., Margaret Elaine. A.B., Stanford University, 1925. Paleontologist Atlantic Oil Prodn. Co., 1925; stratigrapher Sinclair Oil & Gas Co., 1926-30, chief geologist, 1930-32, Sinclair Prairie Oil Co., 1932-45, Sinclair Oil Corp., 1945-50; v.p. Sinclair Can. Oil Co.; dir. Sinclair Oil Corp.; pres., dir. Sinclair Internat. Oil Co.; v.p., dir. Sinclair Petroleum Co., to 1968, Cambridge Royalty Co.; dir. Cambridge Petroleum Royalties Ltd.; Mem. exec. com. bd. advisors paleontol. sect. Am. Mus. Natural History, until 1968; adv. com. Columbia, until 1968; past mem. subcom. future domestic oil and gas availability of Nat. Petroleum Council's Com. on Oil and Gas Availability. Fellow Geol. Soc. Am.; mem. Am. Assn. Petroleum Geologists, Société Geologique de France, Am. Petroleum Inst., Petroleum Exploration Soc., N.Y. Acad. Sci., Audubon Soc., English Speaking Union, Explorers Club. Club: Shenorock Shore (Rye, N.Y.). Home: Upland Dr Greenwich CT 06830

BUSH, FREDERICK MORRIS, government official; b. Newport News, Va., Feb. 6, 1949; s. Morris and Dorothy Montony B.; m. Catherine Marie Murphy, Sept. 10, 1977; 1 son, Alexander Murphy Morris. B.A., U. Colo., 1971; M.A. in Internat. Studies, Am. U., 1974. Clk. Republican policy com. U.S. Senate, 1971-73; legis. asst. Ho. of Reps., 1973; asst. to fin. chmn. Rep. Nat. Com., 1973-74; dep. fin. dir. Pres. Ford Com., 1975-77; nat. fin. dir. George Bush for Pres., 1979-80; asst. sec. commerce for tourism; pres. Frederick Bush & Assocs.; v.p. B. B. Andersen Cos., Inc. Founder Rep. Assos. Chgo.; adv. bd. Am. Council Young Polit. Leaders. Home: 8208 Kerry Rd Chevy Chase MD 20815 Office: 2000 L St NW Suite 702 Washington DC 20036

BUSH, GEORGE HERBERT WALKER, vice president of U.S.; b. Milton, Mass., June 12, 1924; s. Prescott Sheldon and Dorothy (Walker) B.; m. Barbara Pierce, Jan. 6, 1945; children: George W., John E., Neil M., Marvin P., Dorothy W. B.A. in Econs, Yale U., 1948, Adelphi U., Austin Coll., No. Mich. U., Franklin Pierce Coll., Allegheny Coll., Beaver Coll. Co-founder, dir. Zapata Petroleum Corp., 1953-59; pres. Zapata Off Shore Co., Houston, 1956-64, chmn. bd., 1964-66; mem. 90th-91st congresses, 7th Dist. Tex., Ways and Means com.; U.S. ambassador to UN, 1971-72; chmn. Rep. Nat. Com., 1973-74; chief U.S. Liaison Office Peking, People's Republic China, 1974-75; dir. Central Intelligence Agy., 1976-77; adj. prof. Rice U.; v.p. of U.S., 1981—. Chmn. Rep. Party Harris County, Tex., 1963-64; del. Rep. Nat. Conv., 1964, 68; Rep. candidate U.S. senator from, Tex., 1964, 70. Served to lt. (j.g.), pilot USN, World War II. Decorated D.F.C., Air medals (3). Address: The White House 1600 Pennsylvania Ave Washington DC 20501

BUSH, GERALD WILLIAM, corp. exec.; b. San Francisco, Mar. 20, 1937; s. Bernard Joseph and Anne Josephine (Kelly) B.; m. Jean Pond Wentworth, June 15, 1960; children—Michael Joseph, Patrick Kevin, Mark William, Robert Timothy. B.S., U. Santa Clara, 1958; M.A., Claremont Grad. Sch., 1959; postgrad., U. Calif. at Berkeley, 1959-61; Ph.D., No. Ill. U., 1969. Adminstrv. asst. Calif. C. of C., 1958-59; instr., then research asso. U. Calif. at Berkeley, 1959-61; staff mem. Com. Fgn. Affairs Personnel, Washington, 1961-62; dir. tng. in Far East Peace Corps, 1962-64, spl. asst. to dir., exec. sec., 1964-65; mem. dept. polit. sci., dir. Peace Corps programs No. Ill. U., DeKalb, 1965-67; spl. asst. to sec. U.S. Dept. Labor, 1967-68, asst. v.p., 1968; sr. staff Arthur D. Little, Inc.; dir. commerce and manpower, City of Boston, 1972-75; exec. dir. Gulf Co. Mgmt. Inst., 1975—; sr. v.p. Gulf Oil Corp., 1975—. Author: Recent Trends in Government Finances, 1961, Inter-university Case Study: A Business Office for the West, 1965, The Peace Corps: a study in Open Organization, 1965. Bd. dirs. Psychol. Services, Pitts. Mem. Am. Polit. Sci. Assn., Am. Soc. Pub. Adminstrn., Nat. Council on Urban Econ. Devel. (bd. dirs.), Alpha Phi Omega, Phi Sigma Alpha. Office: Gulf Bldg Pittsburgh PA 15219

BUSH, IAN ELCOCK, research scientist; b. Bristol, Eng., May 25, 1928; came to U.S., 1964; s. Gilbert B. and Jean (Elcock) B.; m. Alison Pickard, Aug. 26, 1951 (div. 1966); children: Charles Fabian, Philippa, Caroline; m. Joan Morthland, Sept. 16, 1967 (div. 1972); children: Andrew, Georgia.; m. Mary Johnson, Feb. 15, 1982. B.A., U. Cambridge, Eng., 1949, Ph.D., 1952, M.B., B.Chir., 1957. Med. Research Council scholar Cambridge Nat. Inst. Med. Research, London, 1949-52; Commonwealth fellow U. Utah at Mass. Gen. Hosp., Boston, 1952-53; research asso. St. Mary's Hosp., Boston, 1952-53, St. Mary's Hosp. Med. Sch., London, 1953-56; grad. asst. U. Oxford, Eng., 1956-60; prof., chmn. dept. physiology U. Birmingham, Eng., 1960-64; sr. scientist Worcester Found. Exptl. Biology, 1964-67; prof., chmn. dept. physiology Med. Coll. Va., 1967-70; v.p. research and devel. Cybertek Inc., 1970-71, pres., chief exec. officer, 1971-72; sr. research asso., dept. medicine Dartmouth Med Sch., 1974-77, prof. psychiatry and physiology, 1977—; asso. chief staff research VA Hosp., 1977—; cons. in field, 1949—; past mem. panels NSF, Am. Cancer Soc., Med. Research Council Eng. Author: Chromatography of Steroids, 1961, The Siberian Reservoir, 1983; also papers. Fellow Am. Acad. Arts and Scis.; mem. Am., Eng. physiol. socs., Am., Eng. endocrine socs., AAAS, The Players. Home: PO Box 6 Woodstock VT 05071

BUSH, IRVING M., urological surgeon; b. N.Y.C., Jan. 19, 1934; s. Arthur M. and Mirra (Guttman) B.; m. Jan Lanners, Jan. 27, 1956; children: Alan Michael, Steven Douglas, Aaron Phillip. B.A., NYU, 1954; M.D., Chgo. Med. Sch., 1958. Rotating intern, asst. resident surgery, resident urology Beth Israel Hosp., N.Y.C., 1959-63, asst. adj. urology, 1963-66; fellow Sloan Kettering Inst., 1963-65, asst. clinician, 1965-66; clin. research trainee Meml. Hosp., N.Y.C., 1963-65, clin. asst. surgeon, 1965-66, James Ewing Hosp., N.Y.C., 1965-66; sr. attending urologist Cook County Hosp., Chgo., 1966—, chmn. dept., 1966-76; prin. investigator urology, med. sci. group Hektoen Inst. Med. Research, 1966-76; asst. prof. urology Northwestern U. Med. Sch., 1966-68; clin. prof., chief div. urology Chgo. Med. Sch., 1968-79; attending urologist, chief div. Mt. Sinai Hosp., Chgo., 1968-76, now mem. staff; cons. Oak Forest Hosp., 1968; mem. sci. advisory panel FDA, 1975-76, chmn., 1976-77; staff Sycamore (Ill.) Municipal Hosp., Suburban Med. Center, Hoffman Estates, Ill., Sandwich (Ill.) Hosp., St. Joseph's Hosp., Elgin, Sherman Hosp., Delnor Hosp., St. Charles, Geneva (Ill.) Hosp.; sr. cons. Center for Study GU Diseases, Ltd. Editor-in-chief: Chgo. Med. Sch. Quar, 1958; cons. editor urology: Jour. Student A.M.A, 1966; urology editor: Geriatrics Digest, 1968, Med. Portfolio, 1983. Valentine fellow N.Y. Acad. Medicine, 1964; Mosley scholar, 1958; Recipient Valuable Service citation Chgo. Med. Sch., 1958. Mem. Am. Urol. Assn. (1st prize 1964, grand prize 1965, 1st prize lab. research 1968, Wirt R. Dankin hist. award 1968, 69, 72, 1st prize lab. research 1970, 1st prize new techniques 1979), AMA (John B. Morrisey award 1965, Hektoen medal for research 1970), Ill. Med. Soc., Chgo., North Central urol. socs., James Ewing Soc., ACS, Am. Med. Writers Assn., Am. Soc. Nephrology, Soc. Univ. Urologists, Assn. Acad. Surgery, Assn. Clin. Urologists. Home: Burlington IL 60109 Office: One Chapman Rd Burlington IL 60109

BUSH, MARTIN H., museum official, history educator; b. Amsterdam, N.Y., Jan. 24, 1930; s. Martin J. B.; children: Lisa, Jennifer, Pamela. B.A., State U. N.Y. at Albany, 1958, M.A., 1959; Ph.D., Syracuse U., 1966. Acting sr. historian N.Y. State Edn. Dept., 1961-62, cons., 1962-63; instr. history dept. Syracuse U., 1963-65, asst. dean acad. resources, 1965-70; asso. prof. history dept. Wichita (Kans.) State U., 1970—, asst. v.p. acad. resource devel., 1970-74, v.p., 1974—; dir. Edwin A. Ulrich Mus. Art, 1974—; art cons. Fourth Fin. Corp. (in cooperation with Skidmore, Owings & Merrill), 1974—; vice chmn. Kans. Com. for Humanities, 1971-74, Kans. Pub. Television Service, 1973—, Univ. Press of Kans., 1972-73; dir. Wichita Festivals, Inc., 1971-74, Mid-Am. Art Alliance, 1973-76. Author: Ben Shahn: The Passion of Sacco and Vanzetti, 1968 (Am. Scholar mag. selection 1968), Revolutionary Enigma, 1969, Doris Caesar, 1970, Duane Hanson, 1976, Ernest Trova, 1977, Robert Goodnough, 1982, The Photographs of Gordon Parks, 1983; also various catalogs and brochures.; Contbr. articles to profl. publs. Home: 8201 E Harry St Apt 2204 Wichita KS 67207 Office: Wichita State U Box 46 Wichita KS 67208

BUSH, RAYMOND SYDNEY, physician; b. Toronto, Ont., Can., Apr. 11, 1931; s. Raymond E. and Alice T. (Hampson) B.; m. Margaret J. Bush, Sept. 5, 1959; children—Catherine, Elizabeth, Jennifer. B.Sc., U. London, 1951; M.D., U. Toronto, 1961, M.A., 1964. Physicist No. Electric, 1952-53, Can. AEC, 1953-55; resident Toronto East Gen. Hosp., 1961-62, Princess Margaret Hosp., Toronto, 1962-64, radiation oncologist, 1966—; dir. Ont. Cancer Inst. (incorporating Princess Margaret Hosp.), 1976—; resident Victoria Gen. Hosp., Halifax, N.S., Ca., 1964-65; Richard's fellow, Ont. Cancer Soc. awardee Christie Hosp., Manchester, Eng., other centers, 1965-66; prof. radiology U. Toronto, 1976—, asso. prof. med. biophysics, 1976—; vis. prof. U. London, 1974, U. Manchester, 1974; Lichfield lectr. Oxford (Eng.) U., 1974. Author: Malignancies of the Ovary, Uterus and Cervix, 1979; mem. editorial bd.: Cancer Nursing, 1978—, Internat. Jour. Radiation Oncology, 1977, Clin. and Investigative Medicine, 1979—. Mem. Acad. Medicine (Toronto), Can. Assn. Radiologists (editorial bd.), Can. Oncology Soc., Nat. Cancer Inst. Can., Can. Cancer Soc., Royal Coll. Physicians and Surgeons Can., Am. Soc. Therapeutic Radiologists, Am. Soc. Clin. Oncology. Office: 500 Sherbourne Toronto ON M4X 1K9 Canada

BUSH, ROBERT BENJAMIN, manufacturing company executive; b. Attica, Ind., Jan. 15, 1928; s. Robert Lincoln and Virginia (Leath) B.; m. Patricia Ann Gosnell, Jan. 6, 1951; children: Robert Benjamin II, Anne Elizabeth. B.S. in Elec. Engring, Purdue U., 1949; J.D., Ind. U., 1956. Bar: Ind. 1956. Engr. Naval Ordnance Plant, Indpls., 1950; with Bur. Naval Ordnance, 1951-53; gen. counsel Cummins Engine Co., Inc., 1956-79, v.p. bus. devel., 1979—; dir., v.p. Cummins KH-12, Inc., Cummins Research Ltd. Partnership. Author articles. Pres. Columbus Redevel. Commn., 1965-73; mem. Columbus Central Area Master Plan; pres. City Hall Archt. Facilities Com.; Pres. Commn. Christian Edn. in Higher Edn. Ind., United Ministries Bd. of Ind. U. Campus.; Commr. to 182d Gen. Assembly U.P. Ch., 1970; elder 1st Presbyn. Ch., Columbus.; Bd. dirs. Day Care Bd. Served as lt. (j.g.) USNR, 1951-53. Mem. ABA, Ind. Bar Assn. (bd. dirs., chmn. corp. law sect.), Phi Delta Phi (pres. Foster Inn 1955). Home: 210 Newsom Ave Columbus IN 47201 Office: 432 Washington St Columbus IN 47201

BUSH, ROBERT DONALD, archives and museum director; b. Marshalltown, Iowa, Apr. 9, 1939; s. Donald Dudley and Ruth E. (Lorimer) B.; m. Bonnie Thielges, May 29, 1962; children: Sarah, Susan, Carolyn, Jennifer, David. B.A., U. Dubuque, 1962; M.A., U. Richmond, 1963; Ph.D., U. Kans., 1969. Tchr. history Sch. Dist. 111, Oak Lawn, Ill., 1963-66; asst. instr. U. Kans., Lawrence, 1965-68; asst. prof. Nebr. Wesleyan U., Lincoln, 1968-74; asst. dir. New Orleans Coll., 1974-82; dir. Wyo. State Archives, Cheyenne, 1982—. Editor Memoirs of P. Laussat, 1978; Observations on the. . ., 1979, First Constitution. . ., 1975. Seay grad. fellow, 1963; Regents fellow, 1968; NDEA fellow, 1968-69; recipient Pres.'s award Nebr. Wesleyan U., 1971. Mem. Am. Assn. Museums, Am. Assn. State and Local History, Nat. Trust Hist. Preservation, Wyo. Hist. Soc. (exec. sec.). Home: 6717 Redwood Ct Cheyenne WY 82009 Office: Wyoming State Archives 24th St and Central Ave Cheyenne WY 82002

BUSH, SPENCER HARRISON, metallurgist; b. Flint, Mich., Apr. 4, 1920; s. Edward Charles and Rachel Beatrice (Roser) B.; m. Roberta Lee Warren, Aug. 28, 1948; children: David Spencer, Carl Edward. Student, Flint Jr. Coll., 1938-40, Ohio State U., 1943-44, U. Mich., 1946-53. Registered profl. engr., Calif. Asst. chemist Dow Chem. Co., 1940-42, 46; asso. Engring. Research Inst., U. Mich., 1947-53; research asst. Office Naval Research, 1950-53, instr. dental materials, 1951-53; metallurgist Hanford Atomic Products Operation, Gen. Electric Co., 1953-54, supr. phys. metallurgy, 1954-57, supr. fuels fabrication devel., 1957-60, metall. specialist, 1960-63, cons. metallurgist, 1963-65; cons. to dir. Battelle N.W. Labs., Richland, Wash., 1965-70, sr. staff cons., 1970-83; pres. Rev. & Synthesis Assocs., cons., 1983—; lectr. metall. engring. Center for Grad. Study, U. Wash., 1953-67, affiliate prof., 1967—; chmn., com. study group on pressure vessel materials Electric Power Research Inst., 1974-78; cons. U. Calif. Lawrence Berkeley Labs., 1975-79; chmn. com. on reactor safeguards U.S. AEC, 1971; mem. Wash. Bd. Boiler Rules, 1972—; Gillett lectr. ASTM, 1975; Mehl lectr., 1981, mem. Bd. Nuclear Codes and Standards, 1983—. Contbr. tech. articles to profl. jours. Served with U.S. Army, 1942-46. Recipient Silver Beaver award Boy Scouts Am.; Am. Foundrymens Soc. fellow, 1948-50; Regents prof. U. Calif., Berkeley, 1973-74. Fellow Am. Nuclear Soc. (adv. editorial bd. nuclear applications 1965-77), Am. Soc. Metals (chmn. program council 1966-67, trustee 1967-69, chmn. fellow com. 1968), ASME (Langer award 1983); mem. AIME (chmn. ann. seminar com. 1967-68), ASTM, Nat. Acad. Engring., Sigma Xi, Tau Beta Pi, Phi Kappa Phi. Home: 630 Cedar Ave Richland WA 99352 Office: PO Box 999 Richland WA 99352

BUSH, WALTER LEWIS, JR., hockey team executive; b. Mpls., Sept. 25, 1929; s. Walter Lewis and Ruth (Lyman) B.; m. Mary Wheaton Relf, Dec. 29, 1951; children: Walter Lewis, Steven, Anne. B.A., Dartmouth Coll., 1951; LL.B., U. Minn., 1954. Bar: Minn. 1954. Practiced in, Mpls., 1954-67; ptnr. firm Strong, Tully & Bush, Mpls., 1961; pres. Northstar Fin. Corp., Bloomington, Minn., 1976-77, chmn. bd., 1977-78, v.p., 1978—; bd. govs. Nat. Hockey League. Recipient Lester Patrick Meml. Trophy for outstanding service to hockey in U.S. Nat. Hockey League, 1973. Mem. ABA, Minn. Bar Assn., Hennepin County Bar Assn., Mpls. C. of C., Amateur Hockey Assn. U.S. (dir.), U.S. Olympic Ice Hockey Com. (sec. 1967—). Episcopalian. Clubs: Amateur Sportsmen's, Dunkers, Minneapolis; Minikahda (Mpls.); Decathalon. Office: 7901 Cedar Ave S Bloomington MN 55420 *

BUSH, WILLIAM HENRY TROTTER, banker; b. Greenwich, Conn., July 14, 1938; s. Prescott and Dorothy (Walker) B.; m. Patricia Redfearn, Aug. 15, 1959; children: William P., Louisa R. B.A., Yale U., 1960. With Hartford Nat. Bank and Trust Co., Conn., 1962-78; pres., chief operating officer Boatmen's Nat. Bank of St. Louis, 1978—; dir. Covenant Ins. Group, Valman Corp., Clark and Sullivan Constructors. Chmn. bd. trustees St. Louis U.; Trustee St. Louis Symphony, Mo. Bot. Gardens; bd. dirs. St. Louis Regional Commerce and Growth Assn. Served with C.E. U.S. Army, 1960-62. Mem. Assn. Res. City Bankers, Mo. Bankers Assn. Republican. Episcopalian. Clubs: St. Louis, St. Louis Country., Log Cabin; Links (N.Y.C.). Home: 37 Picardy Ln Saint Louis MO 63124 Office: 100 N Broadway Saint Louis MO 63102

BUSH-BROWN, ALBERT, university administrator; b. West Hartford, Conn., Jan. 2, 1926; s. James and Louise (Carter) Bush-B.; m. Frances Wesselhoeft, Aug. 28, 1948; children: David, Frances, Lesley, Martha. A.B., Princeton U., 1947, M.F.A., 1949, Ph.D, 1948; LL.D, Emerson Coll., 1965; H.H.D., Providence Coll., 1966; D.F.A., Mercy Coll., 1976. Instr. art and archaeology Princeton U., 1949-50; jr. fellow Soc. of Fellows, Harvard U., 1950-53; Lowell lectr. Boston U., 1952; asst. prof. art and architecture Western Res. U., Cleve., 1953-54; asst. prof. architecture MIT, 1954-58, assoc. prof., 1958-62, exec. officer dept., 1958-62; pres. R.I. Sch. Design (Providence), 1962-68; chmn. Research and Design Ctr., Inc., 1964-67; dir. council urban and regional studies SUNY Buffalo, 1968-71, vis. prof., 1968-69, prof., v.p., 1969-71; chancellor L.I.U., 1971—; faculty assoc. Joint Ctr. Urban Studies, MIT-Harvard, 1968-69; dir. Barclays Bank of N.Y.; adviser Brown, Dallas,, Saudi Arabia, 1977—. Author: Louis Sullivan, 1960, (with J.E. Burchard) The Architecture of America: A Social Interpretation, 1961, Books, Bass, Barnstable, 1967, King Khalid Military City, 1978; editor architecture sect: Ency. Brit., 1955—; contbr. articles to profl. jours. Active Providence City Planning Commn., 1962-67; spl. adviser to sec. Dept. of Housing and Urban Devel., 1968-69, U. Mass, 1970-71; mem. White House Nat. Council on Arts, 1965-70; bd. govs. Sch. of Arts, W. Pa., 1975—; bd. dirs. Recording for the Blind, 1976-81; bd. mng. dirs. Met. Opera, 1976—. Woodrow Wilson fellow, Princeton U., 1947-48; Hdoward Found. fellow, Brown U., 1959-60; fellow Inst. Politics, J.F. Kennedy Sch. Govt., Harvard, 1968-69. Mem. AIA (hon.), Conf. Bd., Council on Fgn. Relations. Clubs: Century Assn., Piping Rock; Coffee House (N.Y.C.). Home: Piping Rock Rd Locust Valley NY 11560 Office: Barclays Bank of NY 300 Park Ave New York NY 10022

BUSHEK, JOSEPH ANTHONY, insurance company executive; b. Shenandoah, Pa., Mar. 8, 1924; s. John and Bertha (Kinger) B.; m. Julia Zakarevicz, July 19, 1950; children: Karen, Stephen, Joan, Mark, David. B.S., Mt. St. Mary's Coll., 1949; M.S., Columbia U., 1950. C.P.C.U. With Nationwide Ins., 1950—, ops. controller, Columbus, Ohio, 1975-78, v.p. ops. controls, 1978, v.p., corp. controller, 1978-81, Nationwide Ins. Co. and Affiliates, Columbus, 1981-83, v.p. internal audits, 1983—. Com. chmn. United Way-Catholic Social Services, Franklin County, Ohio, 1978-79; mem. St. Peter's Ch. Parishioners' Club, Worthington, Ohio; troop committeeman Boy Scouts Am.; chmn. United Way Campaign at Nationwide Ins., Columbus, 1979; bd. dirs. ARC, Columbus area, 1982-83; mem. Worthington Hills Civic Assn. Served with U.S. Army, 1943-46. Mem. Soc. C.P.U.s (com. chmn. 1978), Am. Council Life Ins., Life Office Mgmt. Assn., Fin. Execs. Inst. Republican. Roman Catholic. Home: 1614 Tennyson Ct Worthington OH 43085 Office: Nationwide Ins Cos 1 Nationwide Plaza Columbus OH 43216

BUSHINSKY, JAY (JOSEPH MASON), journalist, radio commentator, TV correspondent; b. Buffalo, N.Y., Dec. 8, 1932; s. Joshua M. and Malka (Coralnik) B.; m. Dvora Apte, Dec. 30, 1952; children: Jesse, Aviv, Dahlia. B.A., Queens Coll., 1955; M.S. in Edn, Yeshiva U., N.Y.C., 1959, Columbia U., 1963. Municipal reporter Times Herald/Record, Middletown, N.Y., 1963-64; copy editor Miami (Fla.) Herald, 1964-66; corr. Chicago Daily News Foreign Service, Tel Aviv, spl. corr., Middle East, 1966-78; corr., chief bur. Westinghouse Broadcasting Co. Inc., Tel Aviv, 1967-76, analyst-corr., 1976—; spl. corr. Chgo. Sun-Times, 1978—; corr., Jerusalem bur. chief Cable News Network, 1980—; tchr. social studies Long Island City (N.Y.) High Sch., 1958-59, William C. Bryant High Sch., N.Y.C., 1959-62; lectr. journalism Tel Aviv U., 1966-70; asst. prof. journalism U. Mo., 1978—. Served with AUS, 1955-57. Co-recipient Chgo. Newspaper Guild award for investigative reporting for expose of Nazi war criminals in U.S., 1978, Media award for econ. understanding Amos Tuck Sch. Bus. Adminstrn., Dartmouth Coll., 1979. Mem. Fgn. Press Assn. in Israel (chmn. 1968-71), Overseas Press Club Am. (award for Best Radio Spot News Reporting from Abroad to Group W Foreign News Service for coverage of Oct. War in Mideast, Joint citation 1973, co-recipient media award for econ. understanding 1979). Home: Rehov Hatsafon 5 Savyon Israel Office: Rehov Pinsker 37 Tel Aviv Israel

BUSHNELL, CLARENCE WILLIAM, hospital consultant; b. Lowville, N.Y., Nov. 25, 1916; s. Robert Emmett and Isabelle (Webster) B.; m. Ethel Victoria Loving, Apr. 26, 1943; children: Sandra Lynn, Paul George, Susan Lisa. R.N., Hudson River State Hosp., 1937; A.B., N.Y. U., 1947; M.P.H., Yale U., 1951. Various adminstrv. and indsl. nursing positions, 1937-51; asst. adminstr. Mass. Meml. Hosp., Boston, 1951-62; adminstr. Bridgeport (Conn.) Hosp., 1962-80; hosp. cons., 1980—; lectr. pub. health and hosp. adminstrn. Yale, 1963—. Active United Community Services.; Trustee New Eng. Hosp. Assembly, pres., 1979. Served with USCG, 1942-45. Mem. Conn. Hosp. Assn. (past pres., past trustee). Cong'list. (trustee, deacon). Club: Rotarian. Home: 80 Wianno Circle Osterville MA 02655 Office: Health Strategy Assocs 822 Boylston St Chestnut Hill MA 02617

BUSHNELL, GEORGE E., JR., lawyer; b. Detroit, Nov. 15, 1924; s. George E. and Mary (Bl) B.; m. Elizabeth McLeod Whelden, June 17, 1950; children: George Edward III, Christopher Gilbert Whelden, Robina McLeod. B.A., Amherst Coll., 1948; LL.B., U. Mich., 1951; student, U. Kans., 1943. Assoc. Miller, Candield, Paddock and Stone, Detroit, 1953-60, partner, from, 1960, sr. partner, until 1977; sr. partner firm Bushnell, Gage, Doctoroff & Reizen, Southfield, Mich.; commr. Mich. Jud. Tenure Commn., 1969—, chmn., 1979-80; lectr. in field. Contbr. in field. Elder Grosse Pointe Meml. Ch.; moderator Detroit Presbytery, United Presbyterian Ch. in U.S.A., 1972, pres. program agy. bd., 1972-76; bd. dirs. Econ. Growth Corp. of Detroit, 1978—; trustee New Detroit, Inc., 1972—, chmn., 1974-75. Served with USAR, 1943-46, 51-53. Decorated Bronze Star., Army Commendation medal. Mem. ABA, State Bar Mich. (Pres. 1975-76), Detroit Bar Assn. (pres. 1964-65), Am. Arbitration Assn. (dir. 1970-82), Am. Coll. Trial Lawyers, Am. Bar Found., Am. Judicature Soc. (dir. 1977-82), Internat. Soc. Barristers, Fed. Bar Assn., Trial Attys. Am., Def. Research Inst., Indsl. Relations Research Assn., NAACP, Phi Delta Phi, Psi Upsilon. Democrat. Clubs: Detroit, Country of Detroit; Metropolitan (N.Y.C.). Lodge: Masons. Home: 262 Vendome Ct Grosse Pointe Farms MI 48236 Office: 400 Renaissance Center Suite 2380 Detroit MI 48243 or 3000 Town Center Bldg Suite 1500 Southfield MI 48075

BUSHNELL, JOHN ALDEN, foreign service officer; b. Glen Cove, N.Y., July 26, 1933; s. Richard C. and Emma Lee (Anderson) B.; m. Ann Carolyn Morel, Sept. 2, 1962; children—John M., Mark A., Timothy. B.A., Yale U., 1955; M.A., U. Melbourne, Australia, 1959. Prof. econs. McMurry (Tex.) Coll., 1957-58; joined U.S. Fgn. Service, 1959; assigned Bur. Intelligence and Research, State Dept., 1959-61, Policy Planning Council, 1961-62; econ. officer, Bogota, 1962-64, Santo Domingo, 1964-65, San Jose, Costa Rica, 1965-68; U.S. rep. UN Commn. on Trade and Devel., Geneva, 1969-71; mem. staff NSC, Washington, 1971-74; dep. asst. sec. in internat. affairs Treasury Dept., 1974-76; mem. Sr. Seminar in Fgn. Policy, Dept. State, Washington, 1976-77; dep. asst. sec. of state Bur. Inter Am. Affairs, Washington, 1977-81; minister U.S. embassy, Buenos Aires, Argentina, 1982—; Bd. dirs. Panama Canal Commn., 1980—. Author: Australian Company Mergers, 1946-55, 1961. Served as officer USAF, 1957-59. Recipient Rivkin award State Dept., 1968, Meritorious Honor award, 1967; Exceptional Service award Dept. Treasury, 1976. Mem. Am. Econ. Assn., Fgn. Service Assn., DACOR, Phi Beta Kappa. *It is an honor to serve the people of this great and diverse country. The people's business is never done, never perfect and never dull, at least in foreign affairs. Every day provides opportunities to improve the conduct of the government and the well-being of the people.*

BUSHNELL, NOLAN KAY, business executive; b. Ogden, Utah, Feb. 5, 1943; s. Clarance H. and Delma (Nelson) B.; m. Paula Rochelle, Mar. 21, 1966; children: Alissa, Britta; m. Nancy Nino, Nov. 27, 1977; children: Brent, Tyler, Gavin. B.S.E.E., U. Utah, 1968. Engr. Ampex Corp., Redwood City, Calif., 1968-71; chief engr. Nutting Assocs., Mountain View, Calif., 1971-72; founder Syzygy, Santa Clara, Calif., 1972; founder, chmn. Atari, Inc., Sunnyvale, Calif., 1972-79, Pizza Time Theatre, 1979—; chmn. Androbot, Inc., Sunnyvale, 1981—, ByVideo, Inc., 1981—, Magnum Microwave, Inc., Mountain View, Calif., 1979—, Timbertech, Inc., Sunnyvale, 1981—. Inventor: video game Pong, 1972. Mem. Nat. Adv. Council on Vocat. Edn., Washington, 1982; bd. dirs. High Tech. Mus., Palo Alto, Calif., 1983. Named Disting. Alumnus U. Utah, Salt Lake City, 1982, Bus. Leader of Yr. Santa Clara County Bus. Mag., 1980. Mem. Acad. Disting. Entrepreneurs Babson Coll. Republican. Office: Pizza Time Theatre 1213 Innsbruck Dr Sunnyvale CA 94089

BUSHNELL, WILLIAM STUART, bank executive; b. Oneida, N.Y., May 15, 1930; s. Stanton Joseph and Pauline (Jacobs) B.; m. Dolores Frances McDuffee, Nov. 3, 1950; children: Patricia A., Nancy J., Diane L. B.A., Utica Coll., Syracuse, 1960. Sec.-treas. Oneida (N.Y.) Savs. Bank, 1953-68; pres. Elmira (N.Y.) Savs. Bank, 1968-80, Amoskeag Savs. Bank, Manchester, N.H., 1980—. Bd. dirs. United Way, Manchester, YMCA, Manchester, Federated Arts and Palaca Theatre Trust, Manchester. Mem. N.H. Assn. Savs. Banks (dir.), Nat. Assn. Mut. Savs. Bank (chmn. ins. com.), Manchester C. of C. (dir.). Republican. Presbyterian. Office: Amoskeag Savs Bank 875 Elm St Manchester NH 03105

BUSINGER, JOOST ALOIS, atmospheric scientist, emeritus educator; b. Haarlem, Netherlands, Mar. 29, 1924; came to U.S., 1956; s. Leopold Joost Eduard and Helena Margareta (Schimpt) B.; m. Judith Businger, May 21, 1949 (div. Jan. 1983); children: Ferdi, Steven, Margaret Anne. Candidaats, U. Utrecht, Netherlands, 1947, Doctoraat, 1950, Ph.D., 1954. Sci. officer Inst. Hort. Engring., Wageningen, Netherlands, 1951-56; research assoc. U. Wis., Madison, 1956-58; asst. to prof. atmospheric sci. U. Wash., Seattle, 1958-65, prof. emeritus, 1965—; chmn. dept. atmospheric sci., 1982-83; vis. scientist Nat. Ctr. Atmospheric Research, Boulder, Colo., 1983—. Author: Am. Introduction to Atmospheric Physics, 1963, Am. Introduction to Atmospheric Physics, 2d rev. edit., 1980. Precinct committeeman Democratic Party, Seattle, 1970-71. Sr. fellow NRC, Australia, 1965-66; sr. scientist Konimklyka Meteorologisch Instituut, Netherlands, 1974-75. Fellow AAAS, Am. Meteorol. Soc. (Half Century award 1979); mem. Am. Geophys. Union, Royal Acad. Scis. (Netherlands) (corr.), AAUP (pres. Seattle chpt. 1972-73, nat. councillor 1974-76). Home: 750 Spruce Boulder CO Office: Nat Ctr Atmospheric Research PO Box 30000 Boulder CO 80307

BUSINO, ORLANDO FRANCIS, cartoonist; b. Binghamton, N.Y., Oct. 10, 1926; s. Frank and Rose (Clementi) B.; m. Ann Louise Darlington, Nov. 3, 1951; children—Linda, Christopher, Michele, Andrea, Robert, Frank. B.A., State U. Ia., 1952. Cartoonist, works pub.: other U.S. and fgn. mags. Family Circle; (Named best mag. cartoonist of year Nat. Cartoonists Soc. 1965, 67, 68). Served with AUS, 1945-47. Mem. Nat. Cartoonists Soc., Mag. Cartoonists Guild. Address: 12 Shadblow Hill Rd Ridgefield CT 06877

BUSKIRK, ELSWORTH ROBERT, physiologist, educator; b. Beloit, Wis., Aug. 11, 1925; s. Ellsworth Fred and Laura Ellen (Parman) B.; m. Mable Heen, Aug. 28, 1948; children—Laurel Ann Buskirk Wiegand, Kristine Janet Buskirk Schmidt. Student, U. Wis., 1943; B.A., St. Olaf Coll., Northfield, Minn., 1950; M.A., U. Minn., 1951, Ph.D., 1954. Lab. and teaching asst. Lab. Physiol. Hygiene, U. Minn., 1951-53; research fellow Life Ins. Med. Research Fund, 1953-54; physiologist Environ. Research Center, Natick, Mass., 1954-57, Nat. Inst. for Arthritis, Metabolic and Digestive Diseases, NIH, Bethesda, Md., 1957-63; prof. applied physiology Pa. State U., University Park, 1963—; mem. sci. adv. com. President's Council on Phys. Fitness, 1959-61; mem. applied physiology study sect. div. research grants NIH, 1964-68, 76-80; mem. com. on interplay of engring. with biology and medicine Nat. Acad. Scis.-Nat. Acad. Engring., 1968-74; mem. research com. Pa. Heart Assn., 1970-74; mem. Pa. Gov.'s Council on Phys. Fitness and Sports, 1976-81. Sect. editor: Jour. Applied Physiology, 1974; co-editor: Science and Medicine of Exercise and Sports, 1974; editor: Medicine and Sports, 1973-75; mem. editorial bd.: Physician and Sports Medicine, 1974—; Contbr. over 185 articles on physiology, also revs. to sci. jours. Bd. visitors Sargent Coll., Boston U., 1976—; bd. dirs. Center Community Hosp., Pa., 1966-70, sec., 1971-72, v.p., 1973, pres., 1974-75. Served with U.S. Army, 1943-46; ETO. Recipient dist. alumni award St. Olaf Coll., 1969; research grantee NIH, 1963—, U.S. Olympic Com., 1965-68, U.S. Air Force, 1965-69, Pa. Dept. Health, 1966-67, Pa. Heart Assn., 1966, 76-80, NSF, 1968-70, Nat. Inst. for Occupational Safety and Health, 1969-74; NATO sr. fellow in sci., 1977. Mem. Aerospace Med. Assn., Am. Acad. Phys. Edn., AAHPER, AAAS, Am. Coll. Sports Medicine (citations 1973, 75), Am. Inst. Nutrition, Am. Physiol. Soc., ASHRAE, Am. Heart Assn. (council on epidemiology), N.Y. Acad. Scis., NIH Alumni Assn., Pa. Heart Assn. Lutheran. Club: Centre Hills Country. Home: 216 Hunter Ave State Coll PA 16801 Office: 119 Noll Lab Pa State U University Park PA 16802

BUSKIRK, JOSEPH VAN, lawyer; b. Pitts., June 20, 1929; s. Arthur Bostwick and Katharine (Jones) Van Buskirk; children: Rebecca, Joseph, Mary. A.B., Yale U., 1951; LL.B., U. Mich., 1954. Bar: Pa., Colo. Atty. Gulf Oil Corp., Denver, 1962-64; mem. firm Reed Smith Shaw & McClay, Pitts., 1964—. Office: Reed Smith Shaw & McClay 747 Union Trust Bldg PO Box 2009 Pittsburgh PA 15230

BUSS, CLAUDE ALBERT, history educator; b. Sunbury, Pa., Nov. 29, 1903; s. W. Claude and Clara (Fetter) B.; m. Evelyn Lukens, Jan. 20, 1928; 1 dau., Lynne. A.B., Washington Missionary Coll., Takoma Park, D.C., 1922; M.A., Susquehanna U., 1924; Ph.D., U. Pa.; LL.D., U. So. Calif., 1945; student, Ecole Libre des Science Politiques, Paris, 1927-28; Fulbright scholar, U. Philippines, 1957, 1959. Carnegie teaching fellow in internat. law, Europe, 1927-28; attaché for language study U.S. Legation in China, U.S. Dept. State, 1929-31; U.S. vice consul, Nanking, China, 1931-34; prof. internat. relations U. So. Calif., 1934-41; prof. history Stanford, 1946-69, prof. emeritus, 1969; prof. Inst. Fgn. Studies, Monterey, Calif., 1968-75, Naval Postgrad. Sch., Monterey, 1976—, San Jose State Coll.; Exec. asst. U.S. High Commr. to Philippine Islands, 1941-44; chief San Francisco office O.W.I., 1944-46; exec. cons. petroleum div. U.S. Strategic Bombing Survey, Japan, 1945-46; cons. Civil Information and Edn. Sect., Gen. Hdqrs., Tokyo, 1948; U.S. del. 10th Internat. Conf., Inst. Pacific Relations, 1947, also 12th Conf., 1954; mem. Seminar on U.S. Fgn. Policy, Brookings Instn., Lake Forest (Ill.) Coll., 1949; dir. studies Nat. War Coll., Washington, 1949, mem. civilian faculty, 1963-64; adviser Bur. E. Asia and Pacific Affairs U.S. Dept. State, 1967-68. Author: War and Diplomacy in Eastern Asia, 1941, The Far East, 1955, South-east Asia and World Today, 1958, Arc of Crisis, 1961, People's Republic of China, 1962, Asia in the Modern World, 1964, Contemporary Southeast Asia, 1970, Peoples Republic of China and Richard Nixon, 1972, U.S. and Philippines, 1977, The United States and the Republic of Korea, 1982; also articles in various mags. Home: 1234 Pitman Ave Palo Alto CA 94301

BUSS, JERRY HATTEN, real estate co. exec., sports team owner. B.S. in Chemistry, U. Wyo., M.S., Ph.D., U. So. Calif., 1957. Chemist Bur. Mines; past mem. faculty dept. chemistry U. So. Calif.; mem. missile div. McDonnell Douglas, Los Angeles; partner Mariani-Buss Assos.; former owner Los Angeles Strings; chmn. bd., owner Los Angeles Lakers (Nat. Basketball Assn.); owner Los Angeles Kings (Nat. Hockey League.). Office: care Los Angeles Lakers PO Box 10 The Forum Ingelwood CA 90306

BUSS, WALTER RICHARD, geology educator emeritus; b. Provo, Utah, Nov. 1, 1905; s. Fred Earle and Edith Bliss (Rumsey) B.; m. Edna Taylor, Nov. 30, 1928; children—Richard Taylor, David Walter, Marilyn Ruth (Mrs. John Francis Wilcox), Warren Rumsey, Barbara Ellen (Mrs. J Stephen Jones). Student, San Jose State Coll., 1925-28; B.A., Brigham Young U., 1930, M.A., 1933; postgrad., U. Chgo., 1937; Newell scholar, Stanford, 1937-39, Ph.D., 1964; postgrad., Ind. U., 1961, U. Utah, 1965. Instr., asso. prof., prof. geology and geography Weber State Coll., Ogden, Utah, 1933-74, emeritus, 1974; ranger naturalist U.S. Nat. Park Service, summers 1940-42; geologist Utah State Engr., 1953; engring. technician, geologist U.S. Forest Service, 1955-82. Fellow A.A.A.S., Utah Acad. Scis., Arts and Letters (pres. 1970-71); mem. Utah Geol. Assn. (sec.-treas. 1962-69), Utah Hist. Soc., Assn. Am. Geographers, Nat. Assn. Geology Tchrs., Nat. Council Geog. Edn., Sigma Xi. Mem. Ch. of Jesus Christ of Latter-day Saints (high councilor). Home: 2820 Liberty Ave Ogden UT 84403 *To teach in humility and with understanding, to live so as to be an example to others, to raise an upright and honorable family, to keep myself physically strong, mentally awake, and morally clean, and to serve God and my fellowmen to the best of my ability. These are my goals and principles.*

BUSSARD, CLARENCE LEASE, farm supply company executive; b. Frederick, Md., Feb. 9, 1911; s. Clarence A. and Katharine Elizabeth (Lease) B.; m. Frances Lovina Thomas, June 22, 1935; 1 dau., Jeanne Frances (dec.). B.S., U. Md., 1934; B.E., Western Md. Coll., 1934. Coach, organizer comml. dept. Clearspring (Md.) High Sch., 1934-35; opened fertilizer dept. father's bus. Farmers Supply Co., 1935, added feeds, seeds and insecticides, 1940; built feed processing and plant as Farmers Feed & Supply Co., 1951—, since owner; owner-mgr., operator dairy farm, Frederick County, 1935-51; pres. emeritus Three Springs Fisheries, Lilypons, Md.; founding dir. Francis Scott Key Bank & Trust Co., Frederick. Pres. Frederick County Civil War Centennial, 1961-64; pres. Francis Scott Key Meml. Found.; exec. v.p. Antietam-South Mountain Civil War Centennial, 1962; mem. Md. Bi-Centennial Commn.; treas., charter pres. Central Md. council Girl Scouts U.S.A.; Bd. dirs. Frederick Optimist Boys Found., Big Bros. Balt., Md. Civil War Commn. Centennial, Frederick County Assn. for Retarded Children, Frederick County Hist. Soc.; active YMCA, Community Chest.; Trustee Western Md. Coll. Mem. Mil. Manpower Commn., 2d Corps Area, World War II; 1st lt. Army Res. Mem. Western Md. Alumni Assn. (Alumni award 1957, pres.), U.S. Navy League P.R. (dir. 1982-85), SAR, Gamma Beta Chi. Lutheran. Clubs: Shriners, Order Eastern Star; Rotary (San Juan); Optimist Internat. (internat. pres. 1956-57), Los Angeles Breakfast.). Lodges: Elks; Masons (past master); Shriners; Order Eastern Star; Rotary. Office: E All Saint St Box 310 Frederick MD 21701 also Apt 1601-1602 Condado Del Mar San Juan PR 00907

BUSSARD, RICHARD EARL, newspaper editor and publisher; b. Jacksonville, Fla., Dec. 14, 1934; s. Ernest H. and Mary Gladys (Davis) B.; m. Billee A. Neumann, Aug. 7, 1967; children: Sheryl A. Bussard Weitnaur, Clifford E., Tiffany L., Mary-Lee. Student public schs. Reporter Jacksonville Jour., 1952-53, state editor, then asst. city editor, 1957-59, city editor, 1960-77, mng. editor, 1977-81; sports editor Leesburg (Fla.) Comml., 1953-54; pub. Ocean Beach Reporter, Jacksonville Beach, Fla., 1955-57, Beaches Sun-Times, Jacksonville Beach, 1981—; v.p. Sun-Times, Inc.; editor Seaboard System Railroad. Served with USMCR, 1952. Democrat. Home: 16 Hopson Rd Jacksonville Beach FL 32250 Office: 500 Water St Jacksonville FL 32202

BUSSARD, ROBERT WILLIAM, physicist; b. Washington, Aug. 11, 1928; s. Marcel Julian and Elsa Mathilda (Griesser) B.; m. Dolly H. Gray, 1981; children: Elise Marie Bussard Bright, William Julian, Robert Lee, Virginia Lesley. B.S. in Engring., UCLA, 1950, M.S. in Engring., 1952; A.M. in Physics, Princeton U., 1959, Ph.D. in Physics, 1961. Design engr. Falcon program Hughes Aircraft Co., 1949-51; mech. engr. aircraft nuclear propulsion project Oak Ridge Nat. Lab., 1952-55; alt. group leader nuclear rocket program Los Alamos Sci. Lab., 1955-62, alt. leader laser div., 1971-73; dir. nuclear systems staff, asst. dir. mechanics div. Space Tech. Labs., Thompson-Ramo-Wooldridge, Inc., Redondo Beach, Calif., 1962-64; assoc. mgr. research and engring., corp. chief scientist Electro-Optical Systems div. Xerox Corp., Pasadena, Calif., 1964-69; with CSI Corp., Los Angeles, 1969-70; mgr. Cherokee Assos., Pasadena, Md., 1970-74; asst. dir. div. controlled thermonuclear research U.S. AEC, Washington, 1973-74; founder, pres., chmn. Energy Resources Group, (ERG), Inc., La Jolla, Calif., Alexandria, Va., 1974; Internat. Nuclear Energy Systems Co. (INESCO), Inc., La Jolla and McLean, 1976—; cons. NATO, 1960-64, U.S. Dept. Energy, 1974-78; lectr. UCLA, 1960-69, U. Fla., 1962-64. Author: (with R.D. DeLauer) Nuclear Rocket Propulsion, 1958, Fundamentals of Nuclear Flight, 1965; editor: Nuclear Thermal and Electric Rocket Propulsion, 1967; contbr. articles to profl. jours. Fellow AIAA; mem. Am. Phys. Soc., Internat. Acad. Astronautics. Clubs: Princeton (N.Y.C.); Cosmos, Capitol Hill (Washington). Patentee space nuclear propulsion, power generation, fusion and fission power, solar power systems. Office: 11077 N Torrey Pines Rd La Jolla CA 92037 *The future is constructed in a fashion and to a scale envisioned by those who perceive what it might be, and who work to make these visions happen. At any one time, probably no more than a few thousand dedicated people are actively working to shape the world of tomorrow from the tools, techniques, and ideas of today. I like to think that I have tried to spend my life in this manner, always with the goals of improving the lot of man, and of assisting in ensuring the survival and growth of my people and my country, in order that the freedom of men, as it flourishes under democracy, might be preserved and extended for future generations.*

BUSSE, EWALD WILLIAM, psychiatrist; b. St. Louis, Aug. 18, 1917; s. Frederick Ewald and Emily Louise (Stroh) B.; m. Ortrude Helen Schnaedelbach, July 18, 1941; children: Ortrude Susan Busse White, Barbara Ann, Ewald Richard, Deborah Emily Busse Bragg. A.B., Westminster Coll., 1938, Sc.D. hon., 1960; M.D., Washington U., St. Louis, 1942. Diplomate: Am. Bd. Psychiatry and Neurology, Am. Bd. Qualification in Electroencephalogy. Intern St. Louis City Hosp., 1942; resident in neuropsychiatry and psychiatry McCloskey Gen. Hosp., Temple, Tex., 1943-46, Colo. Psychiat. Hosp., Denver, 1946-48; mem. faculty, head dept. psychosomatic medicine U. Colo., Denver, 1950-53; prof. Duke U. Med. Ctr., Durham, N.C., 1953-65, J.P. Gibbons prof. psychiatry, 1965—, chmn. dept., 1953-74, dir. Ctr. for Study Aging, 1957-70, assoc. provost, dean Sch. Medicine, 1974-82, dean emeritus, 1982—; mem. council Nat. Inst. on Aging, Bethesda, Md., 1979-83; chmn. geriatrics and gerontology adv. com. VA, 1981—. Author-editor: Behavior and Adaptation in Late Life, 1969, (2d edit.) Behavior and Adaptation in Late Life, 1977, Handbook of Geriatric Psychiatry, 1980, (part II) Vol. II—Psychiatry Update, 1983; author: Cerebral Manifestations of Cardiac Dysrhythmias, 1979. Mem. N.C. State Commn. on Care of Elderly, Raleigh, 1968-73, Durham County Commn. in Mental Health, 1971-74; sect. chmn. del. White House Conf. on Aging, 1978-81. Served to maj. U.S. Army, 1943-46. Recipient Brookdale Found. award, 1982. Fellow Am. Psychiat. Assn. (pres. 1971-72, chmn. ethics com. 1981—, Jack Weinberg Meml. award 1983), Am. Geriatrics Soc. (pres. 1975-76, Allen Thewlis award 1967), Gerontol. Soc. Am. (pres. 1967-68, Freeman award 1978), ACP (Menninger award 1971), Southeastern Med. Dental Soc. (pres. 1978-80); mem. Internat. Assn. Gerontology (pres. 1983—, Sandoz prize 1983), N.Y. Acad. Medicine (Salmon award 1980). Clubs: Hope Valley; Beach Mountain (N.C.). Lodges: Rotary/Durham; Masons. Home: 1132 Woodburn Rd Durham NC 27705 Office: Duke U Med Ctr Box 2948 Durham NC 27710

BUSSGANG, JULIAN JAKOB, electronic engineer; b. Lwow, Poland, Mar. 26, 1925; came to U.S., 1949, naturalized, 1954; s. Joseph and Stephanie (Philipp) B.; m. Fay Rita Vogel, Aug. 9, 1960; children: Jessica Edith, Julia Claire, Jeffrey Joseph. B.Sc., U. London, 1949; S.M. in Elec. Engring., MIT, 1951; Ph.D. in Applied Physics, Harvard U., 1955. Registered profl. engr., Mass. Mem. tech. staff Lincoln Lab., M.I.T., Lexington, 1951-55; mgr. applied research RCA, Burlington, Mass., 1955-62; pres. Signatron, Inc., Lexington, 1962—; vis. lectr. Harvard U., 1964; lectr. Northeastern U., Boston, 1962-65; mem. Mass. del. White House Conf. on Small Bus., 1980. Assoc. editor: Radio Sci., 1976-78; contbr. chpts. to books, also articles. Mem. Town Meeting, Lexington, 1975—; mem. alumni council M.I.T., 1965-72. Served with Free Polish Forces, 1942-46. Fellow IEEE; mem. Research Mgmt. Assn., Smaller Bus. Assn. New Eng., Am. Assn. Small Research Cos. Patentee in field. Office: 12 Hartwell Ave Lexington MA 02173 *I was a child-refugee, an adolescent-soldier, a student-immigrant, a young engineer and an adult entrepreneur. In every phase of my life I was blessed with the friendship and support of many wonderful people from various walks of life. Even in the darkest moments I had faith that each of us could improve the world a little.*

BUSSIERES, PIERRE, Can. govt. ofcl.; b. Normandin, Que., Can., July 8, 1939; s. Jean-Baptiste and Therese (Poison) B.; m. Gertrude G. Cloutier, July 18, 1964; children: Denis, Marie-Pierre. Student public schs., Que. Mem. House of Commons for, Charlesbourg, Que., from 1974, parliamentary sec. to minister state for sci. and tech., parlimentary sec. to minister of energy, mines and resources; minister of state for fin., Can., 1980-82, minister of nat. revenue, 1982—. Liberal. Roman Catholic. Office: Connaught Bldg MacKenzie Ave Ottawa ON K1A 0L5 Canada

BUSSMANN, CHARLES HAINES, publisher; b. Pitts., Mar. 9, 1924; s. Amos George and Ann (Haines) B. Student, Colgate U., 1946. With Pit & Quarry Publs., Inc., 1946-63, v.p., 1957-63, dir., 1960-63; pres., dir. Compass Publs., Inc., Arlington, Va., 1963—. Served with USAAF, 1942-43. Fellow Marine Tech. Soc.; Mem. Indsl. Marketers Cleve. (past bd. dirs.), Am. Bus. Press Inc., Marine Tech. Soc., Am. Oceanographic Orgn., Advt. Club Cleve., T.F. Club Cleve. (past pres.), Theta Chi. Office: 1117 N 19th St Arlington VA 22209

BUSTAMANTE, RODRIGO ANTONIO, physician; b. Cienfuegos, Cuba, Oct. 21, 1921; s. Rodrigo Segundo and Carolina Dominga (Marcayda) B.; m. Sara I. Vianello, July 19, 1953; children—Sara M., Carolina, Rodrigo R., Eduardo, Victor. B.S., B.A., Cienfuegos Inst., 1938; M.D., Havana (Cuba) U. Sch. Medicine, 1944. Diplomate: Am. Bd. Internal Medicine, Am. Bd. Cardiovascular Diseases. Intern Havana U. Hosps., 1944-45, resident, 1945-47; practice medicine, specializing in cardiology, Havana, 1950-61, Miami, Fla., 1968—; dir. cardiology dept. Havana U. Hosp., 1959-61; asst. prof. medicine Marquette U. Sch. Medicine, Milw., 1962-66; chief cardiology sect. Wood VA Hosp., Milw., 1963, Miami VA Hosp., 1966-68; sr. attending cardiologist Mercy Hosp., Miami, Cedars of Lebanon Hosp.; clin. prof. medicine Miami U. Sch. Medicine, 1968—; Mem. Fla. Health Planning Council, 1969-70, Fla. Regional Med. Program, 1970-72. Contbr. articles to profl. publs.; Author: (with others) Primer of Cardiac Catherization, 1964. Brit. Council scholar, 1947. Fellow A.C.P., Am. Coll. Cardiology, Am. Coll. Chest Physicians, Royal Coll. Physicians. Club: Key Biscayne (Fla.) Yacht. Home: 320 Harbor Ct Key Biscayne FL 33149 Office: 3661 S Miami Ave Miami FL 33133

BUSTEED, ROBERT CHARLES, educator; b. Milan, Ind., Sept. 4, 1907; s. Robert and Emma (Elble) B.; m. Ada Flora Kohlerman, June 6, 1931; children—Philip Gene, Robert Louis, Richard Charles, Wallace Bruce. Student, Hanover Coll., 1925-27; A.B., Ind. U., 1930, M.A., 1932, Ph.D., 1936. Grad. asst. botany dept. and U., 1930-33, tutor, 1934-35, instr., 1935-36; prof., head dept. biology Appalachian State Tchrs. Coll., 1937-45; prof. botany, chmn. sci. div. U. Ga., Savannah div., 1946-48; prof., head dept. biology, chmn. sci. div., grad. council West Tex. State Coll., 1948—; Faculty sponsor West Tex. State chpt. Tex. Collegiate Acad. Sci.; Mem. adminstrv. council Kilgore Research Center, 1967—. Dir. Am. Brittany Spaniel Club, 1946; Dist. commr. Boy Scouts Am., Boone, N.C., 1944-46. Mem. Texas Coll. Tchrs. Assn., Tex. Panhandle Sci. Council (dir. 1959, pres. 1967- 68), Ind. Acad. Sci., Sigma Xi, Theta Kappa Nu, Alpha Phi Omega (sponsor), Beta Beta Beta (sponsor). Lutheran. Clubs: Mason, Lion (Boone) (pres.). Home: Route 2 Box 68 Canyon TX 79015

BUSTER, EDMOND BATE, metal products company executive; b. Whitt, Tex., Oct. 20, 1918; s. Edmond Bate and Emma Lee (Johnston)

B.; m. Beatrice Keller, Oct. 24, 1939; children: John Edmond, Robert William, Susan Lynn, Steven K., James L., Brian R. A.A., Menlo Jr. Coll., 1937; B.S. in Mining Engring, U. Calif. at Berkeley, 1940. With Tex. Co., Santa Paula, Calif., 1937-40, Tidewater Asso. Oil Co., Ventura, 1940-42; supr. mfg. and engring. Douglas Aircraft Co., Long Beach, 1942-45; pres. Pacific Rivet and Machine Co., Alhambra, 1945-52, Pacific Fasteners, inc., 1951-54; v.p. Milford Pivet and Machine Co., Alhambra, 1952-54; sales mgr. S & C Electric Co., Chgo., 1954-56; v.p. West Coast operations Townsend Co., Santa Ana, 1956-67, exec. v.p., 1967-82; pres. Cherry Textron, 1982—; profl. cons. engr., 1954—; pres. Camalisa, Panama, 1965—; dir. Morehouse Engring. Corp., 1968-74, Orange County regional bd. U.S. Nat. Bank, 1969-73, First Fed. Savs. & Loan Assn., 1974-82; mem. regional bd. Calif. Fed. Savs. and Loan, 1982—. Mem. adv. bd. Calif. State U., Fullerton, 1961-81, chmn., 1971-81; chmn. Disneyland awards Com., 1971-72; Trustee St. Joseph Found., 1970-76, 78—; trustee Chapman Coll., Orange, 1972—, exec. vice chmn., 1976—; trustee Calif. Coll. Medicine of U. Calif. at Irvine, 1973—, vice chmn., 1976-79, chmn., 1979—; chmn. Community Airport Council, 1974—. Recipient Outstanding Humanitarian award NCCJ, 1980. Mem. Am. inst. Elec. Engrs., Nat. Aero. Assn., Mchts. and Mfrs. Assn. (v.p., dir.), Airplane Owners and Pilots Assn., Nat. Pilots Assn., Am. Mgmt. Assn., Theta Tau. Clubs: Santa Ana Country, Balboa Bay., Pacific. Home: 1841 Beverly Glen Dr Santa Ana CA 92705 Office: 1224 E Warner Santa Ana CA 92707 *Credit for whatever success I may have attained is due in great part to a loving, constant wife, six children in need of superior education, and the thought that we as parents should set as well as espouse good examples of human behavior. We believe in a strong, but independent family unit, with love and trust for each other; yet at the same time we recognize the absolute need for each of us to produce something which can contribute to the well-being and happiness of our society.*

BUSTER, WILLIAM ROBARDS, SR., historical society director; b. Harrodsburg, Ky., Oct. 10, 1916; s. John Shelby and Martha Lillard (Nooe) B.; m. Mildred Pine Martin, June 24, 1942; children—William Robards, Kathryn Martin, Martha Lillard. Student, Centre Coll., 1934-35; B.S., U.S. Mil. Acad., 1939; grad., Command and Gen. Staff Sch., 1951, Army War Coll., 1964. Commd. 2d lt. U.S.Army, 1939, advanced through grades to brig. gen., 1960; arty. comdr. (2d Armored Div.), African Middle East and European Theatres, 1945-45, mem. War Dept. gen. staff, European Sect., 1945-47, ret., 1947; mem. USAR, 1947-53, Ky. N.G., 1953-69, corps arty. comdr., dep. adj. gen. of, Ky., 1960-69; ret., 1969; dir. Ky. Hist. Soc., Frankfort, 1973—; farmer, 1947—; dir. United Bank & Trust Co., Versailles, Ky. Editorial bd., Univ. Press of Ky., 1976—. Pres. Woodford County Farm Bur., 1957-59; chmn. ARC Louisville Regional Blood Center, 1954-59, Central Ky. Council Camps and Hosps., 1955-58; trustee Midway Coll. Decorated Legion of Merit, Bronze Star, Silver Star with oakleaf cluster, Air medal. Mem. Ky. Archives and Records Commn., Ky. Adv. Commn. Public Documents, Ky. Hist. Records Adv. Bd. (coordinator), Ky. Oral History Commn. (exec. com.). Democrat. Mem. Christian Ch. Club: Midway Lions (pres. 1948-49). Home: Audubon Farm Midway KY 40347 Office: Kentucky Historical Society Box H Frankfort KY 40601

BUSTIN, EDOUARD JEAN, political scientist, educator; b. Hollogne aux Pierres, Belgium, Apr. 9, 1933; came to U.S., 1961; s. Maurice and Mariette (De Graeve) B.; m. Francine Lekeu, Apr. 13, 1957; children: Denis, Olivier. Cand.Phil., U. Liege, 1953, D. en Droit, 1956, Lic.Sc. Diplomat., 1957. Bar: bar 1956. Asst. in public law and adminstrn. U. Liege, 1956-59; atty. in, Liege, 1956-59; sr. lectr., then vis. prof. U. Officielle du Congo, 1959-71; vis. lectr. polit. sci. UCLA, 1961-63; mem. faculty Boston U., 1963—, prof. polit. sci., 1970—, chmn. dept., 1977-82, asso. African Studies Center, 1963—. Author: Lunda Under Belgian Rule: The Politics of Ethnicity, 1975; co-author: Five African States: Responses to Diversity, 1963. Mem. African Studies Assn., Centre d'Etudes et de Documentation Africaines, Inst. Royal des Relations Internat., Acad. Royale des Scis. d'Outre-Mer. Home: 383 Main St Hingham MA 02043 Office: 125 Bay State Rd Boston MA 02215

BUTCHER, (CHARLES) PHILIP, educator, author; b. Washington, Sept. 28, 1918; s. James William and Jennie Lawrence (Jones) B.; m. Ruth Ann Batch, Dec. 27, 1948; children: Wendy Ann Butcher Samuel, Laurel Ruth Butcher Miles. A.B., Howard U., 1942, M.A., 1947; Ph.D., Columbia U., 1956. Instr. in English Morgan State U., Balt., 1947-49, asst. prof., 1949-56, asso. prof., 1956-59, prof. English, 1959-79, prof. emeritus, 1979—, chmn. div. humanities, 1960-66, dean Grad. Sch., 1972-75; occasional lectr. U. Iowa, U. Pa., U. N.C. at Chapel Hill, N.C.; Central U., Va. State Coll. Author: George W. Cable: The Northampton Years, 1959, George W. Cable, 1962; editor: The William Stanley Braithwaite Reader, 1972, The Minority Presence in American Literature, 1600-1900, 2 vols, 1977, Modern American Literature 1900-1950, 1984; contbr. articles to profl. jours. Served with AUS, 1943-46. Research grantee Am. Philos. Soc., 1968-69, 73; Gen. Edn. Bd. fellow, 1948-49; John Hay Whitney Opportunity fellow, 1951-52. Mem. Modern Lang. Assn., Coll. Lang. Assn. (Creative Scholarship award 1964, asso. editor Jour. 1970-77), Soc. Study of So. Lit. Home: 9326 Mellenbrook Rd Columbia MD 21045

BUTCHER, DEVEREUX, association executive; b. Radnor, Pa., Sept. 24, 1906; s. Henry Clay and Constance (Devereux) B.; m. Mary Frances Taft, Dec. 13, 1935; 1 son, Russell Devereux. Grad., St. George's Sch.; student, Pa. Acad. Fine Arts, 1926-28. Free lance writer, photographer, 1936-39; editorial asst. Am. Forests mag. Am. Forestry Assn., 1941-42; exec. sec. Nat. Parks Assn., 1942-50, field rep., 1950-57; editor Nat. Parks Mag., 1942-57; editor, pub. Nat. Wildlands News, 1959-62; dir. Hawk Mountain Sanctuary Assn., 1963—, John Burroughs Meml. Assn., 1965-80; Mem. adv. com. on conservation Sec. Interior, 1952-53. Author: Exploring Our National Parks and Monuments, 1947, Exploring the National Parks of Canada, 1951, Seeing America's Wildlife in Our National Refuges, 1955, Exploring Our National Wildlife Refuges, 1963, Our National Parks in Color, 1964; Co-author photographer: Knowing Your Trees, 1963-78; painter landscapes nat. parks, nature monuments. Mem. Wilderness Soc., Defenders Wildlife (sec. 1947-59), Nat. Parks Assn. Club: Explorers. Home: 10 Hilltop Pl New London NH 03257

BUTCHER, DONALD FRANKLIN, statistician, computer scientist; b. Parkersburg, W.Va., June 29, 1937; s. John Franklin and Anna Pearl (Hersman) B.; m. Alice Adelia Rosier, July 24, 1959; children: Dianna Lynn, Daniel Bruce, Damon Scott. B.S., W.Va. U., 1960, M.S., 1962; Ph.D., Iowa State U., 1965. Asst. prof. W.Va. U., 1965-69, assoc. prof., 1970-73, chmn. dept., prof. stats. and computer sci., 1973—; asst. prof. Kans. State U., 1969-70; dir. Math. and Statis. Consultants, Inc. Contbr. articles on statis. methodology, exptl. design, Monte Carlo simulation using digital computers to profl. jours. Mem. Assn. Computing Machinery, Am. Statis. Assn., Biometrics Soc., Sigma Xi, Gamma Sigma Delta, Upsilon Pi Epsilon, Mu Sigma Rho. Republican. Methodist. Home: Route 7 Box 464 Morgantown WV 26505 Office: West Virginia University Knapp Hall Morgantown WV 26506

BUTCHER, FRED RAY, biochemistry educator, university administrator; b. Rochester, Pa., Aug. 11, 1943; s. Goble S. and Monnie (Gibson) B.; m. Letty Jean Lytton, June 19, 1965; children: Allen Ray, Amy Jo. B.S., Ohio State U., 1965, Ph.D., 1969. Postdoctoral fellow U. Wis., Madison, 1969-71; asst. prof. Brown U., Providence, 1971-76, assoc. prof., 1976-78; prof. W.Va. U., Morgantown, 1978—, chmn. dept. biochemistry, 1981—, interim assoc. dean Sch. Medicine, 1983—; cons. NIH, Bethesda, Md., 1976—, Cystic Fibrosis Found., Bethesda, 1977—. Contbr. articles to profl. jours. Grantee NIH, Cystic Fibrosis Found., Juvenile Diabetes Found. Mem. Am. Soc. Biol. Chemists. Home: RD 1 Box 242 Independence WV 26374 Office: WVa Univ Med Ctr Morgantown WV 26506

BUTCHER, JAMES WALTER, biologist; b. Pa., Feb. 14, 1917; s. Louis and Mary B.; m. Mary Katharine Culley, June 18, 1944; children: Craig, Mary Helen. B.S., U. Pitts., 1943; M.S., U. Minn., 1949, Ph.D., 1951. With Gulf Research Devel. Corp., 1948, Dept. Agr., 1950-52, Minn. Dept. Agr., 1952-57; mem. faculty Mich. State U., East Lansing, 1957—, prof. biology, 1965—, asst., asso. dean research, 1969-74, chmn. dept. zoology, 1974-81, prof., chmn. emeritus, 1981—, acting dean, 1973; cons. in field. Author papers in field, rev. articles. Served with USAAF, 1943-47. Fulbright sr. research scholar U. Vienna, 1966-67; grantee fed. and state govts., also industry. Mem. Ecol. Soc. Am., Am. Zool. Soc., Entomol. Soc. Am., Phi Beta Kappa, Sigma Xi. Home: 1002 Aragon Saint Augustine FL 32086 Office: 203 Natural Sci Bldg Mich State Univ East Lansing MI 48824

BUTCHER, MICHAEL ANDREW JONATHAN, hospital executive; b. Bexley Heath, Kent, Eng., Nov. 7, 1943; emigrated to Can., 1948; s. Thomas Frederick and Ethel Mabel (Posgate) B.; m. Diane Irene Agopsowicz, June 1, 1968; children: Christine Jennifer, Jonathan David. B.A., U. B.C., 1965; M.H.A., U. Ottawa, 1970. Asst. adminstr. Mississauga Hosp., Ont., Can., 1970-71; asst. exec. dir. Joseph Brant Meml. Hosp., Burlington, Ont., 1971-76, exec. dir., 1976-79; pres., chief exec. officer Royal Jubilee Hosp., Victoria, B.C., Can., 1979—; pres. B.C. Hosps. Shared Systems Soc., Vancouver, 1983—. Bd. dirs. United Way, Victoria, 1982-83, Boys and Girls Club, Victoria, 1981-83. Served to 1st lt. RCAF, 1965-68. Recipient Father Danis award U. Ottawa, 1970. Mem. Can. Coll. Health Service Execs., Brit. Coll. Health Assn., Ont. Hosp. Assn. Anglican. Office: Royal Jubilee Hosp 1900 Fort St Victoria BC Canada V8R 1J8

BUTCHER, WILLARD CARLISLE, banker; b. Bronxville, N.Y., Oct. 25, 1926; s. Willard F. and Helen (Calhoun) B.; m. Sarah C. Payne, Oct. 8, 1949; children: Sarah Carlisle, Helen Catherine; m. Elizabeth Allen, Jan. 28, 1956 (dec. Aug. 1978); children: Barbara Downs, John Carlisle; m. Carole E. McMahon, June 23, 1979; 1 son, Willard Carlisle. Student, Middlebury Coll., 1944; B.A., Brown U., 1947. With Chase Nat. Bank (now Chase Manhattan Bank), N.Y.C., 1947—, asst. treas., 1953-56, asst. v.p., 1956-58, v.p., 1958-60, sr. v.p., 1960-69, exec. v.p., 1969-72, vice chmn., 1972, pres., 1972-81, chmn., 1981—, chief exec. officer, 1980—; dir. ASARCO, Inc. Trustee Am. Enterprises Inst., Brown U. Served with USNR, 1944-46. Mem. Conf. Bd., Bus. Roundtable, Bus. Council, Phi Beta Kappa, Sigma Nu. Conglist. Clubs: Union League, Economic, Links (N.Y.C.); Blind Brook (Port Chester, N.Y.). Home: Wilton CT Office: 1 Chase Manhattan Plaza New York NY 10081

BUTCHKES, SYDNEY, artist; b. Covington, Ky., Oct. 13, 1922; s. Isadore and Bertha (Gussis) B. Student, Cin. Art Acad., 1936-40, Art Students League, N.Y.C., 1940-42, New Sch., N.Y.C., 1957-59. Exhibited one-man shows, Amel Gallery, N.Y.C., 1966, Bertha Schaefer Gallery, N.Y.C., 1969, 71, 73, Benson Gallery, Bridgehampton, N.Y., 1971, Alonzo Gallery, N.Y.C, 1978, Touchstone Gallery, N.Y.C., 1982, group shows, Mus. Modern Art, N.Y.C., 1964, San Francisco Mus., 1967, Inst. Contemporary Art, Boston, 1969;; exhibited group shows, Robert Elkon Gallery, N.Y.C., 1974, 76, 86, 79, Bklyn. Mus, Cin. Mus. Art, Wadsworth Atheneum, Hartford, Conn., Nat. Collection of Smithsonian Inst., Washington, Newark Mus. Served with AUS, 1942-45. Mem. Abstract Am. Artists. Home: Sagg Main St Sagaponack NY 11962

BUTCHVAROV, PANAYOT KRUSTEV, educator; b. Sofia, Bulgaria, Apr. 2, 1933; s. Krustyu Panayotov and Vanya (Tsaneva) B.; m. Sue Graham, Sept. 28, 1954; children: Vanya, Christopher. B.A., Robert Coll., Istanbul, 1952; M.A., U. Va., 1954, Ph.D., 1955. Instr. philosophy U. Balt., 1955-56; asst. prof. U. S.C., 1956-59; asso. prof. Syracuse U., 1959-66, prof., 1966-68; vis. prof. U. Iowa, 1967-68, prof., 1968—, chmn. dept. philosophy, 1970-77; vis. prof. U. Miami, Coral Gables, Fla., 1979-80; Simon lectr. U. Toronto, 1984. Author: The Concept of Knowledge, 1970, Resemblance and Identity, 1966, Being Qua Being, 1979, Midwest Studies in Philosophy; mem. editorial bd.: Philos. Monographs; contbr. numerous articles and revs. to profl. jours. Mem. Am. Philos. Assn. (chmn. program com. 1971, 75, mem. nominating com. 1978), Phi Beta Kappa. Home: 2507 Princeton Rd Iowa City IA 52240

BUTKUS, DICK, former professional football player, actor; b. Chgo., Dec. 9, 1942; m. Helen Butkus; children: Nicole, Richard, Matthew. Ed., U. Ill. With profl. football team Chgo. Bears, 1965-73. Named to Pro-Football Hall of Fame, 1979.

BUTLER, ARTHUR D., economics educator; b. Detroit, Oct. 13, 1923; s. Dwight and Gertrude Mae (Byers) B.; m. Kathleen Lehman, Sept. 3, 1945; children: Terese Kay, Pamela Ann, Sandra Sue. B.A., Manchester Coll., (North Manchester, Inc.), 1944; M.A., U. Minn., 1946; Ph.D., U. Wis., 1951. Lectr. U. Buffalo, 1949-52, asst. prof. econs., 1952-57, assoc. prof., 1957-61, prof., 1961—, acting dean, 1960-63; provost social studies SUNY-Buffalo, 1973-78; cons. U.S. Senate, Washington, 1976-78. Author: Labor Economics and Institutions, 1961, Impact of the Fiscal System, 1968, State and Local Government Payrolls, 1968; editor: Selections in Economics, 1958. Bd. dirs. Housing Opportunities Made Equal, Buffalo, 1983—. Recipient Outstanding Alumnus award Manchester Coll., 1982. Mem. Am. Econs. Assn., Indsl. Relations Research Assn., Econometric Soc., Fedn. Am. Scientists. Home: 32 Bernhardt Dr Apt 5 Amherst NY 14226 Office: SUNY 616 O'Brien Hall Amherst NY 14226

BUTLER, BROADUS NATHANIEL, university administrator; b. Mobile, May 28, 1920; s. John Nathaniel and Mary Lillian B.; m. Lillian P. Rutherford, Dec. 27, 1947; children—Bruce N., Janet Cecile (Mrs. Reid). B.A., Talladega (Ala.) Coll., 1941; M.A., U. Mich., 1947, Ph.D., 1952. Instr. philosophy St. Augustine's Coll., Raleigh, N.C., 1953; dean guidance, asst. prof. humanities Talladega Coll., 1953-56; grad. officer Coll. Liberal Arts, Wayne State U., 1957-68; asst. to dean, 1956-68, asst. to U.S. commr. edn., 1964-65, spl. asst. to asso. commr. for higher edn., 1965-66; dean Coll. Arts. and Scis., Tex. So. U., 1969; pres. Dillard U., New Orleans, 1969-73; dir. Office Leadership Devel. in Higher Edn., Am. Council on Edn., Washington, 1974-77; pres. Robert Russa Moton Meml. Inst., 1977-80; dir. Office Internat. Affairs and Research NAACP Spl. Contbn. Fund, 1981—; acad. v.p. U. D.C.; Dir. New Orleans br. Fed. Res. Bank Atlanta. Author, editor, lectr., research scholar. Mem. New Orleans Mayor's Com. on Internat. Trade Relations, La. Commn. for Performing Arts; commr. La. Ednl. TV Authority, La. Museum Commn.; adv. com. NSF; bd. dirs. Assn. Study Negro Life and History, NAACP, Nat. Merit Scholarship Corp., Internat. Trade Mart, New Orleans Philharmonic Soc., New Orleans Children's Bur., CEMREL St. Louis; trustee Lane Coll., Center for Study of the Presidency, N.Y.C., Internat. Inst. Public Mgmt. Served with USAAF, 1942-45. Named Citizen of Year Mich. Chronicle, 1962, Hon. Citizen New Orleans and Mobile, Ala.; recipient Social Action award Phi Beta Sigma, 1961, Pan-Africa Student Union Service award, 1963; decorated grand comdr. Order Star of Africa, Liberia; recipient numerous awards. Mem. NAACP (life), Assn. U.S. State Dept. (dir.), Nat. Urban League, New Orleans C. of C. (dir.), Hist. Soc. Mich., Am. Acad. Polit. and Social Sci., Assn. Fgn. Service (pub. mem. dir.), Am. Pub. Health Assn., Omega Psi Phi, Sigma Pi Phi., Phi Delta Kappa. Mem. Protestant Episcopal Ch. Clubs: Internat. House (New Orleans); Cosmos (Washington). Home: 10014 Branch View Ct Silver Spring MD 20903 Office: 4200 Connecticut Ave NW Washington DC 20008 *I have been blessed to have a happy, loving, and achieving family. In my personal and professional life, I have tried to be governed by and to sustain in my relationships to others the qualities of altruism and integrity. This has been both costly and rewarding—mostly rewarding, occasionally shattering. I shall continue to strive for those qualities, to pay the cost, to try to transmit the benefits to others, to enjoy the deeper satisfactions—and to hope that more and more others will share those with me.*

BUTLER, CHARLES FREDERICK, lawyer; b. Quincy, Mass., July 10, 1933; s. Percy and Ethel Garrett (Sutermeister) B.; m. Alice Ryan, June 21, 1959; children: Charles Frederick, Colin, Christopher, Alison. A.A., Boston U., 1957, A.B., 1959; J.D. with honors, George Washington U., 1964. Bar: Mass. bar 1965. Air transp. examiner CAB, 1959-63; adminstrv. asst. to Congressman Hastings Keith of, Mass., 1959-65; Washington rep. for internat. proc. Eastern Airlines, 1965-69; cons. to Spl. Asst. to Pres., Harry Flemming, 1969; U.S. rep. Internat. Civil Aviation Orgn., Montreal, 1969-71; dir. Bur. Internat. Affairs, CAB, Washington, 1971-74; pres. Butler Assocs., Inc., Washington, 1974-76, Air New Eng., Boston, 1976-80; mem. firm Hale Sanderson Byrnes & Morton, Boston, 1980—; lectr., external examiner McGill Inst. Air and Space Law. Author symposium report, article. Served with AUS, 1963-65. Recipient award of merit CAB, 1961. Mem. Nat. Aviation Club, Phi Delta Phi. Republican. Home: 136 Linden St South Hamilton MA 01982 Office: One Center Plaza Boston MA 02109

BUTLER, CHARLES M., III, federal agency official; b. Midland, Tex., Feb. 6, 1943; s. Charles M. and Marjorie Clare (Pundt) B.; m. Mary Evalyn Burke, Feb. 25, 1967; children: Evalyn Mary, Marjorie Clare, Anna Colleen. B.A., U. Houston, 1969; J.D., U. Tex., 1971. Bar: Tex. 1971. Assoc. Baker & Botts, Houston, 1971-73; chief legis. asst. U.S. Senator John Tower, Washington, 1974-75, adminstrv. asst., 1979-81; assoc. Kendrick, Kendrick & Bradley, Dallas, 1975-76; atty. Am. Natural Service Co., Detroit, 1976-79; chmn. FERC, Washington, 1981—. Served with U.S. Army, 1964-66. Mem. ABA, Tex. Bar Assn., D.C. Bar Assn., Mich. Bar Assn. Republican. Roman Catholic. Office: FERC 825 N Capitol St NE Washington DC 20426

BUTLER, CHARLES WILLIAM, clergyman; b. Dermott, Ark., May 4, 1922; s. George Jackson and Effie (Russell) B.; m. Helen Odean Scoggins, Aug. 26, 1946; children: Charles, Jr., Beverly, Keith, Kevin. B.A., Philander Smith Coll., 1939; B.D., Union Theol. Sem., 1949, M.Div., 1971; D.D., Interdenominational Theol. Ctr., Morehouse Sch. Religion, 1980, Birmingham Bapt. Bible Sch., 1980. Ordained to ministry Bapt. Ch. Asst. pastor St. James Presbyn. Ch., N.Y.C., 1947-50; released time tchr. N.Y.C. Mission Soc., 1950-51; tchr. Bapt. Center, N.Y.C., 1950-51; tchr. bibl. lit. and religion Morehouse Coll., Atlanta, 1951-54; pastor Met. Bapt. Ch., Detroit, 1954-63, New Calvary Bapt. Ch., 1963—; pres. Mich. Progressive Bapt. Conv., Detroit, 1962—; bd. dirs. Interdenominational Theol. Ctr., Atlanta, 1978—, Morehouse Sch. Religion, Atlanta; 1st v.p. Bapt. Pastor's Council, Detroit, 1983—; pres. Progressive Nat. Bapt. Conv., Washington, 1982—. Dir., organizer First Ind. Nat. Bank, Detroit, 1970; chmn. bd. Police Commn., City Detroit, 1976; mem. adv. bd. Mich. Consol. Gas Co., Detroit, 1980—. Served with U.S. Army, 1943-46; ETO. Named Man of Year Mich. Chronicle, 1962. Mem. Alpha Phi Alpha. Office: New Calvary Baptist Ch 3975 Concord St Detroit MI 48205

BUTLER, EDWARD LEE, retired publishing executive; b. Oklahoma City, Nov. 6, 1915; s. Oscar Edward and Gladys Marie (Dyke) B.; m. Mary-Jean Vecchio, June 26, 1965. B.A., U. Okla., 1935. With New Am. Library, Inc., N.Y.C., 1953-80, asst. sales mgr., 1953-60, v.p., gen. sales mgr., 1960-67, v.p. mktg., 1967-70, sr. v.p., 1970-72, exec. v.p., 1972-79, dir., 1967—; chmn. bd. Mac-Nal, 1975, 79; dir. Internat. Periodical Distbrs. Assn., 1971-79. Clubs: Lords Valley Country (pres., gov.), 25-Year (pres., adv.); Pinnacle Peak Country (Scottsdale, Ariz.)). Home: 8715 Via de La Luna Scottsdale AZ 85258

BUTLER, EDWARD SCANNELL, organization executive; b. New Orleans, Mar. 11, 1934; s. Edward Scannell and Unola (Perrin) B.; m. Elizabeth Gay Bringier Rivet, Dec. 30, 1957 (div. Jan. 1972); children: Edward Scannell IV, Nola Elizabeth, Matthew Franklin Thomson; m. Rosanne Marie Clarkston, Nov. 18, 1972 (div. 1981); children: Dawn Marie, Clarkston James. Student, Loyola U., New Orleans, 1955-57, Nat. Art Acad., Washington, 1959. Account exec. Brown-Friedman Advt., New Orleans, 1960; staff dir. Information Council of Ams., New Orleans, 1961-62, exec. v.p., 1963-69, communications v.p., 1970, exec. v.p., 1971-77, pres., 1978—, Scannell Assocs., Inc., 1967—; Sr. cons. to chmn. bd. Eversharp Inc., 1966-70, Technicolor Inc., 1966-70; speaker to nat. and local bus. edn. and profl. groups, also appearances on radio and TV, 1961—; Mem. nat. adv. com. Cold War Council, 1963-66; mem. adv. com. Friends of Free Asia, 1966-67; mem. adv. bd. Young Ams. for Freedom, 1967-69; Bd. dirs. World Youth Crusade for Freedom, 1967-68. Producer: record album Oswald: Self-Portrait in Red, 1964, Oswald Speaks, 1967; TV spl. Hitler in Havana!, 1967; host: Oswald: Self-Portrait, 1968; TV series The Square World of Ed Butler, 1969-70; host, exec. producer: Spirit '76, 1975-76; radio-TV series Spirit U.S; Author: Revolution Is My Profession, 1968; Contbr. articles to trade, profl. and popular publs. Served with AUS, 1957-59. Mem. Young Men's Bus. Club Greater New Orleans (def. bur. chmn. 1962, editor Action 1963, Americanism award 1963), New Orleans Jaycees (editor Forward 1963, Distinguished Service award, Outstanding Young Man in New Orleans award 1969), Am. Security Council (cold war victory com. 1966-68). Roman Catholic. Clubs: Bienville, Bogalusa Country. Office: care INCA 800 Audubon Bldg New Orleans LA 70112

BUTLER, EUGENE, editor, publisher; b. Starkville, Miss., June 11, 1894; s. Tait and Dell (Bell) B.; m. Mary Britt Burns, June 11, 1921; children: Eugene Britt, Mary Jean. B.S., Miss. Agrl. and Mech. Coll., (now Miss. State U.), 1913, Cornell U., 1915; M.S., Iowa State U., 1917. With Progressive Farmer, 1917—, editor Tex. edit., mgr. Dallas office, pres., 1953-68, chmn. bd. dirs., 1964—, now editor-in-chief; agrl. info. specialist M.S.A. trip to, Europe, 1952; mem. group educators and journalists selected by Carnegie Endowment for Internat. Peace to make goodwill trip to, S.Am., 1941. Bd. dirs. Hill Jr. Coll. History Complex. Recipient Hoblitzelle award for advancement Tex. rural life, 1953; award for outstanding contbn. to Tex. agr. Tex. Cottonseed Crushers Assn., 1957; award for profl. writers Am. Seed Trade Assn., 1961; Tex. Fedn. Co-ops. Agrl. Press award, 1962; Distinguished Service award Nat. Future Farmers Am., 1968; Farm Editor of Year award Tex. Farmers Union, 1975; Centennial award for outstanding contbns. to Tex. agr. Tex. A. and M. U., 1976; Distinguished Service award Miss. State U. Alumni Assn., 1978. Mem. Tex. Agrl. Workers Assn. (pres. 1940-41, Distinguished Service award 1978), Dallas Agrl. Club (pres. 1935), Tex. Forestry Assn., S.C.V., Phi Kappa Phi, Alpha Zeta, Sigma Delta Chi. Clubs: Dallas Hardware and Implement,

Ferndale Fishing. Home: 5514 Ursula Dallas TX 75229 Office: 3737 Noble Suite 390 Dallas TX 75204

BUTLER, FREDERICK GEORGE, retired drug company exective; b. Greenwich, Conn., Mar. 25, 1919; s. Harold Nassau and Rosa (Rhinhart) B.; m. Sarah Lou Allred, Sept. 23, 1945; children: Pamela Sue, Frederick Houston. A.B., Middlebury (Vt.) Coll., 1941; M.B.A., Columbia U., 1947. C.P.A., N.Y. With Price Waterhouse & Co. (C.P.A.'s), 1941-42, 47-49; with McKesson & Robbins, Inc., N.Y.C., 1949-63, asst. comptroller, 1952-61, comptroller, 1961-63; controller Bristol-Myers Co., N.Y.C., 1963-66, v.p., controller, 1966-69, v.p. ops., 1970-76. Village mayor, Briarcliff Manor, N.Y., 1969-71; treas., trustee Phelps Meml. Hosp., North Tarrytown, N.Y., 1976-78. Served to comdr. USNR, 1942-46, 51-52. Mem. Fin. Execs. Inst., Chi Psi. Congregationalist. Club: Marco Island (Fla.) Country. Charter mem. grocery ad hoc com., past chmn. Drug ad hoc com; co-developers compatible universal product code and nat. drug code for super market automated check out scanning and inventory control. Home: 58 N Collier Blvd Apt 2103 Marco Island FL 33937

BUTLER, GEORGE ANDREWS, banker; b. Westmont, N.J., Apr. 14, 1928; s. John T. and Kathryn B.; m. Barbara J. Thomas, June 17, 1950; children—Lynn B., William E. Thomas S., Pamela S. B.S. in Econs, U. Pa., 1950. With First Pa. Banking and Trust Co., 1950—, exec. v.p., 1968—, chief adminstrv. officer, 1976—; exec. v.p. First Pa. Corp., 1973-74, vice chmn., 1975—; also dir.; vice chmn., dir. First Pa. Bank, pres., chief operating officer, 1977—; chmn., pres., chief exec. officer First Pa. Corp., 1979—; dir. Gen. Accident Group Cos. Mem. adv. bd. Salvation Army; bd. dirs. Phila. council Boy Scouts Am. Served with AUS, 1946-47. Clubs: Union League, Mfrs. Golf and Country (Phila.). Home: Ambler PA Office: First Pennsylvania Bank Centre Sq W 39th Floor Philadelphia PA 19101

BUTLER, GEORGE HARRISON, lawyer; b. Jackson, Miss., Mar. 9, 1917; s. George H. and Mamie (Gardner) B.; m. Jean Word Baker, Aug. 25, 1951. B.A., U. Miss., 1938, LL.B. with distinction, 1940. Bar: Miss. bar 1940. Since practiced in, Jackson; partner firm Butler, Snow, O'Mara, Stevens and Cannada, 1954—. Served to capt. AUS, 1941-45. Mem. Am., Miss., Hinds County bar assns., Jackson C. of C., Omicron Delta Kappa, Phi Delta Phi, Sigma Chi. Methodist. Home: 4005 Old Canton Ln Jackson MS 39206 Office: Deposit Guaranty Plaza Jackson MS 39201

BUTLER, GORDON CECIL, biochemist; b. Ingersoll, Ont., Can., Sept. 4, 1913; s. Irvin and Edna M. (Harris) B.; m. Jean S. Meeke, July 3, 1937; children—Judith, Stephen, Gregory, Susan. B.A. in Physiology and Biochemistry, U. Toronto, Ont., 1935, Ph.D. in Biochemistry, 1938. Postdoctoral researcher U. London, 1938-40; research chemist Charles E. Frosst Co., Montreal, Que., Can., 1940-42; with Atomic Energy Project, NRC Can., 1945-47; prof. biochemistry U. Toronto, 1947-57; dir. div. biology and health physics Atomic Energy of Can. Ltd., Chalk River, Ont., 1957-65; dir. div. radiation biology NRC Can., Ottawa, Ont., 1965-68, div. biology, 1968-72, div. biol. scis., 1972-78, group dir., 1974-78, cons. div. biol. scis., Ottawa, 1978—; Can. del. UN Sci. Com. on Effects of Atomic Radiation, 1962-80; mem. coms. Internat. Commn. on Radiol. Protection, 1963-73, 73-77; chmn. com. UN Sci. Com. on Effects of Atomic Radiation, 1967-69; vice chmn. assoc. com. on sci. criteria for environ. quality NRC Can., 1970—, chmn. mgmt. subcom., 1974—, chmn. assoc. com. on toxicology, 1981—; vice-chmn. Can. Nat. Com. for Sci. Com. on Problems of Environment, Internat. Council Sci. Unions, 1972-78, chmn., 1978-82, editor report 12, 1978; vice chmn. exec. com. Sci. Group on Methodologies for Safety Evaluation Chems.; mem. sci. adv. com. UN Environment Programme, Internat. Register Potentially Toxic Chems., 1976-79. Contbr. numerous articles to profl. publs. Served to maj. Can. Army, 1942-45. Fellow AAAS, Royal Soc. Can. (pres. Acad. Sci. 1974-75); mem. Can. Soc. Cell Biology, Health Physics Soc., Can. Physiol. Soc., Can. Biochem. Soc. (pres. 1961-62), Am. Soc. Biol. Chemists, Soc. Internat. Devel., Can. Fedn. Biol. Socs. (chmn. bd. 1967-69), Assn. Advancement Sci. in Can., Internat. Acad. Environ. Safety, Internat. Found. Sci. (v.p. 1975-81, pres. 1982—). Home: 260 Sandridge Rd Ottawa ON K1L 5A2 Canada Office: Nat Research Council Can Ottawa ON K1A 0R6 Canada

BUTLER, JACK FAIRCHILD, laser co. exec.; b. El Centro, Calif., July 18, 1933; s. Jack Orval and Dorothy (Marsh) B.; m. Colette Alice Guerard, Sept. 6, 1959; children—Alice, Jack, Michael, Patricia. Student, San Jose State Coll., 1951-54; B.S., U. Calif., Berkeley, 1959, M.S., 1960, Ph.D., 1962. Research staff mem. Mass. Inst. Tech., Lincoln Lab., Lexington, Mass., 1962-68; staff scientist Gen. Dynamics Corp., Pomona, Calif., 1968-71; sr. staff mem. Arthur D. Little, Inc., Cambridge, Mass., 1971-74; co-founder, co-owner, dir., pres. Laser Analytics, Inc., Lexington, 1974-81; founder, owner, dir., pres. Butler Research and Engring., Inc., 1981—. Contbr. articles to sci. jours. Served with USMC, 1954-57. Mem. IEEE, Am. Inst. Physics, AAAS. Office: 38 Hartwell Ave Lexington MA 02173:

BUTLER, JACK LAWRENCE, newspaper editor; b. Seymour, Tex., Oct. 21, 1917; s. Wash Cain and Margaret (Lawrence) B.; m. Mary Lou Ford, Oct. 26, 1940; children—Lawrence Ford, Helen (Mrs. David Hays). B. Journalism, U. Tex., 1939. Mng. editor Tyler (Tex.) Morning Telegraph, 1940, Gladewater (Tex.) Times Tribune, 1941; news editor Austin (Tex.) Tribune, 1942; mem. staff Ft. Worth Star-Telegram, 1943-80, asst. mng. editor, 1958-63, editor, 1963-75, v.p., 1975-80; disting. prof. Tex. Christian U., 1978—. Chmn. adv. com. dept. communications Tex. Tech. U.; bd. dirs. Tex. Christian U. Research Found. Mem. Am. Soc. Newspaper Editors, A.P. Mng. Editors Assn., Sigma Delta Chi. Home: 1613 Scenery Hill Rd Fort Worth TX 76103 Office: 400 W 7th St Fort Worth TX 76102

BUTLER, JAMES H., educator; b. Cathlament, Wash., Dec. 16, 1908; s. Don Carlos and Maude (Kimball) B.; m. E. Willena Barnhart, June 5, 1937. A.B., Western Wash. Coll. Edn., 1937; A.M., U. So. Calif., 1939, Ph.D., 1948. Tchr. pub. schs., Kelso, Wash., 1934-38, Tulare (Calif.) Union High Sch., 1939-40; asst. prof. speech West Tex. State Coll., Canyon, 1940-42, 43-44, San Jose (Calif.) State Coll., 1945-46; asst. prof. drama U. So. Calif., Los Angeles, 1946-57, prof. drama, 1957-73, head dept. drama, 1953-70, Demille prof. drama, 1953-73, prof. emeritus, 1974—. Author: The Theatre and Drama of Greece and Rome, 1972; numerous filmstrips on history of theater; contbr. articles to theater jours. Served as pvt. U.S. Army, 1942-43. Recipient award of merit Am. Theatre Assn., 1973; award of excellence Am. Coll. Theatre Festival, 1972. Mem. Am. Ednl. Theater Assn. (fellow, pres. 1968), Nat. Coll. Players (past pres.), Western Speech Assn., Am. Legion, Blue Key, Phi Beta Kappa, Phi Kappa Phi, Phi Delta Kappa. Home: 5030 W Slauson Los Angeles CA 90056

BUTLER, JAMES NEWTON, chemist, educator; b. Cleve., Mar. 27, 1934; s. Clyde Henry and Margaret (Manor) B.; m. Nancy Elizabeth Close, Aug. 31, 1957 (div.); 1 son, Christopher J.; m. Rosamond Hatch Bee, Dec. 10, 1966; stepchildren: Alden G. Bee, Kenneth M. Bee. B.S. (Alumni scholar), Rensselaer Poly. Inst., 1955; Ph.D. (NSF fellow, Gen. Electric fellow), Harvard, 1959. Staff scientist NACA Lewis Lab., Cleve., summers 1952-57, Mass. Inst. Tech. Lincoln Lab., summer 1958; instr. U. B.C., Vancouver, 1959-61, asst. prof., 1961-63; sr. scientist Tyco Labs., Inc., Waltham, Mass., 1963-66, dept. head, 1966-71, cons., 1962-63, 71-73; lectr. Harvard, 1970-71, Gordon McKay prof. applied chemistry, 1971—, mem. faculty geol. scis., com. on oceanography, 1972—; Panel chmn., co-author report Petroleum in the Marine Environment, Nat. Acad. Scis.—NRC, 1973-75, 80-82; mem. tech. panel, report drafting com. Com. on Environ. Decision-Making, 1975-77; cons. EPA, 1978—, NOAA, 1981—. Author: Ionic Equilibrium, 1964, Solubility and pH Calculations, 1964, The Calculus of Chemistry, 1965, Problems for Introductory University Chemistry, 1967, Pelagic Tar from Bermuda and the Sargasso Sea, 1973, Carbon Dioxide Equilibria and their Applications, 1982, Studies of Sargassum and the Sargassum Community, 1983; Contbr. articles profl. jours. Trustee Bermuda Biol. Sta. NSF Faculty Sci. fellow, 1977. Mem. Am. Chem. Soc., AAAS, Am. Soc. Limnology and Oceanography, Internat. Soc. Electrochemistry, Electrochem. Soc. N.Y. (chmn. Boston sect.), Gordon Research Conf. on Electrochemistry (chmn.), Assn. Harvard Chemists (pres.), Sigma Xi, Phi Lambda Upsilon. Office: Pierce Hall 29 Oxford St Cambridge MA 02138

BUTLER, JEFFREY ERNEST, educator, historian; b. Cradock, S. Africa, Sept. 27, 1922; came to U.S., 1957, naturalized, 1966; s. Ernest Collett and Alice (Stringer) B.; m. Valerie Joy de la Harpe, Nov. 29, 1947; children—Katherine, Peter, Jonathan. B.A., Rhodes U., S. Africa, 1947; M.A., Oxford (Eng.) U., 1956, D.Phil., 1963. Tchr. Kingswood Coll., S. Africa, 1947-50; tutor Delegacy of Extra Mural Studies, Oxford U., 1953-57; research asso. African studies program Boston U., 1957-64; vis. asso. prof. history U. Calif. at Los Angeles, 1964; faculty Wesleyan U., Middletown, Conn., 1964—, prof. history, 1967—. Author: The Liberal Party and the Jameson Raid, 1968, (with Leonard Thompson) Change in Contemporary South Africa, 1975, (with Robert Rotberg and John Adams) The Black Homelands of South Africa, 1977. Served with S. African Army, World War II. Mem. African Studies Assn., Am. Hist. Assn. Home: 296 Pine St Middletown CT 06457

BUTLER, JOHN, physician, educator; b. Grantham, Eng., Nov. 28, 1923; came to U.S., 1960, naturalized, 1970; s. Percival Williamson and Eileen Mabel (O'Callaghan) B.; m. Sybil Worrall Durham, May 30, 1980; children: Joan, Malcolm, Sarah, James, Charles. M.B.Ch.B., U. Birmingham, Eng., 1946, M.D., 1957. Intern Queen Elizabeth Hosp., Birmingham, Eng., 1947, resident, 1953; intern Postgrad. Med. Sch., London, 1949; chief resident Birmingham United Hosps., 1953-55; research fellow, Rockefeller travelling fellow U. Pa. Hosp., Phila., 1957-59; sr. lectr. in medicine Manchester (Eng.) U., 1959-60; mem. staff cardiovascular research inst., assoc. clin. prof. U. Calif., San Francisco, 1960-65; prof. medicine, chief div. respiratory disease U. Wash., 1965—. Served to capt. Brit. Army, 1950-52. Fellow Royal Coll. Physicians (Edinburgh), Royal Coll. Physicians (London); Mem. Am. Physiol. Soc., Am. Soc. Clin. Investigation, Western Assn. Physicians. Mem. Ch. of England. Research in lung mechs., lung circulation. Home: 3403 Perkins Ln W Seattle WA 98199 Office: U of Wash Hosp Seattle WA 98105

BUTLER, JOHN MUSGRAVE, railroad exec.; b. Bklyn., Dec. 6, 1928; s. John Joseph and Sabina Catherine (Musgrave) B.; m. Ann Elizabeth Kelly, July 9, 1955; children: Maureen, John, Ellen, Suzanne. B.A. cum laude, St. John's U., 1950; M.B.A., N.Y. U., 1951. C.P.A., N.Y. Sr. accountant Lybrand, Ross Bros. & Montgomery (C.P.A.s), N.Y.C., 1953-59; sr. auditor ITT, N.Y.C., 1959-62; asst. to controller Dictaphone Corp., Bridgeport, Conn., 1962-63, controller, Bridgeport, Rye, N.Y., 1964-68; v.p. acctg. Chgo. & Northwestern Ry. Co., Chgo., 1968-69, v.p. fin. and acctg., 1969-72, Chgo. and Northwestern Transp. Co., Chgo., 1972-79, sr. v.p. fin. and acctg., 1979—, dir., 1976—, trustee, 1978-82. Served with USCGR, 1951-53. Mem. Assn. Am. R.R.s, Am. Inst. C.P.A.s, Fin. Execs. Inst. Roman Catholic. Office: Chicago and Northwestern Transportation Co 165 N Canal St Chicago IL 60606

BUTLER, KATHARINE GORRELL, speech pathologist educator; b. Chicago Heights, Ill., Mar. 15, 1925; d. Talbot John Howe and Katharine (Parmenter) Gorrell; m. Joseph Franklin Butler, Sept. 1, 1944; children: Katharine Marie Butler Nunes, Andrew Carlton, Paul Dean. B.A., Western Mich. U., 1950, M.A., 1953, Ed.S., 1961; Ph.D., Mich. State U., 1967. Sch. speech clinician, Portage and Vicksburg, Mich., 1950-52, Kalamazoo, 1954-58; asso. dir. Soc. for Better Hearing, Kalamazoo, 1953-54; pvt. practice speech pathology, Kalamazoo, 1953-64; asst. prof. psychology Western Mich. U., Kalamazoo, 1962-64; asst. prof. San Jose (Calif.) State U., 1964-68, asso. prof., 1968-69, prof., 1969—, dir. speech and hearing center, 1969—, chmn. dept. spl. edn., 1969-74, asso. dean, 1974-75, asso. dean grad. studies and research, 1975-77, acting dean, 1977-78; dir. div. spl. edn. and rehab. Syracuse (N.Y.) U., 1979-83, dir. research, 1983—; chmn. speech pathology and audiology exam. com. Calif. Bd. Med. Examiners, 1973-74, mem., 1973-79; cons. VA Hosp., Palo Alto, Calif., 1969—, HEW, Office of Edn., Bur. Edn. Handicapped. Author: (with C. VanRiper) Speech in the Elementary Classroom, 1955; editor: (with J. Wallach) Language Learning Disabilities in School Age Children, 1983, Topics in Lang. Disorders, 1980—; contbr. articles to profl. jours., chpts. to books. Bd. dirs. Eastfield Center for Emotionally Disturbed, 1964-66. Recipient Disting. Alumnae award Mich. State U. Coll. Communication, 1973, Western Mich. U., 1980; Japan Found. grantee, 1978. Fellow Am. Speech and Hearing Assn. (chmn. sci. and profl. meetings bd. 1974, chmn. conv. 1974, councilor from Calif. 1969-76, pres. 1978, chmn. asso. adv. bd. 1980); mem. Calif. Speech and Hearing Assn. (pres. 1970-71), Am. Psychol. Assn., Internat. Assn. Logopedics and Phonetics (pres. 1983—), Calif. Assn. Profs. Spl. Edn. (pres. 1974-75), Higher Edn. Consortium for Spl. Edn. (pres. 1981-83), Council Exceptional Children (pres. div. children with communication disorders 1977-78). Office: Syracuse Univ 411 Huntington Hall Syracuse NY 13210

BUTLER, LESLIE RICHARD, banker; b. Camden, N.J., Mar. 21, 1940; s. Charles Harvey and Anne Williams (Smith) B.; m. Geraldine Tepper, Aug. 8, 1981; children: Charles H., Lynda E. B.A. in History cum laude, Susquehanna U., 1962; M.B.A., Drexel U., 1970. With First Pa. Bank N.A., Phila., 1963—, asst. to vice chmn. real estate and consumer groups, 1973-74, sr. v.p., head consumer fin. dept., 1974-76, exec. v.p., group head consumer group, 1976-78, exec. v.p. group heald ops. group, 1978-80, group head adminstrv. services group, 1980-83, sr. exec. v.p., head consumer and banking services group, 1983—. Author: The Shopping Center as a Branch Bank Location, 1970; chmn. policy bd.: Jour. Retail Banking. Mem. pacesetter com. U.S. Pro Indoor Tennis Championships, 1976-80; mem. devel. com. Opera Co. Phila.; past pres. Pitman Bd. Edn., 1965-67; mem. council, youth group adv. St. James Lutheran Ch. Mem. Consumer Bankers Assn. (pres. 1979-80), Am. Bankers Assn., Bank Adminstrn. Inst. Home: 108 Burgundy Ct Wenonah NJ 08090 Office: 16th and Market Sts Centre Sq W 39th Floor Philadelphia PA 19101

BUTLER, LEWIS CLARK, univ. dean; b. Hornell, N.Y., July 11, 1923; s. H. McKey and Evelyn (Clark) B.; m. Margaret M. Kelley, June 19, 1948; children—Lewis Clark, Andrew McKey, Charles Kelley, Elizabeth Lee. B.A. cum laude, Alfred (N.Y.) U., 1944; M.S., Rutgers U., 1948; Ph.D., U. Ill., 1957. Research asst. Rutgers U., 1946-47; instr. math. Alfred U., 1947-49, prof. math., dean, 1963—; teaching asst. U. Ill., 1949-54; instr., then asst. prof. math. Pa. State U., 1954-57; asst. prof., then asso. prof. math State U. N.Y. Coll. Ceramics at Alfred, 1957-60; Dir. Inst. Central de Matematicas, U. Concepcion, Chile, 1960-63; cons. in field, 1964—. Served with AUS, 1944-46; ETO. Decorated Bronze Star. Mem. Am. Math. Soc., Delta Sigma Phi, Phi Kappa Phi. Club: Mason. Home: 8 Terrace St Alfred NY 14802

BUTLER, MANLEY CALDWELL, lawyer; b. Roanoke, Va., June 2, 1925; s. W.W.S. Butler Jr.; m. June Nolde, June 26, 1950; children: Manley, Henry, James, Marshall. A.B., U. Richmond, 1948; J.D., U. Va., 1950. Bar: Va. Mem. Va. Ho. Dels., 1962-72, minority leader, 1966-72; mem. 92d-97th Congresses from 6th Va. Dist., Judiciary Com., Com. on Govt. Ops.; mem. firm Woods, Rogers, Muse, Walker & Thornton, 1983—. Mem. Va. State Bar, Am., Roanoke bar assns., Raven Soc., Order of the Coif, Phi Beta Kappa, Tau Kappa Alpha, Omicron Delta Kappa, Phi Gamma Delta. Episcopalian. Home: 845 Orchard Rd SW Roanoke VA 24014 Office: PO Box 720 Roanoke VA 24004

BUTLER, MARGARET KAMPSCHAEFER, computer scientist; b. Evansville, Ind., Mar. 7, 1924; s. Otto Louis and Lou Etta (Rehsteiner) Kampschaefer; m. James W. Butler, Sept. 30, 1951; 1 son, Jay. A.B., Ind. U., 1944; postgrad., U.S. Dept. Agr. Grad. Sch., 1945, U. Chgo., 1949, U. Minn., 1950. Statistician U.S. Bur. Labor Statistics, Washington, 1945-46, U.S. Air Forces in Europe, Erlangen and Wiesbaden, Germany, 1946-48; statistician U.S. Bur. Labor Statistics, St. Paul, 1949-51; mathematician Argonne (Ill.) Nat. Lab., 1948-49, 51-80, sr. computer scientist, 1980—; dir. Nat. Energy Software Center, Dept. Energy Computer Program Exchange, 1960—; cons. AMF Corp., 1956-57, OECD, 1964, Poole Bros., 1967. Editor: Computer Physics Communications, 1969-80; Contbr.: chpt. to The Application of Digital Computers to Problems in Reactor Physics, 1968, Advances in Nuclear Science and Technology, 1976; also articles to profl. publs. Treas. Timberlake Civic Assn., 1958; rep. mem. nominating com. Hinsdale (Ill.) Caucus, 1961-62; coordinator 6th dist. Equal Rights Amendment, 1973-82; del. Republican Nat. Conv. Fellow Am. Nuclear Soc. (mem. publs. com. 1965-71, chmn. math and computation div. 1966-67, dir. 1976-79, exec. com. 1977-78, chmn. bylaws and rules com. 1979-82, reviewer for publs.); mem. Assn. Computing Machinery (exec. com., sec. Chgo. chpt. 1963-65, publs. chmn. nat. conf. 1968, reviewer for publs.). Home: 17W139 Hillside Ln Hinsdale IL 60521 Office: 9700 S Cass Ave Argonne IL 60439 *My goal is the removal of barriers restricting individuals from achieving their full potential and the furtherance of individual rights.*

BUTLER, MICHAEL, producer, development company executive; b. Chgo., Nov. 26, 1926; s. Paul Butler. Ed., U. Colo. V.p. Butler Co.; pres. Butler Communications Corp.; exec. v.p., dir. Butler Engring. & Constrn., Butler Overseas; pres. Oak Brook Devel. Co., Butler Devel. Co.; chmn. Michael Butler Assocs., Natoma Prodns., Inc., Talisman Co.; dir. Butler Paper Corp., Internat. Sports Core, Basic Investment Corp., J.W. Butler Paper Co. Chgo., Intrafi, Overseas Bank Ltd., Oak Brook Utility, Drake Oak Brook Hotel, Oak Brook Landscaping, Ondine Inc. (land devels.), Oak Brook, Sugarbush, Talisman; coal washeries in, India, Dugda I and II, Petherdi; former civic chancellor Lincoln Acad.; pres. Orgn. Econ. Devel.; dir., commr. Chgo. Regional Port Dist.; spl. adviser on India and Middle East affairs to Senator John F. Kennedy. World producer: play Catonsville 9, Hair, motion picture, You Are What You Eat. Pres. Ill. Sports Council. Decorated Order of Lincoln, Order Sword and Cutlass Soc. Colonial Wars. Mem. Oceanographic Inst., Chgo. Hist. Soc., English Speaking Union, Chgo. Natural History Mus., U.S. Polo Assn. (gov.). Clubs: Racquet, Arts (Chgo.); Oak Brook Polo (gov.); Racquet and Tennis, Explorers, Knickerbocker (N.Y.C.); Talisman Corinthian Yacht (Port Antonio) (vice commodore); Guards Polo (U.K.)). Address: Natoma Oak Brook IL 60521 *

BUTLER, NATALIE STURGES (MRS. BENJAMIN BUTLER), author, historian; b. Melrose, Mass., July 13, 1908; d. Dwight Case and Clare (Vaughan) Sturges; m. Benjamin Butler, May 23, 1932; children—Diane-Clare Butler Brinkman, Benjamin Sturges. Student, Vesper George Art Sch., 1926-28; M.A. (hon.), U. Maine at Farmington, 1972. Librarian, decorator Irving & Casson-A. H. Davenport Co., Boston, 1928-31; pres. Sturdia Corp., Farmington, Maine, 1955—; Franklin County chmn. Maine Sesquicentennial, 1970; sec. Maine Citizens for Historic Preservation, 1971, trustee, 1976—; mem. Maine State Mus. Commn., 1974-77. Author: (with Ben Butler) History of Old South Church, Farmington, Maine, 1966, Little Red Schoolhouse, 1971, Dwight C. Sturges: Etcher of an Era, 1974, (with Ben Butler, Don McKeen) Zephaniah Builds a Schoolhouse—Among Other Things!, 1975, (with Ben Butler) Farmington's Musical Heritage, 1975, The Falls: Where Farmington, Maine, Began in 1776, 1976, also Pilgrimage booklets for hist. soc. and articles. Trustee Farmington Pub. Library Assn., 1950—, treas., 1958-74, sec., 1958-77; trustee Franklin County Meml. Hosp., 1963-70; mem. Maine League Hist. Socs. and Museums, 1964—, trustee, 1973-77; curator Red Schoolhouse Mus., 1972—. Recipient certificate of commendation Am. Assn. State and Local History, 1970; Historic Preservation award Maine Historic Preservation Commn., 1972. Mem. Maine Soc. Mayflower Descs., Maine Hist. Soc., John Howland Soc., New Eng. Historic Geneal Soc., Delta Kappa Gamma (Hon.). Republican. Congregationalist (deaconess 1963-68). Home: 93 Main St Farmington ME 04938 *I discovered years ago the necessity of choosing carefully the most important steps to follow to achieve one's goals, but I've never really adhered to that discovery. My goals have always been too ambitious, too varied, too time-consuming, but there's never been a dull or boring moment. That's the way I hope it always will be.*

BUTLER, OWEN BRADFORD, household products company executive; b. Lynchburg, Va., Nov. 11, 1923; s. James Herbert and Ida Virginia (Garbee) B.; m. Erna Bernice Dalton, Mar. 7, 1945; children: Nancy (Mrs. Curt Brown), James. A.B., Dartmouth Coll., 1947. With Procter & Gamble Co., Cin., 1945—, v.p. sales, 1968-70, v.p., group exec., 1970-73, exec. v.p., 1973-74, vice chmn. bd., 1974-81, chmn. bd., 1981—. Trustee Good Samaritan Hosp.; bd. overseers Tuck Sch. Served with USNR, 1941-45, 50-51. Mem. Com. Econ. Devel. (research and policy com.), Phi Beta Kappa. Republican. Clubs: Queen City (Cin.); Metropolitan (Washington). Home: 4346-S State Route 123 Morrow OH 45152 Office: PO Box 599 Cincinnati OH 45201

BUTLER, RHETT WHEELER, publishing company executive; b. Oak Park, Ill., 1940; married. B.A., DePauw U., 1962; M.B.A., Northwestern U., 1964. Sales mgr. Goodyear Tire and Rubber Co., 1964-68; dir. world trade div. Chgo. Assn. Commerce, 1968-71; pres., chief exec. officer Unistruct Corp., 1971-74; v.p. bldg. systems group GTE Sylvania, 1974-78; pres., chief exec. officer GTE Directories Corp., Des Plaines, Ill., 1978—, dir.; pres., dir. Directorio Telefonico Centroamericano S.A., Dominion Directory Co. Ltd., St. Petersburg Printing Co., Directories (Australia) Pty. Ltd., Courtnay's Pty. Ltd. Office: GTE Directories Corp 1865 Miner Des Plaines IL 60016 *

BUTLER, RICHARD COLBURN, banker, lawyer; b. Little Rock, Jan. 1, 1910; s. R. Colburn and Edna (Clok) B.; m. Gertrude Remmel, Mar. 7, 1936; 1 son, Richard Colburn. Student, Little Rock Jr. Coll., 1929; A.B., U. Ark., 1931; LL.D. (hon.), Hendrix Coll. Bar: Ark. bar 1933, U.S. Supreme Ct. bar 1933. Gen. practice law, Little Rock, 1933-63; partner firm House, Holmes, Butler & Jewell, 1941-63; pres., chmn. bd. Comml. Nat. Bank Little Rock, 1963-80, sr. chmn., 1980—; pres., dir. Ark. Nat. Stockyards Co., 1958-78, First Ark. Devel. Finance

Corp.; chmn., dir. Little Rock Abstract Co., 1974-81; chmn. Peoples Savs. & Loan Assn., Little Rock; dir. Kin-Ark Corp., Tulsa, Coca Cola Bottling Co. Ark., Indsl. Devel. Co. of Little Rock. Pres. bd. trustees Little Rock U., 1961-63; bd. dirs. Little Rock Boys Club, pres., 1960; nat. assoc. for Ark. Boys Clubs America, 1964-74; mem. Pillars Club, United Way Pulaski County; trustee Hendrix Coll., Conway, Ark., 1969-81. Served to maj. USAAF, 1942-46; CBI. Decorated Bronze Star. Mem. Am. Judicature Soc., Am., Ark. bar assns., Am. Hemerocallis Soc., Am. Iris Soc. (life, regional v.p. 1960-61), Bookfellows (pres. 1961), Little Rock C. of C. (pres. 1952). Methodist (chmn. bd. trustees). Clubs: Kiwanis, Little Rock Country, Little Rock, XV; Union League (Chgo.). Home: 36 River Ridge Rd Little Rock AR 72207 Office: 123 W 3d St Little Rock AR 72201 *To some, the acquisition of great material wealth, or appearing in "Who's Who" is "success." Fortunately, there are many who still believe that a person is successful if he has "lived well, laughed often and loved much," and who recognize that "Success is in the silences, though fame is in the song."*

BUTLER, RICHARD DEAN, interior designer; b. Lansing, Mich., May 27, 1930; s. Robert Edmond and Grace Marie (Laycock) B. B.A., Mich. State U., 1953; postgrad., Chgo. Acad. Fine Art, 1958, Sch. of Art Inst. Chgo., 1959. With Sears Roebuck & Co., 1948-71, nat. dir. design and home furnishings coordinator, 1959-71; prin. Richard Butler Assos. (design, merchandising, color cons.), Chgo., 1971—; also House Store, Chgo.; mem. industry com. interior design program William Rainey Harper Coll.; exec. sec. Decorative Arts Personnel Agy.; chair holder Color Mktg. Group. Fellow Am. Soc. Interior Designers. Home and office: 548 W Belden St Chicago IL 60614

BUTLER, ROB WILLIAM, company executive; b. London, Apr. 21, 1930; m. Mary Frances Elizabeth Butler, Nov. 21,, 1959; children: Michael, James, Millicent, Katherine, William. Chartered acct., Clarks Coll., Romford, Essex, Eng., 1947. Systems cons. Haskins & Sells, Chile, 1955-57; pub. acct. Clare Henning Co., Toronto, Ont., Can., 1957; comptroller Glidden Co., Ltd., Toronto, 1958-68; treas. SCM Can. Ltd., Toronto, 1968-73; comptroller The de Havilland Aircraft of Can. Ltd., Downsview, Ont., 1973-80, v.p. fin. and adminstrn., 1980. Mem. Air Industries Assn. Can. (contracts and fin. com. 1973—, chmn. 1980). Home: 47 Colin Ave Toronto ON Canada M5P 2B8 Office: The de Havilland Aircraft of Can Ltd Garratt Blvd Downsview ON Canada M3K 1Y5

BUTLER, ROBERT ALLAN, psychologist, educator; b. Pittsfield, Mass., Mar. 29, 1923; s. Thomas Arthur and Beulah Adeline (Combs) B.; m. Caroline Laura Emery, Jan. 19, 1952; children—Amy, Ann, Catherine, Elizabeth. B.A., U. Fla., 1947; Ph.D., U. Chgo., 1951. Instr. dept. psychology U. Wis., Madison, 1951-53; research psychologist Walter Reed Army Hosp., Washington, 1953-57, research asso., 1957-65; assoc. prof. depts. behavioral scis. and surgery U. Chgo., 1965-72, prof., 1972—, chmn. dept. behavioral scis., 1979-82, acting chmn. sect. otolaryngology dept. surgery, 1983—; vis. prof. Erlangen (W. Ger.) U., 1966-68. Contbr. articles to profl. jours. Served with U.S. Navy, 1943-46. Mem. Acoustical Soc. Am., Assn. for Research in Otolaryngology (past pres.), Psychonomics Soc., Midwestern Psychol. Assn. Office: 5848 S University Ave Chicago IL 60637

BUTLER, ROBERT CLIFTON, broadcasting co. exec.; b. Newark, Aug. 29, 1930; s. Thomas C. and Helen V. (Woods) B.; m. Eileen Hudson, Apr. 14, 1956; children—Christopher R., John H., Thomas C. B.S.C., U. Notre Dame, 1952; M.B.A., Wharton Sch. U. Pa., 1956. Dir. planning Gen. Telephone & Electronics Internat., 1965-66; v.p., treas. Isotopes Inc., 1966-67; sr. v.p., controller Inmont Corp., 1967-72; v.p. financial analysis RCA, 1972-76, v.p., controller, 1976-79; exec. v.p. fin. NBC, 1979—. Served with AUS, 1954-55. Home: 146 Rensselaer Rd Essex Fells NJ 07021 Office: 30 Rockefeller Plaza New York NY 10020

BUTLER, ROBERT GEORGE, III, lawyer, business exec.; b. Ft. Mills, Philippines, June 6, 1930; s. Robert George, Jr. and Mary Adeline (Wood) B.; m. Barbara June Barker, Aug. 27, 1955; children—David N., Susan R., Karen L., Deborah L. B.A., Haverford (Pa.) Coll., 1952; J.D., U. Mich., 1957. Bar: N.Y. bar 1957, N.J. bar 1968. Asso. firm Shearman, Sterling & Wright, N.Y.C., 1957-61; with Becton, Dickinson and Co., Paramus, N.J., 1962—, asst. gen. counsel, asst. sec., 1969-77, sec., 1977—. Mem. Am. Bar Assn., Am. Soc. Corp. Secs., N.J. Bar Assn. Office: Becton Dickinson & Co Mack Centre Dr Paramus NJ 07652

BUTLER, ROBERT NEIL, gerontologist, psychiatrist, writer, educator; b. N.Y.C., Jan. 21, 1927; s. Fred and Easter (Dikeman) B.; m. Diane McLaughlin, Sept. 2, 1950; children: Ann Christine, Carole Melissa, Cynthia Lee; m. Myrna I. Lewis, May 19, 1975; 1 dau., Alexandra Nicole. B.A., Columbia U., 1949, M.D., 1953. Intern St. Lukes Hosp., N.Y.C., 1953-54; resident U. Calif. Langley Porter Clinic, 1954-55, NIMH, 1955-56, research psychiatrist, 1955-62; founder geriatric unit Chestnut Lodge, 1958, adminstr., 1958-59; research psychiatrist Washington Sch. Psychiatry, 1962-76; dir. Nat. Inst. on Aging, NIH, 1976-82; Brookdale prof. geriatics and adult devel. Mt. Sinai Sch. Medicine, N.Y.C., 1982; mem. faculty George Washington U. Med. Sch., Washington, 1962—, Howard U. Sch. Medicine; cons. NIMH, 1967-76, U.S. Senate Spl. Com. on Aging. (Recipient Pulitzer prize for gen. nonfiction 1976); Author: (with others) Human Aging, 1963, (with Myrna I. Lewis) Aging and Mental Health, 1973, Why Survive? Being Old in America, 1975, Sex After Sixty, 1976; Mem. editorial bd.: Jour. Geriatric Psychiatry, Aging and Human Development; Contbr. articles to publs. Sec. Nat. Ballet of Washington, 1962-75; chmn. D.C. Advisory Commn. on Aging, 1969-72; bd. dirs. Nat. Council on Aging. Served with U.S. Maritime Service, 1945-47. Leo Laks award, 1976; McIntyre award, 1977; others. Fellow Am. Psychiat. Assn., Am. Geriatrics Soc. (founding mem.); mem. Group for Advancement Psychiatry (trustee 1974-76), Gerontol. Soc., Forum for Profls. and Execs. (founding). Club: Cosmos (Washington). Home: 3815 Huntington St NW Washington DC 20015 Office: Nat Inst on Aging NIH Bldg 31 Room 5L02 9000 Rockville Pike Bethesda MD 20014 *To always stretch the limits of the possible through personal relationships, scholarship, science, writing, action and political activism. To work toward making life a work of art. To do no harm.*

BUTLER, ROBERT THOMAS, advt. exec.; b. Westmont, N.J., Feb. 22, 1925; s. John T. and Kathryn M. (Donehower) B.; m. Eleanore MacIndoe, May 4, 1950; children—R. Mark, Kathryn J., Elizabeth Anne. B.S., Temple U., Phila., 1951. Market research mgr. James Lees Carpet Co., 1951-53; v.p. N.W. Ayer ABH Internat., Phila., 1953-74; pres. Gray & Rogers, Inc., Phila., 1974—. Vestryman St. Martin's Ch., Radnor, Pa. Served with USCG, 1943-46. Republican. Episcopalian. Clubs: Racquet (Phila.); St. David's (Pa.) Golf. Office: 1234 Market St Philadelphia PA 19107

BUTLER, ROY FRANCIS, educator; b. Atlanta, May 4, 1914; s. Roy Edward and Mae (Kenner) B.; m. Barbara Goehring Scott, Nov. 17, 1943; children—Roy Francis, John Scott. A.B. (Chattanooga Times scholar), U. Chattanooga, 1935; M.A. (Latin scholar), U. Tenn., 1938; Ph.D. (Univ. scholar), Ohio State U., 1942. Instr. U. Tenn., 1946, Ohio State U., 1946-47; asst. prof. U. Tenn., 1947, 48, Baylor U., 1947-49, faculty, Waco, Tex., 1947—, prof. classics, 1952—, chmn. dept. classics, 1958—. Author: Vocabulary Building Through Etymology, 1948, Handbook of Medical Terminology, 1957, 71, The Meaning of Agapao and Phileo in the Greek Testament, 1977; editorial cons.: Dorland's Illustrated Medical Dictionary, 1965, 74; contbr. articles to profl. jours. Served with USAAF, 1942-45. Mem. Am. Philol. Assn., Linguistic Soc. Am., Am. Oriental Soc., Classical Assn. Middle West and South, N.Y. Acad. Scis., AAAS, Mensa, Phi Kappa Phi, Blue Key. Home: 2613 Starr Dr Waco TX 76710

BUTLER, SAMUEL COLES, lawyer; b. Logansport, Ind., Mar. 10, 1930; s. Melvin Linwood and Jane Levinia (Flynn) B.; m. Sally Eugenia Thackston, June 28, 1952; children: Samuel Coles, Leigh F., Elizabeth J. B.A. magna cum laude, Harvard U., 1951, LL.B., 1954. Bar: D.C. 1954, Ind. 1954, N.Y. 1957. Law clk. to Justice Minton U.S. Supreme Ct., 1954; assoc. Cravath, Swaine & Moore, N.Y.C., 1956-60, ptnr., 1961—; dir. Ashland Oil, Inc., Geico Corp.; trustee U.S. Trust Co. N.Y. Trustee Vassar Coll., 1969-77, N.Y. Pub. Library, 1979—; chmn. Harvard Coll. Fund.; bd. overseers Harvard U., 1982—; bd. dirs. Culver Ednl. Found., 1981—. Served with U.S. Army, 1954-56. Mem. Council Fgn. Relations. Home: 1200 Park Ave New York NY 10128 Office: Carvath Swaine & Moore 1 Chase Manhattan Plaza New York NY 10005

BUTLER, THOMAS WARWICK, JR., engring. co. exec.; b. Niagara Falls, N.Y., Oct. 9, 1922; s. Thomas Warwick and Genevieve Margaret (Casey) B.; m. Jeanne E. Lindsey, Aug. 24, 1950; 1 son, Thomas W. B.S., M.S., U. Mich., Ph.D., 1961. Research asso. U. Mich., Ann Arbor, 1951-54, research engr., 1960-62, asso. research engr., 1954-60; dir. engring. and research Mech. Products, Inc., Jackson, Mich., 1962-65; asso. prof., dir. Cooley Electronics Lab., U. Mich., 1965-70, dir., prof., 1970-74; v.p., corp. officer engring. and research AMF, Inc., White Plains, N.Y., 1974—; dir. Fed. Screw Works, Detroit, 1978—; chmn. adv. bd. Applied Research Lab., Pa. State U., 1976—; chmn. Nat. Engring. Consortium seminar on product planning, 1978-79; spl. cons. to dir. NSF, 1975; vis. prof. Mich. State U., 1973; advisor fgn. tech. div. USAF, 1962-65. Author book. Served with USAAF, 1942-45. Mem. N.Y. Zool. Soc., Indsl. Research Inst., IEEE, Am. Soc. Engring. Edn., Soc. Profl. Engrs., Sci. Research Club. Clubs: Greenwich Country, Indian Harbor Yacht; Seabrook Island (Charleston, S.C.). Patentee in field. Home: 9 Joshua Ln Greenwich CT 06830 Office: 777 Westchester Ave White Plains NY 10604

BUTLER, VINCENT PAUL, JR., physician, educator; b. Jersey City, N.J., Feb. 16, 1929; s. Vincent Paul and Ruth Eilene (Lynch) B. A.B., St. Peter's Coll., 1949; M.D., Columbia U., 1954. Intern Presbyn. Hosp., N.Y.C., 1954-55, resident, 1955-56, 58-59, asst. physician, 1963-68, asst. attending physician, 1968-71, asso. attending physician, 1971-74, attending physician, 1974—; trainee clin. immunology U. Rochester Med. Center, 1959-61; research fellow immunochemistry dept. microbiology Columbia U., 1961-63, asst. prof. medicine, 1963-70, assoc. prof., 1970-74, prof., 1974—; asst. vis. physician 1st med. div. Bellevue Hosp., N.Y.C., 1963-68, Harlem Hosp., 1968—; mem. VA Merit Rev. Bd. in Immunology, 1974-77, chmn., 1976-77; mem. immunol. sci. study sect. NIH, 1979-83, chmn., 1980-83. Served as lt., M.C. USN, 1956-58. Helen Hay Whitney Found. fellow, 1960-63; Arthritis Found. investigator, 1963-68; Josiah Macy, Jr. Found. scholar dept. zoology Univ. Coll., London, 1979-80; recipient Research Career Devel. award NIH, 1968-73; Joseph Mather Smith prize Columbia U. Coll. Physicians and Surgeons, 1973; Irma T. Hirschl Charitable Trust Career Scientist, 1973-78. Mem. Assn. Am. Physicians, Am. Soc. Clin. Investigation, Am. Assn. Immunologists, Am. Soc. Pharmacology and Exptl. Therapeutics, Am. Heart Assn., N.Y. Heart Assn., Internat. Soc. Thrombosis and Haemostasis, Am. Fedn. Clin. Research, Am. Rheumatism Assn., Harvey Soc. Roman Catholic. Home: 301 E 66th St New York NY 10021 Office: 630 W 168th St New York NY 10032

BUTLER, WENDELL PACE, former state official; b. Sulphur Well, Ky., Dec. 18, 1912; s. Henry and Pearl (Pace) B.; m. Edna Ford, Jan. 15, 1947; children—Rendell and Kendell (twins), Wendell Ford. A.B., Western Ky. State Coll., 1936; M.A., U. Ky., 1950, postgrad., 1951. Tchr. pub. schs., Metcalfe County, Ky., 1931-36, supt. schs., 1938-42; supt. pub. instrn. Ky. Dept. Edn., 1952-55, 60-63; commr. agr. Commonwealth of Ky., 1964-67, 72-75; sec. Edn. and Arts Cabinet, 1976-80, supt. pub. instruction, 1968-71; pres., mgr. Sch. Service Co., Frankfort, Ky., 1956-59. Mem. state senate Ky., 1948-51, mem. com. on edn., 1950. Served with USNR, World War II. Mem. Nat., Ky. edn. assns., Farm. Bur., Am. Legion, Vets. Fgn. Wars, Phi Delta Kappa, Kappa Delta Pi. Methodist. Club: Mason. Home: 121 Crittendon Rd Frankfort KY 40601

BUTLER, WILFORD ARTHUR, association executive; b. Grand Rapids, Mich., Apr. 17, 1937; s. Wilford A. and Dorothy (French) B. B.A., Western Mich. U., 1961; M.B.A., Fla. Atlantic U., 1977. Dir. pub. relations Preferred Ins. Co., Grand Rapids, 1961-62; asst. to chmn. Delta Upsilon Fraternity, N.Y.C., 1962, exec. sec., Indpls., 1963-74, exec. dir., 1974—, Delta Upsilon Ednl. Found., 1979—; chmn. Interfraternity Inst., Ind. U., 1970-74. Editor: Our Record, 1963-80. Mem. steering com. Am. Coll. Fraternity Bicentennial, 1976—; Bd. dirs. Greater Indpls. Republican Fin. Com.; bd. dirs. Indpls. Conv. and Visitors Assn. Named Sagamore of the Wabash. Mem. Am. Assn. Coll. Fraternities (past pres.), Fraternity Execs. Assn. (pres. 1976—), Commn. on Fraternity Research (past treas.), Am. Soc. Assn. Execs. (adv. bd. communications sect. 1977-79, pres. elect 1982-83), Ind. Soc. Assn. Execs. (chmn. cert. study com. 1979-80, editor monthly newsletter Spotlight 1979-81, mem. exec. com. 1980-81), Delta Upsilon (editor quar. 1973—). Club: Columbia (Indpls.) (sec., dir.). Office: PO Box 40108 Indianapolis IN 46240

BUTLER, WILLIAM JOSEPH, lawyer; b. Brighton, Mass., Mar. 22, 1924; s. Patrick Lawrence and Delia (Conley) B.; m. Jane Hays, Dec. 22, 1945; children: Arthur Hays, Patricia. Student, Harvard U., 1946, N.Y. U. Sch. Law, 1949. Bar: N.Y. 1950. Asso. firm Hays, St. John, Abramson & Schulman, N.Y.C., 1949-53; partner firm Butler, Jablow & Geller, N.Y.C., 1953—; spl. counsel ACLU; lectr. Practising Law Inst., 1966; sec., dir., gen. counsel Walco Nat. Corp., FAO Schwarz, N.Y.C. Author: Human Rights and the Legal System in Iran, 1976, The Decline of Democracy in the Philippines, 1977, Human Rights in United States and United Kingdom Foreign Policy; contbr. articles to profl. jours. Mem. commn. on urban affairs Am. Jewish Congress, 1965-70; bd. dirs. N.Y. Civil Liberties Union, Internat. League for Rights of Man; mem. exec. com. League to Abolish Capital Punishment; standing com. on human rights World Peace Through Law Center, Geneva.; chmn. adv. com. Morgan Inst. for Human Rights, U. Cin Sch. Law. Served with U.S. Mcht. Maritime Service, 1942-45. Recipient spl. citation for contbn. to cause of religious freedom, 1962. Mem. Internat. Commn. Jurists (Geneva) (chmn. exec. com., dir., pres. Am. assn., UN rep.), Am. Bar Assn., Assn. Bar City N.Y. (chmn. com. internat. human rights), Council Fgn. Relations, Inter-Am. Assn. Democracy and Freedom, Internat. Law Assn. (Am. br.), Am. Soc. Internat. Law. Clubs: Harvard (N.Y.C.); (Boston). Internat. legal observer Internat. Human Rights Orgn. at trials in Greece, Burundi, Iran, Nicaragua, South Korea, Philippines, and Israel and confs. and seminars in France, Geneva and USSR. Home: 24 E 10th St New York NY 10003 Office: 400 Madison Ave New York NY 10017

BUTLER, WILLIAM ROBERT, university administrator; b. Robinson, Ill., May 10, 1926; s. George Edward and Blondell Etelka (Smith) B.; m. Virginia Lou Ault, Aug. 18, 1951; children—Michael Allan, Barbara Lou, Jennifer Ann, Rebecca Joan. B.S. in Edn, Ohio U., 1950, M.A., 1951; Ed.D., U. Kans., 1956. Teaching fellow human relations U. Kans., 1951-52, research asst., 1952-54, asst. dean men, internat. student adviser, 1953-57; research psychologist USAF, Topeka, summer 1953; dean men, asst. prof. student affairs U. Wis., 1957-59; asst. prof. human relations Ohio U., Athens, 1959-62, dean of men, 1959-62, dean students, 1962-65; v.p. student affairs, prof. edn. U. Miami, 1965—; Corp. officer, pres. WVUM Radio Sta., Coral Gables, Fla., 1965—; pres. Univ. Rathskeller, Inc., 1972—; dir. Central Nat. Bank Miami, 1978; cons. North Central Assn. Colls. and Secondary Schs., 1958-65, So. Assn. Colls. and Secondary Schs., 1965—; research cons. Am. Bar Assn., 1963-65; pres. House Corp. Sigma Chi, Athens, 1959-65. Adv. bd.: Coll. Student Personnel Abstracts, 1972—; editorial bd.: Jour. Coll. Student Personnel, 1973-76. Mem. Fla. Gov.'s Commn. Scholarships and Loans, 1965-74, Fla. Student Fin. Assistance Com., 1978. Served with USNR, 1944-46. Recipient Distinguished Alumni award Ohio U., 1970. Mem. Nat. Vocat. Guidance Assn., Am. Psychol. Assn., Am. Coll. Personnel Assn. (pres. 1971-72), Am. Personnel and Guidance Assn. (dir. 1972-73), Am. Assn. Univ. Adminstrs. (dir. 1972-75), Ohio U. Alumni Assn. (dir., treas. 1962-65), Sigma Chi, Omicron Delta Kappa, Phi Delta Kappa, Alpha Phi Omega, Phi Mu Alpha. Presbyn. Club: Rotarian. Address: U Miami Coral Gables FL 33124

BUTLER, WILLIAM THOMAS, physician, college president; b. Boston, Aug. 10, 1932; s. Albert Quigg and Elizabeth West (Visknisski) B.; m. Marilou Beutel, Apr. 26, 1967; children: Marilyn West, Thomas Charles, Robin Eileen; m. Carol Ann Pike, Nov. 23, 1977. A.B., Oberlin Coll., 1954; M.D., Western Res. U., 1958; grad. program for health systems mgmt., Harvard U., 1974, advanced mgmt. program, 1979. Intern and asst. resident in internal medicine Mass. Gen. Hosp., Boston, 1958-61, resident in internal medicine, 1964-65; clin. asso. Lab. Clin. Investigations, Nat. Inst. Allergy and Infectious Diseases, NIH, Bethesda, Md., 1961-62, chief clin. asso., 1962-63, clin. investigator, 1963-64, acting head clin. immunology sect., 1965-66; asst. prof. Baylor Coll. Medicine, Houston, 1966-68, asso. prof., 1968-71, prof. microbiology and immunology, prof. internal medicine, 1971—, asso. dean, 1973-74, dean admissions, 1974-77, acting exec. v.p., 1976-77, exec. v.p., dean, 1977-79, pres., 1979—; chmn. spl. med. adv. group VA. Hon. trustee Gulf Coast Regional Blood Ctr.; bd. dirs. Gulf Coast Hosp. Fin. Authority Bd.; bd. dirs., past v.p. Harris County Health Facilities Devel. Corp.; mem. forward planning com. Tex. Med. Ctr.; bd. dirs. South Main Ctr. Assn., exec. com., 1980—; mem. nat. adv. bd. Amigos de las Americas; assoc. chmn. key group United Way Campaign; bd. dirs. Blvd. Oaks Civic Assn. Recipient Mosby Scholarship award, Garvin prize in obstetrics and award for excellence in internal medicine Western Res. U., 1958. Mem. Am. Assn. Immunologists, Am. Soc. Clin. Investigation, N.Y. Acad. Scis., Am. Soc. Microbiology, Soc. Exptl. Biology and Medicine, Infectious Diseases Soc. Am., So. Soc. Clin. Investigation, Transplantation Soc., Assn. Acad. Health Centers, Assn. Am. Med. Colls. (council deans, adminstrv. bd.), Tex. Club Internists (hon.), AMA, Harris County Med. Soc., Houston Acad. Medicine, Tex. Med. Assn. (adv. council med. edn.), Houston C. of C. (bd. dirs.), Sigma Xi, Alpha Omega Alpha. Methodist. Clubs: River Oaks Country, Heritage; Doctors' (Houston) (bd. govs. 1979-82); (pres. 1982). Research, numerous publs. on infectious disease and immunology. Office: One Baylor Plaza Houston TX 77030

BUTNER, FRED W., JR., architect; b. Winston-Salem, N.C., Dec. 15, 1927; s. Fred Washington and Katharine (Pritchard) B.; m. Sarah Martha Hinkle, Mar. 25, 1950; children: Fred Raymond, Blain Byerly, David Eugene. B.S. in Archtl. Engring., N.C. State U., 1949. Architect, draftsman Macklin and Stinson Architects, Winston-Salem, 1949-52; propr. Fred W. Butner, Jr., Assocs.-Architects, Winston-Salem, 1952—; mem. N.C. Bd. Architecture, 1962-77. Fellow AIA (past pres. N.C.); mem. Winston-Salem Council Architects (past pres.), Winston-Salem Engrs. Club (past pres.). Democrat. Methodist. Club: Winston-Salem Lions (past pres.). Home: 397 Plymouth Ave Winston-Salem NC 27104 Office: 847 W 5th St Winston-Salem NC 27101

BUTOW, ROBERT JOSEPH CHARLES, history educator; b. San Mateo, Calif., Mar. 19, 1924; s. Frederick W.C. and Louise Marie B.; m. Irene Elkeles; 1 dau., Stephanie Cecile. B.A. magna cum laude, Stanford U., 1947, M.A., 1948, Ph.D., 1953. Instr. history Princeton U., 1954-59, asst. prof., 1959-60, research asso., 1954-60; asso. prof. history and internat. studies U. Wash., 1960-66, prof., 1966—. Author: Japan's Decision to Surrender, 1954, 67, Tojo and the Coming of War, 1961, 69, The John Doe Associates: Backdoor Diplomacy for Peace, 1941, 1974. Served to 2d lt. U.S. Army, 1943-46. Social Sci. Research Council grantee, 1956-57; Rockefeller Found. grantee, 1956-57; Guggenheim fellow, 1965-66, 78-79. Mem. Am. Com. on History of 2d World War, Assn. Mems. of Inst. Advanced Study, Soc. Historians of Am. Fgn. Relations. Office: Sch Internat Studies Thomson Hall DR-05 Univ Washington Seattle WA 98195

BUTOWSKY, DAVID MARTIN, lawyer; b. Phila., Aug. 14, 1936; s. Hyman and Pearl (Berks) B.; m. Lois Tublin, Aug. 18, 1957; children: Michael, Ellen, Edward, Erica. A.B., Temple U., 1958; LL.B., George Washington U., 1962. Bar: Md. 1962, N.Y. 1971. Practice law, N.Y.C., 1971—; chief enforcement atty. SEC, Washington, 1962-70; assoc. firm Breed Abbott & Morgan, N.Y.C., 1970-71; partner firm Butowsky Schwenke & Devine, N.Y.C., 1971-75, Gordon Hurwitz Butowsky Weitzen Shalov & Wein, 1975—. Lectr. orgns.; contbr. articles profl. publs. Mem. Am., Fed., N.Y. County bar assns., City Bar Assn. N.Y. Home: 320 E 46th St #5C New York NY 10017 Office: 101 Park Ave New York NY 10017

BUTSON, ALTON THOMAS, mathematician, educator; b. Lancaster, Pa., Feb. 18, 1926; s. John Thomas and Dorothy Virginia (Coates) B.; m. Doris Jean Brenner, June 13, 1948 (dec. Sept. 1978); children: Alton Thomas, Ronald H., Philip D., Diana L. B.S. magna cum laude, Franklin and Marshall Coll., 1950; M.A., Mich. State U., 1951, Ph.D., 1955. Instr. Mich. State U., 1954-55; asst. prof. U. Fla., 1955-58, asso. prof., 1958-59; research specialist Boeing Co., Seattle, 1959-61; prof. math. U. Miami, Coral Gables, Fla., 1961—. Contbr. articles profl. jours. Served with AUS, 1944-46. Mem. Am. Math. Soc., Math. Assn. Am., Phi Beta Kappa, Sigma Xi, Phi Kappa Phi. Club: University Yacht (commodore). Home: 6860 SW 104th St Miami FL 33156 Office: Dept Math Box 249085 U Miami Coral Gables FL 33124

BUTT, HOWARD EDWARD, JR., chain grocery executive; b. Kerrville, Tex., Sept. 8, 1927; s. Howard Edward and Mary Elizabeth (Holdsworth) B.; m. Barbara Dan Gerber, Mar. 21, 1949; children: Howard Edward III, Stephen William, Deborah Dan. B.A., Baylor U., 1947; postgrad., Southwestern Baptist Theol. Sem., Ft. Worth, 1948. With H.E. Butt Grocery Co., Corpus Christi, Tex., 1948—, v.p., 1951-67, vice chmn. bd., 1967—. Author: The Velvet Covered Brick: Christian Leadership in an Age of Rebellion, 1973, At the Edge of Hope: Christian Laity in Paradox, 1979. Founder Christian Men, Inc., pub. found. for devel. laity, 1959, chmn. bd., 1967—; founder Laity Lodge Found., pub. found. lay edn., 1963, chmn. bd., 1963—; organizer Layman's Leaderships Insts., 1956-76; chmn. N.Am.

Congress of Laity, 1978; Sec.-treas. H.E. Butt Found., 1957, pres., 1982. Named One of Five Outstanding Young Texans Jaycees, 1954. Baptist. Clubs: Corpus Christi Country, Corpus Christi Yacht, Riverhill, Kerrville. Home: 33 Hewit Dr Corpus Christi TX 78404 Office: PO Box 9216 Corpus Christi TX 78408

BUTT, HUGH ROLAND, physician, educator; b. Belhaven, N.C., Jan. 8, 1910; s. Harry Frederick and Maybelle (Jarvis) B.; m. Mary Dempwolf, Apr. 8, 1939; children: Selby, Lucy, Charles, Frances. Student, Va. Poly. Inst., 1927-29; M.D., U. Va., 1933; postgrad., Mayo Found. U. Minn., 1937. Diplomate: Am. Bd. Internal Medicine (mem. bd., subsplty. gastroenterology). Intern St. Luke's Hosp., Bethlehem, Pa., 1933-34; fellow medicine Mayo Found., 1934-37, 1st asst., 1937-38, instr., 1938-43, asst. prof., 1943-47, assoc. prof., 1947-52, prof., 1952-82; cons. physician Mayo Clinic, St. Mary's Hosp., 1938-80; Chmn. sci. counselors Nat. Cancer Inst., 1961-62; mem. Nat. Adv. Cancer Council, 1966—; v.p. Nutrition Found.; chmn. sci. adv. com. Ludwig Inst. Cancer Research, 1971—. Author: (with Snell) Vitamin K, 1941; papers, monographs. Served as lt. comdr. M.C. USNR, 1942-46. Recipient John Horsley Meml. prize U. Va., 1938. Fellow ACP (Alfred Stengel Meml. award 1975), Royal Coll. Physicians; mem. Am. Soc. Clin. Investigation, Am. Gastroent. Assn. (Julius Friedenwald medal 1979), Central Soc. Clin. Research, Assn. Am. Physicians, AMA. Episcopalian. Home: 1014 7th St SW Rochester MN 55901

BUTT, JIMMY LEE, orgn. exec.; b. Tippo, Miss., Oct. 13, 1921; s. H.W. and Jimmie O. (Davis) B.; m. Jane F. Williams, June 23, 1943; children—Janie Lake, Melanie Maryanne, Jimmy Lee. B.S., Auburn U., 1943, M.S., 1949. Registered profl. engr., Ala. Grad. asst. agrl. engring. dept. Auburn U., 1947-48, asst., 1948-50, asso. agrl. engr., 1950-56; exec. v.p. Am. Soc. Agrl. Engrs., 1956—. Served as capt. F.A. AUS, 1943-46. Recipient Ordre du Merite Agricole, France). Fellow Am. Soc. Agrl. Engrs.; mem. Nat. Soc. Profl. Engrs., Council Engring. and Sci. Soc. Execs. (pres. 1977-78), Am. Assn. Engring. Socs. (dir.), Sigma Xi, Tau Beta Pi, Phi Kappa Phi, Gamma Sigma Delta, Alpha Zeta, Omicron Delta Kappa. Clubs: Lions, Economic. Home: 2572 Stratford Dr Saint Joseph MI 49085 Office: 2950 Niles Rd St Joseph MI 49085

BUTT, JOHN BAECHER, educator; b. Norfolk, Va., Sept. 10, 1935; s. Willoughby Joseph and Mary Angela (Baecher) B.; m. Regina Elizabeth Roche, June 29, 1963; 1 son, John Baecher. B.S., Clemson U., 1956; M.Engring., Yale, 1958, D.Engring., 1960. Registered profl. engr., Conn. Instr. chem. engring. Yale, 1959-60, asst. prof., 1960-63, asst. prof. engring. and applied sci., 1963-64, asso. prof., 1964-69; prof. chem. engring. Northwestern U., Evanston, Ill., 1969—, Walter P. Murphy Prof., 1981—; vis. prof. U. Tex., summer 1961, U. Calif. at Davis, spring 1967; Solvay vis. prof. U. Libre, Brussels, Belgium, 1971. Asso. editor: Catalysis Reviews, Indsl. and Engring. Chemistry Process Design and Devel. Quar; editorial bd.: Jour. Catalysis; Contbr. profl. jours. Mem. Am. Chem. Soc. (petroleum research fund adv. bd. 1973), Am. Inst. Chem. Engrs. (A.P. Colburn award 1968, Profl. Progress award 1978, dir. 1975-77), AAAS, Catalysis Soc., Va. Hist. Soc. Patentee applied chemistry. Home: 1917 Greenwood Ave Wilmette IL 60091 Office: Dept Chemical Engring Northwestern Univ Evanston IL 60201

BUTTENHEIM, EDGAR MARION, business executive; b. Yonkers, N.Y., Dec. 23, 1922; s. Edgar J. and Marian R. (Voorhees) B.; m. Mary Elizabeth Robertson, Aug. 22, 1947; children: Margaret Collier, Anne Robertson, Elizabeth Gay, Martha Bradford. A.B. magna cum laude, Princeton U., 1943; M.B.A., NYU, 1955. Instr. Hotchkiss Sch., Lakeville, Conn., 1946-47; with Buttenheim Pub. Corp., Pittsfield, Mass., 1947-74, exec. v.p., 1963-68, pres., 1969—, Buttenheim Pub. Corp. subs. Morgan-Grampian Ltd., 1974-75, Morgan-Grampian Pub. Co. subs. Morgan-Grampian Ltd., 1975-76, Buttenheim Assos., mgmt. and mktg. cons., Pittsfield, 1976-79; exec. v.p. Springhouse Corp., Springhouse, Pa., 1979—; adj. prof. mgmt. Union Coll., Schenectady. Mem., Westchester County, Republican Com., 1957-61; candidate for Mass. Legislature, 1978. Served to 1st lt., F.A. AUS, 1943-46, 51-52. Decorated Bronze Star. Mem. UN Assn., Phi Beta Kappa. Home: 437 Ridgeview Rd Princeton NJ 08540 Office: 1111 Bethlehem Pike Springhouse PA 19477

BUTTENWIESER, BENJAMIN JOSEPH, banker; b. N.Y.C., Oct. 22, 1900; s. Joseph L. and Caroline (Weil) B.; m. Helen Lehman, Oct. 3, 1929; children—Lawrence Benjamin, Carol (dec.), Peter Lehman, Paul Arthur. B.A., Columbia U., 1919, LL.D., 1977. Adv. dir. Lehman Bros. Kuhn Loeb, Inc.; Past U.S. asst. high commr., Germany. Trustee Fedn. Jewish Philanthropic Socs., Columbia, Lenox Hill Hosp., N.Y.C. Police Found., Charles H. Revson Found. Clubs: Midday, Columbia, University (N.Y.C.); Century Country (White Plains, N.Y.). Home: 450 E 52d St New York NY 10022 Office: 660 Madison Ave New York NY 10021

BUTTERBRODT, JOHN ERVIN, real estate exec.; b. Beaver Dam, Wis., Feb. 14, 1929; s. Ervin E. and Josephine M. (O'Mare) B.; m. June Rose Bohalter, Sept. 27, 1952; children—Claire, Daniel, Larry. U. Agriculture short course, 1946-47. Vice-pres. Pure Milk Assn., 1967-69; pres. Asso. Milk Producers, Inc., Chgo., 1969-75, State Brand Creameries, Madison, Wis., 1970—, Wis. Real Estate Co., Wis. Real Estate of Burnett Inc., 1978—, Sunset Hills Golf & Supper Club Inc., 1979—; dir. Town Mut. Ins. Co., Central Milk Sales, Central Milk Producers Coop. Pres. Sch. Bd., 1968; Bd. dirs. Nat. Milk Producers Fedn., Central Am. Coop. Fedn., World Dairy Expo. Recipient Am. Farmer degree Future Farmers of Am., 1949, hon. degree, 1973; Outstanding Wis. Farmer award, 1965; Outstanding Wis. 4-H Alumni award, 1973; named Realtor of Yr., 1979. Mem. United Dairy Industry Assn. Republican. Home: Route 1 Burnett WI 53922 Office: 1708 N Spring St Beaver Dam WI

BUTTERFIELD, ALEXANDER PORTER, business executive, former government official, retired air force officer; b. Pensacola, Fla., Apr. 6, 1926; s. Horace Bushnell and Susan A. (Alexander) B.; m. Charlotte Mary Maguire, Sept. 9, 1949; children: Leslie Carter (dec.), Alexander Porter, Susan Carter, Elisabeth Gordon. B.S., U. Md., 1956; M.S., George Washington U., 1967; Ph.D. (hon.), Embry-Riddle U., 1973. Commd. 2d lt. USAF, 1949, advanced through grades to col., 1966; fighter pilot, fighter-gunnery instr., weapons officer, mem. Skyblazers (U.S. jet aerobatic team), Europe, 1949-53; aide to comdr. 4th Allied Tactical Air Force NATO, 1954-55; operations officer interceptor squadron, 1955-56; asst. prof. USAF Acad., 1957-59; sr. aide to comdr.-in-chief U.S. Pacific Air Forces, 1959-62; comdr. fighter squadron, Okinawa, 1962-63, comdr. tactical reconnaisance task forces, S.E. Asia, 1963-64; tactical air warfare policy planner USAF hdqrs., 1964-65; mil. asst. to spl. asst. sec. def., 1965-66; student Nat. War Coll., 1966-67; sr. U.S. mil. rep., comdr.-in-chief Pacific rep., Australia, 1967-69, ret., 1969; dep. asst. to Pres. Richard M. Nixon, 1969-73; sec. to Cabinet, 1969-73; adminstr. FAA, 1973-75; lectr., sr. mgmt. cons., 1975-76; exec. v.p., chief operating officer, dir. Internat. Air Service Co., Ltd., 1977-79; pres., chief operating officer, dir. Calif. Life Corp., 1979-80; chmn. GMA Corp. and Global Network, Inc., 1981—; dir. Aloha Airlines, Inc. Contbr. articles to profl. jours. Mem. Nat. Armed Forces Mus. advisory bd. Smithsonian Instn., 1970-76; bd. dirs. Internat. Flight Safety Found., Los Angeles County Mus. Natural History, 1981—. Decorated Legion of Merit, D.F.C., Air medal (4), Bronze Star. Mem. Acad. Polit. Sci., Los Angeles World Affairs Council, Am. Film Inst., Center for Study of Presidency., Sigma Nu. Club: Bel-Air Country. Home: 2171 Ridge Dr Los Angeles CA 90049

BUTTERFIELD, JAN VAN ALSTINE (MRS. HENRY T. HOPKINS), art critic; b. Los Angeles, May 27, 1937; d. Ney Henry and Dorothy Virginia (Heath) Van Alstine; 1 dau., Julia Lynn; m. Henry T. Hopkins, July 1972. B.A., U. Calif. at Los Angeles, 1957. Staff Los Angeles County Mus. Art, 1964-70, asst. pub. relations dir., 1968-70; founding mem. Expts. in Art and Tech., West Coast, 1968-70; exec. sec. Am. Pavilion Venice Biennial, Italy, 1970; art corr. Arts Mag., Tex. Report, 1971-73; contbg. editor Arts Mag., 1973—, Art Gallery Mag., 1974—; information and publs. Ft. Worth Art Center Mus., 1970-74; art critic Tex. Observer, Austin, 1971-74, Fort Worth Star Telegram, 1970-74; art critic, writer Am. Art Review, Art News, Art in Am., Mother Jones; asso. editor Images & Issues mag., 1980—; Adviser Northwood Exptl. Art Inst., Dallas, 1971-74; instr. comtemporary art and criticism San Francisco Art Inst., 1974—; also coordinator spl. programs; instr. contemporary art and criticism San Francisco Mus. Art, 1974—, San Jose State U., 1974-76, Mills Coll.; cons. Art Mus. South Tex., 1973. Nat. Endowment for Arts Critics fellow, 1975, 76, 81; Squaw Valley Writers Conf. fellow, 1978. Address: 735 21st Ave San Francisco CA 94121

BUTTERFIELD, SAMUEL HALE, educator, former AID official; b. Moscow, Idaho, Nov. 8, 1924; s. Rolston Samuel and Leone (Hamilton) B.; m. Lois Herrington, Feb. 10, 1948; children: Charles Oliver, Stephen Crandall, Susan Hale. Student, U. Idaho, 1942-43, 46-47; B.S. in Fgn. Service, Georgetown U., 1949; M.A. in Am. History, Georgetown U., 1953. Retail salesman, 1949-50; labor economist Dept. Labor, 1950-53; examiner, fiscal economist, internat. div. Bur. Budget, 1953-58; with AID (and predecessors), 1958-80, dir. office, East and So. Africa, 1960-62, dep. dir. mission to, Tanganyika, 1962-64, Sudan, 1964-65; dir. mission to, Tanzania, 1966-68; mem. sr. seminar in fgn. policy Dept. State, 1968-69; asso. asst. adminstr. for tech. assistance AID, 1969-76; dir. mission to, Nepal, 1976-80; writer/cons. on devel., affiliate prof. U. Idaho, Moscow, 1981—. Served with USAAF, 1943-46. Recipient Superior Honor award AID, 1974, Outstanding Career Achievement award, 1981. Mem. Soc. for Internat. Devel. (pres. Palouse chpt. 1982-83), Fed. Execs. League, Am. Recorder Soc., Beta Theta Pi. Address: 328 N Polk St Moscow ID 83843

BUTTERS, DOROTHY GILMAN *See* **GILMAN, DOROTHY**

BUTTERWORTH, KENNETH W., manufacturing company executive; b. 1925. Grad., Sydney Tech. Coll., 1955; A.M.P., Harvard Bus. Sch. Dir. sales The Timken Co., 1957-68; mng. dir. Bearings, Inc., 1968-76; corp. v.p. and pres. European region Loctite Corp., Newington, Conn., 1976-83, pres., chief operating officer, 1983—. Office: Loctite Corp 705 N Mountain Rd Newington CT 06111

BUTTLAR, RUDOLPH OTTO, coll. dean; b. Chgo., Dec. 31, 1934; s. Otto Robert and Lucille Ann (Blasnig) B.; m. Lois Jacqueline Mercier, June 5, 1955; children—Michael Robert, Andrew Scott, John David. B.S. in Chemistry, Wheaton (Ill.) Coll., 1956; Ph.D. in Inorganic Chemistry, Ind. U., 1962. Mem. faculty Kent (Ohio) State U., 1962—, asso. prof. chemistry, 1971—, dean, 1975—. Mem. Am. Chem. Soc., Am. Sci. Affiliation, Am. Assn. Higher Edn., Am. Conf. Acad. Deans. Baptist. Home: 5936 Horning Rd Kent OH 44240 Office: Coll Arts and Scis Kent State Univ Kent OH 44242

BUTTLE, EDGAR ALLYN, judge; b. N.Y.C., May 7, 1903; s. Norman Alexander and Ella Tice (Collins) B.; m. Erika Lucille Heydolph, Aug. 9, 1931; 1 dau., Dagmar Jo Ann. A.B., Columbia U., 1928; J.D., N.Y. U., 1931, J.S.D., 1935; postgrad., Princeton U., 1945. Bar: N.Y. 1933, D.C. 1948. Spl. asst. atty. gen., N.Y. State, 1933; law asso. George Gordon Battle, 1936-49; N.Y. regional counsel War Assets Adminstrn., 1946-48; spl. asst. to atty. gen. of U.S., antitrust div., 1950-52; trial counsel Finch & Schaefler, N.Y.C., 1952-56; adminstrv. law judge FTC, 1959-73, lectr. fed. trial practice; chmn. bd. Buttle-Baker Chem. Corp., 1953-56; mem. adv. com. on vets. re-employment Dept. Labor; fed. referee Appeals Council Social Security Adminstrn., 1956-59. Author: The Perplexities of Trade Regulation, 1956, The Search for Administrative Justice, published 1958, A Guide to the Law and Legal Literature of Peru, (in collaboration with Library of Congress), 1947, Trial Problems in Antitrust Litigation, 1953; also articles law jours. Served as comdr. USNR, 1942-45; navy liaison officer Selective Service Hdqrs., 1943-45; N.J. and Del. Decorated Army Commendation medal; recipient Distinguished Service award FTC; named hon. adm. Tex. Navy. Mem. S.R., SAR, Fed. Adminstrv. Law Judges Conf. (pres. 1961-62), World Assn. Judges, ABA, Fed. Bar Assn. (exec. council 1947-48, chmn. adminstrv. law com. 1962-63, 65-66), VFW, Delta Sigma Phi, Phi Delta Phi. Episcopalian. Club: Princeton of South Fla. Home: 290 174th St Miami Beach FL 33160

BUTTLES, BRUCE, investment analyst; b. Vienna Twp., Mich., Aug. 26, 1906; s. Cephas and Lillian (Voelker) B.; m. Virginia Lee Gilmer, Oct. 14, 1949; children: Suzanne L. (Mrs. Judson J. McIntire), John S. A.B., U. Calif., 1930; B.S. in Printing, Carnegie Inst. Tech.; M.S. in Journalism, Columbia U., 1936. Staff corr. Christian Sci. Monitor, 1930-38; staff reporter, asst. city editor Pitts. Post-Gazette, 1939-40; assoc. prof. graphic arts, head dept. printing Carnegie Inst. Tech., 1947; chief infor. control br. U.S. Mil. Govt., Berlin, 1948; with Allied Control Commn., Vienna, 1949; asst. officer-in-charge German and Austrian pub. affairs Dept. State, 1949-51; 1st sec. Am. embassy, Belgrade, 1951-53; chief linotype publs., asst. to pres. Mergenthaler Linotype Co., 1953-56; chief div. pub. services Dept. State, 1956-58; consul, Calcutta, India, 1958-63; 1st sec. Central Treaty Orgn., Ankara, Turkey, 1963-66; v.p., dir. George A. Rogers & Co., N.Y.C., 1967—; dir. Timetable & Folder Distbrs., Inc., N.Y.C. Author: America's New Army, 1942. Served to col. USAAF, 1940-47; asst. mil. attachè Am. embassy, 1946-47; Moscow. Decorated Legion of Merit, Bronze Star. Mem. Am. Soc. Internat. Law, Asiatic Soc., N.Y. Soc. Security Analysts, Financial Analysts Fedn., Sigma Chi. Clubs: Army-Navy Country (Arlington, Va.); Royal Calcutta Golf, Swimming, Bengal, Calcutta (Calcutta, India); Oriental (London, Eng.); Sea Bright Lawn Tennis and Cricket (Rumson, N.J.). Home: 3801 SE Fairway W Stuart FL 33494 Office: 66 Ward Ave Rumson NJ 07760

BUTTON, DANIEL EVAN, magazine editor; b. Dunkirk, N.Y., Nov. 1, 1917; m. Rebecca B. Pool; children: Nancy, Sarah, Daniel, Jefferson, Mary; m. Rena P. Posner, 1969. A.B., U. Del., 1938; M.S., Columbia U., 1939. Reporter, editor News-Jour. Papers, Wilmington, Del., also; AP, N.Y.C., 1939-46; dir. public relations U. Del., 1947-51; asst. to pres. SUNY, Albany, 1952-58; mem. staff Rensselaer Poly. Inst., 1959; editorial page editor Times-Union, Albany, 1959-60, exec. editor, 1960-66. Editor-in-chief: Sci. Digest, N.Y.C., 1976-80; editor: Health Protection mag, N.Y.C., 1981—. Exec. dir., pres. Arthritis Found., 1971-75; Mem. 90th, 91st congresses 29th Dist. N.Y., 1967-70. Home and Office: 162 Chestnut St Albany NY 12210

BUTTON, JACK BLAIR, international consultant; b. Lebanon, Kans., Feb. 12, 1926; s. Elgin R. and Mabel (Van Tries) B.; m. Jean Stodard, Dec. 20, 1947; children: Alexander, Van Tries, Margaret Button Nosco, Jonathan. A.B., U. Kans., 1947, M.A., 1948; postgrad., Yale U., 1957-58. Instr. polit. sci. U. Kans., 1947-48; intern Nat. Inst. Pub. Affairs, 1948-49; joined U.S. Fgn. Service, 1949, assigned, Baghdad, Iraq, 1949-51, Berlin, Germany, 1951-56, Tel Aviv, Israel, 1960-63, State Dept., 1956-60, 63-67, asst. chief foodstuffs div., 1964-67; assigned Nat. War Coll., 1967-69, faculty, 1968-69; adviser U.S. delegation UN Gen. Assembly, 1969; econ. counselor AID liaison officer Am. embassy, Tel Aviv, 1970-74; dep. dir. personnel for policy State Dept., Washington, 1974-75; minister for econ. comml. affairs Am. embassy, Tokyo, 1975-79; exec. dir. U.S.-Japan Econ. Relations Group, 1979-81. Home: 3506 Kent St Kensington MD 20895 Office: 3506 Kent S Kensington MD 20895

BUTTON, KENNETH JOHN, physicist; b. Rochester, N.Y., Oct. 11, 1922; s. Kenneth Paul and Ruth Caroline (Wagner) B.; m. Margaret Jane Wells, Dec. 22, 1952 (div. 1971). B.S., U. Rochester, 1950, M.S. in Physics, 1952. Research physicist MIT, Cambridge, Mass., 1952-62, research group leader, 1962-72, sr. scientist, 1972—; organizer, program chmn. Ann. Internat. Conf. on Infrared and Millimeter Waves, 1974—. Author: Microwave Ferrites & Ferrimagnetics, 1962; editor: Infrareds and Millimeter Waves, Vol. 1-12, 1979—, Internat. Jour. Infrared and Millimeter Waves, Vol. 1-5, 1980—. Served with U.S. Army, 1942-46. Decorated Bronze Star with oak leaf cluster. Fellow IEEE (recipient Disting. Service award Microwave Soc. 1980, Cert. of Merit 1981), Am. Phys. Soc. Republican. Episcopalian. Home: 247 Clifton St Belmont MA 02178

BUTTON, RENA PRITSKER, public relations company executive; b. Providence, R.I., Feb. 15, 1925; d. Isadore and Esther (Kay) Pritsker; m. Daniel E. Button, Aug. 16, 1969; children by previous marriage: Joshua, Bruce, David Posner. Student, Pembroke Coll., 1942-45; B.S., Simmons Coll., 1948; postgrad., Albany Law Sch., Union U., 1968-69. Spl. asst. to U.S. Rep., 1967-69; spl. projects coordinator United Jewish Appeal, 1971-74; exec. dir. Nat. Council Jewish Women, Inc., N.Y.C., 1974-76; pres. Button Assos., N.Y.C., 1976—; exec. v.p. Catalyst, N.Y.C., 1980-82; pres. Button & Button, Albany, N.Y., 1982—; mem. adv. council N.Y. State Senate Minority, 1980—. Co-producer, moderator: TV pub. affairs program Speak For Yourself, Albany, N.Y., 1963-66. Past mem. Mohawk-Hudson Council on Ednl. TV.; chmn. pub. affairs com. Marymount Manhattan Coll.; Past bd. dirs. Albany YWCA, Albany Council Chs. Devel. Corp., World Affairs Council, Planned Parenthood Assn. Albany, N.Y. Com. for Integrated Housing.; trustee Jerusalem Women's Seminar, Citizen's for Family Planning. Club: Siasconset Casino (Siasconset, Mass.). Home: 162 Chestnut St Albany NY 12210 Office: 167 Chestnut St Albany NY 12210

BUTTON, RICHARD TOTTEN, TV producer, former figure skating champion; b. Englewood, N.J., July 18, 1929; s. George and Evelyn Bunn (Totten) B.; m. Slavka Kohout, Mar. 10, 1973; children: Edward Totten, Emily Rada. B.A., Harvard U., 1952, LL.B., 1956. Founder, pres. Candid Prodns., Inc., N.Y.C., 1959—; dir. Decorative Arts Trust, 1979-80. Creator, owner: Superstars Sports, ABC-TV; Author: Dick Button on Skates, 1955, Instant Skating, 1964; Contbr. articles to various mags. Pres. Richmondtown Restoration, Inc., 1968-77. U.S. figure skating champion, 1946-52; world figure skating champion, 1948-52; European figure skating champion, 1948; Olympic gold medalist, 1948, 52; recipient James E. Sullivan award, 1949, Emmy award for outstanding sports personality-analyst, 1980-81. Mem. Bar Assn. D.C., Skating Club N.Y., Skating Club Boston, Phila. Skating Club. Club: New York Athletic. Office: 888 7th Ave New York NY 10106

BUTTRICK, JOHN ARTHUR, educator, economist; b. Rutland, Vt., Sept. 12, 1919; s. George Arthur and Agnes (Gardner) B.; m. Ann Tatlow, July 24, 1958; children—Peter M., Hilary J., Michael S. B.S., Haverford Coll., 1941; M.A., Yale, 1947, Ph.D., 1950. Asst. prof. econs. Northwestern U., 1949-53; faculty U. Minn., Mpls., 1953-75, prof. econs., 1958-75, chmn. dept., 1960-63, dir. grad. studies, 1967-69; prof. econs. York U., Toronto, Ont., Can., 1975—, dir. grad. studies, 1979—; Vis. prof. U. Calif. at Berkeley, 1957-59, U. Tokyo, 1963-64, U. de los Andes, Colombia, 1964-66, York U., 1970-74; summer vis. prof. Vanderbilt U., Stanford, Harvard, Singapore; vis. lectr., Govt. Pakistan, 1961. Co-author: Economic Development, 1954, Spanish edit., 1958, Theories of Economic Growth, 1960, Spanish edit., 1964, Consumer, Producer and Social Choice, 1968, Who Goes to University from Toronto, 1977, Educational Problems and Some Policy Options, 1977, Two Views of Aid and Development, 1979. Ont. Council Econs. fellow, 1976-77; fellow Fund for Advancement Edn., 1952-53; Ford Found. fellow, 1959-60; Fulbright fellow, Japan, Singapore, 1963-64. Mem. Am. Econ. Assn., Can. Economic Assn., Can. Civil Liberties Assn., Can. China Soc. Office: Economics Dept York U Toronto ON Canada

BUTTS, DAVID PHILLIP, educator; b. Rochester, N.Y., May 9, 1932; s. George Albert and Susie Bertha (Hicks) B.; m. Velma M. Walton, Aug. 2, 1958; children—Carol Sue, Douglas Paul. B.S., Butler U., 1954; M.S., U. Ill., 1960, Ph.D., 1962. Asst. prof. Olivet Nazarene Coll., Kankakee, Ill., 1961-62; prof. U. Tex., Austin, 1962-74; prof., chmn. dept. sci. edn. U. Ga., 1974—; ednl. cons., writer A.A.A.S. Author: (with A. Lee) Vanilla, 1964, Chocolate, 1965, Watermellon, 1966, The Teaching of Science A Self Directed Guide, 1973, Teaching Science in the Elementary School, 1973, (with Hall) Science and Children, 1976; Editor: Designs for Progress in Science Education, 1970, Research-Development in Science Education, 1971, Jour. of Research in Sci. Teaching, 1974-79. Served to capt. USAF, 1954-57. Fellow A.A.A.S., Tex. Acad. Sci.; mem. Assn. for Edn. Tchrs. Sci. (regional v.p. 1966-68, pres. 1973-75), Nat. Sci. Tchrs. Assn. (dir. 1970-72), Council Elementary Sci. Internat., Am. Ednl. Research Assn., Am. Sci. Affiliation. Home: Deerfield Rd Box 126 Bogart GA 30622

BUTTS, VIRGINIA, corporate public relations executive; b. Chgo. B.A., U. Chgo. Writer, producer, performer CBS-TV, Chgo., 1954, Dave Garroway's radio show NBC, N.Y.C., 1953; midwest dir. pub. relations for mags. Time, Fortune, Life and Sports Illustrated, 1956-63; dir. pub. relations Chgo. Sun-Times and Chgo. Daily News, 1963-74; v.p. pub. relations Field Enterprises Inc., Chgo., 1974—. Contbr.: Lesly's Public Relations Handbook, 1978, 83. Mem. vis. com. to the Coll. U. Chgo. Recipient Clarion award Women in Communications Inc., 1975, 76, Businesswoman of the Yr. award Lewis U., 1976. Mem. Pub. Relations Soc. Am. (dir. Chgo. chpt.), Publicity Club Chgo. (recipient Golden Trumpet award 1968, 69, 75, 76, 80), Fashion Group Chgo., The Chgo. Network. Club: Mid-Am. (Chgo.). Office: Field Enterprises Inc 401 N Wabash Ave Chicago IL 60611

BUTZ, KARL THEODORE, banker; b. Fort Stockton, Tex., Oct. 12, 1931; s. Karl Theodore and Edna (Bennett) B.; m. Constance Carolyn Lee, June 20, 1954; children: Karl Theodore, Lee Anne. B.B.A., U. Tex.-Austin, 1954. With Republic Nat. Bank, Dallas, 1956-61, asst. cashier, 1959-61; with Bank of Southwest N.A., Houston, 1961-70, v.p., 1963-70, mgr. comml. loan dept., 1965-70; sr. v.p. First Nat. Bank, Fort Worth, 1970-76, pres., 1971-76, also dir.; v.p., dir. 1st United Bancorp., Inc., 1972-76; pres., dir. Merc. Nat. Bank, Dallas, 1976-79; with Merc. Tex. Corp., Dallas, 1979—, now pres.; dir. Porta Kamp Mfg. Co., Inc., Houston, W.R. Berkley Corp., N.Y.C. Mem. advisory council Coll. Bus. Adminstrn. Found., U. Tex. at Austin; active various civic orgns. including Meth. Hosp. Served to lt. (j.g.) USNR, 1954-56. Mem. Res. City Bankers Assn., Dallas C. of C.,

Sigma Nu. Methodist. Clubs: Dallas Petroleum, Dallas Country. Office: 1704 Main St Dallas TX 75201 *

BUTZ, OTTO WILLIAM, educator; b. Floesti, Roumania, May 2, 1923; came to U.S., 1949, naturalized, 1959; s. Otto E. and Charlotte (Engelmann) B.; m. Velia DeAngelis, Sept. 13, 1961. B.A., Victoria Coll., U. Toronto, 1947; Ph.D., Princeton, 1953. Asst. prof. polit. sci. Swarthmore Coll., 1954-55; asst. prof. politics Princeton U., 1955-60; asso. editor Random House, N.Y.C., 1960-61; prof. social sci. San Francisco State Coll., 1961-67; academic v.p. Sacramento State Coll., 1967-69, acting pres., 1969-70; pres. Golden Gate U., 1970—. Author: German Political Theory, 1955, The Unsilent Generation, 1958, Of Man and Politics, 1960, To Make a Difference—A Student Look at America, 1967. Recipient Calif. State Colls. Outstanding Tchr. award, 1966. Mem. Am. Polit. Sci. Assn. Home: Wolfback Ridge Sausalito CA 94965 Office: 536 Mission St San Francisco CA 94105

BUTZ, WILLIAM BRINTON, lawyer, banker; b. Alburtis, Pa., Mar. 6, 1902; s. William Brinton and Mary Alice (Ettinger) B. B.A., Yale U., 1926, LL.B., 1928. Bar: Pa. bar and fed. cts 1929. Dir. Lehigh Valley Trust Co., 1946-68, gen. counsel, 1946-70, pres., 1963-68; vice-chmn. bd. dirs. Indsl. Valley Bank & Trust Co., Allentown, Pa., 1968-76; commr., sr. atty. Bd. Econ. Warfare, 1940-42; U.S. asst. to atty. gen., 1943-46; mem. Com. on World Trade, 1946; adviser to Gen. McArthur, Tokyo, 1946. Pres. Allentown Art Mus.; trustee N.Y. Infirmary, Trexler Found.; chmn. William and Alice Butz Found. Mem. Am., Pa., Lehigh County bar assns., Delta Theta Phi. Clubs: Lehigh Country (Allentown); Saucon Valley Country (Bethlehem, Pa.); Racquet (Phila.); Metropolitan Opera, Metropolitan (N.Y.C.). Home: 1411 Hamilton St Allentown PA 18102 also Blickling Hall Norwich Norfolk England Office: 1411 Hamilton St Allentown PA 18101

BUTZEL, ALBERT KAHN, environ. lawyer; b. Detroit, Oct. 1, 1938; s. Martin Leo and Rosalie (Kahn) B.; m. Brenda Sosland, Dec. 27, 1961; children—Laura Elizabeth, Kyra Jane. A.B. magna cum laude, Harvard, 1960, LL.B., 1964. Bar: N.Y. State bar 1965. Asso. firm Paul, Weiss, Rifkind, Wharton & Garrison, N.Y.C., 1964-71; partner firm Berle Butzel Kass & Case, N.Y.C., 1971—. Contbr. articles to profl. publs. Trustee Community Law Offices, N.Y.C., 1969-72. Mem. Bar Assn. City N.Y. (spl. com. power and environ. 1972-74), Am. Bar Assn. Home: 1125 Park Ave New York NY 10128 Office: Berle Butzel Kass & Case 45 Rockefeller Plaza New York NY 10111

BUTZER, KARL WILHELM, archaeology educator; b. Mülheim-Ruhr, Germany, Aug. 19, 1934; s. Paul A. and Wilhelmine (Hansen) B.; m. Elisabeth Schlösser, May 12, 1959. B.Sc. honours Math, McGill U., 1954, M.Sc., 1955; D.Sc., U. Bonn, Germany, 1957. Asst. prof., then assoc. prof. geography U. Wis., 1959-66; prof. anthropology and geography U. Chgo., 1966-80, Henry Schultz prof. environ. archaeology, 1980—; chair prof. human geography Swiss Fed. Inst. Tech., 1981-82. Author: Environment and Archeology, 1964, rev., 1971, Desert and River in Nubia, 1968, History of an Ethiopian Delta, 1971, Geomorphology from the Earth, 1976, Early Hydraulic Civilization in Egypt, 1976, Archeology as Human Ecology, 1982; Editor: After the Australopithecines, 1975, Dimensions of Human Geography, 1978, Jour. Archaeol. Sci., Prehistoric Archeology and Ecology. Recipient Busk medal Royal Geog. Soc., 1979; Fryxell medal Soc. Am. Archeology, 1981; Stopes medal Geologists Assn. of London, 1982; Guggenheim fellow, 1977. Home: Flossmoor IL 60422 Office: Pick Hall Univ Chicago Chicago IL 60637

BUTZNER, JOHN DECKER, JR., circuit judge; b. Scranton, Pa., Oct. 2, 1917; s. John Decker and Bess Mary (Robison) B.; m. Viola Eleanor Peterson, May 25, 1946; 1 son, John Decker III. B.A., U. Scranton, 1939; LL.B., U. Va., 1941. Bar: Va. bar 1941. Practice in, Fredericksburg, 1941-58; judge 15th and 39th Jud. Circuit of Va., 1958-62; U.S. judge Eastern Dist. Va., 1962-67; U.S. circuit judge 4th circuit Ct. Appeals, Richmond, Va., 1967—. Served with USAAF, 1942-45. Home: 5507 Dorchester Rd Richmond VA 23225 Office: PO Box 2188 Richmond VA 23217

BUXEDA, ROBERTO, ophthalmologist; b. Arecibo, P.R., Jan. 4, 1916; s. Miguel and Ambrosina (Velez) B.; m. Helen Dolores Dacri, Apr. 17, 1941; children: Roberto Miguel, Adriano Roberto. Student, U. P.R., 1933-36; M.D., Hahnemann Med. Coll., 1940; M.Sc. in Medicine, U. Pa., 1951. Diplomate: Am. Bd. Ophthalmology. Intern Woman's Hosp., Phila., 1940; resident Ophthalmic Inst. P.R., San Juan, 1948-49, McGuire VA Hosp., Richmond, Va., 1949-51; co. physician South P.R. Sugar Co., Guanica, 1941-43; physician VA Hosp., New Castle, Del., 1946-47; practice medicine specializing in ophthalmology, San Juan, 1951—; chief sect. ophthalmology Presbyterian Hosp., San Juan, 1964-73, cons., 1973—; clin. prof. ophthalmology U. P.R., 1952—; advisor Eye Bank P.R., 1954—; v.p. 10th Panam. Congress Ophthalmology, 1975. Contbr. articles on ophthalmology to med. jours. Pres. fin. campaign P.R. chpt. Am. Cancer Soc., 1961; dir. glaucoma clinics Lions Club P.R., 1960; trustee San Juan Bautista Sch. Medicine, 1979—. Served with M.C. AUS, 1943-46. Recipient Certificate of Admiration for treatment of physically handicapped Antilles Command Personnel, 1964; Recognition award Italian Am. Club P.R., 1967. Fellow Am. Acad. Ophthalmology, ACS, Internat. Coll. Surgeons; mem. Pan Am. Assn. Ophthalmology, Barraquer Inst., P.R. Ophthalmol. Soc. (pres. 1953), P.R. Acad. Arts and Scis. (a founder). Club: Lions. Office: Ashford Med Center San Juan PR 00907 *I think I would attribute my present success to a combination of hard work and perseverance. I might also add that throughout my professional life I have looked at clocks and my own personal watch when strictly necessary only, never habitually.*

BUXTON, CHARLES INGRAHAM, II, ins. co. exec.; b. Owatonna, Minn., Dec. 17, 1924; s. John Anthony and Vera Helen (Moore) B.; m. Norma Pat Lee, Oct. 21, 1950; children—Cynthia Lee, John Anthony II, Sarah, Patricia, Elizabeth. Student, Carleton Coll., 1942-43; B.S. with distinction, U.S. Naval Acad., 1946; postgrad., Wharton Sch. Finance and Commerce, U. Pa., 1949-50. In home office dept. Federated Mut. Ins. Co., 1950- 51, office, personnel mgr., 1953-55, mgr., 1956, v.p., asst. to pres., 1957, pres., dir., 1957—, Federated Life Ins. Co., 1958—, chmn. bd., 1966—; dir., past chmn. Alliance Am. Insurers, Northwestern Nat. Bank & Trust Co., Owatonna; past bd. govs., past pres. Mut. Loss Research Bur.; dir., past pres. Minn. Ins. Information Service; dir., past chmn. Minn. Ins. Fedn. Trustee, past sec. bd. trustees Asso. Ch. Owatonna; bd. govs. Am. Inst. Property and Liability Underwriters. Served as ensign USN, 1946-49; to lt., 1951-53. Mem. Am. Legion. Clubs: Mason, Rotarian., Owatonna Country, Minneapolis Athletic. Office: Federated Mut Ins Co 129 E Broadway Owatonna MN 55060 *

BUXTON, JORGE NORMAN, ophthalmologist; b. Buenos Aires, Argentina, June 21, 1921; came to U.S., 1947, naturalized, 1961; s. Norman G. and Alejandrina B.; m. Gonzalez, Oct. 11, 1947; children: Douglas F., George N. Baccalaureate, St. George's Coll., Buenos Aires, 1940; M.D., Nat. U. of Buenos Aires, 1947; postgrad., N.Y. U. Med. Sch., 1948-49. Diplomate: Am. Bd. Ophthalmology. Intern Ramos Mejia Hosp., Buenos Aires, 1944-47, St. Clare's Hosp., N.Y.C., 1947-48; resident in ophthalmology Newark Eye and Ear Infirmary, 1950, N.Y. Eye and Ear Infirmary, N.Y.C., 1950-51; asst. and assoc. to Ramon Castroviejo, 1953-64; surgeon-dir. N.Y. Eye and Ear Infirmary, 1963—; dir. Corneal Clinic, 1963—; chmn. med. bd., 1983—, practice medicine specializing in ophthalmology, N.Y.C., 1951—; dir. Eye Bank for Sight Restoration, N.Y.C., 1960—, N.J. Eye Bank, 1960—; clin. prof. ophthalmology Coll. of Medicine and Dentistry N.J., Newark, 1977—; mem. panel ophthalmic device classification FDA, 1976—; cons. to various hosps. in, N.J. and N.Y., 1958—. Contbr. articles on eye surgery to profl. jours. Served from capt. to maj. USAF, 1955-57. Fellow A.C.S.; mem. Soc. Eye Surgeons, N.Y. Ophthal. Soc. (sec.-treas. 1975, pres. 1980-81), N.Y. Acad. Medicine (sec. sect. ophthalmology 1978-79, pres. 1980-81), Am. Acad. Ophthalmology and Otolaryngology, Am. Assn. Ophthalmology, Pan Am. Assn. Ophthalmology (vis. prof. Columbia 1973), No. N.J. Ophthal. Soc., Pan Am. Soc. Ophthalmic Microsurgery, Contact Lens Assn. of Ophthalmologists (pres. 1976-77), Am. Intra-Ocular Implant Soc. (sci. adv. bd. 1978-80), Brazilian Inst. Ophthalmology and Prevention of Blindness, Sociedad Hispano Americana de Oftalmologia (pres. 1970-71), Sociedad Dominicana de Oftalmologia (hon. mem.), Sociedad Medica Argentina, AMA, Pan Am. Med. Assn. Clubs: Bathing of Southampton, Meadow of Southampton; Doubles, N.Y. Athletic (N.Y.C.). Office: New York Eye and Ear Infirmary 310 E 14th St New York NY 10003

BUYA, WALLACE JOSEPH, insurance company executive; b. Lawrence, Mass., Jan. 7, 1925; s. Joseph and Antenett (Nevers) B.; m. JoAnn Heinzerling, Aug. 12, 1950; children: Vicki Buya Bruen, Jeffrey. B.S., Ohio State U., 1950. Cert. activity vector analyst. Assoc. dir. mgmt. devel. Nationwide Ins. Co., Columbus, Ohio, 1951-67; dir. Stone-Brandel Ctr., Chgo., 1967-70; sr. v.p., sec. Combined Ins. Co. Am., Northbrook, Ill., 1970—. Active Combined Opportunities, Chgo., 1971—, pres., Chgo., 1976—; chmn. bd. dirs. Chgo. Better Bus. Bur., 1972-74; active Camp Fire Inc., 1960—, mem. nat. exec. bd., 1965—; pres. Helping Hearts and Hands, Chgo., 1970-83; trustee Heinzerling Meml. Found., Columbus, 1965-83; mem. Dr. Martin Luther King Chgo. Boys Club, 1969-72, Mental Health Assn. Greater Chgo., 1970-72. Served with USNR, 1942-46. Mem. Chgo. Assn. Commerce and Industry (World Trade Council 1975-83). Republican. Presbyterian. Lodge: Masons (32) degree. Home: 2910 Hawthorn Ln Wilmette IL 60091 Office: Combined Ins Co Am 707 Combined Ctr Northbrook IL 60062

BUYERS, JOHN WILLIAM AMERMAN, agribusiness and specialty foods company executive; b. Coatesville, Pa., July 17, 1928; s. William Buchanan and Rebecca (Watson) B.; m. Elsie Palmer Parkhurst, Apr. 11, 1953; children: Elsie Buyers Viehman, Rebecca Watson Buyers-Basso, Jane Palmer Buyers-Russo. B.A. cum laude in History, Princeton U., 1952; M.S. in Indsl. Mgmt., MIT, 1963. Div. ops. mgr. Bell Telephone Co. Pa., 1964-66; dir. ops. and personnel Gen. Waterworks Corp., Phila., 1966-68, pres., chief exec. officer, 1971-75; v.p. adminstrn. Internat. Utilities Corp., Phila., 1968-71; pres., chief exec. officer, dir. C. Brewer and Co., Ltd., Honolulu, 1975—, chmn. bd., 1982—; chmn. Calif. and Hawaiian Sugar Co., 1982-84; dir. First Hawaiian Bank, IU Investment Corp.; mem. Gov.'s Adv. Council on China Affairs, U.S. Army Civilian Adv. Group, Hawaii Joint Council Econ. Edn., Japan-Hawaii Econ. Council, Commn. on Jud. Discipline. Pres., trustee U. Hawaii Found.; bd. dirs. Research Corp. U. Hawaii, Pacific Aerospace Mus. Served with USMC, 1946-48. Sloan fellow, 1963. Mem. Hawaiian Sugar Planters Assn. (chmn. bd. dirs. 1980-82, dir.), C. of C. Hawaii (chmn. bd. dirs. 1981-82), Nat. Alliance Bus. (chmn. Hawaii Pacific Metro chpt. 1978), Newcomen Soc. N.Am. Presbyterian. Clubs: Cap and Gown (Princeton); Hilo Yacht, Oahu Country, Pacific, Waialae Country, Prouts Neck (Maine) Country. Home: 148 Poipu Dr Honolulu HI 96825 Home: Buckhaven Farm RD 3 Box 254 Benton PA 17814 Office: C Brewer & Co Ltd 827 Fort St Honolulu HI 96813

BUYSE, EMILE J., film company executive; b. Brussels, Apr. 16, 1927; U.S., 1976; s. Omer J. and Flore G. (Copain) B.; m. Evelyne Mulpas, June 26, 1964. M.A., Ecole Normale Charles Buls, Brussels, 1947. Dir. advt. and publicity for continental Europe and Middle East United Artists Corp., Paris, 1962-66; dir. advt. and publicity 20th Century-Fox Film Corp., 1966-70, v.p. internat. distbn., 1970-76; pres. 20th Century-Fox Internat. Corp., Los Angeles, 1976-81, EBE Internat., Culver City, Calif., 1981—. Mem. Acad. Motion Picture Arts and Scis. Home: 1320 Carla Ln Beverly Hills CA 90210 Office: 10201 W Pico Blvd Los Angeles CA 90035 Office: PO Box 900 Beverly Hills CA 90213

BUZACOTT, JOHN ALAN, engineering educator; b. Sydney, N.S.W., Australia, May 21, 1937; emigrated to Can., 1967; s. Alan Ernest and Jean Elizabeth (Bingle) B.; m. Ursula Schulmerich, Sept. 7, 1963; children: Alan J., Kimberly A. B.Sc., U. Sydney, 1957; M.Sc., U. Birmingham (Eng.), 1962, Ph.D., 1967. Engr. Associated Elec. Industries, Rugby, Eng., 1959-61; ops. research systems officer A.E.I. Hotpoint Ltd., London, 1963-64; asst. prof. U. Toronto, 1967-71, assoc. prof., 1971-77, prof., 1977-83, U. Waterloo, Ont., Can., 1984—. Corr. editor: Canadian Jour. Info. Processing and Ops. Research, 1974-78; author: Scale in Production Systems, 1982. Mem. Canadian Operational Research Soc. (pres. 1983-84), Ops. Research Soc. Am. Home: 68 Divadale Dr Toronto ON Canada M4G 2P2 Office: U Waterloo Faculty of Engring Waterloo ON Canada N2L 3G1

BUZBEE, RICHARD EDGAR, newspaper editor; b. Fordyce, Ark., Aug. 16, 1931; s. Edgar Andrew and Helen Koester (Darling) B.; m. Marie Palmer, Apr. 16, 1955; children: Robert Edgar, William Bruce, James Palmer, John Richard. B.J., B.A., U. Mo., 1954. Mgmt. intern Harris Newspaper Group, Chanute (Kans.) Tribune, Burlington (Iowa) Hawk-Eye, also Olathe (Kans.) News, 1957-63; editor, pub. Olathe News, 1963-79, Hutchinson (Kans.) News, 1979—; partner Radine Enterprises, Olathe. Pres. Olathe C. of C., 1969, Olathe United Way, 1968, Johnson County chpt. ARC, 1978-79; chmn. Johnson County Scholarship Found., 1968; mem. Olathe Public Bldg. Commn. 1, 1964-65, 2, 1978-79; co-chmn. Olathe Home-for-Christmas from Vietnam Project, 1969-72; mem. bd. Hutchinson Public Library, 1980-81, chmn., 1982-83; bd. dirs. Hutchinson Symphony Assn., 1980-83. Served to lt. (j.g.) USNR, 1954-57. Mem. Am. Soc. Newspaper Editors, Internat. Press Inst., Inland Daily Press Assn., William Allen White Found., Phi Beta Kappa. Republican. Methodist. Club: Rotary. (dir. 1981-83). Home: 4 Crescent Blvd Hutchinson KS 67501 Office: 300 W 2d St Hutchinson KS 67501

BUZBY, RUSSELL CONWELL, distilling co. exec.; b. Feb. 13, 1934; s. Leland Stanford and Ethel Mae (McHenry) B.; m. Gloria Jean Landry, July 11, 1953; children—William James, Patricia Ann, Linda Sue, Mary Ellen. B.A. with honors, Lafayette Coll., 1956. Personnel mgr. Armstrong Cork Co., Lancaster, Pa., 1959-64; personnel dir. Celanese Corp., N.Y.C., 1964-72; v.p. Ryder System, Miami, Fla., 1972-75; sr. v.p. ARA Services Inc., Phila., 1975-80; v.p. Brown-Forman Distillers Corp., 1981—. Served to capt., inf. U.S. Army, 1956-58. Mem. Labor Relations Council, Conf. of Personnel Officers. Home: Cave Springs Pl Anchorage KY 40223 Office: 850 Dixie Hwy Louisville KY 40210

BUZBY, SCOTT HAINES, rubber company executive; b. Phila., Feb. 5, 1929; s. Jesse Milton and Helene Eleanore (Geisser) B.; m. Anne Elizabeth Ellis, July 14, 1956; children: Cynthia, Scott Haines. B.A., Middlebury Coll., 1951. With Goodyear Tire Co., Akron, Ohio, 1954-56, Goodyear-Brazil, Sao Paulo, 1957-62; sales mgr. Goodyear-Colombia, Cali, 1962-66; mng. dir. Goodyear-Australia, Sydney, 1966-71; v.p. internat. Goodyear Tire & Rubber Co., Akron, 1971-76, exec. v.p., 1978—; pres. Kelly-Springfield Co., Cumberland, Md., 1976-78. Served with USCG, 1951-54. Mem. Rubber Mfg. Assn. (nominating com. 1981—), Nat. Tire Dealers and Retreaders Assn., Western Highway Inst. Club: Portage Country. Office: The Goodyear Tire & Rubber Co 1144 E Market St Akron OH 44316

BUZICK, WILLIAM ALONSON, JR., business executive, lawyer, educator; b. Sylvan Grove, Kans., Nov. 4, 1920; s. William Alonson and Mildred (Hickman) B.; m. Mary Lee Emerson, Nov. 18, 1954; children: William Alonson III, Bonnie Lee. A.B., Kans. U., 1942; LL.B., Washburn U., 1950. Bar: Kans. bar 1950. Vice pres., dir. Sylvan State Bank, Sylvan Grove, 1946-48; 1st sec. Alcoholic Beverage Bd., Kans., 1948-50; pres. Shasta Water Co., San Francisco, 1950-60, Shasta div. Consol. Foods Corp., Chgo., 1960- 66; dir., v.p. Consol. Foods Corp., 1964, exec. v.p., 1966-68, pres., chmn. bd., chief exec. officer, 1968-75; dean Sch. Bus. and Adminstrv. Sci., Calif. State U., Fresno, 1975-78; dir. Bonner Packing Co., Sambo's Restaurants, Inc., Walter E. Heller Internat. Corp., 1st Savs. and Loan Assn., Berry Holding Co., ICX Corp., Bekins Co., Itel Corp. Trustee U Calif. Med. Edn. Program, Fresno, San Joaquin Coll. Law, Fresno. Served to lt. USNR, 1942-46. Recipient Distinguished Service citation Kans. U., 1972. Mem. Am., Kans. bar assns. Home: 6533 N Van Ness Blvd Fresno CA 93711 Office: 1391 W Shaw Ave Fresno CA 93711

BUZZELL, ROBERT DOW, management educator; b. Lincoln, Nebr., Apr. 18, 1933; s. Dow Alan and Grace (Blomquist) B.; m. Edith F. Moser, June 5, 1953; children: Susan, Robert Dow, Barbara, William. A.B., George Washington U., 1953; M.S., U. Ill., 1954; Ph.D., Ohio State U., 1957. Faculty Ohio State U., 1957-61; faculty Harvard Grad. Sch., Bus. Adminstrn., 1961—, prof., 1967—; Vis. prof. Inst. European d'Adminstrn. des Affaires, 1967; exec. dir. Mktg. Sci. Inst., 1968-72; dir. U.S. Shoe Corp., Chelsea Industries, Inc., VF Corp., Gen. Nutrition, Inc.; cons. in field, 1960—. Author or co-author: Wholesaling, 1959, Mathematical Models and Marketing Management, 1964, Marketing: An Introductory Analysis, 1964, rev., 1972, Marketing Research, 1969. Mem. Am. Mktg. Assn., Phi Beta Kappa. Congregationalist. Home: 15 Swarthmore Rd Wellesley MA 02181 Office: Harvard Bus Sch Boston MA 02163

BUZZI, RUTH ANN, comedienne; b. Westerly, R.I., July 24, 1936; d. Angelo Peter and Rena Pauline (Macchi) B.; m. Basil Keko, Nov. 28, 1965; m. Kent Perkins, Dec. 10, 1979. Student, Pasadena Playhouse, 1954-57; pvt. study dance, drama, voice. Appeared on Broadway in: Sweet Charity; appeared in N.Y. theater prodns. including: Misguided Tour; network TV appearances include: Garry Moore Show; appeared in: Rowan and Martin's Laugh-In, Dean Martin Roasts, Trapper John, M.D., Medical Center, Alice; films Skatetown, U.S.A., 1977, The Villain, 1979, The North Avenue Irregulars, 1979; TV movie In Name Only, 1969; featured commedienne in mus. revues; filmed TV commls. for various sponsors. Recipient Golden Globe award, Image award NAACP; named to R.I. Hall of Fame. Hon. mem. D.A.R. *

BYAM, MILTON SYLVESTER, library consultant; b. N.Y.C., Mar. 15, 1922; s. Charles and Sybil J. (Williams) B.; m. Yolanda Shervington, Jan. 18, 1947; children: Megan, Roger. B.S. cum laude, City Coll., N.Y., 1947; M.S., Columbia U., 1949, postgrad., 1968; postgrad., N.Y. U., 1950-51. With Bklyn. Pub. Library, 1947-68, chief pub. services, 1961-65, dep. dir., 1965-68; chmn. dept. library sci. St. Johns U., 1968-72; dir. D.C. Public Library, 1972-74, Queens Borough Pub. Library, Jamaica, N.Y., 1974-79; pres. Byam et al Consultants Inc., 1979—; tchr. history of libraries, humanities, lit., social sci. lit. Pratt Inst., Sch. Library Sci., Bklyn., 1956-67; tchr. pub. library adminstrn. St. Johns U. Grad. Sch., 1956-68; co-chmn. Bklyn. Citizens Com. for Nat. Library Week, 1959-60; trustee Bookmobile Services Trust, 1968, New York Reference and Resources Council, 1969-72, 74—; cons./adviser to High John, U. Md. Grad. Library Sch., 1969-70; mem. adv. council Cath. Library Assn., 1968-72; mem. adv. com. dept. library sci. Queens Coll.; examiner, dir. positions N.Y. N.J. State Civil Service Dept., 1966—. Contbr. articles to profl. jours. Vestryman Grace Ch., Jamaica, 1968-69; mem. Commn. on Urban Affairs, Diocese of L.I., 1971-72, Flushing Suburban Civic Assn., 1953; pres. Flushing Suburban Civic Assn., 1964, fin. sec., 1983; mem. Community Planning Bd. 15A, 1967-68; bd. dirs. Queens Council on Arts, Queens council Boy Scouts Am.; pres. Queens Council for Social Welfare, 1979—, Jamaica Hosp. Served with AUS, 1943-45. Decorated Bronze Star medal; recipient Savannah State Coll. Library award, 1964, Friends of Library award Bklyn. Pub. Library, 1968, commendation D.C. Library Services and Constrn. Act Adv. Council, 1974, resolution of commendation bd. trustees D.C. Pub. Library, 1974, certificate of appreciation Personnel Dept., City of Phila., 1974, plaque for outstanding community service Queens Alumni chpt. Delta Sigma Theta, 1974, Brotherhood awards NCCJ, 1977, St. Albans Civic Improvement Assn., 1977, award Queens Interfaith Clergy Council, 1977, Municipal Officers Club of D.C., 1974, ARC, 1978, Greater Jamaica C. of C., 1979. Mem. ALA, N.Y. State Library Assn. (chmn. intellectual freedom com. 1968-72), New York Library Club (dir. 1956-57, 69-71). Episcopalian. Clubs: Jamaica Rotary (pres. 1978), Archons of Colophons, Melvil Dui Chowder and Marching Soc. Home and office: 162-04 75th Rd Flushing NY 11366 *Reading is the most important way in which we might improve the warp and woof of society.*

BYARS, WALTER RYLAND, JR., lawyer; b. Birmingham, Ala., Oct. 5, 1928; s. Walter Ryland and Essie (Hopper) B.; m. Mildred Lucile Rhodes, Dec. 22, 1950; children: Debra Leigh, Walter Ryland III, Rebecca Lynn, John Baxter. B.S., U. Ala., 1948, LL.B., 1952, J.D., 1969. Bar: Ala. bar 1952, also U.S. Supreme Ct, U.S. Circuit Ct. of Appeals, 5th Circuit, U.S. Dist. Cts. No., Middle and So. dists. Ala. Practiced in, Troy, 1953-57, Birmingham, 1959-68, Montgomery, 1968—, pvt. practice, 1953-57; atty. legal dept. So. Bell. Tel. & Tel. Co., Atlanta, 1957-59, Ala. atty., Birmingham, 1959-60, gen. atty., 1960-68; partner Steiner, Crum & Baker, 1968—; Mgmt. rep. Ala. Unemployment Bd. Appeals, 1962-63; vice chmn. Ala. chpt. Americans for Constl. Action, 1966—, Montgomery Dist. chmn., 1968—. Bd. editors: Ala. Law Rev, 1951-52. Republican committeeman, Montgomery County, 1970. Served to lt. (j.g.) USNR, 1952-53. Fellow Internat. Soc. Barristers (gov. 1977-83, sec.-treas. 1979-80, 2d v.p. 1980-81, 1st v.p. 1981-82, pres. 1982-83), Am. Coll. Trial Lawyers; mem. ABA (Young Lawyers past mem. exec. council, com. chmn.), Ala. Bar Assn. (com. chmn. 1980-81, pres.-elect 1983-84, past pres. Young Lawyers, past sect. chmn., past com. chmn.), Pike County Bar Assn. (past pres.), Birmingham Bar Assn. (past com. chmn.), Montgomery County Bar Assn. (past com. chmn., bd. dirs. 1976—, v.p. 1978, pres. 1979), Fed. Jud. Conf., Nat. Assn. R.R. Trial Counsel, Ala. Law Inst. (council), Sigma Chi, Phi Alpha Delta. Methodist. Club: Men of Montgomery. Lodges: Masons; Shriners; Kiwanis. Home: 1616 S Hull St Montgomery AL 36104 Office: First Ala Bank Bldg PO Box 668 Montgomery AL 36101

BYBEE, RODGER WAYNE, educator; b. San Francisco, 1942; s. Wayne and Genevieve (Mungon) B.; m. Patricia Brovsky, May 28, 1966. B.A., Colo. State Coll., 1966; M.A., U. No. Colo., 1969; Ph.D., NYU, 1975. Tchr. Pub. Schs. Greeley, (Colo.), 1965-66; sci. instr. U. No. Colo., 1966-70; teaching fellow NYU, 1970-72; instr. in edn. Carleton Coll., Northfield, Minn., 1972-75, asst. prof., 1975-81, assoc. prof., 1981—, chmn. dept., 1981—; cons. D.C. Health Spl. Edn. for

Elem. Sci., Nat. Assessment of Ednl. Progress. Co-author: Becoming a Better Elementary Science Teacher, 1975, Becoming a Secondary School Science Teacher, 1981, Violence, Values and Justice in the Schools, 1982, Piaget for Educator, 1982, Science and Society, 1984; editor, contbr., Jour. Social Issues, 1979, Am. Biology Tchr., 1983. Bd. dirs. Acid Rain Found. Mem. AAAS, Nat. Sci. Tchrs. Assn., Nat. Assn. Biology Tchrs. (editorial bd.), Nat. Assn. Research in Sci. Teaching (exec. bd., publs. adv. bd., editorial bd. Jour. Research in Sci. Teaching), World Future Soc., Assn. Humanistic Psychology. Home: 212 Maple St Northfield NM 55057 Office: Dept Edn Carleton Coll Northfield MN 55057

BYCHKOV, SEMYON, conductor; b. Leningrad, USSR, Nov. 30, 1952; came to U.S., 1975; s. May and Doroteya (Kreizberg) B.; m. Tatiana Rozina, July 3, 1973; children: David, Elizabeth Rachel. Diploma of honor, Clinka Choir Sch., 1970; student, Leningrad Conservatory, 1970-74; diploma, Mannes Coll. Music, N.Y.C., 1976. Music dir., Bonch-Bruyevich Inst. Chorus, Leningrad, 1970-72; condr., Leningrad Conservatory Symphony and Opera Orch., 1972-74; asso. condr., then music dir., Mannes Coll. Music Orch., 1976-80; music dir./condr., Grand Rapids (Mich.) Symphony, 1980—; asso. condr., Buffalo Philharm. Orch., 1979—; prin. guest condr., 1981—; guest condr., Israel Chamber Orch., N.Y. Philharm., Spoleto Festival, Concertebouw Orch., Art Park Festival, Cin. Symphony, San Remo Symphony, Aix-en-Provence Music Festival, Tivoli Symphony, Indpls. Symphony, Bournemouth Symphony, Chautaqua Symphony, Columbus Symphony, Lyon Opera, Seattle Symphony, L.I. Philharm., Minn. Orch., CBS Chamber Orch., Syracuse Orch., Can. Nat. Arts Center Orch., Detroit Symphony, summers 1981-83, N.Y.C. Opera, fall 1981. Recipient 1st prize Rachmaninoff Conducting Competition, 1973. Mem. Am. Fedn. Musicians. Office: Suite 802 Exhibitors Bldg Grand Rapids MI 49503

BYCK, ROBERT SAMUEL, psychiatrist, educator; b. Newark, Apr. 26, 1933; s. Louis and Lucy Ruth (Landau) B.; m. Therese Jaeger, May 4, 1963; children: Carl, Gillian, Lucas; m. Susan Elizabeth Wheeler, Aug. 21, 1976. A.B., U. Pa., 1954, M.D., 1959; M.A. hon., Yale U., 1978. Intern U. Calif.-San Francisco, 1959-60; asst. prof. pharmacology and rahab. medicine Albert Einstein Coll. Medicine, Bronx, N.Y., 1964-69; resident in psychiatry Yale U., New Haven, 1969-72, lectr. in pharmacology, 1969-72, assoc. prof. psychiatry and pharmacology, 1972-77, prof. psychiatry and pharmacology, 1977—; cons. N.Y. Zool. Soc., Bronx, 1968—, Nat. Inst. Drug Abuse, Bethesda, Md., 1976-80, West Haven VA Hosp., Conn., 1972—, Med. Letter on Drugs and Therapeutics, 1970—. Editor: Cocaine Papers: Sigmund Freud, 1974; contbr. (articles to sci. publs.). Recipient Career Devel. award, 1967; Burroughs-Wellcome scholar in clin. pharmacology, Research Triangle Park, N.C., 1972-77. Mem. Am. Soc. Pharmacology and Exptl. Therapeutics, Am. Soc. Clin. Pharmacology and Therapeutics, Am. Coll. Neuropsychopharmacology, AAAS, Sherlock Holmes Soc. Club: Yale (N.Y.C.). Home: 197 McKinley Ave New Haven CT 06515 Office: Yale U Sch Medicine 333 Cedar St New Haven CT 06510

BYE, RANDULPH DEBAYEUX, artist, author; b. Princeton, N.J., June 17, 1916; s. Arthur Edwin and Mary C. (Heldring) B.; m. Mary DuBois McCarty, May 24, 1941 (div. 1981); children: Dennis L., Barbara D., Stephen G., Catherine M.; m. Glenna C. Lange, Oct. 16, 1983. Diploma, Phila. Mus. Sch. Indsl. Art, 1938; student, Art Students League, N.Y.C., 1940-41.. One-man shows Newman Galleries, Phila, Hahn Gallery, Phila, Allerbescht Gallery, Telford,Pa.; group shows Am. Watercolor Soc. ann., 30 yrs., Allied Artists anns., N.Y.C., NAD, 10 yrs., Phila. Waercolor Club, 40 yrs., Woodmere Art Gallery; represented: permanent collections Smithsonian Instn., Davenport, Iowa, Mcpl. Art Gallery, Reading, Pa., Pub. Mus., Temple U. Sch. Pharmacy, Phila., Munson, Williams Proctor Inst., Utica, N.Y.; author, illustrator: The Vanishing Depot, 1973, rev. edit., 1983; author: (with Margaret Bye Richie) Victorian Sketchbook. Served with U.S. Army, 1942-45. Recipient numerous awards various art orgns., Gold medal Nat. Arts Club, 1963. Mem. Am. Watercolor Soc. (4 awards 1964-73), Phila. Watercolor Club, Allied Artists Am., Salmagundi Club (24 awards 1958—), NAD (assoc., cert. of merit 1976). Mem. Soc. of Friends. Home: PO Box 362 Mechanicsville PA 18934 *I fell fortunate in being able to pursue a career of my own choice; painting and interpreting my enviornment in landscape and genre subjects. I am a watercolorist in the tradition of American realism—the impressionist school of Sargent and Homer. My concern for architectural preservation caused me to publish two books on this theme. One with illustrations of bygone railroad stations and another on Victorian structures, hoping to enlighten the public's awareness of our architectural heritage*

BYE, RICHARD EARL, publisher; b. Worcester, Mass., Mar. 12, 1920; s. Terschak Franzoir and Odelie Belle (Johnson) B.; m. Delia Faye Grubb, Feb. 15, 1947; children: Juliana, Jonathan, Matthew, Amelia; m. Nancy Hamilton Carrier, Aug. 23, 1974. B.S. cum laude, Bowdoin Coll., Brunswick, Maine, 1942; grad., Advanced Mgmt. Program, Harvard U., 1965. Project engr. Alonzo J. Harriman (architect/engr.), Portland, Maine, 1942; coll. traveller Ronald Press, 1946-47; advt. salesman, then advt. mgr. Publishers Weekly, 1948-63; dir. R.R. Bowker Co., N.Y.C., 1956-63, v.p., then sr. v.p., 1963-68, pub., 1968-73; pres. L.J. Cards Inc., 1965-70; sr. v.p. Nat. Order Systems Co., N.Y.C., 1973-74; pres. Hector Bye Inc., pubs., N.Y.C., 1973-77; pres., pub. Knapp Press, Los Angeles, 1977-81, chmn. bd., pub., chief exec. officer, 1981—; v.p. Knapp Communications Corp., 1982—. Democratic committeeman, Rockland County (N.Y.), 1961; pres. New City (N.Y.) Library Bd., 1963; mem. Clarkstown (N.Y.) Shade Tree Commn., 1963. Served to lt. USNR, 1942-46; PTO. Mem. Pubs. Ad Club (past pres.), Am. Bach Soc. (past pres.); mem. Pubs. Assn. So. Calif. (pres. 1983); Mem. Theta Delta Chi. Club: Players (N.Y.C.). Office: 5900 Wilshire Blvd Los Angeles CA 90036

BYERLY, THEODORE CARROLL, educator, former government official; b. Melbourne, Iowa, May 3, 1902; s. William Henry and Lulu May (Crook) B.; m. Helen Frances Freeman, May 31, 1929 (dec.); children: Carroll (Mrs. N. Holcomb), David, Nora (Mrs. T.D. Bolita); m. Imogene J. McCarthy, Aug. 7, 1967. A.B., U. Iowa, 1923, M.S., 1925, Ph.D., 1926. Instr. zoology U. Mich., 1926-28, Hunter Coll., 1928-29, Peabody Coll., summers 1927-28; physiologist div. animal husbandry Bur. Animal Industry, Dept. Agr., 1929—, sr. poultry husbandman charge poultry husbandry investigation, 1941—, chief animal husbandry div., 1947—; asst. dir. livestock research Agrl. Research Service, 1955-57, dep. adminstr., 1957-62, adminstr. coop. state exptl. sta. service, 1962-63; adminstr. Coop. State Research Service, 1963-69; coordinator environmental quality activities Dept. Agr., 1969-73, cons., 1973—; prof. U. Md., 1937-41, adj. prof., 1976—; cons. Winrock Internat. Center Livestock Research and Tng., 1975-82; chmn. div. biology and agr. NCR, 1963-65; mem. U.S. Nat. Commn. for UNESCO, 1954-60; chmn. U.S. delegation Internat. Conf. Rational Use Biosphere, 1968, Nat. Com. for Man and Biosphere, 1968-79; tech. adviser to U.S. delegation UN Conf. on Human Environment, Stockholm, Sweden, 1972. Recipient Superior Service award U.S. Dept. Agr., 1953; Disting. Service award, 1965; Spl. award, 1972. Fellow AAAS, Poultry Sci. Assn. (Borden award 1943, pres. 1960-61), Am. Soc. Animal Sci.; mem. Am. Inst. Biol. Scis. (Disting. Service award 1979), Am. Soc. Zoologists, Soc. Exptl. Biology and Medicine, Soc. Growth and Devel., Acad. Medicine D.C., Am. Poultry Hist. Assn. (Hall of Fame 1983). Club: Cosmos (Washington). Home: 6-J Ridge Rd Greenbelt MD 20770

BYERRUM, RICHARD UGLOW, college dean; b. Aurora, Ill., Sept. 22, 1920; s. Earl Edward and Florence (Uglow) B.; m. Claire Somers, Apr. 3, 1945; children: Elizabeth, Mary, Carey. A.B., Wabash Coll., 1942, D.Sc. (hon.), 1967; Ph.D., U. Ill., 1947. Teaching asst. U. Ill., 1942-44; research asso. U.S. Chem. Corps, toxicity dept. U. Chgo., 1944-47; faculty Mich. State U., East Lansing, 1947—, prof. biochemistry, 1957—, acting dir., 1961-62, dean, 1962—. Author: (with others) Experimental Biochemistry, 1956; Editorial bd.: Phytochemistry, 1961-81; Contbr. numerous articles to profl. jours. Mem. Project Hope, 1961—; Trustee Mich. Health Council, 1961—, pres., 1966. Travel grantee Internat. Congress Biochemistry, Vienna, 1958, Internat. Congress Biochemistry, Montreal, 1959. Mem. Am. Chem. Soc. (lectr. vis. scientist program, awards com., visitor for com. profl. tng.), N. Central Assn. Colls. and Secondary Schs., A.A.A.S., Am. Soc. Plant Physiologists (trustee, exec. com.), Am. Soc. Biol. Chemists, Soc. Exptl. Biology and Medicine, Mich. Acad. Arts, Sci. and Letters, Phi Beta Kappa (pres. local chpt. 1962), Sigma Xi (awards com., Jr. Research award Mich. State U. chpt. 1958), Phi Kappa Phi (pres. 1968-69), Phi Lambda Upsilon, Alpha Chi Sigma, Beta Theta Pi. Patentee cancer tumor inhibiting material. Home: 602 Wildwood Dr East Lansing MI 48823

BYERS, BUCKLEY MORRIS, business exec.; b. Pitts., Jan. 7, 1917; s. John Frederic and Caroline Mitchell (Morris) B.; m. Rosamond Farrell Murray, Nov. 19, 1940; children—Buckley Morris, Joseph Murray, Christopher Farrell. A.B., Yale U., 1940. Salesman A.M. Byers Co., Pitts., 1940-42, asst. mgr., Washington, 1942, N.Y.C., 1945-51, mgr. export dept., 1946-51, asst. mgr. steel sales, 1951-53, gen. mgr. wrought iron sales, 1953-54, v.p. charge sales, 1954-57, pres., 1957-62, dir., 1948-70; v.p., spl. asst. to pres. Blaw-Knox Co., Pitts., 1962-64; pres., dir. Byers McManus Assos. Inc., Washington, 1965—. Dep. fin. chmn. Republican Nat. Com., 1976—. Served from ensign to lt. USN Intelligence, 1942-45; overseas 4 major invasions in ETO, PTO. Recipient Presl. citation and Individual commendation. Mem. Nat. Steeplechase and Hunt Assn. Clubs: F St., Capitol Hill, Carlton, Internat., Met. (Washington); Rolling Rock, Duquesne, Allegheny Country (Pitts.); Fence, Book and Snake (Yale); Racquet and Tennis (N.Y.C.). Home: 4212 48th Pl NW Washington DC 20016 Office: 310 1st St SE Washington DC 20003

BYERS, LEX J., association executive; b. San Francisco, Dec. 20, 1926; s. Lex Jasper and Jennie Elizabeth (Kessinger) B.; m. Nancy R. Bischak, Sept. 5, 1965; children—Lex J., Steven Jack, Matthew Jason, Kimberly Jay. B.A., Wash. State U., 1959. Enlisted in U.S. Army, 1944, advanced through grades to lt. col., 1964; service in, Japan, Germany, Korea and, Panama, ret., 1966; gen. mgr. San Francisco C. of C., 1966-78; pres. Oakland (Calif.) C. of C., 1978-82; exec. dir. San Francisco Coalition of Bus. and Labor, 1983—. Decorated Silver Star, Purple Heart, Combat Inf. badge. Clubs: St. Francis Yacht, Masons. Office: 233 SansomeSt San Francisco CA 94104

BYERS, NINA, physics educator; b. Los Angeles, Jan. 19, 1930; d. Irving M. and Eva (Gertzoff) B.; m. Arthur A. Milhaupt, Jr., Sept. 8, 1974. B.A. in Physics, U. Calif., Berkeley, 1950, M.S., U. Chgo., 1953, Ph.D., 1956; M.A., U. Oxford, Eng., 1967. Research fellow dept. math. physics U. Birmingham, Eng., 1956-58; research asso., asst. prof. Inst. Theoretical Physics and dept. physics Stanford, 1958-61; asst. then asso. prof. physics U. Calif. at Los Angeles, 1961-67, prof. physics, 1967—; mem. Sch. Math., Inst. Advanced Studies, Princeton, N.J., 1964-65; fellow Somerville Coll., Oxford, 1967-68, Janet Watson vis. fellow, 1968-76; faculty lectr. U. Oxford, 1967-68, sr. vis. scientist, 1973-74. John Simon Guggenheim Meml. fellow, 1963-64; Sci. Research Council fellow Oxford U., 1978. Fellow AAAS (mem.-at-large physics sect. 1983—), Am. Phys. Soc. (councillor at large 1977-81, Mem., mem. panel public affairs 1980-83, chmn. Forum on Physics and Soc. 1982-83), Fedn. Am. Scientists (nat. council 1972-76, 78-80, exec. com. 1974-76, 78-80). Research theory particle physics and superconductivity. Office: Dept Physics U Calif Los Angeles CA 90024

BYERS, RICHARD GEORGE, oil company executive, lawyer; b. Rimbey, Alta., Can., June 28, 1937; s. John N.C. and Teresa B.; m. Eleanor R. King, May 14, 1960; children: Douglas Richard, Eleanor Diane, Stephen Donald. B.Sc., U. Alta., 1960, LL.B., 1968. Bar: Called to Alta. bar 1969. Gen. counsel, sec. Union Oil Co. Can. Ltd., Calgary, 1973—, dir., 1980—; sec.-treas., dir. Obed Mountain Coal Co. Ltd.; dir. Union Oil Holdings Ltd., 1973—. Mem. Canadian, Calgary bar assns., Alta. Law Soc., Canadian Petroleum Law Found., Calgary C. of C. Clubs: Calgary Petroleum, Pinebrook Golf and Country. Home: 1531 Varsity Estates Dr NW Calgary AB Canada T3B 3Y5 Office: Union Oil Co Can Ltd PO Box 999 Calgary AB Canada T2P 2K6

BYERS, WALTER, athletic assn. exec.; b. Kansas City, Mo., Mar. 13, 1922; s. Ward and Lucille (Hebard) B.; children—Ward, Ellen, Frederick. Student, Rice U., 1939-40, U. Iowa at Iowa City, 1940-43. News reporter United Press Assn. (now U.P.I.), St. Louis, 1944; sports editor U.P.I., Madison, Wis., 1945, Chgo., 1945, asst. sports editor, N.Y.C., 1946-47; also fgn. sports editor; dir. Big Ten Conf. Service Bur., Chgo., 1947-51; exec. asst. Nat. Collegiate Athletic Assn., Chgo., 1947-51, exec. dir., 1951-52, Kansas City, Mo., 1952-73, Shawnee Mission, Kans., 1973—; Pres. Byers Seven Cross Ranch, Inc., Emmett, Kans., 1974—. Served with M.C. AUS, 1944. Home: Box 1525 Mission KS 66222 Office: Box 1906 Shawnee Mission KS 66222

BYINGTON, S. JOHN, lawyer.; b. Grand Rapids, Mich.; m. Sally Ruth Meyer; children: Nancy, Barbara. B.Phar., Ferris State Coll., Big Rapids, Mich.; postgrad., U. Mich. Law Sch.; J.D., Georgetown U., 1963; hon. doctorate, Albany Sch. Pharmacy. Dir. pub. relations Am. Pharm. Assn., 1961-64; asst. pros. atty. Kent County, Grand Rapids, 1964-65; mem. gov.'s staff State of Mich., 1965-68; practice law, Oakland County, Mich., 1968-72; dir. Detroit Office Dept. Commerce, from 1972; dep. dir., nat. export mktg. dir., Washington, until 1974; dep. dir. Office Consumer Affairs HEW, Washington, from 1974; dep. spl. asst. for consumer affairs to Pres. Ford, Washington; chmn. U.S. Consumer Product Safety Commn., 1976-78; partner firm Bushnell, Gage, Reizen & Byington, Detroit, 1978-81, Rogers Hoge & Hills, N.Y.C. and Washington, 1981-83, Pillsbury Madison & Sutro, San Francisco and Washington, 1983—; co-founder, mem. Interagy. Regulatory Liaison Group, Washington, 1976-78; dir. Control Laser Corp.; guest lectr. on product liability George Washington U. Mem. adv. council Ctr. for Study of Presidency; mem. nat. adv. bd. Citizen's Choice, Inc. Mem. ABA, Fed. Bar Assn., D.C. Bar Assn., Mich. Bar Assn., Am. Pharmacists Assn., Mich. Pharmacists Assn., U.S. C. of C. (govt. and regulatory affairs com.). Club: Chemists. Office: 1050 17th St NW Washington DC 20036

BYLINSKY, GENE MICHAEL, magazine editor; b. Belgrade, Yugoslavia, Dec. 30, 1930; s. Michael Ivan and Dora (Shadan) B.; m. Gwen Gallegos, Aug. 14, 1955; children: Tanya, Gregory. B.A. in Journalism, La. State U., 1955. Staff reporter Wall St. Jour., Dallas, 1957-59, San Francisco, 1959-61, N.Y.C., 1961; sci. writer Nat. Observer, Washington, 1961-62, Newhouse Newspapers, 1962-66; asso. editor Fortune Mag., N.Y.C., 1966—. Author: The Innovation Millionaires, 1976, Mood Control, 1978, Life in Darwin's Universe, 1981. Served with AUS, 1956. Recipient 21st Ann. Albert Lasker Med. Journalism award, 1970, Deadline award Sigma Delta Chi, 1970, 72; spl. commendation, 1967, 68, 72; Med. Journalism award, 1974; both A.M.A.; Claude Bernard Sci. Journalism award Nat. Soc. Med. Research, 1973, 74; hon. mention, 1970, 71; James. T. Grady award for interpreting chemistry to public Am. Chem. Soc., 1976. Mem. Nat. Assn. Sci. Writers, N.Y. Acad. Scis. Mem. Russian Orthodox Ch. Office: Time and Life Bldg Rockefeller Center New York NY 10020

BYNUM, BARBARA STEWART, health scientist administrator; b. Washington, June 13, 1936; d. Oliver Walton and Mabel (Easton) Stewart; m. Edward Bynum, Apr. 4, 1959; 1 son, Christian. B.A. in Chemistry, U. Pa., 1957; postgrad. in biochemistry, Georgetown U., 1958-60. Chemist Nat. Cancer Inst.-NIH, Bethesda, Md., 1958-71; adminstrv. asst. office assoc., for adminstrn. NIH, Bethesda, 1971-72, sci. grants program specialist div. research grants, 1972-75, health scientist adminstr. div. research grants, 1975-78, asst. chief for spl. programs, sic. rev. br. div. research grants, 1978-81; dir. div. extramural activities Nat. Cancer Inst., Bethesda, 1981—; reviewer, cons. AAAS, Washington, 1974—. Contbr. articles to profl. jours. Recipient Dirs. award NIH, 1980, Sr. Exec. Service Superior Performance award HHS, 1982. Mem. Am. Assn. Cancer Research, Am. Assn. Pathologists, AAAS, Biophys. Soc. Democrat. Roman Catholic. Office: Nat Cancer Inst 9000 Rockville Pike Bethesda MD 20205

BYRD, BENJAMIN FRANKLIN, JR., surgeon, educator; b. Nashville, May 18, 1918; s. Benjamin Franklin and Ida (Brister) B.; m. Allison Caldwell, Feb. 6, 1950; children: Benjamin Franklin, Barney Duncan, Damon Winston, Andrew Wayne, Evelyn Hope, John W. Thomas. A.B., Vanderbilt U., 1938, M.D., 1941. Intern, Nashville Gen. Hosp., 1941-42, asst. resident, 1942, Vanderbilt U. Hosp., 1945-47, resident, 1947-48; practice medicine, specializing in surgery, Nashville, 1948—; chief surgery St. Thomas Hosp., 1964-70, pres. staff, 1977-79; mem. staff Baptist Hosp.; instr. surgery Vanderbilt U., Nashville, 1947-54, asso. clin. prof. surgery, 1954-71, clin. prof. surgery, 1971—; asso. clin. prof. surgery Meharry Med. Coll., Nashville, 1951-69, prof. clin. surgery, 1969—; dir., mem. trust bd. Commerce Union Bank, 1974-80; dir. NLT Corp. Pres. Tenn. div. Am. Cancer Soc., 1963, nat. bd. dirs., 1965—, nat. exec. com., 1970—, chmn. med. and sci. exec. com., 1973—, nat. pres., 1975-76; pres., mem. exec. bd. Tenn. Bot. Gardens and Fine Arts Center, 1971-73; trustee Sr. Citizens, Hermitage Assn.; bd. dirs. Cumberland Mus. Served to lt. col. M.C., AUS, 1941-45. Decorated Bronze Star with oak leaf cluster, Silver Star, Purple Heart. Fellow ACS (gov. 1973—, chmn. commn. on cancer); mem. Am. Surg. Assn., So. Surg. Assn., Nashville Surg. Soc. (pres. 1962-63), Soc. Surg. Oncology, Tenn. Med. Assn. (mem. council, Disting. Service award), So. Med. Assn. (mem. council), Société International de Chirurgie, Southeastern Surg. Congress (mem. council, pres. 1968-69, Disting. Service award 1977), Nashville Acad. Medicine (pres. 1980, chmn. 1981), Nashville C. of C. (bd. govs. 1967-70, 82—, pres.-elect 1984), Vanderbilt U. Med. Alumni (pres. 1979-81), Sigma Xi. Club: Nashville Exchange. Home: 400 Ellendale Dr Nashville TN 37205 Office: 2122 West End Ave Nashville TN 37203

BYRD, CHARLES DANIELL, manufacturing company executive; b. Atlanta, May 3, 1925; s. Lloyd Porter and Gladys (Daniell) B.; m. Suzanne Ballinger, May 18, 1952; children: Steven Daniel, Cynthia Suzanne. B.S. in Bus. Adminstrn, Ohio State U., 1950. With Dresser Industries, Inc., Columbus, Ohio, 1952—, exec. v.p., Columbus, 1961-65, pres., Dallas, 1965-68, Salisbury, Md., 1968-71, Petroleum Equipment Group, Houston, 1971—; dir. AB Ljungmans Verkstader, Malmo, Sweden, Wayne Pump & Tank Co., Reading, Eng.; v.p. Symington Wayne Internat., Ont., Can., 1974—. Chmn. Greater Salisbury Com., 1975-77; chmn. mfg. div. Combined Arts Corp. Campaign, Houston, 1979-80. Served with USAF, 1943-45. Mem. Am. Petroleum Inst., Am. Lift Inst., Gasoline and Pump Mfrs. Assn., Ohio State U. Assn. Republican. Methodist. Club: Houston Petroleum. Office: 2600 Dresser Tower 601 Jefferson St Houston TX 77002

BYRD, DAVID LAMAR, dentist, educator; b. Houston, June 3, 1922; s. William Leslie and Gabie O. (Cissell) B.; m. Carobeth Weeber, Feb. 1, 1947; 1 dau., Sharon Ann. D.D.S., U. Tex., 1946; M.S.D. in Oral Surgery, Northwestern U., 1949. Diplomate: Am. Bd. Oral Surgery (past mem. examining bd.). Intern Jackson Meml. Hosp., Miami, Fla., 1949-50; resident oral surgery Charity Hosp., New Orleans, 1950-51; prof., chmn. dept. oral and maxillofacial surgery Baylor Coll. Dentistry, Dallas, 1951—; cons. in oral surgery Southwestern Med. Sch. U. Tex.; cons. U.S. Army, Ft. Hood, Tex.; chief dept. dentistry Baylor U. Med. Center; attending staff St. Pauls, Presbyn., Parkland Meml. hosps.; Mem. com. grad. dental edn. Am. Cancer Soc., 1955—, bd. dirs., med. v.p., now pres.; sr. cons. U.S. Army. Author: Emergencies in Dentistry; Editor: Current Therapy in Dentistry, 1st, 2d, 3d, vols; Contbr. articles to profl. jours. Bd. dirs. Dallas chpt. Med. Benevolence Found., Hemophiliac Found.; pres., Central Dallas Unit, Am. Cancer Soc. Served as lt. USNR, 1946-48. Recipient Distinguished Tchr. award Acad. Gen. Practice of Dentistry, 1971, 1st place award Oral Surgery Clinic, various awards Dallas Mid-Winter Clinic. Fellow Internat., Am. colls. dentists, Internat. Soc. Oral Surgeons, mem., Am. Soc. Oral Surgeons, Tex. Soc. Oral Surgeons, S.W. Soc. Oral Surgeons (past pres.), Am., Tex. dental assns., Sigma Xi, Omicron Kappa Upsilon. Home: 1 Cornerstone Pkwy Dallas TX 75225

BYRD, DONALD ARTHUR, county official; b. Dallas, July 27, 1927; s. John Henry and Blanch (Corley) B.; children: Susan R., Linda R., Joyce R. B.S., U. Albuquerque, 1972. Mem., Dallas; Police Dept., 1951-71, 73—, asst. chief police, then exec. asst. chief police, chief of police, 1973-79; pres. Don Byrd Co., from 1979; chief of police, City of Albuquerque, 1971-73; mem. Tex. Gov's. Bd. on Criminal Justice Council, 1982; organizer Crime Prevention Council, Tex.; sheriff, Dallas County, 1980—. Served with USM, U.S. Maritime Service, 1944-46; Served with USN, 1946. Mem. FBI Nat. Acad. Grads., Tex. Municipal Police Assn., Internat. Assn. Chiefs Police, North Tex. Police Chief's Assn., North Tex. Coordinating Council Law Enforcement, New Mex. Arabian Horse Assn. (past pres.), North Tex. Arabian Horse Club (pres. 1977-78). Methodist. Clubs: Masons, Shriners, Jesters. Office: Dallas County Govt Center Dallas TX 75202

BYRD, HARRY FLOOD, JR., former U.S. senator, newspaper executive; b. Winchester, Va., Dec. 20, 1914; s. Harry Flood and Anne Douglas (Beverley) B.; m. Gretchen B. Thomson, Aug. 9, 1941; children: Harry, Thomas Thomson, Beverly. Student, Va. Mil. Inst., 1931-33, U. Va., 1933-35; hon. LL.D., L.H.D., D. Internat. Service. Editor Winchester Evening Star, from 1935; pub. Harrisonburg (Va.) Daily News-Record, 1937—; Pres., dir. Rockingham Pub. Co., 1946; dir. A.P., 1950-66; v.p., mem. exec. com.; mem. Va. Senate, 1947-65; mem. U.S. Senate from Va., 1965-83. Author state automatic tax reduction law. Mem. Va. Democratic Central Com., 1940-66. Served to lt. comdr. USNR, 1942-46. Recipient Honor medal Freedoms Found. Mem. V.F.W., Am. Legion. Clubs: Rotarian., National Press, Army-Navy. Home: Winchester VA 22601 Office: Rockingham Pub Co 213 S Liberty St PO Box 193 Harrisonburg VA 22801

BYRD, ISAAC BURLIN, fishery biologist, fisheries adminstr.; b. Canoe, Ala., Mar. 14, 1925; s. Isaac Britt and Mary Adline (Wright) B.; m. Marjorie Fé Elmore, Sept. 24, 1949; children—Cathy Ann, Teresa Carol, Gary Curtis. B.S., Auburn U., 1948, M.S., 1950. Chief fisheries sect. Ala. Dept. Conservation, 1951-65; fed. aid coordinator fisheries research and devel. Bur. Comml. Fisheries, Dept. Interior, 1965-70; chief div. state-fed. relationships, fisheries research, devel. and mgmt. Nat. Marine Fisheries Service, 1970—; adminstr. Internat. Fisheries Agreement (for U.S. shrimp fishermen to fish Brazilian coastal waters), 1975-76; mem. adv. com. to organize 1st fishery mgmt. councils and to develop initial fed. policies under Fisheries Conservation and Mgmt. Act 1976 (for marine fisheries in fisheries conservation zone of U.S.). Contbg. author: McCanes Standard Fishing Ency., Internat. Angling Guide, 1965; contbr. articles to sci. jours. Served with USAAF, 1943-46. Recipient Gov. Ala. award outstanding tech. accomplishments conservation, 1964. Fellow Am. Inst. Fishery Research Biologists; mem. Am. Fisheries Soc. (pres. So. div. 1958, pres. 1965-66, asso. editor trans. 1955-58), World Mariculture Soc. (dir. 1972-73), Internat. Assn. Fish and Wildlife Agys., Gulf and Caribbean Fisheries Inst., Inland Comml. Fisheries Assn., Phi Kappa Phi, Omicron Delta Kappa, Gamma Sigma Delta, Alpha Zeta, Alpha Gamma Rho. Baptist (Sunday sch. tchr.). Initiated 1st fisheries mgmt. and fisheries research program in state for Ala. Dept. Conservation. Home: 11105 7th St E Treasure Island Saint Petersburg FL 33706 Office: Nat Marine Fisheries Service 9450 Koger Blvd Saint Petersburg FL 33702

BYRD, JAMES ADON, bank economist; b. Houston, Aug. 25, 1924; s. James Amory and Roberta (Lamb) B.; m. Patricia Gay Leatherman, Mar. 15, 1945; children—Douglas Lamb, Pamela, Katherine Ames. Student, Southwestern U., 1941-42; B.B.A., U. Tex., 1950, M.B.A., 1955, Ph.D., 1957. Asst. prof. finance U. Tex., 1957-58; v.p., econ. adviser Tex. Commerce Bank, Houston, 1958-67; asst. to pres., prof. finance U. Houston, 1967-70; sr. v.p., economist First Nat. Bank Dallas, 1970-72; economist First Internat. Bancshares, Inc., Dallas, 1972—; mem. faculty Southwestern Grad. Sch. Banking So. Meth. U., 1960—, Stonier Grad. Sch. Banking Rutgers U., 1969—. Served with USAAF, 1943-46. Mem. Nat. Assn. Bus. Economists, Am. Econ. Assn., Dallas Economists Club. Clubs: Dallas Petroleum, Houston. Home: 3624 Bryn Mawr St Dallas TX 75225 Office: 1201 Elm St Dallas TX 75283

BYRD, MILTON BRUCE, business executive, former college president; b. Boston, Jan. 29, 1922; s. Max Joseph and Rebecca (Malkiel) B.; m. Susanne J. Schwerin, Aug. 30, 1953; children: Deborah, Leslie, David. A.B. cum laude, Boston U., 1948, M.A., 1949; Ph.D., U. Wis., 1953; postgrad. (fellow), U. Mich., 1961-62. Teaching asst. English U. Wis., 1949-53; instr., asst. prof. English Ind. U., 1953-58; asst. prof., asso. prof. humanities So. Ill. U., 1958-62, head div. humanities, 1958-60, supr. acad. advisement, 1959-60, asso. dean, 1960- 62; v.p. acad. affairs No. Mich. U., 1962-66; pres. Chgo. State U., 1966-74; provost Fla. Internat. U., 1974-78; pres. Adams State Coll., Alamosa, Colo., 1978-81; v.p. corp. devel. Frontier Cos., Anchorage, 1981—; Bd. dirs Chgo. Council for Urban Edn., Union for Experimenting Colls. and Univs., Am. Assn. State Colls. and Univs., Resource Devel. Council Alaska, Alaska Commn. Econ. Edn.; sec. Common Sense for Alaska, Inc.; pres. Alaska Support Industry Alliance. Author: (with Arnold L. Goldsmith) Publication Guide for Literary and Linguistic Scholars, 1958; contbr. to profl. jours. Served with USAAF, 1943-46. Mem. MLA, Nat. Council Tchrs. English, Coll. English Assn., Am. Studies Assn., AAUP, Fla. Assn. Univ. Adminstrs. (pres.), Rocky Mountain Athletic Conf. (pres.), Assn. for Higher Edn., Pub. Relations Soc. Am., NEA, Alaska Press Club, Mich. Edn. Assn., Phi Beta Kappa, Phi Delta Kappa. Club: Rotary. Office: PO Box 101616 Anchorage AK 99510

BYRD, RICHARD EDWARD, clergyman, psychologist; b. St. Petersburg, Fla., Jan. 23, 1931; s. Eldo Lawton and Louise (Parker) B.; m. Helen Mandeville Penn, Aug. 31, 1950; children—Jackie Louise, Richard Edward. B.A., U. Fla., 1952; M.S.T., Va. Theol. Sem., Alexandria, 1956; Ph.D., N.Y. U., 1970. Ordained priest Episcopal Ch., 1956; priest-in-charge St. Paul's Ch., Waldo, Fla., also; 1St. Anne's Ch., Keystone Heights, Fla., 1956-57; vicar, then rector Grace Episc. Ch., West Palm Beach, Fla., 1957-60; asst. Trinity Ch., West Palm Beach, 1957-58; founder Ch. of Holy Communion, Hawthorne, Fla., 1957; pres. The Richard E. Byrd Co., Faribault, Minn., 1966—; exec. v.p. Wilson Center for Edn. and Psychiatry, Faribault, 1977-79, also group therapist, individual therapist, supr. group therapy, 1971-75; dir. E.W. Cook Sch. Psychotherapy, 1972-77; past chief exec. Jones & Byrd Inc. (Tng. Cons. Internat.); adj. faculty dept. psychology Antioch Coll., Yellow Springs, Ohio, 1973—, adj. faculty, Columbia, Md., 1976, Am. U., Washington; asso. sec. adult edn. and leadership tng. Exec. Council Episc. Ch., 1961-64; inventor Creative Risk Taking Lab.; cons. tng. Ch. Action Program, St. Martins-by-the Lake, Minnetonka Beach, Minn., 1964-66; vis. lectr. Hamline U.; instr. Cornell Sch. Indsl. Relations. Author: Crises in Faith, 1964, Creative Risk Taking Training Laboratory, Book of Basic Readings, 1967, Communication, 1970, Seize the Times, 1971, A Guide to Personal Risk Taking, 1974, 77, Paperback, 1978; contbr. articles to profl. jours. Co-founder Greenwich (Conn.) Fair Housing Assn., 1963; 1st chmn. Human Rights Commn., Edina, Minn., 1971; dist. chmn. United Fund, 1971. Mem. Am., Minn. psychol. assns., Assn. for Creative Change (1st pres.), Internat. Assn. Applied Social Scientists, NTL Inst., Am. Psychol. Assn. Address: 4900 W Sunnyside Rd Minneapolis MN 55424 *My life has been characterized by an uninterrupted confidence in God and a search for discovering what I do best and how to refine it in service to others.*

BYRD, ROBERT CARLYLE, U.S. senator; b. North Wilkesboro, N.C., Nov. 20, 1917; s. Cornelius Sale and Ada (Kirby) B.; m. Erma Ora James, May 29, 1937; children: Mona Carole (Mrs. Mohammad Fatemi), Marjorie Ellen (Mrs. John Moore). Student, Beckley Coll., Concord Coll., Morris Harvey Coll., 1950-51, Marshall U., 1951-52; J.D., Am. U., 1963. Elected mem. W.Va. Ho. of Dels., 1946-50, W.Va. Senate, 1950-52; mem. 83d-85th Congresses, 6th Dist., W.Va.; U.S. senator from, W. Va., 1959—, Senate majority leader, 1977-79, Senate minority leader, 1980—. Named Most Influential Mem. U.S. Senate U.S. News & World Report Poll, 1979. Mem. Country Music Assn. (hon.). Democrat. Baptist. Lodge: Masons (33°). Office: 311 Hart Senate Office Bldg Washington DC 20510 *

BYRD, STEPHEN FRED, pharmaceutical company executive; b. Charleston, S.C., June 12, 1928; s. Paul Fred and Dorothy B.; m. Margaret A. McAulay, Apr. 15, 1955; children: Owen, Susan. Student, CCNY, 1945-48; LL.B., N.Y. Law Sch., 1951. Bar: N.Y. 1951. Corp. indsl. relations rep. Pan Am. Airways, 1957-62, Sinclair Oil Corp., 1962-64; v.p. employee relations indsl. chems. div. Allied Chem. Corp., 1964-68; v.p. indsl. relations and personnel Internat. Nickel Co., Ltd., 1968-72; sr. v.p. human resources Schering-Plough Corp., Kenilworth, N.J., 1973—. Author: Front Line Supervisors Labor Relations Handbook, 1962, Management Strategy in Collective Bargaining, 1964. Bd. dirs. United Fund Morris County, N.J., Big Bros. Morris County, Morristown YMCA, 1962-63; chmn. Madison council Boy Scouts Am., 1975-76; trustee Drew U., Madison, N.J., 1976-80. Served with AUS, 1952-53; Korea. Mem. Indsl. Relations Research Assn., N.Y. Law Sch. Alumni Assn. Home: 23 Academy Rd Madison NJ 07940 Office: One Giralda Farms Madison NJ 07940

BYRNE, BRENDAN, public affairs consultant; b. N.Y.C., Dec. 28, 1908; s. Thomas J. and Clara (Janson) B.; m. Rena H. Faecher, July 1, 1937; children: Mary P., Michael K., Judith A. A.B. magna cum laude, Fordham U., 1930, M.A., 1936. Chmn. social studies dept. John Adams High Sch., N.Y.C., 1931-42; editor Facts mag., Read mag., New Books Digest, 1946; research dir., copywriter Grady Advt. Agy., 1947; dir. programs Am. Heritage Found., 1947-50, assoc. dir., 1956, exec. dir., 1956, 1957-65; public affairs cons. ITT Fed. Electric Corp., 1965—; pres. Richmond Hill Devel Corp., 1982—; trustee Richmond Hill Savs. Bank, 1969—; Pub. relations dir. Nat. Citizens Commn. for Better Schs., 1950; v.p. Valley Forge Found., 1951-52; exec. v.p. Goldby & Byrne. Inc. (philanthropic cons.), N.Y.C., 1954-55; pub. affairs cons. Author: Guide to the Study of History, 1936, American Heritage Manual, 1950, Alert America Public Relations Guide, 1951, Three Weeks to a Better Memory, 1951, Let's Modernize Our Horse-and-Buggy Election Laws, 1961, How to Help or Hurt Your Country, 1963; Contbr. articles to profl. jours. Mem. Pres.'s Commn. on Registration and Voter Participation, 1962-65; vice chmn. N.Y. Commn. on Hist. Observances, 1960-63; dir. Nat. Conf. on Citizenship, 1962—; dir. nationwide campaign Contribute to Your Polit. Party, 1958-65, nonpartisan program to modernize archaic election laws, 1957-65, Register, Inform Yourself and Vote Program, 1957-65; mem. N.Y.C. Bd. Edn., 1961-64, N.Y.C. Nat. Shrines Com., 1969—. Served from lt. (j.g.) to lt. comdr. USNR, 1942-45; ETO. Decorated Sec. of Navy Letter of Commendation; recipient Freedoms Found. George Washington honor medal for pub. speaking, 1963; S.A.R. Gold Good Citizenship medal, 1948. Mem. Pub. Relations Soc. Am., N.Y. Hist. Soc., Am. Polit. Sci. Assn., Authors League Am., Authors Guild, Am. Mgmt. Assn., Am. Acad. Polit. Scis., Nat. Municipal League, Adult Edn. Assn., Advt. Club N.Y.C., Fordham U. Alumni Assn. (bd. dirs.), Am. Polit. Sci. Assn. Club: Naval Reserve Officers (N.Y.C.). Home: 8405 108th St Richmond Hill NY 11418 Office: 111-27 Jamaica Ave Richmond Hill NY 11418

BYRNE, CHARLES RAYMOND, editor, pub.; b. Bklyn., Mar. 17, 1916; s. Charles Ambrose and Rose Cecilia (Garrity) B.; m. Dorothy Grace Smith, June 30, 1941; children—Anthony Richard, Adrian Michael, Nicholas Charles, Alison Andrea. A.B., Fordham U., 1938, student, 1938-40; postgrad., Columbia, 1948-50, N.Y.U., 1950-52. With N.Y. Post, 1938-40; v.p., editor-in-chief Avon Pub. Co., 1946-54; pres., editor-in-chief Berkley Pub. Corp., 1954-60; editor-in-chief Avon Books (pub. by Hearst Corp.), 1960-61; pub. editor-in-chief paperback book div. Macfadden Publs., Inc., 1961-66, v.p. book div., 1965-66; mgr. subsidiary and fgn. rights, editor Meredith Press div. Meredith Pub. Co., 1966—; dir. gen. trade book pub. Consumer Book div. Meredith Corp.; founder own lit. agy., 1974; dir. Carroland Realty Corp.; Rep. of Macfadden Publs. to Am. Book Pubs. Council. Served to capt., arty. AUS, 1940-45. Clubs: New York Athletic; Racquet (Yonkers, N.Y.); Dutch Treat. Home: 2728 Henry Hudson Pkwy Riverdale New York NY 10463 Office: 128 E 56th St New York NY 10022

BYRNE, DAVID, musician, composer, artist, director; b. Dumbarton, Scotland, May 14, 1952; came to U.S., 1958; s. Thomas and Emily Anderson (Brown) B. Student, R.I. Sch. Design. Performer Talking Heads, N.Y.C., 1975—. Musician, composer, producer LP recs., 1980—; dir., producer: Index Video, N.Y.C., 1983—; songwriter: Talking Heads Group albums, including Talking Heads: 77, 1977, More Songs About Buildings and Food, 1978, Fear of Music, 1979, Remain in Light, 1980, My Life in the Bush of Ghosts, 1981, The Name of This Band Is Talking Heads, 1982, David Byrne: Songs from The Catherine Wheel, 1982, Speaking in Tongues, 1983; dir. videotapes, 1981—; artist stage design, lighting, LP covers and posters, 1977—. Office: Index Music care Overland 1775 Broadway New York NY 10019

BYRNE, DONN ERWIN, psychologist, educator; b. Austin, Tex., Dec. 19, 1931; s. Bernard Devine and Rebecca (Singleton) B.; m. Lois Ann Pugsley, Sept. 12, 1953 (div. 1978); children: Keven Singleton, Robin Lynn; m. Kathryn Kelley, Aug. 17, 1979; 1 child, Lindsey Kelley. B.A., Calif. State U., Fresno, 1953, M.A., 1956; Ph.D., Stanford U., 1958. Instr. psychology Calif. State U., San Francisco, 1957-59; asst. prof. psychology U. Tex., Austin, 1959-62, asso. prof., 1962-66, asst. chmn., 1964-66; vis. prof. psychology Stanford U., Palo Alto, Calif., 1966-67, U. Hawaii, Honolulu, 1968; prof. psychology U. Tex., 1966-69, dir. exptl. personality program, 1963-69; prof. psychology Purdue U., West Lafayette, Ind., 1969-79, chmn. social personality program, 1972-78; prof. psychology SUNY at Albany, 1979—, chmn. social-personality program, 1980—; panel mem. NSF grad. fellowship program NRC, 1972; NIH participant Inst. Sex Research Summer Program, 1974. Author: (with H.C. Lindgren) Psychology: An Introduction to the Study of Human Behavior, 1961, 66, 71, 75, (with P. Worchel) Personality Change, 1964, An Introduction to Personality: A Research Approach, 1966, 74, (3d edit. with K. Kelley), 1981, (with M.L. Hamilton) Personality Research: A Book of Readings, 1966, The Attraction Paradigm, 1971, (with R.A. Baron and W. Griffitt) Social Psychology: Understanding Human Interaction, 1974, (2d and 3d, 4th edits. with R.A. Baron), 77, 81, (with R.A. Baron, B.H. Kantowitz) Psychology: Understanding Behavior, 1977, 80 (with L.A. Byrne), Exploring Human Sexuality, 1977, (with K. Kelley) An Introduction to Personality, 1981, (with W.A. Fisher) Adolescents, Sex, and Contraception, 1983; contbr. numerous articles to psychol. jours. and chpts. to anthologies. Grantee NSF, NIMH, U. Tex. Research Inst., USAF, others.; G. Stanley Hall lectr. Am. Psychol. Assn., 1981. Mem. Midwestern Psychol. Assn. (pres. 1979-80). Invited participant numerous univ. colloquia; numerous presentations to various psychol. assns. Home: 140 Indian Hill Rd Feura Bush NY 12067 *All of us are seeking the ultimately impossible aims of happiness and self-satisfaction. The former is achieved, however fleetingly, by sensual pleasures and by the reaching of a series of challenging but attainable goals. Satisfaction depends not only on attaining such goals, but also on the unoriginal but golden ideal of treating other individuals with the same measure of fairness and kindness that we desire from them.*

BYRNE, EDWARD BLAKE, broadcasting company executive; b. Columbus, Ohio, July 2, 1935; s. John Francis and Naomi Elaine (Hart) B.; m. Mary Frances Bowden, May 28, 1960; children: John, Jocelyn. B.A., Duke U., 1957; M.B.A., Columbia U., 1961. Trainee, fin. analyst, sales service account exec. CBS TV Network, 1961-64; account exec. Edward Petry Co., 1964-67; gen. sales mgr. Sta. KPTV, Portland, Oreg., 1967-73; gen. mgr. Sta. WJAR-TV, The Outlet Co., 1973-74; pres., gen. mgr. Sta KXAS-TV, LIN Broadcasting, Ft. Worth, 1974—; group v.p. TV LIN Broadcasting; dir. Seminary State Bank, Ft. Worth. Bd. dirs. Goodwill Industries, 1975-79, United Way, 1974—. Served with U.S. Army, 1957-59. Mem. Nat. Assn. Broadcasters, TV Bur. Advt., Tex. Assn. Broadcasters, Oreg. Assn. Broadcasters, R.I. Assn. Broadcasters, Young Pres.'s Orgn. (chmn. West Tex. 1978). Episcopalian. Clubs: University (N.Y.C.); Ft. Worth, Rivercrest. Office: PO Box 1780 Fort Worth TX 76101

BYRNE, JAMES HENRY, public relations executive; b. Utica, N.Y., Jan. 14, 1937; s. James Henry and Ruth Evelyn (Jones) B.; m. Carol C. Carville, July 4, 1964; children: James H., Carrie E. B.A. in Journalism and Am. Studies, Syracuse (N.Y.) U., 1959. Mgr. news info. CBS-TV, 1967-70; dir. info. services CBS News, 1970-73; asst. postmaster gen. for communications U.S. Postal Service, 1973-77; sr. v.p., dir. public relations services N.W. Ayer ABH Internat., N.Y.C., 1977-83; dir. communications U.S. Football League, N.Y.C., 1983—. Served with USAR, 1959, 61-62. Mem. Public Relations Soc. Am., Sigma Delta Chi. Home: 107 Hudson Ave Tenafly NJ 07670 Office: 52 Vanderbilt Ave New York NY 10017

BYRNE, JAMES THOMAS, JR., banker, lawyer; b. Queens, N.Y., May 4, 1939; s. James Thomas and Jeanne C. (DiPaola) B.; m. Carolyn M. Vecchio, Jan. 28, 1962; children: Craig Michael, Christopher Thomas. A.B., Adelphi Coll., 1961; LL.B., Bklyn. Law Sch., 1964; grad., Exec. Program, Amos Tuck Sch. Bus. Adminstrn., Darmouth Coll., 1979. Bar: N.Y. 1965. Asso. Mahoney Spohr & Mahoney, N.Y.C., 1964-66, Dillon & O'Brien, 1966-67; with Bankers Trust Co., N.Y.C., 1967—, asst. counsel, asst. sec., 1970-72, asst. gen. counsel, 1972-76, v.p., counsel, 1976-77, v.p., dir. govt. relations, 1977-81, v.p., dir. public affairs, 1981-82, sr. v.p. corp. affairs, 1982—. Vice chmn. bd. trustees, chmn. fin. com. Adelphi U.; bd. govs. Sch. Banking and Money Mgmt.; pres., bd. mgrs. Nassau County Med. Center; bd. dirs. pres. Boys' Athletic League. Mem. ABA, Assn. Bar City N.Y., N.Y. State Bar Assn., Assn. Bank Holding Cos., Am. Bankers Assn., Internat. Mgmt. and Devel. Inst. Republican. Roman Catholic. Club: Capitol Hill (Washington). Home: 110 Kildare Rd Garden City NY 11530 Office: 280 Park Ave New York NY 10017

BYRNE, JEROME CAMILLUS, lawyer; b. Grand Rapids, Mich., Oct. 3, 1925; s. Camillus Abraham and Katherine Blanche (Kelly) B. B.A., Aquinas Coll., 1948; J.D. magna cum laude, Harvard U., 1951. Bar: Calif. 1952. Assoc. firm Gibson Dunn & Crutcher, Los Angeles, 1952-59, partner, 1960—, mem. exec. com., 1981—; spl. counsel to regents U. Calif., 1965. Bd. dirs. Constnl. Rights Found., 1967—, pres., 1971-72; bd. regents Mt. St. Mary's Coll., 1979—. Mem. Am. Bar Assn., Calif. Bar Assn., Los Angeles County Bar Assn., Century City Bar Assn., Am. Judicature Soc., Indsl. Relations Research Assn. Office: 2029 Century Park East Suite 4000 Los Angeles CA 90067

BYRNE, JOHN JAMES, mfg. co. exec.; b. Anaconda, Mont., June 14, 1920; s. Peter J. and Emma (Eakin) B.; m. Florence Rinker, Feb. 11, 1950; children—Katharine Anne, Lael Meredith, Marilyn Rosamond. B.S., Poly. Coll. Engring., 1942. Jr. engr. Richmond (Calif.) Shipbuilding Corp., 1942; mech. engr., sales engr. Adherite Corp., Oakland, Calif., 1946-51; head field service engring. E. W. Bliss Co., Canton, Ohio, 1953-55, mgr. launching and recovery equipment div., 1955-61, dir. research and engring., 1961-64, v.p. research and engring., 1964-69, group v.p. press divs., 1969-70; v.p. engring., research and devel. Gulf & Western Indsl. Products Co., 1970-72; v.p. Advanced Devel. and Engring. Center, G & W Industries, 1972—. Served with USNR, 1942-46; to comdr., 1951-53. Mem. Am. Def. Preparedness Assn., Am. Mgmt. Assn., NAM, Soc. Mfg. Engrs. Club: Merion Golf. Patentee in field. Home: 321 Ellis Rd Havertown PA 19083 Office: 101 Chester Rd Swarthmore PA 19081

BYRNE, JOHN JOSEPH, lawyer; b. Dubuque, Apr. 6, 1925; s. Thomas Edward and Clara (Loes) B.; m. Joan Marie Boyle, Nov. 4, 1950; children: John Joseph, Thomas, Peter, Dennis, Joan, Katherine. B.S., U.S. Mil. Acad., 1946; LL.B., Georgetown U., 1957. Bar: D.C. 1957. Commd. 2d. lt. U.S. Army, 1946, advanced throught grades to capt., 1950, served, Saipan, 1947, Korea, 1947-49, battery comdr., Ft. Meade, Md., 1950-51, ret., 1953; examiner U.S. Patent Office, Washington, 1955-57; assoc. Fisher, Christen & Goodson, Washington, 1957-59, ptnr., 1960-61, Robillard & Byrne, 1962-65, Baker & McKenzie, 1966—; adj. prof. law for intellectual property U. Va., Charlottesville, 1982—. Mem. D.C. Bar Assn., ABA, Fed. Bar Assn., Interam. Bar Assn., Bar Assn. D.C., Am. Patent Law Assn., Lincensing Execs. Soc. Clubs: Met., Army & Navy; Counsellors (Washington). Home: 7718 Savannah Dr Bethesda MD 20817 Office: Baker & McKenzie 815 Conneticut Ave NW Washington DC 20006

BYRNE, JOHN JOSEPH, JR., ins. co. exec.; b. Passaic, N.J., July 11, 1932; s. John Joseph and Winifred (Mohr) B.; m. Dorothy M. Cain, July 22, 1958; children—John Joseph III, Mark James, Patrick Michael. B.S., Rutgers U., 1954; postgrad., Harvard Law Sch., 1957; M.S., U. Mich., 1959. C.L.U. With Lincoln Nat. Life Ins. Co., Ft. Wayne, Ind., 1959-63; exec. v.p. Mass. Life Ins. Co., Boston, 1963-67, Travelers Ins. Cos., Hartford, Conn., 1967-76; chmn. bd., chief exec. officer Geico, 1976—; dir. Martin Marietta, Potomac Electric Power Co. Chmn. Spl. Olympics Premiere, Nat. Symphony Orch. Ann. Fund. Served to maj. USAF, 1954-57. Recipient Boss of Year award Jr. C. of C.; Community Service award United Way. Mem. Soc. Actuaries (asso.), Knights of Malta, Cap and Skull, Zeta Psi. Republican. Roman Catholic. Clubs: Columbia Country (Bethesda, Md.); Univ. (Boston and); (Washington); Burning Tree, Mid Ocean. Home: 7001 Heatherhill Rd Bethesda MD 20034 Office: Geico Plaza Washington DC 20076

BYRNE, JOHN VINCENT, government official; b. Hempstead, N.Y., May 9, 1928; s. Frank E. and Kathleen (Barry) B.; m. Shirley O'Connor, Nov. 26, 1954; children: Donna, Lisa, Karen, Steven. A.B., Hamilton Coll., 1951; M.A., Columbia U., 1953; Ph.D., U. So. Calif., 1957. Research geologist Humble Oil & Refinery Co., Houston, 1957-60; asso. prof. Oreg. State U., Corvallis, 1960-66, prof. oceanography, 1966—, chmn. dept., 1968—, dean, 1972-76, acting dean research, 1976-77, dean research, 1977-81, v.p. for research and grad. studies, 1980-81; adminstr. NOAA, 1981—; Program dir. oceanography NSF, 1966-67. Recipient Carter teaching award, 1964. Fellow AAAS, Geol. Soc. Am.; mem. Am. Assn. Petroleum Geologists, Am. Geophys. Union, Sigma Xi, Chi Psi. Research on oceanography and marine geology. Home: 3355 Quesada St NW Washington DC 20015

BYRNE, JOSEPH WILLIAM, titanium sponge and mill products manufacturing company executive; b. Lawrence, Mass., Apr. 9, 1931; s. Joseph W. and Beatrice M. (MacGregor) B.; m. Estelle McFarland, Jan. 31, 1959; children: Michael, Katherine, Julia. B.S. in Mech. Engring, Cornell U., 1954. With project engring. and mktg. mgmt. depts. Spl. Metals Corp., New Hartford, N.Y., 1956-65; div. gen. mgr., then v.p. ops. Howmet Corp., Greenwich, Conn., 1966-76; pres. TIMET, Pitts., 1977—, TMCA Internat., 1978—; co-chmn. bd. Titanium Metal and Alloys Ltd., London, 1980. Served to lt. U.S. Army, 1954-56. Mem. ASM, AIME. Clubs: Toastmasters, Chartiers Country, Montour Country. Office: PO Box 2824 Pittsburgh PA 15230 *

BYRNE, WILLIAM MATTHEW, JR., federal judge; b. Los Angeles, Sept. 3, 1930; s. William Matthew and Julia Ann (Lamb) B. B.S., U. So. Calif., 1953, LL.B., 1956; LL.D., Loyola U., 1971. Bar: Calif. Became fed. prosecutor, 1966; exec. dir. Pres. Nixon's Commn. Campus Unrest, 1970; now judge U.S. Dist. Ct. (cen. dist.) Calif., Los Angeles. Mem. Los Angeles County Bar Assn. (vice chmn. human rights sect.). Address: US Courthouse 312 N Spring St Los Angeles CA 90012 *

BYRNES, ARTHUR F., federal official; b. N.Y.C., June 28, 1917; s. Arthur I. and Barbara (Young) B.; m. Anne Louise Schug, Dec. 24, 1941; children: Arthur Everett, Sue Anne, John Mitchell. B.S., Manhattan Coll., 1940; student, Springfield (Mass.) Coll., 1942; Ph.D., NYU, 1951. Asst. prof. orgn., adminstrn. and mgmt. Springfield Coll., 1940-42; supt. schs., Monroe, Ind., 1945-49; prof., dir. communications Eastern Ill. State U., Charleston, 1949-53; dir. research, 1953-55; ICA cons. Ministry Edn., Govt. Brazil, 1955-57; div. chief AID, Dept. State, 1957-62, dep. dir. mission, Northeast Brazil, 1962-63, dir. mission, 1963-64, asst. dir. Rio de Janeiro, Brazil,

1964; dep. dir. U.S.; also attaché, econ. and social devel. Am. embassy, Quito, Ecuador, 1965-66; with U.S. Army War Coll., Carlisle, Pa., 1966-67; dir. internat. and regional programs AID, 1967-70, dir. office internat. tng., Washington, 1970—; dir. internat. programs U.S. Dept. Agr. Grad. Sch., 1975—. Mem. Fulbright Brazilian-U.S. Exchange Commn., 1957—; acad. affairs com. Escola Americana, Rio de Janeiro, 1960—. Served to capt. USAAF, 1942-45. Decorated Cruziero do Sul, Brazil, 1960. Mem. Am. C. of C., Am. Soc., AAUP, Fgn. Service Assn., Soc. Internat. Devel., Phi Delta Kappa. Home: 6661 Sorrell St McLean VA 22101 Office: AID U S Dept State Washington DC 20523

BYRNES, GEORGE BARTHOLOMEW, pension-ins. cons.; b. Kansas City, Mo., Oct. 19, 1911; s. James C. and Hannah (Haffey) B.; m. Grace E. Mehren, Apr. 11, 1942; children—Marygrace, Patrick, Robert, Brian, Kathleen. Student, Rockhurst Coll., Kansas City, 1929-31; grad., U. N.Mex., 1935. Rep. Equitable Life Assurance Soc., Albuquerque, 1935-42, dist. mgr., Phoenix, 1942-45, Pasadena, Calif., 1945-54; gen. agt. New Eng. Mut. Life Ins. Co., N.Y.C., 1954-60; cons. pension and profit-sharing planning, bus. and personal estate plans, Los Angeles, 1960—. Pres. Pasadena Tb Assn., 1954, Nat. Epilepsy League, 1960; Bd. dirs. Million Dollar Round Table Found., Des Plaines, Ill.; Mem. bd. fellows U. Santa Clara, Calif.; trustee Little Co. of Mary Hosp. Found. Decorated knight magistral grace Sovereign Mil. Order of Malta; named Honor agt. Equitable Life Assurance Soc., 1949. Mem. C.L.U.'s Assn. Los Angeles (v.p. 1952-53, nat. bd. 1958-60), Life Ins. and Trust Council Los Angeles (sec.-treas. 1951-52, v.p. 1952-53, pres. 1953-54), Million Dollar Round Table (exec. com. 1952-54, pres. 1955), Pasadena C. of C. (mem. bd. 1950, 53, sec.-treas. 1952, 2d v.p. 1953, 1st v.p. 1954), Tournament of Roses Assn., Phi Kappa Phi, Sigma Chi. Roman Catholic. Clubs: California (Los Angeles); Los Angeles Country. Home: 2017 Paseo del Sol Palos Verdes Estates CA 90274 Office: PO Box 953 Palos Verdes Estates CA 90274

BYRNES, JAMES BERNARD, fine arts cons.; b. N.Y.C., Feb. 19, 1917; s. Patrick J.A. and Janet E. (Geiger) B.; m. Barbara A. Cecil, June 10, 1946; 1 son, Ronald L. Student, N.A.D., 1936-38, Am. Artist Sch., 1938-40, Art Students League, 1940-42, U. Perugia, Italy, 1951, Istituto Meschini, Rome, 1952. Art tchr. mus. activity program N.Y.C. Bd. Edn., 1936-40; indsl. designer Michael Saphier Assos., N.Y.C., 1940-42; docent Los Angeles County Mus., 1946-47, asso. curator modern contemporary art, 1947-48, curator, asst. to dir., 1948-53; dir. Colorado Springs Fine Arts Center, 1954-55; asso. dir. N.C. Mus. Art, 1956-58, acting dir., 1958-59, dir., 1959-60, New Orleans Mus. Art, 1962-71, Newport Harbor Art Mus., Newport Beach, Calif., 1972-75, now cons.; vis. lectr. U. Fla., 1961, Newcomb Coll., Tulane U., 1963; art cons. Author: Masterpieces of Art, W.R. Valentiner Memorial, 1959, Tobacco and Smoking in Art, 1960, Fetes de la Palette, 1963, Edgar Degas, His Family and Friends in New Orleans, 1965, Odyssey of an Art Collector, 1966, Art of Ancient and Modern Latin America, 1968, The Artist as Collector of Primitive Art, 1975, also numerous mus. catalogs. Decorated knight Order Leopold II, Belgium. Mem. Western Assn. Art Mus. Dirs. (sec.-treas. 1955), S.E. Assn. Art Mus. Dirs. (council), Am. Soc. Aesthetics, Am. Assn. Museums, Art Mus. Dirs. Assn., Am. Fedn. Arts, Am. Soc. Interior Design (hon.), Am. Soc. Appraisers (sr.), Appraisers Assn. Am. Office: James B Byrnes and Assos 7820 Mulholland Dr Los Angeles CA 90046

BYRNES, JOHN ROBERT, U.S. attorney; b. Washington, Jan. 18, 1948; s. John W. and Barbara (Preston) B.; m. Monica Prueher, Jan. 7, 1977; children: Amy Preston, John Michael. B.A., U. Wis.-Madison, 1970—, J.D., 1973. Bar: Wis. 1973, U.S. Surpeme Ct. 1982. Asst. U.S. atty. U.S. Dept. Justice, Madison, Wis., 1973-76, U.S. atty., 1981—; sole practice law, Green Bay, Wis., 1976-79; adminstr. Worker Compensation div. Dept. Justice, Madison, 1979-81. Republican. Roman Catholic. Club: Exchange. Office: US Atty's Office 215 Monona Ave PO Box 112 Madison WI 53701

BYRNES, JOHN W., lawyer; b. Green Bay, Wis., June 12, 1913; s. Charles W. and Harriet (Schumacher) B.; m. Barbara Preston, 1947; children—John, Michael, Bonnie, Charles, Barbara, Elizabeth. A.B., U. Wis., 1936; LL.B., 1938. Bar: Wis. bar 1939, D.C. bar 1972. Mem. Wis. Senate, 1941-45, 79th-92d Congresses from 8th Wis. Dist.; now with firm Foley, Lardner, Hollabaugh & Jacobs, Washington. Mem. Wis., D.C. bar assns. Republican. Home: 1215 25th St S Arlington VA 22202 Office: Foley Lardner Hollabaugh & Jacobs 1775 Pennsylvania Ave NW Suite 1000 Washington DC 20006

BYRNES, ROBERT FRANCIS, history educator; b. Waterville, N.Y., Dec. 30, 1917; s. Michael Joseph and Pauline (Albecker) B.; m. Eleanor Frances Jewell, June 6, 1942; children: Shaun, Sheila Byrnes Bowles, Sally Byrnes Neylon, Susan Byrnes Wallace, Robin, Charles, James. B.A., Amherst Coll., 1939, D.H.L., 1964; M.A., Harvard U., 1940, Ph.D., 1947; sr. fellow, Columbia U., 1948-50; LL.D., Coe Coll., 1964; D.Litt., St. Mary's Coll., 1967. With Fgn. Econ. Adminstrn., 1943-44; instr. Swarthmore Coll., 1945-46, vis. lectr., 1946-48; asst. to asso. prof. Rutgers U., 1946-53; fellow Inst. Advanced Study, 1950; staff Office Nat. Estimates, CIA, 1951-54; dir. Mid-European Studies Center, N.Y.C., 1954-56; prof. history Ind. U., 1956—, chmn. dept., 1958-65, dir. Russian and East European Inst., 1959-62, 71-75, dir. Internat. Affairs Ctr., 1965-67, Distinguished prof. history, 1967—; scholar in residence Rockefeller Found. Center, 1977; fellow Netherlands Inst. for Advanced Study, 1976-77; chmn. Conf. on Slavic and East European Affairs, 1959; vis. scholar Inst. History Soviet Acad. Scis., 1963, 78; disting. lectr. Chinese Acad. Social Scis., May 1981. Author: Anti-semitism in Modern France; The Prologue to the Dreyfus Affair, 1950, 2d edit., 1969, Bibliography of American Publications on East Central Europe, 1945-57, 1959, The Non-Western Areas in Undergraduate Education in Indiana, 1959, (with others) The College and World Affairs, 1964, Pobedonostev: His Life and Thought, 1967, The United States and Eastern Europe, 1967; editor: East-Central Europe under the Communists, 7 vols, 1956-57, Germany and the East: The Collected Essays of Fritz Epstein, 1973, Communal Families in the Balkans: The Zadruga Essays by Philip E. Mosely, 1975, Soviet-American Academic Exchanges, 1958-1975, 1976, Awakening American Education to the World: The Role of Archibald Cary Coolidge, 1982, After Brezhnev: Sources of Soviet Conduct in the 1980s, 1983; contbr. articles to profl. jours. Bd. dirs. Radio Free Europe/Radio Liberty, 1975-82; trustee Alverno Coll., 1967-76, pres., 1975-76; trustee Boston Coll., 1968-74. Civilian service M.I. AUS, 1944-45. Recipient Centennial medal Boston Coll., 1976, Sesquicentennial award St. Louis U., 1968; Guggenheim fellow, 1953; Am. Council Learned Socs. fellow, 1962-63, 78. Mem. Am. Hist. Assn. (exec. council 1963-67), Am. Assn. Advancement Slavic Studies (pres. 1978-79), Am. Cath. Hist. Assn. (pres. 1961), Commn. Internationale des Etudes Slaves (v.p. 1966-80), Phi Beta Kappa. Home: 402 Reisner Dr Bloomington IN 47401

BYRNES, WILLIAM LEO, investment company executive; b. Boston, Dec. 12, 1921; s. William H. and Marguerite A. (Black) B; m. Mary Elizabeth Cryan; 1 son, Randall William. B.S., Wharton Sch., U. Pa., 1943. Gen. mgr. Hamilton-Lapp Co., Boston, 1946-57; with Fidelity Mgmt. & Research Co., Boston, 1957—, pres., dir., 1969-77, vice chmn., dir., 1977-80; pres. Fidelity Mgmt. & Research Corp., Boston, 1977—; dir. FMR Corp., 1972—; vice chmn., dir. Fidelity Internat. Ltd., 1969—. Trustee Belmont Hill Sch. Served with USAAF. Mem. Inst. Chartered Fin. Analysts, Boston Security Analysts Soc. Office: 25/26 Lovat Ln London EC4 England *

BYRNES, WILLIAM RICHARD, forester, educator; b. Barnesboro, Pa., Oct. 12, 1924; s. William H. and Effie Matilda B.; m. Ellen Jane Thomas, Sept. 10, 1947; children—Jeanette M., Michael R., Alice S., Ellen E., Robert H. B.S. in Forestry, Pa. State U., 1950, M.S., 1951, Ph.D. in Agronomy, 1961. Grad. research asst. Pa. State U., 1950-51, instr. to asso. prof., 1952-62; soil scientist Soil Conservation Service, Bloomsburg, Pa., 1951-52; asso. prof., prof. forestry Purdue U., West Lafayette, Ind., 1962-74, prof., asst. head dept. forestry and natural resources, 1974—. Cubmaster, mem. exec. com. Cub Scouts, 1970-72; mem. exec. com. Boy Scouts Am., 1972-73. Served with USN, 1943-46. Mem. Soc. Am. Foresters, Agronomy Soc. Am., Weed Sci. Soc. Am., Nat. Walnut Council, Central States Forest Soils Conf. Home: 2208 Huron Rd West Lafayette IN 47906 Office: Dept Forestry and Nat Resources Purdue U West Lafayette IN 47907

BYRNS, RICHARD HOWARD, English educator, author, counselor. B.A., U. No. Colo.; M.A., U. Calif. at Berkeley; Ph.D., U. Edinburgh, Scotland, 1955. Cert. marriage and family counselor, Nev. Asst. prof. English U. Alaska, 1947-49, asso. prof., 1949-51, dir. mil. brs., 1950-51; research student U. Edinburgh, 1951-52; prof. English U. Alaska, 1953-57; editorial cons. Geophys. Inst., 1953-57; asso. prof. So. Oreg. Coll., 1957-59, prof. English, 1959-66, head dept. English, 1965-66; prof. English, chmn. dept. U. Nev., 1966-67, prof. English, 1971—, dean Coll. Humanities, 1967-71; pres. Richard H. Byrns MFC, Ltd., 1982—; dir. Carra Corp. Author: Current Research in Alaska, 1954; also short stories.; Contbr. articles scholastic jours. Mem. Modern Lang. Assn., Philol. Assn. Pacific Coast, Am. Comparative Lit. Assn., Rocky Mountain Modern Lang. Assn., Am. Assn. Marriage and Family Therapy (clin.), Alpha Psi Omega, Pi Kappa Delta, Phi Lambda Alpha, Phi Kappa Phi. Home: 3081 Liberty Circle S Las Vegas NV 89121

BYRNSIDE, OSCAR JEHU, JR., association executive; b. Huntington, W.Va., June 2, 1935; s. Oscar Jehu and Eula (Bayliss) B.; m. Patricia Ann Oxley, Aug. 1, 1954; children: Barbara Ann, Brenda Gail, Bethany Lynne. B.S., Concord Coll., Athens, W.Va., 1960; M.S., Va. Poly. Inst. and State U., Blacksburg, 1961; Ph.D., Ohio State U., Columbus, 1968. Tchr. bus. Kanawha County schs., Charleston, W.Va., 1960; coordinator vocat. edn. Danville (Va.) public schs., 1961-63; asst. prof. bus., dir. data processing Longwood Coll., Farmville, Va., 1963-65; state dir. bus. edn. W.Va. Bd. Edn., 1965-66; research asso., cons. Ohio State U., 1966-68; exec. dir. Nat. Bus. Edn. Assn., Reston, Va., 1968—, Future Bus. Leaders Am.-Phi Beta Lambda, Inc., 1968-73; vis. prof. Va. Poly. Inst. and State U., 1969-70, Catholic U. Am., 1969—; pres. Center Ednl. Assns., Reston, 1976-77; treas., bd. dirs. Alliance Assns. Advancement Edn., 1973-74; bd. dirs., exec. v.p. Found. for Teaching Free Enterprise, 1979—; exec. v.p. Assn. Data Mgmt., Inc., Reston, Va.; chmn. Trust for Insuring Educators, 1981—; mem. nat. task force edn. and tng. minority bus. enterprise HEW, 1971-74. Editor: Bus. Edn. Forum, 1968-79; pub., 1979—. Bd. dirs. Reston Soccer Assn., 1979-81, commr. girls travel div., 1979-82; exec. bd. Washington Area Girls Soccer League, 1978-81; co-dir. Reston Internat. Soccer Festival, 1979. Served with USMC, 1953-56. Recipient Centennial award Ohio State U., 1970. Mem. Nat. Bus. Edn. Assn., Am. Vocat. Assn. (life), NEA (life), Internat. Council Small Bus., Am. Soc. Assn. Execs., Nat. Assn. Secondary Sch. Prins., Am. Assn. Sch. Adminstrs., Assn. Supervision and Curriculum Devel., Internat. Soc. Bus. Edn., Phi Kappa Phi, Phi Delta Kappa, Pi Omega Pi, Delta Pi Epsilon, Kappa Delta Pi. Baptist. Home: 2053 Eakins Ct Reston VA 22091 Office: 1914 Association Dr Reston VA 22091

BYROM, FLETCHER LAUMAN, chemical manufacturing company executive; b. Cleve., July 13, 1918; s. Fletcher L. and Elizabeth (Collins) B.; m. Marie L. McIntyre, Feb. 17, 1945; children: Fletcher Lauman, Carol A. Byrom Conrad, Susan J. Byrom Evans. B.S. in Metallurgy, Pa. State U., 1940. Sales engr. Am. Steel & Wire Co., Cleve., 1940-42; procurement and adminstrv. coordination Naval Ordnance Lab., also Bur. Ordnance and Research Planning Bd., Navy Dept., 1942-47; asst. to gen. mgr. Tar Products div. Koppers Co., Inc., Pitts., 1947-54, mgr. ops., 1954-58, v.p., gen. mgr., 1958-60, pres., chief adminstrv. officer, dir., 1960-67, chief exec. officer, 1968—, chmn., 1970-82; dir. N.Y. Stock Exchange, Ralston Purina, Continental Group, Inc., N.Am. Philips Corp., ASARCO, Mex. Desarrollo Indsl. Minero, S.A., Koppers Co. Inc. Co., Lehman Corp.; adv. dir. Unilever., Mellon Nat. Corp., Chem. Bank. Bd. dirs. Allegheny Conf. on Community Devel., v.p.; chmn. Hershey Med. Center, 1970-73, Pres.'s Export Council, 1974-79; chmn. bd. trustees Presbyn.-Univ. Hosp., Kiskiminetas Springs Sch., 1971-82; trustee Carnegie Mellon U., 1975-81, Allegheny Coll., 1969-79, Pa. State U., 1970-73, Inst. Advanced Studies Hudson Inst. Recipient Disting. Civilian Service award U.S. Navy Dept.; recipient Disting. Alumnus Pa. State U. Mem. Conf. Fgn. Relations, Conf. Bd. (chmn. 1975-76); mem. Pa. State U. Alumni Assn. (pres. 1965-66); Mem. Com. Econ. Devel. (chmn. 1978—), Bus. Council, Phi Kappa Psi. Presbyterian. Clubs: Duquesne (Pitts.); Rolling Rock, Laurel Valley Golf (Ligonier, Pa.); Links (N.Y.C.); Little Egg Harbor Yacht (Beach Haven, N.J.); Metropolitan (Washington); Desert Forest Golf, Ranch (Carefree, Ariz.). Home: Box 578 Keystone Dillon CO 80435

BYRON, BEVERLY BUTCHER, congresswoman; b. Balt., July 27, 1932; d. Harry C. and Ruth Butcher; m. Goodloe E. Byron, 1952 (dec.); children: Goodloe E. Jr., Barton Kimball, Mary McComas. Student, Hood Coll., 1962-64. Mem. 96th-98th Congresses from 6th Md. Dist. State treas. Md. Young Democrats, 1962, 65; bd. assocs. Hood Coll.; bd. visitors U.S. Air Force Acad.; bd. dirs. Frederick County chpt. ARC; sec. Frederick Heart Assn., 1974-79; mem. Frederick Phys. Fitness Commn.; chmn. Md. Phys. Fitness Commn.; mem. Frederick County Landmarks Found.; bd. dirs. Am. Hiking Soc. Episcopalian. Home: 306 Grove Blvd Frederick MD 21701 Office: 1216 Longworth House Office Bldg Washington DC 20515

BYRON, FREDERICK WILLIAM, JR., physicist, educator, university dean; b. Manchester, N.H., July 8, 1938; s. Frederick William and Anna (Muir) B.; m. Edith Iselin, June 23, 1961; children: Kenniston, Alexander deNeufville. A.B., Harvard U., 1959; Ph.D., Columbia U., 1963. Acting asst. prof. U. Calif., Berkeley, 1963-65, asst. prof., 1965-66, U. Mass., Amherst, 1966-69, asso. prof., 1969-74, prof., 1974—, head dept. physics and astronomy, 1975-79, dean, 1979—. Author: (with Robert W. Fuller) The Mathematics of Classical and Quantum Physics, 1970; contbr. articles to profl. jours. Alfred P. Sloan Found. fellow, 1965-67; Fulbright research scholar, 1973-74. Fellow Am. Phys. Soc. Office: U Mass Amherst MA 01003

BYRON, WILLIAM JAMES, university president; b. Pitts., May 25, 1927; s. Harold J. and Mary I. (Langton) B. A.B. in Philosophy, St. Louis U., 1955, Ph.L., 1956, M.A. in Econs, 1959; S.T.B., Woodstock Coll., 1960, S.T.L., 1962; Ph.D. in Econs, U. Md., 1969; cert., Harvard U. Inst. Ednl. Mgmt., 1974. Joined S.J., Roman Catholic Ch., 1950, ordained priest, 1961; tchr. math. Scranton (Pa.) Prep. Sch., 1956-58; manpower research fellow Dept. Labor, 1965-66; asst. prof. econs. Loyola Coll., Balt., 1967-69; asso. prof. social ethics Woodstock Coll. and; rector Woodstock Jesuit Community, 1967-73; dean Coll. Arts and Scis., Loyola U., New Orleans, 1973-75; pres. U. Scranton, 1975-82, Catholic U. Am., 1982—; mem. adv. council Center for Constl. Studies, Mercer U. Author: Toward Stewardship: An Interim Ethic of Poverty, Pollution and Power, 1975; editor: Causes of World Hunger, 1982; contbr. numerous articles to profl. jours. Trustee U. Scranton, Georgetown U., Loyola U., Chgo., Loyola U., New Orleans; bd. dirs. Fed. City Council, Bd. Trade Greater Washington. Served with parachute inf. U.S. Army, 1945-46. Mem. Am. Econs. Assn., Am. Soc. Christian Ethics, AAUP, Assn. Cath. Colls. and Univs. (dir.), Am. Council Edn. (govt. relations commn.), Nat. Inst. Ind. Colls. and Univs. (chmn. planning commn.), Phi Beta Kappa, Alpha Sigma Nu. Home: 3901 Harewood Rd NE Washington DC 20064 Office: Catholic Univ of Amer 620 Michigan Ave NE Washington DC 20064

BYSIEWICZ, SHIRLEY RAISSI, lawyer; b. Enfield, Conn.; d. Kyriakos and Anna (Gavala) Raissi; m. Stanley J. Bysiewicz, July 18, 1959; children: Susan, Walter John, Karen, Gail. B.A., J.D., M.S. in L.S, U. Conn. Bar: Conn. 1954. Mem. firm Raissi & Raissi, Enfield, 1954—; faculty U. Conn., West Hartford, 1956—, prof. law, 1965—, law librarian., 1956-83; Mem. Permanent Commn. on Status Women for Conn., 1976-80, pres., 1978-79; mem. Conn. Law Library Adv. Com., 1976—; law revision commr. for, Conn., 1980—. Author: (with Max R. White) Forms of Town Government in Connecticut, 1954, Survey of County Law Libraries in Connecticut, 1967, Dictionary of Legal Terms, 1983; co-author: (with Max R. White) Selected Annotated Bibliography on Education for Professional Responsibility, 1968, (with Price & Bitner) Effective Legal Research, 1979; Bus. mgr.: Law Library Jour, 1968-72; co-editor: Materials on Estate Planning, 1969; Contbr. law articles to profl. jours. Mem. Bar Assn. Conn. (treas. 1975-78), Nat. Assn. Women Lawyers, ABA, Hartford County Bar Assn. (exec. com.), Conn. Bar Assn. (chmn. juvenile justice coms.), Am. Bar Assn. Women Lawyers, Am. Assn. Law Schs. (co-presider sect. on status of women, sect. legal research 1974), Am. Assn. Law Librarians (law library jour. com., sec. 1980-83), U. Conn. Law Sch. Alumni Assn. (exec. sec. 1958-68), New Eng. Law Librarians (pres. 1970), Women's Equity Action League, Delta Zeta. Greek Orthodox. Home: S Plumb Rd Middletown CT 06457 Office: 1800 Asylum Ave West Hartford CT 06117

BYSTEDT, GOSTA PETRUS, manufacturing company executive; b. Haggdanger, Sweden, May 14, 1929; s. Petrus and Anna (Jonsson) B.; m. Kerstin Elmer, May 25, 1958; children: Ingrid Christina, Anna Pernilla, Per Ivar Gosta. M.Engring., Royal Inst. Tech., Stockholm, 1953; B.S., Stockholm Sch. Econs., 1958. Asst. prof. Royal Inst. Tech., Stockholm, 1953-55, asst. lectr., 1955-58; head orgn. and methods dept. AB Electrolux, Stockholm, 1958-65, head Vacuum Cleaner div., 1965-68, dep. mng. dir., 1968-74, mng. dir., 1974-81, chief exec. officer Electrolux group, 1981—. Home: 59 Bergsv Lidingo Sweden S-181 31 Office: Luxbacken Stockholm Sweden S-105 45

BYWATER, WILLIAM HAROLD, labor union official; b. Trenton, N.J., Sept. 10, 1920; s. William Harold and Rose Ann B.; m. Eleanor, 1943; 2 children. Mem. Internat. Union Elec., Radio and Mechine Workers, Washington, 1941—; pres. dist. counsil 3, Internat. Union Elec., Radio and Machine, Washington, 1968-80; sec.-treas. Internat. Union Elec., Radio and Machine workers, Washington, 1980-82, dir. orgn., 1980—, pres., 1982—; chief stewart, shop steward local 425, Internat. Union Elec., Radio and Machine workers, East Rutherford, N.J., 1941-46, v.p., 1947-49, pres., 1949-57, internat. rep., 1957-58, chmn. Sperry Rand conf. bd., 1958-67. Served with U.S. Army. Office: Internat Union Elec Radio and Mechine Workers 1126 16th St NW Washington DC 20036 *

BYWATERS, JERRY, artist, educator, writer, art museum dir.; b. Paris, Tex., 1906; s. Porter A. and Hattie (Williamson) B.; m. Mary McLarry, Nov. 3, 1930; children—Jerry, Dick. B.A., So. Meth. U., 1927; student, Art Students League, N.Y.C., 1927; studied in, Mexico. Europe. Prof. art So. Meth. U., 1936—, head dept. art, 1965-67; dir. Dallas Mus. Fine Arts, 1943-64; painter, printmaker, lectr. art, 1930—; art critic Dallas News, 1933-39; art editor Southwest Rev., Dallas, 1950-60. Home: 3625 Amherst Dallas TX 75225

CAAN, JAMES, actor, director; b. N.Y.C., Mar. 26, 1940; (div.)1 dau., 1 son, Scott. Student, Hofstra Coll. Appeared in: off-Broadway play La Ronde, 1961; film appearances include Lady in a Cage, 1964, The Glory Guys, 1965, Red Line 7000, 1965, Eldorado, 1967, Games, 1967, Journey to Shiloh, 1968, Submarine X-1, 1969, Rain People, 1969, Rabbit, Run, 1970, The Godfather, 1972, Slither, 1973, Freebie and the Bean, 1973, Cinderella Liberty, 1974, The Gambler, 1974, Funny Lady, 1975, Rollerball, 1975, The Godfather-Part II, 1974, The Killer Elite, 1975, Harry and Walter Go to New York, 1976, Silent Movie, 1976, A Bridge Too Far, 1977, Another Man, Another Chance, 1977, Comes a Horseman, 1978, Chapter Two, 1979, Thief, 1982, Kiss Me Goodbye, 1983; dir.: Hide in Plain Sight, 1980; appeared in: TV film Brian's Song, 1971; numerous TV appearances. Office: care Creative Artists Agy 1888 Century Park E Suite 1400 Los Angeles CA 90067 *

CABANA, ALDEE JEAN, science educator, faculty dean; b. Beloeil, Que., Can., July 20, 1935; s. Germain and Marie-Ange (Laquerre) C.; m. Lise Couillard, June 28, 1958; children: Bruno, Marianne, Louise, Yves. B.Sc., U. Montreal, 1958, M.Sc., 1959, Ph.D. in Chemistry, 1962. Research assoc. Princeton U., 1961-63; faculty U. Sherbrooke, (Que.), 1963—, prof. in phys. chemistry, 1971—, dean Faculty of Scis. Editorial bd.: Can. Jour. Spectroscopy, 1970-83; contbr. research papers to profl. lit. Recipient Gerhard Herzberg award in spectroscopy, 1976. Mem. Assn. Canadienne Francaise pour l'Advancement des Sciences, Chem. Inst. Can., Can. Assn. Spectroscopy, Can. Assn. Physicists, Order Chemists Que. Home: 264 Heneker Sherbrooke PQ Canada J1J 3G4 Office: U Sherbrooke Faculte Des Sherbrooke PQ Canada J1K 2R1

CABANA, GEORGES, archbishop; b. Granby, Can., Oct. 23, 1894; s. Joseph and Marie V. (Desgrés) C. Student, St. Charles Coll., Sherbrooke, 1908-10, St. Hyacinthe Sem., 1910-14; B.A., Laval U., 1914; B. Canon Law, Sem. of Theology, Montreal, 1917; D.C.L., Bishop's U.; Doct. Un., U. Sherbrooke; LL.D., Bishop's Univ., Lennoxville, Sherbrooke U. Ordained as priest Roman Catholic Ch., 1918; prof. St. Hyacinthe Sem., 1918-21, St. Augustine's Sem., Toronto, 1921-31; prof., asst. St. Hyacinthe and Sorel, 1931-34; chaplain St. Charles Hosp., 1935; spiritual dir. St. Hyacinthe Sem. of Theology, 1936-41; consecrated archbishop-coadjutor of St. Boniface, Man., Can., 1941-52; archbishop of, Sherbrooke, Que., 1952-68; titular See, 1968—; chancellor Sherbrooke U., 1954-68. Address: Pavillon Mgr Racine 1415 Godbout St Sherbrooke PQ J1K 2C7 Canada

CABELL, WILLIAM DANIEL, lawyer; b. Big Stone Gap, Va., Sept. 1, 1908; s. Mayo and Clara (Cabell) C.; m. Ellen Elspeth Rolston, Dec. 27, 1941; children: Kathleen Rolston (Mrs. Robert A. Hildreth), Willliam Daniel. Grad., Va. Episcopal Sch., 1922-26; B.A., U. Va., 1930. Bar: N.Y. 1936, Va. 1942, also U.S. Supreme Ct. 1942. Practice in, N.Y.C., 1932-42, Richmond, Va., 1942-45; ptnr. firm Cabell, Kennedy & French. A founder United Fund No. Westchester, N.Y., 1958, bd. dirs., sec., 1959- 61; chmn. Chappaqua Community United Fund campaign, 1961, Chappaqua Adv. Council United Fund, 1962; mem. men's com. N.Y.C. campaign United Negro Coll. Fund, 1950-60; mem. interacial conf. Nat. Council Chs., Richmond, 1944-45; mem. com. Washington Irving council Boy Scouts Am., 1959-60; Mem. 5th Dist. Republican Com., New Castle, Westchester County, 1956-62; editor Voters Voice, 1952-53. Served as lt. (j.g.) USNR, 1942. Mem. Am., Va., Westchester County bar assns., Delta Psi. Clubs: Squadron A, St. Anthony, Knickerbocker (N.Y.C.). Home: 255

Quaker St Chappaqua NY 10514 Office: 220 E 42d St New York NY 10017

CABELLE, MONTSERRAT, opera singer, soprano; b. Barcelona, Spain, Apr. 12, 1933; m. Bernabe Marti; 2 children. Ed., Conservatorio del Liceo. Am. debut: in Donizetti's Lucrezia Borgia, Carnegie Hall, N.Y.C., 1965; apperared with, LaScala Opera, Milan, Vienna Staatsoper, Glydebourne Festival, Met. Opera, Chgo. Symphony Orch., Orch. Hall, 1966; recorded by, RCA Victor; performed in works of Richard Strauss, Mozart, de Falla, Luigi Nono; appearance on radio and TV. Decorated Cross of Lazo de Damas, Order Isabel the Catholic, Spain. Address: care Columbia Artists Mgmt Inc 165 W 57th St New York NY 10019 *

CABEZAS, ROBERT THOMAS, advertising executive; b. N.Y.C., May 22, 1940; s. Robert H. and Eleanor (Curley) C. (King); m. Jean A. Raczko, Sept. 25, 1965; children: Diane, Robert, Howard. B.S., St. Peter's Coll., 1965; M.B.A., Fordham U., 1979. With Interpublic, N.Y.C., 1967-80, asst. v.p., asst. controller, 1978-80; v.p., budget dir. McCann-Erickson Inc., N.Y.C., 1980-81, v.p. adminstrn., 1981-82, sr. v.p. fin. and adminstrn., 1982—, dir., N.Y.C. Municipal chmn. Democratic Party, Mountain Lakes, N.J. Named Outstanding Pres. Jr. C. of C., 1968-69. Mem. Nat. Assn. Accts. Democrat. Roman Catholic. Club: K.C. Office: McCann-Erickson Inc 485 Lexington Ave New York NY 10017

CABLE, CHARLES ALLEN, mathematician; b. Akeley, Pa., Jan. 15, 1932; s. Elton Thomas and Margaret (Fox) C.; m. Mabel Elizabeth Yeck, Dec. 19, 1955; children: Christopher A., Carolyn E. B.S., Edinboro State Coll., 1954; M.Ed., U. N.C., 1959; Ph.D. in Math., Pa. State U., 1969. Instr. math. Interlaken High Sch., N.Y., 1954-55, Tidioute High Sch., Pa., 1957-58; asst. prof. math Juniata Coll., Huntingdon, Pa., 1959-67; prof., chmn. dept. math Allegheny Coll., Meadville, Pa., 1969—. Editorial reviewer: Math. Mag., 1975-80; assoc. editor: Focus, 1981—. Served with AUS, 1955-57. Gen. Elec. fellow, 1958; NSF fellow, 1959, 61, 69, 73; NDEA fellow, 1969. Mem. Am. Math. Soc., Math. Assn. Am. (chmn. Allegheny Mountain sect. 1973-75, bd. govs. 1981—, mem. newletter editorial com. 1981—, mem. publs. com. 1983—), AAUP. Republican. Presbyterian. Home: 199 Jefferson St Meadville PA 16335 Office: Allegheny Coll N Main St Meadville PA 16335

CABLE, DONALD AUBREY, lawyer; b. Chgo., Aug. 7, 1927; s. Forbes and Clara (Henderson) C.; m. Joan B. Swanton, June 27, 1953; children—Bruce Cameron, Neil Alexander, Alison Clare. B.A., Lake Forest Coll., 1949; J.D., George Washington U., 1957. Bar: Wash. bar 1957. Staff auditor Main & Co., Washington, 1954-57; agt. IRS, Seattle, 1957-58; mem. firm Short, Cressman & Cable (and predecessor firms), Seattle, 1958-79, partner, 1962-79; mem. firm Cable, Barrett, Lagenbach & McInerney, Seattle, 1980—. Served with USNR, 1945-46, 52-54. Mem. Jr. C. of C. (past nat. bd. dirs.). Club: Rotarian. Home: 6227 83d Ave SE Mercer Island WA 98040 Office: 1900 Fourth and Blanchard Bldg 2121 4th Ave Seattle WA 98121

CABLE, HOWARD REID, composer, conductor; b. Toronto, Ont., Can., Dec. 15, 1920; s. George William and Mary McIntyre (Deverall) C.; m. Peggy Feltmate, June 16, 1973; children by previous marriage: Judy, Linda, Nairn, Greg. A.A., Royal Conservatory Music, Toronto, 1939. Dir. publs. Brassworks Music, Toronto, 1978—; chief arranger Can. Brass, 1976—; music dir. Festival Can., 1977—. Condr., composer, CBC, 1943-60; music dir., Canadian Nat. Exhbn., 1953-68, Broadway shows, 1965-66; theatre producer, Gen. Motors of Can., 1955-66; music dir., Royal York Hotel, Toronto, 1974—; condr., McMaster U., Hamilton, Ont., 1975-76; program head, Mus. Theatre Faculty; music dir., Banff (Alta.) Sch. Fine Arts, 1975—; dir. music and theatre, Humber Coll., Toronto; Composer numerous works for band, orch. and chorus. Bd. dirs. Shaw Festival, Niagara-on-the-Lake, Ont. Mem. Nat. Band Assn. U.S.A., Am. Fedn. Musicians, Actors Equity Assn. (producer mem.), Composers, Authors and Pubs. Assn. Can. (pres. 1968-70). Home: 58 Langmuir Crescent Toronto ON Canada Office: Royal York Hotel 100 Front St W Toronto ON Canada

CABOT, LOUIS WELLINGTON, chemical manufacturing company executive; b. Boston, Aug. 3, 1921; s. Thomas Dudley and Virginia (Wellington) C.; m. Mary Ellen Flynn de Pena Vera, Oct. 19, 1974; children by previous marriage: James Bass, Anne Louise, Godfrey Lowell, Amanda Cabot Kjellerup, Helen. A.B., Harvard U., 1943, M.B.A., 1948; LL.D. (hon.), Norwich U., 1961. With Cabot Corp., 1948—, pres., 1960-69, chmn. bd., 1969—; dir. Owens-Corning Fiberglas Corp., R.R. Donnelley & Sons Co., Wang Labs Inc., New Eng. Tel. & Tel., 1965-82, Fed. Res. Bank Boston, 1970-78, chmn., 1975-78; U.S. rep. 15th Plenary Session UN Econ. Commn. for Europe, 1960; mem. bus. ethics adv. council Dept. Commerce, 1961-63; dir., New Eng. chmn. Nat. Alliance Businessmen, 1970-72, Boston chmn., 1968-69; chmn. Sloan Commn. on Govt. and Higher Edn., 1977-80. Overseer Harvard U., 1970-76; chmn. Harvard Coll. Fund Council, 1963-65; pres. Beverly Hosp., 1958-61; chmn. Com. Corp. Support Pvt. Univs., 1977-83; bd. dirs. Council Fin. Aid to Edn.; vice chmn. Brookings Instn.; trustee Norwich U., 1952-77, Mus. of Sci., Boston; mem. corp., mem. exec. com. M.I.T.; trustee Northeastern U., Nat. Humanities Ctr. Fellow Am. Acad. Arts and Scis.; mem. C. of C. of U.S. (dir., exec. com. 1978-83), Nat. Council for U.S.-China Trade (dir. 1978-82), Bus. Council, Conf. Bd., Mass. Bus. Roundtable, Council Fgn. Relations, Phi Beta Kappa, Sigma Xi. Clubs: Somerset, Commercial (pres. 1970-72), Harvard (Boston); Metropolitan (Washington); Wianno (Osterville); N.Y. Yacht, River. Office: 125 High St Boston MA 02110

CABOT, PAUL CODMAN, investment company executive; b. Brookline, Mass., Oct. 21, 1898; s. Henry B. and Anne M. (Codman) C.; m. Virginia Converse, Sept. 20, 1924; children: Virginia Wood, Elizabeth Minot, Paul C., Frederick C., Edmund C. A.B., Harvard U., 1921, M.B.A. with distinction, 1923, LL.D., 1966; LL.D., Yale U., 1965. Treas. Harvard U., Cambridge, Mass., 1948-65; chmn. bd. State St. Investment Corp., 1924—; sr. ptnr. State St. Research & Mgmt. Co., Boston, 1924—. Served to 2d lt. arty. U.S. Army, World War-I; served with War Production Bd., World War II. Mem. Bus. Council. Republican. Clubs: Harvard (Boston); Porcellian (Cambridge); Dedham Country and Polo (Mass.). Home: 653 Chestnut St Needham MA 02192 Office: State Street Investment Corp 225 Franklin St Boston MA 02110

CABOT, THOMAS DUDLEY, chem. co. exec.; b. Cambridge, Mass., May 1, 1897; s. Godfrey Lowell and Maria Buckminster (Moors) C.; m. Virginia Wellington, May 15, 1920; children—Louis Wellington, Thomas Dudley, Robert Moors, Linda, Edmund Billings. A.B., Harvard, 1919; L.H.D., Tufts U., 1951, Boston U., 1961; LL.D., Northeastern U., 1952, Morris Harvey Coll., 1953, Harvard, 1970. Former pres. United Fruit Co., Boston; pres. Godfrey L. Cabot, Inc. (name changed to Cabot Corp., 1960), chmn. bd., 1960-68, hon. chmn. bd., 1968—; dir. Controlled Risk Ins. Co., Ltd.; former dir. John Hancock Mut. Life Ins. Co., First Nat. Bank of Boston, Am. Mut. Liability Ins. Co.; Chmn. Mass. Aero Commn., 1944-45; dir. office Internat. Security Affairs, Dept. of State, 1951; cons. Spl. Mission to Egypt, 1953. Author: Beggar on Horseback. Bd. overseers Harvard, 1953-59, 62-68; mem. governing bd. Harvard-Mass. Inst. Tech. Div. in Health Scis. and Tech., 1977—; trustee Radcliffe Coll., Escuela Agricola Panamericana; mem. corp. emeritus Mass. Inst. Tech.; hon. trustee Com. Econ. Devel.; trustee Children's Med. Center; hon. bd. dirs. Brigham and Women's Hosp. Served as 2d lt., A.S. U.S. Army; flying instr., 1917-18. Decorated chevalier Legion of Honor, France; commendatore Al Merito della Republica Italiana. Fellow A.A.A.S.; mem. Council Fgn. Relations, Internat. C. of C. (trustee U.S. council). Republican. Unitarian. Home: 31 Farm Rd Weston MA 02193 Office: 125 High St Boston MA 02110

CABRANES, JOSÉ ALBERTO, federal judge; b. Mayaguez, P.R., Dec. 22, 1940; s. Manuel and Carmen (López) C.; m. Susan Beth Feibush, Aug. 1, 1965 (div. 1984); children: Jennifer Ann, Amy Alexandra. A.B., Columbia U., 1961; J.D., Yale U., 1965; M.Litt. in Internat. Law (Kellett research fellow, Humanitarian Trust studentship), Queens' Coll., Cambridge (Eng.) U., 1967. Bar: N.Y. 1968, D.C. 1975, Conn. 1976. Asso. Casey, Lane & Mittendorf, N.Y.C., 1967-71; asso. prof. law Rutgers U. Law Sch., 1971-73; spl. counsel to gov. P.R., also adminstr. Office Commonwealth P.R., Washington, 1973-75; gen. counsel and dir. govt. relations Yale U., 1975-79; judge U.S. Dist. Ct. Dist. Conn., New Haven, 1979—; mem. Pres.'s Commn. Mental Health, 1977-78; founding mem. P.R. Legal Def. and Edn. Fund, 1972, chmn. bd. dirs., 1977-80; counsel Internat. League for Human Rights, 1971-77, v.p., 1977-80; cons. to sec. Dept. State, 1978; mem. U.S. del. Conf. Security and Cooperation in Europe, Belgrade, 1977-78. Author: Citizenship and the American Empire, 1979; also articles on law and internat. affairs. Mem. Commn. White House Fellows, 1980-81; trustee Yale-New Haven Hosp., 1975-80, Colgate U., 1981—; bd. dirs. Aspira of N.Y., 1970-74, chmn., 1971-73; trustee 20th Century Fund, 1983—. Mem. Am. Law Inst., ABA, Conn. Bar Assn., Assn. Bar City N.Y., Council Fgn. Relations. Roman Catholic. Office: US Courthouse 141 Church St New Haven CT 06505

CACCIA, CHARLES L., Canadian government official; b. Milan, Italy, Apr. 28, 1930; married; children: Nicolette, John. Student, Liceo Scientifico Vittoria Veneto, Milan, Italy, Faculty of Forestry U. Vienna. Prin. Caccia & Assocs.; mem. Met. Council Toronto, 1964-66; alderman City of Toronto Council, 1964-69; mem. Can. Ho. of Commons, 1968—, chmn. labour, manpower and immigration com., 1968-69, minister of Labor, 1969-83; minister of the Environ., Ottawa, 1983—; mem. Can. delegation to ILO Conf., Geneva, 1969; parliamentary sec. to Solicitor Gen., Pres. of Treasury Bd., Minister of Manpower and Immigration, 1969-71; chmn. Ont. Caucus, 1977-78; parliamentary observer UN, 1976, Conf. Security and Cooperation In Europe, Belgrade, 1977, Madrid and Brussels, 1980; mem. Inter-Parliamentary Union Confs., Caracas, 1979, Oslo and East Berlin, 1980. Liberal. Roman Cathloic. Office: Environment Canada Ministry Ottawa ON Canada K1A 0H3 *

CACCIATORE, S. SAMMY, JR., lawyer; b. Tampa, Fla., Aug. 2, 1942; s. Sam and Margarita C.; m. Carolyn Michels, Aug. 10, 1963; children: Elaine Michel, Sammy Michel. B.A., Stetson U., DeLand, Fla., 1966, J.D., 1966. Bar: Fla. 1966, U.S. Ct. Appeals (5th Cir.) 1967, U.S. Ct. Appeals (11th Cir.) 1981. Asst. public defender 9th jud. circuit, State of Fla., 1966, assoc. firms, Orlando, Fla., 1966-67, practice in, Melbourne, Fla., 1967—; ptnr Nance, Cacciatore & Sisserson (and predecessors), 1970—; mem. 5th Dist. Appellate Nominating Commn., 1979-83, State of Fla. Med. Malpractice Adv. Com.; lectr. in field, 1971—. Contbr. articles to profl. jours., chpts. to books. Trustee A. Max Brewer Meml. Law Library, Brevard County, Fla., 1972—, chmn., 1972-76; mem. sch. bd. Central Catholic High Sch. Mem. ABA, Am. Law Inst., Am. Trial Lawyers Assn., Fla. Bar (exec. council trial sect. 1975), Acad. Fla. Trial Lawyers (dir. 1970-76, 76—, sec.), Brevard County Bar Assn. (dir., President's award 1975), Melbourne Area Com. of 100. Democrat. Roman Catholic. Club: Eau Gallie Yacht (gov., vice commodore 1981—). Office: 525 N Harbour City Blvd Melbourne FL 32935 *The law is a living, growing institution of our lives. Lawyers need to remember this and nurture its development as one would a child. It should grow straight and strong for the benefit of the people.*

CACHERIS, JAMES C., judge; b. Pitts., Mar. 30, 1933. B.S. in Econs., U. Pa., 1955; J.D. cum laude, George Washington U., 1960. Bar: D.C. 1960, Va. 1962. Asst. corp. counsel, Washington, 1960-62, pvt. practice, Washington and Alexandria, Va., 1962-71; judge 19th Jud. Circuit Ct. Va., Fairfax, 1971-83, U.S. Dist. Ct., Alexandria, 1983—. Mem. ABA, Va. Bar Assn., Fairfax County Bar Assn., Am. Judicature Soc. Office: US Dist Ct 200 S Washington St Alexandria VA 22314

CACHIA, PIERRE JACQUES, language and culture educator, researcher; b. Fayoum, Egypt, Apr. 30, 1921; came to U.S., 1976; s. Francois and Anna Rachel (Axler) C.; m. Phyllis Barbara Oyston, Mar. 20, 1953; children: Susan Margaret, Philip Greville, Helen Frances. B.A., Am. U., 1942; Ph.D., U. Edinburgh, 1951. Mem. faculty Am. U., Cairo, 1946-48, U. Edinburgh, Scotland, 1949-75; prof. Middle East langs. and cultures Columbia U., N.Y.C., 1975—, chmn. dept. Middle East langs. and cultures, 1980-83. Author: Taha Husayn, 1956; co-author: History of Islamic Spain, 1965, 77; compiler: The Monitor-Arabic Grammatical Terms, 1973; editor: The Book of the Demonstration by Eutychius, Vol. 1, 1960, The Book of the Demonstration by Eutychius, Vol. 2, 1961; joint editor: Jour. Arabic Lit., 1970—. Grantee NEH, 1977, Smithsonian Instn., 1979; fellow Am. Research Ctr. in Egypt, Cairo, 1982. Mem. Am. Oriental Soc., Middle East Studies Assn., Am. Assn. Tchrs. Arabic. Office: Columbia U 608 Kent Hall New York NY 10027

CADDELL, JOHN A., lawyer; b. Tuscumbia, Ala., Apr. 23, 1910; s. Thomas Arthur and Florence Lee (Huff) C.; m. Lucy Bowen Harris, Sept. 1, 1935; children—Thomas A., Lucinda Lee, Henry Harris and John A. (twins). A.B., U. Ala., 1931, LL.B., 1933. Bar: Ala. bar 1933. Since practiced in, Decatur.; Sec., dir. Southeastern Metals Co., Inc., Birmingham, 1946-68; chmn. bd. First Nat. Bank Decatur, 1976-81; City atty., Decatur, 1936-59; counsel com. investigating campaign expenditures U.S. Ho. of Reps., 1944; bd. commrs. Ala. State Bar, 1939-54, Jud. Council Ala., 1946-58; mem. bd. Bar Examiners Ala., 1949, 50. Mem. Ala. Democratic Exec. Com., 1938-50; Trustee U. Ala., 1954-79, also pres. pro tem, 1974-78. Fellow Am. Coll. probate counsel, Am. Coll. Trial Lawyers, Am. Bar Found.; mem. ABA, Ala. Bar Assn. (pres. 1951-52), Morgan County Bar Assn., U. Ala. Alumni Assn. (pres. 1953), Decatur C. of C. (pres. 1943-44), Ala. Acad. Honor, Pi Kappa Alpha, Omicron Delta Kappa, Phi Delta Phi. Democrat (mem. Ala. exec. com. 1938-50). Presbyn. (elder). Clubs: Athletic, U. Alabama, Decatur Kiwanis (pres. 1939). Home: PO Box 1727 Decatur AL 35602 Office: 230 E Moulton St Decatur AL 35601

CADDELL, JOHN ALLEN, construction and engineering company executive; b. Montgomery, Ala., Mar. 13, 1930; s. Martin Lesser and Vivian (Deel) C.; m. Lowell Joyce Kirby, Sept. 8, 1951; children: Cathy, Michael, John Kirby, Jeffery, Christopher. B.S., Ga. Inst. Tech., 1952; grad., U.S. Air Force Officer Engr. Sch., 1953; advanced mgmt. program, Harvard U., 1968; postgrad. in basic advanced mgmt., U. Va., 1959. Estimator Blount Bros. Constrn. Co., 1952-55, chief estimator, 1955-61; project mgr. Blount Bros. Corp., Cape Canaveral, Fla., 1961-63, v.p., mgr. constrn. div., 1963-69, pres., chief exec. officer, 1969-78; pres. and chief exec. officer Blount Internat., Ltd., Montgomery, 1978-80, chmn. bd. and chief exec. officer, 1980-83; pres. Caddell Constrn. Co., 1983—; dir. Blount, Inc., Delchamps, Inc. Bd. dirs. YMCA, Montgomery, Bapt. Med. Center, Montgomery, Bapt. Found. Ala. Served with USAF, 1952-54. Mem. Associated Gen. Contractors Am., Moles, Beavers. Clubs: Montgomery Country, Capital City. Home: 145 Bell Rd Montgomery AL 36117 Office: 145 Bell Rd Montgomery AL 36117

CADDELL, PATRICK HAYWARD, public opinion company executive; b. Rock Hill, S.C., May 19, 1950; s. Newton P. and Janie (Burns) C. Grad., Harvard U., 1972. Pres. Cambridge Survey Research, Inc., Mass., 1971—, Cambridge Reports Inc., 1974-80; cons. to presdl. campaigns of Jimmy Carter, George McGovern and Gary Hart, to numerous congl., senatorial and gubernatorial campaigns. Office: Cambridge Survey Research Inc 1750 Pennsylvania Ave Washington DC 20006

CADDEN, JAMES MONROE, oil company executive; b. Williston, S.C., Dec. 19, 1923; s. George Otis and Martha Adilade C.; m. Joanna Craig, Aug. 25, 1947; children: Christine Cadden Macmurphy, Nancy Cadden Wells. B.S. in Chemistry and Math., Tex. A&I U., 1949, 1950; Petroleum Engr., U. Houston, 1957. Registered profl. engr., Tex. With Getty Oil Co., 1950—, gas engr., Palestine, Tex., petroleum engr., Venice, La., petroleum engr. Mid Continent div., Houston, asst. to sr. v.p. corp. office, dist. petroleum engr. Coastal Dist., Ventura, Calif., mgr. computers for supply and transp. div., mktg. and mfg. div. and internat. exploration and prodn. and minerals div., mgr. engring. exploration and prodn. div., Calif., mgr. engring. Mid Continent div., Houston, chief engr., 1950-77, mgr. exploration and prodn. research, 1977-83, spl. assignments for corp. mgr. natural resource tech. services, 1983—. Served with USNR, 1942-45. Mem. Soc. Petroleum Engrs. of AIME, Am. Petroleum Inst. Republican. Episcopalian. Club: Petroleum (Houston). Home: 10219 Briar Dr Houston TX 77042 Office: Getty Oil Co 10201 Westpark Dr Houton TX 77042

CADDY, EDMUND HARRINGTON HOMER, JR., architect; b. N.Y.C., Apr. 17, 1928; s. Edmund Harrington Homer and Glenna Corinne (Garratt) C.; m. Mary Audrey Ortiz, Dec. 22, 1951; children—Edmund Harrington Homer III, Mary Elizabeth. B.A., Princeton, 1952, M.F.A. (grad. sch. fellow), 1955. With firm Louis E. Jallade (architect), N.Y.C., 1949; Eggers & Higgins (architects), N.Y.C., 1953; dir. design Dalton-Dalton Assos. (architects and engineers), Cleve., 1955-60; asso. mem. firm Raymond & Rado (architects), N.Y.C., 1960-68; gen. partner Raymond & Rado and Partners (architects), N.Y.C., 1968-72, Raymond, Rado, Caddy & Bonington (P.C.), 1972-80, pres., 1980—; Mem. adv. com. arts John F. Kennedy Center Performing Arts, 1963-70; mem. archtl. adv. commn. N.Y.C. Community Coll., City U. N.Y., 1979—. Works include Suburban Hosp, Cleve., 1957, J.M. Smucker Co, Salinas, Cal., 1957, Brookpark (Ohio) City Hall, 1959; Cleve. Transit System addition, 1959, adminstrn. bldg., Met. Water Treatment System, Saigon, 1960, Franklin D. Roosevelt High Sch, N.Y.C., 1963, Crown Heights Intermediate Sch, N.Y.C., 1966, J.C. Penney dept. stores in, Kansas City, Mo., 1968, J.C. Penney dept. stores in, Greensburg, Pa., 1969, J.C. Penney dept. stores in, Ft. Wayne, Ind., J.C. Penney dept. stores in, Mpls., 1970, Robinson's dept. stores, Fla., 1972, 73, engring. complex, Stony Brook Campus, State U. N.Y., 1970, Sibley's dept. stores, Syracuse, N.Y., 1973, Rochester Downtown Devel. Study, 1975, Stix, Baer & Fuller dept. stores, St. Louis, 1976, Hahne & Co. dept. stores, Woodbridge and Rockaway, N.J., 1977, R.H. Macy & Co. dept. store, Stamford, Conn., 1979. Pres. bd. trustees Montclair (N.J.) Community Hosp., 1973-80. Served with USMC, 1946-48; Served with USMCR, 52-53. Mem. AIA, Architects Soc. Ohio, N.Y. State Architects Assn. Clubs: Tower (Princeton); Racquet and Tennis (N.Y.C.); Montclair Golf. Home: 2 Wendover Rd Montclair NJ 07042 Office: 150 E 22d St New York NY 10010

CADENHEAD, ALFRED PAUL, lawyer; b. LaGrange, Ga., Oct. 14, 1926; s. Roy E. and Omie (Bishop) C.; m. Sara Davenport, Oct. 14, 1945; children: Steven Paul, David James. Jr. coll. certificate, W. Ga. Coll., 1944; LL.B., Emory U., 1949. Bar: Ga. 1949. Ptnr. firm Hurt, Richardson, Garner, Todd & Cadenhead, Atlanta; dir. various corps.; pres. Atlanta Legal Aid Soc., 1958. Pres. Met. Atlanta Mental Health Assn., 1964-65, Ga. Assn. Mental Health, 1968; trustee Queens Coll., Charlotte, N.C. Served with paratroops U.S. Army. 1944-46. Fellow Am. Coll. Trial Lawyers, Internat. Soc. Barristers; mem. Atlanta Bar Assn. (pres. 1970-71), State Bar Ga. (bd. govs.), Atlanta Estate Planning Council (pres. 1976). Presbyterian. Home: 6305 Riverside Dr NW Atlanta GA 30328 Office: 1100 Peachtree Center Harris Tower 233 Peachtree St NE Atlanta GA 30343

CADER, ARNOLD LEWIS, hotel exec.; b. Toronto, Ont., Can., Aug. 17, 1940; s. David and Natalie C.; m. Paula Sharon Peranson, Dec. 22, 1963; children—Raquel Tracy, Michelle Stacy, Lindsay Jill. B.Comm., U. Toronto, 1962, LL.B., 1965. Bar: Called to Ont. bar 1967. Asso., then partner firm Goodman and Goodman, Toronto, 1968-79; exec. v.p. Four Seasons Hotels Ltd., Toronto, 1979—. Mem. Ont. Bar Assn. (lectr.). Office: 1100 Eglinton Ave E Don Mills ON M3C 1H8 Canada

CADES, JULIUS RUSSELL, lawyer; b. Phila., Oct. 30, 1904; s. Isaac and Ida Frieda (Russell) C.; m. Charlotte Leah McLean, Nov. 28, 1938; 1 son, Russell McLean. A.B., U. Pa., 1925, LL.B. cum laude, 1928, LL.M. (Gowan research fellow corp. law), 1930. Bar: Pa. 1928, Hawaii 1930, U.S. Supreme Ct. 1936. Practice in, Honolulu, 1929—; partner firm Cades Schutte Fleming & Wright (and predecessor), 1934—; Chmn. com. to promote uniformity of legislation of U.S. for, Hawaii, 1949-60, mem., 1962-66, Jud. Council State Hawaii, 1966-71; dir. Universal Corp., Kekaha Sugar Co., Ltd., Lihue Plantation Co., Ltd., Puna Sugar Co., Ltd., Pacific Devel. Co., Ltd., Pacific Concrete & Rock Co., Ltd., Oahu Sugar Co., Ltd., Pioneer Mill Co. Ltd. Writer on taxation, gen. semantics, jurisprudence. Chmn. bd. commrs. Hawaii Bd. Pub. Instrn., 1945; bd. govs., violin and viola player Honolulu Symphony Orch., 1930-65; Chmn. bd. regents U. Hawaii, 1941-43; trustee, bd. dirs. Honolulu Acad. Arts, 1950-51, Watumull Found., 1955—; treas., bd. dirs. Honolulu Art Soc., 1936-50; bd. dirs. Contemporary Art Center of Hawaii, 1967—, chmn., 1980—. Decorated Order Brit. Empire; Order of Distinction for Cultural Leadership, Hawaii . Fellow Am. Bar Found. (life); mem. Am. Bar Assn. (del. Hawaii 1950-53), Bar Assn. Hawaii (pres. 1946-48), Am. Law Inst. (life), Am. Judicature Soc. (dir. 1969-73), Order of Coif. Home: 2186 Round Top Dr Honolulu HI 96822 Office: Bishop Trust Bldg PO Box 939 Honolulu HI 96808

CADES, STEWART RUSSELL, lawyer, communications company executive; b. Phila., Jan. 16, 1942; s. Ralph E. and Lillian G. (Mann) C. B.S. in Econs, U. Pa., 1964; M.Ed., Temple U., 1971; LL.B., U. Pa., 1967. Bar: Pa. bar 1971. Individual practice law, Bala-Cynwyd, Pa. and Phila., 1971—; chmn. bd. Porcupine Communications Co., Phila., 1971—; pres. Nairn U.S. Holdings div. Stewart Nairn Group P.L.C.; mng. dir. Juniper Properties; dir. Cloche Assos., Inc., Corp. Retail Media Corp., Acad. Microforms, Inc., Andrews & Leith, Ltd.; Judge of election, Montgomery County, Pa., 1975-77; ct. vol. probation dept. Ct. Common Pleas of Philadelphia County; bd. dirs. Juvenile Law Center; mem. Montgomery County Planning Commn. Mem. alumni council on admissions, reunion gift chmn. U. Pa.; alumni pres. Class of 1964. Mem. Phila., Montgomery County, Pa., Am. bar assns. Clubs: Locust, Print (Phila.) (bd. govs.). Office: 1317 Filbert St Philadelphia PA 19107

CADGE, WILLIAM FLEMING, photographer; b. Phila., May 5, 1924; s. Arthur and Janet (Fleming) C.; m. Anne Marie English, Feb. 5, 1949; children: Stephen Anthony, Jeffrey John, Catherine Anne. Student, Phila. Mus. Sch. Art, 1945-49. Freelance designer, Phila., 1949-50; asst. art dir. Eve. Bull., Phila., 1950-52, Woman's Home Companion, 1952-56; art dir. Doyle, Dane & Bernbach (advt.), N.Y.C., 1956-57; asso. art dir. McCall's mag., 1959-61; art dir. Redbook mag., 1961-75; owner, mgr. Jeff and Bill Cadge Photography. Photog. covers nat. and European mags., also editorial and advt. illustration. Served with RAF, 1941-43; with USAAF, 1943-45. Recipient 2 gold medals, 8 award distinctive merit Art Director's Club N.Y.; 1 gold medal; 1 award distinctive merit Art Director's Club Phila.; 1 award excellence Art Director's Club N.J.; also N.J. 2 awards of excellence.; 1 award outstanding achievement for 1966 Soc. Illustrators; 1 gold medal, 1971, 72; 5 awards excellence Type Director's Club N.Y.; 1 award excellence for 3 consecutive issues of Redbook in 1966, 1969, Soc. Publ. Designers; also 1 award excellence best typography in 1966, and award distinctive merit for 3 consecutive issues Redbook, 1970; awards excellence CA Mag. Show, 1967, 68, 1968, Soc. Illustrators, 1968, 1977; gold medal Art Dirs. Club Show, 1977. Mem. Soc. Illustrators, Art Dirs. Club N.Y. (exec. bd. 1966-68). Home: 33 Colonial Ave Dobbs Ferry NY 10522 Office: 15 W 28th St New York NY 10001

CADIEUX, R.D., chemical company executive; b. 1937; married. B.S. in Econs. and Acctg., Ill. Inst. Tech.; M.B.A., U. Chgo. Former div. controller internat. ops. Standard Oil Co (Ind.); v.p. adminstrn. and planning Amoco Chems. Corp., Chgo., 1975-81, exec. v.p., dir., 1981—. Office: Amoco Chems Corp 200 E Randolph Dr Chicago IL 60601 *

CADIGAN, GEORGE LESLIE, bishop; b. Mt. Vernon, N.Y., Apr. 12, 1910; s. Edward J. and Christine (Lindbloom) C.; m. Jane Jones, Aug. 15, 1944; children—Peter, David, Rufus, Christine. B.A. cum laude, Amherst Coll., 1933, also D.D.; student, Episcopal Theol. Sch., 1935, Jesus Coll., Cambridge U., 1936; D.D., Hobart Coll., U. South, Hofstra U. Ordained deacon P.E. Ch., 1935, priest, 1936; curate Grace Ch., Amherst; chaplain Amherst Coll.; rector St. Paul's Ch., Brunswick, Maine, 1937-42, Grace Ch., Salem, Mass., 1942-48, St. Paul's Ch., Rochester, N.Y., 1948-59; bishop Diocese of Mo., 1959-75; dir. religious activities Amherst Coll., 1975—. Dep. Episcopal Gen. Convs., 1955, 58; mem. Commn. on Alcoholism, Episcopal Ch., 1955-59; past trustee St. Luke's Episcopal-Presbyterian Hosps., Episcopal-Presbyn. Found. for Aging, Barnard Free Skin and Cancer Hosp., Thompson Retreat and Conf. Center, Mo. Botanical Gardens, all St. Louis; past pres. chpt. Christ Ch. Cathedral, Episcopal City Mission Soc., CARE and Counseling, Inc., Met. Ch. Fedn. Greater St. Louis; past chmn. bd. Grace Hill Settlement House, Neighborhood Health Center, Ednl. Center, all St. Louis; mem. agenda com., chmn. adv. com. to suffragan bishop to armed forces House of Bishops, Episcopal Ch., 1959-75. Named Distinguished Citizen of Yr. St. Louis Jewish Council Community Relations, 1973, St. Louis Urban League, 1974. Address: 44 Chapel Rd Amherst MA 01002

CADIGAN, WILLIAM JOSEPH, utility company executive; b. Boston, Aug. 29, 1919; s. John Joseph and Mary Theresa (Sampson) C.; m. Dorothea Marie Murphy, June 11, 1945; children: Nancy (Mrs. Alan Casden), Christine, Susan (Mrs. Douglas P. Hahn), Paul, Marie, Mark. A.B., Boston Coll., 1942. Asst. editor Textron, Lowell, Mass., 1945-46; reporter Lawrence (Mass.) Eagle, 1946-47; publs. dir. New Eng. Electric System, Boston, 1947-60; asst. to pres. Mass. Electric Co., Worcester, 1960-68, v.p., 1968-72, pres., 1972-82, dir., 1968-82; pres., dir. New Eng. Power Service Co., Westboro, Mass., 1982—. Author: The ICIE File A History of Industrial Journalism, 1958. Dir. Boy Scouts Am., Worcester; mem. Community Services of Greater Worcester, Mass.; Trustee, incorporator St. Vincent Hosp., Worcester; corporator Consumers Savs. Bank. Served with USAAF, 1942-45. Mem. Electric Council of New England (chmn. gen. div. 1975), Worcester C. of C. Home: 12 Elma Circle Shrewsbury MA 01545 Office: New Eng Power Service Co 25 Research Dr Westboro MA 01581

CADMAN, THEODORE WESLEY, chemical engineering educator; b. Osceola Mills, Pa., Feb. 28, 1940; s. Frank B. and Marjorie (Lutz) C.; m. Mary Lou Richardson, June 24, 1961; children: David Scott. B.S. in Chem. Engring., Carnegie-Mellon U., 1962, M.S., 1964, Ph.D., 1966. Instr. Carnegie-Mellon U., Pitts., 1963-65; asst. prof. U. Md., College Park, 1965-68, assoc. prof., 1968-73, prof., 1973-78, prof., chmn. dept. chem. and nuclear engring., 1978—; cons. State of Md. Air Quality, 1970-74, Icarus, 1970-78, SAI, 1980-82; v.p. ENSCI Inc., College Park, 1973—; cons. Univ. Research Found., 1983—. Contbr. articles to profl. jours. NSF grantee, 1968-70; Water Resources Ctr. grantee, 1971-73; State of Md. grantee, 1976-77; NSF grantee, 1976—. Mem. Am. Inst. Chem. Engring., Am. Chem. Soc., Instrument Soc. Am., AAAS. Republican. Methodist. Home: 9110 Saint Andrews Pl College Park MD 20740 Office: U Md College Park MD 20742

CADMAN, WILSON KENNEDY, utility company executive; b. Wichita, Sept. 7, 1927; s. Wilson K. and Ethel Louise (Wheeler) C.; m. Mary Roslyn Rowley, Nov. 22, 1950; children: Elizabeth Louise, Robert Wilson. A.B., Wichita State U., 1951; postgrad., 1953; postgrad., Okla. State U., 1965. With Kans. Gas & Electric Co., Wichita, 1951—, mgr. Wichita div., 1967-70, v.p., 1970-79, pres., 1979—, chief exec. officer, 1981—, also chmn. bd.; dir. Fourth Fin. Corp., Fourth Nat. Bank & Trust Co. Bd. govs. Wichita State U. Endowment Assn.; bd. dirs. St. Frances Hosp., United Way, Music Theatre, Wichita State U. Athletic Scholarship Orgn.; pres. E.S. Edgerton Med. Research Found.; mem. Gov.'s Task Force on High Tech. Devel.; mem. Mayor's Econ. Adv. Council Kans. Water Resources Council. Served with USN, 1945-46. Mem. Mo. Valley Electric Assn. (chmn. gen. mgmt. com.), NAM (bd. dirs.), Edison Electric Inst., Atomic Indsl. Forum (bd. dirs.), Wichita Area C. of C. (bd. dirs.), Wichita Area Devel. (exec. com.), Electric Cos. Assn. Kans. (exec. com.), Missouri Valley Electric Assn., Wichita State U. Endowment Assn., Phi Lambda Phi. Clubs: Wichita, Wichita Country, Petroleum, Kiwanis. Home: 6512 Aberdeen St Wichita KS 67206 Office: 201 N Market St Wichita KS 67202

CADMUS, PAUL, painter, etcher; b. N.Y.C., Dec. 17, 1904; s. Egbert and Maria (Latasa) C. Student, N.A.D., N.Y.C., 1919-26, Art Students League of N.Y., 1926-27. Advt. work, 1928-31, lived and painted in, Europe, 1931-33. First one-man show, N.Y.C., 1937; represented in, Met. Mus. Art, Whitney Mus. Am. Art, Library of Congress, Chgo. Art Inst., Balt. Mus., N.Y. Pub. Library, Seattle Mus., Milw. Mus., Sara Roby Found., Smithsonian Inst.; works include Coney Island, 1934, Gilding the Acrobats, 1935, Sailors and Floosies, 1938, Hinky Dinky Parley Voo, 1939, The Seven Deadly Sins, 1945-49, Bar Italia, 1952-55, Subway Symphony, 1975-76; pub.: Paul Cadmus/Prints and Drawings, 1922-67; subject of: Paul Cadmus Yesterday and Today (by Philip Eliasoph), 1981, Paul Cadmus (Lincoln Kirstein), 1984, Paul Cadmus: Enfant Terrible at 80 (David Sutherland), 1984. Nat. Inst. Arts and Letters grantee, 1961; Recipient purchase award Norfolk Mus. Arts and Scis., 1964. Mem. Soc. Am. Graphic Artists, Am. Acad. and Inst. Arts and Letters, NAD (elected academician 1980). Home: PO Box 1255 Weston CT 06883

CADWELL, FRANCHELLIE MARGARET, advertising agency executive, writer; b. Hamilton, Bermuda, Apr. 23, 1937; came to U.S., 1938; d. Margaret (Roulston) C.; B.S., Cornell U., 1958; M.B.A., NYU, 1973. Pres. Cadwell Davis Advt., N.Y.C., 1960-73, Cadwell Compton (div. Compton Advt.), 1973-75, Cadwell Davis Ptnrs., 1975—; dir. Compton Advt., Kirby Co.-Scott Fetzer, Cleve. Author: The Un-Supermarkets, 1969. Bd. dirs. N.Y. Humane Soc.; bd. govs. N.Y. Arthritis Found., N.Y.C. Recipient Entrepreneurial award Women Bus. Owners of N.Y., 1983. Mem. Advt. Women N.Y., Fashion Group, Cosmetic, Toiletry and Fragrance Assn., Proprietary Assn., Women in Communications (Matrix award 1980). Home: 7 East 94th St New York NY 10028 Office: Cadwell Davis Partners 625 Madison Ave New York NY 10022

CADY, EDWIN HARRISON, English language educator; b. Old Tappan, N.J., Nov. 9, 1917; s. Edwin Laird and Ethel Sprague (Harrison) C.; m. Norma Woodard, Aug. 31, 1939; children: Frances (Mrs. Edward Hitchcock), Elizabeth (Mrs. Larry Saler). A.B., Ohio Wesleyan U., 1939, Litt.D., 1964; M.A., U. Cin., 1940; Ph.D., U. Wis., 1943; Litt.D., Oklahoma City U., 1967. Instr. English U. Wis., 1945, Ohio State U., 1946; from asst. prof. to prof. Syracuse U., 1946-59; Rudy prof. English Ind. U., 1959-73; prof. English Duke U., 1973—, Andrew W. Mellon prof. humanities, 1975—; vis. prof. Am. lit., Uppsala and Stockholm, Sweden, 1951-52. Author: The Gentleman in America, 1949, The Road to Realism, The Early Years, 1837-1885, of William Dean Howells, 1956, The Realist at War: The Mature Years, 1885-1920, of William Dean Howells, 1958, Stephen Crane, 1962, rev. edit., 1980, John Woolman: The Mind of the Quaker Saint, 1965, The Light of Common Day, 1971, The Big Game: College Sports and American Life, 1979; Editor: (with H.H. Clark) Whittier on Writers and Writing, 1950, Literature of the Early Republic, rev. edit, 1969, (with L. Ahnebrink) An Anthology of American Literature, 1953, (with L.G. Wells) Stephen Crane's Love Letters to Nellie Crouse, 1954, (with F.J. Hoffman and R.H. Pearce) The Growth of American Literature, 1956, W.D. Howells, The Rise of Silas Lapham, 1957, Corwin K. Linson, My Stephen Crane, 1958, (with D.L. Frazier) The War of the Critics Over William Dean Howells, 1962, W.D. Howells, The Shadow of a Dream and An Imperative Duty, 1962, William Cooper Howells, Recollections of Life in Ohio, 1963, The American Poets, 1800-1900, 1966, (with D.F. Hiatt) W.D. Howells, Literary Friends and Acquaintance, 1968, Nathaniel Hawthorne, The Scarlet Letter, 1969, W.D. Howells as Critic, 1973, (with C. Anderson and L. Budd) Toward a New American Literary History: Essays in Honor of Arlin Turner, 1980, (with N.W. Cady) Critical Essays on W.D. Howells, 1766-1920, 1983, A Modern Instance, 1984; gen. editor: A Selected Edition of W.D. Howells, 1966-68; assoc. editor: Am. Lit. mag, 1973—; chmn. bd. editors, 1979—. Mem. exec. com. Center Am. Editions, 1964-68; mem. U.S. Nat. Commn. for UNESCO, 1969-71. Served with Am. Field Service, 1943-44; Italy; with USNR, 1945. Guggenheim fellow, 1953-54, 75-76. Mem. MLA (chmn. Am. lit. sect. 1979), Guild Scholars, Am. Antiquarian Soc., Phi Beta Kappa, Omicron Delta Kappa, Phi Gamma Delta. Episcopalian. Home: Box 1056 RFD 4 Hillsborough NC 27278

CADY, ERNEST ALBERT, newspaper editor; b. Newark, Ohio, Oct. 25, 1899; s. Charles Adelbert and Bird Lenore (Bollwine) C.; m. Frances D. Fairchild, June 11, 1923; children—Charles Sherman, Jocelyn Sue (Mrs. Richard Ritter), Judith Ann (Mrs. Alyn Hughes), Jerilou. Student, Ohio State U., 1920-22. Mem. staff Columbus (Ohio) Dispatch, 1922-77, editorial writer, asst. editor of editorial page, 1936-65, lit. editor, columnist, 1948-77; now book reviewer.; Mem. book awards com. Ohioana Library Assn., 1950—, chmn., 1965, 67, 69, 71, 73. Author: We Adopted Three, 1952, (with Frances Cady) How to Adopt a Child, 1956; also articles. Co-incorporator, trustee Ohio Childrens' Soc., pvt. adoption agy., 1953—. Recipient nat. Freedoms Found. award editorial writing, 1971, Ohioana library citation for service to Ohio journalism, 1974. Mem. Nat. Book Critics Circle (charter), Sigma Delta Chi (organizing pres. Central Ohio profl. chpt. 1950, Disting. Service award 1980). Republican. Methodist. Clubs: Ohio Press, Gridiron, Columbus Dispatch Country (Columbus). Home and Office: 3720 Pendlestone Dr Columbus OH 43230

CADY, HOWARD STEVENSON, editor; b. Middlebury, Vt., July 28, 1914; s. Frank William and Marian (Kingsbury) C.; m. Marjory Arnold, Dec. 31, 1938; children: Peter, Janet (Mrs. James Hutchinson), Susan (Mrs. Timothy Y. Hayward), Anne (Mrs. Andrew M. Jackson), Ellen. A.B., Middlebury Coll., 1936. Employed in the editorial dept. of The Macmillan Co., N.Y.C., 1937-41; mng. editor Stephen Daye Press, Brattleboro, Vt., 1941-42; editor Doubleday & Co., Inc., N.Y.C., San Francisco, 1942-52; editor-in-chief Little Brown & Co., Inc., Boston, 1952-54, Henry Holt & Co., N.Y.C., 1954-57; editor-in-chief, v.p., dir. G. P. Putnam's Sons, 1957-62; gen. mgr., editor-in-chief gen. book div. Holt, Rinehart & Winston, Inc., 1962-64; exec. editor David McKay Co., Inc., 1964-68; sr. editor, v.p. Wm. Morrow & Co., Inc., 1968—; Lectr. editing and publishing Sch. Gen. Studies, Columbia, 1958-60. Served with OSS, 1943-45; Served with AUS, 1945-46. Home: 10 Prospect Ave Darien CT 06820 Office: 105 Madison Ave New York NY 10016

CADY, JOHN LODGE, publishing company executive, lawyer; b. Boston, July 17, 1922; s. Joseph Patrick and Mildred (Lodge) C.; m. Margaret Ann Foley, Aug. 8, 1944; 1 son, Robert Lodge. A.B., Harvard U., 1943, J.D., 1948; LL.M., NYU, 1956. Bar: N.Y. 1951. Assoc. Chadbourne Hunt Jaekel & Brown, N.Y.C., 1948-52; atty. Radio Corp. Am., N.Y.C., 1952-57; tax dir. McGraw-Hill, Inc., N.Y.C., 1957-63, v.p. taxes, 1963-73, sr. v.p. taxes, gen. tax counsel, 1973—; v.p. sec., dir. McGraw-Hill Publs. Overseas Corp.; v.p., sec., dir. McGraw-Hill Export Corp., McGraw-Hill Found., Inc.; v.p. treas., dir. Donald C. McGraw Found., Inc.; v.p., dir. Internat. Archtl. Found., 1974-81, pres., 1981—; sec. adv. bd. Tax Mgmt., Inc., Washington, 1979—. Vice pres., dir. Pub. Health Nursing Orgn., Eastchester, N.Y., 1978—; treas., dir. Bronxville Adult Sch., N.Y., 1977-82; village atty. Village of Bronxville, 1973-74; pres. Bronxville PTA, 1967-68. Served to 1st lt. USAAF, 1943-45; ETO. Mem. Tax Execs. Inst. (v.p. N.Y. chpt. 1962-63), N.Y. C. of C. and Industry, NAM, Mag. Pubs. Assn., Assn. Am. Pubs. (chmn. 1978-80), U.S. C. of C., ABA, Bar Assn. City of N.Y., N.Y. State Bar Assn., Knights of Malta. Republican. Roman Catholic. Clubs: Siwanoy Country (gov. 1983—); Bronxville Field (Bronxville, N.Y.); Harvard (N.Y.C.). Home: 46 Summit Ave Bronxville NY 10708 Office: McGraw-Hill Inc. 1221 Ave of Americas New York NY 10021

CADY, JOHN RAMSDEN, manufacturing company executive; b. Rome, N.Y., Nov. 28, 1930; s. Charles William and Mary (Bacchus) C.; m. Margot Lamphier, Sept. 24, 1955; children: Shawn, Kevin, Erin, Colin. Student, Cleve. Coll., 1950-51, LaSalle Extension U., 1955-57. Sales rep. Addressograph-Multigraph Corp., Cleve., 1950-55; diet mgr. Kaiser Jeep Corp., Toledo, 1955-64, v.p., gen. mgr., 1965-70, exec. dir., 1970-71; gen. mgr. packaging div. Kaiser Aluminum, Oakland, Calif., 1971-79, v.p., gen. mgr. mill products, 1980—; dir. Alcan Booth Inc., London, 1975-79. Bd. dirs. Keep Am. Beautiful, N.Y.C., 1981—. Served with USN, 1949-50. Republican. Roman Catholic. Clubs: Commonwealth (San Francisco); Round Hill Country. Office: Kaiser Aluminum and Chem Corp 300 Lakeside Dr Oakland CA 94643

CAEN, HERB, newspaper columnist, author; b. Sacramento, Calif., Apr. 3, 1916; s. Lucien and Augusta (Gross) C.; m. Sally Gilbert, Feb. 15, 1952 (div. 1959); 1 step dau., Deborah; m. Maria Theresa Shaw, Mar. 9, 1963; 1 son, Christopher. Student, Sacramento Jr. Coll., 1934. Daily newspaper columnist San Francisco Chronicle, 1938-50, 1958-; columnist San Francisco Examiner, 1950-58. Author: The San Francisco Book, 1948, Baghdad-by-the-Bay, 1949, Baghdad 1951, 1950, Don't Call It Frisco, 1953, Caen's Guide to San Francisco, 1957, Only in San Francisco, 1960, (with Dong Kingman) City on Golden Hills, 1968, The Cable Car and the Dragon, 1972, One Man's San Francisco, 1976. Served from pvt. to capt. USAAF, 1942-45. Decorated Medaille de la Liberation, France, 1949. Democrat. Club: Calif. Tennis. Office: San Francisco Chronicle Pub Co 925 Mission St San Francisco CA 94103 *

CAESAR, HENRY A., II, sculptor; b. N.Y.C., Oct. 20, 1914; s. Harry I. and Doris (Porter) C.; m. Allison Garver, Mar. 15, 1941; children: Sanderson, Porter Dean, Austin Brewster, John Garver. A.B., Princeton U., 1937; LL.B., Yale U., 1940. Partner H.A. Caesar & Co., N.Y.C., 1946-69; pres., dir. H.A. Caesar & Co., Inc., 1969-73, chmn. bd., 1973-74; cons., 1974-79; former dir. Bank of Manhattan, First Union Nat. Bank of N.C. Sculptor in bronze, marble and alabaster, one-man shows, Jardiniere, Greenwich, Conn., 1978; Carriage Barn, 1978, Waveny Arts Center, New Canaan, 1979, Caravan House, N.Y.C., 1981, other shows include, Audubon Soc., 1979, 80, 82, Avery Fisher Hall, Lincoln Center, 1980, Artist Studio Center, Artist Studio Center, all N.Y.C. Trustee, chmn. bd. trustees N.Y. Inst. Credit, 1971-74; pres., trustee New Canaan Nature Center, 1978-80; trustee Proctor Acad., Andover, N.H.; trustee, v.p. New Canaan Soc. Arts. Served as lt. USNR, World War II. Clubs: New Canaan Country; Hampton Court (London). Studio: Fine Arts Acad Mill Hill Terr Fairfield CT 06430

CAESAR, SID, actor, comedian; b. Yonkers, N.Y., Sept. 8, 1922; s. Max and Ida (Raphael) C.; m. Florence Levy, June 17, 1943; children: Michele, Richard, Karen. Grad., Yonkers High Sch., 1939; studied saxophone and clarinet, N.Y.C. Played in small bands, later orchs. of, Charlie Spivak, Shep Fields and Claude Thornhill, following World War II; toured leading theatres and night clubs as comedian; appeared in: also film version Tars and Spars Revue; in Broadway musical prodn. of Make Mine Manhattan, 1948; on TV as the star of: Admiral Broadway Revue, 1948, Your Show of Shows, 1950-54; star of: own show Caesar's Hour, 1954-57; star and producer: Sid Caesar Invites You, 1958, also, As Caesar Sees It, 1962-63; TV guest appearances include: Robert Morse Show; star of: Broadway musical Little Me, 1962-63; in films It's a Mad, Mad, Mad, Mad World, 1963, The Spirit is Willing, 1967, Ten from Your Show of Shows, 1973, Silent Movie, 1975, Fire Sale, 1977, The Cheap Detective, 1978; films Grease, 1978, Grease 2, 1982; in films History of the World, Part I, 1981, Over the Brooklyn Bridge, 1984; author autobiography: Where Have I Been?, 1982. Recipient Best Comedian on TV award Look mag., 1951, 56, Emmy award, best comedian, 1956, Sylvania award best comedy-variety show, 1958; named to U.S. Hall of Fame, 1967. Club: Old Falls Rod and Gun (Fallsburgh, N.Y.). Office: care Contemporary-Korman Artists Ltd 132 Lasky Dr Beverly Hills CA 90212 *

CAESAR, VANCE ROY, newspaper executive; b. Pa., Dec. 22, 1944; s. Jack Raymond and Norma Norine (Wiles) C.; m. Carol Ann Richards, Apr. 22, 1967; 1 son, Eric. B.S. in Bus. Adminstrn, The Citadel, 1966; M.B.A., Fla. Atlantic U., 1969. From asst. to gen. mgr. to consumer mktg. dir. Miami (Fla.) Herald, 1970-77; assoc. editor Detroit Free Press, 1977-78; gen. mgr. Long Beach (Calif.) Press-Telegram, 1978—. Bd. dirs. Meml. Med. Ctr., Long Beach, Downtown Long Beach Assocs., Region III, United Way; adviser Long Beach Jr. League.; adviser Extended Edn. Dept. Calif. State U.-Long Beach, mem. bus. sch. adv. bd., mem. Bus. Roundtable; exec. com. Am. Cancer Soc.; mem. Long Beach promotion com. 49er Athletic Found.; mem. Long Beach Area Conv. and Tourism Bur. Mem. Long Beach Area C. of C. (dir.), Stanford Bus. Sch. Alumni. Home: 4357 Dogwood Ave Seal Beach CA 90740 Office: 604 Pine Ave Long Beach CA 90844

CAFFEY, GUY HAMILTON, JR., banker; b. Montgomery, Ala., Feb. 16, 1926; s. Guy Hamilton and Mamie Susan (Barber) C.; m. Marjorie Sue Courtney, Dec. 26, 1948; children—Guy Hamilton III, William Courtney, Mamie Susan. B.S., Samford U., 1951; grad., Stonier Sch. Banking, 1963. With Birmingham Trust Nat. Bank, Ala., 1951—, chmn., chief exec. officer, 1969-81; now dir.; chmn., chief exec. officer So. Bancorp., until 1981, now dir.; instr. Am. Inst. Banking, 1961-64; lectr. Banking Sch. South, 1965-67. Mem. met. and devel. bd. Birmingham YMCA; bd. dirs. United Way. Served with USAAF, 1944-46. Named Outstanding Young Banker of Year Ala. Bankers Assn., 1961; récipient Alumnus of Yr. award Samford U., 1976. Mem. Am. Res. City Bankers Assn. (corp. planning exec. com.), Ala. Res. City Bankers Assn. (1st v.p.), Ala. Bankers Assn., Birmingham Area C. of C. (past pres. met. devel. bd., chmn.). Clubs: Quarterback, Relay House, The Club, Vestavia Country, Mountain Brook, Country (Birmingham). Office: 112-118 N 20th St Birmingham AL 35290

CAFFEY, H(ORACE) ROUSE, educational and agricultural research administrator, international rice consultant; b. Grenada, Miss., Mar. 24, 1929; s. C. Horace and Anna Belle (James) C.; children: Brenda, Jerry, Belle, Rex. B.S., Miss. State U., 1951, M.S., 1955; Ph.D., La State U., 1959. Agronomist in charge rice project Miss. Agrl. Exptl. Sta., Stoneville, 1958-62; supt. La. State U. Rice Sta., La. Agrl. Exptl. Sta., Crowley, 1962-70, assoc. dir., prof., Baton Rouge, 1970-79; vice-chancellor adminstrn. La. State U. Agrl. Ctr., 1979-80, vice-chancellor internat. programs, 1980-81, chancellor, 1984—, La. State U.-, Alexandria, 1981-84; internat. rice cons. AID, World Bank, other orgns., 1965—; mem. pub. health study team Nat. Acad. Sci, Washington, 1973-74; mem. adv. bd. Bd. Regents Masters Plan Higher Edn., Baton Rouge, 1977. Contbr. chpts. to books, articles to profl. jours. Pres. Internat. Rice Festival, Crowley, 1968; bd. dirs. Boy Scouts U.S.A., United Way, others. Served to 1st lt. U.S. Army, 1951-54. Recipient Internat. Award of Merit Gamma Sigma Delta, 1970, 81; honoree Internat. Rice Festival, 1974; named Man of Yr. Crowley C. of C., 1969-70. Mem. Am. Soc. Agronomy, Sigma Xi, Gamma Sigma Delta, Phi Delta Kappa, Omicron Delta Kappa, Phi Delta Phi, Phi Zeta. Democrat. Baptist. Club:. Lodges: Masons; Rotary. Home: 10471 Barry Dr Baton Rouge LA 70809 Office: Louisiana State University Agrl Center Baton Rouge LA 70803

CAFFREY, ANDREW AUGUSTINE, U.S. dist. judge; b. Lawrence, Mass., Oct. 2, 1920; s. Augustine J. and Monica A. (Regan) C.; m. Evelyn F. White, June 26, 1946; children: Augustine J., Andrew A., James E., Mary L., Francis J., Joseph H. A.B. cum laude, Holy Cross Coll., 1941, LL.B., Boston Coll., 1948; LL.M., Harvard U., 1948. Bar: Mass. 1948, U.S. Supreme Ct. 1958. Assoc. prof. law Boston Coll. Law Sch., 1948-55; asst. U.S. atty., chief civil div. Dist. Mass., 1955-59, 1st asst. U.S. atty., 1959-60, U.S. dist. judge, 1960—, chief judge, 1972—; Mem. Jud. Panel on Multidist. Litigation, 1975—, chmn., 1980. Served with AUS, World War II; ETO. Mem. Jud. Conf. U.S. (exec. com. 1975-79), Am., Fed., Mass. Boston bar assns., Am. Law Inst., Harvard Law Sch. Assn. Mass., Order of Coif (hon.), Alpha Sigma Nu, Delta Epsilon Sigma. Clubs: Merrimack Valley, Holy Cross Alumni (past pres., dir.). Address: 1629 Post Office Bldg Boston MA 02109

CAFFREY, FRANCIS DAVID, banker; b. Phila., Jan. 18, 1927; s. John Joseph and Hilda Marie (Peterson) C.; m. Nancy R. Distel, Feb. 23, 1952; children—Mark, Eric, Diane. Student, Pa. State U., 1955.

With Continental Bank, Norristown, Pa., 1958—, sr. v.p., treas., 1976—; v.p. Greater Norristown Corp., 1978. Mem. Citizen's Adv. Commn., Norristown, 1973—, Citizens Council Montgomery County, Pa., 1973—, Whitpain Twp. Mcpl. Authority, 1973—; v.p. bd. trustees Sacred Heart Hosp., Norristown; trustee Norristown State Hosp. Served with USMC, 1945-51. Mem. Robert Morris Assos. (trustee 1969-72), V.F.W., Am. Legion, Valley Forge C. of C., Am. Inst. Banking, Bank Adminstrn. Inst., Pa. Soc. Home: 1640 Winchester Dr Norristown PA 19401 Office: Continental Bank Main and Swede Sts Norristown PA 19401

CAFFREY, KENNETH EDWARD, advt. exec.; b. N.Y.C., Sept. 17, 1938; s. Edward Andrew and Ethel (Craig) C.; m. Joan Louise Mennona, Dec. 26, 1959; children—Kenneth, Thomas, Anne Marie. Student, City Coll. N.Y., 1959-63, Pace U., 1965-72. With CBS, N.Y.C., 1959-60; media planner Ted Bates & Co., N.Y.C., 1960-63; with Ogilvy & Mather, N.Y.C., 1963—, v.p., 1968-74, sr. v.p., 1974—, mem. operating com., 1980—, exec. dir. media ops., 1979—; dir. Certified Audit of Circulation, 1980, Nat. Yellow Pages Adv. Bd., 1978—. Contbr. articles to profl. jours. Pres. N. Eastchester Civic Assn., 1969-70. Served with U.S. Army, 1956-58. Mem. Internat. Radio and TV Soc., Am. Assn. Advt. Agys. Republican. Roman Catholic. Office: 2 E 48th St New York NY 10017

CAFRITZ, PEGGY COOPER, commucications executive; b. Mobile, Ala., Apr. 7, 1947; d. Algernon Johnson and G. Catherine (Mouton) C.; m.; 1 child. B.A. in Polit. Sci., George Washington U., 1968, J.D., 1971. Bar: D.C. 1972. Founder Workshops for Careers in Arts, Washington, 1968; developer, chmn. bd. Duke Ellington Sch. Arts., Washington, 1968—; dir. Arrowstreet, Architects and Planners Inc., Cambridge, Mass., 1972-74, Washington, 1972-74; spl. asst. to pres. Post-Newsweek Stas. Inc., Washington, 1974-77; programming exec., producer documentary films Sta. WTOP-TV, Washington, 1974—; cons. arts. Mem. exec. com. D.C. Commn. Arts and Humanities, 1970-75, chmn., 1979—; trustee Am. Film Inst., 1972-74; bd. govs. Corcoran Gallery Art, Washington; exec. dir. great issues program D.C. Bicentennial Commn., 1974; bd. dirs. Washington Performing Arts Soc.; mem. exec. bd. Nat. Assembley State Arts Agys., 1980—; mem. conv. staff Democratic Nat. Com., 1972, 76; mem. steering com. Carter-Mondale, Washington, 1976; mem. nat. panel Arts, Edn. and Ams., 1975—; mem. internat. com. UNICEF, 1976—, bd. dirs. U.S. com., 1978—; bd. dirs. Nat. Guild Coummunity Schs. of Arts, 1976—, Pennsylvania Ave Devel. Corp., Washington; trustee Atlanta U., 1983—; founder Duke Ellington High Sch. for the Arts. Fellow Woodrow Wilson Internat. Ctr. for Scholars, 1971-72; recipient John D. Rockefeller III award, 1972, George F. Peabody award U. Ga., 1976, Emmy award, 1977, 27th Ann. Broadcast Media award, 1977; named Washingtonian of Year Washingtonian Mag., 1972, Woman of Yr. Mademoiselle Mag., 1973. Mem. ABA, D.C. Bar Assn. Home and Office: 2900 44th St NW Washington DC 20016 *Growing up black in the fully segregated city of Mobile, Alabama, instilled in me a youthful passion "to become the wind and not the blown." This passion, from which flows the energy that drives me to achieve has never abated; it has broadened: I do hope that I have done and will continue to do much to help others so that they too can become the wind.*

CAGAN, PHILLIP DAVID, economics educator; b. Seattle, Apr. 30, 1927; s. Herman Solomon and Lillian (Levinson) C.; children: John, Laird, David. A.A., UCLA, 1948; M.A., U. Chgo., 1951, Ph.D., 1954. Research assoc. Nat. Bur. Econ. Research, N.Y.C., 1953-55; asst. prof. econs. U. Chgo., 1955-58; assoc. prof. Brown U., Providence, 1958-62, prof., 1962-65, Columbia U., N.Y.C., 1966—, chmn. dept. econs., Providence, 1981—; vis. scholar Am. Enterprise Inst., Washington, 1972—. Author: (including) Determinants and Effects of Changes in the Money Stock, 1965, The Channels of Monetary Effects on Interest Rates, 1972, Persistent Inflation, 1979. Served with USNR, 1945-46. Fellow Econometric Soc.; mem. Am. Econ. Assn. Office: Dept Econs Columbia U New York NY 10027

CAGE, JOHN, composer; b. Los Angeles, Sept. 5, 1912; s. John Milton and Lucretia (Harvey) C.; m. Xenia Kashevaroff, June 7, 1935. Student, Pomona Coll., 1928-30; pupil, Richard Buhlig, Adolph Weiss, Henry Cowell, Arnold Schoenberg. Faculty Cornish Sch., Seattle, 1936-38, Sch. Design, Chgo., 1941-42; tchr. composition New Sch. for Social Research, N.Y.C., 1955-60; musical dir. Merce Cunningham and Dance Co., N.Y.C., 1944-66; fellow Center Advanced Studies, Wesleyan U., Middletown, Conn., 1960-61; composer-in residence U. Cin., 1967; research prof. and asso. Center Advanced Studies, U. Ill., Urbana, 1967-69; Mem. bd., past pres. Cunningham Dance Found.; mem. Found. for Contemporary Performance Arts. Dir. concert percussion music sponsored by, Mus. Modern Art and League Composers, 1943; commd. by Ballet Soc. to write: The Seasons, 1947; by Donaueschinger Musiktage to write: work for two prepared pianos 34'46. 766 for Two Pianists, 1954; by the Montreal Festivals Soc. to write: work for full orch. Atlas Eclipticalis, 1961; by Serge Koussevitsky Music Found. in Library of Congress to write: Cheap Imitation for Full Orch, 1972; by CBC to write: Lecture on the Weather for 12 speaker-vocalists (tape and film in collaboration with Maryanne Amacher and Luis Frangella), 1975; by Seiji Ozawa and Boston Symphony Orch. in collaboration with, 5 other Am. orchs. and, Nat. Endowment for Arts to write, Renga with Apartment House 1776 for orch; four quartets and eight soloists, 1976; by Metz Centre Europeen pour la Recherche Musicale to write 30 pieces for 5 orchs., 1981; recorded Fontana Mix on magnetic tape for, Studio di Fonologia, Milan, Italy, 1958; organized group of musicians and engrs. for making music directly on magnetic tape, 1951; produced: (with Lejaren Hiller) HPSCHD for seven harpsichords and 52 computer generated tapes, 1967-69; Author: (with Kathleen O'Donnell Hoover) The Life and Works of Virgil Thomson, 1958, Silence, 1961, A Year from Monday, 1967, (with Alison Knowles) Notations, 1969, (with Lois Long and Alexander H. Smith) Mushroom Book, 1972, M, 1973, Writings Through Finnegans Wake, 1978, Empty Words, 1979, For the Birds, Themes and Variations; Graphic works include Not Wanting to Say Anything About Marcel, 1969, (with Calvin Sumsion) Seven Day Diary, Score Without Parts, 17 Drawings by Thoreau, Signals, 1978, Changes and Disappearances, 1979, On the Surface, 1980. Guggenheim fellow, 1949; award for extending boundries mus. art Nat. Acad. Arts and Letters, 1949; recipient first prize Woodstock Art Film Festival for score of Works of Calder, 1951, ann. award from the People to People Com. on Fungi, 1964; Thorne Music Fund grantee, 1967-69; Carl Sczuka prize for Roaratorio, an Irish Circus on Finnegans Wake, 1979. Mem. ASCAP, N.Y. Mycol. Soc. (a founder), also The Nat. Inst. Arts and Letters, Am. Acad. Arts and Scis. Address: 101 W 18th St New York NY 10011

CAGE, JOSEPH SHELBY, JR., lawyer; b. Monroe, La., Feb. 28, 1942; s. Joseph Shelby and Virginia Fern (Ziegler) C.; m. Susan Broadway Sperry, Sept. 7, 1968; children: Susanna, Cynthia, Joseph Shelby. B.A., N.E. La. U., 1966; J.D., U. Houston, 1971. Bar: La. 1973. Asst. U.S. atty. U.S. Dept. Justice, Shreveport, La., 1973-76, 82—; assoc. Johnston, Thornton, Greer & Cage, Shreveport, 1976-79, Brown, Wicker, Cage & Aiman, Monroe, La., 1979-82. Served with USMC, 1963. Republican. Episcopalian. Office: US Atty 500 Fannin St Shreveport LA 71101

CAGGIANO, JOSEPH, advt. agy. exec.; b. N.Y.C., Oct. 22, 1925; s. Daniel Joseph and Lucia (Gaudiosi) C.; m. Catherine Marie Gilmore, Aug. 28, 1948; children—Cathleen, Mary Yvonne. B.B.A., Pace Coll., 1953. Chief accountant Criterion Advt. Co., N.Y.C., 1947-57; treas. Emerson Foote, Inc., N.Y.C., 1957-67; became sr. v.p. Bozell & Jacobs, Inc., N.Y.C., 1967, exec. v.p. finance and adminstrn., Omaha, 1971-74, vice chmn. bd., chief financial officer, 1974—, also dir., mem. exec. com.; dir. Emerson Foote, Inc. Bd. dirs. St. Mary's Coll., Omaha Zool. Soc. Served with USNR, 1943-46; ETO, PTO. Mem. N.Y. Credit and Financial Mgmt. Assn., Omaha Zool. Soc. (dir.). Home: 9731 Fieldcrest Dr Omaha NE 68114 Office: 10250 Regency Circle Omaha NE 68114 *Luck in business is best defined as preparation meeting opportunity while always keeping a positive attitude. Dedication and fairness to a cause is mandatory. There are few short cuts to success in business or meaningful relationships with family and friends; and still fewer gray areas. It would have been impossible to achieve any degree of success without the help and understanding of my wife and family.*

CAGLE, FREDRIC WILLIAM, JR., educator; b. Metropolis, Ill., Dec. 17, 1924; s. Fredric William and Hattimay (Stalcup) C. B.S., U. Ill., 1944, M.S., 1945, Ph.D., 1946. Mem. Sch. Math. Inst. for Advanced Study, Princeton, N.J., 1947-48; fellow in chemistry U. Utah, 1948-49, research asst. prof., 1949-53, asst. prof., 1953-54, asso. prof., 1954-60, prof., 1960—; cons. Pacific Northwest Pipeline Corp., 1958-61, Dow Chem. Co., 1963-67. Mem. Am. Chem. Soc., Am. Crystallographic Assn., Sigma Xi, Phi Kappa Phi, Sigma Pi Sigma. Club: University Club of Salt Lake City. Research X-ray crystallography and crystal structure; chemical thermodynamics. Office: Dept of Chemistry U Utah Salt Lake City UT 84112

CAGLE, WILLIAM REA, librarian; b. Hollywood, Calif., Nov. 15, 1933; s. Howard Clinton and Eunice (Colcord Althouse) C.; m. Terry Lucinda Conrad, Jan. 17, 1975; children by previous marriage: Michael, Stewart, Chantal, Gabrille, Mark Christopher, Monique Antoinette. A.B. in English, UCLA, 1956, M.L.S., 1962; postgrad., Oxford U., 1959-60. Asst. to librarian Henry E. Huntington Library and Art Gallery, San Marino, Calif., 1960-62; librarian for English Ind. U. Libraries, Bloomington, 1962-67, asst. Lilly librarian, 1967-75, acting Lilly librarian, Bloomington, 1975-77; Lilly librarian Ind. U. Liraries, Bloomington, 1977—. Contbr.: Printing and the Mind of Man, 1967; editor: Indiana U. Bookman, 1966—; contbr. articles to profl. jours. Served with U.S. Army, 1956-59. Mem. Benjamin Franklin Guild (bd. govs.), Assn. Internationale De Biliophilie, Lincoln Soc., Alfred Kinsey Inst. Sex Research (trustee). Clubs: Grolier (N.Y.C.); Caxton (Chgo.). Home: 102 F N Park Ridge Bloomington IN 45401 Office: Lilly Lirary Ind U Bloomington IN 47405

CAGNEY, JAMES, actor; b. N.Y.C., July 17, 1899; m. Frances Vernon, 1922. Ed. grammar sch. Began in vaudeville, 1924; worked in motion pictures, 1931-61; pres., Cagney-Montgomery Prodns., Los Angeles; v.p., Cagney Productions, 1942; has appeared in: many pictures among which were Yankee Doodle Dandy (best actor award Critics' Circle 1942), What Price Glory?, A Lion is in the Streets, Run for Cover, Love Me or Leave Me, Mr. Roberts, 1, 2, 3. Johnny Come Lately, Blood on the Sun, The time of Your Life, Never Steal Anything Small, Shake Hands With The Devil, The Gallant Heart, Ragtime, 1981, Terrible Joe Moran, 1984; TV appearances include: Terrible Joe Moran, 1984. Recipient Academy award as best actor, 1942, Life Achievement award Am. Film Inst., 1974. Address: care Paul Jannuzzo ITT Corp Hdqrs 320 Park Ave New York NY 10022 *

CAHAL, MAC FULLERTON, lawyer, publisher; b. Kiowa, Kans., Mar. 28, 1907; s. Frank Bastian and Carrie (Fullerton) C.; m. Wilma Marshall, June 1, 1935; children: Carolyn Holder, William Marshall. A.B., U. Kans., 1931; postgrad., Northwestern U., 1937; J.D., De Paul U., 1942. Bar: Ill. 1942. Newspaper reporter, feature writer Wichita (Kans.) Beacon, 1928; pub. relations dept. Grigsby-Grunow, Kansas City, 1929; 1st exec. sec. Sedgwick Co. (Kans.) Med. Soc., 1931-37; exec. dir. Am. Coll. Radiology, Chgo., 1937-48; exec. v.p. Southwestern Med. Found., Dallas, 1943-44; exec. v.p., gen. counsel Am. Acad. Family Physicians (pub. Am. Family Physician), Kansas City, 1948-73; now pres. Med. Book Club, Inc.; publisher Continuing Edn.; lectr. legal and social medicine U. Kans. Med. Sch.; Cons. Med. Task Force of Hoover Commn. for Orgn. Exec. Br. Govt., 1953-55; founder Med. Soc. Execs. Assn., pres., 1947-48. Author monographs on legal, social and econ. aspects of medicine.; Pres., pub.: Continuing Edn. Jour; Contbr. articles to med. and legal publs. Recipient Gold medal German Inst. Medicine, 1972. Mem. AMA (Distinguished Service award 1972), Mo., Kansas City, Chgo. bar assns., U.S. C. of C. (bd. regents Inst. for Assn. Mgmt., mem. tax council), Am. Soc. Assn. Execs. (dir.), Profl. Conv. Mgrs. Assn. (founder, Disting. Service award 1979), Chartered Assn. Execs. (trustee), Kansas City Soc. Western Art (pres.), C. of C., Acad. Health Profls. (trustee). Episcopalian. Clubs: Indian Hills Country, Kansas City (Kansas City); Wine and Food (pres. 1972); Lawyers (Washington); Bohemian (San Francisco); Mission Valley Hunt, Saddle and Sirloin; University (Chgo.). Home: 6610 Indian Ln Mission Hills KS 66208 Office: 4821 W 83d Overland Park KS 66208

CAHALAN, (JOHN) DONALD, educator; b. Lewistown, Mont., Oct. 3, 1912; s. Daniel Emmett and Emma Cecilia (Robinson) C.; m. Ellen Margaret Johnson, Aug. 19, 1933; children: Carolyn Cahalan Cooper, Michael. B.A., State U. Iowa, 1937, M.A., 1938; Ph.D., George Washington U., 1968. Asso. prof. psychology and social sci., dir. Opinion Research Ctr., U. Denver, 1946-49; research dir. Attitude Assessment, Dept. Army, 1949-52; research cons. to univ. and govt. research groups, 1952-57; chief project dir. W.R. Simmons and Assocs., N.Y., 1957-59; pres. ARB Surveys, Inc., N.Y.C., 1959-62; exec. v.p. Nowland & Co., Greenwich, Conn., 1962-64; program dir. social research group George Washington U., 1964-70; from adj. prof. to prof. behavioral scis. in residence, also dir. social research group Sch. Pub. Health, U. Calif.-Berkeley, 1970-78, prof. pub. health emeritus, 1978—; vis. colleague Sch. Pub. Health, U. Hawaii, 1978-79. Author: Problem Drinkers: A National Survey, 1970, (with Ira H. Cisin and Helen M. Crossley) American Drinking Practices, 1969, (with Robin Room) Problem Drinking Among American Men, 1974; also articles. Mem. Mayor's Commn. Human Relations, Denver, 1947-48. Served with USNR, 1943-46. NIMH grantee, 1970. Mem. Am. Psychol. Assn., Soc. Psychol. Study Social Issues, Am. Sociol. Soc., Soc. Study of Social Problems, Am. Pub. Health Assn., Am. Assn. Pub. Opinion Research (sec.-treas. 1969-73), Sigma Xi. Home: 1338 Grizzly Peak Blvd Berkeley CA 94708

CAHAN, WILLIAM GEORGE, surgeon, educator; b. N.Y.C., Aug. 2, 1914; s. Samuel George and Flora (Gomperts) C.; m. Mary Arnold Sykes, Dec. 26, 1952 (div.); children: Christopher, Anthony; m. Grace Mirabella, Nov. 24, 1974. B.S., Harvard U., 1935; M.D., Columbia U., 1939. Diplomate: Am. Bd. Surgery. Surg. pathology Presbyn. Hosp., N.Y.C., 1939; intern, house surgeon Hosp. Joint Diseases, N.Y.C., 1940-41; fellow cancer surgery Meml. Hosp., N.Y.C., 1942-48; thoracic cons. Strang Clinic, 1949-53, attending surg. staff thoracic service, 1949—; asst. attending surgeon Manhattan Eye, Ear and Throat Hosp., 1950-58, cons. gen. surgeon, 1964—; asso. vis. surgeon James Ewing Hosp., N.Y.C., 1959-68; cons. tumor service Newark Beth Israel Hosp., 1968; instr. surgery Cornell U. Med. Coll., 1950-56, mem. faculty, 1956—, asso. prof. surgery, 1966-74, prof., 1974—; asst. clinician Sloan-Kettering Inst., 1953-68; co-chmn. Internat. Workshop on Multiple Primary Cancers, Meml. Sloan-Kettering Cancer Center; vis. scholar Univ. Center in Va., Richmond, 1967; mem. Lasker Award Jury, 1980-84. Author: (with Hans von Leden) Cryogenics in Surgery, 1971; Editorial bd.: Jour. Cryosurgery; Contbr. numerous articles to med. jours. Pres. Treadwell Farm Hist. Dist., N.Y.C., 1966-69; mem. overseers vis. com. music Harvard, 1968-69; mem. adv. bd. Leeds Castle Found. Served to maj. M.C. USAAF, 1943-46. Recipient Disting. Service award Am. Cancer Soc., 1982. Fellow A.C.S.; mem. Am. Assn. Thoracic Surgery, Am. Cancer Soc., Am. Coll. Chest Physicians, A.M.A., Am. Radium Soc., Internat. Congress Smoking and Health (adv. bd.), N.Y. Cancer Soc. (sec. 1955-58), N.Y. County, N.Y. State med. socs., N.Y. Surg. Soc., N.Y. Soc. Thoracic Surgeons, Royal Soc. Medicine (affiliate), Soc. Cryobiology, Soc. Thoracic Surgeons. Office: 1275 York Ave New York NY 10021

CAHILL, CLYDE S., U.S. judge; b. St. Louis, Apr. 9, 1923; s. Clyde and Effie (Taylor) C.; m. Thelma Newsom, Apr. 29, 1951; children: Linda Diggs, Marina, Valerian, Randall, Kevin, Myron. B.S., St. Louis U., 1949, J.D., 1951. Bar: Mo. Asst. circuit atty., City of St. Louis, 1954-66; regional atty. OEO, 1966-68; gen. mgr. Human Devel. Corp., 1968-72; gen. counsel, dir. Legal Aid Soc., 1972-75; circuit judge, State of Mo., 1975-80; U.S. dist. judge Eastern Dist. Mo., 1980—; lectr. St. Louis U. Law Sch., 1974-79. Bd. dirs. St. Louis Urban League, 1974, Met. YMCA, St. Louis, 1975—, Comprehensive Health Center, St. Louis, 1975, Cardinal Ritter High Sch., St. Louis, 1978. Served with USAAF, World War II. Recipient NAACP Disting. Service award, St. Louis Argus award. Mem. Am. Bar Assn., Nat. Bar Assn., Am. Judicature Soc., Met. St. Louis Bar Assn., St. Louis Lawyers Assn., Mound City Bar Assn. Office: US Court and Custom House 1114 Market St Saint Louis MO 63101

CAHILL, GEORGE FRANCIS, JR., physician, educator; b. N.Y.C., July 7, 1927; s. George Francis and Eva Marion (Wagner) C.; m. Sarah Townsend duPont, Dec. 20, 1949; children: Colleen (Mrs. Thomas P. Remley), Peter duPont, George F. III, Sarah Rhett, Eva Wagner (Mrs. William M. Doll), Elizabeth Anglin. B.S., Yale, 1949; M.D., Columbia U., 1953; M.A., Harvard U., 1966. Intern Peter Bent Brigham Hosp., Boston, 1953-54, resident, 1954-55, 57-58, asso. in medicine, 1962-65, sr. physician, 1983—; research fellow biol. chemistry Harvard U., 1955-57, prof. medicine, 1970—; practice medicine specializing in metabolism, Boston, 1965—; Prin. cons. endocrinology, metabolism VA, 1972-75; investigator Howard Hughes Med. Inst., 1962-68, dir. research, 1978—; mem. research tng. coms. NIH. Contbr. articles to profl. jours. Served with USNR, 1945-47. Recipient Banting medal, U.S., 1971, Eng., 1974, J.P. Hoet award, Belgium, 1973. Mem. Am. Diabetes Assn. (pres. 1975, Lilly award 1965), Endocrine Soc. (Oppenheimer award 1963, Gairdner Internat. award 1979), Nat. Commn. on Diabetes, Am. Soc. Clin. Investigation, Assn. Am. Physicians, Am. Clin. Climatol. Assn., Am. Physiol. Soc., Am. Acad. Arts and Scis. Club: Wellesley Country. Home: Upton Pond Stoddard NH 03464 Office: 398 Brookline Ave Boston MA 02215

CAHILL, JAMES FRANCIS, educator; b. Ft. Bragg, Calif., Aug. 13, 1926; s. James Francis and Mae (Bond) C.; m. Dorothy Dunlap, July 15, 1951; children—Nicholas, Sarah. B.A., U. Calif. at Berkeley, 1950; M.A., U. Mich., 1952, Ph.D., 1958. Curator, Chinese art Freer Gallery Art, Smithsonian Instn., Washington, 1957-65; prof. history of art, curator Oriental art U. Calif. at Berkeley, 1965—; Charles Eliot Norton prof. poetry Harvard U., 1978-79. Author: Chinese Painting, 1960, Fantastics and Eccentrics in Chinese Painting, 1967, Scholar Painters of Japan: The Nanga School, 1972, Hills beyond a River: Chinese Painting of the Yuan Dynasty, 1976. Guggenheim fellow, 1972-73. Mem. Am. Acad. Arts and Scis., Assn. Asian Studies, Coll. Art Assn. Home: 2422 Hillside Ave Berkeley CA 94704

CAHILL, JOSEPH T., university president; b. Phila. Student, Mary Immaculate Sem.; M.A., St. John's U., 1950; LL.D., Niagara U., 1967; Litt.D., China Acad., 1969; LL.D., Nat. Chengchi U., Taipei, Taiwan, 1971, St. Mary's U., San Antonio, 1973; L.H.D., Mercy Coll., 1974. Ordained priest Roman Catholic Ch., 1946; dir. students, mem. faculty St. Joseph's Coll., until 1953, pres., superior, 1962-64; prof. history Niagara U., Niagara Falls, N.Y., 1953-56, dir. dramatics, 1953-56, moderator athletics, 1956-58; dean Grad. Sch. and Sch. Edn., 1958-59; acad. v.p., dean Coll. Arts and Scis., 1959-62; pres. univ., 1964-65, St. John's U., Jamaica, N.Y., 1965—. Address: St John's U Jamaica NY 11439

CAHILL, LAURENCE JAMES, JR., physicist, educator; b. Frankfort, Maine, Sept. 21, 1924; s. Laurence J. and Wilma (Lord) C.; m. Alice Adeline Krieger, Sept. 10, 1949; children: Laurence James III, Thomas G., Daniel A. Student, U. Maine, 1942-43; B.S., U.S. Mil. Acad., 1946, U. Chgo., 1950; M.S., U. Iowa, 1956, Ph.D., 1959. Staff U. Iowa, 1954-59, research asso., 1959; mem. faculty U. N.H., 1959-68, prof. physics, 1965-69; dir. Space Scis. Center, 1966-68; prof. physics U. Minn., Mpls., 1968—, asso. head physics, 1974-77; dir. Space Sci. Center, 1968-74; chief physics NASA Hdqrs., Washington, 1962-63, cons., 1962—; vis. prof. U. Calif. at San Diego, 1965-66; cons. NSF, 1965—. Recipient NASA award for sustained superior performance, 1963; NATO sr. fellow, 1974; vis. scientist Max Planck Inst. Extraterrestrial Physics, W. Ger., 1977-78. Fellow Am. Geophys. Union, Am. Phys. Soc.; mem. AAAS, Sigma Xi. Research and publs. on measurement by rocket-borne magnetometer of elec. currents in ionosphere, measurement boundary between earth's magnetic field and interplanetary medium, ring current of charged particles encircling earth and causing magnetic storms, hydromagnetic waves. Home: Afton MN 55001 Office: U Minn Dept Physics 116 Church St SE Minneapolis MN 55455

CAHILL, THOMAS ANDREW, physicist; b. Paterson, N.J., Mar. 4, 1937; s. Thomas Vincent and Margery (Groesbeck) C.; m. Virginia Ann Arnoldy, June 26, 1965; children: Catherine Frances, Thomas Michael. B.A., Holy Cross Coll., Worcester, Mass., 1959; Ph.D. in Physics; NDEA fellow, U. Calif., Los Angeles, 1965. Asst. prof. in residence U. Calif., Los Angeles, 1965-66; NATO fellow, research physicist Centre d'Etudes Nucleaires de Saclay, France, 1966-67; prof. physics U. Calif., Davis, 1967—; acting dir. Crocker Nuclear Lab., 1972, dir., 1980—; dir. Inst. of Ecology, 1972-75; cons. NRC of Can., Louvre Mus.; mem. Internat. Com. on PIXE and Its Application. Author: (with J. McCray) Electronic Circuit Analysis for Scientists, 1973; Contbr. articles to profl. jours. on physics, applied physics, hist. analyses and air pollution. OAS fellow, 1968. Mem. Am. Phys. Soc., Air Pollution Control Assn., Am. Chem. Soc., Sigma Xi. Democrat. Roman Catholic. Club: Sierra. Home: 1813 Amador Ave Davis CA 95616 Office: Dept Physics U Calif Davis CA 95616

CAHILL, WILLIAM JOSEPH, JR., utility company executive; b. Suffern, N.Y., June. 13, 1923; s. William Joseph and Sophie A. (Scizzafava) C.; m. Edna Kiernan, Oct. 3, 1953; children: William E., Kathleen, Madeleine. B.S. in Mech. Engring., Poly. Inst. Bklyn., 1949. Registered profl. engr., N.Y., La., Tex. Engr. Consol. Edison, N.Y.C., 1949-54, 47-60, nuclear plant engr., 1961-68, v.p., 1969-80; engr. Knolls Atomic Power Lab., Schenectady, N.Y., 1954-56; sr. v.p. Gulf State Utilities Co., St. Francisville, La., 1980—; chmn. safety and analysis task force Electric Power Research Inst., Palo Alto, Calif., 1978-80. Inventor, patentee nuclear reactor vessel, self-activated valve, triggerable fuse. Pres. Queens County Young Republicans, (N.Y.), 1952; bd. dirs. Rockland County Assn. for Retarded, (N.Y.), 1966-67. Served with AUS, 1942-46. Mem. Am. Nuclear Soc. (dir. 1980-81), La. Nuclear Soc. (chmn. 1982—), ASME, Am. Soc. Registered Profl.

Engrs. Republican. Roman Catholic. Club: City (Baton Rouge, La.). Home: PO Box 835 Saint Francisville LA 70775 Office: Gulf States Utility Co PO Box 220 Saint Francisville LA 70775

CAHIR, JOHN JOSEPH, meteorologist, educational administrator; b. Scituate, Mass., Oct. 6, 1933; s. Jeremiah Francis and Mary Eleanor (Duggan) C.; m. Mary Anne Louise Schrott, Dec. 1, 1962; children: Ellen, William, Kathryn, Barton. B.S. in Meteorology, Pa. State U., 1961, Ph.D., 1971. Meteorologist trainee, meteorologist U.S. Weather Bur., 1954-64; instr. meteorology Pa. State U., University Park, 1965-70, asst. prof., 1971-74, assoc. prof., 1975-79, prof., 1980—; assoc. dean Coll. Earth and Mineral Scis., Pa. State U., University Park, 1980—; George J. Haltner research chair U.S. Naval Postgrad. Sch., Monterey, Calif., 1984; dir. research projects on weather analysis and forecasting Nat. Weather Service, Naval Environ. Research Prediction Facility, Air Force Geophys. Lab., NSF, Nat. Earth Satellite Services; vis. prof. St. Augustine's Coll., Va. State Coll.; cons. in field; mem. Nat. Acad Sci. com. to evaluate research program of Nat. Environ. Satellite Service, 1976; participant Nat. Acad. Sci. workshop on atmospheric research, 1978. Co-author: Principles of Climatology, 1969, The Atmosphere, 1975, 78 81; editor: Monthly Weather Rev., 1977-80; contbr. papers, research reports to profl. publs. Served with USN, 1958-60. Fellow Nat. Ctr. Atmospheric Research, 1974. Fellow Am. Meteorol. Soc. (chmn. com. on weather forecasting and analysis 1978-80, seal of approval for TV weathercasting); mem. Royal Meteorol. Soc., Am. Geophys. Union, Nat. Weather Assn. (pres. 1981-82, Service award 1979), Sigma Xi. Home: 269 Osmond St State College PA 16801 Office: 620 Walker Bldg University Park PA 16802

CAHN, DAVID STEPHEN, cement company executive; b. Los Angeles, Jan. 12, 1940; s. Edward Lincoln and Monya (Schuchett) C.; m. Mary Constance Maschio, June 18, 1960 (div. 1972); children: Elizabeth Suzanne, Deborah Jacqueline. B.S. with honors, U. Calif.-Berkeley, 1962, M.S., 1964, D.Eng., 1966. Research engr. Amcord, Inc., Riverside, Calif., 1968-71, dir. environ. matters, Newport Beach, Calif., 1971-77, v.p., 1977-80; dir. environ. affairs Calif. Portland Cement Co., Los Angeles, 1980-82, v.p. regulatoty matters, 1982—. Recipient Rossiter W. Raymond award Soc. Mining Engrs., 1972. Mem. Air Pollution Control Assn., Am. Inst. Mining Engrs., ASTM, Am. Inst. Chem. Engrs. Republican. Office: Calif Portland Cement Co 800 Wilshire Blvd Los Angeles CA 90017

CAHN, JOHN WERNER, metallurgist, educator; b. Germany, Jan. 9, 1928; came to U.S., 1939, naturalized, 1945; s. Felix H. and Lucie (Schwarz) C.; m. Anne Hessing, Aug. 20, 1950; children: Martin Charles, Andrew David, Lorie Selma. B.S., U. Mich., 1949; Ph.D., U. Calif. at Berkeley, 1953. Instr. U. Chgo., 1952-54; with research lab. Gen. Electric Co., 1954-64; prof. metallurgy Mass. Inst. Tech., 1964-78; center scientist Nat. Bur. Standards, 1978—, sr. fellow, 1984—; vis. prof. Israeli Inst. Tech., Haifa, 1971-72, 80; cons. in field, 1963—; chmn. Gordon conf. Phys. Metallurgy, 1964; vis. scientist Nat. Bur. Standards, Gaithersburg, Md., 1977; hon. prof. Jiao Tung U., Shanghai, China, 1980—. Guggenheim fellow, 1960; research fellow Japan Soc. for Promotion of Sci., 1981-82; recipient Dickson prize Carnegie Mellon U., 1981, Gold medal U.S. Dept. Commerce, 1982. Fellow Am. Acad. Arts and Scis., Am. Inst. Metall. Engrs.; mem. AAAS, Nat. Acad. Scis., Am. Phys. Soc. Home: 6610 Pyle Rd Bethesda MD 20817 Office: Nat Bur Standards Washington DC 20234

CAHN, JOSHUA BINION, lawyer; b. N.Y.C., Feb. 11, 1915; s. Edward and Martha (Binion) C.; m. Ruth Hagler Walker, Mar. 6, 1971; children—Deborah (Mrs. T. Richard McIntosh), Nicholas Binion, Martha Binion. A.B., Harvard, 1935; LL.B., Columbia, 1938. Bar: N.Y. State bar 1938. Since practiced in, N.Y.C.; asso. firm Sol A. Rosenblatt & William B. Jaffe, N.Y.C., 1938-43; partner firm Cahn & Mathias (and predecessor firm), N.Y.C., 1950-80; of counsel to James H. Mathias, Esq., N.Y.C., 1980—; Dir. Masback Inc. Author: Artistic Copyright, 1948; Editor: Columbia Law Rev, 1936-38, What Is An Original Print?, 1961; Contbr. articles to profl. publs. Club: Century Assn. Home: 167 E 67th St New York NY 10021

CAHN, JULIUS NORMAN, publishing co. exec.; b. N.Y.C., Oct. 26, 1922; s. Richard David and Frieda (Cohen) C.; m. Ann Foote, Oct. 20, 1946; children—Gary Alan, Glenn Evan, Linda Jan, Carol Diane. B.S.S., CCNY, 1942; M.A., Am. U., 1948. Adminstrv. analyst U.S. Office for Emergency Mgmt., 1942-44; asst. to U.S. Senator Alexander Wiley, 1945-52; cons. U.S. Senate Fgn. Relations Com., 1952-58; staff dir. Govt. Ops. Subcom., 1958-64; asst. to Vice Pres. Hubert Humphrey, 1965-69; pub. asso. Family Health mag., 1969-74; pres., dir. Family Media Enterprises, Inc., N.Y.C., 1975—; bd. dirs. Washingtonian mag., 1974-79; chmn. adv. bd. Futurist mag., 1976—, Fin. Planner mag., 1974-75; lectr. Am. U., 1952-53. Contbr. articles to profl. publs. Dep. nat. chmn. Citizens for Humphrey-Muskie presdl. campaign, 1968. Mem. Soc. Fin. Counseling (past chmn. bd.), Sales Exec. Club N.Y. (dir.), Nat., Washington press clubs. Democrat. Jewish. Club: Atrium (N.Y.C.). Home: 9211 Harrington Dr Potomac MD 20854 Office: 149 Fifth Ave New York NY 10010

CAHN, ROBERT, journalist; b. Seattle, Mar. 9, 1917; s. Adolph and Edna (May) Cahen; m. Patricia Lovelady, Dec. 8, 1951. B.A., U. Wash., 1939; LL.D. (hon.), Allegheny Coll., 1970. Reporter Seattle Star, 1939-41, Pasadena (Calif.) Star-News, 1946-48; corr. Life mag., 1948-51; corr., sr. editor Collier's mag., 1951-56; free-lance mag. writer, 1957-61; Midwest bur. chief Sat. Eve. Post, 1962; White House reporter USIA, 1963-64; staff corr. Christian Sci. Monitor, 1965-69; pres. Council Environ. Quality, 1970-72; environment editor Christian Sci. Monitor, 1973; writer in residence Conservation Found., 1974-77; Washington editor Audubon Mag., 1979—; spl. asst. to pres. Nat. Audubon Soc., 1982—. Author: (with Perle Mesta) Perle, My Story, 1960, Footprints On the Planet: A Search for an Environmental Ethic, 1978, (with Robert Glenn Ketchum) American Photographers and the National Parks, 1981. Mem. Citizens Adv. Com. on Environ. Quality, 1972-76, Coastal Zone Mgmt. Adv. Com., 1976-78; Bd. dirs. Trust for Public Land, Environ. Policy Inst., Inst. Ecology, John Muir Inst., Bolton Inst. Served with AUS, 1942-46; ETO. Decorated Bronze Star; recipient Conservation Service award Dept. Interior, 1968; Pulitzer prize in journalism for nat. reporting, 1969. Mem. Sigma Delta Chi. Christian Scientist. Home: Route 3 Box 316 Leesburg VA 22075

CAHN, SAMMY, lyric songwriter; b. N.Y.C., June 18, 1913; s. Abraham and Alice (Reiss) Cohen; m. Gloria Delson, Sept. 5, 1945 (div. May 1964); children—Steven, Laurie; m. Tita Curtis, Aug. 2, 1970. Student pub. schs., N.Y.C. Violinist since boyhood; organizer of (with Saul Chaplin) a band; songwriter for motion pictures, 1940—; writer for: stage shows Walking Happy, High Button Shoes, Skyscraper; songs written include Love and Marriage (TV Emmy award, Christopher award), Rhythm in My Nursery Rhymes, Bei Mir Bist Schoen, Until the Real Thing Comes Along, Be My Love, Please Be Kind, I've Heard That Song Before, I'll Walk Alone, Shoe Shine Boy, Victory Polka, Because You're Mine, Let It Snow, Let It Snow, Let It Snow, It's Magic, Teach Me Tonight, Three Coins in the Fountain, The Tender Trap; writer for (Acad. award), All the Way, (Acad. award 1957), High Hopes, (Acad. award 1959), Second Time Around, Call Me Irresponsible, (Acad. award 1963). Named to Songwriters Hall of Fame. Office: 2049 Century Park E 2500 Los Angeles CA 90067 *

CAHN, STEVEN M., philosopher, educator; b. Springfield, Mass., Aug. 6, 1942; s. Judah and Evelyn (Baum) C.; m. Marilyn Ross, Mar. 4, 1974. A.B., Columbia U., 1963, Ph.D., 1966. Vis. instr. Dartmouth Coll., Hanover, N.H., 1966; vis. prof. U. Rochester, N.Y., 1967; asst. prof. philosophy Vassar Coll., Poughkeepsie, N.Y., 1966-68, NYU, N.Y.C., 1968-71, dir. grad. studies, 1972, dir. undergrad. studies, 1971-73; prof., chmn. dept. philosophy U. Vt., Burlington, 1973-80, adj. prof. philosophy, 1980-83; program officer Exxon Edn. Found., N.Y.C., 1978-79; assoc. dir. Rockefeller Found., N.Y.C., 1979-81, acting dir. humanities, 1981-82; dir. div. gen. programs NEH, Washington, 1982-83; dean grad. studies, prof. philosophy Grad. Sch. and Univ. Ctr., CUNY, 1983—; pres. John Dewey Found., 1983; cons., panelist NEH, 1975-82. Author: Fate, Logic, and Time, 1967, 82, A New Introduction to Philosophy, 1971, The Eclipse of Excellence: A Critique of American Higher Education, 1973, Education and the Democratic Ideal, 1979; editor: (with Frank A. Tillman) Philosophy of Art and Aesthetics: From Plato to Wittgenstein, 1969, The Philosophical Foundations of Education, 1970, Philosophy of Religion, 1970, Classics of Western Philosophy, 1977, New Studies in the Philosophy of John Dewey, 1977, Scholars Who Teach: The Art of College Teaching, 1978, (with David Shatz) Contemporary Philosophy of Religion, 1982, (with Patricia Kitcher and George Sher) Reason at World: Introductory Readings in Philosophy, 1983. Mem. Phi Beta Kappa. Home: 100 W 57th St New York NY 10019 Office: Grad Sch Univ Ctr of CUNY 33 W 42d St New York NY 10036 *The success of a democratic community depends in great part on the understanding and capability of its citizens. And in our complex world, to acquire sufficient understanding and capability requires a rigorous education. If we fail to provide it, we shall have only ourselves to blame as our schools produce intellectual stagnation instead of contributing to a more vigorous and enlightened society.*

CAHOON, HAROLD PULASKI, manufacturing company executive; b. Salt Lake City, Nov. 24, 1921; s. John B. and Marion Vera (Carlson) C.; m. Priscilla Johnson, Mar. 20, 1943; children: Harvey P., Gary Bruce, Marion Jane, Bradly J., Wendy. B.S., U. Utah, 1949, Ph.D., 1955; M.S., U. Wash., 1950. With Interstate Brick Co., Salt Lake City, 1929—, ceramic engr., plant supr., 1955-66, pres., gen. mgr., 1966—; pres. Fox Clay Co., Salt Lake City, 1976-83. Contbr. articles to profl. jours.; patentee in field. Bd. dirs. Indsl. RElations Council, Salt Lake City, U. Utah Sch. Engring. Served to 1st lt. USMC, 1942-47. Orton fellow, 1950; Naval Research Project fellow, 1952-53. Fellow Am. Ceramic Soc. (Ferro award 1949); mem. Home Builders Assn., Assoc. Gen. Contractors, Producers Council, Nat. Assn. Home Builders, Utah Mining Assn. (dir.), Western States Clay Products Assn. (dir., treas. 1969-82), Tau Beta Pi, Sigma Gamma Epsilon. Club: Willow Creek Country (Salt Lake Beach). Lodge: Sugarhouse Rotary (pres. 1970-71). Office: Interstate Brick Co 9780 S 5200 W West Jordan UT 84084

CAHOON, STUART NEWTON, state health administrator, psychiatrist; b. Avalon, Pa., Dec. 9, 1916; s. Reno McCune and Belle Elizabeth (Newton) C.; m. Myrtle Katherine Opdyke, Sept. 19. 1942; children: Elizabeth Cahoon Knickerbocker, Sandra Cahoon Anderson. B.A., Oberlin Coll., 1939; M.D., Temple U., 1943; postgrad. psychoanalysis, William Alanson White 1st., N.Y.C., 1946-53. Intern Wilmington (Del.) Gen. Hosp., 1943-44; resident in psychiatry N.J. State Hosp., Greystone Park, 1944-47, clin. dir., Skillman, 1949-50; practice medicine specializing in psychoanalysis, Newark, 1950-56, Miami, Fla., 1957-60; mem. staff Jackson Meml. Hosp., Miami, 1957-60; chief mental health clinics, Honolulu; also mem. staff Leahi Hosp., 1961-64; clin. dir. Community Mental Health Center; also mem. staff Halifax Dist. Hosp., Daytone Beach, Fla., 1964-68; assoc. prof. psychiatry U. Fla. Med. Sch., Gainesville, 1968-73, clin. prof., 1974—; dir. community mental health, State of Fla., 1971-74; dir. Fla. Div. Mental Health, Tallahassee, 1974-77; regional dir. mental health, Fort Myers, Fla., 1977—; adv. com. lit. service State Instns. Fla., 1974—. Contbr. profl. jours. Fellow Royal Soc. Health; mem. Mental Health Assn. Fla., Hawaii Psychiat. Soc. (past pres.), Am., Fla. psychiat. assns., Am. Acad. Psychotherapists, AAAS, Am., Fla. med. assns. Home: 511 El Dorado W Cape Coral FL 33904 Office: Dist 8 HRS PO Box 06085 Fort Myers FL 33906 *To listen, to hear and to respond with sensitivity and consideration, this is the key to human administration.*

CAHOUET, FRANK VONDELL, banker; b. Cohasset, Mass., May 25, 1932; s. Ralph Hubert and Mary Claire (Jordan) C.; m. Ann Pleasonton Walsh, July 14, 1956; children—Ann P., Mary G., Frank V., David R. B.A., Harvard, 1954; M.B.A., Wharton Sch. Finance, U. Pa., 1959. Corporate loan asst. Security Pacific Nat. Bank, Los Angeles, 1960-66, v.p., 1966-69, sr. loan adminstr., Europe/Middle East/Africa, 1969-73, exec. v.p., 1978—, vice chmn., 1980—; exec. v.p. Security Pacific Corp., Los Angeles, 1973—, vice chmn., 1980—. Trustee Scripps Coll., Claremont, Calif. Served to 1st lt. AUS, 1954-56. Mem. Calif. Bankers Assn. Clubs: California (Los Angeles); Wharton Alumni of So. Calif., Harvard of So. Calif. (treas., dir. 1966-69); Valley Hunt (Pasadena). Home: 1485 Lomita Dr Pasadena CA 91106 Office: 333 S Hope St Los Angeles CA 90071

CAILLOUETTE, JAMES CLYDE, physician; b. Los Angeles, June 2, 1927; s. Albert F. and Vera Helen C.; m. Joanne Thompson, Dec. 17, 1950; children: Laure, James Thompson, Anne. A.B., Coll. Puget Sound, 1950; M.D., U. Wash., 1954. Diplomate: Am. Bd. Ob-Gyn. Intern Los Angeles Gen. Hosp., 1954-56, resident in Ob-Gyn, 1956-59; instr. U. So. Calif. Sch. Medicine, 1959-64, asst. clin. prof., 1964-69, asso. clin. prof., 1969-78, clin. prof., 1978—; mem. sr. attending staff Los Angeles County-U. So. Calif. Med. Center; sec. med. staff Huntington Meml. Hosp., Pasadena, Calif., 1973—. Contbr. articles to profl. jours. Vice pres. Oak Knoll Property Owners Assn., 1965-75; chmn. ann. drive Nat. Found. March of Dimes, Pasadena, 1966, mem. med. adv. bd., 1966-76; bd. dirs. Pasadena Physicians United Crusade, 1961-63, chmn., 1964; bd. dirs., chmn. med. adv. bd. Pasadena Planned Parenthood World Population, 1970-75; trustee Poly Sch., Pasadena, 1969-78, chmn. devel. com., 1970-76; bd. councilors U. So. Calif. Sch. Medicine, 1978—; bd. dirs. Scripps Home, 1980-83. Served with USNR, 1945-46. Fellow A.C.S., Am. Coll. Obstetricians and Gynecologists; mem. N.Y. Acad. Sci., AMA, Calif. Med. Assn. (past sec., chmn. ob-gyn sect.), Los Angeles County Med. Assn., Pasadena Med. Soc., Pacific Coast Obstetrical and Gynecol. Soc. (dir. 1978—), Los Angeles Obstetrical and Gynecol. Soc. (pres. 1977-78, chmn. Assembly 1981-82), Sigma Chi, Nu Sigma Nu, Phi Sigma, Alpha Omega Alpha. Clubs: Valley Hunt (dir. 1980—, v.p. 1983-84), California. Office: 50 Bellefontaine Pasadena CA 91105

CAIN, CHARLES MARSHALL, lawyer, deputy assistant U.S. attorney general; b. Richmond, Va., July 20, 1934; s. Calvin Howard and Helen Kathryn (Holley) C.; m. Anne Kennedy Hodges, June 24, 1961; children: Julia Summerall, John Marshall, Charles David, Stuart Howard. B.S., U. S.C., 1957, LL.B., 1959. Asst. legis. asst. U.S. Senate, Washington, 1959-60; assoc. Lybrand, Rich, Cain, Aiken, S.C., 1960-81; exec. asst. Gov. S.C., Columbia, 1974-75, 76; dep. asst. atty. gen. U.S. Dept. Justice, Washington, 1981—; mem., minority leader S.C. Ho. of Reps., Columbia, 1968-74, 79-80. Chmn. Gov.s Com. on Criminal Justice, Crime and Delinquency, Columbia, 1974-78. Served with U.S. Air Nat. Guard, 1959. Named Outstanding Young Man of Yr. Aiken Jaycees, 1967. Mem. ABA, S.C. Bar Assn. (regional v.p.), Aiken Bar Assn. (pres. 1980-81). Republican. Am. Baptist. Club: Rotary (Aiken, S.C.) (pres.). Home: 6167 Mori St McLean VA 22101 Office: Dept Justice 10th and Constitution Sts Washington DC 20530

CAIN, DONALD EZELL, judge; b. San Marcos, Tex., Oct. 8, 1921; s. Erie Montclair and Betty Belle (Howell) C.; m. Betty Anne Culberson, June 14, 1952; children: David, Dale Cain Husen, Donald Ezell, Randolph. A.S., North Tex. Agrl. Coll., 1941; B.B.A., U. Tex., 1943, LL.B., 1948. Bar: Tex. 1948. With contracts dept. Convair. Ft. Worth, 1948-50; pvt. practice law, Pampa, Tex., 1951-76, county atty., Gray County, Tex., 1955-68, county judge, 1971-77, dist. judge, 1977—. Pres. Adobe Wells council Boy Scouts Am., 1957-59; bd. dirs. Pampa United Fund, 1956-60. Served from ensign to lt. USNR, 1943-46; as lt., 1950-51. Recipient Silver Beaver award Boy Scouts Am., 1958. Fellow Tex. Bar Found.; mem. ABA, Tex. Bar Assn., Gray County Bar Assn. (pres. 1968), Am. Judicature Soc., Tex. Judges and Commrs. Assn., Panhandle County Judges and Commrs. Assn. (pres. 1975), Pampa C. of C. (dir. 1959-60), Phi Alpha Delta. Democrat. Baptist. Clubs: Masons, Rotary (pres. 1958-59), Pampa Country. Home: 1826 Williston St Pampa TX 79065 Office: Court House PO Box 2160 Pampa TX 79065

CAIN, DOUGLAS MYLCHREEST, lawyer; b. Chgo., Sept. 8, 1938; s. Douglas M. and Louise C. (Coleman) C.; m. Constance Alexis Adams Moffit, Apr. 18, 1970; children: Victoria Elizabeth Moffit, Alexandra Catherine Moffit. A.B., Harvard U., 1960; J.D. with distinction, U. Mich., 1966; LL.M., N.Y. U., 1970. Bar: Colo. 1966. Assoc. Sherman & Howard, Denver, 1966-72, mem., 1972—; adj. prof. law U. Denver, 1972-78; mem. Rocky Mountain Estate Planning Council, pres., 1976-77. Assoc. editor: Mich. Law Rev, 1964-66; contbr. articles to profl. jours. Bd. dirs. Craig Hosp. Found., 1980—, Colo. Children's Chorale, 1983—. Served with USN, 1960-63. Mem. ABA, Colo. Bar Assn. (gov. 1980-82), Greater Denver Tax Counsel Assn., Assoc. Harvard Alumni (regional dir. 1978-81). Clubs: Rocky Mountain Harvard (pres. 1977-78), Denver Country. Lodge: Rotary. Home: 1960 Hudson St Denver CO 80220 Office: 633 17th St Suite 2900 Denver CO 80202

CAIN, E. LEE, banker; b. Iredell County, N.C., Jan. 16, 1928; s. Palmer Dewey and Mina (Wallace) C.; m. Patricia Jones, Sept. 5, 1953; children—Charles Lee, James Palmer, Patrick Eugene. Student, Catawba Coll., 1945-46; B.S. in Bus. Adminstrn, Wake Forest U., 1951; postgrad., U. N.C. Sch. Bus., 1951-52. With Wachovia Bank & Trust Co. (N.A.), 1952—, head Winston-Salem out-of-town div., v.p., 1965-69, sr. v.p., mgr. corporate accounts div., marketing officer, 1969-72, office exec., High Point, 1972—; v.p. Robinson-Humphrey Co., Inc., Winston-Salem, N.C., 1981—. Bd. dirs. United Community Services; trustee Wake Forest U., chmn., 1974-76; bd. advisers Mars Hill Coll., High Point Coll., Southeastern Bapt. Theol. Sem.; trustee annuity bd So. Baptist Conv. Served with USAAF, 1945-48. Mem. Wake Forest U. Alumni Assn. (pres. 1970), Delta Sigma Pi, Pi Kappa Alpha. Home: 1208 Westminster Dr High Point NC 27260 Office: 119 B Reynolda Village Winston-Salem NC 27109

CAIN, EDMUND JOSEPH, teacher educator, emeritus dean; b. Chico, Calif., Mar. 18, 1918; s. Edmund Joseph and Myrtle Ellen (Perdue) C.; m. Virginia Hartigan, Dec. 3, 1944; children: Edmund Joseph III, Mary Ellen, James Michael. B.S., Columbia U., 1946, M.A., 1947, Ed.D., 1950. Tchr. Horace Mann-Lincoln Sch., N.Y.C., 1946-47; research asst. Columbia, 1947-48; asso. prof. edn. Western (Conn.) State Coll., 1948-55; vis. prof. edn. San Francisco State Coll., 1951, San Diego State Coll., summer 1952, U. N.Mex., summers 1953, 54, 58; dir. student teaching programs and grad. and postgrad. program tchr. edn. U. Del., 1955-64; dean Coll. Edn. U. Nev., from 1964, now dean emeritus, disting. prof. internat. edn., also chmn. tchr. edn. bd. and mem. human rights bd.; Expert in edn. UNESCO, Chile, 1961-62; cons. Inst. Internat. Edn., 1962-63; rep. Study Higher Edn. in Yugoslavia, 1967; chmn., vice chmn. bd. dirs. Far West Lab. Ednl. Research and Devel., 1968—; team leader UNESCO Team Higher Edn. in Qatar; rep. Linkages in Higher Edn. project, Kuwait, Jordan, Qatar, and Afghanistan, 1977; AID cons. to Afghanistan, 1978; chmn. Nat. Commn. on Multicultural and Internat. Edn., 1978-81; chmn. subcom. Gov. Nev. Com. Edn.; speaker profl. confs. Contbg. author: Applied Principles of Education Sociology, 1954; Contbr. articles to profl. jours. Mem. Nev. exec. bd. Boy Scouts Am.; bd. dirs. United Way. Served to capt. AUS, 1941-46. Recipient Silver Beaver award Boy Scouts Am. Mem. Am. Assn. Colls. Tchr. Edn. (rep. to S.Am. 1968, 74, also state rep., pres. Nev. chpt.), Nat. Soc. Study Edn., Internat. Council Edn. for Teaching (trustee 1980—), Land Grant Edn. Deans Assn., Phi Delta Kappa (Edn. Leadership award 1971), Kappa Delta Phi. Club: Rotarian. Home: 3710 Clover Way Reno NV 89509

CAIN, GEORGE HARVEY, lawyer, business executive; b. Washington, Aug. 3, 1920; s. J. Harvey and Madeleine (McGettigan) C.; m. Patricia J. Campbell, Apr. 23, 1946; children: George Harvey, James C., John P., Paul J. B.S., Georgetown U., 1942; J.D., Harvard U., 1948. Bar: N.Y. 1949, Ohio 1972, Conn. 1977. Practiced law, N.Y. State, 1949-71, 73—, Ohio, 1972-73; sec., gen. counsel Nat. Carloading Corp., 1949-54; mem. firm Spence & Hotchkiss, 1954-55; gen. atty., asst. sec. Cerro Corp., 1955-68, sec., gen. atty., 1968-72; v.p., gen. counsel Pickands Mather Co., Cleve., 1971-73; v.p., sec., gen. counsel Flintkote Co., White Plains, N.Y., 1973-76, Stamford, Conn., 1976-80; spl. counsel Day, Berry & Howard, Hartford and Stamford, Conn., 1980-82, ptnr., Stamford, Conn., 1983—; sec. Cerro Sales Corp., 1955-71; dir., sec. Leadership Housing Systems, Inc., 1970-71; dir., gen. counsel Atlantic Cement Co., Inc., 1962-71; dir. Hajoca Corp., 1975-79, Polymer Bldg. Systems, Inc.; adj. prof. U. Bridgeport Law Sch., 1983—. Served to 1st lt. USAAF, 1942-46; to capt. USAF, 1951-52. Mem. Am., N.Y. State, N.Y.C., Ohio, Conn. bar assns., Am. Soc. Corp. Secs., Westchester-Fairfield Corp. Counsel Assn., Georgetown U. alumni Assn. (mem. Alumni senate). Club: Harvard of N.Y. Home: 12 Wildwood Dr Greenwich CT 06830 Office: 3 Landmark Sq Stamford CT 06901

CAIN, J. FREDERICK, art dealer, museum cons.; b. Phila., June 24, 1938; s. James Frederick and Helen G. (McCarthy) C. A.B., Assumption Coll., 1960; M.F.A., Tyler Sch. Art, 1962; postgrad. in art history, U. Pa., 1971-72. Curator Lessing J. Rosenwald collection Alverthorpe Gallery, Jenkintown, Pa., 1966-72, Nat. Gallery Art, Washington, 1972-76; curator, acting dir. Charleston (W.Va.) Art Gallery, 1977-78, also author gallery catalogues; art dealer, Washington, 1978—; mem. faculty resident assoc. program Smithsonian Instn., 1972-76; scholar Barnes Found., Merion Sta., Pa., 1961-62; participant opening of Moderna Museet, Stockholm, 1973. Contbr. essays to publs. in field.; prints represented in permanent collections, Los Angeles County Mus. Art, Amon Carter Mus. Art, Mus. Modern Art, N.Y.C., Art Inst. Chgo., Lessing J. Rosenwald Collection, others. Ford Found. curatorial tng. grantee, 1967; English-Speaking Union travel grantee, 1968. Mem. Coll. Art Assn. Am., Am. Assn. Museums. Republican. Club: Peale (Phila.). Home and Office: 301 I St SW Washington DC 20024

CAIN, JAMES CLARENCE, physician; b. Kosse, Tex., Mar. 19, 1913; s. Thomas Marshall and Aileen (Jackson) C.; m. Ida May Wirtz, June 6, 1938; childrenStephaine Cannon (Mrs. Karl H. Van D'Elden), Mary Lucinda (Mrs. William Carleton Moore), Katherine May (Mrs. Jerry Wayne Snider), James Alvin. B.A., U. Tex., 1933, M.D., 1937; M.S., U. Minn., 1948. Diplomate: Pan Am. Med. Assn. Intern Protestant Episcopal Hosp., Phila., 1937-39; instr. pathology U. Tex. Med. Sch., 1939-40; fellow Mayo Found., 1940-41, 46-48; cons.

medicine Mayo Clinic, Rochester, Minn., 1948, head of sect., 1966-70; prof. medicine U. Minn., Mayo Med. Sch.; personal physician to Pres. Johnson, from 1946; Mem. nat. adv. heart council NIH; past pres. Minn. Bd. Med. Examiners; chmn. nat. adv. commn. for selection drs., dentists and allied med. personnel SSS, adviser to dir., 1969-70; mem. Nat. Adv. Commn. on Med. Manpower; cons. to surgeon gen. Dept. Army; mem. spl. med. adv. group to VA, 1976—; mem. adv. com. Bur. Drugs, FDA, 1973-75. Contbr. articles to profl. jours., chpts. to books. Chmn. Johnson for Pres. vols., Minn., 1964. Recipient Ashbel Smith Distinguished Alumnus award U. Tex. Med. Sch., 1969. Mem. Soc. Med. Cons. Armed Forces (pres.), AAAS, AMA (vice chmn. council on nat. security, recipient Billings gold medal award 1963), So. Minn. Med. Assn., Minn. Internal Medicine Soc. (council), A.C.P. (life mem., gov. for Minn.), Am. Gastroenterol. Assn., Am. Assn. Study Liver Disease, Am. Fedn. Clin. Research, Am. Assn. History Medicine, Fedn. State Med. Bds. U.S., U. Tex. Med. Sch., Mayo Clinic alumni assns., IEEE, Am. Radio Relay League, Amateur Radio Emergency Corps, Sigma Xi, Delta Kappa Epsilon, Alpha Kappa, Alpha Epsilon Delta. Baptist. Home: Cain's Mesa Rochester MN 55901 Office: Dept of Medicine Mayo Clinic Rochester MN 55901

CAIN, JAMES MARSHALL, public utility executive; b. Baton Rouge, Aug. 13, 1933; s. James Havard and Louise Josephine (Babin) C.; m. Barbara Ann Hammond, July 2, 1960; children: James Hammond, Beverly Havard. B.B.A., Tulane U., 1955, M.B.A., 1959. With New Orleans Public Service Inc., 1960-75, 78—, v.p. adminstrn., 1971-75, pres., chief exec. officer, dir., 1978—; exec. v.p., then pres., chief exec. officer dir. Middle South Services, Inc., New Orleans, 1975-78; pres., chief exec. officer, dir. La. Power & Light Co., 1983—; dir. Middle South Utilities, Inc., Middle South Services, Inc., System Fuels, Inc., Middle South Energy, Inc., Southeastern Electric Exchange. Bd. dirs. New Orleans and River Region C. of C.; bd. dirs., vice chmn. exec. com. La. Econ. Devel. Council; bd. dirs. New Orleans Met. Area Com., Council Better La.; mem. exec. bd. New Orleans area council Boy Scouts Am., 1980; trustee St. George's Episcopal Sch., New Orleans, Alton Ochsner Med. Found., Dillard U.; trustee Bus. Sch. Council Tulane U.; bd. govs. Tulane U. Med. Center; vis. com. Coll. Bus., Loyola U., New Orleans; mem. met. council continuing higher edn. U. New Orleans. Served with AUS, 1955-57. Mem. Delta Sigma Pi, Beta Gamma Sigma. Episcopalian. Clubs: Boston, Pickwick, Bienville (New Orleans). Address: 317 Baronne St New Orleans LA 70160

CAIN, JAMES NELSON, concert mgr.; b. Arcadia, Ohio, Jan. 6, 1930; s. Alfred Ray and Gladys Eliza (Cruikshank) C.; m. Marthellen Jones, June 12, 1950; children—Nelson, Jennifer, Richard, Elizabeth. A.B., Ohio State U., Columbus, 1955. Dir. Prestige Concerts, Inc., Columbus, 1948-62; exec. dir. Music Assos. Aspen, Inc., Colo., 1962-68; asst. mgr., then mgr. St. Louis Symphony Orch., 1968-80; v.p. St. Louis Conservatory and Schs. Arts, 1980—. Home: 2 Nantucket Ln Saint Louis MO 63132 Office: St Louis Conservatory Trinity at Delmar St Saint Louis MO 63130

CAIN, LEO FRANCIS, educator; b. Chico, Calif., July 30, 1909; s. Edmund Joseph and Myrtle (Perdue) C.; m. Margaret Brennan, Aug. 17, 1940; children: Barbara (Mrs. Richard Miller), Nancy (Mrs. J. Stanley Ahmann), Caroline (Mrs. Peter Detwiler). A.B., Chico State Coll., 1931; M.A., Stanford, 1935, Ph.D., 1939. Tchr., prin. pub. schs., Calif., 1929-40; asst. prof. U. Md., 1940-43; dir. edn. Dept. Justice, 1940-43; prof. U. Okla., 1946-47; dir. spl. edn. San Francisco State Coll., 1947-51, dean ednl. services and summer session, 1951-57, v.p., 1957-62; pres. Calif. State U., Dominguez Hills, 1962-76, pres. emeritus, 1976—; asso. dir. sr. accrediting commn. Western Assn. Schs. and Colls., 1976-78; prof. spl. edn., coordinator doctoral program, dir. Inst. for Research on Exceptionality, San Francisco State U., 1976—; spl. cons. on youth problems, West Germany, 1953, chief of party, ednl. project, Liberia, 1961; mem. Gov.'s Commn. on Mental Retardation, 1963-64; chmn. mental health council Western Interstate Commn. for Higher Edn., 1969-72; cons. Pres.'s Commn. on Mental Retardation, 1970-73, HEW Evaluation Team, Saudi Arabia, 1975, U.S. Office Edn., 1978, U. Riyadh, 1981; mem. task force on handicapped children's edn. project Edn. Commn. of States, 1972—; mem. Calif. Commn. on Tchr. Preparation and Licensing, 1972—; mem. accreditation commn. for sr. colls. and univs. Western Assn. Schs. and Colls., 1972-76; mem. bd. Protection and Advocacy (handicapped) State of Calif., 1978—. Contbr. articles to profl. jours.; author: Cain-Levine Social Competency Scale. Mem. spl. ednl. adv. com. United Cerebral Palsy Assn., 1961; planning council United Way, 1972; bd. dirs. Nat. Easter Seal Soc., 1979—; trustee Easter Seal Research Found., 1981—. Served to lt. USNR, 1944-46. Fellow Am. Assn. Mental Deficiency (Nat. Leadership award 1977); Mem. Council for Exceptional Children (nat. pres. 1961-62, Wallin award 1972), Western Assn. Schs. and Colls. (sr. commn. rep., dir.), Phi Delta Kappa, Kappa Delta Pi. Home: 12 Kenmar Way Burlingame CA 94010 Office: San Francisco State U 1600 Holloway San Francisco CA 94132

CAIN, PAUL W(ILLIS), oil company executive; b. Carlsbad, N. Mex., Jan. 1, 1939; s. Jacob P. and Oma (Martin) C.; m. Dilys Rose, Nov. 18, 1972; chidren: Jon R., Kellie R. B.B.A., U. Houston, 1967. Exec. v.p., gen mgr. Signal Oil of La. (Became Aminoil La. 1976), New Orleans, 1973-76; controller Aminoil Inc., Houston, 1977, asst. to pres., 1978, v.p.-prodn., 1979, exec. v.p.-ops., 1980-82, exec. v.p.-fin. and adminstrn., 1983—. Mem. Am. Petroleum Inst., Fin. Exec. Inst. Office: Aminoil Inc 2800 N Loop W Houston TX 77092

CAIN, WALKER O., architect; b. Cleve., Apr. 14, 1915; s. Oscar Clyde and Meta Mathilde (Gusse) C.; m. Abby Jane Huston, June 1941 (div.); children: Susan Berry Cain Stetson, Tamma Huston Cain O'Mara; m. Elizabeth McCall, July 27, 1973. Diploma in Architecture, Ecole de Beaux Arts Americaine, Fontainebleu, France, 1937; B.Arch., Western Res. U., 1938; M.F.A., Princeton, 1940; fellow, Am. Acad. Rome, 1947-48. With firm McKim, Meade & White, architects, N.Y.C., 1940-51, asso., 1951-61; partner Steinmann, Cain & White (architects), N.Y.C., 1961-65, Steinmann & Cain (architects), 1965-67, Walker O. Cain & Assos., 1967-78, Cain, Farrell and Bell, 1978—. Prin. works include Campus Plan Dormitories, Bethel, Maine, Maine State Cultural Bldg, Schenectady Mus; dormitories, U. Conn., Jafet Library, Engring. Sch; Hosp. addition, faculty apts., Am. U., Beirut, Lebanon, Ballou Hall, Tufts College, campus plan dormitories, Liberal Arts Center, Sci. Center, Union Coll., Schenectady, Museum History and Tech. at Smithsonian Instn; library, field house Computer Center, Princeton, library, Bowdoin Coll., St. Vartan Cathedral and cultural center Armenian Ch. Am, N.Y.C., Casco Bank & Trust Co. office bldg, Portland, Me., additions to, New Eng. Center Hosp., Boston; illustrator archtl. mags. and books. Mem. Manhattan Boro Pres. Community Planning Bd., 1965-67; dir. Park Assn. N.Y.C., 1962-65; chmn. City Parks Week, 1962-63; mem. Taconic State Park Commn., 1966—, Nat. Capitol Com., 1969-70, East Hudson Pkwy. Authority, 1966—; Chmn. Am. Acad. Rome, 1952—; hon. chmn. bd. trustees Garrison's Landing Assn. Museum Transp.; mem. vis. com. visul arts Western Res. U., 1963-66. Served to lt. USNR, 1943-46. Recipient Prix de Rome, 1940. Fellow A.I.A. (chmn. urban design com. N.Y. chpt. 1963-65); mem. N.A.D., Am. Arbitration Assn., Soc. Archtl. Historians, Nat. Inst. Archtl. Edn. Clubs: Century Assn., River (N.Y.C.); Meadow (Southampton, N.Y.). Office: Cain Farrell & Bell 437 Fifth Ave New York NY 10016 *

CAINE, LYNN, author, lecturer; b. N.Y.C.; d. Saul and Sally (Bialkin) Shapiro; children: Jonathan, Elizabeth. Student pub. schs., N.Y.C. Publicity dir. Farrar, Straus & Giroux, N.Y.C., 1955-64; publicity mgr. N.Y.C. office Little, Brown & Co., 1967-76; free lance author, lectr., N.Y.C., 1976—; mem. faculty Human Relations Center, New Sch. Social Research. Author: Widow, 1974, Lifelines: Living Alone Without Being Lonely, 1978. Mem. adv. bd. Women's Center, YWCA, N.Y.C.; trustee New Images for Widows Found. Recipient Christopher award, 1974. Mem. Womens' Media Group, Friends of Scarlett O'Hara, Authors Guild, PEN. Jewish. Office: care Sanford Greenburger Assos Inc 825 3d Ave New York NY 10022

CAINE, MICHAEL, actor; b. London, Mar. 14, 1933; s. Maurice and Ellen Frances Marie Micklewhite; m. Patricia Haines, 1955; 1 dau.; m. Shakira Baksh, 1973. Asst. stage mgr. Westminster Repertory, Horsham, Sussex, U.K., 1953; actor Lowestoft Repertory, 1953-55, Theatre Workshop, London, 1955. Numerous TV appearances, 1957-63; appeared in: play Next Time I'll Sing for You, 1963; films include A Hill in Korea, 1956, How to Murder a Rich Uncle, 1958, Zulu, 1964, The Ipcress File, 1965, Alfie, 1966, The Wrong Box, 1966, Gambit, 1966, Hurry Sundown, 1967, Woman Times Seven, 1967, Deadfall, 1967, The Magus, 1968, Battle of Britain, 1968, Play Dirty, 1968, The Italian Job, 1969, Too Late the Hero, 1970, The Last Valley, 1971, Get Carter, 1971, Zee & Co, 1972, Kidnapped, 1972, Pulp, 1972, Sleuth, 1973, The Black Windmill, Marseilles Contract, The Wilby Conspiracy, 1974, Fat Chance, The Romantic Englishwoman, The Man Who Would be King, Harry and Water go to New York, 1975, The Eagle has Landed, A Bridge too Far, Silver Bears, 1976, The Swarm, 1977, California Suite, 1978, Beyond the Poseidon Adventure, 1979, Dressed to Kill, The Island, 1980, The Hand, Victory, 1981 *

CAINE, RAYMOND WILLIAM, JR., manufacturing company executive; b. Fall River, Mass., June 30, 1932; s. Raymond W. and Emma (Gardella) C.; m. Sharon G. Henry, Nov. 10, 1956; children: Karen, Kimberly, Patrick, Peter. B.S., Providence Coll., 1956. Dir. pub. relations Blue Cross (Blue Shield), Providence, 1974-80; v.p. Trextron, Inc., Providence, 1980—. Bd. dirs R.I. Pub. Transit Authority, Providence, 1981—; mem. exec. adv. com. Bryant Coll., Smithfield,R.I., 1973—; mem. exec. com., trustee Salve Regina Coll., Newport, R.I., 1974—. Served to capt. U.S. Army, 1956-58. Mem. Pub. Relations Soc. Am. (dir. 1971-73), Machinery and Allied Products Inst. (pub. relations council). Roman Catholic. Home: 12 Kay St Newport RI 02840 Office: 40 Westminster St Providence RI 02903

CAIRNCROSS, ALEXANDER KIRKLAND, economist, university chancellor; b. Lesmahagow, Scotland, Feb. 11, 1911; s. Alexander Kirkland and Elizabeth Andrew (Wishart) C.; m. Mary Frances Glynn, May 29, 1943; children: Frances Anne, Philip Wishart, Alexander Messent, David John, Elizabeth Mary. Grad., Hamilton Acad., 1928; M.A., U. Glasgow, 1933; Ph.D., Cambridge U., 1936; LL.D., Mt. Allison U., 1962, Glasgow U., 1966, Exeter U., 1969; D.Litt., Reading U., 1968, Heriot Watt U., 1969; D.Sc., Univ. Coll., Swansea, 1971, Queen's U., Belfast, 1972; D. Univ., Stirling U., 1973. Lectr. U. Glasgow, 1935-39, prof. applied econs., dir. dept. social and econ. research, 1951-61; econ. adviser to Her Majesty's Govt., 1961-64; head of Her Majesty's Govt. Econ. Service, 1964-69; master St. Peters Coll., Oxford, Eng., 1969-78; chancellor U. Glasgow, 1972—; War Cabinet offices Bd. Trade, Ministry Aircraft Prodn., 1939-45; econ. adviser Bd. Trade, 1946-49; head econ. adv. panel, Berlin, 1945-46; staff London Economist, 1946; econ. adviser OEEC, 1949-50; dir. Econ. Devel. Inst., Washington, 1955-56. Author: Introduction to Economics, 1944, Home and Foreign Investment, 1870-1913, 1953, Monetary Policy in a Mixed Economy, 1960, Factors in Economic Development, 1962, Essays in Economic Management, 1971, Control of Long-term International Capital Movements, 1973, Inflation, Growth and International Finance, 1975, Snatches, 1980, (with B. Eichengreen) Sterling in Decline, 1983; Editor: The Scottish Economy, 1954, Scottish Jour. Polit. Economy, 1954-61, The Managed Economy, 1970, Planning and Economic Management, 1970, Britain's Economic Prospects Reconsidered, 1971, others. Bd. govs. London Sch. Econs.; pres. Girls Public Day Sch. Trust, 1972—. Decorated comdr. Order St. Michael and St. George, 1950, knight comdr., 1966; hon fellow St. Peter's Coll., Oxford U., 1978; supernumerary fellow St. Anthony's Coll., 1978; hon. fellow London Sch. Econs., 1981. Fellow Brit. Acad.; mem. Royal Econ. Soc. (v.p.), Scottish Econ. Soc. (v.p.), Am. Acad. Arts and Scis. (fgn. hon.), Brit. Assn. Advancement Sci. (pres. 1971), Nat. Inst. Econ. and Social Research of London (bd. govs.). Home: 14 Staverton Rd Oxford England

CAIRNES, JOSEPH FRANCIS, bldg. constrn. cons.; b. Somerville, Mass., May 26, 1907; s. Edward and Bridget (Shiel) C.; m. Helen Mary Tobin, Sept. 21, 1940; children—Joseph Francis, Edward, Mary Gilberta, Thomas, Anne Clare, Ellen Bernadette. Student, State Steam Engring. Sch., Boston, 1926, Lowell Inst., Cambridge, Mass., 1937-38. Regional engr. Fed. Works Agy., N.Y., Pa., Conn., Mass., N.H., Vt., Me., R.I., 1940-44; commr. pub. works Commonwealth of Mass., 1945-46; bus. mgr. Boston Braves, 1947-51, exec. v.p., 1952, Milwaukee Braves, 1953-56, pres., 1956-60, vice chmn. bd., 1961-63; pres. Perini Westward Developers, Inc., 1958-62; v.p., dir. Perini Corp., 1960-72; constrn. cons., 1973—. Mem. pres.'s adv. council Marquette U., 1956-60; Bd. dirs., chmn. devel. council St. Mary's Hosp., 1974-79; bd. dirs. Mass. Bldg. Congress, 1970-73, Palm Beach Round Table, 1975-79, Salvation Army, West Palm Beach, 1979—. Recipient Meritorious Service awards Nat. Safety Council, 1946, Milw. chpt. Baseball Writers Assn. Am., 1959, Nat. Assn. Home Builders, 1963, Am. Arbitration Assn., 1970. Mem. Nat. Soc. Profl. Engrs., Asso. Gen. Contractors (pres. Fla. East Coast chpt. 1963-64, pres. Mass. chpt. 1967-68, dir. 1966-72), K.C. (4 deg.), Am. Arbitration Assn. Clubs: Engineers (Boston); Sailfish of Fla. (dir.), Old Guard Soc., Palm Beach Rotary (dir.). Home: 2505 S Ocean Blvd Palm Beach FL 33480 Office: 2945 Australian Ave West Palm Beach FL 33402

CAIRNS, ELTON JAMES, chemical engineering educator; b. Chgo., Nov. 7, 1932; s. James Edward and Claire Angele (Larzelere) C.; m. Miriam Esther Citron, Dec. 26, 1974; 1 dau., Valerie Helen; stepchildren: Benjamin David, Joshua Aaron. B.S. in Chemistry, Mich. Tech. U., Houghton, 1955, 1955; Ph.D. in Chem. Engring. (Dow Chem. Co. fellow, univ. fellow, Standard Oil Co. Calif. grantee, NSF fellow), U. Calif., Berkeley, 1959. Phys. chemist Gen. Electric Co. Research Lab., Schenectady, 1959-66; group leader, then sect. head chem. engring. div. Argonne (Ill.) Nat. Lab., 1966-73; asst. head electrochemistry dept. Gen. Motors Corp. Research Labs., 1973-78; asso. lab. dir., head energy and environ. div. Lawrence Berkeley (Calif.) Lab., 1978—; prof. chem. engring. U. Calif., Berkeley, 1978—; Croft lectr. U. Mo., 1979; cons. in field, mem. numerous govt. panels. Author: (with H.A. Liebhafsky) Fuel Cells and Fuel Batteries, 1968; Editorial bd.: Advances in Electrochemistry and Electrochem. Engring, 1974—; div. editor: Jour. Electrochem. Soc, 1970—; Contbr. articles profl. jours. Recipient Case Centennial medal Case Western Res. U., 1980; grantee duPont Co., 1956. Mem. Electrochem. Soc. (chmn. phys. electrochem. div. 1981—, Francis Mills Turner award 1963), Am. Chem. Soc., Am. Inst. Chemists, Am. Inst. Chem. Engrs. (chmn. energy conversion com. 1970—), Internat. Soc. Electrochemistry (chmn. electrochem. energy conversion div. 1977—, U.S.A. nat. sec. 1983—), AAAS, Intersoc. Energy Conversion Engring. Conf. (gen. chmn. 1976, program chmn. 1983—). Patentee in field. Home: 239 Langlie Ct Walnut Creek CA 94598 Office: Lawrence Berkeley Lab Berkeley CA 94720

CAIRNS, H. ALAN C., political scientist, educator; b. Galt, Ont., Can., Mar. 2, 1930; s. Hugh and Lily (Crawford) C.; m. Patricia Ruth Grady, July 17, 1958; children: Lynn Marie, Wendy Louise, Elaine Barbara. B.A., U. Toronto, Ont., 1953, M.A., 1956; D.Phil., Oxford (Eng.) U., 1963. Mem. faculty U. B.C., Can., Vancouver, 1960—, prof. polit. sci., 1971—, head dept. polit. sci., 1973—. Author: Prelude to Imperialism, 1965; contbr. articles to profl. jours. Mem. Canadian Polit. Sci. Assn. (pres. 1976-77), Internat. Polit. Sci. Assn. (council 1976—), Canadian Hist. Assn. Home: 4424 W 2d Ave Vancouver BC V6R 1K5 Canada Office: Dept of Polit Sci U BC Vancouver BC V6T 1W5 Canada

CAIRNS, HUNTINGTON, lawyer, author; b. Balt., Sept. 1, 1904; s. James Duncanson and Helen Huntington (Heath) C.; m. Florence F. Butler, May 29, 1929. Grad., Balt. City Coll., 1922; LL.B., U. Md., 1925; LL.D., N.Y. U., St. Andrews U., Johns Hopkins, U. Md.; L.H.D., Tulane U., Kenyon Coll. Bar: Md. bar 1926, D.C. bar 1943. Asso. Piper, Carey & Hall, 1926-37, partner, 1933-37; spl. legal adviser U.S. Treasury Dept., 1934-37, 43-65; Lectr. taxation U. Md. Law Sch., 1935-37; chmn. radio program Invitation to Learning, 1940-41; asst. gen. counsel U.S. Treasury, 1937-43; mem. com. on practice Treasury Dept., 1944-52; Sec., mem. Am. Commn. for Protection and Salvage of Artistic and Historic Monuments, War Areas, 1943-46; sec., treas., gen. counsel Nat. Gallery Art, 1943-65; James Schouler lectr. polit. sci. Johns Hopkins, 1947, lectr. criticism, 1949-59; mem. Md. Tax Revision Commn., 1938-41. Author: Law and the Social Sciences, 1935, The Theory of Legal Science, 1941, Invitation to Learning, (with Allen Tate and Mark Van Doren), 1941, (with John Walker) Masterpieces of Painting from the National Gallery of Art, 1944, The Limits of Art, 1948, Legal Philosophy from Plato to Hegel, 1949, Law and its Premises, 1962, This Other Eden, 1973; Editor: Tax Laws of Maryland, 1937, Malinowski, A Scientific Theory of Culture, 1944, Saintsbury, French Literature and Its Masters, 1945, Lectures in Criticism, 1949, Great Paintings from the National Gallery of Art, 1952, (with Edith Hamilton) The Collected Dialogues of Plato, 1961, (with John Walker) Treasures from the National Gallery of Art, 1962, H.L. Mencken; The American Scene, A Reader, 1965, What Is Law?, 1970, On Mencken, 1980, Shakespeare's Herbs, 1982; translator: (Plato) Minos, 1970; contbr. to various mags., symposia, Dictionary Am. Biography. Trustee Bollingen Found., Textile Mus.; mem. Dumbarton Oaks adminstrv. com. Harvard; bd. dirs. Jr. History of Ideas; mem.-at-large Am. Council Learned Socs. Benjamin N. Cardozo lectr., 1962; John Randolph Tucker lectr., 1970; Recipient Civic medallion for most significant contbn. to progress of Balt. in field professions and sci., 1935, Rockefeller Pub. Service award. Mem. ABA, D.C. Bar Assn., Md. Bar Assn. (hon. life mem.), Am. Law Inst., Am. Philos. Assn., Am. Acad. Arts and Scis., Phi Beta Kappa. Clubs: Hamilton Street, Maryland, Cosmos, Wranglers. Home: 58 Ocean Blvd Kitty Hawk NC 27949

CAIRNS, JAMES DONALD, lawyer; b. Chesea, Mass., Aug. 7, 1931; s. Stewart Scott and Kathleen (Hand) C.; m. Davida Kahrl Steinbrink, June 27, 1953; children: Douglas S., Timothy H., Pamela S., Heather M.; m. Lydia Smithers, Nov. 13, 1982. A.B., Harvard U., 1952; J.D., Ohio State U., 1958. Bar: Fla. 1974, Ohio 1958, U.S. Dist. Ct. (no. dist.) Ohio 1975, U.S. Tax Ct. 1963. Ptnr. Squire, Sanders & Dempsey, Cleve., 1958—. Served to lt. (j.g.) USNR, 1952-55. Mem. ABA, Fla. Bar Assn., Ohio State Bar Assn., Bar Assn. Greater Cleve. Democrat. Episcopalian. Clubs: Union, Lakeside Yacht. Office: Squire Sanders & Dempsey Suite 1800 Huntington Commerce Bldg Cleveland OH 44115

CAIRNS, JAMES ROBERT, university dean, mechanical engineering educator; b. Indpls., Feb. 4, 1930; s. John Joseph and Agatha Bertha (Krebs) C.; m. Catherine I. DiCicco, Feb. 6, 1954; children: James Robert, Steven J., Michael P., Daniel F., Timothy E., Robert B. B.S. in Mech. Engring, U. Detroit, 1954; M.S. in Engring, U. Mich., 1959, Ph.D., 1963. Registered profl. engr., Mich.; cert. energy mgr. Instr. U. Detroit, 1954-57, U. Mich., Ann Arbor, 1957-63, asst. prof., Dearborn, 1963-65, asso. prof., 1965-68, prof. mech. engring., 1968—, chmn. engring. div., 1964-73, acting dean, 1973-75, dean, 1975—. Contbr. articles to profl. jours. Ford Faculty fellow, 1960-63. Mem. ASME, ASHRAE, Assn. Energy Engrs., Am. Soc. Engring. Edn., Common Cause, Tau Beta Pi, Pi Tau Sigma. Roman Catholic. Home: 836 Dover Dr Dearborn Heights MI 48127 Office: 4901 Evergreen Rd Dearborn MI 48128

CAIRNS, THEODORE LESUEUR, chemist; b. Edmonton, Alta., Can., July 20, 1914; came to U.S., 1936, naturalized, 1945; s. Albert William and Theodora (MacNaughton) C.; m. Margaret Jean McDonald, Aug. 17, 1940; children: John Albert, Margaret Eleanor (Mrs. William L. Etter), Elizabeth Theodora (Mrs. Ernest I. Reveal III), James Richard. B.S., U. Alta., 1936, LL.D., 1970; Ph.D., U. Ill., 1939. Instr. organic chemistry U. Rochester, 1939-41; research chemist central research dept. E.I. duPont de Nemours & Co., Wilmington, Del., 1941-45, research supr., 1945-51, lab. dir., 1951-63, dir. basic scis., 1963-66, dir. research, 1966-67, asst. dir. central research and devel. dept., 1967-71, dir., 1971-79; Regents prof. UCLA, 1965-66; mem. adv. bd. Organic Syntheses, 1958—; mem. Pres.'s Sci. Adv. Com., 1970-73, Pres.'s Com. Nat. Medal Sci., 1974-75; chmn. Office of Chemistry and Chem. Tech., NRC, 1979-81. Editorial bd.: Organic Reactions, 1959—, Jour. Organic Chemistry, 1965-69. Recipient award for creative work in synthetic organic chemistry Am. Chem. Soc., 1968; Perkin medal, 1973; Cresson medal Franklin Inst., 1974. Mem. Nat. Acad. Scis., Am. Chem. Soc. (chmn. organic div. 1964-65), AAAS, Sigma Xi, Phi Lambda Upsilon, Alpha Chi Sigma, Phi Lambda Upsilon (hon.). Office: care EI DuPont de Nemours & Co Exptl Station Wilmington DE 19898

CAJIAO SALAS, TERESA, language educator; b. Iquique, Chile, May 16, 1927; came to U.S., 1963, naturalized, 1972; d. Ramon G. and Donatila L. (Amaya) Cajiao; m. Alberto J. Salas, Nov. 27, 1952; children: Alberto J., Arturo C. Primary edn. degree, Escuela Normal Superior, Santiago, 1954; Profesora de Estado, Tech. U. Chile, 1957; M.Ed. (Fulbright fellow 1959-60), Kent (Ohio) State U., 1960; M.A., Western Res. U., 1965; Ph.D., Case Western Res. U., 1969. Tchr., Chile, 1948-63; instr. Kent State U., 1963-65; mem. faculty SUNY, Buffalo, 1965—, prof. Spanish, 1971—; instr. Peace Corps tng. program U. Notre Dame, summers 1963, 64; dir. jr. semester abroad program U. Costa Rica, 1970; hon. consul of Chile in Buffalo, 1966-72. Author: Temas y símbolos en la obra de Luís Alberto Heiremans, 1969, El teatro de hoy en Costa Rica, 1973, Asedios a la puesía de Nicomedes Santa Cruz, 1982; also articles. Summer research grantee SUNY, Buffalo, 1980. Mem. MLA, Am. Assn. Tchrs. Spanish and Portuguese, Comparative Edn. Soc., Latin Am. Studies Assn., Sigma Delta Pi. Office: Dept Fgn Langs 1300 Elmwood Ave Buffalo NY 14222 *

CAJORI, CHARLES FLORIAN, artist, educator; b. Palo Alto, Calif., Mar. 9, 1921; s. Florian Anton and Marion (Haines) C.; m. Barbara Grossman, June 23, 1967; children: Marion, Nicole. Student, Colo. Coll., 1939-40, Cleve. Art Sch., 1940-42, Columbia, 1946-48, Skowhegan Sch., 1947, 48. Instr. Notre Dame of Md., Balt., 1950-56, Cooper Union, N.Y.C., 1956-59, 60-65; vis. artist U. Calif. at Berkeley, 1959; instr. N.Y. Studio Sch., N.Y.C., 1964-69; prof. Queens Coll.,

N.Y.C., 1965—. Co-founder, Tanager Gallery, N.Y.C., 1952, N.Y. Studio Sch., N.Y.C., 1964; One-man shows, including, Howard Wise Gallery, N.Y.C., 1963, Bennington (Vt.) Coll., 1969, Landmark Gallery, N.Y.C., 1974, 81, Ingber Gallery Ltd., N.Y.C., 1976, Am. U., Washington, 1977, Grass McCleaf Gallery, Phila., 1983; exhibited in numerous group shows, including, Chgo. Art Inst., 1964, Whitney Museum, N.Y.C., 1965, Artists Choice, 1977, 3-man show, Loeb Center, N.Y. U., N.Y.C., 1970; represented in permanent collections including, Am. U., Washington, Del. Art Center, Wilmington, Met. Mus. Art, N.Y.C., Mitchner Collection, Austin, Tex., N.Y. U., N.Y.C., U. N.Mex., Albuquerque, Walker Art Center, Mpls., Whitney Mus., Geigy Chem. Corp., Ardsley, N.Y. Served with USAAF, 1942-46. Recipient Distinction in Arts award Yale, 1959; purchase awards Longview Found., 1962, Ford Found., 1963, Childe-Hassam, 1975, 76, 80; award for painting Inst. Arts and Letters, N.Y.C., 1970; Louis Comfort Tiffany award, 1979; Altman Figure prize Nat. Acad., 1983; Fulbright grantee, 1952-53; Nat. Endowment Arts grantee, 1981. Mem. Coll. Art Assn. Home: Litchfield Rd Watertown CT 06795 Office: Dept Art Queens Coll Flushing NY 11367

CALAFATI, GABRIEL RAFFELE, general contracting company executive; b. Newark, Jan. 14, 1932; s. Pietro and Angelina (Raffele) C.; m. Anna Lucy Giliberti, Apr. 17, 1955; children: Peter, Brian Rodney. With Frank Briscoe Co., Roseland, N.J., 1950—, exec. v.p., mem. exec. com., 1971-79, exec. v.p., asst. to chief exec officer, 1979-81, pres., chief exec. officer, chmn. bd., 1982—, dir. Clubs: Colonia Country (N.J.); Rifle of N.Y. (N.Y.C.). Office: Frank Briscoe Co Inc 3 ADP Blvd Roseland NJ 07068

CALAHAN, DONALD ALBERT, electrical engineering educator; b. Cin., Feb. 23, 1935; s. Joseph Dexter and Loretta Margaret (Reichling) C.; m. Martha Meyer, Aug. 22, 1959; children: Donald Theodore, Patricia Susan, Mary Susan, Judith Lynn. B.S., U. Notre Dame, 1957; M.S., U. Ill., 1958, Ph.D., 1960. Asst. prof. elec. engring. U. Ill., 1961-65; prof. elec. engring. U. Ky., 1965-66; prof. computer engring. U. Mich., Ann Arbor, 1966—; indsl. cons. in high speed computation, 1976—. Author: Modern Network Synthesis, 1964, Computer-Aided Network Design, 1967, rev. edit., 1972, Introduction to Modern Circuit Analysis, 1974. Served to 1st lt. U.S. Army, 1961-62. Fellow IEEE. Roman Catholic. Home: 3139 Lexington St Ann Arbor MI 48105 Office: Dept Elec Engring and Computer Sci U Mich Ann Arbor MI 48109

CALAMAR, GLORIA, artist; b. N.Y.C., Sept. 7, 1921; d. Louis B. and Dina (Cotter) C.; m. R.L. Redgate, Aug. 22, 1950 (div. 1972); children: Chris James, Steven Clay, Michael Cotter. Certificate, Otis Art Inst., Los Angeles, 1943; student, Art Students League, N.Y.C., 1944-45; B.A. in Art History, State Univ. Coll. N.Y. at New Paltz, 1970. Instr. art history and painting Orange County (N.Y.) Community Coll., 1964-69; instr. art history Mt. St. Mary Coll., Newburgh, N.Y., 1968-69; instr. painting Santa Barbara City Coll., 1975—; judge Hallmark Art Contest, N.Y. State, 1968. Artist in water color, oil, acrylic, lithography, etching, pen and ink, 1946—; one woman shows include, Georgetown U., 1974, Portland (Oreg.) Community Coll., 1973, Willamette U., 1972, U. Oreg., 1971-72, U. Calif. at Berkeley, 1969, Santa Barbara (Calif.) Mus., 1950, Mus. d'Art Moderne de la Ville de Paris, 1967, Galerie de la Madeleine, Brussels, Belgium, 1964, Landau Gallery, Beverly Hills, Calif., 1953, Parnassus Sq., Woodstock, N.Y., 1978, Ibiza, Balearic Islands, Spain, Santorini, Greece, 1980, Beaux Arts Ctr., Tunis, Tunisia, 1981, Alkamal Gallery, Jerusalem, Israel, Jaisalmer, India, 1984, group shows include, Delgado Mus., New Orleans, 1950, San Francisco Art Assn., 1953, Los Angeles County Mus. Art, 1954, Bertrand Russel Centenary Invitational, London, 1972-73, Woodstock Art Assn. (N.Y.), 1978; Contbr.: article to Ind. News Alliance. Served with WAAC, World War II. Nat. Endowment for Arts grantee, 1980-81. Mem. Woodstock Art Assn., Alumni Assn. Otis Art Inst., Art Students League N.Y. (life). Home: PO Box 844 Summerland CA 93067 *Many people have told me that I am a strong painter and add in the same breath—like a man. Others have asked me which comes first—my work or my children. I wonder how many male artists have been evaluated or interrogated in the same way. To the former I say thank you for the evaluation of strength but to be a woman artist does not preclude this ingredient. To the latter (I say) one interest supports the other and each is given priority at different times. Much in the same way that food and drink are necessary to the whole person and each is given priority at different times.*

CALAMARAS, LOUIS BASIL, lawyer, assn. exec.; b. Peabody, Mass., Jan. 6, 1908; s. Basil James and Margo (Papalexaton) C.; m. Pauline Spirrison, May 2, 1937; children—Margo, Basil, Georgia. Prep., L'école-Metax a, Athens, Greece; B.A., Columbia, 1931; LL.D., Georgetown U., 1934; postgrad. student law and commerce, Northwestern U. Dept. commr. Ind. Securities Commn., 1935-37; supr. Ill. Labor Dept., 1937-40; counsellor Labor Indsl. Relations, 1940-44; exec. sec. Nat. Electronic Distbrs. Assn., 1944-51, exec. v.p., 1951—; mng. dir. Midwest Elec. Distbrs. Assn.; dir. Montclare Theatre Corp., Elm Theatre Corp., Geo. A. Davis Co.; trustee Nat. Assn. Wholesalers; mgmt. cons. Lawn and Garden Assn., Suburban Restaurant Assn.; Mem. Wholesalers Adv. Com. to Sec. of Commerce; chmn. Radio-TV Industry FTC Trade Practice Conf.; mem. Electronic Coordinating Com. Editor, pub.: Nat. Electronic Distbrs. Assn. Jour; Contbr. articles to profl. jours. Chmn. Park-Recreation Bd., Planning Commn., Zoning Bd., Village of Lincolnwood. Named Man of Yr. of Radio-Electronics Industry, 1975, of Elec. Distbn. Industry, 1975. Mem. Chgo. Exchange, Electric Assn., Am. Acad. Polit. Sci., Phi Delta Theta. Clubs: Rotarian, Mason, K.P., Variety, Tam O'Shanter Country, Lake Shore Athletic (Chgo.); Ridgemore Country (v.p., dir.), Columbia University, Lake Michigan (exec. dir.), Electric Golf, Tower. Established James Calamaras scholarship fund at Ind. U. Law Sch. Home: 6712 N Leroy St Lincolnwood IL 60645 Office: 5901 N Cicero Ave Chicago IL 60646

CALAMARO, RAYMOND STUART, lawyer; b. Cairo, Egypt, May 28, 1944; came to U.S., 1947, naturalized, 1960; s. Albert and Charlotte (Golub) C. A.B., Cornell U., 1966; J.D., N.Y. U., 1969. Bar: N.Y. State 1970, U.S. Supreme Ct. 1975, D.C. bar 1976. Atty. firm Winthrop, Stimson, Putnam & Roberts, N.Y.C., 1969-73; legis. dir. Sen. Gaylord Nelson, Washington, 1973-75; exec. dir. Com. for Public Justice, N.Y.C., 1975-76; adj. faculty New Sch. for Social Research, N.Y.C., 1976; staff profl. Carter/Mondale Transition Team, Washington, 1976-77; dep. asst. atty. gen. Office of Legis. Affairs, Dept. Justice, Washington, 1977-79; of counsel Winston & Strawn, Washington, 1979-80, partner, 1980—; Vol. atty. Community Law Offices, 1970-71; exec. dir. N.Y. State Lawyers for McGovern-Shriver. Mem. Assn. Bar of City of N.Y. (mem. com. on civil rights 1971-73, 75-76, com. on fed. legislation 1980-83). Democrat. Club: Heights Casino (Brooklyn Heights, N.Y.). Home: 1749 Church St NW Washington DC 20036 Office: Winston & Strawn 2550 M St NW Washington DC 20037

CALAME, ALEXANDRE EMILE, emeritus French literature educator; b. Lausanne, Switzerland, Apr. 9, 1913; came to U.S., 1960; s. Jules H. and Hedwig I. (Mittelstenscheid) C.; m. Jeanne M. Burollet, Mar. 29, 1947; children: Isabelle, Beatrice, Mireille, Marianne. D.Lettres, Sorbonne, 1960. Asst. prof. French U. Saarbrucken, W. Ger., 1948-56; assoc. prof. U. Algiers, Algeria, 1956-60; mem. faculty U. Calif., Berkeley, 1960-80, prof. French, 1960-80, emeritus, 1980—, chmn. dept., 1963-68. Author books on seventeenth-century French, 1959-81. Trustee Lycee français, San Francisco, 1967-78. Decorated chevalier Legion of Honor, comdr. Palmes Academiques. Mem. Am. Assn. Tchrs. French. Roman Catholic. Home: 1837 Sonoma Ave Berkeley CA 94707 Office: 4207 Dwinelle Hall U Calif Berkeley CA 94720

CALAME, BYRON EDWARD, journalist; b. Appleton City, Mo., Apr. 14, 1939; s. Harry Franklin and Gladys Verl (Neal) C.; m. Kathryn Lee Boehm, June 9, 1962; children: Christine Lee, Jonathan David. B.J., U. Mo., 1961; M.A. in Polit. Sci, U. Md., 1966. Staff reporter Wall St. Jour., N.Y.C., 1965-67, Los Angeles, 1967-69, Washington, 1969-74, bur. mgr., Pitts., 1974-78, Los Angeles, 1978—. Served to lt. USN, 1961-65. Office: 514 Shatto Pl Los Angeles CA 90020

CALAME, DON L., ret. univ. dean; b. Ft. Scott, Kans., Dec. 22, 1914; s. Arthur B. and Lula N. (Barnett) C.; m. Penelope F. Alexander, Oct. 25, 1936; children—Ross Edwin (dec.), Donna Lou, Betty June. B.S., S.W. Mo. State U., Springfield, 1947; M.A., Northwestern U., 1949, Ph.D., 1956. Tchr. public schs. S.W. Mo., 1935-44, Aurora, Ill., 1946-48; tchr. bus. dept. S.W. Mo. State U., 1948-53; dir. Methodist Men, 1953-62; exec. dir. dept. united ch. mem. Nat. Council Chs., 1962-66; prof., dean Sch. Bus., S.W. Mo. State U., Springfield, 1966-79. Bd. dirs. Religion In Am. Life, 1962—, Am. Leprosy Mission, 1962—. Served to 1st lt. AUS, 1944-46. Mem. AAUP, Pi Omega Pi, Delta Pi Epsilon. Methodist. Club: Kiwanis. Home: 2661 S Belview Ave Springfield MO 65804

CALAME, GERALD PAUL, physicist, educator; b. Lelocle, Switzerland, Nov. 27, 1930; came to U.S., 1935, naturalized, 1953; s. Paul Arnold and Jessie (Beesley) C.; m. Jocelyn Florence Sullivan, July 26, 1958; 1 son, Jeffrey Paul. B.A., Coll. Wooster, 1953; M.A., Harvard, 1955, Ph.D., 1960. Physicist Knolls Atomic Power Lab., 1959-61; asst. prof. Rensselaer Poly. Inst., 1961-63, asso. prof., 1963-66; asso. prof. physics U.S. Naval Acad., 1966-69, prof., 1969—, chmn. dept. physics, 1978-82. Mem. Am. Assn. Physics Tchrs., AAAS, AAUP, Sigma Xi. Research on neutron transport theory, solar system astronomy, theoretical mechanics, optical resonator physics. Home: 74 Gentry Ct Annapolis MD 21403

CALANDRA, JOSEPH CARL, physician, educator; b. Chgo., Mar. 17, 1917; s. Domenic W. and Angela (Palma) C.; m. Patricia Mader, Sept. 9, 1944; children—Carolyn P. (Mrs. Thomas Selsor), Susan J. (Mrs. Thomas Sylvester), Joseph D., David B. B.S., Lewis Inst., 1938; Ph.D., Northwestern U., 1942, M.D., 1950. Diplomate: Am. Bd. Clin. Chemists. Intern Henrotin Hosp., Chgo., 1950-51; asst. prof. biochemistry Northwestern U., Chgo., 1942-50, asso. prof., 1950-53, prof., 1954—; prof. pathology Dental and Med. Sch., 1955—; Pres. Indsl. Bio-Test Labs., Inc., Northbrook, Ill., 1952-76; dir. Nalco Chem. Co., Oak Brook, Ill. Contbr. articles to profl. jours. Bd. dirs. Skokie Valley Community Hosp. Fellow Soc. Clin. Pharmacology and Chemotherapy, Am. Inst. Chemists, AAAS; mem. A.M.A., A.A.A.S., Am. Chem. Soc., Am., European socs. toxicology, Sigma Xi, Phi Lambda Upsilon, Omicron Kappa Upsilon. Roman Catholic. Home: 4630 Elm Terr Skokie IL 60076 Office: 311 E Chicago Ave Chicago IL 60611

CALAPAI, LETTERIO, artist; b. Boston; s. Biagio and Emanuela (Planeta) C.; m. Jean Hilliard, Jan. 5, 1962. Grad., Mass. Sch. Art, Boston Sch. Fine Arts and Crafts, Art Students League N.Y.C. Head graphics Albright Art Sch., Buffalo, 1949-54; became asso. Contemporaries Graphic Art Center, 1956; faculty mem. New Sch. Social Research, N.Y.C., 1957-61; founder, dir. Intaglio Workshop, N.Y.C., 1960-65; lectr. dept. art edn. N.Y.U., 1962-65; asso. prof. Brandeis U., 1964-65; vis. asso. prof. Kendall Coll., Evanston, Ill., 1965-69; lectr. dept. art and architecture U. Ill., Chgo. Circle, 1966; Mem. art adv. com. Field Mus. Natural History, Chgo., 1973-74; mem. adv. panel Ill. Arts Council, 1971-73. Publications: 25 Wood Engravings by Letterio Calapai, 1948, A Portfolio of Wood Engravings: 30 Aesop's Fables Printed by Letterio Calapai from the Original Blocks of Thomas Bewick, 1973, A Negro Bible; wood engravings, 1946; Mural Historical Development of Military Signal Communication; commd. by, Works Progress Adminstrn., 1939; acquired by, U.S. Army Signal Corps Mus., Ft. Gordon, Ga., 1980; One-man shows in, N.Y.C., Nat. Gallery of Art, Smithsonian Instn., Washington, Paris and London; rep. in permanent collections, Met. Mus. Art, Boston Mus. Fine Arts, Chgo. Art Inst., Fogg Mus., Bklyn. Mus., Albright Art Gallery, Library of Congress, N.Y. Pub. Library, Boston Pub. Library, Free Library Phila., Rose Mus., Brandeis U., The Biblioteque Nationale, Paris, Princeton U. Library, The Houghton Library (Harvard), Va. Mus. Fine Arts, Columbia U., Wichita (Kans.) State U., Washington U. Gallery Art, St. Louis, Ill. State Mus., Nat. Mus. of Bezalel, Nat. Mus. Jerusalem, Israel, Tokyo Mus., Japan, Civic Gallery Modern Art, Palermo, Italy, Gorakhpur U. Mus. Art, India, Kunsthaus, Zurich, Switzerland, Rosenwald Collection; illustrator: with wood engravings One Hundred Years Ago. Recipient prize award America In the War Exhibition, 1943; work chosen for Fifty Best Prints of the Year, 1944; Albert H. Wiggins purchase prize First Boston Printmakers Exhbn., 1948; John Taylor Arms prize Soc. Am. Graphic Artists, 1954; Library of Congress purchase prize, 1950, 51, 54; William J. Keller prize Western N.Y. Exhbn., 1954; Tiffany Found. grant in graphic arts, 1959; Audubon Artists medal for creative graphics, 1967; purchase prize 27th Ill. Invitational Exhbn. Ill. State Mus., 1974; purchase awards Art Inst. Chgo., 1972-73; Gold medal for graphics Italian-Am. Artists in U.S.A., 1977, 79; hon. mention Ill. Regional Print Show, 1977; purchase award Northwestern U., 1978, U. Ill., 1978; Excellence award N. Shore Art League, Chgo., 1982; numerous other awards. Mem. Soc. Am. Graphic Artists (hon. mem. council), Print Council Am., Calif. Soc. Etchers, Boston Printmakers, Coll. Art Assn., Internat. Assn. Art, Deer Isle Artists Assn. (pres. 1979—). Office: The Workshop Gallery 344 Tudor Ct PO Box 158 Glencoe IL 60022

CALASIBETTA, JOHN, business executive; b. Newark, June 1, 1905; s. Louis and Anna (Gaspari) C.; m. Josephine Battiato, June 23; 1 son, Louis. Pharm. M., Rutgers U., 1928. Mgr. Whelam Drug, Bloomfield, N.J., 1930-37; owner Phipps Pharmacy, Montclair, Mich., 1937-57; sr. v.p., customer relations,dir. Bergen Brunswing Corp., Los Angeles, 1957—. Mem. Am. Pharm. Assn. Office: Bergen Brunswing Corp 1900 Ave of Stars Los Angeles CA 90067

CALCAGNO, LAWRENCE, painter; b. San Francisco, Mar. 23, 1913; s. Vincent and Anna (de Rosa) C. Student, Calif. Sch. Fine Arts, San Francisco, 1947-50, Academie de la Grande Chaumiere, Paris, Academia degli Belle Arte, Florence, Italy. Asst. prof. art U. Ala., 1955-56, Albright Art Sch. of U. Buffalo, 1956-58; vis. artist in residence U. Ill., 1958-59; part-time tchr. N.Y.U., 1960; Andrew Mellon prof. painting Carnegie Inst. Tech., 1965-68; vis. artist in residence Honolulu Acad. Arts, 1968-69. One man shows, LaBaudt Gallery, San Francisco, 1948, 54, Galleria Numero, Florence, Italy, 1951, 52, Galeria Clan, Madrid, 1955, Studio Paul Fachetti, Paris, France, Martha Jackson Gallery, N.Y.C., 1955, 58, 60, 62, U. Ala., 1956, Albright Art Gallery, Inst. de Arte Contemporaneo, Lima, Peru, 1957, U. Ill., 1959, Fairweather-Hardin Gallery, Chgo., Phila. Art Alliance, 1960, New Arts Gallery, Houston, Ciudad Universitaria, Mexico City, 1961, McRoberts & Tunnard, London, Eng., Carnegie Inst. Tech., 1965, Houston Mus. Fine Arts, Yares Gallery, Scottsdale, Ariz., 1973, 75, 77, Talley Richard Gallery, Taos, N.Mex., 1976, Stables Gallery, Taos, 1978, Ulrich Mus., Wichita, 1979, Lincoln Center, Ft. Collins, Colo., Downtown Gallery, Honolulu, More-Rubin Gallery, Buffalo, 1980, retrospective exhibit, Westmoreland County Mus., Greensburg, Pa., 1967, Honolulu Acad. Arts, 1968-69, Franklin Siden Gallery, Detroit, 1965, 67, 69, Smithsonian Instn. traveling exhbn., 1973-75, Contemporary Art Center, Honolulu, 1976, Roko Gallery, N.Y.C., 1974-77, Stables Gallery, 1978, The New Gallery, Taos, 1981-83, traveling retrospective exhibit, 1982-83; represented in permanent collections, Honolulu Acad. Arts, Santa Barbara Mus., Boston Mus. Fine Arts, Rochester Meml. Gallery, Houston Mus. Fine Arts, Carnegie Inst., Albright-Knox Gallery, Whitney Mus., U. Nebr., Inst. Contemporary Art, Lima, San Francisco Mus. Modern Art, Walker Art Center, U. Ill., Mus. Modern Art, N.Y.U., Calif. Palace of Legion of Honor, Phoenix Art. Mus., Denver Mus. Art, U. Ala., Chase Manhattan Bank, Smithsonian Instn., Balt. Mus., Mus. of N.Mex., Santa Fe, also numerous pvt. collections. Residence fellowships Yaddo Corp., 1965, Ford Found. Humanities Program, 1965, Macdowell Colony, 1967-68, 74-76, Wurlitzer Found., 1972-73; Recipient 2d Drawing prize Nat. Army Arts Contest Nat. Gallery Art, 1945. Taos NM 87571

CALDABAUGH, KARL, holding company executive; b. Salisbury, Md., Nov. 26, 1946; s. Harry Rahr and Eleanor (Long) C.; m. Kay Laws, May 27, 1978; 1 son, Kevin. B.A., W. Va. Wesleyan Coll., 1968; M.B.A., U. Ala., 1973. Asst. v.p. Jacksonville (Fla.) Nat. Bank, 1973-79; v.p., treas. Charter Oil Co., Jacksonville, 1979-81; v.p. corp. devel. The Charter Co., Jacksonville, 1981—. Vice chmn. World Trade Com., Jacksonville, 1976; treas. Jaxport '77 and '78; mem. Leadership, Jacksonville, 1983. Mem. Beta Gamma Sigma. Republican. Methodist. Club: Sawgrass. Home: 1503 Leeward Ln Neptune Beach FL 32233

CALDARELLI, DAVID DONALD, otolaryngologist; b. Chgo., Nov. 7, 1941; s. David D. and Violet (Angus) C.; m. Janna Sue Nowak, Apr. 1, 1967; children: Leslie Ann, Adam David. Student, U. Wis., 1961; M.D., U. Ill., 1965, M.S., 1965. Diplomate: Am. Bd. Otolaryngology. Intern Presbyn. St. Luke's Hosp., Chgo., 1965-66, resident in surgery, 1966-67; resident in otolaryngology U. Ill. Eye and Ear Infirmary and Research and Edn. Hosps., Chgo., 1967-70; practice medicine specializing in otolaryngology, Chgo., 1974—; sr. attending physician, chmn. dept. otolaryngology and bronchoesophagology Rush Med. Coll., Rush-Presbyn.-St. Luke's Med. Center, Chgo., 1974—; attending otolaryngologist U. Ill. Research and Edn. Hosps., Chgo., 1970—, St. Francis Hosp., Evanston, Ill., 1974—; otolaryngologist Center for Craniofacial Anomalies, U. Ill., Chgo., 1970—; asst. otolaryngology Coll. Medicine, U. Ill., Chgo., 1967-70, instr. otolaryngology, 1970—; prof., chmn. dept. otolaryngology and bronchoesophagology Rush Med. Coll., Chgo., 1974—; cons. otolaryngologist Chgo. Contagious Disease Hosp., 1975—. Contbr. articles to profl. jours. and textbooks. Recipient Bordan Found. Undergrad. research award in medicine, 1965; Nat. Inst. Nervous Diseases and Blindness Research trainee, 1967-70; Ford Found. fellow, 1965; NIH grantee, 1963, 65. Fellow ACS; mem. AMA, Am. Acad. Ophthalmology and Otolaryngology, Am. Council Otolaryngology, Am. Cleft Palate Soc., Chgo. Laryngol. and Otol. Soc., Pan Am. Assn. Oto-Rhino-Laryngology and Broncho-Esophagology, Soc. Acad. Chmn. Otolaryngology, Soc. Univ. Otolaryngologists, Am. Broncho-Esophagological Assn., Triological Soc., Am. Soc. Head and Neck Surgery, Soc. Ears, Nose and Throat Advances in Children, Am. Cancer Soc. (unit dir. 1972-75), AAUP. Home: 101 Greenleaf Evanston IL 60202 Office: 1753 W Congress St Chicago IL 60612

CALDECOTT, RICHARD STANLEY, educator, university dean; b. Vancouver, C., Can., Apr. 15, 1924; came to U.S., 1946, naturalized, 1954; s. Godfrey and Ethyl (Snellgrove) C.; m. Lucille Peggy Ingalls, Aug. 16, 1947; children: Richard Robert, Ann Elizabeth, Lisa Barbara. B.S.A., U. B.C., 1946; M.S., Wash. State Coll., 1948, Ph.D., 1951. Research fellow Am. Cancer Soc., 1949-51; asst. prof. U. Nebr., 1951-53; asso. radiobiologist Brookhaven Nat. Lab., 1953-54; geneticist Dept. Agr., 1954-60, 63-65, AEC, 1960-63; prof. genetics, dean Coll. Biol. Scis., U. Minn., 1965-84, univ./bus. tech adv. to pres., 1984—. Editor: Radio-isotopes in the Biosphere, 1960; asso. editor Radiation Research, 1963-66. Del., UN Atoms for Peace Conf., 1955; mem. subcom. radiation biology Nat. Acad. Sci.-NRC, 1965-72; trustee Argonne Univs. Assn., 1970-80, chmn. bd., 1976-78; bd. dirs. Minn. Wellspring, 1982—, Minn. High Tech. Council, 1982—; v.p. Fresh Water Biol. Research Found., 1969—. Fellow AAAS; mem. Radiation Research Soc., Genetics Soc. Am., Am. Inst. Biol. Scis. (chmn. edn. com. 1970—), Orgn. Tropical Studies (dir. 1976), Sigma Xi. Club: Cosmos (Washington). Home: 14743 N Square Lake Trail Stillwater MN 55082 Office: Univ Minn Saint Paul MN 55108

CALDER, ALEXANDER, JR., business executive; b. Bklyn., July 14, 1916; s. Alexander and Adelaide Fancher (Gunnison) C.; m. Rebecca Jane Holmes, Aug. 17, 1940; children: Christie Holmes (Mrs. Richard E. Salomon), Alexander III. A.B., Dartmouth, 1938; M.B.A., Harvard, 1940. With Union Camp Corp., N.Y.C., 1940—, sales trainee, 1940-41, asst. to dir. indsl. relations, 1941-42, 46, asst. to v.p. charge sales, 1947-49, v.p., 1949-52, exec. v.p., gen. mgr., 1952-56, pres., dir., chief exec. officer, from 1956, now chmn. bd., chief exec. officer, chmn. exec. com., dir.; dir. Bank of N.Y. Co., Inc., Bank of N.Y., Burlington Industries, Inc., Ingersoll-Rand Co.; Intelligence analyst Bd. Econ. Warfare, 1942-43; trustee Inst. Paper Chemistry; bd. dirs. Am. Paper Inst. Bd. govs. The Nature Conservancy; trustee The Mountainside Hosp., Montclair, N.J.; mem. The Conf. Bd. and Council on Fgn. Relations, N.Y.C. Served as lt. (j.g.) USNR, 1943-46. Mem. Phi Kappa Psi. Clubs: Montclair (N.J.) Golf, Augusta (Ga.) Nat., Pine Valley (N.J.) Golf, Madison (Conn.) Beach; Oglethorpe (Savannah, Ga.); University (N.Y.C.). Office: 1600 Valley Rd Wayne NJ 07470 *

CALDER, IAIN WILSON, publishing co. exec.; b. Scotland, Feb. 27, 1939; came to U.S., 1967; s. William and Charlotte G. (West) C.; m. Jane Brownlea Bell, Apr. 17, 1965; children—Douglas William, Glen Robert Bell. Student pub. schs., Falkirk, Scotland. Reporter Falkirk Sentinel, 1955-56, Stirling Jour., 1956, Falkirk Mail, 1956-60, Glasgow Daily Record, 1960-64; London bur. chief Nat. Enquirer, 1964-67, articles editor, 1967-73, exec. editor, 1973-75, editor, 1975—, pres., Lantana, Fla., 1976—; dir. Nat. Enquirer Inc. Home: Delray Beach FL 33444 Office: 600 SE Coast Ave Lantana FL 33462

CALDER, KENNETH THOMAS, psychiatrist, psychoanalyst; b. Sault Ste Marie, Mich., Apr. 15, 1918; s. Thomas Kenneth and Margaret Harkness (MacDonald) C.; m. Abbie Ingalls, July 18, 1953; children—Thomas Kenneth, Mary Susannah. A.B., U. Mich., 1941; M.D., Columbia U., 1944. Diplomate: Am. Bd. Psychiatry. Intern Mass. Meml. Hosp., Boston, 1944-45; resident in psychiatry Cin. Gen. Hosp., 1945-46, N.Y. Psychiat. Hosp., 1948-49, Bellevue Hosp., 1949-50; pvt. practice psychiatry and psychoanalysis, N.Y.C., 1949—; faculty N.Y. Psychoanalytic Inst., 1963—, pres., 1980-82; faculty SUNY, Downstate, 1963-80, N.Y. U., 1980—. Contbr. articles to profl. jours. Served to capt. M.C. U.S. Army, 1946-48. Mem. Am. Psychoanalytic Assn. (pres. 1977-78), Internat. Psycho-Analytical Assn. (v.p. 1973-79). Democrat. Presbyterian. Address: 110 E 78th St New York NY 10021

CALDERHEAD, WILLIAM DICKSON, former foreign service officer; b. Carteret, N.J., Feb. 22, 1919; s. William Simpson and Agusta (Graham) C.; m. Elva Jane Alford, Nov. 9, 1942 (dec. July 18, 1971); 1 dau., Billie Jane; m. Norma Jean Willen, Oct. 19, 1974. B.A., U. Tex. at El Paso, 1941. Auditor War Dept., 1941-44; vice consul, Seville, Spain, 1945-49, San Jose, Costa Rica, 1949-51, asst. attache, Guatemala City, 1951-55; assigned Bur. Intelligence and Research, Washington, 1955-59; 2d sec., consul, Quito, Eduador, 1959-61; staff Office Personnel, U.S. Dept. State, 1961-62, 68-70; exec. staff Bur. Inter-Am. Affairs, 1962-63; med. adminstrn. officer Office Personnel, 1963-65, 70, fgn. service insp., 1965-67; assigned Sr. Seminar in Fgn. Policy, 1967-68; exec. dir. Bur. East Asian and Pacific Affairs, 1970-71; counselor for adminstrn. Am. embassy, London, Eng., 1971-74; exec. counselor, Mexico City, 1975-78; exec. dir. Bur. InterAm. Affairs, 1978-79; v.p. mgmt. and contracts Meridian House Internat., Washington, 1979—. Mem. Phi Kappa Tau. Clubs: American, Sesamee Pioneer-Lyceum (London). Home: 2717 Unicorn Ln NW Washington DC 20015 Office: Meridian House 1630 Crescent Pl NW Washington DC 20009

CALDERON, ALBERTO PEDRO, mathematician; b. Mendoza, Argentina, Sept. 14, 1920; s. Pedro and Haydee (Cores) C.; m. Mabel E. Molinelli Wells, Nov. 20, 1950; children: Mary Josephine, Pablo Alberto. Diploma in civil engring., U. Buenos Aires, 1947; Ph.D. in Math, U. Chgo., 1950. Vis. assoc. prof. Ohio State U., 1950-53; mem. Inst. Advanced Study, Princeton, 1953-55; assoc. prof. MIT, Cambridge, 1955-59, prof., 1972-75, U. Chgo., 1959-68, Louis Block prof., 1968-72, Univ. prof., 1975—, chmn., 1970-72; hon. prof. U. Buenos Aires, 1975—. Assoc. editor: Advances in Mathematics; Contbr. articles to math. jours. Recipient Latin Am. prize in Math. I.P.C.L.A.R., Santa Fe, Argentina, 1969; Bôcher Meml. prize Am. Math. Soc., 1979. Mem. Am. Acad. Arts and Scis., Nat. Acad. Scis., Academia Nacional Ciencias Exactas, Buenos Aires, Real Academia de Ciencias, Madrid. Home: Malabia 2791 Buenos Aires Argentina 1425 Office: 1118-32 E 58th St Chicago IL 60637

CALDERONE, MARY STEICHEN, physician; b. N.Y.C., July 1, 1904; d. Edward J. and Clara (Smith) Steichen; m. Frank A. Calderone, Nov. 1941; children: Linda Steichen Hodes, Francesca Calderone-Steichen, Maria S. B.A., Vassar Coll., 1925; M.D., U. Rochester, 1939; M.P.H., Columbia U., 1942; D.Med. Sci. (hon.), Women's Med. Coll., 1967, L.H.D., Newark State Coll., 1971, Jersey City State Coll., 1982, Sc.D., Adelphi U., 1971, Worcester Found. Exptl. Biology, 1974, Brandeis U., 1975, Haverford Coll., 1978, Dickinson Coll., 1981; LL.D., Kenyon Coll., 1972; Ped.D. (hon.), Hofstra U., 1978, D. Hum., Bucknell U., 1982. Intern Bellevue Hosp., N.Y.C., 1939-40; med. dir. Planned Parenthood-World Population, 1953-64; co-founder, dir., pres. Sex Info. Edn. Council U.S., N.Y.C., 1964-82; adj. prof. program in human sexuality NYU, N.Y.C., 1982—; lectr. human sexuality; 33d Lower lectr. Acad. Medicine and Cleve. Clinic, 1970; Rufus Jones lectr. Friends Gen. Conf., 1973; Hundley lectr. gynecology, Balt., 1973; president's disting. visitor Vassar Coll., 1983; 7th ann. Bronfman lectr. Am. Pub. Health Assn., 1968. Author: Release From Sexual Tensions, 1960; co-author: Family Book about Sexuality, 1981; author: Talking with Child about Sex, 1982; Editor: Abortion in U.S, 1958, Manual of Family Planning and Contraceptive Practice, 1964, rev. edit., 1970, Sexuality and Human Values, 1974; Contbr. articles to profl. jours., mags., textbooks, encys. Recipient 4th Ann. award for distinguished service to humanity Women's Aux. Albert Einstein Med. Center, Phila., 1966; Woman of Conscience award Nat. Council Women, 1968; citation Merrill-Palmer Inst. Human Devel. and Family Life, Detroit, 1969; Woman of Achievement award Greater N.Y. chpt. women's div. Albert Einstein Coll. Medicine, Yeshiva U., 1969; Haven Emerson award N.Y.C. Public Health Assn., 1970; Ann. award Soc. Sci. Study of Sex, 1976; Elizabeth Blackwell award for disting. service to humanity Hobart and Wm. Smith Coll., 1977; Margaret Sanger award Planned Parenthood Fedn. Am., 1980; recipient Abram Sachar silver medal Brandeis U. Nat. Women's Com., 1983, Mcdonald House award Univ. Hosps. Women's Com., Cleve., 1983, Human Service award Mental Health Assn. New York and Bronx Counties, 1983, Lifetime Achievement award Schlesinger Library Radcliffe Coll., 1983, Disting. Alumni award Columbia U., 1984, Jake Gimlad hon. lectr. award U. Calif. Sch. Medicine, 1984; named one of America's 75 Most Important Women Ladies Home Jour., 1971; one of 50 most influential women in U.S. Newspaper Enterprises Assn., 1975. Fellow Am. Public Health Assn. (Edward W. Browning award for prevention of disease 1980), Soc. Sci. Study Sex (hon. life mem.); mem. Am. Coll. Sexologists, Am. Assn. Marriage and Family Counselors (hon. life mem.), Am. Assn. World Health, AMA (hon. life), Soc. Sex Therapy and Research, Alpha Omega Alpha. Quaker. Home: 230 E 50th St New York NY 10022 Office: Dept Health Edn NYU 715 Broadway 2d Floor New York NY 10003

CALDERWOOD, STANFORD MATSON, investment management executive; b. Scottsbluff, Nebr., Nov. 6, 1920; s. Herbert Merle and Hazel Emjore (Matson) C.; m. Norma Jean Smith, Mar. 17, 1942. B.A., U. Colo., 1942. Reporter-photographer Manchester (N.H.) Union-Leader, 1946-48; staff corr. U.P.I., 1948-51, bus. rep., 1951-52; pub. relations writer Eastern Gas & Fuel Assos., Boston, 1952-53; with Polaroid Corp., Cambridge, Mass., 1953-70, v.p. advt., 1960-62, v.p. sales and advt., 1962-66, v.p. marketing, 1966-69, exec. v.p., 1969-70; pres., dir. Polaroid of Japan, 1962-70, Polaroid Overseas, 1962-70, Polaroid Can., 1962-70, Polaroid France, 1965-70; pres. Polaroid GmbH, 1965-70, Polaroid (Italia) S.p.A., 1965-70; gen. mgr. dir. Polaroid (Nederlands), N.V., 1962-70; gen. mgr. Polaroid (Internat.) N.V., 1965-70; pres. WGBH Ednl. Found., Boston, 1970-71; cons. Corp. Pub. Broadcasting, 1971-72; vice chmn., dir. Endowment Mgmt. & Research Corp., Boston, 1972-77; pres. Trinity Investment Mgmt. Corp., Boston, 1978—; lectr. econs. Wellesley Coll., 1972-73, vis. prof., 1974—; trustee Eastern Gas & Fuel Assos., 1977—. Bd. dirs. Internat. Student Assn., 1965-69; bd. dirs. MacDowell Colony, also treas., 1973-78; bd. overseers Old Sturbridge (Mass.) Village; trustee Radcliff Coll., 1960-72, Boston Inst. Contemporary Art; corporator Boston Mus. Sci.; vis. com. Center for Internat. Affairs, Harvard, 1976-83. Served to lt. USNR, 1942-46. Mem. Pi Gamma Mu. Club: St. Botolph (Boston). Home: 136 Fletcher Rd Belmont MA 02178 Office: 10 Tremont St Boston MA 02108

CALDWELL, BETTYE MCDONALD, education educator; b. Smithville, Tex., Dec. 24, 1924; d. Thomas Milton and Juanita (Mayes) McDonald; m. Fred T. Caldwell, Jr., June 8, 1947; children: Paul Frederick, Elizabeth Lanier. B.A., Taylor U., 1945; M.A., U. Iowa, 1946; Ph.D., Washington U., St. Louis, 1951. Research assoc. Upstate Med. Ctr., Syracuse, N.Y., 1959-65; prof. edn. Syracuse U., 1965-69; prof. U. Ark.-Little Rock, 1969-78, Disting. prof., 1978—; dir. First Community Bank, Little Rock. Editor: Child Devel. jours., 1968-72, Rev. Child Devel. Research, III, 1973, Infant Education, 1977. Bd. dirs. Ark. Advs., Little Rock, 1977—. Named Woman of Yr. in humanitarian and communit service Ladies Home Jour., 1976, Alumna of Yr. Baylor U., 1980. Fellow Soc. Research in Child Devel. (governing bd. 1977-81); mem. Nat. Assn. for Edn. Young Children (pres. 1982-84). Democrat. Home: 187 Pleasant Valley Dr Little Rock AR 72212 Office: College of Edn U Ark at Little Rock 33d St and University St Little Rock AR 72204

CALDWELL, CARLYLE G., chemical company executive; b. 1914. D. Chemistry, Iowa State Coll., 1939. With Nat. Starch and Chem. Corp., 1940—, pres., 1969—, chief exec. officer, 1975—, chmn. bd., 1978—, also dir.; dir. Research Corp. Trustee Stevens Inst. Tech. Mem. Corn Refiners Assn. (chmn., dir.), Chem. Mfrs. Assn. (past dir.), Soc. Chem. Industry (past chmn. Am. sect.). Address: Nat Starch and Chem Corp 10 Finderne Ave Bridgewater NJ 08807

CALDWELL, CHARLES GAMBILL, univ. dean; b. Radford, Va., Nov. 5, 1915; s. Charles Milton and Ida (Goodykoontz) C.; m. Evelyn Marie Rotenberry, Sept. 6, 1946; children—Charles Gambill, Kate Melissa. A.B., Roanoke Coll., 1937; M.A., U. Chgo., 1947, Ph.D., 1951; postgrad., Coll. William and Mary, also U. Md. Editorial asst. Kellogg Editorial Service, U. Chgo., 1946-49, research asst. com. human devel., 1948-49; asso. prof. Coll. Edn., U. Md., 1947-51; cons. Inst. Child Study; vis. prof. U. Va., Charlottesville, 1952-53; prof. psychology James Madison U., Harrisonburg, Va., 1951-76, head dept., 1955-59, dir. division tchr. edn., 1959-63; dean Sch. Edn., 1966-74, Grad. Sch., 1974—; chmn. careers com. Va. Assn. Mental Health, 1953-59; chmn. parent and family life edn. sect. Va. Congress Parents and Tchrs., 1957-59; pres. Shenandoah Valley chpt. Council Exceptional Children, 1957-58, Va. Commn. Children and Youth, 1962—; vice chmn. Harrisonburg-Rockingham Child Day Care Center, 1966-72; Va. rep. White House Conf. Children and Youth, 1960, conf. co-chmn., 1970; mem. Gov.'s Com. Youth, 1968-73, chmn., 1973-77; pres. VAECE, 1973-75. Contbr. to profl. jours. Bd. dirs. Shenandoah Council Continuing Edn., Valley Program for Aging Services, 1972—, Group Home for Pre-Delinquents, Community Counseling Center, Community Services Council; adv. bd. Massanutten Mental Health Clinic, 1959-73; mem. task force Va. Crime Commn., 1976—. Served with USAAF, 1942-45. Mem. Am. Assn. Colls. Tchr. Edn. (instl. rep.), Va. Edn. Assn., N.E.A., Council Exceptional Children, Va., Am. psychol. assns., Assn. Supervision and Curriculum Devel., Nat. Assn. Edn. Young Children, Va. Assn. Early Childhood Edn. (pres.), So. Assn. Children Under Six, Am. Guild Organists, Psi Chi, Kappa Delta Pi, Phi Delta Kappa. Home: Walnut Cove Farm Pleasant Valley VA 22848 Office: James Madison U Harrisonburg VA 22801

CALDWELL, CLIFFORD DOUGLAS, management consultant company executive; b. Carleton Place, Ont., Can, Jan. 26, 1937; s. Clifford James and Edna Margatet Florence (Jamieson) C.; m. Marilyn Rose French, aug. 25, 1965; children: Douglas Jamieson, Derek Wilson, Susan Alexandra Marion. B.B.A., U. N.B., 1960. With Shell Oil Co., 1960-62, Harding Carpets, 1962-65, Monsanto Fibres, 1965-67, Hickling Johnson, 1967-70; co-founder The Caldwell Ptnrs. Internat., 1970, pres., 1973—. Trustee Lester B. Pearson Coll. of Pacific, lakefield Coll. Mem. Assn. Exec. Search Cons. (dir. 1975-79). Anglican. Clubs: Royal Can. Yacht, Canadian, Badminton and Racquet, Empire. Office: 64 Prince Arthur Ave Toronto ON Canada M5R 1B4

CALDWELL, ELEANOR, artist; b. Kansas City, Mo., May 1, 1927; d. Earl Kendrick and Etta (Clark) C. B.S. magna cum laude in Edn, S.W. Mo. State U., 1948; M.A., Columbia U. Tchrs. Coll., 1953, Ed.D. (Alumni fellow, Dow scholar 1958-59), 1959. Tchr. art high schs., Mo. and Iowa, 1948-52; instr. art S.W. Mo. State U., 1953-54; asst. prof. Ft. Hays (Kans.) State U., 1954-57; instr. Columbia U. Tchrs. Coll.; lectr. art edn. Queen's Coll.; also supr. children's art carnival Mus. Modern Art, N.Y.C., 1957-59; prof., chmn. dept. art N.W. Mo. State Coll., Maryville, 1959-60; asso. prof. Edinboro (Pa.) State Coll., 1960-62, Pa. State U., 1962-63, No. Ill. U., DeKalb, 1963-64, prof. art, 1967—; asso. prof. Ft. Hays State U., 1964-67; dir. Oakbrook (Ill.) Invitational Crafts Exhbn., 1968—; cons., tchr. Arrowmont Sch. Arts and Crafts, Gatlinburg, Tenn., 1974-77. Represented in permanent collections, Denver Public Schs., Colo. Women's Coll., Denver, Ft. Hays State Coll., No. Ill. U., Sheldon Meml. Art Mus., Lincoln, Nebr., Arrowmont Sch. Arts and Crafts.; Editor: Contemporary Jewelry, 1970. Recipient Public Service award Ill. Sesquicentennial Commn., 1968; grantee No. Ill. U., 1968, 70, 74-80. Mem. Soc. N.Am. Goldsmiths, Am. Crafts Council, Artists Equity, AAUP, Delta Kappa Gamma, Pi Lambda Theta, Kappa Delta Pi. Office: Visual Arts Bldg No Ill U DeKalb IL 60115

CALDWELL, ELWOOD FLEMING, food science educator, researcher; b. Gladstone, Man., Can., Apr. 3, 1923; s. Charles Fleming and Frances Marion (Ridd) C.; m. Irene Margaret Sebille, June 13, 1949; children: John Fleming, Keith Allan; m. Florence Annette Zaz, June 23, 1979. B.Sc., U. Man., 1943; M.A. in food chemistry, U. Toronto, 1949; Ph.D. in nutrition, U. Toronto, 1953; M.B.A., U. Chgo., 1956. Chemist Lake of the Woods Milling Co., Can., 1943-47; research chemist Can. Breweries Ltd., Toronto, Ont., 1948-49; chief chemist Christie, Brown & Co. (Nabisco), Toronto, 1949-51; research assoc. in nutrition U. Toronto, 1951-53; with Quaker Oats Co., Barrington, Ill., 1953-72, dir. research and devel., until 1972; prof., head dept. food sci. and nutrition U. Minn., St. Paul, 1972—; chmn. bd. Dairy Quality Control Inst., Inc., St. Paul, 1972—, R.& D. Assocs. for Mil. Food & Packaging, Inc., San Antonio, 1970-71; chmn. evening programing food sci. Ill. Inst. Tech., Chgo., 1965-69. Contbr. articles to sci. jours. Chmn. North Barrington (Ill.) Bd. Appeals, 1966-69, mayor, 1969-72; vice-chmn. Barrington Area Council Govts., 1972; bd. dirs. Family Guidance Barrington, 1971-72. Recipient cert. of appreciation for civilian service U.S. Army Materiel Command, 1970. Fellow Inst. Food Technologists (Chmn.'s Service award Chgo. sect. 1975); mem. Am. Assn. Cereal Chemists, Am. Home Econs. Assn., Phi Tau Sigma, Sigma Xi, Gamma Sigma Delta. Republican. Lutheran. Club: Minnesota Alumni (Mpls.). Office: 1334 Eckles Ave U Minn Saint Paul MN 55108

CALDWELL, ERSKINE, author; b. Moreland, Ga., Dec. 17, 1903; s. Ira Sylvester and Caroline Preston (Bell) C.; m. Helen Lannigan, Mar. 3, 1925; children—Erskine Preston, Dabney Withers, Janet; m. Margaret Bourke-White, Feb. 27, 1939; m. June Johnson, Dec. 21, 1942; 1 son, Jay Erskine; m. Virginia Moffett Fletcher, Jan. 1, 1957. Student, Erskine Coll., S.C., 1920, 21, U. Va., 1922, 25, 26, U. Pa., 1924. Newspaper writer, 1925, cotton picker, stage hand, profl. football player, book reviewer, lectr., editor; motion picture screen writer, Hollywood, Calif., 1933-34, 42-43, corr., Mexico, Spain, Czechoslovakia, 1938-39, China, Mongolia, Turkestan, 1940; editor Am. Folkways, 1940-55; war corr. Life mag., PM, CBS, Russia, 1941. Author: The Bastard, 1929, Poor Fool, 1930, American Earth, 1931, Tobacco Road, 1932, God's Little Acre, 1933, We Are The Living, 1933, Journeyman, 1935, Kneel to the Rising Sun, 1935, Some American People, 1935, (with Margaret Bourke-White) You Have Seen Their Faces, 1937, Southways, 1938, (with Margaret Bourke- White) North of the Danube, 1939, Trouble in July, 1940, Jackpot, 1940, (with Margaret Bourke-White) Say, Is This the U.S.A.?, 1941, All-Out on the Road to Smolensk, 1942, Moscow Under Fire, 1942, All Night Long, 1942, Georgia Boy, 1943, Stories, 1944, Tragic Ground, 1944, A House in the Uplands, 1946, The Sure Hand of God, 1947, This Very Earth, 1948, Place Called Estherville, 1949, Episode in Palmetto, 1950, Call It Experience, 1951, The Courting of Susie Brown, 1952, A Lamp for Nightfall, 1952, The Complete Stories of Erskine Caldwell, 1953, Love and Money, 1954, Gretta, 1955, Erskine Caldwell's Gulf Coast Stories, 1956, Certain Women, 1957, Molly Cottontail, 1958, Claudelle Inglish, 1959, When You Think of Me, 1959, Jenny by Nature, 1961, Close to Home, 1962, The Last Night of Summer, 1963, (with Virginia M. Caldwell) Around About America, 1964, In Search of Bisco, 1965, The Deer at Our House, 1966, In The Shadow of The Steeple, 1966, Writing in America, 1966, Miss Mamma Aimee, 1967, Deep South, 1968, Summertime Island, 1968, The Weather Shelter, 1969, The Earnshaw Neighborhood, 1971, Annette, 1973, (with Alexander Calder) The Sacrilege of Alan Kent, 1976, (with Virginia M. Caldwell) Afternoons in Mid-America, 1976; Contbr. to mags. Recipient Yale Rev. $1,000 award for fiction, 1933. Mem. Authors League Am., Am. Acad. and Inst. Arts and Letters, Internat. P.E.N., Euphemian Lit. Soc., Raven Soc. Clubs: Phoenix Press, San Francisco Press. Home: PO Box 4550 Hopi Station Scottsdale AZ 85258 Office: care McIntosh & Otis Inc 475 Fifth Ave New York City NY 10017 *I am fully aware that my life has not been without fault and error; even so, in my present state of mind, I would hesitate to change anything in the past were I be given the opportunity to do so. My reason for declining an opportunity to change the past is that I am satisfied with myself.*

CALDWELL, GARNETT ERNEST, lawyer; b. Houston, July 2, 1934; s. William Ernest and Ethel Leona (Jones) C. B.A., U. Houston, 1957, J.D., 1959. Bar: Tex. 1958. Pvt. practice law, Houston, 1959-64; partner Ginther, Erwin, Dillard & Caldwell, Houston, 1964-65, Prappas, Caldwell & Moncure, 1965-77, Caldwell & Baggott, 1977-82, Caldwell, Wallis, Pruitt & Baggott, 1982; sole practice, Houston, 1982—; lectr. govt. U. Houston, 1961-62. Republican nominee for State Legislature, 1962; del. Rep. State Conv., 1962, Rep. Dist. Conv., 1974. Served as 2d lt. U.S. Army, 1957; lt. col. Res., 1969-77. Decorated knight and knight comdr. Royal Yugoslavian Order St. John of Jerusalem. Mem. Am., Houston bar assns., Am. Judicature Soc., Res. Officers Assn., Houston Harpsichord Soc., Delta Theta Phi. Roman Catholic. Club: Univ. (Houston). Home: 4471 Yoakum Blvd Houston TX 77006 Office: 1500 Lummus Tower 3000 Post Oak Blvd Houston TX 77056

CALDWELL, JAMES WILEY, lawyer; b. Arkadelphia, Ark., Dec. 14, 1923; s. Joseph Allison and Beulah (Wright) C.; m. Marie Cole, July 11, 1947; children: Susan, Carolyn, James Wiley. B.A., Ouachita Bapt. Coll., 1947; J.D. with honors, U. Tex., 1950. Bar: Tex. Assoc. McGregor & Sewell, Houston, 1950-51; atty. City of Houston, 1951-52; sr. ptnr. Fulbright & Jaworski, Houston. Trustee, gen. counsel Baylor Coll. Medicine; chmn. Houston Tax Research Assn.; originator program for state med. edn. funds Baylor U., 1969; financing for control of pollution on Houston Ship Channel, 1971. Served to 1st lt. inf. AUS, 1943-46; ETO. Named Ouachita Bapt. U. Disting. Alumnus, 1975. Mem. Houston Bar Assn., ABA, Nat. Assn. Bond Lawyers. Am. Baptist. Clubs: River Oaks Country (pres. 1983); Coronado (Houston) (pres. 1975). Office: Fulbright & Jaworski 800 Bank of Southwest Bldg Houston TX 77002

CALDWELL, (JANET) TAYLOR (MRS. WILLIAM ROBERT PRESTIE), author; b. Preswich, Manchester, Eng., Sept. 7, 1900; d. Arthur F. and Anna (Marks) C.; m. William Fairfax Combs, May 27, 1919 (div. 1931); 1 dau., Mary Margaret (Mrs. Gerald Fried); m. Marcus Reback, May 12, 1931 (dec. Aug. 1970); 1 dau., Judith Ann (Mrs. Theodore Roosevelt Goodman); m. William E. Stancell, June 1972 (div. 1973); m. William Robert Prestie, July 1978. A.B., U. Buffalo, 1931; Litt.D., D'Youville Coll., Bufallo, 1964; L.H.D., Niagara U., 1971. Began as stenographer, ct. reporter; ct. reporter Workmen's Compensation Div., N.Y. State Dept. Labor, Buffalo, 1923-24; sec. Bd. Spl. Inquiry, U.S. Immigration and Naturalization Service, Dept. Justice, Buffalo, 1924-31. Author: Dynasty of Death, 1938; latest include Melissa, 1948, Let Love Come Last, 1949, The Balance Wheel, 1951, The Devil's Advocate, 1952, Never Victorious, Never Defeated, 1956 (Grand Prix, Prix Chatrain, Paris), Tender Victory, 1956, The Sound of Thunder, 1957, Dear and Glorious Physician, 1959, The Listener, 1960, A Prologue to Love, 1961, Grandmother and The Priests, 1963, A Pillar of Iron, 1965, No One Hears But Him, 1966, Dialogues with the Devil, 1967, Testimony of Two Men, 1968, Great Lion of God, 1970, Captains and Kings, 1972, Glory and the Lightning, 1974, Ceremony of the Innocent, 1976, Bright Flows the River, 1978, Answer as a Man, 1981; Contbr. to nat. mags. Served as yeomanette USNR, 1918-19. Recipient nat. award D.A.R., 1956; McElligott medal Marquette U., 1964. Fellow Internat. Inst. Arts and Letters; mem. Am. Legion, St. Francis Guild, Nazareth Guild, Legion of Mary. Republican. Roman Catholic. Club: Women's Nat. Republican. Home: Ivanhoe Ln Greenwich CT 06830

CALDWELL, JOHN GILMORE, public utility executive; b. Manor, Pa., Mar. 7, 1931; s. Wayne A. and Mabel M. (Campbell) C.; m. Ellen Sue Baer, July 1, 1979; children from previous marriage: Douglas, Susan, Rebecca, Wayne. B.S., U. Pitts., 1953; postgrad., U. Mich., U. Colo. With Equitable Gas Co., Pitts., 1953, operating mgr., 1976-77, v.p. ops., 1977, exec. v.p., 1978—, also dir.; dir. Ky., W.Va. Gas Co., Ky. Hydrocarbon Co., Phila. Oil Co., Berea Gathering Co., Equitable Gas-Energy Co., KEPCO, Inc. Bd. dirs. ann. giving fund bd. U. Pitts., 1977—; bd. dirs. Big Bros. and Sisters of Greater Pitts., Inc., 1976—. Served with USAF, 1955-57. Mem. Am. Gas Assn., Pa. Gas Assn., Engrs. Soc. Western Pa., W.Va. Oil and Natural Gas Assn. (dir.), Pitts. C. of C. Democrat. Presbyterian. Clubs: Pitts. Athletic Assn., Duquesne. Home: 1420 Centre Ave Pittsburgh PA 15219 Office: 420 Blvd Allies Pittsburgh PA 15219

CALDWELL, JOHN L., company executive; b. Algiers, Algeria, Mar. 5, 1940. B.A., U. Md., 1965; M.A., George Washington U., 1966. Liaison to comdr.-in-chief NATO Fontainebleau, France, 1960-64; exec. sec., staff dir. Task Force World Shortages, Mex.-U.S. Com., East-West Trade Task Force, 1966-73; exec. sec. European Community-U.S. Bus. Council, 1972-75, Adv. Council Japan-U.S. Econ. Relations, 1970-73; dir. Center for Internat. Bus. Relations, 1973-77; mgr. internat. div. U.S. C. of C., 1977-78, v.p. internat., 1978-81; pres. Carl Byoir & Assocs., Washington, 1981-83; mng. dir. U.S. Trading Co., 1983—; bd. advs. Nat. Bank Washington, Landegger Internat. Bus. Diplomacy Program Georgetown U.; dir. Am. Internat. Investments, Inc.; mem. internat. com. Greater Washington Bd. Trade; bd. dirs. Nat. Ctr. Therapeutic Riding. Address: 1605 New Hampshire Ave NW Washington DC 20009

CALDWELL, JOHN THOMAS, JR., communications executive; b. Sewickley, Pa., July 30, 1932; s. John Thomas and Helen Olive (Sheats) C.; m. Margery Eleanor Hill, Dec. 31, 1971. A.B., U. Pitts., 1955; postgrad., Mich. State U., U. Mich., Harvard U. Sch. Bus. Mem. prodn. staff Sta. WKAR-TV, East Lansing, Mich., 1955-56, dir., 1957, producer, 1958, prodn. mgr., 1959-62; distbn. mgr. Nat. Ednl. TV, Inc., Ann Arbor, Mich., 1962-64; v.p. distbn. and ops., 1964-66; ops. mgr. Sta. WGBH, Boston, 1966-70; gen. mgr. Sta. WGBY-TV, Springfield, Mass., 1971-79; pres., gen. mgr. Sta. WTVS-TV, Detroit, 1979-83; dir. electronic communication, corp. pub. affairs Ford Motor Co., Dearborn, Mich., 1983—; bd. dirs. Public Broadcasting Service, 1977-81. Bd. dirs. Detroit Symphony Orch., 1979—, Mich. Cancer Found., 1980—, Boys Clubs Mich., 1981—, Springfield (Mass.) Symphony Orch., 1975-79; mem. U. Mich. Community Adv. Bd., 1979—, Mich. State Film, TV and Rec. Arts Adv. Council. Woodrow Wilson fellow, 1981. Mem. Nat. Acad. TV Arts and Sci., Mich. Corp. Public Broadcasting (dir.). Clubs: Detroit Press, Economic, Recess (Detroit); Grosse Pointe Yacht. Home: 515 Washington Rd Grosse Pointe MI 48202 Office: Ford WHQ The American Rd WHQ Dearborn MI 48121

CALDWELL, JOHN TYLER, political science educator, university chancellor emeritus; b. Yazoo City, Miss., Dec. 19, 1911; s. Joseph Redford and Lilley (Tyler) C.; m. Catherine Wadsworth Zeek, May 16, 1947 (dec. Feb. 1961); children: Alice Beaulieu, Andrew Morton, Charles Franklin, Helen Tyler; m. Carol Schroeder Erskine, June 29, 1963; children: Carol Case Erskine, Melanie Ann Erskine (Mrs. M.F. Johnston). B.S., Miss. State Coll., 1932; A.M., Duke, 1936, LL.D., 1965; Ph.D., Princeton, 1939; student, U. Wis., summer 1938, Naval Sch. Mil. Govt., Columbia, 1943, M.A., 1945; LL.D., Coll. Ozarks, 1955, Wake Forest Coll., 1960, U. Md., 1970, N.C. State U., 1975, U. Montevallo, 1979. Tchr. social scis. and band dir. Holmes Junior Coll., Goodman, Miss., 1932-36; jr. economist U.S. Resettlement Adminstrn., 1936-37; asst. economist, land use planning Bur. Agrl. Econs., U.S. Dept. Agr., summer, 1939; instr. polit. sci. Vanderbilt U., 1939-42, asst. prof., 1942-46; leave of absence, 1942-46, asso. prof., 1946-47; pres. Ala. Coll., Montevallo, 1947-52, U. Ark., Fayetteville, 1952-59; chancellor N.C. State U. at Raleigh, 1959-75, chancellor emeritus, 1975—; prof. politics, 1959—; ednl. cons. Ford Found. in Pakistan, 1954; Ofcl. mem. for Ala. So. Regional Edn. Bd., 1948-52; mem. adv. com. AID-Univ. Relations, 1965-69; trustee Ednl. Testing Service, 1957-60, 65-69, 70-74, chmn. bd., 1966-67, 68-69, 73-74; past mem. com. Advancement Sch. Adminstrn.; past mem. Nat. Commn. on Accrediting; chmn. commn. on internat. edn. Am. Council on Edn., 1967-69; mem. U.S. Nat. Commn. UNESCO, 1968-70; bd. dirs. Overseas Devel. Council, 1969-79; pres. Nat. Assn. State Univs. and Land-Grant Colls., 1962, chmn. internat. affairs com., 1966-69; bd. visitors Air U., Maxwell AFB, 1970-73, chmn., 1972-73; trustee Princeton, 1976-80, Nat. Humanities Center, 1976—; pres. Triangle Univs. Center for Advanced Studies, Inc., 1975-82, dir., 1975—. Served from ensign to lt. comdr. USN, 1942-46. Decorated Bronze Star.; Julius Rosenwald fellow Princeton, 1937-39. Mem. Am. Polit. Sci. Assn., Phi Beta Kappa, Phi Kappa Phi, Blue Key, Pi Kappa Alpha. Democrat. Christian Scientist. Clubs: Rotary, Watauga. Home: 3070 Granville Dr Raleigh NC 27609

CALDWELL, LYNTON KEITH, social scientist, educator; b. Montezuma, Iowa, Nov. 21, 1913; s. Lee Lynton and Alberta (Mace) C.; m. Helen A. Walcher, Dec. 21, 1940; children: Edwin Lee, Elaine Lynette. Ph.B., U. Chgo., 1935, Ph.D., 1943; M.A., Harvard U., 1938; LL.D. (hon.), Western Mich. U., 1977. Asst. prof. govt. Ind. U., Bloomington, 1939-44, Arthur F. Bentley prof. polit. sci., 1956—, dir. advanced studies in sci., tech. and public policy, 1965—; dir. research and publs. Council of State Govts., 1944-47; faculty U. Chgo., 1945-47; prof. polit. sci. Syracuse U., 1947-54; dir. Pub. Adminstrn. Inst. for Turkey and Middle East, UN, Ankara, 1954-55; prof. polit. sci. U. Calif., Berkeley, 1955-56; Mem. environmental adv. bd. C.E., 1970—; mem. sea grant adv. panel Nat. Oceanographic and Atmospheric Adminstrn., 1971—; panel mem. Office Tech. Assessment, 1977—; cons. U.S. Senate Com. on Interior and Insular Affairs, 1969—, UN, 1973-74, UNESCO, 1975—; mem. Nat. Commn. on Materials Policy, 1971—, Nat. Acad. Scis. Com. on Internat. Environ. Programs, 1970—; Chmn. com. internat. law, policy and adminstrn. IUCN, 1969-77. Author: Administrative Theories of Hamilton and Jefferson, 1944, Environment: A Challenge to Modern Society, 1970, In Defense of Earth, 1972, Environmental Policy and Administration, 1975, Citizens and the Environment, 1976, Science and the National Environmental Policy Act, 1982; Bd. editors: Environ. Conservation, 1973—, Natural Resources Jour, 1973—, Sci., Tech. and Soc, 1979—, Environ. Profl., 1981—, Politics and the Life Scis., 1982—. Trustee Inst. of Ecology, Inter Univ. Case Programs, Nature Conservancy., Shirley Heinze Environ. Fund. Recipient Sagamore of Wabash award State of Ind., 1980; Conservation Found. grantee, 1968-69; NSF grantee, 1963—; Conservation and Research Found. grantee, 1969-70; U.S. Office Edn. grantee, 1973; Guest fellow Woodrow Wilson Internat. Center for Scholars Smithsonian Instn., 1971-72; Franklin lectr. Auburn U., 1972; disting. prof. lectr. U. Ala., 1981, U. Aberdeen, 1983; East-West Center fellow, 1981. Fellow AAAS; mem. Am. Soc. Public Adminstrn. (William Mosher award 1966, Laverne Burchfield award 1972, Marshall E. Dimock award 1981), Nat. Acad. Public Adminstrn., Inst. of Ecology (assembly 1973—), Royal Soc. Arts. Club: Cosmos (Washington). Home: 4898 Heritage Woods Rd E Bloomington IN 47401

CALDWELL, OLIVER JOHNSON, educator, former government official; b. Foochow, China, Nov. 16, 1904; s. Harry Russell and Mary Belle (Cope) C.; m. Eda Joslin Holcombe, June 29, 1935; children: Eda Joslyn (Mrs. Edmund Becker), Gail Edna (Mrs. Warren Robinson). Student, U. Wash., 1922-23; A.B., Oberlin Coll., 1926, M.A., 1927; student music, aesthetics, 1927-29; student, Army Civil Affairs Tng. Sch., U. Chgo., 1943; L.H.D., Baldwin-Wallace Coll.; LL.D., Ithaca U., Albright Coll. Head social scis. Harvey Sch., Hawthorne, N.Y., 1929-35; asso. prof. English U. Amoy, China, 1935-36; prof. English U. Nanking, China, 1936-37, acting head dept. fgn. langs., 1937-38; pub. relations officer Asso. Bds. Christian Colls. in China, 1938-43; chief student br., fed. programs br., div. exchange of persons Dept. State, 1947-51; chief program devel. staff ednl. exchange service U.S. Internat. Information Adminstrn., 1951-52; asst. commr. internat. edn., dir. div. internat. edn. U.S. Office Edn., later acting asso. commr., 1952- 64; vis. prof. comparative edn. U. Md., 1964-65; dean internat. services So. Ill. U., Carbondale, 1965-69, prof. higher edn., 1969-73, prof. emeritus, 1973—; author, cons., 1973—. Author: A Secret War-Americans in China 1944-45, 1972; Collaborator: The Task of the Universities in a Changing World; Contbr. 250 articles to profl. and popular jours., also symposium. Mem. sch. bd., Falls Church, 1952-56. Served from capt. to maj., OSS, AUS, 1943-45. Mem. various profl. assns. Methodist. Club: Rotarian. Assisted U. Nanking move through gorges Yangtze River to Chengtu after Japanese attack. Govtl. papers and personal acad. papers in Hoover Instn. for Study of War, Revolution and Peace, Stanford, Calif. Home: Rural Route 2 Box 177 Cobden IL 62920 Office: Dept Higher Edn So Ill U Carbondale IL 62901 *Religion, politics, economics, and race all divide mankind. Unless these divisions are overcome by a new knowledge, a new common sense, mankind is not likely to survive without a miracle. Maybe there is no way out for man. Eventual extinction has been the lot of many life forms since life first appeared in an early ocean. But if education can effectively be used to promote nationalism, ethnic hatred, religious differences, and obedient citizens of Marxist states, then education could be put to a new use: instilling in each human being the wisdom, humility, and compassion required for effective multi-national cooperation necessary for the survival of the tribe of Man.*

CALDWELL, PHILIP, automobile mfg. co. exec.; b. Bourneville, Ohio, Jan. 27, 1920; s. Robert Clyde and Wilhelmina (Hemphill) C.; m. Betsey Chinn Clark, Oct. 27, 1945; children—Lawrence Clark, Lucy Hemphill Caldwell Stair, Desiree Branch Caldwell Armitage. B.A. in Econs, Muskingum Coll., 1940, H.H.D. (hon.), 1974; M.B.A., Harvard U. Grad. Sch. Bus., 1942; D.B.A. (hon.), Upper Iowa U., 1978, L.L.D., Boston U., 1979, Eastern Mich. U., 1979, Miami U., 1980. With Navy Dept., 1946-53, dep. dir. procurement policy div., 1948-53; with Ford Motor Co., 1953—, v.p., gen. mgr. truck ops., 1968-70; pres., dir. Philco-Ford Corp. subs., 1970-71, v.p. mfg. group N. Am. automotive ops., 1971-72; chmn., chief exec. officer Ford of Europe, Inc., 1972-73, exec. v.p. internat. automotive ops., 1973-77, vice chmn. bd., 1977-79, dep. chief exec. officer, 1978-79, pres., 1978-80, chief exec. officer, 1979—, chmn. bd., 1980—; also dir. Ford Motor Co., Ford of Europe, Ford Latin Am., Ford Mid-East and Africa, Ford Asia-Pacific, Ford Motor Credit Co., Ford of Can.; mem. Trilateral Commn.; mem. internat. adv. com. Chase Manhattan Bank; dir. Digital Equipment Corp. Trustee Com. for Econ. Devel., Muskingum Coll.; dir. Harvard U. Assos. Grad. Sch. Bus. Adminstrn., European Inst. Bus. Adminstrn.; vice-chairperson bd. trustees New Detroit Inc.; bd. dirs. Detroit Renaissance, Detroit Symphony Orch. Served to lt. USNR, 1942-46. Recipient 1st William A. Jump Meml. award, 1950; Meritorious Civilian Service award U.S. Navy, 1953. Mem. Bus. Council, Bus. Roundtable, Conf. Bd., Motor Vehicle Mfrs. Assn. (vice-chmn., dir.). Clubs: Detroit, Bloomfield Hills Country, Detroit Athletic, Renaissance. Office: Ford Motor Co American Rd Dearborn MI 48121

CALDWELL, SARAH, opera producer, condr., stage dir. and, adminstr.; b. Maryville, Mo., Mar. 6, 1924. Attended, U. Ark., Hendrix Coll.; studied violin at, New Eng. Conservatory; studied at, Berkshire Music Center, Tanglewood, Mass.; D. Mus. (hon.), Harvard U., Simmons Coll., Bates Coll., Bowdoin U. Mem. faculty Berkshire Music Center; dir. Boston U. Opera Workshop, 1953-57; created dept. music theater Boston U.; founded Boston Opera Group (later became Opera Co. of Boston), 1957, sinced served as artistic dir. and condr. Asst. to Boris Goldovsky in direction of, New Eng. Opera Co.; operatic debut as condr. with, Opera Group of Boston, 1957, Carnegie Hall debut with, Am. Symphony Orch., 1974; condr. and/or dir. maj. opera cos. in U.S., including, N.Y. Met. Opera, Dallas Civic Opera, Houston Grand Opera, N.Y.C. Opera; condr. with maj. orchs. including, Indpls. Symphony, Milw. Symphony, Am. Symphony, N.Y. Philharmonic; condr. at, Ravinia Festival, 1976 (Recipient Rogers and Hammerstein award.); operatic directorial debut with Rake's Progress, Opera Workshop, 1953. Office: care Opera Co Boston 539 Washington St Boston MA 02111 *

CALDWELL, WARREN FREDERICK, investment company executive; b. Braddock, Pa., Nov. 1, 1928; s. Frederick Betts and Ina Maude (South) C.; m. Emma Jewel Wilhite, Sept. 30, 1960; children: Warren Dare, Beth Elaine. B.B.A., North Tex. State U., 1952. Asst. controller Dresser Industries, Dallas, 1955-65; v.p.-control, treas. Lomas & Nettleton, Dallas, 1965—. Mem. Nat. Assn. Corp. Treasures. Presbyterian.

CALDWELL, WARREN W., educator; b. Davenport, Iowa, Dec. 28, 1925; (married); 1 child. B.A., Stanford, 1948, M.A., 1949; Ph.D., U. Wash., 1956. Curator anthropology and history Seattle Mus. History and Industry, 1941-52; asst. curator anthropology State Mus. Wash., Seattle, 1953-54; archaeologist Mo. Basin project Smithsonian Instn., 1956-63, chief, 1963-65; dir. River Basin Survey, 1965—; from asst. prof. anthropology to prof., chmn. dept. anthropology U. Nebr., Lincoln, 1960-78. Contbr. articles to profl. publs. Fellow AAAS, Am. Soc. Archaeology, Am. Anthropology Assn. Office: Dept Anthropology U Nebr Lincoln NE 68553

CALDWELL, WAYNE EUGENE, coast guard officer; b. Springfield, Ohio, July 13, 1923; s. William Arthur and Gladys Fern (Downing) C.; m. Mary Suzanne Jamison, Aug. 5, 1950; children: Mary Suzanne, James Arthur, Lisa Adair. B.S., U.S. Coast Guard Acad., 1948; student, U.S. Naval Postgrad. Sch., 1951-52, Nat. War Coll., 1971-72; M.S., George Washington U., 1972. Served as enlisted man U.S. Army, 1943-44, commd. ensign, 1948, advanced through grades to vice adm., 1976; served in sea duty, North Atlantic, 1948-51, instr. in math., asst. football coach, 1952-57, asst. comdt. cadets, 1965-69, asst. supt. acad., 1975-76, served in sea duty, Alaska, 1957-59, staff duty, Long Beach, Calif., 1959-63, sea duty, Pacific, 1963-65, officer S.E. Asia Market Time, 1969-71, chief officer personnel Coast Guard Hdqrs., Washington, 1972-74, dep. chief office marine environ. and systems Coast Guard Hdqrs., 1974-75, chief, office marine environ. and systems, 1979-82, comdr. Second Coast Guard Dist., St. Louis, 1976-79; comdr. Third Coast Guard Dist. Governor's Island, N.Y., 1982—. Elder United Presbyterian Ch.; bd. dirs. USO, N.Y.C., Seaman's Ch. Inst. Decorated Legion of Merit, Bronze Star, Meritorious Achievement medal (3), Coast Guard Achievement medal., Commandant's Commendation ribbon. Mem. Coast Guard Acad. Alumni Assn.; Mem. Coast Guard Acad. Athletic Hall of Fame; mem. Life Saving Benevolent Assn. N.Y. (bd. dirs.). Home: Quarters One Governors Island NY 10004 Office: COMLANT AREA CCGO Three Governors Island NY 10004

CALDWELL, WILEY NORTH, manufacturing company executive; b. Los Angeles, Apr. 24, 1927; s. Wiley North and Jean (Clarke) C.; m. Joanne Humphrey, Mar. 25, 1950; children: David, Wendy, Charles, Thomas. B.S.M.E., Stanford U., 1950; M.B.A., Harvard U., 1952. Mgr. prodn. control Waste King Corp., Los Angeles, 1952-54; v.p., co-founder Poroloy Equipment, Inc. (became part of Bendix Co. 1957), Van Nuys, Calif., 1954-58, dir. sales and mktg. Bendix Filter div., 1958-60; v.p. Jamieson Labs., Inc., Van Nuys, Calif., 1960-61; v.p. mktg., exec. v.p. McGraw Labs., Am. Hosp. Supply Corp., Los Angeles, Chgo., 1961-69; v.p. internat. McGaw Labs., Am. Hosp. Supply Corp., Los Angeles, Chgo., 1969-72, pres. Midwest Dental div., 1972-77; v.p. ops. distbn. group W.W. Grainger, Inc., Skokie, Ill., 1977-78, pres. distbn. group, 1978-81, exec. v.p., 1981—; dir., trustee Employees Profit-Sharing Trust, 1977—, Group Benefit Trust, 1981—; dir. Am. Sterilizer Co., Erie, Pa. Bd. dirs., vice chmn. Presbyn Home, Evanston, Ill. Served with USN, 1945-46. Club: Indian Hill (Winnetka, Ill.). Home: 125 Woodstock Ave Kenilworth IL 60043 Office: WW Grainger Co 5500 W Howard St Skokie IL 60077

CALDWELL, WILL M., automobile company executive; b. Detroit, Dec. 9, 1925; s. Manly Lee and Marjorie Fern (Meadows) C.; m. Jeanne Boren, Sept. 16, 1950; children: Elizabeth (Mrs. Michael Charles Hatz), Sarah (Mrs. Warren Wilson Stickney), Martha (Mrs. David Michael Muñoz). B.A., U. Mich., 1948, M.B.A., 1949. Credit analyst Chase Manhattan Bank, N.Y.C., 1949-50; mgr. budget analysis Ford Motor Co., Dearborn, Mich., 1952-62, controller Lincoln Mercury div., 1962-66, corp. asst. controller, 1967-68; v.p. fin. Ford of Europe, 1968-72, controller internat. automotive ops., 1973-77, v.p. corp. strategy and analysis, 1977-79, exec. v.p., chief fin. officer, dir., 1979—. Served to ensign USNR, 1943-46; lt., 1950-52; PTO, MTO. Mem. Beta Theta Pi. Baptist. Clubs: Birmingham Athletic, Detroit. Office: The American Rd Dearborn MI 48121

CALDWELL, WILLIAM ANTHONY, editor; b. Butler, Pa., Dec. 5, 1906; s. William Arthur and Johanna Marie (DeLeuw) C.; m. Dorothy C. Alexander, Oct. 22, 1938; children—Toni (Mrs. Daniel Cohen), Alix (Mrs. Thomas McArdle), William Alexander. Litt.D., Rutgers U., 1967; L.H.D., William Paterson Coll., 1972; Litt.D., Fairleigh Dickinson U., 1973. Reporter, editor The Record (formerly Bergen Evening Record), Hackensack, N.J., 1926-72; editorial page columnist Vineyard Gazette, Edgartown, Mass., 1972—. Author: In the Record, 1971; Editor: How to Save Urban America, 1972. Mem. lay judicial com. Bergen County Med. Soc., 1962-72; Pres. Bergen County unit Am. Cancer Soc., 1950-64, pres. N.J. div., 1962-64; chmn. bd. trustees William Paterson Coll. of N.J., 1967-70. Recipient Bronze medal Am. Cancer Soc., 1961, medal for editorial writing Soc. Silurians, 1964, Pulitzer prize for commentary, 1971. Republican. Presbyn. Home: Edgartown Bay Rd Edgartown Box 701 Martha's Vineyard MA 02539 Office: Vineyard Gazette Edgartown MA 02539 *"What do you want your boys to be when they grow up?" an elderly cousin asked my father, and in the next room I could hear his rocking chair creaking. "Decent," he said, and the small boy in the kitchen went back to his reading. I didn't know what the word meant then. I don't know now. Like the Constitution, it is genially agreeable to whatever meaning the time and the exigency require of it. I am obliged to think that as a standard of conduct it is, like the Constitution, sufficient.*

CALDWELL, WILLIAM EDWARD, JR., utility exec.; b. N.Y.C., Mar. 2, 1922; s. William Edward and Hortense Fontain (Storer) C.; m. Alice Wielich, Apr. 15, 1944; children—Ann, Jean, Kim. M.E., Stevens Inst. Tech., Hoboken, N.J., 1943. With Consol. Edison Co., N.Y.C., 1946—, v.p. power supply, 1971-73, sr. v.p. central ops., 1973-75; sr. v.p., chmn. exec. com. PWR Steam Generator Owners Group, 1975—. Served with USNR, 1943-46. Mem. ASME.

CALDWELL, WILLIAM GLEN ELLIOT, geologist; b. Millport, Scotland, July 25, 1932; s. William Harper and Catherine Glen (Elliot) C.; m. Beatrice Ruth North, Aug. 1, 1961; children—Ian Robert, Catherine Jane, Nancy Ileane. B.Sc. in Geology with 1st class honours (Keil Sch. scholar 1947-50), U. Glasgow, 1954, Ph.D.; dept. sci. and indsl. research scholar 1954-56, 1957. Asst. lectr. U. Glasgow, 1956-57; mem. faculty U. Sask., Saskatoon, Can., 1957—, prof. geol. scis., 1970—, head dept., 1971—, dir. div. life scis., 1972-73; cons. to industry, 1958-72, 83—; vis. prof. U. Glasgow, 1968, 79-80, U. London, 1968; chmn. Am. Commn. Stratigraphic Nomenclature, 1976-77; chmn. earth scis. grants selection com. Nat. Research Council Can., 1976-77, adv. bd. sci. publs., 1980—; chmn. sci. publs. grants selection com. Natural Sci. and Engring. Research Council, 1980-81; mem. Sci. Council of Sask., 1981—. Co-author: Cretaceous Rock and their Foraminifera in Manitoba Esceraphment, 1981; editor: Cretaceous System in Western Interior of North America, 1975; assoc. editor: Can. Jour. Earth Scis, 1976-82; editor Can. Jour. Earth Scis., 1982—; assoc. editor: Bull. Can. Petroleum Geology, 1973-81; asso. editor: Geosci. Can, 1974-75; contbr. articles to profl. jours. Fellow Royal Soc. Can., Geol. Soc. London, Geol. Assn. Can. (pres. 1980-81), Geol. Soc. Am.; mem. Palaeontol. Soc., Can. Geosci. Council, Assn. Profl. Engrs. Sask. (bd. examiners 1972—), Geologists Assn., Palaeontol. Assn., Geol. Soc. Glasgow, Can. Soc. Petroleum Geologists, Sask. Geol. Soc., Assn. Earth Sci. Editors. Home: 21 Simpson Crescent Saskatoon SK S7H 3C5 Canada Office: Dept Geol Scis Univ Sask Saskatoon SK S7N 0W0 Canada

CALDWELL, WILLIAM MACKAY, III, furniture co. exec.; b. Los Angeles, Apr. 6, 1922; s. William Mackay II and Edith Ann (Richards) C.; m. Mary Louise Edwards, Jan. 16, 1946; children: William Mackay IV, Craig Edwards, Candace Louise. B.S., U. So. Calif., 1943; M.B.A., Harvard U., 1948. Sec.-treas., dir. Drewry Photocolor Corp., 1957-60, Adcolor Photo Corp., 1957-60; treas., dir. Drewry Bennetts Corp., 1959-60; v.p., chief financial officer Am. Cement Corp., 1960-67, sr. v.p. corp., pres. cement and concrete group, 1967-69; chmn. bd., pres., chief exec. officer Van Vorst Industries, 1969-83; pres. Elgea I, Inc., 1969—, The Englander Co., 1979-83; pres., chief exec. officer Van Vorst Corp., Washington, 1969-77; chmn. bd. Hawaiian Cement Corp., 1967-69; chmn. bd., pres. So. Cross Industries, Inc., 1975-84, U.S. Bedding Co., 1979-83, St. Croix Mfg. Co., 1979-83; pres., dir. Am. Cement Internat. Corp., 1967-69. Bd. dirs. Am. Cement Found., 1966-68. Served as lt. USNR, 1943-46. Mem. Newcomen Soc., Commerce Assos. (dir.), Friends Huntington Library, Internat. Platform Assn., U. So. Calif. Assn., Calif. Mus. Sci. and Industry, Kappa Alpha, Alpha Delta Sigma, Alpha Pi Omega. Presbyn. Clubs: Harvard Business Sch. of So. Calif. (dir. 1960-63); Town Hall, California, Los Angeles Country (Los Angeles); Trojan, Annadale Golf; Marrakesh Golf, Eldorado Country (Palm Springs, Calif.). Office: PO Box 726 Pasadena CA 91102

CALEGARI, MARIA, ballerina; b. N.Y.C., Mar. 30, 1957; d. Richard A. and Marion (Gentile) C. Student, DuPons Dance Sch., Queens., 5 yrs., Ballet Acad., Queens, 6 yrs., Sch. Am. Ballet, 3 yrs. Mem. corps de ballet N.Y.C. Ballet, 1974-82, soloist, 1982-83, prin., 1983—. Office: New York City Ballet 1860 Broadway New York NY 10023

CALENOFF, LEONID, radiologist; b. Vienna, Austria, Aug. 24, 1923; came to U.S., 1957, naturalized, 1962; s. Albert and Anna (Prover) C.; m. Miriam Arnon, Oct. 30, 1955; children—Jean, Deborah. M.D., U. Paris, 1955. Diplomate: Am. Bd. Radiology. Intern Jewish Hosp., Cin., 1958; resident in radiology U. Ill. Med. Center, Chgo., 1959-61; asst. radiologist Ill. Research and Ednl. Hosp., Chgo., 1961-64; chief radiology Chgo. State Hosp., 1963-68; dir. radiology Sheridan Gen. Hosp., Chgo., 1964-68; attending radiologist West Side VA Hosp., Chgo., 1963-68, Rehab. Inst. Chgo., 1964—, chief diagnostic radiology, 1974—; attending radiologist Northwestern Meml. Hosp., Chgo., 1968—, chief outpatient diagnostic radiology, 1979—; chief diagnostic radiology Passavant Pavillion of Northwestern Meml. Hosp., 1972-79; asst. prof. radiology Northwestern U. Med. Sch., 1970-73, asso. prof., 1973-78, prof., 1978—. Author articles in field, chpts. in books.; Editor: Radiology of Spinal Cord Injury, 1981. Fellow Am. Coll. Radiology, Am. Coll. Chest Physicians; mem. Radiol. Soc. N.Am., Am. Roentgen Ray Soc., AMA, Soc. Univ. Radiologists, Soc. Nuclear Medicine, Am. Congress Rehab. Medicine. Home: 1515 Astor St Chicago IL 60610 Office: 250 E Superior St Chicago IL 60611

CALFEE, JOHN BEVERLY, lawyer; b. Cleve., May 2, 1913; s. Robert M. and Alwine (Haas) C.; m. Nancy Leighton, Feb. 8, 1944; children—John Beverly, David L., Peter H., Mark E. Grad., Hotchkiss Sch., 1931; B.A., Yale, 1935; LL.B., Western Res. U., 1938. Bar: Ohio bar 1938. Since practiced in, Cleve.; sr. ptnr. firm Calfee, Halter and Griswold.; Dir. Ajax Mfg. Co., Morrison Products Inc. Dir. civil def., Cleve., 1951; chmn. Cuyohoga County Republican Fin. Com., 1978. Served to maj. AUS, 1942-46. Mem. ABA, Ohio, Cleve. bar assns., Ohio Bar Found., Soc. of Benchers. Presbyterian. Clubs: Masons, Shriners, Rotary; University (N.Y.C.); Chevy Chase (Washington); Mayfield, Union, Pepper Pike (Cleve.). Home: 4892 Clubside Dr Lyndhurst OH 44124 Office: 1800 Central Nat Bank Bldg Cleveland OH 44114 *A person has many guiding principles, but if I am limited to the main one, it would be the motto of Hawken School, my first preparatory institution in Cleveland—"Fair Play." This is a term which for me has become translated into a game goal to be ambitiously sought and achieved by hard work. The effort applied must be honest in thought as well as deed and in achieving it a firm purpose is the motivating concept, tempered by respect for the other person's viewpoint.*

CALFEE, ROBERT CHILTON, educational researcher, psychologist; b. Lexington, Ky., Jan. 26, 1933; s. Robert Klair and Nancy Bernice (Stipp) C.; m. Kathryn Ann McOsker, Dec. 26, 1975; children: Adele, LeeAnn, Janet, Jeffrey, Robert, Elise. B.A., UCLA, 1959, M.A., 1960, Ph.D., 1963. Asst. prof. psychology U. Wis., 1964-66, asso. prof., 1966-69; asso. prof. edn. Stanford U., 1969-71, prof., 1971—; asso. dean research and devel., dir. Center for Ednl. Research, 1976-80; cons and speaker in field. Author: Human Experimental Psychology, 1975, Cognitive Psychology and Educational Practice, 1982; editor: (with P.A. Drum) Teaching Reading In Compensatory Classes, 1979, Jour. Ednl. Psychology, 1984—. Guggenheim Meml. fellow, 1972; fellow Center for Advanced Study in Behavioral Scis., 1981-82. Mem. AAAS, Am. Psychol. Assn., Am. Ednl. Research Assn., Internat. Reading Assn., Nat. Conf. Research in English, Psychonomic Soc., Soc. Research in Child Devel., Nat. Council Tchrs. English, Sigma Xi. Home: 995 Wing Pl Stanford CA 94305 Office: Sch Edn Stanford U Stanford CA 94305

CALFEE, WILLIAM HOWARD, sculptor, painter; b. Washington, Feb. 7, 1909; s. Lee Price and Carrie L. (Whitehead) C.; children—Adriana, Richard, Judy, Helme, William, Alan Edward. Studied sculpture, Beaux Arts, Paris, also Cranbrook Acad., Mich.; L.H.D. (hon.), Am. U., 1979. Instr. spl. skills div. Resettlement Adminstrn., Cumberland Homesteads, Tenn., 1935; executed murals, sculptures, fine arts sect. procurement div. U.S. Treasury Dept., 1936-41; psychotherapy worker St. Elizabeth's Hosp., Washington, 1942-43; Tchr. mural technique Centre d'Art, Port au Prince, Haiti, 1949; guest asso. prof. painting U. Calif. at Berkeley, 1951; chmn. dept. painting and sculpture Am. U., Washington, until 1954, now adj. prof. dept. art. Works exhibited most museums, one-man show painting, Wehye Gallery, N.Y.C., sculpture, Graham Gallery, Balt. Mus., Corcoran Gallery, Philbrook Art Mus., Tulsa; rep. in, Root Collection, Phillips Gallery, Honolulu Acad., Corcoran Gallery, Nat. Collection Fine Arts, retrospective exhbn., Nat. Acad. Scis., 1978; initiated: Watkins Meml. Collection, Watkins Gallery; executed altar, font, candle sticks, St. Augustine's Chapel, Washington, District Columbia, 1968, Rockville (Md.) Civic Center sculpture, 1978. Home: 7206 45th St Chevy Chase MD 20815 *Most of the time I look upon my life as a great privilege.*

CALFEE, WILLIAM LEWIS, lawyer; b. Cleveland Heights, Ohio, July 12, 1917; s. Robert Martin and Alwine (Haas) C.; m. Eleanor Elizabeth Bliss, Dec. 6, 1941; children: William R., Bruce K., Cynthia B. B.A., Harvard Coll., 1939; LL.D., Yale U., 1946. Bar: Ohio 1946. Assoc. Baker & Hostetler, Cleve., 1946-56, ptnr., 1957—. Bd. dirs. Growth Assn. Greater Cleve., 1979—; trustee Greater Cleve. United Appeal; pres. Health Fund Greater Cleve. Served to lt. col. M.I. U.S. Army, 1941-45. Decorated Legion of Merit, Order of Brit. Empire. Mem. Bar Asn. Greater Cleve. (truste, pres. 1979—), Nat. Conf. Bar Pres. (exec. council 1982—), Ohio C. of C. (dir. 1983). Republican. Episcopalian. Clubs: Mayfield Country (pres.), Union, Pepper Pike; Fiddlesticks (Ft. Myers, Fla.). Office: Baker & Hostetler 3200 National City Center Cleveland OH 44114 Home: 21200 Claythorne Rd Shaker Heights OH 44122

CALGAARD, RONALD KEITH, university president; b. Joice, Iowa, July 29, 1937; s. Palmer O. Calgard and Orrie (Beatrice) Nessa-Calgaard; m. Gene Rae Flom, June 14, 1959; children: Lisa Rae, Kent David. B.A., Luther Coll., 1959; M.A., U. Iowa, 1961, Ph.D. in Econs., 1963. Instr. in econs. U. Iowa, 1961-63; asst. prof. econs. U. Kans., Lawrence, 1963-65, assoc. prof., 1967-72, prof., 1972-79, assoc. vice chancellor, 1974-75, vice chancellor acad. affairs, 1975-79; postdoctoral fellow in Latin Am. studies Social Sci. Research Council-Am. Council Learned Socs., Santiago, Chile, 1965-67; pres. Trinity U., San Antonio, 1979—; cons. econs.; dir. Alamo Savs. & Loan Assn. Author: Economic Planning in Underdeveloped Countries, 1963. Bd. dirs. S.W. Research Inst., San Antonio, Learning About Learning Found., San Antonio, United San Antonio; adv. trustee San Antonio Art Inst.; mem. Nexus com. Presbyn. Coll. Union-United Presbyterian Ch. U.S. A. Woodrow Wilson fellow, 1959-60. Mem. Am. Econs. Assn., Midwest Econs. Assn., Western Econs. Assn., Midwest Assn. Latin Am. Studies, AAUP. Lodge: Rotary. Office: 715 Stadium Dr San Antonio TX 78284

CALHOON, JESSE MAYO, labor union ofcl.; b. Belhaven, N.C., Apr. 4, 1923; s. Ephraim Franklin and Nancy (Mayo) C.; m. Jean Nolan, Jan. 9, 1965; children—Richard Earl, Tamara Kay, Ronald Lee, Curtis Sean. Grad., U.S. Merchant Marine Officer Candidate Sch., 1942-43. Service with U.S. Merchant Marine, 1940-55; pres. Marine Engrs. Beneficial Assn., AFL-CIO, 1955—; also chmn. trustee pension and welfare fund; mem. gen. bd., also maritime com. AFL CIO. Office: 17 Battery Pl New York NY 10004 *

CALHOUN, CALVIN LEE, physician; b. Atlanta, Jan. 7, 1927; s. Robert and Mary L. (Huff) C.; m. Evelyn Greene, Feb. 14, 1948; 1 son, Calvin L. B.S., Morehouse Coll., 1948; M.S., Atlanta U., 1950; M.D., Meharry Med. Coll., 1960. Instr. biology Morehouse Coll., 1950-51; intern G.W. Hubbard Hosp., Nashville, 1960-61, resident in medicine, 1961-62; resident in neurology U. Minn. Med. Center, Mpls., 1962-65, fellow in neurology, 1965-66; instr. anatomy Meharry Med. Coll., Nashville, 1951-57, asst. prof. anatomy, 1961-62, asso. prof., 1966-73, prof. medicine, 1973—; dir. div. neurology, 1966—, acting chmn. dept. anatomy, 1968-71, chmn., 1971-81; chief neurology service Meharry Med. Coll.-Hubbard Hosp., 1968, dir. neurodiagnostic lab., 1966; vis. prof. U. W.I., 1975; mem. adv. bd. Epilepsy Found. Am., Davidson County chpt. ARC. Contbr. chpts. to books, articles to profl. jours. Chmn. bd. deacons 1st Baptist Capitol Hill Ch.; mem. life membership com. NAACP; mem. adv. council Pro Musica. Served with U.S. Army, 1945. Fellow Stroke Council of Am. Heart Assn.; mem. Am. Acad. Neurology, Nat. Med. Assn., AAAS, Am. Assn. Anatomists, R.F. Boyd Med. Soc., Tenn. Med. Assn., Tenn. Anatomical Bd., Alpha Omega Alpha, Kappa Alpha Psi. Clubs: Nashville, Sportman's, Apollo. Home: 4217 Kings Ct Nashville TN 37218 Office: 1005 18th Ave N Nashville TN 37208

CALHOUN, DANIEL FAIRCHILD, educator; b. Fairfield, Conn., June 21, 1929; s. Philo Clarke and Doris Antoinette (Wheeler) C.; m. Janet Montgomery McGovern, July 12, 1952; children—Carol Victoria, Philo Clark, Virginia Stuart Blair. Grad., Phillips Exter Acad., 1946; B.A., Williams Coll., 1950; M.A., U. Chgo., 1951, Ph.D., 1959. Instr. Coll. Wooster, O., 1956—, instr. history, 1956-60, asst. prof., 1960-63, asso. prof., 1963-66, prof., 1966—, chmn. dept. history, 1969-72. Author: The United Front: The TUC and the Russians, 1923-1928, 1976. Mem. Am. Hist. Assn., Ohio Acad. History, Phi Beta Kappa. Democrat. Episcopalian. Home: 1150 N Bever St Wooster OH 44691 *I go with Tolstoy: to seek "success" is to guarantee failure. To pursue power is to chase rainbows. What is meaningful, fulfilling and permanent in life is of the spirit, and isn't recorded in Who's Who.*

CALHOUN, DONALD EUGENE, JR., lawyer; b. Columbus, Ohio, May 15, 1926; s. Donald E. and Esther (Cope) C.; m. Shirley Claggett, Aug. 28, 1948; children: Catherine C., Donald Eugene III, Elizabeth C. B.A. in Polit. Sci., Ohio State U., 1949, J.D., 1951. Bar: Ohio 1951. Since practiced in Columbus; partner Folkerth, Calhoun, Webster, Maurer & O'Brien, 1968-82, Guren, Merritt, Feibel, Sogg & Cohen, 1982—; gen. counsel Ohio Conf. United Ch. of Christ, 1964—. Chmn. City-wide Citizens Com. for Neighborhood Seminars on Sch. Program and Finance, 1963; mem. Columbus Bd. Edn., 1963-71, pres., 1966-70. Served with USNR, 1944-46. Mem. ABA, Ohio Bar Assn., Columbus Bar Assn. (pres. 1967-68, Community Service award, pres. 1972), Nat. Conf. Bar Pres., Am. Arbitration Assn., Columbus Jaycees (life). Congregationalist. Club: Masons. Home: 216 W Beechwold Blvd Columbus OH 43214 Office: 88 E Broad St Suite 900 Columbus OH 43215

CALHOUN, FRANK WAYNE, lawyer, former state legislator; b. Houston, Apr. 15, 1933; s. Wilmer Cecil and Ruby Edith (Willis) C.; (div.)children: Michael, David; m. Susan Foscue Ripley, June 24, 1978. B.A., Tex. Tech U., 1956; J.D., U. Tex., 1959. Bar: Tex. 1959, U.S. Supreme Ct. 1965. Partner firm Byrd, Shaw, Weeks & Calhoun, Abilene, 1959-73, Liddell, Sapp, Zivley, Brown & LaBoon, Houston, 1974—; mem. Tex. Ho. of Reps., 1966-75. Contbg.: editor Tex. Lawyers Weekly Letter, 1964. Mem. exec. com. Tex. Film Commn., 1979—; past bd. dirs. Abilene YMCA; trustee, fellow Tex. Tech Law Sch. Found.; trustee Colo. Outward Bound Sch.; del. Tex. Constl. Conv., 1974. Served with U.S. Navy, 1951-53. Named Abilene's Outstanding Young Man Jaycees, 1968; recipient Disting. Service award State Bar Tex., 1969, 71, 73. Mem. Am. Bar Assn., Tex. Bar Assn., Am. Judicature Soc., Tex. Tech U. Ex-Students Assn. (past pres.), Tex. Archeol. Soc., Nat. Audubon Soc., Sierra Club, Nat. Trust for Hist. Preservation, Houston Fine Arts Mus., Sigma Alpha Epsilon, Alpha Kappa Psi. Democrat. Methodist. Clubs: Houston, Austin, Plaza, Inns of Court. Lodge: Rotary. Home: 12917 Trail Hollow Houston TX 77079 Office: 3400 Tex Commerce Tower Houston TX 77002

CALHOUN, HAROLD, architect; b. Mineral Springs, Ark., Oct. 11, 1906; s. Albert Sidney and Willie (Reeder) C.; m. Annie Louise Robertson, Dec. 3, 1932; 1 dau., Nancy Ann. B.A., Rice U., 1932. Freelance delineator and archtl. draftsman, 1925-29; organized firm Wirtz & Calhoun (architects), 1932; with Robert & Co. (architects and engrs. on design of Corpus Christi Naval Air Center), Corpus Christi, Tex., 1940-43; vis. critic, grad. students archtl. dept. Rice U., 1946; with Wirtz, Calhoun, Tungate & Jackson, Houston, 1947-66, Calhoun, Tungate & Jackson, 1966-75, Calhoun, Tungate, Jackson & Dill, 1975—. Served to lt. (s.g.) USNR, 1943-46. Recipient first hon. mention House Beautiful competition, 1946; 3d prize Georgia Builds competition, 1947; certificate of award Houston chpt. A.I.A., 1947; hon. mention, 1953; award of merit Tex. Soc. Architects, 1954; architecture of merit award, 1960. Fellow Am. Inst. Architects; mem. Texas Society of Architects (past president), Houston Engineering and Scientific Soc., La Sociedad de Arquitectos Mexicanos (hon.). Baptist (deacon). Clubs: Mason, Lion., Champions Golf. Home: 1 Concord Circle Houston TX 77024 Office: 7011 Southwest Freeway Suite 600 Houston TX 77074

CALHOUN, JACK ROWLAND, utility exec.; b. Poplar, N.C., Oct. 21, 1919; s. Glenn David and Pearl Wanda C.; m. Jacqueline Capps, Sept. 23, 1944; children—Carol, Patrick, Janice, Susan. B.S.E.E., Tenn. Technol. U., 1949; postgrad., Oak Ridge Sch. Reactor Tech., 1960. With TVA, 1954-80; asst. project mgr. Exptl. Gas-Cooled Reactor, Oak Ridge, 1960-64, asst. chief maintenance br., Chattanooga, 1964-68; supt. Browns Ferry Nuclear Plant, Decatur, Ala., 1968-71, chief nuclear generation br., Chattanooga, 1971-77, dir. nuclear div., 1977-80; sr. v.p. nuclear dept. Pa. Power & Light Co., Allentown, 1980—; cons. on exptl. breeder reactor program Argonne Asso. Univs., 1978-80. Served with USN, 1938-45. Recipient Engr. of Yr. award Chattanooga Engrs. Club, 1980. Mem. Am. Nuclear Soc. (nat. chmn. reactor ops. div. 1977). Methodist. Office: 2 N 9th St Allentown PA 18101

CALHOUN, JERRY L., government executive; b. Ludlow, Miss., Sept. 9, 1943; s. Meshack and Emma (Peterson) C.; m. Robin C. Calhoun, Apr. 24, 1963; children: Shawn P., Hanni E. B.A., Seattle U., 1967; M.A., U. Wash., Seattle, 1975. Mgr. personnel mgmt. The Boeing Co., Seattle, 1964-68, mgr. indsl. relations, 1973-81; dir. nat. manpower The Urban League, Phoenix, 1969-73; dep. asst. Sec. Def. U.S. Dept. Def., Washington, 1981—; adj. lectr. U. Wash., 1975-76; mem. Nat. Congl. Com., Washington, 1981—. Contbr. articles in field. Bd. dirs. Maricopa County Legal Aid Soc., Phoenix, 1969, SOIC, Phoenix, 1969. Mem. Nat. Acad. Pub. Adminstrn., Nat. Soc. for Personnel Adminstrn., Am. Polit. Sci. Assn., Am. Soc. Pub. Adminstrn. Republican. Office: Dept Def The Pentagon Washington DC 20301

CALHOUN, JOSE MACHADO, banker; b. Springfield, Mass., Oct. 13, 1928; s. John Clark and Salome Cecilia (Machado) C.; m. Sallie Newton, Aug. 19, 1950; children: Jose Machado, Cecilia Mary, Nancy Newton. Grad., Hotchkiss Sch., 1946; B.A., Yale, 1950; J.D., Harvard, 1953. Bar: Conn. bar 1953. Partner firm Shipman & Goodwin, Hartford, Conn., 1953-76; exec. v.p. Conn. Bank & Trust Co., Hartford, 1977—; sec. Torin Corp., Torrington, Conn., 1966-76, Waterbury Pressed Metal Co., Conn., 1972-76; dir. Coltsfoot Valley Corp., Sherburne Corp., WPM, Inc.; mem. Hartford asso. bd. Conn. Bank & Trust Co., 1966-76; dir. Dexter Corp., 1971-77. Bd. dirs. Hartford Hosp., 1976—, chmn. exec. com., 1981—; bd. dirs. Child and Family Service of Conn., Inc., 1970-75, Inst. Living, 1972-80; regent U. Hartford, 1961-67, 71-80, 82—, vice chmn., 1972-75, chmn., 1975-80; trustee Hartford Art Sch., 1957-75, pres., 1973-75; bd. corporators Hartford Hosp., Mt. Sinai Hosp., St. Francis Hosp., Inst. Living, Hartford Art Sch. Mem. Am., Conn., Hartford County bar assns., Newcomen Soc. Republican. Conglist. Clubs: Hartford, Twilight, Hartford Golf, Hartford Tennis. Office: 1 Constitution Plaza Hartford CT 06115

CALHOUN, JOSEPH DUKES, lawyer; b. Norwood, Pa., June 25, 1907; s. Joseph Hoe and Mavy Agnes (Dukes) C.; m. Mary Hooton Roberts, Sept. 23, 1939. B.A. with honors, Swarthmore Coll., 1929; B.L., U. Pa., 1932. Bar: Pa., U.S. Supreme Ct. Practice law, Norwood, Pa., asst. dist. atty., Delaware County, 1940-43. Past chmn. Delaware County Welfare Council, Delaware County Housing Authority; asst. gen. counsel Econ. Stablzn. Agy., 1950-51. Fellow Am. Bar Found.; mem. ABA (nat. chmn. jr. bar sect. 1942-43, sec. 1957-63, mem. fellows, life mem. ho. of dels.), Delaware County Bar Assn. (pres. 1963). Home: 210 Mohawk Ave Norwood PA 19074 Office: Carriage House 210 Mohawk Ave Norwood PA 19074

CALHOUN, NOAH ROBERT, oral maxillofacial surgeon, educator; b. Clarendon, Ark., Mar. 23, 1921; s. Noah and Della (Sherman) C.; m. Cecelia Christopher, Oct. 19, 1950; children: Stephen Marc, Cecelia Noel. D.D.S., Dental Sch., Howard U., 1948; M.Dental Sci., Tufts Med. and Dental Sch., 1955. Oral surgeon VA Hosp., Tuskegee, Ala., 1950-52, Kessler AFB, Biloxi, Miss., 1952-53; chief dental service VA Hosp., Tuskegee, Ala., 1955-57, oral surgeon, asst. chief dental surgeon, Washington, 1964-74; chief dental service, oral surgeon VA Med. Center, Washington, 1974—; prof. oral surgery Dental Sch., Howard U., Washington, 1966—, Georgetown U., 1975—; Dir. Tuskegee (Ala.) Red Cross, 1962-64; chmn. Nat. Concerned VA Dentists, 1975. Contbr. articles to profl. jours. Mem. ADA, Am. Soc. Oral and Maxillofacial Surgeons (Audio Visual award 1978), Internat. Coll. Dentistry, Am. Coll. Dentistry, Omicron Kappa Upsilon (chpt. pres. 1974). Roman Catholic. Office: Dental Coll Howard U Washington DC 20059

CALHOUN, RORY, actor, director, producer, writer; b. Calif., Aug. 8. V.p. Ariz. Valley Devel. Corp.; cattle rancher. Appeared in: motion pictures Something for the Boys, 1944, Sunday Dinner for a Soldier, 1944, The Great John L, 1945, Where Do We Go From Here, 1945, Nob Hill, 1945, That Hagen Girl, 1947, Red House, 1947, Massacre River, 1948, Adventure Island, 1948, Return of the Frontiersman, 1949, Sand, 1949, Ticket to Tomahawk, 1950, Rogue River, 1950, Country Fair, 1950, Miraculous Journey, 1951, I'd Climb the Highest Mountain, 1951, Meet Me After the Show, 1951, With A Song in My Heart, 1952, Way of A Gaucho, 1952, The Silver Whip, 1953, Powder River, 1953, Yellow Tomahawk, 1953, How To Marry A Millionaire, 1953, River Of No Return, 1954, Dawn At Socorro, 1954, Four Guns To The Border, 1954, A Bullet Is Waiting, 1954, Aint Mis-Behavin, 1955, The Looters, 1955, Treasure of Pancho Villa, 1955, Raw Edge, 1956, The Spoilers, 1956, Red Sundown, 1956, Flight to Hong Kong, 1956, Utah Blaine, 1957, Domino Kid, 1957, Hired Gun, 1957, The Big Caper, 1957, Ride Out For Revenge, 1957, Apache Territory, 1958, The Saga of Hemp Brown, 1958, Thunder Over Carolina, 1960, The Colossus of Rhodes, 1960, Treasure of Monte Cristo, 1960, Adventures of Marco Polo, 1962, Gun Hawk, 1963, Young and the Brave, 1963, Face in the Rain, 1963, Call Me Bwana, 1963, Black Spurs, 1965, Young Fury, 1965, Finger on The Trigger, 1965, Our Man in Bagdad, 1965, Lady of the Nile, 1966, Apache Uprising, 1966, Dayton's Devils, 1969, Low Price of Fame, 1971, Night of the Lepus, 1973, Koo Lau, 1973, Operation Crosseagles, 1975, Won Ton Ton, 1976, Father Keno Story, 1976, Love and The Midnight Auto Supply, 1976, Mule Feathers, 1977, Now I Lay Me Down to Sleep, 1977, Bitter Heritage, 1978, Revenge of Bigfoot, 1978, Just Not the Same Without You, 1978, Motel Hell, 1982, Angel, 1984; TV shows The Road Ahead, 1950, Ford Theatre, 1954, Day Is Done, 1955, Bet The Wild Queen, 1955, Chrysler Theatre, 1955, Zane Gray Theatre, 1956, Suspicion, 1957, The Texan pilot, 1957; series, 1957-60, U.S. Camera, 1957, Killer Instinct, 1958, Desilu Playhouse, 4 shows, 1958-59, Lands End, 1959, Death Valley Days, 1966, 68; also guest star: TV series, talk shows Death Valley Days; producer, dir., writer: The Texan, 1957-60; star TV series: Capitol, 1982—; screenwriter: film Shotgun, 1955; dir.: films Dominio Kid, 1957, Hired Gun, 1957, Koo Lau, 1973; TV episodes Death Valley Days, 1966; play Belle Star, London, 1969-70; rec. artist; Author: The Man From Padera. Office: care The Light Co 113 N Robertson Blvd Los Angeles CA 90048 *

CALHOUN, WALTER BOWMAN, univ. ofcl.; b. Mt. Olive, Miss., May 19, 1917; s. William Sidney and Fannie (Holloway) C.; m. Eva Burnell Linton, Sept. 23, 1946; children—Eva Suzanne, Mai Fran. B.S., Miss. State U., 1938; M.B.A., La. State U., 1939. Mem. staff La. State U. and A. and M. Coll., 1940—, comptroller, 1958-62, v.p. charge finance, 1962-73, v.p. for employee relations, 1973—. Treas. La. State U. Found.; Mem. exec. bd. Istrouma Area council Boy Scouts Am. Served as aviator USNR, 1942-45. Mem. Am. Legion, Phi Kappa Phi, Beta Gamma Sigma, Beta Alpha Psi, Omicron Delta Kappa. Methodist. Home: 1348 Meadow Lee Dr Baton Rouge LA 70808

CALIFANO, JOSEPH ANTHONY, JR., former sec. HEW; b. Bklyn., May 15, 1931; s. Joseph Anthony and Katherine (Gill) C.; m. Hilary Paley Byers, 1983; children by previous marriage: Mark Gerard, Joseph Anthony III, Claudia Frances; stepchildren: Brooke A. Byers, John Frederick Byers. A.B., Holy Cross Coll., 1952; LL.B., Harvard U., 1955. Bar: N.Y 1955, U.S. Supreme Ct. 1966. With firm Dewey, Ballantine, Bushby, Palmer & Wood, N.Y.C., 1958-61; spl. asst. to gen. counsel Dept. Def., 1961-62; spl. asst. to sec. army, 1962-63; gen. counsel Dept. Army, 1963-64; spl. asst. to sec. and dep. sec. def., 1964-65, spl. asst. to Pres., 1965-69; mem. firm Arnold & Porter, Washington, 1969-71; partner firm Williams, Connolly & Califano, Washington, 1971-76; sec. HEW, 1977-79; partner firm Califano, Ross & Heineman, Washington, 1980-82, Dewey, Ballantine, Bushby, Palmer & Wood, 1983—; dir. Chrysler Corp., Am. Can Co., Automatic Data Processing, Inc; Gen. counsel Democratic Nat. Com., 1970-72. Author: The Student Revolution: A Global Confrontation, 1969, A Presidential Nation, 1975, (with Howard Simons) The Media and the Law, 1976, The Media and Business, 1978, Governing America: An Insiders Report from the White House and the Cabinet, 1981, The 1982 Report on Drug Abuse and Alcoholism, 1982. Trustee Mater Dei Sch., Urban Inst., NYU, Kaiser Family Found. Served to lt. USNR, 1955-58. Recipient Distinguished Civilian Service award Dept. Army, 1964; Man of Year award Justinian Soc. Lawyers, 1966; Distinguished Service medal Dept. Def., 1967; named One of Ten Outstanding Young Men of America, 1966. Mem. Am., Fed., D.C. bar assns., Am. Judicature Soc. Club: Federal City (dir.).

CALIGUIRI, RICHARD S., mayor Pitts.; b. Pitts., Oct. 20, 1931; m. Jeanne Conte; children—Greg, David. Grad., Pitts. Tech. Inst. Mem. City Council, Pitts., 1970-77, pres., 1977; mayor, Pitts., 1977-81. Served with USAF, 1950-54. Office: Office of Mayor City Hall 414 Grant St Pittsburgh PA 15219

CALINGAERT, MICHAEL, foreign service officer; b. Detroit, Sept. 17, 1933; s. George and Dorothy C.; m. Efrem Funghi, June 20, 1962; children: Alexander, Daniel, Nicholas. B.A., Swarthmore Coll., 1955; postgrad., U. Cologne, W. Ger., 1955-56, U. Calif., Berkeley, 1963-64. Commd. fgn. service officer Dept. State, 1956, intelligence research specialist, Washington, 1957-58; vice consul Am. counsulate gen., Mogadiscio, Italian Somaliland, 1959-61, econ. officer Am. consulate gen., Bremen, Ger., 1961-63; econ. officer Am. embassy, Colombo, Ceylon, 1964-68; chief food policy div. Dept. State, Washington, 1968-72; econ. counselor Am. embassy, Tokyo, 1972-75, econ./comml. minister, Rome, 1975-79; dep. asst. sec. for internat. resources and food policy Dept. State, 1979-83; econ. minister Am. Embassy, London, 1983—. Recipient Meritorious Honor award Dept. State, 1971, Superior Honor award, 1981. Mem. Am. Fgn. Service Assn. Office: Am Embassy London England

CALINGER, RONALD STEVE, historian, university dean, educator; b. Aliquippa, Pa., Apr. 6, 1942; s. Thomas H. and Mary (Blicha) C.; m. Betty Jeanne Mikulecky, Dec. 21, 1974; 1 son, John Michael. A.B. summa cum laude, Ohio U., 1963; M.A., U. Pitts., 1964; Ph.D., U. Chgo., 1971. Assoc. editor scis. A.N. Marquis Publ. Co., Chgo., 1966-68; mem. faculty Rensselaer Poly. Inst., Troy, N.Y., 1969—, assoc. prof. history, 1975—, chmn. depts. history and polit. sci., 1977-82, dean Undergrad. Coll., 1982—. Author: Gottfried Wilhelm Leibniz, 1976; editor: Classics of Mathematics, 1982; co-editor: Isis Guide, 1983—; contbr.: Dictionary Sci. Biography, 1971-74, Dictionary Am. Biography, 1977; articles to profl. jours. Mem. Am. Hist. Assn., AAAS, History of Sci. Soc., Soc. Social Studies Sci. (com. future meetings), N.Y. Acad. Scis., Am. Soc. 18th Century Studies. Roman Catholic. Home: 10 Crystal Ln Latham NY 12110 Office: Undergrad Coll Pittsburgh Bldg Rensselaer Poly Inst Troy NY 12181

CALIO, ANTHONY JOHN, scientist, govt. ofcl.; b. Phila., Oct. 27, 1929; s. Antonio and Mary Emma (Cappuccio) C.; m. Cheryll Kay Madison, Feb. 28, 1971. B.A., U. Pa., 1953, postgrad., 1953; postgrad., Carnegie Inst. Tech., 1959; Sc.D. (hon.), Washington U., St. Louis, 1974; postgrad. (Sloan fellow), Stanford U., 1974-75. With Westinghouse Electric Corp., Pitts., 1956-59; chief nuclear physics sect. Am. Machine & Foundry Co., Alexandria, Va., 1959-61; v.p., mgr. ops. Mt. Vernon Research Co., Alexandria, 1961-63; mem. electronic research task group Hdqrs. NASA, Washington, 1963-64, chief research engring., Boston, 1964-65, chief instrumentation and systems integration br., Washington, 1965-67, asst. dir. planetary exploration, 1967-68, dir. sci. and applications, Houston, 1969-75, dep. asso. adminstr., Washington, 1975-77, asso. adminstr., 1977—, acting dep. adminstr., 1981—. Served with U.S. Army, 1954-56. Recipient Group Achievement award (2) NASA, 1969, Exceptional Service medal, 1969, Apollo Achievement award, 1970, Exceptional Sci. Achievement medal, 1971, Lunar Sci. Team award, 1973, Distinguished Service medal, 1973, Exec. Performance award, 1976; presdl. rank of Disting. Exec., 1980. Fellow Am. Astron. Soc., AIAA (asso); mem. AAAS, Am. Geophys. Union, N.Y. Acad. Scis. Home: Nat'l Oceanic and Atmospheric Admn. 19th Between E and Constitution Ave NW Washington DC 20230 Office: Office of Asso Adminstr Space and Terrestiral Applications NASA Washington DC 20546

CALISHER, HORTENSE (MRS. CURTIS HARNACK), author; b. N.Y.C., Dec. 20, 1911; d. Joseph Henry and Hedvig (Lichtstern) C.; m. Curtis Harnack, Mar. 23, 1959; children by former marriage: Bennet Hughes, Peter Heffelfinger. A.B., Barnard Coll., 1932; Litt.D.

(hon.), Skidmore Coll., 1980. Adj. prof. English Barnard Coll., N.Y.C., 1956-57; vis. lectr. State U. Iowa, 1957, 59-60, Stanford U., 1958, Sarah Lawrence Coll., Bronxville, N.Y., 1962, 67; adj. prof. Columbia U., N.Y.C., 1968-70, CCNY, 1969; vis. prof. lit. SUNY, Purchase, 1971-72, Brandeis U., 1963-64, U. Pa., 1965; Regent's prof. U. Calif., 1976; vis. prof. Bennington Coll., 1978, Washington U., St. Louis, 1979; lectr., W. Ger., Yugoslavia, Rumania, Hungary, 1978. Author: short stories In the Absence of Angels, 1951, False Entry; novel Tale for the Mirror, 1961; novella and short stories Textures of Life, 1962; novel Extreme Magic, 1963; novella and short stories Journal from Ellipsia, 1964; novel The Railway Police and The Last Trolley Ride, 1965; novellas The New Yorkers, 1966; novel Queenie, 1969, Standard Dreaming, 1971, Herself, 1972; autobiog. work Eagle Eye, 1972; The Collected Stories of Hortense Calisher, 1975; novel On Keeping Women, 1977, Mysteries of Motion, 1984; Contbr.: short stories, articles, revs. to Am. Scholar; anthologies, others. Guggenheim fellow, 1952, 55; Dept. of State Am. Specialists's grantee to S.E. Asia, 1958; recipient Acad. of Arts and Letters award, 1967, Nat. Council Arts award, 1967. Mem. Am. Acad. and Inst. Arts and Letters. Office: care Candida Donadio 111 W 57th St New York NY 10019 *Going back over one's work, one can see from earliest times certain para-forms emerging. If one is crazy, these are idees fixes: if one is sane these are systemic views. A mind is not given but makes itself, out of whatever is at hand and sticking-tape—and is not a private possession but an offering... I had always had to write everything, no matter the subject, as if my life depended upon it. Of course—it does. (from HERSELF: An Autobiographical Work.)*

CALISTI, LOUIS J. P., dental educator, university administrator; b. Trenton, N.J., Dec. 16, 1925; s. Philip C.; m. Kathryn McEwen, Feb. 14; children: Scott Philip, Bruce McEwen, Robyn T. Student, Rutgers U., 1943-45; D.D.S. with honors, U. Pa., 1949; M.P.H., Harvard U., 1960, grad. Advanced Mgmt. Program, 1971. Pvt. practice dentistry, 1949-50, 52-56; instr. oral diagnosis U. Pa., 1956; dental dir. Brookline (Mass.) Health Dept., 1957-61; mem. faculty Tufts U. Sch. Dental Medicine, 1957-71, asso. prof., chmn. dept. social dentistry, 1961-63, dean, 1963-71, prof. social dentistry, 1967; pres. U. Maine, Portland and Gorham, 1971-72; v.p. Healthco Corp., Boston, 1972—, v.p. univ., govt. and student affairs, 1973-76; asso. dean for adminstrn. Harvard Sch. Medicine and Dental Medicine, 1976—; prof. community and preventive dental health, dir. dental care mgmt. Boston U.; mem. Nat. Bd. Dental Hygiene Examiners.; Mem. dean's com. VA Hosp., Boston; mem. study sect. continuing edn. NIH; mem. Bd. Health, Westwood, Mass., 1970; del., panelist White House Conf. Children and Youth, 1970; cons. to USPHS Hosp., Boston; mem. contract rev. Com. Nat. Inst. Dental Research, HEW, 1972—. Contbr. articles to profl. jours. Served to capt. Dental Corps, USAF, 1950-52. Fellow Am. Pub. Health Assn., Am. Assn. Dental Schs. (dean's council); mem. ADA, Mass. Dental Soc., Dental Gold Inst. (exec. dir. 1982—), Omicron Kappa Upsilon. Home: 30 Orchard Circle Westwood MA 02090

CALKINS, CARROLL CECIL, editor; b. Springfield, Oreg., Oct. 7, 1918; s. Herman Cecil and Gladys (Riggs) C.; m. Ruth Geneva Monroe, Sept. 27, 1947; children: Christopher Carroll, Robin Ruth, Melissa Howard; m. Barbara Pfeffer, Apr. 5, 1981. B.A., U. Oreg., 1946. Self employed comml. photographer, Eugene, 1949-53; N.W. editor Sunset mag., 1953-56, asso. editor, 1956-57, House Beautiful mag., 1957-67; editor-in-chief Home Garden mag., 1967-69; sr. staff editor Readers Digest Books. Author: (with Jerome A. Eaton) How to Garden, 1979. Served to maj. USAAF, 1941-45. Decorated D.F.C., Air medal with 5 oak leaf clusters. Home: 40 W 86th St New York NY 10024

CALKINS, EVAN, physician, educator; b. Newton, Mass., July 15, 1920; s. Grosvenor and Patty (Phillips) C.; m. Virginia McC. Brady, Sept. 9, 1946; children: Sarah Calkins Oxnard, Stephen, Lucy McCormick, Joan Calkins Bender, Benjamin, Hugh, Ellen Rountree, Geoffrey, Timothy. Grad., Milton Acad., 1939; A.B., Harvard U., 1942, M.D., 1945. Intern, asst. resident medicine Johns Hopkins, 1946-47, 48-50; chief resident physician Mass. Gen. Hosp., 1951-52, mem. arthritis unit, 1952-61; NRC fellow med. scis. Harvard, 1950-51, instr., asst. prof. medicine, 1952-61; practice medicine, specializing in rheumatology, Boston, 1951-61, Buffalo, 1961—; prof. medicine SUNY, Buffalo, 1961—, chmn. dept., 1965-77, head div. geriatrics and gerontology, 1978—; head dept. medicine Buffalo Gen. Hosp., 1961-68; dir. medicine E.J. Meyer Meml. Hosp., 1968-78; head geriatrics service Buffalo VA Med. Center, 1978—; head dir. geriatrics/gerontology SUNY-Buffalo, 1978—; founder, pres. Network in Aging of Western N.Y., Inc., 1980-83; cons. Nat. Inst. Arthritis and Metabolic Diseases Tng. Grants Com., 1958-62, Program Project Com., 1964-68, Nat. Insts. Spl. Study Sect. for Health Manpower, 1969-77, for Behavioral Medicine, 1978-79; mem. acad. awards com. Nat. Inst. on Aging, 1979-80; dir. Western N.Y. Geriatrics Edn. Center, 1983—. Editor: Handbook of Medical Emergencies, 1945, Practice of Geriatric Medicine, 1983; Contbr. articles to profl. jours. Served to capt., M.C. AUS, 1943-45, 46-48. Recipient Presdl. citation for Community Service, 1983. Fellow A.C.P.; mem. Am. Assn. Pathologists, Gerontol. Assn., Am. Geriatrics Soc., Am. Rheumatism Assn. (pres.), Am. Clin. and Climatological Assn., Am. Soc. Clin. Investigation, Assn. Am. Physicians, Central Soc. for Clin. Research, Soc. Medicine Argentina (hon.), Alpha Omega Alpha. Home: 3799 Windover Hamburg NY 14075 Office: VA Med Center 3495 Bailey Ave Buffalo NY 14215

CALKINS, FRANCIS JOSEPH, business administration educator; b. Chgo., Oct. 15, 1910; s. Frank M. and Anna (Masilko) C.; m. Rose Marie Schreiber, June 24, 1944; children: Edward J., Richard F., Anne R., Timothy J. A.B., Loyola U., Chgo., 1932, A.M., 1933; Ph.D., Northwestern U., 1947. Statistician, asst. supr. WPA, Chgo., 1933-38; analyst Standard & Poor's Corp., N.Y.C., 1938-39; asst. prof. econs., finance U. Notre Dame, 1939-45; prof. finance Marquette U., 1945-65, chmn., 1949-61; prof., chmn. banking, finance Western Res. U., 1965-67; prof. banking, finance Case Western Res. U., Cleve., 1967-69; prof. finance Cleve. State U., 1969-76, prof. emeritus, 1976—; Hightower prof. bus. adminstrn. Emory U., Atlanta, 1976—; vis. prof. banking and fin. U. Nebr., Omaha, 1978-79, Wichita U., 1979-82. Author: Case and Problems in Investments, 1955, (with Dowrie and Fuller) Investments, 1961. Trustee Cons. Credit Counseling Service Greater Cleve., 1969-76. Mem. Am. Finance Assn., Am. Econ. Assn., Atlanta Soc. Fin. Analysts, Chartered Financial Analysts, Blue Key, Alpha Kappa Psi, Pi Gamma Mu, Beta Gamma Sigma. Home: 2121 Pine Forest Dr NE Atlanta GA 30345

CALKINS, GARY NATHAN, lawyer; b. N.Y.C., Mar. 1, 1911; s. Gary Nathan and Helen R. (Williston) C.; m. Constantia H. Hommann, June 22, 1940 (div. Dec. 1948); m. Susannah Eby, Nov. 19, 1949; children: Helen (dec.), Margaret, Sarah, Abigail. Student, Ecole Internationale, Geneva, Switzerland, 1926-27, Storm King Sch., 1927-29; A.B., Columbia U., 1933; LL.B., Harvard U., 1936. Bar: N.Y. 1936, D.C. 1955, Va. 1981, U.S. Supreme Ct. 1965. Asso. Beekman & Bogue, N.Y.C., 1936-41; staff CAB, 1941-56, chief internat. and rules div., 1947-56; mem. Galland, Kharasch, Calkins & Morse, P.C. (and predecessor firms), Washington, 1956-81, N.Y.C., 1966-77, mng. partner, 1969-80, pres., 1980-81, of counsel, 1981—; of counsel to county atty. Fairfax County (Va.), 1983—; Mem. U.S. sect. Comité Internat. Tecnique d' Experts Juridiques Aériens, 1946-47; Mem. U.S. dels. legal com. Internat. Civil Aviation Orgn., 1947-55; delegation chmn. 1st, 3d, 5th, 9th and 10th meetings; mem. drafting com. Mortgage Conv., Geneva, Switzerland, 1948, Rome Conv. on Surface Damage, 1952; chmn. U.S. delegation internat. Diplomatic Conf. for Revision of Warsaw Conv., The Hague, 1955; chmn. legal div. U.S. Air Coordinating Com., 1955-56; industry observer U.S.-U.K. bilateral air transport talks, London, 1956; asst. sec. Philippine Airlines, 1974—. Asso. editor: United States and Canadian Aviation Reports, 1956-61; asso. editor: Jour. Air Law and Commerce, 1956-58; editor-in-chief, 1958-63; Contbr. articles to profl. jours. Served as lt. USNR, 1943-45. Mem. Am., D.C., Va. bar assns., Am. Judicature Soc., Internat. Platform Assn., Soc. Quiet Birdmen, Psi Upsilon. Club: Georgetown (Washington). Office: Canal Sq 1054 31st St NW Washington DC 20007 Office: County Atty's Office 4100 Chain Bridge Rd. Fairfax VA 20007

CALKINS, SUSANNAH EBY, economist; b. Bucyrus, Ohio, Jan. 16, 1924; d. Samuel L. and Mae (McClure) Eby; m. G. Nathan Calkins, Nov. 19, 1949; children: Helen E. (dec.), Margaret S., Sarah A., Abigail C. A.B., Groucher Coll., 1945; M.S. in Econs. (Univ. scholar 1946-47), U. Wis., 1947. Fiscal analyst U.S. Bur. Budget, 1945-50; economist U.S. Council Econ. Advisors, 1950-51, U.S. Office Price Stabilization, 1951-53, U.S. Bur. Budget, 1953-55; cons. U.S. Adv. Commn. on Intergovernmental Relations, Washington, 1972-73, 74-75, cons. on counter-cyclinical aid programs, 1977-78, sr. analyst, 1979—; cons. revenue sharing Brookings Instn., Washington, 1973-74. Author: (with R. Nathan and A. Manvel) Monitoring Revenue Sharing, 1975. Sponsor S.S. Goucher Victory, Balt., 1945. Mem. Am. Econs. Assn., Phi Beta Kappa. Presbyterian. Home: 6504 Dearborn Dr Falls Church VA 22044 Office: US Adv Com Intergovtl Relations Washington DC 20575

CALL, DAVID LINCOLN, agricultural economics educator, administrator; b. Batavia, N.Y., Feb. 12, 1932; s. Robert Vincent and Lucille (Hale) Call C.; m. Mary Gentry, July 3, 1954; children: Laura, David, Barbara, Carolyn. B.S., Cornell U., 1954, M.S., 1958, Ph.D., 1960. Asst. prof. Mich. State U., East Lansing, 1960-62; H.E. Babcock prof. food Econs. Cornell U., Ithaca, N.Y., 1962-73, dir. Coop. Extension, 1973-78, dean Coll. Agr. and Life Scis., 1978—; vis. prof. MIT, 1968-69; mem. food and nutrition bd. Nat. Acad. Scis., Washington, 1967-73; mem. State Commn. to Revise Social Services Laws, Albany, N.Y., 1971—; trustee Am. Inst. Cooperation, Washington, 1982—; mem. Gov.'s Council on Fiscal and Econs. Priorities, Albany, 1983—. Editor: Nutrition, National Development and Planning, 1973; contbr. articles to sci. jours. Campaign chmn. Tompkins county United Fund, 1973; treas. Am. Agriculturist Found., 1980—. Served to sgt. U.S. Army, 1954-56. Mem. Am. Agrl. Econs. Assn., Phi Kappa Phi, Epsilon Sigma Phi. Republican. Presbyterian. Lodge: Rotary. Home: 108 Comstock Rd Ithaca NY 14850 Office: Coll Agr and Life Scis Cornell U 122 Roberts Hall Ithaca NY 14853

CALL, NEIL JUDSON, corporate executive; b. Detroit, June 15, 1933; s. Judson Francis and Glennys Jean (Amluxen) C.; m. Jane E. Rathslag, Feb. 4, 1956; children: Laura, Keith; m. Eleanor Ann King, Nov. 23, 1978. B.B.A., U. Mich., 1955, M.B.A., 1956. C.P.A., Mich. With Hogan Juengel & Harding (C.P.A.'s), Detroit, 1956-61, Ford Motor Co., Dearborn, Mich., 1961-65; with Ford Motor Credit Co., Dearborn, 1965-67, Gulf & Western Industries Inc., N.Y.C., 1968—, v.p., 1970-79, sr. v.p., 1979-83, exec. v.p., 1983-84. Served with U.S. Army, 1956-58. Mem. Am. Inst. C.P.A.'s. Club: Econ. (N.Y.C.). Home: 906 Castle Point Terr Hoboken NJ 07030 Office: Gulf & Western Industries Inc 1 Gulf & Western Plaza New York NY 10023

CALL, OSBORNE JAY, bus. exec.; b. Afton, Wyo., June 4, 1941; s. Osborne and Janice C.; m. Tamra Compton, Dec. 16, 1977; children—Tad, Crystal. Student, Ricks Coll., Rexburg, Idaho, Brigham Young U., Provo, Utah. Engaged in petroleum mktg., 1960-68; v.p. Caribou Four Corners, Afton, 1964-68; pres. Flying J Inc. (retail and wholesale gasoline and real estate devel. co.), Brigham City, Utah, 1968—; dir. No. div. First Security Bank, Brigham City. Mormon. Address: Flying J Inc 50 West 990 South Brigham City UT 84302

CALLAGAN, DWIGHT A., naval medical officer; b. Sheridan, Ill., Sept. 26, 1917; s. Ralph J. and Amine (Hapeman) C.; m. Anne King, Sept. 26, 1943; children: Sharon Anne, Dwight Allen, Brian King, Wayne Reed. B.S. in Medicine, U. Ill., 1942, M.D., 1942. Diplomate: Am. Bd. Obstetrics and Gynecology. Commd. lt. (j.g.) U.S. Navy, 1942, advanced through grades to capt., 1957; intern U.S. Naval Hosp., Mare Island, 1943; resident in gen. surgery U.S. Naval Hosp., Nat. Naval Med. Center, Bethesda, Md., 1945-46, resident in obstetrics and gynecology, 1945-50, chief obstetrics and gynecology service, 1962-65; chief obstet. and gynecol. service U.S. Naval Hosp., Camp LeJeune, N.C., 1950-51, Guantanamo Bay, Cuba, 1951-53, Bremerton, Wash., 1953-55, Portsmouth, Va., 1955-62, exec. officer, chief profl. services, Great Lakes, Ill., 1966-67, comdg. officers, Subic Bay, 1968-69; with Naval Dispensary, Treasure Island, Calif., 1969—; asst. clin. prof. obstetrics and gynecology George Washington U. Med. Sch., 1962-65. Contbr. numerous articles on diagnosis and mgmt. of multiple pregnancies, sonolining during pregnancy, effect of drugs in pregnancy and ultrasonic doppler diagnostic use. Decorated Bronze Star medal with combat V. Mem. A.M.A., Am. Coll. Obstetricians and Gynecologists, Alpha Omega Pi, Phi Rho Sigma. Inventor ultrasonic doppler fetal heart detection instrument, documented duration of pregnancy and fetal risks of prematurity and prolonged pregnancy. Home: 6385 W Evans Creek Rd PO Box 14 Rogue River OR 97537

CALLAGHAN, J. CLAIR, university president; b. Ebbsfleet, P.E.I., Can., Feb. 21, 1933; s. Harris William Patrick and Cora (Shea) C.; m. Ellen Catherine Mullally, June 14, 1958; children—Kevin, Mary Jane, Jeffrey. B.A. cum laude, St. Dunstan's U., 1953; Diploma in Engring., St. Francis Xavier U., 1954; B.E.E. with honors, N.S. Tech. Coll., 1956; M.S., M.I.T., 1963. Prof. in charge engring. St. Dunstan's U., 1956-58; teaching and research asst. M.I.T., 1958-60; asst. prof. elec. engring. Tech. U. N.S. (name formerly N.S. Tech. Coll.), Halifax, 1960-66, pres., 1977—; assoc. prof. engring. Sir George Williams U., 1966-69, chmn. dept. elec. engring., 1968-70, prof., dean engring., 1969-77; cons. Warnock Hersey, Computing Devices of Can., Fairey Can. Ltd., Chemcell, Can. Internat. Devel. Agy.; mem. com. on scholarship Nat. Research Council, 1975-78, chmn., 1976-78; mem. Can. Engring. Manpower Council, 1976-84; sec. Nat. Com. Deans of Engring. and Applied Sci., 1976-77; dir. Tidal Power Corp. of N.S., 1979—, N.S. Research Found. Corp., 1978—. Contbr. articles to profl. jours. Served to lt. RCAC. Mem. Assn. Profl. Engrs. N.S., Order Engrs. Que., IEEE, Engring. Inst. Can., Assn. Atlantic Univs. (exec. com.), Assn. Univs. and Colls. Can. Roman Catholic. Patentee in field. Office: Tech U NS PO Box 1000 Halifax NS B3J 2X4 Canada

CALLAHAM, BETTY ELGIN, librarian; b. Honea Path, S.C., Oct. 8, 1929; d. John Winfred and Alice (Dodson) C. B.A., Duke U., 1950; M.A., Emory U., 1954, Master Librarianship, 1961. Tchr. public schs. in, N.C., Ga. and S.C., 1951-60; field services librarian S.C. State Library, 1961-64, adult cons., 1964-65, dir. field services, 1965-74, dep. librarian, 1974-79, state librarian, 1979—; Conf. coordinator Gov.'s Conf. on Public Libraries, 1965, S.C. White House Conf. Library and Info. Services, 1978-79; del. White House Conf. Library and Info. Services, 1979; mem. OCLC Users Council, 1979; chair del. SOLINET, 1983-84. Mem. ALA (council 1977-80), S.C. Library Assn. (fed. relations coordinator 1976-80), Southeastern Library Assn., Chief Officers State Library Agys. Home: 1830 St Michael's Rd Columbia SC 29210 Office: PO Box 11469 Columbia SC 29211

CALLAHAM, THOMAS HUNTER, business executive; b. Lynchburg, Va., Nov. 29, 1915; s. Charles Edwin and Celina (Rector) C.; m. Patricia Mae Murphy, Oct. 16, 1953; children: Sandra Colleen (Mrs. Billy C. Herrmann), Thomas Hunter, Kathleen Louise, Michael Merriman. B.S., Va. Poly. Inst., 1937. Accountant Standard Oil Co. N.J., also Godfrey L. Cabot, Inc., Charleston, W.Va., 1937-40; budget officer Office U.S. High Commr. for Germany, 1949-53; budget and programs officer MSA, FOA, ICA, 1953-56; bus. specialist, chief fiscal mgmt., asst. regional dir. for mgmt., regional dir. Ft. Worth regional office Pub. Housing Adminstrn., 1956-66; asst. regional adminstr. HUD, Region V, 1966-72; dir. mgmt. Tulsa Housing Authority, 1972; pres. Callaham & Assos., Inc., Tulsa, 1973—. Served with AUS, 1940-49; col. USAR (ret.). Mem. Nat. Assn. Housing and Redevel. Ofcls. (exec. com. 1968-69), Internat. Platform Assn. Democrat. Club: Elk. Home: 4500-52 NW Blitchton Rd Ocala FL 32675

CALLAHAN, DANIEL JOHN, institute director; b. Washington, July 19, 1930; s. Vincent Francis and Anita (Hawkins) C.; m. Sidney Cornelia de Shazo, June 5, 1954; children: Mark Sidney, Stephen Daniel, John Vincent, Peter Thorn, Sarah Elisabeth, David Lee. B.A., Yale U., 1952; M.A., Georgetown U., 1957; Ph.D., Harvard U., 1965; D.Sc. (hon.), U. Medicine and Dentistry of N.J., 1981. Exec. editor The Commonweal, N.Y.C., 1961-68; staff asso. Population Council, 1969-70; founder, dir. Inst. Soc. Ethics and the Life Scis., The Hastings Center, 1969—; resident scholar Aspen Inst. Humanistic Studies, 1975; vis. asst. prof. religion Temple U., 1964; vis. asst. prof. religious studies Brown U., 1965; vis. prof. theology Marymount Coll., 1966; vis. prof. U. Pa., 1970; cons. med. ethics, jud. council AMA, 1972—, A.C.P., 1979—; spl. cons. Commn. on Population Growth and Am. Future, 1970-71, Nat. Endowment for Humanities, 1979. Author: The Mind of the Catholic Layman, 1963, Honesty in the Church, 1965, The New Church, 1966, Abortion: Law, Choice and Morality, 1970, Ethics and Population Limitation, 1971, The Tyranny of Survival, 1973, The Teaching of Ethics in the Military, 1982; also essays, articles.; Co-editor: Christianity Divided: Protestant and Roman Catholic Theological Issues, 1961, Ethical Issues in Human Genetics, 1973; Editor: Federal Aid and Catholic Schools, 1964, Secular City Debate, 1966, The Catholic Case for Contraception, 1969, The American Population Debate, 1971, Science, Ethics and Medicine, 1976, Knowledge, Value and Belief, 1977, Morals, Science and Sociality, 1978, Knowing and Valuing, 1979, Ethics Teaching in Higher Edn, 1980, Ethical Issues in Population Aid, 1980, The Roots of Ethics, 1981; editor: Ethics in Hard Times, 1981, Ethics, the Social Sciences and Policy Analysis, 1983, Abortion: Understanding Differences, 1984; Mem. editorial adv. bd.: Technology in Soc, 1981—; mem. adv. bd.: Ency. of the Life Scis., 1982, Sci., Tech. and Human Values, 1979—, Bus. and Profl. Ethics, 1981, Criminal Justice Ethics, 1982, Environ. Ethics, 1982. Mem. N.Y. Council for Humanities, 1975-79, Nat. Book Award Com., 1975, N.Y. State Health Adv. Council, 1975-76; selection com. Ford-Rockefeller Program in Population Policy, 1975-78, Rockefeller Found. Program in Humanities, 1980; elector Nat. Medal for Lit., 1979—; pub. mem. Am. Bd. Med. Specialties, 1982—. Served with CIC AUS, 1952-55. Recipient Thomas More medal, 1970; named one of 200 Outstanding Young Am. Leaders Time mag., 1974. Fellow AAAS; Mem. Am. Assn. Advancement Humanities, Inst. of Medicine of Nat. Acad. Scis. Home: 50 Summit Dr Hastings-on-Hudson NY 10706 Office: 360 Broadway Hastings-on-Hudson NY 10706

CALLAHAN, DANIEL JOSEPH, III, banker; b. Washington, May 7, 1932; s. Daniel Joseph and Anne Bailey (Scott) C.; m. Colleen Adrienne Mount, May 5, 1956; children: Daniel Joseph IV, Carey Scott, Caren Anne, Carolyn Patricia, Colleen Gerry. B.A., Williams Coll., 1954. Trainee Riggs Nat. Bank, Washington, 1956-58; v.p. Chase Manhattan Bank, N.Y.C., 1958-69; exec. v.p. Hambro Am. Bank and Trust Co., N.Y.C., 1969-72, also dir.; mng. dir. Merrill Lynch-Brown Shipley Bank Ltd., London, Eng., 1972-73; exec. v.p. Riggs Nat. Bank, Washington, 1973-76, pres., also dir., 1976-83; pres., dir. Am. Security Bank, Washington, 1983—; dir. Genway Corp. Chmn. Mayor's Econ. Devel. Com., Washington, 1980-82; bd. dirs. Washington Area Convention and Visitors Assn., Atlantic Council, Washington; treas. Nat. 4-H Council; trustee Meridian House Internat., Fed. City Council, Capital Children's Mus., Am. Cancer Soc., PanAm. Devel. Found.; bd. dirs. Georgetown U., 1983—. Served to capt. USAF, 1954-56. Mem. Assn. Res. City Bankers, Delta Kappa Epsilon. Republican. Roman Catholic. Clubs: Bucks, Sunningdale, Overseas Bankers (London); Royal and Ancient Golf (Scotland); Alfalfa, Metropolitan (Washington); Chevy Chase; Burning Tree (Md.); Knickerbocker (N.Y.C.). Office: 1501 Pennsylvania Ave NW Washington DC 20013

CALLAHAN, EDWARD WILLIAM, chemical engineer, manufacturing company executive; b. N.Y.C., July 17, 1930; s. William Patrick and Clara (Schultz) C.; children: Susan Lynn, Kevin Foster. B.Ch.E., Cornell U., 1953. Engr. Solvay div. allied Chem. Corp., Syracuse, N.Y., 1953-65; dir. comml. devel. Solvay div. Allied Chem. Corp., Syracuse, N.Y., 1965-66; asst. to exec. v.p. Allied Chem. Corp., N.Y.C., 1966-68, asst. to pres., 1968-70, gen. mgr. environ. services, Morristown, N.J., 1970-78; v.p. health and safety and environ. scis. Allied Corp., Morristown, 1978—. Bd. dirs. Am. Cancer Soc., Morristown, 1982—. Mem. Chem. Industry Inst. Toxicology (dir. 1974—), Am. Indsl. Health Council (dir. 1978), Orgn. Resources Counselors, Synthetic Oraganic Chem. Mfrs. Assn. (bd. govs. 1973-76), Chem. Mfrs. Assn. (chmn. spl. programs adv. com. 1978-82, environ. mgmt. com. 1978-82). Club: Beacon Hill (Summit, N.J.). Home: 78 New England Ave Summit NJ 07901 Office: Allied Corp PO Box 3000R Morristown NJ 07960

CALLAHAN, GEORGE HAROLD, insurance company executive, lawyer; b. Glen Ridge, N.J., July 13, 1920; s. George Leo and Katherine (Higgins) C.; m. Regina Heslin, Feb. 17, 1943; children: Kevin, Jeanne, Jill, Barbara, John. B.S., Seton Hall Coll., 1942; LL.B., Harvard U., 1948. Bar: N.J. 1948. Practice law, Newark, 1948-60; asst. gen. counsel Colonial Life Ins. Co. Am., East Orange, N.J., 1960-62, gen. counsel, 1962-83, sr. v.p., 1970-80, vice chmn., gen. counsel, sec., 1979-83, dir., 1970-83; vice chmn., gen. counsel, sec. dir. Chubb Life Ins. Co. Am., Parsippany, N.J., 1981—, United Life & Accident Ins. Cos., Concord, N.H., 1981—. Mcpl. atty. Glen Ridge, 1958—; asst. counsel Essex County, N.J., 1958-60. Served to lt. USNR, 1942-45; PTO. Decorated Silver Star medal with bar. Mem. ABA, N.J. State Bar Assn., Essex County Bar Assn., Harvard U. Law Sch. Assn. of N.J. (pres. 1963). Democrat. Roman Catholic. Club: Glen Ridge Country. Home: 926 Bloomfield Ave Glen Ridge NJ 07028 Office: Chubb Life Ins Co Am 8 Sylvan Way Parsippany NJ 07054

CALLAHAN, HARRY LESLIE, civil engineer; b. Kansas City, Mo., Jan. 11, 1923; s. B. Frank and Myrtle Lou (Anderson) C.; m. V. June Yohn, Dec. 16, 1944; children: Michael Thomas, Maureen Lynn, Kevin Leslie. B.S. in Civil Engring, U. Kans., 1944; postgrad., UCLA. With Black & Veatch Co., Kansas City, 1946—, mgr. spl. projects, 1970—, partner, 1971-78, exec. partner, 1978—, charge Indsl. div., 1981—; dir. Black & Veatch Internat. Contbr. articles to profl. jours. Served to 1st lt., inf. AUS, 1944-46; Japan. Recipient Mo. Design

Excellence award 1st place, 1972. Fellow ASCE, Am. Cons. Engrs. Council; mem. Am. Nuclear Soc., Nat. Soc. Profl. Engrs., Soc. Mil. Engrs., Am. Concrete Inst., Water Pollution Control Fedn., Combustion Inst., Kappa Sigma. Congregationalist. Clubs: Elephant, Kansas City, Leawood South Country, Homestead, Chancellor, U. Kans. Office: 1500 Meadow Lake Pkwy Kansas City MO 64114

CALLAHAN, HARRY MOREY, photographer; b. Detroit, Oct. 22, 1912; s. Harry Arthur and Hazel (Mills) C.; m. Eleanor Knapp, Nov., 1936; children: Barbara, Mary. D.F.A. (hon.), R.I. Sch. Design, 1979. Mem. faculty Inst. Design, Ill. Inst. Tech., Chgo., 1946-61, head dept. photography, 1949-61; prof., head dept. R.I. Sch. Design, 1971-76. (One-man exhbns.) Mus. Modern Art, N.Y.C., 1976; U.S. rep., Venice Biennial, 1978. Fellow Graham Found., 1956, Guggenheim Found., 1972; grantee Nat. Endowment Arts, 1976; recipient award Gov. R.I., 1969, Citation NASA, 1972. Office: 153 Benefit St Providence RI 02903

CALLAHAN, JAMES FREDERICK, manufacturing company executive; b. Rochester, N.Y., Sept. 15, 1919; s. Maurice and Mary (Pigage) C.; m. Berenice Norman, Mar. 12, 1945; 1 dau., Margaret Callahan Schofield. Diploma, Rochester Bus. Inst., 1939; student, Niagara U., 1941. Cert. internal auditor. With Fasco Industries, Inc., 1939—, v.p., controller, Rochester and Boca Raton, Fla., 1972-76, v.p. fin., Boca Raton, 1976-80, exec. v.p., 1980, pres., vice-chmn. bd., 1981-84, chief exec. officer, 1981—, chmn. bd., 1984—, dir., 1976—; chief exec. officer, chmn. bd. Elmwood Sensors, Inc., Pawtucket, R.I. and Newcastle, Eng., 1981—; dir. Basic Systems Inc., Houston, Westcode Inc., Frazer, Pa. Mem. Nat. Assn. Accts. (past chpt. pres.; nat. dir.). Roman Catholic. Clubs: Royal Palm Yacht and Country, Boca Raton Hotel and Club. Office: 601 N Federal Hwy Boca Raton FL 33432

CALLAHAN, JOSEPH MURRAY, editor; b. Detroit; s. John Hugh and Helen Dorothy (McDonald) C.; m. Halina Anne Sienkiewicz, Oct. 19, 1957; children—Carol, Christopher. B.S. in Journalism, U. Detroit, 1943. Reporter Detroit Times, 1946-53; Engring. editor Automotive News, Detroit, 1953-70; Ed. for Automotive Industries mag., Detroit, 1970—; commentator Sta. WJR, Detroit, 1970—. Served with USNR, 1943-46. Mem. Detroit Auto Writers Group, Soc. Automotive Engrs., Sigma Delta Chi. Roman Catholic. Office: 2600 Fisher Bldg Detroit MI 48202

CALLAHAN, JOSEPH PATRICK, lawyer; b. N.Y.C., Mar. 19, 1945; s. Parnell J.T. and Jane M. (Tubridy) C. B.A., Columbia, 1966; J.D., Albany Law Sch., Union U., Albany, N.Y., 1969. Bar: N.Y. 1969. Ptnr. law firm Callahan & Wolkoff, N.Y.C., 1972—; Chmn., pres. Mackran Assocs., Inc., mortgage brokers, N.Y.C., 1973—; Arbitrator compulsory arbitration program N.Y.C. Civil Ct., 1972—. Mem. Bronx County Bar Assn. Roman Catholic. Club: N.Y. Athletic. Home: 593 7th St Brooklyn NY 11215 Office: 67 Wall St New York NY 10005

CALLAHAN, RALPH WILSON, JR., advertising agency executive; b. Anniston, Ala., Apr. 14, 1942; s. Ralph Wilson and Ida Bell (Price) C.; m. Cathryn Vann Holman, Feb. 16, 1981; 1 dau., Meeghan Crabtree. B.A., U. Va., 1964; M. Fgn. Trade, Am. Grad. Sch. Internat. Mgmt., 1966. Acct. exec. Young and Rubicam, Inc., N.Y.C., 1967-70, v.p., acct. supr., 1971-78; sr. v.p. Henderson Advt., Greenville, S.C., 1978-80, exec. v.p., 1980-81, pres., 1981—; gov. so. region Am. Assn. Advy. Agys., N.Y.C., 1981—; chmn. Carolinas council Am. Assn. Advt. Agys., Greenville, 1982. Vice pres. Met. Arts Council, Greenville, 1982; bd. visitors The McCallie Sch., Chattanooga, 1983. Served to 2d lt. USAR, 1963-65. Mem. Am. C. of C. of Netherlands (pres. 1970), Greenville C. of C. (dir. 1983), Omicron Delta Kappa, Phi Beta Kappa. Episcopalian. Clubs: Union League (N.Y.C.); Apawamis (Rye, N.Y.); Greenville Country. Home: 432 Henderson Rd Greenville SC 29607 Office: Henderson Advertising Inc 60 Pelham Pointe Greenville SC 29602

CALLAHAN, RAYMOND EUGENE, educator; b. St. Louis, Sept. 22, 1921;, 1942; 2 children. B.S., Washington U., St. Louis, 1948, M.A., 1949; Ed.D., Columbia, 1952. Factory worker Anheuser-Busch, Inc., 1939-40, Emerson Electric Co., 1940-41; tchr. Price Sch., Ladue, Mo., 1949-50; asst. prof. edn. Butler U., 1951-52, Washington U., 1952-58, asso. prof., 1958-63, prof., 1963—; Simpson lectr. Harvard, 1964. Author: An Introduction to Education in American Society, 1956, 61, Education and the Cult of Efficiency, 1962, The Superintendent of Schools: An Historical Analysis, 1967; Contbr. articles to profl. jours. Mem. History Edn. Soc. (pres. 1963-64), Am. Ednl. Research Assn. (v.p. 1975—). Address: Grad Inst Edn Washington U St Louis MO 63130

CALLAM, ALEXANDER C., professional baseball team executive. V.p. for fin., sec.-treas. Detroit Tigers, Am. League. Office: care Detroit Tigers Tiger Stadium Detroit MI 48216

CALLAN, JOHN HENRY, univ. dean; b. Lambertville, N.J., Nov. 2, 1920; s. Harry Joseph and Emma (Weiss) C.; m. Nancy Clare Burkle, July 12, 1952; children—John Robert, Jane Marie, Daniel Edward. B.S., Trenton State Coll., 1943; M.A., Columbia, 1949, Ed.D., 1953. Adminstrv. asst., div. higher edn. N.J. Dept. Edn., 1946-49; asso. prof. bus., chmn. div. bus. West Liberty State Coll., 1950-54; dir. tchr. edn. Ferris State Coll., 1954-57; dean Seton Hall U. Sch. Edn., 1957—; chmn. N.J. Adv. Council on Tchr. Edn., 1974-76. Author: Community Resources Handbook in Business Education, 1954; Contbr. chpt. to, Am. Bus. Edn. Yearbook, 1961, also articles to profl. jours. Mem. bd. edn., Lambertville, N.J., 1948-49; mem. bd. Edn. Archdiocese of Newark, 1968-78, pres., 1968-72. Served from pvt. to 1st lt. USMCR, 1943-46; maj. Res. Mem. Nat. Cath. Edn. Assn., Am. Assn. Higher Edn., Am. Assn. Sch. Adminstrs., Nat., N.J. edn. assns., N.J. Council Edn., Internat. Council Edn. Teaching, Nat. Soc. Study Edn., Assn. Supervision and Curriculum Devel., Am.-Israel Friendship League, Kappa Delta Pi, Phi Delta Kappa, Delta Pi Epsilon. Democrat. Roman Catholic. Home: 26 Sherwood Ave Madison NJ 07940 Office: South Orange NJ 07079

CALLAND, DIANA BAKER, broadcasting executive; b. Columbus, Ohio, Oct. 24, 1935; d. Paul Allen and Helene (Schwartz) Baker; m. Frederick Fremont, Sept. 23, 1966. B.A., Ohio State U., 1957, M.A., 1962, postgrad., 1966. Writer, producer WOSU-FM, Columbus, 1957-62; pub. relations dir. Ohio State Nurses Assn., Columbus, 1962-63; research asso., adminstrv. research Ohio State U., Columbus, 1963-66; mgr. cultural affairs programming WFCR-FM, Amherst, Mass., 1966-71; with radio activities dept. Corp. for Pub. Broadcasting, Washington, 1971-81, also, dir. radio activities dept.; radio mktg. mgr. Adler Enterprises, Ltd., McLean, Va., 1981-82; NPR PLUS mktg. dir. Nat. Pub. Radio, Washington, 1982—. Author: (with G.W. Baugham) Writing to People, 1963. Recipient 1st pl. award for children's radio Inst. for Edn. by Radio and TV, 1959; Cris award Film Council of Greater Columbus, 1965; award Council on Internat. Non-Theatrical Events, 1965. Mem. Alpha Epsilon Rho. Office: Corp for Pub Broadcasting 1111 16th St NW Washington DC 20036

CALLANDER, ROBERT JOHN, banker; b. Newark, Feb. 3, 1931; s. George and Mary (Law) C.; m. Marilyn Berg, June 11, 1955; children: Pamela Anne, Robert John Jr., David Webb. A.B. magna cum laude, Dartmouth Coll., 1952, B.D., Yale U., 1955; postgrad., Dartmouth Grad. Sch. Credit and Fin., 1961-62, Harvard Bus. Sch., 1968. Sr. trainee Chem. Bank, N.Y.C., 1957-67, v.p., 1967-72, sr. v.p., 1972-78, sr. v.p., dep. head internat. div., 1978-79, exec. v.p., head internat. div., 1979-81, sr. exec. v.p., head World Banking Group, 1981-83, pres. World Banking Group, 1983—. Bd. dirs. Far East Am. Council Japan Soc. Inc.; trustee Drew U.; mem. adv. bd. Salvation Army Greater N.Y.; trustee YMCA Greater N.Y. Mem. Council Fgn. Relations, Assn. Res. City Bankers, Phi Beta Kappa. Clubs: Univ. (N.Y.C.); Baltusrol (Springfield, N.J.); Somerset Hills Country (Bernardsville, N.J.). Home: Box 29 Oldwick NJ 08858 Office: Chemical Bank 277 Park Ave New York NY 10172

CALLARD, DAVID JACOBUS, investment banker; b. Boston, July 14, 1938; s. Henry Hadden and Clarissa Cooley (Jacobus) C.; children: Owen Winston, Francis Jacobus, Anne Lloyd, Elizabeth Hadden, Samuel Porter. A.B., Princeton U., 1959; postgrad., Union Theol. Sem., 1964-65; J.D., NYU, 1969. With Morgan Guaranty Trust Co., N.Y.C., 1959-61, asst. v.p., 1965-69, v.p., 1970-72; ptnr. Alex Brown & Sons., Balt., 1972—; dep. exec. dir. Pres.'s Commn. on All Vol. Armed Force, 1969-70; dir., mem. exec. com. Waverly Press, Inc.; dir. Hotel Investors Corp.; trustee, chmn. Hotel Investors Trust; dir. U.S. Capital Corp. Treas., trustee Peabody Inst.; bd. dirs. Keswick Home. Served to lt. USMC, 1971-74. Boothe Ferris fellow, 1964-65. Republican. Episcopalian. Clubs: Union, Racquet and Tennis (N.Y.C.); Elkridge (Balt.). Home: 1025 Breezewick Rd Baltimore MD 21204 Office: 135 E Baltimore St Baltimore MD 21202

CALLAS, CHARLIE, comedian, actor; b. Bklyn., Dec. 20; m. Eve; children: Mark, Larry. Profl. drummer, until 1962; profl. comedian, 1962—; played in clubs, throughout U.S.; appearing regularly in, Las Vegas; TV debut on The Hollywood Palace; TV appearances include Dean Martin Celebrity Roast, Love American Style, The Tonight Show; regular on: TV series Switch, The Andy Williams Show; semi-regular on: The Flip Wilson Show; TV appearances include Jerry Lewis Show; appeared in: movies The Big Mouth, 1967, High Anxiety, 1977, Pete's Dragon, 1977; TV movies The Snoop Sisters, 1972, Switch, 1975. Served with U.S. Army. Office: care Metromedia Prodns 5746 Sunset Blvd Hollywood CA 90028 *

CALLAWAY, BEN ANDERSON, journalist; b. Oakland, Calif., Mar. 16, 1927; s. Owen M. and Aulis (Anderson) C.; m. Patricia Hurd, Apr. 7, 1951; children: Randall Owen, Karen Anne. Student, Stanford, 1946-47; B.A., Denison U., 1950. Sports writer, wildlife editor Denver Post, 1950-57; with Phila. Daily News, 1957-80, sports editor, 1961-70, outdoor columnist, 1961-80; outdoor editor Phila. Inquirer, 1980—; exec. editor Metro East Outdoor News, 1973-77; co-editor Penn-Jersey Outdoor Sportsman, 1976-77; free-lance mag. writer-photographer; commentator Sta. KYW, 1972—. Sports chmn. Phila. United Fund, 1966-70; active local Boy Scouts Am., Eagle, 1942. Served with USNR, 1945-46. Recipient Henshall award Am. Fishing Tackle Mfrs. Assn., 1964, Old Salt award N.J. Resort Assn., 1967, Johnson Deep Woods award, 1977; gold medal Pa. Fish and Game Protective Assn., 1978; McCulloch Outdoor Writing award, 1978. Mem. Phila. Sports Writers Assn. (pres. 1968-70), Denver Sports Writers and Broadcasters Assn. (pres. 1957), Outdoor Writers Am. (dir. 1976—), Pa. Outdoor Writers, Boating Writers Internat. (dir. 1976—), Met. N.Y. Rod and Gun Editors, N.J. Outdoor Writers Assn. (v.p. 1982—), Blue Key, Beta Theta Pi, Pi Delta Epsilon, Omicron Delta Kappa. Presbyn. (elder). Home: 420 Kingston Dr Cherry Hill NJ 08034 Office: 400 N Broad St Philadelphia PA 19101 *The only true measure of success is that the world is, and will be, a better place because of his or her presence. As an outdoor writer, I fulfill an important function, in helping others understand and enjoy the great outdoors, and find peace of mind and fitness of body through activity amidst the wonders of woods and waters, with wise use of leisure time.*

CALLAWAY, DAVID HENRY, JR., investment banker; b. N.Y.C., July 3, 1912; s. David Henry and Mary (Sampson) C.; m. Virginia A. Devoe, June 5, 1937; children: Nancy A. (Mrs. Martin L. Lyons), Patricia J. (Mrs. James R. McGrath). A.B., Amos Tuck Sch., Dartmouth, 1934. With Halsey Stuart & Co., Inc., 1934-36; with First Mich. Corp., N.Y.C., 1936—, sr. v.p., 1956-62, pres., 1963-70, chmn. bd., 1970—, also dir.; Pres. Mcpl. Forum N.Y., 1959-60; mem. Am. Stock Exchange, Inc.; allied mem. N.Y. Stock Exchange. Clubs: Bond, Mcpl. Bond, Stock Exchange, Luncheon (N.Y.C.); Detroit, Renaissance (Detroit); Wee Burn Country (Darien). Home: 17 Holly Ln Darien CT 06820 Office: 100 Wall St New York NY 10005 100 Renaissance Center Detroit MI 48243

CALLAWAY, ELY REEVES, JR., golf club manufacturer; b. LaGrange, Ga., June 3, 1919; s. Ely Reeves and Loula (Walker) C.; m. Jeanne Delaplaine Wiler, Oct. 7, 1942 (div. Jan. 1960); children: Ely Reeves III, Louise Wiler, Nicholas Delaplaine; m. Jane Dudley Atkins, Dec. 28, 1961; m. Lucinda Villa, 1983. A.B., Emory U., 1940; D. Textiles, Phila. Coll. Textiles and Sci., 1968. Sales exec. Deering, Milliken & Co., 1946-54; v.p., dir. Amerotron Corp. div. Textron, Inc., 1955-56; joined Burlington Industries, Inc., 1956, successively pres. various divs., then v.p. of corp., 1960, exec. v.p., 1961, pres., 1968-73; also dir., mem. exec. com., mgmt. com.; founder, owner-operator Callaway Vineyard and Winery, Inc., Temecula, Calif., 1973—; founder, owner, operator Callaway Hickory Sticks, Palm Springs, Calif., 1982—. Bd. dirs., chmn. corp. giving United Negro Coll. Fund, 1970-71; bd. Greater N.Y. council Boy Scouts America; board visitors Emory U.; trustee Hampshire Coll., Amherst, Mass., Menninger Found., Topeka, Kan. Served from 2d lt. to maj., Q.M.C. AUS, 1940-45; purchasing and contracting officer cotton clothing Phila. Q.M. Depot. Clubs: University, Blind Brook (N.Y.); Wee Burn Country (Darien, Conn.); Eldorado Country (Palm Desert, Calif.); Pine Valley (N.J.) Golf., Vintage. Address: 27715 Jefferson Suite 205 Temecula CA 92390

CALLAWAY, FULLER EARLE, JR., manufacturer; b. LaGrange, Ga., Jan. 1, 1907; s. Fuller Earle and Ida Jane (Cason) C.; m. Alice Hinman Hand, Aug. 6, 1930; children: Fuller Earle III, Ida Cason Callaway Hudson. Ed., Ga. Inst. Tech., Eastman Bus. Sch. N.Y.; LL.D., LaGrange Coll., 1971; L.H.D., Mercer U., 1980; LL.D., Morris Brown Coll., 1982; D.Sc., U. Ala.-Birmingham, 1984. Treas., Valley Waste Mills, 1927; treas., gen. mgr. Truline, Inc., 1928; dir. Callaway Mills, 1932-46, pres., treas., 1935-36, pres., 1936-45, ret., 1945-59; chmn. bd., chief exec. officer Callaway Mills Co., 1959-61, pres., chief exec. officer, 1961-65, chmn., chief exec. officer, 1965-68; chmn. Callaway Mills, Inc., 1961-68, pres., 1962-65; chmn. Internat. Leasing Corp., 1961-65, pres., 1962-65, Internat. Products & Services, Inc., 1965-70, 76-78, chmn., 1970-78; propr. Hills & Dales; chmn. bd., pres. Charitable Services Co., 1978—. Trustee Callaway Found., 1943-76, Fuller E. Callaway Found., 1923-76, Ga. Tech. Research Inst., Ga. Tech. Found., Callaway Ednl. Assn., 1943-76; past dir. West Ga. council Boy Scouts Am. Commd. capt. Ga. State Guard, 1942; comdg. Troup County Co., lt. col., comdg. 3d Bn., 1943; transferred to D.O.L., 1944; a.d.c., staff gov. Ga., 1943-71. Recipient Silver Beaver award Boy Scouts Am., 1939; Paul Harris fellow. Fellow Textile Inst. (Eng); mem. Ga. Textile Mfrs. Assn. (treas., v.p., pres. 1938-39, dir.), Am. Textile Mfrs. Inst. (chmn. 1945, v.p., dir., chmn. 1947-48), Phi Delta Theta. Democrat. Baptist. Clubs: Masons, Rotary, Field, Long Boat Key Golf, Capital City, Highland Country, Piedmont Driving, Big Eddy. Home: 1200 Vernon Rd LaGrange GA 30240 Office: 200 Ferrell Dr LaGrange GA 30240

CALLAWAY, JAMES THORPE, advertising executive; b. St. Louis, Dec. 10, 1937; s. William F. and Rosemary (Thorpe) C.; m. Elizabeth Ann Neal, Sept. 10, 1960; cildren: David Arthur, John Patrick. B.Journalism, U. Mo., 1959, M.A., 1961. Account exec. Benton & Bowles, Inc., N.Y.C., 1961-64; mgmt. supr. Papert Koenig Lois Inc., N.Y.C., 1965-67; prin., pres. Lois Holland Callaway Inc., N.Y.C., 1967-78, Holland & Callaway Advt., 1978—. Served to capt. AUS, 1960-67. Mem. Sigma Nu. Democrat. Roman Catholic. Home: 605 Park Ave New York NY 10021 Office: 767 3d Ave New York NY 10017

CALLAWAY, JASPER LAMAR, physician, educator; b. Cooper, Ala., Apr. 5, 1911; s. Lucien Adkin and Dora Belle (Robinson) C.; m. Catharine Dater Van Blarcom, Oct. 11, 1941; children: Frederick, Catharine, Elizabeth. B.S., U. Ala., 1935; M.D., Duke, 1932. Diplomate: Am. Bd. Dermatology (pres. 1958-59). Intern Duke Hosp., Durham, N.C., 1933-35, dermatologist, chief dermatology service, 1937—, prof. medicine, specializing dermatology, 1937—, James B. Duke prof. dermatology, 1967—; cons. USPHS, VA, Sec. of War; nat. cons. dermatology to surgeon gen. USAF; mem. spl. med. adv. group to VA, Washington. Co-author: Manual of Clinical Mycology, 1971, Dermatology for Students, 1961; Editorial bd.: Jour. Investigative Dermatology. Fellow A.C.P.; mem. Nat. Adv. Serology Council, Am. Acad. Dermatology (pres. 1971, dir., Gold medal 1972), Am. Assn. Profs. Dermatology (past pres.), So. Med. Assn. (past chmn. dermatology and syphilology), Southeastern Dermatology Assn. (pres. 1950), A.M.A. (chmn. sect. dermatology 1962-63), N.C. Med. Soc. (chmn. sect. dermatology 1968), Am. Dermatol. Assn. (pres. 1958-59), Soc. Investigative Dermatology (pres. 1956, Stephen Rothman award 1982), Balt.-Washington Dermatol. Soc., Am. Assn. Med. Colls., Masters Dermatol. Assn. (pres. 1979-80), Phi Beta Kappa, Sigma Xi, Theta Kappa Psi, Delta Sigma Phi, Alpha Omega Alpha. Home: 26 Stoneridge Circle Durham NC 27705

CALLAWAY, JOHN DOUGLAS, broadcasting executive; b. Spencer, W.Va., Aug. 22, 1936; s. Charles E. and Dorothy (Garwood) C.; m. Shirley A. Andersen, Aug. 16, 1957 (div. Oct. 1978); children: Ann Hampton, Elizabeth Garwood.; m. Patrice Fletcher, 1983. Student, Ohio Wesleyan U., 1954-56, U. Chgo., 1958-59. Gen. assignment reporter WBBM Radio & TV CBS, Chgo., 1957-64, pub. affairs dir., 1964-66, news dir., 1966-68; v.p. program services CBS Radio, N.Y.C., 1968-70, nat. group corr., 1971-73; reporter WBBM-TV, Chgo., 1973-74; dir. news WTTW-TV, Chgo., 1974-83, sr. corr., 1983—; host John Callaway Tonight (formerly John Callaway Interviews), Chgo. Feedback; contbg. editor WLS-TV, ABC, 1981-83; guest lectr. Notre Dame U., Northwestern U., Columbia Coll., Manchester Coll., Loyola U., Chgo., U. Chgo. Div. Sch.; Welles disting. vis. scholar George Williams Coll., 1980-81; bd. dirs. William Benton Fellowships in Broadcast Journalism, U. Chgo., 1983—. Author: (with others) Action on the Streets; contbr. numerous articles to mags. Mem. adv. com. Am. Refugee Commn.; mem. vis. com. student programs and facilities U. Chgo.; bd. dirs. Chgo. Theol. Sem.; mem. Chgo. com. Chgo. Council Fgn. Relations. Recipient Assoc. Press award, NCCJ award, Ohio State Broadcast award, Chgo. Emmy award, 1978, Peabody award, 1980, Emmy award, 1981, 83. Mem. Radio-TV News Dirs. Assn., Soc. Midland Authors, Sigma Delta Chi. Mem. United Ch. Christ. Home: 823 Forest Ave Evanston IL 60202 Office: 5400 N St Louis Ave Chicago IL 60625 *

CALLAWAY, PAUL SMITH, organist; b. Atlanta, Ill., Aug. 16, 1909; s. Ralph Vernon and Mattie (Cubbage) C. Student, Westminster Coll., Fulton, Mo., 1927-29, Mus.D. (hon.), 1959, Washington Coll., Chestertown, Md., 1967. Organist, choirmaster St. Thomas Chapel, N.Y., 1930-35, St. Mark's Ch., Grand Rapids, Mich., 1935-39; organist, choirmaster Washington Cathedral, 1939-77, emeritus, 1977—; organist, choirmaster St. Paul's Ch., Washington, 1979—; condr. Cathedral Choral Soc., Washington, 1942—; mem. faculty Peabody Conservatory, Balt., 1953-57, Coll. Ch. Musicians, Washington, 1962-69, Berkshire Music Center, Tanglewood, Mass., 1965-67, Blossom Music Center, 1968; condr. Opera Soc. Washington, 1956—, Lake George Opera Festival, 1967-77. Composer: An Hymne of Heavenly Love, 1935, The Office of the Holy Communion, 1945, Hark, the Glad Sound, 1946, O Saving Victim, 1947. Served with AUS, 1942-46. Decorated hon. officer Order Brit. Empire. Fellow Am. Guild Organists; mem. Lit. Soc. Wash. Episcopalian. Clubs: Cosmos, City Tavern Assn. (Washington); St. Wilfred (N.Y.C.). Home: 2230 Decatur Pl NW Washington DC 20008 Office: Washington Cathedral Mount St Alban Washington DC 20016

CALLEN, HERBERT BERNARD, physics educator; b. Phila., July 1, 1919; s. Abraham and Mildred (Goldfarb) C.; m. Sara Smith, Jan. 21, 1945; children: Jill Bressler, Jed. B.S. in Edn, Temple U., 1941, M.A., 1942; Ph.D., Mass. Inst. Tech., 1948. With Manhattan Project, N.Y.C., 1944-45; with Guided Missile Project, Princeton, 1945; mem. faculty physics dept. U. Pa., Phila., 1948—, prof., 1956—; cons. Sperry Rand Univac, 1950—; UN cons. Pakistan AEC, 1965; Mem. adv. com. physics NSF, 1966-69, chmn., 1969; mem. adv. com. Nat. Magnet Lab., 1965-68, chmn., 1968; U.S. rep. Commn. on Thermodynamics, Internat. Union Pure and Applied Physics, 1972-78, chmn., 1975-78. Author: Thermodynamics, 1960, also articles. Pres. Am. Profs. for Peace in Middle East, 1976; Bd. dirs. Jewish Community Relations Council Phila., 1970-82. Guggenheim fellow, 1972-73. Fellow Am. Phys. Soc. (council, officer div. solid state physics 1966-69). Home: 612 Cambridge Rd Bala-Cynwyd PA 19004

CALLEN, IRWIN R., physician; b. Chgo., May 3, 1919; s. Harry and Esther (Levey) C.; m. Rose P. Cohen, Aug. 10, 1941; children: Jeffrey P., James Jay. Student, U. Chgo., 1936-39; B.S., U. Ill., 1941, M.D., 1943; M.S., 1949. Diplomate: Am. Bd. Internal Medicine, subsplty. in cardiology. Intern Ill. Research and Ednl. Hosps., U. Ill., 1943, fellow dept. internal medicine, 1946-47, electrocardiographer, asso. attending physician, 1948-51; resident dept. internal medicine McCloskey gen. hosp., Temple, Tex., 1944; dept. of internal medicine and cardiology regional hosp., Camp Maxey, Tex., 1944-45, practice medicine specializing in internal medicine and cardiology, Chgo., 1947-72, North Miami Beach, Fla., 1973—; instr. in medicine U. Health Scis., Chgo., 1951-56, asso. dept. internal medicine, 1956-66, asso. prof. medicine, 1966-72, prof. clin. medicine, 1972-77; prof. medicine and cardiology Cook County (Ill.) Hosp. Grad. Sch., 1958—; mem. staff and bd. of dirs. Miami Heart Inst., Miami Beach, Fla., 1976—; mem. staff Edgewater hosp., Chgo., 1947—, pres., 1967-69, mem. bd. of dirs., 1969-73, dir. of cardiology, 1965-73; Bd. dirs. Fla. Heart Assn., Am. Heart Assn., 1975—. Contbr. numerous articles to med. jours. Served as capt. M.C. AUS, 1944-45. Fellow Am. Coll. Cardiology (sec. Chgo. roundtable 1963), A.C.P., Am. Coll. Chest Physicians, Am. Assn. Bioanalysts; mem. Ill. Soc. Med. Research, Am. Heart Assn. (fellow Council Clin. Cardiology), Chgo. Heart Assn., Greater Miami Heart Assn. (dir. 1975—), Chgo. Diabetes Assn., AMA, Ill. Med. Assn., Chgo. Med. Assn., Dade County (Fla.) Med. Assn., N.Y. Acad. Scis., Fla. Soc. Internal Medicine, AAAS, Brain Research Found. Office: 800 NE 195th St North Miami Beach FL 33179

CALLENBACH, ERNEST, writer, editor; b. Williamsport, Pa., Apr. 3, 1929; s. Ernest William and Margaret Isabel (Miller) C.; m. Christine Leefeldt, May 19, 1978; children: Joanna, Hans. Ph.B., U. Chgo., 1949, M.A., 1953. Editor Film Quar., U. Calif. Press, Berkeley, 1958—, editor books, 1958—. Author: Living Poor with Style, 1971,

Ecotopia, 1975, Ecotopian Encyclopedia for the Eighties, 1981, Ecotopia Emerging, 1981; co-author: screenplay Our New Wife, 1983. Mem. Writers Union. Office: U Calif Press 2120 Berkeley Way Berkeley CA 94720

CALLENDER, JOHN HANCOCK, architect; b. Kansas City, Mo., Jan. 18, 1908; s. Alonzo Lee and Lola (Hancock) C.; m. Mary Carnwath, Aug. 5, 1933; 1 dau., Janet. B.A., Yale, 1928; student, Sch. Architecture, 1928-30; B.Arch., N.Y.U., 1939. Research methods and materials low-cost housing John B. Pierce Found., N.Y.C., 1931-43; individual practice architecture, specializing in residences, 1945—; mem. faculty Columbia U., 1953-54, Princeton U., 1954-57; member faculty Pratt Inst., 1954-73, asso. prof., 1958-63, prof., 1963-73; cons. architect for Nat. Housing Agency, Staff Army Engrs., Manhattan project, Columbia, 1943-45; Vis. prof. Cheng Kung U., Taiwan, China, 1967-68. Author: Before You Buy a House, 1953, (with others) Curtain Walls of Stainless Steel, 1955; Editor-in-chief: Time-Saver Standards for Architectural Design Data, 1982; Contbr. to popular mags., profl. publs. Home: Tobacco St Rural Route 2 Lebanon CT 06249

CALLETON, THEODORE EDWARD, lawyer; b. Newark, Dec. 13, 1934; s. Edward James and Dorothy (Dewey) C.; m. Elizabeth Bennett Brown, Feb. 4, 1961; children: Susan Bennett, Pamela Barritt, Christopher Dewey.; m. Kathy E'Beth Conkle, Feb. 22, 1983. B.A., Yale U., 1956; LL.B., Columbia U., 1962. Bar: Calif. 1963, U.S. Dist. Ct. (so. dist.) Calif. 1963, U.S. Tax Ct. 1977. Asso. firm O'Melveny & Myers, Los Angeles, 1962-69, Agnew, Miller & Carlson, 1969, ptnr., 1970-79; individual practice law, Los Angeles, 1979-83; ptnr. Kindel & Anderson, 1983—; academician Internat. Acad. Estate and Trust Law, 1974—; lectr. Calif. Continuing Edn. bar, 1970—, U. So. Calif. Tax Inst., 1972—, Calif. State U., Los Angeles, 1975—, Practising Law Inst., 1976—; bd. dirs. UCLA Estate Planning Inst. Contbr. articles to legal jours. Chmn. Arroyo Seco Master Planning Commn., Pasadena, Calif., 1970-71; bd. dirs. Montessori Sch., Inc., 1964-68, chmn., 1966-68; bd. dirs. Am. Montessori Soc., N.Y.C., 1967-72, chmn., 1969-72; trustee Walden Sch. of Calif., 1970—, chmn., 1980—; trustee Episcopal Children's Home of Los Angeles, 1971-75. Served as lt. USMC, 1956-59. Fellow Am. Coll. Probate Counsel; mem. Am. Bar Assn., Los Angeles County Bar Assn. (chmn. taxation sect. 1980-81, chmn. probate and trust law sect. 1981-82), State Bar Calif., Aurelian Honor Soc., Beta Theta Pi, Phi Delta Phi. Unitarian. Clubs: Elihu, Univ., Am. Alpine. Home: 301 Churchill Rd Sierra Madre CA 91024 Office: 555 S Flower St Suite 2600 Los Angeles CA 90071

CALLIES, DAVID LEE, lawyer, educator; b. Chgo., Apr. 21, 1943; s. Gustav E. and Ann D. C.; m. Valerie Wayne, June 18, 1966; 1 dau., Sarah Anne. A.B., DePauw U., 1965; J.D., U. Mich., 1968; LL.M.; Mich.-Ford Found. fellow, Nottingham U., 1969. Bar: Ill. 1969. Spl. asst. states atty., McHenry County, Ill., 1969; asso. firm Ross, Hardies, O'Keefe, Babcock & Parsons, Chgo., 1969-75, partner, 1975-78; prof. law Sch. Law, U. Hawaii, Honolulu, 1978—; Mem. transp. adv. com. Oahu Devel. Conf., 1978—; mem. Citizens Adv. Com. on State Functional Plan for Conservation of Lands, 1979—; mem. adv. com. on planning and growth mgmt. City and County of Honolulu Council, 1978—. Author: (with Fred P. Bosselman) The Quiet Revolution in Land Use Control, 1971, (with Fred P. Bosselman and John S. Banta) The Taking Issue, 1973. Mem. Am. Bar Assn. (chmn. com. on land use, planning and zoning 1980-82, council, sect. on urban, state and local govt. 1981—), Am. Planning Assn. (exec. com. Hawaii chpt.), Hawaii Bar Assn., Ill. Bar Assn., Nat. Trust Hist. Preservation, Royal Oak Soc., Sierra Club. Episcopalian. Home: 4621 Aukai Ave Honolulu HI 96816 Office: Richardson Sch Law Dole St Honolulu HI 96822

CALLIGAN, WILLIAM DENNIS, life ins. co. exec.; b. Hibbing, Minn., Mar. 21, 1925; s. Raymond George and Ann Matilda (Olson) C.; m. Aletha E. Cornelius, Dec. 21, 1949; children—Ann M., Timothy M. B.A., Yankton (S.D.) Coll., 1949. With N.Y. Life Ins. Co., 1953—, dir. mass market products, N.Y.C., 1963-77, v.p. pensions, 1977—; mem. Internat. Found. Employee Benefit Plans, Inc. Served with USMC, World War II. Home: 66 Noe Ave Madison NJ 07940 Office: 51 Madison Ave New York NY 10010

CALLIS, CLAYTON FOWLER, research chemist; b. Sedalia, Mo., Sept. 25, 1923; s. Edward J. and Mary L. (Fowler) C.; m. Sara R. Steele, Apr. 9, 1949; children: Joanne, Judy. A.B., Central Meth. Coll., Fayette, Mo., 1944; M.S., U. Ill., 1946, Ph.D., 1984. Research chemist Gen. Electric Co., Richland, Wash., 1948-51, Monsanto Co., Anniston, Ala., 1951-54, Dayton, Ohio, 1951-54; dir. R & D inorganic div., Dayton, St. Louis, 1969-70; dir. R & D detergents and phosphates div. Monsanto Co., Dayton, St. Louis, 1971-75, dir. tech. planning Monsanto Indsl. Chems., Dayton, 1975-83, dir. environ. ops. Monsanto Fibers & Intermediate Co., 1983—. Mem. editorial bd.: Jour. Am. Chem. Soc., 1963-72; co-author: Particle Size, Measurement, Interpretation and Application, 1963; contbr. articles to profl. jours.; patentee. Recipient Disting. Alumni award Central Meth. Coll., 1970. Mem. Am. Chem. Soc. (dir.-at-large 1977—, chmn. bd. 1982, 83, St. Louis award 1971), Soap and Detergent Assn. (steering com. 1975), Am. Inst. Chemists, AAAS, Sigma Xi, Alpha Chi Sigma. Republican. Presbyterian. Club: Clayton (Mo.). Home: 2 Holiday Ln St louis MO 63131 Office: 800 N Lindbergh St Louis MO 63167

CALLIS, J. BRUCE, insurance company executive; b. Sedalia, Mo., Dec. 4, 1939; s. George Elgin and Jo (Trigg) C.; m. Nancy Williams, Nov. 14, 1959; children: Cheryl, Kevin, Kimberly. B.S., U. Mo., 1961. Plant mgr. Boonslick Mfg. Co., Boonville, Mo., 1961-62; field claim rep. State Farm Mut. Automobile Ins. Co., Rolla, Mo., 1963, asst. personnel mgr., Columbia, Mo., 1964-66, various personnel, sales positions, Bloomington, Ill., 1966-76, v.p., personnel, 1976—. Mem. McLean County (Ill.) Bd., 1968-74; chmn. McLean County Republican Com., Bloomington, 1978—; bd. dirs. Brokaw Hosp., Normal, Ill., 1979-82. Recipient appreciation award Am. Compensation Soc., 1969. Mem. Am. Soc. for Personnel Adminstrn. (chmn. adv. com. 1976—), Ins. Inst. for Hwy. Safety (personnel com. chmn. 1977—), McLean County Assn. Commerce. Presbyterian. Home: 1 Crestwood Ct Normal IL 61761 Office: State Farm Mutual Automobile Ins Co 1 State Farm Plaza Bloomington IL 61701

CALLIS, JERRY JACKSON, veterinarian; b. Parrot, Ga., July 28, 1926; s. Samuel Clayton and Sue (Glover) C.; m. Loisanne Roon, July 23, 1964; 1 son, Frederick Allan. Student, North Ga. Coll., 1943-44; D.V.M., Auburn U., 1947; M.S., Purdue U., 1949, D.Sc. (hon.), 1979, Southampton Coll., 1980. With U.S. Dept. Agr., 1948—; veterinarian-in-charge of research Plum Island Animal Center, 1953-56, asst. dir., 1956-63, dir., 1963—; cons. Pan Am. Health Orgn., 1968—; mem. adv. council Vet. Coll. Cornell, 1955—. Mem. AAAS. Home: Paradise Point Southold NY 11971 Office: PO Box 848 Greenport NY 11944

CALLIS, ROBERT, educator; b. Grand Tower, Ill., June 1, 1920; s. Marion J. and Edith (Todd) C.; m. Thelma Lewis, Oct. 23, 1942; children—Ronald W., Steven M.; m. Sharon K. Pope, Sept. 4, 1971. B.Ed., So. Ill. U., 1942; M.A., U. Minn., 1946, Ph.D., 1948. Lic. psychologist, Mo. Mem. faculty U. Mo., 1948—, prof. counseling psychology, 1955—, dir. counseling service, 1953-64, dean extra divisional adminstrn., 1964-69. Author: A Casebook of Counseling, 1955, Minnesota Teacher Attitude Inventory, 1951, Missouri College English Test, 1965, Stanford Achievement Test, High School Level, 1966, Stanford Test of Academic Skills, 1973, 2d edit., 1982; editor: APGA Ethical Standards Casebook, 1976, 2d edit., 1982, Jour. Coll. Student personnel, 1964-70. Served with USNR, 1942-46. Fellow Am. Psychol. Assn.; mem. Am. Coll. Personnel Assn. (pres. 1959-60), Am. Personnel and Guidance Assn. Home: Route 4 Columbia MO 65201

CALLISON, CHARLES HUGH, conservation organization executive; b. Lousana, Alta., Can., Nov. 6, 1913; came to U.S., 1918, naturalized, 1937; s. Guy A. and Dorinda (Stuart) C.; m. Amelia D. Ferguson, June 7, 1951; children: Charles Stuart, Joyce Marie (Mrs. Robert Melville), Karen Sue (Mrs. Glenn Bater), Bettye Ruth (Mrs. Kenneth Palermo). B.Jour., U. Mo., 1937, D.Sc. (hon.), 1979. Editor Garnett (Kan.) Rev., 1937-38, Boonville (Mo.) Advertiser, 1938-41; editor, info. div. chief Mo. Conservation Commn., 1941-46; exec. sec. Conservation Fedn. Mo., 1947-51; asst. conservation dir., then conservation dir. Nat. Wildlife Fedn., 1951-60; asst. to pres. Nat. Audubon Soc., 1960-66, exec. v.p., 1967-77; founder, dir. Pub. Lands Inst., Denver, 1977—; chmn. Nat. Resources Council Am., 1957-59; mem. organizing and exec. coms. 5th World Forestry Congress, 1960; chmn. legis. com. Internat. Assn. Game, Fish and Conservation Commrs., 1955-59; mem. Fed. Water Pollution Control Advisory Bd., 1961-64; mem. of Pres.-Elect's Task Force on Resources and Environment, 1968; mem. N.Y. State Environ. Bd., 1970-75. Author: Man and Wildlife in Missouri, 1952; Editor: America's Natural Resources, rev. edit, 1967. Village trustee, 1969-71. Recipient Frances K. Hutchinson medal Garden Club Am., 1974; Audubon medal Nat. Audubon Soc., 1978; conservation award Dept. Interior, 1980. Mem. Wildlife Soc., Sierra Club, Wilderness Soc., Am. Ornithologists Union, Sigma Delta Chi, Kappa Tau Alpha. Democrat. Mem. Disciples of Christ. Club: Cosmos (Washington). Home: 403 Castle Dr Jefferson City MO 65101

CALLISON, JAMES W., airline executive; b. Jamestown, N.Y., Sept. 8, 1928; s. J. Waldo and Gladys A. C.; m. Gladys I. Robinson, Oct. 3, 1959; children: Sharon Elizabeth, Maria Judith, Christopher James. A.B. with honors, U. Mich., 1950, J.D. with honors (Overbeck award 1952, Jerome S. Freud Meml. award 1953), 1953. Bar: D.C. 1953, Ga. 1960. Atty. firm Pogue & Neal, Washington, 1953-57; with Delta Air Lines, Inc., 1957—, v.p. law and regulatory affairs, 1974-78, sr. v.p., gen. counsel, Atlanta, 1978-81, sr. v.p., gen. counsel, corp. sec., 1981—. Contbr. articles to legal jours.; asst. editor: Mich. Law Rev, 1952-53. Recipient Pro Ecclesia Et Pontifice award, 1966. Mem. Am. Bar Assn. (vice chmn. internat. law sect. 1980-81), State Bar Ga. (co-chmn. corp. counsel com. 1980-81), Atlanta Bar Assn., Corp. Counsel Assn. Greater Atlanta, Am. Soc. Corp. Secs., Order of Coif. Roman Catholic. Clubs: Atlanta Athletic and Yacht, Lawyers (Atlanta); Nat. Aviation (Washington). Lodge: Kiwanis. Home: 950 Crestline Rd NE Atlanta GA 30328 Office: Delta Air Lines Hartsfield Atlanta Internat Airport Atlanta GA 30320

CALLMER, JAMES PETER, architect; b. Aurora, Ill., May 6, 1919; s. Carl L. and Anna (Hegg) C.; m. Sally-Lee Maxwell Young, Mar. 21, 1944; children—Melinda-Lee, Sally Susanne, Shelley Ann. B.S. in Architecture, U. Ill., 1942. Architect with Justement, Elam, Callmer & Kidd, Washington, 1956-66, Justement & Callmer, 1966-68, Callmer & Milstead, 1969-73; asso. Dalton, Dalton, Little, Newport, Inc., Bethesda, Md., 1973-77; constrn. mgr. Eisinger, Kilbane & Assos., Bethesda, 1978—; Bd. govs. Washington Bldg. Congress, 1968-71; pres. Bd. Examiners and Registrars Architects Washington, 1970-77; chmn. design and decoration com. 1969 Inaugural Com.; Mem. panel arbitrators Am. Arbitration Assn.; past pres. Western Bethesda Community Planning Assn. Prin. works include Nat. Guard Meml. Bldg, Washington, Sibley Meml. Hosp, Washington, Pan Am. Health Orgn, Washington; master plan for Judiciary Sq, Washington. Served to lt. comdr. USNR, 1942-46. Mem. A.I.A. (pres. Washington Met. chpt. 1968), Alpha Chi Rho (v.p. Phi Kappa chpt. 1941). Clubs: Cosmos (Washington); Columbia Country (Bethesda). Home: 5625 Huntington Pkwy Bethesda MD 20014 Office: 7315 Wisconsin Ave Bethesda MD 20014

CALLNER, RICHARD, artist, educator; b. Benton Harbor, Mich., May 18, 1927; s. Julius H. and Sarah (Sax) C.; m. Carolyn K. Callner, Apr. 6, 1952; children: David Kei, Joanna Reik. B.S. in Art, U. Wis.-Madison, 1951; certificate in Fine Arts, Academie Julian, Paris, 1949, M.A., Columbia U., 1952. Mem. faculty dept. art Purdue U., 1952-59, Olivet Coll., 1960-64; mem. faculty Tyler Sch. Art, Temple U., 1964-75; dir. Tyler Sch. Art, Rome, 1965-70; prof., chmn. dept. art SUNY, Albany, from 1975; vis. artist, lectr. numerous univs., colls.; vis. artist USIS, Turkey, adviser, Italy. One-man shows include, USIS, Naples, Rome, Munich, Hannover and Heidelberg, Germany, 1968, Gallery 252, Phila., 1971, USIS, Ankara, Istanbul and Ismir, Turkey, 1973, Bristol (R.I.) Mus., 1975, SUNYA Art Gallery, Nat. Acad. Sci., Washington, 1977, Cork (Ireland) Arts Council, 1980; represented in permanent collections, Phila. Mus. Art, Chgo. Art Inst., Olivet Coll., Yale U., Cin. Mus., Detroit Mus. Art, Worchester Mus., Mus. of Painting and Sculpture, Istanbul. Guggenheim fellow, 1959. Mem. Coll. Art Assn. Office: Dept Art SUNY Albany NY 12222 *

CALLO, JOSEPH FRANCIS, advertising agency executive; b. N.Y.C., Dec. 16, 1929; s. Joseph Francis and Mary Ellen (Brennan) C.; m. Susan Catherine Jones, June 10, 1952 (div. Nov. 1978); children: Joseph Francis III, James D., Mary Ellen, Kathleen E., Patricia A.; m. Sally Chin McElwreath, Mar. 17, 1979; 1 stepson, Robert Joseph McElwreath. B.A., Yale U., 1952. Account exec. firm Joseph F. Callo Inc., N.Y.C., 1952-58; vice pres. Potts-Woodbury Inc., N.Y.C., 1958-60, also dir., 1958-60; pres. Callo & Carroll Inc., N.Y.C., 1960-74; chmn. bd. dirs., creative dir. Callo Berger Albanese Inc., N.Y.C., 1974-75; cons., 1975—; TV producer NBC, N.Y.C., also Public Broadcasting Service, 1976-78; exec. v.p. Albert Frank/FCB, Inc., N.Y.C., 1978-81; sr. v.p. Muir Cornelius Moore, Inc., N.Y.C.; partner Leeward Islands Yacht Charters; adj. asso. prof. communication arts St. John's U., N.Y.C., 1970-74; freelance writer/photographer on maritime/nautical subjects; mem. mktg. rev. group USN, 1973. Served with USNR, 1952-54; rear adm. Res. Clubs: Yale of N.Y.; Naval and Military (London); Ski of Gt. Brit. Home: 109-14 Ascan Ave Forest Hills NY 11375 Office: 750 3d Ave Suite 28 New York NY 10017

CALLOW, ALLAN DANA, surgeon; b. W. Somerville, Mass., Apr. 9, 1916; s. Edward Rol and Carrie (Fowles) C.; m. Eleanor M. Magee, Feb. 28, 1943; children—Beverly Ann (Mrs. John C. Nelson, Jr.), Susan Diane (Mrs. John T. Moseley), Allan Dana. B.S., Tufts U., 1938, M.S., 1948, Ph.D., 1952; M.D., Harvard, 1942. Intern Boston City Hosp., 1942-43; research fellow and chief resident surgery Tufts New Eng. Med. Center, Boston, 1946-51, chief gen. and vascular surgery, vice chmn. dept. surgery; spl. fellow vascular diseases Mayo Clinic, Rochester, Minn., 1948-49; instr. to prof. surgery Tufts U. Sch. Medicine, Boston, 1948-64; cons. to surgeon gen. Med. Corps, U.S. Navy, also civilian community hosps.; mem. study com. div. med. scis. NRC, 1969-72. Asso. editor: Jour. Cardiovascular Surgery, 1969—; Contbr. articles on vascular surgery, gen. surgery, med. edn. to profl. jours. Trustee Tufts U., 1971—, chmn. bd., 1977—; trustee Civic Edn. Found., Lincoln Filene Center. Served with M.C., Amphibious Corps USNR, 1943-46; PTO; rear adm. Res. (ret.). Decorated Legion of Merit; recipient award Hellenic Internat. Red Cross. Mem. Internat. Cardiovascular Soc. (sec.-gen. 1967-77, pres. 1977—, pres. N.Am. chpt. 1974-75), A.C.S. (gov. 1974—, pres. Mass. chpt. 1973), New Eng. Surg. Soc., AMA (ho. dels. 1966-70), New Eng. Soc. Vascular Surgery (pres. 1977—), Soc. Vascular Surgery, Boston Surg. Soc. (pres. 1978), Mass. Med. Soc., Am. Surg. Assn., Assn. Med. Consultants to Armed Forces, Navy Inst., Navy League, Navy Res. Officers Assn., Phi Beta Kappa, Sigma Xi, Delta Upsilon; hon. mem. Hellenic, Mexican, Argentine socs. angiology, Italian, Belgian surg. socs., European Soc. Cardiovascular Surgery. Conglist. (chmn. bd. deacons 1962-66). Clubs: Union, Wardroom (Boston). Home: 492 Glen Rd Weston MA 02193 Office: 171 Harrison Ave Boston MA 02111

CALLOW, KEITH MCLEAN, judge; b. Seattle, Jan. 11, 1925; s. Russell Stanley and Dollie (McLean) C.; m. Evelyn Case, July 9, 1949; children: Andrea, Douglas, Kerry. Student, Alfred U., 1943, CCNY, 1944, Biarritz Am. U., 1945; B.A., U. Wash., 1949, J.D., 1952. Bar: Wash. 1952. Asst. atty. gen., Wash., 1952; law clk. Wash. Supreme Ct., 1953; dep. pros. atty. King County, 1954-56; partner firm Little, LeSourd, Palmer, Scott & Slemmons, Seattle, 1957-62, Barker, Day, Callow & Taylor, 1964-68; judge King County Superior Ct., 1969-71, Wash. State Ct. of Appeals, Seattle, 1972—, presiding chief judge, 1980; lectr. bus. law U. Wash., 1956-62; faculty Nat. Jud. Coll., 1980; co-organizer, sec. Council of Chief Judges, 1980. Editor works in field. Bd. dirs. Evergreen Safety Council, Kahumana, pvt. hosp., Hawaii; pres. Young Men's Republican Club, 1957. Served with AUS, 1943-46. Decorated Purple Heart.; recipient Brandeis award Wash. State Trial Lawyers Assn., 1981. Mem. Am. Bar Assn., Wash. State Bar Assn., D.C. Bar Assn., Seattle-King County Bar Assn., Estate Planning Council, Navy League (dir. Seattle chpt.), Psi Upsilon, Phi Delta Phi. Clubs: Rainier (sec. 1978), Forty Nine (pres. 1972), Masons.). Home: 4560 52d NE Seattle WA 98105 Office: One Union Sq 600 University St Seattle WA 98101

CALLOW, WILLIAM GRANT, state supreme court justice; b. Waukesha, Wis., Apr. 9, 1921; s. Curtis Grant and Mildred G. C.; m. Jean A. Zilavy, Apr. 15, 1950; children: William G., Christine S., Katherine H. Ph.B. in Econs, U. Wis., 1943, J.D., 1948. Bar: Wis. Asst. city atty., Waukesha, 1948-52, city atty., 1952-60, county judge, Waukesha, 1961-77; justice Supreme Ct. Wis., Madison, 1978—; mem. faculty Wis. Jud. Coll., 1968-75; asst. prof. U. Minn., 1951-52; Wis. mem. Nat. Conf. Commrs. on Uniform State Laws, 1967—. Served with USMC, 1943-45; Served with USAF, 1948-52. Recipient Outstanding Alumnus award U. Wis., 1973. Fellow Am. Bar Found.; mem. Am. Bar Assn., Dane County Bar Assn. Episcopalian. Office: 231 East State Capitol Madison WI 53702

CALLOWAY, DORIS HOWES, university administrator; b. Canton, Ohio, Feb. 14, 1923; d. Earl John and Lillian Ann (Roberts) Howes; m. Nathaniel O. Calloway, Feb. 14, 1946 (div. 1956); children: David Karl, Candace Calloway Hobbs. B.S., Ohio State U., 1943; Ph.D., U. Chgo., 1947. Head metabolism lab., nutritionist chief div. QM Food and Container Inst., Chgo., 1951-61; chmn. dept. food sci. and nutrition Stanford Research Inst., Menlo Park, Calif., 1961-63; prof. U. Calif., Berkeley, 1963—; provost profl. schs. and colls. Stanford Research Inst., Menlo Park, 1981—; mem. expert adv. panel nutrition WHO, Geneva, 1972—; trustee Internat. Maize and Wheat Improvement Ctr., 1983; cons. FAO, UN, Rome, 1971,74-75,81-83; adv. council NIH, Nat. Inst. Arthritis, Metabolic and Digestive Diseases, Nat. Inst. Aging, Bethesda, Md., 1974-77, 78-82. Author: Nutrition and Health, 1981, Nutrition and Physical Fitness 11th edit., 1984. Recipient Meritorious Civilian Service Dept. Army, 1959; named Disting. Alumna Ohio State U., 1974, Wellcome vis. prof. Fedn. Am. Soc. Exptl. Biol., U. Mo., 1980. Mem. Am. Inst. Nutrition (pres. 1982-83, sec. 1969-72, editorial bd. 1967-72), Am. Diabetic Assn. (editorial bd. 1974-77, Cooper Meml. lectr. 1983), Sigma Xi. Office: U Calif California Hall Berkeley CA 94720

CALLOWAY, JEAN MITCHENER, mathematician, educator; b. Indianola, Miss., Dec. 18, 1923; s. James Earl and Mittie Lou (Mitchener) C.; m. Anne Marie Whitney, June 21, 1952; children—Nancy Lou, Catherine Anne. B.A. with high honors, Millsaps Coll., 1944; A.M., U. Pa., 1949, Ph.D., 1952. With Millsaps Coll., 1944, McCallie Sch., Chattanooga, 1944-47, U. Pa., 1947-52; from asst. prof. to asso. prof., acting chmn. dept. Carleton Coll., 1952-60; Olney prof. math. Kalamazoo Coll., 1960—, chmn. dept., 1960-73; mem. sch. math. study group Inst. Advanced Study, 1959; math. workshop Ednl. Services, Inc., Mombasa, Kenya, 1965. Author: Fundamentals of Modern Mathematics, 1964. Mem. Am. Math. Soc., Math. Assn. Am. (chmn. Mich. sect. 1963-64), AAUP (pres. Kalamazoo Coll. chpt. 1964-65), Sigma Xi. Home: 1341 Bunker Hill Dr Kalamazoo MI 49009

CALLUM, MYLES, editor; b. Lynn, Mass., Apr. 4, 1934; s. Abraham Edward and Ann Edith (Caswell) C.; m. Suzanne Connellis, Apr. 22, 1967 (div. 1974); children—Deborah, Jennifer. Student, U. Conn., 1951-53, N.Y. U., 1958-61. Pvt. investigator, Stamford, Conn., 1958-59; asso. editor Leisure mag., N.Y.C., 1959-60; asst. editor Good Housekeeping mag., N.Y.C., 1961-63, asso. editor, 1963-69, dir. spl. publs. div., 1969-70; mng. editor Better Homes and Gardens, Des Moines, 1971-75; asso. editor TV Guide, Radnor, Pa., 1976—; White House cons., writer Fed. health programs, 1968. Author: Body-Building and Self-Defense, 1961, Body Talk, 1972, also articles. Served with CIC AUS, 1955-57. Mem. Nat. Assn. Sci. Writers, Mensa, U.S. Chess Fedn., Knights of Square Table. Home: 177 Hillside Circle Villanova PA 19085 Office: Radnor PA 19088

CALMAN, ROBERT FREDERICK, corporate executive; b. Mineola, N.Y., May 14, 1932; s. William Arthur and Ida (Alberswerth) C.; m. Susan Jean Raphael, June 20, 1959 (div. 1978); children: Andrew Frederick, Camille, Matthew Alexander; m. Doris Sumerson, June 9, 1979. B.A., Yale U., 1954; M.S., MIT, 1967. With Chase Manhattan Bank, N.Y.C., 1954-61, asst. treas., 1961; with Mobil Oil Corp., N.Y.C., 1961-70, treas. N.Am. div., 1964-68, treas. Internat. div., 1968-69; v.p. finance, treas. IU Internat. Corp., Phila., 1970-72, group v.p. devel., 1972-74, exec. v.p., 1974-78, vice chmn., dir., 1978—; chmn., dir. Echo Bay Mines Ltd.; vice chmn., dir. Gen. Waterworks Corp.; dir. Corp. Cons. Group, Ltd., WHYY, Inc., Western Indsl. Bank; mem. adv. council European Banking Co. Ltd.; lectr. N.Y. U., 1968-69. Author: Linear Programming and Cash Management/ Cash Alpha, 1968. Pres., Phila. chpt. Nat. Found. for Ileitis and Colitis, Inc., 1974-75; pres., mem. bd. govs. Soc. Alfred P. Sloan Fellows; dir. alumni fund, mem. corp. devel. com. Mass. Inst. Tech. Served to 1st lt., arty. AUS, 1955-57. Recipient E.P. Brooks prize Mass. Inst. Tech., 1967. Mem. Phi Beta Kappa, Phi Gamma Delta. Republican. Presbyn. Clubs: Racquet, Union League (Phila.). Home: 11-D Long Beach Blvd North Beach NJ 08008 Office: 1500 Walnut St Philadelphia PA 19102

CALMER, NED, author, journalist; b. Chgo., July 16, 1907; s. Henry Edgar and May (Regan) C.; m. Priscilla A. Hatch, Mar. 1929; 1 dau., Alden; m. Carol Church, Aug. 1957; 1 son, Regan; m. Gloria F. Hercik, Oct. 1974. Student, U. Va., 1930. Reporter, fgn. corr. Chgo. Tribune and N.Y. Herald-Tribune, 1927-34; fgn. news editor in N.Y. for Agence Havas, France, 1934-40; news editor, broadcaster C.B.S., 1940-67; war corr. with U.S. armed forces, Eng., France, Belgium, Germany, Holland, Italy, 1944-45; Mediterranean corr., 1951-53. Author: Beyond the Street, 1934, When Night Descends, 1936, The Strange Land, 1950, All the Summer Days, 1961, The Anchorman, 1970, The Avima Affair, 1973, Late Show, 1974, Madam Ambassador, 1975, The Peking Dimension, 1976, Bay of Lions, The Winds of Montauk, 1980. Club: Players. Home and office: 125 Ocean Ave Lawrence NY 11559

CALOGERO, PASCAL FRANK, JR., state supreme court justice; b. New Orleans, Nov. 9, 1931; s. Pascal Frank and Louise (Moore) C.; children—Deborah Ann Calogero Applebaum, David, Pascal III, Elizabeth, Thomas, Michael, Stephen, Gerald. Student, Coll. Arts and Scis., Loyola U., New Orleans, 1949-51, J.D., 1954. Bar: La. Partner firm Landrieu, Calogero & Kronlage, 1958-69, Calogero & Kronlage, 1969-73; gen. counsel La. Stadium and Expn. Dist., 1970-73; asso. justice La. Supreme Ct., New Orleans, 1973—. Mem. La. Democratic State Central Com., 1963-71; mem. subcom. on del. selection La. Dem. Party, 1971; del. Dem. Nat. Conv., 1968. Served to capt. JAGC U.S. Army, 1954-57. Mem. Am. Bar Assn., La. Bar Assn., New Orleans Bar Assn., Greater New Orleans Trial Lawyers Assn. (v.p. 1967-69). Office: 301 Loyola Ave New Orleans LA 70112

CALTON, JUDGE TERRY, JR., hospital executive; b. Imboden, Va., June 3, 1931; s. Judge Terry and Flora Etta (Southard) C.; children: Michael, Anthony. B.A., Berea (Ky.) Coll., 1953; M.S. in Adminstrv. Medicine, Columbia U., 1959. Adminstrv. asst., asst. adminstr. Miners Meml. Hosp. Assn., Washington, 1955-57, adminstr., 1959-63; research asst. Columbia U., 1963-64; asst. to assoc. hosp. dir. Univ. Hosp., Lexington, Ky., 1965-71, hosp. dir., 1971-77; exec. v.p. Meth. Hosps. of Memphis, 1978-80, pres., 1981—; precepter U. Mich. Program and Bur. Hosp. Adminstrn., Ga. State U. Inst. Health Adminstrs.; chmn. strategic planning com. Tenn. Health Adminstrs.; bd. dirs. Mid-South Med. Center Council; Bd. dirs. U. Tenn. Cancer Clinic., Blue Cross/Blue Shield. Served with M.S.C. U.S. Army, 1953-55. Fellow Am. Coll. Hosp. Adminstrs. (regent adviser to Tenn. regent); mem. Ky. Hosp. Assn. (life), Am. Hosp. Assn., Tenn. Hosp. Assn., Ky. Public Health Assn., Memphis Hosp. Dist. (v.p.), Am. Assn. Med. Colls., Hosp. Alliance Tenn. (bd. dirs.), Health Care Coalition Mem. Methodist. Office: 1265 Union Ave Memphis TN 38104

CALVANO, JAMES FRANCIS, travel and related services executive; b. Chgo., Sept. 24, 1936; s. James V. and Susan (Munno) C.; m. Sharon K. Rickard, May 24, 1964; children—Christine, James, John, Marc, Michael. Student, U.S. Naval Acad., 1954-55, U. Wis., 1955-57, U. Chgo., 1957-59; grad. Advanced Mgmt. Program, Grad. Sch. Bus. Adminstrn., Harvard U., 1978. With Olivetti Corp. Am., 1957-71, Revlon Corp., N.Y.C., 1971-72; from exec. v.p. to pres. and chief exec. officer Avis, Inc., N.Y.C., 1972-81; pres. Payment Systems dir. Am. Express Co., N.Y.C., 1981—. Mem. Businessmen for Performing Arts. Mem. Mktg. Mgmt. Assn., Sales Execs. Assn. Clubs: N.Y. Athletic, Knickerbocker Country, Columbus, Englewood Field; Harvard (N.Y.C.). Office: Am Express Co American Express Plaza New York NY 10004

CALVERLEY, JOHN ROBERT, physician, educator; b. Hot Springs, Ark., Jan. 14, 1932; s. John A. and Della (O'Neill) C.; m. Alice Mae Feller, Dec. 27, 1953; children: Mark (dec.), David. B.S., U. Oreg., 1953, M.D., 1955. Diplomate: neurology Am. Bd. Psychiatry and Neurology (dir. 1977—, sec. 1981-83, v.p. 1983—). Intern U. Iowa, Iowa City, 1955-56, resident in neurology, 1956; resident in internal medicine Mayo Found., Rochester, Minn., 1957, neurology resident, 1957-59; mem. faculty dept. neurology Med. Br. U. Tex., Galveston, 1964—, assoc. prof., 1966-70, prof., 1970—, chief div. neurology, 1967-73, chmn. dept. neurology, 1973—; cons. neurology USAF, 1965—, nat. cons. to surgeon gen., 1976—. Served to capt. M.C. USAF, 1957-64. Mem. AMA (chmn. sect. council on neurology 1974-76), Tex. Med. Assn., Am. Acad. Neurology, Am. Neurol. Assn., Am. Epilepsy Soc., Sigma Xi. Home: 39 Colony Park Circle Galveston TX 77551 Office: Dept Neurology U Tex Galveston TX 77550

CALVERT, DELBERT WILLIAM, business executive; b. Bosworth, Mo., Jan. 29, 1927; s. William McKinley and Ruby Leona (Berrier) C.; m. Mary Lee Brown, Feb. 10, 1947 (div. Mar. 1971); children: Gary D., Danial L.; m. Melva Allen Hurst, Sept. 4, 1971; stepchildren: Holly Hurst, Allen Hurst. B.S. in Civil Engring, U. Mo., 1952. Asst. mgr. supply and transp. div. Phillips Petroleum Co., Bartlesville, Okla., 1952-63; asst. to v.p. Tex. Eastern Transmission Corp., Houston, 1963-65; mgr. diversification dept. No. Natural Gas Co., Omaha, 1965-68; pres. Williams Bros. Pipe Line Co., Tulsa, 1968-71; exec. v.p. The Williams Cos., Tulsa, 1971—; also dir.; chmn. bd. Williams Energy Co., 1975-79; also dir.; chmn., chief exec. officer Agrico Chem. Co., Tulsa, 1977—, also dir.; dir. Williams Exploration Co., Edgcomb Steel Co., Tulsa; mem. fertilizer industry adv. com. FAO. Mem. exec. bd. Indian Nations council Boy Scouts Am., 1969—, pres., 1974-76; bd. dirs. Goodwill Industries Tulsa; mem. U. Mo. Devel. Fund, 1969—, chmn., 1972-73. Served with AUS, 1945-47. Mem. Okla. Petroleum Council (dir. 1968—, pres. 1977-78), Am. Petroleum Inst. (gen. com. div. transp. 1971), Fertilizer Industry Assn. (chmn. bd.), Potash and Phosphate Inst. (dir. 1982—), Tulsa C. of C., Tau Beta Pi, Chi Epsilon, Pi Mu Epsilon. Republican. Clubs: Southern Hills Country, Tulsa, Summit Shangri-La (Afton, Okla.); Garden of Gods (Colorado Springs, Colo.); Castle Pines Golf (Castle Rock, Colo.); Sky (N.Y.C.). Home: 2739 E 69th Pl Tulsa OK 74136 Office: One Williams Center Tulsa OK 74101

CALVERT, GORDON LEE, legal association executive; b. Wardensville, W.Va., Sept. 2, 1921; s. Aaron Lee and Ada (Brill) C.; m. Margaret James, June 9, 1945; children—Gordon R., Roger L., Walter R. B.A. with distinction, George Washington U., 1943, J.D., 1945. Bar: D.C. 1946. Assoc. firm Covington & Burling, Washington, 1944-46; with Investment Bankers Assn. Am., Washington, 1946-71, exec. dir., gen. counsel, 1966-71; exec. v.p., gen. counsel Securities Industry Assn., 1972; v.p., gen. counsel N.Y. Stock Exchange, Washington, 1973-76; exec. dir. comml. collection agy. sect. Comml. Law League Am., Washington, 1976—. Author: Fundamentals of Municipal Bonds, 1959, Digest of Investments of State Pension Funds, 1960, Digest of State Laws Regulating Debt Collection Agencies, 1977, 81. Mem. Am. Bar Assn., Am. Soc. Assn. Execs., Order Coif, Pi Kappa Alpha, Phi Delta Phi, Omicron Delta Kappa. Presbyterian. Clubs: Metropolitan (Washington); Columbia Country (Chevy Chase, Md.). Home: 6712 Michaels Dr Bethesda MD 20817 Office: PO Box 34-531 Washington DC 20817

CALVERT, JACK GEORGE, atmospheric chemist, educator; b. Inglewood, Calif., May 9, 1923; s. John George and Emma (Eschstruth) C.; m. Doris Arlene Breimon, Nov. 8, 1946; children: Richard John, Mark Steven. B.S. in Chemistry, UCLA, 1944, Ph.D., 1949. Mem. faculty Ohio State U., 1950-81, prof. chemistry, 1960-81, Kimberly prof. chemistry, 1974-81, prof. emeritus, 1981—, chmn. dept., 1964-68; sr. scientist Nat. Center Atmospheric Research, Boulder, Colo., 1981—; Cons. air pollution tng. com. USPHS, 1964-66; mem. Nat. Air Pollution Control Manpower Devel. Com., 1966-69, chmn., 1968-69; bd. dirs. Gordon Research Confs., 1969-71; mem. air pollution control research grants com. EPA, 1970-72, chmn., 1971-72, mem. chemistry and physics adv. com., 1973-75; chmn. air pollution com. Conservation Found., 1968-70; mem. air conservation commn. Am. Lung Assn., 1973-75; chmn. EPA environ. chemistry/physics grants rev. panel, 1979-83. Author: (with J. N. Pitts, Jr.) Photochemistry, 1966, Graduate School in the Sciences, 1972; also articles. Served to ensign USNR, 1944-46. Named Honor Prof. of Year Coll. Arts and Scis., Ohio State U., 1957; recipient Alumni award for disting. teaching, 1961, Disting. Research award, 1981; Fellow NRC Can., 1949; Guggenheim fellow, 1977-78. Fellow Ohio Acad. Sci., Am. Inst. Chemists; mem. Am. Chem. Soc. (award for creative research in environ. sci. and tech. 1981, Columbus sect. award 1981), AAUP, Air Pollution Control Assn., Phi Beta Kappa, Sigma Xi, Pi Mu Epsilon, Phi Lambda Upsilon, Alpha Chi Sigma. Spl. research photochemistry, reaction kinetics, environmental chemistry, mechanisms free radical reactions. Office: NCAR Atmospheric Chemistry and Aeronomy Div PO Box 3000 Boulder CO 80307

CALVERT, JAMES FRANCIS, engineering and manufacturing company executive; b. Cleve., Sept. 8, 1920; s. Charles Spence and Grace (Gholson) C.; m. Nancy Ridgeway King, Aug. 9, 1942 (dec. Dec. 1965); children: James, Margaret, Charles; m. Margaretta Sergeant Harrison, Apr. 8, 1968. Student, Oberlin Coll., 1937-39, D.Sc. (hon.), 1960; B.S. in Elec. Engring, U.S. Naval Acad., 1942. Commnd. ensign U.S. Navy, 1942, advanced through grades to vice-adm., 1970; served in submarines, PTO, World War II, comdr. diesel submarine, 1952-55, nuclear power submarine, 1956-59, 1958, 59, 1958, 1958, 1959, dir. politico-mil. policy, 1965-67, comdr., 1967-68, supt., Annapolis, Md., 1968-72, ret., 1973; asst. to chmn. bd. Texaco Inc., N.Y.C., 1973-74; v.p. Combustion Engring., Inc., Stamford, Conn., 1974-75, v.p. ops., 1975-84, dir., 1975-84; dir. Mass. Mut., Springfield, Dexter Corp., Windsor Locks, Conn., Oak Industries Inc., Rancho Bernardo, Calif. Author: Surface at the Pole, 1960, A Promise to Your Country, 1961, The Naval Profession, 1965. Decorated D.S.M. (2), Silver Star (2), Bronze Star (2), Legion of Merit (4), Navy Commendation ribbon, Dept. Def. Commendation medal; French Govt. Merite Maritime. Mem. U.S. Naval Acad. Alumni Assn., U.S. Naval Inst. Clubs: Univ. (N.Y.C.); Mill Reef (Antigua, B.W.I.); N.Y. Yacht, Explorers (N.Y.C.); Wee Burn Country (Darien, Conn.); Employers. Office: One Glendinning Pl Westport CT 06880

CALVERT, JON CHANNING, family practice physician; b. Sonora, Calif., May 17, 1941; s. Floyd Raymond and Aloha Jean (Fernandes) C.; m. Lynnette Laurene Jacobson, June 6, 1970; children: Joshua and Stephen (twins). A.B., Stanford U., 1963; M.S., Baylor U., 1968, M.D., 1968, Ph.D.; postdoctoral fellow in anatomy, 1970. Diplomate: Am. Bd. Family Practice. Intern Meth. Hosp., Houston, 1970-71; pvt. practice medicine, Houston, 1971-73; asst. prof. anatomy and cell biology Baylor U., 1970-73; asst. prof. family practice Med. Coll. Ga., Augusta, 1973-75, asso. prof., 1975-77, prof., 1977-82, chmn. dept., 1976-81; prof. family medicine Oral Roberts U. Sch. Medicine, Tulsa, 1982—, chmn. dept., 1982—; chief dept. community and family medicine City of Faith Hosp. and Research Ctr., Tulsa, 1982—; mem. Gov.'s Joint Bd. Family Practice, 1976-81; chmn. Ga. Fedn. Family Practice Residency Programs, 1976-77; mem. Ga. Dept. Human Resources Adv. Council on Phys. Health Needs of Children and Youth, 1977-78; med. dir. Tri-County Health System, Inc., 1981—; mem. family medicine del. to China, 1983. Bd. deacons Covenant Presbyn. Ch., 1979-81. Fellow Am. Acad. Family Physicians; mem. AMA, AAAS, Am. Assn. Med. Colls., So. Soc. Anatomists, So. Med. Assn. (chmn. family practice sect. 1977-78), Ga. Acad. Family Physicians (Disting. Service award 1975), Soc. Tchrs. Family Medicine, Sci. Research Soc. N.Am., Christian Med. Soc., Richmond County Med. Soc. Office: Oral Roberts U Family Practice Ctr 7306 S Lewis St Tulsa OK 74136

CALVERT, RICHARD WORCESTER, banker; b. Cambridge, Mass., Nov. 18, 1931; s. James Henry and Carolyn Rice C.; m. Margaret Doane, June 15, 1954; children: Karen Baird, Tobin Rice. B.A., Princeton U., 1954; grad., Southwestern Grad. Sch. Banking, 1963. Asst. v.p. Alamo Nat. Bank, San Antonio, 1957-63; with Nat. Bank Commerce San Antonio, 1963—, exec. v.p., 1966-68, pres., 1968-76, chmn. bd., 1976-82; pres. Nat. Bancshares Corp. Tex., San Antonio, 1971-77, chmn. bd., 1977—, chief exec. officer, 1982—; dir. Sigmor Corp., San Antonio. Bd. dirs. United Way, San Antonio and Bexar County, San Antonio Med. Found., Tex. Research League, San Antonio Econ. Devel. Found.; bd. dirs., trustee S.W. Research Inst., San Antonio; vice-chmn. bd. trustees Trinity U. Served with U.S. Army, 1954-56. Recipient Nat. Humanitarian award B'nai B'rith, 1977. Mem. Assn. Res. City Bankers, Greater San Antonio C. of C. (vice-chmn.). Clubs: Tex. Cavaliers, San Antonio German. Home: 224 Allen St San Antonio TX 78209 Office: PO Drawer 121 San Antonio TX 78291 *

CALVERT, STEPHEN EDWARD, oceanography educator; b. London, Dec. 30, 1935; emigrated to Can., 1979; s. Edward George and Pansy Violet (Boxall) C.; m. Helene Marie Flanders, Aug. 30, 1963; children: Bronwen E., Philip F., Alison M., Stephen F. B.Sc., Reading U., Eng., 1958; Ph.D., U. Calif.-San Diego, 1964. Asst. prof. oceanography UCLA, 1964-66; lect. Edinburgh U., Scotland, 1966-72; sr. prin. sci. officer Inst. Oceanographic Scis., Wormley, 1972-79; prof., head dept. oceanography U. B.C., Vancouver, 1979—. Mem. Geochem. Soc., Am. Geophys. Union, Canadian Meterol. and Oceanographic Soc., Scottish Marine Biol. Assn. Office: Dept Oceanography Univ British Columbia Vancouver BCCanada V6P 5K5

CALVIN, ALLEN DAVID, psychologist; b. St. Paul, Feb. 17, 1928; s. Carl and Zelda (Engelson) C.; m. Dorothy VerStrate, Oct. 5, 1953; children—Jamie, Kris, David, Scott. B.A. in Psychology cum laude, U. Minn., 1950, M.A., U. Tex., 1951, Ph.D. in Exptl. Psychology, 1953. Instr. Mich. State U., East Lansing, 1953-55; asst. prof. Hollins Coll., 1955-59, asso. prof., 1959-61; dir. Britannica Center for Studies in Learning and Motivation, Menlo Park, Calif., 1961; prin. investigator Carnegie Found. (grant for automated teaching fgn. langs.), 1960; USPHS grantee, 1960; pres. Behavioral Research Labs., 1962-74; prof., dean Sch. Edn., U., San Francisco, 1974—; Henry Clay Hall prof. Orgn. and leadership, 1978—. Author textbooks. Served with USNR, 1946-47. Mem. Am. Psychol. Assn., AAAS, Sigma Xi, Psi Chi. Home: 1645 15th Ave San Francisco CA 94122 Office: U San Francisco San Francisco CA 94117

CALVIN, DONALD LEE, stock exchange executive; b. Mount Olive, Ill., Nov. 10, 1931; s. Mike H. and Mary Josephine C.; m. Louise Peterson, Mar. 28, 1952; children: Jane Calvin Palasek, Sally Anne. Student, Eastern Ill. U., 1950-55; LL.B., U. Ill., 1956. Bar: Ill. Practiced law, Farmer City, Ill., 1956-57; atty., office of sec. of state State of Ill., 1957-58, securities commr., 1959-62; syndicate mgr. A.C. Allyn & Co., Chgo., 1962-63; atty. F.I. du Pont & Co., Chgo., 1963-64; exec. asst. civic and govt. affairs N.Y. Stock Exchange, N.Y.C., 1964-65, v.p. civic and govt. affairs, 1966-77, sr. v.p., 1977-79, exec. v.p. market devel. and pub. affairs, 1979—; dir. Depository Trust Co., N.Y. Futures Exchange.; Mem. adv. bd. U. Calif. Securities Law Inst. Bd. visitors U. Ill. Coll. Law. Served with USMCR, 1951-56. Mem. Internat. Bar Assn., Am. Bar Assn., Ill. Bar Assn., Chgo. Bar Assn. Clubs: Metropolitan (N.Y.C.); Manhasset Bay Yacht (Port Washington, N.Y.); N.Y. Stock Exchange Luncheon. Home: 4 Knolls Ln Manhasset NY 11030 Office: NY Stock Exchange 11 Wall St New York NY 10005

CALVIN, LARRY O., zoo administrator; (married); 1 son. Formerly curator Dallas Zoo, now dir. Mem. Am. Assn. Zool. Parks and Aquariums. Office: 621 Clarendon Dr Dallas TX 75203 *

CALVIN, LYLE DAVID, statistician, educator; b. Dannebrog, Nebr., Apr. 12, 1923; s. David A. and Muriel (Harvey) C.; m. Shirley Jeanne Schmidt, Apr. 19, 1952; children—James Arthur, Ronald David, Janet Lee. Grad., Parsons (Kans.) Jr. Coll., 1943; B.S. in Meteorology, U. Chgo., 1948, N.C. State U., 1947, Ph.D., 1953. Biometrician G.D. Searle & Co., Chgo., 1950-52; asst. statistician N.C. State U., Raleigh, 1952-53; statistician (Agrl. Expt. Sta.); asso. prof. Oreg. State U., 1953-57, prof., 1957—, chmn. dept. statistics, 1962-81; dir. Survey Research Center, 1974—; dean Grad. Sch., 1981—; vis. prof. U. Edinburgh, 1967, Inst. Stat. Studies and Research, U. Cairo, 1971-72. Served from pvt. to 1st lt. USAAF, 1943-46. Fellow AAAS, Am. Statis. Assn.; mem. Internat. Statis. Inst., Biometric Soc. (pres. WNAR 1964-65, gen. sec. 1980-84), Internat. Assn. Survey Statisticians. Home: 3463 NW Crest Dr Corvallis OR 97330

CALVIN, MELVIN, chemist, educator; b. St. Paul, Apr. 8, 1911; s. Elias and Rose I. (Hervitz) C.; m. Marie G. Jemtegaard, 1942; children: Elin, Karole, Noel. B.S., Mich. Coll. Mining and Tech., 1931, D.Sc., 1955; Ph.D., U. Minn., 1935, D.Sc., 1969; hon research fellow, U. Manchester, Eng., 1935-37; Guggenheim fellow, 1967; D.Sc., Nottingham U., 1958, Oxford (Eng.) U., 1959, Northwestern U., 1961, Wayne State U., 1962, Gustavus Adolphus Coll., 1963, Poly. Inst. Bklyn., 1962, U. Notre Dame, 1965, U. Gent, Belgium, 1970, Whittier Coll., 1971, Clarkson Coll., 1976, U. Paris Val-de-Marne, 1977, Columbia U., 1979. With U. Calif., Berkeley, 1937—, successively instr. chemistry, asst. prof., prof., Univ. prof., dir. Lab. Chem. Biodynamics, 1963-80, assoc. dir. Lawrence Berkeley Lab., 1967-80; Peter Reilly lectr. U. Notre Dame, 1949; Harvey lectr. N.Y. Acad. Medicine, 1951; Harrison Howe lectr. Rochester sect. Am. Chem. Soc., 1954; Falk-Plaut lectr. Columbia U., 1954; Edgar Fahs Smith Meml. lectr. U. Pa. and Phila. sect. Am. Chem. Soc., 1955; Donegani Found. lectr. Italian Nat. Acad. Sci., 1955; Max Tishler lectr. Harvard U., 1956; Karl Folkers lectr. U. Wis., 1956; Baker lectr. Cornell U., 1958; London lectr., 1961, Willard lectr., 1982; Vanuxem lectr. Princeton U., 1969; Disting. lectr. Mich. State U., 1977; Prather lectr. Harvard U., 1980; Dreyfus lectr. Dartmouth Coll., 1981, Berea Coll., 1982; Barnes lectr. Colo. Coll., 1982; Nobel lectr. U. Md., 1982; Abbott lectr. U. N.D., 1983; Gunning lectr. U. Alta., 1983; O'Leary disting. lectr. Gonzaga U., 1984; Eastman prof. Oxford (Eng.) U., 1967-68. Author: (with G. E. K. Branch) The Theory of Organic Chemistry, 1940, Isotopic Carbon, (with others), 1949, Chemistry of Metal Chelate Compounds, (with Martell), 1952, Path of Carbon in Photosynthesis, (with Bassham), 1957, Photosynthesis of Carbon Compounds, 1962, Chemical Evolution, 1969; contbr. articles to chem. and sci. jours. Recipient prize Sugar Research Found., 1950, Flintoff medal prize Brit. Chem. Soc., 1953, Stephen Hales award Am. Soc. Plant Physiologists, 1956, Nobel prize in chemistry, 1961; Davy medal Royal Soc., 1964; Virtanen medal, 1975; Priestley medal, 1978; Am. Inst. Chemists medal, 1979; Feodor Lynen medal, 1983; Sterling B. Hendricks medal, 1983; Oesper award Cin. sect. Am. Chem. Soc., 1981. Mem. Britain's Royal Soc. London (fgn. mem.), Am. Chem. Soc. (Richards medal N.E. sect. 1956, Chem. Soc. Nichols medal N.Y. sect. 1958, award for nuclear applications in chemistry, pres. 1971, Gibbs medal Chgo. sect. 1977, Priestley medal 1978), Am. Acad. Arts and Scis., Nat. Acad. Scis., Royal Dutch Acad. Scis., Japan Acad., Am. Philos. Soc., Sigma Xi, Tau Beta Pi, Phi Lambda Upsilon. Home: 2683 Buena Vista Berkeley CA 94708

CALVO, PAUL MCDONALD, gov. Guam Island; b. Agana, Guam, July 25, 1934; s. Eduardo Torres and Veronica Mariano (McDonald) C.; m. Rosa Herrero Baza, July 28, 1956; children—Dolores, Katherine, Paul, Eduardo, Barbara, Marie, Reyna, Clare. Student, Peacock Mil. Acad., 1954; B.S. in Commerce, U. Santa Clara, 1958. Salesman Studebaker-Packard Motors, Agana, Guam, 1958-60, Am. Nat. Ins. Co., Agana, 1960-63; pres. Calvo's Ins. Underwriters, Agana, 1963-78, Pacific Constrn. Co., 1963-78; v.p. Fed. Bldg., Inc., Agana, 1963-75, Calvo Fin. Corp., 1963-78; sec.-treas. Mid-Pacific Liquor Distbg. Corp., Tamuning, Guam, 1969-78; mem. Guam Senate, 1970-72, minority leader, 1970, 72, chmn. com. on fin. and taxation, 1965, chmn. spl. com. on crime, 1972; gov. Terr. Guam, Agana, 1978—. Chmn. 5th South Pacific Games, 1970—; chmn. fund campaign ARC, Agana chmn. fund campaign ARC, 1970, bd. dirs., 1970-73; co-chmn. fund dr. Chamorro council Boy Scouts Am., 1971; trustee Guam Meml. Hosp., Agana, 1971; mem. Hawaii adv. council CAP, 1979; mem. civilian adv. council Dept. Def.; chmn. Guam Republican Party, 1968. Recipient various awards Am. Internat. Ins. Co., 1969, 71, 72; Disting. Service award Tb and Respiratory Disease Assn.; Eternal Youth award 4th Guam Youth Congress, 1978. Mem. Guam Jaycees. Roman Catholic. Clubs: Rotary (Guam); Elks, Holy Names Soc., Am. Nat. Ins. Co. Pres.'s. Office: Office of Gov Agana GU 96910

CAMACHO, CARLOS SABLAN, physician, govt. ofcl.; s. Luis T. and Ramona (Sablan) C.; 1 child. Grad., U. South Pacific, Fiji Islands, 1962; M.P.H., U. Hawaii. Intern Dr. Jose Torres Meml. Hosp., Saipan, Mariana Islands, 1962-63; mem. staff USPHS, Saipan, 1963-77; co-owner El Cine Theatre, Saipan, 1969-77; mem. Congress Micronesia, 1967-68; pres. Popular Party (name changed to Democratic Party), 1976-77; gov. Commonwealth No. Mariana Islands, 1978—; mem. Micronesian Manpower Devel. Council, 1967-70; del. No. Mariana Islands Constl. Conv., 1976. 96950

CAMACHO FLORES, FELIXBERTO, bishop; b. Agana, Guam, Jan. 13, 1912. Ordained priest Roman Catholic Ch., 1949; apptd. apostolic adminstr. Diocese of Agana, Guam, 1969; apptd. titular bishop of Stonj, 1970, consecrated bishop of Agana, 1970. Office: Bishop's House Cuesta San Ramon Agana GU 96910 *

CAMBEL, ALI B., engr., educator; b. Merano, Italy, Apr. 9, 1923; U.S., 1943, naturalized, 1951; s. H. Cemil and Remziye (Hakki) C.; m. Marion dePaar, Dec. 20, 1946; children—Metin, Emel, Leyla, Sarah. B.S., Robert Coll., Istanbul, Turkey, 1942; postgrad., U. Istanbul, 1942-43, Mass. Inst. Tech., 1943-45; M.S., Calif. Inst. Tech., 1946; Ph.D., U. Iowa, 1950. Instr. State U. Iowa, 1947-50, asst. prof., 1950-53; asso. prof. mech. engring. Northwestern U., 1953-56, prof. mech. engring., 1956-61, Walter P. Murphy distinguished prof., 1961-68, dir. gas dynamics lab., 1953-66, chmn. dept. mech. engring. and astronautical scis., 1957-66; dir. research and engring. support div. IDA, 1966-67, v.p. for research, 1967-68; dean Coll. Engring., Wayne State U., Detroit, 1968-70, exec. v.p. for acad. affairs, 1970-72; v.p. Gen. Research Corp., 1972-74, dir. systems research div., 1972-74; dep. asst. dir. for sci. and tech. NSF, 1974-75; prof. engring. and applied sci. George Washington U., Washington, 1975—, chmn. dept. civil, mech. and environ. engring., 1978-80, dir. energy programs, 1976—; tech. cons. govt. agys., various firms; staff dir. Pres.'s Interdeptl. Energy Study, 1963; engring. scis. adv. com. USAF Office Sci. Research, 1961-63; mem. Commn. Engring. Edn., 1966—, Army Sci. Advisory Panel, 1966-72; nat. lectr. Sigma Xi, 1961-62. Author: Plasma Physics and Magnetofluidmechanics, 1963; co-author: Gas Dynamics, 1958, Real Gases, 1963, Plasma Physics, 1965; Editor: Transport Properties in Gases, 1958, The Dynamics of Conducting Gases, 1960, Second Law Analysis of Energy Devices and Processes, 1980; co-editor: Magnetohydrodynamics, 1962, ACTA Astronautica, 1974-76; asso. editor: Am. Inst. Aeros. and Astronautics jour., Jet Propulsion, 1955-60, Energy, 1975—; Contbr. numerous papers in field. Bd. dirs. YMCA. Recipient leadership award YMCA, 1953; citation for satellite power system evaluation Dept. Energy/NASA, 1981; cert. for patriotic service Sec. of Army; award for excellence NSF/RANN; award for contbns. to sci. and edn. U.S. Immigrants League.; Washburn scholar, 1938; George Westinghouse award, 1966. Fellow AIAA (J. Edward Pendray award 1959, nat. dir.); mem. Am. Soc. Engring. Edn. (Curtiss McGraw award 1960), ASME (founding chmn. energy systems analysis tech. com. 1980—), Sigma Xi, Pi Tau

Sigma, Tau Beta Pi.; Mem. Soc. of Friends. Club: Cosmos (Washington). Home: 6155 Kellogg Dr McLean VA 22101 Office: George Washington U Sch Engring and Applied Sci Office Energy Programs Washington DC 20052

CAMERON, ALASTAIR DUNCAN, cons. engr.; b. Fredericton, N.B., Can., Oct. 28, 1920; s. Adam and Dora Isabel C.; m. Audrey Charlton, May 17, 1951; children: Duncan, Harry, Sheila, Janet. B.Sc. in Civil Engring. U. N.B., 1942; Diploma in Mgmt., McGill U., 1970. Design engr. Dominion Bridge Co. Ltd., Montreal, 1946-47; with Montreal Engring. Co. Ltd., 1947-56, supervising engr., 1949-56; gen. mgr. Maritime Electric Co., Ltd., Charlottetown, P.E.I., Can., 1957-63; with Montreal Engring. Co. Ltd., 1963-71, mgr. econs. and valuation div., 1969-71, v.p., mgr. mgmt. cons. div., 1972—; v.p. Utility Mgmt., Montreal, 1976—; chmn., dir. Maritime Electric Co. Ltd.; chmn., mng. dir. Monenco Jamaica Ltd.; dep. chmn., dir. Nfld. Light & Power Co. Ltd.; v.p., dir. Canelco Services Ltd.; dir. Monenco Ltd., Monenco Holdings Ltd. Served with Can. Army, 1942-45. Decorated mem. Order Brit. Empire. Mem. Order of Engrs. Que., Can. Soc. Civil Engrs., Engring. Inst. Can., Can. Elec. Assn., Can. Nat. Com., World Energy Conf. Clubs: Mt. Stephen, Montreal Amateur Athletic Assn. Office: 2045 Stanley St Montreal PQ H3C 3Z8 Canada *

CAMERON, ALASTAIR GRAHAM WALTER, astrophysicist; b. Winnipeg, Can., June 21, 1925; came to U.S., 1959, naturalized, 1963; s. Alexander Thomas and Airdrie Edna (Bell) C.; m. Elizabeth Aston MacMillan, June 11, 1955. B.Sc., U. Man., 1947; Ph.D., U. Sask., 1952, D.Sc. (hon.), 1977, A.M., Harvard U., 1973. Asst. prof. physics Iowa State Coll., Ames, 1952-54; asst., asso. and sr. research officer Atomic Energy Can., Ltd., Chalk River, Ont., 1954-61; sr. research fellow Calif. Inst. Tech., Pasadena, 1959-60; sr. scientist Goddard Inst. Space Studies, N.Y., 1961-66; prof. space physics Yeshiva U., 1966-73; prof. astronomy Harvard U., Cambridge, Mass., 1973—; chmn. Space Sci. Bd., 1976-82, Nat. Acad. Scis. Contbr. articles to profl. jours. Mem. Nat. Acad. Scis., Am. Acad. Arts and Scis., World Acad. Art and Sci., Royal Soc. Can., AAAS, Am. Phys. Soc., Am. Geophys. Union, Am. Astron. Soc., Royal Astron. Soc., Internat. Astron. Union, Internat. Assn. Geochemistry and Cosmochemistry, Meteoritical Soc. Club: Cosmos. Office: 60 Garden St Cambrioge MA 02138

CAMERON, ALLEN, transportation consultant; b. New Rockford, N.D., Mar. 29, 1911; s. John Stewart and Edith Leslie (Allen) C.; m. Ruth Isabel Trankler, Mar. 15, 1944; children: Suzanne Cameron Schutz, Laurie Cameron Larkin. Successively asst. port capt., v.p., gen. mgr. Pacific Tankers, Inc., San Francisco, 1944-49; v.p. Joshua Hendy Corp., 1949; exec. v.p., dir. Transworld Carriers, Inc.; asst. to exec. v.p. and treas. Nat. Bulk Carriers, Inc., 1959-60, v.p., 1960-67; pres. Rogers, Slade & Hill, Inc., 1968-72, Buckfield Corp., 1972—. Vol. recruiter Internat. Exec. Service Corps. Seaman USN, 1930-34; served with U.S. Mcht. Marine, 1934-44; advancing from able seaman to master. Mem. N.E. Coast Inst. Engrs. and Shipbuilders, Soc. Naval Architects and Marine Engrs., Council Am. Master Mariners, Soc. Maritime Arbitrators, Marine Tech. Soc., Newcomen Soc., Propeller Club. Clubs: Greenwich Country, Bohemian, Circumnavigators, Indian Harbor Yacht. Home: Stanford Hill Rd Essex CT 06426

CAMERON, CHARLES CLIFFORD, banker; b. Meridian, Miss., Jan. 4, 1920; s. Daniel Baker and Bertha (Morris) C.; m. Sara Anderson, Nov. 22, 1978; children—Sheryl, Randolph Morris, Cynthia and Cathy (twins). B.S., La. State U., 1941. Engr. Standard Oil Co. N.J., 1945-49; with Cameron-Brown Co., Raleigh, N.C., 1949—, pres., 1951-66, chmn. bd., 1966—; vice chmn. exec. com., chmn. bd., chief exec. officer First Union Nat. Bank of N.C., from 1966; now exec. v.p., also dir.; chmn. bd., pres. 1st Union Corp., 1968—; dir. Charlotte br. Fed. Res. Bank of Richmond, So. Bell Tel. & Tel. Mem. Gov.'s Council for Econ. Devel.; treas. Bus. Devel. Corp. N.C.; mem. Army Adv. Com. N.C.; Pres. United Fund Raleigh.; Bd. dirs. Raleigh YMCA, Carolinas United Community Service; chmn. bd. trustees U. N.C. at Charlotte, v.p., Chapel Hill; chmn. bd. Dimensions for Charlotte-Mecklenburg; bd. dirs., exec. com. N.C. Citizens Assn. Served to col. AUS, 1941-45; ETO. Decorated Bronze Star.; Named Boss of Year Raleigh Jr. C. of C., 1964. Mem. Assn. Res. City Bankers, Newcomen Soc. N.Am., Nat. Assn. Real Estate Bds. (v.p. 1961), Raleigh Bd. Realtors (past pres.), N.C. Assn. Realtors (past pres., Realtor of year award 1959), Am. Mortgage Bankers Assn. (pres. 1964, Distinguished Service Award 1961), Carolinas Mortgage Bankers Assn. (pres. 1955), Am. Inst. Real Estate Appraisers, U. S. C. of C., Am. Bankers Assn. (exec. com. mktg. div.), Charlotte C. of C. (pres. 1973), Assn. Registered Bank Holding Cos. (dir.), Scabbard and Blade, Alpha Chi Sigma, Phi Lambda Upsilon, Theta Xi (pres. 1941). Baptist (deacon). Clubs: Capital City (Raleigh); Country of N.C. (Pinehurst); Charlotte (N.C.) City, Charlotte Country, Quail Hollow Country. Home: 2633 Richardson Dr Charlotte NC 28211 Office: First Union Corp Charlotte NC 28288

CAMERON, CHARLES METZ, JR., educator; b. Morristown, Tenn., Dec. 20, 1923; s. Charles Metz and Mildred (Brown) C.; m. Vera L. Cheek, Nov. 25, 1948; children—Charles Metz III, Cheryl Lynn, David Alan. Student, U. Tenn., 1942, N.C. State Coll., 1943, U. Ky., 1944, U. Miss., 1945; M.D., Vanderbilt U., 1948; M.P.H., U. N.C., 1955. Rotating intern U.S. Marine Hosp. System, 1949; dist. health officer Tenn. Dept. Pub. Health, 1949-52; physician USPHS, 1951-53; chief communicable disease control sect., accident prevention sect. N.C. Rd. Health, 1953-55; asso. prof., prof. U. N.C. Sch. Pub. Health, 1955-68, acting chmn. dept., 1960-61; dir. N.C. Office Comprehensive Health Planning, 1967-68; prof. dept. health adminstrn. U. Okla. Health Scis. Center, Oklahoma City, 1968—, chmn. dept., 1968-75; also dir. Mid-Continent Comprehensive Health Planning Ednl. Center and Health Resources Information Center. Contbr. papers to profl. lit. Served with AUS, 1943-45. Mem. Delta Omega (nat. pres. 1962). Home: 3132 Goshen Dr Oklahoma City OK 73120

CAMERON, COLIN CAMPBELL, pineapple co. and land devel. exec.; b. Paia, Maui, Hawaii, Feb. 2, 1927; s. J. Walter and Frances (Baldwin) C.; m. Margaret Hartley, Aug. 25, 1951; children—Douglas, Richard, Margaret, Frances. A.B., Harvard, 1950, M.B.A., 1953. Chmn., pres. Maui Land & Pineapple Co., Inc., 1969—; chmn. Kapalua Land Co., Ltd., 1974—, Maui Pineapple Co. Ltd.; v.p., dir. Haleakala Ranch Co., Ltd., Haleakala Dairy, Inc.; pres., dir. Maui Pub. Co. Ltd. (publishers Maui News); dir. Bank of Hawaii, Hawaiian Electric Co., Inc., Maui Electric Co., Ltd. Vice pres., chmn. long-range planning com. J. Walter Cameron Center; bd. dirs., mem. exec. com. Lahaina Restoration Found.; bd. dirs. Hawaii Resort Developers Conf., Maui Philharmonic Soc.; mem. State Coastal Zone Adv. Com.; vice chmn. exec. group Recreation Developers council Urban Land Inst.; chmn. Mayor's Com. on Maui's Econ. Future; bd. visitors Fletcher Sch. Law and Diplomacy; mem. adv. bd. Travel Industry Mgmt. Sch. and Sch. Architecture, both U. Hawaii. Served with USNR, 1945-46. Clubs: Pacific, Plaza, Maui Country. Home: Paia HI 96779 Office: Box 187 Kahului HI 96732

CAMERON, D. PIERRE G., JR., utility company executive, lawyer; b. N.Y.C., Apr. 29, 1934; s. D. Pierre G. and Caroline (Dunbar) C.; m. Katherin MacKie, June 23, 1956; children: David, Raymond, Katherine, Caroline. B.A., Yale U., 1955; LL.B., Duke U., 1958. Bar: Md. 1972, Mass. 1968, Va. 1960. Atty., advisor SEC, Washington, 1958-62; atty. Columbia Gas System, N.Y.C., 1962-66; assoc. corp. counsel Itek Corp., Lexington, Mass., 1966-70; asst. gen. counsel BG & E Co., Balt., 1970-80; v.p., gen. counsel Pub. Service Co. N.H., Manchester, 1980—; mng. dir. PSNH Overseas Fin. N.V., Netherlands Antilles, PSNH Internat. Fin. B.V., PSNH Internat. Fin. N.V., Netherlands Antilles; dir. Properties Inc., N.H. Electric Co., RDC Inc. Chmn. Acton (Mass.) Planning Bd., 1969-70; trustee Mayhew Program, Bristol, N.H., 1981—. Mem. ABA, Am. Corp. Counsel Assn., Edison Electric Inst. (legal com.). Republican. Episcopalian. Office: 1000 Elm St PO Box 330 Manchester NH 03105

CAMERON, DOUGLAS GEORGE, physician; b. Folkestone, Eng., Mar. 11, 1917; emigrated to Can., 1917; s. George L. and Rowena (Shaver) C.; m. Jeanne Sutherland Thompson, Feb. 23, 1946; children—George, Jane, Heather, Bruce, Nancy, Marion. B.S., U. Sask., 1937; M.D., McGill U., 1940; B.S., U. Oxford, 1948. Practice medicine, Montreal, Que., Can.; physician-in-chief Montreal Gen. Hosp., 1957—; dir. McGill U. Med. Clinic, Montreal Gen. Hosp., 1957—; prof. medicine McGill U., 1957—, chmn. dept. medicine, 1964-69, 74—; dir. medicine Baffin Zone and Kenya Med. Projects, 1967—. Contbr. articles to profl. jours. Served to lt. col. M.C. Royal Can. Army, 1940-46. Fellow A.C.P., Royal Coll. Physicians (London), Royal Coll. Physicians and Surgeons Can. (pres.); mem. Am. Clin. and Climatol. Assn., Am., Canadian socs. clin. investigation, Med. Research Soc. London, Internat., Am. socs. hematology, Assn. Am. Physicians, Canadian Med. Assn., Que. Med. Assn. (pres. 1967). Home: 227 Portland Ave Town of Mount Royal Montreal PQ Canada Office: 1650 Cedar Ave Montreal PQ Canada

CAMERON, DUNCAN FERGUSON, museum dir.; b. Toronto, Ont., Can., Feb. 1, 1930; s. Charles Gordon and Winnifred Petrie (Peppderdeane) C.; m. Nancy Tousley, Apr. 24, 1975. Chief info. services Royal Ont. Museum, Toronto, 1956-61; pres. Janus Ltd., Toronto, 1961-70; nat. dir. Can. Conf. Arts, Toronto, 1968-70; dir. Bklyn. Mus., 1971-73; prin. P.S. Ross & Partners, Toronto, 1974-77; dir. Glenbow-Alta. Inst., Calgary, 1977—. Author articles in field. Mem. Internat. Council Museums, Museums Assn., Am. Assn. Museums, Can. Museums Assn., Can. Art Mus. Dirs. Orgn., Commonwealth Assn. Museums, Royal Can. Mil. Inst. Anglican. Club: Ranchmen's (Calgary). Home: 927 19th Ave SW Apt 8 Calgary AB T2T 0H8 Canada Office: Glenbow Museum 130 9th Ave SE Calgary AB T2G 0P3 Canada

CAMERON, DUNCAN HUME, lawyer; b. Brandon, Man., Can., May 26, 1934; s. Donald Ewen and Jean Carruthers (Rankine) C.; m. Caroline I. Gilbert, 1975; children—Sarah, Anne. B.A. cum laude, Harvard, 1956; LL.B., Columbia, 1959, Ph.D., 1965. Asso. firm Paul, Weiss, Rifkind, Wharton & Garrison, 1959-62; atty. office gen. counsel AID U.S. Dept. State, 1963-67, legal advisor mission to Dominican Republic, 1966; partner firms Appleton, Rice & Perrin, 1967-71, Cameron, Hornbostel, Adelman and Butterman, Washington, 1972—; Adj. prof. law Georgetown U. Law Center, 1970-80; lectr. Sch. Fgn. Service, 1973—. Contbr. articles to profl. jours. Mem. Am., Fed., Inter-Am. bar assns. Club: Cosmos. Home: 3616 Davenport St NW Washington DC 20008 Office: 1707 H St NW Washington DC 20006

CAMERON, ELEANOR FRANCES, author; b. Winnipeg, Man., Can., Mar. 23, 1912; d. Henry and Florence Lydia (Vaughan) Butler; m. Ian Stuart Cameron, June 24, 1934; 1 son, David Gordon. Student, UCLA, 1931-33. Clk. Los Angeles Pub. Library, 1930-36, Los Angeles Sch. Book Depository, 1936-42; spl. librarian advt. Foote Cone & Belding, Los Angeles, 1942-43; research asst. Batten, Barton, Durstine & Osborn, Los Angeles, 1956-58; spl. librarian Dan B. Miner Co., Los Angeles, 1958-59; mem. editorial bd. Cricket Mag., LaSalle, Ill., 1973—, Children's Lit. in Edn., 1982—; Mem. adv. bd. Center for Study of Children's Lit., Simmons Coll., Boston, 1977—. (Recipient Nat. Book award for Ct. of the Stone Children 1973); Author: The Unheard Music, 1950, The Wonderful Flight to the Mushroom Planet, 1954, A Room Made of Windows, 1971 (Boston Globe Horn-Book, ALA Notable Book); The Court of the Stone Children, 1973 (ALA Notable Book), To the Green Mountains, 1975 (finalist Nat. Book award; ALA Notable Book), The Green and Burning Tree: On the Writing and Enjoyment of Children's Books, 1969 (Commonwealth Lit. award 1969), Julia and the Hand of God, 1977 (ALA Notable Book), A Spell is Cast (Commonwealth award), Beyond Silence, 1980, That Julia Redfern, 1982 (ALA Notable Book), also others. Mem. Save-the-Redwoods League, Sierra Club, Audubon Soc., Wilderness Soc., Authors League., PEN Internat. Home: Pebble Beach CA 93953 Office: EP Dutton and Co 2 Park Ave New York NY 10016

CAMERON, EUGENE NATHAN, educator; b. Atlanta, Aug. 10, 1910; s. Nathan Massey and Jessie Roberta (Bennett) C.; m. Adrienne M. Macksoud, Aug. 5, 1939; children—Beatrice A., James N., Donald E. B.S., N.Y. U., 1932; M.S., Columbia, 1934, Ph.D., 1939. Lectr., then instr. geology Columbia, 1937-42; asso. geologist U.S. Geol. Survey, 1942-44; geologist, 1944-46, commodity geologist indsl. minerals, 1946-57, sr. geologist, 1956-51; asso. prof. geology U. Wis., 1947-50, prof., 1950-80, prof. emeritus, 1980—, chmn. dept., 1955-60, Van Hise Disting. prof., 1970-80; cons. geologist, 1951—; Chmn. panel raw materials of beryllium Materials Adv. Bd., 1957- 58, vice-chmn. panel raw materials of chromium, 1958-59; cons. NASA, 1965-71; U.S. del. Internat. Commn. on Ore Microscopy, 1964-68; chmn. Panel III com. on mineral resources and the environment, 1973-75; mem. Nat. Com. Geology, 1973-77; chmn. U.S. Nat. Com. for Internat. Geol. Correlation Program, 1974-76. Author: Ore Microscopy, 1961; Editor, contbr.: The Mineral Position of the United States, 1975-2000; Contbr. articles to profl. jours. Fellow Geol. Soc. Am., Soc. Econ. Geologists (sec. 1961-64, pres. 1973, sec. research found. 1966-73, trustee 1977-79), Mineral. Soc. Am. (council 1965-68); mem. Am. Bus. Club (pres. 1953-54). Home: 4414 Rolla Ln Madison WI 53711

CAMERON, J. ELLIOT, univ. pres.; b. Panguitch, Utah, Feb. 9, 1923; s. B.A. and Leonia (Sargent) C.; m. Maxine Petty, Dec. 23, 1942; children—Bruce, Kim, Kerry Lynn, Preston. B.S., M.A., Brigham Young U., 1946-49; Ed. D., 1966. Former high sch. prin., supt. schs., Duchesne, Sevier, Utah; later pres. Snow Coll., Ephraim, Utah; then dean students Utah State U.; former dean of student life, prof. edn. Brigham Young U., Provo, Utah; v.p. student services, now pres. Brigham Young U., Hawaii campus. Served with AUS, World War II. Mem. NEA, Nat. Assn. Student Personnel Adminstrs., Phi Delta Kappa. Mem. Ch. of Jesus Christ of Latter-day Saints. Home: 55-220 Kulanui St Laie HI 96762

CAMERON, JAMES DUKE, state justice; b. Richmond, Calif., Mar. 25, 1925; s. Charles Lee and Ruth M. (Mabry) C.; m. Suzanne Jane Pratt, Aug. 16, 1952 (div. 1982); children: Alison Valerie, Craig Charles, Jennifer Elaine. A.B., U. Calif. at Berkeley, 1950; J.D., U. Ariz., 1954; LL.M., U. Va., 1982. Bar: Ariz. 1954. Practice in, Yuma, 1954-60, 61-65; judge Superior Ct. Yuma County, 1960, Ariz. Ct. Appeals, 1965-70; justice Ariz. Supreme Ct., 1970—, vice chief justice, 1971-75, chief justice, 1975-80; mem. faculty appellate judges seminar Inst. Jud. Adminstrn., 1968-80. Author: Arizona Appellate Forms and Procedures, 1968, also article. Mem. Ariz. Bd. Pub. Welfare, 1961-64, chmn., 1963-64; Mem. Eagle Scout bd. rev. Theodore Roosevelt council Boy Scouts Am., 1968—; Alternate del. Republican Nat. Conv., 1952; treas. Ariz. Rep. Party, 1958-60; Trustee Yuma City-County Library, 1958-67. Served with AUS, World War II. Mem. ABA (chmn. appellate judges conf. Judicial Adminstrn. div. 1977-78), Yuma County Bar Assn. (past pres.), State Bar Ariz., Ariz. Acad., Inst. Jud. Adminstrn., Conf. Chief Justices U.S. (chmn. 1978-79), Am. Judicature Soc., Am. Law Inst., Lambda Chi Alpha, Phi Alpha Delta, Delta Theta Phi. Clubs: Mason, Shriner, Arizona. Home: 5812 N 12th St #20 Phoenix AZ 85014 Office: State Capitol Bldg Phoenix AZ 85007

CAMERON, JAMES WILLIAM, management consultant; b. Chgo., Jan. 16, 1931; s. William D. and Evelyn (Eggers) C.; m. Judi Anderson, July 12, 1971; children—Nancy E. Burnoski, W. Scott, John S., Glenn A., Josie A. B.S. in Bus. Adminstrn, Northwestern U., 1953. Mgr. mgmt. devel. U.S. Gypsum, Chgo., 1968-69; v.p. personnel and indsl. relations Maremont Corp., Chgo., 1969-75; corp. v.p. personnel CNA Ins. Co., Chgo., 1975-76, Levi Strauss & Co., San Francisco, 1976-81; v.p. MSL Internat. Cons., Ltd., San Francisco, 1981—. Bd. govs. Federated Employers of the Bay Area.; Mem. adminstrv. council Mills Coll., Oak, Calif., 1976-81; bd. dirs., mem. personnel and exec. coms. YMCA, San Francisco, 1978—; trustee Golden Gate U., San Francisco, 1979-81, chmn. personnel com., mem. edn. com., 1979-81. Served with U.S. Army, 1953-56. Mem. Am. Soc. Personnel Adminstrn. Club: Bankers (San Francisco). Home: 3961 S Peardale Dr Lafayette CA 94549 Office: One Market Plaza San Francisco CA 94111

CAMERON, JOANNA, actress, director; b. Greeley, Colo., Sept. 20; d. Harold and Erna (Borgens) C.; m. Grant D. Conroy, July 4, 1980. Student, U. Calif., 1967-68, Pasadena Playhouse, 1968. Starred in: weekly TV series The Shazam-ISIS hour, CBS, 1976-78; host, dir.: for TV equipped ships USN Closed Circuit Network Program, 1977, 78, 79, 80; guest star: numerous network TV shows, including Merv Griffin Show, The Survivors, Love American Style, Mission Impossible, The Tonight Show; appeared in numerous commls.; network prime time shows including Name of the Game, Medical Center, The Bold Ones, Marcus Welby, Columbo, High Risk, Switch; motion picture debut in How to Commit Marriage, 1969; other film appearances include The Amazing Spiderman; dir. various commls., CBS Preview Spl.; producer, dir.: documentary Razor Sharp, 1981. Mem. Dirs. Guild Am., Acad. TV Arts and Scis., AFTRA, Screen Actors Guild, Delta Delta Delta. Club: Los Angeles Athletic. Discovered by Walt Disney while spl. tour guide at Disneyland; named In Guinness Book of Records for most nat. network programmed commls. Office: Cameron Prodns PO Box 8569 Universal City CA 91608

CAMERON, JOHN JOSEPH, metals trading company executive, electrical equipment manufacturing company executive; b. Teaneck, N.J., Aug. 16, 1936; s. Edward Henry and Margaret (O'Malley) C.; m. Eileen Louise Hennesey, Nov. 26, 1960; children: Scott, David, Kathryn. B.S., Fordham U. Sr. v.p. Howmet Aluminum Corp., Greenwich, Conn., 1962-83; chmn. Jovic Mfg. Co., Danbury, Conn., 1977—; exec. v.p. Say-Cam Trading Corp., N.Y.C., 1984—; v.p., gen. mgr. Guaranteed Products div. DiGiorgio Corp., Los Angeles, 1983—. Served to sgt. U.S. Army, 1959-61. Republican. Roman Catholic. Club: Stanwich (Greenwich, Conn.).

CAMERON, JOHN LANSING, retired government official; b. Sanford, N.C., Sept. 14, 1916; s. William John and Lena (Rosser) C.; m. Beulah Arena Bradley, Sept. 7, 1940; children: William John, Elizabeth Ann (Mrs. Irvin A. Pearce), David Bradley. A.B., Elon Coll., 1937; M.A., U. N.C., 1947, D.Ed., 1965. Dir. school planning N.C. Dept. Pub. Instrn., 1949-59; with U.S. Office of Edn., Washington, 1959-78, dir. facilities devel. staff, dir. ednl. tech., 1971-72, acting asso. commr., 1972—, dir. program devel., 1972-73, dir. ednl. broadcasting facilities program, 1973-78; dir. public telecommunications facilities program Nat. Telecommunications and Info. Adminstrn., 1978-82; chmn. U.S. del. Internat. Edn. Bldg. Conf., London, 1962, Latin Am. Ednl. Bldg. Conf., Mexico City, 1966. Served to lt. comdr. USNR, 1942-46. Recipient Superior Service award HEW, 1966. Mem. Illuminating Engring. Soc., A.I.A. (hon.), Am. Assn. Sch. Adminstrs., Council Ednl. Facility Planners (pres. 1966-67), Phi Delta Kappa. Methodist (lay leader). Home: 3726 Camley Ave Raleigh NC 27612

CAMERON, JOHN LEMUEL, general surgeon; b. Howell, Mich., Sept. 29, 1936; m. Doris Mae Hood; children: Duncan, Heather, Shannon, Andrew. B.A., Harvard U., 1958; M.D., Johns Hopkins U., 1962. Asst. prof. surgery Johns Hopkins U., Balt., 1971-74, assoc. prof., 1974-78, prof. surgery, 1978—; cons. surgeon Loch Raven Vet. Hosp., Balt., 1978—; cons. gastroenterology Naval Hosp., Bethesda, Md., 1973—; cons. surgery Walter Reed Army Hosp., Washington, 1976—. Editor: Current Surg. Therapy, 1984. Mem. Assn. Acad. Surgery, Soc. for Surgery of Alimentary Tract, Soc. Univ. Surgeons, Balt. Acad. Surgeons, Halsted Soc., So. Surg. Assn., Am. Surg. Assn., Pancreas Club, Surg. Biology Club II, Soc. Clin. Surgery, Societe Internationale de Cirurgie, Internat. Biliary Assn., Am. Assn. Study of Liver Disease. Home: 913 Rolandvue Rd Ruxton MD 21204 Office: Johns Hopkins U Sch Medicine 600 N Wolfe St Baltimore MD 21205

CAMERON, JOHN RODERICK, med. physicist, educator; b. Chippewa Falls, Wis., Apr. 21, 1922; s. Duncan and Mary (O'Connell) C.; m. Lavonda Donovan, Aug. 2, 1947; children—Anne, Carol. B.S., U. Chgo., 1947; M.S., U. Wis., 1949, Ph.D. in Nuclear Physics, 1952. Asst. prof. nuclear physics U. São Paulo, Brazil, 1952-54; project asso. in nuclear physics U. Wis., Madison, 1954-55, faculty radiology, physics, 1958—, prof., 1965—, Farrington Daniels prof. med. physics, 1979—; dir. Biomed. Engring. Center, 1969-76, dir. med. physics div., 1974-81, chmn. dept. med. physics, 1981—; asst. prof. nuclear physics U. Pitts., 1955-58; cons. VA Hosp., Madison, AEC, Washington, IAEA, Vienna, Austria, Bur. Radiation Health, FDA, 1971—; pres. Radiation Measurements, Inc., Middleton, Wis., 1960—. Mem. Am. Assn. Physicists in Medicine (pres. 1968, Coolidge award 1980), Soc. Nuclear Medicine (trustee 1964-67, pres. Central chpt. 1971), Am. Phys. Soc., Biophys. Soc., Radiation Research Soc., AAAS, Internat. Orgn. Med. Physics (sec.-gen. 1969-76), Health Physics Soc. (bd. dirs. 1971-74, pres. N. Central chpt. 1971), Radiol. Soc. N.Am., Brit. Inst. Radiology, Hosp. Physicists Assn. (U.K.); hon. mem. Brazilian Assn. Med. Physicists, Wis. Radiol Soc., Wis. Acad. Scis., Arts and Letters. Research, publs. in radiation dosimetry using thermoluminescence, bone mineral measurement, physics of diagnostic radiology. Home: 118 N Breese Terr Madison WI 53705

CAMERON, NICHOLAS ALLEN, diversified corporation executive; b. Phila., Jan. 6, 1939; s. Nicholas Guyot and Katherine (Rogers) C.; m. Leslie Wood, Dec. 14, 1974; children: Christopher Wilson, Pamela Wilson. B.S., Yale U., 1960. Treas. Allied Corp., Morristown, N.J., 1979-81, v.p. and treas., 1981-82, v.p. fin., 1982-83, v.p. planning and devel., 1983—. Treas., bd. dirs. United Way of Morris County, Morristown, N.J., 1980—. Mem. Morris County C. of C. (bd. dirs. 1975—), Tau Beta Pi. Republican. Episcopalian. Club: St. Elmo Soc. (New Haven, Conn.). Home: Five Noe Ave Madison NJ 07940 Office: Allied Corp Columbia Rd and Park Ave Morristown NJ 07960

CAMERON, PAUL A., business executive; b. Wilmington, Del., Sept. 13, 1921; s. Willard and Mary (Fisher) C.; m. Carol Jean Mikkelson, Jan. 20, 1957; children: Victoria Nan Cameron Carlson, Kim Paul, Paul Karl, Michele Diane. Student, Wilmington public schs. Staff engr. Trans World Airlines, 1946-52; mgr. Milw. div. Allstates Engring. Co., 1952-55; pres., chief exec. officer Feedback Controls, Inc., 1955-63;

with Purolator, Inc., 1963-82, dir., 1967—, exec. v.p., chief operating officer, Piscataway, N.J., 1968-70, pres., chief exec. officer, after 1970, ret. as vice chmn., 1982; chmn. exam. com., dir. Fidelity Union Trust Co.; dir. Mahle, Inc., Exec. Council Fgn. Diplomats. Chmn. trustees Carrier Found.; pres. trustees Animal Medical; mem. adv. council Rockefeller U. Served with USAAF, World War II. Recipient cert. achievement Fin. Eorld, 1979. Office: care Purolator Inc 255 Old New Brunswick Rd Piscataway NJ 08854

CAMERON, PETER ALFRED GORDON, corporate executive; b. Toronto, Ont., Can., Sept. 15, 1930; s. Alfred Gordon C. and Dorothy (Somerville) Hendrick; m. Suzanne M.S. Noble, Oct. 19, 1955; children: Ian, Janet, Patricia. B.Commerce, McGill U., 1953. Mgmt. trainee Ford Motor Co. Can., Windsor, Ont., 1954; asst. to advt. mgr. Brading Breweries, Toronto, Ont., 1954; sales rep. William B. Stewart & Sons Ltd., 1955; asst. advt. mgr. Warner Lambert Can. Ltd., Toronto, 1955, product mgr. Proprietaries div., 1956-58; account exec. MacLaren Advt. Co. Ltd., Toronto, 1958-60, Foster Advt. Co. Ltd., 1960-62, group supr., 1962-65, v.p., Toronot, 1965-69, group v.p., Toronto, 1969; v.p. Can. Industries Ltd., Montreal, Que., 1970-78; pres. Can. Corporate Mgmt. Co. Ltd., Toronto, 1978—; dir. Halifax Ins. Co., Comml. Life Ins. Co. Can., Chromalox Can., Cashway Bldg. Ctrs., RBW Graphics, Regal Greetings and Gifts, Dominion Forge Co. Ltd., Direct Film Inc. Chmn. bd. Appleby Coll., Oakville, Ont.; bd. dirs. Sunnybrook Med. Ctr. Inst., Toronto. Served as lt. col. 48th Highlanders Can., 1967-70. Clubs: Toronto, Univ. Toronto, Toronto Golf, Toronto Racquet; Raquets, St. James, Hermitage (Montreal). Home: 100 Rosedale Heights Dr Toronto Ont Canada M4T 1C6 Office: Canadian Corporate Management Co Ltd PO Box 131 Commerce Court Postal Station Toronto Ont Canada M5L 1E6

CAMERON, RICHARD RAY, psychiatrist; b. Wheeling, W.V., Sept. 17, 1910; s. Albert Ernest and Zoe Shockley (Barker) C.; m. Ellen Irene Jones, Mar. 2, 1935; children—Richard Douglas, Bonnie Jean (Mrs. Ronald L. Arnold), Bruce Robin. Heather Anne, Scott Kenneth. B.A., W.Va. U., 1932; M.D., Jefferson Med. Coll., 1936. Diplomate: Am. Bd. Psychiatry and Neurology. Rotating intern George F. Geisinger Meml. Hosp., Danville, Pa., 1936-37; instr. pathology U. Ark. Sch. Medicine, 1937-38; commd. 1st lt., M.C. U.S. Army, 1938, advanced through grades to col., 1954; assigned, Philippines, 1945-46; resident psychiatry Fitzsimons Army Hosp., 1948-51, chief dept., 1951-52; asst. chief psychiat. cons. div. Office Surgeon Gen., U.S. Army, 1952-53; sr. resident neurology Walter Reed Army Hosp., 1953-54; chief psychiatry and neurology service, Ft. Dix, N.J., 1954-55; chief psychiat. service Brooke Army Hosp., Ft. Sam Houston, Tex., 1955-56, chief dept. neuropsychiatry, 1956-58; ret., 1958; clin. dir. Mental Health Inst., Independence, Iowa, 1958-59; pvt. practice psychiatry and neurology, Cedar Rapids, Iowa, 1959-60; dir. psychiat. services for correctional and juvenile instns. Ia. Dept. Mental Health, 1960-61; also supt. Security Mental Hosp., Anamosa, Ia.; cons. Mich. Dept. Mental Health, 1961-62; med. supt. Newberry (Mich.) State Hosp., 1962-65; dir. Shiawasse County (Mich.) Mental Health Center, 1965-68; clin. dir. edn., tng. and research San Antonio (Tex.) State Hosp., 1968-73; dir. Bexar County Psychiat./Psychologic Office, San Antonio, 1973-81; Professorial lectr. neuroanatomy George Washington Sch. Medicine, 1952- 53, 53-54; asso. clin. prof. psychiatry U. Tex. Med. Sch. at San Antonio, Tex., 1970—; dir. dept. neuropsychiatry, lectr. Army Med. Service Sch., Brooke Army Med. Center, 1956-58. Contbr. articles to profl. jours. Fellow Am. Psychiat. Assn. (life); mem. Phi Beta Kappa, Delta Phi Alpha, Alpha Kappa Kappa, Kappa Beta Phi. Address: 15 Garden Sq San Antonio TX 78209

CAMERON, RONDO, economic history educator; b. Linden, Tex., Feb. 20, 1925; s. Burr S. and Annie Mae (Dalrymple) C.; m. Claydean Zumbrunnen, July 26, 1946; children: Alan, Cindia. A.B., Yale U., 1948, A.M., 1949; Ph.D., U. Chgo., 1952. Instr. Yale, 1951-52; asst. prof. U. Wis. at Madison, 1952-56, asso. prof., 1957-61, prof. econs. and history, dir. grad. program econ. history, 1961-69; William Rand Kenan Univ. prof. Emory U., 1969—; vis. prof. U. Chgo., 1956-57; spl. field rep. Rockefeller Found., S.A., 1965-67. Author: France and the Economic Development of Europe, rev. edit, 1966 (transl. into French and Spanish 1971), Banking in the Early Stages of Industrialization, 1967 (transl. into Japanese 1973, Spanish 1974, Italian 1975), The European World, 2d edit, 1970, Civilization: Western and World, 1975; Editor: Essays in French Economic History, 1970, Civilization Since Waterloo, 1971, Banking and Economic Development, 1972; Am. rev. editor of: Econ. History Rev, 1960-65; rev. editor: Jour. Econ. History, 1968-69; editor, 1975-81; Contbr. articles to profl. jours. Chmn. Council Research Econ. History, 1967-69; bd. dirs. Albert Schweitzer Fellowship. Fulbright scholar, France, 1950-51; Guggenheim fellow, Europe, 1954-55, 70-71; fellow Center Advanced Study Behavioral Scis., 1958-59; Fulbright prof. U. Glasgow, 1962-63; Fellow Woodrow Wilson Internat. Center for Scholars, 1974-75. Mem. Am. Hist. Assn. (co-chmn. program com. 1983), Internat. Econ. Hist. Assn. (exec. com.), Am. Econ. Hist. Assn. (pres. 1974-75), Brit. Econ. Hist. Assn., French Econ. Hist. Assn. Home: 1088 Clifton Rd NE Atlanta GA 30307

CAMERON, ROY EUGENE, scientist; b. Denver, July 16, 1929; s. Guy Francis and Ilda Annora (Horn) C.; m. Margot Elizabeth Hoagland, May 5, 1956 (div. July 1977); children: Susan Lynn, Catherine Ann; m 2d Carolyn Mary Light, Sept. 22, 1978. B.S., Wash. State U., 1953, 54; M.S., U. Ariz., 1958, Ph.D., 1961; D.D. hon., Ministry of Christ Ch., Delavan, Wis., 1975. Research scientist Hughes Aircraft Corp., Tucson, 1955-56; sr. scientist Jet Propulsion Lab., Pasadena, Calif., 1961-68, mem. tech. staff, 1969-74; dir. research Darwin Research Inst., Dana Point, Calif., 1974-75; dep. dir. Land Reclamation Lab. (Argonne Nat. Lab.), Ill., 1975-77, dir. energy resources tng. and devel., 1977—; cons. Lunar Recieving Lab. Baylor U., 1966-68, Ecology Ctr. Utah State U., Desert Biome, 1970-72, U. Alaska Tundra Biome, 1973-74, U. Maine, 1973-76. Contrb. articles to sci. books; participated in 7 Antarctic expdns. Served with U.S. Army, 1950-52; Korea, Japan. Recipient 3 NASA awards for tech. briefs; Paul Steere Burgess fellow U. Ariz., 1959; NSF grantee, 1970-74; grantee Dept. Interior, 1978-80. Mem. AAAS, Soil Sci. Soc. Am., Ecol. Soc. Am., Phycological Soc. Am., Am. Soc. Agronomy, Antarctican Soc., Polar Soc. Am., Am. Scientist Affiliation, World Future Soc., Internat. Soc. Soil. Sci., Ariz. Acad. Sci., Am. Inst. Biol. Sci., Sigma Xi. Mem. Christian Ch. Home: 3433 Woodridge Dr Woodridge IL 60517 Office: 9700 S Case Ave Argonne IL 60439

CAMERON, THOMAS WILLIAM LANE, investment company executive; b. Newton, Mass., Feb. 19, 1927; s. Percy G. and Mary W.D. (Mitchell) C.; m. Carol Louise Soliday, June 17, 1950; children: Helen Delone, Thomas Mitchell. A.B. cum laude, Harvard, 1948, M.B.A., 1951. With sales dept. Procter & Gamble, Boston, 1951-53; with Hopper, Soliday, & Co., Inc., Phila., 1953—, ptnr., 1961—, pres., 1966-72, chmn., 1972-82; dir. Hopper, Soliday & Co., Inc., 1982—; chmn. Sovereign Investors Inc.; dir. Energy Data Systems, D.G. Palmer Co., McCardle Desco, Inc., Disaster Central, Inc., McCarter Corp.; chmn. Phila.-Balt.-Washington Stock Exchange, 1970-74, bd. govs., 1963-75. Chmn. S.E. Pa. chpt. Am. Heart Assn.; bd. mgrs. Franklin Inst., 1970—, chmn., 1978-81. Served with USNR, 1944-46. Mem. Pa. Economy League. Clubs: Waynesborough Country (Paoli, Pa.) (pres. 1965-67); Harvard (pres. 1965-66), Harvard Bus. Sch. (Phila.) (pres. 1962-64). Home: 15 Sugar Knoll Dr Devon PA 19333 Office: 1401 Walnut St Philadelphia PA 19102

CAMICIA, NICHOLAS THOMAS, holding company executive; b. Welch, W.Va., Apr. 23, 1916; s. Anthony and Antonia (Santini) C.; m. Virginia Brown, May 11, 1941; 1 dau., Caren Hollenbeck. B.S. in Mining Engring, Va. Poly. Inst., 1938. Mining engr. Pond Creek Pocahontas Co., 1938-41; supt. Island Creek Coal Co., Holden, W.Va., 1946-49, div. mgr., 1949-53, gen. mgr., 1953-57, v.p., gen. mgr., 1957-63, exec. v.p., 1963-64, dir., 1964; exec. v.p. Freeman Coal Mining Corp., 1965-68, pres., 1968-69, United Electric Coal Cos., 1968-69; pres., dir. Pittston Co., 1969—, chief exec. officer, 1970—, chmn., 1976—; dir. Brink's, Inc., CSX Corp., Ingersoll-Rand Co.; chmn. coal industry adv. bd. Internat. Energy Agy.; mem. White House Coal Adv. Council. Served from 2d lt. to maj. AUS, 1941-45. Decorated Bronze Star; Order Orange-Nassau with swords, Netherlands).; Recipient Man of Conscience award Appeal of Conscience Found., 1975; Erskine Ramsey medal AIME; Americanism award Antidefamation League, 1978. Mem. Am. Mining Congress (dir., past chmn. bd. dirs.), Nat. Coal Assn. (dir., past chmn. bd. dirs.), Bituminous Coal Operators Assn. (past chmn. bd. dirs.), Nat. Mgmt. Assn., W.Va. Coal Mining Inst. (past pres.), Am. Mgmt. Assn., Nat. Mine Rescue Assn. (past pres.), Am. Inst. Mining, Metall., and Petroleum Engrs., Va. C. of C. Republican. Roman Catholic. Clubs: Greenwich Country, Blind Brook, Sky, Indian Harbor Yacht. Home: 224 Round Hill Rd Greenwich CT 06830 Office: One Pickwick Plaza Greenwich CT 06830

CAMINOS, HORACIO, architect, educator; b. Buenos Aires, Argentina, Apr. 5, 1914; came to U.S., 1952, naturalized, 1965; s. Carlos N. and Maria E. (Crottogini) C.; m. Elena Ines Chapman, Sept. 13, 1943; children—Carlos H., José, Miguel, Maria I. Maria P., Ana M. Arquitecto, U. Buenos Aires, 1939. Prof. architecture and town planning U. Tucuman, Argentina, 1946-50; chief architect Univ. City, Tucuman, 1948-50; prof. architecture Archtl. Assn., London, Eng., 1951-52, U. N.C., 1952-61, Harvard, fall 1962, Mass. Inst. Tech., 1962—. Prin. works include univ. campus plans and bldgs., U. Buenos Aires, 1961-67, U. Los Andes-Merida, Venezuela, 1963-67, campus plan, U. Carabobo, Valencia, Venezuela.; Author: (with John Turner and John Steffran) Urban Dwelling Environments, (with Carlos Caminos) Gente, Vivienda, Tierra, (with Reinhard Goethert) Urbanization Primer. Spl. research and design two types of membrane structures, also low cost housing, site and services projects and urban settlements in developing countries. Home: 83 Fairmont Ave Newton MA 02158 Office: Mass Inst Tech Cambridge MA 02139

CAMINOS, RICARDO AUGUSTO, Egyptologist, educator; b. Buenos Aires, Argentina, July 11, 1915; s. Carlos Norberto and Maria (Crottogini) C. M.A., U. Buenos Aires, 1938; Ph.D., U. Chgo., 1947; D.Phil., U. Oxford, 1952. Research asst. Oriental Inst., U. Chgo., 1943-44; Rockefeller Found. fellow U. Chgo. and Oxford (Eng.) U., 1944-46; Oriental Inst. research fellow U. Chgo., 1946-47, epigraphist, expdn. at Luxor, Upper Egypt, 1947-50; asst. prof. Egyptology, Brown U., 1952-57, assoc. prof., 1957-64, prof., 1964-72, Charles E. Wilbour prof. Egyptology, 1972-80, chmn. dept., 1971-80, C.E. Wilbour prof. emeritus Egyptology, 1980—; field dir. Egypt Exploration Soc. and Brown U. expdn. to Gebel es-Silsilah, Upper Egypt, 1955-82, Egypt Exploration Soc. and Brown U. expdn. to, Semna, Sudanese Nubia, 1962-63, Kumma, Sudanese Nubia, 1963-65, Egypt Exploration Soc. expdn. to Wadi el-Shatt el-Rigal, Upper Egypt, 1982-83; Guggenheim Meml. Found. fellow, Europe and Egypt, 1958-59; vis. prof. Egyptology, U. Buenos Aires, 1960; vis. prof. Egyptology U. Leningrad, 1973; vis. lectr. USSR Acad. Scis., Moscow, 1973, Collège de France, Paris, 1981—. Author: Late-Egyptian Miscellanies, 1954, Literary Fragments in the Hieratic Script, 1956, The Chronicle of Prince Osorkon, 1958, Gebel es-Silsilah, Vol. I, 1963, Shrines and Rock-Inscriptions of Ibrim, 1968, The New-Kingdom Temples of Buhen, Vols. I and II, 1974, A Tale of Woe, 1977, (with H.G. Fischer) Ancient Egyptian Epigraphy and Palaeography, 1976; also articles in field. Mem. Oxford Soc., Egypt Exploration Soc., Deutches Archäologisches Institut (corr. mem.). Address: care Egypt Exploration Soc 3 Doughty Mews London WC1N 2PG England

CAMMACK, TRANK EMERSON, university dean; b. Columbus, Kans., July 11, 1919; s. Levi Jackson and Ida Maud (Hull) C. Student, N.E. Okla. Jr. Coll., 1936-37; B.S., U. Okla., 1940, M.A., 1941; Huebner fellow in ins. edn., U. Pa., 1941-43. Fin. statistician SEC, Phila., 1943-48, Washington, 1948-49; prof. fin. U. Ill., Urbana, 1949—; asso. dean charge undergrad. program Coll. Commerce and Bus. Adminstrn., 1968—. Author: (with Robert I. Mehr) The Insurance Contract and Its Analysis, 1950, Principles of Insurance, 1952; Contbr. to: Colliers Yearbook, 1974—. Mem. Champaign County Democratic Central Com., 1962-78; chmn. Champaign Dem. Orgn., 1966-68. Mem. AAUP, Am. Risk and Ins. Assn., Fin. Mgmt. Assn., Midwest Fin. Assn., Royal Econ. Soc., Western Risk and Ins. Assn. Methodist. Home: 1704 W Green St Champaign IL 61820 Office: 214 David Kinley Hall Urbana IL 61801

CAMMAROSANO, JOSEPH RAPHAEL, economist, educator; b. Mt. Vernon, N.Y., Mar. 12, 1923; s. Louis Raphael and Mary Nancy (Sansone) C.; m. Rosalie Nancy Esposito, Nov. 22, 1952; children: Louis, Nancy, Joseph. Student, Stanford U., 1943-44; B.S. cum laude, Fordham U., 1947, Ph.D., 1956; M.A., N.Y.U., 1949. Insp. U.S. Bur. Customs, 1948-50; asst. prof. Iona Coll., 1950-55, Fordham U., Bronx, N.Y., 1956-60, assoc. prof., 1962-67; dir. Inst. Urban Studies, 1964—, prof. econs., 1967—, chmn. dept. econs., 1969, exec. v.p., 1969-75; fiscal economist U.S. Bur. of Budget, Washington, 1961-62; Fiscal cons. N.Y. State Temp. Commn. on Constl. Conv., 1957-58, N.Y. State Spl. Legislative Com. on Revision and Simplification of the Constn., 1958-60, N.Y. State Tax Structure Study Com., 1962-70, N.Y. State Temp. Commn. on the Constn., 1966-67; econ. cons. N.Y. Bell Telephone Co., 1960; cons. N.Y.C. Econ. Devel. Adminstrn., 1969, Community Council Greater N.Y., 1971-74; vice chmn. Regional Manpower Adv. Com. to U.S. Secs. Labor and HEW, 1970-73, chmn., 1973-74; cons. ACTION, Fed. Agy. for Vol. Service, 1976, N.Y.C. Public Devel. Corp., 1979—, Office of Edn. Roman Catholic Diocese of N.Y., 1981—. Author: Highway Finance in New York State, 1958, A Profile of the Bronx Economy, 1967, A Plan for the Redevelopment of the Brooklyn Navy Yard, 1968, The Long Range Forecasting of Telephone Demand, 1960, Industrial Activity in the Inner City: A Case Study of the South Bronx, 1981. Trustee Fordham Rd. Devel. Corp., St. Joseph's Coll., Bklyn., 1974-80, Cathedral Coll., Douglaston, N.Y., Bronx Inter-Neighborhood Housing Corp., AAPC, N.Y.C.; mem. ednl. policies com. bd. trustees L.I. U., Greenvale, N.Y. Served with AUS, 1943-46; ETO. Mem. Am. Econ. Assn., Phi Delta Kappa. Home: 76 N Fulton Ave Mount Vernon NY 10550

CAMP, FRANK HALE, JR., journalist; b. Mobile, Ala., May 26, 1938; s. Frank Hale and Audrey Elizabeth (Field) C.; m. Helen Ann Collier, June 1, 1959; 1 dau., Catherine Eileen. Student. U. Ala., 1959-60, Wayne State U., 1963-64; B.A., U. Mo.-St. Louis, 1968. Asst. to fgn. editor The N.Y. Times, N.Y.C., 1974-77, asst. fgn. editor, 1977-80, asst. news editor, 1980, dep. editor nat. edition, 1980-81, editor nat. edition, 1981-82; dep. editor adminstrn. N.Y. Times mag., 1982—. Home: 400 Central Park W New York NY 10025 Office: The NY Times 229 W 43d St New York NY 10036

CAMP, JAMES DAVID, JR., lawyer; b. Ft. Lauderdale, Fla., Feb. 3, 1928; s. James David and Margueritte (Byrne) C.; m. Suzanne Winterer, June 26, 1954; children: Dorothy Camp McCurry, Marie A., James David III, William M., Suzanne M. B.A., U. Fla., 1949, J.D., 1951. Mem. firm McCune, Hiaasen, Crum Ferris & Gardner, P.A., Ft. Lauderdale, 1951—; mem. Fla. Bd. Bar Examiners, 1980—; dir., chmn. exec. com. Sun Bank-South Fla., Ft. Lauderdale, 1982—; dir. Sun Banks of Fla., Inc., Orlando. Hon. trustee Broward Community Coll., 1975; trustee St. Thomas Aquinas Found., Ft. Lauderdale, 1980—, Holy Cross Hosp., Ft. Lauderdale, 1981—; bd. dirs. U. Fla. Found., Inc., 1981—, 100 Club Broward County, 1982—; mem. U. Fla. Pres. Search Com., 1982—. Named one of Ten Outstanding Young Men in Ft. Lauderdale Ft. Lauderdale Jaycees, 1958; recipient Disting. Service award Broward Community Coll., 1977. Mem. Broward County Bar Assn., Fla. Bar (gov. Young Lawyers Sect.), Am. Judicature Soc., Ft. Lauderdale C. of C. (pres., dir.), Phi Delta Phi. Democrat. Roman Catholic. Clubs: Kiwanis (dir.), Touchdown of Ft. Lauderdale (pres.). Lodges: K.C.; Elks. Office: McCune Hiaasen Crum Ferris & Gardner 25 S Andrews Ave Fort Lauderdale FL 33301

CAMP, JOSEPH SHELTON, JR., film producer; b. St. Louis, Apr. 20, 1939; s. Joseph Shelton and Ruth Wilhelmena (McLaulin) C.; m. Andrea Carolyn Hopkins, Aug. 7, 1960; children: Joseph Shelton III, Brandon Andrew. B.A., U. Miss., 1961. Jr. account exec. McCann-Erickson Advt., Houston, 1961-62; owner Joe Camp Real Estate, Houston, 1962-64; account exec. Norsworthy-Mercer, Dallas, 1964-69; dir. TV commls. Jamieson Film Co., Dallas, 1969-71; founder, pres., writer, producer, dir. Mulberry Square Prodns., Inc.; founder, pres., writer, producer, dir. feature films, Dallas, 1971—. Producer, dir.: films including Benji, 1973, Hawmps, 1976, For the Love of Benji, 1977, The Double McGuffin, 1979, Oh Heavenly Dog, 1980; TV spls. The Phenomenon of Benji, 1978, Benji's Very Own Christmas Story, 1978, Benji at Work, 1980, Benji (Takes a Dive) at Marineland, 1981; TV series Benji, Zax and the Alien Prince. Home: 7272 Stefani Dallas TX 75225 Office: 10300 N Central Expressway 120 Dallas TX 75231 *I hope that I have been able to help people in a troubled time to lose themselves for a moment in a piece of entertainment and, when it's over, to feel better for having done so. I feel that anyone who has been blessed with the ability to affect the emotions of millions of people should always exercise that ability with a great deal of responsibility. I hope that I have done that.*

CAMP, WESLEY DOUGLASS, history educator; b. Bedford Hills, N.Y., Jan. 2, 1915; s. Douglass Fletcher and Edna Mary (Westcott) C.; m. Kathleen Virginia Bamman, Dec. 22, 1936; children: Mary Virginia Camp Smith, Wesley Douglass. A.B., Columbia U., 1936, A.M., 1940, Ph.D., 1957; diplome d'etudes francaises, U. Lille, France, 1937. Asst. d'anglais Lycee Faidherbe, Lille, 1936-37; mem. faculty Monmouth (N.J.) Coll., 1941-60, prof., chmn. social sci. dept., 1946-60; research Bibliotheque Nationale, Paris, 1960-61; asso. prof. history Carnegie Inst. Tech., 1961-62; prof. history Adelphi U., 1962—, chmn. history dept., 1962-74; guest lectr. Hofstra U., Hempstead, N.Y., 1968-69. Author: Marriage and the Family in France: An Essay in the History of Population, 1961; translator: (Jean Egret) The French Prerevolution 1787-1788, 1978; also revs.; editor Roots of Western Civilization, 2 vols., 1983. Mem. Am. Hist. Assn., Société d'Histoire Moderne, Soc. French Hist. Studies, AAUP. Home: 481 Dogwood Ave West Hempstead NY 11552 Office: Adelphi U Garden City NY 11530 *As an educator I have given up trying to "teach"; instead I am trying to "learn them" some appreciation of the past by haranguing, cajoling, and shocking the young into reluctant awareness of the world we have lost.*

CAMP, WOFFORD BENJAMIN, farmer; b. Gaffney, S.C., Mar. 14, 1894; s. John Clayton and Mary Jane (Atkins) C.; m. Georgia Anna App, December, 14, 1921 (dec.); children: Wofford Benjamin, Donald Max; m. Louise Phifer Wise, Jan. 18, 1956; children: Addie Louise Segars, George W. Wise, Sarah Cory. B.S., Clemson Agrl. Coll., 1916; Dr. Agrl. Industries (hon.), 1951; postgrad., U. Calif.; LL.D., Limestone Coll., 1955, Whittier Coll., 1958; H.H.D., Gardner-Webb Coll., 1974. Head coop. testing field crops U.S. Dept. Agr., S.C., 1916-17; founder cotton, San Joaquin Valley, Calif., 1917, agronomist charge cotton breeding and growing expts., San Joaquin Valley, others, 1917-28; established, charge U.S. Expt. Sta., Shafter, Calif., 1922-28; head agr. appraiser Bank of Am. Nat. Trust & Savs. Assn., 1929; mgr. Calif. Lands, Inc., Bank Am. subsidiary, 1929-33; head agrl. economist, asst. dir. cotton div. and So. region A.A.A., Washington, 1933-36; pres., owner Georgianna Farms, Inc., 1937-45; pres. W.B. Camp & Sons, Inc., 1946—; co-owner Calolina Farms and; Calolina Cotton Ginning Co.; founder Calif. Cotton Planting Seed Distbrs.; co-founder Calif. Cotton Coop. Assn.; Mem. com. on conservation and devel. soil and water resources U.S. Dept. Agr.; bd. dirs. Nat. Indsl. Conf. Bd. Author: Calif. One-variety Cotton law; Author several agrl. bulls.; Contbr. articles to mags., newspapers. Founder W.B. Camp Found. (scholarship); bd. dirs. Nat. Rivers and Harbors Congress, co-chmn. com. conversions and uses saline water; trustee Bur. Water Resources, S.C. Conservation Dists. Found., Whittier Coll., Freedom's Found., Valley Forge; exec. com. Religious Heritage Am.; bd. govs. Agrl. Hall of Fame and Nat. Center, also chmn. nat. devel. com.; mem. pres.'s bd. Pepperdine Coll.; mem. adv. bd. Sch. Bus., Am. U.; hon. life dir. Clemson U. Found. Recipient George Washington medal Freedoms Found. at Valley Forge, 1965; Calif. chpt. award Am. Soc. Agronomy, 1974; Agr. award Religious Heritage Am., 1975; Horatio Alger award, 1978; inducted into Order of Knights Hospitallers of St. John Knights of Malta, 1979; Right to Work Com. named its new bldg. in his and his wife's honor, 1980. Mem. Kern County Potato Seed Assn. (founder, pres.), Nat. Potato Council (co-founder, v.p.), Asso. Farmers Calif. (past pres.), Kern County Mus. Assn., Am. Cancer Soc. (Kern County dir.), Crippled Children Soc. Calif., Farm Bur. U.S. C. of C. (v.p., treas., dir., chmn. agrl. com., chmn. vol. unionism com.), Farm Labor Research Com. (chmn.), Right to Work Com. (dir.), Blue Key, Phi Kappa Phi. Baptist. Clubs: Mason, Rotarian., Commonwealth (San Francisco); California (Los Angeles); Capitol Hill (Washington). Founder Camp Irrigation Fund, S.C., and first to urge large scale conservation of water for irrigation in entire rainfall belt. Home and office: 701 Oleander Ave Bakersfield CA 93304 *I learned from my wonderful parents that once I had been given and accepted a certain responsibility, I must never let anything prevent completion of the project. Also early in life I learned the importance of "Seeing what you look at." This led to my coining the other significant piece of advice—Produce a large quantity of quality products on the same acre. Another admonition which I hold strongly is: Freedom is not a physical object. It is a spiritual and moral environment, and it is this that our Constitution was intended to protect.*

CAMPAIGNE, ERNEST EDWIN, chemistry educator; b. Chgo., Feb. 13, 1914; s. John Herbert and Nellie (Daufel) C.; m. Jean Hill White, Jan. 1, 1941; children: David Alan, Claudia Jean (Mrs. Anthony Burris), Barbara Naomi. B.S., Northwestern U., 1936, M.S., 1938, Ph.D. in Biochemistry, 1940. Instr. Bowdoin Coll., 1940-41; research asso. Northwestern U., 1941-42; asso. biochemist M.D. Anderson Hosp. for Cancer Research, Galveston, Tex., 1942-43; mem. faculty dept. chemistry Ind. U., Bloomington, 1943—, prof. chemistry, 1953—; vis. prof. UCLA, 1954-55; cons. NIH, 1960-64, 72-76; indsl. chem. cons., 1952—. Author: (with J. C. Muhler and C. H. Rohrer) Introduction to Chemistry, 1972, Elementary Organic Chemistry, 1962. Fellow N.Y. Acad. Scis., Ind. Acad. Sci.; mem. Am. Chem. Soc., Chem. Soc. (London), AAAS, Internat. Union Pure and Applied

Chemistry (chmn., convenor medicinal chemistry sect. organic div. 1969-75, U.S. del. Munich 1973). Research and publs. on synthesis of drugs, antihistamines, anticonvulsant drugs for treatment of epilepsy, molecular dimensions of drugs to interpret their optimum dimensions and nature of receptor sites. Home: 1240 E Wylie St Bloomington IN 47401

CAMPANELLA, ANTON J., telephone company executive; b. 1932; (married). B.A., Upsala Coll., 1956. Salesman Englishtown Crafts, N.Y.C., 1949-51; asst. traffic mgr. Riedl & Freede Advt., 1955; with N.J. Bell Telephone Co., 1956—, div. traffic mgr., 1963-66, dir. mktg., 1966-68, asst. v.p., 1968-70, gen. mgr., 197-79, v.p. downstate, 1972, v.p, mktg., 1974, then exec. v.p. bus. sers., asst. v.p. mktg. ops., pres., 1983—. Address: NJ Bell Telephone Co 540 Broad St Newark NJ 07101 *

CAMPANELLA, JOSEPH MARIO, actor; b. N.Y.C., Nov. 21, 1927; s. Philip and Mary O. C.; m. Jill Bartholomew, May 30, 1964; 7 sons. Student, Holy Cross Coll., 1944; B.A., Manhattan Coll., 1948; postgrad., Columbia U., 1948-49; acting student, Steffen Zacharias, N.Y.C., Lee Strasberg. Stage debut in Tonight in Samarkand, 1954; other stage appearances include Detective Story, 1954, The Empress, 1955, The Doctor in Spite of Himself, 1955, Mr. and Mrs. North, 1954, Girls of Summer, 1956, House on the Rocks, 1958, The Caine Mutiny Court Martial, 1958, The Teahouse of the August Moon, 1958, Come Back, Little Sheba, 1958, The Country Girl, 1961, A View from the Bridge, 1961, Born Yesterday, 1962, Gypsy, 1962, Mary, Mary, 1965; film appearances include Murder, Inc, 1961, The Young Lovers, 1964, The Saint Valentine's Day Massacre, 1967, Hangar 18, 1981, Earthbound, 1981, My Body, My Child; radio announcer: Voice of Am, 1951, WQXR, N.Y.C.; regular: TV series Mannix, 1967-68, The Lawyers segment The Bold Ones; host: Jacque Cousteau This Is Your Life; narrator: films; numerous TV guest appearances, TV films, TV commls. Served in USNR, 1944-46; PTO. Decorated Knight Order Republic of Italy. Mem. Screen Actors Guild, AFTRA, Actors Equity Assn. Office: care TAT Communications 1901 Ave of Stars Los Angeles CA 90067 *

CAMPANERIA, MIGUEL, dancer; b. Havana, Cuba, Feb. 5, 1951. Student, Nat. Ballet Cuba. Debut with, Nat. Ballet of Cuba, 1968; joined, Harkness Ballet; and became soloist, 1973; with, Dancers, N.Y.C., 1977; prin. dancer, Pitts. Ballet, 1978— *

CAMPANIS, ALEXANDER SEBASTIAN, baseball exec.; b. Greece, Nov. 2, 1916. Student, N.Y. U. Player minor leagues, 1941-43; mgr. Bklyn. Dodger Orgn., Montreal, Nashua, N.H., Lancaster, Pa., Newport News, Va.; dir. scouting Los Angeles Dodgers Orgn., from 1957, now v.p. player personnel. Author: How To Play Baseball. Served with USN, 1943-46. Office: care Los Angeles Dodgers Dodger Stadium 1000 Elysion Park Ave Los Angeles CA 90012 *

CAMPBELL, ALAN KEITH, management services company executive; b. Elgin, Nebr., May 31, 1923; s. Charles E. and Anna (Schneckloth) C.; m. Linna Jane Owen, Mar. 9, 1945; children: Kimberly Ann, Charles Duncan. A.B., Whitman Coll., 1947, LL.D. (hon.), 1972; M.P.A.; Volker fellow, Wayne State U., 1949; Ph.D.; Sheldon Traveling fellow, Harvard U., 1952; L.H.D. (hon.), Ohio State U., 1979. Asst. dir. Harvard U. Summer Sch., 1950-54, instr., 1952-54, vis. lectr., 1957; prof., chmn. polit. sci. dept. Hofstra Coll., Hempstead, N.Y., 1954-60; dep. comptroller adminstrn. State U. N.Y., Albany, 1960-61; vis. prof. Columbia U., 1961-62; prof. polit. sci., dir. met. studies program Maxwell Grad. Sch., Syracuse (N.Y.) U., 1961-68; dean Maxwell Sch. Citizenship and Pub. Affairs, 1969-76, Lyndon B. Johnson Sch., U. Tex., Austin, 1977; chmn. CSC, Washington, 1977-78; dir. U.S. Office Personnel Mgmt., 1979-80; exec. v.p. mgmt. and public affairs, dir. ARA Services, Inc., Phila., 1980—; adj. prof. Wharton Sch., U. Pa., 1981; chmn. Phila. CSC, 1981; mem. staff N.Y. Commn. on Govtl. Ops., N.Y.C., 1959; mem. faculty Salzburg (Austria) Seminar Am. Studies, 1965; mem. com. instrn. and evaluation Am. Council Edn., 1957-68; mem. adv. com. improvement mgmt. in govt. Com. Econ. Devel., 1965-74; mem. com. urban econs. Resources For Future, 1965-70; mem. adv. com. to Sec. HUD, 1967-68; mem. social sci. panel, div. behavioral sci. Nat. Acad. Sci., 1971-74; dir. Sta. WHYY. Author: Case Studies in American Government, 1962, (with Seymour Sacks) Metropolitan America: Governmental Systems and Fiscal Patterns, 1967, The States and the Urban Crisis, 1970, (with Joel Berke and Robert Goettel) Financing Equal Educational Opportunity: Alternatives for State Finance, 1972, (with others) Watergate: Implications for Responsible Government, (with Roy Bahl) Taxes, Expenditures and the Economic Base: The Case of New York City, 1974, The Political Economy of State and Local Government Reform, 1976; contbr. to: Anatomy of a Metropolis; editor: (with Edwin Bock) Case Studies in American Government, 1962, Carnegie-sponsored Study Large City Schs, 1966—; Contbr.: articles to profl. jours. Carnegie-sponsored Study Large City Schs. Mem. Gov.'s Council Econ. Advisers, 1970-74; chmn. adv. platform com. N.Y. State Democratic Com., 1962, co-chmn. platform, resolutions sub-com., 1964; co-chmn. Citizens for Johnson, Humphrey and Kennedy, Syracuse Met. Area, 1964; mem. Temp. N.Y. State Commn. on Revision and Simplification of Constn., 1965-66; del.-at-large N.Y. State Constl. Conv., 1967, chmn. com. on local govt. and home rule, 1967; bd. dirs. Thomas Jefferson U., Pa. Economy League. Served as ensign, CIC USNR, 1943-46. Recipient Alumnus of Merit award Whitman Coll., 1970; Stockberger award for outstanding achievements in personnel mgmt. Internat. Personnel Mgmt. Assn., 1978; Public Service Achievement award Common Cause, 1981; Hubert H. Humphrey Public Service award, 1981; Gunnar and Alva Myrdal award for govt. services, 1981. Mem. Am. Polit. Sci. Assn., Am. Soc. Pub. Adminstrn., Nat. Assn. Sch. Pub. Affairs and Adminstrn. (exec. council 1973—, pres. 1974-75), Nat. Acad. Pub. Adminstrn., Council Nat. Municipal League, Phi Beta Kappa. Office: ARA Services Inc Independence Sq W Philadelphia PA 19106

CAMPBELL, ALAN NEWTON, chemist; b. Halifax, Eng., Oct. 29, 1899; s. Henry and Elizabeth (Newton) C.; m. Alexandra Jean Kerr, Aug. 28, 1931; 1 dau., Morag D.K. Grad., Birkbeck Coll., U. London, 1921, King's Coll., 1924; D.Sc. (hon.), U. Man., 1982. Asst. prof. U. Aberdeen, Scotland, 1925-30; asst. prof. U. Man., Can., Winnipeg, 1930-37, assoc. prof., 1937-45, prof., head dept. chemistry, 1945-69, prof. emeritus, 1969—. Contbr. articles to profl. jours. Fellow Canadian Inst. Chemistry; mem. Royal Inst. Chemistry (London), Royal Soc. Can. Home: 1254 Corydon Ave Winnipeg MB Canada R3M 0Z2 Office: Dept Chemistry U Manitoba Winnipeg MB Canada R3T 2N2

CAMPBELL, ALEXANDER BRADSHAW, provincial supreme court justice Canada; b. Summerside, P.E.I., Can., Dec. 1, 1933; s. Thane Alexander and Cecilia (Bradshaw) C.; m. Marilyn Gilmour, Aug. 19, 1961; children: Blair Alexander, Heather Kathryn, Graham Melville. B.A., Dalhousie U., 1958, LL.B., 1959; LL.D., McGill U., 1967, U. P.E.I., 1979. Bar: P.E.I. 1959, created Queen's counsel 1966. Practice law, Summerside, 1959-66; mem. P.E.I. Legislature, 1965-78; leader Liberal Party, 1965-78, premier, 1966-78, atty.-gen., minister justice, 1966-69, 74-78, minister devel., 1969-72, minister agr., 1972-74, minister responsible for cultural affairs, 1976-78; judge Supreme Ct. P.E.I., 1978—; mem. Privy Council Can., 1967; past sec. Summerside Bd. Trade.; bd. dirs. Can. Inst. Adminstrn. of Justice, 1981—, Internat. Commn. Jurists, 1982. Past v.p. Young Liberal Assn.; past pres. Summerside Y Men's Club; elder Trinity United Ch.; chmn. P.E.I. Electoral Boundaries Commn., 1982; pres. Summerside YMCA, 1980. Office: Sir Louis Davies Law Cts Bldg Charlottetown PE Canada

CAMPBELL, ALISTAIR MATHESON, ins. co. exec.; b. Argyllshire, Scotland, July 3, 1905; s. Peter and Catherine (MacRae) C.; m. Barbara Hampson Alexander, Apr. 2, 1948; children—Michael Alexander, Catherine, Barbara, Jill. Student, Inverness Royal Acad., 1917-23; M.A., U. Aberdeen, 1927. Joined Sun Life Assurance Co. of Can., Montreal, Que., 1928, asst. actuary, 1934-40, asso. actuary, 1940-46, actuary, 1946, asst. gen. mgr. and actuary, 1947, v.p., actuary, 1950, v.p. and chief actuary, 1954, exec. v.p., dir., 1956-62, pres., 1962-70, chmn., 1970-78, chmn. exec. com., 1978-81, chmn. emeritus, 1981—; hon. dir. Royal Trust Ltd., Can. Enterprise Devel. Corp. Ltd.; dir. Royal Trust Co. Mortgage Corp., Digital Equipment Can., Ltd.; Provincial v.p., Que.; Am. Life Conv., 1962-63, mem. exec. com., 1965. Bd. dirs. Can. Safety Council, 1968-73; past mem. bd. divisional trustees, v.p., 1950-53; hon. gov. Que. div. Can. Red Cross Soc., 1975. Served with Royal Canadian Arty., 1940-45. Fellow Inst. Actuaries, Soc. Actuaries (past gov.); mem. Canadian Life Ins. Assn. (pres. 1957-58), Canadian Assn. Actuaries (pres. 1947-48), Life Ins. Assn. Am. (dir. 1968-71). Home: 4 Coltrin Pl Rockliffe Ottawa ON K1M 0A5 Canada

CAMPBELL, ALLAN BARRIE, plant breeder; b. Winnipeg, Man., Can., Mar. 28, 1923; s. Arnold Munroe and Petrina Flora (Wilson) C.; m. Mavis Enid Millar, Dec. 15, 1950; 1 dau., Patricia. B.S.A., U. Man., 1944, M.Sc., 1948; Ph.D., U. Minn., 1954. Research officer wheat breeding Can. Dept. Agr. Research Sta., Winnipeg, 1949—, research scientist, 1965—. Served with RCAF, 1944-45. Recipient Merit award Incentive Award Bd. Public Service Can., 1976; Agronomy Merit award Alta. Wheat Pool and other orgns., 1976. Fellow Royal Soc. Can., Agrl. Inst. Can.; mem. Genetics Soc. Can., Can. Soc. Agronomy, Man. Inst. Agrologists. Devel. eight cultivars of hard red spring wheat. Home: 492 McNaughton Ave Winnipeg MB R3L 1S4 Canada Office: 195 Dafoe Rd Winnipeg MB R3T 2M9 Canada

CAMPBELL, ALLAN MCCULLOCH, educator; b. Berkeley, Calif., Apr. 27, 1929; s. Lindsay and Virginia Margaret (Henning) C.; m. Alice Del Campillo, Sept. 5, 1958; children—Wendy, Joseph. B.S. in Chemistry, U. Calif. at Berkeley, 1950; M.S. in Bacteriology, U. Ill., 1951; Ph.D., 1953, U. Chgo., 1978, U. Rochester, 1981. Instr. bacteriology U. Mich., 1953-57; research asso. Carnegie Inst., Cold Spring Harbor, N.Y., 1957-58; asst. prof. biology U. Rochester, N.Y., 1958-61, asso. prof., 1961-63, prof., 1963-68; prof. biol. sci. Stanford, 1968—; mem. genetics study sect. NIH, 1964-69, mem. DNA recombinant adv. com., 1977-81; mem. genetics panel NSF, 1973-76. Author: Episomes, 1969; co-author: General Virology, 1978; Editor: Gene, 1980—; asso. editor: Virology, 1963-69, Ann. Rev. Genetics, 1969—; editorial bd.: Jour. Bacteriology, 1966-72, Jour. Virology, 1967-75. Served with AUS, 1953-55. Recipient Research Career award USPHS, 1962-68. Mem. Nat. Acad. Scis., Am. Acad. Arts and Scis., Am. Soc. Microbiology, Soc. Am. Naturalists, AAAS. Democrat. Home: 947 Mears Ct Stanford CA 94305 Office: Dept Biol Scis Stanford U Stanford CA 94305 *I've always thought that each individual has some contribution to human knowledge that he is uniquely suited to make. So I try to be organized and to avoid doing things that I expect will get done, anyway, by others. And, of course, everything worthwhile requires hard work.*

CAMPBELL, ANN MORGAN, archivist, association executive; b. Beckley, W.Va., May 15, 1937; d. Thomas and Hazel (Thompson) Morgan; m. Thomas G. Campbell, May 5, 1957. B.A., Old Dominion U., Norfolk, Va., 1967; postgrad., Coll. William and Mary, Williamsburg, Va., 1967-68; M.B.A., Fla. Atlantic U., Boca Raton, 1981. Certified assn. exec. With Nat. Archives and Records Service, 1969-74, archivist John F. Kennedy Library, 1969-71, chief archives br., San Francisco, 1972-74; exec. dir. Soc. Am. Archivists, Chgo., 1974—; adj. lectr. history U. Ill., Chgo. Circle, 1975—; adv. com. Nixon Oral History project Whittier (Calif.) Coll., 1971-74; commr. Nat. Study Commn. Records and Documents Fed. Ofcls., 1975-77; mem. adv. com. Pres.'s Adminstrv. Services Reorgn. Project, 1977—. Contbr. papers in field. Mem. bur. U.S. nat. com. UNESCO Gen. Info. Program, 1977-80; restorer historic houses. Recipient Spl. Achievement award GSA, 1970. Fellow Soc. Am. Archivists (council 1973-74, editor newsletter 1974—); mem. Am. Assn. State and Local History, Orgn. Am. Historians, Am., Chgo. socs. assn. execs., Kappa Delta Pi, Phi Alpha Theta, Zeta Tau Alpha. Home: 1510 W Jackson Blvd Chicago IL 60607 Office: 330 S Wells St Suite 810 Chicago IL 60606

CAMPBELL, ARTHUR ANDREWS, govt. ofcl.; b. Bklyn., Feb. 8, 1924; s. Arthur Monroe and Jo Ethel (Andrews) C.; m. Nancy Elizabeth Pyle, Jan. 28, 1961; children—Julia, Tay. A.B., Antioch Coll., 1948; postgrad., Columbia U., 1947-50. Editorial clk. Met. Life Ins. Co., N.Y.C., 1950-52; statistician U.S. Bur. of Census, Washington, 1952-56; asso. research prof. Scripps Found. for Research in Population Problems, Miami U., Oxford, Ohio, 1956-64; chief natality stats. br. Nat. Center for Health Stats., Washington, 1964-68; dep. dir. Center for Population Research, NIH, Bethesda, Md., 1968—. Co-author: Family Planning, Sterility, and Population Growth, 1959, Fertility and Family Planning in the U.S, 1966, Trends and Variations in Fertility in the U.S, 1968. Served with USN, 1943-46. Recipient Meritorious Service award U.S. Dept. Commerce, 1957; Dir.'s award NIH, 1976. Fellow Am. Statis. Assn.; mem. Population Assn. Am. (pres. 1973-74), Internat. Union for Sci. Study Population. Office: Center for Population Research NICHD/NIH Bethesda MD 20205

CAMPBELL, BRIAN PHILLIP, manufacturing corporation executive; b. Oak Park, Ill., Aug. 23, 1940; s. Andrew Frank and Elizabeth (Gabris) C.; m. Mary Lucina Lincoln, May 28, 1977. B.S.C., Depaul U., 1963, M.S. in Fed. Income Taxation, 1973; M.B.A., Northwestern U., 1966. With No. Trust Co., Chgo., 1963; asst. v.p. Walston & Co., Inc., Chgo., 1963-65; v.p. Glore Forgan Staats Inc., Chgo., 1965-70, DuPont Glore Forgan Inc., 1970-73, Masco Corp., Taylor, Mich, 1974—, group v.p., 1980—; lectr. DePaul U., 1972-73; group v.p. Masco Corp., Taylor, Mich, 1980—. Bd. dirs. Chgo. Boys Clubs, 1972-73; bd. dirs. Boys Clubs Met. Detroit, 1974—. Mem. Inst. Chartered Fin. Analysts, Fin. Execs. Inst., Planning Execs. Inst. Episcopalian. Clubs: Chgo., Univ. Chgo.; Econs. (Chgo.); Barton Hills Country. Office: Masco Corp 21001Van Born Rd Taylor MI 48180

CAMPBELL, BRUCE CRICHTON, hospital administrator; b. Balt., July 21, 1947; s. James Allen and Elda Shaffer (Crichton) C.; m. Linda Page Cottrell, June 28, 1969; children: Molly Shaffer, Andrew Crichton. B.A., Lake Forest Coll., 1969; M.H.A., Washington U., St. Louis, 1973; D.P.H., U. Ill., 1979. Adminstrv. asst. Passavant Meml. Hosp., Chgo., 1970-71; adminstrv. resident Albany (N.Y.) Med. Center Hosp., 1972-73; adminstrv. asst. Rush-Presbyn.-St. Luke's Med. Center, Chgo., 1973-75, asst. adminstr., 1975-77, asst. v.p., 1977-79, v.p. adminstrv. affairs, 1979-83; chmn. dept. health systems mgmt. Rush U., Chgo., 1977-81, dean Coll. Health Scis., 1981-83; exec. dir. U. Chgo. Hosps. and Clinics, 1983—. W.K. Kellogg Found. fellow, 1977. Mem. Young Adminstrs. Chgo. (pres. 1977), Assn. Univ. Programs in Health Adminstrn., Ill. Hosp. Assn., Chgo. Hosp. Council. Office: 950 E 59th St Chicago IL 60637

CAMPBELL, BRUCE EMERSON, JR., banker; b. Hattiesburg, Miss., Mar. 7, 1931; s. Bruce Emerson and Eleanor (Beardslee) C.; m. Judith Fontaine, July 9, 1966; children: Bruce Emerson, Carter Fontaine. Grad., Vanderbilt U., 1953; M.B.A., Harvard U., 1959. Second v.p. Trust Co. Ga., Atlanta; with Nat. Bank Commerce, Memphis, exec. v.p., 1971-74, pres., 1974-76, chmn. bd., chief exec. officer, 1976—, also chief exec. officer, dir.; chmn. Nat. Commerce Bancorp. Trustee William R. Moore Sch.; bd. mem. Memphis Bus. Resource Center, Memphis Arts Council, Memphis-Plough Community Found. Served with USNR, 1953-57. Mem. Assn. Res. City Bankers, Memphis Area C. of C., Future Memphis, 100 Club Memphis. Presbyterian. Clubs: Memphis Country, Univ. *

CAMPBELL, CALVIN ARTHUR, JR., mining, tunneling and plastics molding equipment manufacturing company executive; b. Detroit, Sept. 1, 1934; s. Calvin Arthur and Alta Christine (Koch) C.; m. Rosemary Phoenix, June 6, 1959; 1 dau., Georgia Alta. B.A. in Econs, Williams Coll., 1956; B.S., M.I.T., 1959; J.D., U. Mich., 1961. With Exxon Co., N.Y.C., 1961-69; chmn. bd., treas. John B. Adt Co., York, Pa., N.Y.C., 1969-70; pres. Goodman Equipment Corp., Chgo., 1971—; chmn. bd. Improved Plastics Machinery Corp. (subs. Goodman Equipment Corp.), 1979—; Mem. Econ. Devel. Commn., City of Chgo., 1980—; dir. Ill. Devel. Bd., 1983—. Mem. ABA, N.Y. Bar Assn., Am. Mining Congress (gov. 1972—, chmn. bd. govs. mfrs. div. 1980-83, dir. 1980—), Ill. Mfrs. Assn. (dir. 1978—), Am. Inst Chem. Engrs., Young Pres.' Orgn., Newcomen Soc. N. Am., Psi Upsilon, Phi Delta Phi. Clubs: Racquet, Chicago, Commonwealth (Chgo.); Glen View; Skytop (Pa.). Home: 1320 N State Pkwy Chicago IL 60610 Office: 4834 S Halsted St Chicago IL 60609

CAMPBELL, CARL LESTER, banker; b. Sunbury, Pa., Apr. 10, 1943; s. Claude L. and Viola W. (Voneida) C.; m. Mary E. Bingaman, June 5, 1965; children: Carla L., Craig L. B.S., Susquehanna U., 1965; postgrad., Stonier Grad. Sch. Banking, 1978. Br. mgr. asst. v.p. Tri-County Nat. Bank, Middleburg, Pa., 1965-72; asst. v.p. adminstrn. Pa. Nat. Bank, Pottsville, 1972-74, adminstrv. v.p., 1974-80, sr. v.p., 1980-81, exec. v.p., 1981-82, pres. chief exec. officer, 1982—; dir. Oxford First Corp., Phila. Pres. So. Shuylkill United Way, 1979-80; bd. dirs Shuylkill County Council for Arts, 1982—; mem. exec. com. Hawk Mt. council Boy Scouts Am., 1983—. Club: Kiwanis (Pottsville) (past pres.). Office: 1 S Centre St Pottsville PA 17901

CAMPBELL, CAROL ANN, food service company executive; b. Miller, S.D., Mar. 22, 1940; d. Dick Cort and Meta Viola (Moller) Vitters; m. Joseph Anthony Campbell, Aug. 12, 1961; children: Kimberly, Michael. B.A., Calif. State U.-Fullerton, 1975; M.A., U.S.C., 1977; postgrad., Loyola Law Sch., Los Angeles, 1980. Office mgr. H.B. Devel., Orange, Calif., 1968-70; asst. tax mgr. Denny's Inc., La Mirada, Calif., 1971-75, corp. tax dir., 1975-83, treas., 1980—, v.p., 1983—. Mem. Nat. Restaurant Assn. Fin. and Tax Execs. Group, Tax Execs. Inst. (dir. Los Angeles Chpt. 1982-83), Los Angeles Treas. Club (treas. 1982, v.p. membership 1983). Home: 160 Belleza Ln Anaheim CA 92807 Office: Denny's Inc 16700 Valley View Ave La Mirada CA 90637

CAMPBELL, CARROLL ASHMORE, JR., congressman; b. Greenville, S.C., July 24, 1940; s. Carroll Ashmore and Anne (Williams) C.; m. Iris Rhodes, Sept. 5, 1959; children: Carroll Ashmore, III, Richard Michael. Ed., McCallie Sch., U. S.C., Am. U. Pres. Handy Park Co., 1960-78; mem. S.C. Ho. of Reps., 1970-74, S.C. Senate, 1976; exec. asst. to Gov. S.C., 1975; mem. 96th-98th Congresses from S.C. 4th Dist.; mem. banking, fin. and urban affairs com., com. on House adminstrn., appropriations com., ways and means com., asst. regional whip, Tenn. and Carolinas; farmer, Fountain Inn, S.C. Del. 1976 Republican Conv.; mem. Nat. Republican Congl. Com., Textile Caucus, S.C. Gov.'s Com. on Employment of Handicapped; mem. adv. council White House Conf. on Handicapped Individuals; chmn. March of Dimes; hon. chmn. Arthritis Found. Dr. Recipient Disting. Service award Jaycees; Citizenship award Woodmen of World; K.C. award; Rehab. Assn. Citizenship award; Guardian of Small Bus. award Nat. Fedn. Inst. Bus.; Disting. Service award Ams. for Constl. Action; Watchdog of Treasury award Nat. Associated Businessmen. Episcopalian. Clubs: Sertoma (Citizenship award), Masons, Chowder and Marching. Office: 103 Cannon House Office Bldg Washington DC 20515

CAMPBELL, CHARLES J., fishery biologist; b. Nanton, Alta., Can., Nov. 25, 1915; s. Charles W. and Marion (Joy) C.; m. June C. Mathisen, Oct. 25, 1941. B.S., Wash. State U., 1938. With U.S. Forest Service, summers 1938, 39, 40; with Oreg. Dept. Fish and Wildlife, 1941-78, chief fishery div., 1959-78; with Bur. Land Mgmt., 1978-79, VTN Oreg., Inc., 1979-83, Campbell-Craven, Tigard, Oreg., 1983—; cons. Booz, Allen & Hamilton, 1958. Served with USAAF, World War II. Mem. Am. Fisheries Soc. (pres. 1973), Pacific Fisheries Biologists, Am. Inst. Fishery Research Biologists, Wildlife Soc., Izaak Walton League Am., Phi Beta Kappa, Sigma Phi Epsilon, Phi Kappa Phi. Club: Elk. Home: 921 SW Cheltenham St Portland OR 97201 Office: 9170 SW Elrose St Tigard OR 97223

CAMPBELL, CHARLES JOHN, ophthalmologist; b. Steubenville, Ohio, June 24, 1926; m. Mary Catherine McGuigan, July 2, 1955; children—Catherine Mary, Barbara Irene, Charles Arbuthnot III. B.S., Muskingum Coll., 1949; M.D., George Washington U., 1948; M.S. in Optics, U. Rochester, 1951; Med.Sc.D., Columbia U., 1957. Intern George Washington U. Hosp., 1948-49; resident Edward S. Harkness Eye Inst., 1954-57; practice medicine specializing in ophthalmology, N.Y.C., 1957—; dir. Edward S. Harkness Eye Inst., Ophthalmology Service of Columbia-Presbyn. Med. Center, N.Y.C., 1974—, Knapp Meml. Lab. of Physiol. Optics, 1957—; prof., chmn. dept. ophthalmology Columbia U., 1974—. Served with USAF, 1952-54. Mem. Am. Ophthal. Soc., Am. Acad. Ophthalmology and Otolaryngology, A.C.S., Optical Soc. Am., Assn. U. Profs. Ophthalmology, AMA, N.Y. Ophthal. Soc., Assn. for Research in Vision and Ophthalmology, N.Y. State Med. Soc., N.Y. Acad. Scis. Office: 635 W 165th St New York NY 10032

CAMPBELL, CHRISTOPHER JOHN, process control equipment manufacturing company executive; b. Pittson, Pa., Dec. 8, 1927; s. Earl J. and Tryna (McDermott) C.; m. Anne McHale; children: Christopher J., Martin, Michael, Karen, Lisa, Julie. B.S., Fordham U., 1962. Prodn. planning mgr. AccuRay Corp., Columbus, Ohio, 1959-62, corp. controller, asst. treas., 1962-66, adminstrn. mgr., 1966-69, v.p. leasing and service, 1969-72, group v.p., 1972-73, chief operating officer, exec. v.p., 1973—. Served with U.S. Army, 1946-48. Home: 3977 Lytham Ct Columbus OH 43220 Office: AccuRay Corp 650 Ackerman Rd Columbus OH 43202

CAMPBELL, CLARENCE SUTHERLAND, sports assn. exec.; b. Fleming, Sask., Can., July 9, 1905; s. George A. and Annie M. (Haw) C.; m. Phyllis L. King, Nov. 17, 1955. B.A., LL.B. (Rhodes scholar), U. Alberta, 1926; M.A., Oxford U., 1928, B.C.L., 1929. Bar: Queen's Counsel, Alta. Barrister, Edmonton, Alta., 1929-40; pres. Nat. Hockey League, Montreal, Can., 1946-77, hon. chmn. bd. govs., 1977—. Pres. Lakeshore Gen. Hosp. Found. Served to lt. col. Canadian Army, 1940-

46. Decorated Order Brit. Empire. Mem. Law Soc. Alberta. Home: 3465 Redpath St Montreal PQ Canada Office: 960 Sun Life Bldg Montreal PQ Canada

CAMPBELL, COLIN, obstetrician, gynecologist, medical school dean; b. Washington, June 24, 1927; s. Colin and and Margaret (Kingsland) Masters) C.; m. Catherine Marian Hayden, Aug. 20, 1952; children—Catherine, Janet, Philip. A.B., Stanford U., 1949; M.D., C.M., McGill U., Montreal, Can., 1953; Ed.M., Temple U., 1967. Diplomate: Am. Bd. Obstetrics Gynecology. Gen. practice medicine, Perrine, Fla., 1955-57, practice medicine specializing in obstetrics and gynecology, Balt., 1960-61; instr. obstetrics, gynecology Temple U., Phila., 1961-64; asst. prof. obstetrics, gynecology U. Mich., Ann Arbor, 1964-67, asso. prof., 1967-71, prof., 1971-78, asst. dean Med. Sch., 1972-76, asso. dean, 1976-78; prof. obstetrics and gynecology, dean U. Ala. Sch. Primary Med. Care, Huntsville, 1978-83; prof ob-gyn, provost/dean Northeastern Ohio Univs. Coll. Medicine, Rootstown, Ohio, 1983—. Contbr. numerous articles in obstetrics and med. edn. to profl. jours. Fellow Am. Coll. Obstetricians and Gynecologists. Home: 265 Hampshire Rd Akron OH 44313 Office: Northeastern Ohio Univs Coll Medicine Rootstown OH 44272

CAMPBELL, COLIN, clergyman; b. Antigonish, N.S., Can., June 12, 1931; s. Peter Smyth and Ida (Tompkins) C. B.A., St. Mary's U., Halifax, N.S., 1952; B.Th., Holy Heart Sem., 1956; M.A., U. Montreal, 1964. Ordained priest Roman Cath. Ch., 1956; asst. various parishes, 1956-64; dir. social services Archdiocese of Halifax, 1964-69, vicar gen., 1969-80; also pastor St. Thomas Aquinas Ch., Halifax, 1969-75; pastor St. Anthony's Ch., Dartmouth, N.S., 1975-77, Immaculate Conception Parish, Truro, N.S., 1980-83; columnist Halifax Chronicle-Herald, Halifax Mail-Star; former lectr. social work Dalhousie U.; Pres. N.S. Family and Child Welfare Assn., 1967-69; chmn. Halifax Housing Authority, 1969-74; Chmn. bd. dirs. St. Mary's U., 1978-83; nat. dir. Pontifical Mission Aid Socs. for English-Speaking Can., 1983—. Mem. Profl. Assn. Social Workers N.S. Address: 2661 Kingston Rd Scarboro ON Canada MIM IM3

CAMPBELL, COLIN DEARBORN, economist, educator; b. Cooperstown, N.Y., Feb. 10, 1917; s. James Samuel and Marion (Jennings) C.; m. Rosemary Garst, June 18, 1949; children—William Garst, Janet Adele. B.A., Harvard, 1938; M.A., U. Iowa, 1941; Ph.D., U. Chgo., 1950; M.A., Dartmouth, 1965. Instr. Rensselaer Poly. Inst., 1946-47; asst. prof. Drake U., 1949-51; economist CIA, 1952-54, FRS, 1954-56; mem. faculty Dartmouth, 1956—, prof. econs., 1964-78, Loren M. Berry prof. econs., 1978—, chmn. dept., 1965-66; dir. Dartmouth Nat. Bank, 1961—, Student Loan Mktg. Assn., 1973-75; adj. scholar Am. Enterprise Inst., 1974—; Mem. U.S. Tax Adv. Group to Republic Korea, 1959-60. Author: (with R.G. Campbell) Introduction to Money and Banking, 1981; Contbr. profl. jours. Served to capt., Ordnance Corps AUS, 1941-46, 51-53. Mem. Am. Econ. Assn., Mont Pelerin Soc. Home: 9 N Park St Hanover NH 03755

CAMPBELL, COLIN GOETZE, university president; b. N.Y.C., Nov. 3, 1935; s. Joseph and Marjorie (Goetze) C.; m. Nancy Nash, June 20, 1959; children: Elizabeth, Jennifer, Colin, Blair. A.B., Cornell U., 1957; J.D., Columbia, 1960; M.A. (hon.), Wesleyan U., 1970; LL.D., Williams Coll., 1973, Amherst Coll., 1972, U. Hartford, 1983; D.H.L., Trinity Coll., 1981. Bar: Conn. bar 1961. Atty. Cummings & Lockwood, Stamford, Conn., 1960-62; asst. to pres. Am. Stock Exchange, N.Y.C., 1962-63, sec., 1963-64, v.p., 1964-67; adminstrv. v.p. Wesleyan U., Middletown, Conn., 1967-69, exec. v.p., 1969-70, pres., 1970—; dir. Middlesex Mut. Assurance Co., Pitney Bowes; corporator Liberty Bank Savs.; Bd. dirs. Middlesex Meml. Hosp.; trustee Inst. Architecture and Urban Studies; bd. dirs. Charles E. Culpeper Found. Mem. Psi Upsilon, Phi Delta Phi. Episcopalian. Club: Century Assn. Home: 269 High St Middletown CT 06457

CAMPBELL, COLINE, b. N.S., Can., Sept. 26, 1940. Student, St. Francis Xavier U., Laval U., Ottawa U., Harvard U., Kennedy Sch. Pub. Adminstrn. Lawyer; chmn. Fisheries and Forest Commn.; elected House of Commons, 1974, defeated gen. election, 1979, re-elected, 1980. Liberal. Office: House of Commons Ottawa ON Canada K1A 0A6 *

CAMPBELL, DONALD ALFRED, govt. ofcl.; b. St. Louis, Mar, 31, 1928; s. Clarence Alfred and Dorothy Ethyl (Eggeman) C.; m. Mary Kathryn McKay, June 17, 1951; children—Cynthia Kathleen Campbell Knupp, Jean Elizabeth Campbell DiBlasio. Student, Mercer U., 1945, Ga. Inst. Tech., 1945-46; J.D., George Washington U., 1949. Bar: U.S. Dist. Ct. D.C. bar 1949, U.S. Ct. Appeals D.C. bar 1951, U.S. Supreme Ct. bar 1955. Atty. Office Gen. Counsel Dept. Agr., Washington, 1949-62, asst. to asst. gen. counsel, 1959-62; dir. packers and stockyards div. Consumer and Mktg. Service, 1962-67; adminstr. Packers and Stockyards Adminstrn., 1967-71, judicial officer, 1971—; mem. Adminstrv. Conf. U.S., 1973-76. Contbr. articles to legal jours.; contbg. author Agricultural Law, 1981. Served with USNR, World War II; lt. comdr. Res. ret. Mem. Fed. Bar Assn., Order of Coif. Presbyn. (deacon, elder). Home: Annandale VA Office: Office of Sec Dept of Agriculture Room 250W Washington DC 20250

CAMPBELL, DONALD GUY, journalist, author; b. Brownsburg, Ind., June 27, 1922; s. George Guy and Ella (Menefee) C.; m. Jean Farson, Oct. 15, 1949; children—Scott Guy, Jennifer Lee. A.B. in Journalism, Ind. U., 1948. Reporter, feature writer St. Petersburg (Fla.) Time, 1948-49; writer Nat. Safety Council, 1949-52; reporter Indpls. Star, 1952-54, bus. and financial editor, 1954-65; exec. bus. and financial editor Ariz. Republic, Phoenix, 1965-72; financial editor N.Y. Daily News, 1972-74; chief researcher, writer Dow Theory Trader, 1956-71; columnist The Daily Investor United Feature Syndicate, 1972-79; staffwriter Los Angeles Times, 1979—; columnist real estate Register and Tribune Syndicate, 1968—; editor, pub. Money Views, investment newsletter, 1977-79; hon. lectr. Am. Inst. Fgn. Trade, 1966-72. Contbr., N.Am. Newspaper Alliance, 1967-72; Author: Let's Take Stock, 1959, What Does Daddy Do All Day, 1962, Understanding Stocks, 1965 (Kiplinger Book Club best seller 1965), The Handbook of Real Estate Investment, 1968. Served with AUS, 1942-45; ETO. Mem. Soc. Am. Bus. Writers (v.p.), Author's Guild, Sigma Delta Chi, Phi Gamma Delta. Home: 2236 Micheltorena St Los Angeles CA 90039

CAMPBELL, DONALD RALPH, consultant, former university president; b. Foxboro, Ont., Can., Nov. 14, 1918; s. Fred H. and Florence Pearl (Hollinger) C.; m. Ruth Heron, Feb. 11, 1977; children by previous marriage: Hugh, Catherine, Elizabeth. B.A., U. Toronto, 1949, Oxford (Eng.) U., 1951, M.A., 1958; LL.D., U. Guelph, 1974, U. Winnipeg, 1977; D.C.L. (hon.), St.Andrews Coll., 1981. Lectr., then prof., head agrl. econs. dept. Ont. Agrl. Coll., Guelph, 1951-62; Ford Found. econs. cons. Govt. Jordan, 1962-64, Govt. Kenya, 1970-72; prof., asso. dean U. Toronto, 1964-70; prin. Scarborough Coll., 1972-76; pres. U. Man., Winnipeg, 1976-81; econ. adviser Govt. Kenya, 1981—. Contbr. to profl. jours. Served with RCAF, 1942-45. Decorated D.F.C. with bar. Fellow Agr. Inst. Can. (pres. 1960); Mem. Can. Agrl. Econs. Soc. (pres. 1958), United Ch. Can. Address: care Rockefeller Found PO Box 47543 Nairobi Kenya

CAMPBELL, DONALD THOMAS, psychologist, educator; b. Grass Lake, Mich., Nov. 20, 1916; s. Arthur Lawrence and Hazel (Crafts) C.; m. Lola Sheaff, June 6, 1942 (div. Mar. 1983); children: Thomas Sheaff, Martin Crafts.; m. Barbara Frankel, Mar. 19, 1983. A.B., U. Calif. at Berkeley, 1939, Ph.D., 1947; M.A. (hon.), Oxford, 1969; LL.D., U. Mich., 1974; Sc.D., U. Fla., 1975, U. So. Calif., 1979, Northwestern U., 1983; D.Social Sci., Claremont Grad. Sch., 1978; D.H.L., U. Chgo., 1978. Asst. prof. psychology Ohio State U., 1947-50, U. Chgo., 1950-53; mem. faculty Northwestern U., Evanston, Ill., 1953-79, prof. psychology, 1958-73, Morrison prof., 1973-79; N.Y. State Bd. Regents Albert Schweitzer prof. Maxwell Sch., Syracuse (N.Y.) U., 1979-82; univ. prof. social relations and psychology Lehigh U., 1982—; Fellow Center Advanced Study Behavioral Scis. Stanford, Calif., 1965-66; Fulbright lectr., vis. prof. social psychology Oxford U., 1968-69; William James lectr. Harvard U., 1977; Hovland Meml. lectr. Yale U., 1977. Co-author: Experimental and Quasi-Experimental Designs for Research, 1966, Unobtrusive Measures: Nonreactive Research in the Social Sciences, 1966, The Influence of Culture on Visual Perception, 1966, Ethnocentrism: Theories of Intergroup Conflict, Ethnic Attitudes and Group Behavior, 1972, Social Experimentation: A Method for Planning and Evaluating Social Intervention, 1974, Ethnocentrism and Intergroup Attitudes: East African Evidence, 1976, Quasi-Experimentation, 1979, Nonreactive Measures in the Social Sciences, 1981; also numerous articles. Served to lt. USNR, 1943-46. Recipient Kurt Lewin Meml. award Soc. Psychol. Study Social Issues, 1974; Myrdal Sci. Contbn. award Evaluation Research Soc., 1977; award for disting. contbn. Am. Ednl. Research Assn., 1981. Fellow Am. Acad. Arts and Scis.; mem. Nat. Acad. Scis., Am. Psychol. Assn. (pres. div. personality and social psychology 1968-69, recipient Distinguished Sci. Contbn. award 1970, pres. 1975), Midwestern Psychol. Assn. (pres. 1966-67). Office: Price Hall 40 Lehigh U Bethlehem PA 18015

CAMPBELL, DOUGLASS, banker; b. N.Y.C., Aug. 31, 1919; s. William Lyman and Helene (Underwood) C.; m. Marion Danielson Strachan, Jan. 13, 1962; step-children: Richard and Stephen Strachan. A.B., Yale U., 1941. With N.Y. Central System, 1939-67, timekeeper, traveling car agt., asst. train master, train master, asst. supt. asst. to freight traffic mgr., asst. to pres., supt. exec. rep., 1939-58; v.p. N.Y.C. R.R. (and subs.), 1958-67, also in charge pub. relations and advt. dept., 1960-67, also dir.; chmn. pres. Bowater Paper Co., Inc., 1967-68; pres. Argyle Research Corp. (consultants), N.Y.C., 1968—; v.p. Hambro Am., Inc., subs. Hambros Bank of London, 1983—. Served as maj. AUS, 1942-46. Episcopalian. Clubs: Down Town Assn., River, Yale (N.Y.C.); Chagrin Valley Hunt (Cleve.); Saturn (Buffalo); Chicago. Racquet (Chgo.). Home: 3 E 71st St New York NY 10021 Office: 17 East 71st St New York NY 10021

CAMPBELL, EARL CHRISTIAN, professional football player; b. Tyler, Tex., Mar. 29, 1955; s. Burk and Ann C.; m. Reuna Smith, May 1980. Grad., U. Tex., 1980. Football player Houston Oilers, 1978—; played in AFC Championship Game, 1978, 79; played Pro Bowl, 1978-81. Recipient Heisman trophy, 1977; named Most Valuable Player in NFL, 1978, 79. Office: Houston Oilers PO Box 1516 Houston TX 77001 *

CAMPBELL, EDMUND DOUGLAS, lawyer; b. Lexington, Va., Mar. 12, 1899; s. Henry Donald and Martha Martha (Miller) C.; m. Esther Butterworth, June 9, 1925 (dec. July 1934); children: Edmund D., Virginia (Mrs. Everett W. Holt); m. Elizabeth Pfohl, June 16, 1936; children: H. Donald, Benjamin P. A.B., Washington and Lee U., 1918, LL.B., 1922; M.A., Harvard, 1920. Bar: D.C. 1924, Va. 1924. Practice in, Washington and, Arlington, Va., 1924—; mem. firm Jackson & Campbell, Washington. Pres. Arlington Council Chs., 1949, Arlington Community Chest, 1951; Mem. D.C. Police Complaint Rev. Bd., 1966-69; mem. Arlington County Bd. Suprs., 1941-47; chmn. Arlington Pub. Utilities Commn., 1935, Arlington Civil Service Commn., 1964-67; Democratic candidate for Congress, 1952; Trustee Mary Baldwin Coll., chmn., 1945-62; bd. dirs. Washington Council Chs., 1967. Served as pvt. U.S. Army, 1918. Recipient Algernon Sydney Sullivan award Mary Baldwin Coll., 1949. Fellow Am. Coll. Trial Lawyers; mem. ABA (ho. dels. 1964-75, gov. 1972-75), Va. Bar Assn., D.C. Bar Assn. (Distinguished Lawyers Award 1965, pres. 1961-62, mem. disciplinary bd. 1979—), Order of Coif, Phi Beta Kappa, Omicron Delta Kappa, Phi Delta Phi, Alpha Tau Omega. Episcopalian. Clubs: Metropolitan, Barristers, Lawyers (Washington). Home: 2207 N Tuckahoe St Arlington VA 22205 Office: 1120 20th St NW Suite 300S Washington DC 20036

CAMPBELL, EDWARD FAY, JR., clergyman, educator; b. New Haven, Jan. 5, 1932; s. Edward Fay and Edith Louise (May) C.; m. Phyllis Kletzien, Sept. 4, 1954; children: Thomas Edward, Sarah Ives. Grad., Haverford Sch. Boys, 1949; B.A., Yale, 1953; B.D., McCormick Theol. Sem., 1956; Ph.D., Johns Hopkins, 1959. Ordained to ministry Presbyn. Ch., 1956; asst. pastor 1st Presbyn. Ch., Balt., 1956-58; instr. O.T., archaeology McCormick Theol. Sem., Chgo., 1958-59, asst. prof., 1959-62, asso. prof., 1962-66, prof. O.T., 1966—, Francis McGaw prof., 1972—; acting dir. Am. Sch. Oriental Research, Jerusalem, 1964-65, annual prof., 1965; staff mem. Drew-McCormick Archeol. Expdn. to, Shechem, 1957, 60, 62, 64, asst. dir., 1960-62, treas., 1960—, asso. dir., 1964, archaeol. dir. expdn., 1966, 68; instr. Bibl. Hebrew Harvard, summer 1961; with Presbytery of Chgo., 1956—; Pres. W.F. Albright Inst. Archaeol. Research, 1971-72; trustee Rush-Presbyn. St. Lukes Med. Center, 1978—. Author: The Chronology of the Amarna Letters, 1964, Ruth: A New Translation and Commentary, Anchor Bible, 1975; Editor The Bibl. Archaeologist (quar.), 1959-75, (with David N. Freedman) The Biblical Archaeologist Reader, 2, 1964, 3, 1970; Contbr. to, Shechem, 1965, Magnalia Dei: Essays in Memory of G. Ernest Wright, 1976; contbr. Symposia anniversary collection, Am. Schs. Oriental Research, 1978, Soc. Bibl. Lit. Mem. Am. Schs. Oriental Research (1st v.p. 1967-70, archaeol. v.p. 1974-82). Home: 5465 S Dorchester Ave Chicago IL 60615

CAMPBELL, EDWARD JOSEPH, shipbuilding company executive; b. Boston, Feb. 21, 1928; s. Edward and Mary (Doherty) C.; (div.)children: Gary, Kevin, Diane. B.S. in Mech. Engring, Northwestern U., 1952, M.B.A., 1959. With Am. Brakeshoe Co., 1952-58, Whirlpool Corp., 1958-65; gen. mgr. Joy Mfg. Co., 1965-67; exec. v.p. Tenneco-J.I. Case Co., 1968-78; pres., chief exec. officer Tenneco-Newport News Shipbldg. Co., Va., 1979—; dir. Global Marine Co., Sovran Corp.; Bd. dirs. Webb Inst., Hampden-Sydney Coll. Served with USNR, 1945-48. Mem. Shipbuilders Council Am. (past chmn.), Nat. Maritime Council. Home: 160 Yeardley Dr Apt 26 Newport News VA 23601 Office: 4101 Washington Ave Newport News VA 23607

CAMPBELL, EDWIN DENTON, association executive; b. Boston, June 25, 1927; s. William Edwin and Mildred (Altmiller) C.; m. m. Crystal Cousins Lloyd, 1973; children from previous marriage—Geraldine, Linda, David. Grad., Bentley Coll., Boston, 1948; grad. Advanced Mgmt. Program, Harvard, 1965, 1971; Ed.D., 1975. Diplomate: C.P.A., Mass. Mgr. Arthur Andersen & Co. (C.P.A.'s), Boston, 1948-53; v.p. Lab. for Electronics, Inc., Boston, 1953-62, also dir.; exec. v.p. Itek Corp., Lexington, Mass., 1962-70, dir., 1962-83; pres. Edn. Devel. Center, Newton, Mass., 1971-76, now trustee; pres. Gulf Mgmt. Inst. div. Gulf Oil Corp., Boston, 1976-83; on loan as exec. v.p. Nat. Alliance of Bus., Washington, 1983—; dir. Keystone Apollo Fund, 1969-78, Leesona Corp., 1971-80, Keystone OTC Fund, 1972-78, Keystone Internat. Fund, 1978—, Corp. for Public/Pvt. Ventures, 1980—; mem. faculty Bentley Coll., Boston, 1956-58. Cons. editor: Change, 1980—. Trustee Bentley Coll., 1963—; Vice pres. Mass. Assn. Mental Health, 1965-68, bd. dirs., 1962-73; mem. Mass Commn. Vocational Rehab., 1966-68; mem. vis. com. Harvard Sch. Edn., 1977-83; Mem. finance com. Town of Carlisle, Mass., 1965-68; Trustee Boston Urban Found., 1969-75, Mass. Taxpayers Found., 1962-68, Fenn Sch., 1970-75, OSTI, Inc., 1971-76, Lesley Coll., 1972-76, Mass. Advocacy Center, 1975-76. Served with USMCR, 1943-45. Mem. Asso. Industries Mass. (pres. 1967-69, now dir.). Home: 1416 34th St NW Washington DC 20007 Office: 1015 15th St NW Washington DC 20005

CAMPBELL, F. MARION, professional football coach; b. Chester, S.C., May 25, 1929; s. F. Marion and Ruby (Keller) C.; m. June R. Campbell, Oct. 23, 1958; children: Scott, Alicia. B.S. in Edn., U. Ga. Defensive line coach Boston Patriots, 1962-63; def. coordinator Minn. Vikings, 1964-66; defensive line coach Los Angeles Rams, 1967-68; def. coordinator Atlanta Falcons, 1969-74, head coach, 1975-76, Phila. Eagles, 1983—. Served to 1st lt. U.S. Army, 1952-54. Named to State of Ga. Hall of Fame, 1982. Office: Veterans Stadium Broad St and Pattison Ave Philadelphia PA 19148

CAMPBELL, FINLEY ALEXANDER, geologist; b. Kenora, Ont., Can., Jan. 5, 1927; s. Finley McLeod and Vivian (Delve) C.; m. Barbara Elizabeth Cromarty, Oct. 17, 1953; children—Robert Finley, Glen David, Cheryl Ann. B.Sc., Brandon Coll., U. Man., Can., 1950; M.A., Queen's U., Kingston, Ont., 1956; Ph.D., Princeton U., 1958. Exploration and mining geologist Prospectors Airways, Toronto, 1950-58; asst. and asso. prof. geology U. Alta., Can., Edmonton, 1958-65; prof., head dept. geology U. Calgary, Alta., 1965-69, v.p. capital resources, 1969-71, v.p. acad., 1971-76, prof., 1976—; bd. dirs., vice chmn. Can Energy Research Inst. Contbr. articles on geol. topics to profl. jours. Decorated Queen's Jubilee medal, Can.; Sir James Dunne fellow, 1955-56; Princeton Alumni fellow, 1957-58; Fellow Royal Soc. Can. Mem. Geol. Assn. Can. (council), Mineral. Assn. Can., Soc. Econ. Geologists, Assn. Profl. Geologists Alta., Am. Mineral. Soc., Royal Soc. Anglican. Clubs: Glenmore Yacht, Zig Zag Yacht, Clearwater Bay Yacht. Home: 3408 Benton Dr NW Calgary AB T2L 1W8 Canada Office: Dept Geology U Calgary Calgary AB T2N 1N4 Canada

CAMPBELL, FRANK CARTER, librarian; b. Winston-Salem, N.C., Sept. 26, 1916; s. Joseph Preston and Marvel Inez (Carter) C. B.Mus., Salem Coll., Winston-Salem, N.C., 1938; M.Mus., Eastman Sch. Music, Rochester, N.Y., 1942. Cataloger Eastman Sch. Music, 1943; music librarian Library of Congress, 1943-59; prof. music history Am. U., 1950-53; asst. chief music div. N.Y. Pub. Library, 1959-66, chief, 1966; music critic Washington Eve. Star, 1953-59. Mem. Music Library Assn. (pres. 1967-69, editor jour. 1971-74), Am. Musicol. Soc., Internat. Assn. Music Libraries, The Bohemians, Opera Soc. Washington, Cantata Singers, Festival Orch. Soc., Aston Magna Found. Music., Clarion Music Soc. (v.p.). Home: 1 Nevada Plaza New York NY 10023 Office: Music Div NY Public Library 111 Amsterdam Ave New York NY 10023

CAMPBELL, GEORGE EMERSON, lawyer; b. Piggott, Ark., Sept. 23, 1932; s. Sid and Mae (Harris) C.; m. Joan Stafford Rule; children: Dianne, Carole. J.D., U. Ark., Fayetteville, 1955. Bar: Ark. bar 1955, U.S. Supreme Ct. bar 1971. Law clk. to justice Ark. Supreme Ct., 1959-60; asso. firm Kirsch, Cathey & Brown, Paragould, Ark., 1955; mem. Rose Law Firm (P.A.), Little Rock, 1960—; Del. 7th Ark. Constl. Conv., 1969-70; regional v.p. Nat. Mcpl. League, 1974—; mem. Ark. Ednl. TV Commn. Chmn. Pulaski County Law Library Bd., 1980—; bd. dirs. Ark. Symphony Orch. Soc., 1982—. Mem. Am. Ark., Pulaski County (Ark.) bar assns., Am. Law Inst., Am. Judicature Soc., Ark. Automobile Club (pres. 1977—). Office: 120 E 4th St Little Rock AR 72201

CAMPBELL, GEORGE STUART, educator; b. Sauquoit, N.Y., Nov. 29, 1926; s. Ralph Douglass and Grace Adaline (Dennis) C.; m. Roy Evelyn Stallings, Sept. 21, 1951; children—John Stuart, Robert Douglas. B.S., Rensselaer Polytech. Inst., 1947, B. Aero. Engring., 1949; M.S., Calif. Inst. Tech., 1951, Ph.D. (Douglas Aircraft fellow), 1956. Aero. research scientist NACA, Hampton, Va., 1947-53; research engr. Hughes Aircraft Co., El Segundo, Calif., 1954-59, sr. staff engr., 1959-62, sr. scientist, 1962-63; prof., head, aerospace engring. dept. U. Conn., Storrs, 1963-71, prof., 1972—. Editorial bd. Computers and Edn., 1974-79; Con'br. articles to tech. jours. Served with USNR, 1944-46. Asso. fellow Am. Inst. Aeros. and Astronautics; mem. Internat. Assn. for Math. and Computers in Simulation, Soc. Naval Architects and Marine Engrs. Home: 73 Hillyndale Rd Storrs CT 06268

CAMPBELL, GILBERT SADLER, surgery educator, surgeon; b. Toronto, Ont., Can., Jan. 4, 1924; s. Gilbert S. and Ellen (Thorson) C.; m. Dorothy Jean Nugent, Sept. 18, 1947 (div. 1960); children: Kathryn Ellen, Rebecca Sadler, Thomas Kim, William Riley; m. Joan Louise Hancock, Sept. 28, 1961; children: Susan Hancock, John Gilbert. Student, Hampden Sydney Coll., 1939-40; B.A., U. Va., 1943, M.D., 1946; M.S., U. Minn., 1949, Ph.D., 1954. Intern U. Minn. Hosps., Mpls., 1946-47, tchg. asst., 1947-49, researcher Am. Cancer Soc., 1951-53, sr. surgery resident, 1953-54; instr. physiology U. Minn., Mpls., 1948-49, instr. surgery, 1954-55, asst. prof., 1955-58; prof. surgery U. Okla., Oklahoma City, 1958-65; prof. surgery and thoracic surgery U. Okla. Med. Ctr., Oklahoma City, 1958-65; prof., head surgery, chief thoracic surgery U. Ark. for Med. Scis., Little Rock, 1965—; cons. surgery Little Rock VA Hosp, Little Rock, 1965—, Ark. Children's Hosp., 1973—; mem. courtesy staff Ark. Bapt. Med. Ctr., Little Rock, 1972—. Contbr. articles in field to med. jours. Served to capt. U.S. Army, 1949-51. Decorated Purple Heart U.S. Army, Bronze Star with oak leaf cluster U.S. Army, Silver Star with oak leaf cluster; Mary R. Markle scholar, 1954-59; recipient Horsley prize U. Va., 1954; named Surgery Alumnus of Yr. U. Minn., 1983. Mem. Am. Assn. Thoracic Surgery, AMA (ho. of dels. 1976-82), Am. Physiol. Soc., Am. Surg. Assn., Halsted Soc. (pres. 1978), Internat. Cardiovascular Soc. (v.p. N. Am. Chpt. 1973), Societe Internationale de Chirurgie, Soc. Thoracic Surgeons, Soc. Univ. Surgeons, Soc. Vascular Surgery, So. Surg. Assn. (1st v.p. 1981), Raven Soc., Alpha Omega Alpha. Home: 66 River Ridge Rd Little Rock AR 72207 Office: U Ark Med Scis 4301 W Markham St Little Rock AR 72205

CAMPBELL, GLEN, entertainer; b. Delight, Ark., Apr. 22, 1938; s. Wesley and Carrie (Stone) C.; m. Billie Jean Nunley, Sept. 20, 1959 (div. 1976); children: Debby, Kelli, Travis, Kane. Ed., pub. schs., Ark. and N.Mex. Appearances include: N.Mex.-Bick Bills (uncle), 1953, Hollywood Champs, 1960, 63-64, Shindig, 1964; studio musician, 1962-66; host summer: Smothers Bros. Show, 1968; film appearance in: True Grit, 1969, Norwood, 1970; host: TV show Glen Campbell Good Time Time Hour, 1969-71, Glen Campbell Music Show, 1981; co-sponsor, Glen Campbell-Los Angeles Open Golf Tournament. (Named Entertainer of Year 1968), TV show, Glen Campbell-Los Angeles Open Golf Tournament. (Best Male Vocalist 1968, 69), Glen Campbell-Los Angeles Open Golf Tournament. (TV Personality of Year 1969), Glen Campbell-Los Angeles Open Golf Tournament. (Entertainer of Year), Gt. Britain Country Music Assn. (recipient 5 Grammy awards), Gt. Britain Country Music Assn. (5 Country Assn. awards.); Mem., Nat. Reading Council.; Author: (with Anne Murray) song Less of Me; Recordings include Got It Together, Rhinestone Cowboy, Southern Nights, Gentry and Campbell. Address: care Regency Artists Ltd 9200 Sunset Blvd Suite 823 Los Angeles CA 90069 *

CAMPBELL, GRETNA, painter; b. N.Y.C., Mar. 23, 1922; d. John and Gretna (Koppe) Campbell); m. Louis Finkelstein, Feb. 3, 1945; children—Martha, Henry. Student, Cooper-Union, 1939-43, Art Students League, 1943-45. One man shows, Pyramid Gallery, N.Y.C., 1947, 49, Artists' Gallery, N.Y.C., 1950, 52, 54, Zabriskie Gallery, N.Y.C., 1956-57, Green Mountain Gallery, 1970, 73, 75, Ingber Gallery, N.Y., 1976, 77, 78, 79, 80, 81, N.Y. Studio Sch., 1977, 79, Wright State Mus., Dayton, Ohio, 1980, numerous others, group shows include, Chgo. Art Inst., 1944, Mus. Modern Art, N.Y.C., 1945, Riverside Mus., N.Y.C., 1949, 52, Whitney Mus., 1949, 52, 54, Phila. Mus. Art, 1958, 62, 65, Bklyn. Mus., 1956, Pa. Acad., Phila., 1967, N.Y. Cultural Center, 1973, Fordham U., Ciba-Geigy Collection, 1972, Weatherspoon Gallery, 1974, Queens Mus., Squibb Gallery, 1975, Maine State Mus., Augusta, 1976, Am. Acad. Arts and Letters, 1978, Landmark Gallery, N.Y.C., 1980, 81, others; tchr., Bklyn. Mus., 1959-62, Phila. Coll. Art, 1963-71, N.Y. Studio Sch., 1971-73, 76-80, Md. Art Inst., 1972-73, Pratt Inst., 1980-81, Yale U., 1972—; vis. artist, Ind. U., 1977, Goddard Coll., 1978, U. Houston, 1979, Parson Sch. Design, Wright State U., 1980, others. (Pearl Fund fellow 1946-49), others. (Fulbright fellow), others., France, 1953-54 (Louis Comfort Tiffany Found. fellow 1952).

CAMPBELL, H. STUART, medical products manufacturing executive; b. Phila., Dec. 4, 1929; s. James and Dorothy Baynham (Wilkinson) C.; m. Mildred Lucille Corum, Dec. 2, 1972; children: Constance, Eleanor, H. Stuart, Elizabeth. B.S. in Agr., Cornell U., 1951; grad. Advanced Mgmt. Program, Harvard Grad. Sch. Bus., 1980. Herd mgr. Halo Farms, Perry, N.Y., 1951-52; salesman, asst. mgr. Home Life Ins. Co. N.Y., Phila., 1956-60; with ETHICON, Inc. subs. Johnson and Johnson, Somerville, N.J., 1960-82, v.p. product mgmt. div., 1969-71, v.p. mktg., 1971-72, exec. v.p. mktg., 1972-74, exec. v.p. ops., 1974-75, pres., 1975-78, chmn. bd., 1978-82; dir., 1969-82; also chmn. bd. VASCOR, Inc. subs., Anaheim, Calif., 1978-81; also vice chmn. Johnson and Johnson Internat., 1977-79, co. group chmn., 1979-82, worldwide ETHICON product coordinator, 1978-82; chmn. bd. ETHICON Sutures Ltd. subs., Peterborough, Ont., Can., 1977-82, ETHICON Ltd. subs., Edinburgh, Scotland, 1977-82, ETHICON GmbH subs., Hamburg, W. Ger., 1977-82, ETHICON SpA subs., Rome, 1977-82, ETHNOR, S.A. subs., Paris, 1977-82, ETHICON S.A., Sao Paulo, Brazil, 1980-82, Biomatrix, Inc., Ridgefield, N.J., 1983—; owner, v.p. Drug Concentrates, Inc., Annandale, N.J., 1983—; dir. Berol Corp., Danbury, Conn., Kolff Med., Inc., Salt Lake City, Mesa Med., Inc., Wheat Ridge, Colo. Vice pres. bd. dirs. Somerset Valley YMCA, 1972; bd. govs. Muhlenberg Hosp., Plainfield, N.J., 1977—. Served to lt. USNR, 1952-56. Republican. Episcopalian. Home: 58 Westcott Rd Princeton NJ 08540

CAMPBELL, HENRY CUMMINGS, librarian; b. Vancouver, C., Can., Apr. 22, 1919; s. Henry and Margaret (Cummings) C.; m. Sylvia Woodsworth, Sept. 13, 1943; children—Shiela (Mrs. David Macrae), Bonnie, Robin. B.A., U. B.C., 1940; B.L.S., U. Toronto, 1941; M.A., Columbia, 1949. Librarian, film producer Nat. Film Bd., Can., Ottawa, 1941-46; with Secretariat UN, N.Y., 1946-48, UNESCO, Paris, 1949-56; chief librarian Toronto (Can.) Pub. Library, 1956-78; Lectr. U. Toronto Sch. Library Sci., 1970-71; cons. on information systems and library services Canadian Govt., Social Sci. Research Council Can., UNESCO. Author: How To Find Out About Canada, 1967, Canadian Libraries, 1972, rev. ed, Early Days on the Great Lakes, 1971, Producing Change in Metropolitan Public Library Systems, 1973, The Public Library in the Urban Metropolitan Setting, 1973. Mem. Internat. Assn. Met. City Libraries (pres. 1971—), Canadian Library Assn. (pres. 1973-74), Ont. Continuing Edn. Assn. (pres. 1966), Toronto Hist. Assn. (dir. 1958—). Home: 373 Glengrove Toronto ON Canada M5N 1W4

CAMPBELL, HERBERT PETERKIN, ret. business exec.; b. Ravenswood, W.Va., Nov. 11, 1898; s. Charles Mitchell and Eugenia C. (Fairfax) C.; m. Mary Louise Dyer, June 10, 1920 (dec. Apr. 1980); children—John William, Robert Lee. Student, Marshall U., 1916-17. Salesman wholesale dry goods, 1919-26; sec. Guthrie-Morris-Campbell Co., 1926-41, pres., 1941-72; Hon. trustee Morris Harvey Coll. Served with 38th, 78th Inf. Divs. U.S. Army, 1917-19. Mem. Nat. Assn. Textile and Apparel Wholesalers (past pres.), Nat. Assn. Wholesalers, U.S. (past nat. councilor), Charleston C. of C. (past pres.), W.Va. C. of C. (past pres.). Methodist. Clubs: Mason (Shriner), Rotarian.). Home: 1025 Old Country Club Rd NW Apt 3 Roanoke VA 24017

CAMPBELL, HUGH STEWART, retired lawyer; b. Hartford, Conn., Oct. 29, 1910; s. Frederick Stewart and Anna (Dow) C.; m. Sally Tuttle Moore, Aug. 8, 1936; children: Peter Dow II, Pamela Sanford. B.A., Trinity Coll., 1932; LL.B., Hartford Law Coll., 1937; J.D., U. Conn., 1969. Bar: Conn. bar 1937. With Phoenix Mut. Life Ins. Co., Hartford, 1933—, asst. counsel, 1946, counsel, 1948, sec., counsel, 1951, v.p., counsel, 1958-68, sr. v.p., gen. counsel, 1968-73; counsel firm Murtha, Cullina, Richter & Pinney, Hartford, 1973-80; Former chmn. Wethersfield Library Bd.; mem. Wethersfield Library Survey Com., Town Hall-Library Bldg. Com. Corporator, Inst. of Living; corporator Hartford Public Library; alumni trustee Trinity Coll.; life trustee Watkinson Library. Contbr. articles to profl. jours. Served to lt. USNR, 1943-46. Mem. ABA, Conn. Bar Assn., Hartford County Bar Assn., Assn. Life Ins. Counsel (pres. 1972-73), Am. Life Conv. (chmn. legal sect. 1964), Conn. Hist. Soc., Wethersfield Hist. Soc., Trinity Coll. Alumni Assn. (Alumni medal 1957, past pres.), Wadsworth Atheneum (hon. trustee, past pres. bd. trustees), Antiquarian and Landmark Soc., Phi Beta Kappa, Alpha Chi Rho. Republican. Clubs: 20th Century, University (Hartford); Dauntless (Essex, Conn.). Home: 161 Garden St Wethersfield CT 06109

CAMPBELL, J. JEFFREY, restaurants and holding company executive. Chmn., chief exec. officer Burger King Corp.; v.p. Pillsbury Co. Pffoce: 7360 N Kendall Dr. Miami FL 33156

CAMPBELL, JACK JAMES RAMSAY, microbiology educator; b. Vancouver, C., Can., Mar. 29, 1918; s. Murdoch and Margaret (Campbell) C.; m. Emily Ann Fraser, Sept. 4, 1942; children: Sheila, Merle, Ann, Ross. B.S.A., U. B.C., Vancouver, 1939; Ph.D., Cornell U., 1944. Research assoc. chem. warfare Dept. Def., Kingston, Ont., Can., 1944-46; mem. dairying dept. U. B.C., 1946-65, prof., head microbiology dept., 1965-82. Fellow Royal Soc. Can., AAAS; mem. Am., Can. socs. microbiology, Soc. Gen. Microbiology, Sigma Xi, Phi Kappa Phi, Alpha Delta, Sigma Tau Upsilon. Home: 3949 W 37th St Vancouver BC V6N 2W4 Canada

CAMPBELL, JACKSON JUSTICE, Medievalist, educator; b. Nowata, Okla., Jan. 9, 1920; s. Thomas Bernard and Isis (Justice) C.; m. Margarita Monal, Apr. 24, 1943; children—Catherine, Thomas, Robert. B.A., Yale U., 1941, Ph.D., 1950; M.A., U. Pa., 1946. Tchr. Ruston Acad., Havana, Cuba, 1941-42; instr. English lit. Yale U., 1948-51; asst. prof. English U. Ill., Urbana, 1951-54, prof., 1964—; asst. prof., asso. prof. Princeton, 1954-64; Fulbright lectr. U. Havana, 1952; Annan preceptorship for research in Eng., 1956-57; asso. Recording for the Blind Assn., Princeton, N.J., 1957-64. Author: The Advent Lyrics of the Exeter Book, 1959, Shakespeare's Troilus and Cressida, 1956, Poems in Old English, 1962; Contbr. articles to profl. jours. Served to capt. USAAF, 1942-45. Mem. Medieval Acad. Am., Modern Lang. Assn. Office: 608 S Wright St Urbana IL 61801

CAMPBELL, JAMES ARTHUR, profl. baseball exec.; b. Huron, Ohio, Feb. 5, 1924; s. Arthur A. and Vanessa (Hart) C.; m. Helene G. Mulligan, Jan. 16, 1954 (div. July 1969). B.S., Ohio State U., 1949. Bus. mgr. Thomasville (Ga.) Baseball Club, 1950, Toledo Baseball Club, 61951, Buffalo Baseball Club, 1952; bus. mgr. Detroit Minor League System, 1953; asst. farm dir. Detroit Baseball Club, 1954-56, v.p., farm dir., 1957-61, v.p., gen. mgr., 1962-65; exec. v.p., gen. mgr. Detroit Tigers, 1965-78, pres., gen. mgr., 1978—. Served with AC USNR, 1943-46. Named Maj. League Exec. of Year, 1968. Mem. Ohio State U. Varsity O Assn., Assn., Delta Upsilon. Presbyn. Clubs: Detroit Athletic, Detroit Press, Renaissance. Home: 2121 Trumbull Detroit MI 48216 Office: Tiger Stadium 2121 Trumbull Ave Detroit MI 48216

CAMPBELL, JAMES ARTHUR, chemistry educator; b. Elyria, Ohio, Oct. 1, 1916; s. James Allen and Helen (Metcalf) C.; m. Dorothy Carnell, Nov. 12, 1938; children: Kathleen Annette Campbell Fischer, Christine (Mrs. Richard North). A.B., Oberlin Coll., 1938; M.Sc., Purdue U., 1939; Ph.D., U. Calif., Berkeley, 1942; D.Sc., Beaver Coll., 1972. Instr. U. Calif., Berkeley, 1942-45; prof. Oberlin Coll., 1945-57; program dir. NSF, 1956-57; prof. chemistry Harvey Mudd Coll., Claremont, Calif., 1957—, dir. chem. edn. material study, 1960-63, dean faculty, 1974-75; Sci. adviser UNESCO, Asia, 1969-70; adviser Ford, Sloan, Danforth founds., Research Corp.; lectr. AAAS-Znanlye (USSR) Exchange, 1973; vis. prof. U. Nairobi, 1983; Fulbright lectr. Punjab U., India; AAAS exchange prof. People's Republic China. Author: (with L.E. Steiner) General Chemistry, 1955, Why Do Chemical Reactions Occur?, 1965, Chemical Systems, 1970, Teacher's Guide to Chemical Systems, 1970, (with Barbara Burke) Chemistry, The Unending Frontier, 1978; Columnist Jour. Chem. Edn., 1972-79. Recipient James Flack Norris award N.E. sect. Am. Chem. Soc., 1963; Mfg. Chemists award, 1963; So. Calif. Industry award, 1965; Fund for Advancement Edn. fellow Cambridge U., 1952-53; Guggenheim fellow Kyoto U., also Cambridge U., 1963-64; Nat. Sci. Faculty fellow Harvard, 1970-71; resident scholar Villa Serbeloni, 1972; vis. prof. Chinese U., Hong Kong, 1975-76. Mem. AAAS, AAUP, Am. Chem. Soc. (scientific apparatus makers award 1972), Chem. Soc. Conglist. Home: 4326 Via Padova Claremont CA 91711

CAMPBELL, JAMES FROMHART, former ambassador, co. exec.; b. Lonacoming, Md., May 14, 1912; s. George Dowery and and Eleanor Stirling (Jones) C.; m. Mary Frances Cotton, Sept. 14, 1946; children—Mary Eleanor, James Russell, Margaret Ann. B.A., St. John's Coll., Annapolis, Md., 1932; postgrad. law studies, George Washington U., 1933-34; grad., Naval War Coll., Newport, R.I., 1946. Mem. sales devel. staff Griffith Consumers Co., Washington, 1934-35; mktg. and mgmt. tng. positions Esso Standard Oil Co., Washington, 1935-42; mktg. and mgmt. tng. coordinator Esso Tng. Center, N.Y.C., 1946-49; dir., sales mgr. Esso Standard Oil Co., P.R.), San Juan, 1949-52, pres., dir., 1954-55; asst. regional mgr. Esso Standard of Central Am., Panama City, Panama, 1952-53, Caribbean area Esso Standard of South Am., Ciudad Trujillo, Dominican Republic, 1953-54, regional mgr. Caribbean area, Havana, Cuba, 1955-57, v.p., dir., mgr., Santiago, Chile, 1958-63; chmn. bd., mng. dir. Esso Standard South Africa, Johannesburg, 1963-70; vice chmn., dir. Triomf Fertilizer and Chem. Co., 1963-70; resident dir. Esso Exploration and Prodn. Co., South Africa, 1963-70; cons. Esso Africa, Inc., London, 1970-71; dep. asst. adminstr. for adminstrn. AID, Washington, 1971, asst. adminstr. for program and mgmt. services, 1971-74; ambassador to Republic of El Salvador, 1974-76; pres., dir. Campbell Coal Co., Piedmont, W.Va., Piedmont Hotel Co., ret., 1979; Pres. Am. Soc., Santiago, 1960-61, Johannesburg, 1966-67; pres. Am. Men's Luncheon Club, Johannesburg, 1965-66; bd. dirs. Am. C. of C., Santiago, 1961-63, Johannesburg, 1965-70; Bd. dirs. Rehoboth Beach (Del.) Art League. Served to lt. comdr. USN, 1942-46; MTO, PTO. Decorated Order José MAtias Delgado, Govt. El.Salvador; recipient medallion Internat. House, New Orleans, 1975. Republican. Episcopalian. Clubs: Columbia Country (Chevy Chase, Md.); Rehoboth Beach Country, Henlopen Acres Beach (Rehoboth Beach); John's Island (Vero Beach, Fla.). Home: 500 Beach Rd Apt 105 John's Island Vero Beach FL 32960 also 80 Oak Ave Rehoboth Beach DE *Accept each new assignment as an opportunity to increase your knowledge and experience. Each assignment makes you a more valuable person, broadens your outlook, and makes you more understanding and better prepared to contribute in the world of today.*

CAMPBELL, JAMES ROBERT, banker; b. Rochester, Minn., May 24, 1942; s. Donald William and Alice Marie (Gray) C.; m. Carmen Dawn Starkson, July 11, 1964; children: Peter Ian, Kathryn Ann. B.S. in Bus, U. Minn., 1964. Comml. lending officer Northwestern Nat. Bank, Mpls., 1964-71, sr. v.p. nat. dept., 1975-79; pres., dir. Lease Northwest, Inc., Mpls., 1971-75, U.S. Nat. Bank, Omaha, 1979-82; regional pres. Norwest Corp.-Norwest Banks, Omaha, 1982—; dir. Northwest Computer Services, Inc., Miles Homes, Inc., Nebr. Electronic Transfer System. Trustee Joslyn Art Mus., Omaha; bd. dirs. Jr. Achievement Omaha, St. Joseph Hosp., Omaha., Jr. Achievement Omaha; mem. consultation council SAC. Mem. Young Pres. Orgn., Omaha C. of C. (dir., pres.-elect), Knights of Aksarben (counselor). Presbyterian. Clubs: Omaha; Omaha Country (Minneapolis.). Home: 2223 S 86th Ave Omaha NE 68124 Office: Suite 200 One Central Park Plaza Omaha NE 68102

CAMPBELL, JAMES SARGENT, lawyer; b. Chgo., Sept. 19, 1938; s. E. Riley and Julia (Sargeant) C.; m. Mary Eager, Sept. 3, 1960; children: Catherine, Julia, John. B.A., Yale U., 1960; LL.B., Stanford U., 1964. Bar: D.C. 1966. Carnegie teaching fellow Yale U., 1960-61; law clk. Justice William O. Douglas, U.S. Supreme Ct., 1964-65; spl. asst. antitrust div. Dept. Justice, 1967-68; gen. counsel Nat. Commn. Causes and Prevention Violence, 1968-69; assoc. Wilmer, Cutler & Pickering, Washington, 1965-67, 70-71, ptnr., 1972—; cons. Office Sec. HUD, 1977, 78. Author: (with J. Sahid and D. Stang) Law and Order Reconsidered, 1970. Chmn. exec. com. Eisenhower Found., 1982—; former chmn. bd. tustees Norwood Sch. Mem. ABA, Internat. Bar Assn., Order Coif, Phi Beta Kappa. Office: 166 K St NW Washington DC 20006

CAMPBELL, JAMES WAYNE, biologist; b. Highlandville, Mo., Mar. 2, 1932; s. Frank Pauline and Mable (Kentling) C.; m. Bonnalie Josephine Oetting, Sept. 4, 1960; children—Heather Anne, James Kentling. B.S., S.W. Mo. State Coll., 1953; M.S., U. Ill., 1955; Ph.D. (USPHS fellow), U. Okla., 1958. Nat. Acad. Sci.-NRC fellow Johns Hopkins U., 1958-59; mem. faculty Rice U., Houston, 1959—, prof. biology, 1970—, chmn. dept., 1974-78; vis. asso. prof., USPHS fellow U. Wis. Med. Sch., Madison, 1964-65; program dir. regulatory biology Div. Biol. and Med. Sci. NSF, 1973-74, dir. div. physiology, cellular and molecular biology, 1979—; cons. to govt., 1969—. Editor: Comparative Biochemistry of Nitrogen Metabolism, 2 vols, 1970; co-editor: Nitrogen Metabolism and the Environment, 1972; contbr. profl. jours. Recipient USPHS Career Devel. award, 1966-70; NSF USPHS grantee, 1960—. Fellow AAAS; mem. Am. Physiol. Soc., Am. Soc. Biol. Chemists, Biochem. Soc. Eng., Am. Soc. Zoologists, Sigma Xi, Phi Sigma, Phi Lambda Upsilon. Address: 2628 Fenwood Rd Houston TX 77005

CAMPBELL, JERRY F., insurance company executive; b. Kansas City, Mo., Oct. 10, 1936; s. Dale Elston and Vonna (Fortner) C.; m. Kate Shrago, July 19, 1958; children: Todd, Katherine, Daniel, David. B.B.A., U. Mo.-Kansas City, 1958. C.L.U. Regional group mgr. Phoenix Mut. Life Ins. Co., Pitts., 1965-72, regional dir., 1972-74, v.p. agys., Hartford, Conn., 1974-79, sr. v.p. mktg., 1979-83; sr. v.p.-individual Central Life Assurance Co., Des Moines, 1983—; past dir. Phoenix Holding Co., Hartford, Phoenix Am. Life Ins. Co., Phoenix Gen. Ins. Co., Conn. Savs. and Loan. Active West End Civic Assn., Hartford, 1972-83, pres., Hartford, 1973; dir. Hartford Architecture Conservancy, 1982-83. Mem. Am. Soc. C.L.U.s, Nat. Life Underwriters Assn., Hartford Life Underwriters Assn. Democrat. Office: Central Life AssuranceCo 611 5th Ave Des Moines IA 50306

CAMPBELL, JOHN COERT, author, polit. scientist; b. N.Y.C., Oct. 8, 1911; s. Allan Reuben and Gertrude Helen (DuBois) C.; m. Mary Elizabeth Hillis, Aug. 1, 1936; childrenAllan Reuben II, Alexander Bruce. A.B., Harvard, 1933, M.A., 1936, Ph.D., 1940. Instr. polit. sci. U. Louisville, 1940-41; specialist Eastern Europe State Dept., 1942-46; sec. U.S. delegation, polit. adviser Council Fgn. Ministers, also; Paris (France) Peace Conf., 1946; polit. adviser U.S. delegation Danube Conf., 1948; officer charge Balkan affairs, mem. policy planning staff State Dept., 1949-55; sr. research fellow, dir. studies Council Fgn. Relations, 1955-78; cons. and adv. State Dept., 1963—, mem. policy planning council, 1967-68. Author: The United States in World Affairs, 3 vols, 1947-49, Defense of the Middle East, Problems of American Policy, rev. edit, 1960, American Policy Toward Communist Eastern Europe, The Choices Ahead, 1965, Tito's Separate Road, America and Yugoslavia in World Politics, 1967; Editor: Successful Negotiation, Trieste, 1954, 1976; mem. editorial bd.: Slavic Rev, 1969-76. Gov., v.p. Middle East Inst., 1967-78; mem. joint com. Slavic studies Am. Council Learned Soc. Fellow Middle East Studies Assn.; mem. Council Fgn. Relations, Am. Hist. Assn., Am. Assn. Advancement Slavic Studies (award for disting. contbn. to Slavic studies 1980). Home: 220 S Main St Cohasset MA 02025

CAMPBELL, JOHN KELLY, hotel executive; b. Grand Rapids, Mich., Dec. 22, 1929; s. John A. and Mary (Kelly) C.; m. Mary Lou Payette, Jan. 10, 1953; children: Nancy, John, Mary Kay, Robert, Jane, Peter, David, James. B.S. in Bus. Adminstrn., Mich. State U., 1951. C.P.A., Mich., Calif., Nev. Staff auditor Ernst & Ernst, Grand Rapids, 1954-60, audit supr., Albuquerque, 1960-61, mgr., San Francisco, 1961-63, 65-72; v.p., controller Bankers Mortgage Co., San Francisco, 1963-65; v.p. fin., treas. MGM Grand Hotels, Inc., Las Vegas, 1972—. Served with U.S. Army, 1952-54. Mem. Am. Inst. C.P.A.s, Nev. Soc. C.P.A.s, Nev. Resort Assn. (trustee Health and Welfare Trust 1977—). Republican. Roman Catholic. Office: MGM Grand Hotels Inc 3645 Las Vegas Blvd S Las Vegas NV 89109

CAMPBELL, JOHN LLOYD, oral surgeon, educator; b. Leavenworth, Kans., Jan. 29, 1914; s. Lloyd Gully and Lorena Mary (Starry) C.; m. Ruth Elizabeth Lee, June 15, 1939; children—Margaret Lee (Mrs. John Cremer), Sally Ann (Mrs. Darrel Hicks); m. Eleanor Lois Ingebretsen, Oct. 4, 1947; children—Catherine Louise, John Lloyd Campbell. Student, DePauw U., 1932-33; D.D.S., Ind. U., 1939; M.S., U. Md., 1953. Diplomate Am. Bd. Oral Surgeons. Intern Columbia Presbyn. Med. Center, 1939-40; commd. 1st lt. Dental Corps, U.S. Army, 1940, advanced through grades to lt. col., 1951; ret., 1960; prof. oral surgery, chmn. dept. W.Va. U. Sch. Dentistry, Med. Center, Morgantown, 1960-79, prof. emeritus, 1979—, also asst. chief hosp. dental service; oral surgery cons. VA Hosp., Clarksburg, W.Va., Ireland Gen. Hosp., Ft. Knox, Ky. Bd. dirs. W.Va. chpt. Nat. Hemophilia Found., Friendship Manor, A.R.C., Am. Cancer Soc. Fellow Internat. Coll. Dentists, A.A.A.S., Am. Coll. Dentists, Internat. Assn. Oral Surgeons; mem. Assn. Internat. Dental Research, Assn. Mil. Surgeons, Royal Soc. Health, Am. Assn. Hosp. Chiefs, Am., W.Va. dental assns., Monongahela Valley Dental Soc., Fedn. Dentaire Internat., Pierre Fouchard Acad., Pan Am. Med. Assn., Am., Middle Atlantic, W.Va., Southeastern socs. oral surgeons, Morgantown C. of C., Am. Legion, V.F.W., Omicron Kappa Upsilon, Delta Upsilon, Alpha Phi Omega, Delta Sigma Delta. Presbyterian (elder). Clubs: Mason (Shriner), Kiwanian, Elk. Home: 601 Valley View St Morgantown WV 26505

CAMPBELL, JOHN MORGAN, engineer; b. Virden, Ill., Mar. 24, 1922; S. John M. and Ione Marie (Whittler) C.; m. Gwendolyn Thompson, Aug. 27, 1945; children: John Morgan, Robert, Charles. B.S. in Chem. Engring, Iowa State U., 1943; M.S., U. Okla., 1948, Ph.D., 1951. Devel. engr. and supr. E.I. duPont de Nemours & Co., Inc., 1943-46; spl. instr. chem. engring. U. Okla., 1946-50; tech. adviser to v.p. Black Sivalls and Bryson, Oklahoma City, 1951-54; mem. faculty U. Okla. Sch. Petroleum Engring., 1954-69, chmn. dept., 1956-63, Erle P. Halliburton prof., 1963-69, dir., 1969, Petroleum Research Center, 1964-69; pres. John M. Campbell & Co. (engring. counselors, mgmt. consultants), 1968-82; chmn. bd. Petrotech Ltd., Petroleum Learning Programs Ltd. Author: Oil Property Evaluation, 1959, Effective Technical Communications, 1969, Decision Methods For Petroleum Investments, 1969, Gas Conditioning and Processing, 2 vols., 1970, The Professional - From Puberty to Senility, 1970, Effective Communication for the Technical Man, 1972, Petroleum Reservoir Property Evaluation, 1973, Mineral Property Economics (3 vols.), 1978, Petroleum Evaluation for Financial Disclosures, 1983; also numerous articles, chpts. in books. Mem. Am. Inst. M.E. (exec. com. council edn.), Soc. Petroleum Engrs., Am. Arbtration Assn. (arbitration panel), Internat. Petroleum Inst. (pres. 1968-82), Sigma Alpha Epsilon, Phi Lambda Upsilon, Pi Epsilon Tau. Club: Lion. Home: 6 Rustic Hills Norman OK 73069

CAMPBELL, JOHN RICHARD, pediatric surgeon; b. Pratt, Kans., Jan. 16, 1932; s. John Ross and Laura (Harkrader) C.; m. Susan Charlotte Baker, June 9, 1962; children: Kathryn, John Richard, George Ridgway. B.A., U. Kans., 1954, M.D., 1958. Diplomate: Am. Bd. Surgery. Rotating intern Hosp. U. Pa., 1958-59; resident in gen. surgery U. Kans. Hosp., 1959-63; resident in pediatric surgery Children's Hosp. of Phila., 1965-67; asst. instr. U. Pa. Med. Sch., 1965-67; mem. faculty U. Oreg. Health Scis. Center, Portland, 1967—, prof. surgery and pediatrics, 1972—, chief pediatric surgery; cons. VA, Shriners Crippled Children's hosps., Madigan Gen. Hosp., Tacoma, Wash., Alaska Native Med. Center, Anchorage. Served to lt. comdr. M.C. USNR, 1963-65. Mem. A.C.S., Soc. Acad. Surgeons, Am. Acad. Pediatrics, Am. Pediatric Surg. Assn., Pacific Assn. Pediatric Surgeons, North Pacific Pediatric Soc., North Pacific Surg. Assn., Pacific Coast Surg. Assn., Portland Acad. Pediatrics, Portland Surg. Soc. Presbyterian. Office: U Oreg Health Scis Univ 318 SW Jackson Park Rd Portland OR 97201 *

CAMPBELL, JOHN ROY, animal scientist, educator; b. Goodman, Mo., June 14, 1933; s. Carl J. and Helen (Nicoletti) C.; m. Eunice Vieten, Aug. 7, 1954; children: Karen L., Kathy L., Keith L. B.S., U. Mo., Columbia, 1955, M.S., 1956, Ph.D., 1960. Instr. animal sci. U. Mo., Columbia, 1960-61, asst. prof., 1961-65, asso. prof., 1965-68, prof., 1968—; asso. dean, dir. resident instrn. Coll. Agr., U. Ill., Urbana, 1978-83, dean Coll. Agr., 1983—. Author: (with J.F. Lasley) The Science of Animals That Serve Mankind, 1969, 2d edit., 1975, 3d edit., 1984, In Touch with Students, 1972, (with R.T. Marshall) The Science of Providing Milk for Man, 1975. Recipient Outstanding Tchr. award U. Mo., 1967; Superior Teaching award Gamma Sigma Delta.

Mem. Am. Dairy Sci. Assn. (dir., pres. 1980-81, Ralston Purina Disting. Teaching award 1973), Nat. Assn. Coll. Tchrs. Agr. (Ensminger Interstate Disting. Tchr. award 1973). Home: 1776 Maynard Lake Dr Champaign IL 61821 Office: U Ill Coll Agr 101 Mumford Hall 1301 W Gregory Urbana IL 61801

CAMPBELL, JOHN TUCKER, secretary of state of South Carolina; b. Calhoun Falls, S.C., Dec. 12, 1912; s. John Brown Gordon and Mary (Tucker) C.; m. Gertrude Davis, Jan. 4, 1936; children: James Gordon. Student, U. S.C., 1941-42. Pres. Campbell Drug Stores, Columbia, S.C., 1938—; mem. Columbia City Council, 1954-58, 66-70, mayor, 1970-78; sec. state State of S.C., 1979—. Served with USAAF, 1943-46. Mem. S.C. Pharm. Assn. (dir. 1971-73), Nat. League Cities, S.C. Municipal Assn. (pres. 1972-73). Methodist. Clubs: Mason (Shriner), Optimist Internat. (state gov. 1964-65), Palmetto.). Office: PO Box 11350 Columbia SC 29214 *

CAMPBELL, JOSEPH, author, educator; b. N.Y.C., Mar. 26, 1904; s. Charles William and Josephine (Lynch) C.; m. Jean Erdman, May 5, 1938. Grad., Canterbury Sch., 1921; student, Dartmouth, 1921-22; A.B., Columbia, 1925, M.A., 1927; postgrad., U. Paris, 1927-28, U. Munich, 1928-29. Tchr. Canterbury Sch., 1932-33; mem. faculty dept. lit. Sarah Lawrence Coll., Bronxville, N.Y., 1934-72; lectr. Fgn. Service Inst. Dept. State, Washington, 1956-73, Columbia, 1959. Author: (with Jeff King, Maud Oakes) Where He Two Came to Their Father: A Navaho War Ceremonial, 1943, Grimm's Fairy Tales, Folkloristic Commentary, 1944, (with Henry Morton Robinson) A Skeleton Key to Finnegans Wake, 1944, The Hero with a Thousand Faces, 1949, The Masks of God, Vol. I, Primitive Mythology, 1959, Vol. II, Oriental Mythology, 1962, Vol. III, Occidental Mythology, 1964, Vol. IV, Creative Mythology, 1967, The Flight of the Wild Gander, 1969, Myths To Live By, 1972, The Mythic Image, 1975, Historical Atlas of World Mythology, Vol. I. The Way of the Animal Powers, 1983; Editor: The Viking Portable Arabian Nights, 1952, Papers from the Eranos Yearbooks (vols. 1 to 6), 1954, 55, 57, 61, 64, 68, Myths, Dreams and Religion, 1970, Viking Portable Jung, 1972, (with Heinrich Zimmer) Myths and Symbols in Indian Art and Civilization, 1946, The King and the Corpse, 1948, Philosophies of India, 1951, The Art of Indian Asia, 1955; Contbr. articles to profl. publs. Pres. Creative Film Found., 1954-63, Found. for Open Eye, 1973—; trustee Bollingen Found., 1960-69. Mem. Nat. Inst. Arts and Letters, Soc. for Arts, Religion and Contemporary Culture (dir.), Am. Soc. Study Religion (pres. 1972-75). Home: 2943 Kalakaua Ave Honolulu HI 96815

CAMPBELL, JUDITH MAY, educator; b. Terre Haute, Ind., May 13, 1938; d. O.H. and D. Juanita C. B.S. in Phys. Edn., Ind. State U., 1960, M.S., 1963; D.Phys. Edn., Ind. U., 1978. Recreational dir. Terre Haute Park Dept., summers 1958-60; tchr. St. Louis pub. schs., 1960-61; instr. dept. phys. edn. Ind. State U., Terre Haute, 1961-66, asst. prof., 1968-75, assoc. prof., 1975-79, prof., 1979—, dir. undergrad. preparation; coach volleyball and basketball teams Univ. Sch., 1970-74, girl sports dir., 1974-78; founder Ind. Spl. Olympics, Inc., 1970; chmn. basketball Wabash Valley Bd. Women Ofcls., 1963-65, 68-74; nat. adv. bd. Spl. Olympics, Inc.; mem. nat. adv. bd. Joseph P. Kennedy, Jr. Found., 1972-74, chmn. Contbr. articles to profl. publs.; developer phys. edn. program in sch. curriculums. Bd. dirs. Ind. Spl. Olympics, 1968-74; state co-dir. Ind. Spl Olympics, 1970-74; bd. dirs. State Girls Sports Adv. Bd., 1975-77. Recipient Lambert award Ind. State U., 1960, Outstanding Phys. Fitness Leadership award Vigo County Jaycees, 1968, Service award Vigo County Assn. for Retarded Citizens, 1971, Community Service award Vigo County Jaycees, 1974, Eleanor St. John Disting. Alumni award, 1977; Lilly Found. grantee, 1974; Chismar Found. grantee, 1972. Mem. AAUP (pres. 1981—), AAHPER, Ind. Assn. Health, Phys. Edn. and Recreation (Leadership award 1974), Delta Kappa Gamma (pres. 1980—), Phi Delta Kappa, Delta Psi Kappa. Home: Rural Route 22 PO Box 90 Terre Haute IN 47802

CAMPBELL, KARLYN KOHRS, speech and drama educator; b. Blomkest, Minn., Apr. 16, 1937; d. Meinhard and Dorothy (Siegers) Kohrs; m. Paul Newell Campbell, Sept. 16, 1967. B.A. (Tozer scholar), Macalester Coll., 1958; M.A. (Tozer fellow), U. Minn., 1959, Ph.D., 1968. Asst. prof. SUNY, Brockport, 1959-63, Calif. State U., Los Angeles, 1966-71; asso. prof. SUNY, Birmingham, 1971-72, City U. N.Y., 1973-74; prof. speech and drama U. Kans., Lawrence, 1974—, chairperson women's studies, 1983—; Gladys Borchers lectr. U. Wis., Madison, 1974. Author: Critiques of Contemporary Rhetoric, 1972, Form and Genre, 1978, The Rhetorical Act, 1982, The Interplay of Influence, 1983; editorial bd., Communication Monographs, 1977-80, Quar. Jour. Speech, 1981—; contbr. articles to profl. jours. Mem. Speech Communication Assn., Central States Speech Communication Assn., Nat. Women's Studies Assn., Phi Beta Kappa, Pi Phi Epsilon. Office: Dept Communication Studies U Kans Lawrence KS 66045

CAMPBELL, KENNETH, consulting engineer; b. San Francisco, June 1, 1899; s. William Wallacd and Elizabeth Ballard (Thompson) C.; m. Margaret Bruce Macon, Nov. 8, 1930; children: Janet Bruce, Elizabeth Wallace, Margaret Macon, Martha Madison; m. 2d Miriam N. Frank, Mar. 16, 1972. Grad., Hotchkiss Sch., Lakeville, Conn., 1917; A.B., Harvard U., 1921, S.B., 1923; D.Sc. (hon.), Bard Coll., 1952. Mem. staff Lick Obs. solar eclipse expdn., Kiev, USSR, 1915; mem. eclipse party, Freyburg, Maine, 1932; with various depts. Bethlehem Steel Co., Pa., 1923-26; indsl. engr. Sanderson & Porter, N.Y.C., 1928-33; aircraft power plant research, devel. designer Curtiss-Wright Corp., Wood-Ridge, N.J., 1933-64, dir. research, 1950-55, gen. mgr. research div., 1956-60, chief scientist, 1960-64; cons. Inst. for Def. Analyses, 1964—, others, 1964—; chmn. subcom. compressors and turbines NACA, 1940-45; mem. tech. mission to Germany USN, 1945. Contbr. articles to profl. jours.; patentee in field. Served as ambulance driver ARC, 1918; World War I; served as Lt. RAF; 1918-1919. Decorated Croce di Guerra, Italy; recipient Wright Bros. medal Soc. Automotive Engrs., 1944, Charles Matthews Manley medal, 1945. Fellow Inst. Aero. Sci.; mem. Soc. Automotive Engrs., Harvard Engrs. and Scientist (past pres.). Episcopalian. Home and Office: 896 Oradell Ave Oradell NJ 07649

CAMPBELL, KENNETH EUGENE, JR., vertebrate paleontologist; b. Jackson, Mich., Nov. 4, 1943; s. Kenneth Eugene and Betty Louise (Duffey) C. B.S., U. Mich., 1966, M.S., 1967; Ph.D., U. Fla., 1973. Research asso. Fla. State Mus., Gainesville, 1972-74; asst. prof. zoology U. Fla., Gainesville, 1974-77, asst. prof. geology, 1975-77; curator vertebrate paleontology Natural History Mus. Los Angeles County, Los Angeles, 1977—. Contbr. articles to sci. publs. Mem. AAAS, Am. Ornithologists' Union, Assn. Tropical Biology, Cooper Ornithol. Soc., Soc. Vertebrate Paleontology, Wilson Ornithol. Soc., Sigma Xi. Office: Natural History Mus 900 Exposition Blvd Los Angeles CA 90007

CAMPBELL, LEONARD GENE, university administrator; b. Krebs, Okla., Oct. 15, 1933; s. Thomas Allen and Tempie (Woodall) C.; m. Linda Lou Bailey, May 22, 1958; 1 dau., Kristi Lynn. B.S., Southeastern Okla. State Coll., 1958; M.A., U. Okla., 1964, Ed.D., 1970. Tchr., coach Amarillo (Tex.) pub. schs., 1960-61, Moore (Okla.) High Sch., 1961-63; prin. Moore (Okla.) Jr. High Sch. and Moore High Sch., 1963-65; asst. supt. Moore (Okla.) pub. schs., 1965-70; supt. Western Heights Pub. Schs., Oklahoma City, 1970-75; pres. Southwestern Okla. State U., Weatherford, 1975—. Served with USN, 1952-54. Mem. NEA, Okla. Edn. Assn., Am. Assn. Sch. Adminstrs., Okla. Assn. Sch. Adminstrs., Central Dist. Okla. Edn. Assn. (pres. 1973-74), Okla. Textbook Commn. (chmn. 1972-74). Democrat. Baptist. Lodges: Lions; Kiwanis; Rotary. Office: Southwestern Okla State U Office of Pres Weatherford OK 73096 *

CAMPBELL, LEONARD MARTIN, lawyer; b. Denver, Apr. 12, 1918; s. Bernard Francis and May (Moran) C.; m. Dot J. Baker, Sept. 23, 1944; children: Brian T., Teri Pat, Thomas P. A.B., U. Colo., 1941, LL.B., 1943. Bar: Colo. 1943. Since practiced in Denver; mem. firm Gorsuch, Kirgis, Campbell, Walker & Grover, 1946; cons. pub. utility matters City and County Denver, also Colo. Mcpl. League, 1953—; city atty. Denver, 1951-53. Mem. Denver Charter Com., 1947; mgr. Safety and Excise for Denver, 1947-48; chmn. Denver Com. Human Relations, 1954; mem. Denver Planning Bd., 1950-51, Bd. Water Commrs., Denver, 1965-70; pres. Bd. Water Commrs., 1968-69; mem. Gov.'s Com. on Jud. Compensation, 1972; chmn. U. Colo. Law Alumni Devel. Fund, 1962. Served with USAAF, 1943-46. Mem. ABA, Colo. Bar Assn. (pres. 1978-79), Denver Bar Assn. (pres. 1969), Am. Coll. Trial Lawyers, Cath. Lawyers Guild Denver (pres. 1962), Nat. Inst. Mcpl. Law Officers (v.p. 1952). Democrat. Roman Catholic. Clubs: KC, Denver Athletic (sec. 1960-61, pres. 1962), Cherry Hills Country (Denver)). Home: 3447 S Birch St Denver CO 80222 Office: Alamo Plaza 1401 17th St Denver CO 80202

CAMPBELL, LEVIN HICKS, judge; b. Summit, N.J., Jan. 2, 1927; s. Worthington and Louise (Hooper) C.; m. Eleanor Saltonstall Lewis, June 1, 1957; children—Eleanor S., Levin H., Sarah H. A.B. cum laude, Harvard U., 1948, LL.B., 1951; postgrad., Nat. Coll. State Judiciary, 1970; LL.D. (hon.), Suffolk U., 1975. Bar: D.C. 1951, Mass. 1954. Assoc. firm Ropes & Gray, Boston, 1954-64; mem. Mass. Ho. of Reps., 1963-64; asst. atty. gen. State of Mass., 1965-66, spl. asst. atty. gen., 1966-67, 1st asst. atty. gen., 1967-68; assoc. justice Superior Ct. of Mass., 1969-72; judge U.S. Dist. Ct. Mass., Boston, 1972, U.S. Ct. Appeals (1st cir.), 1972—, chief judge, 1983—; fellow Inst. of Politics; study group leader J.F. Kennedy Sch. Govt., Harvard U., 1980; faculty chmn. law session Salzburg Seminar in Am. Studies, 1981. Pres. Cambridge 9 Neighborhood Assn., 1960-62; treas. Cambridge Center for Adult Edn., 1961-64; campaign chmn. Cambridge United Fund, 1965; mem. bd. overseers Boston Symphony Orch., 1969-75, 77-80; pres. bd. overseers Shady Hill Sch., 1969-70; mem. vis. com. Harvard U. Press, 1958-64; v.p. Cambridge Community Service; corp. mem. SEA Ednl. Assn., 1982—; trustee Colby Coll., Waterville, Maine, 1982—. Served to 1st lt. JAGC, U.S. Army, 1951-54; Korea. Mem. ABA, Mass. Bar Assn., Boston Bar Assn, U.S. Jud. Conf. (ct. adminstrn. com., chmn. subcom. on supporting personnel 1980-83), Salzburg Seminar Alumni Assn. (bd. dirs. 1983—). Office: Room 1618 US Post Office and Courthouse Boston MA 02109

CAMPBELL, LINZY LEON, microbiologist, educator; b. Panhandle, Tex., Feb. 10, 1927; s. Linzy Leon and Eula Irene (McSpadden) C.; m. Alice P. Dauksa, Feb. 7, 1953. B.A. in Bacteriology and Chemistry, U. Tex., 1949, M.A., 1950, Ph.D., 1952. Research scientist U. Tex., 1947-51; predoctoral research fellow NIH, 1951-52; postdoctoral research fellow Nat. Microbiol. Inst., U. Calif. at Berkeley, 1952-54; asst. prof., then asso. prof. Wash. State U., 1954-59; asso. prof. Western Res. U. Sch. Medicine, 1959-62; sr. research fellow USPHS, 1959-62; prof. microbiology U. Ill. at Urbana, 1962-72, head dept., 1963-71; dir. Sch. Life Scis., 1971-72; prof. microbiology, provost and v.p. acad. affairs U. Del. at Newark, 1972—. Editorial bd.: Jour. Bacteriology, 1961-65; editor, 1964-65; editor-in-chief, 1965-77; Contbr. articles to profl. jours. Served with USNR, 1944-46. Fellow Am. Acad. Microbiology; mem. Am. Soc. Microbiology (chmn. publ. bd. 1965-80, councilor at large 1962-64, v.p. 1972-73, pres. 1973-74), Soc. Gen. Microbiology, Am. Soc. Biol. Chemists, A.A.A.S., Am. Chem. Soc. Office: 104 Hullihen Hall U Del Newark DE 19711

CAMPBELL, L(OUIS) LORNE, mathematics educator; b. Winnipeg, Man., Can., Oct. 29, 1928; s. Elgin Smith and Jonina Solveig (Johnson) C.; m. Eha Johanson, June 12, 1954; children: Ian, Barry, Barbara. B.S.C., U. Man., 1950; M.S., Iowa State U., 1951; Ph.D., U. Toronto., 1955. Def. sci. officer Def. Research Bd., Ottawa, Ont., Can., 1954-58; asst. prof., assoc. prof. U. Windsor, Ont., Can., 1963—; assoc. prof., prof. Queen's U., Kingston, Ont., Can., 1963—, head dept. math and stats., 1980—; guest lectr. Instituto di Alta Matematica, Rome, 1971, Institut fur angewandte Mathematik, Heidelberg, Germany, 1978. Contbr. articles to profl. publs. Mem. Can. Math. Soc. (treas. 1982—), Can. Statis. Soc., Can. Applied Math. Soc., IEEE (sr.), Am. Math. Soc., Soc. for Indsl. and Applied Math. Home: 153 Byron Crescent Kingston ON Canada K7L 3N6 Office: Dept Math and Stats Queens Univ Kingston ON Canada

CAMPBELL, MARGARET AMELIA, nursing educator; b. Vancouver, B.C., Can., June 27, 1923; d. Ivan Glen and Helen Kathleen (Davis) C. B.A., U. B.C., 1947, B.A.Sc. in Nursing, 1948, M.S., Western Res. U., 1955; Ed.D., Columbia U., 1970. Staff nurse, asst. head nurse Vancouver Gen. Hosp., 1948-49; instr., sr. adminstrv. instr. Vancouver Gen. Hosp. Sch. Nursing, 1949-54; from instr. to prof. Sch. Nursing, U. B.C., 1955—; cons. curriculum devel. nursing schs. Mem. Registered Nurses Assn. B.C., Can. Nurses Assn., Can. Nurses Found., Can. Assn. Univ. Schs. Nursing. (Western region). Co-developer conceptual models for nursing. Home: 4041 W 27th Ave Vancouver BC Canada V6S 1R6 Office: U BC 2211 Wesbrook Mall Vancouver BC Canada V6T 1W5

CAMPBELL, MARIA BOUCHELLE, banker, lawyer; b. Mullins, S.C., Jan. 23, 1944; d. Colin Reid and Margaret;; d. Colin Reid and Minor (Perry) C. Student, Agnes Scott Coll., 1961-63; A.B., U. Ga., 1965, J.D., 1967. Bar: Ga. bar 1967, Fla. bar 1968, Ala. bar 1969. Practiced in, Birmingham, Ala., 1968; law clk. U.S. Circuit Ct. Appeals, Miami, Fla., 1967-68; assoc. firm Cabaniss, Johnston and Gardner, 1968-73; sec. counsel Ala. Bancorp., Birmingham, 1973-79; sr. v.p., sec., gen. counsel counsel AmSouth Bancorp., 1979—; lectr. continuing legal edn. programs; cons. to charitable orgns. Exec. editor: Ga. Law Rev, 1966-67. Bd. dirs. St. Anne's Home, Birmingham, 1969-74, chancellor, 1969-74; bd. dirs. Children's Aid Soc., Birmingham, 1970—, Positive Maturity, 1976-78, Mental Health Assn., 1978-81, YWCA, 1979-80; commr. Housing Authority, Birmingham Dist., 1980—; trustee Ala. Diocese Episcopal Ch., 1971-72, 74-75, mem. canonical revision com., 1973-75, liturg. commn., 1976-78, treas., chmn. dept. fin., 1979-83, mem. council, 1983—, cons. on stewardship edn., 1981—. Mem. State Bar Ga., Fla. Bar, Am., Ala., Birmingham bar assns., Women's Network. Club: Mountain Brook. Home: 141 Camellia Circle Birmingham AL 35213 Office: PO Box 11007 Birmingham AL 35288

CAMPBELL, MCCOY CLEMPSON, III, banker; b. Spring Hill, Tenn., Apr. 5, 1918; s. McCoy Clempson, Jr. and Annie Elizabeth (Woodard) C.; m. Josephine McHenry, Dec. 2, 1944; children: Lucinda Campbell Peabody, Laura Campbell Peyton. B.A., Vanderbilt U., 1940; grad., Stonier Grad. Sch. Banking, 1957. Mgr. personnel and RFC custody depts. Nashville br. Fed. Res. Bank Atlanta, 1940-50; v.p. First Nat. Bank Atlanta, 1950-68; sr; sr. v.p. human resources Am. Nat. Bank & Trust Co., Chattanooga, 1968-83; mem. faculty Stonier Grad. Sch. Banking, 1969—, Bank Adminstrn. Inst., U. Wis., 1971—, Sch. Banking of South, La. State U., 1983—, Colo. Sch. Banking, 1970, Tenn. Sch. Banking, Vanderbilt U., 1969—. Bd. dirs. Central YMCA, 1969-72. Served to 1st lt. AUS, 1942-46. Mem. Am. Inst. Banking, Ga. Personnel and Guidance Assn. (pres. 1959-61), Bank Adminstrn. Inst. (dir., chmn. personnel commn. 1963-65), So. Coll. Placement Assn. (dir. 1965-68), Greater Chattanooga C. of C., Kappa Alpha. Episcopalian. Home: 308 Henry Ln Lookout Mountain TN 37350

CAMPBELL, MILTON HUGH, chemist; b. Billings, Mont., Sept. 2, 1928; s. John Paul and Natalie Izolia (Bennett) C.; m. Marguerite Ann Herndon, June 8, 1952; children: Chelene, Daniel, Gregory, Cynthia. B.S., Mont. State U., 1951; M.S., U. Wash., 1961. Registered profl. engr., Calif. Process chemist Gen. Electric Co., Richland, Wash., 1955-62, sr. engr., 1962-66, staff engr., 1966-67; chem. lab. mgr. Atlantic Richland Hanford Co., Richland, 1967-73, mgr. waste processing and storage tech., 1973-74; staff chemist Exxon Nuclear Co., Richland, 1974—; mem. chem. tech. adv. com. Seattle Community Coll., 1981—. Editor: Advances in Chemistry, 1976. Served with U.S. Army, 1951-53. Recipient service recognition Richland sect. Am. Chem. Soc., 1979. Mem. Am. Chem. Soc., Am. Nuclear Soc., Inst. Nuclear Materials Mgmt., ASTM. Presbyterian. Office: 2101 Horn Rapids Rd Richland WA 99352 *It has been my experience that respect for the knowledge and dignity of your associates and a willingness to give credit where it is due go far toward creating an innovative and productive work group. When you put yourself in such an environment, you will reap the benefits.*

CAMPBELL, MONA LOUISE, manufacturing company executive; b. Toronto, Ont., Can., Feb. 3, 1919; d. Frederick Kennean and Edna Lillian (Mann) Morrow); m. Kenneth Laidlaw Campbell, Aug. 14, 1967; children: John Morrow, Sarah Alexandra Band, Mary Victoria Band Macrae. Ed. schs., Eng.; LL.D., Dalhousie U. Pres., dir. Dover Industries Ltd., Hamilton, Ont., 1954—, Movisa Securities Ltd.; dir. Toronto Dominion Bank., Rothmans of Pall Mall Can. Ltd., Toronto. Founding mem. renovation expansion fund Royal Ont. Mus.; bd. govs. Mt. St. Vincent U., Dalhousie Coll. and U. Conservative. Anglican. Clubs: Rosedale Golf, Osler Bluffs Ski, Eglinton Hutn. Office: 96 Avenue Rd Toronto ON Canada M5R 2H3

CAMPBELL, NEWTON ALLEN, consulting engineering company executive, consulting electrical engineer; b. Kansas City, Kans., July 2, 1928; s. Edward A. and Sarah A. (Newton) C.; m. Mabel Rose McKinstry, Feb. 18, 1929; children: Elizabeth Anne, Joyce Dianne. Cert., Kansas City Jr. Coll., Mo., 1947; B.S.E.E., U. Ill., 1949; M.B.A., U. Mo.-Kansas City, 1970. Registered profl. in 17 states, including Mo. With Burns & McDonnell, Kansas City, Mo., 1955-83, dep. mgr. elec. dept., 1971-76, v.p., 1976-82, pres., 1982-83, Profl. Services div. Armco Inc., 1983—. Mem. Prairie Village Park Bd., Kans., 1963—; bd. dirs. Linwood United Ch., Kansas City Mo., 1963—. Served with U.S. Army, 1950-52. Recipient Eagle Scout award Heart of Am. council Boy Scouts Am., 1943, Mic-O-Say award Heart of Am. council Boy Scouts Am., 1943; named Man of Yr. Tau Beta Pi. Kans. State U., Manhattan, 1980. Mem. Mo. soc. Profl. Engrs., Nat. Soc. Profl. Engrs., IEEE, Friends of Art, Kansas City C. of C., Eta Kappa Nu, Beta Gamma Sigma. Presbyterian. Home: 7916 Rosewood Prairie Village KS 66208 Office: Armco Profl Services Div 8700 Indian Creek Pkwy PO Box 25548 Overland Park KS 66225

CAMPBELL, NORMAN WILLIAM, advertising executive; b. Dallas, Dec. 29, 1933; s. Earl W. and Jewel Madeline (Smith) C.; m. Barbara Ann Tidwell, Sept. 11, 1959; children: Stephani Lynn, Michael Norman. Student, Arlington State Jr. Coll., 1953; B.J., U. Tex., Austin, 1955. Mem. advt. sales staff Dallas Morning News, 1955; advt. rep. Progressive Farmer Co., Dallas, 1956; account exec. Batten, Barton, Durstine and Osborne, 1956-63; mgr. mktg. services, co-owned plants Pepsi-Cola Co., N.Y.C., 1964-65; also dir. mktg. Pepsi-Cola Met. Bottling Co.; pres., dir. Tracy-Locke Advt. and Pub. Relations Inc., Dallas, from 1965, now chmn. bd.; dir. Tracy-Locke Co., Mktg. and Research Counselors Inc.; Pres. adv. council U. Tex. Sch. Communication, 1977-79. Trustee Nat. Hemophilia Found., Am. Heart Assn.; chmn. Keystone Gifts div., 1979; bd. dirs. Shakespeare Festival, 1979; active United Way. Mem. Nat. Advt. Rev. Bd., Dallas Advt. League, Dallas C. of C., Salesmanship Club Dallas (dir.). Club: Northwood (pres. 1980). Home: 6556 Meadowcreek Dallas TX 75240 Office: Plaza of Americas PO Box 50129 Dallas TX 75250

CAMPBELL, PATRICK J., union official; b. N.Y.C., July 22, 1918; s. Peter James and Mary (Clark) C.; m. Catherine Keane, May 19, 1940; children: Patrick M., Cynthia Campbell McGuire, Kevin. Organizer United Brotherhood of Carpenters and Joiners of Am., Washington, 1955-57, gen. rep., 1957-66, asst. to. gen. pres., 1966-69, gen. exec. bd. mem. 1st dist., N.Y.C., 1969-74, 2d gen. v.p., Washington, 1974-80, 1st gen. v.p., 1980-82, gen. pres., 1982—; dir. Urban Devel. corp., N.Y., 1971-74; v.p. bldg. and constrn. dept. AFL-CIO, Washington, 1982—, mem. exec. council, 1982—. Served with USAF, 1941-45; S. Pacific. Recipient Cert. Merit U.S. Dept. Labor, 1974, Michael J. Quill award Hibernarian Soc., 1974, D. Russell Harlow award Bldg. Contractors Assn. N.Y., 1983; named Gael of Yr. United Irish Counties Assn., 1974. Mem. VFW, Holy Name Soc. Democrat. Roman Catholic. Lodge: K.C. Home: 3445 Mt Burnside Way Woodbridge VA 22180 Office: United Brotherhood of Carpenters and Joiners of Am 101 Constitution Ave NW Washington DC 20001

CAMPBELL, PATTON, designer, educator; b. Omaha, Sept. 10, 1926; s. Ralph Harold and Frances Lorraine (Patton) C. B.A., Yale U., 1950, M.F.A., 1952. Instr. costume design and history Barnard Coll., 1955-57, N.Y. U., 1962-67; assoc. prof. Columbia U., 1967-72, 79-81; asso. prof. SUNY, Purchase, 1975-76; vis. lectr. Bklyn. Coll., 1973-74, 80, Brandeis U., 1975-76, 82-83; assoc. prof. Columbia U., 1979-81, 83—. Designer: costumes for plays and operas including 27 Wagons Full of Cotton, Playhouse Theatre, 1955, Trouble in Tahiti, 1955, Fallen Angels, 1956, A Hole in the Head, Plymouth Theatre, 1957, All American, Winter Garden Theatre, 1962, Wuthering Heights, N.Y.C. Opera, 1959, The Inspector General, 1960, Natalia Petrovna, 1964, Capriccio, 1965, Lizzie Borden, 1965, La Traviata, 1966, 81, Carry Nation, 1969, Susannah, 1971, The Ballad of Baby Doe, 1976, La Belle Helene, 1976, The Student Prince, 1980, La Traviata, 1981, The Mikado, N.Y.C. Center, 1959, The Pirates of Penzance, 1968, Il Tabarro, Juilliard Opera Theatre, N.Y.C., 1964, Katya Kabanova, 1964, Madame Butterfly, Central City (Colo.) Opera, 1964, After The Fall, Nat. Co., Wilmington, Del., 1964, Oliver!, 1964, Man of La Mancha, ANTA Washington Square, 1965, On A Clear Day You Can See Forever, 1966, Tosca, Santa Fe Opera, 1969, Cosi Fan Tutte, 1969, The Fisherman and His Wife, Opera Co. of Boston, 1970, Scarlett, Imperial Theatre, Tokyo, 1970, Gone With The Wind, Drury Lane Theatre, London, 1972, Regina, Houston Grand Opera, 1980; costumes and scenery The Rake's Progress, Santa Fe Opera, 1957, Ariadne auf Naxos, 1957, La Boheme, 1958, Capriccio, 1958, Falstaff, 1958, Fledermaus, 1959, The Abduction From The Seraglio, 1959, The Makropoulos Affair, N.Y.C. Opera, 1970, H.M.S. Pinafore, 1975. Served with USN, 1944-46. Mem. United Scenic Artists. Episcopalian.

CAMPBELL, PAUL BARTON, lawyer; b. Owosso, Mich., Feb. 24, 1930; s. George Wiley and Louise Marian (Pletke) C.; children: Jane, Paul Barton, James. B.B.A., U. Mich., 1951, M.B.A., 1954, J.D., 1954. Bar: Ohio 1955, Mich 1955, Fla. 1978. Assoc. mem. firm Squire, Sanders & Dempsey, Cleve., 1954-66, partner, 1966—; Sec. Ferro Corp., Cleve., 1970—; dir. Huntington Nat. Bank of Northeast Ohio, Cleve., 1975—; sec. Midwest Forge Corp., Cleve., 1979—; sec., dir.

Shelby Paper Box Corp., Cleve., 1980—. Democrat. Home: 12700 Lake Ave Apt 1306 Lakewood OH 44107 Office: 1800 Huntington Bldg Cleveland OH 44115

CAMPBELL, RICHARD ALDEN, electronics executive; b. Bend, Oreg., July 31, 1926; s. Corlis Eugene and Lydia Amney (Peck) C.; m. Edna Mary Seaman, June 12, 1948; children: Stephen Alden, Douglas Niall (dec.), Carolyn Joyce. B.S. in Elec. Engring., U. Ill., 1949, M.S., 1950. With TRW Inc., Redondo Beach, Calif., 1954—, exec. v.p., 1979—; ptnr. Calif. Investment Assos.; dir. Tylan Corp., Cetec Corp. Trustee Nat. Multiple Sclerosis Soc. Served with USN, 1944-46. Recipient Alumni Honor award U. Ill. Coll. Engring. Mem. Am. Electronics Assn. (pres. 1969, dir. 1970), IEEE (sr.), Sigma Xi, Phi Kappa Phi, Tau Beta Pi, Eta Kappa Nu, Sigma Tau, Pi Mu Epsilon, Phi Eta Sigma. Republican. Clubs: Kiwanis (Palos Verdes, Calif.); Rolling Hills Country, Rancheros Visitadores, Los Caballeros. Patentee in radio communications. Office: TRW Inc One Space Park Redondo Beach CA 90278

CAMPBELL, RICHARD ARTHUR, architect; b. Bklyn., May 1, 1930; s. William J. and Dorothy T. (Regan) C.; m. Françoise Marie Botrot, Nov. 14, 1972; children—Scott, Carene. B.Arch., U. Oreg., 1956; M.Arch., Yale U., 1961. Designer Wilmsen, Endicott, Eugene, Oreg., 1956-58, Skidmore, Owings and Merrill, Portland, Oreg., 1958-60, 61-64; prin. Campbell-Yost-Grube, P.C., Portland, 1964—; guest lectr. Yale U., U. Oreg. Grad. Sch., Portland State U., Portland Art Mus., Lewis and Clark Coll., Portland; mem. numerous design award juries. Ian Lewis traveling fellow, 1959-60. Fellow AIA (19 design awards); mem. Nat. Council Archtl. Registration Bds. Democrat. Clubs: Multnomah Athletic, West Hills Racquet. Home: 3186 SW Fairmont Blvd Portland OR 97201 Office: 2040 SW Jefferson St Portland OR 97201

CAMPBELL, RICHARD JOHN, air conditioning manufacturing company executive; b. Rochester, N.Y., Dec. 21, 1929; s. Eugene S. and Margaret (Lurz) C.; m. Mary Ann Hinders, July 18, 1958; children: Richard, Ann, John. Student, Rochester Inst. Tech., 1948-50; B. Welding Engring., Ohio State U., 1955. Registered profl. engr., Wis., Ohio. Welding engr. ACF Industries, Berwick, Pa., 1957-59, Gen. Electric Co., Cin., 1959-61; with Trane Co., La Crosse, Wis., 1962-66, 68—, v.p., gen. mgr. comml. div., 1973-77, pres., chief operating officer, 1977—, also dir.; mfg. mgr. Societe Trane, Epinal, France, 1966-68; dir. Trane Co. Can. Ltd. Bd. dirs. U. Wis.-La Crosse Devel. Found., Aquinas Found., La Crosse. Served to 1st lt. USAF, 1955-57. Hon. recipient James F. Lincoln Welding award Lincoln Electric Co., Cleve., 1961; named Outstanding Engring. Alumnus Ohio State U., 1973. Mem. ASME (boiler code), Am. Welding Soc., Am. Soc. Metals, Nat. Assn. Purchasing Mgmt., Am. Soc. Heating, Air Conditioning, Refrigeration Engrs. Roman Catholic. Office: Trane Corp 3600 Pammel Creek Rd La Crosse WI 54601 *

CAMPBELL, RICHARD RICE, newspaperman; b. Athens County, Ohio, Mar. 25, 1923; s. Arthur Donald and Marguerite (Rice) C.; m. Margaret Jandes, Feb. 9, 1946; children: Christopher, Constant. A.B. summa cum laude, Ohio U., 1947; M.A., Kent State U., 1977—. With Cleve. Press, 1947-77, asst. city editor, 1959-62, chief editorial writer, 1962-66, asso. editor, 1966-68, mng. editor, 1968-77; on leave Scripps-Howard Newspapers rep. to Newspaper Systems Devel. Group, 1975; editor Columbus (Ohio) Citizen-Jour., 1977—. Served with; AUS, 1943-46. Recipient Alumni award outstanding achievement journalism Ohio U., 1962, Carr Van Anda award, 1983. Mem. Am. Soc. Newspaper Editors, Phi Beta Kappa, Sigma Delta Chi, Sigma Pi. Methodist. Clubs: Columbus Athletic, Scioto Country., Kit Kat, Torch. Home: 1243 Kenbrook Hills Dr Upper Arlington OH 43220 Office: Columbus Citizen-Jour 34 S Third St Columbus OH 43216

CAMPBELL, ROBERT BRUCE, retail executive; b. Pitts., July 4, 1936; s. Robert J. and Doris C. C.; m. Betsy White, Aug. 17, 1963; children: Holly, Scott. B.A., Muskingum (Ohio) Coll., 1958; M.B.A., U. Pitts., 1959. With Highbee Co., Cleve., 1959—, sr. v.p., 1975-77, exec. v.p. adminstrn., 1977—; chmn., v.p. personnel Asso. Mdsg. Corp., 1973-74. Mem. Pvt. Industry Council, 1978-80, Leadership Cleve., 1978-81; pres. Found. Community Planning, 1982-84; chmn. bus. adv. com. Stark Coll., Canton, Ohio, 1970-71; chmn. Stark County Better Bus. Bur., 1971, Downtown Cleve. Bus. Council, 1980-81; trustee, v.p. Cleve. Fedn. Community Planning, 1979-81; chmn. No. Ohio Research Info. Center, 1980-81; bd. dirs. United Way Cleve.; trustee Federated Ch. Chagrin Falls, Ohio, 1979-81, Cleve. chpt. Am. Cancer Soc., 1979-81; bd. dirs. Conv. and Visitors Bur. Greater Cleve., 1979-81, Greater Cleve. Growth Assn. Served with USAR, 1959-65. Mem. Nat. Retail Mchts. Assn., Am. Mgmt. Assn., Ohio Retail Mchts. Assn., Greater Cleve. Growth Assn. Republican. Clubs: Hillbrook, Chagrin Valley Racquet, Mid Day. Office: Higbee Co 100 Public Sq Cleveland OH 44113

CAMPBELL, ROBERT CHARLES, clergyman; b. Chandler, Ariz., Mar. 9, 1924; s. Alexander Joshua and Florence (Betzner) C.; m. Lotus Idamae Graham, July 12, 1945; children: Robin Carl, Cherry Colleen. A.B., Westmont Coll., 1944; B.D., Eastern Baptist Theol. Sem., 1947, Th.M., 1949, Th.D., 1951, D.D., 1974; M.A., U. So. Calif., 1959; postgrad., Dropsie U., 1949-51, U. Pa., 1951-52, N.Y. U., 1960-62, U. Cambridge, Eng., 1969; D.Lit., Calif. Bapt. Theol. Sem., 1972; Hum.D., Alderson-Broaddus Coll., 1979; L.H.D., Linfield Coll., 1982. Ordained to ministry Am. Bapt. Ch., 1947; pastor 34th St. Bapt. Ch., Phila., 1945-49; instr. Eastern Bapt. Theol. Sem., Phila., 1949-51; asst. prof. Eastern Coll., St. Davids, Pa., 1951-53; asso. prof. N.T. Am. Bapt. Sem. of West, Covina, Cal., 1953-54, dean, prof., 1954-72; gen. sec. Am. Bapt. Chs. in U.S.A., Valley Forge, Pa., 1972—; Vis. lectr. Sch. Theology at, Claremont, Calif., 1961-63, U. Redlands, Calif., 1959-60, 66-67; Bd. mgrs. Am. Bapt. Bd. of Edn. and Publ., 1956-59, 65-69; v.p. So. Calif. Bapt. Conv., 1967-68; pres. Am. Bapt. Chs. of Pacific S.W., 1970-71; Pres. N.Am. Bapt. Fellowship, 1974-76; mem. exec. com. Bapt. World Alliance, 1972—, v.p., 1975-80; mem. exec. com., gov. bd. Nat. Council Chs. of Christ in U.S.A., 1972—; del. to World Council of Chs., 1975, 83, mem. central com., 1975—. Author: Great Words of the Faith, 1965, The Gospel of Paul, 1973. Home: 1000 Valley Force Circle King of Prussia PA 19406 Office: American Baptist Churches Valley Forge PA 19481

CAMPBELL, ROBERT DALE, educator; b. Omaha, Dec. 2, 1914; s. Robert Ward and Emma Mary Augusta (Klempnauer) C.; m. Ann Elizabeth Abel, Sept. 4, 1941; 1 son, Robert William Duncan. B.A., U. Colo., 1938, M.A., 1940; Ph.D., Clark U., 1949. Prof. geography, chmn. dept. George Washington U., 1947-66; Fulbright lectr. Alexandria (Egypt) U., 1952-53, U. Peshawer (Pakistan), 1957-58; prin. investigator George Washington U.-C.E., U.S. Army, Hist. Records Project, 1953-57, Q.M.C. Intelligence Research Project, 1958-60; Outdoor Recreation Resources Rev. Commn. Shoreline and Beach Recreation Resources Study, 1960; Urban Planning Data Systems Project Md. Nat. Capital Park and Planning Commission, 1961—; pres. AREA, Inc., research, Arlington, Va.; v.p. Matrix Corp., Arlington, 1966-70; prof. geography U. N.Mex., 1970-80, prof. emeritus, 1980—; lectr. Conf. Am. Studies Oxford (Eng.) U., 1955; chmn. theory group Army Logistics Research Project, 1955-56; cons. Office Q.M. Gen., 1947-49, George Washington U.-Office Naval Research Logistics Research Project, 1949—; Spl. Operations Research Office of Am. U., 1959—, Arctic Inst., 1960—; regional planning cons. Ford Found.; Adv. Planning Group Calcutta Met. Planning Orgn., Calcutta, 1964-65. Author: Pakistan, Emerging Democracy, 1963, A Question of Place, (with Fisher and Miller), 1967, also articles, papers. Served with USNR, 1943-46. Mem. Am. Assn. Geographers (pres. Middle Atlantic div. 1948), Phi Beta Kappa, Sigma Xi, Pi Gamma Mu, Kappa Delta Pi. Office: Dept Geography U New Mexico Albuquerque NM 87131 *More than anything else I appreciate the opportunities we have here in America to work at several careers, both sequentially and simultaneously. I feel very fortunate to be able to regard my retirement from university teaching as the beginning of a new career.*

CAMPBELL, ROBERT DOUGLAS, coll. adminstr.; b. Chatham, Ont., Can., Sept. 1938; s. Ernest John and Margaret Elaine (Botting) C.; m. Myrtle Sheron Whittle, June 29, 1967; children—Mireya, Roger, Bryce, Brent. B. Engring. Sci, U. Western Ont., 1961. Quality control engr. Internat. Nickel Co., Thompson, Man., Can., 1961-62; devel. engr. Parke Davis Drug Co., Detroit, 1962-63; tech. instr. St. Clair Coll., Windsor, Ont., 1963-68; adminstr. Niagara Coll., St. Catharines, Ont., 1968—; vice chmn., heads of apprenticeship tng. Western Ont. Region, 1981—; mem. bd. examiners Assn. Profl. Engrs., Ont., 1975-78. Editor: Nutshell mag, 1979—, Song News, 1972—. Mem. Profl. Engrs. Ont. (chmn. 1973-74), Am. Magnolia Soc., No. Nut Growers Assn. (sec.), Can. Rhododendron Soc., Soc. Ont. Nut Growers (editor). Mem. United Ch. Can. Home: Rural Route 1 Niagara-on-the-Lake ON L0S 1J0 Canada Office: PO Box 340 St Catherines ON L2R 6V6 Canada

CAMPBELL, ROBERT GOETZE, physician; b. N.Y.C., Apr. 2, 1932; s. Joseph and Marjorie (Goetze) C.; m. Barbara Helen Yoder, Oct. 30, 1959; children: Robert, Susan, William. A.B., Colgate U., 1954; M.D., Columbia U., 1958. Clin. dir. metabolic unit St. Luke's Hosp.; Inst. Nutrition Scis. Columbia U., 1966-69; dir. endocrine unit Monroe Community Hosp., Rochester, N.Y., 1969—; asst. prof. clin. nutrition Inst. Nutrition Scis. Columbia U., 1966-69; asst. prof. medicine U. Rochester, 1969-72, asso. prof., 1972-79, prof., 1979—, prof. medicine and biochemistry, 1981—; med. dir. Monroe Community Hosp., 1982—; vis. scholar Dunn Nutrition unit Cambridge U., 1979-80. Contbr. articles to profl. jours. Pres., Rochester chpt. Am. Diabetes Assn., 1980—. Served as Peace Corps physician USPHS, 1962-64. Recipient Future Leader award Nutrition Found., 1970-72; Acad. Career award NIH, 1972-76. Mem. Am. Fedn. for Clin. Research, Endocrine Soc., Am. Soc. Clin. Nutrition, Phi Gamma Delta. Presbyterian. Club: Madison Sq. Garden (N.Y.C.). Home: 35 Lime Rock Ln Rochester NY 14610 435 E Henrietta Rd Rochester NY 14603

CAMPBELL, ROBERT KENNETH, utilities company executive; b. Chgo., June 20, 1930; s. Donald E. and Jeanette A. C.; m. Alvina Oblinger; children: John E., Thomas L., Joseph A. B.S. in Engring, Ill. Inst. Tech., 1952; M.S. in Mech. Engring, U. Ill., 1956; M.B.A., U. Chgo., 1958; J.D., Loyola U., 1962. Registered profl. engr., Ill. With Western Electric Co., 1957-77, dir. mfg. Allentown Works (Pa.), 1969-71, gen. mgr. Reading Works (Pa.), 1971-72, gen. mgr. Allentown Works, 1972-76, gen. mgr. adminstrn. mfg. div. corp. hdqrs., N.Y.C., 1976-77; pres., dir. Pa. Power and Light Co., Allentown, 1977—, chief exec. officer, 1979—; dir. Hansco Corp., 1979—. Bd. dirs. Edison Electric Inst., Atomic Indsl. Forum, Sacred Heart Hosp., Allentown, United Way of Lehigh County; bd. assos. Muhlenberg Coll., Allentown, Cedar Crest Coll., Allentown; mem. Pa. Environ. Council, Minsi Trails council Boy Scouts Am., Bus. Council Pa.; gen. chmn. Good Shepherd Home and Rehab. Hosp. Bldg. Fund Campaign, 1978. Served with U.S. Army, 1953-55. Mem. ASME, Pa. Soc. Profl. Engrs. (pres.), Nat. Soc. Profl. Engrs., Ill. Bar Assn., Assn. Edison Illuminating Cos. (exec. com.), Pa. State C. of C. (vice chmn.), Sigma Xi, Tau Beta Pi. Presbyterian. Clubs: Lehigh Country (Allentown); Saucon Valley Country (Bethlehem, Pa.). Office: 2 N 9th St Allentown PA 18101

CAMPBELL, ROBERT M., state supreme ct. justice; b. Mar. 1, 1935. B.A., Tex. Wesleyan Coll.; J.D., Baylor U. Practice law, Waco, Tex.; justice Tex. Supreme Ct., 1981—. Office: Supreme Ct Bldg Austin TX 78711

CAMPBELL, ROBERT NEAL, engineering executive, insurance company executive; b. Greenville, S.C., Feb. 18, 1922; s. Robert Lee and Mary Elizabeth (Heath) C.; m. Karen Elizabeth Smith, Aug. 7, 1943; children: Cheryl, Bob, Candace, Patrice, Russell, Dawn, Heath. B.E.E., Clemson U., 1943. Engr. Huntington & Guerry Inc., Greenville, 1946-49; pres., chmn. bd. AE Engrs., Inc., Greenville, 1949—; dir. Design Profls. Ins. Co., San Francisco, Design Profls. Fin. Corp., Greater Carolinas Realty Co., Columbia, S.C., Greater Carolinas Corp., Columbia, v.p., sec., dir., Columbia. Served to lt. with USNR, 1943-46; PTO. Fellow Am. Cons. Engrs. Council (bd. dirs. 1962-69, v.p. 1969-71); mem. S.C. Cons. Engrs. (pres. 1960-62), S.C. Assn. Cons. Engrs. (sec., treas. 1972-73). Democrat. Presbyn. Club: Green Valley Country (Greenville). Home: 7 Marshall Ct Greenville SC 29605 Office: 1200 S Pleasantburg Dr Greenville SC 29605

CAMPBELL, ROBERT SANDERS, JR., lawyer; b. Boise, Idaho, Sept. 8, 1933; s. Robert Sanders and Edythe Ann C.; m. Karen Hinckley, Aug. 5, 1955; children: Courtney Scott, Randall Sanders, Kristin Ann. B.A., U. Idaho, 1955; J.D., U. Colo., 1958; D.L., Oxford (Eng.) U., 1980. Asst. atty. gen. State of Idaho, 1958; asst. atty. gen. State of Utah, 1959-63, chief trial lawyer, 1962-63; partner firm Parsons, Behle & Latimer, 1964-69; spl. asst. atty. gen. Utah Air Matters, 1969-74; sr. mem. firm Watkiss & Campbell (and predecessor), Salt Lake City, 1969—; chmn. Utah Supreme Ct. Com. on Rules of Civil Procedure, 1968—; mem. bd. bar examiners Utah Bar, 1970-73; chmn. Utah Bar Com. on Ethics and Discipline, 1975-81; chief spl. counsel to Utah Bar on Watergate, 1975-76; scholar in residence Oxford U., 1979-80; bencher Am. Inn of Ct.; chmn. Utah Adv. Com. on Reapportionment, 1981; speaker on internat. antitrust law numerous European seminars. Author thesis on antitrust divestiture in the petroleum industry; contbr. articles to legal jours. Served to capt. Judge Adv. Gen. Corps. U.S. Army. Fellow Internat. Acad. Trial Lawyers, Am. Coll. Trial Lawyers; mem. Am. Inn of Ct., Am. Bar Assn. (mem. select com. on fed. rules of civil procedure 1964-75), Am. Judicature Soc., Salt Lake City Area C. of C. (gov., v.p. govt. affairs), Scabbard and Blade, Sigma Chi. Republican. Office: 310 S Main St Suite 1200 Salt Lake City UT 84101

CAMPBELL, ROLLA DACRES, lawyer; b. Huntington, W.Va., Jan. 5, 1895; s. Charles William and Jennie Elena (Ratliff) C.; m. Ruth Cammack, Jan. 1, 1918 (dec. Sept. 23, 1979); children: Rolla Dacres, William C.; m. Patience McNulty, June 8, 1980. B.A., Harvard, 1917, J.D. cum laude, 1920. Practice law, 1920—; sr. partner firm Campbell, Woods, Bagley, Emerson, McNeer and Herndon (and predecessors), 1935—; pres., dir. Dingess-Rum Coal Co., Huntington, C.W. Campbell Co.; v.p. dir. Caldwell-Campbell Co.; v.p., dir. D-R Stores, Inc.; gen. and cons. counsel Island Creek Coal Co., and affiliated cos., 1935-62; founder, pres., dir. Nat. Council Coal Lessors, Inc., Washington, 1951-71. Mem. editorial bd.: Harvard Law Rev. (vol. 33), 1919-20. Mem. ABA (past chmn. natural resources sect., past mem. ho. of dels.). Episcopalian. Clubs: D.U., Inst. of 1770, Speakers, Varsity (Harvard Coll.); Guyan Golf and Country, City (Huntington); Everglades, Beach, Governor's, Bath and Tennis (Palm Beach, Fla.). Home: 261 Via Bellaria Palm Beach FL 33480 also 419 E Washington St Lewisburg WV 24901 also 1030 Ritter Park Huntington WV 25701 Office: PO Box 386 Huntington WV 25708

CAMPBELL, RONALD NEIL, magazine executive; b. Morristown, N.J., Mar. 7, 1926; s. Carroll Francis and Emily Ruth (Peters) C.; m. Jule Gallina, Sept. 22, 1956; 1 son, Bruce G. B.F.A., R.I. Sch. Design, 1951. With Fortune mag., N.Y.C., 1952-82, art dir., 1974-82; asst. circulation promotion dir. Time Inc., 1982—; freelance writer Sports Illustrated, Case Currents, Graphis mag.; freelance graphic designer, painter, lectr., 1951—; mem. adv. bd. Internat. Editorial Design Forum. Served with USNR, 1944-46. Recipient merit awards Art Dirs. Club N.Y., Communication Arts Mag., Art Direction Mag.; Page One award Newspaper Guild, N.Y. Mem. Soc. Illustrators (Gold and Silver medals), Am. Inst. Graphic Arts (merit awards), Soc. Publ. Designers (hon. bd. dirs., merit awards). Home: RFD 5 Barton Rd Flemington NJ 08822 Office: Time & Life Bldg Rockefeller Center New York NY 10020

CAMPBELL, ROSS, business consultant; b. Toronto, Ont., Can., Nov. 4, 1918; s. William Marshall and Helen Isabel (Harris) C.; m. Penelope Grantham-Hill, June 6, 1945; children: Hugh, Timothy. B.A., U. Toronto, 1940. Can. ambassador to, Yugoslavia, 1964-67, Algeria, 1965-66, NATO, 1967-72, Japan, 1973-75, Republic of Korea, 1973-74; Chmn. bd. Atomic Energy of Can. Ltd., 1976-79; pres. Atomic Energy of Can. Internat., Ottawa, 1979—, Canus Tech. Services Corp.; exec. tech. services co., 1980-82; now ptnr. Inter Con Cons. Served with Royal Can. Navy, 1940-45. Decorated D.S.C. Mem. Can. Inst. Internat. Affairs. Clubs: Rideau (Ottawa); Country (Lucerne, P.Q.).

CAMPBELL, SAMUEL GORDON, veterinary immunology educator, veterinarian; b. Oban, Scotland, Dec. 10, 1933; came to U.S., 1961; s. Charles Peter and Mary Innes (Gordon) C.; m. May Elizabeth Craik, Aug. 25, 1961; children: Rory M., Kyle B., Scott M. B.V.M.S., Glasgow U., 1956; M.V.Sc., Toronto U., 1959; Ph.D., Cornell U., 1964. House physician Glasgow U., 1956-57; grad. asst. Ont. Vet. Coll., Guelph, Ont., 1957-59, Cornell U., Ithaca, N.Y., 1961-64; sr. lectr. Melbourne U., 1964-68; prof. immunology Cornell U., 1968; cons. vet. edn. Rockefeller Found., Brazil, 1968, Peru, 1968; cons. microbiology Tuskegee (Ala.) Inst., 1973; cons. animal disease AID, Colombia, 1975, Kenya, 1975; cons. immunology Pa. State U., College Station, 1980. Pres. Tompkins County Soc. Prevention Cruelty to Animals, Ithaca, 1981. Served to capt. Brit. Army, 1959-61. Mem. Royal Coll. Vet. Surgeons, Am. Suffolk Sheep Soc., Am. Assn. Sheep and Goat Practitioners, Am. Assn. Vet. Immunologists (dir. 1980). Home: 234 Lower Creek Rd Ithaca NY 14850 Office: Cornell U Ithaca NY 14850

CAMPBELL, SCOTT ROBERT, food company executive, lawyer; b. Burbank, Calif., June 7, 1946; s. Robert Clyde and Genevieve Anne (Olsen) C.; m. Thersa Melanie Mack, Oct. 23, 1965; 1 son, Donald Steven. B.A., Claremont Men's Coll., 1970; J.D., Cornell U., 1973. Bar: Ohio 1973, Minn. 1976. Assoc. atty. Taft, Stettinius & Hollister, Cin., 1973-76; atty. Mpls. Star & Tribune, 1976-77; v.p., gen. counsel, sec. Kellogg Co., Battle Creek, Mich., 1977—. Mem. ABA, Ohio Bar Assn., Minn. Bar Assn., Grocery Mfrs. Assn. (exec. legal com.), Am. Soc. Corp. Secs. Office: 235 Porter St Battle Creek MI 49016

CAMPBELL, STEWART FRED, foundation executive; b. St. Louis, June 29, 1931; s. Archibald Stewart and Charlotte (Ehrmann) C.; m. Ann Abbey Hudson, Dec. 18, 1954; children: Karen Ann, Deborah Ann. B.S., Lehigh U., Bethlehem, Pa., 1954; M.B.A., Ny.U., 1961. With Mfrs. Hanover Trust Co., N.Y.C., 1958-64, asst. sec., 1962-64; with Duke Endowment, N.Y.C., 1964-79, asst. treas., 1967-73, treas., 1973-79; treas. Dorris Duke Trust, 1973-79, Angier B. Duke Meml., Inc., 1973-79, Nanaline H. Duke Fund, 1973-79; sec.-treas. Alfred P. Sloan Found., N.Y.C., 1979—; asst. treas. Duke Power Co., 1968-75. Treas. Essex unit N.J. Assn. Retarded Children, 1967-72, trustee, 1966-74. Served to lt. USNR, 1954-58. Mem. Delta Phi. Clubs: Rockefeller Center Luncheon (N.Y.C.); Normandy Beach Yacht (N.J.); Montclair Golf. Home: 3 Wendover Rd Montclair NJ 07042

CAMPBELL, STUART BLAND, JR., lawyer; b. Wytheville, Va., July 30, 1916; s. Stuart Bl and Mary (Miles) C.; m. Janet Reed Sutherland, Aug. 14, 1953; children: Stuart Bland III, Arthur Reed, Martha Miles. A.B., Presbyn. Coll., Clinton, S.C., 1937; LL.B., U. Va., 1941. Bar: Va. 1940. Partner firm Campbell & Campbell, 1941-42; sec. State Dept. Bd. Appeals on Visa Cases, 1942-44; div. dir. UNRRA Greece Mission, 1944-47; U.S. fgn. service officer, 1949-53; partner firm Campbell, Young & Hodges (and predecessor), Wytheville, Va., 1953; mem. advisory bd., dir. Wytheville br. First Nat. Exchange Bank Va., 1971—. Del. Democratic Nat. Conv., 1960; chmn. Wythe County Dem. Com., 1966-70; mem. Wythe County Sch. Bd., 1964—; bd. dirs. Wythe County Community Hosp., pres., 1983; trustee Union Theol. Sem., Richmond, Va., 1972-80. Fellow Am. Coll. Trial Lawyers, Am. Bar Found.; mem. Am. Law Inst., Am. Bar Assn., Va. Bar Assn. Presbyterian (elder). Clubs: Commonwealth, Richmond. Home: Peppers Ferry Rd Wytheville VA 24382 Office: 210 W Main St Wytheville VA 24382

CAMPBELL, THOMAS COLIN, nutritional science educator, consultant; b. Annandale, N.J., Mar. 14, 1934; s. Thomas McIlwain and Bessie Hoagland (DeMott) C.; m. Karen Lee Margaret, Sept. 1, 1962; children: Nelson, LeAnne, Keith, Daniel, Thomas. B.S., Pa. State U., 1956; M.S., Cornell U., 1957, Ph.D., 1962. From asst. prof. to prof. biochemistry and nutrition Va. Inst. Tech., Blacksburg, 1965-75; prof. nutritional sci. Cornell U., Ithaca, N.Y., 1975—; cons. Contbr. 200 articles to sci. jours. Mem. panels Nat. Acad. Scis. NIH grantee; Nat. Cancer Inst. Exchange scholar People's Republic of China, 1981. Mem. Am. Inst. Nutrition, Am. Soc. Pharmacology and Exptl. Therapeutics, Soc. Toxicology. Office: Cornell U Ithaca NY 14850

CAMPBELL, THOMAS CORWITH, JR., educator; b. Enfield, Va., Mar. 19, 1920; s. Thomas Corwith and Pearl (Gravatt) C.; m. Burdine Gordon, Apr. 17, 1943; children—Thomas Corwith III, Maxwell Gordon. A.B., Lynchburg Coll., 1942; M.A., U. Pitts., 1947, Ph.D., 1948; student, U. Wis., summer 1947. Mem. faculty W.Va. U., 1948—, asst. to asso. prof., 1948-58; asst. dean Coll. Commerce, 1955-64, prof., 1958-80, dean, 1964-68; vis. prof. Va. Commonwealth U., 1980—. Contbr. articles to profl. jours. Adviser to Ministry of Econ. Planning and Devel. Govt. of Kenya, 1968-70; economist U.S. Bur. Mines, 1974-77, Dept. of Energy, 1977—; Chmn. Gov's. Council Econ. Advisers, 1963-65; mem. Charleston Regional Export Expansion Council, 1964—. Served to lt. USNR, 1942-46; capt. Res. Mem. Am. Econ. Assn., AAUP, Soc. Cincinnati, Beta Gamma Sigma. Mem. Christian Ch. Home: 4014 Fauquier Ave Richmond VA 23227 Office: Dept of Economics Virginia Commonwealth Univ 1015 Floyd Ave Richmond VA 23284

CAMPBELL, THOMAS JOSEPH, hospital administrator, management consultant; b. Auburn, N.Y., Oct. 8, 1929; s. Thomas Joseph and Barbara Helen (McMahon) C.; m. Jane Elizabeth Brown, Aug. 9, 1952; children: Thomas J., Martha M. Campbell Kutik, Andrew F., Mary T. B.S., LeMoyne Coll., 1951; M.H.A., U. Minn., 1959; L.H.D. hon., N.Y. Coll. Podiatric Medicine, 1981. Adminstrv. resident Johns Hopkins Hosp., Balt., 1958, adminstrv. asst., 1958-59; asst. adminstr. Syracuse (N.Y.) U. Hosp., 1959-63; hosp. adminstr.

Kansas City (Mo.) Gen. Hosp. and Med. Ctr., 1963-68; asst. dir. operational studies Assn. Am. Med. Colls., Washington, 1968-73; adminstr. Univ. Hosp. of Upstate Med. Ctr., Syracuse, 1973—; sec. bd. dirs. Hosp. Exec. Council, Syracuse, 1974-79, 81-83; bd. dirs. Blue Cross Central N.Y., Syracuse, 1974-83, Health Services Assn. Prepaid Health Plan, 1978-83; vice chmn., bd. dirs. Health Mgmt. Services, Syracuse, 1981-83; mgmt. cons. HHS, 1977-81. Author, editor mgmt. study reports; co-author mgmt. reports. TV fund raiser March of Dimes, Syracuse, 1981-82; chmn. hope appeal St. Ann's Ch., Manilus, N.Y., 1982. Served to 1st lt. USAF, 1951-58. Fellow Am. Coll. Hosp. Adminstrs. (Fellow of Yr. award 1983, Fellows Cup 1983); mem. Central N.Y. Hosp. Assn. (chmn. bd. dirs. 1981-83). Roman Catholic. Home: 4895 Edgeworth Dr Manilus NY 13104 Office: State Univ Hosp Upstate Med Ctr 750 E Adams St Syracuse NY 13210

CAMPBELL, WALLACE JUSTIN, aid organization executive, economist; b. Three Forks, Mont., Jan. 25, 1910; s. Alvin Douglas and Julia Etta (MacDonald) C.; m. Helen Marie Gordon, Apr. 11, 1936; children—Bruce Gordon, Gale Ellen Campbell Martin. B.S., U. Oreg., 1932, M.S., 1934. Asst. sec. Coop. League U.S.A., N.Y.C., 1934-48, dir. Washington office, 1948-60; dir. public affairs, asst. to pres. and v.p. Nationwide Ins., Columbus, Ohio, 1960-64; pres. Found. for Coop. Housing, Washington, 1964-75, CARE, U.S.A. 1978—, CARE, Internat. 1982—; cons. D.C. Nat. Bank; permanent rep. Internat. Coop. Alliance to Econ. and Social Council of UN; pres. Internat. Coop. Housing Devel. Assn., Washington, London, 1966-80; dir. Nat. Bur. Econ. Research, N.Y.C., 1956-78; treas., pres., chmn. Internat. Devel. Conf., Washington, 1952-78; mem. Nat. Commn. for UNESCO, 1955-58; adj. prof. Am. U., 1975. Author: (with J. Voorhis) The Morale of Democracy, 1946; Editor Coop. News Service, 1934-42, Consumer Cooperation, 1934-40. Mem. Coop. League U.S.A. (dir.), Soc. Internat. Devel. Democrat. Congregationalist. Home: 560 N St SW Washington DC 20024 Office: Suite 230 1575 Eye St NW Washington DC 20005

CAMPBELL, WESLEY GLENN, economist, educator; b. Komoka, Ont., Can., Apr. 29, 1924; s. Alfred E and Delia (O'Brien) C.; m. Rita Ricardo, Sept. 15, 1946; children: Barbara Campbell Bizewski, Diane Campbell Porter, Nancy. B.A., U. Western Ont., 1944; M.A., Harvard, 1946, Ph.D., 1948. Instr. econs Harvard, 1948-51; research economist U.S. C. of C., 1951-54; dir. research Am. Enterprise Assn., 1954-60; dir. Hoover Instn. War, Revolution and Peace, Stanford, 1960—; program adviser Am. Enterprise Inst. Pub. Policy Research, Washington, 1960—; Co-dir. project on Am. competitive enterprise, fgn. econ. devel. and aid program, spl. com. to study fgn. aid program; U.S. Senate, 1956-57; mem. Pres.'s Commn. on White House Fellows, 1969-74, President's Com. on Sci. and Tech., 1976; mem. personnel adv. com. to Pres., 1980-81; mem. adv. bd. Center for Strategic and Internat. Studies, 1980—; dir. Hutchins Center for Study Democratic Instns., 1981—; bd. dirs. NSF, 1972-78, Com. on Present Danger, 1976—; chmn. Pres.'s Intelligence Oversight Bd., 1981—; mem. Pres.'s Fgn. Intelligence Adv. Bd., 1981—; chmn. Am. panel Joint Com. Japan-U.S. Cultural and Ednl. Coop., 1983—; chmn. Japan-U.S. Friendship Commn., 1983—; mem. UNESCO Monitoring Panel, 1984. Co-author: The American Competitive Enterprise Economy, 1952; Editor, prin. author: The Economics of Mobilization and War, 1952; Contbr. articles to profl. jours. Trustee Herbert Hoover Presdl. Library Assn.; mem. bd. visitors Bernice P. Bishop Mus.; regent U. Calif., 1968—. Fellow Royal Econ. Soc.; mem. Am. Econ. Assn., Phila. Soc. (pres. 1965-67), Mont Pelerin Soc. (dir. 1980—). Clubs: Bohemian, Cosmos, Commonwealth (Cal.). Home: 26915 Alejandro Dr Los Altos Hills CA 94022 Office: Hoover Instn Stanford Stanford CA 94305

CAMPBELL, WILLARD DONALD, lawyer; b. New Philadelphia, Ohio, June 6, 1901; s. Dr. Howard N. and Eloise (Gray) C.; m. Rosanna L. Vance, Nov. 25, 1936 (dec. Dec. 1965); children—Rosanna Vance (Mrs. Michael Guy), Willard Donald. A.B., Muskingum Coll., 1922; student, U. Pitts., 1922-23, Cornell U., 1924; LL.B. (fellow); J.D., Yale, 1925. Bar: Ohio bar 1925, Fla. bar 1926. Acting city solicitor, Cambridge, Ohio, 1928-30, pros. atty., 1930-34; mem. Ohio Senate representing 17th, 18th 19th, 28th dists., 1935-37; chief enforcement counsel O.P.A., Columbus, 1941-46; dir. Bur. Code Revision Oreg., 1946-53; practice law, Columbus, 1953-63; chmn. bd. rev. Ohio Bur. Employment Sers., 1963-81; sr. partner Campbell, Potts, Alban & Watson; spl. asst. atty. gen. Ohio, 1957-58; chmn. Ohio Bd. Rev., Bureau Employment Services Ohio. Author: Ohio Revised Code, 1953, Accumulated Index Attorney General Opinions, 1959. Chmn. Columbus Park Commn., 1963-71, Columbus Tree Commn., 1972-78. Named Fraternalist of Year Ohio Council Fraternal and Service Orgns., 1962. Mem. Am. Judicature Soc., Ohio, Fla., Columbus, Guernsey County bar assns., Cambridge C. of C. (past dir., v.p.), U.S. Navy League, Phi Delta Theta, Delta Theta Phi, Tau Kappa Alpha (hon.). Presbyterian. Clubs: Mason (32 deg., Shriner), Moose (state pres. 1939-40), Moose (supreme councilman 1946-51), Moose (supreme prelate 1951), Moose (supreme gov. 1953), Athletic of Columbus, Agonis, Ohio Commodores, Männerchor. Home and Office: 3249 Tremont Rd Columbus OH 43221

CAMPBELL, WILLIAM BENNETT, Canadian government official; b. Montague, Can., Aug. 27, 1943; s. Wilfred and Edith (Rice) C.; m. Shirley Chaisson, Aug. 1, 1970; children: Kelly, Colin, Grant, Sherri, Grace, Brad. Ed., St. Dunstan's U. Mem. P.E.I. legislature, 1970-81, Minister of Edn., 1972-78, provincial sec., 1974-76, Minister of Fin., 1976-79; chmn. Treas. Bd., 1976-79, Regional Treas. Bd., 1976-77; premier, pres. exec. council, Minister of Fin. Govt. of P.E.I., 1978-79; mem. Ho. of Commons for Cardigan and Minister of Veterans Affairs, Can. Govt., Ottawa, 1981—; leader Loyal Opposition, 1979-81; chmn. Council of Ministers of Edn. for Can., 1975-76. Mem. Liberal Party. Roman Catholic. Home: PO Box 10 Cardigan PE C0A 1G0 Canada Office: Rm 533 Confederation Bldg Ho of Commons Ottawa ON Canada K1A 0A6 *

CAMPBELL, WILLIAM CLARKE, lawyer; b. Haileybury, Ont., Can., Dec. 3, 1918; s. Reuben Yacht and Maude (Moses) C.; m. Kathleen Joan Jenkins, July 3, 1943; children: Kathleen (Mrs. David Thomas), William Clarke, Bryan James. B.A., Victoria Coll., U. Toronto, Ont. Can. Bar: Ont. bar 1943. Partner Day, Wilson, Campbell (and predecessors), Toronto, 1946—; Chmn. bd., dir. Consolidated Canadian Faraday Ltd., Toronto, 1969—; dir. Rubbermaid Can. Inc., Billiton Con. Ltd. Served with Royal Canadian Navy, 1943-45. Mem. Bailli Delegue, Confrerie de la Chaine des Rotisseurs, Engrs. Club (Toronto), Royal Canadian Mil. Inst. Clubs: Eglinton Hunt (Toronto); Metropolitan (N.Y.C.). Home: 33 Elmhurst Ave Willowdale ON Canada M2N 6G8 Office: 33 Yonge St Toronto ON Canada M5E 1T1

CAMPBELL, WILLIAM EDWARD, state hospital school superintendent; b. Kansas City, Kans., June 30, 1927; s. William Warren and Mary (Bickerman) C.; m. Joan Josselyn Larimer, July 26, 1952; children: William Gregory, Stephen James, Douglas Edward. Student, U. Nebr., 1944-45, M.S., 1975, U. Mich., 1945, Drake U., 1948; B.A., U. Iowa, 1949, M.A., 1950; Ph.D. in Psychology, U. Nebr., Lincoln, 1980. Psychologist Dept. Pub. Instrn., State of Iowa, 1951-52; hosp. adminstr. Mental Health Inst., Cherokee, Iowa, 1952-68; dir. planning and research Dept. Social Services, State of Iowa, 1968-69; supt. Glenwood (Iowa) State Hosp. Sch., 1969—, Clarinda (Iowa) Mental Health Inst., 1979—; adj. prof. Coll. Medicine and Health Adminstrn. (Tulane U.); pres., bd. dirs. River Bluffs Community Mental Health Center; founder, chmn. Regional Drug Abuse Adv. Council; adj. prof. Sch. Pub. Health (U. Minn.); also preceptor grad. students in mental health adminstrn.; vis. faculty Avepane U., Caracas, Venezuela. Author works in field. UN spl. cons. to Venezuela for UNESCO.; Bd. dirs. Polk County Mental Health; v.p., bd. dirs. Mercy Hosp., Council Bluffs, Iowa; state pres. United Cerebral Palsy; charter mem. bd. dirs. Public Broadcasting Sta. KIWR, Council Bluffs, Iowa. Served with AUS, 1944-46; col. Res. Decorated Army Commendation medal. Fellow Assn. Mental Health Adminstrs. (nat. com. chmn. 1970); mem. Assn. Med. Adminstrs., Am. Hosp. Assn. (nat. governing bd. psychiat. services sect., charter panelist nat. adv. panel on mental health services, mem. governing body psychiat. services sect.), Iowa Hosp. Assn., Health Planning Council of Midlands, Assn. Univ. Programs in Health Adminstrn. (mem. nat. task force on edn. of mental health adminstrs.), Am. Assn. on Mental Deficiency (chmn. adminstrn. sect. Region 8), Nat. Rehab. Assn., Assn. for Retarded Children, Mental Health Assn., Phi Beta Kappa. Address: Glenwood State Hosp Sch Glenwood IA 51534

CAMPBELL, WILLIAM HENRY, geologist; b. Kansas City, Mo., Sept. 20, 1923; s. Myers D. and Wilma (Morris) C.; m. Virginia Hargus, Oct. 8, 1955; children: Constance Lyn, William Arthur. B.A., Kans. U., 1947; B.S. in Geology, Mo. State U., 1950, M.S., 1960; Ph.D. in Archaeology, U. Biarritz, France, 1965. Cons. geologist and oil field operator various locations, 1951-55, mining engr., Batesville, Ark., 1955-57; geologist, v.p. A.R. Jones Oil & Operating Co., Kansas City, Mo., 1957-58; also dir.; pres. Jones & Campbell, Inc., Shawnee Mission, Kans., 1958—, chmn. bd., 1960; lectr. paleontology Mo. State U., 1960; geologist Lotus & Trojan Oil Co., Kansas City, Mo., 1957-58. Contbr. articles on paleontology and mineralogy to sci. jours. Chmn. United Fund, Kansas City, Mo., 1957; mem. Energy Adv. Council, State of Kans., 1976-78; bd. dirs. Gillis Home for Children. Served to capt. U.S. Army, 1943-46; ETO. AAU 3-meter diving champion, 1940. Mem. Am. Assn. Profl. Geologists (lic.), Am. Assn. Petroleum Geologists, Soc. Mining Engrs., Smithsonian Assos., Aircraft Owners and Pilots Assn., Air Force Assn., Am. Legion, VFW, Sigma Chi, Phi Sigma Epsilon. Episcopalian. Clubs: Univ. (Kansas City, Mo.); Exchange, Bounders, Masons. Office: 9320 Switzer Prairie Village KS 66208 *

CAMPBELL, WILLIAM J., judge; b. Chgo., Mar. 19, 1905; s. John and Christina (Larsen) C.; m. Marie Agnes Cloherty, 1937; children—Marie Agnes (Mrs. Walter J. Cummings), Karen Christina (Mrs. James T. Reid), Heather Therese (Mrs. Patrick Henry), Patti Ann (Mrs. Peter V. Fazio, Jr.), Roxane (Mrs. Wesley Sedlacek), William J., Christian Larsen, Thomas John. J.D., Loyola U., 1926, LL.M., 1928, LL.D., 1955; LL.D., Lincoln Coll., 1960; Litt.D., Duchesne Coll., 1965; J.C.D., Barat Coll., 1966. Bar: Ill. bar 1927. Partner Campbell and Burns, Chgo., 1927-40; Ill. adminstr. Nat. Youth Adminstrn., 1935-39; U.S. dist atty. No. Dist. Ill., 1938-40; judge U.S. Dist. Ct., 1940—; chief judge No. Dist. Ill., 1959-70; Mem. Jud. Conf. U.S., 1958-62; chmn. Jud. Conf. Commn. Budget, 1960-70; asst. dir., chmn. seminars Fed. Jud. Center, 1971—. Mem. nat. exec. bd. Boy Scouts Am., 1934—, mem. regional exec. com., 1937—; mem. exec. bd. Chgo. council, 1930—; Trustee Barat Coll., Lake Forest, Ill.; mem. citizens bd. U. Chgo., Loyola U., Chgo.; bd. dirs. Catholic Charities Chgo. Recipient award of merit Citizens of Greater Chgo., 1966, Lincoln laureate in law State of Ill., 1970; named Chicagoan of Year, 1965. Clubs: Ill. Athletic, Union League, Standard, Mid-America (Chgo.); La Coquille (Palm Beach, Fla.). Home: 400 S Ocean Blvd Manalapan FL 33462 Office: 401 US Courthouse 701 Clematis St West Palm Beach FL 33401

CAMPBELL, WILLIAM STEEN, mag. publisher; b. New Cumberland, W.Va., June 27, 1919; s. Robert N. and Ethel (Steen) C.; m. Rosemary J. Bingham, Apr. 21, 1945; children—Diana J., Sarah A., Paul C., John W. Grad., Steubenville (Ohio) Bus. Coll., 1938. Cost accountant Hancock Mfg. Co., New Cumberland, 1938-39; cashier, statistician Weirton Steel Co., W.Va., 1939-42; travel exec. Am. Express Co., N.Y.C., 1946-47; adminstr., account exec. Good Housekeeping mag., 1947-55; pub. Cosmopolitan mag., 1955-57; asst. dir. circulation Hearst Mags., N.Y.C., 1957-61; gen. mgr. Motor Boating mag., 1961-62, v.p., dir. circulation mags., 1962-67, v.p., asst. gen. mgr. mags., 1967-73, v.p., gen. mgr. mags., 1973-78, v.p., dir. circulation mags., 1978-81; pres. Internat. Circulation Distbrs., 1978-81; with Periodical Pubs. Service Bur. subs. Hearst Corp., Sandusky, Ohio, 1964, v.p., chief exec. officer, then pres., chief exec., 1970—; dir. Audit Bur. Circulations, Periodical Pubs. Service Bur., Nat. Mag. Co., Ltd., London, Randolph Jamaica Ltd., Omega Pub. Corp. Fla., Hearst Can. Ltd.; former chmn. Central Registry, Mag. Pubs. Assn.; Chmn. bd. trustees Hearst Employees Retirement Plan; mem. president's council Brandeis U., 1974—; chmn. nat. corp. and found. com. U. Miami, 1979—. Served to lt. col. USAF, 1942-46; ETO. Recipient Lee C. Williams award Mag. Fulfillment Mgrs. Assn.; Torch of Liberty award Anti-Defamation League, 1979. Mem. Mag. Pubs. Assn. (circulation com.). Club: Mason. Home: 240 Central Park South New York NY 10019 Office: 959 8th Ave New York NY 10019

CAMPBELL, WILLIAM STUART, glass company executive; b. Chatham, Ont., Can., June 1, 1927; s. William S. and Mary (Shannon) C.; m. Della Huff, Sept. 15, 1951; 1 dau., Amy Victoria. M.T.C., U. Western Ont., 1966. With Imperial Bank of Commerce, Chatham, Ont.; div. mgr. Rockwell Internat., Chatham, v.p., gen. mgr. plastics, Toronto, Ont.; v.p., gen. mgr. metals Consumers Glass Co. Ltd., Toronto, exec. v.p. corp. mktg. and devel., Etiobicoke, Ont., Can., 1970—; dir. Dennison Mfg. Ltd., 1982-83. Pres. Licensing Exec. Soc., Inc., U.S.A., Can., 1982-83; mem. exec. council Toronto Bd. Trade, 1980-83; pres. Toronto Area Indsl. Devel. Bd., 1981-83; v.p. On. C. of C., 1978-81; chmn. Econ. Com. Met. Toronto, 1982-83. Recipient CanPlast Leadership award Soc. Plastics Ins., 1980. Mem. SAE, Licensing Execs. Soc. Conservative Party. Anglican. Club: Rotary (dir. 1976-77). Office: Consumers Glass Co Ltd 703 Evans Ave Suite 301 Etobicoke ON Canada M9C 5A6

CAMPEAU, JEAN, investment company executive; b. Montreal, Que., Can., July 6, 1931; s. Elmira and Lucienne (Leduc) C.; m. Rejeanne Rouleau, June 22, 1957; children: Lucie, Louis, Paul. B.A., U. Montreal, 1952; license, Ecole de hautes Etudes Commericiales, 1955. Investment broker Rene T. Leclerc, Montreal, 1955-63; v.p., gen. mgr. Can. Flooring, Montreal, 1963-65, pres., gen. mgr., 1965; head dept. mgmt. Dept. Fin., Quebec, 1971, asst. dep. minister, 1977-80; chmn., gen. mgr. Caisse de depot et placement du Que., Montreal, Quebec, 1980—. Home: 10415 rue Laverdure Montreal PQ Canada Office: Caisse de depot et placement du Que 1981 Ave McGill College Montreal PQ Canada H3A 3C7

CAMPEAU, ROBERT, real estate development company executive; b. Sudbury, Ont., Can., Aug. 3, 1923; m. Ilse Luebbert. Chmn., chief exec. officer, dir. Campeau Corp., Toronto, Ont.; mem. adv. bd. Guaranty Trust Co. Can., Can. Bus. Health Research Inst. Bd. govs. Ashbury Coll., Ottawa, Ont. Clubs: Lambton Golf and Country, Donalda, Rideau, Ottawa Hunt and Golf, Mt. Royal, Rivermead Gold, Aylmer Country, Laval sur-le-lac, Jupiter Hills, Metropolitan. Office: Campeau Corp 320 Bay St Toronto ON Can M5H 2P6

CAMPION, FRANK DAVIS, medical association executive; b. Columbus, Ohio, Oct. 30, 1921; s. Edward Winslow and Ruth Baird (Johnson) C.; m. Georgene A. Haney, July 30, 1964; children—Frank Davis, Ann Baird, Katherine Weller, Geoffrey Mills. B.A. with honors, Yale U., 1943. Corr., bur. chief Life mag., Chgo., 1946-52, bur. chief, Los Angeles, 1952-55, asst. editor, N.Y.C., 1955-60; copywriter Young and Rubicam, N.Y.C., 1960-68; exec. asst. pub. relations N.Y. Stock Exchange, N.Y.C., 1968-70; dir. communications AMA, Chgo., 1970-75, dir. Office of Pub. Relations, 1975-77, spl. asst. pub. relations to exec. v.p., 1978—. Contbr. articles to profl. jours. Trustee Boys Club of N.Y.C., 1955-70. Served with AUS, 1943-45. Decorated Bronze Star. Mem. Pub. Relations Soc. Am., Aurelian Honor Soc. Club: Indian Hill. Home: 679 Hill Rd Winnetka IL 60093 Office: 535 N Dearborn St Chicago IL 60610

CAMPION, ROBERT THOMAS, manufacturing company executive; b. Mpls., June 23, 1921; s. Leo P. and Naomi (Revord) C.; m. Wilhelmina Knapp, June 8, 1946; 1 son, Michael. Student, Loyola U., Chgo., 1939-41, 46-48. C.P.A., Ill. With Alexander Grant & Co., Chgo., 1946-57, ptnr., 1954-57; with Lear Siegler, Inc., Santa Monica, Calif., 1957—, pres. chief exec. officer, dir., 1971—, chmn., 1974—. Served with AUS, 1942-46. Mem. Am. Inst. C.P.A.s, Ill. Soc. C.P.A.s. Republican. Clubs: Bel Air (Cal.) Country; Metropolitan (N.Y.C.); Jonathan (Los Angeles); Burning Tree (Md.). Office: Lear Siegler Inc 2850 Ocean Park Blvd Santa Monica CA 90405

CAMPO, BENJAMIN PAUL, lawyer, company executive; b. Willimantic, Conn., Apr. 3, 1941; s. Paul and Loretta May (Bailey) C.; m. Patricia Reynolds, June 4, 1966; children: Benjamin Paul, Patrick Paul. B.A., Georgetown Coll., 1963; J.D., Columbia U., 1966. Bar: N.Y. 1968, N.J. 1977. Assoc. Spear & Hill, N.Y.C., 1968-73; asst. gen. counsel Engelhard Industries, Iselin, N.J., 1973-80, v.p., assoc. gen. counsel, 1980-82, group v.p., gen. counsel, 1982—. Served to capt. U.S. Army, 1966-68. Mem. ABA. Democrat. Roman Catholic. Club: Bath and Tennis (Monmouth Beach, N.J.). Home: 5 Edwards Point Rd Rumson NJ 07760 Office: Engelhard Industries Div 70 Wood Ave S Iselin NJ 08830

CAMPOBASSO, THOMAS ANTHONY, electronics company executive; b. N.Y.C., June 30.1924; s. Gaetano and Mary (Vavoso) C.; m. Yvonne Mary McTernan, Sept. 5, 1951; children—Thomas Derek, Karl Jeffrey, Michelle Marie, Richard Michael, Laura Ann, Christina Louise. Student, Manhattan Sch. Aviation, 1938-42. With aircraft maintenance div. Am. Overseas Airlines, N.Y.C., Shannon, Ireland and London, 1942-50; with central European maintenance div. Pan Am. World Airways, Frankfurt, W. Ger., 1950-52; v.p. ops. and maintenance Alaska Airlines, Seattle, 1952-57; with Collins Radio Co./Rockwell Internat., 1957—, v.p. mktg., Dallas, 1969-74; v.p., gen. mgr. Collins Internat. Sales and Service div., 1974-77; pres. electronics internat. ops. Rockwell Internat., Dallas, 1977-80, corp. v.p. internat. export mktg., 1980—. Fellow Radio Club Am.; mem. Electronics Industries Assn. (past chmn., bd. govs.), Armed Forces Communications and Electronics Assn. (bd. dirs., past nat. pres.), IEEE, Am. Def. Preparedness Assn. (dir.), Aerospace Industries Assn., Soc. Automotive Engrs., NAM, Am. League Internat. Security Assistance, U.S. C. of C., Nat. Mgmt. Assn. Roman Catholic. Clubs: Internat. of Washington, Washington Golf and Country, Georgetown (Washington); Wings (N.Y.C.); Northwood (Dallas); Duquesne (Pitts.); Pitts. Field. Home: 2829 Shamrock St Allison Park PA 15101 Office: 600 Grant St Pittsburgh PA 15219

CAMPOS, SANTIAGO E., federal judge; b. Santa Rosa, N.Mex., Dec. 25, 1926; s. Ramon and Miquela Campos; m. Patsy Campos, Jan. 27, 1947; children: Teresa, Rebecca, Christina, Miquela Feliz. J.D., U. N.Mex., 1953. Bar: N.Mex. 1953. Asst., ist asst. atty gen. State of N.Mex., 1955-57; judge N.Mex. Dist. Ct.; 1st Jud. Dist., 1971-78; now judge U.S. Dist. Ct. for Dist. N.Mex. Served as seaman USN, 1944-46. Mem. State Bar N.Mex., First Jud. Dist. Bar Assn., ABA, Order of Coif. Democrat. Roman Catholic. Office: US Dist Ct PO Box 2244 Santa Fe NM 87501

CAMPUS, PETER, video artist; b. N.Y.C., 1937. Student, Ohio State U., 1960. Mem. faculty MIT, Cambridge, 1976-78; mem. R.I. Sch. Design, 1982-83. Exhibitor: one man shows Bykert Gallery, N.Y.C., 1972, 73, 75, Everson Mus. Art, Syracuse, N.Y., 1974, Leo Castelli Gallery, N.Y.C., 1976, Hayden Gallery, MIT, Mus. Modern Art, N.Y.C., Ohio State U., Columbus, 1977, Whitney Mus. Am. Art, N.Y.C., 1978, Sarah Lawrence Coll., Bronxville, N.Y., Atlantic Gallery, Boston, Akron Art Inst. (Ohio), 1979, Paula Cooper Gallery, N.Y.C., 1979, 81, 82, Protech-Mcintosh, Washington, 1979, Kolnischer Kunstverein, Cologne, West Germany, Neuer Berliner Kunstverein, West Berlin, Centre Pompidou, Paris, 1980, McIntosh-Draysdale Gallery, Washington, 1981, group shows, Finch Coll., N.Y., 1971, Corcoran Gallery Art, Washington, Whitney Mus. Am. Art, N.Y.C., 1973,75,76, Houston Contemprorary Arts Mus., 1974, Kennedy Ctr., Washington, Walker Art Ctr., Mpls., 1974.79, Leo Castelli Gallery, N.Y.C., 1974,75, Knokke Film Festival, Belgium, 1974, The Kitchen, N.Y.C., Sao Paulo Bienal, Brazil, 1975, Boston Mus. Fine Arts, 1976, San Francisco Mus.Art, Documenta 6/Kassel. Germany, 1977, Venice (Italy) Biennale, 1978, Grand Rapids (Mich.), 1979, Los Angeles Inst. Contemporary Art, U. N.C.-Greensboro, Kaiser Wilhelm Mus., Krefeld, West Germany, Galerie Yvon Lambert, Paris, 1980, Anthology Film Archives, N.Y.C., Aldrich Mus., Ridgefield. Conn., 1980, 82, Nat. Gallery Ireland, Dublin, 1980, U. Calif.-Santa Barbra Mus., 1980,81, Stadtischen Kunsthalle, Dusseldorf, West Germany, 1981, Paula Cooper Gallery, N.Y.C., 1980,81, Muhlenbert Coll., Allentown, Pa., 1983, commn. MIT., 1980. Guggenheim fellow, 1975; grantee Nat. Endowment Arts, 1976. Address: care Paula Cooper Gallery 155 Wooster St New York NY 10012

CAMRAS, MARVIN, engineer, inventor; b. Chgo., Jan. 1, 1916; s. Samuel and Ida (Horwich) C.; m. Isabelle Pollack, 1951; children: Robert, Carl, Ruth, Michael, Louis. B.S., Armour Inst. Tech., (now Ill. Inst. Tech.), 1940; M.S., Ill. Inst. Tech., 1942, LL.D., 1968. Registered profl. engr., Ill. Mem. staff Armour Research Found., Chgo., 1940—, asst. physicist, 1940-45, asso. physicist, 1945-46, physicist, 1946-49, sr. physicist, 1949-58, sr. engr., 1958-65, sci. adviser, 1965-69, sr. sci. adviser, 1969—; Chmn. S-4 com. Am. Nat. Standards Inst., 1966, mem., 1966—. Editor: Inst. of Radio Engrs. Transactions on Audio, 1958-63. Recipient Distinguished Service award Ill. Inst. Tech. Alumni Assn., 1948; Achievement award for outstanding contbn. motion picture photography U.S. Camera mag., 1949; John Scott medal, 1955; Ind. Tech. Coll. citation, 1958; Achievement award I.R.E., 1958; Indsl. Research Mag. Product award, 1966; John S. Potts Meml. Gold Medal award Audio Engring. Soc., 1969; merit award Chgo. Tech. Socs., 1973; Alumni medal Ill. Inst. Tech., 1978; named to Hall of Fame, 1981; Inventor of Yr. award Patent Law Assn., Chgo., 1979. Fellow IEEE (sec.-treas. 1951-53, Consumer Electronics award 1964, nat. chmn. profl. group on audio 1953-54 of I.R.E.), Acoustical Soc. Am. (patent rev. bd.), AAAS, Soc. Motion Picture and Television Engrs.; mem. Nat. Acad. Engring., Western Soc. Engrs. (Washington award 1979), Physics Club Chgo. (dir. 1969—, pres. 1973-74), Radio Engrs. Club Chgo., Chgo. Acoustic and Audio Group (dir. 1967-68), Audio Engring. Soc. (hon.; gov. 1970—), Midwest Acoustics Conf. (dir. 1969—), Sigma Xi (chpt. pres. 1959-60), Tau Beta Pi, Eta Kappa Nu. Patentee in field, devels. in wire and tape recorders and stereo sound reproduction, motion picture sound, video recorders. Home: 560

Lincoln Ave Glencoe IL 60022 Office: Technology Center Chicago IL 60616

CAMRON, ROXANNE, editor; b. Los Angeles, May 16; S. Irving John and Roslyn (Weinberger) Spiro; m. Robert Camron, Sept. 28, 1969; children: Ashley Jennifer, Erin Jessica. B.A. in Journalism, U. So. Calif., 1967. West Coast fashion and beauty editor, Teen mag., Los Angeles, 1969-70, sr. editor, 1972-73, editor, 1973—; pub. relations rep. Max Factor Co., 1970; asst. to creative dir. Polly Bergen Co., 1970-71; lectr. teen groups; freelance writer. Active Homeowners Assn. Mem. Women in Communications., Am. Soc. Exec. Women. Address: 8831 Sunset Blvd Los Angeles CA 90069

CANADA, MARY WHITFIELD, librarian; b. Richmond, Va., June 13, 1919; d. Waverly Thomas and Ruth Bradshaw (Smith) C. B.A. magna cum laude, Emory and Henry Coll., 1940; M.A. in English, Duke U., 1942; B.S. in L.S., U. N.C., 1956. Asst. circulation dept. Duke U. Library, 1942-45, undergrad. librarian, 1945-55, reference librarian, 1956—, asst. head reference dept., 1967-79, head dept., 1979—. Contbr. articles to profl. jours. Mem. exec. com. Friends of Duke U. Library. Duke U. grantee, Can., 1979, 81. Mem. ALA (reference services in large research libraries discussion group, life), Southeastern Library Assn. (sec. coll. and univ. sect., chmn. nominating com. reference services div., also chmn. div.), N.C. Library Assn. (chmn. nominating com., chmn. newspaper com., chmn. coll. and univ. sect.), Alumni Assn. Sch. Library Sci. U. N.C. (pres.), AAUP, Va. Hist. Soc. (life), Va. Geneal. Soc., DAR, Trinity Coll. Hist. Soc., Va. Mus. Beta Phi Mu, Tau Kappa Alpha, Alpha Psi Omega, Delta Kappa Gamma. Methodist. Home: 1312 Lancaster St Durham NC 27701

CANADAY, JOHN EDWIN, writer, art critic; b. Ft. Scott, Kans., Feb. 1, 1907; s. Franklin and Agnes F. (Musson) C.; m. Katherine S. Hoover, Sept. 19, 1935; children: Rudd Hoover, John Harrington. B.A., U. Tex., 1929; M.A., Yale U., 1933. Tchr. art history, dept. architecture U. Va., 1938-50; head sch. art Newcomb Coll. Tulane U., New Orleans, 1950-52; chief div. edn. Phila. Mus. art, 1953-59; art critic N.Y Times, 1959-77; vis. prof. U. Tex.-Austin, 1977. Author: (24 portfolios) The Metropolitan Seminars in Art, Mainstreams of Modern art, 1959, Embattled Critic, 1962, Culture Gulch: Notes on Art and Its Public in the 1960's, 1969, (with katherine H Canaday) Keys to Art: Lives of the Painters, 4 vols., Baroque Painters, 1972, Late Gothic to Renaissance Painters, 1972, Neo-Classic to Post-Impressionist Painters, 1972, Artful Avocado, 1973, What is Art, 1981; 7 mystery novels under pseudonym Matthew Head. Served with USMCR, 1944-45. Home: 25 Sutton Pl S New York NY 10022

CANAPARY, HERBERT CARTON, insurance company executive; b. Bklyn., Dec. 1, 1932; s. Edward Paul and Alice G. (Brennan) C.; m. Mary E. Dolan, May 6, 1961; children: Patrick, Ellen, Ann, Jennifer, Blaine. B.B.A., Manhattan Coll., 1954; M.S., Columbia U., 1957. With Manhattan Life Ins. Co., N.Y.C., 1957-80, asst. sec., 1961-70, 2d v.p., 1970-79, v.p., treas., 1974-80; v.p. investments Union Labor Life Ins. Co., Washington, 1981—. Roman Catholic. Home: One Goshen Ct Gaithersburg MD 20879 Office: 111 Massachusetts Ave NW Washington DC 20001

CANARY, JOHN JOSEPH, physician, educator; b. Roslyn, N.Y., Jan. 9, 1925; s. John Henry and Mary (Keenan) C.; m. Mary Alice Ryan, June 2, 1951; children: Mary Jo, Deirdre P., John J., Andrea G., Brendan R., Christopher C., Hilary E., Joshua F. B.S., St. John's U., Jamaica, 1947; M.D., Georgetown U., 1951. Intern, then resident in medicine Mass. Meml. Hosp., Boston, 1951-52; jr., then sr. resident in medicine Georgetown U. Hosp., 1952-53, Boston City Hosp., 1953-54; trainee in metabolic disease NIH, 1954-55; NIH postdoctoral fellow Georgetown U. Med. Sch., 1955-57, mem. faculty, 1955—, prof. medicine, 1967—, dir. endocrinology and metabolism, 1959—; cons. on endocrine and metabolic disease WHO, Geneva; mem. com. on diabetes in the Caribbean Pan Am Health Orgn./WHO, Washington; cons. in field. Founder, coordinator ballet med. com. Washington Ballet Co., 1978. Author numerous articles in field, chpts. in books. Mem. Am. Soc. Clin. Investigation, So. Soc. Clin. Investigation, Am. Fedn. Clin. Research, Endocrine Soc., Endocrine Soc. Chile, Med. Soc. Punta Arenas, Sigma Xi., Alpha Omega Alpha. Home: 12727 River Rd Potomac MD 20854 Office: 3800 Reservoir Rd NW Washington DC 20007

CANAVAN, JOHN JOSEPH, clergyman; b. Ridgefield Park, N.J., Aug. 18, 1921; s. Frederick Louis and Esther (Buckley) C. A.B., Loyola U., Chgo., 1944, M.A., 1946; Ph.L., W. Baden (Ind.) Coll., 1945; S.T.L., Woodstock Coll., 1952; Ph.D., Cornell U., 1956. Joined Soc. of Jesus, 1938; ordained priest Roman Cath. Ch., 1951; tchr. Latin and English Bklyn. Prep. Sch., 1945-47, Loyola Sch., N.Y.C., 1947-48; prof. Classical langs. Canisius Coll., Buffalo, 1956-65; dean Coll. Arts and Scis., 1965-71, dir. instl. research, 1971-74; acad. v.p. St. Peter's Coll., Jersey City, 1974-78; vice provincial for higher edn. N.Y. province Soc. Jesus, 1978—; Vis. prof. Rome center liberal arts Loyola U., Chgo., 1972-73. Address: 1735 LeRoy Avenue Berkeley CA 94709

CANAVAN, TERENCE COONAN, international banker; b. N.Y.C., Jan. 16, 1934; s. Eugene F. and Josetta (Coonan) C.; m. Mary A. Reynolds, Aug. 1961; children: Terence C., Patricia R., Michael C. B.A., Williams Coll., 1955. With Chem Bank, 1955—; rep. Chem. Bank, Caracas, Venezuela, 1964-68, Mexico City, 1969-70, Madrid, 1971-72, region head Latin Am. div., 1976-78, exec. in charge Latin Am. div., N.Y.C., 1978—, sr. v.p., 1979-82, exec. v.p. world banking group Latin Am. div., 1982—; dir. Sociedad Financiera Exterior, Caracas, 1973-76, Banco Gen. de Negocios, Buenos Aires, Argentina. Bd. dirs. Accion International. Served to capt. USAF, 1956-59. Mem. Pan Am. Soc. U.S. (dir.), Venezuelan-Am. Assn. U.S. (dir.), Hispanic C. of C. of N.Y. (dir. 1983). Club: Canoe Brook Country (Summit, N.J.). Home: 26 Tanglewood Ln Chatham Township NJ 07928 Office: Chem Bank 277 Park Ave New York NY 10172

CANBY, VINCENT, newspaperman; b. Chgo., July 27, 1924; s. Lloyd and Katharine Anne (Vincent) C. B.A., Dartmouth Coll., 1947. Reporter N.Y. Times, 1965-69, film critic, 1969—; tchr. history of film criticism Yale U., 1970-71; assoc. fellow Pierson Coll.; Yale U. Author: Living Quarters, 1975; play End of the War, 1978; novel Unnatural Scenery, 1979; play After All, 1981, The Old Flag, 1984; contbr. film criticism to anthologies. Served with USNR, 1944-46. Office: 229 W 43d St New York NY 10036

CANBY, WILLIAM CAMERON, JR., U.S. judge; b. St. Paul, May 22, 1931; s. William Cameron and Margaret Leah (Lewis) C.; m. Jane Adams, June 18, 1954; children—William Nathan, John Adams, Margaret Lewis. A.B., Yale U., 1953; LL.B., U. Minn., 1956. Bar: Minn. bar 1956, Ariz. bar 1972. Law clk. U.S. Supreme Ct. Justice Charles E. Whittaker, 1958-59; asso. firm Oppenheimer, Hodgson, Brown, Baer & Wolff, St. Paul, 1959-62; asso., then dep. dir. Peace Corps, Ethiopia, 1962-64, dir., Uganda, 1964-66; asst. to U.S. Senator Walter Mondale, 1966; asst. to pres. SUNY, 1967; prof. law Ariz. State U., 1967-80; judge U.S. Ct. Appeals 9th Circuit, Phoenix, 1980—; bd. dirs. Ariz. Center Law in Public Interest, 1974-80, Maricopa County Legal Aid Soc., 1972-78, D.N.A.-People's Legal Services, 1978-80; Fulbright prof. Makerere U. Faculty Law, Kampala, Uganda, 1970-71. Author: American Indian Law, 1981; also articles.; Note editor: Minn. Law Rev, 1955-56. Precinct and state committeeman Democratic Party Ariz., 1972-80; bd. dirs. Central Ariz. Coalition for Right to Choose, 1976-80. Served with USAF, 1956-58. Mem. State Bar Ariz., Minn. Bar Assn., Maricopa County Bar Assn., Phi Beta Kappa, Order of Coif. Office: US Courthouse 230 N 1st Ave Phoenix AZ 85025

CANCRO, ROBERT, psychiatrist; b. N.Y.C., Feb. 23, 1932; s. Joseph and Marie E. (Cicchetti) C.; m. Gloria Costanzo, Dec. 8, 1956; children: Robert, Carol. Student, Fordham U., 1948-51; M.D., SUNY, 1955. Intern Kings County Hosp., Bklyn., 1955-56, resident in psychiatry, 1956-59; attending staff Gracie Sq. Hosp., N.Y.C., 1959-66; clin. instr. SUNY Downstate Med. Center, Bklyn., 1959-66; staff psychiatrist Menninger Found., Topeka, Kans., 1966-69; cons. Topeka State and VA Hosps., 1967-69; prof. dept. psychiatry U. Conn. Health Center, Farmington, 1970-76; prof., chmn. dept. psychiatry N.Y. U. Med. Center, 1976—; dir. M.S. Kline Inst. Psychiat. Research, 1982—; cons. psychiat. edn. br. NIMH; biol. scis. sect. NIMH. Editor 10 books.; Contbr. articles on schizophrenia to profl. jours. Recipient Frieda Fromm-Reichmann award, 1975, Strecker award, 1978, Dean award, 1981. Fellow A.C.P., Am. Coll. Psychiatrists, Am. Psychiat. Assn.; mem. Am. Psychol. Assn., Assn. Am. Med. Colls., Am. Assn. Social Psychiatry (pres.-elect 1982-84), N.Y. Acad. Scis., AAAS, AMA. Home: 118 McLain St Mount Kisco NY 10549 Office: 550 1st Ave New York NY 10016

CANDER, LEON, physician, educator; b. Phila., Oct. 7, 1926; s. Joseph Harry and Anna (Glick) C.; m. Geraldine Piontkowski, Dec. 11, 1954; children—Alan Drew, Harris Scott. M.D., Temple U., 1951. Research fellow in physiology Grad. Sch. Medicine U. Pa., 1952-56; resident in medicine Beth Israel Hosp., Boston, 1956-58; asst. in medicine Harvard U. Med. Sch., 1957-58; practice medicine specializing in internal medicine, Boston, Phila. and San Antonio, 1958—; sr. instr. medicine Tufts U. Med. Sch., Boston, 1958-60; asst. prof. medicine Hahnemann Med. Coll., Phila., 1960-63, asso. prof., 1963-66; prof., chmn. dept. physiology and medicine U. Tex. Med. Sch., San Antonio, 1966-72; chmn. dept. medicine, dir. med. edn. Daroff div. Albert Einstein Med. Center, Phila., 1972-80, head sect. of chest diseases, dir. med. edn., 1980—; prof. medicine Jefferson Med. Coll., Phila., 1972—; mem. nat. adv. council on black lung. Soc. Editor: (with J. H. Moyer) Aging of the Lung, 1963. Research fellow Nat. Acad. Scis., 1954-55. Fellow A.C.P.; mem. Am. Thoracic Soc., Am. Physiol. Home: 317 Cherry Ln Wynnewood PA 19096 Office: 1429 S 5th St Philadelphia PA 19147

CANDIOTTY, MAX, lawyer; b. N.Y.C., May 10, 1923; s. Isaac and Dora (Amira) C.; m. Lillian Steinkeler, Sept. 5, 1948; children—Doreen, Edward, Mark. A.A., U. Calif. at Los Angeles, 1943; B.S., U. So. Calif., 1946, J.D., 1951. Bar: Cal. bar 1951. Pub. accountant Candiotty & Beck, Los Angeles, 1948—; practice in, Los Angeles, 1951-66, Beverly Hills, 1966—; co-founder, sec.-treas. Daylin, Inc., 1960-68, pres., 1968-75; also dir.; sr. partner Adam Assos., 1965; chmn. exec. com., dir. Handy Dan Home Improvement Centers, Inc.; dir. Am. Med. Enterprises; mem. Beverly Hills adv. bd. Union Bank. Mem. Citizens Efficiency Economy Com., Los Angeles County, 1965-69; co-founder Fund for Job Corps Grads., 1965-70; mem. Beverly Hills Mall Com., 1969-80; Bd. dirs., v.p. Jewish Fden. Council; chmn. Los Angeles Bur. Jewish Edn., 1968—; bd. dirs. Am. Friends of Hebrew U.; mem. exec. com. Israel Bonds. Served with AUS, 1943-45. Recipient Israel Freedom medal, 1968, Tower of David award, 1968, Bd. Suprs. commendation County of Los Angeles, 1968, Man of Year award Sephardic Jewish Community, 1964, Prime Minister's medal, 1974, Weitzman award in scis. and humanities Washington Inst. Sci.; Hall of Fame award Am. Jewish Congress, 1978; Hon. fellow Hebrew U. Mem. Soc. Attys. and C.P.A.'s, Sephardic Jewish Community and Brotherhood (pres. Los Angeles). Home: 632 N Arden Dr Beverly Hills CA 90210 Office: 10100 Santa Monica Blvd Suite 2500 Century City Los Angeles CA 90067

CANDLAND, DOUGLAS KEITH, psychology educator; b. Long Beach, Calif., July 9, 1934; s. Horace George and Erma Louise (Downing) C.; m. Mary Homrighausen, June 18, 1959; children: Kevin, Christopher, Ian. A.B., Pomona Coll., 1956; Ph.D., Princeton U., 1959. Research fellow U. Va., 1959-60, Delta Primate Center, 1967-68, Pa. State U., 1968-69, U. Stirling, Scotland, 1972-73, Cambridge (Eng.) U., 1977-78, U. Mysore (India), 1983; asst. prof. psychology Bucknell U., 1960-64, asso. prof., 1964-67, prof., 1967—, Presdl. prof., 1973-80, head program in animal behavior, 1968—, pres. div. teaching of psychology, 1976-77, Class of 1956 lectr., 1971; mem. adv. bd. psychology Princeton U., 1970—. Author: Exploring Behavior, 1961, Psychology: the experimental approach, 1968, 2d rev. edit., 1978, Emotion, bodily change, 1961, Emotion, 1979; contbr. chpts. to profl. books; editor: The Primates, 1968-78, Animal Behavior, 1979—; asso. editor: Animal Learning and Behavior, 1976, Teaching of Psychology, 1976—, Am. Jour. Primatology, 1980—. Recipient award Lindback Found., 1971; Harriman award Bucknell U., 1979. Mem. Brit. Psychol. Assn., Am. Psychol. Assn. (award for disting. contbn. to edn. 1978), Psychonomic Soc., Internat. Soc. Primatologists, Animal Behavior Soc. (chmn. policy and planning). Home: 125 Stein Ln Lewisburg PA 17837 Office: Bucknell U Lewisburg PA 17837

CANDLER, JOHN SLAUGHTER, II, lawyer; b. Atlanta, Nov. 30, 1908; s. Asa Warren and Harriet Lee (West) C.; m. Dorothy Bruce Warthen, June 13, 1933; children: Dorothy Warthen (Mrs. Joseph W. Hamilton, Jr.), John Slaughter. A.B. magna cum laude, U. Ga., 1929; J.D., Emory U., 1931. Bar: Ga. bar 1931. Since practiced in Atlanta; ptnr. firm Candler & Cox, Andrews also other law firms, 1931—; dep. asst. atty. gen., Ga., 1951-68; gen. counsel, sec., dir. The D.M. Weatherly Co.; Dir. Sungas, Inc., Leon Propane, Inc., also others. Pres. Atlanta Estate Planning Council, 1963-64; Trustee Ga. Student Ednl. Fund; trustee Kappa Alpha Scholarship Fund, pres., 1970-72; trustee Lovett Sch., 1953-59; pres. USO Council Greater Atlanta. Served from capt. to col. USAR, 1941-46. Decorated Army Commendation Ribbon. Fellow Am. Coll. Probate Counsel (bd. regents 1968-74), Internat. Acad. Law and Sci.; mem. Am., Atlanta bar assns., State Bar Ga. (chmn. sect. fiduciary law 1964-65), Lawyers Club Atlanta, Nat. Tax Assn.-Tax Inst. Am. (adv. council Tax Inst. Am. 1969-72), Am. Legion (post comdr. 1949-50), Res. Officers Assn. U.S. (state pres. 1946, nat. exec. com. 1947), Am. Judicature Soc., Newcomen Soc., Internat. Platform Assn., Mil. Order World Wars, English Speaking Union, U.S. Power, Squadrons, Phi Beta Kappa, Phi Kappa Phi, Phi Delta Phi, Kappa Alpha Order, Sigma Delta Chi. Episcopalian (vestryman, 1953-56, cathedral trustee 1957-67, lay reader 1971—, sr. warden 1955). Clubs: Atlanta Touchdown, Kiwanis, Piedmont Driving, Capital City, Commerce, Peachtree Racket, Ft. McPherson Officers; Oglethorpe (Savannah); Army-Navy (Washington); Masons. Home: 413 Manor Ridge Dr NW Altanta GA 30305 Office: 610 Eight Piedmont Ctr. Atlanta GA 30305

CANEDY, JAMES ANDREW, hospital administrator; b. Ulysses, Nebr., June 12, 1919; s. Harry and Elsie Lorraine (Andrews) C.; m. Betty Jane Thompson, May 21, 1943; 1 son, James T. B.A. in Econ. Theory and Bus., Hastings Coll., 1950; M.H.A., Washington U., St. Louis, 1952. Resident in adminstrn. Bishop Clarkson Meml. Hosp., Omaha, 1951-52, asst. adminstr., 1952-62, adminstr., 1962-68, exec. adminstr., 1968—; mem. Health Ins. Benefits Adv. Com., Washington, 1975-79. Served to sgt. U.S. Army, World War II; PTO. Fellow Am. Coll. Hosp. Adminstrs. (regent for Nebr. 1974-79); mem. Am. Hosp. Assn. (del.-alt. del. 1971-73, 77-79, 80-82), Mid-West Health Congress (chmn. 1982-83, pres.-elect 1983-84), Nebr. Hosp. Assn. (pres. 1972-73), Omaha Hosp. Assn. (pres. 1964-65). Office: Bishop Clarkson Meml Hosp Dewey Ave at 44th Omaha NE 68103

CANEPA, JOHN CHARLES, financial exec.; b. Newburyport, Mass., Aug. 26, 1930; s. John Jere and Agnes R. (Barbour) C.; m. Marie Olney, Sept. 13, 1953; children—Claudia, John J., Peter C., Milissa L. A.B., Harvard U., 1953; M.B.A., N.Y. U., 1960. With Chase Manhattan Bank, N.Y.C., 1957-63; sr. v.p. Provident Bank, Cin., 1963-70; pres. Old Kent Fin. Corp., also Old Kent Bank & Trust Co., Grand Rapids, Mich., 1970—. Served with USN, 1953-57. Office: Old Kent Bank & Trust Co 1 Vandenberg Center Grand Rapids MI 49503

CANEVARI, CHARLES DANIEL, pharmaceutical company executive; b. N.Y.C., Nov. 6, 1920; s. Peter and Mary (Feeney) C.; m. Mildred C. Madden, Oct. 25, 1948; children: Karen, Kevin, Kathy. B.S., FordhamU., 1943; M.B.A., NYU, 1950. Vice pres. American Home Products Corp., N.Y.C., 1956—; regional analyst IRS, N.Y.C., 1947-56. Served to lt. U.S. Army, 1944-46; ETO. Mem. Tax Exec. Inst., Inst. Fiscal Internat. Assn. Republican. Roman Catholic. Club: KC. Office: American Home Products Corp 685 3d Ave New York NY 10017

CANFIELD, CASS, publishing company executive; b. N.Y.C., Apr. 26, 1897; s. August Cass and Josephine (Houghteling) C.; m. Katharine Emmet, May 24, 1922; children: Cass, Michael Temple; m. Jane White Fuller, May 27, 1938. Student, Groton Sch., 1909-15; A.B., Harvard, 1919; postgrad., Oxford U., Eng., 1919-20; LL.D. (hon.), Wagner Coll. With Harris. Forbes & Co., 1921-22, N.Y. Evening Post, 1922-23, Fgn. Affairs, 1923-24; mgr. London (Eng.) office Harper & Bros., 1924-27, with, N.Y.C., 1927-62, pres., 1931-45, chmn. bd., 1945-55, chmn. exec. com. and editorial bd., 1955-62; chmn. exec. com., and Harper editorial bd. Harper & Row, N.Y.C., 1962-67, sr. editor, 1967—; hon. chmn. Harper's Mag., Inc., 1965-75; Pres. Nat. Assn. Book Pubs., 1932-34. Author: The Publishing Experience, 1969, Up and Down and Around, 1971, The Incredible Pierpont Morgan, 1974, Samuel Adams' Revolution, 1976, The Iron Will of Jefferson Davis, 1978, Outrageous Fortunes, 1981, The Six, 1983. Chmn. exec. com. Planned Parenthood Fedn. Am.-World Population Emergency Campaign, 1962-67; chmn. governing body Internat. Planned Parenthood Fedn., 1963-69, hon. chmn., 1969—; Trustee Woodrow Wilson Fellowship Found.; Mem. N.Y. State Council on Arts, 1960-64; Mem. Bd. Econ. Warfare, Washington, 1942-43; spl. adviser to Am. ambassador, London, in charge Econ. Warfare Div.; dir. O.W.I., France, 1945. Served as 2d lt., World War I. Recipient Albert Lasker award. Mem. Am. Assn. UN (dir.), Phi Beta Kappa (hon.). Club: Century Assn. Home: Bedford Village NY 10506 Office: 10 E 53d St New York NY 10022

CANFIELD, EARLE LLOYD, university dean; b. Des Moines, Oct. 24, 1918; s. Lloyd Angle and Margaret Melissa (Earle) C.; m. Betty Elice Fosher, Jan. 30, 1947; children: Irving Nelson, Ward Evan, Marcia Elice. B.A., Drake U., 1940; M.A., Northwestern U., 1944; Ph.D., Iowa State U., 1950. Math. and sci. tchr. Moorhead (Iowa) High Sch., 1940-42; math. and sci. tchr., prin. Winterset (Iowa) High Sch., 1942-46; mem. faculty dept. math. Drake U., Des Moines, 1946—, prof., 1958—, grad. dean., 1957—; Edn. research adviser Colo. State U., summers 1952-57; Bd. coll. visitors Iowa Synod (Presbyn. Colls.), 1964, chmn., 1967-69, Iowa Coop. Study Post High Sch. Edn., Grad. Instrn. and Research Com., 1965-66; mem. com. on instnl. membership Council Grad. Schs. in U.S., 1971-75, chmn., 1972-75, bd. dirs., 1975, 78-80, mem. task force on transfer and equivalency of grad. credit, 1975-77; mem. com. publs. Midwest Assn. Grad. Schs., 1961-64, mem. grad. standards com., 1964-65, mem. exec. com., 1971-75, chmn., 1973-74. Fellow Iowa Acad. Sci. (chmn. program com. for long range planning 1967-68); mem. Math. Assn. Am. (sec. Iowa 1956-67), Phi Beta Kappa, Phi Delta Kappa, Pi Mu Epsilon. Presbyn. (elder). Club: Mason. Home: 3820 SW 31st St Des Moines IA 50321

CANFIELD, EDWARD FRANCIS, business exec., lawyer; b. Phila., Apr. 7, 1922; s. Frank James and Eunice C. (Sullivan) C.; m. Janet Powell Trotter, Jan. 12, 1952; children—Andrew Trotter, Janet Powell. B.A., St. Joseph's U., 1943; J.D., U. Pa., 1949. Bar: Pa. bar 1949, D.C. bar 1972. Practice in, Phila., 1949-51; with RCA, 1953-60, Philco-Ford Corp., 1960-69, corp. dir. marketing, 1961-63, v.p. govt. planning and marketing, 1964-66, v.p. electronic group marketing, 1966-69; pres. Leisure Time Industries, Inc., 1969; mem. firm Casey, Scott & Canfield, 1971—; adv. bd. 1st Am. Bank, McLean, Va. Served as officer USNR, 1942-46; Served as officer USNR, 51-53. Mem. Fed., D.C., Phila., Am. bar assns. Club: Congressional Country (Bethesda. Md.). Home: 9600 Weathered Oak Ct Bethesda MD 20034 Office: 420 Washington Bldg 1435 G St NW Washington DC 20005

CANFIELD, FRANCIS XAVIER, clergyman, educator; b. Detroit, Dec. 3, 1920; s. Edward and Adelle (Berg) C. B.A., Sacred Heart Sem., Detroit, 1941; M.A., Catholic U., 1945; A.M. in L.S, U. Mich., 1950; Ph.D. U. Ottawa, 1951; spl. courses, Notre Dame U., Wayne U., U. Detroit. Ordained priest Roman Cath. Ch., 1945, named domestic prelate, 1963; with English dept. Sacred Heart Sem., Detroit, 1946—, librarian, 1948-63, rector-president, 1963-70; pastor St. Paul's Parish, Grosse Pointe Farms, Mich., 1971—; Instr. library sci. Immaculate Heart Coll., Los Angeles, summers 1955-61; Chaplain Detroit Police Dept., 1965—. Author: Condensed History of the Catholic Church in the Archdiocese of Detroit, 1984; Editor: Philosophy and the Modern Mind, 1961, Literature and the Modern Mind, 1963, Political Science and the Modern Mind, 1963; Author articles, book revs. Mem. Cath. Library Assn. (chmn. Mich. unit 1950-52, 54-56, exec. council 1957-63, pres. 1961-63), Grosse Pointe Ministerial Assn. (pres. 1972-73), Council Nat. Library Assns. (vice chmn. 1962-63), Am. Friends of Vatican Library (pres. 1981—). Club: First Saturday (spiritual dir. 1952-60). Home: 157 Lake Shore Grosse Pointe Farms MI 48236 *In whatever circumstances of life I find mysejf, I feel called somehow to bring God to man and man to God.*

CANFIELD, FREDERICK WEBER, corporate executive; b. Cambridge, Mass., Feb. 1, 1930; s. Haskins Bishop and Anne (Waterman) C.; m. Janet Billings Littlefield, Sept. 6, 1952; children: Scott Weber, Leigh Pierce, Clarke Bishop, Amanda Billings. A.B., Williams Coll., 1952; postgrad., Boston U. Sch. Law, 1952; M.B.A., Harvard, 1958. Asst. to financial v.p. and chmn. finance coms. Mo. Pacific Corp., N.Y.C., 1957; asst. treas., dir. planning East Tenn. Natural Gas Co., 1958-60; treas. Dysatech Corp., Cambridge, 1960-62; pres. Littlefield Lumber Co., Cambridge, 1962-65; treas. Mississippi River Transmission Corp., St. Louis, 1965-67; asst. to exec. v.p. and pres. Ralston Purina Co., St. Louis, 1967-69; founder, pres., treas., dir. Servicetime Corp., 1969-72; pres. West-Time, Inc., Rock Island, Ill., 1970-72; fin. v.p. Southwide, Inc., Fed. Compress & Warehouse Co., Delta and Pine Land Co., Southwide Devel. Co., Aguanova Inc., P. Brown Co., Inc. (and subs. of each), Memphis, 1973—; dir. E. Ritter & Co., Southwide, Inc. Served to lt. USNR, 1953-56. Mem. Memphis Soc. Security Analysts, Fin. Execs. Inst., Ducks Unltd., Kappa Alpha. Republican. Presbyterian. Clubs: St. Louis; Williams (N.Y.C.); Memphis Petroleum; Chickasaw Country, Summit, Memphis Racquet, Bucks Harbor Yacht (Maine). Home: 6572 Bramble Cove Memphis TN 38119 Office: First Tenn Bldg Memphis TN 38103

CANFIELD, JAMES A., III, public relations company executive; b. Queens, N.Y., Sept. 1, 1943; s. James A. and Muriel C. (Lyons) C.; children: James, Kathleen, Christine. B.A., St. John's U., Jamaica, N.Y., 1965. Vice pres., dir. advt. and public relations Security Nat. Bank, Long Island City, N.Y., 1969-75; dep. dir. corp. public relations Chem. Bank, N.Y.C., 1974-76; dir. corp. public relations Babcock & Wilcox Co., 1976; sr. v.p. Bozell & Jacobs Public Relations, Inc., 1976-79, pres., 1979—, also dir.; bd. dirs. jobs program L.I. chpt. Nat. Alliance Businessmen, 1969. Trustee Stony Brook (N.Y.) Fire Dept. Benevolent Assn., 1978-79; bd. dirs. Impact on Hunger; capt. Stony Brook Fire Dept. Rescue Co., 1974-79; mem. men's com. N.Y. Infirmary/Beekman Downtown Hosp., 1980—. Mem. Public Relations Soc. Am. (counselors acad.), Fin. Communications Soc., Nat. Acad. TV Arts and Scis., Internat. Assn. Bus. Communicators. Office: 1 Dag Hammarskjold Pl New York NY 10017

CANFIELD, WILLIAM NEWTON, editorial cartoonist; b. Orange, N.J., Oct. 8, 1920; s. Walter L. and Mildred (Apgar) C.; m. Dorothy J. Levins., Feb. 23, 1946; children—Craig R., Susan A. Student, Am. Sch. Design, N.Y.C., 1940-41. Cartoonist Morning Telegraph and Racing Form, N.Y.C., 1941-46; with Newark News, 1946-72, sports cartoonist, 1946-60, editorial cartoonist, 1960-72, Newark Star-Ledger, 1972—. Served with USNR, World War II. Home: 143 Wayside Rd Tinton Falls NJ 07724

CANGELOSI, VINCENT EMANUEL, banker; b. Baton Rouge, Feb. 5, 1928; s. Philip Vincent and Angelina Elizabeth (Roccaforte) C.; m. Mary Jean Johnson, Feb. 23, 1952; children: Philip William, Phyllis Ann, Angyln Marie, Mary Jean, Joan. B.S., La. State U., 1954, M.B.A., 1956; Ph.D. in Econs, U. Ark., 1961; postdoctorate, Carnegie-Mellon U., 1964. Instr., then asst. prof. U. Ark., 1956-59; instr. La. State U., 1959-60; asso. prof. U. Ark., 1960-65, U. Tex., 1965-67; prof. La. State U., Baton Rouge, 1967-70, 1970—, chmn. dept. quantitative methods, 1970-74, dean jr. div., 1975-84; pres., chief exec. officer, dir. First Met. Mortgage Corp.; dir. Met. Bank & Trust, First Met. Fin. Corp.; Chmn. bd. vis. Postal Service Inst.; spl. cons. Postmaster Gen., 1968. Editor: Mathematics and Quantitative Methods Series, 1967, Compound Statements and Mathematical Logic, 1967, Basic Statistics—A Real World Approach, 1976, 3d edit., 1983; Contbr. to World Book Ency. Served with AUS, 1950-52. Recipient First Annual Distinguish Service award Am. Inst. Decision Scis., 1970. Fellow Am. Inst. Decision Scis.; mem. Phi Eta Sigma, Phi Kappa Phi; Beta Gamma Sigma Pi Gamma Mu, Pi Tau Pi, Alpha Kappa Psi. Club: Rotary. Home: 2109 Fairway Dr Baton Rouge LA 70809

CANGEMI, JOSEPH PETER, psychologist, consultant, educator; b. Syracuse, N.Y., June 26, 1936; m. Amelia Elena Santaló, Oct. 5, 1962; children: Michelle, Lisa Anne. B.S. in Edn., English and Psychology, SUNY-Oswego, 1959; M.S. in Edn. and Psychology, Syracuse U., 1964; Ed.D., Ind. U., 1974. Cert. sch. psychologist, N.Y. Tchr. English, reading Syracuse Pub. Schs., 1959-60, vocat. rehab. coordinator, research assoc., 1961-65; asst. dir., tchr. Carol Morgan Sch., Santo Domingo, Dominican Republic, 1960-61; asst. head basketball coach SUNY Community Coll., Syracuse, 1962-63, lectr., chmn. dept. psychology evening-extension div., 1962-65, vis. lectr., summer 1966; supr. edn. Orinoco Mining div. U.S. Steel Corp., Ciudad Piar, Venezuela, 1965-66, supr. tng. and devel., Puerto Ordaz and Ciudad Piar, Venezuela, 1966-68; asst. prof. psychology Western Ky. U., Bowling Green, 1968-75, assoc. prof., 1975-79, prof., 1979—; project dir. Universidad de Los Andes, Merida, Venezuela, 1975-77, Inter-Am. Devel. Bank, Washington, 1975-77, Western Ky. U., 1975-77; cons. R.R. Donnelley & Sons, Coca Cola, Gould Corp., Eaton Corp., Firestone Corp., others; host Conversation program Western Ky. U. Div. Radio, TV Film, 1968-71. Author: books la Administracion Participativa, 1983, (with Casimir Kowalski) Perspectives in Higher Education, 1983, (with Casimir Kowalski and Jeffrey Claypool) Participative Management: Employee Mangement Cooperation, 1984; contbr. numerous articles, chpts. to profl. publs.; editor: Educator's Service Bull., 1971-72, Psychology-A Quar. Jour. Human Behavior, 1977—, Jour. Human Behavior and Learning, 1983—; mem. editorial bd.: Archivos Panamenos de Psicologia, 1968—, Coll. Student Jour., 1973—, Faculty Research Bull. of Western Ky. U., 1977—, Jour. Instructional Psychology, 1977—, Am. Biog. Inst., 1978—, Counseling and Values, 1979—, Technol. Horizons in Edn. Jour., 1979—, Edn., 1983—, Jour. Internat. and Comparative Social Welfare, 1983—, Orgn. Devel. Jour., 1983—. Recipient cert. U.S. Army Armor Sch., 1974, Eaton Corp. award, 1974, 76, Brazilian Acad. Humanities medal, 1976, Escudo Nat. Autonomous U. Nicaragua, 1976, cert. ICETEX, Colombia, 1977, Columbian Nat. Assn. Indsl. Engrs. award, 1977, Decreto award State of Santander, Colombia, 1977, cert. City Bucaramanga, Colombia, 1976, 77, Coll. Student Jour. award, 1983, Quality Control Assn. award, 1979, Excellence in Productive teaching award Western Ky. U. Coll. Edn., 1979, Firestone Tire and Rubber Co. award, 1978-81, Profl.-Tech. Socs. award, 1983, Models of Excellence award, 1983, Disting. Pub. Service award, 1983, Excellence in Pub. Service award Coll. Edn., 1983, Disting. Alumnus award SUNY-Oswego, 1983. Fellow World Wide Acad. Scholars; mem. Am. Personnel and Guidance Assn. (regional chmn. com. internat. edn. 1976, life), Am. Psychol. Assn., Am. Assn. Sch. Adminstrs. (life), Nat. Vocat. Guidance Assn. profl., Internat. Council Psychologists (area chmn. Ky.), Assn. Specialists in Group Work (charter), Panamanian Psychol. Assn. (hon.), Southeastern Psychol. Assn., Ky. Acad. Arts and Scis. (life), Internat. Assn. Edn. and Vocat. Guidance, Midwest Assn. Tchrs. Ednl. Psychology, Nat. Assn. Gifted (bd. dirs. 1973), Colombian Nat. soc. Indsl. Engrs. (hon.), Internat. Registry Orgn. Devel. Profls., InterAm. Soc. Psychology, Acad. Mgmt., Japanese Mgmt. Assn. (hon.), Capitol Arts Assn., Alumni Assn. SUNY-Oswego, Ind. U. Alumni Assn. (life), Pi Kappa Delta, Psi Chi, Sigma Delta Psi, Sigma Tau Delta, Phi Delta Kappa. Club: Bowling Green Country. Home: 1305 Woodhurst Dr Bowling Green KY 42101 Office: Dept Psychology Western Ky U Bowling Green KY 42101

CANIFF, MILTON ARTHUR, cartoonist; b. Hillsboro, Ohio, Feb. 28, 1907; s. John William and Elizabeth (Burton) C.; m. Esther Parsons, Aug. 23, 1930. A.B., Ohio State U., 1930, L.H.D., 1974; LL.D. (hon.), Atlanta Law Sch., A.F.D., Rollins Coll., U. Dayton. Began as cartoonist, summer 1921; successively on Dayton (Ohio) Jour.-Herald, Miami (Fla.) Daily News, Columbus (Ohio) Dispatch, A.P. Feature Service, N.Y.C., Chgo. Tribune-N.Y. News Syndicate, 1934-46; now with Field Newspaper Syndicate div. Field Enterprises, Inc., also King Features. Creator of: Male Call, and Steve Canyon. Recipient Scroll of Merit Dayton Art Inst.; War Dept. citation for Male Call; Billy DeBeck Meml. award (now Reuben award), 1947; Distinguished Service award Sigma Delta Chi, 1950; Freedoms Found. award, 1950; certificate of merit, 1953; Medal of Merit award Air Force Assn., 1952; Arts and Letters award, 1953; U.S. Treas. citation, 1953; Ohioana Career medal, 1954; USAF exceptional service award, 1957; Ohio gov.'s award, 1957; Silver Beaver award Boy Scouts Am., 1960; Silver Buffalo award, 1976; Silver medallion N.Y. World's Fair, 1964; Goodwill Industries award, 1965; N.Y. Philanthropic League award, 1965; Aerospace Edn. Council award, 1966; named Man of Yr. USAF Assn., 1966; YMCA Service-to-Youth award, 1966; Freedoms Found. Nat. Service medal, 1967; Freedoms Found. George Washington Honor medal, 1969; Distinguished Eagle award Boy Scouts Am., 1969; Elzie Segar Cartoon award, 1971; Second Reuben award, 1972; San Diego Inkpot award, 1974; Silver Buffalo award Boy Scouts Am., 1977; 4th Estate award; Good Guy award Am. Legion, 1978; Spirit of Am. Enterprise award, 1981; named to Nat. Comic Strip Hall of Fame, 1981. Mem. Newspaper Comics Council, Soc. Illustrators, Nat. Cartoonists Soc. (pres. 1948- 49, now hon. chmn., recipient Golden Scroll 1964), Air Force Assn., Arnold Air Soc. (hon. nat. comdr.), Exec. Order Ohio Commodores (charter), Air Force Assn. (Maxwell Kriendler Man of Yr. 1981, past pres. Iron Gate chpt.), Sigma Chi (Significant Sig 1940, Order of Constantine 1976), Sigma Delta Chi. Clubs: Players, N.Y. Press, Dutch Treat, Silurians (N.Y.C.); Nat. Press, Nat. Aviation (Washington). Milton Caniff Research Library at Ohio State U. named in his honor, 1979. Office: King Features 235 E 45th St New York NY 10017

CANIN, STUART VICTOR, violinist; b. N.Y.C., Apr. 5, 1926; s. Monroe H. and Mary (Becker) C.; m. Virginia Yarkin, June 8, 1952; children—Aram Roy, Ethan Andrew. Student, Juilliard Sch. Music, 1946-49. Asst. prof. violin State U. Iowa, Iowa City, 1953-57, asso. prof., 1957-61; prof. Oberlin Conservatory, 1961-66; concertmaster Chamber Symphony of Phila., 1966-68, San Francisco Symphony Orch., 1970-80; Fulbright prof. Staatliche Musikhochschule, Freiburg, Germany, 1956-57. Chamber music artist, Aspen (Colo.) Summer Music Festival, 1962, 63, 64, Santa Fe Chamber Music Festival, 1975, Spoleto Festival of Two Worlds, Charleston, S.C. and Spoleto, Italy, 1980; concert master, Casals Festival Orch., San Juan, P.R., 1977, 78, Mostly Mozart Summer Festival, Lincoln Center, 1980. Served with U.S. Army, 1944-46. Recipient 1st prize Paganini Internat. Violin Competition, Genoa, Italy, 1959; Handel medal, N.Y.C., 1960.

CANIZARO, PETER CORTE, surgeon, educator; b. Vicksburg, Miss., June 30, 1935; s. Peter Joseph and Masie Nona (Ross) C.; m. Sandra Lou Brian, Dec. 21, 1957 (div. 1981); children: Peter, Carolyn, Vincent, Janet; m. Hana Pospisil, Nov. 1, 1982; children: Martin, Anna. B.A., U. Tex.-Austin, 1956; M.D., U. Tex.-Dallas, 1960. Diplomate: Am. Bd. Surgery. Intern Parkland Meml. Hosp., Dallas, 1960-66, resident, 1964-68; asst. prof. surgery U. Tex.-Southwestern, Dallas, 1968-72, assoc. prof., 1972-74; assoc. prof. surgery U. Wash., Seattle, 1974-76, Cornell U., N.Y.C., 1976-81, prof., 1981-82; prof., chmn. dept. surgery Tex. Tech. U. Health Scis. Ctr., Lubbock, 1982—; mem. Pres.'s Nat. Health Adv. Com., 1972-73. Contbr. articles to profl. jours.; assoc. editor (Circulatory Shock), 1979—; mem. editorial bd. (Tex. Medicine), 1983—. Served to capt. U.S. Army, 1961-63. Recipient Elliot Hochstein Teaching award Cornell U., 1979, Peter C. Canizaro Lectureship Cornell U., 1983; fellow NIH, 1963-64, 71-74; grantee Nat. Inst. Med. Scis., 1974-76. Fellow ACS; mem. Am. Assn. Surgery of Trauma, Soc. Internationale de Chirurgie, Soc. Surg. Chairmen, Soc. Univ. Surgeons, Shock Soc. Republican. Roman Catholic. Office: Dept Surgery Tex Tech U Health Scis Ctr Lubbock TX 79430

CANN, WILLIAM FRANCIS, judge; b. Somerville, Mass., Oct. 10, 1922; s. William Arthur and Frances (Hardy) C.; m. Ellen Catherine Hughes Watts, Sept. 6, 1958; stepchildren—Ellen (Mrs. Dale H. Lockhart), Allan Craig Watts. Student, Tufts U., 1940-42; LL.B., Boston U., 1948; grad., Nat. Coll. State Judiciary, Reno, 1972. Bar: Mass. bar 1948, N.H. bar 1959. Sr. claim examiner Am. Mut. Liability Ins. Co., Wakefield, Mass., 1948-60; law asst. Office Atty. Gen., State N.H., Concord, 1960-61, asst. atty. gen., 1961-67, dep. atty. gen., 1967-71; asso. justice N.H. Superior Ct., 1971—; lectr. trial advocacy Franklin Pierce Law Center. Mem. adv. bd. Community Corrections Center of N.H. State Prison, Franklin Pierce Law Center, Civic Intern Program. Served with USAAF, 1942-45. Mem. Am. Bar Assn., N.H. Bar Assn., Merrimack County Bar Assn., Am. Judicature Soc. Home and Office: 36 Roger Ave Concord NH 03301

CANN, WILLIAM HOPSON, mining company executive; b. Newark, June 17, 1916; s. Howard W. and Ruth (Hopson) C.; m. Mildred E. Allen, Mar. 7, 1942 (dec. 1982); children: William Hopson, Sharon Lee, John Allen, Lawrence Edward. A.B. magna cum laude, Harvard, 1937; LL.B., 1940. Bar: N.Y. 1941, Calif. 1947. Asso. firm Chadbourne, Parke, Whiteside & Wolfe (and predecessors), N.Y.C., 1940-53; asst. to pres. Rockwell Internat. Corp., 1953-60, v.p., sec., 1960-75; coordinator for stockholder relations Cyprus Mines Corp., Los Angeles, 1975-76, corp. sec., 1977—. Mem. adv. bd. Family Service of Los Angeles. Served to 1st lt. USAAF, 1942-45. Mem. Am. Soc. Corporate Secs. (past pres.), Phi Beta Kappa. Episcopalian. Clubs: Rocky Mountain, Harvard (Denver). Home: 5111 Sanford Circle W Englewood CO 80110 Office: Cyprus Mines Corp 7000 S Yosemite St PO Box 3299 Englewood CO 80155

CANNELL, CHARLES FREDERICK, psychologist, educator; b. Antrim, N.H., Sept. 10, 1913; s. William J.B. and Hattie (Morse) C.; m. Martha Phyllis Osgood, Aug. 23, 1937; children—John Charles, Edward Lincoln. A.B., U. N.H., 1936; M.A., Ohio State U., 1940, Ph.D., 1952. Head field sect., div. program surveys Bur. Agrl. Econs., Dept. Agr., 1942-46; mem. faculty U. Mich., 1954—, prof. psychology in journalism, 1962—; mem. staff Inst. Social Research, Survey Research Center, 1946—, program dir., 1963—; cons. Nat. Center for Health Services Research, Nat. Center Health Stats. Author: (with R.L. Kahn) The Dynamics of Interviewing, 1957, Techniques for Evaluating Interviewer Performance, 1975, Experiments in Interviewing Techniques, 1979; contbr.: chpts. to Handbook of Social Psychology, Sociological Methodology Experiments in Interviewing Techniques, 1981, articles to profl. jours. Fellow Am. Psychol. Assn.; mem. Soc. Psychol. Study Social Issues, A.A.U.P., Am. Statis. Assn., Am. Assn. Pub. Opinion Research. Home: 13 Heatheridge St Ann Arbor MI 48104

CANNELL, PETER BEST, investment counselor; b. Glen Ridge, N.J., May 8, 1926; s. John and Hildegarde (Best) C.; m. Ann Eberstadt, June 10, 1950; children: William B., Peter F., Cynthia, Michael, James Carlo. B.A., Princeton, 1949. With ECA, Paris, 1949-50; advt. copywriter Batten, Barton, Durstine & Osborn, Inc., 1951-54; with Merrill, Lynch, Pierce, Fenner & Smith, brokerage, 1954-55, F. Eberstadt & Co., investment bankers, 1955-69, partner, 1959-69; with Chemical Fund, Inc., 1955-64, exec. v.p., 1959-62, pres., chief exec. officer, dir., 1962-64; chmn. Cannell, Breed & Musser, 1969-70; with Wertheim & Co., Co. (investment bankers), 1970-72; sr. v.p. Wertheim Asset Mgmt. Services, Inc., 1972-73; pres. Peter B. Cannell & Co., Inc., N.Y.C., 1973—. Bd. dirs. Fountain House Found., Hosp. for Spl. Surgery, Hurricane Island Outward Bound Sch. Mem. N.Y. Soc. Security Analysts. Clubs: Madison Square Garden, River (N.Y.C.); Piping Rock; Links (N.Y.C.); University Cottage (Princeton, N.J.). Home: 160 E 72d St New York NY 10021 Office: 919 Third Ave New York NY 10022

CANNELL, STEPHEN JOSEPH, TV writer/producer/director; b. Los Angeles, Feb. 5, 1941; s. Joseph Knapp and Carolyn (Baker) C.; m. Marcia C. Finch, Aug. 8, 1964; children: Derek (dec.), Tawnia, Chelsea, Cody. B.A., U. Oreg., 1964. Chief exec. officer Stephen J. Cannell Prodns., 1979—. Creator, writer, producer: TV series Rockford Files, 1974—; creator, producer: Baa-Baa Blacksheep, 1978, Richie Brockelman, 1978, The Duke, 1979, Stone, 1979, The Greatest American Hero, 1981—; creator: Baretta, 1976. Recipient Mystery Writers award, 1975; Emmy award, 1979. Mem. Writers Guild (4 awards), Producers Guild, Dirs. Guild. Episcopalian. Office: 7083 Hollywood Blvd Los Angeles CA 90028

CANNELLA, JOHN MATTHEW, U.S. judge; b. N.Y.C., Feb. 8, 1908; s. Joseph and Laura (Gullo) C.; m. Ida Rutnik, Dec. 26, 1938; children: Lauretta (Mrs. Alfred Kushay), Christine (Mrs. John J. Phelan 3d), John Matthew. B.S., Fordham U., 1930, LL.B., 1933. Bar: N.Y. 1934. Gen. practice, N.Y.C., 1934-40; asst. U.S. atty., 1940-42; commnr. Water Supply Gas and Electricity, N.Y.C., 1946-48, Dept. Licenses, 1948-49; mem. Ct. Spl. Sessions, N.Y.C., 1949-59, Ct. Gen. Sessions, 1957-58, City Ct., 1959-61, Criminal Ct., 1963; U.S. judge So. Dist. N.Y., 1963—, sr. judge, 1977—. Served with USCGR, 1942-45. Mem. Catholic Lawyers Guild, Columbian Lawyers Assn. Home: 240-45 42d Ave Douglaston NY 11363 Office: US Dist Courthouse Foley Sq New York NY 10007

CANNING, FRED FRANCIS, drug store chain executive; b. Chgo., Apr. 1, 1924; s. Fred and Lillian (Popiolek) C.; m. Margaret Luby, Nov. 23, 1944; children: Jeanette, Laura, Debbie, Terry, Patrick, Marggie, Timothy, Kathleen. Registered Pharmacist, Hynes Sch. Pharmacy, 1950. With Walgreen Co., Deerfield, Ill., 1946—, v.p., 1975-76, sr. v.p., 1976-78, exec. v.p., 1978, pres., 1978—, also chief exec. officer, also dir. Served with USCG, 1942-45. Mem. Am. Pharm. Assn., Am. Mktg. Assn. Roman Catholic. Office: Walgreen Co 200 Wilmot Rd Deerfield IL 60015

CANNING, JESSIE MARIE, public relations executive; b. N.Y.C.; d. Robert James and Jessie Murray (Melville) C. B.A., Marymount Coll., Tarrytown, N.Y., 1947; D.Hebrew Letters (hon.), Beth Jacob Tchrs. Coll., N.Y.C., 1969. Exec. asst. to gen. counsel Met. Life Ins. Co., 1948-52; dir. govt. and bus. liaison N.Y.C. Dept. Commerce, 1952-53; asst. city adminstr. N.Y.C., 1953-55; pres. Sydney S. Baron & Co., Inc., N.Y.C., 1955-80; chmn. Baron/Canning & Co., N.Y.C., 1980—; instr. mgmt. sci. St. Francis Coll., N.Y.C., 1958-61; assoc. prof. communications St. Ann's Coll., N.Y.C., 1962-65; Assoc. dir. pub. relations N.Y. State Democratic Com., 1952-60; bd. dirs. Sr. Med. Consultants, Inc., Center for Family Life, Children of Alcoholics Found. Author: Women in American Business, 1967; also articles. Recipient Merit award N.Y.C. Mem. U.S. C. of C., Am. Mgmt. Assn. (pres. council), The Pres.'s Assn. Roman Catholic. Clubs: Westchester Country (White Plains, N.Y.); I.C. 100 (Montclair, N.J.); Georgetown (Washington). Office: 540 Madison Ave New York NY 10022

CANNING, JOHN RAFTON, urologist; b. Evanston, Ill., Dec. 5, 1927; s. Claude E. and Martha C. Canning; m. Elizabeth Learned, Sept. 11, 1948; 1 dau., Sarah Blee; m. Jacqueline Maartense, Apr. 3, 1970; children—John R., Richard, Roberta. B.A., Lake Forest (Ill.) Coll., 1951; M.D., Northwestern U., 1955, M.S., 1956. Diplomate: Am. Bd. Surgery, Am. Bd. Urology. Intern St. Luke's Hosp., Chgo., 1955; resident in gen. surgery VA Hosp., Hines, Ill., 1956-60, resident in urology, 1966-68; chest fellow Presbyn.-St. Luke's Hosp., Chgo., 1963; asst. chief vascular surg. sect. VA Hosp., Hines. 1960-66, asst. chief urology surg. sect., 1968, chief urology, 1969—; asst. prof. urology Loyola U. Stritch Sch. Medicine, Maywood, Ill., 1969—, chmn. dept., 1979—. Fellow A.C.S.; mem. AMA, Am. Geriatrics Assn., Ill. Urol. Soc. (exec. com.), Chgo. Urol. Soc. (exec. com.), Chgo. Med. Soc. Club: Chgo. Yacht. Address: Loyola U Stritch Sch Medicine Dept Urology Maywood IL 60153

CANNON, BRADFORD, surgeon; b. Cambridge, Mass., Dec. 2, 1907; s. Walter Bradford and Cornelia (James) C.; m. Ellen DeNormandie, June 25, 1938; children—Walter Bradford, Philip Yardley, Robert Laurent, Sarah, Woodward. B.S., Harvard, 1929, M.D., 1933. Diplomate: Am. Bd. Surgery, Am. Bd. Plastic Surgery (sec.-treas. 1950-55). Intern, asst. resident, then resident surgery Barnes Hosp., St. Louis, 1933-37, fellow plastic surgery, 1938-39; asst. surgery Washington U., St. Louis, 1934-39; surgeon Mass. Gen. Hosp., Boston, 1941-74, sr. surgeon, 1974—; clin. asso. surgery Harvard U., 1941-73, assoc. clin. prof. surgery, 1973—; clin. prof., 1973-74, emeritus, 1974—; asst. chief, then chief plastic surgery Valley Forge Gen. Hosp., Phoenixville, Pa. Editorial bd. Jour.: Plastic and Reconstructive Surgery, 1958-63; co-editor, 1966-73; mem. editorial bd.: Jour. Surgery of Hand, 1975—; author articles, papers on plastic and reconstructive surgery. Cons. VA, AEC; sr. cons. surgeon Crippled Children's Program, Mass.; Pres. Mass. Med. Benevolent Soc., 1972—; trustee Proctor Acad. N.H. Served from lt. to lt. col., M.C. AUS, 1943-47. Decorated Legion of Merit. Fellow A.C.S.; mem. A.M.A., Am. Surg. Assn., Soc. U. Surgeons, Am. Assn. Plastic Surgeons (pres. 1957-58), Harvard Med. Sch. Alumni Assn. (v.p. 1968-71, pres. 1981-82), Am. Soc. Plastic and Reconstructive Surgery (v.p. 1959-60), New Eng. Surg. Soc., New Eng. Soc. Plastic and Reconstructive Surgery (pres. 1962-63), Am. Soc. Surgery the Hand, Internat. Soc. Burn Injuries, Boston Surg. Soc. (pres. 1978-79), Mass. Med. Soc., Societe Internationale Chirurgie, Soc. Mayflower Descs., Sigma Xi., Unitarian. Clubs: Harvard, Aesculapian (Boston). Home: Silver Hill Rd Lincoln MA 01773 Office: Mass General Acc 353 Boston MA 02114

CANNON, CHARLES DALE, English educator; b. Bruce, Miss., May 27, 1928; s. Walter D. and Eunice K. (Johnson) C.; m. Patricia Faye Capwell, Dec. 25, 1952; children: Patricia Dianne, Charles Dale. Student, Copiah-Lincoln Jr. Coll., 1945-46; B.A., U. Miss., 1951, M.A., 1952; M.A. postgrad, Johns Hopkins U., 1952; Ph.D., U. Mo., 1964. Instr. English Copiah Lincoln Jr. Coll., Wesson, Miss., 1953-55, U. Mo., Columbia, 1955-56, 60-64; investigator U.S. CSC, Dallas, 1956-57; asst. prof. Miss. Coll., Clinton, 1957-59, SE Mo. State Coll., Cape Girardeau, 1965-66, U. Miss., University, 1964-65, 66-68, asso. prof., 1968-71, prof., 1971—, acting chmn. dept., 1976-77, dir. grad. studies, 1979—. Author: A Warning for Fair Women, 1975. Served with U.S. Army, 1946-49. Mem. MLA, Renaissance Soc. Am., Malone Soc., Delta Phi Alpha, Pi Kappa Pi, Eta Sigma Phi, Phi Kappa Phi, Sigma Tau Delta. Club: Oxford Music. Office: Dept English Univ of Mississippi University MS 38677

CANNON, CHARLES NIBLEY, engineering and construction company executive; b. Salt Lake City, May 7, 1922; s. George Mousley and Edna (Nibley) C.; m. Margie Moore, Mar. 2, 1945; children—Carolyn, Martha. Student, U. Utah, 1939-41; B.S. in Chem. Engring, U. Mich., 1947. Process engr. Fluor Corp., Los Angeles, 1947-51, in various sales and engring. positions, N.Y.C., 1961-66, Houston, 1966-68; v.p. FS West Co. (Cons. Engrs.), Whittier, Calif., 1951-60; mng. dir. Fluor Nederland N.V., Haarlem, Holland, 1968-71; pres. Fluor Engrs. & Constructors, Irvine, Calif., 1971-77; dir. and group v.p. Fluor Corp., 1977—. Served to 1st lt. Ordnance Corps U.S. Army, 1942-45. Mem. Am. Inst. Chem. Engrs., Am. Petroleum Inst., Nat. Petroleum Refiners Assn., Orange County Republican Assn. Clubs: Big Canyon Country, Balboa Bay, Eldorado Country., Vintage. Home: 4633 Tremont Ln Corona Del Mar CA 92625 Office: 3333 Michelson Irvine CA 92730

CANNON, DYAN, actress; b. Tacoma, Wash., Jan. 4; m. Cary Grant (div.); 1 dau., Jennifer. Ed., U. Wash.; pupil, Sanford Meisner. Former model; TV appearances include Diane's Adventure; Broadway appearances include Ninety-Day Mistress; with road company How to Succeed in Business Without Really Trying; motion pictures include Bob and Carol and Ted and Alice, 1969, The Anderson Tapes, 1971, Deathtrap, 1982, The Love Machine, 1971, Such Good Friends, 1971, Doctors' Wives, 1971, The Last of Sheila, 1973, Shamus, 1973, Child Under a Leaf, Revenge of the Pink Panther, 1978, Heaven Can Wait, 1978, Coast to Coast, 1980, Honeysuckle Rose, 1980; appeared in: TV movie Virginia Hill Story, 1974, Lady of the House, 1978. Named Best Actress of Year Nat. Assn. Theater Owners. Address: care Creative Artists Agy Inc 1888 Century Park E Suite 1400 Los Angeles CA 90067 *

CANNON, EDMUND RASHA, lawyer; b. Mobile, Ala., Dec. 17, 1926; s. Edmund Rasha and Kate (Davis) C.; m. Lucinda Moore Samford, Aug. 17, 1974 (div. Aug. 1977); 1 son, Edmund Rasha. A.B., U. Ala., 1949, LL.B., 1952. Bar: Ala. bar 1952. Asso. firm Joseph C. Sullivan, Mobile, 1952-55, Hand, Arendall, Bedsole, Greaves & Johnston, 1956-58, partner, 1958—; Bus. mgr. Ala. Law Rev., 1951-52. Served with AUS, 1945-46. Mem. ABA, Ala. Bar Assn., Mobile Bar Assn. (treas. 1962), Am. Legion, V.F.W., Phi Delta Theta, Phi Delta Phi (magister de Graffenried Inn 1951). Democrat. Presbyterian. Clubs: Bienville, Athelstan, Alba Fishing and Hunting, Mobile Country. Home: 4108 Ridgelawn Dr Mobile AL 36608 Office: PO Box 123 Mobile AL 36601

CANNON, GEORGE QUAYLE, savs. and loan exec.; b. Salt Lake City, May 28, 1908; s. William T. and Ada C.; m. Irene Chipman, Oct. 19, 1927; children—George Quayle, Vance C., Mary Jean. Student, U. Utah, Brigham Young U., 1926; postgrad. in Bus, Harvard U., 1955. Pres., chmn. Meadow Gold Dairies, Hawaii, 1961-76; mng. dir. Far East and Pacific ops., Beatrice Foods, 1961-76; chmn. Hawaii group, 1976; chmn., dir. Honolulu Fed. Savs. & Loan, 1950-79; cons. in field. Pres. Honolulu council Boy Scouts Am., 1955-60; chmn. Honolulu Police Commn., 1950-61; v.p., bd. dirs. Polynesian Cultural Center. Decorated Red Cross of Constantine. Mem. Honolulu C. of C. (pres. 1962). Mormon. Clubs: Masons, Rotary, Oahu Country, Scottish Rite, York Rite, Shriners, Jesters. Home: 1778 Ala Moana P H 14 Honolulu HI 96815 Office: PO Box 1518 2115 Davies Bldg Honolulu HI 96809

CANNON, HELEN LEIGHTON, geologist, government official; b. Wilkinsburg, Pa., Apr. 29, 1911; d. Henry and Jessie M. (Cipperley) Leighton); m. Ralph Smyser Cannon, July 6, 1935 (dec. div. 1965); 1 dau., Susan Ellen (Mrs. Richard Enos). A.B., Cornell U., 1932; postgrad., Northwestern U., 1932-33; M.S., U. Pitts., 1934, U. Okla., 1934-35. Geologist Gulf Oil Co., Saginaw, Mich., 1935; geologist U.S. Geol. Survey, Washington and Denver, 1940—. Author govt. bulls.; Contbr. articles on geol. surveys and environ. geochemistry to profl. publs. Recipient Meritorious award Dept. Interior, 1970, Distinguished Service award, 1975. Mem. Geol. Soc. Am. (council 1973-76, chmn. environment and pub. policy 1974-76), Internat. Assn. Geochemistry and Cosmochemistry, Assn. Exploration Geochemists, Colo. Sci. Soc., AAAS (mem. council 1969-71, 76-80, com. on council affairs 1979-80, sect. chmn. 1976), Soc. Environ. Geochemistry, NRC (chmn. subcom. geochem. environment in relation to health and disease 1969-73), Kappa Kappa Gamma. Home: Route 9 Box 77B Santa Fe NM 87501 Office: US Geological Survey Mail Stop 955 Box 25046 Federal Center Denver CO 80225

CANNON, HERBERT SETH, brokerage executive; b. Bklyn., Dec. 3, 1931; s. Joseph and Gertrude (Kimmel) C.; m. Edith Marks, June 20, 1954; children: Naomi Sue, Nina Louise. B.A., Washington and Jefferson Coll., 1953; student, Cornell U. Law Sch., 1953-54; LL.B., Fordham U., 1960. Salesman Manhattan Scalloping & Embroidery Co., N.Y.C., 1956-57; stock broker Hirsch & Co., N.Y.C., 1956-61, Wineman, Weiss & Co., 1961-62; pres. Weis, Voisin, Cannon, Inc., N.Y.C., 1963-70; chmn. bd. Elgin Nat. Industries, Inc., N.Y.C., 1967-70; chmn. bd., pres. Cannon, Jerold & Co., Inc., 1970-73; chmn. bd. PUD Industries, Inc., 1971—, CitiWide Capital Corp., 1984—, CitiWide Securities Corp., 1984—; pres. Herbert S. Cannon & Co. Ltd., real estate devel. and investment bankers, N.Y.C., full service stockbrokerage firm, N.Y.C., Fla., Colo., Pa.; chmn. bd. Holistic Services Corp., 1979—. Past trustee Washington and Jefferson Coll. Served with AUS, 1954-56. Mem. Young Pres. Orgn. Home: 480 Park Ave New York NY 10022 also 3145 Estates Dr Pompano FL 33060 Office: 665 Fifth Ave New York NY 10022 also 6301 NW 5th Way Fort Lauderdale FL 33309 *Make it happen. Don't wait for it to happen.*

CANNON, HOWARD WALTER, former U.S. senator; b. St. George, Utah, 1912; s. Walter and Leah (Sullivan) C.; m. Dorothy Pace, Dec. 21, 1945; children: Nancy Lee, Alan Howard. B.E., Ariz. State Tchrs. Coll., 1933; LL.B., U. Ariz., 1937; LL.D., Ariz. State Coll., 1962. Bar: Ariz. 1937, Utah bar 1938, Nev. bar 1946. Reference atty. Utah Senate, 1939; county atty. Washington County, Utah, 1940-41; city atty., Las Vegas, Nev., 1949-58; U.S. senator from Nev., 1959-83. Mem. Nev. Bd. Bar Examiners, 1950-55; Past chmn. Clark County (Nev.) Democratic Central Com. Served with USAF, 1941-46; maj. gen. Res. ret. Mem. Ariz., Clark County, Nev., Utah bar assns., Air Force Assn., Nat. Space Club, Res. Officers Assn., V.F.W., D.A.V., C. of C. (pres. 1955), Am. Legion. Club: Nat. Aeronautic (Washington) (trustee). Lodges: Lions (pres. 1956-57, past dist. gov., internat. counsellor); Eagles. Home: 6300 Evermay Dr McLean VA 22101 Office: 499 S Capitol St SW Suite 400 Washington DC 20003

CANNON, ISABELLA WALTON, mayor; b. Dunfermline, Scotland, May 12, 1904; d. James and Helen Bett (Seaman) Walton); m. Claude M. Cannon. B.A., Elon Coll., LL.D. (hon.). Tchr. pub. schs.; head dept. stats. French Purchase Commn., Washington; fin. officer UN, Washington; with N.C. State U. Library; mayor of Raleigh, N.C., 1977-79. Vol. Crisis-Intervention Hopeline, Meals on Wheels; v.p. Women in Bus. Adv. Council; mem. N.C. Conservation Council, Women's Polit. Caucus; charter mem. Wake County Democratic Women; bd. dirs. Wake County Friends of Library Systems, N.C. Youth Adv. Council; organizer, pres. Univ. Park Assn., Raleigh; civic sponsor, mem. bldg. com. Raleigh Little Theatre; mem. task force White House Conf. on Aging; bd. dirs., project adv. com. Conserva, Inc. Mem. Nat. League of Cities, U.S. Conf. Mayors, Wake County Hist. Soc., N.C. Sr. Citizens Assn. (pres.), Elon Coll. Alumni Assn. (disting. alumna 1983), Delta Kappa Gamma. Mem. United Ch. of Christ. *The motivation which directs my life and activities is my profound belief in the democratic process and the response each citizen should make to its demands. This response includes taking an active part in political and governmental affairs, whether it be local community service or state or national matters. It is of basic importance for citizens to study the issues before their governmental bodies, communicate with their representatives and then vote faithfully. Only though wide-spread involvement in our communities can we meet the ideals of democratic society, no matter how small a part we play.*

CANNON, J. D., actor; b. Apr. 24, 1922. Student, Am. Acad. Dramatic Arts. Early acting career with, Joseph Papp's N.Y. Shakespeare Festival; appeared: plays Great Day in the Morning, Peer Gynt; appeared in: Great God Brown; films include Raise the Titanic, An American Dream, Cool Hand Luke, Cotton Comes to Harlem, The Lawman, Scorpio; TV appearances include My Love; films include Profiles in Courage, Wedding Bank, Testimony of Two Men, Ike, The Top of the Hill, Pleasure Palace, My Kidnapper; appeared in: TV ser.es McCloud, 1971-76. Office: care The Artists Agy 190 N Canon Dr Beverly Hills CA 90210 *

CANNON, JOHN, actor, performing arts assn. exec.; b. Chgo., Mar. 26, 1927; s. John Thomas and Margaret (Stewart) C.; m. Gertrude (Trudy) Weincek, June 11, 1951; children—Michael, Constance. Student, Western Res. U., 1940-41. Pres. N.Y. chpt. Nat. Acad. TV Arts and Scis., 1969—, nat. vice-chmn. from, 1972, chmn., 1974-76; founder full opportunity com. TV Acad. Encouragement of Minorities Peoples in Television. Free-lance host, interviewer, moderator, narrator, newscaster, actor, writer, producer, numerous network shows, newsreels, comml., feature films, 1947—; appeared: Golden Age of TV, N.Y.C., 1950-60; premier interviewer: NBC's Monitor, 1961—. Served with AUS, 1943-46. Decorated Bronze Star. Mem. Institut Francais, Sommelier Soc. N.Y. Club: West Side Tennis. Home: 110-45 Queens Blvd Forest Hills NY 11375 Office: Nat Acad TV Arts and Scis 110 W 57th St New York NY 10019

CANNON, JOSEPH EDWARD, physician, state official; b. Providence, Aug. 17, 1910; s. Francis and Mary Jane (Milligan) C.; children: Joseph F., David A. Ph.B., Brown U., 1932; M.D. cum laude, Tufts U., 1936, M.P.H., Harvard U., 1954. With Colo. Dept. Health, 1950-58, R.I. Dept. Social Welfare, Providence, 1958-61; dir. R.I. Dept. Health, Providence, 1961—; del. White House Conf. on Aging, 1961, 1963, 1965; mem. Surgeon Gen.'s Task Force on Tb, 1963, 1964-67, Nat. Adv. Health Services Council. Mem. editorial bd.: Control of Communicable Diseases in Man, 1970 edit. Dir. R.I. Health Planning Council, Inc., Hosp. Service Corp. R.I., R.I. Water Resources Bd., R.I. Health Services Research Inc. Served with M.C. U.S. Army, 1937-46. Fellow Am. Pub. Health Assn.; mem. AMA, R.I., Providence med. assns., R.I. Hosp. Assn. (Disting. Service award), Assn. State and Territorial Health Ofcls. (McCormack award). Office: RI Dept Health 75 Davis St Providence RI 02908 *

CANNON, NORMAN LAWRENCE, publishing co. exec.; b. Kansas City, Kans., Oct. 9, 1936; s. William Lawrence and Norma (Purvis) C.; m. Alyce Diane Blanton, Sept. 26, 1964; children—Charlotte Walker, Catherine Shafer. B.A. in Econs. cum laude, Harvard, 1959, M.B.A., 1961. With Johns-Manville Co., 1961-63, W.Va. Pulp & Paper Co., 1963-64; from project dir. to asst. to pres. Air Reduction, Inc., 1964-69; with Harper & Row Publishers, N.Y.C., 1969—, treas., 1970—, v.p., 1977—. Republican. Episcopalian. Home: 5 Winged Foot Dr Larchmont NY 10538 Office: 10 E 53d St New York City NY 10022

CANNON, PETER, elec. and aerospace co. exec.; b. Chatham, Eng., Apr. 20, 1932; U.S., 1956, naturalized, 1958; s. William Douglas and Ena (Bennett) C.; m. Elaine Moosdorf, Aug. 5, 1955; children—Ian Douglas, Adrienne Louise, Eric Milton, Peter Andrew. B.Sc. in Math. and Chemistry with honors, U. London, 1952, Ph.D. in Phys. Chemistry, 1955. Chem. engr. Proctor & Gamble, Cin., 1955-56; mem. tech. staff Gen. Electric Research Lab., Schenectady, N.Y., 1956-64, liaison scientist, 1964-65, mgr. ops. analysis-info. systems bus., Charlottesville, Va., 1965-67, mgr. sensors and microelectronics automation bus. systems, 1967-72, mgr. strategic devel., West Lynn, Mass., 1972-73; v.p. bus. devel. utility and indsl. ops. Rockwell Internat., Pitts., 1973-76; corp. staff v.p. research, v.p. Sci. Center, Thousand Oaks, Calif., 1976—; adj. prof. physics Bklyn. Poly. Inst., 1962-67; lectr. U. Va., 1967, Royal Soc. London, 1978; mem. U.S. Nat. Acad. Sci. vis. team U. Alexandria, Egypt, 1980. Author: (with others) Vacuum Technique, 1961, Reactivity of Solids, 1968; contbr.: articles to profl. jours. Reactivity of Solids. Bd. dirs. Ventura County (Calif.) United Way, 1978-79; campaign chmn. Ventura County Jr. Achievement Program, 1979. Fellow Royal Soc. Chemistry; mem. Nat. Mgmt. Assn. (recipient Silver Knight of Mgmt. award 1980), Am. Phys. Soc., Am. Chem. Soc., Am. Mgmt. Assn. Patentee in field. Office: 1049 Camino Dos Rios Thousand Oaks CA 91360

CANNON, ROBERT EMMET, consumer products manufacturing company executive; b. Greenville, Miss., Nov. 18, 1929; s. Robert Emmet and Louise (Hill) C.; m. Kathryn Gracey, Aug. 28, 1955; children: Katherine, Howard, Hall. B.M.E., Ga. Inst. Tech., 1951. With Procter & Gamble Co., 1954—, group v.p., Memphis, 1981—. Pres. Chickasaw council Boy Scouts Am., 1978-80, bd. dirs., 1975—; bd. dirs. United Way Greater Memphis, Future Memphis, Inc., Lebonheur Children's Hosp.; mem. exec. adv. council Memphis State U. Coll. Bus. Adminstrn.; v.p., mem. exec. com. bd. dirs. Memphis Orchestral Soc.; officer Shady Grove Presbyn. Ch., Memphis. Served with USN, 1951-54. Mem. Am. Paper Inst. (chmn. pulp producers exec. bd. 1977-78), Can. Pulp and Paper Assn. (exec. bd.). Club: Chickasaw Country. Home: 445 Shady Grove Rd Memphis TN 38119 Office: 1001 Tillman St Memphis TN 38108

CANNON, ROBERT HAMILTON, JR., aeronautical engineering educator; b. Cleve., Oct. 6, 1923; s. Robert Hamilton and Catharine (Putnam) C.; m. Dorothea Alta Collins, Jan. 4, 1945; children: Philip Gregory, Douglas Charles, Beverly Jo, Frederick Scott. David John, Joseph Collins, James Robert. B.S., U. Rochester, 1944; Sc.D. (du Pont fellow), MIT, 1950. Research engr. Baker Mfg. Co., Evansville, Wis., 1946-50; instr. MIT, 1949-50; research engr. Bendix Aviation Research Labs., Detroit, 1950-51; with Autonetics div. N.Am. Aviation Inc., Downey, Calif., 1951-57, supr. automatic flight control systems, 1951-54, systems engr. inertial nav. instruments and systems, 1954-57; asso. prof. mech. engring. MIT, 1957-59; mem. faculty Stanford U., 1959-74, prof. aeros. and astronautics, 1962-74, dir. Guidance and Control Lab., 1960-69; chief scientist USAF, 1966-68; asst. sec. Dept. Transp., Washington, 1970-74; chmn. div. engring. and applied sci. Calif. Inst. Tech., Pasadena, 1974-79; Charles Lee Powell prof., chmn. dept. aeros. and astronautics Stanford U., 1979—; chmn. sci. adv. com. Gen. Motors Corp., 1979—; mem. Draper Corp., 1975-81; dir. Parkin Hannifin Corp.; Chmn. research adv. subcom. guidance, control and nav. NASA, 1967-70, chmn. electronics research center adv. group, 1968-69; vice chmn. sci. adv. bd. USAF, 1968-70; chmn. assembly of engring. NRC, 1974-75, chmn. energy engring. bd., 1975-81, mem. aeros. and space engring. bd., 1975-79, mem. governing bd., 1976-78. Author: Dynamics of Physical Systems, 1967; also articles. Served to lt. (j.g.) USNR, 1944-46. Fellow AIAA (chmn. tech. com. guidance and control 1964-66, dir. 1968-70); mem. Nat. Acad. Engring. (councillor 1975-81), Sigma Xi, Theta Chi (chpt. pres. 1943-44), Tau Beta Pi. Presbyterian. Participated devel. hydrofoil boats, automatic flight control, inertial guidance instruments and systems, space vehicle control, drag free satellite, gyro test of gen. relativity, tech. assessment of climatic impact of stratospheric flight, wave-actuated upwelling pump, flexible robot control systems, nat. energy alternatives. Office: Dept Aeros and Astronautics Stanford U Stanford CA 94305

CANNON, ROWLAND MORRELL, retired sugar company executive; b. Logan, Utah, June 2, 1914; s. Clawson Young and Winnifred (Morrell) C.; m. Elithe Fillmore, July 16, 1940; children: Rowland Morrell, Douglas Fillmore, Maurine. B.S., Iowa State U., 1936. With U and I Inc., 1936-81, v.p., prodn. mgr., 1964-67, exec. v.p., 1967-69, pres., also chief exec. officer, 1969-81, also dir., exec. com., pres. emeritus, spl. adviser, 1971—; dir. 1st Security Corp., Standard Ins. Co., Z.C.M.I. Mem. water pollution adv. council Idaho Bd. Health, 1962-64; mem. adv. bd. U. Utah Coll. Bus. Mem. Sigma Chi. Mem. Ch. of Jesus Christ of Latter-day Saints. Clubs: Rotary, Elks, Alta (Salt Lake City). Office: PO Box 11699 Salt Lake City UT 84147

CANNON, WILLIAM BERNARD, university official; b. Cascade, Iowa, Nov. 10, 1920; s. Charles Bernard and Irma (White) C.; m. Jeanne Adair Ketchum, Aug. 16, 1944; children: Julia, Dominic, William, Robert. Ph.B., U. Chgo., 1947; M.A., 1949. Budget examiner Bur. Budget, 1951-54, 59-62; asst. v.p. U. Chgo., 1954-59, v.p. programs and projects, 1968-74; dean Lyndon B. Johnson Sch. Pub. Affairs, U. Tex. at Austin, 1974-75; v.p. bus. and fin. U. Chgo., 1976—; asst. chief, office legislative reference for health, edn. and welfare programs Bur. Budget, 1962-65, chief edn., manpower and sci. div., 1965-67; dep. chmn. Nat. Endowment for the Arts, 1968. Mem. selection com. Rockefeller Pub. Service Awards, 1976—; mem. Midwest selection com. H.S. Truman Scholarship Program; mem. bd. Youthwork Corp., Field Found. N.Y., Nat. Opinion Research Ctr. Served with AUS, 1943-46. Mem. Phi Beta Kappa. Home: 5N135 Hanson Rd St Charles IL 60174 Office: U Chgo 5801 Ellis Ave Chicago IL 60637

CANNON, WILLIAM JOHN, psychologist, editor, educator; b. South Wales, U.K., Sept. 16, 1908; s. Frederick John Harold and Elsie (Caturan) C.; m. Lois Lowry Irwin, Apr. 4, 1971; 1 dau., Ruth (Mrs. Gerald Gelford); stepchildren: Malcolm, Warren, Beverley Ludders and Barbara Orr (twins), Susan, Shelley Lowry. Student, Stanborough Coll., Watford, Eng.; FL.C.th., London Coll. Theology, 1946; M.A., Andrews (Mich.) U., 1954, B.D., 1956; Ph.D., Am. U., 1958. Ordained to ministry Seventh Day Adventist Ch., 1935; minister, educator, adminstrv. psychologist, Gt. Britain, 1931-50, evangelist, D.C. and Va., 1950-52; prof. Andrews U., 1952-59; chmn. dept. psychology, dir. guidance Columbia Union Coll., Takoma Park, Md., 1960-70; psychologist Washington Adventist Hosp., 1954—; pvt. practice psychology, Takoma Park, 1954—; asso. dir. dept. edn. Gen. Conf. Seventh Day Adventists, 1970-75; chmn. dept. psychology, dir. guidance Columbia Union Coll., Takoma Park, Md., 1976-82; cons. World Conf. Seventh Day Adventists. Editor: Adventist Home, 1970-75, Home and School Leader, 1970; Author: Guidelines to Mental Health, 1963; also articles in field. Mem. Am., Eastern, Md., D.C. psychol. assns. Home: 1705 Ritchie Rd Washington DC 20028 Office: 8001 Barron St Takoma Park MD 20012

CANNON, WILLIAM RAGSDALE, bishop; b. Chattanooga, Apr. 5, 1916; s. William Ragsdale and Emma (McAfee) C. A.B., U. Ga., 1937; B.D. summa cum laude, Yale U., 1940, Ph.D., 1942; D.D., Asbury Coll., 1950; LL.D., Temple U., 1955; L.H.D., Emory U., 1962; S.T.D. (hon.), Wesleyan Coll., 1980, Litt.D., La Grange Coll., 1980, Duke U., 1983, D.C.L., N.C. Wesleyan Coll., 1982; D.H., Meth. Coll., 1984. Ordained to ministry Methodist Ch., 1940; pastor Allen Meml. Methodist Ch., Oxford, Ga., 1942-43; prof. ch. history and hist. theology Candler Sch. Theology, Emory U., 1943-68, dean sch. theology, 1953-68; bishop Raleigh area United Meth. Ch., 1968-72, 80—, Richmond area, 1970-72, Atlanta area, 1972-80; lectr. Fondren Found. So. Meth. U., 1948; vis. prof. Garrett Bibl. Inst., summer 1949, Richmond Coll., U. London, 1930; Mem. commn. on ritual and worship Meth. Ch., 1948-64; chmn. bd. ministerial tng. North Ga. Conf., Meth. Ch., 1948-64; del. to gen. and jurisdictional confs. Meth. Ch., 1948, 52, 56, 60, 64, 68; also mem. commn. on worship, commn. ecumenical affairs; del. Ecumenical Conf. Methodism, Oxford, Eng., 1951, World Meth. Conf., Lake Junalaska, N.C., 1956; fraternal del. from World Meth. Council to World Conf. on Faith and Order, Lund, Sweden, 1952, Nairobi, Kenya, 1975; chmn. exec. com. World Meth. Council; pres. World Meth. Conf., 1980—; accredited visitor World Council Chs., Evanston, Ill., 1954; Meth. ch. del. 3d assembly World Council of Chs., New Delhi, 1961, Lund, Sweden, 1968, Nairobi, Kenya, 1976; del. World Meth. Conf., Oslo, Norway, 1961; Meth. Ch. del. Conf. on Faith and Order, Montreal, Can., 1963; pres. N. Am. sect., mem. exec. com. World Methodist Council; mem. presidium; ofcl. protestant observer from council to II Vatican Council of Roman Catholic Church; co-chmn. Conversations of Methodists and Roman Catholics at Internat. Level. Author: A Faith for These Times, 1944, The Christian Church, 1945, The Theology of John Wesley, 1946, Accomplishments to Wesley's Death in Methodism, (edited by W. K. Anderson), 1947, Our Protestant Faith, 1949, The Redeemer, 1931, History of Christianity in the Middle Ages, 1960, journeys after St. Paul, 1963, Evangelism in a Contemporary Context, 1973, A Disciple's Profile of Jesus: On the Gospel of Luke, Jesus the Servant from the Gospel of Mark, 1978, The Gospel of Matthew, 1983; Editor: Selections from Augustine, Table Talk (Martin Luther), 1950. Trustee La Grange (Ga.) Coll., Asbury Coll.; trustee, vice chmn. bd. Emory U.; chmn. trustees Protestant Radio and TV Center, 1953-63. Mem. Oxford Inst. Wesleyan Studies, Phi Beta Kappa, Phi Beta Kappa Assos. (exec. com.), Theta Phi, Phi Kappa Phi. Address: Methodist Bldg 1307 Glenwood Ave PO Box 10955 Raleigh NC 27605 *The principles by which I have tried to live are: complete devotion to Jesus Christ; loyalty to His Church as represented by the United Methodist Church; daily Bible reading and prayer; service to others; and concern for the betterment of humanity. I have pursued scholarship, organized my time and energy, and enjoyed the simple things of life.*

CANON, ROBERT MORRIS, government official, arts adminstrator; b. Winona, Miss., July 26, 1941; s. Booma Sharp and Elizabeth Pauline (Harrison) C. B.A., U. Miss., 1964, M.A., 1967. Artistic dir. Panola Playhouse, 1962-70; instr. opera theatre U. Miss., 1964-66; coordinator performing and fine arts, 1966-72; dir. Galveston Arts Ctr., Tex., 1972-74; exec. dir. Arts Council San Antonio, 1975-83; dir. Nat. Endowment for Arts, Washington, 1983—; program dir., cons. Miss. Arts Commn., Jackson, 1970-72; dir. The Joffrey Workshop, 1973-74; U.S. del. AITA-UNESCO Conf., Monaco, 1969; pres. Nat. Assembly Local Arts Agys., 1981-83; mem. nat. council U.S. Internat. Ballet Competition, 1981—; mem. Miss. Arts Commn., 1967-70; bd. dirs. Tex. Assembly Arts Councils, 1976-79; mem. urban affairs com. Tex. Arts Commn., 1979-82. Contbr. articles to arts jours. Mem. Miss. Theatre Assn. (pres. 1966-68), Southeastern Theatre Assn. (gov. 1969-72), Assn. Am. Dance Cos. (exec. com. 1975-77), Soc. Performing Arts (dir. 1978-81). Home: 1522 Swann St NW Washington DC 20009 Office: 1100 Pennsylvania Ave NW Washington DC 20506

CANRIGHT, SARAH ANNE, artist, educator; b. Chgo., Aug. 20, 1941; d. William and Constance (Clark) C.; m. Edward C. Flood, Apr. 15, 1968 (div. 1979). B.F.A., Art Inst. Chgo., 1964. Vis. artist Sch. of Art Inst. Chgo., 1974, 82, Skowhegan Sch. Painting and Sculpture, Maine, 1980; instr. Princeton U., 1978-80, 83; lectr. Phila. Coll. Art, 1978, 80-81, Sch. Visual Arts, N.Y.C., 1981; sr. lectr. U. Tex., Austin, 1982, 83. Artist: visual books Franklin Furnace, 1979; exhibited one-man shows, Phillis Kind Gallery, Chgo., 1974, 79, Pam Adler Gallery, N.Y.C., 1979, 81, 83, various group shows. Recipient Armstrong award Art Inst. Chgo., 1971; nat. Endowment for Arts grantee, 1975, 78; N.Y. State Council for the Arts grantee, 1977. Home: 161 Mulberry St New York NY 10013 Office: Princeton Univ 185 Nassau St Princeton NJ 08540

CANSLER, LESLIE ERVIN, editor; b. Hickory, N.C., Sept. 16, 1920; s. Leslie Ervin and Mabel Pearl (Braswell) C.; m. Marie Muriel Olwell, Aug. 19, 1944 (div.); children: David, Robert, James.; m. Elizabeth Marie Walters; 1 dau., Leslie Anne. B.A., Wake Forest U., 1941. News editor Daily Advance, Elizabeth City, N.C., 1941; reporter Raleigh (N.C.) Times, 1941-42, 46, city editor, 1946-47; with News-Jour. Co., Wilmington, Del., 1947—, day mng. editor, 1966-68, mng. editor, 1968-76, assoc. Sunday editor, 1976-79, Sunday editor, 1979—, assoc. editor, 1980—. Served with USNR, 1942-45. Mem. Am. Soc. of Newspaper Editors, Hist. Soc. Del., Sigma Phi Epsilon. Republican. Episcopalian. Club: Torch of Delaware. Home: 31 Golfview Dr Apt D-1 Newark DE 19702 Office: 831 Orange St Wilmington DE 19899

CANTALUPO, JAMES RICHARD, restaurant company executive; b. Oak Park, Ill., Nov. 14, 1943; s. James Francis and Eileen Patricia (Goggin) C.; m. Jo Ann Lucero, June 16, 1973; children: Christine,

Jeffrey. B.S. in Acctg., U. Ill.-Champaign, 1966. C.P.A., Ill. Staff acct. Arthur Young & Co., Chgo., 1966-71, mgr., 1971-74; controller McDonald's Corp., Oak Brook, Ill., 1974-75, sr. v.p., controller, 1981—; dir. No. Trust Bank-Oak Brook, 1983—. Treas. McDonald Polit. Action Com., Oak Brook, 1979—; chmn., dir. Nat. Multiple Sclerosis Soc., Chgo.-No. Ill. chpt., 1981—. Mem. Am. Inst. C.P.A.'s, Ill. Soc. C.P.A.'s, Inst. Corp. Controllers. Roman Catholic. Office: McDonald's Corp One McDonald's Plaza Oak Brook IL 60521

CANTARINO, VICENTE, linguist, educator; b. Lerida, Spain, May 12, 1925; came to U.S., 1958, naturalized, 1964; s. Isidro and Carmen C.; m. Baerbel Becker, Aug. 12, 1960; children—Christine, Suzanne, Myra. Licenza, Pontificia Università, Gregoriana, Rome, 1948; Ph.D., U. Munich, Germany, 1957. Instr. U. N.C., 1959-62; asst. prof. Spanish and Arabic, 1962-64, asso. prof., 1964-65, Ind. U., 1965-68, prof., 1968-69; prof. Spanish and Portuguese U. Tex., Austin, 1969—. Author: Der neuaramaeische Dialekt von Gubb "Adin', 1961, Syntax of Modern Arabic Prose, vol. I, 1974, vols. II and III,1975, Arabic Poetics in the Golden Age, 1975, Qasidas de amor, profano y místico Ibn Zaidun, Ibn Arabi, Textos poéticos y estudio, 1977, Entre monjes y musulmanes: El conflicto que fué España, 1978, Civilización y cultura de España, 1981. NDEA summer research fellow, 1960. Mem. Medieval Acad. Am., Am. Oriental Soc., MLA, Am. Assn. Tchrs. Spanish and Portuguese, Dante Soc. Am., Middle East Studies Assn., Asociación de Orientalistas Españoles, Internat. Assn. Comparative Lit. Office: Dept Spanish and Portuguese U Tex Austin TX 78712

CANTELLA, VINCENT MICHELE, stock broker; b. Boston, Oct. 27, 1917; s. Michele and Josephine (Sapienza) C.; m. Josephine R. Castanien, Nov. 19, 1944; children—Betsy Ann, David V., Steven M. B.S., Boston U., 1939. Mng. partner Cantella & Co., Boston, 1963-74; partner Josephthal & Co., Boston, 1974-78; pres. Cantella & Co. Inc., 1979; Mem. Boston Stock Exchange, 1953—, bd. govs., mem. exec. com., 1963-74, 79—, chmn. exec. com., 1971-73, chmn. bd. govs., 1973-74; mem. Midwest Stock Exchange, 1965-72, Pacific Coast Stock Exchange, 1965-78, N.Y. Stock Exchange, 1969-78, Detroit Stock Exchange, 1963-76, P.B.W. Stock Exchange, 1970-73, Am. Stock Exchange, 1972-75; dir. Prince Macaroni Co., 1980—. Served to maj. USMC, World War II. Mem. Boston Fin. Research Assn. Clubs: N.Y. Athletic; Algonguin (Boston). Home: 635 Lewis Wharf Boston MA 02110 Office: One Court St Boston MA 02108

CANTELON, JOHN EDWARD, university official; b. Warroad, Minn., June 20, 1924; s. Arthur Edward and Georgia (Turnbull);; s. Arthur Edward and Georgia (Cantelon); m. Joy Elizabeth Norton, Aug. 16, 1953; children: Barbara Jean, Charles Norton. Student, U. Man., 1941-42; B.A., Reed Coll., 1948; Ph.D., Oxford U., 1951; D.H.L., Hebrew Union Coll.-Jewish Inst. Religion, 1972. Ordained to ministry, 1952; pastor Fairmont Presbyn. Ch., Eugene, Oreg., 1952-53; mem. staff Christian Assn., U. Pa., 1953-57; asso. sec. div. higher edn. United Presbyn. Ch., Phila., 1957-60; univ. chaplain, asso. prof. U. So. Calif., 1960-67, prof., dir., 1967-70, vice-provost, dean, 1970-72, v.p. undergrad. studies, 1972-76, Bicentennial prof., 1976; provost, v.p. for acad. affairs Central Mich. U., Mt. Pleasant, 1976—, distinguished prof., 1976—; pres. Middle Mich. Devel. Corp., 1981—. Author: Higher Education and the Campus Revolution, 1969, a Protestant Approach to the Campus Ministry, 1964. Served with AUS, 1943-45. Recipient Gov. Gen.'s medal acad. excellence Neepawa Collegiate Inst., 1941. Mem. Newcomen Soc., Phi Beta Kappa, Phi Kappa Phi, Blue Key, Skull and Dagger, Sigma Iota Epsilon. Home: 717 Kane St Mount Pleasant MI 48858 Office: Office of Provost: Central Mich U Mount Pleasant MI 48859

CANTER, MILTON ERNEST, lawyer, corp. exec.; b. Poughkeepsie, N.Y., Nov. 21, 1908; s. Jacob and Jennie (Abrams) C. B.A., Union Coll., Schenectady, 1929; LL.B., St. Lawrence U., 1932, J.D., 1967. Bar: N.Y. bar 1935, D.C. bar 1947. Reporter Bklyn. Eagle, 1930-31; editor-in-chief, founder Bklyn. Law Rev., 1932; editor-in-chief Justinian (legal newspaper), 1931-33; pub. relations counsel N.Y.C. Housing Authority, 1934; asst. counsel Joint Legislative Com. Investigate Pub. Utilities State N.Y., 1934-36; gen. practice law, N.Y.C., 1935-37; assn. counsel N.Y. State Pub. Service Commn., 1937-39; spl. prosecutor to investigate N.Y. State Ins. Fund, 1939-40; referee N.Y. State Tax Commn., 1941; dir. priorities div. War Assets Adminstrn., 1945-46; sr. mem. firm Canter, McLaughlin & Urow, Washington, 1947—; dir. Washington-Balt. Helicopter Airways Service, B. Manischewitz Co. (and affiliated cos.), 1960-75; chmn. bd. Am. Rail & Steel Co., 1948-68; pres. Potomac Investment Corp.; Mem. U.S. Expn. of Sci. and Industry; sec. Mayor N.Y.C. Com. Real Property Inventory, 1934; mem. com. investigate 3d degree methods N.Y. Criminal Bar, 1934. Author: Rates and Ratemaking for Public Utilities, 1937, Weather Flying, 1944. Mem. N.Y. State Democratic Pub. Relations Bur., 1929-30; vice chmn. finance com. Dem. Nat. Com., 1946-47; mem. Nat. Dem. Club.; Nat. bd. dirs. Boys' Clubs Am.; bd. dirs., trustee Freedoms Found. at Valley Forge; mem. advisory council George Washington U., 1969-73. Served to capt. USAAF, 1942-45. Mem. Am., N.Y. State, D.C. bar assns., Washington Bd. Trade, Am. Legion (comdr. Nat. Def. Post 1966), Tau Kappa Alpha, Zeta Beta Tau. Clubs: Army and Navy (gov.), Federal City (Washington)). Home: Canterbury Doncaster MD 21914 Office: 1025 15th St NW Washington DC 20005 *While most people measure success in terms of accumulated wealth, and while I have been successful from that point of view, my real success has been the achievement of independence. This has permitted me to assist in the furtherance of my major goals which include the maintenance and improvement of our democracy in its present form, and the preservation of religious institutions of every kind.*

CANTER, STANLEY D., marketing consulting company executive; b. N.Y.C., Dec. 10, 1923; s. Frank and Rose (Posner) Kanter. B.S., Coll. City N.Y., 1944; M.A., Columbia, 1947. Econ. analyst Econometric Inst., N.Y.C., 1944-45; dir. mktg. research McCann-Erickson, 1947-57; sr. v.p., dir. Ogilvy & Mather, 1957-73; pres. Canter, Achenbaum, Assocs., N.Y.C., 1974—. Served with USAAF, 1945-46. Mem. AAAS, Inst. Math. Statistics, Am. Statis. Assn., Am. Mktg. Assn., Market Research Council, Copy Research Council. Home: 10 Waterside Plaza New York NY 10010 Office: 950 3d Ave New York NY 10017

CANTEY, JAMES WILLIS, banker; b. Columbia, S.C., 5Mar. 3, 1917; s. J.M. and Elizabeth (Childs) C.; m. Nancy Moorer, Apr. 19, 1941; children—James Willis, Joseph Moorer, John Childs. B.A., U. S.C., 1938. With Columbia Outdoor Advt., Inc., 1945-58, pres., 1947-58, chmn. bd., 1973—; with Citizens & So. Nat. Bank S.C., Charleston, 1958-74, pres., 1960-71, chmn. bd., 1971-74, also dir.; dir. Liberty Life Ins. Co., Carolina Freight Carriers Corp., State-Record Newspaper, Standard Bldg. & Loan Assn., Charlotte br. Fed. Res. Bank, 1967-72. Chmn. S.C. Ports Authority, 1956-64. Served with inf. AUS, World War II. Decorated Silver Star (3), Bronze Star (4), Legion of Merit, Purple Heart; Croix de Guerre, France). Mem. S.C. Bankers Assn. (pres. 1966—), Sigma Alpha Epsilon. Episcopalian. Club: Kiwanian. Home: 1400 Westminster Dr Columbia SC 29204 Office: PO Box 727 Columbia SC 29202

CANTIENI, GRAHAM ALFRED, art educator; b. Australia, Aug. 26, 1938; emigrated to Can., 1968, naturalized, 1973; s. Alfred Cyril and Meryl Edith (Greenwood) C.; (div.)children: Angela, David. Diploma, Royal Melbourne Tchrs. Coll., 1958. Art master Edn. Dept., Victoria, Melbourne, 1959-65; matriculation art examiner fine arts dept. U. Melbourne, 1964-65; attache de recherche en psychomathematiques U. Sherbrooke, Que., Can., 1968-72; animator Ateliers d'animation culturelle, Sherbrooke, 1969-76; artistic dir. Cultural Center, Sherbrooke, 1976-83; vis. prof. U. Victoria (B.C.), 1983—. Co-founder, Cahiers (art rev.), 1979; founder, dir., 10.5155.20 (art rev.), 1982; Co-author: Mathematique concrète et langue seconde, 1974; Contbr. articles to profl. jours. Que. Ministry Cultural Affairs grantee, 1971, 76. Mem. Found. du Regroupment des Artistes des Cantons de L'Est Sherbrooke (pres. 1973-76), Soc. des Artistes Profls. Que. (v.p. 1977), Darcheu (founding dir. 1982). Address: CP 608 Sherbrooke PQ J1H 5K5 Canada

CANTINI, VIRGIL D., artist; b. Italy, Feb. 28, 1920; 2 children. Student, Manhattan Coll., 1940; B.F.A., Carnegie Inst. Tech., 1946; M.A., U. Pitts., 1948; postgrad., Cleve. Inst. Art, 1947, Alfred U., 1948, Showhegan Sch. Art, 1949, Kalamazoo Inst. Art, 1966; D.F.A. (hon.), Duquesne U., 1981. Partner Tech. Indsl. Models, 1946-48; with Pitts. Public Schs., 1948-52; instr. fine arts U. Pitts., 1952-55, asst. prof., 1955-58, asso. prof., 1948-61, prof., 1961—, chmn. studio arts and art edn., 1968—. Exhibited in group shows including, World's Fair, Brussells, Belgium, 1958, Carnegie Inst., 1964, St. Louis Mus., Pitts. Internat., 1967, Carnegie Mus., 1945-70, U. Pitts., 1968, Pitts. Ctr. for Arts, 1982, one-man shows, Westmoreland County Mus. Art, Greensburg, Pa., 1962; Pitts. Plan for Art, 1962, 71, 75, 79, Mansfield (Pa.) State Coll., 1973, William Penn Meml. Mus., Harrisburg, Pa., 1977, Brookfield (Conn.) Craft Center Gallery, 1981, Philip Dressler Ctr. for Arts, Somerset, Pa., 1982; represented in permanent collections, Carnegie Mus. Art, Pitts., Greensburg County Mus. Art, Greensburg, Pa., Wichita (Kans.) Mus. Art, Duquesne U., Pitts., Mt. Mercy Coll., Pitts., Seton Hill Coll., LaSalle Acad., Phila., also chs., pub. schs., pvt. collections, numerous artistic commns., latest including: Pitts. mural, Oliver Tyrone Co., 1970, sculpture, U. Pitts., Johnstown, 1971 (commemorative medal honoring Roberto Clemente 1973), murals, U. Pitts., 1974, 75, 77, enamel cross, 1st Luth. Ch., Pitts., 1976 (1st prize for sculpture Asso. Artists Pitts.); enamel panel, Armstrong County Meml. Hosp., Kittanning, Pa., 1982, Pitts. Steeler trophy, 1982. Guggenheim fellow, 1958; recipient Pope Paul VI Bishops medal, 1964, 1st prize for sculpture Associated Artists Pitts., 1964, DaVinci medal I.S.D.A. Cultural Heritage Found., 1968, Arts and Scis. award KC, 1971. Address: Dept Studio Arts U Pittsburgh Pittsburgh PA 15260

CANTLAY, GEORGE GORDON, retired army officer; b. Honolulu, Aug. 2, 1920; s. George Gordon and Helen (Reid) C.; m. Wilhelmina Shannon Davison, Apr. 27, 1946; children: George Gordon III, Donald Davison, Carolyn Reid. Student, U. Hawaii, 1938-39; B.S., U.S. Mil. Acad., 1943; grad., Armor Sch., 1952, Command and Gen. Staff Coll., 1955, Army War Coll., 1962; M.A., George Washington U., 1963. Commd. 2d lt. U.S. Army, 1943, advanced through grades to lt. gen., 1977; mem. faculty Army War Coll., 1962-65; brigade comdr. 2d Inf. Div., Korea, 1965-66; chief congl. activities div. Office Chief of Staff of Army, 1966-68; asst. div. comdr. 1st Inf. Div., Vietnam, 1968-69; dep. comdg. gen. Delta Mil. Assistance Command, Vietnam, 1969-70; comdg. gen. U.S. Army Armor Tng. Center, 1970; dep. comdg. gen. U.S. Army Armor Center, Fort Knox, Ky., 1970-71; comdg. gen. 2d Armored Div., Ft. Hood, Tex., 1971-73; dep. U.S. rep. NATO Mil. Com., Brussels, Belgium, 1973-77, dep. chmn. com., 1977-79. Decorated Def. Disting. Service medal, D.S.M., Silver Star medal, Legion of Merit with three oak leaf clusters, D.F.C. with oak leaf cluster, Bronze Star with V device and oak leaf cluster, Air medal with 16 oak leaf clusters, Army Commendation medal with oak leaf cluster, Purple Heart; RVN Army Distinguished Service Order 1st Class; RVN Gallantry Cross with palm; RVN Armed Forces Honor medal 1st Class, Republic Vietnam). Mem. Armor Assn., Assn. U.S. Army, Assn. Grads. U.S. Mil. Acad. Episcopalian. Clubs: Army and Navy, Army Navy Country (Washington). Home: PO Box 1335 Kailua HI 96734

CANTLON, JOHN EDWARD, university official; b. Sparks, Nev., Oct. 6, 1921; s. John Edward and Anna (Riddle) C.; m. Carolyne Irene Riley, Aug. 20, 1944; children: John Edward (dec.), William Howard, Carolyne Ann, Robert Dean. B.S., U. Nev., 1947; Ph.D., Rutgers U., 1950. Asst. prof. George Washington U., 1950-52, asso. prof., 1952-53; sr. ecologist Boston U., 1953-54; asso. prof. Mich. State U. at East Lansing, 1954-58, prof. botany and plant pathology, 1958, provost, 1969-75, v.p. research and grad. studies, 1975—; program dir. environmental biology NSF, Washington, 1965-66, adv. com. div. environmental sci., 1966-69, adv. com. instl. devel. program, 1970-74; adv. com. health physics Oak Ridge Nat. Lab., 1966-69, mem. adv. council, 1970-75; mem. nat. research council, exec. com., div. biology and agr. Nat. Acad. Sci., 1969-71; mem. Commn. on Natural Resources, chmn. environ. studies bd., 1977-80; chmn. sci. adv. bd. EPA, 1978-82; vice chmn. bd. dirs. World Resources Inst., 1982—. Contbr. articles to profl. jours. Served with USNR, 1942-45. Recipient Distinguished Faculty award Mich. State U., 1964. Mem. Ecol. Soc. Am. (sec. 1958-61, v.p. 1965-66, pres. 1968-69), A.A.A.S. (exec. com. 1970-72), Am. Inst. Biol. Scientists (gov. bd. 1962-65), Mich. Energy Resources Research Assn. (chmn. bd. 1979-80). Home: 1795 Bramble Dr East Lansing MI 48823

CANTONE, VIC, political cartoonist; b. N.Y.C., Aug. 7, 1933. Grad., Sch. Art and Design, N.Y.C., 1952, Art Instrn. Schs., Inc., Mpls., 1978; A.A. cum laude, Nassau Coll., Garden City, N.Y., 1978; B.A., Hofstra U., 1979. Cartoonist Newsday, Garden City, N.Y., 1954-59; Polit. cartoonist/caricaturist N.Y. Daily News, 1959—, Editor and Pub. mag., 1973-78, WPIX-TV Wall Street Jour. Report; syndicated polit. cartoonist/caricaturist Rothco Cartoon Syndicate, 1980—; lectr. on media, terrorism. Exhibited widely work in permanent collections. Recipient Bicentennial Trophy award Aux. Am. Legion, 1976; Golden Press award, 1979; Fourth Estate award Am. Legion, 1976; Valley Forge Honor Cert. award Freedoms Found., 1976; Cert. of Recognition award NCCJ, 1977; Patriotic Service award U.S. Dept. Treas., 1978; George Washington honor medal award Freedoms Found., 1978. Mem. Assn. Am. Editorial Cartoonists. Club: N.Y. Press. Office: NY Daily News 220 E 42d St New York NY 10017 *The political cartoonist is a powerful political weapon in that a public image can be shaped. Therefore, the burden of responsibility rests heaviest upon the political cartoonist to triumph in common sense, over myths and hysteria, over nostalgia or paranoia.*

CANTONI, GIULIO LEONARDO, biochemist, grovernment official; b. Milan, Italy, Sept. 29, 1915; s. Umerto L. and Nella (Pesaro) C.; m. Gabriella S. Sobrero, May 29, 1965; children: Allegra, Serena. M.D., U. Milan, 1938. Research asst. dept. pharmacology Oxford U., Eng., 1940; instr. NYU, N.Y.C., 1943-45; asst. prof. L.I. Coll. Medicine, N.Y., 1945-48; sr. fellow Am. Cancer Soc., N.Y.C., 1948-50; assoc. prof. Western Res. U., Cleve., 1950-54; chief lab. cellular pharmacology NIMH, NIH, Bethesda, Md., 1954-56, chief lab. gen. and comparative biochemistry, 1956—. Patentee 3-Deazaaristeromycin and uses. Mem. Nat. Acad. Scis., Am. Acad. Arts and Scis., Am. Chem. Soc., Biochem. Soc. Eng., Am. Soc. Biol. Chemists. Home: 6938 Blaisdell Rd Bethesda MD 20817 Office: NIMH Bldg 36 Room 3A-17 9000 Rockville Pike Bethesda MD 20205

CANTONI, LOUIS JOSEPH, psychologist, poet; b. Detroit, May 22, 1919; s. Pietro and Stella (Puricelli) C.; m. Lucile Eudora Moses, Aug. 7, 1948; children: Christopher Louis, Sylvia Therese. A.B., U. Calif. at Berkeley, 1946; M.S.W., U. Mich., 1949, Ph.D., 1953. Personnel mgr. Johns-Manville Corp., Pittsburg, Calif., 1944-46; social caseworker Detroit Dept. Pub. Welfare, 1946-49; counselor Mich. Div. Vocat. Rehab., Detroit, 1949-50; conf. leader, tchr. psychology, coordinator family and community relations program Gen. Motors Inst., Flint, Mich., 1951-56; from asso. prof. to prof., dir. rehab. counseling Wayne State U., Detroit, 1956—. Author: (with Mrs. Cantoni) books including Counseling Your Friends, 1961, With Joy I Called to You (poetry), 1969, Supervised Practice in Rehabilitation Counseling, 1978; (poetry) Gradually The Dreams Change, 1979; Editor: Placement of the Handicapped in Competitive Employment, 1957; Editor jours.: Mich. Rehab. Assn. Digest, 1961-63, Grad. Comment, 1963-64; Contbr. articles, revs. and poems to jours. Judge Mich. regional and nat. essay and poetry contests, 1965-77; bd. dirs. Mich. Rehab. Assn., 1962-64, 78-79. Served to 2d lt. AUS, 1942-44. Recipient award for leadership and service Mich. Rehab. Assn., 1964; South and West ann. poetry award, 1970; Award for Meritorious Service Wayne State U., 1971, 81. Fellow AAAS; mem. AAUP, Council of Rehab. Counselor Educators (sec. 1957-58, chmn. 1965-66), Am. Psychol. Assn., Am. Personnel and Guidance Assn., Nat. Rehab. Assn., Mich. Rehab. Assn. (pres. 1963-64), Detroit Rehab. Assn. (pres. 1958), World Poetry Soc., Acad. Am. Poets, Detroit Inst. Arts, Poetry Soc. Mich., Phi Kappa Phi, Phi Delta Kappa. Democrat. Episcopalian. Home: 2591 Woodstock Dr Detroit MI 48203 Office: Wayne State Univ Detroit MI 48202 *His destination, when he set out, was pure poetry, although he did not recognize it. He came to cherish the gifts of sun, rain, a walk in the woods, a brightening smile. His wife radiates the clear beauty of mature women. His children, albeit circuitously, have taken on his values. He feels near to man and God and views death as another beginning. He has reached his destination many times and welcomes sunset as well as sunrise, conflict as well as calm. He knows now that much of his life has been pure poetry.*

CANTOR, ARTHUR, theatrical producer, film distributor; b. Boston, Mar. 12, 1920; s. Samuel S. and Lillian (Landsman) C.; m. Deborah Rosmarin (dec.); children: David Jonathan, Jacqueline Hope, Michael Stephen. Producer: plays on and off Broadway, including The Tenth Man, 1961, A Thousand Clowns, All the Way Home (recipient Pulitzer prize and N.Y. Drama Critics Circle award), Vivat: Vivat Regina:, In Praise of Love, Private Lives, The Constant Wife, St. Mark's Gospel, On Golden Pond, The Hothouse; author: (with Stuart Little) The Playmakers, 1970. Jewish. Club: Harvard (N.Y.C.). Home: 1 W 72d St New York NY 10023 Office: Arthur Cantor Inc 33 W 60th St PH New York NY 10023 *After all these years, it is now clear to me that I must accept totalresponsibility for whatever has happened and will happen in my life. Neither blind fate nor stars in their courses nor some unseen and unseeing power can or should guide me. I have complete faith in the dignity of life and in the perfectibility of mankind. If I can achieve a kind of bravery each living day, that is the only success I cherish and that must endure.*

CANTOR, BERNARD JACK, patent lawyer; b. N.Y.C., Aug. 18, 1927; s. Alexander J. and Tillie (Henzeloff) C.; m. Judith L. Levin, Mar. 25, 1951; children—Glenn H., Cliff A., James E., Ellen B., Mark E. B. Mech. Engring., Cornell, 1949; J.D., George Washington U., Washington, 1952. Bar: D.C. bar 1952, U.S. Patent Office bar 1952, Mich. bar 1953. Examiner U.S. Patent Office, Washington, 1949-52; practice patent law, Detroit, 1952—; partner firm Cullen, Sloman, Cantor, Grauer, Scott & Rutherford, Detroit, 1952—; lectr. in field. Contbr. articles on patent law to profl. jours. Mem. Council Detroit Area Boy Scouts Am., 1972—; trustee Fresh Air Soc. of Detroit. Served with AUS, 1944-46. Recipient Ellsworth award patent law George Washington U., 1952; Shofar award Boy Scouts Am., 1975; Silver Beaver award, 1975. Mem. Am. Technion Soc. (v.p. Detroit 1970—), Am., Mich., Detroit bar assns., Mich. Patent Law Assn., Am. Arbitration Assn., Cornell Engring. Soc., Pi Tau Sigma, Phi Delta Phi, Beta Sigma Rho. Home: 5685 Forman Dr Birmingham MI 48010 Office: 3200 City Nat Bldg Detroit MI 48226

CANTOR, CHARLES ROBERT, biochemistry educator; b. Blkyn., Aug. 26, 1942; s. Louis and Ida Dianne (Banks) C. A.B. summa cum laude, Columbia U., 1963; Ph.D., U. Calif., Berkeley, 1966. Asst. prof. chemistry Columbia, N.Y.C., 1966-69, assoc. prof. chemistry and biol. scis., 1969-72; prof. Columbia U., 1972-81; prof., chmn. human genetics and devel. Columbia (Coll. Phys. and Surgs.), 1981—; dep. dir. comprehensive Cancer ctr.; Sherman Fairchild vis. scholar Calif. Inst. Tech., 1975-76; mem. biophysics and biophys. chemistry study sect. NIH, 1971-75; mem. cell and molecular basis of disease rev. com. NIGMS, 1977-81; mem. ozone update com. NRC, 1983; trustee Cold Spring Harbor Lab., 1977—; mem. proposal rev. panel Stanford Sychrotron Radiation Lab., 1976—. Author: (with Paul R. Schimmel) Biophysical Chemistry, I, II, III; assoc. editor: Ann. Rev. Biophysics, 1983—. Alfred P. Sloan fellow, 1969-71; Guggenheim fellow, 1973-74; Recipient Fresenius award Phi Lambda Upsilon, 1972; Eli Lilly award in biol. chemistry Am. Chem. Soc., 1978. Fellow Am. Acad. Arts and Scis.; mem. Am. Soc. Biol. Chemists, Am. Chem. Soc., Biophys. Soc. (mem. council 1977-81), Soc. Analytical Cytology, Harvey Soc. Home: 560 Riverside Dr New York NY 10027 Office: Dept Human Genetics and Devel Coll Physicians and Surgeons Columbia University New York NY 10032

CANTOR, DAVID GEOFFREY, educator; b. London, Eng., Apr. 12, 1935; came to U.S., 1940; s. Joseph and Sally (Heller) C.; m. Hariet Lebedinsky, Dec. 21, 1958; children—Judith, Michael. B.S., Calif. Inst. Tech., 1956; Ph.D., U. Calif. at Los Angeles, 1960. Instr. Princeton, 1960-62; asst. prof. U. Wash., 1962-64; mem. faculty U. Calif. at Los Angeles, 1964—, prof. math. and computer sci., 1969—; cons. to govt. and industry Inst. for Def. Analyses. Author: (with others) A Fortran Program for Elastic Scattering Analyses with the Nuclear Optical Model, 1958; also research papers. Sloan fellow, 1968-70. Sr. mem. I.E.E.E.; mem. Am. Math. Soc., Math. Assn. Am., Assn. for Computing Machinery, Soc. Indsl. and Applied Math. Office: Dept Math Univ Calif Los Angeles CA 90024

CANTOR, EDWARD ALLEN, construction company executive; b. Jersey City, Jan. 23, 1928; s. Harry and Winnie (Levine) C.; m. Janette Linsker, July 15, 1968; children by previous marriage: Cheryl, Michael. Student, N.Y. U., 1945-46. Sales mgr., purchasing agt., v.p., exec. v.p., dir. United Lacquer Mfg. Corp., 1947-63; chmn. bd., pres. Canfield Realty & Constrn. Corp., 1962-66; dir. Gen. Magnaplate Corp., 1967-69; chmn. bd., officer Am. Container Corp., 1967-70; chmn. bd., pres. Haren Holding Corp., 1952-71, Edward Constrn. Corp., Linden, N.J., 1951—, also; Eastern Lumber & Bldg. Supply, Inc., Mileed Industrials, Inc., Edward A. Cantor Affiliated Interests, Inc., N.J. Indsl. Properties, Inc., Mfrs. Office Bldgs., Inc., Camaco, Inc.; chmn. bd., v.p. Continental Plastics & Chems., Inc.; chmn. bd., sec. Prime Photo Labs.; chmn. bd. Deal Products, Inc., DL Scaffolding, DME Energy Systems, Inc.; ptnr. Western Oil & Gas Fields, Gelco Co.; dir., ptnr., founder Halpert, Oberst and Co.; former hon. consul Govt. of Nicaragua. Served with USAAF, 1946-47. Mem. Indsl. Real Estate Brokers Assn., N.J. Home Builders Assn. (past pres.), U.S. Coastal Cadets (rear adm.). Clubs: Masons, Atlantis Yacht (past commodore Monmouth Beach, N.J.); Ocean Reef (N. Key Largo, Fla.)). Home: 70 Crest Dr South Orange NJ 07079 Office: 1203 W St George Ave Linden NJ 07036

CANTOR, GEORGE NATHAN, journalist; b. Detroit, June 14, 1941; s. Harold and Evelyn (Grossman) C.; m. Sheryl Joyce Bershad, Dec. 7, 1975; children: Jaime, Courtney. B.A., Wayne State U., 1962. Reporter, editor Detroit Free Press, 1963-77; columnist Detroit News, 1977—; commentator WWJ-Radio, Detroit, 1981—, WXYZ-TV, 1982—. Author: The Great Lakes Guidebook, 3 vols., 1978-80. Bd. dirs. Greater Detroit Area Hosp. Council, 1983. Recipient Malcolm Bingay Wayne State U., 1962, Paul Tobenaw Meml. Columbia U., 1980, Disting. Achievement UPI, 1982. Mem. Phi Beta Kappa. Jewish. Office: Detroit News 615 W Lafayette Blvd Detroit MI 48231

CANTOR, MURIEL G., sociologist, educator; b. Mpls., Mar. 2, 1923; d. Leo and Bess Goldsman; m. Joel M. Cantor, Aug. 6, 1944; children: Murray Robert, Jane Cantor Shefler, James Leo. B.A., UCLA, 1964, M.A., 1966, Ph.D., 1969. Lectr. dept. econs. and sociology Immaculate Heart Coll., Los Angeles, 1966-68; faculty Am. U., Washington, 1968—, instr., 1968-69, asst. prof. sociology, 1969-72, asso. prof., 1972-76, dept. chmn., 1973-75, 77-79, prof., 1976—; vis. prof. communication studies UCLA, 1982; cons. agencies including NIMH; cons. Corp. for Public Broadcasting, 1974-75, 80-81. Author: The Hollywood TV Producer: His Work and His Audience, 1971, Prime Time Television: Content and Control, 1980, Varieties of Work Experience, 1974, (with Phyllis L. Stewart) Varieties of Work, 1982, (with Suzanne Pingree) The Soap Opera, 1983; editor: Nat. SWS newsletter, 1977-78. Bd. dirs. Population Inst., 1978-80; trustee WETA, 1972-76. NIMH grantee, 1979-81. Mem. Am. Sociol. Assn., D.C. Sociol. Soc. (pres. 1977-78), Sociologists for Women in Society, Eastern Sociol. Soc. (exec. council 1981—), So. Sociol. Soc. Home: 8408 Whitman Dr Bethesda MD 20817 Office: Dept Sociology American U Washington DC 20016

CANTOR, NORMAN FRANK, educator, historian; b. Winnipeg, Man., Can., Nov. 19, 1929; came to U.S., 1957, naturalized, 1968; s. Max W. and Elizabeth (Niznick) C.; m. Mindy Mozart, Aug. 25, 1957; children: Howard, Judith. B.A. with honors, U. Man., 1951; M.A., Princeton U., 1953, Ph.D. (Porter Ogden Jacobus fellow), 1957; postgrad. (Rhodes scholar), Oxford (Eng.) U., 1954-55; LL.D. (hon.), U. Winnipeg, 1973. Instr. Princeton U., 1955-59, asst. prof. history, 1959-60; asso. prof. Columbia U., 1960-65, prof., 1965-66; Leff prof. Brandeis U., 1966-70; disting. prof. SUNY, Binghamton, 1970-76, provost for grad. studies, 1974-75, v.p. acad. affairs, 1975-76; vice chancellor for acad. affairs U. Ill., Chgo., 1976-78; dean faculty Arts and Sci. NYU, 1978-81, prof. history, sociology and comparative lit., 1981—, dir. Inst. Cultural Analysis, 1981—. Author: Church, Kingship and Lay Investiture, 1958, Medieval History, 1963, The English, 1968, Western Civilization, 1972. Am. Council Learned Socs.-Can. Council fellow, 1960. Fellow Royal Hist. Soc. Office: 113 University Place 9th Floor New York NY 10003 *

CANTOR, SAMUEL C., lawyer; b. Phila., Mar. 11, 1919; s. Joseph and Miryl (Ginzberg) C.; m. Dorothy Van Brink, Apr. 9, 1943; children: Judith Ann Stone, Barbara Ann Palm. B.S.S., CCNY, 1940; J.D., Columbia, 1943. Bar: N.Y. 1943, U.S. Dist. Ct. (so. and ea. dists.) N.Y. 1951, U.S. Supreme Ct 1969, D.C. 1971. Asst. dist. atty., N.Y.C., 1943-48; legislative counsel N.Y. State Senate; counsel N.Y.C. Affairs Com. N.Y. State Senate, 1949-59; mem. firm Newcomb, Woolsey & Cantor, Newcomb & Cantor, N.Y.C., 1951-59; 1st dep. supt. ins. State of N.Y., 1959-64, acting supt. ins., 1963-64; 2d v.p., gen. solicitor Mut. Life Ins. Co. N.Y., 1964-66, v.p., gen. counsel, 1967-72, sr. v.p., gen. counsel, 1973-74, sr. v.p. law and external affairs, 1974-75, sr. v.p. law and corporate affairs, 1975-78, exec. v.p. law and corp. affairs, 1978-84; counsel Rogers & Wells, 1984—; dir. Mony Reins. Corp., Monyco, Inc., Key Resources, Inc., Mony Advisors, Inc., Mony Sales, Inc., 1740 Ventures, Inc.; chmn. exec. com. N.Y. Life Ins. Guaranty Corp., 1974—; Mem. spl. com. on ins. holding holding cos. N.Y. Supt. Ins., 1967, N.Y. State select com. pub. employee pensions, 1973. Contbr. to various legal and ins. publs. Fellow Am. Bar Found.; mem. Ins. Fedn. N.Y. (pres. 1967-68), Am. Bar Assn., N.Y. State Bar Assn., Am. Life Conv. (v.p. N.Y. State 1965-70), Am. Council Life Ins. (chmn. legal sect. 1977, chmn. legis. com. 1977-78, N.Y. State v.p. 1977-84), Health Ins. Assn. Am. (chmn. govt. relations com. 1975, chmn. health care com. N.Y. State 1974-80), Assn. Life Ins. Counsel (dir.), Am. Judicature Soc., Bar Assn. City N.Y., N.Y. Law Inst., Nat., N.Y. State dist. attys. assns., Union Internationale des Avocats, Columbia Law Sch. Alumni Assn. (dir.). Clubs: Mason., University (N.Y.C.); Metropolitan, University (Washington); Fort Orange (Albany, N.Y.); Ponte Vedra (Fla.); Confrérie des Chevaliers du Tastevin; Fairview Country (Greenwich, Conn.). Home: Audubon Ln Greenwich CT 06830 Office: 1740 Broadway New York NY 10019

CANTRELL, JOSEPH DOYLE, newspaper company executive; b. Ft. Pierce, Fla., Oct. 18, 1944; s. Joseph C. and Zula (Doyle) C.; m. Carolyn Dearmond, Aug. 12, 1966 (dec. 1966); 1 son, Joseph; m. 2d Sandra Jordan, Aug. 20, 1975; 1 son, Thomas. A.B., Transylvania U., 1967; M.B.A., U. Ky., 1968. Profl. acct. Ernst & Ernst, Louisville, 1969; fin. analyst to dir. fin. Courier-Jour. and Louisville Times Co., 1969-78; exec. v.p., gen. mgr. Sentinel Star Co., Orlanda, Fla., 1978—. Trustee, v.p. Loch Haven Art Centre, Orlando, Fla., 1981—; pres. Orlando-Orange County Conv. and Vistors Bur., 1983-84. Mem. Inst. Newspaper Controllers and Fin. Officers (pres., dir.), Orlando C. of C. (pres., dir., Pres.'s award 1983). Baptist. Lodge: Orlando Rotary. Office: Sentinel Communications Co 633 N Orange Ave Orlando FL 32801

CANTRELL, LANA, singer, actress; b. Sydney, Australia, Aug. 7, 1943; d. Hubert Clarence and Dorothy Jean (Thistlethwaite) C. Singer supper clubs, TV programs, Australia, 1958-62; U.S. debut: TV show The Tonight Show, NBC, 1962; rec. artist, RCA and Polydor Records, 1967—; (Grammy award as Most Promising New Female Artist, Nat. Assn. Rec. Arts and Scis. 1967). Pres. Thrush, Inc.; U.S. rep. Internat. Song Festival, Poland, 1966, UN Internat. Women's Year Concert, Paris, France, 1975. Recipient 1st prize Internat. Song Festival, Poland, 1966; 1st Internat. Woman of Yr. award Feminist Party, 1973. Office: 300 E 71st St New York NY 10021

CANTRELL, ROBERT WENDELL, otolaryngologist, educator; b. Neosho, Mo., Apr. 25, 1933; s. Lloyd L. and Ruby R. C.; m. Lee Y. Cantrell, Feb. 6, 1964; children: Mark L., Elizabeth L., Victoria L., Robert W., Jr. Student, U.S. Naval Acad., 1952-55; A.B., George Washington U., 1956, M.D., 1960. Intern N.Y. Hosp-Cornell U., 1960-61; resident in otolaryngology Nat. Naval Med. Center, Bethesda, Md., 1965-69; chmn. dept. otolaryngology Naval Regional Med. Center, San Diego, 1969-76; Fitz-Hugh prof. dept. otolaryngology-head and neck surgery U. Va., 1976—, chmn. dept., 1976—. Editorial bd.: Laryngoscope, 1976—, Annals of Otology, Rhinology and Laryngology, 1977—, Am. Jour. of Otolaryngology, 1978—, Archives of Otolaryngology, 1979—; Contbr. numerous articles in field to profl. jours. Mayor City of Oakmont, Md., 1968-69. Served to capt. USN, 1961-76. Am. Heart Assn. fellow, 1969; recipient Huron W. Lawson prize, 1960. Mem. AMA, Am. Acad. Otolaryngology, Am. Council Otolaryngology, Am. Acad. Facial Plastic and Reconstructive Surgery (v.p. So. sect. 1980-83), Triological Soc. (Mosher award 1974), Am. Soc. Head and Neck Surgery (treas. 1979—), Soc. Univ. Otolaryngologists (pres. 1982), Am. Broncho-Esophagological Assn., Am. Laryngological Assn., A.C.S., Am. Otol. Soc., Alpha Omega Alpha. Episcopalian. Home: RFD 5 Box 385 Charlottesville VA 22901 Office: Box 430 University of Virginia Medical Center Charlottesville VA 22908

CANTRELL, WILLIAM ALLEN, psychiatrist, educator; b. Everton, Ark., Nov. 6, 1920; s. William E. and Vida (Vinson) C.; m. Joyce LaRee Hobbs, Jan. 17, 1945; children: Mary Elizabeth, William Robert. B.S., McMurray Coll., 1940; M.D., U. Tex., 1943. Rotating intern U.S. Naval Hosp., Corona, Calif., 1943-44; resident neuropsychiatry U. Tex. Med. Br. Hosps., 1947-49; asst. prof. neuropsychiatry U. Tex. Med. Br., 1949-54; practice medicine specializing in psychiatry, Houston, 1951-63; prof. psychiatry Baylor Coll. Medicine, Houston, 1963—; chief psychiatry service Meth. Hosp., Houston, 1966-73. Mem. med. adv. com. Tex. Bd. Mental Health and Mental Retardation, 1965-73, chmn., 1965-69, 72-73; bd. dirs. Tex. Assn. Mental Health, 1965-72. Served to lt. M.C. USNR, 1944-47. Fellow Am. Psychiat. Assn. (br. pres. 1958-59), Am. Coll. Psychiatrists; mem. Tex. Med. Assn., Tex. Neuropsychiat. Assn. (v.p. 1958-59), Central Neuropsychiat. Assn. (v.p. 1974-75), Central Neruopsychiat. Assn. (pres. 1976-77), Tex. Psychiat. Soc. (pres. 1980-81), Houston Psychiat. Soc. (pres. 1956). Home: 5018 Loch Lomond St Houston TX 77096

CANTUS, H. HOLLISTER, manufacturing corporation executive; b. N.Y.C., Nov. 16, 1937; s. Howard J. and Eleanor (Hollister) C.; m. Barbara Jane Park, Feb. 7, 1961; children: Charles Hollister, Jane Scott. B.A., Williams Coll., 1959. Mem. prof. staff Commn. on Armed Services U.S. Ho. Reps., Washington, 1970-74; dep. asst. sec. def. U.S. Dept. Def., Washington, 1974-75; dir. congl. relations U.S. Energy Research and Devel. Adminstrn., Washington, 1975-77; v.p. bldg. systems United Technologies Corp., Washington, 1977—; dir. Nat. Energy Resources Orgn., Washington, 1975—, Nat. Ctr. for a Barrier-Free Environment, 1983—; mem. nat. exec. com. Nat. Inst. for Bldg. Scis., Washington, 1983—. Served to capt. USNR, 1961-83. Republican. Episcopalian. Clubs: Georgetown, Capitol Hill. Home: McLean VA 22102 Office: United Technologies Corp 1825 Eye St NW Suite 700 Washington DC 20006

CANTWELL, JOHN DALZELL, JR., management consultant; b. Davenport, Iowa, July 17, 1909; s. John D. and Mary Edna (Taylor) C.; m. Margaret Jean Simpson, Apr. 30, 1938; children: Cynthia Jean, John Dalzell III. B.S. in Mech. Engring., U. Iowa, 1932; M.B.A., Wharton Sch., U. Pa., 1934. Registered profl. engr., Ill. Planner, Caterpillar Tractor Co., 1935; plants engr. Bettendorf Co. (Iowa), 1936-40; asst. to v.p. Thilmany Pulp & Paper Co., Kaukauna, Wis., 1941-42; div. engr. U.S. Gypsum Co., Chgo., 1943-48; mgr. home appliance div. Murray Corp. Am., 1949-53; v.p. mfg. Trane Co., 1954-61; v.p. Carrier Corp., 1961-74; exec. v.p. Carrier Air Conditioning Co., 1962-74; sr. asso. McCormick & Co., Tarrytown, N.Y. Pres., Cantwell-Conteville Family Assn. Served to lt. (s.g.) USNR, World War II. Mem. Am. Legion, Phi Delta Theta. Republican. Presbyterian. Clubs: Masons, Onondaga Golf and Country. Office: 606 Kimry Moor Fayetteville NY 13066

CANTWELL, JOHN WALSH, advertising executive; b. Fall River, Mass., July 16, 1922; s. William J. and Esther (Walsh) C.; (div.)children—Sharon, Peter, Paul. B.S. in Econs, Holy Cross Coll., 1944; M.A., Georgetown U., 1945; postgrad., Columbia U., 1949-50. Asst. sales mgr. Internat. Milling Co., 1947-48; v.p. mgmt. supr. Compton Advt., N.Y.C., 1948-60; sr. v.p. mgmt. supr. Sullivan, Stauffer Colwell & Bayles, N.Y.C., 1960- 65; pres., chief exec. officer Pritchard, Wood (advt.), N.Y.C., 1965-68, Parkson Advt. Agy., Inc., 1968-69; sr. v.p. J. B. Williams Co., Inc., 1968-69; pres. Jack Cantwell, Inc., 1970—. Home: 139 Maple St Englewood NJ 07631 Office: 532 Sylvan Ave Englewood Cliffs NJ 07632

CANTWELL, MARY, journalist; b. Providence; d. I. Leo and Mary G. (Lonergan) C.; m. Robert Lescher, Dec. 19, 1953 (div.); children: Katherine, Margaret. B.A., Conn. Coll., 1953. Copywriter Mademoiselle, N.Y.C., 1953-58, chief copywriter, 1962-67, mng. and features editor, 1968-77, sr. editor features, 1978-80; mem. editorial bd. N.Y. Times, 1980—. Contbr. articles and fiction to mags. Recipient Conn. Coll. medal, 1983. Office: 229 W 43d St New York NY 10036

CANTWELL, ROBERT, consumer products mfg. co. exec.; b. Buffalo, Sept. 12, 1931; s. Thomas and Helen (Robinson) C.; m. Barbara Hurlbert, Oct. 19, 1963; children—Robert, Helen Virginia, Sara Elizabeth. A.B., Cornell U., 1953, J.D., 1956; LL.M., N.Y. U., 1959. Bar: N.Y. State bar 1956. Asso. firm Jaeckle, Fleischmann & Mugel (and predecessor firm), Buffalo, 1956-62; mem. legal dept. Colgate-Palmolive Co., N.Y.C., 1962-68, London, dep. gen. counsel, 1972-73, v.p., gen. counsel, 1973—, sec., 1974—; v.p., sec., gen. counsel Roblin Industries, Inc., Buffalo, 1968-72. Mem. Am.,N.Y. State, Erie County bar assns., Assn. Bar City N.Y., Am. Soc. Corp. Secs., Brit. Inst. Internat. and Comparative Law. Clubs: Metropolitan (N.Y.); Saturn (Buffalo); Belle Haven (Greenwich, Conn.). Home: 5 Meadow Dr Greenwich CT 06830 Office: 300 Park Ave New York NY 10022

CANTWELL, WILLIAM PATTERSON, lawyer; b. Saranac Lake, N.Y., Dec. 2, 1921; s. Francis Barry and Genevieve (Godfrey) C.; m. Hendrika Antonia Bestebreurtje, June 19, 1947; children: Peter F., Rebecca D., Christopher A. B.A. with highest honors, Williams Coll., 1942; J.D., Yale, 1948. Bar: N.Y. bar 1948, Colo. bar 1953. Assoc. firm Moot, Sprague, Marcy & Gulick, Buffalo, 1948-52; with Holland & Hart, Denver, 1953-64, mem. firm, 1954-64, Sherman & Howard, 1964—; dir. Lobert Press Inc., Colorado Springs, Colo.; Vis. lectr. law U. Denver, 1956- 60, 64-65, U. Colo., 1962; lectr. various continuing legal edn. insts. and legal meetings; mem. Estate Planning Council, Denver; reporter on Uniform Marital Property Act Nat. Conf. Commrs. on Uniform State Laws, 1980-84. Contbr. articles to profl. jours. Bd. visitors U. Colo. Sch. Law. Recipient Trent award Nat. Coll. Probate Judges for Probate Excellence, 1983. Mem. Am. Coll. Probate Counsel (pres. 1975-76), ABA (mem. ho. of dels. 1964-66, 73-78, chmn. real property probate and trust law sect. 1971-72), Colo. Bar Assn. (pres. 1970-71, gov. 1959-65, chmn. taxation law sect. 1959-60, probate and trust law sect. 1960-61), Denver Bar Assn. (pres. 1962-63, award of merit 1969), Greater Denver Tax Counsel Assn. (pres. 1957-58), Internat. Acad. Estate and Trust Law, Order of Coif (hon.). Club: Rotarian. Home: 24386 W Currant Dr Golden CO 80401 Office: First Interstate Tower North Denver CO 80202

CANVIN, DAVID THOMAS, biologist, educator; b. Winnipeg, Man., Can., Nov. 8, 1931; s. Victor Thomas and Maria (Clouston) C.; m. Lois Marie Endershy, July 13, 1957; children—Steven, Paul, Sarah, Robert. B.S.A., U. Man., 1956, M.Sc., 1957; Ph.D., Purdue U., 1960. Asso. prof. biology U. Man., Winnipeg, Can., 1960-65; prof. biology Queen's U., Kingston, Ont., Can., 1965—; cons. in field. Fellow Royal Soc. Can.; mem. Can. Soc. Plant Physiologists, Am. Soc. Plant Physiologists, Can. Biochemical Soc., Can. Botanical Soc. Anglican. Office: Dept Biology Queen's U Kingston ON K7L 3N6 Canada

CAPA, CORNELL, photographer, dir. photography mus.; b. Budapest, Apr. 19, 1918; U.S., 1937, naturalized, 1941; s. David and Julia (Berkowitz) Friedmann; m. Edith Schwartz, Jan. 6, 1940. Ed. public schs. Staff photographer Life mag., 1946-54, contbg. photographer, 1955-67; mem. Magnum Photos, Inc. (a photographers coop.), 1954—; exec. dir. Internat. Center Photography, N.Y.C., 1974—; lectr. in field. Books of photos include Farewell to Eden, 1964, Margin of Life, 1974; editor: others. Israel The Reality. Served with Photog. Intelligence USAF, 1941-45. Recipient N.Y.C. Mayor's award of honor for arts and culture, 1978. Mem. Am. Soc. Mag. Photographers (award for excellence in photo-journalism 1968, honor roll for great and lasting contbns. to photography 1975). Club: Overseas Press Am. Office: 1130 Fifth Ave New York NY 10028

CAPALBO, CARMEN CHARLES, director, producer; b. Harrisburg, Pa., Nov. 1, 1925; s. Joseph and Concetta (Riggio) C.; m. Patricia McBride, July 9, 1950 (div. June 1961); children—Carla, Marc. Student, Yale Sch. Drama, 1945-46. Dir., co-producer: plays Juno and the Paycock, Shadow and Substance, Dear Brutus, Awake and Sing, The Threepenny Opera, The Potting Shed, A Moon for the Misbegotten, The Cave Dwellers; The Rise and Fall of the City of Mahogonny; dir.: plays A Connecticut Yankee, The Good Soldier Schweik, Seidman and Son, The Strangers, The Sign in Sidney Brustein's Window, Enter Solly Gold; also TV prodn. The Power and the Glory; TV prodn. Slowly, By the Hand Unfurled, 1984; story editor: also TV prodn. Studio One, 1951-52; prodn. mgr.: Emlyn Williams as Charles Dickens, 1952-53, Jean-Louis Barrault-Madeleine Renaud Co., 1952; dir., producer, writer 200 radio plays, numerous TV programs; (recipient Tony award 1956, Obie award 1956). Served with AUS, 1944-45. Decorated Bronze Star, Purple Heart. Mem. League N.Y. Theatres, Screen Dirs. Guild, Soc. Stage Dirs. and Choreographers, Dramatists Guild, League OffBroadway Theatres (co-founder 1958, exec. bd. 1958-60), Royal Philatelic Soc. (London). Address: Fitelson Lasky & Aslan care Floria Lasky 551 Fifth Ave New York NY 10176

CAPALBO, RICHARD J., corporation executive; b. N.Y.C., June 24, 1946; s. Salvatore Francis and Louise Ann (Dromes-Hauser) C.; m. Kathleen McCormack, Dec. 8, 1973; children: Kristin Alison, R. Ryan. B.S., Fordham U., 1968; M.A., Wharton Sch. Fin., U. Pa., 1969. First v.p., asst. dir. mktg. Dean Witter, N.Y.C., 1969-76; sr. v.p., dir. mktg. Drexel Burnham Lambert Inc., N.Y.C., 1976—; dir. Kendrick & Stimpfig, San Francisco, DBL Realty Corp., N.Y.C., Jour. Sales and Mktg. Served with U.S. Army. Mem. Securities Industry Assn. (mktg. com.), Internat. Assn. Fin. Planners. Republican. Roman Catholic. Clubs: Indian Trail (Franklin Lakes, N.J.) (tennis chmn. 1981—); Tuxedo (N.Y.); City Midday (N.Y.C.). Home: 607 Orchard Ln Franklin Lakes NJ 07417 Office: Drexel Burnham Lambert Inc 60 Broad St New York NY 10004

CAPARN, RHYS (MRS. HERBERT JOHANNES STEEL), sculptor; b. Onteora Park, N.Y., July 28, 1909; d. Harold ap Rhys and Clara (Jones) C.; m. Herbert Johannes Steel., Sept. 9, 1935. Student, Brearly Sch., N.Y.C., 1918-27, Bryn Mawr Coll., 1927-29, Ecole Artistique des Animaux, Paris, 1929-30, Archipenko Sch. Art, 1931-33. Instr. sculpture, Dalton Sch., 1946-55, 60-72, one-woman show, at Riverside Mus., 1961, Delphic Studios, N.Y.C., 1933, 35, Archtl. League, N.Y.C., 1941, N.Y. Zool. Park, 1942, Wildenstein & Co., 1944, 47, Dartmouth Coll., 1949, 55, John Heller Gallery, 1953, Art Colony Gallery, Cleve., Meltzer Gallery, N.Y.C., 1956, 59, 60, La Boetie Gallery, N.Y.C., 1970, New Bertha Schaefer Gallery, 1973, Phyllis Weil Gallery, N.Y.C., 1980, group shows include, Whitney Annuals, 1941, 53, 54, 56, 60; represented in permanent collections, City Art Mus., St. Louis (Morton May collection), Colorado Springs Fine Arts Center, Dartmouth, Fogg Mus., Whitney Mus. Am. Art, Concoran Gallery Art, Barnard Coll. Library, Bryn Mawr Coll., Mus. City of N.Y., Yale U. Art Gallery, Riverside Mus. Brandeis U., Elvehjem Art Center U. Wis.; also represented in: exhbn. 8 Am. Painters and Sculptors; touring Asia and Europe under auspices, Dept. State, 1957; One of 11 Am. sculptors representing U.S. in competition: Unknown Political Prisoner, Tate Gallery, London, 1953. Recipient 2d prize for Am. sculpture Met. Mus. Art, 1951; medal of honor Nat. Assn. Women Artists, 1960, 61. Fellow internat. Inst. Arts and Letters; mem. Am. Abstract Artists, Fedn. Modern Painters and Sculptors. Office: Taunton Hill Rd Route 1 Newtown CT 06470

CAPASSO, HENRY F., educator. A.B., Brown U., 1938, A.M., 1946; D.M.L., Middlebury Coll., 1960. Prof. Italian emeritus U. R.I., Kingston. Office: Dept Languages U RI Kingston RI 02881

CAPE, RONALD ELLIOT, microbiology company executive; b. Montreal, Que., Can., Oct. 11, 1932; came to U.S., 1967, naturalized, 1972; s. Victor and Fan C.; m. Lillian Judith Pollock, Oct. 21, 1956; children: Jacqueline R., Julie A. A.B. in Chemistry, Princeton U., 1953; M.B.A., Harvard U., 1955; Ph.D. in Biochemistry, McGill U., Montreal, 1967; postgrad., U. Calif., Berkeley, 1967-70. Customs, purchasing and advt. clk. Merck and Co., Ltd., Montreal, 1955-56; pres. Profl. Pharm. Corp., Montreal, 1960-67, chmn. bd., 1967-73; pres. Cetus Corp., Emeryville, Calif., 1972-78, chmn. bd., 1978—; dir., mem. investment com. Dynamic Fund of Can. Ltd., 1958-67; mem. adv. council dept. biochem. scis. Princeton U.; adj. prof. bus. adminstrn. U. Pitts.; dir. Sci. Am., Inc., Neutrogena Corp.; mem. bus. affairs com. Ann. Revs., Inc. Mem. Rockefeller U. Council.; Bd. dirs. U. Calif. Art Museum Council, Berkeley, 1974-76; trustee Head-Royce Schs., Oakland, Calif., 1975-80; bd. dirs. San Francisco Opera Assn. Mem. AAAS, Am. Soc. Microbiology (Found. for Microbiology lectr. 1978-79), Can. Biochem. Soc., Royal Soc. Health, Soc. Microbiology, Soc. Indsl. Microbiology, Indsl. Biotech. Assn. (founding mem., v.p., dir.), N.Y. Acad. Scis., Sigma Xi. Jewish. Clubs: Princeton of N.Y., Commonwealth of Calif. Office: 1400 53d St Emeryville CA 94608

CAPEHART, BARNEY LEE, industrial and systems engineer; b. Galena, Kans., Aug. 20, 1940; s. Samuel Alfred and Mary Jane (Bliss) C.; m. Lynne Carol Fowler, Sept. 2, 1961; children: Thomas David, Jeffrey Donald, Cynthia Diane. B.S.E.E., U. Okla., Norman, 1961, M.E.E., 1962, Ph.D., 1967. Instr. elec. engring. U. Okla., 1965-67; mem. tech. staff Aerospace Corp., San Bernardino, Calif., 1967-68; asst. prof. indsl. and systems engring. U. Fla., Gainesville, 1968-72; assoc. prof. indsl. engring. U. Tenn., 1972-73; assoc. prof. indsl. and systems engring. U. Fla., 1973-79, prof., 1979—; cons. Martin Marietta Corp., U.S. Naval Tng. Device Center.; Chrmn. Regional Energy Action Com., 1977-79; Region IV adv. group on appropriate tech. Dept. of Energy, 1978-80; mem. Local Energy Action Program, 1980-81. Author books in field; Contbr. articles to profl. jours. Served with USAF, 1963-65. Decorated Air Force Commendation medal. Fellow AAAS; sr. mem. Am. Inst. Indsl. Engrs., IEEE; mem. Soc. Computer Simulation, Audubon Soc., Fla. Defenders of Environment, Fla. Conservation Found., Sierra Club, Sigma Xi, Sigma Tau, Alpha Pi Mu, Tau Beta Pi. Home: 1601 NW 35th Way Gainesville FL 32605 Office: Industrial and Systems Engineering Dept University of Florida 303 Weil Hall Gainesville FL 32611

CAPEHART, HOMER EARL, JR., lawyer; b. Green Bay, Wis., Oct. 29, 1922; s. Homer Earl and Irma (Mueller) C.; m. Harriet Jane Holmes, June 17, 1950; children: Craig Earl, Caroline Mary. A.B., DePauw U., 1945; LL.B., Harvard U., 1948. Bar: Ind. 1948. Since practiced in Indpls.; partner Krieg, DeVault, Alexander & Capehart, 1952—; dir. Secured Ins. Co., Indpls., 1950-62; pres. Capehart Corp. and Capehart Farms, Inc., 1979—; Mem. Ind. Bd. Bar Examiners, 1963-67, Ind. Flood Control and Water Resources Commn., 1953-60; pub. mem. Ind. Air Pollution Bd., 1972-79, chmn., 1974-78; mem. Ind. Environ. Mgmt. Bd., 1974-77. Bd. dirs. Indpls. Symphony Orch., 1958-63; bd. dirs. Historic Landmarks Found. Ind., 1976—, vice-chmn., 1979-81, chmn., 1981-84; bd. dirs. Ind. State Mus. Soc., 1982—. Mem.

ABA, Ind. Bar Assn., Indpls. Bar Assn. (v.p. 1972-73), Decorative Arts Soc. (pres. 1979-81), SAR (pres. Ind. 1960), Ind. Hist. Soc., Ind. Soc. Pioneers, Phi Beta Kappa, Beta Theta Pi. Republican. Clubs: Masons (33 deg.), Literary (pres. 1976), Exchange (pres. 1969), Exchange (nat. dist. dir. 1970-71), Columbia, Woodstock, Contemporary (pres. 1975), Portfolio (Indpls.) (pres. 1983-84). Home: 445 Pine Dr Indianapolis IN 46260 Office: 1 Indiana Sq Indianapolis IN 46204

CAPEL, CHARLES EDWARD, mathematician, educator; b. Troy, N.Y., Dec. 26, 1922; s. Charles Edward and Frances (Albert) C.; m. June Arlene Semple, Sept. 22, 1945; children—Janice Roberta, Gail Ann. A.B., N.Y. State Coll. Tchrs., Albany, 1947; M.A., U. Rochester, 1950; Ph.D., Tulane U., 1953. Instr. Geneseo (N.Y.) State Tchrs. Coll., 1947-49; asst. prof. U. Miami (Fla.), 1953-58; mathematician Westinghouse Electric Corp., 1958-60; prof. math. Miami U., Oxford, Ohio, 1960—, chmn. dept. math., 1960-63. Author math. articles; co-author textbook. Served with AUS, 1943-45. Mem. Am. Math. Soc., Math. Assn. Am., AAUP, Sigma Xi, Pi Mu Epsilon. Home: 5 Patrick Dr Oxford OH 45056

CAPELLI, JOHN PLACIDO, nephrologist; b. Hammonton, N.J., May 23, 1936; s. John L. and Marie C.; m. Patricia Ann Verna, Nov. 4, 1961; children: John L., Elizabeth Ann, David S. B.S. in Biology, Villanova U., 1958; M.D., Jefferson Med. Coll., 1962. Diplomate: Am. Bd. Internal Medicine (Nephrology). Intern Michael Reese Hosp., Chgo., 1962-63; resident Thomas Jefferson U. Hosp., 1963-65, NIH fellow in nephrology, 1965-67, Martin E. Rehfuss chief resident internal medicine, 1967-68; practice medicine specializing in nephrology, Haddonfield, N.J., 1968—; dir. div. clin. pharmacology Jefferson Med. Coll., Phila., 1968-69; dir. hemodialysis unit Our Lady of Lourdes Med. Ctr., Camden, N.J., 1969—, dir. div. nephrology and transplantation, 1974—, chief of staff, 1980—; clin. prof. medicine Thomas Jefferson U., Phila., 1974—; mem. chronic renal disease adv. com. N.J. Dept. Health, 1969-79, chmn., 1971-73, 74-75. Discovered hormone Renin, 1968; contbr. articles to med. jours. Mem. Am. Soc. Nephrology, Internat. Soc. Nephrology, Renal Physicians Assn. (pres. 1977-79), AMA, Med. Soc. N.J., Am. Soc. Artificial Internal Organs, Southeastern Organ Procurement Found., Nat. Kidney Found. Roman Catholic. Office: 35 Kings Hwy E Haddonfield NJ 08033

CAPEN, RICHARD GOODWIN, JR., newspaper executive; b. Hartford, Conn., July 16, 1934; s. Richard Goodwin and Virginia Ann (Knowles) C.; m. Joan Lees Lambert, July 13, 1962; children: Christopher Goodwin, Kelly Lambert, Catherine Knowles. A.B., Columbia U., 1956. Asst. to dir. Clay Products Inst., Washington, 1959-60; mgr. William Aldrich Co., San Diego, 1961; dir. pub. affairs Copley Newspapers, La Jolla, Calif., 1961-69, v.p., 1971-76, sr. v.p., 1976-79; sr. v.p. ops. Knight-Ridder Newspapers, Inc., Miami, Fla., 1979-83, mem. operating com., 1979—, mem. exec. com., 1981—; chmn., pub. Miami Herald Pub. Co., 1983—; dep. asst. sec. for public affairs Dept. Def., Washington, 1968; later asst. for legis. affairs; corp. dir., chmn. newspaper adv. bd. UPI, 1977-79; dir. San Diego Trust & Savs. Bank, 1975-79; Vice chmn. San Diego Econ. Devel. Corp., 1978-79. Served to lt. (j.g.) USN, 1956-59. Recipient Disting. Service medal Dept. Def., 1971; Freedoms Found. awards (8); named One of Calif.'s Five Outstanding Young Men, 1969; San Diego's Outstanding Young Man, 1967. Mem. San Diego C. of C. (pres. 1977-79). Republican. Home: Miami FL Office: The Miami Herald One Herald Plaza Miami FL 33101

CAPER, SAMUEL PHILIP, physician, health administrator; b. Los Angeles, July 22, 1938; s. Gene Harold and Anabelle (Cohn) C.; m. Jane Ann Carpenter, Aug. 19, 1973; children: Dana Victoria, Adam, Sara. A.B., UCLA, 1960, M.S., 1963, M.D., 1965. Intern, Harvard Med. Unit, Boston City Hosp., 1965-66, asst. resident, 1966-67, chief resident, 1969-70; research asso. Nat. Cancer Inst., NIH, 1967-69; fellow Harvard Ctr. Community Health and Med. Care, Harvard U. Med. Sch. and Sch. Public Health, 1969-71; mem. prof. staff U.S. Senate Subcom. on Health, 1971-76; prof. medicine, family/community medicine U. Mass. Med. Sch., 1976—, chief med. staff, 1976-78, vice chancellor, 1976-80; research fellow Harvard U., 1980—; vis. prof. Dartmouth Med. Sch., 1983—; mem. Nat. Council on Health Planning and Devel., HEW, 1977-83, chmn., 1980-84, chmn. subcom. on tech. and productivity, 1977-80; mem. Mass. Statewide Health Coordinating Council, 1977-81. Served with USPHS, 1967-69. Recipient Richard H. Schlesinger award Am. Public Health Assn., 1975. Mem. Mass. Med. Soc., Suffolk (Mass.) Dist. Med. Soc. (dir.), Am. Health Planning Assn., Research and Edn. Soc. Boston (dir.), Alpha Omega Alpha. Club: U.S. Power Squadron. Office: John F Kennedy Sch Govt Harvard U Cambridge MA Dartmouth Med Sch Hanover NH 03755

CAPERS, CHARLOTTE, writer, former state official; b. Columbia, Tenn., 1913; d. Walter B. and Louise (Woldridge) C. Student, Millsaps Coll., 1930-32, U. Colo., 1932; B.A., U. Miss., 1934. With Miss. Archives and History, 1938-83, successively sec., research and editorial asst., asst. dir., 1938-55, dir., 1955-69, dir. spl. projects, 1969-71, dir. info. and edn., 1971-83; editor-in-chief Jour. Miss. History, 1955-69; columnist State Times, 1955-57; contbr. book revs. N.Y. Times Book Rev.; prin. exec. for restoration Miss. gov.'s mansion, 1972-75; cons. Center Study So. Culture, 1979—. Editor: (with William D. McCain) Papers of the Washington County Historical Society, 1954, Miss. History News, 1957—; editorial dir.: Mississippi in the Confederacy, 1961; mem. adv. editorial bd.: Jefferson Davis Papers, Rice U.; publs. com.: Mississippi as a Province, Territory and State (J.F.H. Claiborne), 1964; contbg. editor: The Delta Rev., 1966-70; mem. publs. com.: Jour. Miss. History, 1975—; author: The Capers Papers, 1982, 83. Bd. dirs. Miss. Arts Festival, 1970-76, Miss. Inst. Arts and Letters, 1978-82; mem. Gov.'s Mansion Com., 1980—. Named to U. Miss. Alumni Hall of Fame, 1983; Archives and History Bldg., U. Miss. named for her, 1983. Fellow Soc. Am. Archivists; mem. Jr. League Jackson, Miss. Hist. Soc. (sec.-treas. 1955-69, bd. dirs. 1969-72, v.p. 1973-74, pres. 1974-75), Am. Assn. State and Local History (council 1982—), Millsaps Coll. Alumni Assn. (dir. 1977—). Episcopalian. Home: 4020 Berkley Dr Jackson MS 39211 Office: Box 571 Jackson MS 39205

CAPERS, GERALD MORTIMER, JR., educator; b. New Orleans, May 30, 1909; s. Gerald Mortimer and Vivia (Deane) C.; m. Roberta Alford, Dec. 27, 1962. B.A., Southwestern Coll., 1930; Ph.D., Yale, 1936. Tchr. math. Fairview Jr. High Sch., Memphis, 1930-32; instr. history Yale, 1936-40; faculty mem. Tulane U., 1940—; chmn. history dept. Sophie Newcomb Coll., 1941—, prof. history, 1948—. Author: Biography of a Rivertown, 1939, Stephen A. Douglas, Defender of the Union, 1959, John C. Calhoun, Opportunist, 1960, Occupied City, New Orleans Under the Federals, 1862-1865, 1965, The Mississippi River: Before and After Mark Twain, 1977; also articles in hist. jours. Ency. Brit. Served from 2d lt. to capt. USAAF, 1942-45. Recipient Engleston prize Yale, 1936; Guggenheim fellow, 1959-60; Am. Council Learned Socs. fellow, 1952. Mem. So. Hist. Assn., Orgn. Am. Historians, Phi Beta Kappa, Omicron Delta Kappa. Home: 244 Vinet St Jefferson LA 70121

CAPERTON, CHARLES LEE, lawyer; b. N.Y.C., Dec. 25, 1937; s. Albert Helvey and Loraine Emmons (Elston) C.; m. Frances Ann McNatt, Dec. 23, 1963 (div.); children—Kelly Conder, Charles Lee II; m. Marilyn A. Graves, Apr. 14, 1979. B.B.A., So. Methodist U., 1961, J.D., 1964. Bar: Tex. bar 1964. Asst. dist. atty. Dallas County, 1964-68; practiced in, Dallas, 1968—. Contbr. articles to profl. jours. Bd. dirs. Lawyers Involved for Tex.; trustee Nat. Found. Sudden Infant Death, 1974-75. Served with AUS, 1956. Mem. Tex. Trial Lawyers Assn. (dir. 1972-76, chmn. criminal law sect. 1975-76), Dallas Trial Lawyers Assn. (pres. 1975), Assn. Trial Lawyers Am. (committeeman 1975-77), Tex. Criminal Def. Lawyers Assn. (charter), Kappa Alpha, Phi Alpha Delta; asso-in-law Am. Coll. Legal Medicine. Democrat. Methodist. Club: Mason (32 deg., Shriner). Office: 2823 Routh St Dallas TX 75201

CAPES, CHARLES EDWARD, chem. engr.; b. Sarnia, Ont., Can., Feb. 11, 1939; s. George Edward and Alma Jean C.; m. Jennifer Elizabeth Paine, Apr. 15, 1963; children—Michael Edward, Sarah Elizabeth. B.A.Sc., U. Toronto, 1961; Ph.D., Cambridge (Eng.) U., 1964. Registered profl. engr., Ont. With Polymer Corp., Sarnia, 1961; chem. engr. Nat. Research Council Can., 1964—, head chem. engring. sect., 1979—. Author. Fellow Chem. Inst. Can.; mem. Canadian Soc. Chem. Engring. (dir. 1976—, Erco award 1975), Assn. Profl. Engrs. Ont., Soc. Mining Engrs., Am. Inst. Mining Engrs. Patentee in field. Home: 1851 Playfair Dr Ottawa ON K1H 5R9 Canada Office: Div Chemistry Nat Research Council Can Montreal Rd Ottawa ON K1A 0R9 Canada

CAPIAUX, RAYMOND, aerospace co. exec.; b. Lille, France, Aug. 19, 1927; came to U.S., 1953, naturalized, 1959; s. Lucien and Aimee (Maucourt) C.; m. Aimee Cook, Aug. 20, 1960; children—Claude, Frank, Philip, Corinne, Sean. B.S. in Aero. Engring, Swiss Inst. Tech., 1950, M.S., 1951. Research engr. Sulzer Brothers, Winterthur, Switzerland, 1950-53; sr. propulsion-aerodynamics engr. Convair, Ft. Worth, 1953-56; supr. aerodynamic design Curtiss Wright Corp., Princeton, N.J., 1956-57; staff engr. Fairchild Engring. & Airplane Corp., Deerpark, N.Y., 1957-58; research specialist, staff scientist, sr. mem. for aerophysics, mgr. aerospace scis. lab., dir. engring. scis., asst. gen. mgr., dir. research, v.p. research and devel. Lockheed Missiles & Space Co., Inc., Sunnyvale, Calif., 1958—. Mem. Am. Inst. Aeros. and Astronautics, Assn. U.S. Army. Home: 12610 Via Ventana Los Altos Hills CA 94022 Office: 3251 Hanover St Palo Alto CA 94304

CAPITAN, WILLIAM HARRY, college president; b. Owosso, Mich., Feb. 7, 1933; s. Harry and Anthe (Sarris) C.; m. Dolores Marie Randolph, Sept. 19, 1959; children—Rita, Edwin. B.A., U. Mich., 1954; postgrad., Queens U., 1954-55; M.A., U. Minn., 1958, Ph.D., 1960. Instr. philosophy U. Minn., 1959-60, U. Md., 1960-62; asst. prof., assoc. prof., chmn. dept. Oberlin (Ohio) Coll., 1962-70; dean fine arts, v.p. acad. affairs, acting pres. Saginaw Valley State Coll., University Center, Mich., 1970-74; v.p. acad. affairs, dean faculty, acting pres. W.Va. Wesleyan Coll., Buckhannon, 1974-79; pres. Ga. Southwestern Coll., Americus, 1979—; ednl. cons. Sangamon State U., Ill., Evergreen State Coll., Bd. Govs. State Colls. and Univs. Ill. Author: Introduction to the Philosophy of Religion, 1972; editor: (with D.D. Merrill) Metaphysics and Explanation, Art, Religion, and Mind, 1967. Bd. dirs. Saginaw Symphony Orch., 1970-74, Buckhannon C. of C., Sumter County United Way; trustee Charles L. Mix Meml. Fund, Inc. Am. Council Lerned Socs. fellow, Paris, 1967-68. Mem. Am. Soc. Aesthetics, Am. Philos. Assn., Beta Theta Phi, Omicron Delta Kappa, Phi Kappa Phi, Phi Delta Kappa. Episcopalian. Club: Rotary. Office: Ga Southwestern Coll Americus GA 31709 *Clarity of objectives, persistence, and Christian respect for persons have guided me in whatever of value I have accomplished. My failures came when I wasn't very clear about what I was doing. America rewards, supports, and buoys up those with initiative. This is why my parents were able to go from "rags to riches" and I from illiterate to lettered. We Americans help one another, and we shape our institutions to help, too. May we ever remain so.*

CAPLAN, ALBERT JOSEPH, university dean; b. Phila., June 2, 1908; s. Joseph and Frances (Belber) C.; m. Sylvia Fay Bayuk, Mar. 13, 1932; children: Judith Ann Caplan Gould, Jerome Albert, Stephen Bayuk. B.S. in Edn, Temple U., 1929; LL.B., 1933. Account exec. Bayuk Bros. (brokerage firm), Phila., 1929-44, partner, 1944-51; owner, editor South Jersey News, Collingswood, N.J., 1934-40; partner Albert J. Caplan & Co. (brokerage firm), Phila., 1951-60; pres. Charles A. Taggart & Co. Inc. (brokerage firm), Phila., 1960-65; dean Charles Morris Price Sch. of Advt. and Journalism, Phila., 1966-75, dean emeritus, 1976—. Author: For You and Other Poems, 1925, Manuscript Making in the Middle Ages, 1927, A Bibliography of Sir Walter Scott, Bart, 1929; contbr. to newspapers and mags. Bd. dirs. Temple Beth Zion-Beth Israel, Friends of Music, U. Pa.; hon. life bd. dirs. Cheltenham Twp. Art Center, Congregation Adath Jeshurun. Served with USNR, 1944-45. Fellow Library Co. Phila. (shareholder), Royal Soc. Arts (London) (life), AIM (pres.'s council 1967), Am. Philos. Soc. (library), Phila. Mus. Art (donor 1970, asso. 1972); life mem. Acad. Polit. Sci. of Columbia U., Am. Acad. Polit. and Social Scis. (del.), Am. Def. Preparedness Assn., Cruiser Olympia Assn., Franklin Inst. Pa., Hist. Soc. Pa., Navy League U.S., Pa. Assn. Adult Edn., Phila. Orch. Pension Fund Soc., Phila. Public Relations Assn. (hon.), Settlement Sch. Music Alumni, Central High Sch., Temple U. Trustees Assn. (ednl. policies com), Temple U. Gen. Alumni Assn. (dir., com. chmn. Diamond Asso.), U. Pa. Alumni Assn., Chapel Four Chaplins (legion of honor 1966, 77), Am. Legion (adj. Benjamin Franklin Post 405, past comdr. Louis N. Porter Post 224), Beta Sigma Rho (past trustee grand chpt.); mem. Phila. Flag Day Assn. (dir.), Advt. Hall Fame (bd. judges 1964-74), Am. Cancer Soc., Am. Inst. Graphic Arts (past v.p., dir.), Am. Nat. Red Cross (chpt. membership chmn. 1975, 76, 77), Curtis Inst. Music (patron), Friends of Drama Guild (patron), Friends of Free Library (sponsor), Friends of Independence Nat. Hist. Park (patron), Internat. Graphic Arts Assn. (dir. 1955-70), Charles Willson Peale Soc. of Pa. Acad. Fine Arts, Pa. Am. Legion Press Assn., Phila. Orch. Assn. (council), Rosenbach Found. Mus. (asso.), Seamen's Ch. Inst., So. Profl. Journalists, World Affairs Council Phila., Law Alumni Temple U., Zoological Soc. Phila., Pi Lambda Phi, Lambda Sigma Kappa (past trustee). Clubs: Downtown of Temple U. (pres.), Charlotte Cushman, Faculty of U. Pa., Diamond Faculty, Franklin Inn, Phila. Art Alliance, Poor Richard (sch. trustee, past officer, silver medal), Peale, Pen and Pencil, Print (life), Varsity of Temple U. (life), Union League (trustee scholarship fund), B'nai B'rith.). Home: The Wellington 135 S 19th St Philadelphia PA 19103

CAPLAN, FRED HARRY, ret. state justice; b. Clarksburg, W.Va., Dec. 3, 1914; s. Henry A. and Hannah (Siegelman) C.; m. Miriam Kessler, Nov. 12, 1941; 1 dau., Betty Lee. A.B., W.Va. U., 1939; LL.B., U. Richmond, 1941, LL.D., 1971. Bar: W.Va. bar 1941. Practiced in, Clarksburg, 1946-53, asst. atty. gen. W.Va., 1953- 61; chmn. Pub. Service Commn. W.Va., 1961-62; judge Supreme Ct. Appeals W. Va., 1962-80, chief justice, 1977-80, ret., 1980; pres. Supreme Ct. Appeals W.Va., 1966, 71; Mem. W.Va. Legislature from Harrison County, 1949-53. Served with AUS, 1941-46; PTO. Mem. W.Va., Harrison County bar assns., W.Va. State Bar, W.Va. Jud. Assn., B'nai B'rith. Democrat. Jewish. Home: 4218 Noyes Ave SE Charleston WV 25304

CAPLAN, RONALD MERVYN, gynecologist, obstetrician; b. Montreal, Que., Can., Dec. 12, 1937; came to U.S., 1971; s. Philip and Betty (Gamer) C.; m. Marilyn Gail Amdur, Dec. 23, 1962; children: Randy Sue, Gordon. B.Sc., McGill U., Montreal, 1958, M.D., C.M., 1962. Resident Royal Victorial Hosp., Montreal, 1963-67; instr. ob-gyn McGill U., 1968-71; practice medicine specializing in ob-gyn, Montreal, 1968-71, N.Y.C., 1971—; mem. attending staff Royal Victoria Hosp., Montreal, 1968-71; asst. attending physician in ob-gyn N.Y. Hosp., N.Y.C., 1971, now assoc. attending physician; clin. assoc. prof. ob-gyn Cornell U. Med. Coll. Editor: (with William J. Sweeney, III) Advances in Obstetrics and Gynecology (Williams, Wilkins), 1978, Principles of Obstetrics, 1982. Fellow ACS, Am. Coll. Obstetricians and Gynecologists, Royal Coll. Surgeons (Can.); mem. AMA, N.Y. Med. Soc., Que. Med. Assn., N.Y. Gynecol. Soc. Club: Griffis Faculty of Cornell U. Office: 460 E 63d St New York NY 10021

CAPLES, JOHN, advertising agency executive; b. N.Y.C., May 1, 1900; s. Byron H. and Edith Jessie (Richards) C.; m. Dorothy N. Dickes, Feb. 16, 1980. Student, Columbia, 1918-19; B.S., U.S. Naval Acad., 1924. With engring. dept. N.Y. Telephone Co., 24-25; advt. writer Ruthrauff & Ryan, Inc., 1925-27; writer, exec. Batten, Barton, Durstine & Osborn, Inc., 1927-41, v.p., 1941—; tchr. advt. Grad. Sch. Bus. Columbia, 1952-53. Author: Tested Advertising Methods, 1932, rev. 1974, Advertising for Immediate Sales, 1936, Advertising Ideas, 1938, Making Ads Pay, 1957, How to Make Your Advertising Make Money, 1981; co-author: Copy Testing, 1939; Author: two advertisements (including) They Laughed When I Sat Down at the Piano) included in book The 100 Greatest Advertisements; Columnist: book Direct Marketing mag, 1972—; Contbr. to: The Advertising Handbook, 1950, Saturday Rev; various advt. trade jours. Mem. council of judges Advt. Hall of Fame, 1963-72; pub. relations counsel Girl Scouts U.S.A., 1973—; Mem. nat. adv. council Episcopal Ch. Found., 1968—; mem. pub. relations com. Nat. Multiple Sclerosis Soc., 1969—. Served as seaman USNRF, 1918; from lt. comdr. to comdr. USNR, 1942-45. Recipient Ann. award Nat. Assn. Direct Mail Writers, 1969, Ann. Leadership award Hundred Million Club, 1972; named to Copywriters Hall of Fame, 1973; Advt. Hall of Fame, 1977. Mem. Market Research Council N.Y., Copy Research Council N.Y., Direct Mktg. Creative Guild, Naval Acad. Assn., Alpha Delta Sigma. Clubs: Univ., Dutch Treat, Players (N.Y.C.). Home: 35 Park Ave New York NY 10016 Office: 383 Madison Ave New York NY 10017 *My earliest ambition was to make enough money so I could retire at forty. But at twenty-five I had the good fortune to get into work I enjoyed. Now I never want to retire. The secret of happiness is enjoyable work plus helping others.*

CAPLOW, THEODORE, sociologist; b. N.Y.C., May 1, 1920; s. Samuel Nathaniel and Florence (Israel) C.; m. Margaret Mary Pettit, 1981. A.B., U. Chgo., 1939; Ph.D., U. Minn., 1946. Mem. faculty U. Minn., 1945-60; prof. sociology Columbia, 1961-70; chmn. dept. sociology U. Va., Charlottesville, 1970-78, Commonwealth prof., 1973—; vis. prof. U. Bordeaux, France, 1950, U. Aix-Marseille, 1951, U. Utrecht, Netherlands, 1954-55, Stanford, 1957, U. Bogota, Colombia, 1962, Sorbonne, Paris, France, 1968-69, Institut d'Etudes Politiques, Paris, 1983; Pres. Mendota Research Group Inc., 1957-65. Author: Sociology of Work, 1954, The Academic Marketplace, 1957, Principles of Organization, 1964, Two Against One, 1968, L'Enquête Sociologique, 1970, Toward Social Hope, 1975, Middletown Families, 1981, Managing an Organization, 1983, All Faithful People, 1983. Served with AUS, 1943-45; PTO. Decorated Purple Heart. Mem. Tocqueville Soc. (pres. 1979-83), Am. Sociol. Assn. (sec. 1983—). Clubs: Keswick Hunt, Farmington Hunt (Charlottesville); Century (N.Y.C.); Tarratine (Dark Harbor, Maine). Home: Twin Springs Earlysville VA 22936

CAPOBIANCO, TITO, opera director; b. La Plata, Argentina, Aug. 28, 1931; m. Elena Denda; 2 children. Student pub. schs., La Plata; M.A. in Music, U. Buenos Aires. Prof. U. Chile, 1954-56. Art dir., Cin. Opera, 1962-65; artistic dir., Cin. Opera Festival, 1961-65; tech. dir., Teatro Colón, 1958-62; gen. dir., Chile Opera Co., 1967-70, Chile Opera Co., La Plata, 1959-61, San Diego Opera, 1975-83, Pitts. Opera, 1983—; founder, San Diego Opera Center, 1977, Verdi Opera Festival, San Diego, 1978, Young Am. Opera Condrs. Program, 1980; dir., producer maj. opera cos. in, Argentina, Australia, France, Germany, Holland, Italy, Mexico, Spain and, U.S., including, N.Y.C., Phila., Houston, San Francisco, Washington, Met. Opera; prof. acting and interpretation, Acad. Vocal Arts, Phila., 1962-68; founder, gen. dir., Juilliard Sch. Music, N.Y.C., Am. Opera Center, 1967-69; dir. opera studies, Music Acad. West, 1983; dir., Council of Arts, Argentina, 1959-61 (Named One of Ten Best Talents in Argentina 1968); Operatic debut in Aida, Teatro Argentino, La Plata, 1953; theatre debut, State Co., Buenos Aires, 1954. Hon. citizen Balt., New Orleans and; Miami; recipient Cavaliere award, Italy). Office: Pittsburgh Opera Inc 600 Penn Ave Pittsburgh PA 15222 *

CAPOLONGO, JAMES ANTHONY, automotive company executive; b. Syracuse, N.Y., Oct. 28, 1934; s. Frank and Rose (Grillo) C.; m. Barbara Joan Bice, Dec. 27, 1958; children—William David, Carin Maria. B.M.E., Syracuse U., 1956; M.S. in Automotive Engring, Chrysler Inst., 1958; M.B.A., Wayne State U., 1964. Registered profl. engr., Mich. Trainee engr., project engr. Chrysler Corp., Detroit, 1956-61; with Ford Motor Co., Dearborn, Mich., 1961—, v.p. spl. product and mfg. programs, 1974-76, v.p. export ops., 1976, v.p., gen. mgr. truck and recreation products ops., 1976—; pres. Ford of Europe, Inc. Team capt. United Found., 1977. Mem. Soc. Automotive Engrs., Engring. Soc. Detroit, Am. Hist. Truck Mus., Motor Vehicle Mfrs. Assn., Motor Truck Mfrs., Western Hwy. Inst. Office: 20000 Rotunda Dr Dearborn MI 48131

CAPONE, ALPHONSE WILLIAM, industrial executive; b. Pitts., Oct. 22, 1919; s. Aniello and Mary (Manzione) C.; m. Eleanor M. Polis, Aug. 16, 1947 (dec. Nov. 1972); 1 dau., Margaret Ellen; m. Alvira L. Petty, July 5, 1975. B.B.A., Duquesne U., 1942; postgrad., Harvard, 1959, Am. U. Sch. Internat. Service, Washington, 1965, Brookings Instn., 1966. With Koppers Co., Inc., Pitts., 1946—, mgr. fin. dept. internat. ops., 1964-67, asst. treas., 1958-67, v.p., chief fin. officer, treas., 1967-77, sr. v.p., chief fin. officer, 1978—; v.p., dir. Eastern Rock Products, Inc., Erie Sand S.S. Co., Erie Sand & Gravel Co., Honolulu Wood Treating Co., Ltd., Gen. Crushed Stone Co., Kaiser Sand & Gravel Co., Western Paving Constrn. Co., Thiem Corp., Sim J. Harris Co.; dir. Koppers Internat. (Australia), Ltd., Koppers Internat. Can. Ltd., Koppers of Turkey, Inc.; chmn. bd. Gordon Terminal Service Co. Bd. dirs. Duquesne U., chmn., 1979—. Served to lt. USNR, 1943- 46. Mem. Am., Pa. insts. C.P.A.s, Fin. Execs. Inst. (dir., pres. Pitts. chpt. 1974-75), Pitts. C. of C., World Affairs Council Pitts., Duquesne U. Alumni Assn. (past pres., gov.), Am. Mgmt. Assn. (v.p. charge fin. council 1977-79), Machinery and Allied Products Inst. (fin. council), Conf. Bd. (council fin. execs.), Harvard Advanced Mgmt. Assn., Harvard Bus. Sch. Assn. Pitts., Pa. Soc. Clubs: Duquesne, St. Clair Country; University (Pitts.). Home: RD3 Box 66 Eighty-Four PA 15330 Office: Koppers Bldg Pittsburgh PA 15219

CAPONE, LUCIEN, JR., management consultant, former naval officer; b. Fall River, Mass.; s. Lucien and Louise Dolores (Malafronte) C.; m. Charlotte Loretta Lammers, July 22, 1950; children: Lucien, Judith Ann. B.S., U.S. Naval Acad., 1949; grad., Naval Postgrad. Sch., 1955, Indsl. Coll. Armed Forces, 1967; M.S. in Bus. Adminstrn, George Washington U., 1967, postgrad., 1970-71. Commd. ensign U.S. Navy, 1949, advanced through grades to rear adm.; served on destroyers, 1949-54; mem. staff (Office of Chief of Naval Ops., Dept. Navy), 1955-57, exec. officer, 1957-59, staff, comdr.,

Persian Gulf, 1959-61, head plans, programs, and requirements br., Washington, 1961-63, comdg. officer, 1963-64, dep. chief of staff, Washington, 1964-66, comdg. officer, 1967-69, asst. comdr. plans, programs, requirements, Washington, 1969-72, comdg. officer, 1972-73, dep. dir. nat. mil. command system tech. support, Washington, 1974-76, dir. command and control tech. center, 1976-78, dep. dir. command and control, 1976-78, dir., Washington, 1978-79; exec. Booz, Allen & Hamilton, Inc., Bethesda, Md., 1979—, v.p., 1983—. Decorated Legion of Merit, Def. Superior Service medal with oak leaf cluster. Mem. IEEE, Armed Forces Communications and Electronics Assn. (bd. dirs.). Roman Catholic. Home: 110 High St Bristol RI 02809 Office: Booz Allen Hamilton Inc Bethesda MD 20014 Mailing Address: 6225 Greeley Blvd Springfield VA 22152

CAPONIGRO, PAUL, photographer; b. Boston, Dec. 7, 1932. Studied with, Benjamin Chin, Minor White. Instr. photography N.Y. U., 1967-71, Yale U. Author: An Aperture, 1966, Sunflower, 1974, Landscape, 1975; One-man shows include, George Eastman House, Rochester, N.Y., 1958, Mus. Modern Art, N.Y.C., 1968, Focus Gallery, San Francisco, 1969, Princeton U., 1970. Recipient 1st prize Boston Arts Festival, 1961; Guggenheim Found. fellow, 1966; Nat. Endowment Arts grantee, 1971. Mem. Am. Heliographer Assn. Office: Route 3 Box 96D Santa Fe NM 87501 *

CAPONIO, JOSEPH F., government official; b. Canton, Mass., Mar. 25, 1926; s. Francis and Anna (Musci) C.; m. Virginia Sands Hall, Apr. 27, 1957; children: Frank Joseph, Edward Thomas. B.A., St. Anselm's Coll., 1951; Ph.D., Georgetown U., 1959. Instr. in chemistry Georgetown U., Washington, 1951-52; research chemist Harris Research Labs., Washington, 1952-53; sr. reference analyst and bibliographer sci. and tech div. Library of Congress, Washington, 1953-57; chief reference and bibliography br. Armed Services Tech. Info. Agy., Washington, 1957-59; research biochemist Chemo-Med Research Inst., Gerogetown U., 1957-59; chief reference and bibliography br. Office Tech. Services, Dept. Commerce, Washington, 1959-61; dir. tech. info. Def. Documentation Ctr., Dept. Def., Alexandria, Va., 1961-64; sci. and tech. communications officer Nat. Inst. Neurol. Diseases and Stroke, NIH, HEW, Bethesda, Md., 1964-70; assoc. dir. Nat. Agrl. Library, Dept. Agr., Beltsville, Md., 1970-73, acting dir., 1973-75; dir. Environ. Sci. Info. Ctr. NOAA, Dept. Commerce, Washington, 1975-78; acting dir. Environ. Data and Info. Service, Environ. Sci. Info. ctr., NOAA, Dept. Commerce, Washington, 1978-79; dep. dir. Nat. tech. Info. Service, Dept. Commerce, Springfield, Va., 1979-82; acint dir. Ndat. tech. Info. Service, Dept. Commerce, Springfield, Va., 1982-83; dir. Nat. tech. Info. Service, Dept. Commerce, Springfield, Va., 1983—; lectr. Am. U. Grad. Sch., Washington, 1968-70, U. Md. Grad. Sch. Library Sci. and Info. Sci., College Park, 1970-76, McGill U., Montreal, Que., Can., 1972; cons. div. marine scis. UNESCO, 1976—; mem. Interagy Task Force on Chem. Info. Systems, 1965-67; mem. com. sci. and tech. info. Panel on Info. Analysis Ctrs., 1966-72; mem, food and agr. orng. Agr. Research Info. Service, UN, 1973-75; mem. Dept. State Interagy. Com. on UN Environ Info. Service; chmn. joint panel experts on aquatic scis. and fisheries info. FAO, UN. Intergovtl. Oceanographic Commn., 1975—. Served to staff sgt. U.S. Army, 1943-45; ETO. Recipient Silver medal Dept. Commerce, 1981, Sec.'s award of appreciation Dept. Agr., 1973; fellow Georgetown U., 1951-53. Fellow AAAS; mem. Inst. Sci. Info. (editorial adv. bd. 1970-76), Am. Soc. Info. Sci. (chmn. pub. affairs com. 1977-80, sec.-treas. specialized interset group biology and chemistry 1965-66, founder-editor Washington Update Bull. 1976-80), Nat. Inst. Neurol. Disorders and communicative Diseases (sci. info. adv. com. 1976-78), Exec. Library Com. on Integration Libraries and Info. Services (chmn. 1977-79, exec. council 1975-78), Assn. Research Libraries, Nat. Inst. Neurol. Diseases and Blindness NIH (exec. sec. sci. info. program adv. com. 1964-70), Nat. Acad. Sci.; ex officio mem. NSF. Home: 8417 Fort Hunt Rd Alexandria VA 22308 Office: Nat Tech Info Service 5283 Port Royal Rd Springfield VA 22161

CAPORALE, D. NICK, state supreme court judge; b. Omaha, Sept. 13, 1928; s. Michele and Lucia (DeLuca) C.; m. Margaret Nilson, Aug. 5, 1950; children: Laura Diane, Leland Alan. B.A., U. Nebr.-Omaha, 1949, M.Sc., 1954; J.D. with distinction, U. Nebr.-Lincoln, 1957. Bar: Nebr. 1957, U.S. Dist. Ct. Nebr. 1957, U.S. Ct. Appeals 8th cir. 1958, U.S. Supreme Ct. 1970. Mem. firm Stoehr, Rickerson, Sodoro & Caporale, Omaha, 1956-66; ptnr. Schmid, Ford, Mooney, Frederick & Caporale, Omaha, 1966-79; judge Nebr. Dist. Ct., Omaha, 1979-81, Nebr. Supreme Ct., Lincoln, 1982—; lectr. U. Nebr., Lincoln. Pres. Omaha Community Playhouse, 1976. Served to 1st lt. U.S. Army, 1952-54; Korea. Decorated Bronze Star; recipient Alumni Achievement U. Nebr.-Omaha, 1972. Fellow Am. Coll. Trial Lawyers, Internat. Soc. Barristers. Office: Room 2222 State House 1445 K St Lincoln NE 68509

CAPOTE, TRUMAN, author; b. New Orleans, Sept. 30, 1924; s. Joseph G. and Nina (Faulk) C. Ed., Trinity Sch., St. John's Acad. (N.Y.), pub. schs. of, Greenwich, Conn. Writer from early years.; Author: Other Voices, Other Rooms, 1948, Tree of Night; short stories, 1949; Observations, 1949, Local Color, 1950, The Grass Harp, 1953, The Muses Are Heard, 1956, Breakfast at Tiffany's, 1958, Selected Writings, 1963, In Cold Blood, 1965 (Book-of-Month Club selection), A Christmas Memory, 1966, (with H. Arlen) House of Flowers, 1968, Thanksgiving Visitor, 1969, Trilogy: An Experiment of Multimedia, 1971, The Dogs Bark: Private Places and Public People, 1973, Then It All Came Down: Criminal Justice Today Discussed by Police, Criminals and Correction Officers with Comments by Truman Capote, 1976, Music for Chameleons, 1980, (juvenile) Miriam, 1982; Contbr. (with H. Arlen) short stories, non-fiction to nat. mags.; appeared in motion pictures: Murder by Death, CS Blues. Recipient O. Henry Meml. award for short story, 1946, 48, 51; creative writing award Nat. Inst. Arts and Letters, 1959. Mem. Nat. Inst. Arts. and Letters. Office: care Random House 201 E 50th St New York NY 10022 *

CAPOUYA, EMILE, journalist, translator, educator; b. N.Y.C. Ed., Columbia Coll., Oxford (Eng.) U. Editor numerous book pub. cos., 1950—; former asst. prof. lit. Bard Coll., Annandale-on-Hudson, N.Y.; lectr. comparative lit. New Sch. for Social Research, N.Y.C.; assoc. prof. English Baruch Coll. City U. N.Y., 1971—; mem. acad. faculty Juilliard Sch., N.Y.C., 1971—; editorial dir. Hippocrene Books, N.Y.C., after 1980; now mng. dir. Schocken Books Inc., N.Y.C. Translator books from French, German, Italian.; Lit. editor: The Nation, 1970-76; editor: New Am. Rev, 1979—; contbr.: articles to popular mags. including Saturday Rev; also to numerous lit. jours. Guggenheim fellow, 1964-65. Address: Schocken Books Inc 200 Madison Ave New York NY 10016

CAPP, MICHAEL PAUL, physician, educator; b. Yonkers, N.Y., July 1, 1930; s. Michael and Mary (Bybel) C.; m. Ruth Flynn Harrell, July 20, 1957; children: Marianne, Michael, Steven, John. B.S., Roanoke Coll., Salem, Va., 1952; M.D., U. N.C., 1958. Diplomate: Am. Bd. Radiology (treas. 1982—). Lab. instr. physics Roanoke Coll., 1952; teaching asst. Grad. Sch. Physics, Duke, 1952-54; intern pediatrics Duke Med. Center, 1958-59, resident radiology, 1959-62, asso. in radiology, 1962, asst. prof., 1963-66, asso. prof., 1966-70, dir. diagnostic div., dept. radiology, 1967-70, asst. prof. pediatrics, 1968-70, radiologist in charge pediatric cardiology, 1962-70, dir., 1965-70, 1965-66; prof., chmn. dept. radiology U. Ariz. Coll. Medicine, Tucson, 1970—; chief of staff Ariz. Med. Center, Univ. Hosp., 1971-73; Mem. NRC Com. on Radiology, James Picker Found., 1972. Contbr. articles to profl. jours. Mem. Am. Coll. Radiology, AMA, Am. Roentgen Ray Soc., Radiol. Soc. N.Am. (chmn. sci. exhibits com. 1976-79), N.Y. Acad. Scis., Pima County Med. Soc., Soc. for Pediatric Radiology, Eastern Radiol. Soc. (sci. program chmn. 1967, v.p. 1973—), Am. Assn. U. Radiologists (exec. com. 1970—), Soc. for Chmn. Acad. Radiology Depts. (pres. 1977), N.Am. Soc. Cardiac Radiologists (pres. 1975), Am. Heart Assn. (pres. council on cardiovascular radiology 1976-78), Sigma Pi Sigma. Home: 4789 N Via Entrada Tucson AZ 85718 Office: Dept Radiology Univ of Ariz Tucson AZ 85724

CAPPELLO, JUAN C., corporation executive; b. Santiago, Chile, Sept. 4, 1938; s. Giovanni and Celsa (Lora) C.; m. Jean Forrester, 1966; children: Juan Pablo, Jesse Anne, Philip Bruce. B.A. in Journalism, U. Chile, Santiago, M.S., Northwestern U. Reporter for several publs. covering Latin-Am. affairs; v.p., dir. CR&A Telecom, ITT Corp., N.Y.C., 1976-78, dir. pub. info., 1978-80, dep dir. CR&A, 1980—, v.p. ITT Corp, 1980—. Mem. Overseas Press Club, Press Soc. Am., Internat. Press. Assn., Am. Mgmt. Assn., Nat. Guild Journalists Chile. Clubs: Beacon Hill Country, Clearwater Country (Summit, N.J.); Columbus (N.Y.C.). Home: 55 Gloucester Rd Summit NJ 07901 Office: ITT Corp 320 Park Ave New York NY 10022

CAPPIELLO, FRANK ANTHONY, JR., investment advisor; b. Trenton, N.J., Jan. 5, 1926; s. Frank A. and Rose Marie (Clapis) C.; m. Marie Therese Rhodes, June, 1954; children: Frank Rhodes, Annmarie, Elaine. A.B., U. Notre Dame, 1949; postgrad., Cornell U. Law Sch., 1949-50; M.B.A., Harvard U., 1954. Supr. rate research Va. Electric and Power Co., Richmond, 1954-61; mgr. research dept. Alexander Brown & Sons, 1961-67; v.p. Securities Monumental Life Ins. Co., 1968-74; fin. v.p. Monumental Corp., 1970-80; pres. Monumental Capital Mgmt., Inc., Balt., 1974-80, Dowbeaters, Inc., Summit, N.J. and Balt., 1981-83, Highland Advisors Group, Inc., N.Y.C., 1981—, McCullough, Andrews and Capiello, Inc., Balt. and San Francisco, 1983—; TV panelist Wall St. Week, 1970—; prof. fin. Loyola Coll., Balt., 1980—; mem. adv. investment com. Md. State Retirement Systems. Trustee Balt. City Pension System; mem., commr. Md. State Econ. and Community Devel. Commn., 1977—. Served with U.S. Marine Corps, 1950-52. Mem. Fin. Analysts Fedn. (chmn., dir.), Balt. Security Analysts Soc. Roman Catholic. Clubs: Univ., Harvard (N.Y.C.); Hamilton Street (Balt.). Home: 112 Tunbridge Rd Baltimore MD 21212 Office: 1500 Sulgrave Ave Baltimore MD 21209

CAPPON, ALEXANDER PATTERSON, educator; b. Milw., May 11, 1900; s. John, Jr. and Charlotte Curry (Patterson) C.; m. Dorothy Churchill, Nov. 13, 1922; 1 dau., Frances Burney (Mrs. Hardison J. Geer). Student, Milw. State Tchrs. Coll., 1919-20, Harvard, 1921, 1929-31; Ph.B., U. Chgo., 1925, M.A., 1926, Ph.D., 1935. Instr. English U. Tulsa, 1926-27; asso. English lit. U. Wash., 1927-29; lit. editor The New Humanist, 1931-35; instr. English Mont. State. Coll., 1932-33, asst. prof., 1934-37; instr. Western Ill. State Tchrs. Coll., 1934; asso. editor U. Kansas City Rev., 1937, 42-52, editor in chief, 1938-42, 53-70; asst. prof. English U. Kansas City, 1937-41, asso. prof., 1941-45, chmn. dept. English, 1941-44, 48-51, prof. English lang. and lit., 1945-63; prof. English lit., editor in chief Univ. Rev., U. Mo. at Kansas City, 1953-70. Author: About Wordsworth and Whitehead: A Prelude to Philosophy, Aspects of Wordsworth and Whitehead: Philosophy and Certain Continuing Life Problems, 1983; contbr. articles to profl. pubs. Research on Bertrand Russell. Mem. Modern Lang. Assn. AAUP, Phi Kappa Phi. Home: 16 E 52d St Kansas City MO 64112

CAPPON, RENE JACQUES, editor; b. Vienna, Austria, July 2, 1924; s. Lazare and Bertha (Mond) C.; m. Susan E. Brown, Feb. 4, 1960; children: Elizabeth Ann, Rene Jacques. Student, U. Iowa, 1941-44. With AP, 1946-61, 64—, fgn. corr., Berlin, 1951, news features editor, 1957-61, mng. editor, 1964-71, gen. news editor, N.Y.C., 1971—; mng. editor Anchorage Daily News, 1962-64. Author: The Word: An Associated Press Guide to Good News Writing, 1982. Office: Associated Press 50 Rockefeller Plaza New York NY 10020

CAPPS, ETHAN LEROY, oil company executive; b. Sherman, Tex., Dec. 2, 1924; s. Ethen Daniel and Annie Mae (Anderson) C.; m. Emily Ann Tyson, Sept. 8, 1951; children—Richard LeRoy, Nancy Elizabeth. B.S., Tex. A. and M. U., 1948; grad., Advanced Mgmt. Program, Harvard, 1965. C.P.A., Tex. With Tenn. Gas Transmission Co., Houston, 1948-59, asst. treas., budget dir., 1960-61; chief accountant Midwestern Gas Transmission Co., Houston, 1959; v.p. Tenneco Corp., Houston, 1961-63; adminstrv. v.p., controller Tenneco Oil Co., Houston, 1963-73; v.p., treas. Tenneco Inc., 1974—. Treas., bd. dirs. Planned Parenthood, Houston, 1963-69. Served to 1st lt. AUS, 1944-46. Mem. Am. Inst. C.P.A.'s, Tex. Soc. C.P.A.'s. Presbyn. Clubs: Petroleum, Racquet (Houston). Home: 6206 Cedar Creek Houston TX 77057 Office: PO Box 2511 1010 Milam St Houston TX 77001

CAPPS, JOHN PAUL, state legislator, radio station owner; b. Steprock, Ark., Apr. 17, 1934; s. Edwin H. and Vivian Pinegar C.; m. Elizabeth Ann Vaughan, 1955; children: Paula Ann, Kimberly Kay, John Paul. Student, Beebe Jr. Coll. Annoucer Sta.-KWCB, Searcy, Ark., 1955-57, asst. mgr., 1958-64, sta. mgr., 1965—; announcer Sta.-KTHV, Little Rock, 1957-58; v.p., gen. mgr. Sta.-KWCK, Searcy, Ark., 1971-75; owner, operator Sta.-KAPZ Radio, 1980—; mem. Ark. Ho. of Reps., Little Rock, 1963—, now speaker of house. Served with U.S. Army. Recipient Disting. Service award Searcy Jaycees, 1968. Mem. Jaycees, Mental Health Assn., C. of C. Democrat. Mem. Ch. of Christ. Lodge: Lions. Office: Office of Speaker Ark Ho of Reps Little Rock AR 72201 *

CAPPS, RICHARD HUNTLEY, physicist, educator; b. Wichita, Kans., July 1, 1928; s. Charles M. and Anna (Palmer) C.; m. Joan P. Salatino, June 18, 1955; m. Thelma L. Blair, June 3, 1975; stepchildren: Hollis Blair Westler, Patricia L. Blair, Elizabeth B. Spencer. B.A., U. Kans., 1950; M.A., U. Wis., 1952, Ph.D., 1955. Research asso. U. Calif. at Berkeley, 1955-57; faculty U. Wash., 1957-58; research asso. Cornell U., 1958-60; faculty Northwestern U., Evanston, Ill., 1960-67, prof., 1965-67; prof. physics Purdue U., Lafayette, Ind., 1967—. Contbr. articles to profl. jours. Mem. Am. Phys. Soc. Research on theoretical investigation of basic laws of fundamental sub-atomic particles. Home: 2724 Henderson West Lafayette IN 47906 Office: Purdue U Lafayette IN 47907

CAPRA, FRANK, producer and director motion pictures; b. Palermo, Italy, May 18, 1897; came to U.S. at age of 6; s. Salvatore C.; m. Lucille Warner, 1933; 3 children. Ed., Calif. Inst. Tech. Lectr. in field.; Pres. Acad. of Motion Picture Arts and Sciences, 4 times; pres. Screen Dirs. Guild, 3 times. Producer motion pictures, 1921—; produced, directed: The Strong Man, Submarine, Flight, Dirigible, American Madness, Platinum Blonde, Lady for a Day, It Happened One Night, Mr. Deed Goes to Town, Pocketful of Miracles, Mr. Smith Goes to Washington, Lost Horizon, Broadway Bill, You Can't Take It With You, Meet John Doe, Arsenic and Old Lace, It's a Wonderful Life, State of the Union, Riding High, Here Comes the Groom; dir.: TV spl. 50th Anniversary Columbia Pictures, ABC-TV, 1975; made: series of army orientation films Why We Fight; Author: The Name Above The Title, 1971. Bd. dirs. Calif. Inst. Tech. Served as pvt., advancing to 2d lt. U.S. Army, World War I; commd. maj. U.S. Army, 1942; disch. with rank of col., 1945. Decorated D.S.M., Legion of Merit; Order British Empire.; Recipient 3 Academy awards (Oscars) for best direction of year; twice produced pictures which received Acad. award as best of the year.; Lifetime Achievement award Am. Film Inst., 1982. Address: care Acad Motion Picture Arts and Scis 8949 Wilshire Blvd Beverly Hills CA 90211

CAPRA, JACK REMO, wholesale commodity company executive; b. N.Y.C., Oct. 23, 1923; s. Battista J. and Maria (Garlasco) C.; children: Richard, Douglas. B.B.A., CCNY, 1946; student, Fordham U., 1944. Staff acct. Price, Waterhouse & Co., N.Y.C., 1947-48, Peat, Marwick Mitchell & Co., 1949-50; asst. treas. Newmont Oil Co., N.Y.C., 1950-51; sr. acct. Arthur Young & Co., N.Y.C., 1952-53; v.p. fin., dir. Gill & Duffus, Inc., N.Y.C., 1953—; exec. v.p., dir. Gill & Duffus Securities Inc., 1980-81; dir. G & D Energy, Inc. Served with U.S. Army, 1943-46. Office: Gill & Duffus Inc 130 John St New York NY 10038

CAPRA, TOM, TV producer; s. Frank and Lucille (Warner) C. B.A., U. So. Calif.; postgrad. in mgmt, Harvard U., 1968. Reporter UPI, 1963; with Sta. KTLA-TV, Los Angeles, 1964-67; writer, producer, editor; news dir., corr. Sta. KXTV, Sacramento, 1967-70; producer Sta. KABC-TV, Los Angeles, 1970; West Coast field producer NBC Nightly News, 1971; with ABC News, 1972—; sr. producer 20/20, 1979—. (Emmy award 1968). Recipient Peabody award, 1964. Address: ABC Public Relations 1330 Ave of Americas New York NY 10019 *

CAPRANICA, ROBERT RUDY, neuroethologist, electrical engineer, educator; b. Los Angeles, May 29, 1931; s. Rudy P. and Elsie Anna C.; m. Patricia Alna Mullen, Feb. 1, 1958. B.S., U. Calif., Berkeley, 1958; M.S., NYU, 1960; Sc.D., MIT, 1964. Tech. staff Bell Telephone Labs., Murray Hill, N.J., 1958-69; asso. prof. neurobiology and behavior and elec. engring. Cornell U., Ithaca, N.Y., 1969-75, prof., 1975—; vis. zoology U. Witwatersrand, Johannesburg, South Africa, 1982-83. Editor: Jour. Comparative Physiology, 1974—; cons. editor: Jour. Music Perception, 1981—; bd. editorial commentators: Behavorial Brain Scis.; contbr. articles to profl. jours. Served with USN, 1951-54. Communications Devel. fellow Bell Telephone Labs., 1960-64; NATO sr. fellow in sci., 1976-77; Council Sci. Indsl. Research fellow, South Africa, 1982-83; NIH, NSF prin. investigator grantee. Fellow Acoustical Soc. Am., Explorers Club, AAAS; mem. Am. Physiol. Soc., Am. Soc. Zoologists, Am. Soc. Ichthyologists and Herpetologists, Internat. Brain Research Orgn., Soc. Neurosci., Am. Speech-Lang.-Hearing Assn., Assn. Research Otolaryngology, Soc. Animal Behavior, Sigma Xi. Research in animal sound communication, neurophysiol. processing in auditory nervous system. Home: 1397 Ellis Hollow Rd Ithaca NY 14850 Office: Cornell Univ W-255 Seeley GMudd Hall Sect Neurobiology and Behavior Ithaca NY 14853

CAPRARO, ALBERT, fashion designer; b. N.Y.C., May 20, 1943; s. Carmine and Mary C. B.F.A., Parsons Sch. Design, 1964. Critic Parsons Sch. Design, 1974-80. Assoc., Lily Dache, 1964-65; assoc. designer, Oscar de la Renta, 1966-74; clothes designer for numerous celebrities; (Recipient Outstanding Am. Designer award Salvation Army Aux. 1975-76, Fashion award Fashion Sales Guild of N.Y. 1975, Camelia Fashion award Birmingham, Ala. 1975, Internat. award for outstanding contbn. to fashion Girls Town of Italy 1975, named Bicentennial Designer of Year, Balt. County Bicentennial Com. 1976, Designer to Distinguished Women, AAUW, Austin, Tex. 1978). Award for distinguished service to City of N.Y. Boys Town of Italy, 1977. Mem. Fashion Designers Am. (council). Office: Albert Capraro Ltd 550 7th Ave New York NY 10018 *

CAPRON, ALEXANDER MORGAN, lawyer, educator; b. Hartford, Conn., Aug. 16, 1944. B.A., Swarthmore Coll., 1966; LL.B., Yale U., 1969; M.A. (hon.), U. Pa., 1975. Bar: D.C. 1970, Pa. 1978. Law clk. to Chief Judge David L. Bazelon, U.S. Ct. Appeals, D.C., 1969-70; lectr., research asso. Yale U., 1970-72; asst. prof. law U. Pa., 1972-75, asso. prof., 1975-78, prof. law and human genetics, 1978-82, vice dean, 1976; prof. law, ethics and pub. policy Law Ctr. Georgetown U., Washington, 1983-84, inst. fellow Kennedy Inst. Ethics, 1983-84; Topping prof. law, medicine and pub. policy U. So. Calif., 1984—; mem. policy adv. com. Joint Commn. Accreditation of Hosps., 1984—; exec. dir. Pres.'s Commn. for Study of Ethical Problems in Med., Biomed. and Behavioral Research, 1980-83; cons. NIH, Office Tech. Assessment. Author: (with Katz) Catastrophic Diseases: Who Decides What?, 1976, (with others) Genetic Counseling: Facts, Values and Norms, 1979, Law, Science and Medicine, 1984; contbr. articles to profl. jours. Vice chmn. bd. dirs. Washington Sq. West Project Area Com., Phila., 1975-77; bd. mgrs. Swarthmore Coll. Fellow Inst. Soc., Ethics and the Life Scis. (dir.); mem. Inst. of Medicine of Nat. Acad. Sci., Soc. Am. Law Tchrs., AAUP (mem. exec. com. Pa. chpt.), Am. Soc. Law and Medicine (dir.), Swarthmore Coll. Alumni Soc. (v.p. 1974-77). Club: Cosmos (Washington). Office: USC Law Center University Park Los Angeles CA 90089

CAPSALIS, BARBARA DAMON, banker; b. Washington, Apr. 22, 1943; d. Wallace Carver and Gertrude Marie Damon (Larson) Damon; m. John N. Capsalis, Aug. 7, 1965. B.S. cum laude in Math, Ohio U. Dep. commr. N.Y.C. Dept. Gen. Services; sr. v.p. ops. staff adminstrn. wholesale services Chem. Bank, N.Y.C. Recipient Woman of Achievement award YWCA. Office: 55 Water St New York NY 10041

CAPUTO, DAVID ARMAND, political scientist; b. Brownsville, Pa., Aug. 30, 1943; s. Armand and Marie E. (Smalstig) C.; m. Alice M. Glotfelty, June 27, 1964; children—Christopher, Elizabeth, Jeffrey. B.A., Miami U., Oxford, Ohio, 1965; M.A., Yale U., 1967, M.Phil., 1968, Ph.D., 1970. Mem. faculty Purdue U., 1969—, prof. polit. sci., 1977—, head dept., 1978—. Author: Urban America: The Policy Alternatives, 1976; co-author: Urban Politics and Decentralization, 1974; editor: Politics of Policy-Making in America, 1977. Ruling elder Central Presbyn. Ch., Lafayette, Ind., 1981—. Woodrow Wilson nat. fellow, 1965-66; NSF Faculty fellow, 1977. Mem. Am. Polit. Sci. Assn., Am. Soc. Public Adminstrn., Midwest Polit. Sci. Assn., So. Polit. Sci. Assn., Phi Beta Kappa, Omicron Delta Kappa. Home: 5415 Hillside Ln West Lafayette IN 47906 Office: Recitation Hall Purdue U West Lafayette IN 47907

CAPUTO, JOSEPH ANTHONY, university president; b. Jersey City, May 10, 1940; s. Anthony and Virginia (Bennett) C.; m. Linda Mary Ryan, Sept. 4, 1965; children: Christine D., David R. B.S., Seton Hall U., 1962; M.S., Seton U., 1964; Ph.D., U. Houston, 1967. Research assoc. Duke U., Durham, N.C., 1967-68; prof. dept. chemistry SUNY Coll.-Buffalo, 1968-77, chmn. dept. chemistry, 1974-77, v.p. acad. affairs, 1979-81; dean sch. sci. and math. S.W. Tex. State U., San Marcos, 1977-79; pres. Millersville U., Pa., 1981—; dir. Edwards Aquifier Research and Data Ctr., 1979-81; cons. Pearsall Chem. Corp., 1978, Nat. Bur. Standards, 1973. Author: The Thermal Catalytic Equilibration of Cis and Trans Decalone-2, 1964, Studies in Electronic Transmission, 1967. SUNY Research Found. fellow, 1969; grantee, 1968-70; NSF grantee, 1972-73; Am. Chem. Soc. grantee, 1969-72. Fellow AAAS, Chem. Soc., Commn. for State Colls. and Univs., Sigma

Xi, Phi Kappa Phi. Home: 10 Hemlock Ln Millersville PA 17551 Office: Millersville Univ of Pa Millersville PA 17551

CAPUTO, PHILIP JOSEPH, author, journalist; b. Chgo., June 10, 1941; s. Joseph and Marie Ylonda (Napolitan) C.; m. Jill Esther Ongemach, June 21, 1969 (div. 1982); children: Geoffrey Jacob, Marc Anthony.; m. Marcelle Lynn Besse, Oct. 30, 1982. B.A. in English, Loyola U., Chgo., 1964. Mem. staff Chgo. Tribune, fgn. corr., Rome, 1972-74, Beirut, 1974-76, Moscow, 1976-77. Author: A Rumor of War, 1977, Horn of Africa, 1980; author: Del Corso's Gallery, 1983. Served with USMCR, 1964-67; Vietnam. Recipient award Ill. Asso. Press, Ill. United Press; Green Gavel award Am. Bar. Assn.; Overseas Press Club award; Pulitzer prize; Sidney Hillman award. Mem. Authors Guild. Democrat. Roman Catholic. Address: care Holt Rinehart & Winston 521 Fifth Ave New York NY 10017

CAPWELL, RICHARD LEONARD, educator; b. East Greenwich, R.I., May 6, 1920; s. Walter Henry and Grace (Knowles) C.; m. Margaret Ruth Johnston, Dec. 19, 1959; children—Richard Johnston, Alton Robert. A.B., Brown U., 1942; M.A., Yale, 1946; Ph.D., Duke, 1964. Instr. Adm. Billard Acad., New London, Conn., 1942-44; instr. Milton (Mass.) Acad., 1944-45, U. Mo., Columbia, 1946-49, Ohio Wesleyan U., Delaware, 1952-54; asst. prof. East Carolina U., Greenville, N.C., 1957-64, asso. prof., 1964-66; prof. 17th Century English lit., 1966—, dean, 1969-80. Contbg. editor: Abstracts of English Studies, 1961—. Mem. Modern Lang. Assn. Am., South Atlantic Modern Lang. Assn., Renaissance Soc. Am., Southeastern Renaissance Conf., Phi Beta Kappa, Phi Kappa Phi. Methodist. Club: Greenville Golf and Country. Home: 206 Dalebrook Circle Greenville NC 27834

CARALEY, DEMETRIOS, political scientist, educator, author; b. N.Y.C., June 22, 1932; s. Chris and Stella (Psaras) C.; m. Jeanne Louise Benner, Sept. 7, 1957; children: James Christopher (dec.), David Andrew, Anne Leslie. B.A. summa cum laude, Columbia U., 1954, Ph.D., 1962. Mem. faculty Barnard Coll. and Columbia U., N.Y.C., 1959—, prof. polit. sci., 1968—, Janet H. Robb prof. social scis., 1980—; dir. Columbia Grad. Program in Public Policy and Adminstrn., 1978—. Author: Politics of Military Unification, 1966, New York City's Deputy Mayor—City Administrator, 1966, Party Politics and National Elections, 1966, (with R. H. Connery) Governing the City, 1969, City Governments and Urban Problems, 1977, American Political Institutions in the, 1970's, 1976, (with M.A. Epstein) The Making of American Foreign and Domestic Policy, 1978, Doing More With Less, 1982, (with R. H. Connery) National Security and Nuclear Strategy, 1983; contbr.: American Politics and Public Policy, 1978, Urban Policymaking, 1979; editor: Polit. Sci. Quar, 1973—. Mem. North Tarrytown Zoning Bd. Appeals, 1970-71; mem. North Tarrytown Bd. Trustees, 1971-73, dep. mayor and acting mayor, 1972-73; chmn. North Tarrytown Planning Bd., 1977-79; mem. N.Y.C. Police Commr.'s Research Adv. Bd., 1979—. Served with USNR, 1954-56. Mem. Am. Polit. Sci. Assn., Acad. Polit. Sci., Phi Beta Kappa. Democrat. Home: 24 Hemlock Dr North Tarrytown NY 10591 Office: Dept Polit Sci Barnard Coll Columbia U New York NY 10027

CARAMEROS, GEORGE DEMITRIUS, JR., natural gas company executive; b. El Paso, Tex., Mar.1, 1924; s. George Demitrius and Esperanza (Purdy) C.; m. Verna Narcissus Easterling, May 26, 1944; children: Cecille (Mrs. George Shannon), Cynthia (Mrs. John Blevins), Cathy (Mrs. David Patton), George Demitrius III, Carl. B.A., U. Tex., El Paso, 1947. With El Paso Natural Gas Co., 1948—; mgr. new projects devel. subs. El Paso Products Co., 1957-60; mng. dir. El Paso Europe-Afrique, Paris, France, 1960-65, instrv. asst. to chmn. bd., N.Y.C., 1965-66, asst. v.p., 1966-70, v.p., 1970-73, exec. v.p., 1973-75, dir., 1974-80; exec. v.p. The El Paso Co., 1975-78, dir., 1975-80, vice chmn., 1978-80; pres. El Paso LNG Co., Houston, 1975-78, chmn., 1978-80; also dir.; chmn., dir. Internat. Gas Devel. Corp., 1980—; dir. Internat. Energy Devel. Corp., Tex. Commerce Med. Bank. Served with AUS, World War II. Decorated Bronze Star, Combat Inf. badge. Mem. Interstate Natural Gas Assn Am. (dir.). Methodist. Clubs: Ramada, Heritage, Houston, Lakeside Country, Racquet (Houston). Home: 660 Shartle Circle Houston TX 77024 Office: 711 Polk Ave Suite 1030 Houston TX 77002

CARAPETYAN, ARMEN, editor, musicologist; b. Oct. 11, 1908; U.S., 1928, naturalized, 1942; s. Mackertoum and Miriam (Khazarian) C.; m. Harriette Esther Norris, Nov. 4, 1937; children—Francelle, Peter Anthony. Diploma, Am. Coll., Teheran, 1927; student in, Paris, France, then N.Y.C.; M.A., Harvard U., 1940, Ph.D., 1945. Founder, 1945; since dir. Am. Inst. Musicology (specializing Medieval and Renaissance music), Cambridge, Mass.; spl. work in fostering research and publs. in field, directing project. Dir.: Corpus Mensurabilis Musicae, Musicological Studies and Documents; editor, pub.: Musica Disciplina (yearbook); dir.: Renaissance Manuscript Studies, Miscellanea. Hon. mem. Am., Internat. musicol. socs. Home: PO Box 2051 Tubac AZ 85640 Office: Hänssler Verlag Postfach 1220 7303 Neuhausen-Stuttgart Federal Republic of Germany

CARAS, JOSEPH SHELDON, life insurance company executive; b. Lawrence, Mass., Aug. 3, 1924; s. Joseph and Bessie Esther (Kasanoff) C.; m. Adele Salett, June 8, 1947; children: Richard, David, Susan. B.A., Bowdoin Coll., 1948; C.L.U., 1956. With Met. Life Ins. Co., 1949-55, asst. mgr., Waltham, MAss., 1951-55; with New Eng. Mut. Life Ins. Co., 1955—, 2d. v.p. mktg., Boston, 1967-71, sr. v.p. mktg. services, 1971-81, sr. v.p. mktg., 1982—; pres. New Eng. Nat., 1981—; dir. New Eng. Nat. of N.Y., Covenant Life Ins. Co., InterNEL Corp. Mem. Swampscott (Mass.) Town Meeting, 1972-78; past pres. Temple Emanu-El, Marblehead, Mass. Served with USAAF, 1943-45. Decorated Air medal. Mem. Life Ins. Mktg. Research Assn. (past chmn. sales com. and mktg. services com.), Agy. Mgmt. Tng. Council, Assn. Advanced Life Underwriters, Nat. Assn. Life Underwriters, Am. Soc. C.L.U.'s. Home: 4 Driftwood Rd Marblehead MA 01945 Office: 501 Boylston St Boston MA 02117

CARAS, ROGER ANDREW, author, motion picture company executive; b. Metheun, Mass., May 24, 1928; s. Joseph J. and Bessie (Kasanoff) C.; m. Jill Langdon Barclay, Sept. 5, 1954; children: Pamela Jill, Barclay Gordon. Student, Northeastern U., 1948-49, Western Res. U., 1949-50; B.A. in Cinema, U. So. Calif., 1952; Litt.D., Rio Grande Coll., 1979. Asst. to v.p., also nat. dir. merchandising for U.S. and Can., Columbia Pictures Corp., 1955-65; v.p. Stanley Kubrick's Polaris Prodns., N.Y.C., 1965-68, Hawk Films Ltd., London, Eng., 1965-68; coll. lectr. on wildlife and conservation, 1955-65; sci. editor Armed Forces Radio and TV Service, 1963-68; adj. prof. lit. Southampton Coll., 1975—; lectr. U. Pa. Sch. Vet. Medicine, 1978—, bd. overseers, 1981—. Columnist, Register & Tribune Syndicate, Ladies Home Jour., 1977—, Newsday, 1980—; star, CBS radio show, Pets and Wildlife; TV commentator, ABC-TV; Author: Antarctica: Land of Frozen Time, 1962, Dangerous to Man, 1964, Wings of Gold, 1965; pseudonym Roger Sarac: The Throwbacks, 1965, The Custer Wolf, 1966, Mammals of North America, 1966, Last Chance on Earth, 1966, Sarang, 1968, Monarch of Deadman Bay, 1969, Source of the Thunder, 1970, Panther, 1970, Death as a Way of Life, 1971, The Private Lives of Animals, 1974, Venomous Animals of the World, 1974, Sockeye, 1975, The Roger Caras Pet Book, 1976, A Zoo in Your Room, 1975, The Forest, 1979, Mysteries of Nature, 1979, Yankee, 1979, Amiable Little Beasts, 1980, The Roger Caras Dog Book, 1980, A Celebration of Dogs, 1982, A Roger Caras Treasury, 1984; contbg. editor: Geo Mag, 1979—. Asso. curator rare books Cleve. Mus. Natural History; mem. adv. council Ariz.-Sonora Desert Mus.; Mem. adv. bd. Zero Population Growth.; Vice pres. zoo and wildlife com. Morris Animal Found.; v.p. Humane Soc. U.S. Recipient Joseph Wood Krutch medal, 1977; Scroll of Achievement Hai-Bar Soc., Israel, 1977; Arbor Day ann. TV award, 1982; 1st recipient Oryx award Israel, 1983. Fellow Royal Soc. Arts, Rochester Museum and Sci. Center; mem. Authors League, Outdoor Writers Assn., Mensa, Blue Key, Delta Kappa Alpha (past nat. pres.). Home: 46 Fenmarsh Rd East Hampton NY 11937 *Fight as hard as you must, if you are sure of what you believe, and work as hard as you can, but at all costs avoid causing pain, fear or anguish in another living creature—including fellow human beings. There are only three sins—causing pain, causing fear, causing anguish. The rest is window dressing.*

CARAVATT, PAUL JOSEPH, JR., communications co. exec.; b. New Britain, Conn., Dec. 13, 1922; s. Paul Joseph and Bessie (Avery) C.; m. B. Laura Bennett, June 22, 1946; children—Cynthia Diane, Suzanne Laura. A.B., Dartmouth, 1945, M.C.S., 1947. With Nat. Dairy Assn., 1947-49, Young & Rubicam, 1949-50; advt. mgr. Hunting and Fishing mag., 1950-52, Biow Co., 1952-56; v.p. Ogilvy, Benson & Mather, 1956-59; sr. v.p. Foote, Cone & Belding, 1960-64, LaRoche, McCaffrey & McCall (advt. agy.), N.Y.C., 1964-66; pres. Carl Ally, Ind. (advt. agy.), N.Y.C., 1966-67; chmn. bd., chief exec. officer Marschalk Co., Inc. (mem. Interpublic Group of Cos.), N.Y.C., 1967-69; sr. v.p., dir. Interpublic Group Cos., N.Y.C., 1970-72; pres., chief exec. officer, dir. Caravatt Communications, also; Newtel World Communications, N.Y.C., 1971—. Mem. Newcomen Soc., S.A.R., Zeta Psi. Republican. Conglist. Club: University (N.Y.C.). Home: 274 Westport Rd Wilton CT 06897 Office: 551 Fifth Ave New York NY 10017

CARAY, HARRY CHRISTOPHER, sports announcer; b. St. Louis, Mar. 1, 1919; s. Christopher and Daisy (Argint) Carabina; m. Dolores, June 8, 1975; children: Harry, Patricia, Christopher, Michelle, Elizabeth. Student pub. schs., St. Louis. Sports announcer St. Louis Baseball, 1944-69, Oakland (Calif.) A's, 1969-70, Chgo. White Sox, 1970-81; sports announcer Chgo. Cubs, 1982—; broadcaster numerous All-Star, World Series, and Bowl games. Recipient numerous awards. Address: care Chicago Cubs Wrigley Field Chicago IL 60613 *

CARB, STEPHEN AMES, lawyer; b. Bklyn., Nov. 27, 1930; s. Alfred Benjamin and Betty (Pocost) C.; m. Sarah Rover, Dec. 24, 1971; 1 son, Daniel; children by previous marriage—Alison, Brian, Evan. A.B., Colgate U., 1952; LL.B., Columbia, 1955. Bar: N.Y. State bar 1958. Since practiced in, N.Y.C.; asso. firm Carb, Luria, Glassner, Cook & Kufeld, N.Y.C., 1958-61, partner, 1961—; dir., mem. exec. com. N. Atlantic Life Ins. Co. Am.; dir. Seiden & de Cuevas, Inc. Served to lt. (j.g.) USNR, 1955-58. Mem. Am. Bar Assn., Assn. Bar City N.Y., Phi Kappa Tau, Phi Alpha Delta. Club: Players. Home: 254 E 68th St New York City NY 10021 Office: 529 Fifth Ave New York City NY 10017

CARBERRY, JOHN J.CARDINAL, former archbishop of St. Louis; b. Bklyn., July 31, 1904. Recipient D.D., S.T.D., Ph.D., J.C.D., LL.D. degrees. Ordained priest Roman Catholic Ch., 1929; apptd. titular bishop of Elis, coadjutor cum Jure successionis, 1956, consecrated, 1956, succeeded to See, 1957, bishop of, Columbus, Ohio, until 1968, archbishop of, St. Louis, 1968-79; named to Coll. Cardinals, 1969; apptd. apostolic adminstr., 1979; Pres. Center Applied Research in the Apostolate, 1970—. Home: 4445 Lindell Blvd St Louis MO 63108 *

CARBINE, PATRICIA THERESA, magazine publisher; b. Villanova, Pa., Jan. 31, 1931; d. James T. and Margaret (Dee) C. B.A. in English, Rosemont Coll., 1952. With Look mag., 1953-70, mng. editor, 1966-69, exec. editor, 1969-70; editor McCall's mag., 1970-72; pub. Ms. mag., N.Y.C., 1972—. Vice chmn. trustees Rosemont Coll., 1972—; former chmn., now hon. chmn. Advt. Council. Mem. Am. Soc. Mag. Editors (exec. com.), Mag. Pubs. Assn. (bd. dirs. 1973—). *

CARBON, MAX WILLIAM, educator; b. Monon, Ind., Jan. 19, 1922; s. Joseph William and Mary Olive (Goble) C.; m. Phyllis Camille Myers, Apr. 13, 1944; children—Ronald Allen, Jean Ann, Susan Jane, David William, Janet Elaine. B.S. in Mech. Engring, Purdue U., 1943, M.S., 1947, Ph.D., 1949. With Hanford works Gen. Electric Co., 1949-55, head heat transfer unit, 1951-55; with research and advanced devel. div. Avco Mfg. Corp., 1955-58, chief thermodynamics sect., 1956-58; prof., chmn. nuclear engring. dept. U. Wis. Coll. Engring., 1958—; group leader Ford Found. program, Singapore, 1967-68; mem. Adv. Com. on Reactor Safeguards. Served to capt. ordnance dept. AUS, 1943- 46. Mem. Am. Nuclear Soc., AAAS, Am. Soc. Engring. Edn., AAUP, Sigma Xi, Tau Beta Pi. Office: Engring Research Bldg U Wis Madison WI 53706

CARBONE, JOHN VITO, physician; b. Sacramento, Dec. 13, 1922; s. Vito and Prima Marie (Demaria) C.; m. Gene Elizaeth Grinslade, Sept. 1, 1946; children—John Vito, Jerome, James. A.B., U. Calif., Berkeley, 1945, M.D., 1948. Intern San Francisco Gen. Hosp., 1948-49, sr. asst. resident, 1950-51, asst. chief med. service, 1958-60, chief blue med. service, 1960-61; resident dept. metabolism Walter Reed Army Hosp., 1952-54; Giannini fellow in medicine, 1954-55; asst. resident in medicine U. Calif. Med Center, San Francisco, 1949-50, chief resident, 1950-51, instr., 1951-52, fellow, 1954-55, asst. prof., 1955-60, asso. prof., 1960-66, chief gastroenterology div., 1961-66, prof. medicine, 1966—. Contbr. numerous articles to med. jours. Served to capt. M.C. USAR, 1952-54. Recipient Gold Headed Cane award U. Calif. Sch. Medicine, 1948, Acad. Senate Teaching award, 1959, Disting. Teaching award, 1968, 69; named Alumnus of Yr., 1976. Fellow A.C.P.; mem. Am. Fedn. Clin. Research, Calif. Soc. Internal Medicine, Am. Gastroenterology Assn., Western Soc. Clin. Investigation, Soc. Exptl. Biology and Medicine, AMA, Western Soc. Physicians, Phi Beta Kappa, Alpha Omega Alpha. Office: U Calif Med Center San Francisco CA 94143

CARBONE, PAUL PETER, cancer researcher; b. White Plains, N.Y., May 2, 1931; s. Antonio and Grace (Cappelieri) C.; m. Mary Iamurri, Aug. 20, 1954; children—David, Kathryn, Karen, Kim, Paul J., Mary Beth, Matthew. Student, Union Coll., Schenectady, 1949-52; M.D., Albany (N.Y.). Med. Coll., 1956. Diplomate: Am. Bd. Internal Medicine. Joined USPHS, 1956; intern USPHS Hosp., Balt., 1956-57, resident in internal medicine, San Francisco, 1958-60; mem. staff Nat. Cancer Inst., NIH, Bethesda, Md., 1960-76, chief medicine br., 1968-72, asso. dir. for med. oncology, div. cancer treatment, 1972-76, dep. clin. dir., 1972-76; clin. prof. Georgetown U. Med. Sch., 1971-76; lectr. hematology Walter Reed Army Inst. Research, 1962-76; prof. medicine and human oncology U. Wis., Madison, 1976—, dir. div. clin. oncology, 1976—, chmn. dept. human oncology, 1977—; dir. Wis. Clin. Cancer Center, 1978—. Contbr. profl. jours. Decorated USPHS Commendation medal; recipient Trimble Lecture award Md. Chirurgical Faculty, 1968; Lasker award clin. cancer chemotherapy, 1972; Rosenthal award for improvement in clin. cancer care, 1977. Mem. A.C.P., Exptl. Hematology Soc., Am. Soc. Clin. Investigation, Am. Soc. Clin. Oncology (pres. 1972-73), Am. Soc. Clin. Investigation, Am. Soc. Hematology, Am. Assn. Cancer Research (pres. 1978-79), Am. Fedn. Clin. Research, AMA, Alpha Omega Alpha. Home: 6115 N Highlands Ave Madison WI 53705 Office: Univ Hosps 600 Highland Ave Madison WI 53792

CARBONE, ROBERT FRANK, educator; b. Plentywood, Mont., July 27, 1929; s. Charles and Antoinette (Sack) C.; m. Suzanne M. Wirth, Mar. 23, 1968; children: Angela Michelle, Christopher Wirth. B.S., Eastern Mont. Coll., 1953; M.Ed., Emory U., 1958; Ph.D., U. Chgo., 1961. Instr. U. Chgo., 1960-61; asso. Dr. James B. Conant (A Study of Edn. of Am. Tchrs.), 1961-62; asst. prof. Emory U., 1962-65; asst. to pres. U. Wis., 1965-70; dean Coll. Edn., U. Md., College Park, 1970-74, prof. higher and adult edn., 1974—; Mem. Danforth Conf. on Liberal Arts Edn., summer 1964. Author: (with others) The Nongraded School, 1967, Resident or Nonresident, 1970, Students and State Borders, 1973, Alternative Tuition Systems, 1974, Presidential Passages, 1981; Contbr. articles to profl. jours. Served with U.S. Army, 1953-55. Home: 1805 Pelling Ct Silver Spring MD 20904 Office: Coll Edn U Md College Park MD 20742

CARBONNEAU, COME, mining company executive; b. Saint-Jean-des-Piles, Que., Can., Nov. 24, 1923; s. Omer and Edith (Bordeleau) C.; m. Francoise Pettigrew, Sept. 15, 1951; children: Helene, Marie, Jean, Pierre, Lise, Alaine. B.A., Laval U., 1943, 1948, M.A., U. B.C., 1959; Ph.D. in Geology, McGill U., 1953. Assoc. prof. geology Ecole Polytechnique, Montreal, Que., 1951-63; exec. v.p. SOQUEM, Sainte Foy, Que., 1963-65, founding pres., chief exec. officer, 1965-77; prof. Laval U., Quebec City, Que., 1977-81, chmn. dept. geology, 1979-81; pres., chief exec. officer Corp. Falconbridge Copper, Toronto, Ont., Can., 1981—; cons. geologist St. Lawrence Columbium, Oka, Que., 1953-59; chmn., dir. Bachelor Lake Gold Mines Inc., Montreal, 1980—; dir. Les Releves Geophysiques Inc. Decorated officer Order of Can. Fellow Geol. Assn. of Can.; mem. Can. Inst. Mining and Metallurgy (A.O. Dufresne award 1978), Sigma Xi. Clubs: Cercle Universitaire (Quebec); Engineers (Toronto). Home: 2540 Rue Keable Sanite Foy PQ Canada G1W 1L3 Office: Corp Falconbridge Cooper PO Box 40 Commerce Ct W Toronto ON Canada M5L 1B4

CARBTREE, JACK TURNER, lawyer; b. Mountain View, Okla., Feb. 23, 1936; s. Andrew J. and Dorrit (Turner) Crabtree; (div.)children:Elizabeth Kaye, Deborah Anne, Jacqueline Sue, Nancy Lea. Mus.B., Oklahoma City U., 1960, J.D., 1964. Bar: Okla. 1964, U.S. Supreme Ct. 1967. Practice, Oklahoma City, 1964—; mem. firm Matthews, Buck, Cain, Crabtree & Lynn, 1965-67, Buck, Crabtree, Randsdell & Buford, Inc., 1967-79, Jack T. Crabtee & Assocs., P.C., Oklahoma City, 1979—; adj. prof. law Oklahoma City U. Sch. Law, 1972-80; instr. legal asst. program U. Okla., 1980—; dir. Quail Creek Bank N.A.; chmn. Okla. EPA, 1972. Mem. ABA (com. legal assts. 1974-80, council gen. practice sect. 1973-77, 79-80, sec. 1980-81), Okla. Bar Assn. (chmn. legal assts. com. 1975-78), Oklahoma County Bar Assn. (chmn. com. specialization 1975, Outstanding Young Lawyer 1970), Blue Key, Kappa Alpha, Phi Alpha Delta. Democrat. Presbyterian. Home: 6432 Bradywine St Oklahoma City OK 73116 Office: 6242 N Western Suite 201 Oklahoma City OK 73118

CARDAMONE, RICHARD J., federal judge; b. Utica, N.Y., Oct. 10, 1925; s. Joseph J. and Josephine (Scala) C.; m. Catherine Baker Clarke, Aug. 28, 1946; 10 children. B.A., Harvard U., 1948; LL.B., Syracuse U., 1952. Bar: N.Y. 1952. Practice law, Utica, 1952-62; justice N.Y. State Supreme Ct., 1963-71, N.Y. State Supreme Ct. Appellate Div., 4th Dept., 1971-81; judge U.S. Ct. Appeals for 2d Circuit, Utica, 1981—. Trustee Syracuse U. Coll. Law, Slocum Dickson Found., Utica, St. Luke Hosp. Ctr., New Hartford, N.Y. Served as lt. (j.g.) USNR, 1943-46. Mem. Am. Law Inst., N.Y. State Bar Assn., Oneida County Bar Assn. Roman Catholic. Office: US Ct Appeals 2d Circuit US Courthouse 10 Broad St Utica NY 13503

CARDEN, ARNOLD EUGENE, mech. engr.; b. Birmingham, Ala., Apr. 27, 1930; s. Arnold Preston and Susie F. (Robinson) C.; m. Patsy Ruth Walker, June 3, 1952; children—Daniel, Timothy, Evelyn, Rebekah, Benjamin, Elizabeth. B.S. in Mech. Engring, Auburn (Ala.) U., 1952; M.S., U. Ala., 1956; Ph.D. in Metallurgy, U. Conn., 1972. Registered profl. engr., Ala. Research engr. mech. testing div. Alcoa Research Lab., New Kensington, Pa., 1956-58; mem. faculty U. Ala., 1958—, prof. dept. mech. engring., 1972—, acting head dept., 1981—; research engr. metals and ceramics div. Oak Ridge Nat. Lab., summers 1959-64, 66; vis. staff Los Alamos Nat. Lab., 1968, 69-79-81; research asso. U. Conn., 1971-72; mem. fatigue com. Nat. Materials Adv. Bd., 1977—; cons. to industry. Author articles on metallurgy. Served with Signal Corps AUS, 1952-54. NSF fellow, 1969, 70. Mem. ASME, Am. Soc. Engring. Edn., Am. Soc. Metals, Nat. Assn. Corrosion Engrs., Sigma Xi, Pi Tau Sigma. Baptist. Home: 1001 Riverside Dr Tuscaloosa AL 35401 Office: PO Box 2908 U Ala University AL 35486

CARDENAS AREGUILLIN, LORENZO, bishop; b. Ciudad Victoria, Mex., Mar. 7. Ordained priest Roman Cath. Ch.; named aux. bishop Titular Ch. of Crepedula; bishop of Papantla, 1980—. Address: Apartado 27 Tezuitlan Mexico *

CARDENES, ANDRES JORGE, violinist, educator; b. Havana, Cuba, May 2, 1957; came to U.S., 1958; s. Andres Manuel and Arlene (Cuevas) C. Student, Ind. U., 1975-80; diploma, Meisterkurse Zurich, Switzerland, 1977. Asst. prof. music Ind. U., Bloomington, 1980-82; prof. music Espoo Festival, Helsinki, Finland, 1982; prof. U. Utah, Salt Lake City, 1982—; mem. artistic com. Utah Symphony, Salt Lake City, 1983—; cons. in field; bd. dirs. Intermountain-West Music Festival, Salt Lake City, 1984—. Concertmaster, Utah Symphony, Salt Lake City, 1982—; concert violin soloist, 1981—; editor: Concerto by Ramiro Cortes, 1983; performer, Nuclear Arms Freeze, Worldwide, 1980—. Cultural ambassador UNICEF, 1980—. Recipient Bronze medal Queen Elizabeth Internat. Violin Competition, Brussels, 1980, Sibelius Internat. Violin Competition, Helsinki, 1980, Tchaikovsky Internat. Violin Competition, Moscow, 1982. Roman Catholic. Club: Machista (Bloomington) (pres. 1978—). Home: 658 Columbus St Salt Lake City UT 84103 Office: Care Am Internat Artists 275 Madison Ave New York NY 10016

CARDILLI, MICHAEL ANTHONY, transit authority executive; b. Chgo., Aug. 24, 1932; s. Michele and Carmella (Gianfrancisco) C.; m. Arlene Marie Rakoncay, Nov. 27, 1954; children: Michael, Karen, Lois. Student, Chgo. pub. schs. Commr. City of Chgo., 1976-79, internal govt. affairs officer, 1979, mgr. field ops. O'Hare Internat. Airport, 1980-81; chief adminstrv. officer Chgo. Transit Authority, 1981-82, chmn. bd., 1982—; mem. Ill. Transp. Adv. Com., 1981—. Mem. United Cerebral Palsy Fund, Chgo., 1983-84, Citizens Adv. Commn. Selective Service Bd., Ill., 1983; pres. 13th Ward Democratic Orgn., Chgo., 1969—. Served to sgt. U.S. Army, 1952-54; Korea. Mem. Am. Pub. Transp. Assn. (governing bd.), Chgo. Planning Commn., Comto, Am. Legion, Am. Pub. Works Assn. Roman Catholic. Home: 6733 S Tripp Ave Chicago IL 60629 Office: Chicago Transit Authority 734 Merchandise Mart Chicago IL 60654

CARDIN, BENJAMIN LOUIS, state legislator; b. Balt., Oct. 5, 1943; s. Meyer M. and Dora (Green) C.; m. Myrna Edelman, Nov. 24, 1964; children: Michael, Debbie. B.A. cum laude, U. Pitts., 1964; J.D. (1st in class), U. Md., 1967. Bar: Md. 1967. Sole practice law, Balt., 1967—; mem. Md. Ho. of Dels., 1967—, chmn. ways and means com., 1974-79, speaker of house, 1979—; co-chmn. Md. Legis. Policy Com.; mem. Gov.'s Commn. on Domestic Relations Law, State House Trust, Md.

Environ. Trust, Commn. on Quality Teaching, Capital City Planning Commn.; exec. com. Council State Govts.; mem. Democratic State Legis. Leaders Caucus. Contbr. articles to profl. publs. Trustee Balt. Mus. Art, Balt. Fgn. Relations Council; bd. dirs. Cheswolde Neighborhood Assn.; exec. com. Balt. Jewish Community Relations Council. Recipient William Stroble Thomas award U. Md. Sch. Law, also several humanitarian awards. Mem. Am., Md., Balt. City bar assns., U. Md. Alumni Assn. (trustee), Nat. Conf. State Legislators (chmn. state-local task force, chmn. regulatory improvement com. 1981-82, chmn. fiscal affairs com. 1980-81), Order of Coif, Omicron Delta Epsilon. Home: 2509 Shelleydale Dr Baltimore MD 21209 Office: 211 Saint Paul Pl Baltimore MD 21202

CARDIN, PIERRE, fashion designer; b. St. Andre de Barbarama, Italy, July 7, 1922. Ed., St. Etienne, France. Tailor with Manby (men's tailor), Vichy, France, 1939-40; adminstr. with French Red Cross, World War II. Designer with Paquin, Paris, 1945-47, House of Dior, Paris, 1947-50; propr. own design house, Paris, 1950—; owner: Maxim's Restaurants. Decorated chevalier Legion d' Honneur.; recipient Career Achievement award, Cutty Sark Men's Fashion Awards, 1984. Address: 27 rue de Marigny Paris France

CARDINAL, MARCELIN, artist; b. Gravelbourg, Sask., Can., Apr. 26, 1920; s. Stanislas and Eugenie (Michaud) C.; m. Roseline Bernaud, May 14, 1965. One man shows include, Matthiesen Gallery, London, Eng., 1958, Feingarten Galleries, N.Y.C., 1961, Galerie Denyse Delrue, Montreal, Que., Can., 1962, Galerie Don Stewart, Montreal, 1981, group shows include, Boston Mus., 1953, Musée des Ponchettes, Nice, France, 1955, Knox Albright Gallery, Buffalo, 1960, Art Gallery of Ont., Toronto, 1982, Internat. Art Fair, Toronto, Ont., Can., 1981; represented in permanent collection, Mus. Contemporary Art, Montreal, Mus. Modern Art, Dunkirk, France, Musée du Que., Quebec City. Served with Can. Army, 1941-44. Mem. Can. Conf. Arts, Société des Artistes Professionels du Que. Studio: 4897 Queen Mary Rd Montreal PQ H3W 1X1 Canada

CARDINALI, ALBERT JOHN, lawyer; b. N.Y.C., Apr. 24, 1934; s. John and Ines (Clara) C.; m. June DuRose Seaman; children: Kathleen, John, Raymond. B.A., CCNY, 1955; LL.B., Columbia U., 1958; LL.M., NYU, 1965. Bar: N.Y. 1961. Asso. Thacher, Proffitt & Wood, N.Y.C., 1960-68, partner, 1969—. Clk. session Rye Presbyterian Ch. Served with AUS, 1958-60. Mem. ABA (mem. council sect. on corp. banking and bus. law), N.Y. State Bar Assn., Assn. Bar City N.Y. Clubs: Shenorock Shore (Rye, N.Y.); City-Midday, Univ. (N.Y.C.). Home: 9 Franklin Ave Rye NY 10580 Office: 40 Wall St New York NY 10005

CARDON, BARTLEY PRATT, university dean; b. Tucson, Oct. 1, 1913; m. Charlotte M. Cardon, Dec. 17, 1939; children: Bartley L., Joanne Downey, Christine Kronick, Beth de la Houssaye. B.S., U. Ariz., 1935, M.S., 1940; Ph.D., U. Calif.-Berkeley, 1946. Research dir., nutritionist Ariz. Milling, Tucson, 1954-62; pres. Ariz. Feeds, Tucson, 1962-73, chmn. bd., 1973-80; dean Coll. Agr. U. Ariz., Tucson, 1980—; cons. in field. Contbr. articles to profl. jours. Mem. Pres.'s Pvt. Sector Survey Task Force, Washington, 1982, Gov.'s Com. on Groundwater, Phoenix, 1979-80. Served to col. U.S. Army, 1941-46; ETO. Named 1982 Man of Yr. in Service to Ariz. Agr. Progressive Farmer, 1983; recipient Disting. Service award Am. Feed Mfrs. Assn., 1982, Outstanding Service award Ariz. Cotton Growers Assn., 1982, Service Recognition award Agri-Bus. Council of Ariz., 1981. Mem. Am. Agrl. Econs. Assn., Winrock Internat. (dir.), Consortium for Internat. Devel., Ariz. 4-H Youth Found. (dir., past pres.). Home: 3831 Calle Guayamas Tucson AZ 85716 Office: U Ariz Coll Agr Tucson AZ 85721

CARDON, MARRINER PAUL, lawyer; b. Albuquerque, May 17, 1932; s. Louis Sanders and Winnafred (Bellamy) C.; m. Ruth Hanks, Aug. 9, 1957; children: Stephan, Laurie, Roslyn, Bradley, Lamont, Jared. B.A., U. Utah, 1954; LL.B., U. Colo., 1962. Bar: Ariz. 1962. Practice in Phoenix, 1963—; law clk., research asst. Ariz. Supreme Ct., 1962; asso. Kramer, Roche, Burch & Streich, 1963-66; partner Kramer, Roche, Burch, Streich & Cracchiolo, 1966-70, Streich, Lang, Weeks & Cardon, 1970—; Chmn. Phoenix Charter Govt. Com., 1978-79; mem. Phoenix Planning Commn., 1970-73, Phoenix Municipal Aeros. Adv. Bd., 1980-83, chmn., 1983. Co-author: American Law of Mining, 1962; Editor: U. Colo. Law Rev, 1961. Bd. dirs. Phoenix bd. NCCJ. Served to lt. (j.g.) USNR, 1954-57. Mem. Am., Ariz., Maricopa County bar assns., Order Coif, Phi Alpha Delta. Republican. Mormon. Club: Arizona (Phoenix). Office: 2100 First Interstate Bank Plaza Phoenix AZ 85001

CARDONA, RODOLFO, educator; b. San Jose, Costa Rica, Jan. 17, 1924; came to U.S., 1943, naturalized, 1950; s. Jose Ismael and Julia (Cooper) C.; m. Electra Ducas, Aug. 1, 1954; children: Helen Maria, Alexander Xavier, Michael Anthony, Christopher Pericles. B.A., La. State U., 1946; Ph.D., U. Wash., Seattle, 1953. Consul of Costa Rica, San Diego, 1943-44; asst. instr. fine arts and Spanish La. State U., 1946-47; asst. prof. Am. Inst. Fgn. Trade, Phoenix, 1947-48; instr. U. Wash., 1948-53; hon. consul Costa Rica, Seattle, 1948-53, asst. prof. Western Res. U., also hon. consul, Cleve., 1953-56; asst. prof., then assoc. prof. Chatham Coll., Pitts., 1956-60; prof., then chmn. dept. Hispanic langs. U. Pitts., 1961-69; hon. consul Costa Rica, Pitts., 1956-69; prof. Spanish, chmn. dept. Spanish and Portuguese U. Tex., Austin, 1969-78; Univ. prof., dir. Univ. Profs. Program Boston U., 1978—; pres. bd. dirs. Internat. Inst. in Spain. Author: Ramon: A Study of Gomez de la Serna and His Works, 1957, (co-author) Vision del esperpento; Editor: Novelistas espanoles de hoy, 1959, La sombra de E.P. Galdos, 1964, Dona Perfecta, 5th edit., 1984, Novelistas espanoles de posguerra, 1977; (co-editor) Teatro selecto de Galdos, 1973; founder, editor: Anales galdosianos; Contbr. articles to profl. jours. Andrew Mellon postdoctoral fellow, 1960-61; grantee Am. Council Learned Socs., 1967-68, Univ. Research Inst., 1973-74; fellow Nat. Endowment Humanities, 1973-74. Mem. Modern Lang. Assn., Phi Beta Kappa, Phi Kappa Phi, Pi Mu Epsilon, Phi Sigma Iota. Mem. Easthern Orthodox Ch. Office: Univ Prof 745 Commonwealth Ave Boston U Boston MA 02215

CARDONI, HORACE ROBERT, retired lawyer; b. Jessup, Pa., July 24, 1916; s. Louis and Maria (Saldi) C.; m. Florence D'Arienzo, July 2, 1945; children: Mary Clare, Ann, Louise, Robert L., Joseph J., John G. B.A., U. Scranton, 1938; LL.B., U. Pa., 1941. Bar: Pa. 1941. Pvt. practice, Scranton, 1941-42; area rent atty. Office Housing Expediter, OPA, Scranton, 1946-51; with Daystrom, Inc. (name changed to Weston Instruments, Inc. 1964), Newark, 1953-76, sec., 1962-76, gen. counsel, 1963-76; assoc. counsel Schlumberger Ltd., 1976-81, asst. sec., 1977-81, ret., 1981; dir. Weston P.R., Inc.; sec., treas., dir. Cryodynamics Inc., Mountainside, N.J.; dir. Ponce, Weston Caribe, Inc.; Pres., bd. dirs. N.J. Bd. Profl. Engrs. and Land Surveyors, 1978, mem., 1975-80. Mem. Nat. Def. Exec. Res., U.S. Dept. Commerce.; Treas. cub pack Boy Scouts Am., Mountain Side, N.J., 1964-66; active Mountain Side Little League, 1965-66; v.p., trustee Am. Assn. Mentally Handicapped, Elizabeth, N.J., 1981—; mem. planning bd. City of Mountainside, 1982—; Dist. committeeman Democratic Com., 1967—, mcpl. chmn., 1969-74; counsellor Vols. in Probation, Union County, N.J., 1981—. Served with USNR, 1942-45, 51-52. Mem. Am., Pa. bar assns. Home: 326 Short Dr Mountainside NJ 07092

CARDOZIER, VIRGUS R., educator; b. Montgomery, La., Apr. 2, 1923; s. James C. and Lelia M. C.; m. Nancy Pattison Fyfe, Dec. 29, 1955. B.S., La. State U., 1947, M.S., 1950; Ph.D., Ohio State U., 1952; postgrad., U. Mich., 1967. Adult edn. tchr. and supr. La. schs., 1947-50; edn. specialist in industry, 1952-57; asso. prof. Coll. Edn., U. Tenn., Knoxville, 1957-60; prof., chmn. rural edn. U. Md., College Park, 1960-70, prof. higher edn., 1968-70; v.p. for acad. affairs U. Tex. of Permian Basin, Odessa, 1970-74, prof. higher edn. and behavioral sci., 1970-82, pres., 1974-82; sr. acad. policy adviser U. Tex. System, 1982-83; prof. higher Edn. U. Tex., Austin, 1983—; vis. prof. Pa. State U., 1968; vis scholar UCLA, 1983; sec.-treas. Council Coll. and Univ. Presidents, Tex., 1979-81; cons. in field. Contbr. articles to profl. jours. Bd. dirs. Buffalo Trail council Boy Scouts Am., 1976-82. Served with arty. U.S. Army, 1943-45; PTO. Named Outstanding Grad. Ohio State U. Centennial Celebration, 1969. Mem. Am. Sociol. Assn., Am. Assn. for Higher Edn., Acad. Polit. and Social Scis., Assn. for Study of Higher Edn., Am. Ednl. Research Assn., Phi Delta Kappa. Office: Coll Edn U Tex Austin TX 78712

CARDOZO, BENJAMIN MORDECAI, lawyer; b. N.Y.C., May 15, 1915; s. Sidney Benjamin and Eva Cecile (Mordecai) C.; m. Barbara Ruth Schaffer, Sept. 21, 1941; children—Enid Cardozo Lamcn, Ellen Cardozo Sonsino. B.A., Dartmouth Coll., 1937; postgrad., Columbia U., 1938; J.D., N.Y. U., 1941. Bar: N.Y. State bar 1942, U.S. Supreme Ct. bar 1947, Conn. bar 1954. Mem. staff Moreland Commn. Workmen's Compensation Investigation, N.Y. State, 1941, Office Alien Property, U.S. Dept. Justice, Washington, 1946-49; asso. firm Cardozo & Nathan, N.Y.C., 1949-51, Cardozo & Cardozo, 1952—. Mem. Assn. Bar City N.Y., N.Y. County Lawyers Assn., N.Y. Law Inst., Conn. Fed., Am. bar assns., N.Y. State Assn., Trial Lawyers Inst. Dirs., Nat. Arts Club. Home: 325 E 79th St New York NY 10021 Office: 11 E 44th St New York NY 10017

CARDOZO, MANOEL, educator; b. Ribeiras, Pico, Azores, Dec. 24, 1911; came to U.S., 1915, naturalized, 1944; s. José Silveira and Rosalina Soares (de Sousa) C. B.A., Stanford U., 1931, M.A., 1934, Ph.D., 1939. Teaching asst. U. Calif. at Berkeley, 1935-36; curator Oliveira Lima Library, Catholic U. Am., Washington, 1940—, prof. history, 1954-78, head dept., 1961-71; Smith-Mundt lectr., Portugal, 1958, lectr. in, U.S., Brazil, Portugal, Peru, Argentina, Azores; asso. sec.-gen. First Internat. Colloquium Luso-Brazilian Studies, Washington, 1950; participant 13th Internat. Congress of Hist. Scis., Moscow, Russia, 1970, San Francisco, 1975, Internat. Colloquium on 18th Century and Brazil, Brasilia, 1984; lecture tour of Brazil, 1981; lectr. Mus. Diplomacy, Rio de Janeiro, 1984; guest of Alexandre de Gusmão Found., Brasilia, 1984. Author: The Portuguese in America 590 B.C.-1974 A Chronology and Fact Book, 1976; and numerous hist. studies; translator Brazilian poetry.; Contbr. articles to hist. jours., encys. Decorated chevalier Order So. Cross, Brazil; recipient Rio Branco medal Brazilian Fgn. Office, 1945, Benemerenti medal Holy Sea, 1974; Inst. de Alta Cultura fellow, Lisbon, Portugal, 1936-38; Social Sci. Research Council grantee; Am. Philos. Soc. grantee; OAS grantee; Instituto de Alta Cultura (Lisbon) grantee; Gulbenkian Found. travel grantee, 1984. Mem. Am. Cath. (pres. 1962), Am. hist. assns., Sociedade de Geografia (Lisbon), Inst. Histórico (Terceira, Azores), Institute Histórico Geográfico (São Paulo and São Luís do Marahhão), Inst. do Ceará, Cath. Commn. Intellectual and Cultural Affairs, Inter-Am. Council (pres. Washington 1964-65), Sociedad Peruana de Historia. Spl. research Brazilian and Portuguese history, Portuguese overseas expansion. Home: 1004 Sigsbee Pl NE Washington DC 20017

CARDOZO, MICHAEL HART, lawyer; b. N.Y.C., Sept 15, 1910; s. Ernest A. and Emily (Wolff) C.; m. Alice Corneille, July 31, 1937; children: Michael Hart V, Julia Aline (Mrs. Charles R. Eisendrath), Alice Rebecca. Grad., Phillips Acad., Andover, Mass., 1928; A.B., Dartmouth, 1932; LL.B., Yale, 1935. Bar: N.Y. 1936, D.C. 1973. With firm Parker & Duryee., N.Y.C., 1935-38; atty. temporary nat. econ. com., life ins. investigation SEC, 1938-40; atty. U.S. Dept. Justice, 1940-42; with U.S. Lend-Lease and Fgn. Econ. Adminstrns., 1942-45, Lend-Lease rep. in, Turkey, 1943-44, Office of Legal Adviser, Dept. State, 1945-52, asst. legal adviser for econ. affairs, 1950-52; from assoc. prof. to prof. law Cornell U., Ithaca, N.Y., 1952-63; Fulbright and Guggenheim fellow, Belgium, 1958-59; exec. dir. Assn. Am. Law Schs., 1963-73; pvt. practice, Washington, 1973—; vis. prof. law Northwestern U., 1961-62; Vis. prof. law U. Pa., 1964-65, Howard U., 1965-66, Georgetown U., 1966-67, George Washington U., 1980, Am. U., 1981, Salzburg Seminar in Am. Studies, summer, 1968, Temple U., summer 1973; cons. Dept. State, fgn. relations com. U.S. Senate, subcom. on patents, trade marks and copyrights Ho. of Reps., Naval War Coll., Fellowship review bd. HEW, NSF, Adminstrv. Conf. U.S. Author: Diplomats in International Cooperation, 1963; also contbr. articles to jours. Named Officer Order of Orange-Nassau, The Netherlands. Mem. Am., Fed., D.C. bar assns., Washington Fgn. Law Soc. (pres. 1976), Am. Law Inst., Am. Soc. Internat. Law (sec. 1978—). Home: 2602 36th St NW Washington DC 20007 Office: 1001 Connecticut Ave NW Washington DC 20036

CARDOZO, RICHARD NUNEZ, educator; b. Mpls., Feb. 13, 1936; s. William Nunez and Miriam (Honig) C.; m. Arlene Rossen, June 29, 1959; children: Miriam, Rachel, Rebecca. A.B., Carleton Coll., 1956; M.B.A., Harvard U., 1959; Ph.D. (Ford Found. fellow), 1961-63, U. Minn., 1964. Asst. prof. bus. adminstrn. Harvard U., 1964-67; asso. prof. mktg. U. Minn., 1967-71, prof., 1971—; dir. Center for Exptl. Studies in Bus., 1969-73, chmn. dept. mktg., 1975-78; dir. Valspar Corp., Thermo-Rite Sales of Minn.; Fulbright lectr. Hebrew U., Jerusalem, 1980; vis. prof. Hebrew U. Jerusalem, 1980; vis. prof. bus. adminstrn. Harvard U. Grad. Sch. Bus., 1982-83; cons. in field. Author: (with others) Problems in Marketing, 4th edit, 1968, Product Policy: Cases and Concepts, 1979; contbr.: articles to profl. jours. Product Policy: Cases and Concepts. Served with USAR, 1961. Fulbright fellow London Sch. Econ., 1957. Mem. Am. Mktg. Assn., AAAS, Product Devel. and Mgmt. Assn. Home: 1955 E River Rd Minneapolis MN 55414 Office: U Minn 271 19th Ave S Minneapolis MN 55455

CARDUS, DAVID, physician; b. Barcelona, Spain, Aug. 6, 1922; came to U.S., 1957, naturalized, 1969; s. Jaume and Ferranda (Pascual) C.; m. Francesca Ribas, July 19, 1951; children: Hellena Cardus Guerra, Silvia, Bettina, David. B.A., B.S., U. Montpelier (France), 1942; M.D. magna cum laude, U. Barcelona, 1949; diploma in cardiology, U. Barcelona, 1956. Intern Hosp. Clinico, U. Barcelona, 1949-50; resident Sanatorio del Puig de Olena, Barcelona, 1950-53; French Govt. fellow dept. cardiology Hosp. Boucicaut and Hosp. de la Pitié, Paris, 1953-54; Brit. Council fellow Manchester Royal Infirmary U. Manchester, 1957; research assoc. Lovelace Found., Albuquerque, 1957-60; instr. depts. physiology and rehab. Baylor Coll. Medicine, Houston, 1960-61, asst. prof., 1961-65, asso. prof., 1965-73, dir. Biomath. Program, 1966-69, mem. adv. com. computer scis. to chief exec. officer, 1966-68, mem. grad. exec. com., 1968-69, chmn. biomath. com. Sch. Grad. Studies, 1968-69, prof. dept. rehab., 1969—, prof. dept. physiology, 1973—; Research assoc. Tex. Inst. Rehab. and Research, Houston, 1960—, head exercise lab., 1960—, mem. active med. staff, 1960—, pres. staff, 1967-68, dir. research, 1962-66, chmn. library com., 1968—, head cardio-pulmonary lab., 1969—, dir. div. biomath., 1970—; mem. sci. adv. council Common Research Computer Facility, Tex. Med. Center, 1965-66; NIH trainee Summer Inst. Math. for Life Scientists, U. Mich., 1966; adj. prof. math. scis. Rice U., 1970—; cons. USPHS div. health facilities Planning and Constrn. Service, 1967—, Math. Assn. Am., VA Hosp.Houston. Contbr. articles to profl. jours. Chmn. bd. dirs. Inst. Hispanic Culture, Houston; vice chmn. Gordon Conf. on Biomaths., 1970; pres. Am. Inst. Catalan Studies, 1980—. Recipient 1st prize for exhibit Am. Urol. Assn., 1967, August Pi Sunyerprize Institut d'Estudis Catalans, 1968, 1st prize for sci. exhibit 5th Internat. Congress., 1968, Gold medal for demonstration use of computers and telecommunications in rehab. medicine 6th Internat. Congress Phys. Medicine, 1972, Elisabeth and Sidney Licht award for sci. writing Am. Congress Phys. Med. and Rehab., 1980; decorated Commendation of Isabel la Católica (Spain), 1980. Mem. AAAS, AAUP, Am. Coll. Cardiology, Am. Coll. Chest Physicians, Am. Coll. Sports Medicine, Am. Congress Rehab. Medicine (Gold medal for sci exhibit 45th ann. session 1967), AMA, Tex., Harris County, 9th Dist. med. assns., Am. Physiol. Soc., Am. Statis. Assn., Biomed. Engring. Soc., Fedn. Am. Socs. Exptl. Biology, Houston Acad. Medicine, N.Y. Acad. Scis., Postgrad. Med. Assembly South Houston, Soc. Math. Biology, Tex. Heart Assn., Tex. Med. Center Research Soc., Societat Catalana Biologia, Sigma Xi. Home: 14314 Cindywood St Houston TX 77079 Office: 1333 Moursund Ave Houston TX 77030

CARDWELL, HORACE MILTON, hospital administrator; b. Oklahoma City, Feb. 3, 1919; s. Horace M. and Lona (Bridges) C.; m. Billie Jo Cardwell, Sept. 14, 1957; children by previous marriage: Barbara Ann, Beverly Kay, Horace Milton III. B.S. in Econs, Tex. A. and M. Coll., 1941. Asst. adminstr. Herman Hosp., Houston, 1946-48; adminstr. Meml. Hosp., Lufkin, Tex., 1948—; Chmn. Hosp.-Ins.-Physicians Joint Adv. Com. Tex., 1954—; mem. Tex. Commn. Patient Care, 1957-61; pres. Tex. Bd. Vocational Nurse Examiners, 1962-68; dir. Med. Info., 1968-78; mem. Joint Commn. on Accreditation, 1975—; mem. adv. com. on allied health AMA, 1975-82. Chmn. Lufkin United Fund, 1961-76; mem. med. adv. com. Tex. Dept. Pub. Welfare, 1968-70; Bd. dirs. Blue Cross Tex., 1962—. Served with AUS, 1941-46; ETO, PTO. Fellow Am. Coll. Hosp. Adminstrs.; mem. Am. Health Congress (chmn. bd. govs. 1974), Am. Hosp. Assn. (del. 1955-72, chmn. trustees 1974, speaker ho. of dels. 1975, Disting. Service award 1979), Tex. Hosp. Assn. (pres. 1956-57, chmn. bldg. com. 1965-75, Earl M. Collier award 1970), Tex. Assn. Hosp. Accountants (pres. 1953-54), C. of C. Club: Rotarian (local pres. 1969-70). Address: PO Box 1447 Lufkin TX 75902

CARDWELL, KENNETH HARVEY, educator, architect; b. Los Angeles, Feb. 15, 1920; s. Stephen William and Beatrice Viola (Duperrarult) C.; m. Mary Elinor Sullivan, Dec. 30, 1946; children: Kenneth William, Mary Elizabeth, Ann Margaret, Catherine Buckeley, Robert Stephen. A.A., Occidental Coll.; A.B., U. Calif.-Berkeley; postgrad., Stanford U. Lic. architect, Calif. Draftsman Thompsen & Wilson Architects, San Francisco, 1946-48, Michael Goodman, Architect, Berkeley, Calif., 1949; architect W.S. Wellington, Architect, Berkeley, 1950-59; prin. Kolbeck, Cardwell, Christopherson, Berkeley, 1960-66; prof. dept. arch. U. Calif.-Berkeley, 1950-82; prin. Kenneth H. Cardwell Architect, Berkeley, 1982—; assoc. Hall Goodhue Haisley & Barker, San Francisco, 1976—. Author: Bernard Maybeck, 1977. Pres. Civic Art Commn., Berkeley, 1963-65; mem. Bd. Adjustments, Berkeley, 1967-69, Alameda County Art Commn., 1969-72. Served to 1st lt. USAAF, 1941-45. Decorated D.F.C., Air medal with 3 oak leaf clusters; Rehman fellow, 1957; Graham fellow, 1961; recipient Berkeley citation U. Calif., 1958. Mem. AIA, Alpha Rho Chi. Home: 1210 Shattuck Ave Berkeley CA 94709 Office: Hall Goodhue Haisley & Parker 282 2d St San Francisco CA 94105

CARDY, ANDREW GORDON, hotel executive; b. Brockville, Ont., Can.; s. Roland Hastings and Jean Davidson (Gordon) H.; m. Alice Elizabeth Cochrane, Sept. 18, 1948; children: Roland Andrew, Barbara Elizabeth, Rosemary Carlisle, Gordon David. B. Commerce, U. Toronto (Ont.), 1941. Gen. mgr. Prince Edward Hotel, Windsor, Ont., 1951-52, Sheraton Connaught Hotel, Hamilton, Ont., 1952-54, Sheraton Brock Hotel, Niagara Falls, Ont., 1954-55, Sheraton Hotel, Rochester, N.Y., 1955-56, King Edward Sheraton Hotel, Toronto, 1956-68, Royal York Hotel, 1968—; v.p. central region CP Hotels, 1971-78, pres., chief exec. officer, dir., 1978—, chmn., 1980—; Bd. govs. Ryerson Poly. Inst. Served with Royal Canadian Arty., 1942-45. Decorated Mil. Cross (Can.), Knight Grace Mil. and Hospitaller Order St. Lazarus of Jerusalem.; mem. Most Noble Order of Crown of Thailand. Mem. Toronto Hotel Assn., Ont. Hotel and Motel Assn. (pres. 1973-74), Met. Toronto Conv. and Visitors Assn. (hon. dir.), Hotel Assn. Can., Met. Toronto Travel Assn. (hon. dir.). Mem. United Ch. of Can. Clubs: Lambton, Golf and Country, Canadian, Empire. Home: 53 Dunvegan Rd Toronto ON M4V 2P5 Canada Office: 100 Front St W Toronto ON M5J 1E3 Canada

CARELESS, JAMES MAURICE STOCKFORD, history educator; b. Toronto, Ont., Can., Feb. 17, 1919; s. William Roy Stockford and Ada Josephine (de Rees) C.; m. Elizabeth Isabel Robinson, Dec. 31, 1941; children: Anthony, Virginia, Richard, Andrea, James. B.A., U. Toronto, 1940; A.M., Harvard U., 1941, Ph.D., 1950. Asst. naval historian Can. Naval Hist. Sect., 1942-43; wartime asst. Dept. External Affairs Can., 1943-45; lectr. Can. history U. Toronto, 1945-49, asst. prof., 1949-54, asso. prof., 1954-59, prof., 1959—; vis. prof. U. Victoria, 1968-69; sr. vis. research fellow Australian Nat. U., 1978. Author: Canada, Story of Challenge, 1953, Brown of the Globe, 1959, 63, The Union of the Canada, 1967, Colonists and Canadiens, 1971, Pre-Confederationn Premiers, 1980. Chmn. Hist. Sites Bd. Can.; mem. Ont. Postsecondary Edn. Commn., 1970-73; trustee Ont. Sci. Centre, 1965-73. Carnegie fellow, 1958; Govt. Can. grantee, 1978; decorated officer Order of Can. Fellow Royal Soc. Can. (Tyrrell medal 1962); mem. Can. Hist. Assn., Ont. Hist. Soc. Club: Faculty. Home: 121 Ranleigh St Toronto ON M4N 1X2 Canada Office: Dept History Univ Toronto Toronto ON M5S 1A1 Canada

CARELLI, GABOR PAUL, opera singer; b. Budapest, Hungary, Mar. 20, 1915; came to U.S., 1939, naturalized, 1949; s. Bela Krausz and Lenke Deutsch. Dr. Law, U. Budapest, 1937; studied singing, Liszt-Ferenc Acad., Budapest, 1935-36, with Gigli, 1936-39. Mem. Met. Opera Assn., 1950-74; prof. voice Manhattan Sch. Music, N.Y.C.; vis. prof. master classes Franz Liszt Acad., Budapest, Music Conservatory Peking and Shanghai, China, 1981. Made debut in: La Boheme, Florence, Italy, 1938, opera, concert tours in U.S., 1939—; singer with symphonies; recorded with Toscanini: Antal Dorati for, RCA-Victor; also recorded in, Hungary; singer: Am. premiere Puccini-Mass, Chgo., 1951; artistic adviser opera and concerts, San Salvador, 1951—; singer: premiere Requiem-Mass by Verdi, Israel, 1954; regular radio appearances, 1944-51, guest appearances on operatic TV programs, concert opera appearances, Europe, 1958—; radio lectr. on opera and singers, Europe. Mem. Am. Guild Mus. Artists (dir.). Home and Office: 23 W 73d St New York NY 10023

CAREN, ROBERT POSTON, aerospace company executive; b. Columbus, Ohio, Dec. 25, 1932; s. Robert James and Charlene (Poston) C.; m. Linda Ann Davis, Apr. 17, 1963; children: Christopher Davis, Michael Poston. B.S., Ohio State U., 1953, M.S., 1954, Ph.D., 1961. Sr. physicist N. Am. Aviation, Columbus, 1959-60; asso. research scientist research and devel. div. Lockheed Missiles and Space Co., Inc., Palo Alto, Calif., 1962-63, research scientist, 1963-66, sr. mem. research lab., 1966-69, mgr. def. systems space systems div.,

1969-70, mgr. infared tech. research and devel. div., 1970-71, research dir., 1972-76, chief engr., 1976—, v.p., asst. gen. mgr. research and devel. div.; instr. physics Foothill Coll., 1962-65; lectr. U. Santa Clara, 1968—. Contbr. articles to profl. jours. Assoc. fellow AIAA; mem. Am. Def. Preparedness Assn. (chmn. research div.), Am. Phys. Soc., Cryogenic Soc. Am. (pres.-elect 1969), Helium Soc. Am., Sigma Pi Sigma, Pi Mu Epsilon. Patentee in field. Home: 658 Toyon Pl Palo Alto CA 94306 Office: 1111 Lockheed Way Sunnyvale CA 94088

CARES, CHARLES WILLIAM, landscape architect, educator; b. Cleve., Oct. 29, 1918; s. Charles William and Christine Wilson (Cliff) C.; m. Marian Young McKee, Mar. 20, 1948; children: Charles Christian, Susan Young, John Alexander, Alison McKee. A.B., Allegheny Coll., 1939; B.S. in Landscape Architecture, Mich. State Coll., 1950; M.Landscape Architecture, Harvard U., 1958. Landscape architect Ralph Griswold & Assocs., Pitts., 1950-51; faculty floriculture and ornamental horticulture Cornell U., 1951-58; faculty U. Mich., 1958—, chmn. dept., 1969-79; dir. Nichols Arboretum, 1969—; cons. in field. Mem. Ann Arbor (Mich.) Twp. Planning Bd., 1970—; mem. Mich. Landscape Archtl. Registration Bd., 1969-79. Served with USNR, 1941-46. Mem. Am. Soc. Landscape Architects (trustee), AIA (assoc.), Fed. Garden Clubs Mich., Nat. Trust Hist. Preservation, Washtenaw County Hist. Soc. Presbyterian. Club: Rotary. Home: 505 Riverview Ann Arbor MI 48104 Office: Dana Bldg U Mich Ann Arbor MI 48109

CARETTO, ALBERT ALEXANDER, chemist, educator; b. Baldwin, N.Y., May 16, 1928; s. Albert A. and Mary (Magnasco) C.; m. Virginia L. Ahman, Apr. 30, 1960; children—Joseph A., Ann M. B.S., Rensselaer Poly. Inst., 1950; Ph.D., U. Rochester, 1954. Postdoctoral research Brookhaven Nat. Lab., Upton, N.Y., 1954-56, U. Calif. at Berkeley, 1956-57; asst. prof. Carnegie Inst. Tech., Pitts., 1957-58, 59-64, asso. prof., 1964-67; research chemist U. Calif. at Livermore, 1958-59; with CERN (European Lab. for Nuclear Research), Geneva, Switzerland, 1964-65; prof. Carnegie-Mellon U., Pitts., 1967—, chmn. dept. chemistry, 1970-74; with European Lab. Nuclear Research, CERN, Geneva, Switzerland, 1974-75. Contbr. articles to profl. jours. Mem. Am. Chem. Soc., Am. Phys. Soc., A.A.A.S., Sigma Xi, Phi Kappa Phi. Home: 1231 Woodhill Dr Gibsonia PA 15044 Office: Dept Chemistry Carnegie-Mellon U Pittsburgh PA 15213

CARETTO, LAURENCE STEPHEN, engineering educator; b. Los Angeles, Oct. 5, 1939; s. Bert and Katherine (Gaudino) C. B.S. in Engring, UCLA, 1960, M.S., 1963, Ph.D., 1965. Technologist Shell Chem. Co., 1960-61; asst. prof. U. Calif., Berkeley, 1965-70; sr. vis. fellow Imperial Coll. Sci. and Tech., London, 1970; mem. faculty Calif. State U., Northridge, 1971—, prof. engring., 1974—, chmn. dept. mech. and chem. engring., 1974-79; mem. Calif. Air Resource Bd., 1978—; cons. air pollution, combustion and energy. Author articles in field. Mem. Air Pollution Control Assn., Soc. Automotive Engrs., AAAS, Am. Chem. Soc., Combustion Inst. Office: Dept Mech and Chem Engring Calif State U Northridge CA 91330

CAREW, RODNEY CLINE, professional baseball player; b. Gatun, Panama, Oct. 1, 1945; m. Marilynn Levy, Oct. 1970; children: Charryse, Stephanie. Second baseman Minn. Twins (Am. League), 1967-78, Calif. Angels, 1979—. Named Am. League Rookie of Year Sporting News, 1967, Baseball Writers' Assn. Am., 1967; winner Am. League Bathing Title, 1969, 72-75, 77-78. Mem. Am. League All-Star Team, 1967-83, Sporting News, 1967-69, 72-75, 77-78; Am. League Most Valuable Player, 1977. Address: 2000 State College Blvd Anaheim CA 92806 *

CAREY, BRUCE DOUGLAS, lawyer; b. Detroit, July 20, 1923; s. Frederick Arthur and Hazel Eleanor (Whited) C.; m. Catherine Dunwody McKinley, June 23, 1951; children: William M., Elizabeth M., Ann D. B.A., U. Mich., (1947), J.D., 1950. Bar: Mich. 1951. Practiced in, Detroit, 1951—; atty. Chrysler Corp., Detroit, 1950-55, Carey & Carey, 1955—. Served as lt. (j.g.) USNR, 1943-46. Mem. ABA, Mich. Bar Assn., Detroit Bar Assn. Presbyterian. Clubs: Country of Detroit, University. Home: 251 Moran Rd Grosse Pointe Farms MI 48236 Office: Carey & Carey 2153 Penobscot Bldg Detroit MI 48226

CAREY, CHARLES JEREMIAH, assn. exec.; b. N.Y.C., Dec. 31, 1924; s. Daniel Charles and Jessica (Bechtold) C.; m. Gertrude Campbell, Sept. 10, 1949; children—Charles G., Margaret A., Douglas C., Daniel W. B.A., Wesleyan U., 1949; M.B.A., N.Y. U., 1957. Pres. Nat. Food Processors Assn., Washington, 1972—, Food Processors Assurance Ltd., Bermuda, Food Processors Inst., Washington. Served with USMCR, 1943-45. Home: Chevy Chase MD Office: 1133 20th St NW Washington DC 20036

CAREY, DEAN LAVERE, fruit canning co. exec.; b. Biglerville, Pa., Nov. 29, 1925; s. Earl E. and Ann Olivia (Newman) C.; m. Doris M. Dugan, July 21, 1949; children—Philip D., Juanita Ann. B.S., U. Pitts., 1949. With Knouse Foods Corp., Inc., Peach Glen, Pa., 1949—, controller, 1955-59, asst. gen. mgr., 1960-62, gen. mgr., 1963-65, pres., 1966—. Dir. Blue Cross, Harrisburg, Pa. Served with USNR, 1944-46. Lutheran. Clubs: Am. Legion, Masons, Shriners. Home: 60 Franklin St Biglerville PA 17307 Office: Knouse Foods Coop Inc Peach Glen PA 17306

CAREY, EDWARD JOHN, utility executive; b. N.Y.C., Jan. 16, 1944; s. Edward John and Mary Elizabeth (Hopkins) C.; m. Maureen A. McCullough, June 4, 1977. B.A., Fordham U., 1970. With N.Y. Central R.R., 1962-68, mgr. cash accounts, 1965-68; with Consol. Edison Co., N.Y.C., 1968—, asst. to treas., then asst. treas., 1974-76, treas., 1976-80, v.p. Bronx div., 1980—, gen. auditor, 1983—. Bd. dirs. Salvation Army; mem. Manhattan Adv. Bd. Home: 2727 Palisade Ave New York NY 10463 Office: 4 Irving Pl New York NY 10003

CAREY, ERNESTINE GILBRETH (MRS. CHARLES E. CAREY), author, lecturer; b. N.Y.C., Apr. 5, 1908; d. Frank Bunker and Lillian (Moller) Gilbreth; m. Charles Everett Carey, Sept. 13, 1930; children: Lillian Carey Clark), Charles Everett. B.A., Smith Coll., 1929. Buyer R. H. Macy & Co., N.Y.C., 1930-44, James McCreery, 1947-49; lectr., book reviews, syndicated newspaper articles, 1951. Co-recipient (with Frank B. Gilbreth, Jr.) (Prix Scarron French Internat. humor award for Cheaper by the Dozen 1951), (with Lillian Moller Gilbreth) (McElligott medallion Assn. Marquette U. Women 1966); Author: Jumping Jupiter, 1952, Rings Around Us, 1956, Giddy Moment, 1958, (with Frank B. Gilbreth, Jr.) Cheaper by the Dozen, 1949, Belles on Their Toes, 1951; also mag. articles and book revs. Bd. dirs. Right to Read, Inc., 1968—, co-chmn., 1967; lay adv. com. Manhasset (N.Y.) Bd. Edn.; trustee Manhasset Pub. Library, 1953-59, v.p., 1956-59; trustee Smith Coll., 1967-72. Montgomery award Friends of Phoenix Public Library, 1981. Mem. Authors Guild Am. (life mem., mem. guild council 1955-60), P.E.N. Republican. Conglist. Clubs: Smith College (L.I.) (asst. chmn. scholarship com. 1950-59); Smith Coll. (N.Y.); Smith College Phoenix (vice chmn. scholarship com. 1967), 7 College Conf. Council (Phoenix)). Home: 6148 E Lincoln Dr Paradise Valley AZ 85253

CAREY, FRANCIS JAMES, lawyer; b. Balt., Mar.24, 1926; s. Francis James and Marjorie (Armstrong) C.; m. Emily Norris Large, June 8, 1956; children: Francis James III, Elizabeth Page, Henry Augustus, Emily Norris, Frances Whelen. Student, Princeton, 1943-44; A.B., U. Pa., 1945, J.D., 1949. Bar: Pa. 1950. Law sec. to justice Supreme Ct. Pa., 1950-51; with firm Reed Smith Shaw & McClay, Phila., 1951—; mem. firm Reed Smith Townsend & Munson, 1958—; mem. faculty U. Pa., 1946-47; dir. Internat. Leasing Corp., Careybanc Property Corp.; vice chmn., dir. W.P. Carey & Co., Inc.; dir., chmn. exec. com. Carey Corporate Property, Inc. and affiliates, Carey Corporate Property Mgmt., Inc. Mem. Com. of Seventy, Phila., 1957-58; mem. Lower Gwynedd Twp. (Pa.) Planning Commn., 1962-75, sec., 1962-65; Trustee Germantown Acad., 1961—, pres., 1966-72; mgr. Law Alumni Soc. U. Pa., 1962-66. Served to lt. USNR, 1943-45; PTO. Mem. ABA, Pa. Bar Assn. (chmn. real property, probate and trust sect. 1965-66, chmn. conf. group to cooperate with Pa. Land Title Assn. 1970-77, chmn. real property, probate and trust sect. 1971—), Phila. Bar Assn. (chmn. com. civil legislation 1962). Republican. Episcopalian. Clubs: Philadelphia, Fourth Street, St. Anthony (Phila.); Sunnybrook Golf (Plymouth Meeting, Pa.). Home: 485 Lewis Ln Ambler PA 19002 Office: 1600 Ave of Arts Bldg Philadelphia PA 19107

CAREY, GERALD JOHN, JR., former air force officer, university official; b. Bklyn., Oct. 1, 1930; s. Gerald John and Madeline (McNamara) C.; m. Joan Bennett, Apr. 24, 1954; children: Gerald John, III, Cathleen, John Kevin, Daniel. B.S., U.S. Mil. Acad., 1952; M.S. in Aero. Engring, Tex. A&M U., 1961. Commd. 2d lt. U.S. Air Force, 1952, advanced through grades to maj. gen., 1978; pilot trainee, Victoria, Tex., 1953, flight instr., Laredo, Tex., 1954-56, asst. air attache, Tokyo, 1958-61; aero. engr. Air Force Systems Command, Andrews AFB, Md., 1963-66; flight comdr., Seymour Johnson AFB, 1967, ops. officer, Udorn, Thailand, 1969-70; wing comdr. 1st and 56th Tactical Fighter Wings, Tampa, Fla., 1973-75; asst. dep. chief of staff ops. Tactical Air Command Hdqrs., Langley AFB, Va., 1975-78; comdr. USAF Tactical Air Warfare Center, Eglin AFB, Fla., 1978-81; ret., 1981; asso. dir. Engring. Expt. Sta., Ga. Inst. Tech., Atlanta, 1981—. Decorated Legion of Merit, D.S.M., D.F.C. with 2 oak leaf clusters. Mem. Air Forces Assn., Daedalians, Tau Beta Pi, Sigma Gamma Tau. Office: Engring Expt Sta Ga Inst Tech Atlanta GA 30332

CAREY, GERARD V., banker; b. N.Y.C., Nov. 20, 1926; s. George J. and Helen M. (Curley) C.; m. Doris L. Walz, May 23, 1953; 1 dau., Diane L. B.B.A., Adelphi U., 1950. C.P.A., N.Y. Sr. accountant Price, Waterhouse & Co., N.Y.C., 1953-59; asst. controller Stahl-Meyer Corp. of N.Y., 1959-60; mgr. systems and spl. studies Standard Brands, N.Y.C., 1960-65; v.p. audit, accounting and control functions First Pa. Banking & Trust Co., Phila., 1965-68, sr. v.p., chief financial officer, 1968-70, exec. v.p., 1970-72; v.p. First Pa. Corp., 1968-72, pres., 1972-74, exec. vice chmn., 1974-77; also dir.; chmn., pres., chief exec. officer 1st Pa. Mortgage Trust; chmn., chief exec. officer Life Services Corp. Am., Phila., 1978—; dir. First Pa. Bank, N.A., Health Maintenance Orgn. of Pa., Inflight Services, Inc.; Trustee Magee Rehab. Hosp., Phila. Chmn. bd. Manhattanville Coll., Purchase, N.Y. Mem. Am. Inst. C.P.A.s, N.Y. State, Pa. state socs. C.P.A.s, Bank Adminstrn. Inst. (past chmn.), Financial Execs. Inst. Office: 3200 Bensalem Blvd Bensalem PA 19020

CAREY, HARRY, JR., actor; b. Saugus, Calif., May 16, 1921; s. Harry and Olive (Fuller) C.; m. Marilyn Francis Fix, Aug. 12, 1944; children: Steven Harry, Melinda Carey Minoni, Thomas Paul, Cary, Patricia Olive. Student, Black Foxe Mil. Inst. Appeared: in over 80 feature films including 9 for John Ford, over 150 TV episodes, also plays including Wagon Master; film The Searchers; Page, NBC; appeared in stage show, N.Y. Worlds Fair, 1939-40. Served with USNR. Address: 4513 Vista Del Monte Sherman Oaks CA 91403

CAREY, J. EDWIN, lawyer; b. N.Y.C., Aug. 29, 1923; s. Edwin J. and Nora L. (Greene) C.; m. Marian G. Burke, May 23, 1954; children—Brianne, Christopher. Student, Manhattan Coll., 1941-43; LL.B., St. John's U., 1951. Bar: N.Y. bar 1951. Since practiced in, N.Y.C.; sr. partner firm Hill, Rivkins, Carey, Loesberg, O'Brien & Mulroy (and predecessors), 1961—; Lectr. admiralty law Practicing Law Inst., 1959—. Served with inf. AUS, 1943-46; ETO. Mem. Am., N.Y. State bar assns., Maritime Law Assn. U.S. (chmn. membership com. 1958-60, membership sec. 1960-66, sec. 1966-69, 1st v.p. 1970-72, pres. 1972-74, U.S. del. internat. confs. UN), Comité Maritime International (titular mem.), Union Internationale des Avocats, Am. Judicature Soc., Assn. Average Adjusters, Ins. Soc. N.Y., St. Thomas More Soc. (pres. 1948-49), Phi Delta Phi. Clubs: India House, Drug and Chemical (N.Y.C.); Arcola Country (Paramus, N.J.); Seaview Country (Absecon, N.J.). Home: 393 Carriage Ln Wyckoff NJ 07481 Office: 21 West St New York NY 10006

CAREY, JAMES HENRY, banker; b. Elizabeth, N.J., May 22, 1932; s. Charles C. and Adelyne (Bilyeu) C.; m. Nancy Mershon Ferrenz, Aug. 14, 1954; children: Jane Meredith, Christopher James, George Mershon, David James. B.A. cum laude, Brown U., 1953; postgrad., Sch. Bus. Adminstrn., N.Y. U., 1956-59. With Chase Manhattan Bank, N.Y.C., 1955-68, asst. v.p., 1961-63, v.p., 1963-68, exec. v.p., 1976—, Hambro Am. Bank & Trust Co., N.Y.C., 1968-69, pres., 1969-72, dir., 1969-72; pres., chmn. bd. First Empire Bank N.Y. (formerly Hambro Am. Bank & Trust Co.), N.Y.C., 1972-75; exec. v.p. Chase Manhattan Corp., 1976—; dir. Midland Co., Crown Central Petroleum Corp., Airborne Freight Corp. Served to lt. (j.g.) USNR, 1953- 55. Mem. Phi Beta Kappa, Delta Tau Delta. Episcopalian. Clubs: Knickerbocker, Sleepy Hollow Country. Home: 44 Sleepy Hollow Rd Briarcliff Manor NY 10510 Office: 1 Chase Manhattan Plaza New York NY 10081

CAREY, JAMES WILLIAM, educator, university dean, researcher; b. Providence, Sept. 7, 1934; s. Cyril Joseph and Rita Miriam (Lyons) C.; m. Elizabeth Theresa Gilman, Sept. 7, 1957; children: William, Timothy, Daniel, Matthew. B.S., U. R.I., 1957; M.S., U. Ill., 1959, Ph.D., 1963. Prof. U. Ill., Urbana, 1963-67; dir. Inst. Communications Research, U. Ill., Urbana, 1969-76; dean Coll. Communications U. Ill., Urbana, 1979—; prof. Pa. State U., State College, 1967-68, U. Iowa, Iowa City, 1976-79; assoc. mem. Ctr. for Advanced Study, 1975. Book review editor: Communication Research: An Internat. Quar., 1974—; cons. and contbg. editor: Jour. Communication, 1981-83, Communication yearbook I, II, III, 1981-83; editor: Sage Ann. Revs. of Communication Research, 1982—; mem. editorial bd.: Journalism Quar., 1974—, Journalism Monographs, 1974—, Mass Communication Rev., 1974—, Studies in the Anthropology of Visual Communication, 1981—, Can. Communications Jour., 1980-83; contbr. articles to profl. jours. NEH Fellow, 1975. Mem. Assn. Edn. in Journalism (pres. 1978-79), Assn. Schs. and Depts. Journalism (pres. 1982-83), Am. Sociol. Assn. Democrat. Roman Catholic. Home: 711 W Pennsylvania St Urbana IL 61801 Office: U Ill. 810 S Wright St Urbana IL

CAREY, JOHN, lawyer; b. Phila., June 11, 1924; s. Henry Reginald and Margaret Howell (Bacon) C.; m. Patricia F. Frank, Feb. 24, 1951; children: Henry Frank, John, Douglas, Jennifer Patricia. Grad., Milton Acad., 1942; B.A., Yale U., 1947; LL.B., Harvard U., 1949; LL.M. in Internat. Law, N.Y.U., 1965. Bar: Pa. 1950, N.Y. 1957. Practiced in, Phila., 1949-55, N.Y.C., 1956—, asst. dist. atty., Phila., 1952-54; cons. spl. com. fed. loyalty-security program Assn. Bar City N.Y., 1955- 56; partner firm Coudert Bros., 1961—; Dir. Walker & Co.; Mem. Faculty N.Y. U. Law Sch., 1966-73. Author: UN Protection of Civil and Political Rights, 1970. Mem. city council, Rye, N.Y., 1964-68, 72-74, mayor, 1974-82; Alternate mem. UN Subcommn. on Prevention Discrimination and Protection of Minorities, 1966-82, mem., 1983—; alternate U.S. rep. UN Human Rights Commn., 1968; Trustee Little Harbor Chapel, Portsmouth, N.H. Mem. Am., Internat., N.Y. State, Phila. bar assns., Assn. Bar City N.Y. (rep. at UN), Am. Soc. Internat. Law, Council on Fgn. Relations, Phi Beta Kappa. Home: 860 Forest Ave Rye NY 10580 Office: 200 Park Ave New York NY 10166

CAREY, JOHN LEO, lawyer; b. Morris, Ill., Oct.1, 1920; s. John Leo and Loretta (Conley) C.; m. Rhea M. White, July 15, 1950; children: John Leo III, Daniel Hobart, Deborah M. B.S., St. Ambrose Coll., Davenport, Ia., 1941; J.D., Georgetown U., 1947, LL.B., 1949. Bar: Ind. 1954. Legislative asst. Sen. Scott W. Lucas, 1945-47; spl. atty. IRS, Washington, 1947-54; since practiced in, South Bend; partner firm Barnes & Thornburg, 1954—; law prof. taxation Notre Dame Law Sch., 1968—. Trustee LaLumire Prep. Sch., Laporte, Ind. Served with USAAF, World War II; to lt. col. USAF, Korean War. Decorated D.F.C., Air medal. Mem. ABA, Ind. Bar Assn. (pres. 1976-77), St. Joseph County Bar Assn. Club: South Bend Country (seoc.). Home: 1326 Ridgedale Rd South Bend IN 46614 Office: 1st Source Center South Bend IN 46601

CAREY, LARRY CAMPBELL, surgeon; b. Coal Grove, Ohio, Nov. 5, 1933; s. Ralph and Betty C.; m. Christina Greene; children: William, Robert, Anne, Susan. B.S., Ohio State U., 1955, M.D., 1959. Diplomate: Am. Bd. Surgery. Intern in surgery N.Y. Hosp., 1959-60; resident in surgery Milw. County Gen. Hosp., 1960-64; from instr. to asso. prof. surgery Marquette U. Med. Sch., Milw., 1964-69; from asso. prof. to prof. surgery U. Pitts. Med. Sch., 1969-74, vice chmn. dept., 1973-74; prof. surgery, chmn. dept. Ohio State U. Med. Sch., 1975—, Robert M. Zollinger prof., 1977—. Author articles in field. Served to lt. comdr. M.C., USNR, 1966-68; Vietnam. Decorated Navy Commendation medal; John and Mary R. Markle scholar acad. medicine, 1965-70. Mem. ACS, Am. Surg. Assn., Am. Gastroent. Assn., AMA, Central Surg. Assn., Am. Trauma Soc., Internat. Soc. Surgery, James IV Assn. Surgeons, N.Y. Acad. Scis., Pancreas Club, Soc. Clin. Surgery, Soc. Mil. Surgeons, Soc. Surgery Alimentary Tract, Soc. Univ. Surgeons, Pan-Pacific Surg. Assn., Western Surg. Assn. Office: 410 W 10th Ave Columbus OH 43210 *

CAREY, LEWIS STAFFORD, physician, educator; b. Yorktown, Sask., Can., July 9, 1925; s. Edward Hunsdon and Gladys (Stafford) C.; m. Beverly Jane Baxter, Sept. 19, 1950; children—Richard, Mark, John, Susan, David. Student, U. B.C.; M.D., C.M., Queen's U., Kingston, Ont., 1950, M.Sc., 1956; M.S., U. Minn., 1959. Teaching fellow Kingston (Ont.) Gen. Hosp., 1950-51, intern, 1951-52; resident in surgery Kingston Mil. Hosp., 1952-53; resident Mayo Clinic, Rochester, Minn., 1953-56, resident in radiology, 1956-58; instr. diagnostic radiology U. Minn., 1958-60, asst. prof., 1960-62; staff radiologist St. Joseph's Hosp., St. Paul, 1962-71, dir. cardiovascular diagnostic unit, 1962-71; prof., chmn. dept. diagnostic radiology and nuclear medicine Univ. Hosp., U. Western Ont., London. Contbr. in field. Mem. Alumnae Assn. Mayo Found. for Med. Edn. and Research, Am. Coll. Radiology, Am. Roentgen Ray Soc., Assn. Univ. Radiologists, Can. Assn. Radiologist, Can. Med. Protective Assn., Can. Profs. Radiology, Council on Cardiovascular Radiology, Am. Heart Assn., Minn. Radiol. Soc., N. Am. Soc. Cardic Radiologists, Radiol. Soc. N. Am., Solar Energy Soc. Can. Office: 339 Windermere Rd London ON N6A 5A5 Canada

CAREY, MACDONALD, actor; b. Sioux City, Iowa, Mar. 15, 1913; s. Charles S. and Elizabeth (Macdonald) C.; m. Elizabeth Heckscher, May 4, 1941 (div. 1967); children: Lynn, Lisa, Steve, Teresa, Edward Macdonald, Paul. Student. U. Wis., 1931-32; B.A., U. Iowa, 1935, postgrad., 1935-36. Mem., Old Globe Shakespeare Co., 1936-37, NBC Radio Stock Co., Chgo., 1937-38; free lance radio actor, N.Y.C.; stage appearances include Lady in the Dark, 1939, Anniversary Waltz, 1954; films include Dr. Broadway, 1942, Take a Letter, Darling, 1942, Wake Island, 1942, Suddenly It's Spring, 1947, Dream Girl, 1948, Streets of Laredo, 1949, Copper Canyon, 1950, Great Missouri Raid, 1951, Excuse My Dust, 1951, Let's Make It Legal, 1951, My Wife's Best Friend, 1952, Count the Hours, 1953, Fire Over Africa, 1954, Stranger at My Door, 1956, Tammy and the Doctor, 1963, Broken Sabre, 1965, End of the World, 1977, American Gigolo, 1980; star: TV series Lock Up, 1956, Dr. Christian, 1956, Days of Our Lives, 1965—; other TV appearances on The Girl, The Gold Watch and Everything; host-narrator: radio program Heartbeat Theater; (Recipient Emmy award (2) for Best Actor in Daytime Drama Series Acad. TV Arts and Scis. 1974, 75); Author: poetry Out of Heart. Bd. dirs. Cath. Big Bros., 1962-64. Served to 1st lt. USMCR, 1942-45. Mem. Screen Actors Guild (v.p. 1960), Acad. Motion Picture Arts and Scis. (asst. treas. 1970), AFTRA, Actors Equity Assn., Alpha Delta Phi. Democrat. Roman Catholic. Office: care NBC Press Dept 30 Rockefeller Plaza New York NY 10020 *

CAREY, RAYMOND BERNARD, JR., corporate executive; b. Cambridge, Mass., Nov. 13, 1926; s. Raymond Bernard and Irene (Lawton) C.; m. Dennice Frances Rioux, Aug. 18, 1951; children: Sheila Anne, Lisa Anne, Michael Raymond. B.A., Holy Cross Coll., 1948; M.B.A., Harvard U., 1950. Foreman Dewey & Almy Chem. Co., Cambridge, Mass., 1950-51; asst. to v.p. Gen. Dynamics Corp., Groton, Conn., N.Y.C., 1951-54; plant mgr. (Electro-Dynamics Div.), Bayonne, N.J., 1956-59, pres., gen. mgr., 1960-66; group v.p., dir. Robert Morse Corp., Montreal, Can., 1966-70; pres., gen. mgr. Howe Richardson Scale, 1966-68; exec. v.p. Am. District Telegraph Co., N.Y.C., 1970, pres., 1971—, chief exec. officer, after 1972, chmn. bd., 1973—; dir. Collins & Aikman, Kroger Co. Served with USNR, 1944-46. Roman Catholic. Office: One World Trade Center 92 Fl New York NY 10048 *

CAREY, RICHARD EDWARD, retired marine corps officer, state official; b. Columbus, Ohio, Jan. 10, 1928; s. Timothy Francis and Marie Christine (Schlosser) C.; m. Dena Eloise Adcock, Nov. 18, 1961; children: William, Paul, Michael, Robert, Scott, Tamara, Melody. Student, U.S.C., 1959-60, U. Tex., 1964; B.S. with distinction, George Washington U., 1971. Enlisted in U.S. Navy, 1945; in U.S. Marine Corps., 1946-48, advanced through grades lt. gen., 1980; various assignments as platoon leader, co. comdr., squadron comdr., group comdr.; comdr. Marine Amphibious Brigade, 1975, 2d Marine Aircraft Wing, Cherry Point, N.C., 1976-78; dep. chief staff Office Comdr. in Chief Atlantic, Norfolk, Va., 1978-80; comdg. gen. Marine Corps Devel. and Edn. Command, Quantico, Va., 1980-83; dir. Ohio Dept. Liquor Control, Columbus, 1983—. Mem. Marine Corps Aviation Assn., Tailhook Naval Aviation Assn., Purple Heart Assn., Alpha Kappa Psi. Episcopalian. Clubs: Rotary, Mason, Shrine. Planned security and executed evacuation of Saigon and Cambodia, 1975, participated in recapture mcht. ship Mayaguez, 1975. Home: 2288 Brixton Rd Columbus OH 43221 Office: Dept Liquor Control 2288 Brixton Rd Columbus OH 43221

CAREY, RICHARD FREMONT, business executive; b. Chgo., Aug. 11, 1924; s. James August and Monta Rhea (Chessman) C.; m. Cleona Wertz, Nov. 9, 1956. Student, Rutgers U., 1947-49, U. Pa., 1949-50. Sales rep. Material Handling Equipment Co., Phila., 1948-50; sales corr., mgr. distbr. sales, asst. sales mgr., field sales mgr. Hoover Co., Plainfield, N.J., 1950-55; sales mgr. to gen. mgr. Buck Mfg. Co., San

Jose, Calif., 1956-59; gen. mgr., exec. v.p. F.W. Shrader Co., Inc., Los Angeles, 1961-64; pres. Bux Magnetic Products Inc., Los Angeles, 1961-64; exec. v.p. Bux-Shrader Magnetic Products, Los Angeles, 1959-64, Plastomeric Inc., Los Gatos, Calif., 1964-66, Becton Dickinson of Calif., Inc., 1966-70; v.p. ops. Becton Dickinson & Co., Rutherford, N.J., 1970-76, 1976-77, pres., Rochelle Park, N.J., 1977-81, group pres. consumer group., corp. officer, corp. operating com., corp. mgmt. com., 1981—; dir. O.S. Walker Co., Worcester, Mass. Served with USMC, 1943-46. Mem. Am. Mgmt. Assn., Am. Ordnance Assn., Am. Supply and Machinery Mfg. Assn. Patentee in field. Home: 10 Parsons Ct Mahwah NJ 07430 Office: Becton Dickinson & Co Mack Centre Dr Paramus NJ 07652

CAREY, ROBERT WILLIAMS, insurance company executive; b. N.Y.C., July 31, 1918; s. Robert Jay and Sarah (Williams) C.; m. Anne Levangie, May 17, 1969; children: Christine, Noreen, Brian, Donald, Steven. Grad., Advanced Mgmt. Program, Harvard U., 1963. Accident and health underwriter Fireman's Fund, N.Y.C., 1935-45; accident and health sr. underwriter Royal Liverpool Group, N.Y.C., 1946-49; mgr. accident and health dept. Sun Indemnity Co., N.Y.C., 1949-51, N.Y. Life Ins. Co., 1951-56; dir. health ins. John Hancock Mut. Life Ins. Co., Boston, 1956-61, 2d v.p., 1961-71, v.p., 1971-82, sr. v.p., 1982—; lectr. health ins. N.Y. U., City Coll. N.Y. Bd. dirs. Newton Coll. of Sacred Heart, 1967-70. Served with U.S. Army, 1942-45. Mem. Health Ins. Assn. Am. (chmn. individual health subcom.), Home Office Life Underwriters Assn. (exec. council), Inst. Home Office Underwriters. Club: Needham (Mass.) Golf (gov. 1971-76). Home: 65 Livingston Circle Needham MA 02192 Office: John Hancock Mut Life Ins Co John Hancock Pl Boston MA 02117

CAREY, RON (RONALD J. CICENIA), actor; b. Newark, Dec. 11, 1935; s. John and Fanny Cicenia; m. Sharon Boyeronus, Nov. 11, 1967. B.A., Seton Hall U., 1958. Appeared on: numerous TV variety shows including Steve Allen Show; appeared in: TV series Clifton Davis and Melba Moore Show, Jack Paar Show, Merv Griffin Show, Mike Douglas Show, Johnny Carson Show; over 100 TV commls.; appears in: TV series Barney Miller, 1976-82; appeared in: films History of the World Part I, Dynamite Chicken, Silent Movie, High Anxiety, Fatso; recorded: album The Slightly Irreverant Comedy of Ron Carey, 1966. Mem. Screen Actors Guild, AFTRA, Equity. Democrat. Roman Catholic. Office: care Four D Productions 1438 N Gower St Hollywood CA 90028

CAREY, THOMAS HILTON, advertising agency executive; b. Oak Park, Ill., Aug. 31, 1944; s. James Patrick and Caroline Hale (Hilton) C.; m. Barbara Lynn Hardy, Sept. 13, 1969; children: Christopher, Colleen, Jill. B.A., Holy Cross, 1966; M.S. in Journalism, Northwestern U., 1967. Account mgr. Benton & Bowles Inc., N.Y.C., after 1967, now sr. v.p., account mgr. Office: Benton Bowles Inc 909 3d Ave New York NY 10022

CAREY, TOM MAX, oil co. exec.; b. Guthrie, Okla., Sept. 26, 1928; s. Glen T. and Ora Jo (Mitchell) C.; m. E. Joyce Derden, June 18, 1953; children—Ellen, Martha. B.S., Okla. State U., 1950; M.B.A., So. Meth. U., 1957. Accounting mgr. Mobil Oil Co., Dallas, 1954-61; exec. v.p., dir. Koch Industries, Wichita, Kans., 1961—, Koch Engring. Co.; dir. Matador Cattle Co., Koch Refining Co., Koch Chem. Co. Served to 1st lt. USAF, 1952-54. Home: 562 Brookfield St Wichita KS 67206 Office: PO Box 2256 Wichita KS 67220

CAREY, WILLIAM DANIEL, assn. exec., publisher; b. N.Y.C., Jan. 29, 1916; s. Daniel Joseph and Margaret Elizabeth (Galloway) C.; m. Mary Margaret Rhodin, May 20, 1944; children—Eric, Teresa, Jane, Julia, Elizabeth. A.B., Columbia U., 1940, M.A., 1941; M.P.A., Harvard U., 1942. With Bur. Budget, Exec. Office of Pres., Washington, 1942-69, asst. dir., 1960-69; v.p. Arthur D. Little, Inc., Cambridge, Mass., 1969-74; exec. officer AAAS; pub. jour. Science, Washington, 1975—; trustee MITRE Corp., 1978—, Russell Sage Found., 1979—; mem. Nat. Commn. on Research, 1978—; chmn. U.S. sect. U.S.-USSR Sci. Policy Working Group, 1973—. Recipient Exceptional Service award Bur. Budget, 1960; Rockefeller Public Service award, 1964. Fellow AAAS; mem. Inst. Medicine of Nat. Acad. Scis., Nat. Acad. Public Adminstrn., Am. Soc. Public Adminstrn., Phi Beta Kappa. Roman Catholic. Clubs: Cosmos (Washington); Univ. (N.Y.C.). Office: 1515 Massachusetts Ave NW Washington DC 20005 *

CAREY, WILLIAM JOSEPH, financial executive; b. N.Y.C., May 15, 1922; s. Cornelius Montague and Ellen Katherine (Gannon) C.; m. Barbara L. Garrison, Aug. 24,7 1946; children: Kathleen, Eileen, Christine, Robert. B.S., Rider Coll., 1949; postgrad., NYU, 1952-53. C.P.A., N.Y. Mgr. Ernst and Ernst, N.Y.C., 1949-59; controller Reynolds and Co., N.Y.C., 1959-61; exec. v.p. Bache and Co., N.Y.C., 1961-69; exec. ptnr. Goodbody and Co., N.Y.C., 1970-71; v.p. Paine Webber, N.Y.C., 1971-73; controller, treas., and chief fin. officer J. Henry Schroder Bank and Trust Co., N.Y.C., 1973—; arbitration panel mem. Nat. Assn. Securities Dealers, N.Y.C. Served in USN, 1942-45; PTO. Decorated Purple Heart. Mem. N.Y. State Soc. C.P.A.s, Am. Inst. C.P.A.s, Fin. Execs. Inst. (ops. com., internat. com). Clubs: Franklin Lakes, Indian Trail. Home: 861 Huron Rd Franklin Lakes NJ 07417 Office: Schroder Bank and Trust Co One State St New York NY

CAREY, WILLIAM POLK, investment banker; b. Balt., May 11, 1930; s. Francis J. and Marjorie A. (Armstrong) C. Grad., Pomfret Sch., 1948; student, Princeton, 1948-50; B.S. in Econs., Wharton Sch. of U. Pa., 1953. Vice pres., gen. mgr. A. J. Orbach Co., Plainfield, N.J., 1955-58; prin. W. P. Carey & Co., Bloomfield, N.J., 1958-63; pres., dir. Internat. Leasing Corp., N.Y.C., 1959—; prin. Carey Internat., N.Y.C., 1960—; chmn. bd. Carey Internat. (Australia) Pty. Ltd., 1962—; chmn. exec. com., dir. Hubbard, Westervelt & Mottelay, Inc. (now Merrill Lynch, Hubbard, Inc.), N.Y.C., 1964-67; dept. head Loeb, Rhoades & Co. (now Shearson Am. Express Inc.), N.Y.C., 1967-71; vice chmn. investment banking bd., dir. corporate finance duPont Glore Forgan Inc., 1971-73; pres., dir., chief exec. officer W.P. Carey & Co., Inc. and affiliates, N.Y.C., 1973-83; also chmn. W.P. Carey's Co., Inc. and affiliates, N.Y.C., 1983—; gen. ptnr. Corp. Property Assos., 1978—; pres., dir. various financing corps.; partner various partnerships owning property leased to major corps.;, 1972-73. Trustee, treas. Delta Phi Found., 1969-72, chmn., 1972—; mem. nat. execs.' com. Nat. Council on Crime and Delinquency; trustee, mem. exec. com. Rensselaerville (N.Y.) Inst., 1979—; trustee Gilman Sch., Balt., Pomfret Sch., Conn.; chmn. bd. trustees Anglo-Am. Contemporary Dance Found., Oxford Mgmt. Ctr. Assocs. Council; mem. council of trustees Oxford Ctr. for Mgmt. Studies, Templeton Coll., Oxford U. Served to 1st lt. USAF, 1953-55. Mem. Soc. Mayflower Descs., Delta Phi. Episcopalian. Clubs: Racquet and Tennis, Brook (N.Y.C.); University, Pilgrims; St. Anthony (N.Y.C.); St. Elmo (Phila.). Donor William Polk Carey prize in econs. U. Pa., W.P. Carey & Co., Inc. prize in applied math. Calif. Inst. Tech. Home: 525 Park Ave New York NY 10021 also The Manse Rensselaerville NY 12147 Office: 689 Fifth Ave New York NY 10022

CARGILL, OTTO ARTHUR, JR., lawyer; b. Oklahoma City, May 30, 1914; s. Otto Arthur and Delia Ann (Arnold) C.; m. Rebecca Kay; children: Carole Sue Cargill Lash, Henson, Christina Cargill Best, John Russell, Angela Beth, Kima Leigh, Jennifer Ann. LL.B., Cumberland U., 1934. Bar: Okla. 1935, U.S. Dist. Ct. (we. dist.) Okla. 1935, U.S. Dist. Ct. (no. dist.) Okla. 1956, U.S. Dist. Ct. (ea. dist.) Okla. 1957, U.S. Ct. Appeals (10th cir.) 1944, U.S. Supreme Ct. 1938. Sole practice, Oklahoma City, 1935—. Pres. Buffalo Breeders Am. Inc. Served with U.S. Army, 1943. Fellow Internat. Acad. Trial Lawyers; mem. Oklahoma City C. of C., ABA, Okla. Bar Assn., Oklahoma County Bar Assn., Assn. Trial Lawyers Am., Okla. Trial Lawyers Assn. (pres. 1947, 63), Nat. Assn. Criminal Def. Lawyers (co-chmn. membership com. 1971), Am. Judicatue Soc., Law-Sci. Acad. Am. (founding mem., Gold medal award 1969). Democrat. Am. Baptist. Home: 6401 Northwest 164 Oklahoma City OK 73132 Office: Park-Harvey Ctr Oklahoma City OK 73102

CARGO, DAVID FRANCIS, lawyer; b. Dowagiac, Mich., Jan. 13, 1929; s. Francis Clair and Mary E. (Harton) C.; m. Ida Jo Anaya, Sept. 22, 1960; children—Veronica Ann, David Joseph, Patrick Michael, Maria Elena Christina, Eamon Francis. A.B., U. Mich., 1951, M.Pub. Adminstrn., 1953, LL.B., 1957. Bar: Mich., N.Mex. bars 1957, Oreg. bar 1974. Practice in Albuquerque, 1957, asst. dist. atty., 1958-59; mem. N.M. Ho. of Reps., 1962; gov., N.M., 1967-70, practice law, Santa Fe, 1970-73, Portland, Oreg., 1973—. Chmn. Four Corners Regional Commn., 1967-71, Oil and Gas Conservation Commn.; chmn. N.Mex. Young Republicans, 1959-61, Clackamas County Rep. Central Com.; mem. Israel Bond Com. Served with AUS, 1953-55. Named Man of Year Albuquerque Jr. C. of C., 1964; recipient Outstanding Conservationist award N.Mex. Wildlife Assn., 1969, 70. Mem. Mich., N.Mex., Albuquerque bar assns., Issac Walton League (past v.p. N.Mex.), World Affairs Council Oreg. (pres.), Interstate Oil and Gas Compact, Izaak Walton League Oreg. Home: 750 Brier Cliff Lake Oswego OR 97034 Office: 610 SW Alder Suite 705 Oreg Nat Bldg Portland OR 97205

CARGO, WILLIAM IRA, retired foreign service officer; b. Detroit, Feb. 27, 1917; s. Ira Wiles and Nina (Lathrop) C; m. Margaret Grace Ludwig, June 21, 1938; children: David Paul, Ruth. A.B., Albion Coll., 1937, LL.D., 1963; A.M., U. Mich., 1938, Ph.D., 1941; student Russian lang., Naval Tng. Sch., Boulder, Colo., 1944-45; LL.D., Waynesburg Coll., 1970. Instr. polit. sci. U. Mich., 1941-42, Colo. Coll., 1942-43; staff Dept. State, 1943—, Bur. UN Affairs, 1946-53, dep. dir. office dependent area affairs, 1952; assigned Nat. War Coll., 1953-54; adviser U.S. delegations Gen. Assembly, Trusteeship Council Sessions, 1946-53; alternate U.S. rep. UN Com. on Non-self-governing Terrs., 1952; U.S. rep. UN vis. mission Trust Terrs. Tanganyika, Italian Somaliland, Ruanda-Urundi, 1951; assigned to U.S. Mission to NATO and European regional orgns. in connection with spl. internat. trade problems, Paris, 1954-57; dep. dir. Office of UN Polit. and Security Affairs, Dept. State, 1957-58, dir., 1958-61; dep. U.S. rep. Internat. Atomic Energy Agy., Vienna, Austria, 1961-63; dep. chief of mission, minister-counselor Am. embassy, Karachi and Rawalpindi, Pakistan, 1963-67; dep. U.S. rep. to NATO minister, Brussels, 1967-69; career minister U.S. Fgn. Service, 1969; dir. planning and coordination staff Dept. State, Washington, 1969-73; U.S. ambassador to, Nepal, 1973-76; sr. insp. Fgn. Service Inspection Corps., Washington, 1976-78, cons., 1979—; adviser U.S. delegation UN Gen. Assembly, 1957, Gen. Conf. of IAEA, Vienna, 1958, alt. U.S. rep., 1961, 62; adviser U.S. del. Conf. Discontinuance Nuclear Weapons Tests, Geneva, 1959; vice-chmn. U.S. del. Conf. to Amend Single Conv. Narcotic Drugs, Geneva, 1972. Served with USNR, 1944-46. Recipient Meritorious Service award Dept. State, 1958. Mem. AAAS, Phi Beta Kappa. Methodist. Home: 4312 N 39th St Arlington VA 22207

CARIAGA, MARVELLEE DYVONNE (MOODY CARIAGA), mezzo soprano; b. Huntington Park, Calif., Aug. 11, 1942; d. Robert Earl and Marvellee Dyvonne (Hocker) Moody; m. Daniel Philip Cariaga, May 13, 1961; children: Luisa, Daniel Earl. B.A., Calif. State U., Long Beach, 1960-64. Appears with opera cos. including, San Francisco Opera; Appeared with, Netherlands Opera, Rio de Janeiro (Brazil) Opera, Seattle Opera; appeared with orchs. and in festivals, throughout U.S., N.Y. debut with Phila. Orch. in Carnegie Hall, 1977, numerous recitals in, U.S., Can., 1970-83; appeared in: Gian Carlo Menotti's The Consul, PBS-TV, 1978, several other internat. prodns. staged by the composer. Office: Regency Artists 9200 Sunset Blvd Los Angeles CA 90069

CARIDEO, JAMES VINCENT, lawyer, telephone company executive; b. Mt. Vernon, N.Y., Oct. 8, 1935; s. James Vincent and Emily (D'Amato) C.; m. Frances Cappabianca, Dec. 28, 1957; children: Barbara, Jane, James, Laura, Michael. B.A., U. Notre Dame, 1957; J.D., Fordham U., 1963. Bar: N.Y. 1964, Fla. 1972. Assoc. Naylon, Huber, Magill, Lawrence & Farrell, N.Y.C., 1963-68; gen. atty. Geigy Chem. Corp., Ardsley, N.Y., 1968-69; sr. atty. Gen. Telephone and Electronics, N.Y.C., 1969-70; v.p., gen. counsel GTE Data Services, Tampa, Fla., 1970-76, Gen. Telephone Co. Fla., Tampa, 1976—. Bd. dirs. Tampa chpt. ARC, 1971-74, 83—, Meals on Wheels, Tampa, 1978—, Tampa Bay Regional Poison Control Ctr. Found., Tampa, 1983—, New Life Dwelling Place, 1983-84; mem. fin. planning com. Children's Home, Tampa, 1982—, Acad. Holy Name, 1983—. Served to 1st lt. U.S. Army, 1958-59. Recipient Exec. of Yr. award Nat. Secs. Assn., 1975. Mem. ABA, Fla. Bar Assn., N.Y. Bar Assn., Hillsborough County Bar Assn., Am. Corp. Counsel Assn. Roman Catholic. Club: Tower (Tampa) (dir. 1979-84). Office: Gen Telephone Co Fla One Tampa City Center PO Box 110 Tampa FL 33601

CARIOLA, ROBERT JOSEPH, artist; b. Bklyn., Mar. 24, 1927. Student, Pratt Inst. Art Sch., Pratt Graphic Ctr. Art cons. Cath. Youth Orgn., Rockville Center, N.Y., 1967—; art coordinator St. John's Cloister, Queen's, N.Y., 1972-74; instr. art La Salle Acad., Oakdale, N.Y., 1963-65, Cath. Youth summer workshop Huntington Twp. Art League, 1971. Artist exhibitions include, Boston Mus. Printmakers Exhbn., 1962, Corcoran Gallery Art, Washington, 1963, Pa. Acad. Fine Arts, Phila., Vatican Pavilion-N.Y. World's Fair, 1964, Nat. Acad. Design, N.Y.C., 1970; contbr.: Illustrator Writer's Ann., 1958, Sign Mag., 1971; to art mags. Recipient First prize for painting John Kennedy Cultural Center Bankers Trust, 1971, Grumbacher Cash award Silvermine Guild Artists, New Canaan, Conn., 1976, Best in Show award Bayshore C. of C. Art Festival, 1979. Address: 1844 Gormley Ave Merrick NY 11566

CARIOU, LEN, actor, director; b. Winnipeg, Can., Sept. 30, 1939. Student, St. Paul's Coll. Profl. tng., Guthrie Theatre, Mpls., Stratford Shakespeare Festival; Profl. debut Damn Yankees, Winnipeg Rainbow Stage Theatre, 1959; joined, Man. Theatre Center, 1961; appeared in: The Threepenny Opera, Love Labours Lost; mem., Stratford (Ont.) Shakespeare Festival, 1961-65; appeared in: Cyrano de Bergerac, Cariolanus, 1981, Taming of the Shrew, 1981, The Tempest, 1982, Julius Caesar, 1982, Arms and the Man, Timon of Athens, Chichester (Eng.) Festival, 1964; mem., Guthrie Theatre, Mpls., 1966; assoc. dir., 1972; appeared in: The House of Atreus, King Lear; dir.: The Crucible, Of Mice and Men; appeared in: Othello, Goodman Theatre, Chgo., 1969, Much Ado about Nothing, The Three Sisters, Henry V Am. Shakespeare Festival, Stratford, Conn., 1969; Broadway plays include Applause, 1970; Nightwatch, 1972, A Little Night Music, 1973, Cold Storage, 1978, Sweeney Todd, 1979, Dance a Little Closer up from Paradise, 1983; appeared in: film The Four Seasons, 1981; dir.: play The Petrified Forest, 1974; film Don't Call Back, 1975 (Recipient Tony award for best actor in Sweeney Todd 1979). Office: care STE Representation Ltd 888 7th Ave New York NY 10019 *

CARIS, THEODORE, publishing company executive; b. Boston, Mar. 20, 1934; s. Nicholas and Dimitra (Hedgianou) C.; m. Chrysoula Kazantzi, Apr. 1, 1962; children: Chris, Theo. B.S., Northeastern U., 1957. Editor Allyn-Bacon, Boston, 1960-62, Macmillan Co., N.Y.C., 1962-63; v.p. for editorial programs Random House and Knopf, N.Y.C., 1963-70; pres. Xerox Coll. Publishing, Lexington, Mass., 1970-75; sr. v.p., pub. Aspen Systems Corp., from 1975; now sr. v.p. Phillips Pub. Inc., Bethesda, Md. Served to 1st lt. AUS, 1958-60. Mem. Assn. Am. Pubs., Nat. Press Club, Info. Industry Assn. Greek Orthodox. Home: 6213 Mazwood Rd Rockville MD 20852 Office: 191 Spring St Lexington MA 02173

CARITHERS, HUGH ALFRED, physician; b. Winder, Ga., July 21, 1913; s. Hugh A. and Starr (Blasinfame) C.; m. Cornelia Davis Morse, July 27, 1942; children: Susan (Mrs. John F. Callender), Hugh Alfred, Starr (Mrs. Roy W. Waddell). A.B., Emory U., 1933, M.D., 1937. Diplomate: Am. Bd. Pediatrics. Intern Germantown Dispensary, Phila., 1937-39; resident St. Christophers Hosp. of Phila., 1939-40, Bellevue Hosp., N.Y.C., 1940-41; practice medicine specializing in pediatrics, Jacksonville, Fla., 1945—; chief pediatrics Jacksonville Hosps. Edn. Program, 1958-69; chief dept. pediatrics St. Vincent's Hosp., 1952-64, staff pres., 1956-58; clin. prof. pediatrics U. Fla. Coll. Medicine, 1969—. Editorial bd.: Am. Jour. Diseases Children, 1970—. Served with M.C. AUS, 1941-45. Fellow Am. Pub. Health Assn.; mem. Fla. Pediatric Soc. (pres. 1949-50), Duval Med. Soc. (pres. 1963-64), Phi Delta Theta, Alpha Kappa Kappa. Clubs: Fla. Yacht, Timequana Country (Jacksonville). Home: 3010 St Johns Ave Jacksonville FL 32205 Office: 1661 Riverside Ave Jacksonville FL 32204

CARITHERS, JEANINE RUTHERFORD, educator; b. Boone, Iowa, Sept. 26, 1933; d. John Twedt Rutherford and Catherine Elizabeth (Rutherford); m. Robert William Carithers, Sept. 23, 1953; children: Jeffrey Scott, Brian Reid, Douglas Sean. B.S. in Zoology, 1956; M.A. in Physiology, Iowa State U., 1965; Ph.D. in Anatomy, U. Mo., 1968. Tchr. sci. Union pub. schs., Iowa, 1964-65; asst. prof. vet. anatomy Iowa State U., Ames, 1968-72, assoc. prof., 1972-76, prof., 1976—, chairperson vet. anatomy, 1979—; professeur associe Ministre del'Education Nationale, France, 1976. Contbr. articles to profl. jours. Mem. Soc. of Neurosci., Am. Assn. Anatomists, AAAS, Am. Assn. Vet Medicine Colls., Congress of European Comparative Endocrinologists, N.Y. Acad. Scis., World Assn. Vet. Anatomists, Sigma Xi, Gamma Sigma Delta. Office: 1092 Vet Medicine Dept Anatomy Ames IA 50011

CARIUS, ROBERT WILHELM, retired naval officer, mathematics educator; b. Peoria, Ill., Jan. 4, 1929; s. Henry Clarence and Mary Magdalen (Wilhelm) C.; m. Geraldine Mary Sullivan, Mar. 16, 1957; children: Patricia, Mary, Linda, Robert, Daniel, Sara. B.S. in Naval Sci, U.S. Naval Acad., 1951, U.S. Naval Postgrad. Sch., 1958; M.S. in Nuclear Engring, Iowa State Coll., 1959. Commd. ensign U.S. Navy, 1951, advanced through grades to rear adm., 1977; served with (Fighter Squadron 74), 1953-56, 1959-61, project mgr., 1964-65, served with, 1962-63, command officer, 1966-68, exec. officer, 1968-70, research and devel. br. head, 1970-71, command officer, San Diego, 1971-73, mem. staff, 1973-77, comdr., Jacksonville, Fla., 1977-79; with aviation programs Dept. Navy, from 1979; now instr. math. and sci. Ark. Coll.; bd. govs. USO, Jacksonville. Mem. exec. bd. United Way of Jacksonville, N.E. Fla. council Boy Scouts Am. Decorated Legion of Merit, Air medal, Meritorious Service medal; recipient Spl. award United Way of Jacksonville, 1979. Mem. U.S. Naval Acad. Alumni Assn., Assn. Naval Aviation, Naval Helicopter Assn., U.S. Naval Inst., Jacksonville C. of C. (gov.). Roman Catholic. Club: Rotary. *Personal integrity and honesty to oneself have been key elements in my life's philosophy. Attempting to understand the people you work with and treating them as you prefer to be treated were other essential principles. Lastly, always do your very best in all endeavors, and you never have to look over your shoulder with regret.*

CARL, ROBERT LEROY, office furniture, equipment mfg. co. exec.; b. Muscatine, Iowa, Mar. 25, 1923; s. Howard Dale and Marie Frances (Plessy) C.; m. Maryrose Theresa Brown, Nov. 24, 1945; children—Robert LeRoy, Gregory, Christopher, Anthony, Amy. Student schs., parochial, Muscatine. With Hon Industries Inc., Muscatine, 1947—, asst. to pres., 1964-79, corp. sec., 1979—. Served with USN, 1942-46. Mem. Am. Soc. Corp. Secs. Republican. Roman Catholic. Club: Muscatine Elks. Home: 3 Magnolia Circle Muscatine IA 52761 Office: 414 E 3d St Muscatine IA 52761

CARLANDER, KENNETH DIXON, fishery biologist, educator; b. Gary, Ind., May 25, 1915; s. Lester William and Ruth Emelia (Larson) C.; m. Harriet Coleman Bell, June 23, 1939 (dec. July 1973); m. Julia Genevieve Nichols, June 29, 1975. B.A. cum laude, U. Minn., 1936, M.S., 1938, Ph.D., 1943. Ornithologist Panhandle Plains Hist. Soc. Mus., Canyon, Tex., 1933; lab. technician U. Minn., 1936-38; aquatic biologist Minn. Dept. Conservation, 1938-46; asst. prof. Iowa State U., 1946-48, asso. prof., 1948-57, prof., 1957-74, distinguished prof., 1974—; leader Iowa Coop. Fishery Research Unit, 1946-66; vis. prof. Satya Wacana Christian U., Salatiga, Java, 1977-78, Tex. A&M U., 1982; Exec. bd. 15th Internat. Congress Limnology, 1960-68; editorial referee Fisheries Research Bd. Can., 1957; mem. Iowa Natural Resources Council, 1961, Iowa Water Resources Research Inst., 1964-65; mem. panel fishery Experts FAO of UN; Ford Found. assignment, Egypt, 1965-66. Author: Handbook of Freshwater Fishery Biology, 3d edit, 1969, Vol. 2, 1977; Editorial bd.: Progressive Fish Culturist, 1951-52, Jour. Wildlife Mgmt, 1952-53, Am. Fishery Soc. trans, 1956-59; proc. Iowa Acad. Sci, 1957. Research grantee AEC, NSF. Fellow Am. Inst. Fishery Research Biologists (bd. control 1957-61, Outstanding Achievement award 1983), AAAS (council 1963-65); mem. Am. Inst. Biol. Scis., Am. Soc. Ichthyologists and Herpetologists (bd. govs. 1952-56), Am. Soc. Limnology and Oceanography, Wildlife Soc., Am. Fisheries Soc. (pres. 1960-61, award of excellence 1979), Brit. Fisheries Soc., Biometric Soc., Ecol. Soc. Am., Internat. Assn. Theoretical and Applied Limnology (central com. 1962-72), Am. Soc. Naturalists, Nat. Assn. Biology Tchrs., AAUP, Izaak Walton League, United World Federalists (chpt. chmn.), Iowa Acad. Sci. (dir. 1959-64, pres. 1968-69, Disting. fellow 1980), Nature Conservancy, Soc. Population Ecology, Am. Soc. Zoologists, Asian Ecol. Soc., Sigma Xi (chpt. pres. 1963), Phi Kappa Phi, Gamma Sigma Delta. Conglist. Home: 2322 Knapp St Ames IA 50010

CARLBERG, NORMAN KENNETH, sculptor, educator; b. Roseau, Minn., Nov. 6, 1928; s. Carl Gustav and Alma (Forsberg) C.; m. Juanita Nancy Koch Gorman, Aug. 7, 1961; 1 son, Kenneth Gustav. Student, Brainerd Jr. Coll., 1947-49, Mpls. Sch. Art, 1950-51; B.F.A., Yale U., 1958, M.F.A., 1961. Fulbright fellow Cath. U., Santiago, Chile, 1960; artist in residence Rinehart Sch. Sculpture, Md. Inst. Coll. Art., Balt., 1961-78, dir., 1978—; vis. critic U. Pa., 1977-80. One man-shows include, Cath. U., Santiago, 1960, Pa. State U., 1966, Balt. Mus. Art, 1968, group exhbns. include, Galerie Chalette, N.Y.C., 1960, Whitney Mus. Art, 1962, Yale U., 1965, Schenectady Mus., 1977; represented in permanent collections, Addison Gallery, Phillips Acad., Hirshhorn Mus., Washington, Whitney Mus., Balt. Mus. Art. Served with U.S. Air Force, 1951-55. Recipient Ford Found. purchase award,

1962. Office: Md Inst Coll Art 1300 W Mt Royal Ave Baltimore MD 21217

CARLE, LELAND LESTER, food company executive; b. Stuttgart, Ark., Feb. 9, 1929; s. Elmer G. and Mary Margaret (Walters) C.; m. Helen R. Starnes, Aug. 14, 1949; children: Leslie, Timothy. Student, Internat. Accts. Soc. Corr. Sch. Clk., Ark. Rice Growers Coop. Assn. (now Riceland Foods), Stuttgart, 1946-49, asst. office mgr., 1949-59, office mgr., 1959-62, sec.-treas., 1962-71, v.p. fin., sec.-treas., 1971-78, v.p., gen. mgr., 1978-80, v.p. corp. planning and budgeting, 1980—; v.p., dir. 1st Fed. Savs. & Loan. Chmn., Ark. County Heart Fund, 1962, 63; pres., bd. dirs. Stuttgart Pub. Library; vice chmn. North Ark. County Library Bd.; bd. dirs. Central Ark. Radiation Therapy Inst. Mem. Nat. Assn. Accts., Stuttgart C. of C., Nat. Assn. Accts. for Coops. Lutheran. Club: Kiwanis. Home: 1815 Coker Hampton Dr Stuttgart AR 72160 Office: PO Box 927 Stuttgart AR 72160

CARLEN, SISTER CLAUDIA, librarian; b. Detroit, July 24, 1906; d. Albert B. and Theresa Mary (Ternes) C. A.B. in L.S, U. Mich., 1928, A.M., 1938; L.H.D. (hon.), Marygrove Coll., 1981. Asst. librarian St. Mary Acad., Monroe, Mich., 1928-29; asst. librarian Marygrove Coll., Detroit, 1929-44, librarian, 1944-69, library cons., 1970-71; on leave as index editor New Cath. Ency., 1963-67, Catholic Theol. Ency., 1968-70; library cons., Rome, Italy, 1971-72, St. John's Provincial Sem., Plymouth, Mich., 1972—; supr. orgn. and servicing Community Center Libraries staffed by vols.; Bd. dirs. Corpus Instrumentorum, Inc., v.p., 1969-70; Mem. instructional materials com. Mich. Curriculum Study; cons. McGraw Hill Ency. World Biography, 1968-72, World Book Ency., 1969-70. Author: Guide to Encyclicals of the Roman Pontiffs, 1939, Guide to the Documents of Pius XII, 1951, Dictionary of Papal Pronouncements, 1958, Translatio Studii, 1973; editor: Papal Encyclicals, 1740-1981, 1981; Editor: column At Your Service, Cath. Library World, 1950-52, Reference Book Rev. Sect, 1952-64, 66-72, Books for the Home column; monthly news release, Nat. Cath. Rural Life Conf., 1952-61; adv. bd.: The Pope Speaks, 1953—, Pierian Press; contbr.: Catholic Bookman's Guide, 1961, Dictionary Western Chs, 1969, Ency. Dictionary of Religion, 1979, Translatio Stu., 1979. Trustee Marygrove Coll., Detroit, 1976-79, vice chmn. bd., 1977-79. Recipient Disting. Alumna award U. Mich. Sch. L.S., 1974. Mem. ALA (council 1958-61, 68-71), Cath. Library Assn. (chmn. com. membership 1946-49, chmn. Mich. unit 1952-54, chmn. coll. and univ. sect. 1954-56, chmn. publs. com. 1961-62, pres. 1965-67), Bibliog. Soc. Am., Nat. Fedn. Cath. Coll. Students (moderator nat. lit. commn.), Spl. Libraries Assn., Mich. Library Assn. (chmn. coll. sect. 1956-57, chmn. recruiting com. 1959-60), Am. Friends of Vatican Library (v.p.), Phi Beta Kappa, Phi Kappa Phi, Beta Phi Mu. Home: care Marygrove Coll Library Detroit MI 48221 Office: St John's Provincial Seminary Plymouth MI 48170 *To form the habit of reading good books so that reading becomes a necessity in one's life is a sure means of continual development and growth; a means of attaining that poise of spirit and richness of mind that should mark every professional person; a means by which the mind acquires new light, the will new incentives, the heart new desires, and life new ideals.*

CARLEN, RAYMOND NILS, retired steel company executive, consultant; b. Rockford, Ill., May 3, 1919; s. Charles and Hannah (Nystrom) C.; m. Jean Lovejoy, June 15, 1946; children: Cynthia Jean, Susan Joy. B.S. in Metall. Engring, U. Ill., 1942; M.S. in Bus. Adminstrn, U. Chgo., 1950. With Joseph T. Ryerson & Son, Inc., Chgo., 1946—, v.p. Eastern region, 1963-64, exec. v.p., 1964-68, pres., 1968-76, chmn. bd., 1976-78; also dir.; sr. v.p. Inland Steel Co., Chgo., 1976-78, vice chmn., 1978-82; pres. Aarjoy Inc., 1982—; dir. Am. Nat. Bank and Trust of Chgo., Heller Internat., Timshel Inc., Pecker Plada Corp., Ltd., Tel Aviv, Israel, Hinsdale Fed. Savs. & Loan Assn., Ill., Grant Sq. Agy., Kewaunee Sci. Corp., Lindberg Corp. Mem. Ill. Emergency Resources Planning Com., 1964; chmn. Ill. Council on Econ. Edn., 1982-83; Chmn. Hinsdale (Ill.) Community Caucus, 1963-64; chmn. bd. counselors Chgo. Council Boy Scouts Am., 1981—; pres. Chgo. area council Boy Scouts Am., 1970-74; active fund raising U. Chgo., Loyola U., Chgo., Passavant Meml. Hosp., Chgo., Met. Crusade of Mercy.; Bd. dirs. Hinsdale Community House, 1957-60, Hinsdale PTA, 1957-60; mem. adv. council U. Chgo., 1960—; adv. council Coll. Engring., U. Ill., 1952—. Served to maj. C.E. AUS, 1942-45; ETO. Mem. Chgo. Assn. Commerce and Industry, Ill. C. of C. (Leadership award 1961), Exec. Program Club Chgo. Clubs: Chicago Golf (Wheaton, Ill.) (pres. 1965, 66, dir. 1960-67, 74-76, 80—), Hinsdale (Ill.) Golf; Chicago, Commerical, Economic (Chgo.). Home: 6 Oak Brook Club Dr Residence J305 Oak Brook IL 60521 Office: 7634 Nogales Rd Scottsdale AZ 85258

CARLESON, ROBERT BAZIL, corporation executive; b. Long Beach, Calif., Feb. 21, 1931; s. Bazil Upton and Grace Reynolds (Wilhite) C.; m. Betty Jane Nichols, Jan. 31, 1954 (div.); children: Eric Robert, Mark Andrew, Susan Lynn.; m. Susan A. Dower, Feb. 11, 1984. Student, U. Utah, 1949-51; B.S., U. So. Calif., 1953, postgrad., 1956-58. Adminstrv. asst. City of Beverly Hills, Calif., 1956-57; asst. to city mgr. City of Claremont, Calif., 1957-58; sr. adminstrv. asst. to city mgr. City of Torrance, Calif., 1958-60; city mgr. City of San Dimas, Calif., 1960-64, Pico Rivera, Calif., 1964-68; chief dep. dir. Calif. Dept. Public Works, 1968-71; dir. Calif. Dept. Social Welfare, 1971-73; U.S. commr. welfare, Washington, 1973-75; pres. Robert B. Carleson & Assocs., Inc., Sacramento, Washington, 1975-81; spl. asst. to pres. for policy devel., Washington, 1981-84; prin., dir. govt. relations Main Hurdman, KMG, Washington, 1984—; Dir. transition team Dept. Health & Human Services, Office of Pres.-Elect, 1980-81; spl. adviser Office of Policy Coordination; sr. policy advisor, chmn. welfare task force Reagan Campaign, 1980. Served with USN, 1953-56. Mem. Internat. City Mgmt. Assn. Republican. Clubs: Masons, Rotary (pres. 1964). Office: Main Hurdman KMG 1050 17th St NW Washington DC 20036

CARLETON, JIM G., univ. chancellor; b. Stratford, Okla., Aug. 5, 1928; s. Robert Edward and Ethel (Edwards) C.; m. Frances Bee, June 7, 1952; children—Timothy B., Amelia J., Brenda C. B.A., Okla. U., 1949; Ph.D., Syracuse U., 1969. Mem. faculty Syracuse U., 1952-72, dir. financial aids, 1961-63, dean men, 1963-66, dean student services, 1966-69, vice chancellor student affairs, 1969-72, instr. pub. affairs, 1956-69, asst. prof., 1969-72; v.p. student affairs Northwestern U., 1972—, prof., 1972—. Served with AUS, 1954-56. Mem. Nat. Assn. Student Personnel Adminstrs., Am. Acad., Phi Beta Kappa, Phi Eta Sigma, Phi Delta Kappa. Democrat. Methodist. Home: 617 Dartmouth Pl Evanston IL 60201

CARLETON, RICHARD ALLYN, cardiologist; b. Providence, Mar. 15, 1931; s. Russell Francis and Margaret Rexford (Bristol) C.; m. April Michelle Plumb, Jan. 29, 1975; children: Susan, Bradford, Margaret, Jennifer, Mary. A.B., Dartmouth Coll., 1952; M.D., Harvard U., 1955. Intern Harvard Service, Boston City Hosp., 1955-56, resident and fellow in cardiology, 1956-59; from asst. prof. to prof. medicine U. Ill., 1962-68; chief cardiology, prof. medicine Rush-Presbyn.-St. Luke's Med. Center, Chgo., 1968-72; chief med. service and cardiology San Diego VA Hosp., also prof. medicine U. Calif., San Diego, 1972-74; prof., chmn. dept. medicine Dartmouth Coll. Med. Sch., 1974-76; prof. med. sci., chief cardiology div. Meml. Hosp., Brown U. Med. Sch., Providence, 1976—; prin. investigator NIH heart disease prevention program, 1980—; chmn. R.I. Health Coordinating Com., 1979-80, R.I. Health Edn. Study Com., 1978-81. Contbr. articles to med. publs. Served to lt. comdr. M.C. USNR, 1960-62. Mem. Am. Soc. Clin. Investigation, Assn. U. Cardiologists, Am. Coll. Cardiology, Am. Heart Assn., A.C.P., Am. Heart Assn. (council epidemiology). Club: Barrington (R.I.) Yacht. Office: Memorial Hosp Pawtucket RI 02860

CARLETON, WILLARD TRACY, financial economist; b. Boston, May 3, 1934; s. Frank Nagle and Margaret Lally (Parker) C.; m. Stephanie Anne Brown, Mar. 1, 1958; children—James, Sarah, Leslie, Julia. A.B., Dartmouth Coll., 1956, M.B.A., 1957; M.A. in Econs, U. Wis., 1961, Ph.D., 1962. Acct. C.F. Rittenhouse & Co., Boston, 1956; mem. labs. staff Bell Telephone Labs., Inc., N.Y.C., 1957-58; teaching asst. econs. dept. U. Wis., 1958-59, research asst., 1959-61; economist Fed. Res. Bank of St. Louis, 1961-63; asst. prof. fin. Grad. Sch. Bus. Adminstrn., N.Y. U., 1963-65, asso. prof., 1965-66; asso. prof. quantitative methods and managerial econs. Sch. Bus., Northwestern U., 1966-67; asso. prof. fin. and econs. Amos Tuck Sch. Bus. Adminstrn., Dartmouth Coll., 1967-70, prof. fin. and econs., 1970-73, Leon E. Williams prof. banking and fin., 1973-74; William R. Kenan, Jr. prof. bus. adminstrn. U. N.C., Chapel Hill, 1974—. Assoc. editor: Jour. of Fin, 1977-80; Editor: Fin. Mgmt., 1981—; editorial bd.: Jour. of Fin. Research, 1977-80; contbr. articles to various profl. jours. Mem. Am. Econ. Assn., Am. Fin. Assn. (dir. 1976-78), Am. Statis. Assn., Econometric Soc., Inst. Mgmt. Scis., Western Fin. Assn., Fin. Mgmt. Assn. (dir. 1975-77, pres. 1977-78), So. Econ. Assn., So. Fin. Assn., Research Council on Small Bus. and Professions (dir. 1976-79), Nat. Soc. Rate of Return Analysts (dir. 1977-78). Episcopalian. Office: Sch Bus Adminstrn U NC Chapel Hill NC 27514

CARLEY, CHARLES TEAM, JR., nuclear engineer; b. Greenville, Miss., Dec. 27, 1932; s. Charles Team and Ruby (McClendon) C.; m. Shirley Holland, May 28, 1955; children—Karen, Mary McClendon, Charles Team III, Holland. B.S., Miss. State U., 1955; M.S., Va. Poly. Inst., 1960; Ph.D., N.C. State U., 1965. Engr. Gen. Elec. Co., 1955; instr. Va. Poly. Inst., 1958-60; asst. prof. Miss. State U., 1960-61; Ford Found. fellow N.C. State U., 1961-64; assoc. prof. Miss. State U., 1964-68, prof., 1968—, head mech. engring. dept., 1969-80, head mech. and nuclear engring. dept., 1981—; Chmn. Miss. Tech. Adv. Bd. on Boiler and Pressure Vessel Safety, 1974—; mem. ABET Engring. Accreditation Commn., 1981—. Pres. Oktibeha County unit Am. Cancer Soc., 1970-72; sec.-treas. Starkville Park and Recreation Commn., 1968-71; Chmn. Miss. Republican Municipal Exec. Com., 1968—. Served with USNR, 1955-58. Mem. Engrs. Council Miss. (pres. 1970-71), ASME (v.p. Region XI 1972-74), Miss. Acad. Scis. (pres. 1976-77), Sigma Xi, Omicron Delta Kappa, Phi Kappa Phi. Methodist (chmn. N. Miss. Conf. bd. Christian social concerns 1968-72). Home: 213 Windsor St Starkville MS 39759 Office: Drawer ME Mississippi State MS 39762

CARLEY, JAMES FRENCH, chemical and plastics engineer; b. N.Y.C., July 16, 1923; s. Benjamin Lambert and Helen Jeanne (French) C.; m. E. Lucille Heitz, June 6, 1947 (div. Apr. 1955); children: James French, Ben Lewis; m. Marilyn Jo Mullens, July 29, 1955 (div. Apr. 1976); 1 dau., Katherine Jeanne; m. Nancy Kay Paquette, Nov. 7, 1981. B.S. in Chem. Engring., Cornell U., 1944, B.Ch.E. (now M.Ch.E.), 1947, Ph.D., 1951. Research chem. engr. DuPont Co., Wilmington, Del., 1950-55; engring. editor Modern Plastics, N.Y.C., 1955-59; asso. prof. chem. engring. U. Ariz., Tucson, 1959-62; tech. dir. Prodex Corp., Fords, N.J., 1962-64; devel. asso. Celanese Plastics Co., Clark, N.J., 1964; prof. chem. engring. and engring. design and econ. evaluation U. Colo. at Boulder, 1964-76; research engr. oil shale project Lawrence Livermore Nat. Lab. (Calif.), 1976-83, research engr. composites and polymers tech., 1983—; Instr. Cornell U., Ithaca, N.Y., 1949-50; lectr. U. Del. extension at Wilmington, 1952-54. Contbr. articles to profl. jours., books; tech. editor Modern Plastics mag., 1982—. Served to ensign USNR, 1943-46. Mem. Soc. Plastics Engrs. (pres. Rocky Mt. chpt. 1968-69, sr. mem.), Am. Inst. Chem. Engrs., Sigma Xi, Tau Beta Pi. Home: 5173 Willowview Ct Pleasanton CA 94566 Office: Chem and Materials Sci Dept Lawrence Livermore Lab PO Box 808 Livermore CA 94550 *Because work fills so much of life; work that's not fun is slavery, no matter what the pay.*

CARLEY, JOHN BLYTHE, retail grocery executive; b. Spokane, Wash., Jan. 4, 1934; s. John Lewis and Freida June (Stiles) C.; m. Joan Marie Hohenleitner, Aug. 6, 1960; children: Christopher, Kathryn, Peter, Scott. A.A., Boise Jr. Coll., 1955; student, U. Wash., 1956-57, Stanford U. Exec. Program, 1973. Store dir. Albertson's Inc., Boise, Idaho, 1961-65, grocery merchandiser, 1965-70, dist. mgr., 1970-73, v.p. gen. mdse., 1973, v.p. corp. merchandising, 1973-75, v.p. retail ops., 1975-76, sr. v.p. retail ops., 1976-77, exec. v.p. retail ops., 1977—, also dir. Active fund-raising drives United Way. Served with U.S. Army, 1957-59. Mem. Am. Mgmt. Assn., Food Mktg. Inst. Republican. Roman Catholic. Clubs: Arid, Hillcrest Country (Boise). Home: 915 Harrison Blvd Boise ID 83702 Office: Alberrtsons Inc 250 Park Center Blvd Boise ID 83702

CARLHIAN, JEAN PAUL, architect; b. Paris, France, Nov. 7, 1919; came to U.S., 1948, naturalized, 1954; s. Andre and Henriette (Balézeaux) C.; m. Elizabeth Meta Ware, Sept. 17, 1948; children: Marie Penelope, Jerome Andre (dec.), Isabelle Anne, Judith Amelie, Sophie Virginie. Bachelier es Lettres, U. Paris, 1936; Architecte Diplome par le Gouvernement, Ecole des Beaux Arts, 1948; M.City Planning (wheelwright fellow), Harvard, 1947. Designer Harrison and Abramovitz, N.Y.C., 1949, Coolidge, Shepley, Bulfinch and Abbott, Boston, 1950-57; asso. Shepley, Bulfinch, Richardson and Abbott, Boston, 1958-62, partner, 1963-72, v.p., dir., 1972—; instr., asst. prof. Grad. Sch. Design, Harvard, 1948-55; vis. critic Yale, 1958-61, 63-64, R.I. Sch. Design, 1962-63, 77, Rice U., 1965, Harvard U., 1978; architect-in-residence Am. Acad. in Rome, 1974-75; mem. Royal Commn. on Teaching of Architecture Que., 1963-64; Mem. Back Bay Archtl. Commn., Boston, 1966-79; mem. Landmarks Commn., Boston, 1969-76; bd. dirs. Boston Archtl. Center, 1978-80. Contbr. articles to profl. mags.; prin. works include Christian A. Johnson Meml. Bldg, Middlebury Coll., Mather House, Harvard, Baker Hall and McCollum Center of Harvard Bus. Sch, College Center, Vassar Coll., Nat. Acad. Design Academie d'Architecture, Paris. Nat. Endowment Arts design fellow, 1976-77, 78-79. Fellow AIA (chmn. com. on design 1969, chmn. honor awards jury 1976), Royal Soc. Arts; mem. Mass. Assn. Architects, Boston Soc. Architects. Clubs: Century Assn., Cosmos. Home: 219 Heath's Bridge Rd Concord MA 01742 Office: 40 Broad St Boston MA 02109

CARLIN, DONALD WALTER, lawyer, food company executive; b. Gary, Ind., Aug. 27, 1934; s. Walter Joseph and Mabel (Ebert) C.; m. Kathleen Susan McCone, Jan. 21, 1961; children: Michael Scott, Karen Mary, Mark Steven. B.S. in Engring, U. Notre Dame, 1956; LL.B., U. Mich., 1959; student, Advanced Mgmt. Program, Harvard U., 1978. Bar: Ind. bar 1959, Ill. bar 1960. Practice in, Chgo., 1960—; mem. firm Anderson, Luedeka, Fitch, Even and Tabin, 1965-72; sr. atty. Kraft Inc., Glenview, Ill., 1972-73, asst. v.p., asst. gen. counsel, 1973-74, v.p., asst. gen. counsel, 1974-79, sr. v.p., gen. counsel, 1979—; Bd. dirs. Food and Drug Law Inst., 1977—, Food Update, 1978-80. Mem. ABA, Chgo. Bar Assn. (chmn. patent sub-com., anti-trust com. 1964-70), Assn. Gen. Counsel, Assn. Corp. Patent Counsel, Patent Law Assn. Chgo., Am. Soc. Corp. Secs. Clubs: Westmoreland Country, Notre Dame (Chgo.). Home: 3020 Normandy Pl Evanston IL 60201 Office: Kraft Ct Glenview IL 60025

CARLIN, EDWARD AUGUSTINE, educator; b. Gardiner, N.Y., Sept. 21, 1916; s. Edward A. and Mary (Mulligan) C.; m. Eleanor Helen Bigos, Feb. 20, 1943; children—Mary Ellen, Edward Augustine. B.S., N.Y.U., 1946, M.A., 1947, Ph.D., 1950. Instr. econs. and govt. Packard Bus. Coll., 1946-47; asst. prof. Mich. State U., 1947-51, asso. prof., 1952-56, asst. dean, prof., 1956, dean, 1956-78, prof. econs., 1978—; cons. to Coll. Gen. Studies, U. Nigeria, 1961, 62. Co-editor: Curriculum Building in General Education, 1960; Contbr. numerous articles to profl. jours. Served to 1st lt., inf. AUS, 1942-46. Decorated Purple Heart. Mem. Am. Econ. Assn., Assn. Gen. and Liberal Studies (pres. 1963-64), Am. Acad. Polit. and Social Sci., AAUP, Pi Gamma Mu. Home: 834 Rosewood East Lansing MI 48823

CARLIN, GABRIEL S., manufacturing company executive; b. N.Y.C., Mar. 19, 1921; s. Samuel and Lena (Franco) C.; m. Rosalind Goldberg, Apr. 17, 1943; children: Donald B., Beverly J. B.S., N.Y. U., 1951, M.B.A., 1954. Army-Navy purchasing coordinator Dept. Def., 1946-49; gen. sales mgr. Old Town Corp., Bklyn., 1949-60; div. gen. mgr., mem. world planning group Xerox Corp., Rochester, N.Y., 1960-64; exec. v.p. Savin Corp., Valhalla, N.Y., 1964-83, also dir.; chmn. Columbia Bus. Systems, Inc., Westport, Conn., 1983—. Author: The Power of Enthusiastic Selling, 1962, How to Persuade and Motivate People, 1964. Served to 1st lt. U.S. Army, 1942-46. Home: 1807 Long Ridge Rd Stamford CT 06903 Office: Columbia Bus Systems Inc 88 Post Rd W Westport CT 06880

CARLIN, IRA SAUL, advertising executive; b. N.Y.C., Mar. 12, 1948; s. Jack Raymond and Rhoda (Klenetsky) C.; m. Ina. M. Solomon, June 1, 1969; children: Michael, Bryan. A.B., Ind. U., 1969. Media planner Grey Advt., N.Y.C., 1971-73, asst. group head, 1973, v.p., group head, 1974; sr. v.p., media mgr. Marschalk Co., Inc., N.Y.C., 1974-80; exec. v.p., media dir. Kurnhauser & Calene, Inc., N.Y.C., 1980-81; sr. v.p., media dir. McCann-Erickson Inc., N.Y.C., 1981—. Home: 112 Whitewood Dr. Massapequa NY 11762 Office: McCann-Erickson Inc 845 Lexington Ave New York NY 10017

CARLIN, JOHN WILLIAM, gov. Kans.; b. Salina, Kans., Aug. 3, 1940; s. Jack W. and Hazel L. (Johnson) C.; m. Karen Bigsby Hurley, May 29, 1981; children by previous marriage—John David, Lisa Marie; stepchildren—Patrick Jason Hurley, Marcie Lynn Hurley. B.S. in Agr, Kans. State U., 1962. Farmer, dairyman, Smolan, Kans., 1962—; mem. Kans. Ho. of Reps. (from 93d Dist.), 1971-73, 1973-79, speaker of ho., 1977-79; gov., Kans., 1979—. Democrat. Lutheran. Home: Cedar Crest Topeka KS 66606 Office: Office of Gov State House Topeka KS 66612

CARLIN, LEO JOSEPH, lawyer; b. Grodno, Russia, Dec. 25, 1895; came to U.S., 1901, naturalized, 1906; s. Joseph and Rachel (Cohn) C.; m. Celia Cohn, Aug. 15, 1920; children: Florence E. (Mrs. Chester M. Epstein), Jerome Edward. Ph.B., U. Chgo., 1917, J.D., 1919; LL.D., Chgo. Med. Sch., 1969. Bar: Ill. 1919. Since practiced in, Chgo.; with firm Sonnenschein, Carlin, Nath & Rosenthal (and predecessors), 1919—, partner, 1926—. Hon. life dir. Mt. Sinai Hosp. (pres. 1955-58); trustee Chgo. Med. Sch. (vice chmn. bd.), Francis W. Parker Sch., all Chgo., Retina Found., Boston; past pres., life trustee Five Hosp. Homebound Elderly Program, Chgo.; mem. exec. adv. bd. St. Joseph Hosp., Chgo.; mem. vis. com. Div. Sch., U. Chgo., mem. bd. overseers. Recipient nat. award for disting. service Jewish Theol. Sem. Am.; citation for pub. service U. Chgo.; Sundial award Eye Research Inst. of Retina Found.; Dr. Sol B. Kositchek Interfaith award Lake View Council on Religious Action. Mem. Am., Ill., Chgo. bar assns., Order of Coif, Phi Beta Kappa. Jewish (pres. synagogue). Clubs: Bryn Mawr Country (pres. 1941-43), Standard (pres. Chgo. 1952-54). Home: 180 E Pearson St Chicago IL 60611 Office: 8000 Sears Tower Chicago IL 60606

CARLIN, THOMAS L., newspaper publisher; b. Bird Island, Minn., Dec. 19, 1921; s. Leo Joseph and Agnes (Hentschell) C.; m. Dawn Van Eyck, Mar. 31, 1948; children: Thomas, Mark, Paul, Mary, Sara, Andrew. B.S. in Elec. Engring., U.S. Naval Acad., 1943. Account exec. Arnold Niemeyer & Assos., 1949-51; sales corr. Am. Hoist & Derrick, 1951-53; advt. rep. St. Paul Dispatch and Pioneer Press, 1953-56, asst. prodn. mgr., 1956-57, asst. to pub., 1957-58, bus. mgr., 1958-66, gen. mgr., 1966-73, pub., 1973—; pres. Northwest Publs., Inc., Twin Cities Newspaper Service; v.p. Ridder Publs., 1980—. Pres. St. Paul Jr. Achievement, 1965; gen. chmn. St. Paul Arts and Sci. Fund drive, 1965; trustee Coll. St. Catherine, St. Paul, 1974-83, chmn., 1976-79; bd. dirs. Cath. Digest Mag., 1981—. Served with USN, 1943-47. Decorated Silver Star; recipient Outstanding Community Service award St. Paul Jaycees, 1967, Outstanding Alumnus award St. Thomas Acad., 1977. Mem. St. Paul Serra Club (pres. 1967), Navy League. Republican. Roman Catholic. Clubs: Rotary, Minn., St. Paul Athletic, Mendakota Country (St. Paul). Home: 1101 Sibley Meml Hwy #205 St Paul MN 55118 Office: 345 Cedar St Saint Paul MN 55101

CARLINER, DAVID, lawyer; b. Washington, Aug. 13, 1918; s. Louis and Cassie (Brooks) C.; m. Miriam Kalter, Jan. 24, 1944; children: Geoffrey Owen, Deborah Joan (Mrs. Robert Remes). Student, Am. U., 1935-36, U. Va., 1936-38, U. Va., 1938-40; LL.B., Nat. U., 1941. Bar: D.C., Va. Atty. JAG Office Army Dept., Washington, 1946; Washington rep. New Council Am. Bus., Washington, 1946-48; practice law David Carliner, P.C., Washington.; Lectr. Fgn. Service Inst., Dept. State, USIA. Author: Rights of Aliens. Nat. bd. dirs. ACLU, 1965—, gen. counsel, 1976-79; chmn. Internat. Human Rights Law Group, 1980—, Washington Home Rule Com., 1966-70; co-chmn. D.C. Com. for Re-Orgn. Plan, 1967-68; chmn. Washington chpt., mem. nat. exec. council Am. Jewish Com., 1969-71; mem. nat. adv. council Amnesty Internat., 1969—; hon. chmn. Am. Haitian Com., 1976—; Bd. dirs. Am. Council for Nationalities Services, 1977—, Internat. League for Human Rights; trustee Black Student Fund. Served with AUS, 1941-45. Recipient Oliver Wendell Holmes award, 1966. Mem. Am. Bar Assn. (chmn. immigration and nationality com. adminstrv. law sect. 1979-83, mem. council adminstrv. law sect. 1983), Am. Law Inst., Assn. Immigration, Nationality Lawyers (gov.), Fed. Bar Assn. (chmn. com. immigration and naturalization 1961-62), D.C. Bar (vice chmn. opinions com. ethics 1974-76, dir. 1980—), Va. State Bar, Nat. Lawyers Club. Home: 2941 Chesapeake St NW Washington DC 20008 Office: 931 Investment Bldg 1511 K St NW Washington DC 20005

CARLISLE, CAROL WHITT JONES, educator; b. May 11, 1919; m., 1942; 2 children. B.A., Wesleyan Coll., Ga., 1940; M.A., U. N.C., 1941, Ph.D. in English, 1951. Instr. English Pearl River Jr. Coll., Miss., 1942-43; acting asst. prof. Wesleyan Coll. Ga., 1943; from instr. to assoc. prof. U. S.C., Columbia, 1946-69, prof. English, 1969—. Author: Shakespeare from the Greenroom, 1969; contbr. articles to profl. jours.; cons. editor: Explicator, 1977—. Mem. central exec. com. Folger Inst. Renaissance and 18th Century Studies, 1980—. Coop. Program Humanities fellow U. N.C., Duke U. and Ford Found., 1967-68. Mem. Shakespeare Assn. Am., Renaissance Conf. (pres. 1974-75), Am. Soc. for TheatreResearch (exec. com. 1981—). Office: Dept English Univ South Carolina Columbia SC 29208

CARLISLE, ERVIN FREDERICK, educator; b. Delaware, Ohio, Mar. 20, 1935; s. Ervin Frederick C. and Winnifred (Lucas) Pope; m. Jo Ann Katherine, apr. 2, 1955 (div.); children: Lindy, Rebecca, Ginna, Jana; m. Babara, Sept. 28, 1973. B.A., Ohio Wesleyan U., 1956; M.A., Ohio State U., 1957; Ph.D., Ind. U., 1963. Asst. prof. dept. English Mich. State U., East Lansing, 1966-68, assoc. prof., assoc. chmn. dept. English, 1968-72, prof., 1972—, chairperson dept. English, 1979-81, asst. to pres., 1981—; mem. faculty Ohio U., Athens, 1962-63, DePauw U., Greencastle, Ind., 1963-66. Editor: American Poetry and Prose, 1970; author: The Uncertain Self, 1973, Loren Eiseley, 1983. Served to 1st lt. USAF, 1957-60. NEH fellow, 1972-73; NEH grantee, 1978, 80. Mem. MLA (chmn. lit.and sci. div. 1983), Nat. Council Tchrs. English, Philosophy of Sci. Assn. Home: 1546 Walnut Heights Dr East Lansing MI 48823 Office: Office of Pres Mich State U East Lansing MI 48824

CARLISLE, ROBERT BRUCE, history educator; b. Worcester, Mass., Aug. 13, 1928; m. Susan Goodman, Aug. 31, 1954; children: Robert Bruce, Julia Ellen, Christopher Goodman. A.B., Clark U., 1950; postgrad., U. Glasgow, Scotland, 1952-53, U. Paris, 1954-56; Ph.D., Cornell U., 1957. Instr., asst. prof. social relations Boston U., 1956-58; asst. prof., assoc. prof., prof. St. Lawrence U., Canton, N.Y., 1958-72, Charles D. and John D. Munsil prof. history, 1972-83, John Stebbins Lee prof. history, 1983—, chmn. dept. history, 1972—; cons. SUNY Coll. Proficiency Exam. Program; vis. prof. SUNY, Albany, summer 1967. Contbr. articles to publs. Democrat. Faculty trustee St. Lawrence U. Ford Found. Faculty grantee, 1969, 71; Lilly Found. scholar, 1968-69. Mem. Am. Hist. Assn., Soc. French Hist. Studies, Societe d'Histoire Moderne et Contemporaine, Am. Assn. U. Profs., Omicron Delta Kappa, Phi Alpha Theta. Home: 22 Goodrich St Canton NY 13617

CARLISLE, WILLIAM AIKEN, architect; b. West Point, Ga., July 11, 1918; s. Aiken Rast and Sara Allen (Lane) C.; m. Ruth Davidson, Feb. 17, 1945; children: Mettauer Lee, Carolyn Lane, Thomas Aiken, James Timmerman, Margaret Elizabeth. Draftsman R.R. Markley. B.S. in Architecture, Clemson U., 1939. Architect, Durham, N.C., 1939-40, chief draftsman, area engr., Fort Jackson, S.C., 1940-42; v.p. LBC & W, Inc., Columbia, S.C., 1946-77; pres. Carlisle Assos. (Architects-Engrs.), Columbia, 1977—; sec.-treas. State Bd. Archtl. Examiners, 1968-78; chmn. advisory com. to State Fire Marshal, 1966-79; pres. Nat. Archtl. Accreditation Bd., 1983; dir. Nat. Council Archtl. Registration Bds., 1974-77; mem. exec. com. Gov.'s Mgmt. Review Com., 1972. Served with AUS, 1942-45. Fellow AIA (dir. 1972-74, S.C. pres. 1953); mem. Clemson Archtl. Found. (pres. 1964), Columbia C. of C. (past v.p.). Methodist. Clubs: Forest Lake Country (v.p.), Wildewood, Summit, Sertoma (past pres.). Home: 5645 Lake Shore Dr Columbia SC 29206 Office: PO Box 11528 Columbia SC 29211

CARLITZ, LEONARD, educator; b. Phila., Dec. 26, 1907; s. Michael and Anna (Schneyer) C.; m. Clara Skaler, Sept. 1, 1931; children—Michael, Robert. A.B., U. Pa., 1927, M.A., 1928, Ph.D., 1930. Mem. faculty Duke, 1932—, prof. math., 1944—, James B. Duke prof. math., 1964—. Author numerous research papers.; Editor: Duke Math. Jour, 1938-73, Fibonacci Quar, 1963—; asso. editor: Acta Arithmetica, 1958—, Am. Math. Monthly, 1963—, Discrete Math, 1979—. Mem. Am. Math. Soc., Math. Assn. Am., Soc. Indsl. and Applied Math., Fibonacci Assn. Home: 2303 Cranford Rd Durham NC 27706

CARLOS, HILLARD DON, advertising agency executive; b. Bunceton, Mo., Jan. 28, 1922; s. Hillard Don and Bernadine (English) C.; m. Paulina Helen Atwood, July 14, 1948; children: Susan Mary, Sarah Ann, Brian Don. B.J., U. Mo., 1948. Advt. account exec. Des Moines Register & Tribune, 1948-51; account exec. Fairall & Co. Advt. Agy., Des Moines, 1951-55, W.D. Lyon Co., Cedar Rapids, Iowa, 1955-62; account exec., v.p. package goods Bozell & Jacobs, Omaha, 1962—, exec. v.p., gen. mgr., 1968—, dir., 1966—. Mem. lay adv. bd. Bergen Mercy Hosp., Omaha, 1973-79; mem. fine arts adv. com. U. Nebr., Omaha, 1974—, mem. adv. council Coll. Bus. Adminstrn., 1977—; communications chmn. United Way of the Midlands, 1973-74, 80; trustee Nebr. Humane Soc. Mem. Advt. Fedn. Am., Omaha Fedn. Advt. (dir. 1970-76, Silver Medal award 1982), Omaha Better Bus. Bur. (dir. 1976—). Republican. Episcopalian. Club: Highland Country. Office: Regency Circle Omaha NE 68114

CARLOS, MICHAEL C., wine, spirits and linen service wholesale company executive; b. Atlanta, Jan. 14, 1927; s. Chris and Helen (Spanos) C.; m. Thalia Noras, Dec. 25, 1963; 1 son, Chris Michael. Student, Ga. State U. Pres., chief operating officer Nat. Distbg. Co., Inc., Atlanta. Trustee Ga. State U. Found.; bd. visitors Emory U. Woodward Acad.; bd. dirs. Atlanta Arts Alliance/High Mus. Art. Home: 3695 Randall Mill Rd NW Atlanta GA 30327 Office: One National Dr SW Atlanta GA 30336

CARLOUGH, EDWARD J., labor union official. Pres. Sheet Metal Workers' Internat. Assn. Office: 1750 New York Ave NW Washington DC 20006§

CARLQUIST, SHERWIN, biology and botany educator; b. Los Angeles, July 7, 1930; s. Robert William and Helen (Bauer) C. B.A., U. Calif.-Berkeley, 1952, Ph.D., 1956; postgrad, Harvard U., 1956. Assoc. prof. Claremont Grad. Sch., Calif., 1967—, asst. prof. botany, 1956-61; prof. biology Pomona Coll., Claremont, 1976—. Author: Island Life, 1965 (Gleason award N.Y. Bot. Gardens), Comparative Plant Anatomy, 1961, Hawaii: A Natural History, 1970, Island Biology, 1974, Ecological Strategies of Xylem Evolution, 1975; contbr. articles to profl. jours. Recipient career award Bot. Soc. Am., 1977. Office: Dept Biology Pomona Coll Claremont CA 91711 *I would like to be remembered for initiating a fusion between plant ecology and wood anatomy; also for outlining how dispersal to islands occurs and what evolutionary trends occur on islands. In pursuing these interests, the pleasure of attempting creative and original work in scientific discovery and in written and graphic presentation of those discoveries is my chief motivation.*

CARLSBERG, RICHARD PRESTEN, real estate corporation executive; b. Stockton, Calif., Mar. 2, 1937; s. Arthur Walter and Lillian Marie (Presten) C.; m. Barbara Ann Hearn, June 28, 1959; children: David Arthur, Rebecca Jane, Dawn Marie. Student, City Coll. San Francisco, 1954-56, U. San Francisco, 1955; B.A. in Geology, UCLA, 1959. Pres. Carlsberg Corp., Santa Monica, Calif., 1972—; officer and/or dir. various pvt. corps. in fields of real estate, fin., devel., research, petroleum, 1961—. Bd. dirs. UCLA Found., Calif. Pines Youth Found., Soc. of Blue Shield. Served with Army N.G., 1959-65. Recipient awards, Los Angeles County, 1965, resolution Calif. Legislature, 1965, 71, commendations County of Los Angeles, 1971, U.S. Dept. Interior, 1971. Mem. Young Presidents Orgn. (Golden West chpt.). Presbyterian. Clubs: So. Calif. Safari, Safari Club Internat., Game Coin, various conservation groups including Ducks Unlimited. Office: 2800 28th St Santa Monica CA 90405

CARLSEN, ALBERT, ret. utilities exec.; b. St. Paul, June 29, 1910; s. Alfred and Marin (Jensen) C.; m. Frances Elizabeth Nixon, June 19, 1935; children—Richard C., James A., Nancy Ann, Kenneth M. Student, U. Idaho, 1931-34. With Idaho Power Co., 1934-81, dir., 1964-81, pres., 1967-71, chmn., 1971-81, chief exec. officer, 1971-77, ret., 1981; gen. mgr. Idaho Potato Starch Co., Blackfoot, 1941-56, pres., 1956-66; v.p., dir. Safety Savs. & Loan Assn., Blackfoot, Idaho, until 1968; dir. Provident Savs. & Loan, Boise, Frontier Airlines. Chmn. Blackfoot Sch. Bd., 1947-59; Bd. dirs. Rocky Mountain Fedn. States, 1967—. Mem. Idaho Assn. Commerce and Industry (dir., v.p.), Idaho Sch. Trustees Assn. (past pres.). Clubs: Mason (Shriner), Elk, Rotarian. Home: 4120 Hillcrest Dr Boise ID 83705

CARLSEN, JAMES CALDWELL, educator; b. Pasco, Wash., Feb. 11, 1927; s. Theodore N. and Eunice (Caldwell) C.; m. Mary Louisa Baird, May 1, 1949; children—Philip C., Douglas A., Susan A., Kristine L. B.A., Whitworth Coll., 1950; M.A., U. Wash., 1958; Ph.D., Northwestern U., 1962. Pub. sch. tchr., Almira, Wash., 1950-53, Portland, Oreg., 1953-54; mem. faculty Whitworth Coll., 1954-63, U. Conn., 1963-67; prof. music U. Wash., Seattle, 1967—; research asso. Stäatliches Institut fur Musikforschung, West Berlin, Germany, 1973-74; adj. prof. psychology U. Wash., 1979—. Author: Melodic Perception, 1965; Editor: Jour. Research in Music Edn, 1978-81; asso. editor: Psychomusicology, 1980—. Condr. Spokane (Wash.) Symphonic Band, 1957-60. Served with AUS, 1945-47. Danforth tchr. study grantee, 1960-61; Fulbright-Hays grantee, 1973-74. Mem. Music Educators Nat. Conf., Music Edn. Research Council (past chmn.), Coll. Music Soc. (council), AAUP, Internat. Soc. Music Edn. (chmn. research commn. 1976-80). Home: 2235 Fairview E Boat 10 Seattle WA 98102

CARLSMITH, JAMES MERRILL, psychologist, educator; b. New Orleans, Apr. 12, 1936; s. Leonard Eldon and Hope (Snedden) C.; m. Lyn Kuckenberg, July 27, 1963; children—Christopher, Kimberly, Kevin. A.B., Stanford U., 1958; Ph.D., Harvard U., 1963. Asst. prof. Yale U., 1962-64; from asst. prof. to prof. psychology Stanford U., 1964—, asso. dean grad. studies, 1972-75; fellow (Center for Advanced Study in Behavioral Scis.), 1975. Author: Social Psychology, 1970, Methods of Research In Social Psychology, 1976. Dir. Boys Town Center, 1980—. Office: Dept Psychology Stanford U Stanford CA 94305

CARLSON, BILLE CHANDLER, physics educator; b. Boston, June 27, 1924; s. John Rudolph and Henrietta C. (Peabody) C.; m. Louise Winston, May 30, 1947; children: Marian Bille, John Russell. Grad., Phillips Exeter Acad., 1941; A.B. summa cum laude, Harvard U., 1947, A.M., 1947; D.Phil. (Rhodes scholar), U. Oxford, 1950. Mem. staff radiation lab. Mass. Inst. Tech., 1943-44; instr., research asso. Princeton, 1950-54; mem. faculty Iowa State U.; staff mem. Ames Lab., U.S. Dept. Energy, 1954—, prof. physics, sr. physicist, 1961—, prof. math., 1965—; sr. research fellow math. Calif. Inst. Tech., 1962-63; visitor Institut Henri Poincaré, U. Paris, 1971-72; vis. prof. Inst. for Phys. Sci. and Tech., U. Md., 1980-81. Author: Special Functions of Applied Mathematics, 1977. Served with USNR, 1944-46. Fellow Am. Phys. Soc.; mem. Am. Math. Soc., Soc. Indsl. and Applied Math., Math. Assn., AAUP, Phi Beta Kappa, Sigma Xi. Research and publs. on spl. functions of math. physics, especially R-functions and symmetric elliptic integrals. Home: 430 Westwood Dr Ames IA 50010

CARLSON, BRUCE ROBBINS, electronics company executive; b. Chgo., May 4, 1921; s. Earl C. and Elsie (Robbins) C.; m. Rubydonna Joseph, Feb. 27, 1943; children—Lawrence B., Nancy J., Gregg P., Christine A. B.A., Stanford, 1943; postgrad., Northwestern U., 1946-47. Investment analyst Stein Roe & Farnham, Chgo., 1947-53; statis. asst. to pres. Sprague Electric Co., North Adams, Mass., 1953-60, v.p. corporate planning and systems, 1960-65, treas., 1965-68, sr. v.p. finance, 1968, pres., 1968-75; v.p. fin., treas. Mostek Corp., Carrollton, Tex., 1976-77; sr. v.p. fin./adminstrn., dir. Tele/Resources, Inc., Armonk, N.Y., 1977-80; v.p. Kensington Mgmt. Consultants, Inc., Stamford, Conn., 1980-81; sr. v.p. ISIS Systems, Inc., Cambridge, Mass., 1981-83; pres. Info. Control Corp., Bridgeport, Conn., 1983—; dir. Security Ins. Group; instr. bus. stats. Northwestern U., Chgo., 1948-51; Mem. Sch. Com., Williamstown, Mass., 1959-62, Mt. Greylock Regional Dist., 1960-70. Bd. dirs. North Adams YMCA, 1960-66, pres., 1961; bd. dirs. Williamstown Boys' Club, 1957-60; trustee U. Mass., 1974-77. Served to lt. (j.g.) USNR, 1943-45. Mem. Phi Beta Kappa, Theta Xi. Republican. Congregationalist. Home: 5 Hemmelskamp Rd Wilton CT 06897 Office: 706 Bostwick Ave Bridgeport CT 06605

CARLSON, CURTIS LEROY, business executive; b. Mpls., July 9, 1914; s. Charles A. and Leatha (Peterson) C.; m. Arleen Martin, June 30, 1938; children: Marilyn Carlson Nelson, Barbara Carlson Gage. B.A. in Econs., U. Minn., 1937. Salesman, Procter & Gamble Co., Mpls., 1937-39; founder, pres. Gold Bond Stamp Co., Mpls., 1938-72; pres., chmn. bd. Carlson Cos., Inc. (formerly Premium Service Corp.), 1972—; pres. MIP Agy., Inc., Curtis Home Employer, Inc.; chmn. bd. Gold Bond Stamp Co., Radisson Hotel Corp., Radisson Group Inc., Radisson Dallas Corp., Radisson Mo. Corp., Radisson Raleigh Corp., Resort Hotels of Ariz., Colony Resorts, Inc., First Travel, Corp., Carlson Properties, Inc., Carlson Mktg. Group, Inc., Carlson Leasing, Inc., TGI Friday's Inc., Dallas, Commonwealth Premium Sales Ltd., Can., Ardan, Inc., Sports Films & Talents, Mpls., Superior Fiber Products Co., Wis., N.Am. Fin. Corp., CSA, Inc., Prize Incentives Ltd., Can.; dir. Naegele, Inc., Naegele Outdoor Advt. Co. of Charlotte, Premiums Internat. Ltd., Can., Major Media of Midwest Ltd., of Southeast Ltd, of Calif. Ltd., Gold Bond Japan Ltd., Marquette Nat. Bank of Mpls., Bank Shares, Inc., Major Media Mgmt. Corp., Windhorst Outdoor Advt. of Louisville, Nat. Hotel Corp., Radisson Wilmington Corp., Interpersonal Growth Systems, Inc. Sr. v.p. U. Minn. Found.; bd. dirs. Fairview Hosp., Swedish Council Am.; bd. dirs., founder Boys Club Mpls.; bd. dirs. Minn. Orchestral Assn., Mpls. Downtown Council; mem. adv. bd. U. Minn. Exec. Program. Mem. Trading Stamp Inst. Am. (dir., founder, pres. 1959-60), Mpls. C. of C. (dir.), Minn. Alumni Assn., Sigma Phi Epsilon. (nat. trustee). Methodist (mem. fin. adv. bd.). Clubs: Masons (Jesters, Shriners), Minneapolis, Minneapolis Athletic; North Country (Duluth); Minikahda; Ocean Reef Yacht, Palm Bay (Miami). Home: Long Lake MN 55356 Office: 12755 State Hwy 55 Minneapolis MN 55441

CARLSON, CYNTHIA JOANNE, artist, educator; b. Chgo., Apr. 15, 1942; d. Ivan Morris and Ruth (Holmes) C.; m. Mitchell S. Rosen, Apr. 6, 1942. B.F.A., Sch. Art Inst., Chgo., 1965; M.F.A., Pratt Inst., Bklyn., 1967. Instr. Phil. Coll. Art., 1967-72, U. Colo., Boulder, 1972-73; asst. prof. painting Phila. Coll. Art., 1973; assoc. prof. Phila Coll. Art., 1979-82; prof. Phila. Coll. Art., 1982—. Exhibited: one-person shows Allen Meml. Art Mus., Oberlin, Ohio, 1980, Hudson River Mus., Yonkers, N.Y., 1981, Milw. Art Mus., 1982, Pam Adler Gallery, N.Y.C., 1983, The Contemporary Art Ctr., Cin., 1980, Whitney Mus. Art, N.Y.C., 1980, Hayden Art Gallery, MIT, Cambridge, 1981, Jacksonville Art Mus., (Fla.), 1982; represented: permanent collections Guggenheim Mus., N.Y.C., Phila. Mus. Art, Richmond Mus. Fine Arts, (Va.), Denver Art Mus., Allen Meml. Art Mus., Oberlin, Ohio. NEA grantee 1975,78,81; grantee Creative Artists Pub. Service, 1978. Mem. NOW, Amnesty Internat. Home: 139 W 19th St New York NY 10011 Office: Phila Coll Art Broad and Spruce Sts Philadelphia PA 19102

CARLSON, DALE ARVID, univ. dean; b. Aberdeen, Wash., Jan. 10, 1925; s. Edwin C.G. and Anna A. (Anderson) C.; m. Jean M. Stanton, Nov. 11, 1948; children—Dale Ronald, Gail L. Carlson Manahan, Joan M., Gwen D. A.A., Grays Harbor Coll., 1947; B.S. in Civil Engring, U. Wash., 1950, M.S., 1951; Ph.D., U. Wis., 1960. Registered profl. engr., Wash. Water engr. City of Aberdeen, 1951-55; asst. prof., asso. prof., prof., chmn. dept. civil engring. U. Wash., Seattle, 1955-76, dean, 1976-80, dean emeritus, 1980—; vis. prof. Tech. U. Denmark, Copenhagen, 1970, Royal Coll. Agr., Uppsala, Sweden, 1976, 78. Contbr. articles to profl. jours. Mem. exec. bd. Pacific NW Synod Luth. Ch. in Am., chmn. fin. com., 1980—; mem. exec. bd. Nordic Heritage Mus., 1981—; bd. dirs. Valle Scandinavian Exchange Program, 1980—, Evergreen Safety Council, 1980—. Served with AUS, 1943-45. Named Outstanding Grad. Weatherwax High Sch., Aberdeen, 1972, Grays Harbor Coll., 1947; guest of honor, Soppeldagene, Trondheim, 1978. Mem. Water Pollution Control Fedn., ASCE, Am. Water Works Assn., Am. Scandinavian Found., Swedish Water Hygiene Assn. Clubs: Rotary, Cosmos. Home: 9235 41st St NE Seattle WA 98115 Office: 335 More Hall U Wash Seattle WA 98195

CARLSON, DAVID BRET, lawyer; b. Jamestown, N.Y., Aug. 16, 1918; s. David Albert and Gertrude (Johnson) C.; m. Jane Tapley, Apr. 12, 1947; children: Chistopher Tapey, David Kurt. Nancy. A.B., Brown U., 1940; LL.B., Harvard U., 1947. Bar: N.Y. 1947, U.S. Supreme Ct. 1972. Assoc. firm Debevoise & Plimpton, N.Y.C., 1947-53, ptnr., 1953—. Contbr. articles to profl. publs. Mem. ABA, N.Y. State Bar Assn., Bar Assn. City N.Y., Am. Law Inst., Tax Forum. Home: 2700 Redding Rd Fairfield CT 06430 Office: 875 3d Ave New York NY 10022

CARLSON, DAVID EMIL, physicist; b. Weymouth, Mass., Mar. 5, 1942; s. Emil Algot and Anne Alice (Salomaa) C.; m. Mary Ann Lewinski, June, 1966; children: Eric, Darcey. B.S. in Physics, Rensselaer Poly. Inst., 1963, Ph.D., Rutgers U., 1968. Research scientist U.S. Army Nuclear Effects Lab., Edgewood Arsenal, Md., 1968-69; head photovoltaic device research RCA Labs., Princeton, N.J., 1970-83; dep. gen. mgr., dir. research Solarex Thin Film Div., Newtown, Pa., 1983—. Contbr. articles to profl. jours. Served to capt. Signal Corps U.S. Army, 1968-70; Vietnam. Decorated Bronze Star medal; recipient Ross Coffin Purdy award Am. Ceramic Soc., 1976, Outstanding Achievement award RCA Labs., 1973, 1976. Mem. Am. Phys. Soc., Electrochem. Soc., IEEE (co-recipient Morris N. Liebmann award 1984), Am. Vacuum Soc., Sigma Xi. Patentee in field; inventor amorphous silicon solar cell, 1974. Home: 514 Nancy Rd Yardley PA 19067 Office: Solarex Thin Film Div Newtown PA 18940 *My career in science has resulted from a curiosity about the workings of nature and a desire to use the phenomena and materials of nature to benefit society.*

CARLSON, DONALD EARLE, mechanical engineer; b. Sterling, Ill., Mar. 8, 1938; s. Glen Hjalmer and Dorothy Helen (Smith) C.; m. Susan Kay Renkes, Aug. 18, 1961; children: Jeffrey Alan, Jonathan Andrew. B.S., U. Ill., 1960, M.S., 1961; Ph.D., Brown U., 1965. Asst. prof. theoretical and applied mechanics U. Ill., Urbana-Champaign, 1964-67, assoc. prof., 1967-70, prof., 1970—. Co-editor: Jour. Elasticity, 1979-82; Editor, 1982—; editorial bd., 1971—; co-editor: Mechanics, 1973-76; editorial bd.: Jour. Thermal Stresses, 1978—. Mem. Soc. Natural Philosophy, Am. Acad. Mechanics, ASME, Soc. Engring. Sci., Soc. Indsl. and Applied Math., Am. Math. Soc., Sigma Xi. Home: 501 Sherwin Dr Urbana IL 61801 Office: 216 Talbot Lab U Ill Urbana IL 61801

CARLSON, DONALD HERBERT EDWARD, publishing executive; b. Edmonton, Alta., Can., Aug. 25, 1918; s. Theo Gustav and Grace (Ockenden) C.; m. Madeline Frances Beetlestone, Mar. 5, 1941; children: Madeline Anne (Mrs. Desmond P. Ellis), Elizabeth Jane (Mrs. Richard B. Davis), Susannah Pamela Grace, Anthony Ernest Theo, Gustav Donald Michael. B.A., U. Alta., 1940. Reporter and editor Toronto Daily Star, Vancouver Sun, Vancouver Province and Vancouver News-Herald, 1942-53; dir. pub. relations James Lovick & Co., Ltd., 1953-55, Crown Zellerbach Can. Ltd., 1955-59; with Ford Motor Co., Can., 1959-74, v.p., sec., 1966-74; pub. Fin. Times of Can., Toronto, 1974-82, The Northern Spectator, Hamilton, Ont., 1982—; v.p. Southani Inc., Toronto, 1982—. Clubs: Royal Canadian Yacht, National (Toronto); Hamilton (Hamilton). Home: 32 Colonial Crescent Oakville ON Canada Office: 44 Frid St Hamilton ON Canada

CARLSON, EDWARD ELMER, holding co. exec.; b. Tacoma, June 4, 1911; s. Elmer E. and Lula (Powers) C.; m. Nell Hinckley Cox, June 26, 1936; children—Edward Eugene, Jane Leslie. Student, U. Wash., 1928-32. Mgr. President Hotel, Mt. Vernon, Wash., 1936-37, Rainier Club, Seattle, 1937-42; with Western Internat. Hotels, Inc., Seattle, 1946-70, exec. v.p., 1953-61, pres., 1961-69, chmn., 1969-70, dir., 1953—; pres., chief exec. officer, dir. UAL, Inc., Chgo., 1970-74, chief exec. officer, 1975—, chmn. bd., 1979—; pres., chief exec. officer, dir. United Air Lines, 1970-74, chmn., chief exec. officer, 1975-76, also dir.; dir. 1st Nat. Bank of Chgo., Dart Industries, Inc., Deere & Co., Univar Corp., 1st Chgo. Corp., Seafirst Corp., Seattle First Nat. Bank. Pres. Century 21 Expn. Inc., Seattle, 1957-59, chmn. bd., 1959-61; chmn. Wash. World's Fair Commn., 1955-63, Wash. Oceanographic Study Commn.; mem. Pres. Johnson's Industry-Govt. Task Force, 1968, Navy Ship's Store Office advisory com. to undersec. navy, 1965—; hon. chmn. Pacific Sci. Center Found., 1967-68; mem. Henry Kaiser Family Found.; bd. dirs. Virginia Mason Hosp. and Found. Recipient Am. Tourism award New Sch. Social Research, 1978; named 1st citizen of Seattle, 1966; Alumnus summa laude dignatus U. Wash., 1970. Mem. Cornell Soc. Hotelmen (hon.), Am. Soc. Order St. John of Jerusalem. Clubs: Seattle Golf, Univ., Rainier (Seattle); Commercial (Chgo.); Bohemian (San Francisco). Home: Boundary Ln The Highlands Seattle WA 98177 Office: PO Box 66919 Chicago IL 60666

CARLSON, EDWIN FRANCIS, business machines company executive; b. Bklyn., July 26, 1928; s. Victor and Alice Irene C.; m. Mary Ellen Coffey, June 20, 1953; children: Edwin, Robert, Michael, Patricia, Daniel. B.A.A., Pace U., 1955; postgrad., N.Y. U., 1957-58. Pres. Automated Bus. Systems div. Litton Industries, N.Y.C., 1972-74; v.p. mktg. Dictaphone, Corp., Rye, N.Y., 1975-76; pres. Dictaphone Products and Systems, Rye, 1977-79, Victor Bus. Products, Chgo., 1979—. Clubs: Sales Exec. (N.Y.C.); Execs. (Chgo.). Office: Victor Bus Products 3900 N Rockwell St Chicago IL 60618

CARLSON, GEORGE ARTHUR, artist; b. Elmhurst, Ill., July 3, 1940; s. William Emanuel and Mathilda Katherine (Jorgensen) C.; m. Pamela Gustavson Hatzenbiler, May 9, 1981; children: Solon Emil, Andra Sean. Student, Art Inst. Chgo., Am. Acad. Art, Chgo., U. Ariz., Tucson. Author: The Tarahumara, 1977; One-man shows, Indpls. Mus. Art, 1979, Smithsonian Mus. Natural History, Washington, 1982, group shows, Phoenix Fine Art Mus., Denver Art Mus., NAD, N.Y.C., Nat. Acad. Western Art, Okla., Denver Public Library, others; represented in pvt. collections, monument, Washington Park, Denver, 1979; commd.: portrait busts Bill Cosby; illustrator, Vogue-Wright, Krantzen Studios, Anderson Studios, all Chgo. Served with USAR, 1963-69. Recipient Gold medal Nat. Acad. Western Art, 1974, Silver medal, 1976, Gold medal, 1978, 80, Silver medal, 1981, prix de West (Best of Show Purchase award), 1975. Subject of 2 films. Address: PO Box 550 Elizabeth CO 80107

CARLSON, HARRY LEROY, public relations company executive, marketing consultant; b. Des Moines, Mar. 23, 1919; s. Anton and Minnie (Berquist) C.; m. Helen Brutsch, Aug. 7, 1946; children:

Christopher, Marc, Eric. Student, Augustana Coll., Rock Island, Ill., 1937-40. Bur. mgr. UPI, Seattle, 1945-50; acct. exec. Carl Byoir & Assocs., San Francisco, 1950-52; pres. Gen. Pub. Relations subs. Benton & Bowles, Inc., N.Y.C., 1957-64, Wolcott, Carlson & Co., 1964-73, Carlson, Rockey & Assocs., 1973—; chmn. Darcy & Carlson Internat., N.Y.C., 1975—. Mem. Pub. Relations Soc. Am., Internat. Pub. Relations Assn., Internat. Pub. Relations Group of Cos. Clubs: Overseas Press, Metropolitan, World Trade Ctr. (N.Y.C.); Nat. Press (Washington); Wykagyl Country (New Rochelle, N.Y.). Home: 51 Old Orchard Ln Scarsdale NY 10538 Office: Carlson Rockey and Assocs Inc 360 Lexington Ave New York NY 10017

CARLSON, JACK WILSON, association executive; b. Salt Lake City, Nov. 20, 1933; s. Oscar William and Gretta (Wilson) C.; m. Renée Pyott, Mar. 20, 1954; children: Catherine, Cristine, Steven, Diane, John, David, Paul. B.S., U. Utah, 1955, M.B.A., 1957; M.P.A., Harvard U., 1962, Ph.D. in Econs, 1963. Commd. 2d lt. U.S. Air Force, 1955, advanced through grades to maj., 1966; ret., 1966, mem. Res., 1966-78; asst. to sec. of Air Force, 1965-66; sr. staff economist Pres.'s Council Econ. Advisers, 1966-68; asst. dir. U.S. Bur. Budget, Washington, 1968-71; chmn. sr. econ. advisers Econ. Commn. Europe and UN, 1970-72; asst. to dir. Office of Mgmt. and Budget, Washington, 1971-74; asst. sec. Dept. Interior, Washington, 1974-76; v.p., chief economist C. of C. of U.S., Washington, 1976-79; exec. v.p. Nat. Assn. Realtors, Washington, 1979—; Mem. Nat. Commn. Employment and Unemployment Stats; Cons., del. UN Commn. Human Settlements, 1982-83. Contbr. articles to mags., jours., chpts. to books. Candidate for U.S. Senate from Utah, 1976. Mem. Internat. Real Estate Fedn. (officer 1980-83). Office: 777 14th St NW Washington DC 20005

CARLSON, JERRY ALAN, editor; b. Shenandoah, Iowa, May 19, 1936; s. Glenn A. and Lucille C. (Hoxie) C.; m. Jill Marie Clarkson, July 26, 1959; children—Jennifer, Stephanie, Erik. Student, Silliman U., Philippine Islands, 1956-57; B.S., Iowa State U., 1959, M.S., 1971. Farm bus. editor, mng. editor Farm Jour. mag., Phila., 1964-72; Vice pres. Profl. Farmers of Am., Inc., 1972-81, sr. editor, 1981—; editor LandOwner; chmn. bd. Solar Research Inc., Cedar Falls; cons., electronic editing systems. Author: Farming with Tomorrow's Wild Weather; Contbr. articles to profl. jours. Served to capt. SAC USAF, 1961-63. Mem. Phi Eta Sigma, Gamma Sigma Delta, Alpha Theta, Sigma Delta Chi, Farm House Frat. Lutheran. Club: Rotary. Home: 5330 S Union Rd Cedar Falls IA 50613 Office: 219 Parkade Cedar Falls IA 50613 *Today's man yearns to live a whole life; tomorrow's man will increasingly learn how to do it.*

CARLSON, JOHN BERNARD, biologist; b. Virginia, Minn., Jan. 23, 1926; s. Frank N. and Effie C. (Onkka) C.; m. Dolores Mae Makela, Aug. 27, 1949; children—Stephen Ray, John Alan, Janice Lynn, Michael David. B.A., St. Olaf Coll., 1950; Ph.D. (NSF fellow), Iowa State Coll., 1953, postgrad., 1953-54. Instr. biology U. Minn., Duluth, 1954-56, asst. prof. biology, 1956-61, asso. prof., 1961-65, prof., 1965—. Served with USN, 1944-46. Dept. Agr. grantee, 1966-70. Mem. Minn. Acad. Sci., Lake Superior Biologists Assn., Isaac Walton League, Sigma Xi. Lutheran. Research in soybean and wild rice morphology. Home: 3049 Lester River Rd Duluth MN 55804 Office: U Minn Dept Biology Duluth MN 55812

CARLSON, JOHN I., JR., consulting company executive; b. Phila., Feb. 23, 1926; s. John I. and Laura May (Wheeler) C.; m. Doris Elizabeth Garabedian, June 23, 1950; children: Kristen, Laura, John III, Stephanie. A.B. cum laude, Harvard U., 1950. Pres., chief exec. officer The Carlson Group, Inc., Cochituate, Mass., 1950—; dir. Baybank Harvard Trust Co.; exec. dir. Am. Arab Assn. Commerce and Industry; dir. Home Broadcasting SVC. Trustee, vice chmn. New Eng. Deaconess Hosp.; incorporator Goodwill Industries. Served with USNR, 1944-46. Mem. Nat. Constructors Assn., Soc. Harvard Engrs. and Scientists, Am. Mgmt. Assn., World Bus. Council, Middle East Inst., Nat. Council U.S.-Arab Relations. Clubs: Pres. (Bentley Coll., Waltham, Mass.); Pres.' Fellow (Wentworth Inst.). Office: 321 Commonwealth Rd Cochituate MA 01778

CARLSON, JOHN SWINK, lawyer, petroleum co. exec.; b. Ft. Collins, Colo., June 16, 1911; s. George A. and Rosa (Alps) C.; m. Sara A. Mott, June 22, 1940 (div. 1973); children—John Swink, Lucie Pamela, Ann Brockenbrough, Virginia Charles, Thomas (dec.); m. Barbara Carlson, 1973. A.B., U. Colo., 1932; LL.B., Harvard, 1936. Bar: Okla. bar 1937, N.Y. bar 1975. Legal staff Shell Oil Co., 1936-37, Turman Oil Co., 1937-38; legal asso. Yancey & Spillers, Tulsa, 1938-39; legal counselor Chapman, Barnard & McFarlin (oil, cattle and investments), Tulsa, 1939-42; gen. counsel Seismograph Service Corp., Tulsa, 1942-49; practiced in, Tulsa, 1949-51; gen. counsel Okla. Natural Gas Co., 1951-61; sr. partner firm Carlson, Lupardus, Matthews, Holliman & Huffman, Tulsa, 1951-61; head legal firm John S. Carlson, Tulsa, 1961—; Sec., gen. counsel, dir. Century Geophys. Corp., 1951-71, sr. v.p., 1957-71, sec. exec. com., 1951, chmn. exec. com., 1965; dir.; gen. counsel Hayward-Wolff Research Corp., 1951; v.p., sec., dir., gen. counsel Exploration Cons., Inc., 1951-60, Canadian Geophys. Measurements, Ltd., 1954-65, Venezuela Geophys. Measurements (S.A.), 1957-65; pres., dir., gen. counsel Petroleum Research Corp., 1957-65; chmn. bd., gen. counsel Community Merchandisers, Inc., 1959; pres., dir., gen. counsel Western Petroleum Co., Inc., 1960; v.p., sec., dir., gen. counsel Enterprises & Businesses, Inc., 1960; sec., dir. Western Hemisphere Trade & Credit Corp., 1960, v.p., 1961; sec., dir. Hemisphere Constrn. Co., 1960, v.p., 1961-64; v.p., sec., dir., counsel Digital Resources Corp., 1972-76; pres., chmn. bd. Oil Enterprises Inc., 1965—; gen. counsel, sec. Datatrol Inc., 1975—; counsel Applied Devices Corp., 1973-79. Editor: Compendium of Laws Relating to Problems of Men in the Armed Forces, 1943; Contbr. sect. to report on, 34th Nat. Fgn. Trade Council. Pres. Maple Ridge Assn., 1964-70. Mem. ABA, Okla. Bar Assn., Okla. Jr. Bar Assn. (pres. 1943-44), Tulsa County Bar Assn., Am. Judicature Soc., Tulsa C. of C., Am. Soc. Internat. Law, Phi Beta Kappa, Delta Sigma Rho. Clubs: Tulsa, Harvard (Tulsa) (pres. 1949-50). Address: 912 B Woodside Circle Kissimmee FL 32741

CARLSON, LENUS JESSE, baritone; b. Jamestown, N.D., Feb. 11, 1945; s. Samuel J. and Anna M. (Nelson) C.; m. Linda Kay Jones, Aug. 20, 1972. Student, Jamestown Coll., 1963-64; B.A., Moorhead State U., 1967; postgrad., Juilliard Sch. Music, 1970-73. Pvt. vocal tchr., Mpls., 1965-70, N.Y.C., 1970—. Apprentice artist, Central City (Colo.) Opera, 1965-66, debut, Minn. Opera Co., Mpls., 1968; soloist, Mpls. Symphony, 1967-68; appeared in leading roles with, Dallas Opera House, 1972-73, San Antonio Opera House, 1973, Boston Opera, Washington Opera House; debut as Silvio in: I Pagliacci, Met. Opera, N.Y.C., 1974; Netherlands Opera debut as: La Boheme, 1974, U.K. debut with, Scottish Opera, Edinburgh Festival, 1975; soloist, Cin. Symphony, 1972, nationwide tour, U.S., 1975; debut as Valentin in: Faust, Royal Opera House, London, 1976; debut as count in: Marriage of Figaro, Santa Fe Opera Festival, 1976. Served with AUS, 1968-70. Address: care Columbia Artists Mgmt Inc 165 W 57th St New York NY 10019 *

CARLSON, LEROY THEODORE SHERIDAN, telephone holding co. exec.; b. Chgo., May 15, 1916; s. Axel Jacob and Gerda Marie (Swanson) C.; m. Margaret E. Deffenbaugh, Jan. 12, 1945; children—LeRoy Theodore, Prudence Elizabeth, Walter Carl, Letitia Greta. Student, Morgan Park Jr. Coll., 1933-35; B.A., U. Chgo., 1938; M.B.A., Harvard U., 1941. Sales mgr. Midwest McCall Corp., 1933-40; accountant U.S. Army Ordnance, 1941-42; adminstrv. asst. to gen. mgr. Mdse. Mart, Chgo., 1946-49; new products devel. Acme Steel Co., Chgo., 1949-51; chmn. bd., pres. Suttle Equipment Corp., 1949-77; pres. Calvert Telephone Co., 1954-61, Northeastern Telephone Corp., Ky., 1955-61, No. Ill. Telephone Co., 1956-61, Eastern Iowa Telephone Co., 1958-61; co-chmn., sec. Telephones, Inc. (merged with Continental Telephone Co.), 1961-65; pres., chmn. bd. Telephone and Data Systems, Inc., Chgo., 1968—, chief exec. officer, 1981—; founder Telephone Engring. Services, Inc., Suttle Press, TDS Computing Services, Inc., Telephone Systems Service Corp.; dir. Rural Telephone Bank, 1971-72. Served as ensign USN, 1945-46. Named hon. Ky. Col., 1956. Mem. Nat. R.E.A. Borrowers Assn. (dir. 1958—, chmn. fin. planning com.), U.S. Ind. Telephone Assn. (fin. com. 1970—), Ind. Telephone Pioneers Assn. Republican. Lutheran. Clubs: Union League, Harvard, Harvard Bus. Sch. (Chgo.); Harvard (N.Y.C.). Office: 79 W Monroe St Chicago IL 60603

CARLSON, LOREN MERLE, university dean, political science educator, lawyer; b. Mitchell, S.D., Nov. 2, 1923; s. Clarence A. and Edna M. (Rosenquist) C.; m. Verona Gladys Hole, Dec. 21, 1950; children: Catherine Ann, Bradley Reed, Nancy Jewel. B.A., Yankton Coll., 1948; M.A., U. Wis., 1952; J.D., George Washington U., 1961. Bar: S.D. 1961, U.S. Supreme Ct. 1976. Asst. dir. Govt. Research Bur., U. S.D., 1949-51; orgn. and methods examiner Dept. State, Washington, 1951-52; asst. dir. legis. research State of S.D., 1953-55, dir., 1955-59; research asst. to U.S. Senator from S.D., 1959-60, adminstrv. asst., 1960-63; budget officer State of S.D., 1963-68; dir. statewide ednl. services U. S.D., Vermillion, 1968-74, dean continuing edn., 1974—, assoc. prof. polit. sci., 1968-79, prof., 1979—; hwy. laws study dir. Law Sch., 1963; sec. Mo. Valley Adult Edn., 1978-79; Chmn. Model Rural Devel. Commn., Dist. II, State of S.D., 1972-74; chmn. Region VII Planning Commn. on Criminal Justice, S.D., 1969-74. Author: (with W.O. Farber and T.C. Geary) Government of South Dakota, 1979; contbr. articles profl. publs. Mem. Vermillion City Council, 1980—, pres., 1982—. Served with USNR, 1945-46. Named Outstanding Young Man Pierre Jaycees, 1959. Mem. S.D. State Bar, Am. Soc. Public Adminstrn., Midwest Polit. Sci. Assn., Nat. U. Continuing Edn. Assn., S.D. Adult Edn. Assn. (chmn. 1973-74), Vermillion C. of C., Am. Arbitration Assn., Am. Legion, Pi Sigma Alpha, Pi Kappa Delta. Republican. Lutheran. Clubs: Lions, Eagles. Home: 229 Catalina St Vermillion SD 57069 Office: State Wide Educational Services University of South Dakota Vermillion SD 57069

CARLSON, MARVIN ALBERT, educator; b. Wichita, Kans., Sept. 15, 1935; s. Roy Edward and Gladys (Nelson) C.; m. Patricia Alene McElroy, Aug. 20, 1960; children—Geoffrey, Richard. B.S., U. Kans., 1957, M.A., 1959; Ph.D., Cornell U., 1961. Instr. speech and drama Cornell U., Ithaca, N.Y., 1961-62, asst. prof., 1962-66, asso. prof. theatre arts, 1966-73, prof., 1973-79, chmn. dept., 1966-68, 73-78, dir., 1963-64, 65-66; prof. theatre and drama Ind. U., Bloomington, 1979—. Author: Andre Antoine's Memories of the Theatre-Libre, 1964, The Theatre of the French Revolution, 1966, The French Stage in the Nineteenth Century, 1972, The German Stage in the Nineteenth Century, 1972, Goethe and the Weimar Theatre, 1978, The Italian Stage from Goldoni to D'Annunzio, 1981. Guggenheim fellow, 1968. Fellow Am. Theatre Assn.; mem. Am. Soc. Theatre Research, Phi Kappa Phi. Home: 321 N Indiana St Bloomington IN 47401 Office: Dept Theatre and Drama Ind U Bloomington IN 47401

CARLSON, NATALIE SAVAGE, author; b. Winchester, Va., Oct. 3, 1906; d. Joseph Hamilton and Natalie Marie (Villeneuve dit Vallar) Savage; m. Daniel Carlson, Dec. 7, 1929; children: Stephanie Natalie (Mrs. Robert David Sullivan), Julie Ann (Mrs. Walter Erskine McAlpine). Student parochial schs., Calif. Newspaper reporter Long Beach (Calif.) Sun, 1926-29. Author: The Talking Cat and Other Stories of French Canada, 1952 (N.Y. Herald Tribune award Children's Spring Book Festival 1952), Alphonse, That Bearded One, 1954 (in N.Y. Herald Tribune award Children's Spring Book Festival 1954), Wings Against the Wind, 1955, Sashes Red and Blue, 1956, Hortense, the Cow for a Queen, 1957, The Happy Orpheline, 1957, The Family Under the Bridge, 1958 (Newbery honor book), A Brother for the Orphelines, 1959, Evangeline, Pigeon of Paris, 1960, The Tomahawk Family, 1960, The Song of The Lop-Eared Mule, 1961, A Pet for the Orphelines, 1962, Carnival in Paris, 1962, Jean-Claude's Island, 1963, The Empty Schoolhouse, 1965, Sailor's Choice, 1966, Chalou, 1967, Luigi of the Streets, 1967, Ann Aurelia and Dorothy, 1968, Befana's Gift, 1969, The Half Sisters, 1970, Luvvy and the Girls, 1971, Marie Louise and Christophe, 1974, Mary Louise's Heyday, 1975, Runaway Marie Louise, 1977, Jaky or Dodo?, 1978, The Night the Scarecrow Walked, 1979, King of the Cats and Other Tales, 1980, A Grandmother for the Orphelines, 1980; author: Marie Louise and Christophe at the Carnival, 1981, Spooky Night, 1982, Suprise in the Mountains, 1983, The Ghost at the Lagoon, 1984. Republican. Roman Catholic. Home: 3220 Hwy 19 N Lot 17 Clearwater FL 33575

CARLSON, NORMAN A., govt. ofcl.; b. Sioux City, Iowa, Aug. 10, 1933; s. Albert N. and Esther (Hollander) C.; m. Patricia Helen Musser, Sept. 8, 1956; children—Lucinda M., Gary N. B.A., Gustavus Adolphus Coll., 1955; M.A., State U. Iowa, 1957, Princeton, 1965-66. Parole officer Dept. Justice, U.S. Penitentiary, Leavenworth, Kan., 1957-58; casework supr. Fed. Correctional Inst., Ashland, Ky., 1958-60; asst. supr. instl. programs Fed. Bur. Prisons, Dept. Justice, Washington, 1960-62, project officer, 1962-65, exec. asst. to dir., 1966-70; dir. Fed. Bur. Prisons, 1970—; Del. UN Com. Crime Prevention and Control. Recipient Arthur S. Fleming award, 1972, Roger W. Jones award for exec. leadership, 1978, Atty. Gen.'s award for exceptional service, 1981. Mem. Am. Correctional Assn. (past pres., mem. exec. com., E.R. Cass award 1981). Home: 9923 Natick Rd Burke VA 22015 Office: Fed Bur Prisons Dept Justice Washington DC 20534

CARLSON, OSCAR NORMAN, metallurgist, educator; b. Mitchell, S.D., Dec. 21, 1920; s. Oscar and Ruth Belle (Gammill) C.; m. Virginia Jyleen Forsberg, July 30, 1946; children: Gregory Norman, Richard Norman, Karen Virginia. B.A., Yankton Coll., 1943; Ph.D., Iowa State U., 1950. Mem. faculty Iowa State U., 1943—, prof., sr. metallurgist Ames Lab., 1960—, chmn. dept. metallurgy, chief metallurgy div., 1962-66; Vis. scientist Max Planck Institut für Metallforschung, Stuttgart, Germany, 1974-75, 83. Bd. regents Waldorf Coll., 1964-74. Mem. Am. Soc. Metals (chmn. Des Moines 1957-58), Am. Chem. Soc., AIME, Iowa Acad. Scis., Sigma Xi, Phi Kappa Phi, Phi Lambda Upsilon. Club: Lion. Spl. research nuclear metals and alloys, phase studies binary alloy systems, brittle-ductile behavior metals and alloys, mass transport of solutes in metals. Developed process preparing and purifying yttrium, vanadium, zirconium, calcium, hafnium metals. Home: 811 Ridgewood Ames IA 50010

CARLSON, RALPH LAWRENCE, publishing company executive; b. Tulsa, July 8, 1944; s. Henry Arthur and Mary Lucille (Combs) C.; m. Nancy Ellen Grove, July 15, 1979; children: Laura, Julia. B.A., Oklahoma City U., 1966; M.A., Northwestern U., 1968. Mktg. dir. Northwestern U. Press, Evanston, Ill., 1969-71, sr. editor, 1972-74; editor Garland Pub., Inc., N.Y.C., 1975-78, v.p., 1979—. Home: 52 Remson St Brooklyn NY 11201 Office: Garland Pub Inc 136 Madison Ave New York NY 11201

CARLSON, REYNOLD ERLAND, former foundation executive, former ambassador; b. Chgo., Sept. 7, 1912; s. Amel Reynold and Lillian (Evald) C.; m. Patricia Proctor, July 27, 1964; 1 dau., Marie Louise Roehm. B.S., Northwestern U., 1936, M.A., 1937; Ph.D., Harvard U., 1946. Asst. prof. econs. Johns Hopkins U., 1940-48; econ. cons. UN, 1946-47, Econ. Commn. Latin Am., Santiago, Chile, 1948; asso. prof. econs., dir. Inst. Brazilian Studies, Vanderbilt U., 1949-53; economist Joint Brazilian-U.S. Devel. Commn., Inst. Inter-Am. Affairs, Rio de Janeiro, 1951-52; sr. economist Western Hemisphere operations World Bank, 1953-58; prof. econs., dir. grad. program econ. devel. Vanderbilt U., 1958-63, adj. prof., 1978-79; vis. prof. Grinnell Coll., 1979-80, Franklin Pierce Coll., 1980-81; cons. Ford Found., 1959-61, rep. in, Rio de Janeiro, 1961-65, asso. dir., 1965-66; U.S. ambassador to, Colombia, 1966-69; rep. Ford Found. in, Buenos Aires, 1969-72, regional program adviser, Lima, Peru, 1972-75. Served to 2d lt. USAAF, 1942-45. Decorated Cruzeiro de Sul, Brazil). Mem. Am. Econ. Assn., Phi Beta Kappa, Delta Sigma Pi. Clubs: Harvard (N.Y.C.); Cosmos (Washington); University (Nashville). Home: Medomak ME 04551 Rokeby 204 3901 West End Ave Nashville TN 37205 Office: Box 1828 Sta B Vanderbilt U Nashville TN 37235

CARLSON, RICHARD GEORGE, chemical company executive; b. Chgo., Sept. 26, 1930; s. Gustav George and Mildred Elisabeth (Englund) C.; m. S. Diane Russell, Oct. 10, 1948; children—Richard G., Pamela, Kurt D.; m. Barbara Jennie, Nov. 1979. B.S., Ill. Inst. Tech., 1956. With Waterway Terminal, Argo, Ill., 1949-56; with Dow Chem. Co., Midland, Mich., 1956—, bus. mgr. organic chems., 1971-73, dir. process research, 1973—; mem. fossil energy adv. com. Dept. Energy, 1976—; mem. adv. group dept. chem. engring. Ill. Inst. Tech., 1974-77. Adv. Jr. Achievement, 1956-64; Pres. Midland Newcomers Club, 1957-58; scoutmaster Paul Bunyon council Boy Scouts Am., 1956-64; bd. overseers Coll. Engring. Ill. Inst. Tech., 1981—. Inst. Gas Tech. scholar, 1954-56. Mem. Am. Inst. Chem. Engrs., Mich. Energy and Resource Research Assn. (trustee 1974-78), Tau Beta Pi. Methodist. Office: Dow Chem Co Midland MI 48640

CARLSON, RICHARD MERRILL, aeronautical engineer; b. Preston, Idaho, Feb. 4, 1925; s. Carl and Oretta C.; m. Venis Johnson, July 26, 1946; children: Judith, Jennifer, Richard. B.S. in Aero. Engring, U. Wash., M.S.; Ph.D. in Engring. Mechanics, Stanford U. Registered profl. engr., Calif. Chief aero.-structures engr. Hiller Aircraft, Menlo Park, Calif., 1949-64; rotary wing div. engr. Lockheed Calif. Co., Burbank, 1964-72; chief adv. systems research U.S. Army Air Mobility R&D Lab., Moffett Field, Calif., 1972-76; dir. Research and Tech. Labs., 1976—; lectr. Stanford U.; designated engring. rep. FAA. Contbr. articles to profl. jours. Served to lt. (j.g.) AC USN, 1943-46. Consol.-Vultee fellow, 1947; recipient Meritorious Civilian Service award U.S. Army, 1975, 77. Fellow AHS (hon.), AIAA; mem. Swedish Soc. Aeros. and Astronautics, Sigma Xi. Republican. Mem. Ch. Jesus Christ of Latter-day Saints. Lodge: Elks (Preston, Idaho). Office: US Army Research and Tech Lab Ames Research Ctr Moffett Field CA 94035

CARLSON, RICHARD RAYMOND, physics educator, researcher; b. chgo., Sept. 15, 1923; s. Richard Samuel and Anna Johanna (Stahl) C.; m. Evelyn May Crawford, Aug. 24, 1951; children: Judith Ann, Janet Lynn, Richard Divad. S.B., U. Chgo., 1945, S.M., 1949, Ph.D., 1951. Engr. Western Electric Co., Chgo., 1945-46; asst. prof. U. Iowa, Iowa City, 1951-57, assoc. prof., 1957-63, prof. physics, 1963—; scientist Oak Ridge Nat. Lab., 1952, Los Alamos Nat. Lab., 1956; dir. Univs. Research, Washington, 1976-79. Guggenheim fellow Oxford, Eng., 1959-60. Fellow Am. Phys. Soc.; mem. Sigma Xi. Home: 11 Durham Ct Iowa City IA 52240 Office: Dept Physics U Iowa Iowa City IA 52242

CARLSON, ROBERT JOHN, manufacturing company executive; b. Mpls., Sept. 12, 1929; s. Carlyle R. and Helen (Wahl) C.; m. Joann Ferguson, Jan. 12, 1952; children: Jon R., Jodie K., Robert C., Thomas C. B.A. in Bus. Adminstrn, U. Minn., 1952. With Deere & Co., 1950-79, v.p. farm equipment and consumer products div., 1970-71, sr. v.p., 1971-79, dir., 1970-79; group v.p. United Technologies Corp., Hartford, Conn., 1979, exec. v.p., 1979—; also dir.; pres. Pratt & Whitney Aircraft group, 1979—; pres. United Techs. Corp., 1983—; dir. GIGNA Corp. Bd. dirs. Jr. Achievement North Central Conn., Swedish Council in Am., Council on Fgn. Relations; trustee Nat. 4-H Council; bd. govs. Conn. Aero. Hist. Soc.; mem. Council Econ. Devel. Mem. Royal Round Table Swedish Council Am., Aerospace Industries Assn. (bd. govs.). Club: Wings (N.Y.C.).

CARLSON, ROBERT LEE, educator; b. Gary, Ind., May 22, 1924; s. Herman and Eva (Larson) C.; m. Betty Christine Nelson, Oct. 21, 1950; children—David Lee, Richard Ray, Karen Christine, Robert Lee, Carol Lynn. B.S., Purdue U., 1948, M.S., 1950; Ph.D., Ohio State U., 1962. Research engr. Battelle Inst., Columbus, Ohio, 1950-62; research engr. U.S. Steel Research Lab., Monroeville, Pa., 1962-63; research asso., lectr. Stanford, 1963-66; prof. Ga. Inst. Tech., Atlanta, 1966—; invited lectr. Internat. Union Theoretical and Applied Mechanics, 1960; cons. EIMAC div. Varian Assos., USAF Flight Dynamics Lab. Contbr. to: Folke Odquist Vol, 1967; Contbr. articles to profl. jours. Served with AUS, 1943-45. Recipient Charles Dudley medal ASTM, 1959. Mem. Am. Inst. Aeros. and Astronautics, Am. Soc. for Exptl. Stress Analysis (chmn. S.E. chpt. 1968-69), Sigma Xi, Pi Tau Sigma, Tau Beta Pi. Home: 4738 Cambridge Dr Dunwoody GA 30338 Office: Dept Aerospace Engring Ga Inst Tech Atlanta GA 30332

CARLSON, ROBERT OSCAR, business educator; b. Erie, Pa., Dec. 23, 1921; s. Oscar Edward and Mary Gertrude (Wintroath) C.; m. Eileen E. Evers, Oct. 29, 1966. A.B. summa cum laude, U. Pitts., 1943; Ph.D., Columbia, 1952. Research study dir. USPHS and Miss. Bd. Health, 1948-51; Middle East studies dir. Columbia U. Bur. Applied Social Research, 1951-53; overseas pub. relations adviser Standard Oil Co., N.J., 1953-71; pres. Pub. Relations Soc. Am., N.Y.C., 1971-72; v.p., dir. Internat. Research Assos., Inc., N.Y.C., 1972-74; dean Sch. Bus. Adminstrn., Adelphi U., Garden City, N.Y., 1974-82; prof. mgmt. and bus. policy; Mem. men's com. Am. Mus. Natural History; mem. Market Research Council, J.F. Kennedy's Task Force USIA; mem. adv. com. Grad. Sch. Corp. and Polit. Communications, Fairfield U. Chmn. editorial bd.: Public Opinion Quarterly; editor: Communications and Public Opinion, 1975; Contbr. articles to profl. jours. Served to 1st lt. AUS, 1943-46. Mem. Am. Sociol. Assn. (exec. officer), Am. Assn. for Pub. Opinion Research (pres.), China Inst., Am. Petroleum Inst. (chmn. opinion research com.), Inst. for Religious and Social Studies, Jewish Theol. Sem. Clubs: University, Tuxedo, Watch Hill Yacht, New York Skating, Misquamicut, Explorers, Shimecock Hills Golf. Home: West Lake Dr Tuxedo Park NY 10987 Office: Sch Bus Adminstrn Adelphi U Garden City NY 11530

CARLSON, ROBERT SCOTT, educator; b. Chgo., June 16, 1934; s. Robert F. and Helen (Pierce) C.; children—Cynthia Lynn, Scott Edward. S.B., Mass. Inst. Tech., 1956; M.B.A., Stanford U., 1962, Ph.D., 1964. Prodn. engr. E.I. duPont de Nemours & Co., 1956-57; financial analyst Ford Motor Co., 1961, Standard Oil N.J., 1962; instr. Stanford U., 1963-64; asst. prof. Columbia, 1964-66; vis. prof. Robert Coll., Istanbul, Turkey, 1966; asst. prof. Harvard Bus. Sch., 1966-69; dean Babcock Grad. Sch. Mgmt., Wake Forest U., 1969-71, prof. mgmt., 1969—, coordinator London summer program in internat. fin.

1976—; vis. prof. North European Mgmt. Inst., Oslo, Norway, 1972-73; cons. to industry. Contbr. articles to profl. jours. Served from ensign to lt. (j.g.) USNR, 1957-60. Named adminstr. of year Wake Forest U., 1970; M.I.T. Club of Chgo. fellow, 1952-56; Billings fellow, 1953; Ford Found. fellow, 1963. Mem. Am. Finance Assn., Financial Mgmt. Assn., Acad. Internat. Bus. Research on internat. finance and banking. Home: 112 Cedar Cove Ln Winston-Salem NC 27104

CARLSON, ROBERT WILLIAM, JR., rubber mfg. co. exec.; b. Kalamazoo, Mich., Oct. 14, 1947; s. Robert William and Mary Elizabeth (Creswell) C. Student, No. State Coll., Aberdeen, S.D., 1966-67. With Minn. Ruber Co., 1969-75, 77—, salesman, Cleve., 1969-75, chief exec. officer, chmn. bd., 1977—; pres. Tool Products Co., Mpls., 1975-77. Republican. Lutheran. Office: Minn Rubber Co 3630 Wooddale Ave Minneapolis MN 55416

CARLSON, RONALD LEE, lawyer, educator; b. Davenport, Iowa, Dec. 10, 1934; s. Arthur A. and Louise (Sehmann) C.; m. Mary Murphy, Feb. 10, 1965; children: Michael, Andrew. B.A., Augustana Coll., 1956; J.D. (Clarion DeWitt Hardy law scholar), Northwestern U., 1959; LL.M. (E. Barrett Prettyman law scholar), Georgetown U., 1961. Bar: Ill., Iowa 1959, D.C. 1960, U.S. Supreme Ct. 1966. Mem. firm Betty, Neuman, McMahon, Hellstrom & Bittner, Davenport, Iowa, 1961-65; U.S. commr. So. Dist. Iowa, 1964-64; prof. law U. Iowa, Iowa City, 1965-73, Washington U., St. Louis, 1973—; vis. prof. Wayne State U., Detroit, summers 1974, 76, 77, 79, U. Tex., 1978, St. Louis U., 1982, 83; cons. Legis. Com. Criminal Code Revision Iowa, 1969-73; lectr. Nat. Coll. State Judiciary, Reno, 1974, Nat. Coll. Dist. Attys., Houston, 1974, Boston, 1976, West Palm Beach, Fla., 1980, Chgo., 1983, Am. Acad. Jud. Edn., 1980. Author: Criminal Justice, 1978, (with M. Ladd) Cases on Evidence, 1972, (with J. Yeager) Criminal Law and Procedure, 1979, Criminal Law Advocacy, 1982, Successful Techniques for Civil Trials, 1983. Vice pres. alumni bd. Augustana Coll., Rock Island, Ill., 1968. Mem. Am. Assn. Law Schs., Fed. Bar Assn. (chmn. law sch. div. 1978-79, continuing edn. bd. 1977—), Am. Bar Assn., Iowa Bar Assn., St. Louis Bar Assn., Fed. Practice Inst. (dir. 1980, 81, 82, 83). Republican. Home: 7401 Parkdale St Clayton MO 63105 Office: School of Law Washington University Saint Louis MO 63130 *Proper application of law provides the key to resolution of disputes: local, national, and international. As a teacher of law to judges, lawyers and students, it is my goal to contribute to this needed resolution of conflict in a positive way.*

CARLSON, ROY PERRY MERRITT, banker; b. Chgo., May 23, 1923; s. Roy Frank and Elsie (Zornig) C.; m. Margery Vause Raw, Dec. 24, 1955; children: Randall R.F., Warren P.W., Winona M.C. A.M., U. Chgo., 1948. Fgn. service officer U.S. Dept. State, Washington, 1951-55; v.p. Bank of Am., San Francisco, 1955-75; mgn. dir. Melli Indsl. Group, Tehran, Iran, 1975-79; mng. dir. North West Investment Co., Zurich, Switzerland, 1977—; chmn. and pres. Nat. Bank Ga., Atlanta, 1980—; dir. Ga. Bus. and Ind. Assn., Atlanta, 1980, Southeast Bankcard Assn., Inc., 1980, INROADS, Inc., 1981. Served to lt. USN, 1943-46; PTO. Democrat. Christian Scientist. Clubs: Georgian (dir. 1982), Commerce, World Trade (Atlanta) (dir. 1982). Home: PO Box 71 Snellville GA 30278 Office: National Bank Ga PO Box 1234 Atlanta GA 30301

CARLSON, ROY WASHINGTON, cons. civil engr.; b. Big Stone, Minn., Sept. 23, 1900; s. John Carlson and Christine (Olson) C.; m. Eleanor Cutler, Sept. 14, 1927; children—Suzan Carlson Dieden, Sally Carlson Johnson. A.B., U. Redlands, Calif., 1922, Sc.D. (hon.), 1951; M.S., U. Calif., Berkeley, 1933; Sc.D., Mass. Inst. Tech., 1939. Asst. prof. physics U. Redlands, 1924-25; testing engr. So. Calif. Edison Co., Los Angeles, 1925-27; test engr. County of Los Angeles, 1927-31, U. Calif., Berkeley, 1931-34; asst. prof. civil engring. Mass. Inst. Tech., 1934-35, asso. prof., 1936-43, U. Calif., Berkeley, 1935-36, research asso., 1945—; with atomic bomb project U. Calif., Los Alamos, 1943-45; cons. civil engring., Berkeley, 1945—. Author tech. papers. Recipient Outstanding Civilian Service award U.S. Army, 1972; Berkeley citation U. Calif., Berkeley, 1980. Fellow ASCE; hon. mem. Am. Concrete Inst. (Wason medal 1935, Turner medal 1967), Concrete Inst. Brazil; mem. ASTM (Dudley medal 1939), Nat. Acad. Engring., Sigma Xi. Inventor elec. resistance meters for measuring stress, strain, pressure and temperature. Address: 55 Maryland Ave Berkeley CA 94707

CARLSON, SUZANNE OLIVE, architect; b. Worcester, Mass., Aug. 20, 1939; d. Sigfrid and Helga (Larson) C. B.S., R.I. Sch. Design, 1963. Jr. ptnr. Dingnam-Fauteux & Partners, Worcester, 1969-70; ptnr. Richard Lamoureux Asso., Worcester, 1970-75, Herron & Carlson (AIA), 1975—; Guest lectr. Holy Cross Coll., 1969-70. Chmn. Worcester Hist. Commn., 1976—; Trustee Worcester Heritage Soc., 1982—, Performing Arts Sch. of Worcester, 1977—; v.p. Performing Arts Sch. of Worcester, 1980—; trustee Cultural Assembly of Greater Worcester, 1981—, v.p., 1982-83. Recipient European Honors Program grant, Rome, Italy, 1961-62; recipient AIA School medal for excellence, 1963. Mem. AIA (exec. bd. Central Mass. chpt. 1969-71, sec.-treas. 1970-71, v.p. 1971-72, pres. 1972-73), Mass. Soc. Architects (exec. bd. 1972-74, v.p. 1975, pres. 1976), New Eng. Regional Council Architects (pres. 1977), New Eng. Antiquities Research Assn. (membership chmn., graphics dir. jour. 1982—). Home: 2 Oxford Pl Worcester MA 01609 Office: 5 Oxford Pl Worcester MA 01609

CARLSON, THEODORE JOSHUA, lawyer, utility executive; b. Hartford, Conn., Jan. 4, 1919; s. John and Hulda (Larson) C.; m. Jacqueline L. Coburn, Apr. 25, 1953; children: Stephanie, Christopher J., Victoria, Antoinette. A.B., Montclair State Coll., 1940; J.D., Columbia U., 1948, A.M., 1951; postgrad., U. Chgo., 1942. Bar: N.Y. 1948. Asso. firm Gould & Wilkie, N.Y.C., 1948-54, partner, 1954—, sr. partner, 1970—; dir. Central Hudson Gas & Electric Corp., Poughkeepsie, N.Y., 1968—, chmn., 1975—, prin. officer, 1975—; mem., chmn. fin. and audit com. N.Y. State Energy Research Devel. Authority, 1980; dir. Empire State Electric Energy Research Corp., Public Utilities Reports, Inc., Edison Electric Inst., 1976-79; chmn. exec. com. Energy Assn. N.Y. State, 1976-77, 82-83, N.Y. Power Pool, 1977-78; dir., mem. exec. com. Mid-Hudson Pattern, Inc., Poughkeepsie, N.Y. Pres. United Fund Rockville Centre, N.Y., 1966; chmn. Westchester County (N.Y.) advisory bd. Salvation Army, 1977-80, N.Y. State Advisory Bd., 1977—; chmn. bd. trustees King's Coll. Served to capt. USAAF, 1942-46. Mem. Edison Electric Inst., Am., N.Y. bar assns., Bar Assn. City N.Y. (chmn. pub. utility sect. com. on post admissions-legal edn. 1970-73). Club: Rotary (hon.). Home: 52 Dalmeny Rd Briarcliff Manor NY 10510 Office: 284 South Ave Poughkeepsie NY 12601 also 1 Wall St New York NY 10005

CARLSON, WILLIAM DONALD, educator; b. Sandstone, Minn., Jan. 15, 1914; s. C. Oscar and Jennie A. (Bjorklund) C.; m. Marian A. Finseth, Feb. 15, 1942; children—John W., Marcia A., Audrey J., Meridee J. B.E. with high honors, St. Cloud State Teachers Coll., 1939; M.A., U. Minn., 1951, Ph.D., 1955. Tchr. elementary schs., Minn., 1932-36, tchr., prin., secondary schs., 1937-41; with U.S. Bur. Prisons, 1941-42, 46-47; research asst. bur. ednl. research U. Minn., 1947-48, dir. student personnel, 1948-52; dean student affairs U. Nev., Reno, 1952-57, dean so. regional div., Las Vegas, 1957-65, prof. edn., 1952-80, prof. emeritus, 1980—, also grand marshal. Mem. adv. council U.S. Civil War Centennial Commn.; Member U.S. Regional Export Expansion Council. Served to capt. inf. AUS, 1942-46. Decorated Bronze Star with oak leaf cluster. Mem. Clark County Mental Health Assn. (pres.), Nev. Mental Health Assn. (v.p.), Nev. Psychol. Assn., Am. Personnel and Guidance Assn., Am. Coll. Personnel Assn., Higher Edn. Assn., Phi Delta Kappa, Psi Chi, Kappa Delta Pi, Phi Kappa Phi, Tau Kappa Alpha.; mem. Order Eastern Star, Vasa Order Am. Clubs: Mason (33 deg.), Rotarian). Home: 1308 Cashman Dr Las Vegas NV 89102

CARLSON, WILLIAM DWIGHT, hospital executive; b. Denver, Nov. 5, 1928; m. Beverley Ann Bradshaw, 1950; children: Susan Elaine, Earl Dwight. D.V.M., Colo. State U., 1952, M.S., 1956; Ph.D. in Radiology, U. Colo., 1958. Diplomate: Am. Coll. Vet. Radiology (founding mem.). Pres., prof. radiation biology, adminstr. Am. studies program U. Wyo., Laramie, 1968-79; affiliate prof. radiology, radiation biology Colo. State U., Fort Collins, 1968-80; chief exec. officer St. John's Hosp., Jackson Hole, Wyo., 1980—; nat. cons. vet. medicine to surgeon gen. USAF, 1970-75; dir. 1st Wyo. Bank, Cheyenne, E.E. Mitchell & Co., Ft. Collins; trustee Wyo. Blue Shield/Blue Cross, 1976—, chmn. bd. trustees, 1982—; adv. dir. Wyo. Indsl. Devel. Corp., 1967-79; commr. Wyo. Western Interstate Commn. Higher Edn., 1968-79; mem. president's council and senate Assn. Land Grant Colls. and State Univs., 1968-79; pres. council Western Athletic Conf., 1968-79; exec. com. Assn. Western Univs., 1970-79; regional adv. com. Inst. Internat. Edn., 1969-79; mem. scholarship com. Marathon Oil Co., 1977-79. Author: Veterinary Radiology, 3d edit, 1978; Editor: procs. Internat. Symposium on the Effects of Ionizing Radiation of the Reproductive System, 1964; Contbr. articles to profl. jours. Mem. exec. com. Longs Peak council Boy Scouts Am., 1966-80, pres., 1974-76, v.p., North Central region, 1970-74; regional chmn. Nat. Eagle Scout Assn., 1975-80, Silver Beaver award, 1974; bd. dirs. U. Wyo. Found., 1968-79; bd. visitors Air U., Maxwell AFB, 1972-75; mem. Yellowstone Park Library and Mus. Bd., 1974—, vice chmn., 1976-83. Named Outstanding Young Man of Year Colo. Jr. C. of C., 1960, Top Prof. Colo. State U., 1961, U.S. Vet. of Year Am. Animal Hosp. Assn., 1967, hon. alumni Colo. State U., 1971. Fellow AAAS; mem. Laramie C. of C. (dir. 1968-79), Am., Wyo. vet. med. assns., Nuclear Medicine Soc. Am. (nat. trustee 1964-68), Wyo. Med. Soc., Am. Vet. Radiology Soc. (charter, pres. 1965), Wyo. Hosp. Assn. (dir. 1982—, sec.-treas. 1983), Nat. Cowboy Hall of Fame (hon. life mem.). Club: Rotary (dir. 1982—).

CARLSON, WILLIAM ELMER, mil. officer; b. Maitland, Fla., Mar. 5, 1929; s. Olaf and Laura Kassara (Anderson) C.; m. Nancy Virginia Fortner, Apr. 22, 1956; children—William Bradley, Cecile Ann, Paul Akermo. B.S.A., U. Fla., 1951; M.I.A., George Washington U., 1969; postgrad., Command and Gen. Staff Coll., 1963, Armed Forces Staff Coll., 1966, Naval War Coll., 1969. Commd. 2d lt. U.S. Army, 1951, advanced through grades to brig. gen.; served in, Korea, Vietnam; chief staff (25th Inf. Div.), 1974-78, asst. div. comdr., Ft. Ord, Calif., from 1978; now dep. mil. rep. NATO Mil. Command. Neighborhood commr., asst. dist. commr. Nat. Capital Area council Boy Scouts Am.; active Nat. Assn. Retarded Citizens. Recipient D.S.M., Legion of Merit, Silver Star, Bronze Star, others. Mem. Assn. U.S. Army, V.F.W., 1st Cavalry Div. Assn., 7th Inf. Div. Assn., 25th Inf. Div. Assn., Scabbard and Blade. Republican. Lutheran. Clubs: Rotary, Demolay, Key. Home: 9955 Lake Georgia Dr Maitland FL 32751 Office: US Dep NATO MC APO New York NY 09667

CARLSSON, PERCY ALLAN, philosophy educator; b. San Jose, Calif., Feb. 3, 1927; s. Percy Gustav and Esther (Anderson) C.; m. Marian Inga Carlson, June 27, 1952. Student, U. Tex., 1947, U. Nebr., 1947-48; B.A., Wheaton (Ill.) Coll., 1951, M.A., 1956; B.D., Trinity Evang. Div. Sch., 1954; Ph.D., Northwestern U., 1961. Instr. philosophy Wheaton Coll., 1957-58; instr. philosophy and religion, registrar, dir. admissions Trinity Coll., Chgo., 1958-61; prof. philosophy, registrar, dir. institutional research Va. Mil. Inst., Lexington, 1961—. Author: Butler's Ethics, 1964; Contbr. articles to profl. jours. Served with USNR, 1945-46. Mem. Am. Philos. Assn., Soc. for Philosophy of Religion, So. Soc. Philosophy and Psychology, Metaphys. Soc., Va. Humanities Conf., AAUP, Am. Assn. Higher Edn., Am., Va. assns. coll. registrars and admissions officers, Assn. for Institutional Research. Home: Route 2 Box 20 Lexington VA 24450

CARLTON, CHARLES MERRITT, linguistics educator; b. Poultney, Vt., Dec. 12, 1928; s. Clarence Rann and Margaret Louise (Pennell) C.; m. Mary MacDonald, Aug. 31, 1957; children: David, John, Stephen. A.B., U. Vt., 1950; M.A., Middlebury Coll., 1951; Ph.D., U. Mich., 1963. Instr. Mich. State U., East Lansing, 1958-62; asst. prof. U. Mo., Columbia, 1962-66; prof. French and Romance linguistics U. Rochester, N.Y., 1966—; asst. dir. NDEA French Inst., U. Vt., Burlington, summer 1964; lectr. U.S. State Dept Seminars, Brasov, Romania, summer 1972, U. Ky., Cluj, Romania, summer 1977; reader Nat. Endowment for Humanitites, 1974—. Author: Studies in Romance Lexicology, 1965, A Linguistic Analysis of a Collection of Late Latin Documents Composed in Ravenna between A.D. 445-700: A Quantitative Approach, 1973; bibliographer: Romanian Language and Linguistics, 1973, 75—; co-editor: Miorita: A Jour. of Romanian Studies, 1977—; editor: Comparative Romance Linguistics newsletter, 1970-71. Mem. Rennes-Rochester Sister City Com., Am.-Romanian Cultural Found.; bd. dirs. Rochester Internat. Friendship Council. Fulbright fellow, Paris, 1950-51; fellow NSF, summer 1965, Nat. Def. Fgn. Lang., summer 1970; Fulbright lectr., 1971-72; Fulbright grantee, 1974, 78, 82. Mem. Assn. Advancement of Slavic Studies, Am. Assn Tchrs. of French, Am. Assn. Tchrs. of Spanish and Portuguese, Am. Romanian Acad., Linguistic Soc. Am., MLA, N. Am. Catalan Soc., Romanian Studies Assn. Am, Soc. Romanian Studies, L'Amicale (Middlebury, Vt.), Fulbright Alumni Assn., Immigration History Soc., Sigma Delta Pi. Home: 3 Thornfield Way Fairport NY 14450 Office: Univ Rochester Rochester NY 14627

CARLTON, DEAN, lawyer; b. Ft. Worth, Nov. 4, 1928; s. Robert Ardine and Marjorie (Box) C.; m. Mary Ellen Williams, Sept. 9, 1949; s. Robert Mark, Scott Duane, Mary Ann. B.S., Tex. A&M Coll., 1949; LL.B., So. Methodist U., 1952. Bar: Tex. 1952, U.S. Supreme Ct 1968; Certified in civil trial law Tex. Bd. Legal Specialization. Practice in, Dallas, 1952—; propr. The Carlton Firm (attys.), 1970—. Mem. City of Richardson Bd. Adjustment, 1966-67, Tex. Water Code Adv. Com., 1968-70; co-founder, chmn. Dallas Martini Found. and Trust. Mem. ABA, Tex. Bar. Assn., Tex. Aggie Bar Assn. (pres. 1974-75), Dallas Bar Assn., Richardson Lawyers-Pilots Bar Assn., Aircraft Owners and Pilots Assn. Clubs: Aggie (exec. com. 1980-83, pres. elect 1984. Home: 7038 Spring Valley St Dallas TX 75240 Office: 3109 Carlisle Dallas TX 75204

CARLTON, DONALD MORRILL, research and development company executive; b. Houston, July 20, 1937; s. Spencer William and Ruth (Morrill) C.; m. Elaine Yvonne Smith, Jan. 28, 1961; children: Donna Kay, Spencer Frank, Monica Elaine. B.A., U. St. Thomas, Houston, 1958; Ph.D., U. Tex., Austin, 1962. Mem. staff, then group leader Sandia Corp., Albuquerque, 1962-65; with Tracor, Inc., Austin, 1965-69, asst. dir. research, 1968-69; pres., chmn. bd. Radian Corp., Austin, 1969—; dir. Hartford Steam Boiler Insp. and Ins. Co., Interfirst Bank, Austin. Mem. Air Pollution Control Assn., Am. Chem. Soc., Am. Mgmt. Assn. (pres.'s club), Austin C. of C. (past dir.). Home: 4601 Cat Mountain Dr Austin TX 78731 Office: PO Box 9948 Austin TX 78766

CARLTON, PAUL KENDALL, former air force officer; b. Manchester, N.H., Apr. 14, 1921; s. R.W. and Julia Anne (Jameson) C.; m. Helen Sweat, Oct. 4, 1942; children: Paul Kendall, Dorothy E. (Mrs. Peter Alan Sievert). Student, U. Pitts., 1939-40, Ohio State U., 1940-41, George Washington U., 1961; grad., Nat. War Coll., 1962. Commd. 2d lt. USAAF, 1942; advanced through grades to gen. USAF, 1972; aircraft comdr. 468th Bomb Group, 58th Bomb Wing, CBI, 1944; dep. comdr. 93d Bomb Wing, Castle AFB, Calif., 1957-59; comdr. 4126th Strategic Wing, Beale AFB, Calif., 1959-61, 379th Bomb Wing, Wurtsmith AFB, Mich, 1962-63, 305th Bomb Wing, Bunker Hill AFB, Ind., 1963-65; chief operations plans div. SAC Hdqrs., Omaha, 1965-67, asst. dep. chief staff operations, 1967-68; dep. chief staff operations, 1969; comdr. 1st Strategic Aerospace div., Vandenberg AFB, Calif., 1968-69, 15th Air Force, March AFB, Calif., 1969-72; comdr.-in-chief Mil. Airlift Command, Scott AFB, Ill., 1972-77; ret., 1977; cons. SLS div. Martin Marietta Corp., Denver; former dir. Union Pacific MOPAC R.R. Contbr. articles to mil. jours. Decorated D.S.M. (2), Silver Star, Legion Merit with oak leaf cluster, D.F.C., Air medal with 5 oak leaf clusters, Army Commendation medal, Purple Heart. Mem. Air Force Assn. Methodist. Club: Daedalian. Home: 7300 S Jay St Littleton CO 80123 *Leadership in military or civilian life depends on a deep interest in people of all walks of life and an effective channel of communication with each level of command or supervision*

CARLTON, STEVEN NORMAN, professional baseball player; b. Miami, Fla., Dec. 22, 1944. Student, Miami Dade Jr. Coll. Pitcher St. Louis Cardinals, 1965-71, Phila. Phillies, 1972—. Recipient Nat. League Cy Young Meml. award, 1972, 77, 80, 82; named lefthanded pitcher Nat. League All-Star Team Sporting News, 1968, 69, 71, 72, 74, 77, 79, Pitcher of Yr. Sporting News, 1972, 77, 80, 82. Address: care Philadelphia Phillies PO Box 7575 Philadelphia PA 19101

CARLTON, TERRY SCOTT, chemist, educator; b. Peoria, Ill., Jan. 29, 1939; s. Daniel Cushman and Mabel (Smith) C.; m. Claudine Fields, June 11, 1960; children: Brian Douglas, David Britton. B.S., Duke U., 1960; Ph.D. (NSF grad. fellow 1960-63), U. Calif., Berkeley, 1963. Mem. faculty Oberlin (Ohio) Coll., 1963—, prof. chemistry, 1976—, chmn. dept., 1980-83; vis. prof. chemistry U. N.C., Chapel Hill, 1976. Co-author: Composition, Reaction and Equilibrium, 1970. Mem. Am. Phys. Soc., Sigma Xi. Home: 165 Fairway Dr Oberlin OH 44074 Office: Dept Chemistry Oberlin Coll Oberlin OH 44074

CARLTON-JONES, DENNIS, environmental management, company executive;; b. Colwyn Bay, North Wales, G.B., Dec. 11, 1930; came to U.S., 1964; s. Charles Richard and Amy (Slater) Carlton-J.; m. Anne Helen Nixon, Oct. 3, 1955; children: Christopher Richard, Michael John. B.Sc., U. London, 1951. Engr. George Wimpey & Co., London, 1954-57, asst. to v.p., 1957-60; mgr. Custodis Canadian Chimney Co., Ltd., Toronto and Montreal, 1961-64, mgr., v.p. sales and engring., 1964-69; v.p., gen. mgr. Custodis Constrn. Co., Inc., Chgo., 1969-71, Hamon Cooling Tower div. Research-Cottrell, Inc., 1971-73, Air Control Group, 1973-77; pres. Environ. Cos. Research-Cottrell, Inc., 1977-82, pres., chief exec. officer Custodis-Hamon, 1983—. Served with RAF, 1952-54. Mem. Instn. Civil Engrs., Air Pollution Control Assn. Episcopalian. Club: Raritan Valley Country. Office: PO Box 1500 Somerville NJ 08876

CARLUCCI, FRANK CHARLES, III, business executive; b. Scranton, Pa., Oct. 18, 1930; s. Frank Charles, Jr. and Roxanne (Bacon) C.; m. Marcia Myers, Apr. 15, 1976; children: Karen, Frank, Kristin. A.B., Princeton U., 1952; postgrad., Sch. Bus. Adminstrn., Harvard U., 1956, Wilkes Coll., Kings Coll., 1973. With Jantzen Co., Portland, Ore., 1955-56; fgn. service officer Dept. State, 1956, vice consul, econ. officer, Johannesburg, S. Africa, 1957-59, second sec., polit. officer, Kanshasa, Congo, 1960-62, officer in charge Congolese polit. affairs, 1962-64, consul gen., Zanzibar, 1964-65, counselor for polit. affairs, Rio de Janeiro, Brazil, 1965-69; asst. dir. for ops. Office Econ. Opportunity, Washington, 1969; dir., 1970; assoc. dir. Office Mgmt. and Budget, 1971, dep. dir., 1972; undersec. HEW, 1972-74; ambassador to, Portugal, 1975-78; dep. dir. CIA, Washington, 1978-81; dep. sec. Dept. Def., Washington, 1981-82; pres. Sears World Trade, Inc., Washington, 1983—. Served as lt. (j.g.) USNR, 1952-54. Recipient Superior Service award Dept. State, 1972, Superior Honor award, 1969, HEW Disting. Civilian Service award, 1975, Def. Dept. Disting. Civilian award, 1977, Disting. Intelligence medal, 1981, Nat. Intelligence Disting. Service medal, 1981, Presdl. Citizens award, 1983. Office: Sears World Trade Inc 450 5th St NW 10th Floor Washington DC 20001

CARLUCCI, JOSEPH FRANCIS, advertising executive; b. N.Y.C., Nov. 3, 1943; s. Joseph Francis and Delphine Bridget (Iorio) C.; children: Kimberly, Joseph Richard. B.S. in Econs, Fordham U., 1965; M.B.A. in Mktg, Columbia U., 1967. Account exec. Grey Advt. Inc., N.Y.C., 1967-69, William Esty Co., 1969-72; with Benton & Bowles Inc., N.Y.C., 1972-83, sr. v.p., mgmt. supr., 1978-83, D'Arcy-MacManus & Masius, 1983-84; exec. v.p. Geers Gross Advt., 1984—; adj. prof. mktg. Columbia U. Grad. Sch. Bus. Office: 220 E 42d St New York NY 10017

CARLYLE, JACK WEBSTER, computer scientist, educator; b. Cordova, Alaska, Feb. 23, 1933; s. Jack Bartley and Helen Beatrice (Havil) C.; m. Sheila Adele Greibach, Mar. 22, 1970; 1 son, Jay Samuel. B.A., U. Wash., 1954, M.S. in Elec. Engring, 1957; M.A., U. Calif., Berkeley, 1961, Ph.D., 1961. Asst. prof. elec. engring. Princeton U., 1961-63; mem. faculty dept. engring. and applied sci. UCLA, 1963—, prof. computer sci., 1980—, chmn. system sci. dept., 1975-80. Contbr. articles to profl. jours. Mem. IEEE Computer Soc. (chmn. tech. com. founds. of computing 1975-78), Assn. Computing Machinery, Inst. Math. Stats., Am. Math. Soc., Soc. Indsl. and Applied Math, Am. Radio Relay League, Phi Beta Kappa, Sigma Xi, Pi Mu Epsilon. Office: Dept Computer Sci UCLA Los Angeles CA 90024

CARLYON, DON J., college president; b. Chambers, Nebr., Aug. 14, 1924; s. Richard E. and Ruth (Wolters) C.; m. Betty E. Hunley, June 13, 1946; children: Janette, David, Suzanne, Scott, Richard. Student, Nebr. Wesleyan U.; B.S., U. Nebr.; LL.D., Saginaw Valley State Coll., 1975. Dir. U. Nebr. Men's Residence Halls, 1953-56; asst. bus. mgr. U. Kansas City, 1956-57, bus. mgr., 1957-60, acting dean, 1958; bus. mgr. Delta Coll., Mich., 1960-64, pres., 1964—; mem. nat. commn. on Trends in public higher edn. Mem. Gov. Mich. Com. Comprehensive State Health Adv. Planning Council; mem. commn. adminstrn., also comm. on govtl. relations Am. Assn. Community and Jr. Colls.; pres. Mich. Community Coll. Assn.; bd. dirs. Nat. Assn. Pub. TV Stas. Recipient (Norman C. Harris award for nat. leadership in community coll. movement 1983). Served with USNR. Mem. Nat. Assn. Ednl. Buyers, Bay County Mental Health Assn., Phi Kappa Tau, Beta Gamma Sigma. Methodist. Clubs: Torch, Rotary. Office: Delta Coll University Center MI 48710

CARLYSS, EARL WINSTON, musician; b. Chgo., Oct. 27, 1939; s. S. Paul and Evelyn S. (Daniels) C.; m. Ann Schein, May 24, 1969; children—Linnea, Pauline. Student, Paris Conservatoire, 1955-57; B.Music, Julliard Sch. Music, 1963, M.S., 1964. Debut with, Pasadena Symphony Orch., 1955; concertmaster, N.Y. City Ballet Orch., 1965-66; mem., Juilliard String Quartet, 1966—; artist in residence, Mich. State U., 1977—. Bd. dirs. People to People Music Com. Recipient

Rosenberger medal U. Chgo., 1973; Morris Loeb Meml. prize for string, 1964. Clubs: Cosmos (Washington); Scarsdale Golf. Office: Juilliard Sch Lincoln Center Plaza New York NY 10023

CARMACK, GEORGE, newspaper editor; b. Troy, Tenn., Feb. 20, 1907; s. Dan Meacham and Frances (Burnett) C.; m. Bonnie Tom Robinson, Oct. 1943; 1 dau., Judith Anne. Student, Union U., Jackson, Tenn., 1922-24; A.B., U. Tenn., 1927. Reporter, Knoxville Sentinel, 1926-28, Memphis Evening Appeal, 1928-30; city editor Memphis Press-Scimitar, 1930-35; mng. editor, 1935-37; editor Knoxville News-Sentinel, 1937, Houston Press, 1946-64; staff writer Scripps-Howard Newspaper Alliance, 1964-66; editor Albuquerque Tribune, 1966-73; editorial bd. San Antonio Express-News, 1973-75, 80—, asso. editor, 1975-78. Served as pvt. in 6th Cav., 1940; commd., 1942; ETO.; commd.; PTO. Mem. Tex. Philos. Soc., Tex. Hist. Assn. Episcopalian. Home: 7600 Broadway Apt G-4 San Antonio TX 78209 Office: San Antonio Express-News Box 2171 San Antonio TX 78297

CARMAN, GEORGE HENRY, physician; b. Albany, N.Y., Sept. 23, 1928; s. Simon Peter and Mary (Whish) C. B.A., Cornell U., 1948, M.D., 1951. Diplomate: Am. Bd. Internal Medicine, Am. Bd. Cardiovascular Disease. Intern, then asst. resident in medicine Barnes Hosp., St. Louis, 1951-53; asst. resident in medicine Salt Lake County Gen. Hosp., 1955-56; chief resident VA Hosp., Salt Lake City, 1956-57; fellow cardiovascular diseases U. Utah Coll. Medicine, 1957-60; practice medicine specializing in cardiology and internal medicine, Dallas, 1960—; attending physician Baylor U. Med. Center, Gaston Episcopal Hosp.; mem. faculty U. Tex. Southwestern Med. Sch., Dallas, 1960—, clin. prof. internal medicine, 1972—. Served to 1st lt. M.C. AUS, 1953-55. Fellow A.C.P.; mem. AAAS, Am. Fedn. Clin. Research, AMA, Tex. Acad. Internal Medicine, Am. Heart Assn. (fellow council clin. cardiology), Tex. Heart Assn. (dir.), Dallas Heart Assn. (past pres.), Dallas Acad. Internal Medicine, Confrerie de Chaine des Rotisseurs (chevalier), L'Alliance Française, Phi Beta Kappa, Alpha Omega Alpha. Episcopalian. Club: Gun (Dallas). Office: 3600 Gaston Ave Dallas TX 75246

CARMAN, GREGORY WRIGHT, judge; b. Farmingdale, N.Y., Jan. 31, 1937; s. Willis B. and Marjorie (Sosa) C. Exchange student, U. Paris, 1956; B.A., St. Lawrence U., 1958; J.D., St. John's U., 1961; Judge Adv. Gen. honors grad., U. Va. Law Sch., 1962. Bar: N.Y. 1961. Councilman Town of Oyster Bay, N.Y., 1972-81; mem. 97th Congress from 3d Dist. N.Y.; judge U.S. Ct. Internat. Trade, N.Y.C. Served to capt. AUS, 1962-64. Mem. Am. Bar Assn., Nassau County Bar Assn., Nassau Lawyers Assn., Criminal Cts. Bar Assn., N.Y. State Defenders Assn., N.Y. State Bar Assn. Republican. Episcopalian. Club: Rotary. Office: One Federal Plaza New York NY 10007

CARMAN, HOY FRED, agricultural sciences educator; b. Wallowa, Oreg., July 3, 1938; s. Hoy Ransom and Ruth Nina (Weinhard) C.; m. Patricia Marie Gosse, June 4, 1960; children—Susan Marie, Laura Ann. B.S., Oreg. State U., 1960, M.S., 1962; Ph.D., Mich. State U., 1964. Economist Econ. Research Service, U.S. Dept. Agr., East Lansing, Mich., 1964-65; prof. dept. agrl. econs. U. Calif.-Davis, 1967—, assoc. dean Coll. Agrl. and Environ. Scis., 1983—. Contbr. articles to profl. jours. Served to capt. U.S. Army, 1965-67. Found. Econ. Edn. fellow, 1968; Fulbright Research fellow, New Zealand, 1973. Mem. Am. Agrl. Econs. Assn. (internat. travel grantee 1970), Internat. Assn. Agrl. Economists, Western Agrl. Econs. Assn., Alpha Gamma Rho, Alpha Zeta, Phi Kappa Phi. Republican. Home: 1108 Colby Davis CA 95616 Office: Dept Agrl Econs U Calif Davis CA 95616

CARMAN, IAN DOUGLAS, newspaper editor; b. St. Thomas, Ont., Can., June 17, 1927; s. Samuel James and Bertha Lyle (Appleford) C. B.A., McMaster U., 1950. Exec. editor Toronto (Ont.) Globe and Mail. Home: 50 Alexander St Apt 2502 Toronto ON M4Y 1B6 Canada Office: 444 Front St W Toronto ON M5V 2S9 Canada

CARMAN, WILLIAM BRAINERD, lawyer; b. Detroit Lakes, Minn., Oct. 5, 1905; s. William B. and Frances P. (Fritzsche) C.; m. Dorothy J. Day, Sept. 15, 1930; children: Patricia Jeanne McEldowney, Mary Elisabeth Exton. A.B. magna cum laude, Carleton Coll., 1926, LL.B., Harvard U., 1929. Bar: Calif. 1930. Mem. firm O'Melveny & Myers, 1929-40, partner, 1940-70, of counsel, 1970—; instr. law Southwestern U., 1936-39. Mem. editorial bd.: Harvard Law Rev, 1928-29; author: Goodly Heritage, Yeoman's Service; Author numerous legal and hist. articles. Recipient alumni achievement award Carleton Coll., 1954. Mem. Carleton Nat. Alumni Assn. (pres. 1964-66), Harvard Legal Aid Soc. (pres. 1928), Carleton Coll. So. Cal. Alumni Assn. (pres. 1947-50), ABA, Calif. State Bar Assn. (chmn. radio com. 1950-51), Los Angeles Bar Assn., Calif., S.C. hist. socs., Phi Beta Kappa, Phi Delta Epsilon. Clubs: University, El Niguel Country. Home: 31671 Crystal Sands Dr Laguna Niguel CA 92677 also 422 S Orange Grove Blvd Pasadena CA 91105 Office: 400 S Hope Los Angeles CA 90071-2899

CARMEAN, E. A., JR., museum curator; b. Springfield, Ill., Jan. 25, 1945; s. E.A. and Etta Helen (Marker) C.; m. Janet Yantis, June 8, 1969 (dec.); 1 dau., Elizabeth Anne. B.A., MacMurray Coll., Jacksonville, Ill., 1967. Curator 20th century art Mus. Fine Arts, Houston, 1971-74, Nat. Gallery Art, Washington, 1974—; vis. prof. Rice U., Houston, 1971-74, George Washington U., 1974-76. Author: The Collages of Robert Motherwell, 1972, The Subjects of the Artist, 1978, Mondrian: The Diamond Compositions, 1979, Robert Motherwell: Reconciliation Elegy, 1980, Picasso: The Saltimbanques, 1980, Braque: Les Papier Colles, 1982; author: David Smith, 1982; dir. film. Fellow Nat. Endowment Arts, 1974, Guggenheim Found., 1978-79. Mem. Am. Mus. Assn., Coll. Art Assn. Home: 3419 Dent Pl NW Washington DC 20007 Office: Nat Gallery Art Washington DC 20565

CARMEL, ALAN STUART, lawyer, manufacturing company executive; b. Balt., July 24, 1944; s. Isaac and Sylvia (Sirulnik) C.; m. Ellen Freda Hobman, June 29, 1969; children: Shana Miriam, Jason Mark, Jarre Paige. A.A., U. Balt., 1963, J.D., 1966. Bar: Md. bar 1966. Sec., asst. counsel 1st Federated Life Ins. Co., Balt., 1966-69; dir. equity mktg. U.S. counsel Mfrs. Life Ins. Co., Toronto, Ont., Can., 1970-75; v.p., dir. ManEquity, Inc., Denver, 1970-75; pres., dir. ManuLife Holding Corp., 1970-75; v.p., gen. counsel, sec., dir. Atlantic Internat. Corp., Balt., 1975-80, Atlantic Internat. Mktg. Corp., 1975-80, Atlantic Mfg. Corp., 1975-80; dir. Atlantic Industries, Inc.; gen. counsel AI Services (A.G.), Zug, Switzerland, 1976-80; solo practice, 1981—; exec. v.p., dir. Imperial Group (N.A.) Ltd., 1982—; gen. counsel Brooks Shoe Mfg. Co., Inc., Hanover, Pa., Turner Shoe Co., Aguadilla, P.R., Carmen Athletic Industries, Romana Athletic Industries, Dominican Republic, Century Shoe Co., St. Kitts, W.I.; exec. mgr. Atliran, P.J.S.C., Tehran, Iran, to 1980; U.S. arbitrator Internat. C. of C. Ct. Arbitration. Author: Business Entities and Their Taxation in Liechtenstein. Fellow Life Mgmt. Inst.; mem. Internat. Bar Assn., ABA, Md. Bar Assn., Am. Arbitration Assn. (comml. panel). Home: 2425 Diana Rd Baltimore MD 21209 Office: PO Box 142 Stevenson MD 21153

CARMEN, GERALD P., diplomat; b. Quincy, Mass., July 8, 1930; m. Anita Joan Carmen; children: David, Melinda. Grad., U. N.H., 1952. Founder, owner wholesale automotive service co., Manchester, N.H.; adminstr. GSA, Washington, 1981-84; U.S. rep. with rank of ambassador European office of UN, Geneva, 1984—; former mem. Cabinet Council for Mgmt. and Adminstrn. White House Property Rev. Bd.; former mem. Pres.'s Com. on Arts and Humanities, U.S./Saudi Arabian Joint Commn. on Econ. Coop. Past commr. Manchester Housing and Urban Renewal Authority; mem. Republican Nat. Exec. Com., del. Rep. Nat. Conv., 1964, 80, 84; past N.H. chmn. Republican Nat. Com.; chmn. Manchester Heart Fund; dir., chmn. N.H. chpt. NCCJ; dir. N.H. Brotherhood Council.; trustee Fed. City Council; mem. Nat. Capital Planning Commn. Named Retailer of Yr. Downtown Manchester Assn., 1978; recipient Brotherhood award N.H. Brotherhood Council, 1979, award for pub. service Holocaust Meml. Council, 1982. Office: US Mission to UN Geneva Switzerland

CARMER, SAMUEL GRANT, agronomy educator; b. Buffalo, N.Y., Dec. 19, 1932; s. Elton Brown and Eugenia Heloise (Landgren) C.; m. Judith Ann Huisinga, June 25, 1960; children: Kristi Ann, Craig Samuel, Alan Stuart. B.S., Cornell U., 1954; M.S., U. Ill., 1958, Ph.D., 1961. Asst. prof. dept. agronomy U. Ill., 1962-66, asso. prof., 1966-71, prof. biometry, 1971—; cons. in field. Contbr. articles in field to profl. jours. Bd. dirs. Champaign-Urbana Youth Hockey Assn., 1973-76, pres., 1973-75; bd. dirs. Central Ill. Hockey League, 1974-76. Served with Med. Service Corps U.S. Army, 1955-57. Mem. Am. Soc. Agronomy, Am. Statis. Assn., Biometric Soc., Crop Sci. Soc. Am., Sigma Xi, Gamma Sigma Delta, Phi Kappa Phi. Office: 1102 S Goodwin St Urbana IL 61801

CARMI, SHLOMO, mechanical engineering educator, scientist; b. Cernauti, Rumania, July 18, 1937; came to U.S., 1963, naturalized, 1978; s. Shmuel and Haia (Marcovici) C.; m. Rachel Aharoni, Dec. 23, 1963; children: Sharon, Ronen-Itzhak, Lemore. Student, Technion, Haifa, Israel, 1958-60; B.S. cum laude, U. Witwatersrand, Johannesburg, South Africa, 1962; M.S., U. Minn., 1966, Ph.D., 1968. Research engr. W. Rand Gold Mining Co., Krugersdorp, South Africa, 1962-63; research asst., research fellow U. Minn., 1963-68; asst. prof. mech. engring. Wayne State U., Detroit, 1968-70, 72-73, asso. prof., 1973-78, prof., 1978—, chmn. univ. research com., 1982—; sr. lectr. Technion, Israel Inst. Tech., 1970-72, sabbatical I. Taylor chair, 1977-78; research specialist Ford Motor Co., summer 1973, 74, 76, 77, Detroit Edison Co., summer 1983; speaker sci. meetings, Israel, Can. and, U.S. Editor book in field; Contbr. articles and revs. to profl. jours.; Asso. editor: Jour. Fluids Engring, 1981—. Served in Israeli Army, 1956-58. South African Technion Soc. scholar, 1960-62; recipient prize Transvaal Chamber of Mines, 1961, faculty research award Wayne State U., 1970; research grantee Dept. Energy, U.S. Army Research Office. Mem. Am. Phys. Soc., ASME (coms.), AAUP, Sigma Xi, Tau Beta Pi, Pi Tau Sigma. Home: 5270 Hollow Dr Bloomfield Hills MI 48013 Office: Wayne State U Detroit MI 48202 *In bridging the gap between mankind's needs and the preservation of nature's environment, we strive to both formulate the problem, with all its implied scientific abstraction, and subsequently generate a technically feasible and economically sound solution.*

CARMICHAEL, ALEXANDER DOUGLAS, educator; b. Sliema, Malta, July 19, 1929; s. Adam and Jane (Hamilton) G.; m. Rose Margaret Whittaker, Sept. 1, 1951; children—Gillian Ruth, Alison Rose, Peter Stewart. B.Sc., Plymouth Tech. Coll., London U., 1949; Ph.D., Cambridge U., 1958. Chief engr. Dracone Developments Ltd., London, Eng., 1960-61; sr. project engr. No. Research and Engring. Corp., Cambridge, Mass, 1961-64; research fellow Imperial Coll. Sci. and Tech., London, 1964-68; tech. adv. English Elec. Co. Ltd., Rugby, 1968-70; prof. power engring. Mass. Inst. Tech., 1970—. Mem. Soc. Naval Architects and Marine Engrs., Whitworth Soc. (London), Sigma Xi. Home: 69 Otis St Newtonville MA 02160 Office: Mass Inst Tech Cambridge MA 02139

CARMICHAEL, DAVID BURTON, physician; b. Santa Ana, Calif., Sept. 12, 1923; s. David Burton and Phyllis (Adams) C.; m. Ava Louise Smith, Dec. 26, 1944; children: Catherine Ann, Heather Sue, Linda L., Ava L. Student, Graceland Coll., 1940-42; B.A., M.D., State U. Iowa, 1946; postgrad., Harvard U., 1949-50. Diplomate: Am. Bd. Internal Medicine. Clin. and research fellow medicine Mass. Gen. Hosp., Boston, 1949-50; cons. cardiovascular diseases U.S. Naval Hosp., San Diego, Camp Pendleton, U.S. VA; chief dept. medicine Scripps Meml. Hosp., La Jolla, Calif., 1961-63, 65-67, chief staff, 1970-71; clin. prof. medicine U. Calif. at San Diego, 1968—; pres. De Anza Lab. Corp., 1962-72, Carmichael-Carson Med.-Clin. Lab. Corp., 1962-75; sr. partner Med. Clinic. Contbr. articles to profl. jours. Served to rear adm., med. insp. gen. USNR. Decorated Legion of Merit; recipient Alumni Disting. Service award Graceland Coll., 1967. Fellow A.C.P. (gov. So. Calif. region III 1972-76), Am. Coll. Cardiology (dir., sec. 1975, trustee 1979—), Am. Coll. Chest Physicians; mem. AMA, Am. Heart Assn. (chmn. sect. council on clin. cardiology), San Diego County Heart Assn. (pres. 1959-60), San Diego Biomed. Research Inst. (pres. 1958-59, 62-63, vice chmn. residency rev. com. internal medicine 1971-78), San Diego Soc. Internal Medicine (pres. 1959-61). Republican. Mem. Reformed Ch. of Jesus Christ of Latter-day Saints (elder). Home: 8333 Calle Del Cielo La Jolla CA 92037 Office: 9844 Genesee Suite 400 La Jolla CA 92037 also 3737 3737 Moraga Blvd San Diego CA 92117 *This country, with its Christian heritage, gives to the vast majority the opportunity to serve and often, the chance to excel. The guidance of parents and instructors should never be forgotten, nor should the sacrifices of those who have allowed us to preserve our freedom.*

CARMICHAEL, DONALD SCOTT, lawyer, business executive; b. Toledo, February 19, 1912; s. Grey Thornton and Edna Earle (Jaite) C.; m. Mary Glenn Dickinson, May 28, 1940; children: Mary Brooke, Pamela Hastings. A.B., Harvard U., 1935, law student, 1935-37; LL.B., U. Mich., 1942. Bar: Ohio 1942. Staff dept. law City of Cleve., 1938-40; chief renegotiation br. Cleve. Ordnance Dist., War Dept., 1942-46; practiced in, Cleve., 1946; asst. sec. Diamond Alkali Co., 1946-48, sec., 1948-57, gen. counsel, 1957-58; v.p.-gen. counsel Stouffer Corp., 1959-60, exec. v.p., 1960-64; practiced in, Cleve., 1964-71; pres. Schrafft's div. Pet, Inc., N.Y.C., 1971-75, Sportservice Corp., Buffalo, 1975-80, Del. North Cos., Inc., 1980; officer, dir. various corps. Editor: F.D.R; Columnist, 1947; Contbr. to law revs. Mem. Cuyahoga County Charter Commn., 1959—; chmn.; mem. Cleve. Met. Services Commn., 1957-59, President's Task Force on War Against Poverty, 1964; Del. Democratic Nat. Conv., 1960, 64; mem. Cuyahoga County Dem. Exec. Com.; Chmn. bd. trustees Cuyahoga County Hosps., 1958-64, Urban League, Karamu House. Mem. Am., Ohio, Cleve. bar assns., Phi Gamma Delta. Clubs: Union, Chagrin Valley Hunt (Cleve.); Harvard (N.Y.C.); Buffalo; River (N.Y.C.); Crag Burn Golf (East Aurora, N.Y.). Home: 38 Muirfield Rd East Aurora NY 14052 Office: 700 Delaware Ave Buffalo NY 14209

CARMICHAEL, DOUGLAS, philosophy educator; b. Greenwich, Conn., July 24, 1923; s. George Edgar and Helen Gertrude (Fox) C.; m. Helen Sanborn Edgerly, June 26, 1949 (dec. Oct. 1971); children: Douglas Alasdair, Megan Margaret, Elspeth Edgerly; m. Emma Robertson Grant, Jan. 11, 1975. A.B. summa cum laude, Bowdoin Coll., 1947; M.A., Harvard U., 1948; Ph.D., Ind. U., 1954. Tchr. English Loomis Sch., Windsor, Conn., 1948-49; head, English dept. St. Mark's Sch. Tex., Dallas, 1949-52; instr. philosophy U. Mass., 1954-56; instr. philosophy and acad. counselor Ind. U., S.E. Extension, Jeffersonville, 1956-58; asst. prof. philosophy St. Lawrence U., Canton, N.Y., 1958-63, asso. prof., 1963-65, prof., 1965—, chmn. dept., 1964-83. Translator: Pico della Mirandola (Heptaplus), 1965; author: Pendragon, 1977. Served with AUS, 1943-46. Mem. Am. Philos. Assn., Soc. Ancient Greek Philosophy, Phi Beta Kappa, Kappa Sigma. Republican. Home: 14 Elm St Canton NY 13617

CARMICHAEL, EMMETT BRYAN, biochemist, emeritus educator; b. Shelbyville, Mo., Sept. 4, 1895; s. George Frank and Amelia Grant (Tingle) C.; m. Lelah Marie Van Hook. Student, Central Coll., 1914-16; A.B., U. Colo., 1918; M.S., 1922; Ph.D., U. Cin., 1927; D.Sc. (hon.), Central Methodist Coll., 1979, U. Ala., 1981; postgrad. summers, Northwestern, 1935, Harvard, 1936. Instr. organic chemistry U. Colo., 1919-24; biochemistry U. Cin., 1924-26; bacteriologist William S. Merrill Co., Cin., 1926-27; asst. prof., head dept. physiol. chemistry U. Ala., 1927, asso. prof., 1928-32, prof., 1932-45; prof. biochemistry Med. Coll. Ala., 1945-66, Sch. Dentistry, 1948-66; asst. dean Med. Coll. Ala., Sch. Dentistry, 1959-66, prof. biochemistry emeritus, asst. dean emeritus, 1966; Chmn. N. Central Ala. Regional Sci. Fair, 1954-57. Assembler, editor bibliographies of faculty mems. U. Ala., 1934, ann. supplements, 1935-40; mem. editorial adv. bd.: Scalpel of Alpha Epsilon Delta, 1938-40; editor: Phi Beta Pi Quar, 1945-49, Ala. Jour. Med. Scis, 1964-66; cons. to editorial bd., 1966-73; Contbr. articles to sci. jours. Trustee Wesley Found., U. Ala., 1938-58; trustee Gorgas Scholarship Found., 1947-73, chmn., 1957-73, hon. chmn., 1973—; Acting sec.-mgr. So. Med. Assn., 1948. Served in Ordnance Dept. U.S. Army, 1918-1919; 2d lt. Res., 1919-29. Recipient citations Central Coll., 1954, U. Ala., 1966; William Crawford Gorgas award Med. Assn. Ala., 1966; named to Ala. Acad. Honor, 1973; apptd. hon. lt. col. a.-d.-c. Ala. Militia, 1976. Fellow A.A.A.S. (chmn. acad. conf. 1933), Am. Inst. Chemists (hon., nat. councilor 1952-54, pres. Ala. 1962-63, nat. pres. 1967-69, chmn. bd. 1969-71, Gold medal 1971, dir.-at-large 1971-73), Internat. Coll. Anesthetists; mem. A.M.A., Am. Assn. Clin. Chemists (chmn. edn. com. 1954-58, mem. nat. exec. com. 1956-57), Am. Bd. Clin. Chemistry, Am. Chem. Soc. (So. Chemist award Memphis sect. 1965, vice chmn. Ala. sect. 1932-34, chmn. 1934-35), Am. Soc. Biol. Chem., Soc. Exptl. Biology, Med. (past vice chmn. So. sect.), Am. Physiol. Soc., Ala. Acad. Sci. (pres. 1930-31, editor jour. 1942-48, trustee 1970—, now hon. mem.), Am. Assn. Hist. Med., Sigma Phi Epsilon (alumni citation 1967, dist. gov. 1942-46, Order of Golden Heart 1973), Sigma Xi (1st pres. Ala. chpt. 1939-40), Alpha Chi Sigma, Alpha Epsilon Delta (Distinguished Service award 1966, grand pres. 1932-38, So. councilor 1938-40, nat. councilor 1940-51), Gamma Sigma Epsilon, Phi Beta Pi (So. praetor 1934-39, mem. council 1943-67, Man of Year 1954, supreme archon 1950-52). Democrat. Methodist. Clubs: Mason (32 deg., Shriner), Acacia (Order of Pythagoras 1966), Sojourners, Mark Twain. Home: 3501 Redmont Rd Birmingham AL 35213 Office: University Station Birmingham AL 35294 *Much of my success as a scientist is due to the training which I had on a Missouri farm, until I graduated from high school. Although there was always hard work to perform, there was time for relaxation and thought. I had time to decide what I did not wish to do as an adult and made plans to attempt the task of becoming the uncommon person.*

CARMICHAEL, IAN STUART EDWARD, geologist, educator; b. London, Mar. 29, 1930; U.S., 1964; s. Edward Arnold and Jeanette (Montgomerie) C.; m. Dione Gilmore Thatcher, Sept. 12, 1970; 1 dau., Anthea; children by previous marriage—Deborah, Graham, Alistair. B.A., Cambridge (Eng.) U., 1954; Ph.D., Imperial Coll. Sci., London U., 1958. Lectr. geology Imperial Coll. Sci. and Tech., 1958-63; NSF sr. fgn. sci. fellow U. Chgo., 1964; mem. faculty U. Calif. at Berkeley, 1964—, prof. geology, 1967—, chmn. dept., 1972-76, 80-82, assoc. dean, 1976-78. Author: Igneous Patrology, 1974; Editor-in-chief: Contributions to Mineralogy and Petrology, 1973—. Home: 784 Cragmont Ave Berkeley CA 94708

CARMICHAEL, MARY MULLOY, fgn. service officer, educator; b. Miles City, Mont., Aug. 6, 1916; d. John William and Laura (Maher) Mulloy; m. John Buford Carmichael (dec. June 1949); m. Roger Goiran, Mar. 13, 1981. Ph.B., Marquette U., 1939, M.A., 1940; postgrad., Am. U., Washington, 1943-49. Asst. to dean Women Marquette U., 1935-40; dean women Thompson Falls (Mont.) pub. schs., 1940-42; personnel officer War Dept., Washington, 1942-44; chief overseas classification and wage adminstrn. OWI, Washington and, London, 1944-45; successively chief salary adminstrn. sect., asst. planning adviser, asst. chief pay leave and retirement br. State Dept., 1945-56; fgn. service officer, 1956-69, 1st sec., consul, Brussels, Belgium, 1959-64; 1st. sec., econ. officer Am. embassy, Leopoldville, Congo, 1964-65; econ. officer U.S. delegation OECD, Paris, 1964-65; asst. econ. adviser U.S. del. NATO, 1965-66, spl. asst. to ambassador, also U.S. rep. to coordinating com. of govt. experts, 1966-69, also U.S. relocation coordinator, Paris, Brussels, 1967-69; chmn. internat. bus. adminstrn. and econs. dept., vis. prof. Am. Coll. Switzerland, Leysin, 1969—; also cons. Recipient Superior Service award Dept. State, 1968; Merit award Marquette U., 1978. Mem. Fgn. Service Assn., Alpha Kappa Delta. Clubs: Countryside Tennis and Social (Clearwater, Fla.); Dunedin (Fla.); Boat. Office: PO Box 1044 Dunedin FL 33528

CARMICHAEL, VIRGIL WESLY, coal company executive, mining and geological engineer; b. Pickering, Mo., Apr. 26, 1919; s. Ava Abraham and Rosevelt (Murphy) C.; m. Emma Margaret Freeman, Apr. 1, 1939; m. Colleen Fern Wadsworth, Oct. 29, 1951; children: Bonnie Rae, Peggy Ellen, Jacki Ann. B.S., U. Idaho, 1951, M.S., 1956; Ph.D., Columbia Pacific U., Mill Valley, Calif., 1980. Registered geol., mining and civil engr., geologist, land surveyor. Asst. geologist Day Mines, Wallace, Idaho, 1950; mining engr. De Anza Engring. Co., 1950-52; hwy. engring. asst. N.Mex. Hwy. Dept., Santa Fe, 1952-53; asst. engr. U. Idaho, 1953-56; minerals analyst Idaho Bur. Mines, 1953-56; mining engr. No. Pacific Ry. Co., St. Paul, 1956-67; geologist N.Am. Coal Corp., Cleve., 1967-69, asst. v.p. engring., 1969-74, v.p., head exploration dept., 1974—. Asst. chief distbn. CD Emergency Mgmt. Fuel Resources for N.D., 1968—; bd. dirs., chmn. fund drive Bismarck-Mandan Orch. Assn., 1979-83; bd. dirs. Bismarck Arts and Galleries Assn., 1982—; mem. Nat. Def. Exec. Res., 1983—. Served with USNR, 1944-46. Recipient award A for Sci. writing Sigma Gamma Epsilon. Mem. Am. Inst. Profl. Geologists (past pres. local chpt.), Rocky Mountain Coal Mining Inst. (v.p.), N.D. Geol. Soc., AIME (past chmn. local sect.), Am. Mining Congress (bd. govs. western div. 1973—), Sigma Xi. Republican. Lodges: Kiwanis; Masons; Elks. Home: 1013 N Anderson St Bismark ND 58501 Office: Kirkwood Office Tower Bismarck ND 58501 *I have striven, and will continue to strive, to have the geological profession recognized for the benefits it has provided, and will continue to provide, all humanity. I hope to assist in establishing greater use of the profession in the future.*

CARMICHAEL, WILLIAM DANIEL, Foundation official; b. Denver, Sept. 5, 1929; s. Fitzhugh Lee and Anna Devona (Sullivan) C.; m. Faith Young, June 21, 1958; children: Amy, Philip Fitzhugh, Daniel Owen. A.B., Yale, 1950; M.A., M.P.A., Princeton, 1952, Ph.D., 1959; B.Litt. (Rhodes scholar), Oxford (Eng.) U., 1955. Legislative analyst U.S. Bur. Budget, 1955-56, budget analyst, 1956-57; lectr. econs. and pub. affairs Princeton, 1957-60, asst. prof., 1960-62; dir. undergrad. program Woodrow Wilson Sch. Pub. and Internat. Affairs, 1958-62; prof. econ. policy, dean Grad. Sch. Bus. and Pub. Adminstrn., Cornell U., 1962-68; rep. Ford Found., Brazil, 1968-71, head office, Latin Am., Caribbean, and N.Y.C., 1971-77, Middle East and Africa, 1977-81, v.p. for developing country programs, 1981—. Mem. Council on Fgn. Relations, Assn. Am. Rhodes Scholars, Phi Beta Kappa. Home: 523 N Maple Greenwich CT 06830 also Van Hornesville NY 13475 Office: 320 E 43d St New York NY 10017

CARMICHAEL, WILLIAM JEROME, publishing company executive; b. Evanston, Ill., Sept. 27, 1920; s. Wilbur Jerome and Florence Jenny (Varns) C.; m. Doreen Shirley Davis, Jan. 12, 1946; children: Sally Ann Carmichael Wallace, Bruce Richard. A.B., U. Ill., 1942. With Victor div. RCA, 1942-45; with Sales and Mktg. Mgmt. mag., and (predecessor), Chgo., 1945-77, Goldenrod, Fla., 1977—, sr. v.p., 1960—; pub., dir. Survey of Buying Power, 1973—; cons., lectr. in field. Mem. exec. bd. N.E. Ill. council Boy Scouts Am., 1970-71; pres. David Kinley Ednl. Found., 1968-77; trustee U. Ill. YMCA, 1967-77; bd. dirs. Winter Park YMCA, 1978-81. Recipient Disting. Salesman award N.Y. Sales Exec., 1954; Loyalty award U. Ill., 1963; Silver Beaver award Boy Scouts Am., 1968. Mem. Internat. Newspaper Advt. and Mktg. Execs. Assn., Internat. Newspaper Promotion Assn., U. Ill. Alumni Assn. (pres. 1961-63), Sales and Mktg. Execs. Assn. Chgo. (pres. 1970-71), U. Ill. Found., Sales and Mktg. Execs. Internat. (v.p. 1976-77), Winter Park (Fla.) C. of C., Goldenrod Area C. of C., Phi Gamma Delta. Republican. Methodist. Clubs: Univ. of Chgo. (dir. 1974-76), Illini of Chgo. (Chgo.) (pres. 1956-57); Orange County East Rotary (Winter Park), pres. 1982-83); Citrus (Orlando, Fla.)). Home: 4000 Tuskawilla Road South Goldenrod FL 32733 Office: PO Drawer 668 Goldenrod FL 32733-0668

CARMIN, ROBERT LEIGHTON, retired geography educator; b. Muncie, Ind., Nov. 28, 1918; s. Zora and Florelda May (Harrison) C.; m. Marie Jane Carr, Nov. 2, 1940; children—Thomas Nelson, James Harrison. B.S. in Edn, Ohio U., 1940; M.A., U. Nebr., 1942; Ph.D. (Salisbury fellow geography), U. Chgo., 1953. Instr. geography Mich. State U., 1942-44, asst. prof., 1947-50; cartographer OSS, 1944-45; from asst. prof. to prof. geography U. Ill., 1951-62; dir. Center Latin Am. Studies, 1959-62; head Latin Am. studies unit U.S. Office Edn., 1962; dean Coll. Scis. and Humanities, 1962-80; prof. geography Ball State U., from 1962, now ret.; Cons. lang. devel. br. U.S. Office Edn., 1963-64; cons. NSF, 1964-76; internat. programs com. Am. Assn. State Colls. and Univs., 1966-76; com. geography Nat. Acad. Sci.-NRC, 1961-66; sec.-treas. Asso. Univs. for Internat. Edn., Inc., 1968-70, v.p., 1970-72; U.S. del. 6th Gen. Assembly Pan Am. Inst. Geography and History, Buenos Aires, Argentina, 1961. Author: Anápolis, Brazil: Regional Capital of an Agricultural Frontier, 1953; also articles.; Coeditor: Geographic Research On Latin America-Benchmark 1970, 1971. Pan Am. World Airways travel fellow, Brazil, 1948; adviser AID, Brazil, 1965; grantee U.S. Office Edn., Brazil, 1948-49; Office Q.M. Gen., Brazil, 1956; Fulbright scholar U. de Cuyo, Mendoza, Argentina, 1958; grantee U. Ill. Research Bd., Brazil, 1961, Am. Assn. Colls. Tchr. Edn., Peru, 1963. Mem. Ill. Acad. Sci. (geography sect. 1955-56), Conf. Latin Americanist Geographers (co-founder, dir. 1971-72), Ind. Acad. of Social Scis. (dir. 1967-68), Assn. Am. Geographers (past pres. West Lakes div., ofcl. rep. to Internat. Council Edn. for Teaching, Brazil 1963), Assn. Latin Am. Studies (past pres.), Nat. Council Geog. Edn., Assn. dos Geografos Brasileiros, Latin Am. Studies Assn., Sigma Xi, Sigma Delta Pi. Club: Rotarian. Home: 1220 Miramar St Apt 210 Cape Coral FL 33904 Office: Ball State U Muncie IN 47306 *In a time of trial one of my professional mentors taught me the value of the aphorism: "Everything is important, but nothing is important." Give it your best, but don't fret when things aren't perfect—the world doesn't revolve around you alone.*

CARMODY, ARTHUR RODERICK, JR., lawyer; b. Shreveport, La., Feb. 19, 1928; s. Arthur R. and Caroline (Gaughan) C.; m. Renee Aubry, Jan. 26, 1952; children: Helen Bragg, Renee, Arthur Roderick, Patrick, Timothy, Mary, Virginia, Joseph. B.S., Fordham U., 1949; LL.B., La. State U., 1952. Bar: La. 1952. Mem. firm Wilkinson & Carmody, Shreveport, 1952—; dir. Kansas City So. Transport Co., Kansas City, Shreveport and Gulf Terminal Co., Shreveport Captains Baseball Club. Chmn. Met. Shreveport Zoning Bd. Appeals, 1959-72; bd. dirs. Caddo Dem. Assn., Shreveport, 1966—; pres. bd. trustees Jesuit High Sch., Shreveport; trustee Schumpert Med. Ctr., Shreveport; bd. dirs. La. State U. Found., Baton Rouge, Agnew Day Sch., Shreveport, Ridgewood Montessori Sch., Shreveport; mem. adv. council La. State U., Shreveport; nat. bd. dirs. N.Mex. Mil. Inst., Roswell, 1967—. Fellow Am. Coll. Trial Lawyers; mem. ABA, Fed. Bar Assn., La. Bar Assn., Shreveport Bar Assn., Am. Judicature Soc., La. Law Inst., Nat. Assn. R.R. Trial Counsel, La. Assn. Def. Counsel, Nat. Acad. Law and Medicine, Tarshar Soc., Shreveport C. of C. (dir. 1967—), Soc. Hosp. Council, La. Civil Service League, Phi Delta Phi, Kappa Alpha. Roman Catholic. Clubs: Shreveport; Petroleum (Shreveport); University, Pierremont Oaks Tennis. Home: 255 Forest Ave Shreveport LA 71104 Office: Wilkinson & Carmody Beck Bldg Shreveport LA 71166

CARMONY, D(ONALD) DUANE, physicist; b. Indpls., Sept. 16, 1935; s. Donald F. and Edith B. (Hagelskamp) C.; m. Patricia Myrl Palmer, Dec. 29, 1962; children—P. Diane, Debra Jean. B.S. in Physics, Ind. U., 1956; postgrad. (Rotary internat. fellow), U. Gottingen, W. Ger., 1958-59; Ph.D. in Physics, U. Calif., Berkeley, 1962. Research asso. UCLA, 1962-63, U. Calif., San Diego, 1963-66, lectr., Berkeley, 1966; asso. prof. physics Purdue U., 1966-75, prof., 1975—; Sr. Fulbright scholar, Australia, 1979-80, Sr. Alexander von Humboldt fellow, Munich, Germany, 1972-73. Contbr. numerous articles to profl. jours. Fellow Am. Phys. Soc. Office: Dept Physics Purdue U West Lafayette IN 47907

CARMONY, MARVIN DALE, educator, linguist; b. nr. Richmond, Ind., Feb. 27, 1923; s. Harry Edgar and Ellen (Brown) C.; m. Mary Joan Nicholson, May 31, 1947; children—Ronald Dee, Kathryn Lynn. Student, Valparaiso Tech. Inst., 1941-42, Olivet Nazarene Coll., 1947-49; A.B., Ind. State U., 1950, M.A., 1951; Ph.D., Ind. U., 1965. Radio operator Am. Airlines, Chgo., 1942-44; tchr. high schs., Pendleton and Shelbyville, Ind., 1953-59; instr. English Ind. State U., Terre Haute, 1959-63, asst. prof., 1963-66, asso. prof. English and linguistics, 1966-69, prof., 1969—; asso. dean Coll. Arts and Scis., 1970—; Founder, dir. Ind. Place-Names Survey, 1968-70; co-founder Ind. Names (now Midwestern Jour. Lang. and Folklore), 1970, gen. editor, 1970—. Author: (with D.F. Carmony) Indiana Dialects in Their Historical Setting, 1972, rev. edit., 1979, (with Ronald Baker) Indiana Place Names, 1975; also articles. Trustee Olivet Nazarene Coll., 1967-70. Served with U.S. Mcht. Marine, 1944-46. Am. Council Learned Socs. fellow, 1964-65. Mem. AAUP, Am. Dialect Soc. (adv. bd. publs. 1972-77, pres. 1981—), Soc. Wireless Pioneers, Am. Names Soc. (mem. editorial bd. Am. Speech 1977), Linguistic Soc. Am., Modern Lang. Assn., Nat. Soc. XVII Century Colonial Dames (Disting. Ser. award 1975), Phi Delta Lambda, Phi Delta Kappa. Methodist (lay leader 1981—). Home: 227 Madison Blvd Terre Haute IN 47803

CARNAHAN, A. VERNON, lawyer; b. Latrobe, Pa., Jan. 4, 1917; s. Dewey S. and Ella (Rosborough) C.; m. Alice Kellogg, June 2, 1941; children: Jon Stephen, Ellen Denise, Barry Craig, Judith Lynn. B.A., Drew U., 1939, LL.D., 1979; LL.B., Duke U., 1942. Bar: N.Y. 1943, U.S. Dist. Ct. (so. dist.) N.Y. 1954, U.S. Dist. Ct. (ea. dist.) 1960, U.S. Ct. Appeals (2d cir.) 1959, U.S. Dist. Ct. (we. dist.) N.Y. 1947, U.S. Dist. Ct. (no. dist.) Tex. 1978, U.S. Ct. Appeals (7th cir.) 1980, U.S. Ct. Appeals (9th cir.) 1980, U.S. Ct. Appeals (5th cir.) 1981, U.S. Ct. Appeals (11th cir.) 1981, U.S. Supreme Ct. 1962. Assoc. Donovan Leisure Newton & Irvine, N.Y.C., 1942-59, ptnr., 1959—. Served to 1st lt. U.S. Army, 1943-46. Mem. ABA, N.Y. State Bar Assn., Assn. Bar City N.Y. Republican. Club: Circumnavigators (N.Y.C.). Home: 257 Fairmount Ave Chatham NJ 07928 Office: Donovan Leisure Newton & Irvine 30 Rockefeller Plaza New York NY 10112

CARNAHAN, BRICE, chemical engineer, educator; b. New Philadelphia, Ohio, Oct. 13, 1933; s. Paul Tracy and Amelia Christina (Gray) C. B.S., Case Western Res. U., 1955, M.S., 1957; Ph.D., U. Mich., 1965. Lectr. in engring. biostatistics U. Mich., Ann Arbor, 1959-64, asst. prof. chem. engring. and biostatics, 1965-68, asso. prof., 1968-70, prof. chem. engring., 1970—; vis. prof. U. Pa., 1970; Mem., chmn. Curriculum Aids for Chem. Engring. Edn. com. Nat. Acad. Engring., 1974-75. Author: (with H.A. Luther and J.O. Wilkes) Applied Numerical Methods, 1969, (with J.O. Wilkes) Digital Computing and Numerical Methods, 1973; Editorial bd.: Jour. Computers and Fluids, 1971—, Computers and Chemical Engineering, 1974—. Mem. communications com. Mich. Council for Arts, 1977—. Mem. Am. Inst. Chem. Engrs. (Computers in Chem. Engring. award 1980, chmn. CAST div. 1981), Assn. for Computing Machinery, AAAS, Sigma Xi, Sigma Nu. Home: 1605 Kearney Rd Ave Ann Arbor MI 48104

CARNAHAN, FRANCES MORRIS, magazine editor; b. Evergreen, Ala., Oct. 28, 1937; d. Houston DeLeon and Rene Vester (Bass) Morris; m. Peter Malott Carnahan, Feb. 13, 1960; children—Brian Morris, Edmund Malott. Student, U. Ala., 1956-58. With Mobile Press-Register, 1956-58, H.L. Green Co., N.Y.C., 1958-60, J.H. Lewis Advt. Agy., Mobile, 1960-61; with Early Am. Life mag., Hist. Times, Inc., Harrisburg, Pa., 1972—; editor Early Am. Life, 1975—. Costume designer, Harrisburg Community Theatre, 1961-71, Gov. Pa. Sch., 1976-77; Author articles. Mem. Am. Soc. Mag. Editors. Home: 1524 Greening Ln Harrisburg PA 17110 Office: Historical Times Inc 2245 Kohn Rd Harrisburg PA 17105

CARNAHAN, ORVILLE DARRELL, college president; b. Elba, Idaho, Dec. 25, 1929; s. Marion Carlos and Leola Pearl (Putnam) C.; m. Colleen Arrott, Dec. 14, 1951; children: Karen, Jeanie, Orville Darrell, Carla. B.S., Utah State U., 1958; M.Ed., U. Idaho, 1962, Ed.D., 1964. Vocat. dir., v.p. Yakima Valley Coll., Yakima, Wash., 1964-69; chancellor Eastern Iowa Community Coll. Dist., Davenport, 1969-71; pres. Highline Coll., Midway Wash., 1971-76; asso. Utah Commr. for Higher Edn., Salt Lake City, 1976-78; pres. So. Utah State Coll., Cedar City, 1978-81, Utah Tech. Coll., Salt Lake City, 1981—; cons. to various orgns. Active Boy Scouts Am. Served with U.S. Army, 1952-54; Korea. Mem. Am. Vocat. Assn., NEA, Idaho Hist. Soc., Utah Hist. Soc., Alpha Tau Alpha, Phi Delta Kappa. Mem. Ch. of Jesus Christ of Latter-Day Saints. Home: 1088 W Fairhaven Circle Murray UT 84107 Office: 4600 S Redroad Rd Salt Lake City UT 84107

CARNAHAN, ROBERT DEAN, manufacturing company executive; b. Pontiac, Mich., June 14, 1931; s. Clarence A. and Lena Ann (Rose) C.; m. Judith L. Isola, Dec. 29, 1953; children: Michael, Patrick, Kirstina, Kevin. B.S. with honors in Metall. Engring. (univ. scholar 1949-53), Mich. Tech. U., 1953; postgrad., U. Minn., 1957-59; Ph.D., Northwestern U., 1963. Registered profl. engr., Calif. With Honeywell Co., 1956-59, mgr. quality control lab., New Brighton, Minn., 1959; research asso., teaching asst. Northwestern U., 1960-62; with Aerospace Corp., El Segundo, Calif., 1962-68, asst. dept. head, 1966-68; dir. materials sci. lab. Universal Oil Products Co., Des Plaines, Ill., 1968-73; dir. research elec. electronics lab., dir. corp. office tech. devel. Gould Inc., Rolling, Meadows, Ill., 1973-80; sr. v.p. sci. and tech. U.S. Gypsum Co., Chgo., 1980—; mem. NATO spl. program panel for materials sci. NATO Sci. Co., 1982-85, chmn., 1983. Author. Bd. dirs. Ill. Sci. Lectures Assn.; Pres. Barrington (Ill.) Babe Ruth League, 1969-70; treas. Timberlake Civic Assn., 1970-71. Served with USNR, 1953-56; Korea. Recipient Alumni award U. Mich., 1949. Mem. IEEE, AAAS, Electrochem. Soc., Blue Key, Sigma Xi. Lutheran. Club: Masons. Patentee in field. Home: 69 Lakeshore Dr Barrington IL 60010 Office: 101 S Wacker Dr Chicago IL 60606

CARNEAL, GEORGE UPSHUR, lawyer; b. N.Y.C., May 31, 1935. A.B., Princeton U., 1957; LL.B., U. Va., 1961. Bar: Va. bar 1961, D.C. bar 1962. Law clk. to judge U.S. Ct. Appeals, D.C. Circuit, 1961-62; asso. firm Hogan & Hartson, Washington, 1962-68, partner, 1973—; spl. asst. to sec. Dept. Transp., Washington, 1969-70; gen. counsel FAA, Washington, 1970-73; lectr. Georgetown U. Law Center, 1965-68; chmn. bd. trustees D.C. Bar Clients Security Trust Fund, 1973-78. Decisions editor: Va. Law Rev, 1960-61; contbr. articles to legal jours. Mem. Am. Bar Assn., Fed. Bar Assn., Bar Assn. D.C., Raven Soc., Order of Coif. Office: 815 Connecticut Ave NW Washington DC 20006

CARNEAL, JAMES WILLIAM, natural gas corp. exec.; b. McCracken County, Ky., Sept. 22, 1918; s. William Tell and Jeanette (Throgmorton) C.; m. Mary Thrawley, June 22, 1956; children—James William, Jr., Robert Eugene. B.S. in Agr. and Edn, Murray State U., 1940; postgrad., U. Ky., 1946, 48, Columbia U., 1961. Tchr. agr. Hodgenville (Ky.) Bd. Edn., 1947-48; agr. supr. VA, Louisville, 1948-49; with Tex. Gas Transmission Corp., Owensboro, Ky., 1949—, chief conservationist, 1949-53, mgr. co. housing, 1951-53, asst. supt. pipeline, 1953-55, indsl. rep., 1955-56, asst. dir. sales and customer relations, 1956-58, dir. sales and customer relations, 1958-59, asst. to v.p., 1959-63, v.p., 1963-79, sr. v.p. public affairs, 1979—. City commr., Owensboro, 1964-65, 1967-69; mem. exec. bd. Audubon council Boy Scouts Am., 1960—; chmn., bd. dirs. Wendell Foster Center, 1957—; vice chmn. Murray State Bd. Regents, 1975—. Mem. Am. Gas Assn. (chmn. com.), Interstate Natural Gas Assn., Am., Mid-Continent Gas and Oil Assn., So. Gas Assn., Ohio Valley Improvement Assn., Spindletop Research Found. Democrat. Methodist. Clubs: Owensboro Country, Campbell, National Democratic, Masons. Home: 1630 Linden Ave Owensboro KY 42301 Office: 3800 Frederica St Owensboro KY 42301

CARNEGIE, JAMES GORDON, assn. exec.; b. Toronto, Ont., Can., Oct. 22, 1934; s. Frederick Thomas and Helen Weber (Bawden) C.; m. Gail Elizabeth Jarvis, June 25, 1955; children—Elizabeth Anne, Martha Jane, Christopher James. Student, Upper Can. Coll., Forest Hill Collegiate Inst. Bond trader A.E. Ames & Co. Ltd., 1954-56; unlisted trader Wisener & Co. Ltd., Toronto, 1956-62; dir., mgr. trading dept. McConnell & Co. Ltd., Toronto, 1962-67; dir. Wisener, Mackellar & Co. Ltd., Toronto, 1967-72, v.p., 1969-70, exec. v.p., 1970-72; gen. mgr. Ont. C. of C., Toronto, 1972—. Mem. Bd. Trade Met. Toronto. Constable, Met. Toronto Aux. Police, 1955-57; sgt. Met. Toronto Aux. Police, 1957-59, insp., 1959-62, exec. officer, 1962-67, staff supt., comdg., 1967—. Named Policeman of Month Toronto Jr. Bd. Trade, 1970. Mem. C. of C. Execs. of Can., Ont. C. of C. Execs., Internat. Police Assn., Upper Can. Coll. Old Boys Assn. Anglican. Clubs: Empire, Canadian, Royal Canadian Mil. Inst. Home: 191 Yonge Blvd Toronto ON M5M 3H5 Canada Office: 2323 Yonge St Toronto ON M4P 2C9 Canada

CARNELL, PAUL HERBERT, chemist, educator; b. Oakfield, Wis., May 27, 1917; s. Herbert Clyde and Fannie (Carstens) C.; m. Phyllis Martha Whipple, June 21, 1942; children—Nancy, Michael, Cheryl, Beth, Cara. A.B. with high honors, Albion Coll., 1939; Ph.D. (Wyandotte research fellow), Case. Western Res. U., 1943; postgrad (USPHS fellow), Yale, 1959-60. Research chemist Phillips Petroleum Co., 1943-47; dir. research Leonard Refineries, Inc., Alma, Mich., 1947-48; asst. prof. Marietta Coll., 1948-49; faculty Albion Coll., 1949-66, prof. chemistry, chmn. dept., 1954-66; edn. specialist U.S. Office Edn., Washington, 1966-68, asst. dir. div. instl. devel., 1966—; Vis. scientist div. chem. edn. Am. Chem. Soc., 1959-66; in-service inst. dir. NSF, 1961-62; asso. program dir. Acad. Yr. Insts., 1964-65; mem. sci. com. Mich. Dept. Pub. Instrn., 1961-65; vis. scientist Mich. Acad. Sci., Arts and Letters, 1960-66. Contbr. articles to profl. jours. Grantee Research Corp., 1952; NIH, 1959-66. Mem. Am. Chem. Soc., Mich. Coll. Chemistry Tchrs. Assn. (past pres.), Midwest Assn. Chemistry Tchrs., Liberal Arts Colls. (past mem. exec. com., pres. 1963-64), Yale Chemists Assn. Patentee petroleum processing and refining. Home: 1209 Highland Dr Silver Spring MD 20910 Office: Dept Edn Washington DC 20202

CARNER, JOANNE GUNDERSON, profl. golfer; b. Kirkland, Wash., Mar. 4, 1939; m. Donald Carner. Student, Ariz. State U. Profl. golfer Ladies Profl. Golf Assn. tour, 1970—. Winner Women's U.S. Golf Assn. Women's Open, 1971, other including; Colgate Triple Crown; Peter Jackson Classic; Honda Civic Classic; Women's Kemper Open; Lady Keystone Opera; S & H Classic, Ladies Profl. Golf Assn. matchplay championship, 1979, Turnberry Isle Classic, 1982, U.S. Golf Assn. amateur title, 1957, 60, 62, 66, 68 *

CARNE-ROSS, DONALD S., educator. William Goodwin Aurelio Prof. of Greek Lang. and Lit. Boston U., prof. classics and modern langs. Office: Boston U. Dept. Modern Langs Boston MA 02215

CARNES, JAMES ROBERT, retired naval officer, trade association executive; b. Acworth, Ga., Oct. 23, 1909; s. James Erwin and Fannie (McDowell) C.; m. Virginia Richmond, Aug. 20, 1940; 1 son, Thomas Peter. B.S., Ga. Inst. Tech., 1930; J.D., Emory U., 1935; postgrad., George Washington U., 1962-63. Bar: Ga. bar 1935, D.C. bar 1962. Operating mgr. B.F. Goodrich Co., Johnson City, Tenn., 1930-33; practiced in, Columbus, Ga., 1936-41, 46; served to comdr. USNR, 1941-46; commd. USN, 1946, advanced through grades to capt., 1954; asst. judge adv. gen. Navy, 1959-61; ret., 1961; dir. govt. relations Chem. Mfrs. Assn., Washington, 1962-67, sec.-treas., 1967—, v.p., 1972-73; ret., 1973. Decorated Bronze Star. Mem. Alpha Tau Omega, Phi Delta Phi, Phi Kappa Phi. Democrat. Clubs: Army Navy Country (Washington); Farmington Country (Charlottesville, Va.). Home: 5702 Overlea Rd Bethesda MD 20816

CARNES, WILSON WOODROW, magazine editor; b. Albertville, Ala., June 25, 1924; s. Thomas Jefferson and Alice Jeanetta (Chitwood) C.; m. Elizabeth Mae Lynch, Oct. 10, 1951; children: Elizabeth Anne, Alice Sue, Wilson Woodrow. B.S. in Agrl. Edn, Auburn (Ala.) U., 1949, postgrad., 1950, 54. Engaged in farming, 1942-44, tchr. vocat. agr. to vets., Marshall County, Ala., 1949-50; market news analyst Ala. Dept. Agr., Montgomery, 1950-52; part-time farm reporter Sta. WSFA, Montgomery, 1951-52; vocat. agr. Future Farmers Am.; editor Ala. assn. Future Farmers Am., Auburn, 1953-54; asso. editor nat. Future Farmer, Alexandria, Va., 1955-58, editor, 1958-82; adminstrv. dir. Future Farmers Am., 1982—; editor-in-chief Nat. Future Farmer, 1982—. Mem. President's Com. Employment Handicapped, 1975—; mem. nat. agrl. edn. adv. council, agrl. div. Am. Vocat. Assn., 1975-80, Sec., Hybla Valley Civic Assn., 1961-62. Served with inf. AUS, 1944-46. Decorated Combat Inf. badge, Purple Heart; named Hon. State Farmer, A la. assns. Future Farmers Am., 1954; Hon. Am. Farmer Future Farmers Am., 1959. Hon. life mem. Nat. Vocat. Agrl. Tchrs. Assn., Alpha Tau Alpha.; Mem. Am. Agrl. Editors Assn. (pres. 1974-75), Agrl. Relations Council, Agrl. Council Am., Nat. Assn. Suprs. Agrl. Edn., Future Farmers Am. Alumni Assn., Auburn U. Alumni Assn. Presbyterian. Home: 9105 Patton Blvd Alexandria VA 22309 Office: PO Box 15130 5631 Mt Vernon Hwy Alexandria VA 22309

CARNESE, PAUL JOSEPH, JR., publishing company executive; b. N.Y.C., May 21, 1926; s. Paul J. and Anna (Radosta) C.; m. Caroline L. Moccia, July 21, 1951; children: Kathleen, Denise, Paula, Gregory, Patricia, Christopher. Student, Cornell U., 1944, Bucknell U., 1946-48; B.S., N.Y. U., 1950. Mgr. sales promotion McGraw-Hill Book Co., N.Y.C., 1950-54, Caldwell-Clements, pubs., 1954-56; promotion mgr. McGraw-Hill Pub. Co., N.Y.C., 1956-66, marketing service mgr., 1966-70, sales mgr., 1970-73; v.p., pub. R.R. Bowker Co. div. Xerox Pub. Co., N.Y.C., 1973-82; with Patient Care Communications, Inc., Darien, Conn., 1982—. Served with AUS, 1944-46. Mem. Assn. Am. Pubs., Am. Mgmt. Assn., Internat. Platform Assn., Sigma Phi Epsilon., Sigma Delta Chi. Roman Catholic. Club: K.C. Home: 200 Joan Dr Fairfield CT 06430 Office: Patient Care Communications Inc 16 Thorndal Circle Darien CT

CARNEY, ARTHUR WILLIAM MATTHEW, actor; b. Mt. Vernon, N.Y., Nov. 4, 1918; s. Edward M. and Helen (Farrell) C.; m. Jean Myers, Aug. 15, 1940,; remarried Mar. 1977; children—Eileen, Brian, Paul; m. Barbara Isaac. Student pub. schs. Mem., Horace Heidt Orchestra, 1936-39, vaudeville and club entertainer, 1939-40; radio performer, 1942-44, 45-49; TV actor: featured in comedy and dramatic roles with The Chevy Show, Morey Amsterdam, Henry Morgan, Jackie Gleason, Studio One, Kraft Theatre, 1949—, Omnibus, Climax, Playhouse 90, others; Rope Dancers, 1957-58, Harvey, 1958; actor in Broadway play Take Her, She's Mine, 1961-62, Odd Couple, 1965, Lovers, 1968, Prisoner of Second Avenue, 1972-73; actor: in motion picture The Yellow Rolls Royce, 1964, Harry and Tonto, 1974, W.W. and the Dixie Dancekings, 1975, Won Ton Ton, 1976, The Late Show, 1977, Movie Movie, 1978, House Calls, 1978, Sunburn, 1979, Going in Style, 1979, Defiance, 1980, Roadie, 1980, Steel, 1980; appeared in TV movies: Death Scream, 1975, Katherine, 1975, Lanigan's Rabbi, 1976, Scott Joplin, King of Ragtime, 1978; Recipient (1959-60 TV Acad. Emmy award for outstanding humor program 1960, Emmy award for individual achievement 1953, 54, 55, 68); recipient (Sylvania award 1954, 59, Acad. award as best actor Harry and Tonto 1974, Best Actor award Nat. Soc. Film Critics 1977). Served with U.S. Army, 1944-45. Mem. Screen Actors Guild, AFTRA, Actors Equity. Club: Players. Address: care Internat Creative Mgmt 8899 Beverly Blvd Los Angeles CA 90048 *

CARNEY, DENNIS JOSEPH, steel co. exec.; b. Charleroi, Pa., Mar. 19, 1921; s. Walter Augustus and Ann (Nandor) C.; m. Virginia M. Horvath, June 12, 1943; children—Colleen A., Dennis Joseph, Glenn P., Lynn C., Dianne V. B.S. in Metallurgy, Pa. State U., 1942; Sc.D., Mass. Inst. Tech., 1949. With U.S. Steel Corp., Pitts., 1942-74, gen. supt., 1963-65, v.p. long range planning, 1965-68, v.p. applied research, 1968-72, v.p. research, 1972-74; v.p. operations Wheeling-Pitts. Steel Corp., 1974-75, exec. v.p., dir., 1975-76, pres., 1976—, chief operating officer, 1976-77, chief exec. officer, 1977—, chmn. bd., 1978—. Author: (with others) Gases in Metals, 1956. Bd. dirs. Wheeling (W.Va.) Coll. Served to lt. (j.g.) USNR, 1943-46. Fellow Am. Soc. Metals (Grossmann award Pitts. chpt. 1959, trustee 1972—); mem. Am., Brit., Internat. iron and steel insts., Am. Inst. Mining, Metall. and Petroleum Engrs. (McKune award 1951, Benjamin F. Fairless award 1978), Am. Iron and Steel Engrs., Sigma Xi, Tau Beta Pi, Sigma Nu. Clubs: South Hills Country, Duquesne (Pitts.) (dir.); Laurel Valley Country, Fox Chapel Country. Home: 4536 Brownsville Rd Pittsburgh PA 15236 Office: 4 Gateway Center Pittsburgh PA 15230

CARNEY, JAMES F., archbishop; b. Vancouver, C., Can., June 28, 1915; s. John and Ethel (Crook) C. Ed., Vancouver Coll., Jr. Sem. of Christ the King, 1930-38, St. Joseph's Sem., Alta., Can., 1938-42. Ordained priest Roman Catholic Ch., 1942; pastor Corpus Christi Ch., Vancouver, later vicar gen., domestic prelate; consecrated bishop, 1966; aux. bishop of, Vancouver, 1966-69, installed as archbishop for,

1969. Home: 4670 S Piccadilly St West Vancouver BC Canada Office: 150 Robson St Vancouver BC Canada V6B 2A7

CARNEY, PRICE FELTS, retired insurance company executive; b. Nashville, Apr. 28, 1917; s. Herschel Koster and Ida May (Price) C.; m. Lois Jeanne Hudson, Aug. 14, 1954; 1 son, Price Felts. B.A., Vanderbilt U., 1941. Clk. cashier's office Equitable Life Assurance Soc. U.S., Nashville, 1934-37; clk. Life & Casualty Ins. Co., Nashville, 1937-41, asst. sec., 1946-59, sec., 1959-82. Mem. Nashville City Bd. Edn., 1957-62, chmn. vocational and recreation com., 1957-62; mem. Nashville Motion Picture Bd. Censors, 1953-63; hon. mem. bd. dirs., past v.p. Nashville-Davidson County unit Am. Cancer Soc.; bd. dirs. Music City Softball Assn. Served to maj. AUS, 1941-45. Decorated Bronze Star. Mem. Nashville C. of C., 80th Div. Vets. Assn. (vice comdr), Am. Legion, Sigma Nu Alumni Assn. Democrat. Mem. Ch. of Christ. Clubs: Mason (32 deg.); Nat. Commodore; City (Nashville) (v.p. 1964, dir.); Nashville Quarterback (past dir.), Nashville-Vanderbilt, Green Hills Civitan (Nashville) (past lt. gov. valley dist., past pres.); Temple Hills Country.). Home: 733 Richfield Dr Nashville TN 37205

CARNEY, ROBERT ALFRED, hospital administrator; b. Winnipeg, Man., Can., Feb. 24, 1916; s. Thomas Alfred and Opal Edna (Fogle) C. (parents Am. citizens); m. Jacqueline Briscoe, May 15, 1943; children: Thomas A., Roberta L., Richard D. B.A., Denison U., 1938. Accountant Nat. Cash Register Co., 1938-41; accountant, auditor, controller Miami Valley Hosp., Dayton, O., 1941-47; asst. dir. Ochsner Found. Hosp., New Orleans, 1947-48; adminstrv. dir. Jewish Hosp., Cin., 1948-61, asso. exec. dir., 1961-68, exec. dir., 1968-78; cons. mgmt. and employee relations Children's Hosp. Med. Center, Cin., 1979; adminstr. Marjorie P. Lee Home for Aged, Cin., 1980—; adj. asso. prof. hosp. adminstrn. Coll. Pharmacy U. Cin., 1969-78; adj. faculty mem., grad. program hosp. adminstrn. Xavier U., Cin., 1970-78; Trustee Health Careers Greater Cin., 1956—, 1st v.p., 1970—; mem. exec. com., trustee Health Careers of Ohio, 1973-81, treas., 1976-79; trustee Am. Nurses Assn. Nat. Retirement Plan, 1973-75; pres. Withrow High Sch. PTA, 1969-71; mem. bd., pres. Bapt. Home Benevolent Soc., 1974—; mem. bd. Jewish Fedn. Cin., 1969-70, 72-73; mem. racial isolation task force Cin. Pub. Schs., 1972-73, mem. adv. com. for sch. lic. practical nursing, 1973; mem. home health services adv. com. Cin. Dept. Health, 1972—, chmn., 1974-76; mem. adv. com. Lic. Practical Nurse Assn. Ohio, 1979—; mem. Ohio Commn. Nursing, 1973-75, Am. Bd. Med. Specialists, 1977-80; sec. Ohio Council on Nursing Needs and Resources, 1978-81. Recipient Outstanding Preceptor award Xavier U., 1974. Mem. Am. Coll. Hosp. Adminstrs. (life), Am., Ohio hosp. assns., Nat. League for Nursing (dir. 1977-81), Ohio League for Nursing (dir. 1968-76, v.p. 1973-76), Greater Cin. Hosp. Council, Am. Pub. Health Assn., Assembly of Hosp. Schs. Nursing (chmn. bd. 1977-78), Sigma Chi, Phi Mu Alpha. Baptist. Club: Masons. Home: 2721 Grandin Rd Cincinnati OH 45208 Office: 3550 Shaw Ave Cincinnati OH 45208

CARNEY, ROBERT FORREST, lawyer, corporation executive; b. Chgo., Oct. 22, 1905; s. Joseph Michael and Rose Margaret (McShane) C.; m. Lucille Kelly, May 24, 1946 (dec.); children: Michael Kerwin, Robert McShane. Ph.B., U. Wis., 1927; LL.D., Harvard, 1930. Bar: Wis. 1930, Ill. 1937. Sr. partner firm Carney, Crowell & Leibman, Chgo., 1945-51; chmn. bd. Foote, Cone & Belding, Inc., N.Y.C., 1951-66, chmn. finance com., 1967-71. Served with USNR, 1943-45. Decorated chevalier French Legion of Honor. Clubs: Brook, Racquet and Tennis (N.Y.C.); Shinnecock Hills Golf, Southampton (Southampton, N.Y.); Everglades, Seminole Golf, Bath and Tennis (Palm Beach, Fla.). Home: 340 S Ocean Blvd Palm Beach FL 33480

CARNEY, ROBERT JOSEPH, airline executive; b. Worcester, Mass., July 22, 1940; s. Joseph F. and Helen A. (MacVicar) C.; m. Nancy L. Doerr, May 19, 1973. A.B. summa cum laude, Brown U., 1961; M.B.A., Harvard U., 1963. Asso. Dillon, Read & Co., Inc., N.Y.C., 1964-65, S.G. Warburg & Co., Inc., 1965-66; partner Lorenzo, Carney & Co., Inc., N.Y.C., 1966—; pres., dir. Jet Capital Corp., N.Y.C., 1970—; exec. v.p., dir. Tex. Internat. Airlines, Houston, 1972-80, chmn., 1981—; dir., chmn. exec. com. Tex. Air Corp., 1981—; pres. Life Enterprises, Inc. Trustee Mus. Fine Arts, Houston, 1978-81, Brown U., 1982—; bd. dirs. Rice Ctr., 1982—. Served with AUS, 1963. Mem. Phi Beta Kappa. Clubs: Harvard (N.Y.C.); Harvard Bus. Sch. (Houston) (dir. 1979—). Home: 559 Westminster St Houston TX 77024 Office 3 Allen Ctr Houston TX 77002

CARNEY, WILLIAM, congressman; b. Bklyn., July 1, 1942; s. Joseph James and Sarah Gertrude (Regan) C.; m. Barbara Ann Haverlin, May 14, 1966; children: Jackie, Julie. Student, Fla. State U., 1960-61. Service mgr. Spectrum Planned Services, Bohemia, N.Y., 1969-72; field service rep. Cypack Plastic Systems Corp., Farmingdale, N.Y., 1972-76; mem. Suffolk County Legislature, Hauppauge, N.Y., 1976-79, 96th-98th Congresses from 1st N.Y. Dist. Vice-pres. Suffolk County Council of Boy Scouts Am.; v.p. Long Island Loves Bus., Inc.; vice chmn. Smithtown Conservative Party; dir. Suffolk County chpt. Am. Heart Assn. Served with M.C. U.S. Army, 1961-64. Roman Catholic. Office: 1424 Longworth House Office Bldg Washington DC 20515 *

CARNICERO, JORGE, aero. engr., business exec.; b. Buenos Aires, Argentina, July 17, 1921; came to U.S., 1942, naturalized, 1950; m. Jacqueline Damman, Feb. 22, 1946; children—Jacqueline Denise, Jorge Jay. Student, U. LaPlata, Argentina, 1939-41, Aero. Engr., Rensselaer Poly. Inst., 1945. Chief engr. Dodero Airlines, Argentina, 1945, Flota Aerea Mercante, 1945-46; v.p. Air Carrier Service Corp., Washington, 1946, exec. v.p., 1947-55, chmn. bd., dir., 1955—; chmn. bd. Dynalectron Corp. (formerly Calif. Eastern Aviation); chmn. bd., dir. Dytel Ltd., Bahama Islands, Vegas Valley Electric, Inc., Nev., Seeger Electric Co., Del., Griffin Electric Co., Ky., Servair, Inc., Mass., State Electric Co. Ltd., Can., A&A Electric Co., Inc., Colo., Gibson Electric, Inc., Ga., DYN Internat., Inc., Del., Dynaelectric Co., Fla., HMS Electric Corp., Md., Greater Cin. Air Services, Inc., Ky., Solar Insulators, Inc., Air Carrier Service Corp., Hydrocarbon Realty Inc., Nev.; pres., dir. Trans-Am. Aero. Corp., Fla., Finamerica Corp., Del.; dir. Hydrocarbon Research Inc., N.Y., Frazier Elec. Constrn., Inc., Ky., HRI Tech. Services, Inc., Fla., Hydrocarbon Realty, Inc., N.Y., Hart Electric, Inc., Condor S.A. & Cía., Argentina, Huyck Corp., Conn., Riggs Nat. Bank of Washington, Airtech Service, Inc., Fla., Griffin Constrn. Co., Ky., Round Hill Devel. Ltd., Jamaica. Asso. fellow Royal Aero. Soc. Clubs: University; Metropolitan (N.Y.C.). Home: 3949 52d St NW Washington DC 20016 Office: 1313 Dolley Madison Blvd McLean VA 22101

CARNOCHAN, WALTER BLISS, educator; b. N.Y.C., Dec. 20, 1930; s. Gouverneur Morris and Sibyll Baldwin (Bliss) C.; m. Nancy Powers Carter, June 25, 1955 (div. 1978); children—Lisa Powers, Sarah Bliss, Gouverneur Morris, Sibyll Carter; m. Brigitte Hoy Fields, Sept. 16, 1979. A.B., Harvard, 1953, A.M., 1957, Ph.D., 1960. Asst. dean freshmen Harvard, 1954-56; successively instr., asst. prof., asso. prof., prof. English Stanford U., 1960—, dean grad. studies, 1975-80, vice-provost, 1976-80; Trustee, chmn. Athenian Sch.; Trustee Mills Coll.; mem. overseers com. to visit Harvard Coll. Author: Lemuel Gulliver's Mirror for Man, 1968, Confinement and Flight: An Essay on English Literature of the 18th Century, 1977. Home: 25 Pomponio Portola Valley CA 94025 Office: Dept English Stanford U Stanford CA 94305

CARNOY, MARTIN, economics educator; b. Warsaw, Poland, Sept. 9, 1938; s. Alan Leon and Teresa (Holskener) C.; m. Judith Merle Milgrom, Aug. 6, 1961 (div. 1980); children: David, Jonathan. B.S.E.E., Calif. Inst. Tech., 1960; M.A., U. Chgo., 1961, Ph.D., 1964. With Brookings Instn., Washington, 1964-68; mem. faculty dept. edn. Stanford U. (Calif.), 1968—, now prof.; Mem. Comparative Edn. Soc. Author: Education as Cultural Imperialism, 1974, Economic Democracy, 1980; Author A New Social Contract, 1983, The State and Political Theory, 1984. Ford Found. fellow, 1961-64. Mem. Latin Am. Studies Assn. Democrat. Jewish. Office: Sch Education Stanford U Stanford CA 94035

CARO, ANTHONY (ALFRED CARO), sculptor; b. London, Mar. 8, 1924; s. Alfred and Mary (Haldinstein) C.; m. Sheila May Girling, Dec. 17, 1949; children: Timothy Martin, Paul Gideon. M.A., Christ's Coll., Cambridge U., 1943; grad., Royal Acad. Schs., London, 1952; D.Litt. (hon.), East Anglia U., York U., Toronto, Ont., Can., Brandeis U. Asst. to Henry Moore, 1951-53; part-time tchr. sculpture St. Martin's Sch. Art, London, 1953-79; tchr. sculpture Bennington (Vt.) Coll., 1963, 65. Sculpture commd. by Nat. Gallery Art, Washington, 1977; one-man shows include, Galleria del Naviglio, Milan, Italy, 1956, Gimpel Fils Gallery, London, 1957, Whitechapel Art Gallery, London, 1963, Andre Emmerich Gallery, N.Y.C., 1964, 66, 68, 70, 72, 74, 77, 78, 79, 81, 82, Washington Gallery Modern Art, 1965, Kasmin Ltd., London, 1965, 67, 71, 72, David Mirvish Gallery, Toronto, Ont., Can., 1966, 71, 74, Galerie Bischofberger, Zurich, Switzerland, 1966, Kroller-Muller Mus., Netherlands, 1967, Hayward Gallery, London, 1969, Kenwood House, Hampstead, Eng., 1974, 81, Galleria dell'Ariete, Milan, 1974, Richard Gray Gallery, Chgo., 1975, Watson/de Nagy Gallery, Houston, Lefevre Gallery, London, 1976, Mus. Modern Art, N.Y.C., 1975, Everson Mus., Syracuse, N.Y., 1976, Tel Aviv Mus., 1977, Piltzer-Rheims, Paris, Waddington & Tooth, London, Emmerich Gallery, Zurich, 1978, Harkus Krackow Gallery, Boston, 1978, 81, Knoedler, London, 1978, Wentzel, Hamburg, Ace, Venice, Calif., Kahsahara, Japan, 1979, Glasgow, 1980, Acquavella Gelleries, N.Y., 1980, Galerie Andre, Berlin, Downstairs Gallery, Edmonton, Alta, Can., 1981, Gallery One, Toronto, 1982, Knoedler & Waddington Galleries, London, 1983, Galerie de France, Paris, Brit. Council touring exhbn., Tel Aviv, N.Z., Australia, Germany, 1977-79, Mus. Fine Arts, Boston, 1980, exhibited in group shows, 1st Paris Biennale, 1959 (sculpture prize), Battersea Park Open Air Exhbn., 1960, 63, 66, Gulbenkian Exhbn., London, 1964, Documenta III Kassel, 1965, Jewish Mus., N.Y.C., 1966 (David Bright prize), Venice Biennale, 1958, 66, Pitts. Internat., 1967, 68, Met. Mus. Art, 1968, Sao Paulo, 1969 (sculpture prize), U. Pa., Everson Mus., Mus. Modern Art, N.Y.C., 1975, Walker Art Gallery, Minn., Mus. Fine Arts, Houston, Mus. Fine Arts, Boston. Decorated comdr. Order Brit. Empire; presented key to city N.Y.C., 1976. Mem. Am. Acad. and Inst. Arts and Letters (hon.).

CARO, WARREN, theatrical executive, lawyer; b. Bklyn., Feb. 24, 1907; s. Arthur Brinton and Madeline (Davidsburg) C.; m. Nancy Kelly, Nov. 25, 1955 (div. 1965); 1 child, Kelly; m. Elizabeth Rehill, Dec. 9, 1979. B.A., Cornell U., 1927, J.D., 1929. Bar: N.Y. 1930, U.S. Supreme Ct. 1932. Sole practice law, N.Y.C., 1929-39; asst. gen. counsel Fed. Works Agy., Washington, 1940-42; exec. dir. The Theatre Guild-Am. Theatre Soc., N.Y.C., 1946-67; dir. theatre ops. The Shubert Orgn., N.Y.C., 1967-81; exec. dir. The Theatre Guild-NBC-TV Play Series, N.Y.C., 1949; vis. prof. drama and dir. U. Hawaii, 1955; mem. adv. commn. JFK Ctr. for Performing Arts, Washington; v.p., chmn. bd. trustees Am. Acad. Dramatic Arts. Served to lt. comdr., USCG, 1942-45. Recipient Tony award, 1961. Mem. Am. TV Soc. (founder, pres.), Shaw Soc. Am. (founder, lectr.). Home: Riverbend-North Shore Rd Litchfield CT 06759 *I am grateful for having spent a lifetime of diversification in three inter-related fields. Law and government service provided support for my principal career in the theatre during its most creative era. My prime motivation was to achieve innovation and progress through applying standards of excellence to the utmost of my abilities.*

CARO, WILLIAM ALLAN, physician; b. Chgo., Aug. 16, 1934; s. Marcus Rayner and Adeline Beatrice (Cohen) C.; m. Ruth Fruchtlander, June 15, 1959; children: Mark Stephen, David Edward. Student, U. Mich., 1952-55; B.S. in Medicine, U. Ill., 1957, M.D., 1959. Diplomate: Am. Bd. Dermatology, Sub bd. Dermatopathology. Intern Cook County Hosp., Chgo., 1959-60; resident in internal medicine U. Ill. Research and Ednl. Hosps., 1960-61; resident in dermatology Hosp. of U. Pa., 1961-62, 64-66; Earl D. Osborne fellow dermal pathology Armed Forces Inst. Pathology, Washington, 1966-67; asst. in medicine U. Ill. Coll. Medicine, 1960-61; asst. instr. U. Pa. Med. Sch., 1961-62, 64-66; asst. prof. dermatology Northwestern U. Med. Sch., 1967-73, asso. prof. clin. dermatology, 1973-81; practice medicine specializing in dermatology, Chgo., 1967—; attending physician Northwestern Meml. Hosp., 1969—, mem. med. exec. com., 1977-79; attending pathologist, cons. dermatologist VA Lakeside Hosp., Chgo.; cons. Children's Meml. Hosp., Rehab. Inst. Chgo.; Mcpl. Tb Sanitarium of Chgo., 1968-74; affiliate pathologist Evanston (Ill.) Hosp.; prof. clin. dermatology Northwestern U. Med. Sch., 1981—; mem. Am. Bd. Dermatology, 1981—. Editor trans.: Chgo. Dermatol. Soc, 1971-73; editorial bd., Cutis, 1975—; asso. editor Year Book Pathology and Clin. Pathology, 1977-80; contbr. articles to med. jours. Served as capt. M.C. USAR, 1962-64. Mem. Am. Acad. Dermatology (Gold award sci. exhbit 1970), Chgo. Dermatological Soc. (pres. 1983-84), Am. Dermatol. Assn., AMA, Am. Soc. Dermatopathology, Am. Veneral Disease Assn., Internat. Soc. Tropical Dermatology, Pacific Dermatologic Assn., Soc. Investigative Dermatology, Chgo. Dermatol. Soc., U. Ill. Med. Alumni Assn. (exec. bd. 1977-80), Alpha Omega Alpha, Phi Kappa Phi. Office: 233 E Erie St Chicago IL 60611

CAROFF, PHYLLIS M., educator; b. Bklyn., Feb. 22, 1924; d. Harry and Irene (Lesser) Friedman; m. Joseph Caroff, May 16, 1943; children—Michael, Peter. B.A., Douglass Coll., 1944; M.S.W., N.Y. Sch. Social Work, 1947; D.S.W., Columbia U., 1969. Caseworker ARC, 1944-45; caseworker, student supr. Community Service Soc., N.Y.C., 1956-61; from lectr. to asso. prof. Hunter Coll. Sch. Social Work, N.Y.C., 1961-76, prof., 1976—; dir. Postmasters Program in Advanced Clin. Social Work, 1977—; pvt. practice psychotherapy, N.Y.C., 1964—; cons. VA Hosp., N.Y.C., 1977—, USPHS Hosp., S.I., 1974—; mem. adv. bd. Found. Thanatology, 1976—; mem. profl. adv. com. Grad. Program in Social Work Inst. Health Professions, Mass. Gen. Hosp., 1980—. Author: (with others) Before Addiction, 1973; editorial bd.: Clin. Social Work Jour, 1972—, Jour. Gerontol. Social Work, 1978—; editor: Social Work in Health Services: An Academic Practice Partnership, 1980. Mem. exec. com. of bd. Planned Parenthood N.Y.C., 1974-79, chmn. research and evaluation com., 1974-77, bd. dirs., 1971—. NIMH fellow, 1964-65; various grants. Mem. Nat. Assn. Social Wrkers, Nat. Assn. Social Workers (chmn. council, mem. peer rev. adv. com. 1980—), Am. Orthopsychiat. Assn., AAUP, N.Y. State Soc. Clin. Social Work Psychotherapists. Home: 15 W81 St New York NY 10024 Office: 129 E 79 St New York NY 10021 *

CARON, LESLIE (LESLIE CLARE MARGARET CARON), film and stage actress; b. Boulogne, France, July 1, 1931; d. Claude and Margaret (Petit) C.; m. George Hormel, May 1953; m. Peter Reginald Frederick Hall, Aug. 6, 1956; children: Christopher John, Jennifer Caron; m. Michael Laughlin, Jan. 1, 1969. Student, Convent of the Assumption, Paris, France. With, Ballet des Champs Elysees, 1947-50, Ballet de Paris, 1954; films include: American in Paris, Lili, Glass Slipper, Daddy Long Legs, Gigi, The Doctor's Dilemma, The Man Who Understood Women, Fanny, The L Shaped Room, Father Goose, Promise Her Anything, Is Paris Burning, Head of the Family, Chandler, Purple Night, Valentino, The Man Who Loved Women, Golden Girl, Contract; TV appearances include Carola, 1973, QB VII, 1974; also appeared in Renoir play Orvet, Paris, 1955, Gigi, London, 1956, Ondine, 1961. Address: care Blake Agy Ltd 409 N Camden Dr 202 Beverly Hills CA 90210 *

CARONE, FRANK, medical educator, pathologist; b. New Kensington, Pa., Nov. 28, 1927; married, 1952; 5 children. A.B., W.Va. U., 1948; M.D., Yale U., 1952. Cert. pathologist. Intern U. Pa. Hosp., 1952-53; instr. Yale U. Sch. Medicine, 1959-60; from asst. prof. to profl. Northwestern U. Sch. Medicine, 1960-69, Morrison prof. pathology, 1969—; dir. labs. Northwestern Meml. Hosp., Chgo., 1961—. Served to capt. M.C. USAF, 1953-55. Life Inst. Med. Research Fund research fellow, 1957-59; Markle scholar, 1964-69. Mem. Am. Fedn. Clin. Research, Internat. Acad. Pathology, Am. Soc. Exptl. Pathologists. Office: Dept Pathology Northwestern U Sch Medicine Chgo IL 60611

CAROSSO, VINCENT PHILLIP, historian; b. San Francisco, Mar. 19, 1922; s. Vincent G. and Lucia M. (Barale) C.; m. Rose Celeste Berti, Aug. 23, 1952; 1 son, Steven Berti. A.B., U. Calif.-, Berkeley, 1943, M.A., 1944, Ph.D. (Panama-Pacific fellow in History), 1945-46, LeConte Meml. fellow, 1946-47, 1948. Instr. history San Jose (Calif.) State Coll., 1949-50; asst. prof. Carnegie Inst. Tech., Pitts., 1950-53, N.Y. U., N.Y.C., 1953-56, assoc. prof., 1956-62, prof. history, 1962-76, William R. Kenan Prof. History, 1976—; vis. assoc. research prof. Harvard U., 1961-62; vis. lectr., 1963-64; Fulbright-Hays sr. lectr., Italy, 1973, 76. Author: California Wine Industry, 1830-95, 1951, reprinted, 1976, (with George Soule) American Economic History, 1957, (with Henry Parkes) Recent America, 2 vols, 1963, Investment Banking in America, 1970; reprinted 97 More Than a Century of Investment Banking: The Kidder, Peabody & Co. Story, 1979; editor: Wall Street and Security Markets, 1975; The United States in the Twentieth Century, 1979; co-editor: Companies & Men: Business Enterprise in America, 1976, Small Business Enterprise in America, 1979, Rise of Commercial Banking, 1980; asso. editor: Jour. Econ. History, 1955-61; editorial bds. Business Hist. Rev., 1957-61, Jour. Am. History, 1968-71; contbr.: articles to profl. jours. Jour. Am. History. Harvard postdoctoral fellow, 1948-49; Nat. Endowment for Humanities fellow, 1976-77; Am. Council Learned Socs. research grantee, 1978; John Simon Guggenheim fellow, 1980-81; Alfred P. Sloan Found. grantee, 1983. Mem. Am. Hist. Assn., Orgn. Am. Historians, Econ. History Assn., Bus. and Econ. History Conf. (trustee 1973-76). Home: 375 Riverside Dr New York NY 10025

CAROVANO, JOHN MARTIN, educator, college president; b. Tacoma, May 9, 1935; s. John and Elda C. (Martin) C.; m. Barbara Bevins, June 14, 1958; children: Kristen, Kathryn. B.A., Pomona Coll., 1957, LL.D., 1979; M.A., U. Calif. at Berkeley, 1961, Ph.D., 1965; LL.D., Hamilton Coll., 1974. Research asst., teaching fellow U. Calif. at Berkeley, 1959-63; instr. econs. Hamilton Coll., Clinton, N.Y., 1963-65, asst. prof., 1965-68, asso. prof., 1969-74, acting provost, 1971-72, provost, 1972-74, pres. coll., 1974—; financial economist Office Tax Analysis, U.S. Dept. Treasury, Washington, 1968-69; chmn. N.Y. Com. of Selection, Rhodes Scholarship Trust, 1978-82; trustee Commn. on Ind. Colls. and Univs. N.Y., 1980-83. Mem. Democratic Com., Clinton, 1970-74. Served with AUS, 1957-58. Mem. AAUP (pres. chpt. 1970-71). Home: 11 College Hill Rd Clinton NY 13323 Office: Office of President Hamilton College Clinton NY 13323

CAROZZA, DAVY ANGELO, educator; b. Monteneroдomo, Italy, Oct. 10, 1926; came to U.S., 1947, naturalized, 1952; s. Nicola and Maria A. (Mariotti) C.; m. Anna G. Carozza, Feb. 3, 1952; children—Daniel, Walter, Janet, Paolo. B.A. summa cum laude, Cath. U. Am., 1956, M.A. (Woodrow Wilson fellow), 1957, Ph.D., 1964. Tchr. Italian, 1943-47; lectr. summer sessions Cath. U. Am., 1957-65, lectr. in French, 1960-61; instr. Italian and French U. Md., College Park, 1961-64, asst. prof. Italian, 1964-65; lectr. Sch. Advanced Internat. Studies, Johns Hopkins U., 1964-65; asso. prof. comparative lit. U. Wis., Milw., 1965-68, prof., 1968—, chmn. dept., 1967-69, 73-76, coordinator M.A. program in Fgn. Lang. and Lit., 1976—; vis. asso. prof. comparative lit. Northwestern U., Evanston, Ill., 1966; mem. panel discussion on Dante Georgetown U. Forum radio program, 1965; adviser, coordinator Italian program for adults and children Cardinal Stritch Coll., 1971-73; mem. symposia on Baroque U. Ky., 1965, Cath. U. Am., 1975. Author: European Baroque, 1976; contbr. book revs. and articles to lit. jours. Served with AUS, 1948-52. U. Wis. grantee, 1966-69, 72, 73, 74, 78, 81. Mem. Midwest MLA (pres. 1969-70, exec. com. 1970-71), MLA (exec. council 1969-70), Internat., Am. Comparative lit. assns., Renaissance Soc. Am., Dante Soc. Am., Internat., Am. assns. tchrs. Italian, Am. Assn. Tchrs. French, Am. Assn. Tchrs. Spanish and Portuguese, Phi Beta Kappa, Delta Epsilon Sigma, Phi Kappa Phi. Home: 5549 N Berkeley Blvd Milwaukee WI 53217 Office: Dept Comparative Lit U Wis Milwaukee WI 53201

CAROZZI, ALBERT VICTOR, geology educator; b. Genève, Switzerland, Apr. 26, 1925; came to U.S., 1955, naturalized, 1963; s. Luigi and Anna-Maria (Ferrario) C.; m. Marguerite Peier, July 23, 1949; children: Viviane (Mrs. Onoratino Marrocco), Nadine. M.S., U. Geneva, 1947, D.Sc. summa cum laude, 1948. Asst. prof. geology U. Geneva, 1953-57; vis. asst. prof. geology U. Ill., Urbana, 1955-56, asso. prof., 1957-59, prof., 1959—; cons. geologist to industry; asso. mem. Center Advanced Study, U. Ill., 1969-70. Author books on carbonate petrography, history of geol. concepts.; Contbr. articles to profl. jours. Recipient Davy award in geology U. Geneva, 1949, 54; Plantamour-Prévost award U. Geneva, 1955. Fellow Geol. Soc. Am.; mem. Am. Assn. Petroleum Geologists, Soc. Econ. Paleontologists and Mineralogists, AAAS, Ill. Acad. Sci., AIME, Internat., U.S. coms. history of geology, Assn. Geoscientists Internat. Devel., History of Earth Scis. Soc. (pres. 1984), Sigma Xi, Phi Kappa Phi. Home: 709 W Delaware Urbana IL 61801

CARP, GEORGE, mgmt. cons. co. exec.; b. N.Y.C., May 28, 1921; s. Emil Z. and Florence (Singer) C.; m. Bernice Jeanne Levy, Oct. 1, 1944; children—Joy Nina, Michael Harrison. B.S., Coll. City N.Y., 1949, B.A., 1942. Lab. design engr. Ward Leonard Electric Co., Mt. Vernon, N.Y., 1948-50; exec. mgr. elec. controls G. Carp & Co., South Norwalk, 1950-54; dir. engring. York Research Corp., Stamford, Conn., 1954-57, tech. dir., 1959-60; dir. electronic design Sperry Semicondr. div. Sperry Rand Co., 1957-59; dir. engring. Conn. Tel. & Electric Corp., Meriden, 1960-61, exec. v.p., 1961-62, pres., 1962-78; sr. cons. Kensington Mgmt. Cons., Inc., Stamford, 1978-80, v.p., 1980—; pres. Holtzer Cabot Corp., North Attleboro, Mass., 1971-73; evening instr. Brideport Engring. Inst., 1950-57. Served with AUS, 1943-46. Fellow AIM (pres.'s council); mem. IEEE, AAAS, Inst. Environ. Sci., Nat., Conn. socs. profl. engrs. Patentee in field. Office: 25 3d St Stamford CT 06905 *Success and happiness are not achieved by concentration on only one aspect of life. The one bonding element for happiness and success in all of life's good aspects is free time for individual "breathing room," time to reflect and savor the good, and time to examine and possibly alter former goals.*

CARP, RICHARD IRVIN, microbiologist; b. Phila., May 10, 1934; s. Maurice and Sara (Lee) C.; m. Sally E. Bennet, June 26, 1960; children—Daniel, Melissa, Joshua. B.A., U. Pa., 1955, V.M.D., 1958, Ph.D., 1962. Postdoctoral fellow Wistar Inst., Phila., 1958-62, asso., 1964-68; established virus and tissue culture labs., Baroda, India, 1963; vis. prof. Baylor U. Med. Coll., 1965; prin. research scientist dept. microbiology and animal experimentation N.Y. State Inst. Basic Research in Mental Retardation, S.I., 1968—; prof. SUNY-Downstate Med. Center, 1977—; faculty Richmond Coll., N.Y. U., 1969—, Wagner Coll., 1975—; head animal care com. Research Facility and Research Found. Bd. dirs. S.I. Mental Health Soc. Recipient award for outstanding contbns. in multiple sclerosis research Suffolk County chpt. Nat. Multiple Sclerosis Soc., 1976; Community Service award Tottenville Improvement Council, Inc., 1976. Mem. Am. Soc. Microbiologists, AAAS, Phi Zeta. Home: 46 Duncan Rd Staten Island NY 10301

CARPENTER, ALLAN, author, editor, publisher; b. Waterloo, Iowa, May 11, 1917; s. John Alex and Theodosia (Smith) C. B.A., U. No. Iowa, 1938. Founder, editor, publisher Tchrs. Digest mag., 1940-48; dir. pub. relations Popular Mechanics mag., 1943-62; founder, 1962, since pres. Carpenter Pub. House, Chgo.; founder Infordata Internat. Inc., 1970, chmn. bd., dir., 1970—; partner, editor Index to U.S. Govt. Periodicals, 1972—. Author: 176 non-fiction books, including 52 vol. Enchantment of America state series; 42 vol. Enchantment of Africa, 20 vol. Enchantment of Latin America, Land of Lincoln; others; creator, editor 16 vol.: Popular Mechanics Home Handyman Ency., 1962; founder, pub.: Index to Readers Digest, 1980—. Pres., chmn. Chgo. Businessmen's Symphony Orch., 1942-65; founder, 1954; since pres. Music Council Met. Chgo.; prin. bass violist non-profl. symphony orchs., 1935—; chief lay officer Second Presbyn. Ch., Evanston, Ill., 1954-77. Clubs: Arts, East Bank (Chgo.). Home and Office: 175 E Delaware Pl Suite 4602 Chicago IL 60611 *Plain stubbornness, at least rugged determination, has been a dominant element in whatever success I may have achieved. On the many occasions when I have failed or fallen short, I might have done better to have held on longer. When I have been confident of ultimate success and have held on to that confidence without fail, I have generally managed to make it.*

CARPENTER, ANNA-MARY PASSIER, physician, educator; b. Ambridge, Pa., Jan. 14, 1916; d. Samuel V. and Adele M. (Passier) C. B.A., Geneva Coll., 1936, D.Sc. (hon.), 1968; M.S., U. Pitts., 1937, Ph.D., 1940; M.D., U. Minn., 1958. Research asst. U. Pitts., 1938-40; instr. Moravian Coll. Women, Bethlehem, Pa., 1941-42; chmn. biology curricula Keystone Coll., Scranton, Pa., 1942-44; research assoc. pathology Children's Hosp.; lectr. mycology Sch. Medicine, Pitts., 1944-53; instr. Sch. Medicine U. Minn., Mpls., 1954-57, asst. prof., 1957-58, assoc. prof., 1959-65, prof. anatomy, 1965-80; prof. pathology N.W. Center Med. Edn., Ind. U., 1980—. Author: Color Atlas of Human Histology, 1968. Mem. AAAS, Am. Diabetes Assn., Histochem. Soc. (sec. 1974-75, treas. 1975—, pres. 1981—), Am. Assn. Anatomy, Internat. Soc. Mycology, Internat. Soc. Stereology (sec.-treas. 1972—). Home: 6424 Hayes St Merrillville IN 46410

CARPENTER, BRUCE H., college president; b. Rapid City, S.D., Feb. 5, 1932; s. Ralph A. and Anna F. (Davis) C.; m. Kathryn A. West, June 5, 1975. B.A., Calif. State U.-, Long Beach, 1957, M.A., 1958; Ph.D., UCLA, 1962. Prof. Calif. State U.-, Long Beach, 1962-72, assoc. acad. v.p., 1972-75; provost, acad. v.p. Western Ill. U., Macomb, 1975-82; pres. Eastern Mont. Coll., Billings, 1982—. Contbr. articles to profl. jours. Chmn. Macomb United Way, 1982; mem. exec. bd. Billing United Way, 1983. Served to cpl. U.S. Army, 1952-54. NSF research grantee, 1963-70. Mem. AAAS, Am Soc. Plant Physiologists, N.Y. Acad. Scis. Club:. Lodges: Rotary; Elks. Office: Eastern Montana College Billings MT 59101

CARPENTER, CHARLES COLCOCK JONES, physician, educator; b. Savannah, Ga., Jan. 5, 1931; s. Charles Colcock Jones and Alexandra (Morrison) C.; m. Sally R. Fisher, Nov. 29, 1958; children—Charles Morrison, Murray Douglas, Andrew Fisher. A.B., Princeton, 1952; M.D., Johns Hopkins, 1956. Diplomate: Am. Bd. Internal Medicine (mem. bd. 1976—, exec. com. 1980—, chmn. 1983-84). Intern Johns Hopkins Hosp., 1956-57, resident, 1957-59, 61-62; practice medicine, specializing in infectious disease, Balt., 1962-73; asst. prof. medicine Johns Hopkins, 1962-67, asso. prof., 1967-69, prof., 1969-73; physician-in-chief Balt. City Hosps., 1969-73; prof., chmn. dept. medicine Case Western Res. Sch. Medicine, 1973—; physician-in-chief Case Western Res. Univ. Hosp., 1973—; dir. Cholera Research Program, Johns Hopkins Center Med. Research and Tng., Calcutta, India, 1962-64; chmn. cholera panel U.S.-Japan Coop. Med. Sci. Program, 1965-72, mem., 1973—; mem. exec. com. Bd. Sci. and Tech. Nat. Acad. Scis., 1981—; mem. adv. com. Sch. Medicine Johns Hopkins U., 1982—; mem. Am. Bd. Med. Spltys., 1982—. Trustee Internat. Center for Infectious Disease Research, Bangladesh, 1979. Served as sr. asst. surgeon USPHS, 1959-61. Fellow ACP; mem. Am. Soc. Clin. Investigation, Assn. Am. Physicians (sec. 1975-81, councillor 1981-86), Infectious Diseases Soc. Am. Home: 2720 Dryden Rd Shaker Heights OH 44121

CARPENTER, CHARLES CONGDEN, zoologist; b. Denison, Iowa, June 2, 1921; s. Harry Alonzo and Myrtle Ruth (Barber) C.; m. Mary F. Pitynski, Sept. 2, 1947; children—Janet Eleanor, Caryn Sue, Geoffrey Congden. B.A., No. Mich. Coll. Edn., Marquette, 1943; postgrad., Tarleton State Coll., Stephenville, Tex., 1943-44, Stanford U., 1944, Wayne U., 1945; M.S., U. Mich., 1947, Ph.D., 1951. Lab. asst. zoology No. Mich. Coll. Edn., 1941-43; teaching asst. zoology U. Mich., 1946; asst. herpetology and mammalogy Biol. Sta., summer 1948, teaching fellow zoology, 1947-51, instr. zoology, 1951-52; instr. U. Okla. Biol. Sta., Norman, summer 1952, U. Okla., 1953, asst. prof. zoology, 1953-59; asso. prof. zoology, curator reptiles U. Okla. and; U. Okla. Biol. Sta., 1959-66, prof. zoology, curator reptiles, 1966—; research asso. in herpetology Dallas Zoo, 1980; expdns. and field studies U. Mich. Paleontol. Expdn., Kans. and, Colo., 1947, Jackson Hole Research sta., Grand Teton Nat. Park, 1951, field trips throughout, Mexico and; S.W., U.S., 1979—, Galapagos Islands Expdn., 1962; expdns. to islands of Gulf of Calif., 1964; invited scientist mem. Galapagos Internat. Sci. Project to Galapagos Islands, Ecuador and; Cocos Island, 1964—; sec. Animal Research Council, Oklahoma City Zoo, 1972-74, 78—, chmn., 1980. Contbr. articles to profl. jours. Served with AUS, 1943-46. Recipient Disting. Alumni award No. Mich. U., 1972; Regents award U. Okla., 1980; numerous grants NSF, N.Y. Zool. Soc., U. Okla. Alumni Devel. Fund, U. Okla. Research Inst., 1951—. Fellow Animal Behavior Soc. (sec. 1966-68), Okla. Acad. Sci. (pres. 1970), Herpetologist League (v.p. 1972-73, pres. 1974-75); mem. Am. Ornithologists Union, Am. Soc. Zoologists, Am. Inst. Biol. Sci., Ecol. Soc. Am., Am. Soc. Ichthyologists and Herpetologists, Wilson Ornithol. Soc., Southwestern Assn. Naturalists (bd. govs. 1965-68, pres. 1968-69, permanent sec. 1971-76), Am. Soc. Mammalogists, Brit. Ecol. Soc., Soc. Study Amphibians and Reptiles, Explorers Club, Wilderness Soc., Nature Conservancy, Sigma Xi, Phi Kappa Phi, Phi Sigma. Home: 1218 Cruce St Norman OK 73069 Office: Dept Zoology 730 VanVleet Oval U Okla Norman OK 73019

CARPENTER, DAVID BAILEY, educator; b. Webster Groves, Mo., June 4, 1915; s. Fred Green and Mildred (Bailey) C.; m. Yoshi Horikawa, Aug. 6, 1946; children—Marie Yoshiko, Teresa Teiko, Gary Bailey, James Burton. B.A., Wash. U., 1937, M.A., 1938; M.A., Columbia U., 1944; Ph.D., U. Wash., 1951. Instr. sociology U. Wash., 1941-42; civilian chief of stats. div. MacArthur Hdqrs., Tokyo, 1946-48; instr. sociology U. Wash., 1948-49; asst. prof. sociology Wash. U., 1949-52, assoc. prof., 1952-63, prof., 1963-72, dean, 1965-67; chief grad. acad. programs br. U.S. Office Edn., 1967-68; prof. U. Ill. at Chgo., 1972—, head dept. sociology, 1972-76. Author: (with Stuart A. Queen) The American City, 1953, The Social Life of a Modern Metropolis, 1954. Served with USNR, 1942-46. Mem. Ethical Soc. St. Louis (pres. 1969-71), Phi Beta Kappa. Home: 2237 Lake Ave Wilmette IL 60091 Office: Univ Illinois at Chicago Chicago IL 60680

CARPENTER, DAVID ROLAND, life insurance executive; b. Fort Wayne, Ind., Mar. 24, 1939; s. Geary W. and Rita (Ueber) C.; m. Karen Woodard, Oct. 20, 1963 (div. Apr. 1975); children: Kimberly, Clayton; m. Leila E.M. Sjogren, Sept. 20, 1980; 1 dau., Michelle. B.B.A., U. Mich., 1961, M.S., 1962. Sr. v.p. Booz, Allen Cons., Newport Beach, Calif., 1976-77; v.p. Tillinghast, Nelson & Warren, Newport Beach, Calif., 1977-80; chief mktg. officer Transamerica Occidental Life Ins. Co., Los Angeles, 1980-81, exec. v.p., chief mktg. officer, 1981-82, pres., chief operating officer, 1982-83, pres., chief exec. officer, 1983—, dir.; dir. Transam. Life & Annuity Co., Transam. Assurance Co., Transam. Ins. Corp., Transam. Internat. Ins. Services. Mem. exec. com. Steve Garvey Sports Classic-So. Calif. Multiple Sclerosis Soc., Los Angeles, 1981; trustee Griffith Found., Columbus Ohio, 1982; bd. govs. Arthritis found., Los Angeles, 1983; trustee Calif. Hosp., 1983. Fellow Soc. Actuaries (bd. dirs. 1978-81); mem. Am. Acad. Actuaries (v.p. 1981-83). Presbyterian. Home: 346 Poppy Ave Corona del Mar CA 92625 Office: Transamerica Occidental Life Ins Co 1150 S Olive St Los Angeles CA 90015

CARPENTER, DELMA RAE, JR., physicist, educator; b. Salem, Va., Apr. 15, 1928; s. Delma Rae and Gladys (Jamison) C.; m. Jane Augusta Grant, Aug. 2, 1952; children: Delma Rae III, Cita Anne (dec.), Gordon Grant, Barbara Elizabeth. B.S., Roanoke Coll., Salem, 1949; M.S., Cornell U., 1951; Ph.D., U. Va., 1957. Instr. physics Va. Mil. Inst., Lexington, 1951-55, asst. prof., 1955-59, asso. prof., 1959-63, prof., 1963—, head dept. physics, 1969-74; dep. dir. research Research Labs., 1963-66, dir. research, 1966—, bd. dirs., 1966—; industry control, devel. engr. Gen. Electric Co., summer 1962; cons. Army Research Office; summer research Depts. Army and Commerce, 1953—. Trustee Sci. Mus. Va., 1972—, chmn. bd., 1973-78; trustee VMI Found., 1977—, Va. Acad. Sci., 1981—. Recipient Disting. Service award Va. Mil. Inst., 1982. Fellow AAAS; mem. Am. Assn. Physics Tchrs., Va. Acad. Sci. (trustee 1951—, pres. 1969-70, Disting. Service award 1976), Sigma Xi, Sigma Pi Sigma, Phi Kappa Phi, Alpha Chi. Club: Rotary. Home: 401 Overlook Circle Lexington VA 24450

CARPENTER, DOW WHEELER, JR., publishing and communications executive; b. Los Angeles, Oct. 5, 1927; s. Dow W. and Mildred (Matthews) C.; m. Dian S. Carpenter, Aug. 28, 1956; children: Karen E., Carolyn L. A.B., Stanford U., 1950, M.B.A., 1955. Mgmt. cons. McKinsey & Co., Los Angeles, 1955-64; asst. to. to exec. v.p. Times Mirror Co., Los Angeles, 1964-66, group v.p., 1972-76, fin. v.p., 1976-80, sr. v.p., 1980—; pres. Pickett Plan Hold Corp., Santa Barbara, Calif., 1966-72. Clubs: California (Los Angeles); Coral Casino Beach Montecito. Home: 10501 Wilshire Blvd Los Angeles CA 90024 Office: Times Mirror Co Times Mirror Sq Los Angeles CA 90053

CARPENTER, EDMUND MOGFORD, automotive supply company executive; b. Toledo, Dec. 28, 1941; s. Charles N. and Vivian (Mogford) C.; m. Mary Winterhoff, May 20, 1962; children: Susan, Edmund Mogford, Molly. B.S. in Indsl. Engring, U. Mich., 1963, M.B.A., 1964. Dist. plant mgr. Mich. Bell Telephone Co., Detroit, 1964-68; partner Touche Ross & Co. (C.P.A.'s), Detroit, 1968-74; pres. Fruehauf de Brazil, Sao Paulo, 1974-76; pres. auto truck group Kelsey-Hayes Co., Romulus, Mich., 1976-81; group gen. mgr. world wide automotive ops. ITT, Southfield, Mich., 1981-83, exec. v.p., N.Y.C., 1983—. Bd. govs. Cranbrook Schs., Bloomfield Hills, Mich. Mem. Soc. Automotive Engrs. Address: itt worldwide headquarters 320 park ave New York NY 10022

CARPENTER, EDMUND NELSON, II, lawyer; b. Phila., Jan. 27, 1921; s. Walter S. and Mary (Wootten) C.; m. Carroll Morgan, July 18, 1970; children: Mary W., Edmund Nelson III, Katherine R.R., Elizabeth Lea; stepchildren: John D. Gates, Ashley du Pont Gates. A.B., Princeton U., 1943; LL.B., Harvard U., 1948. Bar: Del. 1949, U.S. Supreme Ct. 1957. Assoc. firm Richards, Layton & Finger, Wilmington, Del., 1949-53, partner, 1953-78, dir., 1978—, pres., 1982—; dep. atty. gen. State of Del., 1953-54, spl. dep. atty., 1960-62; chmn. Superior Ct. Jury Study Com., 1963-66; mem. Del. Gov.'s Commn. Law Enforcement and Adminstrn. Justice, 1969; chmn. Del. Agency to Reduce Crime, 1970-71, Del. Supreme Ct. Adv. Com. on Profl. Fin. Accountability, 1974-75, Long Range Cts. Planning Com., 1976—; dir. Bank Del., 1962—. Trustee Wilmington Med. Center, 1965—, U. Del., 1971-77, Princeton U., 1974—, World Affairs Council of Wilmington, 1968—; trustee Lawrenceville Sch., 1953-74, trustee emeritus, 1974—; bd. dirs. Good Samaritan Inc., 1973—; chmn. lawyers adv. com. U.S. Ct. Appeals 3d Circuit, 1975-77; mem. Del Health Care Injury Ins. Study Comm., 1976—. Fellow Am. Coll. Trial Lawyers, Am. Bar Found.; mem. ABA (ho. of dels. 1979—), Del. State Bar Assn., Am. Judicature Soc. (dir. 1974—, exec. com. 1978-80, v.p. 1980-81, pres. 1981—), Am. Trial Lawyers Assn. Office: PO Box 551 One Rodney Sq Wilmington DE 19899

CARPENTER, ELIZABETH SUTHERLAND, journalist, author, equal rights leader; b. Salado, Tex., Sept. 1, 1920; d. Thomas Shelton and Mary Elizabeth (Robertson) Sutherl; m. Leslie Carpenter, June 17, 1944; children: Scott Sutherland, Christy. B.J., U. Tex., 1942; hon. doctorate, Mt. Vernon Coll. Reporter, UP, Phila., 1944-45; propr. with husband of news bur. representing nat. newspapers, Washington, 1945-61; exec. asst. to Vice Pres. Lyndon B. Johnson, 1961-63; pres. sec., staff dir. to Mrs. Johnson, 1963-69; v.p. Hill & Knowlton, Inc., Washington, 1972-76; cons. LBJ Library, Austin, Tex.; asst. sec. Dept. Edn., 1980-81; co-chmn. ERAmerica, 1976-81. Author: Ruffles and Flourishes, 1970. Recipient Woman of Year award in field of politics and pub. affairs Ladies Home Jour., 1977. Mem. Nat. Women's Polit. Caucus (founding mem., nat. policy council 1971—), Women's Nat. Press (pres. 1954-55), Alpha Phi, Theta Sigma Phi (Nat. Headliners award 1962). Clubs: Press (Washington); Headliners (Headliner award) (Austin). Home: 116 Skyline Dr Austin TX 78746 Office: LB Johnson Library 2313 Red River Austin TX 78705

CARPENTER, FRANK MORTON, zoologist; b. Boston, Sept. 6, 1902; s. Edwin Arthur and Maude Frances (Wall) C.; m. Ruth Frances Scace, June 1, 1932; children—Alden Bliss, Ellen Ruth, Cynthia. A.B. magna cum laude, Harvard, 1926, M.S., 1927, D.Sc., 1929. NRC fellow biol. scis., 1928-31; asso. entomology Harvard, 1931-32; research asso. Carnegie Inst., 1931-32; asst. curator invertebrate paleontology Harvard, 1932-36; curator fossil insects Mus. of Comparative Zoology, Harvard, 1936—, asst. prof. palentology, 1936-39, asso. prof. entomology, 1939-45, prof. entomology, Agassiz prof. zoology, 1945-69, Fisher prof. natural history, 1969—. Author tech. articles on insect evolution. Fellow Am. Acad. Arts and Scis. (v.p. 1961-63); mem. Palentol. Soc. (medal 1975), Phi Beta Kappa, Sigma Xi (nat. pres.). Home: 94 Pleasant St Lexington MA 02173 Office: Harvard U Cambridge MA 02138

CARPENTER, FRANK WILKINSON, construction company executive; b. Richmond, Va., Apr. 22, 1931; s. Frank Washington and Sallye Elizabeth (Wilkinson) C.; m. Virginia Allen, Nov. 30, 1952; children: Karen Elizabeth, Susan Scott. B.S. in Civil Engring., Va. Poly. Inst., 1952. Registered profl. engr., Va. Vice pres. Dickerson, Inc., Monroe, N.C., 1963-74, exec. v.p., dir., 1974-81, pres., dir., 1981-82; exec. v.p., dir. The Dickerson Group, Inc., Monroe, 1982—. Served to 1st lt. U.S. Army, 1952-54. Home: Monroe NCOffice: Dickerson Group Inc 1501 Charlotte Ave Monroe NC 28110

CARPENTER, GENE BLAKELY, educator; b. Evansville, Ind., Dec. 15, 1922; s. Leland A. and Juanita (Blakely) C.; m. Elizabeth E. Corkum, Apr. 15, 1949; children—Jonathan R., Anne E. B.A., U. Louisville, 1944; M.A., Harvard U., 1945, Ph.D., 1947. NRC fellow Calif. Inst. Tech., 1947-48, research fellow, 1948-49; instr. Brown U., 1949-52, asst. prof., 1952-56, asso. prof., 1956-63, prof., 1963—; Guggenheim fellow U. Leeds, Eng., 1956-57; vis. prof. U. Groningen, The Netherlands, 1963-64; Fulbright-Hayes lectr. U. Zagreb, Yugoslavia, 1971-72; vis. scientist Oak Ridge Nat. Lab., 1980. Author: Principles of Crystal Structure Determination, 1969; Contbr. articles to sci. jours. Mem. Am. Crystallographic Assn., Am. Chem. Soc. Home: 8 Angell Ct Providence RI 02906 Office: Dept Chemistry Brown U Providence RI 02912

CARPENTER, GEORGE WYMAN, former utilites executive; b. Lexington, Okla., Aug. 27, 1915; s. G.E. and Emma (Witten) C.; m. Erdina Hill, July 3, 1938; children: Judith Carpenter Williamson, Joe David, James Wyman. B.S. in Mech. Engring., U. Okla., 1936. Registered profl. engr., Okla. With Okla. Natural Gas Co., Tulsa, 1936-50, Stone & Webster Service Corp., N.Y.C., 1950-63, Consumers' Gas Co., Toronto, Ont., Can., 1963-79, exec. v.p., dir., to 1979. Home: 170 Roehampton Ave Toronto ON Canada M4P 1R2 Office: Consumers Gas Co 1 First Canadian Pl Toronto ON Canada M5X 1C5

CARPENTER, JAMES EDGAR, banker; b. Springfield, Colo., Aug. 5, 1933; s. James Medray and Jamie Ernestine (Crossfield) C.; m. Z. Jane Nichols, Apr. 6, 1973; 1 dau., Jane Elizabeth. Student, George Washington U., 1951-53, U. Miss., 1952-55; J.D., U. Colo., Boulder, 1957. Bar: Colo. bar 1957. Partner firm Calkins, Kramer, Grimshaw & Carpenter, Denver, 1960-69; pres., dir. Empire Savs., Bldg. and Loan Assn., Denver, 1969—, E.S.L. Corp., 1971—; dir. Fed. Home Loan Bank of Topeka, 1974-75, 78—; dir. MGIC Investment Co. Bd. editors: Rocky Mountain Law Rev, 1955-57. Dir., pres., exec. bd., v.p. Savs. League Colo., Inc.; Mem. Denver Regional Transp. Dist., 1973-74; Mem. adv. panel U. Denver Research Inst., 1974-76. Served with USN, 1957-60. Mem. Colo. Bar Assn., Young Pres.' Orgn., Met. Denver Exec. Club, Nat. Savs. and Loan League (dir. 1980—), Law Club, Phi Delta Phi. Club: Denver Athletic. Office: 1654 California St Denver CO 80202

CARPENTER, JAMES MORTON, art educator, artist; b. Glens Falls, N.Y., Dec. 7, 1914; s. William Morton and Beulah (Mason) C.; m. Dorothy Neal Sauer, Nov. 4, 1939; children: William Morton, Stephen Sparrell, Elizabeth Ashley, Jane Mason. A.B., Harvard, 1937, Ph.D., 1943. Instr., then asst. prof. Harvard, 1943-50; mem. faculty Colby Coll., 1950—, prof. art, chmn. dept., from 1953; now Jetté prof. art emeritus, dir. Colby Coll. Art Mus., 1959-65. One-man retrospective show at, Colby Coll. Mus. Art, 1980; Author: (with others) Maine and Its Role in American Art, 1963, (with Howard T. Fisher) Color in Art, a Tribute to Arthur Pope, 1974, Visual Art: A Critical Introduction, 1982. Home: 1 Edgewood St Waterville ME 04901

CARPENTER, JOHN HOWARD, film writer-dir.; b. Carthage, N.Y., Jan. 16, 1948; s. Howard Ralph and Milton Jean (Carter) C.; m. Adrienne Barbeau, Jan. 1, 1979. Student, U. So. Calif., 1972. Co-writer, editor, composer: The Resurrection of Broncho Billy, 1970; dir.: Dark Star, 1974, Assault on Precinct 13, 1976, Someone's Watching Me; TV movie, 1978, Halloween, 1978, Elvis, 1979, The Fog, 1980, Escape From New York, 1981. Mem. Dirs. Guild Am. West, Writers Guild Am. West. Office: 9454 Wilshire Blvd Beverly Hills CA 90212

CARPENTER, JOHN MARLAND, engr., physicist; b. Williamsport, Pa., June 20, 1935; s. John Hiram and Ruth Edith (Johnson) C.; children: John Marland, Kathryn Ann, Susan Marie, Janet Elaine. B.S. in Engring. Sci, Pa. State U., 1957; M.S. in Nuclear Engring, U. Mich., 1958, Ph.D., 1963. Fellow Oak Ridge Inst. Nuclear Studies, 1957-60; postdoctoral fellow Inst. Sci. and Tech., U. Mich., 1963-64, mem. faculty univ., 1964-75, prof. nuclear engring., 1973-75; vis. scientist nuclear tech. br. Phillips Petroleum Co., 1965; solid state sci. div. Argonne (Ill.) Nat. Lab., 1971-72, 73; physics div. Los Alamos Sci. Lab., 1973; sr. physicist solid state sci. div., mgr. intense pulsed neutron source project Argonne Nat. Lab., 1975-77, program dir., 1977-78, tech. dir., 1978—; cons. in field., mem. U.S. del. to USSR on fundamental properties of matter, 1977. Author; editor. Recipient Disting. Service award U. Mich. Dept. Nuclear Engring., 1967, L.J. Hamilton Disting. Alumnus award, 1977, Disting. Performance award for work at Argonne Nat. Lab. U. Chgo., 1982. Mem. Am. Phys. Soc., Am. Nuclear Soc. (sect. chmn. 1974-75). Patentee nuclear instrumentation, neutron scattering, time dependent neutron thermalization, pulsed spallation neutron sources, neutron scattering instrumentation. Office: Intense Pulsed Neutron Source Program Argonne Nat Lab Argonne IL 60439

CARPENTER, JOHN WILSON, III, management consultant, retired air force officer, educational administrator; b. Starkville, Miss., Aug. 11, 1916; s. John Wilson and Alice Margaret (McBee) C.; m. Dorothy Biglow Goding, June 13, 1939; children: Carol Sue (Mrs. James P. Rogers), John Wilson IV, Jean McBee Carpenter Murray. Student, Okla. State U., 1934, Miss. State U., 1935; B.S., U.S. Mil. Acad., 1939; grad., Air Command and Staff Coll., 1947, Air War Coll., 1954. Commd. 2d lt. USAAF, 1939; advanced through grades to lt. gen. USAF, 1965; vice-comdr. 13th Air Force, 1949-50; plans and programming office, dep. for operations and chief of staff Hdqrs. Air Research and Devel. Command USAF, 1950; vice-comdr. Arnold Air Devel., USAF Center, 1954; insp. gen., chief plans and programming, asst. vice comdr. Air Research and Devel. Command, USAF, 1955, 57-58; comdr. Flight Test Center, USAF, 1959-62; dir. plans, Hdqrs. USAF, 1962-64, asst. dep. chief of staff for plans and operations. (JCS matters), 1964-65; comdr. Air U., Maxwell AFB, Ala., 1965-68; dep. chief staff, personnel Hdqrs. U.S. Air Force, 1968-69; asst. vice chief staff (Hdqrs. U.S. Air Force), 1969-70; supt. Culver Mil. Acad., Ind., 1970-74; pres. Carpenter Assos., Montgomery, Ala., 1974—. Decorated D.S.M. with oak leaf cluster, also; Silver Star with two oak leaf clusters; Legion of Merit with two oak leaf clusters; D.F.C. with two oak leaf clusters; Air Medal with oak leaf cluster; Presdl. Citation (U.S., P.I.). Assoc. fellow AIAA; mem. Ret. Officers Assn. (pres. 1975-79), Soc. Exptl. Test Pilots (asso.), Order Daedalians, Tau Beta Pi, Sigma Alpha Epsilon. Home: 3522 Carter Hill Rd Montgomery AL 36111

CARPENTER, JOT DAVID, landscape architect, educator; b. San Francisco, Mar. 19, 1938; s. Jot Thomas and Gretchen Marie (Johnston) C.; m. Claire Marie Dunn, Aug. 8, 1962; children: Jot David, Sean Michael, Kevin, Patrick. B.L.A., U. Ga., 1960; M.L.A., Harvard U., 1962. Registered landscape architect, N.Y., Ohio. Landscape architect T.J. Wirth Assocs., Billings, Mont., 1965-68; asst. prof. dept. hort. Cornell U., Ithaca, N.Y., 1968-72; assoc. prof., chmn. dept. landscape architecture Ohio State U., Columbus, 1972-76, prof., chmn., 1976—; dir. Landscape Arch. Found., Washington, 1977—, v.p., 1981, sec., 1982-83; mem. Ohio Bd. Landscape Arch. Examiners, 1973-76, CLARB Uniform Nat. Examination Com., Syracuse, N.Y., 1975-77. Author: Landscape Constrn., 1975; editor: Handbook of Landscape Architecture Construction, 1976. Bd. dirs. Columbus Conv. & Visitors Bur., 1977—; mem. Planning Commn., Upper Arlington, Ohio, 1978-82, Ohio Land Use Planning Task Force, 1974. Served to 1st lt. USAF, 1962-65. Recipient pres.'s medal Am. Soc. Landscaper Architecture, 1982, chpt. medal Ohio chpt. Am. Soc. Landscape Architecture, 1982. Fellow Am. Soc. Landscape Architecture (treas. 1973-79, v.p. 1976-78, pres. 1978-79); mem. Council of Educators in Landscape Architecture, Phi Kappa Phi, Sigma Lambda Alpha. Roman Catholic. Home: 1801 Elmwood Ave Columbus OH 43212 Office: Ohio State Univ Dept Landscape Architecture 190 W 17th Ave Columbus OH 43210

CARPENTER, MALCOLM BRECKENRIDGE, neuroanatomist; b. Montrose, Colo., July 7, 1921; s. Grover B. and Haidee (Moritz) C.; m. Carolyn I. Sloan, July 20, 1949; children—Duncan B., Gregory S., Rustin I. A.B., Columbia, 1943; M.D., L.I. Coll. Medicine, 1947. Diplomate: Am. Bd. Psychiatry and Neurology. Intern Bellevue Hosp., N.Y.C., 1947-48; resident neurology Neurol. Inst. N.Y., 1950-53; fellow neurology Columbia Coll. Phys. and Surg., 1948-50, mem. faculty, 1953-76, prof. anatomy, 1962-76; prof. anatomy and medicine Pa. State U., Hershey, 1976-78; prof., chmn. dept. anatomy Uniformed Services U., Bethesda, Md., 1978—; cons. NIH, 1962-66, 1968-72; adviser Parkinson Disease Found., 1962-65. Author: (with R.C. Truex) Human Neuroanatomy, 1964, 69, (with J.C. Madigan) Cerebellum of the Rhesus Monkey, 1971, Core Text of Neuroanatomy, 2d edit, 1978, Human Neuroanatomy, 1976; also articles.; Editorial bd.: Neurology, 1963-72, Neurobiology, 1970-76, Jour. Comparative Neurology, 1971-80; assoc. editor: Am. Jour. Anatomy, 1968-74. Served with M.C. USNR, 1950- 52. Home: 380 E Chocolate Ave Hershey PA 17033 Office: 4301 Jones Bridge Rd Bethesda MD 20014

CARPENTER, MALCOLM SCOTT, astronaut, oceanographer; b. Boulder, Colo., May 1, 1925; s. Marion Scott and Florence Kelso (Noxon) C.; m. Rene Louise Price, Sept. 9, 1948 (div.); children—Marc Scott, Robyn Jay, Kristen Elaine, Candace Noxon; m. Maria Roach, 1972; children—Matthew Scott, Nicholas André. B.S. in Aero. Engring, U. Colo., 1962. Commd. ensign U.S. Navy, 1949, advanced through grades to comdr., 1959; assigned various flight tng. schs., 1949-51, Barbers Point, Hawaii, 1951, also in, Korea, 1951-52, grad., 1954, assigned electronics test div., 1954-57, 1957, 1957-58, air intelligence officer, 1958-59; joined Project Mercury, man-in-space project NASA, 1959; completed 3 orbit space flight mission in spacecraft (Aurora 7), May 1962, mem., 1965-67; retired from U.S. Navy, 1969; now engaged in pvt. oceanographic and energy research business. Fellow Inst. Environ. Scis. (hon.); mem. Delta Tau Delta. Address: 93 Bell Canyon Rd Canoga Park CA 91307

CARPENTER, MYRON ARTHUR, manufacturing company executive; b. Jacksonville, Ill., Nov. 12, 1938; s. Paul Floyd and Margaret Esther (Lewis) C.; m. JoAnn Fisher, June 22, 1963. B.A. in Acctg, U. Ill., 1960. C.P.A., Mo. Staff acct. Arthur Young & Co., St. Louis, 1960-67, audit mgr., 1967-71; controller Bank Bldg. & Equipment Corp., St. Louis, 1972-78; v.p., treas. Bank Bldg. & Equipment Corp. Am., St. Louis, 1978-82, v.p. fin., treas., 1982—. Author: (with Neal W. Beckman) Purchasing for Profit, 1979. Served with U.S. Army, 1961. Mem. Am. Inst. C.P.A.s, Mo. Soc. C.P.A.s, Planning Execs. Inst., Delta Phi. Office: 1130 Hampton Ave Saint Louis MO 63139

CARPENTER, NOBLE OLDS, banker; b. Cleve., May 8, 1929; s. John W. and Maribel (Olds) C.; m. Ann Lindemann, Oct. 13, 1956; children: John L., Noble Olds, Robert W. A.B. cum laude, Princeton, 1951. Vice pres. Central Nat. Bank, Cleve., 1951-65; chmn., pres., chief exec. officer, dir. Central Trust Co. of Northeastern Ohio, N.A., Canton, 1965—; exec. v.p., dir. Central Bancorp., Cin.; treas., dir. Mountain Lake Tree & Land Co., Ltd.; dir. Central Trust Co. Newark, Ohio, Central Trust Co. No. Ohio, Lorain. Dep. sheriff Stark County.; Bd. dirs. Ducks Unlimited; trustee Stark County Found., Aultman Hosp. Devel. Found., Radio Free Europe, United Negro Coll. Fund, Blue Coats, Inc.; adv. bd. Malone Coll. Named outstanding Young Man of Year Jr. C. of C., 1965. Mem. Greater Canton C. of C. (trustee), Ohio Bankers Assn. (past sec., treas., mem. exec. com.), Robert Morris Assos., World Bus. Council. Clubs: Union (Cleve.); Canton, Brookside Country, Canton Athletic (Canton); Sportsman Rod and Gun. Home: 3423 Croydon Dr NW Canton OH 44718 Office: One Central Plaza S Canton OH 44702

CARPENTER, PATRICIA, educator; b. Del Rosa, Calif., Jan. 21, 1923; d. Daniel James and Dorothy Helen (Clock) C. B.A. cum laude, UCLA, 1944; student composition and theory with, Arnold Schoenberg, 1942-49; student piano with, Ethel Leginska, 1943-48; student conducting with, Leon Barzin, 1949-52. Instr. Barnard Coll., N.Y.C., 1964-70, asst. prof., 1970-78, asso. prof., 1978-79, prof. music, 1979—; chmn. undergrad. theory, 1968-69, chmn. grad. theory, 1969—, chmn. dept. music, 1974—. Condr., San Bernardino (Calif.) Community Orch. and Chorus, 1947-48; Author: The Janus-Aspect of Fugue: an Essay in the Phenomenology of Musical Form, 1971, also articles. Alice M. Ditson fellow Columbia U., 1955-56; Ingram Merrill Found. fellow in musicology, 1967-68. Mem. Am. Musicol. Soc., Coll. Music Soc., Am. Soc. Aesthetics (sec. Eastern div. 1966-67), Soc. Music Theory (exec. bd. 1980—). Home: Colonel Greene Rd Yorktown Heights NY 10598 Office: Barnard Coll New York NY 10027

CARPENTER, PAUL LEONARD, lawyer; b. Norwalk, Ohio, Jan. 21, 1920; s. Irving and Myrtle (McCracken) C.; m. Barbara Jane Chambers, Aug. 28, 1948 (dec. Mar. 1982); children: Susan A., Deborah L., Helen C. A.B., Ohio Wesleyan U., 1941; M.B.A., Harvard U., 1943; LL.B., U. Mich., 1948. Bar: Ohio 1948. With firm Doyle, Lewis & Warner, Toledo, 1948-55; ptnr. Carpenter & Paffenbarger, Norwalk, 1955—; dir. Citizens Nat. Bank, Norwalk. Trustee Norwalk City Hosp. Assn., 1959-75, pres., 1966-68. Served to lt. USNR, 1943-46. Recipient joint award Cleve. Toledo chpts. AIA, 1969. Mem. ABA, Ohio Bar Assn. Republican. Methodist. Home: 54 W Main St Norwalk OH 44857 Office: Citizens Nat Bldg Norwalk OH 44857

CARPENTER, RICHARD AMON, chemist; b. Kansas City, Mo., Aug. 22, 1926; s. Harry Russell and Ina Marie (Garver) C.; m. Joanne Fisher, Aug. 14, 1948; children: Stephen Russell, Lynne, Wendy. B.S., U. Mo., 1948, M.A., 1949. Chemist Shell Oil Co., Wood River, Ill., 1949-51; asst. mgr. Midwest Research Inst., Kansas City, 1951-58, trustee, 1964-69, 75-79; mgr. Washington office Callery Chem. Co., 1958-64; sr. specialist in sci. and tech. Congl. Research Service, Library of Congress, Washington, 1964-69, chief environmental policy div., 1969-72; exec. dir. Commn. on Natural Resources, NRC, Nat. Acad. Scis., Washington, 1972-77; research asso. East-West Center, Honolulu, 1977—; vis. prof. environ. studies, Dartmouth, 1976. Editor: Assessing Tropical Forest Lands: Their Suitability for Sustainable Uses, 1981, Natural Systems for Development: What Planners Need to Know, 1983; Contbr. articles to profl. jours. Trustee Inst. Ecology, 1979—; Mem. corp. vis. com. dept. civil engring. M.I.T., 1974—; mem. internat. environ. programs com. NRC-Nat. Acad. Scis., 1980—. Served with USAAF, 1945. Fellow Am. Inst. Chemists, AAAS; mem. Am. Chem. Soc., Ecol. Soc. Am., Sigma Xi, Sigma Chi. Presbyn. Club: Cosmos (Washington). Patentee in field. Home: 2419 Halekoa Dr Honolulu HI 96821 Office: 1777 East West Rd Honolulu HI 96848

CARPENTER, RICHARD LYNN, composer, arranger, singer, pianist; b. New Haven, Oct. 15, 1946; s. Harold Bertram and Agnes Reuwer (Tatum) C. Rec. artist; leader mus. group The Carpenters; producer A&M Records, Hollywood, Calif. Composer: Top of the World, Yesterday Once More; numerous concert tours, numerous TV guest appearances; spls. include Carpenters First TV Spl., 1976, Carpenters at Christmas, 1977, Space Encounters, 1978, Christmas Portrait, 1978, Music, Music, Music, 1980. Recipient 18 gold records in U.S., 46 gold records world wide, 3 Grammy awards, 1 Am. Music award, 15 ASCAP awards. Office: care Mgmt Three 9744 Wilshire Blvd Beverly Hills CA 90212 *

CARPENTER, ROBERT BEACH, advertising executive; b. Bklyn., Apr. 30, 1930; s. Hiram Beach and Melvina Liana (LaPointe) C.; m. Karin Carlson (dec. 1963); children: Robert Beach, John Wesley, Kristin Anne, Scott Thomas, Charles Andrew, James Carl, Todd Charles; m. Sandra Kay Mitchell, July 13, 1963 (div. 1977); m. Elaine Hahn, Oct. 20, 1978. A.B., U. Mich., 1953, M.B.A., 1956. Asst. dir. research Old Republic Ins. Co., Chgo., 1955-56; research account exec. Campbell Ewald, Detroit, 1956-59; exec. v.p. Fink, Carpenter & Rau, 1960-62; pres. Robert B. Carpenter, Advt., Inc., Detroit, 1963-70; chmn. bd. Specialized Communications, Inc., 1971—. Mem. Detroit Bd. Commerce.; Pres. Birmingham (Mich.) Little League, Detroit City Ballet, 1962. Served with USMCR, 1953-54. Mem. Alpha Delta Phi (dir. Penninsular chpt.). Republican. Presbyn. Clubs: University of Michigan (Detroit) (bd. dirs. 1967-68); Oakland Hills Country, Presidents, Victors (Birmingham). Home: 564 Overhill St Birmingham MI 48010 Office: 4120 W. Maple Rd. Birmingham MI 48010

CARPENTER, ROBERT EDDY, ins. co. exec., mayor; b. N.Y.C., Feb. 7, 1924; s. Arthur E. and Olive Mae (Eddy) C.; m. Mildred Louise Davis, Apr. 25, 1949; children—Robert Eddy, Louise Russet and Olivia LeMay (twins), Mary Renée. Student, Milligan Coll., 1942, Duke U., 1942-43, Auburn U., 1946-47. Engaged in farming and chem. sales, Harris County, Ga., 1947-50; with Cotton States Ins. Cos., Atlanta, 1950—, sr. v.p., 1965-76, exec. v.p., 1976-77, pres., 1977—; dir. Cotton States Mut. Ins. Co., Shield Ins. Co., Cotton States Life and Health, Am. Mut. Reins. Co., Chgo., DeKalb Fed. Savs. and Loan Assn.; lectr. Sch. Bus. Adminstrn., U. Ga. Mem. Decatur (Ga.) City Council, 1967-70, 75-78; now chmn. City Commn. and; mayor City of Decatur; mem. adv. bd. Morris Brown Coll., Ga. Better Bus. Bur.; bd. dirs. DeKalb chpt. Am. Cancer Soc., DeKalb South; chmn. retirement bd. trustees City of Decatur; trustee Edn. Found., Inc.; bd. visitors Emory U. Served with USN, 1943-46; PTO. Mem. U.S. C. of C., Ga. C. of C., Atlanta C. of C., DeKalb County C. of C., Nat. Assn. Ind. Insurers (pub. relations com.), Nat. Assn. Life Underwriters, Ga. Bus. and Industry Assn. (gov.). Republican. Methodist. Clubs: Atlanta Athletic, Highlands Country, Druid Hills Golf. Office: 244 Perimeter Center Pkwy NE Atlanta GA 30346

CARPENTER, ROBERT JAMES, health care co. exec.; b. San Diego, Mar. 14, 1945; s. John A. and Carmen E. (Ewbank) C.; m. Alma Lee, July 22, 1967; children—Christine, Catherine. B.S., U.S. Mil. Acad., 1967; M.S. in Computer Sci, Stanford U., 1969; M.B.A. (J. Spencer Love fellow 1973), Harvard U., 1975. With Baxter Travenol Labs., Inc., 1975-81; dir. prodn. planning div. Fenwal Labs., Deerfield, Ill., 1976-78, pres., 1978-81; pres., chief exec. officer Integrated Genetics Inc., Framingham, Mass., 1981—. Served with capt. U.S. Army, 1967-73. Decorated Bronze Star, Army Commendation medal (2). Office: 51 New York Ave Framingham MA 01701

CARPENTER, STANLEY SHERMAN, government official; b. Boston, Feb. 27, 1917; s. Lloyd and Adeline (Sherman) C.; m. Alice Luken, June 7, 1941; children: Wendell Sherman, Terry Ann. A.B., Wheaton Coll., 1940; A.M., U. Ill., 1941, Ph.D., 1943; student, U. Mich., 1943. Fgn. service officer, 1947—, vice consul Am. consulate, Kobe, Japan, 1948-49, consul, 2d sec. Am. embassy, Tokyo, Japan, 1949-52, 1st sec., 1955-59, consul, 2d sec. Am. embassy, London, Eng., 1953-55; assigned Nat. War Coll., 1959-60; dep. chief personnel operations Dept. State, 1960-62; dep. chief mission Am. embassy, Copenhagen, Denmark, 1962-65; dir. Performance Evaluation Program, Dept. State, 1965-67; civil adminstr., Ryukyu Islands, 1967-69; exec. dir. Bur. European Affairs, Dept. State, 1969-71; dept. asst. sec. for territorial affairs Dept. Interior, 1972-74; sr. fgn. service insp., 1974-77; U.S. sr. commr. S. Pacific Commn., 1974-81. Served to 1st lt. AUS, 1943-47. Decorated Disting. Civilian Service award U.S. Army, 1969; Superior Honor award Dept. Interior, 1973, Dept. State, 1977. Mem. Phi Beta Kappa, Sigma Pi Sigma. Home: 3169 N Pollard St Arlington VA 22207 Office: Dept State Washington DC 20520

CARPENTER, THOMAS EARL, publishing co. exec.; b. Nashville, Dec. 1, 1925; s. Charles Hugo and Ethel Powers (Wilson) C.; m. Mildred Ann Reynolds, Dec. 18, 1946; children—Mary Stephanie, Thomas Earl, Emily Reynolds, Laurale. Student, Carson Newman Coll., Jefferson City, Tenn., 1944-45, Duke, 1945-46; B.S., George Peabody Coll., Vanderbilt U., 1947, M.A., 1948. Tchr. math. Springfield (Tenn.) High Sch., 1948-52; gen. mgr. Reynolds Co., Nashville, 1952-58; with Abingdon Press, Nashville and; N.Y.C., 1958-61, 63-70, mgr., 1963-70; sr. v.p. United Methodist Pub. House, Nashville, 1970—. Trustee Martin Coll., Pulaski, Tenn. Mem. Protestant Ch.-Owned Pubs. Assn., Religious Pubs. Group, Assn. Am. Meth. Socs., Coop. Publ. Assn. (officer 1970-74), Nashville Met. C. of C., Phi Delta Kappa. Home: 512 Alta Loma Dr Goodlettsville TN 37072 Office: 201 8th Ave S Nashville TN 37203

CARPENTER, THOMAS EDGAR, III, scientific company executive; b. Durham, N.C., Mar. 29, 1936; s. Thomas Edgar and Elena Corsica (Ewart) C.; m. Emily Hay Babb, Dec. 28, 1962; children: Thomas IV,Stephen Ashby, Caroline Babb. B.S., U.S. Mil. Acad., 1958; M.A., Fletcher Sch. Law and Diplomacy, 1964, M.A.L.D., 1965, Ph.D., 1968. Commd. 2d lt. U.S. Army, 1958, advanced through grades to brig. gen.; spl. asst., Europe, 1974-76; comdr. (3d Brig., 3d Armored Div.), Ger., 1976-78, Army mem., chmn. staff group, 1978-79, dir. enlisted personnel, 1979-81, ret., 1981; spl. asst. program mgmt. Sci. Applications, Inc., McLean, Va., 1981—. Contbr. articles to profl. jours. Decorated D.S.M., Silver Star with oak leaf cluster, Legion of Merit with oak leaf cluster, D.F.C. with oak leaf cluster, Bronze Star with oak leaf cluster, others. Episcopalian. Club: Army-Navy Country. Home: 7012 Hundsford Ln Springfield VA 22153 Office: 1710 Goodridge Dr McLean VA 22102

CARPENTER, THOMAS GLENN, university president; b. Atlanta, Ga., Feb. 27, 1926; s. Walker G. and Loreta (Jackson) C.; m. Oneida Claire Pruette, Oct. 30, 1948; children: Debra Claire, Thomas Glenn. B.S. in Bus. Adminstrn, Memphis State U., 1949; M.A. in Econs, Baylor U., 1950, Ph.D., U. Fla., 1963. Asst. dir. housing U. Fla., Gainesville, 1957-64, instr. econs., 1956-57; dir. auxs. Fla. Atlantic U., Boca Raton, 1964; bus. mgr., v.p. U. West Fla., Pensacola, 1965-69; pres. U. North Fla., Jacksonville, 1969-80, Memphis State U., 1980—; dir. Indsl.-Am. Corp., Jacksonville; trustee First Am. Bank Memphis.; dir. Delta Life & Annuity. Mem. long-range devel. com. Salvation Army, 1980—; bd. dirs. Mid-South Fair, Inc., 1980—; trustee LeBonheur Children's Hosp., 1980—; exec. bd. Chickasaw Council Boy Scouts Am., 1981—. Served with USN, 1944-46. Mem. So. Assn. Colls. and Schs. (chmn. exec. council 1981—), Memphis Area C. of C. (bd. dirs. 1983—), Phi Delta Theta, Phi Kappa Phi, Beta Gamma Sigma, Omicron Delta Kappa. Presbyterian. Office: Memphis State Univ Southern Ave Memphis TN 38152 *

CARPENTER, WILLIAM LEVY, architect, engineer, planner; b. Columbia, S.C., May 26, 1926; s. Levy Leonidas and Lucille (O'Brien) C.; m. Blanche Augusta Owen, Apr. 10, 1948; children—Becky Carpenter Bouton, William Owen, Robert Meadors. Student, N.C. State U., 1943-44; B.S., U.S. Naval Acad., 1947. Registered profl. engr., S.C., La. Staff engr. Celanese Corp., Charlotte, N.C., 1954-56; power plant design engr. J.E. Sirrine Co., Greenville, S.C., 1956-62, v.p. dept. mech. engring., 1962-69; v.p. bus. devel., 1969-74, exec. v.p., 1974-75, pres., chief exec. officer, 1976—; Chmn. Non-Woven Industries, Inc., 1972-77; dir. S.C. Nat. Bank. Bd. dirs. St. Francis Community Hosp., Greenville, 1980; chmn. United Way Campaign, Greenville County, S.C., 1980, pres., Greenville County, S.C., 1983. Served to lt. comdr. USNR, 1947-53. Mem. S.C. Assn. Cons. Engrs., Cons. Engrs. Council (nat. dir. 1966-69), Greater Greenville C. of C. (pres. 1978). Baptist (chmn. bd. deacons 1973-74). Club: Greenville Country. Home: 227 Seven Oaks Dr Greenville SC 29605 Office: PO Box 5456 Station B Greenville SC 29606

CARPINO, LOUIS A., chemist, educator; b. Des Moines, Dec. 13, 1927; s. Pete and Angela (Ortale) C.; m. Barbara Pepe, Aug. 30, 1958; children—Philip, Alexandra, Nicholas, Christine, Elizabeth, Margaret. B.S., Iowa State U., 1950; M.S., U. Ill., 1951, Ph.D., 1953. Mem. faculty U. Mass., Amherst, 1954—, prof. chemistry, 1967—; vis. prof. U. Padova, 1967, U. Mainz, 1960, 74, 78; guest prof. Sonderforschungsbereich, Mainz-Darmstadt, 1975; U.S. Nat. Acad. Scis. Eastern European Exchange scientist, 1975, 77. NATO sr. fellow, 1974; sr. scientist Alexander von Humboldt Found., 1975. Mem. Am., German, Swiss, Japanese chem. socs., Chem. Soc. London. Research, publs. on devel. new synthetic techniques in field of organic chemistry. Home: 11 Mount Pleasant St Amherst MA 01002 Office: Dept Chemistry Univ Mass Amherst MA 01003

CARR, ALLAN, film producer, celebrity representative; b. Chgo., May 27, 1941; s. Albert and Ann (Neimitz) Solomon. B.A., Lake Forest Coll., 1962. Reopened, Civic Theater, Chgo., 1959; formed, Rogallan Prodns., 1966; became mgr., Ann-Margret's career; formed, Allan Carr Enterprises, 1971; mgr. careers of, Petula Clark, Peter Sellers, Marvin Hamlisch, Nancy Walker, Melina Mercouri, others, producer nightclub extravaganzas, TV spls., motion pictures; creative cons. to, Robert Stigwood Orgn. for all motion picture and TV prodn., including, Tommy, 1975; producer: The First Time, 1969, C.C. & Company, 1970, Can't Stop the Music, 1980; co-producer Broadway mus.: Grease, 1977, 1978; producer Broadway play: La Cage Aux Folles, 1983; co-producer motion picture: Survive, 1976; producer motion picture: Grease II, 1982; creative dir. motion picture: Bugsy Malone; co-exec. producer: Ann-Margret TV spectaculars, 1977; pres., AC Enterprises; v.p., Caloric Prodns., Rogallan Prodns. Active NCCJ. Clubs: Whitehall (Chgo.); Crockford (London); Regines (Paris, N.Y.C.). Office: Viewhaven Inc 1775 Broadway Suite 525 New York NY 10019 *

CARR, ARCHIE F., biologist, educator; b. Mobile, June 16, 1909; s. Archibald Fairly and Louise Gordon (Deaderick) C.; m. Marjorie Harris, Jan. 1, 1937; children: Marjorie, Archie III, Stephen, Thomas, David. B.S., U. Fla., 1932, M.S., 1934, Ph.D., 1937. Mem. faculty U. Fla., 1937—; now grad. research prof. zoology. Prof. biology Escuela Agricola Panamericana, Honduras, 1945-49; research asso. Am. Mus. Natural History, 1951—; tech. dir. Caribbean Conservation Corp., 1961, exec. v.p., tech. dir., 1968—; various expdns. to, Panama, Costa Rica, Trinidad, 1953, NSF expdn. Central Am., 1955, Brazil, French West Africa, Portugal and, Azores, 1956, Union of South Africa, Argentina, Chile, 1958, Africa, Madagascar, 1963, Caribbean, yearly 1960—; prin. investigator marine turtle migrations project NSF, 1955—, Office Naval Research, 1961-70; leader marine turtle survey, mariculture assessment Torres Strait for Spl. Minister State, Australia; hon. cons. World Wildlife Fund; mem. Survival Service Commn., Smithsonian Council, 1974—; mem. BOSTID/ACTI panel on wildlife farming Nat. Acad. Scis., 1981. Author: Handbook of Turtles, 1952, High Jungles and Low, 1952, The Windward Road, 1955, (with Coleman Goin) Amphibians and Freshwater Fishes of Florida, 1956, Guideposts of Animal Navigation, 1962, The Reptiles, 1963, Ulendo, 1964, African Wildlife, 1964, So Excellent a Fishe: A Natural History of Sea Turtles, 1967, The Everglades, 1973. Decorated officer Order Golden Ark, Netherlands; recipient Daniel Giraud Elliott medal Nat. Acad. Sci.; O'Henry award for prize stories, 1956; Edward H. Browning award for outstanding achievement in conservation Smithsonian Instn., 1975; John Burroughs medal for exemplary nature writing; 1st ann. research award Sigma Xi, U. Fla.; Merit award Fla. Audubon Soc., 1961; Gold medal World Wildlife Fund, 1973, N.Y. Zool. Soc.; Archie F. Carr medal established in his honor Fla. State Mus., 1979; Archie F. Carr postdoctoral fellowship established in his honor Dept. Zoology, U. Fla., 1983. Fellow Linnean Soc. London; mem. Am. Soc. Ichthyologists and Herpetologists, Am. Soc. Naturalists, Fla. Acad. Sci. (1st Ann. Honors medal 1963), Internat. Union Conservation Nature (chmn. marine turtle specialist group 1966—), Phi Beta Kappa, Sigma Xi. Home: Micanopy FL 32667 Office: U Fla Gainesville FL 32611

CARR, ARTHUR CHARLES, psychologist, educator; b. Buffalo, Nov. 27, 1918; s. John E. and Katherine (Haas) C. B.S., Buffalo State Tchrs. Coll., 1941; M.A., Tchrs. Coll. Columbia U., 1946; Ph.D., U. Chgo., 1952; postgrad., William Alanson White Inst., 1953-54, Inst. Group Therapy, 1957-58, N.Y. Soc. Clin. Psychologists, 1954, 60. Diplomate: Am. Bd. Examiners in Profl. Psychology, N.Y. State Edn. Dept. Trainee clin. psychology VA, 1947-52; sr. clin. psychologist Creedmoor State Hosp., Queens Village, N.Y., 1952-56; prin. clin. psychologist N.Y. State Psychiat. Inst., N.Y.C., 1956—; asst. prof. psychology Adelphi Coll., Garden City, N.Y., 1952-56; asso. prof. med. psychology, dept. psychiatry Coll. Physicians and Surgeons, Columbia U., 1956-71, prof., 1971-78, prof. emeritus, 1978—; prof. psychology in psychiatry Cornell U. Med. Coll., 1978—. Author: (with Shervert Frazier) Introduction to Psychopathology, 1964, (with Herbert Hendin, William Gaylin) Psychoanalysis and Social Research, 1965; author, editor: (with others) Loss and Grief, 1970, Psychosocial Aspects of Terminal Care, 1972, The Terminal Patient, 1973, Anticipatory Grief, 1974, Bereavement: Its Psychosocial Aspects, 1975, Grief, Selected Readings, 1975, The Mouth in Critical and Terminal Illness, 1980, Education of the Medical Student in Thanatology, 1981, Adolescent Marijuana Abusers and their Families, 1981; editor-in-chief: Man and Medicine, 75-80; cons. editor, 1980—; editorial bd., cons. editor: Jour. Projective Techniques, 1967-73; asso. editor: Jour. Abnormal Psychology, 1966 70, Jour. Thanatology,

1971—; contbr. articles to profl. jours. Served to maj. AUS, 1941-46. Fellow Am. Psychol. Assn., Soc. Projective Techniques (dir. 1961-64, pres. 1971-72); mem. Eastern, N.Y. State psychol. assns., N.Y. Soc. Clin. Psychologists. Home: 560 Riverside Dr New York NY 10027 Office: Westchester Div NY Hosp 21 Bloomingdale Rd White Plains NY 10605

CARR, ARTHUR JAPHETH, English educator; b. Bad Axe, Mich., Apr. 21, 1914; s. Arthur Wellesley and Margaret (McAuslan) C.; m. Penelope Gall, Feb. 1, 1964; children by previous marriage: Jennifer (Mrs. John McGee), Adam Fyfe, Daniel Arthur, Alice (Mrs. Jan A. Van den Broek III). A.B., U. Mich., 1935; A.M., Syracuse U., 1937; Ph.D., U. Ill., 1947. Instr. English Syracuse U., 1937-40, U. Ill., 1947-49; mem. faculty U. Mich., 1949-67, prof. English,, 1961-67, Williams Coll., Williamstown, Mass., 1967—, Edward Dorr Griffin prof., 1970-82, also chmn. dept., 1967-74; cons. U.S. Office Edn., 1965-69; Ednl. Testing Service, Coll. Entrance Exam. Bd., 1966-71; dir. NDEA Inst. U. Mich., 1965. Editor: Victorian Poetry; Clough to Kipling, 1959, 2d edit., 1972; co-editor: Norton Anthology of Poetry, 1970, 3d edit., 1983, Masterpieces of the Drama, 4th edit, 1979; Contbr. articles to profl. jours. Served with USNR, 1943-45; PTO. Mem. Modern Lang. Assn., Nat. Council Tchrs. English, AAUP, Tennyson Soc., Phi Beta Kappa, Phi Eta Sigma, Phi Kappa Phi. Home: 65 Jerome Dr Williamstown MA 01267

CARR, BERNADETTE PATRICIA, editor, publisher; b. N.Y.C.; d. Francis and Elizabeth (O'Donnell) C. B.A. in English Lit, Mercy Coll., Dobbs Ferry, N.Y., 1966; M.A. in Am. Lit, Fordham U., 1968. With Pageant mag., 1966-67; mng. editor Photoplay mag., N.Y.C., 1969-70, editor, 1971-73; editor-in-chief MacFadden Fan Titles mag., N.Y.C., 1973-74; editor Weight Watchers mag., N.Y.C., 1975-80; editor-in-chief Every Woman mag., N.Y.C., 1980-82; assoc. pub., editor CPDA News, N.Y.C., 1982—. Mem. Assn. Am. Pubs., Soc. Nat. Assn. Pubs., Am. Soc. Assn. Expcs., Sigma Phi Sigma. Home: 425 E 81st St New York NY 10021

CARR, BERNARD FRANCIS, hospital administrator; b. Wilkes-Barre, Pa., July 13, 1919; s. John Daniel and Marjorie Veronica (Gallagher) C.; m. Mary Ann Reiss, Dec. 30, 1945; children: Bernard, Cathy, Irene, Patricia, Mary Ann. R.N., Rockland State Hosp. Sch. Nursing, 1942; B.S., NYU, 1949; M.B.A. in Hosp. Adminstrn., U. Chgo., 1951; student, Western State U. Coll. Law, 1981—. R.N., Calif., Pa., Va.; lic. nursing home adminstr., Va.; lic. real estate asso., Calif.; lic. comml. aviator. Adminstrv. resident Ind. U. Med. Center, Indpls., 1950-51, adminstrv. asst., 1951-52, asst. adminstr., 1952-53; supt. Altoona (Pa.) Hosp., 1953-72; adminstr. South Coast Community Hosp., South Laguna, Calif., 1972-78, Bedford (Va.) County Meml. Hosp., 1978-79; exec. dir. South Coast Community Hosp. Found., 1976-77; dir., sec.-treas. Bedford Meml. Hosp. Found., 1978-79; regional mgr. Calif., Charter Med. Corp., Macon, Ga., 1978-81, div. mgr., Calif., 1981—; adminstr./chief exec. officer Kellogg Psychiat (Charter Hosp.), Corona, Calif., 1981—; pres., chief exec. officer New Riyadh (Saudi Arabia) Internat. Airport Hosp., 1980-81; dir. physician relations Charter Med. Corp., 1981-84; com. mem. Blue Ridge Emergency Med. Service. Mem. Altoona Redevel. Authority, 1964-70, vice chmn., 1966-70; exec. com. Coordinating Council on Continuing Edn. in Health Care Systems, Pa. State U., 1971-73; mem. Blair County Child Welfare, Blair County Soc. for Crippled Children adv. bds., 1965-72; Blair County Human Devel. Task Force; mem. tech. adv. com. Altoona Community Renewal Program, 1971-73; fund raising chmn. Bedford area Piedmont div. Am. Heart Assn., 1978, White House Council on the Aged. Served with U.S. Navy, 1943-45; to; 1st lt. USMCR, 1945-52. Fellow Am. Coll. Nursing Home Adminstrs., Am. Coll. Hosp. Adminstrs.; mem. Am. Hosp. Assn. (del. 1970—, mem. regional adv. bd., mem. council hosp. schs. nursing 1968-72), Calif. Hosp. Assn., Va. Hosp. Assn. (coms.), Hosp. Assn. Pa. (v.p. 1969-70, pres.-elect 1970-71, pres. 1971-72), Nat. League for Nursing (agy. rep. 1959—), Am. Health Care Assn., Va. Health Care Assn., Assn. Mental Health Adminstrs., Am. Pub. Health Assn., Hosp. Council So. Calif. (committeeman), Hosp. Financial Mgmt. Assn., Nat. Council Community Hosps., Roanoke Area Hosp. Council, Laguna Beach C. of C. (dir.). Clubs: Rotarian (pres. elect Bedford 1979-80, pres. South-Laguna-Niguel 1976-77. Home: 31291 E Nine Dr Laguna Niguel CA 92677 *Throughout my career I've made it clear to my subordinates that I would never stand in the way of their career opportunities, even if I were hard pressed to replace them. Over the years this attitude became a trademark for me and has resulted in an eager supply of key associates. Each has learned a basic philosophy: "What you do is a reflection on you; what your adversaries do is a reflection on them."*

CARR, BOB, Congressman; b. Janesville, Wis., Mar. 27, 1943; s. Milton Raymond and Edna (Blood) C.; m. Susan Baffa, Aug. 15, 1980. B.S., U. Wis., 1965, J.D., 1968. Bar: Wis. 1968, Mich. 1969, U.S. Supreme Ct. 1973. Asst. atty. gen. State of Mich., Lansing, 1969-72; mem. 94th-96th Congress from 6th Mich. Dist., Washington, 98th Congress from 6th Mich. Dist. Office: US House of Reps Washington DC 20515

CARR, CHARLES JELLEFF, pharmacologist, educator, toxicology consultant; b. Balt., Mar. 27, 1910; s. Joshua Barney and Pearl (Jelleff) C.; m. Sallie D. Wenner, May 15, 1980; children: Daniel Jelleff, Noel Edward, Joseph Barney. B.S. (Garvan scholar), U. Md., 1933, M.S., 1934, Ph.D. (Emerson fellow), 1937; D.Sc. (hon.), Purdue U., 1964. Teaching asst. pharmacology Sch. Medicine, U. Md., 1934-35, instr., 1935-37, asst. prof., 1937-39, assoc. prof., 1939-50, prof., 1950-55, adj. prof., 1957—; prof., chmn. dept. pharmacology Sch. Pharmacy, Purdue U., 1955-57; chief pharmacology unit Psychopharmacology Service Center, NIMH, Bethesda, Md., 1957-63; chief sci. analysis br., life scis. div. Army Research Office, Office Chief Research and Devel. U.S. Army, Arlington, Va., 1963-67; dir. Life Scis. Research Office, Fedn. Am. Socs. for Exptl. Biology, Bethesda, 1967-77; exec. dir. Food Safety Council, Columbia, Md., 1977-80, sci. counsellor, 1980-82; spl. lectr. Georgetown U. Sch. Medicine; instr. physicians course chem. warfare Emergency Med. Service, Balt. Third Civilian Def. Region, 1943. Author: (with Krantz) Pharmacologic Principles of Medical Practice, 7th edit, 1969; also numerous sci. articles; mng. editor: Regulatory Toxicology and Pharmacology. Merit badge councilor for chemistry and pub. health Boy Scouts Am., 1957-67. Recipient U.S. Army Meritorious Civilian award, 1965, 68. Fellow N.Y. Acad. Scis., Am. Coll. Neuropsychopharmacology; mem. Am. Soc. Pharmacology and Exptl. Therapeutics, Am. Chem. Soc., Am. Pharm. Assn. (life), Sigma Xi, Kappa Psi. Club: Cosmos (Washington). Home and Office: 6546 Belleview Dr Columbia MD 21046

CARR, CHARLES WILLIAM, biochemist, educator; b. Mpls., July 20, 1917; s. Eugene Dickinson and Emma Joanna (Fogelmark) C.; m. Betty Jane Westman, June 16, 1945; children—Ralph William, George Eugene. B.Chemistry, U. Minn., 1938, M.S., 1939, Ph.D., 1943. Research asso. U. Minn., 1943—, mem. faculty, 1946—, prof. biochemistry, 1964—, asso. dept. head, 1976—. Co-author: Physiological Chemistry, Laboratory Directions, 1951. Lalor summer fellow, 1956; grantee NIH, 1952-74. Mem. Am. Soc. Biol. Chemists, Am. Chem. Soc., Am. Soc. Cell Biology, N.Y. Acad. Scis., Soc. Exptl. Biology and Medicine, Am. Assn. Med. Colls., A.A.A.S., Minn. Med. Found. Conglist. Co-inventor permselective membranes. Home: 6633 Lynnwood Blvd Minneapolis MN 55423

CARR, DAVID TURNER, physician; b. Richmond, Va., Mar. 12, 1914; s. John Ernest and Mary Lela (King) C.; m. Rosemary Rudow, June 18, 1948 (div. 1953); 1 dau., Jennifer Anne Carr Oderkirk; m. Christine Nadeau, Dec. 27, 1979. Student, U. Richmond, 1931-33; M.D., Med. Coll. Va., 1937; M.S. in Medicine, Mayo Grad. Sch. Medicine, 1947. Intern, then asst. resident Grady Hosp., Atlanta, 1937-39; resident chest diseases Bellevue Hosp., N.Y.C., 1940-41; fellow medicine Mayo Clinic, 1943-47, cons. medicine, 1947-79, chmn. dept. oncology, 1975; dir. Mayo Comprehensive Cancer Center, 1975; asso. dir. Center for Cancer Control, 1976-79; prof. medicine Mayo Med. Sch., 1964-79; prof. medicine, head sect. pulmonary medicine M.D. Anderson Hosp. and Tumor Inst., Tex. Med. Center, Houston, 1979—. Mem.-at-large bd. dirs. Am. Lung Assn., 1959-74, v.p., 1971-72; bd. dirs. Rochester Civic Theatre, 1951-70, pres., 1965-67; bd. dirs. at large Am. Cancer Soc., 1967-74, pres. Minn. div., 1974-75. Fellow ACP, AAAS; mem. Central Soc. Clin. Research, Internat. Assn. for Study Lung Cancer (v.p. 1974-76, pres. 1976, treas. 1976-82), Am. Thoracic Soc. (v.p. 1963-64), Rochester C. of C. (pres. 1959-60); hon. mem. Peruvian Anti-Tb Assn. Spl. research on pulmonary diseases. Office: MD Anderson Hosp Tex Med Center Houston TX 77030

CARR, EDWARD ALBERT, JR., physician, educator; b. Cranston, R.I., Mar. 3, 1922; s. Edward Albert and Florence (Hodge) C.; m. Nancy Albosta, Dec. 27, 1952; children: Sharon L., Cynthia F. A.B. summa cum laude, Brown U., 1942; M.D. cum laude, Harvard, 1945. Research fellow, instr. pharmacology Harvard Med. Sch., 1948-51; exchange fellow St. Bartholomew's Hosp., London, Eng., 1952-53; mem. faculty U. Mich. Med. Sch., Ann Arbor, 1953-74, prof. pharmacology, 1962-74, prof. internal medicine, 1967-74, dir. program investigative clin. pharmacology, 1962-74; mem. sr. staff Univ. Hosp., 1957-74; dir. Upjohn Center Clin. Pharmacology, 1966-74; prof. medicine, prof., chmn. dept. pharmacology Med. Sch., U. Louisville, 1974-76; prof. medicine and pharmacology Med. and Dental Sch., State U. N.Y. at Buffalo, 1976—, chmn. dept. pharmacology and therapeutics, 1976—, pres. med. faculty council, 1981-82; mem. sr. staff, chmn. therapeutics com. Louisville Gen. Hosp., 1974-76; lectr. U. Helsinki, 1972, Autonomous U. Barcelona, 1974, Japan Med. Assn., 1977—, Swedish Acad. Pharm. Scis., Stockholm, 1977; cons. Ann Arbor VA Hosp., 1954-74, Louisville VA Hosp., 1974-76, Buffalo VA Hosp., 1976—, Erie County Med. Center, 1978—; hon. vis. prof. Prince Henry and Prince of Wales Hosp., Sydney, Australia, 1973. Co-author: Radioisotopes in Biology and Medicine, 1964; author also articles. Mem. Nat. Joint Commn. on Prescription Drug Use, 1976-80; mem. coop. studies evaluation com. U.S. VA, 1980-83. Fellow A.C.P.; mem. Central Soc. Clin. Research, Am. Thyroid Assn., Soc. Nuclear Medicine, A.A.A.S., Endocrine Soc., Am. Fedn. Clin. Research, Am. Soc. Pharmacology and Exptl. Therapeutics, Am. Soc. Clin. Pharmacology and Therapeutics (pres. 1974-75, Henry W. Elliott award 1981), Royal Soc. Medicine, Phi Beta Kappa, Sigma Xi, Alpha Omega Alpha. Home: 2 Gothic Ledge Lockport NY 14094 Office: Dept Pharmacology and Therapeutics Med Sch State U NY at Buffalo 127 Farber Hall Buffalo NY 14214

CARR, FRANK CHARLES, insurance company executive; b. Chgo., Mar. 4, 1913; s. Harry Landis and Mabel (Teed) C.; m. Elizabeth Frye, Feb. 10, 1940; children: Stephanie, Frank, Victoria. Student pub. schs. With First Nat. Bank, Palm Beach, Fla., 1935-36; with John Nuveen & Co., Chgo., 1936-69; retiring as chmn. bd.; pres. Am. Municipal Bond Assurance Co., Milw., 1971-80, now cons., dir. Mem. Municipal Forums, N.Y. and. Clubs: Bent Tree and West Bend Country; Municipal Bond, Union League (Chgo.). Office: MGIC Plaza Milwaukee WI 53201

CARR, GEORGE C., judge; b. 1929. B.S., B.A., J.D., U. Fla., Gainesville. Bar: Fla. bar 1954. Presently U.S. dist. judge Dist. of Middle Fla., Tampa. Mem. Am. Bar Assn. Office: US Dist Ct PO Box 3309 Tampa FL 33601

CARR, GERALD PAUL, astronaut; b. Denver, Aug. 22, 1932; s. Thomas Ernest and Freda (Wright) C.; (div.)children: Jennifer, Jamee, Jeffrey, John, Jessica, Joshua. B.S. in Mech. Engring., U. So. Calif., 1954, U.S. Naval Postgrad. Sch., 1961, M.S., Princeton U., 1962; D.Sc. (hon.), Parks Coll., St. Louis U., 1976. Registered profl. engr., Tex. Commd. 2d lt. USMC, 1954, advanced through grades to col., 1973, ret., 1975; jet fighter pilot, U.S., Mediterranean, Far East, 1956-65; astronaut NASA, Houston, 1966-77; comdr. 3d Skylab Manned Mission, 1973-74; cons. Applied Research, Inc., Houston.; project mgr. McDonald Obs. 300 inch telescope U. Tex. Bd. dirs. Houston Pops Orch., Sunsat Energy Council, Space Found. Recipient Group Achievement award NASA, 1971, Distinguished Service medal, 1974; Gold medal City of Chgo., 1974, City of N.Y., 1974; Alumni Merit award U. So. Calif., 1974; Distinguished Eagle Scout award Boy Scouts Am., 1974; Robert J. Collier Trophy, 1974; Robert H. Goddard Meml. trophy, 1975; FAI Gold Space medal; others. Fellow Am. Astronautical Soc. (Flight Achievement award 1975); mem. Marine Corps Assn., Marine Corps Aviation Assn., Nat. Soc. Profl. Engrs., Soc. Exptl. Test Pilots, Tex. Soc. Profl. Engrs., Nat. Space Inst., U. So. Calif. Alumni Assn., Tau Kappa Epsilon. Presbyterian. Office: 2138 Colquitt Houston TX 77098

CARR, GILBERT RANDLE, railroad exec.; b. Rockford, Ill., Jan. 4, 1928; s. Audra Clifford and Marjorie (Lantz) C.; m. Marion Minnie Heinemann, Mar. 28, 1953; children—John W., J. Michael. B.S. in Accounting and Mgmt, U. Ill., 1950. With Arthur Andersen & Co. (C.P.A.s), Chgo., 1950-57; with C.& N. W. Transp. Co., 1957—, comptroller, 1967-79, v.p., comptroller, 1979—; dir. Trailer Train Co., Railbox Co. Served with AUS, 1946-47. Lutheran. Home: 1425 S Linden St Park Ridge IL 60068 Office: One Northwestern Center 165 N Canal Chicago IL 60606

CARR, HAROLD NOFLET, airline executive; b. Kansas City, Kans., Mar. 14, 1921; s. Noflet B. and Mildred (Addison) C.; m. Mary Elizabeth Smith, Aug. 5, 1944; children: Steven Addison, Hal Douglas, James Taylor, Scott Noflet. B.S., Tex. A&M U., 1943; postgrad., Am. U., 1945-46. Asst. dir. route devel. Trans World Airlines, Inc., 1943-47; exec. v.p. Wis. Central Airlines, Inc., 1947-52; mem. firm McKinsey & Co., 1952-54; pres. North Central Airlines, Inc., Mpls., 1954-69, chmn. bd., 1965-79, Republic Airlines, Inc., 1979—; dir., 1952—; professorial lectr. mgmt. engring. Am. U., 1952-62; dir. Dahlberg Electronics, Inc., Ross Industries, Inc., Governor's Sound, Ltd., Cayman Water Co., Republic Energy, Inc., Westland Capital Corp., First Nat. Bank Bryan (Tex.), Cayman Mile, Ltd.; Mem. bd. nominations Nat. Aviation Hall of Fame; mem. adv. com. Tex. Transp. Inst., Tex. A&M U. System; mem. exec. adv. council Nat. Register Prominent Americans and Internat. Notables. Trustee Tex. A&M Research Found.; mem. devel. council Coll. Bus. Adminstrn., Tex. A&M U. Mem. Nat. Aero. Assn., World Bus. Council, Am. Mgmt. Assn., Smithsonian Assos., Nat. Trust Historic Preservation, Minn. Execs. Orgn., Nat. Def. Transp. Assn., Pine Beach Peninsula Assn., Am. Econ. Assn., Greater Mpls., St. Paul Area chambers commerce, Tex. A&M Former Students Assn., Beta Gamma Sigma. Episcopalian. Clubs: Nat. Aviation, Aero (Washington); Minneapolis; Aggie (dir.) (College Station) (Tex.); Tex. A. and M. Century; Racquet (Miami); Gull Lake Yacht (Brainerd, Minn.); Wings (N.Y.C.); Stearman Alumnus (Wichita, Kans.); Briarcrest Country (Bryan). Home: PO Box H Bryan TX 77805 Office: 7500 Airline Dr Minneapolis MN 55450

CARR, HOWARD EARL, physicist, educator; b. Headland, Ala., Sept. 16, 1915; s. Samuel Tilden and Annie Bell (Freeman) C.; m. Carolyn Taylor, June 25, 1939; children—Howard Earl, Carolyn Ann. B.S., Auburn U., 1936; M.A., U. Va., 1939, Ph.D., 1941. Research asst. U. Va., 1939-41; asso. prof. physics U. S.C., 1941-43; physicist Ford, Bacon & Davis, Oak Ridge diffusion plant, 1944; asst. prof. physics U.S. Naval Acad., 1946-48; asso. prof. physics Auburn U., 1948-53, prof., 1953-80, head dept., 1953-78; vis. prof. U.S. Mil. Acad., 1979-80; researcher Oak Ridge Nat. Lab., 1950, cons., 1951-55, USAF, 1957-61, U.S. Army, 1966-68. Served with USNR, 1944-46. Recipient Pegram award, 1974. Fellow Am. Phys. Soc. (sec. S.E. sect. 1956-67, chmn. 1968), A.A.A.S.; mem. Ala. Acad. Sci. (pres. 1957), Am. Inst. Physics (counselor Ala. 1962-69), Am. Assn. Physics Tchrs., Ala. Edn. Assn., Raven Soc., Blue Key, Sigma Xi, Phi Kappa Phi, Sigma Pi Sigma. Methodist. Clubs: Kiwanis, Eufaula Yacht. Spl. research separation isotopes, negative ion studies, ion optics, Mossbauer effect. Home: 342 Payne St Auburn AL 36830

CARR, JAY PHILLIP, newspaper critic; b. N.Y.C., Aug. 19, 1936; s. Andrew Joseph and Florence (Glassman) C.; m. Nancy Lou Hutchison, Oct. 27, 1962 (div. Oct. 1978); children: Diane Elizabeth, Richard Joseph, Julia Veronica. B.S., City Coll. N.Y., 1958. Reporter Jersey City Jour., 1957; editorial asst., amusement dept. staff writer N.Y. Post, 1957-64; drama and music critic Detroit News, 1964-83; critic-at-large Boston Globe, 1983. Served with AUS, 1960-62. Recipient George Jean Nathan award for dramatic criticism, 1971-72. Office: Boston Globe Boston MA 02107

CARR, JOHN HOWARD, public health physician; b. Takoma Park, Md., Jan. 6, 1926; s. John Edwin and Katherine (Williams) C.; m. Joan Hersey, Aug. 6, 1949 (div. July 25, 1955); children: Jesse, Jeffrey; m. Loretta Mae Beckman, July 25, 1956 (div. Mar. 27, 1980); children: John Howard, Terence, Bridget.; m. Kathleen Anne McBurney, Dec. 11, 1982. B.A., Stanford U., 1945, M.D., 1948; M.P.H., U. Hawaii, 1970. Diplomate: Am. Bd. Pediatrics, Am. Bd. Preventive Medicine. Intern Alameda County Hosp., Oakland, Calif., 1947-48; resident in pediatrics U. Calif. Hosp., San Francisco, 1948-51; practice medicine specializing in pediatrics, Marin County, Calif., 1953-64, Honolulu, 1964-66; chief bur. maternal and child health Nev. Div. Health, 1968-69, acting state health officer, 1969, state health officer, 1970-83; practice ambulatory medicine Hawaii Permanente Med. Group, Maui, 1982—. Served to lt. (j.g.) USNR, 1951-52. Fellow Am. Acad. Pediatrics, Am. Acad. Preventive Medicine; mem. Naval Res. Assn. Office: 80 Mahalani St Wailuku HI 96793

CARR, JOHN MAURICE, planetarium adminstr.; b. Oak Park, Ill., Sept. 18, 1926; s. Maurice Tipple and Bessie Emeline (Foster) C.; m. Loretto Lescher, Aug. 5, 1971. B.G.E., Morton Jr. Coll., 1946; student, DePaul U., 1947-48; B.S., Springfield Coll., 1953; postgrad., Wheaton Coll., summers 1959-60, Ill. Inst. Tech. Tchrs. In-Service Inst., 1960-63, Ind. State U. Summer Inst., 1961, St. Louis U. Summer Inst., 1962-64, U. Ill., 1965-66. Equipment engr. Western Electric Co., Cicero, Ill., 1953-54; specifications engr. Stewart Warner Corp., Chgo., 1955-58; tchr. physics, gymnastics coach Morton High Sch. and Jr. Coll., 1959-65; lectr. Charles Hayden Planetarium-Museum of Sci., Boston, 1966, asst. dir., 1966-68, dir., 1968—; lectr. in astronomy Northeastern U., Boston, 1980—; host Conf. Dirs. Maj. N. Am. Plantariums, 1974, Conf. on Use of Lasers in Planetariums, 1976, Middle Atlantic Planetarium Soc. Conv., 1980; plantarium cons. Contbr.: revs. on astronomy and sci. to Sky and Telescope. Pres. Midwest Gymnastics Assn., 1958-60; bd. mgrs. Central Dist. AAU, 1958-60; gymnastics program dir. Pan Am. Games, Chgo., 1959; program dir. Nat. Summer Gymnastics Clinic, 1959-67; Discussion leader Gt. Books Found., Franklin Park, Ill., 1955-64, mem. council, 1956-57. Served with U.S. Army, 1945-46; PTO. NSF fellow, 1960-64. Mem. AAAS, Internat. Planetarium Soc., Middle Atlantic Planetarium Soc., Astron. Soc. Pacific, Royal Astron. Soc. Can. Home: 9 Debston Ln Lynnfield MA 01940 Office: Charles Hayden Planetarium Mus of Sci Boston MA 02114

CARR, KENNETH MONROE, naval officer; b. Mayfield, Ky., Mar. 17, 1925; s. Samuel Norman and Nancy Elmore (Monroe) C.; m. Mary Elizabeth Pace, June 10, 1949. Student, U. Louisville, 1944-45; B.S., U.S. Naval Acad., 1949. Served as enlisted man U.S. Navy, 1943-45, commd. ensign, 1949; advanced through grades to vice admiral, 1977, mem. commissioning crew, 1954, comdg. officer, 1964-67, 1967-68, mil. asst. to, 1973-77, comdr. submarine force, Norfolk, Va., 1977-80, vice dir., Offutt AFB, Nebr., after 1980, now dep. comdr., Norfolk, Va. Decorated D.S.M. (2), Legion of Merit (2). Baptist. Clubs: Army Navy Country, Harbor. Home: 439 Dillingham Blvd Norfolk VA 23511 Office: Dep Comdr US Atlantic Fleet Norfolk VA 23511

CARR, LAWRENCE EDWARD, JR., lawyer; b. Colorado Springs, Colo., Aug. 10, 1923; s. Lawrence Edward and Lelah R. (Rubert) C.; m. Agnes Isabel Dyer, Dec. 26, 1946; children—Mary Lee, James Patrick, Lawrence Edward III, Eileen Louise, Thomas Vincent. B.S., U. Notre Dame, 1948, LL.B., 1949; LL.M., George Washington U., 1954. Bar: Colo. bar 1949, D.C. bar 1952, Md. bar 1961. With Travelers Ins. Co., 1949-51; practiced in, Washington, 1952—; sr. partner firm Carr, Jordan, Coyne & Savits. Served with USMCR, 1943-46, 51-52; col. Res.; ret.). Mem. Am. Bar Assn. (ho. of dels. 1973-75), Bar Assn. D.C. (dir. 1969-71, pres. 1974-75), Internat. Assn. Ins. Counsel, D.C. Def. Lawyers Assn. (pres. 1978-79). Home: 12001 Piney Glen Ln Potomac MD 20854 Office: 900 17th St NW Washington DC 20006

CARR, LESTER, coll. pres.; b. Bklyn., Mar. 7, 1935; s. Samuel and Sarah (Berma) C.; m. Courtney Tall, June 2, 1967; children—Lincoln Damian, Sharon Rose. B.A., N.Y. U., 1957; M.A., New Sch. for Social Research, N.Y.C., 1959; Ph.D., Vanderbilt U., 1963. Research and clin. intern Rockland State Hosp., N.Y.C. Dept. Mental Hygiene, 1958-59; cons. clin. psychologist to sr. clin. psychologist Central State Hosp., Nashville, 1962-64; sr. coordinator psychol. services, dept. social welfare, asso. clin. prof. U. R.I., Providence, 1963-68; prof., chmn. psychology dept., dean Summer Sch., Salve Regina Coll., Newport, R.I., 1968-72, v.p. acad. affairs, 1969-71; project dir. Newport Hosp., 1968-72; pres. Lewis U., Lockport, Ill., 1971-76; chmn. bd. dirs., dean of faculty Columbia Pacific U., Mill Valley, Calif., 1978—; dir. 1st Nat. Bank, Lockport, Wholistic Counseling Assos.; ednl. cons. Sultan and Minister Edn. of Oman; past dir. R.I. Bd. Certification for Psychologists. Past chmn. R.I. Gov.'s Task Force on Mental Health Rehab.; mem. nat. adv. council Profl. Childrens Sch., N.Y.C.; past chmn. adv. bd. dirs. Comprehensive Mental Health Center, Newport; past bd. dirs. Regional Ballet Soc., Joliet, Ill., R.I. Rehab. Assn.; past chmn. bd. trustees St. Marys Acad., Nauvoo, Ill.; past mem. exec. com. R.I. Gov.'s Commn. on Vocational Rehab. Served with U.S. Army, 1958. Mem. Am. Psychol. Assn., AAUP, Am. Assn. Presidents Independent Colls. and Univs., Assn. Correctional Psychologists, NEA, Am. Council on Edn., Am. Assn. for Higher Edn., Assn. Am. Colls., Nat. Catholic Edn. Assn. Home: 148 Wilson Hill Rd Petaluma CA 94952

CARR, MARTIN DOUGLAS, TV producer, director, writer; b. Flushing, N.Y., Jan. 20, 1932; s. Irving Conovitz and Isabel (Hochdorf) C. B.A. summa cum laude, Williams Coll., 1953; postgrad., Neighborhood Playhouse Sch. Theatre, 1956. Producer, CBS News, N.Y.C., 1957-69, NBC News, N.Y.C., 1969-71, ABC News, N.Y.C.,

1973-75; producer: The Saturday Night Kid, N.Y.C., 1959; Recipient (Emmy award Nat. Acad. TV Arts and Scis. 1966, 67, 68, 71, Peabody award U. Ga. Sch. Journalism 1968, 70, 71, Robert F. Kennedy Journalism award Robert F. Kennedy Found. 1970, Sidney Hillman Found. award 1971, DuPont/Columbia Journalism award 1971, Gavel award Am. Bar Assn. 1972, Cine Golden Eagle 1980); major TV prodns. Smithsonian World, CBS Reports, Hunger in America, NBC White Paper: Migrant, This Child Is Rated X, The Search for Ulysses, Gauguin in Tahiti, Leaving Home Blues, Five Faces of Tokyo, Dublin Through Different Eyes, ABC Closeup: The Culture Thieves, ABC News-20/20. Served to lt (j.g.) USN, 1953-55. Club: Williams (N.Y.C.). Home: 305 W 86th St New York NY 10024

CARR, MICHAEL HAROLD, geologist; b. Leeds, Eng., May 26, 1935; came to U.S., 1956, naturalized, 1965; s. Harry and Monica Mary (Burn) C.; m. Rachel F. Harvey, Apr. 14, 1961; son, Ian M. B.Sc., London U., 1956; M.S., Yale U., 1957, Ph.D., 1960. Research asso. U. Western Ont., 1960-62; with U.S. Geol. Survey, 1962—; chief astrogeologic studies br. U. Geol. Survey, Menlo Park, Calif., 1973-79; mem. Mariner Mars Imaging Team, 1969-73; leader Viking Mars Orbiter Imaging Team, 1969-80; mem. Voyager and Galileo Jupiter Imaging Teams, 1978—; Mem. com. on planetary exploration Nat. Acad. Sci., 1979-82. Author: The Surface of Mars. Recipient Exceptional Sci. Achievement medal NASA, 1977; Meritorious Service award Dept. Interior, 1979. Mem. Geol. Soc. Am., AAAS, Am. Geophys. Union. Home: 1389 Canada Rd Woodside CA 94062 Office: US Geological Survey Menlo Park CA 94025

CARR, PATRICK E., U.S. judge; b. Jasper County, Miss., Oct. 2, 1922; s. Eugene A. and Sarah (Finnegan) C.; m. Jean Massey, Dec. 20, 1947; children: Karen, Stanley, Judy Janice, Pat, Mary, Brian. Grad., St. Bernard Jr. Coll.; LL.B., Loyola U. Bar: La. 1950. Pvt. practice, Metaire, La., 1950-75; judge La. Dist. Ct., 24th Jud. Dist., 1975-79; now judge U.S. Dist. Ct. (ea. dist.) La., New Orleans. Served with A.C. U.S. Army, 1942-45. Mem. Am. Bar Assn., Jefferson Parish Bar Assn., La. State Bar Assn., VFW (nat. comdr.). Democrat. Office: US Courthouse 500 Camp St Chambers C-376 New Orleans LA 70130

CARR, PAUL HENRY, physicist; b. Boston, May 12, 1935. B.S. in Physics, MIT, 1957, M.S., 1961, Ph.D., Brandeis U., 1966. Solid state research physicist Rome Air Devel. Ctr. (formerly Air Force Cambridge Research Labs.), 1962-67, chief microwave acoustics br., 1967-77, chief radio frequency and suface acoustic wave components sect., Hanscom AFB, Mass., 1977—, asst. chief antennas and radio frequency components br. of electromagnetic scis. div., 1977—; mem. adv. group on electron devices, working group on microwave devices Office Under sec. Def. for Research and Engring. Contbr. sci. papers to profl. publs.; patentee suface wave delay line with quater-wave taps, accoustic surface wave frequency synthesizer. Served to 1st lt. Ordnance Corps U.S. Army, 1960-62. Recipient Marcus D. O'Day Meml. award for best paper, 1967, Guenter Loeser Meml. award for sci. achievement, 1973, Outstanding Tech. Achievement of Quarter award Air Force Systems Command, 1976. Fellow IEEE (chmn. Boston sect. on sonics and ultrasonics 1973-74, mem. tech. program coms. Ultrasonics Symposia 1971-75, chmn. tech. program coms. Ultrasonics Symposia 1976), Am. Phys. Soc. Office: Rome Air Devel Center RADC-EEA Hanscom AFB MA 01730

CARR, RICHARD, clergyman, air force officer; b. El Centro, Calif., Dec. 3, 1925; s. William Henry and Lucy Emma (Montgomery) C.; m. Jeanne Maurcee Robertson, Apr. 29, 1955; children: David Robertson, Catherine Louise, Kevin Richard. B.A. in History, Whitworth Coll., Spokane, Wash., 1949; M.Div., Fuller Theol. Sem., Pasadena, Calif., 1954. Ordained to ministry United Ch. of Christ, 1954. Student missionary, Alaska, 1950; asst. pastor Faith Presbyn. Ch., Los Angeles, 1954; social worker Los Angeles County, 1954-55; served as enlisted man USAAF, from 1943—; now chaplain USAF. Office: Dept Air Force Chief Chaplains The Pentagon Washington DC 10301

CARR, ROBERT ALLEN, finance educator; b. Los Angeles, Sept. 28, 1917; s. Harry Newton and Elvaretta (Wilson) C.; m. Ruth Eleanor Holland, Dec. 7, 1946; children: Nancy Ellen, David Allen. A.B., San Francisco State Coll., 1951, M.A., 1953; Ph.D., U. So. Calif., 1959. Orgn. and methods examiner VA, San Francisco, 1946-48; instr. Golden Gate Coll., 1952, coordinator econ. edn. project, 1952-56; lectr. U. So. Calif., 1956-57; asst. prof. Calif. State U., Fresno, 1957-61, asso. prof., 1961-66, prof., 1966-83, asst. head div. bus., 1964-65, chmn. dept. fin. and industry, 1965-76, prof. emeritus, 1983—, coordinator Somali project, 1983—; cons. economist Fresno Planning Dept., 1962-63; cons. Somali Inst. Devel. Adminstrn. and Mgmt., 1982-83; trustee Fresno Meml. Gardens, 1977—, chmn., 1978-80. Contbr. articles to profl. jours. Mem. Fresno County Econ. Devel. Adv. Council, 1977-80, vice chmn., 1978, chmn., 1979-80. Served to staff sgt. USAAF, 1941-45. Ford Faculty fellow, 1962; E.L. Phillips intern, 1963-64. Mem. Am. Western econ. assns., Am. Fin. Assn., Western Fin. Assn. (exec. com., v.p. 1966-67, pres. 1967-68), Fin. Mgmt. Assn. (dir. 1970-72, v.p. 1973-74), Soc. Internat. Devel., Am. Statis. Assn. (pres. San Joaquin Valley chpt. 1975-77), Regional Sci. Assn., AAUP. Home: 5734 N Bond St Fresno CA 93710

CARR, ROBERT CLIFFORD, merchandising executive; b. Hanover, N.H., July 10, 1940; s. Robert Kenneth and Olive (Grabill) C.; m. Danna Reeder, Dec. 29, 1962; children: Catherine, Deborah, Elizabeth. B.A. in Govt., Harvard U.; M.A. in Internat. Affairs, Johns Hopkins U. With Mobile Oil Corp., N.Y.C., Paris and Singapore, 1964-72, treas., 1972-77, dep. gen. mgr., Melbourne, Australia; treas. mktg. and refining div. Mobil Oil Corp., Melbourne, Australia, 1977-79; exec. v.p., chief fin. officer Montgomery Ward, Chgo., 1982—. Clubs: Econ., Execs., Harvard (Chgo.); Glen View (Golf, Ill.). Office: Montgomery Ward 535 W Chicago Ave Chicago IL 60072

CARR, ROBERT DAVID, newspaper editor; b. Rockford, Ill., Sept. 17, 1948; s. Robert W. and Elaine E. (Hennings) C.; m. Cathy J. Schroeder, Jan. 22, 1972; children: Kristen, Nathan. B.S. in Communications, So. Ill. U., Carbondale, 1971; M.S. in Edn., No. Ill. U., 1974. Reporter Freeport Jour.-Standard (Ill.), 1974-75; copy editor Des Moines Register, 1975-77, Chgo. Sun-Times, 1977-79; editor Living Sect. Chgo. Sun-Time, 1979-80; copy editor Chgo. Tribune, 1980-82, editor Arts Sect., 1982—. Regional pub. info. coordinator Juvenile Diabetes Found., Chgo., 1983—. Office: Chicago Tribune 435 N Michigan Ave Chicago IL 60611

CARR, ROBERT WILSON, JR., chemistry educator; b. Montpelier, Vt., Sept. 7, 1934; s. Robert Wilson and Marie (Soucy) C.; m. Betty Lee Elmer, June 21, 1958; children: Kevin, Terrell, Kathryn. B.S., Norwich U., 1956; M.S., U. Vt., 1958; Ph.D., U. Rochester, 1962. NIH fellow Harvard U., 1963-65; asst. prof. U. Minn., 1965-69, asso. prof., 1969-75, prof. dept. chem. engring. and materials sci., 1975—; vis. prof. U. Cambridge, 1971-72; guest prof. U. Göttingen (Ger.), 1982. Asst. editor: Jour. Phys. Chemistry, 1970-80. Served to 1st lt. U.S. Army, 1963. NSF fellow, 1971-72; Fulbright fellow, 1982. Mem. Am. Chem. Soc., Am. Aviation Hist. Soc., Sigma Xi. Mem. United Ch. of Christ. Home: 5134 Irving Ave S Minneapolis MN 55419 Office: Dept Chem Engring and Materials Scis U Minn Minneapolis MN 55455

CARR, RONALD EDWARD, opthalmologist, educator; b. Newark, N.J., Sept. 17, 1932; s. Frank Edward and Mildred (Sasso) C.; m. Nancy May Gould, June 8, 1957; children: Peter Richardson, Jacqueline Marie, Timothy Edward. A.B., Princeton U., 1954; M.D., Johns Hopkins U., 1958; M.Sc., NYU, 1963. Intern Bellevue Hosp., N.Y.C., 1958-59; resident NYU Med. Ctr., N.Y.C., 1959-63; clin. assoc. NIH, Bethesda, Md., 1963-64, assoc. ophthalmologist, 1964-65; asst. prof. ophthalmology NYU Med. Ctr., 1965-67, assoc. prof., 1967-71, prof., 1971—. Author: Visual Electrodiagnosis, 1981. Served to lt. comdr. USPHS, 1963. Recipient Knapp award AMA, 1966. Fellow Am. Acad. Ophthalmology, ACS; mem. Am Ophthal. Soc., N.Y. Ophthal Soc., Assn. Research in Ophthalmology. Republican. Episcopalian. Clubs: Princeton, Stone Horse Yacht. Home: 130 East End Ave New York NY 10028 Office: NYU Med Ctr 550 1st Ave New York NY 10016

CARR, RONALD GENE, lawyer, government official; b. Chgo., Jan. 19. 1946; s. Harry Bertram and Marion Esther (Adlam) C.; m. Mary Laurie Azcuenago, Aug. 24, 1968. A.B., Stanford U., 1968; M.A., U. Calif.-Berkeley, 1970; J.D., U. Chgo., 1973. Law clk. to chief judge U.S. Ct. Appeals (D.C. cir.), Washington, 1973-74; law clk. to Justice Lewis F. Powell U.S. Supreme Ct., Washington, 1974-75; spl. asst. to Atty. Gen. Edward H. Levi U.S. Dept. Justice, Washington, 1975-76; assoc. ptnr. Morrison & Foerster, San Francisco, 1977-81, ptnr., 1983—; dep. asst. atty. gen. antitrust div. U.S. Dept. Justice, Washington, 1981-83; lectr. fed. jurisdiction Law Sch., U. Calif.-Berkeley, 1978. Editor-in-chief: U. Chgo. Law Rev., 1972-73. Mem. ABA, Order of Coif, Phi Beta Kappa. Home: 5100 Manning Pl NW Washington DC 20016 Office: 1920 N St NW Washington DC 20036

CARR, STEPHEN HOWARD, materials engineer, educator; b. Dayton, Ohio, Sept. 29, 1942; s. William Howard and Mary Elizabeth (Clement) C.; m. Virginia W. McMillan, June 24, 1967; children: Rosamond Elizabeth, Louisa Ruth. B.S., U. Cin., 1965; M.S., Case-Western Res. U., 1967, Ph.D., 1970. Coop. engr. Inland div. Gen. Motors Corp., Dayton, 1960-65; asst. prof. materials sci. and engring. Northwestern U., Evanston, Ill., 1970-73, asso. prof., 1973-78, prof., 1978—; adj. to surg. staff Evanston Hosp.; cons. Contbr. articles to profl. jours. Fellow Am. Phys. Soc.; Mem. Soc. Auto Engrs. (Ralph R. Teetor award 1980), Plastics Inst. Am. (Ednl. Service award 1975), Am. Chem. Soc., Am. Inst. Chem. Engrs., Am. Soc. Metals, Soc. Plastics Engrs. Patentee plastics and textiles fields. Home: 2704 Harrison St Evanston IL 60201 Office: 2145 Sheridan Rd Evanston IL 60201

CARR, VIKKI (FLORENCIA BISENTA DE CASILLAS MARTINEZ CARDONA), singer; b. El Paso, Tex., July 19; d. Carlos and Florence (Martinez) Cardona. Grad. high sch.; hon. doctorate, St. Edwards U., 1974. Soloist with, Pepe Callahan Mexican-Irish Band, Los Angeles, Palm Springs; rec. star 35, Liberty Records, Columbia Records; rec. star: hit records Can't Take My Eyes Off You., It Must Be Him, With Pen in Hand, also; rec. star with: It Must Be; guest appearances on TV, including, Dean Martin, Ed Sullivan, Jackie Gleason, Smothers Bros., Jerry Lewis, Jonathan Winters, Carol Burnett, spls. with, Bob Hope, Jim Nabors, Johnny Carson, hostess of Tonight show several times; appeared in various nightclubs, U.S., Europe, Australia, Japan, toured mil. bases in, Vietnam; debut in mus. comedy as Lt. Nellie Forbush in: South Pacific, Kansas City; appeared in: Unsinkable Molly Brown, Ohio; lead role: I'm Getting My Act Together and Taking It on the Road, St. Louis; starring role on Broadway as: Nora, 1983; debut as TV dramatic star in: Mod Squad, 1972; sang at royal command performance for, Queen Elizabeth, 1967; performance at, Inaugural Celebration, Kennedy Music Center, 1973.; hostess, Mrs. America Pageant, TV, 1981, 82, 83. Founder, pres. Vikki Carr Scholarship Found., 1971. Named Woman of Yr. Los Angeles Time, 1970, Vis. Entertainer of Yr. Mexico City, 1972, Singer of Yr. Am. Guild Variety Artists, 1972, Woman of World, 1974; recipient Humanitarian award Nosotros, 1981; named No. 1 Female Selling Album Artist for CBS Mex., 1982, 83, 84; recipient Woman of Yr. award League United Latin Am. Citizens, 1983, Hispanic Woman of Yr. award Hispanic Women's Council, 1984. Office: Vi-Car Enterprises Inc care Arnold Mills 8721 Sunset Blvd Los Angeles CA 90069

CARR, WILLARD ZELLER, JR., lawyer; b. Richmond, Ind., Dec. 18, 1927; s. Willard Zeller and Susan (Brownell) C.; m. Margaret Paterson, Feb. 15, 1952; children: Clayton Paterson, Jeffrey Westcott. B.S., Purdue U., 1948; LL.B., Ind. U., 1951. Bar: Calif. 1951, U.S. Supreme Ct. 1963. Ptnr. Gibson, Dunn & Crutcher, Los Angeles, 1952—; mem. nat. panel arbitrators Am. Arbitration Assn.; former labor relations cons. State of Alaska; lectr. Bd. visitors Southwestern U. Law Sch.; trustee Calif. Adminstrv. Law Coll.; bd. dirs. Hollywood Presbyn. Med. Ctr., Greater Los Angeles Visitors and Conv. Bur., Mchts. and Mfrs. Assn., Greater Los Angeles Zoo Assn.; mem. Mayor's Econ. Devel. Policies Com.; mem. adv. com. Econ. Literacy Council of Calif. State Univ. and Colls. Found.; trustee, past chmn. Pacific Legal Found.; past chmn. men's adv. com. Los Angeles County-USC Med. Ctr. Aux. for Recuitment, Edn. and Service; past chmn. bd. Wilshire Republican Club; past mem. Rep. State Central Com.; past mem. pres.'s council Calif. Mus. Sci. and Industry; mem. Nat. Def. Exec. Res., Los Angeles World Affairs Council,; bd. dirs., sec. Los Angeles Policy Meml. Found.; past chmn. Los Angeles sect. United Way; mem. adv. com. Los Angeles County Human Relations Commn.; bd. dirs., 1st vice-chmn. ARC; mem. adv. council Southwestern Legal Found., Internat. and Comparative Law Ctr. Fellow Am. Bar Found.; mem. ABA (past chmn. econ. and resources controls com. of corp., banking and bus. law sect.; internat. labor relations law com. of labor and employment law sect., also com. devel. of law under Nat. Labor Relations Act), Internat. Bar Assn. (chmn. labor law com. of bus. law sect.), Calif. State Bar, Los Angeles County Bar Assn., Los Angeles C. of C. (chmn. 1980). Home: 123 N McCadden Pl Los Angeles CA 90004 Office: Gibson Dunn & Crutcher 333 S Grand Ave 49th Floor Los Angeles CA 90071

CARR, WILLIAM, mining corporation executive; b. Durham County, Eng., Aug. 11, 1930; m. Joan West, Aug. 3, 1953; children: Christopher, Alexandra, Elizabeth. B.S. with honors in Mining Engring, U. Durham (Eng.); grad., London Bus. Sch. Gen. mine mgr. Dawdon Mine, Nat. Coal Bd., 1969-75; sr. mining engr. Paul Weir Co., Chgo., 1975-76; v.p. Jim Walter Corp.; pres. mining div. Jim Walter Resources, Inc., Birmingham, Ala., 1976—; invited session chmn. U.S.A. Conf. on Safety, Bur. Mines. Contbr. articles to profl. jours. Bd. dirs. Warrior Tombigbee Devel. Assn.; mem. council mining dept. U. Ala. Mem. Am. Mining Congress, AIME (Tom Seaman scholar 1969), Ala. Mining Inst., Nat. Coal Assn. (dir.). Mem. Ch. of Eng. Home: 1212 Lake Forest Circle Birmingham AL 35244 Office: PO Box C-79 Birmingham AL 35283

CARRA, ANDREW JOSEPH, magazine editor; b. Bklyn., July 30, 1943; s. Andrew Sylvester and Grace (Santoro) C.; m. Eileen Lynn Campbell, Aug. 6, 1966; children: Christopher Andrew, Allison Lynn, Courtney Lauren. B.A., St. Bonaventure U., 1966. Asso. editor Sport Mag., Macfadden-Bartell, N.Y.C., 1967-71; mng. editor publs. div. Spencer Mktg. Services, N.Y.C., 1971-73; assoc. pub. Camping Jour. mag. Davis Publs., N.Y.C., 1973-82; account supr. Robert Marston and Assocs., N.Y.C., 1982-83; v.p., dir. pub. relations Colarossi Griswatt Inc., N.Y.C., 1983—. Author: Complete Guide to Hiking and Backpacking, 1977, How to Go Camping, 1978; Contbr. chpts. to books, articles to periodicals. Mem. Outdoor Writers Assn., Am., Nat. Geog. Soc., Am. Soc. Mag. Editors, Nat. Wildlife Fedn. Democrat. Roman Catholic. Home: 40 Radcliff Dr Huntington NY 11743 Office: 380 Lexington Ave New York NY 10017

CARRADINE, DAVID, actor; b. Hollywood, Calif., Oct. 8, 1940; s. John Carradine. Attended, San Francisco State U. TV appearances in: series Shane, 1966, Kung Fu, 1972; others; appeared on N.Y. stage: motion pictures include Taggert, 1965; Bus Riley's Back In Town, 1965, Too Many Thieves, The Violent Ones, 1967, Heaven With A Gun, 1969, Young Billy Young, 1969, The Good Guys and the Bad Guys, 1969, Gallery of Horrors, The McMasters, 1970, Macho Callahan, 1970, Boxcar Bertha, 1972, Mean Streets, 1972, The Long Goodbye, 1973, Death Race 2000, 1975, Cannonball, 1976, Bound for Glory, 1976, Thunder and Lightning, 1977, The Serpent's Egg, 1977, Mr. Horn, 1978, Gray Lady Down, 1978, Deathsport, 1978, Circle of Iron, 1979, Cloud Dancer, 1980, The Long Riders, 1980, Safari 3000, 1981, Lone Wolf McQuade, 1983, Americana, 1983, Kain of Dark Planet, 1984. Office: PO Box 1469 Hollywood CA 90078 *

CARRADINE, JOHN RICHMOND, actor; b. N.Y.C., Feb. 5, 1906; s. William Reed and Genevieve Winifred (Richmond) C.; children—Bruce John, John Arthur, Christopher John, Keith Ian, Robert Reed. Student, Episcopal Acad., Phila., Graphic Arts Sch., Phila. Debut, St. Charles Theater, New Orleans, 1925; appeared in numerous motion pictures, 1928—, numerous stage plays, 1943—; organizer own repertory co. playing: Othello, Hamlet, Shylock. Mem. AFTRA, Actors Equity Assn., Screen Actors Guild. Clubs: Players, Channel Island Yacht.

CARRADINE, KEITH IAN, actor, singer, composer; b. San Mateo, Calif., Aug. 8, 1949; s. John Richmond Reed and Sonia (Sorel) C.; m. Sandra Will, Feb. 6, 1982; 1 son, Cade Richmond. Student in drama, Colo. State U., 1967. Appeared: on Broadway Hair, Biltmore Theater, 1969-70, Foxfire, 1982-83 (Outer Critics Circle award 1983); films A Gunfight, 1970, McCabe and Mrs. Miller, 1971, Emperor of the North, 1972, Thieves Like Us, 1973, Nashville, 1975, The Duellists, 1976, Pretty Baby, 1977, welcome To L.A., 1977, Old Boyfriends, 1979, An Almost Perfect Affair, 1979, The Longriders, 1980, Southern Comfort, 1981, Choose Me, 1983, Maria's Lovers, 1983; TV films A Rumour of War, CBS, 1981, Chiefs, CBS, 1983; composer I'm Easy (Acad. award for Best Song of a Motion Picture, Hollywood Fgn. Press Assn. Golden Globe award for best song 1975); also rec. artist. Mem. Acad. Motion Picture Arts and Scis., Greenpeace Found., Cousteau Soc., Sierra Club. Democrat. Episcopalian. Office: care ICM 8899 Beverly Blvd Los Angeles CA 90048

CARRAGHER, FRANK ANTHONY, chemical company executive; b. Belleville, N.J., Feb. 4, 1932; s. Frank A. and Margaret R. (Mallack) C.; m. Eunice M. Burns, Oct. 2, 1955; children: Tracey, Phil, Judy, Matt, Susan, Frank, Marybeth. B.S., Rutgers U., 1953; postgrad., Newark Coll. Engring., 1955. Idst. mgr. Ariz. Chem. Co., 1956-58; regional mgr. Humko div. Nat. Dairy Products, 1958-66; sr. v.p. mktg. research and devel. Glyco Chems., Inc., Greenwich, Conn., 1966-76, dir.; exec. v.p. Petrochems. Co., Inc. subs. Chattem Drug & Chem. Co., Ft. Worth, 1976-77; v.p., gen. mgr. Quad Chem. Corp., Long Beach, Calif., 1977-79; group v.p. chems. Ferro Corp., Cleve., 1979—; assoc. dir. MCA. Mem. Wilton Sch. Bd., Conn. Served with USMC, 1953-55. Mem. Oil Chemists Assn., Plastic Engrs. Soc., Soap and Detergent Assn., Am. Textile Assn., Comml. Devel. Assn. Roman Catholic. Clubs: Chemists, Cleve. Athletic, University. Home: 1080 Sheerbrook Dr Chagrin Falls OH 44022 Office: Ferro Corp 1 Erieview Plaza Cleveland OH 44114

CARRARA, ARTHUR ALFONSO, architect, designer, painter, graphic designer; b. Chgo., Apr. 8, 1914; s. Cesare and Georgia (Marcucci) C.; m. Charlotte A. Bartels, Sept. 23, 1944. B.A. in Arch, U. Ill., 1937; apprenticeship, John S. VanBergen, Prairie Sch. Architect, Highland Park, Ill., 1938. Pvt. practice architecture, Chgo., 1946—; tchr., lectr. various archtl. schs. and museums; mem. editorial staff Inland Architect, 1964-67; Mem. Nat. Council Architects Registration Bd. Collector, curator, Prairie Sch. Architects work.; one-man archtl. shows include, Milw. Art Center, 1960, Walker Art Center, Mpls., 1962, Albright-Knox Art Mus., 1965, Munson-Williams-Proctor Mus. Art, Utica, N.Y.; exhibited in group show, Milw. Art Center, 1977-78, introduction hydraulic/moving parts to architecture, Cafe Borranical, Melbourne, Australia, 1944; architect master plan, Manila, P.I., 1944, Cebu, P.I., 1945, 1st magnetic sculpture exhbn., Renaissance Soc., U. Chgo., 1947, design 1st magnetic lamp, 1946; designer, inventor magnet master playtool, 1947, inflata lamp, 1954, transfer print, 1957, one man show prints, Gilman Gallery, 1963; exhibited in: group show An Am. Architecture: Its Roots, Growth and Horizons, Milw. Art Center, 1977; introduction paper flexagon, Chgo. Art Inst., 1957, prin. magnetic and electro-magnetic into modern architecture, 1960; designer sky-spider duct column, Graphic Controls Bldg., 1962, 1st large scale one piece fibre-glass skylite into modern architecture, 1963; introduced air supported forms into architecture, 1964; designed 1st continuous light-rift Architects Workshop, Kettle Moraine, Wis., 1969; introduced large-scale indsl. fiberglass light-rift controles Graficas, S.A., Mexico City, 1970; Work appears in book The Prairie Sch. Tradition, 1979; Contbr. articles to profl. jours. Served to maj. AUS, 1942-45. Mem. A.I.A., Alpha Rho Chi. Pioneer large scale fibreglass archtl. mech. forms; designed 1st stapled plywood furniture, 1st paper-core house with paper-core furniture. Address: Route 2 Townline Rd Whitewater WI 53190

CARRASCO BRICENO, BARTOLOME, archbishop; b. Tlaxco, Mex., Aug. 18, 1918. Ordained priest Roman Cath. Ch., 1945; named bishop of, Huejutla, Mex., 1963; bishop Titular Ch. of Claterna, 1967; bishop of, Tapachula, 1971, named archbishop of, Antequera, Oaxaca, Mex., 1976. Address: Apartado Postal n 31 Oaxaca Oaxaca Mexico

CARRERAS, FRANCISCO JOSÉ, university president; b. San Juan, P.R., May 13, 1932; s. Francisco and Antonia (Muriente) C.; m. Ana Elisa Carreras, Mar. 29, 1964; children: Inés María, María Soledad, Irene María, Marianne, Francisco JoseUTE. Student, Instituto Superior de Estudios Clásicos, Havana, Cuba, 1954-57; B.A., Universidad Pontificia de Comillas, Santander, Spain, 1959; M.A., Fordham U., 1960; Ph.D., Universidad Pontificia Gregoriana, Rome, 1966. Mem. faculty U. P.R., Humacao Regional Coll., 1962-69, acad. asst. to dir., 1967-69, dir. humanities dept., 1967-68; pres. Cath. U. P.R., Ponce, 1969—; academician P.R. Acad. Arts and Scis., 1970; mem. P.R. State Commn. on Post-Secondary Edn., 1973; dir. Banco Popular de P.R. Author: Filosofía de la Coordinación de José Vasconcelos, 1971, Incógnita y Revelación, 1981; also articles. Adv. Sociedad Puertorriqueña para la UNESCO, 1973; pres. Found. for Humanities, P.R. Endowment for Humanist Values in Community Affairs, 1977; bd. dirs. Angel Ramos Found., 1977, Damas Hosp., 1978, P.R. Acad. Arts and Scis., 1980; adv. bd. dirs. Organización de Universidades Católicas de América Latina, 1976. Mem. Ateneo Puertorriqueño, Fundación Puertorriqueña de las Humanidades (pres. 1977), Ponce Sales and Mktg. Execs. Assn., Alpha Phi Omega, Phi Delta Kappa. Roman Catholic. Clubs: Rotary, Lions. Home: 1504 Ashford Ave Apt 12 Condado San Juan PR 00907 Office: Cath Univ PR Ponce PR 00731

CARRERAS, JOSE, tenor; b. Barcelona, Spain, Dec. 5, 1947; s. Jose and Antonio C.; (married); children—Alberto, Julia. Profl. opera debut as: Gennaro in Lucrezia Borgia, Liceo Opera House, Barcelona, 1970-71 season; appeared in: La Bohème, Un Ballo In Maschera and I Lombardi Alla Prima Crociata in Teatro Regio, Parma, Italy, 1972 season; Am. debut as Pinkerton in: Madame Butterfly with, N.Y.C. Opera, 1972; Met. Opera debut as Cavaradossi, 1974; La Scala debut as Riccardo in Un Ballo In Maschera, 1975; appeared in: film Don Carlos, 1980; other appearances throughout the world include, Teatro Colon, Buenos Aires, Argentina, Covent Garden, London, Vienna Staatsoper, Easter Festival, Summer Festival, Salzburg, Austria, Lyric Opera of Chgo.; recs. include Otello (Rossini), Un Ballo in Maschera, La Battaglia di Legnano, Il Corsaro, Un Giorno, I Due Fuscari, Simone Boccauegra, Macbeth, Don Carlo, Tosca, Thais, Aida, Cavalleria, Turandot, Pagliacci, Lucia di Lammer moor, Elisabetta di Inghilterra. Office: care Columbia Artists Mgmt 165 W 57th St New York NY 10019 also care Opera Caballe Via Augusta 59 Barcelona Spain *

CARRET, PHILIP LORD, business exec.; b. Lynn, Mass., Nov. 29, 1896; s. James R. and Hannah (Todd) C.; m. Elisabeth Osgood, Sept. 4, 1922; children—Gerard, Donald, Diane. A.B., Harvard, 1917; student, Harvard Grad. Sch. Bus. Adminstrn., 1916-17. Chmn. bd. Pioneer Fund, Inc.; pres. Carret & Co., Inc.; dir. other corporations. Author: Buying a Bond, 1924, The Art of Speculation, 1926; Contbr. mag. articles to Barron's and other publs. Trustee Scarsdale Bd. Edn., 1941-46. Mem. Nat. Assn. Securities Dealers (past mem. bd. govs.), Am. Legion. Republican. Conglist. Clubs: Rotary; Explorers, Harvard (N.Y.C.); Scarsdale (N.Y.); Golf. Home: 50 Popham Rd Scarsdale NY 10583 Office: 200 Park Ave New York NY 10166

CARRETTA, ALBERT ALOYSIUS, lawyer, educator; b. N.Y.C., Dec. 23, 1907; s. Vincent and Concetta (De Florio) C.; m. Gertrude Elizabeth Lynch, Nov. 29, 1934; children: Albert Aloysius, John Vincent, William Joseph. B.S., CCNY, 1930; J.D., Georgetown U., 1940; postgrad., N.Y. U. Bar: D.C. 1940, Va 1941. Instr. econs., fin. Coll. City N.Y. Sch. Bus. and Civic Adminstrn., 1930-34; fin. analyst, atty. SEC, Washington, 1934-42; instr. finance Columbus U., Washington, 1935-36; bus. specialist OPA, Washington, 1942-44; lectr. corp. law, corp. finance, unfair trade practices, fed. antitrust legislation Catholic U. Am., Wash., 1942-54; instr. fin. U. Calif., 1945; vice chief, bd. mem. services and sales renegotiation sect. Navy Dept., Washington, 1946-47; lectr. accounting dept., sch. fgn. service Georgetown U., 1946-52; practice law, Washington and Arlington, Va., 1947-52; mem. FTC, 1952-54; practice law, Washington, 1954-82. Pres. Cath. Charities No. Va., 1955-57. Served with USN, 1944-45. Decorated knight Order of the Star of Italian Solidarity. Mem. Am., Va. bar assns., Am. Arbitration Assn. (nat. panel). Democrat. Roman Catholic. Club: Belle Haven Country. Lodge: K.C. Home: 1823 N Glebe Rd Arlington VA 22207

CARRICA, JEAN LEON, college dean; b. Albuquerque, June 1, 1931; s. Jean and Marie (Louissena) C.; m. Margaret M. Kiser, Dec. 19, 1959; children: Annette, Brigitte, Michelle, Loren, John. B.A., Creighton U., 1961, J.D., 1961; M.B.A., Ind. U., 1963; Ph.D., U. Nebr.-Lincoln, 1967. Bar: Nebr. 1961. Owner, dir. small loan ins. and real estate bus., N.Mex., 1954-58; faculty Bus. Sch. Creighton U., Omaha, Nebr., 1967-73, dean, 1973-82, Sch. Bus., Loyola Coll. Md., Balt., 1982—; cons. fin. feasibility studies, 1970-83; expert witness State and Fed Dist. Cts., 1970-83; cons. SBA, 1970-83; mem. search com. Omaha Mayor's Fin. Dir., 1981. Contbr. articles to profl. jours. Mem. transp. com. Greater Balt. Com., 1982—, edn. com., 1982—. Served with USAF, 1951-54. Recipient award Excellence in Teaching Creighton U., 1971. Mem. Baltimore County C. of C. (edn. com.), Nebr. Fin. Assn., Am. Fin. Assn., Nebr. Bar Assn., Managerial Fin. Assn., Am. Jesuit Colls. (regional pres. 1978-79), Beta Gamma Sigma. Democrat. Roman Catholic. Home: 1221 Oak Croft Dr Lutherville MD 21093 Office: Loyola Coll Sch Bus and Mgmt 4501 N Charles St Baltimore MD 21210

CARRICO, HARRY LEE, state chief justice; b. Washington, Sept. 4, 1916; s. William Temple and Nellie Nadalia (Willett) C.; m. Betty Lou Peck, May 18, 1940; 1 dau., Lucretia Ann. Jr. certificate, George Washington U., 1938, J.D., 1942; LL.D. (hon.), U. Richmond, Va., 1973. Bar: Va. 1941. With firm Rust & Rust, Fairfax, 1941-43; trial justice, Fairfax County, Va., 1943-51, pvt. practice, Fairfax, 1951-56; judge 16th Jud. Circuit Va., 1956-61; justice Supreme Ct. Va., 1961-81, chief justice, 1981—. Served to ensign USNR, 1945-46. Recipient Alumni Achievement award George Washington U., 1972. Mem. McNeill Law Soc., Order of Coif, Phi Delta Phi., Omicron Delta Kappa. Episcopalian. Office: Supreme Ct Bldg Richmond VA 23210

CARRIER, ESTELLE STACY, drilling company executive; b. nr. Anderson, Tex., Sept. 3, 1913; d. David D. and Rosa (Miller) Mabry; m. Jack Leonard Stacy, Dec. 24, 1933 (dec. May 1963); 1 son, Richard Allen; m. John B. Carrier, Mar. 2, 1974. Grad. high sch. Vice pres. Stacy Drilling Co., Douglas, Wyo., 1948-63, pres., 1963—, Teno United, 1963—; Treas. Converse County (Wyo.) Found., 1952-77; Vice chmn. Wyo. Republican Com., 1960-66; mem. Wyo. Fedn. Rep. Women (past pres.); Rep. nat. committeewoman for, Wyo., 1965-76; sec. Rep. Nat. Com., 1972-76, Rep. Western States Conf., 1974-76; Mem. Def. Adv. Com. for Women in Services, 1970—, chmn., 1972—; mem. U.S. State Dept. Adv. Com., Western area, 1971-73, Nat. Adv. Council Safety in Agr., 1974-76; sec. Def. Adv. Com. on Women in Services, 1970-72, chmn., 1972; pres. bd. trustees Converse County Library, 1965-72; mem. Rep. Nat. Com. Adv. Com. on Energy and Environ. Trustee, legis. council Wyo. Safety Found.; trustee Del. for Friendship Among Women. Mem. C. of C., Epsilon Sigma Alpha., Order Eastern Star (past matron). Clubs: Women of the Moose, Douglas Sorority, Douglas Civic (past pres.), Federated Women's.). Home: 3 Hilltop Rd Douglas WY Office: PO Box 96 Douglas WY 82633

CARRIER, GEORGE FRANCIS, applied mathematics educator; b. Millinocket, Maine, May 4, 1918; s. Charles Mosher and Mary (Marcaux) C.; m. Mary Casey, June 30, 1946; children: Kenneth, Robert, Mark. B.S. in Mech. Engring, Cornell U., 1939, Ph.D., 1944. From asst. prof. to prof. Brown U., 1946-52; Gordon McKay prof. mech. engring. Harvard U., 1952-72, T. Jefferson Coolidge prof. applied math., 1972—; mem. council Engring. Coll., Cornell U. Co-author: Functions of a Complex Variable, 1966, Ordinary Differential Equations, 1968, Partial Differential Equations, 1976; assoc. editor: Quar. Applied Math. Former trustee Rensselaer Poly. Inst., Troy, N.Y. Recipient Von Karman prize ASCE, 1977. Fellow Am. Acad. Arts and Scis.; hon. fellow Brit. Inst. Math. and Its Applications; hon. mem. ASME (Timoshenko medal 1978, Centennial medal 1980); mem. Nat. Acad. Scis. (award applied math. and mumerical analysis 1980), Soc. Indsl. and Applied Math. (Von Karman prize 1979), Nat. Acad. Engring., Am. Philos. Soc. Office: Pierce Hall 311 Harvard Univ Cambridge MA 02138

CARRIER, GLASS BOWLING, JR., banker; b. Lexington, Ky., Sept. 2, 1931; s. Glass Bowling and Margaret (Sexton) C.; m. Dorothy Kay Olsen, June 15, 1957; children: Catherine Anne, David Bowling. B.S. in Bus, U.N.C., 1953. Supr. Allstate Ins. Co., Charlotte, N.C., 1956-61, div. supr., St. Petersburg, Fla., 1961-62; with First Union Nat. Bank, Charlotte, 1962—, sr. v.p. investment div. head, 1968—. Bd. dirs. N.C. Municipal Council. Served with USNR, 1953-56. Mem Dealer Bank Assn. (dir.). Presbyterian (elder). Home: 3635 Severn Ave Charlotte NC 28210 Office: 1 First Union Plaza Charlotte NC 28288

CARRIER, RONALD EDWIN, university president; b. Bluff City, Tenn., Aug. 18, 1932; s. James Murphy and Melissa (Miller) C.; m. Edith Marie Johnson, Sept. 7, 1955; children: Michael Lavon, Linda Lois, Jennine Marie. B.S., E. Tenn. State U., 1955; M.S., U. Ill., 1957, Ph.D., 1960. Assoc. prof. econs. U. Miss., 1960-63; dir. Bur. Bus. and Econ. Research, Memphis State U., 1963-66, provost, prof. econs., 1966-69, v.p. for acad. affairs, 1969-71; pres. James Madison U., Harrisonburg, Va., 1971—; dir. Leader Fed. Savs. & Loan Assn., Memphis, Rockingham Nat. Bank, Harrisonburg, Universal Leaf Tobacco Co., AAA of Va.; cons. Harland Bartholomew & Assocs., Inc., Memphis; chmn. Council Pres.'s Va. Colls., 1975. Author books and articles on econs. and indsl. location. Mem. White House Conf. Balance Economic Growth; mem. Va. Indsl. Facilities Study Commn., 1972-75; chmn. Va. Land Use Adv. Com., 1974-75, Va. Gov.'s Electricity Costs Commn., 1975—; mem. Va. Gov.'s Energy Resource Adv. Commn., 1975-76, Gov.'s Regulatory Reform Adv. Bd., 1983, Joint Subcom. to Study Coal Slurry Pipeline Feasibility, 1983; Bd. dirs. Rockingham Meml. Hosp., WVPT Pub. TV. Earheart fellow, 1958-60; Recipient Ben Franklin award Memphis Printing Industry, 1966; Faculty award East Tenn. State U., 1955; Disting. Service award Jr. C. of C., 1965; Virginian of Yr. award Va. Assn. Broadcasters, 1982; cultural laureate Va. Mem. Assn. Higher Edn. Execs., Omicron Delta Kappa, Omicron Delta Gamma, Sigma Phi Epsilon. Methodist. Home: 916 Oak Hill Dr Harrisonburg VA 22801 office: univ of arkansas office of the chancellor fayetteville ar 72701 *I believe that man is perfectable. We must commit our energy and resources and our humanity to this effort.*

CARRIER, WARREN PENDLETON, retired university chancellor, writer; b. Cheviot, Ohio, July 3, 1918; s. Burly Warren and Prudence (Alfrey) C.; m. Marjorie Jane Regan, Apr. 3, 1947 (dec.); 1 son, Gregory Paul; m. Judy Lynn Hall, June 14, 1973; 1 son, Ethan Alfrey. Student, Wabash Coll., 1937-40; A.B., Miami U., Oxford, Ohio, 1942; M.A., Harvard U., 1948; Ph.D., Occidental Coll., 1962. Asst. prof. English State U. Iowa, 1949-52; assoc. prof. Bard Coll., 1953-57; mem. lit. faculty, Bennington, 1955-58; vis. prof. Sweet Briar Coll. (Va.), 1958-60; prof. Deep Springs Coll. (Calif.), 1960-62, Portland (Oreg.) State U., 1962-64; prof., chmn. English dept. U. Mont., Missoula, 1964-68; assoc. dean. prof. English and comparative lit., chmn. comparative lit. Livingston Coll., Rutgers U., 1968-69; dean Coll. Arts and Letters, San Diego State U., 1969-72; v.p. acad. affairs U. Bridgeport, Conn., 1972-75; chancellor U. Wis.-Platteville, 1975-82. Author: The Hunt, 1952, Bay of the Damned, 1957, Toward Montebello, 1966, Leave Your Sugar For The Cold Morning, 1977; Founder: Quar. Rev. of Lit. Assn.; editor: Western Rev., 1949-51; co-editor: Reading Modern Poetry, 1955, 68; Co-editor: Literature from the World, 1981; editor: Guide to World Literature, 1980; contbr. numerous articles, poems, revs. to lit. mags. Mem. Jud. Commn. Wis. Vol., Am. Field Service attached to Brit. Army, India-Burma, 1944-45. Mem. Nat. Council Tchrs. English, Royal Soc. Arts, Wis. Acad. Arts and Scis., Phi Beta Kappa, Phi Eta Sigma. Home: 69 Colony Park Circle Galveston TX 77551

CARRIERE, SERGE, physiologist, physician, educator; b. Montreal, Que., Can., July 21, 1934; s. Virgile and Angelina (Malouin) C.; m. Irene Lafond, Dec., 1976; children: Sylvie, Brigitte, Alain, Francois. B.A., U. Montreal, 1954, M.D., 1959. Intern Notre Dame Hosp., Montreal, 1958-59, resident in internal medicine, 1959-62; practice medicine specializing in nephrology, Montreal, 1964—; instr. physiology Harvard Med. Sch., Boston, 1962-64; asst. prof. dept. medicine U. Montreal, 1964-70, asso. prof., 1970-74, prof., 1974-80, prof., head dept. physiology, 1980—; mem. staff Maisonneuve-Rosemont Hosp. Contbr. numerous articles on research in physiology and nephrology to sci. and med. jours. Med. Research Council Can. fellow, 1962-64, grantee, 1971-80. Fellow Royal Coll. Physicians; mem. Can. Soc. Physiology, Am. Soc. Physiology, Internat. Soc. Physiology, Am. Soc. Nephrology, Can. Soc. Nephrology, Am. Soc. Clin. Investigation, Can. Soc. Clin. Investigation. Home: 40 Du Chene Vandreuil Sur Le Lac PQ J7V 5V5 Canada Office: 2900 Edouard Montpetit Blvd Montreal PQ H3C 3T8 Canada

CARRIGAN, DAVID OWEN, history educator; b. New Glasgow, N.S., Can., Nov. 30, 1933; s. Ronald and Marion Constance (Hoare) C.; m. Florence Catherine Nicholson, June 21, 1958; children: Nancy, Janet, David, Glen, Sharon, Douglas. B.A., St. Francis Xavier U., 1954; M.A., Boston U., 1955; Ph.D., U. Maine, 1966. Asst. prof. history St. Francis Xavier U., 1957-61, assoc. prof., 1961-67; assoc. prof. history Wilfred Laurier U., 1967-68; prin., dean arts Kings Coll., U. Western Ont., 1968-71; pres. St. Marys U., Halifax, N.S., 1971-79, prof., 1979—. Author: Canadian Party Platforms, 1867-1968, 1968; contbrs. articles to profl. jours. Former trustee Inst. Research on Public Policy; past mem. Can. Council. Mem. Am., Am. Catholic hist. assns., Phi Kappa Phi. Home: 6112 Coburg Rd Halifax NS Canada Office: St Mary's Univ Halifax NS Canada

CARRIGAN, JIM RICHARD, judge; b. Mobridge, S.D., Aug. 24, 1929; s. Leo Michael and Mildred Ione (Jaycox) C.; m. Beverly Jean Halpin, June 2, 1956; children: Sheila, Maura, Patrick, Kathleen, Andrew, Michael. Ph.B., J.D., U. N.D., 1953; LL.M. in Taxation, NYU, 1956. Bar: N.D. 1953, Colo. 1956. Asso. firm Long & Smart, Denver, 1956; asst. prof. law U. Denver, 1956-59; vis. asso. prof. N.Y. U. Law Sch., 1958, U. Wash. Law Sch., 1959-60; jud. adminstr. State of Colo., 1960-61; individual practice law, Denver, 1961-62; prof. law U. Colo., 1962-67; partner firm Carrigan & Bragg (and); (predecessors), Boulder, Colo., Denver, 1967-76; justice Colo. Supreme Ct., 1976-79; judge U.S. Dist. Ct. for Colo., 1979—; mem. Colo. Bd. Bar Examiners, 1969-71; lectr. Nat. Coll. State Judiciary, 1964-77; bd. dirs., mem. exec. com. Nat. Bd. Trial Advocacy, 1978—; bd. dirs., mem. faculty, mem. exec. com. Nat. Inst. Trial Advocacy, 1972, 80—. Editor-in-chief: N.D. Law Rev., 1952-53; editor: DICTA, 1957-59, Internat. Soc. Barristers Quar, 1972-79; contbr. numerous articles to profl. jours. Chmn. Boulder County Democratic Party, 1967-68; Bd. regents U. Colo., 1975-76; bd. visitors U. N.D. Coll. Law, 1983—. Recipient Distinguished Service award Nat. Coll. State Judiciary, 1969; Outstanding Alumnus award U. N.D., 1973; Regent Emeritus award U. Colo., 1977. Fellow Colo. Bar Found.; mem. Am., Colo., Boulder, Denver County bar assns., Cath. Lawyers Guild, Internat. Soc. Barristers, Internat. Acad. Trial Lawyers, Nat. Bd. Trial Advocacy, Order of Coif, Phi Beta Kappa. Roman Catholic. Office: US Dist Ct C-236 1929 Stout St Denver CO 80294

CARRIGAN, RALPH STEPHEN, lawyer; b. Iron Mountain, Mich., Aug. 19, 1924; s. Mark J. and Bertha (Tetzloff) C.; m. Lily Gatzke, Oct. 13, 1951; children—Gay, Stephen, Mark. B.S. in Mech. Engring, La. State U., 1948; LL.B., Harvard U., 1951; M.S., Calif. Inst. Tech., 1952. Bar: Tex. bar 1952. Practice in Houston, 1952—; partner firm Baker & Botts, 1962—. Nat. chmn. Amigos de Los Americas, 1975-76. Served to 1st lt. USAAF, 1943-46. Mem. Am. Coll. Trial Lawyers, Am. Bar Assn., Am. Bar Found., Houston Bar Assn. (past pres.). Baptist. Home: 75 Williamsburg Ln Houston TX 77024 Office: 3000 One Shell Plaza Houston TX 77002

CARRIGER, JOHN SHIELDS, lawyer; b. Morristown, Tenn., Aug. 7, 1902; s. John Stonewall and Elizabeth (Gammon) C.; m. Helen Fletcher, June 25, 1935; children: John Fletcher, William Converse, Martha (Mrs. Gordon P. O'Neill). A.B., U. Tenn., 1925, LL.B., 1927. Bar: Tenn. bar 1927. Ptnr. Strang, Fletcher, Carriger, Walker, Hodge & Smith (and predecessor), Chattanooga, 1933-83, of counsel, 1983—. Mem. ABA, Tenn. Bar Assn., Chattanooga Bar Assn. (pres. 1954-55, bd. govs. 1955-56), World Peace Through Law Center, U. Tenn. Alumni Assn. (past pres. Hamilton County), U. Tenn. Coll. Law Alumni (pres. 1949-50), Order of Coif, Phi Delta Phi, Phi Kappa Phi, Alpha Tau Omega. Methodist (chmn. ofcl. bd. local ch. 1959-60). Clubs: Executives (pres. 1946-47), Mountain City (Chattanooga)). Lodge: Kiwanis. Home: 1009 E Brow Rd Lookout Mountain TN 37350

CARRIGG, JAMES A., utility company executive; b. 1933. B.E.E., Union Coll., 1953; postgrad., Broome Communtiy Coll. Safety cadet N.Y. State Electric & Gas Corp., Ithaca, 1958, safety dir., 1958-61, personnel dir., 1961-63, supr. tng., 1963-64, local mgr., 1964-66, mgr., 1966-69, asst. v.p., 1969-72, area mgr., 1972-73, gen. mgr., 1973-82; v.p. N.Y. Electric & Gas Corp., Ithaca, 1982-83, pres., chief operating officer, dir., 1983—. Bd. dirs. United Way Broome County, N.Y; mem. adv. bd. Broome County Airport, N.Y.; mem. steering com. ACT NOW; chmn. Broome Community Coll. Citizens Com. Served with U.S. Army, 1955-56. Mem. Broome County C. of C. (vice chmen., dir.). Office: NY State Electric & Gas Corp Route 13 Ithaca-Dryden Rd Ithaca NY 14850 *

CARRINGTON, PAUL, lawyer; b. Mexico, Mo., Sept. 24, 1894; s. William Thomas and Mary (Holloway) C.; m. E. Frances DeWitt, Nov. 5, 1921; children: Frances (Lee), Paul DeWitt. A.B., U. Mo., 1914; LL.B., Harvard U., 1917; LL.D. (hon.), So. Meth. U., 1980. Bar: Mo. bar 1917, Tex. bar 1919. Since practiced civil law, Dallas; mem. firm Carrington, Coleman, Sloman & Blumenthal, until 1974, counsel, 1974-82; adj. prof. law So. Meth. U., 1974-80. Author: (with William A. Sutherland) Articles of Partnership for Law Firms, 1962; Contbr. numerous articles on corp. law, arbitrations and legal subjects to profl. jours. Chmn. N. Tex. Com. on Econ. Devel., 1943-46, Allen Enemy Hearing Bd. for North Tex., 1942-45; pres. Greater Dallas Planning Council, 1948-53; chmn. bd. Dallas Council on World Affairs, 1953-54; v.p., nat. councilor Dallas Boy Scouts Am., 1945-63; pres. Dallas YMCA, 1946-49; Trustee S.W. Legal Found., 1948-74, life trustee, 1974—; trustee Dallas Boy Scout Found., 1946-78; bd. dirs. Am. Bar Endowment, 1963-70, dir. emeritus, 1970-79. Served as 2d lt., instr. primary flying U.S. Army, 1918-19. Recipient Hatton W. Sumners award S.W. Legal Found., 1963; Distinguished Alumnus award U. Mo., 1967; 50-yr. award for distinguished service to law profession Am. Bar. Found., 1973. Fellow Am. Bar Found. (chmn. 1965-66); mem. E. Tex. C. of C. (pres. 1950-51), Dallas C. of C. (pres. 1940-42, chmn. legislative com. 1943-70), Tex. Assn. Commerce (pres. 1946-49), ABA (house of dels. 1957-70, assembly del. 1958, 61, 64, 67, chmn. com. postwar planning 1943-45, chmn. sect. corp. banking and bus. law 1955-56, chmn. com. on lawyer referral 1959-63), Dallas Bar Assn. (pres. 1939-40), State Bar Tex. (pres. 1960-61, 50-yr. award for distinguished service to legal profession 1977, 1st chmn. sect. corp. banking and bus. law 1954-55, chmn. com. rev. Tex. corp. law 1948-57), Am. Soc. Internat. Law (exec. council 1961-67), Am. Arbitration Assn. (dir. 1935-75), World Peace Through Law Center (chmn. corporate law commn. 1963-72), Am. Law Inst., Am. Judicature Soc., Harvard Law Sch. Assn. (pres. 1959-61, nat. council 1953—), SAR, Order of Coif (hon.). Independent. Mem. Christian Ch. (elder emeritus). Clubs: Mason (32 deg.), Dallas Country, Petroleum (Dallas); Harvard (N.Y.C.); Metropolitan (Washington). Home: 6315 Lupton Dallas TX 75225

CARRINGTON, PAUL DEWITT, lawyer, educator; b. Dallas, June 12, 1931; s. Paul and Frances Ellen (DeWitt) C.; m. Bessie Meek, Aug., 1952; children: Clark DeWitt, Mary, William James, Emily. B.A., U. Tex., 1952; LL.B., Harvard U., 1955. Bar: Tex. 1955, Ohio 1962, Mich. 1967. Practiced law, Dallas, 1955; teaching fellow Harvard U., 1957-58; asst. prof. law U. Wyo., 1958-60, Ind. U., 1960-62; asso. prof. Ohio State U., 1962-65; prof. U. Mich., 1965-78; dean, prof. Duke U. Sch. Law, 1978—; Mem. Ann Arbor (Mich.) Bd. Edn., 1970-73. Author: (with Meador and Rosenberg) Justice on Appeal, 1977, (with Babcock) Civil Procedure, 1977, 3d edit., 1983. Served with U.S. Army, 1955-57. Mem. ABA, Am. Law Inst. Episcopalian. Club: Cosmos. Office: Duke U Sch Law Durham NC 27706

CARRINGTON, SAMUEL MACON, JR., educator, librarian; b. Durham, N.C., June 22, 1939; s. Samuel Macon and Nellie Grey (Upchurch) C.; m. Virginia Lou Wilson, May 18, 1975; children: Elizabeth Murphy, Samuel Macon III; children by previous marriage: Catherine Grey, Margaret Leigh. A.B. with honors in French, U. N.C., 1960, M.A., 1962, Ph.D., 1965; student, Ecole Francise, Middlebury (Vt.) Coll., 1961. Instr. French U. N.C., 1964-65; asst. prof. U. Colo., 1965-67; mem. faculty Rice U., Houston, 1967—, prof. French, univ. librarian, 1979—. Author: Premieres poesies et Livre Premier, 1975, Vol. II, Livres II, III et IV, 1978; also articles, revs. Fellow Southeastern Inst. Medieval and Renaissance Studies, 1965; research grantee Am. Philos. Soc., 1968. Mem. ALA, Am. Assn. Tchrs. French, Assn. Research Libraries, Houston Philos. Soc., Alliance Francaise Houston (dir., 1976-79). Anglican. Home: 4318 Firestone Houston TX 77035 Office: Fondren Library Rice Univ Houston TX 77251

CARRION, RAFAEL, JR., banker; b. Santurce, P.R., Aug. 27, 1914; s. Rafael and Ernestina (Ruiz) C.; m. Nellie Rexach, Aug. 19, 1935; children—Nellie, Eileen, Marilyn, Rafael, Richard, Janet. Student, Wharton Coll., 1931. With Banco Popular de Puerto Rico, San Juan, 1932—, exec. v.p., dir., 1952, now chmn.; dir. Seaboard Surety Co. Trustee Com. for Econ. Devel.; bd. dirs. Boys' Clubs Am. Mem. Mgmt. Execs. Soc., Am. Bankers Assn. Roman Catholic. Home: N Candina St Santurce PR 00911 Office: Banco Popular de Puerto Rico Gen PO Box 2708 San Juan PR 00936

CARROL, JAMES VAUGHN, textile company executive; b. St. Louis, April 4, 1915; s. Phillip S. and Selma (Wheeler) C.; m. Florence Stephens, Sept. 21, 1938; children: Catherine, Pauline, James. B.A., U. of Judaism, 1934; M.S., U. Pitts., 1936. With Avondale Mills, Sylacauga, Ala., 1936-45; v.p. Gulford Mills, Greensboro, N.C., 1945-57, Burlington Industries, 1957-65, sr. v.p., 1965; v.p. Dan River Inc., Avondale, La., 1972; chmn. 1st Fed. Savs. & Loan Assn., Avondale; dir. Am. South Bancorp.; adv. bd. Chem. Bank, N.Y.C. Past bd. dirs. Greensboro YMCA; trustee Duke U., So. Research Soc.; bd. visitors Wake Forest U. Recipient Silver Beaver award, Silver Antelope award Boy Scouts Am.; Textile award N.Y. Bd. of Trade, 1970. Mem. Am. Textile Mfrs. Inst., Internat. Textile Mfrs. Inst., Greensboro C. of C. (past dir.), N.C. C. of C. Office: Werik Bldg 137 Nicolle Blvd Avondale LA 70094

CARROLL, ALBERT, corp. exec.; b. Phila., Aug. 25, 1914; s. William and Florence (Ley) C.; m. Rhoda Freudenthal, June 20, 1942; children—David William, Barbara Jean. B.S. in Econs, U. Pa., 1936. Advt. copywriter N.W. Ayer & Son, 1936-40; advt. dir. Merck & Co., Inc., Rahway, N.J., 1940-55; v.p. profl. mktg. div. Benton & Bowles, Inc., N.Y.C., 1955-57; v.p. Vick Internat., 1957-60; v.p., spl. products mgr. Lever Bros. Co., N.Y.C., 1960-68; pres. Julius Schmid Inc., N.Y.C., 1968-75, Med. Funding Corp., Westwood, N.J., 1975-79, Wharton Bus. Cons., Inc., White Plains, N.Y., 1979—. Trustee Hartsdale Bd. Edn.; vol. coordinator advt. council Nat. Blood

Program, 1952. Served as 1st lt. USAAF, 1943-45. Mem. Assn. Nat. Advertisers (chmn. chem. group 1953), Bus. Publ. Audit (dir. 1952-55), Pharm. Advt. Club (dir. 1953-55), Am. Marketing Assn., Beta Gamma Sigma, Pi Gamma Mu. Club: Maplewood. Home: 7 Maplewood Rd Hartsdale NY 10530 Office: 202 Mamaroneck Ave White Plains NY 10601

CARROLL, ALEXANDER SPICER, investment broker; b. Scranton, Pa., Feb. 1, 1917; s. James F. and Muriel C.; m. Marilyn Talbott; children—Tracy, Holly, Allen, Alexander Spicer. B.A., Williams Coll., 1939. Salesman Paper Package Co., Indpls., 1939-41; with Holbomb & Hoke Mfg. Co., Indpls., 1945-52, Thomson McKinnon Securities Co., Inc., 1952—, sr. v.p., 1970—, also dir. Trustee Indpls. Children's Mus.; bd. dirs. Indpls. Jr. Achievement, Meth. Hosp., Indpls.; v.p., bd. dirs. Indpls. Symphony Orch.; past vestryman Trinity Episcopal Ch., Indpls. Served to maj. AUS, 1941-45. Mem. Securities Industry Assn., Indpls. Soc. Fin. Analysts (co-founder, past pres.), Nat. Assn. Investment Clubs (trustee), Indpls. Bond Club (past pres.), Indpls. Econ. Club (dir.), Indpls. C. of C. (dir., past chmn.). Address: 200 Circle Tower Indianapolis IN 46204

CARROLL, BERNARD JAMES, psychiatrist; b. Sydney, Australia, Nov. 21, 1940; came to U.S., 1971; s. William Peter and Alice Maude (Webber) C.; m. Sylvia June Sharpe, May 4, 1966; children: Senga Anne, Jeremy Giles. B.Sc. (Commonwealth scholar 1958, Ross scholar 1961), U. Melbourne, 1961, M.B., B.S., 1964, D.P.M., 1969, Ph.D., 1971. House officer Royal Melbourne Hosp., 1965-66; research fellow Nat. Health and Med. Research Council Australia, 1969-72; asst. prof. psychiatry U. Pa. Med. Sch., 1972-73; mem. faculty U. Mich. Med. Sch., Ann Arbor, 1973-83, prof. psychiatry, 1976-83, acting chmn. dept., 1981-83, chief service adult psychiatry, 1980-83; research scientist Mental Health Research Inst., 1973-83, assoc. dir. inst., 1977-83; prof. psychiatry, chmn. dept. Duke U. Med. Sch., Durham, N.C., 1983—; St. Goran's lectr. Karolinska Inst., Stockholm, 1980; Airazian lectr. U. Tenn., 1982; Karl Beyer lectr. U. Wis., 1982; Litchfield lectr. Oxford U., 1983. Assoc. editor: Psychoneuroendocrinology, 1975—. Searle fellow, 1970; C.J. Martin fellow, 1971; research award Anna-Monika Found. (W. Ger.), 1981. Fellow Royal Australian and N.Z. Coll. Psychiatrists; Mem. Soc. Biol. Psychiatry (sec.-treas. 1979-82, v.p. 1982-83, pres.-elect 1983-84), Royal Coll. Psychiatrists, Royal Soc. Medicine, Am. Coll. Neuropsychopharmacology, Collegium Internat. Neuro-Psychopharmacologicum (councillor 1979-83), Am. Psychosomatic Soc., Psychiat. Research Soc. (pres. 1982), Brit. Assn. Psychopharmacology, Internat. Soc. Psychoneuroendocrinology.

CARROLL, BILLY PRICE, artist; b. Memphis, Nov. 27, 1920; d. Robert Ray and Olive (Thomas) Price; m. Robert Ray Hosmer, May 3, 1941 (div. Aug. 1948); 1 dau., Nadia Jan (Mrs. Wayne Shelton); m. David Donald Carroll, Dec. 25, 1964. Student, Memphis Acad. Arts, 1939-40, Farnsworth Sch. Painting, 1949, 50-51, Accademia Delle Belle Arte, Florence, Italy, 1959, also pvt. study. Lectr., Chinese, Western painting. Exhibited one man shows, Fine Arts Mus., Little Rock, 1953, McCaughen and Burr Gallery, St. Louis, 1954, 64, Brooks Meml. Art Gallery, Memphis, 1956, Greenville Art Assn., 1963, Greenville Art Assn., Hong Kong, 1968, Taiwan Nat. Art Center, 1969, others; exhibited group shows, Fla. Artists Group, 1952-53, 57-58, Brooks Meml. Art Gallery, 1953, 61, 66, 67, Painting of Year Exhbn., Atlanta, 1955, 1st Hunter Ann., Chattanooga, 1960; guest artist, Mpls. Aquatennial Festival, 1970; represented in permanent collections, Ct. Appeals, Jackson, Tenn., U. Tenn. at Memphis, Memphis State U., United Chinese Bank, Hong Kong, Taiwan Nat. Art Center, also pvt. collections. Recipient numerous awards.; Jay Hambridge Found. fellow, 1954; Huntington Hartford Found. fellow, 1958. Mem. Brooks Art Gallery League, Penwomen Am. Home: 1956 Central Ave Memphis TN 38104 *Of course all artists must observe painterly disciplines but as the years lengthen, I grow ever more humbly convinced that good painting is a striving for kernel-truth in a sometimes rich, sometimes barren tangle of irrelevancies or contradictions. When both the artist and the subject yield themselves to the simplest statement of reality, art steals upon the canvas from an origin and a power no one knows.*

CARROLL, CLIFFORD ANDREW, clergyman, educator; b. Duluth, Minn., Apr. 23, 1906; s. Andrew P. and Nellie (Beladeau) C. Student, Gonzaga U., 1927-28, A.B., 1933, A.M., 1934, Santa Clara U., 1932; S.T.L., Alma (Calif.) Coll., 1942; Ph.D., St. Louis U., 1946. Entered Soc. of Jesus, 1928; ordained priest Roman Cath. Ch., 1941; instr. Seattle Coll., 1935-38, vis. prof., summer 1942; dean Gonzaga U. Sch. Econs. and Bus., Spokane, Wash., 1945-53, regent, 1953-63, dir. libraries, prof., 1963-73, archivist, 1973—, adj. prof., 1973—. Mem. Indsl. Relations Inst.; chmn. Pacific N.W. Cath. Regional Library Conf., 1961-63; mem. Wash. Gov.'s Adv. Council on Libraries, 1971—. Mem. Am. Arbitration Assn. (nat. panel), Am., Cath. econ. assns., Royal Econ. Soc. Address: Gonzaga Univ Spokane WA 99258

CARROLL, DANIEL THUERING, management consultant; b. Burlington, Vt., Mar. 21, 1926; s. Daniel B. and Viola T. (Thuering) C.; m. Julie Anne Virgo, Aug. 20, 1977; children: Laura L., Lisa D., Daniel K., Grant T. A.B., Dartmouth, 1947; M.A., U. Minn., 1948; postgrad., U. Chgo. Asst. to mgmt. engring. Navy Dept., Washington, 1950-54; with Booz, Allen & Hamilton, Inc., 1954-72; pres., dir. Gould Inc., Chgo., 1972-80; pres., chief exec. officer Hoover Universal, Inc., Ann Arbor, Mich., 1980-82, also dir.; chmn., pres. The Carroll Group, Inc., Ann Arbor, Mich., 1982—; dir. Combined Internat. Corp., Chgo., A.M. Castle & Co., Diebold Inc., Canton, Ohio, Health Resources Corp. Am., Lake Forest, Ill., Wolverine World Wide, Inc., Grand Rapids, Mich., Domino's Pizza Inc., Ann Arbor, Van Straaten Chem. Co., Conrac Corp., Nat. Bank & Trust Co. of Ann Arbor. Bd. overseers Amos Tuck Grad. Sch.; trustee Union Theol. Sem., N.Y.C., Atlanta U. Served with USNR, 1944-46. Office: 2929 Plymouth Rd Ann Arbor MI 48105

CARROLL, DAVID, pharmaceutical company executive; b. Orange, N.J., Sept. 21, 1930; s. Edward S. and Agnes Harriet (McDonough) C.; m. Peggy J. Habisreitinger, Feb. 27, 1960; children: David, Kathlee, Joanne. B.S. in Chem. Engring., Neward Coll. Engring., 1952. Plant mgr. Lederle Labs., Pearl River, N.Y., 1972-73, dir. mfg., 1973-74, mgr. Pharm. div., 1974-77, v.p., 1977-78, pres. Wayne, N.J. div., 1978-80; group v.p. Am. Cyanamid Co., Wayne, 1980—; dir. Robert & Carriere Lederle, The Proprietary Assn. Served with AUS, 1951-53. Mem. Am. Found. for Pharm. Edn. (dir.), Pharm. Mfrs. Assn. (mktg. account exec. com.), Nat. Pharm. Council (dir.). Home: 79 Indian Rd Wayne NJ 07470 Office: American Cyanamid Co 1 Cyanamid Plaza Wayne NJ 07470

CARROLL, DAVID SHIELDS, physician; b. Morristown, Tenn., Jan. 3, 1917; s. Charles Thomas and Zoe Marvin (Wells) C.; m. Mary Kathryn McGuire, Nov. 9, 1941 (dec. May 1960); children—Kathryn (Mrs. Hal W. Canary), Elizabeth Jane (Mrs. Stephen P. Busch), David Shields; m. Peggy Land Leppert, Nov. 10, 1961. B.S., U. Tenn., 1938, M.D., 1940. Diplomate: Am. Bd. Radiology. Intern John Gaston Hosp., Memphis, 1940-41; resident radiology U. Tenn. Hosp., 1946-47; chmn. dept. radiology City of Memphis Hosps., 1947-64; prof., chmn. dept. radiology U. Tenn. Coll. Medicine, 1957-64, clin. prof., 1964—; staff radiologist Meth. Hosp.; cons. Oak Ridge Inst. Nuclear Studies, 1952-62, Le Bonheur Children's Hosp., 1965—, Kennedy VA Hosp., 1959—, Meth. Hosp., 1962—, St. Jude Children's Hosp., 1963—. Conbtr. articles to med. jours. Pres. bd. dirs. Les Passees Treatment Center, 1960-61; pres. Memphis and Shelby County unit Am. Cancer Soc., 1963, bd. dirs. Tenn. div., 1960—; bd. dirs. West Tenn. Cancer Clinic, 1954—. Served to maj. M.C. AUS, 1941-46; ETO. Fellow Am. Coll. Radiology (chmn. bd. chancellors 1963, pres. 1964); mem. Radiol. Soc. N.Am. (v.p. 1956, chmn. bd. 1971, pres. 1973, gold medal 1978), Am., So. med. assns., Tenn. Radiol. Soc. (pres. 1958), Memphis and Shelby County Med. Soc., Am. Radium Soc. Episcopalian. Club: Memphis Country. Home: 4348 W Cherry Pl Memphis TN 38117 Office: 1265 Union Ave Memphis TN 38104

CARROLL, DEWEY EUGENE, univ. dean; b. Monterey, Tenn., Aug. 30, 1926; s. Weaver McNeese and Ivor (DuBois) C.; m. Elizabeth Ann Cade, Aug. 19, 1956; children—Paul Eugene, Bruce Frederick. B.A., U. Chattanooga, 1949; M.L.S. (Grad. fellow), Emory U., 1954; Ph.D. (L.W. Irwin fellow), U. Ill., 1965. Head sci. and industry div. Atlanta Pub. Library, 1955-56; sci. librarian Emory U., 1957-58, asst. prof. div. librarianship, 1960-63; doctoral residence U. Ill., 1959-60, asso. prof., 1965-69; asst. prof. Sch. Info. Sci., Ga. Inst. Tech., 1963-65; dir. libraries U. Tenn. at Chattanooga, 1969-73; dean Sch. Library and Info. Scis., North Tex. State U., Denton, 1973—. Author: Incunabula in the University Library, 1956, Newspaper and Periodical Production in Europe 1600-1950, 1966, Towards a Systems Approach to Subject Literatures, 1969; Editor: Proceedings of Ann. Clinic on Library Applications of Data Processing, 1968-70. Bd. dirs. Adult Edn. Council, Chattanooga, 1969-72. Served with USNR, 1944-46, 51-53. Mem. A.L.A., Am. Soc. for Info. Sci., Beta Phi Mu, Phi Kappa Phi. Episcopalian. Home: 2121 Pembrooke Pl Denton TX 76201

CARROLL, DIAHANN, actress, singer; b. N.Y.C., July 17, 1935; d. John and Mabel (Faulk) Johnson. Student, N.Y. U. Began career as model; actress: motion pictures, including Claudine (Nominated for Acad. award as best actress by the Acad. Motion Picture Arts and Scis. 1974), Carmen Jones, Porgy and Bess, Hurry Sundown, Paris Blues; on Broadway in No Strings, House of Flowers; appeared in: play Same Time, Next Year; TV series Julia, Dynasty, 1984—. Address: care Aaron Spelling Prodns 1041 N Formosa Ave Los Angeles CA 90046 *

CARROLL, DONALD CARY, college dean; b. Durham, N.C., Nov. 5, 1930; s. Dudley Dewitt and Eleanore Dixon (Elliott) C.; children: Curtis James, Leah Anne. B.S., U. N.C., 1954; S.M., Mass. Inst. Tech., 1958, Ph.D. (Ford fellow), 1965; M.A. (hon.), U. Pa., 1972. Staff asst. Pitts. Plate Glass, 1958-59; cons. Westinghouse Electric Corp., Pitts., 1959-60; mem. faculty Mass. Inst. Tech., Cambridge, 1960-71, asst. prof. mgmt., 1960-64, asso. prof. mgmt., 1964-68, prof., 1968-71; pres. TMI Systems Corp., Cambridge, 1969-72, chmn., 1969-82; dean Wharton Sch. Bus., U. Pa., Phila., 1972—, prof. mgmt., 1972-79, Reliance prof. mgmt. and pvt. enterprise, 1979—; dir. Morse Shoe Co., Boston, Vestaur Securities, Inc., Phila., Monsanto Co., St. Louis, Arlen Realty Inc., N.Y.C., SEI Corp., Wayne, Pa., Nat. Ry. Utilization Corp., Phila., MacAndrews and Forbes Group, N.Y.C. Trustee Council on Opportunity for Grad. Mgmt. Edn., 1972—, chmn., 1976-79; trustee Bryn Mawr Coll., 1977-82. Served with USMCR, 1948-49, 54-56. Mem. Assn. Computing Machinery, Inst. Mgmt. Scis., Soc. Mgmt. Info. Systems, Am. Assembly Collegiate Schs. Bus. (dir.), Phi Beta Kappa, Beta Gamma Sigma, Alpha Tau Omega, Tau Beta Pi. Home: 217 Logan Ct Philadelphia PA 19103 Office: Wharton School Univ Pa Philadelphia PA 19104

CARROLL, EDWIN WINFORD, architect; b. Elizabeth, La., Mar. 6, 1912; s. Rupert A. and Maude Marie (Ping) C.; m. Alyce Moter Outlaw, Mar. 27, 1937. B.Arch., U. Tex., 1936. Designer, draftsman Trost & Trost (architects), El Paso, Tex., 1936-41; architect, supt. bldgs. El Paso Pub. Schs., 1941-45; partner Carroll, Daeuble Du Sang & Rand, El Paso, 1945—; cons. architect met. water treatment plant, Salt Lake City.; Chmn. Tex. Bd. Archtl. Exam., 1953; vice chmn. internat. border devel. commn. A.I.A. and; Sociedad de Arquitectos Mexicanos, 1960-63; mem. El Paso Bldg. Code Bd., 1951—, chmn., 1953; pres. Am. delegation XI Congress of Fedn. Pan-Am. Architects, 1965. Prin. works include Engring.-Biol. Sci. Complex, all U. Tex. at El Paso, El Paso Civic Center, Hotel Dieu Sch. Nursing, Tex. hdqrs. bldg. Mountain Bell Co; also others in, N.Mex., Ariz., Tex., Mexico. Mem. exec. bd. Yucca council Boy Scouts Am.; Pres. Tex. Archtl. Found., 1958-59, 78-79; mem. devel. bd. Tex. Christian U.; mem. Tex. Western Coll. Mission 173. Fellow AIA (chmn. nat. border planning com. 1964-66); mem. Tex. Soc. Architects (pres. 1954), Soc. de Arguitectos Mexicanos (hon.), U. Tex. Ex-Students Assn. (chancellor's council). Mem. Christian Ch. (elder, past pres. congregation). Clubs: El Paso Country (pres. bd. govs. 1957), Coronado Country (pres. 1967, 68). Home: 901 Cherry Hills Ln El Paso TX 79912 Office: 250 N Mesa St El Paso TX 79902

CARROLL, ELISABETH, ballerina; b. Paris, Jan. 19, 1937; d. Jean and Suzanne (Beneyton) Pfister; m. Felix Smith, July 18, 1957; 1 dau., Ariane Smith. Ed., Ecole Elementaire de Filles, 1942-47, Coll. de Jeunes Filles, 1948-51. Faculty Harkness House for Ballet Arts, N.Y.C., 1972-76; asst. prof. ballet Skidmore Coll., Saratoga Springs, N.Y., 1976—. Soloist, Monte Carlo Opera Ballet, Monte Carlo, 1952-54; 1st soloist, Am. Ballet Theatre, 1954-61; prin. dancer, Robert Joffrey Co., 1961-63, Harkness Ballet, 1964-70. Recipient hon. award Dance Masters Am., 1969. Address: Skidmore College Saratoga Springs NY 12866

CARROLL, SISTER ELIZABETH, religious order official, educator; b. Pitts., Mar. 24, 1913; d. Edward Joseph and Estelle (Bonner) C. B.A., U. Pitts., 1934, L.H.D., 1964; M.A., U. Toronto, 1939; Ph.D., Cath. U. Am., 1946. Joined Soc. Sisters of Mercy, Roman Catholic Ch., 1935; faculty Carlow Coll. (formerly Mt. Mercy Coll.), Pitts., 1939-66, prof. history, 1949-52, dean, 1952-63, pres., 1963-66; gen. dir. Pitts. Sisters of Mercy, 1964-74, v.p., 1978—; staff asso. Center of Concern, Washington, 1974-78; Lectr. Cath. U. Am., 1947-51, Marquette U., 1959-61, 63. Author: The Venerable Bede: His Spiritual Teaching, 1946; Contbr. articles to profl. jours. Mem. nat. exec. com. Sister Formation Conf., 1958-70, nat. chmn., 1967-70; Am. del. Internat. Union Superiors Gen., Rome, 1967, 70, 73, mem. council, 1970-73; chairperson Sisters Uniting, 1972-73; del. Detroit Call to Action Cath. Conf., 1976; Trustee Washington Theol. Consortium, 1974-78, Carlow Coll., 1978—; bd. dirs. Assn. for Rights of Catholics in the Ch., 1980—. Mem. Leadership Conf. Women Religious (pres. 1971-72, bd. rep. 1967-73), Women's Ordination Conf. (core commn. 1978-81). Home: Apartado 254 Chimbote Peru *Personal faith in God, transcendent yet immanent, is my deepest life stream, source of love, and courage. Belief that every person is created in the image of God; basic respect for persons. Gratitude for educational opportunities, support of many wonderful people. Desire to help others develop to freedom through a loving concern and by opposing oppressive structures.*

CARROLL, FRANCES LAVERNE, educator; b. Scammon, Kans., Dec. 6, 1925; d. Robert Allen and Truda Hilda (Flanagan) C. B.S., Kans. State Tchrs. Coll., 1948; M.A., U. Denver, 1956; postgrad., Western Res. U., 1957; Ph.D., U. Okla., 1970. Bookkeeper Baxter Springs Bank, Kans., 1944; tchr. English and journalism high sch., Caney, Kans., 1947-49; librarian Field Kindley Meml. High Sch., Coffeyville, Kans., 1949-54, Coffeyville Jr. Coll., 1954-62; supr. elem. sch. libraries Coffeyville, 1957-62; asst. prof. library sci. U. Okla., Norman, 1962-67, assoc. prof., 1971-75, prof., 1975—, acting dir. sch. library sci., 1974-75; head library studies Nedlands Coll. Advanced Edn. (formerly Western Australian Secondary Tchrs. Coll.), Perth, 1977-81; guest lectr. Drexel Inst. Tech., Phila., 1964, U. London, 1972, Pahlavi U., Shiraz, Iran, 1976; dir. U.S. Office Edn. Inst., 1966, 67, 69. Author: (with Mary Meacham) The Library at Mount Vernon, 1977, (with Pat Beilke) Guidelines for the Planning and Organization of School Library Media Centers, 1979, Recent Advances in School Librarianship, 1981; nat. series editor: Reading for Young People, 1979—; contbr. articles to profl. jours. U.S. Office Edn. grantee, 1969. Mem. AAUW, AAUP, ALA, Internat. Relations Round Table (chmn. membership 1970-74), Internat. Fedn. Library Assns. (chmn. sect. sch. libraries 1973-77), Southwestern Library Assn., Okla. Library Assn., Delta Kappa Gamma, Phi Delta Kappa, Beta Phi Mu. Office: Sch Library Sci 401 W Brooks St Norman OK 73019

CARROLL, GEORGE JOSEPH, pathologist; b. Gardner, Mass., Oct. 14, 1917; s. George Joseph and Kathryn (O'Hearn) C. B.A., Clark U., Worcester, Mass., 1939; M.D., George Washington U., 1944. Diplomate: Am. Bd. Pathology. Intern Worchester City Hosp., 1944-45; resident in medicine Doctors Hosp., Washington, 1945-46; resident in pathology Sibley Hosp., Washington, 1948-49, VA Hosp., 1949-50; asst. pathologist D.C. Gen. Hosp., 1950-51, asso. pathologist, 1951-52; pathologist Louise Obici Meml. Hosp., Suffolk, Va., 1952—, sec. med. staff, 1956-59, chief of staff, 1959-60, 67-69; pathologist Chowan Hosp., Edenton, N.C., 1952-71, Southampton Meml. Hosp., Franklin, Va., 1952—, Greensville Meml. Hosp., Emporia, Va., 1961—; instr. pathology Georgetown U. Sch. Medicine, 1950-52; instr. bacteriology Am. U., Washington, 1950-51; asso. clin. prof. pathology Med. Coll. Va., Richmond, 1968-70; clin. prof. pathology Va. Commonwealth U., 1970—; prof. dept. pathology Eastern Va. Med. Sch., Norfolk, 1974—; sec.-treas. Va. Bd. Medicine, 1970—. Contbr. articles to med. jours. Served with U.S. Army, 1946-48. Fellow Am. Soc. Clin. Pathologists (dir. 1969—, pres. 1977—), Coll. Am. Pathologists, A.C.P., Internat. Acad. Pathology; mem. AMA, So. Med. Assn. (councilor from Va. 1965-70, pres. 1973-74), Med. Soc. Va. (pres. 4th Dist. 1968-70, del. 1960—), Med. Soc. D.C. (asso.), Seaboard (pres. 1957), George Washington, Tri-County (pres. 1971-73), med. socs), Am. Soc. Clin. Pharmacy Therapeutics, Va. Soc. Pathology (pres. 1973-74), Soc. Nuclear Medicine, Am. Assn. Blood Banks, Am. Cancer Soc. (dir. Va. div. 1955-62), Va. Med. Service Assn. (dir. 1960-71). Club: Rotary (Suffolk). Home: 219 Northbrook Ave Suffolk VA 23434 Office: Louise Obici Meml Hosp Suffolk VA 23434

CARROLL, GLADYS HASTY, author; b. Rochester, N.H., June 26, 1904; d. Warren Verdi and Emma Frances (Dow) Hasty; m. Herbert A. Carroll, June 23, 1925; children—Warren Hasty, Sarah Carroll Watson. A.B., Bates Coll., Lewiston, Maine, 1925, Litt.D., 1945; A.M. (hon.), U. N.H., 1934; Litt.D., U. Maine, 1939; D.H.L., Nasson Coll., 1975. Author: novels and non-fiction, including As the Earth Turns, 1933, new edit., 1978, A Few Foolish Ones, 1935, Neighbor to the Sky, 1937, Head of the Line, 1942, While The Angels Sing, 1947, West of the Hill, 1949, Christmas Without Johnny, 1950, Dunnybrook, 1952, new edit., 1978, One White Star, 1954, Sing Out the Glory, 1957, Come With Me Home, 1960, Only Fifty Years Ago, 1962, To Remember Forever, 1963, The Road Grows Strange, 1965, The Light Here Kindled, 1967, Christmas Through the Years, 1968, Man on the Mountain, 1969, Years Away from Home, 1972, Next of Kin, 1974, Unless You Die Young, 1977, The Book that Came Alive, 1979; also short stories.; Contbr. to mags., stories appearing as screenplays on TV. Mem. Phi Beta Kappa. Home: Earls Rd Box 468 South Berwick ME 03908

CARROLL, GRAYSON, physician, surgeon; b. Dallas, Feb. 10, 1895; s. Washington Irving and Lettie Catherine (Mosher) C.; m. Thelma Hayman, Nov. 20, 1924; children: Gaye (Mrs. Shelton Voges), Elizabeth (Mrs. Robert Hensley). Student, Austin Coll., 1913-14, U. Tex. at Austin, 1914-15; M.D., U. Tex. at Galveston, 1919. Diplomate: Am. Bd. Urology (past pres.). Intern Bellevue Hosp., N.Y.C., 1919-21; urologist U.S. VA Hosp., Jefferson Barracks, Mo., 1921-24; asst. urologist Baylor Univ. Med. Sch., Dallas, 1924-26; asso. with Bransford Lewis (urologist), St. Louis, 1926-41; asst. prof. urology St. Louis U., 1945-50, asso. prof., 1950-58, prof., 1959—; cons. urology St. Louis City Hosp.; urologist St. John's Hosp., 1933—, asso. chief of staff, 1952—, chief urol. staff, 1959—; cons. urologist Jewish Hosp. Mem. A.M.A. (chmn. sect. urology 1947), A.C.S., Am. Urol. Assn. (pres. 1962-63, Hugh Young award 1971, past pres. S. Central sect.), So. Med. Assn. (past chmn. urol. sect.), Soc. Genito Urinary Surgeons (v.p. 1974), Internat. Soc. Urologists, Delta Tau Delta. Presbyn. Clubs: Bellerive Country, Univ. Home: 710 S Hanley Rd Clayton MO 63105 Office: 1035 Bellevue Ave St Louis MO 63117

CARROLL, HOLBERT NICHOLSON, political science educator; b. Charleroi, Pa., June 30, 1921; s. James Russell and Mary Leola (McDonough) C. A.B., U. Pitts., 1943, M.A., 1947; postgrad., Yale U., 1943-44; Ph.D., Harvard U., 1953. Faculty U. Pitts., 1946-48, 50—, prof. polit. sci., 1960—, chmn. dept., 1960-68; teaching fellow Harvard U., 1949-50; Cons. Brookings Instn., 1959. Author: The House of Representatives and Foreign Affairs, 1958, rev. edit., 1966, A Study of the Goverance of the University of Pittsburgh, 1972; contbr. chpt. to: The Congress and America's Future, 1965, rev. edit., 1973; book rev. editor: Am. Polit. Sci. Rev., 1979-81. Served with AUS, 1943-46; CBI. Mem. Am. Polit. Sci. Assn., Phi Beta Kappa, Omicron Delta Kappa. Office: Dept Polit Sci U Pitts Pittsburgh PA 15260

CARROLL, JAMES, author; b. Chgo., Jan. 22, 1943; s. Joseph F. and Mary A. (Morrissey) C.; m. Alexandra Marshall, May 21, 1978; 1 dau., Elizabeth. B.A., St. Paul's Coll., Washington, 1966, M.A., 1968. Author: novels Madonna Red, 1976, Mortal Friends, 1978, Faultines, 1980, Family Trade, 1982. Mem. Authors League, PEN.

CARROLL, JAMES MICHAEL, retailing executive; b. East Chicago, Ind., May 6, 1943; s. Kenneth Victor and Frances (Herod) C.; m. Genevieve Bulfing, July 22, 1967; children: Jennifer Lynn, James Michael. B.S., U.S. Naval Acad., 1965; M.B.A., U. Mich., 1972. C.P.A., Ga. Staff auditor Peat, Marwick, Mitchell, Atlanta, 1972-76; with Munford Inc., Atlanta, 1976—, sr. exec. v.p. fin., sec., 1983—; dir. United Refrigerated Services Inc. Served to lt. USN, 1965-70. Office: Munford Inc 1960-74 Peachtree NW Atlanta GA 30357

CARROLL, J(EFFERSON) ROY, JR., architect; b. Phila., Sept. 25, 1904; s. J. Roy and Mary (Greenaway) C.; m. Doris Hansen Packard, Dec. 15th, 1945 (dec.); children: Spencer Packard Mary Margaret, Patricia.; m. Ann Darlington Haggerty, Oct. 11, 1981. B.Arch., U. Pa., 1926, M.Arch. (fellow), 1928. Registered architect, Pa., N.J., Md., N.Y., Va., Tenn., D.C., R.I. With J. Roy Carroll, Jr., FAIA (architect), 1977—; asst. prof., exec. chmn. design staff U. Pa., 1945; vis. lectr. architecture Pa. State U., 1953-54; archtl. cons. Dept. Army, 1964—; mem. archtl. rev. bd. Dept. Navy, 1965—. Contbr. articles to profl. publs.; Bldgs. designed by firm include Law Sch. Bldg. U. Pa, all Phila., FAA Office Bldg, The Mall, NASA Bldg, both Washington, Lister Hill Nat. Center for Biomedical Communications, NIH, Bethesda, Md., U.S. Army Engrs. Topographic Research and Devel. Labs., Ft. Belvoir, Va., U.S. Courthouse and Fed. Office Bldg, Phila. Chmn. Delaware County Adv. Com. on Housing and Planning, 1947-52; pres. Citizens Council Housing and Planning of Delaware County, 1953-56; mem. Swarthmore Borough Council, 1955-60; Asso. trustee, chmn. fine arts bd. U. Pa.; adv. bd. Temple U. Sch. Architecture. Recipient award Appomattox Monument competition, 1932. Fellow AIA (Phila. pres.

1951-52, gold medal Phila. chpt. 1963, regional dir. 1956, nat. sec. 1959-62, 1st v.p. 1962-63, pres. 1963-64, pres. AIA Found. 1964-68, pres. Phila. architects charitable trust 1968-72, chancellor Coll. of Fellows 1971-72, Benjamin Franklin fellow), Royal Soc. Arts (London, Eng.), Philippine Inst. Architects (hon.), Royal Archtl. Inst. Can. (hon.); mem. Colegio de Arquitectos de Mexico (hon.), Pa. Soc. Architects (gold medal 1963, pres. 1945-46), Phila. Housing Assn. (dir.), Franklin Inst. of Phila. (chmn. Brown medal com.), Archtl. League N.Y., Phila. Numis. and Antiquarian Soc. (pres. 1984), Pa. Acad. Fine Arts, Gen. Alumni Soc. U. Pa. (pres. 1944-46, Alumni award of merit 1948), Sigma Xi, Tau Sigma Delta. Presbyterian (pres. bd. trustees 1952, elder, mem. session 1965-68),deacon 1984. Clubs: Union League (Phila.); Cosmos (Washington); Carpenters Company Phila. (mng. com.); Century Assn. (N.Y.C.)). Home: The Strath Haven Apt 1009 Swarthmore PA 19081

CARROLL, JOHN BISSELL, psychologist, educator; b. Hartford, Conn., June 5, 1916; s. William James and Helen M. (Bissell) C.; m. Mary Elizabeth Searle, Sept. 6, 1941; 1 dau., Melissa (Mrs. F. Stuart Chapin III). B.A., Wesleyan U., 1937; Ph.D., U. Minn., 1941; A.M., Harvard U., 1953. Instr. Mt. Holyoke Coll., 1940-42, Ind. U., 1942-43; lectr. U. Chgo., 1943-44; research psychologist Dept. Army, 1946-49; asst. prof. Harvard Grad. Sch. Edn., 1949-53, asso. prof., 1953-57, prof. edn., 1957-62, prof. ednl. psychology, 1962-67; sr. research psychologist Ednl. Testing Service, Princeton, N.J., 1967-74; prof. psychology U. N.C., Chapel Hill, 1974-82, prof. emeritus, 1982—; Mem. com. aptitude examiners Coll. Entrance Exam. Bd., 1952-65, commn. tests, 1967-70; adv. com. on new ednl. media U.S. Office Edn., 1961-64. Author: The Study of Language, 1953, Modern Language Aptitude Test, 1958, Language and Thought, 1964; Editor: Language, Thought and Reality, 1956, Toward a Literate Society, 1975. Served to lt. (j.g.) USNR, 1944-46. Recipient E.L. Thorndike award for distinguished service to ednl. psychology, 1970; Diamond Jubilee medal Inst. of Linguists, 1970; award Am. Ednl. Research Assn., 1979; Ednl. Testing Service award for disting. service to measurement, 1980; named to Reading Hall of Fame, 1977. Fellow Am. Psychol. Assn.; mem. Psychometric Soc. (pres. 1960-61), Linguistic Soc. Am., Nat. Acad. Edn. (v.p. 1977-81). Home: 409 Elliott Rd Chapel Hill NC 27514

CARROLL, JOHN DOUGLAS, mathematical-statistical psychologist; b. Phila., Jan. 3, 1939; s. John Joseph and Nolie Fay (Godwin) C.; m. Sylvia Stevens Booma, Jan. 2, 1965; children: Gregory Alan, Steven Douglas. B.S. with honors, U. Fla., 1958; Ph.D., Princeton U., 1963. Research asst. dept. psychology Yale U., 1961-63; math.-statis. psychologist Bell Labs., Murray Hill, N.J., 1963-65, 66—; asst. prof. indsl. engrng. and ops. research NYU, 1965-66, adj. prof. mktg., 1968-70; acting prof. psychology U. Calif.-San Diego, 1975-76; acting prof. social sci. U. Calif.-Irvine, 1975-76; adj. prof. mktg. Baruch Coll., CUNY, 1971, U. Pa., 1978-79. Contbr. numerous articles and chpts. to profl. publs.; author computer progrms for multidimensional analysis of behavioral sci. data; assoc. editor: Psychometrika, 1973—, Jour. Exptl. Psychology, 1978-80. Ednl. Testing Service fellow, 1958-61; NIMH fellow, 1959-61. Fellow Am. Psychol. Assn. (chmn. membership and fellowship com. div. 5 1978-81, mem.-at-large exec. com. Div. 5 1982—), Am. Statis. Assn.; mem. Psychometric Soc. (trustee 1971-77, 81-83, pres. 1975-76, mem. editorial council 1975-81), Classification Soc. (governing council 1974-77, pres. 1980-83), Soc. Multivariate Exptl. Psychology (editorial adv. bd. 1978-82, chmn. editorial adv. bd. 1980-81, pres. 1982-83), AAAS, Eastern Psychol. Assn., Psychonomic Soc., Soc. Math. Psychology, Phi Beta Kappa, Sigma Xi. Office: Bell Labs Room 2C-533 600 Mountain Ave Murray Hill NJ 07974

CARROLL, JOHN H., chem. co. exec.; b. N.Y.C., Nov. 16, 1921; s. Charles J. and Mary H. C.; m. Marie G. Tobin, Feb. 4, 1950; children—Charles S., Paul V., Christina M., Denise M., John D. B.A., Fordham U., 1947, LL.B., 1951. Bar: N.Y. bar 1951, Del. bar 1962. Law clk. to judge U.S.; Dist. Ct., 1951-54; asst. U.S. atty. So. Dist. N.Y., 1954-57; with law dept. N.Y. Life Ins. Co., 1957-58; with ICI Americas Inc. (and predecessor), Wilmington, Del., 1958—, gen. counsel, sec., 1968-79, v.p., gen. counsel, 1979—; bd. overseers Del. Law Sch., 1977—. Served with USAAF, 1943-46. Mem. Am. Bar Assn., Del. Bar Assn. Roman Catholic. Office: ICI Americas Inc Wilmington DE 19897

CARROLL, JONATHAN RICHARD, editor, writer; b. Los Angeles, Nov. 6, 1943; s. Richard Francis and Jane (Cooper) C.; children: Rachel, Shana. Student, Webb Sch. Calif., 1961, U. Calif.-Berkeley, 1961-63. Asso. editor, staff writer San Francisco Chronicle, 1965-69; asso. editor Rolling Stone, San Francisco, 1970—; co-editor Rags, San Francisco, 1970-71; editor Oui, Chgo., 1972-73; mng. editor West, Los Angeles, 1972—; cons. editor Women Sports, San Mateo, Calif., 1974-75; west coast editor Village Voice, N.Y.C., 1974-76; editor New West, Beverly Hills, Calif., 1978-81. Contbr. articles to numerous mags. including Playboy; Columnist: San Francisco Examiner, 1976-78, San Francisco Chronicle, 1982—. Recipient Nat. Mag. award, 1978. Office: San Francisco CA 94119

CARROLL, JULIAN MORTON, lawyer, former governor Kentucky; b. Paducah, Ky., Apr. 16, 1931; s. Elvie B. and Eva (Heady) C.; m. Charlann Harting, July 22, 1951; children: Kenneth Morton, Iva Patrice, Bradley Harting, Ellyn Kriston. A.A., Paducah Jr. Coll., 1952; A.B., U. Ky., 1954, LL.B., 1956. Bar: Ky. bar 1956. Mem. firm Reed, Scent, Reed & Walton, Paducah, 1960-71; mem. Ky. Ho. Reps., 1962-71, speaker, from 1968-71; lt. gov., Ky., 1971-74, gov., 1974-79; chmn. Nat. Conf. Lt. Govs., 1974, Nat. Govs. Assn., 1978-79. Trustee Paducah Jr. Coll. Recipient Minerva award U. Louisville, 1977; Man of Yr. award Advt. Club Louisville, 1978. Mem. Am., Ky., Franklin County bar assns., Phi Delta. Clubs: Optimist, Mason (Shriner). Home: 218 Raintree Rd Frankfort KY 40601 Office: 204 W Broadway Frankfort KY 40601

CARROLL, KENNETH KITCHENER, biochemist, nutritionist, educator; b. Carrolls, N.B., Can., Mar. 9, 1923; s. Lawrence and Sarah Della (Estey) C.; m. Margaret Aileen Ronson, Aug. 26, 1950; children: Douglas, Stephen, James. B.Sc., U. N.B., Fredericton, 1943, M.Sc., 1946; Ph.D., U. Western Ont., London, 1949; M.A., U. Toronto, Ont., Can., 1946. Asst. prof. med. research U. Western Ont., 1954-57, assoc. prof., 1957-65, prof. biochemistry, 1965—, acting chmn., 1965-68. Contbr. articles and chpts. to profl. publs.; editor: Progress in Biochemical Pharmacology, vol. 10, 1975. Merck fellow Merck & Co., Cambridge, Eng., 1952; fellow Agrl. Research Council, Cambridge, 1953; career investigator MRC Can., 1963—. Fellow Royal Soc. Can., Chem. Inst. Can.; mem. Can. Biochem. Soc., Can. Soc. Nutritional Scis., Am. Oil Chemists Soc., Can. Fedn. Biol. Socs. (hon. sec. 1967-71), Nutrition Soc. Can. (sec. 1965-67), NutritionSoc. Can. (pres. 1978-79). Baptist. Home: 561 St George St London ON Canada N6A 3B9 Office: U Western Ont Dept Biochemistry London ON Canada N6A 5C1

CARROLL, KENT JEAN, retired naval officer; b. Newton, Iowa, Aug. 22, 1926; s. Lee A. and Mabel E. (McCormick) C.; m. Betty M. Harrington, Mar. 29, 1947; children: Craig, Debra Carroll Rollins, Lanse S., Maureen Burt. Student, U. Notre Dame, 1946; grad., U.S. Naval Postgrad. Sch., 1955, Naval War Coll., 1960, Army War Coll., 1965; B.A. in Internat. Affairs, George Washington U., 1965. Commd. ensign U.S. Navy, 1946, advanced through grades to vice adm., 1974; service in, Korea and Vietnam; comdr. U.S.S. Sablefish, 1959-60, Submarine Div. 81, 1968-69, U.S.S. Blue Ridge, 1970-72, Amphibious Squadron 10, 1972-73, Task Force 65, 1974-75, Naval Inshore Warfare Command, Atlantic Fleet, 1974-75, U.S. Naval Forces Marianas, 1975-77; dir. J-4 OJCS, Washington, 1977-82; comdr. Mil. Sealift Command, Washington, 1982-83. Decorated D.S.M. with cluster; decorated Def. D.S.H.; Decorated Legion of Merit with 2 clusters; recipient John Paul Jones award Navy League, 1977; Presdl. citation for humanitarian service, 1976. Club: N.Y. Yacht. Home: 138 Baltusrol Ln Pinehurst NC 28374

CARROLL, LESTER EDWARD, cartoonist; b. Lancaster, Pa., June 19, 1912; s. Lewis Edward and Cora Belle (Crowl) C.; m. Mary Ruhl, Sept. 30, 1933; 1 son, Lester Edward. Student, Lancaster Bus. Coll., 1931-32. Office worker K-D Mfg. Co., Lancaster, 1932-38; free lance cartoonist, 1938-43; cartoonist Newspaper Enterprise Assn., Inc., Cleve., 1943—. Cartoons: Boots & Her Buddies, 1948-70, Babe 'n Horace, 1944-71, The Tillers, 1944-64, Life With The Rimples, 1964-71, Our Boarding House, 1971—. Methodist. Home: 21100 Beachwood Dr Rocky River OH 44116 Office: 200 Park Ave New York NY 10017

CARROLL, MARK SULLIVAN, publisher, government official; b. Boston, Apr. 25, 1924; s. Francis M. and Barbara (Blum) C.; m. Jane Hartenstein, Apr. 25, 1953; children—Alison, Jeremy, John. A.B., Harvard, 1950. Corr., reporter Boston Post, 1948-50; news editor radio sta. WORL, Boston, 1950- 51; promotion mgr. Yale U. Press, 1951-56; asst. to dir. Harvard U. Press, 1956-59, asso. dir., 1959-67, dir., 1968-72; dir. profl. publs. Nat. Park Service, 1972—; instr. publ. specialist program George Washington U.; cons. Pahlavi U., Shiraz, Iran, 1966, World Bank, Swaziland, Lesotho, 1979-80, Siera Leone, Liberia; chmn. vis. com. Gallaudet Coll. Press, 1981—. Vice pres. Am. Inst. Graphic Arts, 1962-64; mem. exec. com. Assn. Am. Univ. Presses, 1963-64, bd. dirs., 1970-72; bd. dirs., sec. Assn. Am. Pubs., 1970-72; mem. publs. com. Beacon Press, 1962-65, 72-78; mem. U.S. del. book pubs. to, USSR, 1970; nat. bd. dirs. Center for the Book, Library of Congress; trustee U. Pa. Press, 1978—. Served with AUS, 1943-47; ETO. Decorated Purple Heart, Combat Infantryman's badge.; Ford Found. grantee, Turkey, 1966. Mem. Mass. Hist. Soc., Am. Printing History Assn., Washington Book Pubs. (sec. 1976-79), Soc. for Scholarly Pub. (pres. 1978-81). Democrat. Unitarian. Home: 6302 Friendship Ct Bethesda MD 20817 Office: Nat Park Service Dept Interior Washington DC 20240

CARROLL, MARSHALL ELLIOTT, architect; b. Durham, N.C., May 14, 1923; s. Dudley Dewitt and Eleanore (Elliott) C.; m. Dorothy Jane Grune, Mar. 28, 1953; married; children: Jane Dudley, Marshall Elliott, Frederick Grune. A.B., Harvard U., 1943; student, Grad. Sch. Design, 1947-51. Asso. G. Milton Small & Assos. (architects and engrs.), Raleigh, N.C., 1957-60; various positions to dep. exec. v.p. AIA, Washington, 1960-71; partner Vincent G. Kling & Partners (architects, planners and engrs.), Phila., 1971-73; exec. asst. architect U.S. Capitol, 1973—. Project dir., Master Plan for U.S. Capitol, 1976-81, U.S. Senate Office Systems Research Project; restoration studies (Russell and Dirksen senate office bldgs.), 1979-82; Capitol Hill Graphics System, 1977-81; Project dir., Urban Design, the Architecture of Towns and Cities, 1965, Architectural Graphic Standards, 6th edit., 1970. Pres. N.C. Symphony Soc., 1955-60; vice chmn., mem. exec. com. U.S. com. Internat. Commn. on Monuments and Sites, 1978—; mem. exec. com. U.S. com. Internat. Centre for Conservation in Rome; mem. exec. com. and chmn. com. on archtl. conservation Nat. Inst. for Conservation, 1975—, vice chmn., 1983—; chmn. governing bd. Village of Drummond, Md., 1976-77, treas., 1973-76. Served to capt. USNR, 1944-46, 51-53. Fellow AIA (chmn. com. archtl. graphic standards 1976-80, 84—, com. hist. resources 1981—), Assn. Preservation Tech. (pres. 1980-83); mem. Victorian Soc. in Am. (bd. dirs. 1984—). Democrat. Club: Cosmos (Washington). Home: 4621 Drummond Ave Chevy Chase MD 20015 Office: Office of Architect of Capitol Washington DC 20515

CARROLL, MATTHEW EUGENE, manufacturing company executive; b. Chillicothe, Ill., Nov. 8, 1916; s. Henry C. and Anne (O'Bryne) C.; m. Ellen Estep, June 1, 1940; children:Janet (Mrs. Dennis Geraghty), Patricia E. (Mrs. Luis Garcia), Susan (Mrs. Thomas Tremba), Thomas, Molly. Grad., Spalding Inst., Ill., 1934. Vice pres. mktg. Mpls.-Moline Co., 1959-61; pres. dir. Clinton Engines Co., 1961-63; dir. Amalgamated Metal Industries, 1963—; pres., dir. Steego Corp. (name formerly Sterling Precision Corp.), 1965—. Served with USNR, 1945-46. Home: 320 Fairway Ct Atlantis FL 33462 Office: 319 Clematis St West Palm Beach FL 33401

CARROLL, MICHAEL ADRIAN, newspaper designer; b. Mpls., Feb. 25, 1946; s. Harry Marion and Lillian Josephine (Phelps) C.; m. Kay Lynn Willshire, June 14, 1976; children by previous marriage: Kimberlee, Colleen, Shane. B.F.A., Mpls. Coll. Art and Design, 1968. Designer, Mpls. Tribune, 1968-74, design dir., 1974—; instr. U. Minn., 1975-76, Mpls. Coll. Art and Design, 1976-78. Co-author, designer: A Design for News, 1981. Recipient certificate Excellence, 1972, certificate Merit Soc. Pub. Designers, 1973, Best Picture Editing of Year award Nat. Press Photography Assn., 1975, Gold medal Soc. Pub. Designers, Soc. Newspaper Designers, 1980, cert. of excellence, 1981. Home: 57 S Avon 30 Saint Paul MN 55105 Office: 425 Portland Ave Minneapolis MN 55488

CARROLL, PAT, actress; b. Shreveport, La., May 5, 1927; d. Maurice Clifton and Kathryn Angela (Meagher) C.; children—Sean, Kerry, Tara. Student, Immaculate Heart Coll., 1944-47, Catholic U., 1950; Litt.D. (hon.), Barry Coll., Miami, Fla., 1969. Pres. Sea-Ker, Inc., Beverly Hills, Calif., 1979—; bd. dirs. Hyde Park Theatre, N.Y.C. (With Gloria Swanson in) Profl. debut in stock prodn. A Goose for the Gander, 1947; supper club debut at, Le Ruban Bleu, N.Y.C., 1950; appeared on numerous television shows, 1950—, including, Red Buttons Show, 1951, Caesar's Hour, 1956-57 (Emmy award), Danny Thomas Show, 1961-63, Busting Loose, 1977; Broadway debut in Catch a Star, 1955 (Tony award); appeared in: motion picture With Six You Get Eggroll, 1968; producer, actress: Gertrude Stein Gertrude Stein Gertrude Stein for colls. and univs, 1979—, The Last Resort, 1979. Mem. Dist. Atty.'s Citizens Adv. Com., Los Angeles, 1970-75; pres. Center of Films for Children, 1971-73; bd. regents Immaculate Heart Coll., Hollywood, Calif., 1970. Mem. Actors Studio, Actors Fund (life), Actors Equity Assn., Screen Actors Guild, AFTRA, Acad. Television Arts and Scis. (trustee 1958-59), Am. Youth Hostel (life), Del. and Hudson Canal Hist. Soc., George Heller Meml. Found. Office: care LB Sanders 1900 Ave of Stars Suite 510 Los Angeles CA 90067 *

CARROLL, RICHARD SCHOTT, museum director; b. Greenwich, Conn., Feb. 4, 1929; s. Richard Augustine and Eva Virginia (Howell) C.; m. Mary Lou Bush, Apr. 21, 1951; children: Jan Carroll Hicks, Suzanne Bush, Ann Leslie. B.F.A., Yale U., 1953, M.F.A. (Rabinowitz fellow for conservation of paintings), 1955; postgrad. in Art Edn., NYU, 1955. Dir. wonder Workshop Jr. Mus., Bridgeport, Conn., 1955-59; asst. dir. Columbia Mus. Art Sci., S.C., 1959-66, Norfolk Mus. Art Sci., Va., 1966-70; dir. galleries Lowe Art Ctr.; assoc. prof. museology, founder dept. museology studies Syracuse U., N.Y., 1970-73; dir. Ringling Museums, Sarasota, Fla., 1973—. Author numerous mus. publs.; cotbr. articles to profl. jours. Bd. dirs. John and Mable Ringling Mus. Art Found. Served with AUS, 1946-47. Mem. Am. Assn. Museums, South Eastern Mus. Conf. (council 1968-70). Home: 939 Alameda Way Sarasota Fl 33580 Office: John and Mable Ringling Mus Art PO Box 1838 Sarasota Fl 33578 *conservation, restoration of paintings; developer method for microscopic analysis pigments in plant films; designer security system objects of art*

CARROLL, RICHARD STANLEY, publisher; b. Waltham, Mass., Feb. 13, 1929; s. John Anthony and Mary Elizabeth (Stanley) C.; m. Elizabeth Louise Hart, June 18, 1955; children—Elaine, Kathryn, Robert, John, Amy, Susan. B.A., U. N.Mex., 1951; M.Ed., Boston State Coll., 1953. Prodn. control adminstr. Raytheon, Waltham, Mass., 1951-53; tchr. Killingly High Sch., Danielson, Conn., 1953-55; with Allyn and Bacon, Inc., Boston, 1955—, v.p., 1971-78, pres., chief exec. officer, 1978—, also dir.; Mem. Southboro (Mass.) Sch. Com., 1960-61. Club: Algonquin of Boston. Office: 7 Wells Ave Newton MA 02159 *

CARROLL, ROBERT W., business executive; b. Ossining, N.Y., May 29, 1923; s. John Francis and Catherine Veronica (Coyne) C.; m. Mary Bernardine Dugan, June 1, 1946; children: Kevin, Dennis, Terrence, Maura, Monica. Student, Sch. Commerce, N.Y.U., 1952-56, Mgmt. Inst., 1957. With N.Y. Central R.R., 1942-68, asst. sec., 1954-59, sec., 1959-68; sr. asst. sec. Penn Central Transp. Co., 1968-70, sec., 1971-76, also former v.p., sec., dir. several railroad, real estate, trucking and fin.-oriented subsidiaries, 1971-76; exec. dir. adminstrn. Law Offices La Brum and Doak, Phila., 1976—; corp. sec. Pitts. and Lake Erie R.R. Co., 1959-79; v.p., sec., dir. Montour R.R. Co., Montour Land Co., Youngstown and So. Ry. Co., 1959-79; rep. Kissel Blake Orgn., Inc. Served with USCGR, 1942-46. Mem. Nat. Assn. Legal Adminstrs., V.F.W., Soc. Friendly Sons St. Patrick, Pa. Soc. K.C. (4). Club: Overbrook Golf (Bryn Mawr, Pa.). Home: 9 Ridgewood Rd Radnor PA 19087 Office: 700 IVB Bldg 1700 Market St Philadelphia PA 19103

CARROLL, ROBERT WAYNE, mathematics educator; b. Chgo., May 10, 1930; s. Walter Scott and Dorothy (Le Monnier) C.; m. Berenice Jacobs, Sept. 7, 1957 (div. June 1974); children: David Leon, Malcolm Scott; m. Alice von Neumann, Sept. 1974 (div. Mar. 1977); m. Joan Miller, Jan. 1979. B.S., U. Wis., 1952; Ph.D., U. Md., 1959. Aero. research scientist NASA, Cleve., 1952-54; NSF postdoctoral fellow, 1959-60; asst. prof. Rutgers U., 1960-63, assoc. prof., 1963-64, U. Ill., Urbana, 1964-67, prof. math., 1967—. Author: Abstract Methods in Partial Differential Equations, 1969, Transmutation and Operator Differential Equations, 1979, Transmutation, Scattering Theory, and Special Functions, 1982; co-author: Singular and Degenerate Cauchy Problems, 1976; assoc. editor: Jour. Applicable Analysis, 1970—; contbr. 93 articles to math. jours. Served with U.S. Army, 1954-57. Mem. Am. Math. Soc. Home: 1718 Lincoln Rd Champaign IL 61820 Office: Math Dept Univ Ill Urbana IL 61801

CARROLL, STEPHEN JOHN, JR., business educator; b. Boston, Aug. 23, 1930; s. Stephen John and Helene Ann (Roach) C.; m. Donna June Freeman, June 24, 1961; children: Christopher Wayne, Alisa Helene. B.S., UCLA, 1957; M.A., U. Minn., 1959, Ph.D., 1963. Research fellow, instr. U. Minn., 1957-61; asst. prof. Villanova U., 1961-64, U. Md., College Park, 1964-67, asso. prof., 1967-70, prof., 1970—, chmn. faculty organizational behavior and indsl. relations, 1972-77, also chmn. div. personnel/human resources, 1973-74, editorial bd. jour., 1974—. Author: (with Henry L. Tosi) Management by Objectives: Applications and Research, 1973, Management: Contingencies, Structure, and Process, 1976, Organizational Behavior, 1977, Management, 1981, (with Frank T. Paine and John B. Miner) The Management Process: Cases and Readings, 2d edit, 1977, (with Allan N. Nash) The Management of Compensation, 1974, (with Craig C. Schneier) Performance Appraisal and Review, 1982, (with Randall Schuler) Human Resource Management in the 1980s; contbr. articles to profl. jours. Served with USNR, 1947-53. Named Disting. Scholar U. Md., 1979. Fellow Acad. Mgmt.; mem. Am. Psychol. Assn., Alpha Kappa Psi, Beta Gamma Sigma. Home: 3901 Foreston St Beltsville MD 20705

CARROLL, THOMAS CHARLES, lawyer; b. Louisville, Sept. 1, 1921; s. Tarlton Combs and Irene (Crutcher) C.; m. Julianne Kirk, Apr. 23, 1959. B.A., Harvard U., 1942; J.D., U. Ky., 1948. Bar: Ky. bar 1948. Since practiced in, Louisville; partner firm Carroll and Conliffe; dir. Brokerage, Inc., Service Erection & Machine Co., Inc., Roads and Rivers Transp., Inc.; legal counsel Ky. Democratic Com., 1964-75, spl. counsel, 1975—; parliamentarian Dem. Nat. Com., 1973-75; mem. Dem. Charter Com., 1973—, Ky. Dem. Exec. Com., 1964-75. Served to capt. U.S. Army, 1942-46. Mem. Am., Ky., Louisville bar assns., Assn. Trial Lawyers Am., Phi Delta Phi. Clubs: Pendennis, Jefferson (Louisville); Hasty Pudding (Harvard U.); Harvard (N.Y.C.); Nat. Democratic (Washington). Home: 1603 Evergreen Rd Anchorage KY 40223 Office: 310 W Liberty St Suite 600 Louisville KY 40202

CARROLL, THOMAS JOHN, association executive; b. St. Paul, Aug. 15, 1929; s. William H. and Neva (Saller) C.; m. Eleanor Rose Schmid, Aug. 27, 1955; children: David G., Thomas John, Ann Catherine, Robert G., Paul William. B.A., St. Mary's Coll., Winona, Minn., 1952. Pharm. salesman A.H. Robins, Davenport, Iowa, 1955-70; in advt. sales Modern Medicine, Chgo., 1970-72; advt. sec. D'Arcy, McManus & Massius, St. Paul, 1972-73; dir. mktg. communications AMA, Chgo., 1973—, editor Synergy monthly, 1975—; dir. pub. relations St. Francis Xavier Sch. Bd., LaGrange, Ill., 1977-79; organist St. Francis Xavier Ch., LaGrange, 1964—. Served with AUS, 1952-54; Korea. Recipient Cert. Grad. Sch. Mgmt. UCLA, 1977. Mem. A. Guild Organists (hon.), Phar. Ad Club, Midwest Phar. Ad Club (dir.), Med. Mktg. Assn., Chgo. Area Theatre Orgn. Enthusiasts. Republican. Roman Catholic. Clubs: LaGrange Field; LaGrange Tennis Assn. (past pres.); St. Francis Xavier Men's. Home: 333 N Edgewood St Lagrange IL 60525 Office: AMA 535 N Dearborn St Chicago IL 60610

CARROLL, THOMAS SYLVESTER, business executive; b. N.Y.C., Oct. 1, 1919; s. Thomas Jeremiah and Johanna (Mulvihill) C.; m. Sidney Burke, Sept. 27, 1947 (div.); children: Jeffrey Burke, Thomas Jeremiah (dec.), James Francis, Matthew, Charles Laurence.; m. Caroline Wheelwright, May 30, 1981. A.B. cum laude, Catawba Coll., 1941; postgrad., Mass. Inst. Tech., 1941-42; M.B.A. with distinction, Harvard, 1947. Brand man Procter and Gamble Co., 1947-53; product dir. Gen. Foods Corp., 1953-55; mktg. mgr. Colgate-Palmolive Co., 1955-57; v.p. George Fry & Assos., 1957-58; gen. mgr. mktg. services Lever Bros. Co., 1958-59, mktg. v.p., 1959-63, merchandising v.p., 1963-64, dir., 1963—, exec. v.p., 1964-67, pres., chief exec., 1967-80, chmn. fin. com., 1980-83; dir. Am. Airlines Inc., Assoc. Dry Goods Corp. Police commr. City of New Canaan (Conn.), 1963-67; pres. Harvard Bus. Sch. Assn., 1973-74, mem. vis. com. Bus. Sch., 1975-81; bd. dirs. Assocs. Harvard Bus. Sch., 1975—; trustee Mus. Modern Art, 1974—, Catawba Coll., 1967—, Com. Econ. Devel.; bd. dirs. Internat. Exec. Service Corps., 1972—, exec. v.p., 1980-82, pres., chief exec. officer, 1982—. Served from cadet to lt. col. USAAF, 1941-46. Mem. Grocery Mfrs. Am. (chmn. 1978-80); mem. Conf. Bd. Clubs: Country of New Canaan; Racquet and Tennis, Economic (N.Y.C.) (dir. 1970-71); Pilgrims.; Metropolitan (Washington). Home: 67 Benedict Hill New Canaan CT 06840 Office: IESC 8 Stamford Forum Samford CT 06904

CARROLL, VERN, anthropologist; b. Bklyn., Sept. 2, 1933; m. Mireille Raymonde Cohen, Mar. 7, 1961; 1 dau., Tama. B.A., Yale U., 1959, M.A., 1962; B.A. (honors), Cambridge (Eng.) U., 1959, M.A., 1966; Ph.D., U. Chgo., 1966. Asst. prof., then asso. prof. anthropology U. Wash., Seattle, 1966-72; mem. faculty U. Mich., Ann Arbor, 1972—, prof. anthropology, 1975—. Author: Nukuoro Lexicon, 1973, Pacific Atoll Populations, 1975, also articles, monographs; editor: Adoption in Eastern Oceania, 1970. Served with USMCR, 1953-57. Fellow Am. Council Learned Socs., 1967-68; spl. postdoctoral fellow NIMH, 1970-71; sr. fellow East-West Population Inst., East-West Center, 1972-73. Fellow Assn. Social Anthropology in Oceania (chmn. exec. com. 1969—72, editor monograph series 1967-74), Am. Anthrop. Assn., Royal Anthrop. Inst. Gt. Britain and Ireland; mem. Polynesian Soc., Linguistic Soc. N.Z. Home: 560 S 1st St Ann Arbor MI 48103 Office: Dept Anthropology Univ Mich Ann Arbor MI 48109

CARROLL, VINNETTE JUSTINE, actress, stage director, writer; b. N.Y.C.; d. Edgar Edgerton and Florence (Morriss) C. B.A., L.I. U., 1944; M.A., N.Y. U., 1946; postgrad., New Sch. Social Research, 1948-50. Tchr. drama High Sch. Performing Arts, N.Y.C.; former dir. Ghetto Arts Program; former cons. N.Y. State Council on the Arts; dir. Urban Arts Corps, 1967. Actress: roles include Caesar and Cleopatra, 1955, Small War on Murray Hill, 1956, Jolly's Progress, 1959, Mem. of the Wedding, 1960, Moon on a Rainbow Shawl, London, 1962; plays directed include: Dark of the Moon, 1960, Ondine, 1962, Black Nativity, N.Y.C., 1962, Spoleto Festival of Two Worlds, 1963, The Prodigal Son, 1965, The Flies, 1966, 74, Slow Dance on the Killing Ground, 1968, Don't Bother Me I Can't Cope, 1975 (Tony nominee), Step Lively Boy, 1973, Croesus and the Witch, 1973, All the King's Men, 1974, Desire Under the Elms, 1974, Your Arms Too Short to Box with God, 1975 (Tony nominee), Washington, 1976, N.Y.C., Broadway, 1980, Play Mas, 1976, I'm Laughin' But I Ain't Tickled, 1976, The Ups and Downs of Theophilus Maitland, 1976, Alice, 1977, Lost in the Stars, San Francisco Opera, 1980; TV roles include Jubilation, 1964, We the Women, 1974, Sojourner, 1975; movies include One Potato Two Potato, 1964, Up the Down Staircase, 1966, Alice's Restaurant, 1967; dir.: pre-Broadway prodn. Alice, 1978; showcase prodn. But Never Jam Today, 1978; originator, dir.: When Hell Freezes Over I'll Skate, Lincoln Center Black Theatre Festival, 1979, Phila., 1984. Recipient Obie award for distinguished performance, 1962; Emmy award for conception and supervision of Beyond the Blues, 1962; N.Y. Outer Critics Circle award; Los Angeles Drama Critic's awards; NAACP Image award; Golden Circle award, 1979; Black Filmmakers Hall of Fame award, 1979; others. Office: 227 W 17th St Ground Floor New York NY 10011

CARROLL, WALLACE EDWARD, corporation executive; b. Taunton, Mass., Nov. 4, 1907; s. Patrick J. and Katherine (Feely) C.; m. Lelia Holden, Nov. 7, 1936; children: Wallace E., Denis H., Barry J., Lelia K.H. Ph.B., Boston Coll., 1928, LL.D., 1957; postgrad., Mass. Inst. Tech., 1929, Harvard Bus. Sch., N.Y.U., 1933, Northwestern U., 1936; LL.D., DePaul U., 1966. Various positions, 1924-29; with N.Y. Telephone Co., 1930-33, Reed & Barton, 1933-34, Fed. Products, 1934-40; chmn., dir. Wacker Sales, 1940—, Size Control Co., 1941—, Walsh Press & Die Co., 1945—, Am. Gage & Machine Co., 1948—, Simpson Electric Co., 1950—, Standard Transformer Co., 1956—; chmn. bd. Katy Industries, Inc., 1970—, Hawthorne Bank Wheaton; vice chmn., dir. Ludlow Typograph Co.; vice chmn. M.-K.-T. R.R.; treas., dir. G.M. Diehl Machine Co., Champion Pneumatic Machinery Co., 1957—; dir. numerous cos., including Binks Mfg. Co., Katy Industries.; Dir. metal-working equipment div. BDSA, Dept. Commerce, Washington, 1957; with U.S. Trade Mission to India, 1958-59, UAR, 1960, Ireland and Portugal, 1966. Chmn. fed. agys. Community Fund drive, 1959; Bd. dirs. Catholic Charities, 1962, Chgo. Boys Club, Am. Irish Found.; bd. regents Boston Coll.; trustee Christine and Alfred Sonntag Found. Cancer Research, DePaul U. Served as cadet with Air Corps U.S. Army, 1929; with N.Y.N.G., 1930-33. Mem. Tool and Die Inst. (pres. 1952-53), U.S. C. of C., Nat. Machine Tool Builders Assn. (pres. 1962-63). Roman Catholic. Clubs: Chgo. Athletic, Chgo., Mass. Inst. Tech., Harvard, Harvard Bus., Boston Coll., N.Y. U. (Chgo.); Burning Tree (Bethesda, Md.); Exmoor Country (Highland Park, Ill.); Everglades, Bath and Tennis (Palm Beach, Fla.); Edgartown Yacht; Met. (Washington and N.Y.C.). Office: 853 Dundee Ave Elgin IL 60120 *

CARROLL, WALTER WILLIAM, surgeon; b. Chgo., June 25, 1915; s. Emmett P. and Claudia Mary (Flynn) C.; m. Jean Lawler Gayton, June 13, 1942; children—Michael, Christopher; m. Patricia Louise Kimball, Oct. 12, 1979. B.S. magna cum laude, Loyola U., 1936; M.S., Northwestern U., 1944, M.D., 1941. Diplomate: Am. Bd. Surgery. Intern Passavant Meml. Hosp., 1940-41, surg. resident, 1941-42, surg. fellow, 1942-44; surg. asso. Cook County Hosp., 1944-46; surg. attending staff Passavant Meml. Hosp., 1945, VA Research Hosp., 1954; active tchr. Northwestern U. Med. Sch. and; prof. surgery, dir. tumor clinic; asso. dir. research and standards Joint Commn. on Accreditation of Hosps., 1968-74; hosp. cons., Los Angeles, 1974—; clin. prof. surgery U. So. Calif. Med. Sch., Los Angeles and med. dir.; St. Vincent Med. Center, Los Angeles, 1974-77; bd. dirs. Area XXIV, Profl. Standards Rev. Orgn., 1975-77. Cons. editor: Surgery, Gynecology and Obstetrics; contbr. articles to profl. jours. Fellow A.C.S.; mem. Am. Pub. Health Assn., Am. Radium Soc., Ill., Chgo. Los Angeles, Calif. med. socs., AMA, Pan-Pacific, Internat. (sec.), Chgo., Central, Western (past pres.), Pan-Am. surg. assns., Soc. Surgery Alimentary Tract (founder mem.), Halsted Soc., Geriatric Soc., Nat. Fire Protection Assn., Am. Assn. Med. Instrumentation, U.S. Pub. Health Assn., Sigma Xi. Clubs: K.C., Elks, Saddle and Cycle. Address: 67 Agape Village Warner Springs CA 92086

CARROLL, WILLIAM JEROME, civil engr.; b. Los Angeles, Nov. 23, 1923; s. William Jerome and Adeline Marie (Verden) C.; m. Louise May Judson, June 6, 1944; children—Charisse Jean, Charles Gary, Christine Louise, Pamela Ann. B.S., Calif. Inst. Tech., 1948, M.S., 1949. Diplomate Am. Acad. Environ. Engrs. (pres. 1980—). Indsl. waste engr. Los Angeles County Engr., 1949-51; engr. James M. Montgomery (Cons. Engr., Inc.), Pasadena, Calif., 1951-56, v.p., 1956-69, pres., 1969—; pres. Montgomery Engrs. of Nev., Montgomery Engrs. of Va.; chmn. bd. MICSA, Venezuela; dir. Montgomery-Hoskings, Australia, Ambitec, Brazil. Served with USAAF, 1943-46. Recipient Engring. Merit award Inst. Advancement Engring., Los Angeles, 1975. Mem. ASCE (pres. Los Angeles sect. 1967, nat. dir. 1976—), Am. Water Works Assn., Water Pollution Control Fedn., Cons. Engrs. Assn. Calif. (pres. 1972), Alumni Assn. Calif. Inst. Tech. (pres. 1976), Pasadena C. of C. Republican. Clubs: Jonathan (Los Angeles); Univ. (Pasadena). Home: 342 W Starlight Crest La Canada CA 91011 Office: 250 N Madison Pasadena CA 91101

CARROLL, WILLIAM KENNETH, law educator, psychologist, theologian; b. Oak Park, Ill., May 8, 1927; s. Ralph Thomas and Edith (Fay) C.; m. Frances Louise Forgue; children: Michele, Brian. B.S. in Edn., Quincy Coll., Ill., 1950, B.A. in Philosophy, 1950; M.A., Duquesne U., 1964; S.T.L., Catholic U., 1965; Ph.D., U. Strasbourg, France, 1968; J.D., Northwestern U., 1972. Bar: Ill. 1972, U.S. Dist. Ct. (no. dist.) Ill 1972, U.S. Ct. Apls. (7th cir.) 1973; registered psychologist. Asst/ editor Franciscan Press, Chgo., 1955-60; asst. prof. psychology and religion Carlow Coll., Pitts., 1962-65, Loyola U., Chgo., 1968-70; staff atty. Fed. Defender Program, Chgo., 1972-75; prof. law John Marshall Law Sch., Chgo., 1975—; bd. dirs. Am. Inst. Adlerian Studies, 1982—. Author: (with Kosnik et al.) Human Sexuality, 1977; contbg. author: By Reason of Insanity, 1983. Bd. dirs. Chgo. Sch. Profl. Psychology, 1978-82. Recipient Am. Juris award, 1970. Fellow Inst. Social and Behavioral Pathology; mem. ABA, Catholic Theol. Soc. Am., Ill. Psychol. Assn. (ethics com. 1979—), Am. Psychol. Assn., AAUP. Office: John Marshall Law School 315 S Plymouth Ct Chicago IL 60604

CARROTHERS, ALFRED WILLIAM ROOKE, lawyer, educator; b. Saskatoon, Sask., Can., June 1, 1924; s. William Alexander and Agnes Elizabeth (Godber) C.; m. Margaret Jane Macintosh, July 1, 1961; children: Matthew, Jonathan, Alexandra. B.A., U. B.C., 1947, LL.B., 1948; LL.M., Harvard U., 1951, S.J.D., 1966. Lectr. Faculty Law, U. B.C., 1948-50, asst. prof., 1952-55, asso. prof., 1955-60, prof., 1960-64, dir., 1960-62; asst. prof. Faculty Law, Dalhousie U., Halifax, N.S., 1951-52; dean Faculty Law, U. Western Ont., London, 1964-68; pres., vice chancellor U. Calgary, Alta., 1969-74; pres. Inst. for Research on Pub. Policy, 1974-81; prof. common law Faculty of Law, U. Ottawa, Ont., Can., 1981—; founding chmn. Public Service Adjudication Bd., B.C., 1977—; chmn. Commn. of Inquiries into Redundancies and Layoffs, Fed. Dept. Labour, 1978-79; Mem. Adv. Commn. to Minister No. Affairs and Nat. Resources on Devel. of Govt. N.W. Terrs., 1965-66; mem. Prime Minister's Task Force on Labour Relations, 1966-68; pres. Assn. Univs. and Colls. Can., 1972-73. Author: The Labour Injunction in British Columbia, 1956, Labour Arbitration in Canada, 1961, Collective Bargaining Law in Canada, 1965; Contbr. articles to profl. jours. Mem. Law Soc. Upper Can., Law Soc. Alta., Canadian Bar Assn. Clubs: Cercle Universitaire (Ottawa); University (Vancouver). Home: 864 Echo Dr Ottawa ON Canada

CARROTHERS, GERALD ARTHUR PATRICK, educator; b. Saskatoon, Sask., Can., July 1, 1925. B.Arch., U. Man., Can., 1948, M.Arch., 1951; M.C.P., Harvard U., 1953; Ph.D., Mass. Inst. Tech., 1959. Lectr. architecture U. Man., Winnipeg, 1948-52; research asst. regional sci. Mass. Inst. Tech., Cambridge, 1953-56; asst. prof. town and regional planning U. Toronto, Ont., Can., 1956-60; asso. prof. to prof. city planning U. Pa., Phila., 1960-67, chmn. dept. city planning, 1961-65; founding dir. Inst. Environ. Studies, 1965-67; prof. York U., Downsview, Ont., 1968—, dean faculty environ. studies, 1968-76; chmn. U. Toronto-York U. Joint Program in Transp., 1971-77; adviser Central Mortgage and Housing Corp., Can., 1967-77; vis. prof. U. Nairobi, Kenya, 1978-80. Fellow World Acad. Art and Sci., Royal Archtl. Inst. Can.; mem. Am. Inst. Cert. Planners, Regional Sci. Assn. (pres. 1970-71), Can. Inst. Planners (councillor 1968-70). Home: PO Box 216 Postal Station G Toronto ON Canada M4M 3G7 Office: Faculty of Environ Studies York U 4700 Keele St Downsview ON Canada M3J 2R2

CARROW, LEON ALBERT, physician; b. Chgo., Jan. 18, 1924; s. Charles and Mollie (Sachs) C.; m. Joan Twaddell, June 21, 1974; children by previous marriage—Elizabeth, James. B.S., U. Chgo., 1945, M.D., 1947. Intern Cook County Hosp. and Chgo. Lying-in Hosp., 1947-48; resident Chgo. Wesley Meml. Hosp., Chgo. Maternity Center, 1949-51; sr. attending physician in obstetrics and gynecology Northwestern Meml. Hosp., 1954—, also past chief of staff; asso. prof. obstetrics and gynecology Northwestern U. Med. Sch., 1967-73, prof. clin. obstetrics and gynecology, 1973—. Contbr. articles to profl. jours. Served with AUS, 1944-46; to capt. USAF, 1952-53. Fellow A.C.S.; mem. Ill., Chgo. med. socs., AMA, Chgo. Gynecology Soc., Am. Soc. Cytology, Central Assn. Obstetrics and Gynecology. Home: 566 Cedar St Winnetka IL 60093 Office: 251 E Chicago Ave Chicago IL 60611

CARROW, MILTON MICHAEL, lawyer, educator; b. N.Y.C., Sept. 13, 1912; s. Samuel and Ethel (Berlin) C.; m. Betsey Wood Hall, Nov. 2, 1940 (div. 1968); children: David M., Thomas E., Deborah, James H., Emily W.; m. Eve Wagner Cooper; Feb. 28, 1969. A.B., Syracuse U., 1933, postgrad., 1933-34; LL.B., Harvard U., 1937. Bar: N.Y. 1938. Asso. Legal Aid Soc., Rochester, N.Y., 1937-38, Lincoln Epworth & Nathan Sweedler, 1938-42, Emil Schlesinger, 1946-48; pvt. law practice, 1948-53; partner firm Lavine & Carrow, N.Y.C., 1953-59, Landis, Carrow, Benson & Tucker, 1959-70, Carrow, Bernson, Hoeniger, Freitag & Abbey, 1970-73; dir. Center for Adminstrv. Justice, Am. Bar Assn., 1973-77, Nat. Center for Adminstrv. Justice, Consortium of Univs. of Washington Met. Area, 1977-79; pres. Nat. Center for Adminstrv. Justice, 1979—82; adj. asst. prof. N.Y.U. Law Sch., 1964-68; vis. prof. Nat. Law Center, George Washington U., 1973-80; adj. prof. Georgetown U. Law Center, 1980—81; research prof. pub. policy George Washington U., 1983—; mem. faculy appellate judges seminar Inst. Jud. Adminstrn., 1969, 70; cons. Nat. Adv. Com. Civil Disorders, 1967; Vice chmn. Weston (Conn.) Charter Commn., 1965-66; counsel UN We Believe, 1962-72; vis. intervenor XVIII Internat. Congress of Adminstrv. Scis., Madrid, 1980; U.S. rep. to standing Com. on Law and Sci. of Pub. Adminstrn. Internat. Inst. Adminstrv. Scis., 1982. Author: Background of Administrative Law, 1948, The Licensing Power in New York City, 1968, (with J.D. Nyhart) Law and Science in Collaboration, 1983; also articles. Served with AUS, 1943-46. Mem. Am. Arbitration Assn. (panel arbitrators), Assn. Bar City N.Y. (chmn. com. adminstrv. law 1964-67), Am. Bar Assn. (chmn. sect. adminstrv. law 1971-72). Home: 1302 Clayborne House Ct McLean VA 22101 Office: 2000 L St NW Washington DC 20036

CARRUTH, DAVID BARROW, landscape architect; b. Woodbury, Conn., June 28, 1926; s. Gorton Veeder and Margery Barrow (Dibb) C.; m. Enid Fran Levin, Aug. 11, 1979; children by previous marriage—Kathryn Paige, Todd David, Peter Richmond. Grad., U.S. Mcht. Marine Acad., 1946; B.S. in Land Planning, Cornell U., 1951; M.Landscape Architecture, 1952. Lic. landscape architect, N.Y., Conn., Pa., Fla., Mass.; nat. cert. as landscape architect. Landscape architect, asso. Clarke & Rapuano, Inc. (cons. engrs., landscape architects), N.Y.C., 1952-70; pres. Kane and Carruth (landscape architects), Pleasantville, N.Y., 1970—; mem. N.Y. State Bd. Landscape Architecture, 1970-80; pres. Council Landscape Archtl. Registration Bds., 1975, Interprofl. Council on Registration, 1975, Landscape Archtl. Registration Bds. Found., 1976; Trustee Bayard Cutting Arboretum. Mem. Katonah-Lewisboro Sch. Bd., 1963-73. Served with USNR, 1944-46. Fellow Am. Soc. Landscape Architects. Office: 70 Memorial Plaza Pleasantville NY 10570

CARRUTH, GORTON VEEDER, editor; b. Woodbury, Conn., Apr. 9, 1925; s. Gorton Veeder and Margery Tracy Barrow (Dibb) C.; m. Gisele Leliet, Dec. 28, 1955; children: Gorton Veeder III, Hayden III, Christopher Leliet. Ph.B., U. Chgo., 1948; B.A., Columbia U., 1950, M.A., 1954. Editor ref. books Thomas Y. Crowell Co., N.Y.C., 1954-63; exec. editor McGraw-Hill Book Co., N.Y.C., 1963-68; editor-in-chief Funk & Wagnalls, N.Y.C., 1968-71; pres. Morningside Assocs., Pleasantville, N.Y., 1971—; founding mem., v.p. Hudson Group, Inc., Pleasantville. Author: Encyclopedia of American Facts and Dates, 7th rev. ed, 1978; co-author: Where to Find Business Information, 1979, 2d edit., 1982, Oxford Am. Dictionary, 1980, The VNR Dictionary of Bus. and Fin, 1980, The Oxford Literary Guide to the United States, 1982, The Encyclopedia of Historic Places, 1984, The Complete Word Game Dictionary, 1984. Mem. Linnaean Soc., Lab. Ornithology Cornell U. (hon.), Phi Beta Kappa. Home: Box 168 Pleasantville NY 10570

CARRUTH, HAYDEN, poet; b. Waterbury, Conn., Aug. 3, 1921; s. Gorton Veeder and Margery Tracy Barrow (Dibb) C.; m. Sara Anderson, Mar. 14, 1943; 1 dau., Martha Hamilton; m. Eleanore Ray, Nov. 29, 1952; m. Rose Marie Dorn, Oct. 28, 1961; 1 son, David Barrow II. A.B., U. N.C., 1943; M.A., U. Chgo., 1948. Editor-in-chief Poetry mag., 1949-50; asso. editor U. Chgo. Press, 1950-51; project adminstr. Intercultural Publs. Inc., N.Y.C., 1952-53; poetry editor Harper's mag., 1977—; poet-in-residence Johnson State Coll., 1972-74; adj. prof. U. Vt., 1975-78; prof. English Syracuse (N.Y.) U., 1979—. (Annual Poetry award Brandeis U. 1959, Harriet Monroe Poetry prize U. Chgo. 1960); Author: The Crow and the Heart, 1959, Journey to a Known Place, 1961, Norfolk Poems, 1962, Appendix A, 1963, North Winter, 1964, Nothing for Tigers, 1965, Contra Mortem, 1967, After the Stranger, 1965, For You, 1970, The Clay Hill Anthology, 1970, The Voice That is Great Within Us, 1970, The Bird Poem Book, 1970, From Snow and Rock, from Chaos, 1973, Dark World, 1973, The Bloomingdale Papers, 1975, Loneliness, 1976, Aura, 1977, Brothers, I Loved You All, 1978, Almanach du Printemps ViVarois, 1979, Working Papers, 1982, The Mythology of Dark and Light, 1982, The Sleeping Beauty, 1982, If You Call This Cry a Song, 1983, Effluences from the Sacred Caves, 1983; Mem. editorial bd.: Hudson Rev, 1971—. Recipient Vachel Lindsay prize, 1954, Bess Hokin prize, 1956, Levinson prize, 1958; Helen Bullis prize U. Seattle, 1962; Carl Sandburg prize, 1963; Emily Clark Balch prize, 1964; Gov.'s medal State of Vt., 1974; Shelley award Poetry Soc. Am., 1978; Lenore Marshall prize, 1979; Fellow Bollingen Found., N.Y.C., 1962, John Simon Meml. Guggenheim Found., 1965, 79; 10,000 grantee Nat. Found. on Arts and Humanities, 1967; 5000 grantee, 1974; Morton Zabel prize, 1968. Office: Dept English Syracuse U Syracuse NY 13210

CARRUTHERS, GARREY E., government official; b. Alamosa, Colo., Aug. 29, 1939; m. Katherine Carruthers; children: Deborah, Carol, Steven. B.S. in Agr., N.Mex. State U., M.S. in Agrl. Econs.; Ph.D in Econs., Iowa State U. Asst. prof., then assoc. prof. dept. agrl. econs. and agrl. bus. N.Mex. State U., Las Cruces, 1968-71; spl. asst. to U.S. sec. of agr., Washington, 1974-75; acting dir. N.Mex. Water Resources Research Inst., 1976-78; asst. sec. interior for land and water resources Dept. Interior, Washington, 1981—. Contbr. articles to profl. jours. Mem. Am. Agrl. Econs. Assn., Western Agrl. Econs. Assn., Am. Acad. Polit. and Social Services, Sigma Xi, Omicron Delta Kappa. Office: Dept Interior Land and Minerals Mgmt 18th and C Sts NW Washington DC 20240

CARRUTHERS, JOHN ROBERT, scientist; b. Toronto, Ont., Can., Sept. 12, 1935; came to U.S., 1959, naturalized, 1976; s. William Elwood and Florence Isabelle (Dyment) C.; m. Nancy Louisa Millar, May 28, 1957; children: Wendy Ann, Michael John. B.Sc., U. Toronto, 1959, Ph.D., 1966; M.S., Lehigh U., Bethlehem, Pa., 1961. With Bell Labs., Allentown, Pa., 1959-63, Murray Hill, N.J., 1967-77; research asst. and asst. prof. U. Toronto, 1963-67; with NASA, Washington, from 1977; program dir. materials processing in space Office Space and Terrestrial Applications, 1977-81; dept. mgr. Materials Research Lab. Hewlett-Packard, Palo Alto, Calif., 1981—; dir. Microgravity Techs., Inc., Westridge Assocs.; cons. NASA; dir. Starstruck Inc. Author; Assoc. editor: Jour. Crystal Growth. Pres. Berkeley Heights (N.J.) PTA, 1971-72. Recipient Exceptional Service medal NASA, 1981; Ford Found. fellow, 1963-64; McAllister Found. fellow, 1964-65. Mem. Am. Phys. Soc., Am. Assn. Crystal Growth, Sigma Xi. Patentee in field. Home: 22633 Queens Oak Ct Cupertino CA 95014 Office: Hewlett-Packard Labs Palo Alto CA 94304

CARRUTHERS, PAUL MATTHEW, textile co. exec.; b. Greensboro, N.C., Apr. 6, 1921; s. Joseph Tinnie and Ethel (Williamson) C.; m. Carlotta Marsh, Feb. 23, 1957; children—Nora Evelyn, Paul Matthew. A.B., Duke, 1947; M.S., U. Ill., 1948; J.D., U. N.C., 1954. Bar: N.C. bar 1954; C.P.A., N.C. Tax accountant A.M. Pullen & Co., Greensboro, N.C., 1948-52; asst. counsel R.J. Reynolds Tobacco Co., Winston-Salem, N.C., 1955-59; counsel, controller Wunda Weve Carpet Co., Greenville, S.C., 1959-61; sec., gen. counsel Callaway Mills Co., La Grange, Ga., 1961-68; sec. Deering Milliken Inc., Spartanburg, S.C., 1968-71; sec.-treas. Dan River, Inc., Greenville, S.C., 1971-75, v.p., sec., 1975—. Pres. City-County Hosp. Bd., La Grange, Ga., 1967-68. Served to capt. USAAF, 1942-46. Mem. Am. Inst. C.P.A.'s, Am. Bar Assn. Clubs: Poinsett, Greenville Country. Home: 5 Quail Hill Dr Greenville SC 29607 Office: PO Box 6126 Sta B Greenville SC 29606

CARRUTHERS, PETER AMBLER, physicist, educator; b. Lafayette, Ind., Oct. 7, 1935; s. Maurice Earl and Nila (Ambler) C.; m. Jean Ann Breitenbecher, Feb. 26, 1955; children: Peter, Debra, Kathryn; m. Lucy J. Marston, July 10, 1969; m. Cornelia B. Dobrovolsky, June 20, 1981. B.S., Carnegie Inst. Tech., 1957, M.S., 1957; Ph.D., Cornell U., 1960. Asst. prof. Cornell U., 1961-63, asso. prof., 1963-67, prof. physics, atomic and solid state physics, nuclear studies, 1967-73; div. leader, theoretical div. Los Alamos Sci. Lab., 1973-80, sr. fellow, 1980—; vis. asso. prof. Calif. Inst. Tech., 1965, vis. prof., 1969-70, 77-78; mem. physics adv. panel NSF, 1975-80, chmn., 1978-80; Trustee Aspen Center for Physics, 1976—, chmn. exec. com., 1977-79, chmn. bd. trustees, 1979-82; mem. High Energy Physics Adv. Panel, 1978—; mem. com. on U.S.-USSR cooperation in physics Nat. Acad. Scis., 1978-82. Author: (with R. Brout) Lectures on the Many-Electron Problem, 1963, Introduction to Unitary Symmetry, 1966, Spin and Isospin in Particle Physics, 1971. Recipient Merit award Carnegie Mellon U., 1980; Alfred P. Sloan research fellow, 1963-65; NSF sr. postdoctoral fellow U. Rome, 1967-68. Fellow Am. Phys. Soc., AAAS. Home: 1459 46th St Los Alamos NM 87544 Office: T-DO MS B285 Los Alamos Nat Lab Los Alamos NM 87545

CARSEY, MARCIA LEE PETERSON, TV producer; b. South Weymouth, Mass., Nov. 21, 1944; d. John Edwin and Rebecca White (Simonds) Peterson; m. John Jay Carsey, Apr. 12, 1969; children: Rebecca Peterson, John Peterson. B.A. in English Lit., U. N.H., 1966. Exec. story editor Tomorrow Entertainment, Los Angeles, 1971-74; sr. v.p. prime time series; ABC-TV, Los Angeles, 1978-81; founder Carsey Prodns., Los Angeles, 1981; co-owner Carsey-Werner Co., 1982—; co-exec. producer TV series Madeline, 1983. Office: 1130 Westwood Blvd Los Angeles CA 90024

CARSON, CLARICE, soprano; b. Montreal, Que., Can., Dec. 23, 1939; d. Philip and Regina (Singer) Katz; m. Philon Ktsanes, Apr. 30, 1973; children: Melanie Ornstein, Neil Ornstein. Student, Sir George Williams U., Montreal. Debuts include, Met. Opera, 1969, Chgo. Lyric Opera, Scottish Opera, 1970, Houston Grand Opera, 1973; appeared throughout, U.S. and Europe including, San Francisco Opera, Houston Grand Opera, Netherlands Opera, concert appearances include, Montreal Symphony, Toronto Symphony, Israel Philharm., Stratford Festival, Ravinia Festival. Mem. Can. Actor's Equity. Office: care Robert Lombardo Assocs 61 W 62d St Suite 6F New York NY 10023 *

CARSON, DALE GEORGE, sheriff; b. Amsterdam, Ohio, Jan. 16, 1922; s. Dale C. and Lillian A. (George) C.; m. Doris Newell, Sept. 1, 1946; children—Dale, Chris, Cindy. B.A., Ohio State U., 1949; grad., Nat. Execs. Inst., FBI Acad., 1976. Spl. agt. FBI, 1951-58; sheriff, Duval County, 1958-68, Jacksonville and Duval County, 1968—; Vice chmn. Nat. Commn. on Police Standards and Goals, 1971—. Contbr. numerous articles to law enforcement jours. Served with AUS, 1942-

46. Mem. Am. Soc. Criminologists, Fla. Sheriffs Assn. (pres. 1970-71), Nat. Sheriffs Assn. (dir.). Clubs: Masons (Shriner), Civitan.). Home: 1671 Woodmere Dr Jacksonville FL 32210 Office: PO Box 2070 Jacksonville FL 32202

CARSON, EDWARD MANSFIELD, banker; b. Tucson, Nov. 6, 1929; s. Ernest Lee and Earline M. (Mansfield) C.; m. Nadine Anne Severns, Dec. 13, 1952; children: Dawn, Tod. B.S. in Bus. Adminstrn., Ariz. State U., 1951; grad., Stonier Sch. Banking, Rutgers U., 1963. With First Interstate Bank of Ariz., Phoenix, 1951—, exec. v.p., 1969-72, chief adminstrv. officer, 1972-75, vice chmn. bd., 1975-77, pres., chief exec. officer, 1977—, also dir.; dir. Inspiration Resources Corp., Ramada Inns, Inc. Bd. dirs. Am. Grad. Sch. Internat. Mgmt.; bd. dirs. Ariz. U. Found., Central Ariz. Project Assn.; mem. adv. council Coll. Engring., Ariz. State U. Recipient Service award Ariz. State U. Alumni Assn., 1968, named to Hall of Fame, 1977. Mem. Ariz. bankers assns., Am. Inst. Banking. Clubs: Kiva, Paradise Valley Country, Phoenix Country, Thunderbirds. Address: PO Box 20551 Phoenix AZ 85036

CARSON, GERALD HEWES, author; b. Carrollton, Ill., July 6, 1899; s. James Anderson and Minnie (Hewes) C.; m. Lettie Gay, Nov. 28, 1923; children: Nancy Gay Carson Payne, Sara Ann Carson Forden. A.B., U. Ill., 1921, M.A., 1922. Reporter N.Y. Herald, 1922-23; copywriter Calkins & Holden, Inc., 1923-27; with J. Walter Thompson Co., 1928-29, Batton, Barton, Durstine & Osborn, 1929-32; v.p. William Esty & Co., 1933-40; v.p., copy dir. Benton & Bowles, Inc., 1940-47; v.p., dir. Kenyon & Eckhardt, Inc., 1947-51; mem. adv. bd. Am. Heritage mag., 1964-76; mem. usage panel Am. Heritage Dictionary of English Lang., 1969—. Author: The Old Country Store, 1954, Cornflake Crusade, 1957-76, The Roguish World of Doctor Brinkley, 1960, One for a Man, Two for a Horse, 1961, The Social History of Bourbon, 1963, The Polite Americans, 1966, Men, Beasts and Gods: A History of Cruelty and Kindness to Animals, 1972, The Golden Egg: The Personal Income Tax, Where It Came From, How It Grew, 1977, A Good Day at Saratoga, 1978, The Dentist and the Empress: The Adventures of Dr. Tom Evans in Gas-lit Paris, 1983; Contbr. to: Dictionary Am. Biography, Notable Am. Women; Contbr. revs. to mags., jours. Chmn. Francis Parkman award, 1972, 74. Recipient award of merit Am. Assn. State and Local History, 1954; Dunning prize Am. Hist. Assn., 1954. Fellow Soc. Am. Historians (exec. bd. 1974—); mem. Hist. Soc. Pa., S.R., Authors Guild Authors League Am. Club: University (N.Y.C.). Home: Pennswood H 110 Newtown PA 18940

CARSON, GORDON BLOOM, educational administrator; b. High Bridge, N.J., Aug. 1, 1911; s. Whitfield R. and Emily (Bloom) C.; m. Beth Lacy, June 19, 1937; children—Richard Whitfield, Emily Elizabeth (Mrs. Lee A. Duffus), Alice Lacy (Mrs. William P. Allman), Jean Helen (Mrs. Michael J. Gable). B.S. in Mech. Engring, Case Inst. Tech., 1931, D.Eng., 1957; M.S., Yale, 1932, M.E., 1938; LL.D., Rio Grande Coll., 1973. With Western Electric Co., 1930; instr. mech. engring. Case Inst. Tech., 1932-37, asst. prof., 1937-40, asso. prof. indsl. engring. charge indsl. div., 1940-44; with Am. Shipbldg. Co., 1936; patent litigation, 1937; research engr., dir. research Cleve. Automatic Machine Co., 1939-44; asst. to gen. mgr. Selby Shoe Co., 1944, mgr. engring., 1945-49, sec. of corp., 1949-53; sec., dir. Pyrrole Products Co., 1948-53; dean engring. Ohio State U., Columbus, 1953-58, v.p. bus. and finance, treas., 1958-71; dir. Engring. Exptl. Sta., 1953-58; exec. v.p. Albion (Mich.) Coll., 1971-76, exec. cons., 1976-77; asst. to chancellor, dir. fin. Northwood Inst., 1977-82; v.p. Mich. Molecular Inst., 1982—. Editor: The Production Handbook, 1958; cons. editor, 1972—; Author of tech. papers engring. subjects. Trustee White Cross Hosp. Assn., 1960-71; bd. dirs. Cardinal Fund, 1966—, Goodwill Industries, 1959-67; 1st v.p. Goodwill Industries, 1963-64; bd. dirs. Orton Found., 1953-58; v.p. Ohio State U. Research Found., 1958-71; v.p., chmn. adv. council Center for Automation and Soc., U. Ga., 1969-71; Chmn. tool and die com. 5th Regional War Labor Bd., 1943-45; chmn. Ohio State adv. com. for sci., tech. and specialized personnel SSS, 1965-70. Fellow ASME, AAAS, Am. Inst. Indsl. Engrs. (pres. 1957-58); mem. Columbus Soc. Fin. Analysts (pres. 1964-65), Fin. Analysts Fedn. (dir. 1964-65), C. of C. (dir., treas. 1952-53), Am. Def. Preparedness Assn., Am. Soc. Engring. Edn., Asso. U. for Research in Astronomy (dir. 1968-71), Midwestern Univs. Research Assn. (dir. 1958-71), U.S. Naval Inst., Nat. Soc. Profl. Engrs., Sigma Xi (fin. com. 1975—, nat. treas. 1979—), Tau Beta Pi, Zeta Psi, Phi Eta Sigma, Alpha Pi Mu, Omicron Delta Epsilon, Romophos, Sphinx. Club: Mason (32 deg.). Home: 5413 Gardenbrook Dr Midland MI 48640 *Integrity is as essential as health or intelligence. And it cannot be put on and taken off as can a garment. You either have it or you don't. Integrity must be nurtured, bolstered, and reaffirmed, lest the naturally corrupting influences of life destroy it. Without integrity, democracy cannot survive. Without it, government becomes a mutual looting society, with the citizens paying the bills. No society can be free unless a heavy majority of its citizens has integrity, and demands it on the part of all associates.*

CARSON, HAMPTON LAWRENCE, geneticist, educator; b. Phila., Nov. 5, 1914; s. Joseph and Edith (Bruen) C.; m. Meredith Shelton, Aug. 14, 1937; children: Joseph II, Edward Bruen. A.B., U. Pa., 1936, Ph.D., 1943. Instr. U. Pa., 1938-42; mem. faculty Washington U., St. Louis, 1943-70, prof. biology, 1956-70; prof. genetics U. Hawaii, 1971—; vis. prof. biology U. Sao Paulo, Brazil, 1951, 77. Author: Heredity and Human Life, 1963; Contbr. articles to profl. jours. on evolutionary genetics. Trustee B.P. Bishop Mus., Honolulu. Fulbright Research scholar zoology dept. U. Melbourne, Australia, 1961. Mem. Nat. Acad. Scis., Am. Acad. Arts and Scis., Genetics Soc. (pres. 1982), Soc. for Study Evolution (pres. 1971), Am. Soc. Naturalists (pres. 1973), AAAS, Phi Beta Kappa, Sigma Xi. Address: Univ Hawaii at Manoa Dept. of Genetics Honolulu HI 96822 *As a life scientist, I study evolution with the tools of modern biology. Religious mysticism plays no role in either my scientific or philosophical thought. Each biological individual (man, mouse or fly) is unique in both genetic endowment and environmental experience. This fact is central to the ethics of a humanism that values each human life. The differences between us are mostly due to chance; some persons are more fortunate than others. Nevertheless, each has an equal right to be treated with dignity and forbearance.*

CARSON, HARRY ALBERT, lawyer; b. Detroit, Nov. 11, 1913; s. Albert M. and Elizabeth (Mooradian) C.; m. Cynthia Davis, July 28, 1945; children: Lisbeth Carson Jeffries, William Forrestal. A.B., Wayne State U., 1936; J.D., U. Mich., 1941. Bar: Mich. bar 1941, U.S. Supreme Ct. bar 1946. Practiced in, Detroit, 1941—; asso. Vandeveer & Haggerty, Detroit, 1941-42; asso. counsel Office Gen. Counsel, Navy Dept., Washington, 1946-47; asso. firm McClintock Donovan Carson & Roach, Detroit, 1947-55, partner, 1955-80; partner successor firm Donovan Hammond Carson Ziegelman Roach & Sotiroff, 1980-81; partner Carson & Carson, Detroit, 1981—; chmn. hearing panel State Bar Mich. Grievance Bd.; Security Nat. Bank, numerous other corps.; cons. in field. Served to lt. comdr. USNR, 1942-47; PTO. Mem. State Bar Mich., Am., Fed., Detroit bar assns., Ret. Officers Assn., U. Mich. Alumni Assn. Republican. Episcopalian. Club: Univ. (Detroit). Home: 88 Cambridge Rd Grosse Pointe Farms MI 48236 Office: 2612 Buhl Bldg Detroit MI 48226

CARSON, JAMES DONALD, clergyman; b. Sparta, Ill., July 4, 1929; s. Melville Kennedy and Margaret Faith (Coleman) C.; m. Dorothy Jane Mersereau, May 16, 1952; children: Douglas, Kenneth, Thomas, Rebecca. B.A., Geneva Coll., 1950, D.D., 1970; diploma, Reformed Presbyn. Theol. Sem., 1953; D.Min., Calif. Grad. Sch. Theology, 1980. Ordained to ministry Ref. Presbyn. Ch., 1953, pastor, Portland, Oreg., 1953-57, Ref. Presbyn. Ch. of North Hills, Pitts., 1957-73, Ref. Presbyn. Ch. of Los Angeles, 1973—; Pres. bd. Ref. Presbyn. Theol. Sem., 1964-72, guest lectr., 1972-73; pres. bd. corporators Geneva Coll., 1964-72, trustee, 1976—; moderator Synod, Ref. Presbyn. Ch., 1973; trustee Westminster Theol. Sem. Calif., 1981—. Contbr. articles to ch. jours. Mem. Nat. Reform Assn. (sec. 1962-72), Calif. Council on Alcohol Problems (dir. 1973—, pres. 1982—). Home: 230 Cherry Dr Pasadena CA 91105 Office: 3557 Fletcher Dr Los Angeles CA 90065

CARSON, JOHNNY, TV entertainer; b. Corning, Iowa, Oct. 23, 1925; s. Homer and Ruth (Hook) C.; m. Jody Wolcott, 1948 (div. 1963); children: Chris, Ricky, Cory; m. Joanne Copeland, Aug. 1963 (div.); m. Joanna Holland, 1972 (div.). B.A., U. Nebr., 1949. Announcer radio Sta. KFAB, Lincoln, Nebr., 1948; later at Sta. WOW, WOW-TV, Omaha; became announcer Sta. KNXT, Los Angeles, 1950; co-chmn. Garden State Bank, Hawaiian Gardens, Calif. Started: TV show Carson's Cellar, 1951; next became writer for, Red Skelton; emcee: TV quiz show Earn Your Vacation, 1954; star: The Johnny Carson Show, CBS, 1955; emcee: quiz show Who Do You Trust, ABC-TV, 1958-63; U.S. Steel Hour, Joys!, 1976; host: Tonight show, NBC-TV, 1962—; performer, Las Vegas, 1954—; pres. Carson Prodns.; Author: Happiness Is a Dry Martini, 1965. Served with USNR, World War II. Recipient Entertainer of Year award AGVA. Club: Friars (knight). Address: care NBC 3000 W Alameda Ave Burbank CA 91505 *

CARSON, KENT (LOVETT CARSON), paper company executive; b. White Plains, N.Y., June 24, 1930; s. Oswald B. and Frances (Buente) C.; m. Margaret J. Stroker, May 11, 1963; children: Ann Frances, Michael K. B.A., Williams Coll., 1952. Salesman Kimberly-Clark Corp., N.Y.C., 1954-59; with Andrews/Nelson/Whitehead div. Boise Cascade Corp., Long Island City, N.Y., 1959-78, mgr. book pub., 1969-74, div. gen. mgr., 1974-78; exec. v.p., gen. mgr. Ris Paper Co., Inc., N.Y.C., 1978—. Mem. Greenburgh (N.Y.) Republican Town Com. Served with arty. U.S. Army, 1952-54. Mem. The Navigators (pres. 1963-65), Paper Mchts. Assn. N.Y. (treas. 1983-84), Paper Club N.Y. Presbyterian. Clubs: Williams, Westchester Country. Home: 16 Old Farm Ln Hartsdale NY 10530 Office: 45-11 33d St Long Island City NY 11101

CARSON, LEONARD ALLEN, lawyer; b. Lorain, Ohio, Nov. 6, 1940; s. Frank and Josephine (Suleski) Guzewicz; m. Rosa Nelson Houston, Nov. 27, 1976. B.S. in Bus. Adminstrn., U. Fla., 1963, J.D., 1966. Bar: Fla. 1967. Staff acct. Peat, Marwick, Mitchell & Co., N.Y.C., 1963-64; mem. firm Kates and Ress, P.A., Miami, Fla., 1967-70; corp. counsel, asst. to exec. v.p. and treas. Cordis Corp., Miami, 1970-73; judge Indsl. Claims Ct., Ft. Lauderdale, Fla., 1973; mem. Fla. Indsl. Relations Commn., Tallahassee, 1973-74, chmn., 1974-76, Fla. Pub. Employees Relations Commn., 1976-80; of counsel Seyfarth, Shaw, Fairweather & Geraldson, Tallahassee and Miami, 1980-83; sr. ptnr. Carson & Linn, Tallahassee, 1983—; mem. Fla. Law Revision Council, 1976-77, Internat. Assn. Indsl. Accident Bds. and Commns., 1974-76. Served with USMC, 1960. Mem. ABA, Dade County Bar Assn., Tallahassee Bar Assn., Fla. Govt. Bar Assn., Fla. Bar Assn., Am. Arbitration Assn. (nat. panel 1968-73). Democrat. Roman Catholic. Clubs: Governors, Capital Tiger Bay. Home: 3128 Blair Stone Ct Tallahassee FL 32301 Office: Cambridge Centre 253 E Virginia St Tallahassee FL 32301

CARSON, LETTIE GAY (MRS. GERALD H. CARSON), civic worker; b. Rockport, Ill., Jan. 15, 1901; d. William H. and Hattie (Hubbard) Gay; m. Gerald H. Carson, Nov. 28, 1923; children—Nancy Gay Carson Payne, Sara Ann Carson Forden. B.S., U. Ill., 1922. Editor, dir. dept. N.Y. Herald-Tribune, 1924-30; dept. editor Parents Mag., N.Y.C., 1930-38; Vice pres. League Women Voters, N.Y.C., 1941-44, state dir., 1941-45; v.p. Harlem Valley Transp. Assn., 1970-72, pres., 1972—, Northeast Transp. Coalition, 1973—; coordinator N.Y. State Transp. Council, 1972—; dir. Nat. Assn. R.R. Passengers, 1974-80; Sec. Town of Ancram Planning Bd., 1967-80; pres. Newtown (Pa.) Area Rail Action, 1980—; former mem. bd. dirs. Am. Parents Com. Inc., Citizens' Com. for All-Day Neighborhood Schs., N.Y.C.; trustee Mid-Hudson Libraries System, Poughkeepsie, N.Y., 1959-67, pres., 1963-64. Author: (with others) Two Hundred Years of Charleston Cookery, 1930. Trustee Millerton (N.Y.) Free Library, 1955-60, pres., bd. dirs. Mem. Am. Library Trustee Assn. (regional dir. 1964-67), N.Y. Library Assn., Housatonic Audubon Soc. (pub. relations chmn. 1970). Home: Pennswood Village H-110 Newtown PA 18940 *More than ever, the public interest must be served through organized citizen participation at all levels of government—else Democracy ceases to work.*

CARSON, NOLAN WENDELL, lawyer; b. Bucyrus, Ohio, July 10, 1924; s. James Earl and Adelia Lenore (Crooks) C.; m. Nancy Hipp Ashbaugh, Oct. 25, 1952; children: Nolan Wendell, Julia Elaine. A.B., Heidelberg Coll., 1949; J.D., U. Mich., 1951. Bar: Ohio 1951. Asso. firm Dinsmore & Shohl, Cin., 1951-59, partner, 1959—; trustee Cin. So. Ry., 1978-81. Mem. Ohio Ho. of Reps., 1961-62, Ohio Constl. Revision Commn., 1970-78; chmn. Hamilton County Republican Policy Com., 1973-82, Ohio Elections Commn., 1974-78; commr. Hamilton County Park Dist., 1978—, pres., 1980, 83; pres. Cin. Mus. Natural History., 1980-83. Served with U.S. Army, 1943-46. Mem. Am. Bar Assn., Ohio Bar Assn., Cin. Bar Assn., Cincinnatus Assn. (pres. 1970-80), SAR, Assn. Ohio Commodores, Soc. Colonial Wars. Republican. Presbyterian. Clubs: Comml., Commonwealth (sec. 1980—), Queen City, The Lit., Bankers, Coldstream Country (trustee). Office: Dinsmore & Shohl 2100 Fountain Square Plaza Cincinnati OH 45202

CARSON, SAMUEL GOODMAN, banker; b. Glens Falls, N.Y., Oct. 6, 1913; s. Russell M.L. and Mary (Goodman) C.; m. Alice Williams, Oct. 14, 1939; children: Russell L., Frances Elizabeth (Mrs. Thomas E. Brady Jr.), Mary Goodman (Mrs. John A. Fedderke), Kathryn Williams (Mrs. Robert Richards), Samuel Goodman. B.A. magna cum laude, Dartmouth Coll., 1934. With Aetna Life Ins. Co., 1934-68; with Toledo Trust Co., 1967-84, exec. v.p., 1968, pres., 1969-84, chief exec. officer, 1970-84, chmn., 1976-84; chmn., dir. Toledo Trustcorp, Inc., 1976-84; dir. Nat. Family Opinion, Inc., Toledo Edison Co., Bostwick-Braun Co., Toledo Discount Co., Lathrop Co. Mem. Ottawa Hills Bd. Edn., 1954-64; pres. United Appeal Greater Toledo Area, 1969, campaign chmn., 1964; Bd. dirs., trustee Toledo chpt. ARC, 1950—, chmn., 1959-61; trustee Toledo Hosp., 1960—, v.p., 1963-65, pres., 1966-69; bd. dirs. Community Chest Greater Toledo, 1962-65, pres., 1965; pres. Boys' Club Toledo, 1961-64, trustee, 1957—; trustee Toledo Mus. Art, 1967—, sec.-treas., 1969, v.p., 1973-78, pres., 1978-80; trustee U. Toledo Corp. Recipient Service to Mankind award Sertoma Club Toledo, 1965, Man and Boy award Boys' Clubs Am., 1966, Pacemaker of Yr. award U. Toledo Coll. Bus. Adminstrn. Alumni Assn., 1969. Mem. Toledo Area C. of C. (trustee 1961-62, 73-76, pres. 1974-75), Phi Beta Kappa, Phi Gamma Delta. Republican. Conglist. Clubs: Rotarian., Toledo Country, Toledo. Lodge: Rotary. Office: 245 Summit St Toledo OH 43603

CARSON, WALLACE PRESTON, JR., state supreme court justice; b. Salem, Oreg., June 10, 1934; s. Wallace Preston and Edith (Bragg) C.; m. Gloria Stolk, June 24, 1956; children: Scott, Carol, Steven (dec. 1981). B.A. in Politics, Stanford U., 1956; J.D., Willamette U., 1962. Bar: Oreg. 1962, U.S. Dist. Ct. Oreg. 1963, U.S. Ct. Appeals (9th cir.) 1968, U.S. Supreme Ct. 1971, U.S. Cit. Mil. Appeals 1977; lic. comml. pilot FAA. Sole practice, Salem, Oreg., 1962-77; judge Marion County Circuit Ct., Salem, 1977-82; assoc. justice Oreg. Supreme Ct., Salem, 1982—. Mem. Oreg. Ho. of Reps., 1967-71, maj. leader, 1969-71; mem. Oreg. State Senate, 1971-77, minority floor leader, 1971-77; dir. Salem Area Community Council, 1967-70, pres., 1969-70; mem. Salem Planning Commn., 1966-72, pres., 1970-71; co-chmn. Marion County Mental Health Planning Com., 1965-69; mem. Salem Community Goals Com., 1965; Republican precinct commiteeman, 1963-66; mem. Marion County Rep. Central Exec. Com., 1963-66; com. predinct edn. Oreg. Rep. Central Com., 1965; vestryman, acolyte, Sunday Sch. tchr., youth coach St. Paul's Episcopal Ch., 1935—; task force on cts. Oreg. Council Crime and Delinquency, 1968-69; trustee Willamette U., 1970—; adv. bd. Cath. Ctr. Community Services, 1976-77; mem. comporehensive planning com. Mid-Willamette Valley Council of Govts., 1970-71; adv. com. Oreg. Coll. Edn. Tchr. Edn., 1971-75; pres. Willamette regional Oreg. Lung Assn., 1974-75, state dir., exec. com., 1975-77; pub. relations com. Williamette council Campfire Girls, 1976-77; criminal justice adv. bd. Chemeketa Community Coll., 1977-79; mem. Oreg. Mental Health Com., 1979-80; mem. subcom. Gov's Task Force Mental Health, 1980; you and govt. adv. com. Oreg. YMCA, 1981—. Served to col. USAFR, 1956-59. Recipient Salem Disting. Service award, 1968, Good Fellow award Marion County Fire Service, 1974, Minuteman award Oreg. N.G. Assn., 1980; fellow Eagleton Inst. Politics, Rutgers U., 1971. Mem. Marion County Bar Assn. (sec.-treas. 1965-67, dir. 1968-70), Oreg. Bar Assn., ABA, Willamette U. Coll. Law Alumni Assn. (v.p. 1968-70), Salem Art Assn., Oreg. Hist. Soc., Marion County Hist. Soc., Delta Theta Phi. Club: Salem Stanford (pres. 1963-64). Home: 1309 Hillendale Dr SE Salem OR 97302 Office: Oregon Supreme Court Supreme Court Bldg Salem OR 97310

CARSTEN, JACK CRAIG, semiconductor company executive; b. Cin., Aug. 24, 1941; s. John A. and Edith L. C.; m. Mary Ellis Jones, June 22, 1963; children: Scott, Elizabeth, Amy. B.S., Duke U., 1963. Mktg. mgr. Tex. Instruments, Dallas, Houston, 1965-71, integrated circuits gen. mgr., Houston, 1971-75; v.p. sales and mktg. Intel Corp., Santa Clara, Calif., 1975-79, v.p., microcomputer gen. mgr., 1979-82, sr. v.p., components gen. mgr., 1982—; dir. Cimatel, Inc., Paris. Contbr. articles to profl.jours. Mem. Semiconductor Industry Assn., Am. Mgmt. Assn. Office: Intel Corp 3065 Bowers Ave Santa Clara CA 95051

CARSTEN, MARY E., biochemist, educator; b. Berlin, Germany, Mar. 2, 1922; came to U.S., 1940, naturalized, 1946; d. Paul and Frida (Born) C.; m. Don Marlin, Apr. 23, 1964. A.B., N.Y. U., 1946, M.S., 1948, Ph.D., 1951. Instr. N.Y. U., 1951-53; research asso. microbiology Columbia Coll. Physicians and Surgeons, 1953-55; mem. faculty U. Calif. at Los Angeles Med. Sch., 1956—, prof. obstetrics and gynecology, 1970—; established investigator Los Angeles County Heart Assn., 1961-64. Contbg. author: Ion Exchangers in Organic and Biochemistry, 1957, Thyrotropin, 1963, Biology of Gestation, 1968, The Prostaglandins, Clinical Applications in Human Reproduction, 1972, The Biochemistry of Smooth Muscle, 1976, Excitation-Contraction Coupling in Smooth Muscle, 1977, Uterine Physiology, 1979, Initiation of Parturition: Prevention of Prematurity, 1979; Contbr. articles to profl. jours. Nat. Found. Infantile Paralysis fellow, 1954-55; Am. Cancer Soc. fellow, 1955-57; recipient award cardiovascular research Los Angeles County Heart Assn., 1962, 63, 64, Research Career Devel. award USPHS, 1964-74. Mem. Am. Soc. Biol. Chemists, Am. Chem. Soc., N.Y. Acad. Scis., Am. Physiol. Soc., Soc. for Gynecol. Investigation, Sigma Xi. Home: 624 N Highland Ave Los Angeles CA 90036

CARSTENS, HAROLD HENRY, publisher; b. Ft. Lee, N.J., June 20, 1925; s. Henry G. and Johanna L. (Wolf) C.; m. Phyllis M. Merkle, Apr. 25, 1959; children: Rebecca, Heidi, Henry, Harold. Student, Wagner Coll., 1946-48; B.S., Fairleigh Dickinson U., 1951. Asso. editor Model Craftsman Pub. Corps., Penn Publs., Inc. (became Carstens Publs., Inc., 1973), Fredon, N.J., 1951-54, mng. editor, 1954-57, v.p., 1957-63, pres., pub., 1963—; editor Railroad Model Craftsman mag., Carstens Hobby Books, 1952—; staff photographer N.Y. Lumber Trade Jour., 1954; mng. editor Toy Trains mag., 1954; pub. Flying Models mag., 1969—, Creative Crafts mag., Railfan and R.R. mag., 1974—, The Miniature mag., 1977. Chmn. Fredon Bicentennial Com., 1975-77; mem. Sussex County Overall Econ. Devel. Planning Commn., 1977-79; trustee Wagner Coll., 1977—, Wagner Coll. Exec. Com., 1981—. Served with AUS, 1943-46. Recipient Alumni Achievement award Wagner Coll., 1976; Paul Harris fellow. Mem. Acad. Model Aeros., Ramsey C. of C. (dir.), Train Collectors Assn., Inc. (pres. 1964-65), Photog. Soc. Am. (asso. editor jour. 1960-62), Hobby Industry Assn. Am. (dir. 1965-68, 70-76, 77-80, pres. 1971-72, chmn. model r.r. div. 1967-70, 78, chmn. planning com. 1976-78, chmn. public relations com., Meritorious award of Honor 1979), Nat. Model R.R. Assn., Model R.R. Industry Assn. (pres. 1977-79, dir. 1975—), Mag. Pubs. Assn., Phi Sigma Kappa, Sigma Delta Chi. Lutheran. Club: Rotary. Office: PO Box 700 Newton NJ 07860

CARSTENSEN, EDWIN LORENZ, biophysicist, biomedical engineering educator; b. Oakdale, Nebr., Dec. 8, 1919; s. August Hans and Opal Lois (Norwood) C.; m. Pam McDonald, Aug. 1, 1947; children: Richard Lorenz, Allen Brent, Laura Lee, Loretta Dee, Christina Marie. B.S., Nebr. State Tchrs. Coll., 1941; M.S., Case Inst. Tech., 1947; Ph.D., U. Pa., 1955. Mem. sci. staff div. war research Columbia U., 1942-45; head lab. sect. U.S. Navy Underwater Sound Reference Lab., Orlando, Fla., 1945-48; research asso. Moore Sch. Elec. Engring., U. Pa., 1948-55, asst. prof. elec. engring., 1955-56; prin. investigator U.S. Army Biol. Lab., Ft. Detrick, Md., 1956-61; asso. prof. elec. engring. U. Rochester, 1961-73, prof., 1973—, dir. biomed. engring., 1971—, prof. radiation biology and biophysics, 1981—, univ. mentor, 1982—. Contbr. numerous articles to profl. publs. Fellow Acoustical Soc. Am.; mem. IEEE, Biophys. Soc., Biomed. Engring. Soc., Am. Inst. Ultrasound in Medicine. Democrat. Home: 103 Eastland Ave Rochester NY 14618 Office: Dept Elec Engring U Rochester Rochester NY 14627

CARSTENSEN, VERNON, historian, educator; b. Cherokee County, Iowa, Dec. 28, 1907; s. Frederick Herman and Amelia (Kruse) C.; m. Mary Buffum Hill, May 30, 1936 (dec. June 1971); children: Peter Christian, Frederick Vernon; m. Jeannette Davies Sogge, Sept. 9, 1973. B.A., Iowa State Tchrs. Coll., 1928; M.A., State U. Iowa, 1932, Ph.D., 1936. High sch. tchr., Minn. and Iowa, 1928-31; tchr. history Central Wash. Coll. Edn., 1935-42; historian War Dept., 1942-45; research asso. U. Wis., 1945-48, asst. prof., 1948-50, asso. prof., 1950-54, prof., 1954-64, asso. dean, 1960-64; prof. history U. Wash., Seattle, 1964—; Vis. prof. U. Wash., 1941, U. Oreg., summer session 1954, U. Calif. at Berkeley, 1958; vis. prof. under Smith-Mundt grant U. Stockholm, 1956-57; Mem. adv. council Nat. Archives, 1972-78; adv. com. Bicentennial State Histories, 1972-79; bd. curators Wash. State Hist. Soc., 1964—. Author: (with Merle Curti) The University of Wisconsin: A History, 2 vols, 1949, Farms or Forests, 1958, Land of Plenty, 1975; Editor: Letters of George Gibbs, 1954, The Public Lands, 1962, Farmer Discontent, 1974, Agrl. History, 1953-57, Pacific N.W. Quar, 1965-66; bd. editors: Jour. Am. History, 1963-66, Agrl. History, 1965-76, Pacific Northwest Quar, 1966—. Fellow Wis. Hist. Soc.; mem.

Agrl. History Soc. (pres. 1958-59), Orgn. Am. Historians, Western Hist. Assn. (pres. 1980-81), Wash. Hist. Soc. (Robert Gray merit award 1977), Oreg. Hist. Soc., AAUP. Home: 4815 Purdue Ave NE Seattle WA 98105

CARSWELL, BRUCE, electronics executive, lawyer; b. Los Angeles, Mar. 1, 1930; s. David Westwood and Estelle (Van Schaick) C.; m. Cathy L. Tompson, June 19, 1976; children: Meredith David, Douglas; 1 stepson Matthew. B.A., Colby Coll., 1951; LL.B., Cornell U., 1954. Assoc. Davies Hardy & Scheneck, 1954-58; labor counsel Sylvania Electric Products, 1958-69, v.p. indsl. relations, 1969-76; v.p. human resources GTE Products Corp., Stamford, Conn., 1976-77; v.p. human resources adminstrn. GTE Service Corp., 1977-80, v.p. human resources relations, 1980-81; sr. v.p. human resources Gen. Telephone & Electronics Corp., 1981—. Bd. dirs., v.p. White Plains (N.Y.) Hosp.; bd. dirs. St. Joseph Hosp., Electronic Industries Found.; chmn. project with industry Electronic Industries Found. Served with USNR. Mem. Electronic Industry Assn. (bd. govs., chmn. indsl. relations council), Nat. Elec. Mfrs. Assn., NAM, Labor Policy Assn., ABA, Bus. Roundtable, Am. Soc. Personnel Adminstrn. Office: GTE Corp One Stamford Forum Stamford CT 06904

CARSWELL, JOHN WILLIAM, curator, artist, educator; b. London, Nov. 16, 1931; s. John William and Catherine Wilson Lindsay (Thompson) C.; m. Peggy Ann Hedrick, Nov. 10, 1970. A.R.C.A., Royal Coll. Art, London, 1951. Archaeol. draftsman and surveyor in Near East, 1951-56; prof. fine art Am. U. of Beirut (Lebanon), 1956-76; fellow Sch. Oriental and African Studies, London, 1976-77; curator, research asso./prof. Oriental Inst., U. Chgo., 1977—; vis. prof. St. Antony's Coll., Oxford (Eng.) U., 1967. Author: New Julfa, 1968, Kütahya Tiles and Pottery in Armenian Cathedral of St. James, Jerusalem, 1972, (with Bosch and Petherbridge) Islamic Bindings and Bookmaking, 1981; also articles.; one-man shows at, Hanover Gallery, London, 1958, Fischbach Gallery, N.Y.C., 1968. Recipient numerous research awards and grants. Mem. Oriental Ceramic Soc., Royal Asiatic Soc., Palestine Exploration Fund, Am. Inst. Archaeology. Mem. Ch. of England. 3E Carlisle Pl London SW1 1NP England Office: Oriental Inst 1155 E 58th St Chicago IL 60637 *Life is the ordering of chaos.*

CARSWELL, LLOYD BROOKS, hotel exec.; b. Gardner, Mass., June 21, 1910; s. Charles Thomas and Alice Mildred (Lloyd) C.; m. Mrs. Peter Pauline Burton, 1961. Student, Cornell U., 1929. Clk. Blackstone and Drake hotels, Chgo., 1931; clk. Roosevelt Hotel, N.Y.C., 1930, sales promotion, 1937-38; clk. Hotel Wendell, Pittsfield, Mass., 1932-36; exec. asst. mgr. Hotel Sheraton, Pittsfield, 1939-44; gen. mgr. Sheraton Hotels, New Britain, Conn., Springfield and Worcester, Mass., 1945-48, Sheraton Plaza, Boston, 1949-57, Sheraton Hotel, Phila., 1957-59, v.p., gen. mgr., 1970-71, Sheraton Hawaii Corps., Royal Hawaiian, Moana Surf Rider and Princess Kaiulani Hotels, Honolulu, 1959-60, Sheraton Chgo. Hotel, 1960-63; gen. mgr., v.p. P.R. Sheraton Hotel, 1967-70; v.p. nat. and internat. sales Sheraton Corp. Am.; v.p. Sheraton Hotels Ltd., 1971—; gen. mgr. Four Seasons Sheraton, Toronto, Can., 1971-73; area dir. devel. East Coast ITT Sheraton Corp., Hartford, Conn., 1973—; mng. dir. Adams Hotel, Phoenix; dir. Discover Am., Inc. Mem. travel adv. bd. U.S. Travel Service, Dept. Commerce. Club: Rancho Bernardo Golf (pres. 1980). Address: 17135 Pacato Ct Rancho Bernardo San Diego CA 92128

CARSWELL, ROBERT, lawyer; b. Bklyn., Nov. 25, 1928; s. William Brown and Charlotte Edna (Riegger) C.; m. Mary Killeen Wilde, Dec. 28, 1957; children—Kate, William. A.B. magna cum laude, Harvard, 1949, LL.B. cum laude, 1952. Bar: N.Y. bar 1952, Calif. bar 1954. With firm Shearman & Sterling, N.Y.C., 1955-62, ptnr., 1965-77, 81—; spl. asst. to sec. treasury, 1962-65, dep. sec. treasury, 1977-81. Served to lt. (j.g.) USNR, 1952-55. Mem. Am. Bar Assn., Bar Assn. City N.Y., St. Andrews Soc. N.Y., Phi Beta Kappa. Clubs: Harvard, Links (N.Y.C.); Met. (Washington). Home: 40 E 88th St New York NY 10028 Office: Shearman & Sterling 153 E 53d St New York NY 10022

CARTER, ALEXANDER, bishop; b. Montreal, Que., Can., Apr. 16, 1909; s. Thomas and Mary (Kerr) C. M.Th., M.C.L., LL.D., Montreal Coll., 1930; ed., Sem. Philosophy and Grand Sem. Montreal, 1936; M.Th., M.C.L., Canadian Coll., Rome, 1939; LL.D. (hon.), Laurentian U., Sudbury, Ont., 1962. Ordained priest Roman Cath. Ch., 1936; vice-chancellor Diocese of Montreal, 1940-46; chancellor Diocese of Winnipeg, 1946-47; vice-officialis Marriage Tribunal Diocese of Montreal, 1948-53; bishop of, Sault Ste. Marie, 1957—; pres. Ont. Conf. Cath. Bishops, 1977-81; Chancellor U. Sudbury, 1962—. Mem. Vanier Inst., Can. Cath. Conf. Bishops (pres. 1967-69, chmn. episcopal commn. for laity 1978-83), Pontifical Mission Aid Socs. Can. (Nat. dir. 1971-77).

CARTER, ANNE PITTS, university dean, economics educator; b. N.Y.C., May 7, 1925; d. Jacob J. and Julia (Glayser) Pitts; m. Frank Carter, Aug. 9, 1953; children: Franklin CarterIV, Sarah Pitts. A.B., Queens Coll., 1945; Ph.D., Radcliffe Coll., Harvard U., 1949; Sc.D. (hon.), Lowell U., 1975. Instr. Bklyn. Coll., 1947-49; asst. prof. Smith Coll., Northampton, Mass., 1951-53, Harvard U., Cambridge, Mass., 1966-68, dir. research econ. research project, 1968-72; Fred C. Hecht. prof. econs. Brandeis U., Waltham, Mass., 1972—, dean of faculty, 1981—; chairperson Internat. Input-Output Conf. Organizing Com., Switzerland and Austria, 1968—; dir. Resources for Future, Washington, 1976—; cons. Data Resources, Inc., Lexington, Mass., 1977—; mem. Dept. Commerce Tech. Adv. Bd., Washington, 1977-80. Author: Structural Change in the American Economy, 1970, (with W. Leontief and P. Petri) The Future of the World Economy, 1976; editor: (with A. Brody) Contributions to Input-Output Analysis, 1970, Applications of Input-Output Analysis, 1970, Input-Output Techniques, 1972, Energy and the Environment, A Structural Analysis, 1976. Social Sci. Research Council grantee, 1952; U.S. Bur. Labor Stats. grantee, 1964-70, 73-75; Dept. Commerce grantee, 1967-69, 77-78; NSF grantee, 1972-79; UN Econ. and Social Council grantee, 1974-78. Fellow Econometric Soc.; mem. Fedn. Am. Scientists (sponsor), Am. Econ. Assn., AAAS. Office: Brandeis U 415 South St Waltham MA 02254

CARTER, BARRY EDWARD, lawyer, educator; b. Los Angeles, Oct. 14, 1942; s. Byron Edward and Ethel Catherine (Turner) C. A.B. with great distinction, Stanford U., 1964; M.P.A., Princeton U., 1966; J.D., Yale U., 1969. Bar: Calif. 1970, D.C. 1972. Program analyst Office of Sec. Def., Washington, 1969-70; mem. staff NSC, Washington, 1970-72; research fellow Kennedy Sch., Harvard U., Cambridge, Mass., 1972; internat. affairs fellow Council on Fgn. Relations, 1972; pvt. practice law, Washington, 1973-75; sr. counsel Select Com. on Intelligence Activities, U.S. Senate, Washington, 1975; assoc. Morrison & Foerster, San Francisco, 1976-79; asso. prof. law Georgetown U. Law Center, Washington, 1979—; Dir. Arms Control Assn., 1973—; mem. UN Assn. Soviet-Am. Parallel Studies Project.; trustee No. Calif. World Affairs Council, 1978-80. Contbr. articles to profl. jours. Served with AUS, 1969-71. Mem. Council on Fgn. Relations, Am., Calif., D.C. bar assns., Phi Beta Kappa, Phi Delta Phi. Democrat. Home: 1812 Riggs Pl NW Washington DC 20009 Office: 600 New Jersey Ave NW Washington DC 20001

CARTER, BETSY L., magazine editor; b. N.Y.C., June 9, 1945; d. Rudy and Gerda Cohn; m. Malcolm Carter, Oct. 5, 1968. B.A., U. Mich., 1967. Editorial asst. McGraw Hill, 1967-68; editor co. mag. Am. Security and Trust Co., 1968-69; editorial asst. Atlantic Monthly, 1969-70; researcher Newsweek, N.Y.C., 1971-73, asst. editor, 1973-75, assoc. editor, 1975-80; sr. editor Esquire Mag., N.Y.C., 1980-81, exec. editor, 1981-82, sr. exec. editor, 1982—; freelance contbr. to Atlantic, Washington Post, Family Weekly. Office: 2 Park Ave New York NY 10016

CARTER, BETTY (LILLIE MAE JONES), jazz singer, songwriter; b. Flint, Mich., May 16, 1929; d. James and Bertha (Cox) Jones; m. James Redding, 1965 (div.); children: Myles, Kagle. Student, Detroit Conservatory Music. Singer began in nightclubs, with Lionel Hampton Band, 1948-51; formed own record co. and label Bet-Car Prodns., 1969; condr. workshops Harvard U., Goddard Coll., Dartmouth U., others. Performer: various clubswith Thelonius Monk, Muddy Waters, Miles Davis, Moms Mabley, T-Bone Walker, N.Y.C.; Lincoln Ctr., N.Y.C., 1972; play Don't Call Me Man, Billie Holiday Theatre, Bklyn., 1975; singer, Carnegie Hall, 1977, Newport Jazz Festival, 1977, 78, on Broadway, Shubert Theatre, 1978 (1st jazz singer to sing there); writer: compositions include I Can't Help It, Who, What, Why, Where, When, With No Words, Happy, Someone Else Will Soon Grow Old-Too, What Is It?, New Blues, Tight, Sounds, Open The Door, We Tried, I Think I Got it Now, Timeless, Fake; singer: albums include Betty Carter and Ray Bryant, 1955, Out There, 1957, The Modern Sound, 1959, Ray Charles and Betty Carter, 1960, Round Midnight, 1962, Inside Betty Carter, 1963, Finally, 1969, Betty Carter, 1970, The Audience With Betty Carter, 1979 (Grammy nominee 1981), What Ever Happened to Love, 1982; TV appearances include Saturday Nite Live-NBC, 1976, But Then-She's Betty Carter-PBS, 1980, Over Easy-PBS, 1981, The Tomorrow Show-NBC, 1981, Live At Resorts Internat.-Cable, 1981, Call Me Betty Carter-CBS Cable, 1981, A Tribute to Lionel Hampton, Kennedy Ctr., White House-CBS, 1981; radio programs include All Things Considered-Nat. Pub. Radio, Jazz Alive-Nat. Pub. Radio; participant festivals, Europe, U.S., Brazil, Japan. Recipient Spl. award Nat. Assn. Ind. Record Distributors, 1981. Office: c-o Bet-Car Prodns 117 St Felix St Brooklyn NY 11217 *

CARTER, BURDELLIS LAVERNE, university dean; b. Cloverland, Ind., Sept. 5, 1932; d. Charles Lionel and Dosia Vernice (Slack) C. B.A., Ind. Central U., 1954; diploma, Meth. Hosp., 1957; M.S. in Nursing Edn, Ind. U., 1961, Ed.D., 1965. Supr. Meth. Hosp., Indpls., 1957-60; instr. nursing U. Iowa, 1961-63; with Ind. U. Sch. Nursing, Indpls., 1964-79, asst. prof., 1965-68, asso. prof., 1968-72, prof., 1972—, asst. dean student services, 1971-79; asso. dean student services Ind. U.-Purdue U., Indpls., 1980—. Recipient award for outstanding teaching and community service Indpls. Field chpt. Pi Lambda Theta, 1969. Mem. Am. Assn. Univ. Adminstrs., Am. Assn. Higher Edn., Nat. Assn. Student Personnel Adminstrs., Greater Indpls. Choral Co., Am. Personnel and Guidance Assn., Ind. Hist. Soc., Am. Student Personnel Assn., Marion County Hist. Soc., Pi Lambda Theta, Sigma Theta Tau. Mem. Christian Ch. Office: IUPUI Student Services ES 2129 902 W New York St PO Box 647 Indianapolis IN 46223

CARTER, BYRUM EARL, political scientist; b. Shawnee, Okla., Mar. 3, 1922; s. Byrum Earl and Myrtle (Madison) C.; m. Beth Peter, May 14, 1944; children: Terry Elizabeth, Keith M. A.B., U. Okla., 1943; Ph.D., U. Wis., 1951. Wage rate analyst, 1944; mem. faculty Ind. U., Bloomington, 1947—, prof. polit. sci., 1961—, dean Coll. Arts and Scis., 1966-69, chancellor, 1969-75; mem. disting. speakers panel Phi Beta Kappa Assos., 1970-71. Author: The Office of Prime Minister, 1956, The University Ideal and Contemporary Society, 1975. Served with USMCR, 1943. Recipient Frederic Bachman Lieber award distinguished teaching Ind. U., 1957. Mem. Am. Polit. Sci. Assn. (exec. com. 1962), Midwest Conf. Polit. Scientists (v.p. 1965). Home: 1900 Ruby Ln Bloomington IN 47401

CARTER, CARY WARREN, government official; b. Louisville, Apr. 16, 1947; s. Cary Warren and Anita (Bowman) C.; m. Marcia T. Bridgers, Sept. 16, 1978. B.A., Centre Coll., Ky., 1969. Vice-pres. Liberty Nat. Bank & Trust Co., Louisville, 1972-78; v.p. Aubrey G. Lanston, N.Y.C., 1978-82; dep. asst. sec. fed. fin. U.S. Dept. Treasury, Washington, 1982—. Served to 1st lt. U.S. Army, 1969-72. Republican. Presbyterian. Clubs: Creek (Locust Valley, N.Y.); N.Y. Athletic (N.Y.C.). Home: 230 E 73d St Apt 8E New York NY 10021 Office: US Dept Treasury 15th and Pennsylvania Ave Washington DC 200220

CARTER, CHARLES J., forest products company executive; b. 1922; married; 2 children. B.Sc. in Civil Enging. with honors, Queen's U., 1947. With Gt. Lakes Forest Products Ltd. (formerly Gt. Lakes Paper Co., Ltd.), Thunder Bay, Ont., Can., 1947—, successively design engr., asst. plant engr., chief engr., then v.p. enging., 1964-71, pres., 1971—, chmn. bd., 1978—, also dir.; dir. Pacific Forest Products Ltd., Ormiston Mining & Smelting Co. Ltd., IDEA Corp.; mem. Thunder Bay adv. bd. Royal Trust Corp. Can. Mem., past mem. several hosp. bds. Mem. Forest Engring. Research Inst. Can. (dir.), Can. Pulp and Paper Assn. (exec. bd.), Ont. Forest Industries Assn. (dir.), Assn. Profl. Engrs. Ont. Lodges: Masons; Shriners. Office: Great Lakes Forest Products Ltd PO Box 430 Thunder Bay ON Canada P7C 4W3

CARTER, CHARLES MCLEAN, manufacturing company executive; b. Clyde, Ohio, Jan. 17, 1936; s. Howard Ellsworth and Dorothy Louise (McLean) C.; m. Linda Marie Parr, Apr. 24, 1965; children: Suzanne Marie, Debra Jean, Daniel William. B.E.E., Rensselaer Poly. Inst., 1957; postgrad., Georgetown U., 1959-60; J.D., DePaul U., 1963. Bar: Ill. 1963. Sales engr. Trane Co., La Crosse, Wis. and Pitts., 1957-59; patent asso. Western Electric Co., Washington and Chgo., 1959-62; mem. firm Wolfe Hubbard Voit & Osaan, Chgo., 1962-64, Pendleton Neuman Seibold & Williams, 1964-66; dir. corp. planning and legal, asst. sec. Warwick Electronics, Inc., Chgo., 1966-70; with Skil Corp., Chgo., 1970-80, gen. counsel, sec., 1971-80, v.p., 1975-80, corp. v.p., 1977; pres. Skil Internat. Inc., 1973-80; sr. v.p., treas., chief legal officer Stewart-Warner Corp., Chgo., 1980-81; exec. v.p., gen. counsel Reading Co., Chgo., 1981—. Mem. Am. Bar Assn., Ill. Bar Assn., Chgo. Bar Assn., 7th Circuit Bar Assn., Am. Patent Law Assn., Chgo. Patent Law Assn., Licensing Execs. Soc., Tau Beta Pi, Eta Kappa Nu. Lutheran (deacon 1968-70, trustee 1973-76, pres. 1977-81). Club: Chgo. Execs. Office: One Northfield Plaza Northfield IL 60093

CARTER, CLARENCE HOLBROOK, artist; b. Portsmouth, Ohio, Mar. 26, 1904; s. Clarence William and Hettie May (Holbrook) C.; m. Mary B. Griswold, May 4, 1929; children: John Holbrook, Peter Griswold, Clarence Blakesley. Student, Cleve. Sch. Art, 1923-27; studied abroad under, H. Hoffman, Capri, Italy, summer 1927. Instr. Cleve. Mus. Art, 1930-37; asst. prof. painting and design Carnegie Inst. Tech., Pitts., 1938-44; guest instr. painting Cleve. Inst. Art, summer 1948, Mpls. Sch. Art., fall 1949, Lehigh U., 1954, Ohio U., 1955; Atlanta Art Inst., 1957; guest artist U. Iowa, Spring 1970; artist-in-residence Lafayette Coll., 1961-69, cons., 1970-71; guest artist Kent State U., 1975, Iowa State U., Ames, 1975; gen. supt. Fed. Art Project, Cleve. Dist., 1937-38. Represented in permanent collections, Met. Mus., Mus. Modern Art, Whitney Mus. Am. Art, Chase Manhattan Bank, Citibank, all N.Y.C., Bklyn. Mus., Phila. Mus. Art, Prudential Ins. Co. Am., Columbus Mus. Fine Arts, Cleve. Mus. Art, Toledo Mus. Art, Public Service Electric and Gas Co., Newark, Springfield (Mass.) Mus. Fine Arts, New Britain (Conn.) Mus. Am. Art, Arnot Art Mus., Elmira, N.Y., Meml. Art Gallery, Rochester, N.Y., Herbert F. Johnson Mus. Art, Cornell U., Ithaca, N.Y., Newark Mus., Montclair (N.J.) Art Mus., N.J. State Mus., Trenton, Fogg Art Mus. Harvard, Boston Public Library, Corcoran Gallery Art, Washington, Nat. Collection Art, Washington, Nat. Mus. Am. Art, Washington, Hirshorn Mus., Washington, Amherst (Mass.) Coll. Mus., Colgate U., Hamilton, N.Y., Butler Inst. Am. Art, Youngstown, Ohio, Allen Meml. Art Mus., Oberlin Coll., Coll. of Wooster (Ohio) Art Center, Kent (Ohio) State U., Ohio U., Athens, Sheldon Swope Art Gallery, Terre Haute, Ind., Kalamazoo (Mich.) Inst. Arts, Atkins Mus., Nelson Gallery Art, Kansas City, Mo., Okla. Art Center, Oklahoma City, Mus. Art, U. Okla., Norman, U. Tex. Art Mus. at Austin, Philbrook Art Center, Tulsa, Norton Art Mus., West Palm Beach, Fla., Sheldon Meml. Art Gallery, U. Nebr., Lincoln, Pasadena (Calif.) Mus. Modern Art, So. Ohio Mus. and Cultural Center, Portsmouth, Mus. Boymans-Van Beuningen, Rotterdam, Netherlands, Victoria and Albert Mus., London, Eng., Baukunst, Cologne, West Germany; executed murals for sect. of painting and sculpture, Treasury Dept., Portsmouth, Ohio and Ravenna, Ohio Post offices, murals for, Cleve. Pub. Auditorium; represented by, Gimpel and Weitzenhoffer Gallery Ltd., N.Y.C., Hirsch and Adler Galleries, N.Y.C., Fairweather Hardin Gallery, Chgo. (Awarded 13 first prizes, numerous (2d and 3d prizes in ann. exhbns. by Cleve. artists and craftsmen (Cleve. Mus. Art); Pitts. Asso. Artists), Fairweather Hardin Gallery, Chgo.; retrospective one-man shows in largest cities represented in exhibit 200 Years of Am. Painting, Tate Gallery, London, 1946; European tour of Modern Am. Art, 1955-56, Am. Trauma and Depression 1920/40; 10 paintings, Berlin, Hamburg, 1980-81, S.A.; gathering material for series of paintings for, Alcoa S.S. Co., 1944. Recipient 1st prize oils, 1943, 1st prize water color, 1944, Popular prize, Painting in U.S., Carnegie Inst., 1943, First popularity prize, 1936, 1st prize for oils, 1940, 2d prize for oils, 1943, Youngstown, Ohio, Cleve. Creative Arts award, 1972. Mem. N.A.D. Conglist. Home: Box 119 Route 1 Milford NJ 08848 *My desire from early childhood was to be an artist. To this end I dedicated my life. I ordered my life to accomplish the ideals that I set for myself and would never let anything interfere with this end. I would only tolerate my best. I rigidly guarded my health to better perform my work. Part of my credo has always been not to allow myself to repeat any past successes. Rather, I prefer to stimulate myself constantly with new concepts. I never developed any theories, as I knew that they would fence me in. A free mobility is part of my everyday existence. For this reason the zest for creation never seems to flag.*

CARTER, DAN T., educator; b. Florence, S.C., June 17, 1940; s. Dewey L. and Lalla (Lawhon) C.; m. Jane Winkler, Aug. 29, 1964; children—Alicia Lee, David Charles. B.A., U. S.C., 1962; M.A., U. Wis., 1964; Ph.D., U. N.C., 1967. Asst. prof. U. Md., 1967-69, asso. prof., 1970-71, prof., 1971-75; Andrew Mellon prof. Emory U., 1975—; vis. asso. prof. U. Wis., 1969-70; Fulbright lectr. Central Poly. London, 1979-80. Author: Scottsboro: A Tragedy of the American South, 1969, A Reasonable Doubt, 1968, Crisis of Fear, 1976, (with A. Friedlander) Southern Women in the Educational Movement of the South, 1979. Exec. bd. Ga. Endowment for Humanities. Woodrow Wilson fellow, 1962-63; recipient Bancroft prize, 1969, Anisfield-Wolfe award, 1969, Jules Landry prize, 1970, Lillian Smith award, 1969. Mem. Orgn. Am. Historians, Am., So. hist. assns., Soc. Am. Historians. Home: 1121 Springdale Rd NE Atlanta GA 30307 Office: Hist Dept Emory U Atlanta GA 30322

CARTER, DAVID GILES, art historian; b. Nashua, N.H., Nov. 2, 1921; s. Eliot Avery and Edith Berdan (Gardner) C.; m. Louise Belknap, June 2, 1951; children: Deborah Lamont Carter Conroy, Howard Giles, Margaret Belknap, Pamela Hobart. A.B., Princeton U., 1944; M.A., Harvard U., 1949; postgrad., Inst. Fine Arts, NYU, 1949-51. Participant Brussels Art Seminar, 1952; curatorial asst. dept. paintings Met. Mus. Art, N.Y.C., 1952-54; curator paintings and prints, lectr. art history John Herron Art Inst. (now Indpls. Mus. Art), 1955-59; dir. Mus. of Art, R.I. Sch. Design, Providence, 1959-64, Montreal (Que., Can.) Mus. Fine Arts, 1964-76; cons., New Haven, 1977—; U.S. diplomatic courier, 1944-47; vis. lectr. art history Ind. U., 1958-59; bd. dirs. Providence Art Festival, 1963-64, Preservation Trust of New Haven, 1980-84; mem. adv. coms. Pavilion of Can., Fine Arts Pavilion, Expo '67, 1964-67; mem. Commn. des Biens Culturels du Que., 1974-76; trustee Eli Whitney Mus., Hamden, Conn., Met. Mus. Author: exhbn. catalogs including The Young Rembrandt and His Times, 1958; The Painter and the New World, 1967, Rembrandt and His Pupils, 1969, Jan Menses, 1976. Met. Mus. Student fellow, 1951-52; recipient Golden Medal Culture Italian Fgn. Ministry, 1963. Fellow Royal Soc.; mem. Am. Fedn. Arts, Am. Assn. Mus., Can. Mus. Assn., Coll. Art Assn. Am., Grolier Club, Internat. Council Mus., Internat. Inst. Conservation, Internat. Assn. History of Glass, Internat. Center Medieval Art, Armor and Arts Club Am., Arms Club Am., Arms and Armour Soc. Britain (corr.), Mediaeval Acad. Am., Assn. Internat. de Critiques d'Art, DeutscherVerein für Kunstwissenschaft. Republican. Clubs: Terrace (Princeton U.); New Haven Lawn. Home: 100 Edgehill Rd New Haven CT 06511

CARTER, DAVID WARREN, healthcare company executive; b. Chgo., Dec. 27, 1938; s. Rush Warren and Lenore Edith (Jackson) C.; m. Mary Constance Goodknight, Sept. 2, 1961; children: Cara Ann, Benjamin Craig, Danial Warren. A.B., Ind. U., 1960, M.B.A., 1961. Sales rep. Am. Hosp. Supply, Evanston, Ill., 1961-64, regional mgr., 1967-70, v.p. mktg. internat. div., exec. v.p., chief operating officer, 1972-73, pres. info. systems div., 1973-75, group v.p. dental group, 1975-77; pres. Doric Corp. div. Esmark, Evanston, 1977-81; group v.p. Sybron-Healthcare Products Group, Evanston, 1981—. Pres. Chgo. chpt. Am. Refugee Com., 1979-80; pres. Viking Community Hockey Assn., 1980-81. Presbyterian. Office: 820 Church St Evanston IL 60201

CARTER, DEAN, sculptor; b. Henderson, N.C., Apr. 24, 1922; s. Clement Dean and Mary Clegg (Goodrich) C.; m. Rosina McDonnell, Aug. 8, 1950; children: Frances, Katharine, Clement, J. Thomas, Mary. Student, Corcoran Sch. Art, 1940-43; B.A. magna cum laude, Am. U., 1947; M.F.A., Ind. U., 1948, Zadkine's Sch., Paris, 1948-49. Teaching asst. Ind. U., 1948; instr. to prof. art Coll. Architecture, Va. Poly. Inst. and State U., Blacksburg, 1950-69, chmn. art program, 1965-75, head dept. art, 1975-79, prof. art, 1979—; instr. Roanoke Fine Arts Center, U. Va., 1962-63; cons. U.S. Fire Arts Survey, 1972, Polytron Corp., 1969; mem. arts and crafts adv. bd. Mt. Empire Community Coll., 1969-75; chmn. selection com. Class of 1965 art gifts to Va. Tech., 1965. Sculptor works rep. in public collections, Wachovia Bank & Trust Co., 1st Colony Life Ins. Co., Roanoke Meml. Hosp., Drs. Clinic, Annandale, Va., Providence Bldg., Seven Corners, Va., Charlotte (N.C.) Plaza, Japan Kiwanis Internat., U. Va. Biol. Sta.; advisor, participant: Columbus Film Festival (Chris award 1964). Panelist Va. Dept. Edn., 1968; founder Brush Mountain Crafts Fair. Served with USAAF, 1943-46. Recipient Sleicher award Am. U., 1947; purchase award Cranbrook Acad., 1949, Wichita Art Assn., 1953; sculpture award Fellowship Design Conf., Aspen, Colo., 1957, Gallery Contemporary Art, Winston-Salem, N.C., 1958, 64, 68; Cini fellow, Venice, Italy, 1962. Mem. Coll. Art Assn. Am., Southeastern Coll. Art Assn. (pres. 1977), So. Sculptors Assn. (v.p. 1966-68), Am. Crafts Council (state rep. 1965), So. Highlands Handicraft Guild, Phi Sigma Kappa. Methodist. Clubs: University, Blacksburg Country. Office: Art Dept Virginia Polytechnic Institute and State University Owens Hall Blacksburg VA 24061

CARTER, DON EARL, newspaper editor, publisher; b. Plains, Ga., June 22, 1917; s. William Alton and Annie Laurie (Gay) C.; m. Carolyn McKenzie, Oct. 3, 1942. Student, Ga. Southwestern Coll., 1934-36; A.B., U. Ga., 1938; Litt.D. (hon.), St. Bonaventure U., 1975. Reporter Atlanta Jour., 1938-39, farm editor, 1940-41, municipal govt. reporter, asst. city editor, 1946-50, city editor, 1951-59; exec. dir. Newspaper Fund, Wall Street Jour., 1959-61; founding mng. editor Nat. Observer, 1961-67; exec. editor The Record, Hackensack, N.J., 1967-71, Morning Call, Paterson, N.J., 1967-69; v.p. Bergen Evening Record Corp., 1968-71; exec. editor, v.p. Macon (Ga.) Telegraph and Macon News, 1971-75; pub., pres. Lexington (Ky.) Herald and Leader, 1975-77; v.p. Knight-Ridder Newspapers, Inc., 1976-82, cons., 1982—; Tchr. journalism eve. div. Ga. State Coll., 1950-59; lectr. Am. Press Inst., Columbia, also Reston, Va., 1953—, bd. dirs., 1980—; Pulitzer award juror, 1968-70; Bd. dirs. Newspaper Fund; adv. council journalism U. Tex., U. Ga.; founding trustee Ramapo Coll. of N.J., 1969-71. Editor: Baxley (Ga.) News-Banner, 1939-40. Served to capt. AUS, 1941-45. Decorated Bronze Star; recipient citation service to journalism Theta Sigma Phi, 1961, U. Nebr. Sch. Journalism, 1962, Reddick award U. Tex., 1979. Mem. AP Mng. Editors Assn. (pres. 1971), Am. Council on Edn. for Journalism (pres. 1973-83), Am. Soc. Newspaper Editors, Am. Newspaper Pubs. Assn., Phi Beta Kappa, Sigma Delta Chi (pres. Atlanta 1957-59, nat. dir. 1958-59, 66-67, 69-71), Omicron Delta Kappa, Phi Kappa Phi, Phi Delta Epsilon, Kappa Tau Alpha. Clubs: Nat. Press (Washington); Idle Hour Country (Lexington, Ky.); Atlanta Athletic. Home: PO Box 684 244 DeSoto Dr Sea Island GA 31561

CARTER, DONALD, professional basketball team executive. Pres. Dallas Mavericks, N.B.A. Office: Care Dallas Mavericks Reunion Arena 777 Sports St. Dallas TX 75207

CARTER, DONALD PATTON, advt. exec.; b. Richmond, Mo., July 30, 1927; s. R.D. and Lillian (Patton) C.; m. Susan Virginia Wurst, Apr. 22, 1950 (dec. Apr. 1980); children—Jeffrey, Stephen, Carol. Student, U. Louisville, 1945-46; B.S., U. Mo., 1948; M.B.A., Wharton Sch. U. Pa., 1950. With Continental Color Press, Inc., Kansas City, Mo., 1950-52; pres. Nasco, Inc., Kansas City, Kans., 1953-54; v.p., then pres. Biddle Co., Bloomington, Ill., 1955-68; chmn. bd. Cunningham & Walsh, Chgo., 1968—, also dir.; dir. Dearborn Financial Corp., Upper Av. Nat. Bank, Cunningham & Walsh, Inc., Realty World Corp.; Tchr. econs., bus. adminstrn. Kansas City (Mo.) Jr. Coll., 1950-52. Active local fund raising campaigns. Served with USNR, 1945-47. Named Young Man of Year Jr. C. of C., 1951. Mem. Phi Kappa Psi. Presbyn. Clubs: Knollwood Country, Bob O'Link Golf, Bannockburn Tennis. Home: 120 W Westminster Lake Forest IL 60045 Office: 875 N Michigan Ave Chicago IL 60611

CARTER, DUDLEY CHRISTOPHER, sculptor, forest engineer; b. New Westinster, B.C., Can., May 6, 1891; s. Foster Clyde and Sophia (Miller) C.; m. Teresa Williams Easthope, Dec. 19, 1919 (dec. 1975); 1 dau. Mavis Anne Carter Vaughan. Degree in Fine Arts, City Coll., San Francisco, 1983. Forester, construction Western Power Co. of Can., Stave Falls, B.C., 1909-1916; timber cruiser, forest engr. Clark & Lyford B.C.and Pacific N.W., 1919-1928; instr. sculpture U. Wash., Seattle, 1944-45; instr. U. Calif.-Santa Cruz, 1983. Exhibitor: one man shows Sunshine Coast Gallery, Sechelt, B.C. 1982, Carnegie Art Ctr., Vancouver, B.C., 1983; art in action, Golden Gate Internat. Expt., San Francisco, 1939-40, UN Habitat Formus, Vancouver, B.C. 1976. Recipient award HUD, 1973. Mem. B.C. Sculptors Soc. (hon. life pres.). Home: 3075 Bel-Red Rd Bellevue WA 98008 Office: RR4 Gibbons BC Canada V0N 1V0

CARTER, EDWARD CARLOS, II, librarian, historian; b. Rochester, N.Y., Jan. 10, 1928; s. Paul Epler and Elizabeth (Johnston) C.; m. Theresa Howard, Mar. 24, 1951 (div. 1976); 1 dau., Laura Coffin Carter (dec.); m. Louise Devine Bucknell, Oct. 11, 1976. A.B., U. Pa., 1954, M.A., 1956; Ph.D., Bryn Mawr Coll., 1962. Vis. lectr. history U. Pa., Phila., 1962-64; chmn. dept. history St. Stephen's Sch., Rome, 1965-69; prof. history Cath. U. Am., Washington, 1969-80; editor-in-chief Papers of Benjamin Henry Latrobe, Balt., 1970—; adj. prof. history U. Pa., 1980—; librarian Am. Philos. Soc., Phila., 1980—; adv. council Phila. Center Early Am. Studies, 1981. Editorial bd.: Papers of Philip Mazzei, 1978, Papers of William Penn, 1978, Von Steuben Papers, 1976; co-editor: Enterprise and Entrepreneurs in 19th and 20th Century France, 1976; editor: Microfice edit. Papers of Benjamin Henry Latrobe, 1976; Va. Jours. of Benjamin Henry Latrobe, 2 vols., 1977, Jours. of Benjamin Henry Latrobe: From Philadelphia to New Orleans, 1980. Chmn. bd. trustees St. Stephen's Sch., Rome, 1982—. Served with U.S. Army, 1946-47. Mem. Am. Philos. Soc. Democrat. Presbyterian. Clubs: Chevy Chase; Cosmos (Washington); Franklin Inn (Phila.); Merion Golf (Ardmore, Pa.). Home: 15 S Valley Forge Rd Wayne PA 19087 Office: 105 S 5th St Philadelphia PA 19106

CARTER, EDWARD WALTER, III, naval officer; b. Winston-Salem, N.C., Aug. 27, 1928; s. Edward Walter and Geraldine P. (Parrish) C.; m. Billie Jane Waltemeyer, June 1, 1951; children: Betsy Carter Williams, Michael R., Patrick A., Rebecca. B.S., U.S. Naval Acad., 1951; B.E.E., U.S. Naval Postgrad. Sch., 1958; Sc.M., Mass. Inst. Tech., 1959. Enlisted in U.S. Navy, 1945, commd. ensign, 1951, advanced through grades to rear adm., 1974; service in amphibious ships, cruisers and destroyers; commanded guided missile destroyer, guided missile cruiser; mem. staff Chief Naval Ops., 1962-64, 74-76; dep. comdr. weapons systems and engring. NAVSEASYSCOM, 1976-78; comdr. Cruiser-Destroyer Group 3, 1979-81; naval insp. gen., 1981-82; comdr. Operational Test and Evaluation Force, 1982—. Contbr. to mil. jours. Decorated Legion of Merit (4), Bronze Star with V, Navy Commendation medal with V. Mem. U.S. Naval Inst., Am. Ordnance Assn., U.S. Naval Acad. Alumni Assn. Home: 455 Dillingham Blvd Norfolk VA 23511 *God's greatest gift to man is love. The second is the privilege of service. The exercise of either without the other is incomplete.*

CARTER, EDWARD WILLIAM, retail executive; m. Hannah Locke Caldwell, 1963; children: William Dailey, Mrs. Ann Carter Huneke. A.B., UCLA, 1932; M.B.A. cum laude, Harvard, 1937; LL.D., Occidental Coll., 1962. Chmn. bd., dir. Carter Hawley Hale Stores, Inc., Los Angeles; dir. Novacor Med. Corp., Lockheed Corp., Pacific Mut. Life Ins. Co., So. Calif. Edison Co., First Interstate Bancorp. (and its subs. First Interstate Bank.); Regent U. Calif. Trustee Occidental Coll., Brookings Instn., Nat. Humanities Center, Com. Economic Devel.; bd. dirs. Assos. Harvard Grad. Sch. Bus., Stanford Research Inst., James Irvine Found., Santa Anita Found.; mem. vis. com. UCLA Grad. Sch. Mgmt.; mem. Woodrow Wilson Internat. Center Council, Rockefeller U. Council, Harvard Bd. Overseers Com. Dept. Econs., Art Museums and Univ. Resources; bd. dirs. Los Angeles Philharm. Assn.; trustee Los Angeles County Mus. Art, San Francisco Opera Assn. Mem. Bus. Council, Conf. Bd., Council on Fgn. Relations. Clubs: Calif., Los Angeles Country (Los Angeles); Pacific Union, Bohemian, Burlingame Country (San Francisco); Cypress Point (Pebble Beach). Office: 550 S Flower St Los Angeles CA 90017

CARTER, ELLIOTT COOK, JR., composer; b. N.Y.C., Dec. 11, 1908; s. Elliott Cook and Florence (Chambers) C.; m. Helen Frost-Jones, July 6, 1939; 1 son, David. A.B., Harvard, 1930, A.M., 1932, A.M. hon. degree, 1970; Mus. D. (hon.), New Eng. Conservatory Music, 1961, Swarthmore Coll., 1956, Princeton, 1967, Boston U., Yale, Oberlin Coll., 1970. Tutor, chmn. music St. John's Coll., Annapolis, Md., 1939-41; tchr. Greek and math.; tchr. music theory and composition Peabody Conservatory, Balt., 1946-48; tchr. in Am. studies Salzburg Seminars, Austria, 1958; asso. music Columbia, 1948-50; cons. O.W.I., 1942-44; prof. musical composition Yale, 1960—; lectr. Princeton music seminar, 1959-60. Mus. dir., Ballet Caravan, 1937-39; critic: League of Composers Quar. Modern Music, 1937-42; composer in residence, City of West Berlin, 1964; commd. by, N.Y. Philharmonic Orch.; commd. to write: Night Fantasies, 1979; 1st performance: Bath (Eng.) Festival, 1980; featured musician: Biennale Venice, 1981; (Awarded choral prize for To Music, WPA music div. 1938, Am. Composers Alliance prize for Quartet for Four Saxophones 1943, League of Composers commn. for symphony 1952, First prize in internat. music competition for composers, Liege, Belgium 1953, Ford Found. award for piano concerto 1965, Pulitzer prize for music 1960, 73, Music Critics Circle N.Y. award 1962, Creative Arts award Brandeis U. 1965, Premio delle Muse, City of Florence, Italy 1969, Grand Prix Internat. du Disque 1976, Handel medallion City of N.Y. 1978, Elliott Carter Day proclaimed in Los Angeles 27, 1979, Ernst von Siemens award for music, Munich 1980); Composer: Tarantella, 1937, Ballet Pocahontas (Ballet Caravan commn. 1939), 1938 (Julliard Publ. award for suite 1941), Incidental Music for the Merchant of Venice, 1938, The Defense of Corinth, 1941, First Symphony, 1942-43, The Harmony of Morning, 1945, Piano Sonata, 1945, Holiday Overture, 1945 (Ind. Music Pubs. prize 1945); ballet The Minotaur, 1946-47 (Ballet Soc. commn.), Woodwind Quintet, 1947, Sonata for Cello and Piano, 1948, Emblems for men's chorus and piano, 1948, Eight Etudes and a Fantasy for Woodwind Quartet, 1949, String Quartet, 1950-1951, Sonata for Flute, Oboe, 'Cello, Harpsichord, 1952 (Naumburg award 1956), Variations for Orch, 1955 (Louisville commn.), Double Concerto, 1959 (Fromm Foun. commn.), Concerto for Orch, 1969 (N.Y. Philharmonic Soc. commn.), A Symphony of Three Orchestras; world premier with, N.Y. Philharmonic, 1977, European premier, Paris, 1977, String Quartet No. 2, No. 3, Juilliard commn. (Pulitzer prize), Brass Quintet, Duo for Violin and Piano, A Mirror On Which to Dwell, Syringa, (Nat. Endowment grant 1978). Trustee Am. Acad. in Rome. Guggenheim fellow, 1945-46, 50-51. Mem. League Composers (dir. 1939-52), Internat. Soc. Contemporary Music (dir. 1946-52, pres. U.S. sect. 1952), Nat. Inst. Arts and Letters (Gold medal for music 1971), Am. Acad. Arts and Scis., Am. Composers Alliance (dir. 1939-52, treas. 1949-50).

CARTER, ELTON STEWART, educator; b. Castle Hill, Maine, May 6, 1919; s. Percy Claire and Gertrude (Haines) C.; m. Miriam Erickson, June 12, 1946; children—Sandra, Stanley. B.A., U. Maine, 1941; M.A., Ind. State Tchrs. Coll., 1947; Ph.D., Northwestern U., 1950. Grad. asst., traveling hearing cons. Ind. State Tchrs. Coll., 1941-42, 45-46, instr., 1946-47; asst., then asso. prof. speech Pa. State U., 1950-63; prof. speech U. Nebr. at Omaha, 1966—, dean, 1966-75; staff engr., cons.; dir. profl. devel. HRB-Singer, Inc., 1963-66; Chmn. manpower coordination, planning and action coms., Omaha, 1967-68. Author: The Speech Designer's Handbook, 1962, Thinking With Machines, 1961; author: (with Iline Fife) Learning Your Way Through College, 1962. Served with U.S. Army, 1943-46. Mem. Speech Communication Assn., Inst. Gen. Semantics, Internat. Soc. Gen. Semantics, Internat. Communication Assn., Phi Eta Kappa. Home: 1125 S 87th St Omaha NE 68124

CARTER, EVERITT A., electronics executive; b. Phila., May 9, 1919; s. Robert A. and Florence Emma (Everett) C.; m. Mary M. Cragoe, Oct. 9, 1943; children: Nickola Mary, Robert Edward, Timothy John, Susan Catherine. B.S. in Mech. Engring., Duke U., 1940. Engring. and sales positions Wright Aeros. div. Curtiss-Wright Corp., 1940-45, dir. sales west coast, 1952-55; dir. sales and service Hughes Aircraft Co., 1945-47; v.p. Faber Labs., N.Y.C., 1947-52; gen. mgr. Curtiss-Wright Can., Ltd., 1955-56; v.p., gen. mgr. Canadian Curtiss-Wright, Ltd., 1957-59; pres. Oak Industries, Inc., 1959-70, chief exec. officer, 1959—, chmn. bd., 1963—, also dir.; dir. Fed. Signal Corp., Johnson Controls, Inc., Home State Bank Crystal Lake. Mem. No. Ill. U. Pres.'s Council; chmn. pattern gifts bldg. fund campaign Lake Region YMCA, Crystal Lake; mem. Chgo. Crime Commn.; bd. dirs. Crystal Lake Hosp. Assn., Rockford Coll. Mem. Soc. Automotive Engrs., Can. Aero. Inst., World Trade Council, U.S. C. of C. (membership com.), Chgo. Assn. Commerce and Industry (dir.), U.S.-Korea Econ. Council (dir.), Korean-Am. Midwest Assn. (hon. dir.), Chgo. Council Fgn. Relations (Chgo. com.), Midwest-Japan Assn., Phi Kappa Psi, Delta Epsilon Sigma. Republican. Clubs: Inverness Golf, Turnberry Country; Econ., Chgo., Mid-Am., Univ., Met. (Chgo.); Canadian, Barrington (Ill.) Tennis; Racket (Crystal Lake); West Side Tennis (Forest Hills, N.Y.); Balboa Bay (Newport Beach, Calif.); Escondido (Calif.) Tennis. Office: Oak Industries Inc 16935 W Bernardo Dr Rancho Bernardo CA 92127 *

CARTER, GENE, judge; b. Milbridge, Maine, Nov. 1, 1935; s. K.W. and S. Loreta (Beal) C.; m. Judith Ann Kittredge, June 24, 1961; children: Matthew G., Mark G. B.A., U. Maine, 1958; LL.B., NYU, 1961. Bar: Maine 1962. Ptnr. Rudman, Winchell, Carter & Buckley (and predecessors), Bangor, Maine, 1965-80; asso. justice Maine Supreme Jud. Ct., 1980-83; judge U.S. Dist. Ct. Maine, 1983—; chmn. adv. com. on rules of civil procedure Maine Supreme Jud. Ct., 1976-80. Chmn. Bangor Housing Authority, 1970-77. Mem. Am. Trial Lawyers Assn., Internat. Soc. Barristers, Am. Coll. Trial Lawyers. Office: PO Box 7524 DTS Portland ME 04112

CARTER, GERALD EMMETT, archbishop; b. Montreal, Que., Can., Mar. 1, 1912; s. Thomas Joseph and Mary (Kelty) C. B.Th., Grand Sem. Montreal, 1936; B.A., U. Montreal, 1933, M.A., 1940, Ph.D., 1947, L.Th., 1950; D.H.L., Duquesne U., 1963; LL.D. (hon.), U. Western Ont., 1966, Concordia U., 1976, U. Windsor, 1977, McGill U., Montreal, 1980, Notre Dame (Ind.) U., 1981; Litt.D., St. Mary's U., Halifax, 1980. Ordained priest Roman Cath. Ch., 1937; founder, prin., prof. St. Joseph Tchrs. Coll., Montreal, 1939-61; chaplain Newman Club, McGill U., 1941-56; charter mem., 1st pres. Thomas More Inst. Adult Edn., Montreal, 1945-61; mem. Montreal Cath. Sch. Commn., 1948-61; hon. canon Cathedral Basilica Montreal, 1952-61; aux. bishop London and titular bishop Altiburo, 1961, bishop of, London, Ont., 1964-78, archbishop of, Toronto, 1978—, elevated to cardinal, 1979; Chmn. Episcopal Commn. Liturgy Can., 1966-73; mem. Consilium of Liturgy, Rome, 1965, Sacred Congregation for Divine Worship, 1970; chmn. Internat. Com. for English in the Liturgy, 1971; appointee Econ. Affairs Council of Holy See, 1981, Canon Law Commn., 1981; Vice pres. Can. Cath. Conf., 1973, Cath. Conf. of Ont., 1971-73; pres. Canadian Conf. Cath. Bishops, 1975; mem. council Synod of Bishops, 1977. Author: The Catholic Public Schools of Quebec, 1957, Psychology and the Cross, 1959, The Modern Challange to Religious Education, 1961. Decorated companion Order of Can. Office: 355 Church St Toronto ON M5B 1Z8 Canada

CARTER, GRANVILLE WELLINGTON, sculptor; b. Augusta, Maine, Nov. 18, 1920; s. Brooks Eaton and Araletta Tarr (Payne) C.; m. Senta Jacobshagen, Oct. 15, 1955; children—Juliana S., Richard S. Student, Coburn Classical Inst., 1938-39, Portland Sch. Fine and Applied Art, 1944-45, N.Y. Sch. Indsl. Art, 1945-49, N.A.D., 1945-48, Grand Chaumiere de Paris, 1954, Scuolo del Circolare Internazionale di Roma, 1955. Lectr. sculpture Washington Cathedral and Hofstra U., 1966—; instr. Nat. Acad., Sch. Fine Arts, 1967—; Bd. dirs. Am. Artist Socs. Exhibited in, U.S., Paris, Rome, Hofstra Coll., Washington Cathedral, also collections; important works include Toro Malo Bronze Relief, Bullfighter fountain group, Neptune fountain urns, Gilded terra cotta capitals; limestone St. Augustine of Canterbury; heroic size limestone Archangels Michael and Gabriel at South Transept, Washington Cathedral; medals and also Stonewall Jackson portrait medal for, Hall of Fame for Great Ams. at NYU, also George Washington, Thomas Edison, James Fenimore Cooper and Jane Addams portrait medals, Nat. Commemorative Soc., Ofcl. Sesquicentennial medal for, State of Maine; heroic size bust of Charles A. Lindbergh, Garden City Hist. Soc.; heroic size bronze bust Chaing Kai-Shek, St. John's U.; central tower dedication medal also, figures depicting The Passion in central nave, Washington Cathedral, 2 bronze portrait placques for, Edison Nat. Mus., West Orange, N.J.; monumental bronze portrait bust Alexander Stewart at, Garden City, N.Y.; 3-figure heroic-sized West Tex. Pioneer Family in bronze at, Lubbock, Tex., heroic sized equestrian monument of Gen. Casimir Pulaski in bronze, Hartford, Conn.; represented in permanent collections, Smithsonian Instn., Hall of Fame for Gt. Ams., N.Y. U., Am. Numismatic Soc., Mus. for State of Maine, Thomas Edison Nat. Mus., NAD, Morristown Hist. Mus., Wroclaw (Poland) Mus. Medals, St. Pauls Sch., Garden City.; Mem. editorial bd.: Nat. Sculpture Rev. Recipient First prize N.A.D. Art Sch., 1946; Louis Comfort Tiffany fellow, 1954, 55; Lindsey Morris Meml. prize Nat. Sculpture Soc., 1966; Henry Hering Meml. medal for collaborative archtl. sculpture, 1968; Gold medal Am. Artists Profl. League, 1970, 78; J. Sanford Saltus award, 1976; Therese and Edward H. Richard Meml. prize Nat. Sculpture Soc., 1980; academician NAD. Fellow Nat. Sculpture Soc. (dir., pres. 1979—), Am. Artists Profl. League (dir.), Am. Numismatic Soc. (life). Address: 625 Portland Ave Baldwin NY 11510

CARTER, GWENDOLEN MARGARET, educator, author; b. Hamilton, Ont., Can., July 17, 1906; came to U.S., 1935, naturalized, 1948; d. Charles and Nora (Ambrose) C. B.A., U. Toronto, 1929, Oxford (Eng.) U., 1931, M.A., 1936, Radcliffe Coll., 1936, Ph.D., 1938; D.H.L., Wheaton Coll., 1962, Russell Sage Coll., 1963, Northwestern U., 1977; LL.D., Western Coll. for Women, 1964, Goucher Coll., 1964, Carleton U., 1965, Boston U., 1966, McMaster U., 1966, Toronto U., 1970, Smith Coll., 1979, Stetson U., 1981, Dalhousie U., 1984. Instr. McMaster U., Hamilton, 1932-35, Wellesley Coll., 1938-41, Tufts U., 1942-43; asst. prof. Smith Coll., 1943-47, assoc. prof., 1947-52, prof. govt., 1952-64, Sophia Smith prof., 1961-64; Melville J. Herskovits prof. African affairs, dir. program of African studies, prof. polit. sci. Northwestern U., Evanston, Ill., 1964-74; prof. polit. sci. and African studies Ind. U., Bloomington, 1974-84, U. Fla., Gainesville, 1984—; Mem. adv. council for Africa State Dept., 1962-67; Bd. trustees African-Am. Inst., 1964—; mem. joint com. Project 87, 1978-81. Author: British Commonwealth and International Security, 1947, (with John Herz) Major Foreign Powers, 1949, 52, 57, 62, 67, 72, The Politics of Inequality, 1958, 59, Independence for Africa, 1960, Government and Politics in the Twentieth Century, 1961, 66, 72, The Government of United Kingdom, 1964, 68, 72, The Government of Soviet Union, 1964, 68, 72, (with Thomas Karis and Newell Stultz) South Africa's Transkei: The Politics of Domestic Colonialism, 1967, The Government of France, 1968, 72, Which Way is South Africa Going?, 1980; Editor: (with W.O. Brown) Transition in Africa; Problems of Political Adaptation, 1959, African One-Party States, 1962, Five African States; Responses to Diversity, 1963, (with Alan Westin) Politics in Europe, 1965, Politics in Africa, 1966, National Unity and Regionalism, 1966, Africa in the Modern World series, 1968-72, (with Ann Paden) Expanding Horizons in African Studies, 1969, (with Louise Holborn and John Herz) German Constitutional Documents since 1871, 1970, (with Thomas Karis) From Protest to Challenge: A Documentary History of African Politics in South Africa, 1882-64, Vol. I, 1972, Vol. II, 1973, Vol. III, 1977, Vol. IV, 1977, (with Patrick O'Meara) Southern Africa in Crisis, 1977, Southern Africa: The Continuing Crisis, 1979, 2d edit., 1982, (with E. Philip Morgan) From the Front Line: Speeches of Sir Seretse Khama, 1980, (with Patrick O'Meara) International Politics in Southern Africa, 1982. Recipient George V medal pub. service, 1935, Achievement award Radcliffe Coll., 1962, AAUW, 1962, Disting. Tchrs. award, 1962, Disting. Scholar award African Studies Assn., 1978. Fellow Am. Acad. Arts and Scis.; mem. Am. Polit. Sci. Assn. (council 1954-56, v.p. 1963-64), New Eng. Polit. Sci. Assn. (pres. 1959-60), Internat. Polit. Sci. Assn., Canadian Hist. and Polit. Sci. Assns., African Studies Assn. (v.p. 1957-58, pres. 1958-59, mem. policy and plans com. 1963-65), AAUW (internat. relations com. 1951-57, world problems rep., dir. 1967-69), African-Am. Inst. (dir. 1964—), Chgo. Council Fgn. Relations (dir. 1967-74). Home: 190 W Fern Dr Orange City FL 32763

CARTER, HARLON BRONSON, association executive; b. Hood County, Tex., Aug. 10, 1913; s. Horace Bronson and Ila (Baker) C.; m. Maryann Kamus, Feb. 20, 1953; children—Joy Anna, John, William. Student, U. Tex., 1932-36, Emory U. Sch. Law, 1947. Mem. U.S. Border Patrol, 1936-70, chief, Washington, 1950-57; commr. S.W. region, Immigration and Naturalization Service and Border Patrol, 1961-70; pres. Nat. Rifle Assn., Washington, 1965-67, exec. v.p., 1977—; exec. dir. Inst. for Legis. Action, 1975-76. Contbr. numerous articles on law enforcement, legislation, politics to profl., popular mags. Recipient Distinguished Fed. Agy. Support award Internat. Good Neighbor Council, U.S.-Mexico, 1962. Mem. Safari Club Internat., Hunting Hall of Fame (Outstanding Am. Handgunner of Yr. award 1977), Nat. Rifle Assn. (benefactor), Nat. Skeet Shooting Assn. Baptist. Club: Masons (32 deg.). Lodge: Masons (32 deg.). Office: 1600 Rhode Island Ave NW Washington DC 20036 *

CARTER, HARRY TYSON, lawyer; b. Norristown, Pa., Apr. 17, 1924; s. John S. and Katharine M. (Tyson) C.; m. Elizabeth A. Edge, Aug. 25, 1956; children: Harry Tyson, Elizabeth Hamlin, Robert Edge. A.B., Dartmouth Coll., 1944; LL.B., Harvard U., 1949. Bar: D.C. 1949. Legal asst. to chmn. minority policy com. U.S. Senate, 1949-50; atty. ECA (and successors), 1950-53; legal counsel Sen. Smith of N.J., 1953-55; spl. asst. to asst. sec. def. for internat. security affairs, 1955-56; asst. to Pres.'s spl. rep. for Hungarian Refugee Relief, 32264to chmn. Pres.'s Com. for Hungarian Refugee Relief, 1956-57; dep. gen. counsel USIA, 1957-58; gen. counsel, congl. liaison, 1959-60; resident partner Shanley & Fisher, Washington, 1960-71; cons. Dept. State, 1971-72, 74-76; spl. asst. to under sec. state for mgmt., 1972-74, practice law, Washington, 1976—; Pub. mem. 24th Fgn. Service Officer Selection Bd., 1970. Served with USMCR, 1942-46. Mem. Phi Beta Kappa, Zeta Psi. Republican. Episcopalian. Clubs: Chevy Chase, Metropolitan (Washington). Home: 3520 Hamlet Pl Chevy Chase MD 20815 Office: 620 Washington Bldg Washington DC 20005

CARTER, HENRY MOORE, JR., foundation executive; b. Portsmouth, Va., Mar. 10, 1932; s. Henry and Debbie (McCoy) C.; m. Martha Rhea Greene, Aug. 21, 1954; 1 dau., Ann Clair. B.A., Randolph-Macon Coll., 1953; M.A., George Peabody Coll., 1954. Tchr. English, Norfolk County Public Schs., Portsmouth, 1954-59, head dept., 1957-59; headmaster Bollingbrook Sch., Petersburg, Va., 1959-66; dir. public relations Randolph-Macon Coll., Ashland, Va., 1966-68; dir. Randolph-Macon Fund, 1968-69, dir. devel., 1969-77; exec. dir. Winston-Salem (N.C.) Found., 1977—; mem. adv. com. Kate B. Reynolds Trust for Poor and Needy; sec. Donors Forum of Forsyth County, Winston-Salem Campaign Coordinating Com. Chmn. Winston-Salem Crime Stoppers., Emergency Loan Fund. Carnegie fellow, 1953-54. Mem. Council on Founds. (chmn. com. community founds.), Newcomen Soc. N.Am., Southeastern Council of Founds.

(trustee). Republican. Methodist. Clubs: Twin City, Rotary, Torch. Office: 229 1st Union Bldg Winston-Salem NC 27101

CARTER, HERBERT EDMUND, univ. ofcl.; b. Mooresville, Ind., Sept. 25, 1910; s. George Benjamin and Edna (Pidgeon) C.; m. Elizabeth Winifred DeWees, Aug. 30, 1933; children—Anne Winsett, Jean Elizabeth. A.B., DePauw U., 1930, Sc.D., 1952; A.M., U. Ill., 1931, Ph.D., 1934, Sc.D., 1974; Sc.D., U. Ind., 1974; L.H.D., Thomas Jefferson U., 1975. Instr. chemistry U. Ill., 1933-35, asso., 1935-37, asst. prof., 1937-43, asso. prof., 1943-45, prof., 1945-71, acting dean grad. coll., 1963-64, head dept. chemistry and chem. engring., 1954-67, vice chancellor for acad. affairs, 1967-71; coordinator interdisciplinary programs U. Ariz., Tucson, 1971-77, head dept. biochemistry, 1977-81; research fellow Office Arid Lands Studies, 1981—; Mem. Pres.'s Com. on the Nat. Medal of Sci., 1963-66; mem. nat. sci. bd. NSF, 1963-76, chmn., 1970-74; mem. Citizens Commn. Sci., Law and Food Supply.; Mem. exec. com. div. chemistry and chem. tech. NRC, 1949-55, 57-68. Mem. editorial bd.: Bio Chem. Preparations; editor-in-chief, Vol. I.; Contbr. to tech. publs. Trustee Assn. Univs. for Argonne, 1980—, Nutrition Found., 1972—. Awarded Rector Scholarship, Rector Fellowship DePauw U., Eli Lilly & Co.; Annual award ($1,000 and bronze medal to biochemist under 35 years of age showing promise in research), 1943; Am. Oil Chemists Soc. award in lipid chemistry, 1966. Mem. Am. Chem. Soc. (dir., asso. editor Bio-Chemistry 1961—, recipient William H. Nichols medal N.Y. sect., also Spencer award Kansas City sect. 1969), Am. Inst. Nutrition (sec. 1945-47), Am. Soc. Biol. Chemists (editorial bd. 1951-60, editorial com. 1963-66, pres. 1956-57), Nat. Acad. Scis. (chmn. section biochemistry 1963-66, mem. council 1966-69), Blue Key, Phi Beta Kappa, Sigma Xi, Phi Eta Sigma, Lambda Chi Alpha, Gamma Alpha, Alpha Chi Sigma. Democrat. Presbyn.

CARTER, HOWARD GREGORY, automobile industry executive; b. Winnipeg, Man., Can., Apr. 12, 1929; s. Charles Gregory and Edith Charlotte (Rosing) C.; m. Margaret Elizabeth Brisbin, Dec. 8, 1956; children: Elizabeth D., Martha J., James G. Student, U. Man., 1946-49; diploma in bus. adminstrn., Gen. Motors Inst., 1953. Mgr., co-owner Carter Motors Ltd., Winnipeg, 1953-63; pres. Carter GM, Vancouver, B.C., Can., 1963—, Howar Carter Lease, Ltd., Vancouver, 1968—, Howard Distbrs., 1965—, Bitter Automobiles Can., Ltd., Burnaby, B.C., 1983—, Avanti Motors Can., Ltd., Burnary, 1983—; dir. Eureka Coach Co., Toronto, Ont., Can. Vice pres. Vancouver Symphony Soc., 1982—; bd. govs. Vancouver Pub. Aquarium, 1981—; bd. dirs. Arts Scis. and Tech. Centre, Vancouver, 1981—. Recipient Quality Dealer award Time Mag., 1976, 83; named Businessman of Yr. Better Bus. Bur. Greater Vancouver, 1982. Mem. Fedn. Automobile Dealers (v.p. 1983—). Anglican. Clubs: Vancouver; Arbutus (Vancouver). Home: 6011 Churchill St Vancouver BC Canada V6M 3H4 Office: Carter GM 4550 Lougheed Hwy Vancouver BC Canada V5C 3Z5

CARTER, HUGH CLENDENIN, consulting engineer; b. Polk, Nebr., Dec. 7, 1925; s. Daniel Burr and Ruth Clendenin (McGaffin) C.; m. Patricia Moore, Jan. 22, 1971; children: John, Dan, Jim, Lisabeth. B.S., Calif. Inst. Tech., 1949. Job engr. Bechtel Corp., Los Angeles, 1950-53; sr. mech. estimator Div. Architecture, State of Calif., Los Angeles, 1953-56; sr. mech. engr., project engr. Pereira & Luckman, Los Angeles, 1956-57; chmn. bd. Hugh Carter Engring. Corp. div. Lockwood Andrews and New NAM, San Diego, 1957—; instr. Los Angeles City Coll., Long Beach City Coll., 1957-59, U. So. Calif., 1956-58; Bd. dirs. So. Calif. Rapid Transit Dist., Los Angeles, 1973-75. Author: Mechanical Estimating, 1955, Simplified Mechanical Specifications, 1962, Carter's Design Details, 1965, Consultant's Services, 1966; also over 200 articles. Served with USNR, 1943-45. ERDA solar energy grantee, 1977. Fellow Inst. Engrs., Am. Cons. Engrs. Council ASHRAE, Inst. Engring.; mem. ASME, Cons. Engrs. Assn. Calif. (pres. 1964-65). Episcopalian. Clubs: Rotary, Long Beach Yacht, San Diego Yacht, Cuyamaca, Internat. City., San Diego Athletic. Designer 1st sch. solar energy system in Calif., first central sta. heat pump, tankless pump water system for high rise bldgs., Calif., largest solar cooling system in U.S. *Get good at something, let the world know about it, and get better at it.*

CARTER, JAINE MARIE, human resources development company executive; b. Chgo., Oct. 29, 1936; d. Bruno and Louise (Cunningham) Kucinski; m. James Dudley Carter, Apr. 8, 1970; children: Paul, Todd. B.S., Northwestern U., 1958. Pres. Bacherlorette Assn. (discount services and tng. for women), Los Angeles, 1962-64; mgmt. cons. to bus., 1964-69; chmn. bd. Personnel Devel., Inc., Palatine, Ill., 1969—; dir. women's div. Lake Forest (Ill.) Coll. Advanced Mgmt. Inst., 1970—; lectr., tchr., cons. mgmt. devel. programs; mem. faculty AMR Internat., Penton Learning Systems. Author: How to Train for Supervisors, 1969, Career Planning Workshop for Women, 1975, Training Techniques that Bring About Positive Behavioral Change, 1976, Assertive Management Role Plays, 1976, Understanding the Female Employee, 1976, Rx for Women in Business, 1976, New Directions Needed in Management Training Programs, 1980, The Burnout of Retirement, 1983. Mem. Internat. Transactional Analysis Assn., Am. Soc. Tng. and Devel., Screen Actors Guild, AFTRA, AGVA, Exec. Club Am., Am. Mgmt. Assn. (pres.'s assn.). Address: 921 Scott Dr Marco Island FL 33937 *People are only really free when they are able to turn their back on the expectations of others and confidently pursue their own life goals and unlimited dimensions.*

CARTER, JAMES C., chemistry educator, consultant; b. Hardin, Mo., Aug. 19, 1931; s. James B. and Verna (Griffith) C.; m. Louise Ann Fonteine, June 30, 1956; children: James F., Ann V. B.S. in Chemistry, U. Okla., 1953, M.S., U. Mich., 1955, Ph.D., 1961. Instr. U. Mich., Ann Arbor, 1961-62; asst. prof., then assoc. prof. U. Pitts., 1962-74; prof. chemistry Memphis State U., 1974—; v.p. U. Pitts., 1977-78, pres. Wayne, N.J. div., 1978-80; group v.p. Am. Cyanamid Co, Wayne, 1980—. Bd. dirs. Memphis Ballet Soc., 1978-83. 1st lt. USAF, 1955-57. Mem. Am. Chem. Soc. (chmn. Memphis sect. 1983). Presbyterian. Home: 63 Shady Glen Rd Memphis TN 38119 Office: Memphis State U Dept Chemistry Memphis TN 38152

CARTER, JAMES CLARENCE, university president; b. N.Y.C., Aug. 1, 1927; s. James C. and Elizabeth (Dillon) C. B.S. in Physics, Spring Hill Coll., 1952; M.S., Fordham U., 1953; S.T.L. in Theology, Woodstock Coll., 1959; Ph.D. in Physics, Catholic U. Am., 1956. Joined Soc. Jesus, 1947; instr. Loyola U., New Orleans, 1960-63, asst. prof., 1963-67, asso. prof., 1967—, v.p., 1970-74, pres., 1974—; dir. edn. Soc. Jesus, New Orleans Province, 1968-70; Dir. Internat. Trade Mart, 1975; Mem. steering com. Goals Found. for Met. New Orleans, 1971—; mem. higher edn. facilities com. State La., 1971-73; chmn. Mayor's Com. Ednl. Uses CATV, 1972; mem. Council for Better La., 1974—, La. Ednl. TV Authority, 1977—. Contbr. articles to profl. jours. Bd. dirs. Internat. House, 1975—, Boys' Clubs Greater New Orleans, 1974—, Met. Area Com., 1974—; mem. adv. bd. Inst. Politics New Orleans, 1970—; chmn. La. selection com. Rhodes Scholarships, 1978; trustee Regis Coll., Deuveri Xavier U., Cin. Named to Hall of Fame St. Stanislaus High Sch., 1974. Mem. Palmes Academiques, Am. Assn. Higher Edn., A.A.U.P., Assn. Governing Bds. Univs. and Colls., Fgn. Relations Assn. New Orleans, Am. Phys. Soc., Am. Assn. Physics Tchrs., Nat. Catholic Ednl. Assn., Albertus Magnus Guild, Information Council Ams. (internat. dir. 1974—), Assn. Jesuit Colls. and Univs. (chmn. acad. v.p. conf. 1971-74), Nat. Assn. Ind. Colls. and Univs. (bd. dirs. 1977-82), Am. Council Edn., Assn. Am. Colls., Sigma Xi, Beta Gamma Sigma. Club: Plimsol. Home and office: 6363 St Charles Ave New Orleans LA 70118

CARTER, JAMES H., justice state supreme court; b. Waverly, Iowa, Jan. 18, 1935; s. Harvey J. and Ardus (Simonson) C.; m. Jeanne E. Carter, Mar. 1959; children: Carol, James. B.A., U. Iowa, 1956, J.D., 1960. Law clk. to judge U.S. Dist. Ct, 1960-62; assoc. Shuttleworth & Ingersoll, Cedar Rapids, Iowa, 1962-73; judge 6th Jud. Dist., 1973-76, Iowa Ct. Appeals, 1976-82; justice Iowa Supreme Ct., Des Moines, 1982—. Office: Supreme Ct State Capitol Des Moines IA 50319 *

CARTER, JAMES HAL, JR., lawyer; b. Ames, Iowa, Sept. 25, 1943; s. James H. and Louise (Benge) C.; m. Sara N. Meeker, July 27, 1974; children: Janet, Faith. B.A., Yale U., 1965, LL.B., 1969. Bar: N.Y. 1971, U.S. Dist. Ct. (so. dist.) N.Y. 1972, U.S. Dist. Ct. (ea. dist.) N.Y. 1975, U.S. Dist. Ct. Conn. 1981, U.S. Ct. Internat. Trade 1980, U.S. Ct. Appeals (2d cir.) 1971, U.S. Supreme Ct. 1976. Fulbright scholar Cambridge U., Eng., 1965-66; law clk. U.S. Ct. Appeals (2d cir.), 1969-70; with Sullivan & Cromwell, N.Y.C., 1970, ptnr., 1977; lectr. internat. comml. arbitration Practicing Law Inst. Corr. editor: Internat. Legal Materials; contbr. articles in field to publs. Mem. adv. bd. Southwestern Legal Found. Internat. and Comparative Law Ctr. Mem. ABA, N.Y. State Bar Assn. (chmn. internat. law com.), Assn. Bar CitY N.Y., U.S. Council Internat. Bus. (com. on arbitration), Am. Soc Internat. Law. Office: Sullivan & Cromwell 125 Broad St New York NY 10004

CARTER, JAMES JOHNSTON, lawyer; b. Samson, Ala., Apr. 13, 1913; s. Costello L. and Mary Ann (Smith) C.; m. Eva Jane Edwards, Sept. 6, 1947; children: Harold M., David E. (stepsons), James M., Kathy Jane. LL.B., Jones Law Sch., 1934; postgrad., U. Mich., 1940, U. Va., 1941. Bar: Ala. 1934. Atty. Montgomery County Probate Ct., 1935-38; law clk., sec. U.S. circuit judge, Montgomery, Ala., also New Orleans, 1938-47; mem. Hill, Hill, Carter, Franco, Cole & Black, Montgomery, 1947—; spl. judge 15th Jud. Circuit Ala., 1949, 51, 55, 60; spl. asst. atty. gen., Ala., 1969-71, 78-81; judge Ala. Ct. of Judiciary, 1974—; pres. Jones Law Sch., 1964-72. Served to 1st lt. AUS, 1943-46. Recipient Distinguished Service award U.S. Jr. C. of C., 1937. Fellow Am. Coll. Trial Lawyers, Am. Bar Found.; mem. ABA, Fed. Bar Assn., Tenn. Bar Assn. (hon. mem.), Montgomery County Bar Assn. (pres. 1957), Ala. State Bar (pres. 1962-63, mem. bd. bar examiners 1969-76), Jud. Conf. Ala., Jud. Conf. 5th Circuit, Jr. C. of C. (past pres.), Am. Judicature Soc., Ala. Law Inst., Fedn. Ins. Counsel, Sigma Delta Kappa. Presbyn. (elder). Clubs: Country, Beauvoir. Home: 2602 Wildwood Dr Montgomery AL 36111 Office: Hill Bldg PO Box 116 Montgomery AL 36195

CARTER, JAMES LARRY, banker; b. Highpoint, N.C., Apr. 16, 1938; s. Wade V. and Mabel S. C.; m. Mary West Britton, Sept. 5, 1959; children: James Larry, Mary Margaret, Britton Wade. B.A. in Econs, U. N.C., 1960. With First Union Nat. Bank N.C., 1963-75, regional exec., 1974-75; exec. v.p. First Nat. Bank Albuquerque, 1975-77, pres., chief exec. officer, 1977—; sec., bd. dirs. AIDS/IFA; adv. council Robert O. Anderson Grad. Sch. Bus. Bd. dirs., exec. com. Albuquerque Center; bd. dirs. N.Mex. Symphony Orch., Santa Fe Opera, N.Mex. Heart Inst.; mem. Minority Bus. Opportunity Scholarship Com. Mem. Am. Bankers Assn. (chmn. U.S. Savs. Bond Program), Ind. Bankers Am., Bank Mktg. Inst., N.Mex. Bankers Assn. (pres.-elect 1980), Greater Albuquerque C. of C. (dir., v.p. econs.), Albuquerque Assn. Commerce and Industry (2d vice chmn.), U.S. C. of C. Clubs: Albuquerque Country, Tanoan Country, Petroleum, Rio Rancho Country. Home: Star Route Box 339 Placitas NM 87043 Office: PO Box 1305 Albuquerque NM 87103

CARTER, JAY BOYD, economic development executive; b. Turlock, Calif., Apr. 12, 1925; s. Arthur Wesley and Gail Bernice (Jaderberg) C.; m. Mary Louise Cross, Apr. 12, 1946; children—Jay Boyd, Kathleen Susanne, Brian Douglas, Annette Marie, Daniel Edward, Mary Beth, Jeannette Marie, Lawrence Scott. Student, U. N.Mex., 1944-45; B.S. in Elec. Engring, U. So. Calif., 1946, U. So. Calif., 1951; M.A. in Internat. Pub. Policy, Sch. Advanced Internat. Studies, Johns Hopkins, 1974. Engr. City of Los Angeles Dept. Water and Power, 1946-51; engr., supt. various engring., cons. and constrn. firms, 1951-55; with State Dept., ICA, then; AID, power engr., Thailand, 1955-58, gen. engr., Taiwan, 1958-63, power engr., India, 1963-66, gen. engr., Washington, 1966-68, chief engr., Brazil, 1968-73; dir. power, industry and mineral resources, devel. bank dept. Asian Devel. Bank, Manila, Philippines, 1974-79; mgr. internat. Asia ops. Stanley Cons., Inc., 1979-82; pres. Jay B. Carter & Assocs., Islamabad, Pakistan and Khartown, Sudan, 1982—. Served with USNR, 1943-46. Mem. IEEE, Am. Pub. Works Assn., Mgmt. Assn. of Philippines, Soc. Am. Mil. Engrs. Home: 9017 Hamilton Dr Fairfax VA 22030 Office: US Embassy Khartoum Sudan

CARTER, JIMMY (JAMES EARL, JR.), former president of U.S.; b. Archery, Ga., Oct. 1, 1924; s. James Earl and Lillian (Gordy) C.; m. Rosalynn Smith, July 7, 1946; children: John William, James Earl III, Donnel Jeffrey, Amy Lynn. Student, Ga. Southwestern Coll., 1941-42, Ga. Inst. Tech., 1942-43; B.S., U.S. Naval Acad., 1947; postgrad., Union Coll., 1952-53; LL.D. (hon.), Morris Brown Coll., 1972, Morehouse Coll., 1972, U. Notre Dame, 1977, Emory U., 1979, Kwansei Gakuin U., Japan, 1981, Ga. Southwestern Coll., 1981; D.E. (hon.), Ga. Inst. Tech., 1979; Ph.D. (hon.), Weizmann Inst. Sci., 1980, Tel Aviv U., 1983. Peanut farmer, warehouseman, Plains, Ga., 1953-77; mem. Ga. Senate, 1963-67; gov. of Ga., Atlanta, 1971-75, Pres. of U.S., 1977-81; Disting. prof. Emory U., 1982—. Author: Why Not the Best?, 1975, A Government as Good as Its People, 1977, Keeping Faith/Memoirs of a President, 1982. Mem. Sumter County (Ga.) Sch. Bd., 1955-62, chmn., 1960-62; mem. Americus and Sumter County Hosp. Authority, 1956-70; bd. dirs. Ga. Crop Improvement Assn., 1957-63, pres., 1961; mem. Sumter County (Ga.) Library Bd., 1961; pres. Plains Devel. Corp., 1963; chmn. West Central Ga. Area Planning and Devel. Commn., 1964; pres. Ga. Planning Assn., 1968; state chmn. March of Dimes, 1968-70; chmn. congl. campaign com. Democratic Nat. Com., 1974. Served to lt. USN, 1946-53. Recipient Gold medal Internat. Inst. Human Rights, 1979; Internat. Mediation medal Am. Arbitration Assn., 1979; Martin Luther King Jr. Nonviolent Peace prize, 1979. Democrat. Club: Lions (dist. gov. 1968-69). Office: 75 Spring St SW Atlanta GA 30303

CARTER, JOHN BERNARD, insurance company executive; b. Phila., Sept. 21, 1934; s. John Mein and Elise Hoban (Alexander) C.; m. Hope Elliot, Apr. 12, 1958; children—Hope, John, Helen, Charles, Henry, George, Charlotte, Ann, Katherine, Elizabeth, Richard. B.A., Yale U., 1956; M.B.A., Harvard U., 1961. With Equitable Life Assurance Soc. U.S., 1960—, chief ins. officer, 1981-82; pres., chief exec. officer, dir. Equitable Life Holding Corp. Trustee Morehouse Coll., Atlanta, 1980—; Bd. dirs. United Way of Tri-State; bd. dirs. N.Y. Heart Fund Assn. Served with USN, 1956-59. Office: 1285 Ave of Americas New York NY 10019

CARTER, JOHN BOYD, JR., oil operator; b. Ft. Worth, Oct. 19, 1924; s. John Boyd and Enlie (Corder) C.; m. Susie Ann Browne, Feb. 9, 1946 (div. Dec. 1968); children: Catherine Browne Malone, John Mason; m. Winifred Trimble Runnells, Feb. 23, 1970. Student, Kemper Mil. Sch., 1941-43, U. Tex., 1943-46, Babson Coll., 1946-47. Mortgage loan supr. Am. Gen. Investment Corp., 1947; ind. oil operator, 1948-49; sec., treas. Tex. Fund, Inc., 1949-52, mem. investment adv. bd., 1951-58; pres. Tex. Fund Research and Mgmt. Assos., 1950-52; ind. oil operator and fin. cons., 1952-58; Southwestern rep. Lehman Bros., 1959-65, gen. partner, 1965-77, mng. dir., 1970-77; sr. v.p., dir. Pogo Producing Co., 1977—; dir., chmn. exec. com. Capital Bank (N.A.); chmn. bd. B.C.M. Tech., Inc.; pres., dir. Prescott Ranch Co.; dir. Am. Marine Corp., Sea Drilling Corp. Trustee Houston Mus. Fine Arts, Baylor Coll. Medicine. Mem. Ind. Petroleum Assn. Am., Houston Soc. Fin. Analysts, Houston Com. on Fgn. Relations, Sigma Alpha Epsilon. Clubs: Houston Country, St. Charles Hunting, Bayou, Coronado; River, Turf and Field, Brook (N.Y.C.). Home: 3682 Willowick Dr Houston TX 77019 Office: 66th Floor Tex Commerce Towers PO Box 61289 Houston TX 77208 Home: 1 E 66th St New York NY

CARTER, JOHN COLES, legal educator; b. Eolia, Mo., Jan. 21, 1920; s. Charles William and Ollie (Brown) C.; m. Dorothy Mary Strong, Jan. 29, 1944; children: Carolyn L., Charles W. A.B., Lake Forest (Ill.) Coll., 1943, M.A., 1979; LL.B., Chgo.-Kent Coll. Law, 1950. Pub. accountant Price Waterhouse & Co., Chgo., 1946-47, Paul Pettingill Co., Waukegan, Ill., 1950-51; instr. Lake Forest Coll., 1947-50; with Inland Steel Co., Chgo., 1951-79, sec., 1962-79; prof. law Memphis State U., 1979—; instr. John Marshall Sch. Law, 1964. Commr., past pres. Lake Bluff (Ill.) Park Dist.; past pres. Lake Bluff Village Library.; Past bd. dirs. Am. Lung Assn., Chgo. Lung Assn.; bd. dirs. Tenn. Lung Assn., Lake Forest Hosp.; former trustee Village of Lake Bluff, Lake Forest Coll. Served to lt. (j.g.) USNR, 1943-46; PTO. Decorated Presdl. Commendation Medal. Mem. Am., Chgo. Memphis, Shelby County, Tenn. bar assns., Am. Soc. Corporate Secs. (pres. 1964-65, nat. dir. 1966—, nat. v.p. 1967, nat. pres. 1975-76), Lake Forest Alumni Assn. (past pres. exec. bd.), Scholarship and Guidance Assn. (pres. 1972-73, dir.), Am. Iron and Steel Inst. Clubs: Legal, Law, Economic (Chgo.); Farmington (Charlottesville, Va.); Chickasaw (Memphis, Tenn.). Home: 550 E Parkway S Memphis TN 38104 Office: Memphis State U Sch Law Memphis TN 38152

CARTER, JOHN MACK, publishing company executive; b. Murray, Ky., Feb. 28, 1928; s. William Z. and Martha (Stevenson) C.; m. Sharlyn Emily Reaves, Aug. 30, 1948; children: Jonna Lyn, John Mack II. Student, Murray State Coll., 1944-46, LL.D., 1971; B.J., U. Mo., 1948, M.A., 1949; LL.D., St. John's U., 1983. Reporter Murray Ledger & Times, 1945; asst. editor Better Homes & Gardens mag., 1949-51; mng. editor Household mag., Topeka, 1953-57, editor, 1957-58; exec. editor Together, 1958-59; editor Am. Home, 1959-61; exec. editor McCall's, 1961, editor, 1962-65; v.p., dir. McCall Corp., N.Y.C., 1962-65; editor-in-chief Ladies Home Jour., 1965-74, pub., 1967-70; pres., chief operating officer Downe Communications Inc., 1972-73, chmn. bd., editor-in chief, 1973-77; pres. Am. Home Pub. Co., 1974-75; editor-in-chief Good Housekeeping, 1975—. Served as lt. (j.g.) USNR, 1951-53. Recipient Walter Williams award for writing, 1949. Mem. Sigma Delta Chi. Office: 959 8th Ave New York NY 10019

CARTER, JOHN ROBERT, physician; b. Buffalo, Apr. 21, 1917; s. John Harvey and Gertrude Ann (Buckpitt) C.; m. Adelaide Briggs, May 8, 1943; children—Marilyn Anne, Jeanne Catherine. B.S., Hamilton Coll., 1939; M.D., U. Rochester, 1943. Diplomate: Nat. Bd. Med. Examiners. Intern State U. Iowa, 1943-44, resident, 1944-48, asst. dept. pathology, 1944, from instr. to asso. prof., 1944-55, prof., 1955-59; prof., chmn. dept. pathology and oncology U. Kans. Med. Center, 1960-66; prof. pathology dept. orthopedics Case Western Res. U., Cleve., 1966—, dir. Inst. Pathology, chmn. dept. pathology, 1966-81; cons. VA Hosp., U.S. Army Hosp., U.S. Penitentiary, Watkins Meml. Hosp.; Past chmn. pathology study sect. NIH; mem. pathology tng. grant com. Nat. Inst. Gen. Med. Scis.; mem. pathology adv. council Central VA Office; mem. sci. adv. bd. Armed Forces Inst. Pathology.; Bd. dirs. Univs. Asso. Research and Edn. Pathology; past pres. Mem. editorial bd.: Am. Jour. Pathology. Served to lt. USNR, 1946-48. Mem. AMA, AAAS, Cleve. Acad. Medicine, Path. Soc. Gt. Britain and Ireland, Am. Assn. Pathologists and Bacteriologists (past pres.), Internat. Acad. Pathology, Am. Soc. Clin. Pathology, Am. Soc. Exptl. Pathology, Coll. Am. Pathologists, Soc. Exptl. Biology, AAUP, Central Soc. Clin. Research, Phi Beta Kappa, Sigma Xi, Alpha Omega Alpha. Home: 36570 Ridge Rd Willoughby OH 44094 Office: Inst Pathology Case Western Res U Cleveland OH 44106

CARTER, JOSEPH CARLYLE, JR., lawyer; b. Mayfield, Ky., June 3, 1927; s. Joseph Carlyle and Cynthia Elizabeth (Stokes) C.; m. Dianne C. Dinwiddie, July 15, 1949; children: Joseph Carlyle, Hugh D., William H., Henry S., Dianne C. B.A., U. Va., 1948, LL.B., 1951. Bar: Va. 1951. Since practiced in, Richmond; assoc. firm Hunton & Williams, 1951-58, ptnr., 1958-82, mng. ptnr., 1972-82; dir. Va. Fed. Savs. and Loan Assn., Ethyl Corp. Active elder 2d Presbyn. Ch., Richmond, 1962—; chmn. Richmond Pub. Library Bd., 1967-77, mem., 1980—; trustee Colonial Williamsburg Found., 1977—, Med. Coll. Va. Found., 1976—, U. Va. Patent Found., 1975—. Recipient Algernon Sidney Sullivan award, 1948. Mem. Am. Bar Assn., Va. Bar Assn., Richmond Bar Assn., Am. Law Inst., Am. Judicature Soc., Newcomen Soc. Presbyn. Clubs: Commonwealth, Country of Va., Downtown (Richmond); Union League (N.Y.C.). Home: 6102 St Andrew Ln Richmond VA 23226 Office: PO Box 1535 Richmond VA 23212

CARTER, JOSEPH EDWIN, former nickel company executive; b. Jackson, Ga., Apr. 3, 1915; s. Charles Luther and Marilu (Holiman) C.; m. Virginia Meredith Crickmer, Apr. 8, 1939; children: Joseph Charles, Virginia Ann (Mrs. James Allan Colburn). B.S., Ga. Inst. Tech., 1937. Metallurgist Internat. Nickel Co., Huntington, W.Va., 1937-40, various positions, 1940-57, indsl. relations mgr., 1957-58, gen. supt., 1958-60; mfg. mgr. Huntington Alloy Products Div., 1960-62, v.p. mfg., 1962-67, exec. v.p., 1967-70, pres., 1971; v.p. Internat. Nickel Co. Can. Ltd., N.Y.C., 1971, exec. v.p., 1972-73, pres., 1974-77; also dir.; chmn., chief exec. officer INCO Ltd., Toronto, Ont., Can., 1977-80; former dir. Toronto Dominion Bank. Active United Fund; former mem. lay bd. St. Mary's Hosp.; past bd. dirs. Huntington Galleries, Huntington Pediatric Clinic. Served to maj. AUS, 1942-45. Decorated Bronze Star.; Recipient Gold Knight of Industry award Nat. Mgmt. Assn., 1965. Mem. Am. Chem. Soc., W.Va. Mfrs. Assn. (pres. 1970-71), Phi Kappa Phi, Tau Beta Pi. Presbyterian (deacon). Clubs: Guyan Country, Baltusrol Golf, Nashua Country; University (N.Y.C.). Patentee in field.

CARTER, LAUNOR FRANKLIN, former science administrator, consultant; b. Friday Harbor, Wash., Jan. 23, 1914; s. Alvia F. and Hazel Agnes (Shull) C.; m. Mary Ann Wickersham, Feb. 14, 1941; 1 son, James Franklin. B.S., U. Wash., 1936, M.S., 1939; Ph.D., Princeton U., 1941; certicicate Exec. Tng. Program, UCLA, 1961. Chief examiner Wash. State Dept. Social Security Merit System Office, 1937-38; personnel technician Social Security Bd., Washington, 1940-41, Adj. Gen. Office, Dept. Army, 1941-42; research psychologists Aero-Med. Lab., Wright Field, Ohio, 1946; asst., then asso. prof. psychology U. Rochester, 1946-52; dir. research Human Research Unit 2, Continental Army Command, Ft. Ord, Calif., 1952-55; v.p., dir. research System Devel. Corp., Santa Monica, Calif., 1955-62, v.p., mgr. pub. systems div., 1963-73, v.p. civil devel., 1973-81, v.p. studies and evaluation, 1975-81; chief scientist USAF, 1962-63; pvt. cons., 1981—; Mem. USAF Sci. Adv. Bd., 1955-68; adv. com. dept.

psychology Princeton, 1962-68; mem. Nat. Adv. Commn. Libraries, 1966-68; mem. sci. information council NSF, 1965-69; mem. computer sci. and engring. bd. Nat. Acad. Sci.; chmn. com. on socio-econ. research and earthquake prediction; bd. dirs., treas. Council for Applied Social Research, 1977-82. Cons. editor: Psychol. Bull, 1955-60, Jour. Abnormal and Social Psychology, 1955-68, Evaluation Quar, 1976—; asso. editor: Sociometry, 1955-64; Contbr. numerous articles to profl. jours. Served with USAAF, 1942-46. Benjamin Franklin fellow Royal Soc. Arts. Fellow AAAS; mem. Am. Psychol. Assn. (rec. sec., dir. 1955-61, 71, chmn. program com. 1953, chmn. ad hoc conv. com. 1954), Western Psychol. Assn., Soc. for Psychol. Study Social Issues, Am. Fedn. Scientists, Council Applied Social Research (treas. 1976—). Club: Riviera Country. Home: 249 Mantua Rd Pacific Palisades CA 90272 Office: 2500 Colorado Ave Santa Monica CA 90406

CARTER, LISLE CARLETON, JR., univ. pres.; b. N.Y.C., Nov. 18, 1925; s. Lisle Carleton and Eunice (Hunton) C.; m. Emily Ellis, Dec. 29, 1950; children—Eric, Stephen, Leslie, Lisa, John. A.B., Dartmouth Coll., 1944, LL.D. (hon.), 1979; LL.B., St. John's U., 1950; LL.D. (hon.), Bethune Cookman Coll., 1976, George Washington U., 1979. Practiced law, 1950-54, 56-61; exec. dir. Washington Urban League, 1954-56; counsel Nat. Urban League, 1959-61; dep. asst. sec. HEW, 1961-64, asst. sec., 1966-68; asst. dir. OEO, 1964-66; vis. prof. adminstrn., v.p. Cornell U., 1968-71, prof. and dir. public policy, 1970-74; chancellor Atlanta U. Center, 1974-77; pres. U. D.C., 1977—; mem. adv. council Cornell U. Grad. Sch. Bus. and Public Adminstrn., 1974-80; dir. Heublein, Inc., Washington Star Co., Harper's Mag. Found.; mem. adv. bd. internat. fellows program ITT; mem. adv. council to dir. NSF, 1977-80; mem. Pres.'s Commn. on Pension Policy, 1978-81. Trustee Nat. Health and Welfare Mut. Life Ins. Assn., Inc., 1975-81; Chmn. bd. Children's Def. Fund; chmn. Commn. on Future Financing for City of Atlanta, 1974-75; mem. steering com. Nat. Urban Coalition; sr. vice chmn. bd. Nat. Urban League; bd. govs. United Way of Am. Inc., chmn. exec. com., 1981—; trustee Aspen Inst. Humanistic Studies. Mem. Assn. Am. Colls. (dir.), Am. Assn. State Colls. and Univs. (v.p., com. on fed. relations), Am. Council Edn. (Commn. Internat. Ednl. Relations). *

CARTER, LYNDA, actress, entertainer; b. Phoenix, July 24. Student, Ariz. State U. Toured 4 years with, The Garfin Gathering; appeared 4 movies for TV, 5 TV variety spls.; star of: television series Wonder Woman, 1976-77, The New Adventures of Wonder Woman, 1977-79; recording artist: album Portraits. Named Miss World-USA, 1973. Profl. performer since age 15. Office: care Lynda Carter Prodns PO Box 5973 Sherman Oaks CA 91413 *

CARTER, MARSHALL SYLVESTER, foundation executive, former army officer; b. Ft. Monroe, Va., Sept. 16, 1909; s. Clifton Carroll and Mai (Coleman) C.; m. Préot Nichols; children: Josephine Stoney, Marshall Nichols, Mary Coleman. B.S., U.S. Mil. Acad., 1931; M.S., MIT, 1936; grad., Nat. War Coll., 1950. Commd. 2d lt. U.S. Army, 1931; advanced through grades to lt. gen., 1962; with plans and operations div. War Dept. Gen. Staff, 1942-45; dep. and asst. chief of staff G-5, Hdqrs., China Theater, 1945-46; spl. rep. in Washington for Gen. Marshall (China Mission), 1946-47; spl. asst. to sec. state, 1947-49; minister Am. embassy, London, Eng., 1949; comdg. 138th AAA Group and AA officer Air Defs. Central Japan, 1950; dir. exec. office Sec. Def., 1950-52; dep. comdg. gen. U.S. Army, Alaska, asst. div. comdr. 71st Inf. Div., 1952-55, comdg. gen. 5th AA Regional Command, Ft. Sheridan, 1955-56; chief of staff N.Am. Air Def. Command, 1956-59, U.S. 8th Army, Korea, 1959-60; comdg. gen. Army Air Def. Center, Ft. Bliss, Tex., 1961-62; dep. dir. CIA, Washington, 1962-65; dir. Nat. Security Agy., 1965-69; now cons.), ret., 1969; pres. George C. Marshall Research Found., Lexington, Va., 1969—. Trustee Cheyenne Mt. Zool. Soc.; Bd. dirs. Internat. Human Assistance Program, N.Y.C. Decorated Distinguished Intelligence medal, D.S.M. with two oak leaf clusters, Legion of Merit with oak leaf cluster, Bronze Star, U.S.; spl. Breast Order of Yun Hui with Rosette (China), 1945; and oak-leaf cluster, 1947; comdr. Order of Orange Nassau with swords (Netherlands); Order of Service Merit (Korea). Mem. Va. Hist. Soc. (hon., life), Sigma Xi. Clubs: Boone and Crockett (N.Y.C.); Cheyenne Mountain Country, Cooking, Country of Colo. (Colorado Springs); Army-Navy Country (Arlington, Va.); Army-Navy (Washington). Home: 655 Bear Paw Ln Colorado Springs CO 80906 Office: George C Marshall Research Found Lexington VA 24450

CARTER, MARY EDDIE, govt. adminstr.; b. Americus, Ga., Mar. 14, 1925; d. Walker G. and Esther (Stewart) C. B.A., LaGrange Coll., 1946; M.S., U. Fla., 1949; Ph.D., U. Edinburgh, 1956. Tchr. LaGrange (Ga.) Coll., 1946-47; chemist Callaway Mills, LaGrange, 1947-48; microscopist So. Research Inst., Birmingham, Ala., 1949-51; chemist West Point Mfg. Co., Shawmut, Ala., 1951-53; research asso. FMC Corp., Am. Viscose div., Marcus Hook, Pa., 1956-71; lab chief textiles and clothing lab. U.S. Dept. Agr., Knoxville, Tenn., 1971-73; dir. So. Regional Research Center, 1973-80; asso. adminstr. Agrl. Research Service, Washington, 1980—. Recipient Herty medal Ga. sect. of Am. Chem. Soc., 1979. Mem. Am. Chem. Soc., Am. Assn. Textile Chemists and Colorists, Inter-Soc. Color Council, Sci. Research Soc. Am., Fiber Soc., Inst. Food Technologists, Am. Assn. Cereal Chemists. Office: US Dept Agr ARS 14th and Independence Ave SW Washington DC 20250

CARTER, MASON CARLTON, educator; b. Washington, Jan. 14, 1933; s. Mason Franklin and Odessa (Roberts) C.; m. Ida Ruth Bishop, 1953; children—Mason Lee, Daniel Clyde. B.S. in Forestry, Va. Poly. Inst., 1955, M.S. in Plant Physiology, 1957; Ph.D. in Forestry, Duke U., 1959. Research forester S.E. Forest Expt. Sta., Macon, Ga., 1959-60; mem. faculty Auburn (Ala.) U., 1960-73, Alumni prof. forestry, 1966-73; prof. forestry, head dept. forestry and natural resources Purdue U., 1973—; mem. Sec. Agr. Adv. Bd. Coop. Forestry Research, 1975-79; exec. com. Assn. State Coll. and U. Forestry Research Orgns., 1974-77; chmn. Council Forestry Sch. Execs., 1978-79; mem. industry execs./forestry deans com. Forest Industries Council, 1981; cons. mem. forest research council Internat. Paper Co., 1981. Author papers in field. Mem. Auburn City Council, 1965-69; bd. dirs. Auburn Water Works Bd., 1968; mem. White River (Ind.) Park Commn. Adv. Bd., 1979. Mem. Soc. Am. Foresters (award excellence Southeastern sect. 1973), Sigma Xi, Xi Sigma Pi, Alpha Zeta, Phi Sigma, Gamma Sigma Delta. Office: Forestry Bldg Purdue U West Lafayette IN 47907

CARTER, NELL, actress, singer; b. Birmingham, Ala., Sept. 13, 1948; d. Horace L. and Edna (IM.) Hardy. Student, Bill Russells Sch. Drama, 1970-73. Numerous radio and TV appearances in, Ala.; numerous club appearances and concerts including Los Angeles Philharm; appeared in play and film: Hair; appeared in: films Modern Problems, 1981, Back Roads, 1981; TV appearances include: Baryshnikov on Broadway, The Big Show; star: TV series Gimme a Break.; theatrical appearances include: Dude, Don't Bother Me, I Can't Cope, Jesus Christ Superstar, Bury the Dead, Rhapsody in Gershwin, Blues is a Woman, Black Broadway, Ain't Misbehavin'. Recipient Tony award; OBIE award; Drama Desk award; Soho News award for Ain't Misbehavin. Mem. AFTRA, Screen Actors Guild, Equity, NAACP (life). Democrat. Presbyterian. Office: care Richard Astor 119 W 57th St New York NY 10019

CARTER, NEVILLE LOUIS, geophysicist, educator; b. Los Angeles, Aug. 21, 1934; s. Herman Louis and Maribelle (Sheller) C.; m. Kathleen Diane Ablitt, Sept. 8, 1956; children—James Neville, Lindsay Louis, Jenifer June. A.B., Pomona Coll., 1956; M.A., UCLA, 1958, Ph.D., 1963; postgrad. (Fulbright fellow), U. Oslo, Norway, 1958-59. Research asso. Inst. Geophysics, UCLA, 1963; research geologist Shell Devel. Co., Houston, 1963-66; asso. prof. geology and geophysics Yale U., New Haven, Conn., 1966-71; prof. geophysics SUNY, Stony Brook, 1971-78; prof., head dept. geophysics, faculty asso. Center for Tectonophysics, Tex. A&M U., College Station, 1978—; cons. Re/Spec Inc. Author, editor numerous works in field. Mem. Am. Geophys. Union (pres. tectonophysics sect. 1974-76), Geol. Soc. Am., AAAS, Sigma Xi. Home: 2525 Arbor St Bryan TX 77801 Office: Dept Geophysics Tex A&M U College Station TX 77843

CARTER, POWELL FREDERICK, naval officer; b. Los Angeles, June 3, 1931; s. Powell Frederick and Helen June (Shaw) C.; m. Carole Ann Oswald, June 22, 1957; children: Gretchen Kimberly, Janeen Alicia, Heidi Karen. B.S., U.S. Naval Acad., 1955. Commd. ensign USN, advanced through grades to vice adm.; engr. officer Nuclear Submarine USS Haddo, 1965-67, exec. officer Fleet Ballistic Missile Submarine, 1967-70, comdg. officer Nuclear Submarine USS Hammerhead, 1970-73, exec. asst., sr. aide Chief Naval Ops., 1973-76, comdr. Submarine Squadron 16, 1976-78, dep. dir. plans and policy OPNAV, 1978-80, dir. strategic and theater nuclear warfare OPNAV, 1980-81, comdr. Submarine Group Two, 1981-83; vice dir. Joint Strategic Target Planning Staff Offutt AFB, Nebr., 1983—. Decorated Legion of Merit (7), 6 other decorations. Mem. AIAA, U.S. Naval Inst., U.S. Naval Acad. Alumnae Assn., Newcomen Soc. Clubs: Ariston, Rotary. Home: Quarters 3 Offutt AFB NE 68113 Office: Joint Strategic Target Planning Staff Offutt AFB NE 68113

CARTER, RICHARD, author; b. N.Y.C., Jan. 24, 1918; s. Samuel J. and Alice (Kulka) C.; m. Gladys Chasins, Oct. 20, 1945; children—Nancy Jane, John Andrew. B.A., Coll. City N.Y., 1938. Music editor Billboard mag., 1940-46; staff organizer N.Y. Newspaper Guild, 1946-47; writer N.Y. Daily Mirror, 1947-49, N.Y. Daily Compass, 1949-52; pres. Millwood Publs., Inc., 1971—. Author; contbr. mags., 1952—; Author: The Man Who Rocked the Boat, 1956, The Doctor Business, 1958, The Gentle Legions, 1961, Your Food and Your Health, 1964, Breakthrough: The Saga of Jonas Salk, 1966, Superswine, 1967, (with Curt Flood) The Way It Is, 1971, (under pseudonym Tom Ainslie) The Compleat Horseplayer, 1966, Ainslie's Jockey Book, 1967, Ainslie's Complete Guide to Thoroughbred Racing, 1968, The Handicapper's Handbook, 1969, Theory and Practice of Handicapping, 1969, Ainslie's Complete Guide to Harness Racing, 1970, Ainslie's Complete Hoyle, 1975, Ainslie's Encyclopedia of Thoroughbred Handicapping, 1978, How to Gamble in a Casino, 1979, (with Bonnie Ledbetter) The Body Language of Horses, 1980. Served with USAAF, 1942-45; PTO. Recipient George Polk Meml. award, 1952. Mem. Authors Guild, Nat. Assn. Sci. Writers, N.A.A.C.P. Address: 165 Pinesbridge Rd Ossining NY 10562

CARTER, RICHARD DUANE, business educator; b. Canton, Ohio, Feb. 27, 1929; s. Herbert Duane and Edith Irene (Richardson) C.; m. Nancy Jean Cannell, Sept. 3, 1955; 1 son, Erich Richardson. A.B., Coll. William and Mary, 1951; M.B.A., Columbia U., 1960; Ph.D., UCLA, 1968. Sr. advisor, dir. Taiwan Metal Industries Devel. Center (under auspices of ILO), 1966-67; dir. UNDP cons. services, Taiwan, 1966-67; chief exec. officer Human Resources Inst., Baton Rouge, La., 1968-70; liaison advisor Internat. Inst. Applied Systems Analysis, Vienna, Austria, 1975; U.S. rep., dir. indsl. mgmt. and cons. services program UN Indsl. Devel. Orgn., Vienna, 1970-75; mem. East-West Trade and Mgmt. Commn., 1973-75; sr. advisor, dir. Korean Inst. Sci. and Tech. (under auspices of UN), Seoul, 1974-75; dean Sch. Bus., Quinnipiac Coll., Hamden, Conn., 1977-80; chmn. bd. TCG Industries, Inc., N.Y.C., 1980—; prof. mgmt., program coordinator Fairfield (Conn.) U., 1980—; founder, mng. dir. Internat. Mgmt. Consortium, Vienna and N.Y.C., 1975—; asso. mem. Columbia U. Seminar on Orgn. and Mgmt., 1976—, chmn. research and publ. com., 1976—. Editorial bd.: Indian Adminstrv. and Mgmt. Rev, New Delhi, 1974—; Author: Management: In Perspective and Practice, 1970, The Future Challenges of Management Education, 1981; also numerous articles and revs. Trustee Dingletown Community Ch., Greenwich, Conn., 1978—; mem. adv. council Am. Poly. U., Los Angeles, 1978—. Fellow Internat. Acad. Mgmt.; mem. Acad. Mgmt., Am. Mgmt. Assns. (pres.'s council, dir. 1976-77), N.Am. Soc. Corp. Planning, Soc. Internat. Orgn. Devel., Beta Gamma Sigma. Office: Fairfield U Fairfield CT 06430 *Success depends upon the art of optimizing the skills of confrontation, accommodation and cooperation.*

CARTER, ROBERT LEE, judge; b. Caryville, Fla., Mar. 11, 1917; s. Robert and Annie (Martin) C.; m. Gloria Spencer, Dec. 4, 1946 (dec. Nov. 1971); children: John Walton, David Christopher. A.B. magna cum laude, Lincoln U., 1937, D.C.L., 1964; LL.B. magna cum laude, Howard U., 1940; LL.M., Columbia U., 1941. Bar: N.Y. 1945. Assp. spl. counsel NAACP, N.Y.C., 1945-46, gen. counsel, 1956-68; mem. firm Poletti, Freidin, Prashker, Feldman & Gartner, N.Y.C., 1969-72; judge U.S. Dist. Ct. So. Dist. N.Y., N.Y.C., 1972—; dir. vets. affairs Am. Vets. Com., Washington, 1948-49; adj. prof. Law Sch., NYU, 1966-70; spl. asst. U.S. atty. So. Dist. N.Y., 1962; mem. N.Y.C. Mayor's Jud. Com., 1968-72. Editorial bd.: N.Y. Law Jour., 1969-72; contbr. articles to profl. jours. Pres. Nat. Com. Against Discrimination in Housing, 1966-72; mem. N.Y. State Spl. Commn. on Attica, N.Y. State Temp. Commn. on Ct. Reform, 1970-72, Am. del. UN Third World Conf. on Crime and the Treatment of Offenders, Stockholm, 1965; bd. dirs. Northside Center Child Devel. Served to 2d lt. USAAF, 1941-44. Rosenwald fellow, 1940-41; Columbia Urban Center fellow, 1968-69; recipient Howard U. Disting. Alumni award, 1980. Mem. Nat. Conf. Black Lawyers (co-chmn. 1968-72). Home: 65 Central Park W New York NY 10023 Office: US Courthouse Foley Sq New York NY 10007

CARTER, RONALD, musician; b. Royal Oak Twp., Mich., May 4, 1937; s. Lutheran Morris and Willie (Howard) C.; m. Janet Clarice Hosbrouck, June 7, 1958; children: Ronald Carter, Myles. B.Mus., Eastman Sch. Music, 1959; Mus.M., Manhattan Sch. Music, 1962. Faculty Nat. State Bank Camp; tchr. U. Buffalo, 1968; tchr. jazz, ensemble, guidance counselor Washington U., St. Louis, 1969; tchr. jazz history Manhattan Sch. Music, N.Y.C. 1st bassist, Eastman Philharmonia, 1959, Manhattan Symphony Orch., 1960-61; formed own quartet, 1975; leader group performing in colls., night clubs.; albums include New York Slick, Parfait, Pastels, Patrao, Peg Leg, Piccolo, Pick 'Em, Song for You, Super Strings; Author 3 tech. books on jazz and classical bass. Named Internat. Jazz Bassist of Year Internat. Jazz Critics-Downbeat Mag., 1965, Jazz Bassist of Decade Detroit Free Press, 1966; Winner Japan All Star Jazz Poll on bass, 1969-70, Downbeat Readers Poll, 1973, 74, 75, 83. Mem. Jazz Musicians Assn. (adv. bd.). First Negro in Rochester (N.Y.) Philharmonic, 1958-59. *

CARTER, ROSALYNN SMITH, wife of former President of United States; b. Plains, Ga., Aug. 18, 1927; d. Edgar and Allie (Murray) Smith; m. James Earl Carter, Jr., July 7, 1946; children: John William, James Earl III, Donnell Jeffrey, Amy Lynn. Grad., Ga. Southwestern Coll.; D.H.L. (hon.), Morehouse Coll., 1980. Author: First Lady from Plains, 1984. Mem. Ga. Gov.'s Commn. to Improve Service for the Mentally and Emotionally Handicapped, 1971-74; vol. Ga. Regional Hosp., Atlanta; hon. chmn. Ga. Spl. Olympics for Retarded Children, Pres.'s Commn. on Mental Health; hon. chmn. bd. trustees John F. Kennedy Center Performing Arts; bd. dirs. Nat. Assn. Mental Health; campaigned independently during 1976 and 1980 Presdl. Campaigns. Recipient Vol. of Yr. award Southwestern Assn. Vol. Services. Address: Plains Ga 31780

CARTER, ROY ERNEST, JR., journalism educator; b. Ulysses, Kans., Apr. 7, 1922; s. Roy Ernest and Inez (Anderson) C.; m. Ruby Maxine Rice, Mar. 28, 1948; children: Phyllis Diane, Patricia Inez, Susan Dolores. B.A., Ft. Hays State Coll., 1948; M.A., U. Minn., 1951; Ph.D., Stanford U., 1954. Reporter, editor, editorial writer various newspapers, 1942-48, high sch. tchr., Hutchinson, Kans., 1948-50; assoc. prof., chmn. dept. journalism Ohio Wesleyan U., 1951-52; acting assoc. prof. journalism, Stanford U., 1952-54; research prof. journalism, mem. Inst. Research in Social Sci. of U. N.C., 1954-58; prof. journalism, sociology and internat. relations U. Minn., 1958—; cons. to marketing, pub. opinion research firms and internat. orgns.; lectr., Quito, Ecuador, 1961; vis. prof. U. Chile, 1962-63, U. Concepción, Chile, 1964, 66-68, U. Costa Rica, 1971, U. Pernambuco, Brazil, 1972, U. P.R., 1978-79. Author: North Carolina Press-Medical Study, 1957, (with R.O. Nafziger, D.M. White et al.) Introduction to Mass Communication Research, 1963; Assoc. editor of: Journalism, Quarterly, 1958-63; Contbr. articles to sci. jours. Recipient Kellogg Found. grant Stanford, 1952-53, sr. Fulbright-Hays award, Chile, 1962-63, Costa Rica, 1971, Social Sci. Research Council grants, 1962-68. Fellow Am. Sociol. Assn.; mem. Assn. Edn. Journalism, World Assn. Pub. Opinion Research, Sigma Delta Chi, Phi Kappa Phi. Episcopalian. Research in Costa Rica, 1975, El Salvador and Chile, 1976, P.R., 1979, Uruguay, 1982-83. Office: 206 Church St SE Minneapolis MN 55455

CARTER, SAMUEL THOMSON, III, author; b. N.Y.C., Oct. 6, 1904; s. Samuel Thomson and Annie Burnham (Washburn) C.; m. Justine Smith, 1929 (div. 1940); children: Peter Burnham (dec.), Dorothy de Longpre, Margo Alison; m. Alison Bigelow Nott, Mar. 1942. B.A., Princeton, 1927, Oxford (Eng.) U., 1929; postgrad., Sorbonne, Paris, 1932-33. V.p. in charge TV Sullivan, Stauffer, Colwell & Bayles, N.Y.C., 1962-67. Author books including: Man of Two Worlds, 1968, The Boatbuilders of Bristol, 1970, Blaze of Glory: The Fight for New Orleans, 1971, The Siege of Atlanta, 1973, The Riddle of Dr. Mudd, 1974, Cherokee Sunset, 1976, The Last Cavaliers, 1979, The Final Fortress, 1980; writer radio and motion picture scripts, Hollywood, 1940-50; scriptwriter, editor, NBC-TV, 1950-62; radio script writer, J. Walter Thompson, N.Y.C., 1931-40. Bd. dirs. Berkshire Farm, Canaan, N.Y. Club: Princeton (N.Y.C.). Address: 67 Walnut Tree Hill Sandy Hook CT 06482

CARTER, SIDNEY, physician; b. Boston, Dec. 8, 1912; s. Jack and Rose (Laurence) C.; m. Elizabeth M. Crosby, Mar. 24, 1945; children: Jeffrey, Jonathan, Jeremy. A.B., Dartmouth, 1934; M.D., Boston U., 1938. Intern St. Mary's Hosp., Waterbury, Conn., 1938-39; resident psychiatry Westboro (Mass.) State Hosp., 1939-40; resident neurology Boston City Hosp., 1940-42; adj. attending neurologist Montefiore Hosp., N.Y.C., 1946-48; mem. staff Columbia-Presbyn. Med. Center, N.Y.C., 1948—, attending neurologist, 1952—, chief div. pediatric neurology, 1952-78; Dwight D. Eisenhower prof. neurology Columbia Coll. Phys. and Surg., 1962-78, prof. emeritus neurology and pediatrics, 1978—. Author articles in field. Served with AUS, 1943-46. Mem. Am. Acad. Neurology (pres.), A.M.A., Assn. Research Nervous and Mental Disease, Am. Epilepsy Soc., Am. Neurol. Assn. (pres.). Home: 53 Rockland Ave Yonkers NY 10705 Office: Blythedale Childrens Hosp Valhalla NY 10595

CARTER, TERRY (JOHN E. DECOSTE), actor, producer, director; b. Bklyn., Dec. 16, 1928; s. William and Mercedes DeCoste; m. Anna Scratuglia, July 5, 1964; children: Miguel Carter DeCoste, Melinda Carter DeCoste. Student, Northeastern U., 1947-49, St. John's U., 1949-51, Boston U. Sch. Public Communications, 1966-68, UCLA Sch. Theater Arts, 1971-72. Pres. META-4 Prodns., Inc. (film and videotape prodn. co.); mem. Calif. Motion Picture Devel. Council, 1978; pres. Council for Positive Images, Inc. Appeared on Broadway: in male lead: Mrs. Patterson, 1954; in title role: Kwamina, 1961; newscaster, Sta. WBZ-TV, Boston, 1965-68; appeared as Sgt. Joe Broadhurst in: TV series McCloud, NBC-TV, 1969-77; as Col. Tigh in: Battlestar Galactica, ABC-TV, 1978-79. Vice pres. Hollywood (Calif.) Wilshire Fair Housing Council, 1970-71, Westside Fair Housing Council, Los Angeles, 1974-75; bd. govs. United Stroke Program. Mem. Acad. Motion Picture Arts and Scis., Acad. TV Arts and Scis. (gov.), Info. Film Producers Am., Am. Nat. Theater and Acad. Office: 8300 Santa Monica Blvd Suite 203 Los Angeles CA 90069

CARTER, THOMAS SMITH, JR., railroad executive; b. Dallas, June 6, 1921; s. Thomas S. and Mattie (Dowell) C.; m. Janet R. Hostetter, July 3, 1946; children: Diane Carter Petersen, Susan Jean, Charles T., Carol Ruth. B.S. in Civil Engring., So. Meth. U., 1944. Registered profl. engr., Mo., Kans., Okla., Tex., La., Ark. Various positions M.-K.-T. R.R., 1941-44, 46-54, chief engr., 1954-61, v.p. operations, 1961-66; v.p. KCS Ry. Co., L & A Ry. Co., 1966—; pres., dir. K.C.S. Ry., 1973—, chmn. bd., 1981—; pres., dir. L & A Ry. Co., 1974—, chmn. bd., 1981—; dir. Kansas City So. Industries. Served with C.E. AUS, 1944-46. Fellow ASCE; mem. Am. Ry. Engring. Assn., Assn. Am. Railroads (dir. 1978—), Nat. Soc. Profl. Engrs. Clubs: Chgo., Kansas City, Shreveport. Home: 9319 W 92d Terr Overland Park KS 66212 Office: 114 W 11th St Kansas City MO 64105

CARTER, TIM LEE, congressman, physician; b. Tompkinsville, Ky., Sept 2, 1910; s. James Clark and Idru (Tucker) C.; m. Kathleen Bradshaw, Nov. 15, 1931. A.B., Western Ky. U.; M.D., U. Tenn., 1937. Pub. sch. tchr., 1927-32; intern U.S. Marine Hosp., Chgo. Maternity Center; practice medicine, Tompkinsville, 1939-42, 46-65; mem. 89th-96th congresses from 5th Dist. Ky., mem. interstate and fgn. commerce com., small bus. com.; engaged in farming, Tompkinsville; owner T.L. Carter Devel. Co.; chief staff Monroe County Meml. Hosp. Served to capt., M.C. AUS, 1942- 46. Decorated Bronze Star; recipient Benjamin Rush award for citizenship and community service, Tom Wallace award for conservation. Mem. AMA, Ky. Med. Assn., Am., Ky. acads. gen. practice, Alpha Omega Alpha. Baptist. Clubs: Masons (33 deg.), Shriners.). Home: 701 N Main St Tompkinsville KY 42167 Office: House Office Bldg Washington DC 20515

CARTER, WILFRED WILSON, mfg. co. exec.; b. Providence, Feb. 22, 1923; s. Leo and Florence (Wilson) C.; m. Elsa Aulisio, June 17, 1950; children—Linda J., Donald J., Paul J., Gregory J. A.A., Roger Williams Coll., 1951; student, Bryant Coll., 1958-62. Sec., tax mgr. Nicholson File Co., East Providence, 1940-73; controller Columbia Chase Corp., Braintree, Mass., 1973—. Served with USAAF, 1942-46. Mem. Tax Exec. Inst., Adminstrv. Mgmt. Soc. Episcopalian (vestryman 1968-76, treas. 1969-76). Club: Mason. Home: 40 Kennedy Blvd Lincoln RI 02865 Office: 220 Forbes Rd Braintree MA 02184

CARTER, WILLIAM CASWELL, computer scientist; b. Waterville, Maine, Jan. 16, 1917; s. Benjamin Edward and Mary Helen (Caswell) C.; m. Virginia Lee Davis, Aug. 14, 1957; children: Benjamin Everett, Candace, Clark Thomas. B.A. magna cum laude, Colby Coll., 1938; postgrad., Oxford U., 1938-39, U. Chgo., 1939-42; Ph.D. in Math.,

Harvard U., 1947. Mathematician, Aberdeen Proving Ground, Md., 1947-52; computer scientist Raytheon Corp., Waltham, Mass., 1952-55, Honeywell Computer Div., 1955-59, IBM T.J. Watson Research Center, Yorktown Heights, N.Y., 1959—; mem. adv. com. systems tech. NASA, 1982—. Contbr. chpts. to books, articles to profl. jours. Mem. Woodbury (Conn.) Charter Revision Com., 1977; mem. Woodbury Democratic Town Com., 1976-77. Served to lt. USNR, 1942-45; PTO. Rhodes scholar, 1938. Fellow IEEE; mem. Assn. Computing Machinery, Phi Beta Kappa. Democrat. Episcopalian. Patentee in field. Home: 3 Shagbark Ln Woodbury CT 06798 Office: IBM TJ Watson Research Center PO Box 218 Yorktown Heights NY 10598

CARTER, WILLIAM GILBERT, lawyer; b. Chgo., Jan. 15, 1927; s. William Curtis and Maye (Corbin) C.; m. Mary Carlyle Fitzgerald, Aug. 20 1955; children: Elizabeth, Sarah, ZoeUTE. B.A., Yale U., 1948; LL.B., Columbia U., 1952. Bar: N.Y. 1953, D.C. 1971. Asso. firm Hughes, Hubbard, Blair & Reed, N.Y.C., 1952-53, Lewis and MacDonald, 1953-54; asso. Coudert Bros. (Paris office), 1954-60, partner, 1961-62; spl. asst. to dept. adminstr. AID, 1962; spl. asst. internat. space communications to asst. sec. state econ. affairs, 1962-64, chief of private investment div., 1964-65; asso. asst. adminstr. for private enterprise AID, State Dept., Washington, 1965-67; asso. asst. adminstr. Office Pvt. Resources, 1967-68, dep. asst. adminstr., 1968-70; cons. Overseas Pvt. Investment Corp. (agy. of U.S. govt.), 1970-71; partner law firm Nicholson & Carter, Washington, 1971-78, Squire, Sanders & Dempsey, 1979—. Trustee Am. Overseas Meml. Day Assos., Inc., 1959-62, Am. Sch. Paris, 1960-62, Am. Library Paris, 1959-62, Am. Coll. Paris, 1961—; Vol. Am. Field Service, 1945. Recipient Superior Honor award Dept. State, 1964, AID, 1970. Mem. Assn. Bar City N.Y., Am. Soc. Internat. Law, Am. Fgn. Law Assn., Am., D.C. bar assns., Chi Psi, Phi Delta Phi. Clubs: Yale (N.Y.C.); Travellers (Paris); Boodles (London); Metropolitan (Washington). Home: 3450 Ordway St NW Washington DC 20016 Office: 1201 Pennsylvania Ave NW Washington DC 20004

CARTER, (WILLIAM) HODDING, III, television anchorman and reporter; b. New Orleans, Apr. 7, 1935; s. William Hodding and Betty Brunhilde (Werlein) C.; m. Margaret Ainsworth, June 21, 1957 (div. 1978); children: Catherine Ainsworth, Elizebeth Fearn, William Hodding IV, Margaret Lorraine; m. Patricia M. Derian, 1978. B.A., Princeton U., 1957; LL.D., Stetson Coll., 1980; Litt.D., Tusculum Coll., 1983. Reporter Delta Democrat-Times, Greenville, Miss., 1959-62, mng. editor, 1962-65, editor, asso. publisher, 1965-77; asst. sec. state for pub. affairs, dept. spokesman Dept. State, Washington, 1977-80; vis. prof. Am. U., 1980; anchorman and chief corr. Inside Story, PBS, 1981—. Author: The South Strikes Back, 1959; contbr. articles to newspapers and mags.; columnist: Wall St. Jour. Co-chmn. Young Democrat Clubs Miss., 1965-68; founding mem. Loyal Dems. of Miss., 1968; mem. O'Hara Rule Reform Commn. Dem. Party, 1969-72; vice chmn. credentials com. Dem. Conv., 1972; mem. Charter Commn. Dem. Party, 1973-74; del. Dem. Conv., 1968, 72, Dem. Mini Conv., Kansas City, Mo., 1974; mem. campaign staff Johnson for Pres., 1964, Carter for Pres., 1976; mem. exec. com. So. Regional Council, 1969-75, Miss. Dem. Party, 1976-79; trustee Princeton U., 1983—; bd. dirs. Am. Com. on East-West Accord. Served with USMC, 1957-59. Nieman fellow Harvard U., 1965-66; Urban Service award OEO, 1967; Silver Em journalism award U. Miss., 1968; Robert F. Kennedy award Miss. Council on Human Relations, 1970; Distinguished Achievement award U. Calif. Sch. Journalism, 1972. Mem. Atlantic Council, Am. Council Young Polit. Leaders, Com. for Nat. Security, Com. for Pub. Justice, Twentieth Century Fund (N.Y.C.).

CARTER, WILLIAM LEE, former mathematics educator; b. Flora, Ill., Jan. 19, 1925; s. Emerson Lee and Zola (King) C.; m. Phyllis Lee Cisne, Oct. 28, 1944; children: Kanda Sue, William Brand. Student, Kenyon Coll., 1943-44; B.S., Eastern Ill. U., 1948; M.A., Ohio State U., 1949, Ph.D., 1952. Tchr. Ashmore (Ill.) High Sch., 1947-48; research asst. Ohio State U., 1948-50; instr. Western High Sch., Macomb, Ill., 1950-52; prof. Coll. of Guam, Agana, 1952-54; prof. edn. U. Cin., 1954-67, asst. dean faculties, 1963-64, asso. dean faculties, officer acad. planning, 1964-66, acting dean Grad. Sch., 1966-67, dean Coll. Edn. and Home Econs., 1966-67; pres Wis. State U., Whitewater, 1967-71; chancellor U. Wis.-Whitewater, 1971-74, Distinguished prof. math. and chancellor emeritus, 1974—; dir. First Citizens State Bank, Whitewater.; Cons. Hamilton County Schs., Cin., 1957-63; Hon. life mem. Ohio Congress P.T.A.; Trustee Alverno Coll., 1974-81, Meml. Hosp., Ft. Atkinson, Wis., 1975—, Hillsdale-Lotspeich Sch., Cin., 1964-67, Lincoln (Ill.) Bible Coll. and Sem., 1983—. Author: Learning to Teach in the Elementary School, 1959, Learning to Teach in the Secondary School, 1962. Served with USAAF, 1943-46; maj. Res. 33813). Mem. Math. Assn. Am., Phi Sigma Epsilon, Phi Delta Kappa, Kappa Delta Pi, Kappa Mu Epsilon, Iota Lambda Sigma (hon. life), Phi Eta Sigma (hon. life), Phi Kappa Phi. Lodges: Masons; Shriners; Kiwanis. Home: 1232 Court St Whitewater WI 53190

CARTER, WILLIAM MINOR, lawyer, ins. co. exec.; b. Balt., May 24, 1940; s. Robert Eugene and Dorothy Martha (Weiss) C.; m. Susan Richwine, Mar. 23, 1963; children—Paige Susanne, Robin Juliette. B.S., U.S. Naval Acad., 1962; J.D., U. Md., 1970. Bar: Md. bar 1970. Counsel Dept. Legis. Reference, Annapolis, Md., 1970; asso. firm Piper and Marbury, Balt., 1971-73; gen. counsel, v.p., sec. Md. Casualty Co., Balt., 1973-80; v.p., govt. and industry affairs U.S. Fidelity & Guaranty Co., 1980—; instr. U. Md. Law Sch., 1976—. Vice chmn. bd. trustees Md. Environ. Trust; chmn. Md. Capitol City Commn., 1977. Commd. ensign U.S. Navy, 1962; advanced through grades to lt. comdr., 1969; ret., 1969. Mem. Am., Md. bar assns. Home: 39 Southgate Ave Annapolis MD 21401 Office: 100 Light St Baltimore MD 21202

CARTER, WILLIAM WALTON, physicist, government official; b. Pensacola, Fla., Nov. 7, 1921; s. Eugene Hudson and Nannie (Ledyard) C.; m. Elizabeth Jean Dedick, June 11, 1945; children—Carolyn A., Susan J., Judith J., Paul W. B.S., Carnegie Inst. Tech., 1943; M.S., Calif. Inst. Tech., 1948, Ph.D., 1949. Atomic, thermonuclear Weapon research and devel., group leader applied physics group, weapons div. Los Alamos Sci. Lab., 1949-59, project leader 1st thermonuclear weapon to enter regular nat. stockpile, also mem. joint working com.; chief scientist Army Missile Command, Redstone Arsenal, 1959-67; asst. dir. nuclear programs, def. research and engring. Office Sec. Def., Washington, 1967-71; assoc. dir. Harry Diamond Labs. U.S. Army, 1971-74, tech. dir., 1975—, also chmn. staff devel. council; coordinator nuclear adv. panel NATO.; Chmn. steering com. Huntsville Research Inst. Served to lt. USNR, 1944-46. Asso. fellow Am. Inst. Aeros. and Astronautics; mem. Am. Phys. Soc., AAAS, Am. Def. Preparedness Assn., Am. Inst. Physics, Assn. U.S. Army. Home: 1124 Ormond Ct McLean VA 22101 Office: Harry Diamond Labs Adelphi MD 20783

CARTERETTE, EDWARD CALVIN HAYES, psychologist; b. Mt. Tabor, N.C., July 10, 1921; s. John Calvin and Alma Olivia (Fowler) C.; m. Patricia Spidel Blum, Jan. 18, 1955 (dec. Jan. 1977); 1 son, Christopher Edward; m. Noël McSherry, Sept. 27, 1980. Diploma, U.S. Army Command and Gen. Staff Coll., 1943; A.B., U. Chgo., 1949, Harvard U., 1952; M.A., Ind. U., 1954; Ph.D. (NSF predoctoral fellow), Ind. U., 1956. Served as enlisted man U.S. Army, 1937-42; commd. 2d lt., 1942, advanced through grades to lt. col., 1946, served in, Hawaii, 1937-41; dep. dir. personnel Hampton Roads Port of Embarcation, Newport News, Va., 1942-45; adj. gen. 32d Inf. Div., Philippines and, Japan, 1945-46; ret., 1946; mem. research staff acoustics lab. M.I.T., 1952; instr. UCLA, 1956-58, asst. prof. psychology, 1958-63, asso. prof., 1963-68, prof., 1968—; vis. asso. prof. U. Calif., Berkeley, 1966; NSF postdoctoral fellow in physics Royal Inst. Tech., Stockholm and Cambridge (Eng.) U., 1960-61; NSF sr. postdoctoral fellow Inst. Math. Studies in Social Scis., Stanford U., 1965-66; cons. neuropsychology VA Wadsworth Hosp. Center, 1978—; chmn. selection com. Woodrow Wilson Nat. Fellowship Found., 1963-72, chmn., 1966-72; mem. editorial com. U. Calif. Press, 1970-77, co-chmn., 1973-77, mem. bd. control, 1973-77; Disting. visitor Am. Psychol. Assn., 1979—. Author: Brain Function: Speech, Language and Communication, 1966, (with Margaret Hubbard Jones) Informal Speech, 1974; editor: (with M.P. Friedman) Handbook of Perception, 11 vols, 1973-78, Academic Press Series in Cognition and Perception, 1973—; asso. editor: Perception and Psychophysics, 1972—, Music Perception, 1981—. Fellow Acoustical Soc. Am., AAAS (electorate nominating com. 1981—), Am. Psychol. Assn., Soc. Exptl. Psychologists (sec.-treas., mem. exec. com. 1982-85, co-chmn. 1977); mem. IEEE, Psychonomic Soc., Internat. Neuropsychol. Soc., Soc. Math. Psychology, Sigma Xi (sec. 1983—). Club: Harvard Radcliffe of So. Calif. Home: 456 Greencraig Rd Los Angeles CA 90049 Office: Dept Psychology U Calif Los Angeles CA 90024

CARTEY, WILFRED GEORGE ONSLOW, educator, author, poet; b. Port-of-Spain, Trinidad, July 19, 1931; U.S., 1955, naturalized, 1972; s. Samuel and Ada C. B.A., U. W. Indies, 1955; M.A., Columbia U., 1956, Ph.D., 1964. Mem. faculty Columbia U., 1957-69; prof. comparative lit. CCNY, 1969-72, disting. prof., 1973-79, disting. prof. dept. black studies, 1979—; Martin Luther King prof. Bklyn. Coll., 1972; vis. scholar, lectr. U. P.R., summer 1959; vis. prof. U. Vt., summer 1964, U. W. Indies, Jamaica, summer 1965, U. Ghana, Legon, 1967-68; resident prof. extra mural dept. U. W. Indies, Nassau, summer 1973; vis. disting. prof. Romance langs. Howard U., 1976; vis. disting. prof. Afro-Am. studies U. Calif., Berkeley, spring 1979. Author: The West Indies; Islands in the Sun, 1967, Black Images, 1970, Palaver, 1970, Whispers from the Continent, 1971, The House of Blue Lightning, 1973, Waters of My Soul, 1975, Red Rain, 1977, Suns and Shadows, 1978, Fires in the Wind, 1980, others; editor: (with Martin Kilson) Colonial Africa, 1971, Independent Africa, 1971; collaborator: Human Uses of the University: Planning a Curriculum in Urban and Ethnic Affairs at Columbia University, 1970; mem. editorial bds. profl. jours.; contbr. articles to profl. jours. Bernard Van Leer Found. fellow, 1955-56; Fulbright grantee, 1955-59; grantee Urban Center, 1970. Mem. African Heritage Studies Assn., African Studies Assn., AAUP, Am. Friends Service Com., Assn. Black and P.R. Faculty, Black Acad. Arts and Letters, Columbia U. Seminars, Hispanic Inst. U.S., African Am. Heritage Assn., Am. Soc. African Culture, Inst. Caribbean Studies, Inst. Black World, MLA, PEN. Office: City Coll NY 138th St and Convent Ave New York NY 10031

CARTHY, MARGARET, college dean; b. N.Y.C., Oct. 15, 1911; d. Patrick and Ellen (Hosburg) C. A.B., Coll. of New Rochelle, 1933; postgrad., Columbia, 1934-36; M.A., Catholic U. Am., 1948, Ph.D., 1957. Asst. to bus. mgr. Tchrs. Coll., Columbia, 1933-37; asst. registrar Coll. of New Rochelle, 1941-49, dean, 1950-57, pres, 1957-61; staff editor New Cath. Ency., 1962-66; editor Corpus Instrumentorum, Inc., 1966-67; asso. prof., asst. dir. gen. edn. program U. Md., College Park, 1968-71, asst. dean undergrad. studies, 1971-75; dean Grad. Sch., Coll. of New Rochelle, 1975—; lectr. Cath. U. Am., 1963-66. Mem. Am. Cath. Hist. Assn., Phi Kappa Phi. Office: 39 Willow Dr New Rochelle NY 10805

CARTIER, CELINE PAULE, librarian, administrator; b. Lacolle, Que., Can., May 10, 1930; d. Henri Rodolphe and Irene (Boudreau) Robitaille; m. Georges Cartier, Nov. 29, 1952; children: Nathalie, Guillaume. Diplome superieur en pedagogie, U. Montreal, 1948, certificats en litterature et linguistique, 1952; diplome de bibliothecaire-documentaliste, Inst. Catholique, Paris, 1962; maîtrise en adminstrn. publique, Ecole Nationale d'Adminstrn. Publique, 1976; maîtrise en bibliothéconomie, U. Montreal, 1982. Dir. Bibliotheque Centrale, Commn. des ecoles catholiques, Montreal, 1964-73; dir. spl. collections U. Quebec, 1973-76, dir. sector libraries, 1976-77; chief gen. library U. Laval, Que., 1977-78, gen. dir. libraries, 1978—. Contbr. articles to profl. jours. Mem. Corp. des Bibliothecaires Profs. de Quebec, Can. Library Assn., ALA, Fedn. Internat. des Assn. de Bibliothecaires et des Bibliotheques, Assn. pour l'avancement des Scis. et des techniques de la documentation. Office: Univ Laval Bibliotheque Cite Universitaire Ste Foy Quebec PQ G1K 7P4 Canada *The guiding principles of any profl. way of life are to some extent indentical to those which direct the personal life of individual: respect for a human being, dignity, and a sense of responsibility and fairness. Intellectual honesty in all its aspects together with a strong desire to achieve specific objectives or ideals constitute the best guarantee for satisfaction and success.*

CARTIER, DIANA, dancer, educator; b. Phila., July 23, 1939; d. Rocco G. and Emma Saulli. Student public schs., Phila. Mem. permanent faculty David Howard Sch. Ballet, 1979—. Leading dramatic dancer, Joffrey Ballet, N.Y.C., 1964-76; ballet mistress, 1976-79. Office: 36 W 62d St New York NY 10023

CARTLAND, BARBARA, author; b. Eng., July 9, 1901; d. Bertram and Polly (Scobell) Cartl; m. Alexander George McCorquodale, 1927 (div. 1933); m. Hugh McCorquodale, Dec. 28, 1936 (dec. 1963); children: Raine (Countess Spencer), Ian, Glen. Student pvt. girls' schs. in, Eng. Lectr., polit. speaker; TV personality (2 lecture tours), Can., 1940. Author hist. novels; hist. biographer, writer on health and phys. fitness; autobiographer, playwright books include; history The Private Life of Elizabeth, Empress of Austria, 1959, Josephine, Empress of France, 1961, Diane de Poitiers, 1962; biography Ronald Cartland, 1942, Polly, My Wonderful Mother, 1956; autobiography The Isthmus Years, 1943, The Years of Opportunity, 1948, I Search for Rainbows, 1967, We Danced All Night, 1971, I Seek the Miraculous, 1978; non-fiction Be Vivid, Be Vital, 1956, Etiquette, 1963, The Many Facets of Love, 1963, Sex and the Teenager, 1964; novels Jigsaw, 1925, Debt of Honour, 1970, The Queen's Messenger, 1971, No Darkness for Love, 1974, The Castle of Fear, 1975, Sweet Adventure, 1976, Rainbow to Heaven, 1976, The Mysterious Maid-Servant, 1977, Love in Hiding, 1977, The Disgraceful Duke, 1977, A Fugitive from Love, 1978, The Explosion of Love, 1979, From Hell to Heaven, 1980, Dreams Do Come True, 1981, From Hate to Love, 1982; many others. County councillor, Hertfordshire, 9 years, hon. services welfare officer, Bedfordshire, 1941-45. Decorated Dames of Grace of St. John Jerusalem. Mem. Nat. Assn. Health (Eng.) (pres.). Listed in Guiness Book of Records as having sold largest number of books in world (300 million), 1981. Office: care Bantam Books 666 Fifth Ave New York NY 10019 *

CARTLEDGE, RAYMOND EUGENE, paper company executive; b. Pensacola, Fla., June 12, 1929; s. Raymond H. and Meddie (Brookins) C.; m. Gale Perry, June 30, 1962; children: John R., Perri Ann, Susan R. B.S., U. Ala., 1952; postgrad., Harvard Bus. Sch., 1970. With Procter & Gamble Co., 1955-56; with Union Camp Corp., Wayne, N.J., 1956-71, 81—, v.p., gen. mgr. Container div., 1981-82, exec. v.p., 1982—, dir., 1983—; pres., chief exec. officer Clevepak Corp., White Plains, N.Y., 1971-80. Served with U.S. Army, 1952-55. Home: 8 Westwind Ct Saddle River NJ 07458 Office: 1600 Valley Rd Wayne NJ 07470

CARTMELL, PETER, banker; b. Clydebank, Scotland, Apr. 30, 1921; came to U.S., 1924, naturalized, 1942; s. George Jack and Kate Banks (Griffin) C.; m. Constance Wingerter, May 26, 1945; children: Virginia, Peter B., Jennifer B., Elizabeth B., George D. B.S. in Bus. Adminstrn., Rutgers U., 1943. With Fidelity Union Bank, Newark, 1946—, pres., 1969—, chmn., 1980—; chmn., dir. Fidelity Union Bancorp.; dir. Foster Wheeler Corp., Thomas & Betts Corp., United Steel & Aluminum Corp. Mayor Borough of Rumson, N.J., 1958-61; trustee Rutgers, The State U. Served to capt. AUS, 1943-46. Mem. Greater Newark C. of C. (vice chmn., dir.), N.J. Bankers Assn. (hon. v.p.), N.J. Hist. Soc. (trustee, gov.), Phi Beta Kappa. Episcopalian. Office: 100 Fidelity Plaza North Brunswick NJ 08905

CARTMELL, VINTON AIKINS, molded wood products company executive; b. Glen Ridge, N.J., Oct. 11, 1925; s. Nathaniel Madison and Madeline (Aikins) C.; m. Jane Ann Thomson, Feb. 16, 1957; children: Jennifer Anne, Geoffrey Wayne Thomson, Matthew Frederick Lindsay, Barbara Jane. Grad., Phillips Acad., 1944; B.S., Yale U., 1949. With Chase Manhattan Bank, 1949-55; with Westvaco Corp., 1955-76, treas., 1968-76; v.p., chief exec. officer, dir. Souhegan Wood Products Inc., Wilton, N.H., 1977—. Served with inf. AUS, 1944-46, 50-52. Decorated Bronze Star. Mem. Chi Phi. Club: Yale (N.Y.C.). Home: 848 Old Peterborough Rd Hancock NH 03449 Office: Wilton NH 03086

CARTMILL, GEORGE EDWIN, JR., hospital administrator; b. Plover, Wis., Dec. 26, 1918; s. George Edwin and Elsie Evelyn (Dobbie) C.; m. Helen Marie Heimburg, Feb. 20, 1948; children: George Thomas, William Charles, Sara Jane. B.S., Central State Tchrs. Coll., Stevens Point, Wis., 1938; M.S., Columbia, 1947. High sch. tchr., Wis., 1938-41; asst. dir. Harper Hosp., Detroit, 1947-50, asso. dir., treas., 1950-52, dir., 1952—, pres., trustee, 1966-74; pres., chief exec. officer Harper-Grace Hosps., Detroit, 1974—; Mem. adv. com. hosps. div. W.K. Kellogg Found., 1956-61; pres. Greater Detroit Area Hosp. Council, 1952; trustee Blue Cross-Blue Shield of Mich., 1952—, vice chmn. bd., 1962—; v.p. Tri-State Hosp. Assembly, 1958-59; com. adminstrn. Wayne State U. Sch. Medicine, 1953-57, adj. asso. prof., 1972—; trustee, v.p. Community Health, Inc., 1968; bd. dirs. Kresge Found., 1977—; mem. Pres.'s Nat. Adv. Com. Health Facilities, 1968, Task Force on Medicaid and Related Programs, HEW, 1970. Served with AUS, 1941-45. Recipient Award of Merit Tri-State Hosp. Assembly, 1965; Meritorious Service award Mich. Hosp. Assn., 1966. Fellow Am. Coll. Hosp. Adminstrs. (regent 1970-72, Gold medal award 1974), Detroit Acad. Medicine (hon.); mem. Am. Dietetics Assn. (hon. mem., adv. bd. 1963-69), Am. Hosp. Assn. (chmn. council adminstrv. practice 1959-62, trustee 1962-68, pres. 1966, Distinguished Service award 1975), Mich. Hosp. Assn. (pres. 1958, trustee 1952-60), Nat., Mich. leagues nursing, Assn. Am. Med. Colls. (exec. council 1970-72, chmn. council of teaching hosps. 1971-72). Presbyn. Clubs: Rotarian. Clubs, Detroit, Detroit Athletic, Country of Detroit, Economic of Detroit (dir. 1971—). Home: 336 Kercheval Ave Grosse Pointe Farms MI 48236 Office: 3990 John R St Detroit MI 48201

CARTON, JOHN HAZELTON, insurance company executive; b. East Tawas, Mich., Oct. 20, 1906; s. Augustus Ceasar and Grace (Hazelton) C.; m. Helen Elizabeth Shepherd, Nov. 7, 1936 (dec.); children: John Shepherd, Ronda Carton Huber; m. Elizabeth McNicol, Nov. 1, 1980. B.A., Antioch Coll., 1928; J.D., George Washington U., 1931. Bar: Mich. 1931. Practiced in, Lansing, Mich., 1932-36; pres., chmn. bd. Wolverine Ins. Co., Battle Creek, Mich., 1946-69, Mich. Title Co., 1961-69; pres. Fed. Life & Casualty Co., Battle Creek, 1952-70; chmn. bd. Secured Ins. Co., 1952-70, Riverside Ins. Co. Am., 1952-70; vice chmn. Fed. Life & Casualty Co., 1970-79, Transam. Ins. Co. of Mich. and; Transam. Ins. Corp. Am. (formerly Riverside & Wolverine Ins. Cos.), Battle Creek, 1969-74, 79—, chmn., 1974-79; vice chmn. Peoples-Union Life Ins. Co., Battle Creek, 1970-78; dir. Mich. Nat. Bank, Union Pump Co., Bill Knapp's Mich. Inc. Mem. adv. council Leila Y. Post Montgomery Hosp., 1970-79; bd. dirs. Mich. United Fund, 1971-74, Calhoun County Heart Assn., 1974-79. Mem. Nat. Assn. Indsl. Insurers (past pres.), Am., Mich. bar assns., Battle Creek Area Devel. Assn. (past pres.), Calhoun County Bar Assn. Clubs: Mason, Country, Athelstan (Battle Creek); Desert Island Country (Rancho Mirage, Calif.). Home: 33 Lakeside Dr Battle Creek MI 49015 Office: 70 W Michigan St Battle Creek MI 49016

CARTON, LAURENCE ALFRED, lawyer; b. Chgo., Oct. 11, 1918; s. Alfred Thomas and Mildred (Wells) C.; m. Ann Fontaine Schmidt, July 2, 1949; childrenKatherine Lynch, Ellen, John Laurence, Mary, Evelyn. Grad., Hotchkiss Sch., Lakeville, Conn., 1936; A.B., Princeton, 1940; J.D., U. Chgo., 1947. Bar: Ill. bar 1947. Since practiced with Gardner, Carton & Douglas (and predecessors), Chgo., mem. firm, 1952—. Trustee Morton Arboretum, Lake Forest Acad.-Ferry Hall, John G. Shedd Aquarium, James C. King Old Men's Home, Chgo. Sunday Evening Club; trustee, chmn. Presbyn. Home. Served as lt. comdr. USNR, 1942-46. Mem. Am., Ill., Lake County, Chgo. bar assns., Chgo. Zool. Soc., Art Inst. Chgo. (gov.), Orchestral Assn., Chgo. Com. Council Fgn. Relations. Clubs: Chicago, University, Onwentsia. Home: 285 W Laurel Ave Lake Forest IL 60045 Office: 1 First National Plaza Chicago IL 60603

CARTON, MARVYN, investment banking company executive; b. N.Y.C., Nov. 10, 1917; s. Jay and Helen (Hornstein) C.; m. Bernice E. Brand, June 29, 1941; children: Dana (Mrs. Anthony S. Caprio), John. A.B., Brown U., 1938; M.B.A., N.Y.U., 1948. Navigator, chief flight instr. Nav. Sch., Am. Airlines, 1940-45; analyst Am. Securities Corp., N.Y.C., 1946-48; exec. v.p., mem. exec. com., dir. Allen & Co., Inc., N.Y.C., 1948—; chmn. fin. com., dir. Fischbach and Moore, Inc., Syntex Corp.; chmn. finance com., mem. exec. com., mem. audit com., mem. compensation com., dir. Frank B. Hall & Co., Inc.; dir., mem. audit com. Barco of Calif.; mem. audit com., mem. fin. com., dir. Standards Brands Paint Co., Rockcor. Trustee Brown U. Club: Royal Motor Yacht (Poole, Eng.). Home: 2 E 70th St New York NY 10021 Office: 711 Fifth Ave New York NY 10022

CARTWRIGHT, ALTON STUART, electrical manufacturing company executive; b. Casper, Wyo., Oct. 7, 1922; s. Alton Stuart and Blanche Susan (Harper) C.; m. Adelaide Frances Igoe, Dec. 22, 1951; children: Stuart Andrew, Matthew Alton, David Francis, Patrick Harper. B.S. in Elec. Engring, Oreg. State U., 1944; grad., Advanced Mgmt. Program, Harvard U., 1969. Registered profl. engr., Mass. With Gen. Electric Co., 1946—; with Canadian Gen. Electric Co. Ltd., 1970—, exec. v.p., Toronto, Ont., 1972, pres., 1972-77, chmn. bd., chief exec. officer, 1977—, also dir.; dir. Dominion Engring. Works Ltd., Montreal, Que., Can. Bd. dirs. Wellesley Hosp. Research Council. Served to 1st lt. AUS, 1942-46. Mem. Bus. Council on Nat. Issues, Canadian Mfrs. Assn., Elec. and Electronic Mfrs. Assn. Can., Conf. Bd. Inc., Conf. Bd. of Can. (exec. council), Can. C. of C., Newcomen Soc., Sigma Alpha Epsilon. Clubs: Toronto, Canadian, Empire, Toronto Lawn Tennis, No. Lake George Yacht. Home: 259 Dunvegan Rd Toronto ON M5P 2P5 Canada Office: 25 King St W Toronto ON M5L 1J2 Canada

CARTWRIGHT, HOWARD E(UGENE), assn. exec.; b. Kenosha, Wis., Nov. 19, 1924; s. Raymond W.A. and Theresa (Peterson) C.; m. Evelyn Tieckelmann, June 11, 1949; children—Thomas, Mark, Bradley, Jeffrey. B.A., Carthage Coll., 1946; M.S., Northwestern U., 1950. Reporter LaPorte (Ind.) Herald-Argus, 1949-50; editorial writer Lindsay-Schaub Newspapers, Decatur, Ill., 1950-56; speech writer, dept. head AMA, Chgo., 1956-66; communications dir. A.C.S., Chgo., 1966-67; asst. exec. dir. Coll. Am. Pathologists, Skokie, Ill., 1967-72, exec. dir., 1972—; bd. dirs. Coll. Am. Pathologists Found. Mem. Am. Soc. Assn. Execs., Am. Assn. Med. Soc. Execs. Presbyterian. Home: 591 Forest Hill Lake Forest IL 60045 Office: 7400 N Skokie Blvd Skokie IL 60077

CARTWRIGHT, PHILIP WINDSOR, economics educator; b. Pasadena, Calif., Mar. 24, 1919; s. Theodore Carl and Lo Elizabeth (Norris) C.; m. Charlotte Marie Lombardi, Sept. 3, 1941; children: Karen, Morgan, Christine, Theodore. Student, Pasadena Jr. Coll., 1936-38; A.B., Stanford U., 1940, M.A., 1942, Ph.D., 1950. Instr. econs., accounting Stanford U., 1941-42, 46-47; prof. econs. U. Wash., Seattle, 1947—, dean Arts and Scis., 1966-70, exec. v.p., 1970-76, Equal Employment officer, 1976—; Mem. Gov.'s Tax Adv. Council, 1966-70, 82, Gov.'s Council Econ. Advisers, 1968-76, Seattle-King County Econ. Devel. Council, 1972-76; dir. Office Price Stblzn., Seattle Dist., 1951-52. Author: Unemployment Compensation and the Allocation of Resources, 1959, A Measure of the Utilization of Labor in Economy, 1958, The Economics of Deaning: The Care and Feeding of Homo Academicus, 1965. Served with USNR, 1942-46. Ford Found. fellow, 1942-46. Mem. Western Econ. Assn. (pres. 1964), Am. Econ. Assn., Council Colls. Arts and Scis. (pres. 1969), Phi Beta Kappa. Home: The Highlands Seattle WA 98177 Office: University of Washington Seattle WA 98195

CARTWRIGHT, ROBERT EUGENE, lawyer; b. Fresno, Calif., July 9, 1925; s. Joseph Leslie and Isabelle (Jacobsen) C.; m. Dorothy Christopherson, Dec. 5, 1953; children—Robert E., Jr., Caroline. B.S., U. Calif., Berkeley, 1949, LL.B., 1951. Bar: Calif. bar 1952, diplomate: Am. Bd. Trial Advocates (chpt. pres.). Asso. firm Brubeck, Phlege & Harrison, San Francisco, 1951-52, Shirley, Saragan, Cartwright & Peterson, 1952-66; sr. partner firm Cartwright, Sucherman, Slobodin & Fowler, Inc., San Francisco, 1966—. Author: California Products Liability Actions, 1970; Asso. editor: Calif. Trial Lawyers Assn. Quar. Jour, 1970-75; Contbr. articles to legal publs. Served with USAAC, 1944-46. Fellow Internat. Acad. Trial Lawyers, Am. Coll. Trial Lawyers, Internat. Soc. Barristers; mem. San Francisco Trial Lawyers (pres.), Calif. Trial Lawyers Assn. (pres.), Western Trial Lawyers Assn. (pres.), Assn. Trial Lawyers Am. (nat. pres. 1974-75), San Francisco Lawyers Club (pres.), Western Trial Lawyers Assn. (pres.), Calif. Bar Assn. (mem. exec. com.), Am. Judicature Soc., San Francisco Bar Assn. Home: 850 Hayne Rd Hillsborough CA 94010 Office: 160 Sansome St San Francisco CA 94104

CARTWRIGHT, WALTER JOSEPH, educator; b. Carona, Kans., Apr. 26, 1922; s. James William and Agnes (Whitehead) C.; m. Elizabeth Daniel Atkins, June 6, 1948; children: Joseph Daniel, Deborah. Student, Texarkana Coll., 1939-41; A.B., So. Meth. U., 1943, M.Th., 1946; M.A., U. Tex., 1960, Ph.D., 1964. Ordained to ministry Methodist Ch., 1944; pastor, McLeod-Lodi, Tex., 1944-45, Douglassville, Tex., 1945-47, Mount Pleasant, Tex., 1948, Johnson City, Tex., 1948-49, Hebbronville, Tex., 1949-52, Weimar, Tex., 1952-55, Goldthwaite, Tex., 1955-58, Bastrop, Tex., 1958-62; asst. prof. Tex. Tech U., Lubbock, 1962-65, asso. prof., 1965-68, prof., dept. sociology, 1968—, chmn., 1968-74. Author: (with Mhyra S. Minnis) Sociological Perspectives, 1968; contbr. articles to profl. jours. Cons. Tex. Commn. on Alcoholism, 1965-67; mem. South Plains Area Aging Adv. Com., 1973—; mem. projects bd. Internat. Center Arid and Semi-Arid Land Studies, 1968-74, Lubbock Met. Council Govts. Com. Crime Prevention, 1966-70, Tech. Adv. Com. Canyon Lakes Project, Lubbock, 1970-71; manpower com. Lubbock County Community Action Agy., OEO, 1967-70; bd. dirs. Golden Age Home, Lockhart, Tex., Coordinating Bd. Tex. Coll. and Univ. System. Mem. Am., So., Southwestern sociol. socs., Law and Soc. Assn., Rocky Mountain, Southwestern social sci. assns., AAUP, Phi Beta Kappa (hon.). Home: 7904 Joliet Ave Lubbock TX 79423 Office: Dept Sociology Texas Tech Univ Lubbock TX 79409

CARTWRIGHT, WILLIAM HOLMAN, teacher educator emeritus; b. Pine Island, Minn., Sept. 12, 1915; s. William Holman and Ada Caroline (Frisbie) C.; m. Elaine Mary McGladrey, Sept. 3, 1934; children: John Morris, Mary Elaine, Margaret Ann. B.S., U. Minn., 1937, M.A., 1942, Ph.D., 1950. Dairy farmer, 1934-36, tchr. pub. sch., Mabel, Minn., 1937-40, Rochester, Minn., 1940-43; tchr. Univ. High Sch., Mpls., 1943-45; instr. U. Minn., 1943-45, Macalester Coll., 1944; historian Mil. Dist., Washington, 1945-46; asst. prof. edn. Boston U., 1946-50, asso. prof., 1950-51; prof. edn. Duke, 1951-82, prof. emeritus, 1982—, chmn. dept. edn., 1951-65, 67-70, chmn. acad. council, 1969-71; vis. prof. summers U. Calif., 1950, U. Colo., 1957; pres. So. Council on Tchr. Edn., 1959; curriculum cons.; staff James B. Conant Study of Edn. Am. Tchrs., 1961-63. Author: A History of Newburg Township and the Village of Mabel, 1943, The Military District of Washington during the War Years, 1946, (with Arthur C. Bining) The Teaching of History in the United States, 1950, (with Miriam E. Mason) Trailblazers of American History, 1961, rev. 1966, (with Oscar O. Winther) The Story of Our Heritage, 1962, last rev. edit., 1971, (with Edgar B. Wesley) Teaching Social Studies in Elementary Schools, 1968; also chpts. in yearbooks The National Council Social Studies; numerous articles, revs. ednl., hist. publs.; Editor: (with Richard L. Watson, Jr.) Interpeting and Teaching American History, 1961, The Reinterpretation of American History and Culture, 1973. Recipient Army Commendation Ribbon for hist. writing, 1946; Outstanding Achievement award U. Minn., 1959. Mem. Nat. Council Social Studies (pres. 1957), Am. Hist. Assn., NEA, N.E. History Tchrs. Assn. (pres. 1949-50), N.C. Council Social Studies (Distinguished Service award 1976), Phi Delta Kappa, Phi Alpha Theta, Pi Gamma Mu, Kappa Delta Pi. Unitarian. Home: Box 705 Seven Lakes West End NC 27376

CARTY, DONALD JOHN, airline company financial executive; b. Toronto, July 23, 1946; U.S., 1978; s. Roland Kenneth and Catherine Elizabeth Gordon (Matheson) C.; m. Sharon Louise Smith, May 30, 1970; children: Michael Patrick, Catherine Rebecca, William Robert Douglas. B.S., Queen's U., Kingston, Ont., 1968; M.B.A., Harvard U., 1971. With Air Can., Montreal, 1971-74, Cleanese Can. Ltd., 1974-78; sr. v.p. fin. Americana Hotels, N.Y.C., 1978-79; v.p. Am. Airlines, Dallas-Ft. Worth Airport, 1979-83; sr. v.p., controller AMR Corp.-Am. Airlines Inc., 1983—; pres. Caribbean Data Services, Barbados, B.W.I., 1983; DIR. Airline Tariff Pub. Co., 1983—. Elder Woodhaven Presbyterian Ch., Irving, Tex., 1983; mem. univ. council Queen's U., 1981—. Mem. Air Transport Assn. (mem. econs. and fin. council 1981-83, chmn. econs. and fin. council 1983), fin. Execs. Inst. Clubs: Las Colinas Country; Las Colinas Sports (Irving). Home: 509 Balboa Dr Irving TX 75062 Office: Am Airlines PO Box 61616 Dallas-Ft Worth Airport TX 75261

CARUCCI, SAMUEL ANTHONY, lawyer; b. Bronx, N.Y., Dec. 16, 1935; s. Anthony and Rose (Russo) C.; m. Joan Elizabeth Kelly, Aug. 18, 1962; children—Patricia, Caroline, Samuel. B.S., N.Y.U., 1956; LL.B., St. John's U., 1959. Bar: N.Y. bar 1960. Atty. Corp. Trust Co., 1960-63; asst. legal counsel, asst. sec. Royal McBee Corp., 1963-65; counsel office communications equipment group Litton Industries, N.Y.C., 1966-72; counsel Litton Industries Credit Corp., 1965-71; sec., corporate counsel Olivetti Corp. Am., 1972-74; sec., counsel Eutectic Corp., Flushing, N.Y., 1974—. Served with AUS, 1959-60. Mem. Am. Bar Assn., N.Y. State Bar Assn., Bar Assn. City N.Y., Licensing Execs. Soc., U.S. Trademark Assn., Phi Lambda Phi, Delta Theta Phi. Roman Catholic. Home: 34 Country Club Dr Manhasset NY 11030 Office: 40-40 172d St Flushing NY 11358

CARUS, MILTON BLOUKE, chemical company executive, publisher; b. Chgo., June 15, 1927; s. Edward H. and Dorothy (Blouke) C.; m. Marianne Sondermann, Mar. 3, 1951; children: Andre, Christine, Inga. B.S. in Elec. Engring, Calif. Inst. Tech., 1949; postgrad., Mexico City Coll., summer 1949, U. Freiburg, Sorbonne, Paris, 1951. Devel. engr. Carus Chem. Co., Inc., LaSalle, Ill., 1951-55, asst. gen. mgr., 1955-61, exec. v.p., 1961-64, pres., 1964—, Carus Corp., LaSalle, 1967—; editor Open Ct. Pub. Co., LaSalle, 1962-67, pub., pres., 1967—; Chmn. Ill. Valley Community Coll. Com., 1965-67; pres. Internat. Baccalaureat N.Am. Inc., 1977, chmn., 1980; mem. IBO Council, Geneva, 1977—; co-trustee Hegeler Inst., 1968; mem. employment and tng. com. U.S. Chamber Edn., 1981-82; mem. Nat. Council on Ednl. Research Nat. Inst. Edn., Dept. Edn., 1982. Served with USNR, 1945-46. Mem. Ill. Valley Indsl. Assn. (pres. 1970—), Chem. Mfrs. Assn. (dir. 1977-80), Ill. Mfrs. Assn. (dir. 1972-77), LaSalle County Hist. Soc. (dir. 1979—), Phila Soc. Office: 1500 8th St La Salle IL 61301

CARUTHERS, ROBERT MACK, petroleum engr., educator; b. Shreveport, La., Jan. 19, 1938; s. John DeWitt and Veva (Ozley) C.; m. Valleau Renee Resweber, June 25, 1960; children—Carol Renee, Aimee Katharine, Shelton DeWitt. B.S. in Liberal Arts, La. Tech U., 1960, 1961; Ph.D., U. Tex., 1965. Registered profl. engr., La. Reservoir engr. Humble Oil & Refining Co., Dallas, 1965, New Orleans, 1965-67; head dept. petroleum engring. La. Tech U., Ruston, 1967—; Dir. emeritus Homer Nat. Bank; dir. Ruston State Bank. Chmn. Lincoln Parish chpt. A.R.C., 1968-70; treas. Lincoln Parish chpt. La. Assn. Mental Health; chmn., treas. La. Peach Festival, 1973-81; Bd. dirs., pres., treas. Wesley Found.; v.p., pres., bd. dirs. La. Tech Alumni Found.; bd. dirs., v.p. Ruston Civic Symphony. Named Alumnus of Year La. Tech U., 1973. Mem. Am. Inst. M.E. (edn. and accreditation com. of Soc. of Petroleum Engrs. sect.), Am. Soc. Engring. Edn., La. Engring. Soc. Methodist (adminstrv. bd.). Home: 430 Forest Circle Ruston LA 71270

CARVEL, ELBERT NOSTRAND, former governor of Delaware, fertilizer company executive; b. Shelter Island Heights, N.Y., Feb. 9, 1910; s. Arnold Wrightson and Elizabeth (Nostr) C.; m. Ann Hall Valliant, Dec. 17, 1932; children: Elizabeth Nostrand Carvel Palmer, Edwin Valliant, Ann Hall, Barbara Jean Carvel Krahn. Engring. course, Balt. Poly. Inst., 1924-28; J.D., U. Balt., 1931. Sales engr. Consol. Gas and Electric Power and Light Co., Balt., 1931-36; gen. mgr. and dir. Valliant Fertilizer Co., Laurel, Del., 1936-45; dir. Beneficial Corp., Western Auto Co., Kansas City; pres. Valliant Fertilizer Co., 1945-72, chmn. bd., 1972-82, chmn. emeritus, 1982—; dir. Milford Fertilizer Co., Del., 1937—, v.p., 1941-59, chmn. bd., 1959-82, chmn. emeritus, 1982—; chmn. Fischer Enterprises, 1969-75; v.p. Laurel Grain Co., 1965-75; dir. Beneficial Nat. Bank, 1967—; chmn. bd. Peoples Bank and Trust Co., 1975—; dir. Central Gain Co.; lt. gov. Del., 1945-49, gov., 1949-53, 61-65; mem. exec. com. Govs.' Conf., 1950-51, 62-63; mem. Del. Jud. Nominating Commn., 1977—, Del. Com. on Judiciary, 1980—; Vice pres. Del. Safety Council; exec. bd. Delmarva council Boy Scouts Am.; mem. Del. Bicentennial Commn., 1968-71; pres. Del. Bd. Pardons, 1945-49; chmn. Delmarva Ecumenical Council, 1970-72, mem. exec. com., 1970-76; mem. adminstrv. bd., co-chmn. Delawareans for Orderly Devel., 1971—; mem. Del. Bicentennial Medal Commn., 1973-74; del. Continental Congress Bicentennial, Phila., 1974; Chmn. Del. Democratic Com., 1946-47, 54-56; del. Dem. Nat. Conv., 1948, 52, 56, 60, 64; jointly nominated Adlai Stevenson Dem. candidate for pres. nat. conv., 1952; chmn. Del. Dem. Renewal Commn., 1970, Del. Tax Study Commn., 1973-74; Dem. candidate U.S. Senate, Del., 1958, 64; chmn. Del. Const. Revision Commn., 1968-70. Trustee U. Del., 1945—, vice chmn. bd. trustees, 1972—; trustee U. Balt., 1968-74; chmn. March of Dimes of Del., 1952-62; bd. dirs. Del. Wild Lands, Kent Island Heritage Soc., 1975—. Decorated comdr. Order Orange Nassau, Netherlands; recipient Good Govt. award Com. of 39, Wilmington, 1964, Good Citizenship medal Nat. Soc. S.A.R., 1967, Vrooman award Prisoners Aid Soc. Del., 1965, Silver Beaver award Boy Scouts Am., 1970, Del. award NCCJ, 1979, Liberty Bell award Del. Bar Assn., 1982; named Alumnus of Yr. Balt. Poly. Inst., 1979, U. Balt. Law Sch., 1981. Mem. Lewes, Milford hist. socs., Wilmington Savs. Fund Soc. Del. Hist. Soc., Del. Ducks Unlimited, Swedish Colonial Soc. Del., Sigma Delta Kappa, Alpha Zeta. Episcopalian (del. gen. conv. 1946, 52). Clubs: Mason (Shriner) (33 deg.); Lion., Tall Cedars of Lebanon, Antique Automobile of America, Del. Motor (v.p.), Lincoln of Del.). Elbert N. Carvel State Office Bldg. named in his honor, Wilmington, 1980. Address: Box 111 Laurel DE 19956 *We do not always achieve a specific goal, but high goals and high ideals will advance anyone well on the road of success. As governor of Delaware, I determined to follow a course of strict honesty and the dedication to the ideals in which I believed, regardless of political expediency or pressure. Although there were political setbacks when I bucked the will of my political party where I thought they were wrong, in the final analysis, my fight for principle proved to be correct, and my party always supported me when I was a candidate.*

CARVER, CALVIN REEVE, public utility holding company executive; b. East Orange, N.J., Mar. 14, 1925; s. Harry Eugene and Rena Fichter (Reeve) C.; m. Emma G. Carver, Dec. 8, 1951 (dec. 1977); children: Marthanne G., Calvin Reeve, Gilbert H.; m. 2d June G. Carver, Jan. 10, 1982. B.S. in E.E., Cornell U., 1947. Vice pres. Syracuse Sub. Gas Co, East Syracuse, N.Y., 1952-68; v.p., then pres. City Gas Cos., Flemington, N.J., 1952-65, also dir.; v.p., then pres. Penn-Jersey Pipe Line, Elizabeth, N.J., 1952—, also dir.; v.p. Elizabethtown Gas, Elizabeth, 1965-75, also dir., 1965—; chmn. Lenape Resources, Elizabeth, 1981—, also dir.; pres. Pomfret Prodn. Co., Inc., Elizabeth, 1981—, also dir.; exec. v.p. Nat. Utilities and Industries Corp., Elizabeth, 1969—, also dir. Served with USN, 1943-47; served to lt. USN, 1950-52. Republican. Congregationalist. Club: Short Hills. Office: NUI Corp One Elizabeth Plaza Elizabeth NJ 07207

CARVER, DAVID HAROLD, physician, educator; b. Boston, Apr. 18, 1930; s. Elias and Lottie (Jaffe) C.; m. Patricia Jo Nair, Aug. 3, 1963; children: Randolph Nair, Rebecca Lynn, Leslie Allison. A.B. magna cum laude, Harvard U., 1951; M.D., Duke U., 1955. Intern Johns Hopkins Hosp., 1955-56; research fellow pediatrics Cleve. Met. Hosp., 1956-58; jr. asst. resident Children's Hosp. Med. Center, Boston, 1958-59, sr. asst. resident, 1959-60, chief resident, 1960-61, USPHS spl. post doctoral research fellow, 1961-63; asst. prof. pediatrics Albert Einstein Coll. Medicine, 1963-66; assoc. prof., then prof. Johns Hopkins U. Med. Sch., 1966-76; prof. pediatrics, chmn. dept. U. Toronto Med. Sch., 1976—; physician-in-chief Hosp. Sick Children, Toronto, 1976—; mem. study sect. USPHS Ctr. Disease Control, 1971-73; mem. provincial research grants rev. com. Ont. Ministry Health, 1977-83, chmn., 1981-83. Assoc. editor: Textbook of Pediatrics, 14th edit, 1968, 15th edit., 1972, 16th edit., 1977; editorial bd.: Pediatrics, 1973-79. Served with USPHS, 1956-58. Recipient Schaffer award clin. teaching Johns Hopkins U. Med. Sch., 1973, Bain award for clin. teaching Hosp. Sick Children, 1978, Kennedy sr. scholar, 1966-73. Mem. Am. Acad. Pediatrics (Com. on infectious diseases 1973-79), Infectious Disease Soc. Am., Am. Soc. Virology, Internat. Soc. Interferon Research, Canadian Infectious Disease Soc., Am. Soc. Microbiology, Soc. Pediatric Research, Am., Canadian pediatric socs. Club: Harvard of Toronto. Home: 17 Lynwood Ave Toronto ON Canada M4V 1K3 Office: 555 University Ave Toronto ON Canada M5G 1X8

CARVER, KENDALL LYNN, ins. co. exec.; b. Spencer, Iowa, Nov. 4, 1936; s. Marion and Letha G.; m. Carol Lee Spiers, July 1, 1961; children: Merrian, Kendra, Lee, Christine. B.S., U. Iowa, 1958. Rep. field sales Washington Nat. Ins. Co., Evanston, Ill., 1958-73, regional dir., 1974-77, pres., N.Y.C., 1977—, chief exec. officer, 1978—; also mem. exec. com., chmn. fin. com., dir. C.L.U.; chmn. com. seminars Ins. Council N.Y. Fellow Life Mgmt. Inst.; mem. Nat. Assn. Life Underwriters, Am. Coll. Life Underwriters, Life Ins. Council N.Y. (dir. 1979-82). Republican. Home: 5 Tanglewood Tr Darien CT 06820 Office: Washington Nat Life Ins Co NY 500 Fifth Ave New York NY 10036

CARVER, LOYCE CLEO, clergyman; b. Decaturville, Tenn., Dec. 13, 1918; s. Oscar Price and Mae Joanne (Chumney) C.; m. Mary Rebecca Frymire, Dec. 14, 1940; children—Judith Ann Carver Tyson, Linda Carver Sheals, Rebecca Carver Bishop. Ordained to ministry Apostolic Faith, 1947; real estate appraiser, dep. county tax assessor, Klamath County, Oreg., 1943-44; bookkeeper Pacific Fruit Co., Klamath Falls, Oreg. and; Los Angeles, 1945-47; pastor Apostolic Faith Ch., Dallas, Oreg., 1948-49, San Francisco, 1949-52, Los Angeles, 1952-56, Medford, Oreg., 1956-65; gen. overseer Apostolic Faith, Portland, Oreg., 1965—; chmn. bd. dirs. World-Wide Movement, 1965—, trustee, 1959-65, pres., 1965—. Editor: Light of Hope, 1965—. Served with USNR, 1944. Home: 3322 SE Raymond St Portland OR 97202 Office: 6615 SE 52d Ave Portland OR 97206

CARVER, MARTIN GREGORY, manufacturing company executive; b. Muscatine, Iowa, May 10, 1948; s. Roy James and Lucille Avis (Young) C. B.A., U. Iowa, 1970; M.B.A., U. Ind., 1972. Asst. treas. Consol. Foods Corp., 1975-79; Regional v.p. heavy duty parts, then vice chmn. Bandag, Inc. (retreaded tires mfrs.), Muscatine, 1979-81, chmn. bd., chief exec. officer, 1981—; dir. Ring King Visibles. Clubs: Rotary, 33. Address: Bandag Inc Bandag Center Muscatine IA 52761

CARVER, NORMAN F., JR., architect, photographer; m. Joan Willson; children: Norman III, Cristina. Grad., Yale. Practice architecture, Kalamazoo; prof. advanced photography Kalamazoo Inst. Arts, 1971—; vis. lectr., critic Carnegie Inst. Tech., Mich. State U., Yale U., MIT; guest lectr. King Faisal U., Saudi Arabia, 1981. Exhibited photography, U.S. and abroad; photographs pub. in Aperture, House Beautiful, Horizon; others.; Author: photographs of Japan Form and Space of Japanese Architecture, 1955; Silent Cities: Mexico and the Maya, 1966, Italian Hilltowns, 1979, Iberian Villages - Spain and Portugal, 1981, Japanese Architecture, vol. I, 1983. Recipient Fulbright awards to Japan, 1953-54, 64; silver medal Archtl. League, 1962; award Archtl. Record, 1960, 61, 62. Address: 3201 Lorraine Kalamazoo MI 49008

CARVER, RAYMOND, author, educator; b. Clatskanie, Oreg., May 25, 1938; s. Clevie Raymond and Ella Beatrice (Casey) C.; m. Maryann Burk, June 7, 1957 (div. Oct. 1982); children: Christine LaRae, Vance Lindsay. A.B., Humboldt State U., 1963; M.F.A., U. Iowa, 1966. Lectr. creative writing U. Calif., Santa Cruz, 1971-72, vis. prof. English, Berkeley, 1972-73; vis. lectr. Writers' Workshop, U. Iowa, 1973-74; mem. faculty writing program Goddard Coll., 1977-78; vis. disting. writer U. Tex., El Paso, 1978-79; prof. English Syracuse (N.Y.) U., 1980-83. Author: poetry Near Klamath, 1968, Winter Insomnia, 1970, At Night The Salmon Move, 1976; short stories Put Yourself in My Shoes, 1974, Will You Please be Quiet, Please?, 1976, Furious Seasons, 1977, What We Talk About When We Talk About Love, 1981, Cathedral, 1983; essays, poetry, short stories Fires, 1983. Recipient Strauss Living award Am. Acad. and Inst. Arts and Letters, 1983—; Nat. Endowment Arts fellow in poetry, 1971; fellow in fiction, 1980; Wallace Stegner fellow, 1972-73; Guggenheim fellow, 1979-80. Mem. PEN, Author's Guild. Office: Dept English Syracuse U Syracuse NY 13210

CARVER, RICHARD E., mayor; b. Des Moines, Aug. 28, 1937; s. Maurice Swan and Alice Cecilia (Ellison) C.; m. Judith S. Carver, July 18, 1959; children: Kathryn, Stephen, Cynthia, Susan. B.S. in Bus. Adminstrn, Bradley U., 1959. Pres. Carver Lumber Co., Peoria, Ill.; dir. Provident Fed. Savs. & Loan Assn., Peoria, L.R. Nelson Mfg. Co.; alderman, Peoria, 1969-73, mayor of Peoria, 1973—; Mem. U.S. Conf. Mayors, 1973—; chmn. com. on criminal and social justice, past pres.; pres. Nat. Conf. Republican Mayors; v.p., mem. steering com. community devel. Ill. Municipal League; chmn. Ill. Local Govt. Adv. Council; mem. adv. council Nat. League Cities; mem., chmn. housing programs com. Pres.'s Commn. on Housing; del. UN Conf. Human Settlement (Habitat), 1976; bd. dirs. United Rep. Fund. Ill.; del. Rep. Nat. Conv., 1976. Mem. nat. council advisors Bradley U. Coll. Bus. Adminstrn.; mem. exec. com., dir. Ill. State C. of C.; mem. Peoria Area Hosp. Council, Ill. Jobs Training Coordinating Council; dir. Methodist Med. Ctr. Ill., Econ. Devel. Council for Peoria Area. Served to lt. col. USAFR; coordinator admissions counseling U.S. Air Force Acad. Recipient B'nai B'rith Citizenship award, 1974; named Downstate Ill. Tri-county Citizen of Yr., 1974; Magnificent Gentlemen Citizen of Yr., 1974; Peoria's Most Outstanding Man of Yr., 1974; Nat. Disting. Alumnus award Phi Gamma Delta, 1983. Mem. Retail Lumber Dealers Assn., Bradley U. Urban Affairs Inst., Ill. State C. of C. Office: Office of Mayor City Hall 419 Fulton St Peoria IL 61602

CARVER, ROBERT VERNON, research physicist; b. Mpls., June 2, 1932; s. Walter Burdette and Daveda Margaret (Hansen) Garver; m. Shirley Marie Phillips, June 15, 1957; children: Debra, Douglas, Daniel, Mary, Jennifer. B.S., U. Md., 1956; M.E.A., George Washington U., 1968. Physicist Harry Diamond Labs., Washington, 1956-69, supervisory physicist, Adelphia, Md., 1969—; cons. Weinschel Engring., Gaithersburg, Md., 1970-75. Author: Microwave Diode Control Devices, 1976; patentee in field. Elder Presbyn. Ch., Germantown, Md., 1975. Served with U.S. Army, 1953-54. Fellow IEEE (editor Jour. Solid State Circuits 1969-73, mem. nat. adminstrv. com. porfl. group on microwave theory and techniques); mem. Sigma Pi. Republican. Lodge: Toastmasters. Home: 12205 Greenridge Dr Boyds MD 20841 Office: US Army Harry Diamond Labs 2800 Powder Mill Rd Adelphi MD 20738

CARVER, STEVEN, motion picture director; b. Bklyn., Apr. 5, 1945; s. Murray Leonard and Frances C. B.F.A., U. Buffalo, 1966; M.F.A., Washington U., St. Louis, 1968; student, Am. Film Inst.-Center for Advanced Studies, Beverly Hills, Calif., 1970-71. Tchr. film-making, art, photography Florrissant Valley Coll., Mo., 1966-68, Met. Ednl. Council in Arts, St. Louis, 1966-68. Dir.: Lone Wolf McQuade, Orion Pictures, 1983, An Eye for An Eye, Avco Embassy, 1981, Steel, Columbia Pictures, 1979, Moonbeam Rider, Universal Studios, 1977, Drum, Dino DeLaurentiis, 1976, Capone, New World Pictures (20th Century Fox), 1975, Big Bad Mama, 1974, The Arena, 1973; dir., producer, writer, cinematographer, editor: The Tell-Tale Heart, Am.

Film Inst., 1971, Patent, 1970, More Than One Thing for Morton B. May of St. Louis, 1969; dir., producer, cinematographer: Give A Damn for St. Louis Mayor's Council, 1968; asst. to dir.: Dalton Trumbo in Johnny Got His Gun, 1970; dir., cinematographer: Winthrop Rockefeller, NBC, CBS, ABC, 1968-69; dir.: cinematography Hot Connections, Four Winds Enterprises, 1970, World's Greatest Lover, SAE Prodns., 1970, Censorship USA, 1971, Zodiac Couples, 1970; cinematographer: Wide World of Sports, Nat. Football League, St. Louis Cardinals, 1968, others.; Exhibited one-man shows, Schweig Gallery, St. Louis, 1968, Norton Gallery, St. Louis, 1967, Steinberg Mus. St. Louis, 1968, U. Buffalo, 1966; represented in permanent collections, Louisville Mus., Springfield (Mo.) Mus., others; photographer for various publs. Recipient awards Cork Film Festival, N.Y. Film Festival, Nat. Ednl. TV, San Francisco, Chgo. film festivals. Mem. Dirs. Guild Am. Home: 1010 Pacific Ave Venice CA 90291 Office: care Michael Greenfield Charter Mgmt Suite 1112 9000 Sunset Blvd Los Angeles CA 90069

CARVILLE, JOHN WILLIAM, manufacturing company executive; b. Johnstown, Pa., Aug. 6, 1923; s. John F. and Caroline Smith (Adams) C.; m. Nina L. Bosley, Jan. 22, 1944; children: Sharen Lehman, John, Patricia Lubawy, Michele, Carol. B.B.A., U. Pitts., 1949; grad/ Advanced Mgmt. Program, Harvard Bus. Sch., 1965. C.P.A., Pa. Acct. Price Waterhouse & Co., Pitts., 1952-67, H.J. Heinz, 1949-52; acctg. mgr. Mine Safety Appliances Co., Pitts., 1957-67, treas., 1967-68, v.p., treas., 1968—; dir. Catalyst Research Corp., Balt. Bd. dirs. YMCA, Pitts., 1983—. Served with USN, 1942-45. Mem. Fin. Execs. Inst. (dir. 1982—), Pa. Inst. C.P.A.'s, Am. Inst. C.P.A.'s. Republican. Roman Catholic. Clubs: Duquense; Edgewood Country (Pitts.). Office: Mine Safety Appliances Co 600 Penn Center Blvd Pittsburgh PA 15235

CARY, CHARLES OSWALD, flight research laboratory official, educator, aviation consultant; b. Boston, July 10, 1917; s. Charles P. and Adeline J. (Oswald) C.; m. Jean M. Cochran, May 8, 1948. Student, Northeastern U., 1937-39, MIT, 1941-42. With comml. airlines, 1936-44; exec. asst. to chmn. CAB, 1944-46; spl. asst. to asst. sec. navy for air, 1946-48; mem. Civil Transp. Aircraft Evaluation and Devel. Bd., 1948-49; exec. sec. Air Coordinating Com., 1949-54; gen. sec. Air Transp. Moblzn. Survey, Nat. Security Resources Bd., 1950-51; dep. adminstr. Def. Air Transp. Adminstrn., 1951-54; dir. marketing electronics div. Curtiss-Wright Corp., 1954-63; v.p. Hazeltine Corp., 1963-65; asst. adminstr. dept. transp. FAA, 1965-78, spl. rep. of adminstr., Brussels, Belgium, 1978-79; ret., 1979; sr. lectr., dir. internat. studies Flight Transp. Lab., MIT, 1979—; dir. Flight Transp. Assos., Inc., Cambridge; mem. U.S. del. 1st assembly Provisional Internat. Civil Aviation Orgn., 1946, U.S. dels. assemblies, 1947, 51, 53, 70, 74, 77; cons. to adminstr. FAA, 1963; Bd. dirs., exec. com. Flight Safety Found., Washington, 1979—. Asso. fellow AIAA; mem. Acad. Polit. Sci. Clubs: University, Internat. Aviation (Washington). Home: North Rd RD 1 Box 163 Sunapee NH 03782 Office: Flight Transp Lab MIT Cambridge MA 02139

CARY, ELTON MIKELL, insurance company executive; b. Savannah, Ga., Jan. 28, 1929; s. Theron Elton Mikell and Nellie (Johnson) Walker Mikell; m. Betty Laine Jackson, Aug. 5, 1950 (dec. 1967); children: Mikell, James. B.S., U. Ga., 1950. Ins. agt. Adae & Hooper, Miami Beach, Fla., 1951-73; chmn. Gen. Ins. Co., Miami Beach, 1973—; dir. Wometco Enterprises, Inc., Miami, 1972—; chmn. Wometo Enterprises, Inc., Miami, 1983—; dir., exec. com. Fin. Fed. Savs., Miami, 1980—. Trustee Papenicolaou Cancer Research Inst., Miami, 1975—. Democrat. Methodist. Home: 1 Palm Bay Towers Miami FL 33138 Office: Gen Ins Co Wometco Enterprises Inc 1815 Purdy Ave Miami Beach FL 33139

CARY, FRANK TAYLOR, business machines manufacturing executive; b. Gooding, Idaho, Dec. 14, 1920; s. Frank Taylor and Ida C.; m. Anne Curtis, 1943; children: Marshall, Bryan, Steven, Laura. B.S., UCLA, 1943; M.B.A., Stanford U., 1948. With IBM, 1948—, pres. data processing div., 1964—, v.p., group exec., 1966, sr. v.p., 1967, dir., 1968—, pres., from 1971, chmn. bd., chief exec. officer, from 1973, now chmn. exec. com., Armonk, N.Y.; dir. J. P. Morgan & Co., Hosp. Corp. Am., Morgan Guaranty Trust Co. N.Y., ABC, Inc., Merck & Co., Inc., Texaco, Inc. Trustee The Conf. Bd., Brookings Instn., Am. Mus. Natural History, Mus. Modern Art, Rockefeller U.; mem. corp. M.I.T. Served with AUS, 1944-46. Mem. Bus. Council. Office: IBM Corp Old Orchard Rd Armonk NY 10504

CARY, FREEMAN HAMILTON, physician; b. LaGrange, Ga., Sept. 14, 1926; s. Ashton Hall and Edna Gwendolyn (Freeman) C.; m. Ruby I. Samples, July 26, 1951 (div.); children: Robin L., Freeman H., Emily A., Leslie L.; m. Sara Ellen Hunter, Nov. 15, 1971; children: Tim, Alex, Kippen, Eric. Student, Ga. Tech., 1943-45; B.S., Emory U., 1946, M.D., 1950. Diplomate: Am. Bd. Internal Medicine. Intern, resident Grady Hosp., Atlanta, 1950-53, fellow cardiology, 1953-54, instr., 1953-58, dir. cardiac clinic, 1957-60, dir. stroke rehab. clinic, 1958-60; dir. med. edn. Orange Meml. Hosp., Orlando, Fla., 1960-71; asst. attending physician Congress, Washington, 1971-72, attending physician, 1973—; asso. in medicine Emory U. Med. Sch., 1958-60; clin. prof. med. edn. U.S. Fla., Tampa, 1968-71; clin. prof. allied health scis. Fla. Tech. U., Orlando, 1969-71; dir. Central Fla. Blood Bank, Orlando, 1963-71. Served to rear adm. M.C. USNR, 1954-56, 71—. Recipient Bronze medallion Ga. Heart Assn., 1961, Silver medallion Fla. Heart Assn., 1966. Fellow A.C.P., Am. Heart Assn. (council clin. cardiology, bd. dirs.), Am. Coll. Cardiology, Am. Coll. Chest Physicians; mem. Fla. Heart Assn. (pres. 1970-71), Central Fla. Heart Assn. (pres. 1968-69, dir. 1961-71), Washington Heart Assn. (dir. 1972). Clubs: Carolina Trace (Sanford, N.C.); Evergreen Country (Haymarket, Va.). Home: Stonehenge Box 31 Markham VA 22643 Office: Room h-166 US Capitol Washington DC 20515

CARY, JAMES DONALD, journalist; b. Douglas, Ariz., Oct. 7, 1919; s. Leon Barker and Ruth F. (Dunlap) C.; m. Norma Frances Goben, Dec. 18, 1942; 1 son, James Christopher. B.A., U. Ariz., 1941; M.S. in Journalism, Northwestern U., 1948. Reporter Miami Beach Evening Sun, Miami, Fla., 1945-46, Miami Daily News, 1946-47, Ariz. Times, Phoenix, 1947-48; reporter AP, Phoenix, 1949-54, Tokyo Bur., 1954-60, news editor, 1959-60; desk editor Washington Bur., 1960-65; newsman Copley New Service, Washington, 1965-73, bur. chief, 1973-78, sr. corr., 1978-81; vis. prof. Brigham Young U., 1983-84. Author: Japan Today: Reluctant Ally, 1962, Tanks and Armor in Modern Warfare, 1965. Served from 2d lt. to capt. AUS, 1941-46; ETO. Decorated Silver Star, Purple Heart (2).; Recipient Copley Ring of Truth awards, 1966, 72, Ariz. Press Club award., Brigham Young U. Disting. Service cert. Club: Nat. Press. Home: 269 SW 29th Ave Delray Beach FL 33445

CARY, WILLIAM STERLING, church executive; b. Plainfield, N.J., Aug. 10,1927; s. Andrew and Sadie C.; m. Marie B. Phillips; children: Yvonne, Denise, Sterling, Patricia. Ed., Morehouse Coll., also D.D.; student, Union Theol. Sem.; LL.D., Bishop Coll.; D.D., Elmhurst Coll.; L.H.D., Allen U. Ordained to ministry Baptist Ch., 1948; pastor Butler Meml. Presbyn. Ch., Youngstown, Ohio, 1953-55, Interdenominational Ch. of Open Door, Bklyn., 1955-58, Grace Congl. Ch., N.Y.C., 1958-68; area minister Met. and Suffolk assns. N.Y. Conf. United Ch. Christ, 1968-75; pres. Nat. Council Chs., N.Y.C., 1972-75; conf. minister Ill. conf. United Ch. Christ, 1975—; chmn. United Ch. Christ Council Conf. Execs.; mem. governing bd. Nat. Council Chs.; mem. United Ch. Christ Rep. Consultation on Ch. Union, Council on Ecumenism; lectr. Mem. Pres.'s Adv. Com. Refugees. Named One of 100 Most Influential Blacks in Am. for 1974-75 Ebony mag. Address: PO Box 7208 Westchester IL 60153

CASAD, ROBERT CLAIR, legal educator; b. Council Grove, Kans., Dec. 8, 1929; s. Clair L. C. and Eula Imogene (Compton) Casas; m. Sally Ann McKeighan, Aug. 20, 1965; children: Benjamin Nathan, Joseph Story, Robert Clair, Madeleine. A.B., U. Kans., 1950, M.A., 1952; J.D. with honors, U. Mich., 1957; S.J.D., Harvard U., 1979. Bar: Kans. 1957, Minn. 1958, U.S. Dist. Ct. Kans. 1957. Instr. law U. Mich., Ann Arbor, 1957-58; assoc. firm Steater & Murphy, Winona, Minn., 1958-59; asst. prof. law U. Kans., Lawrence, 1959-62, assoc. prof., 1962-64, prof., 1964-81, John H. and John M. Kane prof. law, 1981—; vis. prof. UCLA, 1969-70, U. Ill., 1973-74, U. Calif. Hastings Coll. Law, 1979-80, U. Colo., 1982. Author: Jurisdiction in Civil Actions, 1983, Expropriation Procedures in Central American and Panama, 1975, (with others) Kansas Appellate Practice, 1978, Civil Judgment Recognition and the Integration of Multiple State Associations, 1982, Res Judicata in an Nutshell, 1976; contbr. numerous articles to legal jours. Mem. civil code adv. com. Kans. Jud. Council. Served to 1st lt. USAF, 1952-53. Recipient Coblentz prize U. Mich. Sch. Law, 1957; Ford fellow, 1965-66; fellow in law Harvard U., 1965-66; OAS fellow, 1976; NEH fellow, summer 1978; grantee Dana Fund for Internat. and Comparative Legal Studies; recipient medal Dana Fund for Internat. and Comparative Legal Studies, 1981, Rice prize U. Kans. Law Sch., 1976, 83. Mem. Am. Law Inst., ABA, Kans. Bar Assn. Democrat. Home: 1130 Emery Rd Lawrence KS 66044 Office: U Kans Sch Law Lawrence KS 66045

CASADO, ANTONIO FRANCISCO, city official; b. Puerto Padre, Cuba, Oct. 10, 1913; came to U.S., 1926, naturalized, 1936; s. Miguel and Mercedes (Puig); m. Ardeen Frances Burkett, June 27, 1948; children: Jill Anne, Nancy, Mary Lou. B.A., Friends U., Wichita, Kans., 1937. Auditor Stanley Spurrier & Co. (C.P.A.s); accountant Boeing Airplane Co., Wichita, 1939-42; sec.-treas Casado-McKay Inc. (Realtors and developers), Wichita, 1946-84; dep. dir. U.S. AID, Paraguay, 1970-72; dir. Wichita Bd. Realtors, 1951-58, pres., 1953. Mem. Kans. Ho. of Reps., 1960-64, Kans. Senate, 1964-70; mem. Wichita City Commn., 1975—; mayor of Wichita, 1977, 79. Served with Med. Dept. AUS, 1942-46. Recipient Realtor of Year award, 1962, Lion of Year award, 1964. Mem. Wichita Assn. Home Builders. Republican. Episcopalian. Clubs: Mason (Shriner), Lion.). Home: 714 N Brookfield Wichita KS 67206 Office: 236 S Topeka Ave Wichita KS 67202

CASALS, ROSEMARY, professional tennis player; b. San Francisco, Sept. 16, 1948. Profl. tennis player, 1968—; nat. championships and major tournaments include U.S. Open singles (finalist), 1970, 71, U.S. Open doubles, 1967, 71, 74, 82, U.S. Open mixed doubles, 1975, Wimbledon doubles, 1967, 68, 70, 71, 73, Wimbledon mixed doubles, 1971, 73, finalist with Dick Stockton, 1976, Italian doubles, 1967, 70, Family Circle Cup (winner), 1973, Wightman Cup, 1967, 76-81, Bridgeston doubles championships (finalist), 1975, Spalding mixed doubles, 1976, 77, U.S. Tennis Assn. Atlanta doubles, 1976, Fedn. Cup, 1967, 76-81; winner 1st Virginia Slims tournament, 1970; 3d place Virginia Slims Championships, 1976, 4th place, 1977, 78; winner Murjani-WTA championship, 1980; Fla. Fed. Open doubles, 1980; Mem. Los Angeles Strings team, World Team Tennis, 1975-77; pres. Sportswoman, Inc., Sausalito, Calif., 1981—. Mem. Women's Tennis Assn. (dir.). Home: Sausalito CA Office: Sportswoman Inc. 1505 Bridgeway Suite 208 Sausalito CA 94965 *

CASALS-ARIET, JORDI, physician; b. Viladrau, Girona, Spain, May 15, 1911; came to U.S., 1936, naturalized, 1946; s. Martin and Margarida (Ariet) Casals-A.; m. Ellen Evelyn Brock, Dec. 6, 1941; 1 dau., Christina. B.Ciencias, Instituto Nacional, Barcelona, Spain, 1928; Licenciado en Medicina y Cirurgia con Grado, U. Barcelona, 1934. Intern Med. Sch. Hosp., Barcelona, 1934-36; research asso. Cornell U. Med. Coll., N.Y.C., 1936-38; asso. Rockefeller Inst. Med. Research, N.Y.C., 1938-52; mem. staff Rockefeller Found., N.Y.C., 1952-74; prof. epidemiology, Yale, 1964-81, prof. emeritus, 1981—; vis. prof. dept. neurology Mt. Sinai Sch. Medicine, N.Y.C., 1981—. Contbr. articles to profl. jours. Served with Spanish Army, 1933. Recipient Kimble Methodology award Am. Pub. Health Assn., 1969. Fellow Am. Soc. Tropical Medicine and Hygiene (Taylor award 1968), Royal Soc. Tropical Medicine and Hygiene (hon.); mem. Soc. Exptl. Biology and Medicine, Harvey Soc., AAAS, N.Y. Acad. Medicine, N.Y. Acad. Scis. Home: 25 Claremont Ave New York NY 10027 Office: One Gustave L Levy Pl New York NY 10029

CASANI, JOHN R., electrical engineer; b. Phila., Sept. 17, 1932; s. John Charles and Julia Jean (Bateman) C.; m. Marie Therese Younger, Nov. 12, 1969 (div. 1977); 1 son, John; m. 2d Jerry Lynn Seitz, Dec. 13; children: Jason, Joshua, Drew. B.S. in Elec. Engring., U. Pa. With Jet Propulsion Lab., Pasadena, Calif., 1967—, mgr. guidance and control div., 1975-76, mgr. Voyager project, 1976-78, mgr. Galileo Project, 1978—. Bd. dirs. YMCA, Pasadena, Calif., 1976-82. Recipient Exceptional Service medal NASA, 1965, medal for outstanding leadership NASA, 1964, 81, Dist. Alumni award U. Pa., 1978, Space System award AIAA, 1978, Astronautics Engring. award, 1981. Fellow AIAA. Republican. Roman Catholic. Home: 281 S Orange Grove Blvd Pasadena CA 91105 Office: Jet Propulsion Lab 4800 Oak Grove Dr Pasadena CA 91109

CASANOVA, ALDO JOHN, sculptor; b. San Francisco, Feb. 8, 1929; s. Felice and Teresa (Papini) C.; children: Aviva, Liana. B.A., San Francisco State U., 1950, M.A., 1951; Ph.D., Ohio State U., 1957. Asst. prof. art San Francisco State U., 1951-53; asst. prof. Antioch (Ohio) Coll., 1956-58; asst. prof. art Tyler Sch. Art, Temple U., Phila., 1961-64, Rome, 1968-70; prof. art Scripps Coll., Claremont, Calif., 1966—, chmn. art dept., 1971-73. One-man shows include, Esther Robles Gallery, Los Angeles, 1967, Santa Barbara (Calif.) Mus., Calif. Inst. Tech., 1972, Carl Schlosberg Fine Arts, Los Angeles, 1977; represented in permanent collections, Whitney Mus., San Francisco Mus. Art, Hirshhorn Collection, Cornell U., Columbus (Ohio) Mus., UCLA Sculpture Garden, Calif. Inst. Tech., Pasadena. Recipient Prix-de-Rome Am. Acad. in Rome, 1958-61; Louis Comfort Tiffany award, 1970. Fellow Am. Acad. in Rome; mem. Sculptors Guild. Democrat. Roman Catholic. Home: 691 W 12th St Claremont CA 91711 Office: Scripps Coll Claremont CA 91711

CASARELLA, EDMOND, artist; b. Newark, Sept. 3, 1920; s. Dominick and Natalina (Feliciani) C.; m. Mary Peters, July 21, 1946; 1 dau., Demetra Casarella Sirinek. B.F.A., Cooper Union, 1942. Instr. N.Y. U., 1964, 65, Pratt Inst., 1964, 65, Hunter Coll., 1964, 65, Tchr.'s Coll., Columbia U., 1964-67, Manhattanville Coll., Cooper Union, 1965-68, Finch Coll., 1969-73; Mem. adv. bd. Cooper Union, 1959-60. Exhbns. include, Corcoran Gallery, Washington, 1955, Nat. Print Council Competition, Am. Prints Today, 1959, 62; represented in permanent collections, Whitney Mus. Am. Art, N.Y.C., Bklyn. Mus. Art, N.J. State Mus., Trenton, Speed Mus., Louisville, Library Congress, commd. works include, No. Valley Bank, Cresskill, N.J., Unitarian Ch., Louisville. Served with U.S. Army, 1944-46. Fulbright grantee, 1951-52; Guggenheim Found. fellow, 1959-60. Home: 83 E Linden Ave Englewood NJ 07631

CASARELLA, WILLIAM JOSEPH, physician; b. Dunmore, Pa., Nov. 17, 1937; s. Rocco F. and Madeline M. C.; m. Carolyn A. Hughes, June 18, 1966; children—Jennifer, Gregory. B.A., Yale U., 1959; M.D., Harvard U., 1963. Intern U. Pa. Hosp., 1963-64; resident in medicine Boston City Hosp., 1966-67; resident in radiology Columbia U.-Presbyn. Med. Center, 1967-70, attending radiologist, 1970—; prof. radiology Columbia U. Coll. Physicians and Surgeons, N.Y.C., 1977-81; chmn. dept. radiology Emory U., Atlanta, 1981—. Contbr. articles to med. jours. Served to capt. M.C. USAR, 1964-66. Mem. Soc. Cardiovascular Radiology (pres. 1979), Am. Heart Assn., Radiol. Soc. N. Am., Am. Coll. Radiology, N. Am. Soc. Cardiac Angiography, Assn. U. Radiologists, Eastern Radiol. Soc., N.Y. Roentgen Soc., Soc. Cardiac Angiography. Home: 1943 Starfire Dr NE Atlanta GA 30345 Office: 1365 Clifton Rd NE Atlanta GA 30322

CASARETT, ALISON PROVOOST, university administrator, scientist; b. Richmond Hill, N.Y., Apr. 17, 1930; d. John C. and Edith T. Provoost; m. Louis Casarett, 1958; children: Elissa Ann, Jenet Alison. B.S., St. Lawrence U., 1951; M.S., U. Rochester, 1953, Ph.D., 1957. Lectr., U. Rochester, N.Y., 1957-63; from asst. prof. to asso. prof. Cornell U., Ithaca, N.Y., 1969-79, asso. dean, 1973-79, dean, 1979—, prof. radiation biology, 1979—, vice provost, 1978—; cons. in field. Author: Radiation Biology, 1968; contbr. articles to profl. jours. Recipient Lalor Found. award, 1971; AEC grantee. Mem. Radiation Research Soc., AAAS, Phi Beta Kappa, Sigma Xi, Sigma Delta Epsilon, Sigma Pi Sigma, Pi Mu Epsilon. Club: Zonta (v.p. 1978). Home: 144 Pine Tree Rd Ithaca NY 14850 Office: Sage Grad Center Cornell U Ithaca NY 14853

CASARETT, GEORGE WILLIAM, pathologist, educator; b. Rochester, N.Y., Aug. 17, 1920; s. George William and Caroline Margaret (Rocco) C.; m. Marion Isabelle Wells, June 12, 1944; children: Leslie Gay, Vicki Wells. Student, St. Michael's Coll., U. Toronto, Ont., Can., 1938-41; Ph.D., U. Rochester, 1952. Scientist Manhattan Project, U. Rochester Sch. Medicine, 1941-47, Atomic Energy Project, 1947-53; from instr. to assoc. prof. Radiation Biology, 1953-63; prof. radiation biology, biophysics and radiology Atomic Energy Project, 1963—; Cons. NIH, NRC, others; chmn. adv. com. on biol. effects of ionizing radiations Nat. Acad. Sci.; bd. dirs. Nat. Council on Radiation Protection and Measurements. Author: Clinical Radiation Pathology, 1968, Radiation Histopathology, 1981; Assoc. editor: Radiation Research Jour, 1960-64. Recipient (with others) First award and; Silver medal Am. Roentgen Ray Soc., 1959; First award for fundamental research Radiol. Soc. N.Am., 1959, 64, 71. Fellow Am. Gerontol. Soc.; mem. AAAS, Am. Assn. Anatomists, AAUP, Am. Assn. Pathologists, Soc. Exptl. Biology and Medicine, Radiation Research Soc. (councilor), Phila. Roentgen Ray Soc. (hon.), Sigma Xi. Research, publs. on mechanisms of radiation pathology, aging, cancer induction and cancer therapy. Home: 107 French Rd Rochester NY 14618 Office: U Rochester Med Center 601 Elmwood Ave Rochester NY 14642

CASCIANO, DANIEL ANTHONY, biologist; b. Buffalo, Mar. 1, 1941; s. Frederick James and Rose Ann C.; m. Gertrude Ann Tara, Aug. 22, 1964; children: Anne, Jonathan. B.S., Canisius Coll., 1962; Ph.D., Purdue U., 1971. Research asst. Rosewell Park Meml. Inst., Buffalo, 1963-64; research asst. dept. biol. scis. Purdue U., Lafayette, Ind., 1965-66, teaching asst., 1969, research trainee, 1966-71; postdoctoral investigator U. Tenn., Oak Ridge Nat. Labs., 1971-73; research biologist Nat. Ctr. Toxicol. Research, Jefferson, Ark., 1973—, program dir. div. mutagenesis research, 1976-78, dir. div. mutagenesis research, 1979—; assoc. prof. U. Ark. for Med. Scis., Little Rock, 1974—; trainee NIH, 1966-71. Contbr. articles to profl. jours. Mem. Tissue Culture Assn., Environ. Mutagen Soc., AAAS, Beta Beta Beta. Home: 1921 Romine Rd Little Rock AR 72205 Office: Nat Center Toxilogical Research FDA Jefferson AR 72079

CASCIERI, ARCANGELO, sculptor, educator; b. Civitaquana, Italy, Feb. 22, 1902; came to U.S., 1907, naturalized, 1934; s. Corrado and Marie (Trabucco) C.; m. Eda Di Biccari, Sept. 19, 1943. Student, Sch. Arch., Boston Archtl. Center, 1922-26, Boston U., 1932-36. Tchr. pvt. classes Boston, 1932-37, Craft Center Sch., Boston, 1939-40; tchr. design New London (Conn.) Jr. Coll., 1941-43, Boston Archtl. Center, 1936—, head Sch. Architecture, 1937—; also mem. bd. dirs.; partner with Adio Di Biccari (in studio for sculpture and decorations), Boston and Arlington, 1952—; Mem. Mass. Postsecondary Edn. Commn., 1976—. Sculptor, asst. dir. sculpture and wood carving, W. F. Ross Studio, Cambridge, Mass., 1923-41; sculptor, asst. dir., Schwamb Assos. Studio, Arlington, Mass., 1941-46; sculptor, dir., 1946-52; prin. sculptural works include statues in parts of, Cathedral St. John the Divine, N.Y.C., Washington Cathedral, Cathedral St. John Evangelist, Spokane, Wash., Cathedral Most Holy Redeemer, Cornerbrook, Nfld., Cathedral Mary Our Queen, Balt., Riverside Baptist Ch., N.Y.C., East Liberty Presbyn. Ch., Pitts., St. George's Sch. Chapel, Newport, R.I., Boston U. Chapel, St. Ignatius Ch., Chestnut Hill, Mass., Shrine Immaculate Conception, Washington, also works at, Boston Coll., Holy Cross Coll., Buffalo Courier Express Bldg., Parlin Jr. High Sch., Everett, Mass., Lexington (Mass.) High Sch., Am. War Meml. World War I at Belleau Woods, France, World war II at Margraten, Holland, exterior, Meml. Auditorium, Lynn, Mass., Boys' Stadium, Franklin Field, Dorchester, Mass., sculpture on fountain, Parkman Plaza, Boston, sculpture, Backus Estate, Pointe Rose, Mich.; Author articles. Decorated cavaliere Order Al Merito della Repubblica Italiana; recipient Gold medal citation Nat. Sculpture Soc., 1961; 75th Anniversary citation Boston Archtl. Center, 1964; citation Boston 200, 1975; silver medal Boston U. Alumni Assn., 1976; 1st Visual Communication award New Eng. Sch. Art and Design; also made hon. alumni, 1979; citation Boston 350, 1980. Fellow AIA (chmn. com. collaborative arts); mem. Dante Alighieri Soc. (hon.), Boston Soc. Architects, Mass. Assn. Architects, Assn. Architects and Engrs. Campania Region-Naples (hon.), New Eng. Sculptors Assn. Roman Catholic. Office: 27 Tavern Rd Boston MA 02115 *

CASCORBI, HELMUT FREIMUND, anesthesiologist, educator; b. Berlin, Germany, July 13, 1933; came to U.S., 1958; s. Gilbert and Isa (Ruckert) C.; m. Ann M. Morgan, Aug. 7, 1965; children: Alicia Maria, Kathryn Ann. M.D., U. Munich, W. Ger., 1957; Ph.D., U. Md., 1962. Prof., chmn. dept. anesthesiology Case Western Res. U., Cleve., 1980—. Mem. Am. Soc. Anesthesiologists, AMA, Assn. Univ. Anesthetists, Am. Soc. Pharmacology and Exptl. Therapeutics. Home: 2844 Fairmount Blvd Cleveland Heights OH 44118 Office: Univ Hosps of Cleve 2074 Abington Rd Cleveland OH 44106

CASE, CHARLES CARROLL, retired army officer; b. Raquette Lake, N.Y., Mar. 20, 1914; s. Charles Carroll and Alberta (Williams) C.; m. Mary Frances Young, Jan. 29, 1938; children: Judith (Mrs. James H. Falkenrath), Charles Carroll III. B.A., W.Va. U., 1936; postgrad., Command and Gen. Staff Coll., 1952, Army War Coll., 1957; M.A., Am. U., 1960, Harvard, 1962, George Washington U., 1963. Commd. 2d lt. U.S. Army, 1936, advanced through grades to maj. gen., 1967; support comdr., chief of staff (3d Div.), 1954-56, dir., Washington, 1957-61, comdr., Battle Creek, Mich., 1962-64; q.m. U.S. Army, Europe, 1964-65; chief (U.S. Army Supply and Maintenance Agy.), Europe, 1965-67, dep. comdg. gen., 1965-67, comdg. gen., St. Louis, 1967-69, comdr., Alexandria, Va., 1969-71; dir. Power Brake Co., Inc., Wheeling, W.Va., 1981—; Mem. nat. adv. bd. Am. Security Council. Contbr. articles to profl. jours. Leader, tng. dir. Boy Scouts Am., 1957-

64. Decorated D.S.M., Legion of Merit with 4 oak leaf clusters, Bronze Star, Army Commendation medal, U.S.; Medal of Orleans, France; recipient Delta Tau Delta Disting. Achievement award. Mem. Ret. Officers Assn., Am. Def. Preparedness Assn., Am. Logistics Assn. (past pres. Washington chpt.), Assn. U.S. Army, Delta Tau Delta. Home: 1628 N Harrison St Arlington VA 22205

CASE, CHARLES WARREN, university dean, education educator; b. Rochester, N.Y., May 14, 1938; s. Paul Wilfred and Wava Katherine (Hamlin) C.; m. Diane Elizabeth Barron, Sept. 17, 1960; children: Cathleen Mary Case Baeb, Heather Anne, Scott Charles, Sean Paul. B.S., LeMoyne Coll., 1960; M.S., Syracuse U., 1965; Ed.D., U. Rochester, 1969. Asst. to pres. SUNY Agrl. and Tech. Coll., Morrisville, 1964-66; asst. to dean U. Rochester, 1966-69; assoc. prof., dept. chmn. U. Vt., Burlington, 1969-74; assoc. dean, prof. edn. Cleve. State U., 1974-76; dean Coll. Edn., prof. U. Wis.-, Oshkosh, 1976-80; dean Coll. Edn., prof. edn. U. Iowa, Iowa City, 1980—; cons. State Depts. Pub. Instrn., N.Y., 1968-77, Vt., 1968-77, N.J., 1968-77, N.H., 1968-77, Mass., 1968-77, R.I., 1968-77, Maine, 1968-77, colls., univs., schs., 1968-80, hosps., Vt., 1970-74. Author, editor: (with W.A. Matthes) Trends in Professional Education, (with P.A. Olson) The Future-Create or Inherit, 1974; contbr. chpts. to books, articles to profl. jours. Bd. dirs. United Way, Iowa City, 1980—. Grantee Desegregation Research and Planning Study, Cleve. found., 1975, Ctr. for Comprehensive Planning, Rockefeller Bros., 1974; Deans grantee U.S. Office Edn., 1978-80. Mem. Assn. Colls. and Schs. of Edn. in State Univs. and Land Grant Colls. (sec. 1982, pres.-elect 1983), U.S. Assn. for Club of Rome, Inter-Am. Soc. for Ednl. Adminstrn., Am. Ednl. Research Assn., World Future Soc. Lodge: Rotary. Home: 112 N Westminster St Iowa City IA 52240 Office: N-459 Lindquist Ctr Coll Edn U Iowa Iowa City IA 52242

CASE, EUGENE LAWRENCE, advertising agency executive; b. Knoxville, Tenn., Dec. 6, 1937; s. Harry Lawrence and Elinor Alice (Irish) C.; m. Mary Jane Austin, Apr. 30, 1959 (div. Mar. 1969); children: Christopher Lawrence, Alison Austin, Timothy Punch; m. Ilon Specht, Jan. 28, 1972; 1 son, Brady Geronimo Specht. Student, Cornell U., 1955-59. Copywriter J. Walter Thompson, 1961-62, Foote, Cone & Belding, 1963; asst. copy supr. Doyle, Dane, Bernbach, N.Y.C., 1964; partner, creative dir. Jack Tinker & Partners, N.Y.C., 1966-69; partner, founder Case & McGrath Inc., N.Y.C., 1969—; founder Alamo Prodns., N.Y.C., 1982—. Writer, co-producer: TV film Ohms. Recipient numerous awards for copywriting from advt. clubs. Mem. Advt. Club N.Y. (dir.). Home: 70 W 69th St New York NY 10023 Office: 445 Park Ave New York NY 10022

CASE, EVERETT NEEDHAM, educator, former university president; b. North Plainfield, N.J., Apr. 9, 1901; s. James Herbert and Alice (Needham) C.; m. Josephine Young, June 27, 1931; children: Josephine Edmonds, James Herbert III, Samuel, John Philip. B.A., Princeton, 1922, LL.D., 1947; B.A., Cambridge U., Eng., 1924, M.A., 1938; postgrad., Harvard, 1924-27; LL.D., Syracuse U., 1942, Temple U., 1943, St. Lawrence U., 1945, U. Rochester, 1948, Colby Coll., 1953, N.Y. U., 1962, Clark U., 1967; L.H.D., Hamilton Coll., Union Coll., 1943, Colgate U., 1957, U. Akron, 1962; D.C.L., Bucknell U., 1947. Asst. history Harvard, 1926-27; asst. to Owen D. Young, 1927-33; asst. sec. Gen. Electric Co., 1929-33; exec. sec. Central Banking and Indsl. Com., Washington, 1932-33; investigation, study monetary policies and problems, also problems of N.Y. dairy farmer, 1933-41; asst. dean Harvard Grad. Sch. Bus. Adminstrn., 1939-42; pres. Colgate U., 1942-62, pres. emeritus, 1962—; pres. Alfred P. Sloan Found., N.Y.C., 1962-68; Dir. Fed. Res. Bank N.Y., 1961-68, chmn., 1966-68; cons. on Far Eastern Affairs to sec. state, 1949. Author: (with Josephine Young Case) Owen D. Young and American Enterprise: A Biography, 1982; Contbr. articles to profl. jours. Alumni trustee Princeton, 1957-61; trustee Millbrook Sch., 1944—, pres., 1960-68; bd. dirs. Nat. Ednl. TV, 1958—, chmn., 1963-69; hon. trustee Com. Econ. Devel.; trustee Ednl. Broadcasting Corp., 1964-68; chmn. Am. Council Edn., 1951-52; overseers com. to visit Harvard Coll., 1951-61; mem. adv. com. Lindsay A. and Olive B. O'Connor Found., Hobart, N.Y., 1966-81; bd. dirs. Nat. Commn. on U.S.-China Relations, 1966-75. Democrat. Baptist. Clubs: Century, University (N.Y.C.). Home: Van Hornesville NY 13475

CASE, HADLEY, oil company executive; b. N.Y.C., Mar. 28, 1909; s. Walter Summerhayes and Mary Soule (Hadley) C.; m. Julie Marguerite Ill, June 8, 1935 (dec. Mar. 1975); children: Mary, C. Durham, Julie Anne, Rosalie C. Clark, Deborah Joan; m. Elizabeth M. McCabe, Nov. 8, 1975. Student, Kent (Conn.) Sch., 1924-29, Antioch Coll., 1929-33. Geol. field work, Australia, 1933-34, Tex., 1935-36; with geol. dept. Case, Pomeroy & Co., Inc., 1936-39, v.p., 1939-41, pres., dir., 1941—; pres. chief exec. officer Felmont Oil Corp., 1952-72, chmn. bd., chief exec. officer, 1972—; dir. N.W. Airlines, Inc., 1957-78, Copper Range Co., 1966-77, Nashua Corp., 1965-81, Numac Oil & Gas Ltd. Trustee Kent Sch., 1959-75, Brewster Acad., 1956-63, Boys' and Girls' Camps, Inc., Boston, 1971-76; trustee Hosp. St. Barnabas, Newark, 1942-59, pres. bd. trustees, 1949-52; bd. dirs. Greenwich Boys Club Assn., 1957-73, hon. mem., 1974—; chancellor Kent Sch., 1982—. Mem. Am. Inst. Mining and Metall. Engrs., Am. Petroleum Inst., Ind. Petroleum Assn. Am. (dir.). Office: 6 E 43d St New York NY 10017

CASE, KEITH EDMOND, educator; b. Creston, Iowa, May 11, 1911; s. Roy C. and Eula (Freeman) C.; m. Leah Young, Nov. 2, 1934; children—Leah Ann Keith, Elizabeth Larie, Kenneth. A.M., Colo. State Coll. Edn., 1935; Ph.D., U. Denver, 1948. Dir. forensics Colo. State Coll. Edn., Greeley, 1934-35; chmn. dept. speech and English Garden City (Kans.) Jr. Coll., 1935-41; chmn. dept. speech, dean men Augustana Coll., Sioux Falls, S.D., 1941-44; coordinator basic communication program U. Denver, 1948-63, chmn. dept. basic communication, 1948-63, chmn. communication div., 1951-63, prof. speech and communications, 1961—, univ. fellow in gerontology, 1978; dir. long term care Colo. Found. for Med. Care, 1977—; cons. in communication to bus., industry, edn., religious groups, govt. agys. Author: Basic Debate, 1935, Speech Improvement Guide, 1953, Mastering Reading Skills, 1954, Developing Modern Reading Techniques, 1956, Mastering Speech Skills, 1956, Mastering Vocabulary Skills, 1957, Mature Reading and Thinking, 1960, Communicating Effectively Through Speech, 1964. Served to lt. USNR, 1944-46. Mem. Internat. Soc. Gen. Semantics, Speech Assn. Am., Nat. Soc. Study Communication, Pi Kappa Delta, Alpha Psi Omega, Phi Sigma Pi, Kappa Delta Pi. Lutheran. Home: 4990 Larkspur St Bowmar Littleton CO 80120

CASE, MANNING EUGENE, JR., business executive; b. Sioux City, Iowa, Mar. 1916; s. Manning Eugene and Loretta (Seims) C.; m. Ernestine Bryan, July 26, 1941; children: Douglas Manning, Randall Bryan. A.B., Western Res. U., 1938, J.D., 1941. Bar: Ohio 1941. Asst. counsel B.F. Goodrich Co., Akron, 1941-52; sec., treas., gen counsel, dir. Perfection Industries, 1952-55; sec. Hupp Corp., 1955-57; v.p. service and fin. M&M Candies div. Mars Inc., 1957-60; asst. treas. Standard Brands Inc., N.Y.C., 1961-62, treas., 1962-68, v.p., treas., 1968-77, v.p., chief fin. officer, 1977-78, sr. v.p., chief fin. officer, 1978-80, sr. v.p. personnel and investor relations, 1980-81; sr. v.p. personnel Nabisco Brands, Inc., Parsippany, N.J., 1981-82, sr. v.p., 1983—; dir. Excelsior Income Shares, Inc. Active Boy Scouts Am.; trustee Case-Western Res. U. Served to col., JAGC U.S. Army, 1942-46. Mem. Am. Soc. Corp. Secs., Am. Bar Assn., Phi Beta Kappa, Delta Sigma Rho, Omicron Delta Kappa, Beta Theta Pi, Phi Delta Phi. Clubs: Metropolitan (gov.), Morris County Golf, N.Y. Athletic. Home: 25 Lake End Pl Mountain Lakes NJ 07046 Office: Nabisco Brands Plaza Parsippany NJ 07054

CASE, WILLIAM B., sugar company executive; b. Lihue, Hawaii, Aug. 30, 1922; s. A. Hebbard and Elizabeth (McConnell) C.; m. Anne Goldsmith, July 12, 1952; children: Catherine, William Jr., Peter, Deborah, Mary, Elizabeth, Patricia Anne. B.A., Williams Coll., 1947. Vice pres. C. Brewert & Co., Honolulu, 1971-75, sr. v.p., 1975—; pres., chmn. Hawaiian Agronomics, Honolulu, 1975-77; pres., chief exec. officer Hilo Coast Processing Co., Pekeekeo, Hawaii, 1982—; pres., dir. Olokele Sugar Co., Kauai, Hawaii, 1977—; pres., dir., chmn. bd. Ka'u Sugar Co., Hawaii, 1977—; pres., chief exec. officer, dir. Hilo Coast Processing Co., Hawaii, 1977—; pres. chmn. bd., dir. Wailuku Sugar Co., Maui, 1977—, Mauna Kea Sugar Co., Hilo, 1977—. Chmn. U.S. Dept. Agr. Hawaiian Agr. Stabilization, 1975; mem. exec. bd. Kilauea council Boy Scouts Am., 1972-76; pres. Brantley Rehab. Ctr., 1967-70. Served with USNR, 1943-46. Mem. Internat. Sugar Cane Tech., Hawaiian Sugar Planters Assn. (dir. 1971-81), Hawaiian Sugar Technologists. Clubs: Honolulu, Pacific, Hilo Yacht. Home: PO Box 18 Pekeekeo HI 96783 Office: Hilo Coast Processing Co PO Box 18 Pekeekeo HI 96783

CASEBEER, EDWIN FRANK, JR., English educator; b. Boise, Idaho, July 8, 1933; s. Edwin Frank and Margaret Elaine Foster (Moye) C.; m. Lois Ann Farrington, June 1960 (div. 1966); m. 2d Ann Wendy McGougan, Apr. 1, 1969 (div. 1972); 1 son, John Frank. B.A., Whitman Coll., Walla Walla, Wash., 1955; M.A., Mont. State U., 1958; Ph.D., U. Wash., 1963. Asst. prof. English Purdue U., Indpls., 1963-69; assoc. prof. English Ind. U.-Purdue U., Indpls., 1969-77, dir. writing program, 1971-79, prof., 1977—; chmn. dept. English, 1980—; cons. Anacomp, Inc., Indpls., 1968-70. Author: Writers of the 70's: Hermann Hesse, 1972, How To Survive in College, 1968. Bd. dir. Phoenix Theater, Indpls., 1983—, Broad Ripple Playhouse, 1983, Indpls. Shakespeare Festival, 1982—, Broad Ripple High Sch. Magnet for The Humanities, 1979. Served with U.S. Army, 1956-58. Mem. Ind. Assn. English Depts. (pres. 1982-83), AAUP (pres. Ind. U. chpt. 1978-79, Purdue chpt. 1968-69), MLA, Midwest Modern Lang. Assn., Nat. Council Tchrs. English, Conf. Coll. Composition and Communmication. Office: Dept English Ind Univ-Purdue Univ 425 Agnes St Indianapolis IN 46202

CASEBOLT, VICTOR ALAN, paper company executive; b. Spokane, Jan. 2, 1935; s. Victor Study and Elizabeth Marie (Sheffels) C.; m. Jo Elaine Beeson, Aug. 25, 1956; children: Victor Study, Mark Alan, Bryan Joseph, Elizabeth Virginia. A.B. in Econs, Stanford U., 1956; M.B.A., Harvard U., 1958. Sales and mktg. mgmt. positions Gen. Electric Co., 1958-66; mng. dir. De La Rue Bull Machines Ltd., London, 1966-67; dir. gen. adjoint Cie Bull-Gen. Electric, Paris, 1967-69; mgr. info. systems sales ops. Gen. Electric Co., Phoenix, 1969-70, gen. mgr. utility and process automation dept., Lynn, Mass., 1972-75; v.p. Tampa (Fla.) ops. Honeywell Inc., 1970-72; pres., chief operating officer, dir. Storage Tech. Corp., Louisville, Colo., 1975-77; gen. mgr. Internat. Container div. Internat. Paper Co., 1977-79; gen. mgr. Folding Carton & Label div. (Internat. Paper Co.), 1979-80; v.p., group exec., Splty. Packaging Group Internat. Paper Co., 1980-81, v.p., group exec. Indsl. Packaging Group,, 1981—; dir. Mobex, Inc.; Chmn. Tampa Metro chpt. Nat. Alliance Businessmen, 1971-72. Bd. dirs. Greater Tampa C. of C., 1971-72; chmn. troop com. Boy Scouts Am., 1980—. Served with AUS, 1958. Episcopalian. Clubs: Harvard of N.Y., Masons. Home: 160 Ferris Hill Rd New Canaan CT 06840 Office: Internat Paper Plaza 77 W 45th St New York NY 10036

CASEI, NEDDA, mezzo-soprano; b. Balt.; d. Howard Thomas and Lyda Marie (Graupman) Casey; m. John A. Wiles, Jr., Dec. 1971 (div. May 1979). Grad. high sch., Scarsdale, N.Y., 1950; studied voice with William P. Herman, N.Y.C., Vittorio Piccinini, Milan, Italy, Loretta Corelli; also student piano, langs., ballet. Operatic debut, Theatre Royal de la Monnaie, Brussels, 1960, operatic performances at, Basel (Switzerland) Stadttheater, Gran Liceo, Barcelona, Spain, Teatro Carlo Fenice, Genova, Teatro Carlo Fenice, San Remo, Trieste Opera, Opera du Rhin, Strasbourg, Salzburg Festspielhaus, Teatro San Carlo, Naples, Italy, Chgo. Lyric Opera, Bogota Opera, Caracas Opera, Pitts. Opera, Vancouver (Can.) Opera, Cape Town Opera, Brno, Bratislava, Kosice and Prague operas, Miami, Houston, San Diego, Hartford, Phila., Toledo, Dayton, Memphis, Mobile, Los Angeles, Boston, N.J. State operas, Met. Opera, N.Y.C., performances in various mus. festivals, concert tours, also symphonic concerts, oratorios in, Europe, performances in various mus. festivals and tours, also symphonic concerts, oratorios in, South Africa, Central Am., S. Am., Can., U.S. and Far East; performed on radio and TV in, Holland, Belgium, Leipzig, Japan, U.S., Hong Kong, Singapore; performed at, White House, Washington, 1967; made various recs. Recipient New Orleans Opera award, 1959, Rockefeller Found. award, 1962, 64. Mem. Actor's Equity, AFTRA, Am. Guild Mus. Artists (bd. govs., pres.). Home: 15 W 72d St New York NY 10023 Office: Met Opera New York NY 10023

CASELLI, VIRGIL P., real estate executive; b. San Francisco, May 29, 1940; s. Americo P. and Cressida N. C.; m. Mary T. McKeon, July 18, 1970; children—Monica, Megan, Virgil Paul. B.S., U. Calif., Berkeley, 1963; M.B.A., U. San Francisco, 1973. Security analyst Wells Fargo Bank, San Francisco, 1963-65; purchasing agt. Raychem Corp., Menlo Park, Calif., 1965-70; founding dir., v.p. 1st Montgomery Corp., San Francisco, 1970-72; div. mgr. Kaiser-Aetna Co., Oakland, Calif., 1972-75; exec. v.p., gen. mgr. Ghiradelli Sq., San Francisco, 1975-82; pres. Comml. Property Ventures, Inc., San Francisco, 1982—; Bd. dirs. San Francisco Conv. and Visitors Bur., 1975-83, Cable Car Friends, San Francisco, 1975—, The Guardsmen, Francisco, 1977-79; pres. Fisherman's Wharf Mchts. Assos., 1976-77, San Francisco and Parking Assos., 1977. Founder, pres. Com. to Save The Cable Cars, 1979—; trustee U. Calif., Berkeley Found., 1981—. Served with USCG, 1958. Mem. Soc. Real Property Adminstrs., Bldg. Owners and Mgrs. Inst. Internat. Republican. Roman Catholic. Office: 680 Beach St San Francisco CA 94109

CASERIO, MARTIN JOSEPH, automobile manufacturing company executive; b. Laurium, Mich., July 18, 1916; s. Joseph and Mary (Michela) C.; m. Josephine Spolarich, Oct. 7, 1944; children: Richard, Kathleen, Joseph, Patricia. B.S., Mich. Tech. U., 1936, D.Sc. in Engring. (hon.), 1961. With AC Spark Plug div. Gen. Motors Corp., 1937-58, gen. mgr., 1964-66, 1958-64, v.p. parent corp., 1964—, gen. mgr., 1966-72, v.p., gen. mgr., 1972-75, v.p. and group exec., elec. components divs., 1975-80, v.p., asst. to pres., 1980—; Mem. bd. control Mich. Technol. U. Served to 1st lt. C.E. AUS, World War II. Recipient Silver Knight award Nat. Mgmt. Assn., 1963; Mich. Tech. U. Disting. Service award, 1970; Disting. Alumnus award, 1977; Eli Whitney award Soc. Mfg. Engrs., 1977. Fellow Am. Soc. Metals (chmn. Saginaw Valley chpt. 1956, Gold award for research 1982); mem. Soc. Automotive Engrs. (chmn. Mid-Mich. sect. 1955, mem. fin. com.), Engring. Soc. Detroit (dir., Council Gold award 1984), U.S. Srs. Golf Assn., Tau Beta Pi, Phi Kappa Phi. Clubs: KC, Knights of Malta, Bloomfield Hills Country (past pres.), Flint City; Pres.'s (Oakland U.). Home: 1731 St Johns Ct Bloomfield Hills MI 48013 2001 Sailfish Court Blvd Apt 307 Stuart FL 33494

CASEY, ALBERT VINCENT, airline executive; b. Boston, Feb. 28, 1920; s. John Joseph and Norine (Doyle) C.; m. Eleanor Anne Welch, Aug. 25, 1945; children: Peter Andrew, Judith Anne. A.B., Harvard, 1943, M.B.A., 1948. With S.P. Ry., 1948-61, asst. v.p., asst. treas., San Francisco, 1953-61; v.p., treas. Ry. Express Agy., N.Y.C., 1961-63; v.p. finance Times-Mirror Co., Los Angeles, 1963-64, exec. v.p., dir., 1964-66, pres., mem. exec. com., 1966-74; chmn. bd., pres. Am. Airlines, 1974-80, chmn. bd., 1980—; dir. LTV Corp., Times Mirror Co., Colgate-Palmolive Co.; mem. internat. adv. bd. Morgan Grenfell. Bd. dirs. Alliance to Save Energy; bd. dirs. Dallas Citizens Council; bd. overseers Harvard Coll.; mem. Exec. Council on Fgn. Diplomats; bd. govs. Corp. Dallas Symphony Assn., Fund for Performing Arts of Kennedy Center, Washington; bd. govs. bus. com. Mus. Modern Art, N.Y.C. Served to 1st lt. AUS, 1942-46. Mem. Air Transp. Assn. (dir.), Ft. Worth of C. of C. (bd. dirs.). Clubs: Sky (N.Y.C.); Dallas Petroleum, Dallas Country (Dallas); Bohemian; Eldorado Country (Indian Wells, Calif.). Office: PO Box 61616 Dallas/Fort Worth Airport TX 75261

CASEY, CHARLES FRANCIS, glass company executive; b. Burlington, Vt., Jan. 12, 1927; s. James E. and Helen C.; m. Marie E. Nehring, Sept. 2, 1950; children: Christina, Charles, Susan, Doug, Tom, Anne. B.A., Upsala Coll., 1948. Sr. v.p. mfg. Thatcher Glass Mfg. Co., Elmira, N.Y., 1969-74; exec. v.p. mfg. Chattanooga Glass Co., 1975-78, exec. v.p., 1978-80, pres., 1980-82, chmn. bd., pres., 1982—; pres. C & H Leasing Co., 1983—; dir. Baker-Dixon Co., Chattanooga. Named Disting. Alumni of Yr. Upsala Coll., 1981. Republican. Roman Catholic. Clubs: Walden, Fairland. Office: 400 W 45th St Chattanooga TN 37410

CASEY, CHARLES PHILIP, organic chemist, educator; b. St. Louis, Jan. 11, 1942; s. John Charles and Hildagarde Mary C.; m. Martha Tanya Link, July 20, 1968; 1 dau., Jennifer Martha. B.S. in Chemistry, St. Louis U., 1963; Ph.D., M.I.T., 1968. Asst. prof. organic chemistry U. Wis.-Madison, 1968-73, asso. prof., 1974-77, prof., 1977—; cons. Tenn. Eastman, 1977—. Romnes faculty fellow, 1978. Mem. Am. Chem. Soc., Royal Chem. Soc. Office: Dept Chemistry U Wis Madison WI 53706

CASEY, DONALD MICHAEL, advertising agency executive; b. N.Y.C., sept. 28, 1935; s. William Henry and Mary Louise (Dunn) C.; m. Carole Ann McGrath, Apr. 4, 1959; children: Donald Michael, Lynn M., Gail V. Brian W. A.B., Boston Coll., 1956. Sales rep. Exxon Coro., N.Y.C., 1959-61; asst. brand mgr. Procter & Gamble Co., Cin., 1961-63; product dir. Johnson & Johnson, New Brunswick, N.J., 1963-66; account supr. Doyle Dane Bernback, N.Y.C., 1967-68; sr. v.p. TWA, N.Y.C., 1968-81; exec. v.p. Interpub. Group of Cos., Inc., N.Y.C., 1981—. Served to 1st. lt. U.S. Army, 1956-58. Republican. Roman Catholic. Home: 13 Fox Hunt Rd Holmdel NJ 07733 Office: Interpub Group of Cos Inc 1271 Ave of Americas New York NY 10020

CASEY, DOUGLAS ROBERT, speculator, author; b. Chgo., May 5, 1946; s. Eugene Bernard and Charolotte G. (Sereikas) C. B.A., Georgetown U., 1968. Speculator Internat. Fund Mgmt. Inc., Washington, 1979—. Author: Strategic Investing, 1982 (N.Y. Times Bestseller), Crisis Investing, 1980 (No.1 N.Y. Times Best Seller), International Man, 1978; editor: Investing in Crisis newsletter, 1980—. Home: 1536 32d St NW Washington DC 20007 Office: International Fund Mgmt Inc PO Box 40949 Washington DC 20016

CASEY, EDWARD DENNIS, editor; b. Binghamton, N.Y., Apr. 16, 1931; s. Edwin John and Agnes Mary (Casey) C.; m. E. Jacqueline Wilson, July 13, 1957; children—Daniel, Jeanne, Edward, John. B.A., St. Bonaventure U., 1952; postgrad., Armed Forces Pub. Information Sch., 1953, Syracuse U. Grad. Sch. Journalism, 1954. News editor Sun-Bull., Binghamton, 1960-65; editor Daily Advance, Dover, N.J., 1965-71; exec. editor Evening Capitol, Annapolis, Md., 1971—. Vice pres. Community Chest of Anne Arundel County.; Bd. dirs. Annapolis Symphony Orch. Served with U.S. Army, 1952-54. Recipient Pub. Service award A.P., 1964, Nat. Headliners award, 1965. Mem. A.P. Mng. Editors Assn., Am. Soc. Newspaper Editors, Sigma Delta Chi. Roman Catholic. Club: K.C. Home: 1517 Riverdale Dr Annapolis MD 21401 Office: 213-33 West St Annapolis MD 21401

CASEY, EDWARD PAUL, manufacturing company executive; b. Boston, Feb. 23, 1930; s. Edward J. and Virginia (Paul) C.; m. Patricia Pinkham, June 23, 1950; children: Patricia Casey Shepherd, Lucile Tyler Casey Arnote, Jennifer Paul Casey Schwab, Sheila Pinkham, Casey McManus, Virginia Louise. A.B., Yale U., 1952; M.B.A., Harvard U., 1955. With Davidson Rubber Co., Dover, N.H., 1950—, pres., 1965—, dir., 1950—; pres. McCord Corp., Detroit, 1965-78; also dir.; pres. Ex-Cell-O Corp., Troy, Mich., chief exec. officer, 1981—, chmn., 1983—, also dir.; dir. Mfrs. Nat. Corp., Uniroyal, Inc., Middlebury, Conn. Trustee Henry Ford Health Care Corp., Detroit; bd. dirs. Detroit Symphony Orch.; adv. council Jr. Achievement of Southeastern Mich.; bd. dirs. United Found., Detroit Renaissance, Machinery and Applied Products Inst.; mem. Detroit Area council Boy Scouts Am. Mem. Engring. Soc. Detroit, Soc. Automotive Engrs., Harvard Bus. Sch. Club Detroit. Clubs: Detroit, Detroit Athletic, Yondotega (Detroit); Grosse Pointe; Country Club of Detroit (Grosse Pointe Farms, Mich.); Bloomfield Hills Country; Eastern Yacht (Marblehead, Mass.); Union League (N.Y.C.); Bath and Tennis (Palm Beach, Fla.); Wig and Pen (London, Eng.). Home: 4 Rathbone Pl Grosse Pointe MI 48230 Office: Ex-Cell-O Corp 2855 Coolidge Troy MI 48084

CASEY, ETHEL LAUGHLIN, concert and opera singer; b. Tarboro, N.C., Jan. 14, 1926; d. Maurice Lee and Mary Irene (Williams) Laughlin; m. Willis Robert Casey, May 23, 1946; children: Willis Robert, Walker Laughlin. Student, Va. Intermont Coll., 1944-45; B.A., Greensboro Coll, 1946-47; postgrad., U. N.C., 1948, 62, Meredith Coll., 1949, Northwestern U., 1961. Founder, owner Carolina Records Co.; founder concert series N.C. State Art Mus. Performed at numerous convs. and festivals; oratorio soloist; conv. and mus. comedy performer; author: Claude de France, 1963; composer: Christmas Night, 1971, America Will Endure, 1972, U.S.A., 1972; N.Y. debut, Town Hall, 1961; concert singer performing at, Carnegie Hall, all-Debussy concert, 1961, Tribute to Galli-Curci, 1965, Composer's Showcase, N.Y., 1965, Electronic Concert, Ann Arbor, Mich., 1966, Webern World Premieres Internat. Webern Festivals, Seattle, Buffalo, 1962-66, World Premieres of Graphic Music, 1965, command performance, Greek Royal Princess, 1966, New Vistas, World Premieres of Am. Music, 1968; command performance, electronic concert Philomel, 1968; Gov.'s concerts, Judson Hall, N.Y., 1969, 1970, Nat. Congress, Constn. Hall, Washington, 1970; world premieres Webern and Earls music, Carnegie Hall, 1971, world premieres own music and Webern, Lincoln Center, N.Y.C., 1971, Internat. Platform Assn., Washington, 1972; performed in, Leningrad, USSR, 1975; TV and radio performer, 1936—. Founder, God's Ministry, Christian Broadcast Network, 1981-82. Named Alumna of Year, Va. Intermont Coll., 1967, Singer of Year, Nat. Assn. Tchrs. Singing, 1963; honored as singer All-Am. City Celebrations, Tarboro, N.C., 1978; recipient award Greensboro Coll. Concert, 1980. Mem. N.C. State Music Soc. (founder). Home and Office: 1605 Park Dr Raleigh NC 27605

CASEY, FRANCIS LAWTON, JR., lawyer; b. Ithaca, N.Y., Feb. 2, 1927; s. Francis Lawton and Helen Marie (Conway) C.; m. Roseanne Mary McIlvane, Apr. 11, 1953; children: Francis Lawton, III, Patrick Conway, Thomas Dallahan. B.S., Georgetown U., 1950, J.D., 1952. Bar: D.C. 1953, U.S. Supreme Ct. 1968. Practice in, Washington, 1953—; partner firm Hogan & Hartson, 1964—; mem. com. grievances U.S. Dist. Ct. for D.C.; Mem. presdl. counsellors Georgetown U., also mem. alumni admissions program. Mem. presdl. adv. bd. Weston Sch. Theology. Served with USMCR, 1945-46. Recipient John Carroll medal merit Georgetown U., 1974, Louise C. and Frank G. Warman award Gonzaga Coll. High Sch., 1976, Gridiron Club Service award Georgetown U., 1981, Recognition award Georgetown U. Club of Met. Washington, 1984. Fellow Am. Coll. Trial Lawyers; mem. ABA, Am. Inn of Ct. VI (master bencher), Internat. Assn. Ins. Counsel, Bar Assn. D.C., D.C. Def. Lawyers Assn., Georgetown U. Alumni Assn. (gov., treas., pres., John Carroll award 1984), Newcomen Soc., Phi Delta Phi. Republican. Roman Catholic. Clubs: Counsellors, Hoya Hoop, Lawyers, Nat. Lawyers, Barristers, Georgetown U. Track and Field, Georgetown Gridiron, Hoya Hoop. Office: 815 Connecticut Ave NW Suite 600 Washington DC 20006

CASEY, GENEVIEVE MARY, librarian, educator; b. Mpls., July 13, 1916; d. Eugene James and Cecelia (Malerich) C. B.S., Coll. St. Catherine, St. Paul, 1937; M.A., U. Mich., 1956. Mem. staff Detroit Pub. Library, 1937-46, 48-61, chief extension dept., 1948-61; Mich. State librarian, Lansing, 1961-67; prof. library scis. Wayne State U., 1967-83; Fulbright prof. U. Brasilia, 1979; librarian U.S. Army Libraries, ETO, 1946-47; book reviewer for Choice, Library Jour. Named Mich. Librarian of Year, 1978. Mem. ALA (pres. Assn. Hosp. and Instn. Libraries 1961-62, pres. library edn. div. 1970-72), Pub. Library Assn. (pres. 1976—), Mich. Library Assn., Catholic Library Assn., Am. Assn. Library Schs. (pres. 1979). Address: 373 Rivard Blvd Grosse Pointe MI 48230

CASEY, HARRY WAYNE, performer, songwriter, record producer; b. Miami, Fla., Jan. 31, 1951; s. Harry L. and Jane Ann (Pugliese) C. A.A., Miami-Dade Community Coll., 1969. Founder, pres., dir. Sunshine Sound Enterprises, Miami, 1974—; pres., dir. KC and the Sunshine Band, Inc., 1975—, Harrick Music, Inc.; partner Boogie Man Music, 1978—. Composer: numerous songs including Rock Your Baby, 1974, Get Down Tonight, 1975, That's The Way (I Like It), 1975, Shake Your Booty, 1976, Dance Across the Floor, 1976, Please Don't Go, 1979, Make Me a Star, 1980; rec.: numerous albums including KC and the Sunshine Band, 1975, Part 3, 1976, Who Do Ya Love, 1978, Do You Wanna Go Party, 1979, Space Cadet-Solo Flight, 1980, The Painter, 1981 (Recipient Grammy award Nat. Acad. Recording Arts and Scis. Album of Yr. for Saturday Night Fever 1978, Producer of Year for album Saturday Night Fever 1978, Best Rhythm and Blues Song for Where Is the Love 1975, Am. Music award favorite soul singer for Get Down Tonight 1975, Best Disco Artist of Yr. award Billboard mag. 1976, recipient numerous gold and platinum single and album record awards.). Mem. AFTRA, Am. Fedn. Musicians. Office: 7764 NW 71st St Miami FL 33166 *Determination; the power of positive thinking; total faith in whatever the endeavor may be; and, hard work.*

CASEY, JAMES VINCENT, bishop; b. Osage, Iowa, Sept. 22, 1914; s. James G. and Nina (Nims) C. A.B., Loras Coll, 1936, LL.D., 1959; student, Gregorian U., Rome, Italy, 1936-40; J.C.D., Cath. U. Am., 1949. Ordained priest Roman Cath. Ch., 1939; asst. pastor St. John's Parish, Independence, Iowa, 1940-44; sec. Archbishop Leo Binz, Dubuque, 1946-49; bishop of, Lincoln, 1957-67, archbishop of, Denver, 1967—. Served to lt. Chaplains Corps USNR, 1944-46. Office: 200 Josephine St Denver CO 80206 *

CASEY, JOHN JOSEPH, airline executive; b. Boston, Oct. 3, 1918; s. John Joseph and Norine (Doyle) C.; m. Mary June Reipe, Apr. 21, 1945; children: John Joseph, David Vaughan, Janet Marjorie, Mary June. S.B., M.I.T., 1940, postgrad., 1940; postgrad., Cornell U., 1942. Stress engr. Curtiss-Wright Corp., Buffalo, 1940-42; mgr. air cargo engring. Am. Airlines, St. Joseph, Mo., 1946-47, service engr., N.Y.C., 1947-49, asst. v.p. maintenance, Tulsa, 1950-56; v.p. R. Dixon Speas Assos., Manhasset, N.Y., aviation cons., 1956-62; sr. v.p. operations, dir. Seaboard World Airlines, N.Y.C., 1962-68; group v.p., vice chmn. bd., dir. Braniff Internat., Dallas, 1968-81, pres., chmn. bd., 1981-82; exec. v.p. ops. Pan Am. World Airways, 1982-84; pres., chief exec. officer Am. World Services, 1984—. Vice-pres. Circle 10 council Boy Scouts Am.; also mem. regional bd. N.E. Region Boy Scouts Am., mem. nat. council, internat. com. Served with USAAF, 1942-46; comdg. officer 320th Squadron, 509th Composite Bomb Group, 1945-46. Mem. AIAA, Soc. Automotive Engrs., Mass. Inst. Tech. Alumni Assn. (bd. govs., v.p. N.Y.C. 1959), Air Force Assos. Clubs: Wings (N.Y.C.); Manhasset Bay Yacht, N.Y. Yacht. Home: 100 W 81st St New York NY 10024

CASEY, JOHN P., educator; b. Pitts., May 26, 1920; s. Patrick F. C.; m. Eileen; children: Charles, Carol. B.A., Bethany (W.Va.) Coll., 1949; M.Ed., U. Pitts., 1950; Ed.D. in Secondary Edn., Ind. U., 1963. Cert. tchr., Ill., Ohio. Tchr. Columbus (Ohio) Public Schs., 1950-59; asst. prof. Ill. State U., Normal, 1959-63; div. chmn. dept. social studies Northwestern Coll., Orange City, Iowa, 1963-64; asst. prof. So. Ill. U., Carbondale, 1964-69, asso. prof. dept. spl. edn. and profl. ednl. experiences, 1969-73, prof. curriculum and spl. edn., 1973—, dir. Talent Retrieval and Devel. Edn. Project (TRADE), 1965—. Co-author: Roles in Off-Campus Student Teaching, 1967; contbr. articles to profl. jours. Served with U.S. Army. Mem. Ill. Assn. Curriculum Devel., Ill. Assn. Tchr. Educators, Phi Delta Kappa. Research in supervision, research and teaching of gifted children. Home: 623 Glenview Dr Carbondale IL 62901 Office: Coll Edn So Ill U Carbondale IL 62901

CASEY, JOHN THOMAS, medical center administrator; b. Pensacola, Fla., Oct. 6, 1945; s. J.T. and Sylvia Marie (Bond) C.; m. Gail E., Apr. 30, 1982; children by previous marriage: Christopher Lee, Kathryn Welch. B.S. in Econs, Auburn U., 1967; M.S. in Hosp. Adminstrn, U. Ala., Birmingham, 1972. Asst. dir. Shands Teaching Hosp., U. Fla., Gainesville, 1972-73; adminstr. Cathedral Rehab. Center, Jacksonville, Fla., 1973-76, St. Luke's Hosp., Denver, 1976-79; pres. Presbyn./St. Luke's Med. Center, Denver, 1979—; dir. Colo. Blue Cross-Blue Shield; chmn. bd. Hosp. Shared Services of Colo. Served to lt. (j.g.) USNR, 1968-69. Named Young Hosp. Adminstr. of Yr. Am. Coll. Hosp. Adminstrs., 1981. Mem. Colo- Hosp. Assn. (dir.), Nat. Council Community Hosps., Met. Denver Hosp. Council (pres.). Republican. Episcopalian. Clubs: Denver Rotary, University.

CASEY, JOSEPH LAWRENCE, manufacturing company executive; b. Lawrence, Mass., Dec. 3, 1936; s. Laurence and Nora Casey (Naughton) C.; m. Katherine Milias, May 25, 1963; children: Elizabeth Anne, Katherine Mary, Mark Lawrence, Michael Joseph. B.A., Harvard U., 1958, M.B.A., 1963. Buyer Microwave Assocs., Inc., Burlington, Mass., 1958-60; assoc. purchasing agt. Elliott Idustries, Inc., Cambridge, Mass., 1960-61; research asst. Harvard U., 1963-64; with 1st Nat. Bank of Chgo., 1964-71, v.p. for Europe, Middle East and Africa; pres. Mark Controls Corp., Evanston, Ill., from 1971; also pres. MCC Powers, Skokie, Ill. Mem. Valve Mfrs. Assn. (bd. dirs.). Democrat. Roman Catholic. Club: Economic (Chgo.). Home: 139 Tudor Pl Kenilworth IL 60043 Office: MCC Powers 3400 Oakton St Skokie IL 60076

CASEY, JOSEPH T., corporate executive; b. 1931; married. B.S., Fordham U. With Arrow Surgical Supply Co., 1947-51, Am. Lumberman's Mutual Casualty Co. of Ill., 1951-52, Thoroughbred Racing Protective Bur. Inc., 1952-55; mgr. audits Touche, Ross, Bailey & Smart, 1955-63; controller Litton Industries Inc., Beverly Hills, Calif., 1963-67, v.p. fin., 1967-69, sr. v.p. fin., 1969-76, exec. v.p. fin., 1976—. Office: Litton Industries Inc 360 N Crescent Dr Beverly Hills CA 90210 *

CASEY, KENNETH LYMAN, neurologist; b. Ogden, Utah, Apr. 16, 1935; s. Kenneth Lafayette and Lyzena (Payne) C.; m. Jean Madsen, June 21, 1958; children—Tena Jeanette, Kenneth Lyman, Teresa Louise. B.A., Whitman Coll., Walla Walla, Wash., 1957; M.D. with honors, U. Wash., Seattle, 1961. Diplomate: Am. Bd. Neurology and Psychiatry. Intern in medicine Cornell U. Med. Center-N.Y. Hosp., 1961-62; USPHS officer lab. neurophysiology NIMH, 1962-64; fellow in psychology McGill U. Med. Sch., Montreal, Que., Can., 1964-66; mem. faculty U. Mich. Med. Sch., Ann Arbor, 1966—, prof. neurology and physiology, 1978—; chief neurology service VA Med. Center, Ann Arbor, 1979—. Author articles in field, chpts. in books. Spl. fellow NIH, 1964-66; grantee, 1966—. Mem. Am. Neurol. Assn., Am. Acad. Neurology, Am. Physiol. Soc., Soc. Neurosci., Am. Pain Soc., Internat. Soc. Study Pain, Phi Beta Kappa, Sigma Xi, Alpha Omega Alpha. Unitarian. Home: 2775 Heather Way Ann Arbor MI 48104 Office: Neurology Service VA Med Center Ann Arbor MI 48105

CASEY, MAURICE FRANCIS, air force officer; b. Chgo., June 3, 1920; s. Maurice Francis and Marie (Rowan) C.; m. Dora Belle Neubert, Oct. 12, 1946; children—Faith Maureen, Shirley Marie, M.F. Timothy, Georgeanne, Michael Joseph. Student, U. Chgo., 1939-40, U. Miami, 1948-50, Nat. War Coll., 1962. Commd. 2d lt. USAAF, 1943; advanced through grades to lt. gen. USAF, 1975; leader heavy bomber air armada (8th Air Force), World War II, troop wing comdr., Far East, 1952-54; chief air traffic control USAF, also mem. tech. div., 1954-55; mil. adviser Royal Danish Air Force; also chief air force MAAG, 1958-61; dep. dir. air force information, 1955-58, 62-65; comdr. 60th Mil. Airlift Wing, Travis AFB, 1965-68; dir. transp. Hdqrs. USAF, 1968-73, J-4 dir. strategic mobility, 1977—, also dir. logistics; exec. v.p. Wayne A. Coloney Co. Inc., Tallahassee.; Schedule airline insp. CAA, 1947-50. Vice pres. McLean (Va.) Civic Assn., 1961-65; pres. St. John's Men's Council, 1962-65. Decorated D.S.M. (3), Legion of Merit (5), Bronze star, D.F.C. (3), Air medal (5); Croix de Guerre, France; D.F.C., U.K.; Commendation of Honor, Greece). Mem. S.E. Air Res. Assn. (v.p. 1950), Nat. Def. Transp. Assn. (pres.), Quiet Birdmen, Aviation Space Writers Assn., Greater Eastern Appaloosa Region (pres.), Nat. War Coll. Alumni (pres. 1977-79). Club: Lions. Home: 7017 Union Mill Rd Clifton VA 22024 Office: Headquarters USAF Washington DC 20333

CASEY, RALPH WALDO, banker; b. Guthrie, Okla., Sept. 24, 1899; s. James O. and Jennie (Plummer) C.; m. Gertrude Richard, Nov. 21, 1927; 1 dau., Mary Patricia (Mrs. John C. Burr). A.B., U. Kans., 1931. With Bank Commerce, Tonkawa, Okla., 1919-29; sec.-treas. Williams Iron Works, Tonkawa, 1931-39; partner D. & D. Drilling Co., Dallas, also Den-Tex. Oil Co., 1940-55; ind. oil producer, Tonkawa, 1940—; exec. rep. Colo. State Bank, Denver, 1965—; Okla. loan agt. Smaller War Plant Corp., Oklahoma City, 1942-44; fiscal agt. Okla. to Mfrs. Trust Co., N.Y.C., 1951-55. Dist. chmn. North Okla. council Boy Scouts Am., 1942-43; exec. sec. to Gov. of Okla., 1951-55. Named Ky. col., 1953; hon. chief Kiowa Indians of Okla., 1953. Mem. Tonkawa C. of C. (pres. 1940, 45), Okla. Hist. Soc., Colo. Hist. Soc., Westerners, Acacia. Republican. Presbyterian. Clubs: Mason (32 deg.), City, 26 (Denver). Home: 1888 S Jackson St Apt 1002 Denver CO 80210 Office: Colo State Bank 1600 Broadway Denver CO 80202

CASEY, RAYMOND RICHARD, agri-business executive; b. Wauseon, Ohio, Sept. 18, 1935; s. Raymond John and Esther Elizabeth (Read) C.; m. Clara Jane Patrick, Apr. 26, 1958; children: Patrick, Natalie, Michelle, Brian, Kevin, Eric. B.Sc. in Agrl. Econs, Ohio State U., 1956, M.B.A., 1969; grad. agri-bus. seminar, Harvard U. Bus. Sch., 1971, 80. Research asst. Ohio Agrl. Expt. Sta., 1956-57; dir. research and devel., then asst. to exec. v.p., then adminstrv. asst. and dir. research and devel. Ohio Farm Bur., 1962-78; v.p. corp. planning, treas. Landmark, Inc., Columbus, Ohio, 1978-80, sr. v.p. mktg., 1980—; dir., vice chmn. Peoples Travel Service, Inc.; dir. Silvergrove Fleeting Service, Inc., Mid States Terminals, Inc.; bd. dirs. Central Ohio Center Econ. Devel., Ohio Council Econ. Edn., 1980—, Ohio 4-H Adv. Com., 1980—; Mem. agrl. econs. adv. com. Ohio State U. Pres. bd. dirs. Camp Willson YMCA, 1970-74, PTA, 1970-75, Booster Club, 1974; bd. dirs. Columbus Artist in Sch. Program, 1975-76, Columbus Met. YMCA, 1975—, Internat. Council Mid-Ohio, 1976-81, Zivili, 1980-82. Served to capt. USAF, 1957-62. Recipient commendation Ohio Ho. Reps. Mem. Am. Mktg. Assn. (past pres. Central Ohio chpt.), Nat. Grain and Feed Assn. (dir.), U.S. Feed Grains Council (dir.), Ohio Feed and Grain Assn. (dir.), Am. Mgmt. Assn., Fin. Execs. Inst., Treas.'s Club, Columbus Area C. of C., Ohio State U. Alumni Assn. (life), Scabbard and Blade, Alpha Zeta Alumni Assn. (past chmn. bd. trustees), Gamma Sigma Delta. Republican. Methodist. Club: Ohio State U. Pres.'s. Office: 35 E Chestnut St Columbus OH 43216

CASEY, SAMUEL ALEXANDER, lawyer, paper mfr.; b. Peoria, Ill., Sept. 10, 1914; s. Richard C. and Chloris (Thomason) C.; m. Ardean Alexander, Nov. 7, 1942; children—John A., Suzanne E., Page E. A.B., Bradley U., 1936; J.D., U. Ill., 1939. Bar: Ill. bar 1939, Wis. bar 1946. Practice law, 1939—; asso. Chapman & Cutler, Chgo., 1939-42; exec. v.p., treas. Nekoosa-Edwards Paper Co., Port Edwards, Wis., 1946-61, pres., dir., 1962-70; now dir.; pres., dir. Gt. No. Nekoosa Corp., Stamford, Conn., 1971-78, chief exec. officer, 1972-79, chmn., 1974-80, chmn. exec. com., 1980—; dir. U.S. Trust Co. of N.Y., Gen. Signal Corp., Greyhound Corp., Pitney Bowes. Trustee Bradley U., Peoria, Ill. Home: Wickenburg AZ 85358 Office: 100 Wisconsin River Dr Port Edwards WI 54469

CASEY, WARREN PETER, playwright, composer, lyricist; b. N.Y.C., Apr. 20, 1935; s. Peter Leonard and Signe (Ginman) C. B.F.A., Syracuse U., 1957. Author: (with Jim Jacobs) Grease, 1971 (book, music, lyrics), Mudgett, 1976 (music and Lyrics), Island of Lost Coeds, 1981 (book, music and lyrics). Mem. Dramatists Guild, ASCAP, Joseph Jefferson Com., Sigma Nu. Office: Internat Creative Management 40 W 57th St New York NY 10019

CASEY, WILLIAM JOSEPH, govt. ofcl.; b. Elmhurst, Queens, N.Y., Mar. 13, 1913; s. William J. and Blanche (La Vigne) C.; m. Sophia Kutz, Feb. 22, 1941; 1 dau., Bernadette. B.S., Fordham U., 1934; postgrad., Cath. U. Am.; J.D., St. John's U., 1937. Chmn. bd. editors Research Inst. Am., Washington, 1938-49; with OSS, U.S. Army Intelligence, 1941-46; spl. counsel small bus. com. U.S. Senate, Washington, 1974-48; asso. gen. counsel ECA Mission to France, 1948; lectr. tax law N.Y. U., 1948-62; lectr. Practicing Law Inst., N.Y.C., 1950-62; partner firm Hall, Casey, Dickler & Howley, N.Y.C., 1957-71; chmn. SEC, Washington, 1971-73; undersec. state econ. affairs Dept. State, Washington, 1973-74; pres., chmn. Export-Import Bank U.S., 1974-75; mem. Pres. Ford's Fgn. Intelligence Adv. Bd., Washington, 1976, Task Force on Equality and Venture Capital, SBA, 1976-80; campaign mgr. Ronald Reagan Presdl. Campaign, 1980; dir. CIA, Washington, 1981—. Author: Lawyers Desk Book, 1965, Tax Sheltered Investments, 1952, Estate Planning Book, 1956, Forms of Business Agreements, 1966, Accounting Desk Book, 1967. Trustee Fordham U., 1966-71; pres. L.I. Assn., 1968-71; chmn. Internat. Rescue Com., 1970-71. Mem. Am. Bar Assn., Nassau County Bar Assn., Assn. Bar City N.Y. Office: Office of Dir CIA Washington DC 20905 *

CASEY, WILLIAM L., petroleum and gas exploration executive; b. 1923; married. With Howell Hydrocarbons Inc (subs.), 1974; v.p. Howell Corp., Houston, 1974-78, sr. v.p., 1978—, pres., dir. Office: Howell Corp 1010 Lamar Houston TX 77002 *

CASEY, WILLIAM ROBERT, JR., U.S. ambassador to Niger, mining engineer; b. Denver, Dec. 15, 1944; s. William Robert and Anne Marie (Elliott) C.; m. B. Dionne Davis, Jan. 2, 1976; children: Stephanie Anne, Patrick Thomas, Jennifer Lee, William Robert III. Engr. of Mines, Colo. Sch. of Mines, 1969; postgrad., Queens U., 1972. Systems analyst Kennecott Copper Corp., Salt Lake City, 1969-71; mining engr. Hudson Bay Mining & Smelting, Flin Flon, Man., Can., 1971-72; project engr. Fluor Utah, Inc., San Mateo, Calif., 1972-73; chief field engr. Arthur G. Mekee, Salt Lake City, 1973-74; sr. mining engr. Morrison-Knudson Co., Boise, Idaho, 1974-75, Dravo Corp., Denver, 1975-77; project mgr. CONOCO, Denver and Paris, 1977-79; mgr. Rocky Mountain Energy Co., Broomfield, Colo., 1979-82; ambassador to Rep. of Niger, Niamey, 1982—; cons. to mineral industry, participant community informational seminars. Precinct chmn. Republican Party, Colo., 1978—; county and state del. Colo. primaries. Mem. Am. Inst. Mining, Colo. Mining Assn. Lodge: Lions. Home: 1609 Ithaca Ct Longmont CO 80501 Office: American Embassy Niamey Dept of State Washington DC 20520

CASH, FRANCIS WINFORD, hotel and restaurant executive; b. Buena Vista, Va., Mar. 16, 1942; s. Winsford McKinley and Elsie E. (Yates) C.; m. Judith R. Robey, Dec. 27, 1962; children: Jeri Lynn, Lori Ann, Robin Elaine, David Francis, Judith Kristine. B.S. in Acctg, Brigham Young U., Provo, Utah, 1965. C.P.A., D.C. With Arthur Andersen & Co. (C.P.A.s), Washington, 1965-74; v.p., corp. controller Marriott Corp., Washington, 1974-79, sr. v.p. corp. services, 1979-84, exec. v.p. Roy Rogers div., 1984—; dir. Sailors and Mchts. Bank and Trust. Pres. Hayfield Elem. Sch. PTA, Fairfax, Va., 1973-74; chmn. Washington area Boy Scouts Am. show, 1978; bd. advisers Sch. Accountancy, Brigham Young U., 1978—. Recipient Service award Boy Scouts Am., 1978, Beta Alpha Psi Outstanding Alumnus award Brigham Young U., 1984. Mem. Fin. Execs. Inst. Mormon. Office: Marriott Dr Washington DC 20058

CASH, FRANK ERRETTE, JR., foreign service officer; b. Oriskany, Va., Mar. 7, 1921; s. Frank Errette and Libbie (Adamson) C.; m. Naomi Duncan, Dec. 3, 1947; children: Hal Duncan, Susan Hamilton. B.S., Birmingham-So. Coll., 1941, U.S. Mil. Acad., 1944; postgrad., Harvard U., 1951-52. Commd. 2d lt. U.S. Army, 1944, advanced through grades to capt., 1948; served in, ETO, World War II, resigned, 1948; joined U.S. Fgn. Service, 1948; assigned Am. consulate gen., Stuttgart, Germany, 1948-51; polit. officer Am. embassy, Bonn, Germany, 1952-55, consul, polit. officer, Manila, Philippines, 1955-57; head dept. univ. tng. and area studies Fgn. Service Inst., State Dept., 1958-60; officer charge German polit. affairs, also dep. dir. Berlin task force State Dept., 1960-63; participant Sr. Seminar in Fgn. Affairs, Fgn. Service Inst., 1963-64; counselor for mut. security affairs Am. embassy, Ankara, Turkey, 1964-68; country dir. for Turkey State Dept., 1968-71; Am. minister, dep. chief mission Am. embassy, Bonn, 1971-77; dep. comdt. for internat. affairs U.S. Army War Coll., 1977—. Home: Route 4 Box 310-A Lexington VA 24450 Office: George C. Marshall Found Drawer 1600 Lexington VA 24450

CASH, JAMES BARRETT, JR., assn. ofcl.; b. Hazen, Ark., Nov. 8, 1921; s. James Barrett and Annie Laurie (Graves) C.; m. Teresa O'Connor, Dec. 27, 1968. A.A., George Washington U., 1948, B.A., 1951; certificate emergency mgmt. of nat. economy, Indsl. Coll. Armed Forces, 1956. Adminstrv. positions FHA, 1939-53; policy and procedures officer Civil Service Commn., 1953-55; profl. staff mem. com. banking and currency U.S. Senate, 1955-61; dep. commr. FHA, 1961-62; with AID, Caracas, Venezuela, 1962-64, dir., 1964; profl. staff mem. Select Com. on Small Bus., U.S. Senate, 1964-65; legislative asst. Senator J.W. Fulbright, 1965-70; fed. legislative rep. Am. Bankers Assn., 1970—. Served with USAAF, World War II. Mem. Sigma Alpha Epsilon. Home: 5111 Colebrook Pl Alexandria VA 22312 Office: 1120 Connecticut Ave NW Washington DC 20036

CASH, JOHNNY, entertainer; b. Kingsland, Ark., Feb. 26, 1932; s. Ray and Carrie (Rivers) C.; m. June Carter, Mar. 1, 1968; 1 son, John Carter; children by previous marriage: Rosanne, Kathleen, Cindy, Tara. H.H.D., Gardner-Webb Coll., 1971, Nat. U., San Diego, 1975; L.H.D. (hon.), Nat. U., San Diego, 1976. Pres. House of Cash, Inc., Song of Cash, Inc.; v.p. Family of Man Music, Inc.; Mem. adv. com. Peace Corps, Country Music Assn., John Edwards Meml. Found. Profl. composer, also; rec. artist; TV performer: the Johnny Cash Show, 1969-71; Author: autobiography Man in Black, 1975; Composer: documentary rec. The True West; composer: movie sound tracks Little Fauss and Big Halsy; recs. include Believer Sings the Truth; subject: documentary films Johnny Cash, the Man, His World, His Music; actor: movie A Gunfight; TV documentary film Johnny Cash at San Quentin; promotional film United Way of America, 1972; co-writer, producer narrator: film The Gospel Road. Hon. com. mem. Israel's 25th Anniversary; co-host Muscular Dystrophy Telethon, 1972. Served with USAF. Named to Country Music Hall of Fame, 1980. Address: care Artists Consultants 11777 San Vicente Blvd Los Angeles CA 90049

CASH, JOSEPH HARPER, coll. adminstr., historian; b. Mitchell, S.D., Jan. 3, 1927; s. Joseph R. and Claudia B. (Harper) C.; m. Margaret Ann Halla, Dec. 18, 1952; children—Sheridan Lisa, Joseph Mark, Meredith Ann. B.A., U. S.D., 1949; M.A., 1959; Ph.D., U. Iowa, 1966. Tchr. public schs., S.D., 1951-62; instr. Black Hills State Coll., summer 1961; grad. asst. U. Iowa, 1962-65; asso. prof. history Eastern Mont. Coll., 1965-68; research asso. Inst. Indian Studies, U. S.D., summer 1967, 68, dir. inst. div. Indian research, 1970-77, acting dir. inst., 1976-77, asso. prof., 1970-74, Duke research prof. history, 1972—, prof., 1974—, dean, 1977—; dir. Am. Indian Research Project, State of S.D., 1969-74, S.D. Oral History Project, 1970-74, Oral History Center (merger both projects), 1974-77; chmn. S.D. Bd. Hist. Preservation, 1970-73; chmn. council dirs., cultural pres. div. State S.D., 1975-76; mem. S.D. Council on Humanities, 1975-77, S.D. Hist. Records Adv. Bd., 1976—, S.D. Bd. Cultural Preservation, 1977—, Kampgrounds of Am.-U. Adv. Bd., 1978—. Author: 6 Indian Tribal Series books, 1971-76; author: (with Herbert T. Hoover) To Be An Indian, 1971, Working the Homestake, 1973, The Practice of Oral History, 1974; gen. editor: American Indian Oral History Collection, 1977; bd. editors: Rocky Mountain Rev, 1966-68, Midwest Rev, S.D. History. Served with USMCR, 1945-46. Recipient award of merit Am. Assn. State and Local History, 1975. Mem. Am. Hist. Assn., Oral History Assn., Orgn. Am. Historians, S.D. Hist. Soc. (pres. 1977—), Western History Assn., Phi Beta Kappa, Phi Delta Theta. Republican. Home: 609 Catalina St Vermillion SD 57069 Office: Coll Arts and Scis U SD Vermillion SD 57069

CASH, JUNE CARTER, singer; b. Maces Springs, Va., June 23, 1929; d. Ezra and Maybelle (Addington) Carter; m. John R. Cash; children: Rebecca Carlene, Rozanna Lea, John Carter. L.H.D. (hon.), Nat. U., San Diego, 1977. Propr. June Carter Cash Antiques and Gift Shop, Hendersonville, Tenn. Singer with, Carter Family, 1939-43; with, Carter Sisters (and mother), after 1943; performed on, Sta. XERF, Del Rio Tex., Sta. KWTO, Springfield, Mo.; mem., Grand Ole Opry, Sta. WSM, Nashville, from 1953; TV appearances include John Davidson Show, Tennessee Ernie Show, Johnny Cash Show, others; films include Thaddeus, Rose and Eddie, Country Music Holiday; TV film Gospel Road, Country Music Caravan, Road to Nashville, Tennessee Jamboree, Gospel Road; songs recorded include Love Oh Crazy Love, Let Me Go Lover, Leftover Loving. Recipient Civic award Nashville Women Execs., 1980. Office: PO Box 508 Hendersonville TN 37075

CASH, PAUL THALBERT, physician; b. Lenox, Iowa, July 11, 1911; s. William Henry and Helen (Phalen) C.; m. Reva Lamb, Aug. 16, 1958; 1 step-son, Peter Goodwin. Student, Creston Jr. Coll., 1929-31; M.D., U. Iowa, 1935. Diplomate: Am. Bd. Psychiatry and Neurology. Intern St. Vincents Hosp., Portland, Oreg., 1935-36; resident psychiatry Clarkson Meml. Hosp., Omaha, 1936-37, Albany (N.Y.) Hosp., 1937-38; vol. asst. internal medicine U. Iowa Hosps., Iowa City, 1938; resident neurology Neurol. Inst. N.Y., 1939; practice medicine specializing in psychiatry, neurology, Omaha, 1940-48, Des Moines, 1948—; instr. neurology, psychiatry U. Nebr. Coll. Medicine, 1946-48; chief service neurology and psychiatry Iowa Meth. Hosp., 1953—; hon. staff Iowa Meth. Med. Ctr.; cons. VA Hosp. Contbr. articles to profl. jours. Served to maj. M.C. AUS, 1942-46. Fellow Am. Psychiat. Assn. (life), A.M.A.; mem. Central, Iowa neuropsychiat. assns., Am. Acad. Neurology, Assn. for Research in Nervous and Mental Diseases, Am. EEG Soc. Home: 3315 Waco Ct Des Moines IA 50321

CASH, POLK WRIGHT, dentist; b. Bastrop, Tex., Feb. 24, 1932; s. Polk Wright and Sadie Ray (Gunn) C.; m. Phyllis Jill Whipple, Dec. 20, 1958 (div. June 1971); children: Cara Lynn, Richard Ryan, Christian Lee; m. Michele Denise Farnum, Nov. 25, 1971. B.S. in Bus. Adminstrn, Trinity U., San Antonio, 1958; postgrad. premed., San Antonio Coll., 1961-64; D.D.S., Baylor U. Sch. Dentistry, 1968. Prodn. analyst Jack Ammann Aerial Photogrammetric Engrs., San Antonio, 1958-59; mgr. prodn., purchasing, statistics personnel Westwood Corp. furniture mfg., San Antonio and San Marcos, Tex., 1959-61; practice dentistry, San Antonio, 1968—; founder, chmn. bd. Dentotronics (mfg. electronic med. equipment), San Antonio, 1969—; faculty St. Mary's U. continuing edn., San Antonio, 1978; Exec. bd. Alamo Regional Sci. and Engring. Fair, 1972—; founder, chmn. bd. regents Tex. State Sci. and Engring. Fair, 1975-79. Contbr. profl. jours. Served with USAF, 1950-53; Korea. Recipient 1st Nat. Annual award in creative dentistry Johnson & Johnson dental div., 1972, Founders award Dallas Midwinter Conv., 1973, honor of merit World Dental Congress, 1972. Mem. Internat. Soc. Electronic Endodontology (founder, pres. 1973—), Tex. Dental Assn., San Antonio Dist. Dental Soc., Acad. Gen. Dentistry, Acad. Psychosomatic Medicine, Delta Sigma Delta. Research on technique of root canal therapy by methods of electronics to determine canal length, adequacy of sealant, location of acessory or lateral canals. Patentee endometer. Address: 4499 Medical Dr 110 San Antonio TX 78229

CASH, ROSALIND, actress; d. Jack C. and Curtis (Cash). Student, pub. schs., Atlantic City. Appeared: in films Wrong is Right, The Class of Miss Mac Michael, The Money Hustle, Cornbread, Earl and Me, Uptown Saturday Night, Amazing Grace, Melinda, Hickey and Boggs, The New Centurions, the Omega Man, The All American Boy; in TV shows Go Tell it on the Mountain, Many Mansions, Denmark Vesey, Up & Coming, Teh Guyana Tragedy, The Sophisticated Gents, South By Northwest, Sister, Sister, A Killing Affair, Barney Miller, Starsky & Hutch, Police Woman, Kojak, What's Happening, Good Times, Mary Tyler Moore Show, Ceremonies in Dark Old Men, King Lear; in plays The Visions of Simon Machard, The Sixteenth Round, Evolution of the Blues, Orchids in the Moonlight, Boesman and Lena, Kings Lear, Charlie Was Here and Now He's Gone, The Negro Ensemble Company, The World Theatre Festival, Rosalind Cash in Concert, the Arena Stage, The Harlem Y Little Theatre Group.

CASH, WILLIAM BRADBURY, business consultant; b. Portland, Oreg., Mar. 28, 1915; s. John P. and Irene (Bradbury) C.; m. Nancy Kirkpatrick, June 14, 1941; children: Penelope, Nancy, Louise. B.A. in English, Dartmouth, 1937; grad., Advanced Mgmt. Course, Harvard, 1953. With Gen. Mills, Inc., 1937-63, dir. marketing, 1960-63, v.p., 1960-63; exec. v.p., gen. mgr. operations United Biscuit Co. Am. (became Keebler Co. 1962), 1963-67; pres., chief exec. officer, dir. Hanes Corp., Winston-Salem, N.C., 1967-70; chmn., dir. Turnpike Properties, Inc., Winston-Salem, N.C.; dir. Turnpike Properties Midwest, Inc., Mpls., Ladd Furniture, Inc., High Point, N.C., Bemis Co., Inc., Mpls.; also bus. cons. Winston-Salem Housing Inc. Served to lt. comdr. USNR, 1940-45. Mem. Winston-Salem C. of C., Psi Upsilon. Republican. Episcopalian. Clubs: Rotarian., Minneapolis (Mpls.); Old Town, Twin City (Winston-Salem). Home: 2848 Bartram Rd Winston-Salem NC 27106

CASHEL, THOMAS WILLIAM, lawyer; b. N.Y.C., Feb. 12, 1930; s. Thomas Leo and Vera Lucia (Blattmacher) C.; m. Sarah Ann Strife, Oct. 11, 1958; children: Thomas W., Michael S., Alison K., Colin M. A.B., Cornell U., 1952, LL.B., 1956; diploma in internat. law, Cambridge U., Eng., 1958. Bar: N.Y. 1957, U.S. Supreme Ct. 1963. Assoc. law firm Simpson Thacher & Bartlett, N.Y.C., 1958-65, ptnr., 1965—. Trustee Practising Law Inst., N.Y.C., 1978-81. Served to lt. U.S. Army, 1952-54. Fellow Am. Bar Found.; mem. Am. Soc. Internat. Law, Internat. Bar Assn., ABA, Assn. Bar City N.Y., Order of the Coif, Phi Kappa Phi. Roman Catholic. Clubs: Racquet and Tennis, N.Y. Yacht, Fishers Island Country, Oxford-Cambridge, Hurlingham. Office: Simpson Thacher & Bartlett 99 Bishopsgate London UK EC2M 3XD

CASHEN, HENRY CHRISTOPHER, II, lawyer, former government official; b. June 25, 1939; s. Raymond and Catherine C.; m. Leslie Renchard, June 28, 1967 (div. 1982); children: Raymond II, Hayley Holloway, Henry Christopher III. A.B., Brown U., 1961; grad., U. Mich. Law Sch., 1963. Bar: Mich. 1964, U.S. Supreme Ct. 1969. Mem. firm Dickinson, Wright, McKean & Cudlip, Detroit, 1964-69; dep. counsel to Pres. U.S., Washington, 1969-70, dep. asst. to, 1970-73; mem. firm Dickstein, Shapiro & Morin (and predecessor), Washington, 1973—. Mem. Barristers Soc., D.C., Mich. bar assns., Psi Upsilon, Phi Delta Phi. Republican. Roman Catholic. Clubs: Country of Detroit, Univ., Met., Chevy Chase. Office: 2101 L St NW Washington DC 20037

CASHEN, J. FRANK, professional baseball team executive; m. Jean Cashen; children: Blaise, Stacey, Sean, Brian, Timmy, Terry, Greg. B.A., Loyola Coll.; J.D., U. Md. Formerly sportswriter and columist Balt. News-Am.; gen. mgr. Balt. Raceway and Bel Air Race Track; exec. asst. to pres., dir. advt. Nat. Brewing Co., Balt., 1962-65; exec. v.p. Balt. Orioles, Am. League, 1965-75; sr. v.p. mktg. and sales Carling Nat. Breweries, Balt., 1975-79; adminstr. baseball Commr.'s Office, N.Y.C., 1979-80; exec. v.p., gen. mgr., chief operating officer N.Y. Mets, Nat. League, 1980—; mem. exec. com. Nat. League; bd. dirs. Major League Baseball Promotions Corp. Trustee Mount St. Mary's Coll. Office: care NY Mets Roosevelt Ave and 126th St Flushing NY 11368

CASHIN, BONNIE, designer; b. Oakland, Calif., 1915. Designer ballet co.; costume designer Roxy Theatre, N.Y.C., 1934-37; sportswear designer Adler & Adler, N.Y.C., 1937-43; fashion designer Twentieth Century Fox Studios, Calif., 1943-49, Adler & Adler, 1949-52; own bus. Bonnie Cashin Designs, Inc., N.Y.C., 1952—; major collections for Philip Sills, Inc., N.Y.C.; opened firm The Knittery, 1972. Recipient Nieman Marcus award, N.Y.C. Fashion Critics Winnie, Sports Illus. award, Knitwear Industry award, Phila. Mus. Coll. of Art citation, Woolknit Assn. award, 1961, N.Y. Fashion Critics award, 1961, 68; London Sunday Times Fashion award, 1966; named Woman of Year Lighthouse for Blind, 1961. Invited by Indian govt. to assist in revitalization program for handloom industry, 1956. Office: Bonnie Cashin Designs Inc 866 UN Plaza New York NY 10017 *

CASHIN, RICHARD MARSHALL, govt. ofcl.; b. Boston, Apr. 3, 1924; s. William David and Anna Genevieve (Keefe) C.; m. Mary Catherine Walsh, Nov. 25, 1950; children—Anne Jordan, Richard Marshall, Jane Kevill, Stephen Douglas. A.B., Harvard, 1946; A.M., Boston U., 1949; grad., Sch. Advanced Internat. Studies, Johns Hopkins, 1959. Mgmt. staff Dept. State, 1949-52; staff U.S. Escapee Program, 1952-56; with ICA, 1956—; program officer USOM to, Libya, 1956-59, Ethiopia, 1959-62; dir. Office Central African Affairs, AID, Washington, 1962-66; assigned Sr. Seminar Fgn. Policy, Fgn. Service Inst., Washington, 1966-67; dep. dir. AID mission to, Ghana, 1967-68, dir., 1968-70, AID mission to Indonesia, Jakarta, 1970-75; asso. asst. adminstr. Office Legis. Affairs AID, Washington, 1975-77; dir. AID mission to, Pakistan, 1977-78; dir. project mgmt. div. UN/FAO World Food Programme, Rome, Italy, 1978—. Home: Via di Villa Pepoli 4 00153 Rome Italy Office: UN/FAO World Food Programme Via delle Terme di Caracalla 00100 Rome Italy

CASHMAN, DANIEL VINCENT, investment company executive; b. Phila., Aug. 16, 1939; s. Daniel Vicent and Eleanor Marie (Haddigan) C.; m. Linda Bernard, June 24, 1964 (div.); children: Kristin, Elise, Daniel. B.A., Vallanova U., 1961. Broker Amott Baker & Co., Phila., 1965-69; securities analyst First Pa. Corp., Phila., 1969-73; portfolio mgr. Provident Nat. Bank, Phila., 1973-79; pres. Provident Capital Mgmt., Phila., 1979-80; ptnr. Cashman Farrell & Assocs., Wayne, Pa., 1980—. Served with USMC, 1962. Republican. Office: Cashman Farrell & Assocs 1285 Drummers Ln Wayne PA 19087

CASHMAN, JOHN (JACK) PATRICK, company executive; b. Eng., Nov. 19, 1940; emigrated to Can., 1980; s. John A. and Nora (Keogh) C. With Johns-Manville, 1964-80, mktg. dir. filtration and minerals for Europe, then group mktg. mgr. fiber glass and bldg. products for Europe, until, 1980; pres., gen. mgr. Manville Can. Inc., Etobicoke, Ont., 1980—; v.p., dir. Manville Internat. Corp., Denver; dir. Polymer Internat., Truro, N.S., Can. Mem. Inst. Mktg., Inst. Dirs. Office: Manville Can Inc 295 The West Mall Etobicoke ON Canada M9C 4ZY

CASHMAN, JOHN W., physician, educator; b. St. Joseph, Mo., Apr. 26, 1923; s. John Amos and Marguerite (Helphingstine) C.; m. Helen Feckanin, Oct. 29, 1948; children: John W., Thomas D. Student, U. Rochester, 1940-43, U. Kans., summer 1942; S.B., U. Chgo., 1944, M.D., 1946; M.P.H., Johns Hopkins, 1964. Pvt. practice internal medicine, Kansas City, Mo., 1954-58, 79—; career officer USPHS, 1947-54, 58-71; asst. surgeon gen., dir. community-health service, 1968-71; dir. health State of Ohio, Columbus, 1971-75; prof. medicine U. Mo. at Kansas City, 1975-79, clin. prof. medicine, 1979—; dir. Western Mo. Health Edn. Center., 1977-79. Served with AUS, 1943-46. Recipient Meritorious Service medal USPHS, 1967; Sec.'s Spl. citation, 1971. Fellow Am. Pub. Health Assn. Mem. Ch. of Nazarene. Home: 4100 W 93d St Shawnee Mission KS 66207 Office: 6420 Prospect St Kansas City MO 64132

CASHMAN, ROBERT J., physicist, educator; b. Wilmington, Ohio, Sept. 27, 1906; s. John and Corina (Smithson) C.; m. Agnes Jones, June 8, 1940; children—Linda Lloyd, John Elliott. A.B., Bethany Coll., 1928, D.Sc., 1953; A.M., Northwestern U., 1930, Ph.D., 1935; student, U. Mich., 1931. With Northwestern U., Evanston, Ill., 1930—, successively instr. physics, asst. prof., asso. prof., 1937-47, prof. physics, 1947—; govt. research, 1941-73. Contbr. articles to sci. and profl. jours., books. Recipient certificates of commendation U.S. Navy, Dept. Def., 1947. Fellow Am. Phys. Soc., Am. Optical Soc.; mem. AAUP, Sigma Xi, Kappa Alpha. Club: Mason. Patentee photoconductive cells, photoemissive cells, sound reprodn. and camera tubes. Home: 830 Indian Rd Glenview IL 60025 Office: Northwestern U Evanston IL 60201

CASIANO VARGAS, ULISES, bishop; b. Lajas, P.R., Sept. 25, 1933. Ordained priest Roman Cath. Ch., 1967; elected to bishop, 1976, bishop of, Mayaquez, P.R., 1976—. Address: Apartado 2272 Mayaquez PR 00708

CASIDA, JOHN EDWARD, entomology educator; b. Phoenix, Dec. 22, 1929; s. Lester Earl and Ruth (Barnes) C.; m. Katherine Faustine Monson, June 16, 1956; children: Mark Earl, Eric Gerhard. B.S., U. Wis., 1951, M.S., 1952, Ph.D., 1954. Research asst. U. Wis., 1951-53, mem. faculty, 1954-63, prof. entomology, 1959-63; prof. entomology, pesticide chemist and toxicologist U. Calif. at Berkeley, 1964—; scholar-in-residence Bellagio Study and Conf. Center, Rockefeller Found., Lake Como, Italy, 1978. Author research publs. Served with USAF, 1953. Recipient medal 7th Internat. Congress Plant Protection, Paris, 1970; Haight traveling fellow, 1958-59; Guggenheim fellow, 1970-71; Jeffery lectr., U. New South Wales (Australia), 1983. Mem. Am. Chem. Soc. (Internat. award research pesticide chemistry 1970, Spencer award in agrl. and food chemistry 1978), Entomol. Soc. Am., Am. Chem. Soc. Home: 1570 La Vereda Rd Berkeley CA 94708

CASKEY, JEFFERSON DIXON, educator; b. Lancaster, S.C., July 31, 1922; s. John Lathan and Lessie (Helms) C.; m. Louise Huffaker, June 14, 1957; children—Nora Constance Caskey Huff, Gretchen Louise. A.B., Erskine Coll., 1948; M.S., Syracuse U., 1952; M.A., U. Houston, 1966, Ed.D., 1972. Tchr. English public schs., S.C., 1948-52; catalog librarian, asst. reference librarian Auburn U., 1953-54; asso. librarian, asst. prof. library sci. Shepherd Coll., Shepherdstown, W.Va., 1954-56; head librarian, asso. prof. Pfeiffer Co., Misenheimer, N.C., 1956-60; head librarian asst. prof. Little Rock U., 1960-63; head librarian, asso. prof. Houston Bapt. U., 1963-70; asso. prof., dir. library sci. program Tex. A&I U., Kingsville, 1970-74; asso. prof. library sci. Western Ky. U., Bowling Green, 1974-77, prof., 1977—. Editor: Samuel Taylor Coleridge: A Selective Bibliography of Criticism, 1935-77, 1978; asst. editor: Ky. Libraries, 1979—; contbg. editor: Back Home in Ky, 1979—; contbr. articles to profl. jours. and childrens mags. Served with USN, 1943-45. Mem. ALA, Ky. Library Assn., Nat. Council Tchrs. English, Ky. Sch. Media Assn., Ch. and Synagogue Library Assn. Democrat. Baptist. Office: Dept Library Sci Western Ky U Bowling Green KY 42101

CASKEY, JOHN LANGDON, archaeologist, emeritus educator; b. Boston, Dec. 7, 1908; s. Lacey Davis and Elsie Langdon (Stern) C.; m. Miriam Ervin, 1967. B.A., Yale U., 1931; Ph.D., U. Cin., 1939. Mem. staff excavations at Troy U. Cin., 1932-38, univ. instr. classics, 1939-42, asst. prof., 1946-48, prof. classical archaeology, 1959-79, emeritus, 1979—, head dept. classics, 1959-72, fellow, 1961—, field dir. univ. excavations in Keos, 1960—; asst. dir. Am. Sch. Classical Studies, Athens, 1948-49, dir., 1949-59, vis. prof., 1975-76; field dir. excavations at Heraion of Argos, 1949, Lerna, 1952-58, Eutresis, 1958; Vice chmn. mng. com. Am. Sch. Classical Studies at Athens, 1966-75. Co-author, co-editor: Troy, 1950—; contbr.: chpts. on Early and Middle Bronze Age, Cambridge Ancient History, 3d edit., Vols. I, II, 1971, 73; also articles to profl. jours., reports in field. Served to lt. col. AUS, 1942-46. Decorated Legion of Merit; named comdr. Royal Order Phoenix, Greece; hon. citizen Athens, Greece).; Hon. fellow Archaeol. Soc. Athens. Fellow Am. Acad. Arts and Scis.; mem. Archaeol. Inst. Am. (Gold medal), Am. Philol. Assn., Vergilian Soc., Am. Philos. Soc., Assn. Field Archaeology, Classical Assn. Can., Soc. Promotion Hellenic Studies, German Archaeol. Inst., Soc. Cycladic Studies (hon.) (Greece), Royal Irish Acad. (hon.), Phi Beta Kappa. Address: Dept Classics U Cin Cincinnati OH 45221 *

CASMEY, HOWARD BIRDWELL, state ofcl.; b. Euclid, Minn., Feb. 4, 1926; s. George and Gladys (Birdwell) C.; m. Eva Mae Lee, Aug. 14, 1949; children—Michael, Kim. B.A., Concordia Coll., 1949; M.A., U. N.D., 1956. Tchr. pub. schs., Plummer, Minn., supt. schs., Lake Bronson, Minn., Herman, Minn., Ada, Minn., Golden Valley, Minn., now commr. edn., State of Minn. Served with Armed Forces, World War II. Mem. Chief State Sch. Officers (pres. 1975-76). *

CASNER, ANDREW JAMES, legal educator; b. Chgo., Feb. 7, 1907; s. Andrew James and Margaret Jane (Connell) C.; m. Margaret Snell, June 12, 1926; children—Andrew James, Truman Snell. A.B., U. Ill., 1930, LL.B., 1929; J.S.D., Columbia, 1941; A.M. (hon.), Harvard, 1942, LL.D., 1969; S.J.D. (hon.), Suffolk U., 1970. Bar: Ill. 1929, Md. 1934, Mass. 1940. Instr. law U. Ill., 1929-30, prof. law, 1936-38, U. Md., 1930-35, Harvard, 1938—, asso. dean sch., 1961, acting dean, 1967-68; asso. Ropes, Gray, Best, Coolidge & Rugg, Boston, 1945-58; chmn. law editorial bd. Little, Brown & Co. Author: (with W.B. Leach) Cases and Text on Property, 1950, 2d edit., 1969, supplement, 1982, Estate Planning, 1953, 4th edit. 1980, supplement, 1983; Editor-in-chief: Am. Law of Property, 1951, supplement, 1976; reporter: Restatement of Property; contbr. to legal periodicals. Served as col. USAAF, 1942-45; E.T.O. Decorated Legion of Merit, Bronze star. Mem. Am., Mass., Boston bar assns., Am. Law Inst., Order of Coif, Sigma Chi, Phi Delta Phi, Delta Sigma Rho. Republican. Epsicopalian. Home: 19 Chauncy St Cambridge MA 02138

CASNER, TRUMAN SNELL, lawyer; b. Balt., Oct. 9, 1933; s. A. James and Margaret (Snell) C.; m. Elizabeth Lyons, June 12, 1954; children—Richard Dana, Elizabeth Anne, Abigail Lee. B.A. cum laude, Princeton U., 1955, LL.B., Harvard U., 1958. Bar: Mass. bar 1958. Law clk. to Chief Justice Raymond Wilkins, Mass. Supreme Judicial Ct., 1958-59; asso. firm Ropes & Gray, Boston, 1959-68, partner, 1968—. Mem. Belmont Town Meeting, 1971—; sec., trustee Buckingham Sch., 1964-71; trustee, mem. exec. com. Belmont Hill Sch., 1966—; sec., trustee, mem. exec. com. Pine Manor Coll., 1973-79; trustee, v.p. Boston Mus. of Sci., 1981—. Mem. Am. Bar Assn., Am. Law Inst. Episcopalian. Clubs: New Bedford Yacht; Union, Skating (Boston); Belmont Hill, Longwood Cricket. Home: 140 Clifton St Belmont MA 02178 Office: 225 Franklin St Boston MA 02110

CASO, GASPER, librarian, lawyer; b. Boston, Aug. 30, 1933; s. Gaspere and Maria (Guisto) C.; m. Antonette Conti, June 2, 1957; children: Dean C., David M. B.A., Northeastern U., 1956; J.D., Boston Coll., 1959.. Sole practice, Boston, 1960; legis. reference librarian Mass. State Library, Boston, 1960-66, counsel, asst. state librarian, 1966-81, state librarian, 1982—. Chmn. Mass. Records Conservation Bd., Boston, 1979—. Served to 1st lt. U.S. Army, 1956-57. Mem. Mass. Bar Assn., Am. Assn. Law Librarians. Roman Catholic. Home: 210 Common St Belmont MA 02178 Office: 341 State House Boston MA 02133

CASON, CHARLES MONROE, physicist; b. Chattanooga, July 24, 1933; s. Charles Monroe and Cleo (Stargel) C.; m. Pauline Cavender, July 29, 1979; children—Tara Nanette, Wendy Karen, Lea Valerie, Laura Cavender, Phyllis Cavender, Leslie Cavender, Jim Cavender. B.S., U. Ala., 1954, M.S., 1958. Atomic and molecular physicist Advanced Systems Concepts Office U.S. Army Missile Command, Redstone Arsenal, 1957—; tech. dir. Cason Voting Systems, Inc.; dir. Expon, Inc. Contbr. articles on plasma physics, aerodynamics, electron beams, gas lasers, optics. Ala. state election law commr., 1980; past trustee Arts Council. Served with USAF, 1955-57. Recipient Achievement Certificate, 1969, Research and Devel. Achievement award, 1971; both Dept. Army; Merit citation Madison County Commn., 1971. Asso. fellow Am. Inst. Aero. and Astronautics (Engr. of Yr. Ala. sect.); mem. Am. Phys. Soc., Assn. U.S. Army, Tenn., Ala. archaeol. socs. Episcopalian. Clubs: Elk., Whitesburg Boat and Yacht, Mason-Dixon Toastmasters (past pres.), Civic Opera Soc., Greenwyche (past pres.). Patentee wind tunnels, electronic circuits, laser devices, missile controls, election equipment. Home: 1207 Toney Dr SE Huntsville AL 35802 Office: Advanced Systems Concepts Office Redstone Arsenal AL 35898

CASON, ROBERT BENJAMIN, journalist; b. Worthington Springs, Fla., Aug. 11, 1942; s. James Hardee and Ruth Alaska (Roberts) C.; m. Carol Lampkin Colvard, Dec. 30, 1967; children—David Benjamin, Alexander Colvard. B.S., U. Fla., 1965. News editor St. Petersburg (Fla.) Times, 1966-68; asst. nat. editor Washington Post, 1968, style layout editor, 1969-71, news editor, 1972-76, asst. mng. editor, 1977—. Served with AUS. Home: 1462 Roundleaf Ct Reston VA 22090 Office: 1150 15th St Washington DC 20071

CASPARY, SISTER ANITA, educator, adminstr.; b. Herrick, S.D., Nov. 4, 1915; d. Jacob A. and Marie (Bruch) C. B.A., Immaculate Heart Coll., 1937; M.A., U. So. Calif., 1943; Ph.D., Stanford, 1948. High sch. tchr., 1939-42; mem. faculty Immaculate Heart Coll., Los Angeles, 1948-58, chmn. dept. English, 1950-57, dean, 1950-57, pres. of coll., 1957-63; mother-gen. Sisters of Immaculate Heart, 1963-69; pres. Immaculate Heart Community, 1969-73; asso. prof. Franciscan Sch. Theology; vis. prof. Grad. Theol. Union, Berkeley, Calif., 1975-81, vis. Dillenberger prof., 1978-80; Firestone vis. prof. U. So. Calif., 1977; adminstr. Center for Peace and Justice, Los Angeles, 1980-81; Merrill fellow Harvard Div. Sch., 1971; Religious Leaders Program, Notre Dame U., 1974. Contbr. articles to profl. jours. Mem. Modern Lang. Assn., Assn. Am. Colls., Nat. Council Tchrs. English, Kappa Gamma Pi, Phi Kappa Phi. Address: 435 S Kenmore Apt 305 Los Angeles CA 90020

CASPER, DAVID JOHN, football player; b. Bemidji, Minn., Sept. 26, 1951. B.A., U. Notre Dame, 1974. Tight end Oakland Raiders, 1974—; played in Pro Bowl, 1976-79 *

CASPER, GERHARD, lawyer, university dean; b. Hamburg, Germany, Dec. 25, 1937; s. Heinrich and Hertha C.; m. Regina Koschel, Dec. 26, 1964; 1 dau., Hanna. Legal state exam., Hamburg, 1961; LL.M., Yale U., 1962; Dr.iur.utr., U. Freiburg, Germany, 1964; LL.D. (hon.), John Marshall Law Sch., 1982. Asst. prof. polit. sci. U. Calif., Berkeley, 1964-66; asso. prof. law and polit. sci. U. Chgo., 1966-69, prof., 1969-76, Max Pam prof. law, 1976-80, William B. Graham prof. law, 1980—; dean (Law Sch.), 1979—; vis. prof. law Catholic U., Louvain, Belgium, 1970; Bd. dirs. Am. Bar Found. Author: Realism and Political Theory in American Legal Thought, 1967, (with Richard A. Posner) The Workload of the Supreme Court, 1976; Co-editor: The Supreme Court Rev, 1977—. Fellow Am. Acad. Arts and Scis.; mem. Am. Law Inst. (council 1980—), Chgo. Bar Assn., Chgo. Council Lawyers (bd. govs. 1973-75), Am. Council on Germany. Office: U Chgo Law Sch 1111E 60th St Chicago IL 60637

CASPER, LEONARD RALPH, English literature educator; b. Fond du Lac, Wis., July 6, 1923; s. Louis and Caroline (Eder) C.; m. Linda Velasquez-Ty, June 2, 1956; children: Gretchen Gabrielle, Kristina Elise. B.A., U. Wis., 1948, M.A., 1949, Ph.D., 1953. Grad. asst. U. Wis., 1949-51; instr. Cornell U., 1952-53; asst. prof. U. Philippines, 1953-56, Fulbright lectr., 1962-63, summer 1973; mem. faculty Boston Coll., 1956—, prof. contemporary Am. lit., 1963—; dir. creative writing U. R.I., summer 1958. Author: Robert Penn Warren: The Dark and Bloody Ground, 1960, The Wayward Horizon: Essays on Modern Philippine Literature, 1961, The Wounded Diamond: Studies in Modern Philippine Literature, 1964, New Writing from the Philippines: A Critique and Anthology, 1966, A Lion Unannounced: 12 Stories and a Fable; editor: Six Filipino Poets, 1955; Editor: (with T.A. Gullason) The World of Short Fiction: An International Collection, 1962; editor: Modern Philippine Short Stories, 1962; contbg. editor: Panorama, Manila, 1954-61, Drama Critique, 1959-62, Solidarity Manila, 1966-78, Literature East and West, 1969-81, Aquila, 1975—. Served with F.A., AUS, 1943-46. Stanford creative writing fellow, 1951-52; Bread Loaf creative writing scholar, 1961; research grantee Am. Council Learned Socs.-Social Sci. Research Council, 1965; grantee Asia Soc., 1965; research travel grantee Am. Philos. Soc., 1968-69; Nat. Council on Arts award, 1970. Mem. Nat. Cath. Playwrights Circle, AAUP. Home: 54 Simpson Dr Saxonville MA 01701 Office: Boston Coll Dept English Chestnut Hill MA 02167

CASPER, WILLIAM CECIL, former university chancellor, economics and business educator; b. China Grove, N.C., Aug. 6, 1927; s. Will and Mary Johnson (Goodnight) C.; m. Gladys Hope McSwain, May 25, 1951. B.S., U. N.C., Chapel Hill, 1954; M.A., U. S.C., Columbia, 1965. Instr., registrar Coastal Carolina Jr. Coll. br. Coll. of Charleston, Conway, S.C., 1954-60; resident dir. U. S.C., Coastal Carolina Campus, Conway, 1960-62; dir. U. S.C., Aiken Campus, 1963-78, chancellor, 1979-83, chancellor emeritus, 1983—, prof. econs. and bus., 1983—; mem. adv. bd. So. region Bankers Trust of S.C. Chmn. planning and evaluation com. Aiken County Community Action Commn., 1977-81, bd. mem., 1976-81. Served with USN, 1945-48, 50-51. Clubs: Rotary, Business Men's. Office: 171 University Pkwy Aiken SC 29801

CASPER, WILLIAM EARL, JR., professional golfer; b. San Diego, June 24, 1931; s. William Earl and Isabel Florence (Stanley) C.; m. Shirley Ann Franklin, June 28, 1952; children: Linda, Billy, Bobby, Byron, Judith, Jennifer, Charles, David, Julia, Sarah Beth, Tommy. Ed. pub. schs., Calif.; student, U. Notre Dame, 1950. Profl. golfer, 1954—; competed in Ryder Cup events, 1961-75; capt. Ryder Cup team, 1979. Served with USN, 1951-55. Named player of Yr., 1966, 68, 70; recipient Byron Nelson award, 1966, 68, 70; Player of Yr. award Golf Writers of Am., 1968; Vardon trophy, 1960, 63, 65, 66, 68. Mormon. Winner numerous ofcl. golf tournaments including U.S. Open, 1959, 66, Can. Open, 1967, Masters Tournament, 1970, Lancome Trophy, 1974, Italian Open, 1975, Mexican Open, 1977. Office: care Profl Golfers Assn Am P.O. Box 12458 Palm Beach Gardens FL 33416

CASPERSEN, FINN MICHAEL WESTBY, financial company executive; b. N.Y.C., Oct. 27, 1941; s. Olaus Westby and Freda C.; m. Barbara Caspersen, June 17, 1967. B.A. With honors in Econs., Brown U., 1963; LL.B. cum laude, Harvard U., 1966; LL.D., Hood Coll.; H.H.D., Washington Coll., Chestertown, Md. Bar: Fla. 1966, N.Y. 1967. Assoc. Dewey, Ballantine, Bushby, Palmer & Wood, N.Y.C., 1969-72; assoc. counsel Beneficial Mgmt. Corp., Wilmington, Del, 1972-75; chmn. bd., chief exec. officer, mem. exec. com. Beneficial Corp., 1976—; dir., mem. exec. com. Beneficial Nat. Bank; dir. Beneficial Nat. Bank, U.S.A. Wilmington, Western Auto Supply Co.; chmn. bd., chief exec. officer Beneficial Fin. Internat. Corp.; chmn., dir. Security Trust Co. Ltd.; dir. Beneficial Internat. Ins. Co. Ltd.; dir Am. Centennial Ins. Co.; dir. Consol, Marine Ins., BFC Agy., Inc., BFC Ins. Agy. Am., BFC Ins. Agy. Nev., Guaranty Life Ins. Co. Am.; past dir. Midlantic Nat. Bank (Sussex and Mchts.); dir. Clark Hill Sugary; dir., pres. Tri-Farms Inc.; dir., Westby Corp., Westby Mgmt. Corp.; chmn. 35th Ann. N.J. Bus. Conf., Rutgers U. Grad. Sch. Mgmt. and Sales Execs. Club N.J., 1983; gen. counsel, dir. Central Nat. Life Ins. Co. of Omaha, 1974-76. Former trustee N.J. Coll. Fund Assn., Brown U.; trustee Camp Nejeda Found. for Diabetic Children, Com. Econ. Devel.; mem. nominating com. Morristown Meml. Hosp.; former mem. N.J. Bd. Higher Edn.; bd. dirs., v.p. O.W. Caspersen Found.; chmn. bd. trustees,mem. exec. com. Peddie Sch., Hightstown, N.J.; chmn. bd. Drumthwacket Found.; chmn. Waterloo Found. for Arts. Inc.; trustee James S. Brady Presdl. Found.; pres. Coalition of Service Industries,Inc., Washington; mem. adv. com. to exec. bd. Morris-Sussex Area Council Boy Scouts Am.; mem. corp. Cardigan Mountain Sch. Served to lt. USCG, 1966-69. Recipient President's medal Johns Hopkins U.; named Civic Leader of Yr. YMCA, 1982. Mem. Am. Fin. Services Assn. (trustee, chmn. govt. affairs com.), ABA, Fla. Bar Assn., N.Y. Bar Assn. Clubs: Harvard; Knickerbocker (N.Y.C.); University (Sarasota, Fla.). Office: Beneficial Corp 1100 Carr Rd Wilmington DE 19899

CASS, A. CARL, metallurgical engineer, consultant. B.C.E., Purdue U., 1930; D.Sc. (hon.), U. Nuevo Leon, Mex., 1958; D.Metall.Eng., Fed. U., Rio de Janeiro, 1968. Registered profl. engr., D.C. With Lackawanna Steel Co., 1928-30, Nat. Aniline & Chem. Co., 1930, Wickwire Spencer Steel Co., also Acme Steel Co., 1929-30; asst. to v.p. ops. Erie R.R., 1930-31; engr. Bur. R.R. Valuation, ICC, 1931-33; sr. engr. U.S. Coast and Geodetic Survey, 1933-35; engaged in gen. constrn. bus., 1935-37; engr. RFC, 1938-41; regional metall. engr. Def. Plant Corp., 1941-48; chief metall. engr. Export-Import Bank U.S., Washington, 1948-51, chief engring. div., 1951-77; internat. engr., mgmt. cons., 1977—; Prof. metallurgy Fed. U., Rio de Janeiro, 1968. Contbr. articles to profl. jours. Decorated commendatore dell'Ordine Al Merito della Republica Italiana, 1968. Fellow ASCE (life); hon. mem. Inst. Latinoam del Fierro y El Acero. Office: 37 Nicholson St NW Washington DC 20011

CASS, MILLARD, lawyer, arbitrator; b. Norfolk, Va., Nov. 8, 1916; s. Sigismund and Ridia (Schreier) C.; m. Ruth Claire Marx, July 19, 1943; children: Sandra Cass Burt, Ronald, Pamela Cass Gershkoff. B.S., U. Va., 1938, LL.B., 1940. Bar: Va. 1939. Pvt. practice law, Portsmouth, Va., 1940-41; atty. SEC, 1941, NLRB, 1941-46, legal asst. to gen. counsel, 1945-46; asst. to asst. sec. labor, 1946-47, under sec. labor, 1947-50; spl. asst. to sec. labor, 1950-55, dep. under-sec. labor, 1955-71, moblzn. planning coordinator, 1962-71, liaison officer with state govs., 1969-71; adminstrv. dir. Constrn. Industry Stblzn. Com., 1971-74, Pay Bd., 1971-73; adminstr. Office Wage Stblzn., 1973; counselor to dir. Cost of Living Council, 1973-74; labor relations arbitrator, 1971—, pvt. practice law, 1975—; Exec. officer Manpower Adminstrn., 1963-64; mem. or chmn. numerous departmental coms., internat. delegations; guest speaker U. Va. Law Sch.; nat. arbitrator men's clothing industry ins. and retirement funds; impartial chmn. N.Y. hotel industry; arbitrator U.S. Postal Service; nat. arbitrator men's cotton garment industry; arbitrator handbag industry; impartial chmn. luggage and leather goods industry; impartial umpire eastern ink mfg. Contbr. articles to legal jours., govt. and other publs. Pres. Montgomery County Council P.T.A.s, 1962-64; bd. mgrs. Md. Congress Parents and Tchrs., 1962-64; pres. Washington Hebrew Congregation, 1970-72. Recipient Arthur S. Flemming award for outstanding young men in fed. govt., 1955; Rockefeller Pub. service award, 1966; Dept. Labor Distinguished Service award, 1960; Distinguished Career Service award, 1971, 74; Hornbook award Montgomery County (Md.) Edn. Assn., 1968; Career Service award Nat. Civil Service League, 1969; Distinguished Honor award Pay Bd., 1973; Distinguished Service award Cost of Living Council, 1974. Mem. Am., Va. bar assns., Raven Soc. Univ. Va., Order of Coif, Phi Beta Kappa, Omicron Delta Kappa. Jewish. Home: 5532 Devon Rd Bethesda MD 20814 Office: Suite 1100 1250 Eye St NW Washington DC 20005

CASSADY, JOHN MAC, chemist; b. Vincennes, Ind., Aug. 16, 1938; s. Theodore John and Juanita (McDowell) C.; m. Nancy Lee Earls, Sept. 5, 1959; children—Betsy, Kimberly, Susanna, John, Patricia. B.A., DePauw U., Greencastle, Ind., 1960; M.S., Case Western Res. U., 1962, Ph.D., 1964. NIH postdoctoral fellow Sch. Pharmacy, U. Wis., Madison, 1964-66; asst. prof. medicinal chemistry Purdue U., West Lafayette, Ind., 1966-70, asso. prof., 1970-74, prof., 1974—, acting dept. head, 1979-80, dept. head, 1980—. Co-editor: Anticancer Drugs Based on Natural Product Models, 1980; Contbr. sci. articles to profl. jours. NSF fellow, 1962-64; Rector scholar, 1956-60. Fellow Acad. Pharm. Scis.; mem. Am., Brit. chem. socs., AAAS, Am. Soc. Pharmacognosy, Phytochemical Soc., Sigma Xi, Kappa Psi, Rho Chi, Alpha Tau Omega. Methodist. Home: 818 Sparta St West Lafayette IN 47906 Office: Sch Pharmacy Pharmacal Sci Purdue U West Lafayette IN 47907

CASSARA, FRANK, painter, printmaker, papermaker; b. Partinico, Italy, Mar. 13, 1913; came to U.S., 1913, naturalized, 1936; s. Gaspare and Rosalia (Savarino) C.; m. Gretchen Jean Grathwohl, Dec. 28, 1946; children: Christina, Francesca. Student, U. Iowa, summer 1956, Atelier 17, Paris, summer 1958; M.S. in Design, U. Mich., 1954. Supr. easel painting sect. WPA, 1937; instr. Detroit Sch. Art, 1935-36, Soc. Arts and Crafts, Detroit, 1946-47; prof. U. Mich., Ann Arbor, after 1947, now prof. emeritus; instr. Nat. Music Camp, Interlochen, Mich., summers 1948-49. Illustrated: manuscript published in Artists Proof, A Collectors Edition, 1963; one-man shows, U. Man., Can.), Winnipeg, Flint (Mich.) Inst. Arts, Toledo Mus., 1963, Kalamazoo Art Center, U. Maine, Orono, U. Ill., Urbana, U. Oreg., Corvallis, U. Nebr., Lincoln, group shows include, 7th Internat. Prints, Chgo. Art Inst., Mus. Palace Legion of Honor, San Francisco, Gallerie Nees Morphes, Athens, Greece, Bklyn. Mus., Achenbach Found. Graphic Arts, San Francisco, Oklahoma Art Center, Oklahoma City, group shows inlcude, Internat. Conf. Hand Papermakers, Boston, 1980, group shows include, Internat. Papermakers, Birmingham Art Assn., Hooberman Gallery, Birmingham, Mich., Ella Sharp Mus. and Slusser Gallery; represented in permanent collections, Bibliotecque Nationale, Paris, Stadelijk Mus., Netherlands, Library of Congress, USIA Agency, Washington, Nat. Mus. Am. Art, Smithsonian Instn., Washington; murals executed, East Detroit Post Office, 1939, Sandusky (Mich.) Post Office, 1941, Lansing (Mich.) Water Conditioning Plant. Served with U.S. Army, 1942-46. Decorated 2 Bronze Stars.; Grantee Rackham Research Found., U. Mich., 1957-61, 68; Recipient over 50 awards in National and regional exhibitions. Mem. Ann Arbor Art Assn. (past pres., dir. 1954-62). Innovator one-bite white-etching ground. Address: U Michigan School of Art 1122 Pomona Ann Arbor MI 48103

CASSAVETES, JOHN, actor, director; b. N.Y.C., Dec. 9, 1929; m. Gena Rowlands, Mar. 19, 1958. Ed., Mohawk Coll., Colgate U., N.Y. Acad. Dramatic Arts. Actor in stock co.; asst. stage mgr. Broadway play: Fifth Season; TV credits include Elgin Playhouse; actor in films: Mickey and Nicky, 1976, Taxi, Crime in the Streets, Edge of the City, Fever Tree, The Dirty Dozen, Rosemary's Baby, Two-Minute Warning, 1976, Brass Target, 1978, The Fury, 1978, Whose Life Is It Anyway, 1981, The Incubus, 1982, The Tempest, 1982; writer-dir. films: Shadows, 1960, Faces, 1968, Too Late Blues, 1961, A Woman Under the Influence, 1974, Killing of a Chinese Bookie, 1976, One Summer Night, 1979; writer-dir.-actor: Minnie & Moskowitz, 1971, Opening Night, 1977, Husbands, 1970; dir.: A Child is Waiting, 1962, Gloria, 1980 (Golden Lion award Venice Film Festival); appeared in: TV movie Flesh and Blood, 1979. Address: care Esme Chandee 9056 Santa Monica Blvd 201 Los Angeles CA 90069 *

CASSEL, (JOHN) WALTER, baritone, actor; b. Council Bluffs, Iowa, May 15, 1920; s. Thaddeus William and Grace Hester Cedarburg; m. Gail Manners, Feb. 27, 1955; children—John Walter, Catherine Jean, Mary Martha, William E., Diedrick S. Student, Creighton U. Flour miller, radio singer and announcer, trumpet player for bands and symphonies, 1938-39; prof. voice Ind. U. Sang on, NBC radio and on stage, N.Y.C., 1939; mem., Met. Opera Co., N.Y.C., 1943-73; appeared with numerous light opera cos. and opera cos., through world. Served with N.G. Recipient decoration N.Y.C. Soc. Voice Tchrs., 1957. Mem. Am. Guild Mus. Arts, Actors Equity. Mem. Metaphysical Ch. Office: Sch of Music Ind U Bloomington IN 47401

CASSELL, FRANK HYDE, business educator; b. Chgo., Oct. 12, 1916; s. Frank V. Seymour and Alicia (Robinson) C.; m. Marguerite Ellen Fletcher, Mar. 24, 1940; children: Frank Allan, Thomas E., Christopher B. A.B., Wabash Coll., 1939; postgrad., U. Chgo., 1946-47. Exec. with Inland Steel Co., Chgo., 1948-68; on leave as dir. U.S. Employment Service, Washington, 1966-68; prof. indsl. relations Grad. Sch. Mgmt., Northwestern U., 1968—; vis. prof. Inst. Am. Studies, Salzburg, Austria, 1957, Inst. Mgmt., Northwestern U., Burgenstock (Luzerne), Switzerland, 1975—; cons. to govt. and industry in fields manpower, indsl. relations and mgmt. Author: The Employment Service: An Organization in Change, 1968, (with Weber and Ginsberg) National Manpower Policies, 1969, Collective Bargaining in the Public Sector, A Case Book, 1976; also numerous papers and articles on pub. and pvt. policy. Chmn. Gov. Ill. Com. Unemployment, 1961-63; chmn. Winnetka (Ill.) Planning Commn., 1973-75; chmn. planning and evaluation com. Ill. Gov.'s Manpower Council, 1973-74; chmn. Long Range Econ. Planning Com., Chgo., 1972-74; trustee TRUST, urban systems planning, 1977—; mem. bldg. research adv. bd. NRC, 1975—; bd. dirs. Chgo. Urban League, 1953—; bd. dirs., mem. exec. com. Means Services, Inc., 1974-82; co-chmn. Chgo. Mayoral Transition Com. on Mgmt., 1983. Recipient Distinguished Service awards U.S. Dept. Labor, 1968, 73; Service award Urban League. Mem. Indsl. Relations Assn. Chgo. (pres. 1957-58), Indsl. Relations Research Assn., Am. Econ. Assn., Nat. Planning Assn. (com. pvt. pensions). Club: Internat. (Washington). Home: 128 Church Rd Winnetka IL 60093 Office: Leverone Hall Northwestern U 2001 Sheridan Rd Evanston IL 60601

CASSELL, JOHN WILLIAM, JR., college president; b. Takoma Park, Md., Mar. 3, 1929; s. John William and Jessie (Swart) C.; m. Charlotte Louise Carper, Aug. 13, 1950; children: Janet Louise, John William III. B.A., Columbia Union Coll., 1950; M.Ed., U. Md., 1955; Ph.D., Mich. State U., 1961. Supervising tchr. Columbia Union Coll., 1950-52; acad. prin. Andrews U., 1955-59, dean students, 1960-63; acad. dean So. Missionary Coll., 1963-67, Pacific Union Coll., 1967-72, pres., 1972—. Served with U.S. Army, 1952-54. Mem. Am. Assn. Presidents Ind. Colls. and Univs., Ind. Colls. No. Calif., Assn. Ind. Calif. Colls. and Univs., Nat. Assn. Ind. Colls. and Univs. Club: Rotary. Office: Pacific Union Coll Angwin CA 94508

CASSELL, KAY ANN, librarian; b. Van Wert, Ohio, Sept. 24, 1941; d. Kenneth Miller and Pauline (Zimmerman) C. B.S., Carnegie-Mellon U., 1963; M.L.S., Rutgers U., 1965; M.A., Bklyn. Coll., 1969. Reference librarian Bklyn. Coll. Library, 1965-68; adult services cons. N.J. State Library, Trenton, 1968-71; library cons.-vol. Peace Corps, Rabat, Morocco, 1971-73; adult services cons. Westchester Library System, White Plains, N.Y., 1973-75; dir. Bethlehem Pub. Library, Delmar, N.Y., 1975-81, Huntington (N.Y.) Pub. Library, 1981—; adj. faculty mem. Grad. Sch. Library Sci., SUNY, Albany, 1976-78; chmn. community adv. com. Capital Dist. Humanities Program, Albany, 1980-81; bd. dirs. Literacy Vols. of Suffolk, Bellport, N.Y., 1981—. Active LWV, Huntington, 1982—. Mem. ALA (reference and adult services div. 1983-84), N.Y. Library Assn. (pres. reference and adult services sect. 1975-76), Suffolk County Library Assn., Huntington C. of C. (chmn. human resources com. 1982—), AAUW, Beta Phi Mu. Club: Bus. and Prof. Women's (Huntington). Home: 108 Woodbury Rd Huntington NY 11743 Office: Huntington Pub Library 338 Main St Huntington NY 11743

CASSELL, MARTIN LEROY, r.r. ofcl., lawyer; b. Vincennes, Ind., Oct. 3, 1910; s. Martin L. and Alice (Shively) C.; m. Claudia E. Stone, June 26, 1937; children—Martin Leroy III, Clyde Thomas. A.B., U. Ill, 1933, LL.B., 1935. Bar: Ill. bar 1935, U.S. Supreme Ct. bar 1941. Asso. firm Hamilton, Black & Klatt, Peoria, 1935-40; with C., R.I. & P. Ry., 1940-80, gen. counsel, 1974-80. Mem. Barrington (Ill.) High Sch. Bd., 1957-69, pres., 1958-63, 68-69; exec. com. Tri-County div. Ill. Assn. Sch. Bds., 1960-69, chmn., 1961-63; dir. Ill. Assn. Sch. Bds., 1960-69, pres., 1965-67; mem. Barrington Hills Plan Com., 1971-79, chmn., 1974-79; bd. dirs., v.p. Contemporary Concerts Inc., 1960-80. Mem. Assn. ICC Practitioners (pres. 1962-63), Am., Ill., Chgo. bar assns., Traffic Club Chgo., Beta Theta Pi. Home: Rural Route 5 Box 331 Sutton Rd Barrington IL 60010

CASSELL, WILLIAM COMYN, college president; b. Vallejo, Calif., Oct. 8, 1934; s. Comyn R. and Emily E. (Duckwith) C.; m. Jeanne Taylor, Dec. 27, 1955; children: Paul, Susan, David. B.A., Pomona Coll., 1956; M.A., Claremont Grad. Sch., 1969; L.H.D. (hon.), Lakeland Coll., 1977. Broker Hornblower and Weeks, Inc., Orange, Calif., 1958-64; asst. to treas. Claremont (Calif.) Coll., 1964-65; dir. income trusts and bequests Calif. Inst. Tech., Pasadena, 1965-69; dir. devel. and pub. relations Menninger Found., Topeka, 1969-70; dir. devel. U. Denver, 1970-74; pres. Coll. of Idaho, Caldwell, 1974-80, Heidelberg Coll., Tiffin, Ohio, 1980—; cons. Ford Found., Phelps-Stokes Fund, Congress of No. Marianas Islands, numerous colls. and govt. agys., 1966—. Author: The Case for Deferred Giving, 1966, Deferred Giving Programs: Administration and Promotion, 1972; editorial adv. bd.: Ednl. Record. Mem. Parks and Recreation Commn., Claremont, 1967-69, City Council, Bow Mar, Colo., 1967-69; Mem. adv. bd. Salvation Army, Caldwell, Rudolph Diesel Meml. Found., Western Electric Fund; trustee Caldwell Meml. Hosp., chmn., 1976; mem. Idaho newspaper carrier scholarship selection com. Gannett Found.; chmn. bd. Western Ind. Coll. Funds. Served to 1st lt. AUS, 1957-58. Recipient Brakeley award for Outstanding Coll. Devel. Am. Alumni Council, 1968, Nat. Fund Raising Council award, 1969; named an Idaho Distinguished Citizen, 1977, hon. VIP Sta. KIDO, Boise. Mem. Am. Council on Edn., Council for Advancement and Support of Edn., Caldwell C. of C. (exec. bd., dir.), Internat. Assn. Univ. Presidents (N.Am. council, chmn. food and tech. subcom., mem. internat. coop. com.), Young President's Orgn. Clubs: Rotary, Mohawk Country (Tiffin); Univ. (N.Y.C.). Office: President's Office Heidelberg College Tiffin OH 44883 *

CASSELL, WILLIAM WALTER, accounting-operations consultant; b. Chgo., Apr. 10, 1917; s. Charles F. and E. Margaret (Jackson) C.; m. Rosamond Mary Fisher, May 13, 1944; children: Anne, Gerald, Douglas, Mary. Student, U. Wash., 1936-38, Syracuse U., 1943-44; grad., Am. Inst. Banking, 1957, Grad. Sch. Savs. Banking, 1965, Savs. Banks Mgmt. Devel. Program, U. Mass., 1970. Officer's asst. Syracuse (N.Y.) Savs. Bank, 1959-66, treas., 1966-71, v.p., 1971-75, sr. v.p., controller, 1975-77, exec. v.p., 1977-83, cons., 1983—, dir., State Bank of Chittenango, 1963-73, 83—, Credit Bur. Syracuse, 1976—, Consumer Credit Counseling Service, 1979—; pres. Fin. Execs. Inst., Syracuse, 1971-72. Bd. dirs. Syracuse Symphony Orch., 1979, Opers Theater of Syracuse, 1982—; pres. Madison County Hist. Soc., 1982—. Served with U.S. Army, 1941-45; ETO. Decorated Bronze Star. Mem. Am. Inst. Banking, Fin. Execs. Inst., Planning Execs. Inst., Hunter Archeol Soc. Republican. Methodist. Clubs: Men's Garden of Am., Monarch of Syracuse. Home: 131 W Genesee St Chittenango NY 13037 *To find happiness in little things each day; to be all I am capable of being, judged within the framework of my own real values and to make others glad I came this way— this is the measure of a life worthwhile: contentment, not complacency.*

CASSELLA, WILLIAM NATHAN, JR., organization executive; b. Alton, Ill., July 14, 1920; s. William Nathan and Martha (Stanly) C.; m. Margaret Powers Crowley, June 22, 1946; children: John Woodson, Stephen Rowan, Mark Crowley, William Kent. A.B., U. Ill., 1942; M.S., Syracuse U., 1943; A.M., Harvard, 1951, Ph.D., 1953. Research asst. Pub. Adminstrn. Clearing House, Washington, 1946; instr., then asst. prof. polit. sci. U. Mo., 1948-54; with Nat. Municipal League, 1953—, exec. dir., 1969—; research asso. Govt. Affairs Found., 1954-57; vis. asso. prof. pub. adminstrn. Columbia, 1957, sr. research asso., 1957-61; Mem. adv. com. state and local govt. statistics Bur. Census, 1962-65, chmn., 1963-65; mem. area devel. adv. bd. Com. Econ. Devel., 1964-66; cons. Adv. Commn. Intergovtl. Relations, 1967—. Author: Constitutional Aspects of Metropolitan Government, 1961, also articles.; Contbg. editor: Nat. Civic Rev, 1954—; chmn. editorial bd., 1969—. Mem. Greenburgh (N.Y.) Bd. Edn., 1961-64; mem. Westchester County Planning Bd., 1962—, vice chmn., 1967-72, chmn., 1973—; bd. dirs. Westchester County Indsl. Devel. Agy., 1976—; trustee Pub. Adminstrn. Service, 1969-76; governing bd. Governmental Affairs Inst., 1969-76. Served to lt. USNR, 1943-46. Mem. Am. Polit. Sci. Assn., Am. Soc. Pub. Adminstrn., Govtl. Research Assn., Internat. City Mgmt. Assn., Nat. Acad. Pub. Adminstrn., Regional Plan Assn. N.Y., Phi Beta Kappa, Alpha Kappa Lambda, Delta Sigma Pi, Omicron Delta Kappa. Episcopalian. Club: Harvard (N.Y.C.). Home: 100 Buena Vista Dr Dobbs Ferry NY 10522 Office: 55 W 44th St New York NY 10036

CASSELS-BROWN, ALASTAIR KENNEDY, educator, organist; b. London, May 3, 1927; U.S., 1952, naturalized, 1961; s. Arthur and Kathleen Cassels-B; m. Rosemarie Langguth, Aug. 10, 1957; children: Peter, Elizabeth. B.A., Oxford U., 1948, M.A., 1952; D.Mus., U. Toronto, 1972. Asst. music master Wellington Coll., Crowthorne, Berkshire, Eng., 1950-52; dir. music St. George's Sch., Newport, R.I., 1952-55; asso. organist, choirmaster Cathedral St. John the Divine, N.Y.C., 1955-57; organist, master choristers Grace Ch., Utica, N.Y., 1957-65; asst. prof. Hamilton Coll., Clinton, N.Y., 1965-67; asso. prof. music Episcopal Div. Sch., Cambridge, Mass., 1967-69, prof., 1969—; music dir. Community Choral Soc., Utica, 1957-67; organ recitalist, 1952—; dean Evergreen (Colo.) Music Conf., summers 1979-81; chmn.

music commn. Episcopal Diocese Mass., 1979-81. Composer music. Served as officer RAF, 1949-50. Recipient Coronation medal. Fellow Royal Coll. Organists; mem. Coll. Music Soc., Am. Guild Organists (sub-dean Central N.Y. chpt. 1964, exec. com. Boston chpt. 1973-76), Boston Computer Soc. Episcopalian. Home: 13 Saint John's Rd Cambridge MA 02138

CASSERLY, JOHN JOSEPH, writer, journalist; b. Chgo., Jan. 4, 1927; s. William J. and Hannah (Kane) C.; m. Joy Ruth Price, Sept. 17, 1955; children—Kevin, Terence, Jeffrey, Lawrence. B.A., Marquette U., 1951. Reporter Milw. Sentinel, 1951; bur. reporter Internat. News Service, Chgo., 1952, assigned Tokyo bur., 1952, war corr. Korea, 1952-54, assigned Paris bur., 1954, assigned N.Y.C., 1954-55, bur. mgr., Rome, Italy, 1957-58; with CBS Network News, 1955-56; Rome bur. chief Hearst Headline service, 1958-61; chief Rome bur. ABC News, 1961-64; assigned Washington bur. ABC News, 1964-68; part-time fgn. reporting; overseas pub. info. mgr. Ford Motor Co., Dearborn, Mich., 1968-70; dir. pub. affairs pub. info. Bur. Census, U.S. Dept. Commerce, Suitland, Md., 1970-74; speechwriter White House staff Exec. Office Pres., Washington, 1974-76; free-lance writer, 1976-80; editorial writer Ariz. Republic, Phoenix, 1980—. Author: We, The Americans; The Ford White House... Diary of a Speechwriter; Contbr. articles to nat. lit. mags. Named hon. capt. South Korean Army, 1952-53, hon. cpl. USMC, South Vietnam, 1966; recipient Byline award for disting. reporting Marquette U. Sch. Journalism, 1982. Mem. Pub. Relations Soc. Am., Sigma Delta Chi. Roman Catholic. Clubs: Press (Milw.); (Tokyo); Press (Seoul); (Rome); Press (Denver); (Phoenix); American of Rome. Home: 7644 N 5th Ave Phoenix AZ 85021

CASSERLY, JOSEPH WILLIAM, architect; b. Chgo., Il, Sept. 19, 1929; s. John Joseph and Emma (Warner) C.; m. Mary Frances Brown, Feb. 14, 1953; children: John, Patricia, Kevin, Margaret, Jean. Ed., Ill. Inst. Tech., Chgo. Archtl. designer Holabird & Root, Chgo., Il, 1947-50, City of Chgo., 1954-66, asst. architect, 1966-79, architect, 1979—. Archtl. works include: Fire Sta., Renovation Widow Clark House, Library. Served to 1st lt. U.S. Army, 1950-54. Mem. AIA. Roman Catholic. Home: 2340 W 109th St Chgo. Il. 60643 Office: Bureau of Architecture City of Chicago 320 N Clark Chgo. Il 60610

CASSIBRY, FRED JAMES, U.S. judge; b. D'Lo, Miss., Sept. 26, 1918; s. Reginald E. and Lelia (Garner) C.; m. Lorraine E. Patterson, Dec. 21, 1940; 1 dau., Elizabeth; m. Muriel D. Belsome, Feb. 13, 1974; 1 dau., Cathryn. B.A., Tulane U., 1941, LL.B., 1943. Bar: La. bar 1944. Practice law, New Orleans, 1947-61; mem. firms Cassibry & Zengel, 1946-47, Dymond & Cassibry, 1950-55, Cassibry, Jackson & Hess, 1955-61; judge Civil Dist. Ct., Parish of Orleans, 1961-66, U.S. Dist. Ct., Eastern Dist. La., 1966—; mem. com. on jud. ethics La. Supreme Ct., 1965-66; instr. fed. procedure Tulane U. Mem. city council, New Orleans, 1954-60; mem. bd. commrs. New Orleans City Park, 1962-68; Del. Democratic Nat. Conv., 1956. Served from ensign to lt. (j.g.) USNR, 1944-46. Mem. Am., Fed., La., New Orleans bar assns., La. Dist. Judges (pres. 1963), 5th Circuit Dist. Judges Assn. (pres. 1974-75), Tulane U. Alumni Assn. (exec. com. 1962-65), Blue Key (hon.), Order of Coif (hon.), Sigma Chi. Home: 45 Hawk St New Orleans LA 70124 Office: US Dist Ct 500 Camp St New Orleans LA 70130

CASSIDAY, BENJAMIN BUCKLES, JR., air force officer; b. Honolulu, July 25, 1922; s. Benjamin Buckles and Harriet (Lucas) C.; m. Suzanne Baldwin, Aug. 20, 1983; children: Benjamin Buckles III, Carol Mary. B.S., U.S. Mil. Acad., 1943; grad., Nat. War Coll., 1962. Commd. 2d. lt. USAAF, 1943; advanced through grades to brig. gen. USAF, 1967; fighter pilot, squadron comdr. 79th Fighter Group, 1943-45; group operations officer, comdr. 81st Fighter Group, 1949-54; dep. comdt. USAF Acad., 1955-59; sec. air staff Hdqrs. USAF, 1963-66; comdr. 36th Fighter Wing, 1966-67; chief air force sect. Joint Mil. Mission to, Turkey, 1967-69; commdt. Air Force R.O.T.C., 1969—. Decorated D.S.M. Air Force, Silver Star, D.F.C., Legion of Merit with 2 oak leaf clusters, Soldier's medal with oak leaf cluster, Air medal with 8 oak leaf clusters; Distinguished Flying Cross, Great Britain). Mem. Air Force Assn., Order of Daedalians, Internat. Platform Assn. Clubs: Outrigger Canoe (Honolulu); Culver (Ind.) Legion, African First Shotters, Safari Internat., Waikiki Rod and Gun, Hui Nalu Canoe. Home: 5621 Kalanianaole Hwy Honolulu HI 96821

CASSIDY, CARL EUGENE, physician; b. Salineville, Ohio, Dec. 4, 1924; s. Clifford J. and Dortha (Lance) C.; m. Helen Ruth Skinner Collord, Dec. 21, 1961 (dec. 1975); children—George L. Collord III, Frederick Perkins Collord. A.B., Kenyon Coll., 1946; M.D., Western Res. U., 1948. Intern Youngstown (Ohio) Hosp. Assn., 1948-49; fellow in medicine Cleve. Clinic Found., 1951-54; research fellow in endocrinology Pratt Clinic, New Eng. Med. Center Hosps., Boston, 1954-56, asst. physician, 1956-67, sr. physician, 1968-72; physician-in-chief Med. Center Western Mass., 1972-76; program dir. Postgrad. Med. Inst., Boston, 1978—; asst. in medicine Tufts U. Sch. Medicine, 1954-56, clin. instr. medicine, 1956-58, instr., 1958-59, sr. instr., 1959-62, asst. prof., 1962-68, assoc. prof., 1968-73, clin. prof., 1973—. Co-editor: Clinical Endocrinology II, 1968; contbr. articles to med. jours. Served with USNR, 1943-45; to lt. M.C., 1949-51. Mem. AMA, Mass. Med. Soc., Am. Thyroid Assn., Endocrine Soc. Clubs: Longwood Cricket (Chestnut Hill, Mass.); Badminton and Tennis (Boston). Office: PO Box 68 Prudential Center Boston MA 02199

CASSIDY, CLAUDIA, performing arts critic; b. Shawneetown, Ill.; d. George Peter and Olive (Grattan) C.; m. William John Crawford, June 15, 1929. A.B., U. Ill. Music, dance and drama critic, Chgo. Jour. of Commerce, 1925-41, Chgo. Sun, 1941-42; music, drama critic, Chgo. Tribune, 1942-65; critic-at-large, 1966-69; formerly critic-at-large: weekly program Critic's Choice, WFMT, Chgo.; film critic: The Chicagoan mag. (now Chicago mag.), 1973-74; contbg. editor monthly column On the Aisle: Chicago mag, 1974—; spl. commentator: radio Lyric Opera, Chgo. Named to Chgo. Press Club Journalism Hall of Fame, 1980.

CASSIDY, DAVID BRUCE, actor, singer; b. N.Y.C., Apr. 12, 1950; s. John Edward (Jack) and Evelyn (Ward) C.; m. Kay Lenz, Apr. 3, 1977 (div.). Student pub. schs., Beverly Hills, Calif. Actor, 1969—; rec. artist, 1970—; appeared in: TV series Partridge Family, 1970-74, David Cassidy—Man Undercover, 1978; other TV appearances include A Chance To Live episode of Police Story, 1978 (Emmy nominee), The Night the City Screamed; tour of U.S. in musical Little Johnny Jones, after 1981; Broadway prodn. Joseph and The Amazing Technicolor Dreamcoat, 1983. Mem. ASCAP., Screen Actors Guild, AFTRA, Actors Equity. Office: care William Morris Agy 151 El Camino Beverly Hills CA 90212 *

CASSIDY, FREDERIC GOMES, humanities educator; b. Oct. 10, 1907; s. Walter C. and Camilla (Gomes-Casseres) C.; m. Hélène Lucile Monod, Dec. 26, 1931; children: Frederic Monod, Victor Monod, Claire Monod, Michael Monod. B.A., Oberlin Coll., 1930, M.A., 1932, H.H.D. (hon.), 1983; Ph.D., U. Mich., 1938; D.Litt. (hon.), Meml. U. Nfld., 1982, Ind. State U., 1983. Faculty Oberlin Coll., 1930-31, U. Strasbourg, France, 1935-36, U. Mich., 1936-39; faculty U. Wis., Madison, 1939—, prof. English, 1949-78, prof. emeritus, 1978—; Vis. prof. Columbia, summer 1956, Stanford, 1963-64; editorial cons. Funk & Wagnalls Co., 1964-72. Author: Place Names of Dane County, Wisconsin, 1947, A Method for Collecting Dialect, 1953, Jamaica Talk, 1961, 2d edit., 1971, Dictionary of Jamaican English, 1967, 2d edit., 1980; editor: Dictionary of American Regional English, 1965—. Recipient Silver Musgrave medal Inst. Jamaica, 1962, Centenary medal, 1980; Fulbright research fellow, 1951-52, 58-59; grantee U.S. Office Edn., 1965-70, Nat. Endowment for Humanities, 1970—. Fellow Am. Acad. Arts and Scis.; mem. Am. Dialect Soc. (past pres.), Soc. for Caribbean Linguistics (pres. 1972-76), Wis. Geog. Names Council, Am. Name Soc. (pres. 1980). Home: Route 3 Waunakee WI 53597

CASSIDY, HAROLD GOMES, chemistry educator; b. Havana, Cuba, Oct. 17, 1906; s. Walter Clarence and Camilla (Gomes) C.; m. Kathryn Myra Childs, May 19, 1934. Student, U. Akron, 1923; A.B., Oberlin Coll., 1930, A.M., 1932; Ph.D., Yale U., 1939; D.Sc., St. Thomas Inst., 1972. With B.F. Goodrich Tire & Rubber Co., 1924-28; research fellow Oberlin Coll., 1932-33; research chemist William S. Merrell Co., Cin., 1933-36; instr. Oberlin Coll., 1936-37; former mem. faculty, prof. Yale; sr. fellow in sci. Center Advanced Studies, Conn. Wesleyan U., 1965-66; now prof. at large Hanover (Ind.) Coll.; Cons. Q.M.C., 1954-61; acad. mem.-at-large Gordon Research Council, 1957-63; del. Conn. Tech. Council, 1945-59; seminar leader Danforth Workship Liberal Arts Edn., 1962, 63, 64, 65; Nat. Sigma Xi lectr., 1960, 63, 65, Ayd lectr., 1962, Korzybski Meml. lectr., 1962; lectr. Assn. Am. Colls. Arts Program, 1968, 71; 1st Lewis lecture St. Joseph's Coll., Hartford, 1969; chmn. Gordon Conf. Separation and Purification, 1956; cons. to Coop. Program for Improvement Sci. Edn. in India, 1970; mem. Nat. Humanities Faculty, 1971, 72; Green Honors Chair prof. Tex. Christian U., fall 1974; Research chemist OSRD and Manhattan Engring. Project, 1942-45. Author: (with J. English) Principles of Organic Chemistry, 1949, Adsorption and Chromatography, 1951, Laboratory Book, 1951, Fundamentals of Chromatography, 1957, The Sciences and the Arts, 1962, (with K.A. Kun) Oxidation-Reduction Polymers, 1965, Knowledge, Experience and Action: An Essay on Education, 1969, Science Restated: Physics and Chemistry for the Non-Scientist, 1970; also numerous articles.; Asso. editor: Am. Jour. Sci. 1948-67; adv. bd.: Analytical Chemistry, 1957-60. Bd. dirs. Save the Valley; past trustee Choate Sch. Recipient Third John Prymak service award Conn. Sci. Tchr. Assn., 1968; Excellence in Chemistry Teaching award Mfg. Chemists Assn., 1972. Fellow AAAS; mem. Am. Chem. Soc. (regional lectr. 1952, 56, 59), Conn. Acad. Arts and Scis., Ind. Acad. Sci. (speaker of year 1975, 76), Fedn. Am. Socs. Exptl. Biology, Conn. Sci. Tchrs. Assn., Sigma Xi (chmn. com. on grants-in-aid of research), pres. (1977), Bicentennial lectr. (1975, 76, 77). Home: 605 W 2d St Madison IN 47250

CASSIDY, JAMES JOSEPH, public relations counsel; b. Norwood, Ohio, Dec. 31, 1916; s. Martin D. and Helen (Johnston) C.; m. Rita Hackett, Oct. 18, 1941; children: Claudia, James. Student, U. Cin., 1934-38. Dir. spl. events, internat. broadcasts Crosley Broadcasting Corp., 1939-44, war corr., 1944-45, dir. pub. relations, 1946-50; war corr. NBC, 1944-45; account exec. Hill & Knowlton, Inc., N.Y.C., 1950-53, v.p., 1953-61, sr. v.p., 1961-66, exec. v.p., 1966-71, pres., chief operating officer, 1971-74, vice chmn., 1974-75, Burson-Marsteller, Washington, 1975-81. Trustee Cabrini Health Care Center and Columbus Hosp., N.Y.C. Recipient Variety award, 1944; citation for reporting in combat areas Sec. War, 1945. Mem. Pub. Relations Soc. Am. (past pres. N.Y. chpt.), Aviation Writers Assn., Ohio Soc., Internat. Assn. Bus. Communicators, Profit Sharing Council Am. (past chmn. bd.). Clubs: George Town, 1925 F St., Nat. Press, Sky, Overseas Press; International (Washington). Home: 826 Heritage Village Southbury CT 06488

CASSIDY, PAUL JAMES, radio industry exec.; b. Troy, N.Y., Feb. 11, 1935; s. John J. and Pauline (Bucholtz) C.; m. Marla Jean Cohen, Aug. 6, 1960; children—Kevin, Stephen, Paula, Carolyn. B.A., Mich. State U., 1957. Gen. sales mgr. stas. KDKA, Pitts., WIND, Chgo., KFWB, Los Angeles, Westinghouse Broadcasting Co., 1961-71; gen. mgr. KHJ, Los Angeles, RKO Gen., 1971-72; KSFX, San Francisco, ABC, 1972-74; v.p., gen. mgr. KTNQ/KGBS, Storer Broadcasting Co., Los Angeles, 1974-78; dir. sales Century Broadcasting Co., Los Angeles, 1978—; faculty Harvard U. Bus. Sch., 1966, Ind. U. Bus. Sch., 1967; mem. exec. bd. Billboard mag. Served to 1st lt. U.S. Army, 1957-59. Mem. Calif. Broadcasters Assn., So. Calif. Broadcasters (dir.), Hollywood Radio and TV Soc. (sec.), Variety Club Internat., Am. Fedn. Advt. Roman Catholic. Home: 18070 Rancho St Encino CA 91316 Office: 6430 Hollywood Blvd Los Angeles CA 90028

CASSIDY, RICHARD THOMAS, hotel executive, retired army officer; b. Camp Keathley, Philippines, Aug. 16, 1916; s. William Henry and Lillie Christiana (Bergstresser) C.; m. Annette Nine, June 12, 1940; 1 dau., Camille Gay Loo. B.S., U.S. Mil. Acad., 1940; postgrad., Command and Gen. Staff Coll., 1945, U.S. Army War Coll., 1958. Commd. 2d. lt. U.S. Army, 1940, advanced through grades to lt. gen., 1971; dep. chief staff (Army Air Def. Command), 1956-57, Army attache to, Iraq, 1959-61, comdg. gen., 1963, Arty. Brigade, U.S. Army, Europe, 1963-66; dir. Air. Def., Pentagon, 1966-68; comdg. gen. Air Def. Center, comdt. Air Def. Sch., Ft. Bliss, Tex., 1968-71, Army Air Def. Command, Colorado Springs, Colo., 1971-73; ret., 1973; v.p. pub. relations and advt. El Paso Nat. Bank, 1973; pres. Paso del Norte Hotel Corp., El Paso, 1975—; v.p., dir. Resort Am. Corp., 1973—; v.p. Camelot, Inc., 1976—. Decorated D.S.M., Legion of Merit, Bronze Star, Army Commendation medal with 2 oak leaf clusters. Home: 6006 Balcones Ct 25 El Paso TX 79912 Office: Resort Am Corp 111 S Oregon St Suite 200 El Paso TX 79912

CASSIDY, ROBERT EDWARD, insurance company executive; b. Bklyn., May 2, 1931; s. Joseph John and Anne M. (Clancy) C.; m. Elizabeth Ann Keely, May 19, 1956; children: Robert, Maureen, Michael, Thomas, Joanne, Paul. A.B., Catholic U. Am., 1953; M.B.A., N.Y.C. Grad. Sch. Bus., 1960. Internal cons. W.R. Grace, N.Y.C., 1957-61; with corp. personnel dept. Gen. Foods Corp., White Plains, N.Y., 1961-64, with sales dept., 1964-68, div. personnel dir., 1968-77; sr. v.p. human resources The Continental Corp., N.Y.C., 1977—. Served to lt. (j.g.) USN, 1953-57. Mem. Pi Gamma Mu. Republican. Roman Catholic. Home: 97 Wedgemere Rd Stamford CT 06905 Office: The Continental Corp 80 Maiden Ln New York NY 10038

CASSIDY, THOMAS JOSEPH, JR., naval officer; b. N.Y.C., July 16, 1932; s. Thomas and Winifred (O'Driscoll) C.; m. Marilynn Joan Harley, Dec. 21, 1963; children: Megan Alyssa, Thomas Harley. B.A., Chapman Coll., 1974. Commd. ensign U.S. Navy, 1953, advanced through grades to rear adm., 1980; various aviation fighter squadron assignments, 1953-65, chief projects officer air test and evaluation squadron four, 1965-68; comdg. officer Fighter Squadron 161 USS Coral Sea, 1969-70; air to air weapons coordinator Office of Chief Naval Ops., 1971-73; asst. chief of staff for ops. and plans Carrier Striking Force, Seventh Fleet, 1975-76; comdg. officer Naval Air Station, Miramar, 1977-79; head, aircraft and weapons requirements br. Office of Chief Naval Ops., 1979-80, dir. tactical readiness div., 1980-83; comdr. fighter/airborne early warning wing U.S. Pacific Fleet, 1983—; Pres. Navy Relief Soc., Miramar, Calif., 1977-79. Contbr. numerous articles to tactical publs., tactical manuals. Adv. bd. Armed Forces YMCA, San Diego, 1977-79. Decorated D.F.C., Bronze Star, Air medal., Legion of Merit. Mem. Soc. Exptl. Test Pilots. Roman Catholic. Office: Fighter/Airborne Early Warning Wing US Pacific Fleet NAS Miramar CA 92145

CASSIDY, WILLIAM ARTHUR, geology and planetary science educator; b. N.Y.C., Jan. 3, 1928; s. John and Nellie (Briel) C.; m. Beverly J. Griffith, Aug. 29, 1959; children: Shauna Lynne, Laura Dawn, Brian John. B.S. in Geology, U. N. Mex., 1952; Ph.D. in Geochemistry, Pa. State U., 1961. Seismic computer Superior Oil Co. of Calif., Midland, Tex., 1952-53; research scientist Lamont Geol. Obs., Palisades, N.Y., 1961-67; assoc. to prof. geology and planetary sci. U. Pitts., 1968-80, prof., 1981—; trustee Univ. Space Research Assn., Columbia, Md., 1975-82, chmn., 1978-79; chmn. meteorite working group Lunar and Planetary Sci. Inst., Houston, 1977-83. Contbr. articles to profl. jours. Served with USNR, 1945-46. Recipient Antarctic Service medal NSF, 1978; Fulbright fellow, 1953-54; grantee NSF, NASA. Mem. Am. Geophys. Union, Meteoritical Soc. Clubs: Explorers (N.Y.C.); Antarctican (Washington). Office: University of Pittsburgh 321 Old Engineering Hall Pittsburgh PA 15260

CASSILL, HERBERT CARROLL, artist; b. Percival, Iowa, Dec. 24, 1928; s. Howard Earl and Mary Elizabeth (Glosser) C.; m. Jean Kuniko Kubota, Aug. 23, 1951; children: Sarah Eden, J. Aaron. Student, Purdue U., 1944-45; B.F.A., State U. Iowa, 1948, M.F.A., 1950. Instr. printmaking State U. Iowa, Iowa City, 1953-57; head printmaking dept. Cleve. Inst. Art, 1957—. One man shows, Oakland (Calif.) Art Mus., Ohio State U., Columbus, Cleve. Inst. Art, U. Wis., group shows include, Library of Congress, Washington, Bklyn. Art Mus.; represented in permanent collections, Mus. Modern Art, N.Y.C., Cleve. Mus. Art, Oakland Art Mus., San Francisco Art Mus., and others. Tiffany fellow printmaking, 1953. Mem. Coll. Art Assn. Home: 3084 Coleridge Rd Cleveland Heights OH 44118 Office: 11141 E Blvd Cleveland OH 44106

CASSILL, RONALD VERLIN, author; b. Cedar Falls, Iowa, May 17, 1919; s. Howard E. and Mary (Glosser) C.; m. Karilyn Kay Adams, Nov. 23, 1956; children—Orin, Erica, Jesse. B.A., U. Iowa, 1939, M.A., 1947. Tchr. Writers Workshop, U. Iowa, 1948-52, 60-66; prof. Brown U., 1966—; reviewer for N.Y. Times, Book Week, Chgo. Sun Times. Author: Eagle on the Coin, 1950, Clem Anderson, 1961, Pretty Leslie, 1963, The President, 1964, The Father, 1965, The Happy Marriage, 1966, La Vie Passionnee of Rodney Buckthorne, 1968, In An Iron Time, 1969, Doctor Cobb's Game, 1970, The Goss Women, 1974, Hoyt's Child, 1976, also short stories.; Editor: Norton Anthology of Short Fiction, 1977, Labors of Love, 1980, Flame, 1980. Served to 1st lt. AUS, 1942-46. Mem. Phi Beta Kappa. Methodist. Home: 22 Boylston Ave Providence RI 02906 *More important than talents or intelligence, luck or strength, is the knack for using these things and using weaknesses as well. This knack is a very mysterious thing. Perhaps it is no more than a determination or a strong desire to make use of the good as well as the bad. The creative process, by its nature, can't have any predetermined goals, but a faith in the infinite possibilities for shaping life tends to define and clarify the value of achievement as one goes along.*

CASSILLY, RICHARD, tenor; b. Washington, Dec. 14, 1927; s. Robert Rogers and Vera F. (Swart) C.; m. Helen Koliopulos, 1951; 3 daus., 4 sons. Ed., Peabody Conservatory Music, Balt. With N.Y.C. Opera, 1955-66. Debut, Chgo. Lyric Opera, 1959, San Francisco Opera, 1966, West Berlin, 1965—, Hamburgishce Staatsoper, 1965, Covent Garden, 1968, Vienna Staatsoper, 1969, Munich Opera, 1970, La Scala, Milan, Paris Opera, 1972, Met. Opera, 1973; television performances include Die Meistersinger (Named Kamersanger, Hamburg 1973). Address: care Robert Lombardo Assocs 61 W 62d St Suite 6F New York NY 10023

CASSIMATIS, PETER JOHN, economics educator; b. Greece, Jan. 30, 1928; came to U.S., 1946, naturalized, 1946; s. John G. and Coula N. (Lourantos) C.; m. Margaret Ann Nell, Nov. 30, 1958; 1 son, Gregory. B.C.E., CUNY, 1953, M.B.A., 1961; Ph.D., New Sch. Social Research, 1967. Registered profl. engr., N.Y. Project mgr. several mgmt. and engring. cons. firms, 1953-64; prof. econs. and finance Fairleigh Dickinson U., Teaneck, N.J., 1964—; vis. prof. Center for Planning and Econ. Research, Athens, Greece, 1972-73. Author: Economics of the Construction Industry, 1970, Construction and Economic Development, 1975, The Construction Industry in Greece, 1976; Contbr. articles to profl. jours. Served with AUS, 1946-47. Research fellow Found. Econ. Edn., 1970. Mem. Am. Econ. Assn., Eastern Econ. Assn., Nat. Assn. Bus. Economists, Acad. Internat. Bus., World Future Soc., Am. Statis. Assn. Home: 19 Lorraine Dr Eastchester NY 10709 Office: Fairleigh Dickinson U Teaneck NJ 07666

CASSIN, JAMES ARTHUR, banker; b. Chgo., Aug. 11, 1934; s. Arthur D. and Mary Catherine (Harris) C.; m. Gertrude K. Considins, May 4, 1957; children: Catherine, Mark, Elizabeth. B.S. in Fgrn. Service, Georgetown U., 1956; cert., Internat. Mktg. Inst., Harvard U., 1963. World trade service mgr. Chgo. Assn. Commerce and Industry, 1959-63; dir. export expansion State of Ill. Dept. of Bus. and Econ. Research, Chgo., 1963-67; with 1st Nat. Bank of Chgo., London, Rome and Milan, 1967-74, sr. v.p., Chgo., 1975-79, exec. v.p., 1979—, mgmt. com., 1982—; dir. Internat. Comml. Bank, London, 1981—, Banco Arfina, Buenos Aires, Argentina, 1982—. Mem. Bankers Assn. for Fgn. Trade (dir. 1981—), Chgo. Assn. Commerce and Industry (dir. 1979—). Roman Catholic. Home: 547 Roslyn Rd Kenilworth IL 60043 Office: 1st Nat Bank Chgo 1 1st Nat Plaza Chicago IL 60670

CASSIN, WILLIAM BOURKE, energy company executive; b. Mexico City, Mexico, Sept. 11, 1931; s. William Michael and Elouise (Hall) C.; m. Kristi Shipnes, July 15, 1961; children: Clay Brian, Michael Bourke, Macy Armstrong. A.B., Princeton, 1953; J.D., U. Tex., 1959. Bar: Tex. bar 1959. Law clk. Judge Warren L. Jones, Fifth Circuit U.S., 1959-60; atty. Baker & Botts, Houston, 1960-70; v.p., gen. atty. United Gas Pipe Line Co., Houston, 1970-73, sr. v.p., gen. atty., 1973, group v.p., gen. counsel, dir., mem. exec. com., 1974-76; exec. v.p., gen. counsel, mem. exec. com., dir. United Energy Resources, Inc., 1976—; Gen. counsel Houston Grand Opera Assn., 1961-70, mem. governing council, 1977—, also bd. dirs. Contbr. articles to profl. jours.; Editor-in-chief: Tex. Law Rev, 1959. Gen. counsel Harris County Republican Exec. Com., 1963-64, 67-68; mem. exec. com. Associated Reps. of Tex., 1976—; bd. dirs. Houston Ballet Found., Gulf and Gt. Plains Legal Found., Legal Found. Am.; trustee Arts for Everyone, Harris County Heritage Soc., Armand Bayou Nature Center, Houston Grand Opera, Tex. Mil. Inst.; mem. vestry Christ Ch. Cathedral, 1970-72, 80—. Served to lt. Airborne Arty. AUS, 1953-57; capt. Res. ret. Fellow Tex. Bar Found. (life); mem. Am., Tex., Houston, Fed. Energy, Fed. bar assns., Order of Coif, Phi Delta Phi. Republican. Episcopalian. Clubs: Houston Country, Houston Met. Racquet, Bayou, Ramada, Houston Polo, Texas, Allegro; Army and Navy (Washington); Princeton (N.Y.C.); Princeton Terrace. Home: 1 S Wynden Dr Houston TX 77056 Office: Suite 7500 Texas Commerce Tower in United Energy Plaza Houston TX 77002

CASSINI, OLEG LOLEWSKI, designer, manufacturer; b. Paris, Apr. 11 1913; s. Alexander C. and Marguerite (Cassini) Loiewski; m. Gene E. Tierney, June 1, 1941 (div. Feb. 1952); children: Daria, Christina. Grad., Academia Belle Arti, Florence, Italy, 1934; student, Sch. Polit. Sci., Florence, 1932-34. Free lance designer, Paris, 1935, designer-owner dress studio, Rome, Italy, 1935-36; designer for Jo Copeland, 1936-38, James Rotherberg, Inc., 1938-39; owner studio, N.Y.C., 1939-40; designer Paramount Pictures Inc., 1940-41, 20th Century Fox, 1941-42; head wardrobe dept. Eagle-Lion Studios, 1946-47; owner firm Cassini-Dardick, 1947-50, Oleg Cassini, Inc., N.Y.C., 1950—; named ofcl. White House designer for first lady Jacqueline Kennedy, 1960-63, established ready-to-wear bus., Milan, Italy. Designer: mus. comedy As the Girls Go; other Broadway plays. Served as 1st lt., cav. AUS, 1942-46. Winner five first prizes Mostra Della Moda, Turin, Italy, 1934; Golden Accolade award; Man of Yr. Men's Fashion, 1980; numerous others. Mem. Council of Fashion Designers Am. Clubs: Tennis, Lawn Tennis (Florence, Italy); Parioli (Rome); Town and Tennis (N.Y.C.); Le Club, Deepdale Golf, Nat. Arts. Office: 257 Park Ave S New York NY 10010

CASTAGNA, WILLIAM JOHN, U.S. dist. judge; b. Phila., June 25, 1924; s. Charles and Ninetta C.; m. Carolyn Ann Spoto, Sept. 1, 1954; children—Charles N., William D., Lisa Ann, Catherine Alice. Student, U. Pa., 1941-43; LL.B., J.D., U. Fla., 1949. Bar: Fla. bar 1949. Practice in, Miami, 1949-50, Clearwater, 1951-79; partner firm MacKenzie, Castagna, Bennison & Gardner, 1970-79; U.S. dist. judge Middle Dist. Fla., 1979—. Served with USAAF, 1943-45. Mem. Am. Bar Assn., Fed. Bar Assn., Am. Trial Lawyers Assn., Am. Judicature Soc., Fla. State Bar (bd. govs., seminar lectr.), Acad. Fla. Trial Lawyers, Clearwater Bar Assn. (pres. 1965). Democrat. Club: Masons. Office: US Post Office Bldg Tampa FL

CASTAGNETTA, GRACE SHARP, pianist, piano educator; b. N.Y.C., June 10, 1912; d. Francis and Grace (Sharp) C. Student, Rutherford (N.J.) High Sch.; piano pupil, N. Elsenheimer, N.Y.C.; student, Hochschule fur Musik, Cologne, Germany, 1928-31; study in, Germany. Now pvt. tchr. piano and composition; now instr. advanced piano Trenton State Coll.; Adviser to faculty of music sch. Lighthouse for Blind, N.Y.C. Appeared in, prin. German cities; has played with, N.Y. Philharmonic Symphony, Nat. Symphony, Washington, symphonies of Portland, Oreg., Bridgeport, Conn., and with, Fed. and N.Y.C. symphonies, Columbia and Mut. Broadcasting symphonies; made Scandanavian tour, 1938; radio artist; began improvising at piano recitals in, 1941, in, Town Hall, 1942, 56, N.Y. U., 1974-75, trans-continental tour, 1956-57; Author: (with Hendrick W. Van Loon) The Songs We Sing, 1936, The Christmas Carols, 1937, Folk Songs of Many Lands, 1938, The Last of the Troubadours, 1939, Songs America Sings, 1940, Life and Times of Bach, 1940, Good Tidings, 1941, More Christmas Carols, 1942, Glad Tidings, 1958, Holiday Harmonics, 1959, Concerto series on radio for, Treasury Dept., Jan.-Apr. 1943; Made: concert transcription of Gershwin Concerto in F for; solo piano, 1946; soloist: Music For An Hour, MBS, 1945, Annual N.Y. City recital, 1945-46; made coast to coast concert tour; also appeared in solo recitals and with leading orchs., 1946-47, Am. Canadian concert tour, 1948-49, 58-59; appearing, Piano Playhouse, ABC coast-to-coast program, 1949, Carnegie Hall recital, coast-to-coast tour, 1950, extensive Am. concert tour, Town Hall Recital, 1954-55, concert tour, 1973-74; appearing on radio and TV in, N.Y.C.; soloist with symphony orchs., recitals throughout the, U.S.; Appeared in concerts at camps, canteens and hosps. for armed forces, during World War II; Author: Robin Hood Ballads, 1947, Sonata and 4 preludes, Goods Tidings; enlarged to pantomime of nativity story, pub., 1960; pub. solo version of Chopin Piano Concerto in E Minor, 1977; pub.: Sonata in C Minor for piano, 1976, Six Preludes and Fugues for piano; recorded improvisations on Christmas carols on Siena pianoforte, 1962; ann. recitals for, Ridgewood Concerts, Fairleigh Dickinson U., Hartwick Coll., Records for, Esoteric.; Has 3 vols. of recorded music and miscellaneous records. Mem. Am. Musicol. Soc. Presbyn. First appeared in pub. at age of four; after. Home: 383 Union Ave Wood Ridge NJ 07075 *The Golden Rule remains the best guide to all human endeavor. Under stress I try to remember that circumstances don't matter, only attitudes do.*

CASTALDI, DAVID LAWRENCE, hospital supply company executive; b. Logansport, Ind., Jan. 27, 1940; s. Lawrence J. and Ruth (Speitel) C.; m. Judith A. Pille, June 18, 1966; children: Valerie A., Maria C. B.B.A. maxima cum laude, U. Notre Dame, 1962; M.B.A. with highest distinction, Harvard U., 1966. Sec., dir. Mid-West Spring Mfg. Co., Inc., Chgo., 1961-71; with Baxter-Travenol Labs., Inc., 1971—, exec. v.p. Artificial Organs div., Deerfield, Ill., 1976-77, pres. Hyland Therapeutics div., Glendale, Calif., 1977—. Served with U.S. Army, 1962-64. Republican. Roman Catholic. Office: 444 W Glenoaks Blvd Glendale CA 91202

CASTANEDA, CARLOS, anthropologist, author; b. Sao Paulo, Brazil, Dec. 25, 1931; s. C.N. and Susana (Aranha) C. B.A., U. Calif. at Los Angeles, 1962, M.A., 1964, Ph.D., 1970. Apprentice to Yaqui Indian sorcerer, five years; now anthropologist. Author: The Teachings of Don Juan: A Yaqui Way of Knowledge, 1968, A Separate Reality: The Phenomenology of Special Consensus, 1971, Journey to Ixtlan, 1974, Tales of Power, 1975, The Second Ring of Power, 1977, The Eagle's Gift, 1982. Office: care U Calif Press 2223 Fulton St Berkeley CA 94720 *

CASTANEDA, HECTOR-NERI, philosopher, educator; b. Zacapa, Guatemala, Dec. 13, 1924; came to U.S., 1956, naturalized, 1963; s. Ezequiel V. and Sara (Calderon) C.; m. Miriam Mendez, Dec. 24, 1946; children: Xmucane (Mrs. Gerald Wiebeck), Kicab, Hector Neri, Omar Sigfrido, Quetzil Eugenio. B.A., U. Minn., 1950, M.A., 1952; Ph.D., 1954; Ph.D. Brit. Council fellow, Wadham Coll., Oxford, 1955-56; H.H.D., Governors State U. Instr. U. Minn., 1953-54; vis. asst. prof. Duke, 1956-57; asst. prof. Wayne State U., 1957-61, assoc. prof., 1961-64, prof., 1964-69, acting chmn. philosophy dept., 1965-66, summer 1968, vis. prof. philosophy, 1970; prof. Ind. U., Bloomington, 1969—, Mahlon Powell prof. philosophy, 1974—, 1st dean Latino affairs, 1978-81; prof. U. San Carlos, Guatemala, 1954-55; vis. lectr. U. Tex., Austin, 1962-63, vis. prof., 1966, U. Cin., 1970; vis. mem. U. Mexico Inst. Philosophy, summer 1970; adj. vis. prof. U. Pitts., 1972; dir. summer seminar Nat. Endowment for Humanities, 1974, 76, 78, year-long seminar, 1980-81. Author: Fundamentos de la didáctica del lenguaje, 1948, La Dialectica de la Conciencia de Si Mismo, 1960, The Structure of Morality, 1974, Thinking and Doing: The Philosophical Foundations of Institutions, 1975, La Teoria de Platon sobre las Formas, las Relaciones y los Particulares en el Fedon, 1976, On Philosophical Method, 1980, Sprache und Erfahrung: Texte zu einer neuen Ontologie, 1982; Editor, contbr.: (with G. Nakhnikian) Morality and the Language of Conduct, 1963, Intentionality, Minds and Perception, 1967, Action, Knowledge and Reality, 1974, (with James E. Tomberlin) Agent, Language and Structure of the World: Essays presented to Hector-Neri Castaneda, with His Replies, 1983; Founding editor: Nous, 1966—; Mem. editorial bd.: Critica, 1966—, Manuscrito, 1977—, Brain and Cognition, 1980—; Contbr. numerous articles to profl. jours. Recipient First award in humanities Wayne State Recognition Fund, 1961; Guggenheim fellow, 1967-68; Nat. Endowment for Humanities fellow, 1975-76, 81-82; Center for Advanced Study in Behavioral Scis. fellow, 1981-82. Mem. Aristotelian Soc., Am. Philos. Assn. (v.p. Western div. 1978-79, pres. 1979-80), Am. Soc. Polit. and Legal Philosophy, Soc. for Exact Philosophy (pres. 1971-74). Home: 4370 N Stuart St Bloomington IN 47401

CASTE, JEAN F., business executive; b. Paris, Mar. 19, 1929; emigrated to U.S., 1971; s. Gaston A. and Valentine M. (Gellie) C.; m. Danielle Y. Feron, Dec. 5, 1953; children: Françoise, Philippe, Nathalie. Diploma, Ecole des Hautes Etudes Commerciales, Paris, 1951; Licence en Droit, U. Paris, 1952. Dir. market research, gen. mgr. Nestlé Group, SOPAD, Paris, 1954-63; dir. mktg. and acquisitions, dir. fin., dir. planning and control L'Oreal, Paris, 1963-71; pres., chief exec. officer Cosmair, Inc., N.Y.C., 1971-80, still dir.; chmn., pres. The Nestlé Co., Inc., White Plains, N.Y., 1981-83; dir. gen. Nestlé, S.A., Vevey, Switzerland, 1983—; chmn. Nestlé Enterprises, Inc., N.Y.C., 1983—, Nestlé Enterprises, Ltd., Canada, 1983—. Served as lt. French Army, 1951-52. Decorated chevalier de l'Ordre National du Merite. Mem. Cercle Interallié (Paris), France-Am. Soc. Club: Paris-Am. (N.Y.C.). Office: Nestlé SA 1800 Vevey Switzerland

CASTEL, JEAN GABRIEL, lawyer; b. Nice, France, Sept. 17, 1928; s. Charles A. and Simone (Ricour de Quinsac) C. Lic., U. Paris, 1948; J.D., U. Mich., 1953; S.J.D., Harvard U., 1957. From asst. prof. to asso. prof. law McGill U., 1954-57; now prof. law Osgoode Hall Law Sch., York U., Toronto, Ont., Can.; vis. prof. U. P.R., Auckland U., U. Paris, U. Nice, Laval U.; Mem. Office Revision Civil Code Que.; academic-in-residence Dept. External Affairs, Ottawa. Author: Canadian Conflict of Laws, 3 vols, 1975-78, Public International Law, 1978, Canadian Criminal Law: International and Transnational Aspects, 1981; editor: Can. Bar Rev., 1957-83. Served with French Army, 1943-45. Fellow Acad. Arts and Scis., Royal Soc. Can.; mem. Can. Bar Assn., Assn. Can. Law Schs., Am. Law Schs. Assn., Societe de L'egislation comparee, Law Soc. Upper Can., Internat. Law Assn., Comparative Law Assn. Home: 658 Hillsdale E Toronto ON Canada M4S 1V4 Office: Osgoode Hall Law Sch 4700 Keele St Downsview ON Canada M3J 2R5

CASTEL, NICO, tenor, educator; b. Lisbon, Portugal, Aug. 1, 1935; s. Felix and Margalitt (Castel) Kalinhoff; m. Nancy Benfield, July 13, 1966; 1 dau., Alexandra. B.A., Temple U., 1952. Instr. diction and langs. NYU, Mannes Coll. Music/Am. Inst. Mus. Studies, Graz, Austria; diction coach Met. Opera; stage dir. opera. Author: The Nico Castel Book of Ladino Songs; Debuts include, N.Y. City Opera, 1965, Metropolitan Opera, 1970; permanent artist, Metropolitan Opera, 1972—; extensive concert tours, U.S., S.Am., Europe; tchr. master classes in multilinqual diction. Cantor Scarsdale (N.Y.) Synagogue. Served with U.S. Army, 1952-54. Mem. Am. Guild Mus. Artists. Democrat. Jewish. Home: 170 West End Ave New York NY 10023

CASTELLAN, GILBERT WILLIAM, chemistry educator; b. Denver, Nov. 21, 1924; s. John and Eleanor (Pavella) C.; m. Joan Margaret McDonald, Sept. 8, 1956; children: Stephen Joseph, William Andrew, David Matthew, Susan Marie. B.S. summa cum laude, Regis Coll., 1945, Sc.D., 1967; Ph.D., Cath. U. Am., 1949. Instr. chemistry Cath. U. Am., Washington, 1950-54, asst. prof., 1954-58; asso. prof., 1958-64, asst. head dept., 1963-65, prof. chemistry, 1964-69; asso. dean phys. scis. and engring. U. Md. Grad. Sch., College Park, 1969-74, prof. chemistry, 1969—, asso. chmn. dept. chemistry, 1973-78; Cons. electrochemistry br. U.S. Naval Research Lab., 1956-63, Melpar, Inc., Falls Church, Va., 1963-67. Author: Physical Chemistry, 1964, 3d edit., 1983. Bd. dirs. The Campus Sch., Washington, 1969-70, treas., 1969-70. AEC fellow phys. scis. U. Ill., 1949-50; NSF fellow Max Planck Institut für Physikalische Chemie, Goettingen, Germany, 1962-63. Mem. Am. Chem. Soc., Am. Phys. Soc., A.A.A.S., Albertus Magnus Guild, Electrochem. Soc. (pres. sect. 1964-65), Sigma Xi. Home: 3116 Cheverly Ave Cheverly MD 20785 Office: U Md Chemistry Dept College Park MD 20742

CASTELLAN, N(ORMAN) JOHN, JR., psychologist, educator; b. Denver, Jan. 21, 1939; s. Norman John and Mary Victoria (Biebl) C.; m. Diane Cecile Swift, July 18, 1964; children: Caryn Lynn, Norman John, Tanya Cecile. A.B., Stanford U., 1961; Ph.D., U. Colo., 1965. Prof. psychology Ind. U., Bloomington, 1965—, psychology editor Conduit curriculum com., 1974—, assoc. dean research and grad. devel., 1977—; vis. prof. computer sci. U. Colo., summers 1971-73; vis. research assoc. Oreg. Research Inst., 1972; mem. steering com. Nat. Conf. on Use of On-Line Computers, 1973-76, 83-85, conf. chmn., 1974, pres., 1979-80. Author: (with Hammond and Householder) Introduction to the Statistical Method, 1970; co-editor: Cognitive Theory, Vol. I, 1975, Vol. 2, 1977, Vol. 3, 1978; editor: Judgment/Decision Making Newsletter, 1981—; contbr. sci. articles to profl. jours. Active noise subcom. Bloomington Environ. Commn.; mem. Monroe County Democratic Central Com., 1968-73, 75-78, 80—. Research grantee and fellow NSF, 1971-73, 81-83, NIMH, 1966, 73-75. Fellow AAAS, Am. Psychol. Assn.; mem. Am. Statis. Assn., Psychonomic Soc., Assn. Computing Machinery, Sigma Xi. Home: 703 Ravencrest Bloomington IN 47401 Office: Dept Psychology Ind U Bloomington IN 47405

CASTELLANO, MICHAEL PATRICK, financial executive; b. N.Y.C., July 6, 1941; s. Michael A. and Angela (Alessandrino) C.; m. Theresa C. Anania, Dec. 7, 1963; children: Michael, Stephen, Lauren. B.S., Fordham U., 1962. C.P.A., N.Y. Sr. auditor Arthur Young & Co., N.Y.C., 1963-68; asst. controller-gen. acctg. Avis Inc., N.Y.C., 1968-71, v.p., internat. controller, London, 1971-74, v.p., corp. controller, 1975-76; v.p., corp. budgeting Citibank, N.Y.C., 1976-77; sr. v.p., corp. controller E.F. Hutton & Co. Inc., N.Y.C., 1977—. Mem. Am. Inst. C.P.A.'s, N.Y. Soc. C.P.A.'s, Security Industry Assn. (sec. fin. mgmt. div.). Club: Downtown Athletic. Home: 4 Westbourne Ln Dix Hills, LI. N.Y.11747 y Office: 1 Battery Park Plaza New York NY 10004

CASTELLANO, RICHARD S., actor, producer; b. Bronx, N.Y., Sept. 4, 1933; m. Margaret Tiernan, 1953; 1 dau., Margaret. Attended, Columbia. Starred: off Broadway in A View From the Bridge, 1966; on Broadway in The Investigation, 1967, That Summer, That Fall, 1967; appeared in: other play appearances include Milk Downstairs, 1968, Why I Went Crazy, 1968, Sheep on the Runway, Lovers and Other Strangers (Tony award nominee); film appearances include A Fine Madness, 1966, Lovers and Other Strangers, 1970, The Godfather, 1972 (Acad. award nominee); TV shows include Joe and Sons, 1975-76. Office: care henrick-hungwell ltd 8200 boulevard east north bergen nj 07047 *

CASTELLI, ALEXANDER GERARD, accountant; b. N.Y.C., May 3, 1929; s. Gerard and Carmela (Canzoneri) C.; m. Michelina Castelli, Jan. 8, 1961; children—Gerard, Alexander, JoAnn. B.S., N.Y. U., 1958. C.P.A., N.Y., Md., 1970. Chief accountant Daitch Crystal Dairies, Inc., Bronx, N.Y., 1965-68; asst. controller Alexander's, Inc., N.Y.C., 1968-70; v.p., treas. Bond Stores, Inc., N.Y.C., 1970-73; v.p. fin. McBrides, Inc., Washington, 1973-77; mng. ptnr. Castelli & Catudal, P.A., 1977—; bd. advisers Nat. Bank of Washington. Served with CIC AUS, 1951-53. Recipient Founder's Day award N.Y. U., 1958. Mem. Am. Inst. C.P.A.'s, N.Y. State Soc. C.P.A.'s, Beta Gamma Sigma. Roman Catholic. Home: 10009 Gainsborough Rd Potomac MD 20854 Office: 1738 Elton Rd Silver Spring MD 20903

CASTELLI, LEO, art dealer; b. Trieste, Italy, Sept. 4, 1907; came to N.Y., 1941; s. Ernest Krauss (mother nee Castelli); m. Ileana Schapira (div.); children—Nina, Jean-Christophe; m. Toiny Castelli. Law degree, U. Milan; student, Columbia U., 1942-43. Early career in internat. banking; opened Galerie Rene Drouin, Paris, 1939-49; worked in knit-goods mfg.; dir. Leo Castelli Gallery, 1957—; also owner Castelli Graphics, N.Y.C.,. Served with AUS, 1943-45. Recipient Mayor's award of honor for arts and culture N.Y.C., 1976; Manhattan Cultural Awards prize, 1980. Address: 420 W Broadway New York NY 10012 *

CASTELLI, LOUIS, oil company executive; b. Corbin, B.C., Can., Sept. 14, 1923; s. Giovanni Battista and Santina (Miglienna) C.; m. Rosemarie MacMillan, Aug. 4, 1956; children: Teresa Marie, Elizabeth Anne. B.S. in Elec. Engring., U. Alta., 1946, M.S. in Math and Physics, 1948; postgrad., Sloane Sch. Bus., MIT, 1967. Dist. geophysicist Mobil Oil Can. Ltd., 1950-54, staff gepphysicist, 1955-60, dist. exploration mgr., 1960-64, chief geophysicist, 1964-66; region exploration mgr. Mobil Co. Corp., Denver, 1966-69, gen mgr. Corpus Christi div., Tex., 1969-72, gen. mgr. Exploration Services Ctr., Dallas, 1972-75, v.p. exploration and producing services, 1975-80; pres., chief operating officer Moore McCormack Energy, Inc., Dallas, 1981—; dir. Inst. Petroleum Computation, Colo. State U., Ft. Collins, 1982—, U. Tex. Engring. Found., Austin, 1971—, Marine Sci. Inst., 1978—. Mem. Soc. Exploration Geophysicists (exec. council 1972-80), Dallas Geophys. Soc. (pres. 1980-81). Roman Catholic. Clubs: Dallas Petroleum; Royal Oaks Country (Dallas). Home: 7306 LaManga Dr Dallas TX 75248 Office: Moore McCormack Energy Inc 12790 Merit Dr Suite 800 Dallas TX 75271

CASTELLINO, FRANCIS JOSEPH, univ. dean; b. Pittston, Pa., Mar. 7, 1943; s. Joseph Samuel and Evelyn Bonita C.; m. Mary Margaret Fabiny, June 5, 1965; children—Kimberly Ann, Michael Joseph, Anthony Francis. B.S., U. Scranton, 1964; M.S., U. Iowa, 1966, Ph.D. in Biochemistry, 1968. Postdoctoral fellow Duke U., Durham, N.C., 1968-70; mem. faculty dept. chemistry U. Notre Dame, Ind., 1970—, prof., 1977—, dean, 1979—. Contbr. articles to profl. jours. NIH fellow, 395201968-70. Fellow N.Y. Acad. Scis.; mem. AAAS, Am. Heart Assn., Am. Chem. Soc., Am. Soc. Biol. Chemistry. Roman Catholic. Office: College of Science University of Notre Dame Notre Dame IN 46556

CASTELLINO, RONALD AUGUSTUS DIETRICH, radiologist; b. N.Y.C., Feb. 18, 1938; s. Leonard Vincent and Henrietta Wilhelmina (Geffken) C.; m. Joyce Cuneo, Jan. 26, 1963; children: Jeffrey Charles, Robbin Leonard, Anthony James. Student, Creighton U., Omaha, 1955-58, M.D., 1962. Diplomate: Am. Bd. Radiology. Rotating intern Highland Alameda County Hosp., Oakland, Calif., 1962-63; USPHS/Peace Corps physician, Brazil, 1963-65; resident in radiology Stanford U. Hosp., 1965-68, chief resident, 1967-68; asst. prof. radiology Stanford U. Med. Sch., 1968-74, assoc. prof., 1974-82, prof., 1982—, chief diagnostic oncologic radiology, 1970—, chief CT body scanning, 1979—, dir. div. diagnostic radiology and assoc. chmn. dept. radiology, 1981—; chmn. diagnostic radiology sect. No. Calif. Cancer Program, 1976—; mem. U.S. Cancer del., People's Republic China, 1977. Co-editor: Pediatric Oncologic Radiology, 1977; assoc. editor: Lymphology, 1973—; contbr. over 125 research papers to profl. publs. Recipient T.F. Eckstrom Fund award, 1978; Guggenheim fellow, 1974-75. Mem. Internat. Soc. Lymphology (exec. com. 1975—), Am. Coll. Radiology, Assn. U. Radiologists, Radiol. Soc. N.Am., Soc. Cardiovascular Radiology (charter), Am. Roentgen Ray Soc., Western Angiography Soc. (charter, pres. 1980-81), Calif. Med. Assn. (adv. panel sect. radiology 1972—), Calif. Radiol. Soc., Calif. Acad. Medicine, Alpha Omega Alpha. Office: Dept Radiology S 072 Stanford U Med Center Stanford CA 94305

CASTELLS, SALVADOR, pediatrician, endocrinologist, educator; b. Barcelona, Spain, Dec. 4, 1935; came to U.S., 1962, naturalized, 1967; s. Domingo and Rosa (Cuch) C.; m. Jean Proudfit, Feb. 24, 1962 (div. 1978); children—David, Brewster.; m. Arlene Hurwitz, May 16, 1981. M.D., U. Barcelona, 1960; postgrad., Cambridge (Eng.) U., 1962. Diplomate: Am. Bd. Pediatrics. Clin. asst. dept. pediatrics Barcelona Med. Sch., 1960-62; rotating intern Women's Hosp., Balt., 1963; pediatric intern Sinai Hosp., Balt., 1963-64; resident in pediatrics Jefferson Med. Sch., Phila., 1964-66; NIH fellow in metabolic and endocrine diseases Lab. Devel. Genetics, Dept. Pediatrics, Yale Med. Sch., New Haven, 1966-67; dept. nutrition and food sci. Mass. Inst. Tech., Cambridge, 1967-68, research asso., 1968; asst. prof. pediatrics N.Y. State U. Downstate Med. Center, Bklyn., 1968-71, asso. prof., 1971-77, prof., 1977—; mem. med. staff Yale-New Haven Hosp., 1966-68; asst. attending physician Kings County (N.Y.) Hosp., 1968-71, asso. attending physician, 1971—, Downstate Med. Center, 1968—, dir. unit of growth and metabolism, 1972—, dir. pediatric research., 1976-82. Contbr. articles to profl. jours. Mem. Soc. Pediatric Research, Endocrine Soc., Lawson Wilkins Soc. Pediatric Endocrinology, N.Y. Diabetes Assn. (detection com. 1972—), N.Y. Acad. Sci., AAAS, Bklyn. Acad. Pediatrics, Bklyn. Endocrine and Metabolic Pediatric Assn., Sigma Xi. Home: 3333 Henry Hudson Pkwy Riverdale NY 10463 Office: 450 Clarkson Ave Brooklyn NY 11203 *

CASTILLO, PEDRO ANTONIO, investor; b. Havana, Cuba, Feb. 2, 1926; came to U.S., 1960, naturalized, 1972; s. Pedro Alejandro and Amparo (Perpinan) C.; m. Julia Falla, Dec. 16, 1951; children: Pedro Alejandro, Miguel Angel, Ana Julia. LL.D., U. Havana, 1949; M.B.A., Harvard U., 1951. Partner firm Lazo y Cubas, Havana, 1951-60; v.p. corp. fin. Wertheim & Co., N.Y.C., 1961-71; stockholder Clark, Dodge & Co., N.Y.C., 1972-73; pres. Bus. Devel. Services, Inc., 1976-81, Fairfield Venture Mgmt. Co., Inc., Stamford, Conn., 1981—; partner Fairfield Venture Partners (L.P.), Stamford, 1981—; dir. Computerworks, Inc., Galileo Electro-Optics Corp., Micro-Linear Corp. Past pres., bd. dirs. Darien (Conn.) Library; past treas., trustee Low Heywood-Thomas Sch. Mem. Nat. Venture Capital Assn. (treas., dir. 1977-82). Clubs: Wee Burn Country, Landmark. Home: 18 Linda Ln Darien CT 06820 Office: 999 Summer St Stamford CT 06905

CASTILLO RENTERIA, JOSÉ DE JESÚS, bishop; b. Mexico City, July 2, 1927. Ordained priest Roman Cath. Ch., 1951; elevated to bishop, 1979, now bishop of, Tuxtepec, Mex. Address: Apartado Postal 9 Tuxtepec Mexico

CASTLE, EMERY NEAL, agricultural and resource economist; b. nr. Greenwood County, Kans., Apr. 13, 1923; s. Sidney James and Josie May (Tucker) C.; m. Merab Eunice Weber, Jan. 20, 1946; 1 dau., Cheryl Diana Delozier. B.S., Kans. State U., 1948, M.S., 1950; Ph.D., Iowa State U., 1952; postgrad., N.C. State Coll., 1956. Asst. prof. Kans. State U., 1948-52; agrl. economist Fed. Res. Bank of Kansas City, 1952-54; from asst. prof. to prof. dept. agrl. econs. Oreg. State U., Corvallis, 1954-65, dean faculty, 1965-66, prof., head dept. agrl. econs., 1966-72, dean, 1972-76, Alumni Distinguished prof., 1970; dir. Water Resources Research Inst., 1966-69; vis. prof. Purdue U., 1962; v.p., sr. fellow Resources for the Future, Washington, 1976-79, pres., 1979—; Mem. Water Resources Bd. Oreg., 1964-72, 73—, chmn., 1968-69, 74-75, Oreg. Water Policy Rev. Bd., 1975-76. Author: Farm Business Management, 2d edit, 1971, Water Resources Development, 1964, U.S.-Japanese Agricultural Trade Relations, 1982; Contbr. to profl. jours. and books. Served with USAAF, 1943-45. Decorated Air medal; recipient Alumni Disting. Service award Kans. State U., 1976. Fellow Am. Assn. Agrl. Economists (pres. 1972), Am. Acad. Arts and Scis., AAAS. Club: Cosmos (Washington). Home: 6506 Smoot Dr McLean VA 22101 Office: Resources for Future Washington DC 20036

CASTLE, JOHN KROB, investment banker; b. Cedar Rapids, Iowa, Dec. 22, 1940; s. Clyo F. and Emma (Krob) C.; m. Marianne Sherman, Sept. 20, 1969; children: William Sherman, John Sherman, James Sherman, David Alexander. S.B., M.I.T., 1963; M.B.A. with high distinction (George F. Baker scholar), Harvard U., 1965. Asso. Donaldson, Lufkin & Jenrette, Inc., N.Y.C., 1965-68, v.p., 1968-71, exec. v.p., 1971-73, mng. dir., 1973-80, chief operating officer, 1979—, pres., 1980—; dir. Sealed Air Corp., Baldt, Inc., Children's Place, D.L.J., Inc. Author: Financial Executives Handbook: Dividend Policy and Equity Financing, 1970, The Strategy of Corporate Financing: Packaging a Merger or Acquisition, 1971, Acquisition and Merger Negotiating Strategy, 1971. Bd. dirs., chmn. bd. N.Y. Med. Coll., 1978—; trustee N.Y. Eye and Ear Infirmary; mem. vis. com. dept. econs. MIT. Mem. Young Pres.'s Orgn., Am. Bus. Conf., Soc. Mfg. Engrs. Clubs: Harvard, City Midday, Economic (N.Y.C.). Home: 775 Park Ave New York NY 10021 Office: Donaldson Lufkin Jenrette Inc 140 Broadway New York NY 10005

CASTLE, LATHAM, U.S. judge; b. Sandwich, Ill., Feb. 27, 1900; s. John B. and Mollie (Latham) C.; m. Georgiana Whitcomb, May 1, 1931; 1 son, John W. LL.B., Northwestern U., 1924. Bar: Ill. 1925. City atty., Sandwich, 1925-28, state's atty., DeKalb County, Ill., 1928-40, corp. counsel, Sycamore, Ill., 1933-35, county judge, DeKalb County, 1942, asst. atty. gen., Ill., 1940-42, atty. gen., 1953-59; judge U.S. Ct. Appeals, 7th Circuit, Chgo., 1959-70, sr. judge, 1970—. Served with U.S. Army, 1918. Mem. Am., Ill., DeKalb County bar assns., Phi Kappa Psi, Phi Delta Phi. Republican. Mem. Federated Ch. *

CASTLE, MARIAN JOHNSON, writer; b. Kendall, Ill.; d. Oliver C. and Anna Mary (French) Johnson; m. Edward Carrick Castle, May 24, 1924. Student, Carroll Coll., Millikin U.; Ph.B., U. Chgo., 1920; Litt.D., Carroll Coll., 1950. Publicity work for concert and lectr. tours; gen. sec. Albuquerque YWCA, 1922-23. Author: novel Deborah (serialized in Woman's Home Companion), 1946 (Fiction Book Club choice, reprinted in 7 fgn. countries), The Golden Fury, 1949, also paperback edit. (selection 5 book clubs including alt. selection Lit. Guild), Roxana, 1955, also paperback edit.; Silver Answer, 1960 (made into Talking Books for Blind); Contbr. to: Harper's Mag., Good Housekeeping, Reader's Digest, others. Recipient Alumni Merit award Millikin U., 1962. Mem. Colo. Authors League, Zeta Tau Alpha. Presbyterian. Club: Denver Woman's Press. Home: 933 W Bonita Ave Claremont CA 91711

CASTLE, MICHAEL N., state lieutenant governor, lawyer; b. Wilmington, Del., July 2, 1939; s. J. Manderson and Louisa B. C. B.A., Hamilton Coll., 1961; J.D., Georgetown U., 1964. Bar: Del. 1964, D.C. 1964. Asso. firm Connolly Bove and Lodge, Wilmington, 1964-73, partner firm, 1973-75; dept. atty. gen., State of Del., 1965-66; partner firm Schnee and Castle (P.A.), 1975-80; lt. gov., State of Del., Wilmington, 1981—; prin. Michael N. Castle (P.A.), 1981—; mem. Del. Ho. of Reps., 1966-67, Del. State Senate, 1968-76, minority leader, 1976. Bd. dirs. Geriatric Service of Wilmington, Boys Club of Wilmington. Mem. Del. State Bar Assn., ABA, Council State Govts., Nat. Conf. Lt. Govs. Republican. Roman Catholic. Office: Legislative Hall Dover DE 19901 *

CASTLE, RAYMOND NIELSON, chemist, educator; b. Boise, Idaho, June 24, 1916; s. Ray Newell and Lula (Nielson) C.; m. Ada Necia Van Orden, June 16, 1937; children: Raymond Norman, Dean Lowell, David Elliott, George Leonard, Elizabeth Anne, Edith Eilene, Christian Daniel, Lyle William. Student, Boise Jr. Coll., 1934-35; B.S., Idaho State U., 1939; M.A., U. Colo., 1941, Ph.D., 1944. Instr. chemistry U. Idaho, 1942-43, U. Colo., 1943-44; research chemist Battelle Meml. Inst., Columbus, Ohio, 1944-46; faculty U. N.M., 1946-70, prof. chemistry, 1956-70, chmn. dept., 1963-70; prof. chemistry Brigham Young U., Provo, Utah, 1970-81; grad. research prof. chemistry U. South Fla., 1981—; Research fellow U. Va., 1952-53; pres. First Internat. Congress Heterocyclic Chemistry, N.M., 1967, sec., France, 1969, v.p., Japan, 1971, Utah, 1973, Yugoslavia, 1975, Iran, 1977. Contbr. research articles to profl. jours.; Editor, co-author: Chemistry of Heterocyclic Compounds, Vols. 27, 28, 1973; Editor: Jour. Heterocyclic Chemistry, 1964—, Topics in Heterocyclic Chemistry, 1969, Lectures in Heterocyclic Chemistry, Vol. I, 1972, Vol. II, 1974, Vol. III, 1975, Vol. IV, 1977, vol. V, 1980, Vol. VI, 1982; adv. editor: English transl. Russian Jour. Heterocyclic Compounds. Fellow Chem. Soc. London (Eng.); mem. Am. Chem. Soc., Internat. Soc. Heterocyclic Chemistry (pres. 1973-75, past pres. 1976-77, Biennial award 1983), Sigma Xi. Mem. Ch. of Jesus Christ of Latter-day Saints (bishop 1957-61). Home: 11401 Cerca Del Rio Pl Temple Terrace FL 33617

CASTLE, ROBERT WOODS, advertising agency executive; b. Oak Park, Ill., June 28, 1925; s. Lester D. and Dorothy (Woods) C.; m. Linda Stringer, July 2, 1977; children: Grant Berkeley, Steven Woods, Leslie Leachman. B.A., Dartmouth Coll., 1949, M.B.A., 1950. Asst. dir. market research, account exec. J. Walter Thompson, N.Y.C., 1950-57; chmn. exec. com., dir., mgmt. supr., dir. Belgium, Holland, Spain Ted Bates & Co., N.Y.C., 1958-75; sr. v.p. NW Ayer Internat., N.Y.C., 1975-79; pres. Ayer Baker, Seattle, 1975-78; exec. v.p., dir. NW Ayer ABH Internat., 1978-79; gen. mgr. Ayer/Chgo., 1978-79; pres. Robert Castle Assocs., 1979—. Mem. planning zoning bd., Darien, Conn., 1960-62, chmn. bd. edn., 1972-74. Served with USAAF, 1943-46. Clubs: WeeBurn Country (Darien) (trustee); Northport Point Country (trustee).

CASTLE, WENDELL KEITH, furniture designer; b. Emporia, Kans., Nov. 6, 1932; s. Marvin Oliver and Bernice Louise (Decker) C.; m. Nancy Jurs, May 8, 1971; 1 dau., Alison Courtney. B.F.A., Kans. U., 1958; M.F.A., 1961; M.F.A. hon. doctorate, Md. Inst. Art. Instr. drawing U. Kans., 1959-61; asso. prof. Rochester Inst. Tech., 1961-69; prof. SUNY-Brockport, 1969-76; pres., dir. The Wendell Castle Workshop, Scottsville, N.Y.; vis. prof. Mpls. Coll. Art, 1977; vis. lectr. schs.; juror numerous nat. art shows. Contbr.: numerous articles to Craft Horizons; author: Wendell Castle Book of Lamination; work appears in mags., films., One-man shows, Carl Solway Gallery, N.Y.C., Alexander-Milliken Gallery, N.Y.C., Fendrick Gallery, Washington, Rochester (N.Y.) Meml. Art Gallery, U. Kans. Art Mus., Lawrence, Louisville Art Assn., Wichita (Kans.) Art Mus., SUNY-Cortland; represented in permanent collections, Mus./Contemporary Crafts, Everson Mus., Syracuse, N.Y., Meml. Art Gallery, Rochester, N.Y., Phila. Mus. Art, Met. Mus. Art, N.Y.C., Mus. Modern Art, N.Y.C., Boston Mus. Fine Art, Nordenfieldske Kunstingdustrimuseum, Norway, Bklyn Mus. Art, St. Louis Art Mus.; designer, builder custom furniture, Scottsville, N.Y., 1968—. Served with U.S. Army, 1954-56. N.Y. State research grantee, 1972; Louis Comfort Tiffany Found. grantee, 1972; Nat. Endowment for Arts grantee, 1973, 75, 76; Lillian Fairchild award U. Rochester. Mem. Am. Craft Council. Home: 80 Oakwood Ln Scottsville NY 14546 Office: 18 Maple St Scottsville NY 14546

CASTLE, WILLIAM BOSWORTH, physician, emeritus educator; b. Cambridge, Mass., Oct. 21, 1897; s. William Ernest and Clara Sears (Bosworth) C.; m. Louise Muller, July 1, 1933; children—William Rogers, Anne Louise. Grad., Browne and Nichols Sch., Cambridge, 1914; student, Harvard, 1914-17, M.D., 1921, D.Sc., 1964; M.S., Yale, 1933; M.D., U. Utrecht, Netherlands, 1936; D.Sc., U. Chgo., 1952, U. Pa., 1966, Marquette U., 1969, Mt. Sinai Sch. Medicine, 1972; LL.D., Jefferson Med. Coll., Phila., 1964; D.H.L., Boston Coll., 1966. Intern Mass. Gen. Hosp., Boston, 1921-23; asst. physiology Harvard Sch. Pub. Health, 1923-25; asst. medicine Harvard Med. Sch., 1925-27, alumni asst., 1927-28, asst., 1928-29, instr. to asso. prof., 1929-37, prof., 1937-57, George Richards Minot prof. medicine, 1957-63, Francis Weld Peabody faculty prof. medicine, 1963-68, emeritus, 1968—; hon. curator Harvard Med. Sch. Archives, 1972—; Disting. physician VA, 1968-72; sr. physician West Roxbury (Mass.) VA Hosp., 1972-74, cons., 1974-79; asso. physician Thorndike Meml. Lab., Boston City Hosp., 1929-48, dir., 1948-63, jr. vis. physician, 1933-48, asst. vis. physician, 1948-55, vis. physician, 1956-63; dir. II and IV Harvard Med. Services, 1940-63, cons. physician, 1963-73; dir. Rockefeller Found. Commn. for Study Anemia, P.R., 1931-32; sr. cons. hematology Lemuel Shattuck Hosp., 1955—; cons. medicine Beth Israel Hosp., 1956—. Recipient William Procter Jr. Internat. award for distinguished service in scis. Phila. Coll. Pharmacy and Sci., 1935; Walter Reed medal Am. Soc. Tropical Medicine, 1939; Mead Johnson & Co. award for research on vitamin B complex, 1950; Gordon Wilson medal Am. Clin. and Climatol. Assn., 1961; John M. Russell award Markle Scholars, 1964; ann. hon. lecture award Albany Med. Coll., 1964; Disting. Lecture award Coll. Medicine U. Ky., 1965; Oscar B. Hunter Meml. award Am. Therapeutic Soc., 1965; Joseph Goldberger award AMA and Nutrition Found., 1966; Key to City San Juan, P.R., 1967; Ann. Am. Coll. Nutrition award for distinguished service in field nutrition and metabolism, 1970; Meritorious Service award VA, 1972; Sheen award AMA, 1973; Distinguished Chmn. award Assn. Profs. Medicine, 1978; named perpetual student Med. Coll. St. Bartholomew's Hosp., London, 1970; Am. Coll. Nutrition Fellow, 1973. Master A.C.P. (John Phillips prize 1932, Disting. Tchr. award 1978); fellow emeritus Am. Acad. Arts and Scis.; hon. fellow Royal Coll. Physicians London, Royal Coll. Physicians and Surgeons Can., Royal Australasian Coll. Physicians, Royal Coll. Physicians Edinburgh; mem. Am. Acad. Tropical Medicine, AAAS, AMA, Am. Philos. Soc., Am. Soc. Clin. Investigation (pres. 1940-41, emeritus 1943—), Am. Soc. Exptl. Pathology, Am. Soc. Tropical Medicine and Hygiene, Am. Fedn. Clin. Research, Assn. Am. Physicians (George W. Kober medal 1962, pres. 1959-60, emeritus 1960—), Boston Soc. Biologists, Mass. Med. Soc., Nat. Acad. Scis. (emeritus 1976—); corr. mem. Société Internationale Europeene Hematologie, l'Academie royale de Medecine de Belgique, Am. Soc. Hematology, Am. Clin. and Climatological Assn.; hon. mem. Societas Medicorum Finlandae, Brit. Med. Assn., Royal Soc. Medicine London, Phi Beta Kappa, Alpha Omega Alpha. Home: 22 Irving St Brookline MA 02146

CASTLE, WILLIAM EUGENE, institute technology official; b. Thomas, S.D., Sept. 5, 1929; s. Eugene Albert and Kathryn (Barkley) C.; m. Diane Lee Sklar, Aug. 8, 1963. B.S., No. State Tchrs. Coll., 1951; M.A., U. Iowa, 1958; Ph.D., Stanford U., 1963. Tchr. Faulkton (S.D) High Sch., 1951; instr. St. Cloud (Minn.) Tchrs. Coll., 1958-60, Central Wash. Tchrs. Coll., Ellensburg, 1961; asst. prof. U. Va., 1963-65; asso. sec. for research and sci. affairs Am. Speech, Lang. and Hearing Assn., Washington, 1965-68; dean Nat. Tech. Inst. for Deaf, Rochester (N.Y.) Inst. Tech., 1968-79; v.p. Rochester Inst. Tech., 1979—, dir., 1977—. Author: The Effect of Narrow Band Filtering on the Perception of Certain English Vowels, 1964. Served with USAF, 1952-56. Mem. Am. Speech, Lang. and Hearing Assn., Assn. Am. Sch. Adminstrs., Acoustical Soc. Am., Conf. Edni. Adminstrs. Serving the Deaf, Conv. Am. Instrs. of Deaf, Nat. Assn. of Deaf, Am. Deafness and Rehab. Assn., Am. Assn. Higher Edn., Alexander Graham Bell Assn. for Deaf (pres. 1982-84). Home: 4272 Clover St Honeoye Falls NY 14472 Office: 1 Lomb Memorial Dr Rochester NY 14623 *Though it took more than half of the years I have thus far spent, a great sense of relief from skepticism and cynicism occurred for me when I reasoned within myself that life is the only absolute and that the greatest component of feeling and the finest advocacy are that of love, not just for fellow human beings but for all parts of life that reflect beauty. Without these two prime thoughts and without lifegiven talents, integrity, and flexibility for working cooperatively with others, I would have no sense of success.*

CASTLEBERRY, JAMES NEWTON, JR., legal educator; b. Chatom, Ala., Dec. 28, 1921; s. James Newton and Nellie (Robbins) C.; m. Mary Ann Blcker, Feb. 12, 1944; children: Jean, Nancy, James III (dec.), Elizabeth, Cynthia. J.D. magna cum laude, St. Mary's U., 1952. Bar: Tex. 1952. Asst. atty. gen. State of Tex., 1953-55; prof. law St. Mary's U., San Antonio, 1955—, dean, 1978—; dir. Alamo Bank North, N.A. Co-author: Water & Water Rights, 1970; contbr. articles to law jours. Mem. Com. to Study Hist. Preservation Laws Tex., 1978—. Mem. ABA, Tex. Bar Assn., Phi Delta Phi (internat. pres. 1977-79). Home: 7727 Woodridge San Antonio TX 78209 Office: 1 Camino Santa Maria San Antonio TX 78284

CASTLEBERRY, VIVIAN LOU ANDERSON (MRS. CURTIS WALES CASTLEBERRY), newspaper editor; b. Lindale, Tex., Apr. 8, 1922; d. William Clarence and Jessie Lee (Henderson) Anderson; m. Curtis Wales Castleberry, May 4, 1946; children: Carol Janet (Mrs. Michael Lynn Tate), Chanda Elaine (Mrs. George Philip Robertson), Keeta Shawn (Mrs. Ingo Rudolfo Rupp), Kimberley Diana (Mrs. Michael Craig Easton), Catherine Ann (Mrs. Ian Dennison Tracy). B.S., So. Meth. U., 1944. Editorial asst. Petroleum Engr. Pub. Co., 1944-45; editorial asst. Cousins Pub. Co., 1945-46; women's editor Tex. A. and M. Bn., 1948-51; home editor Dallas Times Herald, 1954-56, women's editor, 1957—, editorial bd., 1974—; Cons. Mgmt. Seminar for Women Execs., 1963—. Mem. women's group Dallas Council World Affairs, 1964—, Dallas Internat. Cultural and Social Circle, 1965—. Recipient awards for womens news reporting U.P.I., 1963, 65, 77; Katie awards Dallas Press Club, 1968, 70, 72; J.B. Marryat Meml. award, 1980; Outstanding Woman award So. Meth. U., 1970; Headliners Club award, 1970; Southwestern Journalism Forum award, 1971; Extra Mile award Bus. and Profl. Women's Club, 1975; Women Helping Women award Soroptimist Club, 1977, Women's Center, Dallas, 1978. Home: 11311 Buchanan St Dallas TX 75228 Office: 1101 Pacific Ave Dallas TX 75202

CASTLEMAN, ALBERT WELFORD, JR., physical chemist, educator; b. Richmond, Va., Jan. 7, 1936; s. Albert W. and Mildred L. C.; m. Heide Gisela Engel, Mar. 10, 1976; children: Sharon Beth, Robert Gill, Clifton Carl. B.Chem. Engring., Rensselaer Poly. Inst., 1957; M.S., Poly. Inst. Bklyn., 1963, Ph.D., 1969. Leader chemistry research group Brookhaven Nat. Lab., 1958-75; adj. prof. atmospheric chemistry depts. earth and space sci. and mechanics SUNY, Stony Brook, 1973-75; prof. dept. chemistry and CIRES fellow U. Colo., Boulder, 1975-82; prof. dept. chemistry Pa. State U., University Park, 1982—; cons. Mfg. Chemists Assn., 1975—, U.S. Nuclear Regulator Commn., 1975-81, Oak Ridge Nat. Lab., 1976—; chmn. subcommn. on ions, aerosols and radioactivity Internat. Commn. Atmospheric Electricity, 1975—; mem. vis. com. Argonne Univ. Assn., 1976-82; guest prof. Physics Inst., Leopold-Franzens U., Innsbruck, Austria, 1981. Contbr. numerous articles on phys. chemistry to sci. jours. Sherman Fairchild Disting. scholar Calif. Inst. Tech., 1977. Mem. Am. Chem. Soc., Am. Phys. Soc., Am. Geophys. Union, Am. Soc. Mass Spectrometry, Sigma Xi, Phi Lambda Upsilon. Home: 425 W Hillcrest Ave State College PA 16801 Office: Dept Chemistry Pa State U University Park PA 16802

CASTLEMAN, LOUIS SAMUEL, educator; b. St. Johnsbury, Vt., Nov. 24, 1918; s. Max and Fannie (Svetkey) C.; m. Mildred Blanche Rubin, Jan. 25, 1948; children—Michael Z., David A., Steven J., Daniel J. B.S., Mass. Inst. Tech., 1939, D.Sc., 1950. Plant metallurgist Sunbeam Electric Mfg. Co., Evansville, Ind., 1939-41; sr. scientist, supr., acting sect. mgr. Westinghouse Atomic Power Div., Pitts., 1950-54; metall. specialist Gen. Telephone & Electronics Labs., Inc., Bayside, N.Y., 1954-64; prof. phys. metallurgy Poly. Inst. N.Y., 1964—; Cons. phys. metallurgy. Served with AUS, 1941-46; lt. col. Ret. Recipient Distinguished Tchr. award Poly. Inst. N.Y., 1975. Fellow AAAS; mem. Am. Soc. Metals (chpt. chmn. 1963-64), Am. Inst. Mining, Metall. and Petroleum Engrs., Am. Phys. Soc., Metal Sci. Club N.Y. (pres. 1973-74), Sigma Xi. Democrat. Jewish religion. Home: 15 Oak St Lynbrook NY 11563 Office: 333 Jay St Brooklyn NY 11201

CASTLES, JAMES B., corporation consultant; b. Missoula, Mont., 1915. LL.B., U. Mont., 1938. Cons., dir. Tektronix, Inc.; dir. Metheus Corp. Bd. dirs. Lincoln Meml. Park, Multnomah Kennel Club; trustee M.J. Murdock Charitable Trust. Home: 1390 SW Orinda Way Portland OR 97225

CASTON, J(ESSE) DOUGLAS, developmental genetics and anatomy educator; b. Ellenboro, N.C., June 16, 1932; s. Lemuel Joseph and Myrtice Elizabeth (Vassey) C.; m. Marry Ann Keeter, June 1, 1958; children: John Andrew, Elizabeth Anne, Mary Susan. A.B., Lenoir Rhyne Coll., 1954; M.A., U. N.C., 1958; Ph.D., Brown U., 1961. Fellow Carnegie Instn., Washington, Balt., 1961-62; asst. prof. developmental genetics and anatomy Case Western Res. U., Cleve., 1962-71, assoc. prof., 1971-76, prof., 1976—, co-dir. Devel. Biology Ctr., 1971-77; cons. Diamond Shamrock Corp., Cleve., 1975-77. Patantee folate assay, methotrexate assay; contbr. numerous articles to sci. jours., 1962—. Served with AUS, 1954-56. Fellow H.W. Wilson, 1956; grantee USPHS, 1963—, Cancer Soc., 1963—. Mem. Am. Chem. Soc., AAAS, Am. Soc. Zoologists and Developmental Biologists, Biophys. Soc., Soc. Cell Biology, Am. Assn. Anatomists. Episcopalian. Office: Case Western Reserve U 2119 Abington Rd Cleveland OH 44106

CASTONGUAY, ROGER J., banker; b. Van Buren, Maine, Nov. 21, 1939; s. Charles Peter and Adeline (Rioux) C.; m. Sandra Elaine Sirois, June 22, 1963; children: Mark, Lisa. B.S. in Acctg., Husson Coll. C.P.A., Maine. Acct., audit mgr. Arthur Andersen & Co., Boston, 1964-75; sr. v.p. and chief fin. officer Northeast Bankshare, Lewiston, Maine, 1975-81, pres. and chief exec. officer, Portland, Maine, 1981—. Trustee Husson Coll., Bangor, Maine, 1981, Mercy Hosp., Portland, 1982; bd. dirs., 1st v.p., chmn. exec. com. Maine Cancer Research and Edn. Found., Portland. Served with U.S. Army, 1958-61. Mem. Maine Soc. C.P.A.s, Am. Inst. C.P.A.s. Republican. Roman Catholic. Club: Cumberland (Portland). Office: Northeast Bankshare Assn 449 Congress St Portland ME 04101

CASTONQUAY, THOMAS TELISPHORE, chemical engineer, educator; b. Lead, S.D., Nov. 20, 1909; s. Anselm and Mary (McNally) C.; m. Florence Virginia Barr; children: Thomas William, Mary Alexina, John Joseph, Margaret Ann, Jo Ann. B.S., U. Detroit, 1931; student, Northwestern U., 1939; Ph.D., Iowa State Coll. Head gen. chemistry dept. U. Detroit, 1931-33; chem. dir. Ames Reliable Products Co., 1933-36; instr. chem. engring. and chemistry Iowa State Coll., 1936-41; successively asst. prof., asso. prof., head chem. engring. dept. U. Kans., 1941-46; prof. and head chem. engring. dept. U. N.Mex., Albuquerque, 1946—, dir. indsl. relations, 1971—; Cons. engr., 1936—; summer cons. Naval Ordnance Testing Labs., China Lake, Calif., 1957—. Contbr. tech. articles to sci. publs. Mem. Am. Chem. Soc., Am. Inst. Chem. Engrs., Am. Soc. Engring. Edn., Nat., N.Mex. socs. profl. engrs., Blue Key, Sigma Xi, Phi Lambda Upsilon, Alpha Chi Sigma, Phi Kappa, Sigma Tau. Roman Catholic. Address: 923 Vassar Dr NE Albuquerque NM 87106

CASTOR, WILLIAM STUART, JR., chemist, laboratory executive, consultant; b. Granville, Ohio, May 23, 1926; s. William Stuart and Ruth (williams) C.; m. Marilyn Anne Hughes, June 19, 1948; children: Jon Stuart, Richard Lee, Suzanne Marie, Cynthia Anne. Student, Coll. St. Thomas, St. Paul, 1944-45, Marquette U., 1945-46, Ill. Inst. Tech., 1946; B.S., Northwestern U., 1947, Ph.D., 1950. With Am. Cyanamid Co., 1940-72, tech. dir. pigments div., Wayne, N.J., 1961-68, dir. product devel., central research, Stamford, Conn., 1969-72, tech. cons., Allendale, N.J., 1973-74; mgr. devel. N.J. Zinc Co., Palmerton, Pa., 1974; mgr. pigments and chem. research Am. Cyanamid Co., Wayne, N.J., 1975-79; mgr. research and devel., tech. service Gulf & Western Industries Natural Resources Group, Bethlehem, Pa., 1980-81; dir. research and devel. Gulf & Western Industries Natural resources Group, Bethlehem, Pa., 1982-83; tech. dir. Parltec Lab., Allendale, 1984—; cons. in field. Patentee titanium dioxide pigment. Mem. No. Highlands Regional Bd. Edn., Alendale, 1967-73; mem. needs assessment adv. council N.J. Bd. Edn., Trenton, 1972-73. Served with USNR, 1944-46. Mem. Assn. Research Dirs. (pres. 1977-78), Am. Chem. Soc., Oil and Colour Chemists Assn., Soc. Chem. Industry, AAAS. Episcopalian. Club: Chemists (N.Y.C.). Home: 111 Schuyler Rd Allendale NJ 07401

CASTRO, ALBERT, medical educator; b. San Salvador, El Salvador, Nov. 15, 1933; came to U.S., 1952; s. Alberto Lemus and Maria Emma (de la Cotera) C.; m. Jeris Adelle Goldsmith, Oct. 19, 1956; children: Stewart, Sandrea, Alberto, Juan, Richard. B.S., U. Houston, 1958; postgrad., Baylor U., 1958; Ph.D., U. El Salvador, 1962; M.D., Cetec U., 1982. Asst. prof. microbiology and biochemistry U. El Salvador, San Salvador, 1958-60, assoc. prof. Dental and Med. schs., 1960-63, prof., head dept. basic sci., 1965-68, dir. rsearch in basic sci. Dental Sch., 1964-68, co-dir. grad. research, 1965-66, bd. dirs. dental sch., 1961-66, mem. research and scholarship com., 1964-65; asst. prof. pediatrics, co-dir. pediatrics metabolic lab. U. Oreg., Portland, 1969-73; dir. endocrinol. dept. and research unit United Med. Lab., Portland, 1970-73; sr. scientist Papanicolauou Cancer Research Inst., Miami, Fla., 1973-75; assoc. prof. pathology and medicine U. Miami, 1973-77, prof. pathology, medicine and microbiology, 1977—; coordinator Inter Am. Tech. Tansfer and Tng. Program, 1976—. Contbr. over 20 publs. to nat. and internat. sci. jours. NIH postdoctoral fellow, 1966-70; Northwest Pediatric Research fellow, 1971; U. Oreg. Med. Sch. grantee, 1966-69. Fellow Am. Inst. Chemists, Royal Soc. Tropical Medicine and Hygiene; mem. N.Y. Acad. Scis., Am. Chem. Assn., Am. Assn. Microbiology, AAAS, Tooth and Bone Research Soc., Acad. Sci. El Salvador. Roman Catholic. Basic research in diabetes, hypertension and immunochemistry. Home: 6275 SW 123d Terr Miami FL 33156 Office: U Miami Sch Medicine Dept Pathology PO Box 016960 Miami FL 33101 *I have tried to help others whenever possible with no expectation of reward except the satisfaction of having been of help.*

CASTRO, JAN GARDEN, association executive, educator, writer; b. St. Louis, June 8, 1945; d. Harold and Estelle (Fischer) C.; 1 son, Jomo Jemal. Student, Cornell U., 1963-65; B.A. in English, U. Wis., 1967; publishing cert., Radcliffe Coll., 1967; M.A.T., Washington U., St. Louis, 1974. Life cert. tchr. secondary English, speech, drama and social studies, Mo. Tchr., writer, St. Louis, 1970—; exec. dir. Big River Assn., St. Louis, 1975—; lectr. Lindenwood Coll., 1980—; co-founder, dir. Duff's Poetry Series, St. Louis, 1975-81; founder, dir. River Styx P.M. Series, St. Louis, 1981-83. Contbg. author: San Francisco Rev. of Books, 1982—; author: books including Mandals of the Five Senses, 1975; editor: River Styx mag., 1975—. Mem. University City Arts and Letters Commn., Mol., 1983—. Mem. MLA. Home: 7420 Cornell Ave Saint Louis MO 63130 Office: Lindenwood College 6314 Forsyth Ave Saint Louis MO 63108

CASTRO, JOSEPH RONALD, physician, oncology researcher; b. Chgo., Apr. 9, 1934; m. Barbara Ann Kauth, Oct. 12, 1957. B.S. in Natural Sci., Loyola U.-Chgo., 1956, M.D., 1958. Diplomate: Am. Bd.

Radiology, 1964. Intern Rockford (Ill.) Meml. Hosp.; resident U.S. Naval Hosp., San Diego; assoc. radiotherapist and assoc. prof. U. Tex.-M.D. Anderson Hosp. and Tumor Inst., 1967-71; prof. radiology/radiation oncology U. Calif. Sch. Medicine, San Francisco, 1971—, vice-chmn. dept. radiation oncology, 1980—; dir. particle radiotherapy Lawrence Berkeley Lab., Calif., 1975—; mem. program project rev. com. NIH/Nat. Cancer Inst. Cancer Program, 1982—. Author sci. articles. Past pres., chmn. bd. trustees No. Calif. Cancer Program, 1980-83. Served to lt. comdr., M.C. USN, 1956-66. Recipient Teaching award Mt. Zion Hosp. and Med. Center, San Francisco, 1972. Mem. Rocky Mountain Radiol. Soc. (hon.), Am. Coll. Radiology, Am. Soc. Therapeutic Radiology. Office: Bldg 55 Lawrence Berkeley Lab Berkeley CA 94720

CASTRO, RAUL HECTOR, lawyer, former ambassador; b. Cananea, Mexico, June 12, 1916; came to U.S., 1926, naturalized, 1939; s. Francisco D. and Rosario (Acosta) C.; m. Patricia M. Norris, Nov. 13, 1954; children—Mary Pat, Beth. B.A., Ariz. State Coll., 1939; J.D., U. Ariz., 1949; LL.D. (hon.), No. Ariz. U., 1966, Ariz. State U., 1972, U. Autonoma de Guadalajara, Mex. Bar: Ariz. bar 1949. Fgn. service clk. Dept. State, Agua Prieta, Mexico, 1941-46; instr. Spanish U. Ariz., 1946-49; practiced in, Tucson, 1949-51, dep. county atty., Pima County, Ariz., 1951-54, county atty., 1954-58; judge Superior Ct., Tucson, 1958-64, Juvenile Ct., 1961-64; U.S. ambassador to, El Salvador, San Salvador, 1964-68, to Bolivia, La Paz, 1968-69, practice internat. law, Tucson, 1969-74, Phoenix, 1980—, gov., Ariz., 1975-77, U.S. ambassador to, Argentina, 1977-80; operator Castro Pony Farm, 1954-64. Pres. Pima County Tb and Health Assn., Tucson Youth Bd., Ariz. Horseman's Assn.; Bd. dirs. Tucson chpt. A.R.C., Tucson council Boy Scouts Am., Tucson YMCA, Nat. Council Christians and Jews, YWCA Camp; Bd. Mem. Ariz. N.G., 1935-39. Recipient Outstanding Naturalized Citizen award Pima County Bar Assn., 1964, Outstanding Am. Citizen award D.A.R., 1964; Pub. Service award U. Ariz., 1966; John F. Kennedy medal Kennedy U., Buenos Aires. Mem. Am. Fgn. Service Assn., Am. Judicature Soc., Inter-Am. Bar Assn., Ariz. Bar Assn., Pima County Bar Assn., Nat. Assn. Trial Judges, Nat. Council Juvenile Ct. Judges, Phi Alpha Delta. Democrat. Roman Catholic. Club: Rotarian. Office: 1433 E Thomas St Phoenix AZ 85014

CASTRODAD ROSADO, JOSE ALBERTO, journalist; b. Cidra, P.R., June 1, 1949; s. Jose A. C. and Aida Angelica (Rosado); m. Elizabeth Sanchez Barrios, Apr. 17, 1971; children: Joel Castrodad Sanchez, Joselly Castrodad Sanchez. B.A., U. P.R., 1969, postgrad., 1970-75. Journalist El Imparcial, San Juan, P.R., 1972-74; press aide to pres. Senate of P.R., San Juan, 1974-77, press aide to minority leader, 1977-80, press dir., 1980-81; journalist El Nuevo Dia, San Juan, 1981—. Pres. Com. for Intergral Edn., San Juan, 1978. Mem. Journalists Assn. (v.p. 1982—), Ateneo de P.R. Roman Catholic. Office: El Nuevo Dia Ponce Leon Ave 404 San Juan PR 00902

CASTRO-KLARÉN, SARA BEATRIZ, educator; b. Arequipa, Peru, June 9, 1942; came to U.S., 1959, naturalized, 1978; d. José Andrés and Zoila Rosa (Rivas) Castro-K.; m. Peter F. Klarén, Sept. 4, 1963. A.B., UCLA, 1962, M.A., 1965, Ph.D., 1968. Teaching asst. dept. Spanish and Portuguese UCLA, 1962-65; instr. Calif. State Coll., Los Angeles, 1968; asst. prof. dept. fgn. langs. U. Idaho, 1968-70; asst. prof. dept. Romance langs. Dartmouth Coll., Hanover, N.H., 1970-75, asso. prof., 1975-80, prof. Spanish and Portuguese, 1980—. Author: El Mundo Mágico de José Maria Arguedas, 1973; Contbr. articles to profl. jours. Recipient Outstanding Women's Teaching award UCLA, 1965; Mellon Found. fellow, 1975-76; Woodrow Wilson fellow, 1977-78. Mem. MLA, Am. Assn. Advancement Humanities, Internat. Assn. Andean Culture (pres.), Instituto International de literature Iberoamericana. Home: 3 Hilltop St Hanover NH 03755 *Never give up on the difference between right and wrong. Hope that the value of all work will always be recognized as essential to the formation of any community.* *

CASTRO RUIZ, MANUEL, archbishop; b. Morelia, Michoacan, Mex., Nov. 9, 1918; s. Pastor Castro Tinoco and Mercedes Ruiz de;; s. Pastor Castro Tinoco and Mercedes (Castro) Ruiz de. Student, Morelia Sem., 1930-37; Pontifical Pius, Latin Am. Coll., 1937-40, Gregorian U., Rome, Italy, 1937-40, Puebla Sem., 1941-43. Ordained priest Roman Cath. Ch., 1943; pvt. sec. to archbishop of Morelia, 1943; prefect of Valladolid Inst.; spiritual dir. Minor Sem., 1947-50; spiritual dir. major Sem. of Morelia, prof. math. and philosophy, 1950-65; aux. bishop of Yucatan, 1965-69, precognized archbishop of Yucatan, 1969—; asst. to Episcopal Synod, 1974. Office: 501 58th Merida Yucatan Mexico *

CASWELL, HERBERT HALL, JR., biology educator; b. Marblehead, Mass., May 21, 1923; s. Herbert Hall and Grace (Parker) C.; m. Ethel Claire Preble, Mar. 28, 1948; children: Hal, Martha, William, Edward, Thomas, Michael. B.S., Harvard U., 1948; M.S., UCLA, 1950; Ph.D, Cornell U., 1956. Prof. biology Eastern Mich. U., Ypsilanti, 1955-74, head dept. biology, 1974—. Served to 1st lt. U.S. Army, 1942-46. Mem. Am. Ornithol. Union, Ecol. Soc. Am., Wilson Ornithol. Soc., Sigma Xi. Home: 952 Sheridan Ave Ypsilanti MI 48197 Office: Dept Biology Eastern Mich U Ypsilanti MI 48197

CASWELL, JOHN BEVERIDGE, retail company executive; b. Hartford, Conn., Dec. 28, 1938; s. Philip, Jr. and Evelyn Gertrude (Beveridge) C.; m. Heather Francis Livingstone, July 11, 1974; children: John Beveridge, Pamela T., Jeffrey F., Philip A., Elizabeth S. B.A., Brown U., 1960; M.B.A., Columbia U., 1961. Adminstrv. asst. R.I. Hosp. Trust Co., Providence, 1961-64; with Stanhome, Westfield, Mass., 1964—, exec. v.p., 1972-75, pres., dir., Westfield, 1975—; dir. Bay Bank Valley Trust Co. Vice chmn., mem. exec. com. Bay State Med. Ctr., Springfield, Mass. Clubs: Longmeadow (Mass.) Country; Colony (Springfield, Mass.). Home: 196 Prynnwood Rd Longmeadow MA 01106 Office: Stanhome 333 Western Ave Westfield MA 01085

CASWELL, PAUL HADLEY, communications company executive; b. Dover, N.H., Aug. 19, 1936; s. Gay E. and Gladys (Joy) C.; m. Barbara Ann Bradley, Jan. 7, 1967; children: Paul B., Philip C., Carolyn A. B.S., U. N.H., 1960. Gen. plant mgr. N.Y. Telephone, Queens, 1973, asst. v.p., N.Y.C., 1974-75, gen. mgr. tech. services, 1975-77, v.p. bus. services, 1979-81, v.p. N.E. Region Bus. Serivices, White Plains, 1981—; dep. dir. ops. City of N.Y., 1977-78. Served with USN, 1954-56. Republican. Club: Country Club of Darien (bd. govs. 1982—). Home: 10 Settlers Trail Darian CT 06820 Office: AT&T Info Systems 411 Theodore Fremd Ave Rye NY 10580

CATACOSINOS, WILLIAM JAMES, former electronics company executive; b. N.Y.C., Apr. 12, 1930; s. James and Penelope (Paleologos) C.; m. Florence Maken, Oct. 16, 1955; children: William, James. B.S., NYU, 1951, M.B.A., 1952, Ph.D., 1962. Asst. editor 20th Century-Fox, N.Y.C., 1951-52; asst. dir. bus. mgmt. and adminstrn. Brookhaven Nat. Lab., Upton, N.Y., 1956-69; pres. Applied Digital Data Systems, Inc., Hauppauge, N.Y., 1969-77, chmn. and chief exec. officer, 1977-83; adj. asst. prof. NYU, 1962-64; mgmt. counselor, 1962-69; chmn. bd. Corometrics Med., 1968-74; dir. L.I. Lighting Co. Mem. Brookhaven Town Indsl. Commn., 1956-77; bd. dirs. Suffolk County chpt. Am. Cancer Soc., 1969-77, Stony Brook Found., 1978—; trustee Poly. Inst. N.Y., 1981—; nat. chmn. Am. Soc. Prevention of Cruelty to Children, 1981—.

CATALFOMO, PHILIP, univ. dean; b. Providence, Dec. 27, 1931; s. Antonio and Frances (Di Giuseppe) C.; m. Magdalena Wettstein, Jan. 8, 1962; children—Kristina, Anthony Werner. B.S., Providence Coll., 1953, U. Conn., 1958; M.S., U. Wash., Seattle, 1960, Ph.D., 1962. Mem. faculty Oreg. State U., 1963-75, prof. pharmacognosy, 1966-75, head dept., 1966-75; prof. pharmacognosy, dean Sch. Pharmacy, U. Mont., Missoula, 1975—. Author research articles fungal metabolism. Served with AUS, 1953-55. Gustavus A. Pfeiffer Meml. research fellow, 1969-70. Mem. Am. Pharm. Assn., Acad. Pharm. Scis., AAAS, Am. Soc. Pharmacognosy, Sigma Xi, Rho Chi. Home: 33 Willowbrook Ln Missoula MT 59802 Office: Sch Pharmacy and Allied Health Scis U Mont Missoula MT 59812

CATALONA, WILLIAM JOHN, physician; b. Cleve., Nov. 14, 1942; s. William and Lucille Evelyn (Glanzer) C.; m. Janet Pauline Flenner, Apr. 15, 1966; 1 son, Alexander Paul. B.S., Otterbein Coll., Westerville, Ohio, 1964; M.D., Yale U., 1968. Intern in surgery Yale-New Haven Hosp., 1968-69; resident in surgery U. Calif. Med. Center, San Francisco, 1969-70; clin. asso. NIH, Bethesda, Md., 1970-72; resident in urology Johns Hopkins Hosp., 1972-76; prof. surgery/urology Washington U. Med. Sch., St. Louis, 1976—. Mem. editorial bds. profl. jours. Recipient award cancer research James Ewing Soc., 1972; C.E. Alken award, Bern, Switzerland, 1979; Am. Cancer Soc. fellow, 1974, 76-79. Mem. A.C.S., Am. Urol. Assn. (Grayson Carroll prize 1975), Am. Assn. Immunologists, Am. Assn. Cancer Research. Office: 4960 Audubon Ave St Louis MO 63110

CATANESE, ANTHONY JAMES, educator, planner; b. New Brunswick, N.J., Oct. 18, 1942; s. Anthony James and Josephine Marlene (Barone) C.; m. Sara Jean Phillips, Oct. 23, 1968; children: Mark Anthony, Michael Scott, Mark Alexander. B.A., Rutgers U., 1963; Ph.D., U. Wis., 1968; M.Urban Planning, N.Y. U., 1965. Asst. prof. city planning Ga. Inst. Tech., Atlanta, 1967-68, asso. prof., 1968-73, chmn. doctoral studies com., 1970-73; mem. faculty U. Miami, Coral Gables, Fla., 1973-75, James A. Ryder prof. transp. and planning, 1973-75, dir. Ryder program in transp., 1973-75; dean Sch. Architecture and Urban Planning U. Wis.-Milw., 1975-82; prof. architecture and urban planning Pratt Inst., N.Y.C., 1982—, provost, 1982—; sr. cons., State Wis., 1965-67, sr. planner, State N.J., 1963-64; pres. A.J. Catanese & Assos., Inc. (Cons. Planners), 1967—; sr. Fulbright prof., Colombia, 1971-72. Author: Scientific Methods of Urban Analysis, 1972, New Perspectives on Urban Transportation Research, 1972, Systemic Planning-Theory and Application, 1970, Planners and Local Politics; Impossible Dreams, 1973, Urban Transportation in South Florida, 1974, Personality, Politics and Planning, 1978, Introduction to Urban Planning, 1979, Introduction to Architecture, 1979; Contbr. articles to profl. jours. Mem. Ga. Dunes Study Commn., 1972-73; bd. dirs. Archtl. Research Centers Consortium, 1976—; chmn. Middle DeKalb County Democratic Party, 1969-71; mem. 5th Congl. Dist. Dem. caucus, 1971; aide-de camp Gov.'s Office, State Ga., 1971-72; mem. Urban Policy Task Force, Carter Presdl. Campaign, 1976, 80; pres. Park West Redevel. Corp., 1976-78; chmn. Milw. City Plan Commn., 1978-82; bd. dirs. Goals for Milw. 2000, 1978-82. Served with U.S. Army Res., 1961-63. Recipient fellowships State N.J. Act of 1927, 1962-63, Werner Hegemann, 1964-65, Wis. Alumni Research Found., 1965-68, Richard King Mellon Trust, 1966-67, Ford Found., 1967, Nat. Endowment Arts, 1980. Mem. Am. Inst. Planners (bd. govs., v.p. 1971-74), Am. Inst. Cert. Planners (mem. exec. com. 1971-74), Am. Planning Assn., Transp. Research Bd., Regional Sci. Assn., Am. Acad. Polit. and Social Scis., Assn. Coll. Schs. Planning. Club: Montauk of N.Y. Office: Thrift Hall Pratt Inst Brooklyn NY 11205

CATANIA, ANTHONY CHARLES, psychology educator; b. N.Y.C., June 22, 1936; s. Charles John and Elizabeth (Lattarulo) C.; m. Constance J. Britt, Feb. 10, 1962; children: William John, Kenneth Charles. B.A., Columbia U., 1957, M.A., 1958; Ph.D. (NSF fellow), Harvard U., 1961. Postdoctoral research fellow Harvard U., 1961-62; sr. pharmacologist Smith, Kline & French Labs., Phila., 1962-64; asst. prof. NYU, 1964-66, asso. prof., 1966-69, prof., chmn. dept. psychology, 1969-73; prof. dept. psychology U. Md. Baltimore County, Catonsville, 1973—; mem. psychobiology com. NSF, 1982—. Author: Learning, 1979, 2d edit., 1984; editor: Contemporary Research in Operant Behavior, 1968; Editor: (with T.A. Brigham) Handbook of Applied Behavior Analysis, 1978; editor: Jour. Exptl. Analysis Behavior, 1966-69; rev. editor, 1969-76, 83—; asso. editor: Behavioral and Brain Scis., 1980—; bd. editors: Behaviorism, 1972—; contbr. articles to profl. jours. Fellow AAAS, Am. Psychol. Assn. (pres. div. 25 1976-79); mem. Assn. Behavioral Analysis (pres. 1982-83), Eastern Psychol. Assn. (dir. 1979-82), Soc. Exptl. Analysis of Behavior (pres. 1966-67, 81-83). Home: 10545 Rivulet Row Columbia MD 21044 Office: Dept Psychology Univ Md Baltimore County 5401 Wilkens Ave Catonsville MD 21228

CATANIA, FRANCIS J(OSEPH), university dean, educator; b. Chgo., Mar. 5, 1933; s. Francis P. and Rose F. (Vizza) C.; m. Zelda F. Schuman, Aug. 18, 1956; children: Catherine, Francis J., Anita, Thomas, Raymond, Robert. A.B., Loyola U., Chgo., 1954, M.A., 1958; Ph.D., St. Louis U., 1959. Instr. Johns Carroll U., 1958-60; asst. prof. philosophy Loyola U., 1960-65, assoc. prof., 1965-77, prof., 1977—, dean, 1977—. Bd. dirs. Edgewater Community Council, Chgo., 1968-70. Mem. Councl Grad. Schs., Am. Acad. Religion, Metaphys. Soc. Am., Am. Am. Catholic Philos. Assn. Office: 820 N Michigan Ave Chicago IL 60611 *

CATANZARO, TONY, dancer; b. Bklyn., Nov. 10; s. Archie Achilles and Elvira (Alessandra) C.; m. Lizette Piedra. Student, Performing Arts, N.Y.C., 1961-64. Mem. dance panel Mass. Council for Arts and Humanities, 1978—; mem. Com. for Pub. Action for the Arts; mem. blue ribbon com. for Mass. arts lottery bill Spl. Commn. on Performing Arts; mem. hon. com. Dance/New Eng. Appeared with modern dance cos., Paul Sanansardo Co., 1963-64, Pearl Lang Co., 1966-70, Norman Walker, 1963-70; appeared with, Harkness Ballet Co. II, 1967, N.J. Ballet Co., 1968-69, Ala. Ballet Co., 1969, Boston Ballet Co., 1969-70, 73-76, Joffrey Ballet, 1970-73, Dennis Waynes Dancers, Boston, 1977—; artistic dir., choreographer, Boston Ballet Ensemble, 1980-81; prin. dancer, Boston Ballet Co., 1980-82; artistic dir., Ballet Acad. of Miami, 1984—; leading dance roles in: Broadway Annie Get Your Gun, 1966, Golden Boy, London Palaedium, 1968. Served with U.S. N.G., 1967-70. Office: 1809 Ponce de Leon Blvd Coral Gables FL 33134

CATE, BENJAMIN WILSON UPTON, journalist; b. Paris, France, Sept. 28, 1931; s. Karl Springer and Josephine (Wilson) C.; children: Christopher, Stephanie. B.A., Yale U., 1955. Reporter St. Petersburg (Fla.) Times, 1955-60; Corr. Time mag., Los Angeles, 1960-61, corr., Detroit, 1961-65, chief Houston bur., 1965-68, corr., Paris, 1968-69, chief Bonn. (W. Ger.) bur., 1969-72, dep. chief of corrs., N.Y.C., 1972-75, chief Midwest bur., Chgo., 1975-81, chief West Coast bur., Beverly Hills, Calif., 1981—. Served with U.S. Army, 1955-57. Mem. Sigma Delta Phi. Club: Chgo. Press. Office: Time Mag 450 N Roxbury Dr Beverly Hills CA 90210

CATE, PHILLIP DENNIS, museum director; b. Washington, Oct. 19, 1944; s. Phillip Harding and Catherine (Watson) C.; children: Phillip Isaac, Anthony David. B.A., Rutgers U., 1967; M.A., Ariz. State U., 1970. Mem. staff Pa. Acad. Fine Arts, Phila., 1967-68, Phila. Coll. Art, 1969-70; dir. Rutgers U. Art Mus., 1970—; pres. Middlesex County Arts Council, 1977—; bd. dirs. Printmaking Council N.J., 1975—. Author: The Color Revolution: Color Lithography in France 1890-1900, 1978, Circa 1800-The Beginnings of Modern Printmaking, 1775-1835, 1981, Theophile Alexandre Steinlen (1859-1923). Mem. Print Council Am., Am. Assn. Museums. Club: Grolier (N.Y.C.). Office: Zimmerli Art Mus Rutgers U New Brunswick NJ 08903

CATE, WESTON ATTWOOD, JR., historical administrator, editor; b. St. Johnsbury, Vt., July 16, 1921; s. Weston Attwood and Arlene (Jeffords) C.; m. Jean Margaret Stetson, June 29, 1944; children: Weston Attwood, Paul S., David W. A.B., Bates Coll., Lewiston, Maine, 1943. Civilian worker U.S. Air Force, Buffalo, 1943-44; tchr. Black River High Sch., Ludlow, Vt., 1944-46; dept. head Hartford High Sch., White River Junction, Vt., 1946-57; dir. Vt. Edn. Assn., Montpelier, 1983—. Mem. Am. Assn. State and Local History. Unitarian. Club: Club of Montpelier (pres. 1976-77). Home: Calais Stage Montpelier VT 05602 Office: Vermont Historical Soc 109 State St Montpelier VT 05602

CATE, WIRT ARMISTEAD, author; b. Hopkinsville, Ky., Nov. 16, 1900; s. James Henry and Mary Lou (Armistead) C. A.B., Emory U., 1923, A.M. (fellow), 1925; postgrad. (Edward Austin fellow), Harvard, 1926-27, 28-29. Instr. Baylor Sch., Chattanooga, 1923-24, Ga. Sch. Tech., 1925-26, 27-28; lectr. English Emory U., summers 1926, 28; Julius Rosenwald fellow Am. history, 1937-38; fellow Colonial Williamsburg, Inc., 1940-43; now engaged in biog., hist. research, writing. Author: Lucius Q.C. Lamar, Secession and Reunion, 1935, 3d edit., 1978, (with Margaret R. Cate) The Armistead Family and Collaterals, 1971; Editor: Two Soldiers, The Campaign Diaries of Thomas J. Key, C.S.A. and Robert J. Campbell, U.S.A, 1938; Contbr. to: hist., philol. and coll. jours. Ency. Brit. Mem. Modern Lang. Assn. Am., So. Hist. Assn., Phi Beta Kappa, Sigma Upsilon, Sigma Chi. Democrat. Methodist. Home: 713 Lynnbrook Road Nashville TN 37215

CATER, DOUGLASS, writer, editor, educator, college president; b. Montgomery, Ala., Aug. 24, 1923; s. Silas D. and Nancy (Chesnutt) C.; m. Libby Anderson, Dec. 20, 1950; children: Silas Douglass III, R. Sage, L. Morrow, Benjamin W. Grad., Phillips Exeter Acad., 1942; A.B., Harvard U., 1947, M.A., 1948. Washington editor Reporter mag., 1950-63, nat. affairs editor, 1963-64; spl. asst. to Pres. Johnson, 1964-68; spl. asst. to sec. army, 1951; cons. to dir. Mut. Security Agy., 1952; Ferris vis. prof. pub. affairs Princeton, 1959; vis. prof. pub. affairs Wesleyan U., Middletown, Conn., 1963; Regent prof. U. Calif. at San Francisco, 1971-72; cons. prof. Stanford, 1972-77; dir. program council Aspen Inst., sr. fellow, 1978—; pres. Washington Coll., Chestertown, Md., 1982—; vice chmn. The Observer, London, 1976-81; pres. Observer Internat., 1976-81. Author: (with Marquis Childs) Ethics In a Business Society, 1953, The Fourth Branch of Government, 1959, Power in Washington, 1964, Dana: The Irrelevant Man, 1970, TV Violence and the Child, 1975. Served with, World War II; OSS. Guggenheim fellow, 1955; Eisenhower exchange fellow, 1957; recipient George Polk Meml. award, 1961; N.Y. Newspaper Guild Page One award, 1961. Mem. Sigma Delta Chi. Presbyn. Clubs: Century Assn., Univ. (N.Y.C.). Office: Washington College Chestertown MD 21620

CATER, JOHN THOMAS, banker; b. Temple, Tex., July 12, 1935; s. B.J. and Guyrene (Thomas) C.; m. Margot Kyle Steenland, Feb. 1, 1969. B.A. in Govt, U. Tex., 1958, B.B.A. in Finance, 1959, LL.B., 1959. With Tex. Commerce Bank, Houston, 1960—, pres., 1972—; also dir.; vice chmn. bd., dir. Tex. Commerce Bancshares, Inc., from 1973; now chmn., chief exec. officer S.W. Bancshares, Inc.; chmn. chief exec. officer Bank of Southwest; dir. Anderson Clayton Co., Houston Industries, Houston Lighting and Power. Bd. dirs. Tex. Med. Center, Retina Research Found.; mem. devel. bd. Inst. Latin-Am. Affairs, U. Tex., Austin, U. Tex. Health Sci. Center, Houston; mem. Houston Com. for Pvt. Sector Initiatives. Served with AUS, 1959. Mem. Tex. Bankers Assn. (legis. com.), Res. City Bankers Assn., Young Pres.'s Orgn., Tex. Bar Assn., Houston C. of C. (bd. dirs.), Alpha Tau Omega, Phi Alpha Delta. Office: SW Bancshares Inc PO Box 2629 Houston TX 77001

CATERORA, PHILIP RENE, marketing and business educator; b. Houston, May 3, 1932; s. Henry and Hattie Mae (Butler) Cateora; m. Nancy Cateora Windham, July 1, 1956; children: Deborah F., Phyllis A., Robert Henry. B.B.A., U. Tex., 1957, M.B.A., 1959, Ph.D., 1962. Asst. prof. U. Tex., Austin, 1961-62, U. So. Calif., Los Angeles, 1962-63; mem. faculty U. Colo., Boulder, 1963—; prof. mktg. and internat. bus., cons. Pepsi-Cola Mgmt. Inst., Purchase, N.Y., 1965—; dir. Proto-Med Inc., Boulder, TDI Inc., Santa Monica, Calif. Author: International Marketing, 5th edit., 1983; editor: Marketing Insights, 3d edit., 1974. Fellow Acad. Internat. Bus.; mem. Am. Mktg. Assn., Beta Gamma Sigma. Home: 440 Erie Dr Boulder CO 80303 Office: U Colo Coll Bus Campus Box 419 Boulder CO 80309

CATES, DON TATE, lawyer; b. Commerce, Tex., June 12, 1933; s. Harry Louis and Bobbye Edith (Tate) C.; m. Stella Evelyn Oates, July 13, 1957; children: William, Margaret, John, Harry. B.A., Baylor U., Waco, Tex., 1955, J.D., 1957. Bar: Tex. 1957. Asst. city atty., Houston, 1957-59; assoc. sec. endowment dept. Baptist Gen. Conv. Tex., 1959-60; asst. dist. atty., Dallas, 1960-62, practice law, 1962—; prin. Law Offices of Don T. Cates. Bd. dirs., past pres. Dallas Soc. Prevention of Cruelty to Animals. Mem. Tex., Dallas, Kaufman County bar assns., Baylor Alumni Assn. (dir.), Baylor Law Alumni Assn. Democrat. Baptist. Clubs: Masons, Lions, Baylor Bears (dir.). Home: 27 Estate Ln Box 152 Forney TX 75126 Office: 1105 Kirby Bldg Dallas TX 75201

CATES, GILBERT, director-producer; b. N.Y.C., June 6, 1934; s. Nathan and Nina (Peltzman) Katz; m. Jane Betty Dubin, Feb. 9, 1957; children: Melissa Beth, Jonathan Michael, David Sawyer, Gilbert Lewis. B.S., Syracuse U., 1955, M.A., 1965. Bd. dirs. Childville, Inc., N.Y.C., 1966-73; mem. com. 1 Syracuse U. Drama Dept., 1969-73. TV producer, dir.: Haggis Baggis, NBC-TV, 1959, Camouflage, ABC-TV, 1961-62, Internat. Showtime, 1962-64; producer-dir.: Hootenanny, ABC-TV, 1962, To All My Friends on Shore, CBS-TV, 1972, The Affair, ABC-TV, 1974, After the Fall, NBC-TV, 1974, Johnny, We Hardly Knew Ye, NBC-TV, 1977, The Kid From Nowhere, NBC-TV, 1982, Faiere Tale Theatre, Hobson's Choice CBS-TV, 1983; film producer, dir.: The Painting, 1962, Rings Around the World, 1967, I Never Sang for My Father, 1970, Summer Wishes, Winter Dreams, 1973, Dragonfly, 1976, The Promise, 1978, The Last Married Couple in America, 1979, Oh God, Book II, 1980; theatrical producer: You Know I Can't Hear You When the Water's Running, 1967, I Never Sang for my Father, 1968, The Chinese and Doctor Fish, 1970, Solitaire-Double Solitaire, 1971; dir.: Voices, 1972, Tricks of the Trade, 1980; film Jamel, Inc, Los Angeles, 1977—. Recipient Best Short Film award Internat. Film Importers and Distbrs., 1962; Chancellor's medal Syracuse U., 1974. Mem. Dirs. Guild Am. (v.p. Eastern region 1965, Western region 1980—, pres. 1983—), League N.Y. Theaters. Club: Friars (Los Angeles) (gov. 1980—). Office: 195 S Beverly Dr Ste 412 Beverly Hills CA 96212 *Craft is freedom.*

CATES, JOHN MARTIN, JR., lawyer; b. Denver, Jan. 20, 1912; s. John Martin and Mary Arden (Randall) C.; m. Mary Perkins

Raymond, July 4, 1942 (div. 1973); 1 son, John Martin III; m. Melia Barletta, Nov. 19, 1976; 1 dau., Nelia M. Barletta. Grad., Phillips Andover Acad., 1932; B.A., Yale, 1936, J.D., 1939. Bar: Calif. bar 1940, D.C. bar 1946, N.Y. State bar 1976. With McCutchen, Olney, Mannon & Greene, San Francisco, 1939-41; labor relations San Francisco Warehousemen's Assn., 1941-42; with U.S. Maritime Commn. and War Shipping Adminstrn., Washington, 1942-47; fgn. affairs specialist U.S. Dept. State, 1947-53, legal adviser Am. embassy, Bonn; also mem. War Criminal Parole Bd., 1953-55; legal advisor, 1st sec. Am. Embassy, Mexico, 1955-57; chief polit. officer Am. embassy, Venezuela, 1957-61; alternate U.S. rep. Council OAS, Washington, 1961-63; counsellor U.S. Mission to UN, 1963-70, U.S. Mission to Geneva, 1970-71; pres., dir. Center for Inter-Am. Relations, 1971-75; cons., atty., 1976—; London counsel firm Pettit & Martin, San Francisco; adj. prof. Fairleigh Dickinson U. Contbr. articles to profl. jours. Mem. Latin Am. adv. council State Dept.; Committeeman Boy Scouts Am., N.Y.C., also Mexico, Venezuela, 1963—; mem. Am. Ch. Council, Bad Godesburg, Germany, 1953-55; mem. council Yale U., 1968-77; bd. dirs. Youth for Understanding, Incon Internat. Inc., Americas' Found., Programme for New World Anthropology, Ecuador; trustee Am. Aid Soc., London; asso.-cons. Phillips Acad. Bicentennial, 1978. Recipient medal of merit Venezuela Boy Scouts, 1960, superior honor award Dept. of State, 1967, gran cruz Vasco Nuñez de Balboa, Panama, 1975; Order Francisco de Miranda, Venezuela, 1976. Mem. Council Fgn. Relations, Am., Inter-Am., Calif. D.C., bar assns., Bar City N.Y., London Law Soc., Bolivian Soc. (dir. 1971—), Pan Am. Soc. (dir. 1974—), Cercle de la Presse et Amitie Etrangere (Geneva), Am. Polit. Sci. Assn., English Speaking Union (London), S.R., Soc. Colonial Wars (exec. com.), Pilgrims, St. Nicholas Soc. (exec. com. 1969), Phelps Assn. Wolfs Head (exec. com.), Phi Delta Phi. Clubs: Mason., Union, Century, Yale, Explorers (N.Y.C.); BUcks, Am., The Pilgrims (London); Metropolitan (Washington); Bohemian (San Francisco). Home: 44 Upper Grosvenor St London W1 England Office: 44 Reeves Mews London W1 England *I have followed the Emersonian principle of "know thyself" and the political beliefs known as "Jeffersonian democracy". I believe one must be prepared to take stands in accord with his own conscience and pay the price such stands entail even if unacceptable to certain sectors of society. I believe strongly in the equality of persons as stated in our Constitution, particularly the concepts of civil liberties and all that is therein implied. The Puritan ethic and, if we may still mention this, the homely New England strictures as to work, loyalty, honesty, and such models of conduct have certainly been part of my upbringing and life. I also believe strongly in international cooperation and the stark necessity of a one-world society without national borders in the future. With Winston Churchill I believe that with all its faults, democracy, representative democracy, is the best system yet devised by which a society may govern itself.*

CATES, MACFARLANE LAFFERTY, JR., textile company executive; b. Spartanburg, S.C., Nov. 9, 1927; s. MacFarlane Lafferty and Mary (DuPre) C.; m. Marguerite McGee, Aug. 12, 1949; children: Marguerite DuPre, Elisabeth Quarles, Kathleen MacFarlane, Mary Lafferty. A.B., Princeton, 1949; M.B.A., Harvard, 1952. Exec. v.p. Arkwright Mills, Spartanburg, 1954-64, pres., treas., 1964—; dir. Sea Pak Corp., 1965-67; mem. gen. bd. Citizens & So. Nat. Bank S.C., 1968-72, adv. bd., 1972—; dir., adv. bd. Liberty Mut. Ins. Co. Mem. Wofford Assos., Wofford Coll.; v.p. United Fund, 1964, pres., 1965; Past bd. dirs. Spartanburg Devel. Assn.; trustee Chatham Hall; bd. dirs. Spartanburg County Found., pres., 1983; bd. dirs. Spartanburg Music Found., pres., 1983. Mem. S.C. C. of C. (past dir.), Am. Textile Mfrs. Inst. (dir. 1983, chmn. safety and health com. 1983), S.C. Textile Mfrs. Assn. (past pres., mem. exec. bd.), Inst. Textile Tech. (mem. bd.), Spartanburg County Hist. Soc. (past pres.), Trout Unlimited S.C. (past v.p.). Clubs: Brook, Princeton (N.Y.C.); Biltmore Forest Country, Piedmont (past pres., dir.), Spartanburg Country.). Home: 1325 Pinecrest Rd Spartanburg SC 29302 Office: PO Box 5628 Spartanburg SC 29301

CATHCART, HAROLD ROBERT, hosp. adminstr.; b. Odebolt, Iowa, Mar. 9, 1924; s. Catham S. and Martha M. (Wells) C.; m. Tressa Bolt, July 20, 1951; 1 dau., Tressa Ann. Student, Drake U., 1941-43; B.A., State U. Iowa, 1947; D.H.A., U. Toronto, Can., 1948. Fellow W.K. Kellogg Found., 1948-49; mem. staff Pa. Hosp., Phila., 1949—, v.p., 1960-70, pres., 1970—; Mem. bd. commrs. Joint Commn. on Accreditation of Hosps.; chmn. Nat. Commn. on Nursing. Served with U.S. Army, 1943-46. Mem. Am. Hosp. Assn. (chmn. council of nursing 1967-68, council on manpower and edn. 1969-71, trustee 1972-74, chmn. bd. trustees 1976, speaker ho. dels. 1977), Am. Coll. Hosp. Adminstrs., Hosp. Assn. Pa. (pres. 1967-68, Distinguished Service award 1977), Delaware Valley Hosp. Council, Greater Phila. Partnership. Address: Pennsylvania Hosp Philadelphia PA 19107

CATHCART, LINDA LOUISE, museum director; b. Lafayette, Ind., Oct. 20, 1947; d. Robert S. and Dolores J. C. B.A. in Fine Arts, Calif. State U., Fullerton, 1969; M.A. in Art History, Hunter Coll., N.Y.C., 1972; Fulbright fellow, Courtauld Art Inst., London, 1973-74. Curatorial asst. Whitney Mus. Am. Art, 1971-73; adj. prof. SUNY, Buffalo, 1975-79; curator Albright-Knox Art Gallery, Buffalo, 1975-79; dir. Contemporary Arts Mus., Houston, 1979—. Author catalogue and mag. essays. Recipient Humanities award Nat. Endowment Arts, 1972. Mem. Am. Assn. Mus., Assn. Art Mus. Dirs. Home: 5216 Montrose Blvd Houston TX 77006 Office: 5216 Montrose Blvd Houston TX 77006

CATHCART, ROBERT STEPHEN, communications educator; b. Los Angeles, Jan. 30, 1923; s. Stephen Joseph and Martha (Morley) C.; m. Dolores June Hawley, July 1, 1944; children: Linda L., Stephen P. A.B., U. Redlands, 1944, M.A., 1947; Ph.D., Northwestern U., 1953. Teaching fellow U. Redlands, 1946-47; instr. Purdue U., 1947-49; teaching fellow Northwestern U., 1949-51; instr. U. Md., 1953-55; prof. rhetorical theory Calif. State U. at Los Angeles, 1955-68; chmn. dept. communication, Queens Coll., 1968-72, prof. communication theory, 1972—; Cons. USN Officer Tng. Corps, U.S. Army Ordnance Center, Carnation Co.; mem. Pres.'s Adv. Commn. of Scholars, 1967; sr. visitor in philosophy Oxford U., 1966; vis. prof. Sophia U., Tokyo, 1974. Author: (with M. Laser and F. Marcus) Ideas and Issues, 1963, (with J. Dahl and M. Laser) Student, School and Society, 1964, Post Communication, 1966, rev. edit., 1980, (with L. Samovar) Small Group Communication, 1970, rev. edit., 1978, (with G. Gumpert) Inter/Media-Interpersonal Communication in a Media World, 1979, rev. edit., 1983. Served to lt. USNR, 1943-46, 51-53. Home: 1 Oakpoint Dr N Bayville NY 11709 Office: Queens Coll Flushing NY 11367

CATHCART, SILAS STRAWN, tool company executive; b. Evanston, Ill., May 6, 1926; s. James A. and Margaret (Strawn) C.; m. Corlene A. Hobbs, Feb. 3, 1951; children: Strawn, James A., Daniel and David (twins), Corlene. Student, U. Notre Dame, 1944-46; A.B., Princeton U., 1948. With Ill. Tool Works Inc., Chgo., 1948—, v.p., 1954-62, exec. v.p., 1962-64, pres., 1964-72; chmn., 1972—; dir. Jewel Cos., No. Trust Co., Am. Hosp. Supply Corp., Quaker Oats Co., Gen. Electric Co., Bethlehem Steel Corp. Bd. dirs. Northwestern Meml. Hosp., Chgo. Served as ensign USNR, 1944-46. Clubs: Onwentsia (Lake Forest); Chicago, Old Elm, Commercial, Chicago Commonwealth, Economic (Chgo.). Home: 1000 Walden Ln Lake Forest IL 60045 Office: 8501 W Higgins Ave Chicago IL 60631

CATHER, DONALD WARREN, civil engineer; b. Chgo., May 16, 1926; s. Leroy Heywood and Evelyn Linnea (Melin) C.; m. Maxine Miller, June 30, 1946 (div. Feb. 1977); children: Terrence, Judy, Donald Warren, Peter, Jeanne, Martha, Bernard, Samantha, Andrew; m. Jacqueline Pillsbury, Aug. 3, 1980. B.S. in Bus. Adminstrn., Northwestern U., 1947; B.S. in Civil Engring., Ill. Inst. Tech., 1953. Registered profl. engr., Ill., N.Y., N.J., Mass., Pa., Md., Ga., Fla. Sales engr. Byron Jackson Co., Los Angeles, Houston, 1949; with DeLeuw, Cather & Co., Atlanta, 1949-78, v.p., 1969-73, sr. v.p., 1973-78, southeastern regional mgr., 1978—; dir. pub. works City of Miami, 1978—; dir. Tech. Projects Ltd.; pres. Cather Aero Ltd.; v.p. Cather Marine, Inc. Served with USNR, 1945-47. Fellow Am. Cons. Engrs. Council, Inst. Transp. Engrs.; mem. ASCE. Clubs: Ansa (N.Y.C.); Sheridan Shore Yacht, Coconut Grove Sailing, Coral Reef Yacht., Palm Bay. Home: 4201 Palm Lane Bay Point Miami FL 33137 Office: 275 NW 2d St Miami FL 33128 *The most important discovery of my life has been the fact that I can only live one day at a time and that I cannot change other people, only myself. Celebrate your existence.*

CATHER, JAMES NEWTON, embryologist; b. Carthage, Mo., Mar. 17, 1931; s. John Ward and Liza Jane (Webb) C.; m. Jane Ruth Julian, July 21, 1951; children: Alicia Ruth, Craig Julian. B.S., So. Meth. U., 1954, M.S., 1955; Ph.D., Emory U., 1958. Instr. U. Mich., Ann Arbor, 1958-60, asst. prof. biol. scis., 1960-65, asso. prof., 1965-73, prof., 1973—, asso. chmn. div. biol. scis., 1976—, asso. dean Coll. Lit., Sci. and the Arts, 1982—; mem. staff embryology course Marine Biol. Lab., Woods Hole, Mass., 1966-67, Bermuda Biol. Sta., 1972-76; vis. prof. Oreg. Inst. Marine Biology, 1969, 74. Served with USMCR, 1950-52. Recipient award for outstanding undergrad. teaching U. Mich. Class of 1923, 1964; Upjohn faculty fellow, 1965. Mem. Internat. Soc. Devel. Biologists, Soc. Devel. Biology, Am. Soc. Zoologists, Malacological Soc. London. Research, publs. in exptl. embryology of invertebrates, especially molluscs. Home: 5830 Warren Rd Ann Arbor MI 48105 Office: Div Biol Sci U Mich Ann Arbor MI 48109

CATHERMAN, BYRON KING, savs. and loan assn. exec.; b. Mifflinburg, Pa., Sept. 26, 1920; s. Milton Carol and Hattie (Dersham) C.; m. Margaret Katharine Kerns, July 19, 1944; children—Diane Kay, Jay King. Student, Pa. State U., 1938-39, Central Pa. Bus. Coll., 1941, U. Ga. Exec. Devel. Sch., 1962-63. With Commonwealth Pa., 1940, Pa. R.R., 1941; treas. Harris Bldg. & Loan Assn., Harrisburg, 1942—, sec., 1956—, mgr., 1963, pres., 1964—; Mem. Pa. Savs. Assn. Bd., 1965—; treas. Pa. Housing Agy., 1970. Mem. Harrisburg Polyclinic Hosp. Council; pres. Harrisburg area YMCA, 1968-71; treas. Dauphin County Tb Assn., 1966, pres., 1973—; treas. Harrisburg Community Theatre, 1975-77; bd. dirs. Polyclinic Med. Center, 1978—, Harrisburg Credit Exchange, 1979—, Central Pa. Blood Bank, 1979—. Mem. Am. Savs. and Loan Inst. and Controllers, Pa. Savs. and Loan League (pres. 1971), Harrisburg C. of C. (dir. 1970, pres. 1973). Clubs: Mason, Lion (named Lion of Year Harrisburg 1959-60), Executives Central Pa. (pres. 1976-77). Home: 2222 Manchester Blvd Harrisburg PA 17112 Office: 205 Pine St Harrisburg PA 17105

CATHERWOOD, CUMMINS, financier, philanthropist; b. Haverford, Pa., Jan. 30, 1910; s. Daniel B.C. and Jessica (Davis) C.; m. Ellengowen Hood, Feb. 3, 1942 (dec. Aug. 1970); children—Virginia Tucker, Cummins; m. Dorothy Smith Littler, Apr. 17, 1971. Prep. edn., St. Georges Sch., Newport, R.I.; student, U. Pa., 1931-33; L.H.D., Pa. Mil. Coll. Asso. various banking firms in, Phila.; partner Roberts, Fleitas & Catherwood, Ins.; dir. Fidelity-Phila. Trust Co., 1933-39; co-owner Evening Pub. Ledger, Phila.; v.p., purchasing agt. Fox Munitions Corp., 1940-52; ltd. partner Jenks, Kirkland & Grubbs, Phila., now; Hallowell, Sulzberger, Jenks, Kirkland & Co., Phila., Oil & Gas Co., Madison, 1946-57; dir. Bryn Mawr Trust Co.; pres., dir. Mineral Prodn. Corp., Bryn Mawr; chmn. Madeira Oil Corp., Bryn Mawr; dir. Mid-Am. Minerals, Inc., Oklahoma City; dir., mem. exec. com. Vision, Inc. Trustee Catherwood Estates; pres. Catherwood Found.; trustee exec. com. Pa. Mill. Coll.; trustee Acad. Music, Phila.; bd. govs. Phila. Mus. Art; bd. dirs. Phila. Orch. Assn. Served to capt. USAAF, 1942-45. Mem. Res. Officers Assn., Am. Ordnance Assn. Home: 341 Conshohocken State Rd Glaywyne PA 19035 Office: Box 80 850 Lancaster Ave Bryn Mawr PA 19010

CATHEY, HENRY MARCELLUS, government official; b. Statesville, N.C., Oct. 23, 1928; s. Carl H. and Emily (McArthur) C.; m. Mary E. Jackson, May 31, 1958; children—Mary Emily, Henry M. B.S., N.C. State U., 1950; M.S., Cornell U., 1952, Ph.D., 1955. Florist, Mooresville, N.C., 1950-51, horticulturist (Fulbright scholar), Wageningen, Netherlands, 1955-56; horticulturist Dept. Agr., Beltsville, Md., 1956-80; D.C. Kiplinger prof. Ohio State U., 1980-81; dir. U.S. Nat. Arboretum, Washington, 1981—. Mem. Am. Hort. Soc. (pres. 1964-68), Am. Soc. Plant Physiologists, Washington Acad. Sci., Am. Soc. Hort. Sci., Am. Assn. Bot. Gardens and Arboreta, Sigma Xi, Alpha Zeta, Phi Kappa Phi, Gamma Sigma Delta, Pi Alpha Xi. Home: 1817 Bart Dr Silver Spring MD 20904 Office: US Nat Arboretum 3501 New York Ave NE Washington DC 20002

CATION, PAUL CURTIS, lawyer; b. Peoria, Ill., Nov. 16, 1924; s. Nathaniel Curtis and Dena M. (Meindirs) C.; m. Muriel M. Sunderlin, Dec. 27, 1947; children: Richard C., Nancy Jean. B.S., U. Ill., 1948, LL.B., 1950. Bar: Ill. 1950. Partner Vonachen, Cation, Lawless, Trager, Slevin, Peoria, 1965—; asst. atty gen., State of Ill., 1968-83; dir. Dunlap State Bank, Ill., Bartonville Bank. Author: Commercial Real Estate Transactions, 1972, 2d edit., 1977, Day to Day Banking Operations, 1974, 3d edit., 1981, Farm Credit and Finance, 1980. Treas. Peoria County Republican Central Com., 1968-74, now sec.; trustee Methodist Med. Center, Peoria, 1970—, mem. exec. com., 1970—, chmn. bd. trustees, 1974-77, trustee found., 1976—, chmn., 1976—; bd. dirs. Forest Park Found., Peoria, 1958—, YMCA, Peoria, 1968-78; chmn. bd. trustees First United Meth. Ch., Peoria. Served with AUS, 1943-45. Decorated Purple Heart, Bronze Star. Mem. ABA, Ill. Bar Assn., Peoria County Bar Assn. (pres. 1981-82), Phi Delta Phi, Delta Upsilon. Clubs: Rotary, Mt. Hawley Country (Peoria). Home: 417 W Giles Ln Peoria IL 61614 Office: 309 Security Savings Bldg Peoria IL 61602

CATLETT, GEORGE ROUDEBUSH, accountant; b. Fairmount, Ill., Aug. 14, 1917; s. Shirley Tilton and Effie (Wehrman) C.; m. Martha Jane Beamsley, May 27, 1944; children—Stanley, Steven, Lawrence, David. B.S., U. Ill., 1939, M.S., 1940. C.P.A., Ill., other states. With Arthur Andersen & Co. (C.P.A.'s), Chgo., 1940—, partner, 1952-75, sr. partner, 1975—; cons. to govt. Contbr. articles to profl. jours. Pres. bd. dirs. U. Ill. Athletic Assn., 1964-65. Served to maj. AUS, 1942-46. Mem. Am. Inst. C.P.A.'s (council 1964-70, 76-79, v.p., dir. 1976-77), Ill. Soc. C.P.A.'s (pres. 1966-67), Am. Accounting Assn., Nat. Assn. Accountants, U. Ill. Alumni Assn. (dir. 1959-65), Beta Theta Pi, Beta Gamma Sigma. Methodist. Clubs: University, Mid-Day (Chgo.); Westmoreland Country (Wilmette, Ill.). Home: 2939 Indian Wood Rd Wilmette IL 60091 Office: 69 W Washington St Chicago IL 60602

CATLETT, MARY JO, actress; b. Denver; d. Robert James and Cornelia Marie (Callaghan) C. B.A. in Drama and Psychology, Loretto Heights Coll., 1960. Tchr. West High Sch., Denver; lectr. UCLA. Appeared: Broadway plays Hello Dolly, 1964, Canterbury Tales, 1970, Different Times, 1971, Lysistrata, 1972, Pajama Game, 1974, Black Flag, 1976—, Play Me a Country Song, 1982; movies Semi Tough, 1977, The Champ, 1978, O'Hara's Wife, 1981; appeared in: plays Come Back Little Sheba, 1977, Philadelphia Here I Come, 1980; mus. prodns. Annie Get Your Gun, 1977, The Boy Friend, 1972, Something's Afoot, 1972, Fashion, 1974. Recipient Washington Drama award, 1974, Los Angeles Drama Critics award, 1977, 80, Drama Critics Circle award, 1977, 80. Mem. Screen Actors Guild, AFTRA, Actors Equity, Am. Guild Variety Artists. Roman Catholic. *I become more and more conscious of the need for man to help his fellow man—not only in the human phyla, but perhaps more especially animals. How sad to see the hundreds of thousands of abandoned cats and dogs—the innocent beings becoming victims of man's selfishness.*

CATLEY-CARLSON, MARGARET YVONNE, Canadian government official; b. Regina, Sask., Can., Oct. 6, 1942a; d. George Lorne and Helen Margaret (Hughes) Catley; m. Stanley Frederick Carlson, Oct. 30, 1970. B.A. with honors, U. B.C., Can., 1966; postgrad., U. W.I., 1970-71. Diplomat Can. Dept. External Affairs, Ottawa, Ont., Can., beginning 1966, Sri Lanka Trinidad, London, until 1978; v.p. Can. Internat. Devel. Agy., Hull, Que., 1978-79, sr. v.p., 1979-80, pres., 1983—; asst. under-sec. Dept. External Affairs, Ottawa, Ont., Can., 1981; asst. sec., gen. UNICEF, N.Y.C., 1981-83. Club: Cosmopolitan (N.Y.C.). Home: 402-333 Chapel St Ottawa ON Canada K1N 6G2 Office: Can Internat Devel Agy 200 Promenade du Portage Hull PQ Canada K1A 0G4

CATLIN, AVERY, engineering educator, researcher; b. N.Y.C., Jan. 29, 1924; s. Randolph and Hannah (White) C.; m. Edith J. Reed, Sept. 7, 1946; children: Avery W., Edith R., Beverly L., Frederick F. B.E.E., U. Va., 1947, M.A., 1949, Ph.D., 1960. Assoc. prof. elec. engring. and anat. sci. U. Va., 1960-67, prof., 1967-82, univ. prof. computer sci., 1982—, assoc. dean engring., 1967-74, exec. v.p., 1974-82. Office: U Va Thornton Hall Charlottesville VA 22901

CATLIN, FRANCIS IRVING, physician; b. Hartford, Conn., Dec. 6, 1925; s. Robert Irving and Frances Rose (Maleski) C.; m. Rebecca Vaughan Graham, June 11, 1948; children: Robert, Andrew, Martha. A.A., Princeton U., 1949; M.D., Johns Hopkins U., 1948, Sc.D., 1959. Diplomate: Am. Bd. Otolaryngology. Intern Union Meml. Hosp., Balt., 1948-49; resident in otolaryngology Johns Hopkins Hosp., 1950, 52-54; from instr. to asso. prof. Johns Hopkins U. Med. Sch., 1956-72; prof. otorhinolaryngology and communicative scis. Baylor U. Med. Sch., Houston, 1972—; chief otolaryngology service Tex. Children's, St. Luke's hosps.; adv. com. Nat. Eastern Seal Soc. Crippled Children and Adults, 1973—. Contbr. articles to med. jours. Served to capt. M.C. USAF, 1950-52. Fellow Am. Speech and Hearing Assn., Am. Otol. Soc.; mem. Am. Acad. Otolaryngology (adv. com. 1972—), Am. Council Otolaryngology (council 1977—), AMA, Am. Laryngological, Rhinological and Otol. Soc., Med. and Chiurigical Faculty Md., Tex. Med. Soc. Republican. Episcopalian. Home: 13307 Queensbury Ln Houston TX 77079 Office: Tex Children's Hosp 6621 Fannin St Houston TX 77030

CATLIN, KARL AYDELOTTE, physician; b. Cherokee, Okla., Mar. 16, 1910; s. Karl Tracey and Olive Fereba (Aydelotte) C.; m. Euniee Fern Gooch, Apr. 1941; children: Sharon Fern, Linda Louise, Karl Eugene. B.A., U. Wichita, 1932; M.D., U. Kans., 1939. Rotating intern Bethany Hosp., Kansas City, Kans., 1939-40; mem. resident staff Topeka State Hosp., 1940-48; asst. supt. Mental Health Inst., Clarinda, Iowa, 1948-55, supt., 1955-67; med. dir. S.W. Iowa Mental Health Center, Atlantic, 1968-81, W. Central Mental Health Ctr., Adel, Iowa, 1983—; cons. psychiatry Cass County Meml. Hosp., Atlantic. Mem. bd. Community Fund Clarinda, 1960-67. Served to capt., M.C. AUS, 1942-46. Recipient Achievement award Mental Hosp. Inst., Salt Lake City, 1960. Fellow Am. Psychiat. Assn. (life); mem. Iowa Psychiat. Soc., Iowa Med. Soc., Page County Med. Soc. (past pres.), Cass County Med. Soc. Home: 501 E 14th St Atlantic IA 50022 Office: 2111 Green St Adel IA 50022

CATO, JERRY MAC, design and marketing communications executive; b. Indpls.; s. Louis M. and Eunice A. (Swartswood) C.; m. Jane R. Replogle, June 24, 1961; children: Christopher Banning, Michael Charles. B.S. in Design, U. Cinn., 1958. Chmn. Cato Johnson, N.Y.C., 1972-83; mng. ptnr. Peterson Blyth Cato, N.Y.C., 1983. Mem. Package Design Council. Republican. Club: D&AO (London). Office: Peterson Blyth Cato 216 E 45th St New York NY 10022

CATOIR, JOHN THOMAS, priest, religious organization executive, author; b. N.Y.C., Sept. 8, 1931; s. John T. and Catherine M. (Caslin) C. B.S., Fordham U., 1953; J.C.D., Catholic U. Am., 1964. Ordained priest Roman Cath. Ch., 1960; chief judge (Diocese Paterson (N.J.) Marriage Tribunal), 1967-73, pres., 1975-77; dir. The Christophers, N.Y.C., 1978—. Author: The Challenge of Love, 1972, The Way People Pray, 1974, Enjoy the Lord, 1978, also articles. Served with U.S. Army, 1953-55. Mem. Canon Law Soc. Am. (bd. govs. 1971), Cath. Press Assn. (bd. dirs.). Address: The Christophers 12 E 48th St New York NY 10017

CATOLA, STANLEY GUY, naval officer; b. Pitts., Dec. 12, 1934; s. Tony and Laura B. C.; m. Helen F. Ivancic, June 15, 1958; 1 son, Steven. B.S., U.S. Naval Acad., 1956; grad., Submarine Sch., 1958, Nuclear Power Sch., 1961, Naval War Coll., 1972. Commd. ensign U.S. Navy, 1956, advanced through grades to rear adm., 1979; weapons officer U.S.S. Southerland, 1956-58; served in submarine U.S.S. Bluegill, 1958-60; served in weapons and engring. billets submarine U.S.S. Triton, 1961-64; engr. officer submarine U.S.S. Andrew Jackson, 1964-67; exec. officer submarine U.S.S. Tautog, 1967-69; comdr. U.S.S. Andrew Jackson, 1970-72, U.S.S. Henry L. Stimson, 1973-74; sr. mem. Staff of the Comdr. in Chief U.S. Atlantic Fleet, Norfolk, Va., 1974-76, mem. nuclear propulsion examining bd., 1975-76; comdr. Submarine Squadron 14, 1976-78; dep. comdr. for fleet support Naval Sea Systems Command, Washington, 1978-79, prin. dept. comdr. for logistics, 1979-81; project mgr. Trident Systems Project, Washington, 1981—. Decorated Legion of Merit. Office: Naval Material Command Washington DC 20362

CATON, CHARLES EDWIN, educator; b. Evanston, Ill., Mar. 21, 1928; s. Harold Dana and Irma (Fruit) C.; m. Elizabeth Robin McReynolds, Feb. 5, 1955; children—Marcia E., Dewey, John H., George H. A.B., Oberlin Coll., 1950; student, Northwestern U., 1949, 53; M.A., U. Mich., 1951, Ph.D., 1956, Oxford (Eng.) U., 1956-57. Instr. philosophy U. Mich., 1957-58; faculty U. Ill., Urbana, 1958—, prof. philosophy, 1968—; Vis. asso. prof. Purdue U., 1968; vis. prof. U. Western Ont., 1969-70. Editor: Philosophy and Ordinary Language, 1963. Mem. Am. Philos. Assn. (chmn. program com. Western div. 1977), Linguistic Soc. Am. Address: Dept Philosophy Univ Ill 810 S Wright St Urbana IL 61801

CATOVIC, SAFFET CATANI, scientist, educator; b. Bilece, Yugoslavia, Apr. 21, 1924; came to U.S., 1958, naturalized, 1965; s. Abid and Dervisa (Cerimagic) C.; m. Sarah Cameron Kerr, Dec. 22, 1961; children—Saffet A., Saffiya, Suada, Saliha, Surayya, Sami. B.S., Zagreb U., 1950; M.S., U. N.H., 1961; Ph.D., Rutgers U., 1964. Fellow in entomology Zagreb U., 1951-52; research and extension plant pathologist Sarajevo & Sisak, Yugoslavia, 1952-57; research entomologist Inst. Plant Protection, Ankara, Turkey, 1957-58; fellow dept. botany U. N.H., 1958-61; dept. plant biology Rutgers U., 1961-64; asst. prof. dept. biology Fairleigh Dickinson U., 1964-69, asso.

prof., 1969-74, prof. biol. scis., 1974—. Mem. AAAS, Mycol. Soc. Am., Med. Mycology Soc. N.Y., N.J. Acad. Scis., N.Y. Acad. Sci., Internat. Mycological Soc., Met. Assn. Coll. and Univ. Biologists, N.J. Soc. Parasitologists, Smithsonian Inst., N.Y. Bot. Garden, Sigma Xi. Office: Dept Biol Scis Fairleigh Dickinson U Teaneck NJ 07666 *

CATRAVAS, GEORGE NICHOLAS, biologist; b. Argostoli, Greece, June 22, 1916; came to U.S., 1955, naturalized, 1961; s. Nicholas George and Palmyra (Pigadiotis) C.; m. Nancy Donohue, Dec. 30, 1963; 1 son, Nikolas. D.Ch., U. Athens, Greece, 1937; postgrad., U. Berlin, Germany, 1938-39; Ph.D., U. Leeds, Eng., 1947; D.Sc., U. Paris, Sorbonne, 1953, U. Chgo., 1955-56. Lectr. organic chemistry U. Athens, 1937-38; research chemist Unilever Port Sunlight Eng., 1947-49; charge des recherches C.N.R.S. France, 1953-55; asst. prof. biochemistry U. Chgo., 1957-63; dir. biochemical research Technicon Corp., N.Y.C., 1964-66; dir. molecular biology Armed Forces Radiobiology Research Inst., Bethesda, Md., 1966-71; head div. neurochemistry Def. Nuclear Agy., Bethesda, 1971-77, chmn. dept. biochemistry, 1977—; adj. prof. dept. biology Am. U., Washington, 1967—. Contbr. articles profl. jours. Decorated Order George I with swords, Mil. Cross, D.S.M. (Greek); recipient Def. Nuclear Agy. Exceptional Civilian Service medal; Alex Von Humbolt fellow U. Berlin, 1938-39; Adel Edwards fellow U. Leeds, 1945-47; U.S. Nat. Acad.-FOA fellow U. Chgo., 1955-57. Patentee in field. Home: 8512 Bradmoor Dr Bethesda MD 20034 Office: Armed Forces Radiobiology Research Inst Def Nuclear Agy Bethesda MD 20014

CATSIMATIDIS, JOHN ANDREAS, supermarket executive; b. Greece, Sept. 7, 1948; came to U.S., 1949, naturalized, 1955; s. Andreas John and Despina (Emmaulides) C.; m. Liba Korn, Aug. 15, 1972. B.S., NYU, 1970. Founder, 1970, since pres., chief operating officer Red Apple Supermarkets, N.Y.C.; Vice-chmn. Capitol Airlines, N.Y.C. Mem. W. Side C. of C. (pres. 1970). Mem. Greek Orthodox Ch. Address: Red Apple Supermarkets 265 W 87th St New York NY 10024

CATTEY, JAMES PAUL, editor; b. Detroit, May 10, 1935; s. Paul Esterline and Edith Pauline (Kime) C.; m. Eudora H. Jen, Feb. 4, 1957; children—Richard, Laura, Jennifer. B.A., U. Mich., 1959, M.A., 1961. Reporter Milw. Jour., 1961-63, copy editor, 1963-67, N.Y. Times, 1967-68; asst. news editor Milw. Jour., 1969-77, met. editor, 1977—. Served with U.S. Army, 1954-56. Ford Found. grantee, 1966. Office: 333 W State St Box 661 Milwaukee WI 53201

CATTO, HENRY EDWARD, JR., former government official, communications executive; b. Dallas, Dec. 6, 1930; s. Henry Edward and Maurine (Halsell) C.; m. Jessica Oveta Hobby, Feb. 15, 1958; children: Heather, John, William, Elizabeth. Student, Tex. Mil. Inst.; B.A., Williams Coll., 1952. Partner ins. brokerage firm Catto & Catto, San Antonio, 1952—; ambassador, dep. U.S. rep. to OAS, 1969-71; U.S. ambassador to El Salvador, 1971-73, U.S. chief of protocol, 1974-76; U.S. rep. with rank of ambassador to European office UN, Geneva, 1976-77; bus. cons., Washington, 1977-81; chmn. bd. IBIS Corp.; founder, pres. Washington Communications Corp.; vice chmn. H & C Communications; pub. Washington Journalism Rev., 1979-81; asst. sec. for public affairs Dept. Def., Washington, 1981—; mem. Inter-Am. Com. on Edn., 1969-70; mem. permanent exec. com. of Inter-Am. Council on Edn., Sci. and Culture, 1969-71; dir. Houston Post Co., Union First Nat. Bank of Washington. Mem. Tex. Adv. Com. to U.S. Civil Rights Commn., 1965-69; commr. San Antonio Housing Authority, 1968-69; pres. United Fund San Antonio and Bexar County, 1969; Bd. dirs. Catto Found. Mem. Center for Inter Am. Relations, Council Fgn. Relations. Republican. Clubs: Met., 1925 F St. (Washington); Argyle, Country (San Antonio). Home: 7718 Georgetown Pike McLean VA 22101 Office: 2233 Wisconsin Ave Suite 442 Washington DC 20007

CATTO, ISABEL GORDON, orgn. exec.; b. N.Y.C., Sept. 2, 1912; d. Baron and Gladys (Gordon) C. Ed. sch. in, Eng., Paris. With Personal Service League, Women's Vol. Services, head Service Welfare Dept., 1941-43; dep. dir YWCA War Services, Middle East, 1943-46, dir. services, Germany, Belgium, France, 1946—; participant YWCA Study Conf., Columbia, 1948; staff hdqrs. YWCA of Gt. Britain, 1951, pres., 1966-72, Nat. Hostels Com., 1951; mem. exec. com. World YWCA, 1951, pres., 1955-63; YWCA rep. UN Status of Women Commn., UNESCO. Bd. dirs. Christian Aid U.K. Decorated Order Brit. Empire. Club: Oriental (London). Home: 61 Cadogan Garden London SW 3 England also Holmdale Holmbury St Mary Surrey England

CATTOI, ROBERT LOUIS, high technology avionics and telecommunications design, mfg. and marketing co. exec.; b. Hurley, Wis., Apr. 18, 1926; s. Louis Charles and Anna (Dahl) C.; m. Mary Frances Obertone, Aug. 30, 1949; children—David, Carol, Robert. B.E.E., U. Wis., 1950. With Collins Radio Group, Rockwell Internat., Dallas, 1950-77, v.p., 1971-77; v.p. engring. Aerospace and Electronics ops. Rockwell Internat., 1977-78, corp. v.p. engring., 1978—. Mem. devel. bd. U. Tex. at Dallas; trustee Assn. Grad. Edn. and Research N. Tex. Served with USAAF, 1944-46. Mem. IEEE, Quadroto della Radio, Tau Beta Pi, Eta Kappa Nu, Phi Eta Sigma, Phi Kappa Phi. Club: Balboa Bay (Newport Beach, Calif.). Home: 7350 Paldao Dr Dallas TX 75240 Office: Rockwell Internat PO Box 10462 Dallas TX 75207

CATTON, IVAN, mech. engr.; b. Vancouver, C., Can., June 29, 1934; came to U.S., 1943, naturalized, 1956; s. John Arthur and Amy (Bowcock) C.; m. Susan Ann Layton, Oct. 1, 1961; children—Mark Douglas, Michael Scott, Craig Mitchel. B.S., UCLA, 1959; Ph.D. (Douglas fellow), 1966. Sr. scientist supr. McDonnel Douglas Corp., Huntington Beach, Calif., 1959-66; asst. prof. engring. UCLA, 1966-72, asso. prof., 1972-75, prof., 1975—; dir. T.E. Hicks Nuclear Energy Facility; cons. in field. Contbr. numerous articles on heat transfer and nuclear safety to profl. jours. Mem. Belmont Scholarship Found.; active energy-related environ. concerns. Served with U.S. Army, 1954-56. NSF grantee, 1969—. Mem. ASME (heat transfer meml. award 1981), Am. Nuclear Soc., Am. Phys. Soc. Republican. Research on nuclear safety. Home: 22436 Gaililee St Woodland Hills CA 91364 Office: 405 Hilgarde Ave Los Angeles CA 90024

CATTON, JACK JOSEPH, aircraft co. exec., ret. air force officer; b. Berkeley, Calif., Feb. 5, 1920; s. Thomas R. and Jane H. (Sharp) C.; m. Jo Elizabeth Nelson, Jan. 14, 1942; children—Jo Elizabeth (Mrs. Thomas W. Williams), Cheryl Lee (Mrs. Thomas G. Walters), John Joseph. A.A., Santa Monica Jr. Coll., 1938; student, Loyola U., Los Angeles, 1939-40; grad., Air Force Manpower Mgmt. Tng. Program, 1952. Joined USAAF, 1940, grad., 1940, commd. 2d lt., 1941; advanced through grades to gen. USAF, 1969; various assignments, U.S. and Guam, 1941-46; aircraft comdr. Task Group 1.5, Kwajalein, 1946; assigned 393d Bomb Squadron, Roswell, N.Mex., 1946; comdr. 65th Bomb Squadron, 444th Bomb Group, Davis-Monthan Field, Ariz., 1946-47, Task Unit 741, Project Sandstone; also asst. chief staff Air Task Group 7, Kwajalein, 1947-48; assigned Hdqrs.; 43 Bomb Wing, Davis-Monthan AFB, 1948; chief policy br., also chief program br., directorate of plans Hdqrs. SAC, Andrews AFB, Md., 1948, chief plans requirements br., programs sect., directorate of plans Hdqrs., Offutt AFB, Nebr., 1948-50; dir. operations and tng. (22d Bomb Wing), March AFB, Calif., 1950-51, dir. operations, March AFB, 1951-52; dep. to CINCSAC, SAC Xray, FEAF, Japan, 1951-52; successively dep. comdr. (92d Bomb Wing); comdr. 814th AB Group, Fairchild AFB, Wash., 1952-55, (43 Bomb Wing), Davis-Monthan AFB, 1955-56; chief requirements div., directorate of operations Hdqrs. SAC, Offutt AFB, 1956-58; chief staff 8th Air Force, Westover AFB, Mass., 1958-59; comdr. (817th Air Div.), Pease AFB, N.H., 1959-61, Turner AFB, Ga., 1961-62, Homestead AFB, Fla., 1962-63, Ellsworth AFB, S.D., 1963-64; dir. operational requirements DCS/P&R. Hdqrs. USAF, 1964-65, dir. operational requirements and devel. plans, 1965-66, dir. aerospace programs, 1966-67, dep. chief staff programs and resources, 1967-68; comdr. 15th Air Force, March AFB, Calif., 1968-69, Mil. Airlift Command, Scott AFB, 1969-72, Air Force Logistics Command, Wright-Patterson AFB, Ohio, 1972-74, ret., 1974; v.p. ops. Lockheed Corp., 1974-79, sr. v.p. bus. devel., 1979—; dir. United Services Life Ins. Co., Howmet Turbine Components Corp., Muskegon, Mich. Bd. dirs. Falcon Found. of U.S. Air Force Acad. Decorated D.S.M. with 2 oak leaf clusters, Legion Merit with oak leaf cluster, D.F.C. with 2 oak leaf cluster, Air medal with 3 oak leaf clusters, Army Commendation medal, Purple Heart; recipient George Washington medal Freedoms Found., Harrison award Am. Def. Preparedness Assn. Mem. Air Force Assn., Nat. Def. Transp. Assn. (hon. life), Am. Def. Preparedness Assn. (hon. life mem., pres.), Nat. Security Indsl. Assn. (hon. life). Home: 17230 Citronia St Northridge CA 91325

CATTON, WILLIAM BRUCE, historian, educator; b. Cleve., Mar. 21, 1926; s. Bruce and Hazel (Cherry) C.; m. F. Lynn Casman, 1978; 1 son, David Bruce. A.B., U. Md., 1951, M.A., 1952; Ph.D., Northwestern U., 1959. Teaching asst. Northwestern U., 1953-54; instr. U. Md., 1955-58, Princeton, 1958-61, asst. prof., 1961-64; asso. prof. history Middlebury (Vt.) Coll., 1964-68, prof., 1968-80, Charles A. Dana prof. history, 1969-80, chmn. div. social scis., 1969-78, prof. emeritus, historian in residence, 1980—. Author: (with Bruce Catton) Two Roads to Sumter, 1963, (with Arthur S. Link) American Epoch, 1963, rev., 1980, (with Bruce Catton) The Bold and Magnificent Dream, 1978. Served with AUS, 1945-46. Home: Otterside C-2 Middlebury VT 05753

CAUDILL, REBECCA (MRS. JAMES AYARS), author; b. Poor Fork, Ky., Feb. 2, 1899; d. George Washington and Susan (Smith) C.; m. James Sterling Ayars, Sept. 8, 1931; children: James Sterling (dec.), Rebecca Jean. A.B., Wesleyan Coll., Macon, Ga., 1920; M.A., Vanderbilt U., 1922. Tchr. Collegio Bennett, Rio de Janeiro, 1922-24; Alumnae trustee Wesleyan Coll., 1949-52; trustee Pine Mountain Settlement School, 1967-74. Author: Barrie & Daughter, 1943, Happy Little Family, 1947, Tree of Freedom, 1949, Schoolhouse in the Woods, 1949, Up and Down the River, 1951, Saturday Cousins, 1953, House of the Fifers, 1954, Susan Cornish, 1955, Schoolroom in the Parlor, 1959, Time for Lissa, 1959, Higgins and the Great Big Scare, 1960, The Best Loved Doll, 1962, The Far-Off Land, 1964 (Friends Am. Writers juvenile award 1965), A Pocketful of Cricket, 1964, A Certain Small Shepherd, 1965 (Soc. Midland Authors juvenile award 1966), Did You Carry the Flag Today, Charley?, 1966, My Appalachia, 1966, (with James Ayars) Contrary Jenkins, 1969, Come Along, 1969, Somebody Go and Bang a Drum, 1974, Wind, Sand, and Sky, 1976. Recipient Nancy Bloch Meml. award Intercultural Library, Downtown Community Sch., N.Y.C., 1956; award for disting. service in children's reading Chgo. Children's Reading Round Table, 1969; Ill. Author of Year award Ill. Assn. Tchrs. English, 1972. Mem. Delta Kappa Gamma, Theta Sigma Phi. Quaker. Address: 101 W Windsor Rd Urbana IL 61801

CAUDILL, ROBERT PAUL, clergyman; b. Dockery, N.C., July 8, 1904; s. Calvin Millard and Lousina Sernetta Elizabeth (Myers) C.; m. Ethel Fern Alderton, Mar. 23, 1929; children: Netta Sue, Robert Paul, Mary Jane (dec.), David Alderton, Mary Fern. Grad., Mars Hill (N.C.) Coll., 1927; B.A. cum laude, Wake Forest (N.C.) Coll., 1929; Th.M., So. Bapt. Theol. Sem., Louisville, 1934, Ph.D., 1942; D.D., Miss. Coll., 1950. Ordained to ministry Bapt. Ch., 1925; pastor rural and village chs., N.C. and Ky., 1927-35, First Bapt. Ch., Carrollton, Ky., 1935-37, Augusta, Ga., 1937-44, pastor, Memphis, 1944-75, emeritus, 1975—; disting. vis. prof. N.T. interpretation and writer in residence Palm Beach Atlantic Coll., 1979—; guest preacher Bapt. Hour, Columbia Ch. of Air; trustee Laubach Lit., Inc., 1964-76; Mem. com. world peace So. Bapt. Conv., 1959—; chmn. relief com. Bapt. World Alliance, 1947-60, mem. exec. com., 1950-60; mem. Bapt. World Missions Commn., 1950-60; pres. Tenn Bapt. Conv., 1957-58, mem. exec. com., 1970-76; pres. Am. Bapt. Relief, 1947-60; trustee annuity bd. So. Bapt. Conv., 1956-59; past chmn. Bapt. World Missions Trust Fund; exec. com., chmn. fin. com. So. Bapt. Conv., 1944-52; pres. Greater Memphis Bapt. Pastors Conf., 1966. Author: ann. commentary Broadman Comments, 1949-54, A Minister Looks at His World, 1955, Harvest of a Quiet Eye, 1975, Changing Life's Style, 1977; syndicated picture strip The Lesson the Bible Teaches, 1955-56; Ephesians: A Translation with Notes, 1979, Letters to Children, 1979, Pastoralia, 1979, Old Fence Rows, 1980, Philippians: A Translation with Notes, 1980, Modern Acts of the Holy Spirit, 1982, Seven Steps To Peace, 1982, I Corinthians: A Translation with Notes, 1983, Songs by the Sea, 1983; Contbr. to: So. Bapt. Ency, 1957; religious jours. Founding pres. Judeo-Christian League for Decency, 1961; bd. dirs. Am. Relief for Korea, 1952-54; mem. Nat. Council U.S. Com. for Refugees, 1960; 24 mission journeys in various parts of world in interest applied Christianity; past pres. bd. trustees, chmn. exec. com. Found. for World Literacy; bd. dirs. United Tenn. League, Inc., 1946—, pres., 1967-70; bd. dirs. Tenn. Bapt. Press, 1957-58; trustee Mercer U., 1940-44, Union U., 1945-58, 65-68, Bapt. Meml. Hosp., 1947-58, 60-66, 70-76, Golden Gate Bapt. Theol. Sem., 1954-56; founding chmn. bd. dirs., chmn. exec. com. Memphis Transitional Center, 1973; chmn. Tenn. Interfaith Com. to Oppose Legalized Gambling, 1973; founding chmn. Memphis Literacy Council, 1974-75; mem. adv. council Hawaii Bapt. Acad., 1975—; chmn. steering com. Memphis 1st War on Poverty Com., 1965. Commd. hon. chaplain with rank of rear adm. Lower Half USN Chaplain Corps, 1969. Named hon. citizen of South Korea. Mem. Alumni Assn. So. Bapt. Theol. Sem. (pres. 1947), Golden Bough Honor Soc., Gamma Epsilon Tau, Pi Kappa Delta. Clubs: Rotary, Crosscut, Execs. (Memphis). Toured occupied zones in Germany, Austria, Italy, 1947, in interest of Bapt. World Alliance relief program; toured Europe, 1948, 1949, 52. Home and office: Parkview Manor Apt 1 1914 Poplar Ave Memphis TN 38104 *An unwavering faith in Jesus Christ as Savior and Lord, and an abiding effort to lead others to know Him and to translate into everyday life the changeless concepts of truth and duty as set forth in our Judeo-Christian heritage.*

CAUDILL, SAMUEL JEFFERSON, architect; b. Tulsa, June 5, 1922; s. Samuel Jefferson and Maymie Starling (Boulware) C.; m. Joy Maxwell, May 31, 1952; children: Jody Caudill Cardamone, Julie Caudill Githens, Samuel Boone, Robert Maxwell, Anne Caudill Cardamone. B.Arch., Cornell U., Ithaca, N.Y., 1946. Registered architech Colo., Calif., Ind., Idaho., Wyo. Prin. architect Samuel J. Caudill, Jr., Aspen, Colo., 1954-59, Caudill Assocs. Architects, 1959-80; pres. Caudill Gustafson & Assocs. Architects, P.C., Aspen, 1980—; mem. Pitkin County Planning and Zoning Commn., Colo., 1955-58; mem. outdoor edn. com. Colo. Dept. Edn., 1966-68; chmn. Pitkin County Bd. Appeals, 1970; mem. Colo. Water Quality Control Commn., 1977-80. Wildlife rep. adv. bd. Bur. Land Mgmt. Dept. Interior, Grand Junction, Colo., 1969-75, 80—; chmn. citizens adv. com. Colo. Hwy. Dept. for I-70 through Glenwood Canyon, 1975-83; chmn. Colo. Wildlife Commn., 1978-79. Recipient Outstanding Pub. Service Bur. Land Mgmt., 1975. Fellow AIA; mem. Council Ednl. Facility Planners Internat., Colo. Soc. Architects (AIA Community Service 1976, pres. 1983), Colo. Council on Arts and Humanities, Aspen C. of C. (pres. 1956-57). Lodges: Masons (Aspen); Shriners (Denver). Home: Maroon Creek Aspen CO 81612 Office: Caudill Gustafson & Assocs Architects P.C. 234 E Hopkins Aspen CO 81612

CAUDLE, JONES RICHARD, JR., oil co. exec.; b. Foraker, Okla., Nov. 1, 1911; s. Jones Richard and Maude Ethel (Rodgers) C.; m. Mary Ann Brownlee, June 11, 1943; children—Mary Ann, Jones Richard III. Student, Tulsa U., 1932, Okla. U., 1934, Tulsa Law Sch., 1937. Sales mgr. N.M. Asphalt & Refining Co., 1946-52, Delta Refining Co., 1952-54; v.p. Eastern States Chem. Corp., 1954-57; sr. v.p. Eastern States Petroleum & Chem. Co., 1957-59; v.p. Signal Oil and Gas Co., 1959—, dir., 1968-69; pres. Apex Investment, Inc., Apex Oil Co., Apex Oil Co. of La., Major Industries, Inc., Apex Oil Co. Miss.; v.p., dir. Haltermann Inc. Democratic candidate for state rep., N.Mex., 1951. Served to capt. USAAF, World War II. Decorated Bronze Star. Mem. Am. Petroleum Inst., Petroleum Industry 25 Year Club, Delta Theta Phi. Presbyn. (elder, deacon). Club: Houston. Home: 11722 Highgrove Dr Houston TX 77077

CAUGHLAN, GEORGEANNE ROBERTSON, educator; b. Montesane, Wash., Oct. 25, 1916; d. George Duncan and Anna (McLeod) Robertson; m. Charles Norris Caughlan, June 21, 1936 (div. 1975); children—Cheryl Karen, Kevin Michael, Kerry Jan, Deirdre Norrine. B.S. in Physics, U. Wash., 1937, Ph.D., 1964. Faculty Mont. State U., Bozeman, 1957—, instr. physics, 1957-61, asst. prof., 1961-65, asso. prof., 1965-74, prof. physics, 1974—, acting dean grad. studies, 1977-78, acting v.p. acad. affairs, 1978; condr. research, cons. in field. NSF grantee, 1965-77. Fellow Am. Phys. Soc.; mem. Am. Astron. Soc., Internat. Astron. Union, Phi Beta Kappa, Sigma Xi. Episcopalian. Home: 1002 E Kagy Bozeman MT 59715 Office: Dept Physics Mont State Univ Bozeman MT 59717

CAULEY, FRANK WILLIAM, architect, lawyer; b. Chgo., Aug. 25, 1898; s. Frank F. and Margaret E. (Byrnes) C.; m. Rosalie Hill, Aug. 26, 1925 (dec. 1966); 1 son, Francis Hill; m. Sarah Smith, Aug. 2, 1966. B.S., Armour Inst. Tech., 1922; LL.B., Chgo. Kent Coll. Law, 1938; J.D. (hon.), Ill. Inst. Tech., 1970. Bar: Ill. bar 1956. Architect Victor C. Carlson Orgn. (hotels, stores and apts.), 1932-34; archtl. office, Evanston, Ill., 1924-41, 46—, practice in, Ill., N.C. and Wis.; pres., dir. Frank W. Cauley, Inc. (architects), 1940—, Waterford Corp. (real estate), 1940—, Delaware Investment Corp. (securities); Evanston, 1946—; asst. works mgr., also mdse. mgr. Victor Mfg. and Gasket Co., Chgo., 1941-45; pres. Ercom Corp. (contracts with Naval Research Lab.), Washington, 1945; Lectr. Northwestern U., 1962; Mem. Nat. Trust for Historic Preservation; chmn. Com. for Restoration Old Market House of Galena, Ill.; chmn. adv. com. on market house restoration State architect of Ill.; preservation officer historic bldgs., State of Ill. Works include numerous residences in classical revival style, Ill., Wis., Va., 1940-50; 1926 apt. bldg. designated Evanston Hist. Landmark. Mem. A.I.A. (preservation officer hist. bldgs. No. Ill. and Chgo.; del.), Nat. Soc. Archtl. Historians, Evanston, Chgo. hist. socs., Scarab (hon.). Republican. Club: University (Chgo.). Office: 1519 Hinman Ave Evanston IL 60201 *It is only through a broad knowledge of the contributions in ideas and accomplishments in the history of "Western Man" that we can achieve a balance of judgment in conducting our own life.*

CAULFIELD, JAMES BENJAMIN, pathologist, educator; b. Mpls., Jan. 1, 1927; s. Linus Joseph and Olive Bell (Curtis) C.; m. Virginia Walsh, Jan. 28, 1950; children—Ann, John, Clare. B.A., Miami U., Oxford, Ohio, 1947; B.S., U. Ill., 1948, M.D., 1950. Intern Henrotin Hosp., Chgo., 1950-51; resident U. N.C., Chapel Hill, 1951-52, U. Kans. Med. Center, Kansas City, 1954-55; vis. investigator Rockefeller Inst., N.Y.C., 1955-56; instr. pathology Harvard U., 1959-64, asst. prof., 1964-70, asso. prof., 1970-75; asst. pathologist Mass. Gen. Hosp., Boston, 1960-64, asso. pathologist, 1964-75; prof., chmn. dept. pathology U. S.C., 1975—; adj. prof. Med. U. S.C., Charleston, 1981—. Contbr. articles to profl. jours. Served with USN, 1944-46, 52-54. Mem. Am. Soc. Cell Biology, Internat. Acad. Pathology, Fedn. Exptl. Pathology, Electron Microscopy Soc., Internat. Study Group for Heart Research (treas. Am. sect. 1972—), N.Y. Acad. Scis., Sigma Xi, Phi Eta Sigma. Clubs: Harvard, Boston Athanaeum. Office: Department of Pathology University of South Carolina Columbia SC 29208

CAULO, RALPH D., publishing company executive. Exec. v.p., dir. Harcourt Brace Jovanovich, Inc. Office: 757 Third Ave New York NY 10017§

CAUNA, NIKOLAJS, scientist, educator; b. Riga, Latvia, Apr. 4, 1914; came to U.S., 1961; s. Nikolajs and Marija (Manika) C.; m. Dzidra Priede, June 23, 1942. M.D., U. Latvia, 1942; M.Sc., U. Durham (Eng.), 1954, D.Sc., 1961. Lectr. anatomy U. Latvia, Riga, 1942-44; gen. practice medicine Sarsted and Eschershausen, West Germany, 1944-46; acting chmn. anatomy dept. Baltic U., Hamburg, Germany, 1946-48; lectr. anatomy Med. Sch. U. Durham (Eng.), 1948-57, reader, 1958-61; prof. anatomy Sch. Medicine U. Pitts., 1961—, chmn., 1975—. Mem. editorial bd.: Anatomical Record, 1969—; Contbr. articles to profl. jours. Recipient Golden Apple award (tchr. of year) U. Pitts., 1964, 67, 73; research grantee Royal Soc. Eng., 1958-60; USPHS grantee, 1962—; Am. Cancer Inst. grantee, 1961. Mem. Anat. Soc. Gt. Britain and Ireland, Am. Assn. Anatomists, Royal Micros. Soc., Anatomische Gesellschaft, Histochem. Soc., A.A.A.S., Am. Soc. Cell Biology, Internat. Assn. for Study Pain. Research in normal and pathol. sensory receptor organs, autonomic control mechanism, devel. and evolution of sense organs and limbs. Home: 129 Hawthorne Ct Pittsburgh PA 15201

CAUNTER, HARRY ALLEN, electronics company executive; b. Cleve., Dec. 21, 1935; s. Harry Albert and Ruth Olive (Woollocott) C.; children: Keith A., Christine A. B.B.A., Western Res. U., 1960. With Clevite Corp. (merger Gould Nat. Battery 1969, renamed Gould, Inc.), Rolling Meadows, Ill., 1957—, sr. v.p. adminstrn., 1977-83, exec. v.p., 1983—. Office: 10 Gould Center Rolling Meadows IL 60008

CAUSA, ALFREDO GUILLERMO, polymer scientist; b. Montevideo, Uruguay, June 25, 1928; came to U.S., 1959, naturalized, 1975; s. Alfredo and Emilia (DeBenedetti) C. B.Sc. with honors, Montevideo Sch. Chemistry and Chem. Engring., 1958; M.S., Case Inst. Tech., Cleve., 1962; Ph.D. in Polymer Sci., U. Akron, 1968. Chemist S.Am. subs. Courtaulds, Ltd., 1952-58; research chemist textile fibres div. Canadian Industries Ltd., Millhaven Research Lab., Kingston, Ont., 1961-64, Tarrytown Tech. Ctr. Union Carbide Corp., Tarrytown, N.Y., 1968-70; prin. chemist Goodyear Tire & Rubber Co., Akron, Ohio, 1970—. Contbr. articles to profl. jours. Fulbright scholar, 1959-61; Phillips Petroleum fellow, 1964-67. Mem. Am. Chem. Soc., AAAS, Sigma Xi, Alpha Chi Sigma. Home: 1255 Ashford Ln Akron OH 44313 Office: 1144 E Market St Akron OH 44316

CAUSEY, DONALD MCDANIEL, JR., publisher, author; b. Whitville, N.C., Nov. 20, 1942; s. Donald McDaniel and Rachel (Bryan) C. B.A., U. N.C., 1968, M.A., 1970. Reporter Raleigh Times, N.C., 1970-71; writer, N.Y.C., 1971-75; asso. editor, sr. editor, then exec. editor Outdoor Life mag., N.Y.C., 1975-81; publisher Newsletter, 1981—; cons. U.S. Dept. Agr.; speaker writer conf. U. Iowa, 1979; judge mag. awards program Assn. Conservation Info., 1981. Author: Killer Insects, 1980; contbr. articles to mags. Served with U.S. Army, 1963-66. Mem. Am. Soc. Mag. Editors, Outdoor Writers Assn. Am. Clubs: Dutch Treat, Campfire (N.Y.C.). Home: 220 W 13th St New York NY 10011

CAUSEY, ROBERT LOUIS, educator; b. Los Angeles, Apr. 13, 1941; s. Robert Vester and Gertrude (Bloom) C.; m. Sandra Lee Shliff, Jan. 25, 1964; children—Britt Ann, Diane Sue. B.S., Calif. Inst. Tech., 1963; Ph.D., U. Calif., Berkeley, 1967. Asst. prof. dept. philosophy U. Tex., Austin, 1967-73, asso. prof., 1973-79, prof., 1979—, chmn. dept. philosophy, 1980—; cons. NSF, 1979-81; speaker on resource recycling Conf. on Environ. Legislation, 66th session Tex. State Capitol, 1978. Author: Unity of Science, 1977; contbr. articles and reviews to philos. and sci. jours. NSF fellow, NSF grantee, 1973-74; U. Tex. Research Inst. grantee, 1979; NSF grantee, 1979-81. Mem. AAAS, Am. Philos. Assn., Philosophy of Sci. Assn. (governing bd. 1980-81), Southwestern Philos. Soc. Office: Dept of Philosophy Waggener Hall 316 Univ Texas Austin TX 78712

CAUTHEN, IRBY BRUCE, JR., educator; b. Rock Hill, S.C., Aug. 24, 1919; s. Irby Bruce and Ruth (Kimbrell) C.; m. Elizabeth Bagby Greear, Aug. 28, 1954; children: Irby Bruce III, James Noah Greear. B.A., Furman U., 1940, Litt.D., 1980; M.A., U. Va., 1942, Ph.D., 1951. Asst. prof. English Hollins Coll., 1951-54; faculty U. Va., Charlottesville, 1954—, prof. English, 1964—, asso. dean, 1958-62, dean coll., 1962-78, asso. dir. summer session, 1958-72; Chmn. regional selection com. Woodrow Wilson Fellowship Found., 1962-72. Editor: Gorboduc, 1970, Two Mementoes from the Poe-Ingram Collection, 1971, (with J.L. Dameron) Edgar Allan Poe: A Bibliography of Criticism, 1827-1967, 1974; contbg. editor: The Dramatic Works in the Beaumont and Fletcher Canon, 1966; Contbr. articles to profl. jours. Served with AUS, 1942-46; MTO. Decorated Bronze Star; recipient Raven Soc. award U. Va., 1963, Thomas Jefferson award, 1977, Algernon Sydney Sullivan award, 1978. Mem. Bibliog. Soc. U. Va. (v.p. 1961-78, pres. 1978—), Modern Lang. Assn., Shakespeare Assn., Phi Beta Kappa (pres. Va. Beta chpt. 1969-71), Omicron Delta Kappa. Democrat. Presbyn. Clubs: Colonnade, Greencroft (Charlottesville). Home: 1824 Winston Rd Charlottesville VA 22903

CAUTHEN, STEVE, jockey; b. Covington, Ky., May 1, 1960; s. Ronald and Myra C. Profl. jockey, 1976—. Rec. artist And Steve Cauthen Sings Too!, 1977. Recipient Seagram prize, 1977; named Sportsman of Year Sports Illustrated mag., 1977; winner Triple Crown, 1978. Races at maj. tracks in U.S., Can. and Gt. Britain, including Aqueduct, Churchill Downs, Arlington Park, River Downs, Santa Anita, Belmont, Saratoga *

CAVA, MICHAEL PATRICK, chemist, educator; b. Bklyn., Feb. 13, 1926; s. Michael R. and Catherine (Lombardo) C.; m. Esther Laden, June 11, 1951; 1 son, John M. B.S., Harvard, 1946; M.S., U. Mich., 1948, Ph.D., 1951. Postdoctoral fellow Harvard, 1951-53; from asst. prof. to prof. Ohio State U., 1953-65; prof. Wayne State U., Detroit, 1965-69; prof. chemistry U. Pa., Phila., 1969—; Cons. Smith, Kline and French, Phila., 1965—; mem. study sect. NIH, 1966-70. Author: (with M.J. Mitchell) Cyclobutadiene and Related Compounds, 1967; also numerous articles. Alfred P. Sloan Found. fellow. Mem. Am. Chem. Soc., Am. Soc. Pharmacognosy. Reserch on organic sulphur, selenium and tellurium compounds; organic condrs., benzocyclobutenes, natural products chemistry. Home: 312 Penn Rd Wynnewood PA 19096 Office: U Pa Dept Chemistry Philadelphia PA 19174

CAVAGLIERI, GIORGIO, architect; b. Venice, Italy, Aug. 1, 1911; came to U.S., 1939, naturalized, 1943; s. Gino and Margherita (Maroni) C.; m. Norma Sanford, Jan. 31, 1942. D. Archtl. Engring, Sup. Sch. Engring., Milan, Italy, 1932; student spl. city planning, Sup. Sch. Architecture, Rome, 1934. Apprenticeship N.Y. office R. Candela, Balt. offices J.O. Chertkof, also; Benjamin Franklin, architect, prior to World War II; propr. own firm, N.Y.C., 1946—; adj. prof. Sch. Architecture, Pratt Inst.; Trustee Nat. Inst. Archtl. Edn., chmn. trustees, 1957-60. Prin. works in, Milan, prior to World War II, prin. works include, Fenton Hall reconstrn. Fredonia (N.Y.) Coll., Astor Library restoration and conversion to N.Y. Pub. Theatre, N.Y. Shakespeare Festival, Jefferson Market Courthouse restoration and conversion to N.Y. Pub. Library, Branch Library, Riverdale, N.Y., Pub. Sch. 32, S.I., Kip's Bay br. library. Served with C.E. AUS, 1943-45. Decorated Bronze Star; recipient Honor award A.I.A., 1968, House Improvement award, 1961; Bard award, spl. citation City Club N.Y., 1968; Illuminated scroll Municipal Art Soc. N.Y., 1966; Clients award N.Y. State Assn. Architects, 1964; Gold medal honor architecture Archtl. League N.Y., 1956; winner 1st prize nat. competition auditorium, Rome, 1935, 3d prize competition city hosp., Cuneo, Italy., 1938, hon. mention Armed Forces bldgs. Rome World's Fair, 1938, 3d prize N.Y.C. Bd. Edn. archtl. competition for modernization Bronx Jr. High Sch., 1967; certificate of merit for excellence in design N.Y. State Assn. Architects, 1976; 1st honor award ALA/AIA, 1976; Sidney L. Strauss Meml. N.Y. Soc. Architects, 1977. Fellow A.I.A. (pres. N.Y. chpt. 1970-71); mem. Municipal Art Soc. N.Y. (pres. 1963-65), Archtl. League N.Y. (v.p. 1961-63), Am. Inst. Interior Designers, Fine Arts Fedn. N.Y. (pres. 1973-75, 77-78), N.Y. Council Arts and Govt. Democrat. Home: 75 Central Park West New York City NY 10023 Office: 250 W 57th St New York City NY 10019

CAVALLO, DIANA, author; b. Phila., Nov. 3, 1931; d. Genuino and Josephine (Petrarca) C.; m. Henry Weinberg, 1954 (div. 1975); m. Karl Hagedorn, 1981. B.A., U. Pa., 1953; M.A., Sarah Lawrence Coll., 1965. Lectr. USIS, 1961-63; tchr. lit. U. Pisa, Italy, 1961-63, 72-74, Drexel Inst. Tech., 1964; lectr. lit. Queens Coll., Flushing, N.Y., 1966-68; dir. Westside Writers Workshop, 1976—; lectr. creative writing U. Pa., 1979—; Sec.-treas. Mt. Desert Music Festival, 1965. Author: novel A Bridge of Leaves, 1961; short stories Certain Fathoms in the Earth, 1964; The Lower East Side: A Portrait in Time, 1971. MacDowell Colony fellow, 1960, 67, 73, 74; Fulbright Teaching fellow, 1961-63. Mem. Authors League, P.E.N., Phi Beta Kappa. Home: 176 Broadway New York NY 10038

CAVALLON, GIORGIO, artist; b. Italy, Mar. 3, 1904; came to U.S., 1920, naturalized, 1929; s. Augusto and Agnese (Scarsi) C.; m. Linda Lindberg, Mar. 25, 1954. Student, Nat. Acad. Design, 1926-30; pupil of, Charles Hawthorne, Hans Hofmann. Artist in residence U. N.C. at Greensboro, 1964; vis. critic art Yale, 1967; painting workshop Columbia, summer 1969. One man exhbns. include, Bottege D'Art, Vicenza, Italy, 1932, Egan Gallery, N.Y.C., 1946-48, 51, 54, Stable Gallery, N.Y.C., 1957-59, Kootz Gallery, N.Y.C., 1961, 63, 65, A.M. Sachs Gallery, N.Y.C., 1969, 71, 74, retrospective exhbn., Neuberger Mus., State U. N.Y., Purchase, 1977, prin. group shows include, Whitney Mus. ann., 1959, 61, 65, Mus. Modern Art, 1963, 69, Pa. Acad. Fine Arts, 1966, Yale, 1967, Am. Geometric Abstraction/1930's, Labriskie Gallery-Am. Fedn. Arts, 1972; represented in permanent collections, Museum of Modern Art, N.Y.C., U. N.C. at Greensboro, Whitney Mus., Albright Art Gallery, Guggenheim Mus., Union Carbide Corp., Continental Grain Corp., Tishman Collection, Michener Collection U. Tex. at Austin, Chase Manhattan Bank, Singer Mfg. Co., Geigy Chem. Corp., N.Y.U., Univ. Art Mus., Berkeley, Calif., Marine Midland Trust Co., Buffalo, Avco Delta Corp., Cleve., Am. Republic Ins. Co., Des Moines, Rose Mus. of Brandeis U., Lavon Corp., N.Y.C. Guggenheim fellow, 1966-67; recipient award in painting Nat. Inst. Arts and Letters, 1970, New Eng. Art Paintings Sculpture Invitational Show, 1971. Address: 178 E 95th St New York NY 10028 also Gruenebaum Gallery Ltd 38 E 57th St New York NY 10021

CAVANAGH, DENIS, physician, educator. M.B., Ch.B. Diplomate: Am. Bd. Obstetrics and Gynecology. Former prof. gynecology and obstetrics, chmn. dept. St. Louis U. Sch. Medicine; now prof. gynecology and obstetrics Am. Cancer Soc.; prof. clin. oncology U. South Fla., Tampa. Fellow ACS, Am. Coll. Obstetricians and Gynecologists, Am. Ob-Gyn Soc., Royal Coll. Obstetricians and Gynecologists; mem. South Atlantic Assn. Obstetricians and Gynecologists, Soc. Gynecol. Oncologists, Soc. Pelvic Surgeons. Office: Coll Medicine U South Fla Tampa FL 33612

CAVANAGH, EDWARD FRANCIS, JR., corp. exec., lawyer; b. N.Y.C., Aug. 18, 1908; s. Edward Francis and Mae (Masterson) C.; m. Nancy Miller, Mar. 26, 1940; children: Edward Francis III, Nannette Christine, Roderick Anthony, Mae Angela. B.A., Georgetown U., 1929; postgrad., Harvard U., 1930-31; LL.B., St. Lawrence U., 1933. Bar: N.Y. 1933, U.S. Supreme Ct. 1938. Practice in, N.Y.C., 1933—; counsel Curtiss-Wright Corp., N.Y.C., Woodbridge, N.J., 1945-47; dep. commr. N.Y.C. Dept. Marine and Aviation, 1947-49, commr., 1950-54; dep. commr., acting commr. Dept. Hosps., 1949-50; commr. Fire Dept., 1954-62; exec. dep. mayor N.Y.C., 1962-65; v.p. Baker Industries, Inc., 1966-71, dir., 1966-79, Wells Fargo Armored Transport Corp., 1966-70, Wells Fargo Armored Service Corp., Tenn., 1966-70, Wells Fargo Armored Service Corp. Miss., 1966-70, Wells Fargo Armored Service Corp. Del., 1966-70; v.p. Wells Fargo Armored Service Corp. Mass., Pacific Plant Protection, Shane & Assocs.; dir. Wells Fargo Armored Service Fla., James Cavanagh Corp., Personal Investments, N.Y.C. Mem. Gov.'s Emergency Adv. Com.; chmn. Mayor's Chaplaincy Bd., Mayor's Com. on Harlem Affairs; mem. Mayor's Task Force on Markets; chmn. Interagy. Relocation Coordinating Com.; mem. exec. com. World's Fair, 1964-65; treas. Mercy Hosp., Hempstead, N.Y., 1950-56; chmn. bd. layman's adv. com. Bellevue Hosp., N.Y.C.; mem. exec. com. Post Coll., L.I. U.; Vice pres., dir. Thannawaga Democratic Orgn., N.Y.C.; chmn. N.Y. County Dem. Com.; Bd. dirs. Neighborhood House, Glen Cove, L.I., Library Presdl. Papers; trustee L.I. U. Served to col. USAAF, 1942-45. Decorated Legion of Merit, U.S.; knight grand cross Order Holy Sepulchre of Jerusalem, Papal; Order St. George, Greece; Order Rebuen Dario, Nicaragua; cavaliere ufficiale Order of Merit, Italy; chevaller Order of Crown, Belgium; Ecomeinda of Order of Isabella Catolica, Spain; medal of Merit, Iran).; Recipient William Randolph Hearst gold medal award Downtown Lower Manhattan Assn., 1954; Cath. War Vet award; Achievement award Interfaith Movement, 1964; Anti-Defamation League award, 1965. Mem. Assn. Bar City N.Y., Nat. Fire Protection Assn., Am. Legion (comdr. Air Service Post 1952-53, Distinguished Service award N.Y. dept. 1955), Phi Delta Phi. Roman Catholic. Clubs: Racquet and Tennis, Lotos, Whitehall (N.Y.C.); Piping Rock, Beaver Dam Winter Sports (Locust Valley, N.Y.); Harvard of N.Y.; Spouting Rock Beach Assn., Clambake (Newport, R.I.). Home: Lake House 875 E Camino Real Boca Raton FL 33432 Home: Bellevue Ave. Newport RI Office: 345 Park Ave New York NY 10022

CAVANAGH, HARRISON DWIGHT, ophthalmic surgeon; b. Atlanta, July 22, 1940; s. William Edwards and Marie Corrine (Logue) C.; m. Lynn Ayres Gantt, Dec. 27, 1964; 1 dau., Catherine DuVal. A.B., Johns Hopkins U., 1962, M.D. (Joseph Collins scholar 1963-65), 1965; Ph.D. in Biology, Harvard U., 1972. Diplomate: Am. Bd. Ophthalmology. Intern Johns Hopkins Hosp., 1965-66, resident in ophthalmology, 1969-73; fellow corneal surgery Mass. Eye and Ear Infirmary, Boston, 1973-75; instr. ophthalmology Johns Hopkins Med. Sch., 1969-73; asst. prof. Harvard U. Med. Sch., 1975-76; mem. faculty Emory U., 1976—, F. Phinizy Calhoun prof. ophthalmology, chmn. dept., 1978—; cons., chmn. visual scis. study sect. A Nat. Eye Inst. Heed Found. scholar, 1973-74. Contbr. articles. to sci. jours. Recipient Heed medal, 1981; named Jean Lacerte medal lectr. Laval U., 1983, Maxwell Boschner medal lectr., 1983. Fellow A.C.S., Internat. Coll. Surgeons, Am. Acad. Ophthalmology (asso. sect. govt. relations and research 1979—); mem. Contact Lens Assn. Ophthalmologists Am. (dir.), Castroviejo Soc. Corneal Surgeons (dir.), Keratorefractive Soc. (dir.), Internat. Eye Found. Eye Surgeons, New Eng. Ophthal. Soc., Assn. Research Vision and Ophthalmology (sec.-treas. 1981—), Phi Beta Kappa. Republican. Episcopalian. Clubs: Harvard (Atlanta and Boston); Johns Hopkins (Balt.). Home: 3094 E Pine Valley Rd NW Atlanta GA 30305 Office: 1365 Clifton Rd NE Atlanta GA 30322

CAVANAGH, HARRY JOSEPH, lawyer; b. Chgo., July 9, 1923; s. John Albert and Mary (Foster) C.; m. Geri Gale, Sept. 5, 1971; children by previous marriage: Kathleen (Mrs. James Barrow), Dianne (Mrs. Charles Abert), Harry Joseph, Patricia, (Mrs. Ernest Clark), Michael, Jamie. LL.B., U. Ariz., 1950. Bar: Ariz. bar 1950. Since practiced in, Phoenix; ptnr. firm O'Connor, Cavanagh, Anderson, Westover, Killingsworth & Beshears, 1965—; dir. J.F. Helmold & Bros., Chgo., Nu West Devel. Corp. Ariz., Century Bank, Dunoco Internat., SamCor. Past pres. Am. Bd. Trial Advocates, Boys Clubs Phoenix.; chmn. bd. dirs. Samaritan Health Service-Samaritan Med. Found., LPGA Classic. Served to capt. USAAF, 1943-46. Decorated Silver Star, D.F.C. Mem. Internat. Assn. Ins. Counsel, Am. Bar Assn., State Bar Ariz., Am. Judicature Soc., Phoenix C. of C., Phi Delta Phi. Home: 7570 N Silvercrest Way Paradise Valley AZ 85253 Office: 3003 N Central Ave Phoenix AZ 85012

CAVANAGH, JOHN CHARLES, advertising agency executive; b. San Francisco, Dec. 19, 1932; s. John Timothy and Alicia Louise (McDowell) C.; m. Mary Ann Anding, Apr. 10, 1959; children: Karen, Brad. Student, U. Hawaii, 1950; B.S., U. San Francisco, 1954. Pub. relations rep. Kaiser Industries Corp., Oakland, Calif., 1956-58; pub. relations mgr. Kaiser Cement & Gypsum Corp., Oakland, 1958-63; pub. relations dir. Fawcett-McDermott Assos. Inc., Honolulu, Hawaii, 1964-66, ops. v.p., 1966-69, exec. v.p., 1969-73, pres., dir., 1973-75, Fawcett McDermott Cavanagh Inc., Honolulu, 1975—, Fawcett McDermott Cavanagh Calif., Inc., San Francisco, 1975—. Served to 1st. lt. 740th Guided Missile Bn. AUS, 1954-56. Mem. Pub. Relations Soc. Am. (accredited, v.p. 1970, pres. Hawaii chpt. 1971), Advt. Agy. Assn. Hawaii (pres. 1973), Am. Assn. Advt. Agys. (chmn. Hawaii council 1980-81), Affiliated Advt. Agys. Internat. (chmn. elect 1983-84). Clubs: Rotarian., Honolulu Press, Honolulu Advt., Outrigger Canoe, Oahu Country, Pacific. Home: 3068 La Pietra Circle Honolulu HI 96815 Office: 1441 Kapiolani Blvd Suite 1500 Honolulu HI 96814

CAVANAGH, JOHN EDWARD, lawyer; b. Winnipeg, Man., Can., Nov. 15, 1918; came to U.S., 1920, naturalized, 1942; s. John and Mary Ann (McGarty) C.; m. Mary Adele Brophy, May 9, 1953; children—John E., Clare Adele, Cathleen Rose, Sally Ann. A.B., U. Ore., 1942; J.D., George Washington U., 1949, LL.M., 1952. Bar: D.C. bar 1949, Calif. bar 1957. Grad. asst. social sci. U. Oreg., 1941-42; hwy. economist U.S. Bur. Pub. Rds., 1946-49; chief congl. investigations br. Q.M.C.; counsel to dep. quartermaster gen. for operations Dept. Army, 1950-56; asst. counsel Lockheed Aircraft Corp., 1956-58, Lockheed Missiles & Space Co., 1958-62, counsel, 1962-68; chief counsel, asst. sec. Lockheed Aircraft Corp., Burbank, Calif., 1968-71, v.p., gen. counsel, 1971-77, sr. v.p., gen. counsel, 1977—; lectr. U. Santa Clara Law Sch., 1960-68; mem. adv. bd. fed. contracts report Bur. Nat. Affairs, 1968—. Served to maj. AUS, 1942-46; CBI. Mem. Am., Fed. bar assns., Nat. Contract Mgmt. Assn., Order of Coif, Delta Theta Phi. Home: 17341 Gresham St Northridge CA 91324 Office: PO Box 551 Burbank CA 91503

CAVANAGH, RICHARD EDWARD, management consultant; b. Buffalo, June 15, 1946; s. Joseph John and Mary Celeste (Stack) C. A.B., Wesleyan U., Conn., 1968; M.B.A, Harvard U., 1970. Assoc. McKinsey & Co., Inc., Washington, 1970-77; exec. dir. fed. cash mgmt. U.S. Office Mgmt. and Budget, Washington, 1977-79; domestic coordinator Pres.'s Reorgn Project The White House, Washington, 1978-79; sr. cons. McKinsey & Co., Inc., Washington, 1979, prin., 1980—; guest lectr. Brookings Inst., 1978-79, mem. bus. adv. com. advanced study program, 1983—; guest lectr. Harvard U., 1982, Yale U., 1982; adviser to nat. govts., EEC, N.Y.C. Partnership, Am. Bus. Conf.; mem. exec. com. Pres.'s Pvt. Sector Survey on Cost Control, 1983—; quoted on pub. issues in Time, Bus, Week, AP, UPI. Mem. staff Carter-Mondale Policy Planning, 1976; cons. Carter-Mondale Presdl. Transition, 1976-77. Served with U.S. Army, 1968. Recipient Presdl. commendation, 1979,80; John Reilly Knox fellow, 1979; Clark fellow, 1979. Mem. Am. Soc. Pub. Adminstrn., Acad. Polit. Sci., Raimond Duy Baird Assn., Beta Theta Pi. Democrat. Roman Catholic. Club: Harvard (N.Y.C.). Home: 664 Massachusetts Ave NW Washington DC 20002 Office: 1700 Pennsylvania Ave NW Washington DC 20006

CAVANAUGH, GORDON, lawyer; b. Phila., Apr. 3, 1928; s. Gordon Aloysius and Margaret Cecelia (McNulty) C.; m. Joan McNichol, Feb. 6, 1960; children: Gordon A., Ann, Sean, Barbara. B.A., Fordham Coll., 1950; LL.B., U. Pa., 1953; LL.D. (hon.), Delaware Valley Coll. Sci. and Agr., Doylstown, Pa. Bar: Pa. 1954. Pvt. practice law, 1953-57, 59-66, asst. city solicitor, City of Phila., 1957-60, commr. licenses and inspections, 1966-67, housing dir., 1968-71; exec. dir. Housing Assistance Council, Inc., Washington, 1972-77; adminstr. Farmers Home Adminstrn., 1977-81; partner firm Roisman, Reno & Cavanaugh, Washington, 1981—. Bd. dirs. Nat. Low Income Housing Coalition, Coop. Housing Found., Nat. Council on Agrl. Life and Labor, Nat. Housing Conf., Nat. Rural Housing Coalition. Mem. Nat. Low Income Housing Coalition. Democrat. Roman Catholic. Home: 10700 Shelley Ct Garrett Park MD 20896 Office: 509 C St NW Washington DC 20036

CAVANAUGH, JAMES HENRY, cons. to Pres.; b. Madison, N.J., Mar. 3, 1937; s. James R. and Madeline R. (McFerren) C.; m. Esther Sally Musselman, Jan. 20, 1962; children—Elizabeth Anne, Michael Patrick. B.A., Fairleigh-Dickinson U., 1959; M.A., U. Iowa, Ph.D., 1964. Mem. adminstrv. staff Princeton Hosp., 1961-62; mem. faculty Coll. Medicine, U. Iowa, Iowa City, 1962-66; dir. Comprehensive Health Planning Office, USPHS, Washington, 1966-68; dep. asst. sec. HEW, Washington, 1969, dep. asst. sec. sci. affairs, 1969-71; staff asst. to Pres. Nixon (on health affairs), 1971-72; asso. dir. White House Domestic Council Staff, 1973, dep. dir., 1974-75; dep. asst. to Pres. Ford (for domestic affairs), 1976; sr. v.p. planning and sci. Allergan Internat., Irvine, Calif., 1977—; spl. cons. to Pres. Reagan, White House, Washington, 1981—. Contbr. articles to profl. jours. Recipient William A. Jump Meritorious award William A. Jump Found., 1969, Disting. Alumnus award Coll. Medicine, U. Iowa, 1970. Office: The White House 1600 Pennsylvania Ave NW Washington DC 20500 *

CAVANAUGH, TOM RICHARD, artist, antique dealer, retired art educator; b. Danville, Ill., July 19, 1923; s. Harry William and Hazel (Brown) C. B.F.A., U. Ill., 1947, M.F.A. (McLellan fellow), 1950. Art and edn!. dir. Springfield (Ill.) Art Assn., 1947-49; mem. faculty Kansas City Art Inst., 1952-55, Washington U. Sch. Art, St. Louis, 1955-56; prof. painting and drawing La. State U., Baton Rouge, 1957-83, ret., 1983; owner, dir. The Bay Street Studio, Boothbay Harbor, Maine, 1950—. One man shows, Chapellier Gallery, N.Y.C., 1963, La. State U., 1963, 78, group shows include, Met. Mus. Art, 1950, Whitney Mus., 1951-58, Corcoran biennials, 1959, 61, Nelson Gallery Art, 1952, Joslyn Mus. Art, 1954, Mulvane Art Mus., 1955, Kans. State Coll., 1956, New Orleans Mus., 1959, Ark. Arts Center, 1961; represented in permanent collections, Mead Corp., N.Y.C., Joslyn Mus. Art, New Orleans Mus., ers. Served with U.S. Army, 1943-45. Fulbright fellow, Italy, 1956-57; McDowell Colony fellow, 1973. Home and Office: 2 Bay St Boothbay Harbor ME 04538

CAVANAUGH, WARD ARTHUR, greeting cards company executive; b. Saratoga Springs, N.Y., Mar. 11, 1930; s. Jesse M. and Helen (Gray) C.; m. Elizabeth Louise Whalen, Sept. 21, 1957; children: Mark, Louise, Duncan. B.Mgmt. Engring., Rensselaer Poly. Inst., 1952; M.B.A., Wharton Sch., U. Pa., 1959. Staff indsl. engr. ALCOA, 1954-57; financial analyst Tex. Instruments, Inc., 1959-61; v.p. Schroder Rockefeller Co., Inc., 1961-67; v.p. fin., treas. Am. Greetings Corp., 1967-78; v.p. fin. The Lionel Corp., N.Y.C., 1978-82; with Gibson Greeting Cards Co., Cin., 1982—. Served with AUS, 1952-54. Recipient N.Y. State Regents Vets. scholarship, 1957. Mem. Financial Execs. Inst. Clubs: Union League (N.Y.C.); Wharton Graduate. Home: 6800 Hammerstone Way Cincinnati OH 45227 Office: 2100 Section Rd Cincinnati OH 45237

CAVANAUGH, WILLIAM THOMAS, assn. exec.; b. Newark, Apr. 24, 1921; s. Daniel John and Anna E. (McGotty) C.; m. Elizabeth Louise McCann, June 24, 1950; children—Mary (Mrs. Ralph Bloom), Dennis, Elizabeth, William, Peter. B.S., Seton Hall U., 1942; postgrad., Columbia, 1947-50. Instr., asst. prof. Seton Hall U., 1947-50; asst. exec. dir. Engrs. Joint Council, N.Y.C., 1953-56; exec. dir. Engring. Manpower Commn., N.Y.C., exec. dir., sec., 1956-59; Adminstrv. Mgmt. Soc., Willow Grove, Pa., 1959-66; exec. dir. Met. Package Stores Assn., N.Y.C., 1966-67; dir. field operations Am. Soc. Testing Materials, Phila., 1967-68, dep. mng. dir., 1968-70, mng. dir., 1970—, pres., 1980—; Mem. council, mem. exec. standards council Am. Nat. Standards Inst. Served to lt. comdr. USNR, 1942-46; to comdr., 1950-53. Mem. Am. Soc. Assn. Execs., United Bus. Schs. Assn. (nat. hon. life), Council Engring. and Sci. Soc. Execs. (exec. com.). Home: PO Box 127 Warrington PA 18976 Office: 1916 Race St Philadelphia PA 19103

CAVAZOS, RICHARD E., army general. Commander U.S. Army Forces Command, Fort McPherson, Ga. Office: CG USH FORSCOM Ft. McPherson GA 30330

CAVE, ALFRED ALEXANDER, coll. dean; b. Albuquerque, Feb. 8, 1935; s. Robert L. and Jane (Harscher);; s. Robert L. and Jane (Cave); m. Mary Sue Deisher, May 26, 1978; children—Ruth, Laurence, Elizabeth, Rachel. B.A., Linfield Coll., 1957; M.A., U. Fla., 1959, Ph.D., 1961. Instr. U. Fla., 1959-61, Coll. City N.Y., 1961-62; asst. prof. U. Utah, Salt Lake City, 1962-66, asso. prof., 1966-68, prof. history, 1968—, honors dir., 1965-67; asso. dean Coll. Letters and Sci., 1967-68, dean for humanities, 1968-70; dean Coll. Humanities, 1970-73, Coll. Arts and Scis., U. Toledo, 1973—. Author: Jacksonian Democracy and the Historians, 1964, American Civilization: a Documentary History, 1966, An American Conservative in the Age of Jackson, 1969. Mem. Orgn. Am. Historians, Phi Beta Kappa. Office: Univ Toledo Toledo OH 43606

CAVE, EDWARD LEE, realty company executive; b. Washington, Aug. 5, 1939; s. Edward Francis and Anne (Culliane) C. B.A., Columbia U., 1963. Head decorative arts dept. Sotheby Parke Bernet, N.Y.C., 1969-72, sr. v.p., 1972—; chmn. Sotheby's Internat. Realty Corp. N.Y.C., 1978-82; pres. Edward Lee Cave, Inc., N.Y.C., 1982—. Clubs: Metropolitan (Washington); The Travellers (Paris). Captains Farm Union CT 06076 Office: 33 E 68th St New York NY 10021

CAVE, JOHN BARNHARDT, corporate officer; b. Salisbury, N.C., Aug. 9, 1929; s. J. Russell and Sarah E. (Barnhardt) C.; m. Deborah Rugg, Nov. 12, 1955; children—Cynthia Barnhardt, Charles Russell, Elizabeth Rugg. B.S., The Citadel, 1950; M.B.A., Harvard, 1955. With Burlington Industries, Inc., 1955-71, treas., 1962-69, v.p., 1965, financial v.p., dir., 1969-71; sr. v.p. White, Weld & Co., Inc., N.Y.C., 1971-74; v.p. finance, treas. Schering-Plough Corp., Kenilworth, N.J., 1974-76, sr. v.p. fin. and adminstrn., 1976-78, sr. v.p. fin., 1977-80; exec. v.p. fin. McGraw-Hill, Inc., N.Y.C., 1980—, also dir.; dir. McGraw-Hill Ryerson Ltd., Scarborough, Ont., Can., Summit and Elizabeth Trust Co. (N.J.), Crompton Co. Inc. Trustee Com. for Econ. Devel. Club: University (N.Y.C.). Home: 113 Whittredge Rd Summit NJ 07901 Office: New York NY

CAVE, MAC DONALD, anatomy educator; b. Phila., May 14, 1939; s. Edward Joseph and Adeline Roberta (MacDonald) C.; div.; children: Eric MacDonald, Heidi Lee. B.A., Susquehanna U., 1961; M.S., U. Ill., 1963, Ph.D., 1965. Instr. dept. anatomy U. Ill. Coll. Medicine, Chgo., 1964-65; asst. prof. U. Pitts. Sch. Medicine, 1967-72; assoc. prof. anatomy U. Ark. Med. Ctr., Little Rock, 1972-79, prof. anatomy, 1979—. Contbr. numerous articles to profl. jours. Am. Cancer Soc.-Swedish Am. exchange fellow, 1966; USPHS postdoctoral fellow Max Planck Inst., Tubingen, W. Ger., 1966-67. Mem. Am. Assn. Anatomists, Am. Soc. Cell Biology, AAAS, Sigma Xi, Pi Gamma Mu. Home: 11143 Bainbridge St Little Rock AR 72212 Office: Dept Anatony U Ark Med Scis 4301 W Markham Little Rock AR 72205

CAVE, RAY, editor. B.A., St. John's Coll., 1949. Asst. city editor, reporter Baltimore Sun, 1952-59; staff writer Sports Illustrated, 1959-62, sr. editor, 1962-70, asst. mng. editor, 1970-74, exec. editor, 1974-75; acting editorial dir. Time Inc., 1975; exec. editor Sports Illustrated, 1976-77; mng. editor Time, 1977. Office: 1271 Ave of the Americas New York NY 10020 *

CAVENY, ELMER LEONARD, physician; b. Kings Mountain, N.C., May 26, 1907; s. Lebanus High and Lydia (Sarratt);; s. Lebanus High and Lydia (Caveny); m. Dorothy Franklin, June 4, 1930; 1 son, Leonard Hugh. M.D., Emory U., 1930. Diplomate: Am. Bd. Psychiatry, Am. Bd. Preventive Medicine. Commd. lt. (j.g.) M.C. USN, 1930, advanced through grades to capt., 1945; specialist psychiatry, 1938—; postgrad. tng. psychiatry Pa. Hosp. and Inst., Phila. Naval Hosp., 1938-41; head psychiatry br. Naval Sch. Aviation Medicine, 1944-47; psychoanalytic tng. Phila. Inst., 1947-52; chief neuropsychiat. center Naval Hosp., Phila., 1948-51; asst. prof. psychiatry Woman's Med. Coll., Phila., 1948-51; head neuropsychiat. service Naval Med. Center, Bethesda, Md., 1951-53; head neuropsychiatry br. Bur. Medicine and Surgery, Navy Dept., 1953-54; clin. prof. psychiatry Georgetown U., 1953-54; prof. psychiatry U. Ala. Med. Coll., 1955—, chmn. dept., 1955-59. Contbr. profl. articles. Fellow Am. Psychiat. Assn., A.C.P.; mem. A.M.A., Group for Advancement Psychiatry, Am. Psychoanalytic Assn., Assn. So. Psychiat. Prof. (pres. 1958-59). Address: 3516 Robin Dr Mountain Brook Birmingham AL 35223

CAVERLY, GARDNER A., foundation executive; b. Tuftonboro, N.H., Aug. 2, 1910; s. Arthur L. and Emma (Lamprey) C.; (div.)Children: Martha, Jon Christian, Jefferson Smith, Nathaniel Eaton, James R., Douglas G. B.S., Northeastern U., 1934; postgrad., Harvard U., 1938; LL.D., Nasson Coll., 1973. With Bond & Goodwin Inc., Boston, 1935-38; pres. Sargent-Roundy Corp., Randolph, Vt., 1939-45; with Tucker Anthony & Co., N.Y.C., 1941-44; reorgn. mgr. Rutland R.R., 1949-50, trustee, dir., 1950-57, sr. v.p., 1951-54, pres., 1954-57; exec. v.p. New Eng. Council, Boston, 1957-66; pres. Crotched Mountain Found., Greenfield, N.H., 1967-73, chmn., 1973-83; Chmn. N.H. Comprehensive Health Planning Council, 1968-71; mem. corp. Joslin Diabetes Found., Boston; former mem. corp. Northeastern U. Named hon. lt. col. R.I. State Police. Mem. Order DeMolay, Legion of Honor. Clubs: Harvard (Boston); Harvard Faculty (Cambridge); Ivy League (Sarasota, Fla.). Home: Box 74 New Boston NH 03070 also Crotched Mountain Found Greenfield NH 03047

CAVERT, HENRY MEAD, physician, educator; b. Mpls., Mar. 30, 1922; s. William Lane and Mary (Mead) C.; m. June Lorraine Sederstrom, Jan. 27, 1946; children: John Mead (dec.), Harlan McCrea, Winston Peter. B.S. in Agrl. Biochemistry, U. Minn., 1942, M.D., 1951, Ph.D. in Physiology, 1952. Postdoctoral research fellow Am. Heart Assn., 1951-54; faculty U. Minn. Med. Sch., 1953—, prof. physiology, 1967—, asso. dean, 1964—, prin. investigator Gen. Clin. Research Ctr., 1978—; Nat. Heart Inst. spl. research fellow and vis. prof. biochemistry U. Edinburgh, Scotland, 1961-62; established investigator Am. Heart Assn., 1954-57; mem. program project com. B, Nat. Heart Inst., 1966-69; cons. Nat. Heart and Lung Inst., 1969—. Author: (with A.J. Carlson and V. Johnson) Machinery of the Body, 5th edit., 1961; also numerous articles. Mem. bd. parish edn. Am. Luth. Ch., 1958-72; mem. met. bd. Mpls. YMCA, 1968-70; bd. mgmt. U. Minn. YMCA, 1955-75, 77-83, chmn., 1968-70; trustee Minn. Med. Found., 1958—, chmn. scholarship and loan com., 1960-68, chmn. honors and awards com., 1970-76. Served to capt. USAAF, 1943-46; CBI. Mem. Assn. Am. Med. Colls. (chmn. com. student aspects internat. med. edn. 1966-68, mem. steering com. group on student affairs 1967-68, mem. com. internat. relations med. edn. 1968-75), Am. Physiol. Soc., AMA, Sigma Xi, Phi Lambda Upsilon, Alpha Omega Alpha, Gamma Sigma Delta. Home: 3328 48th Ave S Minneapolis MN 55406

CAVES, RICHARD EARL, educator, economist; b. Akron, Ohio, Nov. 1, 1931; s. Earl Leroy and Verna Louise (Jobes) C. A.B., Oberlin Coll., 1953; M.A., Harvard, 1956, Ph.D. (Wells prize 1958), 1958. Asst. prof., asso. prof. econs. U. Calif. at Berkeley, 1957-62; prof. econs. Harvard, 1962—, chmn. dept. econs., 1966-69; Cons. Council Econ. Advisers, 1961; dep. to spl. asst. to Pres. U.S. for fgn. trade policy, 1961; cons. Treasury Dept., 1961-62, Bur. Budget, 1963-64; mem. White House Task Force on Fgn. Econ. Policy. Author: (with R.H. Holton) The Canadian Economy: Prospect and Retrospect, 1959, Trade and Economic Structure, 1960, Air Transport and Its Regulators, 1962, American Industry: Structure, Conduct, Performance, 1964, (with J.S. Bain, J. Margolis) Northern California's Water Industry, 1966, (with others) Britain's Economic Prospects, 1968, (with G.L. Reuber) Capital Transfers and Economic Policy: Canada, 1951-62, 1971, (with R.W. Jones) World Trade and Payments, 1973, (with M.J. Roberts) Regulating the Product: Quality and Variety, 1974, (with M. Uekusa) Industrial Organization in Japan, 1976, (with M.E. Porter and M. Spence) Competition in the Open Economy: A Model Applied to Canada, 1980, (with others) Britain's Economic Performance, 1980, Multinational Enterprise and Economic Analysis, 1982; contbr. numerous articles to profl. jours. Recipient Henderson prize Harvard Law Sch., 1967; Ford Found. fellow, 1959-60. Fellow Am. Acad. Arts and Scis.; mem. Am. Econ. Assn. Home: 24 Agassiz St Cambridge MA 02140

CAVETT, DICK, entertainer; b. Gibbon, Nebr., 1936; s. A.B. Cavett; m. Carrie Nye. Grad., Yale U. Former TV comedy writer, then night club performer; host: TV show This Morning, until 1969, Dick Cavett Show, ABC-TV, after 1969, Dick Cavett Show, Pub. Broadcasting Service, 1977-82; occasional host: also spls. ABC Wide World of Entertainment, Pub. Broadcasting Service. (Recipient Emmy award 1972); Author: (with Christopher Porterfield) Cavett, 1974, Eye on Cavett, 1983. Address: Daphne Prodns 228 W 55th St New York NY 10019

CAVIN, F. G., banking exec.; b. McKenzie, Tenn., Sept. 28, 1930; m. Sally Thornton; children—Virginia, Sarah, John, Carol. B.S. in Agr, U. Tenn., Martin. With Martin Bank, to 1968; exec. v.p. Farmers Exchange Bank (became affiliate First Amtenn Corp., holding co. 1973), Union City, Tenn., 1968-71, pres., 1971-74; exec. v.p. First Amtenn Corp., Nashville, 1974-76, vice chmn., 1979, pres., 1979; exec. v.p. in charge of banking adminstrn. First Am. Bank, First Amtenn Corp. lead bank, Nashville, 1976, vice chmn. bd., 1979. Chmn. Tenn. Indsl. Devel. Authority, 1972-78; chmn. adminstrv. bd. Brentwood United Methodist Ch. Clubs: Corinthian Lodge, Masons, Shriners. Office: First Amtenn Corp First American Center Nashville TN 37237

CAVIN, WILLIAM PINCKNEY, chemist, educator; b. Spartanburg, S.C., June 2, 1925; s. Hugh W. and Marie N. (Wright) C.; m. Martha Louise Duckworth, June 17, 1950; children—William P., Carole. B.S., Wofford Coll., 1945; M.A., Duke, 1946; Ph.D., U. N.C., 1953. Instr. chemistry Wofford Coll., Spartanburg, S.C., 1946-48, asst. prof., 1948-53, asso. prof., 1953-56, prof., 1956-62, John M. Reeves prof. chemistry, 1962—, chmn. dept., 1971—; vis. prof. Brown U., 1965-66. Bd. dirs. Spartanburg County unit Am. Cancer Soc., treas., 1971-72. NSF fellow, 1951-52, 65-66. Mem. Am. Chem. Soc., S.C. Acad. Sci., Phi Beta Kappa, Sigma Xi. Methodist. Home: 704 Perrin Dr Spartanburg SC 29302 Office: Dept Chemistry Wofford Coll Spartanburg SC 29301

CAVIOR, WARREN JOSEPH, communications exec.; b. Boston, Sept. 18, 1929; s. Joel H. and Shirley (Miller) C.; m. Mariko Sanjo, Oct. 12, 1969; children—Mayu, Samuel. A.B. cum laude, Harvard, 1951; M.A., Columbia, 1952; postgrad., Oxford U., 1952-53. Asso. editor Forbes Mag., 1956-59; pres. Wall Street Consultants, Inc., N.Y.C., 1959-62, Warren J. Cavior & Co., 1962-67; chmn. bd. Universal Communications Inc., N.Y.C., 1967-74; exec. v.p. Rogers, Cowan & Taplinger, Inc., N.Y.C., 1974-76; sr. v.p. Rogers & Cowan, Inc., N.Y.C., 1976-81; pres. Cavior Orgn., Inc., 1981—; treas., dir. Wako Internat. Corp., 1962-67. Adv. bd.: Present Tense Mag. Chmn. Cavior Found., 1968—. Mem. Am. C. of C. in Japan. Home: 2 Fifth Ave New York NY 10011 Office: 60 E 42d St New York NY 10165

CAWL, FRANKLIN ROBERT, JR., mktg. cons.; b. Phila., Dec. 6, 1920; s. Franklin Robert and Abigail (Pretlow) C.; m. Florence Rainsford, June 15, 1946; children—Annette Susan, Jeannette Florence. B.S., U. Pa., 1942, M.A., 1948. Instr. mktg. Wharton Sch., U. Pa., 1946-48; with plans dept. Hearst Advt. Service, N.Y.C., 1948-56; instr. mktg. Rutgers U., 1948-56; v.p., dir. mktg. Outdoor Advt., Inc., N.Y.C., 1956-61, Million Market Newspapers, 1961-65; pres. Inst. Outdoor Advt., 1965-71, Outdoor Advt. Assn. Am., N.Y.C., 1971-78; mktg. cons., 1978-79; pres. F.R. Cawl & Assos., Inc., Searsport, Maine and N.Y.C., 1980—; dir. Advt. Council; dir., mem. exec. com. Outdoor Advt. Assn. Am. Chmn. bd. Four Winds Hosp. Served with AUS, 1942-46. Mem. Sales Execs. Club, Am. Mktg. Assn., Am. Soc. Assn. Execs., Sigma Phi Epsilon. Club: Waccabuc Country. Home: E Main St Searsport ME 04974 Office: PO Box 79 Searsport ME 04974

CAWLEY, EDWARD PHILIP, physician, educator; b. Jackson, Mich., Sept. 1, 1912; s. Michael and Gertrude (Klein) C.; m. Virginia Anne Cohen, June 17, 1939; children—Janet Anne, Philip Edward. A.B., U. Mich., 1936, M.D., 1940. Diplomate: Am. Bd. Dermatology (pres., dir.). Intern Mercy Hosp., Jackson, 1940-42; teaching fellow, instr. dermatology and syphilology Med. Sch., U. Mich., 1945-48, asst. prof., 1948-51; prof., chmn. dept. dermatology and syphilology Sch. Medicine, U. Va., Charlottesville, 1951—, Disting. prof., 1977; practice medicine, specializing in dermatology and syphilology, Charlottesville, 1951—. Contbr. articles to med. jours. Served from 1st lt. to maj. M.C. AUS, 1942-45. Decorated Bronze Star. Fellow A.C.P.; mem. Assn. Profs. Dermatology (pres.), Am. Dermatol. Assn. (pres., dir.), A.M.A., Va., Albemarle County med. socs., Am. Acad. Dermatology (pres.), Soc. for Investigative Dermatology, Chgo. Dermatology Soc., Balt.-Washington, Southeastern dermatol. socs., So. Med. Assn., Am. Soc. Dermatopathology (pres., dir.), Sigma Xi, Alpha Omega Alpha. Roman Catholic. Club: Farmington Country (Charlottesville). Investigative and research work in skin diseases, fungus diseases, cancer of skin and dermatopathology. Home: Rugby Circle Charlottesville VA 22903 Office: U of Va Hosp Charlottesville VA 22908

CAWOOD, HOBART GUY, national park adminstrator; b. Jonesville, Va., June 15, 1935; s. George Pope and Eula (Graham) C.; m. Shirley Ann Flanary, Dec. 22, 1956 (div. Oct. 1976); 1 son, Stephen Andrew; m. Adelaide Louise Wahlert, Sept. 10, 1977. B.A., Emory and Henry Coll., Emory, Va., 1957; L.H.D. hon., Pa. Coll. Podiatric Medicine, 1980. With Nat. Park Service, 1958—; historian Cumberland Gap Nat. Hist. Park, 1958-60, Ft. Frederica Nat. Monument, 1960-61; supervisory historian Ft. Sumter Nat. Monument, 1961-62, Castillo de San Marcos Nat. Monument, 1962-63, Chickamauga and Chattanooga Nat. Mil. Park, 1963-67; park planner Washington Service Ctr., 1967-69; supt. Richmond Nat. Battlefield, Va., 1969-71, Independence Nat. Hist. Park, Phila., 1971—. Bd. dirs. Greater Phila. Cultural Alliance, Phila. Council for Internat. Visitors, Phila. Conv. and Visitor Bur., 1977-83. Served with USAR, 1958-64. Recipient award for excellence of service Dept. Interior, 1971, 250th Anniversary medal Carpenters' Co., 1976, KC Cardinal Dougherty, 1976, Man of Yr. Chestnut St. Assn., 1976, Legion of Honor Chapel of Four Chaplains, 1976; citation for assistance with visit by Pres. France Pa. Legislature, 1976; recipient Hist. St. George's Gold medal St. George's United Meth. Ch., 1976, Bicentennial PA Soc. DAR, 1976, Unit Dept. Interior, 1977, Phila. Bowl Colonial Phila. Hist. Soc., 1977, Greater Am. Achievements Bicentennial Countil of Original 13 States, 1977, Honor award for Meritorious Service Dept. Interior, 1977, Disting. Service Phila. Flag Day Assn., 1978, Gold medal King of Sweden, 1980, Disting. Service Am. Legion Dept. Fla., 1980, Achievement Communications Charles Morris Price Sch. Journalism, 1983; named Alumnus of Yr. Emory and Henry Coll., 1977. Democrat. Methodist. Office: Independence Nat Hist Park 313 Walnut St Philadelphia PA 19106

CAWS, MARY ANN, educator, critic; b. Wilmington, N.C., Sept. 10, 1933; d. Harmon Chadbourn and Margaret Devereux (Lippitt) Rorison; m. Peter Caws, June 2, 1956; children: Matthew, Hilary. B.A., Bryn Mawr Coll., 1954; M.A., Yale U., 1956; Ph.D., U. Kans., 1962; D.Humane Letters, Union Coll., 1983. Asst. instr. Romance Langs. U. Kans., 1957-62, asst. editor univ. press, 1957-58, vis. asst. prof., spring 1963; lectr. Barnard Coll., 1962-63; mem. faculty Sarah Lawrence Coll., 1963-64, Hunter Coll., N.Y.C., 1966—, prof., 1969—; exec. officer comparative lit. program CUNY Grad. Ctr., 1977-79, exec. officer French program, 1979—, Disting. prof. French and comparative lit., 1983—; Phi Beta Kappa vis. scholar, 1982-83. Author 20 books in field; contbr. articles to profl. jours.; editor: Dada-Surrealism, 1972, Le Siecle eclate, 1974. Decorated officer Palmes Academiques, France; fellow Guggenheim Found., 1972-73, Nat. Endowment Humanities, 1979-80; Fulbright traveling fellow, 1972-73. Mem. MLA (exec. council 1973-77, v.p. 1982-83, pres. 1983-84), Am. Assn. Tchrs. French, Internat. Assn. Philosophy and Lit. (exec. bd. 1982—), Am. Comparative Lit. Assn. (exec. com. 1981—). Home: 140 E 81st St New York NY 10028 Office: CUNY Grad Ctr 33 W 42d St New York NY 10036 *With the general intention of doing as many things as possible which seem to me of value, I would opt for flexibility over perfection and for a multifaceted approach over a linear one, but without sacrificing the passionate commitment to teaching and criticism in which I most vitally believe.*

CAWS, PETER JAMES, philosophy educator; b. Southall, Eng., May 25, 1931; came to U.S., 1953; s. Geoffrey Tulloh and Olive (Budden) C.; m. Mary Ann Rorison, June 2, 1956; children: Hilary, Matthew. B.S., U. London, 1952; M.A., Yale U., 1954, Ph.D., 1956. Instr. natural sci. Mich. State U., 1956-57; asst. prof. philosophy U. Kans., 1957-60, asso. prof., 1960-62, chmn. dept., 1961-62, Rose Morgan vis. prof., 1963; vis. prof. U. Costa Rica, 1961; exec. asso. Carnegie Corp. N.Y., 1962-65, cons., 1965-67; prof. philosophy Hunter Coll., N.Y.C., 1965-82, chmn. dept., 1965-67; exec. officer Ph.D. program in philosophy CUNY, 1967-70, 81-82; Univ. prof. philosophy George Washington U., 1982—; tchr. New Sch. Social Research, 1965-67; mem. adv. bd. Learning Corp. of Am., 1968-74; editorial bd. Philosophy Documentation Center, 1969—; mem. Council Philos. Studies, 1965-71; bd. dirs. Coordinating Council of Lit. Mags., 1969-70; mem. Scientists Inst. for Pub. Info., 1967—, treas., 1969-72, fellow, 1972—, dir., 1975-80, vice chmn., 1975-79; mem. editorial bd. Environment, 1972-78; mem. bd. advisers, history of physics program Am. Inst. Physics, 1966-75; mem. NRC, 1967-70, Assembly Behavioral and Social Scis., 1973-77; nat. lectr. Sigma Xi, 1975-77; dir. Bicentennial Symposium of Philosophy; cons. in humanities LWV, 1978; vis. scholar Phi Beta Kappa, 1983-84. Author: The Philosophy of Science, Systematic Account, 1965, Science and the Theory of Value, 1967, Sartre, 1979; editor: Two Centuries of Philosophy in America, 1980; editorial bd.: Jour. Enterprise Mgmt, 1976—. Am. Council Learned Socs. fellow, Paris, 1972-73; Rockefeller Found. humanities fellow, 1979-80. Fellow AAAS (v.p. 1967); mem. Am. Philos. Assn. (dir., chmn. com. on internat. cooperation 1974—), Fedn. Internat. des Socs. de Philosophie (commn. on policy 1973—, chmn. 1979—, comité dir. 1978—), Philosophy of Sci. Assn. (del.), Soc. Gen. Systems Research (pres. 1966-67). Club: Elizabethan. Home: 140 E 81st St New York NY 10028

CAWTHON, WILLIAM CONNELL, telecommunications company executive; b. Roxton, Tex., Sept. 1, 1922; s. William Arthur and Lura (Denton) C.; m. Flora Keith Campbell, May 31, 1947; children: William Connell, Clark Campbell, Flora Keith. B.M.E., Cornell U., 1944; M.S.M.E., U. Tex., 1947; M. Automotive Engring., Chrysler Inst., Detroit, 1949. Mfg. exec. Chrysler Corp., Detroit, 1955-59, dir. purchasing, 1959-62; v.p. mfg. Am. Standard Corp., N.Y.C., 1962-66; v.p., dir. indsl. engring. and mfg. worldwide ITT, N.Y.C., 1966-68; exec. v.p. Weatherhead Co., Cleve., 1968-70; prin. William C. Cawthon (cons.), Hudson, Ohio, 1970-72; v.p., gen. mgr. parts div., textile machinery div. Rockwell Internat., Hopedale, Mass., 1972-73; v.p. mfg. No Telecom Ltd. (former No. Electric Co., Ltd.), Montreal, Que., Can., 1973-77, No. Telecom Inc., Nashville, 1973-80, v.p. ops., 1980—; mem. chancellor's council U. Tex. Served to lt. comdr. USNR, 1945-46, 51-53; PTO, Korea. Named Distinguished Grad. U. Tex., 1961. Mem. Newcomen Soc. Republican. Mem. Ch. of Christ. Club: Cornell of N.Y.C. Home: 1024 Lynwood Blvd Nashville TN 37215 Office: 259 Cumberland Bend Nashville TN 37228 *If I have made the places I have worked better places to work, and the places I have lived better places to live, I would suppose that would be success.*

CAWTHORN, ROBERT ELSTON, health care executive; b. Masham, Eng., Sept. 28, 1935; came to U.S., 1982; s. Gerald P. and Gertrude E. (Longster) C.; m. H. Susan Marshall, Jan. 15, 1960; children: Amanda, Liza. B.A., Cambridge U., 1959. Exec. v.p. Rorer Group, Inc., Fort Washington, Pa., 1982—; dir. Cytogen Corp., Princeton, N.J., 1983—. Served to lt. Brit. Army, 1954-56. Home: 50 Crosby Brown Rd Gladwyne PA 19035 Office: Rorer Group Inc 500 Virginia Dr Fort Washington PA 19034

CAWTHORNE, KENNETH CLIFFORD, fragrance manufacturing company executive; b. Manistee, Mich., Feb. 13, 1936; s. Clifford Haney and Marie Dorothy (Schimke) C.; m. Martha S. Zielinski, Aug. 23, 1958; children—Steven, Daniel, Cynthia, Thomas. B.S. cum laude, Central Mich. U., 1958. Lic. real estate broker, Ill. Sr. acct. Ernst & Ernst (C.P.A.), Grand Rapids, Mich., 1958-62; controller Grand Rapids Sash and Door Co., 1962-67, Melling Forging Co., Lansing, Mich., 1968-72; v.p. fin. Jovan, Inc., Chgo., 1973—. Mem. Am. Inst. C.P.A.'s, Nat. Assn. Accts. Home: 503 W Haven Dr Arlington Heights IL 60005 Office: 980 N Michigan Ave Chicago IL 60611

CAYNE, BERNARD STANLEY, editor; b. N.Y.C., Nov. 8, 1924; m. Helen M. Burgard, Apr. 11, 1953; children—Claudia Elizabeth, Douglas Andrew. Student, Cornell U., 1940-42; B.S., Moravian Coll., 1945; postgrad., U. Pa., 1945-46; research fellow, Harvard U., 1953-55; M.A., Columbia U., 1947. Head sci. dept. Adelphi Acad., 1946-47; instr. Bklyn. Coll., 1947-49; tchr. N.Y.C. Pub. Schs., 1948-49; head sci. sect., test devel. dept. Ednl. Testing Service, Princeton, N.J., 1949-53; dir. research Boston U. Coll. Basic Studies, 1953-54; sr. sci. editor Ginn & Co., Boston, 1955-61; v.p. Crowell-Collier Ednl. Corp., N.Y.C., 1961-68; exec. editor Collier's Ency., 1963-68, Collier's Ency. Yearbook, 1963-68; editor-in-chief Merit Students Ency., 1961-69, asst. editorial dir. corp., 1963-68; mng. editor, sch. div. Macmillan Co., 1968-69; editor-in-chief Ency. Americana, Danbury, Conn., 1969—; v.p., editorial dir. Grolier, Inc., Danbury, 1980—. Chmn. bd. editors: Harvard Edn. Rev, 1954. Fellow AAAS; mem. N.Y. Acad. Scis., Am Ednl. Research Assn., Phi Delta Kappa. Home: Snark Haven Route 2 Box C-297 Sandy Hook CT 06482 Office: Old Sherman Turnpike Danbury CT 06816

CAYO, RONALD JEAN, movie production company executive; b. Benton Harbor, Mich., Mar. 7, 1933; s. Howard M. and Elizabeth (Kulich) C.; m. Elizabeth French, Apr. 27, 1963; children: Melissa, Alison. B.A., U. Mich., 1955, J.D., 1958. Bar: Mich. 1958, N.Y. 1961, Calif. 1970. Atty. Donovan Leisure Newton & Irvine, N.Y.C., 1958, 60-69; staff atty. legal dept. Walt Disney Prodns., Burbank, Calif., 1969-74, v.p. bus. affairs, 1974-80, sr. v.p. bus. affairs, 1980-82, exec. v.p. bus. and legal affairs, 1982—. Bd. dirs. Big Brothers of Greater Los Angeles. Served with AUS, 1958-60. Mem. ABA, State Bar Calif., Los Angeles County Bar Assn., Order of Coif. Home: 1423 Wembly Rd San Marino CA 91108 Office: Walt Disney Prodns 500 S Buena Vista St Burbank CA 91521

CAZDEN, COURTNEY B(ORDEN), educator; b. Chgo., Nov. 30, 1925; d. John and Courtney (Letts) Borden Adams; m. Norman Cazden (div. 1971); children: Elizabeth, Joanna. B.A., Radcliffe Coll., 1946; M.Ed., U. Ill., 1953; Ed.D., Harvard U., 1965. Elem. tchr. pub. schs., N.Y., Conn., Calif., 1947-48, 54-61, 74-75; asst. prof. edn. Harvard U., Cambridge, Mass., 1965-68, assoc. prof., 1968-71, prof., 1971—; vis. prof. U. N.Mex., summer 1980, U. Alaska, Fairbanks, summer 1982, U. Auckland, N.Z., spring 1983; chairperson bd. trustees Ctr. Applied Linguistics, Washington, 1981—. Author: Child

Language and Education, 1972; co-editor: Functions of Language in the Classroon, 1972; editor: Language in Early Childhood Education, rev. edit., 1981. Trustee Highlander Ednl. and Research Ctr., New Market, Tenn., 1982—; bd. dirs. Feminist Press, Old Westbury, N.Y., 1982—; asst. clk. New Eng. regional office Am. Friends Service Com., Cambridge, 1983—. Fellow Ctr. Advanced Study in Behavioral Scis., Stanford, Calif., 1978-79. Mem. Council on Anthropology and Edn. (pres. 1981), Am. Ednl. Research Assn. (exec. com. 1981—), Am. Assn. Applied Linguistics (pres.-elect). Quaker. Office: Harvard U Grad Sch Edn Appian Way Cambridge MA 02138

CAZIER, STANFORD, university president; b. Nephi, Utah, June 11, 1930; m. Shirley Anderson, 1952; children: David, John, Paul. B.S. in Philosophy, U. Utah, 1952, M.A. in History, 1956, Ph.D., U. Wis., 1964. Reader, U. Utah, 1954-56; teaching asst. U. Wis., 1957-58, research asst., 1959; instr. Bronx Community Coll., 1959-60; mem. faculty Utah State U., 1960-71, instr., 1960-62, asst. prof. history, 1962-67, asso. prof., 1968-69, prof., 1969-71, asst. to pres., 1968-69, chmn. dept. history, 1969, vice provost, 1969-71; Am. Council on Edn. fellow in acad. adminstrn. NYU, 1967-68; pres. Calif. State U., Chico, 1971-79, Utah State U., Logan, 1979—; chmn. council of pres. Calif. State Univs. and Colls., 1978-79, mem. exec. com. council pres., 1976-79. Contbr. articles to profl. publs.; author: Student Discipline in Higher Education, 1973; also articles; bibliography editor history div.: Am. Quar., 1968-71. Served as ensign USN, 1952-53. Named Tchr. of Year, Robin's award, 1966; Danforth Found. asso., 1966—. Mem. Am. Assn. Higher Edn., Nat. Assn. Colls. and Univs., Soc. Coll. and Univ. Planning, Phi Kappa Phi, Phi Alpha Theta. Office: Office of Pres Utah State U Logan UT 84322

CAZORT, MIMI, museum curator. B.F.A., Washington U., St. Louis, 1953; M.A., U. Mich., 1961, Ph.D., 1971. Mem. curatorial staff Nat. Gallery Can., Ottawa, 1967—; now curator drawings; tchr. history of drawings Carleton U.; mem. Internat. Adv. Com. Keepers Public Graphic Collections. Co-author: Bolognese Drawings in North American Collections, 1981; contbg. author: Settecento emiliano: La pittura, L'Academia Clementina, 1979. Can. Council grantee. Mem. Print Council Am. Home: 91 Concord St N Ottawa ON Canada Office: Nat Gallery Can Lorne Bldg Elgin St Ottawa ON Canada K1A 0M8

CEBRA, JOHN JOSEPH, biologist, educator; b. Phila., May 7, 1934; s. John and Jennie (Baran) C.; m. Ethel Reisse, June 15, 1956; children—Judith, Jonathan, Daniel, Christopher. A.B., U. Pa., 1955; Ph.D., Rockefeller U., 1960. Fellow Nat. Found., Weizmann Inst. Sci., Rehovoth, Israel, 1960-61; from instr. to asso. prof. microbiology U. Fla. Coll. Medicine, 1961-66; vis. fellow Wright-Fleming Inst., St. Mary's Hosp., London, 1966-67; mem. faculty Johns Hopkins U., 1967-80, prof. biology, 1969-80; Annenberg prof. natural scis., chmn. dept. biology U. Pa., 1980—. Author articles, chpts. in books. Mem. Am. Assn. Immunologists, Am. Soc. Microbiology, AAAS. Address: 211 Kaplan Wing G/7 U Pa Philadelphia PA 19104

CECCHETTI, GIOVANNI, author, educator, literary critic; b. Pescia, Italy, July 12, 1922; came to U.S., 1948, naturalized, 1954; s. Agostino and Adorna (Fattorini) C.; m. Ruth Elizabeth Schwabacher, Dec. 27, 1953; children: Stephen G., Margaret F. Liceo Machiavelli, Lucca, 1939-40; Liceo Dante, Florence, Italy, 1940-41; Maturità classica, Florence, Italy, 1941; Lit.D., U. Florence, 1947. Lectr. to asst. prof. U. Calif. at Berkeley, 1948-57; asso. prof., prof. Tulane U., 1957-65; prof. Stanford U., 1965-69, charge Italian program, 1965-69; prof. UCLA, 1969—, chmn. dept. Italian, 1969-77; cons. U. Colo., U. Iowa, 1957. Author: La poesia del Pascoli, 1954, G. Verga, The She-Wolf and other stories, 1958, rev., 1973, Leopardi e Verga, 1962, Diario nomade, 1967, Il Verga maggiore, 1968, 73, 75, Impossible scendere, 1978, Giovanni Verga, a critical monograph, 1978, Le Operette morali, Tre studi con un poscritto sui Canti, 1979, G. Verga, Mastró-don Gesualdo, 1979, Il villaggio degli inutili, 1980, Nel cammino dei monti, 1980, G. Leopardi, Operette morali/Dialogues and Essays, 1982, Spuntature e intermezzi, 1983, La danza del deserto, 1984; asso. editor: Forum Italicum; contbr. essays and poems to European and Am. jours. Served with Italian Liberation Army, 1943-45. Decorated Star of Solidarity Italian Govt., knight and cavaliere ufficiale, Presdl. gold medal for spl. cultural and artistic merits Republic of Italy. Mem. Modern Lang. Assn. Am., Am. Assn. Tchrs. Italian, Dante Soc. Am., Leonardo Da Vinci Soc., Patrons of Italian Culture. Home: 1191 Lachman Ln Pacific Palisades CA 90272 Office: Dept Italian U Calif Los Angeles CA 90024

CECI, JESSE ARTHUR, violinist; b. Phila., Feb. 2, 1924; s. Luigi Concezio and Catherine Marie (Marotta) C.; m. Catherine Annette Stevens, Aug. 5, 1979. B.S., Juilliard Sch. Music, 1951; license de conncert, L'Ecole Normale de Musique, Paris, 1952; Mus.M., Manhattan Sch. Music, 1971. Assoc. concertmaster New Orleans Philharmonic Orch., 1953-54; violinist Boston Symphony Orch., 1954-59, N.Y. Philharmonic Orch., N.Y., 1959-62, Esterhazy Orch., N.Y.C., 1962-68; concertmaster Denver Symphony Orch., 1974—; mem. faculty N.Y. Coll. Music, 1961-71, N.Y. U., 1961-71; mem. Zimbler Sinfonietta, Boston, 1957-59; participant Marlboro Festival, Vt., summmers 1960-62, 65, participant European tour., 1965; mem., assoc. concertmaster Casals Festival Orch., San Juan, P.R., 1963-77; violinist Cleve. Orch. fgn. tours, 1967, 73, 78, Cin. Symphony Orch. world tour, 1966; 1st violinist N.Y. String Quartet in-residence at U. Maine, Orono, summer 1969; concertmaster Minn. Orch., summers 1970-71; mem. N.Y. Philharmonia Chamber Ensemble in-residence at Hopkins Ctr., Dartmouth U., summer 1973; recitalist, Paris, 1963, Amsterdam, 1963, Carnegie Recital Hall, N.Y.C., 1963, Town Hall, 1968, 70, Alice Tully Hall, 1972. Served to cpl. U.S. Army, 1943-46; PTO. Fulbright fellow, Paris, 1951-52. Democrat. Roman Catholic. Office: Denver Symphony Orch 910 15th St Suite 300 Denver CO 80202

CECI, LOUIS J., justice state supreme court; b. N.Y.C., Sept. 10, 1927; s. Louis and Filomena C.; m. Shirley; children by previous marriage: Kristin, Remy, Louis, Joseph, Geraldine, David. Ph.D., Marquette U., 1951, J.D., 1954. Bar: Wis. Sole practice, Milw., 1954-58, 63-68; asst. city atty. City of Milw., 1958-63; mem. Wis. Assembly, Madison, 1965-66; judge Milwaukee County Ct., 1968-73, Miw. Circuit Ct., 1973-82; assoc. justice Wis. Supreme Ct., Madison, 1982—; lectr. Wis. Jud. Confs., 1970-79. Lectr. Badger Boys State, Ripon, Wis., 1961, 82, 83; asst. dist. commr. Boy Scouts Am., 1962. Recipient Wis. Civic Recognition PLAV, Milw., 1970, Community Improvement Pompeii Men's Club, Milw., 1971, Good Govt. Milw Jaycees, 1973, Community-Judiciary Pompeii Men's Club, 1982. Mem. ABA, Wis. Bar Assn., Dane County Bar Assn., Am. Legion (comdr. 1962-63). Office: Wisconsin Supreme Court PO Box 1688 Madison WI 53701

CECIL, CHARLES HARKLESS, painter, educator; b. Kansas City, Mo., May 12, 1945; s. Charles F. and Alice (Harkless) C.; m. Isabelle Claude Jeanne Touren, Dec. 30, 1982. B.A., Haverford Coll., 1967; postgrad., Yale U., 1967-69. Co-dir. Sudio Cecil-Graves, Florence, Italy, 1983—; instr. Villa Schifanoia, Grad. Sch. Fine Arts, Florence, 1983—. Exhibited in group shows at, N.A.D., N.Y.C., 1979, 80, N.A.D., Dallas, 1983; represented in permanent collections at, Portrait Gallery, Haverford Coll., Pa., West Bend Gallery Fine Arts, Wis. NDEA grantee, 1967-69; Elizabeth Greenshields Found. grantee, 1970-73; John F. Stacey Found. grantee, 1980; recipient Julius T. Hallgarten First prize for oil painting, 1979, Benjamin Altman Second prize for landscape 155 Ann. Exhbn. Nat. Acad. Design, 1980. Home: 502 S Center St Clinton IL 61727 Office: Via Pandolfini 21 Florence Italy 50121

CECIL, DAVID ROLF, mathematician, educator; b. Tulsa, July 12, 1935; s. Neil McKinley and Ola Ethel (Turner) C.; m. Betty Lou Poe, June 14, 1958; 1 son, Eric Alan. Student (Pitts. Plate Glass Co. scholar), Carnegie Inst. Tech., 1954-55; B.A., U. Tulsa, 1958; postgrad (fellow), Tulane U., 1958-59; M.S., Okla. State U., 1960, Ph.D., 1962. Grad. teaching asst. Okla. State U., 1959-62; sr. research mathematician Atlantic Refining Co., 1962; asst. prof., then asso. prof. math. North Tex. State U., Denton, 1962-69; prof. math. Butler U., Indpls., 1969-70, Tex. A&I U., Kingsville, 1970—, chmn. dept., 1980—; cons. Edn. Service Center Region II, 1979-80; organizer Kingsville Computer Club, 1980; mem. credit com. Tex. A&I U. Fed. Credit Union, 1979—. Contbr. articles to math. jours. Faculty fellow North Tex. State U., 1968-69, Tex. A&I U., 1971-73. Fellow Tex. Acad. Scis.; mem. Am. Math. Soc., Sigma Xi. Methodist. Club: Kingsville Radio (pres. 1974). Office: Dept Math Tex A&I U Kingsville TX 78363

CECIL, JOHN LAMONT, business executive, lawyer; b. Fredricktown, Ky., May 15, 1909; s. Robert Logan and Dorothea Bovard (Griffith) C.; m. Helen Madigan Breen, Sept. 21, 1954; children: Patricia M. (Mrs. Pierre M. Bikai), Elaina M. (Mrs. John W. Coyne), Anita J. (Mrs. William C. O'Donovan) (dec.), Barbara L. (Mrs. Edward F. Peterson), John Lamont. Student, St. Charles Jr. Coll., 1930, Cath. U. Am., 1930; LL.B., Georgetown U., 1935, LL.M., 1937. Bar: D.C. 1935, Md. 1962. Controller Hamilton Hotel, Washington, 1934-35; supr. property mgmt. office of counsel F.H. Smith Bondholders Protective Com., Washington, 1935-36; asst. counsel Fed. Deposit Ins. Corp., Washington, 1936-42, counsel, 1946-53, asst. gen. counsel, 1953-62; v.p., sec., gen. counsel Western Bancorp., Los Angeles, 1962-64, exec. v.p., sec., gen. counsel, 1964-74; cons., sec. Pacific Am. Income Shares, Inc., Pasadena, Calif., 1974—; v.p., asst. sec. United Calif. Bank Internat., 1962-70; mem. staff Alien Property Custodian, Washington, 1941-42. Served to lt. comdr. USNR, 1942-46; capt. Res. Recipient John Carroll Alumni award Georgetown U., 1969, Sr. Citizen award Los Angeles Expo for Life, 1984. Mem. D.C., Am. bar assns., Navy League, Am. Soc. Corporate Secs., Gamma Eta Gamma. Roman Catholic. Clubs: Congressional Country (Washington); Los Angeles Serra (treas. 1968), Stock Exchange, Newman (pres. Los Angeles 1969), Jonathan (Los Angeles)). Home: 5078 W 4th St Los Angeles CA 90020 Office: 707 Wilshire Blvd Los Angeles CA 90017

CEDARBAUM, BERNARD, lawyer; b. New Haven, Sept. 1, 1928; s. William and Elsie (Schuster) C.; m. Miriam Rachel Goldman, Aug. 25, 1957; children—Daniel Goldman, Jonathan Goldman. A.B., Yale, 1950, LL.M., 1956; LL.B., Harvard, 1953. Bar: Conn. bar 1953, N.Y. bar 1960. Practice in, Washington, 1956-59, N.Y.C., 1959—; atty. Dept. Justice, 1956-59; asso. Carter, Ledyard & Milburn, 1959-65, mem. firm, 1965—. Mem. Scarsdale (N.Y.) Bd. Edn., 1979—. Served with AUS, 1953-55. Mem. Am., N.Y. State bar assns., Am. Law Inst., Assn. Bar City N.Y. Clubs: Town (Scarsdale) (pres., 1977-78. Home: 125 Brewster Rd Scarsdale NY 10583 Office: 2 Wall St New York City NY 10005

CEDDIA, ANTHONY FRANCIS, university president; b. Boston, Mar. 4, 1944; s. Antonio John and Marie (Loungo) C.; m. Valerie Ann Mulkern, Apr. 15, 1966; children: Ann-Marie, Michael. B.S. in Edn., Northeastern U., 1965, M.Ed., 1968; Ed. D., U. Mass., 1980. Cert. counselor, secondary sch. tchr., Mass. Tchr. social studies, counselor Melrose High Sch., Mass., 1965-70; fin. aid and admissions ofcl. North Adams State Coll., Mass., 1970-73, dean of adminstrn, 1973-78, exec. v.p., 1978-81; acting pres. North Adams State Coll., Mass., 1979; pres. Shippensburg U., Pa., 1981—; chmn. planning and research and negotiating planning coms. Commn. of Pres., Harrisburg, Pa., 1982—. Exec. bd. Ams. for Competitive Enterprise System, 1982, Keystone Area council Boy Scouts Am., 1983. Recipient Disting. Alumni Northeastern U., 1979. Mem. Am. Assn. State Colls. and Univs, Am. Assn. Higher Edn. Roman Catholic. Lodge: Shippensburg Rotary. Home: PO Box 606 Shippensburg PA 17257 Office: Shippensburg U. Prince St Shippenburg PA 17257

CEDERING, SIV, poet, writer; b. Overkalix, Sweden, Feb. 5, 1939; came to U.S., 1953, naturalized, 1958; d. Hilding and Elvy (Wikstrom) C.; children—Lisa, Lora, David. Lectr. U. Mass., Amherst, 1973; cons. Coordinating Council Lit. Mags., 1972-75. Author: poems and photographs Cup of Cold Water, 1973, Letters from the Island; poems, 1973, Letters from Helge, 1974, Two Swedish Poets, Gost Friberg and Goran Palm (transl. from Swedish), 1974, Mother Is, 1975, The Juggler, 1977, How to Eat a Fortune Cookie, 1977, Color Poems, 1978, The Blue Horse; children's poems, 1979, Lewen i Grishuset, 1980, books transl. into Japanese, Swedish.; Editor, translator: Det Blommande Trädet (The Flowering Tree, collection Am. Indian and Eskimo lyrics), 1973, You and I and the World, Poems by Werner Aspenström, 1980; Poems and prose published in several periodicals, including, Harper's, New Republic, Partisan Rev., Paris Rev., Quar. Rev. Lit., others, exhibited photography, Modernage Galleries, N.Y.C., 1973. Recipient William Marion Reedy award Poetry Soc. Am., 1970, John Masefield Narrative Poetry award, 1969; Annapolis Fine Arts Festival poetry prize Md. Fine Arts Council, 1968; Photography prize Sat. Rev., 1970; Borestone Mountain Poetry award, 1974; Pushcart prize, 1977; Emily Dickinson award, 1978; N.Y. State Council on Arts fellow, 1974; Swedish Writers Union stipend, 1979. Mem. Poetry Soc. Am.

CEDERSTROM, JOHN ANDREW, artist; b. Phila., Apr. 26, 1929; s. Albert Gustav and Emilie (Laessig) C.; m. Eleanor Susanne Ross, June 17, 1960; children—Andrew Eric, Jeffrey David. Pvt. art instrn., 1943-48; student, Phila. Coll. Art, 1948-50, Pa. Acad. Fine Arts, 1950-51. Children's program dir., exec. dir., treas. Bryn Mawr Art Center, 1951-62; art dir. St. Peters Sch., Phila., 1953-55, Episcopal Acad., Merion, Pa., 1955-59; art therapist Inglis House, Home for the Disabled, Phila., 1955-63; chmn. art dir. Friends Central Sch., Phila., 1963-81; chief conservator Hahn Gallery, Phila., 1975—, Erikson Gallery, Reisterstow, Md., 1981—; vis. lectr. art and art history Art Inst., Phila., 1981—; Arts advocate for Rep. Fred Richmond, N.Y. 14th Dist., 1978-80. Represented in permanent collection: Allentown Mus. Art, N.C. Mus. Art, others. Mem. Ind. Sch. Tchrs. Assn. (chmn. art program), Artists Equity Assn. Phila. (chmn. ethics com. 1972-80), Am. Color Print Soc., Print Club, Phila. Water Color Soc., Am. Artists Profl. league, Pa. Acad. Fine Arts Fellowship. Home: 518 Prescott Rd Merion PA 19066 Office: 1245 R Washington St Gloucester MA 01930

CEDRONE, LOUIS ROBERT, JR., journalist; b. Balt., June 25, 1923; s. Louis and Lucia (Mazzola) C.; m. Nancy Nelson, Sept. 11, 1954; children—Linda, David. B.S., U. Md., 1951. With Balt. Eve. Sun, 1951—, drama-film critic, 1963—; corr. Variety, 1957-77, 81—; TV show cablevision Critics Corner, 1982—. Swimming instr. ARC, 1961-68. Served with inf. AUS, 1943-45. Decorated Purple Heart with oak leaf cluster, Bronze Star. Mem. Sigma Nu, Omicron Delta Kappa, Pi Delta Epsilon. Home: 9 Muirfield Ct Lutherville MD 21093 Office: Balt Eve Sun Calvert and Centre St Baltimore MD 21203

CEITHAML, JOSEPH JAMES, educator; b. Chgo., May 23, 1916; s. Joseph F. and Bessie (Nolc) C.; m. Ann J. Bednarik, May 9, 1942; children—Lenore Ann, Eric Lee. B.S., U. Chgo., 1937, Ph.D., 1941. Prof. biochemistry, dean students biol. scis. U. Chgo., 1942-48, 49—. Gosney fellow biology Calif. Inst. Tech., 1948. Mem. A.A.A.S., Am. Soc. Biol. Chemists, Assn. Am. Med. Colls. (nat. chmn. group student affairs 1966-69). Research malaria project OSRD, World War II. Home: 2337 W 108th Pl Chicago IL 60643

CELEBREZZE, ANTHONY J., JR., attorney general Ohio; b. Cleve., Sept. 8, 1941; s. Anthony J. and Anne M. C.; m. Louisa Godwin, June 19, 1965; children: Anthony J. III, Catherine, Charles, David, Maria. B.S., U.S. Naval Acad., 1963; M.S., George Washington U., 1966; J.D., Cleve. State U., 1973. Bar: Ohio 1973. Ptnr. Celebrezze and Marco, Cleve., 1975-79; mem. Ohio State Senate, 1975-79; sec. of state State of Ohio, Columbus, 1979-83, atty. gen., 1983—. Pres. Joint Vets. Commn. of Cuyahoga County, Ohio, 1977—; v.p. Lake Erie Regional Transp. Authority, 1972-74; mem. Gt. Lakes Commn., 1975-78, vice chmn., 1977-78; bd. dirs. Central br. YWCA, Cleve. Served with USN, 1963-68. Decorated Navy Commendation medal; recipient Jeffersonian Lodge award, 1977; Man of Yr. award Delta Theta Phi; Freedoms Found. Honor medal, 1980; named 1 of 5 Outstanding Legislators by 2 Ohio mags., 1978. Mem. LWV. Democrat. Roman Catholic. Office: office of the attorney general state capitol Columbus OH 43215

CELEBREZZE, FRANK D., chief justice Ohio Supreme Court; b. Cleve., Nov. 13, 1928; s. Frank D. and Mary (Delsander) C.; m. Mary Ann Armstrong, Jan. 20, 1949; children: Judith, Frank, Laura, David, Brian, Steven, Jeffrey, Keith, Matthew. Student, Ohio State U., 1948-50; B.S., Baldwin-Wallace Coll., 1952; LL.B., Cleve.-Marshall Coll. Law, 1956; LL.D. (hon.), Capitol U. Bar: Ohio 1957. Began legal practice, Cleve., 1957; judge Ohio Ct. Common Pleas Cuyahoga County, 1964-72; justice Ohio Supreme Ct., 1972-78, chief justice, 1978—; mem. Ohio Senate, 1956-58. Served with parachute inf. U.S. Army, 1946-47. Recipient Jud. Service award Ohio Supreme Ct., 1972; Outstanding Alumnus award Cleve.-Marshall Coll. Law, 1973; Community Service award AFL-CIO, 1973; Disting. Citizen of Parma award, 1976; Unita Civic award of Youngstown, 1976. Mem. Inst. Jud. Adminstrn. of Bar Assn. Greater Cleve., Cuyahoga County Bar Assn., Am. Bar Assn., Cuyahoga County Joint Vets. Adminstrn. (past pres., past trustee), Cleve. YMCA, Catholic War Vets. Democrat. Roman Catholic. Office: Supreme Ct Ohio State Office Tower 30 E Broad St Columbus OH 43215 *

CELEBREZZE, JAMES P., state supreme court justice; b. Cleve., Feb. 6, 1939; s. Frank D. and Mary (Delsander) C.; m. Daria R. Yurkiw, 1967; children: James Patrick Jr., Leslie Ann Rose, Nicholas John. B.S., Ohio State U., 1960; J.D., Cleve. State U., 1967. Bar: Ohio 1967. Tchr. Cleve. Sch. Dist., 1962-68; sole practice law Cleve., 1967-82; assoc. justice. Cuyahoga Common Pleas Ct., 8th Dist. Ct. Appeals; mem. Ohio Ho. of Reps., 1965-74. Mem. Ohio State Democratic Exec. Com.; chmn. Cuyahoga County Legis Delegation. Served with U.S. Army, 1960-62; served to comdr. USNR, 1970—. Mem. Am. Bar Assn., Italian Sons and Daus. Am., Ukranian Profl. Soc., Delta Theta Phi. Roman Catholic. Office: Ohio Supreme Court 30 E Broad St Columbus OH 43215 *

CELENTANO, FRANCIS MICHAEL, artist; b. N.Y.C., May 25, 1928; s. Michael Anthony and Rafaela (Valentino) C. B.A., N.Y. U., 1951, M.A. in Art History, 1957. Lectr. C.W. Post Coll., L.I., N.Y., 1961-63, N.Y. Inst. Tech., Old Westbury, N.Y., 1965-66; from asso. prof. to prof. Sch. Art, U. Wash., Seattle, 1966—. One-man exhbns. include, Foster/White Gallery, Seattle, 1971, 73, 75, 78, Howard Wise Gallery, N.Y.C., 1963, Diane Gilson Gallery, Seattle, 1981, 82; represented in permanent collections at, Mus. of Modern Art, N.Y.C., Albright-Knox Mus., Buffalo, Seattle Art Mus., Fed. Res. Bank of San Francisco. Fulbright scholar Rome, 1958. Office: Sch of Art Univ of Wash Seattle WA 98195

CELESTE, FRANK PALM, lawyer; b. Italy, Mar. 24, 1907; s. Samuel and Carolina (Santora) C.; m. Margaret Salisbury Louis, Oct. 1, 1932; children: Richard F., Mary Patricia Celeste Hoffman, Theodore S. A.B., Wooster Coll., 1928; J.D., Case Western Res. U., 1931. Bar: Ohio 1932. Since practiced in Cleve.; mem. firms Stephenson & Celeste, 1933-38, Celeste & Taber, 1938-57, Fedor & Fedor, 1956—; interim judge Lakewood (Ohio) Mcpl. Ct., 1954; chmn. bd. Nat. Housing Corp., 1963—; partner Moreland Cts., Fairview Village Apts., Indian Hill Colony Apts., Hamilton House Apts., all Cleve. Pres., Protestant Big Bros., 1940-45, Cleve. Ch. Fedn., 1949-50; v.p. Cleve. Safety Council, 1956-59; mem. Pres.'s. Adv. Com. on Housing for Elderly, 1961-64; chmn. Gov. Ohio Task Force for Health Care, 1972-73; now mem. Assn. St. Luke's Hosp.; treas. Lakewood Democratic Club, 1939-45; mayor, Lakewood, 1955-63; mem. exec. com., chmn. com. finance Cuyahoga County (Ohio) Dem. Party Orgn., 1964; bd. dirs. Fairview Gen. Hosp., Am. Heart Assn.; pres. bd. trustees Lakewood Hosp., 1956-63; trustee Interchurch Center Inc., Ohio Council Chs., Ohio Council Chs. Found.; pres. bd. trustees Lakewood United Meth. Ch., 1976-77. Decorated knight officer Order of Merit (Italy). Mem. Am. Soc. Pub. Adminstrn. (pres. chpt. 1962-63), Cuyahoga County Mayors and City Mgrs. Assn. (pres. 1963), Am. Assn. Homes for Aging, Ohio Council Chs. (pres. 1966-67), Greater Cleve. Growth Assn., Lakewood C. of C., Phi Alpha Delta. Clubs: Masons, Shriners, Rotary. Home: 12500 Edgewater Dr Lakewood OH 44107 Office: 12506 Edgewater Dr Lakewood OH 44107

CELL, GILLIAN TOWNSEND, historian, educator; b. Birkenhead, Cheshire, Eng., June 5, 1937; came to U.S., 1962; d. Thomas Edmund and Doris Abigail (Clark) Townsend; m. John Whitson Cell, Oct. 19, 1962; children: Thomas K., Katherine A., John D. B.A., U. Liverpool, Eng., 1959, Ph.D., 1964. Instr. U. N.C., Chapel Hill, 1965-66, asst. prof., 1966-70, assoc. prof., 1970-78, prof., 1978—, affirmative action officer, 1981-83, chmn. dept. history, 1983—. Author: English Enterpise in Newfoundland; 1577-1660, 1969; editor: Newfoundland Discovered, 1982. Office: Dept History Hamilton Hall U NC Chapel Hill NC 27514

CELLA, FRANCIS RAYMOND, economist, research cons.; b. Harrison, N.J., July 16, 1909; s. Frank L. and Kathryn (Hanlon) C.; m. Mildred Russell, Dec. 11, 1944; 1 son, Charles Ronald. A.B, Wesleyan Coll., 1933; A.M., U. Ky., 1937. Statistician Ky. Agrl. Expt. Sta., 1935-37; research dir. Ky. Unemployment Compensation Commn., 1937-42; dir. bur. bus. research U. Okla., 1946-68, prof. bus. statistics, 1946-74; dir. research Bus. Research, Inc., 1968-74; economist Washita Valley Improvement Assn., 1953-56; cons. USAF, 1954-59; mgmt. research cons. Okla. Restaurant Assn., 1966-74; pres. Cella & Assos., Inc., 1974—; cons. U.S. Navy, 1973; Faculty co-ordinator Com. for Econ. Devel., 1951-57; mem. Gov.'s Council Coal Industry, 1964—, Gov.'s Gen. Adv. Com., 1964-66; pres. Assn. Univ. Burs. Bus. and Econ. Research, 1962-64. Author brochures, articles.; Editor: Okla. Bus. Bull, 1946-68. Served as capt. USAAF, 1942-46; lt. col. USAF Res. ret. Mem. Am. Statis. Assn., Am., Inst. for Mgmt. Scis., Beta Gamma Sigma. Episcopalian. Home: 719 Hoover St Norman OK 73069

CELLA, PHYLLIS ANN, insurance company executive; b. Revere, Mass., Aug. 31, 1920; d. Richard and Matilda (Sarno) C. B.S., Boston

U., 1941. With John Hancock Mut. Life Ins. Co., Boston, 1943—, asst. to sr. v.p., 1968-70, gen. dir. spl. projects and research, 1970-72, 2d v.p., 1972-75, v.p., 1975-79, sr. v.p., 1979—; v.p. Hanseco Ins. Co. subs. John Hancock Mut. Life Ins. Co., 1971-75, pres., chief exec. officer, dir., 1975—; also dir. John Hancock Sub.'s, Inc.; chmn. Hanseco Reins. Co., Hanseco Ins. Co. (U.K.) Ltd. Trustee Bentley Coll., Waltham, Mass.; mem. adv. com. grad. program in mgmt. Simmons Coll., Boston. Fellow Life Office Mgmt. Assn. Inst.; mem. Am. Coll. Life Underwriters (C.L.U.). Office: John Hancock Pl Boston MA 02117

CELLAN-JONES, JAMES GWYNNE, film and television director; b. Swansea, Wales, July 13, 1931; s. Cecil John and Lavinia Sophia (Dailey) C.-J.; m. Margaret Eavis, Apr. 2, 1959; children: Simon, Deiniol, Lavinia. B.A., St. Johns Coll., Cambridge U., 1952, M.A., 1977. From callboy to prodn. mgr. BBC-TV, 1955-60, dir., 1960—, head of plays, 1976-79; mng. dir. Lawnsdale Prodns. Dir.: films The Forsyte Saga, 1966, Portrait of a Lady, 1968, The Way We Live Now, 1968, The Creative Impulse, 1970, The Roads to Freedom, 1970, Midsummer Nights Dream, 1971, The Nelson Affair, 1972, Caesar and Cleopatra, 1974, Jennie, 1974, Adams Chronicles, 1975, You Never Can Tell, 1976, School Play, 1977, Unity Mitford, 1980, The Day Christ Died, 1980, A Fine Romance, 1981, Mrs. Sicily, 1982, The Comedy of Errors, Redundant or the Wife's Revenge, 1983. Served to 2d lt. Royal Engrs., 1953-54. Mem. Dirs. Guild Am. (Series award 1976), Brit. Acad. Film and TV Arts (vice chmn. 1979-83, chmn. 1983—), Dirs. Guild Gt. Britain. Mem. Liberal Party. Home: 19 Cumberland Rd Kew Surrey England Office: care William Morris Inc 1350 Ave of Americas New York NY 10019

CELLI, VITTORIO, physicist, educator; b. Parma, Italy, Aug. 13, 1936; came to U.S., 1966; s. Franco and Carolina (Bertazzoli) C.; m. Eija Iris Urpalainen, July 6, 1962; 1 son, Carlo. Dr. Physics, U. Pavia, Italy, 1959; Docent, U. Rome, 1965. Research assoc. U. Ill., Urbana, 1959-61, asst. prof., 1961-62; asst. research physicist U. Calif. at San Diego, La Jolla, 1962-64; lectr. U. Bologna, Italy, 1964-66; asso. prof. U. Va., Charlottesville, 1966-69, prof. physics, 1969—; prof. extraordinary U. Trieste, 1973-74. Fulbright scholar, 1959-62; U.S. sr. scientist Humboldt Found., 1981. Fellow Am. Phys. Soc. Home: 210 Magnolia Dr Charlottesville VA 22901

CELLIER, GERARD PIERRE, journalist; b. Saint-Mande, Seine, France, 1935; emigrated to Can., 1957; s. Pierre and Suzanne (Heldens) C.; m. Carole Tremblay, Oct. 17, 1970 (div. Jan. 1983); children: Yann, Annick; m. Marie Francoise Michon, Nov. 1957 (div. Oct. 1978); children: Irene, Catherine, Gerard Pierre. Grad., Ecole Militaire, Saint Cyr, France. Directeur de l'information Jour. de Montreal, Que., Can., 1964—. Served to lt. Armed Forces. Office: Jour de Montreal 155 Quest Port Royal Montreal PQ Canada H3L 2B1 *

CENA, LAWRENCE, transp. co. exec.; b. San Jose, Calif., Mar. 19, 1922; s. Carl and Teresa (Massetti) C.; m. Patricia H. Hayes, June 19, 1942; children—Lawrie Kathleen, Patrick C., Timothy M., Terry M., Robin Kay. Student, North Central Coll., Naperville, Ill., 1946, Northwestern U., 1947, various mgmt. programs. With A.T.S.F. Ry., 1948—, asst. gen. mgr., Topeka, 1966-68, asst. v.p. ops., Chgo., 1968, v.p. ops., 1968-78, pres., 1978—. Served with U.S. Navy, 1942-45. Home: 820 Edgewater Dr Naperville IL 60540 Office: 80 E Jackson Blvd Chicago IL 60604

CENARRUSA, PETE T., sec. state Idaho; b. Carey, Idaho, Dec. 16, 1917; s. Joseph and Ramona (Gardoqui) C.; m. Freda B. Coates, Oct. 25, 1947; 1 son, Joey Earl. B.S. in Agr, U. Idaho, 1940. Tchr. high sch., Cambridge, Idaho, 1940-41, Carey and Glenns Ferry, Idaho, 1946; tchr. vocat. agr. VA, Blaine County, Idaho, 1946-51; farmer, woolgrower, nr. Carey, 1946—; mem. Idaho Ho. of Reps., 1951-67, speaker, 1963-67; sec. state Idaho, 1967—; mem. Idaho Bd. Land Commrs., Idaho Bd. Examiners; pres. Idaho Flying Legislators, 1953-63; chmn. Idaho Legis. Council, 1964—, Idaho Govt. Reorgn. Com.; Idaho del. Council State Govts., 1963—. Republican adminstr. Hall of Fame, 978. Served to maj. USMCR, 1942-46, 52-58. Named Hon. Farmer Future Farmers Am., 1955; named to Agrl. Hall of Fame, 1973; Idaho Athletic Hall of Fame, 1976. Mem. Blaine County Livestock Mktg. Assn., Blaine County Woolgrowers Assn. (chmn. 1954), Carey C. of C. (pres. 1952), U. Idaho Alumni Assn., Gamma Sigma Delta. Republican. Office: Office of Sec State State Capitol Boise ID 83720

CENNAMO, RALPH, labor union official; b. Bridgeport, Conn., Jan. 19, 1919; m. Anna Mae, 1943; 3 children. Mem. Internat. Leather Goods, Plastics and Novelty Workers Union, N.Y.C., 1937—, dir. orgn., 1961—, gen. sec.-treas., 1980—; sec.-treas. local 22 Internat. Ladies' Handbag, Pocketbook and Novelty Workers Union, Bidgeport, Conn., 1937-39, bus. agt., 1939-41; organizer Pocket and Novelty Workers Union, N.Y.C., 1946-51, internat. rep., 1951-61. Served with U.S. Army, 1941-45. Office: Internat Leather Goods Plastics and Novelty Workers Union 265 W 14th St 14th Floor New York NY 10011 *

CENSITS, RICHARD JOHN, food company executive; b. Allentown, Pa., May 20, 1937; s. Stephen A. and Theresa M. C.; m. Linda A. Malin, June 21, 1958; children: Debra, Mark, David. B.S. in Econs., U. Pa., 1958; M.B.A., Lehigh U., 1964. Sr. auditor Arthur Andersen & Co., C.P.A.s., 1958-62; mgr. acctg. Air Products & Chems., 1962-64; controller Hamilton Watch Co., Lancaster, Pa., 1964-69; v.p., controller IU Internat., Phila., 1969-75; v.p. fin. Campbell Soup co., Camden, N.J., 1975—. Trustee West Jersey Health Systems; class agt. U. Pa. Alumni. Mem. Fin. Execs. Inst., Nat. Food Processors Assn., Am. Inst. C.P.A.s, Pa. Inst. C.P.A.s, N.J. Soc. C.P.A.s. Club: Union League. Home: 120 Partree Rd Cherry Hill NJ 08003 Office: Campbell Soup Co Campbell Pl Camden NJ 08101

CENTIFANTO, YSOLINA MEJIA, microbiologist; b. Panama City, Panama, Aug. 12, 1928; came to U.S., naturalized, 1960; d. Justiniano and Benila (Poveda) Mejia; children by previous marriage: Loraine, James, Anthony, Matthew. B.S., U. Panama; M.S., Western Res. U., 1954; Ph.D., U. Fla., 1964. Asst. prof. U. Panama, 1955-56; instr. East Carolina Coll., 1958; research technologist Kodak Tropical Research Lab., Panama City, 19565-8, 1956-58, Eastman Kodak Research Lab., Rochester, N.Y., 1958-61; abstractor Chem. Abstracts, Rochester, 1960-61; research asst. dept. ophthalmology Med. Coll., U. Fla., Gainesville, 1964-65; instr., 1965-66, asst. prof., 1966-72, asso. prof. ophthalmology and immunology, also med. microbiology, 1972-78; prof. ophthalmology and microbiology Med. Sch., La. State U., New Orleans, 1978—. Contbr. articles to profl. jours. NIH grantee. Mem. Am. Chem. Soc., Am. Soc. Microbiology, AAAS, Assn. Research in Vision and Ophthalmology, N.Y. Acad. Scis., Southeastern Cancer Soc., Am. Assn. Virology, D'Onore Unione Cavalleresca Europea, Sigma Xi. Democrat. Roman Catholic. Office: 136 Roman St New Orleans LA 70112

CERAMI, ANTHONY, biochemistry educator; b. Newark, Oct. 3, 1940; s. Anthony and Hazel (Kirk) C.; m. Helen Vlassara, May 1, 1981; children: Carla, Ethan. B.S., Rutgers U., 1962; Ph.D., Rockefeller U., 1967. Asst. prof. biochemistry Rockefeller U., N.Y.C., 1969-72, assoc. prof., 1972-78, prof., 1978—, head lab. med. biochemistry, 1972—; med. adv. bd. Cooley's Anemia Vols., N.Y.C., 1976-83, Cooley's Anemia Blood and Research Found., 1978-83; mem. research council Pub. Health Research Inst., 1978—. Editor: Jour. Exptl. Medicine. Mem. Am. Soc. Biol. Chemists, Am. Soc. Pharmacology and Exptl. Therapeutics, Am. Soc. Hematology. Office: Rockefeller University 1230 York Ave New York NY 10021

CERF, VINTON GRAY, communication company executive; b. New Haven, June 23, 1943; s. Vinton Thruston and Muriel (Gray) C.; m. Sigrid L. Thorstenberg, Sept. 10, 1966; children—David, Bennett. B.S., Stanford U., 1965; M.S. in Computer Sci, UCLA, 1970, Ph.D., 1972. Systems engr. IBM, 1965-67; prin. programmer UCLA, 1967-72; asst. prof. elec. engring. and computer sci. Stanford (Calif.) U., 1972-76; sr. programmer Jacobi Systems Corp., Santa Monica, Calif., 1968-70; program mgr. info. processing techniques office Def. Advanced Research Projects Agy., Dept. Def., Arlington, Va., 1976-81, prin. scientist, 1981-82; dir. systems devel. MCI Communications Corp., 1982—. Author: A Practical View of Communication Protocols, 1979. Mem. IEEE, Assn. Computing Machinery, Internat. Fedn. Info. Processing, Sigma Xi. Office: MCI Communications Corp 2000 M St NW 3d Floor Washington DC 20036 *My entire working career has been focused on science and technology, in many forms—teaching, research, engineering management. The trait I have come to admire most among technical colleagues is absolute honesty in reporting or assessing results—blemishes and failures as well as successes.*

CERMAK, IVAN A., communication company executive. V.p. ITT Corp. Office: 320 Park Ave New York NY 10022§

CERMAK, JACK EDWARD, engineer, educator; b. Hastings, Colo., Sept. 8, 1922; s. Joseph and Helen (Herman) C.; m. Helen Jane Carlson, Dec. 17, 1949; children: Douglas Karl, Jonathan Joel. B.S., Colo. State U., 1947, M.S., 1948; Ph.D., Cornell U., 1959; NATO postdoctoral fellow, Cambridge (Eng.) U., 1961-62. Mem. faculty Colo. State U., Ft. Collins, 1948—, prof. charge fluid mechanics and wind engring. program, also dir. Fluid Dynamics and Diffusion Lab., 1960—, dir. fluid dynamics and diffusion lab., 1960—, chmn. engring. sci. fluid dynamics and diffusion lab., 1963-72, pres., dir., 1965-72; pres. Cermak/Peterka and Assocs, Inc., 1982—; cons. in field. Mem. bd. mems. Univ. Corp. Atmospheric Research, 1966-67; pres., chmn. 10th Midwestern Mechanics Conf., 1966-67; dir. summer inst. fluid mechanics NSF, 1963, 65, 68, 72; chmn. 2d U.S. Nat. Conf. Wind Engring. Research, 1975, 5th Internat. Conf. Wind Engring., 1979; pres. Wind Engring. Research Council, Inc., 1979—; co-chmn. U.S.-Japan Seminar Lab. Simulation of Stratified Shear Flows; mem. Colo. Gov.'s Sci. and Tech. Adv. Council, Com. on Army Basic Research, NRC, 1979—. Mem. editorial adv. bd.: Indsl. Aerodynamics Abstracts, Mechanics Research Communications; regional editor for: U.S., Internat. Jour. Wind Engring; Contbr. articles to profl. jours. Fellow ASCE, Am. Acad. Mechanics; asso. fellow AIAA; mem. Am. Soc. Engring. Edn. (chmn. mechanics div.), Nat. Acad. Engring. (chmn. com. natural disasters, chmn. panel on wind engring. research), Internat. Assn. Wind Engring. (chmn. bd. 1975-79, regional sec. North and S.Am. 1983—), Am. Meteorol. Soc., Am. Geophys. Union, ASME, AAAS, ASHRAE (mem. com. flow around bldgs.), Air Pollution Control Assn., N.Y. Acad. Scis., Sigma Xi (nat. lectr. 1976-77). Home: 407 E Prospect Rd Fort Collins CO 80525 *My thoughts and actions have been influenced always by a belief and an awareness that man, his near environment, and the far reaches of his universe are influenced by common natural laws. I believe that the order found in natural events, as revealed by scientific investigation, can someday become manifest in the behavior of man. Ultimately, through persistent and directed effort, I am confident that man will shape his religion, science, and technology to achieve harmony of man with man, and man with his environment. For the most part, my achievements and contributions to society can be attributed to the motivation and direction stemming from these convictions.*

CERMINARO, JOHN, horn player; b. Navasota, Tex., Apr. 7, 1947; s. John Cerminaro Frances and Felder C. Student, Julliard Sch. Music, 1965-68. Solo horn N.Y. Philharm. Orch., 1969-79; 1st horn Los Angeles Philharm. Orch., 1980—; prof. horn Aspen Music Festival. Recipient Naumburg award Julliard Sch. Music, 1965. Office: Los Angeles Philharm Orch 135 N Grand Ave Los Angeles CA 90012

CERNAN, EUGENE A., managment company executive, former astronaut; b. Chgo., Mar. 14, 1934; s. Andrew G. C.; m. Barbara Jean Atchley; 1 dau., Teresa Dawn. B.S. in Elec. Engring, Purdue U., 1956; postgrad., U.S. Naval Postgrad. Sch. Joined U.S. Navy, 1956; advanced through grades to capt.; former mem. attack squadrons 126, 113 U.S. Navy, Miramar (Calif.) Naval Air Sta.; now astronaut with Lyndon B. Johnson Space Center, NASA; pilot Gemini 9; lunar module pilot Apollo 10, 1969; space craft comdr. (last man to leave footprints on moon) Apollo 17, 1972; Spl. asst. to program mgr. Apollo-Soyuz project, 1973-76, ret., 1976; exec. v.p. internat. Coral Petroleum, Inc., Houston, 1976-81; pres. Cernan Corp., Houston, 1981—. Recipient NASA Distinguished Service Medal (2), Exceptional Service Medal, Navy Distinguished Service Medal, D.F.C., Gold Space Medal Fedn. Aeronautique Internationale, V.F.W. Space Medal, N.Y.C. Gold medal. Fellow Am. Astronautical Soc.; mem. Soc. Exptl. Test Pilots, Sigma Xi, Phi Gamma Delta., Tau Beta Pi. Address: Cernan Corp 900 Town and Country Ln Suite 210 Houston TX 77024 *

CERNE, WENCE F., multi-industry company real estate executive, village official; b. Chgo., July 21, 1931; s. Wence F. and Leonie (Stranen) C.; m. Alice Joan Rueckert, Aug. 21, 1957; children: Neal, Laura, Wayne. B.B.A., Emory U., 1953; J.D., Northwestern U., 1956. Bar: Ill. 1956. Atty. Ill. Central R.R. Co., Chgo., 1957-66; gen. atty. Ill. Central R.R. co., Chgo., 1966-69; v.p. Ill. Ctr. Corp., Chgo., 1969-77, pres., 1977-79; v.p. real estate IC Industries Inc., Chgo., 1979—. Police magistrate Village of Downers Grove (Ill.), 1963-67, plan commr., 1970-73; trustee Village of Oak Brook (Ill.), 1975-79, pres., 1979—. Repulican. Methodist. Home: 18 Cambridge Dr Oak Brook IL 60521 Office: IC Industries Inc 111 E Wacker Dr. Chicago IL 60601

CERNICA, JOHN N., educator, civil engr.; b. Romania, May 14, 1932; U.S., 1947, naturalized, 1950; s. John and Mary (Ignat) C.; m. Mary Patricia Marinelli, July 25, 1959; children—Mary Kathleen, Mary Judith, Mary Alice, Mary Johanna, Mary Patricia, Mary Sarah. B.S., Youngstown U., 1954; M.S., Carnegie Inst. Tech., 1955, Ph.D. (NSF grantee), 1957. Registered profl. engr., Fla., S.C., Iowa, Mich., Ohio, Pa., Ind., Md., N.Y., N.C., N.J., Va., W.Va., Ky. Asst. prof. civil engring. Youngstown U., 1957-58, asso. prof., 1958-61, prof., 1961—, acting head dept., 1957, head dept., 1958—; prin. asso., co-owner Cernica-Fok & Assos. (cons. engrs.), Youngstown, 1958—; owner John N. Cernica (Cons. Engrs.); Asst. examiner Ohio Bd. Registration Profl. Engrs. and Surveyors. Author: Reinforced Concrete Fundamentals, 1964, Strength of Materials, 2d edit, 1977, Resistencia de Materiales, 1968, Elements of Soil Mechanics, 1981; Contbr. articles to profl. jours. Recipient Distinguished Engrs. award State of Ohio, 1964. Mem. Am. Soc. Engring. Edn., Am. Soc. C.E., Am. Concrete Inst., Nat., Ohio, Mahoning Valley socs. profl. engrs., Sigma Xi, Sigma Tau, Phi Kappa Phi, Sigma Phi Epsilon. Home: 611 Plymouth Dr Youngstown OH 44512

CERNOVITCH, NICHOLAS, theatrical lighting designer; b. Kewanee, Ill., Dec. 5, 1929; s. John and Anna (Matusic) C. Student, Black Mountain Coll., 1948-52. Resident lighting designer Merce Cunningham Dance Co., N.Y.C., 1954-66, Living Theater, 1960-63, Festival of Two Worlds, Spoleto, Italy, 1962, Alvin Ailey Am. Dance Theater, N.Y.C., 1958-70, Les Grand Balles Canadiens (Ballets), Montreal, 1970—; assoc. prof. SUNY. Home: 177 Tour du Lac St Agathe des Monts PQ Canada J8C 1B8 Office: Les Grands Ballets Canadiens 4816 Rue Rivard Montreal PQ Canada H2J 2N6

CERNUGEL, WILLIAM JOHN, manufacturing company executive; b. Joliet, Ill., Nov. 19, 1942; s. William John, Sr. and Catherine Ann (Piechowiak) C.; m. Laurie M. Kusnik, Apr. 22, 1967; children: Debra, James, David. B.S., No. Ill. U., 1964. C.P.A., Ill. Supervising sr. accountant Peat, Marwick, Mitchell & Co., Chgo., 1964-70; asst. corp. controller Alberto-Culver Co., Melrose Park, Ill., 1970-71, corp. controller, 1972-74, v.p. and controller, 1974-82, v.p. fin., controller, 1982—. Bd. govs., treas. Gottlieb Meml. Hosp., Melrose Park. Mem. Nat. Assn. Accountants, Am. Accounting Assn., Am. Inst. C.P.A.s, Ill. Soc. C.P.A.s. Lodge: Lions. Home: 418 Maple Ln Darien IL 60559 Office: 2525 Armitage Ave Melrose Park IL 60160

CERNY, JOSEPH, III, chemistry educator, scientific laboratory administrator; b. Montgomery, Ala., Apr. 24, 1936; s. Joseph and Olaette Genette (Jury) C.; m. Barbara Ann Nedelka, June 13, 1959 (div. Nov. 1982); children: Keith Joseph, Mark Evan; m. 2d Susan Dinkelspiel Stern, Nov. 12, 1983. B.S. in Chem. Engring., Miss.-Oxford, 1957; postgrad. Fulbright scholar, U. Manchester, Eng., 1957-58; Ph.D. in Nuclear Chemistry, U. Calif.-Berkeley, 1961. Asst. prof. chemistry U. Calif., Berkeley, 1961-67, assoc. prof., 1967-71, prof., 1971—, chmn. dept. chemistry, 1975-79, head nuclear sci. div., 1979—, assoc. dir. Lawrence Berkeley Lab., 1979—; mem. nuclear physics panel Nat. Acad. Scis. Physics Commn., 1983—. Editor: Nuclear Reactions and Spectroscopy, 4 vols., 1974; contbr. numerous articles to field to profl. jours. Served with U.S. Army, 1962-63. Recipient E.O. Lawrence award U.S. AEC, 1974; Guggenheim fellow, 1969-70; recipient Nuclear Chemistry award Am. Chem. Soc., 1984. Fellow Am. Phys. Soc., AAAS; mem. Am. Chem. Soc. Democrat. Home: 860 Keeler Ave Berkeley CA 94708 Office: Nuclear Sci Div Lawrence Berkeley Lab Bldg 70a Berkeley CA 94720

CERRONE, WARREN EDWARD, sales and marketing executive, former air force officer; b. N.Y.C., Oct. 5, 1921; s. Edward Joseph and Cecelia (Gardner) C.; m. Barbara Jane Bishop, Sept. 21, 1946; children: Deborah Jane, Lesley Ann. Student, Iona Coll., N.Y., 1947-51; B.S., U. Md., 1958; M.B.A., George Washington U., 1958. Commd. 2d lt. Air Corps Res., U.S. Army, 1942; advanced through grades to col. USAF, 1967; dep. asst. chief staff (4th Allied Tactical Air Force, NATO), 1961-64; prof. aerospace studies U. Detroit, 1964-68; chief res., guard studies Air War Coll., 1968-70, chief dept. mil. capabilities and employment, 1970-71; asst. dean U. Detroit Coll. Engring., 1971-76; assoc. dean Coll. Engring. and Sci., 1976-77; dir. admissions U. Detroit, 1977-78, assoc. v.p. ops., 1978-80, v.p. ops., 1980-81; sales/mktg. mgr. Openings, 1981—. Decorated Legion of Merit with oak leaf cluster, D.F.C. with 2 oak leaf clusters, Air medal with 6 oak leaf clusters; Croix de Guerre with silver star (France). Mem. Air Force Assn., Air Force Hist. Found., Order Daedalians (life), Engring. Soc. Detroit. Club: Economic (Detroit). Home: 294 Linden Rd Birmingham MI 48009 Office: Openings 40 W Howard St Pontiac MI 48058

CERVENAK, EDWARD DAVID, television executive; b. Cleve., May 24, 1925; s. Daverecte Dezso and Anna (Chervenak) Cservenyak; m. Marjorie Leslie Downing, Oct. 11, 1947; children: Sandra Cervenak McHale, James, Charles, Steven. Grad., Am. TV Lab., 1948. With Sta. WEWS-TV, Cleve., 1948—, dir. news ops., then asst. gen. mgr. news and programming, 1968-75, gen. mgr., 1975—; v.p. Scripps Howard Broadcasting Co., 1979—, dir., 1982—; guest instr. Western Res. U., 1964-66, Ashland Coll., 1980-83, John Carroll U., 1982-83. Bd. dirs. Luth. Med. Center. Served with USNR, 1943-46. Recipient Emmy award outstanding news programming Cleve. chpt. Nat. Acad. TV Arts and Scis., 1971-74. Mem. Nat. Assn. TV Program Execs., Nat. Assn. TV Arts and Scis., Nat. Assn. Broadcasters, Greater Cleve. Growth Assn., Exec. Order Ohio Commodores, Cleve. Advt. Club. Club: Cleve. City. Home: 6817 Parkgate Oval Seven Hills OH 44131 Office: 3001 Euclid Ave Cleveland OH 44115

CERVENY, FRANK STANLEY, bishop; b. Springfield, Mass., June 4, 1933; s. Frank Charles and Julia Victoria (Kulig) C.; m. Emmy Pettway, Nov. 1, 1961; children: Frank Stanley, Emmy Pettway, William DeMoville. B.A., Trinity Coll., Hartford, Conn., 1955, M.Div. (hon.), 1977, Gen. Theol. Sem., N.Y.C., 1958, U. of South, 1977. Asst. rector Ch. of Resurrection, Miami, Fla., 1958-60; assoc. priest, dir. Christian edn. Trinity Ch., N.Y.C., 1960-63; rector St. Lukes Ch., Jackson, Tenn., 1963-68, St. Johns Ch., Knoxville, Tenn., 1968-72; dean Fla., rector St. John's Cathedral, Jacksonville, 1972-74; bishop Episc. Diocese of Fla., Jacksonville, 1974—; bd. mem. Com. of 200 of Nat. Ch.; chmn. Presiding Bishops Com. on Renewal; chmn. bd. Episcopal High Sch., Jacksonville; chmn. evangelism House of Bishops; chmn., adviser Center for Christian Spirituality, N.Y.C.; mem. nat. bd., adviser Brotherhood of St. Andrew. Commr. Bicentennial Com. of Jacksonville; mem. Mayor's Com. on Human Relations, Jackson; bd. dirs. Heart Fund, Mental Health Assn., YMCA, Cerebral Palsy Assn., Travelers Aid Soc., Community Planning Council, Jacksonville; trustee Gen. Theol. Sem., N.Y.C., U. of South, Sewanee, Tenn. Club: Rotary. Office: 325 Market St Jacksonville FL 32202 *

CESARI, LAMBERTO, mathematics educator; b. Bologna, Italy, Sept. 23, 1910; came to U.S., 1949; s. Cesare and Amelia (Giannizzeri) C.; m. Isotta Hornauer, Apr. 2, 1939. Ph.D. in Math, U. Pisa, Italy, 1933. Asst. Nat. Research Council Italy, 1935-39; asso. prof. U. Pisa, 1939-42, U. Bologna, 1942-47, prof. math., 1947-48; staff Inst. Advanced Study, Princeton, N.J., 1948; prof. math. U. Cal. at Berkeley, 1949, U. Wis., 1950, Purdue U., 1950-60, U. Mich., Ann Arbor, 1960—, R. L. Wilder prof. math., 1976—; Corr. mem. Accademie delle Scienze di Bologna, Modena, Milano, Accademia Nazionale Lincei, Rome. Author: Surface Area, 1955, Asymptotic Properties, 1959, Optimization, 1983; also articles on differential equations, calculus of variations, real analysis. Asymptotic Properties; Editorial bd.: Applicable Math. Jour, 1970—, Jour. Differential Equations, 1973—, Rendiconti Circolo Matematico di Palermo, 1960—. Mem. Math. Assn. Am., Am. Math. Soc. Home: 2021 Washtenaw Ave Ann Arbor MI 48104

CESARINI, SAL, fashion designer; b. N.Y.C., Sept. 25, 1941. Student, High Sch. of Fashion Industries, Fashion Inst. Tech., N.Y.C. Sportswear designer Bobbie Brooks; fashion coordinator men's wear Paul Stuart, from 1964; mdse. dir. men's and women's apparel Ralph Lauren/Polo, from 1971; founder, owner Cesarini Ltd. (now div. Jaymar-Ruby Inc.), N.Y.C., 1976—. Recipient Coty award, 1974, 75, 82. Office: care Cesarini Ltd 550 7th Ave New York NY 10018 *

CESARIO, VIRGINIA NAILL, librarian; b. Balt., Dec. 9, 1923; d. Richard Young and Lucy (Fitz) Naill; m. Michael J. Cesario, Aug. 14, 1948 (div. 1965). B.A., Coll. William and Mary, 1945; B.S. in Library Service with honors, Columbia U., 1947. Circulation asst. City Coll. Library, City U. N.Y., 1947-64, instr., adminstrv. asst., 1964-68, asst. prof., asst. chief librarian pub. service, 1968-75, asso. prof., dep.

librarian, 1972-75, prof., chief librarian, 1976-80, emeritus, 1980—; asso. Blue Hills Consultants, 1980—. Dir. service vol. Hospice of South Berkshire, 1981—; mem. Monterey Arts Council, 1983—. Mem. ALA (various offices), N.Y. Library Assn., N.Y. Library Club, Spl. Libraries Assn., ACLU, Archons of Colophon, Common Cause, Phi Beta Kappa. Home and office: Blue Hill Rd PO Box 116 Monterey MA 01245

CESNIK, JAMES MICHAEL, union official, newspaperman; b. Marshfield, Wis., Oct. 6, 1935; s. Ignatius Anthony and Mary Catherine (Bayuk) C.; m. Elizabeth Louise Havlik, Aug. 1, 1959; children: Margaret Mary, Sarah Elizabeth, Michael Ignatius. B.A., St. John's U., Collegeville, Minn., 1958. Reporter, Rice Lake (Wis.) Chronotype, 1958; reporter, makeup, layout editor Mpls. Star & Tribune, 1958-64; internat. rep., asso. dir. research and info., dir. research and info. Newspaper Guild, AFL-CIO/CLC, Washington, 1965-75; editor Guild Reporter, 1973—; v.p. Internat. Labor Press Assn., Washington, 1973-79, pres., 1980-82, sec.-treas., 1984—, editor ILPA Reporter, 1983-84; Elijah P. Lovejoy lectr. So. Ill. U., 1970. Mem. Falls Church (Va.) Democratic Com., 1970-84; founding mem. Falls Church Commn. on Status of Women, 1975-76; pres. Montessori Sch. No. Va., 1970. Mem. Slovenian Heritage Com. Washington, Slovenian Choral Soc. Washington, Am. Slovenian Cath. Union. Roman Catholic. Office: care The Newspaper Guild 1125 15th St NW Suite 835 Washington DC 20005

CESS, ROBERT DONALD, atmospheric sciences educator; b. Portland, Oreg., Mar. 3, 1933; s. Harold Francis and Louise Elizabeth (Teasdale) C.; m. Patricia Ann Peirano, Dec. 23, 1953; children: Barbara Ann, Curtis Maxwell. B.S., Oreg. State U., 1955; M.S. (Westinghouse fellow), Purdue U., 1956, Ph.D., U. Pitts., 1960. Research engr. Westinghouse Research Labs., 1956-60; asso. prof. engring. N.C. State U., 1960-61; asso. prof. engring SUNY, Stony Brook, 1961-65, prof. engring., 1965-75, prof. atmospheric scis., 1975-81, leading prof. atmospheric scis., 1981—; adj. prof. U. Pitts., 1959-60; vis. prof. atmospheric physics Leningrad (USSR) State U., 1980; adv. com. climate sensitivity group Nat. Center Atmospheric Research, 1978—; mem. carbon dioxide/climate rev. panel NRC, 1982; cons. Westinghouse Electric Corp., 1960-64, Lawrence Livermore Nat. Lab., 1981—; del. U.S./USSR confs. on protection of environ., 1978, 79. Author: (with E. M. Sparrow) Radiation Heat Transfer, 1966; asso. editor: Jour. Quantitative Spectroscopy and Radiative Transfer, 1978—; contbr. articles to profl. jours. Mem. Brookhaven Town Adv. Com., 1969-75. Recipient Heat Transfer Meml. award ASME, 1977; NSF research grantee, 1960—. Mem. AAAS, Sigma Xi. Home: 22 Woodfield Rd Stony Brook NY 11790 Office: SUNY Stony Brook NY 11794

CETRON, MARVIN JEROME, consulting company executive; b. Bklyn., July 5, 1930; s. Jack Student and Gertrude Leah C.; m. Gloria Rita Wasserman, June 29, 1955; children: Edward Jack, Adam Bruce. B.S. in Indsl. Engring, Pa. State U., 1952; M.S. in Bus. Adminstrn, Columbia U., 1959; Ph.D. in Research and Devel. Mgmt, Am. U., 1970. Civilian with U.S. Navy, 1951-71, chief research and devel. planning Naval Material command, 1963-71; founder, pres. Forecasting Internat. Ltd., Arlington, Va., 1971—; adj. prof. Am. U., M.I.T., Ga. Inst. Tech.; Mem. research and devel. adv. com. USCG, 1974—. Author: Technological Forecasting: A Practical Approach, 1969, Technica; Reource Management: Quantitative Methods, 1970, The Science of Managing Organized Technology, 4 vols, 1971, Industrial Applications of Technological Forecasting: Its Use in Research and Development Management, 1971, The Navy Technological Forcast, 3d edit, 1970, Technology Assessment in a Dynamic Environment, 1972, The Methodology of Technology Assessment, 1972, Quantitative Decision-aiding Techniques for Research and Development Management, 1972, Proc. NATO Advanced Study Insititute on Technology Transfer, 1974, Industrial Technology Transfer, 1977, Encounters with the Future, A Forecast of Life into the 21st Century, 1982, Jobs with a Future, 1984; editor-in-chief: Tech. Assessment Jour, 1971-78. Served with USCG, 1954-56. Mem. Ops. Research Soc. Am., IEEE, Tech. and Indsl. Mgmt. Soc., World Future Soc. Home: 9324 Convento Terr Fairfax VA 22031 Office: 1001 N Highland St Arlington VA 22201

CEY, RONALD CHARLES, baseball player; b. Tacoma, Feb. 15, 1948; s. Frank Louis and Shirley Eleanor (Robinson) C.; m. Frances Louise Fishbein, Sept. 11, 1971; Children: Daniel Elliott, Amanda Beth. Student, Wash. State U., Pullman, 1966-68, Western Wash. State Coll., Bellingham, 1968-69. With Los Angeles Dodgers, 1972-82, with Chgo. Cubs, 1983—; player for Nat. League in All-Star Game, 1974-78. Sports chmn. Am. Lung Assn., 1977; fund raiser Florence Crittenton Services, Pacific Lodge Boys Home, Woodland Hills, Calif. Named Dodger Rookie of Yr., 1973, Dodger Most Valuable Player, 1975; Sportsman of Yr. Westwood Shrine Club, 1977, Encino (Calif.) Shrine, 1978; Man of Yr. and Pro Athlete of Yr., Tacoma, 1977; Nat. League Player of Month, April, 1977; Grad. of Yr. Am. Amateur Baseball Congress, 1975; recipient Babe Ruth award Baseball Writers Assn. Am., 1981, World Series Hero award Baseball Writers Assn. Am., 1981, co-most valuable player award of 1981 World Series Major League Baseball and Sport mag. Mem. Major League Baseball Players Assn., Phi Delta Theta (Lou Gehrig award 1982). Home: 22714 Creole Rd Woodland Hills CA 91364

CHABON, STEVE, law firm executive; b. Gilberton, Pa., Mar. 4, 1931; s. Onufer and Anna (Bobiak) C.; m. Roberta Jean McGuire, Oct. 30, 1954; children: Stephen J., Gregory M. B.A., U. Md., 1968. Enlisted in U.S. Navy and USAF, 1949; commd. 1st lt. U.S. Army, 1962, advanced through grades to maj., 1967; mil. asst. to spl. asst. to sec. def., 1965-67, sec. gen. staff, Vietnam, 1968-69, exec. asst. to asst. sec. army, 1969-71; dir. adminstrn. Def. Systems Mgmt. Coll., Ft. Belvoir, Va., 1971; ret., 1972; mem. profl. staff Gen. Electric Co. Center for Advanced Studies, 1972; adminstr. law firm Williams & Connolly, Washington, 1973-80; dir. adminstrn. law firm Smith Moore Smith Schell & Hunter, Greensboro, N.C., 1980-82; adminstrv. dir. Arnold & Porter Law Firm, Washington, DC, 1982—. Composer: Rhapsody in Notes, 1953. Decorated Legion of Merit, Meritorious Service medal with oak leaf cluster, Joint Service Commendation medal. Club: Army Navy Country (Arlington, Va.). Home: 9313 MacSwain Pl Springfield VA 22153 Office: Arnold & Porter 1200 New Hampshire Ave NW Washington DC 20036

CHABRIER, JACQUES RENE, financial consultant; b. Nancy, France, Jan. 15, 1921; came to U.S., 1946, naturalized, 1954; s. R. Charles and Simone (Huber) C.; m. Marie Anne Smith, May 27, 1948; 1 dau., Yvonne Vasquez. B.A., Rennes U., 1939; B.L., U. Paris, 1942; grad., Ecole des Sciences Politiques, Paris, 1942. Staff asst. S.N. Pathe Cinema, Paris, France, 1942-43, exec. asst. prodn., studio v.p., 1944-45, Am. rep., 1946-47; pres. Pathe Cinema Corp., 1947-51, Paris Theatre Corp. N.Y., 1948-51; mem. staff investment dept. Hartford Nat. Bank & Trust Co., 1951, supr., 1952-55, asst. trust officer, 1956, trust officer, 1956-58, v.p., 1958-1961, exec. v.p., 1961-68; pres., dir. Chappell & Co., Inc., N.Y.C., 1968-73; chmn., dir. Chappell & Co. Ltd., London, 1968-73; exec. v.p., dir. Polygram Corp., N.Y.C., 1973-74; financial cons. N.Am. Philips Corp., N.Y.C., 1974—, Mandes Gans Bank, N.V., Amsterdam, 1975—, Drexel-Burnham-Lambert Group, N.Y.C., 1976—; dir., mem. investment com. Mut. Ins. Co., Hartford, Covenant Ins. Co. Hartford, Ensign Bickford Industries, Inc., Simsbury, Drexel Burnham Lambert Realty Inc., N.Y.C.; dir. Davey-Bickford Smith & Co., Rouen, France, D.B.L. Realty Corp.; v.p., dir. Importers Motion Picture Orgn. N.Y., 1950-51; Film adviser French embassy, Washington, N.Y.C., 1948-52. Trustee Hartford Coll. for Women, Nat. Health and Welfare Retirement Assn., Edward W. Hazen Found.; bd. dirs. Children's Village, Dobbs Ferry, N.Y., Circle Repertory Theatre, N.Y.C. Mem. Nat. Music Pubs. Assn. (dir.), ASCAP (dir. 1968-74), French C. of C. in U.S. (treas. 1949-51). Club: Knickerbocker (N.Y.C.). Home: 605 Park Ave New York NY 10021 Office: North Am Philips Corp 100 E 42d St New York NY 10017

CHACKO, GEORGE KUTTICKAL, systems science educator, consultant; b. Trivandrum, India, July 1, 1930; came to U.S., 1953, naturalized, 1967; s. Geevarghese Kuttickal and Thankamma (Mathew) C.; m. Yo Yee, Aug. 10, 1957; children: Rajah Yee, Ashia Yo. M.A. in Econs. and Polit. Philosophy, Madras (India) U., 1950; postgrad. (Coll. scholar), St. Xavier's Coll., Calcutta, India, 1950-52; B. Commerce, Calcutta U., 1952; cert. postgrad. tng. (Inst. fellow), Indian Stat. Inst., Calcutta, 1951, Princeton U., 1953-54; Ph.D. in Econometrics, New Sch. for Social Research, 1959, UCLA, 1961. Asst. editor Indian Fin., Calcutta, 1951-53; comml. corr. Times of India, 1953; dir. mktg. and mgmt. research Royal Metal Mfg. Co., N.Y.C., 1958-60; mgr. dept. ops. research (Hughes Semicondr. div.), Newport Beach, Calif., 1960-61; staff ops. research cons. Union Carbide Corp., N.Y.C., 1962-63; mem. tech. staff Research Analysis Corp., McLean, Va., 1963-65, MITRE Corp., Arlington, Va., 1965-67; sr. staff scientist TRW Systems Group, Washington, 1967-70; cons. def. systems, computer, space, tech. systems and internat. devel. systems; asso. in math. test devel. Ednl. Testing Service, Princeton, N.J., 1955-57; asst. prof. bus. adminstrn., UCLA, 1961-62; lectr. Dept. Agr. Grad. Sch., 1965-67; asst. professorial lectr. George Washington U., 1965-68; professorial lectr. Am. U., 1967-70, adj. prof., 1970; vis. prof. def. systems Mgmt. Coll., Ft. Belvoir, Va., 1972-73; vis. prof. U. So. Calif., 1970-71, prof. systems mgmt., 1971-83, prof. systems sci., 1983—; sr. Fulbright prof. Nat. Chengchi U., Nat. Taiwan U., Taipei, 1983-84; tech. proposal reviewer NSF, 1972, chmn. tech. evaluation panel, 1976; speaker in field. Author: 13 books in field, including Applied Statistics in Decision-Making, 1971, Computer-aided Decision-Making, 1972, Systems Approach to Public and Private Sector Problems, 1976, Operations Research Approach to Problem Formulation and Solution, 1976, Management Information Systems, 1979, The Metal: Productivity Promises of Robotics and Artificial Intelligence, 1984; contbr. articles to profl. publs.; editor, contbr.: 17 books, including The Recognition of Systems in Health Services, 1969, Reducing the Cost of Space Transportation, 1969, Systems Approach to Environmental Pollution, 1972, National Organization of Health Services—U.S., USSR, China, Europe, 1979, Educational Innovation in Health Services-U.S., Europe, Middle East, Africa, 1979; assoc. editor Internat. Jour. of Forecasting, 1982—. Active Nat. Presbyterian Ch., Washington, 1967—, mem. ch. council, 1969-71, mem. chancel choir, 1967—; co-dean Ch. Family Camp, 1977; coordinator Life Abundant Discovery Group, 1979. Recipient awards, including Gold medal Inter-Collegiate Extempore Debate in Malayalam U. Travancore, Trivandrum, India, 1945, 1st Pl. Yogic Exercises Competition U. Travancore, 1946, 1st prize Inter-Varsity Debating Team, Madras, 1949, NSF internat. sci. lectures award, 1982. Fellow AAAS (mem. nat. council 1968-73, chmn. or co-chmn. symposia 1971, 72, 74, 76, 77, 78), Am. Astronautical Soc. (v.p. publs. 1969-71, editor Tech. Newsletter 1968-72, mng. editor Jour. Astronautical Scis. 1969-75); mem. Ops. Research Soc. Am. (vice chmn. com. of representation on AAAS 1972-78, mem. nat. council tech. sect. on health 1966-68, editor Tech. Newsletter on Health 1966-73), Washington Ops. Research Council (trustee 1967-69, chmn. tech. colloquia 1967-68, editor Tech. Newsletter 1967-68), Inst. Mgmt. Scis. (rep. to Internat. Inst. for Applied Systems Analysis in Vienna, Austria 1976-77, session chmn. Athens, Greece 1977, Atlanta 1977), World Future Soc. (editorial bd. publs. 1970-71), AAUP., N.Y. Acad. Scis. Democrat. Club: Kiwanis (Capital Dist. Div. One Internat. Disting. Service award 1968, 70, Friendship Heights Club Outstanding Service award 1972-73, First Disting. Dir. Taipei-Keystone Club 1978). Office: U So Calif Office 5510 Columbia Pike Arlington VA 22204 *As one who was privileged to be born into a Christian family tracing itself to the founding in the year 52 of the Mar Thoma Syrian Church in Southwest India by Thomas the Doubting Disciple of Jesus Christ, I look upon the exciting encounters I have had with new ideas (such as Theory of Games) and new professions (such as Operations Research) as precious talents over which I exercise stewardship by enjoying excellence of effort and exposition toward a better tomorrow at home and abroad, as an Indian-American blest with a most supportive family.*

CHADDOCK, JACK BARTLEY, mechanical engineering educator; b. Cameron, W.Va., Dec. 6, 1924; s. Clyde Franklin and Helen Booher (Jacobs) C.; m. Helen Mallary McGurk, May 30, 1973; stepchildren: Katherine Mahoney, James Mahoney. B.S. in Naval Sci, U. S.C., 1945; B.S.M.E., W.Va. U., 1948; S.M., M.I.T., 1949, M.E., 1952, Sc.D., 1955. Registered profl. engr., N.C. Asst. prof. mech. engring. M.I.T., 1953-57; asso. prof. Rensselaer Poly. Inst., 1957-59; prof. Purdue U., 1959-66; sr. cons. research div. Carrier Corp., Syracuse, N.Y., 1966, cons., 1966-72; prof., chmn. dept. mech. engring. Duke U., 1966—; Fulbright lectr. Finland Inst. Tech., 1955-56; vis. research fellow Commonwealth Sci. and Indsl. Research Orgn., Melbourne, Australia, 1973; vis. prof. U. New South Wales, Sydney, Australia, 1973, Bldg. Research Establishment, Garston, Eng., 1980; mem. rev. panel Nat. Bur. Standards, 1977—. Author: Introduction to Energy Technology, 1976; contbr. articles to profl. publs. Trustee, pres. John B. Pierce Found., N.Y.C., 1981—. Served to ensign USNR, 1945-46. Recipient Wolverine Pub. award, 1958. Fellow ASHRAE (Disting. Service award 1971, E.K. Campbell award 1972, pres. 1981-82); mem. ASME, Internat. Solar Energy Soc., Internat. Inst. Refrigeration, U.S. Nat. Commn. for Bldg. Research and Documentation, Phi Beta Kappa. Democrat. Mem. United Ch. of Christ. Clubs: Hollow Rock Racquet and Swim, Kerr Lake Yacht. Office: Duke U Durham NC 27706

CHADICK, T. C., state supreme ct. justice; b. Winnsboro, Tex., Sept. 21, 1910; s. Walter Martin and Carrie Ozella (Mars) C.; m. Doris Adyline Scruggs, Apr. 12, 1941; children—Mary Susan, Nancy Doris Ann. Student, Burleson Jr. Coll., 1927-28, So. Meth. U., 1928-31; LL.B., Cumberland U., 1933. Bar: Tex. bar 1933, U.S. Supreme Ct. bar 1938. Individual practice law, 1934, city atty., Winnsboro, 1934-38, county atty., Wood County, Tex., 1939-40; mem. Tex. State Senate, 1941-48, pres. protem, 1947-48; state dist. judge, Quitman, Tex., 1949-56; chief Ct. of Civil Appeals, Texarkana, Tex., 1957-77; justice Supreme Ct. Tex., Austin, 1977—; Mem. Tex. Jud. Council, 1959-77, pres., 1961-63. Mem. Tex. Bar Assn. Democrat. Methodist. Clubs: Rotary, Masons.

CHADIMA, IVAN CHARLES, hotel executive; b. Prague, Czechoslovakia, Oct. 17, 1940; came to Can., 1969, naturalized, 1974. Grad., Hotel Sch., Marienbad, Czechoslovakia, 1958—; student, U. Prague Sch. Hotel Adminstrn., Prague, 1961-64, Cedok Inst. Hotel Mgmt., Prague, 1968. With Cedok Hotels Ltd., Prague, 1958-68; asst. food and beverage mgr. Le Chateau Champlain, Montreal, Que., Can., 1969-72; with Ramada Inns Can. Ltd., 1972-77; gen. mgr. Don Valley, Toronto, Ont., 1975-77, Four Seasons Hotel, Ottawa, Ont., 1977-78, Toronto, 1978-82; v.p., mng. dir. Ritz Carlton, N.Y.C., 1982—. Served as officer Czechoslovakian Army, 1959-61. Roman Catholic. Clubs: Bayview Golf and Country; Skal (N.Y.C.). Office: 112 Central Park S New York NY 10019

CHADWICK, GEORGE ALBERT, JR., retired lawyer; b. Alexandria, Va., Nov. 20, 1911; s. George Albert and Asenath Moore (Graves) C.; m. Eleanor Worthington Margerum, Aug. 10, 1934; children: George Albert III, Charles M.; m. Avaleen Seamans Gazaway, June 14, 1960; stepchildren: Tarillis Jane (Mrs. T. Paul Adams), Dan Lee Seamans. A.B., Princeton, 1932; LL.B., Georgetown U., 1937. Bar: D.C. 1936, Md. 1944. Practiced in, Washington, 1936-75, Rockville, Md., 1975; of counsel firm Chadwick & Whaley, 1975; engaged in farming, 1957—; owner Chadwick Bar Rev. Sch., 1937-43; pres., dir. York & Frederick Ry., 1975-76; dir. Prodelin, Inc., Hightstown, N.J., 1953-64, So. Oxygen Co., Bladensburg, Md., 1955-62; dir., gen. counsel Horsemen's Benevolent and Protective Assn., 1959-75; pres., dir. Md. Midland Ry., 1978-81, chmn. bd., dir., 1981—; pres. Boyds (Md.) Fed. Credit Union, 1962-67, dir., 1962-80. Author articles. Pres. Washington Grove (Md.) PTA, 1947-50, Edward U. Taylor Sch. P.T.A., Boyds, 1961-63; life mem. Md. PTA. Served to capt. AUS, 1943-46. Named to Horsemen's Benevolent and Protective Assn. Hall of Fame, 1976. Mem. Am., Md., D.C., Montgomery County (Md.) bar assns., Phi Alpha Delta. Democrat. Episcopalian (jr. warden, vestryman 1965-68). Clubs: Barristers, Princeton, Army and Navy (Washington); Princeton (N.Y.C.). Home: Huckleberry Hill Boyds MD 20841 Office: Pennsylvania Ave Walkersville MD 21793

CHADWICK, JOHN LLOYD, accountant; b. Windsor, Ont., Can., Aug. 14, 1922; came to U.S., 1951, naturalized, 1957; s. Charles Harvey and Susan (Sullivan) C.; m. Bernice Danaher, Sept. 8, 1945; children—Donald, Cherilynn (Mrs. Lyle Baugh). B.A. with honors, U. Western Ont., 1944. Chartered accountant, Can. Pub. accountant Clarkson Gordon & Co. (chartered accountants), Hamilton, Ont., 1945-50, Lorenzen & Co., Windsor, 1950-51, Peat Marwick Mitchell (C.P.A.s), Detroit, 1951-52; auditor Parke, Davis & Co., Detroit, 1952-55; with Jennings & Jewell (C.P.A.s), Detroit, 1955-56; controller, then treas. Goebel Brewing Co., Detroit, 1956-65; treas. Squirt Bottling Co., Ferndale, Mich., 1965-66; controller Champion Home Builders Co., Dryden, Mich., 1966-70, treas., 1970-77, sec., 1971-80, v.p. fin., 1972-77, sr. v.p., 1977-80, dir., 1972-79; pres., dir. Champion Ventures, Inc., 1977-81; v.p., dir. Clinton Chem. Co., 1977-81; pvt. practice acctg., 1981—. Dist. vice chmn. Detroit area council Boy Scouts Am., 1960-65; Sec.-treas. Clark Fund, George Fund. Served with Canadian Navy, 1944-45. Club: K.C.

CHADY, EDWARD JOSEPH, accountant; b. Whitewater, Wis., Sept. 4, 1924; s. Ernest Edward and Mary Lucile (Daley) C.; m. Doris Lorraine Hollinger, Sept. 25, 1945; children: Edward A., Robert J., Anne, Thomas, Mary Pat, Stephen, William, Susan. B.E., U. Wis.-Whitewater, 1948; M.B.A., U. Louisville, 1969. With Thomas Industries, Inc., Louisville, 1950—, chief acct., asst. sec., 1961-73, chief acct., sec., 1973-76, sec., controller, 1976-78, v.p. fin., sec., controller, 1978—. Mem. exec. bd., treas. Old Ky. Home council Boys Scouts Am.; chmn. Cath. Com. Scouting Archdiocese of Louisville.; treas. K.C. Mental Retardation Found. of Ky.; bd. dirs. Louisville Regional Sci. Fair, Inc. Served with USNR, 1943-46. Recipient Silver Beaver award Boy Scouts Am.; St. George medal Nat. Cath. Com. Scouting; Bronze Pelican Archdiocese of Louisville. Mem. Fin. Execs. Inst. (pres.). Clubs: K.C., Kiwanis. Home: 3532 Dayton Louisville KY 40207 Office: 207 E Broadway Louisville KY 40202

CHAET, BERNARD ROBERT, artist, educator; b. Boston, Mar. 7, 1924; s. David and Golda (Benjamin) C.; m. Ninon Lacey, Dec. 14, 1951; 1 dau., Leah. Student, Sch. Fine Arts, Boston, 1942-44, 48; B.S., Tufts U., 1950. Tchr. Boston Pub. Schs., Inst. Contemporary Art, Boston, 1951—; instr. painting Yale, 1951-56, asst. prof., 1956-59, asso. prof. painting, chmn. dept. art, 1959-62, prof. painting, 1969—, William Leffingwell prof. painting, 1979—, dir. art. div., 1960-66. Contbg. editor: Arts mag, 1956-59; orig. exhbn. 20th Century Drawing, Yale U. Art Gallery, 1955; Represented in permanent colls., Worcester (Mass.) Art. Mus., Bklyn. Mus., DeCordova Mus., Lincoln, Mass., Brandeis U., Addison Gallery Am. Art, Andover, Mass., U. Calif. at Los Angeles, Fogg Mus., Harvard, Mus. Fine Arts Boston, Mus. Art R.I. Sch. Design, Yale Art Gallery, U. Mass., U. Conn., N.Y. U., State U. N.Y. at Cortland, Brown U.; Author: Artists at Work, 1960, The Art of Drawing, 1970, 3d edit., 1983, An Artist's Notebook: Materials and Techniques of Drawing and Painting, 1979; One-man shows, Boston, N.Y.C., White Museum of Cornell U., group exhbns., Corcoran Gallery of Art, Modern Mus., Bklyn., Los Angeles County, Detroit museums, Art Inst. Chgo., Inst. Contemporary Art, Boston, Am. Drawings traveling show of French Museums, others, group shows, Mass. Inst. Tech., U. Ill., U. Nebr., Brandeis U. Recipient grant Nat. Found. Arts and Humanities, 1966-67. Home: 141 Cold Spring St New Haven CT 06511 Office: Yale U New Haven CT 06520

CHAFE, WALLACE L., educator, linguist; b. Cambridge, Mass., Sept. 3, 1927; s. Albert J. and Nathalie (Amback) C.; m. Mary Elizabeth Butterworth, June 23, 1951 (div. 1980); children—Christopher, Douglas, Stephen. B.A., Yale, 1950, M.A., 1956, Ph.D., 1958. Asst. prof. U. Buffalo, 1958-59; linguist Bur. Am. Ethnology, Smithsonian Instn., 1959-62; mem. faculty U. Calif. at Berkeley, 1962—, prof. linguistics, 1967—. Author: Seneca Thanksgiving Rituals, 1961, Seneca Morphology and Dictionary, 1967, Meaning and the Structure of Language, 1970, The Pear Stories, 1980. Served with USNR, 1945-46. Mem. Linguistic Soc. Am., Am. Psychol. Assn., Am. Anthrop. Assn. Home: 636 Beloit Ave Kensington CA 94708 Office: Dept Linguistics Univ Cal Berkeley CA 94720

CHAFEE, JOHN HUBBARD, senator; b. Providence, Oct. 22, 1922; s. John S. and Janet (Hunter) C.; m. Virginia Coates, Nov. 4, 1950; children: Zechariah, Lincoln, John, Georgia, Quentin. B.A., Yale U., 1947; LL.B., Harvard U., 1950; LL.D., Brown U., 1964, Providence Coll., 1965, U. R.I., 1965, Jacksonville U., 1970, Bryant Coll., 1979. Bar: R.I. bar 1950. Practice law, Providence, 1952-62, 73-76; mem. R.I. Ho. of Reps. 3d Dist. Warwick, 1957-62, minority leader, 1959-62; gov., R.I., 1963-69; sec. Navy, 1969-72; mem. U.S. Senate from R.I., 1977—. Chmn. Republican Gov.'s Assn., 1967; Mem. corp. Yale, 1972-78; trustee Deerfield Acad., 1970-79. Served to capt. USMCR, 1942-45, 51-52. Chubb fellow Yale, 1965. Mem. R.I. Bar, Fed. Bar Assn. Office: sd567 dirksen bldg Washington DC 20510 *

CHAFETZ, MORRIS EDWARD, physician; b. Worcester, Mass., Apr. 20, 1924; s. Isaac and Rose (Handel) C.; m. Marion Claire Donovan, Sept. 2, 1946; children: Gary Stephen, Marc Edward, Adam Francis. B.S., Tufts U., 1944, M.D., 1948. Diplomate: Am. Bd. Psychiatry and Neurology. Intern U.S. Marine Hosp., Detroit, 1948-49; resident psychiatry State Hosp., Howard, R.I., 1949-51; fellow in neurophysiology Instituto Nacional de Cardiologia, Mexico, 1951-52; dir. Alcohol Clinic, Mass. Gen. Hosp., 1957-68, dir. acute psychiat. service, 1962-68, dir. clin. psychiat. services, 1968-70, asst. psychiatrist, 1957-58, asso. psychiatrist, 1958-64, psychiatrist, 1964-70; acting dir. div. alcohol abuse and alcoholism NIMH, 1970-71; dir. Nat. Inst. on Alcohol Abuse and Alcoholism, NIMH, 1971-73, Nat. Inst. Alcohol Abuse and Alcoholism, Alcohol, Drug Abuse and Mental Health Adminstrn., Rockville, Md., 1973-75; prin. research scientist, center for met. planning and research Faculty Arts and Scis., Johns Hopkins U., Balt., 1975—; pres. Health Edn. Found., Washington, 1976—; chmn. bd. Health Insts., Washington, 1977-82; asst. in psychiatry

Harvard Med. Sch., 1954-57, asst. clin. prof. psychiatry, 1957-68, asso. clin. prof. psychiatry, 1968-70; clin. prof. psychiatry and behavioral scis. Med. U. S.C., 1980—; adj. prof. Center for Met. Affairs and Public Policy, Coll. of Charleston, 1979—; Asst. surgeon USPHS, 1948-49, sr. asst. surgeon, 1951-52; cons. Pan Am. Health Orgn., 1972—. Author: Alcoholism and Society, 1962, Liquor: The Servant of Man, 1965, The Treatment of Alcoholism: A Study of Programs and Problems, 1967, Frontiers of Alcoholism, 1970, Why Drinking Can Be Good for You, 1976; Editor: Procs. 1st-4th Ann. Alcoholism Confs. of Nat. Inst. on Alcohol Abuse and Alcoholism, 1973, 74; editor: The Encyclopedia of Alcoholism, 1982, The Alcoholic Patient: Diagnosis and Management, 1983; guest editor: Jour. of Nervous and Mental Disease, 1971; editorial adv. bd.: Jour. Alcohol Studies; weekly columnist: Med. Tribune. Recipient Gold medal Internat. Film and TV Festival New York, 1972, Mt. Airy Found., 1974; Maudsley Bequest lectr. U. Edinburgh, 1969; Moses Greeley Parker lectr., 1969; Louis and Amelia Block lectr. Mt. Zion Hosp. and Med. Center, San Francisco, 1969; Corr. mem. Inst. for Study and Prevention of Alcoholism in Zagreb, 1971—. Fellow Royal Soc. Health; mem. Am. Psychiat. Assn., Am. Orthopsychiat. Assn., A.M.A., Am. Hosp. Assn., AAAS, Sigma Xi. Home: 3129 Dumbarton St NW Washington DC 20007 600 New Hampshire Ave Suite 452 Washington DC 20037 *The Only thing of real value in this world is people.*

CHAFFEE, SUZY, skier, sports activist, bus. woman. Student, Denver, Wash., Innsbruck univs., UCLA. Skier; capt. U.S. Olympic Ski Team, Grenoble, France, 1968; co-founder, pres. World Sports Found. (instrumental in passage Amateur Sports Act of 1978), 1972—. Numerous guest appearances nat. TV shows including Dick Clark's Athletes of the Decade Spl, Today Show, Tonight Show, Good Morning America, American Sportsman, Kids Are People Too; co-host: Challenge of Sexes series ABC-TV Wide World of Sports, 1970-76; host: Ski Scene, ABC affiliate, 1979; appeared in: TV movie Ski Lift; Willy Bergner ski films, 1972-76, Chapstick TV commls.; designer Suzy Chaffee ski wear, sport frames, running shoes, rollerskates sportswear lines. Mem. adv. bd. Girl Scouts Am., Healthy Am. Coalition, Women's Sports Found., Women's Campaign Fund; spl. adviser on employee fitness Pres.'s Council on Fitness and Sport, to Soviets and White House on Soviet-U.S. Olympic diplomacy; leader women sports Title IX Opportunities in Schs.; active Kennedy Spl. Olympics; bd. dirs. U.S. Olympic Com., 1973-76. Recipient Blue Cross-Blue Shield award for contbn. to health; B'nai B'rith award for sports contbns.; Big Apple award for women sports; citation as top speaker U.S. Platform Assn.; cited by nat. press as queen of sports and 1st lady of skiing; others. World freestyle ski champion, 1971-73; innovator ski ballet to music; developed double ski ballet with 12 lifts.

CHAFFEE, WALTER BURNS, lawyer; b. Garden Grove, Calif., Oct. 3, 1915; s. Edward Albert and Carrie (Speelman) C.; m. Margaret Nichols, Apr. 6, 1941; children: Douglas, Paul, William, Janet, Richard. A.A., Fullerton Jr. Coll., 1935; B.A., U. Calif. at Berkeley, 1937, J.D., 1940. Bar: Calif. 1940. Practiced in, Oakland, 1940-41; research asst. Calif. Judicial Council, 1941-42; law clk. Justice William O. Douglas, 1942; atty. War Shipping Adminstrn., Washington, 1943; mem. firm Launer, Chaffee, Ward, Rothrock & Schulman, Fullerton, 1946-56, 58—; city atty., 1952-56; judge Municipal Ct., 1956-58; dir. A.J. Industries. Appeal agt. Selective Service Bd. No. 133, 1949-71; Past chmn. Orange County Democratic Central Com.; Past pres., bd. dirs. Fullerton Boys Club, Family Service Assn. Orange County; bd. dirs. Fullerton Coll. Found.; organizer, past sec. North Orange County Hosp. Bldg. Assn. Served with USNR, 1943-46; PTO. Mem. Calif. Bar Assn., Orange County Bar Assn. (past pres.), Order of Coif. Methodist (past chmn. ofcl. bd.). Home: 184 Hillcrest Dr Fullerton CA 92632 Office: 131 W Wilshire St Fullerton CA 92632

CHAFFIN, VERNER FRANKLIN, lawyer, educator; b. Martin, Ga., Sept. 26, 1918; s. Emory Franklin and Mabel Lea (Verner) C.; m. Corinne Ethel Tison, July 17, 1943; children—Ethel, Verner Franklin, Mary Davis, John Edwards. A.B., U. Ga., LL.B., 1942; J.S.D., Yale, 1961. Bar: Ga. bar 1942, Ala. bar 1953, U.S. Supreme Ct. bar 1965. Atty. Dept. Justice, 1946-47; mem. faculty U. Ga., Athens, 1957—, prof. law, 1954-69, Fuller E. Callaway prof., 1969—; mem. nat. labor panel Am. Arbitration Assn., 1957—, mem. pub. employment disputes settlement panel, 1969—; mem. panel arbitrators Fed. Mediation and Conciliation Service, 1973—; trustee Inst. Continuing Legal Edn. Ga., 1969-76. Author: Georgia Annotations to the Restatement (Second) Trusts, 1970, Studies in the Georgia Law of Decedents' Estates and Future Interests, 1979; Contbr. numerous articles to legal jours. Mem. permanent jud. commn. Gen. Assembly, Presbyn. Ch. U.S.A., 1972-75; elder 1st Presbyn. Ch., Athens, 1966-71, 74-79; pres. Athens chpt. Am. Cancer Soc., 1968-69, Athens Community Concert Assn., 1966-67; trustee Athens Hist. Found., 1962—. Served with USNR, 1943-46, 51-53. Sterling fellow Yale, 1950-51. Fellow Am. Coll. Probate Counsel; mem. Am. Law Inst., Internat. Acad. Law and Sci., Am. Judicature Soc., Athens, Western Circuit, Ga., Am. bar assns., Ga. Hist. Soc., Athens-Clarke Heritage Found., Blue Key, Sphinx, Order of Coif, Phi Beta Kappa, Phi Kappa Phi, Phi Delta Phi, Omicron Delta Kappa. Clubs: Athens City, Athens Country, Toccoa (Ga.) Golf and Country. Home: 510 Riverview Rd Athens GA 30606 Office: University of Georgia Law School Athens GA 30602

CHAGALL, DAVID, journalist, market research consultant; b. Phila., Nov. 20, 1930; s. Harry and Ida (Coopersmith) C.; m. Juneau Joan Alsin, Nov. 15, 1957. Student, Swarthmore Center Coll., 1948-49; B.A., Pa. State U., 1952; postgrad., Sorbonne, U. Paris, 1953-54. Social caseworker State of Pa., Phila., 1955-57; sci. editor Jour. I.E.E., 1959-61; pub. relations staff A.E.I.-Hotpoint Ltd., London, 1961-62; mktg. research assoc. Chilton Co., Phila., 1962-63; mktg. research project dir. Haug Assos., Inc. (Roper Orgn.), Los Angeles, 1964-74; research cons. Haug Assos., 1976-79; investigative reporter for nat. mags., 1975—. Author: Diary of a Deaf Mute, 1960, The Century God Slept, 1963, The Spieler For The Holy Spirit, 1972, The New Kingmakers, 1981; pub.: Inside Campaigning, 1983; contbr. syndicated column, articles, revs., stories and poetry to mags., jours., newspapers; contbg. editor: TV Guide. Recipient U. Wis. Poetry prize, 1971; nominee Nat. Book award in fiction, 1972, Pulitzer prize in letters, 1973, Disting. Health Journalism award, 1978; Carnegie Trust grantee, 1964. Home: PO Box 85 Agoura CA 91301

CHAHINE, MOUSTAFA TOUFIC, atmospheric scientist; b. Beirut, Jan. 1, 1935; s. Toufic M. and Hind S. (Tabbara) C.; m. Marina Bandak, Dec. 9, 1960; children: Tony T., Steve S. B.S., U. Wash., 1956, M.S., 1957; Ph.D., U. Calif., Berkeley, 1960. With Jet Propulsion Lab., Calif. Inst. Tech., Pasadena, 1960—, mgr. planetary atmospheres sect., 1975-78, sr. research scientist, mgr. earth and space scis. div., 1978—; vis. scientist MIT, 1969-70; vis. prof. Am. U., Beirut, 1971-72; mem. NASA Space and Earth Sci. Adv. Com., 1982—; cons. U.S. Navy, 1972-76. Contbr. articles on atmospheric scis. to profl. jours. Recipient medal for exceptional sci. achievements NASA, 1969. Fellow Am. Phys. Soc.; mem. Am. Meteorol. Soc., Sigma Xi. Office: 4800 Oak Grove Dr Pasadena CA 91109

CHAI, WINBERG, political science educator, university official; b. Shanghai, China, Oct. 16, 1932; came to U.S., 1951, naturalized, 1973; s. Ch'u and Mei-en (Tsao) C.; m. Carolyn Everett, Mar. 17, 1966; children: Maria May-lee, Jeffrey Tien-yu. Student, Hartwick Coll., 1951-53; B.A., Wittenberg U., 1955; M.A., New Sch. Social Research, 1958; Ph.D., N.Y. U., 1968. Lectr. New Sch. Social Research, 1957-61; vis. asst. prof. Drew U., 1961-62; asst. prof. Fairleigh Dickinson U., 1962-65, U. Redlands, 1965-68, asso. prof., 1969-73, chmn. dept., 1970-73; prof., chmn. Asian studies CCNY, 1973-79; disting. prof. polit. sci., v.p. acad. affairs, spl. asst. to pres. U. S.D., Vermillion, 1979— (on leave 1983-84); chmn. Third World Conf. Workshop Found., Inc., Chgo.; vice chmn. U.S.-Asia Research Inst., N.Y.C.; cons. Software System & Tech., Inc., U.S. Dept. Edn., Iowa Assn. Ind. Colls. and Univs., Saudi Arabia Edn. Mission to U.S., John Glenn Presdl. Com. Author: (with Ch'u Chai) The Story of Chinese Philosophy, 1961, The Changing Society of China, 1962, rev. edit., 1969, The New Politics of Communist China, 1972, The Search for a New China, 1975; editor: Essential Works of Chinese Communism, 1969, (with James C. Hsiung) Asia in the U.S. Foreign Policy, 1981; co-editor: U.S. Asian Relations: The National Security Paradox, 1983; co-translator: (with Ch'u Chai) A Treasury of Chinese Literature, 1965. Ford Found. humanities grantee, 1968, 69; Haynes Found. fellow, 1967, 68; Pacific Cultural Found. grantee, 1978; NSF grantee, 1970; Hubert Eaton Meml. Fund grantee, 1972-73; Field Found. grantee, 1973, 75; Henry Luce Found. grantee, 1978, 80; S.D. Humanities Com. grantee, 1980. Mem. Am. Assn. Chinese Studies (pres. 1978-80), AAAS, AAUP, Am. Polit. Sci. Assn., N.Y. Acad. Scis., Internat. Studies Assn., NAACP. Democrat. Roman Catholic. Home: Rural Route 1 Box 22 Vermillion SD 57069 Office: PO Box 472 Vermillion SD 57069 *Born in China and educated in the United States, I feel privileged to have experienced two rich cultures. My goals include promoting better understanding of all cultures and peoples.*

CHAIET, ALAN HOWARD, advertising agency executive; b. Newark, June 7, 1943; m. Barbara Dean Mellinger, Dec. 26, 1965; children: Lisa, Whitney. B.A., Rutgers U., 1965; M.S.J., Northwestern U., 1967. Media buyer Ted Bates & Co., N.Y.C., 1967-68; media buyer, planner Young & Rubicam, N.Y.C., 1968-69, sr. media buyer, planner, 1969-72, media supr., 1972-73; media dir. N.W. Ayer ABH Internat., Seattle, 1973-74; v.p., media dir. N.W. Ayer ABH Internat., Seattle, 1974-78, J. Walter Thompson, Atlanta, 1979-81, sr. v.p., media dir., 1981—. Contbr. articles to profl. jours. Mem. Atlanta Media Planners Assn. Clubs: Atlanta Advt., Court S. Racquetball. Office: J Walter Thompson USA Inc 2828 Tower Pl 3340 Peachtree Rd NE Atlanta GA 30026

CHAIKIN, SOL CHICK, trade union ofcl.; b. N.Y.C., Jan. 9, 1918; s. Sam and Beckie (Schechtman) C.; m. Rosalind Bryon, Aug. 31, 1940; children—Robert Evan, Eric Bryon, David Reed, Karen. Grad., City Coll. N.Y., 1938; LL.B., Bklyn. Law Sch., 1940; L.H.D., Rutgers U., 1980, Brandeis U., 1980. With Internat. Ladies Garment Workers Union, 1940—, asst. dir. N.E. dept., 1959-65, v.p., 1965-73, gen. sec.-treas., 1973-77, pres., 1975—; v.p. AFL-CIO, 1975—; mem. bd. Trilateral Commn., 1977—; Com. Present Danger Atlantic council, del. ILO, 1976; nat. chmn. Trade Union Council for Histadrut, Nat. Urban Coalition, 1977, 80; dir. N.Y. Convention Center Operating Corp., 1980—. Trustee L.I. Jewish-Hillside Med. Center, 1967—, Fashion Inst. Tech., 1975, Brandeis U., 1980—. Served with USAAF, 1943-46; CBI. Recipient Three Founders Award Am. Vets. Com., 1976; Parsons Award Parsons Sch. Design, 1977; Labor Human Rights award Jewish Labor Com., 1977. Democrat. Office: 1710 Broadway New York NY 10019

CHAILLE, HOWARD ELMER, bus. exec.; b. Indpls., Apr. 8, 1916; s. Howard Theodore and Lola Marie (Patten) C.; m. Naomi Agnes Hardwick, Aug. 3, 1941; children—Claudia Marie, Angela Louise. Student, Kenyon Coll., summers 1934-37; B.S., Ind. U., 1937, postgrad., 1938. Fire ins. underwriter, 1938; comdt. jr. sch. Briarley Mil. Acad., 1939; shipping, receiving mgr. comml. firm, 1940; communications supr. Brit. Supply Council and Brit. Purchasing Commn., 1940; asst. chief communications and records Bd. Econ. Warfare, 1941, U.S. Dept. State, 1945-70; chief message control center (Div. Communications and Records), 1946, asst. chief, 1949-50, chief telegraph br., 1946-49, field operations officer, 1950-52, orgn. and methods examiner, 1952-53, 1953-54, 1954, dir. exec. staff dep. asst. sec. for operations, Washington, 1955-56, consul, sec. in diplomatic corps, 1st sec., consul of embassy, Taipei, Taiwan, 1956-60, Seoul, Korea, 1960-61; chief program mgmt. and analysis staff Office Personnel, Dept. State, 1961-62, chief personnel services div., 1962-65, fgn. service insp., 1965-67; counselor adminstrv. affairs Am. consul, Vientiane, Laos, 1967-70; v.p. Makai Corp., Hawaii, 1970-72; v.p. for adminstrn. Oceanic Found. and Oceanic Inst.; bd. dirs. Oceanic Inst., 1975—, Pacific Banana Coop., 1977—; pres. Hawaii Banana Industry, 1974—. Served at lt. USNR, 1941-46. Mem. Delta Upsilon. Episcopalian. Home: Lono Gardens 41-878 Kaulukanu St Waimanalo HI 96795

CHAIT, ARNOLD, radiologist; b. N.Y.C., Jan. 20, 1930; s. Irving and Tillie (Newman) C.; m. Joan Lois Oppenheim, Mar. 14, 1965; children: Andrea, Elizabeth, Caroline. B.A., N.Y. U., 1951; M.D., U. Utrecht, Netherlands, 1957; M.A. (hon.), U. Pa., 1971. Diplomate: Am. Bd. Radiology. Intern Kings County Hosp., Bklyn., 1958; resident in pathology Manhattan Vets. Hosp., N.Y.C., 1959; radiology Kings County Hosp., 1959-62; instr. radiology State U. N.Y., Bklyn., 1962-64, asst. prof. radiology, 1964-67, asso. prof., 1967; asst. prof. radiology U. Pa., Phila., 1967-70, asso. prof., 1970-74, prof., 1974-76, clin. prof., 1976—; chief vascular radiology Hosp. U. Pa., 1969-76, dir. dept. radiology Grad. Hosp., 1976—, pres. med. staff, 1981-83; cons. radiology Bklyn. VA Hosp., 1962-67, Phila. VA Hosp., 1969—, Phila. Naval Hosp., 1975—. Contbr. articles to profl. jours. Fellow Coll. Physicians Phila., Am. Coll. Radiology; mem. Pa., Phila County med. socs., Am., Roentgen Ray Soc., Phila. Roentgen Ray Soc. (pres. 1983-84), Radiol. Soc. N. Am., N.Y. Roentgen Soc., AAAS, Assn. U. Radiologists, Soc. Cardiovascular Radiology Am. Heart Assn. (council on cardiovascular radiology), Soc. Uroradiology. Home: 835 Chauncey Rd Narberth PA 19072 Office: Grad Hosp Univ Pa 19th and Spruce Sts Philadelphia PA 19142

CHAIT, FREDERICK, lawyer, newspaper exec.; b. Newark, Sept. 20, 1913; s. Boris and Clara (Wolpe) C.; m. Helen Sporn, Sept. 22, 1938. A.B., Coll. City N.Y., 1932; LL.B., Columbia, 1935, J.D., 1967. Bar: N.Y. State bar 1935, Pa. bar 1952. Atty. Social Security Bd., Washington, 1936-37; asso. firm Konta, Kirchwey and Engel, N.Y.C., 1937-42; chief counsel rationing depts. OPA, 1942-44; war legislation litigation and claims div. U.S. Dept. Justice, 1944-45; gen. counsel UNRRA, 1946-48; counsel Triangle Publs., Inc., also Phila. Inquirer, 1948-69; gen. mgr. Phila. Inquirer and Phila. Daily News, 1958-69; pres. Phila. Newspapers, Inc., 1970-75; v.p. Knight-Ridder Newspapers, Inc., spl. counsel, cons., 1981—. Co-author: Monopoly vs. Competition, 1935; legal casebooks Legal Controls on Competitive Practices, 1936, Copyright Law, 1939. Bd. dirs., mem. planning com. Phila. Mus. Art; bd. mgrs. Pa. Hosp. Mem. Pa., N.Y.C. bar assns. Home: Academy House Apt 28K 1420 Locust St Philadelphia PA 19102 Office: 400 N Broad St Philadelphia PA 19101

CHAIT, LAWRENCE G., marketing consultant; b. Scranton, Pa., June 27, 1917; s. Perez and Rebecca (Chait) C.; m. Sylvia Levine, June 12, 1938; children: Martha, Pamela, George. Student pub. schs. Direct mail advt. mgr. Dow Jones Co., Inc., N.Y.C., 1945-49; advt. mgr. Arthur Wiesenberger & Co., mem. N.Y. Stock Exchange, 1950-51; circulation exec. Time, Life, Fortune, 1951-55; v.p. R.L. Polk Co., 1955-58; founder Lawrence G. Chait & Co., Inc. (advt. agy.), N.Y.C., 1957, pres., 1958-67, chmn., 1968-72; founder, chmn. Multi-Media Direct Marketing, Inc., N.Y.C., 1972-74; founder, treas., sec. Internat. Bus. Devel. Corp., N.Y.C., 1973—, pvt. mktg. counsel to corps. and instns., 1974—. Author: Those Little Golden Lists, 1955, Purchasing is Predictable, 1956, Nine Priceless Ingredients of Success in Selling to Businessmen by Mail, 1958, How to Advertise and Sell to the Consumer Market by Mail, 1959, The Case for Legal Regulation of Advertising, 1962, Building business By Mail, 1965, Targeted Marketing-New Science of Advertising and Selling, 1966, Six Elements in the Consumer Credit Revolution, 1967, Four Vital Ingredients of the Coming Revolution in Consumer Marketing, 1968, Multimedia Direct Marketing, 1970, A Businessman's Notes on Opportunities in the South Pacific, 1971, The United States Postal Service: A Total Communications Facility, 1972. Served with U.S. Maritime Service, World War II. Mem. Direct Mail Advt. Assn. (past pres.), Sales Promotion Execs. Assn. (past v.p.), Assn. Direct Mktg. Agys. (founding pres.), Direct Mktg. Creative Guild (dir.), L.I. Direct Mktg. Assn. Clubs: Atrium (N.Y.C.); Sales Execs. of N.Y. (dir.), Hundred Million (past pres.). Address: 32 Lynwood Dr Valley Stream NY 11580 Address: 4 Lake Dr Sunapee Harbor NH 03782 *The profoundly troubled state of our planet and its people results primarily from our willingness, in extraordinary degree, to accept mediocrity of leadership in the politico-economic sphere... conditions will improve to the extent that we exert ourselves to make known a widespread demand for superior performance... as did our superbly vocal and intelligent forbears 200 years ago.*

CHAIT, WILLIAM, librarian; b. N.Y.C., Dec. 5, 1915; s. Max and Mollie (Miller) C.; m. Beatrice L. Faigelman, June 13, 1937; 1 son, Edward Martin. B.A., Bklyn. Coll., 1934; B.L.S., Pratt Inst., 1935; M.S. in L.S, Columbia U., 1938. Library asst., br. librarian Bklyn. Pub. Library, 1935-45; service command librarian 2d Service Command AUS, 1945-46; chief in- service tng., personnel control Milw. Pub. Library, 1946-48; dir. Kalamazoo Pub. Library, 1948-56, Dayton and Montgomery County Pub. Library, 1956-78, dir. emeritus, 1979—; mem. Library Cons., Inc. Pres. Kalamazoo Council Social Agys., 1954-55, Dayton City Beautiful Com., 1968-69; treas. Montgomery County Hist. Soc., 1968-69; Trustee On-Line Computer Library Center, 1974—, treas., 1976-79. Fulbright lectr. library sci. U. Tehran, 1969-70. Mem. Pub. Library Assn. (pres. 1964-65), ALA (treas. 1976-80, council 1981—, chmn. personnel adminstrn. sect. 1958-60), Mich. Library Assn. (pres. 1955-56), Ohio Library Assn. (pres. 1964-65), S.C. Library Assn. Home: 38 Deer Run Ln Hilton Head Island SC 29928 Office: 215 E 3d St Dayton OH 45402

CHAKRABARTY, ANANDA MOHAN, microbiologist; b. Sainthia, India, Apr. 4, 1938; s. Satya Dos and Sasthi Bala (Mukherjee) C.; m. Krishna Chakraverty, May 26, 1965; children—Kaberi, Asit. B.Sc., St. Xavier's Coll., 1958; M.Sc., U. Calcutta, 1960, Ph.D., 1965. Sr. research officer U. Calcutta, 1964-65; research asso. in biochemistry U. Ill., Urbana, 1965-71; mem. staff Gen. Electric Research and Devel. Center, Schenectady, 1971-79; prof. dept. microbiology U. Ill. Med. Center, 1979—. Editor: Genetic Engineering, 1977. Named Scientist of Year Indsl. Research Mag., 1975. Mem. Am. Soc. Microbiology, Soc. Indsl. Microbiology, Am. Soc. Biol. Chemists. Home: 206 Julia Dr Villa Park IL 60181 Office: Dept Microbiology U Ill Med Center 835 S Wolcott St Chicago IL 60612

CHALABI, A. FATTAH, civil engineer, educator; b. Mosul, Iraq, Apr. 12, 1924; came to U.S., 1959, naturalized, 1967; s. Kasim S. and Khad (Hadid) C.; m. Beatrice Austin, Oct. 14, 1956. M.Sc., U. Mich., 1952, Ph.D. in Engring., 1956. Registered profl. engr., Mass. Asst. prof. U. Baghdad, Iraq, 1956-59; mem. faculty Worcester Poly. Inst., 1959—, prof. civil engring., 1966—, George I. Alden prof. engring., 1978. Mem. Am. Soc. Engring. Edn., Am. Concrete Inst., ASCE, Sigma Xi, Chi Epsilon. Home: 3 Rutland Terr Worcester MA 01609

CHALIF, SEYMOUR H., lawyer; b. N.Y.C., Feb. 27, 1927; s. Hyman and Sarah (Short) C.; m. Ronnie Stern, June 13, 1954; children: John, Peter. B.S., NYU, 1948; M.S. in Bus. Adminstrn., Columbia U., 1949, LL.B., 1952. Bar: N.Y. 1953, U.S. Dist. Ct. (so. dist.) N.Y. 1954, U.S. Supreme Ct. 1959, U.S. Ct. Appeals (2d cir.) 1960. Assoc. firm Hale, Kay & Brennan, N.Y.C., 1952-59, Beer, Richards, Lane, Haller & Buttenwieser, 1959-60; ptnr. firm London, Buttenwieser & Chalif, N.Y.C., 1960-75, Kaye, Scholer, Fierman, Hays & Handler, 1975—; dir. U.S. Home Corp., Houston. Served with USN, 1945-46. Mem. ABA, N.Y. State Bar Assn., Assn. Bar City N.Y. Club: University (N.Y.C.). Office: Kaye Scholer Fierman Hays & Handler 425 Park Ave New York NY 10022

CHALK, HOWARD WOLFE, advertising agency executive; b. N.Y.C., Jan. 15, 1922; s. Maurice and Zara (Philips) C.; m. Shirley Fields, June 1, 1947; children: Robin Kim, Russell Jay. Student, NYU, 1939-41. Account exec. Sterling Advt., N.Y.C., 1947-50, v.p., account supr., dir., 1950-55; exec. v.p., account supr. Altman, Stoller Chalk Advt., Inc., N.Y.C., 1955-68; mng. dir. Chalk, Nissen, Hanft Advt. Inc., N.Y.C., from 1968, now pres. Pres. Broadlawn Harbour Assn., 1965-66 pres. Broadlawn Harbour Assn., 1966-67; mem. Non-Partisan Citizens Nominating Com., Great Neck, N.Y., 1966-67; trustee Post Grad. Center Mental Health. Served with inf. AUS, 1942-45; ETO. Decorated Purple Heart, Bronze Star with oak leaf cluster.; Hon. fellow Harry S. Truman Library Inst. Mem. UN Assn. U.S.A., Am. Arbitration Assn., Sales Exec. Club N.Y.C., Internat. Platform Assn. Clubs: Men's Garden City (N.Y.); Jewish Center (founder, past pres.), Old Westbury (L.I.) Golf and Country, Sierra. Home: 265 E 66th St New York NY 10021 Office: 3 E 54th St New York NY 10022

CHALK, JOHN ALLEN, lawyer; b. Lexington, Tenn., Jan. 16, 1937. A.A., Freed-Hardeman Coll., 1956; B.S., Tenn. Tech. U., 1962, M.A., 1967; J.D., U. Tex., 1973. Bar: Tex. 1973, D.C. 1977; ordained to ministry Ch. of Christ, 1956. Pastor chs., Dayton, Ohio, 1956-60, Cookeville, Tenn., 1960-66, Abilene, Tex., 1966-71; assoc. Rhodes and Seamster, Abilene, 1973-74, Rhodes and Doscher, 1974; ptnr. Rhodes, Dosher, Chalk and Heatherly,, Abilene, 1975-78; gen. counsel La Jet, Inc., Abilene, 1978—, also v.p., sec; pres. Equity, Inc., 1982—, Trustcorp., Inc., 1980—. Author: The Praying Christ, 1964, Three American Revolutions, 1970, Jesus' Church, 1970, The Christian Family, 1973, Great Biblical Doctrines, 1973, The Devil, You Say!, 1974; contbr. articles to religious jours. Trustee Albilene Regional Mental Health Retardation Ctr.; chmn. Abilene Bicentennial Com., 1975-76; nat. adv. council Ams. United for Separation of Ch. and State, 1979-82, pres. bd. trustees, 1981-82; nat. devel. council Abilene Christian U.; featured speaker Herald of Truth radio and TV programs, 1966-69. Mem. ABA (acting assoc. editor, editorial bd. Family Advocate 1977-78), Tex. Bar Assn., Abilene Bar Assn., Fed. Bar Assn., Tex. Criminal Def. Lawyers Assn., Assn. Trial Lawyers Am., Tex. Trial Lawyers Assn. Home: 618 Gill St Abileen TX 79601 Office: PO Box 5305 Abilene TX 79608

CHALKER, DURWOOD, utility holding company executive; b. Breckenridge, Tex., Aug. 22, 1923; s. Robert Nathaniel and Leona Blanche (Cook) C.; m. Vada Ray McAdams, Dec. 22, 1953; children: Daniel Joseph, David James, Jason Paul. B.S. in Elec. Engring, Tex. A&M U., 1950; grad., Advanced Mgmt. Program, Harvard U., 1978. Registered profl. engr., Tex. With W. Tex. Utilities Co., Abilene, 1950-79, pres., 1975-79, chief exec. officer, 1976-79; chmn. bd., chief exec. officer Central Power and Light Co., Corpus Christi, Tex., 1979-80,

Central and South West Corp., Dallas, 1980—, Central and South West Services, Inc., 1980—; 2d v.p. Abilene Indsl. Found., 1979-80. Bd. dirs. Hendrick Med. Center Found., Abilene, 1975-79, West Tex. Rehab. Center, Abilene, 1976—, Abilene YMCA, 1978-79; dir. exec. devel. council Tex. A&M U. Coll. Bus. Adminstrn., 1980-81; chmn. big gifts div. United Way Met. Dallas, 1982; mem. Dallas County adv. bd. Salvation Army, 1981; active Circle 10 sustaining membership enrollment Boy Scouts Am., 1981. Served with USNR, 1943-46, 50-52. Named Tex. Bus. Exec. of Year Tex. Bus. Exec. mag.-Tex. A&M U. Coll. Bus. Adminstrn., 1980. Mem. IEEE (past pres. West Tex. sect.), Edison Electric Inst. (adv. com. 1980-81, policy com. on govtl. affairs 1981-82), Nat. Soc. Profl. Engrs., Tex. Soc. Profl. Engrs. (past pres. Abilene chpt., Engr. of Year award Abilene chpt. 1976), Abilene C. of C. (chmn. indsl. mfg. com. 1978-79), Dallas C. of C. (dir. 1981-82). Baptist. Clubs: City, Northwood (Dallas). Office: 2700 One Main Pl Dallas TX 75250 *

CHALKER, WILLIAM ROGERS, chem. co. exec.; b. Atlanta, Feb. 17, 1920; s. Elliott Lamar and Mildred Edna (Crum) C.; m. Joan Windsor King, Feb. 12, 1955; children—William Rogers, Scott King. A.B., U. S.C., 1942, B.S., 1943; diploma engring., U.S. Naval Acad. Postgrad. Sch., 1945; M.S., Mass. Inst. Tech., 1948, Profl. Engr., 1950. Registered profl. engr., Del. Observor U.S. Weather Bur., Petersburg, W.Va., 1946; research asst. Mass. Inst. Tech., 1946-50; cons. meteorologist A.H. Glenn & Assos., New Orleans, 1950-51; with E.I. duPont de Nemours & Co., Inc., 1951—, atmospheric dispersion research, 1951-53, engr., sr. cons., 1965-72, prin. cons., 1972-77, prin. div. cons., 1977—; Mem. Del. Air Pollution Authority, 1957-66; mem. tech. adv. com. Del. Water and Air Resources Commn., 1967-70; mem. air quality com. Mfg. Chemists Assn., 1960—, vice chmn., 1974-76, chmn., 1976-78; chmn. air control com. Chem. Industry Council N.J., 1964-66; mem. petrochem. industry adv. com. U.S. EPA, 1972-74. Contbr. articles to profl. jours. Served to lt. USNR, 1943-46; ETO. Mem. Am., Royal meteorol. socs., Air Pollution Control Assn. (chmn. mid-Atlantic states sect. 1964-65), Am. Acad. Environ. Engrs. (diplomate 1976), Sigma Xi, Omicron Delta Kappa, Sigma Nu, Kappa Sigma Kappa. Republican. Episcopalian. Home: 41 Bridle Brook Ln Newark DE 19711 Office: care E I du Pont de Nemours & Co Wilmington DE 19898

CHALL, LEO PAUL, sociologist, pub.; b. Daugavpils, Latvia, July 28, 1921; came to U.S., 1937, naturalized, 1943; s. Paul and Rose C.; (married). B.A., Ohio State U., 1948, M.A., 1952. Research asst. sociology Bur. Applied Social Research, Columbia U., N.Y.C., 1950-53; founding editor Sociol. Abstracts, N.Y.C., 1953—, pres., 1962—, Essay Press, Inc., N.Y.C., 1957—; lectr. Bklyn. Coll., 1953-61, instr., 1961; pub. Lang. and Lang. Behavior Abstracts, Reading Abstracts; asso. editor Jour. Sex Research, 1961-70. Contbr. articles to profl. jours. Mem. N.Y. County Democratic Com., 1962. Served with AUS, 1942-46. Fellow Am. Sociol. Assn.; mem. Soc. Study Social Problems. Home: 6002 Beaumont Ave LaJolla CA 92037 Office: PO Box 22206 San Diego CA 92122

CHALLINOR, DAVID, scientific institute administrator; b. N.Y.C., July 11, 1920; s. David and Mercedes (Crimmins) C.; m. Joan Ridder, Nov. 22, 1952; children: Julia M., Mary E., Sarah L., D. Thompson. B.A., Harvard U., 1943; M.F., Yale U., 1959, Ph.D., 1966. With Offerman-Anderson, Clayton & Co., Houston, 1947-51; cotton farmer, Culberson County, Tex., 1951-53; asst. sec. First Mortgage Co., Houston, 1953-57; research asst. Conn. Agr. Expt. Sta., New Haven, 1959-60; dep. dir. Yale Peabody Mus., New Haven, 1960-65, acting dir., 1965-66; spl. asst. in tropical biology Smithsonian Instn., Washington, 1966-67, dep. dir. office internat. activities, 1967-68, dir. office internat. activities, 1968-70, asst. sec. sci., 1971—; Am. adminstrv. sec. Charles Darwin Found., 1971—. Contbr. articles to sci. jours. Trustee Manhattanville Coll., 1964-70, Environ. Law Inst., 1975—; bd. dirs. Environ Def. Fund, 1982—, African Wildlife Found., 1980—. Served with USNR, 1943-46. Fellow AAAS; mem. Sigma Xi. Home: 3117 Hawthorne St NW Washington DC 20008 Office: 120 Smithsonian Bldg Smithsonian Institution Washington DC 20560

CHALLIS, THOMAS WILLIAM, radiologist; b. Fairlight, Sask., Can., June 20, 1926; s. Walter George and Marguerite (Flett) C.; m. Mary Carole MacKenzie, May 26, 1951; children: Judith, Diane. M.D., C.M., McGill U., Montreal, Que., Can., 1951. Instr. clin. surgery N.Y. U. Postgrad. Med. Sch., 1957-60; mem. faculty Queens U. Med. Sch., Kingston, Ont., 1960—, prof. radiology, head dept., 1979—. Fellow Royal Coll. Physicians and Surgeons Can., Am. Coll. Radiology; mem. Can. Assn. Radiologists (editorial bd. jour.), Kingston Acad. Medicine, Ont. Med. Assn., Can. Med. Assn., Radiol. Soc. N. Am., Soc. Nuclear Medicine, Can. Assn. Nuclear Medicine. Home: 231 Fairway Hill Crescent Kingston ON Canada K7M 2B5 Office: Queen's U Kingston ON Canada K7L 3N6

CHALLONER, DAVID REYNOLDS, university official; b. Appleton, Wis., Jan. 31, 1935; s. Reynolds Ray and Marion (Below) C.; m. Jacklyn Davnes Anderson, Aug. 30, 1958; children: David Harvey, Laura Reynolds, Britt-Davnes. B.S. cum laude, Lawrence Coll., Appleton, 1956; postgrad., Cambridge (Eng.) U., 1958; M.D. cum laude, Harvard, 1961. Resident in internal medicine Columbia Presbyn. Hosp., N.Y.C., 1961-63; research asso. Nat. Heart Inst., Bethesda, Md., 1963-65; chief med. resident and endocrinology research fellow U. Wash., Seattle, 1965-67; prof. medicine, asst. chmn. dept. Ind. U. Sch. Medicine, Indpls., 1967-75; vis. scholar Inst. Medicine, Nat. Acad. Sci., 1974; dean St. Louis U. Sch. Medicine, 1975-82; v.p. health affairs U. Fla., Gainesville, 1982—; cons. Eli Lilly & Co., NIH. Served to lt. comdr. USPHS, 1963-65. Recipient Harvard Med. Alumni award, 1961, Dr. William Beaumont award AMA, 1982. Mem. Am. Fedn. Clin. Research (pres. 1975), Inst. Medicine, Nat. Acad. Sci., Am. Soc. Clin. Investigation, Endocrine Soc., Am. Diabetes Assn., Assn. Am. Physicians, Boylston Soc., Am. Clin. and Climatol. Assn., Phi Beta Kappa, Alpha Omega Alpha, Beta Theta Pi. Clubs: Racquet (St. Louis); Cosmos (Washington). Home: 52 Lake Forest Rd St Louis MO 63117

CHALMERS, E(DWIN) LAURENCE, JR., art museum executive; b. Wildwood, N.J., Mar. 24, 1928; s. Edwin Laurence and Carolyn (Smith) C.; children: Edwin Laurence III, Thomas Henry; m. Hani Kamp, 1973; 1 son, Timothy Blair. A.B., Princeton U., 1948, M.A., 1950, Ph.D., 1951. Instr. psychology Princeton, 1951-52; research psychologist USAF, Denver, 1952-53, 56-57; mem. faculty Fla. State U., 1957-69, prof. psychology, dean, 1964-66, v.p. acad. affairs, 1966-69; chancellor U. Kans., Lawrence, 1969-72; pres. Art Inst. Chgo., 1972—. Contbr. articles to profl. jours. Served to 1st lt. USAF, 1953-56. Mem. Phi Beta Kappa, Sigma Xi, Omicron Delta Kappa. Home: 525 Kin Ct Wilmette IL 60091 Office: Art Inst of Chicago Chicago IL 60603

CHALMERS, JOHN, univ. adminstr.; b. Fitchburg, Mass., May 25, 1916; s. James Anderson and Bertha Eulalia (Whitcomb) C.; m. Carol Bloom, July 13, 1940; children—James A., Carolyn, Virginia. A.B., Middlebury (Vt.) Coll., 1938; Rhodes scholar, Oxford (Eng.) U., 1938-39; Ph.D., Cornell U., 1943; L.H.D. (hon.), Kans. State U., 1980. Instr. Cornell U., 1940-43; asst. prof. Middlebury Coll., 1946-47; asso. prof. econs. Kenyon Coll., 1947-53; Fulbright prof. econs. U. Philippines, 1951-52; successively asso. prof., prof., chmn. div. social scis. Harpur Coll., State U. N.Y., 1953-61; dean acad. affairs and arts and scis. U. Wyo., 1961-63; dean Coll. Arts and Scis., Kan. State U., Manhattan, 1963-69, v.p. acad. affairs., 1969—; Tax research specialist N.Y. Tax Commn., 1946-47; v.p. econs. div. Ohio Coll. Assn., 1948-50; cons. econ. edn. workshops in, Ohio, N.J., N.Y. and Kan., 1952—; pres. Council Colls. Arts and Scis., 1968—; mem. Commn. Arts and Scis., 1967—. Served to lt. (j.g.) USNR, 1943-46. Mem. Am. Econ. Assn., Beta Gamma Sigma. Home: 1009 Karla Ln Manhattan KS 66502

CHALMERS, THOMAS CLARK, physician, educational and research adminstrator; b. Forest Hills, N.Y., Dec. 8, 1917; s. Thomas Clark and Elizabeth (Ducat) C.; m. Frances Crawford Talcott, Aug. 31, 1942; children: Elizabeth Ducat (Mrs. Daniel G. Wright), Frances Talcott, Thomas Clark, Richard Matthew. Student, Yale U., 1936-39; M.D., Columbia U., 1943. Diplomate: Am. Bd. Internal Medicine. Intern Presbyn. Hosp., N.Y.C., 1943-44; research fellow NYU Malaria Research Unit, Goldwater Meml. Hosp., N.Y.C., 1944-45; resident Harvard Med. Services of Boston City Hosp., 1945-47; asst. physician Thorndike Meml. Lab., 1947-53; chief med. services Lemuel Shattuck Hosp., Boston, 1955-68; asst. chief med. dir. for research and edn. VA, Washington, 1968-70; asso. dir. clin. care NIH, also dir. clin. center NIH, Bethesda, Md., 1970-73; pres. (Mt. Sinai Med. Center), 1973-83; prof. medicine, dean Mt. Sinai Sch. Medicine, N.Y.C., 1973-83, Disting. Service prof., dir. clin. trials unit, 1983—, pres. emeritus, dean emeritus, 1983—; lectr. medicine Harvard; prof. medicine Tufts U., 1961-68, George Washington U., 1970-73; vis. prof. Harvard Sch. Pub. Health, 1983-84; mem. ethics adv. bd., spl. cons. NIH, HHS, 1980. Contbr. numerous articles profl. jours. Bd. dirs. New Eng. Home for Little Wanderers, 1960-65; bd. regents Nat. Library Medicine, 1978-79. Served as capt., M.C. AUS, 1953-55. Mem. Am. Assn. Study Liver Diseases (pres. 1959), Am. Clin. and Climatol. Assn., ACP, Am. Fedn. Clin. Research, Am. Gastroent. Assn. (pres. 1969), Am. Soc. Clin. Investigation, Assn. Am. Physicians, N.Y. Acad. Medicine, Inst. Medicine of Nat. Acad. Scis.; mem. Internat. Physicians for the prevention of Nuclear War; Mem. Eastern Gut Club.; mem. Physicians for Social Responsibility, Am. Acad. Arts and Scis. Office: Mt Sinai Med Center One Gustave L Levy Pl New York NY 10029

CHALMERS, THOMAS SCOTT, paper company executive; b. Bathurst, N.B., Can., Feb. 12, 1925; s. Harris Scott and Loretta Anne (Canning) C.; m. Margaret Winnifred MacDonald, Sept. 17, 1948; children: Fredrick, Louise, David, Andrew, Anne. B.Sc., Mt. Allison U., 1946. Process chemist Consol. Bathurst Inc. (N.B.), 1946-50, prodn. foreman, 1950-60, prodn. supt., Bathurst and New Richamond (Que.), 1960-72; mill mgr. Abitibi-Price, Stephenville, Nfld., 1972-80; v.p. mfg. and tech. services Kimberly-Clark, Terrace Bay, Ont., 1980—; dir. Kimberly-Clark Can., Toronto. Sr. mem. Can. Pulp and Paper Assn. Clubs: Curling Bathurst (pres.) (1968-69); Golf (Terrace Bay)). Lodge: Masons (master 1957). Home: 422 Elizabeth Ave Terrace Bay ON Canada POT 2WO Office: Kimberly-Clark Terrace Bay ON Canada POT 2WO

CHALON, JACK, anesthesiologist, educator; b. Cairo, July 7, 1920; U.S., 1965, naturalized, 1972; s. William and Helen (Hirsch) C.; m. Barbara Elizabeth Coombs, Oct. 22, 1948; children: Mary Coombs, Jonathan William. M.B., B.S., univs. London and Edinburgh, 1946. Diplomate: Am. Bd. Anesthesiology, Soc. Apothecaries of London. Intern Eastern Gen. Hosp., Edinburgh, 1946-47; resident surgery and anesthesiology Sinai Hosp., N.Y.C., 1965-67; instr. to asst. prof. Albert Einstein Coll. Medicine, Bronx, N.Y., 1968-74; assoc. prof. anesthesiology NYU Med. Ctr., 1974-78, prof., 1978—; pvt. practice medicine, Aldershot, Eng., 1949-64; assoc. dir. anesthesiology, dir. lab. pulmonary cytology, chief of labs. NYU Med. Ctr.; cons. anesthesiologist Manhattan VA Hosp.; cons. to chief med. examiner N.Y.C. Assoc. editor: Survey of Anesthesiology; assoc. editor: Sphere; author: Humidification of Anesthetic Gases, 1981; contbr. articles to profl. jours. Served with M.C. Royal Army, 1947-49; Served with M.C. Territorial Army, 1950-58. Fellow Am. Coll. Anesthesiologists, Royal Soc. Medicine, N.Y. Acad. Medicine (chmn. anesthesiology and resuscitation sect. 1978-79), Am. Coll. Chest Physicians; mem. AMA, N.Y. Soc. Anesthesiologists, Am. Soc. Anesthesiologists, AAAS, Brit. Med. Assn., Pan Am. Med. Assn., Internat. Anesthesia Research Soc., Assn. Police Surgeons Gt. Britain, Internat. Acad. Cytology, N.Y. Acad. Scis. Home: 9 Tarryhill Rd Tarrytown NY 10591 Office: 560 1st Ave New York NY 10016

CHALSTY, JOHN STEELE, investment banker; b. Port Elizabeth, S. Africa, Nov. 7, 1933; came to U.S., 1955, naturalized, 1964; s. Frederick H. and Sarah S. (Lamprecht) C.; m. Jennifer Blomefield, Feb. 16, 1957; children: Susan Chalsty Neely, Deborah Ann. B.Sc. in Chemistry and Physics, U. Witwatersrand, 1952, 1953, M.Sc., 1954; M.B.A. (Baker scholar), Harvard U., 1957. Dep. gen. mgr. Exxon Corp., N.Y.C., 1957-69; asst. gen. mgr. Esso Europe, also Esso Internat., 1966-69; mng. dir. investment banking DLJ Securities Corp., Donaldson, Lufkin & Jenrette, Inc., N.Y.C., 1969—; dir. Donaldson, Lufkin & Jenrette, Inc.; past exchange ofcl. Am. Stock Exchange, N.Y.C. Bd. dirs. Teagle Found., Inc., 1974—, Girls' Club N.Y. Mem. N.Y. Soc. Security Analysts (past pres., dir. 1976—), Oil Analysts Group N.Y., Nat. Assn. Petroleum Investment Analysts. Club: Short Hills (N.J.) (gov.). Home: 10 Gap View Rd Short Hills NJ 07078 Office: 140 Broadway New York NY 10005

CHALTIEL, VICTOR MEYER GUY, health care products executive; b. Tunis, Tunisia, Sept. 8, 1941; s. Jean Joseph and Alice C.; m. Rosita Lelievre, Feb. 22, 1976; children: Jean-Jacques, Eric, Lionel. Diploma, Ecole Superieure des Sciences Economiques et Commerciales, Paris, 1965; M.B.A., Harvard U., 1967. With Baxter Travenol Labs., Deerfield, Ill., 1967—, gen. mgr. Travenol France, 1970-74, area mng. dir. Europe, 1975, v.p. internat. div., 1976-77, pres. artificial organs div., 1978-79, corp. v.p., 1979-80, corp. group v.p., 1981—; chmn., pres., chief exec. officer Omnis Surg. Inc. affiliate Baxter Travenol Labs., Inc., 1983—. Recipient Health Advancement award Nat. Kidney Found., 1982; apptd. Conseiller du Commerce Exterieur de la France, 1982. Mem. Pharm. Mfrs. Assn. Internat., Assn. Advancement Med. Instrumentation, Am. Mgmt. Assn., Nat. Kidney Found. Home: 1752 Ryders Ln Highland Park IL 60035 Office: One Baxter Pkwy Deerfield IL 60015

CHAMBERLAIN, ADRIAN RAMOND, corporate executive; b. Detroit, Nov. 11, 1929; s. Adrian and Leila (Swisher) C.; m. Melanie F. Stevens, May 19, 1979; children: Curtis (dec.), Tracy, Thomas. B.S., Mich. State U., 1951, D.Engring., 1971; M.S., Wash. State U., 1952; Ph.D., Colo. State U., 1955; Litt.D., Denver U., 1974. Registered profl. engr., Colo.; lic. real estate broker, Colo. Research engr. Phillips Petroleum Co., 1955; research coordinator, civil engr. Colo. State U., 1956-57, chief civil engr. sect., 1957-61, dean engring., 1959-61, v.p., 1960-66, exec. v.p., treas., governing bd., 1966-69, pres., 1969-80; chmn. bd. dirs. Univ. Nat. Bank, 1964-69, dir., 1964-74; pres., dir. Mitchell & Co., Inc., 1981—; treas., dir. Simons, Li & Assocs., Inc., 1980-82; chmn. bd. Simons,Li & Assoc., Inc., 1982—; dir. Solaron Corp., Inc.; Chmn. NSF Commn. Weather Modification, 1964-66; mem. Nat. Air Quality Criteria Adv. Com., 1967-70; Colo. commr. Western Interstate Commn. on Higher Edn., 1974-78; pres. State Bd. Agr. System, 1978-80. Past pres., 1970-73, Cystic Fibrosis Found., 1971—; trustee Univ. Corp. for Atmospheric Research, 1967-72, 74-81, chmn. bd. trustees, 1977-79; bd. dirs. Nat. Center for Higher Edn. Mgmt. Systems, 1975-80, chmn. bd. dirs., 1977-78; bd. visitors Air U., USAF, 1973-76, chmn., 1975-76; exec. com. Nat. Assn. State Univs. and Land Grant Colls., 1976-81, pres.-elect, 1978-79, chmn., 1979-80; mem. adv. council to dir. NSF, 1978-81; chmn. Ft. Collins-Loveland Airport Authority, 1983—. Fulbright student U. Grenoble, 1955-56. Mem. ASCE, AAAS, Order of Aztec Eagles, Sigma Xi, Tau Beta Pi, Phi Kappa Phi, Chi Epsilon. Club: Rotarian. Home: 1319 Stonehenge Dr St Fort Collins CO 80525 Office: PO Box 1208 Fort Collins CO 80522

CHAMBERLAIN, CHARLES ERNEST, lawyer, former congressman; b. Ingham County, Mich., July 22, 1917; s. Orson W. and Clara Adella (DaFoe) C.; m. Charlotte Mary Craney, Dec. 2, 1943; children: Charlotte Ellen, Christine Clark, Charles Ernest. B.S. in Commerce, U. Va., 1941, LL.B., 1949. Bar: Va. bar 1949, Mich. bar 1949, also D.C. bar 1949. Agt. Internal Revenue Treasury Dept., 1946-47; pvt. practice of law, Lansing, Mich., 1950—, asst. pros., Ingham County, 1950, city atty., East Lansing, 1953-54; legal counsel Mich. Senate Judiciary Com., 1953-54; pros. atty., 1955-56; mem. 85th-93d congresses from 6th Dist. Mich., mem. ways and means com.; ptnr. firm Webster, Chamberlain & Bean, Washington, 1975—. Served as officer USCG, World War II. Mem. Am., Mich., Va., D.C. bar assns., SAR. Republican. Home: McLean VA 22101 Office: 1747 Pennsylvania Ave Washington DC 20006

CHAMBERLAIN, CHARLES JAMES, railroad labor union exec.; b. Ashton, Ill., Aug. 7, 1921; s. Charles Hubert and Katherine (Reitz) C.; m. Joyce Lois Swanson, June 27, 1942; children—Richard B., Charles M. Student pub. schs. With signal dept. C. & N.-W. Ry., 1938-57; grand lodge rep. Brotherhood of R.R. Signalmen, 1957-61, sec.-treas., 1961-67, pres., 1967—; Labor mem. U.S. R.R. Retirement Bd., Chgo., 1977—. Alderman DeKalb (Ill.) City Council, 1949-57. Mem. Ry. Labor Execs. Assn. (chmn. 1970—). Lutheran. Home: 740 Saint Andrews Ln 33 Crystal Lake IL 60014 Office: 844 Rush St Chicago IL 60611

CHAMBERLAIN, DANIEL ROBERT, college pressident; b. Mexico, Mo., Aug. 22, 1932; s. Ray Willis and Marianne Elizabeth (Horine) C.; m. Joyce F. Books, June 22, 1952; children: Rodney, Mark, Anthony, Priscilla, Aletha, Cynthia, Marianne. B.A., Upland Coll., 1953; M.A., Calif. State U., Los Angeles, 1957; postgrad., UCLA, 1958-59; D.Ed., U. So. Calif., 1967. Tchr., adminstr. Western Pilgrim Schs., El Monte, Calif., 1953-59; tchr. English and history Pasadena (Calif.) City Schs., 1959-63; chmn. div. profl. studies, acting pres. Upland Coll., 1963-65; asst. univ. dean for univ. wide activities SUNY, Albany, 1965-68; dean of coll. Messiah Coll., Grantham, Pa., 1968-76; pres. Houghton (N.Y.) Coll., 1976—. Pres. Calif. youth Wesleyan Ch., 1954-64; chmn. bd. dirs. Mile High Camp, Barton Flats, Calif., 1959-65; pres. men's commn. Christian Holiness Assn., 1975-80; bd. dirs. Commn. Ind. Colls. and Univs.; vice chmn. Ind. Coll. Fund N.Y. Mem. Christian Coll. Consortium (chmn.), Council of Mennonite Coll. Deans (chmn.), Am. Assn. Higher Edn., Middle States Assn. Schs. and Colls. (evaluator, team chmn.), Wesleyan Edn. Council (chmn.), Phi Delta Kappa. Republican. Club: Lions. Home: RD 1 Box 32B Houghton NY 14744 Office: Houghton Coll Houghton NY 14744

CHAMBERLAIN, GEORGE ARTHUR, 3D, manufacturing company executive; b. Boston, Sept. 14, 1935; s. George Arthur, Jr. and Mabel G. (Greene) C.; m. Judith Fehr, June 20, 1959; children—G. Randall, Cynthia L. A.B., Wheaton (Ill.) Coll., 1957; M.B.A., Harvard U., 1961. Loan officer Worcester County Nat. Bank, Mass., 1961-65; v.p. fin., treas. Anderson Corp., Worcester, 1966-69; v.p., treas. Digital Equipment Corp., Maynard, Mass., 1969—; trustee Consumers Savs. Bank, Worcester. Trustee Lawrence Acad., Groton, Mass., Met. Center, Boston. Served with AUS, 1957-59. Mem. Fin. Execs. Inst., Treasurers Club Boston, Internat. Soc. Treasurers. Office: 146 Main St Maynard MA 01754

CHAMBERLAIN, (GEORGE) RICHARD, actor; b. Los Angeles, Mar. 31, 1935; s. Charles and Elsa C. B.A., Pomona Coll., 1956; studied voice, Los Angeles Conservatory Music, 1958; studied dramatics with, Jeff Corey. Participated coll. dramatics; appeared in: King Lear, Arms and the Man, Richard II, Hamlet, The Lady's Not for Burning, Night of the Iguana, Cyrano de Bergerac; TV roles in Alfred Hitchcock Presents, Gunsmoke, Bourbon Street Beat, Thriller, Mr. Lucky; TV series Dr. Kildare, 1961-65, Portrait of a Lady, BBC, 1968, Hamlet, 1970; TV special The Woman I Love (portrayed Duke of Windsor), 1973, F. Scott Fitzgerald and The Last of the Belles, 1974, The Lady's Not for Burning, 1974, The Count of Monte Cristo, 1975, The Man in the Iron Mask, 1978, Shogun, 1980 (Golden Globe award); motion pictures include Secret of Purple Reef, 1960, Thunder of Drums, 1961, Twilight of Honor, 1963, Joy in the Morning, 1965, Petulia, 1968, The Madwoman of Chaillot, 1969, The Music Lovers, 1971, Julius Caesar, 1971, Lady Caroline Lamb, 1972, The Three Musketeers, 1974, Towering Inferno, 1974, The Four Musketeers, 1975, The Slipper and the Rose—The Story of Cinderella, 1977, The Swarm, 1978; TV singing debut on Hollywood Melody, 1962; dir.: play The Shadow Box; recs. include 2 albums, also singles.; (Named favorite male performer TV Guide poll 1963). Served to sgt. AUS, 1956-58. Address: care Chasin-Park-Citron Agency 9255 Sunset Blvd Los Angeles CA 90069 *

CHAMBERLAIN, GEORGE W., advertising executive; b. Colorado Springs, Colo., Dec. 25, 1927; m. Constance, Dec. 30, 1957; children: Kimberly Ann, Brad Arthur. B.A., Colo. Coll., 1954. Auditor Arthur Andersen & Co., Chgo., 1954-58; acct. L.M. Berry & Co., Dayton, Ohio, 1958-62, controller, 1962-66, v.p. prodn. and systems, 1967-79; group v.p. adminstrn. L.M. Berry & co., Dayton, Ohio, 1979—. Home: 227 Zengel Dr Centerville OH 45459 Office: L M Berry and Co. 3170 Kettering Blvd Dayton OH 45439

CHAMBERLAIN, JOHN ANGUS, sculptor; b. Rochester, Ind., Apr. 16, 1927. Student, Art Inst. Chgo., 1950-52, U. Ill., Black Mountain Coll., 1955-56. One-man shows include, Cleve. Mus. Art, 1967, New HemisFair, 1968, York U., Toronto, Ont., Can., 1969, Guggenheim Mus., 1971, Indpl. Mus. Art, 1972, Pratt Inst., 1974, Josechoff Gallery U. Hartford, 1977, Flint (Mich.) Inst. Art, 1978, Whitney Mus. Am. Art, 1979, others; films include Wedding Night, 1967, The Secret Life of Hernando Cortez, 1968, Wide Point, 1968, Thumbsuck, 1971. Address: care Leo Castelli Gallery 420 W Broadway New York NY 10012

CHAMBERLAIN, JOHN RENSSELAER, columnist; b. New Haven, Oct. 28, 1903; s. Robert Rensselaer and Emily (Davis) C.; m. Margaret Sterling, Apr. 22, 1926 (dec.); children—Elizabeth, Margaret; m. Ernestine Stodelle, June 29, 1956; 1 son, John. Ph.B., Yale, 1925. Advt. writer, 1925; report N.Y. Times, 1926-28, daily book columnist, 1933-36; editor Fortune Mag., 1936-41; asso. prof. Columbia Sch. Journalism, 1941-44; asst. editor N.Y. Times Book Rev., 1928-33; asso. editor Saturday Rev. Lit., 1933; book editor Scribners Mag., 1936-38, Harper's Mag., 1939-47; lectr. Columbia Sch. Journalism, 1934-35, New Sch. for Social Research, 1935, Columbia U. Summer Sch., 1937; contbg. daily book columnist Times, 1942-44; editor Life mag., 1945-50, The Freeman rev. politics, econs., arts, 1950-52; asso. editor Barron's Mag., 1953-55; staff writer Wall St. Jour., 1955; dean Troy (Ala.) Sch. Journalism, 1972-77; now daily columnist These Days column King Features Syndicate, N.Y.C. Author: Farewell to Reform, 1932, The American Stakes, 1940, MacArthur, 1941-1951, (with General Charles Willoughby) MacArthur, 1954, The Roots of

Capitalism, 1959, The Enterprising Americans: A Business History of the U.S, 1963, Freedom and Independence: The Hillsdale Story, 1979, A Life with the Printed Word, 1982; Contbr. to: Critique of Humanism, 1930, Challenge to the New Deal, 1934, After the Genteel Tradition, 1937, Books That Changed Our Minds, 1939, America Now; leading mags. Home: 855 N Brooksvale Rd Cheshire CT 06410 Office: King Features Syndicate 235 E 45th St New York City NY 10017

CHAMBERLAIN, JOHN VICTOR, theologian; b. Lakeland, Fla., Aug. 26, 1926; s. Victor and Hinda S. (Loson) C.; children: Rachel, Robert, Kenneth. A.B., Fla. So. Coll., 1950; A.M., Duke U., 1953, Ph.D. (Kearns fellow 1954-55), 1955. Vis. instr. Duke U. Div. Sch., 1954-55; mem. faculty Goucher Coll., Balt., 1955—, prof. religion, 1971—, chmn. dept., 1972-80. Author papers in field of bibl. studies and Am. religion. Served with AUS, 1944-46. Decorated Purple Heart, Bronze Star; Fulbright grantee, 1964. Mem. Am. Acad. Religion, Soc. Bibl. Lit., Bibl. Archaeology Soc., Corvair Soc. Am. Republican. Office: Goucher Coll Towson MD 21204

CHAMBERLAIN, JOSEPH MILES, astronomer, educator; b. Peoria, Ill., July 26, 1923; s. Maurice Silloway and Roberta (Miles) C.; m. Paula Bruninga, Dec. 12, 1945; children—Janet Ann, Susan Louise, Barbara Jean. B.S., U.S. Mcht. Marine Acad., 1944; B.A., Bradley U., 1947; A.M., Tchrs. Coll. Columbia, 1950, Ed.D., 1962. Instr. Columbia Jr. High Sch., Peoria, 1943; instr. nav. War Shipping Adminstrn., 1944-45; boys sec. YMCA, Peoria, 1946-47; instr. U.S. Mcht. Marine Acad., Kings Point, N.Y., 1947-50, asst. prof., 1950-52; asst. curator Am. Museum-Hayden Planetarium, N.Y.C., 1952-53, gen. mgr., chief astronomer, 1953-56, chmn., 1956-64; asst. dir. Am. Mus. Natural History, 1964-68; dir. Adler Planetarium, Chgo., 1968—, pres., 1977—; prof. astronomy Northwestern U., 1968-78; professorial lectr. U. Chgo., 1968-71; led eclipse expdns. to, Can., 1954, 79, Ceylon, 1955, Pacific Ocean, 1977, astro-geodetic expdns. to, Can., 1956, 57, Greenland, 1958; dean council of sci. staff Am. Mus. Nat. History, 1960-62. Co-author: Planets, Stars and Space, 1957; author: Time and the Stars, 1964; also articles on popular astronomy. Active Boy Scouts Am., Met. Chgo. YMCA. Served to lt. USNR, 1945-46; staff Naval Res. Officers Sch., 1953-54; N.Y.C. Mem. AAAS, Am. Astron. Soc., Internat. Astron. Union, Internat. Planetarium Dirs. Conf. (vice chmn. 1968-77, chmn. 1977—), Gt. Lakes Planetarium Assn., Internat. Planetarium Soc., Midwest Museums Conf., Am. Polar Soc., Am. Assn. Museums (mem. council 1965-77, v.p. 1971-74, pres. 1974-75), Phi Delta Kappa, Phi Kappa Phi, Kappa Delta Pi. Republican. Presbyn. (elder). Clubs: University, Tavern, Econ., Execs., Metropolitan (Chgo.); Dutch Treat. Home: 1500 Oak Ave Evanston IL 60201 Office: Adler Planetarium 1300 S Lake Shore Dr Chicago IL 60605

CHAMBERLAIN, JOSEPH WYAN, astronomer, educator; b. Boonville, Mo., Aug. 24, 1928; s. Gilbert Lee and Jessie (Wyan) C.; m. Marilyn Jean Roesler, Sept. 10, 1949; children: Joy Anne, David Wyan, Jeffrey Scott. A.B., U. Mo., 1948, A.M., 1949; M.S., U. Mich., 1951, Ph.D., 1952. Project sci. aurora and airglow USAF Cambridge Research Center, 1951-53; research asso. Yerkes Obs., Chgo., 1953-55, asst. prof., 1955-59, asso. prof., 1959-60, prof., 1961-62, asso. dir., 1960-62; asso. dir. planetary scis. div. of Kitt Peak Nat. Obs., 1962-70, astronomer, planetary scis. div., 1970-71; dir. Lunar Sci. Inst., Houston, 1971-73; prof. dept. space physics and astronomy Rice U., Houston, 1971—; Cons. Stanford Research Inst., NASA. Author: Physics of the Aurora and Airglow, 1961, Theory of Planetary Atmospheres, 1978; Editor: Revs. of Geophysics and Space Physics, 1974-80; editorial bd.: Planetary Space Sci. Recipient Warner prize Am. Astron. Soc., 1961; Alfred P. Sloan research fellow, 1961-63. Fellow Royal Astron. Soc. (fgn.), A.A.A.S., Am. Geophys. Union (councilor 1968-70); mem. Am. Astron. Soc. (councilor 1961-64, chmn. div. planetary scis. 1969-71), Am. Phys. Soc., Internat. Astron. Union, Internat. Union Geodesy Geophysics, Internat. Sci. Radio Union, NRC, Assembly Math. and Phys. Scis. (exec. com. 1973-78), Nat. Acad. Sci. (chmn. geophysics sect. 1972-75). Office: Dept Space Physics and Astronomy Rice U Houston TX 77251

CHAMBERLAIN, MARK MUNROE, college president; b. Pawtucket, R.I., Dec. 10, 1931; s. Merle D. and Lois (Munroe) C.; m. Miriam C. Ewing, May 30, 1953; children: David, Douglas, Matthew. B.S., Franklin and Marshall Coll., 1953; Ph.D., U. Ill., 1956. From instr. to vice provost for student services Western Res. U., 1956-69; pres. Glassboro State Coll., 1969—. Commr., East Cleveland, Ohio, 1967-69. Mem. Am. Chem. Soc. (councilor, chmn. chem. safety), AAAS, Nat. Fire Protection Assn., Sigma Xi. *

CHAMBERLAIN, NEIL CORNELIUS WOLVERTON, economist, emeritus educator; b. Charlotte, N.C., May 18, 1915; s. Henry Bryan and Elizabeth (Wolverton) C.; m. Mariam Kenosian, June 27, 1942 (div. June 1967); m. Harriet Feigenbaum, Aug. 9, 1968. A.B., Western Res. U., 1937, M.A., 1939; Ph.D., Ohio State U., 1942. Research fellow Brookings Instn., 1941-42; research dir. Labor and Mgmt. Center, Yale, 1946-49, asst. dir., 1949-54; asst. prof. econs. Yale, 1947-49, asso. prof., 1949-54, prof. econs., 1959-67, Columbia, 1954-59, 67-80, Armand G. Erpf prof. of modern corp., 1969-80, emeritus, 1981—; dir. program in Econ. Devel. and Adminstrn. Ford Found., 1957-60. Author: Collective Bargaining Procedures, 1944, The Union Challenge to Management Control, 1948, Management in Motion, 1950, Collective Bargaining, 1951, rev., 1965, Social Responsibility and Strikes, 1953, The Impact of Strikes, 1954, A General Theory of Economic Process, 1955, Labor, 1958, Source-book on Labor, 1958, The Firm: Micro- Economic Planning and Action, 1962, The West in a World Without War, 1963, The Labor Sector, 1965, rev., 1971, 80, Private and Public Planning, 1965, Enterprise and Environment, 1968, Beyond Malthus, 1970, The Place of Business in America's Future: A Study in Social Values, 1973, The Limits of Corporate Responsibility, 1973, Remaking American Values: Challenge to a Business Society, 1977, Forces of Change in Western Europe, 1980, Social Strategy and Corporate Structure, 1982; editor: Contemporary Economic Issues, 1969, rev., 1978, Business and the Cities, 1970; co-editor: Cases on Labor Relations, 1949, A Decade of Industrial Relations Research, 1958, Frontiers of Collective Bargaining, 1968; mem. editorial bd., editorial cons.: Mgmt. Internat, 1960-70; bd. editors: Am. Econ. Rev, 1957-59. Bd. dirs. Salzburg Seminar in Am. Studies, 1957-78; trustee Columbia Jour. World Bus., 1969-72, 75-80. Served from ensign to lt. USNR, 1942-46. Mem. Am. Econ. Assn., Indsl. Relations Research Assn. (exec. bd. 1955-58, pres. 1967), Phi Beta Kappa. Home: 49 W 24th St New York NY 10010

CHAMBERLAIN, OWEN, nuclear physicist; b. San Francisco, July 10, 1920;, 1943 (div. 1978); 4 children; m. June Steingart, 1980. A.B. (Cramer fellow), Dartmouth Coll., 1941; Ph.D., U. Chgo., 1949. Instr. physics U. Calif., Berkeley, 1948-50, asst. prof., 1950-54, assoc. prof., 1954-58, prof., 1958—; civilian physicist, Manhattan Dist., Berkeley, Los Alamos, 1942-46. Guggenheim fellow, 1957-58; Loeb lectr. at Harvard U., 1959; Recipient Nobel prize (with Emilio Segré) for physics, for discovery anti-proton, 1959. Fellow Am. Phys. Soc., Am. Acad. Arts and Scis.; mem. Nat. Acad. Scis. Address: Physics Dept U Calif Berkeley CA 94720 *

CHAMBERLAIN, ROBERT GLENN, retired engineering executive; b. Cedar Rapids, Iowa, Feb. 17, 1926; s. Glenn Arlie and Ora Margarite (Castle) C.; m. Jane Helen Newlin, June 13, 1946; children: Carole, James, Sue, Patricia, Tracey. B.S.M.E., Iowa State U., 1949; postgrad., U. Wis.Milw. Registered profl. engr., Iowa. With Link-Belt Speeder, Cedar Rapids, 1949-54, Giddings & Lewis, Fond du Lac, Wis., 1954-83, group v.p. indsl. products, 1980-82, exec. v.p. machine tools, 1982-83, ret., 1983. Vice pres. Bay Lakes council Boy Scouts Am., Menasha, Wis., 1982, chmn. in-sch. exploring, Dallas, 1981, chmn. Area 1 NC region, Oak Brook, Ill., 1977. Served with USNR, 1944-46; PTO. Recipient Silver Beaver award Boy Scouts Am., 1974, Silver Antelope award Boy Scouts Am., 1983. Mem. Soc. Mfg. Engrs. Lodges: Rotary; Masons. Home: 894 Golf Vu Dr Fond du Lac WI 54935

CHAMBERLAIN, WILLARD THOMAS, manufacturing company exective; b. New Haven, Nov. 22, 1928; s. Thomas Huntington and Alice Irene (Daley) C.; m. Harriet Halbert Keck, Nov. 20, 1965; children: Huntington Wilson, Amy Thatcher. B.E., Yale U., 1950; postgrad., Ill. Inst. Tech., 1951-53. With Armour Research Found., Chgo., 1951-53; asst. to tech. mgr. Anaconda Brass div. Anaconda Corp., Waterbury, Conn., 1953-56, tech. supr., 1956, metall. mgr., Torrington, Conn., 1960, mgr. devel., Waterbury, 1961, lab. mgr., 1962, mgr. research-tech. ctr., 1964, mgr., Valley Mills, 1967, Ansonia, 1967, mgr.prodn. planning, 1970, v.p. mfg., 1971, exec. v.p. Brass div., 1972, pres., 1974, Anaconda Industries, 1980; sr. v.p. Atlantic Richfield Co., 1980; pres. Arco Metals Co., 1982—, Anaconda Can. Exploration Ltd.; v.p. Anaconda Internat. Corp.; pres. 85818 Can. Ltd., S.A. Investment Co. Inc.; dir. Amaconda Can. Exploration Ltd., Industrias Nacobre S.A. de C.V., Nacional de Cobre S.A., S.A. Investment Co. Inc., Wis. Centrifugal Inc., Internat. Copper Research Assn., Arilan, S.A. de C.V. Mem. exec. bd. Waterbury Republican Town Com., 1964-70; commr. Waterbury Bd. Fin., 1966-67, chmn. charter revision com., 1966-67; mem. exec. bd. Mattatuck council Boy Scouts Am., 1965-72, Waterbury Assn. for Retarded Children, 1965-56; co-chmn. Clergy-Insustry Conf., 1965-56; campaign chmn. Valley United Fund, 1970-71; bd. dirs. United Way, Central Naugatuck Valley, 1974, The Banking Ctr., 1974-81, Western Conn. Indsl. Council, 1974-81. Recipient Outstanding Civic Leader award, 1967. Mem. Copper Devel. Assn., Aluminum Assn. (dir.), Am. Soc. Metals, Yale Engring. Assn, Greater Waterbury C.of C. (bd. dirs. 1974). Presbyterian. Clubs: Copper, Plaza, Yale of Chgo., Meadow. Home: Deepwood Rd Barrington Hills Il 60010 Office: Arco Metals Co 2 Continental Towers1701 Golf Rd Rolling Meadows Il 60008

CHAMBERLIN, JOHN STEPHEN, home furnishing manufacturing company executive; b. Boston, July 29, 1928; s. Stephen Henry and Olive Helen (McGrath) C.; m. Mary Katherine Leahy, Oct. 9, 1954; children:Mary Katherine, Patricia Ann, Carol Lynn, John Stephen, Liane Helen, Mark Joseph. A.B. cum laude, Harvard U., 1950, M.B.A., 1953. Lamp salesman Gen. Electric Co., N.Y.C., 1954-57, mgmt. cons., 1957-60, mgr. product planning TV receiver dept., Syracuse, N.Y., 1960-63, mgr. mktg., gen. mgr. radio receiver dept., Utica, N.Y., 1963-70; exec. v.p., dir. Lenox Inc., Trenton, NJ, 1970-71; v.p., gen. mgr. housewares div. Gen. Electric Co., Bridgeport, Conn., 1971-74, v.p., gen. mgr. housewares and audio div., 1974-76; pres., chief exec. officer, dir. Lenox Inc., Lawrenceville, N.J., 1976-81, chmn., chief exec. officer, 1981—; dir. N.J. Nat. Corp., Trenton, Gulton Industries, Brown-Forman Distillers Corp. Trustee Med. Ctr. Found.; mem. bd. overseers Parson Sch. Design. Mem. N.J.C. of C. Clubs: Bedens Brook; Harvard, Union League (N.Y.C.). Home: 182 Fairway Dr Princeton NJ 08540 Office: Lenox Inc 3190 Princeton Pike Lawrenceville NJ 08648

CHAMBERLIN, WARD BRYAN, JR., public broadcasting executive; b. N.Y.C., Aug. 4, 1921; s. Ward Bryan and Elizabeth Frances (Nichols) C.; m. Lydia Gifford, Oct. 6, 1951; children: Carolyn, Margot. B.A. summa cum laude, Princeton U., 1946; LL.B., Columbia U., 1948. Bar: N.Y.State bar 1949. Practiced in, N.Y.C., 1949-51; asst. counsel Mutual Security Agency, Washington, 1951-53; asso. counsel Def. Materials Procurement Agency, Paris, London, 1953-54, Gen. Dynamics Corp., N.Y.C., 1954-65; v.p., gen. counsel Internat. Exec. Service Corps, N.Y.C., 1965-68; v.p. Corp. for Pub. Broadcasting, N.Y.C., 1968-70; exec. v.p. Sta. WNET-TV, N.Y.C., 1970-72; pres. PACT, Inc., N.Y.C., 1972-73; sr. v.p. Pub. Broadcasting Service, N.Y.C., 1973-75; pres., gen. mgr. Sta. WETA-TV and WETA-FM, Greater Washington Ednl. Telecommunication Assn., Washington, 1975—; chmn. bd. Dial Mag.; Bd. dirs. Pub. Broadcasting Service, 1977-80; bd. dirs. Eastern Ednl. Television Network, 1976—, pres., 1979-81, chmn., 1981—. Trustee Princeton U., 1975-79; ambulance driver Am. Field Service, Africa, Italy, India, 1942-45, bd. dirs., 1946—, chmn. bd., 1967-72, chmn. bd. trustees, 1972-74; bd. dirs. Outward Bound, 1980—; trustee Earthwatch, Inc., 1981—, Nat. Pub. Radio, 1983—. Recipient John Phillips award Phillips Exeter Acad., 1976, Pub. Service award Cath. U. Am., 1982. Democrat. Clubs: Century, University (N.Y.C.); Army-Navy Country (Washington). Home: 3104 P St NW Washington DC 20007 Office: PO Box 2626 Washington DC 20013

CHAMBERS, ANNE COX, newspaper exec., former ambassador; b. Dayton, Ohio, Dec. 1, 1919; d. James Middleton and Margaretta (Blair) Cox; m. Robert William Chambers, Sept. 12, 1955; children—Margaretta Taylor, Katharine Johnson, James Cox. Grad., Finch Coll. Former ambassador to, Belgium; chmn. bd. Atlanta Newspapers; dir. Cox Broadcasting Corp., Cox Enterprises, Inc., Fulton Nat. Bank. Bd. dirs. Atlanta Humane Soc., Atlanta Music Festival Assn., Atlanta Speech Sch.; trustee Atlanta Hist. Soc.; bd. sponsors Atlanta Symphony; 1st pres., founder trustee Forwards Arts Found.; mem. Internat. Council Mus. Modern Art; Founding trustee So. Center Internat. Studies.

CHAMBERS, CLARKE ALEXANDER, historian, educator; b. Blue Earth, Minn., June 3, 1921; s. Winslow Clarke and Anna Easton (Anderson) C.; m. Florence Wood, Feb. 6, 1944; children—Jenny Elisabeth, Katherine Easton, Robert Wood, Sarah Clarke. B.A., Carleton Coll., Northfield, Minn., 1943; M.A., U. Calif. at Berkeley, 1947; Ph.D., 1950. Lectr. history U. Calif. at Berkeley, 1950-51, 61-62; instr. history U. Minn., Mpls., 1951-52, asst. prof., 1952-56, asso. prof., 1956-63, prof., 1963—, dir., 1964—. Author: California Farm Organizations, 1952, Seedtime of Reform, 1963, Paul U. Kellogg and the Survey, 1971; Editor: Century of Concern, 1973; Contbr. articles to profl. jours. Chmn. Minn. Humanities Commn., 1978-80. Served with USAAF, 1943-45. Recipient McKnight prize history, 1972; Rockefeller Found. grantee; Russell Sage Found. grantee; NIMH grantee; Nat. Endowment for Humanities fellow, 1977-78. Home: 2285 Folwell St St Paul MN 55108 Office: 614 Social Sci Bldg U Minn Minneapolis MN 55455

CHAMBERS, CURTIS ALLEN, clergyman, church communications executive; b. Damascus, Ohio, Sept. 24, 1924; s. Binford Vincent and Margaret Esther (Patterson) C.; m. Anna June Winn, Aug. 26, 1946; children: David Lloyd, Curtis Allen II, Deborah Ann, Charles Cloyde. Th.B., Malone Coll., 1946; A.B., Marion Coll., 1947; B.D., Asbury Theol. Sem., 1950; postgrad., Oberlin Grad. Sch. Theology, 1951-53; S.T.M., Temple U., 1955, S.T.D., 1960; D.D. (hon.), Lebanon Valley Coll., 1967. Ordained to ministry Evang. United Brethren Ch., 1954; pastor 1st Ch., Cleve., 1951-53, Rockville Ch., Harrisburg, Pa., 1953-59; editor adult publs. Evang. United Brethren Ch., 1959-65; asso. editor Ch. and Home mag., Dayton, Ohio, 1963-66, editor, 1967-69; asst. editorial dir. Together and Christian Advocate, Meth. Pub. House, Park Ridge, Ill., 1969; editor Together mag., 1969—; acting editorial dir. gen. periodicals United Meth. Ch., 1971-72, editorial dir., 1972-73; gen. sec. United Meth. Communications, 1973—; book editor Evang. United Brethren Ch., 1965-68; co-editor Plan of Union, United Meth. Ch., 1965-68, 1968, chmn. staff com. long range planning, 1969-72, mem. commn. on ch. union, 1965-68; dir. radio-TV relations gen. confs. Evang. United Brethren Ch., 1958, 62, 66, United Meth. Ch., 1966, 68; Chmn. commn. on ednl. media Nat. Council Chs., 1965-66, chmn. com. on audio visual and broadcast edn., 1962-65, exec. com. broadcasting and film commn., chmn. communications commn., 1975-78, v.p., 1975-78; chmn. Religious Communications Congress, 1980; named 1 of 12 editors sent to Middle East on fact-finding trip, 1969. Contbr. articles to religious lit. Served as capt. (chaplain) CAP, 1960-65. Recipient Distinguished Alumni award Malone Coll., 1967, Alumni of Year, 1978. Mem. Aircraft Owners and Pilots Assn., United Meth. Assn. Communicators (v.p. 1968—), World Assn. Christian Communications (central com., chmn. Jour. editorial bd. 1975—, chmn. periodical devel. com., exec. com., sec. 1978—), Asso. Ch. Press (hon. life), Religious Pub. Relations Council. Clubs: Chgo. Press, Torch (Dayton). Home: 4620 Dartford Rd Englewood OH 45322 Office: 601 W Riverview Ave Dayton OH 45406 *When I was young I thought that anything was possible for me and that I had a long, long time to achieve it. With maturity I have come to a recognition of mortality, finitude, a limitation of time and opportunity. Thus my life has taught me three things: 1) Choose the best. Life is too precious to squander it on the second rate. 2) Live for others. The quality of one's life is enhanced rather than diminished as one shares himself/herself with others. 3) Fulfill your dreams. Tomorrow may never come; act now so that life's opportunities may not be lost forever.*

CHAMBERS, DAVID SMITH, statistician, association executive, consultant; b. Clarksville, Tex., Jan. 26, 1917; s. Clifton A. and Eva Ellen (Smith) C.; m. Mary Othella Parsons, Feb. 22, 1941. B.A. in Math, U. Tex., 1939, M.B.A. in Stats., 1947; postgrad., U. Mich. Instr. aero. engring. U. Tex., 1941-42, applied math. and astronomy, 1942-46, bus. stats., 1946-47; asst. prof. stats. U. Tenn., 1947-48, asso. prof., 1948-58, prof. stats., 1958-82; mem. Am. Soc. Quality Control, 1947—, bd. dirs., 1953-56, 65—, exec. sec., 1959-61, chmn. exec. bd. Inst. Edn. and Tng., 1960-63, chmn. exam. com. Tenn. sect. Inst. Edn. and Tng., 1958—, fellow 1954—, chmn. textile and needle trades div., 1967-68, treas. chem. div., 1967-68, chmn. chem. div., 1969-70, pres., 1971-72, chmn. bd. dirs., 1972-73, dir.-at-large, 1975-77, chmn. awards bd., 1976—; quality control cons. AID, Dept. State, 1962—. Author papers in field. Recipient E.L. Grant award for edn. in quality control, 1970. Fellow AAAS; mem. ASTM (com. E-11 1969-82), Am. Statis. Assn., Engrs. Joint Council (dir. 1971-75, mem. awards com. 1977—), Internat. Acad. Quality, Phi Beta Kappa, Phi Kappa Phi, Phi Eta Sigma, Beta Gamma Sigma. 3304 Bunker Hill Dr Knoxville TN 37920 Office: PO Box 140535 Nashville TN 37214

CHAMBERS, EARL DENTON, insurance executive; b. Norwalk, Conn., June 14, 1925; s. Earl Henderson and Florence (Denton) C.; m. Ann Elizabeth Keating, Sept. 9, 1950; children: Sarah A., Lydia D. A.B., Dartmouth Coll., 1948. Chartered fin. analyst. With R.I. Hosp. Trust Co., Providence, 1953-65; with Marine Midland Trust Co., Rochester, N.Y., 1965-70, exec. v.p., 1967-70; v.p. Marine Midland Banks, Inc., 1969-72, Marine Midland-N.Y., 1970-72; sr. v.p. Amica Mut. Ins. Co., Providence, 1972—; dir. Providence Investors Co. Pres. Providence Pub. Library, 1974—; Trustee Women and Infants Hosp., Providence; mem. investment com. R.I. Sch. Design. Served as ensign USNR, 1943-46. Mem. Providence Soc. Security Analysts, Inst. Chartered Fin. Analysts. Club: Agawam Hunt (East Providence, R.I.). Home: 103 Williams St Providence RI 02906

CHAMBERS, EDWARD HIRSCHY, fast food company executive; b. Mt. Kisco, N.Y., Mar. 25, 1937; s. Harry Hirschy and Florence (Hanlon) C.; m. Barbara V. Kossman, Aug. 6, 1960; children: Laurie, Jennifer, Edward. B.S. in Acctg., Lehigh U., 1961. C.P.A., N.Y. Sr. acct. Price Waterhouse, Stanford, Conn., 1961-66; controller S.B. Thomas, Totowa, N.J., 1966-71; with Heublein, Inc., Hartford, Conn., 1971-75; v.p. fin. and control Ky. Fried Chicken Corp., Louisville, 1975-79, sr. v.p., 1979-82, pres. retail, 1982—. Mem. Leadership Louisville, 1980; mem. fin. com. United Way, Louisville; bd. dirs. Ky. Opera Assn., Louisville. Mem. Fin. Execs. Inst. (dir. 1981-82). Republican. Presbyterian. Home: 40 Calumet Rd Louisville KY 40207 Office: Kentucky Fried Chicken Corp 1441 Gardiner Ln Louisville KY 40232

CHAMBERS, EDWARD THOMAS, foundation executive; b. Clarion, Iowa, Apr. 2, 1930; s. Thomas J. and Hazella Mae (Downing) C.; m. Ann L. Martin, 1974; children: Eve, Mae, Joseph, Lily. B.A., U. St. John's, Collegeville, Minn., 1953. With Indsl. Areas Found., Chgo., N.Y.C., 1940—, exec. dir., 1972—, trustee, 1972—. Office: 675 W Jericho Turnpike Huntington NY 11743

CHAMBERS, FRED, electrical engineer; b. Carbon Hill, Ala., Feb. 17, 1912; s. Bunnier Greater and Zora (McCollum) C.; m. Margaret Armstrong, Nov. 29, 1933; 1 son, Fred. B.S. in Elec. Engring, Auburn U., 1930; postgrad., Mass. Inst. Tech., 1930-31. Registered profl. engr., La., Tenn. With Gen. Electric Co., 1930-32, Asso. Gas and Electric Co., Elmira, N.Y., 1932, Tenn. Electric Power Co., 1933-39, Chattanooga Electric Power Bd., 1939; with TVA, 1939-71, asst. mgr. power, 1970-71; with Bovay Engrs., Inc., 1971-73, Pub. Service Commn. State N.Y., Albany, 1973-74; elec. engr., Houston, 1974—. Author tech. papers. Served with USNR, 1943-45. Fellow IEEE; mem. Internat. Conf. Large High Tension Electric Systems, Tenn. Soc. Profl. Engrs., Houston Engring. and Sci. Soc., Houston C. of C. Democrat. Episcopalian. Office: 13815 Britoak Ln Houston TX 77079

CHAMBERS, JACK A., psychologist; b. Hamilton, Ohio, Feb. 26, 1932; s. Glen S. and H. Edna (McCormick) C.; m. A. Ruth Coe, Aug. 24, 1957; children: Melissa Ann, Wendy Colleen. A.B., U. Miami, Fla., 1954; M.A., U. Cin., 1955; Ph.D., Mich. State U., 1964. Lic. psychologist, Calif., Pa. Dir. personnel U. South Fla., Tampa, 1960-66, dir. computer research center, asst. dean adminstrn., 1966-72; prof. psychology, dir. computer ednl. center Mansfield (Pa.) State Coll., 1972-74; prof. psychology, dir. Center Info. Processing, Calif. State U., Fresno, 1974—; dir. Coordination Center for Computer Assisted Instrn. Calif. State U. System, 1982—; sr. partner Chambers, Sprecher & Assos., 1978—, Zeitgeist; cons. NSF, Sci. mag. Co-author: Computer Assisted Instruction: Its Use in the Classroom, 1983; Author articles in field. Grantee James McKeen Cattell Found., 1960, U.S. Office Edn., 1969, Calif. State Dept. Edn., 1977. Mem. Am. Psychol. Assn., AAAS, Assn. Computing Machinery (co-chmn. CAI task force elem. and secondary schs. subcom., communications cons.), Calif. Ednl. Computing Consortium (co-chmn. CAI com.). Home: 1637 W Morris Ave Fresno CA 93711 Office: Center Info Processing Calif State U Fresno CA 93740

CHAMBERS, JACK HENRY, historical architect; b. Omaha, Feb. 15, 1921; s. Jack Adair Chambers and Ruth Wilhelmina (Swenson) Chambers H.; m. Lorraine L. Stevenson, June 4, 1949; children: Donna J., Ann N. B.Arch., Yale U., 1951. With UN Planning Office, 1948-49; architect M.M. Konarski (Architect), Akron, Ohio, 1951-53, Konarski and Chambers, Akron, 1953-63, Chambers and Kritchgau, 1964-66; mng. partner Chambers and Chambers, Cons. Hist.

Architects, Medina, Ohio, 1966—; Mem. Urban Design Commn., Akron, Ohio. Served with USN, 1942-46. Fellow AIA. Republican. Episcopalian. Office: 3668 Allard Rd Medina OH 44256

CHAMBERS, MARY ALICE, government department administrator; b. North Platte, Nebr., June 6, 1941; d. Glen Trego and Lillian Elizabeth (Gaswick) Kepler; m. Ray Benjamin Chambers, Apr. 3, 1966; children: Elizabeth Carolyn, Glen Randall. B.A., Am. U., 1963. Asst. to Congressman F.B. Morse, Washington, 1964-66; legis. and adminstrv. asst. Congressman Marvin Esch, Washington, 1967-76; v.p. Parrish & Chambers Inc., Washington, 1977-82; dep. asst. sec. for legis. U.S. Dept. Edn., Washington, 1982—. Republican. Methodist. Home: 1431 Woodacre Dr McLean VA 22101 Office: US Dept Edn 400 Maryland Ave SW Washington DC 20202

CHAMBERS, MELBER, lawyer; b. N.Y.C., July 20, 1901; s. Walter Albert and Evangeline (Bowers) C.; m. Katherine Audley Heigho, Aug. 4, 1933; children: Ann Audley Chambers Holloway, Robert Alan. A.B., Cornell U.; LL.B., Harvard U. Bar: N.Y. Formerly partner, now of counsel firm Sage, Gray, Todd & Sims, N.Y.C., 1926—; spl. master N.Y. Supreme Ct., 1978—; Dir. Jersey Central Power & Light Co., 1940-44, Am. Radio Co., 1948-71, Concel, Inc., 1965-72. Pres. Correctional Assn. N.Y., 1958-70; Trustee Goddard Coll., 1962-72. Home: 330 E 46th St New York NY 10017 Office: 2 World Trade Center 100th Floor New York NY 10048

CHAMBERS, MERRITT MADISON, educator; b. Knox County, O., Jan. 26, 1899; s. Rufus Ward and Etta Amelia (Miller) C. Student, U. Fla., Harvard; B.A., Ohio Wesleyan U., 1922; M.A., Ohio State U., 1927, Ph.D., 1931; Litt.D., Eastern Ky. U., 1969. Tchr., prin. high schs., 1922-26; with Am. Council on Edn., 1935-42, 45-51; cons. U.S. Office Edn., 1952-53; owner-operator Lafayette Farms, Mt. Vernon, O., 1951-58; vis. prof. higher edn. U. Mich., 1958-63; exec. dir. Mich. Council State Coll. Presidents, 1961-62; prof. higher edn. Ind. U., 1963-69; prof. ednl. adminstrn., cons. on higher edn. Ill. State U., Normal, 1969—; Participant surveys of higher edn., Mass., Ill., 1949, Conn., Wis., Ia., 1950, N.Y.C., 1961, Ky., 1962, Md., 1963; cons. Com. on Govt. and Higher End., 1957; chmn. Long-Range Study Higher Edn. Ky., 1965-66; cons. So. Ill. U. and Mich. State Bd. Edn., 1966. Author: Youth-Serving Organizations, rev. edit, 1947, The Campus and the People, 1960, Voluntary Statewide Coordination in Public Higher Education, 1961, Chance and Choice in Higher Education, 1962, Financing Higher Education, 1963, The Colleges and The Courts Since 1950, 1964, Freedom and Repression in Higher Education, 1965, Bibliography of Higher Education, 1966, The Colleges and the Courts, 1962-66, 1967, Higher Education: Who Pays? Who Gains?, 1968, Higher Education in the Fifty States, 1970, Above High School, 1970, The Developing Law of the Student and the College, 1972, Faculty and Staff Before the Bench, 1973, Higher Education and State Governments, 1974, Keep Higher Education Moving, 1976; Editor: various works including Charters of Philanthropies, 1948, Universities of the World Outside U.S.A, 1950; Contbr. articles to ednl., legal publs. Served to maj. USAAF, 1942-46. Recipient awards Nat. Orgn. on Legal Problems, 1970, Nat. Colloquium on Higher Edn., 1971; presdl. citation Am. Coll. Pub. Relations Assn., 1972; medalha pro mundi beneficio Brazilian Acad. Humanities. Fellow AAAS; mem. Knox County Farm Bur. (pres. 1957-58), NEA (life), Delta Sigma Rho, Phi Delta Kappa, Alpha Sigma Phi. Office: Dept Ednl Adminstrn Illinois State Univ Normal IL 61761 *As a teacher, researcher, and writer on higher education, the theme "Education can free the world" has steady attraction for me. This means high-level technological and scientific training, as well as education in the humanities, the arts, and the social disciplines, made widely accessible to all the people without wrongful discrimination on account of race, religion, sex, national origins, economic disadvantage or financial handicaps. The public value of universal access to higher education is incalculable; it is the most productive possible long-term investment for public funds, for dollar returns, and for intangible benefits to the whole society.*

CHAMBERS, PATRICK JOSEPH, JR., utility executive; b. Cleve., June 3, 1934; s. Patrick J. and Catherine (Green) C.; m. Nancy Carol Prock, June 3, 1956; children: Stephanie, Patrick, Michele. Ed., Case Inst. Tech. Rate engr. E. Ohio Gas, Cleve., 1956-64; with Commonwealth Services, Inc., N.Y.C., Washington, 1965-72; now sr. v.p., dir. Orange and Rockland Utilities, Inc., Pearl River, N.Y. Vice pres. fin. Boy Scouts Am., Rockland County, 1976-79, now trustee and mem. exec. bd.; bd. dirs., treas. Nyack (N.Y.) Hosp.; bd. dirs. United Way Bergen County, chmn. bd. dirs., 1982-83, chmn. campaign, 1983; trustee Bullawa Trust Fund., Ramapo Coll., Mawah, N.J. Mem. Am. Gas Assn. (mem. fin. com.), Edison Electric Inst. (fin. com.). Roman Catholic. Club: Ridgewood Country. Home: 4 Newton Pl Allendale NJ 07401 Office: 1 Bluehill Plaza Pearl River NY 10965

CHAMBERS, RICHARD H., ret. U.S. circuit judge; b. Danville, Ill., Nov. 7, 1906; s. William R. and Lida J. (Spencer) C.; m. Mary Martin, November 24, 1945; children by previous marriage—Martha Chambers Froese, Janet Chambers Crews. A.B., U. Ariz., 1929, LL.D., 1976; LL.B., Stanford, 1932; LL.D., U. Pacific, 1972. Bar: Ariz. bar 1932. Practice law in, Tucson, 1932-41, 45-54; judge Ct. of Appeals, 9th Circuit, Tucson, 1954-77, sr. judge, 1977—. Served from capt. to maj. USAAF, 1942-45. Recipient Law medal Gonzaga U., 1974. Mem. Am. Law Inst., Am. Bar Assn., Phi Gamma Delta. Republican. Club: Old Pueblo (Tucson). Home: 6300 N Campbell Tucson AZ 85718 Office: 55 E Broadway Tucson AZ 85701

CHAMBLIN, ROBERT ANTHONY, association executive; b. Flora, Ill., May 15, 1939; s. Barkley T. and Margaret (Bishop) C.; m. Karen Keith, Sept. 7, 1957; children: Margaret Ann, Keith. B.A., Millikin U., 1960. Sports editor, columnist Evansville (Ind.) Courier and Press, 1961-65; editor, pub. Horsemen's Jour., Rockville, Md., 1965-73, pub., 1965-83; exec. dir., sec.-treas. Horsemen's Benevolent and Protective Assn., Rockville, 1973-83; pres., gen. mgr. Finger Lakes Racing Assn., Canandaigua, N.Y., 1983—. Editor books in field. Mem. Am. Horse Council (exec. com.), Nat. Turf Writers (sec.-treas.), Am. Horse Publs. (past pres., exec. dir.), Ky. Thoroughbred Assn. (exec. dir.), Md. Racing Writers Assn., Nat. Assn. State Racing Commrs., Thoroughbred Club Am. Club: Nat. Press. Office: PO Box 364 Canandaigua NY 14424 *I have been successful because I aspire to be among the best in my profession because I have worked hard to achieve that goal, and because I do not take myself too seriously, I believe in peace and good will love and compassion, laughter, baseball, hot dogs, apple pie and Chevrolet, the Washington Redskins, Willie Nelson and fried okra. It is my considered opinion that right, truth and justice will prevail in the end; hopefully, the end will not be too late.*

CHAMBRÉ, PAUL L., educator; b. Kassel, Germany, Aug. 7, 1918; came to U.S., 1937, naturalized, 1942; s. Ernest and Minna (Rothenberg) C.; m. Jane C. Miller, June 26, 1943 (dec. Mar. 1964); children—Erika Anne, Suzanne, Marianne. B.S., U. Calif. at Berkeley, 1941, Ph.D., 1951; M.S., N.Y. U., 1947. Research engr. Airesearch Mfg. Co., Los Angeles, 1943-44; research scientist Jet. Propulsion Lab., Calif. Inst. Tech., 1944-45, Project Squid, N.Y. U., 1945-47; research scientist low pressure research group U. Calif. at Berkeley, 1947-51, mem. faculty, 1951—, prof. math. and engring. sci., 1962—. Author: Flow of Rarefied Gases, 1961, also articles. Mem. Sigma Xi, Pi Mu Epsilon. Office: Dept Mathematics Univ California Berkeley CA 94720

CHAMPAGNE, JOSEPH ERNEST, university president, industrial psychology consultant; b. Norwich, Conn., May 19, 1938; s. Fred Joseph and Loretta Eva (Lucier) C.; m. Emilie Lind, Dec. 27, 1969; children: Jennifer, Juliana, Johanna. A.B., St. Mary's U., 1960; M.A., Fordham U., 1962; Ph.D., Purdue U., 1966. Lic. cert. psychologist, Tex. Psychology instr., research asst., cons. various orgns., 1962-71; pres. Houston Community Coll. System, 1971-73, pres. emeritus; assoc. dir. Ctr. Human Resources U. Houston, 1969-71, 73-76; coordinator extended acad. and pub. service programs U. Houston System Office, 1977-78, assoc. v.p. office of exec. v.p., 1977-78; prof. dept. organizational behavior and mgmt. U. Houston, 1967-81, v.p. acad. devel. and coordination, 1978-81; pres. Oakland U., Rochester, Mich., 1981—; pres. Houston Area Rehab. Assn., 1971; bd. dirs. Tex. Rehab. Assn., 1971-72; mem. adv. com. Community Colls., Houston, 1970-71; mem. task force U. Houston, 1974-75, State of Tex., 1973-75. Contbr. articles to numerous publs. Bd. dirs. Ctr. Multiple Handicapped Children, 1973-81; trustee Crittenton Hosp., Oakland U.; bd. dirs. Detroit Symphony Orch.; mem. nat. adv. council Ctr. for Study of Presidency. Named Citizen of Yr. Houston Area Rehab. Assn. Mem. Am. Psychol. Assn., Am. Assn. Higher Edn. Roman Catholic. Home: 300 S Adams Rd Rochester MI 48063 Office: Oakland University North Foundation Hall Rochester MI 48063

CHAMPEAUX, JUNIUS JOSEPH, II, architect, city planner; b. New Iberia, La., Jan. 15, 1939; s. Junius Joseph and Isabelle Annette (LeBlanc) C.; m. Rosalie Levegre, July 29, 1961; children: Renee Michelle, Caron Cherise, Marjorie Annette. Student, U. Southwestern La.; B.Arch., Tulane U.; M.Arch. in City Planning, Rice U. Dir. city planning City of Lake Charles, La., 1968-72; ptnr. Barras Breaux Champeaux, archtl. firm, Lake Charles, 1972—. Chmn. ARC, 1971-73; bd. dirs. YMBC. Served with USAF, 1963-66. Decorated Air Force Commendation medal; recipient Service award YMBC; AIA fellow. Mem. La. State Architects Assn., AIA (RUDAT team), Lake Charles C. of C. (pres. 1979). Democrat. Roman Catholic. Office: 800 Bayou Pines Lake Charles LA 70160 *

CHAMPION, (CHARLES) HALE, university dean; b. Coldwater, Mich., Aug. 27, 1922; s. Paul Upham and Ruth Emma (Hungerford) C.; m. Marie Ozine Tifft, Aug. 21, 1952; children: Thomas Paul, Katherine Marie. B.A., Stanford U., 1952. Journalist UPI, Milw. Jour., Sacramento Bee, San Francisco Chronicle, Reporter mag., 1946-49, 52-58; legis. asst. to Congressman Andrew J. Biemiller of Wis., 1950; press and exec. sec. to Gov. Edmund G. Brown of Calif., 1958-60; dir. fin., State of Calif., 1961-66; dir. Boston Redevel. Authority, 1968-69; v.p. fin., planning and ops. U. Minn., 1969-71; fin. v.p. Harvard U., 1971-76; undersec. HEW, Washington, 1977-79; exec. dean John F. Kennedy Sch. Govt., Harvard U., 1980—; mem. Presdl. Task Force Reorgn. Fed. Govt., 1966-67, Presdl. Task Force Role of Univ. in Urban Affairs, 1967-68; chmn. Mass. Joint Legis.-Exec. Com. Fed. Base Conversion, 1973-74; dir. Multibank Fin. Corp., Inc. Served with AUS, 1942-46. Nieman fellow Harvard U., 1956-57; fellow John F. Kennedy Inst. Politics, 1967. Mem. Nat. Acad. Public Adminstrn. (trustee). Democrat. Office: John F Kennedy Sch Govt Harvard U 79 Boylston St Cambridge MA 02138

CHAMPION, MARGE (MARJORIE CELESTE BELCHER), actress, dancer; b. Los Angeles, Sept. 2; d. Ernest and Gladys (Basquette) Belcher; m. Art Babbitt (div.); m. Gower Champion, Oct. 5, 1947 (div. 1973); children: Blake, Gregg; m. Boris Sagal, Jan. 1, 1977. Student pub. schs., Los Angeles. Stage debut, Los Angeles Civic Opera, 1936; movie debut (under name Marjorie Bell) The Castles, 1938; model for cartoon heroines in: Walt Disney prodns. Blue Fairy in Pinocchio, 1938; appeared: Broadway musicals Dark of the Moon, 1945, Beggar's Holiday, 1946; first profl. appearance with Gower Champion as Gower and Bell, Montreal, Can., 1947; first profl. appearance with Gower Champion as Marge and Gower Champion N.Y. debut in, Hotel Plaza, 1947; first profl. appearance with Gower Champion as Gower and Bell night club tours, 1948; weekly show Admiral Broadway Review, Dumont and NBC TV Network, 1949; appeared with Bing Crosby in: movie Mr. Music, Paramount Pictures, 1950; with husband staged dances for revues: Lend an Ear, 1949, Make A Wish, Small Wonder, Broadway, 1951; movies include Showboat, 1951, Everything I Have is Yours, 1952, Give the Girl a Break, 1952, Three for the Show, 1955, Jupiter's Darling, 1955, The Swimmer, 1968, The Party, 1968, The Cockeyed Cowboy of Calico County, 1970, That's Entertainment, Part 2, 1976; various nightclub, TV appearances, including TV show Toast of the Town, 1953; Three for Tonight, 1955, Shower of Stars, 1956, GE Theatre, 1957, Dinah Shore Show, 1958, Telephone Hour, We Four, 1960; acting debut Hemingway and All Those People, Indpls., 1958; title role: Sabrina Fair, 1960; choreographer: Queen of the Stardust Ballroom, 1975 (Emmy award), Day of the Locust, 1975; Author: (with Marilee Zdenek) Catch the New Wind, 1972, God is a Verb, 1974; dialogue coach and choreographer: The Awakening Land, NBC-TV, 1978, Masada, ABC-TV, 1979, Diary of Ann Frank, NBC-TV, 1980, When the Circus Comes to Town, CBS-TV, 1980; appeared: TV series Fame, 1982; dir. choreography: TV prodn. I Do, I Do, 1983; dancer: 5-6-7-8, Dance!, Radio City Music Hall, 1983. Address: care Mercader & Paperny 10889 Wilshire Blvd Suite 1160 Los Angeles CA 90024

CHAMPLIN, CHARLES DAVENPORT, critic, writer; b. Hammondsport, N.Y., Mar. 23, 1926; s. Francis Malburn and Katherine (Masson) C.; m. Margaret Frances Derby, Sept. 11, 1948; children: Charles Davenport, Katherine (Mrs. Timothy Wilde), John, Judith (Mrs. Robert Desmond), Susan, Nancy. A.B. cum laude, Harvard U., 1947. Reporter Life mag., 1948-49, corr., Chgo., 1949-52, Denver, 1952-54, writer, N.Y.C., 1954-59; corr. Time mag., Los Angeles, 1959-62, London, Eng., 1962-65; entertainment editor, columnist Los Angeles Times, 1965—, prin. film critic, 1967-80, book critic, 1981—; commentator KCET-TV, Los Angeles, also ETV Network, 1969—; adj. prof. Loyola-Marymount U., Los Angeles, 1976—. Author: (with C. Sava) How to Swim Well, 1960, The Flicks, 1977, revised as The Movies Grow Up, 1981, also numerous articles. Served with inf. AUS, 1944-46. Decorated Purple Heart; recipient Order Arts and Letters, France, 1977. Mem. Nat. Soc. Film Critics, Nat. Book Critics Circle, Sigma Delta Chi. Home: 2169 Linda Flora Dr Los Angeles CA 90077 Office: Los Angeles Times Times-Mirror Sq Los Angeles CA 90053

CHAMPLIN, MALCOLM MCGREGOR, retired municipal judge; b. San Francisco, Apr. 13, 1911; s. Charles Chaffee and Maude (Fraser) C.; m. Betty Mee Champlin, Dec. 1943 (div.); children: Sarah, William Bradford, Mimi Lisette; m. Virginia Pearson, Dec. 2, 1955. B.S., U.S. Naval Acad., 1934; J.D., U. Calif., 1939; grad., U.S. Naval War Coll., 1944. Bar: Calif. bar 1940. Commd. ensign USN, 1934, served in, 1934-37; practiced in, Oakland, 1940, 45-67; spl. agt. FBI, 1941; partner firm Stark & Champlin, 1947-67; municipal ct. judge, Oakland, 1967-81; Vice pres., dir. Ventura Processors, Inc., 1949-53. Contbr. to: Sea Power and Shipmate mags. Gen. chmn. fund drive Knowland Park Zoo, 1963; Chmn. Speaker's Com. Republican Party, Alameda County, 1949-50; del. Nat. Rep. Conv., 1960-64; chmn. Vets for Eisenhower, Alameda County, 1952, 56. Served as comdr. USNR, 1941-45; capt. Res.; ret.). Decorated Navy Cross, Army Silver Star.; Recipient George Washington Honor Medal award Freedoms Found. at Valley Forge, 1964. Mem. Am., Calif., Alameda County bar assns., Am. Judicature Soc., Am. Legion (past comdr. 10th Dist., judge adv. dept. of Calif. 1953-54, state comdr. 1954-55, Calif. mem. nat. exec. com. 1956-58), Res. Officers Assn., Soc. Former Spl. Agts. FBI, U.S. Naval Acad. Alumni Assn., Phi Delta Phi. Conglist. Clubs: Mason., Commonwealth (San Francisco); Oakland Lions. Home: 485 Ellita Ave Oakland CA 94610

CHAMPLIN, RICHARD H., lawyer, truck transportation executive; b. Enid, Okla., May 12, 1935; s. Paul B. and Adelene Ida (Johnson) C.; m. Katherine Gore, Apr. 4, 1961; children—Kimberly Kay, Margaret Ann, Christian Paul. B.B.A., U. Okla., 1957, J.D., 1961. Bar: Okla. bar. Asst. gen. counsel Lee Way Motor Freight Co., Oklahoma City, 1961-63, asst. sec., 1963-66, gen. counsel, 1966-69, v.p., gen. counsel, 1969-80, sec., 1977—. Vice pres. Oklahoma City All Sports Assn. Served with Signal Corps AUS, 1957-58. Mem. Okla. Bar Assn., Motor Carrier Lawyers Assn. (v.p.). Presbyterian. Club: Oklahoma City Golf and Country. Home: 2300 NW 56th St Oklahoma City OK 73112 Office: PO Box 12750 3401 NW 63d St Oklahoma City OK 73157

CHAN, LO-YI CHEUNG YUEN, architect; b. Canton, China, Dec. 1, 1932; came to U.S., 1942, naturalized, 1954; s. Wing tsit and Wai hing (Lei) C.; m. Mildred Wu, Sept. 1, 1957; children: Christopher, Leighton, Leicia. B.A., Dartmouth Coll., 1954; M.Arch., Harvard U., 1959, postgrad. (Appleton fellow), 1959-60. Asso. firm I. M. Pei & Partners, N.Y.C., 1960-65; practice architecture, N.Y.C., 1965—; Adj. asst. prof. architecture Columbia, 1963-67; vis. critic Coll. Architecture, Cornell U., 1965-68, Harvard U., 1976, 78, 80, Mass. Inst. Tech., 1977; panelist Am. Arbitration Assn., 1972—. Bd. dirs. Parks Council, N.Y.C., 1971—, pres., 1974; trustee Community Service Soc., N.Y.C., 1977—, Henry St. Settlement, 1980. Served with AUS, 1955-57. Nat. Endowment for Arts Design fellow, 1975-76. Fellow AIA (corp.); mem. Phi Beta Kappa. Home: 270 Riverside Dr New York NY 10025 Office: 14E 4th St New York NY 10012

CHAN, SHAU WING, educator; b. Canton, China, Apr. 4, 1907; s. Chan Chi-Tong and Tsui Wan-Ying; m. Anna Mae Chan, July 27, 1935; children—Wayne Lyman, Loren Briggs. A.B., Lingnan U., China, 1927; A.M., Stanford, 1932, Ph.D., 1937. Instr. English Nat. Sun Yat-Sen U., Canton, China, 1927-30; lectr. Chinese Kwangtung Provincial Normal Sch. for Women, Canton, 1928-30; U. fellow in English Stanford, 1932-34; apptd. prof. English Nat. U. Shantung, Taingtao, China, 1937; spl. lectr. Utah State Agrl. Coll., summer 1941; vis. prof. U. Utah, summer 1944; Pomona Coll., summers 1945, 1946, 1950, 1951; instr. in Chinese lang. and lit. Stanford, 1938-39, asst. prof. Chinese and English, 1939-42, asst. prof. Chinese and humanities, 1942-45, asso. prof. Chinese and humanities, 1945-50, prof. Chinese, 1950-72, emeritus, 1972—, acting exec. head, 1958-62; dir. human relations area files China Research Project, Stanford, 1955-56; cons. hist. research Com. for Free Asia, 1951-52; cons. Stanford Research Inst., 1951-53; established soldier-training program in Chinese Stanford, 1943, dir., 1943-45, Chinese-Japanese Lang. and Area Center, 1956—; research asso. Hoover Instn. Lang.; cons. Internat. Secretariat, UN Conf., San Francisco. Author: Chinese Reader for Beginners, 1942, Concise English-Chinese Dictionary, 1946, Elementary Flash Cards, 1944, Elementary Chinese, 1951, 2d edit., 1961; co-author: China's Men of Letters Yesterday and Today. Chmn. bd. library trustees, City of Menlo Park. Mem. Am. Oriental Soc., Phi Delta Kappa. Conglist. Clubs: Kiwanian., Commonwealth of Calif. Home: 751 Live Oak Ave Menlo Park CA 94025 Office: Stanford University Stanford CA 43305

CHAN, SHU-PARK, educator; b. Canton, China, Oct. 10, 1929; came to U.S., 1951, naturalized, 1965; s. Chi-Tong and Shui-Ying (Mok) C.; m. Stella Yok-Sing Lam, Dec. 28, 1956; children: Charlene Li-Hsiang, Yau-Gene. B.E.E., Va. Mil. Inst., 1955; M.E.E., U. Ill., 1957, Ph.D., 1963. Instr. elec. engring. and math. Va. Mil. Inst., 1957-59; instr. elec. engring. U. Ill., 1960-61, research asso., 1961-62, asst. prof. math., 1962-63; asso. prof. elec. engring. U. Santa Clara, 1963-68, prof., 1968—, chmn. elec. engring. and computer sci. dept., 1969—; prin. investigator NSF, NASA.; Univ. fellow U. Ill., 1959-60; vis. spl. chair prof. elec. engring. dept. Nat. Taiwan U., 1973-74; spl. lectr. Academia Sinica, Peking, China, summer 1980; hon. prof. elec. engring. dept. U. Hong Kong, 1980-81; hon. prof. Anhuei U., China, 1982; spl. chmn. Tamkang U., Taipei, Taiwan, 1981. Author: introductory Topological Analysis of Electrical Networks, 1969, (with others) Analysis of Linear Networks and Systems - A Matrix-Oriented Approach with Computer Applications, 1972, (with E. Moustakas) Introduction to the Applications of the Operational Amplifier, 1974; Editor: Network Topology and Its Engineering Applications, 1975, Graph Theory and Applications, 1982. Chmn. bd., pres. Academic Cultural Co., Santa Clara.; Chmn. Santa Clara County Bicentennial Chinese Festival Com.; pres. Chinese Arts and Culture Inst., 1976—; trustee Inst. Sino-Am. Studies, San Jose, Calif., 1971—. Fellow IEEE (past chmn. circuit theory group San Francisco sect., chmn. asilomar conf. circuits and system 1970); Mem. Am. Soc. Engring. Edn., Chineses Alumni Assn. U. Santa Clara (pres.), Sigma Xi, Tau Beta Pi, Eta Kappa Nu, Pi Mu Epsilon, Phi Kappa Phi. Club: U. Santa Clara Faculty (pres. 1971-72). Home: 2085 Denise Dr Santa Clara CA 95050 *I would like to attribute my personal success to the teaching of my father, the late General of the Army Chi-Tong Chan, who taught me the Four Principles of Goodness: Set a good goal in mind; acquire a good wealth of knowledge; exercise good self-discipline; and perform only good deeds.*

CHAN, SUNNEY IGNATIUS, chemist; b. San Francisco, Oct. 5, 1936; s. Sun and Hip-For (Lai) C.; m. Irene Yuk-Hing Tam, July 11, 1964; 1 son, Michael Kenneth. B.S. in Chem. Engring, U. Calif. at Berkeley, 1957, Ph.D. in Chemistry, 1960. Asst. prof. chemistry U. Calif. at Riverside, 1961-63; mem. faculty Calif. Inst. Tech., 1963—, prof. chem. physics, 1968—, prof. biophys. chemistry, 1976—, exec. officer for chemistry, 1977-80, master student houses, 1980-83; cons. in field. Author numerous articles in field. Guggenheim fellow, 1968-69; Sloan fellow, 1965-67; NSF Postdoctoral fellow, 1960-61; Reilly lectr. U. Notre Dame, 1973-74. Mem. AAAS, Am. Chem. Soc., Am. Phys. Soc., Am. Soc. Biol. Chemists, So. Calif. Chinese Engrs. and Scientists Assn. (Progress award 1971), Chinese Collegiate Colleagues So. Calif. (v.p. 1970-71, pres. 1971-72), Phi Beta Kappa, Sigma Xi, Tau Beta Pi, Alpha Chi Sigma, Phi Tau Phi. (pres. 1981—). Home: 327 Camino del Sol South Pasadena CA 91030 Office: Calif Inst Tech Pasadena CA 91125

CHANCE, BRITTON, educator; b. Wilkes Barre, Pa., July 24, 1913; s. Edwin M. and Eleanor (Kent) C.; m. Jane Earle, Mar. 4, 1938 (div.); children: Eleanor, Britton, Jan, Peter; m. Lilian Streeter Lucas, Nov. 1956; children: Margaret, Lilian, Benjamin, Samuel; stepchildren—Ann Lucas, Gerald B. Lucas, A. Brooke Lucas, William C. Lucas. B.S. and M.S., U. Pa., 1936, Ph.D. (E.R. Johnson Found. fellow), 1940, U. Cambridge, 1942, D.Sc., 1952; M.D. (hon.), Karolinska Inst., Stockholm, 1962, Semmel Weis U., Budapest, 1976; D.Sc., Med. Coll. Ohio, 1974, Hahnemann Coll. and Hosp., 1977. Asst. prof. biophysics U. Pa., 1940-48, prof., chmn., 1949—, acting dir. Johnson Found., 1940-41, dir. Johnson Found., 1949-83, Eldridge Reeves Johnson prof. biophysics and phys. biochemistry, 1949, 77-83, emeritus prof. biophysics and phys. chemistry, also univ. prof. emeritus, 1983—; dir. Inst. Structural and Functional Studies, 1982—; staff MIT, 1941-46; Cons. NSF, 1952-55; mem. Pres.'s Sci. Adv. Com., 1959-60; mem. adv. council Nat. Inst. Alcohol Abuse and Alcoholism, 1971-75; mem. molecular control working group Nat. Cancer Inst., 1973—. Author: (with F.C. Williams, V. Hughes, E.F. McNichol, David Sayre) Waveforms, 1949, (with R.I. Hulsizer, E.F. McNichol, F.C. Williams)

Electronic Time Measurements, 1949, Energy-linked Functions of Mitochondria, 1964, (with Q.H. Gibson, R. Eisenhardt, K.K. Lonberg-Holm) Rapid Mixing and Sampling Techniques in Biochemistry, 1964, (with R.W. Estabrook, J.R. Williamson) Control of Energy Metabolism, 1965, (with R.W. Estabrook, T. Yonetani) Hemes and Hemoproteins, 1966, (with others) Probes of Structure and Function of Macromolecules and Enzymes, 1971, Alcohol and Aldehyde, Vol. I, 1974, II, III, 1977, Tunneling in Biological System, 1979; rev. articles Advances in Enzymology, Vo. 12, 1951, Vol. 17, 1956, Ann. Rev. of Biochemistry, 1952, 70, 76, The Enzymes, Vol. II. Part 1, 1952, Vol. XIII, 1976, Ann. Rev. Plant Physiology, 1958, 68; Bd. editors: Physiol. Revs, 1951-54, FEBS Letters, 1973-75, BBA Reviews, 1972—, Photobiochemistry and Photobiophysics, 1979—; Contbr.: articles to Am., Brit., Swedish, German and Japanese Jours. Presdl. lectr. U. Pa., 1975; Julius L. Jackson Meml. lectr. Wayne State U., 1976; Da Costa oration Phila. County Med. Coll., 1976; Recipient Paul Lewis award for enzyme chemistry, 1950; Pres.'s Certificate of Merit for services, 1941-45, as staff mem. Radiation Lab. of M.I.T., 1950; Guggenheim fellow, Stockholm, 1946-48; Harvey lectr., 1954; Phillips lectr., 1955, 65; Pepper lectr., 1957; Exchange scholar to, USSR, 1963; Genootschapps medal Dutch Acad. Scis., 1965; Heineken medal, 1970; Keilin medal Brit. Biochem. Soc., 1966; Harrison Howe award, 1966; Franklin medal, 1966; Overseas fellow Churchill Coll., 1966; Herter lectr. NYU, 1968; Pa. award for excellence in life scis., 1968; Nichols award N.Y. sect. Am. Chem. Soc., 1970; Phila. sect. award, 1969; Redfearn lectr., 1970; Gairdner award, 1972; Post-Congress Festschrift, Stockholm, 1974; Semmelweis medal, 1974; Nat. medal Sci., 1974; Troy C. Daniels lectr. U. Calif.-San Francisco, 1984. Fellow Am. Phys. Soc., IEEE (Morlock award 1961, Phila. sect. award 1984), AAAS, Am. Inst. Chemists; mem. Internat. Union Pure and Applied Biophysics (pres. 1972-75), Chem. Soc., Royal Soc. Arts, Biochem. Soc. Eng., Am. Soc. Biol. Chemists (Sober lectr. 1984), Am. Philos. Soc., Am. Acad. Arts and Sci., Nat. Acad. Sci., Am. Physiol. Soc., Soc. Gen. Physiologists (council 1957-60), Am. Inst. Physics, Soc. for Neurosci., Biophys. Soc. (council 1959-62), Swedish Biochem. Soc., Royal Swedish Acad. Scis., Royal Acad. Arts and Scis., Sweden, Bavarian Acad. Scis., Acad. Leopoldina DDR, Max-Planck Gesellschaft fü Forerung der Wissenschaften (fgn.), Argentine Nat. Acad. Sci., Royal Soc. London (fgn.), Harvey Soc., Sigma Xi, Tau Beta Pi. Clubs: Corinthian Yacht (Phila.); St. Anthony. Holder numerous patents on automatic steering devices, also spectrophotometric devices, radar circuitry. Gold medal winner (yachting) 1952 Olympics. Home: 4014 Pine St Philadelphia PA 19104

CHANCE, HENRY MARTYN, II, engineering executive; b. Pottsville, Pa., Jan. 16, 1912; s. Edwin M. and Eleanor (Kent) C.; m. Suzanne Sharpless, June 12, 1934; children: Edwin M. Suzanne, Barbara; m. Elizabeth Reese, Aug. 19, 1944; children: Steven K., James M., Henry Martyn III, Mark Raymond. Grad., Haverford Sch., 1930; B.S. in Civil Engring., U. Pa., 1934; LL.D. (hon.), U. Pa., 1983. Registered profl. engr., 7 states. Chemist, assayer Am. Smelting & Refining Co., 1934-36; with United Engrs. & Constructors, Inc., Phila., 1936—, pres., 1954-71, chmn., 1972-77, dir., cons., 1977—. Life trustee, mem. exec. bd. U. Pa., until 1982, emeritus trustee, 1982—; pres. Haverford Sch., 1962-70, mem. bd., 1962-72, life dir., 1974—; bd. mgrs. emeritus Franklin Inst.; mem. bd. overseers U. Pa. Mus. Named Engr. of Year Del. Valley, 1964. Former Mem. ASME. Clubs: Corinthian Yacht; Union League (Phila.). Home: PO Box 432 Malvern PA 19355 Office: United Engrs Bldg 30 S 17th St Philadelphia PA 19101

CHANCELLOR, JOHN WILLIAM, news correspondent; b. Chgo., July 14, 1927; s. Estil Marion and Mollie (Barrett) C.; m. Constance Herbert; 1 dau., Mary; m. Barbara Upshaw, Jan. 25, 1958; children—Laura, Barnaby. Student, DePaul Acad., Chgo., U. Ill. Reporter Chgo. Sun-Times; staff NBC News, 1950-65, newswriter, gen. assignment reporter U.S., 1953-58, Vienna Corr., 1958, with London bur., 1959-60, Moscow Corr., 1960-61, staff N.Y.C. office, 1961-63, Brussels corr., 1963-65; communicator TV program Today, 1961-62, staff corp., 1962-65; dir. Voice of Am., Washington, 1966-67; network nat. affairs corr. NBC, 1967—; anchorman NBC Nightly News, 1970-81; commentator NBC News, 1981—. Address: care NBC 30 Rockefeller Plaza New York City NY 10020 *

CHANDIS, HARRY THOMAS, airline company executive; b. Astoria, N.Y., Apr. 2, 1934; s. Thomas and Hrisanthe (Tsohara) C.; m. Janice Ellen Mitravich, June 19, 1939; children: Christina, Thomas. B.B.A., CUNY, 1971; M.B.A., Columbia U., 1972. Dir. sales planning and spl. market sales Am. Airlines, N.Y.C., 1973-74, dir. gen. sales, 1974-75; v.p. mktg. U.S. Air, Inc., Washington, 1975-77, sr. v.p. mktg., 1977-80; pres., gen. mgr. Tex. Internat. Airlines, Houston, 1980-81; sr. v.p. mktg. Western Airlines, Inc., Los Angeles, 1983—; cons. in field. Recipient Alumni award Acad. Aeronautics, 1960. Mem. Columbia U. Grad. Sch. Bus. (adv. bd. 1977-80). Greek Orthodox. Office: Western Airlines 6060 Avion Dr Los Angeles CA 90045

CHANDLER, ALBERT BENJAMIN, lawyer, former governor; b. Corydon, Ky., July 14, 1898; s. Joseph and Callie (Sanders) C.; m. Mildred Watkins, Nov. 12, 1925; children: Marcella (Mrs. Thomas D. Miller), Mildred (Mrs. James J. Lewis), Albert Benjamin, Joseph Daniel. A.B., Transylvania Coll., 1921, LL.D., 1936; student, Harvard, 1921-33; LL.B., U. Ky., 1924, LL.D., 1937. Football coach Centre Coll., Danville, Ky., 1922-24; began law practice, Versailles, Ky., 1924; apptd. master commr. Circuit Ct., Woodford County, 1928; elected mem. Ky. Senate, from 22d Dist., 1929; lt. gov., Ky., 1931-35, gov., 1935-39, 55-59, resigned, 1939; apptd. U.S. senator (to fill vacancy caused by death of Marvell Mills Logan); elected, 1940, to fill remainder term, to Jan. 1943, re-elected for 6 year term, 1942; high commr. of baseball, 1945-51; pres. Internat. Baseball Congress, Wichita; commr. Continental Profl. Football League, 1965—, Global Internat. Baseball League; v.p., dir. First Flight Golf Co., Chattanooga; dir. Coastal States Life Ins. Co. Ga.; Receiver for Inter-So. Life Ins. Co., Louisville, 1932; an organizer Ky. Home Life. Ins. Co., Louisville, 1932. Mem. athletic com. U. Ky., 1966—, life trustee, 1981—; Chmn. Woodford County Democratic Exec. Com.; Dem. nat. committeeman for, Ky.; Trustee Ty Cobb Found.; trustee U. Ky., mem. athletic com., 1967—; chmn. bd. trustees and fund raising com. Transylvania Coll. Served with U.S. Army, 1918; capt. J.A.G. Dept. Res.; ret.). Named Kentuckian of Year Ky. Press Assn. and Ky. Broadcasters Assn.; named to Ky. Sports Hall of Fame, 1957; recipient Bishop's medal Episcopal Ch., 1959; Cross of Mil. service U.D.C., 1959; Jefferson Davis medal, 1975; U. Ky. Med. Center named in his honor, 1959; honored at spl. lecture Transylvania U., 1980; named to Nat. Baseball Hall of Fame, 1982, award NCCJ, 1983. Mem. Am. Legion, 40 and 8, Pi Kappa Alpha. Episcopalian. Clubs: Mason (32 deg., K.T., Shriner), Ky. Mountain (hon.), Lexington Country, Idle Hour Country (Lexington). One of five senators designated by U.S. Senate to visit world battle fronts in 1943, at which time they made the first landplane flight ever made across the Indian Ocean from Ceylon to Australia. Home: Versailles KY 40383

CHANDLER, ALFRED DUPONT, JR., educator, historian; b. Guyencourt, Del., Sept. 15, 1918; s. Alfred Dupont and Carol (Ramsay) C.; m. Fay Martin, Jan. 8, 1944; children: Alpine Douglass Chandler Bird, Mary Morris Chandler Watt, Alfred Dupont III, Howard Martin. A.B., Harvard U., 1940, A.M., 1947, Ph.D., 1952; Ph.D. (hon.), U. Leuven, Belgium, 1976, U. Antwerp, Belgium, 1979, L.H.D, Babson Coll., 1982. Research asso. Mass. Inst. Tech., 1950-51, from instr. to prof., 1951-63; prof. history Johns Hopkins, 1963-71, chmn. dept., 1966-70, dir. Center for Study Recent Am. History, 1964-71; Straus prof. bus. history Harvard Bus. Sch., 1971—; vis. fellow All Souls Coll., Oxford U., 1975; vis. prof. European Inst. Advanced Studies in Mgmt., Brussels, 1979; Walker-Ames vis. prof. U. Wash., 1981; dir. Landmark Communications, Inc.; Cons. U.S. Naval War Coll., 1954; mem. Nat. Adv. Council on Edn. Professions Devel., 1970-71; Chmn. adv. hist. com. U.S. AEC (renamed ERDA 1974), 1969-77. Author: Henry Varum Poor, 1956, Strategy and Structure, 1962 (Newcomen award 1964), Giant Enterprise, 1964, The Railroads, 1965, (with Stephen Salsbury) Pierre S. duPont, 1971, The Visible Hand (Pulitzer and Bancroft prizes for 1978), (with Herman Daems) Managerial Hierarchies, 1980; Editor: Papers of Dwight D. Eisenhower, 5 vols, 1970; asst. editor: The Letters of Theodore Roosevelt, 4 vols, 1950-53. Trustee Park Sch., Brookline, Mass., 1957-63, chmn. bd., 1961-63; trustee Brookline Pub. Library, 1959-63, Roland Park Sch., Balt., 1964-70, Johns Hopkins, 1971-81, Eleutherian Mills-Hagley Found., 1981—. Served to lt. comdr. USNR, 1940-45. Recipient Pulitzer prize for history, 1978; Guggenheim fellow, 1958-59; Research fellow Harvard U., 1955. Mem. Econ. History Assn. (trustee 1966-70, pres. 1971-72), Orgn. Am. Historians (exec. bd. 1969-72), Soc. for History Tech. (exec. council 1972-75), Am. Hist. Assn., Am. Antiquarian Soc., Soc. Am. Historians, Mass. Hist. Soc. (council 1977-83), Bus. History Conf. (pres. 1977-78), Am. Acad. Arts and Scis., Am. Philos. Soc. Episcopalian. Clubs: St. Botolph (Boston); Nantucket (Mass.) Yacht; Harvard (N.Y.C.); Hamilton Street (Balt.). Home: 1010 Memorial Dr Cambridge MA 02138

CHANDLER, ALICE, university president, educator; b. Bklyn., May 29, 1931; d. Samuel and Jenny (Meller) Kogan; m. Horace Chandler, June 10, 1954; children: Seth, Donald. A.B., Barnard Coll., 1951; M.A., Columbia U., 1953, Ph.D., 1960. Instr. Skidmore Coll., 1953-54; lectr. Barnard Coll., 1954-55, Hunter Coll., 1956-57; from instr. to prof. CCNY, 1961-76, v.p. instl. advancement, 1974-76, v.p. acad. affairs, 1974-76, provost, 1976-79, acting pres., 1979-80; pres. SUNY, New Paltz, 1980—; Mem. higher edn. adv. com. N.Y. State Edn. Dept., 1979; bd. dirs. Revson Found., 1979. Author: The Prose Spectrum: A Rhetoric and Reader, 1968, The Theme of War, 1969, A Dream of Order, 1970, The Rationale of Rhetoric, 1970, The Rationale of the Essay, 1971, From Smollett to James, 1980. Lizette Fisher fellow. Mem. Wave Hill Center Environ. Studies, MLA, Lotos, Phi Beta Kappa. Office: Office of Pres SUNY New Paltz NY 12561

CHANDLER, ARTHUR BLEAKLEY, pathologist, educator; b. Augusta, Ga., Sept. 11, 1926; s. Clemmons Quillian and Mary Isabella (Bleakley) C.; m. Jane Stoughton Downing, Sept. 2, 1953; children—Arthur Bleakley, John Downing. Student, U. Ga., 1943-44; M.D., Med. Coll. Ga., Augusta, 1948. Diplomate: Am. Bd. Pathology. Intern Baylor U. Hosp., Dallas, 1948-49; resident in pathology, trainee in cancer, dept. pathology Med. Coll. Ga., 1949-51, asst. in pathology, 1949-50, mem. faculty, 1949—, prof. pathology, 1962—, chmn. dept., 1975—; attending physician Augusta VA Hosp., 1957—; cons. Eisenhower Army Med. Center, Augusta, 1977—; mem. coms. Nat. Heart, Lung and Blood Inst., 1969—. Author papers in field, chpts. in books; mem. editorial bd.: Haemostasis. Trustee Young Mens Library Assn. Fund, 1962-72, Historic Augusta, Inc., 1966-69, Augusta-Richmond County Mus., 1965—; also chmn. med. adv. com. Augusta-Richmond County Mus.; mus. rep. Greater Augusta Arts Council, 1968-76. Served as officer M.C. AUS, 1951-53. Commonwealth Fund fellow, Norway, 1963-64. Mem. Internat. Acad. Pathology, Internat. Soc. Thrombosis and Haemostasis; mem. Am. Assn. History Medicine, Coll. Am. Pathologists, Am. Assn. Pathologists, Am. Soc. Hematology, Am. Heart Assn. (fellow council arteriosclerosis, chmn. council on thrombosis, dir. 1979-80, chmn. com. on coronary lesions and myocardial infarctions 1980-82), Ga. Assn. Pathologists (pres.-elect 1983-84), AMA, Ga. Heart Assn., Med. Assn. Ga., Richmond County Med. Soc., Alpha Omega Alpha. Episcopalian. Home: 803 Milledge Rd Augusta GA 30904 Office: Dept Pathology Med Coll Ga Augusta GA 30912

CHANDLER, B.J., educator, superintendent schools; b. Bluffton, Ark., July 23, 1921; s. J.V. and Edna (McCreight) C.; m. E. Ursula Bieder, 1978; children: Brenda (Mrs. Thomas Dexter Barbour), Robert W., Cynthia (Mrs. Patrick Bost), Maria, Michael, Bobby Joe. B.A., U. Tex., 1948, M.Ed., 1949; Ed.D., Columbia, 1951. Asst. prof. edn. U. Va., Charlottesville, 1951-54, asso. prof., 1954-56; asso. prof. edn. Northwestern U., 1956-59, prof. edn., 1959—, dean, 1963-78, dean emeritus, 1978—; supt. schs., Dardanelle, Ark., 1981—; ednl. cons. State Farm Ins. Cos., 1953-70; cons. Nat. Bd. Med. Examiners, 1978-79, Nat. Sch. Bds. Assn., 1978-80; Co-chmn. Gov.'s Com. on Literacy and Learning, 1963-67; cons. River City Ednl. Program, Chgo.; Chmn. adv. council, trustee Aerospace Edn. Found., 1964-69; mem. adv. council Kellogg Found., 1963-65; mem. Gov.'s Task Force on Edn., 1965-67; pres. Ill. Council on Econ. Edn., 1969-73; chmn. Ill. Task Force on Tchr. Edn.; mem. Ill. Tchr. Certification Bd.; Bd. dirs. Films, Inc., Law in Am. Soc. Found., 1971—, Citizens Sch. Com. Chgo.; mem. Carter-Mondale Task Force on Edn., 1976; trustee Chgo. Y Community Coll., Evanston Roycemore Sch., North Shore Country Day Sch. Author: Education and the Teacher, 1961, (with Lindley J. Stiles and John I. Kitsuse) Education in Urban Society, 1962, (with Paul V. Petty) Personnel Management in School Administration, 1955, (with Daniel Powell and William Hazard) Education and the New Teacher, 1971; Gen. editor: Introduction to Teaching, 8 vols, 1969—, Free Press Series; mem. editorial adv. bd.: Edn. and Urban Society; cons. editor: Standard Edn. Almanac, 1980-81, Acad. Media, 1980—; Contbr. articles to profl. jours. Served with USAAF, 1942-44. Fulbright-Hays sr. scholar, Rumania, 1975-76, Moscow, spring 1979. Mem. Nat. Cath. Edn. Assn. (dir. 1972), Internat. Council of Scholars (chmn. adv. com. 1979—). Home: Route 2 Dardanelle AR 72834

CHANDLER, C(HARLES) Q(UARLES), bank executive; b. Wichita, Kans., Sept. 1, 1926; s. C.J. and Alice (Cromwell) C.; m. Georgia Johnson, Aug. 22, 1948; children: Jeannette Colleen Chandler Randle, C.Q. IV, Robert Paul. B.S., B.A., Kans. State U., 1949; postgrad, Wis. Sch. Banking, Madison, 1958. With First Nat. Bank in Wichita, 1950—, exec. v.p., 1958-71, pres., 1971-75, pres., chmn. bd., 1975-83, chmn. bd., 1983—; v.p., dir. First Bank of Newton, (Kans.); dir. K.G. & E., Wichita, Fidelity State Bank & Trust, Topeka, Chandler Bank of Lyonst, (Kans.). Pres. Kans. Soc. Crippled Children, Wichita; chmn. Wesley Med. Endowment Found., Wichita; trustee Kans. State U. Found., Manhattan; bd. dirs. Wichita State U. Endowment Assn., Manhattan. Mem. Kans. Bankers Assn. (bd. dirs.), Am. Bankers Assn. (exec. com. comml. lending div.). Republican. Clubs: Wichita (bd. dirs.), Wichita Country). Office: First Nat Bank in Wichita Box One Wichita KS 67201

CHANDLER, COLBY H., photography equipment company executive. B.S., U. Maine, 1950; postgrad., MIT. With Eastman Kodak Co., Rochester, N.Y., 1950—, mem. sales estimating council, then corp. asst. v.p., until 1972, exec. v.p., 1972-77, pres., 1977—, chmn. chief exec. officer, 1983—, also dir.; exec. dir. Lincoln 1st Bank, Rochester.; dir. Continental Group, Inc., Ford Motor Co., J.C. Penney Co. Bd. dirs. Indsl. Mgmt. Council Rochester; bd. dirs. Congl. Award Com.; Bd. dirs. United Way of Greater Rochester; bd. dirs. Rochester-Monroe County Conv. and Visitors Bur., Nat. Orgn. on Disability; exec. dir. Rochester Civic Music Assn.; trustee Rochester Inst. Tech., Colgate Rochester Div. Sch., U. Rochester, Nat. 4-H Council, Internat. Mus. Photography at George Eastman House; mem. MIT Corp. Mem. Soc. Sloan Fellows (bd. govs. 1964, pres. 1966-68), Tau Beta Pi, Sigma Pi Sigma, Phi Kappa Phi, Beta Gama Sigma. Address: Eastman Kodak Co 343 State St Rochester NY 14650 *

CHANDLER, DAVID LEE, journalist; b. Covington, Ky., May 26, 1937; s. James L. and Beatrice L. (Chippendale) C. Student, Boston U. Investigative reporter News-Herald, Panama City, Fla., 1959-61, States-Item, New Orleans, 1962-64; So. corr., then investigative reporter Life mag., 1964-71; engaged in writing, 1972-78; investigative reporter Ledger-Star, Norfolk, Va., 1978—. Author: The Criminal Brotherhoods, 1975, Natural Superiority of Southern Politicians, 1977, 100 Tons of Gold, 1978. Recipient Pulitzer prize, 1962, Delta Chi award nat. mag. reporting, 1971, Willis Scripps 1st Amendment award, 1980. Address: 910 Colonial Ave Norfolk VA 23507

CHANDLER, ELISABETH GORDON (MRS. LACI DE GERENDAY), sculptor, harpist; b. St. Louis, June 10, 1913; d. Henry Brace and Sara Ellen (Sallee) Gordon; m. Robert Kirkland Chandler, May 27, 1946 (dec.); m. Laci de Gerenday, May 12, 1979. Grad., Lenox Sch., 1931; pvt. study sculpture and harp. Mem. Mildred Dilling Harp Ensemble, 1934-39, 42-45; instr. portrait sculpture Lyme Acad. Fine Arts, 1976—; dir. Abbott Coin Counter Co., Inc., 1941-55. Exhibited sculpture, NAD, Nat. Sculpture Soc., Allied Artists Am., Nat. Arts Club, Pen and Brush, Lyme Art Assn., Mattatuck Mus., Catherine Lorillard Wolfe Art Club, Am. Artists Profl. League, Hudson Valley Art Assn., USIA, 1976-78, Lyme Art Ctr., 1979; represented permanent collections, Aircraft Carrier USS Forrestal, Gov. Drummer Acad., James Forrestal Research Ctr. of Princeton U., Lenox Sch., James L. Collins Parochial Sch., Tex., Storm King Art Ctr., Columbia U., Forrestal Meml. Medal, Timoschenko Medal for Applied Mechanics, Benjamin Franklin Medal, Albert A. Michelson Medal, Jonathan Edwards Medal, Shafto Broadcasting Award Medal, Woodrow Wilson Sch. of Princeton U., Ga. Pacific Bldg., Atlanta and Portland, Oreg., Messiah Coll., Grantham, Pa., Adlai E. Stevenson High Sch., Ill., Queen Anne's County, Md., Pace U., N.Y.C., pvt. collections. Chmn. Associated Taxpayers Old Lyme, 1969-72; trustee The Lenox Sch., 1953-55; with mus. therapy div. Am. Theatre Wing. Recipient 1st prize Bklyn. War Meml. competition, 1945, 1st prize sculpture Catherine Lorillard Wolfe Art Club, 1951, 58, 63, Gold medal, 1969, Founders prize Pen & Brush, 1954, 76, 78, Gold medal Pen and Brush, 1957, 61, 63, 69, 74, 76, Am. Heritage award, 1968; rcipient Solo Show award Pen and Brush, 1961, 69, 75; recipient Thomas R. Proctor prize NAD, 1956, Dessie Geer prize NAD, 1960, 79, Sculpture prize Nat. Arts Club, 1959, 60, 62, Gold medal, 1971, Am. Artists Profl. League, 1960, 69, 73, 75, prize, 1981, Anna Hyatt Huntington prize, 1970, 76, Harriet Mayer Meml. prize, 1961, Gold medal Hudson Valley Art Assn., 1956, 69, 74, Mrs. John Newington award, 1976, 78, Lindsey Morris Meml. prize Allied Artists Am., 1973, Gold medal, 1982, sculpture prize Acad. Artists, 1974, Sydney Taylor Meml. prize Knickerbocker Artists, 1975, New Netherlands DAR Bicentennial medal, 1976, Tallix Foundry award, 1979, award Nat. Sculpture Soc., 1979. Fellow Nat. Sculpture Soc. (council 1976—), Am. Artists Profl. League, Internat. Inst. Arts and Letters; mem. Nat. Arts Club, Allied Artists Am., Pen and Brush, Catherine Lorillard Wolf Art Club, Lyme Art Assn. (pres. 1973-75), Council Am. Artists Socs. (dir. 1970-73), Am. Artists Profl. League (dir. 1970-73), NAD, Lyme Acad. Fine Arts (trustee 1976—). Home and Studio: 2 Mill Pond Ln Old Lyme CT 06371

CHANDLER, GEORGE ALFRED, shipbuilding executive; b. Cleve., Aug. 15, 1929; s. George Alfred and Doris Beatrice (Datson) C.; m. Sally Jane Topping, Apr. 10, 1954; children: Nancy, David, James, Elizabeth. B.A., Princeton U., 1951; M.B.A., Harvard U., 1956. With brass div. Olin Corp., East Alton, Ill., 1956-67, v.p., gen. mgr. Aluminum Group, Stamford, Conn., 1967-71, pres. Winchester Group, New Haven, 1971-77; pres. Am. Productivity Ctr., Houston, 1978, Indsl. Products group Amstar Corp., N.Y.C., 1978-82; pres., chief exec. officer Am. Ship Bldg. Co., Tampa, Fla., 1983—; dir. The Allen Group, Melville, L.I., Peabody Internat. Corp., Stamford. Mem. Alton Bd. Edn., Ill., 1963-67, Darien Bd. Edn., Conn., 1969-72. Served to 1st lt. arty. U.S. Army, 1951-53; Korea. Republican. Episcopalian. Home: 1109 Culbreath Isles Dr Tampa FL 33629 Office: American Ship Building Co 2502 Rocky Point Rd Tampa FL 33607

CHANDLER, HARRY EDGAR, author, editor; b. Springfield, Ill., May 11, 1920; s. Harry Edgar and Theresa Augusta (Fromm) C.; m. Mary Louise Becker, June 6, 1946; children: Susan Becker Ballard, Jay Michael, Teresa Ann, Stephen Ross, Julia Elizabeth. A.B. in Sci, U. Evansville, 1942; A.M. in Journalism, Ind. U., 1949, LL.B., 1949. Courthouse reporter, asst. to editor Peru (Ind.) Daily Tribune, 1949-52; tech. editor, writer Armour Research Found., Chgo., 1952-53; asso. editor Steel Mag., Cleve., 1953-54, copy editor, 1954-67; editor Materials Today (monthly materials mag. Am. Soc. for Metals), Metals Park, Ohio, 1967-68; mng. editor Metal Progress, 1968-72, editor, asst. dir. periodical publs., 1968—; Lectr. bus. mag. journalism and article writing Western Res. U., 1963-65; cons. and speaker to bus. mag. pubs., pub. relations agys. Author: The How to Write What Book, Technical Writers Handbook, 1983; Contbr. articles to profl. jours. Served to capt. USMCR, 1942-46. Mem. Sigma Delta Chi. Office: Am Soc for Metals Metals Park OH 44073

CHANDLER, HUBERT THOMAS, army officer; b. Charleston, W.Va., Dec. 8, 1933; s. Hubert Paris and Eleanor Lee (Gay) C.; m. Mary Frances Ritter, June 4, 1955; 1 son, Thomas Ritter. Student, Morris Harvey Coll., Charleston, 1951-52, U. Louisville, 1952-53; D.D.S., Balt. Coll. Dental Surgery, 1957; grad., Army War Coll., 1974. Diplomate: Am. Bd. Prosthodontics. Commd. Dental Corps, U.S. Army, 1957; advanced through grades to maj. gen.; dep. to chief U.S. Army Dental Corps, 1975-78; dep. comdr. U.S. Army Med. Command; also dental surgeon U.S. Army, Europe, 1979-82; asst. surgeon gen., chief U.S. Army Dental Corps, 1982—; dir. personnel U.S. Army Med. Dept., 1983—. Exec. com. Transatlantic council Boy Scouts Am., 1980—; chmn. trust fund Girl Scouts Europe, 1981—; pres. European Assn. Rod and Gun Clubs, 1981—, Am. German Friendship Club, Heidelberg, W. Ger., 1981—. Decorated Bronze Star, Meritorious Service medal, Army Commendation medal. Fellow Am. Coll. Prosthodontists; mem. ADA, Am. Assn. Mil. Surgeons, Fedn. Dentaire Internat., Fedn. Prosthodontic Orgns. Address: Office of Surgen Gen DASG-DC US Army Washington DC 20310

CHANDLER, JAMES E., banker; b. Keene, N.H., July 2, 1924; s. Harold I. and Blanche C.; m. Christine L. Wilder, Feb. 25, 1945; children: Carolyn, Harold I. B.S., Wharton Sch. of U. Pa., 1945; grad., Stonier Grad. Sch. Banking, Rutgers U., 1954. With Keene Nat. Bank, 1945, Phila. Nat. Bank, 1945, First Nat. Bank Phila., 1953; with Indian Head Nat. Bank, Nashua, N.H., 1953—, exec. v.p., 1956-58, pres., 1958-75, chmn. bd., 1976—; chmn. I.H. Banks Inc.; dir. Pratt Read Corp., Edgcomb Steel New Eng., Allen-Rogers Corp., Asso. Grocers of New Eng., Pole & Wood Treating Co.; chmn. Indsl. Devel. Authority. Chmn. bd. Crotched Mountain Found.; mem. adv. council Daniel Webster council Boy Scouts Am. Mem. Nashua C. of C., New Eng. Council, Stonier Grad. Sch. Banking Alumni Assn., Gen. Alumni Assn. U. Pa., Newcomen Soc. Clubs: Kataska (Que., Can.); Nashua Country, Manchester Country. Home: Town Crier Rd Amherst NH 03031 Office: One Indian Head Plaza Nashua NH 03060

CHANDLER, JAMES JOHN, surgeon; b. Dayton, Ohio, Nov. 13, 1932; s. James Kapp and Margaret Bertha (Paulson) C.; m. Fleur Elizabeth Varney, July 23, 1955; 1 dau., Jennifer Fleur. A.B., Dartmouth Coll., 1954, diploma in medicine, 1955; M.D. cum laude, U. Mich., 1957. Diplomate: Am. Bd. Surgery. Intern Harvard Surg. Service, Boston City Hosp., 1957-58, jr. asst. resident, 1958; resident, chief resident in surgery, clin. fellow Am. Cancer Soc. U. Oreg. Hosps., Portland, 1961-64, instr. surgery, 1964; attending staff, chmn. surgery Med. Center at Princeton, N.J., 1972—; clin. prof. surgery Coll. Medicine and Dentistry N.J.-Rutgers Med. Sch., Piscataway, 1975—; cons. in surgery Princeton U. Contbr. chpt. to book, articles to profl. jours. Bd. dirs. Trinity Counseling Service, 1968-82, chmn., 1968-72, 79-81; pres. Princeton Day Sch. PTA, 1976-78, trustee, 1976-81; active All Saints Episcopal Ch., Princeton, 1965—; mem. alumni adv. com. Dartmouth Med. Sch., 1981—; mem. alumni council Darmouth Coll., 1983—. Served to lt. comdr. USN, 1958-60; Served to lt. comdr. USNR, 1960-61. Fellow A.C.S. (pres. N.J. chpt. 1976-77, gov. 1981—), Soc. Surgery Alimentary Tract, Am. Coll. Chest Physicians; mem. Pan-Pacific Surg. Assn., Soc. Surgeons N.J., Med. Soc. N.J. (sec., chmn. surgery sect. 1967-69), Mercer County Med. Soc., Collegium Internationale Chirurgiae Digestivae, Soc. Surg. Oncology, Oncology Soc. N.J., Acad. Medicine N.J., Alpha Omega Alpha. Republican. Clubs: Nassau Gun, Bedens Brook, Gatineau Fish and Game, Sea Pines. Home: 95 Russell Rd Princeton NJ 08540 Office: 253 Witherspoon St Princeton NJ 08540

CHANDLER, JAMES RYAN, physician; b. Charleston, S.C., July 30, 1923; s. James R. C. B.S., Duke U., 1943, M.D., 1947; postgrad., U. Mich. Diplomate: Am. Bd. Otolaryngology. Intern Protestant Episcopal Hosp., Phila., 1947-48; resident Roxborough Meml. Hosp., Phila., 1948-49, U. Mich. Hosp., 1951-55; mem. faculty U. Miami (Fla.) Med. Sch., 1957—, prof. otolaryngology, since 1962, chmn. dept., 1962—; mem. staff Jackson Meml. Hosp. Contbr. articles to med. jours. Served to capt. M.C. AUS, 1955-57. Fellow A.C.S., Am. Laryngological, Rhinological and Otol. Soc., Am. Soc. Head and Neck Surgery (pres. 1980), Soc. Head and Neck Surgeons, Am. Laryngological Assn., Am. Otol. Soc.; mem. AMA., Am. Acad. Otolaryngology, Otosclerosis Study Group, Soc. U. Otolaryngologists. Republican. Episcopalian. Club: Riviera Country (Coral Gables). Office: Univ Miami Med Sch PO Box 016920 Miami FL 33101

CHANDLER, JAMES WILLIAMS, securities company executive; b. Adairville, Ky., Feb. 4, 1904; s. James Avery and Mary Nell (Williams) C.; m. Lelia Elizabeth Roemele, June 29, 1932. A.B., Centre Coll., Danville, Ky., 1925. With Stein Bros. & Boyce, Louisville, 1926-48, N.Y.C., 1948-49; with W.L. Lyons & Co., 1950-55, ptnr., 1955-65; partner J.J.B. Hilliard, W.L. Lyons & Co., Inc., Louisville, 1965—, sr. v.p., 1965—. Trustee emeritus, past alumni dir. Centre Coll., Danville, Ky.; past jr. warden, sr. warden and treas. Calvary Episcopal Ch., Louisville. Recipient Disting. Alumni award Centre Coll., 1983. Mem. Investment Bankers Assn. Am. (nat. committeeman 1954-67), Soc. Colonial Wars (trustee), Delta Kappa Epsilon. Republican. Clubs: Pendennis (Louisville); Gulfstream Bath and Tennis (Delray Beach, Fla.); Yale (N.Y.C.). Home: 6209 Wolf Pen Branch Rd Harrods Creek KY 40027 also 1028 Vista del Mar Delray Beach FL 33444 Office: 545 S 3d St Louisville KY 40202

CHANDLER, JOHN HERRICK, college president; b. San Francisco, Aug. 7, 1928; s. Ralph William and Gwen Thornton (Herrick) C.; m. Nancy Gordon Phillips, Dec. 10, 1955; children: John, Seth, Will. A.B., U. Calif., Los Angeles, 1952; B.D. (Danforth fellow), U. Chgo., 1958; Ph.D. (fellow), U. Chgo., 1963. Instr. English Dartmouth Coll., 1961-63; asst. prof. U. Calif., Los Angeles, 1963-64; asso. prof., dean spl. programs Ohio U., 1964-67; v.p. Danforth Found., St. Louis, 1967-71; pres. Salem Coll. and Acad., Winston-Salem, N.C., 1971-76, Scripps Coll., Claremont, Calif., 1976—; ordained to ministry Episcopal Ch., 1960. Trustee Newton Coll. Sacred Heart, 1970-75, Thacher Sch., 1977—; dir. Clayton (Mo.) Bd. Edn., 1970-71. Clubs: University (Los Angeles); Twilight, Bohemian. Office: Scripps College Balch Hall Claremont CA 91711

CHANDLER, JOHN WESLEY, college president; b. Mars Hill, N.C., Sept. 5, 1923; s. Baxter Harrison and Mamie (McIntosh) C.; m. Florence Gordon, Aug. 25, 1948; children: Alison, John, Jennifer, Patricia. Student, Mars Hill Coll., 1941-43; A.B., Wake Forest Coll., 1945, L.H.D. (hon.); B.D., Duke, 1952, Ph.D., 1954; LL.D., Hamilton Coll., 1968, Colgate U., 1968, Williams Coll., 1973, Amherst Coll., 1974, Wesleyan U., 1978, North Adams State Coll., 1983; L.H.D., Wake Forest U., 1968, Trinity Coll., 1982, Middlebury Coll., 1983, Bates Coll., 1983. Instr. philosophy Wake Forest Coll., 1948-51, asst. prof., 1954-55; asst. prof. religion Williams Coll., 1955-60, asso. prof., chmn. dept., 1960-65, Cluett prof. religion, 1965-68, acting provost, 1965-66, dean faculty, 1966-68; pres. Hamilton Coll., Clinton, N.Y., 1968-73, Williams Coll., Williamstown, Mass., 1973—. Contbg. author: Miscellany of American Religion, 1963, Masterpieces of Religious Literature, 1963, also jour. articles and revs. Trustee Williams Coll., 1969-73; bd. visitors Wake Forest Coll., 1971-77, 79—; bd. dirs. Williamstown Theatre Festival, Sterling and Francine Clark Art Inst.; pres. New Eng. Assn. Schs. and Colls., 1977-78, Assn. Ind. Colls. and Univs. Mass., 1977—; chmn. New Eng. Colls. Fund, 1978. Fulbright fellow, India, 1963; Kent fellow. Mem. Am. Acad. Religion, Soc. for Sci. Study Religion, Phi Beta Kappa. Mem. United Ch. of Christ. Clubs: University, Williams, Century Assn. (N.Y.C.). Office: Williams Coll Williamstown MA 01267

CHANDLER, JOHN, JR., retired educational consultant; b. Clinton, Mass., Oct. 18, 1920; s. John and Katherine (Fassett) C.; m. Fay Cowgill, Sept. 21, 1942; children: Darthea Marentette, Abigail Norling, Rebecca Cuthbert, John III, William C. Grad., Groton Sch., 1938; B.A., Yale, 1942, M.A., 1949. Asst. dean Yale, 1946-49; headmaster Grosse Pointe (Mich.) U. Sch., 1949-63; ednl. cons., Boston, 1964-66; v.p. Nat. Assn. Ind. Schs., Boston, 1966-81. Bd. dirs. Chewonki Found., Wiscasset, Maine. Served to lt. USNR, 1942-46; ETO. Mem. Headmasters Assn., Country Day Sch. Headmasters Assn. Clubs: Union Boat, Yale (Boston); Small Point Yacht (Maine). Home: 6 Brookmere Way Brunswick ME 04011

CHANDLER, MARGARET KUEFFNER, business educator; b. St. Paul, Sept. 30, 1922; d. Otto Carl and Marie (Schaedlich) Kueffner; m. Louis Chandler, Apr. 8, 1943. B.A. in Polit. Sci, U. Chgo., 1942, M.A. in Econs, 1944, Ph.D. in Sociology, 1948. Mem. faculty U. Ill. at Urbana, 1947-62, asso. prof. sociology and indsl. relations, 1954-62; asso. prof. sociology U. Ill. at Chgo., 1962-63, prof., 1963-65; prof. bus. Columbia U., 1965—, mem. pres.'s arbitration panel, 1977—; Fulbright research prof. econs. Keio U., Tokyo, Japan, 1963-64; lectr. Rutgers U., 1958, McGill U., 1963, Emory U., 1966, Columbia, 1962; Labor arbitrator nat. labor panel Am. Arbitration Assn., 1965—, mem. collective bargaining methods study group., 1964—; asso. mem. Center Advanced Study, U. Ill. Grad. Coll., 1964-65; asso. dir. Program Mng. Complex Techs., 1967—; mem. women's salary rev. bd., also affirmative action Commn. Columbia, 1976—; dir. program for Study Collective Bargaining in Higher Edn., 1975—; mem. N.Y. Gov.'s Panel for Dispute Resolution, 1977—; arbitrator, fact-finder N.J. Pub. Employment Relations Commn., 1975—; adminstrv. bd. Bur. Applied Social Research, 1975—; mem. spl. panel interest arbitrators, State of N.J., 1978—; mem. nat. adv. com. Nat. Center Study of Collective Bargaining in Higher Edn., 1978—; mem. state adv. council Inst. Mgmt. and Labor Relations, Rutgers U., 1982—. Author: Labor Management Relations in Illini City, vols. 1 and 2, 1953, 54, Management Rights and Union Interests, 1964 (McKinsey Found. book award 1965), Managing Large Systems, 1971 (McKinsey Found. book award 1972); Editor-in-chief: Columbia Jour. World Business, 1972—; Contbr. articles, monograph to profl. lit. Postdoctoral fellow statistics Yale, 1953-54; Ford Found. Faculty research fellow social sci. and bus. U. Chgo., 1960-61; Ford Found. grantee, 1967—; Fulbright prof. Central U. Planning and Statistics, Warsaw, Poland, 1974; Recipient Recognition award Ill. Nurses Assn., 1960. Fellow Am. Sociol. Assn., Soc. Applied Anthropology; mem. Am. Statis. Assn., Am. Econ. Assn., Indsl. Relations Research Assn. (editor research vol. 1960). Address: Uris Hall Grad Sch Business Columbia U New York NY 10027

CHANDLER, OTIS, publisher; b. Los Angeles, Nov. 23, 1927; s. Norman and Dorothy (Buffum) C.; m. Marilyn Brant, June 18, 1951 (div.); children: Norman, Harry, Cathleen, Michael, Carolyn; m. Bettina Whitaker, Aug. 15, 1981. Grad., Andover Acad., 1946; B.A., Stanford U., 1950. Joined Times Mirror Co., 1953; Los Angeles Times pub. Mirros Co. Times, 1960-80; chmn. bd., editor-in-chief Times Mirror Times Mirror Co., Los Angeles, 1980—. Served to 1st lt. USAAF, 1951-53. Mem. Am. Soc. Newspaper Editors, Am. Newspaper Pubs. Assn. Club: California. Office: Times Mirror Sq Los Angeles CA 90053

CHANDLER, REUBEN CARL, packaging company executive; b. Lawrenceville, Ga., Oct. 25, 1917; s. Reuben C. and Florine (Doster) C.; m. Sarah Megee, Oct. 27, 1940; children: Carla Evalynee (Mrs. Gurkin), Robert Megee, David Pratt, Craig D. Grad., Marist Coll., Atlanta, 1935; student, Ga. Inst. Tech., 1935-37; A.B., Emory U., 1941, Atlanta Law Sch., 1946-48; D.Sc. in Bus. Adminstrn. (hon.), Detroit Inst. Tech., 1960. Sales rep. Gen. Motors Acceptance Corp., Atlanta, 1941-42; asst. dir. tng. Southeastern Shipbldg. Corp., Savannah, Ga., 1942-43; prodn. mgr. Mead-Atlanta Paper Co., 1946-49; salesman Union Camp Corp. (formerly Union Bag & Paper Corp.), 1949-50, dist. sales mgr., Trenton, N.J., 1950-51, Eastern div. sales mgr., 1951-52, dir. corrugated container and bd. sales, N.Y.C., 1952, v.p. sales, 1952-55; chmn., chief exec. officer, chmn. exec., finance coms. Standard Packaging Co., N.Y.C., 1955-66; chmn. bd. Crowell-Collier Pub. Co., N.Y.C., 1957; ltd. partner Elliott & Co. (investment bankers), N.Y.C., 1960-62; chmn bd. J.D. Jewell, Inc., Gainesville, Ga., 1962-72, pres., 1969—; also chmn. exec. com., dir.; pres. Identiseal Systems, Atlanta, 1972—, Perkins-Goodwin Mgmt. Services Co., N.Y.C., 1973—, Am. Resources Corp.; chmn. bd. Lanier Mortgage Corp., Gainesville, Ga., 1973—; pres., chief exec. officer Duncan & Copeland, Inc., 1976-79, Va. Packaging Supply Co., McLean, 1979—, Berles Carton Co., Paterson, N.J., Morris Paperboard; dir. Am. Agy. Life Ins. Co., Atlanta, Berry Steel Corp., Edison, N.J., Jones & Presnell, Charlotte, N.C. Trustee Detroit Inst. Tech., 1960—, Christ Ch. Sch., Short Hills, N.J., 1963—, Brenau Coll., 1968—, Emory U., Atlanta, 1972—, Ga. Found. for Ind. Colls., 1969—; bd. dirs. Am. Soc. Indsl. Security Found. Served as lt. (s.g.) USNR, 1943-46; Lt. col. aide de camp Gov.'s staff Ga., 1951-52, 70-72. Recipient Man of Year award Am. Jewish Com., 1964; Horatio Alger award, 1965; Achievement award Delta Tau Delta, 1966. Mem. Savannah Jr. C. of C. (v.p. 1942-43), Gainesville C. of C., Navy League (life), Def. Orientation Conf. Assn., Am. Pulp and Paper Mill Supts. Assn. (life), Emory U. Alumni Assn. (pres. 1965, Honor award 1968), Ga. Tech. Nat. Alumni Assn. (nat. adv. bd. 1964 —), Ga. Poultry Fedn. (mem. round table 1970—), Tenn. Wesleyan Coll. Parents Assn., U.S. Navy Supply Corps Assn. (trustee 1972—), Delta Tau Delta (life), Alpha Delta Sigma, Omicron Delta Kappa. Baptist. Clubs: Mason., Elk., Atlanta Athletic, Commerce (Atlanta); N.Y. Area Emory (pres. 1964), Sky, University, Union League, Economic (N.Y.C.); Chattahoochee Country (Gainesville); Sea Pines Plantation (Hilton Head Island, S.C.); Washington Golf and Country (Arlington, Va.). Address: 4101 Dunwoody Club Dr Apt 25 Dunwoody GA 30338 *1) Belief in the right of an individual to enjoy and improve his happiness and standard of living through American way of life. (2) Necessity of a strong philosophy of life respecting integrity and rights of others. (3) Necessity of working diligently and in a dedicated manner to prepare one's self for those goals of life he has established. (4) Set about then with confidence and a firm determination to succeed.*

CHANDLER, ROBERT, TV news executive; b. Bklyn., Sept. 25, 1928; s. Louis and Minnie (Gurin) Zuckerkandle; m. Eleanor Reiff, Sept. 29, 1951; children: Douglas Jay, Lawrence Mark. B.Social Sci., CCNY, 1949. Reporter, critic Variety, Chgo., N.Y.C., Los Angeles, 1950-61; dir. TV publicity Metro-Goldwyn-Mayer, N.Y.C., 1961-63; dir. info. services CBS News, N.Y.C., 1963-65, mgr. program adminstrn., 1965-67, dir. ops. Election Unit, 1967-68, dir. Election Unit, 1969-72, v.p. public affairs broadcasts, 1973-75, v.p. adminstrn., asst. to pres., 1975-76, v.p., dir. public affairs broadcasts, 1977-81, sr. v.p. administrn., 1981-82, sr. v.p. documentaries and ops., 1983—; bd. mgrs. News Election Service, 1967-72. Author: Public Opinion, 1972. Served with Signal Corps, U.S. Army, 1951-52. Recipient Alfred P. Sloan Radio-TV award, 1967; CEBA award, 1980. Mem. Internat. Radio-TV Soc. Jewish. Home: care CBS News 524 W 57th St New York NY 10019 Office: 524 W 57th St New York NY 10019

CHANDLER, ROBERT FLINT, JR., consultant international agriculture; b. Columbus, Ohio, June 22, 1907; s. Robert F. and Harriet Clark (Loring) C.; m. Eunice Copeland, May 22, 1931 (div. 1955); children: David, Ralph Hewitt, Sara Eunice; m. Muriel Boyd, Oct. 4, 1957. B.S., U. Maine, 1929, LL.D., 1951; Ph.D., U. Md., 1934; postgrad (NRC fellow), U. Calif., 1935; LL.D., Notre Dame U., 1971; Litt.D., U. Singapore, 1971; L.H.D., Central Luzon (Philippines) State U., 1971; Sc.D., Punjab (India) Agrl. U., 1971, U. Philippines, 1972, U. N.H., 1972, U. Md., 1975. State horticulturist Maine Dept. Agr., 1929-31; grad. asst. U. Md., 1931-34; asst. prof. forest soils Cornell U., 1935-41, asso. prof., 1941-46, prof., 1946-47; dean coll. agr. U. N.H., 1947-50, pres., 1950-54; asst. dir. div. natural scis. and agr. Rockefeller Found., N.Y.C., 1954-57, asso. dir. agrl. scis., 1957; dir. Internat. Rice Research Inst., Manila, Philippines, 1959-72, Asian Vegetable Research and Devel. Center, Taiwan, 1972-75; cons. internat. agr., 1972—; Vis. prof. agronomy Tex. A. and M. Coll., summer 1940; soil sci. Rockefeller Found., Mexico, 1946-47. Author: Rice in the Tropics, 1979, An Adventure in Applied Science—The Early History of the International Rice Research Institute, 1982. Trustee Internat. Council for Research in Agroforestry, Ottawa, Ont., Can.; bd. dirs. Near East Found., N.Y.C. Decorated Star of Merit, Indonesia; recipient Gold medal award Govt. India, 1966; Sitara-I-Imtiaz award Govt. Pakistan, 1968; Golden Heart award Govt. Philippines, 1972; Internat. Agronomy award, 1972. Fellow Am. Acad. Arts and Scis.; mem. Crop Sci. Soc. Am., Soc. for Internat. Devel., Royal Agrl. Soc. (hon.). Home: Petersham Rd Templeton MA 01468

CHANDLER, (ROBERT) LEWIS, lawyer; b. Ft. Worth, May 1, 1920; s. LeRoy Wallace and Edna (Lewis) C.; m. Judy Clark Hickman, Dec. 1, 1978; children by previous marriage: Jerry G., Gay Edna, Ann, Elizabeth. Student, Rice Inst., 1938-39; J.D., U. Tex., 1942. Bar: Tex. Atty. reviewer govt. agy., 1946-50; partner firm Pace, Chandler & Rickey, and predecessors, Dallas; pres. RLC Oil Corp.; counsel Western Gulf Oil & Gas Inc.; pres. Silverhorn Operating Corp.; sec. Mid-Am. Petroleum, Inc. Served in USAAF, 1942-45. Mem. Dallas, Tex., Am. bar assns. Episcopalian. Clubs: Cipango, Chaparral. Home: 4303 University Blvd Dallas TX 75205 Office: 2720 Fairmount St Dallas TX 75201

CHANDLER, ROD D., congressman; b. La Grande, Oreg., July 13, 1942; s. Robert John and Edna Pearl (Hagey) C.; m. Joyce Elaine Laremore, Aug. 3, 1963; children: John Gifford, Amanda Joy. B.S., Oreg. State U., 1968. News corr. Sta. KOMO-TV News, Seattle, 1968-73; mktg. officer Wash. Mut. Savs. Bank, Seattle, 1973—; mem. Wash. State Ho. of Reps., 1975-82, 98th Congress from 8th Wash. Dist., mem. King County Metro Council, 1973-75. Recipient Sigma Delta Chi award, 1972. Republican. Methodist. Lodge: Rotary. Office: 216 Cannon House Office Bldg Washington DC 20515

CHANDLER, STEPHEN S., judge; b. Blount County, Tenn., Sept. 13, 1899; s. Stephen Sanders and Evelyn Amelia (Johnson) C.; m. Margaret Patterson, 1922 (dec.); children—Frances Patterson (Mrs. Sim K. Sims), Stephen Sanders III, Frank Patterson. Student, U. Tenn., 1917-18; J.D., U. Kans., 1922. Pvt. law practice in, Oklahoma City, 1922-43, U.S. dist. judge for, Western Okla., 1943—, chief judge, 1956-69; Mem. law faculty Oklahoma City U., 1957-60. Recipient Hatton Sumners award, 1961; named to Okla. Hall of Fame, 1960. Mem. various bar and other legal assns., Sigma Alpha Epsilon, Phi Delta Phi, Order of Coif. Democrat. Methodist. Clubs: Mason (Shriner), Oklahoma City Golf, Lotus, Petroleum, Rotary (pres. 1940-41); Nat. Press (Washington)). Home: Oklahoma City OK 73101 Office: US Court House PO Box 895 Oklahoma City OK 73101 *Keep in mind the Golden Rule.*

CHANDLER, WALLACE LEE, tobacco company executive, lawyer; b. Mecklenburg County, Va., Oct. 18, 1926; s. Joseph Beale and Esma (Clement) C.; m. Nita Hodnett, Feb. 25, 1950; children: Elizabeth Hardy, Brenda Lee, Jacqueline Blair. A.B., Elon Coll., N.C., 1949, D.C.S. (hon.), 1983; LL.B., Smithdeal Coll. Law, Richmond, Va., 1953; LL.D. (hon.), James Madison U., 1983. Bar: Va. 1954. With Universal Leaf Tobacco Co., Inc., Richmond, 1949—, sec., counsel, 1963-66, gen. counsel, dir., 1966-69, v.p., gen. counsel, 1969-74, sr. v.p., mem. exec. com., 1974—, also dir.; mem. capital bd. Bank of Va. Trustee James Madison U., Harrisonburg, Va., bd. dirs. found.; trustee Elon Coll., N.C., chmn. fin. com. Served with AUS, 1944-46; ETO. Chander Hall at Elon Coll. named, 1983. Mem. ABA, Va. Bar Assn., Richmond Bar Assn. (exec. com. corp. counsel sect. 1964-68), Elon Coll. Alumni Assn. (dir. 1960-66), Tobacco Assn. U.S. (bd. govs.), Alpha Phi Delta. Baptist (chmn. bd. adminstrn., chmn. finance com.). Clubs: Willow Oaks Country (past dir.), Country of Va., Commonwealth (Richmond); Princess Anne Country (Virginia Beach, Va.). Home: (Richmond): Home: 2 Raven Rock Rd Richmond VA 23229 Office: Hamilton at Broad St Richmond VA 23260

CHANDLER, WILLIAM KNOX, physiologist; b. Chgo., Oct. 13, 1933; s. William Knox and Margaret Belle (Colston) C.; m. Caroline Hardee Teague, June 6, 1957; children—William Knox, Janet Colston, Caroline Louise, Margaret Teague. A.B., U. Louisville, 1955, M.D., 1959. Postdoctoral fellow Physiol. Lab., Cambridge, Eng., 1962-65; staff asso. Lab. Biophysics, Nat. Inst. Neurol. Diseases and Blindness, Bethesda, Md., 1965-66; asso. prof. physiology Yale U. Sch. Medicine, 1966-72, prof., 1973—. Editor: Physiol. Revs, 1968-74, Jour. Physiology, 1974-81. Served with USPHS, 1959-61, 65-66. Mem. Biophys. Soc., Physiol. Soc., Am. Physiol. Soc. Democrat. Home: 594 County Rd Guilford CT 06437 Office: 333 Cedar St New Haven CT 06510

CHANDLER, WYETH, city ofcl.; s. Walter C.; 4 children. Grad., Memphis State U.; J.D., U. Tenn. Bar: Tenn. bar. Practiced in, Memphis; spl. judge Memphis City Ct.; mem. Memphis City Council, 1967-71, chmn., 1971; mayor, City of Memphis, 1972—; del. Tenn. Constl. Conv., 1959, 65. Bd. dirs. Memphis and Shelby County Youth Guidance Commn., Boys' Club Memphis; mem. citizens adv. bd. Memphis Juvenile Ct. Served with USMC; Korea. Mem. Tenn., Memphis bar assns. Club: Phoenix. *

CHANDOR, STEBBINS BRYANT, pathologist; b. Boston, Dec. 12, 1933; s. Kendall Stebbins Bryant and Dorothy (Burrage) C.; m. Mary Carolyn White, May 30, 1959; children: Stebbins Bryant, Charlotte White. B.A., Princeton U., 1955; M.D., Cornell U., 1960. Diplomate: Am. Bd. Pathology. Intern Bellevue Hosp., N.Y.C., 1960-61, resident, 1965-66, Stanford U. Med. Ctr., Palo Alto, Calif., 1962-65; instr. Cornell U., Ithaca, N.Y., 1966; asst. prof. U. So. Calif. Med. Ctr., Los Angeles, 1969-73, assoc. prof., 1974-76, SUNY-Stony Brook, 1976-80; prof., chmn. dept. pathology Marshall U Sch Medicine, Huntington, W.Va., 1981—; pathologist Tripler Army Med Ctr, Honolulu, 1966-69; dir. immunopathology U. So. Calif., Los Angeles County Med. Ctr., 1969-76; dir. clin. lab. Univ. Hosp., Stony Brook, N.Y., 1978-80; dir. JMMS Labs., Huntington, W.Va., 1981—. Contbr. articles to profl. jours. Pres. San Marino Tennis Found., 1975. Served to maj. USAR, 1966-69. Decorated Army Commendation medal; recipient Physicians Recognition award AMA, 1983. Fellow Am. Soc. Clin. Pathologists (chmn. council on immunopathology), Coll. Am. Pathologists; mem. Calif. Soc. Pathologists (sec.-treas. 1974-75), Assn. Am. Pathologists. Republican. Episcopalian. Clubs: Guyan Country; Princeton (N.Y.C.); Valley (v.p. 1975). Home: 530 10th Ave Huntington WV 25701 Office: Marshall U Sch Medicine 1542 Spring Valley Rd Huntington WV 25704 *Have fun and make life enjoyable for those around you.*

CHANDRA, ASHOK KUMAR, computer scientist; b. Allahabad, India, July 30, 1948; s. Harish and Sushila C.; m. Mala, Sept. 17, 1974; children: Ankur, Anuj. B.Tech., Indian Inst. Tech., 1969; M.S., U. Calif.-Berkeley, 1970; Ph.D., Stanford U., 1973. Mem. research staff IBM Thomas J. Watson Research Center, Yorktown Heights, N.Y., 1973-83, mgr. theoretical computer sci., 1981-83; tech. adv. office of v.p. and chief scientist IBM, Armonk, N.Y., 1983—. Editor: Jour. Computing Soc. Indsl. and Applied Math, 1982; contbr. articles to profl. jours. Recipient Pres.'s Gold medal Indian Inst. Tech., 1969, IBM Outstanding Innovation award, 1980, Invention Achievement award, 1977, 81. Mem. ACM, Soc. Indsl. and Applied Math. Patentee magnetic bubble tech. (2). Office: PO Box 218 Yorktown Heights NY 10598

CHANDRA, PRAMOD, educator; b. Varanasi, India, Nov. 2, 1930; came to U.S., 1964; s. Moti and Shanti (Devi) C.; m. Mary Carmen Lynn, 1981; children: Abhijit, Sasanka. B.S., Georgetown U., 1951; Ph.D., U. Bombay, 1964; M.A. honoris causa, Harvard U., 1980. Asst. curator Prince of Wales Mus. of Western India, Bombay, 1954-60, curator art and archaeol. sects., 1960-64; asso. prof. U. Chgo., 1964-71, prof., 1971-80; George P. Bickford prof. Indian and South Asian art Harvard U., Cambridge, Mass., 1980—; dir. Am. Acad. Benares, 1965-71; pres. Am. Com. South Asian Art. Author: Bundi Painting, 1959, Stone Sculpture in the Allahabad Museum, 1971, Studies in Indian Temple Architecture, 1974, The Cleveland Tuti-nana and the Origins of Mughal Painting, 1976. Nat. Endowment for Humanities grantee, 1976-80.

CHANDRASEKHAR, BELLUR SIVARAMIAH, physics educator; b. Bangalore, India, May 24, 1928; came to U.S., 1952. B.Sc. with honours, U. Mysore, (India), 1947; M.Sc., U. Delhi, 1949; D. Phil., Oxford U., (Eng.), 1952. Research assoc. physics U. Ill., Urbana, 1952-54, vis. prof., 1977-78; vis. scientist Oxford U., (Eng.), 1954-55;

research physicist Westinghouse Research Labs., Pitts., 1955-59, fellow Physicist, 1959-61, mgr. cryophysics sect., 1961-63, cons., 1963-64; prof. Western Res. U., Cleve., 1963-67; Perkins prof. physics Case Western Res. U., 1967—, dir. labs., dept. physics, 1964-65, chmn. dept. physics, 1965-67, co-dir. Condensed State Ctr., 1965-67, co-chmn. dept. physics, 1967, dir. labs., 1967-69, dean sci., 1969-70, chmn. dept. biology, 1969-70, chmn. Univ. faculty senate, 1970-71, dean Western Res. Coll., 1972-76; mem. NSF vis. com. (Nat. Magnet Lab), 1973-76; vis. prof. Tata Inst. Fundamental Research, Bombay, 1980, Eidgenossische Technische Hochschule, Zurich, 1980-81; cons. in physics. Rhodes scholar Oxford U., (Eng.), 1949-52; sr. vis. research fellow Imperial Coll. Sci. and Tech., London, 1961; Fulbright research scholar Imperial Coll., U. Cambridge, London, 1978. Fellow Am. Phys. Soc. (mem. numerous coms., chmn. condensed matter physics div. 1975, councillor-at-large 1984—); mem. AAUP (v.p. Cleve. chpt. 1979-80), Clevel. Physics Soc. (pres. 1965-66), sigma Xi (chpt. v.p. 1965-66), Sigma Xi (pres. 1966-67). Office: Dept Physics Case Western Res U Cleveland OH 44106

CHANDRASEKHAR, SUBRAHMANYAN, theoretical astrophysicist; b. Lahore, India, Oct. 19, 1910; came to U.S., 1936, naturalized, 1953; m. Lalitha, Madras, India, Sept. 1936. M.A., Presidency Coll., Madras, 1930; Ph.D., Trinity Coll., Cambridge, 1933, Sc.D., 1942; Sc.D., U. Mysore, India, 1961, Northwestern U., 1962, U. Newcastle Upon Tyne, Eng., 1965, Ind. Inst. Tech., 1966, U. Mich., 1967, U. Liege, Belgium, 1967, Oxford (Eng.) U., 1972, U. Delhi, 1973, Carleton U., Can., 1978, Harvard U., 1979. Govt. India scholar in theoretical physics Cambridge, 1930-34; fellow Trinity Coll., Cambridge, 1933-37; research asso. Yerkes Obs., Williams Bay and U. Chgo., 1937, asst. prof., 1938-41, assoc. prof., 1942-43, prof., 1944-47, Disting. Service prof., 1947-52, Morton D. Hull Disting. Service prof., 1952—; Nehru Meml. lectr., Padma Vibhushan, India, 1968. Author: An Introduction to the Study of Stellar Structure, 1939, Principles of Stellar Dynamics, 1942, Radiative Transfer, 1950, Hydrodynamic and Hydromagnetic Stability, 1961, Ellipsoidal Figures of Equilibrium, 1969, The Mathematical Theory of Black Holes, 1983; Mng. editor: The Astrophysical Jour, 1952-71; Contbr. various sci. periodicals. Recipient Bruce medal Astron. Soc. Pacific, 1952, gold medal Royal Astron. Soc., London, 1953; Rumford medal Am. Acad. Arts and Scis., 1957; Nat. Medal of Sci., 1966; Nobel Prizein Physics, 1983. Fellow Royal Soc. (London) (Royal medal 1962); mem. Nat. Acad. Scis. (Henry Draper medal 1971), Am. Phys. Soc. (Dannie Heineman prize 1974), Am. Philos. Soc., Cambridge Philos. Soc., Am. Astron. Soc., Royal Astron. Soc. Club: Quadrangle (U. Chgo.). Address: Lab for Astrophysics and Space Research 933 E 56th St Chicago IL 60637

CHANDY, KANIANTHRA MANI, computer sciences educator, consultant; b. Kottayam, Kerala, India, Oct. 25, 1944; came to U.S., 1965; s. Kanianthra Thomas and Rebecca (Mani) C.; m. Jean Marie Collaco, May 5, 1969; children: Christa Rebecca, Mani K. B.Tech., Indian Inst. Tech., Madras, 1965; M.S., Poly. Inst. Bklyn., 1966; Ph.D., MIT, 1969. Engr. Honeywell, Waltham, Mass., 1966-67; scientist IBM Cambridge Sci. Ctr., Mass., 1969-70; asst. prof. computer scis. U. Tex., Austin, 1970-73, assoc. prof., 1973-78, prof., 1978—; cons. in field; bd. regents Inst. for Software engring., Sunnyvale, Calif.; program chmn. Internat. Symposium on Computer Performance Modelling, Yorktown Heights, N.Y., 1977. Author: Computer Systems Performance Modeling, 1980; co-editor: Computer Performance, 1977, Current Trends in Programming Methodology, 1978; editorial bd.: IEEE Transactions on Software Engring., 1984. Grantee NSF, 1974—, USN, 1979-81, USAF, 1981—, IBM, 1981—. Mem. Assn. Computing Machinery; sr. mem. IEEE. Home: 105 W 32d St Austin TX 78705 Office: U Tex Dept Computer Scis Austin TX 78712

CHANE, GEORGE WARREN, cons. engr.; b. Gloucester, Mass., June 15, 1910; s. Daniel T. and (MacDonald) C.; m. Frances D. Howard, June 22, 1940; children—Peggy Howard, George Warren. B.S. in Mech. Engring, Tufts U., 1934. Indsl. engr. Boston Woven Hose & Rubber Co., 1934-38, Eastman Kodak Co., Rochester, N.Y., 1938-42; mgr. mgmt. services div. Eastern dist. Ernst & Ernst, 1942-58; v.p. finance and mgmt. engring. RCA, 1958-60, v.p. finance and adminstrn., 1960-62; exec. v.p. finance Olin Mathieson Chem. Corp., 1962-65; also dir.; financial v.p. Uniroyal, Inc., N.Y.C., 1965-70; also dir., mem. operating policy com.; pres. George W. Chane, Inc. (cons. engrs.), 1970—; Macrodyne Industries Inc. Author: Motion and Time Study, 1940. Bd. dirs. Deafness Research Found. Mem. Financial Execs. Inst., Nat., Conn., Tex., N.Y. State socs. profl. engrs., Operations Research Soc., Air Force Assn., Am. Soc. M.E., Profl. Golfers Assn. (mem. adv. com. 1960—). Clubs: Wings, University (N.Y.C.); Lost Tree (North Palm Beach, Fla.). Address: 1284 Lake Worth Ln Lost Tree Village North Palm Beach FL 33408

CHANEN, FRANKLIN ALLEN, lawyer; b. Burlington, Iowa, Mar. 12, 1933; s. Sam and Sonia C.; m. Doralu Kohlman, Sept. 9, 1956; children: Gregory, Stuart, Bruce. B.B.A., Northwestern U., 1954, J.D., 1957. Bar: Ill. 1957; C.P.A., Ill. Assoc. Leibman, Williams, Bennett, Baird & Minow, Chgo., 1957-64, ptnr., 1964-72; consol. with Sidley & Austin, 1972, ptnr., 1972—. Contbr. articles to profl. jours. Pres. Ill. Soc. Prevention of Blindness, 1983. Mem. Chgo. Bar Assn., Order of Coif, Beta Gamma Sigma. Club: Birchwood of Highland Park (Ill.) (sec.). Office: Sidley & Austin One 1st National Plaza Chicago IL 60603

CHANEY, JAMES BYRON, petroleum services company executive; b. Van Buren, Ark., July 22, 1926; s. Adrian Byron and Ruth (Jolly) C.; m. Betty Lea Swinea, Aug. 22, 1948; 1 son, William Byron. B.S. in Mining Engring., Mo. Sch. Mines and Metallurgy, 1948, M.S., 1949; Engr. of Mines, U. Mo.-Rolla, 1983. Mgr. domestic prodn. ops. Baroid div. NL Industries, Inc., Houston, 1970-73, plant mgr. Titanium Pigments div., Sayreville, N.J., 1973-74, gen. mgr. NL Magnesium div., Salt Lake, 1974-80, pres. NL McCullough div., Houston, 1980-83, asst. to group pres. Info. Services Group, 1983—. Mem. AIME, Internat. Magnesium Assn. (dir. 1975-80), Utah Mining Assn. (dir. 1979-80). Republican. Presbyterian. Club: Houston. Lodge: Masons. Home: 16218 Chipstead Dr Spring TX 77379 Office: NL Industries Inc 3000 N Belt Houston TX 77032

CHANEY, VERNE EDWARD, JR., surgeon, foundation executive, educator; b. Kansas City, Mo., July 16, 1923; s. Verne Edward and Adelaide (Hafner) C.; (div.)children: Christopher Edward, Steven Wood. B.S., Va. Mil. Inst., 1951; M.D., Johns Hopkins U., 1948, M.P.H., 1972. Diplomate: Am. Bd. Surgery, Am. Bd. Thoracic and Cardiac Surgery. Intern surgery Johns Hopkins U. Hosp., 1948-49, asst. resident, 1949-50, instr. anatomy, 1950-53; surg. resident N.C. Meml. Hosp., Chapel Hill, 1953-56; chief of surgery Albert Schweitzer Hosp., Deschappeles, Haiti, 1956-58; practice medicine specializing in thoracic surgery, Monterey, Calif., 1958-61; pres. and founder Thomas A. Dooley Found.-INTERMED-USA, Inc., N.Y.C., 1961—; clin. prof. surgery U. Miami, 1976—, clin. prof. epidemiology and pub. health, 1977—; founder, pres. INTERMED, Geneva, 1976—. Patentee in field. Served from pvt. to capt. M.C. U.S. Army, 1944, 51-53. Decorated Silver Star medal, Bronze Star medal with V, Purple Heart U.S., Croix de Guerre France, Order of Million Elephants Laos. Fellow ACS, Am. Coll. Chest Physicians; mem. N.Y. State Med. Soc., N.Y. Acad. Medicine, Am. Pub. Health Assn., Internat. Health Soc., Nathan A. Womack Surg. Soc., Intenat. Soc. Surgeons, Nat. Soc. Fund Raising Execs., Explorers Club. Republican. Episcopalian. Clubs: N.Y. Athletic, Sky, West Side Tennis, 7th Regiment Armory Tennis. Home: 520 E 76th St Apt 14E New York NY 10021 Office: 420 Lexington Ave Room 2428 New York NY 10017

CHANEY, WILLIAM ALBERT, educator; b. Arcadia, Calif., Dec. 23, 1922; s. Horace Pierce and Esther (Bowen) C. A.B., U. Calif. at Berkeley, 1943, Ph.D., 1961. Mem. faculty Lawrence U., Appleton, Wis., 1952—, George McKendree Steele prof. Western culture, 1966—, chmn. dept. history, 1968-71; vis. prof. Mich. State U., summer 1958. Author: The Cult of Kingship in Anglo-Saxon England: The Transition from Paganism to Christianity, 1970; Contbr. profl. jours., encys. Jr. fellow Harvard Soc. Fellows, 1949-52; grantee Am. Council Learned Socs., 1966-67. Fellow Royal Soc. Arts; mem. Am. Hist. Assn., Mediaeval Acad. Am., Am. Soc. Ch. History, Modern Lang. Assn., Conf. British Studies, AAUP, Archeol. Inst. Am. Episcopalian. Home: 215 E Kimball St Appleton WI 54911

CHANEY, WILLIAM R., cosmetic company executive; b. Satanta, Kans., July 31, 1932; s. Alva Ross and Irene (Reeves) C.; m. Carolyn Keenan; children: Carole Babette, Diana. B.A. in Bus. Adminstrn., U. Kans., 1953. With Avon Products, Inc., N.Y.C., 1955—, dir. personnel adminstrn., 1966-67, v.p. personnel, 1967-68, group v.p. field ops., 1968-69, sr. v.p. ops., 1969-72, exec. v.p., 1972-77, pres., 1977—, also dir.; dir. Tiffany & Co., Irving Trust Co., Conn. Mut. Life Ins. Co. Chmn., Nat. Minority Supplier Devel. Council. Served to 1st lt. AUS, 1953-55. Mem. Advt. and Sales Execs. Club, Lambda Chi Alpha. Office: Avon Products Inc 9 W 57th St New York NY 10019

CHANG, CHEN CHUNG, mathematician, educator; b. Tientsin, China, Oct. 13, 1927; came to U.S., 1944, naturalized, 1959; s. P.C. and S.T. (Tsai) C.; m. Marjorie Galvan, Aug. 1, 1951 (div. 1975); children: Ann, Alice, Peter, Julia; m. Sharon Elizabeth Myers, July 24, 1977. B.A., Harvard, 1949; M.A., U. Calif.-Berkeley, 1950, Ph.D., 1955. Instr. Cornell U., 1955-56; asst. prof. U. So. Calif., 1956-58; asst. prof. math. UCLA, 1958-61, asso. prof., 1961-64, prof., 1964—; tchr., contbr. Edn. for Human Values Program, Sri Sathya Sai Baba movement, 1978—. Author: (with H.J. Keisler) Model Theory, 1973; Cons. editor: Jour. Symbolic Logic, 1968-77; editor: Annals Math. Logic, 1969-75, Algebra Universalis, 1971-77. Sr. postdoctoral fellow NSF, 1962-63; sr. Fulbright research scholar Oxford (Eng.) U., 1966-67; also vis. fellow All Souls Coll. Oxford (Eng.) U. Mem. Phi Beta Kappa, Sigma Xi, Pi Mu Epsilon. Address: 26332-C N Oak Highland Dr Newhall CA 91321

CHANG, CLARENCE HOO YUEN, banker; b. Honolulu, Dec. 7, 1931; s. Shar Chong and See Moi (Chun) C.; m. Irene S.H. Choy, May 25, 1958; children: Duane H., Mark A. B.B.A., U. Hawaii, 1953. Asst. v.p. Finance Factors, Ltd., Honolulu, 1956-62; sr. v.p. Am. Security Bank, Honolulu, 1962-83, First Interstate Bank Hawaii, 1983—; pres. Hawaiian Lenders Exchange, 1970; v.p. Consumer Credit Counseling Service Hawaii, 1970. Treas. Hawaii div. Am. Cancer Soc., 1970. Served to 1st lt. USAF, 1954-56. Mem. Chinese C. of C. Home: 1072 Kamaole St Honolulu HI 96825 Office: 1314 S King St Honolulu HI 96814

CHANG, DAVID CHUNG-CHING, electrical engineering educator; b. Hupeh, China, Sept. 9, 1941; s. Tao-ming and Hsiao-I (Tsai) C.; m. Cecelia M. Chang, Aug. 21, 1965; 1 son, Stephen. B.Sc.E.E., Nat. Cheng-Kung U., Taiwan, 1961; M.Sc. in Applied Physics, Harvard U., 1963, Ph.D., 1967. Postdoctoral research asst. Harvard U., Cambridge, Mass., 1967; asst. prof. U. Colo., Boulder, 1967-71, assoc. prof., 1971-75, prof., chmn. dept. elec. and computer engring., 1975—; vis. prof. Queen Mary Coll., London, 1972; vis. scientist Nat. Telecom Lab., Taiwan, 1974, 82; cons. Bur. Standards, 1972, Kaman Sci. Corp., Colorado Springs, Colo., 1974-78, 78—, Arthur D. Little, Inc., Acorn Park, Mass., 1978-79, Teledyne Micronetics, San Diego, 1983—. Contbr. articles to tech. jours. Sr. mem. IEEE, Am. Phys. Soc. Office: University of Colorado Campus Box 425 Boulder CO 80020

CHANG, DAVID PING-CHUNG, architect; b. Shanghai, China, Dec. 10, 1929; came to U.S., 1941, naturalized, 1956; s. Hsin-Hai and Siang-Mei (Han) C.; m. Lorna Mickle, Jan. 22, 1955; children: Pamela R., Christopher R., David R., Jennifer R. Grad., Hotchkiss Sch., 1947; A.B., Princeton U., 1951, M.F.A., 1953. Pvt. practice architecture, N.Y.C., 1956-59, San Juan, P.R., 1959-68; v.p. ITT-Levitt & Sons, Inc., N.Y.C., 1969-71; pres. ESI Assos., Inc., N.Y.C., 1971; pvt. practice David Chang Assos., 1972-81; v.p. NIKE Inc., 1981—; guest lectr. seminar indsl. housing MIT, 1971; dir. Huntington Comprehensive Service Center. Contbg. editor: Jour. Indsl. Designers Soc. Am, 1969-70; Prin. works include: Academia San Jose, P.R., WAPA-TV Studios and Offices, P.R., City of Glen Cove (N.Y.) downtown renewal. Bd. dirs. Huntington Citizens Task Force; chmn. Suffolk County Schs. Com., Princeton U., 1975—; bd. govs. Hotchkiss Sch.; trustee Heckscher Mus., Huntington. Recipient 1st prize U. P.R. indsl. design seminar, 1961, 1st prize for best comml. bldg. Urbe award, P.R., 1966, 1st prize best ednl. bldg. Urbe award, P.R., 1971; Archi award, N.Y., 1972, 79. Mem. Colegio de Ingenieros de P.R. Democrat. Clubs: Lloyd Harbor Bath, Winter (Huntington); Century Assn., Anglers, Princeton (N.Y.C.). Home: Breyman Ave Portland OR 97219 also East Barnard VT 05068 Office: Nike Inc 3900 SW Murray Blvd Beaverton OR 97005

CHANG, HENRY CHUNG-LIEN, library administrator; b. Canton, China, Sept. 15, 1941; came to U.S., 1964, naturalized, 1973; s. Ih-ming and Lily (Lin) C.; m. Marjorie Li, Oct. 29, 1966; 1 dau., Michelle. LL.B., Nat. Chengchi U., 1962; M.A., U. Mo., 1966, U. Minn., 1968; Ph.D., 1974. Book selector Braille Inst. Am., Los Angeles, 1965-67; reference librarian U. Minn., Mpls., 1968-70, instr., librarian, 1970-72, asst. head govt. document div., 1972-74; library dir., lectr. social scis. Coll. of the V.I., St. Croix, 1974-75; dir. bur. libraries, museums and archeol. services V.I. Dept. Conservation and Cultural Affairs, 1975—; dir. V.I. Library Tng. Inst., 1975-76; coordinator, chmn. V.I. State Hist. Records Adv. Bd., 1976—; chmn. microfilm com. ACURIL, 1977—; coordinator V.I. Gov.'s Library Adv. Council, 1975—; mem. V.I. Bicentennial Commn., 1975-77, Ft. Frederik Commn., 1975-76; mem. adv. com. on research tng. Caribbean Research Inst., 1974-75; coordinator Library Conf., 1977—; project dir. cultural heritage project Nat. Endowment for Humanities, 1979—. Author: A Bibliography of Presidential Commissions, Committees, Councils, Panels and Task Forces, 1961-72, 1973, Taiwan Democraphy, 1964-71: A Selected Annotated Bibliography of Government Documents, 1973, A Selected Annotated Bibliography of Caribbean Bibliographies in English, 1975, A Survey of the Use of Microfilms in the Caribbean, 1978, Long-Range Program for Library Development, 1978, Institute for Training in Library Management and Communications Skill, 1979; contbr. numerous articles and book revs. on library sci. to profl. jours. Served to 2d lt. Taiwan Army, 1962-63. Recipient Library Adminstrs. Devel. Program fellowship award, 1972; named Mem. Staff of Year Coll. V.I., 1974-75; Nat. Commn. on Libraries and Info. Sci. grantee. Mem. ALA, AAUP, Population Assn. Am., Am. Sociol. Assn., Assn. Carribean Univ. and Research Libraries, V.I. Library Assn. Club: Rotary. Home: PO Box 818 Kingshill Saint Croix VI 00850 Office: PO Box 390 Saint Thomas VI 00801

CHANG, JEFFREY PEH-I, scientist, educator; b. Changteh, Hunan, China; came to U.S., 1945, naturalized, 1952; m. Sulaine Tang; children—Betty, Kaidy, Joann, Landy, Peter. B.S., Nat. Central U. China, 1941; M.S., U. Ill., 1946, Ph.D., 1949. Acting chief sect. exptl. pathology U. Tex. M.D. Anderson Hosp. and Tumor Inst., Houston, 1959-64, prof. biology, also mem. faculty, 1964-72; prof. cellular biology U. Tex. Med. Br., Galveston, 1972—; symposium chmn. 1st Internat. Congress Histochemistry and Cytochemistry, Paris, 1961, session chmn., Japan, 1972; chmn. Internat. Cancer Congress, Japan, 1961, U.S., 1970; vis. prof., lectr. Vanderbilt U., U. Kans. Med. Sch., U. Taiwan, Chin Hwa U., Med. Coll. of Dept. Def., Republic of China; Academician Academia Sinica. Contbr. articles to profl. pubs. Research on tumors, electron microscopy, histochemistry, reproductive biology. Developer of open-top cryostat, sect. freeze substitution. Address: Div Cell Biology Univ Tex Med Branch Galveston TX 77550

CHANG, KWANG-CHIH, anthropologist, educator; b. Peking, China, Apr. 15, 1931; came to U.S., 1955, naturalized, 1970; s. Wo-chûn and Hsin-hsiang (Lo) C.; m. Hwei Li, May 17, 1957; children: Julian Po-keng, Nora Chung-chi. B.A., Nat. Taiwan U., 1954; Ph.D., Harvard U., 1960. Lectr. anthropology Harvard U., 1960-61, prof. anthropology, 1977—; instr. anthropology Yale U., 1961-63, asst. prof., 1963-66, asso. prof., 1966-69, prof., 1969-77, dir. grad. studies anthropology, 1966-69, chmn. dept. anthropology, 1970-73, chmn. Council on East Asian Studies, 1975-77. Author: The Archaeology of Ancient China, 1963, rev. edits., 1968, 77, Rethinking Archaeology, 1967, Settlement Archaeology, 1968, Fengpitou, Tapenkeng and the Prehistory of Taiwan, 1969, Early Chinese Civilization, 1976, Food in Chinese Culture, 1977, Shang Civilization, 1980, Art, Myth, and Ritual, 1983. Fellow Am. Acad. Arts and Scis., London Soc. Antiquaries, Am. Anthrop. Assn.; mem. Nat. Acad. Scis., Assn. Asian Studies, Chinese Acad. Scis. (Taiwan). Office: 58-B Peabody Museum Harvard U Cambridge MA 02138

CHANG, MIN CHUEH, experimental biologist; b. Taiyuan, Shansi, China, Oct. 10, 1908; came to U.S., 1945, naturalized, 1952; s. Gin Shu and Shih (Laing) C.; m. Isabelle C. Chin, May 28, 1948; children—Francis Hugh, Claudia, Pamela. B.Sc., Tsing Hua U., Peking, 1933; Ph.D., Cambridge (Eng.) U., 1941, Sc.D., 1969; D.Sc. h.c., Worcester Poly. Inst., 1982, U. Nottingham (Eng.), 1982. Researcher Cambridge U. Sch. Agr., 1941-45; research asso. Worcester Found., Shewsbury, Mass., 1945-50, sr. and prin. scientist, 1954, 70-82, prin. scientist emeritus, 1982—; mem. faculty Boston U., 1951—, prof. reproductive biology, 1961—; hon. prof. Shanghai Inst. Physiology (China), 1979. Contbr. to profl. jours. Recipient Ortho award Am. Soc. Study Sterility, 1950; Lasker Found. award, 1954; Ortho medal and award Am. Fertility Soc., 1961; Research Career award USPHS, '1962; Hartman award Am. Soc. Study Reprodn., 1970; Marshall medal Brit. Soc. Study Fertility, 1971; Francis Amory prize Am. Acad. Arts and Scis., 1975; Pioneer award Internat. Embryo Transfer Soc., 1983; medal Italian Agrl. Acad., 1978. Mem. Am. Phys. Soc., Am. Anat. Assn., Am. Acad. Arts and Scics., Brit. Soc. Study Fertility, Am. Fertility Soc. Home: 15 Fiske St Shrewsbury MA 01545 Office: Worcester Found Shrewsbury MA 01545 *Wealth and fame do not make one happier than the peace of mind.*

CHANG, MING ERH, naval officer; b. Shanghai, China, Apr. 20, 1932; came to U.S., 1946; s. Yu Ching and Yu May (Yien) C.; m. Charlotte Yu-Jen Chung, Apr. 7, 1956; children: Daniel W., Donalda C. B.S. in Physics, Coll. William and Mary, 1955, U.S. Naval Postgrad. Sch., Monterey, Calif., 1962. Commd. ensign U.S. Navy, advanced through grades to rear adm., 1982; head surface Anti-Submarine Warfare Br. Office Chief of Naval Ops., Washington, 1974-77; comdg. officer U.S.S. Reeves, Pearl Harbor, Hawaii, 1977-79; chief of staff, comdr. Carrier Group Three, Alameda, Calif., 1979-80; comdr. Third Fleet, Pearl Harbor, 1980-81; dir. tactical air, surface and electronic devel. div. Office Chief Naval Ops., Washington, 1981-83; comdr. Cruiser-Destroyer Group Two, Charleston, S.C., 1983—. Decorated Legion of Merit with combat V, Bronze Star, Iron Cross of Merit, (W.Ger.), Hon. medal 1st class Vietnamese Armed Forces. Home: Quarters G Naval Base Charleston SC 29408 Office: Commander Cruiser-Destroyer Group Two Bldg NS 1 Naval Base Charleston SC 29408 *I attribute my success entirely to the fact that I came to the United States of America. It is only in America that I am able to achieve the goals and successes I have had the privilege to enjoy.*

CHANG, PARRIS HSU-CHENG, political science educator, writer; b. Chikou, Chiayi, Taiwan, Dec. 30, 1936; came to U.S., 1961; s. Chao and Liu (Chen) C.; m. Shirley Hsiu-chu Lin, Aug. 3, 1963; children: Yvette, Elaine, Bohdan. B.A., Nat. Taiwan U., 1959; M.A., U. Wash., 1963; postgrad., Pa. State U., 1963-64; Ph.D., Columbia U., 1969, cert. Asian studies, 1966. Research polit. scientist U. Mich., Ann Arbor, 1969-70; asst. prof. polit. sci. Pa. State U., University Park, 1970-72; vis. fellow Australian Nat. U., Canberra, 1978; vis. scholar Inst. Sino-Soviet Studies, George Washington U., Washington, 1979; assoc. prof. polit. sci. Pa. State U., University Park, 1972-76, prof., 1976—; cons. The Rand Corp., Santa Monica, Calif., 1975-82, BDM, Vienna, Va., 1975—, Voice of Am., Washington, 1982—, Dept. State, 1983-84; assoc. China council Asia Soc., N.Y.C., 1976—. Author: Radicals and Radical Ideology in China's Cultural Revolution, 1973, Power and Policy in China, 1975, 2d edit. 1978, Elite Conflict in the Post-Mao China, 1981, 2d edit. 1983. Fellow Fulbright Council Internat. Exchange of Scholars, 1977; research grantee Social Sci. Research Council, 1972; travel grantee Internat. Research Exchange Council, 1982. Mem. Assn. Asian Studies (pres. Mid-Atlantic region 1976-77), Inter-Univ. Seminar on Armed Forces and Soc., Am. Polit. Sci. Assn. Office: Dept Polit Sci Pa State U University Park PA 16802

CHANG, PHIL ZANGFEI, utilities exec.; b. Shanghai, China, Nov. 14, 1925; came to U.S., 1952, naturalized, 1962; m. Karyl A. Middlesworth, Aug. 21, 1964; 1 dau., Jenifer Ann. B.S. in Civil Engring, St. Johns U., Shanghai, 1943; M.B.A., UCLA, 1952. Asst. mgr. China Investment Bank, Shanghai, 1943-49; spl. fin. officer China Mchts. Steam Navigation Co., Taipei, Tokyo, 1949-52; teaching asst. U. Calif., Los Angeles, 1953-55; sr. accountant Haskins & Sells, Los Angeles, 1955-58; treas., asst. sec. Ariz. Pub. Service Co., Phoenix, 1958-75; treas. Hawaiian Electric Co., Honolulu, 1975—. Mem. State Treas.'s Economy Com., 1974-75; mem. Mayor's Adv. Com. on Fin. Affairs, City and County of Honolulu, 1976-77; treas., bd. dirs. Maricopa County Assn. Retarded Children, Am. Cancer Soc., Salvation Army; bd. dirs. Better Bus. Bur., 1973-75, Friends of East West Center, 1980—; trustee Tax Found. of Hawaii. Mem. Am. Inst. C.P.A.'s, Hawaii Soc. C.P.A.'s, Fin. Execs. Inst., Am. Gas Assn. (mng. com., depreciation com., award of accounting merit 1973), Edison Electric Inst. (finance com., depreciation com., taxation com.), Am. Contract Bridge League (unit pres. 1965-66). Home: 1717 Mott-Smith Dr Apt 2104 Honolulu HI 96822 Office: 900 Richards St Box 2750 Honolulu HI 96840 *I have always followed the principle that one should never entertain the thought of harm to others, but can never be too careful as to what other people can do to harm you.*

CHANG, RICHARD KOUNAI, physicist, educator; b. Hong Kong, June 22, 1940; s. Chia Chu and Siao-Mei C.; m. Sung-Wen Pu, Sept. 30, 1961; children: Pang-Hua, Pang-Mei, Pang-Yuan. B.S. in Elec. Engring., M.I.T., 1961; M.S. in Applied Physics, Harvard U., 1962, Ph.D., 1965. Postdoctoral fellow Harvard U., 1965-66; mem. faculty dept. applied physics Yale U., New Haven, 1966—, asso. prof., 1970-76, prof., 1976—; cons. Sandia Nat. Labs., Sanders Assos., Wyatt

Technologies, Inc. Contbr. articles to profl. jours. Alfred P. Sloan Found. fellow, 1967-69. Fellow Am. Phys. Soc., Optical Soc. Am.; mem. IEEE. Office: Yale U PO Box 2157 Yale Station New Haven CT 06520

CHANG, SHELDON SHOU LIEN, electrical engineer; b. Peking, China, Jan. 20, 1920; came to U.S., 1945, naturalized, 1954; s. Hsiang Ping and Lucy (Tao) C.; m. Bridget Hsiao Mei Chou, Feb. 6, 1965; children: Theodore Ching-Chien, Kathleen Ching Hsin, Andrew Ching-Hung, Edward Ching Hsing, Ingrid Jeanette. B.S., Nat. Southwestern Asso. U., Kunming, China, 1942, M.S., 1944; Ph.D., Purdue U., 1947. Design engr. Central Radio Works, Kunming, China, 1943-45; research and devel. engr. Robbins & Myers, Inc., Springfield, Ohio, 1946-52; from asst. prof. to prof. elec. engring. N.Y. U., 1952-63; prof. elec. engring. SUNY-Stony Brook, 1963—; vis. Mackay prof. U. Calif.-Berkeley, 1969-70; cons. to industry, 1952—. Author: Synthesis of Optimum Control Systems, 1961, Energy Conversion, 1963; Editor-in-chief: Fundamentals Handbook of Electrical and Computer Engineering, Vol. 1, 1982, Vol. 2, 1982, Vol. 3, 1983; Author also articles. Fellow IEEE (Fellow award 1962); mem. Sigma Xi (N.Y. U. lectr. 1963), Tau Beta Pi, Eta Kappa Nu. Spl. research feedback communications systems, optimum control theory. Home: 5 Seaside Dr Belle Terre NY 11777 Office: State U NY Stony Brook NY 11794

CHANG, TEH-KUANG, political scientist, educator; b. Changting, Fukien, China, Sept. 15, 1925; came to U.S., 1956, naturalized, 1981; s. Tsan-Yao and Mantii (Chang-Wu) C.; m. Grace Kuo-chang Chin, Oct. 1, 1959; children: Angelo, Angelin, Angelina, Angel. B.A., Nat. Taiwan U., 1950; M.A., U. Wash., 1968; Ph.D., Am. U., 1966. Asst. prof. polit. sci. Ball State U., Muncie, Ind., 1966-70, asso. prof., 1970-74, chmn. Asian studies com., 1970-72, 76-77, prof., 1975—, prof. London Centre, winter, 1975-76; nat. vis. prof. Chengchi U., Nat. Taiwan U., Rep. China, 1972-73; vis. prof. Inst. Am. Culture, Academia Sinica, Taiwan, 1982-83; adj. prof. Tam Kang U., Chung-Yuan Christian U., Taiwan, 1982-83. Author: Organization and Achievement of United Nations, 1953, Foreign Ministers' Conference of Four Powers after World War II, 1955, The Cultural Revolution and Political Modernization of Communist China, 1970, The Party Congress and the Political Development: A Comparison of National and Communist China, 1971, Political Science: United States of America and China, 1973, Special Feature of Communist China's 1975 Constitution, 1975, Presidential Power in Foreign Policy: Expansion and Contraction, 1977, Development of Political Science in Asia, 1979; author: The Rainbow of World Civilization: Chinese Culture and Islamic Culture, 1980, The Policy Science: Scope, Method and Development, 1983. Recipient prize Chinese Assn. for UN, 1952; Cultural award Am. Inst. Chinese Culture, 1979; Nat. Endowment for Humanities fellow, 1977, 84; NSF internat. travel grantee, 1979; UNESCO grantee, 1981; Candido Mendes univ. travel grantee, 1983. Fellow Fukien Fellowship Assn. Taiwan; Mem. Am. Polit. Sci. Assn., Internat. Polit. Sci. Assn. (chmn. Asian polit. studies research com.), Assn. Asian Studies, Pi Sigma Alpha, Pi Gamma Nu. Home: 1015 W Wayne St Muncie IN 47303 *The significance of life is not what one receives from the world, but what one can offer to the world. If everyone is offering, in turn, everyone will receive. The progress of civilization is not merely the continuation of the past, but also the development of the future. The essence of education is not only the transfer of knowledge but also the inspiration of creativity.*

CHANG, THOMAS MING SWI, physician, medical scientist; b. Swatow, Kwantang, China, Apr. 8, 1933; s. Henry Sue-Yue and Frances Hue-Soo (Lim) C.; m. Lancy Yuk Lan, June 21, 1958; children: Harvey, Victor, Christine, Sandra. B.Sc., McGill U., 1957, M.D., C.M., 1961, Ph.D., 1965, F.R.C.P.(C), 1972. Intern Montreal (Que.) Gen. Hosp., 1961-62; research fellow McGill U., Montreal, 1962-65, lectr. dept. physiology, 1965, asst. prof., 1966-69, asso. prof., 1969-72, prof. physiology, 1972—, prof. medicine, 1975—, dir. artificial organs research unit, 1975-79, dir. artificial cells and organs research center, 1979—; practice medicine specializing in med. scis., Montreal, 1962—; staff Royal Victoria Hosp.; hon. cons. Montreal Chinese Hosp., 1970—; cons. Montreal Children's Hosp., 1979—; Med. Research Council fellow, 1962-65, scholar, 1965-68, career investigator, 1968—. Inventor artificial cells; Author: Artificial Cells, 1972, Biomedical Application of Immobilized Enzymes and Protiens, Vols. I and II, 1977, Artificial Kidney, Artificial Liver and Artificial Cells, 1978, Hemoperfusion-Kidney and Liver Supports and Detoxification, 1980, Hemoperfusion, 1981, Past Present and Future of Artificial Organs, 1983; sect. editor: Internat. Jour. Artificial Organs, 1977—; asso. editor: Jour. Artificial Organs, 1977—; editorial bd.: Jour. Biomaterial Med. Devel. and Orgn, 1972—, Jour. Membrane Soc, 1975—, Jour. Bioengring, 1975-79, Jour. Enzyme and Microbial Tech, 1978—. Fellow Royal Coll. Physicians Can.; mem. Biophysic Soc., Am., Canadian physiology socs., Internat. Soc. Artificial Organs (trustee), Can. Soc. Artificial Organs (pres. 1980-82), Canadian Med. Assn. Office: Artificial Cells and Organs Research Centre McGill U 3655 Drummond St Montreal PQ H3G 1Y5 Canada

CHANG, UCK, II, engineer; b. Seoul, Korea, Mar. 23, 1941; s. Suk Don and Who Hyum (Kim) C.; m. Haekyung Park, Mar. 20, 1969; children: Sylvia, Sarah. B.S.E., Seoul Nat. U., 1965; M.S., U. Calif.-Berkeley, 1968, Ph.D., 1970; M.B.A., U. Mich.-Ann Arbor, 1978. Mech. engr. Samsung Moolsen Co., Seoul, 1964-66; research asst. U. Calif., Berkeley, 1966-70; welding devel. engr. mgf. devel. ctr. Ford Motor Co., Detroit, 1971-75, welding devel. engr., engring. and research, 1975-77; mfg. devel. project engring and research, 1977—. Contbr. articles to profl. jours.; expert laser material processing. Mem. Am. Welding Soc., Am. Soc. Metals, Laser Inst. Am., Soc. Mfg. Engrs., Korean Scientists and Engrs. Assn. Home: 3053 Bloomfield Park Dr West Bloomfield MI 48033 Home: Ford Motor Co Mfg Processes Lab 24500 Glendale Ave Detroit MI 48239

CHANG, WILLIAM SHEN CHIE, electrical engineering educator; b. Nantung, Kiangsu, China, Apr. 4, 1931; s. Tung Wu and Phoebe Y.S. (Chow) C.; m. Margaret Huachen Kwei, Nov. 26, 1955; children: Helen Nai-yee, Hugh Nai-han, Hedy Nai-lin. B.S.E., U. Mich., 1952, M.S.E., 1953; Ph.D., Brown U., 1957. Lectr., research asso. elec. engring. Stanford, 1957-59; asst. prof. elec. engring. Ohio State U., 1959-62, asso. prof., 1962-65; prof. dept. elec. engring. Washington U., St. Louis, 1965-76, chmn. dept., 1965-71; dir. Applied Electronic Scis. Lab., 1971-79, Samuel Sachs prof. elec. engring., 1976-79; prof. dept. elec. engring. and computer scis. U. Calif., San Diego, 1979—. Author: Principles of Quantum Electronics, 1969; Contbr. articles to profl. jours. Mem. Am. Optical Soc., Am. Phys. Soc., AAUP, IEEE. Research on quantum electronics and optics. Home: 763 Santa Olivia Solana Beach CA 92075

CHANG, Y. AUSTIN, metallurgical engineering educator; m. P. Jean Ho, Sept. 15, 1956; children: Vincent D., Lawrence D., Theodore D. B.S. in Chem. Engring. U. Calif., Berkeley, 1954; Ph.D. in Metallurgy, U. Calif.-Berkeley, 1963; M.S. in Chem. Engring. U. Wash., 1955. Chem. engr. Stauffer Chem. Co., Richmond, Calif., 1956-59; postdoctoral fellow U. Calif.-Berkeley, 1963; metall. engr. Aerojet-Gen. Corp., Sacramento, 1963-67; assoc. prof. U. Wis.-Milw., 1967-70, prof., 1970-80, chmn. materials dept., 1971-78, assoc. dean research Grad. Sch., 1978-80; prof. dept. metall. and mineral engring. U. Wis.-Madison, 1980—; chmn. dept. U. Wis., Madison, 1982—; with Sandia Labs., Livermore, Calif., 1971. Author: (with others) Phase Diagrams and Thermodynamic Properties of Ternary Copper-Metal Systems, 1979, Phase Diagrams and Thermodynamic Properties of Ternary Copper-Sulfur-Metal Systems, 1979, Thermodynamic Data on Metal Carbonates and Related Oxides, 1982; editor: (with J.F. Smith) Calculation of Phase Diagrams and Thermochemistry of Alloy Phases, 1979, (with Danver and Cigan) Energy: Use and Conversion in the Metals Industry, 1975; contbr. articles to various publs. Mem. bd. Goodwill Residential Community, Inc., Milw., 1978-80; mem. Wis. Gov.'s Asian Am. Adv. Council, 1980-82. Recipient Outstanding Instr. award U. Wis., 1972. Fellow Am. Soc. Metals (trustee 1981-84); Mem. Orgn. Chinese Ams. (chpt. pres. 1979-81), Nat. Assn. Corrosion Engrs., Electrochem. Soc., Metall. Soc. AIME, Sigma Xi, Tau Beta Pi, Phi Tau Phi. Office: 1509 University Ave Madison WI 53706

CHANGNON, STANLEY A., JR., research exec.; b. Donovan, Ill., Apr. 14, 1928; s. Stanley A. and Delphine E. (Hoobler) C.; m. Phyllis J. Williams, Nov. 22, 1950; children—Marc, David, Chris. B.S., U. Ill., 1951, M.S., 1955. Field supr. Cloud Physics Project, U. Chgo., 1952-54; dir. Ill. Weather Card Project, Ill. Water Survey, Champaign, 1955-57; climatologist Ill. Water Survey, 1958-69, head atmospheric scis. sect., Urbana, 1970-79, chief water survey, 1980—; prof. geography U. Ill., 1973—; chmn. Ill. Weather Modification Bd. Served with USMCR, 1946-47. Recipient award for spl. contbn. to bldg. industry Bldg. Research Inst.; Best Paper award Am. Water Works Assn., 1977. Fellow Am. Meteorol. Soc. (councilor 1975-78), AAAS (sec. sect. W 1974-78); mem. Am. Geophys. Union (Horton award 1964), Weather Modification Assn. (pres. 1976-77), Am. Water Resources Assn. (Boggess award 1978), Am. Assn. State Climatologists (pres. 1980-81), Sigma Xi. Home: 39 Sherwin St Urbana IL 61801 Office: Box 232 Urbana IL 61801

CHANIN, MICHAEL HENRY, lawyer; b. Atlanta, Nov. 11, 1943; s. Henry and Herma Irene (Blumenthal) C.; m. Margaret L. Jennings, June 15, 1968; children: Herma Louise, Richard Henry, Patrick Jennings. A.B., U. N.C., 1965; J.D., Emory U., 1968. Bar: Ba. 1968, D.C. 1981. Dir. So. Ctr. for Studies in Pub. Policy, Atlanta, 1968-69; asst. and acting legal officer 1st Coast Guard Dist., Boston, 1969-72; atty. Powell, Goldstein Frazer & Murphy, Atlanta, 1972-77; spl. asst. sec. U.S. Dept. Commerce, Washington, 1977-78; dep. asst. to pres. The White House, Washington, 1978-81; ptnr. Powell, Goldstein, Frazer & Murphy, Washington, 1981—. Served to lt. USCGR, 1969-72. Mem. ABA, D.C. Bar Assn., State Bar Ga. Democrat. Office: Suite 1050 1110 Vermont Ave NW Washington DC 20005

CHANNELL, ORVILLE P., JR., labor union official; b. Des Moines, Sept. 30, 1922; s. Orville P. and Lillian Katherine C.; m. Wanda Maureen, 1945. Rec. sec. local 71 Brotherhood Ry. Carmen U.S. and Can., 1951-63; gen. chmn. Milw. Joint Protective Bd., 1963-69; pres. System Fedn. 76, 1965-69; asst. to pres. Ry. Employee Dept AFL-CIO, 1969-72; gen. sec.-treas. Brotherhood Ry. Carmen U.S. and Can., Kansas City, Mo., 1972—. Served with USMC, 1942-45. Office: Brotherhood of Ry Carmen US and Can 4929 Main St Carmen's Bldg Kansas City MO 64112 *

CHANNING, CAROL, actress; b. Seattle, Jan. 31, 1923; d. George and Adelaide (Glaser) C.; m. Charles F. Lowe, Sept. 5, 1956; 1 son, Channing George. Student, Bennington Coll. Appeared: Broadway prodns. No for an Answer, 1941, Let's Face It, 1941, Proof Through the Night, 1942, So Proudly We Hail, Lend an Ear, 1948, Show Business, 1959, Show Girl, 1961, George Burns-Carol Channing Musical Revue, 1962, The Millionairess, 1963, Carol Channing with Her Stout-Hearted Men, 1970 (London Critics award), Four on a Garden, 1971, Cabaret, 1972, Festival at Ford's, 1972, Carol Channing and Her Gentlemen Who Prefer (Blondes (revue), 1972; star of: Gentlemen Prefer Blondes, 1949, 51-53, Wonderful Town, 1953, Pygmalion, 1953, The Vamp, 1955, Hello Dolly, 1964-67, 77—; actress with, RKO Studios, Hollywood, Calif.; pictures include First Traveling Saleslady; appeared in: Thoroughly Modern Millie, 1967, Skidoo, 1968; TV prodns. Crescendo; also guest star appearances; toured with: play Lorelei, 1973-75 (Recipient Theatre World award, Critics Circle award for play Lend an Ear, award for Best Night Club Act of 1957, 1964 Tony award and N.Y. Drama Critics award as starring actress in Hello Dolly, Golden Globe award as best supporting actress in Thoroughly Modern Millie, 1967, Tony Spl. award 1968). Bronze medallion City of N.Y., 1978. Christian Scientist. Office: care William Morris Agy 151 El Camino Blvd Beverly Hills CA 90212 *

CHANNING, MARK GUNTHER, mgmt. cons.; b. Berlin, Germany, July 5, 1925; came to U.S., 1941, naturalized, 1943; s. Jacob and Maria (Pilger) C.; m. Lila Lang, Apr. 12, 1951; children—Candace Leslie, Stacey Lisa. B.S., Columbia, 1950, M.A., 1952. Various financial positions Ford Motor Co., Dearborn, Mich., 1953-56; managerial positions in finance and planning, dir. market rep. Chrysler Corp., Highland Park, Mich., 1956-61; v.p. Pratt & Whitney Co., Inc., West Hartford, Conn., 1961-64; v.p. finance Precision Instrument Co., Palo Alto, 1964-65; treas. Am. Comml. Lines, 1965-68; exec. v.p. Computer Applications, Inc., N.Y.C., 1968-70; pres. Channing Assos., Inc., Westport, Conn., 1970—. Mem. Am. Mgmt. Assn., Am. Econ. Assn. Home: 39 Soundview Dr Easton CT 06612 Office: 225 Main St Westport CT 06880

CHANNING, ROSE MARIE, coll. pres.; b. Adrian, Pa.; d. Paul A. and Josephine (Bugala) Manger; m. James Gordon Channing, Jan. 24, 1954 (dec. 1973); children—Rose Marie Channing Buhrman, Lorraine Channing Genieczko. Diploma, Jersey City Hosp. Sch. Nursing, 1949; B.S., N.Y. U., 1954; M.A., Columbia U., 1961, M.Ed., 1971, Ed.D., 1973. Staff nurse, asst. supr. Public Health Nursing Service, Jersey City, 1949-55; dir. health and recreation, clin. coordinator, asso. dir. nursing edn. Charles E. Gregory Sch. Nursing, Perth Amboy (N.J.) Gen. Hosp., 1958-66; chmn. dept. nurse edn., dir. health techs., dean div. health techs. Middlesex County Coll., Edison, N.J., 1966-78, pres., 1978—; Mem. Middlesex County Comprehensive Health Planning Council, 1973-75, N.Y. Com. Regents External Degree in Nursing, 1972-80, Council on Continuing Edn. for Allied Health Personnel, N.J.; Regional Med. Program, 1968-71; chmn. N.J. Health Professions Edn. Adv. Council, N.J. Dept. Higher Edn., 1979—, chmn. nursing subcom., 1975-78; mem. health careers com. J.F. Kennedy Hosp., 1972-75; chmn. Middlesex County Coll. Assembly, 1975-77; mem. Pres.'s Adv. Com. Sch. Allied Health, Coll. Medicine and Dentistry of N.J., 1976-79; commr. Middle States Assn. of Colls. and Schs., Commn. High Edn., 1978—; mem. liaison com. Am. Assn. Community and Jr. Colls. and Nat. League for Nursing, 1978—; chmn. acad. affairs com. N.J. Council of Community Coll.; Pres., 1978—; bd. trustees Nat. Bank of N.J., 1979—; exec. com. Acad. Pres.'s, Am. Assn. Community and Jr. Colls.; also exec. com. Internat./Intercultural Consortium. Contbr. articles to profl. jours. Recipient award for excellence in Tb nursing Jersey City Hosp. Sch. Nursing, 1954; Am. Nurses Assn. pin N.J. Nurses Assn., 1973. Mem. Council of County Coll. Presidents, Am. Nurses Assn., Nat. League for Nursing, Am. Soc. Allied Health Professions, Am. Council on Edn., Am. Assn. Community and Jr. Colls., Coll. Consortium for Internat. Studies., Jersey City Sch. Nursing Alumni Assn., N.Y. U. Alumni Assn., Tchrs. Coll., Columbia Alumni Assn., Kappa Delta Pi. Home: 105 Hof Rd Edison NJ 08817 Office: Middlesex County Coll Edison NJ 08817 *An important principle, accepted early in my life, was that education is the key to a successful professional and personal life. I believe in goal-setting on a short term achievable basis, leading gradually to a higher long term goal. Upon making a decision regarding further study or accepting a position, total commitment is essential to success. I take my study and work seriously, but not myself. I truly enjoy all people and working with them.*

CHANNING, STOCKARD (SUSAN STOCKARD), actress; b. N.Y.C.; m. David Debin, 1976. B.A. cum laude, Radcliffe Coll., 1965. Performed in exptl. drama with, Theatre Co. of Boston, 1967; numerous stage appearances including Two Gentlemen of Verona, N.Y.C., San Francisco, Los Angeles, 1972-73, No Hard Feelings, Martin Beck Theatre, N.Y.C., 1973, Vanities, Mark Tapen Forum, Los Angeles, 1976; appeared in: films, including Comforts of Home, 1970, The Fortune, 1975, Sweet Revenge, 1975, The Big Bus, 1976, Grease, 1978, The Cheap Detective, 978, The Fish that Saved Pittsburgh, 1979; TV films include The Girl Most Likely To, 1973, Silent Victory: The Kitty O'Neil Story, 1979; star of: TV series The Stockard Channing Show, 1979-80. Office: Care Creative Artists Agy Inc 1888 Century Park E Suite 1400 Los Angeles CA 90067 *

CHANT, DONALD ALFRED, zoologist, educator; b. Toronto, Ont., Can., Sept. 30, 1928; s. Sperrin N. Fulton and Nellie Irene (Cooper) C.; m. Karen Merle, Oct. 17, 1975. B.A. with honors, U. B.C., Can., 1950, M.A., 1952; Ph.D., U. London, 1956; LL.D. (hon.), Dalhousie U., 1976, Trent U., 1983. With Can. Dept. Agr., summers 1943-44, 49-50, research officer entomology lab., Vancouver, 1951-56, Entomology Research Inst., Belleville, Ont., 1956-60, dir. research lab., Vineland, Ont., 1960-64; chmn. dept. biol. control U. Calif., Riverside, 1964-67; chmn. dept. zoology U. Toronto, 1967-75, prof. zoology, 1967—, v.p., provost, 1975-80; dir. Joint Study Centre for Toxicology, 1980—; pres. Ont. Waste Mgmt. Corp., 1980—; bd. dirs. Can. Environ. Law Research Found., 1972-79; mem. sci. adv. com. World Wildlife Fund of Can., 1972—, chmn., 1977—; mem. Can. Environ. Adv. Council, Can. Dept. Environ., Ottawa, 1972-74, 75—, chmn., 1979-81; cons. expert Rachel Carson Trust, Washington, 1974—; mem. environ. assessment bd. Ont. Ministry of Environ., 1976-78; chmn. steering com. to advise Premier Davis on drafting of regulations for Environ. Assessment Act, 1976-80; cons. on sci. and environ. programming CBC, CTV; pres. Pollution Probe Found., 1969-80. Author 8 books; contbr. articles to profl. jours. and popular publs.; editor: Pesticide Research, 1961, Pollution Probe, 3d edit, 1972. Recipient Alumni award of merit U. B.C., 1970, White Owl Conservation award Imperial Tobacco Co. Ltd., 1973, Disting. Public Service award Fedn. Ont. Naturalists, 1975, Alumni Faculty award U. Toronto, 1980. Fellow Royal Soc. Can., Entomology Soc. Can.; mem. Can. Soc. Zoologists (pres. 1974-75), Univ. Biology Chairmen (chmn. Can. com. 1971-74). Home: 9 Beaumont Rd Toronto ON M4W 1V4 Canada Office: 2 Bloor St 11th Floor Toronto ON M4W 3E2 Canada

CHAO, BEI TSE, mechanical engineering educator; b. Soochow, China, Dec. 18, 1918; came to U.S., 1948, naturalized, 1962; s. Tse Yu and Yin T. (Yao) C.; m. May Kiang, Feb. 7, 1948; children: Clara, Fred Roberto. B.S. in Elec. Engring. with highest honor, Nat. Chiao-Tung U., China, 1939; Ph.D. (Boxer Indemnity scholar), Victoria U., Manchester, Eng., 1947. Asst. engr. tool and gage div. Central Machine Works, Kunming, China, 1939-41, asso. engr., 1941-43, mgr. tool and gage div., 1943-45; research asst. U. Ill., Urbana, 1948-50, asst. prof. dept. mech. engring., 1951-53, asso. prof., 1953-55, prof., 1955—, head thermal sci. div., 1971-75, head dept. mech. and indsl. engring., 1975—, assoc. mem., 1963-64; cons. to industry and govtl. agys., 1950—; Russell S. Springer prof. mech. engring. U. Calif.-Berkeley, 1973; mem. reviewing staff Zentralblatt für Mathematik, Berlin, 1970-82; mem. U.S. Engring. Edn. Del. to Visit People's Republic of China, 1978; mem. adv. screening com. in engring. Fulbright-Hays Awards Program, 1979-81, chmn., 1980, 81; mem. com. U.S. Army basic sci. research NRC, 1980-83. Author: Advanced Heat Transfer, 1969; contbr. numerous articles on mech. engring. to profl. jours.; tech. editor: Jour. Heat Transfer, 1975-81; mem. adv. editorial bd.: Numerical Heat Transfer, 1977—. Recipient Outstanding Tchr. award Ill. Mech. Engring. Alumni, 1978, Max Jakob Meml. award ASME/Am. Inst. Chem. Engring., 1983. Fellow ASME (Blackall award 1957, Heat Transfer award 1971); mem. Am. Soc. Engring. Edn. (Outstanding Tchr. award. 1975, Western Electric Fund award 1973), Nat. Acad. Engring., Am. Soc. Engring. Edn. (Benjamin Garver Lamme award 1984), Soc. Engring. Sci., Chiao-Tung U. Alumni Assn. (pres. Mid-West sect. 1975-76), Sigma Xi, Tau Beta Pi, Pi Tau Sigma. Home: 704 Brighton Dr Urbana IL 61801 Office: 148 Mechanical Engineering Bldg Univ Ill Urbana IL 61801

CHAO, CHONG-YUN, mathematics educator; b. Kunming, China, July 5, 1931; came to U.S., 1949; m. Theresa Dao, June 23, 1956; children: Karl, Evelyn. B.S., U. Iowa, 1952, M.S., 1954; Ph.D., U. Mich., 1961. Research mathematician IBM Research Ctr., Yorktown Heights, NY, 1961-63; assoc. prof. math. U. Pitts., 1963-66, prof., 1966—. Home: 621 Driftwood Dr Pittsburgh PA 15238 Office: Dept Mathmatics NL University of Pittsburgh PA 15260

CHAO, KANG, economist, educator; b. Harbin, China, Mar. 23, 1929; s. Hsi-meng and Teh-lan (Chang) C.; m. Jessica Chung-yee Chen, Feb. 18, 1956; children—Tonia Chao, Connie Chao. B.A. in Econs, Nat. Taiwan U., 1951; M.A., U. Mich., 1957, Ph.D. in Econs, 1962. Asst. prof. econs. U. Rochester, 1960-62, U. Mich., 1962-65; vis. asst. prof. econs. U. Calif., Berkeley, 1965-66; asst. prof. econs. U. Wis., Madison, 1966-67, asso. prof., 1967-69, prof., 1969—. Author 7 books; contbr. articles to profl. jours. Office: Social Sci Bldg U Wisconsin Madison WI 53706

CHAO, KWANG-CHU, educator, chemical engineer; b. Chongqing, China, June 7, 1925; came to U.S., 1954, naturalized, 1969; s. Chung-Pu and Jui-Pu (Chou) C.; m. Jiun-Ying Su, May 2, 1953; children: Howard Honshuen, Albert Honchi, Bernard Honwei. B.S., Nat. Chekiang U., 1948; M.S., U. Wis., 1952, Ph.D., 1956. Chem. engr. Taiwan Alkali Co., 1948-51, 52-54; research engr. Chevron Research Co., Richmond, Calif., 1957-63; asso. prof. Ill. Inst. Tech., Chgo., 1963-64, Okla. State U., 1964-68; prof. Purdue U., West Lafayette, Ind., 1968—; cons. to industry, 1964—. Author: (with R.A. Greenkorn) Thermodynamics of Fluids, 1975; Editor: Applied Thermodynamics, 1968, Equations of State in Engineering and Research, 1979. Fellow Am. Inst. Chem. Engrs. (editorial bd. jour., also Ind. Engring. Chem. Ann. Revs.); mem. Am. Chem. Soc., AAUP, Sigma Xi, Omega Chi Epsilon. Home: 2909 Henderson Ave West Lafayette IN 47906

CHAO, MARSHALL S., chemist; b. Changsha, Hunan, China, Nov. 20, 1924; came to U.S., 1955; s. Heng-ti and Hwei-yng C.; m. Patricia Hu, July 20, 1968; 1 dau., Anita J. B.S., Nat. Central U., Nanking, China, 1947; M.S., U. Ill., 1958, Ph.D., 1961. Tech. asst. Taiwan Fertilizer Co., Taipei, 1949-55; research chemist Dow Chem. Co., Midland, Mich., 1960-72, research specialist, 1973-80; research leader Dow chem. Co., Midland, Mich., 1980—. Author: Taiwan Fertilizers, 1951; articles; patentee in field. Deacon 1st Baptist Ch., Midland, 1974-76. Univ. fellow U. Ill., 1957-60. Fellow Am. Inst. Chemists; mem. Am. Chem. Soc., Electrochem. Soc. (sect. chmn. 1973-74, 83—, 1974-76), Soc. Electronanalytical chemistry (charter), Mensa, Sigma Xi, Phi Lambda Upsilon. Clubs: Midland Chinese (chmn. 1975-76), Tittabawassee Toastmasters (sec.-treas. 1976-77). Home: 1206 Evamar Minland MI 48640 Office: Dow Chem Co 1776 Bldg Midland MI

48640 *A man's intrinsic worth is measured by the good he has done his fellow men. As for outward signs of success, such as recognition or rewards, he should much rather have people wondering why he didn't get them than have people wondering why he got them at all.*

CHAPANIS, ALPHONSE, psychologist, educator; b. Meriden, Conn., Mar. 17, 1917; s. Anicatas and Mary (Barkevich) C.; m. Marion Rowe, Aug. 23, 1941 (div. 1960); children: Linda and Roger (twins); m. Natalia Potanin, Mar. 25, 1960. B.A., U. Conn., 1937; M.A., Yale U., 1942, Ph.D., 1943. Psychologist Tenn. Dept. Pub. Health, 1939-40; asst. psychologist Aero. Med. Lab., Wright Air Devel. Center, 1942-43; asst. prof., research fellow Johns Hopkins, 1946-49, assoc. prof., 1949-56, research contract dir., 1952-53, 55-83, prof. psychology, indsl. engring., 1956-63, prof. psychology, 1963—; mem. tech. staff Bell Telephone Labs., 1953-54; Cons. exec. council Joint Services Human Engring. Guide to Equipment Design, 1953-60; mem. panel on tng., com. on undersea warfare NRC, 1953-57; adv. panel behavioral scis. research Air Force Office Sci. Research, 1956-59; sci. liaison officer Am. embassy Office Naval Research Br. Office, London, Eng., 1960-61. Author: (with W.R. Garner, C.T. Morgan) Applied Experimental Psychology: Human Factors in Engineering Design, 1949, The Design and Conduct of Human Engineering Studies, 1956, Research Techniques in Human Engineering, 1959, Man-Machine Engineering, 1965; Editor: Ethnic Variables in Human Factors Engineering, 1975; corr. editor: Jour. Applied Psychology, 1955-60; co-editor: (with C.T. Morgan, J.S. Cook, M.W. Lund) Human Engineering Guide to Equipment Design, 1963; editorial adv. bd.: Jour. Systems Engring, 1969-70; mem. editorial bd.: Behaviour and Info. Tech, 1980—; Contbr. articles to profl. jours. Mem. NRC, 1971-74, mem. com. on human factors, 1980—. Served from 2d lt. to capt. USAAF, 1943-46. Recipient Franklin V. Taylor award, 1963, Paul M. Fitts award, 1973, Distinguished Contbn. for Applications in Psychology award, 1978, Outstanding Sci. Contbns. to Psychology award, 1981, Polish Ergonomics Soc. award, 1982. Fellow AAAS, Am. Psychol. Assn., Human Factors Soc. (pres. 1963-64), Soc. Engring. Psychologists (pres. 1959-60), Soc. Exptl. Psychologists; mem. Ergonomics Soc. (hon.), Internat. Assn. Applied Psychology, Eastern Psychol. Assn., Systems Safety Soc., Internat. Ergonomics Assn. (mem. council 1967-73, pres. 1976-79, award 1982), Phi Beta Kappa, Sigma Xi. Address: Suite 210 Ruxton Towers 8415 Bellona Ln Baltimore MD 21204

CHAPIN, CHARLES FISHER, manufacturing executive; b. Providence, June 9, 1929; s. Robert Crins and Helen Gertrude C.; m. Genevieve W. Brown, Feb. 15, 1952 (dec. Mar. 1980); children: M. Anne, Nancy A., Betsy J.; m. Mary Kay Tinker, Apr. 29, 1981. B.A., Amherst Coll., 1951. Registered rep. Kidder, Peabody Inc., Providence, 1953-62, co-mgr., 1962-64; asst. treas. Textron Inc., Providence, 1964-68, v.p., 1968, v.p. corp. devel., 1969-72, v.p. investment mgmt., 1972-74, group v.p., 1974—; dir. Ionics, Inc., Keystone Liquid Trust, People's Trust Co.; trustee People's Savs. Bank, Keystone Bond Trust, Keystone Money Trust, Masters Reserves Trust, Keystone Tax Free Fund, Keystone Stock Trust; dir. Money Market/Options Investments. Chmn., trustee Indsl. Found. R.I. Served with USCGR, 1951-53. Republican. Clubs: Turks Head, Barrington Yacht, New Bedford Yacht, Providence Art. Home: 10 Blount Circle Barrington RI 02806 Office: Textron Inc 40 Westminster St Providence RI 02903

CHAPIN, DWIGHT LEE, pub.; b. Wichita, Kans., Dec. 2, 1940; s. N. Spencer and Betty June (Helena) C.; m. Susan Howland, Aug. 18, 1963; children—Kimberly Susan, Tracy Helena. B.A., U. So. Calif., 1962. Account rep. J. Walter Thompson Advt. Agy., 1963-66; personal aide to Richard Nixon, 1967-69; appointment sec. The White House, 1969-73; dir. market planning United Airlines, 1973; mktg. cons. W. Clement Stone, 1974-76; pres., pub. Success Unlimited Mag. & Co., Chgo., 1976—. Bd. dirs. Santa for the Very Poor. Mem. U.S. C. of C. (mem. adv. bd. citizen's choice 1979), Mag. Pubs. Assn., Direct Selling Assn. Republican. Presbyterian. Office: 401 N Wabash Chicago IL 60611

CHAPIN, ELLIOTT LOWELL, retired bank executive; b. N.Y.C., Mar. 5, 1917; s. Gilbert Elliott and Elizabeth Lowell (Black) C.; m. Sarah Louise Root, Feb. 12, 1942; children: Bruce Elliott, Gilbert Russell. Student, NYU, 1935-36. Clk. S.I. Savs. Bank, N.Y., 1937-41, officer to pres., 1942-82, trustee, 1974—; dir. Instns. Group Info. Corp., N.Y.C., 1979-82. Bd. dirs. United Way of S.I. Served to capt. U.S. Army, 1941-46; to lt. col. USAFR. Clubs: Richmond County Country, Richmond County Yacht, Staten Island. Lodge: Rotary. Home: 55 Westminster Ct Staten Island NY 10304 Office: SI Savs Bank 15 Beach St Staten Island NY 10304

CHAPIN, FRANCIS STUART, JR., urban planning cons.; b. Northampton, Mass., Apr. 1, 1916; s. Francis Stuart and Nellie Estelle (Peck) C.; m. Mildred Louise Canfield, Oct. 10, 1941; children—F. Stuart III, Alison L. Chapin Henderson, Steven W. A.B., U. Minn., 1937; B.Arch., M.I.T., 1939, M.City Planning, 1940. Regional planner TVA, Knoxville, Tenn., 1940-42, community planner, 1946-47; intelligence analyst War Dept., Washington, 1942-43; dir. planning City of Greensboro, N.C., 1947-49; asso. prof. planning U. N.C., Chapel Hill, 1949-54, prof., 1954-69, Alumni disting. prof., 1969-78, prof. emeritus, 1978—; dir. Urban Studies Program, Inst. for Research in Social Sci., 1957-62; founder, dir. Center for Urban and Regional Studies, 1962-70; advisor div. of slum clearance HHFA, 1950-52; chmn. com. on land use evaluation Hwy. Research Bd., Nat. Acad. Scis., 1964-67; mem. Pres.'s Task Force on Cities, 1966-67. Author: Communities for Living, 1941, Urban Land Use Planning, 1957, 2d edit., 1965; co-author 3d edit. (with E.J. Kaiser), 1979; editor (with S.F. Weiss); contbr.: Urban Growth Dynamics, 1962, Urban Life and Form, 1963, Urban Development Models, 1968, The Quality of the Urban Environment, 1969, Ency. Urban Planning, 1974, Timing Space and Spacing Time, Vol. 2, 1978; author: Human Activity Patterns in the City, 1974; co-author: (with R.B. Zehner) Across the City Line, 1974. Served to lt. USNR, 1943-46. Recipient Disting. Service award Am. Inst. Planners, 1968; Guggenheim fellow, 1972-73. Mem. Am. Inst. Planners (v.p. 1957, sec.-treas. 1954-56, dir. 1951-53, 58-61), Assn. Collegiate Schs. Planning (pres. 1964-65), Regional Sci. Assn. (v.p. 1961), Am. Soc. Planning Ofcls., Am. Planning Assn. Home: Rt 5 Box 90 White Salmon WA 98672

CHAPIN, FREDERIC LINCOLN, fgn. service officer; b. N.Y.C., July 13, 1929; s. Selden and Mary Paul (Noyes) C.; m. Cornelia Bonner Clarke, Aug. 2, 1952; children—John Clarke Noyes, Anne Cornelia, Grace Selden, Edith Clarke. Grad., St. Paul's Sch., Concord, N.H., 1946; student, Stanford, 1948-49; B.A., Harvard, 1950. Econ. analyst ECA, Paris, France, 1950-52; joined U.S. Fgn. Service, 1952; assigned, Vienna, Austria, 1952-55, State Dept., 1956-59, Managua, Nicaragua, 1959-61; charge d'affaires embassy, Fort Lamy, Chad, 1961; assigned State Dept., 1962-63; spl. asst. to under-sec. for polit. affairs, 1963-65; exec. sec. AID, 1965-66; Fgn. Service examiner, 1966-67, Fgn. Service insp., 1967, country dir. for, Bolivia and Chile, 1968-70, dep. asst. sec. for mgmt. for, Latin Am., 1970-72, consul gen., São Paulo, Brazil, 1972-78, U.S. ambassador to, Ethiopia, 1978-80; dep. asst. sec. Dept. Def., 1980-81; chargé d'affaires Am. embassy, San Salvador, El Salvador, 1981; ambassador to, Guatemala, 1981-84; sr. insp. Dept. State, 1984—; Sec.-treas. Am. Fgn. Service Protective Assn., 1970-71. Editorial bd.: Fgn. Service Jour, 1962-66. Recipient Dept. Def. D.S.M., 1981; Grand Cross Jose Mathias Delgado, El Salvador). Mem. Phi Beta Kappa. Office: Dept State Washington DC 20521

CHAPIN, HUGH A., lawyer; b. Whitesville, N.Y., Sept. 3, 1925; m. Judith A. Kinne, 1951; children: Arthur Lyman, David Chester, Samuel R., Sarah A. B.C.E., Cornell U., 1948; LL.B., Harvard U., 1951. Bar: N.Y. 1951. Now mem. firm Kenyon & Kenyon, N.Y.C.; prof. patent law N.Y. Law Sch., 1957-59. Mem. Am. Patent Law Assn. (chmn. com. jud. selections and presdl. appointments 1972-76), N.Y. Patent Law Assn. (pres. 1968-69), Am. Coll. Trial Lawyers, ABA, N.Y. State Bar Assn., Assn. Bar City N.Y., Fed. Bar Council, Tau Beta Pi. Office: One Broadway New York NY 10004

CHAPIN, MELVILLE, lawyer; b. Boston, Dec. 14, 1918; s. Edward Barton and Jeannette (Thomas) C.; m. Elizabeth Ann Parker, Sept. 6, 1940; children: Allan M., Elizabeth M., Chapin Klaussmann. B.A., Yale U., 1940; J.D., Harvard U., 1943. Bar: Mass. 1943. Chmn, ptnr. Warner & Stackpole, Boston, 1954—; dir. H.B. Smith Co., Inc.; chmn. Security Capital Corp, SMI Investors; pres., trustee Phillips Acad. Trustee Frederick J. Kennedy Meml. Found. Inc.; chmn. Mass. Eye and Ear Infirmary; mem. distbn. com. Cambridge Found.; bd. dirs. Chewonski Found. Inc. Served to lt. USNR, World War II. Fellow Am. Bar Found., Mass. Bar Found.; mem. ABA, Boston Bar Assn., Mass. Bar Assn., Internat. Bar Assn. Home: 15 Traill St Cambridge MA 02138 Office: 28 State St Boston MA 02109

CHAPIN, RICHARD, consultant; b. Boston, Dec. 25, 1923; s. Vinton and Elizabeth (Higgins) C.; m. Maryan Gainor Fox, Nov. 3, 1956; children: Aldus Higgins II, Margery Rodman, Marya Marsh, Richard Dickinson. Grad., Milton Acad., 1942; S.B., Harvard U., 1944, M.B.A., 1949; LL.D., Emerson Coll., 1972. Asst. to treas. Anderson, Davis & Platt, Inc., 1946; journeyman machinist Yale & Towne Co., 1947; various adminstrn. and instnl. positions Harvard Grad. Sch. Bus. Adminstrn., 1949-67; pres. Emerson Coll., Boston, 1967-75; cons., 1975—; exec. dir. Cheswick Center, 1976—; dir. Norton Co., Liberty Bank & Trust Co., Advanced Mech. Tech., Inc., Nickerson Lumber Co.; Mem. panel Am. Arbitration Assn., N.Y. Stock Exchange, 1975—. Bd. dirs. Mass. affiliate Nat. Soc. for Prevention of Blindness, pres., 1973-75, 79—; nat. del. Nat. Soc. Prevention Blindness, 1982—; trustee Wheelock Coll., Concord Acad., Coll. Center, Boston, TMCA Found. Served with USNR, 1942-46. Clubs: N.Y. Yacht, Harvard, Century Assn. Home: 13 Kennedy Rd Cambridge MA 02138 Office: Cheswick Center 11 Newbury St Boston MA 02116

CHAPIN, RICHARD EARL, librarian; b. Danville, Ill., Apr. 29, 1925; s. Harry W. and Lula May (Briggs) C.; m. Eleanor Jane Lang, Aug. 15, 1949; children: Robert Lang, David Brian, Rebecca Anne. A.B., Wabash Coll., 1948; M.S., U. Ill., 1949, Ph.D., 1954. Reference asst. Fla. State U., 1949-50; library asst. U. Ill., 1950-53, vis. prof., 1957; asst. dir., asst. prof. U. Okla. Sch. Library Sci., 1953-55; assoc. librarian, assoc. prof. Mich. State U., East Lansing, 1955-59, dir. libraries, prof. journalism, 1959—; cons. to govts., founds., colls., and univs.; bd. dirs. Center for Research Libraries, 1978-83; pres. OCLC Users' Council, 1980—. Author: Mass Communications, A Statistical Analysis, 1957; Contbr. articles library periodicals and encys. Mem. East Lansing Human Relations Commn., 1966-69, chmn., 1969; mem. East Lansing Bd. Edn., 1970-74, 75, pres., 1973-74. Served to lt. (j.g.) USNR, 1943-46. Mem. ALA, Mich. Library Assn. (pres. 1967), Blue Key, Sigma Chi, Phi Kappa Phi. Home: 614 Camelot Dr East Lansing MI 48823

CHAPIN, ROY DIKEMAN, JR., automobile company executive; b. Detroit, Sept. 21, 1915; s. Roy Dikeman and Inez (Tiedeman) C.; m. Ruth Mary Ruxton, Oct. 29, 1937 (div.); children: Roy D., Christopher K., William R., Cicely P.; m. Loise Baldwin Wickser, July 19, 1965; children: Alexandra, Robert L., Loise B., Hope B. A.B., Yale U., 1937. With Hudson Motor Car Co., Detroit, 1938-54, dir., 1946-54; asst. sales mgr. Hudson div. Am. Motors Corp., 1954-55; asst. treas., dir. Am. Motors Corp., 1954-55, v.p., treas., 1955, exec. v.p., 1956-66, exec. v.p., gen. mgr., 1966-67, chmn., 1967-78, now dir.; dir. Whirlpool Corp., Gould Inc., Am. Natural Resources Co. Bd. dirs. Ruffed Grouse Soc.; trustee Ducks Unltd. Found. Clubs: Elihu Soc. (New Haven); Links (N.Y.C.); Country of Detroit, Detroit (Detroit); Pacific Union (San Francisco); Sankaty Head (Nantucket, Mass.). Office: 333 W Fort St Detroit MI 48226

CHAPIN, SCHUYLER GARRISON, impresario, university dean; b. N.Y.C., Feb. 13, 1923; s. L.H. Paul and Leila H. (Burden) C.; m. Elizabeth Steinway, Mar. 15, 1947; children: Henry Burden, Theodore Steinway, Samuel Garrison, Miles Whitworth. Student, Longy Sch. Music, 1940-41; L.H.D. (hon.), N.Y. U., 1974, Hobart/William Smith Coll., 1974, D.Litt., Emerson Coll., 1976. Spot sales NBC-TV, N.Y.C., 1947-51; gen. mgr. Tex and Jinx McCary Enterprises, N.Y.C., 1951-53; booking dir. Judson, O'Neill & Judd div. Columbia Artists Mgmt., 1953-59; dir. masterworks Columbia Records div. CBS, 1959-62, v.p. creative services, 1962-63; v.p. programming Lincoln Center for the Performing Arts, 1964-69; exec. producer Amberson Enterprises, N.Y.C., 1969-71; acting gen. mgr. Met. Opera, N.Y.C., 1972-73, gen. mgr., 1973-75; dean Faculty of Arts, Columbia, 1976—; cons. Carnegie Hall Corp., 1979—. (Emmy awards 1972, 76, 80); Author: autobiography Musical Chairs, 1977. Chmn. Bagby Music Lovers Found., 1959—, Am. Symphony Orch. League; Trustee Naumburg Found., 1959, Richard Tucker Found., 1975, Stuart Ostrow Found., 1974, Am. Inst. for Verdi Studies, 1975, Bklyn. Philharmonic, 1978; mem. Pres.'s Com. on Arts and Humanities. Recipient N.Y. State Conspicuous service cross, 1951, Christopher award, 1971. Clubs: Coffee House, Century Assn. (N.Y.C.). Home: 901 Lexington Ave New York NY 10021 *Throughout my career, and indeed my life, I have been fortunate to make my avocation my vocation. I've worked in, around, about and for the arts in a variety of ways. That, I hope, has brought as much happiness to others as it has to me. I have been privileged to be part of what a poet once called the Arts: the Signature of man.*

CHAPLIN, ANSEL BURT, lawyer; b. Deerfield, Ill., June 12, 1931; s. Robert Tappan and Ruth (Burt) C.; m. Maud Denise Hazeltine, Feb. 14, 1959; children: Rawson, Margaret, Jane. B.A. magna cum laude, Princeton U., 1953; postgrad., Inst. Polit. Sci., Paris, U. Algiers; J.D., Harvard U., 1959. Bar: Mass. 1959. Law clk. to chief justice Mass. Supreme Ct., 1959-60; practice in, Boston, 1960—; ptnr. Chaplin & Miestein; owner Cape Cod Fishnet Industries, North Truro, Mass., 1980—; chmn. spl. com. legal edn. Mass. Supreme Ct., 1979—, mem. com. lawyer advt., 1979-82; mem. U.S. Dist. Ct. Adv. Practice Com., 1981—. Author papers in field. Pres. Truro Neighborhood Assn., 1979—; mem. corp. Perkins Sch. for Blind, Watertown, Mass., 1973—, Winsor Sch., Boston, 1980—. Served with AUS, 1954-56. Fulbright fellow, 1953-54. Fellow Am. Bar Found., Mass. Bar Found.; Mem. ABA, Am. Law Inst., Mass. Bar Assn. (chmn. law practice sect. 1978-80), Boston Bar Assn. Democrat. Unitarian. Club: Harvard (Boston). Office: 40 Winter St Boston MA 02108

CHAPLIN, GEORGE, editor; b. Columbia, S.C., Apr. 28, 1914; s. Morris and Netty (Brown) C.; m. Esta Lillian Solomon, Jan. 26, 1937; children—Stephen Michael, Jerry Gay. B.S., Clemson Coll., 1935; Nieman fellow, Harvard, 1940-41. Reporter, later city editor Greenville (S.C.) Piedmont, 1935-42; mng. editor Camden (N.J.) Courier-Post, 1946-47, San Diego Jour., 1948-49; mng. editor, then editor New Orleans Item, 1949-58; asso. editor Honolulu Advertiser, 1958-59, editor, 1959—; Pulitzer prize juror, 1969, 83; mem. selection com. Jefferson fellowships U. Hawaii.; Chmn. Gov.'s Conf. on Year 2000, 1970; chmn. Hawaii Commn. on Year 2000, 1971-74; co-chmn. Conf. on Alt. Econ. Future for Hawaii, 1973-75; charter mem. Goals for Hawaii, 1979—; alt. U.S. rep. South Pacific Commn., 1978—. Editor, officer-in-charge: Mid-Pacific edit. Stars and Stripes; Editor: (with Glenn Paige) Hawaii 2000, 1973. Bd. dirs. U. Hawaii Research Corp., 1970-72, Inst. for Religion and Social Change, Hawaii Jewish Welfare Fund; bd. govs. East-West Center, Honolulu, 1980—; Am. media chmn. U.S.-Japan Conf. on Cultural and Ednl. Interchange, 1978—. Served as capt. AUS, 1942-46. Decorated Star Solidarity, Italy).; Recipient citations Overseas Press Club, 1961, 72; Headliners award, 1962; John Hancock award, 1972, 74; Distinguished Alumni award Clemson U., 1974; E.W. Scripps award Scripps-Howard Found., 1976; Champion Media award for Econ. Understanding, 1981. Mem. Soc. Nieman Fellows, Honolulu Symphony Soc., Pacific and Asian Affairs Council (dir.), Internat. Press Inst., World Future Soc., Am. Soc. Newspaper Editors (dir., treas. 1973, sec. 1974, v.p. 1975, pres. 1976), Nat. Conf. Editorial Writers, Friends of East-West Center, Sigma Delta Chi. Clubs: Pacific, Waialae Country. Home: 4437 Kolohala St Honolulu HI 96816 Office: care Honolulu Advertiser Advertiser Sq Honolulu HI 96802

CHAPLIN, GERALDINE, actress; b. Santa Monica, Calif., 1944; d. Charles and Oona (O'Neill) C.; 1 son, Shane. Ed. pvt. schs., Royal Ballet Sch., London. Motion pictures include Doctor Zhivago, 1965, Stranger in the House, 1967, I Killed Rasputin, 1968, The Hawaiians, 1970, Innocent Bystanders, 1973, Buffalo Bill and the Indians or Sitting Bull's History Lesson, The Three Musketeers, 1974, The Four Musketeers, 1975, Nashville, 1975, Welcome to L.A, 1977, Cria, 1977, Roseland, 1977, Remember My Name, 1978, A Wedding, 1978, The Mirror Crack'd, 1980, Voyage en Douce, 1981, Bolero (Double 13), 1982. Address: care William Morris Agy 1350 Ave of Americas New York NY 10019 *

CHAPLIN, HUGH, JR., physician, educator; b. N.Y.C., Feb. 4, 1923; m. Alice Dougherty, June 16, 1945; 4 children. A.B., Princeton, 1943; M.D., Columbia, 1947. Diplomate: Am. Bd. Internal Medicine, Nat. Bd. Med. Examiners. Intern Mass. Gen. Hosp., Boton, 1947-48, resident, 1948-50; fellow in hematology Brit. Postgrad. Med. Sch., London, 1951-53; physician in charge Clin. Center Blood Bank, NIH, Bethesda, Md., 1953-55; Commonwealth Fund fellow Wright Fleming Inst. Microbiology, London, 1962-63, Josiah Macy Faculty scholar, 1975-76; instr. in medicine Washington U. Sch. Medicine, St. Louis, 1955-56, asst. prof. medicine and preventive medicine, 1956-62, asso. dean, chmn. admissions com., 1957-62, asso. prof., 1963-65, prof., 1965, William B. Kountz Prof. preventive medicine, 1965—; dir. IWJ Inst. of Rehab., St. Louis, 1964-72, Barnes Hosp. Blood Bank, 1983; Mem. Am. Standards Com. for Blood Transfusion Equipment; mem. subcom. on transfusion problems NRC, 1959-62, mem. com. on blood and transfusion problems, 1963-67; chmn. ad hoc blood program research com. ARC, 1967-73, bd. govs., 1978—. Asso. editor: Transfusion, 1960—; contbg. editor: Vox Sanguinis, 1960-79. Served with USNR, 1942-45. Mem. Am. Fedn. Clin. Research, Central Soc. Clin. Research, Am. Soc. Clin. Investigation, Assn. Am. Physicians, Am., Internat. socs. hematology, Brit. Med. Research Soc., Brit. Royal Soc. Medicine, Am. Assn. Blood Banks (sci. program com. 1959-60), Phi Beta Kappa, Alpha Omega Alpha, Sigma Xi. Office: Washington U Sch Medicine 4566 South Ave St Louis MO 63110

CHAPLIN, JAMES CROSSAN, IV, securities firm executive; b. Sewickley, Pa., Mar. 20, 1933; s. James Crossan III and Gretchen (Brown) C.; m. Martha A. Tinker, May 19, 1956 (div. Jan. 1980); 1 son, W. Craig II; m. Carol C. Mullaugh, Apr. 12, 1980. Grad., Phillips Acad., 1951; A.B., Princeton, 1955. With firm Chaplin McGuiness & Co. Inc. (now part of Parker/Hunter, Inc.), Pitts., 1959-74, v.p. retail ops., 1971-73, sr. v.p. mktg., 1973-82, sec.-treas., also dir., mem. exec. com., 1973-82; v.p. Parker/Hunter, Inc., 1974-82; chmn., treas. dir. Chaplin-Mullaugh, Inc., 1982—. Corporator Sewickley Cemetary; treas. Leet Twp. Mcpl. Authority, 1975—. Served to 1st lt. USAF, 1956-59. Mem. Bond Club Pitts. (pres. 1971-72). Clubs: Duquesne (Pitts.); Allegheny Country (Sewickley). Home: Camp Meeting Rd Sewickley PA 15143 Office: 435 Beaver St PO Box 567 Sewickley PA 15143

CHAPLINE, GEORGE FREDERICK, JR., theoretical physicist; b. Teaneck, N.J., May 6, 1942; s. George Frederick Chaplaine and Ferne Louise (Copeland) C.; m. Marie Jeanne Hjort, Mar. 5, 1968; 1 son, Michael. B.A., UCLA, 1961. Teaching asst. Calif. Inst. Tech., 1962-64; asst. prof. physics U. Calif.-Santa Cruz, 1967-69; physicist Lawrence Livermore Lab., Livermore, Calif., 1969—; adj. prof. U. Calif., Santa Cruz, 1978. Patentee x-ray laser. Recipient E.O. Lawrence award Dept. Energy, 1983. Office: Dept Physics Lawrence Livermore Nat Lab Livermore CA 94550

CHAPMAN, ALAN JESSE, educator; b. Los Angeles, June 22, 1925; s. Wallace Webster and Isabel (Smith) C.; m. Marjorie Bray, June 8, 1950; children—Alan Jesse, Katherine Lynn. B.S. in Mech. Engring, Rice U., 1945; M.S., U. Colo., 1949; Ph.D., U. Ill., 1953. Registered profl. engr., Tex. Faculty Rice U., Houston, 1946—, prof. mech. engring., 1954-69, chmn. dept. mech. and aerospace engring. and materials sci., 1954-69, v.p., 69-70; dean G.R. Brown Sch. Engring., 1975-80, Harry S. Cameron prof. mech. engring., 1980—; cons. to Manned Spacecraft Center, NASA, Houston, 1961—. Author: Heat Transfer, 3d edit, 1974, Introductory Gas Dynamics, 1970. Pres. S.W. Athletic Conf., 1965-67; mem. council Nat. Collegiate Athletic Assn., 1968-73, pres., 1973-74. Served with USNR, 1942-45. Fellow Am. Inst. Aeros. and Astronautics (asso.), ASME; mem. Am. Soc. Engring. Edn., Am. Soc. Heating, Refrigeration and Air Conditioning Engring., Sigma Xi, Tau Beta Pi. Home: 10031 Doliver St Houston TX 77042

CHAPMAN, ALVAH HERMAN, JR., newspaper executive; b. Columbus, Ohio, Mar. 21, 1921; s. Alvah Herman and Wyline (Page) C.; m. Betty Bateman, Mar. 22, 1943; children: Dale Page (Mrs. Dennis Webb), Chris Ann (Mrs. Robert Hilton). B.S., The Citadel, 1942. Bus. mgr. Columbus Ledger, 1945-53; exec. v.p., gen. mgr. St. Petersburg (Fla.) Times, 1953-57; pres., pub. Morning News and Evening Press, Savannah, Ga., 1957-60; pres. Savannah News-Press, Inc., 1957-60; exec. Knight-Ridder Newspapers, Inc., Miami, Fla., 1960—, exec. com., 1960—, exec. v.p., 1967-73, pres., 1973—, chief exec. officer, 1976—, chmn., 1982—; v.p., gen. mgr. Miami Herald, 1962-70, pres., 1970—; lectr. Am. Press Insts., Columbia. Served from 2d lt. to maj. USAAF, World War II. Decorated D.F.C. with 2 oak leaf clusters, Air medal with 5 clusters, U.S.; Croix de Guerre; named one of five outstanding young men in Ga., 1951, Outstanding Young Man Columbus Jr. C. of C., 1952, Dade County's Outstanding Citizen of 1968-69. Mem. Am. Newspapers Pubs. Assn., So. Newspapers Pubs. Assn. (pres. 1976). Methodist. Home: 4255 Lake Rd Miami FL 33137 Office: Miami Herald Miami FL 33101

CHAPMAN, ANTHONY JAY, physician; b. Covington, Va., Jan. 1, 1939; s. Jay Pierpoint and Thelma Juanita (Sipple) C. B.S. cum laude, Carson-Newman Coll., Jefferson City, Tenn., 1960; M.D., Bowman Gray Sch., Winston-Salem, N.C., j1964. Intern in pathology N.C. Bapt. Hosp., Winston-Salem, 1964-65; resident in pathology Baylor U. Med. Center, Dallas, 1965-68, Am. Cancer Soc. fellow, 1966-67; fellow in legal medicine and forensic pathology Office Chief Med. Examiner Va.-Med. Coll. Va., 1968-70; lectr., registrar forensic medicine St. George's Hosp. Med. Sch., London, 1969; chief med. examiner State of Okla., Oklahoma City, 1971-82; clin. prof. forensic pathology U. Okla. Health Sci. Center, Oklahoma City, 1971-82; forensic pathologist Sonoma County and Napa County,, Okla.; staff Oscar Rose Jr. Coll. Palm Dr. Hosp, Sebastopol, Calif., Vallejo Gen. Hosp. (Calif.), Brookwood Hosp., Santa Rosa, Calif. Contbr. articles to med. publs. Mem. Internat. Acad. Pathologists, Am. Acad. Forensic Scis., Nat. Assn. Med. Examiners. Office: 901 N Stonewall St Oklahoma City OK 73117

CHAPMAN, BRUCE KERRY, government official; b. Evanston, Ill., Dec. 1, 1940; s. Landon Lincoln and Darroll Jessamine (Carlson) C.; m. Sarah G. Williams, Aug. 22, 1976; 1 son, Adam Winthrop. B.A., Harvard Coll., 1962. Pub. Advance mag., Washington, 1960-64; editorial writer New York Herald Tribune, 1965-66; pub. affairs cons., Seattle, 1966-71; mem. City Council, Seattle, 1971-75, chmn. parks and pub. grounds com., 1972-75, co-chmn. planning and urban devel. com., 1974-75; sec. state State of Wash., Olympia, 1975-81; dir. Bur. of Census, Washington, 1981-83; dep. asst. to the Pres. and dir. Office of Planning and Evaluation The White House, Washington, 1983—; Exec. dir. Wash. Commn. on Causes and Prevention Civil Disorders, 1968-69; mem. Gov.'s Urban Affairs Council, 1968-71. Author: The Party That Lost Its Head, 1965, The Wrong Man in Uniform, 1966, The Market; film, 1979; author-narrator: A Memory for the Future, 1975. Chmn. Wash. State Govt. Bicentennial Commn., 1975-76; mem. Pres.'s Adv. Council on Historic Preservation, 1976-81, Metro Council, Seattle; bd. dirs. Nat. Trust for Historic Preservation; mem. adv. council Am. Youth Exchange, 1983—; bd. dirs. Partners for Livable Places, 1982—. Mem. Am. Statis. Assn., Wash. Trust Historic Preservation (hon.). Republican. Episcopalian. Home: 4109 17th St NW Washington DC 20011 Office: The White House Washington DC 20500

CHAPMAN, C. NORMAN, business executive. Chmn. bd. Emco Ltd., London, Ont., Can. Office: Emco Ltd 1108 Dundas St London ON Canada N6A 4N7§

CHAPMAN, CARL HALEY, anthropology educator; b. Steelville, Mo., May 29, 1915; s. William M. and Estelle Madolin (Haley) C.; m. Eleanor Eliza Finley, Mar. 14, 1942; children: Richard Carl, Stephen Finley. A.B., U. Mo., 1939; M.A., U. N.Mex., 1946; Ph.D. (Horace H. Rackham fellow), U. Mich., 1959. Instr. sociology U. Mo., Columbia, 1946-48, dir. Am. archeology, 1946-65, instr. sociology and anthropology, 1948-50, asst. prof. anthropology, 1951-57, assoc. prof. anthropology, 1957-60, prof., 1960—, dir. archeology research activities, 1965-75, research prof. Am. archaeology, 1975—; dir. Mus. Anthropology, 1949-50, 51-56; mem. steering com. Miss. Alluvial Valley Archaeol. Program, 1968-72; chmn. adv. council on archaeology to Mo. State Park Bd., 1959-70; ex-officio mem. Adv. Council on Archaeology and History, 1970-72, Adv. Council on Hist. Preservation, 1977—. Author: (with Eleanor Chapman) Indians and Archaeology of Missouri, 1964, The Origin of the Osage Indian Tribe, 1974, Archaeology of Missouri, I, 1975, II, 1980, (with David Evans and John Cottier) Investigation and Comparison of Two Fortified Mississippi Tradition Sites in Southeastern Missouri, 1977; contbg. author: The Indomitable Osage in Spanish Illinois, 1973, Cultural Change and Continuity, 1976; contbr. articles on Am. Archaeology to scholarly jours. Gov.'s rep. to Lewis and Clark Trail Commn. meetings State of Mo., 1966-68; sec. Mo. Lewis and Clark Trail Commn., 1966-67; Democratic committeeman 3d Ward, Columbia, 1970-72; bd. dirs. Mo. Heritage Trust, 1977—. Served with USAAF, 1942-45. Decorated Air medal; Nat. Park Service grantee, 1952-63; NSF grantee, 1961-63; Nat. Endowment Humanities grantee, 1971-75, 82-85. Fellow Am. Anthrop. Assn., AAAS; mem. Soc. Am. Archaeology (Disting. Service award 1975), Am. Soc. Conservation Archaeology (Conservation award 1980), Soc. Profl. Archaeologists (pres. 1978-79), Mo. Archaeol. Soc. (sec., Honor award 1981), Soc. Hist. Archaeology, Central States Anthrop. Assn., Am. Ethnol. Soc., AAUP, Phi Beta Kappa, Sigma Xi, Phi Kappa Phi. Democrat. Unitarian. Home: 211 Edgewood Columbia MO 65201 Office: 205 Swallow Hall University of Missouri Columbia MO 65211

CHAPMAN, CARLETON BURKE, physician; b. Sycamore, Ala., June 11, 1915; s. John G. and Mary (Anderson) C.; m. Ruth Horine, Aug. 30, 1940; children: Nancy C. Chapman Collins, John G., Mary A. A.B., Davidson Coll., 1936; B.A. in Physiology (Rhodes scholar), Oxford (Eng.) U., 1939, M.A., 1950; M.D., Harvard U., 1941, M.P.H., 1944; M.A. (hon.), Dartmouth Coll., 1968; LL.D., Davidson Coll., 1968; D.Med.Sc. (hon.), Brown U., 1972. Diplomate: Am. Bd. Internal Medicine. Intern 2d and 4th med. services Boston City Hosp., 1941-42, asst. resident, then resident, 1942-44; intern Mallory Inst. Pathology, Boston City Hosp., 1946; asst. medicine Harvard Med. Sch., 1946; faculty U. Minn., 1947-53, asso. prof. medicine, 1950-53; prof. medicine U. Tex. Southwestern Med. Sch., 1953-66; dean Dartmouth Med. Sch., Hanover, N.H., 1966-73; v.p. Commonwealth Fund, 1973-74, pres., 1974-80; prof. history of medicine Albert Einstein Coll. Medicine, 1980—; mem. staff Parkland Hosp., Dallas, 1953—; cons. VA and USAF hosps. Author articles in field; editor: Am. Oxonian, 1963-64. Mem. com. 50 So. Meth. U., 1963; adviser Bishop Coll., 1962-63. Served with USPHS, 1944-46. Rockefeller fellow, 1944-46; recipient Career Professorship award USPHS, 1963; Guggenheim fellow, 1964. Fellow A.C.P., Am. Coll. Cardiology, Am. Heart Assn. (pres. 1964-65); mem. Am. Soc. Clin. Investigation, Assn. Am. Physicians, Am. Acad. Arts and Scis. Club: Century. Spl. research cardiovascular physiology, human exericse. Home: 39 E 75th St New York NY 10021 Office: 1300 Morris Park Bronx NY 10461

CHAPMAN, CHARLES J., JR., consumer products company executive; b. Buffalo, Sept. 27, 1938; s. Charles J. and Eleanor (Waterman) C.; m. Kristin J. Chapman, June 17, 1961; children: Charles Kristin, Peter, Scott. B.A., Dartmouth Coll., 1961, M.B.A., 1962. Various product mgmt. positions Gen. Foods Corp., White Plains, N.Y., 1962-67; in various mktg. and gen. mgmt. positions Chesebrough Ponds Inc., Greenwich, Conn., 1967—, also dir.; dir. Welch Foods Inc., Concord, Mass., 1980—. Mem. Cosmetic Toiletries and Fragrance Assn. (bd. dirs. 1982—). Republican. Home: 52 Lords Hwy Weston CT 06883 Office: Chesebrough Ponds Inc 33 Benedict Pl Greenwich CT 06883

CHAPMAN, CHRISTIAN ADDISON, foreign service officer; b. Paris, Sept. 19, 1921; s. Percy Addison and Marthe Aline (Simon) C.; m. Anita Ioas, Apr. 2, 1960; children: Catherine, Hillary, Jennifer. A.B., Princeton U., 1948; postgrad., Sorbonne, 1946-47, U. Calif.-Berkeley, 1948. Fgn. service officer, 1950—, vice consul, Casablanca, Morocco, 1951-53, 3d sec., Beirut, 1953, 2d sec., Tehran, Iran, 1953-56, 2d sec., acting chief polit. sect., Saigon, Viet Nam, 1957, 2d sec., chief polit. sect., Vientiane, Laos, 1958-59; officer-in-charge Laos affairs Dept. State, 1959-61; mem. Viet Nam Task Force, chief Far East placement br. personnel, 1962-63; assigned to Nat. War Coll., 1963-64; counselor, dep. U.S. rep. High Authority European Coal and Steel Community, 1964-66; chargé d'affaires Am. Embassy, Luxembourg; dep. asst. sec. gen. polit. affairs NATO, Paris, 1966-67, Brussels, 1968; dir. mil. assistance and sales policy Dept. State, 1968-73; dir. regional affairs Bur. Asian Affairs, 1973-74; minister-counselor, dep. chief mission Am. Embassy, Vientiane, Laos, 1974-75; dep. asst. sec. Bur. Ednl. and Cultural Affairs, Dept. State, Washington, 1975-78; minister-counselor, dep. chief mission Am. embassy, Paris, 1978-82; assigned Dept. State, Washington, 1983—. Decorated Legion of Honor, Mil. medal, Croix de Guerre, Medal of the Resistance, France; Meritorious Service award Dept. State, 1960. Mem. Am. Fgn. Service Assn. Club: Univ. (N.Y.C.). Home: 1527 33d St NW Washington DC 20007 Office: Dept State Washington DC 20520

CHAPMAN, DONALD D., lawyer, ret. navy officer; b. Thalia, Tex., Dec. 9, 1917; s. William Gardner and Bertha (Brown) C.; m. Norene Vernetta Elam, Dec. 30, 1942; children—Ronald Warren, Randall Douglas. B.A., Tex. Tech. Coll., 1939; LL.B., U. Tex., 1942; grad., Army Judge Adv. Sch., 1959. Bar: Tex., Va. bars. Commd. ensign U.S. Navy, 1942, advanced through grades to rear adm., 1968; gen. line duty, 1942-45, comdg. officer, 1945-46, asst. dist. legal officer, New Orleans, 1946-49, staff legal officer to comdr., 1949-51, atty., 1951-55, staff legal officer to comdr. in chief, 1955-58, dir. adminstrv. law div., 1959-63, dist. legal officer, Pearl Harbor, Hawaii, 1963-66, chmn. bd. rev., 1966-67, dir. adminstrv. law div., 1967-68, dep. judge adv. gen., 1968-71. Decorated Legion of Merit and; numerous service and area ribbons; recipient Distinguished Alumnus award Tex. Tech. Coll., 1968. Mem. Va., Tex. state bars, Judge Advocates Assn. (pres. 1975-76), Am., Fed., Inter-Am. bar assns. Home: 3400 N Piedmont St Arlington VA 22207 Office: 2060 14th St N Arlington VA 22201

CHAPMAN, DOUGLAS KENNETH, office equipment executive; b. Toronto, Ont., Can., Jan. 10, 1928; s. Alfred D. and Isabel (Jones) C.; m. Doreen E. Lowe, June 29, 1950; children: Laura Chapman Kohler, Dawna Chapman Bailey, Kevin. Student, U. Toronto, 1946-48, Victoria Coll., 1946-48. Chmn., chief exec. officer ACCO World Corp., Chgo., 1971—; chmn. bd. pres., dir. ACCO Canadian Co. Ltd., Toronto; chmn. bd., dir. ACCO Co. Ltd., Eng., ACCO Nederland N.V., Holland; chmn. Internat. Bus. Controls B.V., Holland; v.p., dir. ACCO mfg. C.A., Venezuela, ACCO Mexicana, S.A. de C.V., Mexico; dir. ACCO Jamaica Ltd., Kingston, Dentsply Internat. Inc., York, Pa. Bd. dirs. Evanston (Ill.) Hosp Corp. Mem. Canadian Office Products Assn. (past pres.), Toronto Stationers Assn. (past pres.), Bus. Record Mfrs. Assn. (past pres., dir.), Wholesale Stationers Assn. (dir.), Nat. Office Products Assn. (past chmn. mfrs. div., dir.). Clubs: Sarasota Surf and Racquet (dir.); (Siesta Key, Fla.); North Shore Country (Glenview, Ill.) (gov.); Bob-O-Link Golf (Highland Park, Ill.); Scarborough Golf and Country (Scarboro, Ont.); Mid-Am., Met. (Chgo.); East India, Devonshire and Pub. Sch. (London); Gator Creek Golf (Sarasota, Fla.). Home: 175 Dickens Rd Northfield IL 60093 Office: 2215 Sanders Rd Suite 250 Northbrook IL 60062

CHAPMAN, EDWARD WILLIAM, communications co. exec.; b. Watrous, Sask., Can., Sept. 30, 1925; s. Edward Russel and Ruth Hester (Nichol) C.; m. Natalie Hrudko, Apr. 20, 1966. Student, U. Man. Pres. Sta. CFCN-TV, Calgary, Alta., Can., 1966—, Sta. CFCN Radio, 1974—; pres., chief exec. officer CFCN Communications, Ltd., 1975—; Vice-chmn. Fed. Cultural Policy Rev. Com. Pres. Theatre Calgary, 1966-78; asso. dir. Calgary Stampede. Club: Calgary Petroleum. Office: CFCN Communications Postal Sta E Calgary AB Canada *

CHAPMAN, ERSKINE CLIFFORD, construction company executive; b. Huntington, W.Va., Apr. 4, 1920; s. Charles Corbett and Hazel Mae (Weekly) C.; m. Helen Frances Naisen, Nov. 27, 1948; children: Richard, David, Janet. B.S. in Civil Engring., U. Cin., 1942. With Caterpillar Tractor Co., 1945—; pres. Caterpillar Overseas S.A., Geneva, 1963-65; v.p. Caterpillar Tractor Co., Peoria, Ill., 1965-78, exec. v.p., 1978—, also dir.; dir. Prospect Nat. Bank, Peoria, Beloit (Wis.) Corp. Served with C.E. U.S. Army, 1942-45. Decorated Bronze Star, Purple Heart. Office: Caterpillar Tractor Co 100 NE Adams St Peoria IL 61629

CHAPMAN, EVELETH WINSLOW, city ofcl.; b. Memphis, Dec. 28, 1939; s. Charles Simonton and Mary (Winslow) C.; children—Evelth Winslow, Susan Louise. B.S., U.S. Naval Acad., 1961; M.S., So. Ill. U., 1981. Commd. lt. U.S. Army; provost marshal (U.S. Army Mil. Police), Ansbach, Ger., 1962-64; command sgt. patrol div. Shelby County (Tenn.) Sheriff's Dept., 1965-70; exec. asst. Office of Mayor, Memphis, 1972-76; dir. police, Memphis, 1976—; Mem. Presdl. Adv. Commn. Law Enforcement. Author: Police Isolation, 1979, Developing Police In-Service Training, 1980. Mem. Nat. Council Christians and Jews, S.A.R., Internat. Assn. Chiefs Police. Episcopalian. Home: 4066 James Rd Memphis TN 38128 Office: 128 Adams Room 276 Memphis TN 38103

CHAPMAN, G. ARNOLD, educator; b. Fresno, Calif., June 26, 1917; s. George Arnold and Marie (Homsy) C.; m. Marguerite M. Nickerson, Aug. 7, 1957; children: John, Anna, Mary. A.B., Fresno State Coll., 1939; M.A., U. Wis., 1941; Ph.D., U.Wis., 1946. Instr. Romance langs. Oberlin Coll., 1945-46; from instr. to prof. Spanish U. Calif., at Berkeley, 1946—. Author: The Spanish American Reception of United States Fiction, 1920-1940, 1966; Contbr. articles to profl. jours. Mem. Instituto Internacional de Literatura Iberoamericana, Assn. Tchrs. of Spanish and Portuguese, Philol. Assn. Pacific Coast. Home: 231 Yale Ave Kensington CA 94708 Office: Dept Spanish and Portuguese Univ California Berkeley CA 94720

CHAPMAN, GRAHAM, performer, writer; b. Leicester, Eng., Jan. 8, 1941; s. Walter and Edith (Towers) C. M.A., Emmanuel Coll., Cambridge U., 1962; M.B., B.Chir., St. Bartholomews Hosp. Med. Sch., 1966. Dir. Python (Monty) Pictures Ltd., Python Prodns., Ltd., Kay-Gee-Bee Music, Ltd., Sea Goat Prodns. Ltd., Oversea Goats, Ltd. Appeared in: revue Cambridge Circus, Broadway, 1964, Ed Sullivan Show; TV series include At Last the 1948 Show, 1967, Monty Python's Flying Circus, 1969—; films include Monty Python and the Holy Grail, 1978, Monty Pythons Life of Brian, 1980, Monty Python Live at the Hollywood Bowl, 1981, The Secret Policeman's Other Ball, 1982; Author: Monty Python and the Holy Grail, 1978, Monty Python's Life of Brian, 1980, A Liar's Autobiography, 1981. Fellow World Wildlife Trust. Mem. Gen. Med. Council, Brit. Actors Equity, AFTRA. Club: St. James. Office: Monty Python Pictures Ltd 6-7 Cambridge Gate 2d Floor London NW 1 England *

CHAPMAN, GROSVENOR, architect; b. Paris, July 9, 1911; s. Frederick Burnham and Helen Grosvenor (Kenyon) C.; m. Rose-Marie de Foix Edmunds, Sept. 25, 1937; children: Alexander Kenyon, Eleanor Preston (Mrs. Edmund Randolph). B.A., Yale, 1934, M.Arch., 1937. Pvt. practice architecture, N.Y.C., 1940-41, Washington, 1946-54; partner Brown, Chapman, Taher & Miller, Washington, 1954-63, Chapman & Miller, 1963-76; mem. NRC, 1965-68; participant Symposium on Nat. Capital, 1979. Mem. Washington Urban Renewal Council, 1957-58; pres. Georgetown Planning Council, 1968-69, Citizens' Assn. Georgetown, 1950-51, 73-76; chmn. Com. of 100 of Federal City, 1968-70; mem. Georgetown Adv. Neighborhood Commn., 1976-77; mem. D.C. steering com. Whitehurst Freeway Corridor Study, 1983-84. Served to lt. comdr. USNR, 1942-45. Recipient award in architecture Washington Bd. Trade, 1960, 63, 68, Am. Assn. Sch. Adminstrs.-AIA, 1969, 74; Excellence in Architecture award Sec. Def., 1972. Fellow AIA (pres. Washington Met. chpt. 1957, local awards 1954, 55, 56, 74); mem. Constrn. Specifications Inst. (dir. 1953-57), Soc. Archtl. Historians. Clubs: Cosmos, Chevy Chase (Washington). Home: 3335 Que St NW Washington DC 20007

CHAPMAN, HOWARD STUART, lawyer; b. Chgo., Oct. 16, 1941; s. I. Philip and Freda (Mostow) C.; m. Diane Nelson, Aug. 12, 1978; children—Michael, David. B.S. in Accountancy with honors, U. Ill., 1963, J.D. with honors, 1967. Bar: Ill. bar 1968, U.S. Supreme Ct. bar 1971; C.P.A., Ill. Asst. to Chgo. atty. John J. Kennelly, 1967-69; asso. firm Altheimer & Gray, Chgo., 1969-71; asst. prof. law Chgo. Kent Coll. Law, Ill. Inst. Tech., 1971-73, asso. prof., 1973-76, prof., 1976—, asso. dean of coll., 1973-79; lectr. De Paul U., 1976—; Arbitrator Better Bus. Bur., Chgo., 1976—. Mem. Chgo. Bar Assn., Ill. Bar Assn., Am. Bar Assn., Decalogue Soc. Lawyers. Home: 516 W Aldine Chicago IL 60657 Office: 77 S Wacker Chicago IL 60606

CHAPMAN, HUGH MCMASTER, banker; b. Spartanburg, S.C., Sept. 11, 1932; s. James Alfred and Martha (Marshall) C.; m. Anne Allston Morrison, Dec. 27, 1958; children: Anne Allston, Rachel Buchanan, Mary Morrison. B.S. in Bus. Adminstrn, U. N.C., 1955. With Citizens & So. Nat. Bank S.C., 1958—, exec. v.p. charge Eastern area S.C., 1965-68, asst. pres., Columbia, 1968-71, pres., 1971-74, chmn. bd., 1974—; also dir.; chmn. bd. C & S Corp., 1974—; mem. Fed. Res. Bd., Charlotte, N.C.; Mem. S.C. Commn. on Higher Edn., 1971-75. Pres. Carolinas United Community Services, 1966; Trustee Benedict Coll., Columbia, S.C. Found. Ind. Colls., Presbyn. Coll., Clinton, S.C., 1973-82, Com. for Econ. Devel., Duke Endowment; ruling elder Presbyn. Ch. Served to 1st lt. USAF, 1955-57. Named Distinguished Eagle Scout Palmetto council Boy Scouts Am., 1972. Mem. S.C. Bankers Assn. (pres. 1976-77), Zeta Psi. Club: Augusta Nat. Golf. Home: 5033 Wittering Dr Columbia SC 29206 Office: PO Box 727 Columbia SC 29222

CHAPMAN, JAMES ALFRED, JR., textile manufacturing company executive; b. Inman, S.C., Sept. 30, 1921; s. James Alfred and Martha (Marshall) C.; m. Martha LeNoir Cloud, June 2, 1945; children: Mary Chambless Chapman Webster, Martha Marshall, Dorothy Dryer, James Alfred IV. B.S. in Chemistry, Davidson Coll., 1943; L.H.D. (hon.), Presbyn. Coll., 1975; LL.D., Wofford Coll., 1976. Plant mgr. Inman Mills, 1946-54, v.p., 1954-64, pres., treas., chief exec. officer, 1964-78, chmn. bd., chief exec. officer, 1978—; also dir.; dir. Fed. Res. Bank Richmond, Textile Hall Corp., Greenville, S.C. Moderator Enoree Presbytery, 1963; Trustee Presbyn. Coll., Clinton, S.C., 1964-73, chmn., 1970-73; trustee Spartanburg County Found., 1964-70, chmn., 1970; trustee Inman-Riverdale Found., 1948—, vice chmn., 1964-79, chmn., 1979—; trustee J. E. Sirrine Textile Found., 1964—, S.C. Found. Ind. Colls., 1965—; chmn. S.C. Found. Ind. Colls., 1974-79. Mem. So. Textile Assn. (pres. 1955-56), S.C. Textile Mfrs. Assn. (pres. 1972-73), Am. Textile Mfrs. Inst. (dir. 1968-70, 74-77, 78—, pres. 1983-84), N.A.M. (dir. 1968-71, 74-76), Phi Delta Theta, S.C. C. of C. (pres. 1964-65). Presbyn. (ruling elder). Home: 825 Plume St Spartanburg SC 29302 Office: Inman Mills Inman SC 29349

CHAPMAN, JAMES LEE, college president; b. Manifest, La., Sept. 19, 1932; s. Randolph and Ida (Manchester) C.; m. Mary Bonita Morgan, July 28, 1956; 1 son, Ronald Scott. A.B., Greenville Coll., 1956; M.A., U. Mich., 1960; Ph.D., Mich. State U., 1966. Dean of men Spring Arbor (Mich.) Jr. Coll., 1956-57; coordinator pub. relations Spring Arbor Coll., 1959-61, dean of students, asso. prof., 1964-67; head resident adviser Mich. State U., 1961-64; asso. dean of students, asst. prof. edn. U. Iowa, 1967-69; higher edn. cons. Cresap, McCormick & Paget, N.Y.C., 1969-70; pres. West Liberty (W.Va.) State Coll., 1970—; dir. First Nat. Bank, Wheeling, W.Va. Contbr. articles to profl. jours. Active Boy Scouts Am., Young Life. Served with AUS, 1957-59. Recipient Young Leader award Spring Arbor Coll. Alumni Assn., 1971; award of recognition Greenville Coll. Alumni Assn., 1971; George Washington Honor medal Freedoms Found. at Valley Forge, 1982; named Speaker of Year, State of W.Va., 1971. Mem. North Central Assn. (dir.). Methodist. Clubs: Rotary, Blue Pencil, Short Circuit. Home: President's Manor West Liberty WV 26074

CHAPMAN, JANET CARTER GOODRICH (MRS. JOHN WILLIAM CHAPMAN), educator, economist; b. Bklyn., May 26, 1922; d. Carter and Florence (Nielsen) Goodrich; m. John William Chapman, Feb. 10, 1943; 1 dau., Hazel Perry. B.A., Swarthmore Coll., 1943; M.A., Columbia, 1951, Ph.D., 1963. Analyst Nat. War Labor Bd., Phila., 1943; economist Bd. of Govs. Fed. Res. System, 1945-46; cons. econ. dept. RAND Corp., Santa Monica, Calif., 1949-69; asso. prof. U. Pitts., 1964-67, prof. econs., 1967—, chmn. econs. dept., 1978—; chmn. com. Russian and East European studies, 1965—, dir., 1970—; vis. lectr. econs. Swarthmore Coll., 1962-63; vis. fellow Australian Nat. U., 1964; Mem. fellowship com. AAUW, 1974-78. Author: Real Wages in Soviet Russia Since 1928, 1963, Wage Variation in Soviet Industry: The Impact of the 1956-60 Wage Reform, 1970; Contbr. to: Economic Trends in the Soviet Union, 1963, The Soviet Economy: A Book of Readings, 1966, 70, The Socialist Price Mechanism, 1977, Women in Russia, 1977, Industrial Labor in the USSR, 1979, Income Inequality, 1979; Asso. editor: Soviet Union, 1975-77; exec. com.: Economic Books: Current Selections, 1978—; Contbr. articles profl. jours. Hannah Leedom fellow, 1946-47; Garth fellow, 1946-47; Russian Inst. grant, 1947-48; N.Y. State fellow AAUW, 1948-49; Am. Council Learned Socs. grant for Soviet studies, 1973; NSF research grant, 1973-74; Nat. Council for Soviet and E. European Research grant, 1982-83. Mem. Am. Econ. Assn., Assn. Advancement Slavic Studies (dir. 1974-79), Assn. for Comparative Econ. Studies (exec. com. 1976-79, pres. 1983), Phi Beta Kappa. Home: 223 Gladstone Rd Pittsburgh PA 15217

CHAPMAN, JOHN STEWART, physician; b. Sweetwater, Tex., Jan. 30, 1908; s. Alfred A. and Ollie (Johnson) C.; m. Marianne Ryan, Nov. 12, 1932; 1 dau., Carolyn. B.A., B.S., So. Methodist U., 1927, M.A., 1928; M.D., U. Tex., Galveston, 1932. Pvt. practice medicine specializing in chest diseases, Dallas, 1943-52; mem. faculty U. Tex. Health Sci. Center, Dallas, 1952-83; prof. medicine Southwestern Med. Sch., 1952-83, prof. emeritus, 1983—; dir. lab. investigation E. Tex. Chest Hosp., Tyler, 1971—; cons. Tb and chest diseases; mem. Gov. Tex. Adv. Bd. Tb, 1965-77, Internat. Exec. Com. Sarcoidosis; Tb credentials com. Tex. Dept. Health Resources.; Mem. bd. publs. So. Meth. U. Author: Byron and the Honourable Augusta, 1975, The History of Southwestern Medical School, 1976, The Atypical Myobacteria and Human Mycobacteriosis, 1977; chief editor: Archives Environ. Health, 1970-76. Mem. com. Am. Assn. Indian Affairs.; mem. Tex. Gov.'s Research Adv. Com. Tex. Air Control Bd., 1982—. Recipient Distinguished Alumnus award So. Meth. U., 1972; Hon. mem. Tex. Pediatric Soc. Mem. Am. Thoracic Soc. (pres. 1966-67), Phi Beta Kappa, Sigma Xi, Alpha Omega Alpha. Home: 3606 Lovers Ln Dallas TX 75225

CHAPMAN, JOSEPH EDGAR, JR., lawyer; b. Columbus, Ga., Sept. 6, 1902; s. Joseph Edgar and Eula (Averett) C.; m. Mary Edwina Smenner, June 8, 1927; children: Joseph Edgar III, Daniel McNeil, Mary Edwina (Mrs. Charles L. Dodds, Jr.); m. Jean Murray Smenner, Jan. 15, 1978. A.B. magna cum laude, U. Ga., 1923; pvt. law tutoring, 1923-24. Bar: Ga. bar 1924. Practiced with father, 1924-42; partner firm Swift, Page & Chapman (P.C.), Columbus, 1942-71; mem. firm Page, Scrantom, Harris, McGlamry & Chapman (P.C.), Columbus, 1971—. An organizer, pres. appeals rev. bd. United Givers, Columbus, 1951-52; Chmn. Muscogee County Democratic Com., 1944-56. Mem. Am. Ga. bar assns., Am. Judicature Soc., Am. Coll. Probate Counsel, Columbus Lawyers Club (pres. 1936), Columbus Execs. Clubs (charter), Columbus C. of C. (dir. 1953), Phi Beta Kappa. Presbyterian (elder 1958). Clubs: Masons, Lions (pres. 1952-53). Defendant in civil rights voting case Primus King vs. Chapman et al, 1941. Home: 1423 Forest Ave Columbus GA 31906 Office: 1043 3d Ave Columbus GA 31901

CHAPMAN, LORING, psychologist, neuroscientist; b. Los Angeles, Oct. 4, 1929; s. Lee E. and Elinore E. (Gundry) Scott; m. Toy Farrar, June 14, 1954; children: Robert, Antony, Pandora. B.S., U. Nev., 1950; Ph.D., U. Chgo., 1955. Lic. psychologist, Oreg., N.Y., Calif. Research fellow U. Chgo., 1952-54; research asso., asst. prof. Cornell U. Med. Coll., N.Y.C., 1955-61; asso. prof. in residence, mem. Neuropsychiat. Inst., UCLA, 1961-65; research prof. U. Oreg., Portland, 1965; br. chief NIH, Bethesda, Md., 1966-67; prof., chmn. dept. behavioral biology Sch. Medicine U. Calif., Davis, 1967-79, prof. psychiatry, 1977—, prof. neurology, 1977—, prof. human physiology, 1979—; vice chmn. div. of sci. basic to medicine, 1976-79; vis. prof. U. Sao Paulo, Brazil, 1959, 77, Univ. Coll., London, 1970, U. Florence, Italy, 1979-80; clin. prof. Georgetown U., 1966-67; mem. Calif. Primate Research Center, 1967—; dir. research Fairview Hosp., 1965-66; cons. Nat. Inst. Neurol. Disease and Stroke, 1961—, Nat. Cancer Inst., 1977—, Nat. Inst. Child Health Devel., 1967—, mem. research and tng. com., 1968-72; cons. NASA, USN, USAF, Calif. State Dept. Corrections. Author: Pain and Suffering, 3 vols, 1967, Head and Brain 2 vols, 1971, (with E.A. Dunlap) The Eye, 1981; contbr. sci. articles to publs. Recipient Thornton Wilson prize, 1958, Career award USPHS, 1964, Commonwealth Fund award, 1970; grantee NASA, 1969—, NIH, 1956—, Nat. Inst. Drug Abuse, 1971—; Forgarty Sr. Internat. fellow, 1980. Mem. Am. Acad. Neurology, Am. Physiol. Soc., Am. Psychol. Assn., Royal Soc. Medicine (London)., Am. Neurol. Assn., Am. Assn. Mental Deficiency, Aerospace Med. Assn., Soc. for Neurosci. Condr. research in field of behavioral and sensory physiology, brain function, neuropharmacology, psychopharmacology. Home: 756 Sycamore St Davis CA 95616 Office: Sch Medicine U Calif Davis CA 95616 *The first taste of the forbidden fruit in the distant gardens of genesis evoked a most deeply human question, beautifully phrased in antiquity, "And we, who are we, anyway?". I have been privileged to spend my working life sharing in the search for this understanding. The pace of progress has seemed rapid, but evil has come along with good, and now the terrible fragility of ourselves and our planet lies bare before us. We feel the need for immediate, practical, and wise answers ever more urgently, for our utmost yearning is to see the full flowering of who we, we human beings, are and can become.*

CHAPMAN, ORVILLE LAMAR, chemist, educator; b. New London, Conn., June 6, 1932; s. Orville Carmen and Mabel Elnora (Tyree) C.; m. Faye Newton Morrow, Aug. 20, 1955 (div. 1980); children: Kenneth, Kevin; m. Susan Elizabeth Parker, June 15, 1981. B.S., Va. Poly. Inst., 1954; Ph.D., Cornell U., 1957. Prof. chemistry Iowa State U., 1957-74; prof. chemistry UCLA, 1974—; Cons. Mobil Chem. Co. Recipient John Wilkinson Teaching award Iowa State U., 1968, award Nat. Acad. Scis., 1974; Founders prize Tex. Instruments; George and Freda Halpern award in photochemistry N.Y. Acad. Scis., 1978. Mem. Am. Chem. Soc. (award in pure chemistry 1968, Arthur C. Cope award 1978, Midwest award 1978, Havinga medal 1982). Home: 1213 Roscomare Rd Los Angeles CA 90024 Office: Dept Chemistry U Calif 405 Hilgard Ave Los Angeles CA 90024

CHAPMAN, REID GILLIS, broadcasting company executive; b. Indpls., July 27, 1920; s. Arthur Reid and Esther Mary (Gillis) C.; m. Janet K. Passwater, Oct. 20, 1942 (dec.); children: Arthur II, Martha Chapman Shull, Mark, Rosalie Chapman Hanfield, James.; m. Mary A. Ayers. Student, Butler U., 1938-40. With radio sta. WAOV, Vincennes, Ind., 1943; with WISH, WISH-TV, Indpls., 1943-56; mgr. WANE Radio, Ft. Wayne, Ind., 1956-58; v.p., gen. mgr. WANE-TV, 1958-82; v.p., dir. Ind. Broadcasting Corp., Ft. Wayne, 1959—, Anthony Wayne Bank. Hon. chmn. Cancer Crusade Month, 1971; mem. Com. of 24, 1967—; Bd. dirs. United Way, Conv. Bur., Parkview Meml. Hosp., Martin Luther King Meml. Fund, Asso. Chs. Ft. Wayne, YMCA, Legal Aid Soc., Ft. Worth Art Mus.; bd. dirs. Jr. Achievement, Ft. Wayne, 1958—, pres., 1962-64; bd. dirs., v.p. Better Bus. Bur., 1962-65; bd. dirs. Goodwill Industries, 1959-65, v.p., 1964-65; adv. bd. Ind. U.-Ft. Wayne. Named to Ind. Broadcast Pioneer Hall of Fame. Mem. Ft. Wayne Advt. Club (past pres., Silver medal award 1971), Ft. Wayne Press Club (past pres., roastmaster and chmn. Gridiron Show), Ft. Wayne C. of C. (past v.p., dir.), Nat. Assn. Broadcasters (dir.), Ind. Broadcasters Assn. (past pres.), Broadcast Pioneers (pres.). Presbyterian (elder). Clubs: Summit, Ft. Wayne Country, Quest (Ft. Wayne). Lodges: Masons; Shriners. Home: 4620 Merriam Creek Dr Fort Wayne IN 46816 Office: 2915 W State Blvd Fort Wayne IN 46808

CHAPMAN, ROBERT B., III, high technology company executive; b. Balt., May 12, 1917; s. Robert B. and Mary (McCord) C.; m. Audrey Lee Frank, Apr. 5, 1941; children: Linda Lee (Mrs. Russell W. Fabiszak), Robert B. IV. B.Engring. with honors, Johns Hopkins, 1938. Registered profl. engr., Md. Structural engr. John E. Greiner Co., Balt., 1938-41; structural engr., missile project mgr., bus. mgr. spl. weapons sales Glenn L. Martin Co., Balt., 1941-50; chief contracts AAI Corp., Balt., 1950-52, dir., 1952-75, exec. v.p., 1956-67, pres., chief exec. officer, 1967-75; prof., v.p. institutional planning and devel. Coppin State Coll., Balt., 1975-82; v.p. contracts and procurement AMAF Industries, Inc., 1982—. Past chmn. Vol. Council for Equal Opportunity; past mem. exec. bd. Balt. area council Boy Scouts Am.; past chmn. Md. Commn. on Dyslexia; past chmn. indsl. adv. council Opportunities Industrialization Center Balt.; past chmn. Met. Balt. Nat. Alliance Businessmen. Served to lt. col. USAAF, 1941-46. Assoc. fellow AIAA; mem. Nat. Security Indsl. Assn. (exec. com., past chmn. bd. trustees, trustee emeritus, hon. life mem.), Nat. Contracts Mgmt. Assn. (cert. profl. contracts mgr.), Orton Dyslexia Soc. (past nat. treas., past nat. dir.), World Future Soc., Alpha Tau Omega (past pres. Johns Hopkins Psi chpt., also Balt. alumni chpt.). Presbyn. (ordained elder). Home: 1505 Cranwell Rd Lutherville MD 21093 *The position which we occupy in society is important to the extent that it furnishes power to accomplish our purpose. The one great purpose in life, which we all share, is to love, help, and support one another.*

CHAPMAN, ROBERT FOSTER, federal judge; b. Inman, S.C., Apr. 24, 1926; s. James Alfred and Martha (Marshall) C.; m. Mary Winston Gwathmey, Dec. 21, 1951; children: Edward, Foster, Winston. B.S., U. S.C., 1945, LL.B., 1949. Bar: S.C. bar 1949. Asso. firm Butler & Moore, Spartanburg, 1949-51; partner firm Butler, Chapman & Morgan, Spartanburg, 1953-71; U.S. dist. judge for S.C., 1971-81, U.S. Circuit judge, 1981—. Chmn. S.C. Republican Party, 1961-63. Served to lt. USNR, 1943-46, 51-53. Fellow Am. Coll. Trial Lawyers. Presbyn. (ruling elder). Home: 1822 Fair St Camden SC 29020 Office: Federal Court House Columbia SC 29202

CHAPMAN, ROBERT MAXWELL, research psychologist; b. Chgo., Aug. 29, 1932; s. Maxwell C. and Margaret (Adkinson) C.; m. Susan Erganian, Apr. 20, 1958; 1 son, Eric Robert Ian. B.A., Oberlin Coll., 1954; M.Sc., Brown U., 1956, Ph.D., 1960. Teaching asst. Brown U., 1954-56, research asst., 1958-59; USPHS, NIMH Walter Reed Army Inst. Research fellows, 1960-61, research asso., 1961—; research scientist Inst. Behavioral Research, 1961-68, Eye Research Found., Bethesda, Md., 1968-74; professorial lectr. Am. U., 1970-71; vis. prof. psychology Northeastern U., 1973-74; prof. psychology U. Rochester, 1974—; dir. Center Visual Sci., 1978—; lectr. mil. medicine and allied sci. course Walter Reed Inst. Reasearch, 1961-62; mem. vision com. NRC. Contbr. articles to profl. jours. Served with AUS, 1957-58. Internat. Congress EEG and Clin. Neurophysiology grantee, 1961; Internat. Congress Psychology grantee, 1966. Fellow AAAS; mem. Optical Soc. Am., Psychonomic Soc., Animal Behavior Soc., Assn. Research Vision and Opthalmology, Eastern Psychol. Assn., Sigma Xi. Home: 310 Canterbury Rd Rochester NY 14607

CHAPMAN, SAMUEL GREELEY, educator; b. Atlanta, Sept. 29, 1929; s. Calvin C. and Jane (Greeley) C.; m. Patricia Hepfer, June 19, 1949 (dec. Dec. 1978); children: Lynn Randall, Deborah Jane. A.B., U. Calif. at Berkeley, 1951, M.A., 1959. Officer Police Dept., Berkeley, 1950-56; police cons. Pub. Adminstrn. Service, Chgo., 1956-59; asst. prof. Sch. Police Adminstrn., Mich. State U., East Lansing, 1959-63; police chief Multnomah County, Portland, Oreg., 1963-66; asst. dir. Pres.'s Commn. on Law Enforcement and Adminstrn. of Justice, Nat. Crime Commn., Washington, 1966-67; prof. dept. polit. sci. U. Okla., Norman, 1967—, chmn. athletic council, 1971-72, 79-80. Author: Dogs in Police Work, 1960, The Police Heritage in England and America, 1962, Police Patrol Readings, 1964, rev. edit., 1970, Perspectives on Police Assaults in the South Central United States, 1974, Short of Merger, 1976, Police Murders and Effective Countermeasures, 1976, Police Dogs in America, 1979; contbr. chpts. to books, articles to profl. jours. Mem. Norman City Council, 1972—, mayor pro-tem, 1975-76, 79-80, 81—. Mem. Alpha Delta Phi. Republican. Home: 2421 Hollywood St Norman OK 73069 Office: Dept Polit Sci U Okla 455 Lindsey St Room 205 Norman OK 73019

CHAPMAN, THOMAS WILLIAM, hospital administrator; b. Providence, May 17, 1945; s. Thomas Leon and Alice (Bridgeforth) C.; m. Erica Lynne Battle, July 29, 1972; children: Justin Marc, Stacee Nichole, Darrian Anthony. B.A., St. Anselm's Coll., Manchester, N.H., 1968; M.P.H., Yale U., 1971. Adminstrv. resident Children's Hosp. Med. Center, Boston, 1971-72; health care cons. Arthur D. Little Inc., Cambridge, Mass., 1973-75, now sr. cons., Lester Gorsline Assos., San Rafael, Calif., 1975-76; asst. exec. dir. Group Health Assn., Washington, 1976-78; pres. Provident Hosp., Inc., Balt., 1978—; lectr. Howard U. Sch. Bus., Washington, Johns Hopkins Sch. Health and Hygiene. Mem. adv. bd. Md. Public Broadcasting Network; bd. dirs. Hilltop Green Maintenance Corp., Richmond, Calif., 1973-74. Named to Ebony mag. Success Library, 1974. Mem. Am. Hosp. Assn., Md. Hosp. Assn., Am. Public Health Assn., Am. Coll. Hosp. Adminstrs. Home: 8993 Wetbanks Ct Columbia MD 21045 Office: 2600 Liberty Heights Ave Baltimore MD 21275 *There are many people in the world who are extremely intelligent, but so very few who are effective.*

CHAPMAN, WARREN HOWE, urologist; b. Chgo., Oct. 30, 1925; s. Frank Amos and Katharine (Howe) C.; m. Barbara E. Brueggeman, Sept. 16, 1950; children—Frank, Arthur, Katharine, Marney, Phillip. B.S., Mass. Inst. Tech., 1946; M.D., U. Chgo., 1952. Intern St. Luke's Hosp., Chgo.; resident in urology U. Chgo., 1953-57; practice medicine specializing in urology, Bellingham, Wash., 1957-66; asst. prof. to prof. urology U. Wash., Seattle, 1966—. Author: The Urinary System, an Integrated Approach, 1973; Editorial bd.: Jour. Urology, 1977; Contbr. articles to sci. jours. Served with USNR, 1944-46. Mem. AMA, Wash., King County med. assns., Am. Urol. Assn., Western Urol. Forum. Unitarian. Home: 1212 E Hamlin St Seattle WA 98102 Office: Dept of Urology RL 10 University of Washington Seattle WA 98195

CHAPMAN, WAYNE ELLSWORTH, lawyer; b. Chgo., Aug. 30, 1932; s. John William and Eva (Reece) C.; m. Helen M. Boyes, Sept. 23, 1961; children: Steven, Karen, Paul, Emily. B.A., U. Mich., 1954; LL.B., Columbia U., 1957. Bar: N.Y. 1957. Mem. Cravath, Swaine & Moore, N.Y.C., 1957-64, ptnr., 1965—. Mem. ABA, Assn. Bar City N.Y., N.Y. State Bar Assn. Clubs: Wall St. (N.Y.C.); Quogue Beach, Shinnecock Yacht; Quogue Field (Quogue, N.Y.).

CHAPMAN, WILLIAM A., business executive; b. County of Essex, Eng., 1924;, 1943. With Ranco Inc., 1960—, mng. dir. U.K. ops., 1969, mng. dir., Europe, 1975, exec. v.p. European ops., 1976, vice chmn. bd., 1978, pres., chief operating officer, dir., 1979—. Address: 555 Metro Pl N Suite 550 Dublin OH 43017

CHAPMAN, WILLIAM CLOUD, baritone; b. Los Angeles, Apr. 30; s. William Cloud and Augusta Jane (Kiel) C.; m. Irene Veronica Meyer, Sept. 15, 1957; children—Alexa Maria, Teren Cloud. B.A. in Drama, U. So. Calif. Propr. vocal studio, Los Angeles, 1967—; mem. faculty U.S. Internat. U. Performing Arts Sch., San Diego, 1971-79. Leading baritone, N.Y.C. Opera, 1956—, also other opera houses, U.S. and Europe; opened, Spoleto Festival as; Macbeth in: Macbeth, 1957, Broadway appearances as; Charlie in: Shenandoan, 1978-79; also in: N.Y.C. Center revival of South Pacific; appeared as Frank Maurrant for, N.Y.C. Opera, also PBS-TV; TV appearances on Wonderful World of Disney; Columnist: the Singing Actors' Notes, Voice Mag. Rockefeller grantee; recipient various certs. appreciation. Mem. Screen Actors Guild, Actors Equity, Am. Guild Variety Artists, AFTRA, Nat. Assn. Tchrs. Singing.

CHAPMAN, WILLIAM PAUL, automatic control manufacturing company executive; b. Oakland, Calif., Oct. 19, 1919; s. William Porteus and Lucy Agnes (McCarthy) C.; m. Beth Hartley, June 26, 1943; children: Bruce H., Craig S., Brian A., Dean O. B.S., U. Calif. at Berkeley, 1943; M.S., Purdue U., 1947. Registered profl. engr., Pa., Wis. Research engr. U.S. Steel Co., Pitts., 1947-50, field engr., 1950-56; adminstrv. dir. research Johnson Controls Inc. (formerly Johnson Service Co.), Milw., 1956-58, dir. research and devel., 1958-64, v.p. ops., 1964-80, v.p. tech., 1980—; dir. Johnson Brass and Machine Foundry, Sohweiger Industries.; mem. adminstrv. bd. Mgmt. Resources Assn. (formerly Employers Assn. Milw.), 1973-78; mem. steering com. Milw. Mayor's Sci. and Tech. Utilization Council; mem. panel for bldg. tech. Nat. Bur. Standards, 1980-83; mem. adv. council Coll. Engring., Marquette U.; mem. tech. adv. com. Milw. Sch. Engring.; chmn. dist. econ. progress authority Met. Milw. Sewerage Dist. Contbr. articles to profl. jours. Mem. adv. bd. St. Michael's Hosp., Milw., pres., 1978-80; bd. dirs. U. Wis.-Milw. Found., St. Joseph's and St. Michael's Hosp., Milw., Milw. Urbaan League. Served to capt. AUS, 1943-45; ETO. Decorated Purple Heart with cluster, Silver Star; named Engr. of Yr. Engrs. and Scientists of Milw., 1977. Fellow ASHRAE (dir. 1969-77, officer 1971-77, pres. 1976-77, Distinguished Service award 1969, F. Paul Anderson medal 1983); mem. Nat. Soc. Profl. Engrs., Sigma Xi. Clubs: Town, Univ. (Milw.). Patentee in field. Home: 8260 N Gray Log Ln Milwaukee WI 53217 Office: PO Box 591 Milwaukee WI 53201 *Set your goals in terms of measurable accomplishments that are attainable and worthwhile, then strive for excellence in all your endeavors.*

CHAPOTON, JOHN EDGAR, lawyer, government official; b. Galveston, Tex., May 18, 1936; s. Otis Byron and Grace Donaldson (Wayman) C.; m. Sarah Eastham, Jan. 5, 1963; children: John Edgar, Clare Eastham. Student, Washington and Lee U., 1954-55; B.B.A. with honors, U. Tex., 1958, LL.B., 1960. Bar: Tex. 1960. Asso. firm Andrews, Kurth, Campbell & Jones, Houston, 1961-69; with Dept. Treasury, Washington, 1969-72, tax legis. counsel, 1970-72, asst. sec. for tax policy, 1981—; partner firm Vinson & Elkins, Houston, 1972-81; officer sect. of taxation State Bar of Tex. Mem. asso. bd. Tex. Children's Hosp., Houston. Served as 2d lt. U.S. Army, 1960-61. Mem. ABA (sect. taxation), Am. Law Inst. Republican. Episcopalian. Office: Room 3120 Dept Treasury Washington DC 20220

CHAPPELEAR, CLAUDE KEPLAR, data systems corporation executive; b. Macomb, Ill., Mar. 1, 1937; s. Claude S. and Fannie Virginia (McCall) C.; m. Carol Charlene Pearson. B.A., Northwestern U., 1959, J.D., 1965. Bar: Tex. With Breed, Abbott & Morgan, N.Y.C., 1965-69, LTV Corp., Dallas, 1969-70; sec., v.p., gen. counsel Ramada Europe, Inc., Brussels, 1971-73; gen. counsel, v.p., sec. Ramada Inns, Inc., Phoenix, 1973-78; v.p., gen. counsel, sec. Electronic Data Systems Corp., Dallas, 1978—. Served to lt. USNR, 1955-73. Mem. ABA, N.Y. State Bar Assn., Am. Assn. Corp. Secs., Pi Kappa Alpha. Republican. Methodist. Office: Electronic Data Systems Corp 7171 Forest Ln Dallas TX 75230

CHAPPELL, ANNETTE M., university dean; b. Washington, Oct. 31, 1939; d. Joseph John and Annette B. (Harley) C.; m. Brian Thomas Flower, Sept. 3, 1960 (div. Mar. 1983). B.A. in English, U. Md., 1962, M.A., 1964, Ph.D., 1970. Lectr. European div. U. Md., Eng., 1965-66, instr. English, College Park, 1966-69; asst. prof. English Towson (Md.) State U., 1969-72, assoc. prof., 1972-79, prof., 1979—, spl. asst. to pres., affirmative action officer, 1974-77, dean humanistic, social and managerial studies, 1977-82, dean Coll. Liberal Arts, 1982—. Contbr. articles to profl. jours. and book revs. to Ms Mag., Balt. Sun. Lay reader, chalicist All Saints Episcopal Ch., Reisterstown, Md., 1973—; pres. Baltimore County Commn. for Women, 1977-79; bd. dirs. Baltimore County Sexual Assault and Domestic Violence Center, 1978—, pres., 1980-82. Mem. AAUP, MLA, Am. Assn. Higher Edn., Council Colls. Arts and Scis., Exec. Women's Council Md. (1st v.p. 1980, pres. 1981). Home: 200 Towsontown Ct Towson MD 21204 Office: Towson State U Towson MD 21204

CHAPPELL, CLOVIS GILLHAM, JR., lawyer; b. Waverly, Tenn., Sept. 13, 1911; s. Clovis Gillham and Cecil (Hart) C.; m. Pauline Mikell LaRoche, Oct. 28, 1938; children: Carolyn (Mrs. D.W. Light III), Polly (Mrs. F. Ferrell Davis), Marian (Mrs. David Scott Miles). Student, Southwestern at Memphis, 1929-30; B.A., So. Methodist U., 1934, LL.B., 1936. Bar: Tex. 1936. Landman Humble Oil & Refining Co., 1938-44; atty. Baker & Botts, Houston, 1944-50; partner firm Stubbeman, McRae, Sealy & Laughlin, Midland, 1950-59, Lynch, Chappell, Allday & Alsup, 1959—; Past sec., dir. Tex. Am. Oil Corp., Midland; dir. Comml. Bank & Trust Co., Midland. Contbr. articles to profl. jours. Past mem. bd. visitors So. Methodist U. Law Sch. Fellow Am. Coll. Probate Counsel; mem. Am., Tex., Midland County bar assns., Pi Kappa Alpha. Methodist. Home: 1605 Bedford Dr Midland TX 79701 Office: First Nat Bank Bldg Midland TX 79701

CHAPPELL, FRED DAVIS, English language educator, author; b. Canton, N.C., May 28, 1936; s. James Taylor and Anne Mae (Davis) C.; m. Susan Nicholls, Aug. 2, 1959; 1 son, Christopher. B.A., Duke U., 1961, M.A., 1963. Prof. English U. N.C., Greensboro, 1964—. Author: It Is Time, Lord, 1963, The Inkling, 1965, Dagon, 1968, The World Between the Eyes, 1971, The Gaudy Place, 1972, Midquest, 1981, Moments of Light, 1982, Castle Tzingal, 1984; adv. editor: Skyhook, 1958-59, Red Clay Reader, 1964-65, Greensboro Rev, 1964-81, Appalachian Heritage, 1977-81. Recipient Roanoke-Chowan Poetry prize N.C. Lit. Assn., 1979, Prix de Meilleur Des Lettres Etrangers, 1973, N.C. award in lit. State of N.C., 1980; NDEA fellow, 1961-63; Rockefeller grantee, 1967-68; Nat. Acad. Arts and Letters grantee, 1968. Democrat. Office: English Dept U NC Greensboro NC 27412 *There is no success in literary composition, only guaranteed failure. One perseveres because the discipline itself is endlessly interesting.*

CHAPPELL, JOHN CHARLES, lawyer; b. Minden, Nebr., Jan. 28, 1935; s. Charles Arthur and Eletta Hope (Pattison) C.; m. Joyce Joan Dawson, Sept. 1, 1957; children: Laura, Pamela, James, Allegra. B.S. in Edn., U. Nebr., 1956; LL.B., NYU, 1960. Bar: N.Y. 1960. Summer assoc. firm Dewey, Ballantine, Bushby, Palmer & Wood, N.Y.C., 1959; assoc. Dewey, Ballentine, Bushby, Palmer & Wood, N.Y.C., 1960-68; ptnr. Dewey, Ballantine, Bushby, Palmer & Wood, N.Y.C., 1968—. Served to 1st lt. U.S. Army, 1957. Root-Tilden scholar NYU, 1956. Mem. ABA, N.Y. State Bar Assn., Assn. Bar City N.Y. Club: Down Town Assn. (N.Y.C.). Lodge: Masons. Home: 2 Galloping Hill Circle Holmdel NJ 07733 Office: Dewey Ballantine Bushby Palmer & Wood 140 Broadway New York NY 10005

CHAPPELL, ROBERT HARVEY, JR., lawyer; b. Clarksville, Va., Nov. 28, 1926; s. Robert Harvey and Edna Kathryn (Lumpkin) C.; m. Ann Marie Callahan, Nov. 25, 1950; 1 son, Robert Harvey III. B.S., Coll. William and Mary, 1948, B.C.L., 1950. Bar: Va. 1949. Partner firm Christian, Barton, Epps, Brent & Chappell, Richmond, Va., 1950—; dir., gen. counsel Thalhimer Bros., Richmond. Editor: Ins. Counsel Jour, 1963-72. Mem. Richmond Independence Bicentennial Commn., 1971-80; bd. dirs. Crippled Children's Hosp., pres., 1974-76; bd. dirs. Richmond Eye Hosp.; trustee Westminster-Canterbury, 1979-83; rector Coll. William and Mary, 1972-76, bd. visitors, 1968-76. Served with USAAF, 1944-46. Recipient Alumni Medallion Soc. of Alumni of Coll. of William and Mary, 1968. Mem. Va. State Bar (pres. 1977-78), Va. Bar Assn., Am. Bar Assn. (gov. 1978-81, chmn. standing com. on fed. judiciary 1977-78), Richmond Bar Assn. (pres. 1969-70), Am. Law Inst., Am. Bar Found., Am. Coll. Trial Lawyers (bd. regents 1979—), Internat. Assn. Ins. Counsel, Soc. of Alumni Coll. of William and Mary (pres. 1963-64), William and Mary Law Sch. Assn. (pres. 1951-52), Soc. Sons of the Revolution Va. (pres. 1970-72), Order of Coif, Phi Beta Kappa (pres. chpt. 1978-81), Omicron Delta Kappa, Pi Kappa Alpha. Clubs: Country, Commonwealth, Downtown (pres. 1976-77). Home: 4607 Menokin Rd Richmond VA 23225 Office: 1200 Mutual Bldg Richmond VA 23219

CHAPPELL, VERE CLAIBORNE, philosophy educator; b. Rochester, N.Y., Mar. 22, 1930; s. Vere Chambers and Edyth (Brown) C.; m. Sally Anderson, June 7, 1951 (div. June, 1963); children: Jennifer Helen, Jonathan Claiborne, David Lincoln; m. Sheryl Berglund, July 31, 1963; children: Vere Chambers II, Melissa, Addison Ward; step-children: Clayton Scott Templin, Jaime Templin Strandberg. B.A., Yale U., 1951, M.A., 1953, Ph.D., 1958; student, U. Heidelberg, Germany, 1953-54. Instr. Yale, 1954-57; instr. U. Chgo., 1957-61, asst. prof., 1961-63, assoc. prof., 1963-68, prof. philosophy, 1968-70, acting chmn. philosophy dept., 1964-65; prof., head philosophy U. Mass., 1970-74, acting assoc. provost, dean, 1974-76, assoc. provost, 1977-78, prof. philosophy, 1978—; vis. prof. Ind. U., 1967, U. Ill. at Chgo., 1967, U. Ill. at Urbana, 1968, Notre Dame U., 1969, U. So. Calif., 1969-70, Smith Coll., 1973, 74, Mt. Holyoke Coll., 1982, 83; Mem. Council for Philos. Studies, 1973-78. Editor: The Philosophy of Mind, 1962, The Philosophy of David Hume, 1963, Ordinary Language, 1964, Hume, 1966; mng. editor: Rev. Metaphysics, 1954-56; asst. editor: Ethics, 1958-61; asst.-treas.: Philos. Quar, 1959-69; cons. editor, Random House-Knopf, 1963-74. Fulbright fellow, 1953-54; Nat. Endowment for Humanities fellow, 1970. Mem. Am. Philos. Assn. (chmn. research and publs. subcom.), Aristotelian Soc., Royal Inst. Philosophy. Home: 17 Harkness Rd Pelham MA 01002 Office: Philosophy Dept Bartlett U Mass Amherst MA 01003

CHAPPELL, WALTER, photographer, artist; b. Portland, Oreg., June 8, 1925; s. Elmer and Margaret Louise (Willis) C.; m. Nancy Dickinson Barrett, Jan. 1960 (div. 1974); children: Dharma Chakravarty, Theo, Aryan, Piki, Robin; m. Suzanne Marie Lichau, Aug. 1977 (div. Aug. 1983); 1 dau., Riversong. Student of Minor White. Curator exhbns. and prints George Eastman House of Internat. Mus. Photography, Rochester, N.Y., 1957-61; founder, dir. Assn. of Heliographers Gallery Archives, N.Y.C., 1962-65. One-man shows include, George Eastman House of Internat. Mus. Photography, 1957, one-man shows including, Smithsonian Instn., Washington, 1959, one-man shows include, Mus. de Vill de Paris, 1973, One-man shows include, Volcano Art Gallery, Hawii, 1976, one-man shows include, Vision Gallery, Boston, 1978, Phila. Mus. Art, Santa Fe Ctr. for Photography, 1979, Nicholas Potter Gallery, Santa Fe, 1980, Nicholas Potter Gallery, Santa Fe, New Gallery, Tacos, N.Mex., 1982, Scheinbaum & Russek Gallery of Photography, Santa Fe, 1983; numerous others; 25 yr. retrospective, Colo. Ctr. for Photog. Art, Denver, 1980, exhibited in group shows at, George Eastman House Mus., 1959, Mus. Modern Art, N.Y.C., 1960, 79-81, Whitney Mus. Am. Art, 1974, travelling exhbn., Europe, 1981-84, represented in permanent collections, Smithsonian Instn., George Eastman House Internat. Mus. Photography, Mus. Modern Art, N.Y.C., U. Los Angeles, MIT, Polaroid Corp., Cambridge, Mass., Exchange Nat. Bank of Chgo., Ind. U., Whitney Mus. Am. Art, U. Nebr., Houston Mus. Fine Arts, Fogg Mus., Harvard U., Cambridge, Stanford Mus. Art, U. Ariz.; also others; author: Logue and Glyphs 1943-49, 1951; author-designer: Gestures of Infinity, 1957, Under the Sun, 1960; author-artist: Aperture Quar., 1957-81, Metaflora Portfolio, 1980, Collected Light: The Body of Work, 1984. Served with U.S. Army, 1943-47. Recipient peer awards in creative photography Friends of Photography, Carmel, Calif., 1980-83; Frank Lloyd Wright Taliesin fellow, Ariz., 1953-54; Nat. Endowment for Art photographers fellow, Hawaii, 1977, N.Mex., 1980. Address: PO Box 35 Embudo NM 87531

CHAPPELL, WARREN, artist, author; b. Richmond, Va., July 9, 1904; s. Samuel Michael and Mary Lillian (Hardie) C.; m. Lydia Anne Hatfield, Aug. 28, 1928. B.A., U. Richmond, 1926, D.F.A. (hon.), 1968; student, Art Students League, N.Y.C., 1926-30, Offenbacher Werkstatt, Ger., 1931-32. Tchr. Art Students League, 1932-35, mem. bd. control, 1927-30; instr. Colorado Springs Fine Arts Center, 1935-36; artist-in-residence U. Va., 1979—. Typographic and decorative designer for mags., 1926-35; book designer and illustrator, 1936—; prin. works illus. include: Adventures of Don Quixote, 1939, The Temptation of St. Anthony, 1943, A History of Tom Jones, 1982, Shakespeare: Tragedies, 1944, The Complete Novels of Jane Austen, 1950, Moby Dick, 1976, Gulliver's Travels, 1977, The Complete Adventures of Tom Sawyer and Huckleberry Finn, 1979, The Magic Flute, 1962, Bottom's Dream, 1969, Anatomy of Lettering, 1934, A Short History of the Printed Word, 1970, The Living Alphabet, 1975, They Say Stories, 1960; designer of typefaces: Lydian, 1938, Trajanus, 1940. Recipient Goudy award Rochester Inst. Tech., N.Y., 1970. Mem. Master Drawings Assn., Lawn Soc. of U. Va., Chilmark Assos. (Mass.), Phi Beta Kappa. Home: 500 Court Sq Charlottesville VA 22901 Studio: Alderman Library U Va Charlottesville VA 22903

CHAPPELL, WILLIAM VENROE, JR., congressman; b. Kendrick, Fla., Feb. 3, 1922; s. William Venroe and Laura (Kemp) C.; children: Judith Jane Chappell Gadd, Deborah Kay Chappell Bond, William Venroe 3d, Christopher Clyde. B.A., U. Fla., 1947, LL.B., 1949, J.D., 1967. Bar: Fla. 1949. Mem. Sturgis and Chappell (and predecessors), Ocala, Fla., 1949—; prosecuting atty., Marion County, 1950-54; mem. Fla. Ho. of Reps. from Marion and other counties, 1955-65, 67-68, speaker, 1961-63; mem. 91st-98th congresses from 4th Dist. Fla. Served with USNR, 1942-46. Named Most Valuable Mem. Fla. Ho. Reps., 1967, Most Effective in Debate, 1967. Mem. Am., Fla., Marion County, Inter-Am. bar assns., Am. Trial Lawyers Assn., Acad. Fla. Trial Lawyers, Am. Legion. Democrat. Methodist. Lodges: Masons; Shriners; Lions; Elks. Office: 2468 Rayburn House Office Bldg Washington DC 20515

CHAPPIE, GENE A., congressman, rancher; b. Sacramento, Mar. 28, 1920; children: Susan Thomas, Eugene A. II, John, Tina McClendon, Linda Reilly. Grad., Sacramento High Sch., 1938. El Dorado County supr., 1950-64; mem. Calif. Legislature, from 1964; chmn. Republican Caucus, from 1964; mem. 97th Congress from 1st Dist. Calif., 98th Congress from 2d Dist. Calif. Served to capt. AUS; PTO, Korea. Mem. Am. Legion, Sons of Italy, VFW. Club: Rotary.

CHAPPLE, JOHN THAYER, insurance company executive; b. San Francisco, Feb. 11, 1920; s. William T. and Dora (Thayer) C.; m. Betsy Ann Gordon, Apr. 29, 1945; children: David T., Gordon D. B.A., Stanford U., 1942, M.B.A., 1947. Cert. rev. appraiser and registered mortgage underwriter. Successively mortgage loan rep., supr., dist. mgr., regional dir., asst. v.p. Pacific Mutual Life Ins., Newport Beach, Calif., 1955-74, v.p. mortgage loans, 1974-80, v.p. realty investments, 1980-81, sr. v.p., 1981—. Vice pres., bd. dirs. Orange County Assn. Mental Health, Santa Ana, Calif., 1981—. Served to lt. USN, 1942-46. Mem. Am. Inst. Real Estate Appraisers, Calif. Mortgage Bankers Assn., Nat. Assn. Rev. Appraisers and Mortgage Underwriters, Urban Land Inst. (council and com. mem.), Internat. Council Shopping Centers, Nat. Assn. Corp. Real Estate Execs., Mortgage Bankers Assn. Club: Balboa Bay. Home: 1852 Las Brisas Dr Santa Ana CA 92705 Office: 700 Newport Center Dr Newport Beach CA 92660

CHAPPLE, THOMAS LESLIE, lawyer; b. Canandaigua, N.Y., Nov. 28, 1947; s. Howard Leslie and Elizabeth (Stearns) C.; m. Shelly Smith, July 17, 1982; children: Adam Roger, Hannah Elizabeth. B.A., Cornell U., 1970; J.D., Albany Law Sch., 1973. Bar: N.Y. 1974, U.S. Supreme Ct. 1981. Atty assoc. Nixon, Hargrave, Devans & Doyle, Rochester, N.Y., 1973-76; sec., asst. gen. counsel Gannett Co., Inc., Rochester, N.Y., 1977-79, assoc. gen. counsel., sec., 1979-81, v.p., assoc. gen. counsel, sec., 1981—; sec. The Gannett Found., 1983—; dir. Newspaper Printing Corp., Nashville, 1980—. Mem. ABA, Assn. Corp. Counsel, N.Y. State Bar Assn., Sigma Pi. Republican. Methodist. Office: Gannett Co Inc Lincoln Tower Rochester NY 14604

CHARACHE, SAMUEL, hematologist; b. N.Y.C., Jan. 12, 1930; s. Herman and Deborah (Simmons) C.; m. Patricia Connamacher, June 11, 1951; 1 dau., Barbara Elizabeth. B.A., Oberlin (Ohio) Coll., 1951; M.D., N.Y. U., 1955. Diplomate: Am. Bd. Internal Medicine (hematology), Am. Bd. Pathology (hematology). Intern Mt. Sinai Hosp., N.Y.C., 1955-56; clin. asso. Nat. Cancer Inst., 1956-58; resident in internal medicine U. Pa. Hosp., 1958-60; mem. faculty Johns Hopkins U. Med. Sch., 1966—, prof. medicine, 1978—, dir. hematology div., dept. lab. medicine, 1979—. Mem. A.C.P., Assn. Am. Physicians, Am. Soc. Hematology. Office: B 119 PNC Bldg Johns Hopkins Hosp Baltimore MD 21205

CHARANIS, PETER, educator; b. Lemnos, Greece, Aug. 15, 1908; s. George and Chresanthy (Stroumtsos) C.; m. Madeleine Schiltz, Aug. 5, 1939; children—Alexandra, Anthony. B.A., Rutgers U., 1931, LL.D. (hon.), 1980; Ph.D., U. Wis., 1935; postgrad., U. Brussels, Belgium, 1936-38, U. Thessalonica, 1972. Faculty Rutgers U., 1938—, prof., 1949-63, Voorhees prof. history, 1963-76, emeritus, 1976—, chmn. dept., 1964-66; Vis. prof. U. Wis., 1950-51; vis. scholar Harvard at Dumbarton Oaks, 1956-57, 78-79, former mem. bd. scholars; mem. Am. Nat. Com. Byzantine Studies, 1963—; editorial staff Byzantinoslavica; former mem. com. Gennadeion, Am. Sch. Classical Studies, Athens. Author: monographs on history Byzantine Empire and medieval Near East; Editorial adv. bd.: Greek-Roman and Byzantine Studies, 1956-68, The Greek Orthodox Theological Rev, Neo-Hellenika; cons. editor: Comparative Studies in Society and History, 1958-73; gen. editor: Rutgers Byzantine series. Trustee Holy Cross Greek Orthodox Theol. Sch. Guggenheim fellow, 1956-57; Decorated comdr. Royal Order of Phoenix, Greece).; Recipient Distinguished Research award Adv. Bd. Research and Grad. Edn.; Lindback Found award for distinguished teaching. Mem. Soc. Macedonian Studies (hon.), Am. Hist. Assn., Acad. Athens (corr.), Medieval Acad. Am., Soc. Ch. History. Home: 105 N 7th Ave Highland Park NJ 08904 Office: Rutgers U New Brunswick NJ 08903

CHARD, CHESTER STEVENS, archeologist, educator; b. N.Y.C., Sept. 15, 1915; s. Walter Goodman and Kathleen (Stevens) C.; m. Jeanne W. Bell, Apr. 16, 1974; children by previous marriage—Carleton S., Kenneth W., Frederick H., Robert L., Alan D., Susan L. A.B., Harvard, 1937; Ph.D., U. Calif. at Berkeley, 1953. Vis. lectr. anthropology U. Wash., 1954-56; faculty U. Wis., 1958—, prof. anthropology, 1963—, chmn. dept., 1962-64; founder, editor Arctic Anthropology, 1962-74; cons. Russian translation program Arctic Inst. N.Am., 1960—. Author: Kamchadal Culture, 1961, Northeast Asia in Prehistory, 1974, Man in Prehistory, 1969. Served to lt. USNR, 1942-46. Fellow Am. Anthrop. Assn., AAAS, Royal Anthrop. Inst., Explorers Club of N.Y.; mem. Prehistoric Soc., Soc. Am. Archaeology, Arctic Inst. N.Am., Far Eastern Prehistory Assn., Sigma Xi. Office: Dept Anthropology U Wis Madison WI 53706

CHARD, ROLAND TURNER, banker; b. Falmouth, Eng., Oct. 7, 1907; came to U.S., 1908, naturalized, 1918; s. Edward Turner and Ethel (Reader) C.; m. Kathleen Mabel Cottell, Aug. 31, 1931; children—John T., David E., Kathleen Susan; m. Annette Buckley Everett, June 23, 1979. Student, Rutgers U., 1925-26. With Nat. State Bank, Elizabeth, N.J., 1928—, v.p., 1956—, dir., 1959—; also cashier; pres., dir. Rosedale & Linden Cemetery, Linden, N.J.; sec.-treas., dir. Central Dist. Holding Co., Elizabeth; sec.-treas. Garden State Bancorp, Inc.; pres. Caleb Devel. Corp., 1978—; exec. sec. Elizabeth Devel. Co.; dir. Nat. State Corp., United Armored Carrier, Eldib Engrng. & Research, Inc., Summit, N.J. Mem. Bd. Edn., Roselle, N.J., 1954-65, pres., 1959-60; mem. Commn. Recreation, Roselle, 1958-63; treas., dir. Elizabeth Community Action for Econ. Opportunity, 1964-67; treas. United Fund, Elizabeth, 1964-69, pres., 1969—; treas. N.J. Citizens Transp. Council, 1973—; Bd. dirs. N.J. Taxpayers Assn.; pres., bd. mgrs. St. Elizabeth Hosp. Clubs: Suburban Golf (Union, N.J.); Elizabeth Town and Country; Elmora Country (Elizabeth). Home: 219 W 6th Ave Roselle NJ 07203 Office: 68 Broad St Elizabeth NJ 07207

CHARDON, CARLOS EUGENIO, lawyer, edn. and mgmt. cons., govt. ofcl. P.R.; b. Maracay, Venezuela, Jan. 17, 1939; s. Carlos E. and Dolores (Lopez) C. B.A. magna cum laude, U. P.R., 1961; postgrad. fellow, U. P.R. to Syracuse (N.Y.) U., 1962-65; grad. research asst. social studies, Syracuse U., 1962-65. Instr., research asst. social studies U. P.R., Mayaguez, 1965-68; spl. aide to gov. P.R., 1969; exec. dir. P.R. Bd. Edn., 1969-71; liaison rep. HEW-P.R. office, 1971-76; dir. fed. programs Commonwealth Office Gov. P.R., 1977; sec. edn. of P.R., 1977-81; asst. sec. for tax policy Dept. Treasury, Washington, 1981—; pres. Atlantic Coll., 1980—, Interam. Acad. of P.R., 1980-81, P.R. Conservatory of Music, 1980—, Technos Corp., 1980—; pres. Conf. Ministers Edn. Iberoam., 1977, Commn. for Accreditation Pvt. Schs., 1981; del. White House Conf. Children, 1970; cons. Ponce Mus. of Art, 1980—. Pres. campaign P.R. Heart Assn., 1977-78, bd. dirs., 1977—, pres., 1981; bd. dirs. Festival Casals P.R., 1979. Decorated Isabel La Católica medal, Spain, 1978; recipient Edn. medal Office Ibero-Am. Edn., 1978. Mem. Edn. Commn. States, Council Chief State Sch. Officers, Caribbean Studies Assn., Iberoam. Office Edn., Inst. Ednl. Leadership (adv. bd. 1978—).

CHARFOOS, LAWRENCE SELIG, lawyer; b. Detroit, Dec. 7, 1935; s. Samuel and Charlotte (Salkin) C. Student, U. Mich., 1953-56; LL.B., Wayne State U., 1959. Bar: Mich. 1959, Ill. 1965. Pvt. practice, Detroit, 1960-63; pres., partner Charfoos, Christensen, Gilbert & Archer (P.C.), Detroit, 1967—; theatrical producer, legitimate theater mgr., Chgo., 1963-67; Cons. med.-legal problems Mich. Med. Soc., Mich. Hosp. Council, State Bar Mich., Am. Trial Lawyers Assn.; dir., trustee Sta. WTVS. Author: The Medical Malpractice Case: A Complete Handbook, 1974, Daughters at Risk, 1981; Contbr. articles to profl. jours. Trustee Lawrence S. Charfoos Found. Elected to Inner Circle of Advocates, 1973. Mem. ABA, Mich. Bar Assn., Detroit Bar Assn. (dir.), Am. Bd. Profl. Liability Attys. (founder, past pres.), Am. Coll. Legal Medicine (asso.), Internat. Acad. Trial Lawyers, Am. Acad. Forensic Scis. Office: City Nat Bank Bldg 40th Floor Detroit MI 48226

CHARGAFF, ERWIN, biochemistry educator; b. Austria, Aug. 11, 1905; came to U.S., 1928, naturalized, 1940; s. Hermann and Rosa C.; m. Vera Broido; 1 son, Thomas. Dr. Phil., U. Vienna, 1928; Dr. phil. h.c, U. Basel, 1976; Sc.D. (hon.), Columbia U., 1976. Research fellow Yale U., 1928-30; asst. U. Berlin, Germany, 1930-33; research assoc. Inst. Pasteur, Paris, France, 1933-34; faculty Columbia U., 1935—, prof. biochemistry, 1952-74, prof. emeritus, 1974—, chmn. dept. biochemistry, 1970-74; vis. prof., Sweden, 1949, Japan, 1958, Brazil, 1959, Coll. de France, 1965, Naples, Palermo, Cornell, 1966, Stazione biologica, 1969. Author: Essays on Nucleic Acids, 1963, Voices in the Labyrinth, 1977, Heraclitean Fire, 1978, Das Feuer des Heraklit, 1979, Unbegreifliches Geheimnis, 1980, Bemerkungen, 1981, Wernungstafeln, 1982, Kritik der Zukunft, 1983; numerous articles in field, other lit. work in English and German.; Editor: The Nucleic Acids, 3 vols, 1955, 60. Guggenheim fellow, 1949, 58; recipient Pasteur medal Soc. Biol. Chemistry, Paris, 1949; Neuberg medal Am. Soc. European Chemists, 1958; Bertner Found. award, Houston, 1965; C.L. Mayer prize French Acad. Scis., 1963; Dr. H.P. Heineken prize Netherlands Acad. Scis., 1964; Gregor Mendel medal German Acad. Scis. Leopoldina, 1973; Nat. Medal of Sci., 1975; medal N.Y. Acad. Medicine, 1980; Disting. Service award Columbia U., 1982. Fellow Am. Acad. Arts and Scis.; mem. Nat. Acad. Scis., Am. Philos. Soc.; fgn. mem. Royal Swedish Physiographic Soc., German Acad. Scis. Leopoldina. Home: 350 Central Park W New York NY 10025

CHARLAP, GUY JOSE, laboratory equipment manufacturing company executive; b. Paris, Oct. 25, 1921; s. Samuel and Charlotte (Albert) C.; m. Genia Baltakse, Mar. 29, 1944; children: Jean-Paul, Elizabeth, Berthe Charlap Hurst, Francoise, Marie-Helene. Master's degree, Faculte' Pharmacie, Paris, 1946, Faculte' Scis. Economiques, Paris, 1954; student, Inst. Internat. Mgmt., Northwestern U., 1969. Tech. dir. Labs. la Biomaine, Dieppe, France, 1946-53; asst. gen. mgr. mgf. plants SIFA, Paris, 1953-61; with Technicon Corp., Paris, 1961-66, Geneva, 1966-72, pres., Paris, 1972—. Mem. adv. council NYU Sch. Arts; mem. adv. com. Maison Francaise, Columbia U.; bd. dirs. Center for Internat. Mgmt. Studies; councilor Rockefellor U. Served to lt. French Army, 1942-46. Mem. French-Am. C. of C. (sec.-gen. councillor). Home: 118 Weavers Hill Greenwich CT 06830 Office: 511 Benedict Ave Tarrytown NY 10591

CHARLES, ALLAN G., physician, educator; b. N.Y.C., Nov. 15, 1928; s. Harry G. and Alice (Grotzky) C.; m. Phyllis V. J. Vail, June 28, 1957; children: Della Marie, Aaron Joseph, David Jonathan. A.B. cum laude, N.Y. U., 1948, M.D., 1952. Diplomate: Am. Bd. Obstetrics and Gynecology. Intern Phila. Gen. Hosp., 1952-53; resident in obstetrics and gynecology Mt. Sinai Hosp., N.Y.C., 1955-57, Michael Reese Hosp., Chgo., 1957-60, clin. asst., 1960-61, assoc. attending physician, 1961-69, attending physician, 1969—, co-dir., 1963—, vice-chmn. dept. obstetrics and gynecology, 1971, pres. staff, 1978, bd. dirs., 1981—; practice medicine specializing in obstetrics and gynecology, Chgo., 1960—; courtesy staff Chgo. Lying-In-Hosp.; clin. asst. prof. obstetrics and gynecology U. Ill. Coll. Medicine, Chgo., 1960-64, Chgo. Med. Sch., 1964-72; clin. prof. Pritzker Sch. Medicine, U. Chgo., 1972—; prof. clin. obstetrics and gynecology Northwestern U., 1983. Author: Rh Iso Immunization and Erythroblastosis Fetalis, 1969; Contbr. articles to profl. jours. Fellow Am. Coll. Obstetricians and Gynecologists, Internat. Coll. Surgeons (chmn. Am. sect. obs. and gynec. 1979-83), Central Assn. Obstetricians and Gynecologists, Am. Fertility Soc.; mem. AMA, Ill., Chgo. med. socs., Chgo. Gynecol. Soc. (v.p. 1980—). Developer substitute for uterine tube, Rh-sensitization. Home: 6854 S Bennett Ave Chicago IL 60649 Office: 30 N Michigan Ave Chicago IL 60602

CHARLES, BERTRAM, radio broadcasting executive; b. Boston, Jan. 26, 1918; s. Jacob H. and Annie L. (Kanter) Fein; m. Alberta Marie Carpenter, Sept. 4, 1948; children—Meredith Ann Trapp, Blair Carpenter Adams. Student, N.Y. U., 1935-38. Reporter Bklyn. Daily Eagle, 1938-39, N.Y. Post, 1939-40; news and sports announcer Sta. WAOV, Vincennes, Ind., 1945; sportscaster Sta. WIRE, Indpls., 1945; dir. sports and pub. service Sta. WAKR, Akron, Ohio, 1946-48; program and sports dir. Sta. WVKO-AM-FM, Columbus, Ohio, 1948-49, sta. mgr., 1949-53, v.p., 1953-71, pres., gen. mgr., 1971—; dir. Food Products Co. Trustee Columbus Zoo, Opera/Columbus; patron Columbus Art Gallery; past pres., chmn. bd. Charity Newsies. Served with USAF, 1942-45. Named Columbus Father of Year, 1961. Mem. Columbus Better Bus. Bur. (dir.), Ohio Radio and TV Execs. (pres. 1957), Columbus Radio Broadcasters, Ohio Assn. Broadcasters, Soc. Profl. Journalists (dir.), Ohio Sportscasters Assn., Nat. Football Found. Hall of Fame, Columbus Advt. Fedn. Clubs: Athletic of Columbus, York Temple Country, Maennerchor, Rotary, Agonis. Home: 2548 West Lane Ave Columbus OH 43221 Office: 4401 Carriage Hill Ln Columbus OH 43220 *Although I've prayed to God as if everything depended upon Him, I've worked all my life as if everything depended upon me.*

CHARLES, CAROL MORGAN, educator; b. Loraine, Tex., Jan. 11, 1931; s. Joe M. and Lois F. C.; m. Ruth M. Kimbell, June 3, 1951; children: Gail, Timothy. B.A., Eastern N.Mex. U., 1953, M.A., 1957; Ph.D., U. N.Mex., 1961. Tchr., Estancia (N.Mex.) Schs., 1953-59; research asst., vis. prof. U. N.Mex., 1959-61; prof. edn. San Diego State U., 1961-66, 68—; prof. Tchrs. Coll., Columbia U., 1967-68; cons. govts. Brazil and Peru. Author: Educational Psychology, 1972, 76, Individualizing Instruction, 1976, 80, Schooling, Teaching Learning: American Education, 1978, The Special Student, 1980, Building Classroom Discipline, 1981, Elementary Classroom Management, 1983; contbr. articles to profl. jours. Recipient Disting. Teaching award, Outstanding Prof. award. Mem. Assn. Supervision and Curriculum Devel., Assn. Tchr. Educators, AAUP, Phi Delta Kappa. Home: 1830 Brabham St El Cajon CA 92020 Office: Coll Edn San Diego State U San Diego CA 92182

CHARLES, E. OTIS, bishop; b. Norristown, Pa., Apr. 24, 1926; s. Jacob Otis and Elizabeth Francis (Abraham) C.; m. Elvira Latta, May 26, 1951; children: Christopher, Nicholas, Emilie, Timothy, Elvira. B.A., Trinity Coll., Hartford, Conn., 1948; S.T.B., Gen. Theol. Sem., N.Y.C., 1959, D.D., 1983. Ordained deacon Episcopal Ch., 1951, priest, 1951, bishop, 1971; curate St. Johns Ch., Elizabeth, N.J., 1951-53; priest-in-charge St. Andrews Ch., Beacon, N.Y., 1953-59; rector St. Johns Ch., Washington, Conn., 1959-68; assoc. dir. Montford House Ecumenical Center, 1968-69; exec. sec. Asso. Parishes, Inc., 1968-71; bishop Episcopal Diocese Utah, Salt Lake City, 1971—; bishop in charge Navajo Episc. Ch., 1976-79; mem. Episcopal Standing Liturgical Commn., 1970-79; dir. Epis. Ch. Pub. Co. Trustee Episcopal Radio TV Found., 1972-78; pres. bd. trustees St. Marks Hosp., Rowland Hall St. Marks Sch.; trustee Hospice of Salt Lake, 1978-80; adviser U. Utah Coll. Nursing, 1980-83; mem. Utah State Health Coordinating Council, 1981—; adviser Utah Camp Fire Council, 1980-82; bd. dirs. Episcopal Urban Caucus, 1981, Planned Parenthood of Utah, 1980-83; Mem. Utah Arts Festival Council, 1981—, Utah Assn. Autism, 1980—; mem. Health Systems Agy. Governing Body, 1981—, State Health Coordinating Council, 1981—; exec. com. Utahns United Against the Arms Race, 1982—. Served with USNR, 1943-46; PTO. Recipient Washington Community Fund grants, 1962, 68. Club: Alta (Salt Lake City). Office: 231 E 1st S Salt Lake City UT 84111 *My personal and professional life may be described in words attributed to Prince William, Founder of the House of Orange: "Even without hope to undertake; even without success to persevere." The motivating desire of my life is to make a difference in the continuing evolution of this planet earth. Ecumenism provides the principal focus of this desire—the harmony of diverse spiritual and political experience lending toward unity and peace.*

CHARLES, ISABEL, university administrator; b. Bklyn., Mar. 10, 1926; d. James Patrick and Isabel (Roney) C. B.A., Manhattan Coll., 1954; M.A., U. Notre Dame, 1960, Ph.D., 1965; postgrad., U. Mich., 1968-69. Chmn. dept. English Bishop Watterson High Sch., Columbus, Ohio, 1954-59, St. Mary of the Springs Acad., Columbus, 1959-62; asst. prof. English Ohio Dominican Coll., Columbus, 1965-68, acad. dean, exec. v.p., 1969-73; asst. dean Coll. Arts and Letters, U. Notre Dame, 1973-75, acting dean, 1975, dean, 1976-82, asst. provost, 1982—. Contbr. articles to profl. jours. Mem. MLA, Am. Assn. Acad. Deans, Am. Assn. Higher Edn. Home: 1802 Stonehedge Ln South Bend IN 46616

CHARLES, JACK, petroleum company executive; b. Ft. Worth, Jan. 20, 1933; s. William Lewis and Maurene Mildred (Hodges) C.; m. Barbara Jean Morris, May 29, 1953; children. B.B.A., U. Tex. at Arlington, 1961; postgrad., Tex. Christian U., 1962-63; M.B.A., U. Tex. at San Antonio, 1978. Tng. dir. Tex. Electric Service Co., Ft. Worth, 1952-62; personnel dir. Acme Brick Co., Ft. Worth, 1962-66; mgmt. cons. Peat, Marwick, Mitchell & Co., Dallas, 1966-70; group v.p. Tesoro Petroleum Corp., San Antonio, 1970—; pres. Land & Marine Rental Co., Tesoro Drilling Co., Tesoro Petroleum Distbg. Co. Served with USCG, 1949-52. Mem. Am. Soc. Tng. Dirs. (pres. chpt. 1965-66), So. Tex., No. San Antonio chambers commerce. Home: 103 Village Circle San Antonio TX 78232 Office: 8700 Tesoro Dr San Antonio TX 78286

CHARLES, RAY (RAY CHARLES ROBINSON), musician, singer, composer; b. Albany, Ga., Sept. 23, 1930; s. Bailey and Areatha Robinson. Student music at sch. for blind, St. Augustine, Fla. Played with bands, in South; organized trio; played on TV in, Seattle; formed own band, 1954; rec. artist, Atlantic Records, 1952-59, ABC-Paramount, 1959-65, Tangerine Records, 1965-73, Crossover Records Co., 1973—, numerous TV, concert appearances.; Recent recs. include Rockin' With Ray. Recipient New Star award Down Beat Critics poll, 1958, 61-64; named number 1 male singer 16th Internat. Jazz Critics Poll, 1968; 10 Grammy awards; named to Playboy Jazz and Pop Hall of Fame; Songwriters Hall of Fame; hon. life chmn. Rhythm and

Blues Hall of Fame; gold records include Ray Charles' Greatest Hits, 1962, Modern Sounds in Country and Western Music, Vol. 1 1962, Vol. 2, 1963, Ray Charles: A Man and His Soul. Address: care Buddy Lee Attractions 38 Music Sq East Suite 300 Nashville TN *

CHARLES, RAYMOND ALANSON, investment banker; b. Knoxville, Ill., Mar. 3, 1919; s. John H. and Leona (Lotts) C.; m. Lois D. Sekora, Oct. 6, 1951; children: Margaret Anne, Alanson J. A.B. summa cum laude, Knox Coll., 1941; postgrad., MIT, 1942; M.B.A., U. Chgo., 1947. With bond dept. Prudential Ins. Co. Am., 1947-50; mem. finance staff Ford Motor Co., 1950-56; mem. securities investment dept. Equitable Life Assurance Soc., N.Y.C., 1956-58; with corp. fin. dept. Prudential Ins. Co. Am., 1958—, v.p., 1962-65, sr. v.p., 1965-81; mng. dir. Lehman Bros. Kuhn Loeb Inc., 1981—. Trustee Knox Coll., 1966, Westminster Choir Coll., 1975—. Served with USAAF, 1943-46. Mem. Am. Econ. Assn., Am. Finance Assn., Phi Beta Kappa, Beta Gamma Sigma, Tau Kappa Epsilon. Presbyn. (mem. bd. pensions U.P. Ch. U.S.A.). Home: 16 Hilltop Circle Morristown NJ 07960 Office: 55 Water St New York NY 10041

CHARLIER, ROGER HENRI, oceanographer, geographer, educator; b. Antwerp, Belgium, Nov. 10, 1921; came to U.S., 1946, naturalized, 1948; m. Patricia Mary Simonet, 1958; children: Constance C.P., Jean-Armand. Ph.D., U. Erlangen, 1947; Litt.D., U. Paris, 1956, Sc.D., 1958. Prof. geography and history Coll. Baudouin, Brussels, Belgium, 1941-42; student asst. U. Liège, Belgium, 1943-44; newspaper corr., Europe, 1945-50; dep. dir. assembly centers UNRRA, 1946-48; tech. advisor 20th Century Fox Corp., 1948; research analyst Internat. War Crimes Commn., Nurenberg, Germany, 1948-49; tchr. Berlitz Sch., Newark, 1950-51; assoc. prof. dept. geography, chmn. dept. Polycultural U., Washington, 1951-52; chmn. dept. phys. scis. Finch coll., 1952-55; tchr. New Brunswick (N.J.) Sr. High Sch., 1955; chmn. dept. geology and geography Hofstra U., 1955-58; professeur suppléant U. Paris, France, 1958-59; vis. prof. edn. U. Minn., 1959-60; prof. earth scis. Parsons Coll., Fairfield, Iowa, 1960-61; prof. geology, geography and oceanography Northeastern Ill. U., Chgo., 1961—, resident scholar in oceanography, 1962-65, vice-chmn. dept. geography, 1964-70, dir. oceanography program, 1962—; prof. extraordinary U. Brussels, 1971—; vis. prof. DePaul U., 1965-67, U. Bordeaux, 1970-74, 83-84; exchange scientist Internat. Research Exchange Com., 1968-69, Nat. Acad. Sci., 1967-68, NSF, 1968, Acad. of Romania, 1978-79, Nat. Acad. Scis. Bulgaria, 1979. Assoc. editor: U. So. Fla. Lang. Quar, 1956-77, Hexagon, 1961-63; cons. editor: Oceanic Abstracts, 1965—. Decorated chevalier Order of Léopold, Belgium; chevalier Ordre des Palmes Academiques, France; recipient Médaille du Mérite Touristique, Belgium, 1970; Médaille de vermeil des Lettres, Arts et Sciences, 1970; Grande Médaille d'Or, 1979; France; Gold medal Encouragement à l'Advancement du Progrès, 1973; Grande Médaille U. Bordeaux, 1974; Presdl. Merit award, 1980; Belgian Nat. Found. for Sci. Research grantee, 1977-79; Belgian Govt. grantee, 1976-78; Inst. for River and Estuarine Studies grantee, 1976-78; Fulbright scholar, 1975-76; NATO grantee, 1969-70; French Govt. fellow, 1967-69; Institut Océanographique de Monaco grantee, 1967-68; Colruyt Engring. grantee, 1982-84. Office: Northeastern Ill U 5500 N St Louis Ave Chicago IL 60625 *Perhaps my refusal to accommodate and to bend principles so as to please superiors has won me their respect.*

CHARLSON, ROBERT JAY, educator, scientist; b. San Jose, Calif., Sept. 30, 1936; s. Rolland Walter and Harriet Adele (Stucky) C.; m. Patricia Elaine Allison, Mar. 16, 1964; children: Daniel Owen, Amanda Marcella. B.S. in Chemistry, Stanford U., 1958, M.S., 1959; Ph.D. in Atmospheric Scis., U. Wash., 1964; postgrad. (Fulbright scholar), London U., 1964-65. Research engr. Boeing Co., Seattle, 1959-62; research asst. prof. dept. civil engring. U. Wash., Seattle, 1965-69, asso. prof. atmospheric chemistry, 1969-71, asso. prof. civil engring. and geophysics, 1971-74, prof. atmospheric chemistry in civil engring. geophysics and environ. studies, 1974—, adj. prof. atmospheric scis., 1974—. Author: (with S.S. Butcher) An Introduction to Air Chemistry, 1972; asso. editor: Jour. Applied Meterology, 1971-73; mem. editorial bd.: Jour. Boundary Layer Meterology, 1971—, Water, Air and Soil Pollution, 1971—; contbr. articles on atmosphere chemistry to profl. jours. Grantee USPHS, EPA, NSF, NASA, NOAA. Mem. Am. Chem. Soc., Am. Meterol. Soc., Am. Geophys. Union, AAAS, Sgma Xi, Phi Lambda Upson (hon.). Patentee in field. Office: FC-05 U Wash Seattle WA 98195

CHARLTON, JANET SHIELDS, assn. exec.; b. Geneva, N.Y., Feb. 26, 1954; d. John Francis and Barbara Gene (O'Brien) Shields; m. Richard Morrell Charlton, Apr. 15, 1978; 1 son, Richard. B.A., U. Mass., Amherst, 1975; M.A., Georgetown U., 1977. Congressional legis. intern, 1974; research asst. Kennedy Inst., Washington, 1975-76; public relations asst. Am. Bankers Assn., Washington, 1977-78; research dir. Nat. Leased Housing Assn., Washington, 1978-80, exec. dir., 1980—. Editor coursebooks. Mem. Women in Housing and Fin.; bd. dirs. Nat. Low Income Housing Coalition. State of Mass. Women's Clubs scholar, 1975-76. Mem. Am. Acad. Polit. and Social Sci., Acad. Polit. Sci. Roman Catholic. Home: 818 Devon Pl Alexandria VA 22314 Office: 2300 M St NW Suite 260 Washington DC 20037

CHARLTON, JESSE MELVIN, JR., management educator; b. Livonia, La., May 12, 1916; s. Jesse Melvin and Anna Lela (Medlin) C.; m. Mary Camp, Oct. 4, 1941; children: Jesse Melvin, Frances Anne. B.S., La. State U., 1938, M.B.A., 1938; J.D., Harvard U., 1951. Bar: U.S. Ct. Mil. Appeals 1952, U.S. Supreme Ct 1963, D.C. 1951. Instr. U. Ala., 1938-40; commd. 2d lt., inf. U.S. Army, 1940, advanced through grades to col., 1951; dep. comdr. Judge Adv. Gen. Sch., Charlottesville, Va., 1962-64; ret., 1964; mem. faculty U. New Orleans Coll. Bus., 1964-83, prof. mgmt., 1971-83, prof. emeritus, 1983—, dean, 1978-80. Author handbook; co-editor: Statistical Abstract of Louisiana, 5th edit, 1974. Decorated Bronze Star, Commendation medal, Combat Inf. badge. Mem. AAUP, D.C. Bar Assn., So. Bus. Law Assn. (pres. 1969-70). Republican. Methodist.

CHARNAS, (MANNIE) MICHAEL, supermarket executive; b. Cleve., Sept. 24, 1947; s. Max and Eleanor (Gross) C.; m. Constance Cheney, June 1, 1974. B.B.A., Ohio State U., 1969, M.B.A., 1971. Fin. analyst Addressograph-Multigraph, Inc., Cleve., 1971-73; asst. to pres., dir. planning and budget 1st Nat. Supermarkets, Inc. (Pick-N-Pay), Cleve., 1975-78, asst. to pres., v.p. planning and budgets, 1978-79, sr. v.p. fin., adminstr., 1979-81, sr. v.p., chief fin. officer, adminstrv. officer, Hartford, Conn., 1981—. Jewish. Office: First Nat Supermarkets Inc 500 North St Windson Locks CT 06096

CHARNES, ABRAHAM, mathematics educator, researcher; b. Hopewell, Va., Sept. 4, 1917; s. Harry and Rebecca (Levatin) C.; m. Kathryn Francis, May 1950; children: Deborah, Daniel, William. A.B., U. Ill.-Urbana, 1938, M.Sc., 1939, Ph.D., 1947; cert. applied math., Brown U., 1941. Asst. prof. math. Carnegie Inst. Tech., Pitts., from 1948, assoc. prof., to 1955; prof. math. and econs. of transp. Purdue U., 1955-57; prof. math. and engring. scis. Northwestern U., 1957-68; prof. U. Tex. System, Austin, 1968—, dir. Ctr. Cybernetic Studies, 1968—; cons. in field. Author books and articles. Mem. final expert rev. com. NSF for U.S. Congress, Laxenburg, Austria, 1978. Served to lt. USNR, 1942-46. Ford Found. fellow, 1960; recipient von Neumann Theory award ORSA-TIMS, 1982, Disting. lectr. Soviet Acad. Scis., 1976, Chinese Acad. Sci., 1981, Technion-Israel Inst. Tech., 1982, Highest Civilian award U.S. Navy, 1977. Fellow AAAS, Econometric Soc., Ops. Research Soc. Am.; mem. Inst. Mgmt. Scis. (pres.), Nat. Acad. Engring. Mex. (sec. internat. affairs 1974-77). Office: Center for Cybernetic Studies U Tex Bldg BEB 454C Austin TX 78712 *

CHARNIN, MARTIN JAY, theatrical producer and director, lyricist; b. N.Y.C., Nov. 24, 1934; s. William and Birdie (Blakeman) C.; m. Lynn Ross, Mar. 2, 1958 (div.); 1 son, Randy; m. Genii Prior, Jan. 8, 1962; 1 dau., Sasha. B.A., Cooper Union, 1955. Acting stage debut West Side Story, 1957; also appeared in: The Girls Against the Boys, 1959; writer: lyrics and sketches Fallout Revue, 1959; lyricist: revue Pieces of Eight, 1959, Little Revue, 1960, Hot Spot, 1963, Zenda, 1963, Mata Hari, 1967; lyricist, dir.: Ballad for a Firing Squad, 1968; lyricist: Two by Two, 1970; conceived and directed: Nash at Nine, 1973; dir.: Music! Music!, 1974; lyricist, dir., creator: Annie (Tony award for lyrics), 1977 (2 Drama Desk awards for lyrics and direction); dir. 3 nat. cos., 1978, also London prodn., 1978; Bar Mitzvah Boy, London, 1978; lyricist: I Remember Mama, 1979; lyricist, dir.: The First, 1981; wrote and staged material for nightclub acts of, Anna Marie Alberghetti, Leslis Uggams, Nancy Wilson, Larry Kert, Dionne Warwick, Abbe Lane, Jose Ferrer, Jack Cassidy, Shirley Jones, Mary Travers, Tom Posten, others; lyricist: TV spl. Feathertop, 1961, Jackie Gleason Show, 1961; conceived and produced: the Women in the Life of a Man, 1970 (2 Emmy awards); conceived, produced and directed: TV spls. George M, 1970, Jack Lemmon in 'S Wonderful, 'S Marvelous, 'S Gershwin (2 Emmy awards), 1972 (Peabody award for Broadcasting), Jack Lemmon in Get Happy—The Music of Harold Arlen, 1973, Dames at Sea, 1972, Cole Porter in Paris, 1973, Annie and the Hoods, 1974, The Annie Xmas Show, 1977, C'mon Saturday, 1977; author: The Giraffe Who Sounded Like Ol' Blue Eyes, 1976, Annie: A Theatre Memoir, 1977. Office: care Beam One Ltd 850 7th Ave New York NY 10019 *

CHARNY, ISRAEL W., psychologist, author; b. N.Y.C., July 18, 1931; s. Bernard and Anna (Aichenbaum) C.; m. Phyllis B. Ellen, Apr. 14, 1957 (div. June 1981); children: Adam Shalom, Rena S., Anna L.; m. Judith Schott Katz, Oct. 13, 1982. A.B. in Psychology with distinction, Temple U., 1952; Ph.D. in Clin. Psychology, U. Rochester, 1957. Diplomate: clin. psychology Am. Bd. Profl. Psychology. Clin. psychologist Rochester (N.Y.) Bd. Edn., 1956-58; chief Oakbourne Hosp., West Chester, Pa., 1958-62; pvt. practice, dir. Guidance Cons., Paoli, Pa., 1962-73; prof. psychology, cons. counseling Reconstructionist Rabbinical Coll., Phila., 1971-73; asso. prof. Tel Aviv U., 1973—; sr. cons. Kibbutz Child and Family Clinic, Ramat Aviv, Israel, 1973-80; sr. researcher, co-dir. Genocide Early Warning System Project, Nat. Inst. Research Behavioral Scis., Jerusalem, 1973-82; Mem. adv. council Consortium on Peace Research, Edn. and Devel., U. Colo., 1970-74; chmn. 3d Internat. Congress Family Therapy, 1979; exec. dir. Inst. of Internat. Conf. on Holocaust and Genocide.; chmn. 1st Internat. Conf. on Holocaust and Genocide, 1982. Author: Individual and Family Developmental Review, 1969, Maritial Love and Hate, 1972, Strategies Against Violence, 1978, How Can We Commit the Unthinkable: Genocide—The Human Cancer; Contbr. articles to profl. publs. Fellow Am. Orthopsychiat. Assn. (chmn. study group mental health aspects aggression, violence and war 1970-74); fellow Internat. Soc. Study Aggression; mem. Internat. Peace Research Assn., Israel Assn. Marital and Family Therapy (pres. 1977-78), Am. Psychol. Assn., Assn. Humanistic Psychology. Address: PO Box 3027 Herzliya Israel also 216 Upland Ave Wayne PA 19087

CHARPIE, ROBERT ALAN, physicist; b. Cleve., Sept. 9, 1925; s. Leonard Asbury and Dorothy (McLean) C.; m. Elizabeth Downs, July 12, 1947; children: Richard Alan, Carol Elizabeth, David Wayne, John Robert. B.S. with honors, Carnegie Inst. Tech., 1948, M.S., 1949, D.Sc. in Theoretical Physics, 1950; D.H.L., Denison U., 1965; D.Sc., Alderson-Broaddus Coll., 1967; LL.D., Marietta Coll., 1975; D.Sc., Boston Coll., 1982. With Westinghouse Electric Corp., 1947-50; with Oak Ridge Nat. Lab., 1950-51, tech. asst. to research dir., 1952-54, asst. research dir., 1954-58, dir. reactor div., 1958-61; mgr. adv. devel. Union Carbide Corp., 1961-63, gen. mgr. devel. dept., 1963-64, dir. tech., 1964-66, pres. electronics div., 1966-68; pres. Bell & Howell Co., Chgo., 1968-69; pres., dir. Cabot Corp., Boston, 1969—; trustee Mitre Corp., Boston, 1966-82, chmn., 1972-82; dir. Federated Dept. Stores, Inc., Boston, Champion Internat. Corp., Schlumberger Ltd., Northwest Airlines, Inc.; sec. gen. adv. com. AEC, 1959-63; mem. Nat. Sci. Bd., 1969-76; sci. sec., editor-in-chief proc., also asst. U.S. mem. 7 nation adv. com. 1st Internat. Conf. Peaceful Uses Atomic Energy, 1955; coordinator U.S. fusion research exhibit, 2d Conf., 1958; chmn. invention and innovation panel U.S. Dept. Commerce, 1965-67. Gen. editor: Internat. Monograph Series on Nuclear Energy, 1955-60; editor: Progress Series in Nuclear Energy, 1955-60, Jour. Nuclear Energy, 1955-60. Mem. Oak Ridge Bd. Edn., 1957-61; pres. Byram Hills Central Sch. Dist., 1966-68; trustee Carnegie Inst. Tech., 1962—. Recipient Alumni Merit award Carnegie Inst. Tech., 1957. Fellow Am. Phys. Soc., Am. Nuclear Soc. (dir.); mem. N.Y. Acad. Sci., Nat. Acad. Engring., Sci. Research Soc. Am., Sigma Xi, Tau Beta Pi, Phi Mu Epsilon. Home: 45 Ridgeway Rd Weston MA 02193 Office: 125 High St Boston MA 02110

CHARREN, PEGGY, consumer activist; b. N.Y.C., Mar. 9, 1928; d. Maxwell and Ruth (Rosenthal) Walzer; m. Stanley Charren, June 17, 1951; children: Deborah, Claudia. B.A., Conn. Coll., 1949; LL.D. (hon.), Regis Coll., 1978. Founder, owner Art Prints, Inc., Providence, 1951-53, Quality Book Fairs, Newton, Mass., 1960-65; dir. Creative Arts Council, Newton, 1966-68; founder, pres. Action for Children's Television, Inc., Newtonville, Mass., 1968—; mem. Carnegie Commn. on Future of Public Broadcasting, 1977—; mem. task panel on public attitudes and use of media for promotion of health President's Commn. on Mental Health, 1977—; mem. Mass. Council on Arts and Humanities, 1980—; mem. adv. bd. project on TV advt. and children NSF; mem. adv. bd. project on devel. of programs for children with spl. needs Am. Inst. Research; bd. dirs. Child Devel. Consortium, Media Access Project. Co-author: Changing Channels: Living Sensibly with Television, 1983; Joint editor: Who is Talking to Our Children, 1973; contbr. articles to profl. publs. Bd. dirs. Boston U. Inst. for Democratic Communication, Women's Campaign Fund., Tufts Lincoln-Filene Ctr. Citizen Participation, Young Audiences of Mass.; mem. adv. bd. Am. Repertory Theater. Recipient Disting. Public Info. Service award Am. Acad. Pediatrics, hon. award Motion Picture Assn.; Disting. Service award Mass. Radio and TV Assn., 1974; hon. medal Conn. Coll., 1974; Helen Homans Gilbert award Radcliffe Coll. Democrat. Home: 33 Hancock Ave Newton Centre MA 02159 Office: Action for Children's TV 46 Austin St Newtonville MA 02160

CHARRY, MICHAEL, musician, conductor; b. N.Y.C., Aug. 28, 1933; s. Harold Paul and Sylvia C.; m. Jane Thoms, Mar. 31, 1956; children: Stephen Walter, Barbara. Student, Oberlin Conservatory Music, 1950-52; B.S., Juilliard Sch. Music, 1955, M.S. in Orch. Conducting, 1956. Chairperson, Music Consortium of Nashville, 1977-79; chairperson Nashville Inst. Arts, 1979-80. Condr., pianist, José Limón Modern Dance Co. tours, Europe, 1957, José Limón Modern Dance Co. tours, South and Central Am., 1960, José Limón Modern Dance Co. tours, Far East, 1963; asst. condr., prin. oboist, R.I. Philharmonic, 1960-61; music dir., condr., Canton Symphony Orch., 1961-74; apprentice condr., Cleve. Orch., 1961-65; asst. condr., Cleve. Orch., 1965-72; music dir., condr., Nashville Symphony Orch., 1976-82, Peninsula Music Festival, 1978-82; guest condr. concerts, operas, U.S. and Europe; assoc. prof. orchestral conducting, dir. orchestral activities, Syracuse U. (N.Y.), 1983—; prof., mus. dir. orchestral program (dir. ensembles), Boston U. Sch. Music, 1984—; bd. dirs., Condrs. Guild Am. Symphony League. Served with U.S. Army, 1958-60. Fulbright scholar, 1956-57; Martha Baird Rockefeller grantee, 1975; recipient Alice M. Ditson award Columbia U., 1981, Spl. Merit award Tenn. Arts Commn., 1982. Mem. Am. Symphony Orch. League.

CHARTERIS, LESLIE, author; b. Singapore, May 12, 1907; naturalized, 1946; m. Pauline Schishkin, 1931 (div. 1937); 1 dau., Patricia Ann; m. Barbara Meyer, 1938 (div.); m. Elizabeth Bryant Borst, 1943 (div.); m. Audrey Long, 1952. Student, Cambridge U., 1926; studied art in, Paris. Author: numerous books from Meet the Tiger, 1928, to, Saint to the Rescue, 1959, Trust the Saint, 1962, The Saint in the Sun, 1963, Vendetta for the Saint, 1964, The Saint on TV, 1968, The Saint Returns, 1968, The Saint Abroad, 1969, The Saint in Pursuit, 1971, Catch the Saint, 1975, The Saint and The Hapsburg Necklace, 1976, Send for the Saint, 1977, The Saint in Trouble, 1978, The Saint and the Templar Treasure, 1978, Count on the Saint, 1980; collection The Fantastic Saint, 1981; Salvage for the Saint, 1983; Contbr. to numerous mags.; also written several motion picture plays. Fellow Royal Soc. Arts; mem. Mensa. Clubs: Savage, Yacht de Cannes. Inventor Paleneo, universal sign language. Office: care Thompson Levett and Co 3/4 Great Marlborough St London W1V 2AR England

CHARTERS, ANN, educator; b. Bridgeport, Conn., Nov. 10, 1936; d. Nathan Danbert and Kate (Schultz) Danberg; m. Samuel B. Charters, Mar. 14, 1959; children: Mallay, Nora Lili. A.B., U. Calif.-Berkeley, 1957; M.A., Columbia U., 1960, Ph.D., 1965. Mem. faculty Colby Jr. Coll., New London, N.H., 1962-64; lectr. Columbia U., 1964-65; asst. prof. Am. lit. N.Y.C. Community Coll., 1967-70; prof. Am. lit. U. Conn., Storrs, 1974—. Author: Noboby-Life and Times of Bert Williams, 1967, Kerouac, 1973, I Love-Story of Vladimir Mayakovsky and Lili Brik, 1979, The Story and Its Writer, 1983, The Beats: Literary Bohemians in Post-war America, 1983. Address: Dept English Univ Conn Storrs CT 06268

CHARTERS, ROBERT BURNS, corporate executive; b. Toronto, Ont., Can., May 9, 1923; s. Clarence Victor and Ida Mary (Harcourt) C.; m. Kathleen McKillop, Mar. 13, 1947; children: Thomas Victor, Lorie Louise. Student, pub. schs. With Armbro Holdings, Ltd., Brampton, Ont., exec. v.p., 1966-71, pres., 1971-83, chmn. bd., 1978-83, dir., 1966—, Armstrong Holdings Ltd., 1966—. Served as flight lt. Royal Can. Air Force, 1941-46; ETO. Decorated D.F.M. RAF, Croix de Guerre, France. Mem. RAF Escaping Soc. (Can. br.), Ont. Golf Assn. (2d v.p. 1983). Progressive-Conservative. Anglican. Club: Toronto Golf. Home: 1400 Dixie Rd Mississauga ON Canada L5E 3E1

CHARTIER, DONALD MORRIS, grain company executive; b. Dallas Center, Iowa, Sept. 7, 1933; s. William Melvin C. and Esther Fae (Good) Chariter; m. Patricia O'Donnell, Aug. 16, 1955; children: John, Mary Pat. B.S. in Agrl. Bus. Econs., Iowa State U., 1958. Gen. mgr. Farmers Coop., Terril, Iowa, 1958-62; mgmt. cons. Farmland Industries, Kansas City, Mo., 1962-68, gen. mgr. Okla.-Ark. sales div., 1968-70, div. gen. mgr. Kansas City feed and soybean ops., 1970-79; pres. FAR*MAR*CO Inc., Hutchinson, Kans., 1979—, chief exec. officer; dir. Soy-Cot Sales Inc., Farmers Export Co.; bd. dirs. Kansas City Bd. Trade. Served with U.S. Army, 1953-55. Mem. U.S. Feed Grains Council (dir.), Nat. Soybean Processors Assn. (bd. dirs.), Kansas City Terminal Assn. (pres., bd. dirs.), Gamma Sigma Delta. Disciple of Christ. Home: 222 Apache Trail W Lake Quivira KS 66106 Office: FAR-MAR-CO Inc 3315 N Oak Trafficway Kansas City MO 64116

CHARTOFF, ROBERT IRWIN, film producer; b. N.Y.C.; s. William and Bessie C.; m. Vanessa Howard, July 3, 1970; children: Jenifer, William, Julie, Charley. A.B., Union Coll., 1955; LL.B., Columbia U., 1958. Producer: numerous films including The Split, 1968, Leo the Last, 1969, They Shoot Horses, Don't They, 1969, The Strawberry Statement, 1970, The Gang That Couldn't Shoot Straight, 1971, The New Centurions, 1972, Up the Sandbox, 1972, Peeper, 1975, The Gambler, 1975, Rocky, 1976 (Acad. award for best picture), Nickelodeon, 1976, New York, New York, 1977, Valentino, 1977, Comes A Horseman, 1978, Uncle Joe Shannon, 1978, Rocky II, 1979, Raging Bull, 1980, Rocky III, 1982, The Right Stuff, 1983. Office: Chartoff-Winkler Prodns Inc 10125 W Washington Blvd Culver City CA 90230 *

CHARTON, MARVIN, chemist, educator; b. Bklyn., May 1, 1931; s. William and Elsie (Halpern) C.; m. Barbara Israel, Aug. 28, 1955; children—Michael, Sarah, Deborah. B.S., Coll. City N.Y., 1953; M.A., Bklyn. Coll., 1956; Ph.D., Stevens Inst. Tech., 1962. Instr. chemistry Pratt Inst., Bklyn., 1956-61, asst. prof., 1961-64, asso. prof., 1964-67, prof., 1967-70, chmn. dept., 1969—. Contbr. articles to profl. jours., also chpts. in books. Fellow Intrasci. Research Found.; mem. Am. Chem. Soc., Internat. Soc. Heterocyclic Chemistry, Chemometric Soc., Royal Chem. Soc. London, N.Y. Acad. Scis., AAAS, Sigma Xi. Home: 1 Grace Ct Brooklyn NY 11201

CHARTOUNI, ADIB ELIAS, beverage company executive; b. Beirut, Mar. 24, 1938; s. Elias Dib and Mary A. (Naaman) C.; m. Rona D. Allan, Oct. 15, 1970; children: Vanessa, Sandra. Ed., Lycée Francais, 1960. Rep. in Middle East and Africa for Pepsi Cola Co. Internat., 1961-62; regional mgr. Pepsico Internat., Mex., 1962-67; v.p. acquisition dept. for snack foods, juices and soft drink cos.; v.p. Middle East and African div. Royal Crown Cola Co. Internat., 1967-70, pres. internat. div., Columbus, Ga., 1975—. Mem. Am. Mgmt. Assn., Nat. Soft Drink Assn. Clubs: Columbus Country, Lebanon Golf. Office: 1000 10th Ave Columbus GA 31902

CHARTRAND, MARK RAY, III, astronomer; b. Miami, Fla., Aug. 2, 1943; s. Mark Ray, Jr. and Barbara Dunaway (Wilkins) C. B.S. in Astronomy, Case Inst. Tech., Cleve., 1965; Ph.D., Case Western Res. U., 1970. Asst. to dir. Mueller Planetarium, Cleve., 1965-66; research asst. Warner and Swasey Obs., Cleve., 1966-70; edn. coordinator, asst. astronomer Am. Museum-Hayden Planetarium, N.Y.C., 1970-74, chmn., asso. astronomer, 1974-80; exec. dir. Nat. Space Inst., Washington, 1980—; dir. Scientia, Inc.; speaker colls., public groups. Co-author: Astronomy, 1975; columnist: Omni mag, 1979—; contbr. articles to mags., newspapers; host, producer: radio program What's Up?, 1977-78. Fellow Brit. Interplanetary Soc.; mem. AAAS, Am. Astron. Soc., Am. Astronautical Soc., Explorers Club, N.Y. Acad. Scis., Internat. Planetarium Soc., AIAA, Nat. Space Club, Sigma Xi. Home: 2801 Park Center Dr Apt A1602 Alexandria VA 22302 Office: National Space Inst 600 Maryland Ave SW West Wing Suite 203 Washington DC 20024

CHARTRAND, ROBERT LEE, govt. ofcl.; b. Kansas City, Mo., Mar. 6, 1928; s. Joseph Sterling, Jr. and Isabel Christine (Doherty) C.; m. Eleanor Salmon, Oct. 9, 1967; children: Leslie, Kevin; stepchildren: James, Jennifer. B.A., U. Mo., 1948, M.A., 1949; postgrad., La. State U., 1949-50. Mem. tech. staff Ramo-Wooldridge (TRW), Denver and Canoga Park, Calif., 1959-61; with fed. system div. IBM Corp., Bethesda, Md., 1961-64, mgr. advanced systems mktg., 1964; mgr. applications devel. Planning Research Corp., Washington, 1964-66;

specialist in info. sci. Congressional Research Service, Library of Congress, Washington, 1966-77, sr. specialist in policy and technology, 1977—; Fulbright-Hays lectr., 1968, UN lectr., 1979—; cons. Pres.'s Com. on Population Growth and Am. Future, 1970-71, U.S. Commn. Civil Rights, 1972—, George Washington U., 1975-77, UNESCO, 1977—, Exec. office of Pres., 1977—, Office of Tech. Assessment, 1979—; adj. prof. Am. U., 1974—; mem. adv. com. U.S. CSC, 1973—, White House Conf. on Library and Info. Services, 1979-80; adv. NSF, 1977—; mem. adv. panel Dept. State, 1978—; mem. adv. bd. Chem. Abstracts Service, 1979—. Author: Systems Technology Applied to Social and Community Problems, 1971, Computers and Political Campaigning, 1972, (with others) State Legislature Use of Information Technology, 1978; also congl. studies.; editor, contbg. author: Information Support, Program Budgeting and the Congress, 1968; Editor, contbg. author: Computers in the Service of Society, 1972; editor: Hope for the Cities: A Systems Approach to Human Needs, 1971; co-editor, contbg. author: Information Technology Serving Society, 1979; editorial bd.: Law and Computer Tech, 1968—, The Information Society, 1979—, Hazard, 1979—; editorial adviser: Rutgers Jour. Computers and the Law, 1970-72, ASK, 1982—; cons. editor: Info. Storage and Retrieval, 1969-74, SIAM News, 1976-79; Contbr. articles to profl. jours. Trustee Windham Coll., 1974-76, Engring. Index, 1980—, Capital Children's Mus., Friends of Montgomery County Library. Served to lt. U.S. Navy, 1951-59. Decorated Cavaliere Ufficiale, Italy; recipient Interagy. Com. on ADP award, 1976; Test of Time award, 1979. Fellow AAAS (sect. chmn. 1983—); mem. Am. Soc. Info. Sci. (cons. editor bull. 1974—), Washington Ops. Research Council. Unitarian. Clubs: Cosmos (Washington); Kenwood Golf and Country. Home: 5406 Dorset Ave Chevy Chase MD 20815 Office: 1st and Pennsylvania Ave SE Washington DC 20540

CHARYK, JOSEPH VINCENT, satellite telecommunications company executive; b. Canmore, Alta., Can., Sept. 9, 1920; came to U.S., 1942, naturalized, 1948; s. John and Anna (Dorosh) C.; m. Edwina Elizabeth Rhodes, Aug. 18, 1945; children: William R., J. John, Christopher E., Diane E. B.Sc. in Engring. Physics, U. Alta., 1942, LL.D., 1964; M.S., Calif. Inst. Tech., 1943, Ph.D., 1946; D.Engring. (hon.), U. Bologna, 1974. Sect. chief Jet Propulsion Lab., Calif. Inst. Tech., 1945-46, instr. aeros., 1945-46; asst. prof. aeros. Princeton, 1946-49, asso. prof., 1949-55; dir. aerophysics and chemistry lab., missile systems div. Lockheed Aircraft Corp., 1955-56; dir. aero. lab. Aeronutronic Systems, Inc. subs. Ford Motor Co., 1956-58, gen. mgr. space tech. div., 1958-59; asst. sec. Air Force (for research and devel.), 1959, under sec., 1960-63; pres., dir. Communications Satellite Corp., 1963—, chief exec. officer, 1979—, chmn., 1983—; chmn. bd. Comsat Gen. Corp., Environ. Research and Tech., Inc., Satellite TV Corp.; mem. partners' com. Satellite Bus. Systems; dir. Am. Security Corp., Abbott Labs.; mem. corp. C. S. Draper Lab., Inc. Fellow AIAA, IEEE; mem. Nat. Acad. Engring., Internat. Acad. Astronautics, Nat. Inst. Social Scis., Nat. Space Club, Sigma Xi. Clubs: 1925 F Street, Chevy Chase, Burning Tree, Met. Home: 5126 Tilden St NW Washington DC 20016

CHARYN, JEROME, author; b. N.Y.C., May 13, 1937; s. Sam and Fannie (Paley) C. B.A. cum laude, Columbia, 1959. Former recreation leader Dept. Parks, N.Y.C.; English tchr. High Sch. Music and Art, Sch. Performing Arts, N.Y.C., 1962-64; asst. prof. English, vis. writer Stanford, 1965-68; asst. prof. English Herbert Lehman Coll., City U. N.Y., 1968-71, asso. prof., 1971-78, prof., 1978-80; vis. Mellon prof. English Rice U., spring 1979; vis. prof. creative writing Princeton U., spring 1980, lectr. creative writing, 1981—; vis. prof. English U. Tex., fall 1980. Author: Once Upon a Droshky, 1964, On the Darkening Green, 1965, The Man Who Grew Younger, 1967, Going to Jerusalem, 1967, American Scrapbook, 1969, Eisenhower, My Eisenhower, 1971, The Tar Baby, 1973, Blue Eyes, 1975, Marilyn the Wild, 1976, The Education of Patrick Silver, 1976, The Franklin Scare, 1977, Secret Isaac, 1978, The Seventh Babe, 1979, The Catfish Man, 1980, Darlin' Bill, 1980, Panna Maria, 1982, Pinocchio's Nose, 1983; also short stories.; Editor: The Single Voice, 1969, The Troubled Vision, 1970; co-editor: The Dutton Review, 1970-72; exec. editor: Fiction, 1972—. Guggenheim Found. fellow, 1982; Recipient Rosenthal award Am. Acad. and Inst. Arts and Letters, 1981. Mem. P.E.N., Phi Beta Kappa.

CHASE, ALLEN, diversified investment executive; b. Los Angeles, Sept. 11, 1911; s. Edward Tilden and Lenna (Prather) C.; children: Charlene, Diane Chase Randolph. B.S., UCLA, 1933; postgrad., London Sch. Econs., U. London, Eng., 1934. Salesman Chase Securities Co., Los Angeles, 1934-39; pres. Standardized Aircraft Co., Los Angeles, 1939—; chmn. bd. dirs. Esperence Plains Pty. Ltd., Australia, 1956—, Agra Paraguay, 1967—; pres. Allen Chase & Co., 1964—; dir. Allied Pastoral Co. Enterprises, Pty. Ltd., Australia, Australian Ocean Products, Pacific Basin Industries, Pty. Ltd. Clubs: University, Riviera Country, Bel Air Country, Beverly Hills Wine and Food Soc., Coronado Yacht, Kaneoe Yacht. Conceived establishment over one million virgin acres to agr. in single area by pvt. enterprise. Office: Marina City Club PH38 4337 Marina City Dr Marina del Rey CA 90291 *

CHASE, ANTHONY GOODWIN, lawyer; b. San Francisco, Feb. 15, 1938; s. Goodwin and Gudrun M. (Mack) C.; m. Mary Costa, Mar. 22, 1981; children by previous marriage: Betsy Marie, Whitney Marie, Goodwin Samuel, Anthony Joseph. B.A., U. Wash., 1960; J.D., Georgetown U., 1967. Bar: D.C. 1967, Wash. 1969. Nat. bank examiner U.S. Treasury Dept., 1962-65; asst. to U.S. Comptroller of Currency, 1965-67; individual practice law, 1967-69; asst. to U.S. sec. of commerce, 1969-70; gen. counsel SBA, Washington, 1970-71, dep. adminstr., 1971-73; partner firm Brownstein, Zeidman Schomer and Chase, Washington and Los Angeles, 1973-78; firm Tufo, Johnston, Zuccotti & Chase, Washington and N.Y.C., 1978-80, Drinker Biddle & Reath, Washington, Phila. and N.Y.C., 1980-82; mng. ptnr. firm Trammell, Chase, Lambert & Martindale, Washington, 1982—; adj. prof. corp. law Georgetown U., lectr., 1971—; Wharton Sloan lectr. Wharton Sch. Bus., U. Pa., 1973; lectr. Sr. Bank Mgmt. Seminar, Columbia U., 1971—, N.Y. Law Jour., 1974—, Am. Law Inst., 1980—; dir. VSE Corp., Alexandria, Va., Digital Switch Corp., Dallas, 1980-81; sec. Nat. Adv. Com. on Banking Policies and Practices, 1966; mem. Adminstrv. Conf. U.S., Fed. Adv. Council Regional Econ. Devel.; adv. com. on indsl. issuers SEC, 1972-73; fed. state programs coordinator State of Wash., 1967; Mem. nat. devel. com. Georgetown U., 1970—; mem. bd. control U. Wash., 1960. Author: Small Business Financing, 1983; Co-editor: Wests Fed. Practice Manual, 1974—; mem.: Georgetown Law Rev, 1964-65; Contbr. articles to profl. jours. Served as lt. USMC, 1960-62; capt. Res. Named Outstanding Young Man of Year Wash. Jr. C. of C., 1968; recipient Fed. Silver medal for meritorious service, 1970, Fed. Gold medal for disting. service, 1971; Disting. Service to Am. Bus. award Nat. Assn. Small Bus. Investment Cos., 1972; Outstanding Service to Am. Small Bus. Community award Nat. Small Bus. Assn., 1974. Mem. Am. Bar Assn., Fed. Bar Assn., Pa. Bar Assn., D.C. Bar Assn., Wash. Bar Assn., Am. Judicature Soc., Nat. Lawyers Club, Beta Theta Pi. Republican. Episcopalian. Clubs: Union League (N.Y.C.); Pisces (Chevy Chase, Md.); Georgetown; Mid-Ocean (Tuckerstown, Bermuda). Home: 2404 Wyoming Ave NW Washington DC 20008 Office: 1000 Potomac St NW Washington DC 20007

CHASE, AURIN MOODY, JR., educator; b. Syracuse, N.Y., June 2, 1904; s. Aurin Moody and Bertha (Bucklin) C.; m. Osmunde Olcott Phillips, Dec. 31, 1937; 1 dau., Elise Phillips Chase Dennis. A.B., Amherst Coll., 1926, A.M., 1929; Ph.D., Columbia, 1935. Asst. biology Amherst Coll., 1926-28; asst. biophysics Columbia, 1929-34, instr., research asst., 1934-38; research asso. biology Princeton, 1939-45, asst. prof. biology, 1945-48, asso. prof., 1948-61, prof., 1961-67, prof. biology emeritus, 1967—; Instr. Marine Biol. Lab., Woods Hole, Mass., summers 1945-46, life mem. corp., trustee, 1950-58, 59-67, sec. bd. trustees, 1956-58, trustee emeritus, 1979—; mem. corp. Bermuda Biol. Sta. Contbr. articles to profl. books, jours. Fellow AAAS, N.Y. Acad. Scis. (life mem.); mem. Am. Physiol. Soc., Am. Soc. Photobiology, Am. Soc. Zoologists, N.J. Acad. Scis., Soc. Gen. Physiologists (exec. council 1951-53, treas. 1957-59, hon. mem.), Am. Soc. Biol. Chemists, Am. Soc. Cell Biology, Thoreau Soc. (life), Sigma Xi. Episcopalian. Club: Nassau (Princeton). Research on gen. physiology, biochemistry of vision and bioluminescence, human blood storage, enzyme action. Home: 31 Adams Dr Princeton NJ 08540

CHASE, BRANDON LEE, film company executive, producer, director, writer; b. N.Y.C., Mar. 17, 1932; s. Bernard and Vera C.; m. Marrianne Illona, Oct. 20, 1971; children: Andrea, Barry, Cibbie. B.J., U. Conn. News dir. Sta.-WDSU-TV, NBC, New Orleans, 1952-57; pres. Cahse Assocs., New Orleans, 1958-63, Group 1 Films, Los Angeles, 1964—. Producer: numerous films, including Alligator, The Sword and The Sorcerer; dir., writer films. Recipient Best Picture award Atlanta Film Festival, 1975, others. Office: Group L Films 9200 Sunset Blvd Los Angeles CA 90069

CHASE, CHEVY (CORNELIUS CRANE), performer, author; b. N.Y.C., Oct. 8, 1943; s. Edward Tinsley and Cathalene Crane (Widdoes) C.; m. Jacqueline Carlin, Dec. 4, 1976 (div. 1980); m. Jayni Chase; 1 dau., Cydney Cathalene. B.A. in English, Bard Coll., 1967; CCS, Inst. Audio Research, 1970; M.A., MIT. Artist, MGM Records, 1968; writer: Mad mag., 1969; actor: Groove Tube, Pasta Prodns., 1967-71; writer, actor: Gt. Am. Dream Machine, 1971; dir., writer, actor, Nat. Lampoon Theatre Co., 1972-74; writer, actor: Sat. Night TV show, 1975-76; appeared on: TV in Paul Simon Spl.; appeared in: films Foul Play, 1978, Oh Heavenly Dog, 1980, Caddyshack, 1980, Seems Like Old Times, Under the Rainbow, 1981, Modern Problems, 1981, Vacation, 1983, Deal of the Century, 1983. Recipient award for best script in comedy variety spl. Writers Guild, award best supporting actor in comedy variety series Nat. Acad. TV Arts and Scis. Mem. Am. Fedn. Musicians, Stage Actors Guild, Actors Equity, AFTRA. Democrat. Office: care William Morris Agy 151 El Camino Beverly Hills CA 90212 *

CHASE, CLINTON IRVIN, university official educator; b. Aug. 14, 1927; m. Patricia Cronenberger; 1 child. B.S. in Psychology with honors, U. Idaho, 1950, M.S. in Adminstrn., 1951; Ph.D. in Ednl. Psychology, U. Calif.-Berkeley, 1958. Asst. to dean students Wash. State U., 1951-52; sch. psychologist Piedmont Pub. Schs., Calif., 1957-58; asst. prof. ednl. psychology Idaho State U., 1958-61, Miami U., Oxford, 1961-62, Ind. U., Bloomington, 1962-64, assoc. prof., 1964-68, prof., 1968—, assoc. dir. Bur. Evaluative Studies and Testing, 1962-70, dir., 1970—, chmn. dept. ednl. psychology, 1970-74. Author: (with H. Glenn Ludlow) Readings in Educational and Psychological Measurement, 1966, Elementary Statistical Procedures, 1967, Elementary Statistical Procedures 3d edit., 1984, Measurement for Educational Evaluation, 1974, Measurement for Eudcational Evaluation 2d edit., 1978. Served with USN, 1945-46; to capt. USAF, 1952-55. Mem. Am. Psychol. Assn., Am. Ednl. Research Assn., Nat. Council on Measurement in Edn., Phi Beta Kappa, Kappa Delta Pi. Office: Bur of Evaluative Studies and Testing Indiana Univ 3d St and Jordan Ave Blooming IN 47405 *The careful establishment of objectives, and the persistant pursuit of objectives, are the primary ingredients of achievement.*

CHASE, COCHRANE, advertising agency executive; b. Berwyn, Ill., Feb. 6, 1932; s. Henry Cochrane and Roselyn (Scott) C.; m. Janis Valeria Kueber, June 19, 1954; children—Katherine Ann, Anthony Scott, Lisa Marie. B.A., Wesleyan U., 1954. With steel warehousing div. Jessop Steel Co., Broadview, Ill., 1956-62, mgr. sales, 1961-62; with Jessop Steel Calif., Santa Fe Springs, 1963-64; asst. mgr. market research Ducommun Metals & Supply Co., Los Angeles, 1964-65; v.p. Newport Advt. Inc., Newport Beach, Calif., 1965; pres. Cochrane Chase, Livingston & Co., Inc., Irvine, Calif., 1966, chmn. bd., chief exec. officer, 1966—. Co-author: Marketing Problem Solver, 973. Served with USNR, 1954-56. Mem. Am. Assn. Advt. Agys., Western States Assn. Advt. Agys. (Advt. Leader of Yr 1982). Home: 2162 Papya Dr La Habra CA 90631 Office: 19600 Fairchild Ave Irvine CA 92715

CHASE, DORIS TOTTEN, sculptor, video artist and, filmmaker; b. Seattle, 1923; d. William Phelps and Helen (Feeney) Totten; m. Elmo Chase, Oct. 20, 1943 (div. 1972); children: Gregary Totten, Randall Jarvis Totten. Student, U. Wash., 1941-43. Artist, exhibited in one-woman shows, Seligman Gallery, Seattle, 1959, 61, Gallery Numero, Florence, Italy, 1961, Internat. Gallery, Italy, 1962, Hall Coleman Gallery, Seattle, Formes Gallery, Tokyo, 1963, 70, Bangkok Center Mus., Thailand, 1963, Bolles Gallery, San Francisco, 1964, Suffolk (N.Y.) Mus., 1965, Smolin Gallery, N.Y.C., Gallery Numero, Rome, 1962, 66, Collectors Gallery, Seattle, 1964, 66, 69, Tacoma Art Mus., 1967, Ruth White Gallery, N.Y.C., 1967, 69, 70, Fountain Gallery, Portland, Oreg., 1970, U. Wash. Henry Gallery, 1971, 77, Wadsworth Atheneum, Hartford, Conn., 1973, Hirshhorn Mus., Washington, 1974, 77, Anthology Film Archives, N.Y.C., 1975, 80, 83, Donnell Library, N.Y.C., 1976, 79, 83, Performing Arts Mus. at Lincoln Center, 1976, Mus. Modern Art, N.Y.C., 1978, 80, High Mus., Atlanta, 1978, Herbert Johnson Mus., 1982, A.I.R. Gallery, N.Y.C., 1983, circulating exhbt., Western Mus. Assn., 1970-71; represented in permanent collections, Finch Coll. Mus., N.Y., Seattle Art Mus., Ashai Shimbum, Tokyo, Battelle Inst., Mus. Fine Arts Boston, Milw. Art Inst., Art Inst. Chgo., Mus. Fine Arts Houston, Frye Art Mus., Seattle, Nat. Collection Fine Arts, Smithsonian Inst., Washington, Wadsworth Atheneum, N.C. Mus. Art, Raleigh, Mus. Modern Art, Kobe, Japan, Pa. Acad. Art, Phila., Portland Art Mus., Vancouver (B.C.) Art Gallery, N.Y.C., Montgomery (Ala.) Mus. Fine Art, Hudson River Mus., N.Y.C., works reproduced in various art mags. and books; executed monumental kinetic sculpture, Kerry Park, Seattle, Anderson, Ind., Expo '70, Osaka, Japan, Sculpture Park, Atlanta, Lake Park, Ind., Met. Mus. Art, N.Y.C., Montgomery Mus. Fine Arts, multi-media sculpture for 4 ballets, Opera Assn. Seattle; included in, Sculpture in Park program N.Y.C., Playground of Tomorrow ABC-TV, Los Angeles; included in films: Moon Refined; work in video, TV Exptl. Lab., WNET; TV prodns. Lies, 1980; Window, 1980, Doris Chase Dance Series produced at Bklyn. Coll, WCET-Cin., WGBH, Boston, WNYC, N.Y., NET; producer, Doris Chase Dance Series, 1971-81, Concept Series, 1980-83. Recipient honors and awards at numerous festivals in U.S. and fgn. countries; grantee Nat. Endowment for Arts, N.Y. State Council for Arts, Mich. Arts Council. Address: 222 W 23 St New York NY 10011

CHASE, FRANK RALPH, mfg. co. exec.; b. Mpls., Nov. 10, 1925; s. Frank Ralph and Virginia (Nickerson) C.; m. Jean Ann Fosdick, Sept. 18, 1948; children—Sally, Frank Ralph, Anne, Barbara. B.B.A., U. Minn., 1947. Prodn. coordinator Gould/Nat. Battery Corp., St. Paul, 1947-49; asst. sales mgr. Multi-Clean Products, Inc., St. Paul, 1950-55; sales mgr. Torit Corp., St. Paul, 1955-68, pres., 1968-73; v.p., gen. mgr. Donaldson Indsl. Group, St. Paul, 1974—; dir. Econo-Therm Energy Systems, Inc., Mpls., E. D. Bullard Co., Sausalito, Calif., Tescom Corp., Mpls. Served with USNR, 1944-46. Mem. ASHRAE. Republican. Congregationalist. Patentee in field. Office: 1400 W 94th St PO Box 1299 Minneapolis MN 55440

CHASE, GILBERT, writer, educator; b. Havana, Cuba, Sept. 4, 1906; s. Gilbert P. and Edelmira (Culmell) C.; m. Kathleen Barentzen, Dec. 27, 1929; children—Paul, Peter John. Student, Columbia U., 1926; B.A., U. N.C., 1950; D.Litt. (hon.), U. Miami, 1955; pvt. study music with, Max Wald, Paris. Music critic Continental Daily Mail, Paris, 1929-35; asso. editor Internat. Cyclopedia of Music and Musicians, N.Y.C., 1936-38; editor G. Schirmer, Inc., N.Y.C., 1939-40; Latin Am. specialist music div. Library of Congress, 1940-43; music supr. NBC U. of the Air, 1943-48; mgr. edn. dept. RCA Victor, Camden, N.J., 1948-49; cultural attache Am. embassy, Lima, Peru, 1951-53, Buenos Aires, 1953-55; dir. Sch. Music U. Okla., 1955-56, acting dean, 1956-57; cultural attaché Am. embassy, Brussels, 1958-60; prof. music and Latin Am. studies Tulane U., 1960-66; dir. Inter-Am. Inst. for Musical Research, 1961-69; sr. research fellow Inst. Studies in Am. Music, Bklyn. Coll., City U. N.Y., 1972-73; Ziegele vis. prof. music State U. N.Y. at Buffalo, 1973-74; vis. prof. comparative studies, history and music U. Tex. at Austin, 1975-79; Paris corr. Mus. America, N.Y.C., 1930-35, Mus. Times, London, 1931-35; adviser, reviewer Book of Month Club, 1936-49; lectr. history Am. music Columbia, 1946-48; Mem. adv. com. on music U.S. Dept. of State, 1943-45; mus. cons. Pan Am. Union, 1943-45; cons. for music loan libraries in Latin Am. Library of Congress, 1944-46; mem. U.S. Adv. Com. on Cultural Info., 1957-58; mem. bicentennial com. Nat. Music Council, 1974—. Author: Cities and Souls: Poems of Spain, 1929, The Music of Spain, 1941, 2d rev. edit., 1959, A Guide to Latin American Music, 1945, 2d rev. edit., 1962, America's Music: From the Pilgrims to the Present, 1955, 2d rev. edit., 1966, 3d rev. edit., 1983, The American Composer Speaks, 1966; Transl.: A Concise History of Latin American Culture, 1966; Author: Contemporary Art in Latin America, 1970; Editor: Music in Radio Broadcasting, 1946; music editor: Handbook of Latin Am. Studies, 1963-67, Inter-Am. Mag, 1940-43; editor: yearbook for Inter-Am. Mus. Research, 1964-76; contbg. editor: Yearbook for Arts in Soc, 1965-75. Hon. prof. faculty philosophy, letters U. Buenos Aires. Mem. Am. Musicol. Soc., Soc. for Ethnomusicology (1st v.p. 1963-65), Inter-Am Music Council (pres. 1960-63), Latin Am. Studies Assn. (constituent mem.), Société Francaise de Musicologie, Instituto Español de Musicología, Music Library Assn., Am. Studies Assn. Address: 154 Lake Ellen Dr Chapel Hill NC 27514 *My lack of specialized training (my academic study ended with a B.A.) has been both a handicap and an advantage. A handicap because I was not qualified for any of the prestigious professional careers; an advantage because I was receptive to any kind of job that offered a challenge and an opportunity for achievement. I always wanted to be a writer, and my books helped me to achieve an academic career, beginning as full professor at age 50. I gave all I had to every job, and learned from each.*

CHASE, GOODWIN, retired banker; b. Los Angeles, June 30, 1911; s. Goodwin and Laurene G. (Crosthwaite) C.; m. Gudrun M. Mack, May 9, 1936; children: Anthony G., Christine M. (Mrs. Payne Kenyon Kellogg), Stephen M. Ed., U. So. Calif., 1930-31, Inst. Econs., Brookings Instn., 1933-34. With Wash. Nat. Bank, Ellensburg, 1939-58, v.p., 1940-56, pres., 1957-58; with Nat. Bank of Wash., Tacoma, 1958-70, exec. v.p., 1958, pres., chmn., 1959-70; pres. Pacific Nat. Bank of Wash. (consolidation of Nat. Bank of Wash. and Pacific Nat. Bank of Seattle 1970) (now First Interstate Bank of Wash.), 1970-72, also dir.; pres. Central Wash. Broadcasters, Inc., 1947-58, N.W. Chems., Inc., 1951-55; mem. adv. com. to U.S. comptroller currency, 1962-63; mem. U.S. Renegotiation Bd., Washington, 1973—, chmn., 1977-79. Mem. Western Internat. Trade Group, Dept. Commerce, 1966—, Pres.'s Nat. Citizens Com. on Community Relations, 1964-66; chmn. Wash. State Council on Higher Edn., 1969— chmn. Wash. State Council on Higher Edn., 1969-70, Wash. council Nat. Council Crime and Delinquency, 1964—, Wash. council Nat. Council Crime and Delinquency, 1965-67; mem. Seattle Regional Export Expansion Council, 1962—, chmn., 1967-69; mem. Pacific N.W. Ballet Assn., chmn., 1966-69; Bd. dirs. Adlai E. Stevenson Inst. Internat. Affairs, 1966-73, Tacoma Gen. Hosp., 1968-73; chmn. United Good Neighbor Fund Pierce County, 1964—, Tacoma Gen. Hosp., United Arts Council Puget Sound, 1968-72; trustee Tacoma Art Mus., 1959—, pres., 1959-61; trustee Wash. State Internat. Trade Fair, 1960—, Tacoma Athletic Commn., 1960-73; chmn. Tacoma Philharmonic, Inc., 1960—; bd. regents Pacific Lutheran U., 1970—; mem. vis. com. Coll. Arts and Scis., U. Wash., 1962—; mem. lay adv. bd. St. Jospeh's Hosp., 1966-72. Recipient Distinguished Service award Ellensburg Jr. C. of C., 1945, Sigurd S. Larmon award Nat. Council on Crime and Delinquency, 1969; Lamplighter award NAACP, 1972. Mem. Am., Wash. bankers assns. Club: Tacoma Country and Golf. Home: 11417 Gravelly Lake Dr SW Tacoma WA

CHASE, JAMES KELLER, artist museum dir., educator; b. Logansport, Ind., May 18, 1929; s. James Howard and Agnes (Keller) C.; m. Marcelle Pierard, Dec. 29, 1969; 1 son, Henrik Clovis. B.S., Ball State U., Muncie, Ind., 1952, doctoral fellow, 1972-74; M.A., Mich. State U., 1963. Art supr. Chili (Ind.) schs., 1952-53, Sturgis (Mich.) schs., 1953-57; asst. prof. Western Mich. U., 1957-60; tchr. edn. TV on camera Central Mich. U., 1960-65; prof., chmn. fine arts dept. Northwood Inst., Midland, Mich., 1964-74; dir. Saginaw (Mich.) Mus., 1975-77, Ariz. Capitol Mus., Phoenix, 1978—; extension tchr. Western Mich. U., Saginaw Valley Coll., Delta Coll., Saginaw; mem. Mich. Higher Edn. Com., 1967, Mich. Creativity Com., 1966; bd. dirs. Midland Center Arts, 1967-71. Author: Nine Fine, 1977; contbr. articles to edn. jours., newspapers; exhibiting artist state, regional and nat. shows. Mem. Am. Assn. Museums, Ariz. Adminstrs. Assn., Central Ariz. Museums Assn., Ariz. Hist. Assn. Home: 8754 E Devonshire St Scottsdale AZ 85251 *Creating, sharing and understanding art and beauty adds truth and vibrance to life.*

CHASE, JAMES RICHARD, college official; b. Oxnard, Calif., Oct. 7, 1930; s. James Warren and Nina Marie (Fiscus) C.; m. Mary Corinne Sutherland, Dec. 16, 1950; children: Kenneth, Richard, Jennifer Corinne. B. Theology, Biola Coll., 1951; B.A., Pepperdine U., 1953, M.A., 1954; Ph.D., Cornell U., 1961. Instr. Biola Coll., La Mirada, Calif., 1953-57, prof., chmn. dept. humanities, 1959-65, v.p. acad. affairs, 1965-70, pres., 1970—; teaching asst. Cornell Univ., Ithaca, N.Y., 1957-59; bd. dirs. World Christian Tng. Ctr., 1970—; Bd. dirs. Christian Coll. Coalition, 1977-79, chmn. bd., 1977-79; bd. dirs. Mission Aviation Fellowship, 1975-81, chmn. bd., 1978-81; Western Coll. Assn., 1980-82. Mem. Nat. Assn. Ind. Colls. and Univs. (dir. 1980), Assn. Ind. Calif. Colls. and Univs. (mem. exec. com. 1978-82), Am. Assn. Bible Colls. (dir. 1974-80), Nat. Assn. Intercollegiate Athletics (pres. adv. com. 1976-82), Nat. Assn. Evangelicals (com. higher edn., bd. adminstrn. 1982), Western Assn. Schs. and Colls. (sr. commn. 1981—), Am. Assn. Presidents of Ind. Colls. and Univs. (dir. 1980—, v.p. 1982—), Speech Communication Assn. Baptist. Club: Rotary. Office: Wheaton Coll Wheaton IL 60187

CHASE, JAMES STATON, historian, educator; b. Richmond, Va., July 2, 1932; s. Francis Seabury and Sue Wilbourne (Elder) C. A.B., Coll. William and Mary, 1953; M.A., U. Chgo., 1957, Ph.D., 1961.

Asst. prof. U. Tex., Austin, 1961-68; asso. prof. history U. Ark., Fayetteville, 1968-73, prof., 1973—, chmn. dept., 1970-76; Mem. Ark. Bicentennial Commn., 1970-76; bd. dirs. Ark. Nat. Endowment for Humanities, 1973-76. Author: Emergence of the Presidential Nominating Convention, 1789-1832, 1973; adv. editor: Social Sci. Quar, 1968—; contbr. articles to profl. jours., ency., chpts. in books. Mem. Washington County (Ark.) Democratic Central Com., 1970—; alt. del. Dem. Nat. Conv., 1976. Served with AUS, 1954-55; Korea. Mem. Ark. Assn. Coll. History Tchrs. (pres. 1974-76), Am. Hist. Assn., Orgn. Am. Historians, So. History Assn., Southwestern Social Sci. Assn., Phi Alpha Theta. Democrat. Episcopalian. Office: History Dept Ozark Hall 12 University of Arkansas Fayetteville AR 72701

CHASE, JOHN DAVID, physician, university dean; b. Detroit, Sept. 24, 1920; s. Clyde Harrison and Bonnie Lucille (Fogas) C.; m. Margaret Julia Chamberlain, July 25, 1942; 1 son, Robert Winslow. A.B., Wabash (Ind.) Coll., 1942; M.D., Western Res. U., 1945. Diplomate: Am. Bd. Internal Medicine. Intern Detroit Receiving Hosp., 1945-46; resident in internal medicine Wayne State U. Hosp., 1948-52; teaching fellow Nat. Heart Inst., 1952; with VA, 1952-78, dep. asso. chief med. dir. academic affairs, Washington, 1970-73; chief med. service VA Hosp., Tacoma, 1973-74; chief med. dir. VA Central Office, Washington, 1974-78; asso. dean clin. affairs U. Wash. Sch. Med., Seattle, 1978—, dean Sch. Medicine, 1981-82; mem. nat. adv. council Heart and Lung Inst., 1968-70, Regional Med. Programs, 1970-73, Nat. Library Medicine, 1972-73; mem. Nat. Adv. Council VA Edn., 1973, Nat. Adv. Council Health Services Planning and Resources, 1976, Fed. Coordinating Council Sci., Engring. and Tech., 1976-78, Nat. Adv. Council Health Planning and Devel., 1976—; bd. govs. Armed Forces Inst. Pathology, 1976-78. Trustee Chgo. Med. Sch., 1978—. Served with M.C. USNR, 1946-48. Recipient Distinguished Service award Wayne State U. Med. Sch., 1976. Fellow ACP, Am. Coll. Chest Physicians; mem. Assn. Mil. Surgeons U.S., AMA (ho. dels.), Am. Hosp. Assn. (trustee 1976-78). Home: 3700 Soundview Dr W Tacoma WA 98466 Office: U Wash AA316 Health Sci Bldg Seattle WA 98195

CHASE, KENNETH HUNTINGTON, lawyer; b. N.Y.C., July 17, 1944; s. Hollis H. and Beverly Huntington (Seaman) C.; m. Jeanne-Nicole Ledoux, Feb. 14, 1971. A.B., U. Pa., 1966, LL.B., 1969. Bar: N.Y. 1970. Asst. sec. Am. Investors Fund, Inc., Greenwich, Conn., 1969-70; asst. sec. Am. Gen. Funds, N.Y.C., 1971-77; asst. sec., asso. counsel Am. Gen. Capital Mgmt., Inc., N.Y.C., 1972-77; sec., counsel The Reserve Fund, Inc., N.Y.C., 1977-80; asso. Davis, Polk & Wardwell, N.Y.C., 1980—. Vice pres., trustee Bar Harbor Festival, 1970—; counsel Mendelssohn Glee Club, 1979—; sec., dir. Conductor's Club, 1975—; deacon, cemetery treas. English Neighborhood Reformed Ch., Ridgefield, N.J., 1978—. Mem. Assn. Bar City N.Y., SR (chmn. color guard 1979-81, bd. mgrs. 1982—), St. Nicholas Soc., Soc. Cincinnati, Soc. Colonial Wars, St. George's Soc., Colonial Order of Acorn, Phi Kappa Psi. Republican. Club: U. Pa. (N.Y.C.) (pres., bd. govs.). Home: 8200 Boulevard E North Bergen NJ 07047 Office: 1 Chase Manhattan Plaza New York NY 10005

CHASE, LUCIA, ballet dancer; b. Waterbury, Conn.; d. Irving Hall and Elizabeth Hosmer (Kellogg) C.; m. Thomas Ewing, Jr.; children: Thomas III, Alexander Cochran. Student, St. Margaret's Sch., Waterbury, Theatre Guild Sch., N.Y.C.; L.H.D. (hon.), U. Wis., 1969, D.F.A., Williams Coll., 1977, L.I.U., 1979. Ballerina, Mordkin Ballet, 1937-39; ballerina, Am. Ballet Theatre, N.Y.C., 1940-60; co-dir., from 1945 (Recipient Dance Mag. Award 1957), 1945-80. 17th ann. Capezio Dance award, 1968; Mayor's Arts and Culture award N.Y.C. Commn. Cultural Affairs, 1978. Office: Am Ballet Theatre 890 Broadway New York NY 10003 *

CHASE, LUCIUS PETER, retired corporate executive, lawyer; b. Rochester, N.Y., Jan. 1, 1902; s. Lucius A. and Beatrice (Tucker) C.; m. Virdelle Simpson, June 13, 1925. A.B., U. Wis., 1923, J.D., 1925; LL.D., Lakeland Coll., 1972. Former spl. asst. to atty. gen. U.S.; former gen. counsel, sr. v.p. Kohler Co., Wis., now dir.; practice law as of counsel Chase, Olsen, Kloet & Gunderson, Sheboygan; dir. emeritus Citizens Bank of Sheboygan.; Trustee, chmn. emeritus Lakeland Coll., Sheboygan. Contbr. articles profl. jours. Served as col. AUS, World War II. Decorated Silver Star, Legion of Merit with oak leaf cluster, Purple Heart; Croix de Guerre with palm, France; officer Order of Leopold, Belgium). Mem. Am., Wis., Sheboygan County bar assns., Am. Legion, V.F.W., Mil. Order Purple Heart, Order of Coif, Scabbard and Blade, Alpha Sigma Phi, Gamma Eta Gamma. Methodist. Clubs: Rotarian., Country (Sheboygan). Home: 624 School St Kohler WI 53044 Office: 602 N 6th St Sheboygan WI 53081 *Take your objective seriously; believe in it. Believe in your ability to accomplish it. That won't insure success, but it is the essential first step. If you think you may fail, you probably will.*

CHASE, MERRILL WALLACE, educator, immunologist; b. Providence, Sept. 17, 1905; s. John Whitman and Bertha H. (Wallace) C.; m. Edith Steele Bowen, Sept. 5, 1931 (dec. 1961); children: Nancy Steele (Mrs. William W. Cowles), John Wallace, Susan Elizabeth; m. Cynthia Hambury Pierce, July 8, 1961. A.B., Brown U., 1927, Sc.M., 1929, Ph.D., 1931, Sc.D. honoris causa, 1977, M.D., U. Münster, West Germany, 1974. Instr. biology Brown U., 1931-32; staff mem. Rockefeller Inst. Med. Research, 1932-65; prof. immunology and microbiology, head lab. immunology and hypersensitivity Rockefeller U., 1956-79; med. adv. council Profl. Ednl. and Research Task Force, Asthma and Allergy Found. Am., 1955-82. Editor: (with C.A. Williams) Methods in Immunology and Immunochemistry, Vol. 1, 1967, Vol. 11, 1968, Vol. III, 1970, vols. IV, 1977, and V, 1976. Hon. fellow Am. Acad. Allergy (distinguished service award 1969), Am. Coll. Allergists; fellow Am. Acad. Arts and Scis.; mem. Am. Assn. Immunologists (pres. 1956-57), Am. Soc. Microbiology (program chmn. 1959-61), AAAS, Harvey Soc., N.Y. Acad. Scis., N.Y. Allergy Soc. (hon.), Nat. Acad. Sci. Republican. Universalist-Unitarian. Spl. research hypersensitivity to simple chem. allergens, studies Kveim antigen in sarcoidosis, studies tuberculins and mycobacterial antigens. Office: Rockefeller U 1230 York Ave New York NY 10021

CHASE, MORRIS, internat. mgmt. cons.; b. N.Y.C., May 19, 1918; s. Samuel and Bessie (Rabinowitz) Cherkasky; m. Claire Pernitz, Mar. 14, 1942; children—Sylvia, Viviane. B.B.A., Coll. City N.Y., 1939; student econ. sci., U. Paris, 1959. C.P.A., N.Y. State. Mem. staff several C.P.A. firms, 1939-42; asst. to dir. finance and accounting Am. Joint Distbn. Com., 1946-48; dep. controller Marshall Plan mission to France, 1949; controller, finance officer U.S. spl. econ. mission to Cambodia, Laos and Vietnam, 1950; controller U.S. spl. econ. mission to Yugoslavia, 1951; economist Office U.S. Rep. in Europe, Paris, 1952-53; chmn. Internat. Bd. Auditors for Infrastructure, NATO., Paris, 1954-60, dir. infrastructure program, 1961-68, chmn. def. installations com., 1966-68, chmn. payments and progress com; cons. NATO Air Def. Ground Environment Consortium, 1968—. Served to capt. USAAF, 1942-46; maj. Res. Mem. Am. Inst. C.P.A.'s, N.Y. State Soc. C.P.A.'s, Fed. Accountants Assn. (pres. Paris 1961-62), Fed. Govt. Accountants Assn. Paris (pres. 1964-65), Beta Gamma Sigma. Home: Flaminia C Crans-sur-Sierre Valais Switzerland also 163 Ave Winston Churchill Brussels 1180 Belgium

CHASE, NICHOLAS JOSEPH, lawyer, educator; b. Windsor, Conn., Jan. 9, 1913; s. Michael and Lucy A. (Sinsigalli) C.; m. F. Louise Dooley, Dec. 27, 1936; children: Stephen Edward, Mary Ann, Michael Dooley, Clare Lucia, Martha Louise. A.B., Catholic U. Am., 1933, A.M. Columbian fellow, 1934; student, Brookings Instn., 1935; J.D. magna cum laude, Georgetown U., 1940. Bar: D.C. 1939, U.S. Ct. Appeals and Ct. Claims bars 1940, Supreme Ct. bar 1943, Md. bar 1950. Practiced in, Washington, 1939—; adminstrv. asst. PWA, 1935-40; prof. law Catholic U., 1943-45, Georgetown U., 1946-66; Mem. D.C. Council Law Enforcement, 1958-59; arbitrator Am. Arbitration Assn., 1970—. Contbr. articles on trials, tax and real estate law and practice in law jours. Chmn. bd. trustees Hawthorne Sch., Washington. Mem. Am. Bar Assn., Bar Assn. of D.C. (1st v.p., dir. 1958-63), Georgetown Alumni Assn. (bd. govs. 1958-62), Catholic U. Alumni (pres. 1952-54), Columbia Hist. Soc. (chmn. memls. and plaques com.), Phi Delta Phi. Clubs: Congressional Country, Nat. Press, Counsellors (founder), Touchdown (Washington) (founder); Kenwood Country, Rehoboth Country. Home: 5205 Oakland Rd Chevy Chase MD 20815 Rehoboth DE 19971

CHASE, NORMAN ELI, radiologist, educator; b. Cin., June 29, 1926; s. Oscar and Irene (Gindy) C.; m. Joan Salkover, Oct. 1, 1954; children: Stephen Owen, Diana Stephanie. Student, Ohio U., 1946; B.S., U. Cin., 1950, M.D., 1953. Intern Kings County Hosp., Bklyn., 1953-54; resident radiology Columbia Presbyn. Med. Center, 1956-58, instr., asso., 1959-61; asst. prof. N.Y. U. Med. Center, 1961-64, asso. prof., 1964-67, prof. radiology, 1967—, chmn. dept. radiology, 1969—; dir. radiology Bellevue Hosp., 1965-73, asso. dir. radiology, 1973—; sr. cons. radiology Manhattan VA Hosp., 1969—; cons. St. Vincent's Hosp., 1968—, N.Y. Infirmary, 1971—, New Rochelle Hosp., 1975—, Booth Meml. Hosp., 1976—. Served with USAAF, 1944-45. Fellow N.Y. Acad. Medicine, Council Cerebrovascular Disease; mem. Harvey Soc., Assn. Univ. Radiologists, Am. Coll. Radiology (pres. N.Y. state chpt. 1983), Am. Soc. Neuroradiology (pres. 1971), Am. Heart Assn., Am. Assn. Neurol. Surgeons, N.Y. Roentgen Soc. (pres. 1978-79), Radiol. Soc. N.Am. (2d v.p. 1980—). Research and publs. cerebrovascular disease. Home: 1725 York Ave New York NY 10028 Office: 550 1st Ave New York City NY 10016

CHASE, RICHARD LIONEL ST. LUCIAN, geology and oceanography educator; b. Perth, Australia, Dec. 25, 1933; s. Conrad Lucien Doughty and Vera Mabel (Saw) C.; m. Mary Malcolm Nafe, Aug. 28, 1965; children: Sarah, Samuel, Elijah. B.Sc. with honors, U. Western Australia, 1956; Ph.D., Princeton U., 1963. Geologist Geosurveys of Australia, Adelaide, 1956-57; sr. asst. geologist Ministere des Mines, Que., Can., 1959; geologist Ministerio de Minas, Venezuela, 1960-61; postdoctoral fellow Woods Hole (Mass.) Oceanographic Instn., 1963-64; asst. scientist, 1964-68; asst. prof. U. B.C., Vancouver, 1968-73, assoc. prof., 1973-78, prof. dept. geol. scis., 1978-80, prof. deps. geol. scis. and oceanography, 1980—. Contbr. articles to profl. jours. Mem. Am. Geophys. Union, Geol. Assn. Can., Geol. Soc. Club: Faculty U. B.C. Home: 4178 W 12th Ave Vancouver BC V6R 2P6 Canada Office: U BC Vancouver BC V6T 2B4 Canada

CHASE, ROBERT ARTHUR, surgeon, educator; b. Keene, N.H., Jan. 6, 1923; s. Albert Henry and Georgia Beulah (Bump) C.; m. Ann Crosby Parker, Feb. 3, 1946; children: Deborah Lee, Nancy Jo, Robert N. B.S. cum laude, U. N.H., 1945; M.D., Yale, 1947. Diplomate: Am. Bd. Surgery, Am. Bd. Plastic Surgery. Intern New Haven Hosp., 1947-48, asst. resident, 1949-50, sr. resident surgery, 1952-53, chief resident surgeon, 1953-54; mem. faculty Yale Sch. Medicine, 1948-54, 59-62, asst. prof. surgery, 1959-62; mem. faculty U. Pitts., 1957-59, resident plastic surgeon, also teaching fellow, 1957-59; attending surgeon VA Hosp., W. Haven, Conn., 1959-62, Grace New Haven Community Hosp., 1959-63; prof., chmn. dept. surgery Stanford Sch. Medicine, 1963-74, Emile Holman prof. surgery, 1972—; prof. surgery U. Pa., 1974-77; attending surgeon Pa. Hosp., Hosp. U. Pa., Grad. Hosp., Phila., 1974-77; pres., dir. Nat. Bd. Med. Examiners, Phila., 1974-77; prof. anatomy Stanford (Calif.) U., 1977—; Cons. plastic surgery Christian Med. Coll. and Hosp., Vellore, S. India, 1962; cons. to surgeon gen. USAF, 1970—; Benjamin K. Rank prof. Australasian Coll. Surgeons, 1974. Author: Atlas of Hand Surgery; Editor: Videosurgery, 1974—; editorial bd.: Med. Alert Communication; Contbr. articles to profl. jours. Served to maj. M.C. AUS, 1949-57. Recipient Francis Gilman Blake award Yale Sch. Medicine, 1962, Henry J. Kaiser award Stanford U. Sch. Medicine, 1978-79. Fellow A.C.S., Australasian Coll. Surgeons (hon.); mem. Am. Soc. Plastic Surgery, Calif. Acad. Medicine (pres.), San Francisco Surg. Soc., Am. Surg. Assn., Santa Clara County, Com. med. socs., Am. Soc. Surgery Hand (pres.), Am. Soc. Cleft Palate Rehab., Am. Assn. Surgery Trauma, Plastic Surgery Research Council, AMA, Soc. Clin. Surgery, Western Surg. Assn., Pacific Coast Surg. Soc., Am. Assn. Plastic Surgery, James IV Assn. Surgeons, Am. Cancer Soc. (clin. fellowship com.), Found. Am. Soc. Plastic and Reconstructive Surgery (dir.), Soc. Univ. Surgeons, Inst. Med. (exec. com. 1976), Nat. Acad. Scis., Am. Soc. Most Venerable Order Hosp., St. John of Jerusalem, Halsted Soc., South African Soc. Surgery Hand (hon.), South African Soc. Plastic and Reconstructive Surgery (hon.), Sigma Xi. Home: 797 N Tolman Ln Stanford CA 94305 Office: Dept Surgery Stanford U Stanford CA 94305

CHASE, SYLVIA B., journalist; b. St. Paul, Feb. 23, 1938; d. Kelsey David and Sylvia (Bennett) C. B.A., UCLA, 1961. Aide to Calif. State Assembly Com. on Fin. and to Senator Thomas Rees, 1961-65; active polit. campaigns, Calif., 1961-68; coordinator Kennedy for Pres., 1968; advance person Atty. Gen. Tom Lynch of Calif., 1966; action reporter Sta. KNX Los Angeles, 1969-71; corr. and anchorwoman CBS News, N.Y.C., 1971-77, ABC News, 1977—. (Emmy award 1978, 80). Recipient Public Service award Am. Trial Lawyers Assn., 1970; Headliners award, 1979, 83; Front Page award, 1979; Gainsrugh award, 1979; consumer award Nat. Press Club, 1982; Pinnacle award, 1983; Russel C. Cecil award, 1983; TV pub. affairs unity awards in media Internat. Rehab. Film Festival, 1983. Office: ABC News 157 Columbus Ave New York NY 10023

CHASE, THOMAS GEORGE, judge, mayor; b. Memphis, Sept. 28, 1911; s. James P. and Fanny (George) C.; m. Ellender Stribling, Oct. 23, 1941; children: Thomas George, Davis Stribling, James P. III. B.S., U. Ark., 1934, LL.B., 1936, J.D., 1969. Bar: Ark. 1936, Tenn. 1937, Tex. 1956. Practice law, Memphis, 1936-41; pres. Chase Beverage Co., Waco, Tex., 1945-56; partner Naman, Howell, Smith & Chase, Waco, 1956—; Pres. Runnymede Land & Cattle Co., Valley Mills, Tex., 1967; pres. Hacienda Valle del Viento S.A., San Jose, Costa Rica, 1972—, Corilco, S.A., San Jose; sec.-treas. RuLacco S.A., San Jose; mayor City of Waco, 1980—; assoc. justice Ct. Appeals 10th Supreme Jud. Dist. Tex., 1982—. Pres. Friends Waco Pub. Library, 1967; mem. Waco-McLennan County Library Commn., chmn., 1973; mem. Waco City Council, 1978—; Chmn. exec. com. Republican Party, McLennan County, 1954; Bd. dirs. Waco Legal Aid Clinic; chmn. Waco Airports Bd. Served with USNR, 1942-45. Fellow Tex. Bar Found.; mem. ABA, Waco-McLennan County Bar Assn. (pres. 1965), Assn. Ins. Atty., Internat. Assn. Ins. Attys., Tex. Assn. Def. Counsel (dir. 1968—), Kappa Alpha. Episcopalian. Clubs: Rotary, Ridgewood Country, Ridgewood Yacht (Waco). Home: 3524 Carondolet Dr Waco TX 76710 Office: Texas Center Waco TX 76703

CHASE, THOMAS NEWELL, neurologist, researcher, educator; b. Westfield, N.J., May 23, 1932; s. Newell Adams and Gudrun Margarethe (Eskesen) C.; children: Thomas Newell, Robert Adams. B.S., M.I.T., 1954; postgrad., Columbia U., 1957-58; M.D., Yale U., 1962, Harvard U., 1963-66. Engr. Singer Mfg. Co., Bridgeport, Conn., 1954-55; technician Columbia U. Coll. Phys. and Surgs., 1957-58; intern in internal medicine Yale-New Haven Med. Center, 1962-63; asst. resident in neurology Mass. Gen. Hosp., Boston, 1963-64, resident, 1965-66; fellow in neuropathology Harvard U. Med. Sch., 1964-65; guest worker NIMH, Bethesda, Md., 1966-68, chief unit on neurology, 1968-70, chief sect. exptl. therapeutics, 1970-74; chief lab. of neuropharmacology Nat. Inst. Neurol. and Communicative Disorders and Stroke, Bethesda, 1974-76, dir. intramural research, 1974—; clin. assoc. prof. dept. neurology Georgetown U. Sch. Medicine; mem. sci. adv. bd. Com. to Combat Huntington's Disease, Found. for Research in Hereditary Disease; chmn. adv. bd. Tourette Syndrome Assn.; chmn. Nat. Parkinson Found.; mem. exec. com. Amyotrophic Lateral Sclerosis Soc. Am.; mem. adv. bd. Am. Parkinson Disease Assn., Nat. ALS Found., Nat. Ataxia Found. Mem. editorial bd.: Archives of Neurology Progress in Neuro-Psychopharmacology; Contbr. articles to med. jours. Served with Signal Corps U.S. Army, 1955-57. Recipient Winternitz prize in pathology, 1960, Ramsay prize for clin. medicine, 1961, diploma of recognition of merit for humanitarian services Govt. of Bolivia, 1974, USPHS Meritorious Service medal, 1978; Nutrition Found. summer fellow, 1959; NSF summer fellow, 1960; USPHS summer fellow, 1961; Nat. Inst. Neurol. Diseases and Blindness spl. fellow, 1966-68. Fellow Am. Coll. Neuro-Psychopharmacology; Mem. Am. Neurol. Assn., Am. Acad. Neurology, Soc. Neurosci., Internat. Soc. Neurochemistry, Am. Soc. Neurochemistry, Assn. for Research in Nervous and Mental Disease, Internat. Brain Research Orgn. Office: 9000 Rockville Pike Bethesda MD 20205

CHASE, WILLIAM HOWARD, executive search firm executive, educator; b. Omaha, Jan. 30, 1910; s. Charles Herbert and Pauline (Kottal) C.; m. Elizabeth Coykendall, Oct. 25, 1935; children: Anne Coykendall, Alison Howard, Thomas Howard. A.B., U. Iowa, 1932; postgrad., London Sch. Econs., 1932-33, Harvard U., 1934-36; Ph.D. (hon.), Dong-Guk U., Seoul, Korea, 1968. Instr. internat. relations Harvard U., 1935-36; exec. Am. Retail Fedn., Washington, 1939-40; editor Whaley-Eaton Letter, Washington, 1941; dir. pub. services Gen. Mills, Mpls., 1941-45; dir. pub. relations Gen. Foods, N.Y.C., 1945-52; v.p., gen. exec. McCann-Erickson; pres. Communications Counselors, Inc., Howard Chase Assocs., 1959-68; chmn. Council Mgmt. Change, Inc., 1965—; pub. Innovation and Mgmt. of Change Letter, 1965-76; v.p. Am. Can Co., Greenwich, Conn., 1970-75, asst. to chmn., 1970-75; pres. Howard Chase Enterprises, Inc., 1974—; prof. Grad. Sch. Bus. Adminstrn., U. Conn., 1974-82, Poly. Inst. N.Y., 1975-78; dir. Inst. for Pub. Issue Mgmt., 1976—; editor Corp. Pub. Issues, 1976—; asst. to sec. commerce, asst. to dir. Office Def. Moblzn., 1950-51; Mem. dental adv. com. NIH, 1962-65; mem. nat. com. on community health HEW, 1965—; info. policy cons. Pres.'s Food for Peace Council; mem. Exec. Res. USIA; v.p. strategic planning Council N.E. Econ. Action, 1979-81. Editorial writer, Des Moines Register & Tribune, 1936-39; Author: By Any Other Name, Issue Management: Origins of the Future, 1984. Trustee Wellesley Coll., 1948-60; bd. dirs. Stamford Mus., 1977—, Mannes Coll. Music, North Conway Inst.; Vice chmn. Nat. Citizens for Eisenhower campaign, 1952. Recipient Profl. Proficiency award Pub. Relations Soc. Am., 1948, 81, 82; named One of Ten Distinguished Young Men of Year U.S. Jr. C. of C., 1943. Mem. N.Y. Council Fgn. Relations, Acad. Polit. Sci., Pub. Relations Soc. Am. (past pres.), Issues Mgmt. Assn. (founder, chmn. 1981), Phi Beta Kappa, Alpha Tau Omega. Clubs: Landmark (Stamford, Conn.); Harvard (N.Y.C.); Metropolitan (Washington). Home: 333 Mayapple Rd Stamford CT 06903 *Goals: Literacy; Self-pride; Consideration for others; Self-discipline.*

CHASE, WILLIAM ROWELL, corporation executive; b. Brookline, Mass., Jan. 22, 1904; s. Harry Everett and Florence Ardelia (Rowell) C.; m. Katharine Knox Kingsbury, Feb. 15, 1936 (dec. Nov. 1975); children: Rowell Kingsbury, Alison Mason. A.B., Harvard U., 1926, M.B.A., 1928. Mdse. mgr. Sears, Roebuck & Co., 1928-31; with Procter & Gamble, 1931-70, mgr. brand promotion div., 1936-51, advt. mgr., 1951-54, v.p. charge advt., 1955-57, v.p. charge soap products div., 1957-60, exec. v.p., 1960-70; also dir.; v.p. Kingsbury Inc., Phila., 1945-70, chmn., 1970-75, chmn. exec. com., 1975—. Mem. adv. council Cin. Zoo; hon. dir. Cin. Planned Parenthood Assn.; trustee Cin. Nature Center, Shakertown at Pleasant Hill, Ky., Cin. Mus. Natural History. Mem. NAM (hon. vice-chmn. for life). Clubs: Commonwealth, Harvard, Commercial, Country, Queen City (Cin.). Home: 3424 Paxton Rd Cincinnati OH 45208 Office: 105 W 4th St Cincinnati OH 45202

CHASE, WILLIAM THOMAS, III, museum conservator; b. Boston, May 31, 1940; s. William Thomas and Rhoda Louise (Young) C.; m. Linda Wishart Smith, Sept. 1, 1962; children: Katharine Louise, Samuel Jewett, Ellen Wishart. B.A., Oberlin U., 1962; M.A., N.Y. U., 1967. Conservation certificate, 1967. Summer intern Wadsworth Athenaeum, Hartford, Conn., 1962, 63; conservator Nemrud Dagh Excavations, Turkey, 1964; intern tech. lab. Freer Gallery Art, Smithsonian Instn., Washington, 1965, asst. conservator, 1966-68, head conservator, 1968—; Chester Dale fellow dept. conservation Met. Mus. Art, N.Y.C., 1966; scholar Hebrew Tech. Inst. at N.Y. U., N.Y.C., 1963, 64; mem. archaeology del., People's Republic of China, 1973, 81; alt. to rep. of Smithsonian Instn. to Nat. Conservation Advisory Council, chmn. by-laws com., 1974-77; chmn. Smithsonian Council of Conservators, 1978—; chmn. study group on care of works of art in traveling exhbns., mus. interchange subcom. U.S.-Japan Conf. on Cultural and Ednl. Interchange.; Chmn. bd. Christian edn. Westmoreland Ch., 1974-75. Author: catalogue Bronze Disease and its Treatment, Bangkok Nat. Mus., 1975; contbr. articles to profl. publs.; editor: Corrosion and Metal Artifacts, 1977. JDR 3d Fund travel grantee, 1971. Fellow Internat. Inst. for Conservation Hist., Artistic Works (council 1974-83, editor Art and Archaeology Tech. Abstracts 1976—), Am. Inst. Conservation; mem. Washington Conservation Guild (pres. 1970), Hist. Metallurgy Soc., AAAS. Democrat. Congregationalist. Office: Freer Gallery Art Smithsonian Instn Washington DC 20560

CHASEMAN, JOEL, television exec.; b. Feb. 18, 1926; m. Marlene Meyerson, Sept. 11, 1955; children: Martha Hope, Joanne Amy. A.B., Cornell U., 1948. Pres. Post-Newsweek Stas., Washington, 1973—; v.p. Washington Post Co., 1973—; chmn. Nat. Acad. TV Arts and Scis., 1980-82; Bd. dirs. Assn. Maximum Service Telecasters, 1976—. Office: 1150 15th St NW Washington DC 20071

CHASEN, ROBERT E., business executive; b. Newark, July 3, 1916; s. Julius and Mary (Horland) C.; m. Laura Etta Brown, Apr. 15, 1962; children—Julie Beth, Ellie Brook. B.S., Benjamin Franklin U., 1943; postgrad., Columbia, 1947-48, N.Y. U., 1949-50. Spl. agt. FBI, Washington, 1943-52; coordinator plant security, asst. to v.p. indsl. relations Internat. Tel. & Tel. Corp., N.Y.C., 1952-55; dir. indsl. relations Fed. Labs., Nutley, N.J., 1955-58, v.p. for adminstrn., 1958-63, v.p. parent co., 1970—; exec. v.p., gen. mgr. ITT Kellogg's Communications Systems div., Chgo., 1963-64; pres. Fed. Electric Corp. (subsidiary ITT), Paramus, N.J., 1964-70, chmn. bd., chief exec. officer, 1970—; group gen. mgr. ITT Govt. and Comml. Services Group, 1970—; pres. Robert E. Chasen and Assocs., Inc., 1983—; pres., chmn. bd. ITT Tech. Services, Inc., 1964-69, chmn. bd., chief exec. officer, 1969—; pres., chmn. bd. Intelex Systems, Inc. subsidiary,

1966—; chmn. bd., chief exec. officer ITT Fed. Support Services, 1966—; bus. mgr. Fed Elec. GmbH, German subsidiary, 1965-69; pres., chmn. bd. Base Services, Inc., 1965-69, chmn. bd., 1970—; chmn. bd., chief exec. officer ITT Arctic Services, Paramus, 1969—; pres., dir. ITT Comml. Services, Inc., Paramus, 1969—; chmn. bd. ITT Space Communications, Inc., Ramsey, N.J., 1969-77; U.S. commr. customs Treasury Dept., Washington, 1977-80. Mem. Internat. Assn. Chiefs of Police (dir., exec. com.), Soc. Former Spl. Agts. FBI, Columbia Grad. Sch. Bus. Execs. Assn. Home: 8124 SW 158th Terr Miami FL 33157 Office: 5915 Ponce de Leon Blvd Coral Gables FL 33146

CHASEN, SYLVAN HERBERT, computer applications consultant, educator; b. Richmond, Va., May 19, 1926; s. Nathan and Hanna (Pass) C.; m. Catherine Hudlow, Mar. 25, 1946; children: Deborah Wyatt, Dianne Lipsey, Jane Morrison, Susan. Student, Va. Poly. Inst., 1943-44; B.S. in Engring, Ga. Inst. Tech., 1946, B. Chem. Engring., 1946; M.S., Emory U., 1951, 1951. Math. instr. Ga. Inst. Tech., Atlanta, 1946-50; head computer facility Naval Air Test Ctr., Patuxent, Md., 1951-58; dir. advanced computing CAD and interactive graphics Lockheed-Ga. Co., Marietta, 1958—; pres. Center CAD/CAM Tech., Inc.; cons. Author: Geometric Principles and Procedures for Computer Graphics Applications, 1978, The Guide for the Evaluation and Implementation of CAD/CAM Systems, 1980, 2d edit., 1983. Served as ensign USN, 1944-46. Recipient Outstanding Contbns. award Gov. Md., 1957, Disting. Contbns. award Soc. Mfg. Engrs., 1982. Mem. ASME, Soc. Mfg. Engrs., SIGGRAPH, NCGA. Home: 760 Starlight Ct NE Atlanta GA 30342 Office: PO Box 76042 Atlanta GA 30328

CHASE-RIBOUD, BARBARA DEWAYNE, sculptor, writer; b. Phila., June 26, 1939; d. Charles Edward and Vivian May (West) Chase; m. Marc Eugene Riboud, Dec. 25, 1961; children: David, Alexis. M.F.A., Yale U., 1960; hon. doctorate, Temple U., 1981. Exhibited in one-woman shows at, Berkeley (Calif.) Mus., 1973, Mass. Inst. Tech., Detroit Art Inst., Indpls. Art Mus., Mus. Modern Art, Paris, 1974, Kunstmuseum Dusseldorf, Bronx Mus., 1979; exhibited in group shows at, Whitney Mus., N.Y.C., Smithsonian Mus., Washington, Mus. Modern Art, N.Y.C., Carnegie Inst., Pitts., Centre Pompidou, Paris; represented in permanent collections at, Met. Mus., Mus. Modern Art, Lannan Found., Fla., Centre Pompidou, others.; (recipient Kafka Prize for best fiction written by an Am. woman in 1979); Author: From Memphis and Peking, Poems, 1974, Sally Hemings, A Novel, 1979, Love Perfecting, Poems, 1980, A German Lover (novel 1982), Study of a Nude Woman as Cleopatra, Poems, 1983; author: novel Naksh-l-Dil, 1984. John Hay Whitney Found. fellow, 1958; Nat. Endowment for Arts fellow, 1973; Academic of Italy with Gold medal, 1979. Mem. Yale Alumni Assn. Home: 3 Rue Auguste Comte Paris 07506 France

CHASIN, LAWRENCE ALLEN, biological sciences educator, geneticist; b. Willmantic, Conn., July 2, 1941; s. Solomon Dove and Grace (Krubitsky) C.; m. Phyllis Leah Ostin, Nov. 7, 1961 (div. 1975); children: Lisa Gail, Emma Nicole; m. 2d Gail Susan Urlaub, Nov. 2, 1975. B.S. in Chemistry, Brown U., 1962; Ph.D. in Biology, MIT, 1967. Research assoc. Centre National de la Recherche Scientifique, Gif-sur-Yvette, France, 1966-68; sr. instr. U. Colo. Med. Ctr., Denver, 1968-70; asst. prof. biol. scis. Columbia U., N.Y.C., 1970-75, assoc. prof., 1975-81, prof., 1981—; cons. NIH, Bethesda, Md., 1975-79. Research, numerous publs. in field, 1963—; assoc. editor: Somatic Cell Genetics, 1977—, Jour. Cellular Physiology, 1979—, Molecular and Cellular Biology, 1980—. Grantee Am. Cancer Soc., 1971—, NIH, 1975—. Mem. AAAS, Genetics Soc. Am., Am. Soc. Microbiology, Am. Soc. Cell Biology. Office: Dept Biol Scis Columbia U 902A Fairchild Ctr for Life Scis New York NY 10027

CHASINS, EDWARD A., communications company executive; b. N.Y.C., Dec. 31, 1920; s. Charles L. and Ruth (Lessem) C.; m. Harriett Sue Mellett, Jan. 18, 1947; children—Margaret M. (Mrs. Nurhan Arman), Daniel B., Harriett Brooks. B.A., Swarthmore Coll., 1941. Advt. and sales promotion mgr. Melville Corp., N.Y.C., 1949-66; v.p., creative supr. Muller, Jordan, Herrick, Inc., N.Y.C., 1966-74; pres. Producers Row, Inc., 1974-76, Chasins Communications div. Reeves Communications Corp., N.Y.C., 1977-82; v.p. parent co. Life mem. Archville Vol. Fire Dept., 1952—; mem. Ossining (N.Y.) Democratic Com., 1956-70, chmn., 1964-66. Served to 1st lt. AUS, 1942-46. Home: South Mountain Pass Garrison NY 10524

CHASIS, HERBERT, physician, educator; b. N.Y.C., Nov. 9, 1905; s. Joel Morris and Annie (Kutner) C.; m. Barbara Ann Parker, Jan. 19, 1943; children: Joel, Anne, Sarah. B.A., Syracuse U., (N.Y.), 1926; M.D., NYU, 1930, D.Sc. in Medicine, 1937. Am. Bd. Internal Medicine. Intern Bellevue Hosp., N.Y.C., 1930-31, resident, 1931-38; instr. dept. medicine NYU, 1934-39, asst. prof., 1939-49, assoc. prof., 1949-64, prof., 1964—; cons. Phelps Meml. Hosp., North Tarrytown, N.Y., 1962—, VA Hosp., N.Y.C., 1951—. Author: (with William Goldring) Hypertension and Hypertensive Disease, 1944, Homer William Smith, His Scientific and Literary Achievements, 1965. Recipient Responsible Investigator award USPHS Nat. Heart Inst., 1957-72, Sci. Achievement award NYU Sch. Medicine Alumni Assn., 1965. Mem. N.Y. Heart Assn. (pres. 1963-65), Am. Heart Assn. (chmn. sect. on circulation 1959-61), Am. Physiol Soc., Am. Soc. Clin. Investigation, N.Y. Acad. Medicine (chmn. sect. medicine 1959-60), Sigma Xi, Alpha Omega Alpha. Home: 465 W 23d St New York NY 10011 Office: NYU Med Center 550 1st Ave New York NY 10016

CHASON, JACOB (LEON CHASON), neuropathologist; b. Monroe, Mich., May 12, 1915; s. Ben and Ida (Beiser) C.; m. Helen Pelok, May 19, 1942; children—Steven, Ellen, David. A.B., U. Mich., 1937, M.D., 1940. Intern Wayne County Gen. Hosp., 1940-41, resident, 1941-42, 46-49, asst. pathologist, 1949-50; dir. lab. VA Hosp., Allen Park, Mich., 1950-52; asst. prof. neuropathology Wayne State U., 1952-54, asso. prof., 1954-57, prof., 1958—, chmn. dept. pathology, 1964-78, asso. dean, 1970-72; neuropathologist Henry Ford Hosp., Detroit; cons. in field. Contbr. articles to profl. publs. Served with U.S. Army, 1942-46. NIH sr. fellow, 1959-60; grantee, 1961-63. Mem. Am. Assn. Neuropathologists, Am. Soc. Clin. Pathologists, Coll. Am. Pathologists, Internat. Acad. Pathology, Am. Acad. Neurology. Home: 4862 Keithdale Ln Bloomfield Hills MI 48013 Office: 2799 W Grand Blvd Detroit MI 48202

CHASSLER, SEYMOUR MURRAY, editor, writer, publishing company executive; b. Bklyn., Nov. 8, 1919; s. David and Henrietta (Becker) C.; m. Natalie Elizabeth Goldfarb, Apr. 2, 1943; children: Joseph Holland, Philip Isaac, Deborah Louise. B.A., N.Y. U., 1941; M.A., Columbia, 1942. Picture editor Pageant mag., 1948-50, mng. editor, 1955-57, exec. editor, 1957-59; asso. editor, picture editor Collier's mag., 1950-55; v.p. Hillman Periodicals, Inc., 1959; editorial dir. This Week mag., 1959-60; exec. editor Redbook mag., 1960-65, editor, 1965-70, editor-in-chief, 1970-81; also sr. v.p. Redbook Pub. Co.; v.p. McCall Pub. Co., 1965-73; Mem. joint com. Mag. Pubs. Assn.-N.E.A.; cons. editor Parade mag.; instr. New Sch. for Social Research, N.Y.C. Writer: film March of Time, 1942-45; asso. editor: Coronet mag, 1945- 48. Mem. Nat. Commn. on Observance Internat. Women's Year, 1977—, Nat. Adv. Com. for Women, 1978; bd. dirs. Nat. Bus. Council for Equal Rights Amendment; adv. bd. Nat. Women's Polit. Caucus, Inst. Edn. and Research on Women and Work, First Women's Bank N.Y.; hon. trustee Elizabeth Cady Stanton Found.; mem. nat. adv. council pub. relations Conn. Coll.; bd. dirs. Abortion Rights, Moblzn.; trustee Advancement Fund of Women in Communications. Recipient Graflex award for contbns. photojournalism in color, 1952; Headliner award Women in Communications, 1979. Mem. Am. Soc. Mag. Editors (mem. exec. com., pres. 1980-82), NOW, Women in Communications, Advt. Women N.Y. (hon.). Office: Redbook Mag 230 Park Ave New York NY 10017

CHASSMAN, LEONARD FREDRIC, labor union administrator; b. Detroit, Sept. 30, 1935; s. Joachim and Lillian (Abrams) C.; m. Phyllis Perlman, Aug. 25, 1957; children: Mark, Cheryl, Gregory. B.A., UCLA, 1957. Rep. AFTRA, Los Angeles, 1959-63, Screen Actors Guild, 1963-65; staff exec. Writers Guild Am., West, Inc., Los Angeles, 1965-77, exec. dir., 1978-82; nat. exec. sec. Screen Extras Guild Inc., 1982—; 4th v.p. Associated Actors & Artistes of Am. (AFL-CIO); v.p. Los Angeles County Fedn. Labor. Office: 3629 Cahuenga Blvd W Los Angeles CA 90068

CHASTAIN, ELIJAH DENTON, JR., educator; b. Pickens, S.C., Sept. 26, 1925; s. Elijah D. and Ida (Hendricks) C.; m. Dr. Marian B. Faulkner, Aug. 25, 1956; children—Gwen Caroline, Philip William. B.S., Clemson U., 1947; M.S., Cornell U., 1948; postgrad., Va. Poly. Inst., 1950, Duke, 1961, U. Chgo., 1964; Ph.D., Purdue U., 1956. Asso. prof. Va. Poly. Inst., 1949-56; research asst. Purdue U., 1954-56; asso. prof. econs. Auburn U., 1956-63, prof., 1963—, dir. grad. studies Sch. of Bus., 1967-70; chmn. Gen. Faculty and Univ. Senate, 1970-71; econ. and managerial cons. Editor: Jour. Ala. Acad. Sci, 1962-65; Contbr. articles to profl. and semi-popular jours. Served to capt. C.E. U.S. Army, 1944-46, 47, 50-52. Mem. Am., So. econs. assns., Am. Agrl. Econ. Assn., Ala. Acad. Sci. (v.p.), Sigma Xi, Omicron Delta Epsilon, Delta Sigma Pi, Gamma Sigma Delta, Phi Delta Kappa, Omicron Delta Kappa. Home: 1104 S Gay St Auburn AL 36830

CHATEAU, JOHN PETER D(AVID), economics and finance educator, mining company executive; b. Brussels, Oct. 10, 1942; s. Eugene Chateau. B.A. in Econs., U. Liege, Belgium, 1965, M.A., U. Montreal, Que., Can., 1967, M.Sc., U. Grenoble, France, 1968; Ph.D. in Econs. summa cum laude, U. Paris I, 1970. Fin. analyst Bank of Montreal, 1966; lectr. in econs. U. Montreal, 1966-67, 68-70, asst. prof. econs., 1970-74; lectr. in econs. U. Grenoble, 1967-68; assoc. prof. U. Orleans, France, 1973-74; prof. econs. and fin. McGill U., Montreal, 1974—; pres., chief exec. officer Bachelor Lake gold Mines, Montreal, 1980—; dir. Chema Scutum Inc., Montreal; econ. adviser Societe General de Banque, Brussels, 1978. Can. Council fellow, 1969-70; Research Council Can. research fellow European Inst. for Advanced Studies in Mgmt., Brussels, 1978-79, 81-82. Mem. Am. Econ. Assn., European Fin. Assn., Can. Econs. Assn. Home: 3445 Drummond Sutie 1004 Montreal PQ Canada H3G 1X9 Office: McGill U 1001 Sherbrooke St W Montreal PQ Canada H3A 1G5

CHATER, SHIRLEY SEARS, educational association official; b. Shamokin, Pa., July 30, 1932; d. Raymond Sears and Edna (Shamp) Swars; m. Norman Chater, Dec. 5, 1959; children: Cris, Geoffrey. Diploma, U. Pa., 1953, B.S., 1960; M.S., U. Calif.-San Francisco, 1960; Ph.D., U. Calif.-Berkeley, 1964. Asst. vice chancellor acad. affairs U. Calif.-San Francisco, 1974-77; prof. dept. social and behavioral scis. Sch. Nursing, 1973—, vice chancellor acad. affairs, 1977-82; commr. Am. Council Edn., Washington, 1977-82, council assoc., 1983—. Contbr. articles to profl. jours. Mem. adv. com. City and County San Francisco Health Dept., 1980—; mem. citizens adv. com. Coll. Marin, 1964-80; mem. Pacific Southwest Regional Med. Library Adv. Com., 1976-80. Mem. AAAS, Assn. Acad. Health Ctr., Am. Council Edn., Am. Acad. Nursing, Am. Nurses Assn., Women's Forum West. Republican. Office: Am Council Edn One Dupont Circle Washington DC

CHATLAND, HAROLD, systems analysis cons.; b. Hamilton, Ont., Can., Nov. 13, 1911; s. Albert and Sarah (Hewitt) C.; m. Alice Young, Dec. 28, 1937; children—Anne Young, Clare Lillian, Marilyn Lee. A.B., McMaster U., 1934; M.S., U. Chgo., 1935; Ph.D., 1937. Instr. math. Mont. State U., 1937-41, asst. prof., dept., also dean, 1954-56, dean faculty, 1956-57, acad. v.p., 1957-59; asst. prof. Ohio State U., 1946-49; engring. specialist Sylvania Electric Products Co., Moutain View, Calif., 1959-63; prof. math., acad. dean Western Wash. State Coll., Bellingham, 1963-64; mgr. propagation research dept. Electronic Def. Labs., Mountain View, Calif.; pres. QRC Systems, Inc.; cons. in systems analysis.; Chmn. aero. com. State of Mont., 1945-46. Mem. Am. Math. Soc., Am. Math. Assn. Address: 10566 Blandor Way Los Altos Hills CA 94022

CHATTERJEE, PRANAB, educator; b. Betiah, India, Oct. 15, 1936; came to U.S., 1959, naturalized, 1972; s. Paritosh and Uma (Mukherjee) C. M.S.W., U. Tenn., 1961; M.A., U. Chgo., 1963, Ph.D., 1967. Asst. prof. Sch. Applied Social Scis., Case Western Res. U., Cleve., 1967-71, asso. prof., 1971-76, prof., 1976—. Mem. Soc. Study of Social Problems, Bengali Cultural Soc. Cleve., Nat. Assn. Social Workers, Soc. Study Social Problems. Office: Sch Applied Social Sciences Case Western Reserve U Cleveland OH 44106

CHATTERJI, DEBAJYOTI, metallurgical engineer; b. Puri, India, Aug. 4, 1944; came to U.S., 1967, naturalized, 1980; s. Kumud Chandra and Mrinmoyee (Mukherji) C.; m. Smee Banerjee, July 11, 1968; children: Ananya, Kooheli, Miabi. B.S. with honors, Utkal U., India, 1963; B.Metall. Engring., Indian Inst. Tech., Kharhagpur, India, 1966; M.S., Purdue U., 1968, Ph.D., 1971. Vis. scientist Wright-Patterson AFB, Ohio, 1971-73; with Research & Devel. Center, Gen. Electric Co., Schenectady, 1973—, mgr. electrochemistry br., 1975-79; mgr. Chem. Systems and Tech. Lab., 1979-80, Inorganic Materials and Structures Lab., 1980-83; v.p. tech. affairs AIRCO, Inc., Murray Hill, N.J., 1983—. Contbr. articles to profl. jours. Mem. Am. Soc. for Metals (Geisler award 1979), Electrochem. Soc., Sigma Xi. Patentee in field. Office: 100 Mountain Ave Murray Hill NJ 07974

CHAUDHRY, ANAND, pathologist, educator; b. Jhang, India, Oct. 19, 1922; came to U.S., 1950, naturalized, 1963; s. Jagdish C. and Kirpa (Devi) C.; m. Barbara L. Christiansen, Aug. 10, 1957; children: Anita Lee, Tina Marie, Rajan Andrew, Jay Curtis. B.S., Punjab (India) U., 1942, B.Dental Surgery, 1947; M.S. in Oral Surgery, U. Mich., 1953; Ph.D. in Pathology, U. Minn., 1956. Instr. oral pathology U. Minn., Mpls., 1959-61, prof. oral pathology, 1961-66, chmn. pathology and oral pathology, 1966; prof. pathology SUNY Sch. Medicine, Buffalo, 1966-79; prof., chmn. dept. pathobiology and oral pathology N.Y. U. Dental Center, 1979—, adj. prof. pathology, 1979—; cons. VA Hosp., Bklyn., VA Hosp., N.Y.C., 1980—. Assoc. editor: Jour. Oral Medicine, 1982—; Contbr. articles to profl. jours. Home: 90 Clent Rd Great Neck NY 11021 Office: NY U Dental Center 421 1st Ave New York NY 10010

CHAUT, ROBERT, investment banker; b. N.Y.C., Nov. 12, 1925; s. Abraham and Rita (Abramowitz) C. B.S., City Coll. N.Y., 1945. Exec. v.p. M.A. Schapiro & Co., Inc., N.Y.C., 1963-65, pres., 1965-68; v.p. Kidder, Peabody & Co., Inc., N.Y.C., 1968-76; 1st v.p. Blyth Eastman Dillon & Co. Inc., N.Y.C., 1976-79; sr. v.p. A.G. Becker Paribas Inc., N.Y.C., 1979—; dir. Manhattan Life Corp., N.Y.C. Clubs: Broad Street, Bond (N.Y.C.). Home: 200 E 33d St New York NY 10016 Office: 55 Water St New York NY 10041

CHAVANNE, JOHN HUNTER, utility executive; b. Lake Charles, La., May 6, 1941; s. Michael Charles and Elizabeth Ford (Hunter) C.; m. Bonnie Anne Beaud, Oct. 19, 1963; children: Cherie, Michelle, Hunter. B.B.A., Loyola U. of South, 1963, M.B.A., 1967, J.D., 1971; C.P.A., Tulane U., 1974. C.P.A., notary pub., La., La. 1971. Credit analyst Nat. Bank of Commerce, New Orleans, 1965-66; mgr. fin. planning New Orleans Pub. Service, 1975-77, asst. to v.p. fin., 1977-78, controller, 1978-80, v.p. fin., treas., asst. sec., 1978-80; v.p. corp. control, asst. sec. La. Power & Light Co., New Orleans, 1983—. Chmn. trustees fin. com. Eye, Ear, Nose and Throat Hosp., 1981—; trustee St. Mary's Dominican Coll., 1976—, Internat. Trade Mart, 1983. Served to 1st lt. U.S. Army, 1963-65. Mem. ABA, La. Bar Assn., Am. Inst. C.P.A.'s, La. Soc. C.P.A.'s, Notary Pubs. of La. Roman Catholic. Home: 2257 New York St New Orleans LA 70122 Office: New Orleans Pub Service Inc 317 Baronne St New Orleans LA 70112

CHAVANNES, ALBERT LYLE, electric utility exec.; b. Knoxville, Tenn., Dec. 19, 1897; s. Adrian Leon and May (Sharp) C.; m. Margaret Florence McCown, June 19, 1923; children—Adrian E., Dorothy W. (Mrs. John A. Flynn), Theodore E. B.S. in Elec. Engring, U. Tenn., 1918, grad. student, 1919-22; grad. student, U. Chgo., 1920; extension student bus. adminstrn., U. Calif., 1943. Prodn. engr. Westinghouse Electric Corp., 1919; instr. math. U. Tenn., 1919-22; instr. elec. engring. U. Ill., 1922-23; with So. Calif. Edison Co., Los Angeles, after 1923, gen. auditor, 1947-49, asst. treas., mgr. ins., 1949-59, sec., after 1959, Rea Investment Co., Los Angeles. Mem. Pacific Coast Electric Assn., Electric Club Los Angeles, Phi Gamma Delta, Phi Kappa Phi, Tau Beta Pi. Republican. Presbyn. Clubs: Mason (Shriner, K.T.), Breakfast (Los Angeles)). Home: 1615 Santa Barbara Ave Glendale CA 91208

CHAVES, JOSÉ MARÍA, educator, lawyer, diplomat; b. Bogotá, Colombia, Aug. 19, 1922; s. Carlos Chaves and María García de C.; (Elena Gómez); children—Cristina María, Tomás José. Bachiller, Bogotá, 1939; certificate in anthropology, Bogotá, 1942; J.D., Bogotá, 1945; D.Sc. (hon.), U. Antióquia, 1948; M.A., Columbia, 1951, Ph.D., 1953; LL.D., U. Popayán, Colombia, 1957. Editor-in-chief Revista Colegio del Rosario (arts and letters mag.), Colombia; gen. legal duties specializing in public adminstrn.; asst. atty. gen., Colombia, Bogotá, 1942-45; instr. Romance langs. Columbia U., N.Y.C., 1945-48, 50-51; founder, 1st dean faculty U. Andes, Bogotá, 1948-49; head area studies Queens Coll., N.Y. U., 1951-53; counselor Colombian Embassy, Washington, 1953-55; prof. internat. law U. Colombia, 1955-58, U. Paris, 1957; guest prof. internat. law and relations Brit. Council, various univs. Eng., Scotland, 1957; dir., chief exec. Am. Found. for Cultural Popular Action, Inc. (pvt. internat. orgn. for mass edn. by radio), N.Y.C., 1958—; dir. Center Latin Am. Studies, City U. N.Y.; chmn. Hispanic Am. editorial bd. Grolier, Inc., 1971—; ambassador extraordinary, permanent del. Iberoam. Bur. Edn. to UN; A.E. and P., permanent rep. Grenada to OAS; alt. gov. World Bank and Internat. Monetary Fund, 1974-77; chmn. C.I.P., 1972—; Organizer, dir. tech. assistance mission Unitarian Service Com. in Latin Am.; dir. gen. Nat. Univ. Fund, Colombia, 1955-58. Editor-in-chief: Grolier Spanish Universal Ency; author: Chaves Plan for settlement religious conflict between Caths. and Protestants in Latin Am; Author: Francisco de Vitoria. Founder International Law, 1945, Intergroup relations in the Spain of Cervantes, 1953, University Reform in Colombia, 1957. Decorated Legion of Honor, France; gran cruz Order of St. Constantine the Gt.; comdr. Grand Order Isabel the Catholic; knight comdr. Alfonso El Sabio; knight comdr. Grand Order Isabella, Spain; recipient medaglia universitaria U. Pro Deo. Rome, 1957; medalla de los Andes U. Andes, 1958; grand cross Nasco Núnez de Balboa, Panama, 1970; grand cross Juan P. Duarte Sanchez y Meila, Dominican Republic, 1970; Medal of Jerusalem, Israel, 1972; grand cross Order of Malta, 1976; grand cross Order Justice Law and Peace of Mex., 1977. Mem. Internat. Law Assn., Inter-Am. Bar Assn., Acad. Polit. Sci., MLA, Academia Hispano Americana, Phi Delta Kappa. Clubs: Metropolitan, Columbia U. (N.Y.C.); Quill of U.S.A. (pres.). Home: 118 E 60th St New York NY 10022 Office: 1 E 60th St New York NY 10022 *Faith in God is also faith in man. Service of man is also service of God. As we enter a new period of peace in the world, our faith can sustain our peace building efforts and help create a better life for all mankind.*

CHAVEZ, CESAR, union ofcl.; b. nr. Yuma, Ariz., Mar. 31, 1927; (married); 8 children. Mem. staff Community Service Orgn., Calif., 1952-58, gen. dir., 1958-62; organized Nat. Farm Workers Assn., 1962; (merged with Agrl. Workers Organizing Com. of AFL-CIO), 1966, Delano, Calif., dir., 1966-73; now pres. United Farm Workers Am. AFL-CIO, Keene, Calif. Served with USNR, 1944-45. Roman Catholic. Address: La Paz Keene CA 93531

CHAVEZ, EDWARD A., artist; b. Wagonmound, N.Mex., Mar. 14, 1917; s. Cornelio and Beatrice (Martinez) C.; m. Jenne Magafan, July 28, 1941; m. Eva Van Rijn, 1962; 1 dau., Maia. Student, Colorado Springs Fine Arts Center, 1935-38; studied with, Frank Mechau, Boardman Robinson, Peppino Mangravite, Arnold Blanch. Instr. drawing and painting Art Students League N.Y., 1954, summer sch., 1955-58; vis. prof. art Colo. Coll., 1959; asst. prof. art Syracuse U., 1960-61; instr. art Dutchess Community Coll., Poughkeepsie, 1963. Executed murals, post offices, service clubs, schs., hosps., one-man shows, Denver Art Mus., 1938, Asso. Am. Artists N.Y., 1948-49, Ganso Gallery, N.Y.C., 1950, 52-54, Il Camino Gallery, Rome, 1951, Mus. N.Mex., 1954, Alexandre Rabow Gallery, San Francisco, Annie Werbe Galleries, Detroit, 1957, John Heller Gallery, N.Y.C., 1955, 56, 58, 59, 60, N.Y. State Coll. Tchrs., Albany, 1960; exhibited, Chgo. Art Inst., NAD, Nat. Inst. Arts and Letters, Whitney Mus., Met. Mus., N.Y.C., Pa. Acad. Art, Carnegie Inst., Pitts., Corcoran Bienniel, Washington, others; represented in collections, Mus. Modern Art, N.Y.C., Newark Mus. Art, Library of Congress Print Collection, other museums, galleries and pvt. collections. (Recipient Pepsi-Cola art prize 1947); (Felton Internat. Sculpture award Silvermine Guild of Artists 1977, Bronze Sculpture prize Renaissance Foundry 1981). Lathrop prize Print Club of Albany, 1948; Hermine Kleinert award, 1952; Childe Hassam Purchase award, 1953; 1st prize Albany Inst. History and Art, 1966; Louis Comford Tiffany 2000 fellow, 1948; Fulbright grantee, Italy, 1951; academician NAD. Mem. Nat. Soc. Mural Painters (hon.), Woodstock Art Assn. (sec). Home: 370 John Joy Rd Woodstock NY 12498 *For me, my life's work, my art, has always been a means of giving some semblance of dignity - and even sanity - and meaning to a world too often obsessed with material concerns, with false values and meaningless goals; a world beset with social ills and follies, with frustrations, pain and suffering, and, as a consequence, too often seemingly determined to seek its own destruction.*

CHAYES, ABRAM, educator, lawyer; b. Chgo., July 18, 1922; s. Edward and Kitty (Torch) C.; m. Antonia Handler, Dec. 24, 1947; children: Eve, Abigail, Lincoln, Sarah Prudence, Angelica. A.B., Harvard U., 1943, LL.B., 1949. Bar: D.C. 1953, Conn. 1950, Mass. 1958. Legal adviser to Gov. of Conn., 1949-50; asso. gen. counsel Pres.'s Materials Policy Commn., 1951; law clk. to Justice Felix Frankfurter, 1951-52; with Covington & Burling, Washington, 1952-55, Ginsburg & Feldman, Washington, 1964-65; asst. prof. law Harvard, 1955-58, prof., 1958-61, 65-76, Felix Frankfurter prof. law,

1976—; guest scholar Brookings Instn., 1977-78; chmn. coordinating Com. Internat. Nuclear Fuel Cycle Evaluation, 1977-80; mem. U.S. nat. group Permanent Ct. Arbitration, 1980—; Staff dir. Democratic Platform Com., 1960; legal adviser, asst. sec. Dept. State, 1961-64; dir. fgn. policy task forces Democratic Campaign, 1972. Author: (with others) The International Legal Process, 2 vols, 1968, ABM, An Evaluation of the Decision to Deploy an Antiballistic Missile System, 1969, The Cuban Missiles Crisis: International Crises and the Role of Law, 1974. Served to capt. F.A. AUS, 1943-46. Decorated Bronze Star. Fellow Am. Acad. Arts and Scis. Home: 3 Hubbard Park Rd Cambridge MA 02138 Office: Harvard Law Sch G-404 Cambridge MA 02138

CHAZANOFF, JAY DAVID, investment company executive; b. N.Y.C., Oct. 28, 1945; s. Irving and Sylvia (Hershkowitz) C.; m. Lucille Louise DeSantis, May 17, 1970. B.B.A., Pace U., 1967; M.B.A., L.I.U., 1969. C.P.A., N.Y. Acct. Ernst & Whinney, N.Y.C., 1967-73; sr. exec. v.p. Integrated Resources, Inc., N.Y.C., 1973—. Office: Integrated Resources Inc 666 3d Ave New York NY 10017

CHEATHAM, GLENN WALLACE, university dean, consultant, researcher; b. Salem, Oregon, Oct. 13, 1934; s. Harold Edwin and Myrtle Esther (Crane) C.; m. Kaye Swindoll Adams, Sept. 12, 1952 (div. 1968); children: Dennis Glenn, Jannette Kaye, Diane LaRae; m. Cheryl Elyse Sanders, Nov. 30, 1968. A.A., Modesto Jr. Coll., 1964; B.A. summa cum laude, San Francisco State U., 1967, M.S., 1968; Ph.D., U. Minn., 1973. Registered recreation adminstr. Recreation supr. City of Modesto, (Calif.), 1962-64; ctr. dir. St. Agnes Parish, San Francisco, 1964-68; instr. San Francisco State U., 1968; instr., program coordinator U. Minn., Mpls., 1968-73, asst. prof., 1973-75; prof. leisure studies, dept. chmn. Ariz. State U., Tempe, 1975-83, assoc. dean Coll. Pub. Programs, 1983—; planning cons. Ariz. Outdoor Recreation Coordinating Commn., Phoenix, 1977-78, Ariz. State Lands Dept., 1981-82, Ariz. Office of Tourism, 1982—; research cons. U.S. Bur. Reclamation, Boulder City, Nev., 1975-81, U.S. Army C.E., Los Angeles, 1981-82. Prin. researcher, author: (13 tech. reports) Recreation Use of Lower Colorado River, 1975-81; planner, co-author: Master Plan, Mgmt. Plan for Significant Pre-historic Indian Sites in Arizona, 1982; editor: book reviews Jour. Leisure Research, 1977-80; reviewer: edn. resources, publs., articles Jour. Park-Recreation Adminstrn., 1983. Bd. dirs. G.F. Miller Am. Humanics Chpt., Phoenix, 1977-83; coordinator Legislator's Day, Ariz. State U., 1980-82; mem. State of Ariz. Com. on Prevention, 1977-80, Long Range Planning Com., City of Tempe, 1981. Co-recipient grants U.S. Bur. Reclamation and U.S. Army C.E., 1975-82. Mem. AAHPER, Nat. Recreation and Park Assn., Minn. Parks and Recreation Assn. (sect. chmn. 1974-75), Ariz. Parks and Recreation Assn. (sect. chmn. 1976-79), World Leisure Recreation Assn., Alpha Gamma Sigma. Republican. Office: Coll Public Programs Ariz State U 204 Wilson Hall Tempe AZ 85287

CHEATHAM, JOHN BANE, JR., mech. engr.; b. Houston, June 29, 1924; s. John Bane and Winnie (Carr) C.; m. Juanita Faye Burns, July 19, 1947; children—Preston, Curtis. B.M.E., So. Methodist U., 1948, M.S., 1953; M.E., M.I.T., 1954; Ph.D., Rice U., 1960. Registered profl. engr. Design engr. Linkbelt Co., Dallas and Houston, 1949-50; research engr. Atlantic Refining Co., Dallas, 1950-53; research asso., head drilling research Shell Devel. Co., Houston, 1954-63; prof. mech. engring. Rice U., 1963—; pres. Cheatham Engring. Inc., Houston, 1977—, Techaid Corp., 1978—; cons. in field. Contbr. to profl. jours.; tech. editor: Jour. Energy Resources Tech, 1979-81. Served to 2d lt. USAAF, 1943-45. Tex. Fellow ASME; mem. Am. Inst. Mining and Petroleum Engrs., Am. Soc. Engring. Edn., Sigma Xi. Address: 4402 Briarbend St Houston TX 77035

CHEATHAM, JOHN MCGEE, former textile manufacturing executive; b. Easley, S.C., May 15, 1913; s. John Henry and Janye (Jackson) C.; m. Elizabeth Mathis, June 15, 1939; children: John McGee, Elizabeth M., Harvey M., Jackson Kelley. Student, Furman U., 1930-32, Ga. Tech., 1932-33. With Dundee Mills, Griffin, Ga., 1933-83, successively clk., jr. salesman, asst. to pres., v.p., 1941-50, pres., 1950-79, chmn., chief exec. officer, 1979-83; chmn. Hartwell Mills, Ga.; dir. Trust Co. Ga., Bibb Co. Served as lt. (j.g.) USNR, 1944-46. Mem. Am. Textile Mfrs. Inst., Inc (pres. 1960-61). Baptist. Lodge: Rotary. Office: Dundee Mills Inc PO Box E Griffin GA 30224

CHECCHI, VINCENT, economist; b. Calais, Maine, Nov. 25, 1918; s. Arthur R. and Dina I. (Pisani) C.; m. Mary E. Pate, Aug. 2, 1941; children—Dina Ann, Mary Jane, Vincent Arthur. A.B., U. Maine, 1940; postgrad., Harvard, 1941; M.A., George Washington U., 1942. Statistician-economist WPB, 1941-45; dep. dir. requirements br. Allied Mil. Govt. in Italy, 1945-46; dir. program coordination UNRRA, Italy, then asst. to chief mission in China, 1946-47; loan officer Internat. Bank Reconstrn. and Development, 1947; dir. China econ. br., later dir. East-West trade br. ECA, 1947-49, spl. rep. in Philippines, 1950-51; econ. editor Reporter mag., 1950; founder, 1951; since chmn. bd., chief exec. officer Checchi and Co., Washington; also dir. various subsidiaries; exec. com., dir. FCH Services, Inc.; Trustee, exec. com. Mut. Investing Found. Co-author: Honduras, A Problem in Economic Development; author articles on econs. Home: 9206 Watson Rd Silver Spring MD 20910 Office: 1730 Rhode Island Ave NW Washington DC 20036

CHECKET, EVERETT S., oil company executive; b. Balt., Oct. 15, 1918; s. Benjamin P. and Edith (Booker) C.; m. Kathleen Agnes Kramer, May 31, 1947; 1 dau., Kathy Checket Moranto. B.S., Drexel Inst. Tech., 1939; A.M.P., Harvard U., 1958. Pres. Mobil South Inc., N.Y.C., 1971-72, Mobil East Inc., 1972-73, Mobil Europe Inc., London, 1973-75; v.p. Mobil Oil Corp., N.Y.C., from 1975, exec. v.p., to 1982, exec. v.p., pres. M&R div., 1983—, also dir.; mem. Adv. Council Japan-U.S. Econ. Relations, 1977—, ASEAN-U.S. Bus. Council, 1979—; vice chmn., dir. Banco Central of N.Y., 1981—. Trustee Drexel U., 1977—. Served to lt. col. U.S. Army, 1940-46. Recipient Order of Sacred Treasure, Japan, 1965. Mem. Am. Bur. Shipping (bd. mgrs.), Japan Soc. (dir.). Episcopalian. Club: West Side Tennis (Forest Hills, N.Y.). Office: Mobil Oil Corp 150 E 42d St New York NY 10017 *

CHECKLEY, DAVID MILTON, architect; b. Mattoon, Ill., Aug. 26, 1917; s. Horace R. and Mildred L. (Lemert) C.; m. Dorothea Stinson, Oct. 18, 1941; children—Leslie Ruth, David Milton, Elizabeth. B.S. in Architecture and Bus. Adminstrn., U. Ill., 1940. Archtl. designer, Chgo., 1940-41; indsl. engr. N.Am. Aviation, Inc., 1941-44; project mgr., v.p., gen. mgr. J. Gordon Turnbull, Inc., cons. engrs., Cleve., 1944-54; gen. mgr. indsl. div. Arthur G. McKee & Co., Cleve., 1954-59; pres. Vitro Engring. Co., N.Y.C., 1959-61; pvt. cons. practice, 1961-64, 70—; mng. dir. John Graham & Co., Seattle, 1964-69, pres., 1969-70; cons. architect/designer, 1970—; pres. Kite Factory, Seattle, 1960-64; dir. Olivetti-Underwood, N.Y.C., Creation Co., Hamamatsu, Japan. Mem. AIA, Am. Watercolor Soc., Puget Sound Group N.W. Painters. Episcopalian. Club: Rotary (Seattle). Home: 678 W Prospect Seattle WA 98119

CHECOTA, JOSEPH WOODROW, business executive; b. Watertown, Wis., May 6, 1939; s. Joseph Woodrow and Rachael Cecilia C.; m. Ellen McNamara, Sept. 7, 1963; children—Benjamin David, Nicholas Forbes. B.S., U. Wis., 1963. Wis. area coordinator Area Redevel. Adminstrn., U.S. Dept. Commerce, 1963-64; area supr. Econ. Devel. Adminstrn., Washington, 1965-66; co-founder, pres., dir. Am. Med. Bldgs., Inc., Milw., 1968—, chmn. bd., 1975—; chmn. bd., chief exec. officer The Am. Network, Inc., 1981—; dir. Mid-Continental Bancorp., Continental Bank & Trust Co. Treas. Wis. Democratic Com., 1969-70, chmn., 1979-81; Vice pres. Port of Milw. Bd. Harbor Commrs., 1978-80, pres., 1980-81. Office: 735 N Water St Milwaukee WI 53202

CHEEK, CHARLES WALL, investment co. exec.; b. Lexington, N.C., Mar. 20, 1921; s. John Merritt and Maud (Wall) C.; m. Betty Green Johnson, Dec. 28, 1944; children—Mary Charles Cheek Armstrong, Catherine, Alexander. B.S., Wake Forest U., 1941. Prodn. mgr. Cheek-Holton Co., Durham, N.C., 1946-50; trust officer Fidelity Bank, Durham, 1952-56; v.p. Wachovia Bank, Durham, 1956-60, 1st Nat. Bank of S.C., Charleston, 1960-63; pres. Piedmont Fin. Co., Greensboro, N.C., 1963-73; pres., dir. Lexington Income Fund, Inc., Englewood, N.J., Lexington Tax Free Income Fund, Lexington Growth Fund, Lexington Research Fund, Lexington Money Market Fund; chmn. bd., dir. Templeton Dobrow and Vance; chmn. bd. Lexington Mgmt. Corp.; dir. Richardson Corp., Piedmont Mgmt. Co., Richardson Vicks Inc., Reinsurance Corp. N.Y. Pres. Charleston Civic Ballet, 1962, Greensboro Civic Ballet, 1965; pres., bd. dirs. United Arts Council, 1968; pres. Gen. Greene council Boy Scouts Am., 1975—; chmn. bd. trustees Greensboro Day Sch., 1975—; trustee Wake Forest U., 1971—, Smith Richardson Found., 1965—, Weatherspoon Art Gallery, 1969—, Bowman Gray Med. Center, 1973-75. Served to capt. USNR, 1950-52. Mem. Greensboro C. of C. (bd. dirs. 1974—). Clubs: Greensboro Country, Greensboro City, Carolina Yacht; Union League (N.Y.C.). Home: 804 Sunset Dr Greensboro NC 27408 Office: 201 N Elm St Greensboro NC 27402

CHEEK, GEORGE C(URTIN), forest products co. exec., public affairs specialist; b. Seattle, Jan. 23, 1931; s. George C. and Evelyn K. (Kinvig) Abel; m. Nancy M. Powers, June 13, 1953; children—Allison A., David G., Sarah E., Jennifer T. A.B., Gonzaga U., 1954. Reporter, editor The Spokesman-Rev., Spokane, Wash., 1951-59; with Am. Plywood Assn., Tacoma, 1959-68, public relations mgr., 1962-64, dir. info. services, 1964-68; account supr. Cole & Weber, Seattle, 1968-69; dir. plans and programs Nat. Forest Products Assn., Washington, 1969-70; exec. v.p. Am. Forest Inst., Washington, 1970-78; sr. v.p. public affairs Potlatch Corp., San Francisco, 1978—. Home: 606 Crescent Ave San Mateo CA 94403 Office: PO Box 3591 San Francisco CA 94119

CHEEK, JAMES EDWARD, university president; b. Roanoke Rapids, N.C., Dec. 4, 1932; s. King Virgil and Lee Ella (Williams) C.; m. Celestine Juanita Williams, June 14, 1953; children: James Edward, Janet Elizabeth. B.A., Shaw U., 1955, H.H.D., 1970; B.D., Colgate Rochester Div. Sch., 1958; Ph.D.; Rockefeller doctoral fellow, Drew U., 1962, LL.D., 1971; L.H.D., Trinity Coll., 1970; LL.D., A&T U., 1971, Del. State Coll., 1972; D. honoris causa, L'Universite d'Etat d'Haiti, 1972; Ed.D., Providence Coll., 1972, N.Y. Inst. Tech., 1980, U. N.C., 1981; H.H.D., U. Md., 1975; D.Div., Bucknell U., 1975. Teaching asst. hist. theology Drew Theol. Sch., Madison, N.J., 1959-60; instr. Western history Union Jr. Coll., Cranford, N.J., 1959-61; vis. instr. Christian history Upsala Coll., East Orange, N.J., summer 1960; asst. prof. N.T. and hist. theology Sch. Religion, Va. Union U., Richmond, 1961-63; pres. Shaw U., Raleigh, N.C., 1963-69, Howard U., Washington, 1969—; dir. First Am. Bank (N.A.), Nat. Permanent Fed. Savs. and Loan Assn.; mem. Pres.'s Commn. on Campus Unrest, 1970; spl. cons. to Pres. on Black Colls. and Univs., 1970; Mem. ad hoc com. univ. and coll. presidents Citizens Exchange Corps Congress Internat. Edn. Citizens; mem. adv. com. Woodrow Wilson Internat. Center Scholars; mem. com. internat. edn. Coll. Entrance Exam. Bd., Vilberforce U. Pres.'s Devel. Council; mem. adv. com. AAAS-Smithsonian Instn.; mem. adv. bd. Colgate-Rochester Div. Sch.; mem. nat. adv. council Independent Found.; mem. coll. scholarship program IT&T Corp.; mem. nat. adv. council Minorities in Engring.; mem. adv. council Nat. Archives; mem. nat. coordinating council Drug Abuse, Edn. and Info., Inc.; mem. nat. adv. com. Nat. Council for Black Studies; bd. advisors Washington Urban League; mem. TV career awareness adv. rev. bd. Nat. Urban League and Booker T. Washington Found.; bd. educators Center for Study of Presidency; mem. exec. com. Mid-Eastern Athletic Conf.; hon. mem. Washington Cornaro Tercentenary Com.; hon. mem. fundraising steering com. Virgin Islands Dept. Health; mem. Task Force on Internat. Affairs, D.C. Govt., Nat. Com. for Full Employment, Mordecai Wyatt Johnson Meml. Fund; mem. com. of sponsors Minority Legis. Edn. Program; mem. Am. Found. for Negro Affairs; mem. task force for women's equity AAUW; bd. dirs. Joint Center for Polit. Studies. Bd. editors: Black Forum, Inc; hon. chmn.: Jour. Religious Thought; bd. editorial assos.: Washington Star. Bd. dirs. Nat. Capital area council Boy Scouts Am., Nat. Symphony Orch. Assn., People United to Save Humanity (PUSH); bd. dirs., mem. adv. com. Capital area div. UN Assn.; hon. trustee Choral Arts Soc. Washington; bd. trustees Consortium of Univs. of Washington Met. Area, Fed. City Council, N.Y. Inst. Tech., United Way of Nat. Capital Area, Washington Center for Met. Studies; hon. bd. trustees Inst. Internat. Edn.; mem. coll. adv. bd. Black Sports; mem. nat. adv. bd. Sch. Rev.; bd. advisors Close Up, Nat. Black Monitor, Speak Out. Served with USAF, 1950-51. Colgate-Rochester grad. fellow, 1958; Lily Found. fellow, 1958-59. Mem. Am. Acad. Religion AAUP, Am. Soc. Ch. History, Nat. Assn. Bibl. Instrs., Nat. Soc. Lit. and the Arts, Religious Research Assn., Soc. Bibl. Lit. and Exegesis, Nat. Assn. for Equal Opportunity in Higher Edn. (dir.), Continental African C. of C. (dir.), Alpha Theta Nu, Alpha Phi Alpha, Sigma Pi Sigma. Office: Office of the Pres Howard U Washington DC 20059

CHEEK, JAMES HOWE, III, lawyer; b. Nashville, Nov. 28, 1942; s. James H. and Anne H. C.; m. Sigourney Woods, June 1, 1968; children—James Howe, IV, Daniel W., Matthew H. A.B., Duke U., 1964; J.D., Vanderbilt U., 1967; LL.M., Harvard U., 1968. Bar: Tenn. bar 1967. Assoc. firm Shearman & Sterling, N.Y.C., 1967; asst. dean, asst. prof. law Vanderbilt U. Law Sch., 1968-70, mem. adj. faculty, 1970—; ptnr. firm Bass, Berry & Sims, Nashville, 1970—; lectr. on continuing legal edn. at seminars, insts; trustee Elliott E. Cheatham Fund.; Nat. chmn. Vanderbilt U. Law Sch. Devel. Com., 1978-80. Contbr. articles to law jours. Mem. Am. Law Inst., Am. Bar Assn. (chmn. subcom. on 1933 Act, fed. regulation of securities com., sec. com. on corp. law), Tenn. Bar Assn. (chmn. com. on corp. laws), Nashville Bar Assn., U.S. Tennis Assn., Order of Coif. Clubs: Belle Meade Country, Cumberland. Home: 4404 Honeywood Dr Nashville TN 37205 Office: First American Center Nashville TN 37238

CHEEK, KING VIRGIL, JR., lawyer, ednl. adminstr.; b. Weldon, N.C., May 26, 1937; s. King Virgil and Lee Ella (Williams) C.; m. Annette Walker, Aug. 10, 1968; children—King Virgil III, Kahlil. A.B., Bates Coll., Lewiston, Maine, 1959, LL.D., 1970; M.A.; Jessie Smith Noyes scholar, U. Chgo., 1960, postgrad., 1960-61, J.D., 1964; LL.D., Del. State Coll., 1970, U. Md., 1972. Bar: Ill. bar 1964, N.C. bar 1965. With Midwest Inter-Library Loan Center, Chgo., 1959-64; asst. prof. econs. Shaw U., Raleigh, N.C., 1964-65, acting dean of coll., 1965-66, dean, 1966-67, v.p. acad. affairs, 1967-69; lectr. Citizenship Lab., 1968-69, pres., 1969-71, Morgan State Coll., Balt., 1971-74; v.p. for planning and devel. Union for Experimenting Colls. and Univs., Cin., 1974-76, pres., 1976-78; exec. dir. Washington Center, N.Y. Inst. Tech./Nova U. Fedn., 1978—; practice in, Raleigh, 1965-71; Cons. U.S. Office Edn., 1967, Instl. Studies Commn. Kittrell (N.C.) Coll., 1967; cons., program evaluator U.S. Office Edn. and U.S. Office Econ. Opportunity.; Mem. Mayor's Com. on UN Observance, 1967-71; mem. Task Force, The Vital Univ. (sponsored by Sci. and Soc. Program, N.C. State U.), 1968-69; chmn. N.C. Adv. Com. to U.S. Civil Rights Commn., 1969-70; mem. adv. council N.C. Regional Med. Program, 1968-69; mem. Md. adv. com. U.S. Civil Rights Commn. Bd. dirs. GROW, Inc., Ednl. Resources Inst., East St. Louis, Ill., Balt. Urban League, Balt. Mus. Art; mem. adv. bd. W.H. Trentman Mental Health Center of Wake County.; Mem. New Eng. Forensic Championship Team, 1967-68. Mem. N.C. Assn. Colls., Assn. Eastern N.C. Colls., Acad. Polit. and Social Sci., Raleigh Bus. and Profl. League, Southeastern Lawyers Assn., Delta Sigma Rho. Address: Washington Center NY Inst Tech/Nova U Fedn 1511 K St NW Suite 624 Washington DC 20005

CHEEVER, DANIEL SARGENT, international affairs educator, editor; b. Boston, Dec. 19, 1916; s. David and Jane Welles (Sargent) C.; m. Olivia Thorndike, Aug. 10, 1940 (div. 1954); children: Daniel Sargent, Olivia Lowell, Mary Helen; m. 2d Mary Luce Bryant, Jan. 20, 1956. A.B., Harvard U., 1939, A.M., 1947, Ph.D., 1948; L.H.D., Meadville Theol. Sch., U. Chgo., 1983. Mem. faculty St. Mark's Sch., Southboro, Mass., 1939-42; internat. security analyst U.S. Dept. of State, Washington, 1945-46; lectr., tutor, asst. to pres. Harvard U., Cambridge, Mass., 1948-61; vis. prof. Fletcher Sch. of Law and Diplomacy, Medford, Mass., 1960-61; prof. internat. affairs U. Pitts., 1961-82; assoc. dir. Center Internat. Relations, Boston U., 1982—; vice-chmn. Commn. to Study Orgn. of Peace N.Y., 1955—; pres. Harvard U. Grad. Soc. for Advanced Study, 1969-76; trustee Meadville Theol. Sch., Chgo., 1976-82; mem. council fgn. relations Ocean Policies Studies, N.Y.C., 1975—. Author: (with H.F. Haviland) American Foreign Policy and the Separation of Powers, 1952, Organizing for Peace, 1954, (with M.J. Esman) Common Aid Effort, 1967; editor-in-chief: Ocean Development and Internat. Law N.Y., 1979. Spl. asst. to Sec. Gen. UN Conf. on Internat. Orgn., San Francisco, 1945; faculty Nat. War Coll., Washington, 1950; program com. chmn. Unitarian-Universalist Service Com., Boston, 1956-69; mem. Fgn. Affairs Task Force of Hoover Com. Exec. Br. Reorganization, Washington, 1948; mem. Internat. Marine Sci. Affairs Panel Nat. Acad. Scis., 1968-73; mem. Pub. Adv. Com. on Law of the Sea U.S. Dept. of State, 1980—. Served to lt. USNR, 1942-45. Recipient Chase Prize Harvard U., 1948; Rockefeller Found. grantee, 1963-64; vis. resident scholar Carnegie Endowment for Internat. Peace N.Y., 1967-68; Distng. Service prof. U. Pitts., 1981. Mem. Am. Polit. Sci. Assn. (chmn. W. Wilson Essay Internat. Peace award com. 1963), Internat. Studies Assn. (regional v.p. 1965-67), Am. Soc. Internat. Law, AAUP, Internat. Polit. Sci. Assn., Am. Soc. Pub. Adminstrn. Democrat. Unitarian. Clubs: Somerset (Boston); Harvard (N.Y.C.). Home: 158 Brattle St Cambridge MA 02138 Office: Boster U Center for Internat Relations 152 Bay State Rd Boston MA 02215

CHEEVERS, GERALD MICHAEL, professional hockey coach; b. St. Catherine, Ontario, Canada, Dec. 7, 1940; m. Betty Cheever; 3 children. Hockey goaltender minor league teams of Toronto Maple Leafs, 1961-65; hockey golatender Boston Bruins, NHL, 1965-72, 1976-80; hockey goaltender Cleve. Crusaders, World Hockey Assn., 1972-76; coach Boston Bruins, 1981—; owner Gerald M. Cheever's Thoroughbred Racing Stables; operator Hockey Sch., St. Catherine, Ont., Can. With Boston Bruin Stanley Cup Champion, NHL, 1970, 72; recipient Harry Holmes Meml. Trophy, 1964-65. Office: Boston Bruins 150 Causeway St Boston MA 02114 *

CHEH, HUK YUK, electrochemist, engineering educator; b. Shanghai, China, Oct. 27, 1939; s. Tze Sang and Sue Lang (Che) C.; m. An-li, July 26, 1969; children: Emily, Evelyn. B.A.Sc. in Chem. Engring, U. Ottawa, Can., 1962; Ph.D., U. Calif.-Berkeley, 1967. Mem. tech. staff Bell Telephone Labs., N.J., 1967-70; asst. prof. chem. engring. Columbia U., N.Y.C., 1970-73, assoc. prof., 1973-79, prof., 1979—, Ruben-Viele prof., 1982—, chmn. dept., 1980—; program dir. NSF, 1978-79; vis. research prof. Nat. Tsinghua U., Taiwan, 1977. Contbr. articles to sci. jours. Recipient Harold C. Urey award, 1980. Mem. Am. Inst. Chem. Engrs., N.Y. Acad. Scis., Electrochem. Soc., Am. Electroplaters Soc., Sigma Xi. Office: Columbia U New York NY 10027

CHEIFETZ, DAVID ISRAEL, psychologist; b. South Bend, Ind., Dec. 31, 1922; s. Samuel and Miriam (Lichten) C.; m. Evelyn Kahn, Jan. 21, 1943; children—Daniel, Paul, Davina; m. Laurann Norvell, July 22, 1967. Ph.B., Herzl Jr. Coll., 1942; student, U. Ill., 1942-43; M.A., U. Chgo., 1948, Ph.D., 1955. Diplomate Am. Bd. Profl. Psychology. Psychologist Ill. Dept. Public Safety, 1948-50, Ill. Mental Health Centers, Chgo., 1951-54; NIMH clin. psychology tng. grantee, 1949-50; research asso. U. Chgo., 1950-51; instr., asst. prof., asso. prof. U. Ill., Chgo., 1955-71; lectr. Ill. Psychopathic Inst., Chgo., 1959-60; prof. psychology, sr. scientist Rush-Presbyn.-St. Luke's Med. Center, Chgo., 1955—, chmn. dept. psychology and social scis., 1971-75; asso. dean Rush Med. Coll., 1973-75; dean Coll. Health Scis., v.p. sci. affairs, 1975-81. Served with U.S. Army, 1943-46. Mental Health fellow, 1949-50. Mem. Am. Psychol. Assn., Ill. Psychol. Assn., Phi Beta Kappa, Sigma Xi. Office: 1753 W Congress Pkwy Chicago IL 60612

CHEIT, EARL FRANK, economist, univ. dean; b. Mpls., Aug. 5, 1926; s. Morris and Etta (Warshavsky) C.; m. June Doris Andrews, Aug. 28, 1950; children—Wendy, David, Ross, Julie. B.S., U. Minn., 1947, LL.B., 1949, Ph.D., 1954. Research economist, prof. Sch. Bus. Adminstrn., U. Calif., Berkeley, 1960—, exec. vice chancellor, 1965-69, dean, 1976—; also dir. Inst. Indsl. Relations; program officer in charge higher edn. and research Ford Found., 1972-73; asso. dir., sr. research fellow Carnegie Council on Policy Studies in Higher Edn., 1973-75; dir. Consol. Freightways, Inc., Shaklee Corp. Author: The Useful Arts and the Liberal Tradition, 1975, The New Depression in Higher Education, 1971, Foundations and Higher Education, 1979; Editor: The Business Establishment, 1964. Trustee Chatham Coll., Pitts., 1975—, Richmond (Calif.) Unified Sch. Dist., 1961-65, Russell Found., N.Y.C., 1979—; chmn. State of Calif. Wage Bd. for Agrl. Occupations. Home: 50 Lenox Rd Kensington CA 94707 Office: Sch of Bus Adminstrn U Calif Berkeley CA 94720

CHELAPATI, CHUNDURI VENKATA, civil engineering educator; b. Eluru, India, Mar. 11, 1933; came to U.S., 1957, naturalized, 1971; s. Lakshminarayana and Anjamma (Kanumuri) Chunduri. B.E. with honors, Andhra U., India, 1954; M.S., U. Ill., 1959, Ph.D., 1962. Jr. engr. Office of Chief Engr., State of Andhra, India, 1954-55; asst. prof. structural engring. Birla Coll. Engring., Pilani, India, 1956-57; research asst. dept. civil engring. U. Ill., 1957-62; asst. prof. engring. Calif. State U., Los Angeles, 1962-65, asso. prof., 1965-70, prof. civil engring., 1970—, vice chmn. dept., 1971-73, chmn. dept., 1973-79, coordinator profl. engring. rev. programs, 1972-81, dir. continuing engring. edn., 1982—; pres. C.V. Chelapati & Assos., Inc., Huntington Beach, Calif., 1979—; cons. U.S. Navy Civil Engring. Lab., 1962-68, 75—, Holmes & Narver, Inc., Anaheim, Calif., 1968-73. Contbr. articles to profl. jours. Mem. ASCE, Am. Soc. Engring. Edn., Structural Engrs. Assn. So. Calif., Earthquake Engring. Research Inst., Seismol. Soc. Am., Am. Concrete Inst., Am. Inst. Steel Constrn., Sigma Xi, Chi Epsilon, Tau Beta Pi, Phi Kappa Phi. Home: 16292 Mandalay Circle Huntington Beach CA 92649 Office: Dept Civil Engring Calif State U Long Beach

CA 90840 *When a person is indeed fortunate enough to reach a position of responsibility, that person should even more zealously follow the path of truth and justice, keeping in mind the good of humanity. One should look for long range objectives and not be deterred by minor setbacks.*

CHELF, ROY L., business executive. Chmn. bd. Farmland Industries, Inc., Kansas City, Mo., CRA, Inc. Office: 3315 N Oak Trafficway Kansas City MO 64116

CHELL, BEVERLY C., lawyer; b. Phila., Aug. 12, 1942; d. Max M. and Cecelia (Portney) C.; m. Robert M. Chell, June 21, 1964. B.A., U. Pa., 1964; J.D., N.Y. Law Sch., 1967; LL.M., N.Y. U., 1973. Bar: N.Y. bar 1967. Asso. firm Polur & Polur, N.Y.C., 1967-68, Thomas V. Kingham, Esq., 1968-69; v.p., sec., asst. gen. counsel, dir. Athlone Industries, Inc., Parsippany, N.J., 1969-81; asst. v.p., assoc. gen. counsel, asst. sec. Macmillan Inc., N.Y.C., 1981—; dir. Goodall Rubber Co., Trenton, N.J. Mem. Assn. Bar City N.Y., Am. Soc. Corporate Secs. Clubs: U. Pa., N.Y. U. Home: 31 Lynnfield Dr Morristown NJ 07960 Office: 866 3d Ave New York NY

CHELLGREN, PAUL WILBUR, petroleum company executive; b. Tullahoma, Tenn., Jan. 18, 1943; s. Wilbur E. and Kathryn L. (Berquist) C.; m. Shelia Mary McManus, Nov. 21, 1970; children: Sarah, Matthew, Jane. B.S., U. Ky., 1964; M.B.A., Harvard U., 1966; diploma in Devel. Econ., Univ. Coll., Oxford, Eng., 1967. Assoc. McKinsey & Co., Washington and London, 1967-68; ops. analyst Office Sec. Def., Washington, 1968-70; adminstrv. asst. Boise Cascade Corp., Idaho, 1970-71, div. gen. mgr., Los Angeles, 1971-72; pres. Universal Capital Corp., Kansas City, Mo., 1972-74; exec. asst. to chmn. Ashland Oil Inc., Ky., 1974-77, sr. v.p., group operating officer, 1980—; adminstrv. v.p. Ashland Chem. Co., Columbus, Ohio, 1977-78, group v.p., 1978-80; chmn. bd. Ashland Coal Inc., South Point Ethanol Inc.; dir., v.p. Huntington Galleies, (W. Va.). Served to 1st lt. AUS, 1968-70. Mem. Am. Petroleum Inst., Nat. Petroleum Refiners Assn., Soc. Chem. Industry, Univ. Ky. Fellows. Club: Bellefonte Country (Ashland). Home: 608 Sunset Dr Ashland KY 41101 Office: Ashland Oil Inc PO Box 391 Ashland KY 41114

CHEMECHE, GEORGE, painter, sculptor; b. Basrah, Iraq, May 11, 1934; came to U.S., 1972, naturalized, 1980; s. Zion and Galia (Greatt) Saige; m. Mira Gitta Kalichak (div. 1980). Student, Avni Sch. Art., Tel Aviv, Israel, 1956-59, Ecole des Beaux Arts, Paris, 1960-63. Exhibited one-man shows, Louis K. Meisel Gallery, N.Y.C., 1977, Saidye Bronfman Mus., Montreal, Que., Can., 1982, Grey Art Gallery, NYU, 1983, group shows, Lillian Haidenberg Gallery, N.Y.C., 1980, Aldrich Mus. Art, Ridgefield, Conn., 1981, Deicas Art Gallery, La Jolla, Calif., 1982. Served with Israeli Army, 1951-53. Jewish. Address: 222 W 23d St New York NY 10011

CHEMEROW, DAVID IRVING, financial company executive; b. Washington, July 12, 1951; s. Ben-ami S. and Elynor (Pollay) C.; m. Doreen L. Conforti, Dec. 16, 1972. A.B., Dartmouth Coll., 1973, M.B.A., 1975. Fin. analyst Am. Can Co., Greenwich, Conn., 1975-77, mgr. mergers and acquisitions, 1977-78, dir. corp. fin., 1978-80, asst. treas., 1980-82, v.p., treas., 1982—. Mem. Fairchester Treasurers Group, Am. Mgmt. Assn., Nat. Assn. Corp. Treasurers. Club: Stamford Dartmouth (treas.). Office: American Can Company American Ln Greenwich CT 06830

CHEN, CHUAN FANG, educator; b. Tientsin, China, Nov. 15, 1932; came to U.S., 1950, naturalized, 1963; s. Kwang Yuan and Chin Han (Wang) C.; m. Frances Ya-Kiang Liu, Aug. 10, 1957; children: Peter Peishan, Paul Peichuan, Philip Peihai. B.Sc., U. Ill., 1953, M.Sc., 1954; Ph.D., Brown U., 1960. Asst. to chief engr. Hydronautics, Inc., Laurel, Md., 1960-63; asst. prof. mech. and aerospace engring. Rutgers U., New Brunswick, N.J., 1963-66, asso. prof., 1966-69, prof., 1969—, chmn. dept., 1976-80; prof., head aerospace and mech. engring. dept. U. Ariz., Tucson, 1980—; cons. Vitro Labs., Silver Spring, Md., Hydronautics, Inc., Laurel, C.R. Bard, Inc., Murray Hill, N.J.; Am. Soc. Engring. Edn.-NASA fellow, summers 1968, 69, Rutgers Research Council Faculty fellow, 1971-72; sr. visitor DAMTP, Cambridge (Eng.) U.; vis. fellow Research Sch. Earth Scis., Australian Nat. U., Canberra, summer 1978. Contbr. articles to profl. jours. Fellow Am. Inst. Aeros. and Astronautics (asso.); mem. ASME, AAAS, Am. Phys. Soc., Am. Soc. Engring. Edn., Sigma Xi, Tau Beta Pi, Pi Tau Sigma. Home: 4266 E Coronado Dr Tucson AZ 85718 Office: Dept Aero and Mech Engring U Ariz Tucson AZ 85721

CHEN, JAMES TSUNG-TSUN, radiologist; b. Shantung, China, Jan. 11, 1924; came to U.S., 1959, naturalized, 1971; s. Yi and Chung-yu (Wang) C.; m. Alice Wu, June 29, 1963. M.D., Nat. Def. Med. Center, Taipei, Taiwan, 1950. Resident in medicine 1st Gen. Hosp., Taipei, 1950-52, resident in radiology, 1952-55, Hosp. of U. Pa., Phila., 1955-56, 61-62, resident in radiation therapy, 1960-61; resident in radiology Mt. Sinai Hosp., Chgo., 1959-60; intern Presbyn. Hosp., Phila., 1962-63; resident in pediatric radiology St. Christopher Hosp. for Children, Phila., 1963-64; asst. instr. radiology U. Pa., 1956-57, 60-62; instr. radiology Nat. Def. Med. Center, 1957-59; asso. dept. radiology Duke U., Durham, N.C., 1965-68, asst. prof., 1968-71, asso. prof., 1971-75, prof., 1975—, dir. cardiopulmonary radiology, 1976—. Contbr. in field. Named Tchr. of Yr. of Radiology Dept. Duke U., 1974. Fellow Am. Coll. Radiology and Cardiology, Am. Heart Assn.; mem. Radiol. Soc. N.Am., Am. Roentgen Ray Soc., Assn. Univ. Radiologists, Alpha Omega Alpha (faculty mem.). Presbyterian. Office: X-Ray Dept Duke Hospital Durham NC 27710

CHEN, JOSEPH TAO, historian, educator; b. Shanghai, China, Jan. 30, 1925; came to U.S., 1951, naturalized, 1964; s. Hung Chun and Wei Tseng (Sze) C.; m. Marjorie Anne Wong, July 10, 1965; children: Barbara Joanne, Cynthia Anne. B.A., Coll. Emporia, Kans., 1953; M.A., U. Calif., Berkeley, 1958, Ph.D., 1964. Head librarian Center for Chinese Studies U. Calif., Berkeley, 1963-64; asst. prof. history Calif. State U., Northridge, 1964-68, asso. prof., 1968-71, prof., 1971—; guest lectr. history U. Calif., Santa Barbara, 1970-73, Immaculate Heart Coll., Los Angeles, 1965-79. Author: The May Fourth Movement in Shanghai, 1971, (transl. into Chinese) The May Fourth Movement in Shanghai, 1981; contbr. articles to profl. jours. Served with Chinese Navy, 1944-45. Grantee Social Sci. Research Council, Am. Philos. Soc., Calif. State U. Found., Northridge; asso. Danforth Found. Mem. Assn. Asian Studies. Office: Dept History Calif State U Northridge CA 91330 *In this great land of America, with unfailing faith, perseverance and hard work, one has the ability and the power to influence and determine one's own destiny.*

CHEN, KAO, consulting electrical engineer; b. Shanghai, China, Mar. 21, 1919; came to U.S., 1947; s. Chi-son and Wei C. (Hsu) C.; m. May Yee Yoh, Nov. 14, 1948; children: Jennifer H., Arthur B., Carlson s. B.S. in Elec. Engring., Jiao Tong U., Shanghai, 1942; postgrad., rit. Industries scholar, Rugby, Eng., 1945-47; M.S. in Elec. Engring., Harvard U., 1948; postgrad., Bklyn. Poly. Inst., 1950-53. Registered profl. engr., N.J., N.Y. Relay specialist Am. Power Corp., N.Y.C., 1950-52; project leader Ebasco Internat., N.Y.C., 1953-55; sr. project engr. Westinghouse Electric Corp., Bloomfield, N.J., 1956-67, fellow engr., 1968-83, N.Am. Philips Lighting Corp., 1983—; pres. Carlsons Cons. Engrs., West Orange, N.J., 1981—; cons. in field. Contbr. chpts. to 6 books, 60 articles to profl. jours.; patentee in field. Exec. PTA, Cedar Grove, N.J., 1960-62, Essex council Boy Scouts Am., West Orange, 1966-70. Fellow IEEE (del. to visit China 1982, vice chmn. idsl. utilization systems dept. 1981—, chmn. prodn. and application of light com. 1983—, recipient best paper award, Centennial medal 1984); mem. Illuminating Engring. Soc., Nat. Soc. Profl. Engrs., Industry Applications Soc. of IEEE (mem. transactions adv. bd. 1981—), U.S. Nat. Com. Internat. Commn. on Illumination Jiao Tong Alumni Assn. (v.p. 1962-63). Club: Harvard (mem. sch. com. 1975—). Home: 11 Barone Rd West Orange NJ 07052 Office: North American Philips Corp 1 Westinghouse Plaza Bloomfield NJ 07003 *Hard and honest work is the surest way to success. To be able to leave a small imprint of success on this earth can be the most satisfying life goal.*

CH'EN, KENNETH KUAN-SHENG, educator, historian; b. Honolulu, Sept. 20, 1907; s. Hua-hsiu Ch'en and Chu See; m. Chao-ying Tan, Aug. 3, 1935 (dec.); children: Sylvia Hsiao-wei (dec.), Leighton Lo-tung; m. Man Hing Yue Mok, June 12, 1970. B.A., U. Hawaii, 1931; M.A., Yenching U., 1934; postgrad., U. Calif.-Berkeley, 1940-41; Ph.D., Harvard U., 1946. Research asso. Tsinghua U., 1934-35; instr. history Yenching U., 1935-36, prof., 1947-50; instr. Chinese, U. Hawaii, 1936-40, vis. prof. history, summer 1950; fellow Harvard Yenching Inst., 1941-46, asst. dir., 1947-50, exec. sec. Peking office, 1947-50; research fellow Harvard U., 1946-47; vis. lectr. Far Eastern langs. and Buddhism, 1950-58; vis. prof. history Lingnan U., 1949; prof. Oriental langs. UCLA, 1958-61, prof., chmn. dept. Oriental langs., 1971-76, prof. emeritus, 1976—; prof. Buddhism, Princeton U., 1961-71, Stewart lectr. history of religion, 1961, William H. Danforth prof. religion, 1968-71. Author: Buddhism in China, A Historical Survey, 1964, Buddhism, the Light of Asia, 1968, The Chinese Transformation of Buddhism, 1973; contbr. articles to profl. jours. and encys. Fulbright research scholar, Japan, 1964-65; Guggenheim fellow, 1964-65; McCosh faculty fellow, 1969-70; Recipient grant-in-aid Am. Council Learned Socs., 1960; Lindback award Princeton U., 1963. Mem. Am. Oriental Soc., Assn. Asian Studies, Am. Soc. Study of Religions, Phi Beta Kappa, Phi Tau Phi, Phi Kappa Phi, Pi Gamma Mu. Office: Dept Oriental Langs U Calif Los Angeles CA 90024

CHEN, KUN-MU, educator; b. Taiwan, China, Feb. 3, 1933; came to U.S., 1957, naturalized, 1969; s. Tsa-Mao and Che (Wu) C.; m. Shun-Shun Chen, Feb. 22, 1962; children—Margaret, Katherine, Kenneth, George. B.S., Nat. Taiwan U., 1955; M.S., Harvard, 1958, Ph.D., 1960. Research asso. U. Mich., 1960-64; vis. prof. Chao-Tung U., Taiwan, 1962; asso. prof. elec. engring. Mich. State U., 1964-67, prof., 1967—, dir. elec. engring. grad. program, 1969-73. Author articles on electromagnetic radiation, plasma physics, electromagnetic bioeffects. Recipient Distinguished Faculty award Mich. State U., 1976; C.T. Loo fellow, 1957; Gordon McKay fellow, 1958-60. Fellow IEEE, AAAS; mem. Internat. Union Radio Sci. (commn. A, B and C), AAUP, Sigma Xi, Phi Kappa Phi, Tau Beta Pi. Home: 4608 Tacoma Blvd Okemos MI 48864 Office: Dept Elec Engring Mich State U East Lansing MI 48824

CH'EN, LI-LI, Chinese language and literature educator, writer; b. Peking, China, Apr. 6, 1934; came to U.S., 1951, naturalized, 1963; d. Shujen and Yu-wu (Kuan) C. B.A. magna cum laude, Wilson Coll., 1957, Litt.D., 1980; M.A., Radcliffe Coll., 1958; Ph.D. (Harvard-Yenching Inst. fellow, Ford Found. fellow), Harvard U., 1969. Prof. Chinese lang. and lit. Tufts U., Medford, Mass., 1972—. Translator: Master Tung's Western Chamber Romance, 1977 (Nat. Book Award for Transl.); Contbr. articles to profl. jours. Am. Council Learned Socs. grantee, 1976-77; MacDowell Colony fellow, 1980; Michael Karoly Found. fellow, 1980; Recipient Nat. Mag. Award for Fiction, Criticism, and Belles Lettres for short story Peking! Peking, 1977. Mem. Phi Beta Kappa. Home: 186 Upland Rd Cambridge MA 02140 Office: East Hall 102 Tufts U Medford MA 02155

CHEN, MARTIN FRANCIS, government executive; b. Hong Kong, Sept. 5, 1941; came to U.S., 1950; s. Kenneth and Kwan Sau (Chu) C.; m. Elizabeth Rebecca Elliott, June 9, 1969; 1 dau., Jennifer. B.S., Fordham U., 1965; M.S., Columbia U., 1967. Engr. Naval Surface Weapons tr., Washington, 1967-75; adv. Office Sec. of Def., Washington, 1975-76, sr. adv., 1980-81; dir. systems engring, Naval Material Command, Washington, 1976-80; dep. asst. sec. systems, asst. sec. Air Force Research, Devel. and Logistics, Washington, 1981-83; prin. dep. asst. sec. asst. sec. Air Force, Washington, 1983—. Recipient Exceptional Service medal Air Force, 1982. Office: US Air Force Room 4E964 Pentagon Washington DC 20330

CHEN, MICHAEL MING, engr., educator; b. Hankow, China, Mar. 10, 1933; came to U.S., 1953, naturalized, 1965; s. Kwang Tzu and Hwei Chuing (Deng) C.; m. Ruth Hsu, Oct. 15, 1961; children—Brigitte (dec.), Derek, Melinda. B.S., U. Ill., 1955; S.M., M.I.T., 1957, Ph.D., 1961. Sr. staff scientist research and devel. Avco Corp., Wilmington, Mass., 1960-63; asst. prof. engring. and applied sci. Yale U., 1963-69; asso. prof. mech. engring. N.Y. U., 1969-73; prof. mech. engring. and bioengring. U. Ill., Urbana-Champaign, 1973—; cons. A.D. Little Co., NIH, Argonne Nat. Lab. Asso. editor: Jour. Biomech. Engring; contbr. to profl. publs. Mem. ASME, Am. Phys. Soc., Sigma Xi, Phi Kappa Phi, Tau Beta Pi, Pi Tau Sigma. Home: 311 Eliot Dr Urbana IL 61801 Office: 144 MEB Univ Ill 1206 W Green St Urbana IL 61801

CHEN, MING MAO, educator; b. China, Apr. 23, 1919; came to U.S., 1947, naturalized, 1963; s. Kwang C. and Liao (Shih) C.; m. Frances Cheng, Dec. 22, 1948; children—Elizabeth F., Leon L. B.S. in Mech. Engring; Generalissimo Chiang Kai-shek scholar, Nat. Wu-han U., 1941; M.S., U. Ill., 1948, U. Wash., 1952; Ph.D., U. Ill., 1952. Research engr. Rep. Aviation Corp., 1952-53; mem. research staff Mass. Inst. Tech., 1953-60; asso. prof. Boston U., 1960-66, prof. aero. engring., 1966—, chmn. dept. aerospace engring., 1968-73, chmn. dept. aerospace and mech. engring., 1974—; vis. prof., acting dean acad. affairs Nat. Cheng-Kung U., Taiwan, 1966-67; cons. in field. Trustee U. Lowell, Mass. Contbr. articles to profl. jours. Fellow Am. Inst. Aeros. and Astronautics (asso.); mem. AAUP, Am. Soc. Engring. Edn., Soc. Exptl. Stress Analysis, Greater Boston Chinese Cultural Assn. (pres. 1962), Sigma Xi. Methodist. Home: 6 Redcoat Ln Lexington MA 02173 Office: Dept of Aerospace Engring Boston Univ Boston MA 02215

CHEN, PAUL E., scientist; b. Hangchow, China, June 29, 1925; came to U.S., 1951, naturalized, 1963; s. Johnson T. F. and Von N. (Kao) C.; m. Lydia S. M. Chung, Dec. 1, 1952; children—Susan, Michael. B.S., Nat. Chiao Tung U., China, 1947; M.S., Purdue U., 1953; D.Sc., Washington U., St. Louis, 1962. Instr. Nat. Taiwan U., Taipei, 1947-51; engr. Mississippi Valley Structural Steel Co., Melrose Park, Ill., 1953-55; sr. engr. Sverdrup & Parcel Engring. Co., St. Louis, 1955-59; research scientist Monsanto Co., St. Louis, 1959-70; mgr. Bell Telephone Labs., Naperville, Ill., 1970—; dir. Unisystems, Inc., 1969—; affiliate prof. materials sci. Washington U., 1965-69; prof. engring. mechs. U. Mo. at Rolla St. Louis Grad. Engring. Center, 1966-70; adj. full prof. Ill. Inst. Tech., 1975—; lectr. internat. confs.; invited lectr. univs. People's Republic of China, 1980. Contbr. articles to profl. publs. and books. Bd. dirs. Chinese Christian Ch., River Forest, Ill., 1976—. Mem. ASME, ASCE, Am. Inst. Physics, Soc. Rheology, Sigma Xi, Tau Beta Pi. Designer maj. bridges, U.S. and abroad. Home: 22 W 131 Glen Park Dr Glen Ellyn IL 60137 Office: Bell Telephone Labs Naperville IL 60566 *Truly believe in the democratic principle that all people are created equal and treat them likewise. Always grateful for material blessings and never content with own ability and knowledge. Plan for the future but work as if there is no tomorrow. Always seek His guidance and have complete trust in Him.*

CHEN, SHOEI-SHENG, engineer; b. Taiwan, Jan. 26, 1940; s. Yung-cheng and A-shu (Fang) C.; m. Ruth C. Lee, June 28, 1969; children: Lyrice, Lisa, Steve. B.S., Nat. Taiwan U., 1963; M.S., Princeton U., 1966, M.A., 1967, Ph.D., 1968. Research asst. Princeton U., 1965-68; asst. mech. engr. Argonne (Ill.) Nat. Lab., 1968-71, mech. engr., 1971-80, sr. mech. engr., 1980—; cons. to Internat. Atomic Energy Agy. to assist developing countries in research and devel. of nuclear reactor systems components, 1977, 79,80. Contbr. articles to profl. jours. Mem. ASME, Am. Acad. Mechanics, Accoustical Soc. Am., Sigma Xi. Home: 6420 Waterford Ct Willowbrook IL 60521 Office: 9700 S Cass Ave Argonne IL 60439

CHEN, WAYNE H., electrical engineer, university dean; b. Soochow, China, Dec. 13, 1922; came to U.S., 1947, naturalized, 1957; s. Ting Li and Yung-Chin (Hu) C.; m. Dorothy Teh Hou, June 7, 1957; children: Avis Shirley and Benjamin Timothy (twins). B.S. in E.E, Nat. Chiao Tung U., China, 1944; M.S., U. Wash., 1949; Ph.D., 1952. Registered profl. engr., Fla. Electronic engr. cyclotron project Applied Physics Lab. U. Wash., 1949-50, asso. in math, 1950-52; mem. faculty U. Fla., Gainesville, 1952—, prof. elec. engring., 1957—, chmn. dept., 1965-73, dean Coll. Engring., dir. Engring. and Indsl. Expt. Sta., 1973—; vis. prof. Nat. Chiao Tung U., Nat. Taiwan U., spring 1964; vis. scientist Nat. Acad. Scis. to USSR, 1967; mem. tech. staff Bell Tel. Labs., summers 1953, 54, cons., 1955-60; mem. tech. staff Hughes Aircraft Co., summer 1962; vis. prof. U. Caraboho, Venezuela, summer 1972. Author: The Analayis of Linear Systems, 1963, Linear Network Design and Synthesis, 1964, The Robotosyncrasies (pseudonym Wayne Hawaii), 1976, The Year of the Robot, 1981. Recipient Fla. Blue Key Outstanding Faculty award, 1960, Outstanding Publs. award Chia Hsin Cement Co. Cultural Fund, Taiwan, 1964, Tchr.-Scholar award U. Fla., 1971. Fellow IEEE; mem. AAUP, Am. Soc. Engring. Edn., Fla. Engring Soc., Nat. Soc. Profl. Engrs., Blue Key, Sigma Xi, Sigma Tau, Eta Kappa Nu, Tau Beta Pi, Epsilon Lambda Chi, Omicron Delta Kappa, Phi Tau Phi., Phi Kappa Phi. Club: Rotary. Patentee in field. Home: 2065 19th Ln NW Gainesville FL 32605 Office: Coll Engring U Fla Gainesville FL 32611

CHENEA, PAUL FRANKLIN, retired automobile manufacturing company executive; b. Milton, Oreg., May 17, 1918; s. Paul Francis and Gladys Martha (Welch) C.; m. Katherine Louise Bullock, Jan. 17, 1941; children: Susanne, Paul Franklin. B.S., U. Calif., 1940; M.S., U. Mich., 1947, Ph.D., 1949; D.Eng., Purdue U., 1968, Drexel U., 1971; D.Sc., Rose Hulman Inst. Tech., 1968; D.Engring. Sci., Tri-State Coll., 1968; D.H.L., Clarkson Coll. Tech., 1971. Project engr. contractors Pacific naval air bases, 1940-41; instr. to asso. prof. engring. mechanics U. Mich., 1946-52, prof., chmn. dept. engring. mechanics, 1952-54, head div. engring. sci., 1954-57, asst. dean engring., 1954-56; asso. dean engring. Purdue U., 1956-58, acting head dept. gen. engring., 1954, acting head sch. elec. engring., 1957-58, head sch. mech. engring., 1959-61, acting head div. math. scis., 1960-61, v.p. acad. affairs, 1961-67, acting dean, 1962-63; Edwin Sibley Webster prof. elec. engring. Mass. Inst. Tech., 1958-59; sci. dir. research lab. Gen. Motors Corp., Warren, Mich., 1967-69, v.p. research labs., 1969—; Mem. adv. panel engring. scis. NSF, 1956-59, chmn., 1958-59; cons. Gen. Motors Corp., E.I. duPont de Nemours Co., RCA; mem. Pres.'s Com. Nat. Medal Sci., 1966-68; mem. energy research and adv. council U.S. Energy Policy office, 1973-75; mem. Tech. Adv. Bd. U.S. Dept. Commerce, 1974-76; cons. ERDA, 1976-77; dir. Commn. Engring. Edn., 1960-70, chmn., 1960-63; civilian cons. Army Sci. Adv. Panel, 1968-71; chmn. steering com. Kanpur Indo-Am. Program, 1960-63; Mem. vis. coms. dept. mech. engring. Mass. Inst. Tech., 1966-77, div. engring. and applied sci. Calif. Inst. Tech., 1970—; Sch. Engring., Oakland U., 1968—, dept. mech. engring. U. Mich., 1968-70, Schs. Engring., Purdue U., 1973-75, engring. bd. visitors Duke, 1973—; trustee Thomas Alva Edison Found., 1971-75, Rensselaer Poly. Inst., 1972-82. Author: Mechanics of Vibration, 1952, also articles, tech. papers. Served from 2d lt. to lt. col., ordnance dept. AUS, 1941-46. Recipient Outstanding Achievement award U. Mich., 1968, Distinguished Profl. Achievement award Coll. Engring., 1978. Fellow Am. Acad. Arts and Scis., ASME, AAAS; mem. Soc. Automotive Engrs., Am. Inst. Physics, Am. Soc. Engring. Edn., Indsl. Research Inst. (dir. 1972-75), Nat. Acad. Engring. Address: PO Box 1121 2550 Copper Basin Rd Prescott AZ 86302

CHENERY, HOLLIS BURNLEY, economics educator; b. Richmond, Va., Jan. 6, 1918; s. Christopher Tompkins and Helen Clementina (Bates) C.; m. Louise Seamster, 1942 (div. 1964); children: Hollis Ann, Teresa; m. Mary Montgomery, Aug. 13, 1970. B.S., U. Ariz., 1939, U. Okla., 1942; M.S., Calif. Inst. Tech., 1943; M.A., U. Va., 1947; Ph.D., Harvard, 1950,; hon., Netherlands Sch. Econs., 1968. Prof. econs. Stanford U., 1952-61; prof. econs. Harvard U., 1965-70, 82—; asst. adminstr. U.S. AID, 1961-65; econ. adviser to pres. World Bank, Washington, 1970-72, v.p. devel. policy, 1972—; Mem. vis. com. for dept. econs. Mass. Inst. Tech., Boston U. Author: co-author: Arabian Oil, 1949, Interindustry Economics, 1959; Author or co-author: Patterns of Development, 1975, Structural Change and Development Policy, 1979; editor: Studies in Development Planning, 1971, Redistribution with Growth, 1974. Served to capt. AUS, 1942-46; ETO. Guggenheim fellow, 1961. Fellow Econometric Soc.; mem. Am. Econ. Assn., Royal Econ. Soc., Am. Acad. Arts and Scis. Clubs: Cosmos (Washington); Cambridge Tennis (Belmont Hill, Mass.). Office: Harvard Univ 1737 Cambridge St Cambridge MA 20138

CHENEY, DANIEL LAVERN, magazine publisher; b. Vernon, N.Y., May 26, 1928; s. Luke Lavern and Estella Mae (Clinch) C.; m. Eleanora Louise Stevenson, Aug. 8, 1959; stepchildren: Patricia Dinsmore Walter, Nancy Dinsmore Fulcher, Jon Dinsmore. A.B., Colgate U., 1950. Cost acctg. clk. Gen. Electric Co., Auburn, N.Y., 1955-58; mng. editor Consultant, Phila., 1958-70; founder, pres. Nursing; co-owner Springhouse Corp., Jenkintown, Pa., 1970—; founder, pres. Skillbooks, 1977—; founder, pub. Photobooks. Served with AUS, 1950-52. Methodist. Home: 445 Westminster Ave Haddonfield NJ 08033 Office: Spring House PA

CHENEY, ELLIOTT WARD, mathematics educator; b. Gettysburg, Pa., June 28, 1929; s. Elliott Ward and Carleton (Pratt) C.; m. Elizabeth Jean Helsley, Sept. 5, 1952 (div. Apr. 1974); children: Margaret, Elliott, David; m. Denise Vargo, June 17, 1974. B.A., Lehigh U., 1951; Ph.D., U. Kans., 1957. Instr. U. Kans., 1954-56; research engr., design specialist Convair-Astronautics, San Diego, 1956-59; mem. tech. staff Space Tech. Labs., Los Angeles, 1959-61; asst. prof. Iowa State U., 1961-62, U. Calif. at Los Angeles, 1962-64, asso. prof., 1964-65; vis. asso. prof. math. U. Tex., Austin, 1964-65, asso. prof., 1965-66, prof., 1966—; vis. prof. Lund U., Sweden, 1966-67, Mich. State U., 1969-70; cons. aerospace industry. Author: Introduction to Approximation Theory, 1966, (with D.R. Kincaid) Numerical Mathematics and Computing, 1980; editor: Approximation Theory III, 1980; asso. editor: Jour. Approximation Theory, 1968—, S.I.A.M. Jour. Numerical Analysis, 1964—. Mem. Am. Math. Soc., Math. Assn. Am., Soc. Indsl. and Applied Math. Home: 504 Harris Ave Austin TX 78705

CHENEY, FRANCES NEEL, librarian, educator; b. Washington, Aug. 19, 1906; d. Thomas Meeks and Carrie (Tucker) Neel; m. Brainard Cheney, June 21, 1928. B.A., Vanderbilt U., 1928; B.S. in L.S, Peabody Library Sch., 1934; M.S., Columbia, 1940; Litt.D., Marquette U., 1966. Librarian, chemistry library Vanderbilt U., 1928-29, circulation asst., 1929-30, reference librarian, 1930-37, Joint U. Libraries, 1937-43, head reference dept., 1945-46; asst. prof. Peabody Library Sch., Nashville, 1946-49, asso. prof., 1949-50, 52-67, prof., 1967-75, prof. emeritus, 1976—, also asso. dir.; asst. to chair of poetry Library of Congress, 1943-44, bibliographer gen. reference div., 1944-45; vis. faculty Japan Library Sch., Tokyo, 1951-52. Mem. Cath. Commn. on Intellectual and Cultural Affairs. Recipient Beta Phi Mu award for outstanding teaching, 1959, Mudge award for reference service, 1962; Constance Lindsay Skinner award, 1976; Mary V. Rothrock award, 1979; award Japan Library Assn., 1982. Mem. ALA (exec. bd., hon.), S.E. Library Assn. (pres. 1960-62), Tenn. Library Assn. (past pres.), Tenn. Hist. Assn., Tenn. Folklore Soc., Bibliog. Soc. Am., Assn. Am. Library Schs. (past pres.), Delta Delta Delta. Home: 112 Oak St Smyrna TN 37167 Office: Peabody Library Sch Nashville TN 37203

CHENEY, RICHARD BRUCE, Congressman; b. Lincoln, Nebr., Jan. 30, 1941; s. Richard Hebert and Marjorie Lauraine (Dickey) C.; m. Lynne Anne Vincent, Aug. 29, 1964; children—Elizabeth, Mary Claire. B.A., U. Wyo., 1965, M.A., 1966; postgrad., U. Wis., 1966-68. Staff aide to Gov. Warren Knowles, Wis., 1966; mem. staff Congressman William A. Steiger, 1969; spl. asst. to dir. OEO, Washington, 1969-70; dep. to counsellor to Pres., 1970-71; asst. dir. Cost of Living Council, 1971-73; partner Bradley, Woods and Co., 1973-74; dep. asst. to Pres., 1974-75, asst. to Pres., 1975-77; mem. 96th-97th Congresses from Wyo. at large; chmn. Republican policy com. Named one of 10 outstanding young men in Am. U.S. Jaycees, 1976; Congl. fellow Am. Polit. Sci. Assn., 1968-69. Mem. Am. Polit. Sci. Assn. Republican. Office: US Ho of Reps 225 Cannon House Office Bldg Washington DC 20515

CHENEY, RICHARD EUGENE, public relations executive; b. Pana, Ill., Aug. 30, 1921; s. Royal F. and Nelle E. (Henke) C.; m. Betty L. McCray, Oct. 17, 1943; children: R. Christopher, Elyn G. Cheney McInnis; m. 2d Virginia B. Burns, Jan. 23, 1966; children: Benjamin, Anne. A.B., Knox Coll., Galesburg. Ill., 1943; M.A., Columbia U., 1960. Assoc. editor Tide Mag., 1953; dir. pub. relations Tri Continental Corp., 1953-55; asst. mgr. pub. relations dept. Mobil Corp., 1955-60; vice chmn. bd. Hill & Knowlton, Inc., N.Y.C., 1960—. Served to lt. (j.g.) USNR, 1943-47; PTO. Clubs: Univ, Dutch Treat (N.Y.C.); Edgewood (Tivoli, N.Y.). Home: 25 W 81st St Apt 5A New York NY 10024 Office: Hill & Knowlton Inc 420 Lexington Ave New York NY 10706

CHENEY, THOMAS WARD, insurance company executive; b. Union, Nebr., Dec. 17, 1914; s. Gilbert Ward and Vernie (Barnum) C.; m. E. Margaret Phillippe, Oct. 15, 1938; children—Patricia Kay Cheney Keim, Thomas Charles. B.S., U. Nebr., 1936; student, Life Ins. Mktg. Inst., U. Kans., 1950. With Modern Woodmen of Am., 1935-79, dir., asst. to pres., Rock Island, Ill., 1954-60, pres., 1960-79, also dir.; dir. 1st Nat. Bank Rock Island. Bd. dirs. Rock Island Community Chest, 1956-58, 65-66, YMCA, Rock Island, 1965-69; v.p. Blackhawk Indsl. Devel. Assn., Rock Island County, 1959; mem. bus. advisory com. Coll. Bus. U. Ill., 1969-81; bd. dirs. Augustana Coll., 1970-78, mem. exec. com., 1972-78, chmn. devel. com., 1972-78; bd. govs. Rock Island Found., 1967-76; trustee, mem. exec. com. Rock Island Franciscan Med. Center, 1971-78, chmn. bd. trustees, 1974-75; mem. lay advisory bd. St. Anthony's Hosp., Rock Island, 1965-72. Served to lt. col. USAAF, 1941-46. Decorated Legion of Merit.; Recipient Distinguished Service award U.S. Jaycees, 1940. Mem. Fraternal Ins. Counsellors Assn., Life Underwriters Assn., Gen. Agents and Mgrs. Conf., Nat. Fraternal Congress Am. (mem. exec. com. 1961-62, pres. 1967-68), Ill. Fraternal Congress, Ill. (dir. 1966-72, mem. exec. com. 1967-72, vice chmn. 1971-72), Ill. C. of C., Rock Island C. of C. (pres. 1965), Delta Upsilon. Republican. Presbyterian (elder, trustee, deacon). Clubs: Rock Island Arsenal Golf (bd. govs. 1975-81, pres. 1979), Rock Island Arsenal Golf (exec. com.). Home: 2205 22 1/2 Ave Rock Island IL 61201

CHENG, DAVID HONG, mechanical engineering educator; b. I-Shing, China, Apr. 19, 1920; came to U.S., 1945, naturalized, 1956; s. Tze Kuen and Tseng Sun (Sheng) C.; m. Lorraine Hui-Lan Yang, Sept. 4, 1949; children: Kenneth, Gloria. M.S., U. Minn., 1947, Ph.D.; William Richmond Peters, Jr. fellow, Columbia U., 1950. Instr. Rutgers U., 1949-50; structural engr. Ammann & Whitney, N.Y.C., 1950-52; sr. engr. M.W. Kellogg Co., N.Y.C., 1952-55; lectr. Coll. City N.Y., 1955, asst. prof. civil engring., 1955-58, asso. prof., 1959-65, prof., 1966—, dir. grad. studies and exec. officer Ph.D. programs in engring., 1977-78, dean engring., 1979—; cons. M.W. Kellogg Co., Inst. Def. Analyses, N.Y.C. Transp. Adminstrn., 1976—. Author: Nuclei of Strain in the Semi-infinite Solid, 1961, Analysis of Piping Flexibility and Components, 1973. Hon. research fellow Harvard, 1967; Recipient 125th Anniversary medal Coll. City N.Y., 1973; Am. Soc. Engring. Edn.-NASA Faculty fellow, 1964-65. Mem. ASCE, ASME, Am. Soc. Engring. Edn., Chinese Inst. Engrs. (dir.), Sigma Xi, Tau Beta Pi (Outstanding Tchr. award 1972), Chi Epsilon, Phi Tau Phi. Home: 200 Old Palisade Rd Fort Lee NJ 07024 Office: Coll City NY Convent at 139th St New York NY 10031

CHENG, FRANKLIN YIH, civil engineering educator; b. Shanghai, China, July 1, 1936; came to U.S., 1960, naturalized, 1973; s. Jai Ho and Pailam (Ho) C.; m. Pi-Yu Chang, Sept. 15, 1962; children: George Chen-Hsin, Deborah Wen-Hsin. B.S., Taiwan Nat. Cheng-Kung U., 1960; M.S., U. Ill., 1962; Ph.D., U. Wis., 1966, hon. fellow, 1968. Structural engr. Sargent & Lundy, C.F. Murphy, Chgo., 1962-63; research asst. U. Wis., 1963-66; asst. prof. civil engring. U. Mo., Rolla, 1966-69, asso. prof., 1969-74, prof., 1974—; cons. engr. Buchmueller, Whitworth & Foust, Inc., Mo., Arnold & O'Sheridan Engrs., Wis., Sargent and Lundy Engrs., Los Alamos Sci. Lab.; dir. insts. computer methods of optimum structural design and matrix computer methods in structural mechanics sponsored by U. Mo., Rolla; dir. Internat. Symposium of Structural Earthquake Engring.; hon. prof. Harbin Civil Engring. Inst., China. Author: Dynamic Structural Analysis, 1973; contbr. articles to profl. jours. Served with Chinese R.O.T.C., 1956-60. Research grantee NSF and U. Mo., 1967—. Mem. ASCE, Am. Soc. Engring. Edn., Sigma Xi, Chi Epsilon. Home: 1307 Highland Dr Rolla MO 65401

CHENG, KUANG LU, chemist; b. Yangchow, China, Sept. 14, 1919; came to U.S., 1947, naturalized, 1955; s. Fong Wu and Yi Ming (Chiang) C.; children: Meiling, Chiling, Hans Christian. Ph.D., U. Ill., 1951. Microchemist Comml. Solvents Corp., Terre Haute, Ind., 1952-53; instr. U. Conn., Storrs, 1953-55; engr. Westinghouse Electric Corp., Pitts., 1955-57; asso. dir. research metals div. Kelsey Hayes Co., New Hartford, N.Y., 1957-59; mem. tech. staff RCA Labs., Princeton, N.J., 1959-66; prof. chemistry U. Mo., Kansas City, 1966—. Recipient Achievement award RCA, 1963; N.T. Veatch award for disting. research and creative activity U. Mo., Kansas City, 1979; cert. of recognition U.S. office of Naval Research, 1979, Coll. Engring., Tex. A&M U., 1981. Fellow AAAS, Chem. Soc. London; mem. Am. Chem. Soc., Electrochem. Soc., Soc. Applied Spectroscopy, Am. Inst. Physics. Home: 34 E 56th Terr Kansas City MO 64113 Office: Dept Chemistry U Mo Kansas City MO 64110 *Part of the art of research is to simplify complex phenomena and to elaborate the simple observations. Scientific research resembles gold prospecting — staying away from the spots crowded by people, exploring new territories.*

CHENG, TSUNG O., physician, educator; b. Shanghai, China, Mar. 30, 1925; came to U.S., 1950, naturalized, 1960; s. Keith S. and Fanny (Wang) C.; m. Marie Ellen Roe, June 18, 1955; children: Mark Dudley, Yvonne Joyce. B.S., St. John's U., China, 1945; M.D., U. Pa., 1950, M.S., 1956. Diplomate: Am. Bd. Internal Medicine (cardiovascular disease), Nat. Bd. Examiners. Intern St. Barnabas Hosp., Newark, 1950-51; resident Cook County Hosp., Chgo., 1952-55; fellow in cardiovascular disease George Washington U., D.C. Gen. Hosp., Washington, 1955-56; instr. cardiology Havard Med. Sch. Mass. Gen. Hosp., Boston, 1956-57; fellow in cardiorespiratory physiology Johns Hopkins U. Sch. Medicine and Hosp., 1957-59; practice medicine specializing in cardiology, Washington, 1970—; asst. prof. medicine SUNY, 1959-70; asso. prof. medicine George Washington U., 1970-72, prof., 1972—; chief cardiology D.C. Gen. Hosp., 1971-72; dir. cardiac catheterization lab. George Washington U. Med. Center, 1972-78, assoc. dir. cardiology, 1972-75; asst. physician Cardiac Clinic, Johns Hopkins Hosp., 1957-59, mem. staff cardiac catheterization lab., 1957-59; dir. cardiopulmonary lab. Bklyn. Hosp., 1959-66; co-chief Pediatric Cardiac Clinic, 1959-66; chief Adolescent Cardiac Clinic, 1961-66; attending physician Adult Cardiac Clinic, 1959-66; chief pediatric cardiac clinic Cumberland Hosp., Bkly., 1963-66; asst. chief cardiology VA Hosp., Bklyn., 1966-69; chief Cardiovascular Lab., 1966-70, chief cardiology, 1969-70; asst. vis. physicians Kings County Hosp. Med. Center, Bklyn., 1964-70; attending physician Univ. Hosp., SUNY, Bklyn., 1967-70; cons. Beth Israel Med. Center, N.Y.C.; guest lectr. Chinese Med. Assn., China, 1972, 73, 75, 77, 79, 83; vis. prof. medicine Shanghai Second Med. Coll., 1983—. Sr. editor: Vascular Medicine, 1983—; Contbr. numerous articles to sci., med. jours. Fellow A.C.P., Am. Coll. Chest Physicians, Am. Coll. Cardiology (ofcl. rep. to standards com. on catheters Assn. Advancement Med. Instrumentation 1971—), Am. Heart Assn., Council Clin. Cardiology, Soc. Cardiac Angiography, Internat. Coll. Angiology, Am. Coll. Angiology; mem. Am. Fedn. Clin. Research, Am. Heart Assn., Washington Heart Assn., AAAS, D.C. Med. Soc., AMA. Home: 7508 Cayuga Ave Bethesda MD 20817 Office: George Washington U Med Center 2150 Pennsylvania Ave NW Washington DC 20037 *My goal in life is to serve the people the best way that I know, that is, through medicine which knows no international boundary. Perseverance, patience, hard work and selflessness will always be rewarded by the satisfaction of a job well done.*

CHENHALL, ROBERT GENE, museum consultant; b. Maurice, Iowa, Jan. 24, 1923; s. Raymond Ernest and Lillian Georgia (Clark) C.; m. Carol Ann Vandercook, Feb. 26, 1943 (div. 1972); children: Raymond E., Donald R., Doris Chenhall Flenniken; m. Barbara Phyliss Von Lenz, Nov. 16, 1972. B.A., San Diego State U., 1946; M.A., Ariz. State U., 1965, Ph.D., 1972. Accountant Price Waterhouse & Co. (C.P.A.'s), Los Angeles, 1951-55, Fisher Contracting Co., Phoenix, 1955-63, Del E. Webb Corp., 1963-66; mem. faculty dept.anthropology U. Ark., Fayetteville, 1969-74; mem. staff Strong Museum, Rochester, N.Y., 1974-79; dir. Buffalo Mus. Sci., 1979-80, N.Mex. Mus. Natural History, Albuquerque, 1980-82; mus. cons., 1980—; mem. commn. archaeol. data banks Internat. Union Prehistoric and Protohistoric Scis., 1977-80; mem. trustees vis. com. Internat. Mus. Photography, Rochester, 1978-80; treas. N.E. Museums Conf., 1979-80; mem. mus. aid panel N.Y. State Council Arts, 1979-80; reviewer operating support grants Inst. Mus. Services, 1980-81. Author: Computers in Anthropology and Archeology, 1971, Museum Cataloging in the Computer Age, 1975, Nomenclature for Museum Cataloguing: A System for Classifying Man-Made Objects, 1978; also articles, revs., chpts. in books; founder, editor: Newsletter Computer Archaeology, 1965-71; editor: archaeol sect. Computers and the Humanities, 1967-70; corr. editor: Computers in the Humanities, 1968-71. Served with AUS, 1944-46. Fellow Am. Anthrop. Assn.; mem. Soc. Am. Archaeology, Am. Assn. Museums, Internat. Council Museums (dir. documentation com. 1971—), Assn. Sci. Mus. Dirs., Council Mus. Anthropology.

CHENNAULT, ANNA CHAN (MRS. CLAIRE LEE CHENNAULT), aviation executive, author, lecturer; b. Peking, China, June 23, 1925; U.S., 1948, naturalized, 1950; d. Y.W. and Isabel (Liao) Chan; m. Claire Lee Chennault, Dec. 21, 1947; children: Claire Anna, Cynthia Louise. B.A., Ling Nan U., Hong Kong, 1944; Litt.S., Chungang, Seoul, Korea, 1967; LL.D., Lincoln U., 1970; H.H.D., Manahath Ednl. Center, 1970, St. Johns U., 1982, U. Caribbean, 1982. War corr. Central News Agy., 1944-48, spl. Washington corr., 1965—; with Civil Air Transp., Taipei, Taiwan, 1946-57, editor bull., 1946-57, pub. relations officer, 1947-57; chief Chinese Sect. Machine Translation Research, Georgetown U., 1958-63; broadcaster Voice of Am., 1963-66; U.S. corr. Hsin Shen Daily News, Washington, 1958—; v.p. internat. affairs Flying Tiger Line, Inc., Washington, 1968-76; pres. TAC Internat., 1976—; cons. various airlines and aerospace corps.; lectr., writer, fashion designer, U.S. and Asia.; Dir. D.C. Nat. Bank. Feature writer: Hsin Ming Daily News, Shanghai, 1944-49; Author: Chennault and the Flying Tigers: Way of a Fighter, 1949; best seller A Thousand Springs, 1962; Education of Anna Chennault, 1981; also numerous books in Chinese including Song of Yesterday, 1961, M.E.E. 1963, My Two Worlds, 1965, The Other Half, 1966, Letters from U.S.A., 1967, Journey Among Friends and Strangers, Chinese edit, 1978, China Times, Chinese-English Dictionaries, The Education of Anna Chennault. Mem. Pres.'s adv. com. arts John F. Kennedy Center Performing Arts, 1970—; Pres. Nixon's spl. rep. Philippine Aviation Week Celebration, 1973; mem. women's adv. com. on aviation to sec. transp.; v.p. Air and Space Bicentennial Organizing Com.; spl. asst. to chmn. Asian-Pacific council AmChams; mem. spl. com. transp. to sec. transp., 1972, chmn. com. for spl. transp. activities, 1972; mem. U.S. nat. com. for UNESCO, 1970—; mem. adv. council Am. Revolution Bicentennial Adminstrn., 1975-77, also mem. ethnic racial council; advisor Nat. League Families of Am. Prisoners and Missing in S.E. Asia; presdl. appointee Pres.'s Export Council, 1981; Pres. Chinese Refugee Relief, Washington, 1962-70, Gen. Claire Chennault Found., Washington, 1960—; hon. chmn. Chinese-Am. Nat. Fedn., 1974—; Committeewoman Washington Republican Party, 1960—; mem. Nat. Rep. Finance Com., 1969—; cons. heritage groups, nationalites div. Asian affairs Rep. Nat. Com., 1969—; chmn. Nat. Rep. Heritage Council, 1979; bd. govs. Am. Acad. Achievement, Dallas; trustee Center Study Presidency, Library Presdl. Papers, 1970—, Helping Hand Found.; bd. visitors Civil Air Patrol. Recipient Woman of Distinction award Tex. Tech. Coll., Lubbock, 1966; Freedom award Order Lafayette, Washington, 1966, Free-China Assn., Taipei, 1966; Golden Plate award as champion of democracy and freedom Am. Acad. Achievement, 1967; Lady of Mercy award, 1972; Republican of Yr. award D.C. Rep. Fedn., 1974; award of honor Chinese-Am. Citizens Alliance, 1972. Fellow Aerospace Med. Assn. (hon.); mem. Nat. League Am. Pen Women, Writers Assn., Free China Writers Assn., 14th Air Force Assn. (chmn. awards com. 1969—), U.S. Air Force Wives Club, Flying Tiger Assn., U.S. C. of C. (dir. internat. policy com., council on trends and perspective), Am. Newspaper Women's Club Washington, Theta Sigma Phi. Clubs: Overseas Press (N.Y.C.); Pisces, 1925 F Street, Internat., Capitol Hill, Nat. Press, Aero, George Town (Washington); Army-Navy. Home: 2510 Virginia Ave NW Washington DC 20037 Office: 1511 K St NW Washington DC 20005

CHENOK, PHILIP BARRY, assn. exec., acct.; b. N.Y.C., Oct. 21, 1935; s. Irving and Anna C.; m. Judith Chenok, Aug. 4, 1972; children—David, Dan; stepchildren—Justin Jackson, Adam Jackson. Student, N.Y. U., 1957; postgrad., Grad. Sch. Bus., 1962. Staff acct. Pogson, Peloubet & Co., 1957-61; mgr. spl. projects Am. Inst. C.P.A.'s, N.Y.C., 1961-63, pres., 1980—; partner Main Hurdman, N.Y.C., 1963-80. Mem. Am. Inst. C.P.A.'s, Conn. Soc. C.P.A.'s, N.Y. State Soc. C.P.A.'s, Am. Acctg. Assn. Office: 1211 Ave of Americas New York NY 10036 *

CHEQUER, JOHN HAMILTON, oil company executive; b. N.Y., May 19, 1935; s. L. Hamilton and Frances (Dunham) C.; m. Nan Guthrie Budde, May 30, 1963; children: Elizabeth, Anne, Laura. B.Engring., Yale U., 1957; M.B.A., Harvard U., 1963. Vice pres. First Nat. Bank of Boston, 1963-76; exec. v.p. Tosco Corp., Los Angeles, 1976—. Served to lt. (j.g.) USNR, 1958-61. Office: 10100 Santa Monica Blvd Los Angeles CA 90067 *

CHER, singer; b. El Centro, Calif., May 20, 1946; d. Georgia and; d. Gilbert LaPiere; m. Sonny Bono, Oct. 27, 1964 (div.); 1 dau., Chastity; m. Gregg Allman, June 1975 (div.); 1 son, Elijah Blue. Student drama coach, Jeff Corey. Singer with husband as team, Sonny and Cher, 1964-74; star: TV show Cher, 1975-76, The Sonny and Cher Show, 1976-77; concert appearances with husband, 1977, numerous recs., TV, concert and benefit appearances with, Sonny Bono, TV appearances, ABC-TV, 1978, appearance with, Sonny Bono in motion picture, Good Times, 1966, Chastity, 1969; helped form rock band, Black Rose, 1979; recorded: album Black Rose, 1980; supporting role: Silkwood, 1983. Office: care International Creative Mgmt 40 N 57th St New York NY 10019

CHERBERG, JOHN ANDREW, lt. gov. Wash.; b. Pensacola, Fla., Oct. 17, 1910; s. Fortunato and Annie (R) C.; m. Elizabeth Ann Walker, Aug. 17, 1935; children—Kay Elizabeth (Mrs. Ray Cohrs), Barbara Jean (Mrs. Dean Tonkin), James Walker. B.A., U. Wash., 1933. Hign sch. tchr., athletic coach, 193446; football coach U. Wash., 1946-56; lt. gov., Wash., 1957—; Chmn. Nat. Conf. Lt. Govs., 1968-69. Mem. NEA, AFTRA, Nat. Acad. TV Arts and Scis., Wash. State Assn. Broadcasters (hon. life), Sigma Nu. Club: Variety. Home: 515 Howe St Seattle WA 98109 Office: Legislative Bldg Olympia WA 98504

CHERCOVER, MURRAY HOWARD, TV executive; b. Montreal, Que., Can., Aug. 18, 1929; s. Max Meyer and Betty (Pomerance) C.; m. Barbara Ann Holleran, Aug. 8, 1953; children: Hollis Denny, Sean Peter. Grad., Acad. Radio TV Arts, Toronto, Ont., Can., Neighborhood Playhouse Sch. Theatre, N.Y.C. With Radio Sta. CFPA, Port Arthur, Ont., 1944-46, New Play Soc., Toronto, 1946-48; exec. dir. Equity Library Theatre, N.Y.C., 1948-52; producer, dir. stock cos. in, Eastern U.S., 1948-52, Louis G. Cowan Agy., N.Y.C., 1950; with Canadian Broadcasting Co., 1952-60; v.p., dir. programming Sta. CFTO-TV, Toronto, 1960, dir. programming, 1961, v.p. programming, 1962; exec. v.p., gen. mgr. CTV TV Network Ltd., Toronto, 1966—, pres., mng. dir., 1969—, producer, dir. network TV; pres., dir. Avanti Mgmt. Ltd., 1969—, Lancer Teleprods. Ltd., 1966—; dir. Internat. Council Nat. Acad. TV Arts and Scis., Toronto Arts Prodn., Futures Secretariat; Mem. adv. com. theatre arts George Brown Coll. Applied Arts and Tech.; Adv. council film/TV prodn. program Humber Coll. Served with Royal Canadian Air Cadets, 1941-45. Mem. Canadian Assn. Broadcasters (dir.), Broadcast Execs. Soc.; mem. Internat. Platform Assn., Internat. Press Inst.; Mem. Central Canadian Broadcasters Assn. (former dir.), Radio Control Club, Model Aeros. of Can., Antique and Classic Car Club, Morgan Owners Club, MGT Registry, Ferrari Car Club. Clubs: Royal Canadian Yacht, Bloor Park, Parkview, Dunfield. Office: 42 Charles St E Toronto ON M4Y 1T4 Canada

CHERESKIN, ALVIN, advertising executive; b. Bklyn., May 16, 1928; s. Benjamin and Jessie (Levine) C.; m. Susan Barocas, June 3, 1956; children—Jessica, Benjamin, Sara. Student, Pratt Inst., 1947-48, Parsons Sch. Designing, 1948, Art Students League, 1948-50. Asst. to Joseph Binder; art asst. Hockaday Assos., Inc., 1950-55, v.p., creative dir., 1955-60, pres., 1960-65; established AC & R, 1965-66; (wholly-owned subsidairy of Ted Bates, Inc.), 1966—; now pres., treas., dir. Ted Bates Inc. Active anti-smoking campaign Am. Cancer Soc., Jewish Fedn. Philanthropies, 1970; bd. dirs. United World Colls., Princeton, N.J., Merce Cunningham Dance Found. Served with AUS, 1945-47. Home: 170 E Rockaway Rd Hewlett NY 11557 Office: 16 E 32d St New York NY 10016

CHERKASKY, MARTIN, physician; b. Phila., Oct. 6, 1911; s. Samuel and Sarah (Kosharsky) C.; m. Sarah Griffin, Feb. 3, 1941; children—Marny, Michael. M.D., Temple U., 1936. Pvt. med. practice, Phila., 1939-40; exec. home care dept. Montefiore Hosp., 1947; dir. Med. Group, 1948-51, chief div. social medicine, 1950; dir. Montefiore Hosp. and Med. Center, 1951-75, pres., 1975-81, cons. to hosp. and to bd. trustees, 1981—; Atran prof. dept. community health Albert Einstein Coll. Medicine, 1967-77; cons. N.Y. State Joint Hosp. Rev. and Planning Council; cons. to commr. hosps. N.Y.C. Dept. Hosps., 1961-62; exec. com. Health Research Council of N.Y.C., 1968-74; regional health adv. bd. Region II, Dept. Health, Edn. and Welfare, 1970-72; chmn. profl. adv. com. Joint Distbn. Com., N.Y.C., 1969-78; com. of 100 for Nat. Health Ins., 1969—; dir. Asso. Hosp. Service, 1969—; mem. Gov.'s Steering Com. Social Problems, 1970-72. Editorial bd. jour.: Chronic Diseases, 1957—, Commonwealth and Internat. Library Sci. Tech. and Engring; Contbr. articles to various publs.; Lectr. Served as lt. col. M.C. AUS, 1940-46. Fellow N.Y. Acad. Medicine; mem. Am. Pub. Health Assn., Am. Hosp. Assn., Greater N.Y. Hosp. Assn. (past pres.), Nat. Acad. Scis. (sr. mem. inst. medicine 1971—, mem. council of inst. 1972-74), Assn. Am. Med. Colls. Office: 111 E 210th St Bronx NY 10467

CHERMAYEFF, IVAN, graphic designer; b. London, June 6, 1932; s. Serge Ivan and Barbara Maitland (May) C.; m. Sara Anne Duffy, July 15, 1956; children: Catherine, Alexandra, Maro; m. Jane Clark, Sept. 24, 1978; 1 son, Sam. Grad., Phillips Acad., Andover, Mass., 1950; student, Harvard, 1950-52, Ill. Inst. Tech., 1952-54; B.F.A., Yale, 1955. Asst. to Alvin Lustig (designer), 1955; asst. art dir. Columbia Records, 1956; partner Brownjohn, Chermayeff & Geismar Assos., 1956-59, Chermayeff & Geismar Assos., Inc., N.Y.C., 1959—, Cambridge Seven Assos., 1965—; bd. dirs. Internat. Design Conf., Aspen, Colo.; bd. dirs. Municipal Art Soc., N.Y.; trustee Mus. Modern Art, N.Y.C. Recipient awards Art Dirs. Club, N.Y., Am. Inst. Graphic Arts, Type Dirs. Club., Indsl. Arts, medal AIA, 1967, Gold medal Phila. Coll. Art, 1971; Claude M. Fuess medal Phillips Acad., 1980; Pres.'s award R.I. Sch. Design, 1981; named to N.Y. Art Dirs. Club Hall of Fame, 1982. Mem. Am. Inst. Graphic Arts (pres. 1963-66, dir., Gold medal 1979), Nat. Soc. Indsl. Designers, Alliance Graphique Internat., Royal Soc. Arts (Benjamin Franklin fellow). Clubs: Harvard, Century Assn. (N.Y.C.); SPEE (Cambridge, Mass.). Home: 140 E 81st St New York NY 10028 also Sheep's Hill North Salem NY Office: 830 3d Ave New York NY 10022

CHERMAYEFF, PETER, architect; b. London, May 4, 1936; s. Serge Ivan and Barbara (May) C.; M. Andrea Petersen, Mar. 25, 1983;

children by previous marriage: John Batchelder, Benjamin Batchelder, Nicholas. A.B., Harvard U., 1957, M.Arch., 1962. Prin., v.p. Cambridge Seven Assocs., Inc., Mass., 1962—. Archtl. works include, New Eng. Aquarium, Boston, 1969, San Antonio Mus. Art, 1981, Nat. Aquarium, Balt.; producer: films including Orange and Blue, 1962, Cheetah, 1971, Wildebeest, 1984, others. Mem. Mass. Council on Arts and Humanities, 1969-72; mem. bd. advisers Sch. Visual Arts, Boston U., 1975-80; bd. design cons. U. Pa., Phila., 1976-80; mem. vis. com. R.I. Sch. Design, Providence, 1969-75. Recipient Claude M. Fuess award for disting. pub. service Phillip Acad., Andover, 1979. Fellow AIA. Office: Cambridge Seven Assocs Inc 1050 Massachusetts Ave Cambridge MA 02138

CHERN, SHIING-SHEN, emeritus mathematics educator; b. Kashing, Chekiang, China, Oct. 26, 1911; s. Lien Ching and Mei (Han) C.; m. Shih-ning Chern, July 28, 1939; 1 son, Paul May. B.S., Nankai U., Tientsin, China, 1930; M.S., Tsing Hua U., Peiping, 1934; D.Sc., U. Hamburg, Germany, 1936, 1972; LL.D. honoris causa, Chinese U., Hong Kong, 1969; D.Sc. (hon.), U. Chgo., 1969, Dr. Math, Eidgenossische Technische Hochschule, Zurich, Switzerland, 1982. Prof. math. Nat. Tsing Hua U., China, 1937-43; mem. Inst. Advanced Study, Princeton, N.J., 1943-45; acting dir. Inst. Mathematics, Academia Sinica, China, 1946-48; prof. math. U. Chgo., 1949-60, U. Calif., Berkeley, 1960-79, prof. emeritus, 1979—; dir. Math. Scis. Research Inst., 1981—. Hon. prof. various fgn. univs.; Recipient Chauvenet prize Math. Assn. Am., 1970, Nat. Medal of Sci., 1975. Mem. Am. Math. Soc. (Steele prize 1983), Nat. Acad. Scis., Am. Acad. Arts and Scis., Indian Math. Soc. (hon.), Brazilian Acad. Scis. (corr.), Academia Sinica. Home: 8336 Kent Ct El Cerrito CA 94530

CHERNE, LEO, economist; b. N.Y.C., Sept. 8, 1912; s. Max and Dora (Bailin) C.; m. Julia Rodriguez Lopez, June 7, 1936 (div. 1967); 1 dau., Gail (Mrs. Richard Gambino); m. Phyllis Abbott Brown, Apr. 13, 1968. Grad., N.Y. U., 1931; LL.B., N.Y. Law Sch., 1934; LL.D., Pace Coll., 1967, N.Y. Law Sch., 1967; L.H.D., Northeastern U., 1977; D.F.A., Manhattan Coll., 1982. Bar: N.Y. 1934. Exec. dir. Research Inst. Am., Inc.; hon. mem. faculty, mem. bd. advisers Indsl. Coll. of Armed Forces; lectr. New Sch. for Social Research, 1946-52; chmn. bd. dirs. Internat. Rescue Com., 1951—; adviser on taxation and fiscal policy to Gen. MacArthur, 1946; chmn. bd. Lawyers Co-op. Pub. Co.; dir. Viacom. Internat. Inc., Oppenheimer Funds; Bd. dirs. Willkie Meml.; bd. dirs. Freedom House, 1946—, chmn. exec. com., 1946-75, hon. chmn., 1977—; mem. select commn. Western Hemisphere Immigration, 1967-68; mem. U.S. Adv. Commn. on Internat. Ednl. and Cultural Affairs, 1971-76, Pres.'s Fgn. Intelligence Adv. Bd., 1973-76, chmn., 1976-77; mem. Intelligence Oversight Bd., 1976-77, Commn. on Critical Choices for Ams., Panel on Internat. Info., Edn. and Cultural Relations, 1974-75; adv. bd. Center for Strategic and Internat. Studies, 1975—, chmn., exec. bd., 1980-81; bd. visitors Nat. Def. U., 1976-79; chmn. Citizens Commn. on Indochinese Refugees, 1978—; vice chmn. Pres.'s Fgn. Intelligence Adv. Bd., 1981—. Author: Adjusting Your Business to War, 1939, M-Day and What it Means to You, 1940, The Rest of Your Life, 1944; Sculptor: Bronze of John F. Kennedy, Berlin Germany; bronze portrait Lyndon B. Johnson at Lyndon Baines Johnson Library; bronze of Abraham Lincoln, White House; bronze portrait of Boris Pasternak, Am. Acad. Arts and Letters; represented at, Smithsonian Instn., Phoenix Art Mus., Sibelius Mus., Helsinki, UCLA, U. Bahia, Brazil, Lincoln Mus., Washington, Presdl. Palaces, New Delhi, India, Mexico City, U.S. Pavilion, N.Y. World's Fair, 1964-65, Winston Churchill Meml., Fulton, Mo. Decorated Comdr.'s Cross of Order of Merit, Fed. Republic of Germany; Grand Order Merit, Austria; Kim Khanh Medal, Vietnam; Nat. Order Legion Honor, French Republic; recipient Human Rights award Am. Fedn. Tchrs., 1977; Internat. Platform Assn. award, 1981; named one of Ten Outstanding Young Men of Am. U.S. Jaycees, 1940. Mem. Council on Fgn. Relations., Nat. Sculpture Soc. Clubs: Lotos, Key Biscayne Yacht. Office: 589 Fifth Ave New York NY 10017

CHERNER, MARVIN, judge; b. Bessemer, Ala., Oct. 21, 1924; s. Kaciel and Rachel (Spivak) C.; m. Leona Roth Cherner, Mar. 8, 1953; children—Anne, Amy, Nancy, Ellen, Daniel. B.S. in Chem. Engring, Northwestern U., 1947; LL.B., Harvard U., 1951. Bar: Ala. bar 1951. Individual practice law, Birmingham, Ala., 1953-77; circuit judge 10th Jud. Circuit Ala., 1977—. Mem. Am. Law Inst., ABA, Ala. Bar Assn. (vice chmn. com. unauthorized practice law 1976), Birmingham Bar Assn. (co-chmn. com. profl. ethics 1970-71, chmn. unauthorized practice law 1966). Office: Jefferson County Courthouse Room 414 Birmingham AL 35263

CHERNEV, MELVIN, business executive; b. Bklyn., Nov. 29, 1928; s. Irving and Selma (Kulik) C.; m. Noemi Dohnert, May 29, 1955; 1 dau., Celia Ann. A.B., Cornell U., 1950. Chief statistician Eversharp, Inc., N.Y.C., 1951-52, sales adminstr., 1952-55, asst. gen. sales mgr., 1955-58; sales promotion mgr. Internat. Latex Corp. (Playtex), N.Y.C., 1959-64, product mgr., 1964-66; pres. Snow White Corp., San Jose, Calif., 1966-67; dir. planning and research Fromm and Sichel, Inc. (distbrs. Christian Bros. wines and brandy), San Francisco, 1967-70, dir. mktg. services, 1970-73, v.p. mktg. services, 1973-76, sr. v.p. mktg., 1976-77, exec. v.p., 1977-78, pres., chief operating officer, 1978—, chief exec. officer, 1978-84, also dir. Bd. dirs., trustee Cogswell Coll., San Francisco, 1976—, chmn., 1983—. Mem. Corp. Planners Assn. (dir.), San Francisco Ad Club (dir.). Clubs: Commonwealth, Cornell No. Calif. Home: 1506 Edgewood Rd Redwood City CA 94062

CHERNIACK, NEIL STANLEY, physician; b. Bklyn., May 28, 1931; s. Max and Rebecca (Roulnik) C.; m. Sandra Lebowitz, Dec. 31, 1954; children: Evan, Andrew, Emily. A.B. with honors, Columbia U., 1952; M.D., SUNY, 1956; M.A., U. Pa., 1972. Intern U. Ill., Chgo., 1956-57, resident, 1957-58, 60-62; resident, fellow Columbia Presbyn. Hosp., N.Y.C., 1962-64; practice medicine specializing in pulmonary disease, Chgo., 1964-69, Phila., 1969-77, Cleve., 1977—; asst. prof. medicine U. Ill., Chgo., 1964-68, asso. prof., 1968-69, U. Pa., Phila., 1969-73, prof., 1973-77, Case Western Res. U., 1977—, chief pulmonary service, 1977—, prof. physiology, 1982—, assoc. dean, 1983—; chief pulmonary service, sr. attending physician Phila. Gen. Hosp., 1969—; asso. dir. pulmonary service, attending physician U. Pa. Hosp., 1973-77, U. Hosps. of Cleve., Cleve. VA Med. Center; vis. prof. Karolinska U., Stockholm, 1976-77. Mem. editorial bd.: Handbooks of Physiology; assoc. editor: Jour. Applied Physiology, Handbooks of Physiology. Served to capt. USAF, 1958-60. Mem. Am. Assn. Physicians, Am. Soc. Clin. Investigation, Am. Thoracic Soc., Am. Lung Assn., Am. Physiol. Soc., Bioengring. Soc., Central Soc. Clin. Research, Phi Beta Kappa, Alpha Omega Alpha, Beta Sigma Rho. Home: 2700 Endicott Blvd Shaker Heights OH Office: University Hosp 2065 Adelbert Rd Cleveland OH 44120

CHERNIACK, REUBEN MITCHELL, physician; b. Canora, Sask., Can., June 15, 1924; s. Nathan and Rose (Alpert) C. M.D., U. Man., 1948, M.Sc. Intern, then sr. resident in medicine Winnipeg (Man.) Hosp., 1947-51; fellow in medicine Presbyn. Hosp., N.Y.C., 1951-52; mem. faculty U. Man. Med. Sch., 1952—, prof. medicine, 1966—, head dept., 1974—; chmn. dept. medicine Nat. Jewish Hosp., Denver, 1978—; asst. physician Winnipeg Gen. Hosp., 1955—; cons. respiratory diseases D.V.A. Deer Lodge Hosp., Winnipeg, 1955—; physician in chief dept. med. U. Man. Health Scis. Centre, 1974—. Contbr. articles to med. jours. Recipient Prowse prize U. Man., 1951; Drewery prize, 1952-53; fellow medicine Johns Hopkins U. Med. Sch., 1953-54; Life Ins. fellow, 1953-54; Markle scholar med. sci., 1954—. Fellow Royal Coll. Physicians (Can.), Royal Coll. Physicians (London), ACP, Am. Coll. Chest Physicians; mem. Canadian Med. Assn., Canadian Soc. Clin. Investigation (pres. 1963), Am. Soc. Clin. Investigation, Royal Coll. Physicians and Surgeons Can., Am. Physiol. Soc., Am. Thoracic Soc., Royal Soc. Medicine, Johns Hopkins Soc. Scholars (charter), Assn. Profs. Medicine (pres. 1976), Fleischner Soc., Am. Heart Assn. Home: 30 Clermont St Denver CO 80220 Office: Dept Medicine Nat Jewish Hosp 3800 E Colfax Denver CO 80206

CHERNIAVSKY, P. A., sugar products company executive. Pres. B.C. Sugar Refinery Co., Can. Office: BC Sugar Refinery Co PO Box 2150 Vancouver BC Canada V6B 3V2§

CHERNICK, VICTOR, educator, pediatrician; b. Winnipeg, Man., Can., Dec. 31, 1935; s. Jack and Mina (Tapper) C.; m. Norma Fordman, May 19, 1957; children—Maria, Sharon, Richard, Lisa. M.D., U. Man., 1959. Intern Winnipeg Gen. Hosp., 1959-60; postdoctoral tng. in pediatrics Johns Hopkins U., 1960-64, instr. dept. pediatrics, 1964-65, asst. prof., 1965-66; asst. prof. depts. pediatrics and physiology U. Man. Med. Sch., 1966-67, asso. prof., 1967-71, prof. pediatrics, 1971—, chmn. dept. pediatrics, 1971-79; vis. prof. dept. pediatrics Harvard U. and Children's Hosp. Med. Center, Boston, 1976-77; dir. respiratory service Winnipeg Children's Hosp., 1966-71, pediatrician-in-chief, 1977-79, dir. respiratory service, 1979—; mem. cardiorespiratory grant rev. com. Med. Research Council Can., 1974-76, sci. officer heart and lung com., 1978—; mem. med. adv. bd. Can. Found. Sudden Infant Death, 1973-75. Editor: (with E. Kendig) Disorders of the Respiratory Tract in Children, 1977; editorial bd.: Pediatrics, 1971-77, Jour. Applied Physiology, 1973-76, Jour. Pediatrics, 1978—; contbr. articles to profl. jours. Trustee Queen Elizabeth Research Fund, 1973—. Recipient Queen Elizabeth II scientist award for research, 1967-73. Fellow Am. Acad. Pediatrics; mem. Royal Coll. Physicians and Surgeons Can. (council 1974—), Soc. Pediatric Research, Am. Physiol. Soc., Can. Pediatric Soc. (medal for research 1970), Can. Soc. Clin. Investigation, Am. Thoracic Soc. Home: 14 Montcalm Crescent Winnipeg MB R2V 2N4 Canada Office: Childrens Hosp 685 Bannaty NE Ave Winnipeg MB R3E 0W1 Canada

CHERNOFF, AMOZ IMMANUEL, hematologist, govt. adminstr.; b. Malden, Mass., Mar. 17, 1923; s. Isaiah and Celia (Margolin) C.; m. Renate R. Fisher, Jan. 25, 1953; children—David F., Susan N., Judith A. B.S. in Chemistry with honors, Yale U., 1944, M.D. cum laude, 1947. Diplomate: Am. Bd. Internal Medicine. Med. intern Mass. Gen. Hosp., Boston, 1947-48; asst. resident in medicine Barnes Hosp., St. Louis, 1948-49; fellow in hematology Michael Reese Hosp., Chgo., 1949-51, asst. dir. hematology research lab., 1950-51; A.C.P. fellow Washington U. Sch. Medicine, St. Louis, 1951-52; USPHS spl. research fellow, 1952-53, instr. in medicine, 1952-54, asst. prof., 1954-56; asso. prof. medicine Duke U., 1956-58; chief sect. hematology VA Hosp., Durham, N.C., 1956-58; research prof. U. Tenn. Meml. Research Center, Knoxville, 1958-79, dir., 1964-77; asso. vice chancellor for acad. affairs Center Health Scis., 1977-79; prof. medicine Coll. Medicine, Memphis, 1966-79; med. dir. Cystic Fibrosis Found., Atlanta, 1975-77; dir. div. blood diseases and resources Nat. Heart Lung and Blood Inst., NIH, Bethesda, Md., 1979—; cons. med. program devel. Contbr. articles to profl. jours. Served with U.S. Army, 1943-45. Recipient Campbell award Yale U. Sch. Medicine, 1947, Research Career award USPHS, 1962-77. Fellow A.C.P.; mem. Am. Soc. Clin. Investigation, Am. Soc. Hematology, Internat. Soc. Hematology, Central Soc. Clin. Research, So. Soc. Clin. Investigation, Soc. Exptl. Biology and Medicine, Am. Fedn. Clin. Research, Sigma Xi, Alpha Omega Alpha. Home: 9417 Copenhaver Dr Potomac MD 20854 Office: NIH Fed Bldg Room 518 Bethesda MD 20205

CHERNOFF, DANIEL PAREGOL, patent lawyer; b. Washington, Jan. 24, 1935; s. Bernard M. and Goldie S. (Paregol) C.; m. Nancy M. Kuehner, June 17, 1965; children: Scott, Graham. B.E.E. with distinction, Cornell U., 1957, LL.B., 1959. Bar: N.Y. 1959, D.C. 1959, Oreg. bar 1968. Instr. Cornell U., 1957-59, Oreg. Bd. Higher Edn., Portland, 1970-72; practiced in, N.Y.C., 1959-67, Portland, 1967—; patent counsel Polarad Electronics Corp., Long Island City, N.Y., 1959-61; asso. firm Fish, Richardson & Neave, N.Y.C., 1961-67, Davies, Biggs, Strayer, Stoel & Boley, Portland, 1967-70; patent atty., sr. mem. Chernoff, Vilhauer, McClung, Birdwell & Stenzel, P.C., Portland, 1970—; Bd. dirs. Cardio-Pulmonary Research Inst.; bd. dirs. Learning Resource Center, Inc., chmn., 1975-79; mem. adv. council Cornell Law Sch., 1981—. Mem. Oreg. Bar Assn., N.Y. Bar Assn., D.C. Bar Assn., Am. Patent Law Assn., N.Y. Patent Law Assn., Oreg. Patent Law Assn. (pres. 1973-74), U.S. Trademark Assn., Cornell U. Law Assn., Cornell U. Council, Order of Coif, Tau Beta Pi, Eta Kappa Nu. Clubs: Multnomah Athletic.; Cornell (N.Y.C.). Home: 710 NW Winchester Terr Portland OR 97210 Office: 200 Wilcox Bldg Portland OR 97204

CHERNOFF, HERMAN, educator; b. N.Y.C., July 1, 1923; s. Max and Pauline (Markowitz) C.; m. Judith Ullman, Sept. 7, 1947; children—Ellen Sue, Miriam Cheryl. B.S., CCNY, 1943; Sc.M., Brown U., 1945, Ph.D., 1948. Research asso. Cowles commn. for research in econs. U. Chgo., 1948-49; asst. prof. U. Ill., Urbana, 1949-51, asso. prof., 1951-52, Stanford (Calif.) U., 1952-56, prof. stats., 1956-74; prof. applied math. M.I.T., Cambridge, 1974—. Author: (with L.E. Moses) Elementary Decision Theory, 1959, Sequential Analysis and Optimal Design, 1972. Recipient Townsend Harris medal CCNY Alumni Soc., 1981. Mem. Nat. Acad. Scis., Inst. Math. Stats. (pres. 1967-68), Am. Acad. Arts and Scis. Research in large sample theory, optimal design of expts., sequential analysis, pattern recognition. Home: 75 Crowninshield Rd Brookline MA 02146

CHERNOFSKY, JACOB L., trade magazine editor, publisher; b. Bklyn., Apr. 11, 1928; s. Max and Bertha (Cohen) C.; m. Ellen Esther Jung, Mar. 6, 1955; children: Meir, Michael, Brynna, Eva. Student, Poly. Inst., Bklyn., 1947-49; B.A., NYU, 1953. Editor Every Friday (community weekly), Cin., 1956-58; with Maxson Assos. (pub. relations), N.Y.C., Miami, Fla., 1959-67; dir. publicity Garber and Goodman Advt., Inc., Miami, 1968-72; mng. editor AB Bookman's Weekly, Clifton, N.J., 1973-74, editor, pub., 1975—; mem. nat. adv. bd. Ctr. for the Book, Library of Congress. Mem. Bibliog. Soc. Am., Manuscript Soc., Am. Printing History Assn. Office: 103 Central Ave Clifton NJ 07011

CHERNOW, BURT, artist, educator, writer; b. N.Y.C., July 28, 1933; s. Abe and Selma (Schnieder) C.; m. Tamara Sackman, Jan. 1, 1957 (div. July 1970); children: Perrin, Paul, Paige; m. Ann Levy, Dec. 12, 1970. B.S., N.Y. U., 1958, M.A., 1960. Tchr. art pub. schs. Valley Stream, L.I., N.Y., 1958-60, Westport, Conn., 1960-66; prof., chmn. art dept., dir. art museum Housatonic Community Coll., Bridgeport, Conn., 1966—; tchr. Mus. Modern Art, N.Y.C., 1967-70, Silvermine Guild, New Canaan, Conn., 1970-79, Stamford (Conn.) Mus., 1967-68; art critic Fairpress, Westport and Stratford (Conn.) News, 1972-73, 78-79, Art New Eng.; art cons., writer Ednl. Directions, Westport, 1968—; mem. staff Higher Edn. Center for Urban Studies, 1968-71; cons. ABCD Cultural Arts Center, 1970-71; cons., writer Model Cities, Bridgeport, summer 1969. Author: Milton Avery Drawings, 1973, Paper, Paint and Stuff, 2 vols, 1969, Lester Johnson Paintings, 1974, Contemporary Graphics, 1977, Francisco Zuniga, 1978, Abe Ajay, 1978, Will Barnet Paintings, 1980, Gabor Peterdi Paintings, 1982, The Drawings of Milton Avery, 1984; contbr. to profl. jours.; one man shows include, Mus. Art, Sci. and Industry, Bridgeport, 1972, others; exhibited in group shows, N.Y. World's Fair, 1964-65, UNESCO and USIA traveling shows; represented in permanent collection, Jacksonville (Fla.) Mus., Bridgeport Mus., Coll. Art Mus., Hampton, Va., Le Musee de l'art Contemporain, Skopje, Yugoslavia. Mem. Westport Edn. Assn., 1965-67; Bd. dirs. Westport Weston Arts Council, 1969—, Bridgeport Commn. Arts, 1972—, Art Resources of Conn., 1976-79, ABCD Cultural Arts Center, 1969; Pres. Westport Ctr. for Arts, 1983—. Served with AUS, 1953-55. Recipient 1st prize Barnum Festival, Bridgeport Mus., 1966. Mem. Appraisers Assn. Am., Nat. Art Edn. Assn. (Conn. Art Assn., exec. com. 1965-67), Westport Art Assn. (exec. com. 1962-64); mem. Silvermine Guild Artists (bd. dirs. 1972-80), Internat. Assn. Art Critics (bd. dirs.). Home: 2 Gorham Ave Westport CT 06880 Office: 510 Barnum Ave Bridgeport CT 06608

CHERNOW, DAVID A., distillery exec.; b. N.Y.C., Mar. 10, 1922; s. James and Rose (Rothstein) C.; m. Shirley Kalman, Apr. 11, 1948. A.B., Coll. City N.Y., 1941; M.B.A., Harvard, 1946. Faculty dept. econs. Coll. City N.Y., 1941-42; sec.-treas. Sunrise Curtain Co., Inc., 1946-50; sec. Ky. Distilling Co., Inc., 1950-54; with Schenley Industries, Inc., 1954—, v.p., 1958-65, v.p. finance, 1965-69, exec. v.p., 1969-75, sr. exec. v.p., 1975—, also dir.; mem. adv. bd. Mfrs. Hanover Trust Co., N.Y.C.; Mem. grad. adv. bd. Bernard M. Baruch Coll., City U. N.Y. Served to lt. USNR, 1942-46; lt. comdr. Res. (ret.). Mem. Am. Mgmt. Assn., Phi Beta Kappa, Beta Gamma Sigma. Clubs: Harvard (N.Y.C.); Key Biscayne (Fla.); Yacht. Home: 203 E 72d St New York NY 10021 Office: 888 7th Ave New York NY 10106

CHERNOW, FRED, electrical engineer, communications company executive; b. Bklyn., Sept. 13, 1932; s. Jack and Lillian (Slutsky) C.; m. Phyllis Mack; children: Hillari, Harneen, Andrew, Alexis. B.A. in Physics, Bklyn. Coll., 1955, Ph.D., N.Y. U., 1961. Asst. prof. dept. elec. engring. M.I.T., Cambridge, 1962-66; asso. prof. elec. engring. U. Colo., Boulder, 1966-70, prof., 1970—; interim dir. Computing Center, 1975, asst. to v.p. for ednl. resources, 1976-78, asst. to chancellor for ednl. resources, 1976-78; pres. Chernow Communications Inc., Boulder, 1979—; cons. Electro-Tec. Co., Ormand Beach, Fla., 1962-67, Coors Corp., Golden, Colo., 1971-73, STW, Vienna, Austria, 1971-74, KDI, Cin., 1967-71, ADL, Cambridge, 1969, Friedman & Sons, Denver, 1974-75, Varian Co., Palo Alto, Calif., 1970. Mem. Internat. Com. on Ion Implantation, 1976—; organizer 1st U.S./China Symposium on Ion Implantation, Peking, 1976. Ford Found. fellow, 1962-64; NASA grantee, 1973-75; Air Force Office Sci. research grantee, 1969-73. Mem. Am. Phys. Soc., Am. Vacuum Soc. (pres. Rocky Mountain chpt. 1969-70). Home: 7750 Spring Dr Boulder CO 80303

CHERPACK, CLIFTON, educator; b. New Britain, Conn., Nov. 4, 1925; s. Andrew Nicholas and Olive (Anderson) C.; m. Margaret Grace Bryan, Jan. 30, 1948; children: Mark, Peter. B.A., Trinity Coll., Hartford, Conn., 1950; M.A., Johns Hopkins, 1951, Ph.D., 1953. Asst. prof. Romance langs. Johns Hopkins, 1954-58; mem. faculty Duke U., 1958-67, 68-70, prof. Romance langs., 1962-70, Wesleyan U., Middletown, Conn., 1967-68, U. Pa., Phila., 1970—; cons., lectr. in field, 1954—. Author: The Call of Blood in French Classical Tragedy, 1958, An Essay on Crebillon Fils, 1962, Logos in Mythos, 1983; also articles. Served with AUS, 1944-46; PTO. Mem. Modern Lang. Assn., Am. Assn. Tchrs. French. Home: 218 Windermere Ave Wayne PA 19087 Office: Dept Romance Langs U Pa Philadelphia PA 19174

CHERRICK, HENRY MORTON, oral and maxillofacial surgery educator, college administrator; b. Bklyn., Dec. 4, 1939; s. Nathan and Rhoda (Karmiol) C.; m. Naomi Strichard, June 11, 1961; 1 son, Andrew. A.A., U. Fla.-Gainesville, 1961; D.D.S., Med. Coll. Va., 1965; cert. oral and maxillofacial surgery, U. Cin. Med. Ctr., 1968; M.S.D., Ind. U.-Indpls., 1970. Am. Bd. Oral Pathology. Asst. Prof. oral pathology Washington U., St. Louis, 1970-71; asst. prof. oral pathology UCLA, 1971-72, assoc. prof., 1973-77, prof., 1977-78; dean, prof. Sch. Dentistry-So. Ill. U., Edwardsville, 1978-81; dean Coll. Dentistry-U. Nebr., Lincoln, 1981—; cons. VA Hosp., Lincoln, 1981—, U.S. Surgeon Gen.-USAF, Washington, 1982—. Assoc. editor: Jour. Oral Medicine, 1976—; mem. editorial bd.: Colo. Oral Cancer Bull., 1978—; contbr. chpts. to books. Advisor Los Angeles City Coll., 1977-78; com. chmn. Am. Heart Assn., Lincoln, 1983. Grantee NIH, 1979; recipient Alumni Disting. Teaching Award UCLA, 1977. Fellow Am. Coll. Dentists, Am. Soc. Oral and Maxillofacial Surgery, Am. Acad. Oral Pathology (Samuel Charles Miller Meml. award 1981), Am. Dental Assn. Office: U Nebraska Med Ctr Coll of Dentistry 40th St and Holdrege St Lincoln NE 68583

CHERRINGTON, BLAKE EDWARD, engineering educator; b. Belleville, Ont., Can., Mar. 16, 1937; s. George Edward and Maywin Eileen (Waters) C.; m. Marilyn Mildred McClure, Oct. 8, 1960; children: Graham Blake, Andrea Susan. B.A.Sci., U. Toronto, 1959, M.A.Sci., 1961; Ph.D., U. Ill., 1965. Registered profl. engr., Fla. Mem. faculty U. Ill., Urbana, 1966-79, prof. elec. and nuclear engring., 1974-78, research prof., 1978-79; prof., chmn. dept. elec. engring. U. Fla., Gainesville, 1979—; cons. Zenith Radio Co., Chgo., 1972-78. Author: Gaseous Electronics and Gas Lasers, 1979; contbr. articles to profl. jours. Active Boy Scouts Am., Champaign, Ill., 1973-79; troop com. chmn. Champaign, Ill., 1974-79. Ford Found. teaching fellow U. Ill., 1961-63; Am. Council on Edn. fellow U. Minn., 1977-78. Mem. IEEE (chmn. Gainesville sect. 1982-83, sr.), Am. Soc. for Engring. Edn. (chmn. elec. engring. div. Southeastern sect. 1980-81), Am. Phys. Soc., Sigma Xi, Tau Beta Pi, Eta Kappa Nu. Episcopalian. Lodge: Kiwanis. Home: 3530 NW 26th Terr Gainesville FL 32605 Office: Dept Elec Engring U Fla Gainesville FL 32611

CHERRIX, JOHN ELDER, paper company executive; b. Nassawadox, Va., Nov. 1, 1929; s. Eldred J. and Viola W. (Hill) C.; m. Monica Donoghue, July 8, 1961; 1 son, James Christopher. B.S., U. Md., 1956. C.P.A., Md., Va., D.C. Accountant Price Waterhouse & Co., Washington, 1956-67; asst. treas. Brown Co., N.Y.C., 1967-68, treas., Los Angeles, 1968-76, v.p., treas., 1976-77, v.p. fin., treas., 1977-81, also dir.; pres. JEM Assocs., Inc., La Canada, Calif., 1981—. Served with AUS, 1950-52. Mem. Financial Execs. Inst., Am. Inst. C.P.A.'s, Omicron Delta Kappa, Beta Gamma Sigma, Phi Kappa Phi, Beta Alpha Psi, Delta Sigma Pi. Home: 5165 Gould Ave La Canada CA 91011 Office: 5165 Gould Ave La Canada CA

CHERRY, HAROLD, ins. co. exec.; b. Bronx, N.Y., June 20, 1931; s. Isidor and Esther C.; m. Maida Welt, Aug. 12, 1961; children—Gina, Joshua. B.S. cum laude, CCNY, 1953. With N.Y. Life Ins. Co., N.Y.C., 1956—, 2d v.p., actuary, 1972-78, v.p., actuary, 1978—. Served with U.S. Army, 1954-56. Fellow Soc. Actuaries; mem. Am. Acad. Actuaries, Nat. Assn. Watch and Clock Collectors (past pres. L.I. chpt.). Jewish. Office: NY Life Ins Co 51 Madison Ave New York NY 10010

CHERRY, HERMAN, poet, artist; b. Atlantic City, N.Y., Apr. 10, 1909; s. Israel and Rose (Rotkovitz) C.; m. Regina S. Schneider, Nov. 29, 1976. Student, Otis Art Inst., Los Angeles, 1927-28, Art Students League, N.Y.C., 1930, Students Art League, Los Angeles, 1928, 30-31. Prof. painting U. Calif.-Berkeley, 1959-65; prof. U. Minn., Mpls., 1969, U. Ky., 1966-67, U. Miss., 1957, New Palz Coll., 1970. Author:

Poems of Pain and Other Matters, 1976; contbr. numerous articles and essays to art jours.; exhibited one-man shows, Stanley Rose Galleries, Hollywood, Calif., 1942, Gastine Gallery, Los Angeles, 1943—, Weyhe Gallery, N.Y.C., 1947, 48—, Gasso Gallery, N.Y.C., 1951—, Stable Gallery, N.Y.C., 1955—, Poindexter Gallery, N.Y.C., 1959, 61—, Tanager Gallery, N.Y.C., 1956—, Oakland Art Mus., Calif., 1961—, Pasadena Art Mus., U. Miss., 1958—, So. Ill. U., 1968—, U. Ky., 1967—, U. Oreg., 1969—, Benson Gallery, Bridgehampton, N.Y., 1972—, Kingsborough Community Coll., Nobe Gallery, N.Y.C., 1979, group shows maj. museums, including, Met. Mus., Mus. Modern Art, Weyhe Gallery, Kootz Gallery, Stable Gallery, Nobe Gallery, Landmark Gallery, Newberger Mus., Arbeu Gallery, all N.Y.C., Pa. Acad., Phila., Denver Art Mus., U. Ill., U. Nebr., Walker Art Center, Minn., Los Angeles Mus., Benson Gallery, Bridgehampton, N.Y., U. Tex. Geigy Collection, U. Sask., Wichita Mus., Colo. Coll., group shows maj.museums, including, Corcoran Gallery, Washington, group shows maj. museums, including, numerous others; represented in permanent collections, Bklyn. Mus., U. Calif.-Berkeley, U. Iowa Mus., U. Tex. Mus., So. Ill. Mus., Worcester Mus., Walker Art Mus., Santa Monica Library, Guild Hall Collection, World Trade Center, Western Electric Co., Union Carbide, Ciba Geigy, Best Products, Numerous others. Address: 121 Mercer St New York NY 10012

CHERRY, JAMES DONALD, physician; b. Summit, N.J., June 10, 1930; s. Robert Newton and Beatrice (Wheeler) C.; m. Jeanne M. Fischer, June 19, 1954; children—James S., Jeffrey D., Susan J., Kenneth C. B.S., Springfield (Mass.) Coll., 1953; M.D., U. Vt., 1957. Diplomate: Am. Bd. Pediatrics. Intern, then resident in pediatrics Boston City Hosp., 1957-59; resident in pediatrics Kings County Hosp., Bklyn., 1959-60; research fellow in medicine Harvard U. Med. Sch.-Thorndike Meml. Lab., Boston City Hosp., 1961-62; instr. pediatrics U. Vt. Coll. Medicine, also asst. attending physician Mary Fletcher DeCoesbriand Meml. hosps., Burlington, Vt., 1960-61; asst. prof., then asso. prof. pediatrics U. Wis. Med. Sch., Madison, 1963-66; assoc. attending physician Madison Gen., U. Wis. hosps., 1963-66; dir. John A. Hartford Research Lab., Madison Gen. Hosp., 1963-66; mem. faculty St. Louis U. Med. Sch., 1966-73, prof. pediatrics, 1969-73, vice chmn. dept., 1970-73; mem. staff Cardinal Glennon Meml. Hosp. Children, St. Louis U. Hosp., 1966-73; prof. pediatrics, chief div. infectious diseases center Health Scis. UCLA Med. Sch., 1973—; acting chmn. dept. pediatrics center for Health Scis., 1977-79; attending physician, chmn. asepsis com. UCLA Hosp. and Clinics; cons. Project Head Start; vis. worker Common Cold Research Center, 1969-70; mem. immunization adv. com. Los Angeles County Dept. Health Services, 1978—. Co-editor Textbook of: Pediatric Infectious Diseases, 1981; Author numerous papers in field; editorial reviewer profl. jours. Bd. govs. Alexander Graham Bell Internat. Parents Orgn., 1967-69. Served with USAR, 1958-64. John and Mary R. Markle scholar acad. medicine, 1964. Mem. Am. Acad. Pediatrics (exec. com. Calif. chpt. 2 1975-77, mem. com. infectious diseases 1977-83, assoc. editor 14th Ann. Red Book 1982), Am. Soc. Microbiology, Am. Fedn. Clin. Research, AAAS, Soc. Pediatric Research, Infectious Diseases Soc. Am., Am. Pediatric Soc., Los Angeles Pediatric Soc., Assn. Practitioners in Infection Control, Soc. Exptl. Biology and Medicine. Home: 1402 San Vicente Blvd Santa Monica CA 90402 Office: UCLA Sch Medicine Los Angeles CA 90024

CHERRY, PETER BALLARD, electrical products corporation executive; b. Evanston, Ill., May 25, 1947; s. Walter Lorain and Virginia Ames (Ballard) C.; m. Crissy Hazard, Sept. 6, 1969; children: Serena Ames, Spencer Ballard. B.A., Yale U., 1969; M.B.A., Stanford U., 1972. Analyst Cherry Elec. Products Corp., Waukegan, Ill., 1972-74, data processing and systems mgr., 1974, treas., 1974-77; v.p. fin. and bus. devel. Cherry Elec. Products Corps., Waukegan, Ill., 1977-80; exec. v.p. Cherry Elec. Products Corp., Waukegan, Ill., 1980-82, pres., chief operating officer, 1982—. Trustee Lake Forest Coll., Ill., 1982—, Lake Forest Hosp., Ill., 1982—. Mem. IEEE, Computer Soc., Am. Inst. C.P.A.s. Clubs: Economic (Chgo.); Onwentsia (Lake Forest). Office: Cherry Electrical Products Corp 3600 Sunset Ave Waukegan IL 60087

CHERRY, ROBERT EARL PATRICK, food company executive; b. Geneseo, Ill., Sept. 4, 1924; s. Earl Patrick and Kathryn (Brady) C.; m. Lily Anise Rasmussen, June 28, 1947; children: Christine, Kevin, Tol, Kelly. Grad. pub. shcs. Asst. mgr. Cherry's Sporting Goods, Geneseo, 1946-50, mgr., 1950-53, owner, 1953—; sec., dir. Illini Beef Packers, Inc., Geneseo, 1968-80, Illini Contract Carriers, Inc., 1973-80; sec., dir., mem. exec. com. Imark Industries, Inc., Geneseo, 1980—; cons. Colt's Firearms, Buffalo Bill Mus., Harrington & Richardson Arms Co., High Standard Sporting Firearms Co., Winchester-Western; sec., dir. Schweigert Meat of Illini, Inc., Mpls., 1977—, Copeland Sausage of Illini, Inc., Alachua, Fla., 1977-79; dir. Nat. Buying Syndicate, Ft. Worth, 1974-77, Lea Foods, Albert Lea, Minn., Midwest Resources, Inc., Denver. Bd. dirs., sec. Geneseo Community Park Dist., 1973-77. Served with USMC, 1942-46. Decorated Air medal with gold star. Mem. Colt's Commemorative Gun Collectors Assn. (nat. pres. 1967-68), Colt Hist. Soc. (sec., dir. 1970—), Am. Soc. Corp. Secs., Nat. Sporting Goods Assn. (chmn. bd. 1981-82, mem. exec. com. 1979—, dir. 1978—), Ill. Retail Mchts. Assn., Nat. Rifle Assn. (life), Geneseo C. of C. (dir. 1978-81, pres. 1967), Geneseo Hist. Soc. (life), Ill. Rifle Assn. (life), Henry County Hist. Soc. (life), Internat. Platform Assn., Izaak Walton League Am. Home: 420 N Stewart St Geneseo IL 61254 Office: 1041 S Oakwood Ave Geneseo IL 61254

CHERRY, RUSSELL CATHER, economist; b. Raymondville, Tex., Aug. 3, 1940; s. Russell C. and Flora Ysabel (Jones) C.; m. Janet Weller, June 15, 1963; children: Deborah, Laura. B.S., Cornell U., 1963; M.S., Tex. A&M U., 1965; Ph.D., Brown U., 1972. Instr. econs. Roger Williams Coll., Bristol, R.I., 1969-70; asst. prof. Holy Cross Coll., Worcester, Mass., 1970-75; sr. economist Transp. Systems Ctr., U.S. Dept Transp., 1975-79; sr. cons. Arthur D. Little, Inc., Cambridge, Mass., 1979-83; group leader econs. and regulation Tech. Research Ctr., Arthur D. Little, Inc., Washington, 1983—. Contbr. in field. NDEA fellow, 1967-68. Mem. Am. Econ. Assn., Econometric Soc., Alpha Delta Phi. Home: 174 Laurel Ave Providence RI 02906 Office: 600 Maryland Ave SW Suite 805 Washington DC 20024

CHERRY, WALTER LORAIN, electrical products corporation executive; b. Cedar Rapids, Iowa, Jan. 31, 1917; s. Walter Lorain and Laura Fox (White) C.; m. Virginia Ames Ballard, May 31, 1941; children: Walter Lorain, Peter B. Catherine Cherry Moore. B. Chem. Engring., Yale U., 1939. Research engr. Cherry-Burrell Corp., Chgo., 1939-42, Zenith Radio Corp., 1946-69; co-founder Cherry-Channer Corp., Highland Park, Ill., 1949-53; founder, chmn., chief exec. officer Cherry Elec. Products Corp., Waukegan, Ill., 1953—; dir., past pres. Midwest Indsl. Mgmt. Assn., Westchester, Ill., 1969-79. Zoning bd. Village of Winnetka, (Ill.), 1959-71, village caucus, 1958-59, park bd., 1962-68, chmn., 1967-68, planning commn., 1967-68, trustee, 1970-75; assoc. Rehab. Inst., 1978—; trustee Presbyterian Home, 1980—; pres. Allendale Sch. for Boys, 1975-79, trustee, 1973—; trustee Ill. Inst. Tech., 1977—, chmn. bus. and industry devel. council, 1979-82, vice chmn. devel., 1983—; trustee Mus. Sci and Industry. Served with U.S. Army, 1943-46. Mem. Am. Electronics Assn., IEEE, Physics Club. Republican. Congregationalist. Clubs: Econ., University (Chgo.). Home: 848 Tower Rd Winnetka IL 60093 Office: Cherry Elec Products Corp 3600 Sunset Ave Waukegan IL 60078

CHERRY, WENDELL, corporate exec.; b. Riverside, Ky. B.S., U. Ky., 1957, LL.B., 1959. Bar: Ky. bar 1959. Founder Humana Inc., pres., chief operating officer, dir., 1969—. Named one of Am.'s Outstanding Young Men U.S. Jaycees, 1970. Home: Speed Ave and Sulgrave Rd Louisville KY 40205 Office: 1800 1st Nat Tower PO Box 1438 Louisville KY 40202

CHERRY, WILLIAM ASHLEY, surgeon, state health officer; b. Halls, Tenn., Oct. 25, 1924; s. and Bessie R. C.; m. Flora Finch, June 9, 1949; children: Neal, Darrell, Philip, Susan. B.S., Tulane U., 1946, M.D., 1949. Diplomate: Am. Bd. Surgery. Rotating intern Phila. Gen. Hosp., 1949-51; resident gen. surgery La. State U. div. Charity Hosp., New Orleans, 1953-56, resident thoracic surgery, 1956-57, asst. chief fracture service, 1963-65; practice medicine specializing in gen. and thoracic surgery, New Iberia, La., 1957-63; commd. med. officer USPHS, 1963; mem. surg. staff USPHS Hosp., New Orleans, 1963-66, dir., 1966-71, asst. chief surgery dept., 1963-65, dep. chief, 1965-66, dir., 1966-71; regional health dir. Health Services and Mental Health Adminstrn., HEW, USPHS, Region VI, Dallas, 1971-74; sec., state health officer La. Dept. Health and Human Resources, Baton Rouge, 1977—; commd. ensign U.S. Navy, 1946, advanced through grades to comdr., 1963; sr. surgeon, comdr. USPHS, 1963; advanced through grades to asst. surgeon gen., admiral; comdg. officer Naval Res. Med. Co. 8-32, 1953-55; ret., 1963; chief med. officer USCG, Washington, 1974-77; asst. clin. dir. surgery Charity Hosp., 1956-57, vis. surgeon, 1963—; chief of surgery Iberia Parish Hosp., 1959-61; chief of staff Dauterive Hosp., New Iberia, 1962-63; clin. asso. instr., surgery dept. La. State U. Sch. Medicine, 1953-57, clin. instr., 1963-66, clin. asst. prof. surgery, 1966-67; clin. asso. prof. surgery Tulane U. Sch. Medicine, 1967-70, adj. asso. prof. health services adminstrn., 1969-70, adj. prof., 1970-73, clin. prof. surgery, 1970—. Contbr. articles to med. jours. Chmn. ofcl. bd. First Methodist Ch., New Iberia, 1960-62; mem. ofcl. bd. Carrollton Meth. Ch., New Orleans, 1964-66; chmn. La. Inter-Agy. Council for Tb, 1966-70; mem. exec. com. New Orleans Poison Control Center, 1966-71; mem. Health Goals Task Force, State of La., 1969-70, Fed. Exec. Bd., New Orleans, 1970-71, Fed. Exec. Bd., Dallas, 1972-73; med. adv. to sec. Dept. Transp., 1974-77; pres. So. Inst. Human Resources, Atlanta, 1979-80; mem. La. Gov.'s Adv. Com. on Edn. of Handicapped Children, 1977-80. Recipient Querens-Rives-Shore award Tulane U. Sch. Medicine, 1949; USPHS Commendation medal, 1969; USPHS Meritorious Service medal, 1974; USPHS Disting. Service award, 1980; USCG Meritorious Service award, 1977; cert. of merit State of La., 1980; Grace A. Goldsmith Disting. Alumnus lectr. Tulane U. Med. Alumni Assn., 1974. Fellow A.C.S.; mem. USPHS Clin. Soc., Nat. Tb Assn., James D. Rives Surg. Soc., Commd. Officers Assn., Mil. Order World Wars, La. Heart Assn., La. Tb and Respiratory Disease Assn. (dir. 1964—), La. Thoracic Soc., La. Pub. Health Assn., Assn. Mil. Surgeons of U.S., Phi Beta Kappa, Alpha Omega Alpha, Delta Omega. Home: 12674 S Highmeadow Ct Baton Rouge LA 70816 Office: Suite C 2041 Silverside Dr Baton Rouge LA 70808

CHERRYH, CAROLYN JANICE, writer; b. St. Louis, Sept. 1, 1942; d. Basil L. and Lois Ruth (Van Deventer) Cherry. B.A. in Latin, U. Okla., 1964; M.A. in Classics, Johns Hopkins U., 1965. Cert. tchr., Okla. Tchr. Oklahoma City Pub. Schs., 1965-77; artist-in-residence Central State U., Edmond, Okla., 1980-81; lectr. in field. Author: novel Gate of Ivrel, 1976, Well of Shiuan, 1978, Brothers of Earth, 1976, Hunter of Worlds, 1976, The Faded Sun: Kutath, 1979, Sunfall, 1981, Star Crusade, 1980, Downbelow Sation, 1981 (Hugo award for best novel 1982), The Pride of Chanur, 1982, Merchanter's Luck, 1982, Port Eternity, 1982, The Dreamstone, 1983, The Tree of Swords and Jewels, 1983; contbr. short stories to numerous mags. Woodrow Wilson fellow, 1965; recipient Hugo award for best short story, 1979. Mem. Sc. Fiction Writers Assn., L-5 Soc. (bd. advisors), Phi Beta Kappa. Methodist.

CHERRYHOLMES, JAMES GILBERT, construction consultant; b. El Dorado, Kans., July 5, 1917; s. James Ralph and Loy Eunice (Wall) C.; m. Joyce L. Busbice, June 25, 1965; children—Scott, Leslie, Lon. A.S., El Dorado Jr. Coll., 1937; student, U. Kans., 1938-39. Constrn. mgr. Missouri Valley Constructors, Inc., Amarillo, Tex., 1948-72; constrn. mgr. Mid Valley, Inc., Houston, 1972-74, v.p., 1974—82, ret., 1982; now constrn. cons. Presbyn. Club: Elk. Home: 10818 Chevy Chase Houston TX 77042

CHERTOK, JACK, theatrical producer; b. Atlanta, July 13; s. Isadore and Annie (Rouglin) C.; m. Florence Murray, July 14, 1933; children—Vivian, William Irving, Mary Barbara (Mrs. Lewis M. Terman II). Pres. Jack Chertok TV, Inc., 1949-, Apex Film Corp., 1945—. Exec. producer all short subjects, Metro-Goldwyn-Mayer, Culver City, Calif., 1925-42; short subjects produced include Crime Does Not Pay, Robert Benchley series, Pete Smith series, The Passing Parade, Historical Mysteries; feature motion pictures produced at Metro-Goldwyn-Mayer and Warner Bros. include The Corn is Green, Joe Smith, American, Eyes in the Night; also formed own prodn. company Northern Pursuit, in Hollywood, 1945; which produced The Strange Woman and Dishonored Lady; producer films for TV, 1948-; series include My Favorite Martian, Lone Ranger, Sky King, Cavalcade series, Private Secretary, My Living Doll, Western Marshall, The Lawless Years; producer: animated film My Favorite Martian, 1973 (Recipient Acad. award 1935, 36, 37 (2), 38, 40 (2), 41 (2), 43). 415 S Beverly Glen Blvd West Los Angeles CA 90024 *

CHERVOKAS, JOHN VINCENT, advertising executive; b. Norwood, Mass., Nov. 14, 1936; s. Bronius John and Anna A. (Kudirka) C.; m. Roseanna Conti, Feb. 23, 1963; children: Jason, Joshua, Jessica. B.A., Fordham Coll., 1959. Copywriter Benton & Bowles, N.Y.C., 1961-66; copy group head Grey Advt., N.Y.C., 1966-71; creative dir. McCann-Erickson, N.Y.C., 1971-72, William Esty, 1972-75; vice chmn., chief creative officer Warwick Advt., N.Y.C., 1975—. Pres. sch. bd. Ossining Free Sch. Dist., N.Y., 1971-74. Mem. Fordham Coll. Alumni Assn. (v.p., bd. govs.). Democrat. Roman Catholic. Office: Warwick Advt 875 3d Ave New York NY 10022

CHESAREK, FERDINAND JOSEPH, business executive, former army officer; b. Calumet, Mich., Feb. 18, 1914; s. Joseph and Mary (Pontello) C.; m. Martha Jayne Rullman, Sept. 1, 1938 (dec. 1979); 1 son, John Laymon; m. Joan Tepe. B.S., U.S. Mil. Acad., 1938; M.B.A., Stanford, 1950, Nat. War Coll., 1956, Advanced Mgmt. Program, Harvard U., 1958. Commd. 2d lt. U.S. Army, 1938, advanced through grades to gen., 1968; comdg. officer (28th F.A. Bn., 8th Inf. Div.), ETO, World War II, Korean War, comdg. gen., Europe, 1959-62; asst. dep. chief staff logistics Dept. Army, 1962-66; comptroller of army, 1966; asst. vice chief staff Army, 1967-68, comdg. gen., 1968-70; ret., 1970; now owner Chesarek Industries, Inc.; pres. Consol. Investment & Devel. Corp., Luxembourg. Decorated Silver Star, Legion of Merit, Bronze Star, Commendation medal, Air medal, Purple Heart, D.S.M.; Legion of Honor; Croix de Guerre, France, Luxembourg; Order Ulchi, Korea; Order of Republic, Italy). Home: 25706 Elena Rd Los Altos Hills CA 94022

CHESHIRE, MAXINE (MRS. HERBERT W. CHESHIRE), columnist; b. Harlan, Ky., Apr. 5, 1930; d. M.F. and Sylvia (Cornett) Hall; m. Herbert W. Cheshire, Apr. 25, 1954; children—Marc, Hall, Paden, Leigh. Student, Union Coll., Barbourville, Ky., 1951-52, U. Ky., 1949-50. Reporter Knoxville (Tenn.) News-Sentinel, 1951-54; reporter Washington Post, 1954-65; columnist Los Angeles Times Syndicate, 1965—. Author: (with John Greenya) Maxine Cheshire, Reporter, 1978; contbr. articles to popular mags. Office: Times Mirror Square Los Angeles CA 90053 *

CHESHIRE, RICHARD DUNCAN, university president; b. Mineola, N.Y., Aug. 12, 1936; s. Leslie G. and Catherine C. C.; m. Roberta Ann Jeans, Sept. 6, 1958; children: Jennifer, Jonathan, Camilla. A.B., Colgate U., 1958; M.Ed., U. N.H., 1961; Ph.D., N.Y. U., 1973. Tchr. Am. history Chatham (N.J.) High Sch., 1959-60; asst. to v.p., alumni fund sec. Colgate U., 1960-62; dir. devel. Dickinson Coll., 1963-65; asst. to pres., v.p. univ. relations Drew U., Madison, N.J., 1966-73; v.p. public affairs, lectr. edn. Colgate U., 1973-77; pres., prof. history U. Tampa (Fla.), 1977—; cons. Ford Found., 1968-69. Div. editor: Handbook of Institutional Achievement, 1976. Pres. N.J. Shakespeare Festival, 1972; bd. dirs. Fla. Gulf Coast Symphony, Tampa Museum Fedn., Tampa Bay Arts Center, Tampa Prep. Sch., Greater Tampa United Way; mem. Fla. Council 100, Tampa Bay Area Com. Fgn. Relations. Mem. Greater Tampa C. of C. (dir.). Clubs: Univ. (N.Y.C. and Tampa); Palma Ceia Country, Tower (Tampa). Office: 401 W Kennedy Blvd Tampa FL 33606 *

CHESKI, RICHARD MICHAEL, library director; b. Canton, Ohio, Sept. 29, 1935; s. Sigmund and Henrietta (Makowski) Hiczewski; m. Mary Ella Sica, Aug. 23, 1958; children: Karen, Valerie. B.A., Kent State U., B.S. in Edn, M.A. in L.S. Asst. state librarian State Library of Ohio, Columbus, 1970-74; asst. commr. libraries Colo. State Library, Denver, 1974-76; dir. Oceanside (N.Y.) Free Library, 1976-78, State Library of Ohio, Columbus, 1978—; vis. prof. Kent State U., Denver U.; chmn. legis. com. Chief Officers State Library Agys. Chmn. Ohio Humanities Council; mem. Columbus Cable TV Adv. Commn. Recipient Disting. Alumni award Kent State U. Mem. ALA, Ohio Library Assn., Beta Phi Mu, Tau Kappa Epsilon. Office: 65 S Front St Columbus OH 43215 *

CHESKIN, BERNARD SAMUEL, lawyer, elec. equipment mfg. co. exec.; b. Phila., July 16, 1928; s. Nathan and Betty (Goldberg) C.; m. Rheta S. Freeman, Sept. 25, 1958; children—Abbe Beth, Susan, Bruce. B.S., Temple U., 1950, LL.B., 1955. Bar: Pa. and D.C. bars 1955. Trial atty. U.S. Dept. Justice, criminal div., 1955-57; asst. city solicitor, City of Phila., 1957-60; partner Weiner, Basch, Lehrer & Cheskin, 1960-68; sec., gen. counsel Fed. Pacific Elec. Co., Newark, 1968-73, Warner Co., Phila., 1973-77; owner, developer shopping centers. Author: The Philadelphia Home Rule Charter and Annotations, 1958. Active YMCA. Mem. Phila. Bar Assn. Club: Germantown Cricket (Phila.). Home: 1412 June Ln Narberth PA 19072 Office: 1721 Arch St Philadelphia PA 19103

CHESNEY, JOHN LESTER, association executive; b. Cadomin, Alta., Can., June 3, 1931; s. John Kavin and Fouletta (McLeod) C.; m. Mary, May 11, 1955; children: Sharon, Susan, Seanna. Student, U. Alta., United Mgmt. Inst. N.Y., Inst. for Orgn. Mgmt., McMaster U. Employed in coal mines, Cadomin, employed in food industry, Edmonton, Alta.; membership salesman Edmonton C. of C., 1969-74, gen. mgr., 1974—. Chmn. Federated Community Leagues of Edmonton. Mem. C. of C. Execs. Can. (pres.). Club: Ind. Order Foresters. Lodge: Rotary. Office: Edmonton C of C 10123 99th St Suite 600 Edmonton AB Canada T5J 3G9

CHESNEY, JOHN RAYMOND, lawyer, motor freight company executive; b. Cleve., Oct. 24, 1942; s. Robert Alfred and Anne B. (Hopkins) C.; m. Barbara M. Bond, Sept. 16, 1967; 1 dau., Abigail R. B.B.A., Kent (Ohio) State U., 1968; J.D., U. Akron, Ohio, 1973. Bar: Ohio 1973, Nebr. 1974, Tex. 1975. Line haul controller Roadway Express, Inc., Akron, 1968-71; transp. analyst Firestone Tire & Rubber Co., Akron, 1971-73; atty. Herman Bros., Inc., Omaha, 1973-74, E. Tex. Motor Freight Lines, Inc., Dallas, 1974-80; v.p., gen. counsel, sec. Spector Red Ball, Inc., 1981—. Served with USAF, 1961-65. Pilot Freight Carriers scholar, 1967. Mem. Tex., Dallas bar assns., Motor Carrier Lawyers Assn., Assn. ICC Practitioners. Address: 3177 Irving Blvd PO Box 47407 Dallas TX 75247

CHESNEY, LEE ROY, JR., artist; b. Washington, June 1, 1920; s. Lee Roy and Rena Ruth (Beach) C.; m. Betty J. Lamb, Jan. 28, 1943; children: Lee Roy III, Terril Ann. B.F.A., U. Colo., 1946; M.F.A., U. Iowa, 1948; postgrad., U. Michoacan, Mex., 1950-51. Instr. drawing U. Iowa, 1947-50; prof. art, dir. printmaking, head grad. printmaking and painting U. Ill., Urbana, 1950-67; asso. dean fine arts So. Calif. U., 1967-72; prof. art, chmn. grad. art programs U. Hawaii, Honolulu, 1972—; Louis D. Beaumont vis. disting. prof. Washington U.; vis. artist Otis Art Inst., Los Angeles, U. Colo., U. Wash., Mich. State U., Honolulu Acad. Arts Sch., Visual Arts Center, Anchorage; mem. com., nat. juror Sr. Fulbright Research Awards, 1968-71, com. chmn., 1969-71. One-man shows include, Newman Brown Gallery, Chgo., U. Fla., U. Louisville, U. Mich., U. Wis., Madison, Ohio State U., Ill. State U., Yoseido Gallery, Tokyo, Atrium Gallery, Seattle, Visual Arts Center, Anchorage, Washington U., St. Louis, U. Utah, U. Alaska, Fisher Galleries, U. So. Calif., 1968, Honolulu Acad. Arts, 1973, Comsky Gallery, Beverly Hills, Calif., 1970-76, Downtown Gallery, Honolulu, 1975, BIMC Galerie, Paris, 1979, 81, 83, Galerie Sandoz, Paris, 1979, Cité Internat. des Arts, Paris, Contemporary Arts Center, Honolulu, 1980, 25 yr. retrospective exhbn. of prints circulated by U. Fla., 1977-80; exhibited in group shows including, Am. Fedn. Arts traveling exhbn., Mus. Modern Art traveling exhbn., Am. Cultural Center, Paris, 1964, USIS traveling exhbn., Soc. Am. Graphic artists traveling exhbns., 1973-77, Nihon Sosaku Hanga Kyokai, 1967-84, Contemporary Am. Painting, Bucharest, 1977, Hawaii Nat. Biennial Print Exhbn., Honolulu Acad. Arts, 1971, 73, 75, 77, 78, 80, 83, BIMC Galerie, 1978, 79, 80, 81, 82, 83; represented in permanent collections including, Nat. Gallery Art, Washington, Biblioteque Nationale, Paris, Victoria and Albert Mus., London, Tokyo U. Fine Art, Tokyo Mus. Modern Art, Nat. Gallery Art, Stockholm, Tate Gallery, London, USIS, State Dept., Washington, Library of Congress, Washington, Bklyn. Mus., Mus. Modern Art, N.Y.C., Phila. Mus., Denver Mus., Dallas Mus., Pasadena Mus., Honolulu Acad. Arts, Hawaii Council for Arts, Art Inst. Chgo., Oakland Mus., Los Angeles County Mus., Seattle Mus., Am. Embassy, Bonn, Bank of Am., United Calif. Bank, U. Hawaii, IBM, Litton Industries Corp., Hartford Ins. Co., Fuji Bank Calif., Northrop Corp., 1st Hawaii Trust Bank. Served to capt. AUS, 1942-45. Recipient Francis G. Logan medal Art Inst. Chgo., 1962, Pauline Palmer award, 1966; Concora Found. prize, 1963; Vera List award Soc. Am. Graphic Artists, Am. Acad., Rome, 1964; appointee Cité Internat. des Arts, Paris, 1970, 78-83; Fondation Gardilanne-Moffat Studio award, 1978-80; purchase award Epinal (France) Biennial Invitational Exhbn.; awards Hawaii State Found. for Culture and Arts, 1972, 74, 75, 78, 80, Honolulu Acad. Arts, 1973, 78; Fulbright sr. research award, 1956-57; U. Ill. research grantee, 1963-64; Ford Found. faculty enrichment award, 1978, 82; U. Hawaii Research grantee, 1982. Mem. Coll. Art Assn. Am., Calif. Soc. Printmakers, Northwest Print Council (bd. dirs.), Japan Print Assn., Soc. Am. Graphic Artists, Color Print Soc., World Print Council, Los Angeles Printmaking Soc. (hon. dir.), Honolulu Printmakers (past v.p., pres.), Painters and Sculptors League Hawaii, Hawaii Artists League. Address: 446 Mesa Rd Santa Monica Canyon CA 90402

CHESNEY, MURPHY ALVIS, JR., physician, air force officer; b. Knoxville, Tenn., Nov. 29, 1927; s. Murphy Alvis and Thelma

Constance (Acuff) C.; m. Mary Ann Wilson, June 23, 1950; children—Murphy Alvis III, Charles A., Carol J., John L. B.S., U. Tenn., 1947, M.D., 1950. Intern Scott and White Clinic, Temple, Tex., 1950-51; practice medicine specializing in family practice, Rule, Tex., 1951-55; resident in internal medicine City of Memphis Hosps., 1957-60; commd. capt. U.S. Air Force, 1955, advanced through grades to maj. gen., 1979; comdr. (Air Force Med. Service Center), Brooks AFB, Tex., 1978-80; dep. surgeon gen. U.S. Air Force, Bolling AFB, Washington, 1980—; chmn. Def. Med. Materiel Bd., 1979-80. Decorated D.S.M., Legion of Merit; Spanish Legion of Merit. Fellow A.C.P.; mem. AMA, Tex. Med. Assn., Soc. Air Force Physicians, Aerospace Med. Assn. Methodist. Office: Bldg 5681 Bolling AFB Washington DC 20332

CHESNUT, DONALD BLAIR, educator; b. Richmond, Ind., Dec. 27, 1932; s. James Lyons and Naomi Irene (Wright) C.; m. Deborah Berry, Dec. 21, 1954; children—Lauren, Blair, Lynn. B.S., Duke U., 1954; Ph.D., Calif. Inst. Tech., 1958. Postdoctoral fellow, instr. physics Duke, Durham, N.C., 1957-58, asso. prof. chemistry, 1965-71, prof. chemistry, 1971—; research chemist E.I. duPont de Nemours, Inc., Wilmington, Del., 1958-65. Mem. Am. Chem. Soc., Am. Phys. Soc., Sigma Xi. Home: 4404 Malvern Rd Durham NC 27707 Office: Dept Chemistry Duke U Durham NC 27706

CHESNUT, FRANKLIN GILMORE, clergyman; b. Bowling Green, Ky., Mar. 2., 1919; s. Walter Franklin and Fannie (Meador) C.; m. Laurelyn Travillian, Aug. 19, 1950; children: Franklin Gilmore, Kathryn Lynne. Student, W. Ky. State Tchrs. Coll., Bowling Green, 1937-39; B.A., Bethel Coll., 1941; B.D., Cumberland Presbyn. Theol. Sem., 1943. Ordained to ministry Cumberland Presbyn. Ch., 1940; pastor in, Brunswick, Tenn., 1943-44, denominational youth dir., 1944-53; mgr. Cumberland Presbyn. Book Store, Memphis, 1953-54; pastor, Callco Rock, Ark., 1954-58, Russellville, Ark., 1958-75, Booneville, Ark., 1975—; moderator Logan Presbytery, Ky. Synod, 1941, White River and Ewing presbyteries, Ark. Synod, 1956, 59, 61, 64, W. Tenn. Synod, 1945, Cumberland Presbyn. Gen. Assembly, 1963-64, Porter Presbytery, Caulksville, Ark., 1975, stated clk., 1977—, Ark. Synod, 1956—; mem. Denominational Commn. on the Ministry, 1975-84; trustee Cumberland Presbyn. Children's Home, 1962-71. Address: PO Box 163 1108 Dogwood Ln Booneville AR 72927

CHESROWN, MELVA ANITA, pub. relations cons.; b. Watauga, S.D., Aug. 12, 1911; d. Joseph Dodge and Mathilda Pauline (Mielke) C.; m. Robert E. Laffin, Aug. 22, 1942 (div. Nov. 1947). Student, U. Minn., 1930-38. Sec., asst. publicity dir. Minn. Petroleum Industries Com., 1936-40; dir. women"s programs Tax Found., 1940-42; pub. relations dept. Gen. Motors Corp., 1942-44, Fred Eldean Orgn., 1944-53; owner Melva Chesrown Orgn., N.Y.C., 1960—, The Gift Box, Inc., Nantucket, Mass. Pres. Nantucket Devel. Bd., 1964—. Mem. Pub. Relations Soc. Am. (chmn. edn. com. 1954-55, chmn. publicity com. 1957, treas., mem. bd. 1961—), Com. Women in Pub. Relations (chmn. 1953-54). Republican. Presbyterian. Address: 11 S Water St Nantucket MA 02554

CHESSER, AL H., union official; b. Pettis County, Mo., Feb. 26, 1914; s. James A. and Mary Pearl (Dirck) C.; m. Rose Burns. Grad. high sch. Brakeman-condr. Santa Fe Ry., Amarillo, Tex., 1941; sec.-treas., legis. rep. Brotherhood R.R. Trainmen, Local 608, 1945-56; chmn. Tex. legis. bd., 1956-62, nat. legis. rep., Washington, 1962-70, United Transp. Union, 1969-71, pres., Cleve., 1971-79, pres. emeritus, 1979—; v.p., mem. exec. council AFL-CIO; chmn. Congress of Ry. Unions, 1972—; Chmn. Amarillo Labor Polit. Council, 1954-56; mem. Gov.'s Indsl. Commn., 1957-61, Fed. Task Force on R.R. Safety, 1964-69, Pres.'s Consumers Adv. Council, 1964-68, Greater Cleve. Growth Bd. and Transp. Study Group of Domestic Affairs Task Force, 1973—; mem. adv. panel U.S. Congress Office of Tech. Assessment, 1976; hon. co-chmn. Internat. Guiding Eyes, Inc., 1976. Author: Transportation and Energy, 1975, Economic Advantages of Transporting Coal by Rail, 1976. Bd. dirs. Democratic Nat. Com., 1973; mem. transp. adv. com. Fed. Energy Adminstrn., 1975; co-chmn. R.R. Safety Research Bd., 1975; Chmn. bd. Civil Service Commn.; bd. dirs. Amarillo Community Chest, Maverick Boys Club.; Hon. staff mem. U.S. Army Transp. Sch. Mem. Nat. Def. Execs. Res. Club: Mason (Shriner). Office: United Transp Union 116 Bon Air Dr Heavenly Point Hot Springs AR 70901

CHESTER, ARTHUR NOBLE, physicist; b. Seattle, Aug. 5, 1940; s. Arthur Malbridge and Marjorie (Stenberg) C.; m. Cynthia Anne Ashford, Sept. 6, 1961 (div. June 1968); m. Catherine Rogers Buchanan, Aug. 10, 1969. B.S. in Physics, U. Tex., 1961; Ph.D. in Theoretical Physics, Calif. Inst. Tech., 1965. Mem. tech. staff Bell Labs., Murray Hill, N.J., 1965-69, Hughes Research Labs., Malibu, Calif., 1969-73, mgr. laser dept., 1973-75, assoc. dir., 1975-80; program mgr. very high speed integrated circuits Hughes Aircraft Co., El Segundo, Calif., 1980-83, mgr. tactical engring. div., 1984—; cons. U.S. Dept. Def., Washington, 1975-79; co-dir. Internat. Sch. Quantum Electronics, Erice, Sicily, Italy, 1980—. Co-editor: Integrated Optics: Physics and Applications, 1983, Free Electron Lasers, 1983; contbr. articles to publs. Pres. Masterwork Chorus, Morristown, N.J., 1968-69; chmn. Turrell Exhbn. Fellows Contemporary Art, Los Angeles, 1981—. Recipient A.A. Bennett Calculus prize U. Tex., 1959, Nat. Merit scholar, 1957; NSF fellow, 1961; Howard Hughes doctoral fellow, 1963. Fellow IEEE (chmn. com. 1982—); mem. IEEE Quantum Electronics and Applications Soc. (pres. 1980), Optical Soc. Am., Am. Phys. Soc., AAAS, Sigma Xi. Office: Hughes Aircraft Co 2000 E El Segundo El Segundo CA 90245

CHESTER, EDWARD WILLIAM, historian, author, educator; b. Richmond, Va., Nov. 9, 1935; s. Edward William and Mary Elizabeth (Lewis) C. A.B. summa cum laude, Morris Harvey Coll., 1956; M.A., U. Pitts., 1958, Ph.D., 1961. Asst. prof. history Lambuth Coll., Jackson, Tenn., 1961; instr. history U. Ky., Covington, 1962; asst. prof. history Inter-Am. U., Hato Rey, P.R., 1964, U. Tex.-Arlington, 1965-68, assoc. prof., 1968-82, prof., 1982—. Author: Europe Views America: A Critical Evaluation, 1962, Issues and Responses in State Political Experience, 1968, Radio, Television and American Politics, 1969, Clash of Titans: Africa and U.S. Foreign Policy, 1974, A Guide To Political Platforms, 1977, Sectionalism, Politics and American Diplomacy, 1975, The U.S. and Six Atlantic Outposts: The Military and Economic Considerations, 1979, U.S. Oil Policy and Dimplomacy, 1982; contbr. articles to profl. jours. Summer research grantee Earhart Found., 1977, 78. Mem. Ctr. fir Study of Presidency, Am. Hist. Assn., So. Hist. Assn., Orgn. Am. Historians, Soc. Historians of Am. Fgn. Relations, Caribbean Studies Assn., AAUP, Am. Assn. State and Local History, Soc. Spanish and Portuguese Studies, Soc. Advancement of Scandinavian Studies, Western Assn. Africanists. Republican. Methodist. Home: 800 Tanglewood Ln Arlington TX 76012 Office: Dept History U Tex Box 194277 UTA Sta Arlington TX 76019

CHESTER, GIRAUD, television executive; b. N.Y.C., Apr. 4, 1922; s. Harry and Minnie (Lachman) C.; m. Marjorie J. Fatt, 1962; children: Christopher, Katherine. B.A., Bklyn. Coll., 1942; M.A., U. Wis., 1943, Ph.D., 1947; D.C.S. (hon.), St. John's U., 1980. Asst. prof. speech Cornell U., 1947-49, U. Mich., summers 1947-49, Queens Coll., 1949-53; gen. program exec. NBC-TV, 1954-57; asso. Sylvester L. Weaver, Jr., 1957; dir. new TV program devel. Ted Bates & Co., Inc., 1958; v.p. charge network daytime programming ABC-TV, 1958-62; v.p. charge network program adminstr. NBC-TV, 1962-64; exec. v.p. Goodson-Todman Prodns., N.Y.C., 1964—. Author: Embattled Maiden: The Life of Anna Dickinson, 1951, (with G.R. Garrison) Radio and Television, 1950, Television and Radio, 1956, (with G.R. Garrison and E.E. Willis) Television and Radio, 1963, 1971, 78, The Ninth Juror, 1970; also articles.; Asso. editor: Quar. Jour. Speech, 1948-54. Trustee Guild Hall, East Hampton. Served to lt. (j.g.) USNR, 1943-46. Recipient Edgar Allan Poe award Mystery Writers Am., 1971; H. V. Kaltenborn radio news scholar, 1946-47; Ford Found. fellow, 1953-54. Mem. Nat. Assn. Ind. TV Producers and Distbrs. (chmn. exec. com.), Internat. Radio and TV Soc. (pres. 1977-80), AAUP, Speech Communications Assn., Acad. Television Arts and Scis. Clubs: City Athletic, East Hampton Tennis. Terbell Ln Box 49 East Hampton NY 11937 Home: 1010 Fifth Ave New York NY 10028 Office: 375 Park Ave New York NY 10022

CHESTNUT, HAROLD, foundation executive, electrical engineer; b. Albany, N.Y., Nov. 25, 1917; s. Harry and Dorothy (Schulman) C.; m. Erma Ruth Callaway, Aug. 24, 1944; children: Peter Callaway, H. Thomas, Andrew T. B.S. in Elec. Engring, Mass. Inst. Tech., 1939, M.S., 1940; D.E. (hon.), Case Western Res. U., 1966, Villanova U., 1972. With Gen. Electric Co., 1940-83; cons. systems engr., aeros. and ordnance dept. Advanced Tech. Lab., Schenectady, 1956-66; mgr. Research and Devel. Center, 1966-71; cons. systems engr., 1972-83; pres. SWIIS Found., Inc., 1983—. Editor: Systems Engring. and Analysis, John Wiley and Sons, 1965—; author: Servomechanisms and Regulating Systems Design, Vol. I, 1951, Vol. II, 1955, Systems Engineering Tools, 1965, Systems Engineering Methods, 1967; editor: Jour. Automatica, 1961-67. Mem. commn. sociotech. systems NRC, 1975-78. Case Western Res. U. Centennial scholar, 1980. Fellow IEEE (v.p. tech. activities 1970-71, v.p. regional activities 1972, pres. 1973, exec. com. 1967-75), AAAS, Instrument Soc. Am.; mem. Nat. Acad. Engring., Internat. Fedn. Automatic Control (pres. 1957-58), World Federalists Assn. (bd. dirs. 1980—), Am. Automatic Control Council (pres. 1962-63, Honda prize 1981), Nat. Soc. Profl. Engrs. Home: 1226 Waverly Pl Schenectady NY 12308

CHESTNUTT, GEORGE ALEXANDER, JR., investment company executive; b. Helena, Mont., July 16, 1914; s. George Alexander and Edna (Mueller) C.; m. Sara Marchiano, Jan. 20, 1953; children by previous marriage: Mark M. (adopted), Karen (Mrs. Jon J. Driessen). Student, Mont. State Coll., 1933-35, 37-38. With Mont. Power Co., 1935- 37, 38-46; gen. partner Mansfield Mills Co. (investment adviser), Larchmont, N.Y., 1946-51, Am. Investors Co., Larchmont, 1951-60; pres., dir. Am. Investors Corp., Larchmont, 1961-66, Am. Investors Fund, Inc., Greenwich, Conn., 1957—, Chestnutt Corp., Greenwich, 1966-69, Am. Investors Corp., 1969—; chmn. Am. Investors Income Fund, Inc., Greenwich, 1975—. Author: Stock Market Analysis, Facts and Principles, 1952-74; Editor: weekly publ. Am. Investors Service, 1951-79. Republican. Clubs: Rotarian (past pres. Larchmont); Stanwich. Originator geometric stock market averages and percentage-strength Stock rating system. Home: 944 Lake Ave Greenwich CT 06830 Office: 88 Field Point Rd Greenwich CT 06830

CHESTON, CHARLES EDWARD, forestry educator; b. Princeton, N.J., Nov. 23, 1911; s. Byron Major and Lula Augusta (Smalley) C.; m. Catherine Goe, Sept. 6, 1938; children: Mary Catherine, Lawrence Byron. Jr. B.S., N.Y. State Coll. Forestry, 1933; M.F., Yale, 1940. Forester U.S. Forest Service, also Dept. Interior, 1933-39; asst. state forester, N.J., 1940-42; chmn. dept. forestry U of South, 1942—, prof., 1948—, Annie B. Snowden prof., 1948—; Sec. Keep Tenn. Green Assn., 1956—; also editor publ. and chmn. publs. com.; mem. Forest Protection Com., 1958—; mem. Tenn. Conservation Commn., 1963-69; resource cons.; committeeman Tree Farm of Tenn., 1978. Co-author: Rehabilitation of Hurricane Damaged Forests in New England, 1940; also papers.; reviewer: Choice (publ. Assn. Coll. and Research Libraries). Pres. Sewanee Civic Assn., 1946—; Adv. com. Sewanee Research Center, 1956—. Mem. Soc. Am. Foresters (chmn. Ky.-Tenn. sect. 1964-65), Tenn. Forestry Assn. (pres. 1972-73), Alumni Assn. Yale Sch. Forestry (sec. 1940 class), Franklin County C. of C. (chmn. ednl. com.), Robin Hood, Ecce Guam Bonum Club, Yale Alumni Bd., Sigma Pi Sigma, Xi Sigma Pi, Sigma Nu, Theta Pi. Episcopalian. Home: 1 Florida Ave Sewanee TN 37375

CHESTON, GEORGE MORRIS, lawyer; b. Phila., Aug. 18, 1917; s. Radcliffe and Sydney (Ellis) C.; m. Winifred Dodge Seyburn, May 5, 1955; 1 dau., Sydney. A.B., Harvard U., 1939, LL.B., 1947. Bar: Pa. bar 1947. Since practiced in, Phila.; atty. firm Ballard, Spahr. Andrews & Ingersoll, Phila., 1947-52; farmer, Georgetown, S.C., 1968—; Treas. Nat. Citizens for Eisenhower, 1955-56. Pres. Phila. Soc. to Protect Children, 1959-69; trustee United Fund, Phila., 1958-69; bd. dirs. Phila. Zool. Soc., Phila. Orch. Assn., Saratoga Performing Arts, Am. Fedn. Arts; trustee Phila. Mus. Art, 1962—, pres., 1968-76. Served to lt. comdr. USNR, 1941-46; PTO. Mem. S.C. Plantation Soc. Home: 229 Spruce St Philadelphia PA 19106 Office: Public Ledger Bldg Philadelphia PA 19106

CHESTON, WARREN BRUCE, research institute administrator; b. Rochester, N.Y., Mar. 15, 1926; s. George L. and Clara (Hoesterey) C.; m. Roberta Bohrod, Nov. 1, 1950; children: Stephen, Rebecca, Dena, Nicolas. B.S., Harvard U., 1947; Ph.D., U. Rochester, 1951. Asst. prof. Washington U., St. Louis, 1951-53; mem. faculty U. Minn., 1953-71, prof. physics, 1961-71, dir. Space Sci. Center, 1965-68, dean Inst. Tech., 1968-71; chancellor U. Ill.-Chgo., 1971-76; asso. dir. Wistar Inst., 1976—; sci. attache Am. embassy, London, 1963-65; Fulbright prof. U. Utrecht, Netherlands, 1958-59. Author: Elementary Theory of Electric and Magnetic Fields, 1964. Bd. dirs. Minn. Opera Co., 1965-71, Civic Orch., Mpls., 1966-67, Settlement Music Sch., 1979—; pres. Phila. Cancer Coordinating Assn., 1978-80. Served with AUS, 1944-46. Fellow Am. Phys. Soc. Home: 406 S Van Pelt St Philadelphia PA 19146 Office: Wistar Inst 3601 Spruce Philadelphia PA 19104

CHETKOVICH, MICHAEL N., accountant; b. Angels Camp, Calif., May 7, 1916; s. Nick M. and Anna (Metkovich) C.; m. Alice Virginia Roosma, Mar. 20, 1947; children: Carol, Mark, John, Kathryn. B.S., U. Calif. at Berkeley, 1939, M.S., 1940. C.P.A., Calif., N.Y. With McLaren, Goode & Co. (C.P.A.'s), San Francisco, 1940-52; partner Deloitte Haskins & Sells, San Francisco and N.Y.C., 1952-78, mng. partner, 1970-78, ret., 1978; dir. Phillips Petroleum Co., Am. Internat. Group Inc., McDonnell Douglas Corp.; Regents' prof. Sch. Bus. U. Calif. at Berkeley, 1979, lectr., dir. external affairs, 1980—. Pres. U. Calif. at Berkeley Found., 1981-83; bd. dirs. Internat. House, Berkeley; chmn. Exec. Service Corps Bay Area. Served to lt. USNR, 1942-46. Mem. Am. Inst. C.P.A.s (chmn. 1976-77), Calif. Soc. C.P.A.s (v.p. 1965-66), N.Y. State Soc. C.P.A.s, Am. Acctg. Assn. (v.p. 1975-76), Fgn. Policy Assn., UN Assn. U.S.A., U. Calif. at Berkeley Alumni Assn., Accountants Club Am., Phi Beta Kappa, Beta Gamma Sigma, Beta Alpha Psi. Clubs: Stock Exchange, Board Room, Commonwealth. Home: 93 Serrano Dr Atherton CA 94025

CHEVALIER, HAAKON MAURICE, author; b. Lakewood, N.J., Sept. 10, 1901; s. Emile and Therese (Roggen) C.; m. Ruth Bosley, 1922 (div. 1931); 1 son, Jacques Anatole; m. Barbara Lansburgh, 1931 (div. 1950); children—Suzanne Andrée, Haakon Lazarus; m. Carol Lansburgh, 1952; 1 dau., Karen Anne. Student, Stanford, 1918-20; A.B., U. Calif., 1923, A.M., 1925, Ph.D., 1929. Prof. French U. Calif., 1929-46. Author: Anatole France and His Time, 1932, For Us the Living, 1949, The Man Who Would be God, 1959, Oppenheimer: The Story of a Friendship, 1965, The Last Voyage of the Schooner Rosamond, 1970; Translator: Andre Malraux's Man's Fate, 1934, Days of Wrath, 1936, Louis Aragon's Bells of Basel, 1936, Louis Aragon's Residential Quarter, 1938, The Secret Life of Salvador Dali, 1942, Vladimir Pozner's The Edge of the Sword, 1942, First Harvest, 1943, Gontran de Poncins' Home is the Hunter, 1943; André Maurois' Seven Faces of Love, 1943, Salvador Dali's Hidden Faces, 1944, Joseph Kessel's Army of Shadows, 1944, Denis de Rougemont's Devil's Share, 1944, Vercors' Three Short Novels, 1947, Simon Gantillon's Vessel of Wrath, 1947, Salvador Dali's 50 Secrets of Magic Craftmanship, 1948, Salvador Dali: On Modern Art, 1957, Stendhal's A Roman Journey, 1957, René Grousset's Chinese Art and Culture, 1959, Michel Seuphor's The Sculpture of This Century, 1960, Aragon's Holy Week, 1961, Michel Seuphor's Abstract Painting, 1962, Henri Michaux's Light Through Darkness, 1962, Michel Seuphor's Abstract Painting in Flanders, 1963, Bob Claessen's and Jeanne Rousseau's Our Bruegel, 1969, Pierre Galante's André Malraux, 1971, Jerzy Szablowski's Flemish Tapestries, 1972; others.; Contbr. to various mags. Mem. P.E.N., Authors League Am., Assn. Internationale des Interprètes de Conférence, Assn. des Traducteurs Littéraires de France. French interpreter U.N. Conf., San Francisco, 1945, War Criminals Trials, Nurnberg, 1945-46, UN, Lake Success, N.Y., 1946. Home: 19 rue du Mont-Cenis Paris 18 France

CHEVALIER, LEO CHARLES, fashion designer; b. Montreal, Que., Can., Oct. 8, 1934; s. Leo John and Mary Ellen (Whitten) C. Student, Loyola Coll., 1948-52, Sch. Art Design Montreal Mus. Fine Arts, 1951-53; grad., Ecole Des Beaux Arts de Montreal, 1955, Ecole Des Metiers Commerciaux, 1955. Asst. mgr. Henry Morgan Co. Ltd., 1955-59; designer, costumer Montreal Ballet, 1958; asst. mgr. Robert Simpson Co., 1959-60; freelance fashion designer and interior designer, 1960-61; mgr., buyer Fraid's Co., Montreal, 1961-63; European buyer, designer De St. Victor, 1963-65; owner, mgr. Cheval Botique, Montreal, 1966—; fashion designer numerous cos. including Brooks-Burnett Co., 1968-71, Van Essa Loungewear and Sleepwear, 1972, Brodkin Industries Ltd., 1973—; fashion designer numerous cos.including Boros, 1975; fashion designer numerous cos. including Dalie div. Toptown, 1976, Nacos Ltd., 1978—, Natural Furs, 1978—, Modern Neckwear, 1979—, Monarch Wear Ltd., 1979—; permanent designer, cons. Air Can.; bd. dirs. Can. Colour Council. Named Designer of Yr. Internat. Ladies' Garment Union, 1967; decorated Order of Can. Mem. Fashion Designers' Assn. (pres.), Fashion Can., Designer Devel. Com. (dir.). Office: Montroy Coat Co 140 Cermenzie Blvd Montreal PQ Canada H3A 2K7

CHEVINS, ANTHONY CHARLES, advertising agency executive; b. Frackville, Pa., Apr. 1, 1921; s. Charles A. and Mary (Swade) C.; m. Margaret Macy, Sept. 18, 1948; children: Cheryl L., Christopher M., Cynthia M. A.B. magna cum laude, Syracuse U., 1947; postgrad., Columbia U., 1948-49. Writer Batten, Barton, Durstine & Osborn (advt.), 1948-51; with Cunningham & Walsh, 1951—, sr. v.p., 1959-61, creative dir., 1958-61, exec. v.p., 1961-68, pres., 1968-79, pres., chief operating officer, 1979—. Mem. Nat. Advt. Rev. Bd. Served to lt. USNR, 1941-45. Mem. Am. Assn. Advt. Agys. (dir.), Phi Beta Kappa, Alpha Delta Sigma, Sigma Phi Epsilon. Clubs: Sky, Union League (N.Y.C.); Woodway Country (Darien, Conn.); Nat. Golf Links Am.; Ocean Reef, Card Sound (Key Largo, Fla.). Home: 135 Nearwater Ln Darien CT 06820 Office: 260 Madison Ave New York NY 10016

CHEVRAY, RENE, physics educator; b. Paris, Feb. 6, 1937; U.S., 1962; s. Robert and Marie-Louise (Fracher) C.; m. Keiko Uesawa, Aug. 9, 1964; children: Pierre-Yves Masaki, Veronique Mie. B.S., U. Toulouse, France, 1962; Dipl. Ing. (French Govt. Highest scholar), Ecole Nationale Supérieure d'Electronique, d'Electrotechnique et d'Hydraulique de Toulouse, 1962; M.S. (Alliance Française of N.Y. fellow), U. Iowa, 1963, Ph.D., 1967; D.Sc., U. Claude Bernard, Lyon, France, 1978. Product and mfg. engr. Centrifugal Pumps Worthington, Paris, 1963-64; research asso. Iowa Inst. Hydraulic Research, Iowa City, 1964-67; postdoctoral fellow, lectr. aeronautics Johns Hopkins U., 1967-69; asst. prof. SUNY, Stony Brook, 1969-72, asso. prof., 1972-79, prof., 1979-82; prof. dept. mech. enging. Columbia U., N.Y.C., 1982—; cons. physics of fluids and instrumentation; vis. prof. Japan Soc. for Promotion Sci., 1975; vis. prof., von. Humboldt fellow U. Karlsruhe, 1975-76. Fulbright scholar, 1962-63; NSF grantee, 1970-73, 1973—; Research Found. State U. N.Y. Faculty Research fellow, 1970-71; Dept. Energy grantee, 1979—. Mem. Internat. Assn. Hydraulic Research, Am. Phys. Soc., N.Y. Acad. Scis., Sigma Xi. Research and publs. on transport processes in fluids. Home: 445 Riverside Dr New York NY 10027 Office: Mech Enging Columbia U New York NY 10027

CHEVRIER, JEAN MARC, psychologist, publisher; b. Cheneville, St. Felix de Valois, Que., Can., Mar. 2, 1916; s. Joseph H. and Olevina (Mallette) C.; m. Madeleine Bourassa, Jan. 4, 1941; children: Marie-Paule Chevrier Goulet, Marcel, Claudette Chevrier Houle, Madeleine Chevrier Taylor, Robert. B.A., U. Montreal, 1938, high sch. tchr. diploma, 1939, lic. sc. ped., 1942, Ph.D., 1949; Ph.D. didactic psychoanalysis, 1958. Diplomate: in counselling psychology Am. Bd. Examiners in Profl. Psychology. Tchr. Noranda (Que.) High Sch., 1940-42; prof., dir. studies Arts and Crafts Sch., Octave-Cassegrain, 1942-47; dir. guidance Provincial Govt. Que., 1947-53; prof. U. Montreal, part-time, 1950-62; dir. psychology dept. Rehab. Inst. Montreal, 1953-62; dir. guidance Commission des Ecoles Catholiques de Montreal, 1962-64; pres., dir. gen. Inst. Psychol. Research, Inc., Montreal, 1964—; exec. dir. JMC Press, Ltd., Montreal, 1968—; v.p. Centre de Psychologie et de Pedagogie, 1945-57. Author numerous sci. papers, textbooks and psychol. tests. Recipient Bronze medal for service to Province of Que., 1958; award Edn. Council of Graphic Arts Md., U.S.A., 1960; Cert. of Honor Assn. of Hong Kong Overseas Psychologists, 1979. Mem. l'Association des Psychologues du Quebec (past pres.), Corp. Psychologists Province Que., Can. Psychol. Assn., Am. Psychol. Assn., Am. Cath. Psychol. Assn., Nat. Council on Psychol. Aspects of Disability, Corps Guidance Counsellors Que., Can. Guidance and Counseling Assn., Ont. Sch. Counselors Assn., Ont. Psychologists Assn., Nat. Sci. Tchrs. Assn. Home: 524 De Marigny Laval-des-Rapides Ville de Laval PQ H7N 5A3 Canada Office: 34 Fleury St W Montreal PQ H3L 1S9 Canada

CHEVRIER, RAYMOND MAURICE, development company executive; b. Casselman, Ont., Can., Mar. 18, 1936; s. Emery and Theodora (Dicaire) C.; m. Rachel Y. St. Louis, June 21, 1958; children: Rock, Stephan. Student pub. schs., Casselman. With Campeau Corp., Ottawa, Ont., 1958—, v.p. constrn. adminstrn., 1974—. Roman Catholic. Home: 9 Wick Crescent Gloucester ON Canada K1J 7H1 Office: Campeau Corp 2932 Baseline Rd Ottawa ON Canada K1N 8R9 *Honesty, hard work, and willingness to learn are the keys to anyone's sucess and goals.*

CHEW, DAVID LEWIS, government official; b. Chester, Pa., July 13, 1952; s. Walter G. and Marjorie (Lewis) C.; m. Sheila P. Burke, Jan. 8, 1983. B.S. in Fgn. Service, Georgetown U., 1974. Spl. asst. U.S. Senator Bill Brock, Washington, 1970-73; dep. dir. spl. projects Distributive Edn. Clubs Am., Reston, Va., 1973-75; dir. research Timmons & Co., Washington, 1975-79; adminstrv. asst. U.S. Senator

Robert Dole, Washington, 1979; v.p. Citizen's Choice U.S. C. of C., Washington, 1980-81; exec., asst. to sec. U.S. Treasury Dept., Washington, 1981—. Republican. Presbyterian. Home: 1602-C Beekman Pl Washington DC 20009 Office: Treasury Dept 15th and Pennsylvania Ave NW Washington DC 20220

CHEWNING, ROBERT WILLS, retired naval officer; b. Orange, Va., Dec. 23, 1929; s. Carroll Wills and Vivienne (Akers) C.; m. Virginia Louise Harvey, June 6, 1953; children: Carol-Winter, Virginia Sue, Rush. B.S. in Engring., U.S. Naval Acad., 1953; student, U. Va., 1948-49. Commd. ensign U.S. Navy, 1953, advanced through grades to rear admiral, 1975; chief Navy sect. Joint U.S. Mil. Assistance, Ankara, Turkey, 1974-76, dir. politico-mil. affairs and current plans, Washington, 1976-79, comdr. Middle East Force, 1979-81, dir. plans and policy CINCPAC, Camp Smith, Hawaii, 1981-83; sr. mil. rep. for 1983 Philippine Base Negotiations Joint Chief of Staff, Washington, 1983, ret., 1983. Decorated Dept. Def. Disting. Service medal, U.S. Navy Disting. Service medal. Address: Wicomico View Route 2 Box 185H Heatherville VA 22473

CHEY, WILLIAM YOON, physician; b. Ki Jang, Korea, Jan. 21, 1930; s. Kee Bok and Myungkwon (Lee) C.; m. Fan K. Tang, May 21, 1959; children: William D., Donna C., Richard D., Laura C. M.D., Seoul (Korea) Nat. U., 1953; M.Sc., U. Pa., 1962, D.Sc., 1966. Intern, N.Y.C. Hosp., 1954-55, resident, 1955-56; resident in pathology Mount Sinai Hosp., N.Y.C., 1956-57; fellow Seton Hall Med Coll., Jersey City, 1957-58; practice medicine specializing in gastroenterology, Phila., 1967-71; attending physician Temple U. Med Center, Phila., 1963—; research fellow Samuel S. Fells Research Inst., 1959-60, research asso., 1961, instr. medicine, 1961, asso., 1963, asst. prof., 1965-68, asso. prof., 1968-71; prof. medicine U. Rochester, N.Y., 1971-77, clin. prof., 1977—; sr. attending physician, dir. Isaac Gordon Center for Digestive Diseases and Nutrition, Genesee Hosp., 1971—; physician Strong Meml. Hosp., Rochester, 1971—; cons. gastroenterologist Canandaiqua (N.Y.) VA Hosp., 1977—; hon. prof. Catholic Med. Coll., Seoul, Korea, 1983; clin. prof. medicine Yunsei U. Sch. Medicine, Seoul, Korea, 1984. Contbr. articles to profl. and sci. jours and textbooks; mem. editorial bd.: Peptes. Mem. AAAS, Am. Fedn. Clin. Research, Am. Gastroent. Assn., Am. Physiol. Soc., Am. Assn. Study Liver Disease, Am. Pancreatic Assn., Am. Soc. Gastrointestinal Endoscopy, Sigma Xi. Home: 18 Denonville Ridge Rochester NY 14625 Office: 224 Alexander St Rochester NY 14607

CHEYETTE, FREDRIC LAWRENCE, history educator, writer; b. N.Y.C., Jan. 13, 1932; s. Irving and Ruth Elsie (Netter) C.; m. Shlomit Sambursky, Aug. 15, 1957 (div.); children: Oren, Dina, Tamara. A.B., Princeton U., 1953; Ph.D., Harvard U., 1959; M.A. (hon.), Amherst Coll., 1974. Instr. Stanford U., Palo Alto, Calif., 1959-60, asst. prof., 1960-61, Oberlin Coll., (Ohio), 1962-63; asst. prof. history Amherst Coll., (Mass.), 1963-68, assoc. prof., 1968-74, prof., 1974—; vis. prof. University' d'Aix-en-Provence, (France), 1981-82. Author essays; editor: Lordship and Community, 1968; asst. editor: Speculum, 1978—. Mem. Amherst Sch. Com., 1974-76. Recipient Arthur Cole prize Econ. History Assn., 1977, W.P. Webb prize U. Tex., 1977; Guggenheim fellow, 1981. Mem. Medieval Acad. Am., Am. Hist. Assn. Democrat. Jewish. Office: Amherst Coll Amherst MA 01002

CHEZ, RONALD AUGUST, obstetrician/gynecologist, educator; b. Chgo., Aug. 17, 1932; s. Maurice Rene and Florence Sylvia (Atlas) C.; m. Bonnie Lee Flood, Sept. 14, 1976; children: Nancy Lynn, Kenneth Philip. A.B., Johns Hopkins U., 1953; M.D., Cornell U., 1957. Resident UCLA Med. Center, 1958-64; fellow biophysics Harvard U. Med. Sch., Boston, 1964-66; prof. ob-gyn., asso. dean acad. affairs U. Pitts. Sch. Medicine, 1966-71; chief pregnancy research br., clin. dir. Nat. Inst. Childhood Diseases-NIH, Bethesda, Md., 1971-78; prof., chmn. ob-gyn Pa. State U. Sch. Medicine, Hershey, 1978-82; now chief exec. officer Health Learning Systems. Served with M.C. USAF, 1959-61. Mem. Am. Coll. Ob-Gyn, Am. Fertility Soc., Am. Gynecol. Soc., Am. Physiol. Soc., Am. Profs. Ob-Gyn, Endocrine Soc., Soc. Gynecol. Investigation, Soc. Perinatal Obstetricians, Phi Beta Kappa. Home: 817 Harmon Cove Towers Secaucus NJ 07094 Office: Health Learning System Inc 1290 Wall St W Lyndurst NJ 07071

CHEZEM, CURTIS GORDON, retail executive; b. Eugene, Oreg., Jan. 28, 1924; s. Clinton Daniel and Vera Veneta (Forrester) C.; children: Joanne, David. B.A. in Math, U. Oreg., 1951, M.A. in Physics, 1952; Ph.D., Oreg. State U., 1960. Registered profl. engr.; licensed clockmaker, Oreg. Flight radio officer Pan Am. World Airways, Seattle, San Francisco, 1942-44; chief radio officer Hammond S.S. Lines, San Francisco, 1944-45; telegrapher Western Union, Eugene, 1946; announcer, engr. KUGN-KASH Eugene, 1946-51; staff physicist Los Alamos Sci. Lab., 1952-67; br. chief AEC, 1967-69; head nuclear engring. dept. Kans. State U., Manhattan, 1969-72, Black & Veatch prof. nuclear engring., 1971-72; partner Casa Tlaloc, Los Alamos, 1960-68, Manhattan, 1969-72; dir. nuclear activities Middle South Services, Inc., New Orleans, 1972-77; mgr. Waterman, Inc., Amarillo, Tex., 1978-79; pres. Seven Seas Gifts, Inc., Nantucket, Mass., 1980—; supr. reactor program U.S. Atoms for Peace program, Bogota, Colombia, 1963; vis. prof. Tex. A. and M. U., 1966-67; adj. prof. U. N.Mex., 1962-65; Kans. State U. rep. Atomic Indsl. Forum, 1969-72, Middle South Utilities Inc. rep., 1973-77; chmn. profl. tng. com. Inst. Nuclear Materials Mgmt., 1968-70, mem. profl. standards and certification, 1970-72, mem. exec. com., 1973-74, editor jour., 1972-74; instr. airplane and instrument flight, 1966—; Del. Assembly Border States U.S.-Mexico, Santa Fe, 1966; chmn. adv. council on edn. Atomic Indsl. Forum, 1972-77, mem. com. on reactor licensing and safety, 1974-77; mem. Kans. Nuclear Energy Council, 1969-72. Editor: (with W.H. Kohler) Coupled Reactor Kinetics, 1967; Contbr. articles to profl. jours. Bd. control Tau Kappa Epsilon, Kans. State U., 1969-72. Served with Oreg. N.G., 1939-40; Served with USNR, 1945-46. Fellow Washington Acad. Scis.; mem. Am. Nuclear Soc., Nat. Soc. Profl. Engrs., La. Nuclear Soc., La. Engring. Soc., Electric Power Research Inst. (geothermal program com. 1975-77, new energy resources task force 1976-77), Am. Radio Relay League, Sierra Club, Nat., Orleans Audubon socs., Sigma Xi, Pi Mu Epsilon, Sigma Pi Sigma, Tau Kappa Epsilon. Home: 46 Centre St Nantucket Island MA 02554 Office: PO Box 396 Nantucket Island MA 02554 *I do not know who I am nor why I am here, yet I believe that I am an honest man at peace with God and generations past and future. What more can I say? For what more can I ask*

CHI, RICHARD SEE-YEE, educator; b. Peking, China, Aug. 3, 1918; came to U.S., 1965; s. Mi Kang and Pao (Ten) C. B.S., Nankai U., China, 1937; M.A., Oxford (Eng.) U., 1962, D.Phil., 1964; Ph.D., Cambridge (Eng.) U., 1964. Exec. industry, China and Hong Kong, 1938-56; instr. Air Ministry, Eng., 1957-60; lectr. Cambridge (Eng.) U., 1960-62; univ. lectr. Oxford (Eng.) U., 1962-65; curator Oriental art City Art Gallery, Bristol, Eng., 1965; asso. prof. Ind. U., Bloomington, 1965-71, prof., 1971—, acting chmn., summer, 1972; asso. adviser Centro Superiore di Logica e Scienze Comparate, Italy, 1972—; vis. asso. prof. U. Mich., summer 1968; fellow participant Linguistic Inst., UCLA, 1966; contbg. specialist Summer Faculty Seminar on Buddhism, Carleton Coll., Minn., 1968; mem. Workshop in Problems on Meaning and Truth, Oakland U., 1968; adviser film Buddhism in China, N.Y.C., 1972; cons. Inst. Advanced Studies World Religions, 1972—; session chmn. East-West Philosophers' Conf., 1973; panelist Internat. Conf. on Indian Philosophy, U. Toronto, 1974, 5th Internat. Symposium Multiple-valued Logic, Ind. U., 1974, Internat. Seminar on History of Buddhism, U.Wis., 1976, 30th Internat. Congress Human Scis. in, Asia, Mexico City, 1976; mem. sub-com. Buddhist philos. materials Nat. Endowment for Humanities, 1974; rep. State of Ind. Nat. Reconstrn. Conf., China, 1975. Author: The Bracket Complex in Chinese Architecture, 1946, Palatial Architecture of the Ching Dynasty, 1947, A General Theory of Operators, 1967, Buddhist Formal Logic, 1968, A Comparative Study of Propositions in the Western and Indian Logic, 1972, Topics on Being and Logical Reasoning, 1974, A Semantic Study of Propositions, East and West, 1976, The Art of Chinese Calligraphy, 1977, Dignaga and Post-Russell Logic, 1983, The Art of War of Sun Tzu, 1983; editor: Jour. Buddhist Philosophy, 1978—; editorial bd.: History and Philosophy of Logic, 1978—; dir.: Classical Chinese Architecture, 1978—; reviewer: Nat. Endowment Humanities, 1979—. Fellow China Acad., 1969. Mem. Cambridge U. Buddhist Soc. (v.p. 1961-62), Royal Asiatic Soc., Aristotelian Soc., Decorative Art Soc. Indpls., Mind Assn., Assn. Brit. Orientalists, Assn. for Symbolic Logic, Linguistic Soc. Am., Soc. Asian and Comparative Philosophy (bd. mem.-at-large 1975—), Oriental Art Soc. (founding mem.), Kings Coll. Assn. (Eng.), Asian Studies Inst. (mem. adv. com. 1975—), Indpls. Mus. Art. Club: Lake Havasu Golf and Country. Lodge: Rotary. Home: PO Box 2717 Bloomington IN 47402

CHIA, FU-SHIANG, university dean, zoology educator; b. Shantung, China, Jan. 15, 1931; emigrated to Can., 1969, naturalized, 1975; s. Chien-Ming Chia and Hsu-Tsie Chang; m. Sharon Simonds, Apr. 27, 1963; children: Alisa, Maria. B.Sc., Taiwan Normal U., 1955; M.Sc., U. Wash., 1962, Ph.D., 1964. Asst. prof. biology Sacramento State U., 1964-66; sr. research officer U. Newcastle upon Tyne and Dove Marine Lab., Eng., 1966-69; asst. prof. zoology U. Alta. (Can.), Edmonton, 1969-71, asso. prof., 1971-75, prof., 1975—, also chmn. dept. zoology., dean Faculty of Grad. Studies and Research, 1983—. Editor: (with M.E. Rice) Settlement and Metamorphosis of Marine Invertebrate Larvae, 1978. Fellow AAAS; mem. Am. Soc. Zoologists, Can. Soc. Zoologists, Sigma Xi. Office: Dept Zoology U Alta Edmonton AB T6G 2E9 Canada

CHIA, PEI-YUAN, banker; b. Hong Kong, Jan. 27, 1939; U.S., 1962, naturalized, 1970; s. Dewey T.H. and Kitty C.; m. Frances T.C. Yen, Feb. 20, 1965; children: Katherine, Douglas, Candice. B.A., Tunghai U., Taiwan, 1961; M.B.A., U. Pa., 1965. Products group mgr. Gen. Foods Corp., White Plains, N.Y., 1965-73; mktg. dir. Citibank (N.A.), N.Y.C., 1974-75, head br. automation project, 1976-77; mng. dir. Famibank, Belgium, 1978-80; pres. chief exec. officer Carte Blanche Corp., Los Angeles, 1980; chief exec. officer Diners Club, Inc., 1981—; Mem. adv. bd. China Inst. in Am. Office: The Diner's Club Inc 575 Lexington Ave New York NY 10043

CHIANG, CHIN LONG, biostatistician, educator; b. Chekiang, China, Nov. 12, 1916; came to U.S., 1946, naturalized, 1963; s. Tse Shang and (Chen) C.; m. Fu Chen Shiao, Jan. 21, 1945; children: William S., Robert S., Harriet W. B.A. in Econs, Tsing Hwa U., 1940; M.A., U. Calif.-Berkeley, 1948, Ph.D. in Stats, 1953. Teaching asst. U. Calif., Berkeley, 1948, research asst., 1950-51, asso., 1951-53, instr., 1953-55, asst. prof. biostatistics, 1955-60, assoc. prof., 1960-65, prof., 1965—, chmn. div. measurement scis., 1970-75, chmn. faculty Sch. Public Health, 1975-76, chmn., 1970—, co-chmn. group in biostats., 1971—; vis. prof. U. Mich., 1959, U. Minn., 1960, 61, Yale U., 1965-66, Emory U., 1967, U. Pitts., 1968, U. Wash., 1969, U. N.C., 1969, 70, U. Tex., 1973, Vanderbilt U., 1975, Harvard U., 1977; cons. WHO, HEW, NIH, others. Author: Introduction to Stochastic Processes in Biostatistics, 1968, Life Table and Mortality Analysis, 1978, An Introduction to Stochastic Processes and Their Applications, 1979, The Life Table and its, Applications, 1984; Assoc. editor: Biometrics, 1972-75; Asso. editor: Math. Biosciences, 1976—; editorial bd.: WHO World Health Statis. Quar, 1979—. Nat. Heart Inst. fellow, 1959-60; Fulbright sr. lectr., 1964. Fellow Am. Statis. Assn., Inst. Math. Stats., Am. Public Health Assn., Royal Statis. Soc. London; mem. Internat. Statis. Inst., Biometric Soc. Democrat. Home: 844 Spruce St Berkeley CA 94707 Office: School Public Health U Calif Berkeley CA 94720

CHIANG, HUAI CHANG, educator, entomologist; b. Sunkiang, China, Feb. 15, 1915; came to U.S., 1945, naturalized, 1953; s. Wentse Chiang and Hsiu Hsiu C.; m. Zoh Ing Shen, Sept. 8, 1946; children: Jeanne, Katherine, Robert. B.S., Tsing Hua U., Peking, China, 1938; M.S., U. Minn., 1946, Ph.D., 1948; D.Sc. (hon.), Bowling Green State U., 1979. Asst. instr. entomology Tsing Hua U., Peking, 1938-40, instr., 1940-44; asst. prof. U. Minn., St. Paul, 1954-57, asso. prof., 1957-60, prof., 1960—; cons. FAO, U.S. Dept. Agr.; mem. sci. del. Am. Entomol. Soc., 1974, Nat. Acad. Sci., 1975, U.S. Dept. Agr./EPA, 1978, 81, Dept. Agr., 1979, 81, FAO, 1980, 82; sci. panel Council Environ. Quality, 1977, U.S. Internat. Communication Agy., 1979, Internat. Centre Insect Physiology and Ecology, Nairobi, Kenya, 1980, Chinese Ministry Agr., 1982. Editor 3 publs.; contbr. over 190 research papers to profl. jours. Guggenheim fellow, 1955; named Tchr. of Year Student Assn. U. Minn., 1961; recipient cert. Dept. Agr., 1975, AIBS Disting. Service award, 1979; Phi Kappa Phi nat. scholar, 1983. Mem. Can., Royal (London) entomol. socs., Am. Entomol. Soc. (hon.), Japanese Soc. Population Research, Internat. Assn. Ecologists, Internat. Orgn. Biol. Control, AAAS, Minn. Acad. Sci., Sigma Xi, Gamma Sigma Delta. (award of merit Minn. chpt. 1983), Phi Kappa Phi (scholar of yr. award Minn. chpt. 1982). Home: 1896 Carl St Saint Paul MN 55113 Office: U Minn Saint Paul MN 55108

CHIARELLA, PETER RALPH, corporate executive; b. Bklyn., Dec. 6, 1932; s. C. Ralph and Catherine (Zinzi) C.; m. Frances M. Crane, Oct. 10, 1953; children: Ralph, Thomas, John, Karen. B.B.A., St. John's U., 1957. C.P.A., N.Y. Sr. accountant Peat, Marwick, Mitchell & Co., N.Y.C., 1957-61; asst. controller Bonwit Teller, N.Y.C., 1961-62; financial coordinator internat. div. Merck & Co., N.Y.C., 1962-63; accounting mgr. plastics div. Celanese Corp., Newark, 1963-67; v.p., controller Clairol, Inc., N.Y.C., 1967-72; pres., dir. Kleinert's, Inc., Kutztown, Pa., 1972-77; v.p., corp. controller United Brands Co., N.Y.C., 1977-79; sr. v.p., chief fin. officer Max Factor & Co., Hollywood, Calif., 1979-83; sr. v.p. fin. and adminstrn. Syncor Internat., Sylmar, Calif., 1983—; lectr. Am. Mgmt. Assn. Mem. budget com. United Fund, Stamford, Conn., 1970—. Served with USN, 1952-54. Mem. Am. Inst. C.P.A.s, N.Y. State Soc. C.P.A.s, Financial Execs. Inst., Delta Mu Delta. Home: 2620 E California St San Marino CA 91108 Office: 12847 Arroyd St Sylmar CA 91342

CHIARELLI, JAMES JOSEPH, architect; b. Spokane, July 3, 1908; s. Joseph and Josephine (Dematteis) C.; m. Patricia Alice Bradwell, May 3, 1947; children: Randall Gennaro, Diana Maria, Mark Angelo, Teresa Allegra. B. Arch., U. Wash., 1934. Pvt. practice architecture, Seattle, 1945—. Architect: Seattle Center Opera House, 1961, Thomas Burke Meml, Wash. State Museum, 1962, Herzl-Ner Tamid Conservative, Sanctuary, Social Hall and Offices, 1970. Chmn. Bd. Adjustment Seattle Planning Commn., 1959-60; chmn. Citizens Recreation and Park Com. King County, Wash., 1957-58; chmn. performing arts div. Cultural Arts Bd. for Century 21 Seattle World's Fair, 1960-62; Trustee St. Martin's Coll. Fellow A.I.A. (pres. Wash. State chpt. 1956-58); mem. Tau Sigma Delta. Home and office: 6500 NE Windermere Rd Seattle WA 98105 *Places to work and play should relate to human scale, and human needs, lacking in ostentatiousness but filled with objectivity. Spaces warm and receptive to human experience should engender an excitement and joy for the good life.*

CHIARELLO, DONALD FREDERICK, lawyer; b. Balt., May 27, 1940; s. Vittorio Joseph and Mary Gertrude (Beall) C.; (div.)children: Victoria Lee, Christine G. Student, Drexel Inst. Tech., 1959-60; A.A., U. Balt., 1964, J.D., 1967. Bar: Md. 1967. Account exec. Burroughs Corp., 1963-67; asso. firm Levin & Hochberg, 1968-70; mem. firm Levin, Hochberg & Chiarello, 1970—, Hochberg, Chiarello, Costello & Dowell, 1982—; Vice pres. Edna Gardens Lakeside Civic Assn., 1970, Greater Northwood Community Council, 1970-71. Mem. 3d Dist. Citizens for Good Govt., 1968-74, Md. Polit. Studies Commn., 1969-72; pres. 3d Dist. Young Democratic Club, 1970-71; Bd. dirs. Northwood Assn., 1969-71. Mem. ABA, Md. State Bar Assn., Balt. City Bar Assn. (chmn. coms.), Md. Trial Lawyers Assn. (bd. dirs., chmn. coms.), Am. Trial Lawyers Assn., Theta Chi, Sigma Delta Kappa. Clubs: Balt. Ski (treas. 1974-75, pres. 1981-83. Home: 33 E Montgomery St Baltimore MD 21230 Office: The Professional Bldg 330 N Charles St Baltimore MD 21201

CHIARENZA, CARL, art historian, critic, educator; b. Rochester, N.Y., Sept. 5, 1935; s. Charles and Mary Rose (Russo) C.; m. Heidi Faith Katz, Aug. 13, 1978; children: Suzanne Mari, Jonah Katz, Gabriella Christine. B.F.A., Rochester Inst. Tech., 1957; M.S., Boston U., 1959; M.A., 1964; Ph.D., Harvard U., 1972. Lectr. Boston U., 1963—, 1963-64, instr. dept. fine arts, 1964-68, asst. prof., 1968-72, univ. prof., 1972-73, assoc. prof., 1973-80, prof. dept. art history, 1980—, acting chmn. dept., 1973-74, chmn. dept., 1976-81; adj. vis. prof. Visual Studies Workshop, SUNY, 1972-73; Harnish vis. artist Smith Coll., 1983-84; mem. Artists Adv. Panel, Artists Found., Boston, 1977-81; guest curator Inst. Contemporary Art, Boston, 1980-81; cons. Nat. Endowment for Arts, 1978-80, mem. Artists' Fellowships panel, 1982; bd. dirs. Photographic Resource Ctr.; trustee Visual Studies Workshop. Works represented in permanent collections, Mpls. Inst. Arts, Fogg Art Mus., works represented in permanent collections, Internat. Mus. Photography, Rochester, Ctr. for Creative Photography, Tucson, Addison Gallery Am. Art, Princeton U. Mus., Yale U. Art Gallery, Mus. Fine Arts, Houston, Worcester Art Mus.; author: Aaron Siskind: Pleasures and Terrors, 1982; co-author: (James Enyeart, editor) Heinecken, 1980; contbg. author: Reading Into Photography: Selected Essays, 1959-80, 1982, Kenneth Josephson, 1983. Served with U.S. Army, 1960-62. Mass. Art and Humanities Found. fellow, 1975-76; Nat. Endowment for Arts fellow, 1977-78. Mem. Soc. Photographic Edn., AAUP, Coll. Art Assn., Assn. Historians Am. Art. Office: 725 Commonwealth Ave Boston MA 02215 *I am a switch-hitter. I have always made, written about, or lectured about pictures. Because I seem to do each best when working in a concentrated spurt, I am often torn between these modes of communication. I work intuitively and in a state of agitation until things find their rightful place on a page or in a picture. It is as if I am reaching for a place of equilibrium or understanding as I move through the world from a position of essential ignorance about the meaning of life.*

CHIARENZA, FRANK JOHN, educator; b. New Britain, Conn., Dec. 10, 1926; s. Sebastian X. and Josephine (Spoto) C. A.B., Yale, 1949, Ph.D. in Medieval Lit, 1956; M.A. in English, Rutgers U., 1950; certificate, Inst. for Ednl. Mgmt.; Sloan Found. grantee, Harvard, 1970. Lectr. English U. Conn., 1954-55; instr. English Hillyer Coll., Hartford, Conn., 1955-57; from asst. prof. to prof. chmn. dept. English U. Hartford, 1958-67, acad. dean, 1967-78, prof. English, 1978—; Cons., reader English Coll. Entrance Exam. Bd., 1959—; reader advanced placement tests Ednl. Testing Service, Princeton, N.J., 1961—; chmn. for Conn., Nat. Council Coll. Publs. Advisers, 1966-67; adv. council Career Opportunity Program, 1970—; resource cons. Conn. Commn. for Higher Edn., 1972-73; chief reader Coll. Level Exam. Program, Ednl. Testing Service, N.J., 1978—. Author articles. Trustee Watkinson Sch., West Hartford, Conn. Served with USNR, 1944-46. Fulbright grantee U. Rome, 1953-54. Mem. Modern Lang. Assn., AAUP (pres. Hartford 1962-64), Am. Assn. Higher Edn., N.E.A., Am. Conf. Acad. Deans, Am. Council Edn. Club: Yale (New Britain). Home: 80 Crestview Dr Newington CT 06111 Office: Univ Hartford West Hartford CT 06117

CHIASSON, DONAT, archbishop; b. Paquetville, N.B., Can., Jan. 2, 1930. Ordained priest Roman Catholic Ch., 1956; archbishop of Moncton, N.B., 1972—. Office: PO Box 248 Moncton NB E1C 8K9 Canada *

CHIAT, JAY, advertising agency executive; b. N.Y.C., Oct. 26, 1931; s. Sam and Min (Kretchmer) C.; children: Debra, Marc, Elyse. B.S., Rutgers U. Vice-pres., creative dir. Leland Oliver Co., Los Angeles; pres., chief exec. officer Jay Chiat & Assocs., Chiat-Day, Inc., Advt., Los Angeles, Seattle. Served with USAF. Mem. Am. Assn. Advt. Assn. Advt. Agys., Western States Assn. Advt. Agys. Club: Riviera Country. Office: Chiat-Day Inc 517 S Olive St Los Angeles CA 90013

CHIAZZE, LEONARD, JR., biostatistician, epidemiologist; b. Falconer, N.Y., June 19, 1934; s. Leonard and Jennie (Bondi) C.; m. Ellen Anne Bergman, June 12, 1954; children: Kathleen, Caroline, Michael, Ellen. A.A., SUNY, Jamestown, 1953; B.S., U. Buffalo, 1955, M.B.A., 1957; Sc.D., U. Pitts., 1964. Instr. stats. U. Buffalo, 1955-57; biostatistician Nat. Cancer Inst., 1957-66; dir. div. biostats. and epidemiology Georgetown U. Sch. Medicine, Washington, 1966, asst. prof., 1966-69, assoc. prof., 1969-77, prof., 1977—, dir. grad. program in biostats., 1970—; chief epidemiology and stats. Vincent T. Lombardi Cancer Research Ctr., 1982—; acting chief biometry br. Nat. Cancer Inst., Bethesda, Md., 1975-76. Contbr. articles to profl. jours. Served with USPHS, 1957-66. Fellow Am. Coll. Epidemiology, Am. Pub. Health Assn.; mem. Am. Statis. Assn., Soc. Occupational and Environ. Health (pres. elect, governing council), Soc. Epidemiologic Research, Internat. Epidemiol. Assn., Internat. Assn. Sci. Study Population, Population Assn. Am., Assn. Tchrs. Preventive Medicine, Sigma Xi, Beta Gamma Sigma. Home: 11237 Waycross Way Kensington MD 20895 Office: Georgetown U. 3750 Reservoir Rd Washington DC 20007

CHICAGO, JUDY, artist; b. Chgo., July 20, 1939; d. Arthur M. and May (Levenson) Cohen. B.A., U. Calif. at Los Angeles, 1962, M.A., 1964. Co-founder Feminist Studio Workshop, Los Angeles, 1973. Author: Through the Flower: My Struggle as a Woman Artist, 1975, The Dinner Party: A Symbol of Our Heritage, 1979, Embroidering Our Heritage: The Dinner Party Needlework, 1980; One-woman exhbns. include, Pasadena (Calif.) Mus. Art, 1969, Jack Glenn Gallery, Corona del Mar, Calif., 1972, JPL Fine Arts, London, 1975, Quay Ceramics, San Francisco, 1976, San Francisco Mus. Modern Art, 1979, Bklyn. Mus., 1980, Parco Galleries, Japan, Fine Arts Gallery, Irvine, Calif., 1981, Musee d'Art Contemporain, Montreal, 1982, group exhbns. include, Jewish Mus., N.Y.C., 1966, 67, Whitney Mus., 1972, Winnipeg Art Gallery, 1975; coordinator art project: Dinner Party. Address: PO Box 842 Benica CA 94510 *I am an artist, a feminist, committed to balancing the excesses of masculine culture with feminine values through my art.* *

CHICHESTER, CLINTON OSCAR, food scientist; b. N.Y.C., Feb. 11, 1925; s. Clinton Oscar and Anna M. (Hartmann) C.; m. Irma Lopez de Haro; children: Clinton, Catherine, Christine, Cecile, Charles. B.S., Mass. Inst. Tech., 1949; M.S., U. Calif., Berkeley, 1951,

Ph.D., 1954. Prof. dept. food sci. and tech. U. Calif., Davis, 1954-67, chmn. dept. food sci. and tech., 1967-70; prof. dept. food sci. and tech., nutrition and dietetics, dir. Internat. Center Marine Resource Devel. U. R.I., Kingston, 1970—; exec. chmn. Consortium for Devel. of Tech., Kingston, 1968—; v.p. Nutrition Found., N.Y.C., 1972—; cons. govt. agys. and industry. Sr. editor: Advances in Food Research; co-editor: Research in Pesticides, Microbial Safety of Fishery Products; Contbr. sci. articles to research publs. Bd. dirs. Snell Meml. Found. Served to 2d lt. USAAF, 1942-46. Recipient Bernardo O'Higgins award Govt. Chile, 1967; Gold medal Czech. Nat. Acad. Sci., 1969, Czech. Ministry Agr., 1969; Plaque of Tribute ICAITI, Guatemala, 1974; award Govt. Guatemala; medal State of Sao Paulo, Brazil, 1979. Mem. Am. Chem. Soc., Inst. Food Tech. (Babcock-Hart award 1973, Internat. award 1976, Nicholas Appert award Chgo. chpt. 1982), Chemists Club, Am. Pub. Health Assn., Am. Inst. Chem. Engrs., AMA, Latin Am. Soc. Nutrition, Am. Soc. Biol. Chemists, Am. Inst. Nutrition, Soc. Exptl. Stress Analysis, Assn. Automotive Medicine, Am. Soc. Clin. Nutrition, Soc. Toxicology. Club: Cosmos. Home: PO Box 443 Wakefield RI 02880 Office: Nutrition Found 888 17th St NW Washington DC 20006 Dept Food Sci U RI Kingston RI 02881

CHICKERING, ALLEN LAWRENCE, JR., lawyer; b. Oakland, Calif., Apr. 20, 1907; s. Allen L. and Alma (Sherman) C.; m. Caroline C. Rogers, May 23, 1931 (dec.); children: Caroline (Mrs. George A. Fish), Joan (Mrs. Richard C. Volberg), Howard Allen; m. Pauline C. Fisher, Jan. 2, 1973. A.B., U. Calif., 1929; student, Harvard U., 1929-30; LL.B., Hastings Coll. Law, 1933. Bar: Calif. bar 1934. Since practiced in, San Francisco; mem. Chickering & Gregory. Mem. Calif. Bar Assn., Delta Kappa Epsilon. Republican. Club: Pacific Union. Home: 255 Mt Wood Ln Woodside CA 94062 Office: Three Embarcadero Center Suite 2300 San Francisco CA 94111

CHICOINE, LIONEL MASON, automotive co. exec.; b. Detroit, Apr. 21, 1927; s. Lionel Mason and Ann P. (Hester) C.; m. Marian Elizabeth Bennett, Feb. 10, 1951; children: Carolyn, John. A.B., U. Mich., 1950; M.S., Mass. Inst. Tech., 1967. With Ford Motor Co., 1953—, asst. gen. mgr. supply assembly div., 1974-75, dir. body and assembly purchasing, 1975-76, v.p. purchasing, 1976-79, v.p. purchasing and supply, 1979—. Bd. dirs. Jr. Achievement S.E. Mich., Nat. Jr. Achievement. Served with U.S. Army, 1945-47. Alfred P. Sloan fellow, 1966-67. Mem. Automotive Info. Council (bd. dirs.). Clubs: Grosse Pointe, Detroit Country, Renaissance. Home: 15 Stratton Pl Grosse Pointe Shores MI 48236 Office: 12th Floor Dearborn MI 48121

CHICOREL, MARIETTA S., publisher; b. Vienna, Austria, May 22, 1924; came to U.S., 1939, naturalized, 1945; d. Paul and Margaret (Gross) Selby. A.B., Wayne State U., 1951; M.L.S., U. Mich., 1961. Asst. chief library acquisitions div. U. Wash., Seattle, 1962-66; project dir. Macmillan Info. Scis., Inc., N.Y.C., 1968-69; pres. Chicorel Library Pub. Corp., N.Y.C., 1969-79, Am. Library Pub. Co., Inc., 1979—; asst. prof. dept. library sci. City U. N.Y. (Queens Coll.); Mem. edn. com. Gov.'s Commn. on Status of Women, State of Wash., 1963-65. Chief editor: Ulrich's International Periodicals Directory, 1966-68; Editor: Chicorel Indexes, 1969—; Contbr.: chpt. to Library Statistics: A Handbook of Concepts, Definitions and Terminology, 1966. Mem. ALA (exec. bd. tech. services div. 1965-68, chmn. library materials price index com. 1965-68, chmn. serials sect. nominating com. 1968-69, councillor 1969-73), Book League N.Y. (bd. govs. 1975-79), Am. Soc. for Info. Sci., Canadian, Pacific N.W. library assns., New York Library Club, New York Tech. Services Librarians. Office: 275 Central Park W New York NY 10024

CHIEN, CHIH-YUNG, physics educator; b. Sichuan, China, Aug. 5, 1939; s. Bins C. and Yinlow C.; (married); children: Chi-Bin, Chi-Kai, Chi-An. B.S., Taiwan U., 1960; M.A., Yale U., 1963, Ph.D., 1966. Asst. prof. in residence UCLA, 1966-69; asst. prof. Johns Hopkins U., 1969-73, assoc. prof., 1973-77, prof., 1977—; hon. prof. Nanjung U., 1980—, Beijing Inst. Tech., 1983. Mem. Am. Phys. Soc. Home: 1823 Notre Dame Ave Lutherville MD 21093 Office: Dept Physics Johns Hopkins U Baltimore MD 21218

CHIERI, PERICLE ADRIANO C., educator, consulting mechanical and aeronautical engineer, naval architect; b. Mokanshan, Chekiang, China, Sept. 6, 1905; came to U.S., 1938, naturalized, 1952; s. Virginio and Luisa (Fabbri) C.; m. Helen Etheredge, Aug. 1, 1938. Dr. Engring., U. Genoa, Italy, 1927; M.E., U. Naples, Italy, 1927; Dr. Aero. Engring., U. Rome, 1928. Registered profl. engr., Italy, N.J., La., S.C.; chartered engr., U.K. Naval architect. mech. engr. research and exptl. divs., submarines and internal combustion engines Italian Navy, Spezia, 1929-31; naval architect, marine supt. Navigazione Libera Triestina Shipping Corp., Libera Lines, Trieste, Italy, 1931-32, Genoa, 1933-35; aero. engr., tech. adviser Chinese Govt. commn. aero. affairs Nat. Govt. Republic of China, Nanchang and Loyang, 1935-37; engring. exec., dir. aircraft materials test lab., supt. factory's tech. vocational instrn. SINAW Nat. Aircraft Works, Nanchang, Kiangsi, China, 1937-39; aero. engr. FIAT aircraft factory, Turin, Italy, 1939; aero. engr. and tech. sec. Office: Air Attache, Italian Embassy, Washington, 1939-41; prof. aero. engring. Tri-State Coll., Angola, Ind., 1942; aero. engr., helicopter design Aero. Products, Inc., Detroit, 1943-44; sr. aero. engr. ERCO Engring. & Research Corp., Riverdale, Md., 1944-46; asso. prof. mech. engring. U. Toledo, 1946-47; asso. prof. mech. engring., faculty grad. div. Newark (N.J.) Coll. Engring., 1947-52; prof., head dept. mech. engring. U. Southwestern La., Lafayette, La., 1952-72; cons. engr., Lafayette, 1972—; research engr., adv. devel. sect., aviation gas turbine div. Westinghouse Electric Corp., South Philadelphia, Pa., 1953; exec. dir. Council on Environment, Lafayette, 1975—. Instr. water safety ARC Nat. Aquatic Schs., summers 1958-67; Bd. dirs. Lafayette Parish chpt. ARC. Fellow Royal Instn. Naval Architects London (life); asso. fellow Am. Inst. Aeronautics and Astronautics; mem. Soc. Naval Architects and Marine Engrs. (life mem.), AAAS, AAUP (emeritus), Am. Soc. Engring. Edn. (life), Am. Soc. M.E., Soc. Automotive Engrs., Instrument Soc. Am., Soc. Exptl. Stress Analysis, Nat. Soc. Profl. Engrs., N.Y. Acad. Scis., La. Engring. Soc., La. Tchrs. Assn., AAHPER, La. Acad. Scis., Commodore Longfellow Soc., Cons. Engrs. Council La., Phi Kappa Phi., Pi Tau Sigma (hon.). Home: 142 Oak Crest Dr Lafayette LA 70503 Office: PO Box 52923 Lafayette LA 70505

CHIGAS, VESSARIOS GEORGE, electronics company executive; b. Athens, Greece, June 8, 1922; came to U.S., 1925, naturalized, 1940; s. George V. and Aristea (Rhangos) C.; m. Filitsa Papathanasiou, Apr. 19, 1960; children: Diana V., Daphne V. B.S. in Elec. Engring, Northeastern U., 1944. With Sylvania Electric Products, Inc.; founder M/A-COM, Inc., Burlington, Mass., 1950; chmn. bd. Microwave Assos., Inc.; dir. Microwave Assos. Ltd., Luton, Eng., Analogic Corp., Wakefield, Mass., Blue Cross of Mass., Courier Corp.; mem. corp. Northeastern U., Boston; adv. bd. Center Mgmt. Devel., 1965-68; also dir. nat. council; chmn. exec. com., trustee Am. Coll. of Greece, Athens. Mem. corp. Goodwill Industries, Boston; trustee Lowell (Mass.) Gen. Hosp., NE Deaconess Hosp., Boston. Mem. Am. Mgmt. Assn., Eta Kappa Nu (hon.), Tau Beta Pi. Home: 62 Bartlett St Chelmsford MA 01824 Office: M/A-Com Inc 7 NE Executive Park Burlington MA 01803

CHIGIER, NORMAN, mechanical engineering educator; b. Frankfort, South Africa, Aug. 2, 1933; came to U.S., 1981. B.S. in M.E., U. Wilwatersrand, 1952; M.A., U. Cambridge, 1960, Ph.D., 1961, Sc.D., 1977. With Brit. Thompson Houston Co., Rugby, Eng., 1953-56; asst. in research Engring. Labs U. Cambridge, 1956-60; sr. investigator Internat. Flame Research Found., Ijmuiden, Holland, 1961-63; sr. lectr. aero. engring. Technion, Israel, 1964-66; sr. research assoc. NASA-Ames Research Ctr., Calif., 1970-71; lectr. dept. chem. engring. and fuel tech. U. Sheffield, Eng., 1966-68, sr. lectr., 1968-73, reader, 1973-81; Benedum prof. mech. engring. Carnegie-Mellon U., Pitts., 1981-82, William J. Brown prof. mech. engring., 1982—; vis. cons. Sandia Labs, Livermore, Calif., 1976; vis. prof. Stanford U., 1977, Ecole Centrale, Lyon, 1977-78, U. Calif.-San Diego, 1979. Author: (with J.M. Beer) Combustion Aerodynamics, 1972, Energy, Combustion and Environment, 1981; editor: Progress in Energy and Combustion Science, Vols. 1-7, 1977-82, Collective Phenomena, 1975; mem. editorial adv.* bd.: Combustion and Flame; assoc. editor: Energy-The Internat. Jour., 1979—. Fellow Inst. Fuel (Lubbock-Sambrook award 1968, 75), AIAA (assoc.); mem. ASME (Lewis F. Moody awards Fluids Engring. div. 1965), Inst. Mech. Engrs. Office: Carnegie-Mellon Univ Pittsburgh PA 15213

CHIGOS, DAVID, university president; b. Scranton, Pa., Mar. 29, 1933; s. Andrew D. and Emma (Kossmann) C.; m. Ruth Elizabeth Chamberlain, May 22, 1954; children: Catherine Mary Chigos Bradley, Carla Jane Chigos Sotelo, Lisa Anne, Laura Elizabeth. B.S. in Chemistry, W.Va. Wesleyan Coll., 1954, LL.D., 1980; M.A. in Counseling and Guidance, U.S. Internat. U., 1968, Ph.D., 1971. Teaching asst. U. Tex., 1954-56; commd. ensign USN, 1957, advanced through grades to lt. comdr., 1967, capt. Res., 1976; indsl. relations Convair Aerospace div. Gen. Dynamics Corp., San Diego, 1967-70; faculty U. Calif. Extension at San Diego, 1967—, San Diego State U. Extension, 1968-71, San Diego Evening Coll., 1967-71; pres., chief exec. officer Nat. U., San Diego, 1971—; cons. in field. Mem. Nat. Mgmt. Assn. (Golden Knight award 1979), Convair Nat. Mgmt. Assn. (hon. life), San Diego Safety Council (hon.), AAAS, Am. Assn. Presidents of Ind. Colls. and Univs., Nat. Ind. Colls. and Univs., Personal Mgmt. Assn., Am. Soc. Tng. and Devel., Naval Res. Assn. (life), Navy League U.S. (life, nat. dir.; Scroll of Honor 1979), Res. Officers Assn. (life). Clubs: San Diego Yacht, Kona Kai, Cuyamaca, University (San Diego); Army-Navy (Washington). Home: 651 Silvergate Ave San Diego CA 92106 Office: 4141 Camino del Rio S San Diego CA 92108

CHIHARA, PAUL SEIKO, composer; b. Seattle, July 9, 1938; s. Isao George and Nobue Mary (Fushiki) C. B.A. in English, U. Wash., 1960; M.A., Cornell U., 1961, D.M.A. in Music, 1965. Asso. prof. music UCLA, 1966-75; tchr. composition Calif. Inst. Arts, 1975; composer-in-residence San Francisco Ballet, 1981—. Composer: Symphony in Celebration, 1975, Missa Carminum, 1975; ballet The Tempest, 1980, Concerto for Saxophone and Orch, 1980, Concerto for String Quartet and Orch, 1981; symphony Birds of Sorrow, 1982. Fulbright fellow, 1965; Guggenheim fellow, 1975. Mem. ASCAP.

CHILCOTE, LUGEAN LESTER, architect; b. Oklahoma City, Jan. 14, 1929; s. Mark H. and Myrita A.J. (Lugeanbeal) C.; m. Clara Bernice Dudis, Dec. 18, 1953; children—Martin L., Frederick M., David L., Bradley R. B.Arch., U. Ark., 1951. Designer, draftsman Ken Cole, Jr. (Architect), 1953-54; architect Swaim & Allen Architects, 1954-58; architect, dir. Blass Chilcote Carter Lanford & Wilcox (and predecessor firms), 1958; all Little Rock; Judge City Beautiful Commn., 1967-68. Prin. works include, First Christian Ch., 1962, Continental bldg., 1969, Main Toll and Dial bldg. Southwestern Bell Telephone Co., 1968, Bapt. Med. Center Complex, 1971-73, U. Ark. Med. Sci. Campus, 1973—, U.S. Gen. Mail Facility, Conv./Exhibit/Excelsior-Trust House Forte Complex, 1978—, Ark. Children's Hosp., all Little Rock, U.S. Post Office and Courthouse, Pine Bluff, Ark., 1967, Nat. Center for Toxicological Research, Pine Bluff, 1973—. Mem. com. Ark. Art Festival, 1968, West Little Rock YMCA, 1969; mem. Ark. Arts Center, 1965—; bd. dirs., mem. exec. com. Ark. Community Found.; bd. dirs. Ark. Sports Hall of Fame, 1983—; dist. chmn., mem. exec. bd. of council Boy Scouts Am. Served to capt. USAF, 1951-53. Recipient Wood badge tng. award, Silver Beaver award., Dist. award of Merit Boy Scouts Am. Fellow AIA (pres. Ark. chpt. 1967, trustee ednl. endowment fund 1970-72, gen. chmn. gulf states regional conf. 1966, nat. del. 1967, chmn. nat. profl. interest com. 1982, bd. dirs. nat. polit. action com. 1983—); Mem. Phi Eta Sigma, Theta Tau., Christian Ch. (mem. exec. com., chmn. bd., elder; v.p. Ark. Christian men's orgn.). Clubs: Pleasant Valley Country (bd. govs.), Little Rock, Capital (Little Rock). Home: 806 Carywood Ln Little Rock AR 72205 Office: Blass Chilcote Carter Lanford Wilcox PA PO Drawer 3019 Little Rock AR 72203

CHILCOTE, SAMUEL DAY, JR., assn. exec.; b. Casper, Wyo., Aug. 24, 1937; s. Sam D. and Juanita C. (Cornelison) C.; m. Ellen Sheridan Spear, Nov. 11, 1966. B.S., Idaho State U., 1959. Adminstrv. asst. Continental Oil Co., Glenrock, Wyo., 1960-63; asst. supt. public instrn. Wyo. Dept. Edn., 1963-67; supr. N. Central region Distilled Spirits Inst., Cheyenne, Wyo., 1967-71, exec. dir., Washington, 1971-73; exec. v.p. Distilled Spirits Council, Inc., Washington, 1973-77, pres., 1978-81, Tobacco Inst., Washington, 1981—. Bd. dirs. Nat. Council on Alcoholism, 1977—; Pres. Sky Ranch Found. for Boys, 1975-81, pres. emeritus, 1981—. Mem. U.S. C. of C. Clubs: George Town, Congressional Country (bd. govs.), Nat. Press, Capitol Hill, Masons, Elks, Shriners. Office: 1875 Eye St Washington DC 20006

CHILCOTE, THOMAS FRANKLIN, college president; b. Dayton, Pa., May 25, 1918; s. Thomas Franklin and Emma Jane (Peters) C.; m. Margaret Virginia Mossor, Sept. 18, 1943; children: Wayne Leslie, Deborah Jean. Student, Taylor U., 1936-38; A.B., U. Pitts., 1940; postgrad., Western Theol. Sem., 1940-41, Harvard Inst. Ednl. Mgmt., 1973; M.Div., Boston U. Sch. Theology, 1943; D.D., Chattanooga U., 1955. Ordained to ministry Methodist Ch., 1945, pastor, Cresson, Pa., 1943, First Meth. Ch., Chattanooga, 1948-55, Maryville, Tenn., 1958-62, Fountain City United Meth. Ch., Knoxville, 1962-68, First United Meth. Ch., Oak Ridge, 1968-70, First Broad St. United Meth. Ch., Kingsport, Tenn., 1970-73; supt. Abingdon (Va.) dist. Meth. Ch., 1955-58; pres. Emory and Henry Coll., Emory, Va., 1973—; Mem. theol. study commn. on doctrine and doctrinal standards United Meth. Ch., 1968-72. News editor: The Christian Advocate, Chgo., 1943-45; mng. editor: New Life Mag, Nashville, 1945-48; Author: Youth Courageous, 1947, Jesus and Worship, 1949, The Excellence of Our Calling, 1954, Christ Makes the Difference, 1962, The Methodist Articles of Religion, 1960, Man's Spiritual Pilgrimage, 1965, Quest for Meaning, 1972, Creation and Liberation, 1973, Hoofbeats and Heartbeats, 1975, Behold Your Savior, 1977, God's Twenty-Two, 1983. Del. World Meth. Conf., 1951, 61, Meth. Uniting Conf., 1968, Gen. Conf., 1970; mem. exec. com. Council Ind. Colls. Va., Assn. Va. Colls.; participant Pacific Rim Ednl. Seminar, 1980. Mem. Alpha Pi Omega. Republican. Home: PO Box II Emory VA 24327 Office: Emory and Henry Coll Emory VA 24327

CHILD, ARTHUR JAMES EDWARD, food company executive; b. Guildford, Eng., May 19, 1910; s. William Arthur and Helena (Wilson) C.; m. Mary Gordon, Dec. 10, 1955. B.Commerce, Queen's U., 1931, LL.D., 1983; grad., Advanced Mgmt. Program, Harvard, 1956; M.A., U. Toronto, 1960, LL.D., 1984; LL.D., U. Calgary, 1984. Chief auditor Can. Packers Ltd., 1938-52, v.p., 1952-60; pres. Intercontinental Packers Ltd., 1960-66; pres., chief exec. officer, dir. Burns Foods Ltd., Calgary, Alta., 1966—; chmn. bd., dir. Palm Dairies Ltd., Scott Nat. Co., Ltd.; pres., dir. Ajex Investments Ltd., Jamar Inc.; dir. La Verendrye Mgmt. Corp.; chmn. Canbra Foods Ltd., Stafford Foods Ltd., Food Services Ltd.; dir. Can. Life Assurance Co., Newsco Investments Ltd., Nova, an Alta., Corp., Canoe Cove Mfg. Ltd., Grove Valve & Regulator Co., Nova Energy Systems Inc., Detroit Marine Terminals Inc., Hydroblaster Inc., Ronalds-Federated Ltd., Imperial Trust Co.; asso. prof. U. Sask., 1964-65. Author: Economics and Politics in United States Banking, 1965, (with B. Cadmus) Internal Control, 1953. Fellow Chartered Inst. Secs.; mem. Meat Packers Council Can. (past pres.), Inst. Internal Auditors (past pres.), Am. Mgmt. Assn., Inst. for Strategic Studies. Home: Calgary AB Canada Office: PO Box 2520 Calgary AB T2P 2M7 Canada

CHILD, CHARLES GARDNER, surgeon; b. N.Y.C., Feb. 1, 1908; s. Charles Gardner and Helen (Francis) C.; m. Margaret MacCrae Austin, June 14, 1941; children—Caroline, Helen, Cleland, Charles, Elizabeth. B.A., Yale U., 1930; M.D., Cornell U., 1934. Intern in surgery N.Y. Hosp., N.Y.C., 1934-35, resident in surgery, 1936-42; asst. prof. surgery Cornell U. Med. Sch., N.Y.C., 1942-43, assoc. prof., 1946-52; prof. surgery, chmn. Tufts U. Med. Sch., Boston, 1952-58; prof. surgery U. Mich., Ann Arbor, 1978, prof. emeritus, 1978—; clin. prof. surgery Emory U. Med. Sch., Atlanta, 1978—; assoc. chief staff for edn. VA Med. Center, Atlanta, 1980—. Author: The Liver and Portal Hypertension, 1954, The Portal Circulation, 1965, Portal Hypertension, 1975; contbr. articles to profl. jours. Served with USNR, 1944-46. Mem. Soc. Univ. Surgeons, Am. Surg. Assn., Soc. Clin. Surgeons, Inst. Medicine. Office: VA Med Center 1670 Clairmont Rd Decatur GA 30033

CHILD, FRANK CLAYTON, educator, economist; b. Salt Lake City, Aug. 21, 1921; s. Charles William and Alveretta Gertrude (Clayton) C.; m. Eva Lorraine Clough, Sept. 22, 1948; children: Charles William, Matthew Daniel, Tracy, Suzanne. B.A., U. Utah, 1941; M.A., Stanford, 1947, Ph.D., 1954. Instr. econs. Stanford, 1950, Williams Coll., 1950-52; asst. prof. Pomona Coll., 1952-56; asst. prof., asso. prof. econs. Mich. State U., 1956-59; adviser Mich. State U. Adv. Group, Saigon, Viet Nam, 1959-61; vis. asso. prof. econs. Stanford U., 1961-62; from asso. prof. to prof. U. Calif.-Davis, 1962-82, chmn. dept., 1963-82; dean social sci. div., prof. econs. U. Calif.-Santa Cruz, 1983—; econs. cons., Sabah, Malaysia, 1965, AID, Pakistan, 1966; sr. economist, mission to Vietnam, Devel. and Resources Corp., 1967; research adviser Pakistan Inst. Devel. Econs. (Yale-Pakistan project), Karachi, 1967-69; vis. prof. Inst. for Devel. Studies, U. Nairobi, Kenya, 1972-73; also cons.; coordinator Agrl. Devel. Systems Project/Egypt, 1979—; cons. Devel. and Resources Corp., Brazil, 1972, Pakistan Inst. Devel. Econs., Islamabad, 1975, 76. Author: Theory and Practice of German Exchange Control, 1958, Toward a Policy for Economic Growth (in Viet Nam), 1963, Small-Scale Industry in Rural Kenya, 1977; Contbr. articles to profl. jours. Served from 2d lt. to capt. AUS, 1942-46. Decorated Bronze Star; Croix de Guerre, France). Mem. Am. Econ. Assn. Home: 118 Limestone Lane Santa Cruz CA 95060

CHILD, IRVIN LONG, psychologist, educator; b. Deming, N.Mex., Mar. 11, 1915; s. Arthur Henry and Martina Avila (Long) C.; m. Alice Dukes Blyth, Mar. 29, 1941; children: Richard Blyth, Pamela Colman. B.A., UCLA, 1935; Ph.D., Yale U., 1939. Instr. psychology Harvard U. and Radcliffe Coll., 1939-41; with Yale U., 1941—, successively Latin-Am. research fellow, asst. prof., asso. prof., prof. psychology, 1954—. Author: Italian or American? The Second Generation in Conflict, 1943, Child Training and Personality: A Cross-Cultural Study, (with J.W.M. Whiting), 1953, Humanistic Psychology and the Research Tradition: Their Several Virtues, 1973. Mem. Parapsychol. Assn., Internat. Assn. for Empirical Aesthetics, Assn. for Humanistic Psychology, Phi Beta Kappa, Sigma Xi. Home: 2 Cooper Rd North Haven CT 06473 Office: 2 Hillhouse Ave New Haven CT 06520

CHILD, JULIA MCWILLIAMS (MRS. PAUL CHILD), author, TV performer, cooking expert; b. Pasadena, Calif., Aug. 15, 1912; d. John and Julia Carolyn (Weston) McWilliams; m. Paul Child, Sept. 1, 1945. B.A., Smith Coll., 1934. With advt. dept. W. & J. Sloane, N.Y.C., 1939-40; with OSS, Washington, also, Ceylon, China, 1941-45. Condr.: TV program The French Chef, WGBH-TV, Boston, 1962—, Julia Child & Co, 1978-79, Julia Child & More Co., 1980, Dinner at Julia's, PBS, 1983; weekly cooking segment Good Morning America, ABC-TV, 1980—; Author: (with Simone Beck and Louisette Bertholle) Mastering the Art of French Cooking, 1961, The French Chef Cookbook, 1968, Mastering the Art of French Cooking, Vol. II, 1970, (with Simone Beck) From Julia Child's Kitchen, 1975, Julia Child & Company, 1978, Julia Child & More Company, 1979, Revision Mastering the Art of French Cooking I & II, 1983; monthly columnist: McCall's Mag., 1975-82, Parade Mag., 1982—. Recipient Peabody award, 1964, Emmy award, 1966, French Ordre de Merite Agricole, 1967, Ordre National de Merite, 1974. Office: WGBH 125 Western Ave Boston MA 02134

CHILDERS, NORMAN FRANKLIN, horticulture educator; b. Moscow, Idaho, Oct. 29, 1910; s. Lucius Franklin and Frances M. (Norman) C.; 4 children. B.S. in Horticulture, U. Mo., 1933, M.S. in Horticulture (Gregory scholar 1933-34), 1934; Ph.D. in Pomology, Cornell U., 1937. Grad. asst. pomology. Cornell U., 1934-37; asst. prof. horticulture, asst. research specialist Ohio State U. and Ohio Agr. Expt. Sta., 1937-39; asso. in research Ohio Agr. Expt. Sta., 1939-44; asst. dir., sr. plant physiologist fed. expt. sta. U.S. Dept. Agr., Mayaguez, P.R., 1944-47; prof. horticulture, research specialist Rutgers U., New Brunswick, N.J., 1948-81, chmn. dept., 1948-66, Maurice A. Blake distinguished prof., 1966-81; adj. prof. U. Fla., Gainesville, 1981—. Publisher, co-author 9 horticulture books.; Contbr. numerous articles to profl. jours. Councilman, Milltown, N.J., 1953-56. Recipient Best Tchr. award Alpha Zeta, Rutgers U., 1980, award Nat. Peach Council, 1981, Disting. Service award to N.J. agr., 1982; recipient Internat. Dwarf Fruit Tree award, 1982. Fellow Am. Soc. Hort. Sci. (L.M. Ware Distinguished Teaching award in horticulture 1969); mem. N.J. Hort. Soc. (pres. 1971, Distinguished award 1976), Columbus Hort. Soc. (pres. 1941-43), N.J. Garden Club (hon., Distinguished award 1977). Discoverer relationship between nightshades (tobacco, tomato, potato, eggplant and peppers) and arthritis. Office: Fruit Crops Dept U Fla Gainesville FL 32611

CHILDRESS, ALICE, playwright; b. Charleston, S.C., Oct. 12, 1920. Student public schs. Joined, American Negro Theatre, Harlem, 1941; appeared in: On Strivers Row, 1940, Natural Man, 1941, Anna Lucasta, 1944, others; appeared: first play Florence, 1949; other plays include Trouble in Mind, 1955, Wedding Band, 1966, Wine in the Wilderness; TV, 1969, Mojo, 1971, String, 1969; plays and stories for children include Black Scenes, 1971, A Hero Ain't Nothin But a Sandwich, 1973, When the Rattlesnake Sounds, 1975, Let's Hear It for the Queen, 1976, Seal Island Song, 1979; playwright, scholar, Radcliffe Inst., 1966-68 (Recipient Obie award 1956), Radcliffe Inst. (Paul Robeson award), Radcliffe Inst. (Black Filmmakers Hall of Fame award 1977). Mem. PEN, Harlem Writers Guild, Dramatists Guild, Writers Guild Am.

CHILDRESS, GARY ALAN, diversified manufacturing company executive; b. Los Angeles, Feb. 28, 1934; s. Henry H. and Gladys (Holtberg) C.; m. Jacqueline Benton, June 22, 1963; children: Susannah, Richard, Elizabeth. B.A. in Econs., Stanford U., 1957; M.B.A. in Fin., U. So. Calif., 1962. Pres. Dart Industries, Los Angeles, 1963-76, dir.; sr. v.p., chief operating officer Nat. Can Corp., Chgo., 1977-79; chmn., pres., chief exec. officer Warner Co., Phila., 1979-81; chief exec. officer Gulf Resources, Houston, 1982; pres., chief operating officer The Scott Fetzer Co., Lakewood, Ohio, 1982—, dir.; dir. Anta Corp., Oklahoma City, O'Connor Engring., Costa Mesa, Calif. Mem. Sch. Bd., Madison, Conn., 1968-71; mem. fin. com. Blind Children's Ctr., Los Angeles, 1973-76. Served with U.S. Army, 1957-63. Republican. Office: The Scott Fetzer Company 14600 Detroit Ave Lakewood OH 44107

CHILDRESS, WILLIAM STEPHEN, mathematics educator; b. Houston, Oct. 5, 1934; s. Virgil and Doris C.; m. Brigitte Cormier, Sept. 1960 (div. 1970); children: Christine Carol, Jeffrey Robinson; m. 2d Diana Thomas, June 18, 1971; children: Lilian Isabelle, Lucy Elizabeth. B.S.E., Princeton U., 1956, M.S.E., 1958; Ph.D., Calif. Inst. Tech., 1961. Staff scientist Jet Propulsion Lab., Pasadena, Calif., 1961-64; vis. mem. Courant Inst., N.Y. U., N.Y.C., 1964-66, mem. faculty, 1966—. Author: Mechanics of Swimming and Flying, 1981. Guggenheim fellow, 1976. Mem. SIAM, Am. Math. Soc., Sigma Xi. Home: 94 Bank St New York NY 10014 Office: Courant Inst Math Scis 251 Mercer St New York NY 10012

CHILDS, BARTON, educator, physician; b. Chgo., Feb. 29, 1916; s. Robert William and Katherine Sayles (Barton) C.; m. Eloise L.B. MacKie, Mar. 29, 1950; children—Anne Lloyd, Lucy Barton. A.B., Williams Coll., 1938; M.D., Johns Hopkins, 1942. Successively intern, asst. resident, resident pediatrics Johns Hopkins Hosp., 1942-43, 46-48; research fellow Children's Hosp., Boston, 1948-49; Commonwealth Fund fellow Univ. Coll., London, Eng., 1952-53; mem. faculty Johns Hopkins Sch. Medicine, 1949—, prof. pediatrics, 1962—; Mem. NIH Cons. Coms., 1959-63, 63-67, 67-69, 70-74, 78—. Served to capt., M.C. AUS, 1943-46. John and Mary Markle scholar, 1953-58; Grover F. Powers Distinguished scholar, 1960-62; recipient Research Career award NIH, 1962, Meade Johnson award pediatrics, 1959. Mem. Am. Pediatric Soc., Soc. Pediatric Research, Am. Acad. Pediatrics, Am. Soc. Human Genetics, Genetics Soc. Am., Inst. Medicine, Am. Acad. Arts and Scis. Home: 1019 Winding Way Baltimore MD 21210

CHILDS, BREVARD SPRINGS, educator; b. Columbia, S.C., Sept. 2, 1923; s. Richard A. and Reaux (Jones) C.; m. Ann Taylor, Aug. 7, 1954; children—John, Catherine. B.A., U. Mich., 1946, M.A., 1948; B.D., Princeton, 1950; D.Theol., U. Basel, Switzerland, 1955. Ordained to ministry Presbyn. Ch., 1958; prof. O.T., Mission House Sem., Plymouth, Wis., 1954-58, Yale, New Haven, 1958—. Author: Myth and Reality in the Old Testament, 1960, Memory and Tradition in Israel, 1962, Isaiah and the Assyrian Crisis, 1967, Biblical Theology in Crisis, 1970, The Book of Exodus, 1974, Old Testament Books for Pastor and Teacher, 1977, Introduction to the Old Testament as Scripture, 1979. Served with AUS, 1943-45. Guggenheim fellow, 1963-64; Nat. Endowment for Humanities fellow, 1977-78; Fulbright-Hays fellow, 1981. Home: 508 Amity Rd Bethany CT 06525 Office: 409 Prospect St New Haven CT 06511

CHILDS, JAMES WILLIAM, lawyer, legal educator; b. Muncie, Ind., Sept. 20, 1935; s. Dexter William and Marcelle (Mericle) C.; m. Sally Johnston, June 9, 1978; children: Elizabeth, Anne, James William, Dylan Rhys, Karrin Aleen. Student, Denison U., 1953-55; A.B., U. Mich., 1957, J.D., 1960. Bar: Ohio bar 1960, Ind. bar 1980. Practiced in, Van Wert, Ohio, 1960—; pres. firm Childs Childs & Fortney Co. (L.P.A.), 1962-83; v.p. Wise Childs & Rice, L.P.A., 1983—; dir. Kennedy-Kuhn Inc., P.P.A. Inc.; adj. prof. Western Ohio br. Wright State U.; vis. prof. law U. Akron Sch. Law, 1983—; Mem. Starr Commonwealth Adv. Bd., 1962—, pres., 1970; mem. Van Wert County Hosp. Assn., 1963—. Cons. writer: Farm Jour. mag; co-author: Estate Planning Idea Book. Mem. Ohio Comprehensive Health Planning Adv. Council, 1976, chmn. environ. health com., 1976; Bd. dirs. Van Wert County Heart Assn. Mem. ABA, Ohio Bar Assn., Northwestern Ohio Bar Assn. (pres. 1976), Van Wert County Bar Assn. (pres. 1969-71), Van Wert C. of C. (pres. 1976). Republican. Methodist (lay leader 1966-70). Clubs: Kiwanian (pres. Van Wert 1968, lt. gov. div. 2 1972), Shriner.). Home: 12930 Williamsburg Ave NW Uniontown OH 44685 Office: C Blake McDowell Law Ctr U Akron Akron OH 44325 *It has been my goal to try to the very best of my ability over the years to raise the level of knowledge in the very important field of federal taxation as it applies to agricultural enterprises.*

CHILDS, JOHN FARNSWORTH, investment banker; b. N.Y.C., Nov. 24, 1909; s. Albert Ewing and Amelia (McGraw) C.; m. Mary Elizabeth Cardozo, Apr. 21, 1950; 1 dau., Susan Elizabeth. B.S., Trinity Coll., Hartford, Conn., 1931, M.S., 1932; M.B.A., Harvard, 1933; LL.B., Fordham U., 1946. Bar: N.Y. bar 1946. Analyst Dick & Merle-Smith, N.Y.C., 1935-40; sr. v.p., head corporate services div. Irving Trust Co., N.Y.C., 1941-74; v.p. Kidder-Peabody Inc., 1974—; Mem. tech. adv. com. on finance Fed. Power Commn., 1973-74. Author: Long-Term Financing, 1961, Profit Goals and Capital Management, 1968, Earnings Per Share and Management Decisions, 1971, Encyclopedia of Long Term Financing and Capital Management, 1976, Corporate Finance and Capital Management for the Chief Executive Officer and Directors, 1979; Contbr. articles to profl. publs. Past treas., trustee Lenox Sch.; bd. dirs. N.Y. Council on Econ. Edn. Served as lt. comdr. USNR, World War II. Mem. Am. Mgmt. Assn. (pres. council past dir.), Atomic-Indsl. Forum (past dir.), N.Y. Soc. Security Analysts. Clubs: Harvard Business School (past pres.); Pine Valley Golf (Clementin, N.J.)). Home: 15 Washington Pl New York NY 10003 Office: 10 Hanover Sq New York NY 10005

CHILDS, LUCINDA, choreographer; b. N.Y.C., June 26, 1940; d. Edward Patterson and Lucinda Eustis (Corcoran) C. B.A., Sarah Lawrence Coll., 1962. Choreographer, dancer, Judson Dance Theatre, N.Y.C., 1962-66; choreographer, dancer, artistic dir., Lucinda Childs Dance Co., N.Y.C., 1973—; choreographer, dancer: Einstein on the Beach, 1976, Dance, 1979; dancer I Was Sitting On My Patio This Guy Appeared I Thought I Was Hallucinating, 1977-78; choreographer: Mad Rush, 1981; actress: film 21:12 Piano Bar, 1981 (Recipient Village Voice Obie award for Einstein on the Beach 1977). Fellow Creative Artist Public Service Program, 1974-78, Guggenheim Found., 1979, Nat. Endowment Arts. Address: Performing Art Services Inc 463 West St New York NY 10014

CHILDS, MARQUIS WILLIAM, journalist; b. Clinton, Iowa, Mar. 17, 1903; s. William Henry and Lilian Malissa (Marquis) C.; m. Lue Prentiss, Aug. 26, 1926 (dec.); children: Prentiss, Malissa Elliott (dec.); m. Jane Neylan McBaine. A.B., U. Wis., 1923, Litt.D., 1966; A.M., U. Iowa, 1935, Litt.D., 1969; LL.D., Upsala Coll., 1943. With UPI, 1923, 25-26; with St. Louis Post-Dispatch, 1926-44, spl. corr., 1954-62, chief, 1962-68; columnist United Feature Syndicate, 1944-54; made 3 month tour battlefronts, 1943; lectr. Columbia Sch. Journalism; Eric W. Allen Meml. lectr. U. Oreg., 1950. Author: Sweden The Middle Way, 1936, They Hate Roosevelt, 1936, Washington Calling, 1937, This Is Democracy, 1938, This Is Your War, 1942, I Write From Washington, 1942, The Cabin, 1944; Editor, writer: evaluation new edit. Brooks Adams' America's Economic Supremacy, 1947, The Farmer Takes a Hand, 1952, Ethics in Business Society, (with Douglass Cater), 1954, The Ragged Edge, 1955, Eisenhower, Captive Hero, 1958, The Peacemakers, 1961, Taint of Innocence, 1967, Witness to Power, 1975, Sweden The Middle Way on Trial, 1980; Co-editor: Walter Lippmann and His Times, 1959, Mighty Mississippi: Biography of a River. Decorated Order of North Star, Sweden; Order of Merit Fed. Republic of Germany; Order of Aztec Eagle Mex.; recipient Sigma Delta Chi award for best Washington corr., 1944; award for journalism U. Mo.; Pulitzer prize for commentary, 1969. Mem. Kappa Sigma, Sigma Delta Chi. Clubs: Overseas Writers (pres. 1943-45); Century (N.Y.C.); Washington Press, Gridiron (pres. 1957), Metropolitan, Cosmos (Washington). Office: 1701 Pennsylvania Ave NW Washington DC 20036

CHILDS, MORRIS ELSMERE, mech. engr., educator; b. Yellville, Ark., Mar. 30, 1923; s. Ray Elsmere and Izella Mae (Henson) C.; m. Marian Elsa Tolbert, 1952; children—Robert Edward, Mary Evelynne, Ruth Esther, Amy Elsmere. Student, Murray State Sch. Agr., 1941-43; B.S.M.E., U. Okla., 1944; M.S.M.E., U. Ill., Urbana, 1947, Ph.D., 1956. Research asso. mech. engring. U. Ill., 1947-54; asst. prof. mech. engring. U. Wash., 1954-57, asso. prof., 1957-61, prof., 1961—, chmn. dept. mech. engring., 1973-80. Served with USNR, 1943-46. Research grantee. Fellow ASME; mem. Am. Soc. Engring. Edn., Am. Inst. Aeros. and Astronautics. Research, publs. on supersonic boundary layer flow. Office: Dept of Mech Engring FU-10 U of Wash Seattle WA 98195

CHILDS, ORLO ECKERSLEY, educator, petroleum geologist; b. Loa, Utah, Mar. 28, 1914; s. DeVere and Alice (Eckersley) C.; m. Elizabeth Catharine Swisher, Oct. 31, 1945; children: Bradley, Barry, Elizabeth. Student, Weber Coll., 1931-33; B.S., U. Utah, 1935, M.S., 1937; Ph.D., U. Mich., 1945. Instr. Weber Coll., 1937-42; geologist Sinclair Wyo. Oil Co., 1945-46; asst. prof. Colgate U., 1946-48, U. Wyo., 1948-49; dir. exploration projects Phillips Petroleum Co., Denver, 1949-62; marine geologist U.S. Geol. Survey, 1962-63; pres. Colo. Sch. Mines, Golden, 1963-70; v.p. research and spl. programs Tex. Tech U., Lubbock, 1970-74, Univ. prof., 1974-79, Univ. prof. emeritus, 1979—; adj. prof. geology Ariz. State Geol. Survey, 1979—; dir. Mining and Mineral Resources Research Inst. U. Ariz., 1980—; Mem. regional bd. White House Fellows; mem. Colo. Fulbright Com. Editor: Backbone of America, 1961; Author numerous articles in field. Fellow Geol. Soc. Am.; mem. Am. Inst. M.E., Intermountain Assn. Petroleum Geologists, Am. Assn. Petroleum Geologists (hon., pres. 1965), Am. Inst. Profl. Geologists, Rocky Mountain Assn. Geologists (hon.), Sigma Xi. Address: 7020 N Camino de Fray Marcos Tucson AZ 85718

CHILDS, THOMAS WARREN, co. dir.; b. Butler, Mo., Nov. 21, 1906; s. Edward Bruglar and Gertrude (Clay) C.; m. Isabel Lockward, Jan. 30, 1934; children—Thomas Warren, Henry Clay, William Arthur Purvis. B.S. in Engring. summa cum laude, Princeton, 1928; Rhodes scholar, Oxford, 1928-31, B.A., 1930, B.C.L., M.A., 1938; J.S.D., Yale, 1932. Bar: N.Y. State bar 1932. Practiced with Sullivan & Cromwell, N.Y.C., 1932-40, Paris, 1937-38; gen. counsel to Brit. Supply Council in N.Am.; and exec. asst. to minister resident in U.S., Washington, 1940-45; asso. Lazard Freres, N.Y.C., 1945-48; with Am. Metal Climax, Inc., N.Y.C., 1948-62, v.p., 1953-62, dir., 1961-62; chmn. Internat. Nickel Ltd. (formerly Internat. Nickel Co. (Mond) Ltd.), London, Eng., 1963-68; v.p. Internat Nickel Co. of Can., Ltd., 1963-68; pres. Inco Projects Ltd., 1969-71, chmn., 1971—; dir. Bank of N.T. Butterfield & Sons Ltd., Schroders (Bermuda) Ltd., Butterfield Executor & Trustee Co. Ltd., Aegis Indemnity Ltd., all Bermuda. Mem. council Ditchley Found., Eng., 1964-68; Served as gen. counsel for Brit. Govt. War Supply Orgn. in U.S. and; mem. Anglo-Am. Patent Com., 1940-45. Decorated comdr. Order Brit. Empire. Mem. Phi Beta Kappa. Republican. Episcopalian. Clubs: Royal Bermuda Yacht, Pilgrims; Brooks (London, Eng.). Home: Stancombe Paget Bermuda Office: PO Box 1560 Hamilton Bermuda

CHILDS, WYLIE JONES, metall. engr.; b. Columbia, S.C., Feb. 25, 1922; s. Richard Austin and Reaux (Jones) C.; m. dau., Rebecca Jones. B.Metall. Engring., Rensselaer Poly. Inst., 1943, M.Metall. Engring., 1945, Ph.D., 1948. Research metallurgist Mass. Inst. Tech., 1948-49; asso. prof., then prof., head dept. metall. engring. Lafayette Coll., 1949-57; mem. faculty Rensselaer Poly. Inst., 1957-70, prof. metall. engring., 1960-70; cons. to industry, 1948—; tech. rep. Duffers Assos., Inc., Troy, 1962-70; v.p. Reel Vortex, Inc., Troy, N.Y., 1968-72, pres., 1972-74; v.p. Air Cushion Vehicles, Inc., Troy, 1969-71; prin. engr., nuclear energy div. Gen. Electric Co., San Jose, Calif., 1976-80; project mgr. Electric Power Research Inst., 1980—. NSF fellow U. Birmingham, Eng., 1959. Mem. Sigma Xi, Tau Beta Pi, Phi Lambda Upsilon. Home: 10053 Long Oak Ln Cupertino CA 95014 Office: Electric Power Research Inst 3412 Hillview Ave Palo Alto CA 94303

CHILES, EDDIE, professional sports team executive, company executive. B.S. in Petroleum Engring., U. Okla. Founder, chmn. bd. Western Co. N. Am., Seagraves, Tex.; chmn. bd., pres., chief exec. officer Tex. Rangers Baseball Team, Arlington, Tex., 1980—. Office: Tex Rangers Arlington Stadium PO Box 1111 Arlington TX 76010 *

CHILES, LAWTON MAINOR, U.S. senator; b. Lakeland, Fla., Apr. 3, 1930; s. Lawton Mainor and Margaret (Patterson) C.; m. Rhea May Grafton, Jan. 27, 1951; children: Tandy M., Lawton Mainor III, Edward G., Rhea Gay. B.S., U. Fla., 1952; LL.B., 1955; LL.B. hon. degrees, Fla. So. Coll., Lakeland, 1971, Jacksonville U., 1971. Bar: Fla. bar 1955. Practiced in, Lakeland, 1955-70, U.S. senator from, Fla., 1971—; Mem. Fla. Ho. of Reps., 1958-66, Fla. Senate, 1966-70. Trustee U. Fla. Law Center, 1968—, Fla. So. Coll., 1971—, Eckerd Coll., St. Petersburg, Fla., 1971—. Served as 1st lt. AUS, 1952-54. Mem. Phi Delta Phi, Alpha Tau Omega. Presbyterian. Office: 250 Russell Senate Office Bldg Washington DC 20510 *

CHILINGARIAN, GEORGE VAROS, engineering educator; b. Tbilisi, Ga., July 22, 1929; s. Varos and Klavdia (Gorchakova) C.; m. Yelba Maria, June 12, 1953; children: Modesto George, Mark Steven, Eleandre Elizabeth. B.E. in Petroleum Engring., U. So. Calif., 1949, M.S., 1950, Ph.D. in Geology and Petroleum Engring., 1954; postgrad., Pepperdine U., 1976. Profl. geologist, Calif.; cert. Am. Assn. Petroleum Geologists. Prof. petroleum engring. U. So. Calif., Los Angeles. Contbr. articles to profl. jours.; author books in field. Fellow Geol. Soc. Am., Am. Chem. Soc.; mem. Soc. Petroleum Geologists of AIME, Am. Assn. Petroleum Geologists, Soc. Econ. Paleontologists and Mineralogists, AAUP, Am. Soc. Engring. Edn., Calif. Acad. Sci., N.Y. Acad. Sci., Sigma Xi, Phi Kappa Phi, Tau Beta Pi, Pi Epsilon Tau. Office: Univ So Calif Dept Petroleum Engring Los Angeles CA 90007 *

CHILLRUD, FRANKLIN CHESTER, JR., financial executive; b. Atlanta, June 20, 1930; s. Franklin C. and Ella (Gardner) C.; m. Tatiana Padwa Hunold, Jan. 26, 1963; 1 stepson, Michael S. Hunold; 1 dau., Joanna. B.A., Union Coll., Schenectady, 1954. Investment mgr. bond dept. Prudential Ins. Co. Am., 1954-65; v.p., dir. finance operations bowling products group AMF Inc., 1965-67, group exec. finance services group, 1967-70, v.p., treas., 1970-82; v.p. fin./ adminstrn. Advanced Computer Communications, Santa Barbara, Calif., 1983—. Home: 5680 Via Salerno Goleta CA 93117 Office: Advanced Computer Communications 720 Santa Barbara St Santa Barbara CA 93101

CHILLSON, CHARLES WHITE, aerospace engr.; b. Los Angeles, Mar. 12, 1910; s. Charles Foster and Mary Boone (White) C.; m. Rosa Grey deWaard, Oct. 23, 1944. B.S., Stanford, 1931; postgrad., Cal. Inst. Tech., 1931-35. Design, test, controllable pitch propellers Green Assos., Los Angeles, 1931-36; with propeller div. Curtiss Wright Corp., 1936-71, chief engr. in rocket dept., 1945-50, tech. dir., 1963-71; on leave to assist tech. monitoring mil. satellite program U.S. Dept. Def., Inst. Def. Analysis, Advanced Research Projects Agy., Washington, 1959-60; aerospace cons. engr., 1971—. Served as col. a/s Tech. Intelligence Corps USAAF, 1945. Fellow Am. Inst. Aeros. and Astronautics (nat. dir. Am. Rocket Soc. 1950-52, pres. 1952, dir. N.Y. sect. 1953-56, pres. 1955). Patentee propellers, multi-engine synchronizers, rocket engines, other aircraft components. Home: 15 Chase Dr Santa Barbara CA 93108 *It has been my good fortune to enjoy my vocation. For the most part, I would have done what I did without pay, if I could have afforded to do so. And the times made me feel wanted, a most effective incentive to endeavor.*

CHILMAN, CATHERINE EARLES STREET, educator; b. Cleve., Sept. 20, 1914; d. Elwood Vickers and Augusta (Jewitt) Street; m. C. William Chilman, Sept. 27, 1936 (dec. 1977); children: Margaret Chilman Carpenter, Jeanne Chilman Klovdahl, Catherine Chilman Brown. A.B., Oberlin Coll., 1935; M.A., U. Chgo., 1938; Ph.D., U. Syracuse, 1958. Caseworker United Charities Chgo., 1937-39, Family Services, Roanoke, Va., 1939-40; psychiat. cons. ARC, Syracuse, N.Y., 1943-44; tchr. dept. child devel., family relations Syracuse U., 1947-49, instr., 1949-57, asst. prof., 1957-61; sr. social worker N.Y. State Mental Health Research Unit, Syracuse, 1955-57; parent edn. specialist Children's Bur. HEW, Washington, 1961-64; research adminstr. U.S. Welfare Adminstrn., 1964-69; dean faculty Hood Coll., Frederick, Md., 1969-71; curriculum dir. Internat. Population Planning and Social Work Edn. Project, U. Mich., Ann Arbor, 1971-72; prof. Sch. Social Welfare, U. Wis., Milw., 1972—; pres. Nat. Groves Conf. on the Family, 1975-78; speaker, cons. on research, family life, public policy to univs., fed. govt. and profl. orgns. Asso. editor: Jour. of Marriage and the Family, 1963-69; Author: (with others) Mental Health Crises and the Nation's Children, Your Child: 6 to 12, Moving into Adolescence; author: Adolescent Sexuality in a Changing American Society, Growing Up Poor, Adolescent Childbearing; Contbr. articles to profl. jours. U.S. Office Edn. grantee, 1960-62; Wis. State grantee, 1973-75; Nat. Inst. Child Devel. grantee, 1976-77; recipient Hon. Alumni award Sch. Social Services Adminstrn., U. Chgo., 1978. Fellow Am. Psychol. Assn.; mem. Nat. Council on Family Relations (exec. com.), Council on Social Work Edn. (adv. bd.), Nat. Assn. Social Workers, Internat. Conf. on Social Welfare (exec. com. on U.S. com.). Home: 4424 N Fredrick Milwaukee WI 53211 *Although I have experienced many tragedies and hardships and have lived through tumultuous times, I am continuously surprised and grateful for the many blessings of my life: dear friends and family, the excitement of teaching and research, the marvels of aesthetic creations, and the beauty and wonder of our natural world.*

CHILSON, OLIN HATFIELD, U.S. judge; b. Pueblo, Colo., Nov. 22, 1903; s. Leonard and Annie (Mills) C.; m. Marian Cole, Aug. 18, 1929; 1 son, John Hatfield. LL.B., U. Colo., 1927. Bar: Colo. bar 1927. Practiced in, Greeley, Loveland and Denver, 1927-36, city atty., Estes Park, 1928-56, Loveland, 1931-36; dist. atty. 8th Jud. Dist. Colo., 1940-48; mem. firm Grant, Shafroth, Tell, Chilson & McHendrie, Denver, 1959-60; U.S. dist. judge Colo., Denver, 1960—; Mem. Colo. Bd. Law Examiners, 1951-54. Organizer, sec. 2Big Thompson Soil Conservation Dist., 1940-47; asst. sec. pub. land mgmt. Dept. Interior, 1956-57, under sec. interior, 1957- 58; dir. No. Colo. Water Conservancy Dist., 1951-55; legal cons. Colo. Water Conservation Bd., 1954-56; mem. Loveland Sch. Bd., 1945-55; Trustee Boettcher Found. Mem. ABA, Colo. Bar Assn. (past pres.), Larimer County Bar Assn. (past pres.), Alumni Assn. U. Colo. (past pres.), Phi Alpha Delta, Alpha Tau Omega. Methodist. Clubs: Mason, Rotarian., Denver Country. Home: 2101 S Garfield Ave Apt 424 Loveland CO 80537 Office: US Courthouse Denver CO 80202

CHILTON, ARTHUR BOUNDS, nuclear engineering educator; b. Montgomery, Ala., Sept. 22, 1918; s. Arthur Bounds and Fannylu (Wheeler) C.; m. Charlotte Ann Presler, Sept. 5, 1942; children: Stephen P., Sara D., Geoffrey P. B.S., U.S. Naval Acad., 1939; B.C.E., Rensselaer Poly. Inst., 1942, M.C.E., 1943; student, U.S. Naval Postgrad. Sch., 1949; M.S., Ohio State U., 1951, Ph.D., 1953. Commd. ensign U.S. Navy, 1939, advanced through grades to capt., 1958; dir. research Bur. Yards and Docks, 1957-59, dir. U.S. Naval Civil Engring. Lab., 1959-62, ret., 1962; mem. faculty U. Ill.-Urbana, 1962—, prof. civil and nuclear engring., 1965; asso. chmn. nuclear engring. program U. Ill., 1975-78, prof. emeritus, 1983—; cons. to govt. and industry, 1962—; mem. adv. com. CD, Nat. Acad. Sci.-Nat. Acad. Engring.-NRC, 1960-68, chmn. subcom. radiation shielding, 1965-68. Co-editor: Engineering Compendium on Radiation Shielding, 1968; contbr. articles to profl. jours. Mem. Nat. Council Radiation Protection, 1973—. Fellow Am. Nuclear Soc. (chmn. shielding div. 1968-69, dir. 1970-73); mem. Am. Phys. Soc., Health Physics Soc., Chi Epsilon, Tau Beta Pi, Sigma Pi Sigma. Home: 805 W Michigan Ave Urbana IL 61801

CHILTON, HORACE THOMAS, pipeline company executive; b. San Antonio, June 18, 1923; s. Horace Thomas and Lear Isabel (Word) C.; m. Betty Jane Gray, Oct. 18, 1947; children: Thomas G., William D. B.S. in Mech. Engring., U. Tex., 1947, B.A. in Bus. Adminstrn., 1947; grad., Advanced Mgmt. Program, Harvard U., 1958. Engr. Stanolind Pipe Line Co., Tulsa, 1947; div. chief engr. Service Pipe Line Co., Lubbock, 1950-52, supt. maintenance and constrn., 1956-60, asst. gen. mgr., 1960; mil. pipe line cons. U.S. Govt., Paris, 1955; mgr. products pipelines, lake tankers and barges Amoco Oil Co., Chgo., 1963-68; mgr. transp. ops., v.p. Amoco Pipeline, 1969-71, gen. mgr. transp., pres., chief exec. officer, 1971-74; pres., chief exec. officer Colonial Pipeline, Atlanta, 1974—. Mem. U. Tex. Engring. Advisory Found. Bd., 1977—. Served with USN, 1944-46. Mem. Assn. Oil Pipe Lines (mem. exec. com. 1973—, chmn. 1983—), Am. Petroleum Inst. (mem. gen. com. div. transp. 1971—, dir. 1975—), Nat. Petroleum Council, Transp. Assn. Am. (dir. 1975—), Beta Theta Pi. Presbyterian. Club: Cherokee Town and Country (Atlanta). Home: 8920 River Landing Way Atlanta GA 30338 Office: 3390 Peachtree Rd NE Atlanta GA 30326 also Box 18855 Atlanta GA 30326

CHILTON, ST. JOHN POINDEXTER, educator; b. Phila., Feb. 3, 1909; s. St. John P. and Helen Frances (McGloin) C.; m. Alice Pleasance Hunter, Mar. 2, 1935. B.S., La. State U., 1935, M.S., 1936; Ph.D., U. Minn., 1938. Agt. plant pathology U.S. Dept. Agr., 1938-40; faculty La. State U., 1940—, prof., 1948—, chmn. dept. botany and plant pathology, 1950-70; plant pathologist, head dept. plant pathology La. Agr. Expt. Sta., 1950-76; rep. div. biology and agr. NRC, 1952-57; pres., dir. LaPlace Enterprises, Inc.; pres., mgr. Esperanza Farms; cons. Nicaraque Sugar Estates, Ingenio San Antonio. Fellow AAAS; mem. Am. Phytopath. Soc. (ex-counselor), Internat. Soc. Sugarcane Technologists (vice chmn. 10th congress), Am. Soc. Sugarcane Technologists (past pres.), SAR (past pres. Phil Thomas chpt.), La. Acad. Sci. (past pres.), La. Geneal. and Hist. Soc. (pres. 1972-76), Hist. Assn. Central La. (pres. 1980-82), Am. Sugarcane

League U.S. (life). Club: Rotarian. Home: Route 2 Box 431 Boyce LA 71409

CHILTON, WILLIAM EDWIN, III, journalist; b. Kingston, N.Y., Nov. 26, 1921; s. William Edwin and Louise (Schoonmaker) C.; m. Elizabeth Easley Early, Apr. 5, 1952; 1 dau., Susan Carroll. B.A., Yale U., 1950; H.H.D. (hon.), W.Va. State Coll., 1966, Colby Coll., 1982. Promotion mgr. Charleston Gazette, 1952-55, asst. to pub., 1955-61, pub., 1961—; pres. Daily Gazette Co., 1961—; gen. mgr. Charleston Newspapers, 1962-68, chmn. bd., 1968—; Mem. W.Va. Ho. of Dels., 1952-60; 1st vis. prof. journalism W.Va. U., 1969; weekly guest commentator WCHS-TV, 1971-72, W. Va. Pub. Broadcasting Radio, 1982. Mem. W.Va. Centennial Commn., 1956-64; chmn. W.Va. Lincoln-Kennedy Meml. Commn.; mem. Kanawha County Library Bd., 1957-71, Kanawha County Parks and Recreation Commn., 1967-70, Citizens Adv. Commn. on W.Va. Legislature, 1967-70, Worth Bingham Meml. Found.; W.Va. dir. Crusade for Freedom, 1958; mem. exec. com. Com. of 100.; W.Va. del. at large Democratic Nat. Conv., 1960; mem. Dem. nat. platform com., 1964; Trustee Morris Harvey Coll.; mem. adv. bd. Handgun Control Affiliation. Served with USAAF, 1941-45; CBI. Recipient Elijah Lovejoy award, 1982. Mem. Chi Phi. Episcopalian. Clubs: Edgewood; Pink Sands (Harbour Island, Bahamas). Home: 1 Scott Rd Charleston WV 25314 also Chatterbox Harbour Island Bahamas Office: 1001 Virginia St E Charleston WV 25330

CHIMY, JEROME ISIDORE, bishop; b. Radway, Alta., Can., Mar. 12, 1919; s. Stanley and Anna (Yahnij) C. J.C.D., Lateran U., Rome, 1966. Ordained priest Ukrainian Cath. Ch., 1944; consecrated bishop, 1974; consultor to Provincial Superior, 1958-61; sec. to Superior Gen. of Basilian Order, Rome, 1961-63, consultor, 1963-74; rector St. Josaphat Ukrainian Pontifical Coll., Rome, 1966-74; former consultor to Sacred Congregation for Eastern Chs.; former commissario for matrimonial cases at Sacred Congregation for Doctrine of Faith; bishop of New Westminster, B.C., Can., 1974—; consultor to Pontifical Comm. for Revision Oriental Canon Law. Author: De Figura Luridica Archiepiscopi Maioris in Iure Canonico Orientali Vigenti, 1968. Home and office: 502 5th Ave New Westminister BC Canada V3L 1S2

CHIN, CAROLYN SUE, communications company executive; b. Washington, Nov. 28, 1947; d. Tin Wah and Donna Grace (Ho) C.; m. Gerald Bingham Sweeney, Sept. 18, 1976; 1 dau., Patricia Chin-Sweeney. B.S. in Mgmt. Engring, Rensselaer Poly. Inst., 1969; M.B.A., Harvard U., 1971. Buyer R.H. Macy's, N.Y.C., 1971-74, merchandise adminstr., 1974-75; mktg. mgr. AT&T, Morristown, N.J., 1976-78; spl. asst. to sec HUD, Washington, 1978-79; asst. to sec. and exec. sec. HEW, 1979-80; mgr. strategic planning AT&T, Basking Ridge, N.J., 1980-82; mgr. CIS consumer products Am. Bell, Parsipanny, N.J., 1983—; cons. Boston Model Cities, 1971, N.Y. State Emergency Fin. Control Bd., 1975; chmn. Task Force on Asian Women Bus. Owners, 1978; mem. South Orange Econ. Devel. Com., 1978. Mem. exec. bd. Pacific Asian Coalition, 1978; sec. bd. dirs. exec. com. Albert Einstein Peace Prize Found., Chgo., 1979—; bd. dirs. Ind. Sector, Washington, 1980—, Rensselaer Council, 1982-85. Named 1 of 10 Outstanding Young Working Women Glamour mag., 1977, Outstanding Young Woman for State of N.J. Outstanding Young Women Am., 1977; White House fellow, 1978-79; recipient Award of Excellence HUD, 1979; elected to YWCA Acad. of Women Achievers, 1980. Mem. Harvard Bus. Sch. Alumni Assn., Rensselaer Alumni Assn., Am. Mgmt. Assn., Orgn. Chinese-Ams., NOW, Alliance for Women, Common Cause. Home: Llewellyn Park West Orange NJ 07052 Office: 5 Woodlawn Rd Parsipanny NJ 07054

CHIN, GILBERT YUKYU, metallurgist; b. Kwangtung, China, Sept. 21, 1934; s. George Shee Ng and Liawah (Gee) C.;; s. George Shee Ng (father Am. citizen) and C.; m. Ginie Wong, June 26, 1960; children—Patrick Ken, Michael Philip, Grace Fay, Karen Jean. S.B., MIT, 1959, Sc.D., 1963. Mem. tech. staff Bell Telephone Labs, Murray Hill, N.J., 1962—, head phys. metallurgy and crystal growth research dept., 1973-75, head phys. metallurgy and ceramics research and devel. dept., 1975—. Author. Recipient Achievement award Chinese Inst. Engrs. of U.S.A., 1980, 83. Fellow Inst. Metall. Engrs. (Mathewson Gold medal 1974); mem. Am. Soc. Metals, Nat. Acad. Engring., Metall. Soc. Am., Am. Ceramics Soc., Magnetics Soc. of IEEE, N.Y. Acad. Scis., AAAS, Sigma Xi, Tau Beta Pi, Phi Lambda Upsilon. Episcopalian. Patentee in field. Office: Bell Telephone Labs Mountain Ave Murray Hill NJ 07974

CHINARD, FRANCIS PIERRE, physician, physiologist; b. Berkeley, Calif., June 30, 1918; s. Gilbert and Emma (Blanchard) C.; m. Josephine L. Wise, June 23, 1943; children: Suzanne F., Jeanne M., Marc F. A.B., U. Calif., Berkeley, 1937; M.D., Johns Hopkins U., 1941. Intern, jr. asst. resident in medicine Presbyn. Hosp., N.Y.C., 1941-42; asst. physician Hosp. Rockefeller Inst., N.Y.C., 1945-49, NRC fellow, 1945-46; Markle scholar Johns Hopkins Sch. Medicine, Balt., 1949-54; instr. to asso. prof. medicine and physiol. chemistry, 1949-63; asst. prof. medicine U. Md., 1954-62, asso. prof., 1962-63; prof. exptl. medicine McGill U., 1963-64; prof. medicine N.Y. U., 1964-68, adj. prof., 1968-70; career scientist N.Y.C. Health Research Council, 1964-68; prof. medicine, chmn. dept. Coll. Medicine and Dentistry N.J., N.J. Med. Sch., Newark, 1968-75, prof. exptl. medicine, 1975-77, prof. research medicine, 1977—, prof. physiology, 1978—; physician-in-chief Balt. City Hosp., 1962-63; physician Johns Hopkins Hosp., 1956-63; dep. dir. McGill U. Med. Clinic, Montreal Gen. Hosp., 1963-64; acting physician-in-chief Goldwater Meml. Hosp., N.Y.C., 1965-67; dir. med. service Martland Hosp., Newark, 1970-71; cons. physician VA Hosp., East Orange, N.J., 1971-79; mem. staff Balt. City Hosps., 1953-63; cons. in field. Author: (With J.W. Bauman Jr.) Renal Function, 1975; editorial com.: Jour. Clin. Investigation, 1954-59, Jour. Applied Physiology, 1959-65, Am. Jour. Physiology, 1959-65, Circulation Research, 1967-72, Microvascular Research, 1981; contbr. articles on indicator-dilution techniques, membrane permeability and transport, pulmonary and renal function to med. jours. Mem. profl. adv. com. Martha's Vineyard Guidance Center, 1968—; mem. pulmonary disease adv. com. Nat. Heart and Lung Inst., 1971-75, chmn., 1974-75, mem. bd. sci. counselors, 1976-80, chmn., 1978-80. Served to maj. M.C. USAAF, 1942-45. Decorated Legion of Merit. Fellow A.C.P., N.Y. Acad. Scis., AAAS; mem. Am. Chem. Soc., Am. Soc. Biol. Chemists, Am., Canadian socs. clin. investigation, Harvey Soc., Interurban Clin. Club, Soc. Exptl. Biology and Medicine, Assn. Am. Physicians, Am. Physiol. Soc., Peripatetic Soc., Acad. Medicine N.J. (trustee 1972-78), Am. Heart Assn. (research com. N.J. affiliate 1975-81), Microcirculatory Soc. (Landis award), Am. Thoracic Soc., Soc. Scholars (Johns Hopkins), Sigma Xi, Alpha Omega Alpha. Democrat. Club: Century Assn. (N.Y.C.). Home: 40 Warren Pl Montclair NJ 07042 Office: NJ Med Sch 100 Bergen St Newark NJ 07103

CHING, FRANCIS F. T., horticulturist; b. Honolulu, May 30, 1930; s. Akui C. and Ruth C.; m. Elaine Young., Dec. 27, 1958; children—Byron Alan, Daryl Lane. B.S., Mich. State U., 1951, M.S., 1956. Mem. staff Los Angeles State and County Arboretum, 1956-70, supt., 1967-70; dir. Los Angeles County Dept. Arboreta and Bot. Gardens, 1970—; Mem. U.S. Nat. Arboretum Adv. Council. Mem. sci. adv. council Calif. Poly. State U.; panelist Sunset Mag. and Book Co. Served with USAR, 1953-55. Mem. Am. Assn. Bot. Gardens and Arboreta (pres. 1979-81), Am. Hort. Soc., Am. Soc. Hort. Scis., Zool. Soc. San Diego, Los Angeles Beautiful. Clubs: Men's Garden (Los Angeles); Arcadia Rotary. Home: 821 St John Pl Claremont CA 91711 Office: 301 N Baldwin Ave Arcadia CA 91006 *The Arboretum is not all trees and if it were, there would be little reason for its existence. People and trees go together—they are enmeshed in cobwebs of togetherness and as history tells us, any time man misuses trees and plants as one of his natural resources, he pays for it in many different ways and for a long time.*

CHINN, HERMAN ISAAC, biochemist; b. Connellsville, Pa., Apr. 8, 1913; s. Alex and Anna (Blumberg) C.; m. Rowena Carter, July 22, 1945; children: Susan, Stephen, Nancy. B.S., Pa. State Coll., 1934; M.S., Northwestern U., 1935, Ph.D., 1938. Instr. Med. Sch. Northwestern U., 1938-42; prin. chemist Fla. Bd. Health, 1946-47; chief dept. pharmacology Sch. Aviation Medicine, 1947-55; sci. liaison officer Office Naval Research, London, 1955-57; chief biol. scis. Air Force Office Sci. Research, 1957-60; dep. sci. attache Am. embassy, Bonn, Germany, 1960-63; sci. officer Office Internat. Sci. Affairs, State Dept., Washington, 1963-65; sci. attache Am. embassy, Tehran, Iran, 1965-67; sci. officer State Dept., 1967-71; sci. attache Am. embassy, Stockholm, Sweden, 1971-73, Tel Aviv, 1973-75; sr. scientist Fedn. Am. Socs. for Exptl. Biology, 1976-81. Served to maj. AUS, 1942-46; col. USAF Res. Recipient Sir Henry Wellcome award; Dist. Civilian award USAF; Commendation medal U.S. Army; Superior Honor award Dept. State. Mem. Am. Soc. Pharmacology, Biochem. Soc., Am. Physiol. Soc., Am. Chem. Soc., AAAS, Soc. Exptl. Biology and Medicine, Sigma Xi. Home: Route 3 Box 7380 Waterford TX 76086

CHINN, ROBERT CARSON, computer company executive, lawyer; b. Biloxi, Miss., July 30, 1916; s. Roy and Lula (Carson) C.; m. Twila Thompson, Jan. 1, 1944 (div. 1955); children: Robert Carson, Bennett Thompson; m. Eleanor Wyatt Walker, Aug. 31, 1957; children: Elizabeth Wyatt, Meredith Walker. B.A., La. State U., 1939, J.D., 1942. Bar: La. 1942; cert. mfg. engr. Labor atty. Ford Motor Co., Dearborn, Mich., 1946-48, staff exec., Atlanta, 1948-58, mgr. assembly ops., various locations, 1959-68; v.p. mfg. and ops. Control Data Corp., Mpls., 1969-73, sr. v.p., group exec., 1974-75, sr. v.p., asst. to chief exec. officer, 1976-83; pres. Control Data of Caribbean Basin, 1984—; chmn. bd. Control Data Netherlands B.V., Rijswijk, 1978—, Elbit Computers Ltd., Haifa, Israel, 1973-81; chmn. exec. com. Jamaica Opportunity for Bus. Success, Kingston, 1981—; dir. Elron Electronic Industries, Ltd., Haifa, Fibronics Internat. Trustee Am. Farmland Trust, Washington, 1982—. Served to maj. U.S. Army, 1942-46. Mem. ABA, La. Bar Assn., Am. Soc. Mfg. Engrs (cert engr.), Soc. Automotive Engrs., Engring. Soc. Detroit, St. Paul Area C. of C. (chmn., pres. 1972-73), U.S.-Israel C. of C. (bd. dirs. N.Y.C. 1979—). Presbyterian. Clubs: Minnesota, Baton Rouge Country. Lodges: Masons; Shriners. Home: 1645 Applewood Rd Baton Rouge LA 70808 Office: Control Data Corp 8100 34th Ave S Minneapolis MN 55440

CHINNI, CHARLES ROSS, retail executive; b. Hackensack, N.J., Feb. 1, 1944; s. Carl A. and Grace C.; m. Joan Scandone, Sept. 4, 1966; children: Colleen, Carey. B.A., Rutgers U., 1966; M.B.A., 1971. Sales mgr., asst. buyer Bamberger's, Newark, 1966-69, buyer, 1969-72, mdse. mgr., Paramus, 1972-73, store mgr., Cherry Hill, 1973-74, v.p. mdse. adminstr. home furnishings, 1974-75, sr. v.p., Newark, 1975-80, sr. v.p., dir. mdse. home store and childrens, lingerie and cosmetics, 1980—. Trustee City Hope Pilot Med. Center. Recipient Spirit of Life award City of Hope, 1979. Roman Catholic. Office: 131 Market St Newark NJ 07101

CHINNI, PETER ANTHONY, artist; b. Mt. Kisco, N.Y., Mar. 21, 1928; s. Antonio and Carmella Catherine (Lampo) C.; m. Elisabeth Angela Cott, Aug. 17, 1970; children—Christine Elizabeth, Megan Margaret. Student, Art Students League N.Y., 1947-49, Accademia di Belle Arti, Rome, 1949-50. One-man shows include, Albert Loeb Gallery, N.Y.C., 1966, Loeb-Krugier Gallery, N.Y.C., 1969, A. Monett Gallery, Brussels, 1976, Gallery Bouma, Amsterdam, group exhbns. include, Whitney Mus., N.Y.C., 1962, 63, 64, 65, 75, Carnegie Internat., Pitts., 1964-65, Biennale di Roma, 1969; represented in permanent collections, Whitney Mus., New Orleans Fine Arts Mus., Nat. Gallery Art, City Art Mus., Colo., M.I.T., Beeckestijn (Netherlands) Mus., Denver Art Mus., Rockefeller collection. Served with U.S. Army, 1951-53. Mem. N.Y. Sculptors Guild, Artists Equity.

CHINOY, HELEN KRICH, theater historian; b. Newark, Sept. 25, 1922; d. Benjamin and Anne (Kalen) Krich; m. Ely Chinoy, June 6, 1948 (dec.); children: Michael, Claire Nicole. B.A., NYU, 1943, M.A., 1945; certificate in Elizabethan drama, U. Birmingham, Eng., 1947; Ph.D., Columbia U., 1963. Mem. faculty English dept. N.Y. U., 1944-45, Queens Coll., 1945, 50, Rutgers U., Newark Coll., 1946-48; mem. faculty English dept. Smith Coll., Northampton, Mass., 1952-55, dept. theater, 1956-60, prof. theater, 1965—; lectr. colls., cultural instns. Author: (with Toby Cole) Actors on Acting, 1949, Directors on Directing, 1953, Reunion: A Self Portrait of the Group Theatre, 1977, (with Linda Walsh Jenkins) Women in American Theatre, 1981; contbr. chpts. to books, articles to profl. jours., program for ednl. TV.; assoc. editor: Theatre Jour., 1975—. AAUW fellow, 1962-63; NEH fellow, 1979-80. Fellow Am. Theatre Assn. (research commn. 1977—); mem. Am. Soc. Theatre Research (exec. com. 1972—, program chmn. 1973-74, chmn. research com., Am. Council Learned Socs. rep. 1975), Nat. Theatre Conf., League Women Voters, AAUW. Home: 230 Crescent St Northampton MA 01060 Office: Smith Coll Center for Performing Arts Northampton MA 01060

CHIOGIOJI, MELVIN HIROAKI, government official; b. Hiroshima, Japan, Aug. 21, 1939; came to U.S., 1939; s. Yutaka and Harumi (Yamasaki) C.; m. Eleanor Nobuko Oura, June 4, 1960; children: Wendy A., Alan K. B.S. in Elec. Engring., Purdue U., 1961; M.B.A., U. Hawaii, 1968; D.Bus. Adminstrn., George Washington U., 1972. Registered profl. engr., Hawaii. Head weapons gen. component div. Quality Evaluation Lab., Oahu, Hawaii, 1965-69; dir. weapons evaluation and engring. div. Naval Ordinance Systems Command, Washington, 1969-73; dir. Office Indsl. Analysis Fed. Energy Adminstrn., Washington, 1973-75; asst. dir., div. bldg. and community systems Dept. Energy, Washington, 1975-79, dir. fed. program div., 1980—, dep. asst. sec. state and local assistance program, 1980—; prof. mgmt. sci. George Washington U., 1972—. Author: Industrial Energy Conservation, 1979, Energy Conservation in Commercial and Residental Buildings, 1982; contbr. articles to profl. jours. Mem. Md. State Adv. Com. on Civil Rights, 1976—, Nat. Naval Res. Policy Bd., 1977—; vestryman Grace Episcopal Ch., Silver Spring, Md., 1982—. Served with USN, 1961-65. Decorated Navy Commendation medal. Mem. IEEE (sr.), Nat. Soc. Profl. Engrs., Acad. Mgmt., Naval Res. Assn., Assn. for Sci., Tech. and Innovation (pres. 1979-81), Soc. Am. Mil. Engrs., Armed Forces Mgmt. Assn., Purdue U. Alumni Assn. Home: 15113 Middlegate Rd Silver Springs MD 20904 Office: 1000 Independence Ave NW Washington DC 20585

CHIOKE, CHRISTOPHER EKEMEZIE, marketing company executive; b. Enugu, Nigeria, Dec. 25, 1941; came to U.S., 1968, naturalized, 1975; m. Felixberta M. Chioke; children: Michael A., Faye U. B.S. in Econs., U. London, 1965; MA.A in History, Yeshiva U., 1971; Ph.D., Southeastern U., Greenville, S.C., 1975; postgrad., Harvard U. Sch. Bus., 1979. Dept. mgr. Lloyds & Scottish Bankers, London, 1964-67; ins. underwriter London & Overseas Ins. Co., 1967-68; sr. cost acct. Automatic Data Processing Co., Clifton, N.J., 1968-69; fin. and credit officer Fgn. Credit Ins. Assn., N.Y.C., 1969-71; chmn. bd., chief exec. officer Chioke Internat. Corp., N.Y.C., 1971—; dir. One America Ins. Co., Inc., Elmwood Tool & Machine Co. Inc., Hartford, Conn. Bd. dirs. Deux Youth Found., N.Y.C., 1978—; mem. U.S. Senatorial Bus. Adv. Bd.; co-founder Republican Presdl. Task Force. Recipient cert. recognition Black Enterprise mag., 1974,75,76,77,78,79,80,81, citation for bus. and community service Pres. Carter, 1978. Mem. Brit.-Am. C. of C., UN Assn., U.S.-Arab C. of C., N.Y. C. of C. and Industry. Republican. Roman Catholic. Home: 3001 Henry Hudson Pkwy Riverdale NY 10463 Office: Chioke Internat Corp 200 Park Ave New York NY 10166

CHIOU, GEORGE CHUNG-YIH, pharmacologist, educator; b. Taoyuan, Taiwan, July 11, 1934; came to U.S., 1964, naturalized, 1973; s. Chang and Mei (Wei) C.; m. Tricia Ten-Sian Cheng, Sept. 23, 1961; children: Linda Y., Faye Y. B.S. in Pharmacy, Nat. Taiwan U., 1957, M.S. in Pharmacology, 1960; Ph.D., Vanderbilt U., 1967. Instr. pharmacology China Med. Coll., Taiwan, 1962-64; research assoc. Vanderbilt U., 1967-68, U. Iowa, 1968-69; from asst. prof. to prof. pharmacology and therapeutics U. Fla., Gainesville, 1969-78; prof. pharmacology, head dept. med. pharmacology and toxicology Tex. A&M U., College Station, 1978—; vis. scientist NIH, 1975—; cons. in field. Author articles, revs. in field. Served as 2d lt. Chinese Air Force, 1961-62. Recipient Health Scis. Advancement award NIH, 1967, U. Fla. Faculty Devel. award, 1975, Disting. Achievement award Tex. A&M U., 1984; Mead Johson & Co. fellow, 1964-67; Pfizer scholar, 1955; grantee NIH, Am. Cancer Soc., Cooper Vision Labs., Merck, Sharp & Dohme, Merrell-Dow Pharm. Inc. Mem. Am. Soc. Pharmacology and Exptl. Therapeutics, Soc. Exptl. Biology and Medicine, N.Y. Acad. Scis., Assn. Research Vision and Ophthalmology, Assn. Med. Sch. Pharmacology, Sigma Xi. Republican. Buddhist. Office: Dept Med Pharmacology Tex A&M U Coll Medicine College Station TX 77843 *Life can last longer by utilizing time more efficiently and life can last forever by sacrificing it for the right cause.*

CHIPMAN, GORDON LEIGH, JR., government executive; b. Newport News, Va., May 12, 1942; s. Gordon L. and Arta (Leon) C.; m. Geraldine J. Frankhauser, Dec. 3, 1965. B.S.E.E., U. Nebr., 1965. Resident engr. Westinghouse Electric Corp., Pitts., 1970-72; sect. leader U.S. Nuclear Regulatory Commn., Washington, 1972-79; tech. cons. U.S. Ho. of Reps., Washington, 1979-81; dep. asst. sec. for breeder reactor programs U.S. Dept. Energy, Washington, 1981—. Served to lt. USN, 1965-70. Recipient Nat. Def. Service medal spl. achievement award U.S. Nuclear Regulatory Comm., 1979. Mem. Am. Nuclear Soc., Scientists and Engrs. for Secure Energy. Republican. Home: 6953 B Linganore Rd Frederick MD 21701 Office: US Dept of Energy Dep Asst Sec for Breeder Reactor Programs NE-50 Washington DC 20545

CHIPMAN, JOHN SOMERSET, economist, educator; b. Montreal, P.Q., Can., June 28, 1926; s. Warwick Fielding and Mary Somerset (Aikins) C.; m. Margaret Ann Ellefson, June 24, 1960; children: Thomas Noel, Timothy Warwick. Student, Universidad de Chile, Santiago, 1943-44; B.A., McGill U., Montreal, 1947, M.A., 1948; Ph.D., Johns Hopkins U., 1951; postdoctoral, U. Chgo., 1950-51. Asst. prof. econs. Harvard U., Cambridge, Mass., 1951-55; asso. prof. econs. U. Minn., Mpls., 1955-60, prof., 1961-81, Regents' prof., 1981—; fellow Center for Advanced Study in Behavioral Scis., Stanford, Calif., 1972-73; Guggenheim fellow, 1980-81, vis. prof. econs. various univs. Author: The Theory of Intersectoral Money Flows and Income Formation, 1951; editor: (with others) Preferences, Utility, and Demand, 1971, (with C.P. Kindleberger) Flexible Exchange Rates and the Balance of Payments, 1980; co-editor: Jour. of Internat. Econs, 1970-76; editor, 1977-82; asso. editor: Econometrica, 1956-69, Canadian Jour. Stats, 1980—. Recipient James Murray Luck award Nat. Acad. Scis., 1981. Fellow Econometric Soc. (council 1971-76, 81-83), Am. Statis. Assn., Am. Acad. Arts and Scis.; mem. Am. Econ. Assn., Inst. Math. Stats., Can. Econ. Assn., Royal Econ. Soc. Office: Dept Econs 1122 Mgmt and Econs Bldg U Minn 271 19th Ave S Minneapolis MN 55455

CHIRIAEFF, LUDMILLA GORNY, ballet dancer, choreographer; b. Riga, Latvia, Jan. 10, 1924; s. Alexandre and Catherine (Abrahmoff-Radziwill) Gorny; m. Uriel Luft, Aug. 9, 1962; children—Ludmilla, Catherine; children from previous marriage—Anatasie, Avde, Glebe. Grad., Russian German High Sch., Berlin. Founder Les Ballets Chiaeff, Montreal, Que., Can., 1958—; founder, dir. L'Academie and l'Ecole Superieure des Grands Ballets Canadiens. Made debut with, Ballets Russes, 1936; soloist, Berlin Opera Ballet, 1939-41; prima ballerina, choreographer, Mcpl. Theater Lausanne, Switzerland, 1945-47. Recipient award for best prodn. of ballets on TV in Montreal Can. Broadcasting Co., 1955; Can. Montreal Ballet Assn. award, 1957; Centennial medal, 1967; medal Order Can., 1969; Parchemin Honorifique de l'Accord, 1969; Concert Soc. award, 1970. Mem. Union des Artistes, Can. Actors Equity Assn. Address: Academie des Grands Ballet Canadiens 5010 Coolbrook St Montreal PQ H3X 2K9 Canada

CHIROVSKY, NICHOLAS L., economics educator, author; b. North Ukraine, Aug. 5, 1919; came to U.S., 1949, naturalized, 1955; s. Nicholas and Zenobia (Zarycky) Freishyn;; adopted son Leonid C. and; m. Iwanna Smishkewych, Sept. 21, 1947; children: Leo, George, Andrew, John. J.S.D., M.A., U. Graz, Austria; D.Pol.Econ., Ukranian Free U. Instr. Ukranian Grad. Sch. Econs., Munich, Germany, 1947-49; faculty Seton Hall U., South Orange, N.J., 1949—, prof. econs., 1955—, chmn. dept., 1963-74, chmn., 1952-62; adj. prof. Ukrainian Cath. U., Rome. Author: The Economic Factors in the Growth of Russia, 1957, Old Ukraine, 1963, The Ukrainian Economy, 1965, An Introduction to Russian History, 1967, Philosophy in Economic Thought, 1972, A History of the Russian Empire, Vol. I, 1973, (with others) Ukraine and the European Turmoil, 1973; co-Author: Philosophical Foundations of Economic Doctrines, 1977, 3d edit., 1981; Author: An Introduction to Ukrainian History, Vol. I, 1981, Vol. II, 1983; editor: On the Historical Beginnings of Slavic Eastern Europe, 1976; contbr. numerous articles to profl. jours. Mem. Shevchenko Sci. Soc. (sec.-gen. 1974-80). Home: 7 Madison Ave Maplewood NJ 07040 Office: Seton Hall U South Orange NJ 07079 *Confidence in God, hard work, responsibility before pleasure, respect for moral values tested by centuries and rooted in Christianity.*

CHISHOLM, DONALD ALEXANDER, telecommunications communications executive; b. Toronto, Ont., Can., May 7, 1927; s. Douglas Alexander and Daisy Pretoria (Smith) C.; m. Marilyn Bayliss, May 16, 1953; children—Leslie Megan, Christopher Andrew. B.S. in Engring. Physics, U. Toronto, 1949, M.A. in Physics, 1950, Ph.D., 1952; D. Engring. (Hon.), U. Waterloo, 1979; D.Sci. (hon.), U. Toronto, 1980, U. Quebec, 1983. Dir. Bell Telephone Labs., Murray Hill, N.J., 1953-68; mng. dir. Bellcomm, Inc., Washington, 1968-69; v.p. research and devel. No. Electric Ltd., Ottawa, Ont., 1969-70; pres. Bell No. Research Co., Ottawa, Ont., 1971-76; exec. v.p. tech. No. Telecom Ltd., Mississauga, Ont., 1976-81, pres. innovation and devel., 1981—. Chmn. bd. BNR Ltd.; mem. Can. Sci. Council.; v.p. Ont. Research Found. Fellow Rejerson Poly. Inst. Fellow IEEE. Clubs:

Country of Ottawa; Mt. Royal (Montreal); Mississauga Golf and Country. Home: 1523 Knareswood Dr Mississauga ON Canada

CHISHOLM, LESLIE LEE, educator; b. Cairo, Ill., Dec. 6, 1900; s. William Eli and Minnie (Edwards) C.; m. Lila Cates, Aug. 27, 1927 (div. Nov. 1956); children: Leslie Lee, George; m. Neva Joy, Aug. 3, 1963; 1 dau., Sheila Jo. A.B., So. Ill. State U., 1929; A.M., U. Chgo., 1932; Ph.D., Columbia, 1935. Pub. sch. prin., supt., Ill., 1919-31; asst. prof. edn. Wash. State U., 1935-36, asso. prof., 1936-45, acting dean, 1942-43, acting dir. summer session, 1943-45; mem. summer staff U. Mich., 1941, U. Calif., 1948-49, U. Tex., 1952, U. Wash., 1958; prof. edn. U. Nebr., Lincoln, 1945-69, prof. emeritus, 1969—; asst. dean edn., 1953-58, acting chmn. ednl. adminstrn. dept., 1967-68; vis. prof. Tex. A. and I. U., 1970-71; Coordinator Midwest Adminstrn. Center, U. Chgo., 1952-55; co-organizer, mem. Nat. Commn. on Sch. Reorgn., 1947-50; mem. White House Conf. on Edn., 1944 (chmn. sch. finances sect); adviser Nat. Citizens Commn. for Pub. Sch., 1948-54; cons. state edn. groups, legislatures. Author: The Economic Ability of the States to Finance Public Schools, 1936, The Shifting of Federal Taxes and Its Implications for the Public Schools, 1939, Guiding Youth in the Modern Secondary School, 1945, 50, The Work of the Modern High School, 1953, The School District Reorganization Program, 1957, (with Reeves and Dawson) Your School District, 1948, (with Johns and Morphet) Problems and Issues in Public School Finance, 1952; also numerous bulls., articles, chpts. in books. Mem. NEA, Am. Ednl. Research Assn. (recipient Annual award 1941), AAUP (pres. Wash. State U. chpt. 1944-45), Am. Assn. Sch. Adminstrs., Phi Kappa Phi (pres. Wash. State U. chpt. 1943-44), Phi Delta Kappa. Home: 14501 Winter Dr Lutz FL 33549

CHISHOLM, RICHARD LEROY, food company executive; b. Great Falls, Mont., Mar. 13, 1932; s. Joseph Francis and Genevieve Lena (Allum) C.; m. Marilyn Ruth Wadsworth, Apr. 3, 1955; children: Linda Marie Chisholm Wiley, David Richard, Dean Daniel. B.A., Coll. of Great Falls, 1954; postgrad., La Salle Extension U., 1954-56, Harvard U. Bus. Sch., 1978. Gen. mgr. BeaTRICE Foods, Missoula, Mont., 1963-71; group pres. Beatrice Foods, Honolulu, 1971-74, Denver, 1974-81, regional pres., Chgo., 1981—, corp. v.p., div. pres., sr. v.p., 1983—. Coach Little League Baseball, Denver; bd. dirs. St. Patrick's Hosp., Missoula, Jr. Achievement, Missoula, 1965-69, Honolulu council Boy Scouts, Oahu Land Devel., Honolulu. Recipient Boss of Yr. award Missoula Credit and Profl. Women Internat., 1967. Mem. Milk Industry Found. (dir. 1982), United Dairy Industries Assn (dir. 1982—), Missoula Shippers Assn. (co-founder), Missoula C. of C. (v.p.), Mont. Taxpayers Assn. Republican. Baptist. Clubs: Waialae Golf and Country; Pacific (Honolulu); Missoula Country; Valley Country, Brown Palace (Denver); Monroe (Chgo.); U. Mont. Century (pres., treas. Missoula); Toastmasters Internat. (pres., treas. Great Falls). Lodge: Rotary. Office: Beatrice Foods Co 2 N La Salle St Chicago IL 60602

CHISHOLM, SHIRLEY ANITA ST. HILL, congresswoman; b. Bklyn., Nov. 30, 1924; d. Charles Christopher and Ruby (Seale) St. Hill; m. Conrad Chisholm, Oct. 8, 1949 (div. Feb. 1977); m. Arthur Hardwick, Jr., Nov. 26, 1977. B.A. cum laude, Bklyn. Coll.; M.A., Columbia U.; LL.D. (hon.), Talladega (Ala.) Coll., Hampton (Va.) Inst., LaSalle Coll., Phila., U. Maine, Portland, Capital U., William Patterson Coll., Pratt Inst., Coppin State Coll., N.C. Coll., Kenyon Coll., Wilmington (Ohio) Coll., Acquinas Coll., Grand Rapids, Mich., Reed Coll., Portland, Oreg., U. Cin., Smith Coll., Northampton, Mass. Former nursery sch. tchr., dir. nursery sch.; ednl. cons. Div. Day Care, Bur. Child Welfare, N.Y.C.; mem. N.Y. State Assembly, 1964-68, 91st-97th congresses from 12th Dist. N.Y. Author: Unbought and Unbossed, 1970, The Good Fight, 1973. Hon. mem. bd. dirs. Cosmopolitan Young People's Symphony Orch., N.Y.C.; adv. bd. Fund. for Research and Edn. in Sickle Cell Disease; bd dirs. Bklyn. Home for Aged; mem. Central Bklyn. Coordinating Council; mem. nat. adv. council Inst. for Studies in Edn., Notre Dame; mem. adv. com. Washington Workshops; nat. bd. dirs. Ams. for Democratic Action; mem. adv. council NOW; hon. com. mem. United Negro Coll. Fund. Named Alumna of Year Bklyn. Coll. Alumni Bull., 1957; recipient award for outstanding work in field of child welfare Women's Council of Bklyn., 1957, Key Woman of Year award, 1963, Woman of Achievement award Key Women, Inc., 1965. Mem. Nat. Assn. Coll. Women, Bklyn. Coll. Alumni, LWV, Key Women, NAACP, Delta Sigma Theta. Methodist.

CHISHOLM, TOMMY, utlity company executive; b. Baldwyn, Miss., Apr. 14, 1941; s. Thomas Vandiver and Rubel (Duncan) C.; m. Janice McClanahan, June 20, 1964; children: Mark Alan (dec.), Andrea, Stephen Thomas, Patrick Ervin. B.S.C.E., Tenn. Tech. U., 1963; J.D., Samford U., 1969; M.B.A., Ga. State U., 1984. Bar: Ala. 1969; Registered profl. engr., Ala., Fla., Ga., Miss., Del., N.C., S.C., Tenn., La., W. Va., Va., Ky., P.R. Civil engr. TVA, Knoxville, Tenn., 1963-64; design engr. So. Co. Services, Birmingham, Ala., 1964-69, coordinator spl. projects, Atlanta, 1969-73, sec., house counsel, 1977-82, v.p., sec., house counsel, 1982—; asst. to pres. So. Co., Atlanta, 1973-74, sec., asst. treas., 1977—; mgr. adminstrv. services Gulf Power Co., Pensacola, Fla., 1975-77; sec. So. Electric Internat., Atlanta, 1981-82, v.p., sec., 1982—. Mem. Am. Bar Assn., State Bar Ala., ASCE, Am. Soc. Corp. Secs., Phi Alpha Delta. Club: Rotary. Home: 1611 Bryn Mawr Circle Marietta GA 30067 Office: PO Box 720071 Atlanta GA 30346

CHISHOLM, WILLIAM HARDENBERGH, consultant; b. N.Y.C., Apr. 24, 1917; s. Hugh J. and Sara Clark (Hardenbergh) C.; m. Alice Jensen, Nov. 7, 1942; children: Barbara Maud Chisholm Young, Margo Jensen. A.B., Yale, 1940. With Oxford Paper Co., N.Y.C., 1940-71, asst. to pres., 1946-50, v.p., dir., 1950-56, pres., 1956-69, chmn., 1969-71; exec. v.p., dir. Ethyl Corp., 1967-71; pres., dir. Boardroom Consultants, Inc., 1975—; dir. Phelps Dodge Corp.; Dep. dir. pulp and paper div. NPA, Washington, 1951. Trustee, treas. W.T. Grant Found.; trustee Westminster Kennel Found.; v.p., trustee Episcopal Ch. Bldg. Fund; pres. Animal Med. Center, 1970-74. Clubs: Westminster Kennel (pres., gov.), Links, Sky, Blind Brook, Round Hill; Yale, Economic (N.Y.C.). Home: 118 Glenwood Dr Greenwich CT 06830 Office: 230 Park Ave New York NY 10169

CHITTICK, ELIZABETH LANCASTER, association executive, women's rights activist; b. Bangor, Pa., Nov. 11, 1918; d. Benjamin and Flora Mae (Mann) Lancaster. Student, Columbia U., 1944-45, N.Y. Inst. Fin., 1950-51, Hunter Coll., 1952-56, Upper Iowa U., Fayette, 1976. Adminstrv. asst. to comdg. officer and chief clk. U.S. Naval Air Syas., Seattle and Banana River, Fla., 1941-45; v.p., treas. W.A. Chittick & Co., Manila, 1945-52, real estate sales, La Jolla, Calif., 1949; registered rep. Bache & Co., N.Y.C., 1950-62, Shearson & Hamil, 1950-62; investment adviser, 1962-65; revenue officer IRS, N.Y.C., 1965-72; pres. Nat. Women's Party, Washington, 1971—, Woman's Party Corp., 1978—, Sewall-Belmont Restoration Fund Inc., 1976—; dir. Wexita Corp., N.Y.C.; bd. dirs. D.C. Commn. for Women, Nat. Council Women U.S., Pan Am. Liason Com. of Women's Orgns. Inc. Lectr., TV commentator on Equal Rights Amendment; author: Answers to Questions About the Equal Rights Amendment, 1973, 1976. Mem. Coalition for Women in Internat. Devel., Internat. Women's Yr. Continuing Com., 1978—, Women's Campaign Fund, Washington, 1975-80; mem. U.S. com. of cooperation to Inter-Am. Commn. of Women, OAS, 1974-80; del. U.S. World Conf. of Internat. Women's Yr., Mexico City, 1975; mem. women's history ctr. task force Am. Revolution Bicentennial Adminstrn., 1973-76; mem. adv. com. U.S. Ctr. for Internat. Women's Yr., 1973-76; chmn. UN Drive for war orphans and widows, Manila, 1949. Mem. Nat. Fedn. Bus. and Profl. Women's Clubs, Gen. Fedn. Women's Clubs. Clubs: Order Eastern Star; Women's Press (N.Y.C.); Am. Newswomen's; Nat. Press (Washington). Office: Nat Women's Party 144 Constitution Ave NE Washington DC 20002

CHITTIM, RICHARD LEIGH, mathematician, educator; b. Easthampton, Mass., Dec. 2, 1915; s. Harry and Lulu (Hodges) C.; m. Mary Elizabeth Young, July 22, 1949; children—David Bateman, Wendy, Nancy Hodges. A.B., Bowdoin Coll., 1941; postgrad., Princeton, 1941-42, U. London, 1961-62; B.A. (Rhodes scholar), Merton Coll., Oxford U., 1950, M.A., 1954. Faculty, chmn. math. Bowdoin Coll., Brunswick, Maine, 1942—, prof., 1963—, Wing prof. math., 1977—, clk. faculty, 1966—; dir., faculty NSF Summer and In-Service Insts., 1959—; Mathematician-programmer U.S. Geol. Survey, summers 1952-55, 57, IBM, summer, 1956. Troop committeeman Boy Scouts Am., 1952-53; campaign worker A.R.C. NSF sci. faculty fellow, 1961-62. Mem. Am. Math. Soc., Am. Assn. Rhodes Scholars, Assn. Tchrs. Math. in Maine, Nat. Council Tchrs. Math., Phi Beta Kappa, Theta Delta Chi. Episcopalian (past vestryman). Home: 11 Potter St Brunswick ME 04011 Office: Seth Adams Hall Bowdoin Coll Brunswick ME 04011

CHITTY, ARTHUR BENJAMIN, JR., educational consultant; b. Jacksonville, Fla., June 15, 1914; s. Arthur Benjamin and Hazel T. (Brown) C.; m. Elizabeth Nickinson, June 16, 1946; children: Arthur Benjamin III, John Abercrombie Merritt, Em Turner, Nathan Harsh Brown. B.A., U. of South, 1935; M.A., Tulane U., 1953; L.H.D., Canaan (N.H.) Coll., 1969; LL.D., Cuttington (West Africa) Coll., 1974. Vice pres., sales mgr. Chitty & Co., Jacksonville, 1935-45, chmn. bd., 1962-67; pres. Assn. Episcopal Colls., N.Y.C., 1965-70, 74-79; dir. pub. relations U. of South, 1946-65, 70-73, historiographer, 1954—; Am. coordinator Oxford scholar program Keble Coll., Eng., 1969—. Author: Reconstruction at Sewanee, 1954, Sewanee Sampler, 1978, Eli and Ruth Lilly, 1979, (with Moultrie Guerry) Men Who Made Sewanee, 1980; editor: Sewanee News, 1946-65, Ely: Too Black Too White, 1969; Contbr. articles to profl. jours.; Iconographer hist. windows, All Saints Chapel, Sewanee, 1957; dir.: documentary film Education in West Africa, 1974. Pres. Sewanee (Tenn.) Civic Assn., 1948-49; historian, Franklin County, Tenn., 1965-69; sr. warden Episc. Ch., 1956-65; trustee U. South, 1944-45, St. Andrews Sch., Tenn., 1970-72, St. Augustine's Coll., N.C., 1971-80, St. Paul's Coll., Va., 1974-82; cons. Trinity Coll., Quezon City, 1974—, Voorhees Coll., S.C., 1979—. Served with USNR, 1942-45. Named hon. paramount chief Kpelle Tribe, Liberia, 1974. Mem. Ch. Hist. Soc. (dir. 1964—), English-Speaking Union (pres. Hudson Stuck chpt. 1972—, mem. nat. bd. 1973—), N.Y. Acad. Scis., Newcomen Soc., Nat. Inst. Social Scis., Brotherhood St. Andrew (nat. v.p. 1969-74), St. George's Soc., Sigma Nu (pres. Ednl. Found. 1969-79), Phi Beta Kappa, Pi Gamma Mu, Sigma Upsilon, Phi Alpha Theta. Episcopalian. Clubs: Century, St. George's (N.Y.C.); E.Q.B. (Sewanee). Home: 100 South Carolina Ave Sewanee TN 37375 Office: 815 2d Ave New York NY 10017

CHITWOOD, JULIUS RICHARD, librarian; b. Magazine, Ark., June 1, 1921; s. Hoyt Mozart and Florence (Umfrid) C.; m. Aileen Newsom, Aug. 6, 1944. A.B. cum laude, Ouachita Bapt. Coll., Ark., 1942; M.Mus., Ind. U., 1948; M.A., U. Chgo., 1954. Music supr. Edinburgh (Ind.) Pub. Schs., 1946-47; music and audiovisual librarian Roosevelt Coll., Chgo., 1948-51; humanities librarian Drake U., 1951-53; spl. cataloger Chgo. Tchrs. Coll., 1953; asst. circulation librarian Indpls. Pub. Library, 1954-57, coordinator adult services, 1957-61; dir. Rockford (Ill.) Pub. Library, 1961-79, No. Ill. Library System, Rockford, 1966-76; chmn. subcom. library system devel. Ill. Library Adv. Com., 1965—; adv. com. U. Ill. Grad. Sch. Library Sci., 1964-68; cons. in field, participant workshops. Pres. Rockford Regional Academic Center, 1974-76; Mem. history com. Ill. Sesquicentennial Commn.; mem. Mayor Rockford Com. for UN, 1962-70; sect. chmn. Rockford United Fund, 1966-70; exec. Rockford Civic Orch. Assn., 1962-70. Served to maj., inf. AUS, 1942-45; ETO. Recipient Ill. Librarian of Year award, 1974. Mem. ALA (chmn. subcom. revision standards of materials, pub. library div. 1965-66, pres. bldg. and equipment sect. library adminstrn. div. 1967-68, chmn. staff devel. com. personnel adminstrn. sect., library adminstrv. div. 1964-68, pres. library adminstrn. div. 1969-70), Ill. Library Assn. (v.p. 1964-65, pres. 1965-66), Rockford Area C. of C. Unitarian (pres. 1965-67). Clubs: Rotarian (exec. bd. Rockford 1965-66), Rockford University.). Home: 916 Paris Ave Rockford IL 61107 Office: 115 7th St Suite 209 Rockford IL 61104

CHITWOOD, ROBERT HODSON, oil company executive; b. Pratt, Kans., Oct. 2, 1930; s. Joe Vern and Blanche Katherine (Hodson) C.; m. Barbara Ann Johnson, Mar. 10, 1952; children: Catherine Chitwood Hurst, Thomas Randall, Nancy Chitwood Ryan, Amalie Ann. B.S. in Bus. Adminstrn, Okla. State U., 1952; grad. exec. devel. program, Cornell U., 1970. With Cities Service Co., Tulsa, 1952—, v.p. supply and transp., 1970-74; pres., dir. Cities Service Gas Co., 1974-76, exec. v.p. parent co., pres. petroleum products group, 1976-81, pres., chief operating officer, 1982—; pres. Cities Service Oil & Gas Co.; dir. Cities Service Co., Columbian Chems. Co. Trustee Philbrook Art Center, Holland Hall, Okla. Safety Council; mem. adv. bd. trustees Tulsa Philharm.; bd. dirs. Industries for Tulsa, Inc.; bd. govs. Okla. State U. Served with AUS, 1952-53. Named to Okla. State U. Hall of Fame, Okla. State U. Coll. Bus. Adminstrn. Assocs. Mem. Tulsa, Okla. chambers commerce, Nat. Petroleum Refiners Assn. (chmn. bd.), Am. Petroleum Inst., Mid-Continent Oil and Gas Assn., Okla. Petroleum Council, Transp. Assn. Am. (dir.). Republican. Episcopalian. Clubs: Internat. (Washington); Tulsa, So. Hills Country, Petroleum (Tulsa); Beacon (Oklahoma City). Home: 2108 E 29th St Tulsa OK 74114 Office: PO Box 300 Tulsa OK 74102

CHIU, HUNGDAH, lawyer, legal educator; b. Shanghai, China, Mar. 23, 1936; came to U.S., 1960; s. Han-ping and Ming-non (Yang) C.; m. Yuan-yuan Hsieh, May 14, 1966; 1 son, Wei-hsueh. LL.B., Nat. Taiwan U., 1958; M.A. with honors, L.I. U., 1962; LL.M., Harvard U., 1962, S.J.D., 1965. Asso. in research East Asian Research Center, Harvard U., 1964-65; asso. prof. internat. law Nat. Taiwan U., 1965-66; research asso. in law Harvard U., 1966-70, 72-74; vis. prof. law Nat. Chengchi U., Taipei, Taiwan, 1970-72; asso. prof. law U. Md., Balt., 1974-77, prof., 1977—. Author: The Capacity of International Organizations to Conclude Treaties, 1966, The People's Republic of China and the Law of Treaties, 1972, (with J.A. Cohen) People's China and International Law, 2 vols, 1974 (certificate of merit Am. Soc. Internat. Law 1976), Normalizing Relations with China: Problems, Analysis and Documents, 1978, China and the Taiwan Issue, 1979, Agreements of the People's Republic of China, 1966-80, A Calendar of Events, 1981; contbr. numerous articles to profl. jours., chpts. to books; gen. editor: Contemporary Asian Studies, 1976—. Del. UN Conf. Law of the Sea, 1976-82; chmn. Immigration Commn. Asian-Am. Assembly Policy Research. Served to 2d lt. Chinese Army, 1958-60. Named One of 10 Outstanding Young Men Jr. C. of C. of Republic of China, 1971; Social Sci. Research Council fellow, 1968; recipient Cultural award Inst. Chinese Culture, 1980, Toulmin medal Soc. Am. Mil. Engrs., 1982; Nat. Reconstrn. award Chinese Profl. Assn. Mid-Am., 1980; Toulmin medal Soc. Am. Mil. Engrs., 1981—. Mem. Am. Soc. Internat. Law (panel on China and internat. order 1969-74), Assn. for Asian Studies (com. on Asian law 1976-79). Home: 6168 Devon Dr Columbia MD 21044 Office: U Md Law Sch 500 W Baltimore St Baltimore MD 21201

CHIU, YAM TSI, space physicisr; b. Canton, China, Sept. 5, 1940; came to U.S., 1955, naturalized, 1960; s. Wah Shing and Shui May (Lee) C.; m. Frances M.C. Lee, Dec. 21, 1974. B.A., Yale U., 1961, M.S., 1963, Ph.D., 1965. Henry Ford fellow Oxford U., Eng., 1962; research assoc. Enrico Fermi Inst., U. Chgo., 1965-67; mem. tech. stff Aerospace Corop., El Segundo, Calif., 1967-76; staff scientist Aerospce Corp., El Segundo, Calif., 1972-74; research scientist Aerospace Corp., El Segundo, Calif., 1974-80, sr. scientist, 1980—; prin. investigator contracts Dept. Energy, NASA, Air Force, NSF. Contbr. articles to profl. jours., chpts. to books. Mem. Am. Phys. Soc., Am. Geophys. Union, Meteorol. Soc., Phi Beta Kappa. Episcopalian. Office: 2350 E El Segundo Blvd El Segundo CA 90245

CHLUSKI, JOHN J., bus. exec.; b. Warsaw, Poland, Aug. 12, 1923; (married), 1948; 1 son, John. Ed. in France and Eng.; degrees in mercantile law, commerce and econs, France and Eng. From dir. planning and procurement U.K. ops. and gen. mgr. French ops. to pres. Massey Ferguson Industries, Ltd., and Massey Ferguson Inc., Massey Ferguson Ltd., Toronto, Ont., Can., 1947-67; group v.p. internat. ops., group v.p. Tractomotive group Allis Chalmers Corp., Milw., 1968-71; with ITT, 1972—; exec. asst. and pres. ITT Europe and; group gen. mgr., automotive products, Europe, 1972-73; v.p. ITT, 1977; sr. v.p. ITT and group exec. engineered products Europe, 1979—. Served with Brit. and U.S. paratroop forces, 1943-45. *

CHO, ALFRED YI, electrical engineer; b. Peking, China, July 10, 1937; came to U.S., 1955, naturalized, 1962; s. Edward I-Lai and Mildred (Chen) C.; m. Mona Lee Willoughby, June 16, 1968; children: Derek Ming, Deidre Lin, Brynna Ying, Wendy Li. B.S. in Elec. Engring., U. Ill., 1960, M.S., 1961, Ph.D., 1968. Research physicist Ion Physics Corp., Burlington, Mass., 1961-62; mem. tech. staff TRW-Space Tech. Labs., Redondo Beach, Calif., 1962-65; research asst. U. Ill., Urbana, 1965-68, vis. prof. dept. elec. engring., vis. research prof. coordinated sci. lab., 1977-78, adj. prof. dept. elec. engring. adj. research prof. coordinated sci. lab., 1978—; dir. Instruments S.A., Metuchen, N.J. Contbr. articles to profl. jours.; developer molecular beam epitaxy. Recipient Disting. Tech. Staff award AT&T Bell Labs., 1982, Morris N. Liebmann award, 1982. Fellow IEEE; mem. Am. Phys. Soc. (Internat. prize for new materials 1982), Am. Vacuum Soc., Electrochem. Soc. (electronic div. award 1977), N.Y. Acad. Scis., AAAS, Sigma Xi, Tau Beta Pi, Eta Kappa Nu, Sigma Tau. Home: 11 Kenneth Ct Summit NJ 07901 Office: AT & T Bell Labs 600 Mountain Ave Murray Hill NJ 07974 *I learned early in my life that hard work is a major ingredient for success. We can always do more than we think we are able to do. I drive myself to my utmost capacity so that I will not have regrets later that I did not try my best. My first love is art but I earn my living as an engineer. In my work as a research scientist, the secret for success is that I combine Oriental patience with Western technology. We should always try to enhance the best part of what we have and not be afraid to change.*

CHO, CHENG TSUNG, pediatrician, educator; b. Kaohsiung, Taiwan, Dec. 2, 1937; came to U.S., 1964, naturalized, 1976; s. R.E. and S.M. (Chou) C.; m. Chiou-shya Chen, Dec. 14, 1968; children: Jennifer, Julie. M.D., Kaohsiung Med. Coll., 1962; Ph.D., U. Kans., 1970. Diplomate: Am. Bd. Pediatrics. Intern Norwegian-Am. Hosp., Chgo., 1964-65; resident U. Kans. Med. Center, 1965-67, fellow, 1967-70, asst. prof. pediatrics and microbiology, 1970-74, assoc. prof., 1974-78, prof., 1978—, acting chmn. dept. pediatrics, 1978-79, chief sect. pediatric infectious disease, 1972—; vis. prof. Tri-Service Gen. Hosp. and Nat. Def. Med. Sch., Taiwan, 1980. Co-author: Pediatric Infectious Diseases; author articles on virology and infectious diseases. Recipient Outstanding Pediatric Teaching award U. Kans. Med. Center, 1975. Fellow Am. Acad. Pediatrics, Infectious Disease Soc. Am.; mem. AAAS, Am. Soc. Microbiology, Am. Pediatric Soc., Soc. Pediatric Research, Soc. Exptl. Biology and Medicine, Kans. Med. Soc., Midwest Pediatric Research Soc., Kaohsiung Med. Coll. Alumni Assn. Am. (pres. 1978), Sigma Xi. Home: 10215 Howe Ln Leawood KS 66206 Office: Dept Pediatrics U Kansas Medical Center Kansas City KS 66103

CHO, HYUN JU, research scientist; b. Chinju, Korea, June 12, 1939; s. Gil Rae and Sun Gae (Park) C.; m. Kim Bok Mee, June 13, 1967; children—Jae Shin, Elisa, Jane. D.V.M., Chinju Nat. Agrl. Coll., 1963; M.Sc., Seoul Nat. U., 1966; Ph.D., U. Guelph, 1973. Vet. research scientist Inst. Vet. Research, Anyang, Korea, 1965-70; vis. scientist Wallaceville Animal Research Center, New Zealand, 1968; research scientist Animal Diseases Research Inst. Can. Dept. Agr., Lethbridge, Alta., Can., 1973—. Contbr. articles to profl. jours. Mem. Am. Soc. Microbiology, Can. Soc. Microbiology, Conf. Research Workers in Animal Diseases. Discovered virus of Aleutian disease of mink and developed practical diagnostic test for it. Home: 1040 Fern Crescent Lethbridge AB Canada Office: Animal Diseases Research Inst PO Box 640 Lethbridge AB Canada *A combination of persistent and repeated experimentation, original ideas and thinking and the ambition to succeed where others may have failed, tempered with loyalty and dedication to sound research principles, has been the key to my scientific achievements.*

CHO, LEE-JAY, sociologist, demographer; b. Kyoto, Japan, July 5, 1936; came to U.S., 1959; s. Sam-Soo and Kyung-Doo (Park) C.; m. Eun-Ja Chun, May 20, 1973; children—Yun-Kyong, Sang-Mun. B.A., Kookmin Coll., Seoul, Korea, 1959; M.A. in Public Adminstrn, Geroge Washington U., 1962, U. Chgo., 1964, Ph.D., 1965. Statistician Korean Census Council, 1958-61; fellow Population Research and Tng. Center, U. Chgo., 1962, research asso., asst. prof. sociology, 1965-66; asso. dir. Community and Family Study Center, 1969-70; sr. demographic adv. to Malaysian Govt., 1967-69; asso. prof. U. Hawaii, 1969-73, prof., 1973-78; asst. dir. East-West Population Inst., East-West Center, Honolulu, 1971-74, dir., 1974-80; pres. protem East-West Center, 1980-81; cons. in field; mem. Nat. Acad. Scis. Com. on Population and Demography; mem. U.S. 1980 Census Adv. Com., Dept. Commerce. Author: (with others) Differential Current Fertility in the United States, 1970, Estimates of Current Fertility for the Republic of Korea and Its Geographical Subdivisions: 1959-1970, 1975; editor: Introduction to Censuses of Asia and the Pacific: 1970-74, 1976, (with Kazumasa Kobayashi) Fertility Transition in East Asian Populations, 1979, (with Suharto, McNicoll and Mamas) Population Growth of Indonesia, 1980; contbr. numerous articles on population to profl. jours. Bd. dirs. Planned Parenthood Assn., Hawaii, 1976-77. Ford Found. grantee, 1977-79; Population Council grantee, 1973-75; Dept. Commerce grantee, 1974-78. Mem. Internat. Statis. Inst. (tech. adv. com. World Fertility Survey), Internat. Union Sci. Study Population, Population Assn. Am., Am. Statis. Assn., Am. Sociol. Assn. Home: 1718 Halekoa Dr Honolulu HI 96821 Office: 1777 East-West Rd Honolulu HI 96848 *The survival and welfare of the future generations will depend largely upon what we do today to plan and manage human population growth and movements.*

CHOATE, JOSEPH, lawyer; b. Santa Ana, Calif., Jan. 14, 1900; s. Walter Addison and Nellie E. (Jurd) C.; m. Dorothy Drew, 1939; 1 son, Joseph. A.B., LL.B., U. So. Calif., 1925; LL.M. in Internat. Law, Harvard U., 1936; postgrad. intramural session, Oxford U., Internat.

Law Seminar, U. Mich., 1937; LL.D., Salem (W.Va.) Coll., 1937. Bar: Calif. 1927, U.S. Supreme Ct. 1935. Dep. dist. atty., Los Angeles County, Calif., 1927-34, in gen. practice of law, Los Angeles; pvt. internat. law; mem. Choate & Choate & Assocs. Author: Qualifying for Destiny, 1937; also numerous legal articles. Mem. pub. panel War Labor Bd. Mem. Am., Los Angeles County, Internat. bar assns., Japan-Am. Soc. So. Calif., Am. Soc. Internat. Law, U.S. Naval Inst., Internat. Platform Assn., SR (life), Delta Theta Phi. Presbyn. Clubs: Mason (Shriner, K.T.), Lincoln (Los Angeles); Harvard of Calif. Mem. Lindblad Explorer Expdn. to Antarctica to observe penquins and seals, 1981-82. Home: 450 S Serrano Ave Los Angeles CA 90020 Office: Choate & Choate & Assocs Five Ten Bldg 6th and Olive Sts Los Angeles CA 90014 *Life, to me, has never been merely an economic treadmill for the acquisition of the "good things" of life alone, but rather a challenge to pursue and adopt as far as possible those fundamental, spiritual values which help sustain a man in the inevitable, frequent crises of life and which can be the source of a man's greatest achievement, personal satisfaction and contentment on this pilgrimage called Life. Ambition alone tends to destroy the man. Aspiration tends to ennoble the man and thus thereby also to please and honor his Maker.*

CHOATE, ROBERT ALDEN, lawyer; b. Grand Rapids, Mich., May 24, 1912; s. Frederick Cherington and Kate (Alden) C.; m. Eileen McManus, June 5, 1937; children—Alan G., Elizabeth (Mrs. Leroy Sloas), Christina (Mrs. Sean Austin), Alison (Mrs. Gary Benjamin). B.S.E., U. Mich., 1934, LL.B., 1936. Bar: Mich. bar 1936. Patent practice with firm Barnes, Kisselle, Raisch & Choate, 1936—; with Office of Judge Adv., Wright Field, Ohio, 1945-46; lectr. patent law U. Mich., 1960-80, emeritus, 1980—. Author: Case Book on Patent Law, 1973, 2d edit., 1981; contbr. articles to profl. jours. Mem. bd. mgmt. YMCA, 1950—, pres., 1964-67. Mem. Mich. Patent Law Assn. (past pres.), Tau Beta Pi. Conglist. Home: 8817 Marseilles St Detroit MI 48224 Office: 1520 Ford Bldg Detroit MI 48226

CHOATE, ROBERT BURNETT, consultant, educator; b. Boston, Nov. 6, 1924; s. Robert B. and Katherine S. (Crosby) C. Student, Harvard U., 1943-44, Ed.M., 1981; B.S.C.E., U. Calif., Berkeley, 1949. Engring. positions with constrn., engring. cos., 1949-53; Western regional mgr. Preload Constrn. Corp., San Francisco, 1953-54; civil engr. Sika Chem. Corp., 1955; pub. Reveille mag., Phoenix, 1965-66; officer real estate investments corp., 1957—, cons. poverty, food, nutrition, television issues, 1966-78; founder Careers for Youth, Phoenix, 1958, bd. dirs., 1958-66; cons. Pres. Kennedy's Nat. Ser. Corp., 1962, Citizens' Crusade Against Poverty, 1966-69, HEW, 1969; chmn. Council on Children, Media and Merchandising, 1970-80; adminstrv. staff mem. White House Conf. on Food, Nutrition and Health, 1969; lectr. Wharton Sch. Bus., U. Pa., 1973-74. Author works in field; speaker, lectr. in field. Bd. dirs. Nat. Com. Effective Congress, 1974—; vis. com. Food and Nutrition Bd., Nat. Acad. Scis., 1977; mem. adv. bd. FDA, 1976-78; mem. adv. com. Consumers Product Safety Commn., 1979—; testifier to Congress and govt. agys. 56 times in 13 years; fellow Inst. Politics, Kennedy Sch. Govt., 1979-80; exec. dir. Inst. for Gender Equity, 1980—; fellow Woodrow Wilson Found., 1980—; Former bd. dirs. Urban League, Alice Lloyd Coll. Outreach Program. Address: 826 Capistrano Pl San Diego CA 92109

CHOBANIAN, ARAM VAN, physician; b. Pawtucket, R.I., Aug. 10, 1929; s. Van and Marina (Arsenian) C.; m. Jasmine Goorigian, June 5, 1955; children: Karin, Lisa, Aram. B.A., Brown U., 1951; M.D., Harvard U., 1955. Intern, resident Univ. Hosp., Boston, 1955-59, cardiovascular research fellow, 1959-62; asst. prof. Boston U. Sch. Medicine, 1964-67, assoc. prof., 1967-70, prof. medicine, 1970—, prof. pharmacology, 1975—, dir. U.A. Whitaker Labs. for Blood Vessel Research, 1973—, dir. Hypertension Specialized Ctr. of Research, 1975—, dir. Cardiovascular Inst., 1975—; chmn. FDA Cardiovascular and Renal Adv. Com., 1978-80, NIH Hypertension and Arteriosclerosis adv. com., 1977-78; chmn. Cardiovascular Study Sect. B. NIH, 1982-84. Author: Heart Risk Book, 1982. Pres. Am. Heart Assn., Boston, 1974-75; trustee Armenian Library of Am., 1975—; bd. dirs. Armenian Culture Soc., 1976—. Served to capt. USAF, 1956-57. Recipient Community Edn. and Disting. Service Am. Heart Assn., Boston, 1975, 78. Fellow ACP, Am. Heart Assn., Am. Coll. Cariology; mem. Assn. Am. Physicians, Am. Soc. Clin. Investigation, Am. Physiol. Soc., AAAS, Phi Beta Kappa, Sigma Xi, Alpha Omega Alpha. Home: 5 Rathbun Rd Natick MA 07162 Office: 80 E Concord St Boston MA 02118

CHODOROW, MARVIN, physicist, educator; b. Buffalo, July 16, 1913; s. Isidor and Lena (Cohen) C.; m. Leah Ruth Turitz, Sept. 19, 1937; children: Nancy Julia, Joan Elizabeth. B.A., U. Buffalo, 1934; Ph.D., Mass. Inst. Tech., 1939; LL.D., U. Glasgow, 1972. Research asso. Pa. State Coll., 1940-41; instr. physics Coll. City N.Y., 1941-43; sr. project engr. Sperry Gyroscope Co., 1943-47; faculty Stanford, 1947—, prof. physics, 1947-54, prof. applied physics and elec. engring., 1954-78, Barbara Kimball Browning prof. applied physics, 1975-78, prof. emeritus applied physics and elec. engring., 1978—; dir. Edward L. Ginzton Lab., 1959-78, chmn. dept. applied physics, 1962-69; Cons. Def. Dept., Rand Corp.; vis. lectr. Ecole Normale Superieure, Paris, France, 1955-56; vis. research asso. U. Coll. London, 1969-70. Co-author: Fundamentals of Microwave Electronics, 1964; Contbr. articles to profl. jours. Fulbright fellow Cambridge (Eng.) U., 1962-63. Fellow IEEE (W.R.G. Baker award 1962, Lamme medal 1981), Am. Acad. Arts and Scis., Am. Phys. Soc.; mem. Nat. Acad. Scis., Nat. Acad. Engring., Am. Assn. Physics Tchrs., AAAS, AAUP, Phi Beta Kappa, Sigma Xi. Designed 1st klystron for microwave relay systems, 1946, 1st megawatt klystron, 1949, 1st megawatt traveling-wave tube, 1952-57. Home: 809 San Francisco Terr Stanford CA 94305 Office: Edward L Ginzton Lab Stanford U Stanford CA 94305

CHOI, BYUNG HO, neuropathologist; b. Korea, Oct. 16, 1928; came to U.S., 1954, naturalized, 1973; s. Poong Chick and Young Ai (Lee) C.; m. Chan Ock Park, Oct. 20, 1956; children: Theodore Kyu, Sue Yun. M.D., Severance Union Med. Coll., Seoul, 1953; D.Med. Sci., Yonsei U., 1963. Asst. in pathology Severance Union Med. Coll., 1953-54; resident in pathology Univ. Hosps. of Cleve., 1954-57; fellow in neuropathology Western Res. U., Cleve., 1957-59; from instr. to asso. prof. neuropathology Yonsei U. Med. Sch., 1959-65; asst. prof. Albany (N.Y.) Med. Coll., 1967-69; asso. prof. pathology St. Louis U. Med. Sch., 1969-72, U. Rochester (N.Y.) Sch. Medicine and Dentistry, 1972-77, prof., 1977-81; mem. staff Strong Meml. Hosp.; prof. neuropathology U. Calif. Coll. Medicine, Irvine, 1981—. Author papers in field. Served as officer M.C. Korean Army, 1954, 63-64. NIH grantee. Mem. Am. Assn. Neuropathologists, Am. Soc. Clin. Pathologists, Coll. Am. Pathologists, Am. Assn. Pathologists, Internat. Acad. Pathology, Tissue Culture Assn., Sigma Xi. Office: Dept Pathology U Calif Coll Medicine Irvine CA 92717

CHOLLET, JEAN LOUIS, paper co. exec.; b. Que., Can., June 29, 1930; s. Louis and Jeanne (Lacroix) C.; m. Renee Painchaud, Dec. 9, 1953; children—Denis, Andre, Caroline. B.Sc. in Chem. Engring, Laval U., 1953. With Anglo Can. Pulp & Paper Mills Research Labs., 1955-61, Reed Paper, Eng., 1961-64; with Rolland, Inc., Montreal, Que., Can., 1964—, successively v.p. research and tech. services, v.p. mfg., now exec. v.p. fine papers div., 1972—. Recipient F. G. Robinson award, 1970. Mem. Can. Pulp and Paper Assn. (chmn. tech. sect.), Can. Environ. Adv. Council, Can. Mfrs. Assn., TAPPI. Home: 772 Carre Thibault Ste Therese en Haut PQ J7E 4C3 Canada Office: 800 Place Victoria Suite 3620 Montreal PQ H4Z 1H3 Canada

CHOMSKY, AVRAM NOAM, educator; b. Phila., Dec. 7, 1928; s. William and Elsie (Simonofsky) C.; m. Carol Doris Schatz, Dec. 24, 1949; children: Aviva, Diane, Harry Alan. B.A., U. Pa., 1949, M.A., 1951, Ph.D., 1955, D.H.L. (hon.), 1984, U. Chgo., 1967, Loyola U. Chgo., 1970, Swarthmore Coll., 1970, Bard Coll., 1971, U. Mass., 1973; D.Litt., U. London, Eng., 1967, Delhi (India) U., 1972, Visva-Bharati U., Santiniketan, West Bengal, 1980. Faculty Mass. Inst. Tech., 1955—, prof. modern langs., 1961—, Ferrari P. Ward prof. modern lang. and linguistics, 1966—, Inst. prof., 1976—; Vis. prof., Columbia, 1957-58; mem. Inst. Advanced Study, Princeton, 1958-59; Linguistic Soc. Am. prof. U. Calif. at, Los Angeles, summer 1966; Beckman prof. U. Calif. at Berkeley, 1966-67; John Locke lectr., Oxford, 1969; Shearman lectr. U. London, 1969; Bertrand Russell Meml. lectr. Cambridge, 1971; Nehru Meml. lectr. New Delhi, 1972; Huizinga lectr. Leiden, 1977. Author: Syntactic Structures, 1957, Current Issues in Linguistic Theory, 1964, Aspects of the Theory of Syntax, 1965, Cartesian Linguistics, 1966, Topics in the Theory of Generative Grammar, 1966, (with Morris Halle) Sound Pattern of English, 1968, Language and Mind, 1968, American Power and the New Mandarins, 1969, At War with Asia, 1970, Problems of Knowledge and Freedom, 1971, Studies on Semantics in Generative Grammar, 1972, For Reasons of State, 1973, (with Edward Herman) Counterrevolutionary Violence, 1973, Peace in The Middle East?, 1974, Logical Structure of Linguistic Theory, 1975, Reflections on Language, 1975, Essays on Form and Interpretation, 1977, Human Rights and American Foreign Policy, 1978, (with Edward Herman) The Political Economy of Human Rights, 2 vols, 1979, Rules and Representation, 1980, Lectures on Government and Binding, 1981, Concepts and Consequences of the Theory of Government and Binding, 1982, Fateful Triangle, 1983. Jr. fellow Soc. Fellows, Harvard, 1951-55; research fellow Harvard Cognitive Studies Center, 1964-67. Fellow A.A.A.S.; corr. fellow Brit. Acad.; mem. Nat. Acad. Scis., Am. Acad. Arts and Scis., Linguistic Soc. Am., Deutsche Akademie der Naturforscher Leopoldina, Am. Philos. Assn., Aristotelian Soc. Gt. Britain, Utrecht Soc. Arts and Scis. Home: 15 Suzanne Rd Lexington MA 02173 Office: Mass Inst Tech Massachusetts Ave Cambridge MA 02139

CHOMSKY, MARVIN, television director; b. N.Y.C., May 23, 1929. B.S., Syracuse U.; M.A., Stanford U. Dir.: films including Good Luck Miss Wyckoff; dir.: TV shows King Crab (Recipient Emmy awards for Holocaust 1978, Attica 1980). Office: care Plant Cohen & Co 10900 Wilshire Blvd Suite 900 Los Angeles CA 90024 *

CHON, MYRON EDWARD, advertising executive; b. Chgo., Dec. 12, 1901; s. Benjamin W. and Anna (Bransky) C.; m. Bernice Larson, July 30, 1937 (dec. 1959). A.B., U. Mich., 1923. Copywriter J. Walter Thompson, Chgo., 1923-25; copy dir. William H. Rankin Co., Chgo., 1926-33; exec. creative dir. Arthur Meyerhoff Assos., Inc., Chgo., 1934—, exec. v.p., 1962—; owner Jade House.; Music and advt. cons. Composer musicals, compositions and commls.; saxophone performer. Recipient numerous awards for mus. commls. Mem. ASCAP, Composers Hall of Fame. Home: 1300 Lake Shore Dr Chicago IL 60610 Office: Jade House 166 Superior St Chicago IL 60611

CHONG, THOMAS, comedian, writer, director, musician; b. Edmonton, Alta., Can., May 24, 1938; s. Stanley and Lorna Jean (Gilchrist) C. Ed. public schs. Co-founder: rhythm and blues band The Shades; mem.: group Bobby Taylor and the Vancouvers, until, 1968; founder: improvisational theater troupe City Works; formed: comedy duo with Cheech Marin called Cheech and Chong; appeared in nightclubs, Can., Los Angeles; recs. include Sleeping Beauty; co-writer, co-star: film Up in Smoke, 1978, Things Are Tough All Over, 1982; writer, actor, dir.: Cheech & Chong's Next Movie, 1979, Cheech & Chong's Nice Dreams, 1981; co-writer: title song Up in Smoke (Recipient with Cheech Grammy award for Best Comedy recording Los Cochinos 1973). Office: care Monterey Peninsula Artists PO Box 7308 Carmel CA 93921 *

CHOOK, PAUL HOWARD, marketing and advertising research executive; b. N.Y.C., Oct. 17, 1929; s. Abraham and Etta (Cohen) C. M.S., Columbia U, 1950; B.B.A., CCNY, 1949. Quality control cons. Philip Morris, Inc., N.Y.C., 1951-55; pres. media studies div. Alfred Politz Research, Inc., N.Y.C., 1955-66; v.p., dir. communications info. services Young & Rubicam, Inc., N.Y.C., 1966-74; pres. W.R. Simmons Research Assocs., N.Y.C., 1974-75; v.p. Ziff Corp., N.Y.C., 1975—; exec. v.p. mktg. and circulation Ziff Davis Pub. Co., N.Y.C., 1975—; instr. CCNY, 1951-63. Chmn. Advt. Research Found. Mem. Am. Statis. Assn., Am. Mktg. Assn., Radio and TV Research Council, Am. Assn. Pub. Opinion Research, Market Research Council, Media Research Dirs. Assn. Home: 65-65 Wetherole St Forest Hills NY 11374 Office: 1 Park Ave New York NY 10016

CHOPE, HENRY ROY, inventor, engineer; b. Louisville, July 19, 1921; s. Henry Roy and Amelia (Gutermuth) C.; m. Lois Elizabeth Sherman, June 11, 1954; children: Elizabeth Ann, David Roy, Amelia Louise, Charles Sherman. B.E.E., Ohio State U., 1948; M.S., Cal. Inst. Tech., 1948; S.M., Harvard, 1950. Registered profl. engr., Ohio. Electronic scientist rocket devel. USAF, 1949-50; atomic scientist, 1950-53; exec. v.p., dir. AccuRay Corp., Columbus, Ohio, 1952-81, dir., 1981—, mem. exec. com., tech. adv. com.; dir. AccuRay Internat., Bell P.A. Systems, Columbus, 1968-79, Medicon Corp., 1978-79, Danninger Med. Tech., Inc., 1983—; Mem. labor-mgmt. adv. com. AEC, 1965-70, adv. com. isotopes and radiation devel., 1966-67; mem. Ohio Atomic Energy Adv. Bd., 1967-69; mem. adv. com. innovation Pres.'s Office Sci. and Tech., 1964; mem. adv. com. state tech. services Ohio Bd. Regents, 1967-70; mem. adv. com. on health care Am. people AMA, 1970-72; mem. engring. steering com., com. for tomorrow Ohio State U. Coll. Engring. Contbr. tech. papers to profl. lit. Trustee Riverside Meth. Hosp., Columbus; trustee Riverside Meth. Hosp. Med. Research Found., Ohio Wesleyan U., Delaware, 1971-79, Columbus Mus. Art, Columbus Symphony orch., Center Sci. and Industry; commr. Franklin County Hosp. Commn., 1978—; bd. dirs. Buckeye Boys Ranch, Grove City, Ohio, 1976-77, Ohio State U. Research Found., 1969-74. Recipient Dist. Alumnus award Ohio State U., 1961, Alumni Centennial award, 1970. Fellow AAAS, Instrument Soc. Am. (Albert F. Sperry award 1972); sr. mem. IEEE (Morris E. Leeds award 1967), Am. Nuclear Soc.; mem. Nat. Soc. Profl. Engrs., U.S. C. of C. (dir. 1967-72, chmn. sci. and tech. com. 1968-70), Ohio C. of C. (dir.), Columbus C. of C. (dir. 1967-74), Newcomen Soc. N.Am., Tau Beta Pi (pres., chmn. exec. com. 1966-70), Eta Kappa Nu, Theta Tau, Pi Kappa Alpha. Clubs: Scioto Country (Columbus); Harvard (N.Y.C., Central Ohio); Rotary. Patentee nuclear energy, instrumentation, process control. Home: 3885 Woodbridge Rd Columbus OH 43220 Office: 1625 Bethel Rd Columbus OH 43220

CHOPER, JESSE HERBERT, law educator; b. Wilkes-Barre, Pa., Sept. 19, 1935; s. Edward and Dorothy (Resnick) C.; m. Sonya Rae Schwartz, June 27, 1961; children: Marc Steven, Edward Nathaniel. B.S., Wilkes Coll., 1957, D.H.L., 1967; LL.B., U. Pa., 1960. Bar: D.C. 1961. Instr. Wharton Sch., U. Pa., 1957-60; law clk. Chief Justice Earl Warren, U.S. Supreme Ct., 1960-61; asst. prof. U. Minn. Law Sch., 1961-62, asso. prof., 1962-65; prof. U. Calif. Law Sch. at Berkeley, 1965—, dean, 1982—; vis. prof. Cath. U. Law Sch., 1967, Harvard U., 1970-71. Author: Constitutional Law: Cases-Comments-Questions, 5th edit., 1980, The American Constitution, Cases and Materials, 5th edit., 1980, Constitutional Rights and Liberties, Cases and Materials, 5th edit., 1980, Corporations, Cases and Materials, 2d edit., 1977, Judicial Review and the National Political Process, 1980; contbr. articles to profl. jours. Mem. AAUP, Am. Law Inst., Am. Acad. Arts and Scis., Order of Coif. Democrat. Jewish. Home: 118 Alvarado Rd Berkeley CA 94705

CHOPPIN, PURNELL WHITTINGTON, virology researcher, educator, internist; b. Baton Rouge, July 4, 1929; s. Authur Richard and Eunice Dolores (Bolin) C.; m. Joan Harriet Macdonald, Oct. 17, 1959; 1 dau., Kathleen Marie. M.D., La. State U., 1953. Diplomate: Am. Bd. Internal Medicine. Intern Barnes Hosp., St. Louis, 1953-54, asst. resident, 1956-57; postdoctoral fellow, research assoc. Rockefeller U., N.Y.C., 1957-60, asst. prof., 1960-64, assoc. prof., 1957-60, prof., sr. physician, 1970—, Leon Hess prof. virology, 1980—, v.p. acad. programs, 1983—; mem. virology study sect NIH, 1968-72, chmn. virology study sect., 1975-78; bd. dirs. Royal Soc. Medicine Found. Inc., N.Y.C., 1978—; mem. adv. com. fundamental research Nat. Multiple Sclerosis Soc., 1979-84; chmn. adv. com. fundamental research, 1983-84; mem. adv. council Nat. Inst. Allergy and Infectious Deseases, 1980-83; mem. bd. scis. cons Meml. Solan-Ketting Cancer Ctr., N.Y.C., 1981—; chmn. bd. sics. cons Mem. Sloan-Kettering Cancer Ctr., N.Y.C., 1983-84; mem. commn. on life scis. NRC, Wahington, 1982—; mem. sci. rev. com. Scripps Clinic and Research Found., La Jolla, Calif., 1983—, chmn. sci. rev. com., Lfa Jolla, Calif., 1984; mem. council for research and clin. investigation Am. Cancer Soc., N.Y.C., 1983—; mem. com. priotities for vaccine devel. Inst. Medicine, Washington. Contbr. numerous articles to profl. pubs., 1958—, chpts. on virology, cell biology, infectious deseases to profl. publs., 1958—; editor: Procs. Soc. Exptl. Biology and Medicine, 1966-69; assoc. editor: Virology, 1969-72; editor, 1973—; assoc. editor: Jour. Immunology, 1968-72, Jour. Supramolecular Structure, 1972-75; editorial bd.: Jour. Birology, 1972, Comprehensive Virology, 1972; overseas adv. panel: Biochem. Jour., 1973-77. Served as capt. USAF, 1954-56; Japan. Recipient Howard Taylor Ricketts award, U. Chgo., 1978; named to alumni Hall of Distinction La. State U., Baton Rouge, 1983. Fellow N.Y. Acad. Scis., AAAS; mem. Nat. Acad. Scis. (chmn. Class IV 1983—), Assn. Am. Physicians, Am. Soc. Clin. Investigation, Am. soc. Microbiology (chmn. virology div. 1977-79), Am. Soc. Microbiology (divisional group councilor 183—), Harvey Soc., Am. Inst. Biol. Scis., Am. Assn. Immunologists, Soc. Exptl. Biology and Medicine, Am. Soc. Cell Biology, Infectious Diseases Soc. Am., Practitioners Soc. N.Y., Am. Clin. and Climatological Assn., Am. Soc. Virology, Sigma Xi (pres. chpt. 1980-81), Alpha Omega Alpha. Home: 530 E 72 St New York NY 10021 Office: Rockefeller U 1230 York Ave New York 10021

CHOPRA, ANIL KUMAR, civil engineering educator; b. Peshawar, India, Feb. 18, 1941; came to U.S., 1961, naturalized, 1977; s. Kasturi Lal and Sushila (Malhotra) C.; m. Hamida Banu, Dec. 7, 1976. B.Sc. in Engring, Banaras Hindu U., Varanasi, India, 1960; M.S., U. Calif., Berkeley, 1963, Ph.D., 1966. Design engr. Standard Vacuum Oil Co., New Delhi, India, 1960-61, Kaiser Engrs. Overseas Corps, India, 1961; asst. prof. civil engr. U. Minn., Mpls., 1966-67; mem. faculty U. Calif., Berkeley, 1967—, prof. civil engring., 1976—; vice chmn. Div. Structural Engring. and Structural Mechanics, 1980-83; dir. Applied Tech. Council, Palo Alto, 1972-74; mem. com. natural disasters NRC, 1980—, chmn., 1982-83; cons. earthquake engring. to govt. and industry. Author over 100 publs. in structural dynamics and earthquake engring.; mem. adv. bd., M.I.T. Press, Series in Structural Mechanics. Recipient Gold medal Banaras Hindu U., 1960, Disting. Alumnus award, 1980; certificate of merit for paper Indian Soc. Earthquake Tech., 1974. Mem. ASCE (Walter L. Huber prize 1975, Norman medal 1979, chmn. EMD tech. com. on dynamics 1975-77, mem. EMD exec. com. 1981—, sec. EMD exec. com. 1981-83), Seismol. Soc. Am. (bd. dirs. 1982-83), Structural Engrs. Assn. Calif., Earthquake Engring. Research Inst., U.S. Com. Large Dams. Home: 635 Crossridge Terr Orinda CA 94563 Office: Dept Civil Engring Univ Calif Berkeley CA 94720

CHOQUETTE, PAUL JOSEPH, JR., building company executive; b. Providence, July 24, 1938; s. Paul Joseph and Virginia Josephine (Gilbane) C.; m. Elizabeth Walsh, Aug. 18, 1962; children: Jeanne Marie, Denise Elizabeth, Suzanne, Christine Noell, Paul Joseph. B.A., Brown U., 1960; LL.B., Harvard U., 1963. Assoc. firm Edwards & Angell, Providence, 1963-65; gov.'s legal counsel State of R.I., Providence, 1965-67; assoc. Edwards & Angell, 1967-69; gen. counsel Gilbane Bldg. Co., Providence, 1969-71, v.p., 1971-75, exec. v.p., 1975-81, pres., 1981—, dir.; dir. Fleet Bank, Fleet Fin. Group; chmn. bd. Gilbane Properties Inc., Taco Inc. Nat. Football Found. scholar, 1959. Mem. Providence C. of C. (past pres., dir.). Roman Catholic. Clubs: Dunes, Hope, Univ. Home: 57 Forge Rd Warwick RI 02818 Office: Gilbane Bldg co 7 Jackson Walkway Providence RI 02940

CHORIN, ALEXANDRE JOEL, mathematician, educator; b. Warsaw, Poland, June 25, 1938; came to U.S., 1962, naturalized, 1971; s. Joseph and Hannah (Judowicz) C.; m. Alice Louise Jones, Aug. 11, 1965; 1 son, Ethan Daniel. Ing.Dipl., EPFL, 1961; M.Sc., NYU, 1964, Ph.D., 1966. Research scientist NYU, 1966-69, asst. prof. math., 1969-71; assoc. prof. U. Calif.-Berkeley, 1972-73, prof., 1973—, Miller research prof., 1971-72, 82-83, dir. Ctr. Pure and Applied Math., 1980-82; sr. staff scientist Lawrence Berkeley Lab., 1980—. Author: (with J. Marsden) A Mathematical Introduction to Fluid Dynamics, 1979; contbr. articles to profl. jours. Sloan Found. fellow, 1972-74. Home: 2501 Hawthorne Terr Berkeley CA 94708 Office: Dept Mathematics U California Berkeley CA 94720

CHOROVER, STEPHAN LEWIS, psychologist; b. N.Y.C., July 17, 1932; s. Aaron and Ann Ruth (Schumacher) C.; m. Beatrice Feinstein, May 21, 1954; children—Nora, Jon, Katya. A.B., Coll. City N.Y., 1955; Ph.D., N.Y. U., 1960. Asst. in pharmacology Albert Einstein Coll. Medicine, N.Y.C., 1956-58; asst. in physiology N.Y. U. Sch. Medicine, N.Y.C., 1958-60; NSF fellow Inst. Neurology London, Cambridge (Eng.) U., 1960-61; research asso. dept. psychology and brain sci. Mass. Inst. Tech., Cambridge, 1961-62, asst. prof., 1962-65, asso. prof., 1965-68, prof., 1968—; cons. in neuropsychology NIMH, NSF; vis. scientist Jackson Lab., Bar Harbor, Maine, U. Calif., Berkeley, Institut Marey, Paris. Author: From Genesis to Genocide: The Meaning of Human Nature and the Power of Behavior Control, 1979; contbr. articles on neuropsychology, neurosci., and psychotech. and soc. to profl. jours. USPHS grantee, 1963—. Mem. AAAS, Internat. Brain Research Orgn., Brit. Psychol. Soc. (hon.), Soc. Neurosci., Am. Psychol. Assn. (fellow div. physiology and comparative psychology). Home: 262 Clinton Rd Brookline MA 02146 Office: 77 Massachusetts Ave Cambridge MA 02139

CHORPENNING, NANCY ELLEN, publishing company executive; b. Columbus, Ohio, Nov. 29, 1953; d. Harry Row and Margaret Ellen (Hayes) C. B.A., Denison U., 1975; postgrad. in mgmt., Northwestern U., 1979—. Ednl. rep. Year Book Med. Pubs. subs. Times Mirror Inc., Chgo., 1975-77, field editor, 1977-79, med. editor, 1979-82; dir., exec. editor G.K. Hall Med. Pubs. subs. ITT Pub., Boston, 1982—. Mem. Nat. Assn. Female Execs., Chgo. Women in Pub., Denison U. Alumni Assn., Alpha Phi. Republican. Congregationalist. Home: 26 Linden Sq Wellesley MA 02181 1415 North View Dr Westlake Village CA 91362 Office: 70 Lincoln St Boston MA 02111

CHOU, CLIFFORD CHI FONG, research engineer; b. Taipei, Taiwan, Dec. 19, 1940; U.S., 1966, naturalized, 1978; s. Ching piao and Yueh li (Huang) C.; m. Chu hwei Lee, Mar. 23, 1968; children: Kelvin Lin yu, Renee Lincy. Ph.D., Mich. State U., 1972. Research asst. Mich. State U., East Lansing, 1967-70, Wayne State U., Detroit, 1970-72, research assoc., 1972-76; research engr. Ford Motor Co., Dearborn, 1976-81, sr. research engr., 1981-82, prin. research engr. assoc., 1982—; tchr. in field. Contbr. articles to profl. jours. Recipient Safety Engring. Excellence award Nat. Hwy. Traffic Safety Adminstrn., 1980; grantee Soc. Automotive Engrs. Mem. ASME, AIAA, Soc. Automotive Engrs., Sigma Xi. Club: Detroit Chinese Am. Assn. Home: 45228 Patrick Dr Canton MI 48187 Office: Scientific Research Lab Ford Motor Co Room E 3184 PO Box 2053 Dearborn MI 48121

CHOU, PEI CHI, mech. engr.; b. Ichang, Hupei, China, Dec. 1, 1924; s. Hung Lieh and Shiu Lan (Kao) C.; m. Rosalind Chen, June 23, 1956; children—James C.Y., George C.H., Arthur C.P., William C.T. B.S., Nat. Central U., China, 1946; M.S., Harvard U., 1949; D.Sc., N.Y. U., 1951. Cons. Budd Co., Phila., 1955-57; Prewitt Aircraft Co., Clifton Heights, Pa., 1957-58, Kellet Aircraft Corp., Willow Grove, Pa., 1958-62, Allegheny Ballistics Lab., Cumberland, Md., 1961-63; Billings prof. mech. engring. Wave Propagation Inst., Drexel U., Phila., 1953—; cons. Air Force Materials Lab., Wright Patterson AFB, Dayton, Ohio, 1966-70, Dyna East Corp., Wynnewood, Pa., 1968—, now v.p. Author: Elasticity: Tensor, Dyadic, and Engineering Approaches, 1967, Dynamic Response of Materials to Intense Impulsive Loading, 1973; asso. editor: Jour. Composite Materials. Pres. Assn. Chinese Schs.; bd. dirs. Rho Psi Found. Mem. Am. Inst. Aero. and Astronautics, ASME, Am. Soc. Engring. Edn., ASTM, Am. Def. Preparedness Assn., Sigma Xi, Phi Tau Sigma, Phi Kappa Phi, Tau Beta Pi, Rho Psi (trustee 1964-71). Republican. Episcopalian. Home: 227 Hemlock Rd Wynnewood PA 19096 Office: 32d and Chestnut Sts Philadelphia PA 19104

CHOU, SHELLEY NIEN-CHUN, neurosurgeon, medical educator; b. Chekiang, China, Feb. 6, 1924; s. Shelley P. and Tse-tsun (Chao) C.; m. Jolene Johnson, Nov. 24, 1956 (div. 1977); children: Shelley T., Dana, Kerry; m. remarried, 1979. B.S., St. John's U., Shanghai, China, 1946; M.D., U. Utah, 1949; M.S., U. Minn., 1954, Ph.D., 1964. Diplomate: Am. Bd. Neurol. Surgery (mem. bd.). Resident U. Minn. Hosps., 1950-55; practice medicine, specializing in neurosurgery, Salt Lake City, 1955-58, Bethesda, Md., 1959, Mpls., 1960—; clin. asst. Coll. Medicine U. Utah, 1956-58; vis. scientist Nat. Insts. Neurol. Diseases and Blindness NIH, 1959; mem. faculty U. Minn., 1960—, asso. prof. neurosurgery, 1965-68, prof. neurosurgery, 1968—, head dept. neurosurgery, 1974—; mem. Am. Bd. Neurol Surg., 1974-79. Contbr. numerous articles to profl. jours.; Publs. on studies of intracranial lesions using radioactive angiography techniques; malformations of cerebral vasculature; neurol. dysfunctions of urinary bladder. Mem. AMA, A.C.S., Congress Neurol. Surgery, Soc. Neurol. Surgeons (pres. 1978-79), Am. Acad. Neurol. Surgery, Soc. Nuclear Medicine, Am. Assn. Neurol. Surgeons (bd. dirs. 1980-83), Neurosurg. Soc. N.Am. (pres. 1977-78), N.Y. Acad. Medicine, Forum Univ. Neurosurgeons (pres. 1968-69), AAAS, Phi Rho Sigma. Home: 12 S Long Lake Trail North Oaks MN 55110 Office: B-590 Mayo Meml 420 SE Delaware St Minneapolis MN 55455

CHOUINARD, JULIEN, judge Can. Supreme Ct.; b. Quebec, Que., Can., Feb. 4, 1929; s. Julien and Berthe (Cloutier) C.; m. Jeannine Pettigrew, Sept. 6, 1956; children—Julien, Lucie, Nicole. B.A., U. Laval, Quebec, 1948, LL.L., 1951; M.A. in Law, U. Oxford, Eng., 1953. Bar: Called to Que. bar 1953, created queen's counsel 1965. Ptnr. firm Prevost, Gagne, Flynn, Chouinard & Jacques, Quebec city, 1953-65; dep. minister of justice, Province Que., Quebec, 1965-68, sec. gen. of exec. council, 1968-75; judge Ct. of Appeal, 1975-79, Supreme Ct. of Can., Ottawa, Ont., 1979—; lectr. in corp. law U. Laval, 1959-66. Co-commr. Royal Commn. of Inquiry into Bilingual Air Traffic Services in, Que., 1976-79. Decorated Centennial medal, officer Order Can.; recipient Vanier medal Inst. Public Adminstrn. Can., 1972; Rhodes scholar, 1951. Office: Supreme Ct Can Wellington St Ottawa ON K1A 0J1 Canada

CHOUINARD, YVON VINCENT, mountaineer, mountaineering equipment manufacturing company executive; b. Lewiston, Maine, Nov. 9, 1938; m. Malinda, 1971; children: Fletcher, Claire. Asst. pvt. investigator with Gerald Chouinard, Los Angeles; mountaineer, climbing equipment mfg.-designer, 1956—; founder, owner The Chouinard Equipment Co., Ventura, Calif., 1966—, Gt. Pacific Iron Works, 1973—. Designer: Shoenard, Chouinard frost ice axe, Realized Ultimate Reality Piton. Served with U.S. Army, 1962-64. Mountaineer 1st ascents, including North Wall of El Capitan, Yosemite, 1964, Nose Route, El Capitan, 1973, South Face, Mt. Watkins, Yosemite, 1964; mountaineer ascents worldwide, including Creag Dhubh, Scotland, Fitzroy Massif, Patagonia, South Island Glaciers, N.Z., Diamond Couloir, Mt. Kenya, Kenya, Gong-ga Shan, China, 1980, Los Frailes, Baja, Calif. Office: Gt Pacific Iron Works PO Box 150 Ventura CA 93002 *

CHOW, ANTHONY WEI-CHIK, physician; b. Hong Kong, May 9, 1941; s. Bernard Shao-Ta and Julia Chen (Fan) C.; m. Katherine Cue, May 20, 1967; children: Calvin Anthony, Byron Calbert. Student, Brandon (Man., Can.) Coll., 1961-63; M.D., U. Man., 1967. Intern Calgary (Atla., Can.) Gen. Hosp., 1967-68; resident in internal medicine Winnipeg (Man.) Gen. Hosp., 1968-70; fellow in infectious disease UCLA Harbor Gen. Hosp., 1970-72, assoc. prof., assoc. head div. infectious disease; practice medicine specializing in infectious disease; prof. medicine, head div. infectious disease U. B.C., Vancouver Hosp., 1979—. Contbr. articles to profl. jours. Med. Research Council Can. grantee, 1979—. Mem. Am. Soc. Microbiology, Am. Fedn. Med. Research, Am. Venereal Disease Assn., Western Assn. Physicians, Infectious Disease Soc. Am., Am. Soc. Clin. Investigation, Coll. Phys. and Surg. B.C., Can. Soc. Clin. Investigation. Roman Catholic. Home: 1119 Gilston Rd West Vancouver BC Canada Office: 700 W 10th Ave Vancouver BC V5Z 1M9 Canada

CHOW, GREGORY CHI-CHONG, educator, economist; b. Macau, South China, Dec. 25, 1929; came to U.S., 1948, naturalized, 1963; s. Tin-Pong and Pauline (Law) C.; m. Paula K. Chen, Aug. 27, 1955; children: John S., James S., Jeanne S. B.A., Cornell U., 1951; M.A., U. Chgo., 1952, Ph.D., 1955. Asst. prof. MIT, 1955-59; asso. prof. Cornell U., 1959-62, vis. prof., 1964-65; staff mem., mgr. econ. models IBM Research Center, Yorktown Heights, N.Y., 1962-70; prof. and dir. econ. research program, 1970—; Class of 1913 prof. polit. economy Princeton, 1979—; adj. prof. Columbia U., 1965-70; vis. prof. Harvard U., 1967, Rutgers U., 1969. Author: Demand for Automobiles in the United States: A Study in Consumer Durables, 1957, Analysis and Control of Dynamic Economic Systems, 1975, Econometric Analysis by Control Methods, 1981; author Econometrics, 1983; The Chinese Economy, 1984; co-editor: Evaluating the Reliability of Macro-Economic Models, 1982; Contbr. to: The Demand for Durable Goods, 1960; also articles to profl. jours.; co-editor: Jour. Econ. Dynamics and Control. Fellow Econometric Soc., Am. Statis. Assn., Academia Sinica; mem. Am. Econ. Assn., Inst. Math. Statistics, Soc. for Econ. Dynamics and Control (pres. 1979-80). Home: 30 Hardy Dr Princeton NJ 08540 Office: Dept Econs Princeton U Princeton NJ 08544

CHOW, KAO LIANG, neurobiologist, educator; b. Tientsin, China, Apr. 21, 1918; came to U.S., 1946, naturalized, 1963; s. Su Tau and Tau Yu (Tsau) C.; m. Margaret W.C. Zee, May 2, 1964. B.S., Yenching U., China, 1943; Ph.D., Harvard, 1950. Staff Yerkes Lab. Primate Biology, Orange Park, Fla., 1947-54, research asso., 1947-54; faculty U. Chgo., 1954-61; mem. faculty Stanford Med. Sch., Palo Alto, Calif., 1961—, prof. neurology, 1965—. Contbr. articles profl. jours. Mem. Internat. Brain Research Orgn., Am. Physiol. Assn., A.A.A.S., Sigma Xi. Home: 101 Alma St Apt 805 Palo Alto CA 94301

CHOW, RITA KATHLEEN, government official; b. San Francisco, Aug. 19, 1926; d. Peter and May (Chan) C. B.S., Stanford U., 1950, nursing diploma, 1950; M.S., Case Western Res. U., 1955; profl. diploma in nursing edn. adminstrn, Columbia U., 1961, Ed.D., 1968. Asst. in teaching Stanford (Calif.) U., 1951-52; instr., dir. student health Fresno (Calif.) Gen. Hosp. Sch. Nursing, 1952-54; instr. Wayne State U. Coll. Nursing, Detroit, 1957-58; research asso., project dir. cardiovascular nursing research Ohio State U., Columbus, 1965-68; commd. officer USPHS, 1968, advanced through grades to nurse dir., 1974; spl. asst. to dep. dir. Nat. Center Health Services Research, Health Services and Mental Health Adminstrn., HEW, Rockville, Md., 1969-73; dep. dir. manpower utilization br., 1970-73; dep. dir. Office Long Term Care; dep. chief nurse officer USPHS, Rockville, 1973-77; chief quality assurance br. div. long-term care Office of Standards and Certification, Health Standards and Quality Bur., Health Care Fin. Adminstrn., HHS, 1977-82; health sci. analyst Office Health Tech. Assessment Nat. Ctr. Health Services Research, OASH, HHS, 1982—. Author: Identifying Nursing Action with the Care of Cardiovascular Patients, 1967, Cardiosurgical Nursing Care: Understandings, Concepts, and Principles for Practice, 1975; Editorial bd., HPEER Am. Ednl. Research Assn., 1973-77; Contbr. to publs. in field. Served with Nurse Corps U.S. Army, 1954-57; commd. officer USPHS, 1968; advanced through grades to nurse dir., 1974. AAUW scholar; Nat. League Nursing fellow, 1959-61; recipient research grant Sigma Theta Tau, 1966; Fed. Nursing Service award Assn. Mil. Surgeons U.S., 1969; citation for outstanding contbn. to cardiovascular nursing Am. Heart Assn., 1972, 79; Nursing Edn. Alumni Assn. award for distinguished achievement in nursing research Columbia U. Tchrs. Coll., 1973; Meritorious Service medal USPHS, 1977; Disting. Alumnus award Case Western Res. U. Sch. Nursing, 1979. Home: US PO Box 163 Annandale VA 22003 Office: Nat Ctr Health Services Research Park Bldg 310-2 5600 Fishers Ln Rockville MD 20857

CHOW, TSE-TSUNG, educator, author; b. Kiyang, Hunan, China, Jan. 7, 1916; s. P'eng-Chu and Ai-Ku (Tsou) C.; m. Nancy N. Wu; children: Lena Jane, Genie Ann. B.A., Cheng-Chih U., 1942; M.A., U. Mich., 1950, Ph.D., 1955. Editor-in-chief New Understanding monthly, Chungking, China, 1942-43; dir. dept. research and supervision Chungking Municipal Govt., 1943-44; editor-in-chief City Govt., monthly, 1943-44; editor New Critic monthly, 1945; dean Chungking Coll. Pub. Adminstrn., 1944; sec. to Pres. Republic China, 1945-47; research asst. U. Mich., 1955; research fellow Harvard U., 1956-60, research assoc., 1961-62; vis. lectr. U. Wis., Madison, 1963, assoc. prof., 1964-65, prof., 1966—, chmn. dept. East Asian langs. and lit., 1973-79. Author: Election, Initiative, Referendum and Recall: Charter Provisions in Michigan Home Rule Cities, 1958, The May Fourth Movement: Intellectual Revolution in Modern China, 1960, Research Guide to The May Fourth Movement, 1963, Hai-yen (Stormy Petrel) (collected poems), 1961, On the Chinese Couplet, 1964, A New Study of the Broken Axes in the book of poetry, 1969, An Index to Mathews' Chinese-English Dictionary with a New Method of Arranging Chinese Words, 1971; Editor: Wen-Lin: Studies in the Chinese Humanities, 1968, On Wang Kuo-wei's Tz'u Poetry, 1971; Chinese transl. Rabindranath Tagore's Fireflies, 1971, Stray Birds, 1971, Odyssey (1st part), 1972; Papers on Dream of the Red Chamber, 1982. Recipient medal of honor Chinese Govt., 1946; Guggenheim fellow, 1966-67. Mem. MLA, Assn. Asian Studies, Island Soc. Singapore (hon. pres.), Singapore Assn. Writers (hon. pres.). Home: 1101 Minton Rd Madison WI 53711

CHOY, HERBERT YOUNG CHO, judge; b. Makaweli, Kauai, Hawaii, Jan. 6, 1916; s. Doo Wook and Helen (Nahm) C.; m. Dorothy Helen Shular, June 16; 1945. B.A., U. Hawaii, 1938; J.D., Harvard U., 1941. Bar: Hawaii bar 1941. Practiced in, Honolulu, 1946-57, 58-71, atty. gen., Ter. Hawaii, 1957-58; judge U.S. Ct. Appeals, 9th circuit, Honolulu, 1971—. Trustee Hawaii Loa Coll., 1963-79. Served with AUS, 1942-46. Decorated Order Civil Merit, Korea). Fellow Am. Bar Found.; mem. Am., Hawaii bar assns., World Peace Through Law Center. Home: 3964 Monterey Pl Honolulu HI 96816 Office: US Courthouse Honolulu HI 96850

CHOY, WILBUR WONG YAN, bishop; b. Stockton, Calif., May 28, 1918; s. Lie Yen and Ida (Lee) C.; m. Grace Ying Hom, Sept. 26, 1940 (dec. Dec. 1977); children: Randolph W., Jonathan W., Phyllis W. (Mrs. Lawrence Uno), Donnell W. A.A., Stockton Jr. Coll., 1944; B.A., Coll. of Pacific, Stockton, 1946; M.Div., Pacific Sch. Religion, Berkeley, Calif., 1949, D.D., 1969; L.H.D., U. Puget Sound, Tacoma, 1973. Ordained deacon Methodist Ch., 1947, elder, 1949; asso. pastor Chinese Meth. Ch., Stockton, 1943-49, pastor, 1949-54, St. Marks Meth. Ch., Stockton, 1954-59; asso. pastor Woodland (Calif.) Meth. Ch., 1959-60; pastor Oak Park Meth. Ch., Sacramento, 1960-69; also Chinese Meth. Ch., Sacramento, 1968-69; dist. supt. Bay View Dist., Calif.-Nev. Conf., United Meth. Ch., 1969-72, resident bishop, Seattle Area, 1972-80, San Francisco Area, 1980—; mem. exec. com. World Meth. Council; mem. Gen. Bd. of Ch. and Soc., United Meth. Ch., 1972-80, Gen. Bd. of Global Ministry, 1980—; v.p., chmn. div. gen. welfare, 1972-76; chaplain Calif. Senate, 1967; del. United Meth. Western Jurisdictional Conf., 1952, 56, 60, 64, 72, alt., 1968; del. United Meth. Gen. Conf., 1972; mem. Meth. Gen. Bd. of Temperance, 1952-56; mem. adv. com. Asian-Am. Ministries, 1968-72; mem. exec. com. Nat. Conf. Chinese Chs., 1971-74; Rep. Chinese Assn. of Stockton to Nat. Conf. Chinese Communities in U.S.A., 1954; cons. Pacific and Asian Center Theology and Strategies, Berkeley, Calif., 1972—. Bd. dirs. Goodwill Industries, Stockton, 1958-59, Family Service Agy., Stockton, 1958-59, Family Service Agy., Woodland, 1959-60, Center for Asian-Am. Ministries, Sch. Theology at Claremont (Calif.), 1977—; trustee Pacific Sch. Religion, Berkeley, U. Puget Sound, Tacoma, 1972-80; mem. exec. com. Oak Park Neighborhood Council, Sacramento, 1964-67. Club: Press (San Francisco). Office: 330 Ellis St PO Box 467 San Francisco CA 94101 *

CHRENCIK, FRANK, chemical company executive; b. Osage, Iowa, Jan. 6, 1914; s. Tom and Agnes (Walashek) C.; m. Edith Jo Phelps, July 27, 1935; children: Charles Frank, James Phelps (dec.). B.S. in Chem. Engring, State U. Iowa, 1937; grad., Advanced Mgmt. Program, Harvard, 1955. Plant engr., prodn. and constrn. supr. gen. chem. div. Allied Chem. & Dye Corp., 1937-40; mgr. various plants Diamond Shamrock Chem. Co., Cleve., 1946-56, gen. mgr. electrochems. div., 1956-60, co. v.p., sr. officer, 1960-72; dir., chmn. exec. com. Terra Chem. Internat., Inc., Sioux City, Iowa, 1969-72; exec. v.p. chems. and metals group Vulcan Materials Corp., Birmingham, Ala., 1972-77, vice chmn. bd., 1977-79, also dir., mem. exec. com., emeritus, dir. and cons., 1979—; bd. govs. Gulf Coast Devel. Co., Pasadena, Tex., 1955; Past mem. adv. council Coll. Engring., State U. Iowa.; bd. dirs. Chlorine Inst., 1968-72. Mem. internat. adv. bd.: Ency. of Chem. Processing and Design. Past trustee Nat. Hemophilia Found., N.Y. Served to lt. col. Chem. Corps AUS, 1940-46. Recipient Disting. Alumni Achievement award U. Iowa, 1977. Mem. Am. Inst. Chem. Engrs. (Outstanding Chem. Engr. Award Ala. sect. 1983), Mfg. Chemists Assn., U. Iowa Pres.'s Club. Clubs: The Club, Vestavia Country (Birmingham). Home: 3401 Westbury Rd Birmingham AL 35223 Office: 1 Metroplex Dr Birmingham AL 35209

CHRETIEN, JEAN, Canadian government official; b. Shawinigan, Que., Can., Jan. 11, 1934; s. Wellie and Marie (Boisvert) C.; m. Aline Chaine, Sept. 10, 1957; children: France, Hubert, Michel. Law degree, Laval (Que.) U., 1958. Bar: Called to Que. bar 1958. Mem. firm Chrêtien, Landry, Deschênes, Trudel & Normand; mem. Canadian Ho. of Commons from St. Maurice, 1963—; Parliamentary sec. to prime minister, 1965, to minister of finance, 1966, minister without portfolio, 1967, of nat. revenue, 1968, of Indian affairs and No. devel., 1968-74; pres. Treasury Bd. Can., 1974-76; minister of industry, trade and commerce, 1976-77, finance, 1977-79, justice; atty. gen. of Can., minister of state responsible for constl. negotiations, 1980-82; minister of energy, mines and resources, 1982. Mem. Shawinigan Sr. C. of C. (dir. 1962). Mem. Liberal Party. Office: House of Commons Ottawa ON Canada K1A 0R6 *

CHRIEN, ROBERT EDWARD, physicist; b. Cleve., Apr. 15, 1930; s. Friedrich and Anna (Goros) C.; m. Susan Varga, June 6, 1953; children: Robert Edward, Katherine, Elizabeth, Thomas. B.S. in Physics, Rensselaer Poly. Inst., 1952; M.S., Case Inst. Tech., 1955, Ph.D., 1958. Research assoc. Brookhaven Nat. Lab., Upton, N.Y., 1957-59, asst. physicist, 1959-61, asso. physicist, 1961-65, physicist, 1965-72, sr. physicist, 1972—, group leader, mem.; Group leader, sci. writer specializing in nuclear physics Grolier, Harper & Rowe, Plenum Press, Pergamon Press, N.Y.C., 1966; chmn. sec. U.S. Nuclear Data Com., 1967-74; mem. European-Am. Nuclear Data Com., 1971—; chmn. Nuclear Energy Agy. Nuclear Data Com., 1978—. Editor: Nuclear Sci. and Tech. Series, Pergamon Press; contbr. articles to profl. jours. Fellow Am. Phys. Soc., N.Y. Acad. Scis., AAAS; mem. Am. Chem. Soc. (nuclear chemistry div.), Sigma Xi. Lutheran. Home: 51 S Country Rd Bellport NY 11713 Office: Dept Physics Brookhaven Nat Lab Upton NY 11973

CHRIST, CARL FINLEY, educator, economist; b. Chgo., Sept. 19, 1923; s. Jay Finley and Maud (Trego) C.; m. Phyllis Tatsch, Mar. 16, 1951; children: Alice Trego, Joan Elizabeth, Lucy Martha. Student, Colo. Coll., 1940-42; B.S. in Physics, U. Chgo., 1943; Ph.D. in Econs., 1950. Jr. physicist Manhattan Project, 1943-45; instr. physics Princeton, 1945-46; research asso. Cowles Commn. Research Econs., 1949-50; asst. prof., asso. prof. polit. economy Johns Hopkins, 1950-55; asso. prof. econs. U. Chgo., 1955-61; prof. polit. economy Johns Hopkins U., 1961—, Abram G. Hutzler prof., 1977—; chmn. dept., 1961-66, 69-70; Vis. prof. U. Tokyo, 1959; Keynes vis. prof. econs. U. Essex (Eng.), 1966-67; lectr. Kyoto (Japan) Am. Studies Summer Seminar, 1977, Brazilian Econometric Soc., 1981; Chmn. Univs.-Nat. Bur. Com. for Econs. Research, 1967-74; mem. Md. Gov.'s Council Econ. Advisers, 1969-77; bd. dirs. Nat. Bur. Econ. Research, 1975—; mem. econ. adv. panel NSF, 1965-66, 67-68; cons. Fed. Res. Bd., 1979. Author: Econometric Models and Methods, 1966; Bd. editors: Am. Econ. Rev., 1969-73; adv. bd.: Jour. Monetary Econs., 1983—. Sr. Fulbright research scholar U. Cambridge, Eng., 1954-55; fellow Center Advanced Study Behavioral Scis., Palo Alto, Calif., 1960-61. Fellow Econometric Soc. (Council 1976-82), Am. Statis. Assn.; mem. Am. Econ. Assn. (v.p. 1980), Am. Fin. Assn. Address: Political Economy Dept Johns Hopkins Univ Baltimore MD 21218

CHRIST, CHARLES FREDERICK, manufacturing executive; b. Saginaw, Mich., Mar. 5, 1939; s. Frederick Arthur and Irene (Mooney) C.; m. Judith Kay Ploetz, Aug. 6, 1960; children: Geoffrey, Matthew, Rachel, Jonathan. B.Indsl. Engring., Gen. Motors Inst., 1962; M.B.A., Harvard U., 1964. Strategic planning mgr. Xerox Corp., Stamford, Conn., 1971-72, mfg. mgr., 1972-73, mgr. mfg. ops., 1974-76, v.p. mfg. tech., 1976-81, v.p. transition program, 1981, pres. Reprographic Mfg. Group, 1981—; mem. adj. faculty U. Rochester, N.Y., 1972—; mem. adv. com. Lab. for Productivity, MIT, Cambridge, 1980—. Contbr. articles to profl. jours. Republican. Office: Reprographic Mfg Group 800 Phillips Rd Webster NY 14580 *

CHRISTENBERRY, GEORGE ANDREW, coll. pres.; b. Macon, Ga., Sept. 3, 1915; s. Thomas Edwin and Jessie Gertrude (Earnhardt) C.; m. Elizabeth Reid, Sept. 4, 1937; children—Becky Anne, George A., John Reid. B.S., Furman U., 1936; A.M., U. N.C., 1938, Ph.D., 1940. Mem. faculty Meredith Coll., Raleigh, N.C., 1940-43, prof. biology and head dept., 1942-43; mem. faculty Furman U., Greenville, S.C., 1943-44, 46, prof. biology, dean men's coll., 1948-53, v.p. for devel., adminstrv. dir., 1958-64; pres. Shorter Coll., Rome, Ga., 1953-58; prof., chmn. dept. biology Ga. Coll. at Milledgeville, 1964-65, dean coll., 1965-70; pres. Augusta (Ga.) Coll., 1970-79, 80—; vice chancellor Univ. System of Ga., 1979-80. Contbr. papers on mycology. Bd. dirs. United Way; trustee Richmond County Mus.; Active A.R.C. campaigns; pres. bd. dirs. Traveler's Aid Soc., 1950; chmn. edn. commn. Ga. Bapt. Conv.; mem. exec. com. Bapt. World Alliance, 1965-70. Served as lt. USNR, as radar officer aboard attack transport, 1944-46. Mem. A.A.A.S., Mycol. Soc. Am., Assn. Ga. Colls. (pres. 1957-58), Ga. Edn. Assn. (pres. dept. higher edn. 1955-56), Assn. Southeastern Biologists, S.C. Acad. Sci., Greater Augusta C. of C. (dir.), Am. Inst. Biol. Scis., Ga. Acad. Scis. Baptist (deacon). Clubs: Torch (pres. Western S.C. 1952-53), Rotary (pres. Milledgeville 1968-69), Rotary (pres. Augusta 1976-77). Home: Augusta College 2500 Walton Way Augusta GA 30910

CHRISTENSEN, A(LBERT) KENT, anatomy educator; b. Washington, D.C., Dec. 3, 1927; s. Albert Sherman and Lois (Bowen) C.; m. Elizabeth Anne Reynolds Sears, Aug. 26, 1952; children: Anne, Kathleen Martha, Albert David, Jennifer, John Sears. A.B., Brigham Young U., 1953; Ph.D., Harvard U., 1958. Instr. dept. anatomy Harvard Med. Sch., Boston, 1960-61; asst. prof. dept. anatomy Stanford Sch. Medicine, Palo Alto, Calif., 1961-68, asso. prof., 1968-71; prof., chmn. dept. anatomy Temple U. Sch. Medicine, Phila., 1971-78; prof. anatomy U. Mich. Med. Sch., Ann Arbor, 1978—, chmn. dept. anatomy and cell biology, 1978-82. Contbr. articles to profl. jours. Served with USMC, 1946-47. Postdoctoral fellow Cornell Med. Coll., 1958-59, Harvard Med. Sch., 1959-60. Mem. AAAS, Am. Soc. Cell Biology, Am. Assn. Anatomists, Endocrine Soc., Soc. for Study of Reprodn. Office: Dept Anatomy and Cell Biology Med Sci II Bldg U Mich Med Sch Ann Arbor MI 48109

CHRISTENSEN, ALBERT SHERMAN, judge; b. Manti, Utah, June 9, 1905; s. Albert H. and Jennie (Snow) C.; m. Lois Bowen, Apr. 4, 1927; children: A. Kent, Karen D., Krege B. Student, Brigham Young U., intermittently 1923-27; J.D., Nat. U., 1931. Bar: D.C. 1932, Utah 1933. Asst. bus. specialist U.S. Dept. Commerce, 1930-32; practiced in, Provo, Utah, 1933-42, 45-54, U.S. dist. judge, Salt Lake City, 1954—; mem. com. on revision laws Jud. Conf. U.S., 1960-68, com. on ct. adminstrn., 1968-75, mem. adv. com. rules of civil procedure, 1972-82, mem. rev. com., 1977-78, jud. ethics com., 1978—; mem. Temporary Emergency Ct. Appeals, 1972—; mem. bd. Utah Bar Examiners, 1939-42. Republican congressional candidate, 1939. Served from lt. to lt. comdr. USNR, 1942-45. Mem. ABA, Utah Bar Assn. (pres. 1951-52), Utah Jr. Bar Assn. (pres. 1937-38), Utah County Bar Assn. (pres. 1936-37, 47-48). Mem. Ch. Jesus Christ of Latter-day Saints. Office: Federal Bldg Salt Lake City UT 84138

CHRISTENSEN, CARL ROLAND, business administration educator; b. Tyler, Minn., Aug. 17, 1919; s. Thomas P. and Marie (Dahm) C.; m. Dorothy Isabell Smith, Dec. 26, 1943; children: Philip, Steven, Ann, Joan. A.B., U. Iowa, 1941; M.B.A., Harvard, 1943; D.C.S., Harvard, 1953. From instr. to assoc. prof. Harvard Bus. Sch., 1946-58; prof. Harvard Grad. Sch. Bus., 1958—, Robert Walmsley prof. bus. adminstrn., 1963—; Vis prof., Stanford, 1955, Imede, Lausanne, Switzerland, 1963-64, Sloan Sch. Mgmt., M.I.T., 1977-79; dir. lInternat. Register Co., Chgo., Cabot Corp., Boston, Arthur D. Little, Inc., Cambridge, Mass., Bank of New Eng. N.A., New Eng. Mchts. Bank, Cooper Industries. Author: Management Succession in Small and Growing Enterprise, 1953, (with G.A. Smith, Jr.) Policy Formulation and Administration, 1955, 9th edit., 1982, (with A. Zaleznick, F. J. Roethlisberger) Motivation, Productivity and Satisfaction of Workers, 1959, (with E.P. Learned, K.R. Andrews) Problems in General Management, (with others) Business Policy: Text and Cases, 1965, 4th edit., 1976; rev., 1977. Served from cpl. to captain AUS, 1943-46. Mem. Am. Soc. Pub. Adminstrn., Acad. Polit. Sci., Soc. Applied Anthropology, Am. Sociol. Soc., Phi Beta Kappa. Home: 4 Oakmount Circle Lexington MA 02173 Office: Harvard Bus Sch Boston MA 02163

CHRISTENSEN, CLYDE MARTIN, educator; b. Sturgeon Bay, Wis., Aug. 8, 1905; s. Peter Karl and Christine Ann (Christensen) C.; m. Katherine Wallace Barry, Sept. 27, 1935; children—Sarah Ellen (Mrs. William R. Nelson), Melanie Barry, Jane Martin (Mrs. Gary Thompson Vance). B.S., U. Minn., 1929, M.S., 1930, Ph.D., 1937; postgrad., U. Halle, Halle an der Saale, Germany, 1932-33. Instr. U. Minn., 1929-37, asst. prof., 1937-46, asso. prof., 1946-48, prof. plant pathology, 1948—, Regents' prof., 1973—; Cons. various grain storage and processing firms. Author: Common Edible Mushrooms, 1943, Common Fleshy Fungi, 1946, The Molds and Man, 1953; Spanish edit. Los Hongos y El Hombre, 1964, (with H.H. Kaufmann) Grain Storage: The Role of Fungi in Quality Loss, 1969, Molds, Mushrooms and Mycotoxins, 1975; also articles. Fellow Am. Phytopath. Soc., Am. Coll. Allergists (hon.); mem. Am. Soc. Microbiology, Mycol. Soc. Am., Sigma Xi. Home: 12619 Skyview Dr Sun City West AZ 85375

CHRISTENSEN, CRAIG WANE, university dean, legal educator; b. Lehi, Utah, Mar. 11, 1939. B.S., Brigham Young U., 1961; J.D. magna cum laude, Northwestern U., 1964. Bar: Ill. 1965, U.S. Supreme Ct. 1973. Assoc. Kirkland, Ellis, Hodson, Chaffetz & Masters, Chgo., 1964-66; exec. asst. to chmn. and pres. C & N.W. Ry. Co., Chgo., 1966-67; dir. Nat. Inst. for Edn. in Law and Poverty, Chgo., 1967-70; assoc. prof. law, legal adviser to pres. U. Mich., 1970-71; dean, prof. law Cleve. State U., 1971-75, Syracuse U., 1975—. Trustee Law Sch. Admission Council, 1979—; chmn. fin. com., 1983—; asst. to chmn. White House Civil Rights Conf., 1966; mem. legal services nat. adv. com. OEO, 1968-70. Mem. ABA (vice chmn. div. state adminstrv. law 1977-81, mem. Right to Legal Services Com. 1970-71), N.Y. State Bar Assn., Order of Coif. Home: 949 Maryland Ave Syracuse NY 13210 Office: Syracuse U Coll Law Ernest I White Hall Syracuse NY 13210

CHRISTENSEN, DAN, painter; b. Lexington, Nebr., 1942. B.F.A., Kansas City Art Inst., 1964. Guest artist Whitney Mus. Sch., 1969, San Francisco Art Inst., 1971, Provincetown Workshop for Artists and Writers, 1972; instr. Ridgewood Sch. Art., 1975, 76, 77, Sch. Visual Arts, N.Y.C., 1976-82. Exhibited one-man shows, Noah Goldowsky Gallery, N.Y.C., 1967, Galerie Ricke, Cologne, Germany, 1968, 71, Andre Emmerich Gallery, N.Y.C., 1969, Nicholas Wilder Gallery, Los Angeles, 1970, Edmonton Art Gallery, Alta., 1973, Greenberg Gallery, St. Louis, 1974, Andre Emmerich Gallery, N.Y.C., 1975, Douglas Drake Gallery, Kansas City, 1976, B.R. Kornblatt Gallery, Balt., 1977, Meridith Long Contemporary Gallery, N.Y.C., 1978, 79, 80, U. Nebr. at Omaha Art Gallery, 1980, Salander-O'Reilly Galleries Inc., N.Y.C., 1981, 82, 83, Ivory Kimpton gallery, San Francisco, 1982, Lincoln Ctr. Gallery, N.Y.C., 1983, group shows, Oberlin Coll., Ohio, 1966, Whitney Annual, N.Y.C., 1967, Whitney Mus. Am. Art, N.Y.C., 1968, 71, 72, 73, Galerie Ricke, Kassel, Germany, 1968, Corcoran Mus. Biennial, Washington, 1969, Guggenheim Mus., N.Y.C., Albright-Knox Gallery, Buffalo, N.Y., 1970, Balt. Mus. Art, 1971-72, Milw. Art Ctr., 1972, Boston Mus. Fine Arts, Aldrich Mus. Contemporary Art, Ridgefield, Conn., 1973, Greenberg Gallery, St. Louis, 1974, Museo Bellas Artes, Curacus, 1975, Lehigh U., Bethlehem. Pa., 1976, Edmunton Art Gallery, 1977, U. Nebr., Omaha, 1978, Zolla Liberman Gallery, Chgo., 1979, Carson-Sapiro Gallery, Denver, 1980, Mus. Modern Art, N.Y.C., 1981, Mus. Fine Arts, Houston, La Jolla Mus. Contemporary Art, Calif., Spl. Projects at PSI, N.Y.C., 1983; represented permanent collections, Albright-Knox Gallery, Boston Mus. Fine Arts, Chgo. Art Inst., Dayton Art Inst., Denver Mus. Art, Edmunton Art Gallery, Guggenheim Mus., Hirshhorn Mus. and Sculpture Garden, Washington, Houston Mus. Fine Arts, Wallraf-Richartz, Cologne, Germany, Met. Mus. Art, N.Y.C., Mus. Contemporary Art, Chgo., Mus. Modern Art, N.Y.C., St. Louis Art Mus., Toledo Mus., Whitney Mus. Am. Art. Recipient Theodoron award, 1969; Nat. Endowment grantee, 1968; Guggenheim fellow, 1969. Mem. Kansas City Art Inst. (gov. 1981). Office: care Salander-O'Reily Gallery 22 E 80th St New York NY 10021 *

CHRISTENSEN, FRANK L., drill manufacturing company executive. Chmn. Christensen Inc. Office: Christensen Inc. 365 Bugatti St Box 26185 Salt Lake City UT 84126

CHRISTENSEN, GEORGE CURTIS, university official; b. N.Y.C., Feb. 21, 1924; s. Carl Lee and Marie (Larsen) C.; m. Janeth M. Reid, July 19, 1947; children: Curtis Lee, Joyce Janeth, William George, Cheryl Reid. D.V.M., Cornell U., 1949, M.S., 1950, Ph.D., 1953; D.Sc. (hon.), Purdue U., 1978. Instr. vet. anatomy Cornell U., 1949-53; asso. prof. vet. anatomy Iowa State U., 1953-58; prof. vet. anatomy, head dept. Purdue U., 1958-63; dean Iowa State U. Coll. Vet. Medicine, Ames, 1963-65; v.p. acad. affairs Iowa State U., Ames, 1965—; chmn. council on internat. programs, commr. North Central Assn. Colls. and Secondary Schs.; chmn. Iowa Instnl. Com. Ednl. Coordination; mem. com. on costs of educating med. profls. Nat. Acad. Sci.-NRC. Co-author: Anatomy of the Dog, 1964. Vice pres. Iowa Bd. Health.; Bd. dirs. Quad Cities Grad. Center, State Hygienic Lab., Iowa, Center for Research Libraries. Served with AUS, 1942-43. Mem. Am. Assn. Anatomists, Am. Assn. Vet. Anatomists, AVMA (past chmn. council on edn.), AAAS, Mid-Am. State Univs. Assn. (v.p., governing council), Nat. Adv. Council on Research Resources, Conf. Research Workers Animal Diseases, Am. Assn. for Accreditation of Lab. Animal Care (chmn.), Nat. Assn. State Univs. and Land Grant Colls. (chmn. council acad. affairs, chmn. com. on open learning, mem. exec. com., com. on ednl. telecommunications, exec. com. council on internat. programs), N.Y. Acad. Scis., Sigma Xi, Phi Kappa Phi, Phi Zeta, Lambda Chi Alpha, Alpha Psi, Gamma Sigma Delta, Cardinal Key. Lutheran. Club: Rotarian. Research numerous publs. cardiovascular system, genito-urinary system, history vet. med. edn., higher edn. Home: 1025 Gaskill Dr Ames IA 50010

CHRISTENSEN, HALVOR NIELS, educator, biochemist; b. Cozad, Nebr., Oct. 24, 1915; s. Niels and Matena (Smidt) C.; m. Mayme Matthews, Aug. 28, 1939; children—Haldan, Carl, Karen. B.S., Nebr. State Tchrs. Coll., (now Kearney State Coll.), 1935; M.S., Purdue U., 1937; Ph.D., Harvard, 1939. Asst. chemistry Purdue U., 1935-37; asso. chemistry, Harvard, 1939-40; biochemist Lederle Labs., 1940-42; instr. biol. chemistry Harvard Med. Sch., 1942-44, Asst. prof., 1947-49; Biochemist Mary Imogene Bassett Hosp., 1944-47; Dir. dept. chem. research Children's Hosp., Boston, 1947-49; prof., head dept. biochemistry and nutrition Tufts Coll. Med. Sch., 1949-55; prof. biol. chemistry U. Mich. Med. Sch., Ann Arbor, 1955—, head dept., 1955-70, Russel lectr., 1980; Guggenheim fellow Carlsberg Lab., Copenhagen, 1952; Nobel guest prof. U. Uppsala, Sweden, 1968-69; cons. USPHS.; Mem. Unitarian Service Com. Med. Mission to Germany, 1950. Author: Neutrality Regulation in the Living Organism, Dissociation, Enzyme Kinetics and Bioenergetics, pH and Dissociation: Body Fluids and the Acid-Base Balance, Introduction to Bioenergetics, Thermodynamics for the Biologist; (with R.A. Cellarius) programmed texts, monograph Biological Transport, 1962-75; Contbr. numerous articles to profl. jours. Recipient Distinguished Service award Kearney State Coll., 1978. Mem. Am. Soc. Biol. Chemists, Am. Chem. Soc., Am. Acad. Arts and Scis., Biophys. Soc., Am. Inst. Nutrition, Sigma Xi. Home: 2200 Devonshire Rd Ann Arbor MI 48104

CHRISTENSEN, HAROLD GRAHAM, lawyer; b. Springville, Utah, June 25, 1926; s. Harold and Ruby (Graham) C.; m. Gayle Sutton, June 17, 1950; children: Steven H., David S., Susan. A.B., U. Utah, 1949; J.D., U. Mich., 1951. Bar: Utah 1952. Partner firm Skeen, Worsley, Snow & Christensen (and successor firms), Salt Lake City; chmn. bd. Snow Christensen & Martineau, P.C., Salt Lake City, 1972—. Served with USNR, 1944-46. Fellow Am. Coll. Trial Lawyers; mem. Am. Bar Found., Fedn. Ins. Counsel, Utah State Bar (pres. 1975-76), Utah Bar Found. (trustee 1978), Salt Lake County Bar (pres. 1972-73). Home: 2269 Pheasant Way Salt Lake City UT 84121 Office: 10 Exchange Pl 11th Floor Salt Lake City UT 84111

CHRISTENSEN, HARVEY DEVON, aerospace and mech. engr., educator; b. Challis, Idaho, Apr. 6, 1920; s. Haireld H. and Ethel S. (James) C.; m. Dolores M. Spelbrink, June 9, 1951; childrenJeannette Marie, Karen Cozette, Denise Annette, Christopher Benton, Amy Elizabeth. B.S. in Mech. Engring, U. Wash., 1943; M.S., Oreg. State U., 1950; Ph.D., Stanford, 1960. Registered profl. engr., Ariz., Oreg. Prof. aerospace and mech. engring. U. Ariz., Tucson, 1958—, head dept., 1958-70; Cons. to industry, 1948—. Contbr. articles to profl. jours. Recipient Anderson prize for recognizing accomplishment in engring. of edn., 1976—. Mem. Am. Soc. Engring. Edn., ASME, Soc. Automotive Engrs., Sigma Xi, Pi Tau Sigma. Spl. research individual paced interactive ednl. systems, nonlinear mechanics, structures, exptl. stress analysis, engring. mechanics, applied math. Home: 5714 E S Wilshire St Tucson AZ 85711

CHRISTENSEN, HOWARD ALAN, investor relations consultant; b. Atlantic, Iowa, Aug. 15, 1933; s. J. Chris and S. Christena (Gustafsen) C.; m. Verla Suhr, May 10, 1953; children—Debra, Jo Elyn, Jeffrey. B.S., State U. Iowa, 1959. C.P.A., Kans., Mo. Mgr. Arthur Andersen & Co., Kansas City, Mo., 1959-65; v.p., sec. St. Joseph Light & Power Co., St. Joseph, Mo., 1965-76; treas. Mich. Wis. Pipe Line Co., Detroit, 1976-78; dir. investor relations Am. Natural Resources Co., Detroit, 1978-80, v.p. corp. planning and investor relations, 1980-82; with Christensen & Langs Inc., investor relations cons. Bd. dirs. United Fund, 1972-76. Served with U.S. Army, 1953-55. Mem. Am. Inst. C.P.A.s, Fin. Analyst Soc., Nat. Investor Relations Inst., C. of C. (dir. 1972-76, 1st v.p. 1975-76). Lutheran. Clubs: Savoyard, City Midday, Rotary (dir. 1968-76), Rotary (pres. 1974-75), Detroit Athletic, Renaissance. Home: 748 Woodchester Dr Bloomfield Hills MI 48013 Office: Christensen & Langs Inc 1800 Guardian Bldg 500 Griswold St Detroit MI 48226

CHRISTENSEN, JOHN WILLIAM, lawyer; b. Roselawn, Ind., Mar. 14, 1914; s. Henry Julius and Caroline Belle (Conrad) C.; m. Eleanor Schwerak, Sept. 2, 1939; children—William J., Amy Christensen Fox, Martha Christensen Rand, Nancy Christensen Couyoumjian. A.B., DePauw U., 1935; J.D., U. Ind., 1939. Bar: Ind. bar 1939, Ohio bar 1947. Accountant Gen. Electric Co., Schnectady, 1936-37; atty. SEC, 1939-44; spl. counsel Utilities div., 1944-46; asso., then partner firm Dargusch, Caren, Greek & King, Columbus, Ohio, 1946-53; v.p., gen. counsel, dir. Brodhead-Garrett Co., Cleve., 1955—, Columbus Mut. Life Ins. Co., 1962—; v.p., sec., dir. O.M. Scott & Sons Co., Marysville, Ohio, 1951—; partner firm Gingher & Christensen, Columbus, 1953—; chmn., pres., chief exec. officer, dir. Nat. Extrusion and Mfg., Bellefontaine, Ohio, 1978—; dir. Barry Equipment Co., United McGill Corp.; adj. prof. law Ohio State U., 1964-72. Trustee DePauw U., Greencastle, Ind., 1962—. Served with USCGR, 1943-45. Mem. Am., Ohio, Columbus bar assns., Order of Coif, Phi Beta Kappa, Phi Delta Phi. Presbyterian. Home: 2475 Onandaga Dr Columbus OH 43221 Office: 311 E Broad St Columbus OH 43215

CHRISTENSEN, LEW FARR, choreographer, ballet director; b. Brigham City, Utah, May 6, 1909; s. Chris and Mary Isabelle (Farr) C.; m. Giselle Caccialanza, May 10, 1941; 1 son, Chris. Soloist, ballet master Ballet Caravan, N.Y.C., 1936-41, Am. Ballet, 1941, Ballet Soc., N.Y.C. Ballet, 1946-52; dir. San Francisco Ballet, 1952—; Mem. Adv. Com. on Arts, Washington, 1963-69, Cal. Arts Commn., 1963-66. Served with AUS, 1942-46. Recipient Capezio Dance award, 1984. Office: 378 18th Ave San Francisco CA 94121 *

CHRISTENSEN, LYDELL LEE, telephone company executive; b. Walnut, Iowa, Nov. 16, 1934; s. Hans J. and Alma P. C.; m. Barbara M. Pearsall, June 1, 1974; children: Brent, Amy, Paul, Jeffrey. B.S., U. Nebr., Omaha, 1959; postgrad., Pace Coll. With Northwestern Bell Telephone Co., Omaha, 1959-80, asst. treas., then treas., 1972-80; dir. fin. planning AT&T Co., N.Y.C., 1980-82, asst. treas., 1982—. Active local Boy Scouts Am. Mem. Fin. Mgmt. Assn., Fin. Execs. Inst., Am. Fin. Assn., Western Fin. Assn., Omaha/Lincoln Soc. Fin. Analysts, Nat. Soc. Rate of Return Analysts. Republican. Mem. United Ch. of Christ. Office: 195 Broadway New York NY 10007

CHRISTENSEN, NIKOLAS IVAN, geophysicist, educator; b. Madison, Wis., Apr. 11, 1937; s. Ivan Rudolph and Alice Evelyn (Ethen) C.; m. Karen Mary Luberg, June 18, 1960; children—Kirk Nathan, Signe Kay. B.S., U. Wis.-Madison, 1959, M.S., 1961, Ph.D., 1963. Research fellow in geophysics, Harvard, 1963-64; asst. prof. geol. scis. U. So. Calif., 1964-66; prof. U. Wash., 1966—; Mem. Pacific adv. panel Joint Oceanographic Instns. for Deep Earth Sampling, Seattle, 1973-75, mem. igneous and metamorphic petrology panel, 1973-75, mem. ocean crust panel, 1974-77; mem. adv. panel on oceanography NSF, 1976-78; mem. adv. panel on continental lithosphere NRC, 1979—; mem. adv. panel Internat. Assn. Geodesy, 1980—. Contbg. author: Geodynamics of Iceland and the North Atlantic Area, 1974; Contbr. numerous articles to profl. jours. NSF grantee, 1968-80. Fellow Geol. Soc. Am.; mem. Am. Geophys. Union, Seismol. Soc. Am. Research on nature of Earth's interior. Home: 30 Bridlewood Circle Kirkland WA 98033 Office: Dept of Geol Scis U of Wash Seattle WA 98195

CHRISTENSEN, PAUL WALTER, JR., gear manufacturing company executive; b. Cin., Jan. 31, 1925; s. Paul Walter and Lucy (Sickler) C.; m. Sarah Ernst, Nov. 22, 1947; children: Delle (Mrs. Charles W. Gay), Sarah (Mrs. William McC. Reynolds), Lucy (Mrs. Craig M. Davis). B.S. in Mech. Engring, Cornell U., 1945. With Cin. Gear Co., 1946—, v.p., 1947-58, pres., 1958-78, chmn. bd., 1978—, Cin. Steel Treating Co., 1961-68, pres., 1968—; dir. Potter Shoe Co., Central Trust Co., Eagle Picher Industries, Inc., Central Bancorp., Ohio Nat. Life Ins. Co., Cin. Bell Inc. Trustee U. Cin.; commr. Hamilton County Park Dist. Mem. Am. Gear Mfrs. Assn. (past pres.), Ohio Mfrs. Assn. (past pres.). Clubs: Queen City, Commonwealth, Camargo, Commercial (Cin.). Home: 4660 Drake Rd Cincinnati OH 45243 Office: Cincinnati Gear Co Wooster Pike Cincinnati OH 45227

CHRISTENSEN, RAY RICHARDS, lawyer; b. Salt Lake City, July 7, 1922; s. E.R. and Carrie (Richards) C.; m. Carolyn Crawford, July 9, 1954; children: Carlie, Paul Ray, Joan, Eric. LL.B., U. Utah, 1944. Bar: Utah 1944. Enforcement atty. OPA, 1946; clk. to Utah Supreme Ct. Justice Wolfe, 1947-48; practice in, Salt Lake City, 1949—; partner firm Christensen, Jensen & Powell (and predecessors), 1949—; Mem. Utah Bar Commn., 1963-66. Bd. dirs. Salt Lake City Jr. C. of C., 1949-53, v.p., 1950-52. Served with AUS, 1943-46. Fellow Internat. Acad. Trial Lawyers (dir. 1982—), Am. Coll. Trial Lawyers (state chmn. 1984—); mem. ABA (mem. council jr. bar conf. 1952-56, ho. of dels. 1966-68, 73-79, mem. council bar activities sect. 1967-70), Utah Bar Assn. (pres. 1965-66, Lawyer of Yr. 1981), Salt Lake County Bar Assn., Western States Bar Conf. (pres. 1969-70), Internat. Assn. Ins. Counsel, Fedn. Ins. Counsel, Phi Eta Sigma, Phi Kappa Phi. Home: 861 Monument Park Circle Salt Lake City UT 84108 Office: 900 Kearns Bldg Salt Lake City UT 84101

CHRISTENSEN, WILLIAM HAROLD, gas transmission company executive; b. Wilmot, S.D., Aug. 26, 1909; s. Albert Rasmus and Emma Elenora (Christensen) C.; m. Flora M. MacRae, June 30, 1938; children: Jon Alexander, William James, Kerry MacRae. Student, Dublin U., Trinity Coll., 1950-51. Clk. Am. Consulate, Winnipeg, Can., 1926; vice consul, Barbados, B.W.I., 1940-43, Toronto, 1943, Sarnia, 1943; vice consul, officer charge Am. Consulate, Antigua, B.W.I., also, Curacao and Martinique, 1944; consul, Martinique, F.W.I., 1945, Marseilles, France, 1947; 2d sec., consul Am. embassy, Dublin, Ireland, 1950; assigned staff Dept. State, Washington, 1952-56, desk officer, Ireland and Caribbean; dep. chief mission counselor Am. Embassy, Luxembourg, 1956-58; also chargé d'affairs; consul gen. St. John's, Nfld., Can., 1958-60; consul gen. Am. consulate gen., Port of Spain, Trinidad, W.I., 1961; counselor of embassy, dep. chief mission Am. embassy, Port of Spain, 1962-63; assigned State Dept., 1963; consul gen. for, Alta., Calgary, 1963-64, ret., 1964; exec. Gt. Lakes Gas Transmission Co., Detroit, 1965—; cons. Am. Natural Resources Co., Washington.; Adviser U.S. delegation 15th Session Caribbean Commn., 5th Session West Indian Conf., Montego Bay, Jamaica, 1952, 20th Session Caribbean Commn., 6th Session West Indian Conf., San Juan, P.R., 1955. Mem. commn. for selection sculptor and design statue of Commo. James Barry, for gift to people of Ireland, 1953; bd. dirs. U. Windsor Inst. Canadian-Am. Studies. Recipient Silver medal City of Sete, Herault, France, 1948; Meritorious Service award Dept. State, 1960; decorated comdr. Oak Crown Luxembourg, 1958. Mem. Am. Fgn. Service Assn., Diplomatic and Consular Officers Ret. Lutheran. Home: 2841 29th Pl NW Washington DC 20008 also 100 Chestnut Plain Rd Whately MA 01093 Office: Suite 500 1899 L St NW Washington DC 20036

CHRISTENSEN, WILLIAM ROZELLE, physician, educator; b. Salt Lake City, Nov. 20, 1917; s. Niels Christian and DeVere (Rozelle) C.; m. Mary Beeley, June 24, 1942; children—William B. (dec.), Ellen Ann, Eric Peter. B.A., U. Utah, 1938; M.D., Harvard, 1942. Intern Mass. Gen. Hosp., Boston, 1942-43; research fellow Harvard Med. Sch., 1946-48; resident radiology Peter Bent Brigham Hosp., Boston, 1948-51; prof. radiology, chmn. dept. U. Utah Coll. Medicine, Salt Lake City, 1952-70; radiologist-in-chief Salt Lake City Gen. Hosp., 1952-65, U. Hosp., 1965-70; radiologist Valley West Hosp., Granger, Utah, 1970—; Cons. U.S. Army, VA. Contbr. articles to profl. jours. Served to maj. M.C. AUS, 1943-46. Fulbright scholar U.K., 1951-52. Fellow Am. Coll. Radiology; mem. Am. Roentgen Ray Soc., Utah State Med. Assn. (pres. 1973), Harvard Med. Alumni Assn. (pres. 1978-79), Am. Radium Soc., Assn. U. Radiologists, A.M.A., Radiol. Soc. N.Am., A.A.A.S., Phi Beta Kappa, Phi Kappa Phi, Phi Delta Theta. Home: 1469 Harvard Ave Salt Lake City UT 84105

CHRISTENSON, CHARLES JOHN, educator; b. Chgo., Sept. 25, 1930; s. John Edward and Ethel Dagmar (Osterberg) C. B.S., Cornell U., 1952; M.B.A., Harvard, 1954, D.B.A., 1961. Mem. faculty Harvard Grad. Sch. Bus., 1957-58, lectr., 1959-61, asst. prof., 1961-63, asso. prof., 1963-68, prof., 1968-74, Jesse Isidor Straus prof., 1974-79, Royal Little prof., 1980—; prin. Mgmt. Analysis Center, Inc., Cambridge, 1966—. Author: Strategic Aspects of Competitive Bidding for Corporate Securities, 1965, (with J.L. Bower) Public Management: Cases and Readings, 1978, (with W.L. Berry and J.S. Hammond III) Management Decision Sciences: Cases and Readings, 1979. Treas. Telluride Assn., Ithaca, N.Y., 1973—; dir. and treas. Banchetto Musicale, 1980—; dir. U.S. Windpower, Inc., 1979—. Served with AUS, 1955-57. Mem. Inst. Mgmt. Scis. Home: 1 Chauncy Ln Cambridge MA 02138 Office: Soldiers Field Boston MA 02163

CHRISTENSON, GORDON A., university dean, lawyer; b. Salt Lake City, June 22, 1932; s. Gordon B. and Ruth Arzella (Anderson) C.; m. Katherine Joy deMik, Nov. 2, 1951 (div. 1977); children: Gordon Scott, Marjorie Lynne, Ruth Ann, Nanette; m. Fabienne Fadeley, Sept. 16, 1979. B.S. in Law, U. Utah, 1955, J.D., 1956; S.J.D., George Washington U., 1961. Bar: Utah bar 1956, U.S. Supreme Ct. bar 1971, D.C. bar 1978. Practiced in, Salt Lake City, 1957-58; law clk. to chief justice Utah Supreme Ct., 1956-57; asso. firm Christenson & Callister, Salt Lake City, 1956-58; atty. Dept. of Army, Nat. Guard Bur., Washington, 1957-58; atty., acting asst. legal adviser Office of Legal Adviser, U.S. Dept. State, Washington, 1958-62; asst. gen. counsel for sci. and tech. U.S. Dept. Commerce, 1962-67, spl. asst. to undersec. of commerce, 1967, counsel to commerce tech. adv. bd., 1962-67, chmn. task force on telecommunications missions and orgn., 1967, counsel to panel on engring. and commodity standards, tech. adv. bd., 1963-65; assoc. prof. law U. Okla., Norman, 1967-70, exec. asst. to pres., 1967-70; univ. dean for ednl. devel., central adminstrn. State U. N.Y., Albany, 1970-71; prof. law Am. U. Law Sch., Washington, 1971-79, dean, 1971-77; on leave, 1977-79; Charles H. Stockton prof. internat. law U.S. Naval War Coll., Newport, R.I., 1977-79; dean, Nippert prof. law U. Cin. Coll. Law, 1979—; vis. scholar Harvard U. Law Sch., 1977-78; asso. professorial lectr. in internat. affairs George Washington U., 1961-67; participant summer confs. on internat. law Cornell Law Sch., Ithaca, N.Y., 1962, 64; cons. in internat. law U.S. Naval War Coll., Newport, R.I., 1969; faculty mem., reporter seminars for experienced fed. dist. judges Fed. Jud. Center, Washington, 1972—. Author: (with Richard B. Lillich) International Claims: Their Preparation and Presentation, 1962, The Future of the University, 1969; Contbr. articles to legal jours. Cons. to Center for Policy Alternatives Mass. Inst. Tech., Cambridge, 1970—; mem. intergovtl. com. on Internat. Policy on Weather Modification, 1967; Vice pres. Procedural Aspects of Internat. Law Inst., N.Y.C., 1962—. Served with intelligence sect. USAF, 1951-52; Japan. Recipient Silver Medal award Dept. Commerce, 1967; fellow Grad. Sch. U. Cin. Mem. Am. Soc. Internat. Law (mem. panel on state responsibility 1957—), D.C. Bar Assn., Am. Bar Assn., Utah Bar, Order of Coif, Phi Delta Phi, Kappa Sigma. Clubs: Literary (Cin.); Cosmos (Washington). Home: 3465 Principio Ave Cincinnati OH 45226 Office: U Cin Coll Law Cincinnati OH 45221

CHRISTIAN, ALMERIC LEANDER, chief judge; b. Christiansted, St. Croix, V.I., Nov. 23, 1919; s. Adam Emmanuel and Elena (Davis)

C.; m. Virginia Cecilia Sterling, Sept. 13, 1943 (div. Sept. 1962); 1 dau., Donna Marie; m. Shirley Camille Frorup, Aug. 31, 1963; children—Adam, Rebecca. Student, U. P.R., 1937-38; A.B., Columbia, 1941, J.D., 1947. Bar: V.I. bar 1947. Practiced law, V.I., 1947-62, U.S. dist. atty. for, V.I., St. Thomas, from 1962; now chief judge U.S. Dist. Ct. for V.I., St. Thomas. Dist. commr. Boy Scouts Am., V.I., 1962—; adv. bd. St. Dunstan's Episcopal Sch., St. Croix.; Mem. V.I. Bd. Edn., 1961—; Bd. visitors Columbia Law Sch. Served to 1st lt. AUS, 1942-46; ETO; Served to 1st lt. AUS; PTO. Mem. V.I. Bar Assn. Democrat. Home: Parcel 19-0 Solberg St Thomas VI 00801 Office: US Dist Court Charlotte Amalie St Thomas VI 00801 *

CHRISTIAN, BETTY JO, lawyer; b. Temple, Tex., July 27, 1936; d. Joe and Mattie Manor (Brown) Wiest; m. Ernest S. Christian, Jr., Dec. 24, 1960. B.A. summa cum laude, U. Tex., 1957, LL.B., 1960. Bar: Tex. bar 1961, U.S. Supreme Ct. bar 1964. Law clk. Supreme Ct. Tex., 1960-61; atty. ICC, 1961-68, asst. gen. counsel, Washington, 1970-72, asso. gen. counsel, 1972-76, commr., 1976-79; partner firm Steptoe & Johnson, Washington, 1980—; atty. Labor Dept., Dallas, 1968-70. Mem. ABA, Fed. Bar Assn. (Younger Fed. Lawyer award 1964), Tex. Bar Assn., Am. Law Inst., Adminstrv. Conf. U.S., City Tavern Assn. Office: 1250 Connecticut Ave NW Washington DC 20036

CHRISTIAN, CHARLES DONALD, physician, educator; b. Parker, Kans., Nov. 28, 1930; s. O.L. and Vivian L. (Brown) C.; m. Sarah J. Andrews, June 21, 1956; children: Charles Donald, Van Andrews, Sarah Elizabeth. Ph.D in Anatomy, Duke U., 1955, M.D., 1958. Diplomate: Am. Bd. Ob.-Gyn. Teaching and research asst. dept. anatomy Duke U., 1953-55, intern, 1959; resident in ob-gyn Columbia-Presbyn. Med. Ctr., N.Y.C., 1959-62, Josiah Macy Jr. fellow, 1959-62; asst. prof. ob-gyn U. Fla., Gainesville, 1962-64; assoc. prof. Duke U., Durham, N.C., 1964-69, dir. reproductive endocrinology, 1964-69; prof. ob-gyn and anatomy Ariz. Health Sci. Ctr., Tucson, 1969—; head dept. ob-gyn Ariz. Health Scis. Ctr., Tucson, 1969—, U. Ariz. Coll. Medicine. Author: Controversies in Obstetrics and Gynecology, 1974, 1983; contbr. articles to profl. jours. Recipient Disting. Alumnus award Duke U. Med. Ctr., 1973. Mem. Soc. Gynecologic Investigation (pres. 1973-74), Am. Coll. Obstetricians and Gynecologists, Am. Gynecologic Soc., Central Assn. Ob-Gyn, Pacific Coast Ob-Gyn Soc., Assn. Profs. Ob-Gyn, AMA, S.W. Ob-Gyn Soc., Am. Assn. Anatomists, Sigma Xi, Alpha Omega Alpha. Republican. Club: Old Pueblo. Office: Dept Ob-Gyn Coll of Medicine U Ariz 1501 N Campbell Ave Tucson AZ 85724

CHRISTIAN, CHARLES LEIGH, physician, educator; b. Wichita, Kans., July 10, 1926; s. Robert V. and Anna (Vezie) C.; m. Diane Collings, Nov. 13, 1954; children—Victoria Anne, Jennifer Diane, Matthew Middleton. B.S., U. Wichita, 1949; M.D., Western Res. U., 1953. Diplomate: Am. Bd. Internal Medicine. Mem. faculty Columbia Coll. Phys. and Surg., 1958-70, asso. prof. medicine, 1964-69; prof. medicine, 1969-70, Cornell U. Sch. Medicine, 1970—; adj. prof. Rockefeller U., 1970—; physician-in-chief Hosp. Spl. Surgery; attending physician N.Y. Hosp. and Meml. Hosp. Editor: Arthritis and Rheumatism, 1970-76. Chmn. Nat. Arthritis Adv. Bd., 1977—; trustee Helen Hay Whitney Found., Burke Found. Served with USNR, 1944-46. Mem. Am. Rheumatism Assn. (pres. 1976). Club: Century Assn. (N.Y.C.). Research in immunology. Home: 149 Cedar St Englewood NJ 07631 Office: Cornell U Sch Medicine 1300 York Ave New York NY 10021

CHRISTIAN, ERNEST SILSBEE, JR., lawyer; b. Gonzales, Tex., Jan. 15, 1937; s. Ernest Silsbee and Ruby Ruth (Hamon) C.; m. Betty Jo Wiest, Dec. 24, 1960. LL.B. cum laude, U. Tex., 1961. Bar: Tex. bar 1961, D.C. bar 1961, U.S. Supreme Ct. bar 1978. Asso. firm Covington & Burling, Washington, 1961-68, Wynne & Jaffe, Dallas, 1968-70; atty. Treasury Dept., Washington, 1970-72, tax legis. counsel, 1973-74, dep. asst. sec. treasury (tax policy), 1974-75; partner firm Patton, Boggs & Blow, Washington, 1975—. Mem. Am. Law Inst., Am. Bar Assn. Republican. Clubs: City Tavern, Met. (Washington). Home: 3750 Fordham Rd NW Washington DC 20016 Office: 2550 M St NW Washington DC 20037

CHRISTIAN, GARY DALE, chemistry educator; b. Eugene, Oreg., Nov. 25, 1937; s. Roy C. and Edna Alberta (Trout) Gonier; m. Suanne Byrd Coulbourne, June 17, 1961; children: Dale Brian, Carol Jean. B.S., U. Oreg., 1959; M.S., U. Md., 1962, Ph.D., 1964. Research analytical chemist Walter Reed Army Inst. Research, Washington, 1961-67; asst. prof. U. Md., College Park, 1965-66, U. Ky., Lexington, 1967-70, assoc. prof., 1970-72; prof. chemistry U. Wash., Seattle, 1972—; vos. prof. Universite Libre de Bruxelles, Brussels, 1978-79; invited prof. U. Geneva, 1979; cons. Ames Co., 1968-72, Beckman Instruments, Inc., 1972—, Westinghouse Hanford Co., 1977—. Author: Analytical Chemistry, 3d edit., 1980, Instrumental Analysis, 1978, Atomic Absorption Spectroscopy, 1970; contbr. articles to profl. jours.; editorial bd.: Analytical Letters, 1971—, Can. Jour. Spectroscopy, 1974—, Chem. Instrumentation, 1974—, Talanta, 1980—; instrumentation panel: Analytical Chemistry, 1977-80. Fulbright Hays scholar, 1978-79; recipient Medal, U. Brussels, 1978. Mem. Am. Chem. Soc. (sect. chmn.), Soc. Applied Spectroscopy (chmn. 1982), Spectroscopy Soc. Can., Am. Inst. Chemists (cert.). Republican. Home: 7827 NE 12th St Medina WA 98039 Office: U Wash Dept Chemistry BG-10 Seattle WA 98195

CHRISTIAN, GEORGE EASTLAND, pub. relations exec.; b. Austin, Tex., Jan. 1, 1927; s. George Eastl and Ruby (Scott) C.; m. Elizabeth Anne Brown, July 30, 1950 (dec. 1957); m. Jo Anne Martin, June 20, 1959; children—Elizabeth, Susan, George Scott, Robert Bruce, John, Brian. B. Journalism, U. Tex. Sports editor Temple (Tex.) Daily Telegram, 1949; corr. Internat. News Service, 1949-56; asst. to Senator Price Daniel, Washington, 1956, to Gov. Price Daniel, Austin, 1957-63, to Gov. John Connally, 1963-66; press sec., spl. asst. to Pres. Johnson, Washington, 1966-69; pres. George Christian, Inc. Author: The President Steps Down. Served with USMC, 1944-46. Mem. Sigma Delta Chi. Democrat. Episcopalian. Clubs: Citadel, Headliners (Austin); Federal City (Washington). Home: 6800 Rockledge Cove Austin TX 78731 Office: Am Nat Bank Bldg Austin TX 78701

CHRISTIAN, GEORGE LLOYD, JR., writer, editor; b. Houston, May 27, 1937; s. George Lloyd and Hazel Margaret (Singleton) C.; m. Mary Frances Blount, Sept. 22, 1956; children—Scott, Karen, Devin. B.S. in Journalism and English, U. Houston, 1952. Drama and film critic Houston Post, 1950-66, mag. editor, 1966-67, asst. mng. editor, 1968-75; freelance syndicated columnist, 1975, syndicated comic strip writer, 1977; book rev. editor Houston Chronicle, 1977—; editorial cons. First lt. CAP, 1976-79. Syndicated newspaper column, 1976-77, comic strip, 1978. Served with U.S. Army, 1945-46. Democrat. Home: 1108 Danbury St Houston TX 77055 Office: Houston Chronicle 801 Texas Ave Houston TX 77002

CHRISTIAN, JOHN CATLETT, JR., lawyer; b. Springfield, Mo., Sept. 12, 1929; s. John Catlett and Alice Odelle (Milling) C.; m. Peggy Jeanne Cain, Apr. 12, 1953; children: Cathleen Marie, John Catlett, Alice Cain. A.B., Drury Coll., 1951; LL.B., Tulane U., 1956. Bar: La. 1956, Mo. 1956, U.S. Supreme Ct. bar 1975. Asso. firm Porter & Stewart, Lake Charles, La., 1956-58, Wilkinson, Lewis, Wilkinson & Madison, Shreveport, La., 1958-62, partner, 1962-64; partner firm Milling, Benson, Woodward, Hillyer, Pierson & Miller, New Orleans, 1964—; pres. Sherburne Land Co., 1974-83; dir. Emerald Land Corp. Pres. Kathleen Elizabeth O'Brien Found., 1963—. Served with USMCR, 1951-53. Fellow Am. Coll. Trial Lawyers; mem. Am. Bar Assn., Am. Judicature Soc., Mo. Bar Assn., Fed. Bar Assn., La. Bar Assn., La. Landowners Assn. (bd. dirs. 1983—), Kappa Alpha Order, Omicron Delta Kappa, Phi Delta Phi. Clubs: Boston, Essex, Plimsoll, Petroleum (New Orleans); Timberlane Country. Home: 5 Fernwood St Gretna LA 70053 Office: 1100 Whitney Bldg New Orleans LA 70130

CHRISTIAN, JOHN EDWARD, educator; b. Indpls., July 12, 1917; s. George Edward and Okel Kandus (Waltz) C.; m. Catherine Ellen Spooner, July 23, 1948; 1 dau., Linda Kay. B.S., Purdue U., 1939, Ph.D., 1944. Control chemist Upjohn Co., 1939-40; faculty Purdue U., Lafayette, Ind., 1940—, prof. pharm. chemistry, 1950-59, head dept. radiol. control, 1956-59, prof. bionucleonics, head dept., 1959—; chmn. adminstrv. com. Trace Level Research Inst., 1960—; dir. Inst. for Environmental Health, 1965—; head Sch. Health Scis., 1979—, Hovde Disting. prof., 1979—; vis. prof. radiation therapy Ind. U. Sch. Medicine, 1970—; Harvey Washington Meml. lectr. Purdue U., 1955; Edward-Kremers Meml. lectr. U. Wis., 1956; vis. lectr. U. Tex., 1959, Taylor U. Ann. Sci. Lecture Series, Upton, Ind., 1960; Julius A. Koch Meml. lectr. U. Pitts., 1961. Asso. editor: Radiochem. Letters. Mem. revision com. U.S. Pharmacopeia, 1950-60, mem. adv. panel on radioactive drugs, 1960-70; adv. com. isotope distbn. AEC, 1952-58, mem. med. adv. com., 1967-75; mem. radiation and chem. def. sect. Ind. Dept. Civil Def., 1954—; vice chmn. Radiation Control Adv. Commn., Ind., 1958—; mem. exec. com. Ind. Comprehensive Health Planning Council, 1972-76; mem. adv. com. radiopharms. FDA, 1970-75; mem. Ind. Gov.'s Pesticide Council, 1970-73; Alumni research councilor Purdue Research Found., 1964—; mem. Ind. Environmental Mgmt. Bd., 1972—, Nat. Energy Policy Task Force, Dept. Energy, 1981—. Recipient award Chilean Iodine Ednl. Bur., 1956; Julius Sturmer award Phila. Coll. Pharmacy and Sci., 1958; Leather medal Purdue U., 1971. Fellow AAAS (past sec. and chmn. pharm. sci. sect., mem. council), Ind. Acad. Sci.; mem. Am. Assn. Colls. Pharmacy (past mem. exec. com., chmn. conf. tchrs., chmn. conf. grad. study and grad. tchrs., chmn. com. study grad. edn. in pharmacy), Am. Chem. Soc. (past chmn. Purdue sect.), Am. Pharm. Assn. (Ebert medal 1957, Justin L. Powers Research Achievement award 1963, past chmn. sci. sect.), Acad. Pharm. Sci. (past v.p.), Ind. Pharm. Assn., Am. Pub. Health Assn., A.M.A. (spl. affiliate), Am. Nuclear Soc., Am. Soc. Bacteriology, Health Phys. Soc., AAUP, Sigma Xi (past pres. Purdue chpt., research award Purdue chpt. 1950), Rho Chi, Phi Lambda Upsilon, Sigma Pi Sigma., Eta Sigma Gamma, Gamma Sigma Delta. Home: 1301 Woodland Ave West Lafayette IN 47906 Office: Sch Health Scis Bionucleonics Dept Purdue U West Lafayette IN 47907

CHRISTIAN, JOHN KENTON, orgn. exec., publisher; b. Pana, Ill., Nov. 6, 1927; s. Ben Ross and Ruth (Stevenson) C.; m. Marjorie Adair Pollock, Nov. 28, 1958; children—Jefrey, Dwane, Kevin. Student, Westminster Coll., 1945, Colo. Coll., 1948, Emerson Coll., 1949; B.S., Boston U., 1951, Am. U., 1954-55. Relief editor, rep., columnist St. Louis Daily Record, 1950-51; reporter Commerce Clearing House, Washington, 1952; with U.S. News and World Report, 1953-68, regional sales mgr., Los Angeles, 1960-63, mktg. mgr., Washington, 1964-68; pub. Nation's Cities Mag., Washington, 1968-76; mem. U.S. Fed. Preparedness Agy. mission to Iran, 1975-76; pres. Internat. Center for Emergency Preparedness, Washington, 1977-80; also pub. Emergency Preparedness News, 1977-79; v.p. Nat. Radio Broadcasters Assn., 1979—. Served with USAAF, 1945-48. Mem. Nat. Press Club, Am. Mktg. Assn., Delta Tau Delta. Presbyn. Home: 9001 Logan Dr Potomac MD 20854 Office: 2033 M St NW Washington DC 20036

CHRISTIAN, JOSEPH JOHN, city government housing official; b. Woonsocket, R.I., Dec. 5, 1915; s. Joseph Casimir and Barbara Veronica (McDonald) C.; m. Agnes Josephine Noreyko, Apr. 20, 1940 (dec. Feb. 1983); children: Kathleen Mary Christian Gallo, Joseph John. Student, Poly Inst. Bklyn., 1951, NYU Grad. Sch. Pub. Adminstrn., 1962-63. Clk. Dept. Housing and Bldgs, Queens, N.Y., 1938-49, plan examiner, 1949-56, chief plan examiner, acting dep. commr., exec. asst., N.Y.C., 1956-62; dir. program planning N.Y.C. Housing Authority, 1962-67, gen. mgr., 1967-70; commr. devel. Housing Devel. Adminstrn., N.Y.C., 1970-73; chmn. N.Y.C. Housing Authority, 1973—. Author: booklet You and Your Landlord, 1961. Mem. Citizens Housing and Planning Council, N.Y.C., 1973; bd. dirs. Community Council Greater N.Y., N.Y.C., 1973—; bd. dirs., treas. Catholic Interracial Council N.Y., N.Y.C., 1973—; mem. N.Y.C. Housing Authority br. NAACP, 1969—. Served to lt. col., arty. AUS, 1942-46; ETO. Recipient City of N.Y. Mayor's Disting. Performance medal, 1969, Pub. Service Fund for City N.Y., 1974, Appreciation for Leadership cert. U.S. Dept. NUH, 1975. Mem. Nat. Assn. Housing Redevel. Ofcls., Citizens Housing and Planning Council (award 1978), Res. Officers Assn., Am. Mgmt. Assn., Lambda Alpha Land Use Frat. (award 1972). Democrat. Roman Catholic. Home: 16-06 212th St Bayside NY 11360 Office: NYC Housing Authority 250 Broadway New York NY 10007 Z *Entered government service during the "great depression" primary to obtain a job that offered security. Soon realized that the public perception of the majority of civil servants as lazy, indifferent workers was wrong. Determined to strive not only to disprove that evaluation but also to achieve as high a position within the system as my talents would permit without resources to political influence. Realization that this was possible without compromising one's principles is ample reward for many years of hard work in serving the needs of the residents of our city.*

CHRISTIAN, JOSEPH RALPH, physician; b. Chgo., June 15, 1920; s. Ralph F. and Anna M. (Across) Co; m. Marcia Pomeroy, Sept. 25, 1944; children—Patricia Ann, Joseph Ralph. A.A., U. Chgo., 1941; M.D., Loyola U., Chgo., 1944. Diplomate: Am. Bd. Pediatrics. Intern Cook County Hosp., Chgo., 1944-45, resident, 1945-46, 48-49; faculty Stritch Sch. Medicine, Loyola U., Chgo., 1948-61, prof., 1957-61, exec. com. chmn. dept., 1960-61; attending pediatrician Loyola Service at La Rabida Sanitarium, 1948-61; chmn. dept. pediatrics Mercy Hosp., 1960-61; chief pediatrics Lewis Meml. Maternity Hosp., 1951-61; chmn. dept. pediatrics Rush Presbyn.-St. Luke's Med. Center, Chgo., 1961—; prof. pediatrics U. Ill. Coll. Medicine, Chgo., 1961-70; prof., chmn. dept. pediatrics Rush Med. Coll., Chgo., 1970—; sr. attending pediatrician children's div. Cook County Hosp., 1959-65. Editor: Pediatrics Digest, 1962-78; Mem. editorial bd.: Childcraft, 1963—; Contbr. articles to med. jours. Chmn. poison control com. Chgo. Bd. Health, 1961-69; chmn. med. com. Infant Welfare Soc., Chgo., 1958-61; chmn. 9th Ill. Congress Meternal and Infant Health, 1962; Chmn. bd. trustees Holy Cross Chgo., 1970-75. Served to capt. M.C. AUS, 1946-47. Recipient Clin. Faculty award Stritch Sch. Medicine, 1954, 57. Fellow Am. Coll. Chest Physicians, Am. Acad. Pediatrics (chmn. film rev. com. 1963-73, chmn. com. residency fellowships 1964-67), Am. Pub. Health Assn., A.C.P.; mem. A.M.A., Am. Fedn. Clin. Research, Am. Pediatric Soc., Am. Heart Assn., Ambulatory Pediatric Assn., Am. Assn. Poison Control Centers, Am. Assn. Maternal and Infant Health, Ill. Assn. Maternal and Infant Health (pres. 1964), Am. Pediatric Soc., Chgo. Pediatric Soc. (pres. 1964-65), Midwest Soc. Pediatric Research, Assn. Med. Sch. Pediatric Dept. Chairmen. Home: 3 Oak Brook Club Dr Oak Brook IL 60521 Office: 1753 W Congress Pkwy Chicago IL 60612

CHRISTIAN, LEARD HUGHES, broadcasting co. exec.; b. Bogart, Ga., Feb. 28, 1919; s. Robert Franklin and Katie Lee (Norris) C.; m. Sara Bradbury, Oct. 30, 1938; children—Carolyn, Hugh, Frank, Charles. Chief engr. Sta. WGAU, Athens, Ga., 1937-38; chief engr., mgr. Sta. WGGA, Gainesville, Ga., 1941-48; pres., gen. mgr. Sta. WRFC, Athens, 1948-78; pres. Radio Athens, Inc., Stas. WRFC-WFOX-FM, 1978—. Served with USN, 1944-46. Mem. Ga. Assn. Broadcasters (past pres.). Clubs: Kiwanis (past pres.), Elks (past exalted ruler). Office: 255 S Milledge Athens GA 30605

CHRISTIAN, MICHAEL WOOD, bank and finance company executive; b. Boston, June 10, 1938; s. Frank Sharp and Martha (Wood) C.; m. Anthea Myra Kirton, Sept. 23, 1967; 1 son, James Michael. A.B., Harvard U., 1960, LL.B., 1964; student, Trinity Coll., Cambridge (Eng.) U., 1961. Bar: Mass. 1967. Asst. legal sec. E. African Common Services Co., Nairobi, 1964-67; asso. firm Goodwin, Procter & Hoar, Boston, 1967-70; v.p. Sprague Assos. Inc., Boston, 1970-73; pres. M.W. Christian Inc., Boston, 1973-77, Johnston Mut. Fund Inc., 1979—; exec. v.p. Boston Co., 1978—; chmn. Boston Co. Fund, 1978; exec. v.p., vice chmn. Boston Safe Deposit and Trust Co., 1980—; dir. Atlantic Monthly. Vice chmn. Mass. Port Authority, 1973-80; trustee Emerson Hosp., 1981—, World Peace Found., 1975—, Boston Ballet Co., 1978—. Mem. Mass. Bar Assn. Republican. Unitarian. Office: 1 Boston Pl Boston MA 01620

CHRISTIAN, PERCY WILLIS, educator; b. Viborg, S.D., Jan. 8, 1907; s. John Willis and Tillie Victoria (Peterson) C.; m. Evelyn Anna deVries, June 25, 1931 (dec.); 1 son, John Willis.; m. Ellen Louise Gibson, Dec. 27, 1881. B.A., Broadview Coll., 1926; B.S., Lewis Inst., Chgo., 1928; M.A., Northwestern U., 1929, Ph.D., 1935; LL.D., Walla Walla Coll., 1967. Instr. history Chgo. Acad., 1926-28, Broadview Coll., 1931-33; asst. prof. history Walla Walla Coll., 1933-35, asso. prof., 1935-38, prof., 1938-43, pres., 1955-64; dean Pacific Union Coll., Angwin, Cal., 1943-45, pres., 1945-50, prof. history, 1964—; pres. Emmanuel Missionary Coll., 1950-55; vis. prof. Eastern Wash. Coll. Edn., summer 1934, State Coll. Wash., summer 1942, Loma Linda U., summer 1962, Andrews U., summer 1966, Seminaire Adventiste, Collonges, France, 1968-69; dir. pub. relations Taiwan Adventist Hosp., Taipei. Mem. Am. Hist. Assn., Assn. Western Adventist Historians (pres. 1972), Orgn. Am. Historians. Home: 160 White Cottage Rd Angwin CA 94508 *A sincere interest in helping others to develop their potentialities by offering advice (often by "just listening") has resulted in success and has paid rich dividends in satisfaction.*

CHRISTIAN, RICHARD CARLTON, advertising agency executive; b. Dayton, Ohio, Nov. 29, 1924; s. Raymond A. and Louise (Gamber) C.; m. Audrey Bongartz, Sept. 10, 1949; children: Ann Christian Carra, Richard Carlton. B.S. in Bus. Adminstrn, Miami U., Oxford, Ohio, 1948; M.B.A., Northwestern U., 1949; postgrad., Denison U., The Citadel, Biarritz Am. U. Mktg. analyst Nat. Cash Register Co., Dayton, 1948, Rockwell Mfg. Co., Pitts., 1949-50; exec. v.p. Marsteller Inc., Chgo., 1951-60, pres., 1960-75, chmn. bd., 1975-84, chmn. emeritus, 1984—; assoc. dean Medill Sch. Journalism Northwestern U., 1984—; dir., chmn. Bus. Publs. Audit Circulation, Inc., 1969-75; dir. First Ill. Corp.; Speaker, author marketing, sales mgmt., marketing research and advt. Trustee Northwestern U., 1970-74, Nat. Coll. Edn., Evanston, Ill., James Webb Young Fund for Edn., U. Ill., 1962—; pres. Nat. Advt. Rev. Council, 1976-77; bd. adv. council mem. Miami U.; Mem. adv. council J. L. Kellogg Grad. Sch. Mgmt., Northwestern U.; dir. Mus. Broadcast Communications. Served with inf. AUS, 1942-46; ETO. Decorated Bronze Star, Purple Heart; recipient Ohio Gov.'s award, 1977, Alumni medal, Alumni Merit and Service awards Northwestern U. Mem. Am. Mktg. Assn., Indsl. Marketing Assn. (founder, chmn. 1951), Bus./Publs. Advt. Assn. (life mem. Chgo., pres. Chgo. 1954-55, nat. v.p. 1955-58, G.D. Crain award 1977), U. Ill. Found., Northwestern U. Bus. Sch. Alumni Assn. (founder, pres.), Am. Mgmt. Assn., Am. Assn. Advt. Agys. (dir., chmn. 1976-77), Northwestern U. Alumni Assn. (nat. pres. 1968-70), Council Better Bus. Burs. Chgo. (dir.), Council Fgn. Relations, Chgo. Assn. Commerce and Industry, Alpha Delta Sigma, Beta Gamma Sigma, Delta Sigma Pi, Phi Gamma Delta. Baptist (trustee). Clubs: Sky (N.Y.C.); Mid-America, Chicago, Executives, Economic (Chgo.) (dir., sec., mem. exec. com.); Kenilworth; Westmoreland Country (Wilmette, Ill.); Pine Valley Golf (Clementon, N.J.). Home: 132 Oxford Rd Kenilworth IL 60043 Office: Medill Sch Journalism North Western U Fisk Hall Evanston IL 60201

CHRISTIAN, ROBERT HENRY, architect; b. Cin., Feb. 28, 1922; s. Richard Dudley and Lillian Emma (Huber) C.; m. Marjorie Ann Ruff, Apr. 12, 1947; children—Carol Ann, Robert Alan. B.S. in Architecture, U. Cin., 1952. Color matcher Interchem. Corp., Cin., 1945-46; draftsman various cos., 1946-54; asso. architect Sullivan, Isaacs & Sullivan, Cin., 1954-62, L.P. Cotter & Assos., 1962-67, partner, 1967-72; v.p. devel. D.C. Peterson Co. Inc., Hilton Head Island, S.C., 1972—; pres. Hilton Head/Beaufort Council Architects, 1976. Mem. Hamilton County Regional Planning Commn., Cin., 1963—; active Boy Scouts Am.; artist and archtl. rep. Cin. Archdiocesan Liturgical Commn., 1970—; tech. adviser to Village Woodlawn, Ohio, 1963—; mayor Village, 1957-63; Mem. Edgecliff Coll. Acad. Fine Arts Found., 1961-69, chmn., 1963-66. Served with USAAF, 1942-45. Mem. AIA, U.S. Tennis Assn. Tennis Umpires, Hilton Head Profl. Tennis Umpires Assn. (pres.), Nat. Rifle Assn., Scarab. Club: K.C. (4 deg.). Home: 8 Liberty Pl Hilton Head Island SC 29928 Office: Suite N Craig Bldg Hilton Head Island SC 29928

CHRISTIAN, SHERRIL DUANE, chemistry educator; b. Estherville, Iowa, Sept. 28, 1931; s. Carl B. and Elverna E. (Kuhlman) C.; m. Dolores L. Gabriel, Jan. 7, 1956; children: Dale Warren, Ian Mark, Lani Aloha. B.S. in Math, Iowa State U., 1952, Ph.D. in Phys. Chemistry, 1956. Asst. prof. chemistry U. Okla., Norman, 1956-60, assoc. prof., 1960-65, prof., 1965-69, George Lynn Cross research prof., 1969—; asst. dean Coll. Arts and Scis., 1963-66, chmn. chemistry dept., 1963, 68-69; Participant Oak Ridge Inst. for Nuclear Studies, Tenn., summer 1956; employed summers at research div. Hawaiian Dole Pineapple Co., Honolulu, 1957, IBM Glendale Lab., Endicott, N.Y., 1959; guest prof., research assoc. U. Oslo, Norway, 1966-67, 74-75, U. Trondheim, 1979-80; pres. CET Research Group, Ltd., Norman. Contbr. articles to sci. jours. Recipient U. Okla. Found. Research award, 1956, U. Okla. Research Inst. Project Dirs.' Research award, 1966; Fulbright fellow U. Ceylon, 1961; Norwegian Council for Sci. and Indsl. Research fellow, 1966; recipient Citation of Merit Coll. of Scis. and Humanities, Iowa State U., 1980. Mem. Am. Chem. Soc., AAUP, U.S. Lawn Tennis Assn., Sigma Xi (Faculty Research award 1968), Phi Kappa Phi, Phi Lambda Upsilon, Pi Mu Epsilon. Home: 1900-10 Rock Creek Rd Norman OK 73071

CHRISTIAN, WINSLOW, judge; b. Caldwell, Idaho, Apr. 12, 1926; s. John L. and Bernice (Christian); m. Donna Margaret Hammond, June 12, 1948; children—Megan, Jason, Sidonie. B.A., Stanford U., 1947, LL.B., 1949. Bar: Calif. bar 1949. Fulbright teaching fellow (Law Faculty), Rangoon U., Burma, 1950; dep. atty. gen., Calif., 1951-52, individual practice law, Loyalton, Calif., 1952-54, city atty., Loyalton and Portola, 1952-54, dist. atty., Sierra County, 1954-58; judge Superior Ct., 1958-63; adminstr. Calif. Health and Welfare Agy., Sacramento, 1963-64; exec. sec. to Gov. Edmund G. Brown, 1964-66; justice Calif. Ct. of Appeal, San Francisco, 1966—; exec. dir. Nat. Center for State Cts., 1971-73; mem. Calif. Jud. Council, 1971-72. Contbr. articles to profl. jours. Pres. Found. for Jud. Edn., 1978—; pres., bd. trustees French-Am. Bilingual Sch., San Francisco, 1972-76.

Served with USN, 1944-46. Fellow Am. Bar Endowment; mem. Am. Bar Assn. (chmn. com. implement standards jud. adminstrn. 1975-78, chmn. appellate judges conf. 1979-80), Am. Law Inst. Home: 2335 Hyde St San Francisco CA 94109 Office: Ct of Appeal 455 Golden Gate Ave San Francisco CA 94102

CHRISTIANSEN, CHRISTIAN CARL, JR., banker; b. York, Pa., May 17, 1933; s. Christian Carl and Anna Marie C.; m. Nancy Louise Sheffer, Sept. 29, 1956; children: David, Melinda. B.S. in Bus. Adminstrn, Pa. State U., 1955. C.P.A., Pa. Auditor Ernst & Whinney, Pitts., 1955-56, 58-59; controller Sealtest Foods div. Kraft Foods, Washington, Phila. and N.Y.C., 1959-70, Bergen Record, Hackensack, N.J., 1970-72; v.p. Bankers Trust Co., N.Y.C., 1972-80, sr. v.p., 1980-82, gen. auditor, 1982—. Mem. Ramsey (N.J.) Bd. Edn., 1976-79. Served with U.S. Army, 1956-58. Mem. Fin. Execs. Inst. (dir., v.p. N.Y.C. chpt.), Am. Inst. C.P.A.s, N.Y. Soc. C.P.A.s. Clubs: Ramsey Golf and Country (pres. 1973-74); Brookside Racquet (Allendale, N.J.)). Office: 280 Park Ave New York NY 10015

CHRISTIANSEN, DONALD DAVID, editor, publisher, electrical engineer; b. Plainfield, N.J., June 23, 1927; s. David Carsten and Rita (Holmes) C.; m. Joyce Ifill, Jan. 1, 1951; children: Jacqueline, Jill. B.E.E., Cornell U., Ithaca, N.Y., 1950; postgrad., Mass. Inst. Tech., 1951, 54, U. Wis.-Madison, 1966, 68, 71. Registered profl. engr., Mass. Engr. Philco Corp., Phila., 1948-50; engr. CBS, Danvers, Lowell and Newburyport, Mass., 1950-62; solid-state editor Electronic Design, Hayden Pub. Co., N.Y.C., 1962-63; sr. editor EEE-Circuit Design Engring. Mactier Pub. Co., N.Y.C., 1963-66; sr. asso. editor Electronics McGraw-Hill Pub. Co., N.Y.C., 1966, sr. editor, 1966-67, asso. mng. editor, 1967-68, editor-in-chief, 1968-70, mgr. planning, devel. electronics publs., 1970-71; gen. mgr. Electronics in Medicine, 1971; editor and pub. Spectrum, jour. I.E.E.E., N.Y.C., 1971—, chmn. editorial bd., 1972—; I.E.E.E. rep. to UN, 1974—; speaker in field.; Lectr. Newark Coll. Engring., 1967, U. Mich., Ann Arbor, 1973, Walla Walla (Wash.) Coll., 1973, Ga. Inst. Tech., 1976, NASA Goddard Space Flight Center, 1981. Editor: Electronic Engineers' Handbook, 2d edit, 1981; Contbr. articles to profl. jours. Bd. dirs. YMCA, Newburyport, Mass., 1962, Broadband Info. Services, N.Y.C., 1970—. Served with USNR, 1945-46. Fellow IEEE; mem. N.Y. Acad. Sci., Cornell Soc. Engrs., Council Engring. and Sci. Soc. Execs., Am. Soc. Assn. Execs., Am. Soc. Mag. Editors, Soc. Nat. Assn. Publs. (dir. 1976—, chmn. editorial com. 1976-79, pres. 1981-83), N.Y. Bus. Press Editors (dir. 1978-79), Delta Club, Union Internationale de la Presse Radiotechnique et Electronique, Deadline Club, Nat. Conf. Electronics in Medicine (chmn. 1971), IEEE (co-founder, charter exec. com. chpt. 1958), Soc. for History Tech., Jovians, Antique Wireless Assn., Franklin Inst., Eta Kappa Nu (chmn., outstanding elec. engr. award 1976-78, dir. 1982—), Mu Sigma Tau, Sigma Delta Chi. Clubs: Cornell, Nat. Press. Office: 345 E 47th St New York NY 10017

CHRISTIANSEN, ERNEST BERT, educator; b. Richfield, Utah, July 31, 1910; s. Ernest C. and Sarah (Nielsen) C.; m. Susan Mann, Sept. 6, 1935; children—David Ernest, Susan Catherine, Gale Ann, Alan Grant, Philip Arne, Richard Lee, Lisa Beth. B.S., U. Utah, 1937; M.S., U. Mich., 1939, Ph.D., 1945. Registered profl. engr., Utah. Chem. engr. E.I. DuPont de Nemours Co., 1941-46; prof. chem. engring. U. Idaho, 1946-47, U. Utah, 1947—, head dept., 1947-75, distinguished research prof., 1977-78. Contbr. articles to profl. jours. Fellow Am. Inst. Chem. Engrs. (nat. dir. 1966-68, Founders award), Utah Acad. Sci., Arts and Letters; mem. Am. Chem. Soc., Am. Soc. Engring. Edn., Am. Soc. Rheology, Tau Beta Pi, Sigma Xi, Phi Kappa Phi. Home: 3025 S 1935 E St Salt Lake City UT 84106

CHRISTIANSEN, JOHN REES, educator, sociologist; b. Wales, Utah, Aug. 17, 1927; s. ElRay Lavar and Lewella (Rees) C.; m. Lucele Kartchner, Sept. 18, 1951; children: David, Steven, ElRay, Carol, Daniel. B.S., Utah State U., 1949, M.S., 1952; Ph.D., U. Wis., 1955. Asst. rural sociologist U. Ky., 1954-55; social sci. analyst Dept. Agr., 1955-57; mem. faculty Brigham Young U., 1957—, prof. sociology and social work, 1963—; vis. prof. Tex. A. and M. U., 1963-64, Mich. State U., 1969; U. Wis., 1970-71; collaborator Dept. Agr., 1963-65; cons. Teamwork Found., 1967—, Rivkin/Carson, 1973, Center for Planning and Research, 1978, Far West Labs., 1978—. Author: Introductory Sociology, 1963; also monographs, articles.; Bull. index editor: Rural Sociology, 1969-76. Served with USNR, 1945-47. Fellow Am. Sociol. Assn.; mem. Nat. Council Family Relations, Rural Sociol. Soc., Sigma Xi, Phi Kappa Phi, Pi Kappa Alpha, Alpha Kappa Delta. Home: 1161 Holly Circle Provo UT 84604 Office: Dept Social Work Brigham Young Univ Provo UT 84602

CHRISTIANSEN, KENNETH ALLEN, educator, biologist; b. Chgo., June 24, 1924; s. Christian Peder and Ethel (Robinson) C.; m. Phyllis Jean Smith, June 7, 1947; children—Karen, Eric, Paula, Diane. B.A., Boston U., 1948; Ph.D., Harvard, 1951. Teaching fellow Harvard, 1949-51; asst. prof. biology Am. U. Beirut, Lebanon, 1951-54; instr. zoology Smith Coll., 1954-55; faculty Grinnell (Iowa) Coll., 1955—, prof. biology, 1962—; Instr. Harvard Summer Sch., 1956, 59; vis. researcher Le Lab. Souterrain, Moulis, France, 1962, 67-68. Author: Collembola North America, 1980; Contbr. articles to profl. jours. Mem. Iowa Gov.'s Sci. Adv. Council. Served with AUS, 1942-45. Decorated Bronze Star with oak leaf cluster; recipient award for merit Iowa Acad. Sci., 1976; research grantee Sigma Xi, 1950-55, Bache Fund, 1955, Am. Philos. Soc., 1957, NSF, 1957-78. Fellow AAAS, Nat. Speleological Soc., Explorers Club; mem. Soc. for Study Evolution, Soc. Systemic Zoology, Internat. Soc. Soil Zoology, Am., Cambridge entomol. socs., Mus. of Paris (corr.), Phi Beta Kappa, Sigma Xi. Home: 1402 Main St Grinnell IA 50112

CHRISTIANSEN, NORMAN JUHL, newspaper publisher; b. Isle, Minn., Apr. 30, 1923; s. Arthur Theodore and Ingeborg Hansena (Clemensen) C.; m. Margaret Eleanor Whorton, June 13, 1948; children—Gregory Lowell, Susan Joy. B.A. in Journalism, Drake U., Des Moines, 1947. Reporter Bloomington (Ill.) Pantagraph, 1947; spl. agt. FBI, 1948-54; mem. labor relations staff Am. Newspaper Pubs. Assn., 1954-59; with Gannett Newspapers, 1959-67; asst. gen. mgr. Westchester-Rockland Newspaper Group, 1965-67; with Knight-Ridder Newspapers, Inc., 1967-80, group v.p. ops., Miami, Fla., 1975-80; pres., pub. Wichita (Kans.) Eagle and Beacon, 1980—. Bd. dirs. William Allen White Found., United Way, Wichita and Sedgwick, Wichita State U., Endowment Assn. Served with AUS, 1943-45. Mem. Am. Newspaper Pubs. Assn., Inland Daily Press Assn. (dir.). Clubs: Wichita, Wichita Country. Home: 626 N Doreen St Wichita KS 67206 Office: 825 E Douglas St Wichita KS 67201

CHRISTIANSEN, RICHARD DEAN, journalist; b. Berwyn, Ill., Aug. 1, 1931; s. William Edward and Louise Christine (Dethlefs) C. B.A., Carleton Coll., Northfield, Minn., 1953; postgrad., Harvard U., 1954. Reporter, critic, editor Chgo. Daily News, 1957-73, 74-78; editor Chicagoan mag., 1973-74; critic-at-large Chgo. Tribune, 1978—. Served with U.S. Army, 1954-56. Recipient award Chgo. Newspaper Guild, 1969, 74. Mem. Am. Theatre Critics Assn., Chgo. Acad. TV Arts and Scis. Republican. Lutheran. Clubs: Headline, Arts (Chgo.) (dir.). Home: 666 Lake Shore Dr Apt 1109 Chicago IL 60611 Office: Chgo Tribune 435 N Michigan Ave Chicago IL 60611

CHRISTIANSEN, ROBERT LESTER, advertising executive; b. Chgo., July 2, 1927; s. Clarence Martin and Leta (Covey) C.; m. Annemarie Gabor, Sept. 7, 1952 (dec.); children: Eric Robert, Clarence Martin II; m. Joy Flodin, Jan. 23, 1965. B.S., Northwestern U., 1949; student, Law Sch., 1949-50. Sec.-treas. C.M. Christiansen Co., Phelps, Wis., 1949-51, pres., 1957—; with Cramer-Krasselt Co. (advt.), Milw., Chgo. and Phoenix,, 1951—, exec. v.p., 1961-68, pres., 1968-79, chief exec. officer, 1971—, chmn. bd. and treas., 1979—, also dir.; v.p. Sylvan Products Corp., Phelps, 1959—; dir. Smoky Lake Corp., Lake Shore Inc., Iron Mountain and Kingsford, Mich. Former mem. Nat. Advt. Review Bd.; Former trustee Milw. Art Center; mem. Greater Milw. Com.; past bd. dirs. St. Joseph's Hosp., St. Michael Hosp.; former v.p.; dir. Florentine Opera Co., Milw.; asso. chmn., 1966, Milw. United Fund; bd. corp. Citizens' Govtl. Research Bur., Milw. Boys Clubs, Milw. Symphony Orch., Wis. Coll.-Conservatory, Milw.; bd. dirs., past chmn. Better Bus. Bur., Milw.; former mem. bd. dirs. Council Better Bus. Burs., Inc., Wis. Soc. Prevention Blindness; bd. regents Northwestern U., 1971; bd. govs. Mt. Mary Coll. Named Communicator of Year Wis. Advt. and Graphic Arts Industry, 1975. Mem. Am. Assn. Advt. Agys. (sec.-treas. 1977-78, dir., trustee group ins. trust, past chmn. central region bd. govs.), U.S. Navy League (dir. Milw. council). Clubs: Milwaukee (pres. 1979—), University, Milwaukee Country (Milw.); Chippewa (Iron Mountain, Mich.); Confrerie des Chevaliers du Tastevin. (Grand Genechal sous-commanderie de Milwaukee 1982—). Home: 9370 N Lake Dr Milwaukee WI 53217 Office: 733 N Van Buren St Milwaukee WI 53202

CHRISTIANSEN, TED LEO, educator; b. Chgo., Sept. 6, 1922; s. Ted and Minnie (Scholl) C.; m. Marjorie Lee Miner, Aug. 10, 1951; 1 dau., Karen Lee. B.S., U. N.Mex., 1951, M.A., 1959; Ph.D., Utah State U., 1966. Tchr., counselor N.Mex. pub. schs., 1952-63; prof. spl. edn. Highlands U., 1966-67, U. N.Mex., 1967-69; prof., chmn. dept. spl. edn. James Madison U., Harrisonburg, Va., 1969-74; dir. Center for Retarded, Las Vegas, N.Mex., 1966-67; spl. edn. cons., N.Mex., 1966-67, W.Va., 1969—; Mem. Gov. N.Mex. Com. Vocat. Edn. Handicapped, 1968-69; pres. Project Concern, Va., 1970—. Editor: N.Mex. Council for Exceptional Children Jour, 1968-69; book reviewer Coll. Library Jour., 1971—. Bd. dirs. Friendship Industries, Va. Served with AUS, 1942-45. Decorated Bronze Star. Mem. Council Exceptional Children (pres. N.Mex. fedn. 1968-69, treas. Va. fedn. 1972-73), Am. Assn. Mental Deficiency, Nat. Assn. Retarded Children, Assn. Retarded Children Va., Phi Delta Kappa. Club: Elk. Home: 94 Laurel St Harrisonburg VA 22801

CHRISTIANSEN, WALTER HENRY, aeronautics educator; b. McKees Rocks, Pa., Dec. 14, 1934; s. Walter Henry and Elizabeth (Miller) C.; m. Joan Marilyn Swisler, Aug. 5, 1960; children: Walter, Audrey. B.S.M.E., Carnegie Inst. Tech., 1956; M.S.A.E., Calif. Inst. Tech., 1957, Ph.D., 1961. Sr. scientist Jet Propulsion Lab., Pasadena, Calif., 1961-62, 1963-67; research assoc. prof. aeros. and aeronautics U. Wash., Seattle, 1967-70, assoc. prof., 1970-74, prof., 1974—; cons. Boeing Sci. Research Lab., 1967-69, Math. Scis. N.W., 1970—. Contbr. articles to profl. jours.; patentee in field. Com. mem. Directions for 70's Bellevue (Wash.) Sch. Dist., 19670. Served to capt. U.S. Army, 1961-63. NASA grantee, 1980-83; NSF grantee, 1977, 80; Dept. Def. grantee, 1970-83; Boeing, Convair, Mesta Machine fellows., 1952-56, 58, 60. Mem. AIAA (mem. tech. com. recipient Pacific N.W. sect. award for contbn. to aerospace tech. 1972), Am. Phys. Soc., Sigma Xi, Tau Beta Pi, Pi Tau Sigma, Theta Xi. Home: 1405 Evergreen Point Rd Bellevue WA 98004 Office: Dept Aeronautics and Astronautics FS 10 U Wash Seattle WA 98195

CHRISTIANSON, LLOYD FENTON, management consultant; b. Watertown, S.D., Jan. 6, 1914; s. Charles J. and Pearl Ellen (Auchampach) C.; m. Sergie A. Dannenberg, Dec. 25, 1935; children: George Fenton, Charles John, Lloyd Fredrick, Sergie Ann. B.S., U. Kans., 1935, Chem.E., 1940; postgrad., Harvard, 1941, Mass. Inst. Tech., 1942. Asst. chemist Kans. Bd. Health, Lawrence, 1933-35; petroleum engr. U.S. Bur. Mines, Bartlesville, Okla., 1935-41; pres. Electronic Assos., Inc., 1945-70; now mgmt. cons. Trustee Howards Savs. Bank.; Past pres. Monmouth County United Fund.; Bd. dirs. Monmouth County council Boy Scouts Am.; mem., past chmn. bd. trustees Monmouth Coll., 1972-76. Served to capt. Signal Corps AUS, 1941-45. Mem. Armed Forces Communications and Electronics Assn., Long Branch C. of C. (past pres.), U.S. Army Assn., Theta Tau., Rotarian (past pres.). Address: 99 Rumson Rd Rumson NJ 07760

CHRISTIANSON, RICHARD LINDBERGH, mortgage banker; b. Des Moines, May 21, 1927; s. Marion Sanford and Grace Alverda (Alleman) C.; m. Jeanne Lee Carpenter, Sept. 4, 1953; children: Nancy, Deborah, Thomas. B.S., U. Oreg., 1951; postgrad., U. Colo., 1952-53. Exec. v.p. M.S. Christianson Mortgage & Investment Co., Eugene, Oreg., 1953-68; v.p., div. mgr. 1st Nat. Bank of Oreg., Portland, 1968-72; sr. v.p., div. mgr. Pacific Nat. Bank of Wash., Seattle, 1972-79; pres., chief exec. officer Western Bancorp Mortgage Co., Denver, 1979-80; chmn., chief exec. officer 1st Interstate Bank of Idaho, Boise, 1980-83; pres., chief exec. officer, chmn. CalFed Mortgage Co. subs. Calif. Fed. Savs. & Loan, Los Angeles, 1983—. Trustee Coll. of Idaho. Served with U.S. Army, 1945-47. Mem. Mortgage Bankers Assn. Am., Calif. Mortgage Bankers Assn., Kappa Sigma. Republican. Clubs: Rotary., Multnomah Athletic. Office: 5615 Wilshire Blvd Los Angeles CA 90036

CHRISTIE, CLARENCE J., insurance brokerage executive; b. Ironton, Wis., Mar. 24, 1930; s. Leslie H. and Clementine C.; m. Delores Clary, Dec. 29, 1951; children: Michael, Patti, Kay, Pamela, Jeffrey. B.A. in Bus., U. Wis., 1952. C.P.A., Ill., Ind. Audit mgr. Arthur Andersen & Co. (C.P.A.s), 1954-69; v.p., treas. Fred S. James & Co., Inc., Chgo., 1970—. Served with U.S. Army, 1952-54. Mem. Fin. Execs. Inst. (dir. 1979—, v.p. 1981-82, pres. 1983-84), Am. Inst. C.P.A.s, Ill. Soc. C.P.A.s, Ind. Assn. C.P.A.s. Office: Fred S James & Co Inc 830 Morris Turnpike Short Hills NJ 07078

CHRISTIE, DOUGLAS HEWSON, lawyer; b. Winnipeg, Man., Can., Apr. 24, 1946; s. Douglas H. and Norma (McIntosh) C. B.A., United Coll., 1967; LL.B., U. B.C., 1970. Bar: B.C. 1971, Yukon Terr. 1979. Pres. Progressive Conservative Constituency, Victoria, B.C., 1974-75; founder, pres. Com. for Western Independence, Victoria, 1975-80; founder, leader Western Can. Concept, Victoria, 1980—; sole practice law, Victoria, 1971—. Founder A Polit. Party, Western Can. Concept, 1980—. Mem. Com. for Western Independence. Roman Catholic. Office: 810 Courtney St Victoria BC Canada V8W 1C4

CHRISTIE, GEORGE CUSTIS, legal educator, author; b. N.Y.C., Mar. 3, 1934. A.B., Columbia U., 1955, J.D., 1957; diploma in internat. law (Fulbright scholar), Cambridge (Eng.) U., 1962; S.J.D., Harvard U., 1966. Bar: N.Y. 1957, D.C. 1958. Assoc. Covington & Burling, Washington, 1958-60; Ford Found. fellow in law teaching Harvard U., 1960-61; asso. prof. law U. Minn., Mpls., 1962-65, prof., 1965-66; asst. gen. counsel for Near E. and S. Asia, AID, Dept. State, 1966-67; prof. law Duke U., 1967-79, James B. Duke prof. law, 1979—; vis. prof. U. Witwatersrand, South Africa, 1980; fellow Nat. Humanities Center, 1980-81; scholar-in-residence McGuire, Woods & Battle, Richmond, Va. Author: Jurisprudence: Text and Readings on the Philosophy of Law, 1973, The Sum and Substance of the Law of Torts, 1980, Law, Norms & Authority, 1982; contbr. Cases and Materials on the Law of Torts, 1983, articles to legal jours.; mem. bd. editors: Am. Jour. Legal History, 1971-76, Law and Philosophy, 1982—. Served with U.S. Army, 1957. Mem. ABA, Am. Law Inst., Am. Soc. Internat. Law, Phi Beta Kappa. Office: Duke U Sch Law Durham NC 27706

CHRISTIE, JULIE, actress; b. Chukua, India, Apr. 14, 1940; d. Frank St. John and Rosemary Ramsden C. Student, Central Sch. Dramatic Art, London, Brighton Coll. Tech. Profl. Debut in: Brit. television series A is for Andromeda, 1962; films include: Crooks Anonymous, 1962, The Fast Lady, 1963, Billy Liar, 1963, Young Cassidy, 1964, Darling, 1965, Dr. Zhivago, 1965, Farenheit 451, 1966, Far From the Madding Crowd, 1967, Petulia, 1968, In Search of Gregory, 1969, The Go-Between, 1971, McCabe and Mrs. Miller, 1971, Don't Look Now, 1974, Shampoo, 1975, Demon Seed, 1977, Heaven Can Wait, 1978, The Return of the Soldier, 1981, Heat and Dust, 1983; appeared with, Birmingham Repertory Co., 1963, Royal Shakespeare Co., 1964. Recipient Academy award for best actress in Darling, 1965; N.Y. Film Critics Circle award, 1965; Best Dramatic Actress Laurel award and Herald award, 1967. Office: care Internat Creative Mgmt 40 W 57th St New York NY 10019 *

CHRISTIE, MARION FRANCIS, educator; b. Emerson, Ark., Dec. 10, 1922; s. Scott T. and Milbra (Pafford) C.; m. Joann Finley, Aug. 23, 1944; children—Catherine Ann, Christine, John Finley. B.A., Hendrix Coll., 1944; B.D., So. Meth. U., 1947, M.A., 1947; Ph.D. (Carre fellow, Hillel fellow), Vanderbilt U., 1952. Instr. phys. edn. So. Meth. U., 1944-45, instr. religion, 1946-49; tchr. English, Terrill Prep. Sch., Dallas, 1945-46; prof. religion Birmingham-So. Coll., 1951-57; dean Simpson Coll., Indianola, Ia., 1957-59; head dept. philosophy and religion Mt. Union Coll., Alliance, Ohio, 1959-60, dean, 1960-65; acad. dean Hendrix Coll., Conway, Ark., 1965-76, distinguished prof. philosophy and religion, 1976—; dean acad. affairs Graz (Austria) Center, summers 1970, 71, spl. adviser, summer 1972; vis. lectr. Bible, Perkins Sch. Theology, Candler Sch. Theology, Emory U., Div. Sch. Vanderbilt U.; Ordained to ministry Meth. Ch., 1947. Contbr. articles to profl. jours. Chmn. N. Ala. Conf. Commn. Christian Vocations, 1955-57, chmn. bd. ch. and soc. for conf., 1978—. Mem. Blue Key, Alpha Psi Omega. Home: Route 7 Box 266 Conway AR 72032 *I am most characterized by a continual and deepening desire for learning and an overwhelming concern to share this with others.*

CHRISTIE, ROBERT WAYNE, business executive; b. Marion, Ky., Aug. 3, 1929; s. Elliot and Charlotte C.; m. Arden Furlong, Aug. 2, 1974; children: Susan Lynn, David, Robert, Elizabeth, Mark. Grad., Robert Morris Coll., 1951. Joined Pitts. Nat. Bank, 1960, asst. cashier, 1961-62, asst. comptroller, 1962-63, comptroller, 1963-65, v.p., comptroller, 1965-68, sr. v.p., comptroller, 1968-71, sr. v.p., adminstrv. asst. to chmn., pres., 1971-75; exec. v.p. Pitts. Nat. Corp., 1972-82; vice chmn., chief exec. officer The Kissell Co., Pitts., 1975-76; pres., chief exec. officer Kissell Co., 1976-78, chmn., pres., chief exec. officer, 1978-81, chmn., chief exec. officer, 1981—, also dir.; dir. PNC Funding Corp., PINACO, Inc., Pitts. Nat. Life Ins. Co. Mem. Am. Inst. C.P.A.s, Pa. Inst. C.P.A.s, Fin. Execs. Inst. Clubs: Duquesne, St. Clair Country, Springfield Country. Home: 740 Somerville Dr Pittsburgh PA 15243 Office: 30 Warder St Springfield OH 45501

CHRISTIE, THOMAS PHILIP, govt. ofcl.; b. Pensacola, Fla., May 28, 1934; s. Joseph Aloysius and Margaret Gabriel (Donaldson) C.; m. Kathleen Ann Lawson, June 27, 1964; children—Kevin Patrick, Stephanie Marie. B.S., Spring Hill Coll., 1955; M.S., N.Y. U., 1962. Dir. analysis div. Air Force Armament Lab., Eglin AFB, Fla., 1970-73; dir. Tactical Air Div., Office of Sec. of Def., Pentagon, 1973-77, dep. asst. sec. of Def. for operational test and evaluation, 1977-79, dep. asst. sec. of Def. for gen. purpose forces, 1979—. Roman Catholic. Home: 2117 Freda Dr Vienna VA 22180 Office: Room 2-E 330 Pentagon Washington DC 20301

CHRISTINE, VIRGINIA FELD, actress; b. Stanton, Iowa, Mar. 5, 1920; d. George Allen Ricketts and Helga (Ossian) Kraft; m. Fritz Feld, Nov. 10, 1940; children: Steven, Danny. Student, UCLA, 1939-40. Actress appearing in Edge of Darkness, Mission to Moscow, The Killers, Cover Up, High Noon, The Mummy's Curse, Not as a Stranger, Cyrano, The Men, Three Brave Men, Cobweb, Body Snatchers, The Spirit of St. Louis, Johnny Tremaine, Judgement at Nuremberg, Guess Who's Coming to Dinner?, the Prize, Rage to Live, Four for Texas, 300 TV shows; spokeswoman Proctor & Gamble (role of Mrs. Olson, Folgers coffee commercial), Cin., 1964-83. Hon. mayor, Brentwood, Calif.; bd. dirs. Family Planning Centers Greater Los Angeles; judge Am. Coll. Theatre Festival. Recipient 1st place award Forensic League, 1937, Hall of Fame award Long Beach City Coll., 1977, citation-cultural award City of Los Angeles, 1979. Democrat.

CHRISTISON, MURIEL BRANHAM, emeritus museum administrator; b. Mpls.; d. Harold D. and Helen (Ferguson) Branham;, 1933; children: Evelyn, Carolyn. B.A., U. Minn., 1933, M.A., 1940; diplome, U. Paris, 1936, U. Brussels, 1938. Curatorial researcher Mpls. Inst. Arts, 1936-42, head edn., 1944-47; assoc. dir. Va. Mus. Fine Arts, 1948-61; assoc. dir., operating dir. Krannert Art Mus., U. Ill., 1962-74; dir. Krannert Art Mus. U. Ill., 1975-82, emeritus dir., 1982—; vis. prof. fine arts Coll. William and Mary, 1983; vis. prof. fine arts Coll. William and Mary; lectr. cons. in field. Contbr. articles to profl. jours., mags. Fellow Belgian-Am. Ednl. Found.; Carnegie scholar. Mem. Am. Assn. Museums (council, sr. examiner), Internat. Council Museums, Assn. Art Mus. Dirs., Midwest Museums Conf., Assn. Preservation Va. Antiquities. Club: Cosmopolitan (N.Y.C.). Home: 1184 Jamestown Rd Apt 5 Williamsburg VA 23185 Office: Dept Fine Arts Coll William and Mary Williamsburg VA 23185

CHRIST-JANER, ARLAND FREDERICK, college president; b. Garland, Nebr., Jan. 27, 1922; s. William Henry and Bertha Wilhelmina (Beckman) C.-J.; m. Sally Johnson Grice, Sept. 4, 1975. B.A., Carleton Coll., 1943; B.D., Yale, 1949; J.D., U. Chgo., 1952; LL.D., Coe Coll., 1961, Carleton Coll., 1967, Colo. Coll., 1971; L.H.D., Monmouth Coll., 1967, Curry Coll., 1972. Asst. to pres. Lake Erie Coll., Painesville, Ohio, 1952-53; asst. to pres. St. John's Coll., Annapolis, Md., 1953-54, tutor, treas., 1954-59, v.p., tutor, 1959-61; pres. Cornell Coll., Mt. Vernon, Iowa, 1961-67, Boston U., 1967-70, Coll. Entrance Exam. Bd., N.Y.C., 1970—73, New Coll., Sarasota, Fla., 1973-75, Stephens Coll., Columbia, Mo., 1975—; Trustee New Coll. Found., U. South Fla., Sarasota; mem. nat. identification program for advancement of women in higher edn. adminstrn. Am. Council on Edn.; mem. bd. Mus. Assos., U. Mo., Columbia. Exhibiting artist. Served with USAAF, 1943-46. Mem. Am. Acad. Arts and Scis., Newcomen Soc. N.Am., Phi Beta Kappa (hon.). Clubs: Rotary of Columbia, Century Assn., University (N.Y.C.). Home: President's Home Stephens Coll Columbia MO 65215

CHRISTMAN, HENRY MAX, author, state official; b. Kansas City, Mo., Jan. 21, 1932; s. Henry Max and Irene Blanche (McBride) C. B.A. in History and Govt, U. Mo. at Kansas City, 1953; Ph.D., U. Belgrade, 1971. Pub. info. cons. Fund for Republic, 1956-62; past dir. city record, City N.Y., 1966-74; adj. prof. polit. sci. L.I. U., 1971-74; mem. Worker's Compensation Bd., State of N.Y., 1977—; Mem. com. candidates Citizens Union, City N.Y., 1961-66; vice-chmn. N.Y. County, Liberal Party, 1974—. Author: The Public Papers of Chief Justice Earl Warren, 1959, The Mind and Spirit of John Peter Altgeld, 1960, A View of the Nation, 1960, Walter P. Reuther-Selected Papers, 1961, This is our Strength-Selected Papers of Golda Meir, 1962, Walt

Whitman's New York, 1963, Peace and Arms-Reports from the Nation, 1964, The South As It Is, 1965, One Hundred Years of the Nation, 1965, The Essential Works of Lenin, 1966, The American Journalism of Marx and Engels, 1966, Communism in Practice: A Documentary History, 1969, The State Papers of Levi Eshkol, 1969, The Essential Tito, 1970, Neither East Nor West: The Basic Documents of Non-alignment, 1973, Indira Gandhi Speaks: On Democracy, Socialism, and Third World Nonalignment, 1975, Mahout, 1982; Editor: (Myers) The History of Bigotry in the United States, 1960, (La Guardia) The Making of an Insurgent, 1961, (Garland) A Son of the Middle Border, 1962; also Contbr. articles to profl. jours., mags. Decorated Star Yugoslavia 1st class, 1970; recipient gold medal City of Athens, 1976. Mem. Am. Ethical Union, Soc. Am. Historians, League Indsl. Democracy (past dir., nat. council), Ams. for Democratic Action (N.Y. State vice chmn. 1963-67, dir., chmn. Greenwich Village chpt. 1965-66), A.A.U.P., Am. Polit. Sci. Assn., Phi Alpha Theta, Pi Gamma Mu, Sigma Delta Chi. Home: 453 Franklin D Roosevelt Dr New York NY 10002 Office: 2 World Trade Center New York NY 10047

CHRISTMAN, JOHN FRANCIS, university official; b. Terre Haute, Ind., Feb. 17, 1924; s. Fred Garland and Josephine Louise (Vesque) C.; m. Emma Neale Slover, June 7, 1950; children: John Benton, Claudia Anne. B.S. in Chemistry, U. Notre Dame, 1944; M.A., Ind. U., 1946; M.S., U. Tenn., Knoxville, 1948, Ph.D., 1950. Mem. faculty La. State U., Baton Rouge, 1950-66, prof. biochemistry, 1966, Loyola U., New Orleans, 1966—, dir. acad. grants, 1966-67, v.p. acad. affairs, 1967-68, dir. research, 1968-71, dir. research and grad. studies, 1971—; pres. Aurora Research Inc., 1980—; research participant biology div. Oak Ridge Nat. Labs., 1954-55; asso. program dir. student and coop. programs NSF, 1964-65; dir. student sci. tng. program, 1959-73; mem. La. Commn. Extension and Continuing Edn., 1966-75. Author articles in field.; Editorial bd.: New Orleans Rev, 1974—. Recipient Spl. Public Service citation U.S. Dept. Commerce, 1979; predoctoral research fellow USPHS, 1948-50. Fellow Am. Inst. Chemists; mem. Am. Chem. Soc. (regional tour speaker 1979-83), Soc. Research Adminstrs., Conf. So. Grad. Schs., Assn. Jesuit Colls. and Univs., Am. Assn. Affirmative Action, Sigma Xi, Delta Epsilon Sigma (nat. pres. 1974-77), Phi Lambda Upsilon, Alpha Chi Sigma (dist. counselor 1954-59), Tau Kappa Epsilon. Democrat. Roman Catholic. Home: 5730 Norland Ave New Orleans LA 70114 Office: Box 47 Loyola Univ New Orleans LA 70118 *One must learn, somehow, that independence of self is achieved from faith in others; dependence on others does not diminish oneself. Confidence in one's ability comes not only with success, but equally from failure. These concepts cannot be learned from a single source. They are the influences of family, teachers, colleagues, students, and writers. It is my belief that what talents I have are from a divine source. The ultimate judgement will consist of how I have developed and applied them. I try, then, to extend my doing beyond what I have done before, and never pass an opportunity to continue to learn.*

CHRISTMAN, LUTHER PARMALEE, university dean; b. Summit Hill, Pa., Feb. 26, 1915; s. Elmer and Elizabeth (Barnicott) C.; m. Dorothy Mary Black, Dec. 5, 1939; children: Gary, Judith, Lillian. Grad., Pa. Hosp. Sch. Nursing for Men, 1939; B.S., Temple U., 1948, Ed.M., 1952; Ph.D., Mich. State U., 1965; L.H.D., Thomas Jefferson U., 1980. Cons. Mich. Dept. Mental Health, Lansing, 1956-63; asso. prof. psychiat. nursing U. Mich., 1963-67; research asso. Inst. Social Research, U. Mich., 1963-67; prof. nursing and sociology, dean nursing Vanderbilt U., 1967-72; prof. sociology Rush Coll. Health Scis.; sr. scientist Rush-Presbyn.-St. Luke's Med. Center; prof. nursing, dean, v.p. nursing affairs Coll. Nursing, Rush U., 1972—; cons. community services and research br. NIMH, 1963-66; psychiat. research project So. Regional Edn. Bd., 1964-67; Chmn. planning com. 1st Midwest Conf. Psychiat. Nursing, Mpls., 1956; mem. team to survey mental health facilities of Colo. NIMH, 1962, of Ga., 1964; mem., workshop leader White House Conf. on Children, 1970; mem. nursing panel Nat. Commn. for Study Nursing and Nursing Edn., 1968-70; mem. regional med. programs rev. com. Health Services and Mental Health Adminstrn., HEW, 1968—; cons. dept. medicine and surgery VA Central Office, 1968-71, 74—; mem. panel nurse consultants to com. on nursing AMA, 1968-71; mem. health services adv. com. Am. Assn. Med. Colls., 1968-71; mem. action com. pub. health Am. Health Found., 1970-72; mem. membership com. Inst. Medicine, Nat. Acad. Sci., 1972-73, mem. com. on edn. in health professions, 1973-75; participant numerous confs. in field; mem. S.D. Bd. Nursing, Tenn. Bd. Nursing. Contbr. numerous articles to profl. jours. Fellow AAAS, Am. Acad. Nursing, Inst. Medicine Chgo., Soc. Applied Anthropology; mem. Am. Nurses Assn. (3rd v.p.), Mich. Nurses Assn. (pres. 1961-65), Am. Sociol. Assn., Soc. Gen. Systems Research, Inst. Medicine, N.Y. Acad. Scis., Biomed. Engring. Soc., Sigma Theta Tau, Alpha Omega Alpha (hon.), Alpha Kappa Delta. Home: 19141 Loomis Homewood IL 60430

CHRISTO, artist; b. Gabrovo, Bulgaria, June 13, 1935; came to U.S., 1964; s. Vladimir Ivan and Tzveta (Dimitrova) C.; m. Jeanne-Claude de Guillebon; 1 son, Cyril. Student, Fine Arts Acad., Sofia Bulgaria, 1952-56, Vienna (Austria) Fine Arts Acad., 1957. Stacked oil drums, Cologne Harbor (Germany), 1961, Paris, 1962, Phila. Mus. Contemporary Art, 1968, air package and wrapped tree, Stedelijk van Abbemuseum, Eindhoven, Netherlands, 1966, air package, Walker Art Center, Mpls. Sch. Art, 1966, Kassel, Germany, 1968; wrapped fountain and tower, Spoleto, Italy, 1968; packaged pub. bldgs., Kunsthalle, Bern, Switzerland, 1968, Mus. Contemporary Art, Chgo., 1969; stacked hay, Phila. Inst. Contemporary Art, 1969; wrapped monuments to Vitorio Emanuele and Leonardo da Vinci, Milan, Italy, 1970; wrapped coast, Little Bay, Sydney, Australia, 1969; Valley Curtain Grand Hogback, Rifle, Colo., 1970-72; wrapped Roman wall Porta Pinciana, Rome; Ocean Front, Newport, R.I., 1974; running fence, Sonoma and Marin Counties, Calif., 1972-76; wrapped Walk Ways, Kansas City, Mo., 1977-78; Surrounded islands, Biscayne Bay, Miami, Fla., 1980-83. Address: 48 Howard St New York NY 10013

CHRISTOFERSON, LEE ALLEN, neurosurgeon, educator; b. Bemidji, Minn., June 9, 1921; m. Nancy A. Nelson, June 12, 1943; children: Karen, Lee Allen, Eric, Jeanne, Joel, Nancy Lee. B.Sc., U. Minn., Mpls., 1943, M.D., 1945; M.S., Mayo Grad. Sch., 1950. Diplomate: Am. Bd. Neurol. Surgery. Intern Cleve. Clinic Found., 1944-45; resident in neurosurgery Mayo Clinic, Rochester, Minn., 1947-51; neurosurgeon Neurologic Assos., Neuropsychiat. Inst., Fargo, N.D., 1951—; mem. faculty U. N.D. Med. Sch., Grand Forks, 1951—, prof. neurology and neurosurgery, 1971-73, chmn. dept. neurosci., prof. neurosurgery, 1973—, acting chmn. dept. surgery, 1979-80; program dir. neurol. surgery residency tng. program Neuropsychiat. Inst., U. N.D. Med. Sch., 1972-80; mem. cons. staff Neuropsychiat. Inst.; sponsor Mayo Clinic; mem. cons. staff St. Luke's, St. Ansgar, St. John's, Dakota VA Hosp., United Hosp.; mem. Pres.' Com. on Mental Retardation; cons. in field, mem. various govtl. med. coms.; dir. Fargo Nat. Bank. Contbr. articles to med. jours. Served with M.C. AUS. Mem. Am. Assn. Neurol. Surgeons, Soc. Neurol. Surgeons, Neurosurg. Soc. Am. (v.p. 1978—), A.C.S. (chmn. N.D. com. trauma), Congress Neurol. Surgeons, Assn. U. Prof. Neurology, AMA, Minn. Soc. Neurol. Scis. (past pres.), N.D. Med. Assn. (speaker ho. dels. 1966-71), 1st Dist. Med. Soc. (treas. 1972), Minn. Soc. Neurol. Scis., N.D. Acad. Sci., Mayo Clinic Alumni Assn., Fargo-Moorhead Med. Found., Sigma Xi., Alpha Omega Alpha. Home: Rural Route 1 Chrisan Fargo ND 58103 Office: 700 1st Ave S Fargo ND 58102

CHRISTOFFERSEN, RALPH EARL, chemist; b. Elgin, Ill., Dec. 4, 1937; s. Arthur Henry and Mary C.; m. Barbara Hibbard, June 10, 1961; children: Kirk Alan, Rachel Anne. B.S., Cornell Coll., 1959; Ph.D., Ind. U., 1963. Asst. prof. chemistry U. Kans., Lawrence, 1966-69, assoc. prof., 1967-72, prof., 1972-81, asst. vice chancellor for acad. affairs, 1974-75, assoc. vice chancellor for acad. affairs, 1976-79, vice chancellor for acad. affairs, 1979-81; pres. Colo. State U., Ft. Collins, 1981-83; dir. biotech. Upjohn Co., Kalamazoo, 1983—; chmn. sci. adv. bd. U.S. Solar Energy Research Inst., 1981—; bd. dirs. Mich. Biotech. Inst. Contbr. articles to profl. jours. NIH fellow, 1962-63, 64-66. Fellow Am. Inst. Chemists; mem. Am. Chem. Soc., Am. Phys. Soc. (v.p. theoretical div. 1981), AAUP, Internat. Soc. Quantum Biology (pres. 1977-79), Sigma Xi, Phi Lambda Upsilon. Office: The Upjohn Co Kalamazoo MI 49002

CHRISTOFIDES, CONSTANTINE GEORGE, art history educator; b. Alexandria, Egypt, Mar. 31, 1928; s. George Emmanuel and Mary C.; m. Koren Grayum, 1983; children by previous marriage: Alix, Philip. B.A., Columbia Coll., 1948; M.A. in French, U. Mich., 1949, U. Mich., 1950, Ph.D., 1956. Asst. prof. U. Iowa, 1956-59; asso. prof. Syracuse U., 1959-66; prof. comparative lit. and art history U. Wash., Seattle, 1966—, head art history dept., 1978—, dean humanities, 1975-78. Author: Bossuet and Jansenism, 1956, Introduction to French Literature, 1958, Medieval and Renaissance Art, 1978; asso. editor: Symposium and Modern Lang. Quar; contbr. articles to profl. jours., one person photographic exhbns. Decorated chevalier Order Palmes Académiques, (France). Mem. MLA, Coll. Art Assn., AAUP. Office: Sch Art U Wash Seattle WA 98195

CHRISTOFORIDIS, A. JOHN, radiologist, educator; b. Greece, Dec. 24, 1924; s. John P. and Ada A. C.; m. Ann Dimitriadis, Nov. 11, 1961; children: John, Gregory, Alex, Jimmy. M.D. summa cum laude, Nat. U. Athens, Greece, 1949; M.M.Sc., Ohio State U., 1957; Ph.D., Aristotelian U., Greece, 1969. Instr. to prof. Ohio State U., Columbus, 1956-74, clin. prof., 1974—; chmn. dept. radiology Aristotelian U., Salonika, Greece, 1971; prof., chmn. dept. radiology Med. Coll. Ohio, Toledo, until 1982, Ohio State U., Columbus, 1982—; cons. Greek Ministry Health, Batelle Meml. Inst., Columbus. Contbr. to textbook for med. students. Served to lt. M.C. Greek Army, 1950-52. Recipient Silver award Ohio Med. Assn., 1969, awards Heart Assn., 1960, Batelle Meml. Inst., 1965, Astra Co., 1967, Lung Assn., 1970-71; named Hon. Citizen City of Thessalonike, 1973; Ohio Geriatrics Med. grantee, 1980; NSF grantee, 1980. Fellow Am. Coll. Chest Physicians, Am. Coll. Radiology; mem. Ohio Radiol. Soc., Assn. Univ. Radiologists, AAAS, Radiol. Soc. N. Am., AMA, Soc. Chmn. Acad. Radiology Depts., AAUP, Fleishner Soc. (charter), Am. Hellenic Ednl. Progressive Assn., Greek-Am. Progressive Assn. Greek Orthodox. Research in chest and gastrointestinal radiology. Office: Ohio State Univ 410 W 10th Ave Columbus OH 43210

CHRISTOL, CARL QUIMBY, lawyer, educator; b. Gallup, S.D., June 28, 1914; s. Carl and Winifred (Quimby) C.; m. Jeannette Stearns, Dec. 18, 1949; children: Susan Quimby, Richard Stearns. A.B., U. S.D., 1934, LL.D. (hon.), 1977; A.M., Fletcher Sch. Law and Diplomacy, 1936; postgrad., Institut Universitaire des Hautes Etudes Internationales, Geneva, 1937-38, U. Geneva, 1937-38; Ph.D., U. Chgo., 1941; LL.B., Yale U., 1947, Acad. Internat. Law, The Hague, 1950. Bar: Calif. bar 1949, S.D. bar 1948. Assoc. firm Guthrie, Darling and Shattuck, Los Angeles, 1948-49; of counsel Fizzolio, Fizzolio & McLeod, North Hollywood, 1949—; assoc. prof. polit. sci. U. So. Calif., 1949-59, prof., 1959—, chmn. dept. polit. sci., 1960-64, 75-77; Stockton chair internat. law U.S. Naval War Coll., 1962-63, cons., 1963—, World Law Fund; mem. Los Angeles Mayor's Adv. Com. Human Relations, Commn. to Study Orgn. of Peace; mem. adv. panel on internat. law Dept. State, 1970-76; v.p. Ct. of Man Found., 1971-77. Author: Transit by Air in International Law, 1941, Introduction to Political Science, 1957, 4th edit., 1982, Readings in International Law, 1959, The International Law of Outer Space, 1966, The International Legal and Institutional Aspects of the Stratosphere Ozone Problem, 1975, The Modern International Law of Outer Space, 1982; bd. editors: Western Polit. Quar, 1970-75, Internat. Lawyer, 1975—; contbr. articles on legal, polit. and mil. subjects to profl. jours. Bd. dirs. Los Angeles County Heart Assn., 1956-61. Served to lt. col. AUS, 1941-46; col. Res. ret. Decorated Bronze Star medal; recipient Dart award U. So. Calif., 1970, Assos. award for excellence in teaching, 1977, Raubenheimer award, 1982; Rockefeller Found. fellow, 1958-59. Mem. Am., Los Angeles, Internat. bar assns., Am. Soc. Internat. Law (exec. council 1973-76), Internat. Studies Assn. (chmn. internat. law sect. 1977-78), Internat. Acad. Astronautics (corr. mem.), State Bar Calif., UN Assn. Los Angeles (pres. 1961-63), Am. Polit. Sci. Assn., Internat. Inst. Space Law (pres. Am. br. 1973-75), Town Hall, AIAA, Internat. Law Assn., UN Assn. U.S. (dir. 1967-71), Blue Key, Skull and Dagger, Phi Beta Kappa, Alpha Tau Omega. Republican. Presbyterian. Club: Masons. Home: 1041 Anoka Pl Pacific Palisades CA 90272 Office: Univ So Calif Los Angeles CA 90089 *Teaching allows me to explore the realities of the 21st century while experiencing those of the 20th with the most delightful people I know—my students. Through these relationships I am fulfilling the work that God has designed for me.*

CHRISTOPH, JAMES BERNARD, educator; b. Waukesha, Wis., Aug. 17, 1928; s. Floyd Howard and Esther (Orvis) C.; m. Natalie Ann Kunz, Dec. 22, 1955; children—Lesley Schafer, Ian Howard, Alison Hunt, Nancy Kunz, Megan Campbell. B.A., U. Wis., 1950; postgrad., Harvard, 1950-51; M.A., U. Minn., 1952, Ph.D., 1956, London Sch. Econs. and Polit. Sci., 1953-54. Instr. to prof. polit. sci. Ohio State U., 1955-67, postdoctoral fellow, 1957-58, asst. dean, 1959-61; prof. polit. sci. Ind. U., Bloomington, 1967—, chmn., 1967-71, acting chmn., 1975-76, dir. undergrad. studies, 1977-80, chmn., 1973-74, dir. learning support services, 1981—; Fulbright fellow to, U.K., 1953-54, Social Sci. Research Council faculty research fellow, 1962-63; Fulbright prof. Johns Hopkins Sch. Advanced Internat. Studies, Bologna, Italy, 1966-67; mem. award com. Woodrow Wilson Found., 1979. Author: Capital Punishment and British Politics, 1962, Britain At the Crossroads, 1967; Editor: Cases in Comparative Politics, 1965, 69, 76; Contbr. articles to profl. jours. Recipient Pi Sigma Alpha award Am. Polit. Sci. Assn., 1965; Disting. Teaching award Ind. U., 1980. Mem. Am. Polit. Sci. Assn. (council 1976-78), Midwest Polit. Sci. Assn), Brit. Politics Group (pres. 1978-80, exec. council 1976—), Polit. Studies Assn., AAUP, Phi Beta Kappa. Democrat. Home: 4875 E Heritage Woods Rd Bloomington IN 47401

CHRISTOPHER, FLOYD HUDNALL, JR., tobacco company executive; b. Franklin, Va., Dec. 9, 1933; s. Floyd Hudnall and Dorothy Eberwine (Ames) C.; m. Claire Penn Cannon, Feb. 11, 1961; children—John H., Ashley Penn, David Ames. B.Chem.Engring., U. Va., 1955; S.M., MIT, 1959. With R.J. Reynolds Industries, Inc., 1959; v.p. R.J. Reynolds Tobacco Co., Winston-Salem, N.C., 1976-79, sr. v.p., 1981-83, exec. v.p., 1983—, dir., 1981—; pres., chief exec. officer RJR Archer, Inc., 1979-81, dir., 1979—. Bd. dirs. United Way Forsyth County, 1978—, Children's Center Physically Handicapped.; Bd. visitors Wake Forest U., Winston-Salem; Bd. overseers Sweet Briar Coll. (Va.). Served to lt. (j.g.) USN, 1955-57. Mem. Aluminum Assn. (dir. 1979-81), Winston-Salem C. of C. Republican. Episcopalian. Clubs: Old Town (Winston-Salem) (bd.-govs.); Rotary). Home: 2837 Reynolds Dr Winston-Salem NC 27104 Office: 401 N Main St Winston-Salem NC 27102

CHRISTOPHER, JAMES WALKER, architect, educator; b. Phila., Nov. 5, 1930; s. Arthur Bailey and Cornelia (Slater) C.; m. Carolyn Kennard, July 9, 1955; children: William W., Kathryn A., Kimberley, James S., Pamela W. B.A., Rice U., 1953, B.S. in Architecture, 1953; M.Arch., MIT, 1956. Registered architect, Utah, Colo., Nev., Idaho, Wyo. Asst. prof. architecture U. Utah, Salt Lake City, 1956-60, adj. prof. architecture, 1983; archtl. designer various firms, Salt Lake City, 1960-63; founding prin. Brixen & Christopher Architects, Salt Lake City, 1983—. Architect, Phase I, Snowbird, Alta Canyon, Utah (AIA Western Mountain Region award 1971), Numemaker Place Chapel, Salt Lake City 1977, Congregation Kol Ami, Salt Lake City 1977, Block 53 Master Plan, Salt Lake City (Utah chpt. AIA award 1979). Mem. Utah Environ. Transp. Council, Salt Lake City, 1970-77, vice chmn., Salt Lake City, 1970-75; mem. Big Cottonwood Citizens Planning Com., Salt Lake County, Utah, 1975, Salt Lake City Downtown Planning Com., 1981, Utah Transit Authority Transplan, Salt Lake City, 1982. Served to lt. (j.g.) USNR, 1953-55. Fellow AIA (pres. Utah Soc. 1970, 12 Utah Soc. Design awards 1966-83, 12 Western Mountain Region Design awards 1968-83, 8 nat. Design awards 1975-83, Presdl. citation 1982). Episcopalian. Club: Alta (Salt Lake City). Home: 2954 Millcreek Rd Salt Lake City UT 84109 Office: Brixen & Christopher Architects 252 S 2d East Salt Lake City UT 84111

CHRISTOPHER, JOHN BARRETT, educator; b. Phila., Nov. 20, 1914; s. John and Gertrude (Barrett) C.; m. Marjorie Gilles, Dec. 21, 1957. A.B., Haverford Coll., 1935; A.M., Harvard U., 1936, Ph.D., 1942. Instr. history Haverford Coll., 1938; teaching fellow Harvard U., 1938-41; instr. Duke U., 1941-42; analyst U.S. Dept. State, 1945-46; asst. prof. history U. Rochester, 1946-52, asso. prof., 1952-65, prof., 1965-80, emeritus, 1980—. Author: (with others) A History of Civilization, 1955, rev. edit., 1976, Modern Civilization, 1957, rev. edit., 1973, Civilization in the West, 1964, rev. edit., 1981, Lebanon Yesterday and Today, 1966, The Islamic Tradition, 1972. Served with U.S. Army, 1942-45. Fund for Advancement of Edn. fellow, 1955-56. Mem. Am. Hist. Assn., AAUP, Middle East Inst., Middle East Studies Assn., Soc. for French Hist. Studies (v.p. 1960), N.Y. State Assn. European Historians (pres. 1957). Democrat. Home: 2105 Clover St Rochester NY 14618

CHRISTOPHER, MAURINE BROOKS, writer, editor; b. Three Springs, Tenn.; d. John Davis and Zula (Pangle) Brooks; m. Milbourne Christopher, June 25, 1949. B.A., Tusculum Coll., 1941. Reporter, feature writer Balt. Sun, 1943-45; TV radio Editor Advt. Age, 1947-51, sr. editor, head broadcast dept., 1951-77, dep. exec. editor, N.Y.C., 1977-79, dep. exec. editor, Videotech columnist, 1979—; producer-moderator Adbeat, syndicated radio show, 1970-78. Author: America's Black Congressmen, 1971, Black Americans in Congress, 1976. Mem. Am. Women in Radio and TV (past pres. N.Y.C. chpt., cert. of merit), Women in Communications, Women's Econ. Council, Assn. Study Afro-Am. Life and History. Home: 333 Central Park W New York NY 10025 Office: 220 E 42d St New York NY 10017

CHRISTOPHER, ROBERT ALLAN, manufacturing company executive; b. Cin., May 21, 1929; s. Robert Stewart and Joy Sunshine (Allan) C.; m. Martha A. Surnbrock, Aug. 12, 1950; children: Robert J., James H., John S. B.S. in Bus. Adminstrn, U. Cin. Dir. mfg. Philip Carey Co., Cin., 1950-68; v.p., gen. mgr. Evans Products Co., Portland, Oreg., 1968-75; pres., chief exec. officer Susquehanna Corp., Denver, 1975-80, Globe Industries, Chgo., 1980—. Mem. Beta Gamma Sigma. Republican. Episcopalian. Clubs: Olympia Fields (Ill.); Country, Masons. Office: Globe Industries Inc 2638 E 126th St Chicago IL 60633

CHRISTOPHER, ROBERT ARTHUR, mechanical engineering educator and administrator, consultant; b. Port Depoist, Md., Jan. 31, 1929; s. Arthur Bailey and Cornelia (Slater) C.; m. Mary Louise Brown, Mar. 28, 1953; chidlren: Thomas, John, Julie. B.A. in Math., U. Colo.-Boulder, 1951, B.S. in Mech. Engring., 1957, M.S., 1958, Ph.D., 1971. Registered profl. engr., Colo. Instr. mech. engring. U. Colo., Boulder, 1954-60, asst. prof., 1960-71, assoc. prof., 1972-78, prof., 1978—, chmn. dept. mech. engring., 1980—; cons. Automotive Specialists, Denver, 1976—. Served to lt. USNR, 1951-54. Recipient Ralph R. Teetor award Soc. Automotive Engrs., 1980. Mem. ASME, Am. Acad. Mechanics, Nat. Soc. Profl. Engrs., Am. Acad. Forensic Scis., Sigma Xi, Tau Beta Pi, Pi Tau Sigma. Home: 971 Crestmoor Dr Boulder CO 80303 Office: U Colo Mech Engring PO Box 427 Boulder CO 80309

CHRISTOPHER, ROBERT COLLINS, journalist; b. Thomaston, Conn., Mar. 3, 1924; s. Gordon Newton and Ruth Mignon (Adams) C.; m. Rita Joan Goldstein, May 17, 1970; children—Alistair David, Gordon Francis Benjamin; children by previous marriage—Ulrica Boyd, Thomas Adams, Valerie, Nicholas. B.A. with exceptional distinction, Yale, 1948. Staff Investment Dealers Digest, 1949-50; with Time mag., 1950-63, asso. editor, 1956-61, sr. editor, 1961-63; dir. fundamental econ. research Corning Glass Works, N.Y.C., 1963; fgn. editor Newsweek mag., 1963-69, exec. editor, 1969-72, editor internat. edit., 1972-77, contbg. editor, 1977-79; mng. editor GEO mag., 1979-80, contbg. editor, 1980-81; adminstr. Pulitzer Prizes, 1981—. Author: The Japanese Mind: The Goliath Explained. Trustee African-Am. Inst., Corrs. Fund. Served with AUS, 1942-46, 51-52; CBI. Mem. Council on Fgn. Relations, Phi Beta Kappa. Episcopalian. Clubs: Century (N.Y.C.); Elizabethan (New Haven). Home: 6 Rose Ln Old Lyme CT 06371 Office: 702 Journalism Bldg Columbia Univ New York NY 10027

CHRISTOPHER, RUSSELL LEWIS, baritone; b. Grand Rapids, Mich., Mar. 12, 1930; s. Russell Stewart and Violet (Jurewicz) C.; m. Gail B. Eldredge, Aug. 24, 1963; 1 son, Russell Frederick. A.A., Grand Rapids Jr. Coll., 1950; Mus.B., U. Mich., 1953, Mus.M., 1954. Music librarian NBC, N.Y.C., 1955-58. Prin. artist, N.Y.C. Opera Co., 1958-60, San Francisco Opera Co., 1962, 63, Met Opera Assn., N.Y.C., 1963—; soloist, 2Los Angeles, Montreal, Chgo., Richmond symphony orchs.; sang role Maecenas in: world premiere Antony and Cleopatra at new, Met. Opera House, 1966; also appeared with, Miami Beach Symphony, Hollywood Bowl, Balt. Civic Opera, Central City Opera, Dayton Opera Assn., Phila. Lyric Opera Assn., Met. opera tour, Japan, 1975; concert soloist, Spoleto (Italy) Festival, 1977. Recipient award Martha Baird Rockefeller Fund for Music, 1961; auditions winner Am. Opera, 1962, Met. Opera, 1963; Mrs. Frederick K. Weyerhaeuser award, 1963; Distinguished Alumni award Grand Rapids Jr. Coll., 1964. Home: 314 W 77th St New York NY 10024 Office: Met Opera Assn Lincoln Center Plaza New York NY 10023

CHRISTOPHER, THOMAS WELDON, legal educator, administrator; b. Duncan, S.C., Oct. 8, 1917; s. William Arthur and Ruby (Thomas) C.; m. Evelyn Montez Hawkins, Oct. 25, 1950; 1 son, Thomas Heflin. A.B., Washington and Lee U., 1939; LL.B., U. Ala., 1948; LL.M., NYU, 1950, J.S.D., 1957; LL.D., U. Ala., 1978. Bar: Ala. 1948, Ga. 1955, N.Y. 1961, N.C. 1963, N.Mex. 1968. From asst. prof. to prof. law Emory U. Law Sch., 1950-61, assoc. dean, 1954-61; atty.

Corn Products Co., 1959-60; prof. law U. N.C., 1961-65; dean U. N.Mex. Law Sch., 1965-71; prof. U. Ala. Sch. Law, 1971—, dean, 1971-81, dir., 1981—; Mem. nat. adv. food and drug council HEW, 1968-70; v.p. Food and Drug Law Found., 1974-78. Author: Poems from a Carolina Farm, 1948, (with Dunn) Special Federal Food and Drug Laws Annotated, 1951, (with others) Georgia Procedure and Practice, 1957, Constitutional Questions in Food and Drug Law, 1960, Cases and Materials on Food and Drug Law, 1966, (with Goodrich), 2d edit., 1973. Served with USAAF, World War II. Mem. Am. Bar Assn. Club: North River Yacht. Home: 7 Pinehurst Tuscaloosa AL 35401 Office: Univ Ala Sch Law Box 1435 University AL 35486

CHRISTOPHER, WARREN MINOR, lawyer, govt. ofcl.; b. Scranton, N.D., Oct. 27, 1925; s. Ernest W. and Catharine Anna (Lemen) C.; m. Marie Josephine Wyllis, Dec. 21, 1956; children—Lynn, Scott, Thomas, Kristen. Student, U. Redlands, 1942-43; B.S. magna cum laude, U. So. Calif., 1945; LL.B., Stanford, 1949; LL.D. (hon.), Occidental U., 1977, Bates Coll., 1981, Brown U., 1981, Claremont Coll., 1981. Bar: Calif. bar 1949, U.S. Supreme Ct. bar 1949. Law clk. U.S. Supreme Ct. Justice William O. Douglas, Washington, 1949-50; practice in Los Angeles, 1950-67, 69-76, 81—; mem. firm O'Melveny & Myers, 1950-67, 69, partner, 1958-67, 69-76, 81—; dep. atty. gen. U.S., Washington, 1967-69; dep. sec. of state Dept. State, Washington, 1977-81; spl. counsel to Gov. Calif., 1959; cons. Office Under Sec. State, 1961-65; mem. bd. bar examiners State Bar Calif., 1966-67; dir. So. Edison Co., First Interstate Bank.; Mem. Calif. Coordinating Council for Higher Edn., 1960-67, pres., 1963-65; vice chmn. Gov.'s Commn. on Los Angeles Riots, 1965-66; chmn. U.S. delegations to U.S.-Japan Cotton Textile Negotiations, 1961, Geneva Conf. on Cotton Textiles, 1961; civilian aid to sec. army, So. Calif. area, 1962-66; spl. rep. sec. state for Wool Textile Meetings, London, Rome, Tokyo, 1964-65; mem. Trilateral Commn., 1975-77, 81—. Trustee Stanford U., 1973-77, 81—. Served to lt. (j.g.) USNR, 1943-46. Decorated Medal of Freedom; recipient Harold Weill award N.Y. U., 1981; Louis Stein award Fordham U., 1981. Fellow Am. Bar Found., Am. Coll. Trial Lawyers; mem. ABA (ho. of dels. 1975-77, chmn. standing com. fed. judiciary 1975-77), Calif. Bar Assn. (gov. 1975-77), Los Angeles County Bar Assn. (pres. 1974-75), Am. Law Inst., Order of Coif, Phi Kappa Phi. Clubs: Calif., Chancery, Bohemian. Office: O'Melveny & Myers 611 W 6th St Los Angeles CA 90017

CHRISTOPHER, WILFORD SCOTT, public relations consultant; b. Enid, Okla., Feb. 8, 1916; s. W. Scott and Mary Elizabeth (Heaton) C.; m. Marjorie Lois Lester, Dec. 30, 1941; 1 son, Scott Douglas. B.A., Phillips U., 1938; M.A., U. Iowa, 1941. Asst. prof. speech Phillips U., 1939, assoc. prof. sociology, 1940-42; pub. relations dir. Miami (Fla.) C. of C., 1946-51; gen. mgr. Greater Tampa C. of C., 1951-64, exec. v.p., 1964-76, pres., 1976-78; dir. community relations U. Tampa, Fla., 1978-81; pres. W. Scott Christopher & Assos. (public relations), 1981—; dir. Automotive Mgmt. Services; spl. asst. to chmn. Nat. Exec. Services Corp., N.Y.C., 1980-82, Tampa, Fla.; Chmn. Nat. Adv. Council Urban Devel., 1959-60; mem. tech.-occupation adv. com. Hillsborough Jr. Coll., 1969-76, chmn. advanced mgmt. curriculum com., 1958-59; mem. Adv. Group on Continuing Edn. for Urban Leadership, 1967-68; mem. internat. com. C. of C. U.S., 1972-75, sr. adv. council, 1978—, dir., 1976-78. Contbr. to, Chamber of Commerce Administration. Bd. dirs. Tampa Philharmonic Orch. Assn., Tampa Oral Sch. for Deaf, 1971-74; Trustee U. South Fla. Found., 1959-65; mem. president's adv. bd. U. South Fla., 1975-78; mem. exec. com. Fla. Eye Inst. U. South Fla. Coll. Medicine, 1982—; v.p. Fla. Found. Eye Research; trustee, mem. exec. com. U. Tampa, 1977-78; trustee Berkeley Prep. Sch., 1963-71, v.p., 1967-71; bd. fellows U. Tampa, 1974, chmn., 1976—, sec.-treas., 1981—; trustee H.B. Plant Mus., 1979—. Named Tampa Citizen of Year, 1972, Tampa Humanitarian of Year, 1973. Mem. Fla. C. of C. Execs. Assn. (pres. 1954), Southeastern Inst. C. of C. Execs. (pres. 1956), So. Assn. C. of C. Execs. (pres. 1972), Inst. Orgn. Mgmt. (bd. regents 1975-77), Am. C. of C. Execs. (sec.-treas., v.p. 1960, pres. 1961-62, chmn. nat. panel on exec. certification 1966). Clubs: Tampa Exchange (pres. 1956), Executive (past pres.), University (dir.), Tampa Yacht and Country, Ye Mystic Krewe of Gasparilla. Home: 10701 Carrollwood Dr Tampa FL 33618 Office: 700 N Dale Mabry Tampa FL 33609

CHRISTOPHER, WILLIAM, actor; b. Evanston, Ill., Oct. 20; m. Barbara Christopher; children—John, Edward. Grad., Wesleyan U., Middletown, Conn. Former stage mgr., The Barnstormers, Tamworth, N.H.; acting debut in My Three Angels; appeared in: Off-Broadway play The Hostage; Broadway play and touring co. of Beyond the Fringe; semi-regular appearances on TV series Gomer Pyle; regular appearances on TV series MASH; other TV appearances include Alias Smith and Jones, Hogan's Heroes, That Girl, The Andy Griffith Show, The Patty Duke Show, The Men from Shiloh; film appearances include Hearts of the West, The Fortune Cookie, With Six You Get Eggroll, The Shakiest Gun in the West, The Private Navy of Sgt. O'Farrel *

CHRISTOPHERSON, PAUL, lawyer; b. Long Prairie, Minn., Aug. 12, 1902; s. Conrad H. and Effie (Jacobsen) C.; m. Edna M. Belgum, Jan. 11, 1945; children—Paul Conrad, David Lee, John Alfred. B.A., Carleton Coll., 1923, Oxford (Eng.) U., 1926, B.C.L., 1927, M.A., 1953; student, U. Minn. Law Sch., 1927-28. Bar: Minn. bar 1928. Practiced in Mpls. until retirement; partner firm Faegre & Benson, from 1935; Trustee Carleton Coll., 1951-68; Spl. asst. Office Surgeon Gen., War Dept., 1943-44. Mem. Am., Minn. bar assns., Inner Temple (London), Phi Beta Kappa, Phi Delta Phi. Republican. Episcopalian. Clubs: Minneapolis, Minneapolis Athletic, Minikahda (Mpls.). Home: 2250 W Lake of Isles Blvd Minneapolis MN 55405 Office: 2300 Multifoods Tower 33 S 6th St Minneapolis MN 55402

CHRISTOPHERSON, WESTON, retail chain company executive; b. Walum, N.D., May 5, 1925; s. Carl and Ermie (Larsen) C.; m. Myrna Christensen, June 8, 1951; children: Mia Karen, Mari Louisa, Kari Marie. B.S., U. N.D., 1949, J.D., 1951. Bar: N.D. 1951, Ill. 1952. With Jewel Cos., Inc., Chgo., 1951—; v.p., gen. mgr. Jewel Home Shopping Service, 1963-67, pres., 1967-70; exec. v.p., gen. mgr. Osco Drug, Inc., 1965-67, pres., 1967-70; pres. parent co. Jewel Cos., Inc., 1970-80, chief exec. officer, 1979—, chmn. bd., 1980—, also dir.; dir. Ill. Tool Works, Borg-Warner, Aurrera, S.A., Mexico City, Continental Ill. Corp., Continental Ill. Nat. Bank & Trust Co., Ill. Bell Telephone Co., GATX Corp. Vice chmn. bd. trustees U. Chgo.; Mem. Bus. Roundtable, The Bus. Council, Northwestern U. Assocs., Chgo. Com., Chgo. United, Met. Chgo. United Way/Crusade of Mercy. Presbyn. Clubs: Economic, Chicago, Lake Forest Winter, Onwentsia, Old Elm, Commercial, Commonwealth. Home: 200 N Green Bay Rd Lake Forest IL 60045 Office: 5725 N East River Rd Chicago IL 60631

CHRISTOPHERSON, WILLIAM MARTIN, physician; b. Salt Lake City, July 2, 1916; s. George Walter and Myrtle (Jack) C.; m. Kathryn Donley, July 24, 1943; 1 son, George Walter. Student, U. Utah, 1938; M.D., U. Louisville, 1942. Intern Akron (Ohio) City Hosp., 1942-43, resident, 1946-48, U. Louisville Hosp., 1948-49; fellow pathology Meml. Hosp., N.Y.C., 1949-50; mem. faculty U. Louisville Grad. Sch., 1950—, prof. pathology, 1956—, chmn. dept., 1956-74; spl. cons. Nat. Cancer Inst., bur. state service USPHS, adv. com. cancer control program, 1963-67; cons. Oak Ridge Inst. Nuclear Studies, 1956-68, Louisville VA Hosp.; mem. panel experts on cancer WHO.; Pres., bd. dirs. Ky. div. Am. Cancer Soc., 1970—; mem.-at-large bd. dirs. Nat. Am. Cancer Soc., 1967-72, exec. com., 1968-70; mem. council on pathology AMA, 1970-77. Mem. editorial bd.: Am. Jour. Surg. Pathology, Am. Jour. Clin. Pathology, Internat. Jour. Gynecologic Pathology and Cancer; nat. editor: Acta Cytologica. Served to capt. AUS, 1943-46. Mem. Am. Soc. Cytology (pres. 1966-67), Am. Assn. Cancer Edn. (pres. 1967-68), Soc. Exptl. Pathology, Internat. Acad. Pathology (pres. 1971-72), Am. Soc. Surg. Pathology (pres. 1981), Arthur Purdy Stout Soc. Surg. Pathology (pres. 1981-82), Internat. Acad. Cytology, Pathol. Soc. Gt. Britain and Ireland, European Soc. Pathology, Assn. Pathologists and Bacteriologists, Am. Soc. Clin. Pathology, Sigma Xi, Alpha Omega Alpha. Home: 2211 Cherokee Pkwy Louisville KY 40204

CHRISTY, ARTHUR HILL, lawyer, scrimshander; b. Bklyn., July 25, 1923; s. Francis Taggart and Catherine Virginia (Damon) C.; m. Gloria Garvin Osborne, Feb. 14, 1980; children by previous marriage: Duncan Hill, Alexandra. A.B., Yale U., 1945; LL.B., Columbia U., 1949. Bar: N.Y. bar 1950. Asso. firm Baldwin, Todd & Lefferts, N.Y.C., 1950-52; spl. asst. atty. gen. Saratoga Investigation, N.Y., 1952-53; asst. U.S. atty. So. Dist. N.Y., 1953-54; chief prosecutor spl. asst. atty. gen. Saratoga and Columbia County Investigations, 1954-55; asst. atty. gen., N.Y., 1955; chief criminal div. U.S. atty.'s Office, So. Dist. N.Y., 1955-57; chief asst. U.S. atty., 1957-58, U.S. atty., 1958-59; partner firm Christy & Viener (and predecessors), N.Y.C., 1959—; spl. asst. to Gov. Rockefeller, 1959-61; apptd. 1st spl. prosecutor Under Ethics in Govt. Act of 1978 to investigate charges against White House Chief of Staff, 1979-80; trustee Met. Savs. Bank. Artist in scrimshaw. Trustee, v.p. Bklyn. Hosp., Community Service Soc.; mem. council N.Y. Heart Assn. Served as lt. USNR, 1944-46. Mem. Am., N.Y. State, Fed. bar assns., Assn. Bar City N.Y. (chmn. exec. com. 1966-67), Am. Coll. Trial Lawyers. Republican. Episcopalian. Clubs: Century Assn., Rockefeller Luncheon, Univ., Town Tennis (N.Y.C.); Mastigouche Fish and Game (Que., Can.). Home: 430 E 57th St New York NY 10022 Office: 620 Fifth Ave New York NY 10020

CHRISTY, JAMES WALTER, astronomer; b. Milw., Sept. 15, 1938; s. Walter Witald and Mary (Nistor) C.; m. Charlene Mary Crockett, Nov. 22, 1975; children—David James, Teresa Elizabeth, James Randolph, Nola Marie. B.S., U. Ariz., 1965, postgrad., 1965-67. Astronomer U.S. Naval Obs., Washington, 1962-82. Mem. Astron. Soc. of the Pacific, Am. Astron. Soc., Internat. Astron Union. Research on spectrography and distances of nearby stars, color photography of galaxies. Discovered Charon, moon of Pluto, June 1978. Home: 11720 W Niona Pl Tucson AZ 85704 Office: Hughes Aircraft Co *Discovery is the end result; first, of allocating one's mental effort to personal understanding of where knowledge disguises one's own ignorance; and finally, of focusing on nature through that understanding only.*

CHRISTY, JOHN GILRAY, diversified company executive; b. Silver Creek, N.Y., Aug. 27, 1932; s. John Van Vlack and Ruth (Gilray) C.; m. Sally Roesser, Dec. 23, 1955 (dec. 1984); children: Andrew, Jennifer. B.A., Dartmouth Coll., 1954; M.A. in Asian Studies, U. Calif., Berkeley, 1960. Loan officer U.S. Devel. Loan Fund, 1960-61; with AID, New Delhi and Washington, 1961-65, chief extended risk guaranty div., 1965; with ITT, N.Y.C., 1965-72, treasury dept., 1965-68, v.p. internat. communications, 1968-69, asst. group exec. internat. communications, 1969-70; pres. ITT World Directories, Inc., N.Y.C., 1970-72; group v.p. land transp. IU Internat., Inc., Phila., 1972-76, exec. v.p., 1976-78; pres. and chief exec. officer IU Internat. Corp., 1978-80, Chmn., pres., 1982, also dir.; dir. Pennwalt Corp., Fidelcor, Inc. Trustee Colby Coll., Univ. Mus.; bd. dirs. Phila. Orch., Phila. Contributionship. Served to lt. as aviator USNR, 1958. Recipient Disting. Service award AID, 1965. Office: 1500 Walnut St Philadelphia PA 19102

CHRISTY, MARIAN, syndicated columnist; b. Ridgefield, Conn., Nov. 9; d. Peter and Anna (Saba) C. Asso. degree in Journalism, Boston U., 1951-58. Former reporter Boston bur. Women's Wear Daily; fashion, style columnist Boston Globe-Los Angeles Times Syndicate, Los Angeles, 1979—; columnist Conversations, 1983—; columns syndicated Boston Globe-Los Angeles Times Syndicate. Numerous TV appearances, Boston, N.Y.C., Chgo. Decorated cavaliere al merito Republica Italiana; recipient citations Men's Fashion Assn., N.Y., 1965-68, 70-72, Am. Footwear Assn., 1966-72, including Golden Slipper awards, J.C. Penney-U. Mo. Journalism Hall of Fame awards for fashion editorials, 1966, 68, 70, Fashion Reporter's award, N.Y., 1967, Prestige award, France, 1969, 2d prize internat. competition; Italian Fashion Press award, 1970; Humor prize for UPI story, 1972; named Woman of Achievement Mass. Bus. and Profl. Women's Club, 1965, 1st Lady of Fashion Mass. chpt. Nat. Assn. Cystic Fibrosis, 1972, Woman of Year New Woman mag., 1973, Best Columnist New Eng. Women's Press Assn., 1977, One of Five Top Women Journalists Cosmopolitan mag., 1979. Home: 135 Morrissey Blvd Boston MA 02107 *My mother's faith in her god and stoicism when facing cruel death by cancer continues to inspire me.*

CHRISTY, NICHOLAS PIERSON, physician; b. Morristown, N.J., June 18, 1923; s. Leroy and Elizabeth (Baker) C.; m. Beverly Vairin Morris, June 21, 1947; children—Nicholas Pierson, Martha Vairin. A.B., Yale, 1945; M.D., Columbia, 1951. Diplomate: Am. Bd. Internal Medicine. Asst. vis. physician Delafield Hosp., N.Y.C., 1955-66, vis. physician, 1966-75; asst. vis. physician 1st med. div. Bellevue Hosp., N.Y.C., 1958-66; asso. attending physician Presbyn. Hosp., N.Y.C., 1962-78, attending physician, 1978—; dir. med. service Roosevelt Hosp., N.Y.C., 1965-79; faculty Columbia Coll. Phys. and Surg., N.Y.C., 1956—, asso. prof. medicine, 1962-65, asso. clin. prof., 1965-67, clin. prof. medicine, 1967-71, prof. medicine, 1971-79, lectr. in medicine, 1979—; prof. medicine, asso. dean vets. affairs Downstate Med. Center, SUNY, Bklyn., 1979—; chief staff Bklyn. VA Med. Center, 1979—; asso. Nat. Humanities Center, Research Triangle Park, N.C., 1979; cons. NIH, FDA, 1980. Editor, co-author: The Human Adrenal Cortex, 1971; editor-in-chief: Jour. Clin. Endocrinology and Metabolism, 1963-67; asso. editor: Beeson-McDermott Textbook of Medicine, 1968-75; cons. editor, 1975-79; mem. adv. bd.: Am. Jour. Medicine, 1971—; Contbr. numerous papers to profl. lit. Served to lt. (j.g.) USNR, 1943-46; PTO. Recipient Borden award, Joseph Mather Smith prize Columbia; John and Mary R. Markle scholar. Mem. Harvey Soc., AAAS, Soc. Exptl. Biology and Medicine, Am. Soc. Clin. Investigation, Am. Fedn. Clin. Research, A.C.P., N.Y. Acad. Medicine, Laurentian Hormone Conf., Am. Physiol. Soc., N.Y. State, N.Y. County med. socs., Am. Clin. and Climatol. Assn. (recorder 1977—), Am. Assn. Study Liver Diseases, Endocrine Soc. (sec.-treas. 1978—), N.Y. Clin. Soc., N.Y. Med. and Surg. Soc., Assn. Am. Physicians, Interurban Clin. Club, Hosp. Grads. Club, Peripatetic Soc., Practitioners Soc. Clubs: Elizabethan, Colony (Yale); Century Assn., Church. Home: 8 Peter Cooper Rd New York NY 10010 Office: Bklyn VA Med Center Brooklyn NY 11209

CHRISTY, ROBERT WENTWORTH, physicist, educator; b. Chgo., Nov. 2, 1922; s. Walter Christian and Ruth Adele (Seifried) C. A.A., U. Chgo., 1942, M.S., 1949, Ph.D., 1953. Mem. faculty Dartmouth, 1953—, prof. physics, 1962—, Appleton prof., 1980—, chmn. dept. physics and astronomy, 1963-67, 78-80; cons. Motorola, Inc., 1952-53, TRW Systems, 1958-70. Author: (with A. Pytte) Structure of Matter, 1965, (with J.R. Reitz and F.J. Milford) Foundations of Electromagnetic Theory, 1979. Served to lt. (j.g.) with USNR, 1943-46. Fellow AAAS; mem. Am. Phys. Soc., Sigma Xi, Alpha Delta Phi. Home: Bragg Hill Rd Norwich VT 05055 Office: Wilder Physics Lab Dartmouth Coll Hanover NH 03755

CHRISTY, WILLIAM O., food products company executive; b. 1931. With Certified Grocers of Calif. Ltd., 1952-60; owner Rancho Mirage, Calif., 1960-62; with Certified Grocers of Calif., 1962—, asst. treas., 1971-72, treas., 1972-74, sr. v.p., 1974-75, exec. v.p. ops., 1975-77, chief exec. officer, 1977, dir. Office: Certified Grocers of Calif 2601 S Eastern Ave Los Angeles CA 90054 *

CHRONLEY, JAMES ANDREW, franchise executive; b. Springfield, Mass., July 31, 1930; s. Robert Emmett and Eleanor Agnes (Sullivan) C.; m. Monique Mary Delpech, July 29, 1955; children: Mary Elizabeth, James Michael, Jean Louise, Patricia, Joseph Patrick, John Peter, Robert Emmett. A.B., Brown U., 1952; diploma in real estate, U. R.I., 1963. With Arco Co., 1954-74, Eastern area mgr., until 1972; nat. real estate dir. Atlantic Richfield Co., Los Angeles, 1972-74; v.p. restaurant ops. and real estate Marriott Corp., Washington, 1974-78; exec. v.p. Burger Chef Systems, Inc., Indpls., 1978-82, pres., 1982; v.p. devel. Taco Bell, Irvine, Calif., 1983—. Served with AUS, 1952-54. Mem. Nat. Assn. Corp. Real Estate Execs. (chpt. pres. 1979), Nat. Assn. Rev. Appraiser, Am. Right of Way Assn., Internat. Council Shopping Centers. Roman Catholic. Office: Taco Bell 16808 Armstrong Ave Irvine CA 92714

CHROSNIAK, THOMAS D., JR., distilling company executive; b. South St. Paul, Minn., July 4, 1925; s. Thomas D. and Anna E. (Matras) C.; m. Marian L. Blais, June 28, 1947; children: Thomas D. III, Cheryl, Jeanne, Robert, Mary Beth, Ann Marie. B.B.A., U. Minn., 1959; student, U. Minn. Exec. Program, 1974-75. With IRS, St. Paul, 1949-66; tax mgr. Hamm Brewing Co., 1966-68; dir. taxes Heublein, Inc., Farmington, Conn., 1968-81, treas., 1981—. Served with USMCR, 1942-45. Mem. Tax Execs. Inst., Fin. Execs. Inst. Roman Catholic. Office: Heublein Inc Munson Rd Farmington CT 06032

CHRUDEN, HERBERT JEFFERSON, educator; b. Roswell, N.Mex., Oct. 3, 1918; s. Lawrence B. and Elizabeth (FitzGerald) C.; m. Marie Schwartz, Sept. 9, 1944; 1 dau., Mary Beth. A.B., San Diego State Coll., 1940; M.B.A., Stanford, 1947, Ed.D., 1949. Tchr. Cajon Valley Union Sch., El Cajon, Calif., 1940-41; faculty N. Tex. State U. Sch. Bus., 1949-52, Sacramento State Coll., 1952-81, prof. bus. adminstrn., 1961—, chmn. div. bus. adminstrn., 1963-64; mgmt. cons., 1955—. Co-author: Personnel Management, 1959, 6th edit., 1980, Readings in Personnel Management, 1961, 5th edit., 1980, Personnel Practices of American Companies in Europe, 1972. Served to lt. comdr. USNR, 1941-45. Mem. Am. Arbitration Assn. (labor panel), Calif. Conciliation Service (labor panel), Acad. Mgmt., Beta Gamma Sigma, Delta Sigma Pi. Home: 251 Bancroft Way Sacramento CA 95825

CHRYSLER, WALTER P., JR., art collector; m. Marguerite Sykes, Apr. 29, 1933 (div.); m. Jean Esther Outland, Jan. 13, 1945. Ed., Dartmouth, 1933. Organizer York Pub. House, 1926; dir. Madison Sq. Garden Corp., 1929-55; pres., chmn. bd. Cheshire House, Inc. (Pubs.), N.Y.C., 1930; founded Airtemp div. Chrysler Corp., 1934, dir. corp., 1935-56; pres. Chrysler Bldg., N.Y.C., 1935-53, dir., 1932-53; pres. Chrysler Mus. Provincetown, Mass., 1958; chmn., trustee Chrysler Mus., Norfolk, Va., 1971—, dir., 1971-77; dir. Va. Opera Assn., 1971—; trustee Norfolk Mus. Arts and Scis., 1969-71; cons. on comml. relations Office Coordinator Inter-Am. Affairs, Washington, 1941; corp. mem. Mus. Modern Art, N.Y.C. Presented: Broadway prodn. The Strong are Lonely; Eng. prodn. The Hanging Judge; movie The Joe Louis Story; paintings and sculpture in collections, shows in, Richmond, Va. and Phila., 1941, Old Masters and Modern French Sch., Portland, Oreg., Seattle, San Francisco, Los Angeles, Mpls., St. Louis, Kansas City, Mo., Detroit, Boston, 1956-57, Flemish, Dutch and German paintings, Washington, Atlanta, Dallas, New Orleans, West Palm Beach, Chattanooga, 1957-58, Inaugural Exhbn., Provincetown, Mass., 1958, French paintings 1789-1929, Dayton, Ohio, 1960, The Controversial Century 1850-1950, Provincetown, Mass., Ottawa, Can., 1962, Italian Renaissance and Baroque paintings, Norfolk, 1967-68. Mem. SAR, SR, Beta Theta Pi. Clubs: N.Y. Athletic, N.Y. Yacht, Harbor, Norfolk Yacht and Country, Virginia, Cedar Point, Princess Anne Country. Began collecting art at age 14 with Renoir landscape, later small Picasso. Address: care Chrysler Museum at Norfolk Norfolk VA 23510

CHRYSSA, sculptor; b. Athens, Greece, 1933. Student, Academie de la Grande Chaumiere, Paris, France, 1953-54, Calif. Sch. Fine Arts, 1954-55. One-woman shows include, Guggenheim Mus., N.Y.C., 1961, Cordier and Ekstrom Gallery, N.Y.C., 1962, Betty Parsons Gallery, N.Y.C., 1961, Mus. Modern Art, N.Y.C., 1963, Inst. Contemporary Arts, Phila., 1965, Pace Gallery, N.Y.C., 1966, 68, Walker Art Center, Mpls., 1968, Harvard, Obelisk Gallery, Boston, 1969, Gallery der Spiegel, Cologne, Germany, Gallery Rive-Droite, Paris, Whitney Mus., N.Y.C., 1972, Mus. d'Art Contemporain, Montreal, 1974, Mus. d'Art Modern de la Ville de Paris, 1979, group shows include exhbns., Whitney Mus. Am. Art, N.Y.C., 1960, 61, 62, 64, 66, 69, Mus. Modern Art, 1960-61, 63, 64, 66, 67, 72, Carnegie Instn., 1961, 64, Seattle World's Fair, 1963, VII Biennial, São Paolo, Brazil, 1963, 1963, Stedjlik van Abbemuseum, Eindhoven, Holland, 1966, Inst. Contemporary Art, Boston, Art Inst. Chgo., Yale Art Gallery, 1967, Los Angeles County Mus., Phila. Art Mus., Documenta, Kassel, Germany, 1968; represented in permanent collections, Mus. Modern Art, Whitney Mus., Guggenheim Mus., Chase Manhattan Bank, Met. Mus. Art, all N.Y.C., Albright-Knox Gallery, Buffalo, Walker Art Center, Mpls., Boise Cascade Corp., Idaho, Hirshhorn Mus., Corcoran Gallery of Art, both Washington, Tate Gallery, London. Address: 15 E 88th St New York NY 10028 *

CHRYSSAFOPOULOS, NICHOLAS, cons. civil engr.; b. Istanbul, Turkey, Apr. 23, 1919; came to U.S., 1951, naturalized, 1959; s. John and Despina (Hondropoulos) C.; m. Hanka Wanda Sobczak, Sept. 6, 1956. B.S. in Civil Enging, Robert Coll., Istanbul, 1940; M.S., U. Ill., 1952, Ph.D., 1956. Registered profl. engr., Calif., Ill., N.Y., N.J., Mo., Pa., Kans. Design and constrn. work in, Turkey, 1940-51; mem. faculty U. Ill., 1951-59, asst. prof., 1956-59; chief engr., mng. prin., exec. v.p. Woodward, Clyde, Sherard, Kansas City, Mo. and Los Angeles, 1959-68; partner Dames & Moore (cons. engrs.), N.Y.C., 1968—, regional mgr. for, Latin Am., Boca Raton, Fla., 1978—; asso. Transp. Research Bd. Author reports, tech. papers. Served with Turkish Army, 1941-44. Fulbright scholar, 1951-52. Fellow ASCE, Am. Cons. Engrs. Council; mem. Am. Soc. Testing and Materials, Am. Assn. Enging. Socs., Sigma Xi. Greek Orthodox. Home: 6642 Patio Ln Boca Raton FL 33433 *Freedom, fair opportunity and treatment, and the chance to work for a good and happy life are principles I was taught at home and have cherished and pursued all my life.*

CHRYST, GARY, ballet dancer; b. La Jolla, Calif., Nov. 28, 1949. Student, Jaime Rodgers, Nina Popva, Matteo, Am. Ballet Center. With, Norman Walker Co.; then, Utah Ballet; summer stock prodns. Milk and Honey, 1968; with, Joffrey Ballet, 1968—; created: roles Deuce Coupe; guest artist, José Limon Dance Co., N.Y.C., 1978. Office: care Peter S Diggins Assos 133 W 71st St New York NY 10023 *

CHRYSTIE, THOMAS LUDLOW, investment banker; b. N.Y.C., May 24, 1933; s. Thomas Witter and Helen (Duell) C.; m. Eliza S. Balis, June 9, 1955; children: Thomas W., Alice B., Helen S., Adden B., James MacD. B.A., Columbia U., 1955; M.B.A., N.Y. U., 1960. With Merrill Lynch, Pierce, Fenner & Smith, Inc., N.Y.C., 1955-75, dir. investment banking div., 1970-75; sr. v.p. Merrill Lynch & Co., 1975-78, chief fin. officer, 1976-78; chmn. Merrill Lynch White Weld Capital Markets Group, 1978-81, Merrill Lynch Capital Resources, 1981-83; adv. on strategy Merrill Lynch & Co. Inc., 1983—; dir. Philips Industries, Signode Industries. Trustee Am. Health Found., Columbia U. Served to capt. USAF, 1955-58. Mem. Down Town Assn. Club: Short Hills. Home: 77 Knollwood Rd Short Hills NJ 07078 Office: 1 Liberty Plaza 165 Broadway New York NY 10080 *Whatever you are involved in, see it as part of a larger picture.*

CHU, C.K., applied mathematician, educator; b. Shanghai, China, Aug. 14, 1927; came to U.S., 1948; s. Ju-Tang and Ping (Wh) C.; m. Anne Loomis, Dec. 23, 1978; children by previous marriage: Barbara M., David C., Anne M. B.S. in M.E., Chiao-Tung U., 1948, M.S., Cornell U., 1950; Ph.D. in Math., Courant Inst., NYU, 1959. Engr. Gen. Electric Co., 1950-53; asst. prof. Stevens Inst. Tech., 1953-57; assoc. prof. Pratt Inst., 1957-59, NYU, 1959-63; research assoc. Columbia U., 1963-65, assoic. prof., 1965-68, prof. engring. sci., 1968—, chmn. dept. applied physics and nuclear engring., 1982—, chmn. applied math. com., 1979—; vis. prof. U. Strathclyde, U. Oxford, U. Uppsala, U. Paris, Shanghai Jiao-Tong U., Academia Sinica, Peking, Princeton Plasma Physics Lab., Los Alamos Nat. Lab. Assoc. editor: Physics of Fluids, 1973-75; contbr. chpts. to books, atricles to profl. jours. Trustee Chubb Found. Named Sherman Fairchild disting. shcolar Calif. Inst. Tech., 1983; Guggenheim fellow, 1971-72. Fellow Am. Phys. Soc., Japan Soc. for Promotion of Sci.; mem. Soc. Indsl. and Applied Math., AIAA, Am. Phys. Soc. (div. plasma physics), Univ. Fusion Assn. Home: 227 Millwood Rd Chappaqua NY 10514 Office: Dept Applied Phys and Nuclear Engring Columbia U New York NY 10027

CHU, FUN SUN, food toxicology educator; b. Jukao, China, May 7, 1933; came to U.S., 1957; s. Yun-Chung C. and Liu (Chu); m. Doris Yun-chen Ni, Nov. 1, 1958; children: Paul, Sandra, Mary. B.S., Chungshin U., Taichung, Taiwan, 1954; M.S., W. Va. U., Morgantown, 1959; Ph.D., U. Mo.-Columbia, 1964. Research assoc. U. Chgo., 1963-66; asst. prof. food toxicology U. Wis., Madison, 1966-72, assoc. prof., 1972-78, prof., 1978—. Office: U Wis 1925 Willow Dr Madison WI 53706

CHU, KUANG-HAN, structural engineer, educator; b. Kashan, Chekiang, China, Nov. 13, 1919; came to U.S., 1946, naturalized, 1962; s. Chih Hsien and Yu-Po (King) C.; m. Janie Lee, Aug. 18, 1962. B.S., Nat. Central U., China, 1942; M.S., U. Ill., 1947, Ph.D., 1950. Structural designer Ammann & Whitney, N.Y.C., 1950-51, D.B. Steinman, 1951-55; acting asso. prof. civil engring. State U. Iowa, 1955-56; asso. prof. dept. civil engring. Ill. Inst. Tech., 1956-63, prof., 1963-84, prof. emeritus, 1984—; cons. structural analysis, buckling, dynamic analysis, plates and shells, 1958—. Contbr. articles to profl. jours. Fellow ASCE (Collingwood prize 1953); mem. Am. Concrete Inst., Internat. Assn. Bridge and Structural Engring., Am. Soc. Engring. Edn., Sigma Xi. Home: 730 Washington St San Francisco CA 94108

CHU, TSANN MING, immunochemist; b. Kaohsiung, Taiwan, Apr. 18, 1938; came to U.S., 1963, naturalized, 1971; s. Tsi Fa and Su Lian (Sun) C.; m. Bonnie Diane Covert, Sept. 28, 1967; children: Nancy, Daniel. B.S., Nat. Taiwan U., 1961; M.S., N.C. State U., 1965; Ph.D., Pa. State U., 1967. Fellow Med. Found. Buffalo, 1967-69, Buffalo Gen. Hosp., 1969-70; asso. chief cancer research scientist, dir. diagnostic immunology and clin. chemistry Roswell Park Meml. Inst., Buffalo, 1970-76, dir. cancer research in diagnostic immunology research and biochemistry, 1976—; asst. prof. exptl. pathology State U. N.Y. at Buffalo, 1970-74, asso. prof., 1974-77, prof., 1977—; cons. nat. prostatic cancer project Nat. Cancer Inst., NIH, 1973—, mem. com. cancer immunodiagnosis, 1978-79, mem. tumor immunology com., 1979-81; mem. immunology and immunotherapy com. Am. Cancer Soc., 1979-81; research cons. Nat. Sci. Council, Republic of China, 1976—; adv. council Internat. Soc. Oncodevelopmental Biology and Medicine, 1978—. Contbr. articles to profl. jours. United Health Found. Western N.Y. fellow, 1968-69. Mem. Am. Chem. Soc., Am. Assn. Clin. Chemists, Nat. Acad. Clin. Biochemistry, Am. Assn. Cancer Research, Am. Fedn. Clin. Research, Am. Assn. Immunologists, Am. Soc. Biol. Chemists, Am. Assn. Pathologists, Phi Lambda Upsilon. Home: 117 Old Orchard Dr Williamsville NY 14221 Office: 666 Elm St Buffalo NY 14263 *Good science requires hard work, and both are enjoyable to me. My goal is to add a brick of knowledge to the house of science.*

CHU, WEN-DJANG, Chinese lang. and literature educator; b. Peking, Republic of China, Feb. 15, 1914; came to U.S., 1946; s. King (Ching-nung) and Zingshan (Yang) C.; m. Liu-ch-ing Shao, Dec. 25, 1938 (dec. Sept. 1942); m. 2d Helen Yu-li Chao, Sept. 12, 1954; children: Otto He-chang, Patricia P'ei-chang, Lily Lei'chang. B.A., Cheeloo U., Tsinan, China, 1935; M.A., Peking U., 1937, U. Wash., 1950, Ph.D., 1956. Instr. Seattle Pacific U., 1937; research assoc. U. Wash., Seattle, 1955-56; instr. Yale U., New Haven, 1956-61; from asst. prof. to profl. Chinese lang. and lit. U. Pitts., 1961—. Author: The Biography of Shik K'e-fa, 1943, The Moslem Rebellion in Northwest China, 1862-1878, 1966, Hai-t'ao-chi, 1969. Recipient award Ministry Edn. Republic China, 1945. Mem. Assn. Asian Studies, Am. Assn. Chineses Studies (2d v.p. 1979-81, rec. sec. 1981-83). Home: 152 Tanglewood Dr Pittsburgh PA 15221 Office: Dept East Asian Lang and Literatures Univ Pitts Oakland Pittsburgh PA 15260

CHU, WESLEY WEI-CHEN, computer science educator, consultant; b. Shanghai, China, May 5, 1936; came to U.S., 1958; s. Lai Fei and Yen Yen (Chung) C.; m. Julia Nee, Dec. 26, 1960; children: Milton, Christina. B.S. in Elec. Engring., U. Mich., 1960, M.S., 1961; Ph.D., Stanford U., 1966. Engr. computer dept. Gen. Electric, Phoenix, 1961-62; engr. IBM, San Jose, Calif., 1962-66; mem. tech. staff Bell Tech. Lab., Holmdel, N.J., 1966-69; asst. prof. computer sci. UCLA, 1969-72, assoc. prof., 1972-75, prof., 1975—; cons. to industry and govt.; exec. cons. Western Union, Upper Saddle River, N.J., 1982—. Editor: books Advances in Computer Communications, 1976, Advances in Computer Communications 3d edit., 1979, Centralized and Distributed Data Base System, 1969; contbr. articles to profl. jours.; patentee stat. multiplexing. Fellow IEEE (Meritorious Service award 1983); mem. Assn. Computing Machinery (chmn. SGICOM 1973-77). Office: 3731 Boelter Hall UCLA Los Angeles CA 90024

CHUBB, PERCY, III, insurance company executive; b. N.Y.C., Oct. 14, 1934; s. Percy, 2d and Corinne Roosevelt (Alsop) C.; m. Sally Gilady, Dec. 29, 1956; children—Percy Lee, Sarah Caldecot, Lucy Alsop. B.A., Yale U., 1956. With Chubb & Son Inc., N.Y.C., 1958—, dir., 1965—; sr. v.p., dir. Chubb Corp., 1979-81, exec. v.p., dir., 1981—; dir. Colonial Life Ins. Co. Am., Fed. Ins. Co., United Life & Accident Ins. Co., Safeway Stores Inc., Fidelity Union Bancorp. Pres. Victoria Found. Served with AUS, 1956-58. Mem. Am. Bur. Shipping, Downtown Assn. Club: N.Y. Yacht (N.Y.C.). Home: Bernardsville NJ 07924 Office: 15 Mountain View Rd Warren NJ 07061

CHUBB, STEPHEN DARROW, medical corporation executive; b. Newton, Mass., Mar. 16, 1944; s. Phillip Darrow and Clarissa Stoddard (Nye) C.; m. Kathleen Alice Zimmerman, Mar. 24, 1973. B.S., U.S. Naval Acad., 1965; M.B.A., Northwestern U., 1974. C.P.A., Ill. Plant engr. Am. Can Co., Oakland, Calif., 1970-73, devel. engr., Barrington, Ill., 1972-73; product mgr. Baxter Travenol Labs., Deerfield, Ill., 1974-75, corp. dir. sterilization, 1976-77, asst. to exec. v.p., 1978; also mem. chmn.'s sr. mgmt. com., pres. Hyland Diagnostics, 1978-81; pres., chief exec. officer, dir. Cytogen Corp., 1981—. Bd. dirs. Sherwood Community Assn., 1978-79, v.p., 1979-80. Served with USN, 1965-70; comdr. Res. Mem. Ill. C.P.A. Soc., Northwestern U. Mgmt. Alumni Assn. (bd.). Club: U.S. Naval Acad. Alumni Assn. Home: 145 Philip Dr Princeton NJ 08540 Office: 201 College Rd E Princeton NJ 08540

CHUBB, TALBOT ALBERT, physicist; b. Pitts., Nov. 5, 1923; s. Charles F. and Mary Clare (Albert) C.; m. Martha Capps, Oct. 24, 1947; children: Mary Carroll, Nancy Henderson, Talbot Spence, Constance Lamont. A.B., Princeton U., 1944; Ph.D., U. N.C., 1950. Physicist, U.S. Naval Research Lab., 1950-58, head upper air physics br., 1958-82; pres. Research Systems, Inc., Oxon Hill, Md., 1982—. Recipient Elisha Mitchell Soc. award U. N.C., 1951, E.O. Hulbert award Naval Research Lab., 1963, Pure Sci. award Naval. Research Lab.-Research Soc. Am., 1970, Disting. Civilian Service award Dept. Navy, 1978. Fellow Am. Geophys. Union, Am. Phys. Soc.; mem. Am. Astron. Soc. Research on solar flare x-rays, x-ray stars, UV aurora, cosmology, solar thermal power. Home: 5023 N 38th St Arlington VA 22207 Office: Research Systems Inc 5410 Indian Head Hwy Suite 203 Oxon Hill MD 20745

CHUCK, WALTER G(OONSUN), lawyer; b. Wailuku, Maui, Hawaii, Sept. 10, 1920; s. Hong Yee and Aoe (Ting) C.; m. Marian Chun, Sept. 11, 1943; children: Jamie Allison, Walter Gregory, Meredith Jayne. Ed.B., U. Hawaii, 1941; J.D., Harvard U., 1948. Bar: Hawaii 1948. Navy auditor, Pearl Harbor, 1941; field agt. Social Security Bd., 1942; labor law insp. Terr. Dept. Labor, 1943; law clk. firm Ropes, Gray, Best, Coolidge & Rugg, 1948; asst. pub. prosecutor, City and County of Honolulu, 1949; with Fong, Miho & Choy, 1950-53; ptnr. Fong, Miho, Choy & Chuck, 1953-58; pvt. practice law, Honolulu, 1958-65; ptnr. Chuck & Fujiyama, Honolulu, 1965-74; ptnr. firm Chuck, Wong & Tonaki, Honolulu, 1974-76, Chuck & Pai, 1976-78; sole practice, Honolulu, 1978-80; pres. Walter G. Chuck Law Corp., Honolulu, 1980—; dist. magistrate Dist. Ct. Honolulu, 1956-63; treas., dir. M & W, Inc.; gen. ptnr. Tripler Warehousing Co., Kapalama Investment Co.; dir. Pacific Resources, Inc., Gasco, Inc., Aloha Airlines, Inc., Hawaiian Ind. Refinery, Inc., Honolulu Painting Co., Ltd., Enerco, Inc., Ala Moana Volkswagen, Inc. Chmn. Hawaii Employment Relations Bd., 1955-59; bd. dirs. Nat. Assn. State Labor Relations Bd., 1957-58, Honolulu Theatre for Youth, 1977-80; chief clk. Ho. of Reps., 1951, 53; chief clk. Hawaii senate, 1959-61; govt. appeal agt. SSS, 1953-72; mem. jud. council, State of Hawaii; exec. com. Hawaiian Open; mem. Friends of Judiciary Mus.; former bd. dirs. YMCA. Served as capt. inf. Hawaii Territorial Guard. Fellow Internat. Acad. Trial Lawyers (dir.); mem. ABA, Hawaii Bar Assn. (pres. 1963), Am. Trial Lawyers Assn. (editor), U. Hawaii Alumni Assn. (Distinguished Service award 1967, dir.), Law Sci. Inst., Assoc. Students U. Hawaii, Am. Judicature Soc., Internat. Soc. Barristers, Am. Inst. Banking, Chinese C. of C. Republican. Clubs: Harvard of Hawaii (pres. 1975), Waialae Country (pres. 1975), Pacific (bd. dirs.), Oahu Country.). Home: 2691 Aaliamanu Pl Honolulu HI 96813 Office: Suite 1814 745 Fort St Honolulu HI 96813

CHUNG, CONSTANCE YU-HWA, journalist; b. Washington, Aug. 20, 1946; d. William Ling and Margaret (Ma) C. B.S., U. Md., 1969; D.J. (hon.), Norwich U., Northfield, Vt., 1974. TV news reporter WTTG-TV, Metromedia Channel 5, Washington, 1969-71; corr. CBS News, Washington, 1971-76; TV news anchor sta. KNXT-TV, CBS, Los Angeles, 1976-83; anchor NBC News, NBC News at Sunrise, NBC Nightly News (Saturday), NBC News Digests, NBC News, N.Y.C., 1983—. Recipient Emmy award for individual achievement Acad. TV Arts and Scis., 1978, 80, Metro Area Mass Media award AAUW, 1971, cert. of achievement for series of broadcasts which enhanced pub. awareness of cruelties of seal harvesting U.S. Humane Soc., 1969; award Atlanta chpt. Nat. Assn. Media Women, 1973; Oustanding Excellence in News Reporting and Pub. Service award Chinese-Am. Citizens Alliance, 1973; hon. award for news reporting Boston chpt. Chinese YMCA, 1974; nominated Woman of Yr. award Ladies Home Jour., 1975; named Outstanding Young Woman of Yr., 1975; award for best TV reporting Los Angeles Press Club, 1977; award for outstanding TV broadcasting Valley Press Club, 1977; Women in Communications award Calif. State U., Los Angeles, 1979; George Foster Peabody award for programs on environment Md. Center Public Broadcasting, 1980; hon. mem. Pepperdine U. Broadcast Club, 1981; Newscaster of Yr. award Temple Emanuel Brotherhood, 1981; Portraits of Excellence award B'nai B'rith, Pacific S.W. Region, 1980; First Amendment award Anti-Defamation League of B'nai B'rith, 1981. Office: NBC 30 Rockefeller Plaza New York NY 10020

CHUNG, DAE HYUN, geophysicist; b. Jeongup, Korea, Dec. 6, 1934; came to U.S., 1956, naturalized, 1974; s. Mynn and Mockdaan (Rhee) C.; m. Inhan Choi, Oct. 19, 1963; children: Henry H., Gene H. A.B., Alfred U., 1959, M.Sc., 1961; Ph.D., Pa. State U., 1966. Postgrad. research fellow MIT, Cambridge, 1967-68, research asso. geophysics, 1968-74; prof. geophysics, dir. Weston (Mass.) Obs., 1972-74; geophysicist, coordinator geophysics progams, dept. applied sci. U. Calif. and Lawrence Livermore Nat. Lab., 1974-80; staff geophysicist Lawrence Livermore Nat. Lab., 1980—; pres. Livermore Associated Research Group, 1982—; sr. fellow and Inst. prof. Internat. Ctr. Peace Studies, Internat. Assn. Univ. Pres., 1980—; instr., researcher Pa. State U., MIT, U. Calif.; cons. MIT Lincoln Lab.; staff councillor to Minister Sci. and Tech. Republic of Korea, 1969-70; sr. fellow, inst. prof. Internat. Ctr. Peace Studies (Kyung Hee U.), 1980—; mem. seismic expert panel IAEA, Vienna, 1982—; mem. field mission to Turkish Govt., Ankara and Istanbul, 1982; cons. Atomic Energy Bd., Pretoria, South Africa, 1982; seismic cons. Korea Advanced Research Inst., Seoul, 1984—. Contbr. articles to profl. jours. and chpts. to textbooks. Recipient Maj. Edward Holmes award SUNY-Alfred, 1959; recipient achievement citation Geol. Survey, Korea, 1970; decorated Order of Confrerie des Vignerons de St. Vincent, 1977. Mem. AAAS, Am. Geophys. Union, Am. Acad. Mechanics, N.Y. Acad. Scis., Sigma Xi. Presbyterian. Club: M.I.T. Faculty. Home: 4150 Colgate Way Livermore CA 94550 Office: Mail Code L-95 U Calif PO Box 808 Livermore CA 94550

CHUNG, EDWARD KOOYOUNG, cardiologist, educator, author; b. Seoul, Korea, Mar. 3, 1931; came to U.S., 1958, naturalized, 1971; s. Il-Chun C.; m. Lisa Sang-In Lee, May 28, 1958; children: Linda, Christopher. B.S., Seoul Nat. U., 1953, M.D., 1957. Intern St. Louis City Hosp., 1958-59; resident in medicine St. Louis County Hosp., 1959-60, St. John's Hosp., St. Louis, 1960-62; fellow in cardiology Washington U. Sch. Medicine, Barnes Hosp., St. Louis, 1962-64; asst. prof. medicine, dir. heart sta. Meharry Med. Coll., Nashville, 1964-66, asso. prof., 1966-68; vis. investigator in cardiology Vanderbilt U. Sch. Medicine, Nashville, 1965-68; asso. prof. W.Va. U. Sch. Medicine, Morgantown, 1968-70, prof. medicine, 1970-73, dir. heart sta., 1968-73; prof. medicine, dir. heart sta. Jefferson Med. Coll., Thomas Jefferson U., Phila., 1973—. Author: 37 med. textbooks including Non-Invasive Cardiology, 1976, Controversy in Cardiology, 1976, Principles of Cardiac Arrhythmias, 3d edit, 1980; 45 med. textbooks including Electrocardiography - Practical Applications with Vectorial Principles, 2d edit, 1980; 37 med. textbooks including Artificial Cardiac Pacing - Practical Approach, 1979, Exercise Electrocardiolraphy - Practical Approach, 1979, Ambulatory Electrocardiography, 1979, Cardiac Emergency Care, 2d edit, 1980, One Heart... One Life, 1982, Heart Attack... Health Guide for Executives, 1982; contbr. numerous articles to profl. jours., Cardiac Arrhythmias: Self Assessment, Vol. II, 1982, Introduction to Clinical Cardiology, 1983, Quick Reference to Cardiovascular Diseases, 3d edit., 1983; editorial cons., Williams & Wilkins Co., 1969—, Harper & Row Pubs., 1971—, Lea & Febiger Pubs., Springer-Verlag Pubs., 1974—, J.B. Lippincott Co., 1975—, Medcom, Inc., 1972—, AMA Jour. Questions and Answers, 1973—; book reviewer: Annals of Internal Medicine, 1969—, Am. Jour. Cardiology, 1971—, New Eng. Jour. Medicine, 1971—, Cardiology, 1975—; manuscript reviewer: Am. Heart Jour, 1972—, Heart and Lung, Chest, 1973—, Cardiology (Switzerland), 1973—, J.A.M.A, 1974—, Circulation, 1978—; editorial bd.: Heart and Lung, 1973—, Jour. Electrocardiology, Cardiology, 1975—, Primary Cardiology, Drug Therapy, 1976—, Hosp. Physician, 1978—. Fellow Am. Coll. Cardiology (gov. W.Va. 1970-73), A.C.P., Philippine Heart Assn. (hon.), Philippine Coll. Cardiology (hon.); mem. AMA, Am. Heart Assn., Am. Fedn. for Clin. Research, Pa. Med. Soc., Philadelphia County Med. Soc. Home: 777 Woodleave Rd Bryn Mawr PA 19010 Office: Room 5611 Thomas Jefferson U Hosp 111 S 11th St Philadelphia PA 19107

CHUNG, FRANK HUAN-CHEN, chemist; b. Kiangsi, China, July 20, 1930; came to U.S., 1964, naturalized, 1974; s. Koe-yie and Chi-ming (Hsu) C.; m. Doris Chu-feng Wen, Dec. 26, 1959; children: Susan, Shirley, Sonia. B.S. in Chem. Engring, Chung Cheng Inst. Tech., Taiwan, 1953; M.S. (NSF fellow), Kent State U., Ohio, 1966; Ph.D. (NASA fellow), 1968; postdoctoral studies, Ill. Inst. Tech., 1977. Instr. indsl. chemistry Chung Cheng Inst. Tech., 1954-57, lectr., 1960-63; liaison officer, guided missile sch. U.S. Army, Tex., 1958-59; research fellow phys. chemistry Kent State U., 1964-68; sr. scientist Sherwin Williams Research Center, Chgo., 1968—. Contbg. editor, Marcel Dekker Inc., 1979; contbr. articles to sci. jours. Recipient Internat. Achievement award Kent State U., 1967; Commendation letter U.S. Army, 1959. Mem. Am. Chem. Soc. (reviewer audio course on X-ray flourescence spectrometry 1977, reviewer Jour. Environ. Sci. and Tech. 1979), Soc. Applied Spectroscopy (program co-chmn. X-ray Symposium 1980, chmn. tech. session on x-ray fluorescence 1982, 83), Am. Crystallographic Assn., Midwest Assn. Chinese Engrs. Scientists. Formulator of Matrix-Flushing Theory for quantitative interpretation of x-ray diffraction patterns of mixtures. Office: Sherwin Williams Research Center 10909 S Cottage Grove Ave Chicago IL 60628 *The truth is usually hidden under a mass of confusing facts. Integrate wits, logic and faith to discover it. Once the truth is found, it is simple and pretty, and compatible with all facts. The stroke of luck greatly favors the prepared mind. A prepared mind catches inspiring flash, accepts challenge, explores the impossible, and generates clear thought beyond existing concepts.*

CHUNG, JOSEPH SANG-HOON, economics educator; b. Unmun-myon, Chongdo-kun, Kyongbuk, Korea, Oct. 11, 1929; came to U.S., 1953; s. Anthony Dosent and Martha (Cho) C.; m. Louise Carol Guenther, Aug. 17, 1957; children: Vincent, Sara, Melissa. Student, Seoul Nat. U., Korea, 1949-51; B.S. in Econs., Marquette U., 1956, M.A., 1958; Ph.D., Wayne State U., 1964. Lectr. in econs. Marquette U., Milw., 1958-60; from instr. to asst. prof. Kalamazoo Coll., 1962-63, 63-64; asst. prof. Ill. Inst. Tech., Chgo., 1964-68, chmn. dept. econs., 1975-82, assoc. prof., 1968-73, prof. econs., 1973—; Fulbright prof. Seoul Nat. U., Korea, 1966-68; cons. Hoover Instn., 1964-66, Dept. Def., 1969; assoc. Asia Sci. Research Assocs., Menlo Park, Calif., 1968—. Author: Evolution of the Japanese Electronics Industry, 1980, The North Korean Economy: Structure and Development, 1974; editor: Patterns of Economic Development: Korea, 1966. Social Sci. Resrch Council fellow, 1962; Stanford U. Hoover Instn. grantee, 1964-65; Fulbright lectr. Dept. State, 1966-68; Gen. Electric Found. grantee, 1975. Mem. Am. Econs. Assn., Assn. Asian Studies, Assn. Comparative Econ. Studies, Midwest Econs. Assn. Roman Catholic. Home: 5455 Lee Ave Downers Grove IL 60515 Office: Ill Inst Tech Dept Econs IIT Ctrq Chicago IL 60616

CHUNG, KYUNG CHO, educator, author; b. Seoul, Korea, Nov. 13, 1921; s. Yang Sun and Kyung Ok (Peng) C.; m. Yosi S. Chung, Oct. 10, 1958; children: In Kyung, In Ja. Student, Waseda U., Tokyo, 1941-43; B.A., Seoul Nat. U., 1947; postgrad., Columbia U., 1948-49; M.A., N.Y. U., 1951; LL.D., Pusan Nat. U., 1965; Litt.D., Sungkyunkwan U., 1968; M.A., Monterey Inst. Fgn. Studies, 1974. Mem. faculty U.S. Def. Lang. Inst., Monterey, Calif., 1951—, Monterey Inst. Fgn. Studies, 1973-74, Hartnell Coll., Salinas, Calif., 1974—; Dir. Korean Research Council; adviser Korean Assn., Monterey, 1974—, Am.-Korean Found.; treas. Korean Research Bull.; hon. prof. Kunkuk U.; Pres. South Carmel Hills Assn., 1962-63. Author: Korea Tomorrow, 1957, New Korea, 1962, Seoul (Ency. Americana), 1965, Naeil Hankuk, 1965, Sae Hankuk, 1968, Korea: The Third Republic, 1972, Korean Unification, 1973, Korea Reunion and Reunification, 1974. Recipient Superior Performance award U.S. Govt., 1964, Korean Prime Minister citation, 1965; cert. of achievement U.S. Def. Lang. Inst., 1976; Outstanding Performance award U.S. Def. Lang. Inst., 1980. Mem. AAUP, Am. Assn. Asian Studies, Am. Assn. Modern Langs., Am.-Korean Polit. Assn. Democrat. Mem. Korean Ch. Home: 25845 S Carmel Hills Dr Carmel CA 93923 Office: PO Box 5834 Presidio of Monterey CA 93940 *Dedicate and contribute toward better relations among the nations and the lasting peace in the world, teaching other languages to meet the other nations half way by speaking the same language.*

CHUNG, PAUL MYUNGHA, educator, mechanical engineer; b. Seoul, Korea, Dec. 1, 1929; came to U.S., 1947, naturalized, 1956; s. Robert N. and Kyungsook (Kim) C.; m. E. Jean Judy, Mar. 8, 1952; children: Maurice W., Tamara P. B.S. in Mech. Engring, U. Ky., 1952, M.S., 1954; Ph.D., U. Minn., 1957. Asst. prof. mech. engring. U. Minn., 1957-58; aero. research scientist Ames (Calif.) Research Center, NASA, 1958-61; head fluid physics dept. Aerospace Corp., San Bernardino, Calif., 1961-66; prof. fluid mechanics U. Ill. at Chgo., 1966—; head dept. energy engring. U. Ill. at Chgo. Circle, 1974-79, dean engring., 1979—; mem. nat. tech. com. AIAA on Plasmadynamics, 1972-74, com. on propellants and combustion, 1976—; mem. tech. adv. com. Ill. Inst. Environ. Quality, 1975-77; corp. mem. Underwriters Lab., 1983—; cons. to industry, 1966—. Author numerous papers in field; author: Electric Probes in Stationary and Flowing Plasmas, 1975, Russian edit., 1978. Bd. govs. Redlands (Calif.) YMCA, 1965-67. Fellow AIAA (assoc.); mem. Am. Soc. Engring. Edn. (exec. bd. engring. deans' council 1983—); Mem. Sigma Xi, Tau Beta Pi, Pi Tau Sigma, Phi Kappa Phi. Home: 2003 E Lillian Ln Arlington Heights IL 60004 Office: Univ Ill Chicago IL 60680

CHUNG, T. J., mechanical engineering, educator; b. Sunchon, Korea, May 20, 1929; came to U.S., 1960, naturalized, 1971; s. Ku Taik and Yon Ah (Kim) C.; m. Wharan Kim, June 24, 1964; children: Arleen, Jason. Diploma in engring, Seoul Nat. U., 1949; M.S., Okla. State U., 1961, Ph.D., 1964. Asst. prof., then asso. prof. mech. engring. Tenn. Tech. U., 1964-70; mem. faculty U. Ala., Huntsville, 1970—, prof.

mech. engring., 1975—, chmn. dept., 1978, dir. engring., 1981-82. Author: Finite Element Analysis in Fluid Dynamics, 1978; editor: Developments in Theoretical and Applied Mechanics, 1982. Mem. Am. Acad. Mechanics, AIAA, ASME, Sigma Xi. Office: U Ala Huntsville AL 38899

CHUNG, YOUNG-IOB, educator; b. Bihyun, Korea, June 28, 1928; came to U.S., 1950; s. Moon-chul and Yoon-sun (Choi) C.; m. Oke Kim, July 2, 1960; children—Jee-Won, Jinwon. B.S., U. Calif. at Los Angeles, 1952; M.A., Columbia, 1955, Ph.D., 1965. Instr. econs. Moravian Coll., Bethelehem, Pa., 1961-63, asst. prof., 1963-66; asso. prof. Eastern Mich. U., Ypsilanti, 1966-70, prof., head dept., 1970—. U. Calif. at Los Angeles Alumni scholar, 1950-52; Rotary scholar, 1950-52; Phi Beta Kappa alumni scholar, 1950-52. Mem. Am. Econ. Assn., Assn. Asian Studies, Midwestern Econ. Soc., Midwest Asian Affairs Soc., Mich. Acad. Arts and Sci., Mich. Econ. Soc. Home: 1625 Gregory St Ypsilanti MI 48197

CHUPKA, WILLIAM ANDREW, chemical physicist; b. Pittston, Pa., Feb. 12, 1923; s. William and Antoinette C.; m. Olive Augusta Pirani, May 21, 1955; children: Jocelyn Terese, Marc William. B.S., U. Scranton, 1943; M.S., U. Chgo., 1949, Ph.D., 1951. Instr. Harvard U., 1955-58; asso. physicist Argonne (Ill.) Nat. Lab., 1958-67; sr. physicist, 1967-75; prof. chemistry Yale U., 1975—. Research, numerous publs. in chem. physics. Served with U.S. Army, 1943-46. Guggenheim fellow, 1961-62. Mem. Am. Chem. Soc., Am. Phys. Soc. Office: 225 Prospect St PO Box 6666 New Haven CT 06511

CHURCH, ALONZO, educator; b. Washington, June 14, 1903; s. Samuel Robbins and Mildred Hannah Letterman (Parker) C.; m. Mary Julia Kuczinski, Aug. 25, 1925 (dec. Feb. 1976); children—Alonzo, Mary Ann, Mildred Warner. A.B., Princeton, 1924, Ph.D., 1927; D.Sc., Case Western Res. U., 1969. Faculty Princeton, 1929-67, prof. math., 1947-61, prof. math. and philosophy, 1961-67; prof. philosophy and math. UCLA, 1967—. Author: Introduction to Mathematical Logic, vol. I, 1956; Editor: Jour. Symbolic Logic, 1936-79; contbr. articles to math. and philos. jours. Mem. Am. Acad. Arts and Scis., Assn. Symbolic Logic, Am. Math. Soc., AAAS, Nat. Acad. Scis., Brit. Acad. (corr.), Am. Philos. Assn. (pres. Pacific div. 1973-74). Address: Dept Philosophy U Calif Los Angeles CA 90024

CHURCH, C. HOWARD, artist, educator; b. South Sioux City, Nebr., May 1, 1904; s. Charles Cyrus and Della (Pilgrim) C.; m. Ila Hamer, 1933. B.F.A., Sch. Art Inst. Chgo., 1935; student with, John Norton, Wm. P. Welsh, Boris Anisfeld, 1928-32; A.B., U. Chgo., 1938; M.A., Ohio State U., 1939, postgrad., 1939-40. Dir. Morgan Park Sch. Art, Chgo., 1933-36; head dept. art and dir. Mulvane Art Mus., Washburn U., Topeka, 1940-45; head dept. art Mich. State U., East Lansing, 1945-60, prof. art, 1960-72; Mem. Mich. Gov.'s Cultural Commn., 1960-68. Executed mural project for, Morgan Park Mil. Acad., Chgo., 1932-36; exhibited group and one-man shows, 1932—, one man print exhbn., Hackley Gallery, Muskegon, Mich., Mich. State U. Gallery, 1970; Free-lance artist, 1928-33. Recipient prizes Kansas Artists, 1940-41, Six State Exhbn. Omaha, 1941, 42; Print Purchase award Mich. Artists Exhbn., Mich. Edn. Assn., 1969, 70. Mem. Mich. Acad. Sci., Arts and Letters (Fine Arts medal 1963, 1st purchase award mems. exhbn. 1966), Midwestern Coll. Art Assn. (pres. 1959-60), AAUP, Phi Beta Kappa. Home: 271 Lexington Ave East Lansing MI 48823

CHURCH, DALE WALKER, lawyer, former government official; b. Portland, Oreg., Dec. 17, 1939; s. Floyd Walker and Lydia Belle (Barnette) C.; m. Mollie Ann Harper, Apr. 11, 1964; 1 son, Forrest Gregory. B.S., Oreg. State U., 1961; J.D., George Washington U., 1967. Bar: D.C. 1968, Calif. 1971. Contracting officer, exec. sec. Contract Rev. Bd., CIA, 1963-69; corp. counsel, asst. sec., dir. contracts ESL, Inc., Sunnyvale, Calif., 1969-77; dep. under sec. of Def. for research and engring. Dept. Def., Washington, 1977-80; pvt. practice specializing in internat. govt. contracts; counsel U.S.-Egyptian Bus. Council, U.S.-Pakistan Alliance; lectr. on acquisition and contract policy to profl. orgns. and univs.; counsel Egypt-U.S. Bus. Council, U.S.-Pakistan Alliance; mem. task force on industry-to-industry cooperation Def. Sci. Bd.; mem. def. orgn. project Ctr. for Strategic and Internat. Studies. Contbr. articles to profl. jours. Bd. advisors Am. U. Bus. Sch. Mem. Fed. Bar Assn., Calif. Bar Assn., D.C. Bar Assn., Santa Clara Bar Assn., Nat. Contract Mgmt. Assn., Soc. Logistics Engrs.; mem. Am. Def. Preparedness Assn., Nat. Security Indsl. Assn. (chmn. internat. com.), Nat. Contract Mgmt. Assn. (bd. advisors, bd. editors Jour.); Mem. Sigma Phi Epsilon, Delta Theta Phi. Home: 4087 Ridgeview Circle Arlington VA 22207 Office: 1250 Eye St NW Washington DC 20005

CHURCH, GEORGE LYLE, botanist, educator; b. Boston, Dec. 19, 1903; s. William R. and Anna Marie (Lind) C.; m. Margaret Fobes, June 16, 1934; 1 son, Robert Fobes. Sc.B., U. Mass., 1925; A.M., Harvard, 1927, Ph.D., 1928. Mem. faculty Brown U., 1928—, prof. botany, 1951-59, became Stephen T. Olney prof. natural history, 1959, now emeritus prof., also curator herbarium, 1951—, chmn. dept. botany, 1958-65. Contbr. articles to profl. jours. Fellow AAAS; mem. Bot. Soc. Am., Growth Soc., Soc. Study of Evolution, New Eng. Bot. Club, Soc. Am. Plant Taxonomists, Sigma Xi, Phi Kappa Phi, Alpha Gamma Rho. Home: 278 Doyle Ave Providence RI 02906

CHURCH, HERBERT STEPHEN, JR., construction company executive; b. Framingham, Mass., July 24, 1920; s. Herbert Stephen and Edith L. (Shaw) C.; m. Carol S. Orzech, Apr. 2, 1945; children: Carolyn, David, Kathryn, Patricia, Virginia. B.S. in Civil Engring, Northeastern U., Boston, 1943. Constrn. insp. N.Y., New Haven & Hartford R.R., 1940-43; with Turner Constrn. Co., 1943; from gen. supt. to v.p., gen. mgr. Chgo. terr., 1965-73, sr. v.p. Western region, Chgo., 1974-80, sr. v.p. Central region, 1980—; dir., 1972—. Trustee Nat. Commn. for Coop. Edn., 1981. Mem. Contractors Mut. Assn. (dir. 1974—), Builders Assn. Chgo. (dir. 1969-74). Methodist. Clubs: Chgo.; Inverness Golf (Palatine, Ill.). Home: 811 W George St Arlington Heights IL 60005 Office: 55 W Monroe St Chicago IL 60603

CHURCH, JOHN TRAMMELL, retail stores company executive; b. Raleigh, N.C., Sept. 22, 1917; s. Charles Randolph and Lela (Johnson) C.; m. Emma Thomas Rose, Dec. 31, 1943; children: John Trammell, Elizabeth Church Bacon. Student, Catawba Coll., 1936-37; B.S., U. N.C., 1942. With Rose Co., Henderson, N.C., 1945—, asst. sec., dir., 1948-49, buyer several depts., 1949-54, v.p., sec., 1954-57; mdse. mgr. Rose's Stores Inc., 1957—, sr. v.p., 1963-73, chmn. bd., 1973—; dir. Peoples Bank and Trust Co. Past mem. Tax Study Commn. N.C., Legis. Pay Commn., Exec. Residence Bldg. Commn., Legis. Services Commn.; mem. State Art Mus. Bldg. Commn.; chmn. Kerr Reservoir Devel. Commn., 1967; mem. N.C.-Va. Water Resources Mgmt. Com.; sec. N.C. Ports Authority; pres. United Fund, 1955; trustee, mem. exec. com. Carolinas United, 1955-59; sec. Vance-Granville Community Coll.; mem. adv. bd. Salvation Army, 1959-65; v.p., mem. exec. bd. Occoneechee council Boy Scouts Am., 1955-69, pres., 1969-70; adv. bd. S.E. regional council; seal chmn. Tar River Lung Assn., 1976; Mem. Henderson City Council, 1965-66, N.C. Ho. of Reps., 1967-69, 77, 79, 81, N.C. Senate, 1971; past chmn. N.C. Exec. Democratic Com.; past mem. Nat. Dem. Com.; vice-chmn. bd. trustees Maria Parham Hosp., Henderson, N.C., chmn. doctors procurement com.; trustee N.C. Symphony Soc.; bd. visitors, past trustee U. N.C. at Chapel Hill; past mem. Morehead Scholarship selection com.; bd. dirs. Bus. Found., Order of Tar Heel One Hundred; chmn. utilities study commn. Order of Tar Heel One Hundred; trustee Vance-Granville Community Coll.; past chmn. bd. visitors; trustee Peace Coll., Raleigh; vice chmn. bd. trustees Louisburg (N.C.) Coll. Served to capt., aviator USMCR, 1942-45. Decorated D.F.C. with 2 oak leaf clusters (3), Air medal (10); recipient Silver Beaver award, Disting. Citizen award Boy Scouts Am.; O.B. Michael Distinguished Alumnus award Catawba Coll., 1973; named Tarheel of Week, 1962; Man of Year Henderson-Vance County, 1977. Mem. N.C. Mchts. Assn. (pres. 1962, 64, dir., exec. com), Assn. Gen. Mdse. Chains (sec., exec. com.), N.C. Citizens Assn. (dir.), Am. Retail Fedn. (vice chmn. 1965), Am. Legion, 40 and 8, Henderson-Vance County C. of C. (dir. 1959-63, pres. 1976), Jr. C. of C. (pres. 1950-51), Nat. Retail Mchts. Assn. (past dir.), U. N.C. Alumni Assn. (dir., pres. 1980), Newcomen Soc. N.C. Methodist (chmn. bd. trustees, past chmn. adminstrv. bd.). Clubs: Mason (Shriner), Elk, Rotarian (pres. Henderson Club 1964-65), Henderson Country (pres. 1956-57); Hound Ears Lodge and Club (Blowing Rock, N.C.); Grandfather Golf and Country (Linville, N.C.); Sphinx, Capital City (Raleigh). Home: 420 Woodland Rd Henderson NC 27536 Office: Garnett St Henderson NC 27536

CHURCH, KENNETH ROBERT, mfr. gas turbine engines; b. Ottawa, Ont., Can., Mar. 20, 1921; s. George Alexander and Ethel (Turley) C.; m. Elsie May Chambers, Dec. 9, 1944; children—Kenneth Edward, Thomas Robert. B. Comm., Queen's U., 1942. Chartered accountant Price Waterhouse & Co., Toronto, Ont., 1942-50; chief accountant A.V. Roe Can. Ltd., 1950-51; comptroller, v.p. finance Orenda Engines Ltd., Toronto, 1952-60; finance mgr. Hawker Siddeley Can. Ltd., Toronto, 1961-66; treas. Orenda Ltd., Toronto, 1967—. Mem. Univ. Council Queen's U., 1969—. Mem. Air Industries Assn. Can. Club: Weston Golf and Country (Toronto). Home: 30 Cedarland Dr Islington ON Canada Office: Box 6001 Toronto Internat Airport ON Canada

CHURCH, MARTHA ELEANOR, college president; b. Pitts., Nov. 17, 1930; d. Walter Seward and Eleanor (Boyer) C. B.A., Wellesley Coll., 1952; M.A., U. Pitts., 1954; Ph.D., U. Chgo., 1960; D.Sc. (hon.), Lake Erie Coll., 1975, Litt.D., Houghton Coll., 1980, L.H.D., Queens Coll., 1981, Ursinus Coll., 1981, St. Joseph Coll., 1982, Towson State U., 1983. Instr. geography Mt. Holyoke Coll., S. Hadley, Mass., 1953-57; lectr. geography Ind. U. Gary Center, 1958; instr., then asst. prof. geography Wellesley Coll., 1958-60, 60-65; dean coll., prof. geography Wilson Coll., 1965-71; assoc. exec. sec. Commn. Higher Edn., Middle States Assn. Coll. and Secondary Sch., 1971-75; pres. Hood Coll., Frederick, Md., 1975—; Cons. for Choice: Books for Coll. Libraries; adv. bd. Project Noncollegiate-Sponsored Instruction, 1974-76; dir. Farmers and Mechanics Nat. Bank. Author: The Spatial Organization of Electric Power Territories in Massachusetts, 1960; Co-editor: A Basic Geographical Library: A Selected and Annotated Book List for Am. Colls, 1966; cons. editor, Change mag., 1980—. Bd. dirs. Four-Year Servicemen's Opportunity Project, 1973-75; bd. dirs. Council for Internat. Exchange of Scholars, 1979-80, Japan Internat. Christian U. Found., 1977—, Nat. Center for Higher Edn. Mgmt. Systems, 1980—, Am. Council on Edn., 1976-79; vice chmn. Am. Council on Edn., 1978-79; mem. nat. identification panel, 1977—; bd. advisors Fund for Improvement of Postsecondary Edn., HEW, 1976-79; mem. Sec. of Navy's Adv. Bd. on Edn. and Tng., 1976-80; chmn. Md. Panel on Civil Rights, 1981-82; trustee Bradford Coll., Mass., 1982—, Peddie Sch., N.J., 1983—; mem. pub. adv. com. Bus. and Profl. Women's Found., 1982—. Recipient Christian R. and Mary F. Lindback Found.; Disting. Teaching award Wilson Coll., 1971. Mem. AAUW, Am. Assn. Advancement of Humanities (dir. 1979—), Am. Assn. Higher Edn. (chmn. 1980, dir), Md. Ind. Colls. and Univs. Assn. (pres. 1979-81), Assn. Am. Colls. (adv. com. project on status and edn. of women 1980—), Women's Coll. Coalition (exec. com. 1976-80), Am. Conf. Acad. Deans (sec., editor 1969-71), Council Protestant Colls. and Univs. (bd. dirs. 1969-71), Soc. Coll. and Univ. Planning (editorial bd. 1976-84), Sigma Delta Epsilon. Home: President's House Hood Coll Frederick MD 21701

CHURCH, RUSSELL MILLER, educator; b. N.Y.C., Dec. 24, 1930; s. Donald E. and Pearl (Friedman) C.; m. Ruth Kutz, Apr. 4, 1954; children—Kenneth, Emily. B.A., U. Mich., 1952; M.A., Harvard U., 1954, Ph.D., 1956. Mem. faculty Brown U., 1955—, prof. psychology, 1965—, chmn. dept. psychology, 1980—. Editor: (with E.E. Boe) Punishment: Issues and Experiments, 1968; editor: (with B.A. Campbell) Punishment and Aversive Behavior, 1969. Fellow Am. Psychol. Assn. Home: 20 Abbotsford Ct Providence RI 02912

CHURCH, SAMUEL MORGAN, JR. (SAM CHURCH), labor union ofcl.; b. Matewan, W.Va., Sept. 20, 1936; m. Patti, Mar. 23, 1978. Student, Berea Coll. Warehouse maintenance mechanic Domino Sugar Co., Balt.; active United Packing House Workers Union; with Clinchfield Coal Co.; electrician-mechanic Westmoreland Coal Co., Va.; ofcl. United Mine Workers Am.; field rep. United Mine Workers Assn. Dist. 28, 1973-75, internat. rep. nat. hdqrs., Washington, 1975-76; dep. dir. United Mine Workers Am., Washington, from 1976; exec. asst. to Arnold Miller, pres., 1979—. Office: United Mine Workers Am 900 15th St NW Washington DC 20005

CHURCH, THOMAS TROWBRIDGE, former steel company executive; b. N.Y.C., Nov. 21, 1919; s. William Bowen and Agnes Mansfield (Curtis) C.; m. Sylvina Williams, Sept. 20, 1943; children: Donald C., Martha C., Thomas N., Sara C., Warren B., Minette C. B.A., Yale U., 1941. With Bethlehem Steel Corp. (Pa.), 1941-82, gen. traffic mgr., 1968-71, asst. v.p., 1971-75, v.p. transp., 1975-82. Pres. Bach Choir of Bethlehem. Served with USAAF, 1942-44, to capt. Transp. Corps., 1944-46. Mem. Am. Iron and Steel Inst. (chmn. traffic com. 1978-80), Nat. Freight Transp. Assn., Transp. Assn. Am. (dir., chmn., user panel, chmn. transp. data coordinating com.). Episcopalian. Club: Saucon Valley Country (Bethlehem). Office: Bach Choir Bethlehem 423 Heckewelder Pl Bethlehem PA 18018

CHURCHILL, JAMES PAUL, judge; b. Imlay City, Mich., Apr. 10, 1924; s. Howard and Faye (Shurte) C.; m. Ann Muir, Aug. 30, 1950; children: Nancy Ann Churchill Nyquist, David James, Sally Jo. B.A., U. Mich., 1947, J.D., 1950. Individual practice law, Vassar, Mich., 1950-65; circuit judge 40th Jud. Circuit Mich., 1965-74; U.S. dist. judge Eastern Dist. Mich., Detroit, 1974—. Served with U.S. Army, 1943-46. Mem. State Bar Mich., Am. Bar Assn. Office: US Courthouse Room 853 Detroit MI 48226 *

CHURCHILL, NEIL CENTER, educator; b. Bismarck, N.D., Sept. 6, 1927; s. Neil Orr and Helen (Center) C.; m. Marjorie Ann Shipman, June 28, 1952; children: Neil T., Gregory S., Christopher S. B.S., UCLA, 1951, M.B.A., 1954; Ph.D., U. Mich., 1962. C.P.A., Calif. Staff accountant Haskins & Sells (C.P.A.s), Los Angeles, 1951-53; instr. San Diego State Coll., 1954-56; assoc. prof. Carnegie Mellon U., 1958-67; prof. Harvard Grad. Sch. Bus. Adminstrn., 1967—, Royal Little prof. bus. adminstrn., 1970-80; Disting. prof. acctg. So. Meth. U., Dallas, 1980—; dir. Nimrod Press, D.L. Martin Co., Top Yield Industries, Controlonics Corp., Shelco Steel Works; cons. Gen. Motors, Gen. Electric; others. Author: (with others) Computer-Based Information Systems in Management, 1968, Measuring Corporate Social Performance, 1976. Served with USNR, 1945-46. Mem. Am. Inst. C.P.A.s, Am. Acctg. Assn. Home: 12002 Browning Ln Dallas TX 75230 Office: Southern Meth U Cox Sch Dallas TX 75275

CHURCHILL, RUEL VANCE, mathematician; b. Akron, Ind., Dec. 12, 1899; s. Abner C. and Meldora (Friend) C.; m. Ruby F. Sicks, 1922 (dec. 1969); children: Betty Churchill McMurray, Eugene S.; m. Alice B. Warren, 1972. B.S., U. Chgo., 1922; M.S., U. Mich., 1925, Ph.D., 1929. Faculty U. Mich., Ann Arbor, 1922—, prof. math., 1942-65, emeritus, 1965—; vis. lectr. U. Wis., 1941; research U. Freiburg, Germany, 1936, Calif. Inst. Tech., 1949; research specialist USAAF, 1944; mem. NRC, 1947-50. Author: books including Complex Variables and Applications, 1948, 4th edit. (with J.W. Brown),1984, Japanese edit., 1975, Spanish edit., 1978; Operational Mathematics, 1944, Japanese edit. 1950, Fourier Series, 1941, 3d edit. (with J.W. Brown) 1978, Japanese edit., 1960, Spanish edit., 1966, Portuguese edit., 1978. Chmn. bd. visitors Sch. Pub. Affairs U. Md. Mem. Am. Math. Soc. (council 1946-49, mem. com. on applied math. 1948-49, 51-54, chmn. editorial com. Procs. Symposia in Applied Math. 1949), Math. Assn Am. (asso. editor Am. Math. Monthly 1952-56, v.p. 1956-57, gov. 1959-61, 74-77), Phi Beta Kappa, Sigma Xi. Home: 1231 Wisteria Dr Ann Arbor MI 48104

CHURCHILL, STUART WINSTON, chemical engineering educator; b. Imlay City, Mich., June 13, 1920; s. Howard Heenan and Faye Erma (Shurte) C.; m. Donna Belle Lewis, Feb. 22, 1946 (div.); children: Stuart Lewis, Diana Gail, Cathy Marie, Emily Elizabeth; m. Renate Ursula Treibmann, Aug. 3, 1974. B.S. in Math, U. Mich., 1942, 1942, M.S., 1948, Ph.D., 1952; M.A. honoris causa, U. Pa., 1972. Technologist Shell Oil Co., 1942-46; tech. supr. Frontier Chem. Co., 1946-47; mem. faculty U. Mich., 1949-67, prof. chem. engring., 1957-67, chmn. dept. chem. and metall. engring., 1962-67; Carl V.S. Patterson prof. chem. engring. U. Pa., 1967—; chmn. region 2 edn. and accreditation com. Engrs. Council Profl. Devel., 1961-65, mem. nat. council, 1965-71, exec. com., 1968-71; cons. heat transfer and combustion. Recipient S. Reid Warren, Jr. award for distinguished teaching U. Pa., 1976; Max Jakob Meml. award for heat transfer ASME/Am. Inst. Chem. Engrs., 1979; Japan Soc. for Promotion of Sci. grantee, 1977. Fellow Am. Inst. Chem. Engrs. (nat. council 1962-64, pres. 1966, Profl. Progress award 1964, William H. Walker award 1969, Warren K. Lewis award 1978, Founders award 1980); mem. Nat. Acad. Engring., Combustion Inst., Am. Chem. Soc., Verein Deutscher Ingenieure (Corr. mem.), Sigma Xi, Phi Kappa Phi, Phi Lambda Upsilon (award U. Mich. chpt. 1961), Tau Beta Pi. Unitarian. Home: 137 Pole Cat Rd Glen Mills PA 19342

CHURCHWELL, CHARLES DARRETT, librarian; b. Dunnellon, Fla., Nov. 7, 1926; s. John Dozier and Leeannah (DeLaughter) C.; m. Yvonne Ransom, Aug. 25, 1957; children: Linda Louise, Cynthia Diane. B.S., Morehouse Coll., 1952; M.S., Atlanta U., 1953; Ph.D., U. Ill., 1966. Instr. library sci. Prairie View A&M Coll., (Tex.), 1953-57; reference librarian circulation dept. N.Y. Pub. Library, 1959-61; asst. circulation librarian U. Ill., 1965-67; asst. dir. libraries U. Houston, 1967-69; dir. libraries Miama U., Oxford, Ohio, 1969-72; assoc. provost Miami U., Oxford, Ohio, 1972-74; univ. librarian Brown U., Providence, 1974-78; dean library services Washington U., St. Louis, 1978—. Served with USAAF, 1945-47. Mem. Am. Library Assn. (life), Council Library Resources (dir.), NAACP (life), So. Assn. Colls. and Univs., Mo. Library Assn. Home: 6408 Forsyth Blvd Saint Louis MO 63105 Office: Washington U Library Saint Louis MO 63130

CHURG, JACOB, physician; b. Dolhinow, Poland, July 16, 1910; came to U.S., 1936, naturalized, 1943; s. Wolf and Gita (Ravich) C.; m. Vivian Gelb, Oct. 18, 1942; children: Andrew Marc, Warren Bernard. M.D., U. Wilno, Poland, 1933, 1936. Diplomate: Am. Bd. Pathology. Intern City Hosp., Wilno and State Hosp., Wilejka, Poland, 1933-34; asst. in gen. and exptl. pathology U. Wilno, 1934-36; asst. in bacteriology Mt. Sinai Hosp., N.Y.C., 1938, fellow in pathology, 1942-43, research asso., 1946—, attending physician, 1966-81, cons., 1982—; resident in pathology Beth Israel Hosp., Newark, 1939-40; pathologist Barnert Meml. Hosp., Paterson, N.J., 1946—; prof. pathology and community med. Mt. Sinai Sch. Med., N.Y.C., 1966-81, prof. emeritus, 1982—; cons. pathologist VA Hosp., Bronx, N.Y., Nassau County Med. Center, East Meadow, N.Y., St. Barnabas Med. Center, Livingston, N.J., N.J. Valley Hosp., Ridgewood; chmn. mesothelioma reference panel Internat. Union Against Cancer, 1965-81; chmn. com. for histologic classification renal diseases WHO, 1975—; Lady Davis vis. prof. pathology, Jerusalem, 1975; former mem. sci. adv. group NIH, Bethesda, Md.; mem. Internat. Union Against Cancer, 1982—. Author: Histological Classification of Renal Diseases, Renal Disease—Present Status, Glomerular Diseases, Tubulo-Interstitial Diseases, Tumors of Seresal Surfaces; also numerous articles in sci. jours. Served to capt., M.C. AUS, 1943-46. Fellow Coll. Am. Pathologists; mem. AMA, Am. Assn. Pathologists, Am. Soc. Nephrology, N.Y. Acad. Medicine, Internat. Acad. Pathology, Harvey Soc., Internat. Soc. Nephrology, Alpha Omega Alpha. Research in vascular diseases and renal structure, pneumokonioses. Co-describer syndrome of allergic granulomatosis (Churg-Strauss syndrome). Address: 711 Ogden Ave Teaneck NJ 07666

CHUSID, PAUL, advertising executive; s. Abraham Bernard and Mija (Braunstein) C.; m. Laure Anne Cote, Dec. 26, 1951; children: Marc, Eric. B.A., U. Vt.; grad., Amos Tuck Sch. Bus., Dartmouth Coll. Sr. v.p. Klemtner Advt., Inc.; pres. Grey Med. Advt., Inc., N.Y.C. Bd. dirs. Pharm. Advt. Club, N.Y.C., pres., 1978. Home: 68 Deertrack Ln Irvington-on-Hudson NY 10533 Office: 800 3d Ave New York NY 10022

CHUTE, MARCHETTE, author; b. Wayzata, Minn., Aug. 16, 1909; d. William Young and Edith Mary (Pickburn) C. A.B., U. Minn., 1930; Litt.D., Western Coll. for Women, 1952, Carleton Coll., 1957, Dickinson Coll., 1964. Author: Rhymes About Ourselves, 1932, The Search for God, 1941, Rhymes About the Country, 1941, The Innocent Wayfaring, 1943, Geoffrey Chaucer of England, 1946, Rhymes About the City, 1946, The End of the Search, 1947, Shakespeare of London, 1950, An Introduction to Shakespeare, 1951, Ben Jonson of Westminster, 1953, The Wonderful Winter, 1954, Stories from Shakespeare, 1956, Around and About, 1957, Two Gentle Men: The Lives of George Herbert and Robert Herrick, 1959, Jesus of Israel, 1961, (with Ernestine Perrie) The Worlds of Shakespeare, 1963, The First Liberty: A History of the Right to Vote in America, 1619-1850, 1969, The Green Tree of Democracy, 1971, P.E.N. American Center: A History of the First Fifty Years, 1972, Rhymes About Us, 1974; Exec. com., Nat. Book Com.; judge non-fiction Nat. Book Awards, 1952, 59. Recipient Author Meets the Critics award for best non-fiction of, 1950; Chap-Book award Poetry Soc. Am., 1954; N.Y. Shakespeare Club award, 1954; Secondary Edn. Bd. book award, 1954; Outstanding Achievement award U. Minn., 1957. Fellow Royal Soc. Arts, Soc. Am. Historians; mem. Am. P.E.N. (pres. 1955-57), Am. Acad. Arts and Letters, Renaissance Soc. Am., Phi Beta Kappa. Home: 450 E 63d St New York NY 10021

CHUTE, ROBERT MAURICE, biologist, educator; b. Bridgton, Maine, Feb. 13, 1926; s. James Clevel and Elizabeth Ellen (Davis) C.; m. Virginia Hinds, June 24, 1946; children: David Christopher, Dian Leslie. B.A. in Zoology, U. Maine, Orono, 1950; Sc.D., Johns Hopkins U., 1953. Asst. prof. biology Middlebury (Vt.) Coll., 1953-59, San Fernando Valley State Coll., Northridge, Calif., 1959-61; asso. prof.

Lincoln (Pa.) U., 1961-62; prof. biology Bates Coll., Lewiston, Maine, 1962—, Dana prof., 1975—, chmn. dept., 1962-83, chmn. div. natural scis., 1983—. Author: Environmental Insight, 1971, Introduction to Biology, 1975; poetry Quiet Thunder, 1975, Uncle George Poems, 1977, Voices Great and Small, 1977, Thirteen Moons, 1978; also French-English bilingual edit., 1981, 275 poems in jours.; founder, editor: lit. mag. The Small Pond, 1963; also articles. Served with USAAF, 1944-46. NIH grantee. Fellow AAAS; mem. Maine Biologists Assn. (hon. life), Phi Beta Kappa, Sigma Xi, Phi Kappa Phi. Office: Dept Biology Bates Coll Lewiston ME 04240 *Such success as I have enjoyed comes from following my interests—frequently the course of least resistance—making use of what is at hand and not seeking out opportunities.*

CHUTKOW, JERRY GRANT, neurologist, educator; b. Denver, June 14, 1933; s. Samuel and Yvette (Robinson) C.; m. Melicent Kratz Rupp, June 14, 1957; children—Dawn Michelle, Cyanne Tamar, Mark Daniel Rupp, William Alexander. A.B., U. Chgo., 1952, B.S., 1954, M.D., 1958. Diplomate: Am. Bd. Internal Medicine, Am. Bd. Psychiatry and Neurology. Intern Columbia-Presbyn. Hosp., N.Y.C., 1958-59; resident in internal medicine U. Chgo., 1959-62, resident in neurology, 1964-67, instr. internal medicine, 1962-64, asst. prof., 1967-69; research asst. Argonne Cancer research Hosp., 1961-63; cons. neurology Mayo Clinic, 1969-77; asst. prof. Mayo Med. Sch., 1970-74, asso. porf., 1974-77; prof., chmn. dept. neurology SUNY, Buffalo, 1977—; dir. dept. neurology Erie County (N.Y.) Med. Center, 1979—; chief neurology service VA Med. Center, Buffalo, 1979—; cons. in field. Contbr. chpts. to books and articles in field. Served with U.S. Army, 1967-69. Nat. Insts. Neurologic Disease spl. fellow, 1965-67; Schweppe found. fellow, 1967-69. Mem. Am. Neurologic Assn., Am. Acad. Neurology, A.C.P., Assn. Univ. Profs. Neurology, Am. Coll. nutrition, Am. Psychiat. Assn., Soc. Neurosci., Central Soc. Neurologic Research, Phi Beta Kappa, Sigma Xi, Alpha Omega Alpha. Office: Department of Neurology SUNY at Buffalo 3435 Main St Buffalo NY 14214

CHYLA, DAVID RAYMOND, executive search company executive; b. Chgo., July 28, 1944; s. Raymond Walter and Helen Marie (Gradek) C.; m. JoAnne Marie Jalovecky, June 11, 1966; children: Kimberly Anne, Stacy Lynn. B.S. in Chemistry, Purdue U., 1966; postgrad., Law Sch., U. Notre Dame, 1966-68; M.B.A., Ind. U., 1969; profl. acctg. cert., Northwestern U., 1970. C.P.A., Ill. Sr. acct. Arthur Young & Co., Chgo., 1969-72; analyst Gould, Inc., Chgo., 1972-73; sr. cons. Peat Marwick Mitchell & Co., Chgo., 1973-76; v.p. William H. Clark Assos., Inc., Chgo., 1976-81; sr. v.p., mgr. Eastman & Beaudine Inc., Chgo., 1981—; asso. prof. Keller Grad. Sch. Mgmt., Chgo., 1975—. Mem. Am. Inst. C.P.A.'s, Assn. Exec. Recruiting Consultants, Ill. Soc. C.P.A.'s, Hazel Crest Jaycees (charter, treas. 1974-75). Clubs: Young Execs., University (Chgo.). Office: 111 W Monroe St Suite 2150 Chicago IL 60603

CHYTIL, FRANK, biochemist; b. Prague, Czechoslovakia, Aug. 28, 1924; came to U.S., 1965, naturalized, 1971; s. Frantisek and Ruzena (Vitouskova) C.; m. Lucie Scheinost, Nov. 26, 1949; children: Frank, Anna, Helena. M.S., Sch. Chem. Tech., Prague, 1949, Ph.D., 1952; C.Sc., Czechoslovak Acad. Sci., Prague, 1956. Research biochemist Charles U., Prague, 1949-51; research fellow Inst. Human Research, Prague, 1952-63; sr. scientist Czechoslovak Acad. Sci., Prague, 1956-64; sr. research fellow Brandeis U., Waltham, Mass., 1964—, sr. research assoc., 1965-66; head sect. enzymology S.W. Found. Research and Edn., San Antonio, 1966-69; mem. faculty Vanderbilt U., 1969—, prof. biochemistry, 1975—; adj. assoc. prof. U. Tex., San Antonio, 1968-69. Editor: Vitamins and Hormones, 1983; mem. editorial bd.: Analytical Biochemistry, 1980—, Jour. Biol. Chemistry, 1982—; contbr. profl. jours. Recipient Osborne-Mendel award; USPHS grantee, 1967—. Mem. Am. Chem. Soc., Am. Soc. Biol. Chemists, Am. Inst. Nutrition (chmn. (nomenclature) 1982, 83, Osborne Mendel award 1983), Endocrine Soc., Sigma Xi. Address: 914 Lynnwood Blvd Nashville TN 37205 Office: Vanderbilt U Sch Medicine Nashville TN 37232

CIAMPI, MARIO JOSEPH, architect, planner; b. San Francisco, Apr. 27, 1907; s. Guido and Palmira (DiVita) C.; m. Loretta Keane, Sept. 26, 1939 (dec. 1972); m. Carolyn Smith, June 1, 1983. Grad., Harvard Sch. Architecture, 1932; D.F.A. (hon.), Calif. Sch. Arts and Crafts, 1980. Lic. architect, Calif. Design critic San Francisco Archtl. Club, 1935-40; practice architecture Mario J. Ciampi and Assos. (Urban Design Consultants), San Francisco, 1945—; lectr. various orgns. and univs. Urban cons. San Francisco projects including, Market St. Devel. Plan, 1963-79, Waterfront Study, 1958, Golden Gateway Project, Freeway Study, 1966, Market St. Beautification Project, 1968-79, Yerba Buena Center Study, 1973-75, N.Waterfront, Port Commn., 1980, South of Market Design Plan, 1983. Bd. trustees San Francisco Art Inst.; bd. regents St. Mary's Coll.; bd. dirs. Museo Italiano; mem. San Francisco Symphony Assn., Ballet Soc., Opera Soc. Recipient honors and awards including; collaborative medal of honor Archtl. League N.Y., 1960; gold medal of honor, 1962; Albert John Evers Environ. award, San Francisco, 1972; San Francisco Art Festival award, 1973; one man show of works winner nat. competition Arts Center U. Calif., 1965; recipient certificate of honor Bd. Suprs. City of San Francisco, 1973. Fellow AIA (mem. nat., state, local orgns., first honor awards state and nat. awards programs, awards for Market St. Beautification, 1970-79, Univ. Art Mus., Berkeley, San Francisco Junipero Serra Freeway, Seton House, Los Altos, various schs. and churches San Francisco area). Clubs: Harvard, Family, Olympic, Serra, Laqunitas. Traveler, research and study urban design, architecture N.Am., Europe, S.Am., Orient, Middle East, 1950-66; works published N.Am., S.Am., Europe, India. Home: 520 Woodland Rd Kentfield CA Office: 617 Front St San Francisco CA 94111

CIANCI, VINCENT ALBERT, JR., mayor Providence; b. Providence, Apr. 30, 1941; s. Vincent Albert and Esther (Capobianco) C.; m. Sheila Ann Bentley, Sept. 30, 1973. Grad., Moses Brown Sch., Providence, 1958; B.S., Fairfield (Conn.) U., 1962, Dr. Pub. Service (hon.), 1978; M.A. in Polit. Sci, Villanova U., 1965; J.D., Marquette U., 1966; LL.D. (hon.), Roger Williams Coll., D.B.A., Johnson and Wales Coll. Bar: R.I. bar 1967. Spl. asst. atty. gen., R.I., Providence, 1969-73, spl. asst. atty. gen. in charge of organized crime unit, 1973-74, mayor, Providence, 1975—; lectr. in govt. Bryant Coll., Providence, 1969—. Served to 1st lt. U.S. Army, 1966-69. Decorated Order Merit, Italy). Mem. R.I. Bar Assn., Bar U.S. Ct. Mil. Appeals, Nat. Dist. Attys. Assn., Am. Judicature Soc., Phi Delta Phi. Clubs: Italo-Am. (Providence); Alpine Country (Cranston, R.I.); K.C. Home: 145 Blackstone Blvd Providence RI 02906 Office: Office of Mayor City Hall 25 Dorrance St Providence RI 02903

CIANCIMINO, MATTHEW RUDOLPH, banker; b. N.Y.C., Dec. 21, 1925; s. Philip and Eleanor (Tasca) C.; m. Eleanor A. Osborn, June 5, 1948; children: Paul Henry, Eugene Philip, Kenneth Matthew. B.A., St. Johns U., 1949; M.A., Columbia U., 1950. With Irving Trust Co., 1951-52, Bank of Am., N.Y., 1952-55; with bank exams. div. Fed. Res. Bank, N.Y.C., 1955-61; sr. v.p. banking activities in Latin Am. Marine Midland Bank, N.Y.C., 1961-74; sr. v.p., head internat. div. First Nat. State Bank N.J., 1974—. Served with AUS, 1944-46. Mem. Bankers Assn. for Fgn. Trade, U.S.-Mexican C. of C. (nat. dir.). Clubs: Essex (Newark, N.J.); Essex County Country (West Orange, N.J.). Home: 31 Parkway Montclair NJ 07042 Office: First Nat State Bank NJ 550 Broad St Newark NJ 07102

CIANCIO, SEBASTIAN GENE, periodontist, educator; b. Jamestown, N.Y., June 21, 1937; m. Marilyn Bonfiglio; children: Michele Ann, Sebastian. D.D.S., SUNY-Buffalo, 1961. Diplomate: Am. Bd. Periodontology; cert. periodontist, 1965. Postdoctoral fellow depts. pharmacology and periodontology SUNY-Buffalo, 1963-65, instr., 1964-65, asst. clin. prof. pharmacology, asst. prof. periodontology, 1966, acting co-chmn. dept. periodontology, 1967-68, acting chmn., 1968, chmn. dept. periodontology, 1969-72, prof., chmn. dpet. periodontics-endodontics, 1972—, clin. prof. dept. pharmacology, 1973—; vis. faculty Sch. Dentistry, U. Zurich, Switzerland, 1976; dental chmn. com. on revision U.S. Pharmacopeia, 1981—; cons. in field. Contbr. numerous articles to profl. jours., chpts. to books. Served to capt. U.S. Army Dental Corps, 1961-63. Recipient George B. Snow prize in Prosthetic dentistry, 1961; named Alpha Omega Dental Educator of Yr., 1971; recipient hon. citation U. Chile, 1980. Fellow Internat. Coll. Dentist; mem. ADA, Internat. Assn. Dental Research, Nat. Soc. Dental Research (bd. dirs. 1981—), Royal Soc. Health (London), Am. Acad. Periodonology (spl. citaion 1983), 8th Dist. Dental Soc., Erie County Dental Soc., Federation Dentaire Internationale, Omicron Kappa Upsilon. Office: SUNY Buffalo Amherst NY 14260

CIARDI, JOHN, poet; b. Boston, June 24, 1916; s. Carmin and Concetta (di Benedictis) C.; m. Myra Judith Hostetter, July 28, 1946; children—Myra Judith, John Lyle, Benn. Student, Bates Coll., 1934-36; A.B. magna cum laude, Tufts U., 1938, D. Litt., 1960; M.A., U. Mich., 1939; H.D., Wayne U., 1963; LL.D., Ursinus Coll., 1964; L.H.D., Kalamazoo Coll., 1964, Bates Coll., 1970, Washington U., 1971, Ohio Wesleyan Coll., 1971; D.H.L., Kean U., 1975, U. Mo.-Kansas City, 1983. Instr. English U. Kansas City, 1940-42, 46; instr. Harvard, 1946-48, Briggs Copeland asst. prof., 1948-53; lectr. Am. poetry Salzburg Seminar in Am. Studies, 1951; staff lectr. poetry Bread Loaf Writers Conf., 1947-73, dir., 1955-72; lectr. English Rutgers U., 1953-54, assoc. prof. English, 1954-56, prof. English, 1956-61. Poetry editor, Saturday Rev., 1956-73; contbg. editor, World Mag., 1972-73; Author: Homeward to America, 1940, Other Skies, 1947, Live Another Day, 1949, Mid-Century American Poets; anthology, 1950, From Time to Time, 1951, The Inferno of Dante; translation, 1954, As If, Poems New and Selected, 1955, I Marry You, 1958, The Reason for the Pelican, 1959, 39 Poems, 1959, How Does a Poem Mean?, 1959, Scrappy the Pup, 1960; children's poems I Met A Man, 1961, The Man Who Sang the Sillies, 1961, You Read to Me, I'll Read to You, 1962, Someone Could Win a Polar Bear, 1970; poems In the Stoneworks, 1961, In Fact, 1962, This Strangest Everything, 1966, Lives of X, 1971; translation Dante's Purgatorio, 1961, Dante's Paradiso, 1970, The Divine Comedy, 1977; story for children The Wish-Tree, 1962; poems for children J.J. Plenty and Fiddler Den, 1963, You Know Who, 1964, Fast and Slow, 1975; critical essays Dialogue with an Audience, 1963; poems Person to Person, 1964; for children The Monster Den, The King Who Saved Himself From Being Saved, 1965; poems An Alphabestiary, 1966, The Little that is All, 1974; occasional pieces Manner of Speaking, 1972, (with Isaac Asimov) Limericks, 1978, For Instance, 1979, A Browser's Dictionary, 1980. Served with USAAF, 1942-45. Recipient Avery Hopwood award in Poetry, 1939; Blumenthal prize Poetry mag., 1944; Eunice Tietjens award, 1945; Levinson prize, 1947; Harriet Monroe Meml. award, 1955; Prix de Rome; Am. Acad. Arts and Letters, 1956. Fellow Am. Acad. Arts and Scis., Nat. Inst. Arts and Letters; mem. Nat. Coll. English Assn. (dir. 1955-57, pres. 1958-59), N.E. Coll. English Assn, past dir.), Phi Beta Kappa. 725 Windsor Lane Key West FL 33040 359 Middlesex Ave Methuchen NJ 08840 *There is no success. There is only engagement. Any man who believes he has succeeded has settled for a limited engagement. At any time in one's life there is only the process of engaging more fully. If there is achievement, it is to put by. Achievement is only what brings into view the next thing to be engaged. Stop that process of engagement and the man is stopped dead. Let him go on breathing: he is dead.* *

CICCONI, JAMES W., presidental assistant. J.D., U. Tex. Issues coordinator James A. Baker, Ill, campaign for atty. gen. Tex., 1978; adminstrv. asst. to gov. Tex., 1979-80; gen. counsel to sec. of state Tex., 1980-81; spl. asst. to Pres., Washington, 1981—; asst. to chief of staff, Washington, 1981—. Republican. Office: Office of Chief of Staff 1600 Pennsylvania Ave NW Washington DC 20500 *

CICERO, CARMEN LOUIS, artist, educator; b. Newark, N.J., Aug. 14, 1926; s. Carmen and Mae C.; m. Carol Baldwin. B.S. in Fine Arts Edn., Newark State Coll., 1951; postgrad., Hunter Coll., N.Y.C., 1953. Tchr. elem. sch., Paterson, N.J., 1951-54, tchr. secondary sch., Roselle Park, N.J., 1954-57; prof. Sarah Lawrence Coll., Bronxville, N.Y., 1959-68, Montclair Coll., N.J., 1969—. Exhibited various one-man shows, New Orleans, 1969-71, N.Y.C., 1971-74, 1982, Los Angeles, 1978, Provincetown, Mass., 1979, 81, groups shows, Rome-N.Y. Art Found., Premiere Bienale De Paris, France, Mus. des 20 Jahrunderts, Austria, Roosevelt House, New Delhi, N.Y. World's Fair; represented in permanent collections, Guggenheim Mus., N.Y.C., Mus. Modern Art, N.Y.C., N.J. State Mus., Trenton, Worcester Mus., Mass., Whitney Mus. Am. Art, N.Y.C., Art Gallery of Toronto, Can., Newark Mus., Larry Aldrich Mus., Conn., Mus. Boymaus Van Beuningen, Holland, Hirschhorn Mus., Washington, Neuberger Mus., Purchase, N.Y., Exeter Acad., N.H., Cornell U., Springfield Mus., Mass., Mint. Mus., Charlotte, N.C. Guggenheim fellow, 1957, 63. *

CICIRELLI, VICTOR GEORGE, psychologist; b. Miami, Fla., Oct. 1, 1926; s. Felix and Rene (DeMaria) C.; m. Jean Alice Solveson, Aug. 9, 1954; children: Ann Victoria, Michael Felix, Gregory Sheldon. B.S., Notre Dame U., 1947; M.A., U. Ill., Urbana, 1950; M.Ed., U. Miami, 1956; Ph.D. (Univ. fellow), U. Mich., 1964, Mich. State U., 1971. Asst. prof. ednl. psychology U. Mich., 1963-65; dir. student teaching for elem., secondary and M.A.T. programs U. Pa., 1965-67; assoc. prof. early childhood edn. Ohio U., 1967-68; dir. research Nat. Evaluation of Head Start Westinghouse Learning Corp. at Ohio U., 1968-69; Office Edn. postdoctoral fellow U. Wis. Inst. Cognitive Learning, 1969-70; prof. human devel. Purdue U., 1970-73, prof. devel./aging psychology, 1974—, dir. devel. psychology program, 1977-78, 80-81, 82-83; cons. in field; mem. research adv. bd. Calif. Commn. for Tchr. Preparation and Licensing, 1973-78; scholar NSF Inst., Ohio U., 1956, Am. U., 1958, U. Fla., 1960; Gerontology Soc. fellow, summer 1983. Author: Helping Elderly Parents: Role of Adult Children, 1981; Contbr. numerous articles to profl. publs. OEO grantee, 1968-69, 71-73; U.S. Office Edn. grantee, 1971-73; Nat. Inst. Edn. grantee, 1973-74; NIH grantee, 1973-74; Office Child Devel. grantee, 1973-74; Nat. Ret. Tchrs. Assn./Am. Assn. Ret. Persons Andrus Found. grantee, 1978-82. Fellow Am. Psychol. Assn.; mem. Gerontol. Soc., Am. Ednl. Research Assn., Soc. Research in Child Devel., Phi Kappa Phi. Roman Catholic. Home: 1221 N Salisbury St West Lafayette IN 47906 Office: Purdue U Dept Psychol Sci West Lafayette IN 47907

CIELEWICH, DONALD EUGENE, banker; b. Medina, N.Y., Feb. 4, 1923; s. John W. and Mary (Crowley) C.; m. Ruth M. Feltz, Nov. 25, 1947; children: Scott Paul, Donald Eugene. Degree comml. banking, Rutgers U., 1958. With Marine Midland Bank-Western, Buffalo, 1946—, v.p., asst. to sr. v.p., 1961-64, v.p., asst. sr. loan officer, 1964-68, sr. v.p. charge retail banking depts., 1968-72, exec. v.p., 1972—, Marine Midland Banks, Inc., 1976; regional pres. Marine Midland Bank-Western, 1976-77, also chmn. exec. bd., 1976-77; chmn. bd., pres. Girard Bank of Del. N.A. (Subs. Mellon Nat. Corp.), Wilmington, 1977-80; chmn., chief exec. officer Farmers Bank of Del., 1980—; pres., chief exec. officer Marine Midland Bank (Del.), 1984—; dir., mem. exec. com. Niagara Frontier Housing Devel. Corp., to 1977; dir. Interbank Card Assn.; faculty Consumer Bankers Sch., U. Va., 1966-76. Treas. N.Y. State fin. com. Am. Cancer Soc., 1972-77, bd. dirs. N.Y. State fin. com., Wilmington, 1977—, chmn. bd. Del. div., 1983-84; bd. dirs., unit rep. Assembly Erie County, 1972-77; mem. citizens adv. group Assembly Subcom. on Econ. Devel. N.Y. State, 1970-77; pres. Western N.Y. Traffic Safety Council; mem. Erie County Traffic Safety Bd., 1972-77; trustee Trocaire Coll., Greater Buffalo Devel. Found., 1976-77, Buffalo Found., 1976—; bd. dirs. Del. div. Boy Scouts Am., 1977—; mem. Bishop's Catholic Appeal, 1977—; vice-chmn. United Way campaign, 1980, chmn., 1983-84; bd. dirs. Blue Cross/Blue Shield Del., 1982; mem. adv. bd. NCCJ, 1984; mem. Gov.'s Task Force on Edn. for Econ. Growth. Served to 1st lt. USAAF, 1942-45; ETO. Home: 3803 Ardleigh Dr Wilmington DE 19807 Office: 824 Market S Mall Excelsior Centre Wilmington DE 19801

CIERESZKO, LEON STANLEY, chemistry educator; b. Holyoke, Mass., July 31, 1917; s. Albert Wojciech and Valerie Ann (Keller) C.; m. Esther Wynona Martin, May 1, 1943; 1 son, Leon Stanley. B.S. in Chemistry magna cum laude, Mass. State Coll., 1939; Ph.D. in Physiol. Chemistry, Yale, 1942. Research biochemist med.-research div. Sharp & Dohme, 1942-45; instr. biol. chemistry U. Utah Sch. Medicine, 1945-46; instr. chemistry U. Ill., 1946-48; mem. faculty U. Okla., Norman, 1948—, prof. physics, 1956—, chmn. dept. chemistry, 1969-70; research participant Oak Ridge Inst. for Nuclear Studies, 1951-52; vis. research asso. Brookhaven Nat. Lab., summmer 1953; ofcl. participant U.S. Program in Biology, Internat. Indian Ocean Expdn., 1963; cons. prof. U. Okla. Health Scis. Center, 1967-79; vis. research prof. Coll. V.I., 1971; vis. prof. marine scis. Port Aransas Marine Lab. U. Tex., summer 1978; mem. Nat. Acad. Scis. exchange program with Council of Acads. Yugoslavia, 1978; vis. investigator various marine labs. Lalor fellow Marine Biol. Lab., Woods Hole, Mass., 1951, 52; Fulbright fellow Stazione Zoologica, Naples, Italy, 1955-56; recipient Regents' award U. Okla., 1967. Fellow AAAS, Explorers Club; mem. Am. Chem. Soc., Geochem. Soc., Sigma Xi, Phi Kappa Phi, Phi Sigma, Lambda Tau, Phi Lambda Upsilon. Research and publs. in comparative biochemistry of marine invertebrates, chemistry of coelenterates, biogeochemistry of coral reefs. Home: 639 S Lahoma Ave Norman OK 73069

CIFELLI, JOHN LOUIS, lawyer; b. Chicago Heights, Ill., Aug. 19, 1923; s. Antonio and Domenica (Liberatore) C.; m. Irene Romandine, Jan. 4, 1948; children—Carla, David, John L., Bruce, Thomas, Carol. Student, Bowdoin Coll., 1943, Norwick Mil. Acad., 1943, Mt. Piliar Acad., 1943, U. Ill. Extension Center, 1946-47; LL.B., DePaul U., 1950; J.D. (hon.), DePaul U., 1975. Bar: Ill. bar 1950, U.S. Supreme Ct. bar 1960. Partner firm Piacenti, Cifelli & Sims and (predecessor firms), Chicago Heights, 1950—; spl. counsel City of Chicago Heights, 1961-72; village atty. Village of Richton Park, Ill., 1962-77; counsel Maj. League Umpires Assn., 1973—, Ill. High Sch. Baseball Coaches Assn., 1975—. Sec. Bd. Fire and Police, Chicago Heights, 1959-65; co-founder Small Fry Internat. Basketball, 1969, pres., 1969—; coach, baseball coordinator Chicago Heights Park Dist., 1970-75; coach Babe Ruth League Baseball, 1972, 74, 75, asst. Ill. dir., 1973; dir. Ill. tournament, 1973. Served to 2d lt. USAAF, 1942-45; ETO. Mem. Ill. State, Am., South Suburban bar assns., Ill. Trial Lawyers Assn., Assn. Trial Lawyers Am., Am. Soc. Ecol. Edn., Justinian Soc. Lawyers, Am. Judicature Soc., Roscoe Pound/Am. Trial Lawyers Found., Chicago Heights C. of C., DePaul U. Devel. Program, Isaac Walton League, Italo Am. Vets. Group, VFW (judge adv. 1951-72), Cath. War Vets. (judge adv. 1951-70), Am. Legion, Delta Theta Phi. Clubs: Chicago Heights Country, Pike Lake Fishing and Gun, U. N.Mex. Lobo, Moose, DeMolay. Home: 879 D'Amico Dr Chicago Heights IL 60411 Office: 450 W 14th St Chicago Heights IL 60411

CIKOVSKY, NICOLAI, JR., curator, art history educator; b. N.Y.C., Feb. 11, 1933; s. Nicolai and Hortense (Hilbert) C.; m. Sarah Eden Greenough, June 17, 1978; 1 dau., Emily Hilbert. A.B. magna cum laude, Harvard Coll., 1955; A.M., Harvard U., 1958, Ph.D., 1965. Asst. prof. Skidmore Coll., Saratoga Springs, N.Y., 1961-63; chmn., assoc. prof. Pomona Coll., Claremont, Calif., 1964-68; vis. assoc. prof. U. Tex., Austin, 1969-70; dir. art gallery, assoc. prof. Vassar Coll., Poughkeepsie, N.Y., 1971-74; prof., chmn. dept. art U. N.Mex., Albuquerque, 1974-83; curator Am. art Nat. Gallery Art, Washington, 1983—. Author: Sanford Robinson Gifford; editor Lectures on the Affinity of Painting with the Other Fine Arts (Samuel F.B. Morse), 1983; exhbn. catalogue, 1970, George Inness, 1971, The Life and Work of George Inness, 1977; also articles on William Merritt Chase, George Inness, Winslow Homer, Am. landscape painting. Am. Council Learned Socs.-Smithsonian Instn. postdoctoral research fellow, 1968-69; Guggenheim fellow, 1978-79; Kress sr. fellow Nat. Gallery Art, 1983. Mem. Coll. Art Assn., Phi Beta Kappa. Club: Harvard (N.Y.C.). Office: Nat Gallery Art Washington DC 20565

CIMINO, JAMES ERNEST, physician; b. N.Y.C., July 7, 1928; s. Ernest S. and Rose (Gorga) C.; m. Dorothy Hilary Naperkoski, June 5, 1954; children: James, Ernest, Christopher, Peter, Paul, Maria. Student, Syracuse U., 1946-48; A.B., N.Y. U., 1950, M.D., 1954. Diplomate: Am. Bd. Internal Medicine. Intern, resident E.J. Meyer Meml. Hosp., Buffalo, 1954-58; research fellow physiology U. Buffalo, 1957-58; practice medicine specializing in internal medicine; dir. renal service Bronx VA Hosp., 1960-68; chief medicine, me, dir. Calvary Hosp., 1963-80, attending, 1961—; cons. medicine St. Joseph's Hosp., Yonkers, N.Y., Holy Name Hosp., Teaneck, N.J., VA Hosp., Bronx, N.Y., 1970-77, dir. hemodialysis unit, 1960-70; asst. clin. prof. medicine Mt. Sinai Sch. Medicine, N.Y.C., 1970-73; now clin. prof. medicine N.Y. Med. Coll.; adj. prof., cons. nutrition NYU; cons. internal medicine N.Y.C. Dept. Health, 1971-74; also chmn. com. advanced cancer, 1971-74; mem. instl. biohazards com. Albert Einstein Coll. Medicine. Editorial bd., N.Y. Med. Quar.; contbr. articles to med. jours. Bd. dirs. Bronx chpt. Am. Cancer Soc.; mem. med.-moral ethical bd. Archdiocese of N.Y. Served with USAF, 1958-60. Recipient commendation VA, 1968, Dialysis Pioneering award Nat. Kidney Disease Found., 1982—; Ann. Merit award N.Y.C. Public Health Assn., 1979; 1st ann. Catherine McParlan Humanitarian award, 1980; co-recipient Good Samaritan award Nat. Cath. Devel. Conf., 1981—. Fellow ACP; mem. AMA, N.Y. Acad. Scis., Am. Heart Assn., Internat. Soc. Nephrology, Am. Soc. Nephrology. Office: 1740-70 Eastchester Rd Bronx NY 10461

CIMINO, JOSEPH ANTHONY, educator, physician; b. N.Y.C., Jan. 1, 1934; m. Peggy; 7 children. B.A. in Am. History, Harvard U., 1956, M.I.H., 1964, M.P.H., 1965; M.S. in Biology, Fordham U., 1958; M.D., U. Buffalo, 1962. Diplomate: Am. Bd. Preventive Medicine. Intern Grasslands Hosp., Valhalla, N.Y., 1962-63; AEC fellow in environ. medicine Harvard U. Sch. Public Health, 1963-65; research asso., health officer N.Y.C. Dept. Health, 1965-66; dir. Bur. Community Safety and Occupational Health, 1968-71, dep. commr. health, 1971-72, commr. health, 1972-74; chief med. officer N.Y.C. Dept. Sanitation, 1966-69; med. dir. N.Y.C. Poison Control Center, 1966-72; dir. health and safety N.Y.C. Environ. Protection

Adminstrn., 1968-71; commr. hosps. Westchester County, N.Y., 1974-78; pres., chief exec. officer N.Y. Med. Coll., 1978-81, clin. prof. preventive medicine, 1976—, chmn. dept. preventive medicine, 1980—; asso. prof. environ. medicine and public health N.Y. U., 1971-76; prof. community dynamics Pace U., 1977-78; adj. prof. public health and tropical medicine Tulane U., 1972-76; lectr. in public health Columbia U., 1973-76; vis. prof. community health Albert Einstein Coll. Medicine, 1973-76; bd. govs. Greater N.Y. Hosp. Assn.; pres. bd. Dominican Sisters Family Health Services, Inc.; bd. dirs. Westchester Artificial Kidney Center, N.Y. State Environ. Facilities Corp., Westchester Cancer Soc. Author: Safety: Protection from Injury, 1969, Medical Service Manual, 1971, Drug Abuse Treatment Agencies in New York City, 1972; author numerous profl. monographs; contbr. articles to profl. publs. Mem. Westchester Community Services Council; chmn. Catholic Interracial Council of Westchester County; mem. med. adv. com. Westchester Rockland-Putnam chpt. March of Dimes; mem. adv. council Grad. Sch. Social Service, Fordham U., Tarrytown, N.Y.; chief med. cons. N.Y.C. CSC, 1966-71. Served with M.C. U.S. Army, 1964-65. Fellow Am. Coll. Preventive Medicine; mem. Human Factors Soc., Am. Public Health Assn., N.Y.C. Public Health Assn., Indsl. Med. Assn., Assn. Govtl. Hygienists, Aerospace Med. Assn., Westchester County Med. Soc., N.Y. State Med. Assn., AMA, Westchester Heart Assn. Home: 50 Willard Ave North Tarrytown NY 10591 Office: NY Med Coll Valhalla NY 10595

CIMINO, MICHAEL, film director, writer; b. N.Y.C., 1948. Screenwriter: Silent Running, 1972, Magnum Force, 1973; screenwriter, dir.: Thunderbolt and Lightfoot, 1974; producer, writer, dir.: The Deer Hunter, 1978 (Acad. awards Best Dir. and Best Producer); writer, dir.: Heaven's Gate, 1980. Office: care Internat Creative Mgmt 8899 Beverly Blvd Beverly Hills CA 90048

CINADER, BERNHARD, scientist, immunologist, educator; b. Vienna, Austria, Mar. 30, 1919; s. Leon and Adele (Schwarz) C.; 1 dau., Agatha. B.Sc., U. London, 1945, Ph.D., 1948, D.Sc., 1958. Research asst. Jenner Meml. student Lister Inst. Preventive Medicine, London, 1945-46, Beit Meml. fellow, 1949-53; fellow immunochemistry Inst. Pathology, Western Res. U., Cleve., 1948-49; prin. sci. officer, dept. exptl. pathology Inst. Animal Physiology, Babraham Hall, Cambridge; also hon. lectr. biochemistry dept. U. Coll., London, 1955-58; head subdiv. immunochemistry, div. biol. research Ont. (Can.) Cancer Inst., Toronto, 1958-69; assoc. prof. depts. med. biophysics and pathol. chemistry U. Toronto, 1958-67, prof. dept. med. biophysics, 1967—, prof. dept. med. cell biology, 1969—; dir. Inst. Immunology, 1971-81; mem. governing body U. Toronto, 1980—; vis. prof. U. Man., 1967, U. Alta., 1968, U. Sask, 1970, U. Western Ont., 1972, U. Bombay, 1981; chmn. immunology con. Biol. Council Can., 1967—; mem. WHO Expert Adv. Panel on Immunology, 1970—; chmn. adv. bd. Internat. Immunology Tng. and Research Center, Amsterdam, 1975-80; mem. adv. bd. dept. basic and clin. immunology Med. U. S.C., 1974; mem. adv. bd. Research in Immunology and Immunobiology, 1972-74; chmn. nomenclature com. WHO/Internat. Union Immunol. Socs., 1980—; lectr. numerous instns., profl. meetings, confs. and seminars. Editor: Antibody to Enzymes - A Three Component System, 1964, Antibodies to Biologically Active Molecules, 1967, Regulation of the Antibody Response, 1968, Immunological Response of the Female Reproductive Tract, 1976, Immunology of Receptors, 1976-77; Series editor: Receptors and Ligands in Intercellular Communication, 1983—; editorial bd.: Immunochemistry, 1965-70; editorial bd. Immunology, Serology, Transplantation sect., Excerpta Medica Found., 1966—; editorial bd.: Can. Jour. Biochemistry, 1967-71, Immunol. Methods, 1970-74, Bolletino dell-istituto sieroterapico Milanese, 1972—, Immunol. Communication, 1973—, Jour. Immunogenetics, 1973—, Immunology Letters, 1978—, Jour. Receptor Research, 1979—, Asian Pacific Jour. Allergy and Immunology, 1983—; contbr. articles to numerous profl. publs.; also catalogues and articles on Canadian Indian art. Recipient Old Student prize, London, 1944; medal Société de Chimie Biologique, Paris, 1954; Pfizer fellow Institut de Recherches Cliniques de Montreal, 1972; Jubilee medal, Ottawa, 1977; Ignác Semmelweis medal, Budapest, 1978. Fellow Royal Inst. Chemistry (U.K.), Royal Soc. Can. (Thomas W. Eadie medal 1982), N.Y. Acad. Scis.; mem. Internat. Union Immunol. Socs. (chmn. 1970—, pres. 1969-74), Can. Soc. Immunology (pres. 1967-69, 79-81), Nat. Com. Immunology (chmn. 1981—), Can. Fedn. Biol. Socs. (chmn. 1976-77), Internat. Council of Sci. Unions (mem. council and assembly 1980—). Home: 73 Langley Ave Toronto ON M4K 1B4 Canada Office: Inst Immunology Rm 4366 Med Scis Bldg U Toronto Toronto ON M5S 1A8 Canada

CIOFFI, LOUIS JAMES, news corr.; b. N.Y.C., Apr. 30, 1926; s. Louis and Lucy (Migliori) C.; m. Naomi Waki, Apr. 7, 1954; children: Louis George, Marc James. Student, CCNY, 1942-43, Muhlenberg Coll., Allentown, Pa., 1943-44. Copy boy, writer, editor CBS News, 1947-52, war corr., Korea, Paris corr., 1952-61; chief European corr.; Far East corr. ABC News, 1961-65; fgn. corr. German Bur., Paris Bur., 1965-77, UN Bur. chief, N.Y.C., 1977—. Served with USN, 1943-46. Decorated Purple Heart; recipient Overseas Press Club awards for radio and television news coverage, 1970, 74, Nat. Headliners Club award, 1970, Emmy award for news and documentary, 1980-81. Mem. UN Corrs. Assn., Assn. Radio and Television News Analysts, AFTRA, White House Corrs. Assn., Soc. Profl. Journalists, Sigma Delta Chi. Office: Satellite News Channel 1111 18th St NW Washington DC 20036 *Everyone has to realize early that it's the striving that's important. The fortunate ones are those who realize their own mountain to climb. The unfortunate ones get to the top without ever knowing why or how they got there.*

CION, RICHARD M., lawyer; b. Hartford, Conn., July 27, 1943; s. Irving and Anne (Miller) C.; 1 dau., Stephanie Lee. A.B., Princeton U., 1965; LL.B., Harvard U., 1968. Assoc., ptnr. Kaye, Scholer, Fierman, Hays & Handler, N.Y.C., 1968-81; v.p., gen. counsel Condec Corp., Old Greenwich, Conn., 1981-82, v.p. fin. and legal affairs, 1982—, dir., 1983—. Mem. ABA, N.Y. State Bar Assn., Assn. Bar City N.Y. Home: 1520 York Ave Apt 27B New York NY 10028 Office: Condec Corp 1700 E Putnam Ave Old Greenwich CT 06870

CIOTTI, EUGENE BARNEY, paper packaging company executive; b. Wierton, W. Va., July 9, 1928; s. Sirio Dante and Jennie (Principini) C.; m. Mary Jane Robertson, Sept. 3, 1955; children: Mary Carol, Robert Barney. Student, Lincoln Meml. U., Harrogate, Tenn., 1949-50; B.S., Ind. U., 1955. Plant gen. mgr. Inland Container Corp., Louisville, 1966-70, civ. v.p., mgr., Indpls., 1970-75, v.p. mfg., 1975-77, sr. v.p., 1980—; pres. Anderson Box Co., Indpls., 1977—. Served with USMC, 1946-48, 50-52. Republican. Roman Catholic. Clubs: Woodland Country (Carmel, Ind.); Racquet. Home: 3710 Brian Pl Carmel IN 46032 Office: Anderson Box Co PO Box 1851 Indianapolis IN 46206

CIPLIJAUSKAITE, BIRUTE, humanities educator; b. Kaunas, Lithuania, Apr. 11, 1929; came to U.S., 1961; d. Juozas and Elena (Stelmokaite) C. B.A., Lycee Lithuanien Tubingen, 1947; M.A., U. Montreal, 1956; Ph.D., Bryn Mawr Coll., 1960. Permanent mem. Inst. Research in Humanities U. Wis., Madison, 1974, asst. prof., 1961-65, assoc. prof., 1965-68, prof., 1968-73, fJohn Bascom prof. Inst. for Research in Humanities, 1973—. Author: El poeta y la poesia, 1966, Baroja, un estilo, 1972, Los noventayochistas y la historia, 1981, La mujer insatisfecha, 1984; editor: Lusi de Gongora, Sonetos. Guggenheim fellow, 1968. Mem. Assn. For Advancement Baltic Studies (v.p. 1981). Office: Inst for Research in Humanities U Wis Madison WI 53706

CIPRIANI, FRANK ANTHONY, college president; b. N.Y.C., Sept. 28, 1933; s. Domenico and Maria (DiGiesi) C.; m. Judith Pellathay, Aug. 9, 1959; children: Maria, Frank, Michael, Dominique. A.B. in Polit. Sci., Queens Coll., 1955; M.A. in Edn., NYU, 1961, Ph.D., 1969. Adminstrv. asst. to v.p. bus. affairs NYU, 1961-64; prof. history SUNY Coll., Farmingdale, 1964; asst. dean Evening Coll., 1964-67, asst. to pres., 1966-69, v.p. adminstrn., 1969-78, pres., 1978—; chmn. L.I. Regional Adv. Council on Higher Edn. Chmn. bd. dirs. Regional Indsl. Tech. Edn. Council. Served to capt. USAF, 1955-57. Mem. Middle States Assn. Colls. and Secondary Schs. Roman Catholic. Office: SUNY Melville Rd Farmingdale NY 11735

CIPULLO, ALDO MASSIMO FABRIZIO, jewelry designer; b. Naples, Italy, Nov. 18, 1938; came to U.S., 1959, naturalized, 1966; s. Giuseppe and Italia (D'Alessio) C.; m. Patricia McMahon, Apr. 10, 1961. Student, U. Florence, 1956-59. Designer David Webb, N.Y.C., 1961-63, Tiffany, 1963-69, Cartier, 1969-74; jewelry designer, N.Y.C., 1974—; lectr. Fashion Inst. Tech. Served with Italian Air Force, 1955-56. Recipient Pearl award, 1971, Coty award, 1974; winner Diamonds Today Competition, 1977. Club: N.Y. Athletic. Commd. to design 1st N.Am. gemstone jewelry collection Smithsonian Instn. permanent collection, 1978. *Designing for me is a continuous process...in flight, at the theatre, on the street. The world is my workroom and I use my surroundings to the utmost. The most important concept to keep in mind is always to reflect the present in designs that endure.*

CIRCUIT, HAROLD THEODORE, soft drink company executive; b. Tampico, Mex., July 31, 1924; s. Harold and Emma (Rivers) C.; m. Yvette Delagrave, Dec. 19, 1948; children: Michael, Alexander, Monica, Jacqueline. B.S., Syracuse U., N.Y., 1948; postgrad., Harvard U. Bus. Sch. Field rep. Latin Am., Pepsico, 1948-50; from asst. sales mgr. to gen. mgr. Pepsico Bottling Co., Mexico City, 1950-56; mgr. Mexico City br. United Shoe Machinery Co., Boston, 1957-62; mgr. for Mex., N. Latin Am. Coca-Cola Co., 1962-81; pres. Coca-Cola, Latin Am., Mexico City, 1981—; pres. Coca-Cola Bottling Co., P.R. Dir. Profl. Soccer Club, Mexico City.; Bd. dirs. Mexican Govt. Tourist Bur., 1972-78. Served with RCAF, 1943-45. Recipient Hon. award Fedn. Internat. Football Assn., 1970. Mem. Brit. Ex-Service Assn., Am. Benevolent Soc. Clubs: Univ., Chapultepec Golf (Mexico City). Home: 285 Saratoga St Mexico City 10 DF Mexico Home: 3530 Piedmont Rd Atlanta GA 30305 Office: 43 Amazonas Mexico City 5 DF Mexico Office: PO Drawer 1734 Atlanta GA 30301

CIRE, GEORGE EDWARD, U.S. dist. judge; b. Houston, Sept. 29, 1922; s. Jorda Michael and Ida Marie (Melancon) C.; m. Mary Margaret Scott, July 12, 1954; children—Scott Edward, George Edward, Mary Margaret Cire Hicks, Stephen Edward, Jennifer Elizabeth. B.S. in Commerce, St. Edward's U., Austin, Tex., 1946; LL.B., U. Tex., Austin, 1948. Bar: Tex. bar 1948. Partner firm Cire & Jamail, Houston, 1956-64; judge 165th Dist. Ct. Tex., 1964-76, 14th Ct. Civil Appeals Tex., 1976-79; U.S. dist. judge So. Dist. Tex., 1979—. Servedto capt. USMCR, 1943-46, 50-52. Decorated Silver Star, Purple Heart. Mem. State Bar Tex. (chmn. dist. grievance com. 1958), Houston Bar Assn., Phi Delta Phi. Democrat. Roman Catholic. Address: 515 Rusk St Houston TX 77002

CIRIACY, EDWARD WALTER, physician, educator; b. Phila., Feb. 12, 1924; s. William Frederick and Elizabeth Jane (McGettigan) C.; m. Adele L4rge Wallis, Sept. 9, 1942; children—Adele, Edward, Walter, Deborah, Melissa Jane, Timothy. B.S., Pa. State Coll., 1948; M.D., Temple U., 1952. Diplomate: Nat. Bd. Med. Examiners, Am. Bd. Family Practice (chmn. recertification com. 1972-76). Intern Frankford Hosp., Phila., 1952-53, surg. resident, 1953-54, Temple Hosp., Phila., 1953-54; practice medicine specializing in family practice, Ely, Minn., 1954-57, 58-71, Miami, Fla., 1957-58; mem. staffs Ely-Bloomenson Community Hosp.; prof. U. Minn., 1971—, chmn. dept. family practice, 1971—; Mem. adv. panel for subcom. on patient care Cancer Coordinating Com. for Health Scis. Contbr. articles to med. jours. Served with USAAF, 1944-46. Recipient Merit award Minn. Acad. Gen. Practice, 1963. Fellow Am. Acad. Family Physicians (charter); mem. Minn. Acad. Family Physicians (pres. 1975—), Minn. Med. Assn. (mem. com. med. services 1970—), Range Med. Soc. (pres. 1961), Babcock Surg. Soc., Assn. Am. Med. Colls., Alpha Omega Alpha. Club: Mason. Home: 17 E Beacon Hill Rd Ely MN 55731 Office: Phillip Wagensteen Bldg U Minn Minneapolis MN 55455

CIRKER, HAYWARD, publisher; b. N.Y.C., June 1, 1917; s. Solomon and Sadie (Goodman) C.; m. Blanche Brodsky, Aug. 11, 1939; children—Steven, Victoria Cirker Fremont. B.S. in Social Studies, Coll. City N.Y., 1936. Salesman Crown Pubs., N.Y.C., 1936-43; pres. Dover Publs. Inc., N.Y.C., 1943—. Served with USNR, 1945. Home: 199 Woodside Dr PO Box 53 Hewlett NY 11557 Office: 180 Varick St New York NY 10014

CIRUTI, JOAN ESTELLE, educator; b. Ponchatouia, La., Aug. 8, 1930; d. Joseph Aloysius and Olga (Jordan) C. B.A., Southeastern La. Coll., 1950; M.A., U. Okla, 1954; Ph.D., Tulane U., 1959. Instr. modern langs U. Okla., Norman, 1957-59; asst. prof. U. Okla, Norman, 1959-63; research asst. U.S. Office Edn., Washington, 1959-60; asst. prof. Spanish Mt. Holyoke Coll., South Hadley, Mass., 1963-66; assoc. prof. Mt Holyoke Coll., South Hadley, Mass., 1966-71; chmn. dept. Spanish Mt. Holyoke Coll., South Hadley, Mass., 1965-71, prof., 1971—, Helen Day Gould prof. Spanish, South Hadley, Mass., 1977—, dean studies, 1971-74, chmn. dept, Spanish and Italian, 1975-81; cons. Ednl. Testing Service, 1968-79. Co-author: Modern Spanish, 2d edit., 1966, Continuing Spanish, 1967; contbg. editor, Handbook of Latin-American Studies, vol. 28, 1966, Handbook of Latin-American Studies vol. 30, 1968, Handbook of Latin-American Studies, vol. 32, 1970. Named Disting. Alumnus Southeastern La. Coll., 1973. Mem. Am. Council on Teaching Fgn. Langs., MLA (nomination adv. com. 1962-64, nominating com. 1979-80, acad. freedom com. 1980-83), Latin Am. Studies Assn. (mem. steering com. consortium Latin Am. studies program 1969-72, com. on women 1973-74, nominating com. 1975), New Eng. Modern Lang. Assn., Am. Assn. Tchrs. Spanish and Portuguese, AAUW, Phi Sigma Iota. Home: 21 Jewett Ln South Hadley MA 01075 Office: Mt. Holyoke Coll Dept Spanish and Italian South Hadley MA 01075

CISLER, WALKER LEE, consultant; b. Marietta, Ohio, Oct. 8, 1897; s. Louis H. and Sara S. (Walker) C.; m. Gertrude Demuth Rippe, July 28, 1939 (dec. 1975); adopted children: Richard Rippe, Jane Rippe Cisler Eckhardt. M.E., Cornell U., 1922; Eng.D., U. Mich., Stevens Inst. Tech., S.D. Sch. Mines and Tech.; LL.D., U. Detroit, Wayne State U., Marietta Coll., U. Akron, No. Mich. U., Mich. State U., Detroit Coll. Law; D.Sc., U. Toledo, Ind. Tech. Coll., Mich. Technol. U.; L.H.D., Shaw Coll., Detroit; D.Econs., Tan Kook U., Korea; D.Pub. Service, Detroit Inst. Tech.; H.H.D., Lawrence Inst. Tech. Various engring. positions Pub. Service Electric & Gas Co., Newark, 1922-41; with WPB, Washington, 1941-43; chief public utility sect. SHAEF, 1944; chief engr. power plants Detroit Edison Co., 1945-47, exec. v.p., 1948-51, pres., 1951-64, chmn. bd., 1964-75; also dir.; chmn. exec. com. of bd. Freuhauf Corp.; chmn. Overseas Adv. Assocs., Inc. Mem. Bus. Council; chmn. Thomas Alva Edison Found.; hon. chmn. internat. exec. council World Energy Conf.; mem. Nat. Acad. Scis.-Nat. Acad. Engring.; trustee emeritus Cornell U., Cranbrook Inst. Sci., Marietta Coll.; hon. trustee Atomic Indsl. Forum. Served to col. AUS, 1943-45. Decorated by several fgn. govts., U.S.; recipient Henry Lawrence Gantt Gold medal ASME, AMA, 1955; Washington award W. Soc. Engrs., 1957; Hoover medal Engring. Founders Soc., 1962; John Fritz medal, 1967; William Metcalf award Engring. Soc. Western Pa., 1963. Fellow IEEE (Edison medal 1965), ASME (pres. 1960, hon. mem., George Westinghouse Gold medal 1954), Am. Inst. Mgmt., Engring. Soc. Detroit, Am. Ordnance Assn., Soc. Am. Mil. Engrs. (pres. 1961, George W. Goethals award 1958), Edison Electric Inst. (pres. 1964), Engrs. Joint Council (pres. 1964), Newcomen Soc. N.Am. (hon. chmn. Mich. chpt.). Clubs: Detroit, Detroit Econ. (chmn. 1954-74), Country, Athletic (Detroit); Met. (Washington); Engrs., Univ., Cornell, Brook (N.Y.C.). Home: 1071 Devonshire Rd Grosse Pointe Park MI 48230 Office: 3000 Book Bldg Detroit MI 48226 *It is possible to share the experience that we all have together in making energy available and then in utilizing that energy well.*

CISNEROS, HENRY G., mayor, educator; b. San Antonio, June 11, 1947; s. J. George and Elvira (Munguia) C.; m. Mary Alice Perez; children: Teresa Angelica, Mercedes Christina. B.A., Tex. A&M U., 1969, M. Urban and Regional Planning, 1970; M.P.A., Harvard U., 1973; D.Public Adminstrn., George Washington U., 1975. Adminstrv. asst. to city mgr., San Antonio, 1968, Bryan, Tex., 1968, asst. dir. dept. model cities, San Antonio, 1969-70; asst. to exec. v.p. Nat. League Cities, Washington, 1970-71; White House fellow asst. Sec. of HEW, Washington, 1971-72; teaching asst. dept. urban studies and planning M.I.T., 1972; mem. faculty div. environ. studies U. Tex., San Antonio, 1974—, asst. prof., 1974—; mem. City Council, San Antonio, 1975-81; mayor City of San Antonio, 1981—. Trustee City Pub. Service Bd., City Water Bd., San Antonio; chmn. Fire and Police Pension Fund, San Antonio; mem. strategy council Nat. Democratic Party; mem. Twentieth Century Fund Ednl. Task Force, Eisenhower Found., com. on visual arts Tex. A & M U., bus. adv. com. Trinity U.; tri-chmn. United San Antonio; bd. dirs. San Antonio Symphony Soc., 1974-75. Office: Office of the Mayor PO Box 9066 San Antonio TX 78285

CISSELL, JAMES CHARLES, lawyer; b. Cleve., May 29, 1940; s. Robert Francis and Helen Cecelia (Freeman) C.; m. Carol Javana Justes, Sept. 7, 1964; children: Denise, Helen-Marie, Suzanne, James. A.B., Xavier U., 1962; postgrad., Sophia U., Tokyo, summer 1961; J.D., U. Cin., 1966, Ohio State U., 1973-74; hon. degree, Cin. Tech. Coll., 1979. Bar: Ohio bar 1966. Practice law, 1966-78; U.S. atty. So. Dist. Ohio, Cin., 1978-82; first v.p. Cin. Bd. Park Commrs., 1973-74; mem. council City of Cin., 1974-78, vice mayor, 1976-77; mem. Cin. Recreation Commn., 1974, Cin. Planning Commn., 1977. Editor, contbr.: Proving Federal Crimes; author: Federal Criminal Trials. Mem. Am. Bar Assn., Ohio Bar Assn., Cin. Bar Assn., Fed. Bar Assn., Lawyers Club Cin. Home: 45 Rawson Woods Circle Cincinnati OH 45220 Office: 505 Gwynne Bldg Cincinnati OH 45202

CITRIN, MARTIN EARLE, real estate and investment company executive; b. Detroit, Nov. 16, 1928; s. Jacob Abraham and Matilda (Beiner) C.; m. Myra Arons, Nov. 3, 1968; children: Alise, Michael, Jacob, Samantha. Student, Wayne State U. Pres. Citrin Oil Co., Detroit, 1966-70; ptnr. J.A. Citrin Sons Co., Detroit, 1970—; dir. Total Petroleum Denver, Allied Supermarkets Inc.; mem. nat. adv. bd. SBA, 1968. Pres. Nat. Oil Jobbers Council, Washington, 1966, Council Jewish Fedns., N.Y.C., 1982-83. Recipient Disting. Service award Nat. Oil Jobbers Council, 1967. Mem. Nat. Petroleum Council, Am. Petroleum Inst. Clubs: Franklin Hills Country (Franklin Mich.); Detroit. Office: J A Citrin Corp 28001 Citrin Dr Romulus MI 48174

CITRON, DAVID SANFORD, physician; b. Atlanta, Jan. 8, 1920; s. Morris and Ida (Levine) C.; m. Doris Berman, Feb. 14, 1946; children: Michael, Dennis, Lynn, Steven. A.B., U.N.C.-Chapel Hill, 1941, cert. in medicine, 1943; M.D., Washington U., St. Louis, 1944. Lic. physician, N.C.; cert. Am. Bd. Internal Medicine, Am. Bd. Family Practice. Intern Barnes Hosp., St. Louis, 1944-45; resident Barnes Hosp, St. Louis, 1945-46, 48-49, USPHS Hosp, Boston, 1949-50; gen. practice medicine, Charlotte, N.C., 1952—; dir. family practice residency Charlotte Meml. Hosp. & Med. Ctr., 1973—; mem. N.C. Bd. Med. Examiners, 1974-83, physician, 1980-83. Served with USPHS., 1946-52. Recipient Disting. Service award U.N.C. Sch. Medicine, 1975. Fellow ACP; mem. Nat. Acad. Sci., Inst. Medicine, AMA, N.C. Med. Soc., Mecklenburg County Med. Soc. (pres. 1972-73). Democrat. Jewish. Clubs: Raintree, Masons (Charlotte). Home: 8117 Rising Meadow Rd Matthews NC 28105 Office: Charlotte Meml Hosp and Med Ctr 1000 Blythe Blvd Charlotte NC 28232

CIVILETTI, BENJAMIN R., lawyer, former attorney general U.S.; b. Peekskill, N.Y., July 17, 1935; m. Gaile Lundgren. A.B., Johns Hopkins U., 1957; LL.B., Columbia U. and U. Md., 1961; LL.D. (hon.), U. Balt., 1978, N.Y. Law Sch., 1979, Tulane U., 1979, St. Johns U., 1979, U. Notre Dame, 1980, U. Md., 1983. Bar: Md. 1961. Law clk. to judge U.S. Dist. Ct. for Md., 1961-62; asst. U.S. atty., 1962-64; mem. firm Venable, Baetjer & Howard, 1964-77; asst. atty. gen., criminal div. U.S. Dept. Justice, Washington, 1977-78; dep. atty. gen. U.S., 1978-79, atty. gen., 1979-81; practice law, Balt. and Washington, 1981—. Trustee Johns Hopkins U.; chmn. Md. Legal Services Corp.; chmn. bd. visitors Sch. Pub. Affairs U. Md.; chmn. Gov.'s Task Force for Funding of Pub. Edn. Recipient Herbert H. Lehman ethics award. Fellow Am. Coll. Trial Lawyers, Am. Law Inst., Am. Bar Found., Md. Bar Found.; mem. Am., Md., Balt. City, D.C. bar assns., Am. Judicature Soc. (dir.), Order of Coif, Phi Alpha Delta. Office: 1800 Mercantile Bank & Trust Bldg 2 Hopkins Plaza Baltimore MD 21201 1301 Pennsylvania Ave NW Suite 704 Washington DC 20004 *

CIZIK, ROBERT, manufacturing executive; b. Scranton, Pa., Apr. 4, 1931; s. John and Anna (Paraska) C.; m. Jane Morin, Oct. 3, 1953; children: Robert Morin, Jan Catherine, Paula Jane, Gregory Alan, Peter Nicholas. B.S., U. Conn., 1953; M.B.A., Harvard U., 1958; LL.D. (hon.), Kenyon Coll., 1983. Acct., Price Waterhouse & Co. (C.P.A.s), N.Y.C., 1953-54, 56; fin. analyst Exxon U.S.A., N.J., 1958-61; with Cooper Industries, Inc., Houston, 1961—, exec. asst. corp. devel., treas., controller, 1963-67, v.p. for planning, 1967-69, exec. v.p., 1969-72, pres., 1972—, chief exec. officer, 1975—, chmn. bd., 1983—, also dir.; dir. First City Bancorp. Tex., NBC, Inc., Temple Inland Inc., RCA Corp., N.Y.C.; v.p. Machinery and Allied Products Inst. Bd. dirs. Central Houston, Inc., Nat. Bus. Com. for Arts, Catalyst; co-chmn. Houston Lyric Theater Found.; mem. Houston Bus. Com. for Arts; trustee Center for Internat. Bus., Conf. Bd.; mem. exec. com. Houston Grand Opera; trustee Com. Econ. Devel.; bd. overseers Exec. Council Fgn. Diplomats; mem. Soc. Founders, Am. Leadership Forum. Served to 1st lt. USAF, 1954-56. Clubs: Coronado, Houston Petroleum, River Oaks Country, Ramada, Forum of Houston (founding). Office: PO Box 4446 Houston TX 77210

CLAAR, JOHN BENNETT, former university administrator; b. Watson, Ill., Aug. 9, 1922; s. Harry Burnett and Ollie (Bryant) C.; m. Charlotte Lucille Wismer, Feb. 16, 1946; children: Nancy Jill Claar Flom, Bonnie Gail Claar, Richard Corbin. Student, Blackburn Coll., 1939-40; B.S., U. Ill., 1947, M.S., 1948, Ph.D., 1959. Engaged in farm mgmt. service Sangamon Valley Assn., 1948-51; farm mgmt. specialist

U. Ill. at Urbana, 1951-55; chief farm mgmt. br. Fed. Extension Service, Dept. Agr., 1955-58, adminstrv. field rep., 1958-60; asso. dir. Coop. Extension Service, U. Ill., 1960-65, dir., 1965; asso. dean Coll. Agr., U. Ill., Champaign, 1965-79; asso. v.p. for pub. service, 1973-82; dir. Interpaks, 1982—; vis. prof. U. Wis., 1957; cons. AID projects in India, Sierra Leone, Somalia, Iran, Indonesia, Egypt and the Carribean; chmn. extension com. orgn. and policy Nat. Assn. State Univs. and Land Grant Colls., 1968. Contbg. author: Goals and Values in Agriculture Policy, 1963, Cooperative Extension Service in the U.S, 1965. Bd. dirs. Nat. 4-H Found., v.p., 1978-79. Served with USAAF, 1943-45. Recipient award Farm Credit System, 1968; Wakefield award for high profl. achievement, 1975; Distinguished Service award Ill. Farm Bur., 1976; Weber award Coop. Extension, 1979; Edn. award Pork Producers Assn., 1980. Mem. Phi Kappa Phi, Gamma Sigma Delta, Epsilon Sigma Phi. Home: 2211 Briarhill Circle Champaign IL 61820

CLAAS, GERHARD, religious orgn. exec.; b. Wetter, Germany, Aug. 31, 1928; s. Ernst and Anna (Schroeder) C.; m. Irmgard Lydia Saffran, July 29, 1954; children—Regina, Gabriele, Martin. Diploma, Bapt. Theol. Sem., Rüschlikon, Switzerland, 1951, 1953; D.D., Ouachita Bapt. U., Ark., 1974. Ordained to ministry German Bapt. Union, 1953; pastor 1st Bapt. Ch., Duesseldorf, W. Ger., 1953-58; youth sec. German Bapt. Union, Hamburg, 1958-64, gen. sec., 1967-76; pastor J. G. Oncken Bapt. Ch., Hamburg, 1964-67; asso. sec. for Europe, Bapt. World Alliance, 1976-80, gen. sec., Washington, 1980—; tchr. religion Jacobi Gymnasium, Dusseldorf, 1953-58; dir. Youth Leaders Sem., 1958-64; chmn. exec. bd. Bapt. Theol. Sem., Ruschlikon, 1975-80. Author: Missionary Church Work, 1960; editor: b to y: Working Material for Youth Workers, 1958-64. Mem. exec. bd. Bread for the World, 1967-76; bd. dirs. Albertinen Hosp., Hamburg, 1964-80; chmn. exec. bd. Evang. Free Ch., Social Work, Hanover, W. Ger., 1967-80. Mem. Evang. Free Ch. Pastors Assn. Office: 1628 16th St NW Washington DC 20009

CLABBY, WILLIAM ROBERT, editor; b. Waterloo, Iowa, Feb. 12, 1931; s. James Francis and Pearl Marie (Bloes) C.; m. Joann Alma Carroll, Aug. 9, 1952; children—Theresa, Joseph, Dennis, Carolyn, Kathleen, Maureen, Timothy, Margaret, Brigid, Erin. Student, No. Iowa U., 1949-51; B.A., U. Iowa, 1953. With Dow Jones & Co., N.Y.C., 1953—; bur. mgr. Wall St. Jour., N.Y.C., 1966-71; mng. editor AP-Dow Jones, 1971-77; v.p. Dow Jones News Services, 1977—. Mem. Omicron Delta Kappa, Sigma Delta Chi. Roman Catholic. Home: 25 Tulip St Summit NJ 07901 Office: 22 Cortlandt St New York NY 10007

CLABORN, JAMES RICHARD, banker; b. Chgo., Oct. 24, 1942; s. James B. and Mary (Hauser) C.; m. Marjorie Bartmess, May 4, 1973; 1 son, James B. B.B.A., U. Okla., 1965; M.A., U. Wis., 1980. Acctg. mgr. Apco Oil Corp., Oklahoma City, 1965-74; exec. v.p., chief fin. officer, dir. 1st Okla. Bancorp., Inc., Oklahoma City, 1974—; dir. Okla. Nat. Bank and Trust Co. Mem. Nat. Assn. Accts. (v.p., dir.), Fin. Exec. Inst., Oklahoma City C. of C. Republican. Clubs: The Greens Country, Oak Tree Country, Young Mens Dinner. Office: Box 25189 Oklahoma City OK 73125

CLAFLIN, BEECHER NEVILLE, lawyer, former engineering and construction company executive; b. Lancaster, Ohio, Mar. 14, 1919; s. Walter Neville and Margretta (Steele) C.; m. Dorothy J. Kromer, Jan. 26, 1946; children: Edward, Helen. A.B., Miami U., Oxford, Ohio, 1941; LL.B., Columbia U., 1947. Bar: Conn. 1947, Ohio 1966. Atty. firm Maguire & Cole, Stamford, Conn., 1947-58; sec., counsel Fafnir Bearing Co., New Britain, Conn., 1959-64; sec., gen. counsel Chase Brass & Copper Co., Cleve., 1964-74; sec., assoc. gen. counsel Davy Inc., Cleve., 1974-84; dir. New Britain Fed. Savs. & Loan Assn., 1961-63. Chmn. New Britain Zoning Bd. Appeals, 1962; v.p. Orange Bd. Edn., Cleve., 1969-70. Served to capt. AUS, 1942-46. Mem. Am. Bar Assn. (Ross Essay award 1956), Ohio Bar Assn. Club: Cleve. Racquet. Home: 29980 Bolingbrook Rd Pepper Pike OH 44124 Office: 24200 Chagrin Blvd Cleveland OH 44122

CLAFLIN, ROBERT MALDEN, educator; b. Flint, Mich., Nov. 11, 1921; s. Robert Hugh and Kathryn Elizabeth (Ruhl) C.; m. Barbara Ellen Garrison, June 21, 1957; children—Deborah Ann, Blair Lawrence, Kathryn Elizabeth. D.V.M., Mich. State U., 1952; M.S., Purdue U., 1956, Ph.D., 1958. Faculty Purdue U., Lafayette, Ind., 1952—, prof. vet. pathology, 1959—, head dept. vet. microbiology, pathology and pub. health, 1959—. Mem. AVMA, Internat. Acad. Pathology, Conf. Research Workers Animal Diseases N.A., Sigma Xi, Phi Zeta, Phi Kappa Phi. Home: 706 Carrolton Blvd West Lafayette IN 47906 Office: Purdue U Lafayette IN 47907

CLAGETT, MARSHALL, historian, educator; b. Washington, Jan. 23, 1916; s. M. Brice and Claire (Manning) C.; m. Susan M. Riley, Feb. 2, 1946; children: Kathleen A., Dennis M., Michael R. Student, Calif. Inst. Tech., 1933-35; A.B., George Washington U., 1937, A.M., 1938; Ph.D., Columbia U., 1941. Instr. history Columbia, 1946-47; asst. prof. history of sci. U. Wis., 1947-49, asso. prof., 1949-54, prof., 1954-64, Inst. Research in Humanities, 1959-64; mem. Inst. Advanced Study, Princeton, 1958-59, 63, prof., 1964—; Fellow Medieval Acad. Am. Author: Giovanni Marliani and Late Medieval Physics, 1941, (with Ernest Moody) The Medieval Science of Weights, 1952, Greek Science in Antiquity, 1956, Mechanics in the Middle Ages, 1959, Archimedes in the Middle Ages, I, 1964, II, 1976, III, 1978, IV, 1980, V, 1984, Nicole Oresme and the Medieval Geometry of Qualities, 1969. Mem. History of Sci. Soc. (1st v.p. 1958-62, pres. 1962-64), Am. Philos. Soc. (v.p. 1969-71), Acad. Internat. History Sci. Home: 30 Maxwell Ln Princeton NJ 08540 Office: Inst for Advanced Study Princeton NJ 08540

CLAGETT, OSCAR THERON, surgeon; b. Jamesport, Mo., Oct. 19, 1908; s. Oscar Frederic and Effie (Stevens) C.; m. Alicia M. Eames, Nov. 3, 1934; children—Mary Alice, Nancy Jane, Barbara Joan, Martha Eleanor, James Stevens, Robert Scott. M.D., U. Colo., 1933, D.Sc., 1962; M.S., U. Minn., 1938, postgrad., 1935-40. Intern Colo. Gen. Hosp., Denver, 1933-34; practice medicine, Glenwood Springs, Colo., 1934-35; fellow in surgery Mayo Found. Grad. Sch., 1935-38; asst. surgeon Mayo Clinic, 1938-40; head sect., div. of surgery, 1940; prof. surgery Mayo Found. Grad. Sch. U. Minn., 1951—; vis. prof. surgery Johns Hopkins Hosp., 1957; Past sec.-treas. Am. Bd. Thoracic Surgery. Recipient Norlin medal U. Colo., 1947; Clement Price Thomas award Royal Coll. Surgeons Eng., 1968. Fellow A.C.S., Am. Assn. for Thoracic Surgery (past pres.), Am. Surg. Assn., Central Surg. Assn., Western Surg. Assn. (past pres.), Mexican Nat. Acad. Surgery, Royal Coll. Surgeons Eng. (hon.); hon. mem. Royal Australasian Coll. Surgeons, Royal College Surgeons in Ireland, Thoracic Soc. (Eng.), Soc. Thoracic Surgeons Gt. Britain and Ireland, Royal Coll. Surgeons Eng., Societa Italiana di Chirurgia (corr.). Home: 2011 Merrihills Dr Rochester MN 55901 Office: Mayo Clinic Rochester MN 55901

CLAGGETT, WILLIAM MORGAN, food products company executive; b. Los Angeles, Dec. 8, 1930; s. William Nathaniel and Dorothy (Morgan) C.; m. Barbara Clark, June 8, 1976; children: Carolyn Raney, Susan Elizabeth, M. Weldon Rogers IV, Debra English Rogers. Student, U. Va., 1950-51; B.A., Ohio State U., 1954. Account supr. Gardner Advt. Co., St. Louis, 1956-66, v.p., 1967; v.p. advt. Ralston Purina Co., St. Louis, 1967-70, v.p. mktg. services and new food enterprises, 1970-77, v.p. advt. and mktg. services, 1977—. Served to 1st lt. U.S. Army, 1955-56. Named Advt. Man of Year, Media Decisions mag., 1978. Mem. Assn. Nat. Advertisers (past chmn. bd.), Audit Bur. Circulations (past chmn. bd.), Advt. Council (dir.), Nat. Advt. Rev. Bd. (charter). Episcopalian. Clubs: St. Louis Country, St. Louis Racquet; N.Y. Univ., Brook (N.Y.C.). Home: 2500 S Warson Rd Saint Louis MO 63124 Office: Ralston Purina Co Checkerboard Sq Saint Louis MO 63164

CLAIBORNE, CRAIG, editor, author cookbooks; b. Sunflower, Miss., Sept. 4, 1920; s. Lewis Edmond and Kathleen (Craig) C. B.J., U. Mo., 1942; student, Ecole Hoteliere, Lausanne, Switzerland, 1953-54. With ABC, Chgo., 1946-49; now food editor N.Y. Times. Author: Classic French Cuisine, 1970, Cooking with Herbs and Spices, rev. edit, 1970, New York Times International Cook Book, 1971, Craig Claiborne's Kitchen Primer, 1972; Editor: New York Times Cook Book, 1961, New York Times Menu Cook Book, 1966, (with Virginia Lee) The Chinese Cook Book, 1972, Craig Claiborne's Favorites From The New York Times, Vol. I, 1975, Vol. II, 1976, Vol. III, 1977, Vol. IV, 1978, (with Pierre Franey) Time/Life Books' Classic French Cookery, 1970, Veal Cookery, 1978, The New New York Times Cook Book, 1979, The Gourmet Diet Cook Book, 1980, A Feast Made for Laughter, a memoir with recipes, 1982. Served to lt. USNR, 1942-45, 50-53. Decorated chevalier Ordre du Merite Agricole. Mem. La Tripiere d'Or, Commanderie des Cordons Bleus. Home: 15 Clamshell Ave East Hampton NY 11937 Office: New York Times 229 W 43d St New York NY 10036

CLAIBORNE, LIZ (ELISABETH CLAIBORNE), women's clothing designer; b. Brussels, Mar. 31, 1929; U.S., 1934; s. Omer Villere and Louise Carol (Fenner) C.; m. Arthur Ortenberg, July 5, 1957; 1 son by previous marriage, Alexander G. Schultz. Student, Art Sch., Brussels, 1947, Academie, Nice, France, 1948. Asst. Tina Lesser, N.Y.C., 1949-50; Omar Khayam, Ben Reig, Inc., N.Y.C., 1950-52; designer Juniorite, N.Y.C., 1952-54, Dan Keller, 1955-60, Youth Guild Inc., 1960-76; designer, pres. Liz Claiborne Inc., N.Y.C., 1976—; guest lectr. Fashion Inst. Tech., Parsons Sch. Design. Recipient Designer of Yr. award Palciode Hierro, Mexico City, 1976, Dayton Co., Mpls., 1978. Mem. Fashion Group. Roman Catholic. Office: 1441 Broadway New York NY 10018 *

CLAIBORNE, MARY LYNN, assn. exec.; b. McRae, Ark., Mar. 9, 1937; d. W.W. and Mildred Pauline C. Diploma, Draughon Sch. Bus., Little Rock, 1956. Sec. Ins. Service Offices Ark., 1956-60; sec., bookkeeper, then dir. public relations Ark. Ind. Ins. Agts. Assn., 1960-67; adminstrv. asst., then. v.p. Marrs Ins. Services, Ft. Smith, Ark., 1967-78; exec. dir. Nat. Assn. Ins. Women, Tulsa, 1978—. Mem. Am. Soc. Assn. Execs., Nat. Assn. Female Execs. Democrat. Baptist. Address: 1847 E 15th St PO Box 410 Tulsa OK 74104

CLAIRBORNE, HARRY EUGENE, judge; b. McRae, Ark., July 2, 1917. Student, Ouachita U., 1934-37; LL.B., Cumberland U., 1941, J.D., 1969. Bar: Ark. 1942, Nev. 1946, U.S. Supreme Ct. 1965. Individual practicee law, Las Vegas, Nev., after 1946; now chief judge U.S. Dist. Ct., Nev.; mem. Nev. Assembly, 1949; chmn. judiciary com.; asst. dist. atty. Clark County, Nev., 1946-48; city atty. City North Las Vegas, 1948-55. Fellow Am. Coll. Trial Lawyers; mem. Nat. Assn. Trial Lawyers, Am. Assn. Criminal Def. Lawyers, Am. Bar Assn., Am. Bd. Trial Advisors (adv.). Office: US Dist Ct 300 Las Vegas Blvd S 3d Floor Las Vegas NV 89101 *

CLAIRE, FRED, professional baseball team executive. A.A., Mt. San. Antonio Coll.; B.A. in Journalism, San Jose State Coll., 1957. Formerly sports writer and columnist Long Beach Ind. Press Telegram and Whittier News; sports editor Pomo Progress-Bull, Calif., until 1969; dir. publicity Los Angeles Dodgers, Nat. League, 1969-75, v.p. pub. relations and promotions, 1975-82, exec. v.p., 1982—; bd. dirs. Major League Baseball Promotion Corp. Bd. dirs. Greater Los Angeles Vistors and Conv. Bur. Mem. Echo Park C. of C. Lodge: Los Angeles Rotary. Office: Los Angeles Dodgers 1000 Elysian Park Ave Los Angeles CA 90012

CLANCY, GILBERT THOMAS, sports announcer; b. N.Y.C., May 30, 1922; s. Gilbert Francis and Veronica C.; m. Nancy Theresa Sheehan, May 24, 1947; children: Patricia, Gilbert, Joan, John, Kathleen, Nancy. B.S., M.A., NYU. Tchr. phys. edn. N.Y. Sch. System, N.Y.C., 1950-61; boxing coach Police Athletic League, N.Y.C., 1949-53; boxing trainer and mgr., N.Y.C., 1953-76; matchmaker Madison Sq. Garden, N.Y.C., 1976-79; boxing announcer CBS Sports, N.Y.C., 1979—; trainer CYO, N.Y.C., 1953-56. Served to cpl. USAAF, 1942-46. Recipient Al Buck Meml. award as mgr. of yr. N.Y. Boxing Writers, 1967, 73, Timex award as boxing announcer of yr. Guantes Mag., 1983. Republican. Roman Catholic. Home: 47 Morris Ave W Malverne NY 11565 Office: CBS Sports 51 W 52d St New York NY 10019

CLANCY, JOSEPH PATRICK, lawyer; b. Washington, July 10, 1931; s. Patrick J. and Esther M. (Crowley) C.; m. Margaret E. Kennedy, May 22, 1965; children—Susan, Kevin, Kathleen, Megan. A.B., U. Notre Dame, 1953, LL.B., 1959; LL.M., Georgetown U., 1962. Bar: D.C. bar 1960, Md. bar 1966. Law clk. to chief judge U.S. Dist. Ct. for D.C., 1960-61; practiced in, Washington, 1961—; partner firm Clancy & Pfeifer, 1971—. Trustee Montgomery County (Md.) Heart Assn., Catholic Youth Orgn. Served to capt. USMCR, 1954-56. Mem. Am., D.C., Montgomery County bar assns., Jud. Conf. for D.C. Circuit, Nat. Conf. Lawyers and Realtors. Republican. Roman Catholic. Clubs: K.C., Notre Dame (Washington) (pres.); Kenwood Country.). Home: 5004 Overlea Ct Sumner MD 20016 Office: 5454 Wisconson Ave Chevy Chase MD 20815

CLANCY, LOUIS JOHN, journalist; b. Utrecht, Netherlands, Aug. 10, 1946; emigrated to Can., 1946, naturalized, 1946; s. John Joseph and Maria Wilhelmina (Van Dommelen) C.; m. Rhonda Darlene Jackson, Apr. 7, 1969; children—Robin, Jamie. Student, Centennial Coll., Can., 1967-69. Copy boy Toronto (Ont.) Star, 1964-65; sports editor Simcoe (Ont.) Reformer, 1965-66; reporter, news editor Owen Sound (Ont.) Sun-Times, 1969-71; copy editor Kitchener-Waterloo (Ont.) Record, 1971-73; mem. staff Toronto Star, 1974—, asst. nat. editor, asst. city editor, then week in rev. editor, 1977-78, nat. editor, 1978-81; Sunday editor, 1981—. Club: Arctic Circle Press. Home: 141 Blantyre Ave Scarborough ON M1N 2R6 Canada Office: 1 Yonge St Toronto ON M5E 1E6 Canada

CLANCY, MAURICE LEE, pharm. co. exec.; b. Carter, Okla., Dec. 8, 1915; s. Byron Hall and Lilly (Finch) C.; m. DeAnn Peterson, Dec. 31, 1966; children—Maurice Lee, Brian Carl. B.A., U. Okla., 1937; Ph.D. (hon.), Colo. Christian Coll., 1973. Product mgr. Westvaco Chem. Co., 1939-44; with Wyeth Internat. Ltd., 1944—, v.p., then exec. v.p., 1952-69, pres., chief exec. officer, Phila., 1969—; dir. Wyeth Japan Corp., Wyeth Labs., Eng.; Bd. dirs. Pa. Mental Health Assn., 1952-53; bd. govs. Pa. Export Corps, 1954. Mem. Phila. Advt. Golf Assn. (pres. 1979-80), Phi Beta Kappa, Delta Tau Delta. Republican. Presbyterian. Clubs: Merion Cricket (Haverford, Pa.); Overbrook Golf (Bryn Mawr, Pa.). Home: 1956 Montgomery Ave Villanova PA 19085 Office: PO Box 8616 Philadelphia PA 19101

CLANCY, RAYMOND WENDELL, automatic temperature controls co. exec.; b. Chgo., June 28, 1925; s. Mark Wendell and Ida May (Warn) C.; m. Mary Alice Urich, Jan. 5, 1952; children—Lizbeth Ann, Warne R., Amy U. B.S. in Elec. Engring, Purdue U., 1950. With Therm-O-Disc, Inc., Mansfield, Ohio, 1950—, sales mgr., 1969-72, v.p. product and market devel., 1972-75, v.p. engring. and mfg., 1975-79, exec. v.p., 1979-80, pres., 1980—. Served with USNR, 1943-46. Mem. Nat. Electric Mfrs. Assn., Gas. Appliance Mfrs. Assn. Club: Westbrook Country. Office: Therm-O-Disc Inc 1320 S Main St Mansfield OH 44907

CLANON, THOMAS LAWRENCE, hospital administrator; b. Detroit, Sept. 17, 1929; s. William John and Wilhelmina T. (Francis) C.; m. Esther Theresa Giffin, June 11, 1955; children—John P., Kathleen A., Paul A., David L., Daniel J. B.S., U. Detroit, 1951; M.D., U. Mich., 1955. Diplomate: Am. Bd. Psychiatry and Neurology. Intern St. Mary's Hosp., Grand Rapids, Mich., 1955-56; grad. tng. Meninger Sch. Psychiatry, Topeka, 1956-59; resident psychiatrist in tng. Kans. Boys Indsl. Sch., Topeka, 1958-59; psychiatrist U.S. Med. Center for Prisoners, Springfield, Mo., 1959-61; mem. staff Calif. Med. Facility, Vacaville, 1961-66, 72—, asst. supt. psychiat. services, 1972, supt., 1972-80; med. asst. Broadmoor Spl. Security Hosp., Crowthorne, Eng., 1971-72; staff psychiatrist San Francisco Parole Outpatient Clinic; asst. clin. prof. U. Calif. Med. Sch., Davis, 1969. Contbr. articles to med. jours. Mem. community adv. bd. dept. psychiatry San Francisco Gen. Hosp. Served with USPHS, 1958-61. Fellow Am. Psychiat. Assn.; mem. Am. Correctional Assn., Am. Acad. Psychiatry and Law, Calif. Correctional Psychiatrists and Psychologists Assn., San Francisco Med. Soc. Roman Catholic. Club: Vacaville Kiwanis (past pres.). Office: 1580 Valencia #406 San Francisco CA 94110

CLAPMAN, PETER C., insurance company executive; b. N.Y.C., Mar. 11, 1936; s. Jack and Evelyn (Clapman); m. Barbara Posen, May 8, 1966; children: Leah, Alice. A.B., Princeton U., 1957; J.D., Harvard U., 1960. Bar: N.Y. State bar 1961, Conn. bar 1972. Asso. firm Sage, Gray, Todd & Sims, N.Y.C., 1961-63; asst. counsel Stichman Commn., N.Y.C., 1964; legal cons. OEO, Washington, 1965; asso. counsel Equitable Life, N.Y.C., 1965-72; asst. counsel Tchrs. Ins. and Annuity of Am., N.Y.C., 1972, counsel, 1973-74, asst. gen. counsel, 1975, 2d v.p., asso. gen. counsel, 1976-78, v.p., asso. gen. counsel, 1978-79, sr. v.p., asso. gen. counsel, 1980—. Bd. dirs. Scarsdale Greenacres Assn., 1981-83. Served with U.S. Army, 1960. Mem. N.Y. State Bar Assn., Am. Life Ins. Counsel (chmn. com. securities law, vice chmn. investment sect.), Am. Bar Assn. (mem. com. devels. in bus. financing), Bar Assn. City N.Y. (mem. corp. law dept. com.). Home: 3 Valley Rd Scarsdale NY 10583 Office: 730 3d Ave New York NY 10017

CLAPP, EUGENE HOWARD, II, manufacturing executive; b. Brookline, Mass., Sept. 22, 1913; s. George Allen and Sarah Lillian (Clapp) C.; m. Maud Millicent Greenwell, Apr. 10, 1943; children: Eugene Howard III, Candace Millicent. B.S., Lafayette U., 1936. With Penobscot Co., Great Works, Maine, 1937-68, treas., 1946-50, pres., 1950-65, chmn. bd., 1960-67, dir., 1946-68; also gen. mgr.; with Tileston & Hollingsworth Co., Mattapan, Mass., 1946-67, treas., 1946-53, chmn. bd., 1953-68, dir., 1946-68; pres., dir. Penobscot Capital Investment Co., Pine Tree Land Co.; treas., dir. King Spruce Co.; dir. Am. Mut. Ins. Co., Am. Mut. Ins. Co. Boston, AM Life Ins. Co., Am. Mut. Corp., Fidelity Funds. Justice of peace. Bd. dirs. Asso. Industries Mass., Newton-Wellesley Hosp., Mass. div. Am. Cancer Soc.; trustee Children's Hosp. Med. Center, Lafayette Coll.; pres. Phi Gamma Delta Ednl. Found., 1972—. Served with OSS, 1942-46. Mem. Phi Gamma Delta (chmn. bd. trustees 1970-72). Republican. Episcopalian. Club: Masons. Home: 37 Autumn Rd Weston MA 02193 Office: 10 High St Boston MA 02110

CLAPP, JAMES FORD, JR., architect; b. Cambridge, Mass., Nov. 18, 1908; s. James Ford and Leonora (Fanshawe) C.; m. Grace G. FitzGerald, June 3, 1933; children: James Ford III, Susan Fanshawe, Deborah FitzGerald. A.B., Harvard Coll., 1931; M.Arch., Harvard Grad. Sch. Design, 1935. Architect, Coolidge Shepley Bulfinch & Abbott, Boston, 1953; asso. architect Shepley, Bulfinch Richardson & Abbott, Boston, 1953-60, partner, 1960-72; pres. Shepley Bulfinch Richardson & Abbott Inc., Boston, 1972-75, prin., v.p., 1975-83, cons., 1983—; archtl. cons. Acadia U.; also to Keyes D. Metcalf for book Planning Academic and Research Library Buildings, 1965; pres. Boston Archtl. Center, 1955-56. Mem. Cambridge Hist. Commn., 1969—; permanent sec. John Worthington Ames Scholarship, 1966—. Fellow AIA, Am. Numis. Soc.; mem. Boston Soc. Architects (sec. 1957, centennial chmn. 1967), Mass. State Assn. Architects (v.p. 1958-59), Boston Numis. Soc. (pres. 1949-50, 63-64), New Eng. Numis. Assn. (pres. 1956-57), Am. Numis. Assn. (gen. chmn. 1960, Numismatic Ambassador award 1980). Home: 20 Bellevue Ave Cambridge MA 02140 Office: 40 Broad St Boston MA 02109

CLAPP, LEALLYN BURR, educator; b. Paris, Ill., Oct. 13, 1913; s. Ivan Burr and Blanche (Tate) C.; m. Florence Cottingham, Aug. 28, 1940; children—Peter, Jean. B.Ed., E.Ill. U., 1935, Pd.D. (hon.), 1956; M.A., U. Ill. at Urbana, 1939, Ph.D., 1941; LL.D. (hon.), R.I. Coll., 1964. Tchr. math. Paris (Ill.) High Sch., 1935-38; mem. faculty Brown U., 1941—, prof. chemistry, 1956—; lectr. chemistry, Chile, 1961, Nigeria, 1962, India, 1965, 68, 71, Uruguay, 1967, Pakistan, 1970, S. Korea, 1974, Mex., 1976. Author: Chemistry of the Covalent Bond, 1957, Chemistry of the OH Group, 1967, Portuguese edit. 1967, Japanese 1968, French 1969; co-author: General, Organic, and Biochemistry, 1980; Editor: Organic Modules, 1972—. Recipient award Mfg. Chemists Assn., 1973; Sci. Apparatus Makers award in chem. edn., 1976; Disting. Alumnus award Eastern Ill. U., 1978. Mem. New Eng. Assn. Chemistry Tchrs. (sec. 1952-57, pres. 1961-63, John Timm award 1974), Am. Chem. Soc. (vis. scientist 1956-67, com. prof. tng. 1958-67, chmn. div. chem. edn. 1959-60, award western Conn. sect. 1969). Home: 125 Congdon St Providence RI 02906

CLAPP, NORTON, building materials company executive; b. Pasadena, Calif., April 15, 1906; s. Eben Pratt and Mary Bell (Norton) C.; m. Mary Cordelia Davis, July 8, 1929 (dec.); children: James Hayes (dec.), Matthew, Ralph (dec.), Roger (dec.); m. Evelyn Beatrice Booth, Jan. 15, 1941 (dec.); children—William Hayes, Stephen Gilbert; m. Jane Bumiller, Apr. 19, 1952. A.B., Occidental Coll., 1928, LL.D., 1958; Ph.B., U. Chgo., 1928, J.D., 1929; D.C.L., U. Puget Sound, 1958. Bar: Calif., Wash. bars 1929. Practiced in, Tacoma, 1929-42; chmn. Met. Bldg. Corp., Seattle, 1954-75; pres. Pelican (Alaska) Cold Storage Co., 1947-60, chmn., 1960-77; pres. Boise (Idaho) Payette Lumber Co., 1949-55, Laird Norton Co., bldg. materials, Winona, Minn., 1950-60, chmn., 1960—; v.p. Weyerhaeuser Co., 1956-57, chmn. bd., 1957-60, 66-76, pres., 1960-66. Mem. nat. adv. bd., hon. v.p. Boy Scouts Am., nat. pres., 1971-73; Chmn. bd. trustees U. Puget Sound, Tacoma; life trustee U. Chgo.; trustee Menninger Found., Episcopal Ch. Found. Served as lt. comdr. USNR, 1942-46. Mem. Seattle C. of C. (pres. 1970-71). Republican. Episcopalian. Clubs: Harbor, Rainier, University, Overlake Golf and Country, Yacht, Tennis (Seattle); Tacoma, Country and Golf, Yacht (Tacoma). Home: PO Box 99 Medina WA 98039 Office: Norton Bldg Seattle WA 98104

CLAPP, ROGER ALVIN, lawyer; b. Balt., Dec. 17, 1909; s. Clyde Alvin and Lillian Adele (Dickason) C.; m. Harriet Reid, Aug. 15, 1936; children: Thomas R., Martha T. (Mrs. Robert McDorman). A.B., Oberlin (Ohio) Coll., 1931; LL.B., Harvard U., 1934. Bar: Md.

1934. Asso. firm Hershey, Donaldson, Williams & Stanley, Balt., 1934-40, partner, 1940-63; partner firm Hinkley & Singley (name later changed to Clapp, Somerville, Black & Honemann), Balt., 1964-82; of counsel Clapp, Somerville, Honemann & Beach, 1982—; dir. Worcester Wire Mfg. Co. Contbr. articles to profl. jours. Trustee Congregational Summer Assembly. Fellow Md. Bar Found.; mem. Balt., Md. State, Am. bar assns. Republican. Presbyterian. Clubs: Merchants, Center, Hamilton Street (Balt.). Home: 10518 Pot Spring Rd Cockeysville MD 21030 Office: 1700 First Nat Bank Bldg Baltimore MD 21202

CLAPP, ROGER HOWLAND, newspaper advertising executive; b. Scarsdale, N.Y., May 11, 1928; s. Kenneth John and Louise (Allen) C.; m. Patricia Anne Townshend, June 26, 1954; children: Roger Howland, Georgia Louise, Sarah Townshend. B.A. cum laude, Amherst Coll., 1954. Vice pres., asso. media dir. Benton & Bowles, Inc., N.Y.C., 1954-67; v.p., media dir. Rumrill-Hoyt, Inc., N.Y.C., 1967-72; advt. dir. Richmond Newspapers, Inc. div. Media Gen., Inc., Richmond, Va., 1972—. Served with USN, 1948-52. Mem. Internat. Newspaper Advt. and Mktg. Execs., Sales and Mktg. Execs. Internat. (dir.), Mid-Atlantic Newspaper Advt. Execs. Assn. (dir.), Advt. Club Richmond, Theta Delta Chi. Clubs: Bull and Bear, Brandermill Country. Home: 13705 Harbour Bluff Ct Midlothian VA 23113 Office: 333 E Grace St Richmond VA 23219 *A strong belief in the essential goodness of other people; a desire to respect this in others and attempt to practice it myself.*

CLAPPER, HOMER WALTER, corp. exec.; b. Swissvale, Pa., May 12, 1916; s. Homer Linhart and Marie Cecilia (Traynor) C.; m. Betty M. Stagg, May 16, 1941; 1 dau., Barbara. M.E., Rutgers U., 1938, postgrad. bus. adminstrn., aero, 1942. Registered profl. engr., N.J. With Curtiss-Wright Corp., 1938-46, Reeves Internat. Inc., 1946-48; with Bergen Wire Rope Co., 1948-69; former chmn. bd. dirs.; with Reeves Industries, Inc., 1952-70, pres., 1965-70, Mercury Industries, Inc., 1970—, Conveyors & Dumpers (both Park Ridge, N.J.), Chatham Labs. Inc., 1970-74; v.p. Conti Causeway Ford, Mercury, Lincoln, Manahawkin, N.J., 1969-76, Toms River Lincoln Mercury, N.J., 1971-78, Toms River Am. Motors, Jeep, 1974-78; founder, dir. Ramapo Bank. Mem. Am. Inst. Banking. Home: 152 Pines Lake Dr E Wayne NJ 07472 Office: Mercury Industries Inc Hawthorne Ave Park Ridge NJ 07656

CLAPTON, ERIC, musician; b. Ripley, Surrey, Eng., Mar. 30, 1945; m. Patricia Anne Boyd, 1979. Student, Kingston Art Sch. Former mem. rock music groups, Yardbirds, John Mayall's, Bluesbreakers, Cream, Blind Faith, Delaney & Bonnie & Friends, Derek & the Dominoes; now solo performer; films A Concert for Bangladesh, 1972, Tommy, 1975; composer: Badge, Let It Rain, Layla; albums include: Eric Clapton, 1970, Rainbow Concert, 1973, There's One in Every Crowd, 1974, No Reason to Cry, 1976, Slowhand, 1977, Backless, 1978, Another Ticket, 1981, Money and Cigarettes, 1983. Address: care Warner Bros Record 3300 Warner Blvd Burbank CA 91510 *

CLARDY, JESSE V., educator; b. Olney, Tex., Feb. 15, 1929; s. Jesse Ellis and Tiny (Pringle) C. B.S., Tex. A&I U., 1949, M.S., 1951; Ph.D., U. Mich., 1961. Mem. faculty U. Tex., Arlington, 1961-62, U. Mo., Kansas City, 1963—, asso. prof. Russian history, 1964-68, prof., 1968—. Author: Philosophical Ideas of Alexander Radishchev, 1964, G.R. Derzhavin, a Political Biography, 1967, the Superfluous Man in Russian Letters, 1980. Served with AUS, 1951-54. Mem. S.W. Slavic Assn. (pres. 1964-65), Bi-Slavic Assn. (sec. 1970-71), Assn. Advancement Slavic Studies. Republican. Home: 1004 Broad St Warrensburg MO 64093 Office: Dept History U Mo Kansas City MO 64110

CLARE, CARL PETER, elec. engr.; b. Rossland, C., Can., May 25, 1903; s. Peter and Hattie (Stenson) C.; m. Ethel May Johnson, Jan. 22, 1926; 1 dau., Valdine (Mrs. Richard A. Cameron). Student, U. Mich., 1921-24; B.Sc. in Elec. Engring, U. Ida., 1927, D.Sc., 1962; grad., advanced mgmt. program, Harvard, 1956; D.Engring., S.D. Mines and Tech., 1970. Registered profl. engr., Ill. Engr. Automatic Electric Co., Chgo., 1927-32, Automatic Electric Labs., 1932-37; founder C.P. Clare & Co., Chgo., 1937, pres., chmn. bd., 1937-72, chmn. bd., 1972—; dir. C.P. Clare Internat. NV, Tongeren, Belgium, Gen. Instrument Corp., Dor-O-Matic. Mem. Northwestern U. Assos.; Bd. dirs. Dickinson Coll., Carlisle, Pa., Northwest Community Hosp., Arlington Heights, Ill.; chmn. bd. dirs. Northwest Community Hosp. Found. Fellow IEEE; mem. Am. Soc. Metals, Western Soc. Engrs., Tau Beta Pi, Sigma Tau, Sigma Chi (grand trustee, pres. found.). Presbyn. (elder). Clubs: Mason (Shriner), Union League, Mid-Am., Executives, Harvard (Chgo.); Bob O'Link Country (Highland Park, Ill.); Medinah (Ill.) Country, University of Mich. Home: 22 Park Ln Park Ridge IL 60068 Office: 3101 Pratt Blvd Chicago IL 60045

CLARE, DAVID ROSS, pharmaceutical executive; b. Perth Amboy, N.J., July 21, 1925; s. Robert Linn and Helen M. (Walsh) C.; m. Margaret Mary Corcoran, July 5, 1947; children: Lynne Clare Ferree, Carol Clare Brown, David Ross, Christopher E. B.S. in Mech. Engring., MIT, 1945. With Johnson & Johnson, New Brunswick, N.J., 1946—, pres. domestic operating co., 1970, corp. pres., 1976—, dir., 1971—, mem. exec. com., 1971—, chmn. exec. com., 1976—. Mem. corp. Mass. Inst. Tech.; bd. dirs. Overlook Hosp. Served as lt. (j.g.) USNR, 1944-46. Roman Catholic. Clubs: Echo Lake Country (Westfield, N.J.); Lost Tree (North Palm Beach, Fla.). Office: 501 George St New Brunswick NJ 08903

CLARE, STEWART, research biologist, educator; b. nr. Montgomery City, Mo., Jan. 31, 1913; s. William Gilmore and Wardie (Stewart) C.; m. Lena Glenn Kaster, Aug. 4, 1936. B.A. (William Volker scholar), U. Kans., 1935; M.S. (Rockefeller Research fellow, teaching fellow), Iowa State U., 1937; Ph.D. (Univ. fellow), U. Chgo., 1949. Dist. survey supr. entomology bur. entomology and plant quarantine CSC, 1937-40, tech. cons., 1941-42; instr. meteorology USAAF Weather Sch., 1942-43; research biologist Midwest Research Inst., Kansas City, Mo., 1945-46; spl. study, research Kansas City Art Inst., U. Mo., 1946-49; instr. zoology U. Alta., 1949-50, asst. prof. zoology, lectr.-instr. sci. color, dept. fine arts, 1950-53; interim asst. prof. physiology Kansas City Coll. Osteopathy and Surgery, 1953; lectr. zoology U. Adelaide, S. Australia, 1954-55; sr. research officer and cons. entomology Sudan Govt. Ministry Agr., Khartoum, Sudan and Gezira Research Sta., Wad Medani, Sudan, N.Africa, 1955-56; sr. entomologist and cons. Klipfontein Organic Products Corp., Johannesburg, Union S.Africa, 1957; prof., head dept. biology Union Coll., 1958-59, chmn. sci. div., prof., head biology, 1959-61, spl. study grantee, 1960; prof., head dept. biology Mo. Valley Coll., Marshall, 1961-62, research grantee, 1961-62; lectr., instr. biology, meteorology, sci. of color Adirondack Sci. Camp and Field Research Sta. at Twin Valleys, SUNY, Plattsburgh, 1962-66; dir. acad. program SUNY, 1963-66, research facilities grantee, 1963-66; Buckbee Found. prof. biology Rockford (Ill.) Coll., lectr. biology evening coll., 1962-63, spl. research grantee, 1962-63; prof., chmn. dept. biochemistry, mem. research div. Kansas City (Mo.) Coll. Osteopathy and Surgery, U. Health Scis., 1963-67; also NIH basic research grantee, 1963-67; prof. biology Coll. of Emporia, Kans., 1967-74, dir. biol. research, 1972-74, prof. emeritus, 1974—; research biologist, cons., 1974—; research study grantee, 1967-74, spl. research grantee study in, Arctic, 1970, 72, C. Am. and Mexico, 1973; cons. VITA, 1962—, Adirondack Research Sta., 1962-66, Nat. Referral Center for Sci. and Tech., other orgns. Contbr. over 100 papers and monographs on capillary movement in porous materials, physiology and biochemistry of arthropoda; numerous local, nat., internat. exhbns. on color, also articles to profl. jours. Mem. adv. bd. Fine Art Registry Soc. N.Am. Artists. Served with USNR, 1943-45. Recipient Certificate of Service Vols. Internat. Tech. Assistance, 1970; Creativity Recognition award Internat. Personnel Research, 1972; Distinguished Achievement and Service awards for edn. and research in biology; Certificate of Merit in Art Internat. Biog. Centre, Cambridge, 1968, 72, 73, 76; Outstanding Service to Community award Am. Biog. Inst., 1975, 76, 77, 79-80; Notable Ams. of Bicentennial Era award, 1976; Book of Honor award, 1978; named Outstanding Educator Coll. of Emporia, 1973; research grantee Alta. Research Council, 1951-53; research facilities grantee U. Alaska, 1970, No. Research Survey Arctic Inst. N.Am., 1970, 72. Fellow Internat. Biog. Assn. (life), Am. Biog. Inst., Explorers Club, Anglo-Am. Acad. (hon.); mem. N.Y. Acad. Scis. (life), Brit. Assn. Adv. Sci. (life), Am. Entomol. Soc. (life), Nat. Assn. Biology Tchrs., AAUP, Arctic Inst. N.Am., Am. Polar Soc., Inter-Soc. Color Council, Sigma Xi, Phi Sigma, Psi Chi, numerous others. Spl. research sci. of color and design of color. Home: 405 NW Woodland Rd Indian Hills in Riverside Kansas City MO 64150

CLARENS, JOHN GASTON, investment executive; b. Bordeaux, France, July 16, 1924; s. Pierre Maurice and Cecile (Dupreuilh) C.; m. Francoise Legrand, Aug. 7, 1948. Engr., Ecole Polytechnique, Paris, 1948; M.B.A. (Am. Field Service scholar), Harvard U., 1950. Chartered fin. analyst, N.Y. Vice-pres. Lepercq, de Neuflize & Co., Inc., N.Y.C., 1970-75, pres., chief exec. officer, 1975-76; pres. Istel Fund, N.Y.C., 1975-76; chmn., pres. Clarens Assos., Inc., N.Y.C., 1976—. Served to lt. French Army. Mem. France-Am. Soc. Clubs: Knickerbocker, Harvard (N.Y.C.). Home: 51 Fox Run Rd Redding CT 06896 Office: 41 E 57th St New York NY 10022

CLARIE, T. EMMET, federal judge; b. Killingly, Conn., Jan. 1, 1913; children: D'Arcy R., Marilyn Ann, Thomas C. LL.B., Hartford Coll. Law, (now U. Conn. Sch. Law), 1938. Bar: Conn. 1940. Individual practice law, Danielson, Conn., 1940-61; sr. judge U.S. Dist. Ct. Conn., Hartford.; chmn. Com. for Operation of Jury System; mem. Conn. Gen. Assembly, 1937-43. Mem. Killingly Bd. Edn., 1938-61. Mem. U.S. Jud. Conf. (exec. com.). Office: US Dist Ct 450 Main St Hartford CT 06163 *

CLARIZIO, JOSEPHINE DELORES, manufacturing and engineering company executive, foundation executive; b. Montclair, N.J., Dec. 15, 1922; d. Thomas and Raffaels (Caruso) D'Andrea; m. N. Robert Clarizio, June 3, 1951. Cert., Katharine Gibbs Sch., 1942; B.S., Seton Hall U., 1947; postgrad., Fordham U. Sch. Law, 1947-48, N.Y. Inst. Fin., 1964. Registered rep. Drexel, Burnham & Co., N.Y.C., 1965-70; asst. to pres. Wheelabrator-Frye Inc., Hampton, N.H., 1970-78, corp. sec., 1981—; pres. Wheelabrator Found. Inc., Hampton, 1978—. Mem. Seton Hall U. Alumni Assn. Republican. Roman Catholic. Club: Club at the Top of the World (N.Y.C.). Home: 943 Ocean Blvd Hampton NH 03842 Office: Wheelabrator-Frye Inc Liberty Ln Hampton NH 03842

CLARK, ALAN F., physicist; b. Milwaukee, June 29, 1936. B.S. in Physics, U. Wis., Madison, 1958, M.S. in Nuclear Engrin., 1959; Ph.D. in Nuclear Sci., U. Mich., Ann Arbor, 1964. NAS-NRC postdoctoral assoc. Nat. Bur. Standards, Boulder, Colo., 1964-66, physicist, 1966-78, chief products of solids and superconductors, 1978-80, group leader magnetics materials, 1981—; chmn., founder Internat. Cryogenic Materials Conf. Bd., Boulder, Colo., 1975—; chmn. ASTM Commn. Superconductors, Phila., 1980—. Contbr. articles to profl. jours.; editor, conf. proceedings. Recipient Superior Research Nat. Bur. Standards, 1967, 74, 82, 83. Mem. Am. Phys. Soc., IEEE, Am. Soc. Testing and Materials. Office: Nat Bur Standards 325 S Broadway Boulder CO 80302

CLARK, ALFRED, JR., educator; b. Elizabethton, Tenn., May 5, 1936; s. Alfred and Winifred (Gardner) C.; m. Patricia Ann Andre, Sept. 11, 1960; 1 dau., Alice Susan. B.S., Purdue U., 1958; Ph.D., Mass. Inst. Tech., 1963. Registered profl. engr., N.Y. Asst. prof. mech. and aerospace scis. U. Rochester, N.Y., 1964-67, asso. prof., 1968-74, prof., 1974—, chmn. dept., 1972-77; vis. fellow Joint Inst. for Lab. Astrophysics, U. Colo., 1970-71. Mem. editorial bd.: Geophysical Astrophysical Fluid Dynamics, 1977-80; Contbr. articles to profl. jours. Mem. ASME, Internat. Astron. Union, Am. Phys. Soc., Microcirculatory Soc., Internat. Soc. Oxygen Transport to Tissue. Home: 210 Chelmsford Rd Rochester NY 14618 Office: Dept Mech Engring U Rochester Rochester NY 14627

CLARK, ALLEN MINOTT, advertising agency executive; b. Albany, N.Y., Feb. 28, 1936; s. William Minott, Jr. and Betty (Murray) C.; m. Whitney Olson, Oct. 1, 1960; children: Anthony Pierce, Margot Elizabeth, Robinson Gill. B.A. cum laude, Amherst Coll., 1958. Account exec. B.B.D.O., N.Y.C., 1959-61; account supr. Grey Advt., N.Y.C., 1962-67; v.p., mgmt. supr. Ogilvy & Mather, N.Y.C., 1968-75; sr. v.p., mgmt. supr. S.S.C.&B., Inc., N.Y.C., 1976-77; partner, exec. v.p. Della Femina, Travisano & Partners, N.Y.C., 1977—. Home: 740 Soundview Dr Mamaroneck NY 10543 Office: 625 Madison Ave New York NY 10022

CLARK, ANITA LOUISE, journalist; b. Flint, Mich., Mar. 18, 1950; d. Arthur James and Mary Lydia (Peacock) C. B.A., U. Mich., 1972; M.S. in Journalism, Northwestern U., 1973. Reporter intern Chgo. Today, 1973; reporter Suburban Trib, Hinsdale, Ill, 1973-75, Wis. State Jour., Madison, 1975—. Recipient Nat. Headliner award Atlantic City (N.J.) Press Club, 1978. Mem. Investigative Reporters and Editors. Home: 821 W Lakeside St Madison WI 53715 Office: Wis State Jour 1901 Fish Hatchery Rd Madison WI 53708

CLARK, ARTHUR WATTS, insurance company executive; b. Seattle, Nov. 28, 1922; s. Irving Marshall and Nell (Watts) C.; m. Mary Dick Cannon, Nov. 21, 1942; children: Arthur Watts, Claiborne Marshall, Johnston Jewell. A.B., U. N.C., 1943; M.A., U. Calif., 1948. Dir. planning Home Security Life Ins. Co., Durham, N.C., 1952-58, v.p., 1959-63, exec. v.p., 1964-67, pres., 1967-75, chmn., chief exec. officer, 1975—, also dir.; chmn., chief exec. officer Peoples Life Ins. Co. of Washington, D.C., 1983—; dir. Central Carolina Bank & Trust Co.; mem. Res. Forces Policy Bd., Office Sec. Def., 1975-78. Treas. Research Triangle Regional Planning Commn., 1959-63; mem. N.C. Health Ins. Adv. Bd., 1966-70; chmn. bd. dirs. N.C. Central U. Found. Served with USAAF, 1942-46; with USAF, 1950-52; maj. gen. USAFR ret. Decorated D.S.M., Legion of Merit with oak leaf cluster, Bronze Star, Meritorious Service medal, Air Force Commendation medal. Mem. Am. Life Ins. Assn. (dir. 1973-75, 83—), Life Office Mgmt. Assn. (dir. 1973-76), Am. Council Life Ins. (dir. 1976), Life Insurers Conf. (exec. com. 1972-75), Am. Life Conv. (dir. 1972), Phi Beta Kappa, Sigma Xi. Home: 3540 Rugby Rd Durham NC 27707 Office: Box 61 Durham NC 27702

CLARK, BIRGE MALCOLM, architect; b. Palo Alto, Calif., Apr. 16, 1893; s. Arthur B. and Grace (Birge) C.; m. Lucile Townley, June 15, 1922; children—Richard Townley, Dean Townley, Birge Gaylord, Malcolm Mallory. A.B., Stanford, 1914; M. Arch., Columbia, 1917. Practicing architect, 1921—; vice chmn. bd. No. Calif. Savs. & Loan Assn.; lectr. in architecture Stanford, 1950-71. Served to capt. USAAF, 1917-18; comdg. officer 3d Balloon Co. Decorated Silver Star; named Palo Alto Citizen of Yr., 1981. Fellow AIA. Club: Kiwanian. Home: 1490 Edgewood Dr Palo Alto CA 94301 Office 3200 Hanover St Palo Alto CA 94304

CLARK, BLAIR, journalist; b. East Hampton, N.Y., Aug. 22, 1917; s. William and Marjory (Blair) C.; children—Timothy Blair, Cameron, Ian R. Grad., St. Marks Sch., Southborough, Mass., 1935; A.B., Harvard, 1940. Reporter St. Louis Post-Dispatch, 1940-41; pub. N.H. Sunday News, Manchester, 1946-48; editorial writer Boston Herald-Traveler, 1950-52; fgn. corr. CBS News, Paris, France, 1953-56, N.Y.C., 1957-60, gen. mgr., v.p., 1961-64; asso. pub. N.Y. Post, 1965-66; campaign mgr. for Senator Eugene J. McCarthy, 1968; editor The Nation mag., 1976-78; Ferris prof. Princeton U., 1979-80; fellow N.Y. Inst. for Humanities, N.Y. U., 1980. Trustee Harvard Crimson. Home: 229 E 48th St New York NY 10017

CLARK, BLAKE, author, business executive; b. Howell, Tenn., July 11, 1908; s. Thomas B. and Ethel (Harris) C.; m. Deena Speliakos (div. 1972); 1 dau., Nikia; m. Gretta Clark (div. 1979). B.A., Vanderbilt U., 1929, M.A., 1930, Ph.D., 1938; student, U. London, 1933-34. Instr., U. Hawaii, 1930-34, asst. prof., 1934-42; information officer U.S. Office Civilian Def., Washington, 1942-43, OSS, 1943-46; roving editor Reader's Digest, 1946-77; pres. Classic Motor Cars. Author: Oriental England, 1939, Omai, First Polynesian Ambassador to England, 1940, Paradise Limited, 1941, Remember Pearl Harbor, 1942, Advertising Smoke Screen, 1943, (with George Tweed) Robinson Crusoe, USN, 1945, (with Nicol Smith) Into Siam, 1945, Hawaii, The 49th State, 1947, (with Morris Frank) First Lady of the Seeing Eye, 1957; Contbr. articles to popular mags. Clubs: Met., Univ., Chevaliers de Tastevin, Cosmos (Washington); Burning Tree (Bethesda, Md.). Home: 5101 River Rd Apt 1818 Bethesda MD 20816 Office: 1930 West St Annapolis MD 21401

CLARK, BRONSON PETTIBONE, former economic development official; b. Cleveland Heights, Ohio, Oct. 6, 1918; s. Sheldon P. and Hazel (Baker) C.; m. Eleanor Meanor, Dec. 21, 1940; children: Mallory (Mrs. George Waldman, Jr.), Jennifer (Mrs. Robert Kahn), Melissa (Mrs. Thomas Scheffey), Alison. A.B. in Polit. Sci, Antioch Coll., 1941; Dr. Human Reconstrn., Wilmington (Ohio) Coll., 1974. New Eng. sec. Fellowship of Reconciliation, 1941-42; served in U.S. penitentiaries as conscientious objector, 1943-44; with Am. Friends Service Com., 1945-50, 61—, mem. nat. bd., 1964-67; program asso. Spl. Vietnam Effort, 1967-68, exec. sec., 1968-74; sec.-treas. Community Devel., Inc., 1951-60; v.p. Gilford Instrument Labs., Inc., Oberlin, Ohio, 1964-67, dir., 1958-80, chmn. bd., 1979-80; sec. Penobscot Bay Fish and Cold Storage Co., 1978-82; dir. Coastal Enterprises Inc. Co-author: Peace in Vietnam: a New Approach in Southeast Asia, 1966. Charter mem. Bus. Execs. Move for Vietnam Peace, 1967; selectman Vinalhaven, Maine, 1978-81; mem. Mid-Coast Monthly Meeting of Friends, Damariscotta, Maine, 1982—; trustee Wilmington (Ohio) Coll., 1970-75. Mem. ACLU, Council Fgn. Relations. Home: Box 483 Rockport ME 04856

CLARK, BRUCE BUDGE, educator; b. Georgetown, Idaho, Apr. 9, 1918; s. Marvin E. and Alice (Budge) C.; m. Ouida Raphiel, Nov. 7, 1946; children—Lorraine, Bradley, Robert, Jeffrey, Shawn, Sandra. B.A., U. Utah, 1943, Ph.D., 1951; M.A., Brigham Young U., 1948. Teaching fellow Brigham Young U., 1946-47, U. Utah, 1947-50; asst. prof. Brigham Young U., 1950-55, asso. prof., 1955-58, prof., 1959—, dir. humanities program, 1958-60, chmn. dept. English, 1960-65; dean Coll. Humanities, 1965—. Author: The Spectrum of Faith in Victorian Literature, 1966, The Challenge of Teaching, 1966, Romanticism through Modern Eyes, 1968, Oscar Wilde, A Study in Genius and Tragedy, 1970, Brigham Young on Education, 1970, Idealists in Revolt, 1975; Editor: Richard Evans Quote Book, 1971; anthology (Out of the Best Books, vol. 1, 1964, vol. II, 1966, vol. III, 1967, vol. IV, 1968, vol. V, 1969, Great Short Stories for Discussion and Delight, 1979; Contbr. articles to profl. jours. Served with AUS, 1944-46. Recipient Karl G. Maeser Teaching Excellence award, 1972. Mem. Nat. Council Tchrs. English, Modern Lang. Assn., Rocky Mountain Modern Lang. Assn., Coll. Conf. on Composition and Communications, Phi Kappa Phi. Mem. Ch. of Jesus Christ of Latter-day Saints. Home: 365 E 1655 South St Orem UT 84057 Office: Brigham Young U Provo UT 84602

CLARK, BURTON ROBERT, sociologist, educator; b. Pleasantville, N.J., Sept. 6, 1921; s. Burton H. and Cornelia (Amole) C.; m. Adele Halitsky, Aug. 31, 1949; children: Philip Neil, Adrienne. B.A., UCLA, 1949, Ph.D., 1954. Asst. prof. sociology Stanford U., 1953-56; research asso., asst. prof. edn. Harvard U., 1956-58; asso. prof., then prof. edn. and asso. research sociologist, then research sociologist U. Calif. at Berkeley, 1958-66; prof. sociology Yale U., 1966-80, chmn. dept., 1969-72; chmn. Higher Edn. Research Group, 1973-80; prof. sociology Allan M. Cartter prof. higher edn. UCLA, 1980—. Author: Adult Education in Transition, 1956, The Open Door College, 1960, Educating the Expert Society, 1962, The Distinctive College, 1970, The Problems of American Education, 1975, Academic Power in Italy, 1977, The Higher Education System, 1983; co-author: Students and Colleges, 1972, Youth: Transition to Adulthood, 1973, Academic Power in the United States, 1976, Academic Power: Patterns of Authority in Seven National Systems of Higher Education, 1978. Served with AUS, 1942-46. Mem. Internat., Am., Pacific sociol. assns., Am. Ednl. Research Assn. (Am. Coll. Testing award 1979), Assn. Study Higher Edn. (pres. 1979-80), Am. Assn. Higher Edn. Home: 201 Ocean Ave Santa Monica CA 90402 Office: Dept Edn UCLA Los Angeles CA 90024

CLARK, BYRON BRYANT, pharmacologist; b. Temple, Tex., Apr. 5, 1908; s. Oscar W. and Ida (Hansen) C.; m. Gladys Lawson, Jan. 26, 1931; children—Barbara (Mrs. Edward Riter), Jack, Kenneth. B.A., Baylor U., 1930; M.S., State U., Iowa, 1932, Ph.D., 1934. Instr. physiology, pharmacology Albany Med. Coll., 1936-39, asst. prof., 1939-40, asso. prof., 1940-47; became prof. pharmacology, chmn. dept. Med. Sch. Tufts U., 1947; dir. pharmacology and chemotherapy Mead Johnson Research Center, Evansville, Ind., 1957-62, v.p., 1962-68; dir. pharmacology-toxicology program Nat. Inst. Gen. Med. Scis., NIH, Bethesda, Md., 1968-79; cons. pharmacologist N.E. Center Hosp.; mem. com. on drug safety, drug research bd. Nat. Acad. Scis.-NRC. Contbr. chpts. in books, articles profl. jours. Recipient NIH Dir.'s award, 1977; Sec. HEW cert. merit, 1979. Fellow AAAS; mem. Am. Soc. Pharmacology and Exptl. Therapeutics, Soc. Exptl. Biology and Medicine, Soc. Toxicology, N.Y. Acad. Scis. Home: 9612 Linfield Dr Cincinnati OH 45242

CLARK, CANDY, actress; b. Norman, Okla., June 20; d. Thomas Prest and Ella Lee (Padberg) C. Student public schs., Ft. Worth. Appeared in: movies Fat City, 1971, American Graffiti, 1973 (nominated for best supporting actress), The Man Who Fell To Earth, 1975, Citizens Band, 1976, The Big Sleep, 1977, When Ya' Coming Back Red Ryder, 1978, More American Graffiti, 1978, National Lampoon Goes To The Movies, 1981, Blue Thunder, 1981, Amityville 3-D, 1983; appeared in: TV movies Amateur Night at the Dixie Bar and Grill, 1978, Where The Ladies Go, 1980, Rodeo Girl, 1980; appeared: in off-Broadway show A Coupla White Chicks Sitting Around Talking, 1981. Office: care Pat McQueeney 146 N Almont Dr Apt 8 Los Angeles CA 90048

CLARK, CAROLYN COCHRAN, lawyer; b. Kansas City, Mo., Oct. 30, 1941; d. John Rogers and Betty Charleston (Holmes) Cochran; m. L. David Clark, Jr., Dec. 29, 1967; children: Gregory David, Timothy Rogers. B.A., U. Mo., 1963; LL.B., Harvard U., 1968. Bar: N.Y. 1968, Fla. 1979. Assoc. Milbank, Tweed, Hadley & McCloy, N.Y.C., 1968-76, ptnr., 1977—. Mem. deferred giving com. Harvard Law Sch. Fund; mem. vis. com. Harvard Law Sch., 1982—; trustee Madison Ave. Presbyn. Ch., 1984—. Fellow Am. Coll. Probate Counsel; mem. Assn. Bar City N.Y. (sec. com. philanthropic orgns. 1976-82, mem. com. trusts, estates and surrogates cts. 1977-80), N.Y. State Bar Assn. (com. estate planning, trusts and estates sect. 1978—), ABA (chmn. subcom. income taxation of charitable trusts 1976-78, vice chmn. com. charitable instns.), Am. Law Inst., Harvard Law Sch., Assn. Greater N.Y. (trustee 1978-80, v.p. 1980-81, pres. 1981-82), Nat. Harvard Law Sch. Assn. (exec. com. 1978—), Soc. Colonial Dames Am. in Mo. Clubs: Wall Street, Cosmopolitan (N.Y.C.). Home: 161 E 79th St New York NY 10021 Office: 1 Chase Manhattan Plaza New York NY 10005

CLARK, CHAMP, journalist, author, educator; b. St. Louis, Aug. 24, 1923; s. Bennett Champ and Miriam (Marsh) C.; m. Mizzell Phillips, Feb. 2, 1949; children—Genevieve, Jane, Champ, Julia. Grad., Kent Sch., 1940; student, U. Mo., 1940-42, 46-47. Reporter Kansas City (Mo.) Star, 1947-51; writer Time mag., 1951-74, sr. editor, 1960-74, Chgo. bur. chief, 1969-72; sr. corr., 1972-74; tchr. journalism U. Va., Charlottesville, 1976—. Author: The Badlands, 1974, Flood, 1983. Chmn. 7th dist. Va. Republican Party. Served with USMCR, 1942-46. Mem. Sigma Chi. Home: Box 308 RFD 1 Ruckersville VA 22968

CLARK, CHAPIN DEWITT, law educator; b. Lawrence, Kans., Dec. 27, 1930; s. Carroll DeWitt and Pearl (Holl) C.; m. Dorothy L. Becker, May 25, 1952; children—Julia Kay, Jeffrey Becker. A.B., U. Kans., 1952, LL.B., 1954; LL.M., Columbia U., 1959. Bar: Kans. 1954, Oreg. 1965. Asst. prof. law U. S.D., 1959-62; asso. prof. law U. Oreg., 1962-67, prof., 1967—, dean, 1974-80; vice chmn. Oreg. Water Policy Rev. Bd., 1975-77, chmn., 1977-79; vis. prof. U.S. Mil. Acad., West Point, N.Y., 1980-81. Contbr. articles to profl. jours. Pres. Planned Parenthood Lane County, 1975-76; mem. Gov.'s Commn. on Oceanography, 1967-68. Served with JAGC U.S. Army, 1954-58. Mem. Am. Bar Assn., Am. Judicature Soc., AAUP (pres. U. Oreg. chpt. 1970-71). Club: Masons. Home: 3565 Knob Hill Eugene OR 97403 Office: U Oreg Sch of Law Eugene OR 97405

CLARK, CHARLES, judge; b. Memphis, Sept. 12, 1925; s. Charles and Anita (Massengill) C. Student, Millsaps Coll., 1943-44, Tulane U., 1944; LL.B., U. Miss., 1948. Bar: Miss. bar 1948. Mem. firm Wells, Thomas & Wells, Jackson, Miss., 1948-61, Cox, Dunn & Clark, Jackson, 1961-69; spl. asst. to atty. gen. State of Miss., 1961-66; judge U.S. Ct. Appeals, 5th Circuit, Jackson, 1969—, chief judge, 1981—. Served to lt. USNR, 1943-46, 51-52. Mem. Miss. Bar Assn., Am. Coll. Trial Lawyers, Jud. Conf. U.S. (chmn. com. budget). Episcopalian. Home: Jackson MS Office: US Courthouse Jackson MS 39205

CLARK, CHARLES DAVID, food company executive; b. Hamilton, Ont., Can., Mar. 22, 1939; s. Charles Henry and Marguerite Sandell (Waller) C.; m. Mary Edna Kelly (Aug. 25, 1965); children: Alexandra, Sarah, Hazel Ann. B.A., McMaster U., 1963; M.B.A., U. Western Onst., 1966. Dir. mktg. Dominion Seven-Up, Toronto, Ont., Can., 1970-72; vp.p mktg.l SThomas J. Lipton Inc., Toronto, 1972-76; exec. v.p. Thomas J. Lipton Inc., Toronto, 1976-78, pres., chief ops. officer, 1978-82; pres., chief exec. officer thomas J. Lipton Inc., Toronto, 1982-83, Campbell (Soup Co. Ltd.), 1983—; dir. Irving Bank Can. Bd. govs. YMCA met. Toronto, 1979-83; provincial exec. council Boy Scouts Can., Ont., 1977-83. Fellow Inst. Dirs. Can.; mem. Grocery Products Mfrs. Can. (dir., exec. com., chmn. food policy task force), Can. Food Porcessors Assn. (dir.). Clubs: Donalda, Granite (Toronto). Home: 25 Farmigton Crescent Agincourt ON Canada MIS 1E9 Office: Campbell Soup Co. Ltd 60 Birmingham St Toronto ON Canada M8V 2B8

CLARK, CHARLES EDWIN, communications company and private foundation executive; b. Cuyahoga Falls, Ohio, June 1, 1920; s. Robert McCleaf and Nellie Lois (Marsh) C.; m. Marvel Gale Bonesteel, Aug. 7, 1944; children: William Charles, Robert M. B.S. in Bus. Adminstrn., Kent State U., 1942. C.P.A., Ohio, 1951. Agt. IRS, Akron, Ohio, 1945-52; auditor Beacon Jour. Pub. Co., Akron, 1952-63, bus. mgr., 1963-67; treas. Knight-Ridder Newspapers Inc., Akron, 1967-74, Miami, Fla., 1967-74, corp. sec., 1974—; trustee, sec.-treas. Knight Found., Akron, 1969—. Served to lt. (s.g.) USN, 1942-45; PTO. Mem. Am. Soc. Corp. Secs. Republican. Clubs: Miami; La Gorce Country (Miami Beach, Fla.). Home: 2233 Brickell Ave Apt 1117 Miami FL 33129 Office: Knight-Ridder Newspapers Inc One Herald Plaza Miami FL 33101

CLARK, CHARLES GILBERT, state official; b. Los Angeles, Jan. 13, 1923; s. Charles J. and Josephine (Ballard) C.; m. Mary Alice Burns, Feb. 11, 1950; children: Douglas, Athline, Betty-Jo, Charles Gilbert, Thomas. B.A. in Edn, U. Calif., Santa Barbara, 1945. Tchr. Kamehameha Schs., Honolulu, 1945-47; vice prin. Farrington High Sch., Honolulu, 1947-50; prin. Maunaloa Sch., Molokai, Hawaii, Pearl Harbor Intermediate Sch., Oahu, Hawaii, Kailua High Sch., Oahu, to 1958; civil service dir., then mng. dir. City and County Honolulu, 1958-62; propr. Clark Realty Co., Honolulu, 1962-68; with Office Personnel Service, Hawaii Dept. Edn., 1968-76, supt. edn., 1976-82; dir. Hawaii Dept. Health, 1982—. Active local Boy Scouts Am., YMCA, John Howard Assn. Mem. Oahu Edn. Assn., Pub. Personnel Assn., Soc. Personnel Adminstrn., Am. Soc. Pub. Adminstrn. Roman Catholic. Home: 84 Kailuana Pl Kailua HI 96734 Office: PO Box 2360 Queen Liliokalani Bldg Honolulu HI 96813

CLARK, CHARLES JOSEPH, mem. Canadian Parliament, former prime minister; b. High River, Alta., Can., June 5, 1939; s. Charles A. and Grace R. (Welch) C.; m. Maureen McTerr, June 30, 1973; 1 dau., Catherine Jane. B.A. in History, U. Alta., 1960, M.A. in Polit. Sci., 1973; LL.D. hon., U. N.B., 1976. Lectr. polit. sci. U. Alta., 1965-67; journalist CBS Radio and TV, Calgary (Alta.) Herald, Edmonton Jour., 1966; dir. provincial orgn. Peter Lougheed, 1966; exec. asst. in Ottawa to Robert L. Stanfield, Ont., 1967-70, M.P. for Rocky Mountain, Ottawa, 1972-79, M.P. for Yellowhead, 1979—; leader Progressive Conservative Party, 1976-83; prime minister Can., 1979-80. Roman Catholic. Office: Room 163 East Block House of Commons Ottawa ON Canada K1A 0A6

CLARK, CHARLES LESTER, educator; b. San Jose, Calif., Nov. 17, 1917; s. Charles James and Minnie Bethiah (Lester) C.; m. Jean Show, Sept. 8, 1940; children—Charles Dennis, Robert Keith, Jeffrey Craig. Student, San Jose State Coll., 1935-38; A.B., Stanford, 1939, A.M., 1940; Ph.D., U. Va., 1944. Instr. math. U. Va., 1942-44, vis. prof., 1955-56; from asst. prof. to prof. Oreg. State Coll., 1944-57; prof. math. Calif. State U., Los Angeles, 1957—, head math. dept., 1957-64, 71-77, dir. instl. research, 1964-71, dir. coll. computing center, 1961-71, chmn. acad. senate, 1968-69; cons. edn., industry, legis. groups, 1958—; info. privacy and security advisor Calif. State Univ. and Coll. System, 1977—. Royall Victor fellow Stanford, 1940-41; du Pont fellow U. Va., 1941-42. Mem. Am. Math. Soc., Math. Assn. Am., AAAS, Assn. Computing Machinery, AAUP, Phi Beta Kappa, Sigma Xi. Home: 23000 Sierra Dr PO Box 1006 Twain Harte CA 95383

CLARK, CHARLES MARTIN, JR., investment banker; b. Summit, N.J., Nov. 2, 1905; s. Charles Martin and Bessie (Milligan) C.; m. Valerie Graham, Aug. 1, 1939 (dec. Apr. 1971); children: Ann Valer (Mrs. Josiah T. Austin), Cecily Martin, John Sheldon; m. Helen M. Lonergan, Aug. 3, 1972. Grad., Hotchkiss Sch., 1924; B.S., Harvard U., 1928; hon. diploma, U.S. Mcht. Marine Acad., 1945. Reporter Bradstreet Co., 1928-29; statistician Second Nat. Bank, Boston, 1930-33; pres. Martin Co. (printers), Boston, 1934-35; partner Charles Clark & Co.; mems. N.Y. Stock Exchange, 1937-47; engaged in estate mgmt. and directorship cos., 1948-61; partner Sullivan & Co.; mems. N.Y. Stock Exchange, 1962-64; ltd. partner Estabrook & Co., 1965-69; chmn. bd. Estabrook & Co., Inc., 1970-72; pres., dir. Sherwood Investors, Inc.; dir. Dun & Bradstreet, Inc., 1935-76; U.S. adviser N. Atlantic Planning Bd. Ocean Shipping, 1952. Trustee Kips Bay Boys Club, N.Y.C.; trustee, v.p. Hewitt Sch., N.Y.C., to 1983. Served to lt. (s.g.) U.S. Maritime Service, 1942-44. Presbyn. Clubs: Down Town Assn., Union (N.Y.C.); Piping Rock (Locust Valley, L.I.); Seawanhaka Corinthian Yacht (Oyster Bay); Jupiter Island (Hobe Sound, Fla.); Everglades (Palm Beach, Fla.); Portmarnock Golf (Dublin, Ireland). Home: E Main St Oyster Bay NY 11771 Office: 120 Broadway Suite 3044 New York NY 10005 *There are many complicated formulas for success. I have found one word sufficient - Integrity.*

CLARK, CHARLES T(ALIFERRO), business statistics educator; b. Danville, Ill., Mar. 18, 1917; s. Charles A. and Kathryn S. (Gentry) C.; m. Pearl W. DuBose, Oct. 6, 1943; children: Charles A., Mary D., Robert S. B.B.A., U. Tex., 1938, M.B.A., 1939, Ph.D., 1956. Asst. mgr. Austin C. of C., Tex., 1940-41; dir. personnel U. Tex., Austin, 1946-59, asst. prof. bus. stats., 1959-60, assoc. prof., 1961-79, prof., 1979—; bd. dirs. Tex. Student Publs., Austin, 1964-69, Tex. Union, 1969-83, Univ. Fed. Credit Union, 1977—, Univ. Coop. Soc., 1980—. Author numerous text books; (with L.L. Schkade) textbooks Statistical Analysis for Adminstrative Decision, 1969, 4th edit., 1983, (with John R. Stockton) Introduction to Business and Economic Statistics, 1971, 3d edit., 1980; contbr. articles to profl. jours. Served to 2d lt. USAAC, 1941-46; PTO. Recipient 11 teaching awards U. Tex., 1960-80. Mem. Coll. and Univ. Personnel Assn. (pres. 1959), Austin Personnel Assn. (pres. 1950), Austin Stat. Assn. (pres. 1975). Lodge: Rotary (Austin). Home: 4106 Farhills Dr Austin TX 78731 Office: U Tex Austin TX 78712

CLARK, CLIFFORD D., university president; b. Moulton, Iowa, Feb. 26, 1925; s. Artie Seymour and Myrtle Ida (Severs) C.; m. Margery Blair Miller, June 19, 1949; children—Geoffrey, Kathyrn. A.B. in Econs, U. Kans., 1948; M.A., U. Chgo., 1950, Ph.D., 1953. Instr. stats. Loyola U., Chgo., 1950-51; fgn. affairs officer research div. CIA, 1951-55; asst.; prof. econs. N.C. State U., Raleigh, 1955-57; assoc. prof. econs. Grad. Sch. Bus. Adminstrn. N.Y. U., 1957-62, prof., 1962-68, head, research office, 1963-64, assoc. dean, 1964-65, vice dean, 1965-68; dean Sch. Bus., prof. econs. U. Kans., 1968-73; v.p. acad. affairs SUNY, Binghamton, 1973-74, acting pres., 1974-75, pres., 1975—; dir. 1st City div. Lincoln 1st Bank N.A., Security Mut. Life Ins. Co. N.Y., Transitional Opportunities Corp. Contbr. articles to profl. jours. Bd. dirs. Broome County Urban League, 1979—, Wilson Hosp., 1980—. Served with U.S. Army, 1943-46. Decorated Bronze Star. Mem. Am. Council Edn., Am. Assn. Higher Edn., Nat. Assn. Land Grant Univs. and Colls., Broome County C. of C. (dir. 1978—). Club: Live Wire (Binghamton). Office: Vestal Pkwy E Binghamton NY 13901

CLARK, CLIFTON BOB, physicist; b. nr. Fort Smith, Ark., July 8, 1927; s. Clifton Breckenridge and Coly (Stroud) C.; m. Sue Magruder, Sept. 1, 1950; children—Carol Jane, Charles Brian, Richard Thomas. B.A., U. Ark., 1949, M.A., 1950; Ph.D., U. Md., 1957. Asst. prof. sci. Florence State Tchrs. Coll., 1950-51; asst. prof. physics U.S. Naval Acad., 1951-55; asso. prof., 1956-57; physicist U.S. Naval Research Lab., 1955-56; asso. prof. physics So. Meth. U., Dallas, 1957-61, prof., 1961-65, head dept., 1962-65; physicist, head dept. U. N.C., Greensboro, 1965-75, prof., 1965—; vis. prof. physics Fla. State U., 1975-76. Served with USNR, 1945-46. Mem. Am. Assn. Physics Tchrs. (pres. S. Atlantic Coast sect. 1974-75, 76-77), Am. Phys. Soc. (treas. Southeast sect. 1974—), AAAS, N.C. Acad. Sci., Phi Beta Kappa, Sigma Xi, Sigma Pi Sigma, Pi Mu Epsilon, Kappa Mu Epsilon, Omicron Delta Kappa. Home: 800 Montrose Dr Greensboro NC 27410 Office: Physics Dept U NC Greensboro NC 27412 *I believe people who are happy are those who accept doing things they do not enjoy as the price they pay for getting to do the things they enjoy. The most pleasant of experiences is the completion of a task which demanded extremely hard work. The most unhappy people I have known are those who cheated themselves of this satisfaction, because they tired of hard work and quit before they completed an endeavor.*

CLARK, COLIN WHITCOMB, mathematics educator; b. Vancouver, B.C., Can., June 18, 1931; s. George Savage and Irene (Stewart) C.; m. Janet Arlene Davidson, Sept. 17, 1955; children: Jennifer Kathleen, Karen Elizabeth, Graeme David. B.A., U. B.C., 1953; Ph.D., U. Wash., 1958. Instr. math. U. Calif., Berkeley, 1958-60; asst. prof. math., U. B.C., 1960-65, assoc. prof., 1965-68, prof., 1968—; Vis. prof. math. N.Mex. State U., 1970-71; vis. scientist Fisheries and Oceanography div. C.S.I.R.O., Cronulla, Australia, 1975-76. Author: The Theoretical Side of Calculus, 1972, Mathematical Bioeconomics, 1976, Elementary Mathematical Analysis, 1982; Contbr. articles to profl. jours. Mem. Can. Applied Math. Soc. (pres. 1981—), Soc. Indsl. and Applied Math. Home: 9531 Finn Rd Richmond BC Canada V7A 2L3 Office: Math Dept U British Columbia Vancouver BC Canada V6T 1W5

CLARK, DAVID DELANO, physicist; b. Austin, Tex., Feb. 10, 1924; s. David Lee and Grace (Delano) C.; m. Gladys Braunstein, Dec. 27, 1949; children: Marcia Susan, Gordon Richard, Janet Mirella. Student, U. Tex., 1941-42, 46; A.B. in Physics, U. Calif. at Berkeley, 1948; Ph.D. (AEC predoctoral fellow 1950-52), U. Calif. at Berkeley, 1953. Research asso. Brookhaven Nat. Lab., 1953-55, vis. scientist, summers, 1957, 58, 64, 73, fall 79; mem. faculty engring. physics Cornell U., 1955—, asso. prof., 1958-65, prof., 1965—, dir. Ward Lab. Nuclear Engring., 1960—; cons. Gen. Atomic Co., summer 1959; vis. prof. Tech. U., Munich, W. Ger., 1976. Contbr. articles to profl. jours. Served with USAAF, 1942-46. Euratom fellow Euratom Research Center, Ispra, Italy, 1962; Guggenheim Found. fellow Niels Bohr Inst., 1968-69. Mem. Am. Phys. Soc., Phi Beta Kappa, Sigma Xi. Home: 105 Needham Pl Ithaca NY 14850

CLARK, DAVID HATHAWAY, steel co. exec.; b. Canton, Ohio, June 9, 1928; s. Lyman H. and Mary M. (McClell) C.; m. Barbara Noaker, June 19, 1948; children—Charles H., Deborah Clark Batchelder, Steven N., Constance S. B.S. in Mech. Engring, U. Mich., 1949; postgrad. program for sr. execs, M.I.T., 1974. Registered profl. engr., Ohio. With Republic Steel Corp., Cleve., 1956—, asst. v.p. steel ops., 1975-79, v.p. ops., 1979-80, exec. v.p., 1980—. Mem. Am. Iron and Steel Inst., Nat. Soc. Profl. Engrs., Assn. Iron and Steel Engrs. Republican. Episcopalian. Clubs: Cleve. Yachting, Union, Cleve. Athletic. Office: Republic Steel Corp PO Box 6778 Cleveland OH 44101

CLARK, DAVID LEIGH, marine geologist educator; b. Albuquerque, N.Mex., June 15, 1931; s. Leigh William and Sadie (Ollerton) C.; m. Louise Boley, Aug. 31, 1951; children: Steven, Douglas, Julee, Linda. B.S., Brigham Young U., 1953, M.S., 1954; Ph.D., U. Iowa, 1957. Geologist Standard Oil Calif., Albuquerque, 1954; asst. prof. So. Meth. U., Dallas, 1957-59; assoc. prof. Brigham Young U., Provo, Utah, 1959-63; prof. geology and geophysics U. Wis.-Madison, 1963—, chmn. dept. geology and geophysics, 1971-74. Author Fossils, Paleontology, Evolution, 1968,72; author and coordinator: Treatise on Invertebrate Paleontology-Conodonts, 1981. Recipient Fulbright award, Bonn, W.Ger., 1965-66; Disting. Professorship U. Wis., 1974. Fellow Geol. Soc. Am.; mem. Paleontol. Soc., Am. Assn. Petroleum Geologists, Soc. Econ. Paleontologists and Mineralogists, Am. Geophys. Union, Pander Soc., Paleontologisches Gesselschaft, Paleontol. Assn., N.Am. Micropaleontology Soc., AAAS. Mormon. Home: 2812 Oxford Rd Madison WI 53705 Office: Dept Geology and Geophysics U Wis Madison WI 53706

CLARK, DAVID LOUIS, teacher educator, author; b. Binghamton, N.Y., Nov. 14, 1929; s. Ralph Keeler and Catherine (Hartigan) C.; m. Elsie Edith Shaw, June 28, 1952; children: Patricia, Michael, Timothy, Catherine. B.A., N.Y. State Coll. Tchrs., Albany, 1951, M.A., 1952; Ed.D., Columbia Tchrs. Coll., 1954. Research asst. N.Y. State Tchrs. Assn., 1954-56; asst. to supt. Garden City (N.Y.) Pub. Schs., 1956-58; dir. coop. research program U.S. Office Edn., 1958-62; asso. dean, prof. edn. Ohio State U., 1962-66; prof. edn. Ind. U., 1966—, dean, 1966-74. Author: (with John E. Hopkins) Educational Research, Development, and Diffusion Manpower, 1969, Federal Policy in Educational Research and Development, 1975, (with Egon G. Guba) The Configurational Perspective: A New View of Educational Knowledge Production and Utilization, 1974, Teacher Education Institutions as Innovators, Knowledge Producers and Change Agencies, 1977, (with Gerald Marker) The Institutionalization of American Teacher Education, 1975, (with Mary A. Amiot) The Impact of the Reagan Administration on Federal Educational Policy, 1981, (with Linda S. Lotto) Educational Knowledge Dissemination and Utilization, 1978, (with Linda S. Lotto and Martha M. McCarthy) Secondary Source Study of Exceptionality in Urban Elementary Schs, 1980, (with McKibbin and Malkas) Alternative Perspectives for Viewing Educational Organizations, 1981, In Consideration of Goal-Free Planning: The Failure of Traditional Planning Systems in Education, 1981; also reports in field. Mem. Am. Ednl. Research Assn., NEA, Am. Assn. Sch. Adminstrs., Phi Delta Kappa. Home: 1243 Matlock Rd Bloomington IN 47401

CLARK, DAVID RANDOLPH, wholesale grocer; b. Columbia, S.C., Mar. 25, 1943; s. Joseph Wilbur and Josephine (Timberlake) C.; m. Carole Jane Cooper, Aug. 21, 1965; 1 dau., Catherine. B.A., Wofford Coll., 1965; M.B.A., U. S.C., 1966. Vice pres., gen. mgr. Thomas & Howard Co., Spartanburg, S.C., 1969-77, pres., Columbia, S.C., 1977—; pres. T & H Ins. Agy., Inc.; dir. Timberlake Grocery Co. Mem. campaign cabinet United Way, 1975. Served with U.S. Army, 1967-68. Mem. Nat. Am. Wholesale Grocers Assn., S.C. Assn. Convenience Food Stores (dir.), Scabbard and Blade, Phi Beta Kappa, Pi Gamma Mu, Pi Kappa Alpha. Episcopalian. Clubs: Rotary, Forest Lake. Office: PO Box 947 Columbia SC 29202

CLARK, DAVID WILLARD, hosp. adminstr.; b. Rockford, Ill., May 17, 1930; s. Willard Wilbur and Arline Marie (Anderson) C.; m. Barbara Ardel Boyd, June 18, 1955; children—Deborah Jean, Alan Boyd. B.S., Beloit (Wis.) Coll., 1952; M.B.A., U. Chgo., 1955. Mem. adminstrv. staff Univ. Hosps., Cleve., 1955—, asst. adminstr., then asso. adminstr., 1960-67, adminstr., 1967-79, sr. v.p., 1979—; pres. Hosp. Fin. Corp., 1975-76, Med. Center Co., 1976—. Chmn. hosp. div. United Torch, Cleve. Served with AUS, 1952-53. Recipient Kate Baron Sci. award, 1952. Mem. Am. Hosp. Assn., Ohio Hosp. Assn. (trustee, dist. chmn.), Am. Coll. Hosp. Adminstrs., Council Teaching Hosps., Phi Beta Kappa. Episcopalian. Club: Masons. Home: 25459 Bryden Rd Beachwood OH 44122 Office: Univ Hosps 2074 Abington Rd Cleveland OH 44106

CLARK, DICK, performer, producer; b. Mt. Vernon, N.Y., Nov. 30, 1929; m. Kari Wigton; children—Richard, Duane, Cindy. Grad., Syracuse U., 1951. Announcer, Sta. WRUN, summer 1950; then staff announcer, Sta. WOLF; rejoined, Sta. WRUN; then joined, Sta. WKTV; announcer, Sta. WFIL, Phila., 1952; host: 32d Ann. Emmy Awards, 1981, Daytime Emmy Awards; formed, Dick Clark Prodns., 1956; exec.: TV producer Natalie Cole Spl; Dick Clark Cinema Prodns. produced Because They're Young, 1960, The Young Doctors, 1961, Psych-Out, 1968, The Savage Seven, 1968, Killers Three, 1969, The Man in the Santa Claus Suit, 1979, The Birth of the Beatles, 1979, Elvis, 1979, The Dark, 1979, Murder in Texas, 1981; host-producer Dick Clark's Rock 'n Roll Revue; also Dick Clark's Nifty 50's; for concert appearances; Author: Your Happiest Years, 1959, To Goof or Not To Goof, 1963, Rock, Roll and Remember, 1976, Looking Great, Staying Young, 1981, Dick Clark's First 25 Years of Rock 'N Roll, 1981; contbr. articles on teenage problems to nat. publs. Recipient daytime emmy award as host $50,000 Pyramid, 1979. Address: care Dick Clark Prodns 3003 W Olive Ave Burbank CA 91505

CLARK, DICK CLARENCE, former U.S. Senator; b. Paris, Iowa, Sept. 14, 1929; s. Clarence and Bernice (Anderson) C.; m. Julie Kennett, 1977; children—Julie Ann, Thomas Richard, Kennett. Student, U. Md. at Wiesbaden, Germany, 1950-52; B.A., Upper Iowa U., Fayette, 1953, LL.D. (hon.), 1973; M.A., U. Iowa, 1956; L.H.D. (hon.), Parsons Coll., 1973, Mt. Mercy Coll., Drake U., Cornell Coll., Haverford Coll., St. Ambrose Coll. Teaching asst. State U. Iowa, 1956-59; asst. prof. history and polit. sci. Upper Iowa U., 1959-64; adminstrv. asst. to Congressman, 1965-72; U.S. senator from, Iowa, 1973-79; ambassador-at-large U.S. coordinator refugee affairs, 1979; sr. fellow Aspen Inst.; Mem. World Food Conf., 1974; also conf. on European history, conf. on Slavic and East European history. Chmn. Iowa Civil Def. Adminstrn., 1963-65, Office Emergency Planning in Iowa, 1963-65; Trustee Upper Iowa Coll., 1972-75. Served with AUS, 1951-52. Mem. Am. Hist. Assn., Am. Assn. Advancement Slavic Studies, AAUP. Home: 4424 Edmunds St NW Washington DC 20007 Office: Aspen Inst 2010 Massachusetts Ave NW Washington DC 20036

CLARK, DONALD CAMERON, diversified company executive; b. Bklyn., Aug. 9, 1931; s. Alexander and Sarah (Cameron) C.; m. Jean Ann Williams, Feb. 6, 1954; children: Donald, Barbara, Thomas. B.B.A., Clarkson Coll., 1953; M.B.A., Northwestern U., 1961. With Household Corp., Chgo., 1955—, asst. sec., 1964-65, sec., asst. treas., 1965-72, treas., 1972-74, sr. v.p., office of chief exec. officer, 1974-76, exec. v.p., 1976, chief fin. officer, 1976—, pres., dir., 1977—; also pres., dir. holding co. Household Internat., Inc., 1981—, chief exec. officer, 1982—; dir. Burch Co., Sq. D. Co. Bd. dirs. Evanston Hosp.; trustee Clarkson Coll., Northwestern U. Served to lt. U.S. Army, 1953-55. Mem. Chgo. Assn. Commerce and Industry (dir.), Econ. Club Chgo. (dir.), Chgo. Council Fgn. Relations. Clubs: Westmoreland Country, Mid-Am.; Commercial (Chgo.). Home: 2828 Blackhawk Rd Wilmette IL 60091 Office: 2700 Sanders Rd Prospect Heights IL 60070

CLARK, DONALD MALIN, assn. exec.; b. Buffalo, Feb. 11, 1929; s. Jack Malin and Louise Mary C.; m. Joan Marie Coyle, Dec. 27, 1958; children—Kevin Malin, Michael John, Elizabeth Anne. B.S., Canisius Coll., Buffalo, 1950, M.A., 1952; Ed.D., SUNY, Buffalo, 1961. Dir. Center for Econ. Edn., SUNY, Buffalo, 1966-70; exec. dir. Niagara Falls (N.Y.) Area Industry-Edn. Council, 1970-79; pres. Nat. Assn. Industry-Edn. Coop., Buffalo, 1979—; pres. Consumer Credit

Counseling Service, Buffalo, 1973, edn. chmn., 1974—; bd. dirs. Nat. Assn. Career Edn., N.Y. State Council Econ. Edn.; radio and TV public info. news commentator, 1962-78. Author: Meeting the Challenge of a Free Society, 1965, also handbooks. Served with Army N.G.; to col. USAR, 1948—. Recipient Kazanjian Found. teaching award, 1968, Freedoms Found. medal, 1965; fellow NAM, 1965. Mem. Am. Soc. Tng. and Devel., Assn. Supervision and Curriculum Devel., AAUP, Nat. Mil. Intelligence Assn., Res. Officers Assn., Phi Delta Kappa. Republican. Roman Catholic. Club: Buffalo Tennis. Home: 235 Hendricks Blvd Buffalo NY 14226 *Being in the vanguard of change has been the most exciting aspect of my professional career. To participate in effecting change, particularly in education and human resources development requires risk taking and the determination to gain support for one's ideas.*

CLARK, DONALD OTIS, lawyer; b. Charlotte, N.C., May 30, 1934; s. Erwin and Ruby Lee (Church) C.; m. Jo Ann Hager, June 15, 1957 (div. 1980); children: Deborah Elise, Stephen Merritt; m. Anja Maria Smith, Nov. 5, 1983. A.B., U. S.C., 1956, J.D. cum laude, 1963; M.A., U. Ill., 1957. Bar: S.C. 1963, Ga. 1964. Practice law, Atlanta, 1963-83; mem. Candler, Cox, McClain & Andrews, 1968-70, McClain, Mellen, Bowling & Hickman, 1970-75; ptnr. King & Spalding, 1975-78; sr. ptnr. Hurt, Richardson, Garner, Todd & Cadenhead, 1978-83; ptnr. Debevoise & Liberman, Washington, 1983—; mem. dist. export council U.S. Dept Commerce, 1974—; adj. prof. law Emory U., 1970—, U.S.C., 1974; lectr. Ga. State U., 1972; lectr. numerous internat. trade seminars and workshops. Author: German govt. study on doing bus. in Southeastern U.S., 1974; editor-in-chief: S.C. Law Rev., 1963; contbr. articles to profl. jours. Served to capt. USAF, 1957-60. Decorated knight Order St. John of Jerusalem, Knights of Malta, knight and minister of justice Order of New Aragon, Sungrye medal Korea; recipient Nat. Leadership medal Air Force Assn., 1956, Coll. award Am. Legion, Outstanding Sr. award U. S.C., 1956, hon. consul Republic of Korea, 1972—. Mem. Atlanta Bar Assn., ABA, S.C. Bar Assn., Ga. Bar Assn., Lawyers Club Atlanta, Am. Judicature Soc., Am. Soc. Internat. Law, Atlanta C. of C., Ga. C. of C. (exec. com. Internat. Councils), Inst. Internat. Edn. (chmn. Southeastern regional adv. bd. 1974—, nat. trustee), So. Consortium Internat. Edn. Inc. (dir.), Wig & Robe, Sigma Chi (pres. 1956, Province Balfour award 1956), Omicron Delta Kappa, Kappa Sigma Kappa, Phi Delta Phi (pres. 1963, Province Grad. of Yr. award 1963). Home: 3010 Ellicott St NW Washington DC Office: Debevoise & Liberman 1200 17th St NW Washington DC 20036

CLARK, DONALD ROBERT, insurance company executive; b. Chgo., Jan. 19, 1924; s. Sherman Fred and Frieda (Grossklags) C.; m. Lora Marie Steiner, Aug. 11, 1945; children: Gregory Wayne, Sharon Louise. Student, Northwestern U., 1941-43, U. Wis., 1943-44. With div. Kemper Ins. Cos., 1941—; now v.p. Fed. Kemper Ins. Co.; sec., treas. Am. Motorists Ins. Co., Am. Mfrs. Mut. Ins. Co., Kemper Corp., Lumbermen's Mut Casualty Co.; treas. Am. Protection Ins. Co., Fed. Kemper Life Assurance Co., Fidelity Life Assn., Kemper Conservation Industrielle S.A., Belgium, Kemper Europe Reassurances, Kemper S.A., Kemper Mgmt. Co., Ltd., Bermuda, Kemper Ins. Co., Australia, Kemper Reins. Co., Kemper Internat. Ins. Co., Kemper County Mut. Ins. Co., Seven Continents Ins. Co. Ltd., Bermuda; asst. treas., asst. sec. Iowa Kemper Ins. Co., Sequoia Ins. Co., Economy Fire & Casualty Co.; dir. Fed. Kemper Ins. Co., Economy Fire & Casualty Co. Former, Iowa Kemper Ins. Co., Am. Protection Inc. Co.; adviser Chgo. Jr. Achievement.; dir. Kemper Internat. Ins. Co., Kemper Reinsurance Co. Contbr. to: Insurance Accounting Fire and Casualty, 2d edit, 1965, Property-Liability Insurance Accounting, 1974. Mem. Ins. Accounting and Statis. Assn. (pres. 1968-69). Lutheran (past chmn. congregation and fin. com.). Home: 704 Juniper Dr Palatine IL 60067 Office: Kemper Center Long Grove IL 60049

CLARK, DUNCAN WILLIAM, physician, educator; b. N.Y.C., Aug. 31, 1910; s. William H. and Lillian (Keating) C.; m. Carol Dooley, Jan. 30, 1943 (dec. 1971); children: Carol Ann, Duncan William, James Fenton (dec.).; m. Ida O'Grady, June 10, 1972. A.B., Fordham U., 1932. Diplomate: Am. Bd. Internal Medicine, Am. Bd. Preventive Medicine. With L.I. Coll. Medicine, Bklyn., 1936, dir. student health, 1941-49, dean, 1948-50; asst. prof. medicine, 1948-50; prof., chmn. dept. environ. medicine and community health State U. Coll. Medicine at N.Y.C., 1951-78, prof. preventive medicine, 1978-82, prof. emeritus, 1982—; intern Bklyn. Hosp., 1936-38; also cons. physician, medicine; resident in medicine, coll. div. Kings County (N.Y.) Hosp., 1938-40; cons. USPHS, 1961-81, NIH, 1961-65, NRC, 1965-68; chmn. health services research tng. com. USPHS, 1965-69, mem. health services research study sect., 1961-65, 73-77; WHO traveling fellow, 1952; vis. prof. Med. Sch., U. Birmingham, Eng., 1961. Co-editor, co-author: Textbook of Preventive Medicine, 1967, 2d edit., 1981; Contbr. articles on med. edn., pub. health and medicine. Bd. dirs. Health Ins. Plan of N.Y.C., 1953-71; chmn. N.Y. Study Com. Research Accident Prevention in Children, 1958-60, Assn. Aid Crippled Children; Bd. dirs. Health Systems Agy., N.Y.C., 1980—, Kings County Health Care Rev. Orgn., 1980—; mem. Gov.'s Adv. Council to N.Y. State Health Dept., 1984—; chmn. Nat. Adv. Com. on Local Health Depts., 1960-61. Recipient Fordham Alumni award, 1958, Fordham Coll. Encaenia award, 1962; Frank L. Babbott award Downstate Med. Center Alumni Assn., 1974; 1st Duncan W. Clark award Assn. Tchrs. Preventive Medicine, 1974; medallion for disting. service to Am. medicine SUNY Coll. at N.Y.C., 1982. Fellow Am. Pub. Health Assn., N.Y. Acad. Medicine (trustee 1975, v.p. 1976-78, council 1979—, pres. 1983-84), ACP, Am. Coll. Preventive Medicine; mem. N.Y. Pub. Health Assn. (pres. 1954-55), Conf. Profs. Preventive Medicine (chmn. 1953-54), Assn. Tchrs. Preventive Medicine (pres. 1954-56, editor Newsletter 1959-70), Com. to Protect Our Children's Teeth (pres. 1957-60), AAAS, Am. Arbitration Assn., AMA (alt. del. 1984, 85), N.Y. State Med. Soc. (del. 1978—), Kings County Med. Soc. (chmn. community medicine com. 1975-83, pres. 1983-84, trustee 1978—, v.p. 1981—), Harvey Soc., N.Y. Acad. Sci., Internat. Epidemiological Assn., Alpha Omega Alpha (faculty councillor 1948-76). Roman Catholic. Home: 35 Prospect Park W Brooklyn NY 11215 Office: 450 Clarkson Ave Brooklyn NY 11203

CLARK, DWIGHT EDWARD, professional football player; b. Kingston, N.C., Jan. 1, 1957. B.A., Clemson U., 1980. Wide receiver San Francisco 49ers, NFL, 1979—, played in Super Bowl, 1981. Mem. NSF All-Star Team, 1981, 82. Office: care San Francisco 49ers 711 Nevada St Redwood City CA 94061 *

CLARK, EARL WESLEY, maritime consultant, political scientist; b. Cadwell, Ill., Aug. 10, 1901; s. Charles Wesley and Mary Comfort (Harding) C.; m. Mary Eudora Bracken, June 28, 1922 (dec. 1972); 1 dau., Mrs. Joan C. Hoover. A.B., Eureka Coll., 1928; A.M., U. Ill., 1931. Instr. high sch., El Paso, Ill., 1928-32; vocat. dir. Bur. Pub. Welfare, Chgo. and Cook County, Ill., 1933; dist. and later state rep. Ill. Emergency Relief Comm., 1934-35; Peoria dist. dir., regional exec. officer, dep. regional adminstr., regional adminstr. (covering Ill., Wis., Minn., Nebr., Iowa, S.D., N.D.) Chgo. OPA Region, 1943-46; asst. and later nat. commr. OPA, 1947; mem. War Contracts Price adjustment Bd., 1947; nat. liquidation officer Office of Temporary Controls (included OPA, Civilian Prodn. Adminstrn., Office War Moblzn. and Reconversion, Office Econ. Stablzn.), 1947; dir. div. of liquidation Dept. Commerce (included OPA, Civilian Prodn. Adminstrn., Office War Moblzn. and Reconversion, Office Econ. Stablzn., Office Temp. Controls, Fgn. Econ. Adminstrn.), 1947-48; chief deptl. moblzn. staff, later dir. Office of Industry Cooperation, 1948-49; chmn. bd. appeals-employee grievances Dept. Commerce; also pub. hearing officer Office of Industry Cooperation; spl. asst. to sec. of commerce, 1949-50; dep. maritime adminstr. Maritime Adminstrn., 1950-53; pres. N.Y. & Cuba Mail S.S. Co.; maritime cons. Mem. Nat. Cargo Bur., Inc., 1954; co-dir. Labor-Mgmt. Maritime Com., 1955-80; lectr. Fla. State U., 1952; mem. nat. adv. bd. Operation Ship Shape, Inc., 1968-71; Mem. adv. com. on requirements Dept. Commerce, 1949; adv. com. on tech. assistance Dept. State, 1949-50; industry adviser Intergovtl. Maritime Consultatory Orgn. of UN, London, 1965; mem. Radio Tech. Commn. Maritime Services; co-chmn. spl. com. Bridge-to-Bridge Communication, 1958. Author: O.P.A. reports, Div. of Liquidation reports, Industry Voluntary Agreements Reports, 1949, Cathedral, 1952, Program Imperatives for Strengthening the U.S. Merchant Marine, 1965, Bread Upon the Waters, 1970, Reply to the Rockefeller Report, 1970, Merchant Marine March, 1978; co-author: State Pilotage in America, 1960, 2d edit., 1978, Medical and Hospital Care for Merchant Seamen, 1964, A Dialogue on Maritime Policy, 1966, The U.S. Merchant Marine Today, 1970, The American Passenger Ship Fleet, 1970, Dual U.S.-Foreign Flag Shipping Interests, 1970. Red Cross div. chmn., 1947, Com. Fund div. chmn., 1947; Mem. Gt. Lakes Pilotage Adv. Com., 1960-70; Past bd. dirs., chmn. fgn. relations com. United Seamans Service. Recipient Spl. award United Seamen's Service, 1969; Recognition plaque P.R. Propeller Club, 1970; Hall of Fame award Sullivan, Ill., 1974. Former mem. Soc. Naval Architects and Marine Engrs., Nat. Def. Transp. Assn., Navy League; mem. Pi Kappa Delta, Lambda Chi Alpha. Episcopalian. Clubs: Propeller (pres. Washington, nat. bd. dirs. 1964-66, chmn. positions and resolutions com. of U.S. 1964-74), Propeller (vice chmn. 1974-79), Propeller (mem. nat. exec. com. 1966-79), Propeller (nat. finance com. 1971-76), Propeller (mem. nat. constn. and by-laws com. 1966-74), Propeller (nat. conf. com. 1966-80). Home: 3209 Wood Ave Burtonsville MD 20866 *I consider the welfare of my country, its institutions and my family the greatest motivation for the giving of myself in the best way I know how, within the time frame God has allotted me.*

CLARK, EARNEST HUBERT, JR., tool company executive; b. Birmingham, Ala., Sept. 8, 1926; s. Earnest Hubert and Grace May (Smith) C.; m. Patricia Margaret Hamilton, June 22, 1947; children—Stephen D., Kenneth A., Timothy R., Daniel S., Scott H., Rebecca G. B.S. in Mech. Engring, Calif. Inst. Tech., 1946, M.S., 1947. With Baker Oil Tools, Inc. (now Baker Internat.), Los Angeles, 1947—, v.p., asst. gen. mgr., 1958-62, pres., chief exec. officer, 1962-69, pres., chmn. bd., 1969—; dir. CBI Industries, Inc. Bd. dirs. Downey (Calif.) YMCA, YMCA for, Met. Los Angeles; mem. nat. council YMCA; chmn. bd. trustees Harvey Mudd Coll. Served with USNR, 1944-46, 51-52. Mem. Am. Inst. M.E., Am. Petroleum Inst. (dir.), Petroleum Equipment Suppliers Assn. (dir.), Calif. C. of C. (1st v.p.), Tau Beta Pi. Office: Baker Internat 500 City Parkway W Orange CA 92668

CLARK, EDWARD, lawyer, banker, former ambassador; b. San Augustine, Tex., July 15, 1906; s. John David and Leila (Downs) C.; m. Anne Metcalfe, Dec. 27, 1927; 1 dau., Leila Downs Clark Wynn. LL.D., Southwestern U., 1966; D.Sc., Cleary Coll., 1972. Bar: Tex. 1928. County atty., San Augustine County, 1929-30, asst. atty. gen., Tex., 1931-34, pvt. practice law, Austin, 1939—; sr. partner Clark, Thomas & Winters, 1939—; chmn. bd. Tex. Commerce Bank, Austin, 1960—, First Nat. Bank, San Augustine, 1959—; U.S. ambassador to Australia, Canberra, 1965-68; fed. commr. for HemisFair, San Antonio, 1968; Am. exec. dir. Inter-Am. Devel. Bank, Washington, 1968-69; gen. adv. com. U.S. ACDA, 1974-77; dir. Telecom Corp., Houston San Benito Bank & Trust Co., Tex, Employers Casualty Ins. Co., Dallas, Employers Nat. Life Ins. Co., Tex. Commerce Bank, Tex. Commerce Bancshares; sec. to gov. Tex., 1935-36, sec. of state Tex., 1937-39. Trustee U. Tex. Law Sch. Found.; bd. regents U. Tex. System for State Tex., 1973-79; chmn. devel. bd. Inst. Texan Cultures, San Antonio; mem. devel. bd. U. Tex. Med. Br., Galveston; mem. adv. council McDonald Obs., U. Tex. Served to capt. AUS, World War II. Mem. ABA, State Bar Tex., Tex. Philos. Soc., Tex. Hist. Assn. (pres.), SAR, Knights San Jacinto, Sons Republic Tex., Kappa Sigma, Phi Delta Phi. Episcopalian. Clubs: Capital, Headliner, Citadel (Austin); Ramada (Houston). Collector Tex. books and documents. Home: 47 Woodstone Sq Austin TX 78703 Office: Tex Commerce Bank Bldg PO Box 1148 Austin TX 78767

CLARK, EDWARD ALOYSIUS, university president; b. Jersey City, Jan. 28, 1934; s. Edward Aloysius and Ellen K. (Dalton) C.; m. Anne B. Riedy, June 9, 1956; children: Edward, Jennifer, Patrick, Timothy, Jeremy. B.S., Holy Cross Coll., 1955; M.S., Fordham U., 1960, Ph.D., 1966. Instr. physics L.I. U. (Bklyn. Center), 1960, chmn. physics dept., 1962-69, asst. to pres., 1970; dean Coll. Liberal Arts and Scis., 1971-74, prof. physics, acad. v.p., pres., 1974—; Mem. faculty N.Y. State Regents External B.A. Degree; mem. Regents Task Force on Full Utilization of Resources; cons. N.Y. State Dept. Edn. Served to 1st lt. USMCR, 1955-58. Recipient Nugent Physics award, 1955; NSF Faculty fellow, 1964-65. Mem. Am. Phys. Soc., Am. Assn. Physics Tchrs., Sigma Xi. Office: 385 Flatbush Ave Ext Brooklyn NY 11201

CLARK, EDWARD FERDNAND, lawyer; b. Delaware, Ohio, May 10, 1921; s. Daniel John and Lillian (Holdgreve) C.; m. Helen Ruth Swick, Feb. 10, 1945; children—Pamela Ann (Mrs. James R. Hanser), Michael E., Steven J., Philip J., Joseph W., Edward C., Nicholas J. J.D., Ohio No. U., 1953. Bar: Ohio bar 1953. Claims examiner Central Mut. Ins. Co., Van Wert, Ohio, 1954-63; asso. firm Lindeman-Shenk-Clark, Delphos, 1963—; Sec., treas. M.I. Clark, Inc. Past pres. Citizens for Delphos Com.; mem. exec. com. Mental Health and Retardation Bd., Van Wert, Mercer and Paulding Counties; pres. St. John's Parochial Sch. Bd. Served to capt. AUS, 1942-47. Mem. Van Wert County (sec.-treas., pres.), Allen County, Ohio, N.W. Dist. bar assns., Delphos C. of C., V.F.W., Am. Legion, Am. Fedn. Musicians (v.p. local 1949-50), Home and Sch. Assn. (pres. 1959). Democrat. Roman Catholic. Clubs: Kiwanian (pres. Delphos 1964-65), K.C. (4 deg.). Home: 425 N Clay St Delphos OH 45833 Office: 214 W 2d St Delphos OH 45833

CLARK, ELEANOR, author; b. Los Angeles; d. Frederick Huntington and Eleanor (Phelps) C.; m. Robert Penn Warren, Dec. 7, 1952; children: Rosanna, Gabriel. B.A., Vassar Coll. Bd. dirs. Corp. of Yaddo. Author: novels The Bitter Box, 1946, Baldur's Gate, 1971, Dr. Heart, A Novella, and Other Stories, 1975, Gloria Mundi, 1979; for children The Song of Roland, 1960; non-fiction Rome and a Villa, 1952, expanded edit., 1975, The Oysters of Locmariaquer, 1964, Eyes, Etc., A Memoir, 1977; translator: Dark Wedding (R. Sender), 1943; contbr. stories, essays and revs. to numerous publs. Served with OSS, 1943-45. Guggenheim fellow, 1946-47, 49-50; recipient Nat. Book Award, 1965. Mem. Nat. Inst. Arts and Letters (award 1946). Address: 2495 Redding Rd Fairfield CT 06430 *My only regret: living in the age of TV. Otherwise have been awfully lucky.*

CLARK, ELIAS, law educator; b. New Haven, Aug. 19, 1921. B.A., Yale U., 1943, LL.B., 1947, M.A., 1957. Bar: N.Y. 1948, Conn. 1950. Assoc. Cleary, Gottlieb, Friendly & Cox, N.Y.C., 1947-49; mem. faculty Law Sch., Yale U., New Haven, 1949—, prof., 1958—, Lafayette S. Foster prof., 1968—; master Stillman Coll., 1962-81. Co-author: Gratuitous Transfers, 1977, Cases and Materials on Federal Estate and Gift Taxation, 1984; contbr. articles to legal jours. Bd. dirs. Mental Health Conn., 1957-67, New Haven Found., 1969-76. Mem. Conn. Bar Assn. (Disting. Pub. Service 1959). Home: 155 Bradley St New Haven CT 06511 Office: Yale U Law Sch New Haven CT 06520

CLARK, ELMER J., educator; b. Wixom, Mich., Dec. 17, 1919; s. Elmer E. and Ella S. (Decker) C.; m. children—Janet Elizabeth, Thomas Allen; m. Grace Ella Cruse, Nov. 9, 1968. A.B., U. Mich., 1941, M.A., 1943, Ph.D., 1949. Tchr. Pontiac (Mich.) Pub. Schs., 1941-43; grad. asst. U. Mich., 1946-48; asso. prof. edn. Central Mo. State Coll., 1948-49; asst., then asso. prof. edn. Ind. State Coll., Terre Haute, 1949-55, dean grad. studies, prof. edn., 1955-64; dean Coll. Edn., So. Ill. U., Carbondale, 1964-81, dir. office of regional research and service, prof. ednl. leadership, 1981—. Contbr. articles to profl. jours. Served with USAAF, 1943-46. Mem. NEA, Am. Ednl. Research Assn., Nat. Soc. Study Edn. Democrat. Home: Rural Route 1 Anna IL 62906 Office: Dir Regional Research and Service Anthony Hall Room 213 So Ill U Carbondale IL 62901

CLARK, ELOISE ELIZABETH, biologist, university official; b. Grundy, Va., Jan. 20, 1931; d. J. Francis Emmett and Ava Clayton (Harris) C. B.A., U. Va., 1951; Ph.D. in Zoology, U. N.C., 1958; D.Sc., Kings Coll., 1976; postdoctoral research, Washington U., St. Louis, 1957-58, U. Calif. at Berkeley, 1958-59. Research asst., then instr. U. N.C., 1952-55; instr. physiology Marine Biol. Lab., Woods Hole, Mass, summers 1958-62; mem. faculty Columbia U., 1958-69, asso. prof. biol. sci., 1966-69; with NSF, Washington, 1969-83, head molecular biology, 1971-73, div. dir. biol. and med. scis., 1973-75, dep. asst. dir. biol., behavioral and social scis., 1975-76, asst. dir. biol., behavioral and social scis., 1976-83; v.p. acad. affairs Bowling Green State U. (Ohio), 1983—. Contbr. articles to profl. jours. Mem. alumnae bd. Mary Washington Coll., U. Va., 1967-70; bd. regents Nat. Library of Medicine; mem. policy group competitive grants program U.S. Dept. Agr.; mem. White House interdepartmental task force on women and interagy, 1978-80; task force for conf. on families, 1980, mem. com. on health and medicine, 1976-80, vice chmn. com. on food and renewable resources, 1977-80. Named Distinguished Alumnus Mary Washington Coll., 1975; Wilson scholar, 1956; E.C. Drew scholar, 1956; USPHS postdoctoral fellow, 1957-59; recipient Disting. Service award NSF, 1978. Mem. Soc. Gen. Physiology (sec. 1965-67, council 1969-71), AAAS (council 1969-71, dir. 1978—), Biophys. Soc. (council 1975-76), Am. Soc. Cell Biology (council 1972-75), Am. Inst. Biol. Scientists, Phi Beta Kappa, Sigma Xi. Home: 1222 Brownwood Dr Bowling Green OH 43403 Office: McFall Center Bowling Green State U Bowling Green OH 43403

CLARK, ERNEST JOHN, consulting civil engineer; b. Worcester, Mass., Sept. 5, 1905; s. William A. and Flora (Milton) C.; m. Ruth I. Bohlman, Sept. 21, 1929; 1 dau., Jeanne Clark Saulnier. C.E., Rensselaer Poly. Inst., 1928; M.C.E., Poly. Inst. N.Y., 1942. Estimator Habirshaw Electric Cable Co., 1922-24; engring. asst. Westchester County (N.Y.) Park Commn., 1924-25, asst. engr., 1928-30; park engr. L.I. (N.Y.) State Park Commn., 1930-34; structural engr. N.Y.C. Dept. Parks, 1934-36; bridge engr. N.Y. World's Fair, 1936-38; structural engr., chief engr. W. Earle Andrews (Engr.), N.Y.C., 1938-45; partner Andrews & Clark (Cons. Engrs.), N.Y.C., 1945—; cons. Triborough Bridge and Tunnel Authority, Jones Beach Authority, Port of N.Y. and N.J. Authority, N.Y. State Dept. Transp., N.Y. Thruway Authority, City of N.Y. Prin. works include UN Plaza along 1st Ave. and 42d St, N.Y.C., Flushing Meadows-Corona Park, Brooklyn Heights Pedestrian Promenade. Fellow ASCE, Am. Cons. Engrs. Council; mem. Nat. Soc. Profl. Engrs., N.Y. State Assn. Cons. Engrs., Rensselaer Alumni Assn., Delta Phi. Club: East Hills Golf. Home: 189A Heritage Hills Somers NY 10589 Office: 49 W 37 St New York City NY 10018

CLARK, ESTHER FRANCES, legal educator; b. Phila., Aug. 29, 1929; d. John and Lucy (Scapula) Giaccio; m. John H. Clark, Jr., June 12, 1954; 1 dau., Jacqueline. B.A., Temple U., 1950; J.D., Rutgers U., 1955. Bar: Pa. 1956. Practiced in, Chester, until 1976; prof. law Del. Law Sch., Widener U., Wilmington, 1976—. Assoc. editor: Rutgers U. Law Rev, 1954-55. Bd. dirs. Taylor Hosp., Ridley, Pa., Pa. Bar Inst., Lindsay Law Library. Recipient Citizenship award Chester NAACP, 1973. Fellow Am. Bar Found.; mem. ABA, Pa. Bar Assn. (chmn. com. legal edn. and bar admission), Delaware County Bar Assn. (pres. 1982), Am. Trial Lawyers Assn., Delaware County Legal Assistance Assn. (dir. 1972-77, pres. bd. dirs. 1974-76). Roman Catholic. Club: Soroptimists. Home: 207 Knoll Rd Wallingford PA 19086 Office: PO Box 7474 Wilmington DE 19803

CLARK, EUGENIE, zoologist; b. N.Y.C., May 4, 1922; m. Hideo Umaki, 1942; m. Ilias Konstantiou, 1949; 4 children; m. Chandler Brossard; 1966; m. Igor Klatzo; 1969. B.A., Hunter Coll., 1942; M.S., N.Y. U., 1946, Ph.D. (Pacific Sci. Bd. fellow 1949), 1950. Research asst. in ichthyology Scripps Instn. Oceanography, 1946-47; with N.Y. Zool. Soc., 1947-48; research asst. in animal behavior Am. Museum Nat. History, N.Y.C., 1948-49, research asso., 1950—; instr. Hunter Coll., 1954; exec. dir. Cape Haze Marine Lab., Sarasota, Fla., 1955-67; asso. prof. biology City U. N.Y., 1966-67; asso. prof. zoology U. Md., 1968-73, prof. zoology, 1973—; vis. prof. Hebrew U., 1972. Author: Lady with a Spear, 1953, The Lady and the Sharks, 1969; subject of biography, Shark Lady (Ann McGovern), 1978. Recipient Myrtle Wreath award in sci. Hadassah, 1964; Nogi award in art Underwater Soc. Am., 1965; Dugan award in aquatic sci. Am. Littoral Soc., 1969; Diver of Year award Boston Sea Rovers, 1978; David Stone medal, 1984; Stoneman Conservation award, 1982; Fellow AEC, 1950; Fulbright scholar, Egypt, 1951; Saxton fellow, 1952; Breadloaf Writer's fellow; recipient Alumnae award, Hall Fame award Hunter Coll. Fellow AAAS; mem. Am. Soc. Ichthyology and Herpetology (life), Soc. Women Geographers (Gold medal 1975), Internat. Soc. Profl. Diving Scientists, Nat. Parks and Conservation Assn. (vice chmn. 1976), Am. Littoral Soc. (v.p.). Spl. research reproductive behavior fishes, morphology and taxonomy marine fishes, isolating mechanisms poecillid fishes. Home: 7817 Hampden Ln Bethesda MD 20814 Office: Dept of Zoology Univ of Md College Park MD 20742

CLARK, FRANK RINKER, JR., retired pipe line executive; b. Washington, May 4, 1912; s. Frank Rinker and Theresa Louise (Burton) C.; m. Evelyn Crews, June 27, 1943 (dec. July 1972); children: Theresa Lynn, Frank Robert; m. Annelle Macon Beaty, June 3, 1973. Student, Northwestern U., 1930-33, U. Tulsa, 1933-35, Harvard Law Sch., 1935-36, U. Okla. Law Sch., 1936-38, U. Tulsa, 1939-42, 45-47. Bar: Okla. 1938, U.S. Supreme Ct. 1938. Claims adjuster Travelers Ins. Co., 1938; trainee Helmerich & Payne, Tulsa, 1938-39; law clk. Settle, Monnet & Clammer, Tulsa, 1939-42; prodn. planning Douglas Aircraft Co., 1942-45; tax acct. Exxon Pipeline Co. (formerly Interstate Oil Pipe Line, later Humble Pipe Line Co.), 1945-50, tax atty., 1950-63, sec., 1955-77, treas., 1958-61, 63-77; past treas. Dixie Pipeline Co., 1966-76, sec., 1972-76. Mem. Am., Okla. bar assns., Am. Soc. Corp. Secs., Houston Soc. Fin. Analysts, Sigma Chi. Republican. Presbyterian (elder). Club: East Ridge Country (Shreveport, La.). Home: 125 Harpeth Trace Dr Nashville TN 37221 *I am firmly convinced that as we yield our will to the Lord's, we fit into His plan for us individually and into His ongoing plan for the universe. When we are thus in rhythm there is nothing we cannot accomplish.*

CLARK, FREDERICK R., banker; b. Rochester, N.Y., July 22, 1916; s. Roy M. and Laura (Gamble) C.; m. Anne M. Murray, Sept. 3, 1950; children: Paul, Douglas, Stephen, Mary, Cynthia, Pamela. M.B.A., Harvard U.; LL.B., Bklyn. Law Sch. Bar: N.Y. 1940. Since practiced in, Rochester, commr. taxation, State of N.Y., Albany, 1957-60; spl. rep. IBM Corp., 1960-61; exec. v.p. State Bank Albany, 1961-72, Key Banks, Albany, 1972—; chmn. N.Y. State Power Authority, 1977-79; trustee KBI Capital Corp., 1973—; chmn. FCB Life Ins. Co., Ltd., 1975—. Served with AUS, 1940-45. Decorated Order Crown Italy; recipient Conspicuous Service medal State N.Y., 1945. Clubs: Schuyler Meadows, Sky Top. Home: 19 Princess Ln Loudonville NY 12211 Office: 2 Colvin Ave Albany NY 12206

CLARK, GEORGE L., banker; b. 1938; m. B.B.A., U. Tex., 1961; M.B.A., Stanford U., 1963. Exec. v.p. Schneider, Bernet & Hickman, 1967-75; v.p. Merc. Nat. Bank, Dallas, 1975-76, sr. v.p., head metroplex banking, 1976-78, exec. v.p. adminstrn., 1978-79; pres. Merc. Nat. bank, Dallas, 1979-81; chmn. bd., chief exec. officer Merc. Nat. Bank, Dallas, 1981—, dir., 1981—; v.p. Merc. Tex. Corp. Office: Merchantile Nat Bank Dallas 1704 Main St Box 225415 Dallas TX 75265 *

CLARK, GEORGE ROBERTS, instn. exec.; b. Cynwyd, Pa., Jan. 12, 1910; s. Percy H. and Elizabeth (Roberts) C.; m. May Denckla Howe, Sept. 18, 1937. A.B., Harvard U., 1932, M.B.A., 1934. With Corn Exchange Nat. Bank & Trust Co., Phila., 1935-51, asst. cashier, 1939-43, asst. v.p. charge consumer credit, 1946-47, v.p., spl. asst. to pres., 1947-49, v.p. charge personnel and ops., 1949-50, exec. v.p., dir., 1951; sr. v.p. comml. and banking dept. Girard Trust Corn Exchange Bank, Phila., 1951-60; also vice chmn. bd. Girard Trust Bank, 1960-74; vice chmn. Acad. Natural Scis., Phila., 1974—. Trustee Acad. Natural Scis. Phila. Mem. Am. Philos. Soc. (chmn. fin. com.), Pa. Hort. Soc. Clubs: Phila., Harvard, Rabbit (Phila.); Fly (Cambridge, Mass.); Pohoqualine Fish Assn. Home: 519 Auburn Ave Chestnut Hill PA 19118 Office: 1518 Walnut St Suite 1302 Philadelphia PA 19102

CLARK, GEORGE WHIPPLE, educator, physicist; b. Evanston, Ill., Aug. 31, 1928; s. Robert Keep and Margaret (Whipple) C.; m. Elizabeth Kister, Dec. 18, 1954; children—Katherine, Jacqueline. B.A., Harvard, 1949; Ph.D., Mass. Inst. Tech., 1952. Instr. physics Mass. Inst. Tech., 1952-54, asst. prof., 1954-60, asso. prof., 1960-65, prof., 1965—; bd. dirs., past mem. vis. com., past mem. space telescope inst. council Asso. Univs. for Research in Astronomy. Mem. Nat. Acad. Scis. (mem. space astronomy subcom. of space sci. bd., mem. astron. survey com., chmn. panel high energy astrophysics), Am. Acad. Arts and Scis., Internat. Astron. Union (nat. com.), Am. Astron. Soc., Am. Phys. Soc. (past chmn. div. cosmic physics). Research on high energy astronomy. Home: 177 Gardner Rd Brookline MA 02146 Office: Mass Inst Tech Cambridge MA 02139

CLARK, GERALD LAMONT, architect; b. Tempe, Ariz., Feb. 16, 1932; s. Arthur Allen and Jessie Milisa (LeMont) C.; m. Jane McBurnett, Apr. 23, 1954; children: Steven, Stephenie, Stuart; m. Rosemary Fullerton, Jan. 4, 1981. B.S. in Architecture, Ariz. State U., 1958. Exec. v.p. Schwenn & Clark Architects, Inc.; now prin. Clark-Van Voorhis Architects, Inc., Phoenix; chmn. design jury Colo. Soc. Architects Ann. Award, 1977; mem. jury Nev. State Soc. AIA, 1978; chmn. design jury S.W. Oreg. Ann. Awards, 1979. Patentee structural framing system. Founder, first chmn. Constrn. Industry Council Ariz.; bd. dirs. Ariz. Community Coll. Facilities Adv. Council; mem., chmn. Phoenix Planning Commn.; bd. dirs. Phoenix Symphony Assn., Phoenix Men's Symphony Council; chmn. audience devel. com. Phoenix Symphony. Served with USCG, 1949-52. Recipient 1st Disting. Achievement award State U. Coll. Architecture. Fellow AIA (pres. Central Ariz. chpt., bd. dirs. Ariz. Soc., nat. bd. dirs., nat. v.p., v.p. western states mahour data bank), Am. Planning Assn. (charter mem. Ariz. chpt.); mem. Lambda Alpha (charter mem. Phoenix chpt.). Home: 1740 E Butler Phoenix AZ 85020 Office: 1130 E Missouri Suite 206 Phoenix AZ 85014

CLARK, GILBERT EDWARD, diplomat; b. Thompson Ridge, N.Y., Jan 15, 1917; s. Theodore Gilbert and Kathryn Cornelius Morgan (Jones) C.; m. Lyla Elaine Sween, Apr. 7, 1943; children: Bonnie Lee, Theodore Edward, George Kirsten. B.A., Syracuse U., 1938, M.A., 1940. Reporter Middletown (N.Y.) Times Herald, 1937; grad. asst. instr. Syracuse U., 1938-39; prodn. mgr. Whitney Graham Pub. Co., Buffalo, 1940-41; asst. prof. Syracuse U., 1946; with Dept. State, 1946—, info. officer, vice consul Am. consulate gen., Bombay, India, 1946-49, consul, 1949-51; pub. affairs staff Bur. Near Eastern, South Asia and African Affairs, 1951-53; 2d sec., consul, 1st sec. Am. legation, Tangier, Morocco, 1953-56; detailed to Bur. Budget, Exec. Office of Pres., 1956-57, Dept. State, 1957-58; assigned to Nat. War Coll., 1958-59; Am. consul gen., Amsterdam, Netherlands, 1959-61; counselor of embassy, dep. chief of mission Am. embassy, Pretoria, Transvaal, Republic South Africa, 1961-65; dir. Office West Africa Affairs, Dept. State, 1965-66; country dir. So. Africa Affairs, 1966-68; ambassador to, Mali, 1968-70, to, Senegal and The Gambia with residence in Dakar, 1970-73, fgn. service insp., 1974, sr. insp., 1975-81; fgn. affairs cons. Congl. Research Service, 1975—. Bd. dirs. Washington Internat. Coll., Leopold Senghor Found.; mem. adv. com. Sister Cities Internat.; mem. vestry St. Patrick's Episcopal Ch. Served as lt. col. Signal Corps AUS, 1941-45; CBI. Decorated Bronze Star; grand officer Nat. Order Lion, Senegal). Mem. Am. Fgn. Service Assn., Nat. War Coll. Alumni Assn., Assn. Diplomatic and Consular Officers Ret., Sigma Delta Chi, Alpha Phi Omega. Home: 4421 Hawthorne St NW Washington DC 20016

CLARK, GILBERT MICHAEL, lawyer, association executive; b. Madison, Wis., July 26, 1944; s. Joseph Gilbert and Jeanne Marie (Stromberg) C.; m. Claudia Suzanne Trimble, Oct. 24, 1954; children: Joseph Colin, Brendan Michael. B.S., U. Ill., 1967; J.D., Detroit Coll. Law, 1973. Bar: Mich., D.C., U.S. Dist. Ct. (Ea. dist.) Mich. Sr. law clk. U.S. Dist. Ct., Detroit and Bay City, Mich., 1973-75; legis asst. Sen. Robert F. Griffin, Washington, 1975-77; dir. govt. affairs Am. Assn. Blood Banks, Washington, 1977-81, exec. dir., 1981—. Editor: Medicolegal Aspects of Blood Transfusion and Collection, 1983. Pres. Rockville PTA, 1977-79. Mem. Am. Soc. Assn. Execs., Kappa Delta Pi. Unitarian. Home: 4813 Cherry Valley Dr Rockville MD 20853 Office: Am Assn of Blood Banks 1117 N 19th St Suite 600 Arlington VA 22209

CLARK, GLENWOOD, naval officer; b. Shreveport, La., Dec. 18, 1926; s. Glenn Wood and Grace Witherspoon (Hawkins) C.; m. Myrtle Marie Conrad, June 9, 1949; children—John, Pamela. Student, La. State U., 1943-44; B.S. in Engring, U.S. Naval Acad., 1949; M.S. in Physics, U.S. Naval Postgrad. Sch., 1957. Commd. ensign, 1949, advanced through grades to rear adm., 1978; nuclear devel. officer Def. Atomic Support Agy., 1963-66; with Strategic Systems Projects Office, 1966-80, dir. strategic systems projects, 1980—. Decorated Legion of Merit.; Recipient Navy League of U.S. William S. Parsons award for sci. and tech. progress, 1980. Republican. Roman Catholic. Club: Army Navy Country. Home: 3608 Tupelo Pl Alexandria VA 22304 Office: Navy Department Washington DC 20376

CLARK, H. SOL, lawyer; b. Savannah, Ga., Dec. 29, 1906; s. Sam and Ella (Raskin) C.; m. Matilda Shapiro, May 14, 1933; children: Fred Stephen, Janet (dec.). A.B., Cornell U., 1928, LL.B., 1930. Bar: Ga. 1929. Practice law, Savannah, 1930-72; mem. Brannen Clark & Hester, 1945-70, Brannen & Clark, 1970-72; judge Ct. Appeals Ga., Atlanta, 1972-77; mem. firm Lee & Clark, 1977—; asst. city atty., Savannah, 1944-47; Mem. Ga. Indsl. Loan Adv. Bd., 1955-59; founder Savannah Legal Aid Office, 1946; mem. Chatham County Civil Service Bd., 1968-70, Ga. State Jud. Council, 1974-75; founder Authors Ct., Ga. State Bar. Compiler: Ga. Masonic Code, 1954; co-author: Settlements-Law and Strategies. Trustee Telfair Art Acad., 1959-62, v.p., 1983-84. Recipient Reginald Heber Smith Legal Aid award, 1961, Arthur von Briesen Legal Aid award, 1970, plaque Harvard Law Sch. Assn. Ga., 1971; created H. Sol Clark award Ga. State Bar, 1983. Fellow Am. Bar Found. (50 Yr. award 1982), Internat. Acad. Trial Lawyers (dean 1969-70, dir. 1967-71, 78—), Am. Coll. Probate Counsel, Internat. Soc. Barristers; mem. Am. Judicature Soc. (dir. 1960-64), Savannah Bar Assn. (pres. 1952), Nat. Legal Aid Assn. (dir. 1960-64), Scribes (pres. 1979). Jewish. Club: Mason (33 deg.). Home: P O Box 8205 Savannah GA 31412

CLARK, HAROLD FLORIAN, economics educator; b. Lancaster, Ky., Aug. 29, 1899; s. William Leslie and Cora (Dunn) C.; m. Anne Beth Price, Dec. 25, 1931; 1 son. A.B., Asbury Coll., 1920, LL.D., 1939; A.M., Columbia U., 1922, Ph.D., 1923; postdoctoral, London Sch. Econs., 1926-27. William Price. Asst. prof. ednl. finance Ind. U., 1923-25, assoc., prof., 1925-27, prof., 1927-28; prof. ednl. econs. Columbia U., 1928-65; prof. econs. Trinity U., San Antonio, 1965-66; Vernon Taylor prof. econs., chmn. dept., 1966—; dir. and mem. investment com. Am. Security Life Ins. Co.; cons. to spl. asst. for Air Force Acad. Matters; also to Nat. Manpower Council, Teloprograms, Inc., School Exec. mag. econ.; cons. Challenge mag.; study of edn. costs for Ford Found., 1957. Author: books including Economics, 1948, rev. 1951, Classrooms in the Factories, 1958, Classrooms in the Stores, 1961, Classrooms in the Military, 1964, Classrooms on Main Street, 1966, Cost and Quality in Edn; Co-author: Yearbook of Am. Assn. of Sch. Adminstrs, 1947, Financing Higher Education, 1959, Developing the Nation's Work Force, 1975; Editor: Yearbook Econ. Edn. for Nat. Council for Social Studies; co-editor: Social Backgrounds of Education; contbr. to: Ency. of Edn, Ency. of Social Scis.; author numerous tech. articles. Co-chmn. Bogota Conf. Edn. and Econ. Devel. Latin Am. for OAS; chmn. exec. bd. Social Education; apptd. by Am. Hist. Assn., 1929-41; dir. and v.p. Am. Provident Soc.; chmn. Com. on Coops. NEA, 1941-43; mem. exec. com. Nat. Occupation Conf., 1932-39; co-ordinator Sloan project in applied econs., to get exptl. evidence of what schs. can do to improve econ. conditions in low income communities, 1939-49; Pres. Am. Assn. Gifted Children, 1948; mem. adv. com. and co-ordinating com. Consumer div. N.Y. Civilian Def. Vol. Office, 1942-43. Served in U.S. Army, World War I; mem. 51st Regt. N.Y. Guard, World War II. Fellow AAAS (v.p., chmn. Sect. Q. 1941, 42), Royal Econ. Soc., Nat. Council Edn.; mem. NEA, Am. Assn. Sch. Adminstrs. (mem. yearbook commn. on sch. curriculum 1947), Am. Ednl. Research Assn., Am. Econ. Assn., Nat. Council for Social Studies, Nat. Soc. Coll. Tchrs. Edn., Consumer Edn. Assn. (chmn. coll. div., pres. 1941, 42), Phi Delta Kappa. Democrat. Address: Trinity U San Antonio TX 78284

CLARK, HENRY, financial executive, consultant; b. Phila., Mar. 21, 1932; m. Nancy J. Taffler, Jan. 28, 1956; children: Stephen H., Douglas A., Lisa A., Paul T. B.S., Temple U., 1958. C.P.A., D.C., Pa. Vice pres., treas. RLC Corp., Wilmington, Del., 1972—; vice chmn. fin. com. Rollins Environ. Services Inc, Wilmington, 1982—; dir. Transrisk Ltd., Hamilton, Bermuda. Mem. Am. Inst. C.P.A.s, Fin. Execs. Inst. Home: 460 Tavistock Blvd Haddonfield NJ 08033 Office: RLC Corp PO Box 1791 Wilmington DE 19899

CLARK, HENRY BENJAMIN, JR., food company executive; b. Chevy Chase, Md., Oct. 8, 1915; s. Henry Benjamin and Lena (Sefton) C.; m. Geraldine D. Putman, July 25, 1942; children: Putman D., Sefton R. B.C.S., Northwestern U., 1937; M.B.A., Harvard U., 1940. Analyst Castle & Cooke, Inc., Honolulu, 1946-50, asst. sec., 1950-58, asst. treas., 1956-58, treas., 1958-70, v.p., 1962-70, exec. v.p., dir., 1970—, vice chmn. bd., 1980-81, chmn. bd., 1981—; dir. Hawaiian Telephone Co., Honolulu Gas Co., Pacific Resources, Inc., Hawaiian Ind. Refinery, Inc., Hawaiian Airlines, Bunker Hill Income Securities. Pres. Honolulu Acad. Arts; bd. dirs. Honolulu YMCA, Hawaii Loa Coll.; pres. Honolulu Symphony Soc., McInerny Found.; chmn. Goodwill Industries, Palolo Chinese Home, Pacific and Asian Affairs Council, Rehab. Hosp. Pacific, Aloha United Way. Served to lt. comdr. USNR, 1940-45. Mem. C. of C., Phi Kappa Psi. Clubs: Pacific, Outrigger, Pacific-Union. Home: 3003 Kalakaua Ave Honolulu HI 96815 Office: PO Box 2990 Honolulu HI 96802

CLARK, HOWARD LONGSTRETH, lawyer, business executive; b. Pasadena, Calif., Mar. 14, 1916; s. W.D. and Florence (Longstreth) C.; m. Jean Beaven; 4 children, 5 step-children. B.A., Stanford U., 1937; J.D., Harvard U., 1942. Bar: N.Y. bar 1942; C.P.A., N.Y. With Price-Waterhouse & Co., 1937-39; practiced law with firm Sullivan & Cromwell, N.Y.C., 1941; v.p. Am. Express Co., 1948-49, sr. v.p., dir., 1952-56, exec. v.p., dir., 1956-60, pres., chief exec. officer, 1960-68, chmn., chief exec. officer, 1968-77, chmn. exec. com., dir., 1979-83; dir. Xerox Corp., Mobil Corp., Cluett, Peabody & Co., Stone & Webster, Inc., Gen. Foods Corp. Trustee U.S. Trust Co. N.Y.; Trustee Wooster Sch.; Chmn. bd. trustees Am. Mus. Natural History; Trustee Presbyn. Hosp., N.Y.C.; mem. adv. bd. Sch. Orgn. and Mgmt., Yale U.; Bd. dirs. Central Park Conservancy; bd. govs. Fed. Hall Meml. Assos., Inc. Mem. Internat. Golf Assn. (dir., pres.), Harvard Law Sch. Assn., Bus. Council, Bus. Roundtable, Downtown Lower Manhattan Assn. (exec. com.), U.S. Golf Assn. (exec. com.). Clubs: Links, River (N.Y.C.); Augusta (Ga.) Nat. Golf, Pacific Union; Blind Brook (Port Chester, N.Y.); Round Hill (Greenwich, Conn.); Seminole Golf (Riviera Beach, Fla.); Royal and Ancient Golf of St. Andrews (Fife, Scotland); Hon. Co. Edinburgh Golfers. Home: Box 10 Riverview Rd Hobe Sound FL 33455 Office: 660 Madison Ave Suite 1805 New York NY 10021

CLARK, HOWARD LONGSTRETH, JR., financial executive; b. N.Y.C., Feb. 1, 1944; s. Howard Longstreth and Elsie (Dancaster) C.; m. Sandra Little, Aug. 27, 1966; 1 son, Howard Longstretch, III. B.S.B.A., Boston U., 1967; M.B.A., Columbia U., 1968. Exec. v.p., chief investment officer Am. Express Co., N.Y.C., 1981—; dir. Palm Beach Co., Sherson-Am. Express, Fireman's Fund Can., Magic Chief, Inc. Episcopalian. Clubs: River, Racquet and Tennis, Round Hill, Blind Brook, Links. Home: 1112 Park Ave New York NY 10028 Office: Am Express Co Am Express Plaza New York NY 10004

CLARK, IAN CHRISTIE, Canadian diplomat; b. Toronto, Ont., Can., Apr. 17, 1930; s. Christie Thomas and Gwyneth (Shannon) C.; m. Nancy Cynthia Blachford, Aug. 28, 1958; children: Graeme Christie, Brenda Trenholme. B.A., McGill U., Montreal, 1953, M.A., 1958. Fgn. service officer Can. Dept. External Affairs, 1958-72, cultural counsellor, Paris, 1968-70, London, 1970-72; dir. museums and visual arts Dept. Sec. State, Ottawa, 1972-74; spl. adv. to sec. state, 1974-76; chmn. Can. Cultural Property Export Rev. Bd., 1977-78; sec. gen. Nat. Museums Can., Ottawa, 1978-83; ambassador and permanent del. of Can. to UNESCO, Paris, 1983—, mem. exec. bd., 1983—; spl. advisor Can. Cultural Property Export Rev. Bd., Paris, 1983—. Author: Indian and Eskimo Art of Canada, 1970; contbr. articles to critical revs. Mem. Que. Anthrop. Assn. (a founder), Can. Museums Assn., Internat. Council Museums, Que. Archeol. Assn. (founding mem.), Zeta Psi. Presbyterian. Clubs: Tennis, Rockliffe Lawn, Five Lakes (Ottawa); Cercle de l'Union Interalliée (Paris). Home: 40 ave Foch 75016 Paris France Office: Permanent Del Can to UNESCO Irue Miollis 75015 Paris France *To preserve, conserve and maintain the National Heritage is not a one man job*

CLARK, J. KENT, English educator; b. Blue Creek, Utah, Sept. 29, 1917; s. Ernest E. and Adelaide (Kent) G.; m. Ora Christensen, Sept. 15, 1939 (dec. 1970); children: Karen Marie, Jeffrey Kent, Don Alan; m. Joanne Straub Goldmann, Aug. 28, 1972. A.B., Brigham Young U., 1939; Ph.D., Stanford U., 1950. Instr. English, Stanford U., 1942-43, 46-47; instr. English, Calif. Inst. Tech., Pasadena, 1947-50, asst. prof., 1950-54, asso. prof., 1954-60, prof., 1960—, chmn. faculty com. on programs, 1967-72. Author: The King's Agent, 1958, Dimensions in Drama, 1964, Goodwin Wharton, 1984; musicals Take Your Medicine, 1958, Organization Woman, 1962. Mem. edn. com. Pasadena Art Mus., 1968-73; chmn. Calif. Liaison Com. on Creative Arts, 1972-75; Life mem. PTA, 1957. Served to 1st lt. USAAF, 1943-46; PTO. Home: 2251 Suree Ellen Ln Altadena CA 91001

CLARK, JACK, hospital company executive, accountant; b. Munford, Ala., Feb. 23, 1932; s. Raymond E. and Ora (Camp) C.; m. Louise Omega Lackey, jan. 30, 1951; 1 son, Terry Wayne. B.S., Springhill Coll., Mobile, Ala., 1960. Staff acct. Max E. Miller, C.P.A., Mobile, 1960-62; comptroller Mobile Gen. Hosp., 1962-67; assoc. adminstr. fin. Univ. Med. Ctr., Mobile, 1967-74; regional mgr. Humana Inc., Mobile, 1974-75, v.p., 1975-80, sr. v.p., 1980—; trustee Mid-South region Humana Hosps., 1974—. Bd. dirs. Agape of S. Ala., Mobile, 1983. Served in USAF, 1952-56; Korea. Mem. Hosp. Fin. Mgmt. Assn. (assoc.), Am. Hosp. Assn., Ala. Hosp. Assn., Ala. Hosp. Assn. Accts. (pres. so. council, dir. 1967-68), Mobile C. of C. Democrat. Mem. Ch. of Christ. Home: 1100 Lucerne Dr Mobile AL 36608 Office: Humana Inc 4 Winthrop Sq 800 Hillcrest Rd Mobile AL 36608 *To always be God-fearing, fair, honest with myself and others, striving to succeed in every endeavor of life in order that my associates will recognize and remember me as a desire example.*

CLARK, JAMES EDWARD, physician; b. Elkins, W.Va., Nov. 19, 1926; s. Orda and Fannie May C.; m. Virginia Arvold, Aug. 19, 1977; children: David William, Stephen Edward, Anne Woodburn, Kristen Oberdiek, Anne, Heidi, John F. K. A.B., W. Va. U., 1948; M.D., Jefferson Med. Coll., 1952. Diplomate: Am. Bd. Internal Medicine. Intern Jefferson Med. Coll. Hosp., Phila., 1952-53; resident in medicine Jefferson Me. Coll. Hosp., Phila., 1953-55; chief resident in medicine Jefferson Med. Coll. Hosp., Phila., 1955-56; asst. in medicine Jefferson Med. Coll., Phila., 1956-58, instr. medicine, 1958-62, assoc. medicine, 1962-64, asst. prof., 1964-67, assoc. prof., 1968-69; prof. medicine Hahnemann Med. Coll., Phila., 1969—; chmn. dept. medicine, chief sect. nephrology Crozer-Chester Med. Ctr., 1968—; cons. nephrology Riddle Meml. Hosp.; cons. Taylor Hosp., Sacred Heart Hosp., Chester County Hosp., Brandywine Hosp., Paoli Meml. Hosp., 1968—; cons. internal medicine Elwyn Inst., 1971—; dir. health services Swarthmore Coll., 1972—; corp. med. dir. Franklin Mint, Franklin Center, 1974—; cons. health care financing adminstrn. HEW, 1978—; cons. home dialysis evaluation project Orkand Med. Adv. Panel, 1980—. Contbr. articles to profl. jours. Trustee Thomas Jefferson U., 1979—; bd. govs. Southeastern Pa. chpt. Am. Heart Assn., 1981—. Served with USN, 1944-46. Recipient Citizen of Yr. award HEW, 1974. Mem. Internat. Soc. Artificial Organs, Internat. Soc. Nephrology, ACP (gov. Eastern Pa. region 1980—), Am. Fedn. Clin. Research, Am. Heart Assn., AMA, AAAS, Am. Soc. Artificial Internal Organs, Am. Soc. Nephrology, Assn. Hosp. Med. Edn., European Dialysis and Transplant Assn., Nat. Kidney Found., Royal Soc. Medicine, Delaware County Med. Soc., Coll. Physicians Phila., Indsl. Med. Soc. Phila., Inc., Pa. State Med. Soc., Physiol. Soc. Phila., Bernard J. Alpers Silver Stick Soc. Nephrology, Katahdin Med. and Philos. Soc., J. Aitken Meigs Med. Assn., Sigma Xi. Clubs: Union League; Corinthian Yacht (Phila.). Home: 5 Wellesley Rd Swarthmore PA 19081 Office: 15th and Upland Ave Upland Chester PA 19013

CLARK, JAMES GORDON, consulting engineer, author; b. Kansas City, Mo., Dec. 23, 1913; s. John Arthur and Stella (Wright) C.; m. Jeannette Hazel McKinstry, May 8, 1937; children: Nannette, Diana; m. Janice Elizabeth Winters, Nov. 28, 1952; children: Mary, Jane, James. A.S., Kansas City Jr. Coll., 1933; B.S. with honors, U. Ill., 1935, M.S., 1939. Instr. civil engring. Oreg. State Coll., 1935; jr. engr. U.S. Bur. Reclamation, Denver, 1936; from instr. to prof. civil engring. U. Ill., 1936-56; assoc. Harry Balke Engrs.; owner James G. Clark (cons. engr.); partner Clark, Daily & Dietz (cons. engrs.), 1957-62; pres. Clark, Daily, Dietz & Assocs., 1962-63, Clark, Dietz, Painter & Assocs., Urbana, Carlyle, Waukegan (Ill.), Memphis, 1963-65, Leffler, Clark, Dietz & Assocs., Sanford, Fla., 1963—, Clark, Dietz and Assocs. (engrs.), Urbana, Chgo., Carbondale, St. Louis, Memphis, Jackson and Sanford, 1965-80; partner Clark, Daily, Smith & Assocs., 1962-63, Clark, Altay & Assocs. (structural engrs. and architects), 1963-78; pres. ESCA Cons., Inc., 1981—; interim profl. work in structural engring. Am. Bridge Co., Bethlemen Steel Co., Howar, Needles, Temmen & Bergendoff, Curtiss Wright Corp., Consol. Vultee Aircraft Corp.; partner Balke & Clark; asso. Harry Balke Engrs.; emeritus mem. Profl. Engrs. Exam. Com. State of Ill.; chmn. James F. Lincoln Arc Welding Found. Award Programs. Author: Elementary Theory and Design of Flexural Members, 1950, Welded Deck Highway Bridges, 1950, Welded Highway Bridge Design, 1952, Comparative Bridge Designs, 1954, Welded Interstate Highway Bridges, 1959. Trustee, v.p. Ill. Bapt. Student Found., 1954-84. Mem. Nat., Ill. socs. profl. engrs., ASCE (past pres. Central Ill. sect.), Am. Soc. Engring. Edn., Am. Ry. Engring. Assn., Am. Welding Soc., Am. Ry. Bridge and Bldg. Assn., Ill. Assn. Cons. Engrs., ASTM, Hwy. Research Bd., Greater Champaign-Urbana Devel. Assn. (chmn.), Sigma Xi, Tau Beta Pi, Chi Epsilon. Home: 716 W Florida Urbana IL 61801 Office: 1606 Willow View Rd Urbana IL 61801 *Spend time in a meaningful way. Enjoy play time. Relax when time is meant for resting. Achieve concentration when making decisions and doing other work. Work as much as you wish or need to, then stop working and apply yourself to other endeavors. Your authority requires responsibilities of you. Live up to your responsibilities or relinquish your authority.*

CLARK, JAMES HENRY, publishing company executive; b. Chgo., Aug. 30, 1931; s. James Henry and Mildred Beth (Rutledge) C.; children: Garrette Elizabeth, James Henry. A.B., U. Calif.-Berkeley, 1959. With personnel dept. Fireman's Fund, San Francisco, 1959-60; coll. textbook salesman Prentice-Hall Inc., Berkeley, 1960-63, regional editor, 1963-64, editor, Englewood Cliffs, N.J., 1964-67; dir. Western editorial office, Belmont, Calif., 1967-68; asso. pub. Aldine Pub. Co., Chgo., 1969; editor-in-chief coll. div. Harper & Row Pubs., Inc., N.Y.C., 1969-70, pub., v.p., 1970-77; dir. Univ. Press, U. Calif.-, Berkeley, 1977—. Served with USAF, 1949-53. Mem. Am. Assn. Univ. Presses (pres. elect.). Home: 6th Ave San Francisco CA 94116 Office: Univ Press U Calif Berkeley CA 94720

CLARK, JAMES MILFORD, coll. pres.; b. Mich., Apr. 11, 1930; s. Roy Wesley and Florence (Grice) C.; m. Patricia Ann Haynes, Mar. 11, 1960; children—Pamela, Matthew, Timothy. B.A., U. Mich., 1952, Ph.D. (Horace H. Rackham fellow), 1962; M.A., U. Philippines, 1955. Fulbright travel grantee, France, 1955-56; teaching fellow U. Mich., 1957-59; asst. prof. polit. sci. U. Maine, Orono, 1960-64, asso. prof., 1964-79, asst. to pres., 1966-68, v.p. for acad. affairs, 1968-79; pres. SUNY Coll., Cortland, 1979—; Fulbright lectr. U. Toulouse, France,

1965-66; dir. Dime Fed. Savs., Cortland. Author: Teachers and Politics in France, 1967. Chmn. Maine Health Planning Council, 1970-72, mem. exec. com., 1972-76; bd. dirs. Penobscot Valley United Fund, 1972-77, Cortland County United Way, 1979—. Served with U.S. Army, 1952-55. Mem. Am. Polit. Sci. Assn., Nat. Assn. State Univs. and Land-Grant Colls. (exec. com. council for acad. affairs 1971-76, sec. council 1974-76), Am. Assn. State Colls. and Univs. (N.Y. rep. 1979-81), Phi Beta Kappa, Phi Kappa Phi, Phi Eta Sigma, Pi Sigma Alpha. Office: SUNY Cortland NY 13045

CLARK, JAMES WHITLEY, food company executive; b. Springfield, Mo., Nov. 23, 1930; s. Henry Burrow and Dorothy (Demuth) C.; m. Frances Ann Seibert, July 5, 1952; children: Anne Louise, Janet Susan, John Demuth. B.J., U. Mo., 1952; postgrad., Harvard Bus. Sch., 1970. Advt. mgr., sales mgr. Fleming Cos., Inc., Oklahoma City, 1959-64, dir. advt., 1965-71, dir. corp. communications, 1972-75, corp. sec., 1975-80, v.p., sec., 1980—. Served with USAF, 1952-53. Mem. Am. Soc. Corp. Secs., Nat. Investors Relations Inst. Republican. Methodist. Home: 1912 Westridge Dr Edmond OK 73034 Office: 6301 Waterford Blvd Oklahoma City OK 73126

CLARK, JOAN M., government official; b. Ridgefield Park, N.J., Mar. 27, 1922. Attended, Katharine Gibbs Sch., N.Y.C. With Fgn. Service, Dept. State, 1945—, clk., then adminstrv. asst., Berlin, beginning in 1945; econ. asst., London, 1951-53, adminstrv. asst., Belgrade, 1953-57; placement officer Dept. State, beginning in 1957, adminstrv. officer, to 1962, Luxembourg, 1962-68; coordinator adminstrv. tng. Dept. State Sch. Profl. Studies, 1968-68; personnel officer, then adminstrv. officer Bur. Inter-Am. Affairs, Dept. State, 1969-71; dep. exec. dir., then exec. dir. Bur. European Affairs, 1971-77; dir. Office Mgmt. Ops., Dept. State, 1977-79; AEP, Republic of Malta, 1979-81; dir. gen., dir. personnel Fgn. Service, 1981-83; asst. sec. of state for consular affairs Dept. State, 1983—. Office: Dept State 2201 C St NW CA Room 6811 Washington DC 20520 *

CLARK, JOE, Canadian government official, former prime minister; b. High River, Alta., Can., June 5, 1939; s. Charles A. and Grace R. (Welch) C.; m. Maureen McTeer, June 30, 1973; 1 dau., Catherine Jane. B.A. in History, U. Alta., 1960, M.A. in Polit. Sci, 1973; LL.D. (hon.), U. N.B., 1976. Lectr. polit. sci. U. Alta., 1965-67; journalist for CBC Radio and TV, Calgary Herald, Edmonton Jour., 1966; dir. provincial orgn. Peter Lougheed, 1966; exec. asst. in Ottawa to Robert L. Stanfield, 1967-70; mem. Parliament for Rocky Mountain, 1972—; leader Progressive Conservative Party, 1976—; prime minister, Can., 1979-80, leader of opposition, 1980—. Roman Catholic. Office: House of Commons Room 448-N Ottawa ON K1A 0A6 Canada *

CLARK, JOHN ALDEN, mechanical engineering educator; b. Ann Arbor, Mich., July 9, 1923; s. Ellef Syver and Esther (Baker) C.; m. Ethel Marie Mountain, July 8, 1945; children: David W., Eloise M., Peter M. Student, Lawrence Inst. Tech., 1941-43; B.M.E., U. Mich., 1948; M.S., Mass. Inst. Tech., 1949, Sc.D., 1953. Research engr. Research Center, United Aircraft Corp., East Hartford, Conn., 1948; research assoc. Research Center, U. Mich., 1947-48; instr. Mass. Inst. Tech., 1949-52, asst. prof. mech. engring., 1952-57; prof. mech. engring. U. Mich., 1957—, chmn. dept., 1966-74; guest prof. tech. univs., Munich and Berlin, 1965-66, 72-73; sr. partner Solarcon, Inc., Ann Arbor, 1977; pres. Central Solar Energy Research Corp., 1978-80; research dir. StarPak Solar Systems, 1982—; engring. cons. thermal scis. and tech., cyrogenics, solar energy. Editor: Theory and Fundamental Research in Heat Transfer, 1963, Environmental and Geophysical Heat Transfer, 1972; contbr. numerous articles to tech. jours. Vice-pres. Conservative Fedn. Mich., 1963-65. Served to lt., pilot USAAF, 1942-45. Decorated Air medal with 5 oak leaf clusters; Croix de Guerre with palm, France; NSF sr. postdoctoral fellow, 1965-66. Fellow ASME (chmn. heat transfer div. 1964-65, asso. tech. editor Jour. Heat Transfer 1966-71, sr. editor 1978, Internat. Heat Transfer Conf., Pi Tau Sigma gold medal award 1956, heat transfer div. meml. award 1978), Tau Beta Pi, Pi Tau Sigma, Phi Kappa Phi. Home: 2214 Avalon Pl Ann Arbor MI 48104

CLARK, JOHN DESMOND, anthropology educator; b. London, Eng., Apr. 10, 1916; U.S., 1961; s. Thomas John Chown and Catherine (Wynne) C.; m. Betty Cable Baume, Apr. 30, 1938; children: Elizabeth Ann (Mrs. David Miall Winterbottom), John Wynne Desmond. B.A. Hons, Cambridge U., 1937, M.A., 1942, Ph.D., 1950, Sc.D., 1974. Dir. Rhodes-Livingstone Mus., No. Rhodesia, 1938-61; prof. anthropology U. Calif., Berkeley, 1961—, faculty research lectr., 1979; Raymond Dart lectr. Inst. for Study Man, Africa, 1979; Sir Mortimer Wheeler lectr. Brit. Acad., 1981. Author: The Stone Age Cultures of Northern Rhodesia, 1950, The Prehistoric Cultures of the Horn of Africa, 1954, The Prehistory of Southern Africa, 1959, Prehistoric Cultures of Northeast Angola, 1963, Distribution of Prehistoric Culture in Angola, 1966, The Atlas of African Prehistory, 1967, Kalambo Falls Prehistoric Site, Vol. I, 1968, Vol. II, 1973, The Prehistory of Africa, 1970. Served with Brit. Army, 1941-46. Decorated comdr. Order Brit. Empire; comdr. Nat. Order Senegal; Huxley medallist Royal Anthrop. Inst., London, 1974; Ad personam internat. Gold Mercury award, Addis Ababa, 1982. Fellow Am. Acad. Arts and Scis., Brit. Acad., Royal Soc. S. Africa, Soc. Antiquaries London, AAAS; mem. Pan-African Congress Prehistory, Geog. Soc. Lisbon, Istituto Italiano di Preistoria e Protostoria, Body Corporate Livingstone Mus. Zambia. Office: Dept Anthropology U Calif Berkeley CA 94720

CLARK, JOHN EIGNUS, foreign service officer; b. Balt., Oct. 16, 1939; s. John Evans and Aileen (Olson) C.; m. Martha Dorman, Dec. 28, 1968; children: John, Jean. B.A., U. Notre Dame, 1961; postgrad, U. Madrid, 1961-62; postgrad., NYU, 1962-63. Commd. U.S. Fgn. Service, 1969; adminstrv. officer Dept. State, Washington, 1972-75, Dept. State, Am. Embassy, Wellington, New Zealand, 1975-77, Dept. State, Washington, 1977-79; congl. fellow Am. Polit. Sci. Assn., Washington, 1979-80; consul gen. Am. Consulate, Seville, Spain, 1982—. Served to capt. U.S. Army, 1963-67. Recipient Superior Honor award U.S. Dept. State, 1982. Roman Catholic. Home: Paseo de las Delicias No 7 Seville Spain Office: Am Consulate Gen Paseo de las Delicias No 7 Seville Spain

CLARK, JOHN F., engineer; industrial executive; b. Reading, Pa., Dec. 12, 1920; s. John F. and Edith Dix (Long) C.; m. June Teubner Schweiger, July 14, 1974; children from previous marriage—Linda J., James C. B.S. in Elec. Engring. with honors, Lehigh U., 1942, E.E., 1947; M.S. in Math, George Washington U., 1946; Ph.D. in Physics, U. Md., 1956. Registered profl. engr., N.J. Electronic engr. Naval Research Lab., 1942-47, physicist, atmospheric electricity br. head, 1948-58; asst. prof. elec. engring. Lehigh U., 1947-48; dir. physics and astronomy programs NASA, 1958-63, dep. asso. adminstr. space sci. and applications (scis.), 1963-65, chmn. space sci. steering com., 1963-65; dir. Goddard Space Flight Center, 1965-76; dir. space applications and tech. RCA Corp., Princeton, N.J., 1976—; part-time lectr. math. George Washington U., 1956-58; part-time cons. research Grad. Council, 1960-66; part-time lectr. physics U. Md., 1958; mem. indsl. and profl. adv. council Pa. State U., 1963-65; mem. vis. com. physics Lehigh U., 1966-74. Contbr. numerous articles to profl. jours.; cons. editor space tech.: McGraw-Hill Ency. Sci. and Tech, 1977—. Pres. Indian Springs Citizens Assn., Silver Spring, Md.; mem. Com. on Fed. Labs., 1971-75, Md. Gov.'s Sci. Adv. Council, 1972-76, N.J. Gov.'s Sci. Adv. Com., 1980—, Am. Geophys. Union-URSI Bd. Radio Sci., 1974-78; mem. study panel Office Telecommunications, Nat. Assembly Engring., 1976-77; chmn. adv. com. FCC, 1981—. Recipient NASA medals for Distinguished Service, Outstanding Leadership, Exceptional Service, Collier trophy Nat. Aero. Assn. Fellow Am. Astronautical Soc., AIAA (gen. chmn. Communications Satellite System Conf. 1984), IEEE, Explorers Club; mem. Am. Geophys. Union, Am. Physics Tchrs., Internat. Sci. Radio Union, Phi Beta Kappa, Sigma Xi, Pi Mu Epsilon, Tau Beta Pi, Sigma Phi Epsilon, Sigma Pi Sigma. Patentee electronic circuits and systems. Office: RCA Corp PO Box 432 Princeton NJ 08540

CLARK, JOHN H., JR., lawyer; b. Chester, Pa., June 6, 1928; s. John H. and Emma E. (Higler) C.; m. Esther F. Giaccio, June 12, 1954; 1 dau., Jacqueline Ann. B.A. with honors, U.Pa., 1948, J.D. cum laude, 1951. Bar: Pa. 1951. Partner firm Clark & Breslin, Ridley Park, Pa., 1973—. Pres. Historic Delaware County, Inc., 1972; del. Democratic Nat. Conv., 1960; solicitor Tinicum Twp., 1960-64, Folcroft Borough Sch. Dist., 1959-63, Norwood Borough, 1972-76, Folcroft Borough, 1973-74. Served with USAF, 1952-53; to maj. Res. Mem. ABA, Pa. Bar Assn. (ho. of dels. 1972—), Delaware County Bar Assn., Pa. Trial Lawyers Assn. Roman Catholic. Home: 207 Knoll Rd Wallingford PA 10986 Office: 204 E Chester Pike Ridley Park PA 19078

CLARK, JOHN HALLETT, III, consulting engineer; b. Bristol, Va., Oct. 31, 1918; s. John Hallett, Jr. and Shirley (Winston) C.; m. Suzanne North Hazelet, Sept. 19, 1942; children: Craig Winston (Mrs. Michael A. Kah), John Hallett IV, Philip Winston. Student, Williams Coll., 1937-38, Colo. Coll., 1938-42; B.S. in Civil Engring, U. Ky., 1948. Registered profl. engr., Ky., Miss., D.C., S.C.; registered land surveyor, Ky. Jr. engr. Austin Co., 1942; with Hazelet & Erdal, Louisville, 1942-43, 47—, partner, 1956—, mng. partner, 1973-82, pres., 1982—; co-designer major hwy. and bridge projects. Mem. Louisville and Jefferson County Planning and Zoning Commn., 1957-64, vice chmn., 1962-64; bd. dirs. Better Bus. Bur. Louisville, 1965-68; Mem. town council, Anchorage, Ky., 1969-71. Fellow ASCE (pres. Ky. 1954); mem. Am. Inst. Cons. Engrs. (councilor 1970-73), Am. Rd. Builders Assn. (dir. engring. div. 1958, 65-68, 69-72), Internat. Assn. Bridge and Structural Engrs., Nat., Ky. socs. profl. engrs., Cons. Engrs. Council U.S. (dir. Ky. 1968-70, pres. Ky. 1967), Tau Beta Pi, Delta Kappa Epsilon. Episcopalian. Clubs: Red Lantern (Colo. Coll.); Harmony Landing Country (Goshen, Ky.); Tavern (Louisville). Home: 520 Old Stone Ln Louisville KY 40207 Office: 304 W Liberty St Louisville KY 40202

CLARK, JOHN HAMILTON, chemist; b. San Gabriel, Calif., Nov. 22, 1949; s. Charles Warren and Nellie May (Hamilton) C.; m. Piyanud Ruth Hyssey, June 12, 1971. A.B. with highest honors, U. Calif.-Santa Barbara, 1971; Ph.D., U. Calif.-Berkeley, 1976. J. Robert Oppenheimer research fellow Los Alamos Sci. Lab, 1976-79; asst. group leader laster photochemistry Los Alamos Sci. Lab., 1979; asst. prof. chemistry U. Calif.-Berkeley, 1979—, prin. investigator chem. biodyanamics div. Lawrence Berkeley Lab., 1979—. Co-author: Laser Chemistry, 1977, Chemical and Biochemical Applications of the Laser, 1980; contbr. numerous articles to profl. jours.; patentee laser chemistry. Nat. Merit Scholar, 1967-71; Regents scholar, 1967-71; Pres.'s fellow, 1970-71; Chancellor's Sci. fellow; Kofoid Eugenics fellow; grantee Research Corp., 1980-81, Dept. Energy, 1980-83, Am. Heart Assn., 1980-82, Dow Chem. Co., 1981-84, Gen. Atomic Co, 1981, Office Naval Research, 1982—, Gas Research Inst., 1982—; Alfred P. Dean research fellow, 1982-84; Camille and Henry Dreyfus tchr.-scholar, 1981—. Mem. Am. Chem. Soc., Am. Phys. Soc., AAAS, Optical Soc. Am., Phi Beta Kappa, Sigma Xi. Office: Dept of Chemistry University of California Berkeley CA 94720

CLARK, JOHN HENRY, surgeon; b. Moab, Utah, Apr. 7, 1910; s. Robert Cecil and Alice Elberta (Gaines) C.; m. Doris Mildred Colburn, June 14, 1935; children: Cecile Clark Hultquist, John Henry II. A.B., U. Utah, 1932; M.D., U. Chgo., 1935. Am. Bd. Surgery. Practice medicine specializing in surgery, Salt Lake City; asst. surgeon Tulane U. Med. Sch., New Orleans, 1945-47; assoc. clin. prof. surgery U. Utah, 1955—; bd. dirs. St. Mark's Hosp., Salt Lake City, 1969—; chmn. Utah Physicians Licensing Bd., 1968-80. Contbr. articles to profl. jours. Bd. dirs. Am. Cancer Soc., Utah Chpt., 1948-52; mem. regional adv. group Intermountain Regional Med. Program, Salt Lake City, 1964-69. Served to lt. col. M.C. AUS, 1941-45; PTO. Decorated Legion of Merit, Purple Heart; recipient Best Vis. Physician award U. Utah, 1958-59. Fellow ACS (pres. Utah chpt. 1962-63), Southwestern Surg. Congress (pres. 1968-69); mem. Fedn. State Med. Bds. (flex test com. 1968-81, bd. dirs. 1977—, pres. 1982-83), Western Surg. Assn. (sr. v.p. 1980), Salt Lake Surg. Soc. (pres. 1960), Utah Med. Assn. (trustee 1959-66, 76-80), Salt Lake County Med. Soc. (pres. 1960). Republican. Episcopalian. Clubs: Ambassador, Alta. Lodges: Masons; K.T.; Shriners. Home: 2557 Beacon Dr Salt Lake City UT 84108 Office: Western Surg Assocs Suite 2-D 1220 East 3900 South Salt Lake City UT 84108

CLARK, JOHN J., educator; b. N.Y.C., June 21, 1924; s. John J. and Mary E. (Taylor) C.; m. Margaret T. Norton, July 1, 1965; 1 dau., Patricia Ann. B.B.A. magna cum laude, St. John's U., 1948; M.B.A., Coll. City N.Y., 1950; Ph.D., N.Y. U., 1959. Prof. econs. Coll. Bus. Adminstrn., St. John's U., 1950-69, chmn. dept., 1959-62, dean, 1962-70; now prof. fin. Drexel U., Phila.; lectr. econs. Bklyn. Poly. Inst., 1954-58. Co-author: The Impact of the Foundation Reports on Business Education, 1963, Business Fluctuations, Growth and Economic Stabilization, 1963, Professional Education for Business, 1964, The New Economics of National Defense, 1966, Financial Management: A Capital Market Approach, 1976, Management of Capital Expenditures, 1979, Lease/Buy Decision, 1980, A Statistics Primer for Managers, 1980; also numerous articles.; Editor: Business and The Liberal Arts, 1962; Contbg. editor: Fin. Mgmt. Jour, 1972-82. Mem. Borough Pres.'s Planning Com., Queens County, N.Y.C., 1964-69; economist joint legislative com. banking law N.Y. State Legislature, 1965-68. Mem. Am. Econ. Assn., Eastern Fin. Assn. (exec dir. 1974-77), U.S. Naval Inst. (medal 1969), Royal United Service Inst. for Def. Studies (Mil. Rev. award 1964), Beta Gamma Sigma, Delta Mu Delta, Omicron Delta Epsilon. Home: 1704 Brigantine Ave Brigantine NJ 08203 Office: Coll Bus Adminstrn Drexel U Philadelphia PA 19104 *To live is to function.*

CLARK, JOHN P., distilling company executive; b. Chgo., Mar. 13, 1935; m. Donna Clark; children: Erin, Sean, Patrick, Michael. Student, Loras Coll., 1954-55, De Paul U., 1955-56. Sales promotion mgr. Wilson Jones Co., Chgo., 1966-70, v.p., gen. sales mgr., 1970-71, v.p., sales mktg., 1971-72, exec. v.p., 1972-76, pres., chief exec. officer, 1976-79; v.p., dir. Am. Brands, Inc., N.Y.C., 1979—; dir. Am. Franklin Co., N.Y.C., James B. Beam Distilling Co., Chgo., Sunshine Biscuits, Inc., N.Y.C., Wilson Jones Co., Chgo.; chmn. bd., chief exec. officer, dir. Swingline, Inc., Long Island City, N.Y., 1980—. Served with U.S. Army, 1956-58; Korea. Mem. Nat. Office Products Assn. (dir., mem. exec. com.), Bus. Records Mfrs. Assn. (dir.), Wholesale Stationers Assn. (dir.). Home: 16 Sherry Ln Darien CT 06820 Office: American Brands Inc 245 Park Ave New York NY 10167

CLARK, JOHN RUSSELL, ecologist; b. Seattle, Apr. 11, 1927; s. Donald Hathaway and Mildred (Taylor) C.; m. Catherine Lockner; children: John M., Jeffry R., George K., Linda J., Kerry S. B.S., U. Wash., Seattle, 1949. Research biologist Woods Hole (Mass.) Fishery Lab., Dept. Interior, 1950-59; asst. dir. Sandy Hook (N.J.) Marine Lab., Dept. Interior, 1960-70; dir. Narragansett (R.I.) Marine Lab., Dept. Interior, 1971; dir. water programs Conservation Found., Washington, 1972-81; with Nat. Park Service, Washington, 1982—; exec. dir. Nat. Wetlands Tech. Council. Author: Fish and Man, 1968, Through the Fish's Eye, 1973, Shark Watch, 1975, Coastal Ecosystems Management, 1977, The Sanibel Report, 1977, Small Seaports, 1979, Wetland Functions and Values, 1979, California Coastal Catalog, 1980, Coastal Environment Management, 1980, The Coastal Catalog, 1980, Wetlands of Bottomland Hardwood Forests, 1981. Served with USNR, 1945-46. Named Conservationist of Year Am. Motors Corp., 1968; recipient Meritorious Publ. award U.S. Fish and Wildlife Service, 1969. Mem. Am. Littoral Soc. (dir., past pres.). Home: Hickory Landing Box 99 Hollywood MD 20636 Office: 1100 L St Suite 2115 Washington DC 20240

CLARK, JOHN STEVEN, state atty. gen.; b. Leachville, Ark., Mar. 21, 1947; s. John Willis and Elizabeth Jean (Bearden) C.; m. Kathryn Marie Fairchild, Dec. 20, 1968; children—Donna Marie, Anna Kathryn. B.A. in Polit. Sci, Ark. State U., 1968; J.D., U. Ark., 1971. Bar: Ark. bar 1971, U.S. Supreme Ct. bar 1978. Asso. firm Sharp & Sharp, Brinkley, Ark., 1971-73; asst. prof., asst. dean of Sch. of Law, U. Ark., Fayetteville, 1973-76; exec. sec. to Gov. David Pryor, State of Ark., 1976-78; partner firm Clark & Nichols, Little Rock, 1978-79; atty. gen. State of Ark., Little Rock, 1979—. State chmn. Multiple Sclerosis campaign, 1979—. Recipient Employer of Year award Ark. Council Blind, 1979; named Ark. Outstanding Young Man, 1979. Mem. Nat. Assn. Attys. Gen., Ark. Bar Assn., Am. Bar Assn. Democrat. Methodist. Office: Justice Bldg Little Rock AR 72201

CLARK, JOHN WALTER, JR., shipping company executive; b. Mobile, Ala., Oct. 21, 1919; s. John Walter and Mae (Kappner) C.; m. Evelyn Ruth Hamilton, Aug. 29, 1941 (dec.); children: Ann Hamilton, Ruth Kappner, Susan Jay; m. Sandra L. Sharp, June 21, 1977; stepchildren—Kirsten L. and Heidi G. Jahncke. Grad., U.S. Mcht. Marine Acad., 1940; postgrad., Tulane U., 1950-55. Served from cadet to master mariner U.S. Mcht. Marine, 1936-46; port capt., then spl. rep. in W.Africa Delta Steamship Lines, Inc., 1946-50, asst. to pres., New Orleans, 1950-53, v.p., 1953-59, pres., 1959-79, chmn. bd., 1979-80; pres. Clark Maritime Assos., Inc., 1980—; Bd. dirs. Panama Canal Commn., 1980-83; past pres., mem. exec. com., bd. dirs. New Orleans Internat. Trade Mart; maritime arbitrator New Orleans Bd. of Trade; commr., pres. Port of New Orleans, 1978-82; exec. dir. Miss. State Port Authority; mem. Nat. Security Adv. Com. on Law of Sea. Decorated knight Order of Crown of Belgium; Order of Star of Africa, Liberia; Order of So. Cross, Brazil; comendador de la Orden de Mayo, Argentina; Order de Isabel La Catolica, Spain; named Maritime Man of Year Port of New Orleans Propeller Club, 1965. Mem. U.S. Mcht. Marine Acad. Alumni Assn. (Alumnus of Yr. 1975). Methodist. Clubs: Plimsoll, New Orleans Country, So. Yacht, Pickwick, Gulfport Yacht, Circumnavigators, New Orleans Internat. House. Mississippi State Port Authority Post Office Box 40 Gulfport MS 39502 Office: 1441 Jackson Ave New Orleans LA 70130

CLARK, JOHN WHITCOMB, diagnostic radiologist; b. Walkerton, Ind., Aug. 14, 1918; s. John and Minnie (Whitcomb) C.; m. Mary Louise Dormady, Apr. 15, 1961. Student, U. Chgo., 1936-39; M.D., Harvard, 1943. Diplomate: Am. Bd. Radiology. Intern Presbyn. Hosp., Chgo., 1943-44, resident radiology, 1946-49, asst. attending radiologist, 1949-50, asso. attending, 1950-55; attending radiologist div. radiology and nuclear medicine Presbyn.-St. Luke's Hosp., Chgo., 1955-70, attending radiologist, 1970—, head radioisotope dept., 1955-65, chmn. radioisotope com., 1956-70; mem. faculty U. Ill. Sch. Medicine, Chgo., 1948-70, prof. radiology, 1963-70, Rush Med. Coll., Chgo., 1970—, dir. computed tomography and nuclear magnetic resonance, 1982—; asso. scientist div. biol. and med. research Argonne Nat. Lab., Lemont, Ill., 1952-56, cons. scientist, 1956-62; mem. radiation study sect. NIH, 1962-66; mem. com. community health Inst. Medicine, Chgo., 1968—; cons. in field. Author numerous articles in field.; Mem. editorial bd.: Radiology Jour, 1966—. Served to capt. AUS, 1944-46. Fellow Am. Coll. Radiology; mem. Radiol. Soc. N.Am., Chgo. Roentgen Soc. (pres. 1963-64), AMA, Am. Roentgen Ray Soc. Patentee ultrasonic rapid sector scan imaging system. Home: 3740 N Lake Shore Dr Chicago IL 60613 Office: 1753 W Congress Pkwy Chicago IL 60612

CLARK, JOSEPH S., former U.S. senator; b. Phila., Oct. 21, 1901; s. Joseph S. and Kate R. (Avery) C.; m. Iris Richey; children by previous marriages: Joseph S., Noel C. Miller. Student, Chestnut Hill Acad.; grad., Middlesex Sch., 1919; B.S. magna cum laude, Harvard U., 1923; LL.B., U. Pa., 1926; LL.D., Temple U., Harvard U., 1952, Drexel Inst., 1957, U. Pa., 1963, Haverford Coll., 1966, Franklin and Marshall Coll., 1967; D.C.L., Susquehanna U., 1961; L.H.D., Lincoln U., 1961. Bar: Pa. 1926. Practiced in, Phila., 1926-51, city controller, 1949-51, mayor, 1952-56, U.S. senator from Pa., 1957-68; founder, pres. Mems. of Congress for Peace through Law. Pres. World Federalists U.S.A., 1969-71; chmn. Coalition on Nat. Priorities and Mil. Policy, 1969-73. Author: The Senate Establishment, 1963, Congress: The Sapless Branch, 1964, 66, Readings in Congressional Reform, 1966. Mem. bd. overseers Harvard, 1953-59; trustee Fund for Peace. Served to col. USAAF, 1941-45; CBI; Served to col. USAAF, 1943-45; CBI. Decorated Bronze Star, Legion Merit, U.S.; Order Brit. Empire.; Recipient; Bok award, Phila., 1956. Fellow Am. Acad. Arts and Scis.; mem. Am. Acad. Polit. and Social Scis. (v.p.), Am. Philos. Soc., Arms Control Assn. (bd. dirs.), Phi Beta Kappa. *

CLARK, KENNETH BANCROFT, educator, psychologist; b. Canal Zone, July 24, 1914; s. Arthur Bancroft and Miriam (Hanson) C.; m. Mamie Phipps, Apr. 14, 1938 (dec. 1983); children: Kate Miriam, Hilton Bancroft. A.B., Howard U., 1935, M.S., 1936; Ph.D., Columbia U., 1940. Staff psychology dept. CCNY, 1942—, prof., 1960-70, Disting. U. prof., 1970-75, prof. emeritus, 1975—; vis. prof. psychology Columbia U., summer 1955, U. Calif.-Berkeley, summer 1958, Harvard U., summer 1965; research dir. Northside Center for Child Devel., 1946—; social sci. cons. legal and ednl. div. NAACP, 1950—; cons. personnel div. U.S. Dept. State, 1961-68, 76-77, mem. com. on fgn. affairs personnel, 1961-62; Pres. Met. Applied Research Center Corp., 1967-75; chmn. bd., pres. Clark, Phipps, Clark & Harris Inc., 1975—; dir. Harper & Row, Presdl. Life Ins., Lincoln Savs. Bank. Author: Desegregation: An Appraisal of the Evidence, 1953, Prejudice and Your Child, 1955, Dark Ghetto, 1965, A Possible Reality, 1972, The Pathos of Power, 1974; co-author: A Relevant War Against Poverty, 1968, How Relevant is Education in America Today?, 1970; co-editor: The Negro American, 1966. Bd. regents State of N.Y.; trustee U. Chgo., Woodrow Wilson Internat. Center for Scholars. Recipient Springarn, 1974, 79. 1961; Kurt Lewin award, 1965; Sidney Hillman Prize Book award, 1965; Coll. Bd. medal for disting. service to edn., 1980. Fellow Am. Psychol. Assn. (dir. 1969, pres. 1970-71); mem. Soc. Psychol. Studies Social Issues (council 1954—, pres. 1959-60), Phi Beta Kappa, Sigma Xi. Episcopalian. Club: Century Assn. Home: 17 Pinecrest Dr Hastings-on-Hudson NY 10706 Office: Clark Phipps Clark & Harris Inc 60 E 86th St New York NY 10028 *Probably the most difficult value for me to live by, rather than to just verbalize, is that of maintaining a genuine and functional compassion for those human beings who do not share my values.*

CLARK, KENNETH COURTRIGHT, geophysics educator; b. Austin, Tex., Sept. 30, 1919; s. Evert Mordecai and Grace (Courtright) C.; m.

Eleanor Lorraine McKenna, June 10, 1947; children: David Templeton, Gracia Courtright. B.A., U. Tex., 1940; A.M., Harvard U., 1941, Ph.D., 1947. Spl. research assoc. nat. def. research project Electro-Acoustic Lab., Harvard, 1942-45, instr. physics, 1947-48; mem. faculty U. Wash., Seattle, 1948—, asso. prof., 1955-60, prof., 1960—, chmn. geophysics, 1967-69; research asso. prof. Geophys. Inst., U. Alaska, Fairbanks, 1957-58, mem. sci. adv. bd., 1972-76; vis. prof. div. theoretical and space physics LaTrobe U., Melbourne, Australia, 1979-80; cons. AID, State Dept. and Ministry Edn. India, Varanasi, 1964, Udaipur, 66; dir. aeronomy program NSF, Washington, 1969-70; cons. Boeing Co., Seattle, 1964, Los Alamos (N.Mex.) Sci. Labs., 1961, Aerospace Corp., Los Angeles, 1964, Battelle Meml. Inst., Richland, Wash., 1965—. Fellow Am. Phys. Soc., Optical Soc. Am.; mem. Am. Geophys. Union, Am. Assn. Physics Tchrs., Phi Beta Kappa, Sigma Xi. Methodist. Home: 5211 17th Ave NE Seattle WA 98105

CLARK, KENNETH EDWIN, psychologist, dean; b. New Madison, Ohio, Dec. 18, 1914; s. Harry H. and Nellie B. (Tremps) C.; m. Helen Titelmaier, June 29, 1942; children: Patricia Storm, Virginia, Joyce Marie. B.S., Ohio State U., 1935, M.A., 1937, Ph.D., 1940. Tchr. Ashtabula County (Ohio) Schs., 1935-37; asst. dept. psychology Ohio State U., 1937-40; instr. U. Minn., 1940-42, asst. prof., prof., 1946-60, chmn. dept. psychology, 1957-60; assoc. dean Grad. Sch., 1960; dean U. Colo. Coll. Arts and Scis., Boulder, 1961-63; prof. psychology U. Rochester, N.Y., 1963-83; dean Coll. Arts and Sci., 1963-80; Mem. Pres.'s Com. on Nat. Medal of Sci., 1962-64; cons. Office Sci. and Tech., 1961-69; mem. Army Sci. Bd., 1966—. Author: America's Psychologists, 1957, Vocational Interests of Nonprofessional Men, 1961, (with G.A. Miller) Psychology, 1970; Editor: Jour. Applied Psychology, 1961-70. Trustee Am. Psychol. Found., 1966-73; chmn. bd. govs. Center for Creative Leadership, 1974-81, pres., 1981—; chmn. Am. Conf. Acad. Deans, 1976-77. Served with USAAF, 1942-44; lt. (j.g.) USNR, 1944-46. Mem. AAAS, Am., Midwestern psychol. assns., Assn. Advancement Psychology (trustee 1974-78, chmn.); 974-75 Am. Bd. Examiners in Profl. Psychology (pres. 1959-63), Psi Chi, Phi Delta Kappa, Phi Beta Kappa. Home: 24-C Fountain Manor Dr Greensboro NC 27405

CLARK, KENNETH SEARS, architect; b. Lamont, Okla., Jan. 21, 1909; s. Allen Sears and Alice (Lumsden) C.; m. Betty M. Cullen, Jan. 25, 1936; children: Kay Melicent, William K., Susan Sears; m. Ellen Montgomery, Feb. 15, 1964; children—Bridget Sharon, John Brion. B.Arch., Okla. State U., 1932, M.A., 1933. With U.S. Coast and Geodetic Survey, 1933-35; asst. state architect N.Mex. W.P.A., 1935-38; pvt. archtl. practice, Santa Fe, 1938—. Works include missile research structures, White Sands Missile Range, N.Mex. Pres. Santa Fe United Fund, 1959. Served to capt. C.E. AUS, 1942-45. Recipient civilian service award Dept. Army, 1960. Fellow AIA; mem. Am. Arbitration Assn., ASTM, Soc. Am. Mil. Engrs., Bd. Examiners Architects N.Mex., N.Mex. Soc. Architects (pres. 1968), Santa Fe C. of C. (dir. 1953-54). Methodist (trustee). Club: Santa Fe Kiwanis (lt. gov. SW dist. 1957). Office: 208 Delgado St Santa Fe NM 87501

CLARK, LARRY, photographer; b. Tulsa, Jan. 19, 1943. Photographer, N.Y.C. Author book of photographs, 1971; photographs and tes Teenage Lust, 1983. Served with U.S. Army, 1956-66. Nat. Endowment for Arts photographers fellow, 1973; Creative Arts Pub. Service grantee, N.Y.C., 1980. Office: Box 171 70 Greenwich Ave New York NY 10011

CLARK, LARRY DALE, educator; b. Gainesville, Mo., Sept. 18, 1932; s. Wolford W. and Doris Evelyn (Looney) C.; m. Yvonne Lou Murray, June 6, 1954. B.S. in Edn., S.W. Mo. State U., 1956; M.A., U. Mo., 1961; Ph.D., U. Ill., 1963. Tchr. Mo. Pub. Schs., 1950-52, 56-61; asst. prof., mng. dir. Iowa Repertory Theatre, U. Iowa, 1963-66; asst. prof. U. Mo., Columbia, 1966-68, asso. prof., dir. Theatre, 1968-70, prof., 1970—, chmn. dept. speech and drama, 1970-73, asst. provost acad. affairs, 1973-77, asso. provost, 1977-82, dir. Theatre, 1982—; Mem. joint Speech Assn. Am.-Nat. Council Tchrs. English ad hoc com. on preparation of tchrs. of rhetoric, 1964-66; mem. theatre adv. com. Mo. Council on Arts; regional chmn. Am. Coll. Theatre Festival, 1970-71. Contbr. articles to profl. jours. Served with USAF, 1952-56. Recipient Am. Oil Co. award of excellence for outstanding contbn. to ednl. theatre in Am., 1973; Summer fellow U. Ill., Urbana, 1962-63. Mem. Central States Speech Assn. (pres.), Am. Theatre Assn. (pres.), Univ. Coll. Theatre Assn. (pres.), Alpha Psi Omega. Club: Rotary. Home: 820 Bourn Ave Columbia MO 65201

CLARK, LEIGH MALLET, judge; b. Auburn, Ala., May 16, 1901; s. George Samuel and Willie Gertrude (Little) C.; m. Evelyn Staggers, Aug. 8, 1928; 1 dau., Eva Jean (Mrs. Frank C. Marshall, Jr.). Student, Ala. Poly. Inst., 1917-19; A.B., U. Ala., 1921, LL.B., 1923. Bar: Ala. bar 1923. Practice in, Tuscaloosa, 1923-25, Birmingham, 1925-43, 51—; circuit judge 10th Jud. Circuit Ala., 1935-51; mem. firm Cabaniss, Johnston, Gardner & Clark (and predecessor), 1951-73; supernumerary circuit judge 10th Jud. Circuit Ala., Birmingham, 1973—; spl. chief justice Supreme Ct. Ala., 1976; instr. Birmingham Sch. Law, 1927—. Served to lt. col. AUS, 1943-45; col. Res. Fellow Am. Coll. Trial Lawyers; mem. ABA, Ala. Bar Assn., Birmingham Bar Assn. (Outstanding Lawyer of Year award 1974), Ala. Assn. Circuit Judges (past pres., hon. life), Phi Alpha Delta. Democrat. Mem. Ch. of Christ (elder). Club: Mason (Shriner). Home: 215 Sheridan Ln Birmingham AL 35216 Office: 716 N 21st St Birmingham AL 35203

CLARK, LEO J., food company executive; b. 1921; married. With Godfrey Co. Inc., Waukesha, Wis., 1946—, with credit corp., 1946-48, salesman, Waukesha, Milw., 1948-54, dist. mgr., 1954-65, dir. personnel, 1965-67, dir. corp. retail ops., 1967-72, v.p., 1972-79, exec. v.p., 1979-82, pres., chief operating officer, 1982—, dir.; pres. Sentry Markets Inc., dir. Office: Godfrey Co Inc 1200 W Sunset Dr Box 298 Waukesha WI 53187 *

CLARK, LEONARD VERNON, aerospace engineer; b. Newport News, Va., June 27, 1938; s. Lenwood Vernon and Catherine Elizabeth (Brady) C.; m. Doris Nerine Foster, June 9, 1962; children: Jeffrey Lee, Alan Bradley. B.S., Va. Poly. Inst., 1961, M.S. in Engring. Mechanics, 1966; M.B.A. in Aviation, Embry-Riddle Aero. U., 1981. With NASA (and predecessor), 1957—; surface sampler team leader Viking flight team, Hampton, Va. and Pasadena, Calif., 1975-76; dep. dir. sci. analysis and mission planning Viking extended mission flight team, Pasadena, 1976-77; with Terminal Configured Vehicle Program Office, Langley, 1977-83, tech. asst. to dir. for electronics, 1983—; instr. math. NASA/Langley Apprentice Sch., 1967, Coll. William and Mary extension, 1967-68. Author papers in field. Recipient Spl. Achievement award NASA, 1972, 77, Exceptional Service medal, 1977. Methodist. Home: 103 Artillery Rd Yorktown VA 23692 Office: NASA Langley Research Center M/S 117 Hampton VA 23665

CLARK, LESTER WILLIAM, lawyer; b. Hallowell, Maine, Oct. 24, 1911; s. Harlan Eugene and Maude (Ordway) Keyes; m. Etta Marie Stephenson, Jan. 24, 1935; children: Arthur Keyes, Mary Elizabeth (Mrs. Roland L. Roehrich). B.S. in Elec. Engring, George Washington U., 1937; J.D., U. Conn., 1947. Bar: Conn. 1947, N.Y. 1950. Examiner U.S. Patent Office, 1938-39; patent agt. Honeywell, Inc., 1939-43; patent atty. Chandler-Evans div. Colt Industries, 1943-47, Union Switch div. Westinghouse Air Brake Co., 1947-49; atty. George H. Corey, N.Y.C., 1949- 52; mem. firm. Cooper, Dunham, Clark, Griffin & Moran, N.Y.C., 1952—. Mem. Am. Bar Assn., N.Y. Patent Law Assn., N.Y. County Lawyers Assn., IEEE, AAAS, Licensing Exec. Soc., Phi Eta Sigma, Sigma Tau. Clubs: Sleepy Hollow Country, Scarborough, N.Y. Home: 9 Birch Close North Tarrytown NY 10591 Office: 30 Rockefeller Plaza New York NY 10112

CLARK, LYNWOOD EDGERTON, air force officer; b. Delhi, N.Y., Mar. 1, 1929; s. Ralph Scott and Lena Belle (Edgerton) C.; m. Joan Ann Symons, Feb. 22, 1960; children: Catherine Anne, Christopher Lynn. Student, Rensselaer Poly. Inst., Troy, N.Y., 1947-49. Commd. 2d lt. USAF, 1950, advanced through grades to lt. gen., 1981; combat duty, Korea, 1951-52, comdr. F-111 Wing, 1972-73, comdr. 327th Air Div., Taiwan, 1974-75, comdr. 313th Air Div., Okinawa, 1975-76; dep. chief staff logistics Pacific Air Forces, 1976-77; comdr. San Antonio Air Logistics Ctr., 1977-81, Alaskan Air Command, 1981—; mem. USAF Sci. Adv. Bd., 1964-65. Decorated D.S.M., Legion of Merit with oak leaf cluster, D.F.C. with oak leaf cluster, Bronze Star, Air medal with oak leaf cluster, Air Force Commendation medal; named USAF Mgr. of Year, 1973. Mem. Air Force Assn., Order Daedalians. Presbyterian. Home: 5-504 5th St Elmendorf AFB AK 99506 Office: Hdqrs Alaskan Air Command Elmendorf AFB AK 99506 *As supervisors we are often reluctant to demand excellence from ourselves or our subordinates. We establish or tolerate marginal standards that reflect only modest concern for success. Consequently, no one is challenged, least of all the potentially superior individual. The conscientious supervisor can readily correct this all-too-common situation by simply raising his expectations. It is my experience that people respond to a "request" for improved performance and ultimately produce at a level that surprises everyone. Thus, the supervisor who practices great expectations, who applies and enforces high standards in a consistent, complementary manner can expect his job to grow ever easier.*

CLARK, MARTIN, journalist; b. Beaumont, Tex.; s. John Franklin and Katherine (Hooper) C.; m. Nancy Linda Grayson, Dec. 26, 1958 (div. 1970); m. Maria P. Grant, Aug. 15, 1975. B.A., U. Tex.; postgrad., San Francisco Conservatory Music. Mng. editor Sandy (Oreg.) Post, 1951-53; wire service Enterprise-Courier, Oregon City, Oreg., 1953-55; staff writer UP Internat., Portland, 1955-56; music editor, daily columnist Oreg. Jour., Portland, 1956-82; music critic The Oregonian (merger Oregonian and Oreg. Jour.), Portland, 1982—. Tenor, San Francisco Opera, (1946-48), recitalist in personal appearances, also on radio, 1949-51; radio talk show, Sta. KLIQ-AM-FM, Portland, 1966-70. Served with AC, amphibious forces USNR, 1942-46; PTO. Home: 3461 NW Thurman St Portland OR 97210 Office: Oregon Journal 1320 SW Broadway Portland OR 97201 *It was helpful to me when I learned that, generally speaking, the most superficial persons I met usually had the most profound expressions on their faces. I came to realize that humor is an indispensable element of genuine intelligence.*

CLARK, MARY HIGGINS, author, business executive; b. N.Y.C., Dec. 24, 1929; d. Luke J. and Nora C. (Durkin) Higgins; m. Warren Clark, Dec. 26, 1949 (dec. Sept. 1964); m. Raymond C. Ploetz, Aug. 8, 1978; children: Marilyn, Warren, David, Carol, Patricia. B.A., Fordham U., 1979. Advt. asst. Remington Rand, 1946; stewardess Pan Am., 1949-50; radio scriptwriter, producer Robert G. Jennings, 1965-70; v.p., partner creative dir., producer radio programming Aerial Communications, N.Y.C., 1970-80; chmn. bd., creative dir. D. J. Clark Enterprises, N.Y.C., 1980—. Author: Aspire to the Heavens, A Biography of George Washington, 1969, Where Are the Children, 1976, A Stranger is Watching, 1978, The Cradle Will Fall, 1980, A Cry in the Night, 1982. Recipient Grand Prix de Litterature Policiere, France, 1980. Mem. Mystery Writers Am. (dir.), Authors League, Am. Soc. Journalists and Authors, Acad. Arts and Scis. Republican. Roman Catholic. Office: 200 Central Park S New York NY 10019

CLARK, M(ARY) MARGARET, anthropology educator; b. Amarillo, Tex., Jan. 9, 1925; d. Columbus Andrew and Myrtice (Neal) C. B.S. in Chemistry, So. Meth. U., 1945; postgrad., Southwestern Med. Coll., 1945-48; Ph.D. in Anthropology, U. Calif., Berkeley, 1957. Research anthropologist USPHS, Washington, 1957-58; research coordinator, lectr. Navaho Health Edn. Project, Sch. Public Health, U. Calif., Berkeley, 1958-59; research specialist Langley Porter Neuropsychiat. Inst., San Francisco, 1960-73; prof., chmn. med. anthropology dept. epidemiology and internat. health U. Calif., San Francisco, 1975—; faculty lectr. U. Calif.-San Francisco, 1980; cons. NIH, VA, other health related agencies. Author: Health in the Mexican-American Culture, 1959, 70, (with Barbara G. Anderson) Culture and Aging: An Anthropological Study of Older Americans, 1967; contbr. articles to profl. publs. Fellow Center for Advanced Study in Behavioral Sci., 1978-79; research awards NIMH, 1968-71, NIA, 1972-76. Fellow Am. Anthrop. Assn. (exec. bd. 1974-77, pres. 1981-82), Gerontol. Soc. (v.p. 1974-75, exec. council 1973-76), Soc. for Applied Anthropology (exec. bd. 1974-77); mem. Soc. Med. Anthropology (pres. 1972-73), AAAS (sect. H exec. com. 1977—), Sigma Xi. Home: 1 Phoenix Rd Kentfield CA 94904 Office: 1320 3d Ave San Francisco CA 94143

CLARK, MATT, magazine editor, science writer; b. Chgo., Feb. 3, 1930; s. Matthew and Kathryn (Speckman) C.; m. Ellen Ann Mitchell, Aug. 23, 1952 (dec. 1978); children: Thomasin, Geoffrey Beach, Douglas Mitchell. Grad., Hill Sch., 1947; A.B., Wesleyan U., Middletown, Conn., 1951. Reporter Boston Traveler, 1953-56, sci. editor, 1956-58; writer Med. News, N.Y.C., 1958- 61; medicine editor Newsweek mag., 1961—; free-lance contbr. to publs. in field, 1958—. Served with USNR, 1951-53. Recipient Albert Lasker Med. Journalism award, 1964, 67; Howard W. Blakeslee award Am. Heart Assn., 1965, 68, 73, 83; Editorial award Assn. Advancement Med. Instrumentation, 1967; Penney-Mo. mag. award in health, 1967, 71, 75; med. journalism award AMA, 1969; spl. citations, 1966, 70; Claude Bernard Sci. Journalism award Nat. Soc. for Med. Research, 1971; hon. mention, 1972; Page One award Newspaper Guild N.Y., 1974, 83; Media award (mag.) Am. Cancer Soc., 1976; N.Y. Deadline Club award, 1977; James T. Grady award Am. Chem. Soc., 1983; Am. Med. Writers Assn.-Searle Labs. journalism award, 1983. Fellow AAAS; mem. Nat. Assn. Sci. Writers. Clubs: Century, Coffee House, Players (N.Y.C.). Home: 201 E 87th St Apt 12-K New York NY 10028 Office: 444 Madison Ave New York NY 10022

CLARK, MATTHEW HARVEY, bishop; b. Troy, N.Y., July 15, 1937; s. M. Harvey and Grace (Bills) C. B.A., Coll. Holy Cross, Worcester, Mass.; student, St. Bernard's Sem., Rochester, N.Y.; S.T.L., N. Am. Coll., Rome; J.C.L., Gregorian U., Rome. Ordained priest Roman Catholic Ch., 1979—; vice chancellor Diocese of Albany, N.Y.; Cath. chaplain Albany Law Sch.; mem. faculty Vincentian Inst.; chmn. personnel bd. Diocese of Albany; spiritual dir. N. Am. Coll.; bishop Diocese of Rochester, 1979—. Address: Chancery Office 1150 Buffalo Rd Rochester NY 14624

CLARK, MELVIN EUGENE, chemical company executive; b. Ord, Nebr., Oct. 2, 1916; s. Ansel B. and Ruth Joy (Bullock) C.; m. Virginia May Hiller, Sept. 16, 1938; children—John Robert, Walter Clayton, Dale Eugene, Merry Sue. B.S. in Chem. Engring. cum laude, U. Colo., 1937; grad. exec. program, Columbia U., 1952, Advanced Mgmt. Program Harvard U., 1961. Asst. editor Chem. Engring., McGraw-Hill, N.Y.C., 1937-41; mktg. staff Wyandotte Chem. Corp., Mich., 1941-53; chief program br. War Prodn. Bd., Washington, 1942-44; v.p. mktg. Frontier Chem. Co., Wichita, 1953-69; exec. v.p. chems. div. Vulcan Materials Co., Birmingham, Ala., 1969-81, v.p. planning, chems. and metals group, 1981-82; cons., 1982—; pres. Chlorine Inst., 1977-80. Contbr. numerous articles to profl. jours. Recipient U. Colo. Alumni Recognition award, 1962; named Chem. Market Research Assn. Man of Year, 1963. Mem. Am. Inst. Chem. Engrs., Chem. Mktg. Research Assn., Am. Chem. Soc., Tau Beta Pi, Pi Mu Epsilon. Republican. Mem. Christian Disciples. Clubs: Inverness Country, Relay House, Shoal Creek Country (Birmingham). Home: 3200 Kiltie Ln Birmingham AL 35243 Office: PO Box 7497 Birmingham AL 35253

CLARK, MEREDITH KAYE PLIER (MRS. PHILIP C. CLARK), mem. Republican National Committee; b. Oconto Falls, Wis., Jan. 14, 1927; d. Arnold W. and Herasa (Boyce) Plier; m. Philip Cannady Clark, June 24, 1950; children: James William, Meriwether Kaye. B.A. in Psychology, Lawrence U., 1948; postgrad., N.Y. Sch. Social Work, 1949. Head stock dept. Saks Fifth Ave., N.Y.C., 1948-49; psychiat. social worker Bklyn. State Hosp., 1949-50; clk. U.S. Govt., 1951-53; clk.-typist V.I. Telephone Co., St. Croix, 1956, V.I. law firm, 1956-57; v.p. Petheny, Ltd., 1973-75, pres., 1975—; treas. Young-Clark Ins., Ltd., 1974—; Mem. St. Croix Bd. Appeals for Med. Assistance, 1972-75, 78—; treas. St. Croix br. Republican Party V.I., 1963-65, pres., 1974; mem. Rep. Territorial Com. V.I., 1964—, sec., 1964-68, exec. sec., 1978-82; charter mem., treas. V.I. Republican Women, St. Croix-Nat. Fedn. Rep. Women, 1975-78; charter mem. V.I. League Women Voters, 1969; mem. task force V.I. Comprehensive Health Planning Council, 1969, V.I. Inauguration Com. for Pres. Nixon, 1969; V.I. publicity chmn. 17th Ann. Rep. Women's Conf., 1969; mem. Rep. Nat. Com. for V.I., 1968—; adviser inaugural com. 1st elected Gov. V.I., 1971; chmn. V.I. housing, mem. arrangements com. Rep. Nat. Conv., 1972, 76, 80; spl. asst. to gov., V.I., 1969-75; mem. V.I. Civil Rights Commn., 1976-83. Trustee Good Hope Sch., 1977-83. Mem. Nat. Fedn. Bus. and Profl. Women's Club, St. Croix Landmarks Soc., Navy League U.S., Roger Williams Family Assn., Christiansted Bus. and Profl. Women (2d v.p.), St. George Bot. Gardens, Kappa Delta (pres. Lawrence U. chpt. 1946-47). Methodist. Clubs: St. Croix Tennis, St. Croix Forum, St. Croix Island Center, St. Croix Yacht, Capitol Hill. Home: Estate the Sight PO Box 788 Christiansted St Croix VI 00820

CLARK, MONTAGUE GRAHAM, JR., former college president; b. Charlotte, N.C., Feb. 25, 1909; s. Montague G. and Alice C. (Graham) C.; m. Elizabeth Hoyt, May 2, 1933; children: Elizabeth (Mrs. Joe Embser), Alice (Mrs. Harold Davis), Margaret (Mrs. William Miller), Julia (Mrs. Cecil Hampton). Student, Ga. Inst. Tech. Sch. Engring.; LL.D., Drury Coll., 1957; Ed.D., S.W. Bapt. Coll., 1972; Litt.D., Sch. of the Ozarks, 1975; D.D., Mo. Valley Coll., 1977. Vice pres. Hoyt & Co., Atlanta, 1934-46; v.p. Sch. of Ozarks, Point Lookout, Mo., 1946-52, pres., 1952-81, sec. bd. trustees, 1957-71; now chmn.; ordained to ministry Presbyn. Ch., 1950; past dir. Bank of Taney County.; Past mem. Commn. on Colls. and Univs., North Central Assn. Colls. and Secondary Schs.; former moderator Lafayette Presbetery and Synod of Mo., Presbyn. Ch. of U.S.; Past mem. nat. adv. council on health professions edn. NIH; dir. Empire Gas Corp. Mem. Nat. council Boy Scouts Am.; also mem. adv. bd. Ozarks Empire Area council; mem. Wilson's Creek Battlefield Nat. Commn., 1961—; mem. bd., exec. com., sec. Blue Cross; hon. mem. Mo. Am. Revolution Bicentennial Commn.; former v.p., dir. Am. Heart Assn., mem. exec. com., chmn. fund raising adv. and policy com., Gt. Plains regional chmn.; chmn. Mo. Heart Fund; Past chmn. Mo. Heart Assn.; mem. adv. council Council on Am. Affairs.; mem. South Central/Lakes County Med. Services System; mem. security panel Aircraft War Prodn. Council, N.Y.; v.p. Thomas Hart Benton Homestead Meml. Commn.; bd. dirs. St. Louis Scottish Towers Residence Found.; chmn. burns prevention com. Shrine of N.Am.; hon. chmn. So. Mo. div. Am. Cancer Soc.; pres. Youth Council Atlanta; mem. exec. com. Atlanta Christian Council; mem. Park and Recreation Commn. Fulton County; chmn. planned giving and legacies Mo. div. Am. Cancer Soc. Served to maj. Internal Security, World War II. Named Ark. traveler, 1962; recipient Silver Beaver award Boy Scouts Am., Gold Heart award Am. Heart Assn., George Washington certificate Freedoms Found., 1974, 78, In God We Trust award Family Found., Red Cross of Constantine York Rite, Disting. Service award Am. Legion Dept. of Mo., numerous other awards; named to Ozark Hall of Fame. Mem. Royal Order Scotland; Mem. S.A.R. (past pres. gen. nat. soc., hon. v.p. Mo. Soc., Nat. Soc. Good Citizenship medal, Patriot medal, Minute Man award, Va. Soc. medal), Acad. Mo. Squires, Navy League U.S., Mo. C. of C., Branson C. of C. (econ. devel. com.), Assn. Grand Jurors of Fulton County, Atlanta Sunday Sch. Supts. Assn. (pres., treas.), Mo. Pilots Assn. (1st chmn. bd.), Civil Air Patrol (dir. adv. bd.), White River Valley Hist. Soc. (past pres.), Soc. Colonial Wars, Order Founders and Patriots Am., Air Force Assn., Assn. U.S. Army, Mo. Assn. State Troopers Emergency Relief Soc., Internat. Assn. Chiefs of Police. Clubs: Masons (33 deg., awards, grand chaplain 1980-81), Shriners (past imperial chaplain), K.T., Rotary (past local pres., dist. gov. 1966-67), DeMolay.). Address: Sch of the Ozarks Point Lookout MO 65726

CLARK, PEGGY, theatrical lighting designer; b. Balt., Sept. 30, 1915; d. Eliot Round and Eleanor (Linton) C.; m. Lloyd R. Kelley, Jan. 28, 1960. A.B. cum laude, Smith Coll., 1935; M.F.A., Yale U., 1938. Designer theatrical costumes, 1938—; instr. lighting Lester Polakov Studio & Forum of Stage Design, Inc., 1965—; lectr. lighting design Smith Coll., 1967-69, Yale Drama Sch., 1969-70; Bd. counselors Smith Coll., 1961-69, pres. class of, 1935, 1970-75, 80-85; mem. adv. com. Internat. Theatre Inst. Designer settings and lighting Gabrielle, 1941, High Ground, 1951, Curtain Going Up, 1952, Agnes de Mille Dance Theatre, 1953-54; designer stage lighting: numerous plays, including Beggar's Holiday, 1946, Song of Norway, 1952; Peter Pan, 1954, Will Success Spoil Rock Hunter, 1955, Kiss Me Kate, 1955, No Time for Sargeants, 1956; designer decor: Stage Door Canteen; tech. dir.: Am. Theatre Wing; lighting and tech. dir.: other plays including Connecticut Yankee, 1942; Brigadoon, 1946, High Button Shoes, 1947, Along Fifth Avenue, 1948, Gentlemen Prefer Blondes, 1949, Pal Joey, 1951, Mr. Wonderful, Auntie Mame, Bells Are Ringing, 1956, N.Y.C. Center Musical Revivals, 1956-58, 63-68, Say Darling, 1957; prodns. Wonderful Town, Carousel, Susannah, Flower Drum Song at, Brussels Internat. Expn., 1958; lighting tech. supr.: Goodbye Charlie, 1959, Bye Bye Birdie, Unsinkable Molly Brown, Under the Yum Yum Tree, 1960, Show Girl, Mary Mary, 1961, Sail Away, 1961, Romulus, 1962, Girl Who Came to Supper, 1963, Around the World in 80 Days, 1963-64, Bajour, Poor Richard, 1965, The Rose Tattoo, 1966; designer lighting: Darling of the Day, 1968, South Pacific, 1968, Rosalinda, 1968, Jimmy, 1969, Last of the Red Hot Lovers, 1969, Sound of Music, 1970, How the Other Half Loves, 1971, The King and I, 1972, Bil Baird's Bandwagon, 1973, Bil Baird's Whistling Wizard and the Sultan of Tuffet, Pinochio, 1973, Jones Beach's Carousel, 1973, Alice in Wonderland, 1974, Winnie the Pooh, Davy Jones' Locker for Bil Baird Theatre, 1976, Student Prince and Merry Widow for Light Opera of Manhattan, 1976, Mlle. Modiste Grand Duchess, Babes in Toyland, 1978. Recipient Smith medal, Disting. Alumnae award, 1977. Fellow U.S. Inst. Theatre Tech. (vice commr. engring. commn.); mem. United Scenic Artists (rec. sec. 1942-47, trustee 1948-51, pres. 1968-69, v.p. 1974-76, pension and welfare trustee 1970-80), ANTA, Illuminating Engring. Soc., Yale Drama Alumni Assn. (Eastern v.p. 1970-77, pres. 1977-83), Woods Hole Protective Assn. (pres. 1978-81). Clubs: French Bull Dog of Am. (pres. 1972—), Smith (Bklyn., N.Y.C. and Cape Cod); Woods Hole Yacht (sec. 1978-80, vice commodore 1980-81), Woods Hole Yacht (commodore 1981-83). Home: 36 Cranberry St

Brooklyn NY 11201 Summer Home: 23 Albatross St Woods Hole MA 02543 *I have always tried to do anything I undertook, however big or small, to the best of my ability. I was especially lucky to have parents and a husband who loved and believed in me and my ability and talent, and who encouraged me with inspiration and enthusiasm. I have found that the quotation "Freedom is the recognition of necessity" suits the way I work as a designer and, combined with patience, tolerance of others and a sense of humor, works for every day of living in this complicated world.*

CLARK, PETER BRUCE, newspaper executive; b. Detroit, Oct. 23, 1928; s. Rex Scripps and Marian (Peters) C.; m. Lianne Schroeder, Dec. 21, 1952; children: Ellen, (Mrs. Fowler M.S. Brown), James. B.A., Pomona Coll., 1952, LL.D. (hon.), 1972; M.P.A., Syracuse U., 1953; Ph.D., U. Chgo., 1959; H.H.D., Mich. State U., 1973; LL.D. (hon.), U. Mich., 1977. Research assoc., then instr. polit. sci. U. Chgo., 1957-59; asst. prof. polit. sci. Yale, 1959-61; with Evening News Assn., Detroit, 1960—, sec., v.p., 1961-63; pres. Detroit News, 1963—, chmn. bd., dir., 1969—, pres., 1963-81, pub., 1963-82, also dir.; chmn. Fed. Res. Bank Chgo., 1975-77. Bd. dirs. United Found. Met. Detroit, Harper-Grace Hosps. Detroit; trustee Pomona Coll., 1981—. Served with AUS, 1953-55. Mem. Am. Newspaper Pubs. Assn. (dir. 1966-74), Am. Polit. Sci. Assn., Am. Soc. Newspaper Editors, Adcraft Club Detroit, Econ. Club Detroit, Pi Sigma Alpha. Clubs: Detroit Country, Detroit, Detroit Athletic. Office: 615 Lafayette Blvd Detroit MI 48231

CLARK, R. BRADBURY, lawyer; b. Des Moines, May 11, 1924; s. Rufus Bradury and Gertrude Martha (Burns) C.; m. Polly Ann King, Sept. 6, 1949; children: Cynthia Clark Maxwell, Rufus Bradbury, John Atherton. B.A., Harvard U., 1948, J.D., 1951; diploma in law, Oxford U., Eng., 1952; D.H.L., Ch. Div. Sch. Pacific, San Francisco, 1983. Bar: Calif. Assoc. firm O'Melveny & Myers, Los Angeles, 1952-62, sr. ptnr., 1961—; dir. First Charter Fin. Corp., So. Calif. Water Co., Econ. Resources Corp., Brown Internat. Corp., Automatic Machinery & Electronics Corp. Editor: California Corporation Laws, 6 vols, 1976—. Pres. John Tracy Clinic, Los Angeles; chancellor Episcopal Diocese of Los Angeles, 1967—, hon. canon, 1983—. Served to capt. U.S. Army, 1943-46. Decorated Bronze star with oak leaf cluster, Purple Heart with oak leaf cluster; Fulbright grantee, 1952. Mem. ABA, State Bar Calif. (chmn. corp. Com. 1976-77, chmn. drafting com. on gen. corp. law 1973-81), Calif. State Bar (chmn. drafting com. on nonprofit corp. law 1980—), Los Angeles County Bar Assn. Republican. Clubs: Califonia, Harvard, Chancery (Los Angeles); Alamitos Bay Yacht (Long Beach). Office: O'Melveny & Myers 400 S Hope St Los Angeles CA 90071

CLARK, RAMSEY, lawyer; b. Dallas, Dec. 18, 1927; s. Tom C. and Mary (Ramsey) C.; m. Georgia Welch, Apr. 16, 1949; children: Ronda Kathleen, Thomas Campbell. B.A., U. Tex., 1949; A.M., J.D., U. Chgo., 1950. Bar: Tex. 1951, U.S. Supreme Ct. 1956, D.C. 1969, N.Y. 1970. Practiced law, Dallas, 1951-61, N.Y.C., 1970—; asst. atty. gen. U.S. Dept. Justice, 1961-65, dep. atty. gen., 1965-67, atty. gen. U.S., 1967-69; Adj. prof. Howard U., 1969-72, Bklyn. Law Sch., 1973-81. Author: Crime in America. Served with USMCR, 1945-46. Home: 37 W 12th St New York NY 10011 Office: 113 University Pl New York NY 10003

CLARK, RANDALL LIVINGSTON, tire manufacturing company executive; b. Syracuse, N.Y., Sept. 13, 1943; s. Chester Edmond and Ruth Alice (Randall) C.; m. Suzanne Drane Jones, Jan. 8, 1966; children: Randall L., Karen Ann, Robert Dewitt. B.A., U. Pa., 1965, M.B.A., 1968. Mktg. assoc. B.F. Goodrich Co., Akron, 1968-70, product mgr., 1971-73; dir. mktg. Dunlop Tire and Rubber Corp., Buffalo, 1973-75, v.p. mktg. and sales, 1975-80, pres. tire div., 1980-83; pres. tire div., exec. v.p. corp.; dir. Dunlop Tire and Rubber Corp., Buffalo. Mem. Rubber Mfrs. Assn. (exec. com.), Young Presidents Orgn., Buffalo C. of C. Club: Park Country. Home: 26 Heritage West Williamsville NY 14221 Office: Dunlop Tire & Rubber Corp PO Box 1109 Buffalo NY 14240

CLARK, RAYMOND SKINNER, transportation and distribution company executive; b. N.Y.C., Dec. 31, 1913; s. Raymond Skinner and Helen Ashton (Burt) C.; m. Marjorie Armstron Pendleton, Oct. 6, 1947. A.B. cum laude, Harvard U., 1936; LL.B., Yale U., 1939. Bar: Md. 1940. Assoc. Venable, Baetjer & Howard, Balt., 1939-41, 46-50; counsel The Davidson Chem. Corp., Balt., 1951-54; sr. atty., asst. sec. W.R. Grace & Co., N.Y.C., 1954-61; pres. Canton Co. of Balt., Canton R.R., 1951-76; chmn. W.P. Carey & Co., N.Y.C., 1973—. Treas. various Republican candidates, 1950-64; chmn. Md. Indsl. Financing Authority, 1971-73. Served with USNR, 1941-46. Club: Elkridge. Home: 4 Middleton CT Baltimore MD 21212 Office: WP Carey & Co 67 Wall St New York NY

CLARK, RICHARD MCCOURT, lawyer; b. Bridgewater, Mass., Nov. 10, 1937; s. Robert G. and Louise (Balboni) C.; m. Patricia Holmes, May 7, 1983; m. Diane P. Kennard, June 7, 1960 (dec. 1977); children: Carolyn, Lauren. A.B., Coll. Holy Cross, Mass., 1959; LL.B., Cornell U., 1962. Bar: N.Y. 1962. Assoc. Milbank Tweed Hadley & McCloy, N.Y.C., 1962-67; counsel corp. devel. Olin Corp., Stamford, Conn., 1967-68; asst. gen. counsel, asst. sec. Indian Head Corp., N.Y.C., 1968-69; v.p., asst. gen. counsel Grolier Inc., Danbury, Conn., 1970-73, v.p., corp. counsel, sec., 1973-75, sr. v.p., gen. counsel, sec., 1977—, dir., 1978—, officer subs. Trustee Cancer Care Inc., Nat. Cancer Found. Inc. Mem. ABA, N.Y. State Bar Assn., Assn. Bar City N.Y., Conn. Bar Assn., Am. Corp. Counsel Assn., Westchester-Fairfield Corp. Counsel Assn., Am. Soc. Corp. Secs. Clubs: American Yacht; Manursing (Rye, N.Y.) (bd. govs.); University, Oyster Harbor, Hyannisport (Mass.). Office: Grolier Inc Sherman Turnpike Danbury CT 06816

CLARK, ROBERT ARTHUR, educator, mathematician; b. Melrose, Mass., May 3, 1923; s. Arthur Henry and Persis (Kidder) C.; m. Jane Burr Crofut Kinder, June 25, 1966. Student, Colo. Coll., 1940-42; B.A., Duke, 1944; M.S., MIT, 1946, Ph.D., 1949. Instr., research asso. MIT, 1946-50, vis. asst. prof., 1956-57; faculty Case Inst. Tech. (now Case Western Res. U.), Cleve., 1950—, prof. math., 1964—, acting head dept. math., 1960-61, asso. chmn. dept. math., 1974-79, 82—, exec. officer, 1981-82; vis. mem. U.S. Army Math. Research Center, Madison, Wis., 1961-62. Mem. Am. Math. Soc., Math. Assn. Am., Soc. Indsl. and Applied Math., A.A.A.S., Am. Assn. U. Profs., Phi Beta Kappa, Sigma Xi. Spl. research asymptotic integration theory of differential equations and theory thin elastic shells. Office: Dept Math Case Western Reserve Univ Cleveland OH 44106

CLARK, ROBERT CHARLES, lawyer, educator; b. New Orleans, Feb. 26, 1944; s. William Vernon and Edwina Ellen (Nuessly) C.; m. Kathleen Margaret Tighe, June 1, 1968; children—Alexander Ian, Matthew Tighe. B.A., Maryknoll Sem., 1966; Ph.D., Columbia U., 1971; J.D., Harvard U., 1972. Bar: Mass. bar 1972. Asso. firm Ropes & Gray, Boston, 1972-74; asst. prof. Yale U. Law Sch., New Haven, 1974-76, asso. prof., 1976-77, prof., 1977-78; prof. law Harvard U., Cambridge, Mass., 1978—. Contbr. articles to profl. jours. Mem. Am. Bar Assn. Office: Harvard Law Sch Cambridge MA 02138

CLARK, ROBERT EDWARD, journalist; b. Omaha, May 14, 1922; s. Charles Wright and Lulu (Wilson) C.; m. Ruth Sylvia Kanianen, Oct. 21, 1945. B.S., U. Minn., 1945, M.A., 1948. White House corr. INS, Washington, 1952-57; Supreme Ct. and nat. staff reporter Washington Evening Star, 1958-61; White House and Congl. corr. ABC, Washington, 1961-75, host, chief corr., 1975-81, Washington corr., 1981—. Served to ensign USNR, 1942-46. Mem. Radio-TV Corrs. Assn. (past pres.). Home: 420 N Park Dr Arlington VA 22203 Office: 1717 De Sales St Washington DC 20036

CLARK, ROBERT EUGENE, savs. and loan exec.; b. Lansing, Mich., Apr. 6, 1926; s. Roy W. and Ruth (McCall) C.; m. Anne Abbott, June 16, 1950; children—Linda, Thomas, David, Robert. B.A., Mich. State U. With Capitol Savs. & Loan Assn., Lansing, 1952—, treas., 1961-67, exec. v.p., then pres., 1967—; dir. Mich. Millers Mut. Ins. Co. Bd. dirs. Sparrow Hosp., Jr. Achievement of Mid-Mich., Lansing Symphony Assn. Served with USAAF, 1944-46. Mem. U.S. League of Savs. Assns. (exec. com. 1976-78), Mich. Savs. and Loan League (pres. 1972), C. of C., Downtown Bus. Assn. Clubs: Lansing Country, Automobile, City, Elks, Masons. Office: Capitol Savs & Loan Assn 112 E Allegan St Lansing MI 48901

CLARK, ROBERT HENRY, JR., holding company executive; b. Manchester, N.H., Mar. 4, 1941; s. Robert Henry and Elva C. (Stearns) C.; m. Rosalie Foster Case, Dec. 21, 1963; children: Robert Henry III, Hilary Eagan, Hadley Case. B.S. in Bus. Adminstrn., Boston U., 1964. Mcpl. bond underwriter Merrill Lynch, Pierce, Fenner & Smith, N.Y.C., 1964-70; v.p. Case, Pomeroy & Co., Inc., N.Y.C., 1971-75, exec. v.p., 1975—, also dir.; v.p. fin. Felmont Oil Corp., 1972-79, exec. v.p., 1979—; dir. Langdon P. Cook & Co., Inc., Case-Pomeroy Oil Corp., Essex Offshore, Inc., MEMTEC Corp.; chmn. bd. Hazeltine Corp. Mem. Sigma Alpha Epsilon. Clubs: Downtown Assn.; University (N.Y.C.); Leash; Bald Peak Colony (Melvin Village, N.H.); Round Hill. Office: Case Pomeroy & Co Inc 6 E 43d St New York NY 10017

CLARK, ROBERT LEE, investment banker; b. Yuba, Calif., Jan. 19, 1943; s. Forrester Andrew and Katharine (Burrage) C.; m. Carroll Taylor, June 21, 1963; children: Robert Lee, David Taylor, Carroll Nicholson, Daphne Lee. B.A., Harvard U., 1966. Gen. ptnr. H.C. Wainwright & Co., Boston, 1970—, Alex Brown & Sons, 1977—. Office: Alex Brown & Sons 1 Boston Pl Boston MA *

CLARK, ROBERT LLOYD, JR., librarian; b. McAlester, Okla., Sept. 12, 1945; s. Robert Lloyd and Fairel Ruth (Nelson) C.; children: Roberta, Johnathan. B.A., U. Okla., 1968, M.L.S., 1969. Dir. div. archives and records Okla. Dept. Libraries, Oklahoma City, 1968-72, data processing coordinator, 1972-73, dir., 1976—; asst. dir. pub. services Jackson (Miss.) Met. Library System, 1973-74; dir. Mid-Miss. Regional Library, Kosciusko, 1974-76; sec. Okla. Archives and Records Commn., 1976—; ex officio sec. Okla. Arts and Humanities Council, 1976-81; sec. adv. council Library Services and Constrn. Act., 1976—. Author: Archive-Library Relations, 1976. Robert L. Clark, Jr. Day proclaimed by Gov. of Okla., Nov. 15, 1982. Mem. ALA (chmn. pub. library assn. interlibrary coop. com. 1974-77, mem. standards com. 1979-82), Okla. Library Assn., Southwestern Library Assn. (pres. 1980-82), Amigos Bibliog. Council (exec. bd. 1977-80), Assn. State Libraries (bd. dirs. 1977-80), Assn. Chief Officers of State Library Agys. (chmn. legis. com. 1979-81, chmn. 1982—). Home: 2001 Cedar Ridge Edmond OK 73034 Office: 200 NE 18th St Oklahoma City OK 73105

CLARK, ROBERT NEWHALL, electrical engineering educator, consultant; b. Ann Arbor, Mich., Apr. 17, 1925; s. Ellef S. and Esther (Baker) C.; m. Mary Quiatt, Aug. 20, 1949; children: Charles W., John R., Timothy J., Franklin T. B.S. in Elec. Engring., U. Mich., 1950, M.S., 1951; Ph.D., Stanford U., 1969. Registered profl. engr., Wash., Minn. Research engr. Honeywell, Inc., Mpls., 1951-57; lectr. Stanford U., 1968; prof. elec. engring. U. Wash., Seattle, 1957—; vis. scientist Fraunhofer Gesellschaft, Karlsruhe, W.Ger., 1976-77; guest prof. U. Duisburg, W.Ger., 1983-84; cons. analyst Boeing Aerospace Co., Seattle, 1971—. Author: Introduction to Automatic Control System, 1962. Served with USMC, 1943-46. NSF fellow, 1966-68. Fellow IEEE, AIAA (assoc.). Home: 3900 50th Ave NE Seattle WA 98105 Office: Univ of Wash FT-10 Seattle WA 98195

CLARK, ROBERT PHILLIPS, newspaper editor; b. Randolph, Vt., Dec. 3, 1921; s. James S. and Gladys M. (Phillips) C.; m. Jeanne Orr Rice, Dec. 14, 1949; children: Patricia Orr Clark Thorpe, Elizabeth Phillips Clark Christiansen. A.B., Tufts U., 1942; M.A., U. Mo., 1948. Reporter Owensboro (Ky.) Messenger & Inquirer, 1948-49; reporter, sci. writer Courier-Jour., Louisville, 1949-62, Washington corr., 1958; mng. editor Louisville Times, 1962-71; exec. editor Courier-Jour. and Louisville Times, 1971-79; editor Fla. Times Union and Jacksonville Jour., 1979-82; v.p/news Harte-Hanks Newspapers, 1983—. Served to capt. AUS, World War II. Nieman fellow Harvard U., 1960-61; Decorated Bronze Star. Mem. Am. Soc. Newspaper Editors (dir., v.p.), AP Mng. Editors Assn. (past pres.), Internat. Press Inst. (dir. Am. com.), Sigma Delta Chi, Delta Tau Delta. Democrat. Presbyterian. Clubs: San Antonio City, Ponte Vedra. Home: 3506 Elm Knoll San Antonio TX 78230

CLARK, ROBERT WILSON, manufacturing executive; b. Greeley, Colo., Jan. 7, 1925; s. Edgar Wilson and Florence Mary (Huntington) C.; m. Margaret Ella Swope, Aug. 20, 1950; children: Matthew Wilson, John Huntington. B.S. in Mech. Engring, U. So. Calif., 1945; postgrad., Stanford U. With Goodyear Aerospace Corp., 1946—, v.p. ops., 1977-80, exec. v.p., chief operating officer, Akron, Ohio, 1980-81, pres., chief exec. officer, 1981—. Sr. warden Episcopal Ch., Dayton, Ohio, 1966. Mem. Nat. Security Indsl. Assn. (trustee 1979-80), Aviation Distbg. and Mfg. Assn. (trustee 1976-77), Aerospace Industries Assn. Office: 1210 Massillon Rd Akron OH 44315 *

CLARK, ROGER ARTHUR, lawyer; b. Chgo., May 23, 1932; s. Frank Arthur and Alice Rita (Mahoney) C.; m. Kate Dawson, June 24, 1961; children: Alice Anne, John, Michael. B.S., U. Ill., 1954, LL.B., 1958. Bar: Ill. 1958, N.Y. 1961, D.C. 1962, U.S. Supreme Ct. 1967. Trial atty. Antitrust div. U.S. Dept. Justice, Washington, 1958-60; assoc. Donovan, Leisure, Newton & Irvine, N.Y.C., 1960-61; sr. ptnr. Rogers & Wells, Washington, 1961—; adj. prof. law Georgetown U., Washington, 1961-67; dir. Cafritz Cos., Washington; spl. counsel U.S. Architect of the Capitol, 1963-64; trustee, gen. counsel Fed. City Council, Washington, 1969—; dir., gen. counsel Fed. City Housing Corp., Washington, 1972—; gen. counsel Presdl. Inaugural Com., 980-81. Nationalities coordinator Citizens for Nixon-Agnew, Washington, 1968. Served to 1st lt. U.S. Army, 1955-57. Mem. ABA, D.C. Bar Assn., Nat. Health Lawyers Assn., Order of the Coif. Republican. Clubs: Chevy Chase, Metropolitan. Home: 4 E Kirke St Chevy Chase MD 20815 Office: Rogers & Wells 1737 H St NW Washington DC 20006

CLARK, ROGER HARRISON, architecture educator, architect; b. Cin., Nov. 20, 1939; s. Roy Harrison C. and Lillian (Elfrieda) Warneke (Clark); m. Judith Elizabeth Engel, June 23, 1962; children: Kyla Paige, Andrew Harrison. B.S. in Architecture, U. Cin., 1962; M.Arch., U. Wash., 1963. Registered architect, N.C., Ohio. Instr. Sch. Architecture, U. Va., Charlottesville, 1964-65, asst. prof., 1965-69, Sch. Design N.C. State U., Raleigh, 1969-72, assoc. prof., 1972-78, asst. dean, 1977-79, prof. architecture, 1978—; design architect Obrien/Atkins Assocs., Chapel Hill, N.C., 1978—, John D. Latimer & Assocs., Durham, N.C., 1970-78; profl. adviser Bespak, Cary, N.C., 1983-84, King's Lynn, Eng., 1983-84; guest lectr. various univs., 1971—. Author: Kinetic Architecture, 1970, Analysis of Precedent, 1979, Precedent in Architecture, 1984. Youth league coach YMCA, Raleigh, N.C., 1974-78; mem. pub. adv. panel Region IV GSA, Atlanta, 1975; trustee Kamphoefner Fund Recognition of Excellence in Architecture, Raleigh, N.C., 1982—; coach Capitol Area Soccer League, Raleigh, N.C., 1979-81. Recipient award of Merit Design Award program South Atlantic Regional Council, AIA, 1978, 79, honor award, design award N.C. chpt. AIA, 1973, 75, 77, 79, cert. Excellence Design award, 1981; grantee Graham Found. Advanced Studies in Fine Arts, 1983. Fellow AIA (chmn. design com. 1982); mem. Nat. Trust Hist. Preservation, Nat. Endowment for Arts. Democrat. Home: 301 Hillcrest Rd Raleigh NC 27605 Office: Sch Design NC State U Raleigh NC 27695

CLARK, ROMANE LEWIS, philosopher, educator; b. Waverly, Iowa, Dec. 3, 1925; s. Fred G. and Mildred L. (Cole) C.; m. Marilyn Jean Cash, Aug. 8, 1948; children—Ronald, Carolee, Cathleen, John. A.B., State U. Iowa, 1949, Ph.D., 1952. Instr. State U. Iowa, 1953; successively asst. prof., asso. prof., prof. Duke U., 1953-70; prof. philosophy Ind. U., Bloomington, 1970—. Contbr. articles to acad. philos. jours. and anthologies. Served with USAAF, 1944-45. Sr. fellow Nat. Endowment for Humanities, 1974; Fulbright sr. scholar, 1981. Mem. Am. Philos. Assn., AAUP. Office: Philosophy Dept Ind U Bloomington IN 47401

CLARK, ROY, singer, musician, business executive; b. Apr. 5, 1933; m. Barbara Joyce. D.H.L. (hon.), Baker U., 1978. Partner Jim Halsey Properties, Halark Music Pub. Co., Tulsa Drillers Baseball Team; v.p., dir. Am. Entertainment Corp. Appearances include: host and guest others; host TV spl.; star TV show Hee-Haw; ann. appearances, Frontier Hotel, Las Vegas, Carnegie Hall, N.Y.C.; appeared in, USSR, 1976, Cannes, France, 1979, Montreux Internat. Jazz Festival, Millenium Celebration, Brussels, Belgium, rec. artist for, MCA Records. Named Entertainer of Year Country Music Assn., 1973, Acad. Country Music, 1973-74; Instrumentalist of Year Country Music Assn., 1977, 78, 80; Guitarist of Year Guitar Player Mag. and Playboy Poll, 1977, 78

CLARK, ROY CLYDE, bishop; b. Mobile, Ala., July 24, 1920; s. Clyde Columbus and Lelia B. (Cochran) C.; m. Esther Maddox, June 7, 1945; children: Lynn B., Susan. B.A., Millsaps Coll., 1941, D.D., 1962; B.D., Yale U., 1944; H.H.D., Columbia Coll., S.C., 1981. Ordained deacon Meth. Ch., 1944, elder, 1946, bishop, 1980. Pastor various chs., Pasacagoula and Wesson, Miss., 1944-49, Centreville and Forest, Miss., 1949-53, Captial Street Meth. Ch., Jackson, Miss., 1953-63, St. John's Meth. Ch., Memphis, 1963-67, West End United Meth. Ch., Nashville, 1967-80; bishop United Meth. Ch., Columbia, 1980—; dir., pres. Assn. Christian Tng. and Service, Nashville, 1977-83; dir. gen. bd. global ministries United Meth. Ch., N.Y.C., 1980—; trustee Lake Junaluska Assembly, N.C., 1980—. Author: Expect a Miracle, 1976. Mem., chmn. Jackson Appeal Rev. Bd., 1957-61; pres. Family Service Assn., Jackson, 1963; dir. Council Community Services, Nashville, 1976-80; trustee Emory U., Atlanta, 1980—. Named Alumnus of Yr. Millsaps Coll., 1957. Mem. World Meth. Council. Office: United Methodist Ch Columbia Area 4908 Colonial Dr 08 Columbia SC 29203

CLARK, RUSSELL GENTRY, U.S. dist. judge; b. Myrtle, Mo., July 27, 1925; s. William B. and Grace Frances (Jenkins) C.; m. Jerry Elaine Burrows, Apr. 30, 1959; children—Vincent A., Viki F. LL.B., U. Mo., 1952. Bar: Mo. bar 1952. Mem. firm Woolsey, Fisher, Clark, Whiteaker & Stenger, Springfield, Mo., 1952-77; U.S. dist. judge Western Dist. of Mo., Kansas City, 1977—. Served to 2d lt. U.S. Army, 1944-46. Mem. Aba, Mo. bar assn. (continuing legal edn. com. 1969), Greene County bar assn. (dir. 1968-71). Democrat. Methodist. Club: Kiwanis (past pres. Springfield chpt.). Office: 654 US Courthouse 811 Grand Ave Kansas City MO 64106 *

CLARK, SAMUEL DELBERT, emeritus sociology educator; b. Lloydminster, Alta., Canada, Feb. 24, 1910; s. Samuel David and Mary Alice (Curry) C.; m. Rosemary Josephine Landry, Dec. 26, 1939; children—Ellen Margaret, Samuel David, William Edmund. B.A., U. Sask., 1930, M.A., 1931; M.A., McGill U., 1935; Ph.D., U. Toronto, 1938; LL.D., U. Calgary, 1978, Dalhousie U., 1978; D.Litt., St. Mary's U., 1979, Lakehead U., 1982. Lectr. sociology U. Man., 1937-38; lectr. U. Toronto, 1938-44, asst. prof., 1944-48, asso. prof., 1948-53, prof., 1953-76; vis. prof. U. Calif., Berkeley, 1960-61, U. Sussex, 1970-71; McCulloch prof. Dalhousie U., 1972-74; vis. prof. U. Guelph, 1976-78, Lakehead U., Thunder Bay, Ont., 1978-80, Tsukuba U., Japan, spring 1980, U. Edinburgh, 1980-81. Author: Canadian Manufacturers' Association, 1939, The Social Development of Canada, 1942, Church and Sect in Canada, 1948, Movements Political Protest in Canada, 1957, The Suburban Society, 1963, The Developing Canadian Community, 1968, The Canadian Society in Historical Perspective, 1976, The New Urban Poor, 1978. Guggenheim fellow, 1943-44; officer Order of Can., 1978. Fellow Royal Soc. Can. (pres. 1975-76); mem. Am. Acad. Arts and Scis., Can. Polit. Sci. Assn. (pres. 1958-59), Can. Assn. Sociology and Anthropology (hon. pres.). Home: 9 Lamont Ave Agincourt ON M1S 1A8 Canada

CLARK, SAMUEL INGALLS, political science educator; b. Oak Park, Ill., June 3, 1923; s. Lincoln R. and Ellen N.F. (Lethin) C. A.B. in Polit. Sci, U. Chgo., 1943, Ph.D., 1949. Faculty Western Mich. U., 1948—, prof. polit. sci., 1961—, dir. honors coll., 1962—, pres. faculty senate, 1971-73, 78-79; co-dir. seminars in, India, 1963, 67, People's Republic of China, 1975, 78, 80; asso. Danforth Found., 1973—; Mem. exec. com. Nat. Collegiate Honors Council, 1971-73, 77-79, v.p., pres., past pres., 1983-85. Author: (with Jerome Manis) Man and Society, 1961. Commr. Mich. Crippled Children Commn., 1958-65; Democratic candidate for U.S. Congress, 1956, 60. Served with AUS, 1943-44. Fulbright fellow U. Louvain, Belgium, 1950-51; Ford Found. fellow, India, 1957-58; Fulbright prof., Japan, 1961. Mem. Am. Polit. Sci. Assn., Assn. Asian Studies, AAUP, Internat. House Japan. Roman Catholic. Home: 1819 Greenlawn St Kalamazoo MI 49007

CLARK, SAMUEL SMITH, urologist; b. Phila., Sept. 2, 1932; s. Horace E. and Jane (Mullin) C.; m. Heather Jean Ogilvy, June 21, 1957; children: Ross Angus, Erin, Brian Mullin. B.S., McGill U., 1954, M.D., 1958, C.M., 1958. Diplomate: Am. Bd. Urology. Intern Bethesda (Md.) Naval Hosp., 1958-59; resident Royal Victoria Hosp., Montreal, Can., 1962-67; practice medicine specializing in urology, Munster, Ind., 1967-68, Chgo., 1969—; attending urologist Central DuPage Hosp., Winfield, Ill., 1976—; asst. prof. urology Abraham Lincoln Sch. Medicine, U. Ill., 1968-71, asso. prof., 1971-73, prof., 1973-81, head div. urology, 1971-77; chief urology West Side VA Hosp., Chgo., 1969-77, U. Ill. Hosp., 1971-77; clin. prof. urology Loyola U., Chgo., 1981—; med. dir. Crescent Counties Found. Med. Care, 1979-83; dir. urol. services, dir. neurologic bladder clinic Marianjoy Rehab. Hosp., Wheaton, Ill., 1983—, bd. dirs., 1979—. Contbr. articles to profl. jours. Served to lt. MC USNR, 1958-6211. Fellow ACS, Inst. Medicine Chgo.; mem. Am. Urol. Assn. (exec. com. North Central sect. 1974-77), Ind. Med. Soc., DuPage Med. Soc., AMA, Chgo. Urol. Soc. (pres.). Episcopalian. Club: Glen Oak Country. Home: 592 Turner St Glen Ellyn IL 60137 Office: 399 Schmale Rd Carol Stream IL 60187

CLARK, SUSAN (NORA GOULDING), actress; b. Sarnia, Ont., Can., Mar. 8, 1944; d. George Raymond and Eleanor Almond (McNaughton) C. Student, Toronto (Ont.) Children's Players, 1956-59, Royal Acad. Dramatic Art, London. Partner Georgian Bay Prodns. Producer: Jimmy B. and Andre, 1979, Word of Honor, 1980, Maid in America, 1982; appeared in play Silk Stockings; mem. London Shakespeare Festival Co.; mem. Brit. Repertory Co.; appeared in Brit. TV prodns.; co-star: Brit. premiere of play Poor Bitos; appeared in Can. TV prodns., including Heloise and Abelard, Hedda Gabler; starred in Taming of the Shrew; appeared in Sherlock Holmes,: Williamstown Theatre Festival, (taped for HBO), 1981; appeared in: Getting Out, Mark Taper Forum, Los Angeles, 1978; films include The Apple Dumpling Gang, Disney Studios, Night Moves, The North Avenue Irregulars, Airport '75, Midnight Man, Porky's, Murder by Decree, Tell Them Willie Boy is Here, Skin Game, City on Fire, Madigan, Coogan's Bluff, Skullduggery, Promises in the Dark, Valdez is Coming, Skin Game, Showdown, Double Negative; appeared in segments of TV series Columbo; appeared in Double Solitaire, Pub. Broadcasting System, Babe, MGM-CBS TV spl., 1975 (Emmy award), Amelia Earhart (Emmy nomination), The Choice. Mem. ACLU, Am. Film Inst. (Julian Bond Group). Office: care Georgian Bay Prodns 3620 Fredonia Dr 1 Hollywood CA 90068

CLARK, SYDNEY PROCTER, geophysics educator; b. Phila., July 26, 1929; s. Sydney P. and Isabella L. (Mumford) C.; m. Elizabeth Frey, 1963; 4 children. A.B., Harvard U., 1951, M.A., 1953, Ph.D. in Geology, 1955. Research fellow in geophysics Harvard U., 1955-57; geophysicist, geophys. lab. Carnegie Inst., 1957-62; Weinberg prof. geophysics Yale U., New Haven, 1962—. Fulbright scholar, Australian Nat. U., 1963. Office: Yale U Dept Geology PO Box 6666 New Haven CT 06511

CLARK, THOMAS DIONYSLUS, emeritus history educator, author; b. Louisville, Miss., July 14, 1903; s. John Collingsworth and Sallie (Bennett) C.; m. Martha Elizabeth Turner, June 10, 1933; children: Thomas Bennett, Ruth Elizabeth. A.B., U. Miss., 1928; postgrad., U. Va., 1928; M.A., U. Ky., 1929, Litt.D., 1969; Ph.D., Duke U., 1932; D.Litt., Lincoln Meml. U., 1949, Washington and Lee U., 1963; LL.D., U. Louisville, 1964; D.H.L., Berea Coll.; D.Litt., Eastern Ky. U., 1976; Litt.D., Ind. U., 1978, Transylvania U., 1980. Tchr. history Western State Tchrs. Coll., Memphis, 1930; vis. instr. U. Tenn., 1931; vis. prof. U. Rochester, Duke U., U. N.C., U. Chgo., Claremont Grad. Sch., U. Vienna; faculty U. Ky., 1931-68, instr., asst. prof., assoc. prof., 1939-42, prof. history, 1942-65, Hallam prof., 1965-68; head dept. 1942-65; now fellow; Sesqui-centennial prof. Am. history Ind. U., 1966, distinguished prof. history, 1968-73, emeritus prof. Am. history, 1973—; distinguished prof. Eastern Ky. U., 1973—; vis. prof. U. Wis.; adj. prof. Winthrop Coll., 1977-78. Author: books, latest being Pills, Petticoats and Plows, 1944, The Southern Country Editor, 1948, The Rural Editor and the New South, 1948, The Bluegrass Cavalcade, 1956, Frontier America, 1959, The Emerging South, 1961, Gold Rush Diary, 1967, Mid-Western Pioneer, 1970, Indiana University in Mid-Passage, 1973, The Great American Frontier, 1975, The Metes and Bounds of Kentucky, 1979; editor: Southern Travel Series, 1950-56, Three Paths to the Modern South, 1965; (with A.D. Kirwan) The South Since Appomattox, 1965; books, latest being South Carolina, the Grand Tour, 1973, Off at Sunrise: The Overland Journal of Charles Glass Gray, 1976, Indiana University, The Realization, 1976, Agrarian Kentucky, That Far-Off Land, 1976, Historic Maps of Kentucky, 1980, The Second National Bank, a Century of Banking in the Blue Grass, 1983; mng. editor.: Jour. So. History, 1948-54; contbr. to hist. jours. Trustee U. Ky. Guggenheim fellow, 1963-64; recipient Merit award Assn. State and Local History, 1966; Distinguished Teaching award and Research award U. Ky., 1968; Ind. Author's award, 1971; Citizenship gold medal award SAR, 1980. Mem. Am. Hist. Assn., So. Hist. Assn. (hon. mem.; pres. 1947), Orgn. Am. Historians (hon. mem.; exec. sec. emeritus; pres. 1957), Phi Beta Kappa, Phi Pi Phi, Phi Alpha Theta (nat. hon. mem., nat. pres. 1957-59), Omicron Delta Kappa. Democrat. Baptist. Clubs: Kiwanis; Filson (Louisville) (hon. mem.); Bradford (Lexington)). Home: 248 Tahoma Rd Lexington KY 40503

CLARK, THOMAS GARIS, rubber products mfr.; b. Norristown, Pa., Jan. 30, 1925; s. George W. and Esther (Garis) C.; m. Dolores M. DeBolt, Feb. 18, 1956; children—Kimberley, Valerie. A.B., Gettysburg Coll., 1947; M.B.A., U. Pa., 1949. Gen. accountant Firestone Tire & Rubber Co., Akron, Ohio, 1949-57; successively supr., gen. accountant, asst. sec.-treas., sec.-treas., v.p. and sec.-treas. sr. v.p., chief fin. officer Rubbermaid, Inc., Wooster, Ohio, 1957-80; dir. 1st Fed. Savs. & Loan Assn. Served from ensign to lt. USNR, 1944-61. Former mem. Am. Soc. Corporate Secs., Ohio Mfrs. Assn. (trustee), Cleve. Treasurers' Club, Phi Beta Kappa, Beta Gamma Sigma, Phi Sigma Kappa. Republican. Presbyterian. Clubs: Mason, Rotarian. Home: 1838 Pine Cove Dr Wooster OH 44691

CLARK, THOMAS WILLARD, poet; b. Oak Park, Ill., Mar. 1, 1941; s. Arthur Willard and Rita Mary (Kearin) C.; m. Angelica Louise Heinegg, Mar. 21, 1968 (div. 1 dau., Juliet). B.A., U. Mich., 1963; student, Cambridge (Eng.) U., 1963-65, U. Essex, Eng., 1965-67. Poetry editor Paris Rev., 1963-74; instr. Am. poetry U. Essex, 1966-67. Author: 30 books of poetry, including Stones, 1969, Air, 1970, Blue, 1974, Suite, 1974, Chicago, 1975, At Malibu, 1975, When Things Get Tough on Easy Street (Selected Poems 1963-78), 1978, The End of the Line, 1980, A Short Guide to the High Plains, 1981, Paradise Resisted (Selected Poems 1978-84), 1984, The Border, 1984; prose includes Champagne and Baloney, 1976; (with Mark Fidrych) No Big Deal, 1977, The World of Damon Runyon, 1978; play The Emperor of the Animals, 1966, One Last Round for the Shuffler, 1979; novel Who Is Sylvia?, 1979, The Master, 1979; The Great Naropa Poetry Wars, 1980, The Last Gas Station and Other Stories, 1980, A Life of Jack Kerouac, 1984, Property, 1984. Fulbright fellow, 1963-65; Rockefeller fellow, 1967-68; Guggenheim fellow, 1970-71. Address: 822 Windsor Way Santa Barbara CA 93105

CLARK, WALLACE HENDERSON, pathologist, dermatologist; b. La Grange, Ga., May 16, 1924; s. Wallace Henderson and Sue Brown (Vaughan) C.; m. Patricia Ann Denoncour, Apr. 28, 1973; children: Wallace H., James M., Ann H., Carol V., Kristin D., Kathryn L. Student, The Citadel, 1940-43; B.S., Tulane U., 1944, M.D., 1947. Diplomate: Am. Bd. Pathology, Am. Bd. Dermatopathology. Rotating intern Touro Infirmary, New Orleans, 1948-49, resident in pathology, 1947-48, Tulane U. Sch. Medicine, New Orleans, 1949-52, instr. dept. pathology, 1949-52, asst. prof., 1954-58, asso. prof., 1958-61, prof., 1961-62; asst. prof. dept. pathology Harvard Med. Sch. at Mass. Gen. Hosp., 1962-68, clin. asso. prof., 1968-69; mem. Fels Research Inst., Temple U. Sch. Medicine, Phila., 1969-78, prof. dept. pathology, 1969-78, chmn. dept., 1974-78; research prof. dept. dermatology and pathology U. Pa. Sch. Medicine, 1978—; Shelley Meml. lectr. and vis. prof. Johns Hopkins U. Sch. Medicine, Balt., 1981. Author: (with R. J. Reed and D. F. Richfield) Dermatopathology, 1977, (with L. I. Goldman and M. J. Mastrangelo) Human Malignant Melanoma, 1979; co-editor: Dermatology in General Medicine, 1971. Served with USNR, 1944-47; M.C. U.S. Army, 1952-54. Recipient First Sci. award Am. Cancer Soc., Phila. Div., 1975, Arnold Ungerman, Robert I. Lubin cancer research award, 1979; named Outstanding Alumnus Tulane U., 1981; Markle scholar, 1954-60; USPHS sr. research fellow, 1954-60; NIH postdoctoral fellow, 1960-62. Mem. Am. Soc. Exptl. Pathology, Am. Acad. Dermatology, Am. Acad. Dermatology and Syphilolgy (Gold award 1958, Lila Gruber award for outstanding research on cancer 1983), AAAS, Am. Soc. Cell Biology, Am. Soc. Dermatopathology, Internat. Acad. Pathology, Am. Assn. Cancer Research, Am. Assn. Pathology and Bacteriology, Internat. Acad. Pathology (mem. adv. council), Soc. Surg. Oncology (Lucy Wortham James award 1975), James Ewing Soc., Sigma Pi Sigma. Republican. Club: Harvard (Boston). Home: 358 Yellow Springs Rd Malvern PA 19355 Office: U Pa Sch Medicine 250 Med Edn Bldg 36th and Hamilton Walk Philadelphia PA 19104 *A genuine joy in sharing discovery and learning with others (teaching) has paralleled my research. I never desired success but found happiness and reward while going through the days of life with curiosity, teaching and love.*

CLARK, WARD CHRISTOPHER, hosp. adminstr.; b. Springfield, Ill., Sept. 19, 1939; s. William Wallace and Portia Savage (Ward) C.; m. Linda Joyce Garrett, Dec. 28, 1963; children—Paul Christopher, Karen Lynne. B.A., Vanderbilt U., 1962; M.B.A., U. Chgo., 1964. With N.C. Baptist Hosp., Winston-Salem, 1963-71, sr. v.p., 1966-71; asso. adminstr. Northside Hosp., Atlanta, 1971-73, chief exec. officer, 1973—; asso. in career devel. U. Chgo., 1965—; preceptor, instr. Ga. State U. Trustee Blue Cross/Blue Shield of Ga., 1980—; Mem. Leadership Atlanta, 1980-81. Mem. Am. Coll. Hosp. Adminstrs. Baptist. Club: Rotary. Home: 1464 Stratfield Circle NE Atlanta GA 30319 Office: 1000 Johnson Ferry Rd NE Atlanta GA 30342

CLARK, WESLEY CLARKE, educator, editor; b. Cleve., Sept. 17, 1907; s. William Chester and Mabel Ruth (Clark) C.; m. Frances Grace Stiles, Oct. 9, 1931 (dec. Sept. 1969); children: Sally Lee (Judd), William Standish; m. Rhea Doyle Eckel, Feb. 9, 1974. A.B., Marietta Coll., 1930; M.A., U. Pa., 1937, Ph.D., 1942. Reporter Marietta Times, 1930, Phila. Evening Bull., 1930-41; instr. polit. sci. Wharton Sch. U. Pa., 1937-41; asst. prof. Syracuse U., 1941-43, prof., 1947-73; dean Sch. Journalism, 1952-73, John Ben Snow prof. newspaper research, 1972-73; pres. Syracuse U. Press, 1954-55; asst. to Sec. of Interior, 1943-46; research dir. H.L. Ickes, 1946-47; v.p., treas. Skaneateles Press, N.Y., 1963-69, asso. editor, 1978—; pres. Teasel, Ltd., 1976—; vis. prof. Am. U., Cairo, 1973-74, Sweetbriar Coll., 1981; cons. Caribbean Commn., 1950. Author: Some Economic Aspects of a President's Popularity, 1942, El Derecho a la Information, 1966; editor: Journalism Tomorrow, 1959. Mem. N.Y. Gov.'s Com. on Minority Group Employment in News Media, 1968-69. Mem. Inter-Am. Press Assn., N.Y. State Soc. Newspaper Editors, N.Y. State Press Assn., Caribbean Conservation Corp., Delta Upsilon. Clubs: Sedgwick, University (Syracuse); Cosmos (Washington). Home: 56 E Genesee St Skaneateles NY 13152 *As a small boy, I was told by my grandfather that God put us here to make the world a better place in which to live. Most of my life I have tried.*

CLARK, WILLIAM GEORGE, judge; b. Chgo., July 16, 1924; s. John S. and Ita (Kennedy) C.; m. Rosalie Locatis, Nov. 28, 1946; children: Merrilee, William George, Donald, John Steven, Robert. Student, Loyola U., Chgo., 1942-43, 44; J.D., DePaul U., 1946, John Marshall Law Sch., Chgo., 1962. Bar: Ill. 1947. Mem. firm Crane, Kearney, Korzen, Phelan & Clark (and predecessor), Chgo., 1947-56; atty. for Pub. Adminstr. Ill., 1949-53; mem. Ill. Ho. of Reps. from Austin Dist. of Chgo., 1952-54, 56-60, Senate, 1954-56, majority leader, 1959; atty. gen., Ill., 1960-69; partner firm Arvey, Hodes & Mantynband, Chgo.; justice Supreme Ct. Ill., 1976—. Served with AUS, 1942-44. Mem. Ill., Chgo., bar assns., AMVETS, Celtic Legal Soc., Am. Legion, Irish Fellowship Club (pres. 1961-62), Catholic Lawyers Guild Chgo., Delta Theta Phi. Office: Ill Supreme Ct Richard J Daley Center Chicago IL 60602

CLARK, WILLIAM HARTLEY, educator; b. Pitts., Apr. 29, 1930; s. Arthur Tillotson and Ruthanna Frame (Anderson) C.; m. Barbara Jean Rockne, June 27, 1953; children—Heather Anderson, Jill Eleanor, Robert Hartley, Edward Kirtland. B.A., Carleton Coll., 1952; M.A., N.Y. U., 1955, Ph.D., 1960. Researcher for Carnegie Endowment for Internat. Peace, Brookings Instn., N.Y. U., 1953-54; instr. polit. sci. Western Coll., Oxford, Ohio, 1954-55; instr. internat. relations Carleton Coll., 1955-60, asst. prof., 1960-66, asso. prof., 1966-70, prof., 1970—, chmn. dept. polit. sci., 1972-76, Frank B. Kellogg prof. internat. relations, 1973—; lectr. U. Minn., 1970; dir. Geneva Seminar on Internat. Instns., 1975—. Author: The Politics of the Common Market, 1967; contbr. articles and revs. to profl. publs. Fulbright research fellow, 1961-62; Ford Found. research fellow, 1967; NSF research fellow, 1970, 71, 79. Mem. Internat. Studies Assn., Council Fgn. Relations (St. Paul-Mpls. Com. Fgn. Relations), UN Assn. Home: 216 Nevada St Northfield MN 55057 Office: Carleton Coll Northfield MN 55057

CLARK, WILLIAM HAWLEY, bishop; b. Escanaba, Mich., May 10, 1919; s. William James and Katherine Elsie (Hawley) C.; m. Rosemary Ellen Lehman, June 12, 1943; 3 children. B.A., U. Mich., 1942; postgrad., Chgo. Theol. Sem., 1942-44; B.D., Episc. Theol. Sch., 1945; S.T.M., Yale U., 1952, St. Augustine's Coll. Eng., 1960-61. Ordained deacon, 1945, priest, 1946; asst. rector St. Pauls Ch., Flint, Mich.; and vicar Trinity Ch., Flushing, Mich., 1945-49; priest in charge St. Peters Ch., Monroe, Conn., 1949-51; rector Trinity Ch., Concord, Mass., 1951-62; asso. sec. World Council Chs., Geneva, 1962-65; rector St. Andrew's Ch., Wellesley, Mass., 1965-73; now bishop Diocese Del., Wilmington; tutor Episc. Theol. Sem., 1951-56; exchange preacher Brit. Council Chs., 1969. Adminstrv. bd. Delmarva Ecumenical Agy., 1975—; bd. dirs. Wilmington Devel. Council, 1980—; governing bd. Nat. Council Chs., 1976-82; adv. bd. NCCJ, 1978—. Office: 2020 Tatnall St Wilmington DE 19802

CLARK, WILLIAM JAMES, insurance company executive; b. Kansas City, Mo., Oct. 1, 1923; s. William LeRoy and Margaret (Theobald) C.; children: Holly, Jane Clark Truden, Nancy, Patty. Student, Kansas City Jr. Coll., 1941-42; B.S., U. Mo., 1947. With Mass. Mut. Life Ins. Co., Springfield, 1947—, v.p. sales, 1967-70, sr. v.p., 1971-74, pres., mem. exec. com., dir., 1974—, chief exec. officer, 1980—; dir. Bank of Boston, Bank of Boston Corp. Bd. dirs. Springfield Coll.; trustee Clarke Sch. for Deaf; v.p. Pioneer Valley United Way; mem. com. on field relations ACLI. Served to 1st lt. USAAF, 1943-45. Mem. Life Ins. Mktg. and Research Assn., Life Ins. Assn. Mass., Am. Soc. C.L.U.s, Greater Springfield C. of C. (chmn.), Conf. Bd. (mem. com. on re-elections and admissions). Clubs: Longmeadow (Mass.) Country; Colony (Springfield). Home: 101 Woodsley Rd Longmeadow MA 01106 Office: 1295 State St Springfield MA 01111

CLARK, WILLIAM KEMP, neurological surgeon; b. Dallas, Sept. 2, 1925; s. James and Florine (Kemp) C.; m. Fern Blair, Mar. 30, 1952; children: Elizabeth, Sarah, Florine, Blair, Peter, Jonathan. B.A., U. Tex., 1945, M.D., 1948. Diplomate: Am. Bd. Neurol. Surgery (bd., sec. 1972-76, chmn. 1976-78). Intern Ind. U. Hosp., 1948-49; resident Neurol. Inst., N.Y.C., 1953-56; practice medicine specializing in neurosurgery, Dallas, 1956—; prof. div. neurosurgery Southwestern Med. Sch., Dallas, 1956—; dir. neurosurg. service Parkland Meml., Children's Meml. hosps., 1956—; cons. VA Hosp., 1956—; nat. cons. U.S. Navy Surgeon Gen., 1977—, USAF Surgeon Gen., 1980; mem. nat. adv. council neurol. surgery VA, 1974—; chmn. Nat. Manpower Com. Neurosurgery, 1971-80; mem. Linz Award Com., 1972, Am. Bd. Med. Specialists, 1972-78, Residency Rev. Com. Neurol. Surgery, 1972-78, chmn., 1978-80. Bd. dirs. Tex. div. Am. Cancer Soc., 1976; Mem. lay advisory bd. St. Michael's Sch., Dallas, 1973—. Served to capt. M.C. USAF, 1950-52. Mem. Soc. Neurol. Surgeons (sec. 1979—1979-82), Soc. Neurl. Surgeons (pres.-elect 1982-83), Am. Assn. Neurol. Surgeons (dir. 1978-80, pres. 1981-82, mem., chmn. Washington liaison com.-joint com. with Congress Neurol. Surgeons 1982-83); Mem. Am. Neurol. Assn., ACS (gov. 1983-84). Clubs: Brookhollow Golf, City (Dallas). Home: 3909 Euclid St Dallas TX 75205 Office: 5323 Harry Hines Blvd Dallas TX 75235

CLARK, WILLIAM PATRICK, govt. ofcl., rancher; b. Oxnard, Calif., Oct. 23, 1931; s. William Pettit and Bernice (Gregory) C.; m. Joan Brauner, May 5, 1955; children—Monica, Peter, Nina, Colin, Paul. Ed., Stanford U., 1949-51, Loyola U. Law Sch., Los Angeles, 1955. Bar: Calif. bar 1958. Sr. partner firm Clark, Cole & Fairfield, Oxnard, Calif., 1958-66; chief of staff Gov. Ronald Reagan, Sacramento, 1966-69; judge Superior Ct. San Luis Obispo County, Calif., 1969-71; justice Ct. of Appeals, Los Angeles, 1971-73, Supreme Ct. Calif., San Francisco, 1973-81; dep. sec. Dept. State, Washington, 1981—; pres. Clark Land & Cattle Co., Ventura, Calif., 1963-73. Mem. Gov. Reagan's Task Force on Govtl. Reorganization, 1966-67. Served with U.S. Army, 1951-53. Mem. Calif. Cattlemen's Assn. Roman Catholic. Office: National Security Affairs 1600 Pennsylvania Ave NW Washington DC 20500

CLARK, WILLIAM STRATTON, physician; b. Dayton, Ohio, Nov. 24, 1914; s. Clyde Melvin and Hazel Marie (Walker) C.; m. Vivien Ranschburg, June 25, 1971; children: William Stratton, Judith Ann, Robin Walker, James Pennell. B.S., U. Dayton, 1932; M.D., St. Louis U., 1938. Diplomate: Am. Bd. Internal Medicine. Intern Miami Valley Hosp., Dayton, 1938-39; gen. practice medicine, Dayton, 1939-44; asst. in pathology Tulane U., 1944-45; clin. fellow medicine Mass. Gen. Hosp., 1945-48; research, tchr. Mass. Gen. Hosp., Med. Sch. Harvard, 1948-53; asst. prof. medicine Western Res. U., 1953-56, asso. prof. medicine, 1956-58; dir. med. dept. Nat. Found., 1958-64; pres., chief exec. officer Arthritis Found., N.Y.C., 1964-70, cons., 1970—; attending physician St. Luke's Hosp., 1974—, acting dir. dept. medicine, 1975-76, dir. dept. medicine, 1977-79, chief div. rheumatic diseases, 1979—; prof. clin. medicine Columbia U. Coll. Physicians and surgeons, 1975—. Former editor-in-chief: Arthritis and Rheumatism (ofcl. jour. Am. Rheumatism Assn.); contbr. articles to profl. jours. Fellow ACP; mem. AMA, Am. Fedn. Clin. Research, Am. Rheumatism Assn. Episcopalian. Club: Century Assn. (N.Y.C.). Home: 1349 Lexington Ave New York NY 10028 Office: 15 W 72d St New York NY 10023

CLARKE, ALLEN BRUCE, educator; b. Saskatoon, Sask., Can., Sept. 8, 1927; came to U.S., 1947, naturalized, 1953; s. Arthur Roy and Florence (Clarke) C.; m. Florence Myres, Sept. 14, 1949; children—David John, Richard Neil, Deborah Lynn. B.A. with Honours, U. Sask., 1947; M.Sc., Brown U., 1949, Ph.D., 1951. From instr. to prof. U. Mich., 1951-67; Fulbright lectr. U. Turku and U. Abo, Finland, 1959-60; prof., chmn. dept. math. Western Mich. U., 1967-78; dean Coll. Arts and Sci., 1978—; cons., lectr. probability and random processes. Author: Elementary Statistics, 1961, (with R.L. Disney) Probability and Random Processes for Engineers and Scientists, 1970; Contbr. articles to profl. jours. Mem. Math. Assn. Am. (sect. chmn. 1969-70), Am. Math. Soc., Inst. Math. Statistics, AAUP, ACLU. Home: 2016 Greenbriar Dr Kalamazoo MI 49008

CLARKE, BOBBY *See* **CLARKE, ROBERT EARLE**

CLARKE, BOWMAN LAFAYETTE, educator; b. Meridian, Miss., Sept. 19, 1927; s. Alvin Merritt and Mamie Edna (Blakeley) C. B.A., Millsaps Coll., 1948; B.D., Emory U., 1951, M.A., 1952, Ph.D., 1961; M.A., U. Miss., 1957. Ordained to ministry Methodist Ch., 1952; minister to Meth. students Ga. State Coll. for Women, 1953-54, U. Miss., 1954-57; instr. philosophy U. of South, 1959-60; asst. prof. philosophy U. Ga., Athens, 1961-65, asso. prof. philosophy, 1965-67, prof., 1967—, head dept. philosophy and religion, 1972-79. Author: Language and Natural Theology, 1966; Editor: Internat. Jour. Philosophy Religion, 1970; Contbr. articles to profl. jours. Danforth grantee, 1957; Cokesbury award, 1958; research grantee Ella Lyman Cabot Trust Fund, 1960. Mem. Am. Philos. Assn., Am. Acad. Religion, Soc. for Philosophy of Religion, Soc. for Advancement Am. Philosophy, Metaphys. Soc. Am., Internat. Soc. Metaphysics, So. Soc. for Philosophy and Psychology. Home: 18 S Stratford Dr Athens GA 30605

CLARKE, CHARLES FENTON, lawyer; b. Hillsboro, Ohio, July 25, 1916; s. Charles F. and Margaret (Patton) C.; m. Virginia Schoppenhorst, Apr. 3, 1945; children: Elizabeth, Margaret, Jane, Charles Fenton, IV. A.B. summa cum laude, Washington and Lee Coll., Lexington, Va., 1938; LL.B., U. Mich., 1940; LL.D. (hon.), Cleve. State U., 1971. Bar: Mich. 1940, Ohio 1946. Pvt. practice, Detroit, 1942, Cleve., 1946—; partner firm Squire, Sanders & Dempsey, 1957—, adminstr. litigation dept., 1979—; trustee Cleve. Legal Aid Soc., 1959-67; pres. Nat. Assn. R.R. Trial Counsel, 1966-68; life mem. 6th Circuit Jud. Conf.; chmn. legis. com. Cleve. Welfare Fedn., 1961-68; dir. Found. Equipment Corp., W.M. Brode Co., Park Mfg. Co. Pres. alumni bd. dirs. Washington and Lee U., 1970-72; pres. bd. dirs. Free Med. Clinic Greater Cleve., 1970—; trustee Cleve. Citizens League, 1956-62; bd. dirs. citizens adv. bd. Cuyahoga County (Ohio) Juvenile Ct., 1970-73; bd. dirs. George Jr. Republic, Greenville, Pa., 1970-73, Bowman Tech. Sch., Cleve., 1970—; vice chmn. Cleve. Crime Commn., 1973-75; exec. com. Cuyahoga County Republican Orgn., 1950—; councilman Bay Village, Ohio, 1948-53; pres., trustee Cleve. Hearing and Speech Center, 1957-62; trustee Laurel Sch., 1962-72. Served to 1st lt. AUS, World War II. Fellow Am. Coll. Trial Lawyers; mem. Greater Cleve. Bar Assn. (trustee 1983—), Cleve. Civil War Round Table (pres. 1968), Cleve. Zool. Soc. (dir. 1970), Phi Beta Kappa. Presbyterian. Clubs: Skating, Union (Cleve.); Tavern. Home: 2262 Tudor Dr Cleveland Heights OH 44106 Office: Huntington Bldg Cleveland OH 44115

CLARKE, CHARLES ROBERT, trust company executive; b. London, Ont., Can., Mar. 13, 1920; s. Charles John and Margaret (McPhail) C.; m. Joyce Norris, Aug. 25, 1951 (dec. July 1982); children: Robert, John, Margaret. B.A., U. Western Ont., 1941; LL.B., Osgoode Hall Law Sch., Toronto, Ont., 1949. Bar: Ont. 1949. With Can. Trustco Mortgage Co., London, 1949—, gen. counsel, 1966—, sec., 1970—, v.p., 1975—. Served with Can. Army, 1941-46. Mem. Can. Bar Assn. Anglican. Clubs: London, London Hunt and Country. Home: 1022 Hunt Club Mews London ON N6H 4R7 Canada Office: 275 Dundas St London ON N6A 4S4 Canada

CLARKE, CLIFFORD MONTREVILLE, health foundation executive; b. Ludowici, Ga., July 20, 1925; s. Clifford Montreville and Lella Bertrue (Hightower) C. A.B. in Polit. Sci, Emory U., 1951. Radio engr., announcer WSAV, Savannah, 1941-43; pub. relations dir. Ga. dept. Am. Legion, 1945-47; instr. Armstrong Coll., Savannah, 1947-48; asst. supt. Savannah Park and Tree Commn., 1951; instr., supr. tng. dept. Lockheed Aircraft Corp., Marietta, Ga., 1951-52, mgr. employee services dept., 1952-53; exec. v.p. Asso. Industries, Ga., 1953-68; pres. Ga. Bus. and Industry Assn., Atlanta, 1968-73; exec. dir. Bicentennial Council Thirteen Original States, Atlanta, 1973-75; pres. Arthritis Found., 1975—; mem. Am. Soc. Assn. Execs., 1955—, bd. dirs., 1958-67, mem. exec. com., 1960-67, treas., 1962-64, sr. v.p., 1964-65, pres.,

1965-66, Ga. Soc. Assn. Execs., 1958-60; v.p., chmn. state assn. group Nat. Indsl. Council, 1970-72. Mem. Ga. Urban and Tech. Assistance Adv. Council, 1965-70, Ga. Intergovtl. Relations Commn., 1966; mem. Ga. Ednl. Improvement Council, 1964-69, chmn., 1967-69, vice chmn., 1970-71; mem. Forward Ga. Commn., 1969-72; vice chmn. Ga. Commn. for Nat. Bicentennial Celebration, 1969-72, chmn., 1973—; chmn. Chartered Exec. Chartering Bd., 1969-71; mem. Cert. Assn. Exec. Bd., 1978—; mem. policy com. U. Ga. Grad. Sch. Bus.; adv. bd. Ga. Vocat. Rehab.; mem. Nat. Arthritis Adv. Bd., 1977—; Bd. dirs. Arthritis Found. Ga., 1965-71, Atlanta Community Services to Blind, Coop. Services for Blind, 1964-71, Atlanta Sch. Art, Atlanta Conv. Bur., 1968-71, Nat. Health Council, 1978—; trustee Am. Soc. Assn. Execs. Found. Served with inf. AUS, World War II. Decorated Purple Heart with 2 oak leaf clusters. Office: 1314 Spring St. NW Atlanta GA 30309

CLARKE, CORDELLA KAY KNIGHT MAZUY, insurance company executive; b. Springfield, Mo., Nov. 22, 1938; d. William Horace and Charline (Bentley) Knight; m. Logan Clarke, Jr., July 22, 1978; children by previous marriage—Katharine Michelle Mazuy, Christopher Knight Mazuy. A.B. with honors in English, U. N.C., 1960; M.S. in Statistics, N.C. State U., 1962. Statistician Research Triangle Inst., Durham, N.C., 1960-63; statis. cons. Arthur D. Little, Inc., Cambridge, Mass., 1963-67; mktg. research project mgr. Polaroid Corp., Cambridge, 1967, dir. mktg. research, 1968-69, mgr. mktg. planning and analysis, 1969-70; dir. mktg. and bus. planning Transaction Tech., Inc., Cambridge, 1970-72; pres. Mazuy Assos., Boston, 1972-73; v.p. Nat. Shawmut Bank, Boston, 1973-74; sr. v.p., dir. mktg. Shawmut Corp., 1974-78; sr. v.p., dir. retail banking Shawmut Bank, 1976-78; v.p. corp. devel. Arthur D. Little, Inc., 1978-79; v.p. Conn. Gen. Life Ins. Co., 1979—; faculty Williams Sch. Banking; adv. com. Bur. of Census, 1978—; dir. Blue Shield of Mass, 1976-79, McGraw Hill, 1976—, Data Terminal Systems, 1978-82; tchr. Amos Tuck Grad. Sch. Bus., Dartmouth Coll., 1964-65, exec.-in-residence, 1978, 80; now bd. overseers; exec.-in-residence Wheaton Coll., 1978; vis. prof. Simmons Grad. Sch. Mgmt., 1978; mem. schs. adv.council Bank Mktg. Assn., 1976-78; mem. corp. adv. bd. Hartford Nat. Bank & Trust Co., 1980—. Columnist Am. Banker, 1976-78. Mem. Mass. Gov.'s Commn. on Status of Women, 1977-79; bd. corporators Babson Coll., 1977-80; adv. bd. Boston Mayor's Office Cultural Affairs, 1977-79; bd. dirs. Greater Hartford Arts Council, 1979—; trustee Children's Mus. Hartford, 1980-82; corporator Inst. of Living, 1981—. Mem. Am. Statis. Assn., Am. Mktg. Assn., Phi Beta Kappa, Phi Kappa Phi, Kappa Alpha Theta. Home: 31 Main St Farmington CT 06032 Office: Conn Gen Life Ins Co Hartford CT 06152

CLARKE, DAVID HOWELL, aluminum company executive; b. Wei Hai Wei, Shantung, China, Nov. 4, 1925; came to Can., 1980; s. Arthur Gladstone and Nellie Sophia (Pettifer) C.; m. Margaret Doris Swonnell, July 11, 1953; children: Evangeline Margaret Clarke Miller, Alison Ruth Clarke Wilson, Heather Joy Clarke Barnes. Assoc., Royal Inst. Brit. Architects, Waltham Forest, London, 1951. Architect Tooley & Foster, Buckhurst Hill, Essex, Eng., 1951-53, Norman & Dawbarn, London, 1953-54, Hannen & Markham, 1954-57, Aluminio Arquitechonico, Mexico City, 1958-60; townsite engr. Sprostons Constrn. Co., Mackenzie, Guyana, 1957-58; with Alcan Aluminum Ltd., U.S., Argentina, Hong Kong, Can., 1960-80, v.p. personnel, Montreal, Que., Canada, 1980—; dir. Alcan Adminco Inc., Montreal, 1981—, Alcan Fiduciaries Ltd., 1981—, Toyo Aluminum K.K., Osaka, Japan, 1980—. Office: Alcan Aluminum Ltd 1188 Sherbrook St W Montreal PQ Canada H3A 3G2

CLARKE, DAVID MARSHALL, college president; b. Chewalah, Wash., Nov. 28, 1927; s. Melvin L. and Louise M. (Van Bibber) C. B.S., Gonzaga U., 1949, M.S. in Organic Chemistry, 1949, Licentiate in Philosophy, 1958; Ph.D. in Phys. Chemistry, Northwestern U., 1953; Licentiate in Sacred Theology, Weston Coll., 1965. Instr., asst. prof. chemistry and math. Gonzaga U., Spokane, Wash., 1949-50, 56-61, asst. prof. chemistry, 1966-68, asso. prof., 1968-70, acad. v.p., 1968-69, exec. v.p., 1969-70; research scientist Weston Obs., Boston Coll., 1961-65; provost, acad. v.p. St. Francis Coll., Joliet, Ill., 1970-72; pres. Regis Coll., Denver, 1972—. Commr. Denver Commn. Community Relations, 1975-83; trustee, mem. exec. com. N.W. Assn. Pvt. Colls. and Univs., 1968-70; trustee Gonzaga U., 1968-70, Coll. Holy Cross, 1969-78, Regis Coll., 1972—, Inst. Health, Denver; trustee, chmn. acad. com. Loyola U., Chgo., 1971-80, trustee, New Orleans, 1982—; bd. dirs. Assn. Jesuit Colls. and Univs., 1973—; mem. adv. bd. Colo. Youth Leadership Seminar. Mem. Am. Chem. Soc., Pres.'s Assn., Sigma Xi, Delta Epsilon Sigma, Phi Lambda Upsilon, Alpha Sigma Nu. Research and publs. in field. Address: 3539 W 50th Pkwy Denver CO 80221

CLARKE, DONALD DUDLEY, biochemistry educator; b. Kingston, Jamaica, B.W.I., Mar. 20, 1930; came to U.S., 1948, naturalized, 1961; s. Izett Dudley and Ivy (Burrowes) C.; m. Marie B. Burrowes, Sept. 5, 1953; children: Carol, Stephen, Paula, David, Ian, Sylvia, Peter. B.S., Fordham U., 1950, M.S., 1951, Ph.D., 1955. Postdoctoral research fellow U. Toronto, 1955-57; sr. research scientist N.Y. Psychiat. Inst., N.Y.C., 1957-62; research asso. biochemistry dept., Columbia, 1959-61; adj. asso. prof. Fordham U., N.Y.C., 1961-62, asso. prof., 1962-70, prof. biochemistry, 1970—, chmn. chemistry dept., 1978—; cons. preclin. psycho pharmacology research rev. com. NIMH, 1972-76; mem. behavioral and neuroscis. study sect. NIH, 1982-85. Contbr. articles to profl. jours. Fellow N.Y. Acad. Scis.; mem. Am. Chem. Soc. (chmn. N.Y. sect. 1977-78, councillor sect. 1981—), Am. Soc. Biol. Chemists, Biochem. Soc. (London), AAAS, N.Y. Acad. Sci., Internat., Am. socs. for neurochemistry, Soc. for Applied Spectroscopy, Sigma Xi, Phi Lambda Upsilon. Democrat. Roman Catholic. Club: K.C. Home: 2528 Grand Ave New York NY 10468

CLARKE, EDWARD NIELSEN, educator; b. Providence, Apr. 25, 1925; s. Edward O.A. and Edith (Nielsen) C.; m. Vivian Constance Bergquist, July 23, 1949; children—Sandra J., David E., Allan R., Jeffrey B. B.S., Brown U., 1945, Ph.D., 1951; M.S., Harvard, 1947, M.Engring. Sci., 1948. Mem. tech. staff, sect. head for semiconductors, physics lab. Sylvania Electric Products Co., Bayside, N.Y., 1950-56; group head for research Sperry Semiconductor div. Sperry Rand Corp., Norwalk, Conn., 1956-59; v.p. ops. and dir. Nat. Semiconductor Corp., Danbury, Conn., 1959-65; asso. dean faculty, asso. dean grad. studies, dir. research Worcester Poly. Inst., 1965—; also tri-coll. coordinator research Clark U.-Holy Cross Coll.-Worcester Poly. Inst., 1974—. Trustee Upsala Coll., East Orange, N.J., 1971-74. Served with USNR, 1943-46. Mem. Research Soc. Am. (past br. pres.), IEEE, Am. Phys. Soc., AAAS, Am. Soc. Engring. Edn., Sigma Xi (past chpt. pres.), Tau Beta Pi. Lutheran. Clubs: Rotarian., Torch (Worcester). Home: 85 Richards Ave Paxton MA 01612 Office: Worcester Poly Inst Worcester MA 01609 *Helping others to achieve has been my own principal achievement. Retain mobility and be willing to use one's skills wherever they are needed. Do not become too comfortable and secure. Move on to find new challenges. Stay young with variety in one's life and a healthy use of the out-of-doors.*

CLARKE, EDWIN CAMERON, college pres. emeritus; b. Beaver Falls, Pa., Oct. 30, 1913; s. Robert and Bernice Mehard (Wilson) C.; m. Agnes Currie Thorburn, Feb. 29, 1944; children: Robert Thorburn, Carolyn Wilson. B.A., Geneva Coll., 1935, D.H., 1980; postgrad., Princeton U., 1935-37, U. Colo., summer 1938; Ph.D., U. Pitts., 1949; LL.D., Grove City Coll., 1972; L.H.D., Westminster Coll., 1979. Faculty Geneva Coll., 1937—, asso. prof. econs. and bus. adminstrn., acting head dept., 1947-49, prof., head dept., 1949-56, v.p. devel., 1950-56, pres., 1956-80; dir. Pitts. Tubular Shafting Corp. Pres. Youth Tennis Found., Pitts.; bd. dirs. Beaver County Heart Assn., Beaver County br. Pa. Assn. for Blind; trustee Ref. Presbyn. Theol. Sem., Pitts. Served with AUS, 1941-46. Named Man of Year Beaver Falls Jr. C. of C., 1953. Mem. Am. Econs. Assn., Pa. Edn. Assn., Beaver Falls C. of C. Mem. Ref. Presbyterian Ch. (elder). Club: Kiwanis. Home: 1622 21st Ave Beaver Falls PA 15010

CLARKE, ELIOT CHANNING, banker; b. Boston, Sept. 22, 1928; s. James Freeman and Aleen Victoria (Hughes) C.; m. Susanne Murray Low, Jan. 18, 1975; 1 son, Eliot C.L.; children by previous marriage—Amory Y., Laughlin H., Victoria A.L. A.B., Harvard, 1951, M.B.A., 1955. With Morgan Guaranty Trust Co., N.Y.C., 1958-78, sr. v.p., 1970-78; pres. Travelers Asset Mgmt. Internat. Corp., N.Y.C., 1978-80, Internat. Power Devel. Corp., 1980—; dir. Boorum & Pease Co., Atlantic Energy & Devel. Corp., Consol. Gemstones Ltd. Served to capt. AUS, 1952-54. Club: Knickerbocker (N.Y.C.). Home: Lithgow Millbrook NY 12545 Office: 1 E 62d St New York NY 10021

CLARKE, ERIC THACHER, physicist; b. Rochester, N.Y., Nov. 27, 1916; s. Hans Thacher and Frieda (Planck) C.; m. Elizabeth Hewitt, Oct. 9, 1944; children—Rebecca, Hans, Heidi, Benjamin, Abigail. S.B., Harvard U., 1938; Ph.D., Mass. Inst. Tech., 1944. Physicist U.S. Antarctic Service, 1939-40; research asso. Mass. Inst. Tech., Cambridge, 1944-48; asso. tech. dir. Tracerlab, Boston, 1949-50; with Tech. Ops. Inc., Boston, 1951—, v.p., sec., 1953—. Mem. Lexington (Mass.) Planning Bd., 1968-78. Mem. Am. Phys. Soc., Am. Nuclear Soc. Home: 29 Moon Hill Rd Lexington MA 02173 Office: Technical Operations Inc One Beacon St Boston MA 02108

CLARKE, ERWIN BENNET, banker; b. Troy, Tenn., Apr. 23, 1922; s. Homer Bruce and Grace (Erwin) C.; m. Janet Sue McCray, June 18, 1952; children—Daniel B., Gary B., Richard T. B.A., Vanderbilt U., 1947; postgrad., Rutgers U., 1966. With 3d Nat. Bank, Nashville, 1947-76, sr. v.p., sr. loan officer met. div., to 1976; exec. v.p. exec. div. Nashville City Bank, 1976—; instr. Am. Inst. Banking. Bd. dirs. Big Bros. of Nashville; treas. bd. trustees; mem. exec. com. Scarritt Coll.; trustee Sr. Citizens, Inc., Nat. Meth. Found. for Christian Higher Edn. Served to capt. USMCR, 1946, 50-51. Mem. Am. Inst. Banking (dir., past pres. Nashville chpt.), Nashville Credit Mens Assn., Sales and Mktg. Execs. Nashville, Nashville Area C. of C. (econ. devel. com.), Am. Bankers Assn., Tenn. Bankers Assn., Kappa Sigma. Methodist. Clubs: Mason (Shriner, Jester), Cumberland, City, Vanderbilt. Home: 6018 Ashland Dr Nashville TN 37215 Office: 315 Union St Nashville TN 37201

CLARKE, FRANK ELDRIDGE, govt. ofcl.; b. Brunswick, Md., Dec. 26, 1913; s. Frank Dorsey and Mary J. (McKenzie) C.; m. Doris Mae Booth, Aug. 20, 1934; children—Virginia Mary (Mrs. G. Robert Blakley), Ernest Eldridge. A.B. in Chemistry with honors, Western Md. Coll., 1935; M.S. equivalent in Phys. Chemistry, U. Md., 1942. With U.S. Naval Engring. Expt. Sta., 1941-61; with U.S. Geol. Survey, 1961-76, asst. dir., 1968-71; dep. under sec. for sci. engring. Dept. Interior, 1971-72; sr. scientist U.S. Geol. Survey, 1972-76; Cons. in corrosion field, 1961-79. Recipient Gordon research certificate of award, 1966; Dept. Interior Distinguished Service award, 1971. Mem. ASTM (pres. 1974-75, dir., v.p. water com. D-19, award of merit 1961, Max Hecht award 1964), Am. Chem. Soc. (certificate merit 1953), Am. Inst. Chem. Engrs., AAAS. Lutheran (pres. 1957-63). Clubs: Elk., Cosmos (Washington). Patentee in field. Home and Office: 165 Williams Dr Annapolis MD 21401

CLARKE, FREDERIC B., III, risk analysis consultant; b. Portsmouth, N.H., Aug. 31, 1942; s. Fredric B. and Elizabeth Jane (Leach) C.; m. Janice Freeman, Feb. 25, 1962; children: Frederic B., Claire Evan. Student, U. Mo., 1960-62; A.B., Washington U., 1966; A.M., Harvard U., 1968, Ph.D., 1971. Research chemist Monsanto Co., 1971-73; mktg. supr., 1973-74; asst. to dir. Center for Fire Research, Nat. Bur. Standards, Dept. Commerce, 1974-76, dep. dir., 1977-78; dir. Center for Fire Research, Nat. Engring. Lab., 1978-81; pres. Benjamin/Clarke Assocs. Inc., 1981—. Contbr. articles to profl. jours. Legis. asst. to Sen. John C. Culver, 1976-77. NSF fellow, 1966-69; Congl. fellow, 1976-77. Mem. Am. Chem. Soc., ASTM, Nat. Fire Protection Assn., Congl. Fellows Assn. (pres. 1981), Phi Beta Kappa, Sigma Xi. Patentee in field. Home: 14501 Carrolton Rd Rockville MD 20853 Office: 10605 Concord St Kensington MD 20895

CLARKE, FREDERICK JAMES, civil engr.; b. Little Falls, N.Y., Mar. 1, 1915; s. Edward James and Grace Ellen (Zoller) C.; m. Isabel Morrison Van Slyke, Sept. 15, 1938; children—Warren E., Isabel V., Nancy S. B.S., U.S. Mil. Acad., 1937; M.S.C.E., Cornell U., 1940; postgrad., Harvard U. Bus. Sch., 1954; grad., Nat. War Coll., 1957. Commd. 2d lt. U.S. Army, 1937, advanced through grades to lt. gen., 1969; mgr. Hanford Ops., Richland, Wash., 1945-47; dist. engr., Pakistan, 1957-59, engr. commr., D.C., 1960-63; comdt. U.S. Army Engring. Sch., Ft. Belvoir, Va., 1965-66; chief engr. U.S. Army, Washington, 1969-73; ret., 1973; exec. dir. Nat. Commn. on Water Quality, Washington, 1973-76; cons. engr. Tippetts-Abbett-McCarthy-Stratton, Washington, 1973-79. Decorated Legion of Merit, D.S.M. with oak leaf cluster. Mem. Nat. Acad. Engring., Nat. Soc. Profl. Engrs., ASCE, Am. Acad. Environ. Engrs., Am. Public Works Assn. (hon.), Am. Water Resources Assn. (hon.), U.S. Com. on Large Dams, Soc. Am. Mil. Engrs. (hon.), Assn. U.S. Army, AIA, Permanent Internat. Assn. Navigational Congresses. Clubs: Chevy Chase, Cosmos. Home: 4801 Upton St NW Washington DC 20016 Office: 1101 15th St NW Washington DC 20005

CLARKE, GARRY EVANS, educator, musician, composer; b. Moline, Ill., Mar. 19, 1943; s. Clarence Henderson and Gladys Arlene (Hokinson) C.; m. Melissa Jane Naul, May 24, 1975; 1 dau., Catharine van Gelder. B.Mus. summa cum laude, Cornell Coll., Iowa, 1965; M.Mus., Yale U., 1968. Asst. prof. music Washington Coll., Chestertown, Md., 1968-73, assoc. prof., 1973-79, prof., 1979—, dean coll., 1977-83, acting pres., 1981-82. Concert pianist, U.S., Europe, 1972—; composer symphonic, chamber, vocal, piano and organ music and opera; lectr. and recitalist: Am. music; condr. piano workshops; opera coach; organist and choir master, St. Paul's Episcopal Parish, Centerville, Md., 1975—; author: Essays on American Music, 1977; contbr. articles, revs. to profl. jours.; co-editor: Varied Air and Variations (Ives), 1971; editor: Charles Ives. Soc. publs. Trustee Council Econ. Edn. Md. Ford Found. fellow, 1965; Woodrow Wilson fellow, 1965; Carnegie Found. research grantee, 1964; NEH research grantee, 1970. Mem. Soc. Music Theory, Sonneck Soc., Council Higher Edn. in Music, Am. Conf. Acad. Deans, Nat. Assn. Schs. Music, Am. Assn. Higher Edn., AAUP, Yale Sch. Music Alumni Assn. (exec. com. 1975-80), Assn. Yale Alumni, Pi Kappa Lambda, Omega Delta Kappa. Episcopalian. Club: Yale (N.Y.C.). Home: Kentmere-Quaker Neck Chestertown MD 21620 Office: Washington Coll Chestertown MD 21620

CLARKE, HAROLD G., justice Supreme Ct. Ga.; b. Forsyth, Ga., Sept. 28, 1927. J.D., U. Ga., 1950. Bar: Ga. 1950. Mem. Ga. State Legislature, 1961-71; chmn. Ga. Inst. for Continuing Legal Edn.; justice Ga. Supreme Ct., 1979—. Fellow Am. Coll. Trial Lawyers, Am. Bar Found.; mem. ABA, Flint Circuit Bar Assn. (pres. 1960-61), Am. Judicature Soc. (bd. dirs.), State Bar Ga. (gov. 1971—, exec. com. 1973—, pres. 1976-77), Omicron Delta Kappa. Office: Supreme Ct Judicial Bldg Atlanta GA 30334

CLARKE, HENRY LELAND, composer; b. Dover, N.H., Mar. 9, 1907; s. Ward Robinson and Annie Leland (Barber) C.; m. Julia Newbold Keasbey, June 24, 1937; 1 dau., Anne Newbold (dec.). A.B., Harvard U., 1928, M.A., 1929, Ph.D., 1947; student of, Nadia Boulanger, 1929-31, Gustav Holst, 1932, Hans Weisse, 1933-34, Otto Luening, 1936-38. Asst. N.Y. Pub. Library, 1932-36; teaching asst. Bennington Coll., Vt., 1936-38; chmn. grad. faculty Westminster Choir Coll., Princeton, N.J., 1938-42; lectr. U. Calif. at, Los Angeles, 1947-48; asst. prof. Vassar Coll., 1948-49, U. Calif. at, Los Angeles, 1949-58; asso. prof. U. Wash., Seattle, 1959-75, prof., 1975-77, prof. emeritus, 1977-80; lectr. Brattleboro (Vt.) Music Center, 1977—; vis. prof. Boston U., summer 1949, Harvard U., 1956, UCLA, 1962, Columbia U., 1963. Composer: The Loafer and the Loaf, 1951, Lysistrata, 1969, Monograph, 1948, No Man Is an Island (chorus and band), 1951, A Game That Two Can Play (flute and clarinet), 1959, To See the Earth, 1973, Patriot Primer, 1974, Mass for All Souls, 1975, The Mountain and the Squirrel, 1976, The Bounty of Athena, 1978, Listen to Me, 1980, Choose Life, 1983. Served with AUS, 1944. John Harvard Traveling fellow, 1929-30; Am. Council Learned Socs. grantee, 1936; recipient Wash. Music Educators prize award, 1964; fellow Mac Dowell Colony, 1966, 67. Mem. Am. Composers Alliance, Am. Musicol. Soc. (past chpt. pres.), Am. Soc. Aesthetics (past chpt. pres.), Coll. Music Soc. (past v.p.), Phi Mu Alpha. Unitarian. Club: Harvard (N.Y.C.). Home: One Wapping Rd Deerfield MA 01342 *What I believe, I set to music: Freedom is a noble thing (but) No man is an island. Winter is a cold thing (and) These are the times that try men's souls. (Yet) Wonders are many and none is more wonderful than Man.*

CLARKE, J. CALVITT, JR., federal judge; b. Harrisburg, Pa., Aug. 9, 1920; s. Joseph Calvitt and Helen Caroline (Mattson) C.; m. Mary Jane Cromer, Feb. 1, 1943; children: Joseph Calvitt III, Martha Tiffany. B.S. in Commerce, U. Va., 1944, LL.B., 1944. Bar: Va. 1944. Practiced in, Richmond, Va., 1944-74; partner firm Bowles, Anderson, Boyd, Clarke & Herod, 1944-60; firm Sands Anderson, Marks and Clarke, 1960-74; judge U.S. Dist. Ct. Eastern dist. of Va., 1975—; mem. 4th Circuit Judicial Conf., 1963; hon. consul for Republic of Bolivia, 1959-75. Chmn. Citizen's Advisory Com. on Joint Water System for Henrico and Hanover counties, Va., 1968-69; mem. Mayor's Freedom Train Com., 1948-50; del. Young Republican Nat. Conv., Salt Lake City, 1949 del. Young Republican Nat. Conv., Boston, 1951; chmn. Richmond (Va.) Republican Com., 1952-54; candidate for Congress, 1954; chmn. Va. 3d Dist. Rep. Com., 1955-58, 74—, Va. State Rep. Conv., 1958—; co-founder Young Rep. Fedn. of Va., 1950, nat. committeeman, 1950-54; chmn. Speakers Bur., Nixon-Lodge campaign, 1960, mem. fin. com., 1960-74; chmn. Henrico County Republican Com., 1956-58; fin. chmn. 1956; pres. Couples Sunday Sch. class Second Presbyn. Ch., Richmond, Va., 1948-50, mem. bd. deacons, 1948-61, elder, 1964—; bd. dirs. Family Service Children's Aid Soc., 1948-61, Gambles Hill Community Center, 1950-60, Christian Children's Fund, Inc., 1960-67, Children, Inc., 1967-75, Norfolk Forum, 1978—; mem. bd. of chancellors Internat. Consular Acad., 1965-75; trustee Henrico County Pub. Library, chmn., 1971-73. Mem. Va. State Bar (mem. 3rd dist. com. 1967-70, chmn. 1969-70), Am. Judicature Soc., ABA, Va. Bar Assn. (vice chmn. com. on cooperation with fgn. bars 1960-61), Richmond Jr. C. of C. (dir. 1946-50), Delta Theta Phi. Clubs: Windmill Point Yacht, Westwood Racquet (pres. 1961-62), Commonwealth.). Office: 325 US Courthouse Norfolk VA

CLARKE, JACK ALDEN, educator, librarian; b. Bay City, Mich., Feb. 20, 1924; s. Harry and Olivia (Bence) C.; m. Anna Holler, Feb. 1, 1951; children—David, Cynthia. B.A., Mich. State U., 1949; postgrad., U. Poitiers, France, 1949; M.A., U. Wis., 1950, 1952, Ph.D. in History, 1954. Intern Library of Congress, 1952-53; dir. Washington Cathedral Library, 1953-55, Doane Coll. Library, 1955-56; asst. librarian U. Wis., 1956-62; dir. libraries, chmn. dept. library sci. Wis. State U., Eau Claire, 1962- 66; asst. dir. U. Wis. Grad. Sch. Library Sci., Madison, 1966-68, acting dir., 1968-69, 70-71, prof., 1967—. Author: Gabriel Naudé 1600-1653; compiler: Research Materials in the Social Sciences, 1967, Modern French Literature: A Bibliography of Homage Studies, 1976; editor: Reader's Advisor, 1976; contbr. articles to profl. jours. Mem. AAUP, ALA, Wis. Library Assn. (chmn. coll. sect. 1963- 64), Assn. Coll. Reference Librarians. Home: 4326 Herrick Ln Madison WI 53711

CLARKE, JACK GRAEME, petroleum company executive; b. N.Y.C., Aug. 7, 1927; s. Jack Arnold and Jessie Alva (Murray) C.; m. Dorothea Jean Snyder, Feb. 3, 1951; children—David Dean, Douglas Graeme, Kathryn Alva. B.A. in Polit. Sci, Hofstra U., 1949; LL.B., Cornell U., 1952; LL.M. in Internat. Law, Harvard U., 1953. Bar: N.Y. bar 1953. With firm Sullivan & Cromwell, N.Y.C., 1953-56; atty. Creole Petroleum Corp., N.Y.C., 1957, Venezuela, 1957-59; counsel Standard Oil Co. (N.J.), N.Y.C., 1959-65; dep. Middle East rep., London, 1965-66, Middle East rep., 1966-68, asst. gen. counsel, N.Y.C., 1968-69, asso. gen. counsel, 1969-72, gen. counsel, 1972-73; exec. v.p. Esso Europe Inc., London, 1973-75; dir. Amstar Corp., N.Y.C.; dir., sr. v.p. Exxon Corp., N.Y.C., 1975—; mem. investment policy adv. com. Office of U.S. Trade Rep. Bd. dirs. Am. Ditchley Found.; bd. dirs., assoc. mem. exec. com. NAACP Legal Def. and Ednl. Fund; trustee Hofstra U., Hempstead, N.Y., YMCA Greater N.Y., Carnegie Corp. N.Y.; exec. com. Aspen Inst.; adv. bd. Georgetown Ctr. Strategic and Internat. Studies; bd. dirs. N.Y. Philharm. Mem. Nat. Council Fgn. Langs. and Internat. Studies, Am.-Saudi Bus. Roundtable, Council on Fgn. Relations, Internat. C. of C. (trustee and exec. com. of U.S. council), Fgn. Policy Assn. (bd. govs.), UN Assn. U.S.A. (dir.), Nat. Planning Assn. (trustee, exec. com.). Office: Exxon Corp Room 5107 1251 Ave of Americas New York NY 10020

CLARKE, JAMES MCCLURE, congressman; b. Manchester, Vt., June 12, 1917; m. Elspeth McClure, 1945; children: Susie, Jim, Annie, Dumont, Mark, Billy, Ambrose (dec.), Doug. Assoc. editor Asheville Citizen Times, N.C., 1960-69; asst. to pres. Warren Wilson Coll., 1969-81; dairy farm and apple orchard operator; mem. 98th Congress from 11th Dist. N.C. Chmn. Buncombe County Bd. Edn., 1969-76; sec. James G.K. McClure Found., 1956-82; mem. N.C. Ho. of Reps., 1977-80, N.C. State Senate, 1981-82, Gov.'s Crime Commn.; bd. dirs. Eckerd Wilderness Ednl. Systems; trustee Thoms Rehab. Hosp., Southeastern Council Founds.; hon. trustee N.C. Symphony; former bd. dirs. Fairview Vol. Fire Dept.; former elder Warren Wilson Presbyterian Ch. Served to lt. USNR, 1942-45. Democrat. Club: Asheville Civitan. Office: 415 Cannon House Office Bldg Washington DC 20515 *

CLARKE, JAMES THOMPSON, business exec., accountant; b. Petoskey, Mich., May 18, 1937; s. James H. and Imogene (Thompson) C.; m. Patricia W. Kemp, July 6, 1968; children—Timothy, Jonathan, Christian. B.A. with honors, Coll. of Wooster, 1959; M.B.A., U. Mich., 1961. C.P.A. Partner Coopers & Lybrand, 1965-73, 76—; asst. sec. Dept. of Interior, Washington, 1973-76; bd. dirs. Am. Revolution Bicentennial Adminstrn., 1973-76, Archtl. and Transp. Compliance Bd., 1973-76, Fed. Law Enforcement Tng. Center, 1973-76. Trustee

Conservation Trust of P.R., 1973-76, Coll. Wooster, 1977—. Served with USNR, 1962-65. Mem. Am. Inst. C.P.A.'s. Club: Stock Exchange. Home: 45 Bel Aire Ct Hillsborough CA 94010 Office: Coopers & Lybrand 333 Market San Francisco CA 94105

CLARKE, JOHN CLEM, artist; b. Bend, Oreg., June 6, 1937; s. Eugene and Wilma Mary (Owen) C.; m. Jane Dee Purucker, Apr. 7, 1979. B.S., U. Oreg., 1960; student, Oreg. State U., U. Mexico, Mexico City Coll. Exhbns. include, Whitney Mus., N.Y.C., 1967-73, Realism Now, N.Y. Cultural Center, Tokyo Biennale, Mus. Modern Art, N.Y.C., USA Bicentennial, U.S. Dept. Interior, represented in permanent collections, Whitney Mus. Am. Art, Met. Mus., Mus. Modern Art, Dallas Mus. Fine Arts, Va. Mus. Fine Arts, William Rockhill Nelson Gallery Art, Kansas City, Mo., Balt. Mus. Fine Arts. Address: 465 W Broadway New York NY 10012

CLARKE, JOHN FREDERICK GATES, entomologist; b. Victoria, C., Can., Feb. 22, 1905; came to U.S., 1916, naturalized, 1934; s. Robert Wilson and Ida Charlotte (Gates) C.; m. Thelma Blanche Canterbury Miesen, June 14, 1929; children: John Frederick Gates, Carol Canterbury. Student, U. Wash., 1923-24; Ph.C. in Pharmacy, Wash. State U., 1926; B.S. in Zoology, Wash. State U., 1930; M.S. in Entomology, Wash. State U., 1931, postgrad., 1935-36, U. Paris, 1945-46; Ph.D. in Entomology, U. London, 1953. Pharmacist Offerman Drug Co., Bellingham, Wash., 1926-29; instr. biology Wash. State Coll., 1931-35; entomologist Dept. Agr., 1936-54; curator div. insects U.S. Nat. Mus., Smithsonian Instn., 1954-62, chmn. dept. entomology, 1963-65; sr. entomologist Smithsonian Instn., 1965-75, research asso., 1975—; field expdns. to, Pacific Islands, Micronesia, 1952-53, 76, W.I., V.I., 1956, 58, Eng., Austria, 1957, 60, S.Am., 1958-59, Yucatan, 1960, S. Pacific, Polynesia, 1961, Tahiti, Raivavae, Tubuai, Rapa, Fiji, 1963, Dominica, 1965, Marquesas Islands, Tuamotus Islands, 1968, Argentina, 1973, Ponape, 1976, St. Eustatius, Cayman Islands, 1981, Queen Charlotte Islands, 1982; vis. prof. entomology Oreg. State U., 1970; Dept. Agr. del. 8th Entomol. Conf., Stockholm, 1948; presented papers numerous internat. confs. Author: Giant Golden Book on Butterflies, 1963; contbr. numerous articles to profl. jours. Served to capt. AUS, 1942-46; ETO. Decorated Bronze Star; recipient Karl Jordan medal, 1979; NRC grantee, 1934, 35; Smithsonian Instn. grantee, 1947; Am. Philos. Soc. grantee, 1950; NSF grantee, 1958, 61; Office Naval Research grantee, 1961, 62; Smithsonian Research Found. grantee, 1967-68. Fellow Royal Entomol. Soc., Entomol. Soc. Am. (chmn. com. proposal establish Nat. Inst. Entomology 1957); mem. Lepidopterists Soc. (pres. 1973), Entomol. Soc. Washington (chmn. program com. 1955-58, pres., mem. exec. com. 1960), Soc. Brit. Entomology, Biol. Soc. Washington, Washington Biologists Field Club, Sigma Xi, Phi Kappa Phi, Rho Chi, Phi Sigma, Phi Delta Theta; hon. mem. Soc. Crucena de Ciencias Naturales (Bolivia), Entomol. Soc. Peru. Club: Cosmos (Washington). Inventor philatelic tool. Home: 5115 72d Ave Glenridge Hyattsville MD 20784 Office: Dept Entomology US Nat Mus Smithsonian Instn Washington DC 20560

CLARKE, JOSEPH BRIAN, manufacturing company executive; b. Toronto, Ont., Can., Dec. 2, 1938; s. Kirkwood Johnson and Ethel May (Thomas) C.; m. Odette Hamel, July 24, 1972; children: Johanna, Krystina. Student, Ryerson Inst. Tech., 1957-61. Sales supr. Moore Bus. Forms, Toronto, 1961-65; v.p. mktg. Deluxe Reading Corp., Toronto, 1966; exec. v.p. Coleco (Can.) Ltd., Montreal, 1967-78, pres., 1978-81, chmn., pres., chief exec. officer, 1981—; v.p. internat. mktg. Coleco Industries, Inc., Hartford, Conn., 1970-81, exec. v.p., 1981—. Mayor City of Barkmere, Que. Mem. Can. Toy Mfrs. Assn. (dir.). Office: 4000 St Ambroise St Montreal PQ Canada H4C 2C8 99 Quaker Ln S West Hartford Conn. 06110

CLARKE, KENNETH KINGSLEY, electrical equipment company executive; b. Miami, Fla., June 7, 1924; s. Kenneth Kingsley and Mary (Coffin) C.; m. Nona Nelme, Sept. 15, 1945; 1 son, Kenneth Stephen. Student, Cornell U., 1941-43; M.Sc. in Elec. Engring, Stanford, 1948; D.Elec.Engring., Bklyn. Poly. Inst., 1959. Research fellow Bklyn. Poly. Inst., 1949-50; asst. prof. Madras (India) Inst. Tech., 1950-52; lectr. U. Ceylon, Colombo, 1952-54; asst. prof. Clarkson Coll. Tech., Potsdam, N.Y., 1954-55; faculty Bklyn. Poly. Inst., 1955-69, prof. elec. engring., 1965-69, dir. grad. elec. engring. div., 1967-69; pres. Clarke-Hess Communication Research Corp., N.Y.C., 1969—; Cons. to govt., industry, 1952—; vis. prof. Middle East Tech. U., Ankara, Turkey, 1961-62; dir. Julie Research Labs., 1966-71. Author: (with M.V. Joyce) Transistor Circuit Analysis, 1961, (with D.T. Hess) Communication Circuit Analysis, 1971. Served to 2d lt. USAAF, 1943-46. Mem. IEEE, AAUP, AAAS, Sigma Xi, Tau Beta Pi. Co-inventor frequency locked loop. Home: 300 Riverside Dr New York NY 10025 Office: 17 W 17th St New York NY 10011

CLARKE, KENNETH STEVENS, sports medicine adminstr.; b. South Bend, Ind., Aug. 18, 1931; s. Walter Robert and Mattie Marie (Boley) C.; m. Vivian Elizabeth Long, July 5, 1958; children—Patrick Stevens, Mary Elizabeth, Margaret Christine, Daniel. M.S., U. Ill., 1957, Ph.D., 1963. Whitman. Program cons. Chgo. Heart Assn., 1957-59; supr. recreation and athletics U. Ill. div. rehab.-edn., 1959-63; cons. health and fitness AMA, Chgo., 1963-68; coordinator continuing edn. Am. Acad. Orthopedic Surgeons, 1968-70; prof. health scis. Mankato (Minn.) State U., 1970-73; prof., chmn. health edn. Pa. State U., 1973-77; dean Coll. Applied Life Studies U. Ill., Urbana, 1977-81; dir. sports medicine U.S. Olympic Com., Colorado Springs, Colo., 1981—; cons. athletic injury prevention; founder Nat. Athletic Injury/Illness Reporting System. Active Pa. Emergency Med. Services Council, 1974-77, Ill. Gov.'s Council on Health and Fitness, 1978—; bd. dirs. Nat. Safety Council. Editor: Standard Nomenclature of Athletic Injuries, 1966, (with J.C. Hughston) Bibliography of Sports Medicine, 1970, Fundamentals of Athletic Training, 1971, Drugs and the Coach, 1972, 2d edit., 1976; Contbr. profl. articles to ednl. and med. jours. Served with CIC U.S. Army, 1953-55. Recipient Spl. citation Nat. Fedn. State High Sch. Assns. Mem. Am. Coll. Sports Medicine, AAHPER, Am. Acad. Phys. Edn., Assn. for Advancement Health Edn., Am. Orthopedic Soc. for Sports Medicine (hon.), U. Ill. Alumni Assn. (Merit award). Roman Catholic. Club: Rotary Internat. Home: 2813 Country Club Circle Colorado Springs CO 80909 Office: 1750 E Boulder St Colorado Springs CO 80909

CLARKE, LEWIS JAMES, landscape architect; b. Eng., Mar. 10, 1927; s. Rol and May (Pringle) C.; children: Lewis Nigel, Jennifer Kay, Rachel May, Lisa Elaine. Dip. Arch., Sch. Architecture, Leicester, Eng., 1950; Dip. L.D., Kings Coll, U. Durham, 1951; M.L.A., Harvard U., 1952. Prof. Sch. Design N.C. State Univ., Raleigh, 1952-68; sr. partner Lewis Clarke Assos., Raleigh, 1952—. Served with Corps Royal Engrs., 1945-48. Smith Mundt and Fulbright awards, 1951-52. Fellow Inst. Landscape Architects, Am. Soc. Landscape Architects; mem. Royal Inst. Brit. Architects. Office: 1701 Glen Eden Dr Raleigh NC 27612

CLARKE, LOGAN, JR., banker; b. Atlanta, May 28, 1927; s. Leonard Warner Moore and Marion (Ray) C.; children: Logan III, Jeffrey Reed, Jonathan, Lisa Beth; m. Cordelia Kay Knight Mazuy. Student, U. Okla., 1944; La., State U., 1945; Stonier Grad., Sch. Banking, 1960; B.A., U. Pa., 1949; M.S., Hartford Grad. Center, 1981. Salesman Liberty Mut. Ins. Co., Boston, 1949-52; with Nat. Shawmut Bank Boston, 1952-70, asst. v.p., 1955-58, v.p., 1958-70; exec. v.p. County Bank NA, Cambridge, Mass., 1970-71, pres., dir., 1971—, Shawmut Corp., 1975-78; alt. dir. Atlantic Internat. Bank Ltd., London; alt. rep. Internat. Monetary Conf., 1976-78; lectr. Hartford (Conn.) Grad. Center, 1979—, dean Sch. Mgmt., 1983—; cons. Arthur D. Little, Inc., 1979—. Mem. Town Meeting Lexington, Mass., 1961-70, appropriations com., 1960-66, sch. com., 1966-70; bd. overseers Children's Hosp. Med. Center, Boston, 1967—; trustee Lesley Coll., Cambridge, 1971—; corporator Northeastern U., Boston, 1976—. Served with AUS, 1945-47. Recipient Outstanding Young Man award Boston Jr. C. of C. Episcopalian. Lodge: Masons. Home: 31 Main St Farmington CT 06032

CLARKE, MICHAEL FRANCIS, insurance company executive; b. N.Y.C., Mar. 10, 1942; s. Frank Joseph and Mary (Hodgins) C. B.S., Fairfield U., 1969. Reins exec. Gen. Reins Corp., Greenwich, Conn., 1969—, v.p., 1979—. Served to lt. comdr. USNR, 1964-68. Mem. Conn. Property and Casualty Mgrs. Assn. (pres. 1980-81). Home: Bushnell Plaza Hartford CT 06103 Office: Gen Reins Corp 600 Steamboat Rd Greenwich CT 06830

CLARKE, PHILIP REAM, JR., banker; b. Chgo., Feb., 10, 1914; s. Philip Ream and Louise (Hildebr) C.; m. Valerie Mead, Oct. 20, 1939 (dec. Sept. 1965); children: Barbara Foster, Philip Ream III; m. Jan Finan, Dec. 2, 1967; m. Barbara Schroeder, Apr. 15, 1977. A.B., U. Chgo., 1937. With Glore, Forgan & Co., Chgo., 1937-42; with City Nat. Bank & Trust Co., Chgo., 1946-57, asst. v.p., 1947-51, v.p., 1951-57; with Lehman Bros., Chgo., 1957-65, mgr. indsl. dept., 1959-62, dir. new bus., 1962-65; v.p., treas., dir. Hinsdale Cemetery Co., 1946-66; sr. v.p. Chgo. Corp., 1965-72, mem. exec. com., 1968-75, exec. v.p., 1972, vice chmn., 1973—, dir., 1965—; pres., chief exec. officer Hollymatic Corp., 1978-79, chmn., chief exec. officer, 1979-81, dir., 1969-81; dir. Sun Electric Corp., Duckwall-Alco Stores Inc., 1st Fed. Savs. & Loan Assn. Chgo.; Mem. Midwest Stock Exchange, 1954-56; Pres., treas., dir. Bronswood Cemetery, Inc., 1966—. Bd. dirs., exec. com. Cook County Sch. of Nursing, 1958-68, v.p., 1965-68; treas., dir. Chgo. Com. on Alcoholism, 1952-56, v.p., 1957, exec. v.p., 1958, pres., 1959, chmn., 1960-61; charter mem. bd. assos. Chgo. Theol. Sem., 1980—; vice chmn. Chgo. Non Partisan Com. to Bring Republican Nat. Conv. to Chgo.; Mem. Republican Nat. Conv., 1959-60; treas. Citizens Com. to Bring Republican and Democratic convs. to Chgo., 1952, 56; bd. govs. Hinsdale Community House, 1968-70, vice chmn., 1969, chmn., 1970; trustee, chmn. finance com. Village of Clarendon Hills, Ill., 1956-60, pres., 1961-65, dep. village treas., 1965-68; bd. govs. United Rep. Fund of Ill., 1948-74, treas., 1948-62, v.p., exec. com., 1955-69; bd. dirs. Ill. council Trout Unltd., 1972-75; trustee U. Chgo. Alumni Found., 1958-61, citizens bd., 1955—; mem. exec. com. Citizens of Greater Chgo., 1960-61. Served as lt. comdr. USNR, 1942-45. Mem. Chgo. Assn. Commerce and Industry (dir., treas. 1952-53), Chgo. Zool. Soc. (governing mem. 1956-69, 79—), Nat. Council on Alcoholism (v.p. 1959-62), Alpha Delta Phi. Republican. Episcopalian. Clubs: Chicago, Monroe, Bond (Chgo.); Hinsdale Golf; Coleman Lake (Wis.) (dir., v.p. 1982—. Home: 404 Burr Ridge Club Dr Burr Ridge IL 60521 Office: 208 S LaSalle St Chicago IL 60604

CLARKE, RICHARD ALAN, electric and gas utility company executive; b. San Francisco, May 18, 1930; s. Chauncey Frederick and Carolyn (Shannon) C.; m. Mary dell Fisher, Feb. 5, 1955; children: Suzanne, Nancy, Douglas, Alan. A.B. cum laude, U. Calif.-Berkeley, 1952, LL.B., 1955. Bar: Calif. 1955. Atty. Pacific Gas and Electric Co., San Francisco, 1955-60, 69, sr. counsel, 1970-74, asst. gen. counsel, 1974-79, v.p., asst. to chmn., 1979-82, exec. v.p., gen. mgr. utility ops., 1982—; ptnr. Rockwell, Fulkerson and Clarke, San Rafael, Calif., 1960-69. Bd. dirs. Ind. Colls. No. Calif., San Francisco, 1980—; mem. steering com. Citizens for Adequate Energy, San Francisco, 1980—; mem. State Solid Waste Mgmt. Bd., Sacramento, 1980—. Served to capt. USAR, 1952-60. Mem. Calif. State Bar Assn., Pacific Coast Elec. Assn., Pacific Coast Gas Assn., San Francisco C. of C. (dir. 1983—). Club: Marin Tennis (San Rafael). Office: Pacific Gas and Electric Company 77 Beale St San Francisco CA 94106

CLARKE, ROBERT BRADSTREET, publishing company executive; b. Mountainside, N.J., Oct. 31, 1928; s. Bert and Antoinette (Bartlett) C.; m. Roberta Powell, Aug. 26, 1950; children—William, Cynthia. Student, U. Miami (Fla.). Exec. v.p. Grolier Enterprises, Inc., 1960-67, pres., dir., 1967—, Am. Peoples Press, Westmont, Ill., 1965-70; v.p. mail order, then exec. v.p. Grolier Inc., N.Y.C., 1974-76, pres., chief exec. officer, 1976-78, chmn., pres., chief exec. officer, 1978—, also dir. Advisory bd. Union Trust Co., Stamford, Conn.; Trustee Danbury (Conn.) Hosp., 1974-78; vice chmn. Danbury United Way, 1972; bd. dirs. Western Conn. Corp. Coll. Council, 1978—; trustee Direct Mktg. Assn. Ednl. Found., 1981—. Named Direct Mktg. Man of Year Direct Mktg. Day in N.Y., Inc., 1977. Mem. Direct Selling Assn., Am. Mgmt. Assn. (gen. mgmt. council), Direct Mktg. Assn. (dir., past chmn.), Danbury C. of C. (past chmn.), Cousteau Soc (dir. 1974-81), Tower Fellows. Club: Saugatuck Harbor Yacht (past commodore). Home: 705-D Weed St New Canaan CT 06840 Office: Grolier Inc Sherman Turnpike Danbury CT 06816

CLARKE, ROBERT EARLE (BOBBY CLARKE), hockey player; b. Flint, Mich., Aug. 12, 1949. With Phila. Flyers, 1969—. Winner Bill Masterton Meml. trophy, 1972; Hart Meml. trophy, 1973, 75, 76; co-winner Lester Patrick award, 1981. Office: care Phila Flyers Pattison Pl Philadelphia PA 19148 *

CLARKE, ROGER CHETWODE, farm machinery company executive; b. Norwich, Eng., Aug. 10, 1938; s. Pete and Dorothy (Hilborne) C.; m. Vivien Hare, Aug. 18, 1961; children: Dominic Windham, Cleone Rachel. M.A., U. Cambridge, Eng., 1960. Mem. staff Perkins Engines Ltd., Peterborough, Eng., 1960-69; exec. Massey-Ferguson Ltd., Toronto, Ont., Can., 1980—; chmn. Verity Assocs. Inc., Toronto, 1982—. Office: Massey-Ferguson Ltd 595 Bay St Toronto ON Canada M5G 2C3

CLARKE, STANLEY MARVIN, musician, composer; b. Phila., June 31, 1951; s. Marvin and Blanche (Bundy) C.; m. Carolyn Helene Reese, Nov. 29, 1974; 1 son, Christopher Ivanhoe. Student, Phila. Musical Acad., 1968-71. Mem., Horace Silver Band, 1970, Joe Henderson Band, 1971, Stan Getz Band; charter mem., Return to Forever; leader, Stanley Clarke Group, 1976—; charter mem., Clarke/Duke Project, 1980—; composer: Life is Just A Game (Grammy nominee 1976), Stanley Clarke Songbook, 1977, I Wanna Play for You Songbook, 1979; rec. artist, Epic/CBS Records. (Recipient numerous awards 1973), Epic/CBS Records. (including: Bassist of Yr. award Down Beat Internat. Critics Poll 1973), Epic/CBS Records. (Electric Bassist of Yr. award 1974, 75), Epic/CBS Records. (Acoustic Bassist of Yr. award 1974), Epic/CBS Records. (Electric Bassist of Yr. Down Beat Internat. Readers Poll 1976), Epic/CBS Records. (named Jazz Artist of Yr., Rolling Stone Mag. Music Critics Poll 1977), Epic/CBS Records. (Bassist of Year, Playboy Poll 1976, 77, 78, 79, 80), Epic/CBS Records. (named to Gallery of Greats, Guitar Player mag. 1980), Epic/CBS Records. (Grammy award nominee for album Modern Man 1978), Epic/CBS Records. (Grammy award nominee for album Clarke/Duke Project 1981). Mem. Musicians Local 802 Union, Nat. Acad. Rec. Arts and Scis., AFTRA, Screen Actors Guild, Hubbard Assn. Scientologists Internat., Scientologist. Office: 8817 Rangely Ave Los Angeles CA 90048

CLARKE, T. DEXTER, lawyer; b. New Bedford, Mass., July 23, 1910; s. Ronald B. and Ruth (Dexter) C.; m. Anne M. Hatheway, Sept. 28, 1940; children—David A., Catherine A. Clarke Bermon, Richard D. A.B., Brown U., 1932; LL.B., Yale U., 1935. Bar: R.I. bar 1935. With firm Greenough, Lyman & Cross, Providence, 1935-41; atty. Narragansett Electric Co., Providence, 1941-42, sec.-counsel, 1946-58, v.p., 1958-68, pres., 1968-73; dir. Old Stone Trust Co., Old Stone Corp., Providence, to 1980. Served to lt. comdr. USNR, 1942-46. Mem. R.I. Bar Assn. Home: 2020 Gulf Shore Blvd N Naples FL 33940 Office: 111 Westminster St Providence RI 02903

CLARKE, THOMAS HAL, lawyer; b. Atlanta, Aug. 10, 1914; s. James Caleb and Mary Cox (DeSaussure) C.; m. Mary Louise Hastings, July 12, 1951; children: Thomas Hal, Mary Katherine, Rebecca DeSaussure. LL.B., Washington and Lee U., 1938. Bar: Ga. 1939. Practiced law, Atlanta, 1946-69, 73—; mem. firm Mitchell, Clarke, Pate, Anderson & Wimberly, 1948-69, 73—. Mem. Fed. Home Loan Bank Bd., Washington, 1969-73; Past pres., bd. dirs. Atlanta Hist. Soc.; past bd. visitors Emory U.; trustee Washington and Lee U.; mem. Hibernian United Service Club, Dublin, Ireland. Served with USNR, 1942-46; ETO. Mem. Internat. Bar Assn. (vice chmn. savs. and bldg. socs. com.), ABA (past chmn. sect. corp., banking and bus. law, mem. ho. of dels. 1974-80), Ga. Bar Assn., Atlanta Bar Assn., Am. Law Inst., Atlanta Lawyers Club (past pres.), Selden Soc., English Speaking Union (past pres., chmn. bd.). Clubs: Piedmont Driving, Commerce (Atlanta). Home: 186 15th St NE Atlanta GA 30309 Office: 20 Marietta St Atlanta GA 30335

CLARKE, WALTER SHELDON, diplomat; b. Washington, Dec. 28, 1934; s. Walter Clowes and Lena Phoebe (Lovejoy) C.; m. Chantal Aubert, Dec. 26, 1974; children: Philippe, Quentin, Aurélie; 1 stepson, Nicolas Lance. B.A., Yale U., 1957; cert. African studies, Northwestern U., 1968. Commd. fgn. service office Dept. State, 1958; served in Ruanda-Urundi (Later Kingdom of Burundi), 1960-62, Am. embassy, San Jose, Costa Rica, 1963-65, Bogota, Colombia, 1965-67; desk officer West African affairs Dept. State, 1968-70; chief polit. sect. Am. embassy, Abidjan, Ivory Coast, 1970-72; consul Am. consulate, Douala, Cameroon, 1972-74; desk officer Latin Am. affairs Dept. State, 1974-76; info. programmer A/OASIS, 1976-77; consul gen., Djibouti, French Ter. of Afars and Issas, 1977, became charge d'Affaires upon independence of, 1977-80, polit. counselor Am. embassy, Lagos, Nigeria, 1980-83, Spl. asst. Bur. Intelligence and Research, 1983—. Contbr. bibliog. and hist. research articles to profl. jours. Mem. African Studies Assn., Internat. African Inst., Info. Mgmt. Assn. Home: 7517 Spring Lake Dr Bethesda MD 20814 Office: Dept State Washington DC 20520

CLARKE, WILLIAM HENRY, lawyer; b. Washington, Oct. 8, 1916; s. Alexander Sidney and Ruth Marie (Doyle) C.; m. Ruth Lee Thompson, Jan. 15, 1944; children—William Henry, Patricia (Mrs. Jerry White), Christine Ann, Robert A. B.S. in Bus. Adminstrn, U. Fla., 1939; J.D., Georgetown U., 1947. Bar: D.C. 1947, Md. 1952. Partner firm Galiher, Clarke, Martell & Donnelly, Washington and Rockville, Md., 1960-83, Galiher, Clarke & Galiher, 1983—. Past pres. PTA, Fire Bd., Hamlet Citizens Assn. Served with USNR, 1942-46. Fellow Am. Coll. Trial Lawyers; mem. Am., D.C., Md., Montgomery County bar assns., Internat. Assn. Ins. Counsel, Def. Research Inst., Counsellors Club (past pres.), Am. Legion (past pres.), Barristers Club, Beta Theta Phi, Delta Theta Phi. Roman Catholic. Club: Columbia Country. Home: 8309 Kerry Rd Chevy Chase MD 20015 Office: 5 N Adams St Rockville MD 20850

CLARKE, WILLIAM HILLARY, member Canadian Parliament; b. Toronto, Ont., Can., July 5, 1933; s. James Reginald and Eleanor (Aubin) C.; m. Sandra Baxter, Jan. 23, 1954 (div. 1977); children: Alan, Hillary, John; m. 2d Shelagh McGonigle, July 16, 1977; children: Elizabeth, Simon. Chartered acct., Can., 1956. Student in accounts Price Waterhouse, Vancouver, B.C., Can., 1951-46; pvt. practice acctg., Vancouver, 1957-60; chief fin. officer Vancouver Mgmt. Group Cos., 1960-72; mem. House Commons for Vancouver Quadra, Ottawa, Ont., 1972—, chmn. pub. accounts com., 1980—, chmn. fin. trade and econ. affairs com., 1979-80. Fellow Inst. Chartered Accts. B.C. Progressive Conservative. Anglican. Clubs: University (pres. 1966-67), Vancouver Lawn Tennis (Vancouver)). Home: 702 - 6060 Balsam St Vancouver BC Canada V6M 4C1 Office: House of Commons Ottawa ON Canada K1A 0A6

CLARKE, WILLIAM JAY, insurance company executive; b. Elizabethtown, Pa., Sept. 5, 1937; s. Luther J. and Kathryn L. C.; children—William Jay, Cheryl L., Bryan R. B.S., Elizabethtown Coll., 1963. C.P.A., Pa. Mgr. acctg., auditing and SEC staff Coopers & Lybrand, Phila., 1963-75; v.p., treas. Reliance Ins. Co., Phila., 1975-81; exec. v.p. Ideal Mut. Ins. Co., N.Y.C., 1981—. Mem. Am. Inst. C.P.A.s, Soc. Ins. Accts., Fin. Exec. Inst., Pa. Inst. C.P.A.s, Phila. Treas. Club., Planning Execs. Inst. Office: 260 Madison Ave New York NY 10016

CLARKE, WILLIAM NEASE, lawyer; b. Washington, Pa., Aug. 23, 1917; s. William Nease and Adelaide (McCoy) C.; m. Andree Marconnet, Aug. 30, 1947; children: Claudine, Jean Marie. A.B., Washington and Jefferson Coll., 1939; J.D., U. Pa., 1942. Bar: Pa. 1943, N.Y. 1947. Assoc. Cadawalader, Wickersham & Taft, N.Y.C., 1946-58; ptnr. Cadawalader, Wickersham & Taft, N.Y.C., 1959—; dir. Holiday Inns Inc., Memphis, 1961—. Trustee Washington & Jefferson Coll., 1975—. Served to capt. inf. U.S. Army, 1944-45; ETO. Decorated Silver Star. Mem. ABA, Assn. Bar City N.Y., Fed. Bar Council. Republican. Presbyterian. Clubs: Union, Downtown. Home: 164 E 72d St New York NY 10021 Office: 1 Wall St New York NY 10005

CLARKE, WILLIAM NORRIS, educator; b. N.Y.C., June 1, 1915; s. Richard Henry and Frances (Chew) C. Ph.L., Coll. St. Louis, Jersey, Eng., 1939; M.A., Fordham U., 1940; Th.L., Woodstock Coll., 1946; Ph.D., Louvain U., 1949. Joined S.J.; instr. philosophy Woodstock Coll., 1949-52; asst. prof. philosophy Bellarmine Coll., Plattsburg, N.Y., 1952-55; asst. prof. Fordham U., Bronx, N.Y., 1955-60, asso. prof., 1960-66, prof. philosophy, 1966—. Author: The Philosophical Approach to God, 1980; founder, editor-in-chief: Internat. Philos. Quar, 1961; Contbr. articles to profl. jours. and chpts. to books. Mem. Metaphys. Soc. Am. (pres. 1967), Am. Cath. Philos. Assn. (pres. 1968), Jesuit Philos. Assn. (pres. 1960). Address: Fordham U Bronx NY 10458

CLARKSON, ANDREW MACBETH, retail executive; b. Glasgow, Scotland, July 9, 1937; s. Robert Gibson and Josephine Abigail (Anderson) C.; m. Carole Frances Grant, June 4, 1966; children: Jennifer Mary, William MacBeth. B.A., Oxford (Eng.) U., 1960, M.A., 1980; diploma in agr., Mcgill U., 1961; M.B.A., Harvard U., 1966. Various positions to asst. v.p. First Nat. Bank, Chgo., 1966-72; corp. asst. treas. Gen. Foods Corp., White Plains, N.Y., 1972-78; fin. dir. Gen. Foods Ltd., U.K., 1978-80; asst. corp. controller and controller Gen. Foods Internat., 1980-81; v.p. and treas. F.W. Woolworth co., N.Y.C., 1981-83; sr. v.p. fin. and adminstrn. Malone & Hyde, Memphis, 1983—; lectr. internat. fin. U. Conn., 1976. Served to 2d lt. Brit. Army, 1955-57. Fellow Assn. Corp. Treas.; mem. Fin. Execs. Inst. Club: Field (New Canaan). Office: Malone & Hyde 1990 Corporate Ave Memphis TN

CLARKSON, GEOFFREY PENISTON ELLIOTT, educator; b. London, Eng., May 30, 1934; came to U.S., 1957; s. George Elliott and Alice Helen (Mannaberg) C.; m. Eleanor Micenko, Feb. 19, 1960; children—Julia, Elizabeth. B.Sc., Carnegie-Mellon U., 1958, M.Sc., 1959, Ph.D., 1961. Asst. prof. Mass. Inst. Tech., 1961-65, asso. prof., 1965-67; prof. bus. fin. U. Manchester, Eng., 1967-77; dean Coll. Bus. Adminstrn., Northeastern U., Boston, 1977-79, prof. bus. adminstrn., 1979—; fin. cons. dir. pub. and pvt. cos. Author: Portfolio Selection, 1962, Theory of Consumer Demand, 1963; Managerial Economics, 1968, Managing Money and Finance, 1969; novel Jihad, 1981; Contbr. articles to profl. jours. Ford Found. fellow, 1960-61; Social Sci. Research Council fellow, 1962. Mem. Am. Econ. Assn., Econometric Soc., Inst. Mgmt. Sci. Home: 99 Old Colony Rd Wellesley Hills MA 02181 Office: Northeastern U Coll Business Administration 360 Huntington Ave Boston MA 02115

CLARKSON, JAMES, savings and loan association executive; b. Wigan, Lancshire, Eng., May 7, 1924; came to U.S., 1926, naturalized, 1945; s. Caleb and Nellie (Hart) C.; m. Ione Magdeline Luebbers, July 6, 1946; children: Jerome James, James Michael, Kathleen Diane. Student, Wayne State U., 1946-50, U. Mich., 1950-51, Met. U.; grad., Am. Inst. Banking, 1952. Asst. v.p. Wabeek State Bank & Trust Co., Detroit, 1946-52; pres., chief exec. officer 1st Fed. Savs. Bank & Trust, Pontiac, Mich., from 1952; now pres. and chmn. bd. 1st Fed. Savs. and Loan Assn. of Oakland, 1960—; mem. Fed. Savs. and Loan Adv. Council. Chmn. Pontiac Stadium Authority, Waterford Twp. Zoning Bd., 1960-69, Waterford Twp. Bd. Appeals, 1960-69; commr. Huron-Clinton Met. Authority; bd. dirs. United Way of Pontiac. Served with USAAF, 1943-45. Recipient certificate of appreciation SSS, 1975, Distinguished Pub. Service medal U.S. Navy, 1976; Man and Boy award Boys' Club, 1971; bronze medallion, 1972. Mem. Mich. Savs. and Loan League (2d v.p., immediate past chmn., Community Service award 1966), Soc. Residential Appraisers, Nat. Assn. Rev. Appraisers (certified rev. appraiser), Pontiac Bd. Realtors (past pres.), Detroit Controllers Soc. (past pres.), Pontiac Downtown Bus. Assn. (dir.), Pontiac Fedn. Musicians (life mem.), Navy League U.S. (founder, pres. Oakland County council), Fraternal Order Police. Republican. Presbyterian. Clubs: Elks, Masons, Shriners. Home: 3111 St Jude Dr Drayton Plains MI 48020 Office: 761 W Huron St Pontiac MI 48053

CLARKSON, KENNETH WRIGHT, economics educator; b. Downey, Calif., June 30, 1942; s. William Wright and Constance (Patch) C.; m. Mary Jane Purdy, June 20, 1965; children: Steven Wright, Thomas David. A.B., Calif. State U., 1964; M.A., UCLA, 1966, Ph.D., 1971. Economist Office Mgmt. and Budget, Washington, 1971-72, assoc. dir., 1982-83; asst. prof. econs. U. Va., 1969-75; prof. econs. U. Miami, Coral Gables, Fla., 1975—, dir. Law & Econs. Ctr., 1981—; mem. Pres.'s Task Force on Food Assistance, 1983-84; cons. in field; mem. governing bd. Credit Research Ctr., Purdue U., 1981—. Author: Food Stamps and Nutrition, 1975, Intangible Capital and Rates of Return, 1975; co-author: Correcting Taxes for Inflation, 1975, Distortions in Official Umemployemtn Statistics, 1979, Industrial Organization: Theory, Evidence and Public Policy, 1982, West's Business Law, 1980, (2d edit.) West's Business Law, 1983, The Federal Trade Commission Since 1970, 1981, Economics Sourcebook of Government Statistics, 1983; contbr. numerous articles to profl. jours. Mem. Regan-Bush Transition Team, Washington, 1980. NSF grantee, 1972-74; Heritage Found. scholar, 1977—. Mem. Am. Econ. Assn., Am. Bus. Law Assn., Western Econ. Assn., Sigma Xi. Home: 15925 SW 77th Ct Miami FL 33157 Office: 1541 Brescia Ave Coral Gables FL 33146

CLARKSON, MARK H., educator; b. Lafayette County, Mo., Sept. 27, 1917; s. Julius A. and Frances (Anderson) C.; m. Florence Johnston, Mar. 14, 1941; children—David, Michael, Linda. B.S. in Aero. Engring, U. Minn., 1939; M.S., U. Tex., 1948; Ph.D., Tex., 1953. With Douglas Aircraft Co., 1939-41, Consol. Vultee Co., 1942-45; research engr., research mathematician Def. Research Lab. U. Tex., 1945-53; supr. theoretical aerodynamics Chance Vought Aircraft Corp., 1953-59, supr. aerophysics, 1959-61; prof. aerospace engring. U. Fla., 1961—, chmn. dept., 1961-72; mem. part-time grad. faculty So. Meth. U., 1954-59; cons. to industry, 1961—; NRC sr. asso. Ames research center NASA, Moffett Field, Calif., 1973-74. Contbr. articles to profl. jours. NRC fellow U. Manchester, Eng., 1951-52. Asso. fellow Am. Inst. Aeros. and Astronautics; mem. Tau Beta Pi, Phi Kappa Phi, Sigma Xi. Home: 2400 NW 18th Pl Gainesville FL 32605 Office: Dept Aerospace Engring U Fla Gainesville FL 32611

CLARKSON, MAX BOYDELL ELLIOTT, printing company executive, business educator; b. Lenzie, Scotland, Oct. 14, 1922; s. George Elliott and Helene (Mannaberg) C.; m. Madeleine Earls, June 5, 1948; children: Max Adam, Helene Edith. B.A., U. Toronto, 1944, M.A., 1946. Vice pres. Tech. Charts, Inc., Buffalo, 1947-50; pres. Clarkson Press Inc., Buffalo, 1950-57, Graphic Controls Corp., 1957-70, chmn. bd., 1970-75; dean faculty mgmt. studies U. Toronto, Ont., Can., 1975-80, prof. mgmt., 1975—; dir. Eastern Utilities Ltd., Am. Consumer Industries, Inc., Tymshare, Inc., Suncor Inc., Transcan. Freezers Ltd., Mentholatum Co., Buffalo, N.Y.; pres. Printing Industries Am., 1962-63; mem. council Bd. Trade Met. Toronto, 1978—. Chmn. Mayor Buffalo Citizens Adv. Com. on Community Improvement, 1964-75; pres. Allentown (N.Y.) Assn., 1963-75; Bd. dirs. Shaw Festival, Niagara Inst., Niagara-on-the-Lake, Ont., 1969-79. Served to lt. Royal Canadian Navy, 1942-45. Recipient Man of Year award, Buffalo Council World Affairs, 1974; Community Service award D'Youville Coll., 1974. Mem. Can. Fedn. Deans Mgmt. and Adminstrv. Studies (chmn. 1976-80). Episcopalian. Clubs: Buffalo; Metropolitan (N.Y.C.); Naval and Mil. (London, Eng.); York, Queens (Toronto). Home: 71 Old Forest Hill Rd Toronto ON Canada M5P 2R3 Office: 246 Bloor St W Toronto ON Canada M5S 1V4

CLARKSON, THOMAS WILLIAM, toxicologist, educator; b. Eng., Aug. 1, 1932; came to U.S., 1957; s. William and Olive (Jackson) C.; m. Winifred Browne, Mar. 4, 1957; children: Ian, Jean, Ann. B.Sc., U. Manchester, 1953, Ph.D., 1956. Sci. officer tox research unit Med. Research Council U.K., Carshalton, Surrey, 1962-64; sr. fellow polymer sci. Weizmann Inst. Sci., Rehovot, Israel, 1964-65; mem. faculty U. Rochester (N.Y.) Med. Sch., 1958—, prof. toxicology, 1971—, head div., 1980—; mem. Inst. Medicine-Nat. Acad. Sci., 1980—. Mem. editorial bds. profl. jours.; author articles in field. Mem. Internat. Assn. Occupational Health, Soc. Toxicology, AAAS, Brit. Pharm. Soc., Royal Inst. Chemistry. Address: Div Toxicology U Rochester Med Sch Rochester NY 14642

CLARO, JAIME, metal trading company executive; b. Santiago, Chile, Mar. 14, 1936; came to U.S., 1971; s. Gumecindo and Emma (Valdes) C. B.C.E., U. Chile, 1959. Engr., gen. advisor comml. matters Dept. del Cobre, Chile, 1960-64; v.p. Cerro Exploration Co., Chile, 1964-70; also dep. gen. mgr. Cia. Minera Andina; pres. Cerro Sales Corp., N.Y.C., 1971—; asst. prof. Engring. Sch., U. Chile, 1960-62; dir. Cerro Metals, U.K. Mem. Chilean Am. C. of C. (v.p., dir.). Clubs: Yale (N.Y.C.); Copper, Golf Los Leones, Union (Chile). Home: 118 E 60th St New York NY 10022 Office: Cerro Sales Corp 250 Park Ave New York NY 10017

CLARSON, JOHN JULIUS, real estate company executive; b. N.Y.C., Feb. 27, 1921; s. John F. and Martha (Nichols) C.; m. Ruth Ann Beck, Apr. 28, 1945; children: Dorothy, John, Donna, Patrick. B.B.A., Pace Coll., 1953. With Champion Internat. Corp., N.Y.C., 1949-77, v.p. fin. services, 1970-77, v.p. real estate, 1977—; pres. Champion Realty, Houston, 1977—; dir. Tex. Commerce Bank, Greens Crossing. Served with AUS, 1942-45. Home: 13707 Chelwood Pl Houston TX 77069 Office: Suite 500 16855 Northchase Dr Houston TX 77060

CLARY, EVERETT BURTON, lawyer; b. San Francisco, Dec. 1, 1921; s. William Webb and Elizabeth Augusta (Foss) C.; m. Mary Marjorie DeFriest, May 6, 1944; children—Ann Clary Judy, Carter DeFriest. B.A., Stanford U., 1943, LL.B., 1949. Bar: Calif. 1949. Practiced in, Los Angeles; partner firm O'Melveny & Myers, 1960—, adminstrv. head litigation dept., 1977—, mem. mgmt. com., 1977—. Contbr. articles to legal jours. Bd. visitors Stanford U. Law Sch.; trustee Pacific Oaks Coll. and Children's Sch., Pasadena, Calif.; bd. fellows Claremont U. Center; vestryman Episcopal Ch. of Angels, Pasadena. Served with USNR, 1943-46. Fellow Am. Bar Found., Am. Coll. Trial Lawyers; mem. Am. Bar Assn., Los Angeles County Bar Assn. Clubs: Calif., Stock Exchange (Los Angeles); Annandale (Calif.), Golf. Office: 400 S Hope St Los Angeles CA 90071

CLASEN, CLAUS-PETER, historian, educator; b. Berlin, Feb. 8, 1931; U.S., 1962, naturalized, 1969; s. Will and Senta (Caspar) C. Student, Hamilton Coll., 1950-51; Statsexamen, Free U., Berlin, 1957, Dr. Phil. magna cum laude, 1962; student, St. Anthony's Coll., Oxford, Eng., 1959-62. Instr. history Yale U., 1962-64, asst. prof., 1964-66, UCLA, 1966-68, asso. prof., 1968-73, prof., 1973—. Author: Die Wiedertaufer im Herzogtum Wurtemberg und benachbarten Herrschaften, 1966, Anabaptism: A Social History 1525-1618, 1972, Die Augsburger Steuerbucher um 1600, 1976, The Anabaptists in South and Central Germany, Switzerland and Austria, 1978; mem. editorial bd.: Central European History, 1974-78. Recipient Marquis of Lothian prize essay Oxford U., 1962; Fulbright-Hays research scholar Germany, 1974-75. Mem. Soc. Reformation Research. Office: Dept History UCLA Los Angeles CA 90024 *

CLASTER, JILL NADELL, University dean, history educator; d. Harry K. and Edith Lillian Nadell; m. Millard L. Midonick, May 24, 1979; 1 dau. from previous marriage, Elizabeth Claster (dec.). B.A., NYU, 1952, M.A., 1954; Ph.D., U. Pa., 1959. Instr. history U. Pa., 1956-58; instr. ancient and medieval history U. Ky., Lexington, 1959-61, asst. prof., 1961-64; adj. asst. prof. classics N.Y. U., N.Y.C., 1964-65, asst. prof. history, 1965-68, asso. prof., 1968—, acting undergrad. chmn. history, 1972-73, dir. M.A. in liberal studies program, 1976-78; asso. dean Washington Sq. and Univ. Coll., 1978, acting dean, 1978-79, dean, 1979—. Author: Athenian Democracy: Triumph or Travesty, 1967, The Medieval Experience, 1982; Contbr. articles to profl. jours. Danforth grantee, 1966-68; Fulbright grantee, 1958-59. Mem. Am. Hist. Assn., Medieval Acad. Am., Archaeol. Inst. Am., Medieval Club N.Y. Home: 32 Washington Sq W New York NY 10011 Office: NY Univ Washington Square and University Coll 910 Main Bldg New York NY 10003

CLATWORTHY, HARRY WILLIAM, JR., physician; b. Denver, Oct. 2, 1917; s. Harry William and Freda Althea (Miller) C.; m. Rovena Louise Conn, Aug. 31, 1940 (div.); children—Harry William, Diana Ro, John Conn, Susan Honor; m. Betty Jones (dec. 1960); m. Nancy Moore Krueger, Dec. 1961. B.S., Stanford U., 1939; M.D., Harvard U., 1943; M.Sc., U. Minn., 1950. Diplomate: Am. Bd. Surgery. Student asst. children's pathology Boston Children's Hosp., 1942, surg. intern, 1943-44, asst. resident surgery, 1946-47, chief surg. resident, 1947-48; asst. surgery Harvard Med. Sch., 1946-48; sr. surg. fellow Univ. Hosp. U. Minn. Med. Sch., 1948-50; asst. prof. pediatric surgery Ohio State U. Coll. Medicine, 1950-52, asso. prof., 1952-60, dir. div. pediatric surgery, 1952-72, prof. pediatric surgery, 1960—; attending surgeon Univ. Hosp., 1950—, Children's Hosp., Columbus, 1950—, chief surg. service, 1953-72; Felton Bequest vis. prof. Royal Children's Hosp., Melbourne, Australia, 1964; Munroe lectr., Regina, Sask., Can., 1972, Horace Smithy lectr., Charleston, S.C., 1974, David Hutchinson lectr., Sheffield, Eng., 1976, Robert E. Gross lectr., 1979; chmn. 27th Ross Pediatric Conf. Contbr. articles to profl. jours., chpts. to books; asso. editor: Am. Jour. Surgery; editorial bd.: Surg. Techniques Illus. Pres. Saratoga Land & Cattle Co.; dir. The Clatworthy Co. Med.; adv. bd. Ohio Crippled Children, mem. residency rev. com. surgery. Served as capt., M.C. AUS, 1944-46. Named Horseman of Yr. Touchdown Club, 1976. Fellow A.C.S., Am. Acad. Pediatrics (Ladd medalist 1979); mem. AMA, Ohio Med. Assn., Ohio, Columbus (pres. 1978-79), Central, Am. surg. assns., Brit. Assn. Pediatric Surgeons, Soc. Univ. Surgeons, Am. Assn. Thoracic Surgery, Am. Pediatric Surg. Assn. (pres. 1972-73), Sigma Xi, Phi Gamma Delta, Am. Hereford Assn. Episcopalian. Home: Fireside Farms 6400 Dublin Rd Delaware OH 43015 Office: Childrens Hosp Columbus OH 43205

CLAUD, JOSEPH GILLETTE, banker; b. Norfolk, Va., Apr. 14, 1927; s. Joseph Gillette and Miriam Elanor (Jones) C.; m. Mary Ann Medford, May 12, 1962; children: Elizabeth, John. A.B. in History, Maryville (Tenn.) Coll., 1950; grad. student, U. N.C. at Chapel Hill, 1952. With NCNB Nat. Bank, Charlotte, 1955—; sr. v.p. N.C. Nat. Bank, 1965—, Tryon city exec., 1977—; dir. Brenner Cos. Trustee, sec. St. Luke's Hosp., Inc.; vestryman Episcopal Ch. of Holy Cross. Served with USNR, 1945-46. Mem. Am. Bankers Assn., Tryon C. of C. (past pres.). Democrat. Clubs: Red Fox Country, Rotary (Tryon) (pres.). Home: PO Box 127 Tryon NC 28782 Office: PO Box 1000 Tryon NC 28782

CLAUDE, INIS LOTHAIR, JR., educator, political scientist; b. Yellville, Ark., Sept. 3, 1922; s. Inis Lothair and Parilla Jane (Pledger) C.; m. Marie Stapleton, Aug. 1, 1943; children: Susan, Robert Burr, Cathy. B.A. with high honors, Hendrix Coll., 1942; M.A., Harvard U., 1947, Ph.D. (Chase prize), 1949. Instr., then asst. prof. govt. Harvard U., 1949-56; asso. prof. polit. sci. U. Del., 1956-57, U. Mich., 1957-60, prof., 1960-68; Edward R. Stettinius Jr. prof. govt. and fgn. affairs U. Va., Charlottesville, 1968—; mem. Center Advanced Study, 1968-71; vis. research scholar Carnegie Endowment Internat. Peace, 1960-61; faculty chmn. course internat. relations Inst. Social Studies, The Hague, 1964-65; vis. professorial fellow U. Wales, 1973-74; vis. prof. Hebrew U. Jerusalem, 1981; mem. exec. com. Center Research Conflict Resolution, 1959-63; chmn. com. internat. orgn. Social Sci. Research Council, 1962-69; mem. research group UN financial problems Brookings Instn., 1962-63, adv. com. UN policy study program, 1963—; occasional lectr. Nat., Army, Navy war colls., Air Command and Staff Colls., U.K. Nat. Def. Coll., Inter-Am. Def. Coll., UN Fgn. Service Tng. Seminar; cons. Dept. State, 1962-71, mem. adv. com. fgn. relations publs., 1968-72. Author: National Minorities: An International Problem, 1955, Swords Into Plowshares: The Problems and Progress of International Organization, 4th edit, 1971, Power and International Relations, 1962, The Changing United Nations, 1967; bd. editors: Internat. Orgn., 1960-74; chmn. bd. editors: Jour. Conflict Resolution, 1961-63; cons. editor internat. affairs: Random House, Inc, 1962-73; editorial bd.: Polit. Sci. Quar., 1973, Orbis, 1975, Am. Jour. Internat. Law, 1975-80, Strategic Rev., 1977, Global Perspectives, 1982. Served with AUS, 1942-46. Faculty fellow Fund Advancement Edn., 1951-52; Rockefeller research grantee, 1958-59; Horace H. Rackham Grad. Sch. research grantee, 1963; Guggenheim fellow, 1964-65; Fulbright research grantee, 1964-65; recipient Disting. Alumnus award Hendrix Coll., 1968. Mem. Am. Polit. Sci. Assn. (Woodrow Wilson Found. award 1963), Internat. Polit. Sci. Assn. (rapporteur gen. internat. orgn. 1964), So. Polit. Sci. Assn. (exec. council 1970), Am. Soc. Internat. Law, Commn. Study Orgn. Peace (exec. com. 1957-66). Home: 103 Melissa Pl Charlottesville VA 22901

CLAUS, CLYDE ROBERT, banker; b. East Orange, N.J., June 21, 1931; s. Clyde Emil and Ruth Ida (Hanks) C.; m. Eleanor Louise Graham, Aug. 22, 1956. Student, Dartmouth Coll., 1949-52; postgrad., Amos Tuck Sch., 1963-65; B.A., Boston U., 1956; M.B.A., Babson Coll., 1958. With Marine Midland Bank-N.Y., N.Y.C., 1958-77, v.p., 1967, v.p. exec. devel., 1969-71, sr. v.p. human resources, 1971-72, sr. adminstrv. officer, 1974-77; exec. v.p., dir. Dreyfus-Marine Midland, Inc., N.Y.C., 1972-74; dir. Marine Midland, Ltd., London; exec. v.p., chief adminstrv. officer BA Investment Mgmt. Corp., San Francisco, 1978-82, dir., 1982—; v.p. Montgomery Street Income Securities, San Francisco, 1978-82; sr. v.p. adminstrn. and mktg./trust Bank of Am., 1981-82, exec. v.p. trust/worldwide, 1982—; dir. Pacific Clearing Corp., Pacific Trust Co.; chmn. Bank Am. Trust & Banking Corp. (Bahamas) Ltd., Bank Am. Trust & Banking Corp. (Gibraltar) Ltd., Bank Am. Trust Corp. (Hong Kong) Ltd., Bank Am. Trust Co. (Jersey) Ltd., Bank Am. Trust & Banking Corp. (Cayman) Ltd. Bd. dirs. YMCA, Clear Water Children's Ranch; trustee Boston U. Served with U.S. Army, 1952-55. Mem. San Francisco Soc. Security Analysts, Phi Sigma Kappa. Clubs: Met. (N.Y.C.); Commonwealth of Calif., Bankers. Home: 6301 Bullard Dr Oakland CA 94611 Office: Bank of Am Center 555 California St San Francisco CA 94104

CLAUSEN, ALDEN WINSHIP, banker; b. Hamilton, Ill., Feb. 17, 1923; s. Morton and Elsie (Kroll) C.; m. Mary Margaret Crassweller, Feb. 11, 1950; children: Eric David, Mark Winship. B.A., Carthage Coll., 1944, LL.D., 1970; LL.B., U. Minn., 1949; grad., Advanced Mgmt. Program, Harvard U., 1966. Bar: Minn. bar 1949, Calif. bar 1950. With Bank Am. (NT & SA), San Francisco, 1949-81, v.p., 1961-65, sr. v.p., 1965-68, exec. v.p., 1968-69, vice chmn. bd., 1969, pres., chief exec. officer, 1970-81; pres. World Bank, 1981—; past pres. Internat. Monetary Conf., San Francisco; Clearing House Assn. Past pres. Fed. Adv. Council, 1972; past chmn. Bay Area Council; past bd. govs. United Way of Am.; past chmn. United Way of Bay Area; past mem. Bus. Roundtable; mem. Bus. Council; past mem. Japan-U.S. Adv. Council; past bd. dirs. Conf. Bd., San Francisco Opera; past bd. dirs., mem. adv. council SRI Internat.; mem. adv. council Stanford U. Grad. Sch. Bus.; bd. dirs. Harvard Bus. Sch.; trustee Carthage Coll., Brookings Instn. Mem. Res. City Bankers Assn. (hon.), Calif. Bar Assn. Clubs: Bankers of San Francisco, Pacific Union, Burlingame Country; Bohemian, Links (N.Y.C.); Metropolitan (Washington); Chevy Chase (Md.). Office: 1818 H St NW Washington DC 20433 *

CLAUSEN, HENRY CHRISTIAN, lawyer, Masonic executive; b. San Francisco, June 30, 1905; s. Louis and Lena (Clausen); m. Virginia Palmer, Aug. 17, 1935; children—Henry Christian, Florian Clausen Elliot, Donald, Karen Clausen Freeman. J.D., U. San Francisco, 1927; postgrad., U. Calif., San Francisco, 1927-32, U. Mich., 1942-43. Bar: Calif. bar 1927. Since practiced in, San Francisco; asst. U.S. atty. for No. Dist. Calif.; chief counsel for chief engr. Joseph B. Strauss during constrn. Golden Gate Bridge, 1931-33; law asso. Judge E. Crothers, Thomas G. Crothers, Francis V. Keesling and his sons, 1947-67. Author: Emergence of the Mystical; contbr. articles to publs. Pres. San Francisco YMCA; trustee George Washington U. Served to lt. col., JAGC AUS, 1942-45. Decorated Legion of Merit. Mem. Calif. Jr. C. of C. (pres.), Nat. Lawyers Club Washington. Congregationalist. Clubs: Masons, K.T., Shriners (sovereign grand comdr. Supreme Council Ancient and Accepted Scottish Rite of Freemasonry, So. Jurisdiction U.S.A. 1949—), Shriners (editor in chief monthly mag. The New Age), Bohemian, San Francisco Golf; Met., Columbia Country, Burning Tree (Washington). Office: 1733 16th St NW Washington DC 20009

CLAUSEN, HUGH JOSEPH, army officer; b. Mobile, Ala., Dec. 25, 1926; s. Hugh Martin and Elizabeth Hazel (Orrell) C.; m. Betty Sue Richards, June 7, 1949; children: Melinda, Joseph. LL.B., U. Ala., 1950; grad., Advanced Mgmt. Program, Harvard U., 1970. Bar: Ala. 1950, U.S. Supreme Ct. 1959, U.S. Ct. Mil. Appeals 1959. Commd. 1st lt. U.S. Army, 1951, advanced through grades to maj. gen.; various assignments, U.S. and Europe, 1951-62; asst. staff judge adv. (8th Army), Korea, 1962-64; judge adv. U.S. Disciplinary Barracks, Ft. Leavenworth, Kans., 1964-66; instr. U.S. Army Command and Gen. Staff Coll., 1966-68; staff judge adv. 1st Inf. Div., Vietnam, 1968-69; assigned Office Legis. Liaison, Dept. Army, Washington, 1969-71; chief mil. justice div. Office JAG, 1971-72, exec. officer, 1972-73; staff judge adv. III Corps and Ft. Hood, Tex., 1973-76; chief judge U.S. Army Ct. Mil. Rev., Falls Church, Va., 1976-78; asst. judge adv. gen. for mil. law Dept. Army., 1978-79, asst. judge adv. gen., 1979-81, judge adv. gen., 1981—. Decorated Bronze Star with 3 oak leaf clusters, Meritorious Service medal, Legion of Merit with oak leaf cluster, Air medal with oak leaf cluster, Army Commendation medal with oak leaf cluster; RVN Honor medal; RVN Gallantry Cross with palm; Civic Action Honor medal with palm, Vietnam). Mem. Am., Ala. bar assns., Phi Alpha Delta, Phi Kappa Sigma. Office: Office Judge Adv Gen Dept Army Pentagon Washington DC 20310

CLAUSEN, WENDELL VERNON, classics educator; b. Coquille, Ore., Apr. 2, 1923; s. George R. and Gertrude (Johnson) C.; m. Corinna Slice, Aug. 20, 1947; children: John, Raymond, Thomas; m. Margaret W. Woodman, June 19, 1970. A.B., U. Wash., 1945; Ph.D., U. Chgo., 1948; A.M. (hon.), Harvard U., 1959. Mem. faculty Amherst Coll., 1948-59, assoc. prof. classics, 1955-59; prof. Greek and Latin Harvard U., 1959—, Victor S. Thomas prof. Greek and Latin, 1982—; chmn. dept. classics Harvard, 1966-71; vis. prof. Univ. Coll., London, 1971; Sather prof. U. Calif., Berkeley, 1982. Editor: Persius, 1956, Persius and Juvenal, 1959, Appendix Vergiliana, 1966; editor, contbr.: The Cambridge History of Latin Literature, 1981; assoc. editor: Am. Jour. Philology, 1976-81; Contbr. articles in classical philology. Fellow Am. Acad., in Rome, 1952-53, Am. Council Learned Socs., 1962-63; fellow commoner Peterhouse, Cambridge. Fellow Am. Acad. Arts and Sciences; mem. Am. Philol. Assn., Cambridge Philol. Soc., Phi Beta Kappa. Home: 8 Kenway St Cambridge MA Office: Harvard U Cambridge MA 02138

CLAUSER, DONALD R., musician; b. Fort Worth, Mar. 2, 1941; s. Donald Milton and Selina Almira (Sizer) C. B.F.A., U. N.M., 1962; Mus.M., Boston U., 1964; diploma, Curtis Inst. Music, 1967. Mem. viola sect., Phila. Orch., 1966—. Home: 224 Hickory Ln Haddenfield NJ 08033 Office: Acad of Music Philadelphia PA 19102 *It is my conviction that music is a universal medium of communication—a factor which is surely of distinct value in these troubled times. Keeping this in mind has constantly been uppermost in the pursuit of my career, wherever this may have led me.*

CLAUSER, FRANCIS H., educator; b. Kansas City, Mo., May 25, 1913; s. Claude H. and Celeste (Horton) C.; m. Catharine McMillan, July 30, 1937; children—Caroline, John. B.S., Calif. Inst. Tech., 1934, M.S., 1935, Ph.D., 1937. Research aerodynamicist Douglas Aircraft Co., Santa Monica, Calif., 1937-46; chmn. dept. aeros. Johns Hopkins, 1946-60, prof. mechanics, 1960-64; acad. vice chancellor U. Calif. at Santa Cruz, 1965-66, vice chancellor sci. and engring., 1966-68, prof. applied sci., 1968-69; Clark B. Millikan prof. engring. Calif. Inst. Tech., Pasadena, 1969-80, Clark B. Millikan prof. emeritus, 1980—; chmn. div. engring. and applied sci., 1969-74. Contbr. articles to tech.

publs. Fellow AIAA, Am. Phys. Soc., Am. Acad. Arts and Scis.; mem. Nat. Acad. Engring., Sigma Xi, Tau Beta Pi. Address: 4072 Chevy Chase Flintridge CA 91011

CLAUSON, ANDREW GUSTAF, JR., banker; b. S.I., N.Y., July 1, 1895; s. Andrew Gustaf and Maria (Olson) C.; m. Esther Larsen, Sept. 25, 1920; children—Ralph Andrew, Barbara C. A.A.S., State U., N.Y., 1947; LL.D., Upsala Coll., 1948, Wagner Coll., 1950. C.P.A., N.Y. State. Accountant Richmond Light and R.R. Co., 1913-17; with Haskins & Sells (C.P.A's), 1919-23; comptroller J.H. Schroeder Banking Corp., 1924-27, United Wallpapers, Inc., 1928; founder, partner firm Bayer & Clauson (C.P.A.'s), 1929-64, ret., 1964; chmn. bd., pres. Richmond County Savs. Bank, S.I., 1964-73; pres. Obelisk Trading Corp. Trustee, chmn. emeritus Richmond County Savs. Bank.; Mem. N.Y.C. Bd. Edn., 1945-61, pres., 1946-49, 51-53; Chmn. emeritus bd. trustees S.I. Hosp.; trustee emeritus Wagner Coll.; pres. Wingate Meml. Found.; chmn. adv. bd. Salvation Army, S.I. Served as ensign U.S. Navy, 1917-19. Decorated Legion of Honor, France; knight 1st class Royal Order N. Star, Sweden; recipient Distinguished Citizenship award Wagner Coll., 1948. Mem. N.Y. State Soc. C.P.A.'s, Am. Inst. C.P.A.'s, Naval Order U.S., Am. Legion, N.Y. Acad. Pub. Edn., S.I. Inst. Arts and Scis., S.I. Hist. Soc., S.I. Tchrs. Assn. (life), Am.-Scandinavian Found., LaGuardia Meml. Found., Richmond County Grand Jurors Assn., John Erickson Soc., Tall Cedars of Lebanon, Beta Alpha Psi, Tau Phi Sigma. Methodist. Clubs: Mason., Lawyers (N.Y.C); Richmond County Country. Home: 244 Lawrence Ave Staten Island NY 10310 Office: 1214 Castleton Ave Staten Island NY 10310

CLAUSON, JAMES WILSON, accountant; b. N.Y.C., Aug. 2, 1913; s. James Earl and Bertha Vivian (Stickney) C.; m. Mary Penelope Parrish, Oct. 6, 1939; children: James W., Judith P., Andrew S. B.A., Amherst Coll., 1934; postgrad., N.Y. U., 1936-37. Pub. acct. Price, Waterhouse & Co., N.Y.C., 1934-41; with United Aircraft Corp., 1941-45, Heyer Industries, Inc., 1945-51; v.p., treas. S. P.R. Sugar Co., 1951-69; treas. Ethan Allen, Inc., N.Y.C., 1969-74; controller Indonesian State Oil and Gas Mining Enterprise, N.Y.C., 1975—. Author: Investments and Taxes, 1968. Mem. Am. Inst. C.P.A.'s, N.Y. State, N.J. socs. C.P.A.'s, Newcomen Soc. N.Am., Delta Kappa Epsilon. Clubs: Montclair Golf, Yale. Home: 73 Buckingham Rd Upper Montclair NJ 07043 Office: 20 E 42d St New York NY 10165

CLAUSS, ALFRED, architect; b. Munich, Germany, Aug. 23, 1906; came to U.S., 1930, naturalized, 1936; s. Walter and Clara (Osburg) C.; m. Jane West, Dec. 22, 1934; children—Peter Otto, Carin Ann, Carl Alex. B.S., Munich Archtl. Sch., 1926. Chief design architect, partner Bellante & Clauss, Phila., 1947-67, Bellante, Clauss, Miller & Partners, 1968—; chief architect DiLullo, Clauss, Ostroski & Partners, Bridgewater, N.J., 1956; asso. prof. Yale U., 1950. Contbr. numerous articles to profl. jours. Mem. AIA. Home: 314 Copples Ln Wallingford PA 19086 Office: Widener Bldg-Concourse Chestnut St at Broad Philadelphia PA 19107

CLAVELL, JAMES, author, screenwriter, producer-director, playwright; b. Sydney, Australia, Oct. 10, 1924; came to U.S., 1955, naturalized, 1963; s. Richard Charles and Eileen (Collis) C.; m. April Stride, Feb. 20, 1951. Student, Birmingham U., 1946-47. Screenwriter: films The Fly, 1956, Watussi, 1957, The Great Escape, 1962, 633, Squadron, 1963, The Satan Bug, 1963; writer, producer-dir.: Five Gates to Hell, 1957; Walk Like A Dragon, 1958; writer, producer-dir.: films The Great Escape (Writers Guild award for screenplay 1963); To Sir With Love, 1966, Where's Jack, 1968, The Last Valley, 1970; dir. various TV programs.; Author: novellette The Children's Story, 1981; novels King Rat, 1962; Taipan, 1966; novels Shogun, 1975, Noble House, 1981; play Countdown at Armegeddon, 1966; also poetry. Served to capt. Royal Arty., 1941-46 *

CLAVER, ROBERT E., television director, producer; b. Chgo., May 22, 1928; s. Louis E. and Sara M. (Sosna) C.; 1 dau., Nancy Beth. B.S. in Journalism, U. Ill., 1950. Dir.: Welcome Back Kotter, ABC-TV, 1977-78, All's Fair, CBS-TV, Housecalls, 1979-80, Mork & Mindy, ABC-TV, 1981-82; producer-dir.: Gloria, CBS-TV, 1982-83, Partridge Family, 1970-74, Here Come The Brides, 1968-70, The Interns, 1970-71, numerous other film series; producer-writer first 1000: Captain Kangaroo shows. Served with U.S. Army, 1951-53. Recipient Sylvania award, Peabody award, both for Captain Kangaroo. Mem. Dirs. Guild Am. Jewish. Home: 2254 Chelan Pl Los Angeles CA 90068 Office: 10989 Rochester Ave Los Angeles CA 90024

CLAWSON, DAVID KAY, orthopedic surgeon; b. Salt Lake City, Aug. 8, 1927; s. David J. and Elva (Gundry) C.; m. Janet Dorothy Smith, June 1, 1952; children: Kim Debra, David Roger. Student, U. Utah, 1944-45, 47-48; M.D., Harvard U., 1952. Diplomate: Am. Bd. Orthopedic Surgery. Intern Stanford U. Hosp., 1952-53, resident gen. surgery, 1953-54; resident orthopedic surgery Stanford U. Hosp., also San Francisco City and County Hosp., 1954-57; fellow in orthopedics Nat. Found. Infantile Paralysis, 1955-58; hon. sr. registrar Royal Nat. Orthopedic Hosp., London, Eng., 1957-58; asst. prof. U. Calif. at Los Angeles Med. Sch., 1958; asst. prof. surgery, head div. orthopedic surgery U. Wash. Med. Sch., 1958-61, asso. prof. surgery, head div. orthopedic surgery, 1961-65, prof., 1964—, chmn. dept. orthopedics, 1964-75; dean Coll. Medicine, U. Ky., 1975—, vice chancellor for clin. profl. services, 1982—; chmn. residency rev. com. orthopedic surgery, 1981-82; mem. Accreditation Council for Grad. Med. Edn., 1982—. Contbr. med. jours.; Mem. editorial bd.: Clin. Orthopedics and Related Research, 1964—, Rev. Surgery, 1971—; bd. editorial advisors: Orthopaedic Rev, 1972-75; asso. editor: Jour. Bone and Joint Surgery, 1973-75. Served with USNR, 1945-46. Exchange fellow Am. Orthopedic Assn., 1967. Fellow A.C.S.; mem. Am. Acad. Orthopedic Surgeons, Assn. Bone and Joint Surgeons (sec. 1972-75, pres. 1977), Assn. Orthopedic Chairmen (pres. 1973), Am. Orthopedic Assn., Ky. Med. Assn., Fayette County Med. Soc. Home: 810 Delong Rd Lexington KY 40502 Office: U Ky Coll Medicine MN-140 Med Center Lexington KY 40506 *Look to the past only for the lessons we can learn, live today for the joy of being alive, plan to the future to insure that what should be, will be.*

CLAWSON, ELDON RICHARD, lawyer; b. Tucson, May 15, 1926; s. Leslie Vern and Ethel (Skousen) C.; m. Luana W. Willis, June 14, 1950; children—Byde Wayne, Reed Eldon, Leslie Ann, Ross Willis, Bruce Arthur. LL.B., U. Ariz., 1952; LL.M., Columbia, 1955. Bar: Calif. bar 1955, Ariz. bar 1952. Clk. to Ariz. Supreme Ct. justice, 1952-53; asst. atty. gen., Ariz., 1953-54, pvt. practice, Los Angeles, 1955-57; with Bekins Co., 1957-75, exec. v.p. bus. services group, 1974-75; mem. firm Tscharner & Douglas, Clawson, White, Glendora, Calif., 1975-80; chief exec. officer Baker Ins. Brokerage Co., 1981—; Past mem. bd. dirs. Transport Underwriters Assn., Am. Movers Conf., Calif. Trucking Assn., Los Angeles chpt. Am. Soc. Ins. Mgmt. Served with USNR, 1944-46. Mem. ABA, Calif., Ariz., Los Angeles bar assns. Home and Office: 14 Sage Canyon Rd Pomona CA 91766

CLAWSON, JOHN ADDISON, chemical company executive; b. Monaco, Pa., June 4, 1922; s. Ralph S. and Elsie (Winnett) C.; m. Patricia Harmon, July 5, 1947; children: Christine (Mrs. Deane P. Higgs), Hunter Winnett. B.S. Miami U, 1943; LL.D., 1979; postgrad., Harvard, 1968. Vice pres., nat. mgr. bus. and labor reports div. Prentice-Hall, N.Y.C., 1948-55; with DuBois Chems. div. Chemed Corp., Cin., 1955-78, dist. mgr., N.Y.C., 1955-60, regional mgr. Eastern div., 1960-64, divisional mgrs. v.p., 1964-66, exec. v.p., dir. sales, 1966-70, gen. mgr., 1968-70, pres., chief exec. officer, 1970-79, group exec., 1975-79; cons. Chemed Corp., 1979; chmn. Whitehall Mgmt. Corp., Cin., Driftwood Resorts, Inc., Vero Beach. Dir. Suburban Fed. Savs. & Loan Assn., Cin.; Trustee Providence Hosp., 1974-76; dean's assoc. Miami U., 1973—. Served to lt. (j.g.) USNR, 1943-46. Mem. Cin. C. of C. (city and county planning com. 1971-74), Soap and Detergent Assn. (vice chmn. bd. 1971-73, chmn. bd., chief exec. officer 1974-75, mem. exec. com., bd. dirs. 1976-79), Delta Sigma Phi, Sigma Alpha Epsilon. Presbyterian. Clubs: Queen City, Kenwood Country (Cin.); John's Island, Riomar Bay Yacht (Fla.); Cay Cay, Ltd. (Bahamas). Home: 6525 Given Rd Indian Hill Cincinnati OH 45243 Office: Whitehall Park 8040 Hosbrook Rd Cincinnati OH 45236

CLAWSON, JOHN GIBBS, manufacturing company executive; b. Seattle, Feb. 19, 1928; s. J.H. and Leora (Gibbs) C.; m. Cherie M. Marcil, June 11, 1953; children: Carla Henderson, Martha Abell, John D., Curtis J., Craig S., Scott G., Caroline C. M.B.A., Harvard U., 1955. Vice pres. mfg. Educator's Mfg. Co., Tacoma, 1956-68; pres. Thonet Industries, York, Pa., 1968-72, DeSoto Furniture Group, Jackson, Miss., 1972-76, Hill-Rom Co. Inc., Baresville, Ind., 1976—; bd. dirs. Miss. Eaton Co., Pontotoc, Wausita Fertilizer, Monroe, La. Pres., bd. dirs. Tacoma YMCA, 1964-68; bd. dirs. Jackson (Miss.) YMCA, 1973-76. Republican. Mormon. Lodge: Kiwanis. Home: RR 4 PO Box 20 Batesville IN 47006 Office: Hill-Rom Co Inc Hwy 46 Batesville IN 47006

CLAY, ALBERT GREENE, tobacco company executive; b. Mt. Sterling, Ky., May 27, 1917; s. William Caldwell and Kathryn (Greene) C.; m. Lorraine Case Newlin, Oct. 28, 1939; children: Robert Newlin, John William, Charlotte Newlin. B.A., Duke U., 1938; M.B.A., Harvard U., 1939. Pres. Clay Tobacco Co., Mt. Sterling, Burley Auction Warehouse Assn., 1946-65, chmn. bd., 1965—; dir. Fed. Res. Bank Cleve., 1964-72, chmn. bd., 1968-72; mem. Nat. Tobacco Adv. Com., 1962—; mem. agr. policy adv. com. U.S. Dept. Agr., 1977—; vice chmn. Nat. Tobacco Council, Washington, 1982—; sec. tobacco tax council Burley and Dark Leaf Tobacco Export Assn., 1957-69, Am. Horse Council, 1969—; mem. adv. com. on horse industry IRS, 1970—. Active Boy Scouts Am.; chmn. exec. com. U. Ky., 1969—, chmn. bd. trustees, mem. Devel. Council, 1982—; mem. bd. curators Transylvania Coll., Lexington, 1969—; mem. Gov.'s Adv. Council on Agr., 1982—. Served to lt. USNR, 1939-42. Mem. Ky., Mt. Sterling chambers commerce, Montgomery County Farm Bur., Am. Legion, Am. Horse Council, Alpha Tau Omega. Christian Scientist. Home: Fairway Farm Mount Sterling KY 40353 Office: Clay Tobacco Co PO Box 363 Mount Sterling KY 40353 *Any success that I might have received in life is due to my many loyal friends and associates and the divine guidance of a Supreme Being.*

CLAY, CAROLYNE, metallurgist; b. Chgo., Apr. 30, 1952; d. Calvin and Leanet (May) C. B.S., Rensselaer Poly. Inst., 1974; M.S., MIT, 1976, Metall. Engr., 1978. Research asst. MIT, Cambridge, 1975-77; research metallurgist Ford Motor Co. Sci. Research Lab., Dearborn, Mich., 1977-79; sr. metallurgist Kaiser Aluminum & Chem. Co.-Trentwood Works, Spokane, Wash., 1979—; vis. com. MIT Material Sci. and Enging. Corp., 1978. Recipient Karl T. Compton award, 1977, Scott MacKay award, 1974. Mem. Am. Soc. Metals, AIME, Nat. Soc. Profl. Engrs., NAACP, Sigma Xi, Delta Sigma Theta. Congregationalist. Office: Trentwood Works PO Box 15108 Spokane WA 99215

CLAY, CASSIUS MARCELLUS *See* **ALI, MUHAMMAD**

CLAY, CECIL DAVID, union official; b. Cairo, Ga., Apr. 17, 1916; s. Green Monroe and Essie (Jordan) C.; m. Opal Carler, Aug. 27, 1937; 1 dau., Maxine Clay Cutts. Sheet metal worker, Charleston, S.C., 1941-54; bus. mgr. Sheet Metal workers Internat. Assn., Charleston, 1954-81, gen. sec.-treas., Washington, 1981—. Mem. Charleston County Council, 1979-81; chmn. Charleston County Democratic Party, 1974-78; pres. Charleston Labor Council, 1970-80. Home: 4501 Withers Dr Charleston Heights SC 29405 Office: Sheet Metal Workers Internat Assn 1750 New York Ave NW Washington DC 20000

CLAY, CHARLES HORACE, railroad executive; b. Troy, Mont., Aug. 5, 1925; s. Charles Horace and Helen Ethel C.; m. Audrey Jorgenson, Mar. 17, 1951; children—John Sheldon, Janis Marie, Steven Charles. B.B.A., U. Minn., 1948, LL.B., 1950. Atty. Soo Line R.R. Co., Mpls., 1952-59, gen. atty., 1959-72, gen. freight traffic mgr., 1972-73, asst. to pres., 1973-77, v.p., 1977-78, exec. v.p., 1978—. Office: Soo Line RR Co 800 Soo Line Bldg Box 530 Minneapolis MN 55440

CLAY, DISKIN, classicist; b. Fresno, Calif., Nov. 2, 1938; s. Norman and Florence Patricia (Diskin) C.; m. Sara Christine Clark, Oct. 28, 1978; children: Andreia, Hilary. B.A., Reed Coll., 1960; postgrad. (Fulbright fellow), France, 1960-61; M.A. (Woodrow Wilson fellow), U. Wash., 1963; Ph.D., Am. Sch. Classical Studies, Athens, Greece, 1963-64. Asst. prof. classics and humanities Reed Coll., 1966-69; jr. fellow Center for Hellenic Studies, 1969-70; asst. prof. classics Haverford Coll., 1970-73, assoc. prof., 1973-76; prof. classics Johns Hopkins U., 1976—, Francis White prof. Greek, 1980—, chmn. dept. classics, 1976-83; vis. prof. Universite de Lille, France, 1972. Author: Oxyrhynchan Poems, 1973, (with Stephen Berg) Oedipus the King, 1978, Lucretius and Epicurus, 1983; Mem. editorial bd.: Jour. of Modern Greek Studies, 1983—; contbr. articles on Greek lit. and philosophy to profl. jours.; mem. editorial bd.: Am. Jour. Philology, 1975—; editor, 1982—. Nat. Endowment for Humanities fellow, 1974-75. Mem. Am. Philol. Assn., Am. Inst. Archeology, Soc. Ancient Greek Philosophy, Modern Greek Studies Assn., Phi Beta Kappa. Roman Catholic. Home: 206 Hawthorn Rd Baltimore MD 21210 Office: Dept of Classics Johns Hopkins U Baltimore MD 21218

CLAY, GEORGE HARRY, financial company executive, lawyer; b. Kansas City, Kans., Feb. 14, 1911; s. G. Harry and Linnie Winn (Phillips) C.; m. Harriett Hawley, Feb. 17, 1940; children: Constance Lucille (Loosli), Martha Linnie (McDermott), Charles Hawley, Catherine Louise (Winston), James Nicholas. A.B., LL.B., U. Mo., 1934. Bar: Mo. 1934. Gen. practice law Borders, Borders & Warrick, 1935, Parker & Knipmeyer, 1935-40, Winger, Reeder & Barker, 1940-44; exec. asst. Trans World Airlines, Inc., Kansas City, Mo., 1944-47, sec., 1947-54, v.p., sec., 1954-57, v.p. adminstrv. service, 1957-58, dir., 1956-58; v.p., gen. counsel Fed. Res. Bank Kansas City, 1958-61, pres., 1961-76; chmn. bd., dir. ISC Fin. Corp., 1980—; dir. Ameribanc, Inc., Carter-Waters, Inc. Pres. Regional Health and Welfare Council, 1965-67; asso. mem. Civic Council Kansas City, 1960-76; bd. dirs. Kansas City (Mo.) YMCA, 1950-58, 71-74, pres., 1955-56; bd. dirs. Starlight Theatre Assn., pres., 1968-69; bd. dirs. U. Mo.-Columbia Devel. Fund, 1969-74, United Funds, Mid-Am. Regional Council, 1968—, Helping Hand Inst., Urban Reinvestment Task Force; mem. adv. bd. Salvation Army; bd. govts. Am. Royal Live Stock and Horse Show; trustee Conservatory Music chmn., 1967-75. Mem. Mo., Kansas City bar assns., Chancery, Kansas City C. of C., Nat. Alliance Businessmen, Phi Gamma Delta. Presbyterian (elder). Clubs: Kansas City, Mission Hills Country, Rotary, Mercury. Home: 6201 High Dr Shawnee Mission KS 66208 Office: ISC Financial Corp 310 Parkway 80 Bldg Kansas City MO 64114

CLAY, HENRY JONES, lawyer; b. Jamaica, N.Y., July 13, 1915; s. George H. and Amelia S. (Jones) C.; m. Mary Belle Trent, Aug. 14, 1948 (div.); children: Marcia Clay Hamilton, Henry Jones, Jonathan. A.B., Union Coll., Schenectady, 1939; LL.B., U. Va., 1942. Bar: N.Y. bar 1946, D.C. bar 1952, Vt. bar 1964. Practiced in, N.Y.C.; gen. partner Abberley, Kooiman, Marcellino & Clay; also mem. firm DeWitt, Lockman & DeWitt; asst. atty. gen. N.Y. State, 1947-48; gen. counsel Workman's Compensation Bd. State N.Y., 1948-50; exec. dir. N.Y. State Labor Relations Bd., 1950-52; enforcement commr. Nat. Enforcement Commn. of; Fed. Wage Stblzn. Bd., 1953; acting chmn. Internat. Claims Commn. U.S., 1954; mem. Fgn. Claims Settlement Commn. U.S., 1954-59; dir. Integrated Resources, Inc., Pandick Press, Manchester Printing Co. Contbr. articles to profl. jours. Bd. dirs. Preventive Medicine Inst. Served from ensign to lt. comdr. USNR, 1941-46. Mem. ABA (chmn. fgn. claims com.), Internat. Bar Assn., N.Y. Bar Assn., Vt. Bar Assn., Assn. Bar City N.Y., Am. Arbitration Assn. (panel). Republican. Episcopalian. Clubs: Union (pres. 1983—), Brook; Piping Rock (N.Y.C.); Univ. (Washington); Landsdowne (London); Masons. Home: 160 E 65th St New York NY 10021 also Wolverhollow Rd Upper Brookville NY Office: 521 Fifth Ave New York NY 10017

CLAY, JOHN ERNEST, lawyer; b. Kansas City, Mo., Nov. 27, 1921; s. Ernest Worman and Gertrude Marie (Turfler) C.; m. Theodora Summerfield Buchman, Mar. 11, 1944 (div. Aug. 1973); children: Peter Worman, Robert Scott; m. Mary A. Dailey, Oct.20,1973. B.A., Carleton Coll., 1943; J.D., Harvard U., 1948. Bar: Ill. 1948. Assoc. Taylor, Miller, Busch & Magner, Chgo., 1948-51, Mayer, Brown & Platt, 1951-58, ptnr., 1959—; dir. Pub. Interest Law Internship, Chgo., 1982—. Chmn. Ill. Com. for Eugene McCarthy, Chgo., 1976, vice presdl. running mate in Ill., Chgo., 1976; chmn. Glencoe Bd. Edn., Ill., 1966-68; treas. 1st Nat. Conf. Optimum Population and Environ., Chgo., 1970. Served to 2d lt. U.S. Army, 1945-46. Mem. Chgo. Bar Assn., Chgo. Council Lawyers, Phi Beta Kappa. Clubs: Law, Monroe (Chgo.). Home: 229 6th St Wilmette IL 60091 Office: Mayer Brown & Platt 231 S LaSalle St Chicago IL 60604

CLAY, JOHN WILLIAM, banker; b. nr. Americus, Ga., Dec. 5, 1913; s. Charles Clifford and Zerelda (Martin) C.; m. Eleanor Eakin Reed, Oct. 2, 1939; children: John William, James Reed. B.A., Vanderbilt U., 1937. With Third Nat. Bank, Nashville, 1937—, v.p., 1951-63, sr. v.p., 1963-65, exec. v.p., 1965-70, pres., 1970-72, chmn. bd., 1972-74, sr. chmn. bd., 1974-78, chmn. exec. and fin. coms., 1974-78, dir., 1970-78, ret., 1978; sr. chmn. bd., chmn. exec. com. 3d Nat. Corp., 1973-77, pres., 1977-79, also dir.; dir. Marquette Co., 1974—, Thomas Nelson Pubs., 1979—, mem. exec. com., 1980—. Co-chmn. Nashville Com. for Am. Industry Nat. Fund for Med. Edn., 1956-64; gen. chmn. Middle Tenn. Heart Assn. campaign, 1951, dir., 1954-57; gen. chmn. United Way for Nashville and Davidson County campaign, 1958-59, also trustee; gen. alumni reunion chmn. Vanderbilt U., 1962; chmn. Vanderbilt Nashville Living Endowment Program, 1964-66, nat. chmn., 1968-69; Trustee Nashville Meml. Hosp.; former asso. bd. dirs. St. Thomas Hosp.; bd. dirs. Tenn. Council Econ. Edn., 1975-76. Mem. Am. Bankers Assn., Tenn. Taxpayers Assn. (pres. 1974—), Nashville Area C. of C. (past pres., dir., mem. exec. com.), Vanderbilt U. Alumni Assn. (past trustee, mem. exec. com.), Sigma Alpha Epsilon. Methodist (steward). Clubs: Belle Meade Country (past dir.), Cumberland (Nashville)). Home: 4422 Harding Pl Nashville TN 37205 Office: 201 4th Ave N Nashville TN 37244

CLAY, LANDON THOMAS, investment co. exec.; b. N.Y.C., Mar. 12, 1926; s. Cassius Marcellus and Emily (Thomas) C. A.B., Harvard, 1949. Security analyst Bank of N.Y., N.Y.C., 1949-54; investment officer Mass. Investors Trust, Boston, 1954-68; v.p., chmn. Eaton Vance, Inc., Boston, 1968—. Trustee Museum Fine Arts, Boston, Middlesex Sch., Concord, Mass. Served with USAAF, 1944-46. Clubs: Harvard (Boston and N.Y.C.); Somerset (Boston); Knickerbocker (N.Y.C.). Home: Old Dublin Rd Hancock NH 03449 Office: 24 Federal St Boston MA 02110

CLAY, LYELL BUFFINGTON, communications company executive; b. Balt., Dec. 15, 1923; s. Buckner and Juliet Lyell (Staunton) C.; m. Patricia Kennedy, Dec. 3, 1949 (dec.); children: Whitney Kennedy, Ashton deLashmet, Leslie Staunton, Courtney Buffington. B.A., Williams Coll., 1944; LL.B., U. Va., 1948; M.A., Marshall U., W.Va., 1956; M.B.A., W.Va. U., 1975; grad., Advanced Mgmt. Program, Harvard U., 1967. Bar: W.Va. bar 1948. Chmn. bd. Clay Communications, Inc., Charleston, W.Va., 1970—; co. pubs. Charleston Daily Mail, Beckley (W.Va.) Post Herald, Shelby (N.C.) Daily Star, Raleigh (W. Va.) Register, Enquirer Jour., Monroe, N.C.; operator TV stas. in, N.C., Miss. and Tex., also WCHV-WWWV radio, Charlottesville, Va.; pres. Clay Realty Co., Charleston, 1957—; dir. Territorial Ins. Co., Mut. Ins. Co., Ltd., Mut. Reins. Co. Trustee U. Charleston, 1967—; city solicitor, Charleston, 1951-56. Served in USMC, 1945; comdr. JAGC USNR; ret. Mem. Am. Newspapers Pubs. Assn. (past dir.), W.Va. State Bar, Charleston Area C. of C. (past pres.), W.Va. Press Assn. (past pres.). Presbyterian. Clubs: Edgewood Country, Charleston Rotary (past pres.). Home: 1230 Staunton Rd Charleston WV 25314 Office: 1001 Virginia St Charleston WV 25301

CLAY, ORSON C., insurance company executive; b. Bountiful, Utah, July 26, 1930; s. George Phillips and Dorothy (Cliff) C.; m. Dianne Jones, June 13, 1961; children: Orson Cliff, Charles Kenneth, Elizabeth Temple. B.S., Brigham Young U., 1955; M.B.A. with distinction (Donald Kirk David fellow), Harvard, 1959. With Continental Oil Co., various locations in, U.S.; mng. dir. Conoco A.G., Zug, Switzerland, 1962-63; dir. econs. div. Continental Oil Co. Ltd., London, Eng., 1964-65; gen. mgr. adminstrn. and operations Continental Oil (U.K.) Ltd., London, 1965-66; asst. mgr. marine transp., N.Y.C., 1966-68; exec. asst. fin. Pennzoil United, Inc., Houston, 1968-70; exec. v.p. fin., treas. Am. Nat. Ins. Co., Galveston, Tex., 1970-73, sr. exec. v.p., treas., 1973-76, pres., 1977—, chief exec. officer, 1978—, also dir.; chmn. bd., dir. Standard Life & Accident Ins. Co., Oklahoma City, 1976—; chmn. bd., pres., chief exec. officer, dir. Commonwealth Life & Accident Ins. Co.; dir. Am. Printing Co.; dir., chmn. bd. Am. Nat. Property & Casualty Co., Am. Nat. Gen. Ins. Co; dir. First City Nat. Bank of Houston, Dillard Dept. Stores, Little Rock; chmn. bd., pres. Am. Nat. Life Ins. Co. of Tex., Galveston; v.p., dir. Am. Nat. Real Estate Mgmt. Corp.; mem. exec. com., dir. Securities Mgmt. & Research, Inc., Galveston; dir. Galveston Indsl. Devel. Corp., Am. Nat. Bond Fund, Am. Nat. Growth Fund, Am. Nat. Income Fund, Am. Nat. Money Market Fund. Bd. dirs. Tex. Research League; trustee United Way of Galveston; mem. investment adv. com. for permanent univ. fund U. Tex. System.; trustee, mem. fin. com. William Temple Found. Served to 1st lt. USMCR, 1955-57. Mem. Tex. Guaranty Assn. (dir.); mem. Tex. Life, Accident, Health and Hosp. Service Ins. Guaranty Assn. (vice chmn.); Mem. Tex. Life Ins. Assn. (v.p.), Alumni Assn. Brigham Young U. (bd. dirs.). Mormon (missionary in Can. 1951-53). Home: 2619 Christopher Sq Galveston TX 77550 Office: 1 Moody Plaza Galveston TX 77550

CLAY, WILLIAM DANE, lawyer; b. Fort Smith, Ark., Feb. 1, 1928; s. W. Wesley and Ina (Stephens) C.; m. Mary Ann Smith, Nov. 5, 1961. A.A., Fort Smith Jr. Coll., 1947; LL.B. (J.D.), U. Ark., 1951. Bar: Ark. bar 1951. Asso. firm Rose, Nash, Williamson, Carroll, Clay & Giroir, Little Rock, 1953-58, partner, 1958-70, sr. partner, 1970—. Served to 1st lt. JAGC USAF, 1952-53. Mem. Little Rock Philharmonic Assn.

(pres. 1961), Am. Contract Bridge League (nat. goodwill, charity coms., pres. Ark. 1962-64), Phi Alpha Delta, Omicron Delta Kappa. Democrat. Home: 12010 Fairway Dr Little Rock AR 72212 Office: 120 E 4th St Little Rock AR 72201

CLAY, WILLIAM LACY, congressman; b. St. Louis, Apr. 30, 1931; s. Irving C. and Luella (Hyatt) C.; m. Carol A. Johnson, Oct. 10, 1953; children: Vicki, Lacy, Michelle. B.S. in Polit. Sci, St. Louis U., 1953. Real estate broker, from 1964, mgr. life ins. co., 1959-61, alderman 26th Ward, St. Louis, 1959-64, bus. rep. state, county and municipal employees union, 1961-64; edn. coordinator Steamfitters local 562, 1966-67; mem. 91st-98th congresses from 1st Mo. Dist. Dist. Served with AUS, 1953-55. Mem. NAACP (past exec. bd. mem. St. Louis), CORE, St. Louis Jr. C. of C. Democrat. Office: 2470 Rayburn House Office Bldg Washington DC 20515

CLAYBURGH, JILL, actress; b. N.Y.C., Apr. 30, 1944; d. Albert Henry and Julia (Door) C.; m. David Rabe, Mar., 1979. B.A., Sarah Lawrence Coll., 1966. Former mem., Charles Playhouse, Boston; Off-Broadway plays include: The Nest; Broadway debut in: The Rothschilds, 1970; stage appearances include: In the Boom Boom Room; film appearances include: Portnoy's Complaint, 1972, The Thief Who Came to Dinner, 1973, The Terminal Man, 1974, Gable and Lombard, 1976, Silver Streak, 1976, Semi-Tough, 1977, An Unmarried Woman, 1978, Luna, 1979, Starting Over, 1979, It's My Turn, 1980, I'm Dancing as Fast as I Can, 1982, Hannah K, 1983, First Monday in October, 1981; appeared in TV films: Hustling, 1975, Griffin and Phoenix, 1976. Recipient Best Actress award for An Unmarried Woman, Cannes Film Festival; Golden Apple award for best film actress in An Unmarried Woman. Office: care Press Relations Universal Pictures 445 Park Ave New York NY 10022 *

CLAYCAMP, HENRY JOHN, educator, consultant; b. Ogallah, Kan., Mar. 12, 1931; s. Henry John and Jenny Katherine (Armbruster) C.; m. Joanne Hillman, Aug. 20, 1950; children: Eric, Gregg, Jan, Jill. B.A. magna cum laude in Econs., Washburn U., 1956; M.A., U. Ill., 1957, Ph.D., 1961. Asst. prof. mktg. MIT, Cambridge, 1961-65; assoc. prof. Stanford U., Calif., 1965-69; vis. prof. IMEDE Mgmt. Devel. Inst., Lausanne, Switzerland, 1969-70; sr. v.p. advanced methods and research N.W. Ayer & Son, N.Y.C., 1970-73, dir.; v.p. corp. mktg. Internat. Harvester Corp., Chgo., 1973-77; v.p. corp. planning Internat. Harvest Corp., Chgo., 1977-82; prof. mgmt. Purdue U., West Lafayette, Ind., 1983—. Mem. editorial bd.: Jour. Mktg. Research, 1975-79, Research on Consumer Behavior Jour., 1977, Strategic Mgmt. Jour., 1979; contbr. articles to profl. jours.l. Chmn. Coll. Mktg. Instn. of Mgmt. Scis., 1973. Mem. Am. Mktg. Assn. (v.p. 1975-76). Office: Purdue U 430 Krannert Lafayette IN 47906

CLAYCOMB, CECIL KEITH, biochemist, educator; b. Twin Falls, Idaho, Oct. 19, 1920; s. Cecil R. and Frilla E. (Reams) C.; m. Elizabeth Jane Gregg, Mar. 10, 1943; children: John K., Mary E. B.S., U. Oreg., 1947, M.S., 1948, Ph.D., 1951. Prof., head dept. biochemistry Dental Sch. U. Oreg., Portland, 1951-82, dir. minority recruitment, 1971—, coordinator basic sci. curriculum, 1951-77, chmn. admissions com., 1959-69. Contbr. articles to sci. jours. Served to 1st lt. AUS, 1943-46. Scholar dental bd. New South Wales, Sydney, Australia, 1970. Mem. Am. Chem. Soc., Internat. Assn. Dental Research, AAAS, Res. Officers Assn., Sigma Xi. Home: 3324 SW 13th Ave Portland OR 97201 Office: 611 SW Campus Dr Portland OR 97201

CLAYDON, SISTER MARGARET, college president; b. N.Y.C., July 19, 1923; d. George Thomas and Susan (Murray) C. A.B., Trinity Coll., 1945; M.A., Catholic U. Am., 1953, Ph.D., 1960, L.H.D., 1975; postgrad., Oxford U., summer 1958; L.H.D., Georgetown U., 1970. Tchr. Latin St. Hubert's High Sch., Phila., 1948-51, Trinity Prep. Sch., Ilchester, Med., 1951-52; faculty dept. English Trinity Coll., Washington, 1952-59, pres., 1959—, prof. English, 1976—; exchange lectr. English Notre Dame Coll., Glasgow, Scotland, 1958-59; psotdoctoral research fellow, resident guest fellow Timothy Dwight Coll., Yale, 1975-76; Mem. Commn. on Instl. Affairs, A.A.C. Mem. D.C. Commn. Arts and Humanities.; Trustee Greater Washington Ednl. TV Assn. Mem. NEA, Nat. Cath. Edn. Assn. (pres. coll. and univ. dept. 1968-70), Washington Opportunities for Women. Address: Trinity Coll Washington DC 20017

CLAYPOOLE, ROBERT EDWIN, distribution service company executive; b. Elizabeth, N.J., July 6, 1936; s. Nelson A. and Mary J. (Fox) C.; m. Nancy P. Tetzlaff, May 12, 1962; children: Patricia, N. Catherine, Kimberly, Christine, Robert, Michael. B.C.E., Cornell U., 1959, M.B.A., 1961. Plant mgr. GATX Terminals, Carteret, N.J., 1964-66, mgr. European Ops., Barcelona, Spain, 1966-68, GATX European Ops., Antwerp, Belgium, 1968-70; asst. mgr. ops. GATX Terminals, Chgo., 1970-78, v.p. ops., 1978-80, chief exec. officer, pres., 1980—; treas., dir. Chgo. Dist. Waterways Assn., 1974-77; dir., treas. Ind. Liquid Terminals Assn., Washington, 1981-83, vice chmn., 1983—. Chmn. GATXGood Govt. Program, Chgo., 1981—; pres. Fairhaven Civic Assn., Barrington, Ill., 1976. Recipient Profl. Mgmt. award Cornell Sch. Bus. and Pub. Adminstrn., Ithaca, N.J., 1981. Mem. Cornell Bus. and Pub. Adminstrn. Assn. Republican. Roman Catholic. Clubs: Beefeater, Biltmore Country, Barrington Tennis, The Tower. Lodge: K.C. Office: GATX Terminals Corp 120 S Riverside Plaza Chicago IL 60606

CLAYTON, BILLY WAYNE, consultant, former state legislator; b. Olney, Tex., Sept. 11, 1928; s. William and Myrtle C.; m. Delma Jean Dennis; children: Brenda Jean Clayton Smith, Thomas Wayne. B.S. in Agrl. Econs., Tex. A&M, 1950; LL.D. (hon.), Tex. Wesleyan U., 1979, Tex. Tech U., 1983. Farmer, rancher, Springlake, Tex., 1950—; exec. dir. Water, Inc., Lubbock, Tex., 1968-72; pres. Springlake Enterprises, Inc., Texhold Inc.; mem. Tex. Ho. of Reps., 1962-82, chmn. aero. com., counties com., livestock com., interim water com., vice chmn. banks and banking com., speaker of ho., 1975-82; pres. Capital Cons., bus. and polit. cons., Austin, 1983—, Distbrs. of Tex., 1983—; mem. West Tex. adv. com. Water Devel. Bd.; chmn. Interstate Conf. Water Problems, 1973, Council State Govts., 1977-78; mem. exec. bd. West Tex. Water Inst.; mem. exec. com. So. Environ. Resources Conf., 1973-74; chmn. intergovtl. relations com. Nat. Legis. Conf., 1973; mem. for Tex. Nat. Water Congress; chmn. So. States Speakers Conf., 1975-76; mem. exec. com. So. Legis. Conf., 1973-74, chmn., 1975-76. Mem. adv. bd. Young Ams. for Freedom; trustee High Plains Research Found., Halfway, Tex.; former deacon 1st Baptist Ch., Springlake. Named Outstanding Farmer in Lamb County, Lamb County Farm Bur., 1967; Hon. Water Well Digger Tex. Water Well Assn., 1968; recipient Distinguished Service to People of Tex. award Progressive Farmer Mag., 1967; Outstanding Service to Farmers in Lamb County award Earth C. of C., 1973; Distinguished Service award Democratic Party Tex., 1968; commendation Tex. Water Rights Commn., 1970; Outstanding Service award in water conservation Ft. Worth Press Club, 1972; 1st award West Tex. Water Inst., 1971. Mem. West Tex. C. of C. (exec. com., water resources com.), West Tex. Water Inst. Club. Lodges: Lions (past pres. Springlake club); Masons (33 deg.). Home: PO Box 38 Springlake TX 79082 Office: 1108 Lavaca St Suite 100 Austin TX 78701

CLAYTON, CHARLES CURTIS, journalist; b. Cambridge, Nebr., June 3, 1902; s. Curtis Stanton and Clara Clyde (Richardson) C.; m. Elizabeth Elliott, June 3, 1925; children—Carol Roma (Mrs. William G. Hill), Charles Stephen. Student, U. Nebr., 1919-22; B.J., U. Mo., 1925. Reporter St. Louis Globe Democrat, 1925-29, asst. city editor, 1929-39, lit. editor, 1937-39, city editor, 1939-40, editorial writer, 1940-54, exec. asst. to publisher, 1954-55; prof. journalism So. Ill. U., 1956—; on leave to establish Sch. Journalism and Mass Communications Center at Chinese U. of Hong Kong, 1965-66; lectr. journalism Washington U., St. Louis, 1928-29, Webster Coll., 1937-40, Lindenwood Coll., St. Charles, Mo., 1940-52, sch. journalism U. Mo., 1947-50; chmn. publ. bd. Quill, 1951-53; editor The Quill, 1956-61; vis. prof. journalism, grad. sch. journalism Nat. Chengchi U., Taipei, Formosa, 1961-62, 70-71; hon. prof. for life; dir. Yenching Inst., 1970-71; leader Seminar Chinese Studies, 1976. Author: books including Newspaper Reporting Today, 1947, Fifty Years for Freedom, 1959, Little Mack: Joseph McCullah of the St. Louis Globe-Democrat, 1969, (with others) The Asian Newspapers' Reluctant Revolution, 1971, A Twinge of Nostalgia, 1979; also mag. articles. Bd. dirs. Walter Williams Found. in Journalism, 1936-38. Recipient U. Mo. Honor Medal for distinguished service to journalism, 1952; Ministry Def. medal Republic China, 1976. Mem. U. Mo. Journalism Alumni Assn. (pres. 1936-38), State Univs. Annuitants Assn. Ill. (pres. 1977-78, dir. 1977—), Sigma Delta Chi (exec. council 1947—, chmn. 1952-53, nat. pres. 1951-52), Kappa Tau Alpha, Alpha Epsilon Rho. Clubs: Circumnavigators, Rotary. Home: 805 Taylor Dr Carbondale IL 62901 *Adversity is not only the sternest test of a man, but it can also be the key that opens new opportunities and challenges.*

CLAYTON, DONALD DELBERT, astrophysicist, nuclear physicist, educator; b. Shenandoah, Iowa, Mar. 18, 1935; s. Delbert Homer and Avis (Kembery) C.; children: Donald, Devon, Alia. B.S., So. Meth. U., 1956; Ph.D., Calif. Inst. Tech., 1962. Research fellow in physics Calif. Inst. Tech., 1961-63; staff scientist Aerospace Corp., El Segundo, Calif., 1961-63; mem. faculty Rice U., Houston, 1963—, assoc. prof. physics and space sci., 1965-69; prof. physics and space sci. and faculty assoc. Wiess Coll., 1969-77, Andrew Hays Buchanan prof. astrophysics, 1975—; vis. assoc. physics Calif. Inst. Tech., 1966-67; vis. fellow Inst. Theoretical Astronomy, Cambridge, summers 1967-72. Author: Principles of Stellar Evolution and Nucleosynthesis, 1969, The Dark Night Sky, 1975; also articles. Sloan fellow, 1966-70; Humboldt awardee Max Planck Inst., Heidelberg, 1977, 82; Fulbright fellow, Heidelberg, 1979-80. Fellow Am. Phys. Soc.; mem. Am. Astron. Soc., AAAS, Phi Beta Kappa, Sigma Xi. Office: Dept Space Physics and Astronomy Rice U Houston TX 77001 *My life centers on love of nature. As a cosmologist studying the universe, I find the truth to be stranger than fiction, and the commonplace to be the spectacular. To share this joy with laymen, I wrote a personal memoir, The Dark Night Sky.*

CLAYTON, FRANCES ELIZABETH, educator; b. Texarkana, Tex., Nov. 6, 1922; d. Carl C. and Louise (Heath) C. A.A., Texarkana Coll., 1942; B.A., Tex. Womens U., 1944; M.A., U. Tex., 1947, Ph.D., 1951. Instr. U. Ark., Fayetteville, 1950-51, mem. faculty, 1954—, prof. zoology, 1961—; instr. U. Tex., Austin, 1951-52, Rosalie B. Hite Postdoctoral fellow, 1952-53, research scientist, 1953-54; vis. colleague in genetics U. Hawaii, 1963-64. Contbr. articles to tech. jours. Fellow AAAS; mem. Am. Genetic Assn., Evolution Soc., Soc. for Exptl. Biology and Medicine, Am. Soc. Zoologists, Am. Micros. Soc., Soc. Am. Naturalists, Soc. Cell Biology. Research on devel. eye mutants in Drosophila, genetic irradiation effects during different stages cell division and devel., cytology species of Drosophila. Home: 665 Lindell Fayetteville AR 72701

CLAYTON, HUGH NEWTON, lawyer; b. Ripley, Miss., Aug. 22, 1907; s. Ira L. and Nancy (McCord) C.; m. Cathryn Rose Carter, June 26, 1939; children: Rose Clayton Cochran, Hugh Carter. A.B., U. Miss., 1929, J.D., 1931. Bar: Miss. 1931, Tenn. 1931. Practiced in, Memphis, 1931-33, Ripley, 1933-36, city atty., 1933-36, New Albany, Miss., 1937-75, 76-82; atty. New Albany Sch. Bd., 1937; dir. Bank of New Albany. Editor: Miss. Law Jour, 1931; asso. editor: New Orleans Christian Advocate, 1941-42; contbr. articles to profl. jours. Chmn. Union County chpt. ARC, 1945-51, nat. com. on internat. ops., 1946-47, chmn. nat. conv., 1959, mem. nat. exec. com. and chmn. nat. chpt. relations com., 1954-56, vice chmn. and parliamentarian, 1948; nat. conv.; chmn. area adv. com. Southeastern U.S., 1949-51; nat. bd. govs., 1950-56, vol. field cons., 1956—, chmn. nat. conv., 1959, chmn. state conv., 1961, mem. state div. council, 1979—; mem. exec. bd. Yocona Area council Boy Scouts Am., 1955—, pres., 1963-65, chmn. com. on advancements, 1956-57, chmn. com. on orgn. and extension, 1958-60; chmn. com. on trust fund promotion Region 5, 1968-72, chmn. fin. com., 1972-73, mem. nat. council, 1959—, mem. regional exec. com., 1966—, mem. nat. ann. meeting com., 1970-72, mem. nat. com. on local council fin., 1973—, chmn. trust fund com. S.E. region, 1974-80, vice chmn. adminstrn. com. S.E. region, 1973-75; chmn. adminstrn. com. 1975-77; pres. Union County Tb Assn., 1937-40, New Albany Planning Com., 1945-49; mem. nat. conf. Commrs. on Uniform State Laws, 1956—; mem. Miss. Democratic Exec. Com., 1952-56, Nat. Dem. Com., 1956-60; mem. exec. com. Nat. Dem. Com., 1958-60; mem. Dem. Nat. Adv. Council, 1959-60; Founder, 1st pres. Miss. Jr. Bar, 1936. Served from lt. to lt. comdr. USNR, 1942-45; served as acting comdg. officer Naval Air Sta., 1945; New Orleans. Recipient Silver Beaver award Boy Scouts Am., 1962, Silver Antelope award, 1968; Paul Harris award Rotary Internat., 1976; Disting. Alumnus award U. Miss., 1983; named Outstanding Law Alumnus U. Miss., 1977-78. Fellow Am. Coll. Trial Lawyers, Miss. Bar Found. (trustee), Am. Bar Found. (State chmn. fellows 1980—), Am. Coll. Probate Counsel, Internat. Acad. Law and Sci.; mem. Am. Judicature Soc. (dir. 1962-65), Internat. Platform Assn., Internat. Bar Assn. (patron), Fed. Bar Assn., Am. Counsel Assn. (bd. dirs. 1980-83), ABA (mem. various coms., mem. ho. dels. 1966-81, state del. 1974-80, chmn. communications com. 1967-68, chmn. standing com. on membership 1973-78, chmn. standing com. on jurisprudence, tenure and compensation 1980-81, gov. 1981—, bd. govs. fin. com. 1981-84, chmn. bd. govs. fin. com. 1983-84, bd. govs. coms. long range fin. planning, planning and mgmt. systems, relocation 1983-84, mem. exec. com. 1983-84), Miss. Bar Found. (trustee 1963-65, pres. 1965-66), Miss. Def. Lawyers Assn. (bd. dirs. 1980-83), Miss. State Bar (1st v.p. 1958-59, pres. 1959-60), Miss. Law Jour. Assn. (bd. dirs. 1978—), 3d Miss. Circuit Bar Assn. (pres. 1963-68), Jud. Conf. U.S. 5th Circuit, U. Miss. Alumni Assn. (dir. 1962-65, founder, 1st pres. law alumni chpt. 1964-65), Am. Acad. Polit. and Social Sci., Miss. Assn. Meth. Ministers and Laymen (pres. 1958), Am. Bar Retirement Assn. (bd. dirs. 1981-82), Inst. Jud. Adminstrn., Am. Legion, Scribes (dir. 1969-73), Omicron Delta Kappa, Phi Delta Theta, Phi Alpha Delta, Tau Kappa Alpha, Sigma Upsilon. Methodist (treas. North Miss. Conf. bd. missions 1938-60, trustee North Miss. Conf. 1960—, chmn. bd. trustees Miss. Conf. 1973—, treas. Lewis Meml. Hosp. Fund Miss. 1938-49, nat. emergency com. 1940). Clubs: Masons, Rotary (dist. gov. 1965-66), Oaks Country (New Albany, Miss.)). Office: Clayton Bldg PO Box 157 New Albany MS 38652

CLAYTON, JAMES EDWIN, journalist; b. Johnston City, Ill., Nov. 14, 1929; s. John Herman and Vinnie Ethyl (Black) C.; m. Elise Brookfield Heinz, June 3, 1961; children—Jonathan Brown, David Lake. B.S., U. Ill., 1953; M.P.A., Princeton, 1956. Reporter So. Illinoisan, Carbondale, Ill., 1951-52; reporter Washington Post, 1956-64, asst. mng. editor, 1964-67, 72-74, editorial writer, 1967-72, asso. editor, 1974—; Vis. lectr. Northwestern U., 1966-67, Johns Hopkins, 1970. Author: The Making of Justice, 1964. Served to 1st lt. AUS, 1951-52. Recipient Interpretive Reporting awards Washington Newspaper Guild, 1959, 62, 63, Distinguished Washington Correspondence award Sigma Delta Chi, 1960, Worth Bingham prize, 1970, George Polk Meml. award for editorial writing, 1970. Baptist. Club: Princeton (Washington). Home: 2728 N Fillmore St Arlington VA 22207 Office: 1150 15th St NW Washington DC 20071

CLAYTON, JAMES LEROY, university dean; b. Salt Lake City, July 28, 1931; s. Ernest Clarence and Olita (Melville) C.; m. Geraldine Horsley, June 13, 1957; children: John Creed, Catherine, Andrea. B.A., U. Utah, 1958; Ph.D., Cornell U., 1964. Instr. history Hamilton Coll., Clinton, N.Y., 1962-63; mem. faculty U. Utah, 1964—, prof. history, 1971—, Univ. Disting. Honors prof., 1977-78, dean, 1979—; vis. asst. prof. Dartmouth Coll., 1966-67; Reynolds lectr., 1976; mem. admissions bd. U. Utah Med. Sch., 1968-69. Author: A Farewell to the Welfare State, 1976, Does Defense Beggar Welfare, 1979, On the Brink: Defense Deficits and Welfare Spending, 1984; editor: The Economic Impact of the Cold War, 1970. Served with AUS, 1954-55. Recipient Solon J. Buck prize Minn. Hist. Soc., 1967. Mem. Council Grad. Schs. U.S., Western Assn. Grad. Schs. (pres. 1981-82), Phi Kappa Phi. Home: 1445 Arlington Dr Salt Lake City UT 84103 Office: 310 Park Bldg U Utah Salt Lake City UT 84112

CLAYTON, JOE TODD, educator; b. Etowah, Tenn., Oct. 2, 1924; s. Joe Madison and Onye (Rymer) C.; m. Helen Deane Harris, Aug. 30, 1946; children—Jeffrey Todd, Jill Elaine, Joel Harris. B.S. in Agrl. Engring, U. Tenn., 1949, postgrad., 1949-50; M.S., U. Ill. at Urbana, 1951; Ph.D. (NSF sci. faculty fellow), Cornell U., 1962. Registered profl. engr., Ill., Mass. Instr. U. Ill. at Urbana, 1951-54, asst. prof., 1955-57, U. Conn., 1954-55; asso. prof. U. Mass. at Amherst, 1957-61, prof. agrl. engring., 1961-66, prof., head dept. food engring., 1966—; vis. prof. bioengring., NATO sr. fellow sci. U. Reading, Eng., 1971—; chmn. sci. devel. Research & Devel. Assos., 1981—. Contbr. numerous articles to nat. and internat. profl. jours. Served with AUS, 1943-46. Japan Soc. for Promotion of Sci. fellow U. Tokyo, 1981. Fellow AAAS; mem. Am. Soc. Agrl. Engrs. (sr. mem., dir. 1976—), Inst. Food Technologists (profl. mem.), Internat. Soc. Biometeorology, N.Y. Acad. Scis., Sigma Xi, Gamma Sigma Delta, Phi Tau Sigma. Home: N Silver Ln Sunderland MA 01375 Office: U Mass Dept Food Engring Amherst MA 01003

CLAYTON, JON KERRY, holding company financial executive; b. Cin., Dec. 29, 1945; s. Lawrence and CharlotteMarie (Miller) C.; m. Mary-Paige Royer, Aug. 27, 1983; 1 dau. from previous marriage, Margaret Allyn. B.I.E., Ga. Inst. Tech., 1968; M.B.A., Harvard U., 1970. Asst. treas. Am. Security Ins. Co., Atlanta, 1970-76, treas., 1976-78; v.p., treas. Am. Security Inc. Co., Atlanta, 1978-80; v.p.-fin. AMEV Holdings, Inc., N.Y.C., 1980—. Served to 1st lt. U.S. Army, 1970. Home: 217 E 60th St Apt 203 New York NY 10022 Office: A NEV HoldingsInc 2 World Trade Ctr Suite 9766 New York NY 10048

CLAYTON, JONATHAN ALAN, banker; b. New Brunswick, N.J., Jan. 20, 1937; s. Llewellyn H. and Florence E. (Denton) C.; m. Carole Elaine Jolly, Sept. 23, 1961; children—David Alan, Susan Beth. B.A. in History, Lafayette Coll., 1959; postgrad., N.Y. U. Law Sch., 1959, N.Y. U. Grad. Sch. Bus. Adminstrn., 1961-64; grad., Robert Morris Loan Mgmt. Seminar, 1973. Trainee mgmt. program Mfrs. Hanover Trust Co., N.Y.C., 1961-64, asst. sec., 1966-69, asst. v.p., 1969-71, v.p., 1971-80, officer in charge credit and fin. group, 1972-74, officer in charge hdqrs. br., 1974-76, dep. officer in charge, Upper Manhattan, Westchester, Bronx and Orange counties, 1976-78, Bklyn. and S.I. brs., 1978-80, sr. v.p. corp., comml. and retail banking, 1980-83; officer in charge comml. and retail Stonier Grad. Sch. Banking, Rutgers U., Manhattan br., 1983—, instr. comml. banking, New Brunswick, 1973—, N.Y. State Bankers Assn. Exec. Devel. Schs., West Point, 1973-81, Syracuse, 1979-81; mem. bd. govs. N.Y. chpt. Robert Morris Associates, 1979-81. Vice pres. bd. trustees, treas., chmn. fin. com. Rutgers Preparatory Sch., Somerset, N.J., 1975-78; bd. regents St. Francis Coll., Bklyn., 1981—; elder First Presbyn. Ch., Cranbury, N.J., 1981-83; v.p. Men's Fellowship, 1981-83; bd. dirs. Bklyn. Borough Hall Restoration Found. Served from 2d. lt. to capt. U.S. Army, 1959-66. Mem. N.Y. State Bankers Assn. (mem. edn. com. 1975-81), Downtown Bklyn. Devel. Assn. (vice chmn., dir. 1981—), N.Y.C. C. of C., Bklyn. C. of C. (dir. 1980-82), Am. Arbitration Assn. (arbitrator 1971—). Republican. Clubs: Lions (Cranbury) (dir. 1981—); Bklyn., Mcpl. of Bklyn., Marco Polo, Candy Execs. and Affiliated Industries. Office: 270 Park Ave New York NY

CLAYTON, MARY JO, advertising agency executive; b. Georgetown, Ky., Dec. 29; d. Jesse L. and Nettie (Lutz) C. B.A. in English And Math., Meredith Coll. Copy supr. Foote, Cone & Belding, N.Y.C., 1960-66; copy group head Grey Advt., N.Y.C., 1967-70; v.p., copy supr. Ketchum, MacLeod & Grove, Inc., N.Y.C., 1970-76; sr. v.p., creative group head Benton & Bowles, Inc., N.Y.C., 1976-83; with Wells, Rich, Greene, Inc., N.Y.C., 1983—; writer TV commls. for Digital Equipment Corp.; writer Procter & Gamble, Shiseido Cosmetics, Revlon Cosmetics, Clairol, Johnson & Johnson. Democrat. Baptist. Office: Wells Rich Greene Inc 767 Fifth Ave New York NY 10153

CLAYTON, PRESTON COPELAND, lawyer; b. Eufaula, Ala., Sept. 21, 1903; s. Lee Johnston and Caroline E. (Copel) C.; m. Jewel Gladys Robinson, July 20, 1933; children—Mary Elliott (Mrs. Robert Mack Dixon), Sarah Hunter (Mrs. Thos. S. Lawson, Jr.), Preston Copeland. B.A., U. Ala., 1924; LL.B., Jones Law Sch., 1935. Bar. Ala. bar 1931. Cotton mcht., Quanah, Tex., 1927-32, pvt. practice in, Clayton and Eufaula, 1932—; aso. justice Supreme Ct., Ala., 1953-54; instr. econs. U. Ala., 1923-24; dir., atty. Clayton Banking Co., 1946-53; organizer, atty. Pea River Electric Coop., 1937-53, Wiregrass Electric Coop., 1938-42; Breeder Arabian horses. Contbr. articles on Arabian and Barb horses of No. Africa to mags. City atty., Clayton, 1933-39; Mem. Ala. Bd. Vets. Affairs, 1946-50; Chmn. Barbour County Democratic Exec. Com., 1937-53; mem. Ala. Senate, 1938-53; Pres. Ala. Cattlemens Assns. Served to lt. col. AUS, World War II. Mem. Internat. Arabian Horse Assn. (dir.). Episcopalian. Club: Rotarian. Home: 1 mile South of Clayton AL 36016 Office: 210 E Broad St Eufaula AL 36027

CLAYTON, RICHARD REESE, fastener manufacturing company executive; b. St. Louis, Aug. 26, 1938; s. Lester Cox and Gladys Caroline (Reese) C.; m. Leigh Ila Smith, Feb. 25, 1961; children: Mark, Catherine, Christine. B.S. in Indsl. Econs, Purdue U., 1960. With Trane Co., 1960-73, mng. dir., Sydney, Australia, 1970-73; pres. Hallowell div. Standard Pressed Steel Co., Hatfield, Pa., 1973-77; exec. v.p. domestic ops. SPS Technologies Inc., Jenkintown, Pa., 1977—, also dir. Mem. Am. Mgmt. Assn., Conf. Board, Indsl. Fastener Inst., NAM, Machinery and Allied Products Inst., Pa. Soc., Ross-Ade Found. Republican. Presbyterian. Office: Benson East SPS Technologies Newtown PA 18940

CLAYTON, ROBERT NORMAN, chemist, educator; b. Hamilton, Ont., Can., Mar. 20, 1930; came to U.S., 1952; s. Norman and Gwenda (Twist) C.; m. Cathleen Shelburne, Jan. 30, 1971; 1 dau., Elizabeth Jane. B.Sc., Queens U., 1951, M.Sc., 1952; Ph.D., 1955. Research fellow Calif. Inst. Tech., 1955-56; mem. faculty Pa. State U., 1956-58, U. Chgo., 1958—, prof. chemistry and geochemistry, 1966—. Fellow Royal Soc. (London), Royal Soc. Can., Am. Acad. Arts and Scis.; fellow Am. Geophys. Union, Meteoritical Soc.; mem. AAAS. Research distbn. stable isotopes of light elements in nature, application to problems in geology. Home: 5201 S Cornell Ave Chicago IL 60615

CLAYTON, ROSS, university dean. Dean pub. adminstrn. U. So. Calif., Los Angeles. Office: Office of Dean Pub Adminstrn U So Calif University Park Los Angeles CA 90089§

CLAYTON, SHARON, publisher; b. Bunkerville, Nev., Jan. 26, 1935; d. Hyram and Edith (Bunker) Potter; m. Charles Carlton Clayton, Sept. 12, 1952; 1 son, James Brian. Student, E. Los Angeles Coll., 1952-53. Mgr. Olin-Mathieson Co., City of Commerce, Calif., 1960-62; gen. mgr. J & R Engring. Co., El Monte, Calif., 1962-65; comptroller, sec., treas. Cycle News Inc., Long Beach, Calif., 1965-73, pub., sec., treas., 1973—. Vice-pres. Kiefer Meml. Fund, found. sports medicine, 1979—. Recipient Rolf Tibbins award Motorcycle Industry Council, 1976. Mem. Am. Motorcycle Assn. (dirt track racing bd.). Republican. Club: Mormon. Home: 711 Hillside St Long Beach CA 90815 Office: 2201 Cherry Ave Long Beach CA 90806

CLAYTON, THOMAS (SWOVERLAND), humanities educator; b. New Ulm, Minn., Dec. 15, 1932; s. Robert Schoonmaker and Vida Virginia (Swoverl) C.; m. Ruth Barbara Madson, Sept. 24, 1955; children—Pamela Alison, Katherine Anne, John Robert Madson, David Montgomery. Student, U. Chgo., 1949-51; B.A. summa cum laude, U. Minn., 1954; D.Phil. (Rhodes scholar), Oxford U., Eng., 1960. Instr. Yale U., 1960-62; asst. prof., asso. prof. UCLA, 1962-68, Humanities Inst. fellow, 1966-67; assoc. prof., then prof. English U. Minn., Mpls., 1968—, chmn. Classical Civilization Program, 1982—. Editor: The Non-Dramatic Works of Sir John Suckling, 1971, Cavalier Poets, 1978; Author: Shakespearean addition in Book of Sir Thomas More, 1969. Served with U.S. Army, 1955-57. Recipient Disting. Teaching award Coll. Liberal Arts, U. Minn., 1971, Horace T. Morse-Amoco award U. Minn., 1982; Guggenheim fellow, 1978—; Am. Council Learned Socs. grantee, 1962. Mem. Internat. Shakespeare Assn., Am. Assn. Rhodes Scholars, Modern Humanities Research Assn., MLA, Renaissance English Text Soc., Renaissance Soc. Am., Shakespeare Assn. Am. Home: 1866 Portland Ave Saint Paul MN 55104 Office: Dept English U Minn Minneapolis MN 55455

CLAYTON, WILLIAM HOWARD, university president; b. Dallas, Aug. 16, 1921; s. William Howard and Blanche (Phillips) C.; children: Jill, Gregory. B.S., Bucknell U., 1949; Ph.D., Tex. A & M U., 1956. Instr. Bucknell U., 1949; grad. asst. Ohio State U., 1949, U. N.Mex., 1949-50; research asst. oceanography and meteorology Tex. A&M U., College Station, 1950-51; asst. oceanography Tex. A. and M. U., 1951-54; asso. oceanography, instr. math. Tex. A&M U., 1954-56, micrometeorologist U. Research Found., instr. math., 1956-58, faculty oceanography, meteorology, 1958—, prof. oceanography, 1965—, prin. investigator Research Found., 1956-65; asso. dean Coll. Geoscis. Tex. A & M U., 1970-71; dean Moody Coll., Galveston, 1971-74, provost, 1974-77, pres. coll., 1977-79; pres. Tex. A&M U., Galveston, 1979—; sec.-treas. Tex. Coastal Higher Edn. Authority, 1981—; vis. prof. U. Hawaii, 1963-64; tech. dir. Project Themis, U.S. Army Electronics Command, 1967-74; chmn. field observing facility adv. panel Nat. Center for Atmospheric Research, 1973-74. Contbr. articles to profl. lit., chpts. to books. Dir. Bank of West. Commr., Galveston Police and Fire Dept. CSC, Galveston Marine Affairs Council; trustee Gulf Univs. Research Consortium, 1971—, chmn., 1977-79. Served with RCAF, 1940-44; Served with USAAF, 1944-45; rear admiral U.S. Maritime Service. Mem. Am. Geophys. Union, Am. Meteorol. Soc. (dir.), Galveston C. of C. (dir.), Sigma Xi, Pi Mu Epsilon, Sigma Pi Sigma, Phi Kappa Phi, Sigma Phi Epsilon. Home: 54 Adler Circle Galveston TX 77550 Office: Tex A and M U at Galveston PO Box 1675 Galveston TX 77553

CLAYTON, WILLIAM L., investment banking executive; b. Tenafly, N.J., Oct. 27, 1929; s. Walter I. and Emily A. (Caverly) C.; m. Carol L. Farmer, June 23, 1951; children: Andrew L., Robin L., Kathleen L., Kevin L., Susan L., Christopher L. B.S., Lehigh U., 1951; postgrad. in Bus., NYU, 1953-56. Asst. portfolio mgr. Marine Midland, N.Y.C., 1953-54; account exec. E.F. Hutton, N.Y.C., 1954-64, v.p., 1964-71, sr. v.p., 1971-81, exec. v.p., 1981—; dir. Stabler Cos., Harrisburg, Pa., Eastern Industries. Trustee Lehigh U., 1980—. Recipient Nat. Mktg. Club, 1980; named Outstanding Alumnus Lehigh U., 1971. Mem. Lehigh U. Alumni Assn. (pres. 1980—), Beta Gama Sigma, Chi Phi (treas. 1951). Clubs: Baltusrol (Springfield, N.J.); India House (N.Y.C.). Home: One Slope Dr Short Hills NJ 07078 Office: E F Hutton 1 Battery Park Plaza New York NY 10004

CLAYTOR, ROBERT BUCKNER, railroad executive; b. Roanoke, Va., Feb. 27, 1922; s. William Graham and Gertrude Harris (Boatwright) C.; m. Frances Tice, Sept. 25, 1943; children—Jane Gordon (Mrs. Samuel J. Webster), Robert Harris, John Preston. A.B. cum laude, Princeton U., 1944; J.D., Harvard U., 1948; L.H.D., Hollins Coll., 1982. Bar: Mass. bar 1948, N.Y. bar 1949, Va. bar 1952. Atty. AT&T, 1948-51; solicitor Norfolk & Western, Roanoke, 1951-54, asst. gen. solicitor, 1954-56, asst. gen. counsel, 1956-60, gen. solicitor, 1960- 64, v.p. law, 1964-68, sr. v.p., 1968-70, exec. v.p., 1970-80, pres., chief exec. officer, 1980—, also dir.; dir. Piedmont Aviation Inc., Norfolk, Va. Nat. Bankshares, Richardson-Wayland Elec. Corp., Ga.-Pacific Corp. Chancellor Episcopal Diocese Southwestern Va., 1969-74, trustee diocese funds.; trustee Hollins Coll.; bd. visitors Va. Poly Inst.; bd. regents Mercersburg Acad. Served to 1st lt. AUS, 1943-46. Mem. Am., Va., Roanoke bar assns., Phi Beta Kappa. Episcopalian. Clubs: Princeton (N.Y.C.); Metropolitan (Washington); Harbor (Norfolk); Norfolk Yacht and Country; Shenandoah (Roanoke); Duquesne (Pitts.); Laurel Valley Golf (Ligonier, Pa.); Sky, Links (N.Y.C.). Home: 7300 Woodway Ln Norfolk VA 23505 Office: PO Box 3609 Norfolk VA 23514

CLAYTOR, WILLIAM GRAHAM, JR., lawyer, railroad executive, government official; b. Roanoke, Va., Mar. 14, 1912; s. William Graham and Gertrude Harris (Boatwright) C.; m. Frances Murray Hammond, Aug. 14, 1948; children: Frances Murray, William Graham III. B.A., U. Va., 1933; J.D. summa cum laude, Harvard, 1936. Bar: N.Y. 1937, D.C. 1938. Law clk. U.S. Judge Learned Hand, 1936-37, Mr. Justice Brandeis, 1937-38; asso. firm Covington & Burling, Washington, 1938-47, partner, 1947-67, counsel, 1981—; v.p. law So. Ry. Co., 1963-67, chief exec. officer, 1967-77, pres., 1967-76, chmn. bd., 1976-77; former chief exec. officer, dir. various cos. comprising So. Ry. System; sec. Navy, Washington, 1977-79, acting sec. Transp., 1979, dep. sec. Def., 1979-81; bd. dirs. Assn. Am. Railroads, 1967-77. Pres.: Harvard Law Rev, 1935-36. Trustee Episcopal Home Children, Washington, 1960-65, v.p., 1960-63; govs. Beauvoir Sch., Washington, 1958-61, St. Albans Sch., Washington, 1961-67; mem. adv. bd. Center for Advanced Studies, U. Va., 1974-80; trustee Eisenhower Fellowships, Inc., 1981—; mem. adv. com. Mt. Vernon (Va.) Ladies Assn. of the Union, 1980—. Served to lt. comdr. USNR, 1941-46. Mem. Am. Bar Assn., Am. Law Inst., Am. Judicature Soc., Harvard Law Sch. Assn., Am. Soc. Corp. Execs. (asso. mem.). Democrat. Episcopalian. Clubs: Metropolitan, City Tavern Assn. (Washington) (bd. govs. 1961-64); Chevy Chase, Gibson Island (Md.); Shenandoah (Roanoke). Home: 2912 N St NW Washington DC 20007 Office: National Railroad Passenger Corp 400 N Capital St NW Washington DC 20001

CLEARFIELD, HARRIS REYNOLD, physician; b. Phila., Aug. 8, 1933; s. Samuel and Rae (Lewis) C.; m. Louis Libby, June 30, 1957; children: Andrea, Jonathan. B.S., Franklin and Marshall Coll., 1955; M.D., Jefferson Med. Coll., 1959. Intern Grad. Hosp. U. Pa., Phila., 1959-60, resident in internal medicine, 1960-62, resident in gastroenterology, 1962-63, mem. staff, 1963-72, Episcopalian Hosp., 1967-72, head sect. gastroenterology, until 1972; sr. attending physician Phila. Gen Hosp., 1972-77; mem. faculty U. Pa. Med. Sch., Phila., 1963-72; clin. asst. prof. medicine Temple U. Med. Sch., Phila., 1967-71, clin. assoc. prof., 1971-72; dir. div. gastroenterology Hahnemann Hosp., Phila., 1972—, prof. medicine, 1972—; editorial cons. Am. Jour. Proctology, 1976—; lectr., cons. Naval Regional Med. Center, Phila., 1976-78; sr. cons. Phila. Gen. Hosp., 1972-74; chmn. sci. adv. bd. Nat. Found. Iletis and Colitis, 1976-80; mem. gov.'s adv. com. of ACP, 1980—. Contbr. articles to profl. jours.; author: (with Dinoso) Gastrointertinal Emergencies, 1979. Named Physician of the Yr. Phila. chpt. Nat. Found. Iltetis and Colitis, 1980—; recipient Lindback award for execellence in teaching Phila. chpt. Nat. Found. Iletis and Colitis, 1979. Fellow ACP, Phila. Coll. Physicians; mem. Am. Gastroenterologic Assn., Bockus Internat. Soc. Gastroenterology (trustee), Phila. Gastrenterology Group (pres. 1974-75), Am. Soc. Gastrointestinal Endoscopy, Am. Coll. Gastroenterology, Deleware Valley Soc. Gastrointestinal Endoscopy, Phila. Gastrointestinal Research Forum, Pa. Soc. Gastroenterology. Home: 720 Oxford Rd Bala Cynwyd PA 19004 Office: 230 N Broad St Philadelphia PA 19102

CLEARY, BEVERLY ATLEE (MRS. CLARENCE T. CLEARY), author; b. McMinnville, Oreg.; d. Chester Lloyd and Mable (Atlee) Bunn; m. Clarence T. Cleary, Oct. 6, 1940; children—Marianne Elisabeth, Malcolm James. B.A., U. Calif., 1938, U. Wash., 1939. Children's librarian, Yakima, Wash., 1939-40; post librarian Regional Hosp., Oakland, Calif., 1942-45. Author: Henry Huggins, 1950, Ellen Tebbits, 1951, Henry and Beezus, 1952, Otis Spofford, 1953, Henry and Ribsy, 1954, Beezus and Ramona, 1955, Fifteen, 1956, Henry and the Paper Route, 1957, The Luckiest Girl, 1958, Jean and Johnny, (1959) The Real Hole, 1960, Hullabaloo ABC, 1960, Two Dog Biscuits, 1961, Emily's Runaway Imagination, 1961, Henry and the Clubhouse, 1962, Sister of the Bride, 1963, Ribsy, 1964, The Mouse and the Motorcycle, 1965, Mitch and Amy, 1967, Ramona the Pest, 1968 (Georgia Children's Book award 1970), Runaway Ralph, 1970, Socks, 1973, Ramona the Brave, 1975, Ramona and her Father, 1977 (Honor Book for U.S., Internat. Bd. and Books for Young People), Ramona and her Mother, 1979, Ramona Quimby, Age 8, 1981 (Recipient Young Reader's Choice award Pacific N.W. Library Assn. 1957, 60, 68, 71, 80, Dorothy Canfield Fisher Children's Book award Vt. Congress of Parents and Tchrs. 1958, 66, Nene award Hawaii Assn. Sch. Librarians and Hawaii Library Assn. 1968, 69, 71, 72, 79, Sue Hefley award La. Assn. Sch. Librarians 1973, William Allen White award Kans. Assn. Sch. Librarians and Kans. Tchrs. Assn. 1968, 75, Sequoyah Children's Book award Okla. Library Assn. 1971, Charlie May Simon award Ark. Elem. Sch. Council 1973, Laura Ingalls Wilder award Children's Services div. ALA 1975, Golden Archer award U. Wis. 1977, Newbery Honor Book 1978, Regina medal Cath. Library Assn. 1980, Utah Children's Book award Children's Lit. Assn. Utah 1980, Tenn. Children's Book award Tenn. Library Assn. 1980, Garden State award N.J. Library Assn. 1980, Tex. Bluebonnet award Tex. Library Assn.-Tex. Assn. Sch. Librarians 1981, Am. Book award 1981). Mem. Authors Guild of Authors League Am. Address: care William Morrow 105 Madison Ave New York NY 10016

CLEARY, JAMES FRANCIS, securities executive; b. Boston, Oct. 27, 1927; s. Charles F. and Catherine (Quinn) C.; m. Barbara M. Coliton, July 27, 1961; children: Kara Lyn, James Francis, Kristin Coliton. Grad., Boston Coll., 1950; M.B.A., NYU, 1956. With Eastman Dillon (Union Securities Co.), 1951-72, mgr., 1959-68, mng. partner sales and br. offices div., 1968-71, exec. v.p., dir., mem. exec. com., 1971-72; with Blyth Eastman Dillon & Co., Inc., N.Y.C. and Boston, 1972—, formerly pres., chief operating officer, now vice-chmn.; dir. Eastdil Realty, Inc.; past gov. Boston Stock Exchange. Bd. dirs., past chmn. Mass. div. Am. Cancer Soc.; vice chmn. United Cerebral Palsy Campaign; trustee Boston Coll. Served with USN, 1944-46. Mem. Securities Industry Assn. (past bd. govs.), Bond Club N.Y., AIM, Conf. Bd. Clubs: Algonquin, Madison Sq. Garden (Boston) (trustee); River (N.Y.C.); Weston Country, Wianno, Oysters Harbor in Cape Cod, Hundred of Mass. Office: Blyth Eastman Paine Webber 100 Federal St Boston MA 02110

CLEARY, JAMES ROY, lawyer; b. Springville, Ala., July 16, 1926; s. Bereman Leroy and Bertie (Jones) C.; m. Miriam Voncille James, Apr. 10, 1960; children: Johanna, Susan. B.A., Birmingham-So. Coll., 1948; J.D., Northwestern U., 1951. Bar: Ala. 1951. Practiced in, Huntsville, 1956—; atty. Dept. Army, Redstone Arsenal, 1951-55; mem. firm Cleary, Lee, Morris, Evans & Rowe, 1956—. V.p., dir. Security Fed. Savs. Assn.; dir. Am. Nat. Bank, Huntsville.; Trustee Birmingham-So. Coll. Named Young Man of Year Huntsville, 1957. Mem. Jr. Chamber Internat. (life mem., senator), Am. Coll. Mortgage Attys. (bd. regents). Club: Ala.-Miss. Dist. Optimist Internat. (past lt. gov.). Home: 1902 Chippendale Dr SE Huntsville AL 35801 Office: PO Box 68 300 Clinton Ave W Huntsville AL 35804

CLEARY, JAMES W., university president; b. Milw., Apr. 16, 1927; (married), 1950. Ph.B., Marquette U., 1950, M.A., 1951; Ph.D. (Univ. fellow 1954-55), U. Wis., 1956. Instr., dir. forensics high sch., Wis., 1949-51; instr. speech, head coach debate Marquette U., 1951-53; from instr. to prof. speech U. Wis., 1956-63, vice chancellor academic affairs, 1966-69; pres. Calif. State U., Northridge, 1969—. Author: books in field including Robert's Rules of Order Newly Revised, 1970, 80; editor: John Bulwer's "Chirologia... Chironomia," 1644, 1974; co-editor: Bibliography of Rhetoric and Public Address, 1964. Served to 2d lt. AUS, 1945-47. Mem. Speech Assn. Am., Am. Assn. State Colls. and Univs. (chmn. 1983). Address: 18111 Nordhoff St Northridge CA 91330

CLEARY, JOHN JOSEPH, journalist; b. Cleve., Mar. 7, 1905; s. John Joseph and Susan Ann (MacLain) C. L.H.B., Cath. U. Am., 1927. Asst. fin. editor Cleve. News, 1928-36, marine editor, 1936-46, bus. editor, 1946-49, fin. editor, 1949-60, columnist, 1946-60; gen. bus. editor Cleve. Plain Dealer, 1960-72; account exec. Dix & Eaton, Inc., Cleve., 1972-76; freelance writer, 1976—. Served to 1st lt. AUS, 1942-46. Mem. Sigma Delta Chi (pres. Cleve. chpt. 1957-58). Home: 11820 Edgewater Dr Lakewood OH 44107 Office: Ten Ten Euclid Bldg Cleveland OH 44115

CLEARY, JOHN WASHINGTON, lawyer; b. Milw., Feb. 22, 1911; s. Peter A. and Mathilda A. (Borning) C.; m. Alice M. Shinners, Jan. 15, 1938; children: Terrence P., Mary E., Peter J., Margaret A., John T., Catherine A. J.D., Marquette U., 1933. Bar: Wis. 1933. Since practiced in Milw.; partner Erbstoeszer, Cleary & Misey, 1936-82, Fiorenza & Hodan, 1982—; sec. Hopkins Savs. & Loan Assn., Milw., 1936-65, pres., 1965—; faculty Savs. and Loan Inst., Milw., 1961-63. Vice chmn. Milw. Commn. Community Relations, 1959-63; savs. and loan commr., Wis., 1963-65; mem. pres.'s senate Marquette U., 1977—; bd. dirs. Greater Milw. chpt. ARC, pres., 1961-63; trustee Marquette U. High Sch.; gov. nat. ARC. Mem. Wis. Legis. Council, Milw. Savs. and Loan Council (pres. 1948-50), Wis. Savs. and Loan League (pres. 1954-55), U.S. Savs. and Loan League (dir. 1962-63). Home: 2728 N 98th St Milwaukee WI 53222 Office: 7901 W Burleigh St Milwaukee WI 53222

CLEARY, MARTIN JOSEPH, real estate company executive; b. N.Y.C., July 27, 1935; s. Patrick Joseph and Kathleen Theresa (Costello) C.; m. Peggy Elizabeth McIntyre, June 22, 1957; children: Patrick Francis, Eileen Ann, Michael Thomas, Kathleen Marie, Maureen Elizabeth. B.S., Fordham U., 1960; M.B.A., N.Y. U., 1963. With Tchrs. Ins. and Annuity Assn. and Coll. Retirement Equities Fund, N.Y.C., 1953-81; pres. Jacobs, Visconsi, Jacobs, Westlake, Ohio, 1981—; Mem. mortgage adv. com. N.Y. State Tchrs. Retirement System, 1981—; trustee Internat. Council Shopping Centers, 1980—, pres., 1983-84. Office: 25425 Center Ridge Rd Westlake OH 44145

CLEARY, ROBERT EDWARD, educator; b. East Orange, N.J., Feb. 27, 1932; s. Charles A. and Mary J. (Solomon) C.; m. Marilyn F. Jacoby, Apr. 21, 1956; children—Barbara, Kevin, Charles. B.A. in Social Sci, Montclair (N.J.) State Coll., 1953; M.A. in Polit. Sci, Rutgers U., 1959, Ph.D., 1962; LL.D., Am. U., 1977. Asst. dir. secondary sch. project Eagleton Inst. Politics, Rutgers U., 1959-61; asst. prof. George Peabody Coll. for Tchrs., 1961-64; asst. dir. Am. Polit. Sci. Assn., 1966-67; asso. prof., asso. dean Sch. Govt. and Pub. Adminstrn., Am. U., Washington, 1965-70, prof. govt. and public adminstrn., 1970—, dean acad. devel., 1970-72, provost, 1972-76, acting pres., 1975-76, dean, 1980—. Contbr. articles to profl. jours. Exec. sec. Harry S. Truman Scholarship Found., 1976-78. Mem. Am. Polit. Sci. Assn. (Congl. fellow 1964-65). Club: Cosmos (Washington). Home: 7503 Elmore Ln Bethesda MD 20817

CLEARY, RUSSELL GEORGE, brewing company executive; b. Chippewa Falls, Wis., May 22, 1933; s. George and Ruth (Halseth) C.; m. Gail J. Kumm, Jan. 8, 1955; children: Kristine Hope, Sandra Gay. LL.B., U. Wis., 1957. Bar: Wis. bar 1957. Individual practice law, La Crosse, Wis., 1957-58; atty., dir. sales Hoeschler Realty Co., La Crosse, 1958-60; v.p., atty., asst. to pres. G. Heileman Brewing Co., Inc., La Crosse, 1960-71, pres., chmn. bd., chief exec. officer, 1971—, also dir.; dir. 29th Dist. Fed. Res. Bank, Mpls., The Trane Co., Protection Mut. Ins. Co., Econs. Lab. Inc., Northwestern Nat. Bank Mpls., Ill.-Wis. adv. bd. Am. Mut. Ins. Co., 1971—. Bd. dirs., past v.p. La Crosse Festivals; bd. dirs. La Crosse Interstate Fair Assn., U. Wis.-La Crosse Found., Inc.; trustee Hamline U., St. Paul; past chmn. La Crosse Redevel. Authority; past pres. United Fund La Crosse Area. Named Man of Year La Crosse Area C. of C., 1975, Exec. of Year Corporate Report mag., 1980. Home: 1111 Cedar Rd Dr La Crosse WI 54601 Office: 100 Harborview Plaza La Crosse WI 54601

CLEARY, TIMOTHY FINBAR, government official; b. Cork, Ireland, Sept. 30, 1925; s. John Francis and Nora (Riordan) C.; m. Patricia Agnes Hanley, June 21, 1947; children: Timothy F. X., Maureen P., Therese A., Richard S., Gail P., Eileen P. B.S., Fordham U., 1955, J.D., 1959. Bar: N.Y. 1959, D.C. 1980. Atty. N.Y.C. Police Dept., 1959-67; asst. counsel Fair Labor Standards div. U.S. Dept. Labor, Washington, 1967-71, chief counsel, 1971-73, mem., 1973—; chmn. U.S. Occupational Safety and Health Rev. Commn., Washington, 1977-81; mem. Adminstrv. Conf. U.S.; lectr. labor law Practising Law Inst., U. Wis., Washington and Lee U., Cumberland Sch. Law, Ohio No. U., Brookings Instn., AFL-CIO Center for Labor Studies, Gompers-Murray Inst., numerous others. Contbr. articles to profl. jours. Served with USN, 1943-45. Home: 5709 Cheshire Dr Bethesda MD 20814 Office: Occupational Safety and Health Review Commission 1825 K St NW Washington DC 20006

CLEASBY, JOHN LEROY, civil engineer, educator; b. Madison, Wis., Mar. 1, 1928; s. Clarence Allen and Othelia Amanda (Swanson) C.; m. Donna Jean Haugh, Sept. 2, 1950; children: Teresa, Richard, Lynne. B.S., U. Wis., 1950, M.S., 1951; Ph.D., Iowa State U., 1960. Diplomate: Am. Acad. Environ. Engrs.; registered profl. engr., Iowa. Inspection engr. Standard Oil Co. Ind., Whiting, 1951-52; project engr. Consoer Townsend & Assocs., Chgo., 1952-54; instr. Iowa State U., Ames, 1954-56, asst. prof., 1956-61, assoc. prof., 1961-65, prof., 1965—; vis. prof. Univ. Coll. London, 1975-76; cons. World Bank, Washington, Pan Am. Health Orgn., WHO, U. Sao Paulo. Co-author: Water Supply Engineering, 1962; contbr. articles to profl. jours. Served with USN, 1945-46. Recipient Outstanding Tchr. award Iowa State U., 1977; named Disting. Prof. Engring. Iowa State U., 1983. Mem. ASCE (sec. Environ Engring. div. 1969-73, pres. Iowa sect. 1966), Nat. Acad. Engring., Am. Water Works Assn. (trustee Water Quality div. 1981—, chmn. Iowa sect. 1982). Am. Baptist. Lodge: Kiwanis (Ames). Home: 1730 Coolidge Dr Ames IA 50010 Office: Iowa State U 492 Town Engring Bldg Ames IA 50011

CLEAVER, VERA ALLEN, author; b. Virgil, S.D., Jan. 6, 1919; d. Fortis Alonzo and Beryl Naiome (Reininger) Allen; m. William Joseph Cleaver, Oct. 4, 1945. Student pub. schs. Freelance pub. accountant, 1945-54; with U.S. Air Force, Tachikawa, Japan, 1954-56, Chaumont, France, 1956-58. Author: (with Bill Cleaver) Ellen Grae, 1967, Lady Ellen Grae, 1968, Where the Lilies Bloom, 1969 (Nat. Book award nominee), Grover, 1970 (Nat. Book award nominee), The Mimosa Tree, 1970, I Would Rather Be a Turnip, 1971, The Mock Revolt, 1971, Delpha Green & Company, 1972, Me Too, 1973, The Whys and Wherefores of Littabelle Lee, 1973 (Nat. Book award nominee), Dust of the Earth (Western Writers of Am. Spur award Best Western Juvenile Novel, Lewis Carroll Bookshelf award), Trial Valley, 1977, Queen of Hearts, 1978 (Nat. Book award nominee), A Little Destiny, 1979, The Kissimmee Kid, 1981. Office: care Bantam Books Inc 666 Fifth Ave New York NY 10103 *I cannot believe that at some exciting future time my literary art, if that is what it may be termed, will be dug from a ruin and used again in the shaping of opinions and tastes. Yet the creation of it now, this awful and wonderful endeavor with its inherent interests and concerns and mysteries growling from every corner, brings me my own kind of peace and I thank God for it.* *

CLEAVER, WILLIAM PENNINGTON, cons., retired sugar refining company executive; b. Newark, Nov. 13, 1914; s. Chester H. and Mildred (Day) C.; m. Virginia Whaley, Apr. 15, 1938; 1 dau., Jane P. A.B., Princeton U., 1937. With Amstar Corp. (formerly Am. Sugar Co.), N.Y.C., 1937—, raw sugar buyer, 1954-57, v.p., 1957-79, div. pres., 1975-79; cons., 1979—. Presbyterian. Home: 38 Manor Ave Cranford NJ 07016

CLECAK, PETER EMMETT, humanities educator, author; b. Oakland, Calif., July 22, 1938; s. Nicholas Peter and Jean Anne (Peter) C.; m. Dvera Vivian Bozman, Feb. 26, 1966; children: Aimée Elizabeth, Lisa Nicole. B.A. in English, U. Calif. at Berkeley, 1960; Ph.D. (Woodrow Wilson fellow), Stanford U., 1964. Asst. prof. English U. Calif., Irvine, 1966-72, asso. prof. comparative culture, 1972-76, prof. social thought and comparative culture, 1976—, assoc. dean, 1981-83, also past dir. program in comparative culture.; Mem. nat. bd. cons. Nat. Endowment for the Humanities, 1976—. Author: Radical Paradoxes: Dilemmas of the American Left, 1973 (Choice award), Crooked Paths: Reflections on Socialism, Conservatism, and the Welfare State, 1977, (with others) Investment in Learning, 1977, America's Quest for the Ideal Self: Dissent and Fulfillment in the 60s and 70s, 1983; editorial bd.: (with others) Book Forum; contbr. essays and criticism to scholarly jours., essays translated into Italian and Spanish. Bd. dirs. Shepherd of the Hills United Ch. Christ; mem. religion and socialism com. Democratic Socialist Organizing Com. Served with U.S. Army, 1964-66. Humanities Inst. fellow, summer 1967; Am. Council on Edn. fellow in higher adminstrn. Claremont Grad. Sch., 1974-75; Phi Beta Kappa bicentennial fellow, 1975-76;

Nat. Endowment Humanities fellow, 1979-80. Fellow (assoc.) Internat. Coll. Applied Nutrition; Mem. Am. Studies Assn., Am. Hist. Assn., Orgn. Am. Historians, Am. Council on Edn., Am. Assn. Higher Edn. Home: 1486 Morningside Circle Laguna Beach CA 92651

CLEE, JAN EVERT, educator, consultant, executive; b. Amsterdam, Holland, June 24, 1928; came to U.S., 1960; s. Jacobus J. S. W. and Johanna Josephine (Schultz) C. Diploma, Social Acad., Amsterdam, 1953; M.S./Ph.D., Case Inst. Tech., 1967. Scientist, dept. mental health Netherlands Inst. Preventive Medicine, Leyden, 1953-60; grad. asst. in orgn. behavior Case Inst. Tech., 1960-63, instr. in organizational behavior, 1963-67; asso. prof. orgn. devel. Whittemore Sch. Bus. and Econs. U. N.H., 1967-70, adj. prof., 1970—; dean Whittemore Sch. Bus. and Econs., U. N.H., 1967-77; pres., chief exec. officer Genetics Engring., Inc.; cons. in field.; mem. adv. com. Internat. Ctr. for Integrative Studies; prof. postgrad. studies Interuniv. Inst. Mgmt., Delft, Netherlands; prof. econs. faculty Erasmus U., Rotterdam, Netherlands; bd. advisors Marine Assocs. U. H.H.; dir. Portsmouth Holdings Ltd., Panatech Inc. Mem. art adv. com. Phillips Exeter Acad. Served with Royal Dutch Navy, 1948-50. Fellow Nat. Tng. Labs.; charter mem. Internat. Inst. Applied Social Scientists., Organizational Devel. Network. Clubs: Netherland of N.Y., Netherlands Soc. Phila., Denver Athletic. Office: 401 State St Suite 505 Portsmouth NH 03801

CLEGHORN, JOHN EDWARD, banker; b. Montreal, Que., Can., July 7, 1941; m. Pattie E. Hart; children: Charles, Ian, Andrea. B.Comm., McGill U., Montreal, 1962. Articled with Clarkson Gordon, Montreal, 1964; sugar buyer and futures trader St. Lawrence Sugar Ltd., Montreal, 1964-66; with Merc. Bank of Can., Montreal br., 1966, asst. mgr., 1967, mgr. Winnipeg br., 1969, regional gen. mgr. Western Can., Vancouver, 1970-72, v.p. Western div., 1972-74; mgr. project financing Corp. Banking div. Royal Bank of Can., Montreal, 1974, asst. gen. mgr. project financing, 1975, dep. gen. mgr. corp. lending, 1976-78, v.p. nat. accounts, 1978-79, sr. v.p. planning and mktg. Internat. div., 1979-80, sr. v.p. and gen. mgr. B.C. and Yukon, Vancouver, 1980-83, exec. v.p. internat. banking div., Toronto, 1983—; dir. Pacific Forest Products Ltd., Victoria, B.C., Royal Bank of Can. A.G., Frankfurt, Ger., Western Trust & Savs. Ltd., Plymouth, Eng. Club: Vancouver. Home: 275 Oriole Pkwy Toronto ON M5P 2H4 Canada Office: Royal Bank Plaza Toronto ON M5J 2J5 Canada

CLEGHORN, REESE, journalist, educator; b. Lyerly, Ga., Apr. 9, 1930; s. John Storey and Nona (Reese) C.; m. Cheree Briggs, 1975; children by previous marriage: Nona Elizabeth, John Michael. M.A. in Pub. Law and Govt, Columbia U., 1956; B.A., Emory U., 1950. Gen. assignments reporter Atlanta Jour., 1950-51, 52-54; reporter editor AP, 1954-58; editor, co-pub. Calif. Courier, Fresno, 1958-60; asst. city editor, state news editor Atlanta Jour., 1960-63, editorial writer, 1963-64, asso. editor, 1964-69; dir. Leadership Project, So. Regional Council, editor, 1969-71; editor, editorial pages Charlotte (N.C.) Observer, 1971-76; asso. editor Detroit Free Press, 1976-81; dean Coll. Journalism, U. Md., College Park, 1981—; part-time tchr. journalism Ga. State U., 1963-65; mem. exec. bd. Nat. Conf. Editorial Writers, 1974-81, sec., 1977, treas., 1978, v.p., 1979, pres., 1980; trustee Nat. Conf. Editorial Writers Found., 1981—, v.p., 1982—. Author: (with Pat Watters) Climbing Jacob's Ladder, 1967; also articles. Served with USAF, 1951-52. Mem. Assn. Edn. in Journalism and Mass Communication, Am. Soc. Journalism Sch. Adminstrs., Assn. Schs. of Journalism and Mass Communication, Sigma Delta Chi (pres. Atlanta 1966), Omicron Delta Kappa, Chi Phi. Presbyterian. Home: Washington DC Office: Coll Journalism U Md College Park MD 20742

CLELAND, GEORGE L., ednl. adminstr.; b. Hoyt, Kans., Feb. 9, 1904; s. Frank Estel and Laura Elizabeth (White) C.; m. Virginia Penick, July 27, 1930; children—John David, Joseph Le. A.B., Baker U., 1926, Pd.D., 1959; A.M., Columbia, 1935; Ed.D., Kans. U., 1958. Country sch. tchr., Whiting, Kans., 1922-24, math. tchr., coach, Effingham, Kans., 1926-31, dir. extra class activities, Atchison, Kans., 1931-35; prin. Atchison Jr.-Sr. High Sch., 1935-52; dir. secondary edn. Kans. Dept. Edn., 1952-65, asst. commr. edn., 1965-71; vis. lectr. Kans. State Coll., Manhattan, summer 1948-49; mem. Nat. Com. on Secondary Edn., 1965—. Contbr. articles to profl. publs. John Hay fellow U. Oreg., 1962. Mem. Kans. State Activities Assn. (legis. council 1944-48), Kans. Activities Assn. (Bd. control 1952), Kans. Prins. Assn. (pres. 1949), Nat. Assn. Secondary Sch. Prins. (exec. com. 1952-58, pres. 1956-57, field cons. 1973-80), NEA, Nat. Com. Devel. Sci. and Engrs., Council Advancement Secondary Edn., Nat. Com. Exptl. Projects Secondary Edn., Phi Delta Kappa, Kappa Sigma. Republican. Methodist. Clubs: Mason, Kiwanian (lt. gov. 1948), Educators.). Address: 1256 Wayne Ave Topeka KS 66604

CLELAND, JOSEPH MAXWELL, government official; b. Atlanta, Aug. 24, 1942; s. Joseph Hugh and Juanita (Kesler) C. B.A., Stetson U., Deland, Fla., 1964; M.A., Emory U., 1968, LL.D., 1979. Mem. Ga. Senate, Atlanta, 1971-75; cons. Com. on Vets. Affairs, U.S. Senate, Washington, 1975, profl. staff mem., 1975-77; adminstr. VA, Washington, 1977-81; now sec. of state State of Ga., Atlanta. Served with U.S. Army, 1965-68. Decorated Bronze Star, Silver Star; recipient Gt. Georgian award WSB Radio, award for gallantry Easter Seal Soc., 1973, Jefferson award for greatest pub. service by individual under 35 Am. Inst. Pub. Service, 1977, Inspiration award Assn. U.S. Army, Atlanta, 1978, AMP of Year award, 1978, Life Inspiration award Religious Heritage Am., 1978, Golden Key award Am. Assn. Sch. Adminstrs., 1978, Gold medallion Chapel of Four Chaplains, 1979, Am. Patriot's medal Valley Forge Freedom's Found., 1979, J.O. Wright award, 1979, Neal Pike award, 1979; named One of Five Outstanding Young Men in Ga. Ga. Jr. C. of C., Distinguished Alumnus Stetson U., 1972, Outstanding Handicapped Citizen in Ga., 1973, Outstanding Disabled Vet. DAV. Democrat. Office: Sec of State 214 State Capital Atlanta GA 30334

CLELAND, ROBERT ERSKINE, plant physiologist; b. Balt., Apr. 30, 1932; s. Ralph Erskine and Elizabeth (Shoyer) C.; m. Mary Love, Sept. 2, 1957; children: Thomas Andrew, Alison Anne. B.A., Oberlin Coll., 1953; Ph.D., Calif. Inst. Tech., 1957. Postdoctoral fellow U. Lund, Sweden, 1957-58, King's Coll., London, 1958-59; asst. prof. botany U. Calif.-Berkeley, 1959-64; assoc. prof. botany U. Wash., Seattle, 1964-68, prof., 1968—; mem. life scis. adv. com. NASA, Washington, 1983—, mem. space biology panel, 1979—. Editorial bd.: Plants, 1977—, Plant Sci. Letters, 1981—; contbr. articles to profl. jours. Fellow AAAS; mem. Am. Soc. Plant Physiologists (pres. 1974-75). Methodist. Office: Botany Dept KB15 Univ Wash Seattle WA 98195

CLELAND, ROBERT LINDBERGH, educator; b. St. Francis, Kans., June 10, 1927; s. Robert Earl and Dorothy (Voss) C.; m. Monique Cecile Tremege, Aug. 20, 1956; children—Chantal C., Maryke A., Andrew N., Francis A. B.S., A. and M. Coll. Tex., 1948; M.Ch.E., Mass. Inst. Tech., 1951, Ph.D., 1956. Research asso. Cornell U., 1956-58; Fulbright research scholar U. Leiden, The Netherlands, 1958-59; USPHS Spl. Research fellow Retina Found., Boston, 1959-60; asst. prof. chemistry Dartmouth, 1960-65, asso. prof., 1965-71, prof., 1971—; professeur associe U. Strasbourg, France, 1968-69; vis. prof. U. Uppsala, Sweden, 1977-78. Asso. editor: Macromolecules, 1974-76. Mem. ACS, AAAS. Office: Dept Chemistry Dartmouth Coll Hanover NH 03755

CLELAND, SHERRILL, college president; b. Galion, Ohio, Sept. 21, 1924; s. Fred Burr and Doris Louise (Gregg) C.; m. Betty Irene Chorpenning, July 6, 1946; children: Ann Denise Houtrow, Douglas Stewart, Sarah McDermott Gold, Scott Cameron. A.B., Oberlin Coll., 1949; M.A., Princeton, 1951; Ph.D. in Econs., 1957. Instr. econs. Princeton, 1951-55; asst. prof. U. Richmond, 1955-56; mem. faculty Kalamazoo Coll., 1956-73, acad. v.p., 1964-67; pres., prof. econs. Marietta (Ohio) Coll., 1973—; econs. adviser Hashemite Kingdom Jordan, 1963-64; Ford Found. vis. prof. econs. and devel. adminstrn. Am. U., Beirut, Lebanon, 1967-69; cons. examiner N. Central Assn. Colls., 1960—; dir. Cleve. Fed. Res. Bank, Cin. br. Co-editor, author: Continuity and Change in the World Oil Industry, 1970; contbg. author: Linear Programming and Theory of Firm, 1962; Contbr. profl. jours. Pres. Kalamazoo chpt. Human Relations Council, 1958-60; Bd. dirs. Marietta Meml. Hosp., Tuition Exchange, Inc., Ohio Student Loan Funding Corp.; past pres. Ohio Coll. Assn., East Central Coll. Consortium; trustee Oberlin Coll. Served with AUS, 1944-46. Decorated Bronze Star, Purple Heart.; Recipient Kazanjian Found. teaching award econs., 1971; Leadership tng. fellow N. Central Assn. Colls., 1959. Fellow Middle East Studies Assn.; mem. Am. Econ. Assn., AAAS, AAUP (asso.), Comparative Internat. Edn. Soc., UN Assn. (past pres. Kalamazoo chpt.). Home: 301 5th St Marietta OH 45750

CLELAND, W(ILLIAM) WALLACE, biochemistry educator; b. Balt., Jan. 6, 1930; s. Ralph E. and Elizabeth P. (Shoyer) C.; m. Joan K. Hookanson, June 18, 1967; children: Elsa Eleanor, Erica Elizabeth. A.B. summa cum laude, Oberlin Coll., 1950; M.S., U. Wis., 1953, Ph.D., 1955. Postdoctoral fellow U. Chgo., 1957-59; asst. prof. U. Wis.-Madison, 1959-62, assoc. prof., 1962-66, prof., 1966—, M.J. Johnson prof. biochemistry, 1978—, Steenbock prof. chem. sci., 1982—. Contbr. articles to profl. biochem. and chem. jours. Served with U.S. Army, 1957-59. NIH grantee, 1960—; NSF grantee, 1960—. Mem. Am. Acad. Arts and Scis., Am. Soc. Biol. Chemists, Am. Chem. Soc. Office: Dept Biochemistry U Wis Madison WI 53706

CLELLAND, RICHARD COOK, statistics educator, university administrator; b. Camden, N.Y., Aug. 23, 1921; s. Ford John and Beryl (Cook) C.; m. Anne Chapin Buel, June 16, 1963; children: Richard Buel, Susan Elizabeth. B.A., Hamilton Coll., 1944; A.M., Columbia U., 1949; Ph.D., U. Pa., 1956. Asst. prof. U. Pa., Phila., 1956-61, asso. prof., 1961-66, prof., 1966—, chmn. dept. stats. and ops. research, 1966-71, acting dean Wharton Sch., 1971-72, assoc. dean Wharton Sch., 1975-80, acting assoc. provost, 1981, dep. provost, 1982—; statis. cons. bus., govt. and research orgns. Author: (with M.W. Tate) Nonparametric and Shortcut Statistics, 1957, (with J.B. O'Hara) Effective Use of Statistics in Accounting and Business, 1964, (with others) Basic Statistics with Business Applications, 1966, 2d edit., 1973, Library Planning and Decision Making Systems, 1974. Served with Signal Corps, AUS, 1944-46. Fellow Am. Statis. Assn.; mem. Ops. Research Soc. Am., Inst. Mgmt. Scis., Inst. Math. Stats., AAUP. Home: 530 Hilaire Rd Saint Davids PA 19087

CLELLAND, ROD, hospital administrator; b. Imperial, Calif., Oct. 17, 1916; s. George Andrew and Laura (Miller) C.; m. Nathel Stapley, Dec. 21, 1936; children: Jean Boghossian, Rick A., Michael Dow, Marty Kathleen (Mrs. Michael Abercrombie), Jacquelyn Dee McDonald, Christine Anne Archer, Jeffrey George, Shelly Gay. B.F.A. with high distinction, U. Ariz., 1937; M.B.A., Ariz. State U., 1966; postgrad., U. Ga., 1970-73, U. Ala., 1975; D.P.A., Nova U., 1983. Exec. sec. Ariz. Council Assns., Phoenix, 1947-52; bus. adminstr. Ariz. State Hosp., Phoenix, 1952-64; adminstr. Maryvale Samaritan Hosp., Phoenix, 1964-67; adminstrv. supt. Central State Hosp., Milledgeville, Ga., 1967-72; supt. Bryce State Hosp., Tuscaloosa, Ala., 1972-75, Larned (Kans.) State Hosp., 1975-79, Massillon (Ohio) State Hosp., 1979—; Mem. bd. Bapt. Hosp., Scottsdale, Ariz., 1962-63. Author: The Human Side of Hospital Administration, 1974; Contbr. articles profl. jours. Served with USNR, World War II. Fellow Am. Coll. Hosp. Adminstrs., Assn. Mental Health Adminstrs. (past pres.), Nat. Assn. Hosp. Purchasing Agts. (past pres.), Am. Hosp. Assn., Nat. Assn. Purchasing Agts. (past dir.), Iota Sigma Alpha, Alpha Mu Gamma, Delta Psi Omega. Home: Box 540 Massillon OH 44648 *Man can find the satisfaction of accomplishment within himself, even when there is no acclaim from other sources.*

CLEM, ALAN LELAND, political scientist; b. Lincoln, Nebr., Mar. 4, 1929; s. Remey Leland and Bernice (Thompson) C.; m. Mary Louise Burke, Oct. 24, 1953; children: Andrew, Christopher, Constance, John, Daniel. B.A., U. Nebr., 1950; M.A., Am. U., 1957, Ph.D., 1960. Copywriter, research dir. Ayres Advt. Agy., Lincoln, 1950-52; press sec. to Congressman Carl Curtis of Nebr., 1953-54, Congressman R. D. Harrison of Nebr., 1955-58; info. specialist Fgn. Agrl. Service, Dept. Agr., 1959-60; asst. prof. polit. sci. U. S.D., Vermillion, 1960-62, asso. prof., 1962-64, prof., 1965—; asso. dir. Govtl. Research Bur., 1962-76, chmn. dept. polit. sci., 1976-78; partner Opinion Survey Assos., 1964—; state analyst Comparative State Elections Project, U. N.C., 1968-73; dir. Mt. Rushmore Presdl. Inst., 1970-71; mem. U.S. Census Bur. Adv. Com. on State and Local Govt. Stats., 1970-74. Author: several books, including Prairie State Politics: Popular Democracy in South Dakota, 1967, The Making of Congressmen: Seven Campaigns of 1974, 1976, American Electoral Politics: Strategies for Renewal, 1981, Law Enforcement: The South Dakota Experience, 1982; contbr. articles to profl. jours.; editor: Contemporary Approaches to State Constitutional Revision, 1969. Mem. Vermillion City Council, 1965-69; sr. warden St. Paul's Episcopal Ch., Vermillion, 1971-73. Nat. Conv. faculty fellow, 1964. Mem. Mensa, Midwest Polit. Sci. Assn. (exec. council 1979-82, editorial bd. Am. Jour. Polit. Sci. 1971-72), Am. Polit. Sci. Assn., Phi Beta Kappa, Phi Alpha Theta, Pi Sigma Alpha, Sigma Delta Chi. Republican. Club: Vermillion Golf Assn. Home: 902 Valley View Vermillion SD 57069 Office: Dept Polit Sci U SD Vermillion SD 57069 *Avoid haste, anxiety, contentiousness, and self-centeredness. Care, clarity, persistence, honesty, and grace will prevail in the long run.*

CLEMENCE, ROGER DAVIDSON, architecture educator; b. Worcester, Mass., Jan. 20, 1936; s. Luther Davidson and Dorothy (Kay) C.; m. Margaret Weinandy; 3 children. A.B. cum laude, Amherst Coll., 1957; M.Arch. with honors, U. Pa., 1960, M.L.A., 1962. Instr. Coll. of Architecture and Design U. Mich., 1962-64, asst. prof., 1964-66; asso. prof. U. Minn., 1966-73, prof., 1973—, dir. Grad. Studies in Architecture,, 1978—; cons. in field. Mem State of Minn. Designer Selection Bd., 1980—; bd. dirs. Community Design Center of Minn., 1969-72. Contbr. articles in field. Chandler fellow, 1960-62; recipient Amoco Morse Distinguished Tchr. award, 1974. Mem. Am. Soc. Landscape Architects, Minn. Soc. AIA, Tau Sigma Delta. Democrat. Unitarian. Home: 1904 Girard Ave S Minneapolis MN 55403 Office: School of Architecture and Landscape Architecture University of Minnesota Minneapolis MN 55455

CLEMENS, WILLIAM ALVIN, vertebrate paleontology educator; b. Berkeley, Calif., May 15, 1932; s. Vincent Alvin and Estella (Osborn) C.; m. Dorothy Elise, Jan. 22, 1955; children: Catherine, Elisabeth, Diane, William. B.A., U. Calif.-Berkeley, 1954, Ph.D., 1960. Instr. to assoc. prof. dept. zoology U. Kans., Lawrence, 1961-67, curator Mus. Natural History, 1961-67; assoc. prof. dept. paleontology U. Calif.-Berkeley, from 1967, now prof., curator Mus. Paleontology, 1967—; Miller research prof. Miller Inst., 1982-83. Contbr. articles to profl. jours. Served with U.S. Army, 1954-56. NSF fellow U. London, 1960-61; sr. postdoctoral fellow Royal Holloway Coll., 1968-69; Guggenheim fellow, 1974-75; Humboldt-Pries, A. von Humboldt Stiftung U. Munich, 1978-79. Fellow Zool. Soc. London, Linnean Soc. London, Geol. Soc. Am., Calif. Acad. Sci. Home: 920 Spruce St Berkeley CA 94707 Office: Dept Paleontology Univ Calif Berkeley CA 94720

CLEMENT, ALVIS MACON, former utilities exec.; b. Norfolk, Va., July 5, 1912; s. Benjamin Bullock and Lorene Ramuth (Jackson) C.; m. Frances Kent Harvie, Nov. 18, 1939; children—Alvis Macon, Edwin Harvie. B.S., U. Richmond, 1939. C.P.A., Va. With Fed. Res. Bank, Richmond, Va., 1929-36, Bank of Va., Richmond, 1936-39; with Va. Electric & Power Co., Richmond, 1939—, v.p., 1975—; instr. accounting U. Richmond, 1947-53. Mem. Service Corps Ret. Execs. (chmn. Richmond chpt. 1979), Va. Soc. C.P.A.'s, Edison Electric Inst. (chmn. taxation accounting com. 1959), Phi Beta Kappa. Presbyterian. Club: Bull and Bear. Home: 2211 Buckingham Ave Richmond VA 23228

CLEMENT, HOPE ELIZABETH ANNA, librarian; b. North Sydney, N.S., Can., Dec. 29, 1930; d. Harry Wells and Lana (Perkins) C. B.A., U. of King's Coll., 1951; M.A., Dalhousie U., 1953; B.L.S., U. Toronto, 1955. With Nat. Library of Can., Ottawa, Ont., 1955—, chief nat. bibliography div., 1966-70, asst. dir. research and planning br., 1970-73, dir. research and planning br., 1973-77, asso. nat. librarian, 1977—. Editor: Canadiana, 1966-69. Mem. Can. Library Assn., Can. Assn. Info. Sci. Office: Nat Library Can 395 Wellington St Ottawa ON K1A 0N4 Canada

CLEMENT, HOWARD WHEELER, lawyer; b. Greencastle, Ind., Apr. 27, 1917; s. John A. and Clara Caroline (Wheeler) C.; m. Carol L. Ege, Aug. 22, 1942; children: John Jeffrey, Patricia Louise, Martha Anne. B.A., U. Ill., 1938, J.D., 1942. Bar: Ill. 1942. Assoc. Wilkinson, Huxley, Byron & Hume, 1946-51, partner, 1952-56, 1956-70; pres. Hume, Clement, Brinks, Willian & Olds, Ltd., 1970-81; Mem. grad. faculty John Marshall Law Sch., 1955-60; Tech. adv. bd. Dept. Commerce, 1964-65; mem. Pres.'s Commn. on Patent System, 1965-67, Ill. Bd. Higher Edn., 1959-71; Trustee U. Ill., 1959-71, pres., 1962-67; bd. dirs. U. Ill. Found., 1975—, Ill. Bar Found., 1974-78, pres., 1975-78. Served 1st lt. USAAF, 1942-45. Decorated Air medal. Fellow Am. Coll. Trial Lawyers; mem. Am. Judicature Soc., Phi Gamma Delta, Phi Delta Phi. Democrat. Unitarian. Clubs: Law (Chgo.); Lake Delavan (Wis.); Yacht, Wicket and Racket. Home: 8 Holly Ct Sugarmill Woods Homosassa FL 32646 Turtle Cove 3135 S Shore Dr Delavan WI 53115

CLEMENT, JOSEPH DALE, educator; b. Kalamazoo, Jan. 7, 1928; s. William S. and Bernadette C. (Rynne) C.; m. Elizabeth Viola Boyd, July 28, 1956; children—Steven Louis, Mark Robert. B.S., Western Mich. U., 1949; M.S., U. Wis., 1953, Ph.D. (Knapp fellow), 1957. Sr. scientist Westinghouse Bettis Atomic Power Lab., Pitts., 1957; supervisory engr. Martin Co., Balt., 1959-60; sr. scientist Westinghouse Astronuclear Lab., Pitts., 1960-62; mgr. nuclear engring. dept. Nuclear Materials & Equipment Corp., Apollo, Pa., 1962-65; asso. prof. nuclear engring. Ga. Inst. Tech., Atlanta, 1965-68, prof., 1968—; Dir. Sci., Tech. & Research, Inc.; cons. Nuclear Assurance Corp. Contbr. articles profl. jours. Served with U.S. Army, 1953-55. Recipient McCraken award in chemistry Western Mich. U., 1949. Mem. Am. Nuclear Soc., Sigma Xi. Patentee in field. Home: 2484 Burnt Leaf Ln Decatur GA 30033 Office: Sch Nuclear Engring Ga Inst Tech Atlanta GA 30332

CLEMENT, MEREDITH OWEN, educator, economist; b. Colusa, Calif., June 7, 1926; s. Eldon Wilford and Lillian (Ohm) C.; m. Jacqueline Parker, Apr. 10, 1955; children—William, Christopher. Student, Yuba Coll., Marysville, Calif., 1946-48; B.S., U. Calif. at Berkeley, 1950, Ph.D., 1958. Research economist CIA, 1954-56; mem. faculty Dartmouth, 1956—, prof. econs., 1967—; vis. asst. prof. U. Calif. at Berkeley, 1961-62; Brookings research prof. Brookings Instn., 1964-65; Fulbright lectr. Robert Coll., Istanbul, Turkey, 1969-70. Author: (with others) Theoretical Issues in International Economics, 1967, An Economic Evaluation of the Federal Grant-in-Aid Programs in New England, 1961, also articles. Served with USMCR, 1944-46. Mem. Am., So. econ. assns., Royal Econ. Soc., Econometric Soc. Unitarian. Home: Star Route Etna NH 03750 Office: Dept Econs Dartmouth Coll Hanover NH 03755

CLEMENT, RICHARD FRANCIS, business exec.; b. Chgo., Nov. 29, 1906; s. Robert Fawne and Jennie (Halvorson) C.; m. Margaret Buchanan, Aug. 11, 1934; children—Richard Bradley, Jane Elizabeth (Mrs. David L. Wilemon), Charles Frederic. B.S., U. Wis., 1928. Men's furnishings merchandiser Wilson Bros., Chgo., 1935-39; sportswear merchandiser Ely & Walker, St. Louis, 1939-47, v.p., dir., 1949-65, dir. sales, 1954-63, dir. marketing and planning, 1963-65; partner Yates & Co. (investments), St. Louis, 1965-69; v.p. Newhard, Cook & Co. (investments), St. Louis, 1970—; chmn. C & B Investment Assos., Inc., Los Alamos, Precious Metals, Inc., Webster Groves, Mo., 1979—; operator Rippling River Ranch, Steelville, Mo.; chmn. Champion Springs Ranch, Annapolis, Mo. Chmn. adv. bd. Midland div. Salvation Army, 1979-80. Mem. Alpha Tau Omega. Conglist. Clubs: Algonquin, Kiwanis. Home: 55 S Gore Ave Webster Groves MO 63119 Office: 300 N Broadway Saint Louis MO 63102

CLEMENT, WILLIAM ALEXANDER, life ins. co. exec.; b. Charleston, S.C., May 6, 1912; s. Arthur John and Sadie (Jones) C.; m. Josephine Dobbs, Dec. 24, 1941; children—Alexine C. (Mrs. Aaron G. Jackson), William Alexander. Wesley Dobbs, Arthur John, Kathleen O., Josephine M. Student, Talladega Coll., 1934. With N.C. Mut. Life Ins. Co., Durham, 1934-78, agy. dir., 1961-62, v.p., 1962-66, v.p. charge field ops., 1966, agy. v.p., 1967-69, sr. v.p., 1969-76, exec. v.p., 1976-78; also dir.; pres. William A. Clement and Assos. Inc., 1978—; vis. prof. N.C. Coll., 1960; mem. Durham bd. Wachovia Bank & Trust Co. Chmn. dist. Boy Scouts Am., v.p. Occoneechee council, 1971—, spl. dep. grand master, 1959-75, dep. grand master, 1975-80, grand master, 1980—; pres. Durham United Fund, 1970; mem. Raleigh-Durham Airport Authority, 1979—; bd. dirs. Durham Devel. Corp., 1980—; trustee Durham County Hosp. Corp. Recipient Silver Beaver award, 1966. Mem. Life Ins. Agy. Mgmt. Assn. (dir. 1970), Durham C. of C. (dir. 1970), Am. Coll. Life Underwriters (dir.), Am. Soc. C.L.U.'s, Sigma Pi Phi, Alpha Phi Alpha. Baptist. Club: Masons (grand master N.C. 1980). Home: 206 Pekoe St Durham NC 27707

CLEMENTE, CARMINE DOMENIC, anatomist; b. Penns Grove, N.J., Apr. 29, 1928; s. Ermanno and Caroline (Friozzi) C.; m. Juliette Vance, Sept. 19, 1968. A.B., U. Pa., 1948, M.S., 1950, Ph.D., 1952; postdoctoral fellow, U. London, 1953-54. Asst. instr. anatomy U. Pa., 1950-52; faculty U. Calif. at Los Angeles, 1952—, prof., 1963—, chmn. dept. anatomy, 1963-73, dir. brain research inst., 1976—; hon. research asso. Univ. Coll., U. London, 1953-54; cons. Sepulveda VA Hosp., NIH; mem. med. adv. panel Bank Am.-Giannini Found.; chmn. sci. adv. com., mem. bd. dirs. Nat. Paraplegia Found. Author: Aggression and Defense: Neurol Mechanisms and Social Patterns, 1967, Physiological Correlates of Dreaming, 1967, Sleep and the Maturing Nervous System, 1972, Anatomy, An Atlas of the Human Body, 1975, 2d edit., 1981; editor: Gray's Anatomy, 1973—, also Exptl. Neurology; asso. editor: Neurol. Research; contbr. articles to sci. jours. Recipient award for merit in sci. Nat. Paraplegia Found., 1973.

Mem. Pavlovian Soc. N.Am. (Ann. award 1968, pres. 1972), Brain Research Inst. (dir. 1976—), Am. Physiol. Soc., Am. Assn. Anatomists (v.p. 1970-72, pres. 1976-77), Am. Acad. Neurology, Am. Acad. Cerebral Palsy, Am. Neurol. Assn., AMA-Assn. Am. Med. Colls. (exec. com. 1978—, disting. service mem. 1982), Council Acad. Socs. (adminstrv. bd. 1973-81, chmn. 1979-80), Assn. Anatomy Chairmen (pres. 1972), Biol. Stain Commn., Inst. Medicine of Nat. Acad. Scis., Internat. Brain Research Orgn., Med. Research Assn. Calif. (dir. 1976—), N.Y. Acad. Sci., Nat. Bd. Med. Examiners, Nat. Acad. Sci. (mem. com. neuropathology, BEAR coms.), Japan Soc. Promotion of Sci. (Research award 1978), Sigma Xi. Democrat. Home: 11737 Bellagio Rd Los Angeles CA 90049

CLEMENTS, B. GILL, business exec.; b. 1941; (married). B.B.A., So. Meth. U., 1963. Loan officer First Nat. Bank Dallas, 1963-68; treas. Sedco Inc., Dallas, 1968-73, pres., 1973—, chief exec. officer, 1977—, also dir. Office: Sedco Inc 1901 N Akard St Dallas TX 75201 *

CLEMENTS, HARVEY WILLIAM, advertising agency executive; b. Oak Park, Ill., Dec. 7, 1921; s. Harvey William and Florence (Ryan) C.; m. Barbara Marie Crafts, Aug. 18, 1951; children: Shannon, Scott. Student journalism, U. Wis., Madison, 1943. Copywriter Buchanan Advt., Chgo., 1946, Dancer-Fitzgerald-Sample, 1946-48; copywriter Foote, Cone & Belding Advt., Inc., Chgo., 1948-53, account supr., 1953-68, sr. v.p., group mgmt. supr., 1968-79, sr. v.p., dir. adminstrn. and human resources, 1979—. Active Glenkirk Assn. Retarded Children, Am. Cancer Soc., United Way/Crusade Mercy. Served to 1st lt. inf. U.S. Army, 1943-46. Decorated Silver Star, Bronze Star with oak leaf cluster, Purple Heart with 2 oak leaf clusters. Mem. U. Wis. Found. (dir.), Chgo. Council Fgn. Affairs, Psi Upsilon, Alpha Delta Sigma. Mem. Glenview Community Ch. Clubs: Dairymen's Country, North Shore Country, Tavern. Office: 401 N Michigan Ave Chicago IL 60611

CLEMENTS, JAMES DAVID, med. cons., physician; b. Pineview, Ga., May 7, 1931; s. Marcus Monroe and Dewey Thelma (Gammage) C.; m. Janet Collier Swan, Aug. 25, 1952; children—Leiliar Ann, David Marcus. B.A., Emory U., 1952; M.D., Med. Coll. Ga., 1956. Intern Temple U., Phila., 1956-57, resident in pediatrics, 1957-59; fellow mental retardation Sch. Medicine, Yale U., 1959-60; med. dir. Gracewood (Ga.) State Sch. Hosp., 1960-62, asst. supt., 1963-64; dir. planning mental retardation Ga. Dept. Pub. Health, Atlanta, 1964-65; dir. Ga. Retardation Center, Atlanta, 1964-79; med. cons. mental retardation Ga. Dept. Human Resources, 1979-81; clin. asst. prof. pediatrics and psychiatry Emory U., Atlanta, 1964—; asso. clin. prof. neurology, asst. clin. prof. pediatrics Med. Coll. Ga., Augusta, 1970—; spl. cons. neurology mental retardation dept. pediatrics Ga. Bapt. Hosp., 1965—; mem. adv. com. program exceptional children Ga. Dept. Edn., 1968-70; mem. adv. bd. Sch. Allied Health Sci., Ga. State U., 1971-76; mem. accreditation council mental retardation council Joint Commn. on Accreditation Hosps., Chgo., 1975-79; del. White House conf. Ga. com. children youth, 1970; mem. Pres.'s Com. on Mental Retardation, 1975-78; chmn. Willowbrook rev. panel Fed. Ct. Eastern Dist. N.Y.; reviewer NSF; cons. Inst. Society, Ethics and Life Scis., Hastings Center; commr. Am. Bar Assn., 1976—. Contbr. articles to profl. jours., anthologies, seminars. Mem. adv. bd. Arbor Acad., DeKalb County (Ga.) Dept. Edn., 1973-75; mem. bd. founders, adv. com. Ashdun Hall, 1965-70; trustee Gatchell Sch., Mental Health Law Project; adv. com. Kennedy Center, Johns Hopkins U. Recipient Leadership award Am. Assn. Mental Deficiency, 1980. Fellow Am. Acad. Pediatrics (cons. head start med. cons. service), Am. Assn. Mental Deficiency (pres. 1974-75), Pan Am. Med. Assn., Am. Geriatrics Soc.; mem. Ga. Pediatric Soc., Nat. Assn. Supts. Pub. Residential Facilities Mentally Retarded, Nat. Assn. Retarded Citizens (legal advocacy adv. com. 1975), Internat. Assn. Sci. Study Mental Deficiency (chmn. local organizing com. 4th internat. congress, mem. council 1976—). Home: 1247 Mt Vernon Rd Atlanta GA 30338 Office: 1247 Mt Vernon Rd Atlanta GA 30338 also Willie M Revie Panel Albemarle Bldg Room 406 325 N Salisbury St Raleigh NC 27611

CLEMENTS, JOHN ALLEN, physiologist; b. Auburn, N.Y., Mar. 16, 1923; s. Harry Vernon and May (Porter) C.; m. Margot Sloan Power, Nov. 19, 1949; children—Christine, Carolyn. M.D., Cornell U., 1947. Research asst. dept. physiology Cornell U. Med. Coll. N.Y., 1947-49; commd. 1st lt. U.S. Army, 1941, advanced through grades to capt., 1951; asst. chief clin. investigation br. (Army Chem. Center), 1951-61; asso. research physiologist U. Calif. at San Francisco, 1961-64, prof. pediatrics, 1964—, mem. staff, 1961—; career investigator Am. Heart Assn., 1964—; mem. group in biophysics and med. physics U. Calif. at Berkeley, 1969—; cons. Surgeon Gen. USPHS, 1964-68, Surgeon Gen. U.S. Army, 1972-79; sci. counselor Nat. Heart and Lung Inst., 1972-75; Bowditch lectr. Am. Physiol. Soc., 1961; 2d ann. lectr. Neonatal Soc., London, 1965; Distinguished lectr. Can. Soc. Clin. Investigation, 1973. Mem. editorial bd.: Jour. Applied Physiology, 1961-65, Am. Jour. Physiology, 1965-72, Physiol. Reviews, 1973—, Jour. Developmental Physiology, 1979—; assoc. editor: Am. Rev. Respiratory Diseases, 1973-79; chmn. publs. policy com.: Am. Thoracic Soc., 1982—. Recipient Dept. Army Research and Devel. Achievement award, 1961; Modern Medicine Distinguished Achievement award, 1973; Howard Taylor Ricketts medal and award U. Chgo., 1975; Mellon award U. Pitts., 1976; Calif. medal Am. Lung Assn. of Calif., 1981; Trudeau medal Am. Lung Assn., 1982; Internat. award Gairdner Found., 1983. Hon. fellow Am. Coll. Chest Physicians; mem. N.Y. Acad. Scis., Western Assn. Physicians, Western Soc. Clin. Research, Perinatal Research Soc. (councillor 1973-75), Nat. Acad. Scis., Am. Lung Assn. (hon., life). Office: U Calif Sch Medicine Cardiovascular Research Inst 3d and Parnassus Ave San Francisco CA 94143

CLEMENTS, NEAL WOODSON, corporation executive, former naval officer; b. Crockett, Tex., Aug. 5, 1926; s. Neal William and Alberta Mildred (Hager) C.; m. Ann Buck, June 11, 1949; children: Neal Woodson, Mark Henley, Lisa Ann. B.S., U.S. Naval Acad., 1949; B.C.E., Rensselaer Poly. Inst., Troy, N.Y., 1951; M.S. in Physics, Naval Postgrad. Sch., 1960; grad., Advanced Mgmt. Program, Harvard Bus. Sch., 1977. Commd. ensign U.S. Navy, 1949, advanced through grades to rear adm., 1976; service in, Vietnam, 1965-66, dir. installations office Sec. of Navy, 1969-72, comdr. naval constrn. bns. U.S. Atlantic Fleet, Davisville, R.I., 1972-74, dep. comdr. facilities acquisition, 1974-76, dep. comdr. for planning, 1976-77, comdr. Pacific div., also comdr. naval constrn. bns. U.S. Pacific Fleet, 1977-81, ret., 1981; sr. v.p. Riedel Internat., Inc., Portland, Oreg., 1981—. Decorated D.S.M., Legion of Merit, Meritorious Service medal, Navy Commendation medal. Fellow Soc. Am. Mil. Engrs.; mem. Sci. Research Soc. Am., Am. Pub. Works Assn., Sigma Xi, Tau Beta Pi, Chi Epsilon. Home: 2644 Marland Wood Circle Temple TX 76501 Office: Riedel Internat Inc Portland OR 97208 *I believe in establishing goals which are beyond what one might expect to achieve - then making the effort not only to achieve them - but to exceed them.*

CLEMENTS, OMAR RANDOLPH, chemicals and plastics executive; b. Ida, La., Aug. 14, 1925; s. Quilla Zedoic and Josephine LaVada (Slay) C.; m. Lovenia Holder, Dec. 22, 1950; 1 son, Terence Christopher. B.S. in Ch. E., La. Tech. U., 1950. Registered profl. engr., Tex. Plant engr. S.W. Gas Producing Co., Dubach, La., 1950-51; field service engr. Western Co., Midland, Tex., 1951-52, Henderson Engring. Co., Shreveport, La., 1952-53; sr. process engr. El Paso Natural Gas Co., Tex., 1953-54, asst. chief process engr., 1954-56, chief process engr., 1956-60; ops. supr. El Paso Products Co., Odessa, Tex., 1960-64, ops., maintenance mgr., 1965-66, complex mgr., 1966-67, gen. mgr., mfg., 1967-69, asst. v.p., 1969-72, v.p., 1972-77, sr. v.p., 1979-82, pres., 1982—. Served with AUS, 1943-45. Mem. Tex. Mfg. Assn. (dir., regional chmn. 1974-76, exec. com. 1976-78), W. Tex. C. of C. (dir., v.p. 1970-76), Odessa C. of C. (dir. 1970-76, 83—), Tex. Assn. Bus. (dir. 1982—). Republican. Presbyterian. Clubs: Odessa Country, Odessa Petroleum, Santa Teresa Country, Mission Hills Country. Home: 2927 Kirkwood St Odessa TX 79762 Office: El Paso Chem Co PO Box 3986 Odessa TX 79760

CLEMENTS, ROBERT, ins. brokerage exec.; b. Chgo., Sept. 7, 1932; s. John and Mildred L. (Chapman) C.; m. Marilyn Trexler, Dec. 27, 1955; children—Paula J., John, Jeffrey, Ben T. B.A., Dartmouth Coll., 1954. Underwriter Royal Ins. Co., N.Y.C., 1956-59; sr. v.p. Marsh & McLennan, Ltd., Toronto, Ont., Can., 1959-75; pres., chief exec. officer Marsh & McLennan Inc., N.Y.C., 1975—, also dir.; dir. various Marsh & McLennan cos., Lynwood Mgmt. Ltd. Served with U.S. Army, 1954-56. Mem. Nat. Assn. Ins. Brokers, Am. Risk and Ins. Assn., Ins. Inst. Can. Democrat. Office: 1221 Ave of Americas New York NY 10020

CLEMENTS, ROBERT JOHN, educator; b. Cleve., Oct. 23, 1912; s. Earl W. and Mildred (Warner) C.; m. Helen Louise Card, Sept. 3, 1940 (div.); children—Caird Robert, Cleveland Warner; m. Lorna Levant, July 19, 1975; 1 dau., Erin June. A.B., Oberlin Coll., 1934; Ph.D., U. Chgo., 1939; postgrad., U. Bordeaux, U. Florence, Harvard; Litt. D., U. Rome, Italy, 1961; H.H.D., Philathea Coll., Can., 1966. Instr. U. Chgo., 1937-39, U. Ill., 1939-40; instr., asst. prof. Harvard, 1940-47; prof., chmn. dept. Romance langs., lits. Pa. State U., 1947-54; prof. Romance langs. and lits. Grad. Sch., N.Y. U., 1954-56, also chmn. comparative lit. dept., grad. sch., 1956—; lectr. U. Madrid, 1953; univ. asso. Columbia, 1955—; Fulbright Research scholar, Rome, 1960-61; Mellon prof. lit. U. Pitts., 1968; screening com. for langs. and lit. Fulbright office, Washington, 1965-68; adv. modern lang. editor Ginn & Co., Boston, 1944-57; cons. Juilliard Sch., 1971—; adv. bd. Nat. Endowment Humanities, 1978. Author: Critical Theory and Practice of the Pléiade, 1942 (rev. as Critical Theory of Pléiade 1968), (co-author) Pennsylvania Curriculum Revision for Modern Languages, 1952, Platonism in French Renaissance Poetry, 1957, The Peregrine Muse; Studies in Renaissance Comparative Literature, 1959, rev., 1968, Picta Poesis, Literary and Humanistic Theory in Renaissance Emblem Books, 1960, Michelangelo's Theory of Art, 1960, Michelangelo, A Self-Portrait, 1962 (rev. as Michelangelo, Self Portrait 1968), Michelangelo Scultore, 1964, The Poetry of Michelangelo, 1964, Renaissance Letters, 1976, Anatomy of the Novella, 1977, Comparative Literature as Academic Discipline, 1978; Corr. editor: Boletín de Filología Espanola, Madrid, Romantisches Jahrbuch, Hamburg; asso. editor: Gotham Library, 1962—; co-editor: Renaissance Letters, 1976; editorial bd.: Modern Internat. Drama, 1967—; Contbr. chpts. to books and bibliographies, many articles, revs. to profl. periodicals, newspapers.; Columnist: Literary Scene in Europe, Saturday Rev, 1964-71. Co-organizer Civil Affairs Tng. Program, Harvard, 1940-44. Decorated knight cavaliere ufficiale, Italy). Mem. Phi Beta Kappa Assos. (nat. bd. 1954-62), Modern Lang. Assn. Am. (chmn. French, Italian, Portuguese, Romance sects.), Am. Council Learned Socs. (mem. editorial bd., Renaissance com. 1944—), Société des Amis du Louvre, Dante Alighieri Soc., Accademia dell' Arcadia Rome, Mazzini Soc., Mediaeval Acad. Am. (sec. pub. 1940-47), Internat. Assn. for Study of Italian Lang. and Lit. (v.p. 1962-73, co-pres. 1973-79), Am. Comparative Lit. Assn. (adv. bd. 1965-68, 77-80), Am. Assn. Tchrs. Italian (pres. 1960-62), Phi Beta Kappa. Home: 8 E 8th St New York NY 10003 also Box 826 Mahopac NY 10541

CLEMENTS, THOMAS, consulting geologist; b. Chgo., June 7, 1898; s. George Henry and Caroline Barbara (Nathan) C.; m. Lydia Pryce Brooks, Oct. 14, 1922; 1 dau., Anne. E.M., Tex. Sch. Mines, 1922; M.S., Calif. Inst. Tech., 1929, Ph.D., 1932. Metallurgist Compañia Minera de Peñoles, S.A., Torreón, Mexico, 1922-25; engr. Security Title Ins. & Guarantee Co., Los Angeles, 1925-28; teaching fellow Calif. Inst. Tech., 1928-29; teaching staff U. So. Calif., Los Angeles, 1929-64, Hancock prof. geology, 1945-64, head dept., 1933-63; chmn. com. research Hancock Found., 1952-60; curator of mineralogy and petrology Los Angeles County Mus., 1955-60; condr. research in Mexico on source of ancient Mexican jade, 1957—; geologist Los Angeles County Mus. Expdn. to Lake Chapala, Jalisco, Mexico, 1956, Nat. Geog. Soc. archeol. site, Calico, Calif., 1964—; cons. mining engr., geologist, 1930—; cons. geologist Dept. Petroleum, Ministerio de la Economia Nacional, Bogotá, Colombia, 1939; mem. geol. hazards com., City Los Angeles, 1957-63; mem. grading cons. bd. Bldg. and Safety Commn., 1963-73; pres. Qualifications Bd. Engring. Geologists, 1960-70; mem. Adv. Com. on Engring. Geology, 1979—. Author: Geological Story of Death Valley, 1954, 11th edit., 1982; contbr. tech. articles to sci. jours. Served with USN, 1917-19. Fellow Geol. Soc. Am., So. Calif. Acad. Scis.; mem. Sociedad Geológica Mexicana, Death Valley Fortyniners (dir., past pres. 1955), Los Angeles Mineral. Soc. (founding, 1st pres. 1932), Soc. Econ. Geologists, Am. Inst. Mining and Metall. Engrs., Am. Assn. Petroleum Geologists, Assn. Engring. Geologists, Branner Geol. Club (hon. life, past pres.), Phi Kappa Phi, Acacia. Home: 2171 Vista del Mar Ave Hollywood CA 90068 Office: 1710 N La Brea Ave Los Angeles CA 90046 *Such success as I have achieved has come as the result of: (1) an abiding faith in God and His son Jesus Christ; (2) an attempt to treat my fellowman and woman as I should like to be treated; and (3) the ever-present help and encouragement of my wife, Lydia. We grew up in a time of respect for law and order and for moral decency. The ideals instilled into us by our parents and teachers, whom we respected, have remained with us throughout our lives.*

CLEMENTS, VASSAR CARLTON, fiddle player; b. Kinard, Fla., Apr. 25, 1928; s. Preston and Mary E. (McQuage) C.; m. Millie Gandy, Nov. 30, 1965. Student pub. schs., Kissimmee, Fla. Worked at various odd jobs. Appeared with, Grand Ole Opry, Nashville, 1949; mem., Monroe's Bluegrass Boys, 1950; recorded: Will The Circle Be Unbroken with, Nitty Gritty Dirt Band, Nashville, 1971; performed with, Dickie Betts, Grateful Dead, Monkees, Hot Tuna, Elvin Bishop, Papa John Creach and Marshall Tucker Band, others, 1971-75; performed with own group, Vassar Clements Band, 1975—. Served with U.S. Army, 1952-54

CLEMENTS, WILLIAM PERRY, JR., former governor of Texas, corporate executive; b. Dallas, Apr. 13, 1917; s. William Perry and Evelyn (Cammack) C.; m. Rita Crocker, Mar. 8, 1975; children by previous marriage: B. Gill, Nancy Seay. Student, So. Meth. U., D.H.L., 1974. Chmn. bd., chief exec. officer, founder SEDCO, Inc., Dallas, 1947-73, 77; chmn. bd. SEDCO Inc., Dallas, 1983—; dep. sec. of Def. U.S. Dept. Def., Washington, 1973-77; gov., State of Tex., 1979-83. Bd. trustees, bd. govs. So. Meth. U.; mem. nat. exec. bd. Boy Scouts Am. Office: 190 N Akard St Dallas TX 75201

CLEMENTS, WOODROW WILSON, beverage company executive; b. Tuscaloosa, Ala., July 30, 1914; s. William Houston and Martha (Christian) C.; m. Eloise Davis, Mar. 20, 1937; 1 son, Wayne Wilson.; m. Virginia Thomas, 1982. Student, Howard Coll., Birmingham, Ala., 1932-33, U. Ala., 1933-35; L.H.D. (hon.), U. Ala., 1974. Began as route salesman advancing to sales mgr. Dr Pepper Bottling Co., Tuscaloosa, 1935-42; with Dr Pepper Co., 1942—, successively dist. mgr., sales promotion mgr., asst. mgr. bottler service, gen. sales mgr., 1942-49, 49-51, v.p., gen. sales mgr., 1951-58, v.p. mktg., 1958-67, exec. v.p., dir., 1967-68, pres., 1969-80, chief exec. officer, 1970—, chmn., 1974—; chmn. Dr. Pepper Bottling Co. and Dr. Pepper Bottling Co. of Calif., Dallas; chmn., pres. Dr Pepper Bottling Co., Waco, San Antonio, Corpus Christi and Houston, Tex., SW Dr Pepper Beverage Sales Co.; dir. Dr. Pepper Japan Ltd., Tokyo, Dr. Pepper Bottling Co. of So. Calif., First Internat. Bancshares, Inc., First Nat. Bank Dallas. Past dir. Council Opportunities Selling; exec. council Internat. and Comparative Law Center; mem. Cotton Bowl Council; gen. chmn. Dallas Salute to Vietnam Vets., 1973; devel. council Tex. Sports Hall of Fame; adv. council Nat. Alliance Businessmen, Council Religious Heritage Am., Salvation Army; mem. alumni council Pres.'s Cabinet U. Ala.; Bd. visitors U. Ala. Coll. Commerce and Bus. Adminstrn.; bd. dirs. North Tex. Commn., Internat. Trade Conf. S.W. So. Meth. U., State Fair of Tex., Dallas Council World Affairs, Dallas Civic Opera, Dallas Citizens' Council, Grocery Mfrs. AM., Boy Scouts Am., Better Bus. Bur. Met. Dallas; trustee Council on Opportunities in Selling; Inc.; chmn. bd. govs. Jr. Achievement Dallas. Recipient Mktg. Man of Decade award Am. Mktg. Assn., 1970, Golden Plate award Am. Acad. Achievement, 1970, George Washington certificate Freedoms Found. at Valley Forge, 1975, Entrepreneur of Yr. award So. Meth. U. Sch. Bus., 1975, Beverage Industry Man of Yr. award Beverage Industry publ., 1976, Chief Exec. Officer of Yr. in Beverage Industry award Fin. World, 1977, Horatio Alger award, 1980, Disting. Am. award Nat. Football Hall of Fame, 1980; named Beverage World Hall of Fame, 1982. Mem. Sales and Marketing Execs. Internat. (regional v.p., pres. 1968-69, chmn. bd. 1969-70, Distinguished Salesman award 1972), Dallas Personnel Assn. (dir.), S.W. Sales Execs. Council (pres., named Distinguished Sales Exec. 1969), Dallas Sales Exec. Club (pres. 1957), Dllas C. of C. (dir.). Baptist. Clubs: Rotarian., Dallas Country., Chaparral, City, Tower. Office: PO Box 225086 Dallas TX 75265

CLEMETSON, CHARLES ALAN BLAKE, physician; b. Canterbury, Eng., Oct. 31, 1923; came to U.S., 1961, naturalized, 1972; s. Charles Harold and Gwendoline Maude Winefred (Blake) C.; m. Helen Cowan Forster, Mar. 27, 1947; children: Claudia, Charles, David, Andrew. B.M., B.Ch., Oxford (Eng.) U., 1948. Research asst. Obstetric Hosp., Univ. Coll. Hosp., London, 1950-52; Nichols research fellow Royal Soc. Medicine, 1951-52; house surgeon obstetrics W. Middlesex Hosp., 1952-53; resident med. officer obstetrics Queen Charlotte's Hosp., 1953; house surgeon gynecology Hammersmith Hosp., 1953-54; obstetric and gynecol. registrar Lake Hosp., Ashton-under-Lyne, Lancashire, Eng., 1954-56; lectr. obstetrics and gynecology Univ. Coll. Hosp., London, 1956-58; asst. prof. obstetrics and gynecology Univ. Hosp., Saskatoon, Sask., Can., 1958-61, U. Calif., San Francisco, 1961-67; dir. dept. obstetrics and gynecology Methodist Hosp., Bklyn., 1967-81; prof. obstetrics and gynecology Tulane U., Huey P. Long Meml. Hosp., Pineville, La., 1981—; asso. prof. Downstate Med. Center, State U. N.Y., Bklyn., 1967-72, prof., 1972—; mem. obstetric adv. com. N.Y.C. Dept. Health, 1968; cons. in field; mem. med. adv. com. Planned Parenthood N.Y.C., Inc., 1971; mem. physicians rev. com. Blue Cross-Blue Shield N.Y.C., 1975; lectr. obstetrics and gynecology London U., 1956-58; lectr. maternal health U. Calif., Berkeley, 1964-65. Contbr. articles to med. jours. Served with RAF, 1948-50. Recipient Research Career Devel. award NIH, 1965-67. Fellow Am. Coll. Nutrition, Am., Royal colls. obstetricians and gynecologists, Royal Coll. Physicians and Surgeons Can.; mem. Brit. Med. Assn., N.Y. Acad. Scis., N.Y. Obstet. Soc., Bklyn. Gynecol. Soc. (pres. 1977-78), Med. Soc. Kings County. Office: Huey P Long Mem Hosp Pineville LA 71360 *Certainty of knowledge is the antithesis of progress.*

CLEMINSHAW, FRANK FOSTER, electronic company executive; b. Bklyn., July 21, 1911; s. Frank V. and Virginia (Foster) C.; m. Gertrude Niclas, Feb. 21, 1934 (dec.); children: Lenore (Mrs. Walter J. Lekki), Theresa (Mrs. John McAuliffe), Catherine; m. Marguerite Rogge, Feb. 1, 1979. Ed., St. Thomas Coll., 1928-30, Columbia, 1931-36; grad., Advanced Mgmt. Program Harvard, 1957. Vice pres., gen. mgr. U. R.I. Bond Tabulating Corp., N.Y.C., 1938-40; mgr. data processing, cost accounting Am. Car & Foundry Co., N.Y.C., 1940-48, dir. methods, 1948-52, asst. comptroller, 1952-54, comptroller, 1954-59; v.p., gen. mgr. Diebold Assos., N.Y.C., 1959-60; cons. mgmt. controls Internat. Paper Co., N.Y.C., 1960-61; v.p., treas. Gen. Instrument Corp., Clifton, N.J., 1961—; officer, dir. various U.S. and fgn. cos. Author: International Management Controls. Mem. Fin. Execs. Inst., Harvard Advanced Mgmt. Assn. Episcopalian. Clubs: Harvard (N.Y.C.); St. George Soc. Home: 4 Scotchwood Glen Scotch Plains NJ 07076 Office: Gen Instrument Corp 225 Allwood Rd Clifton NJ 07012

CLEMMONS, JIMMIE RUSSELL, psychiatrist; b. Spur, Tex., Nov. 24, 1955; s. Jeff Dave and Rilla Ruth (Brashers) Clemons; m. Mary Ann Strobel, June 5, 1960 (div. 1975); children: Anne, David; m. Melodie Ann Turner, Dec. 23, 1977. Assoc.Sci., Arlington State Jr. Coll., 1956; student, U. Tex., 1957; M.D., U. Tex. Med. Br., Galveston, 1961. Diplomate: Am. Bd. Psychiatry and Neurology. Practice medicine specializing in psychiatry, Austin, Tex., 1968-75; acting dir. mental health Travis County Mental Health Mental Retardation Ctr., Austin, 1968; teaching cons. residency program Austin State Hosp., 1969-75; psychiat. cons. Theol. Sem. of S.W. Austin, 1973-75; unit chief Terrell State Hosp., Tex., 1977, clin. cir., 1977-78, supt., 1981—; dep. commr. mental health State of Tex., Austin, 1978-81; assoc. prof. clin. psychiatry U. Tex. Health Sci. Ctr., Dallas, 1981—. Mem. Knights of Symphony, Austin, 1969-75, Heritage Soc., Friends of Library, Terrell, 1982—. Served to capt. M.C. AUS, 1966-68; Vietnam. Mem. AMA (Physicians Recognition award 1981), Am. Psychiat. Assn. (Self Assessment Skills award 1980), Tex. Med. Assn., Tex. Psychiat. Soc., Titus Harris Psychiat. Soc., Tex. Neuropsychiat. Assn. (pres. 1970-71), Am. Assn. Psychiat. Adminstrs. Club: Physicians (Austin) (pres. 1982—). Office: Terrell State Hosp PO Box 70 Terrell TX 75160 *

CLEMON, U. W., federal judge; b. Birmingham, Ala., Apr. 9, 1943; m. Barbara Lang; children: Herman Issac, Addine Michele. Bar: Ala. Partner firm Adams and Clemon and predecessor, Birmingham, 1969-80; fed. judge U.S. Dist. Ct., No. Dist. Ala., Birmingham, 1980—. Mem. Ala. Senate, 1974-80. Recipient Law and Justice award SCLC, 1980. Mem. Am. Bar Assn. (exec. council 1976-79), Alpha Phi Alpha. Office: 305 Fed Courthouse Birmingham AL 35203

CLEMONS, WALTER, JR., journalist; b. Houston, Nov. 14, 1929; s. Walter C. and Margaret (Ewing) C. A.B., Princeton U., 1951; M.A. (Rhodes scholar), Magdalen Coll., Oxford U., 1953. Free lance writer, 1955-65; editor McGraw-Hill Book Co., N.Y.C., 1966-68, New York Times Book Rev., 1968-71; editor, book critic Newsweek, N.Y.C., 1971-77, sr. writer, 1978-82; editor, writer Vanity Fair mag., N.Y.C., 1982—; Writer-in-residence Alley Theater, Houston, Ford Found. Program for Poets and Fiction Writers, 1963-64; dir. Nat. Book Critics Circle, 1978-83; Hodder fellow Princeton, 1959-60. Author: The Poison Tree and Other Stories, 1959. Recipient Prix de Rome Am. Acad. in Rome, 1960-62. Mem. Century Assn., The Players. Home: 21-12 45th Ave Long Island City NY 11101 Office: Vanity Fair 350 Madison Ave New York NY 10017

CLENDENIN, JOHN L., telephone company executive; b. El Paso, Tex., May 8, 1934; s. Thomas Pipes and Maybelle Baumann C.; m. Margaret Ann Matthews, Aug. 30, 1954; children: Elizabeth Ann, Linda Susan, Mary Kathryn, Thomas Edward. B.A., Northwestern U., 1955. With Ill. Bell Telephone Co., 1955-78, v.p., 1975-78; v.p. ops. Pacific Northwest Bell, Seattle, 1978-79; v.p. AT&T, 1979-81; pres. So. Bell Tel. & Tel. Co., Atlanta, 1981-82, chmn. bd., 1982-84, BellSouth Corp., 1984—; dir. 1st Atlanta Corp., 1st Nat. Bank Atlanta., Nat. Service Industries Inc., Equifax Inc., Capital Holding Corp., Louisville. Pres.-elect Atlanta council Boy Scouts Am.; v.p. United Way Met. Atlanta; trustee Atlanta Arts Alliance; Chmn. Atlanta Pvt. Industry Council. Served with USAF, 1956-59. Mem. Atlanta C. of C. (pres.-elect). Presbyterian. Clubs: Commerce (dir.), Cherokee Town and Country (Atlanta)). Office: BellSouth 675 W Peachtree St NE Atlanta GA 30375

CLENDENNING, WILLIAM EDMUND, dermatologist; b. Waynesburg, Pa., June 23, 1931; s. William Burdette and Anna Marie (Schellhase) C.; m. Elizabeth Woodbury Bennett, Sept. 6, 1958; children—William Alan, Joy Marie, Bruce Bennett, Sarah Elizabeth. B.S., Allegheny Coll., Meadville, Pa., 1952; M.D., Jefferson Med. Coll., Phila., 1956. Diplomate: Am. Bd. Dermatology, Am. Bd. Dermatopathology. Intern St. Luke's Hosp., Cleve., 1956-57; resident in dermatology Univ. Hosps. of Cleve., 1957-60; sr. investigator dermatology br. Nat. Cancer Inst., USPHS, 1961-63; asst. prof. dermatology Western Res. U. Med. Sch., 1963-67; prof. clin. dermatology Dartmouth Coll. Med.; also mem. staff Mary Hitchcock Meml. Hosp., Hitchcock Clinic, 1967—; mem. Nat. Mycosis Fungoides Coop. Group, N.Am. Contact Dermatitis Group. Author articles in field, chpts. in books. Nat. Cancer Inst. grantee, 1963-67. Mem. Am. Acad. Dermatology, Soc. Investigative Dermatology, Am. Dermatol. Assn., Am. Soc. Dermatopathology, New Eng. Dermatol. Soc., Am. Fedn. Clin. Research, N.H. Med. Assn., AMA. Home: 7 Pleasant St Hanover NH 03755 Office: 2 Maynard St Hanover NH 03755

CLENDINEN, JAMES AUGUSTUS, newspaper editor; b. Eufaula, Ala., Dec. 1, 1910; s. Thomas A. and Katherine M. (Powell) C.; m. Barbara Harrison, May 22, 1943; children: James Dudley, Melissa Louise. Student, U. Fla., 1929-30. Reporter, then mng. editor Clearwater (Fla.) Evening Sun, 1930-35; mem. staff Tampa (Fla.) Tribune, 1935-42, 46—, editor, 1958—, chmn. editorial bd., 1974—; pres. Nat. Conf. Editorial Writers, 1966; mem. Pulitzer Prize Jury, 1967, 68. Mem. Gov.'s Commn. on Edn., 1971-73; mem. Fla. Jud. Commn., 1975—. Served with USAAF, 1942-45. Recipient 1st prize for editorial writing Fla. Daily Newspaper Assn., 1953, 57, 58, 60, 64, 66, 68, 70, 71, 76, 78, 83; traveling fellow to study conditions in Spain So. Assn. Nieman Fellows, 1953; Freedoms Found. award for editorial writing, 1961, 62; Fla. Edn. Assn. award, 1963; Nat. Headliners Club award, 1964; Pub. Service award Fla. Bar, 1965; Distinguished Service award U. Fla. Coll. Journalism, 1974; Pub. Service award Am. Bar Assn., 1977, Fla. Legislature, 1965. Mem. Am. Soc. Newspaper Editors (mem. del. to Red China 1972, dir.), Fla. Soc. Editors (founder, 1st pres. 1955), Sigma Delta Chi (award editorial writing 1962), Phi Kappa Tau. Episcopalian. Clubs: Tampa Yacht and Country, Univ., Exchange (Tampa); Gasparilla Krewe. Home: 3000 Schiller Ave Tampa FL 33629 Office: Tampa Tribune 202 S Parker St Tampa FL 33606

CLEPPER, HENRY EDWARD, forester; b. Columbia, Pa., Mar. 21, 1901; s. Martin Neil and Charlotte (Keech) C.; m. Clorinda McFerren, Aug. 14, 1921 (dec.); children—Charlotte Mae, Albert Lynn. B.Forestry, Pa. State Forest Acad. (Pa. State U.), 1921. Forester Pa. Dept. Forests and Waters, 1921-36; forest service U.S. Dept. Agr., 1936-37; mng. editor jour. Forestry, 1937-66; exec. sec. Soc. Am. Foresters, 1937-66; dir. Am. forestry history project Forest History Soc., Inc., 1966-69; tech. cons. (lumber) WPB, 1942-44; U.S. del. World Forestry Congress, 1960, 66. Author: (with A.B. Meyer) World of the Forest, 1965, Origins of American Conservation, 1966; Author, editor: American Forestry; Six Decades of Growth, 1960, Careers in Conservation, 1963, 79, Leaders of American Conservation, 1971, Professional Forestry in the United States, 1971, Crusade for Conservation, 1975, (with C.E. Randall) Famous and Historic Trees, 1976, (with R.H. Stroud) Marine Recreational Fisheries, 1976-80, Predator-Prey Systems in Fisheries Management, 1979. Recipient Gifford Pinchot medal, 1957, John Aston Warder medal, 1977. Fellow Soc. Am. Foresters; hon. mem. Am. Forestry Assn., Can. Inst. Forestry, Natural Resources Council Am., Soil Conservation Soc. Am. Club: Cosmos (Washington). Home: 4545 Connecticut Ave NW Apt 514 Washington DC 20008 Office: American Forestry Assn 1319 18th St NW Washington DC 20036

CLERGUE, LUCIEN GEORGES, photographer; b. Arles, Frances, Aug. 14, 1934; s. Etienne and Jeanne (Grangeon) C.; m. Yolande Wartel, Jan. 10, 1963; children: Anne, Olivia. Dr. es Letters in Photography, U. Provence, 1979. Tchr. workshops New Sch., N.Y.C., other U.S. univs. and colls. Freelance photographer, 1959—; artistic dir., Arles Festival, 1971-75; artistic adv., Manitas de Plata, 1965; founder, Rencontres Internationales de la Photographie, Arles, 1970; one-man exhbns. include, Kunstgewerbe Mus., Zurich, 1958, 63, Mus. Modern Art, N.Y.C., 1961—, Musee Arts Decoratifs, Paris, 1962—, Moderna Museet, Stockholm, 1969—, Art Inst. Chgo., 1970—, Kunsthalla, Düsseldorf, Ger., Gallery Witkin, N.Y.C., 1972-79, Bruxelles Musee d'Ixelles, 1974—, Israel Mus., Jerusalem, Centre Pompidou, Paris, 1980—, Nude Workshop, N.Y., 1982, works rep. books, movies. Decorated chevalier Nat. Order Merit, 1980; recipient Louis Lumiere prize, 1966. Mem. Assn. Nat. Photographers Createurs, Parc Regional Camargue, Ste. des Amis Jean Cocteau, Rencontres Internat. de la Photographie Arles. Roman Catholic. Address: 17 A Briand Arles Cedex 13632 France

CLEVELAND, JAMES, gospel singer, composer, minister; b. Chgo., Dec. 5, 1931. D. (hon. doctorate), Temple Bible Coll. Minister, Los Angeles, 1961—; pastor New Greater Harvest Baptist Ch., Los Angeles; founder, pastor Cornerstone Instnl. Baptist Ch., Los Angeles; founder Gospel Music Workshop of Am., 1968; organizer So. Calif. Community Choir, 1969, Gospel Girls, 1969. Singer: with various groups The Caravans, Gospelaires, Roberta Martin Singers, Mahalia Jackson, Meditation Singers of Detroit; Gospel Chimes; singer, former of group: Cleveland Singers; singer: James Cleveland Singers; actor: film Save The Children, 1973; composer: hundreds of gospel songs including Grace is Sufficient, God Specializes, He's Using Me, The Man, Jesus; recorded: over 70 albums including All You Need, At The Cross, Bread of Heaven, Christ Is The Answer, Down Memory Lane, Free At Last, Give Me My Flowers, Peace Be Still, I'll Do His Will, Lord, Do It, I Stood on the Banks, Lord Help Me, Jesus Is The Best Thing. Recipient Grammy award, numerous gold albums, Image award NAACP, 1976, award Nat. Assn. Negro Musicians, 1975, numerous musical awards. Office: Co Ed Smith Gospel Artists Assn PO Box 4632 Detroit MI 48243

CLEVELAND, JAMES COLGATE, congressman; b. June 13, 1920; s. Mather and Susan (Colgate) C.; m. Hilary Paterson, Dec. 9, 1950; children—Cotton Mather, James Colby, David Paterson, Lincoln Mather, Susan Sclater. Student, Deerfield Acad., 1933-37; B.A. magna cum laude, Colgate U., 1941; LL.B., Yale, 1948. Bar: N.H. bar 1948. Practice law, Concord, New London, 1949—; sr. partner Cleveland, Waters & Bass; now of counsel; mem. 88th-96th congresses from 2d N.H. dist.; Organizer, incorporator, officer, dir. New London Trust Co.; Rep. 7th Dist. to N.H. Senate, 1950-62. Co-author: We Propose A Modern Congress, 1966. Served with AUS, World War II, Korean War. Decorated Bronze Star for Valor. Mem. Am. Legion, VFW, Phi Beta Kappa. Home: New London NH 03257 Office: Cleveland Waters & Bass New London NH 03257

CLEVELAND, (JAMES) HARLAN, political scientist, public official; b. N.Y.C., Jan 19, 1918; s. Stanley Matthews and Marian Phelps (Van Buren) C.; m. Lois W. Burton, July 12, 1941; children: Carol Zoe (Mrs. Palmer), Anne Moore (Mrs. Kalicki), Alan Thorburn. Grad. cum laude, Phillips Acad., Andover, Mass., 1934; A.B. with high honors in politics, Princeton U., 1938; Rhodes scholar, Oxford U., 1938-39, Intern Nat. Inst. Pub. Affairs, 1939-40; writer information div. Farm Security Adminstrn., Washington, 1940-42; ofcl. Bd. Econ. Warfare and its successor, Fgn. Econ. Adminstrn., Washington, 1942-44; exec. dir. econ. sect. Allied Control Commn., Rome, Italy, 1944-45; mem. U.S. delegation 3d session UNRRA Council, London, 1945; acting v.p. in charge econ. sect. Allied Commn., Rome, 1945-46; dept. chief of mission UNRRA Italian Mission, Rome, 1946-47, dir. China office, Shanghai, 1947-48; dir. China program ECA, Washington, 1948-49, dept. asst. adminstr., 1949-51; asst. dir. for Europe Mut. Security Agy., 1952-53; exec. editor Reporter, N.Y.C., 1953-56, pub., 1955-56; prof. polit. sci., dean Maxwell grad. sch. citizenship and pub. affairs Syracuse U., 1956-61; chmn. Citizens for Kennedy, Central N.Y., 1960; asst. sec. for internat. orgn. affairs Dept. State, 1961-65; chmn. Cabinet Com. on Internat. Cooperation Yr., 1965; U.S. ambassador, rep. to NATO, 1965-69; prof. polit. sci., pres. U. Hawaii, Honolulu, 1969-74; dir. program in internat. affairs Aspen Inst. Humanistic Studies, Princeton, N.J., 1974-80; chmn. U.S. Weather Modification Adv. Bd., 1977-78; disting. vis. Tom Slick prof. world peace LBJ Sch. Public Affairs, U. Tex., Austin, 1979; prof. public affairs, dir. Hubert H. Humphrey Inst. Public Affairs, U. Minn., Mpls., 1980—; Vice chmn. Atlantic Council U.S., Global Perspectives in Edn.; bd. dirs. Inst. for Future; trustee Internat. Council Ednl. Devel., Univ. Corp. Atmospheric Research; mem. nat. adv. council Expt. in Internat. Living. Author: The Obligations of Power, 1966, NATO: The Transatlantic Bargain, 1970, The Future Executive, 1972 (Louis Brownlow award 1975), China Diary, 1976, The Third Try at World Order, 1977, (co-author) The Overseas Americans, 1960, Humangrowth, 1978; Editor: The Promise of World Tensions, 1961, The Management of Sustainable Growth, 1980, Energy Futures of Developing Countries, 1980; Co-editor: The Art of Overseasmanship, 1957, The Ethic of Power, 1962, Ethics and Bigness, 1962, Bioresources for Development, 1980. Decorated U.S. Medal of Freedom, 1946; grand knight officer Order of Crown of Italy, Italian govt., 1946; gold star Order Brilliant Star, China, 1948; recipient Woodrow Wilson award Princeton, 1968, Prix de Talloires, 1981. Mem. Am. Polit. Sci. Assn., Am. Soc. for Pub. Adminstrn. (pres. 1970-71), Council on Fgn. Relations, Phi Beta Kappa. Clubs: Century, Princeton (N.Y.C.); Internat. (Washington); Waikiki Yacht (Honolulu). Home: 5720 Camelback Dr Edina MN 55436 Office: U Minn 267 19th Ave S Minneapolis MN 55455 *If you try too carefully to plan your life, the danger is that you will succeed—succeed in narrowing your options, closing off avenues of adventure that cannot now be imagined, perhaps because they are not yet technologically possible. When a student asks me for career advice, I can only suggest that he or she opt for the most exciting "next step" without worrying where it will lead, and then work hard on the job in hand, not pine for the one in the bush. When your job no longer demands of you more than you have, go and do something else. Always take by preference the job you don't know how to do. If you build into your life enough variety of experience, you will be training for leadership in the role I have called The Public Executive.*

CLEVENGER, SARAH, botanist; b. Indpls., Dec. 19, 1926; d. Cyrus Raymond and Mary Beth (Stevens) C. A.B., Miami U., 1947; Ph.D., Ind. U., 1957. Tchr. Sci. Radford Sch., El Paso, Tex., 1949-51, Hillsdale Sch., Cin., 1951-52; asst. prof. Berea (Ky.) Coll., 1957-59, 61-63, Wittenberg U., Springfield, Ohio, 1959-60, Eastern Ill. U., 1960-61, Ind. State U., Terre Haute, 1963-66, asso. prof., 1966-78, prof., 1978—. Mem. AAAS, Am. Inst. Biol. Sci., Am. Soc. Plant Physiologists, Am. Soc. Plant Taxonomists, Bot. Soc. Am., Internat. Assn. Plant Taxonomy, Phytochem. Soc. N.Am. (past sec.), World Future Soc. Home: 717 S Henderson St Bloomington IN 47401 Office: Dept Life Sciences Indiana State Univ Terre Haute IN 47809

CLEVER, LINDA HAWES, physician; b. Seattle; d. Nathan Harrison and Evelyn Lorraine (Johnson) Hawes; m. James Alexander Clever, Aug. 20, 1960; 1 dau., Sarah Lou. A.B. with distinction, Stanford U., 1962, M.D., 1965. Diplomate: Am. Bd. Internal Medicine. Intern Stanford U. Hosp., Palo Alto, Calif., 1965-66, resident, 1966-67, fellow in infectious disease, 1967-68; fellow in community medicine U. Calif., San Francisco, 1968-69, resident, 1969-70; med. dir. Sister Mary Philippa Diagnostic and Treatment Center, St. Mary's Hosp., San Francisco, 1970-77; chmn. dept. occupational health Presbyn. Hosp. of Pacific Med. Center, San Francisco, 1977—; assoc. clin. prof. medicine U. Calif. Med. Sch., San Francisco; NIH research fellow Stanford U. Sch. Medicine, 1967-68; mem. San Francisco Comprehensive Health Planning Council, 1971-76, dir., 1974-76; mem. Calif.-OSHA Adv. Com. on Hazard Evaluation System and Info. Service, 1979—, Calif. Statewide Profl. Standards Rev. Council, 1977-81, San Francisco Regional Commn. on White House Fellows, 1978-81, 83, chmn., 1979-81. Contbr. articles to profl. jours. Trustee Stanford U., 1972-76, 81—, Marin Country Day Sch., 1978—; bd. dirs. Sta. KQED, 1976-83, chmn., 1979-81; bd. dirs. Independent Sector, 1980—. Fellow A.C.P.; mem. Inst. Medicine of Nat. Acad. Scis., Calif. Med. Assn., Am. Public Health Assn., Am. Occupational Medicine Assn., Western Occupational Medicine Assn., Am. Acad. Occupational Medicine, Chi Omega. Club: Stanford U. Women's (San Francisco) (dir. 1971-80). Office: 2351 Clay St San Francisco CA 94115

CLEVER, W(ARREN) GLENN, editor, publishing executive, poet, writer; b. Champion, Alta., Can., Feb. 10. 1918; s. Martin George and Florence (Anderson) C.; m. Elizabeth Hall, June 13, 1942; 1 dau., Christine Susan. B.A., U. Ottawa, Ont., Can., 1964, M.A., 1966, Ph.D., 1969. Joined Canadian Army, 1939, advanced through grades to maj., 1955, served, U.K., Sicily, Italy, Netherlands; staff Surgeon Gen. of Can. Forces, 1952-55, 61-66, ret., 1966; lectr. U. Ottawa, 1967-70, asst. prof. English lit., 1970-72, assoc. prof.,·1972-80, prof., 1980-83, gen. editor U. Ottawa Short Story Series, 1971-81, chmn. dept. English, 1972-75, coordinator symposia series, 1977-83; v.p. Borealis Press Ltd., Ottawa, 1972—; pres. Techumseh Press Ltd., Ottawa, 1972—. Co-editor: Jour. Can. Poetry, Ottawa, 1978—; editor: books including Selected Short Stores of Cuncan Campbell Scott, 1972, Selected Poetry of Duncan Campbell Scott, 1974; author: 5 vols. of poetry, including Alberta Days, 1974 (Ont. Arts Council award 1976); On E.J. Pratt, 1977; bd. dirs., Can. Writers' Found., Ottawa, 1974—; v.p., Can. Writers' Found., Ottawa, 1976—. Can. Council grantee, 1974-75. Mem. Am. Soc. 18th-Century Studies, Assn. Can. Univ. Tchrs. English, Assn. Can. and Que. Lit. Home: 9 Ashburn Dr Nepean ON Canada K2E 6N4 Office: Dept English U Ottawa 175 Waller St Ottawa On Canada K1N 6N5

CLEWETT, KENNETH VAUGHN, college official; b. Pomona, Calif., June 3, 1923; s. Heber Hovey and Thelma Lela (Sikes) C.; m. Margery Marie Haas, July 10, 1949; children: Richard A., Bruce D., Curtis L., Janet M. A.A., Pomona Jr. Coll., 1943; student naval tng., U. Redlands, 1943-44, Columbia U., 1944; B.A., Stanford U., 1947. Gen. clk. So. Counties Gas Co., Pomona, 1947; personnel examiner Calif. Personnel Bd., Sacramento, 1947-50; asst. personnel officer Calif. Dept. Mental Hygiene, Sacramento, 1950-52; personnel dir. Sonoma State Hosp., Eldridge, Calif., 1952-60, hosp. adminstr., 1960-72, Fairview State Hosp., Costa Mesa, Calif., 1972-75, 76; acting exec. dir. Patton (Calif.) State Hosp., 1975-76, exec. dir., 1976-78; bus. mgr. So. Calif. Coll., 1978-82, dir. planning and corp. relations, 1982—; preceptor George Washington U., Grad. Sch. Health Care Adminstrn., 1962-78, Northwestern U. Grad. Sch. Mgmt., 1975-78, U. Minn. Program Mental Health Adminstrn., 1976-78. Vice pres. Sonoma-Mendocino council Boy Scouts Am., 1968-71, bd. dirs., 1965-72; v.p. Sonoma County United Crusade, 1969-70; chmn. Sonoma Valley Council Edn. Com., 1969-71; founding chmn. bd. dirs. Sonoma Valley United Crusade, 1969-70, bd. dirs., 1969-72; vice chmn. bd. dirs. Big Sisters Orange County, Calif., 1975-77; bd. dirs. So. Calif. Coll., 1977-78, Goodwill Industries Inland Counties, 1978; mem. adv. bd. Orange County Rescue Center, 1980—; trustee Sonoma Valley Unified Sch. Dist., 1971-72; pres. Redwood Empire Hosp. Conf., 1967, bd. dirs., 1966-68; elder United Presbyterian Ch. in U.S.A., 1949-74; deacon Newport-Mesa Christian Center, Costa Mesa, Calif., 1975-76, 79-83. Served to lt., j.g. USN, 1943-46; PTO. Recipient Citizens award of Year Valley Moon Tchrs. Assn., 1970, Outstanding Service award Redwood Empire Hosp. Conf., 1972. Fellow Royal Soc. Health, Assn. Mental Health Adminstrs. (pres. 1976); mem. Am. Acad. Med. Adminstrs., Am. Assn. Mental Deficiency, Am. Soc. Public Adminstrn., Assn. Western Hosps., Inland Area Personnel Mgmt. Assn., Internat. Personnel Mgmt. Assn., Sonoma Valley C. of C. (pres. 1964, dir. 1962-65), Costa Mesa Rotary C. of C., Alpha Gamma Sigma (hon. life). Lodge: Rotary. Home: 2501 W Manly Ave Santa Ana CA 92704 Office: 55 Fair Dr Costa Mesa CA 92626 *Each additional personal achievement further confirms the weakness of depending upon myself alone and that real success is dependent upon truly following the leading of God, our heavenly Father.*

CLEWETT, RICHARD MONROE, marketing educator; b. San Diego, Feb. 1, 1911; s. George E. and Marie E. (Rees) C.; m. Mary Jane Roby, Dec. 24, 1941; children: Richard Monroe, Barbara Jane. B.A., U. Nev., 1934; M.A., U. Pa., 1942, Ph.D., 1948. With Universal Credit Co., 1934-36, Gen. Motors Acceptance Corp., 1936-37; asst. econs. U. Calif., 1937-39; instr. mktg. U. Pa., 1939-42, 45-48; asst. prof. sch. bus. Northwestern U., 1948-51, asso. prof., 1951-54, prof., 1954—, chmn. dept. mktg., 1953-58, 65-77; faculty Internat. Inst. Mgmt., Lucerne; participant Pres.'s Conf. on Tech. and Distbn. Research for Small Bus., 1957; cons. Orgn. European Econ. Cooperation, 1958-59. Author: Marketing Channels for Manufactured Products, 1953; Co-author: Cases in Marketing Strategy, 1958, rev. edit., 1964, Vertical Marketing Systems, 1970; Co-editor: Contemporary American Marketing, 1957, rev. edit., 1963; editorial staff: Jour. Mktg., 1950-58. Bd. dirs. Lake Forest Sch. Mgmt., 1980—. Served with USNR, 1942-45. Mem. AAAS, Am. Econ. Assn., Am. Mktg. Assn., Am. Inst. Baking (dir.; ednl. adv. com. 1963-68), Phi Kappa Phi, Delta Sigma Pi, Beta Gamma Sigma. Baptist. Club: University. Home: 2320 Central St Evanston IL 60201

CLEWLOW, CARL WILLIAM, govt. ofcl.; b. Evansville, Ind., June 25, 1916; s. Leonard Lucius and Ruby Lee (Jacobs) C.; m. Beulah Hutchinson, Feb. 22, 1941; children—Carl William, Sybil Derrington Clewlow Bouett, Theresa Ann Whitley. A.B., George Washington U., 1949, M.A., 1951; postgrad., Am. U., 1951-56. With War Dept., Washington, 1939-48; dep. for programs Exec. Office Pres., Washington, 1948-52; spl. asst. to sec. Army, Washington, 1952-60; dep. asst. sec. Treasury, 1961-63; prin. Arthur Young & Co., Washington and N.Y.C., 1963-67; dep. asst. sec. Def., 1967-80; cabinet advisor on personnel mgmt. to Govt. of Lesotho, 1980—; vis. lectr. Syracuse U., 1957-64, Fla. Atlantic U., Boca Raton, 1965-71, others. Contbr. articles to profl. jours. Mem. adv. bd. Fla. Atlantic U., 1967-71, George Washington U., 1968-71. Served with Q.M.C. U.S. Army, 1945. Recipient meritorious award Dept. Army, 1960, Treasury Dept., 1963; Arthur S. Flemming award U.S. Jaycees, 1964; Disting. Service award Dept. Def., 1973, 77, 80; IPMA ann. award, 51979; U.S. Civil Service League award, 1980. Clubs: Masons, Univ. (Washington). Office: care US AID Masero Air Pouch Dept State Washington DC 20520

CLIBURN, VAN (HARVEY LAVAN, JR.), concert pianist; b. Shreveport, La., July 12, 1934; s. Harvey Lavan and Rildia Bee (O'Bryan) C. Studied music with, mother, 1937-51; studied with, Mme. Rosina Lhevinne; grad. with highest honors, Julliard Sch. Music, 1954; H.H.D. (hon.), Baylor U., 1958. Pub. appearances, Shreveport, 1940, debut, Houston Symphony Orch., 1947; appeared with, Dallas Symphony Orch., 1952, N.Y. Philharmonic Orch., Carnegie Hall, 1954, 58; concert pianist on tour, U.S., 1955-56, Soviet Union, 1958, recs., RCA Victor; guest TV shows, concert with, Symphony of the Air, Carnegie Hall, 1958, concert, Brussels Fair, Belgium, 1958, other appearances include, Phila., Chgo., Hollywood, Denver, London, Amsterdam, Paris; nation-wide tour U.S., 1958—; Composer classical music. Recipient Tex. State prize, 1947, Nat. Music Festival award, 1948, G.B. Dealy award, Dallas, 1952, Koscluszko Found. Chopin award, 1952; Grand Olga Samaroff Found., 1953; 1st pl. Julliard Concerto concert, 1953; Edgar M. Leventritt Found. award, 1954; Carl M. Rosder Meml. award Julliard Sch. Music, 1954; 1st prize Internat. Tschaikovsky Piano Competition, Moscow, Russia, 1958; citation Am. Assn. Sch. Adminstrs., 1959; named number in classical field Top Artists on Campus Poll (album sales), 1968. Mem. Am. Guild Mus. Artists. Baptist. Clubs: Thespian (Kilgore, Tex.) (pres.); Rotary (hon.), Lotus (life). Home: 455 Wilder Pl Shreveport LA 71104 Office: care Shaw Concerts Inc 1995 Broadway New York NY 10023 *

CLIETT, CHARLES BUREN, educator; b. Montpelier, Miss., July 10, 1924; s. James Thomas and Sallie Lou (Saul) C.; m. Grace Holland Campbell, Dec. 25, 1946; children—Susan Marie, Charles Buren. B.S. in Aero. Engring, Ga. Inst. Tech., 1945, M.S., 1950. Registered profl. engr., Miss. Faculty Miss. State U., 1947—, prof. aero. engring., 1957—, chmn. dept., 1960—. Served to lt. (j.g.) USNR, 1943-46. Mem. Am. Soc. Engring. Edn., AIAA, Am. Legion, Nat. Soc. Profl. Engrs., Miss. Engring. Soc., Aerospace Dept. Chairpersons Assn. (pres. 1979), Tau Beta Pi, Sigma Gamma Tau. Mem. Christian Ch. (elder). Home: 638 Commerce St West Point MS 39773 Office: PO Drawer A Mississippi State MS 39762

CLIFF, WALTER CONWAY, lawyer; b. Detroit, Jan. 2, 1932; s. Frank V. and Virginia L. (Conway) C.; m. Ursula McHugh, Nov. 5, 1960; children: Walter C., Mary F., Catherine C. B.S., U. Detroit, 1955, LL.B., 1955; LL.M., NYU, 1956. Bar: Mich. 1956, N.Y. 1958. Assoc. firm Cahill Gordon & Reindel, N.Y.C., 1958-66, ptnr., 1966—; chmn. bd. Shakespeare & Co., Lenox, Mass., 1983—. Bd. dirs. Florence Gould Found., N.Y.C., 1983—, Austen Riggs Center, Stockbridge, Mass., 1983—. Served with U.S. Army, 1956-58. J.K. fellow NYU, 1955-56. Mem. ABA, N.Y. Bar Assn., Assn. Bar City N.Y. Democrat. Roman Catholic. Clubs: Down Town, Stockbridge Golf. Office: Cahill Gordon & Reindel 80 Pine St New York NY 10005

CLIFFORD, CLARK MCADAMS, lawyer; b. Fort Scott, Kans., Dec. 25, 1906; s. Frank Andrew and Georgia (McAdams) C.; m. Margery

Pepperell Kimball, Oct. 3, 1931; children—Margery Pepperell Clifford Lanagan, Joyce Carter Clifford Burland, Randall Clifford Wight. LL.B., Washington U., St. Louis, 1928. Assoc. firm Holland, Lashly & Donnell, St. Louis, 1928-33; with Holland, Lashly & Lashly, 1933-37; ptnr. Lashly, Lashly, Miller & Clifford, 1938-43; sr. ptnr. Clifford & Miller, Washington, 1950-68; sec. Dept. Def., Washington, 1968-69; sr. ptnr. Clifford & Warnke, Washington, 1969—; chmn. bd. First Am. Bankshares, Inc.; dir. Knight-Ridder Newspapers; spl. counsel to Pres. U.S., 1946-50. Served from lt. (j.g.) to capt. USNR, 1944-46; naval aide to Pres. U.S., 1946. Recipient medal of Freedom. Mem. Fed., Am., Mo., D.C., St. Louis bar assns., Kappa Alpha. Clubs: Racquet (St. Louis); Burning Tree, Metropolitan, Chevy Chase (Washington). Home: 9421 Rockville Pike Bethesda MD 20814 Office: 815 Connecticut Ave Washington DC 20006

CLIFFORD, DONALD JOSEPH, newspaper publisher; b. Rutland, Vt., Jan. 23, 1925; s. John M. and Ethel LeClair C.; m. Helen Connell, Nov. 9, 1950; children—Stephen F., Thomas J., Martha L., Daniel J., Donald J., Sarah F. Pub. The Star, Oneonta, N.Y., 1968-74, The Record-Eagle, Traverse City, Mich., 1974-79; pres. The Standard Times Pub. Co.; pub. The Standard Times, Daily and Sunday, New Bedford, Mass., 1979—; dir. Mechanics Exchange Savs. Bank, Oneonta, N.Y.; lectr. Am. Press Inst., 1959-61. Trustee Fox Hosp., Oneonta. Served with USAF, 1942-45. Mem. Am. Newspaper Pubs. Assn., New Eng. Daily Newspaper Assn. Office: 555 Market St New Bedford MA 02742

CLIFFORD, EARLE WINCHESTER, JR., banker; b. Rutland, Vt., Sept. 12, 1925; s. Earle Winchester and Florence U. (Phillips) C.; m. Marie T. Mondella, Nov. 15, 1952; children: Karen, Philip. Student, U. Me., 1943; diploma with highest honors, Rutland Jr. Coll., 1948; A.B. magna cum laude, Syracuse U., 1950, M.S., 1951, postgrad., 1951; LL.D., St. Peter's Coll., 1968; L.H.D., Monmouth Coll., N.J., 1974. Mem. staff Syracuse U., 1952-57, 61-63, dean men, 1961-63, instr. citizenship dept., 1954-57, 62-63; dean men U. Vt., 1957-61, instr. evening div., 1958-61; dean student affairs Rutgers U., 1963-70, v.p. for student affairs, 1970-72; pres. Assn. Ind. Colls. and Univs. in N.J., 1972-74; v.p. univ. resources and pub. affairs Fairleigh Dickinson U., 1974-78; exec. asst. to pres. Eckerd Coll., 1978-82; v.p. trust services Royal Trust Bank Fla., N.A., 1982—; lectr. sociology dept. and Grad. Sch. Edn. Rutgers U., New Brunswick, N.J., 1963-73. Mem. adv. bd.: Coll. Student Personnel Abstracts, 1972—; Contbr. articles to learned publs. Mem. Gov. Vt. Com. Youth Fitness, 1958-60; div. chmn. govt. and edn. Burlington (Vt.) United Fund, 1960-61; vice chmn. Consortium on Community Coll., 1972-75; chmn. ednl. div. United Hosp. Appeal; chmn. New Brunswick Adv. Com. on Recreation; mem. Gov.'s Task Force on Econ. Edn. in N.J., 1972-73; com. chmn. Cub Scout Pack 178, Cranford, N.J.; bd. dirs. Burlington Boys Club, 1959-61, v.p., 1960-61; bd. dirs. New Brunswick chpt. ARC, St. Peter's Hosp., Lakewood Baseball Assn., 1981—. Served with AUS, 1943-46. Mem. Am. Acad. Polit. and Social Sci., Nat. Assn. Student Personnel Adminstrs. (exec. com., pres. 1970), Am. Assn. U. Adminstrs. (pres. 1973-75), Am. Personnel and Guidance Assn., N.J. Assn. Colls. and Univs. (dir., v.p. 1973-75, pres. 1975-77), Am. Coll. Personnel Assn. (chmn. resolutions com. 1966-67), Tampa Bay Estate Planning Council, Phi Beta Kappa, Kappa Phi Kappa (nat. councillor 1950-52), Phi Delta Kappa, Pi Gamma Mu, Alpha Phi Omega (nat. dir.), Omicron Delta Kappa (hon.), Alpha Delta Kappa, Tau Theta Upsilon. Congregationalist. Home: 1128 Pinellas Point Dr S Saint Petersburg FL 33705 Home: Chittenden Rd Rutland Town VT 05701

CLIFFORD, EDWARD, psychologist, educator; b. Phila., June 29, 1921; m. Miriam Wittelle, Aug. 14, 1949; children—Jeanne Francis, Ralph Douglas. B.A., Roosevelt Coll., 1949; M.A., U. Chgo., 1950; Ph.D., U. Minn., 1957. Asst. prof. U. Colo. Sch. Medicine, Denver, 1958-62; research psychologist Children's Asthma Research Inst. and Hosp., Denver, 1962-63; research asso. U. Colo., Boulder, 1963-65; prof. med. psychology, co-dir. Facial Rehab. Center, Duke U. Med. Center, Durham, N.C., 1965—. Served with AUS, 1942-46. Home: 2535 Sevier St Durham NC 27705 Office: Duke U Med Center Box 3098 Durham NC 27710

CLIFFORD, FREDERICK BURR, educator; b. Samaria, Mich., June 3, 1914; s. Frederick Jesse and Genevieve Clara (Burr) C.; m. Doris Jean Jones, Aug. 26, 1943; children—John Frederick, David Burr, Jeanne Ellen. A.B., No. Mich. Coll., 1935; M.A., U. Mich., 1937, Ph.D., 1943; B.D., Oberlin Coll., 1946. Ordained to ministry Methodist Ch., 1943; pastor in Dearborn, Mich., 1943-47; prof. English Adrian (Mich.) Coll., 1947-53; asso. prof. humanities Emory-at-Oxford, Emory U., 1953-58; prof. English, chmn. dept. Southwestern U., 1958-62, dean, 1962-77, prof. classics and humanities, 1977-81. Mem. Central Tex. Conf. Meth. Ch., Am. Philol. Assn., Classical Assn. Middle West and South. Home: 1407 Hutto Rd Georgetown TX 78626

CLIFFORD, GEORGE ORR, medical educator, consultant hematologist; b. Akron, Ohio, Apr. 30, 1924; s. George Orr and Mary Adams (Mitchell) C.; m. Nancy Easley, Aug. 8, 1948 (div. July 1978); children: Mitchell, George, John; m. Marie Anderson, Aug. 25, 1978. Student, Harvard U., 1942-44; M.D., Tufts U., 1949. Diplomate: Am. Bd. Internal Medicine, Nat. Bd. Med. Examiners. Intern Henry Ford Hosp., Detroit, 1949-50; resident in internal medicine Detroit Receiving Hosp., 1950-52, 54-55; from instr. to assoc. prof. medicine Wayne State U., Detroit, 1955-63; assoc. prof. medicine Cornell U., 1968-72; prof., chmn. dept. medicine Creigton U., Omaha, 1972—; researcher Am. Cancer Soc., mem. personnel com., 1964-68, 70-74; health resource com. NIH, Bethesda, Md., 1968-71. Served to 1st lt. M.C. U.S. Army, 1952-54; Korea. Markle scholar in medicine, 1959-64. Fellow ACP; mem. Assn. Profs. Medicine, Central Soc. Clin. Research, Am. Soc. Hematology, Am. Fedn. Clin. Research. Democrat. Home: 5333 Raven Oaks Dr Omaha NE 68152 Office: Creighton U Med Sch 601 N 30th St Omaha NE 68131

CLIFFORD, GERALDINE MARIE JONCICH (MRS. WILLIAM F. CLIFFORD), educator; b. San Pedro, Calif., Apr. 17, 1931; d. Marion and Geraldine (Mustacich) Joncich; m. William F. Clifford, July 12, 1969. A.B., UCLA, 1954, M.Ed., 1957; Ed.D., Columbia U., 1961. Tchr., San Lorenzo, Calif., 1954-56, Maracaibo, Venezuela, 1957-58; researcher Inst. Lang. Arts, Tchrs. Coll., Columbia, 1958-61; asst. prof. edn. U. Calif. at Berkeley, 1962-67, asso. prof., 1967-74, prof., 1974—, asso. dean, 1976-78, chmn. dept. edn., 1978-81, acting dean Sch. Edn., 1980-81, 82-83. Author: The Sane Positivist: A Biography of Edward L. Thorndike, 1968, The Shape of American Education, 1975. Macmillan fellow, 1958-59; Guggenheim fellow, 1965-66; Rockefeller fellow, 1977-78. Mem. Am. Hist. Assn., History Edn. Soc., Am. Ednl. Studies Assn., Phi Beta Kappa, Pi Lambda Theta. Home: 2428 Prince St Berkeley CA 94705

CLIFFORD, MAURICE CECIL, physician, college president; b. Washington, Aug. 9, 1920; s. Maurice C. and Rosa P. (Linberry) C.; m. Patricia Marie Johnson, June 15, 1945; children: Maurice Cecil III, Jay P.L., Rosemary Clifford McDaniel. A.B., Hamilton Coll., 1941, Sc.D., 1982; A.M., U. Chgo., 1942; M.D., Meharry Med. Coll., 1947; L.H.D., LaSalle Coll., 1981. Diplomate: Am. Bd. Ob-Gyn. Intern Phila. Gen. Hosp., 1947-48, resident in ob-gyn, 1948-51, asst. chief service ob-gyn, 1951-60; mem. faculty Med. Coll. Pa., Phila., 1955—, prof. ob-gyn., 1975—, v.p. for med. affairs, 1978-80, pres., 1980—; bd. mgrs. Germantown Savs. Bank. Contbr. articles to profl. jours. Trustee Meharry Med. Coll., Phila. Award, Phila. Art Mus., Phila. Coll. Textiles and Sci., Phila. Acad. Natural Scis.; former alumnus trustee Hamilton Coll.; bd. dirs. University City Sci. Center, Urban Coalition, Urban Affairs Partnership, Allegheny West Found.; mem. nat. med. com. Planned Parenthood, 1975-78; mem. adv. com. on arts John F. Kennedy Center for Performing Arts, 1978-80. Served to capt. M.C., U.S. Army, 1952-54. Recipient Dr. Martin Luther King, Jr. award PUSH, 1981; Dr. William H. Gray, Jr. award Educators Roundtable Assn., 1981; Ann. award Phila. Tribune Charities, 1981; Disting. Am. award Edn. and Research Fund Am. Found. for Negro Affairs, 1980; Outstanding Service award Phila. br. NAACP, 1965; others. Fellow Am. Coll. Obstetricians and Gynecologists (life); mem. Nat. Med. Assn., Pa. Med. Soc., Med. Soc. Eastern Pa., Philadelphia County Med. Soc., Phi Beta Kappa, Alpha Omega Alpha. Office: 3300 Henry Ave Philadelphia PA 19129

CLIFFORD, NICHOLAS ROWLAND, educator, college administrator; b. Radnor, Pa., Oct. 12, 1930; s. Henry and Esther (Rowl) C.; m. Deborah Pickman Clifford, June 22, 1957; children: Mary Rowland, Sarah, Susannah, Rebecca Harrison. B.A., Princeton U., 1952; M.A., Harvard U., 1957, Ph.D., 1961. Instr. history MIT, 1961-62; instr. Princeton U., 1962-66; asst. prof. Middlebury (Vt.) Coll., 1966-68, asso. prof., 1968-75, William R. Kenan Jr. prof., 1976-81, acad. v.p., 1979—, provost, 1980—. Author: Retreat from China: British Policy in the Far East, 1937-41, 1967, Shanghai, 1925: Urban Nationalism and the Defense of Foreign Privilege, 1979. Served with USN, 1953-56. Mem. Am. Hist. Assn., Assn. Asian Studies, Soc. Historians of Am. Fgn. Relations. Democrat. Roman Catholic. Club: Am. Alpine. Office: Dept History Middlebury College Middlebury VT 05753

CLIFFORD, PETER, college president; b. N.Y.C., Feb. 17, 1925; s. Peter and Mary (Lynch) C. A.B., Manhattan Coll., 1951; M.A., Fordham U., 1957; Ed.D., Harvard U., 1980; postgrad., U. Santo Tomas, Philippines, 1957-61, NYU, 1962-64, Center Internat. Religious Studies, Rome, 1965-66. Joined Bros. of the Christian Schs., 1943; tchr. Cath. elem. schs., N.Y.C., 1947-52, prin., 1952-57; acad. dean De La Salle Coll., Manila, 1957-61, dean, 1958-61, dir., 1960-61; sr. tchr. Bishop Loughlin High Sch., Bklyn., 1962-63, asst. prin., 1963-65; asst. supt. secondary schs. Cath. Schs. Office, Bklyn., 1968-71; exec. sec. secondary sch. dept. Nat. Cath. Ednl. Assn., Washington, 1971-74; v.p. edn. Christian Bros., Narragansett, R.I., 1972-74; asso. dean Sch. Edn., St. John's U., Jamaica, N.Y., 1974-76; pres. St. Mary's Coll., Winona, Minn., 1976—; dir. Norwest Bank of Winona; dir. workshops various Cath. instns. of learning, 1971-76; mem. Nat. Commn. Reform of Secondary Edn., 1972-73. Contbr. articles to jours. in edn. Vice chmn. Minn. Pvt. Coll. Council, 1979-81; trustee La Salle Mil. Acad., Oakdale, N.Y., 1969-81, Coll. Santa Fe. Mem. Nat. Soc. Study of Edn., Am. Assn. Univ. Adminstrs., Nat. Assn. Ind. Colls. and Univs., Assn. Cath. Colls. and Univs., Am. Assn. Higher Edn., Winona C. of C. (dir. 1979-82), Phi Delta Kappa. Home: Terrace Heights Office: Saint Mary's College Winona MN 55987

CLIFFORD, ROBERT L., supreme ct. justice N.J.; b. Passaic, N.J., Dec. 17, 1924; s. John P. and Elizabeth E. C.; m. Joan Sieben, Oct. 20, 1951; children—Robert L., John P. II, Michael A. B.A., Lehigh U., 1947; LL.B., Duke U., 1950. Bar: N.J. bar 1950. Law sec. to Hon. William A. Wachenfeld, N.J. Supreme Ct., 1953-54; practice law, Newark, 1954-62, Morristown, N.J., 1962-70, commr. of banking and ins., State of N.J., 1970-72, commr. of instns. and agys., 1972-73; asso. justice N.J. Supreme Ct., 1973—. Served with USNR, 1943-46. Recipient Trial Bar award Trial Attys. N.J., 1970. Fellow Am. Coll. Trial Lawyers, Am. Bar Found.; mem. Am. Judicature Soc., Morris County Bar Assn., N.J. State Bar Assn. (officer 1968-70), Am. Bar Assn. Democrat. Office: State Courthouse Trenton NJ 08625 *

CLIFFORD, SYLVESTER, educator; b. Forgan, Okla., May 17, 1929; s. William St. Ledger and Ella Opal (Street) C.; m. Betty Alice Gregory, June 10, 1949; children—Bradford William, Opal Alice. B.A., Northwestern State Coll., Alva, Okla., 1951; M.A., U. Denver, 1957, Ph.D., 1959. High sch. tchr., Hazelton, Kans., 1951-52, Anthony, Kans., 1952-53; exec. dir. Wallace Sch. for Brain Damaged Children, Denver, 1957-61; faculty U. S.D., Vermillion, 1961—, prof., chmn. dept. communication, 1969-80, Harrington lectr., 1976, dir. Speech and Hearing Center, 1961-80; cons. S.D. Dept. Pub. Instruction, 1962—, North Brown Multi-Dist. Spl. Correction Program, 1970—. Editor: S.D. Speech and Hearing Jour, 1963-65, 70-72. Bd. dirs. S.D. Easter Seal Soc., Children's Developmental Disabilities Center of U. S.D. Served with AUS, 1953-55. Mayo Clinic fellow, 1968-69. Mem. AAUP, Am. Heart Assn., Am. Cancer Soc., Assn. for Retarded Children, Nu Voices Club S.D., Am. Speech and Hearing Assn., Internat. Communication Assn., S.D. Speech and Hearing Assn. (pres. 1966-67). Democrat. Methodist. Club: Rotarian. Home: 424 E Main St Vermillion SD 57069 *I believe the directions I've taken in life, and the way I have lived were determined by early family influences, which taught me, simply, the worth of every person and every thing.*

CLIFFORD, THOMAS JOHN, university president; b. Langdon, N.D., Mar. 16, 1921; s. Thomas Joseph and Elizabeth (Howitz) C.; m. Florence Marie Schmidt, Jan. 25, 1943; children: Thomas John, Stephen Michael. B.C.S., U. N.D., 1942, J.D., 1948; M.B.S., Stanford, 1957, Stanford exec. fellow, 1958. C.P.A., 1949. Instr. accounting U. N.D., 1946-47, counselor men, 1947-49, head accounting dept., 1948-49, dean sch. commerce, 1950-71, pres. univ., 1971—; dir. Red River Nat. Bank, Grand Forks, N.D., Ottertail Power Co., Fergus Falls., Western States Life Ins. Co. Bd. dirs. Greater N.D. Assn., Fargo, Bush Found., St. Paul, Minn.; pres., No. Lights council, Boy Scouts Am., 1981—. Served from 2d lt. to maj. USMC, 1942-45. Decorated Purple Heart, Bronze Star medal, Silver Star. Mem. N.D. C.P.A. Soc. (pres. 1953-54), A.I.M., Am. Inst. Accountants, Am. Bar Assn., Beta Gamma Sigma, Beta Alpha Psi, Phi Eta Sigma, Kappa Sigma, Blue Key, Order Coif. Club: K.C. Office: Univ North Dakota Grand Forks ND 58201

CLIFT, WILLIAM BROOKS, III, photographer; b. Boston, Jan. 5, 1944; s. William Brooks C. and Anne (Pearmain) Thomson; m. Vida Regina Chesnulis, Aug. 8, 1970; children: Charis, Carole, William. Free lance comml. photographer in partnership with Steve Gersh under name Helios, 1963-71; pres. William Clift Ltd., Santa Fe, 1980—; cons. Polaroid Corp., 1965-67. Photographer one-man shows, Carl Siembab Gallery, Boston, 1969, Mus. Art, U. Oreg., Eugene, New Boston City Hall Gallery, 1970, U. Mass., Berkshire Mus., Pittsfield, Mass., William Coll., Addison Gallery of Am. Art, Wheaton Coll., Mass., Worcester Art Mus., 1971, Creative Photography Gallery, MIT, 1972, St. John's Coll. Art Gallery, Santa Fe, 1973, Wiggin Gallery, Boston Pub. Library, 1974, Australian Ctr. for Photography, Sydney, 1978, Susan Spiritus Gallery, Newport Beach, Calif., 1979, MIT Creative Photography Gallery, 1980, William Lyons Gallery, Coconut Grove, Fla., Eclipse Gallery, Boulder, Colo., Atlanta Gallery of Photography, Phoenix Art Mus., 1981, Jeb Gallery, Providence, Portfolio Gallery, Images Gallery, Cin., 1982, Boston Atheneum, 1983, group shows, Gallery 216, N.Y., N.Y. Grover Cronin Gallery, Waltham, Mass., 1964, Carl Seimbab Gallery, Boston, 1966, Lassall Jr. Coll., 1967, Hill's Gallery, Santa Fe, Tyler Mus. Art, Austin, Tex., Dupree Gallery, Dallas, 1974, Quindacqua Gallery, Washington, 1978, Zabriskie Gallery, Paris, Am. Cultural Ctr., Paris; photograher, many others; photographer, AT & T Project-Am. Images, 1978, Seagram's Bicentennial Project, Courthouse, 1975-77; author: Photography Portfolios, Old Boston City Hall, 1971, Photography Portfolios, Old Boston Courthouse, 1979, Photography Portfolios, New Mexico, 1975. Nat. Endowment for Arts photography fellow, 1972, 79; Guggenheim fellow, 1974, 80. Home: PO Box 6035 Santa Fe NM 87502 Office: William Clift Ltd PO Box 6035 Santa Fe NM 87502

CLIFTON, BUEL, fin. co. exec.; b. Sulphur Springs, Tex., Sept. 28, 1924; s. Oscar C. and Della S. (White) C.; m. Charlotte G. Fischer, Apr. 6, 1945; children—Guy, Sandra, Karen, Rita, Mary, Greg, Brian, Patricia. Student, Paris Jr. Coll., 1940-42. With Household Fin. Corp., Prospect Heights, Ill., 1946—, now exec. v.p. U.S. ops. Served with USN, 1942-43. Mem. Nat. Consumer Fin. Assn. (ops. com., bankruptcy task force com.), Nat. Second Mortgage Assn. (dir.), North Barrington Plan Commn. Republican. Roman Catholic. Clubs: Turnberry Country, Horseshoe Bay Country, K.C. Office: 2700 Sanders Rd Prospect Heights IL 60070

CLIFTON, CHESTER VICTOR, JR., public relations executive, former army officer; b. Edmonton, Alta., Can., Sept. 24, 1913; s. Chester Victor and Minnie (Corbett) C.; m. Anne Bodine, Oct. 16, 1937. Student, U. Wash., 1931-32; B.S., U.S. Mil. Acad., 1936; M.A., U. Wis., 1948; grad., Nat. War Coll., 1954. Newspaper reporter Seattle Post Intelligencer, 1930-32, N.Y. Herald Tribune, summer 1936; commd. 2d lt. U.S. Army, 1936, advanced through grades to maj. gen., 1961; operations officer Hdqrs. 22d F.A. Group, Ft. Bragg, N.C., 1942-43; comdg. officer 193d F.A. Group, 1943, 698th F.A. bn., Ft. Bragg, then Italy, France, Germany, 1943-45; pub. relations officer Hdqrs. Army Ground Forces, Washington, 1945-47; asst. sec. gen. staff Office Chief of Staff, Washington, 1948-49; asst. to chmn. Joint Chiefs Staff, 1949-53; exec. officer Hdqrs. 2d Armored Div. Arty., Germany, 1954-55; chief joint plans J-3 Div., European Command, France, 1955-56; dep. chief, then chief of information Dept. Army, 1956-61; mil. aide to Pres. Kennedy, 1961-63, Pres. Johnson, 1963-65; pres. Thomas J. Deegan Co., Inc., 1965-67, Clifton-Raymond Assos., Inc., 1967-68, Clifton Counselors, Inc., Washington, 1968—. Author: The Memories 1961—JFK-1963; Contbr. articles to mags.; Korean War history in Ency. Brit. Mem. Assn. Grads. U.S. Mil. Acad. (trustee 1975—), Sigma Delta Chi, Delta Upsilon. Clubs: Nat. Press, Federal City, Burning Tree (Washington). Home: 2339 Massachusetts Ave NW Washington DC 20008 Office: 1607 New Hampshire Ave NW Washington DC 20009

CLIFTON, JAMES ALBERT, physician; b. Fayetteville, N.C., Sept. 18, 1923; s. James Albert, Jr. and Flora M. (McNair) C.; m. Katherine Rathe, June 25, 1949; children—Susan M. (dec.), Katherine Y., Caroline M. B.A., Vanderbilt U., 1944, M.D., 1947. Diplomate: Am. Bd. Internal Medicine (mem. 1972-81, mem. subsplty. bd. gastroenterology 1968-75, chmn. 1972-75, mem. exec. com. 1978-81, chmn. 1980-81). Intern U. Hosps., Iowa City, Iowa, 1947-48, resident dept. medicine, 1948-51; staff dept. medicine Thayer VA Hosp., Nashville, 1952-53; asst. clin. medicine Vanderbilt Hosp., Nashville, 1952-53; cons. physician VA Hosp., Iowa City, 1965—; asso. medicine dept. internal medicine Coll. Medicine, U. Iowa, 1953-54, chief div. gastroenterology, 1953-71, asst. prof. medicine, 1954-58, asso. prof., 1958-63, prof., 1963—, traveling fellow, 1964, vis. prof. dept. physiology, 1964, vice chmn. dept. medicine, 1967-70, chmn. dept. medicine Coll. Medicine, 1970-76, Roy J. Carver prof. medicine, 1974—; investigator Mt. Desert Isle Biol. Lab., Salisbury Cove., Maine, 1964; vis. faculty mem. Mayo Found. and Mayo Clinic, 1966; vis. prof. dept. medicine U. N.C., Chapel Hill, 1970; cons. gastroenterology and nutrition tng. grants com. Nat. Inst. Arthritis and Metabolic Diseases, NIH, 1964-68, chmn., 1965-68; mem. Nat. Adv. Arthritis and Metabolic Diseases Council, 1970-73; mem. gastroenterology tng. com. VA, Washington, 1967-71, chmn. tng. grants com., 1971-73; mem. med. adv. bd. Digestive Disease Found., 1969-73. Mem. internat. editorial bd.: Italian Jour. Gastroenterology, 1970—, Gastroenterology, 1964-68. Phi Connell scholar Vanderbilt U., 1943-44; spl. research fellow NIH, USPHS, 1955-56; fellow in medicine Evans Meml. Hosp., Mass. Meml. Hosps., also Boston U. Sch. Medicine, 1955-56. Fellow A.C.P. (bd. regents 1972-79, pres. 1977-78); mem. Inst. Medicine of Nat. Acad. Scis., Am. Gastroent. Assn. (pres. 1970-71), AMA (liaison com. grad. med. edn. 1976-77), Am. Heart Assn., Am. Assn. Study Liver Disease, Am. Soc. Internal Medicine, AAAS, Am. Fedn. Clin. Research, Am. Clin. and Climatol. Assn., Assn. Am. Physicians, AAUP, Soc. Exptl. Biology and Medicine, Am. Physiol. Soc., Assn. Am. Med. Colls., Assn. Profs. Medicine (councillor 1972-73, sec.-treas. 1973-75), Internat. Soc. Internal Medicine (exec. com. 1978—). Home: Rural Rt 2 Iowa City IA 52240

CLIFTON, LUCILLE THELMA, author; b. Depew, N.Y., June 27, 1936; d. Samuel Louis and Thelma (Moore) Sayles; m. Fred James Clifton, May 10, 1958; children—Sidney, Fredrica, Channing, Gillian, Graham, Alexia. Student, Howard U., 1953-55, Fredonia (N.Y.) State Tchrs. Coll., 1955. Poet-in-residence, Coppin State Coll., Balt., 1972-76; Jerry Moore vis. writer, George Washington U., 1982-83; Author: Good Times, 1969, Good News About The Earth, 1972, An Ordinary Woman, 1974, Generations, 1976, Two-Headed Woman, 1980; Everett Anderson books and other books for children Two-Header Woman; co-author: Free to Be You and Me, 1974 (Emmy award). Trustee Enoch Pratt Free Library, Balt. Named Poet Laureate, State of Md., 1979; Recipient Discovery award Poetry Center, 1969; YMHA grantee, 1969; Nat. Endowment Arts grantee, 1970, 72. Mem. Authors League, Author Guild, P.E.N. Office: care Curtis Brown Ltd New York NY

CLIFTON, RODNEY JAMES, engineering educator, civil engineer, consultant; b. Orchard, Nebr., July 10, 1937; s. James Edward and Minnie Gertrude (Williamson) C.; m. MercaDee Bonde, Dec. 28, 1958; children: Mark Bradford, Jeffrey John, Gregg Andrew, Anne Michelle. B.S.C.E., U. Nebr., 1959; M.S.C.E., Carnegie Inst. Tech., 1961, Ph.D. in Civil Engring., 1964. Registered profl. engr., R.I. Interdisciplinary fellow Brown U., Providence, 1964-65, asst. prof. engring., 1965-68, assoc. prof., 1968-71, prof., 1971—, chmn. exec. com. div. engring., 1974-79; vis. prof. materials sci. and engring. Stanford U., Calif., 1979-80; cons. in field; mem. Nat. Materials Adv. Bd. Commn. on Personnel Armor, 1968, Nat. Materials Adv. Bd. Commn. on Material Response to Ultra-High Loading Rates, 1978. Research, numerous publs. in solid mechanics with emphasis on dynamic plasticity, plate impact expts., hydraulic fracturing; assoc. editor: Jour. Applied Mechanics, 1980—. NSF sci. faculty fellow, Southampton, Eng., 1971; NDEA fellow, 1960-63; grantee Army Research Office, 1973—, NSF, 1972—. Fellow Am. Acad. Mechanics; mem. ASCE, ASME (Melville medal 1981), Soc. Engring. Sci. (pres. 1982-83), AAAS, Sigma Xi, Phi Kappa Phi, Pi Mu Epsilon, Sigma Tau. Presbyterian. Home: 18 Starbrook Dr Barrington RI 02806 Office: Brown U Div Engring Providence RI 02912

CLIFTON, RUSSELL B., financial executive; b. Maroa, Ill., Jan. 16, 1930; s. Russell Thomas and Clara Leoda (Luckenbill) C.; m. Mary Joyce Hartline, Oct. 10, 1948; 1 son, Steven Shawn. B.S., Mich. State U., 1957. Bank auditor Arthur Andersen & Co., Detroit, 1957-59; v.p. Mich. Nat. Bank, Lansing, 1959-65; sr. v.p. Assoc. Mortgages Co., Kansas City, Mo., 1965-69; v.p. Fed. Nat. Mortgage Assn., Washington, 1969—; mem. adv. com. Home Owner's Warranty Corp., Washington, 1978-81; dir., mem. exec. com. Nat. Acad. Conciliators,

Washington, 1979—. Served with U.S. Army, 1952-54. Named disting. fellow Nat. Assn. Cert. Mortgages Bankers, 1975. Assoc. mem. Mortgage Bankers Assn., Nat. Savs. and Loan League, Nat. Assn. Home Builders, U.S. League Savs. Assn., Nat. Assn. Mut. Savs. Banks, Am. Bankers Assn., Nat. Assn. Realtors, Am. Savs. and Loan League, Community Assn. Inst.; mem. Phi Kappa Phi, Beta Alpha Psi, Beta Gamma Sigma, Tau Sigma. Methodist. Club: University (Washington). Office: Fed Nat Mortgage Assn 3900 Wisconsin Ave NW Washington DC 20016

CLIMAN, DAVID A(RTHER), automotive dealership executive; b. Montreal, Que., Can., Nov. 25, 1926; s. Louis and Anne C.; m. Mara, Nov. 21, 1948; children: Richard, Douglas. B.Sc., McGill U., 1947; M.B.A., U. Pa., 1952. With Allied Chem. Corp., 1952-73, v.p. internat. ops., N.Y.C., 1970-73; v.p., treas. No. Telecom Co., Montreal, 1973-75; v.p. fin. Phelps Dodge Internat. Corp., N.Y.C., 1976-78; pres. Superscope Inc., Chatsworth, Calif., 1979-81; exec. v.p., chief fin. officer Cadillac fairview Corp. Ltd., Toronto, 1981—; dir. Cadillac Fairview Corp. Ltd. Office: Cadillac Fariview Corp Ltd 20 Queen St W Toronto ON Canada M5H 3R4

CLIMENHAGA, ARTHUR MERLIN, clergyman, church administrator; b. Grantham, Pa., Feb. 21, 1916; s. John Arthur and Emma Light (Smith) C.; m. Arlene Brubaker, Aug. 27, 1937 (dec.); m. Lona Brubaker, Sept. 27, 1969. B.S.L., Upland (Calif.) Coll., 1936; B.A. magna cum laude, Pasadena Coll., 1937; M.A. in Theology, Taylor U., 1938; postgrad., Claremont Grad. Sch., 1942-43; S.T.D., Los Angeles Baptist Theol. Sem., 1944; LL.D., Houghton Coll., 1965. Ordained to ministry Brethren in Christ Ch., 1938; religious dir. Upland Coll., 1938-39, pres., 1939-44; dist. supt. Wanezi mission, So. Rhodesia, Africa, 1945-50; bishop Brethren in Christ Ch., Rhodesia, gen. supt. missions in, So. and No. Rhodesia, 1951-60; pres. Messiah Coll., Grantham, 1960-64; exec. dir. Nat. Assn. Evangelicals, Wheaton, Ill., 1964-67; bishop Western confs. Brethren Christ Ch., 1967-72; v.p., dean Western Evang. Sem., Portland, Oreg., 1972-78; dir. acad. affairs Ashland (Ohio) Theol. Sem., 1978-82; adminstr. Upland Manor (Calif.), 1982—; gen. sec. Brethren in Christ Ch., 1981—; Treas. bd. young people's work Brethren in Christ Ch., 1941-44, mem. bd. adminstrn., 1960—, gen. sec., 1973—; sec. So. Rhodesia Missionary Conf., 1948-50; pres. So. Rhodesia (Africa), Christian Conf., 1954-60; Mem. Pa. Gov.'s Prayer Breakfast Com., 1962-64; Bd. dirs. Rhodesia Christian Press, 1956- 60, Council for Advancement Small Colls., 1960-64; mem. So. Rhodesia Edn. Adv. Bd., 1952-60, mem. standing exec. com., 1954-60; chmn. theol. commn. World Evang. Fellowship, 1976-80, vice chmn., 1980—. Author: (with Frank McConnell) Draw Nigh Unto God, 1952; Contbr. to: Facing Facts in Modern Mission, 1963, Further Insights into Holiness, 1963, The Word and The Doctrine, 1965. Mem. Phi Delta Kappa. Republican. Club: Rotarian. Home and Office: 1125 W Arrow Hwy #14 Upland CA 91786 . . .*The best way to achieve success is never to give up one minute too soon. . . The three definitives for life are: to know, to do, to be. Know your God. Do his will in your life. Be the person you always want to see in the mirror.*

CLIMENKO, JESSE, lawyer; b. N.Y.C., Apr. 3, 1904; s. Hyman and Rose (Busky) C.; m. Pearl Siegel, July 3, 1929; 1 dau., Jane Climenko Gottschalk. B.A. magna cum laude, Harvard U., 1924, LL.B., 1927. Bar: N.Y. bar 1927. Since practiced in, N.Y.C.; mem. firm Shea Gould Climenko & Casey, and predecessors, 1944-79; of counsel Shea & Gould, 1979—; spl. asst. to atty. gen. U.S., 1943-44, 48. Mem. Am., Fed. bar assns., Assn. Bar City N.Y., N.Y. County Lawyers Assn., Am. Law Inst. Home: 190 E 72d St New York NY 10021

CLINARD, MARSHALL BARRON, educator; b. Boston, Nov. 12, 1911; s. Andrew Marshall and Gladys (Barron) C.; m. Ruth Blackburn, Aug. 28, 1937; children: Marsha Clinard Schacht, Stephen Andrew. B.A., Stanford U., 1932, M.A., 1934; Ph.D., U. Chgo., 1941. Instr. U. Iowa, 1937-41; chief criminal statistics U.S. Bur. Census, 1941-43; chief analysis report, enforcement dept. OPA, 1943-45; asso. prof. Vanderbilt U., 1945-46; mem. faculty U. Wis., 1946—, prof. sociology, 1951-79, prof. emeritus, 1979—; Fulbright research prof. U. Stockholm, 1954-55; vis. prof. Makerere U. Coll., Kampala, Uganda, 1968-69; cons. urban community devel. Ford Found., India, 1958-60, 62-63; UN expert Asian Seminar Urban Community Devel., Singapore, 1962; rapporteur 3d UN Congress Prevention Crime and Treatment Offenders, Stockholm, 1965; panel expert 4th UN Congress, Kyoto, 1970; cons. 5th UN Congress, Geneva, 1975, Dept. Labor, 1966-67, Dept. Justice, 1980—. Author: The Black Market: A Study of White Collar Crime, 1952, (with Robert F. Meier) Sociology of Deviant Behavior, 5th edit, 1979; editor, contbr.: Anomie and Deviant Behavior: A Discussion and Critique, 1964, Slums and Community Development: Experiments in Self-Help, 1966, (with Richard Quinney) Criminal Behavior Systems: A Typology, 1967, 2d edit., 1973, (with Daniel J. Abbott) Crime in Developing Countries: A Comparative Perspective), 1973, Cities with Little Crime: The Case of Switzerland, 1978, Illegal Corporate Behavior, 1979, (with Peter C. Yeager) Corporate Crime, 1980, Corporate Ethics and Crime: The Role of Middle Management, 1983. Recipient Sutherland award Am. Soc. Criminology, 1970; NSF research grantee, Switzerland, 1973. Mem. Soc. Study Social Problems (exec. com. 1959-60, 62-63, 65-67, pres. 1961-62), Midwest Sociol. Soc. (pres. 1965-66), Am. Sociol. Assn. (council mem. at large 1966-68). Home: 808 Juniper Dr Santa Fe NM 87501

CLINCH, JOHN HOUSTOUN MCINTOSH, management company executive, lawyer; b. Danville, Ill., Aug. 18, 1902; s. John Houstoun McIntosh and Edna L. (Wilber) C.; m. Frances S. Bell, June 25, 1927; children: Frances Clinch Jones, J. Houstoun M. Student, U. Ill., 1920-22, John Marshall Law Sch., 1942; A.B., U. Chgo., 1924. With Chgo. North Shore & Milw. Ry. (now Susquehanna Corp.), 1925-57, pres., 1948-57, Consol. Mgmt. Co., 1957—; v.p. Middle West Service Co., 1963-74; lectr., instr. Grad. Sch. Bus., U. Chgo., 1958-63; spl. asst. atty. gen., State of N.Mex., 1969-70; spl. cons. Ill. Commerce Commn.; spl. counsel Iowa Commerce Commn., Minn. Pub. Service Commn., 1971. Mem. Winnetka Caucus Com. Mem. Chgo. Bar Assn., Sigma Alpha Epsilon. Episcopalian. Clubs: University (Chgo.); Sheridan Shore Yacht (Wilmette, Ill.); Skokie Country (Glencoe, Ill.); Bird Key Yacht (Sarasota, Fla.). Home: 623 N Owl Dr Bird Key Sarasota FL 33577

CLINCHY, EVERETT ROSS, clergyman, educator; b. N.Y.C., Dec. 16, 1896; s. James Hugh and Lydie (Stagg) C.; m. Winifred Marcena Mead, Sept. 21, 1918; children—Ross, Eleanor Marcena, Barbara Rex. Student, Wesleyan U., Middletown, Conn., 1916-18, D.D., 1950; B.S., Lafayette Coll., 1920, D.D., 1951; postgrad., Union Theol. Sem., 1920-21, Yale, 1922-23; M.A., Columbia, 1921; Ph.D. in Edn, Drew U., 1934; LL.D., Fla. So. Coll., 1946, Washington U., 1955; L.H.D., Missouri Valley Coll., 1949, Wilberforce Coll., 1958, Hartwick Coll., 1959; Litt.D., St. Mary's Coll., 1981. Ordained to ministry Presbyn. Ch., 1921; minister Ch. of Christ, Wesleyan U., 1923-28; sec. Fed. Council Chs. of Christ Am., 1928-33; pres. NCCJ, 1928-58, Council on World Tensions, World Brotherhood; v.p., exec. dir. Roger Williams Straus Found.; mem. extension winter faculty U. Calif., Riverside, 1968-71; Mem. Joint Army and Navy Com. on Welfare and Recreation, Washington.; Originated Seminar confs. for study Cath.-Protestant-Jewish relations; also priest-rabbi-minister trio dialogue teams; dir. Williamstown Inst. Human Relations, summers 1935, 37, 39, 41; founder Inst. Man and Sci., Rensselaerville, N.Y., 1963, pres., 1963-72, chmn. exec. com., 1972—; gen. sec. program Improving Understanding Between Islam and West under auspices UNESCO, 1977—, v.p., 1979—. Author: All in the Name of God, 1934, The World We Want to Live In, 1942, A Handbook on Human Relations, 1949, Intergroup Relations Center, 1950; Contbr. articles to religious, ednl. publs. Chmn. Harlem Sch. Arts, 1972-75. Served as 2d lt. F.A. U.S. Army, World War I. Mem. Council on Fgn. Relations, Am. Sociol. Soc., Am. Acad. Polit. Sci., AAAS, Alpha Delta Phi. Clubs: Cosmos (Washington); Yale (N.Y.C.). Home: Little Meadow Guilford CT 06437 Office: Inst on Man and Sci Rensselaerville NY 12147

CLINE, CHARLES WILLIAM, poet; b. Waleska, Ga., Mar. 1, 1937; s. Paul Ardell and Mary Montarie (Pittman) C.; m. Sandra Lee Williamson, June 11, 1966; 1 son, Jeffrey Charles. Student, Conservatory of Music-U. Cin., 1957-58; A.A., Reinhardt Coll., 1957; B.A., George Peabody Coll. for Tchrs., 1960; M.A., Vanderbilt U., 1963. Asst. prof. English Shorter Coll., Rome, Ga., 1963-64; instr. English West Ga. Coll., Carrollton, 1964-68; manuscript procurement editor Fideler Co., Grand Rapids, Mich, 1968; assoc. prof. English Kellogg Community Coll., Battle Creek, Mich., 1969-75, prof. English and resident poet, 1975—; chmn. creative writing sect. Midwest Conf. on English, 1976; condr. poetry readings and workshops. Author: Crossing the Ohio, 1976, Questions for the Snow, 1979, Ultima Thule, 1984; editor: Forty Salutes to Mich. Poets, 1975; contbr. poems to jours. and anthologies. Recipient Poetry awards Modus Operandi, 1975, Internat. Belles-Lettres Soc., 1975, Poetry Soc. Mich., 1975, N.Am. Mentor, 1977,78. Fellow Internat. Acad. Poets (founding, prize 1983), Internat. Biog. Assn., Internat. Soc. Lit. (life); mem. Tagore Inst. Creative Writing Internat. (life), Midwest Conf. on English, NEA, Mich. Edn. Assn., Mich. Assn. Higher Edn., World Poetry Soc. Intercontinental, Centro Studi e Scambi Internazionali (poet Laureate award), Centro Studie Scambi Internazionali (Diploma di Benemerenza), Accademia Leonardo da Vinci, Poetry Soc. Am. (assoc. writing programs). Presbyterian. Office: Kellogg Community Coll 450 North Ave Battle Creek MI 49016

CLINE, CLARENCE LEE, educator; b. Belton, Tex., Jan. 6, 1905; s. William Edwin and Permilla (Mitchell) C.; m. Henriette Fechenbach, June 12, 1933; children—Patricia Holmes, Judith Harrison. B.A., Baylor U., 1926; M.A., U. Tex., 1931, Ph.D., 1938. Mem. faculty U. Tex., 1938—, prof. English, 1952—, chmn. dept., 1949-52, 62-68, Ashbel Smith prof. English, 1971-75, Ashbel Smith prof. emeritus, 1975—; vis. asso. prof. Harvard, summer 1952. Author: Byron, Shelley and Their Pisan Circle, 1952, also articles, chpts. in books.; Editor: Rinehart Book of Short Stories, 1952, Rinehart Book of Short Stories, alternate edit, 1964, The Letters of George Meredith, 1970, The Ordeal of Richard Feverel (George Meredith), 1971, The Owl and the Rossettis, 1978. Guggenheim fellow, 1974-75. Mem. Modern Lang. Assn., AAUP, S. Central Modern Lang. Assn., Coll. Conf. Tchrs. English, Modern Humanities Research Assn. Home: 1401 Hardouin Ave Austin TX 78703

CLINE, DOUGLAS, physicist, educator; b. York, Eng., Aug. 28, 1934; came to U.S., 1963; s. William Patrick and Annie Rita C.; m. Lorraine Van Meter, Dec. 28, 1975; children: Julia Van Meter, Geoffrey Karl. B.Sc. with 1st class honours, Manchester U., 1957, Ph.D., 1963. Mem. faculty U. Rochester, N.Y., 1963—, prof. physics, 1977—. Author papers in field. Address: Dept Physics U Rochester Rochester NY 14627

CLINE, MARTIN JAY, physician, educator; b. Phila., Jan. 12, 1934; s. David and Rose C.; m. Evelyn Helen Cohen, June 19, 1955; children—Eric, Avril, David. Student, U. Pa., 1951-54; M.D., Harvard U., 1958. Intern Peter Bent Brigham Hosp., Boston, 1958-59, resident in medicine, 1959-60; asst. prof. medicine U. Calif. Sch. Medicine, San Francisco, 1964-67, asso. prof., 1968-73; asso. dir. Cancer Research Inst., 1968-73; Bowyer prof. med. oncology UCLA, 1973—, chief div. hematology-oncology dept. medicine, 1973-81; Wright Meml. lectr. Ohio State U., 1980; 1st Dameshek lectr. Tufts U., 1981. Author 4 books in field; contbr. articles to profl. jours. Served with USPHS, 1960-62. Mem. Assn. Am. Physicians, Am. Soc. Clin. Investigation, AAAS, Am. Soc. Hematology, A.C.P., Internat. Soc. Exptl. Hematology. Republican. Office: Div Hematology and Oncology Dept Medicine UCLA Center Health Scis Los Angeles CA 90024

CLINE, PAUL CHARLES, educator; b. Clarksburg, W.Va., Dec. 26, 1933; s. Kemper Price and Irene (Neff) C.; m. Diane Chilcote, Aug. 10, 1958; children—Alice J., Camille N. A.A., Potomac State Coll., 1953; A.B., W.Va. U., 1956, J.D., 1957, M.A., 1961; Ph.D. in Govt, Am. U., 1968. Bar: W.Va. bar 1957. Practice in, Huntington, 1959-60; asst. prof. polit. sci. James Madison U., Harrisonburg, Va., 1961-68, asso. prof., 1968-70, coordinator fed. grants and program, 1966-67, exec. asst. to pres., 1967-69, head dept. polit. sci. and geography, 1969-71, prof. polit. sci., 1970—. Chmn. Harrisburg City Planning Commn., 1971-72; mem. Harrisonburg City Council, 1972-76; chmn. Harrisonburg Redevel. and Housing Authority, 1979-80. Served with AUS, 1957-59. Mem. Am. Polit. Sci. Assn., Shenandoah Valley Folklore Soc., W.Va. State Bar, Phi Alpha Delta, Phi Alpha Theta, Sigma Phi Omega, Phi Sigma Alpha, Pi Sigma Nu. Home: 221 Dixie Ave Harrisonburg VA 22801

CLINE, RAY STEINER, world affairs educator and administrator; b. Anderson, Ill., June 4, 1918; s. Charles and Ina May (Steiner) C.; m. Marjorie Wilson, June 4, 1941; children: Judith, Sibyl. A.B., Harvard U., 1939, M.A., 1941, Ph.D., 1949; Ph.D. (Henry prize fellow), Balliol Coll., Oxford (Eng.) U., 1939-40. Jr. fellow Harvard U., 1941-42; with OSS, 1943-46, Office Chief Mil. History, Dept. Army, 1946-49, CIA, 1949-51; attaché Am. embassy, London, 1951-53; with CIA, 1954-58; dir. U.S. Naval Aux. Communications Center, Taipei, 1958-62; dep. dir. for intelligence CIA, 1962-66; spl. adviser Am. embassy, Bonn, Germany, 1966-69; dir. Bur. Intelligence and Research, Dept. State, 1969-73; dir. world power studies Georgetown U. Center Strategic and Internat. Studies, Washington, 1973—; pres. Nat. Intelligence Study Center, Washington, Com. for Free China. Author: Washington Command Post, 1951, World Power Assessment, 1975, Secrets, Spies and Scholars, 1976, World Power Assessment-1977, 1977, World Power Trends and U.S. Foreign Policy for the 1980's, 1980, The CIA: Reality vs. Myth, 1982, (with Herbert Block) The Planetary Product in 1982, 1983, (with Yonah Alexander) Terrorism: the Soviet Connection, 1984; contbr. articles to publs. Mem. Oxford Soc., Council Fgn. Relations, Washington Inst. Fgn. Affairs, Acad. Polit. and Social Sci., Phi Beta Kappa. Clubs: Internat. (Washington); Harvard of N.Y.C. Home: 3027 N Pollard St Arlington VA 22207 Office: Center Strategic and Internat Studies Georgetown U Washington DC *Because of World War II and the international problems besetting America in the ensuing thirty-five years, I have combined a life of scholarship with a life of government service. This combination of the world of thought and the world of action has seemed to me congenial, rewarding and, from time to time, useful to the nation. The 1980's seem to require more careful thinking and more patriotism than ever.*

CLINE, RICHARD GORDON, distribution company executive; b. Chgo., Feb. 17, 1935; s. William R. and Katherine A. (Bothwell) C.; m. Carole J. Costello, Dec. 28, 1957; children: Patricia, Linda, Richard, Jeffrey. B.S., U. Ill., 1957. With Jewel Cos., Inc., Chgo., 1963—; pres. Osco Drug, Inc. subs., 1970-79, sr. exec. v.p., 1979, vice chmn., 1979, pres., 1980—, also dir.; dir. NICOR Inc., No. Ill. Gas Co., Aurrera, S.A. de C.V., Mexico City. Trustee Rush-Presbyterian-St. Luke's Med. Center; gov. and former chmn. bd. Central DuPage Hosp.; mem. U. Ill. Found. Presbyterian. Clubs: Econ., Chgo., Commercial, Commonwealth, Chgo. Golf. Office: Jewel Cos Inc 5725 East River Rd Chicago IL 60631

CLINE, ROBERT STANLEY, air freight company executive; b. Urbana, Ill., July 17, 1937; s. Lyle Stanley and Mary Elizabeth (Prettyman) C.; m. Judith Lee Stucker, July 7, 1979; children: Lisa Andre, Nicole Lesley, Christina Elaine, Leslie Jane. B.A., Dartmouth Coll., 1959. Asst. treas. Chase Manhattan Bank, N.Y.C., 1960-65; v.p. fin. Pacific Air Freight Co., Seattle, 1965-68; exec. v.p. fin. Airborne Freight Corp., Seattle, 1968-78, vice chmn., chief fin. officer, dir., 1978-84, chmn., chief exec. officer, dir., 1984—. Trustee Seattle Repertory Theatre, 1974—, Children's Orthopedic Hosp. Found., 1983—; chmn. bd. Seattle Repertory Theatre, 1979-83. Served with U.S. Army, 1959-60. Home: 10058 SE 16th St Bellevue WA 98004 Office: 190 Queen Anne Ave N Seattle WA 98009

CLINE, WILLIAM RICHARD, economist; b. Denver, Oct. 30, 1941; s. John Russell and Marian Alice (Franklin) C.; m. Ruth Eleanor Harwood, June 10, 1967; children: Alison Margaret, Marian Harwood. A.B., Pub. Affairs summa cum laude, Princeton U., 1963; M.A. in Econs., Yale U., 1964, Ph.D., 1969. Lectr. Princeton U., 1967-69, asst. prof., 1969-70; Ford Found. vis. prof. Brazilian Planning Ministry and U. Sao Paulo, 1970-71; dep. dir. trade and devel. research U.S. Treasury Dept., Washington, 1971-73; sr. fellow Brookings Instn., Washington, 1973-81, Inst. for Internat. Econs., 1982—; pres. Internat. Econ. Analysis, Inc., Washington, 1981—. Author: Economic Consequences of a Land Reform in Brazil, 1970, Potential Effects of Income Redistribution, 1976, Trade Negotiations in the Tokyo Round, 1978, World Inflation and the Developing Countries, 1981, International Dept: Systemic Risk and Policy Response, 1983. Woodrow Wilson fellow, 1964; Ford Found. fellow, 1965. Mem. Am. Econ. Assn. Episcopalian. Hoem: 5315 Oakland Rd Chevy Chase MD 20815 Office: Inst for Internat Econs 11 Dupont Circle NW Suite 620 Washington DC 20036

CLINGER, WILLIAM FLOYD, JR., congressman; b. Warren, Pa., Apr. 4, 1929; s. William Floyd and Lella May C.; m. Julia Whitla, Aug. 2, 1952; children: Eleanore, William Floyd, James, Julia. B.A., Johns Hopkins U., 1951; J.D., U. Va., 1965. Bar: Pa. 1965, U.S. Supreme Ct. 1975. Advt. exec. New Process Co., Warren, 1955-62; partner firm Stone and Harper, and successor firm Harper, Clinger & Eberly, Warren, 1965-78; mem. 96th-98th Congresses from 23d Pa. Dist., mem. com. on public works and transp., 1979, com. on govt. ops., 1981; chief counsel Econ. Devel. Adminstrn., 1975-77; del. Pa. Constl. Conv., 1968. Editorial bd.: U. Va. Law Rev, 1964-65. Chmn. Kinzua Dam Dedication Com., 1966; del. Republican Nat. Conv., 1972; pres. Warren Library Assn., 1957-62, 67-70, Warren Hosp. Bd., 1971-75. Served with USN, 1951-55. Decorated Spirit of Honor medal; named Man of Year Pa. Jaycees, 1960. Mem. Am. Bar Assn., Pa. Bar Assn., Warren County Bar Assn., Warren Jaycees (pres. 1959-60). Presbyterian. Office: 1122 Longworth House Office Bldg Washington DC 20515

CLINGMAN, ALLEN EDWARD, music educator; b. Newton, Iowa, June 19, 1929; s. Van Dyke and Helen Aileen (Bishop) C.; m. Shirley Lee Patterson, Dec. 27, 1950. B.M.E., Drake U., 1951, M.Mus. Edn., 1954; M.A., Columbia U., 1956, Ed.D., 1958. Prof., head music dept. Eastern Ky. U., Richmond, 1964-65; prof. music edn. U. B.C., Vancouver, 1966—, chmn. music edn. program, 1979—; Cana. rep. XI Internat. Conf., Internat. Soc. Music Edn., Perth, Australia, 1974; cons. Australian Council for Arts, 1974; bd. dirs. Community Arts Council, Vancouver, 1980—, pres., 1982—. Editor: B.C. Music Educator, 1960-64, 65-67; contbr. profl. jours. Served with AUS, 1951-53. Lydia Roberts fellow Columbia, Tchrs. Coll., 1955-56. Mem. B.C. Music Educators Assn. (pres. 1963-64), Can. Music Educators Assn. (pres. 1971-73), Phi Mu Alpha Sinfonia, Pi Kappa Lambda. Clubs: Masons, Shriners. Home: 3235 Quesnel Dr Vancouver BC V6S 1Z7 Canada

CLINK, STEPHEN H., lawyer; b. Muskegon, Mich., Jan. 26, 1911; s. Stephen H. C. A.B., U. Mich., 1933, J.D., 1936; LL.M. in Taxation, N.Y.U., 1949. Bar: Mich. bar 1936. Pros. atty., Muskegon County, 1939-41, judge of probate, 1941-48; now mem. firm Landman, Luyendyk, Latimer, Clink & Robb, Muskegon, 1950—; Teaching fellow N.Y.U., 1948-49. Contbr. articles to profl. jours. Pres. Muskegon Area Child Guidance Clinic, 1942; chmn. Mich. Juvenile Inst. Commn., 1945-47; pres. Mich. Welfare League, 1951-53, Timber Trails council Boy Scouts Am., 1965-66; chmn. bd. trustees Timber Trails council Boy Scouts Am., 1962-74; pres. Muskegon County Community Found., 1972-74; sec. Fremont Area Found., 1970-76; chmn. United Appeal Planning and Research Council, 1968-69; pres. Muskegon County United Appeal, 1970-71; Mem. com. of visitors U. Mich. Law Sch., 1963-64; bd. dirs. numerous charitable founds. Named Young Man of Year Jr. C. of C., 1940, Muskegon's Outstanding Citizen, 1978; recipient Silver Beaver award, Distinguished Eagle award Boy Scouts. Fellow Am. Coll. Probate Counsel (regent 1967-76); mem. ABA (chmn. probate judges com. 1946), Muskegon County Bar Assn. (pres. 1952-53), State Bar Mich. (chmn. taxation sect. 1958-59, chmn. probate and trust law sect. 1968-69, ethics com. 1958-70). Congregationalist (chmn. bd. deacons). Club: Muskegon Kiwanis (pres. 1958). Office: 400 Terrace Plaza Muskegon MI 49443

CLINTON, GORDON STANLEY, JR., lawyer; b. Medicine Hat, Alta., Can., Apr. 13, 1920; s. John H. and Gladys (Hall) C.; m. Florence H. Vayhinger, Dec. 19, 1942; children: Barbara H. Clinton Tompkins, Gordon Stanley, Deborah. A.B. in Polit. Sci., U. Wash., 1942, J.D., 1947; spl. student, Harvard Grad. Sch., 1945; LL.D. (hon.), Coll. Puget Sound, 1957, Seattle Pacific Coll., 1960. Bar: Wash. 1947. Spl. agt. FBI, 1942-44; pvt. practice, Seattle, 1949—; firm Clinton, Fleck & Glein; dep. pros. atty., King County, 1947-49; judge pro-tem Mcpl. Ct., Seattle, 1949-52; spl. atty. City Council of Seattle, 1954; mayor City Council of, 1956-64; chmn. exec. com. Japan-Am. Conf. Mayors; adv. bd. U.S. Conf. Mayors, 1956-64; mem. Presdl. Commn. Intergovtl. Relations, 1959-60; v.p. Western region, civic com. People to People; chmn. Kobe-Seattle Affiliation Com., Marine Employees Commn. Mem. Wash. Bd. Edn., 1969-70; Trustee Seattle Pacific Coll., 1964-70; bd. dirs. YMCA, Wesley Found., 1968—, Town Affiliation Assn.; pres. Asso. Methodist Home, 1969-72; del. Gen. Conf. Meth. Ch. Served from apprentice seaman to lt. (j.g.) USNR, 1944-46. Recipient Silver Beaver award, Disting. Service award Chief Seattle council Boy Scouts Am.; Disting. Grad. award Roosevelt High Sch., 1960; Newsmakers of Tomorrow award Time Mag. and Seattle C. of C., 1953; citation of honor Wash. State chpt. AIA, 1957; Human Relations award Seattle Civic Unity Commn., 1963; citation NCCJ, 1964; Outstanding Pub. Ofcl. award Mcpl. League, 1964; Decorated Order of Sikatunah (Philippines), 3d Class Order of Rising Sun (Japan). Mem. Am. Mcpl. Assn. (exec. com. 1957—, pres. 1962), ABA, Wash. State, Seattle bar assns., NCCJ, Japan-Am. Soc. Seattle (pres. 1973), Phi Delta Phi. Republican. Methodist (bd. missions). Clubs: Masons (32 deg.), Shriners, KC. Home: 7733 58th Ave NE Seattle WA 98115 Office: Third-Lenora Bldg Seattle WA 98121

CLINTON, JOHN HART, lawyer, publisher; b. Quincy, Mass., Apr. 3, 1905; s. John Francis and Catherine Veronica (Hart) C.; m. Helen Alice Amphlett, Feb. 18, 1933 (dec. 1965); children: Mary Jane (Mrs. Raymond Zirkel), Mary Ann (Mrs. Christopher Gardner, Jr.), John Hart; m. Mathilda A. Schoorel van Dillen, Feb. 22, 1969. A.B., Boston Coll., 1926; J.D., Harvard U., 1929. Bar: Calif. 1930, Mass. 1930. Since practiced in, San Francisco; assoc. Morrison, Foerster, Holloway, Clinton & Clark, and predecessor, 1929-41, ptnr., 1941-72; of counsel Morrison & Foerster, 1972—; Vice pres., gen. counsel Indsl. Employers and Distbrs. Assn., Emeryville, 1944-72; pres. Leamington Hotel, Oakland, Calif., 1933-47, Amphlett Printing Co., San Mateo, Calif., 1943—; pub. San Mateo Times, 1943—, editor, 1960—. Hon. mem. exec. com. San Mateo County council Boy Scouts Am.; bd. dirs., pres. Calif. Jockey Club Found.; regent emeritus Notre Dame Coll., Belmont, Calif. Decorated Knight Equestrian Order of Holy Sepulchre of Jerusalem. Mem. FCC, Am., San Francisco, San Mateo County bar assns., State Bar Calif. (past chmn. fair trial/free press com., past co-chmn. Calif. bench/bar media com.), Am. Judicature Soc., Nat. Lawyers Club, Am. Law Inst., San Mateo County Devel. Assn (pres. 1963-65), San Mateo County Hist. Assn. (pres. 1960-64), Calif. Press Assn. (pres. 1970, chmn. membership com.), Am. Newspaper Pubs. Assn. (govt. affairs com., press/bar relations com.; Am. Bar Assn.-Am. Newspapers Pubs. Assn. task force), Calif. Newspaper Pubs. Assn. (pres. 1969), Wine and Food Soc. San Francisco, Am. Soc. Newspaper Editors, Assn. Cath. Newsmen, Nat. Press Photographers Assn., Internat. Platform Assn., Newcomen Soc. Clubs: Commonwealth of Calif. (past pres.), San Francisco Comml., Bohemian (San Francisco); Bombay Bicycle Riding (Burlingame, Calif.); Sequoia (Redwood City, Calif.). Lodges: Elks; Rotary (San Mateo past pres.). Home: 131 Sycamore Ave San Mateo CA 94402 Office: 1080 S Amphlett Blvd San Mateo CA 94402

CLINTON, MARIANN HANCOCK, assn. exec.; b. Dyersburg, Tenn., Dec. 7, 1933; s. John Bowen and Nell Maurine (Johnson) Hancock; m. Harry Everett Clinton, Aug. 25, 1956; children—Carol, John Everett. B.Mus., Cin. Conservatory Music, 1956; B.S., U. Cin., 1956; M.Mus., Miami U., Oxford, Ohio, 1971. Tchr. music public schs., Hamilton County, Ohio, 1956-57, tchr. voice and piano, Butler County, Ohio, 1964—; instr. music Miami U., 1972-75; exec. dir. Music Tchrs. Nat. Assn., Cin., 1977—; Mng. dir. Am. Music Tchr., 1977—. Mem. adminstrv. bd. Middletown (Ohio) 1st United Methodist Ch., 1968-72. Mem. Music Educators Nat. Conf., Am. Ednl. Research Assn., Am. Soc. Assn. Execs., Nat. Fedn. Music Clubs, Pi Kappa Lambda, Kappa Delta Pi, Mu Phi Epsilon, Phi Mu. Republican. Home: 6543 Niderdale Way Middletown OH 45042 Office: 2113 Carew Tower Cincinnati OH 45202 *I have found that a consideration for the interrelatedness of all parts so necessary in the presentation of music and a warm regard for the feelings of others which is implicit in the practice of good manners in daily observance create success in one's personal and professional lives.*

CLINTON, ROBERT L., assn. adminstr.; b. Putnam, Tex., Nov. 27, 1923; s. Robert L. and Eva Frances (Park) C.; m. Wanda Merle Lowry, Oct. 14, 1944; children—Robert Lowry, David Reagan, Ronald Dale. B.M., North Tex. State U., 1948; Mus.M., 1950; Ed.D., Tex. Tech U., 1962. Dir. music Cisco Jr. Coll., 1949-53; supr. music Snyder (Tex.) Public Schs., 1953-60; grad. asst. Tex. Tech U., 1960; prin. Snyder Ind. Sch. Dist., 1961-63, supt., 1964-67; asst. commr. jr. coll. coordinating bd. Tex. Coll. and Univ. System, 1967-70; pres. Western Tex. Coll., 1970-81; dir. Tex. Public Community/Jr. Coll. Assn., Austin, 1981—. Served with USAAF, 1943-46. Mem. Phi Mu Alpha, Alpha Chi, Phi Delta Kappa. Methodist. Office: 406 E 11th St Austin TX 78701

CLINTON, WILLIAM J., lawyer, governor of Arkansas; b. Hope, Ark., Aug. 19, 1946; (married); 1 dau. B.S. in Internat. Affairs, Georgetown U., 1968; postgrad. (Rhodes scholar), U. Coll., Oxford (Eng.) U., 1968-70; J.D., Yale U., 1973. Prof. law U. Ark. Sch. Law at Fayetteville and ltd. individual practice law, 1973-76; atty. gen., Ark., 1977-79; gov. State of Ark., 1979-81, 83—; of counsel firm Wright, Lindsey & Jennings, Little Rock, 1981-82. Chmn. bd. Ark. Housing Devel. Corp.; chmn. state and local election div. Dem. Nat. Com. Mem. Am., Ark. bar assns., Nat. Assn. Attys. Gen. Democrat. Office: State Capitol Little Rock AR 72201

CLIVE, JOHN LEONARD, educator; b. Berlin, Germany, Sept. 25, 1924; came to U.S., 1940, naturalized, 1943; s. Bruno and Rose (Rosenfeld) C. Student, Buxton Coll., Derbyshire, Eng., 1937-40; A.B., U. N.C., 1943; M.A., Harvard, 1947, Ph.D., 1952. From teaching fellow to asst. prof. history Harvard U., 1948-60, prof. history and lit., 1965-75, prof. history, 1975-79, William R. Kenan, Jr. prof. history and lit., 1979—; Vernon vis. prof. biography Dartmouth Coll., 1979; asst. prof., then asso. prof. history U. Chgo., 1960-65; vis. fellow All Souls Coll. Oxford, 1977-78; spl. Ford lectr. Oxford U., 1978. Author: Scotch Reviewers: The Edinburgh Review, 1802-1815, 1957, Macaulay: The Shaping of the Historian, 1973; Gen. editor: Classics of British Historical Literature. Served to 2d lt. AUS, 1943-46. Recipient Nat. Book award, 1974; Robert Livingston Schuyler prize Am. Hist. Assn., 1976. Fellow Royal Hist. Soc., Am. Acad. Arts and Scis.; mem. Mass. Hist. Soc., Phi Beta Kappa. Club: Century Assn. Home: 38 Fernald Dr Cambridge MA 02138

CLIVER, DEAN OTIS, virologist, educator; b. Oak Park, Ill., Mar. 2, 1935; s. Milton Clarence and Ivy Ada (Erb) C.; m. Carolyn Elaine Parker, Aug. 13, 1960; children—Blanche Irena, Frederick Lajos, Carl Milan, Marguerite Estelle. B.S., Purdue U., 1956, M.S., 1957; Ph.D., Ohio State U., 1960. Postdoctoral research Ohio State U., 1960; resident research asso. Nat. Acad. Sci.-NRC, U.S. Army Biol. Labs., Ft. Detrick, Md., 1961-62; research asso., instr. Food Research Inst., U. Chgo., 1962-66; asst. prof. dept. food microbiology and toxicology, dept. bacteriology Food Research Inst., U. Wis., Madison, 1966-67, asso. prof., 1967-76, prof., 1976—; prin. investigator, head WHO Collaborating Centre on Food Virology, Madison. Contbr. articles to profl. jours. and chpts. to books. Served as 2d lt. U.S. Army Res., 1957. Recipient Borden undergrad. award Purdue U., 1956; Ralston-Purina grad. fellow, 1956-57. Mem. Am. Soc. Microbiology, Sigma Xi. Home: 653 Pickford St Madison WI 53711 Office: Food Research Inst Dept Food Microbiology and Toxicology U Wis 1925 Willow Dr Madison WI 53706

CLOAK, FRANK THEODORE, educator; b. Detroit, Aug. 13, 1904; s. Frank V.C. and Harriet A. (White) C.; m. Zoe Comer, June 11, 1930; children—Frank Theodore, Andrea Louise (Mrs. Raymond Mihok), Nathaniel Healy; m. Evelyn Campbell, Jan. 8, 1965 (dec. Oct. 1971). B.A., Wesleyan U., Middletown, Conn., 1925; M.A., Northwestern U., 1927, Yale, 1937-39; M.F.A., Lawrence U., 1969. Prodn. mgr. Evanston Childrens Theatre, 1925-26; instr. theatre Northwestern U., 1926-28; tchr. speech and theatre Benton Harbor (Mich.) High Sch., 1928-29; asst. prof. theatre Lawrence U., Appleton, Wis., 1929-35, asso. prof., 1935-40, prof., 1940—, Evangeline Bergstrom prof. fine arts, 1966—; founder, dir. Berkshire Playhouse Drama Sch., summers 1932-42. Author: Allardyce Nicoll Forbidden Fruit and Other Plays, 1940. Served with OSS, 1943-45. Recipient Rockefeller Found. grants for study, 1938-39, 45-46, 57. Fellow Royal Soc. Arts. Home: 1015 Jardin Street Appleton WI 54911

CLOAR, CARROLL, artist; b. Earle, Ark., Jan. 18, 1913; s. Charles W. and Eva (David) C. A.B., Southwestern Coll., Memphis, 1934, 1978; student, Memphis Acad. Art, 1935, Art Students League, N.Y.C., 1936-40. Author: Hostile Butterflies and Other Paintings, 1977; Contbr. to: Delta Rev; One man shows include, Alan Gallery, N.Y.C., 1956, 58, 60, 62, 64, 66, Brooks Meml. Gallery, Memphis, 1955, High Mus., Atlanta, 1959, M. H. De Young Gallery, San Francisco, 1967, Ark. Art Ctr., Little Rock, 1956, exhbns. include, Pitts. Internat., 1955, Whitney Ann., 1960, Phila. Ann., 1962, retrospective exhbn., N.Y. State U., 1968; represented in permanent collections, Met. Mus., Mus. Modern Art, Whitney Mus., Library of Congress, Wadsworth Atheneum, others, also pvt. collections. Former trustee Brooks Meml. Gallery Art, Memphis. Served with USAAF, 1942-45. Guggenheim fellow, 1946; named Ark. traveller, 1956. Hon. mem. Phi Beta Kappa. Address: 235 S Greer St Memphis TN 38111

CLODIUS, ROBERT LEROY, educator, economist; b. Walla Walla, Wash., Mar. 10, 1921; s. Hans Frederick and Emma (Wellman) C.; m. Joan Elizabeth Coyle, Aug. 27, 1949; children: Catherine, Mark. Student, Whitman Coll., 1938-40, LL.D., 1970; B.S., U. Calif. at Berkeley, 1942, Ph.D., 1950. Lectr. econs. U. Calif. at Berkeley, 1949-50; mem. faculty U. Wis., 1950—, prof. agrl. econs., 1958—, chmn. dept., 1960-62, v.p. univ., 1962-71, acting pres., 1970, prof. econs., 1971—, prof. ednl. adminstrn., 1971—, prof. univ., 1971—; on leave as pres. Nat. Assn. State Univs. and Land Grant Colls., 1979—; vis. asso. Harvard Bus. Sch., 1954; lectr. Am. Council Edn., Inst. Coll. and U. Adminstrs.; State Dept. specialist in, S.Am., 1961; cons. dept. Agr., 1961; mem. com. agr. scis. to sec. agr., 1961-69; cons. Rockefeller Found., 1963-67; adviser U. East Africa, 1963-67; chmn. Com. Instnl. Coop., 1968; cons. Ford Found., Philippines, 1970; chmn. exec. bd. commn. instns. higher edn. N. Central Assn., 1972-74; v.p. Midwest Univs. Consortium Internat. Activities, Inc., 1964-70, chmn. bd., 1970-71; mem. Commn. on Higher Edn., Govt. Sierra Leone, 1969; adminstr. Indonesian Higher Agr. Edn. Project, 1971-77; adv. commr. Edn. Commn. of the States, 1980—; mem. Nat. Commn. on Higher Edn. Issues, 1981-82. Author articles, monographs, chpts. in books; editor: Jour. Farm Econs, 1958-60. Bd. dirs. Univ. Corp. Atmospheric Research, 1962-67, Center for Research Libraries, 1969-71, Argonne Univ. Assos., 1978—. Served to lt. USNR, 1942-46. Decorated Commendation medal; recipient Kiekhofer Teaching award U. Wis., 1953. Mem. Am. Econs. Assn., Am. Agrl. Econs. Assn. (v.p. 1960, Thesis award 1951), AAUP (pres. Wis. 1957), Phi Beta Kappa, Alpha Zeta, Phi Kappa Phi. Home: 3828 Klingle Pl NW Washington DC 20016

CLOGAN, PAUL MAURICE, educator; b. Boston, July 9, 1934; s. Michael J. and Agnes J. (Murphy) C.; m. Julie Sydney Davis, June 27, 1972; children: Michael Rodger, Patrick Terence, Margaret Murphy. B.A., Boston Coll., 1956, M.A., 1957; Ph.D., U. Ill., 1961; F.A.A.R., Am. Acad. in Rome, 1966. Asst. prof. Duke U., 1961-65; assoc. prof. Case Western Res. U., Cleve., 1965-72; prof. English N. Tex. State U., Denton, 1972—; vis. prof. U. Keele, Eng., 1965, U. Pisa, Italy, 1966; vis.prof. U. Tours, France, 1978; vis. mem. Inst. Advanced Study, Princeton, N.J., 1970, 77; cons. Library of Congress, Ednl. Testing Service, NEH, Nat. Acad. Scis., NRC Commn. Human Resources, Am. Council Learned Socs., Nat. Enquiry into Scholarly Communication, Chilton Research Services; mem. Am. Arts Assn., Inst. Internat. Edn. Author: The Medieval Achilleid of Statius, 1968, Social Dimensions in Medieval and Renaissance Studies, 1972, In Honor of S. Harrison Thomson, 1970, Medieval and Renaissance Studies in Review, 1971, Medieval and Renaissance Spirituality, 1973, Medieval Historiography, 1974, Medieval Hagiography and Romance, 1975, Medieval Poetics, 1976, Transformation and Continuity, 1977, Byzantine and Western Studies, 1983; editor: Medievalia et Humanistica: Studies in Medieval and Renaissance Culture, 1970; contbr. articles to profl. jours. Grantee Duke Endowment, 1961-62, Am. Council Learned Socs., 1963-64, 70-71, Philos. Soc., 1964-69; sr. Fulbright-Hays postdoctoral research fellow, Italy, 1965-66; Fulbright-Hays research grantee, France, 1978; fellow Prix de Rome, 1966-67, Bollingen Found., 1966, NEH, 1969-70; N. Tex. State U. Faculty grantee, 1972-75, 80-81. Mem. Internat. Assn. Univ. Profs. English, MLA (exec. com. 1980—, del. assembly 1981—), Internat. Comparative Lit. Assn., Internat. Arthurian Soc., Modern Humanities Research Assn., Medieval Acad. Am. (nominating com. 1975-76, John Nicholas Brown Prize com. 1980—). Democrat. Roman Catholic. Office: PO Box 13348 North Texas Sta Denton TX 76203

CLOHERTY, JOHN JOSEPH (JACK CLOHERTY), journalist; b. Chgo., Nov. 2, 1949; s. John Joseph and Grayce (Mulvenna) C.; m. Barbara Joan Campbell, Apr. 19, 1980. B.S. in Journalism, U. Mont., 1972. Congressional aide, 1972; investigative reporter Jack Anderson's column, 1972-76; columnist Los Angeles Times Syndicate, 1976-78; investigative reporter Sta. WRC-TV, Washington, 1978—. Co-producer, reporter story on potential dangers of asbestos in hand-held hairdryers. Recipient George Polk award for nat. TV reporting, 1980, Ohio State award for public service reporting, 1980, Nat. Press Club citation for consumer reporting, 1980, Gavel award cert. of merit Am. Bar Assn., 1980. Mem. Investigative Reporters and Editors (Gold medallion for reporting 1980), Nat. Acad. TV Arts and Scis. Roman Catholic. Office: 4001 Nebraska St Washington DC 20016

CLOKEY, FRANK R., marketing communications company executive; b. Bryn Mawr, Pa., Mar. 29, 1939; s. James D. and Amy Lucille (Frost) C.; m. Elizabeth Adele Seay, Apr. 8, 1972. A.B., Washington and Jefferson Coll., 1961; LL.B., U. Pitts., 1964. Bar: Pa. 1965. Pvt. practice, Pitts. and Waynesboro, Pa., 1965-68; mgr. contract adminstrn. NBC, N.Y.C., 1968-72; spl. asst. atty. gen. for environ. affairs, Commonwealth of Pa., Harrisburg, 1972-74; asso. gen. counsel Leo Burnett Co., Chgo., 1974-78; v.p., gen. counsel Ketchum Communications, Inc., Pitts., 1979—. Bd. dirs., pres. Islamorada S. Condominium Assn. Served with U.S. Army, 1964. Recipient Class of 1933 Legal Aid award U. Pitts. Sch. Law, 1964. Mem. Am. Assn. Advt. Agencies (legal affairs com.). Republican. Presbyterian. Clubs: Highland Country, Gateway Center. Office: 4 Gateway Center Pittsburgh PA 15222

CLONEY, WILLIAM THOMAS, JR., former athletic association executive; b. Boston, Oct. 29, 1911; s. William T. and Elizabeth Anne (McLaughlin) C.; m. Arline Patricia Lynch, June 29, 1937; children: Mary E. (Mrs. William D. Benjes, Jr.), Kathleen (Mrs. N. Phillips Dodge III), Martha (Mrs. W. Brooke Hamilton, Jr.) (dec.), William Thomas (killed in action). A.B., Harvard U., 1933, student Grad. Sch. Edn., 1934-35. With Boston Herald, 1930-53; sports editor Boston Post, 1953-56; jr. master Roxbury Latin Sch., 1935- 36; instr. to assoc. prof. English and journalism Northeastern U., 1937-53; pub. relations counsel, 1956-59; asst. to pres. Keystone Custodian Funds, 1956-62, v.p., 1962-78; pres. Boston Athletic Assn.; dir. Boston Marathon, 1946-82; pres. emeritus Assn. Internat. Marathons Inc., 1982—. Author: The Story of a New England Industrialist, James Lorin Richards, 1952; also mag. articles. Served to lt. col. AUS, 1942-46. Home: 17 Elm Park Scituate MA 02066

CLOONAN, CLIFFORD B., electrical engineer, educator; b. Chugwater, Wyo., Aug. 28, 1928; s. Clifford Brokaw and Jessie Fern (Dowler) C.; m. Ann Jean Worstell, Mar. 23, 1951; children: Clifford Cameron, Alison Ann, Kevin Allen. Student, S.D. State Coll., 1945-46; B.S., U. Colo., 1955; M.S., Mont. State Coll., 1961; postgrad., Utah State U., 1964, Colo. U., 1967-69, Ph.D., 1975. Systems engr. Collins Radio Co., Cedar Rapids, Iowa, 1955-57; asst. prof. Calif. Poly. State U., San Luis Obispo, 1957-62, asso. prof., 1962-67, prof. elec. engring., 1967—; research asso. Mont. State Coll., 1960-61; electronic scientist Environ. Sci. Services Adminstrn., Boulder, Colo., 1966-68; cons. McDonnell Aircraft Co., St. Louis, TRW, Redondo Beach, Calif., Hewlett-Packard, Santa Rosa, Calif. Served with inf. AUS, 1946-47; Served with Signal Corps, 1951-53. NSF fellow, 1968-69. Mem. IEEE, Am. Radio Relay League, Mensa, Sigma Xi, Phi Kappa Phi. Republican. Baptist. Home: 650 Lilac Dr Los Osos CA 93402 Office: Elec Engring Dept Calif Poly State U San Luis Obispo CA 93407

CLORE, ALAN E., chemical company executive; b. 1943. Chmn. bd., dir. Gulf Resources & Chem. Corp., Houston, 1982—. Office: Gulf Resources & Chem Corp 1100 Milam Bldg Houston TX 77002

CLOSE, CHARLES MOLLISON, engineering educator; b. Ilion, N.Y., Mar. 15, 1927; s. Charles M. and Marion (Young) C.; m. Ann V. Hasbrouck, June 8, 1957; children: Douglas A., Kimberly A., Scott C. B.S., Lehigh U., 1950; M.S., Stevens Inst. Tech., 1953; Ph.D., Rensselaer Poly. Inst., 1962. Devel. engr. Westinghouse Electric Corp., 1950-52; grad. asst. Stevens Inst. Tech., 1952-54; mem. faculty Rensselaer Poly. Inst., 1954—, prof. elec. engring., 1967—, assoc. chmn. elec. engring., 1972-74, chmn. elec. engring., 1974—. Author: (with others) State Variables for Engineers, 1965, The Analysis of Linear Circuits, 1966, (with D.K. Frederick) Modeling and Analysis of Dynamic Systems, 1978. Vestryman St. John's Ch., Troy, N.Y.; mem. council YMCA Silver Bay (N.Y.) Assn. Served with USNR, 1945-46. Mem. IEEE, Am. Soc. Engring. Edn., Phi Beta Kappa, Sigma Xi, Tau Beta Pi, Eta Kappa Nu, Pi Mu Epsilon. Republican. Episcopalian. Home: 18 Berkshire Dr Clifton Park NY 12065

CLOSE, CHARLES THOMAS, painter; b. Monroe, Wash., July 5, 1940; s. Leslie Durwood and Mildred Emma (Wagner) C.; m. Leslie Rose, Dec. 24, 1967; children: Georgia Molly, Maggie Sarah. B.A., U. Wash., 1962; B.F.A., Yale U., 1963, M.F.A., 1964; postgrad. (Fulbright grantee), Akadamie der Bildenen Kunste, Vienna, Austria, 1964-65. Faculty U. Mass., 1965-67, Sch. Visual Arts, N.Y.C., 1967-71, N.Y. U., 1970-73; mem. Bykert Gallery, N.Y.C., 1969-74, Pace Gallery, 1975—. One-man shows, Los Angeles County Museum, 1971, Mus. Contemporary Art, Chgo., 1972, 81, Mus. Modern Art, N.Y.C., 1973, San Francisco Mus. Art, 1975, Balt. Mus. Art, 1976, Georges Pompidou Centre/Musée Nationale d'Art Moderne, Paris, 1979, retrospective) Walker Art Center, Mpls., 1980, St. Louis Art Mus., 1981, Whitney Mus., N.Y.C., group shows include, Whitney Mus., N.Y.C., 1969, 70, 72, 77, 79, Documenta 5 & 6, Kassel, W.Ger., 1972, 77, Tokyo Biennale, 1974. Nat. Endowment for Arts grantee, 1973. Home: 271 Central Park West New York NY 10024

CLOSE, DAVID PALMER, lawyer; b. N.Y.C., Mar. 16, 1915; s. Walter Harvey and Louise De Arango (Palmer) C.; m. Margaret Howell Gordon, June 26, 1954; children: Louise, Peter, Katharine, Barbara. B.A., Williams Coll., 1938; J.D., Columbia U., 1942. Bar: N.Y. State bar 1942. Practice law, Washington, 1946—; partner Dahlgren & Close; dir. Nat. Savs. and Trust Co., Washington. Mem. adv. council Nat. Capital area Boy Scouts Am., 1961—; Bd. dirs. Nat. Soc. Prevention Blindness, 1961-63, Internat. Humanities, Inc., 1960—, Internat. Eye Found., 1965—; bd. dirs. D.C. Soc. Prevention of Blindness, 1957-63, pres., 1961-63; bd. dirs. Marjorie Merriweather Post Found., 1974—; trustee Williams Coll., 1963-68, Hill Sch., 1965—; chmn. Hill Sch., 1974—; trustee Mount Vernon Coll., 1963—, pres., 1971-74. Served with USN, 1942-46. Mem. Am., Inter-Am., D.C. bar assns., Assn. Bar City N.Y., Assn. Trial Lawyers Am., World Assn. Lawyers of World Peace Through Law Center, Pilgrims, Order of St. John. Clubs: Chevy Chase (Md.); Taconic Golf (Williamstown, Mass.); University (Washington). Home: Hungry Run Farm Route 1 PO Box 600 Amissville VA 22002 Office: 1000 Connecticut Ave NW Washington DC 20036

CLOSE, ELIZABETH SCHEU, architect; b. Vienna, Austria, June 4, 1912; came to U.S., 1932, naturalized, 1938; d. Gustav and Helene (Riesz) C.; m. Winston A. Close, 1938; children—Anne Miriam (Mrs. Milton Ulmer), Roy Michel, Robert Arthur. Student, Technische Hochschule, Vienna, 1931-32; B.Arch., Mass. Inst. Tech., 1934, M.Arch., 1935. Draftsman Oscar Stonorov, Architect, Phila., 1935-36; designer Magney & Tusler, Mpls., 1936-38; partner, architect Elizabeth and Winston Close (changed to Close Assos., Inc., 1969), Mpls., 1938—; instr. Mpls. Sch. Art, 1936-37; instr. design U. Minn. Sch. Architecture, 1938-39. Prin. works include Garden City Devel, Brooklyn Center, Minn., 1957, Duff House, variety structures Met. Med. Center Complex, 1960-75, Golden Age Homes, 1960, Peavey Tech. Center, Chaska, Minn., 1970, Gray Freshwater Biol. Inst., Orono, Minn., 1974. Bd. dirs. Civic Orch. Mpls., 1951-68; bd. dirs. Minn. Opera Co.; past pres. New Friends Chamber Music; mem. Commn. on Minn.'s Future. Recipient Honor award Pub. Housing Adminstrn., 1964; hon. mention F.D. Roosevelt Meml. competion, 1960; named Outstanding Woman of Yr. YWCA, 1983. Fellow AIA (dir. Mpls. chpt. 1964-69); mem. Minn. Soc. Architects (pres., Honor award 1975). Home: 1588 Fulham St St Paul MN 55108 Office: Close Assos Inc 3101 E Franklin Ave Minneapolis MN 55406

CLOSE, WINSTON ARTHUR, architect; b. Appleton, Minn., Apr. 27, 1906; s. Arthur Edwin and Clara (Michel) C.; m. Elizabeth Hilde Scheu, Apr. 11, 1938; children—Ann Miriam (Mrs. Milton Ulmer), Roy Michel, Robert Arthur. B.Arch., U. Minn., 1927; M.Arch., Mass. Inst. Tech., 1935. Draftsman and designer, 1927-38; partner firm Elizabeth and Winston Close, Mpls., 1938—; prof. architecture U. Minn., 1946-71, adv. architect, 1950-71. Prin. works include Duluth campus, U. Minn., 1949; coordinator planning: W. Bank campus, U. Minn., Mpls., 1956-61. Past pres. bd. Civic Orch., Mpls.; bd. dirs. New Friends Chamber Music, Mpls.; past mem. bd. Walker Art Center, Mpls.; mem. bd. Artspace Re-Use Com.; mem. arts adv. com. Met. Council. Fellow A.I.A. (past pres. Mpls.); mem. Assn. U. Architects (past pres.), Minn. Soc. Architects (sec.), Sigma Phi Epsilon, Grey Friars, Scarab. Home: 1588 Fulham St St Paul MN 55108 Office: 3101 E Franklin Ave Minneapolis MN 55406

CLOSS, MAURICE JOSEPH, automotive company executive; b. Toronto, Ont., Dec. 14, 1927; s. Wilfred Clinton and Kathleen Rose (Skelly) C.; children: Paul Maurice, Patricia Lynn. Student, U. Western Ont., Queen's U., Kingston, Ont., Wayne State U. With Gen. Motors, 1943-55, Ford Motor Co., 1955-59; with Chrysler Can., 1959—, exec. v.p., 1980, pres., 1980—; sales mgr. West Chrysler Corp., Detroit, 1979-80, v.p., 1981—; dir. Ont. Land Corp., Chrysler Credit Can. Ltd., Chrysler Ins. Can. Ltd. Clubs: Beach Grove Golf & Country, Windsor; Renaissance (Detroit). Office: 2450 Chrysler Centre Windsor ON Canada N9A 4H6

CLOTFELTER, BERYL EDWARD, educator; b. Prague, Okla., Mar. 23, 1926; s. Cecil F. and Velma Z. (Stringer) C.; m. Mary Lou Hixson, Aug. 16, 1951; children—Anne Elizabeth, David Blake, Susan Katherine. B.S., Okla. Baptist U., 1948; M.S., U. Okla., 1949, Ph.D., 1953; postgrad., Ohio State U., 1950-51. Research physicist Phillips Petroleum Co., Bartlesville, Okla., 1953-55; asst. prof. physics U. Idaho, Moscow, 1955-56, Okla. Baptist U., Shawnee, 1956-58, asso. prof., 1958-61, prof., 1961-63; asso. prof. physics Grinnell (Iowa) Coll., 1963-68, prof., 1968-73, Williston prof. physics, 1973—. Author: Reference Systems and Inertia, 1970, The Universe and Its Structure, 1976; Contbr. articles to profl. jours. NSF Faculty fellow, 1968-69.

Mem. Am. Phys. Soc., Am. Assn. Physics Tchrs., A.A.A.S., Iowa Acad. Sci. Democrat. Mem. United Ch. of Christ. Home: 1421 6th Ave Grinnell IA 50112

CLOTHIER, GIRARD S., professional baseball team executive; b. Wilmington, Del., Oct. 1, 1945; s. Robert Baird and Eleanor Elizabeth (Perry) C.; m. Sharon Lee Riggs, Aug. 31, 1968; children: Amy Rebecca, Kelly Harding. B.S., U. Del., 1967; M.B.A., Wharton Sch., 1973. Cert. mgmt. cons.; C.P.A. Staff acct. Price Waterhouse, Phila., 1970-71, sr. cons., 1973-76, mgr., 1976-79, sr. mgr., 1979-81, ptnr., Dallas, 1981-82; v.p. fin. Phillies, Phila., 1982—. Active fund raising Common Pleas Ct. and Pa. gov. candidates; mem. Wharton Exec. Centennial Com., U. Pa., 1980. Served to lt. (j.g.) USN, 1967-70. Mem. Inst. Mgmt. Cons., Am. Inst. C.P.A.s, Pa. Inst. C.P.A.s, Sigma Phi Epsilon (pres. alumni bd. 1974), Omicron Delta Kappa. Republican. Presbyterian. Clubs: Germantown Cricket (Phila.); Wharton of Phila. (pres. 1979-80). Office: Phillies Vets Stadium Broad St and Pattison Ave Philadelphia PA 19148

CLOTWORTHY, JOHN HARRIS, oceanographic executive; b. Balt., Mar. 23, 1924; s. Harris A. and Violet (Klein) C.; m. Martha D. Wilson, Mar. 22, 1947; 1 son, John S. B.E.E., U. Va., 1946; certificate, Harvard Bus. Sch., 1956. Registered profl. engr., Md. With Westinghouse Electric Corp., 1948-67, v.p. def. and space center, gen. mgr. underseas div., 1963-67; chmn. div. ocean engring. U. Miami, Fla., 1967-68; cons. to oceanographic industry, 1967-68; founder, pres. Oceans Gen., Inc., Miami, 1968-71; dir. office congl. and legislative affairs NOAA, Washington, 1971-78; v.p., gen. mgr. Joint Oceanographic Instns. Inc., Washington, 1978—; Sec., v.p. Oak Bldg. & Savs. Assn., 1946-56; Bd. govs. Va. Engring. Found., 1965-68, 72-78. Fellow Marine Tech. Soc. (founding mem., dir. 1966-69); mem. Nat. Oceanography Assn. (pres. 1966-69), Am. Guild Organists, Soc. Naval Engrs., Alpha Tau Omega. Clubs: Annapolis (Md.) Yacht, Explorers; Cosmos (Washington). Home: 7225 Van Ness Ct McLean VA 22101 Office: 2100 Pennsylvania Ave Washington DC 20037

CLOUD, BRUCE BENJAMIN, constrn. co. exec.; b. Thomas, Okla., Feb. 15, 1920; s. Dudley R. and Lillian (Sanders) C.; m. Virginia Dugan, June 5, 1944; children—Sheila Marie Cloud Kiselis, Karen Susan Cloud Faris, Bruce Benjamin, Deborah Ann Cloud Mixon, Virginia Ann. B.C.E., Tex. A. and M. U., 1940. Registered profl. engr., Tex. With H.B. Zachry Co., San Antonio, 1940-42, 55—, exec. v.p., 1963—; also dir.; partner Dudley R. Cloud & Son, constrn., San Antonio, 1946-55. Mem. adv. council Boysville Inc., 1978-79. Served to lt. col. C.E. AUS, 1942-46; ETO. Recipient Pro Deo Et Juventute award Nat. Council Catholic Youth. Mem. Tex. Asso. Gen. Contractors (dir. hwy. and heavy br. 1947-48, 72-76, pres. 1974), Am. Concrete Paving Assn. (v.p. 1970-74, dir. 1970—, 1st v.p. 1975-75, pres. 1976), Nat. Asphalt Paving Assn., Tex. Hotmix Paving Assn. (dir. 1972), Nat. Asso. Gen. Contractors (dir. 1976—, mem. exec. com. 1978-79, chmn. heavy div. 1979), San Antonio Livestock Assn. (life), Nat., Tex. socs. profl. engrs., Tex. Good Rds.-Transp. Assn. (dir. 1974-79, exec. com. 1975-81), AIM, Am. Mgmt. Assn., San Antonio C. of C. (chmn. better roads task force 1978-79), Cons. Contractors Council Am., Holy Name Soc. (v.p. 1962-63), Noctural Adoration Soc. Club: K.C. (3 deg.). Home: 127 Cave Ln San Antonio TX 78209 Office: PO Box 21130 San Antonio TX 78285

CLOUD, PRESTON, geologist, author, consultant; b. West Upton, Mass., Sept. 26, 1912; s. Preston E. and Pauline L. (Wiedemann) C.; m. Janice Gibson, 1972; children by previous marriage: Karen, Lisa, Kevin. B.S., George Washington U., 1938; Ph.D., Yale U., 1940. Instr. Mo. Sch. Mines and Metallurgy, 1940-41; research fellow Yale U., 1941-42; geologist U.S. Geol. Survey, 1942-46, 48-61, 74-79, chief paleontology and stratigraphy br., 1949-59; research geologist, 1959-61, 74-79; asst. prof., curator invertebrate paleontology Harvard U., 1946-48; prof. dept. geology and geophysics U. Minn., 1961-65, chmn., 1961-63; faculty geology dept. UCLA, 1965-68; prof. biogeology and environ. studies dept. geol. scis. U. Calif., Santa Barbara, 1968-74, prof. emeritus, 1974—; vis. prof. U. Tex., 1962, 78; H.R. Luce prof. cosmology Mt. Holyoke Coll., 1979-80; Sr. Queens fellow Baas-Becking Geobiology Lab., Canberra, Australia, 1981; internat exchange scholar Research Council Can., 1982; hon. vis. prof. U. Ottawa (Ont. Can.), 1982; Nat. Sigma Xi lectr., 1967; Emmons lectr. Colo. Sci. Soc.; Bownocker lectr. Ohio State U.; French lectr. Pomona Coll.; Dumaresq-Smith lectr. Acadia Coll., N.B., Can.; A.L. DuToit Meml. lectr. Royal Soc. and Geol. Soc. of South Africa; mem. governing bd. NRC, 1972-75; mem. Pacific Sci. Bd., 1952-56, 62-65; del. internat. sci. congresses; cons. to govt., industry, founds. and agys. Author: Terebratuloid Brachiopoda of the Silurian and Devonian, 1942, (with Virgil E. Barnes) The Ellenburger Group of Central Texas, 1948, (with others) Geology of Saipan, Mariana Islands, 1957, Environment of Calcium Carbonate Deposition West of Andros Island, Bahamas, 1962, Resources and Man, 1969, Cosmos, Earth and Man, 1978; editor and co-author: (with others) Adventures in Earth History, 1970; Author articles. Recipient A. Cressey Morrison prize natural history, 1941; Rockefeller Pub. Service award, 1956; U.S. Dept. Interior Distinguished Service award and gold medal, 1959; medal Paleontol Soc. Am., 1971; Lucius W. Cross medal Yale U., 1973; Penrose medal Geol. Soc. Am., 1976, J.S. Guggenheim fellow, 1982-83. Fellow Am. Acad. Arts and Scis. (com. on membership 1978-80, council 1980-83); mem. Am. Philos. Soc., Nat. Acad. Scis. (com. on sci. and pub. policy 1965-69, mem. council 1972-75, exec. com. 1973-75, chmn. com. on resources and man 1965-69, chmn. ad hoc com. nat. materials policy 1972, chmn. study group on uses of underground space 1972, chmn. com. mineral resources and environment 1972-73, chmn. com. geology and climate 1977, chmn. sect. geology 1976-79, mem. assembly math. and phys. scis. 1976-79, C.D. Walcott medal 1977), Polish Acad. Scis. (fgn. assoc.), Geol. Soc. Am. (council 1972-75), Paleontol. Soc. Am., Paleontol. Soc. India (hon.), AAAS, Geol. Soc. Belgium (hon. fgn. corr.), Phi Beta Kappa, Sigma Xi, Sigma Gamma Epsilon. Field work 6 continents and 2 oceans. Home: 400 Mountain Dr Santa Barbara CA 93103 Office: Dept Geol Scis U Calif Santa Barbara CA 93106

CLOUDMAN, HARRY HOWARD, JR., retired book publisher; b. Oklahoma City, July 23, 1917; s. Harry Howard and Maebelle (Burnell) C.; m. Hazel Marcellus Clay, June 1, 1947; 1 dau., Ruth Howard. B.A. Letters, U. Okla., 1939, M.A., 1941. Grad. asst. English U. Okla., 1940-42; coll. rep. Macmillan Co., 1942, 46-52, editor coll. dept., 1952-55, asst. dir. coll. dept., 1955-59, dir. coll. dept., 1959-61, dir. of co., 1957-60, 66-69, dir. coll. and profl. div., 1961-69, sr. v.p., 1965-69, 75-82, pres. div., 1969-80. Served from pvt. to staff sgt. AUS, 1942-46. Mem. Coll. Pubs. Group (chmn. 1962-63), Delta Upsilon. Unitarian. Home: 8033 N New Braunfels #600F San Antonio TX 78209

CLOUGH, CHARLES ELMER, corporation executive; b. Concord, N.H., Aug. 7, 1930; s. Harold Roland and Roelene (Sawyer) C.; m. Rosemary Todd, Jan. 29, 1960; children: Martha, John, David, Benjamin, Thomas. A.B., Dartmouth Coll., 1952, M.B.A., 1953. Mem. rectifier dept. Gen. Electric Co., Lynn, Mass., 1956-57; pres. Nashua Corp., N.H., 1957—. Served to lt. USN, 1953-56. Republican. Club: Dartmouth (N.Y.C.). Home: Box 417 Hollis NH 03049 Office: 44 Franklin St Nashua NH 03060

CLOUGH, JOHN PAUL THOMAS, railway company executive; b. Toronto, Aug. 20, 1934; s. John and Florence Osborne (Deane) C.; m. Catherine Galagher, May 17, 1958. B.Commerce in Acctg. and Econs., U. Toronto, 1956. With Can. Pacific Ltd., Montreal, 1956—, acctg. trainee, 1956, statistician, 1965-69, asst. gen. auditor, 1969-70, dir. corp. accounts, 1970-75, comptroller, 1975-77, asst. v.p. fin. and acctg., 1977-79, v.p. fin. and acctg., 1979—; dir. Can. Pacific Cons. Services Ltd., Owwawa, Ont., Can., 1979—, Can. Pacific Express & Transport Ltd., Toronto, 1979—, Can. Pacific Securities Ltd., Calgary, Alta., Can., 1982—, Can. Pac. Car Inc., Wilmington, Del., 1979—, CanPac Terminals Ltd, Toronto, 1979—, Centennial Shipping Ltd., Hamilton, Bermuda, 1981—, CHEP Can. Inc., Toronto, 1979—, CNCP Telecommunications, 1980—, Provident Properties Co., Cleve., 1982—, Shawinigan Terminal Ry. Co., Que., 1979—, Toronto, Hamilton and Buffalo Ry. co., Hamilton, Ont., Can., 1979—, Toronto Terminals Ry. Co., 1979—. Mem. Council Fin. Execs. of Conf. Bd. in Can. Home: 137 Easton Ave Montreal West PQ Canada H4X 1L4 Office: Can Pacific Ltd 910 Peel St PO Box 6042 Sta A Montreal PQ Canada H3C 3E4

CLOUGH, RALPH NELSON, research scholar; b. Seattle, Nov. 17, 1916; s. Ray William and Mildred (Nelson) C.; m. Mary Lou Sander, Nov. 1, 1941 (dec. Mar. 1950); m. Awana Alene Stiles, Sept. 5, 1952; children: Frederick William, Marshall Sander, Laurie, Drusilla. A.B., U. Wash., 1939; student, Lingnan U., 1936-37; M.A., Fletcher Sch. Law and Diplomacy, 1940. Vice consul, Toronto, Ont., Can., 1941-42, 3d sec. embassy, vice consul, Tegucigalpa, Honduras, 1942-45, vice consul, successively, Kunming, Chungking, Peiping, China, 1945-47, 3d sec. embassy, vice consul, Nanking, China, 1947-49, 2d sec., consul, 1949-50, consul, Hong Kong, 1950-54; assigned Nat. War Coll., 1954-55; dep. dir. office Chinese affairs Dept. State, 1955-57, dir., 1957-58; counselor Am. embassy, Bern, Switzerland, 1958-59, 1st sec., London, 1959-61, became dep. chief of mission, Taipei, Taiwan, 1961, also consul gen., to 1965; fellow Center for Internat. Affairs, Harvard U., 1965-66; mem. policy planning council Dept. State, 1966-69; sr. fellow Brookings Instn., Washington, 1969-75, guest scholar, 1975-77; fellow Woodrow Wilson Internat. Center for Scholars, Washington, 1978—, Inst. Sino-Soviet Studies, George Washington U., 1980—; professorial lectr. Sch. Advanced Internat. Studies, Johns Hopkins U., 1974, 83; adj. prof. Am. U., 1975-76. Author: Island China, East Asia and U.S. Security; Co-author: Japan, Korea and China: American Perceptions and Policies. Trustee Lingnan U. Mem. Assn. for Asian Studies, Nat. Com. on U.S.-China Relations, Asia Soc., Phi Beta Kappa, Theta Delta Chi. Club: Rotarian (Hong Kong). Home: 4540 N 41st St Arlington VA 22207

CLOUGH, RAY WILLIAM, JR., educator; b. Seattle, July 23, 1920; s. Ray William and Mildred (Nelson) C.; m. Shirley Claire Potter, Oct. 30, 1942; children—Douglas Potter, Allison Justine, Meredith Anne. B.S. in Civil Engring, U. Wash., 1942; M.S., Calif. Inst. Tech., 1943; S.M., Mass. Inst. Tech., 1947; Sc.D., MIT, 1949; D.Tech. (hon.), Chalmaers U., Goteborg, Sweden, 1979, U. Tron d heim, (Norway). Registered profl. engr., Wash. Faculty U. Calif.-Berkeley, 1949—, prof. civil engring., 1959—, chmn. div. structural engring. and structural mechanics, 1967-70, dir., 1973-76, Nish Kran prof. structural engr., 1983—; Cons. in field, 1953—; Mem. Nat. Acad. Scis.-Nat. Acad. Engring. adv. com. Environmental Sci. Services Adminstrn., 1967-70; mem. dynamics panel Nat. Acad. Scis. adv. bd. on hardened electric power system, 1964-70; mem. U.S. C.E. Structural Design Adv. Bd., 1967—. Served to capt. USAAF, 1942-46. Fulbright fellow Ship Research Inst., Trondheim, Norway, 1956-57; Overseas fellow Churchill Coll., Cambridge (Eng.) U., 1963-64; hon. researcher Laboratorio Nacional de Engenharia Civil, Lisbon, Portugal, 1972; Fulbright fellow Tech. U. Norway, Trondheim, 1972-73. Fellow ASCE (chmn. engring. mechanics div. 1964-65, Research award 1960, Howard award 1970, Newmark medal 1979, Moissieff medal 1980); mem. Structural Engrs. Assn. No. Calif. (dir. 1967-70), Earthquake Engring. Research Inst. (dir. 1957-60, 70-73), Seismol. Soc. Am. (dir. 1970-73), Nat. Acad. Scis., Nat. Acad. Engring., Det Kongelige Norske Videnskabers Selskab. Home: 576 Vistamont Ave Berkeley CA 94708

CLOUGH, RICHARD HUDSON, civil engineering educator; b. Springer, N.Mex., Aug. 25, 1922; s. Richard Buckley and Minnie (Caldwell) C.; m. Ethel J. Lamb, Oct. 19, 1945; children: Kenneth Richard, Janet Louise. B.S. in Civil Engring, U. N.Mex., 1943, M.S., U. Colo., 1949; Sc.D., MIT, 1951. Registered profl. engr., N.Mex. Mem. faculty civil engring. U. N.Mex., 1946-49; researcher Mass. Inst. Tech., 1949-51; exec. v.p. Lembke, Clough & King, Inc., gen. contractors, Albuquerque, 1951-57; faculty civil engring. U. N.Mex., 1957-60, dean, 1960-68, dir. Bur. Engring. Research,, 1960-68, prof. civil engring., 1968—; Mem., chmn. N.Mex. State Bd. for Profl. Engrs. and Land Surveyors; mem., sec.-treas. Albuquerque Met. Arroyo Flood Control Authority. Author: Construction Contracting, 1960, 4th edit., 1981, Construction Project Management, 1972, 2d edit., 1979. Served with USNR, 1943-46; PTO. Recipient Sir award N.Mex. Bldg. br. Asso. Gen. Contractors Am., 1973. Fellow ASCE; Mem. Nat. Soc. Profl. Engrs., Am. Soc. Engring. Edn., Sigma Xi, Sigma Tau, Chi Epsilon. Clubs: Mason (Shriner), Rotarian.). Home: 1025 Pueblo Solano NW Albuquerque NM 87107

CLOUSTON, ROSS NEAL, food and related products co. exec.; b. Montreal, Que., Can., Sept. 13, 1922; came to U.S., 1965, naturalized, 1973; s. Alan Roy and Maude (Neal) C.; m. Brenda Kerson, Feb. 12, 1944; children: Robert, Brendan. B.Sc., McGill U., 1949; M.B.A., Harvard U., 1951. With fisheries plant, N.S., Can., from 1940; founder LaSalle Foods Ltd., 1953, Blue Water Sea Food Ltd., Montreal, 1959,; pres. Gorton Group div. Gen. Mills, Inc., 1969—, corp. v.p. parent co., 1970—; v.p. Gen. Mills Can. Ltd.; pres. Nat. Fisheries Inst., 1975, Fisheries Council Can., 1962; dir. Bank of New Eng., Boston, Cape Ann Bank and Trust Co.; chmn. bd. Cape Ann Bank & Trust Co. Served with RCAF, 1941-45. Home: R104 Hesperus Ave Magnolia MA 01930 Office: 327 Main St Gloucester MA 01930

CLOUTIER, GILLES GEORGES, research executive; b. Quebec, Que., Can., June 27, 1928; m. Colette Michaud, May 1954; children: Hetine, Suzanne, Pierre, Benoit, Nathalie. B.A., Laval U., 1949, B.A.Sc., 1953; M.Sc., McGill U., 1956, Ph.D., 1959. With RCA Research Lab., 1959-63; asso. prof. U. Montreal, 1963-67, prof., 1967-68; dir. basic scis., then dir. research, asst. dir. Hydro Que. Inst. Research, 1968-78; pres., chief exec. officer, Alta. Research Council, Edmonton, 1978—; mem. NRC Can., 1972-77. Bd. govs. U. Montreal. Roman Catholic. Home: 926 Rice Rd Edmonton AB T6R 1A1 Canada Office: 4445 Calgary Trail S Edmonton AB T6H 5R7 Canada

CLOUTIER, LEONCE, chemical engineering educator; b. Quebec City, Que., Can., Feb. 5, 1928; s. Napoleon and Eugenie (Langevin) C.; m. Jeannine Fillion, Aug. 4, 1951; children—Denise, Pauline, Gaston. B.Sc.A., Laval U., 1950, D.Sc., 1964. Prodn. engr. Can. Packers Ltd., Montreal, Que., 1950-52; design engr. C. D. Howe Co., Montreal, 1952-55; mem. faculty Laval U., 1955—, prof. chem. engring., 1967—, dir. dept., 1969-75, sec. faculty sci. and engring., 1980—; tchr. summer courses to engrs. Alcan Co., Arvida, 1965, Demerara Bauxite Co., Guyana, 1968; vis. prof. material sci. and engring. dept. U. Calif., Berkeley, 1975-76; v.p. Valmiro Ltd., 1965-70, Caisse Populaire St. Thomas D'Aquin, 1965-75, 77-81; mem. asso. com. automatic control NRC, 1971-75. Local pres., provincial v.p. Quefratec, 1969-72. Recipient Mgr. Vachon prize Faculty Sci., Laval U., 1960; NRC Can. grantee, 1959-78. Mem. Chem. Inst. Can. (prize 1949), Corps Engrs. Que., Soc. Canadienne de Genie Chimique. Research and publs. in mixing, chem. reactors, simulation and control. Home: 880 Lienard St Quebec PQ G1V 2W5 Canada

CLOUTIER, SYLVAIN, export devel. co. exec.; b. Trois Rivieres, Que., Can., Nov. 4, 1929; s. Edmond and Helene (St. Denis) C.; m. Denyse Sauvé, 1953; children—Guy, Sylvie. B.A., B.Phil., U. Ottawa, 1949; M.Comm., U. Montreal, 1953; M.B.A., Harvard U., 1955. Chartered acct. Staff Can. govt., 1955-65; mem. Public Service Commn. Can., 1965-67; dep. sec. Treasury Bd. Can., 1967-70; dep. minister taxation Dept. Nat. Revenue, 1970-71; dep. minister nat. def., 1971-75, dep. minister transport, 1975-79; chmn. bd., pres. Export Devel. Corp., 1979—. Mem. exec. com. Nat. Joint Council Public Service Can., 1966-67; bd. govs. Algonquin Community Coll., 1969—, Exec. Council Intern-Am. Centre Tax Adminstrs., 1971; mem. adv. bd. Can. Mil. Colls., 1971-75; bd. dirs. Montfort Hosp., Ottawa, 1973-79. Mem. Inst. Public Adminstrn. Can. Roman Catholic. Home: 2307 Orlando Ave Ottawa ON K1H 7JH Canada Office: 110 O'Connor St Ottawa ON K1P 5T9 Canada

CLOVIS, ALBERT L., lawyer; b. Canton, Ohio, Oct. 20, 1935; s. Oscar R. and Bess (Jeffrey) C.; m. Judith Nikodym, June 24, 1961; children: Charles B., Sarah C. B.A., Yale U., 1957; M.A., U. Mich., 1959; LL.B., Harvard U., 1962. Bar: Ohio 1962. Asso. firm Day, Ketterer, Raley, Wright & Rybolt, Canton, 1962-65; asst. prof. law Ohio State U., Columbus, 1965-67, asso. prof., 1967-70, prof., 1970-82, Newton D. Baker prof., 1982—; vis. prof. U. Va., 1978-79; of counsel firm Porter, Wright, Morris & Arthur, Columbus, 1972—. Author: (with Robert J. Nordstrom) Commercial Paper, 1972, (with John E. Murray and Robert J. Nordstrom) Sales, 1982. Recipient Distinguished Teaching awards Ohio State U., 1968, 74, 82. Mem. Am. Bar Assn., Ohio Bar Assn., Am. Law Inst. Home: 397 Green Hollow Pataskala OH 43062 Office: Ohio State University College of Law 1659 N High St Columbus OH 43210

CLOWARD, RICHARD ANDREW, educator; b. Rochester, N.Y., Dec. 25, 1926; s. Donald Bernard and Esther (Fleming) C.; m. Ethelmarie McGaffin, Mar. 25, 1951 (div. 1979); children—Leslie Anne, Mark, Kevin, Keith. B.A., U. Rochester, 1948; M.S.W., Columbia, 1950, Ph.D., 1958. Mem. faculty Columbia, 1954—, prof. social work, 1961—; dir. research Moblzn. for Youth, N.Y.C., 1958-65. Author: Social Perspectives on Behavior, 1958, Delinquency and Opportunity, 1960 (Dennis Carroll award Internat. Soc. Criminology 1965), Regulating the Poor: The Functions of Public Welfare, 1971 (C. Wright Mills award Soc. Study Social Problems 1972), The Politics of Turmoil: Essays on Race, Poverty and the Urban Crisis, 1974, Poor People's Movements: Why They Succeed, How They Fail, 1977, The New Class War, 1982. Trustee Abbott House for Children, N.Y.C., 1965-69, Northside Center Child Devel., N.Y.C., 1964-68, Citizens Crusade Against Poverty, Washington, 1964-68, Poverty/Rights Action Center, Washington, 1966—; bd. dirs. N.Y. Civil Liberties Union, 1968-80. Served with USNR, 1944-46; as officer AUS, 1951-54. Mem. Nat. Assn. Social Workers, Am. Sociol. Assn., AAUP. Home: 35 Claremont Ave New York NY 10027 Office: 622 W 113th St New York NY 10025

CLOWER, ROBERT WAYNE, economics educator, consultant; b. Pullman, Wash., Feb. 13, 1926; s. Fay Walter and Mary Valentine (Gilchrist) C.; m. Frances Hepburn, Jan. 7, 1946 (div. July 1975); children: Alisa, Leslie, Robert, Stephanie, Valerie; m. Georgene Helen Thousendfriend, Jan. 30, 1976; children: Anastasia, Kathryn. B.A in Econs., Wash. State U., 1948, M.A., 1949, M.Litt., Oxford U., Eng., 1952, D.Litt., 1978. Asst. prof. econs. Wash. State U., Pullman, 1952-56; prof. econs. Northwestern U., Evanston, Ill., 1957-70; prof. econs., dean Sch. Social Studies Essex U., Wivenoe, Eng., 1968-69; prof. econs. UCLA, 1971—; cons. editor Penguin Books, Ltd., London, 1967—. Author: Introduction to Mathematical Economics, 1957, Microeconomic Analysis, 1972, Essays in Monetary Theory, 1984; editor: Readings in Monetary Theory, 1968; mng. editor: Am. Econ. Rev., 1981—. Served with AUS, 1973-76. Rhodes scholar, 1949; Guggenheim fellow, 1965; hon. fellow Brasenose Coll., Oxford, Eng., 1978. Fellow Econometric Soc.; mem. Am. Econs. Assn. (exec. com. 1978-81), Royal Econ. Soc., Western Econ. Assn. Internat. (editor econ. inquiry 1973-80, v.p. elect 1984). Office: Dept Econs UCLA Los Angeles CA 90024

CLOWER, WILLIAM DEWEY, association executive; b. Salem, Va., Oct. 9, 1935; s. Alton Oliver and Addie Vane (Young) C.; m. Shirley Carol Tuttle, Sept. 1, 1956; children—Candice Denise, Michael DeWayne, Catherine Dione. B.S., U. Va., 1958, M.S., 1958. Applications engr. ITT, Nutley, N.J., 1958-60; regional mktg. mgr. Litton Industries, Washington, 1960-61; propr. W.D. Clower Co., Gt. Falls, Va., 1961-70; spl. asst. to Pres. of U.S., 1970-75; exec. v.p. CISPI, Washington, 1975-76; pres. Food Processing Machinery and Supplies Assn., Washington, 1976—; dir. Food Processors Inst., 1977-80. Mem. campaign services steering com. Republican Nat. Com., 1977; mem. Pres. adv. council Peace Corps, 1982—; mem. Industry Policy Adv. Council for Export Policy, 1982—. Served with USAF, 1959-60. Va. Gen. Assembly scholar, 1954-58. Mem. Am. Soc. Assn. Execs., Washington Soc. Assn. Execs., Aircraft Owners and Pilots Assn., Food Group, Gamma Delta Epsilon. Presbyterian. Clubs: Sertoma (Vienna, Va.) (pres. 1963-64); Capitol Hill, River Bend Golf and Country. Home: 1098 Fairbank St Great Falls VA 22066 Office: 1828 L St NW Washington DC 20036

CLOWES, ROYSTON COURTNEY, microbiologist, educator; b. Swansea, Wales, Sept. 11, 1921; came to U.S., 1965; s. William John and Prudence Alice (King) C.; m. Janet Shopland, Apr. 5, 1952; children: Martin Anthony, Christopher Tobias, David Malcolm. B.S., U. Birmingham, Eng., 1942, Ph.D., 1951, D.Sc., 1965. Research assoc. St. Mary's Hosp. Med. Sch., London, 1951-57; mem. staff Med. Research Council's Microbial Genetics Research Unit, Hammersmith Hosp., London, 1958-65; prof. biology S.W. Center Advanced Studies, Dallas, 1965-69; prof. div. biology U. Tex., Dallas, 1969—, chmn., 1969-74, 79—; vis. prof. microbiology U. Calif., Berkeley, 1961-62; mem. microbial chemistry study sect. HEW-NIH, 1971-73; mem. Recombinant DNA adv. com. NIH, 1983—; chmn. HEW-NIH, 1973-75. Author: The Structure of Life, 1964; editor: Experiments in Microbial Genetics, 1968, Plasmid, 1979—; editorial bd.: Jour. Gen. Microbiology, U.K, 1960-65, Jour. Bacteriology, 1970-72, Antimicrobial Agents and Chemotherapy, 1973—. Served to capt. Brit. Army, 1943-47. Damon Runyon Cancer Research fellow, 1955-56; recipient numerous grants. Address: 7148 Meadowcreek Dr Dallas TX 75240 Office: Div Biology U Tex at Dallas PO Box 688 Richardson TX 75080

CLOWNEY, WILLIAM D., insurance company executive; b. Atlantic City, Nov. 18, 1923; s. Frank Sherman and Mabel Erskine (Eastlake) C.; m. Mary, Dec. 11, 1954; children: Lester, Elizabeth, William, Michael, Janet. A.B., Princeton U., 1948; postgrad., U. Pa., 1948, Exec. Sch. Bus., Columbia U. C.L.U. With prudential Ins. Co. Am., 1952—; exec. dir. group sales and services Prudential Ins. Co. Am., 1966-67, exec. dir. group ins. Eastern home office, 1967-73, v.p. group ins., 1973-75; v.p. Prudential Ins. Co., 1975-78; pres. Eastern ops. Prudential Ins. Co. Am., South Plainfield, N.J., 1978—. Vice chmn. bd. trustees Morristown Meml. Hosp., N.J.; mem. adv. bd. Center Alcohol

Studies, Rutgers U., New Brunswick, N.J.; v.p., trustee Morristown-Beard Sch. Served to capt. U.S. Army, 1942-46, 50-51. Mem. Nat. Assn. Life Underwriters. Republican. Episcopalian. Clubs: Morris Country Golf, Morristown Field; Princeton (N.Y.C.); Essex (Newark). Home: Hunter Dr New Vernon NJ 07976 Office: Prudential Ins Co Am 745 Broad St Newark NJ 07101

CLUBB, BRUCE EDWIN, lawyer; b. Blackduck, Minn., Feb. 6, 1931; s. Ernest and Abigail (Gordy) C.; m. Martha Lucia Trapp, Dec. 19, 1954; children: Bruce Allen, Christopher Wade. B.B.A., U. Minn., 1955, LL.B. cum laude, 1958. Bar: D.C. bar 1959. Atty. Covington & Burling, 1958-61, Devel. Loan Fund, 1961-62, Chapman, DiSalle and Friedman, 1962-67; commr. U.S. Tariff Commn., 1967-71; ptnr. firm Baker & McKenzie, Washington, 1971—; disting. lawyer in residence U. Minn. Law Sch., 1981-82. Contbr. law revs. Served with AUS, 1952-54. Mem. D.C. Bar Assn., Am. Judicature Soc., Order of Coif. Republican. Clubs: Cosmos, Metropolitan, Army Navy. Home: 100 Quay St Alexandria VA 22314 Office: 815 Connecticut Ave NW Washington DC 20006

CLUFF, EDWARD FULLER, chemist; b. Dedham, Mass., Feb. 14, 1928; s. Laurance Webster and Frances Violet (Patten) C.; m. Margaret Lee Hill, June 30, 1956; children—Stephen Laurance, Christopher Wallace. B.S., Mass. Inst. Tech., Cambridge, 1949, Ph.D., 1952. With E.I. duPont de Nemours & Co., Inc., 1952—, research chemist, 1952-68, research div. head, 1968-74, gen. supt. research and devel., Deepwater, N.J., 1974-77, gen. process supt., 1977-80, research mgr., 1980—. Contbr. articles to sci. jours. Served with AUS, 1952-54. Mem. Am. Chem. Soc. Patentee in field. Home: 706 Hertford Rd Wilmington DE 19803 Office: DuPont Exptl Sta Wilmington DE 19803

CLUFF, LEIGHTON EGGERTSEN, physician, foundation executive; b. Salt Lake City, June 10, 1923; s. Lehi Eggertsen and Lottie (Brain) C.; m. Beth Allen, Aug. 19, 1944; children: Claudia Beth, Patricia Leigh. B.S., U. Utah, 1944; M.D. with distinction, George Washington U., 1949; Sc.D. (hon.), Hahnemann Med. Sch., 1979. Intern Johns Hopkins Hosp., 1949-50, asst. resident, 1951-52; asst. resident physician Duke Hosp., 1950- 51; vis. investigator, asst. physician Rockefeller Inst. Med. Research, 1952-54; fellow Nat. Found. Infantile Paralysis, 1952-54; mem. faculty Johns Hopkins Sch. Medicine; staff Johns Hopkins Hosp., 1954-66, prof. medicine, 1964-66, physician, head div. clin. immunology, allergy and infectious diseases, 1958-66; prof., chmn. dept. medicine U. Fla., 1966-76; exec. v.p. Robert Wood Johnson Found., 1976—; U.S. del. U.S.-Japan Coop. Med. Sci. Program, 1972-81; mem. council drugs A.M.A., 1965-67; mem. NRC-Nat. Acad. Sci. Drug Research Bd., 1965-71; mem. expert adv. panel bacterial diseases (coccal infection) WHO; mem. council Nat. Inst. Allergy and Infectious Diseases, 1968-72; cons. FDA; tng. grant com. NIH, 1964-68. Author, editor books on internal medicine, infectious diseases, clin. pharmacology.; Contbr. articles to profl. jours. Markle scholar med. scis., 1955-62; recipient Career Research award NIH, 1962. Mem. Inst. Medicine-Nat. Acad. Scis., Am. Soc. Clin. Investigation, Assn. Life Scis.-Nat. Acad. Scis., Assn. Am. Physicians, Soc. Exptl. Biology and Medicine, Am. Assn. Immunologists, Am. Fedn. Clin. Research, Harvey Soc., N.Y. Acad. Sci., Infectious Disease Soc. Am. (pres. 1973), So. Soc. Clin. Investigation, A.C.P. (Fla. gov. 1975-76, Mead-Johnson postgrad. scholar 1954-55, Ordronaux award med. scholarship 1949), Am. Clin. and Climatological Assn., Alpha Omega Alpha. Home: 7 Beechtree Ln Princeton NJ 08540

CLUMECK, JACK REGINALD, business exec.; b. Singapore, Nov. 22, 1913; s. Victor and Marie (Frankel) C.; m. Lois Lees, May 30, 1934; children—Jack Reginald, Jill Marie (Mrs. J. Freidenrich). Student, Stanford, 1933. Exec. v.p. Hunt Foods & Industries, Inc., 1956-61, dir., vice chmn. finance com., 1961-68; partner L.C.L. Co., real estate and investments, 1948-77; dir., mem. finance com. Norton Simon, Inc., 1968—, chmn. finance com., 1970—. Home: PO Box 116 Ross CA 94957 *What you are to be, you are now becoming.*

CLURMAN, RICHARD MICHAEL, public policy advisor; b. N.Y.C., Mar. 10, 1924; s. Will N. and Emma (Herzberg) C.; (m) (div.); children: Susan Emma, Carol Mae; m. Shirley Potash, Apr. 13, 1957; 1 son, Richard Michael. Ph.B., U. Chgo., 1946, postgrad., 1946-48. Asst. editor Commentary mag., 1946-49; press editor Time mag., 1949-55; editorial dir. Newsday, 1955-58; dep. chief corrs. Time and Life Mag., N.Y.C., 1958-60, chief, 1960-69; v.p. Time Inc., 1969-72; chmn. bd. Time-Life Broadcast, 1971-72; adminstr. Parks, Recreation and Cultural Affairs Adminstrn. and Commn. Parks, City N.Y., 1973-74; cons. Am. Revolution Bicentennial Adminstrn., 1974; dir. E.M. Warburg, Pincus & Co., Inc., 1976-81; pres. Richard M. Clurman Assos., Inc., 1975—; public policy advisor Office of Chmn., Joseph E. Seagram & Sons, Inc., 1980-84. Chmn. bd. N.Y.C. Center Music and Drama, Inc., 1968-75; pres. N.Y. Found. for Arts, Inc., 1971-72; bd. dirs. Lincoln Center for Performing Arts, 1968-75, Sch. Am. Ballet, 1970-76, Parks Council, 1975-77; chmn. Gov.'s Task Force on Arts and Cultural Life, 1975; mem. adv. council N.Y. U. Sch. of Arts, 1974—; chmn. adv. com. WNCN, chmn., 1975-76; bd. dirs. Citizens Com. N.Y.C., 1976—; chmn. bd. govs. Columbia U. Grad. Sch. Journalism media and society seminars, 1981—. Served with AUS, 1942-46. Mem. Council Fgn. Relations. Clubs: Federal, City (Washington); Century Assn. (N.Y.C.). Home: 40 E 66th St New York NY 10021 Office: 200 Park Ave New York NY 10166

CLUTTER, BERTLEY ALLEN, management company executive; b. Oskaloosa, Iowa, Oct. 21, 1942; s. Bertley Allen and Dorothy A. (Martin) C.; m. Elizabeth Ann Jaska, Aug. 26, 1967; children: Allen, Julie. Student, Macalester Coll., 1960-62, 64-66, B.A., 1966; M.A., Eastern Mich. U., 1973. Asst. prof. U.S. Air Force Acad., Colo., 1973-76; exec. dir. Minn. Ethical Practices Bd., St. Paul, 1976-80; staff dir. Fed. Election Commn., Washington, 1980-83; v.p. Owners Mgmt. Co., Cleve., 1983—. Contbr. articles to prof. jours. Pres. North End Homeowners Assn., Colorado Springs, Colo., 1975-76; v.p. Lowery Hill Residents' Assn., Mpls., 1977-80, Blvd. Assn., Shaker Heights, Ohio. Served to capt. USAF, 1976. Decorated Bronze Star; USAF scholar Eastern Mich. U., 1972; endowed scholar Macalester Coll., 1961, 65, 66. Mem. Am. Mgmt. Assn. Club: Calhoun Beach (Mpls.). Home: 2929 Warrington Rd Shaker Heights OH 44120 Office: Owners Mgmt Co 25250 Rockside Rd Cleveland OH 44146

CLUTZ, WILLIAM HARTMAN, artist, educator; b. Gettysburg, Pa., Mar. 19, 1933; s. Paul Alexander and Catherine (Hartman) C. B.A., U. Iowa, 1951-55. Instr. drawing, painting Parsons Sch. Design, N.Y.C., 1969—. One-man shows include, Condon Riley Gallery, N.Y.C., 1959, David Herbert Gallery, N.Y.C., 1962, Triangle Gallery, San Francisco, 1967, Bertha Schaefer Gallery, N.Y.C., 1963, 64, 66, 69, Bklyn. Coll., 1969, Graham Gallery, N.Y.C., 1972, Mercersburg (Pa.) Acad., Lamont Gallery, Phillips Exeter (N.H.) Acad., 1973, Addison Gallery Am. Art, Phillips Acad., Andover, Mass., Moravian Coll., Bethlehem, Pa., 1977, Brooke Alexander Gallery, N.Y.C., 1973, Alonzo Gallery, N.Y.C., 1977, 78, 79, Walther-Rathenau-Saal, Rathaus Kunstamt Wedding, Berlin, 1978, Mellon Art Center, Wallingford, Conn., 1979, Gallery 333, Dayton, Ohio, 1980, Tatistcheff & Co., N.Y.C., 1981, 82, John C. Stoller & Co., Mpls., 1983; exhibited in group shows including, Mus. Modern Art, N.Y.C., 1956, 62, Am. Fedn. Arts Traveling Exhbn., 1961-62, Contemporary Arts Mus., Houston, 1961, Am. Fedn. Fine Arts Traveling Exhbn., 1963-64, Pa. Acad. Fine Arts, Phila., 1964, 65, 66, U. Wis., 1967, Purdue U., 1968, Tweed Gallery, U. Minn., Duluth, Ringling Mus. Art, Sarasota, Fla., 1969, Columbus (Ohio) Gallery Fine Arts, 1970, Hall Gallery, Miami, Fla., 1972, Brooke Alexander Gallery, 1973, Smithsonian Traveling Exhbn., 1976-79, Westmoreland County Mus., Greensburg, Pa., 1979, Hirschl & Adler, N.Y.C., 1980, Aaron Berman Gallery, N.Y.C., Stoller Gallery, 1980, 81, Tatistcheff & Co., Corcoran Gallery Art, Washington, 1982, Bklyn. Mus., 1983; represented in permanent collections, Addison Gallery Am. Art, Ball State U. Art Gallery, Muncie, Ind., Bklyn. Coll., Fogg Art Mus., Harvard U., Cambridge, Mass., Guggenheim Mus., N.Y.C., Hirshhorn Mus. and Sculpture Garden, Washington, Dayton Art Inst. (Ohio), Mercersburg Acad., Miles Coll., Atlanta, Milw. Art Center, Mus. Modern Art, N.Y.C., Met. Mus. Art, N.Y.C., N.Y. Sch. Interior Design, N.Y.C., N.Y. U. Art Collection, Newark Mus., Minn. Mus., St. Paul, Sheldon Meml. Art Gallery, Lincoln, Nebr., U. Mass., Amherst, Tweed Mus., Duluth, Washington County Mus. Fine Arts, Hagerstown, Md., also, AT&T, Ashland Oil, Inc., Chase Manhattan Bank, Schroder Bank, Topseal Corp., Wausaw Ins. Co., Lehman Bros., Milbank Tweed, Minn. Mut. Ins. Co., Simpson Thatcher & Bartlett, Solomon Bros., Third Nat. Bank, Dayton. Home: 370 Riverside Dr New York NY 10025 Office: care Tatistcheff Gallery 50 W 57th St New York NY 10022

CLYDE, LARRY FORBES, banker; b. Heber, Utah, Nov. 19, 1941; s. Don and Kathryn (Forbes) C.; m. Barbara Eliason, Dec. 23, 1963; children: Lynne, Karen Lee. B.A., Utah State U., 1963, M.S., 1965. With Pitts. Nat. Bank, 1965-68; with Crocker Nat. Bank, San Francisco, 1968—, mgr. investment banking, 1973-75, mgr. portfolio, money market and bond trading div., 1975—, sr. v.p., 1976-78, exec. v.p., mem. policy com., 1978—; dir. Crocker Investment Mgmt. Corp.; bd. dirs. Pub. Securities Assn., 1976—, mem. govt. borrowing com. vice chmn., 1981, chmn., 1982; treas., dir. No. Calif. chpt. Invest-In-Am., 1975. Mem. Am. Bankers Assn. (vice chmn.-bank investment and funds mgmt. div. com. 1982, chmn. com. 1983), San Francisco Bond Club. Clubs: Round Hill Country, San Francisco Tennis. Home: 3336 Rowland Dr Lafayette CA 94549 Office: One Montgomery St 25 West Tower San Francisco CA 94104

CLYMER, ELEANOR, author; b. N.Y.C., Jan. 7, 1906; d. Eugene and Rose (Fourman) Lowenton; m. Kinsey Clymer, Mar. 7, 1933; 1 son, Adam. Student, Barnard Coll., 1925; B.A., U. Wis., 1927; postgrad., NYU, Bank St. Coll., N.Y.C. Author: 58 juvenile books, including My Brother Stevie, 1968 (Woodward Sch. Book award); 56 juvenile books, including Luke Was There, 1974 (Child Study Assn. Children's Book award), The Spider, the Cave and the Pottery Bowl, 1971 (Jr. Lit. award Border Regional Library Assn.), The Trolley Car Family, 1947, Search for a Living Fossil, 1963, The Second Greatest Invention, 1969, We Lived in the Almont, 1970, Me and the Eggman, 1972, Santiago's Silvermine, 1973, The Get-Away Car, 1978 (Sequoyah Book award 1980), My Mother is the Smartest Woman in the World, 1982, The Horse in the Attic, 1983. Mem. Authors Guild (past mem. council, chmn. children's book com.). Address: 11 Nightingale Rd Katonah NY 10536 *When I write a book for children, I am telling them something about the world and about life. I have a responsibility to tell them the truth, whether the story is realistic or a fairy tale. If the book holds the children's interest and helps them cope with their world, I shall have succeeded.*

CLYMER, JOHN FORD, artist; b. Ellensburg, Wash., Jan. 29, 1907; s. John Perkepin and Elmira Elizabeth (Ford) C.; m. Doris E. Schnebly, Mar. 4, 1932; children: David J., Jo Lorraine Clymer Tatum. Student, Vancouver Sch. Art, 1925-28, Ont. Coll. Art, 1930, Wilmington Acad. Art, 1931-32, Grand Central Sch. Art, 1936. Illustrator stories for munerous mags. in Can. and U.S., 1925-64; painted more than 80 covers for Saturday Evening Post, 1942-62; exhibited group shows, Nat. Acad. Western Art Cowboy Hall of Fame, Oklahoma City, 1972-81, Cowboy Artists Am. Ann. Show, Phoenix, 1969-83, Cowboy Artists Am. Mus., Kerrville, Tex., 1983; represented in permanent collections, Mont. Hist. Soc., Helena, Buffalo Bill Hist. Ctr., Cody, Wyo., Nat. Cowboy Hall of Fame, Oklahoma City, Rockwell Corning Mus., Corning, N.Y., The Glenbow Found., Calgary, Can., Grand Teton Nat. Park Vis. Ctr., Moose, Wyo. Recipient Franklin Mint Gold medal for western art, 1973, Gold medal in oil Nat. Acad. Western Art, 1974; featured in PBS Profiles in Am. Art, 1982. Mem. Cowboy Artistsof Am., Nat. Acad. Western Art, Soc. Animal Artists, Ont. Soc. Artists, Hudson Valley Art Assn. Home: PO Box 369 Teton Village WY 83025

CLYMER, WAYNE KENTON, bishop; b. Napoleon, Ohio, Sept. 24, 1917; s. George Arnold and Grace Susan (Hulvey) C.; m. Helen Eloise Graves, Sept. 3, 1939; children: Kenton James, Richard George. A.B., Asbury Coll., 1939; M.A., Columbia, 1942; B.D., Union Theol. Sem., 1944; Ph.D., N.Y. U., 1950; LL.D., Westmar Coll., 1969; D.Litt., Hamline U., 1975; D.D., Iowa Wesleyan Coll., Rust Coll., Garrett-Evang. Theol. Sem. Ordained to ministry Evang. Ch., 1942; pastor Emanuel Ch., Ozone Park, N.Y.C., 1939-41, St. Paul's Ch., Forest Hills, N.Y.C., 1941-46; prof. Evang. Theol. Sem., Naperville, Ill., 1946-57, dean, 1957-67, pres., 1967-72; bishop United Meth. Ch., Mpls., 1972-80, Des Moines, 1980—; lectr. St. Andrews Theol. Coll., Manila, 1966, Trinity Coll., Singapore, 1967; pres. United Meth. Com. on Relief, 1976—. Author: Affirmation, 1971, Membership Means Discipleship, 1976; Contbr. to: Ency. Religious Edn. Pres. Naperville Sch. Bd., 1959-63; Mem. bd. Naperville Community Fund, 1966; pres. Chgo. Pastoral Counseling Center. Mem. Soc. Sci. Study Religion, Kappa Delta Pi. Club: Kiwanian. Office: 1019 Chestnut St Des Moines IA 50309

CLYNE, JOHN VALENTINE, lawyer, retired business executive; b. Vancouver, C., Can., Feb. 14, 1902; s. Henry and Martha A. (Dillon) C.; m. Betty V. A. Somerset, Dec. 14, 1927; children—Valentine, (Mrs. Anthony W. Gamage), J. Stuart. B.A., U. B.C., 1923; postgrad. student law, London Sch. Econs., King's Coll., London; LL.D. (hon.), McGill U., 1981. Bar: Can. 1927. With E.P. Davis & Co., Vancouver, 1923-25, 27, Blake & Redden, legal firm, London, 1925-27, William & Mason, lawyers, Prince Rupert, Can., 1928-29; ptnr. Macrae, Duncan & Clyne, Vancouver, 1929-46, Campney, Owen, Clyne & Murphy, 1947-50; pres. Park S.S. Co. (Crown Co.), 1945-50; chmn. Can. Maritime Commn., 1947-50; judge Supreme Ct., B.C., 1950-57; chmn. bd. MacMillan and Bloedel Ltd., 1957-60; now hon. dir.; chmn. bd. MacMillan, Bloedel and Powell River (now MacMillan Bloedel Ltd.), 1960-73, chief exec. officer, 1960-72; Royal commr. Land Expropriation in B.C., 1961; rep. Can. sub-coms. UN and NATO dealing with shipping; chmn. prep. com. inter-govtl. Maritime Consultative Orgn., Lake Success, 1948-50; royal commr. to investigate Whatshan Power House Disaster, 1954; royal commr. on Milk Inquiry, 1954-55; chmn. adv. group Exec. Compensation Pub. Service, 1968-71; past provincial pres. St. John Ambulance Assn.; bd. dirs. Nat. Indsl. Conf. Bd., Can., 1961-73, Nat. Indsl. Conf. U.S., 1962-73; chmn. selection com. Royal Bank Award, 1967—; hon. patron Can. Inst for Advanced Legal Studies, 1977—; hon. mem. C. D. Howe Inst.; chmn. B.C. Heritage Trust, 1978-81; gov. Consortium for Atlantic-Pacific Affairs, 1977—; chancellor U B.C., 1978—; chmn. Consultative Com. on Implications of Telecommunications for Can. Sovereignty, 1979-80; chmn. roundhouse adv. com., 1981—. Mem. Cultural Heritage Adv. Com., 1981—. Decorated comdr. Order Knights St. John, companion Order of Can. Mem. Can. Bar Assn., Law Soc. B.C. Clubs: The Vancouver, University, The Shaughnessy Golf and Country (Vancouver); Union (Victoria, B.C.); Rideau (Ottawa); Mt. Royal (Montreal); Bohemian (San Francisco). Home: 3738 Angus Dr Vancouver BC V6J 4H5 Canada Office: 1075 W Georgia St Vancouver BC V6E 3R9 Canada

CLYNE, ROBERT MARTIN, physician; b. Bridgeport, Conn., July 23, 1918; s. Charles August and Loretta Elizabeth (Reilly) C.; m. Mary Theresa Angst, Aug. 14, 1943; children—Robert M., Richard M., Roger M. B.S., Fordham U., 1939; M.D., Cornell U., 1943. Diplomate: Am. Bd. Internal Medicine. Intern Lenox Hill Hosp., N.Y.C., 1943; resident Lincoln Hosp., N.Y.C., 1944-45, VA Hosp., 1946-47; practice medicine, specializing in internal medicine, Bronx, N.Y., 1948-52; cons., clin. physician Am. Cyanamid Co., Wayne, N.J., 1948-67, corporate med. dir., 1967-81; Lectr. on alcoholism Rutgers U., U. Utah, U. Miami; lectr. occupational health Colby Coll. Contbr. articles to profl. jours. Served with AUS, 1945-46. Fellow A.C.P., Am. Occupational Med. Assn. (award of spl. recognition 1972, dir.), Am. Acad. Occupational Medicine (dir.), Am. Coll. Preventive Medicine. Republican. Roman Catholic. Home: 18 Kitchell Lake Dr West Milford NJ 07480

COADY, JOHN MARTIN, dental association executive; b. Minooka, Ill., Apr. 2, 1927; s. John Jay and Mildred Schuyler (Brinckerhoff) C. A.S., Joliet (Ill.) Jr. Coll., 1949; D.D.S., Loyola U., Chgo., 1953, M.S., 1960; D.Sc. (hon.), Georgetown U. Sch. Dentistry, 1980. Mem. faculty Loyola U. Sch. Dentistry, 1954-63; pvt. practice dentistry, Morris, Ill., 1953-57, Chgo., 1957-63; mem. adminstrv. staff ADA, Chgo., 1963—, asst. exec. dir. edn. and hosps., 1972-78, acting exec. dir. assns., 1978-79, exec. dir., 1979—; asst. sec. (Council on Dental Edn.), 1963-70, sec., 1970-72; mem. adv. com. hosp. sponsored ambulatory dental services Robert Wood Johnson Found.; mem. task force on dental medicine Commn. on the Future of Washington U. Dental Sch., St. Louis. Author papers in field. Served with USNR, 1945-46. Recipient ann. Dental Alumni award Loyola U. Sch. Dentistry, 1982. Fellow Pierre Fauchard Acad. (Pierre Fauchard medal 1983), Internat. Coll. Dentists, Am. Coll. Dentists; mem. ADA, Am. Assn. Dental Schs., Am. Assn. Oral and Maxillofacial Surgeons (hon.), Am. Acad. Oral Medicine (hon.), Ill. State Dental Soc., Chgo. Dental Soc., Acad. Gen. Dentistry (hon.), Blue Key, Omicron Kappa Upsilon, Delta Sigma Delta. (meritorious award 1983). Republican. Episcopalian. Home: 1550 N Lake Shore Dr Chicago IL 60610 Office: 211 E Chicago Ave Chicago IL 60611

COAKLEY, JOSEPH CHARLES, lawyer; b. Cleve., June 10, 1928; s. John A. and Marie (Beckman) C.; m. Patricia Hunkin, July 6, 1949; children—Patricia H. (Mrs. Harvey Oppmann), Joseph Charles, M. Sean, Lisa F. B.S., John Carroll U., 1948; LL.B., Cleve. State U., 1951. Bar: Ohio bar 1951. Pvt. practice law, Cleve., 1951—; partner firm Squire, Sanders & Dempsey, Cleve., 1961-73; Chmn. bd. dirs. Union Commerce Corp., 1970-81; dir. Minster Machine Co., Marjon Co.; pres. M-F Securities Inc.; v.p. Cleve. Industries Inc. Trustee Musical Arts Assn.; chmn. bd. trustees John Carroll U., 1975-79. Clubs: Union, Kirtland, Tavern, Chagrin Valley Hunt (Cleve.); Brook (N.Y.C.); Rolling Rock (Ligonier, Pa.). Home: Berkshire Rd Gates Mills OH 44040 Office: 1500 Union Commerce Bldg Cleveland OH 44115

COALE, ANSLEY JOHNSON, economics educator; b. Balt., Nov. 14, 1917; s. James Johnson and Nellie Ansley (Johnson) C.; m. Sarah Hamilton Campbell, Oct. 18, 1941; children—Ansley Johnson, Robert Campbell. B.A., Princeton, 1939, M.A., 1941, Ph.D., 1947; D.honoris causa, U. Louvain, Belgium, 1979, U. Liege, Belgium. Research asst. Office Population Research, Princeton, 1941-42; instr. elec. communications M.I.T., 1943-44; sec. com. social implications atomic energy Social Sci. Research Council, 1946-47; faculty Princeton, 1947—, prof. econs., 1959—, dir., 1959-75; U.S. rep. UN Population Commn., 1961-67; Social Sci. Research Council-Nat. Sci. Research Council fellow Inst. Advanced Study, 1947-49; chmn. com. on population and demography Nat. Acad. Scis., 1977-82; fellow Ctr. Advanced Study Behavioral Scis., 1982-83. Author: The Problems of Reducing Vulnerability to Atomic Bombs, 1947, (with Edgar M. Hoover) Population Growth and Economic Development in Low Income Countries, 1958, (with Melvin Zelnik) New Estimates of Population and Births in the United States, 1963, (with Paul Demeny) Regional Model Life Tables and Stable Populations, 1966, The Growth and Structure of Human Populations, 1972, (with B. Anderson and E. Härm) Human Fertility in Russia Since the Nineteenth Century, 1979; also articles. Served with USNR, 1942-46. Recipient Mindel Sheps prize in math. demography, 1974. Fellow AAAS, Am. Statis. Assn.; mem. Population Assn. Am. (pres. 1967-68), Am. Econ. Assn., Am. Philos. Soc., Internat. Population Union (pres. 1977-81), Am. Acad. Arts and Scis., Nat. Acad. Scis. Home: 155 Edgerstoune Rd Princeton NJ 08540

COAN, GAYLORD O., agribusiness executive; b. Franklin County, Ala., Oct. 12, 1935; s. E.H. and Dallas M. C.; m. Sandra Garrison, Nov. 28, 1957; children: Anna Patricia, Gregory Michael, Mark Douglas. B.S. in Agrl. Scis., U. Ga. Mgr. FMX Gold Kist, Inc., Waycross, Ga., 1959-61, dir. field services, Atlanta, 1961-62, dir. oil products and grain depts., 1962-72, 72-73, asst. v.p. mktg. group, 1973-78, group v.p. agricommodities, 1978—; mem. agrl. policy adv. com. U.S. Dept. Agr., 1982-83. Bd. dirs. DeKalb C. of C., Atlanta, 1977-80, Ga. Fgn. Trade Zone, 1980-81; active Ga. C. of C., Atlanta, 1980-81. Served with U.S. Army, 1957. Mem. Nat. Soybean Processors Assn. (chmn. 1981-83), Nat. Soybean Processors Asn. (dir. 1975-83). Baptist. Office: Gold Kist Inc 244 Perimeter Center Pkwy Atlanta GA 30346 *

COAN, STEPHEN SAMUEL, investment banker; b. N.Y.C., Apr. 15, 1942; s. George B. and Jean (Rubin) C.; m. Carol L. Marks, July 8, 1967; children: Garrett, Peter. B.S., Wharton Sch., U. Pa., 1963. Investment researcher Empire Trust Co., N.Y.C., 1963-65; mktg. exec. A.G. Becker & Co., N.Y.C., 1965-69, Stern, Frank, Meyer & Fox, 1969-71; gen. ptnr. investment banking Bear, Stearns & Co., N.Y.C., 1971—; grad. advisor Wharton Sch., U. Pa., 1977—. Exec. dir. United Jewish Appeal-Fedn., N.J., 1982—; fund raiser Am. Israel Pub. Affairs Com., Washington, 1982—; cons. community affairs N.J., 1977—. Mem. Nat. Assn. Security Dealers, Fedn. Charities (dir.). Club: Montammy Golf. Office: Bear Stearns & Co 55 Water St New York NY 10041

COASE, RONALD HARRY, economist; b. Willesden, Eng., Dec. 29, 1910; came to U.S., 1951; s. Henry Joseph and Rosalie (Giles) C.; m. Marian Ruth Hartung, Aug. 7, 1937. B. 85708Commerce, London (Eng.) Sch. Econs., 1932, D.Sc. in Econs, 1951. Sir Ernest Cassel Travelling scholar, 1931-32; asst. lectr. Dundee Sch. Econs., 1932-34, U. Liverpool, 1934-35; asst. lectr., lectr., then reader London Sch. Econs., 1935-51; prof. U. Buffalo, 1951-58, U. Va., 1958-64, U. Chgo., 1964—, now Clifton R. Musser prof. emeritus; statistician, then chief statistician Central Statis. Office, Offices War Cabinet, Eng., 1941-46. Author: British Broadcasting, A Study in Monopoly, 1950; Editor: Jour. Law and Econs, 1964-82. Rockefeller fellow, 1948; fellow Center for Advanced Study Behavioral Scis., 1958-59; sr. research fellow Hoover Instn., Stanford U., 1977. Fellow Am. Acad. Arts and Scis., Am. Econ. Assn. (Disting.); mem. Royal Econ. Soc., Mont Pelerin Soc. Home: 1515 Astor St Chicago IL 60610 Office: Laird Bell Law Quadrangle U Chgo 1111 E 60th St Chicago IL 60637

COATES, CLARENCE LEROY, JR., educator, research engineer; b. Hastings, Nebr., Nov. 5, 1923; s. Clarence Leroy and Mildred (Creighton) C.; m. Henrietta Hoff, Jan. 1, 1943; children: Catherine Anne, Christopher John; m. Lila M. Mustola, Mar. 5, 1969; 1 son, Randall Lee; m. Henrietta Coates, July 17, 1972. B.S. in Elec. Engring. U. Kans., 1944, M.S., 1948; Ph.D., U. Ill., 1954. Instr. elec. engring. U. Kans., 1946-48; instr., then asso. prof. elec. engring. U. Ill., 1948-56; research scientist Gen. Electric Research Labs., 1956-63; prof. elec. engring. U. Tex., 1963-71, chmn. dept., 1964-66, dir., 1967-71, (Coordinated Sci. Lab.); prof. U. Ill., 1971-72; head Sch. Elec. Engring., Purdue U., 1973—; Cons. NSF, 1969-70, mem. sci. info. council, 1972-75; mem. research adv. com. NASA, 1971-76. Author: Threshold Logic; Cons. editor, Blaisdell Pub. Co., 1968-70; Contbr. articles in field to profl. jours. Served as officer USNR, 1944- 46. Fellow IEEE (v.p. publ. activities, dir. 1971-72), AAAS; mem. Sigma Xi, Phi Kappa Phi, Tau Beta Pi, Eta Kappa Nu, Sigma Tau. Home: 116 Glen Court West Lafayette IN 47906

COATES, DONALD ROBERT, scientist, educator; b. Grand Island, Neb., July 23, 1922; s. Frank Jefferson and Harriet (Ferris) C.; m. Jeanne Louise Grandison, Mar. 18, 1944; children: Cheryl D., Donald Eric, Lark J. B.A., Coll. Wooster, 1944; M.A., Columbia U., 1948, Ph.D., 1956. Mem. faculty Earlham Coll., Richmond, Ind., 1948-51; geologist, project chief U.S. Geol. Survey, Tucson, 1951-54; faculty Harpur Coll. (now State U. N.Y.), Binghamton, 1954—, chmn. dept. geology, 1954-63, prof., 1963—; Soil scientist Charles Kettering Found., Richmond, Ind., 1948-51; research geologist U.S. Geol. Survey, Vestal, N.Y., 1958-61; vis. geoscientist Am. Geol. Inst., 1963-65; cons. Consol. Edison N.Y., Niagara Mohawk Power Corp., U.S. Army C.E., Town of Islip, N.Y. State Atty. Gen., Broome County, Town of Vestal, N.Y., also pvt. cos. Editor: Geology of South-Central New York, 1963, Environmental Geomorphology and Landscape Conservation, 3 vols., Coastal Geomorphology, Glacial Geomorphology, Geomorphology and Engineering, Landslides, Thresholds in Geomorphology, Urban Geomorphology; editor, Author: Environmental Geology; contbr.: Science - A Process Approach, 1965; also articles, reports. Recipient award for Sustained Superior Performance NSF, 1964; research grantee NSF, U.S. Dept. Commerce, U.S. Geol. Survey, N.Y. State Atomic and Space Devel. Authority, Research Found. SUNY, 1958-61. Fellow AAAS, Geol. Soc. Am. (cert. of merit engring. geology div. 1980); mem. Assn. Engring. Geologists, Nat. Assn. Geology Tchrs. (pres. Eastern sect. 1962, Ralph Digman award 1972, Coll. Tchr. of Yr. award 1971), Am. Inst. Profl. Geologists, N.Y. State Geol. Assn. (pres. 1963, 81), Phi Beta Kappa. Home: Box 268 A RD 3 Endicott NY 13760 Office: Dept Geol Scis State U NY Binghamton NY 13901

COATES, JAMES OTIS, lawyer; b. Cin., Feb. 13, 1914; s. Charles Houston and Bessie Lee (Becraft) C.; m. Shirley Jane Ripley, Sept. 4, 1937 (dec. May 1973); children: James Houston, Thomas Ripley, Virginia Lee; m. Clare M. Haller, Mar. 15, 1974. A.B., Princeton U., 1935; J.D., Harvard U., 1938; postgrad., Columbia U., 1958. Bar: Ohio 1939. Since practiced in, Cin.; assoc. firm Dinsmore, Shohl, Sawyer & Dinsmore, 1938-43, ptnr., 1946-61; sr. ptnr. Dinsmore, Shohl, Barrett, Coates & Deupree, 1961-67, Dinsmore, Shohl, Coates & Deupree, 1967-82, Dinsmore & Shohl, 1982—; counsel South-Western Pub. Co., Senco Products Inc., 1975—; dist. atty. L. & N. R.R. Co. Dist. chmn. United Appeal, 1958-59; pres. local chpt. Am. Field Service, 1962-64; trustee Legal Aid Soc., Cin., 1970-74. Served to lt. (j.g.) USNR, 1943-46. Decorated Bronze Star. Mem. Internat., Am., Ohio, Cin. bar assns., Princeton Alumni Assn. So. Ohio, Cin. Hist. Soc., Am. Soc. Internat. Law, Harvard Law Sch. Assn., Phi Beta Kappa. Presbyn. Clubs: Literary, Torch, University, Cincinnati Country, Hyde Park Country. Home: Deupree House East Apt 512 3939 Erie Avenue Cincinnati OH 45208 Office: 2100 Fountain Sq Plaza Cincinnati OH 45202

COATES, JESSE, ret. chem. engr.; b. Baton Rouge, Mar. 12, 1908; s. Charles Edward and Ollie (Maurin) C.; m. Judith Mills Williams, Apr. 16, 1938; children—Judith Mills, Jesse, Victor Maurin (dec.). B.S., La. State U., 1928; postgrad., Mass. Inst. Tech., 1930-31; M.S., U. Mich., 1932, Ph.D., 1936. Mem. La. Bd. for Registration Profl. Engrs. Chemist, treating engr. Nat. Lumber & Creosoting Co., 1928; chemist Internat. Paper Co., 1928-29, Meeker Sugar Refinery, 1930-31, Punta Alegre Sugar Co., 1931; chem. engr. Tex. Pacific Coal & Oil Co., 1932-33, United Gas Pub. Service, 1933-36; asst. prof. chem. engring. La. State U., Baton Rouge, 1936-42, asso. prof., 1942-47, prof., 1947-78, chmn. dept., 1955-67, 69-70, Alumni prof., 1969-78, ret., 1978; cons. chem. engr. Contbr. articles to profl. jours. Recipient Technol. Accomplishment medal La. Engring. Soc., 1958; Charles E. Coates meml. award Am. Chem. Soc.-Am. Inst. Chem. Engrs., 1958; named Man of Month Chem. Engring. mag., Apr. 1958; Distinguished Service certificate Nat. Council Engring. Examiners, 1977. Fellow Am. Inst. Chemists, Am. Inst. Chem. Engrs.; mem. Am. Chem. Soc., Am. Soc. Engring. Edn., La. Acad. Scis., Sigma Xi, Phi Kappa Phi, Alpha Chi Sigma, Phi Lambda Upsilon, Kappa Alpha. Episcopalian. Home: 333 Lee Dr Apt 344 Baton Rouge LA 70808

COATES, JOSEPH FRANCIS, chemist; b. Bklyn., Jan. 3, 1929; s. Joseph Marcellus and Elizabeth Claire (Jones) C.; m. Vary Ellen Taylor, Feb. 2, 1952; children—Marcy (Mrs. Richard Canavan), Peter, Matthew, Anna, Vary Elizabeth. B.A., Poly. Inst. Bklyn., 1951; M.S., Pa. State U., 1953; postgrad., U. Pa., 1953-55. Research chemist Atlantic Refining Co., Phila., 1953-60; chief chemist Onyx Chem. Co., Jersey City, 1960-61; staff scientist Inst. Def. Analyses, Arlington, Va., 1961-70; project mgr. NSF, Washington, 1970-74; asst. to dir. Office Tech. Assessment, U.S. Congress, Washington, 1974-79; pres. J. F. Coates, Inc., Washington, 1980—; adj. prof. Am. U., Washington, 1972-73, George Washington U., 1974—; lectr. Author. Patentee in field. Home and Office: 3738 Kanawha NW Washington DC 20015

COATES, ROBERT CARMAN, lawyer, govt. ofcl.; b. Amherst, N.S., Can., Mar. 10, 1928; s. Frederick Carman and Rita Bridget (O'Brien) C.; m. Mary Blanche Wade, Dec. 27, 1954; children—David, Amy Marijo. B.A., Mt. Allison U., 1951; LL.B., Dalhousie U., 1954. Mem. Parliament of Can., Ottawa, Ont., 1957—; pres. John G. Diefenbaker Meml. Found., Inc. Author: Night of the Knives, 1969; contbr. to newspapers. Mem. N.S. Barristers Soc. (Queens Counsel 1979), Commonwealth Parliamentary Assn., NATO Parliamentary Assn., Can.-Korea Parliamentary Group, Can.-U.S. Parliamentary Group, Progressive Conservative Assn. Can. (pres. 1977-81). Anglican. Home: 46 Regent St Amherst NS Canada Office: House of Commons Ottawa ON Canada

COATES, ROBERT JAY, electronic scientist; b. Lansing, Mich., May 8, 1922; s. Archie Louis and Ruth Agnes (Hutchings) C.; m. Gladys Buchhorn, Aug. 17, 1946; 1 dau., Bonnie. B.S.E.E., Mich. State U., 1943; M.S.E.E., U. Md., 1948; Ph.D., Johns Hopkins U., 1957. Registered profl. engr., D.C. Electronic scientist U.S. Naval Research Lab., Washington, 1943-49, 52-59; instr. physics Johns Hopkins U., Balt., 1949-52; asso. chief tracking systems div., chief space data acquisition div., chief advanced devel. div., chief advanced data systems div. Goddard Space Flight Center, Greenbelt, Md., 1959-79, mgr. crustal dynamics project, 1979—. Served with USN, 1944-45. Recipient Group Achievement award NASA, 1973, 1968, Apollo Achievement award, 1969, Exceptional Performance award Goddard Space Flight Center, 1971; Outstanding Performance award NRL, 1959. Fellow IEEE; mem. Am. Phys. Soc., Am. Geophys. Union, AAAS, Sigma Xi, Phi Kappa Phi, Tau Beta Pi. Home: 529 Whittingham Dr Silver Spring MD 20904 Office: Code 904 Goddard Space Flight Center Greenbelt MD 20771

COATES, ROBERT MERCER, chemist; b. Evanston, Ill., May 21, 1938; s. John Mercer and Mary (Abbott) C.; m. Linda Lee LaRue, July 11, 1964; children—John M., Anne E., Christina D. B.S., Yale U., 1960; Ph.D., U. Calif., Berkeley, 1963. Postdoctoral fellow Stanford U., 1964-65; asst. prof. chemistry U. Ill., Urbana, 1965-71, asso. prof., 1971-75, prof., 1975—. Editor: Organic Syntheses, vol. 59, 1979. A. P. Sloan fellow, 1971-73; Guggenheim fellow, 1980. Mem. Am. Chem. Soc., Chem. Soc. (London), AAAS, AAUP. Home: 2202 Combes St Urbana IL 61801 Office: Dept Chemistry U Ill Urbana IL 61801

COATS, DANIEL R., congressman; b. Jackson, Mich., May 16, 1943; s. Edward R. and Vera E. C.; m. Marcia Crawford, Sept. 4, 1965; children: Laura, Lisa, Andrew. B.A., Wheaton (Ill.) Coll., 1965; J.D. cum laude, Ind. U., 1971. Bar: Ind. 1972. Mem. 97th-98th Congresses from 4th Dist. Ind. Pres., Big Bros./Big Sisters, Ft. Wayne, Ind. Served with U.S. Army, 1966-68. Mem. Ind. Bar Assn., Allen County Bar Assn. Home: 7251 Springside Way McLean VA 22101 Office: 1427 Longworth House Office Bldg Washington DC 20515

COATSWORTH, ELIZABETH (MRS. HENRY BESTON), author; b. Buffalo, May 31, 1893; d. William T. and Ida (Reid) C.; m. Henry Beston, June 18, 1929; children: Margaret Coatsworth (Mrs. Dorik Mechau), Catherine Maurice (Mrs. Richard Barnes). Prep. edn., Buffalo Sem.; A.B., Vassar Coll., 1915; M.A., Columbia U., 1916; Litt.D., U. Maine, 1955; L.H.D., New Eng. Coll., 1958. (Recipient Newbery medal 1931, Golden Rose award New Eng. Poetry Club 1967, Maine Arts and Sci. award, 1st runner-up Hans Christian Anderson award 1968); Author: 7 other books of verse Mountain Bride, and; 4 other novels; 3 books essays, numerous childrens books including The Cat Who Went to Heaven; the 5 Sally books beginning with Horses, Dogs and Cats, 1957; book of collected verse, 1957; novel The White Room, 1958, The Peaceable Kingdom, The Cave, 1958, Indian Encounters, 1960, Lonely Maria, 1960, Desert Dan, 1960, The UNICEF Christmas Book, 1960, The Noble Doll, 1961, Ronnie and the Chief's Son, 1962, The Princess and the Lion, 1963, Jock's Island, 1963, Cricket and the Emperors Son, 1965, The Secret, 1965, The Hand of Apollo, 1965, The Sparrow Bush; poetry, 1966, The Fox Friend, 1966, The Place, 1966, (with Henry Beston) Chimney Farm Bedtime Stories, 1966, Maine Memories, 1968, Bess and the Sphinx, 1968, Lighthouse Island, 1968, George and Red, 1969, Indian Mound Farm, 1969, Grandmother Cat and the Hermit, 1970, Good Night, 1972, The Wanderers, 1972, Daisy, 1973, Pure Magic, 1973, All of a Sudden Susan, 1974, Marra's World, 1975, Personal Geography of Elizabeth Coatsworth, 1976, Books pub. in, England, Germany, Norway, Sweden, other countries.; Editor: Henry Beston's Especially Maine, 1970. Fellow Internat. Inst. Arts and Letters; mem. Phi Beta Kappa. *At least, make a beginning.* *

COBB, BRIAN ERIC, broadcasting executive; b. Berlin, N.H., Jan. 3, 1945; s. Everett Bryan and Eleanore (Bouchard) C.; children—Jennifer Kay, Heather Christine. B.A. in Bus, U. Nev., 1967. Gen. sales mgr. Sta. WNGE-TV, Nashville, 1972, mktg. mgr., 1973-76, v.p., gen. mgr., 1977, also Sta. WSIX AM/FM, Nashville, 1977, Gen. Electric Broadcasting of Colo., stas. KOA-AM, KOAQ, KOA-TV, Denver, 1978-81; with Chapman Assocs., Denver, 1982—. Comml. chmn. Mile-Hi United Way, 1980; bd. dirs. Vanderbilt Children's Hosp., 1976-77. Mem. Nat. Assn. Broadcasters, Nat. Assn. Program TV Execs., Colo. Assn. Broadcasters (dir.), Denver Advt. Fedn. Republican. Roman Catholic. Club: Rotary. Home: 415 Josephine Denver CO 80206 Office: 1044 Lincoln Denver CO 80210

COBB, CHARLES ELVAN, resort and community development company executive; b. Fresno, Calif., May 9, 1936; s. Charles Elvan and Mildred (Kerr) C.; m. Sue McCourt, Feb. 28, 1959; children: Christian, Tobin. B.A., Stanford U., 1958, M.B.A., 1962. Investment counselor Dodge & Cox, San Francisco, 1962-64; with Kaiser Aluminum & Chem. Corp., various locations, 1964-72; pres. Arvida Corp., Miami, Fla., 1972-80, chmn., chief exec. officer, 1980—; also dir.; pres. living/leisure group Penn Central Corp., Miami, 1980-83; dir. Southeast First Nat. Bank of Miami; trustee Bankers Life Ins. Co., Nebr. Trustee U. Miami, 1975—, also vice chmn.; mem. Fla. Gov.'s Task Force for Econ. Devel., 1978—, Fla. Council of 100. Served with USNR, 1958-60. Recipient Brotherhood award medallion NCCJ, 1981. Mem. Fla. C. of C. (dir. 1980—). Republican. Presbyterian. Clubs: Miami, Bankers, Royal Palm Tennis (Miami); Ocean Reef (Key Largo, Fla.); Boca Raton (Boca Raton, Fla.); Olympic (San Francisco). Mem. 1960 U.S. Olympic Team. Office: 5550 Glades Rd Boca Raton FL 33432

COBB, G. ELLIOTT, JR., lawyer; b. Franklin, Va., July 11, 1939; s. Gardner E. and Thelma L. (Whitley) C.; m. Betty Minor, July 15, 1961; children: Polly, Susan, Gardner. B.S., U. Va., 1960, LL.B., 1966. Bar: Va. 1966, Supreme Ct. U.S 1974. Asso. counsel Union Camp Corp., Wayne, N.J., 1967-74, counsel, mgr. adminstrn., 1974-76, gen. counsel, asst. sec., 1976, v.p., gen. counsel, sec., 1976-78; ptnr. Moyler, Moyler, Rainey & Cobb, Franklin, 1978—; mem. adv. bd. United Va. Bank, Franklin. Mem. Franklin City Council, 1980—; vice mayor of Franklin, 1982—; bd. dirs. Southampton Meml. Hosp. Served with USMC, 1960-61. Mem. ABA, Va., Southampton-Franklin bar assns. Episcopalian. Clubs: Cypress Cove Country, Rotary. Home: 913 Clay St Franklin VA 23851 Office: Moyler Moyler Rainey & Cobb 506 N Main St Franklin VA 23851

COBB, GEORGE HAMILTON, oil, mineral consultant; b. St. Louis, Aug. 16, 1911; s. George H. and Julia L. (Middleton) C.; m. Esther Victoria Preston, Nov. 30, 1957; children: Carolyn Rozella Martinson, David Dean (dec.). Student, Okla. State U., 1929-30, U. Nebr., 1934; B.S., U. Kans., 1939. Registered profl. engr., Okla., Tex. Petroleum engr. Kerr-McGee Corp., Oklahoma City, 1939-41, prodn. supt., 1942-47, prodn. mgr., 1948-53, asst. to pres., 1953-56, v.p. exploration, 1959-60, v.p. minerals div., 1960-63, v.p. exploration research, 1964-67, sr. v.p., 1968-71, exec. v.p., 1968-76, chmn. operating com., 1968-76, cons., 1976—; owner Three Forks Ranch, Wagoner County, Okla.; exec. v.p. Kermac Nuclear Fuels Corp., Oklahoma City, 1956—; asso. dir.; dir. Community Bank of Warr Acres, Oklahoma City. Named to Nat. Cowboy Hall of Fame. Mem. Am. Inst. M.E., Am. Petroleum Inst., Am. Assn. Petroleum Geologists, N.Mex., Colo. mining assns., Western Heritage Center. Home: 6425 N Grandmark Dr Oklahoma City OK 73116 Office: PO Box 25861 Oklahoma City OK 73125

COBB, HENRY NICHOLS, architect; b. Boston, Apr. 8, 1926; s. Charles Kane and Elsie Quincy (Nichols) C.; m. Joan Stewart Spaulding, June 5, 1953; children: Sara Quincy, Emma Trow, Pamela Codman. A.B., Harvard, 1947, M. Arch., 1949. Designer in office Hugh Stubbins, 1949-50; mem. archtl. div. Webb & Knapp, Inc., 1950-55; partner I.M. Pei & Partners, 1955—; vis. critic Yale U., 1963-66, Bishop vis. prof. architecture, 1973, 78, Davenport vis. prof., 1975; chmn. dept. architecture Harvard U. Grad. Sch. Design, Cambridge, Mass., 1980—. Prin. works include Pl. Ville Marie, Montreal, Can., 1962; acad. center and residence halls, State U. Coll., Fredonia, N.Y., 1967, John Hancock Tower, Boston, 1972, Collins Place, Melbourne, Australia, 1976, Wilson Commons, U. Rochester, 1976, World Trade Center, Balt., 1977, Dallas Center, 1979, Johnson & Johnson World Hdqrs., New Brunswick, N.J., 1981, Mobil Research Lab., Farmers Branch, Tex., 1983, Portland Mus. Art, Portland, Maine. Trustee Am. Acad. in Rome, 1972—, Brearley Sch., 1975-80. Served with USNR, 1944-46. Recipient Arnold W. Brunner Meml. prize in architecture Am. Acad. and Inst. Arts and Letters, 1977. Fellow AIA (Medal of honor N.Y. chpt. 1982); mem. Am. Acad. and Inst. Arts and Letters. Office: Harvard U Grad Sch Design Cambridge MA 02138 also I M Pei & Partners 600 Madison Ave New York NY 10022

COBB, HENRY VAN ZANDT, psychologist; b. East Orange, N.J., Feb. 22, 1909; s. Sanford Ellsworth and Margaret Brown (Macleish) C.; m. Florence Ruth Crozier, Aug. 3, 1932; children: Margaret Alice, Judith Helen, Catherine Macleish, Peter Van Zandt, David Crozier. A.B., Pomona Coll., 1930; Ph.D., Yale, 1936. Acting prof. psychology and philosophy Furman U., Greenville, S.C., 1934-35; instr. philosophy Carleton Coll., Northfield, Minn., 1936-41, asst. prof., 1941-44; prof. philosophy and psychology, head dept. U. S.D., 1946-58, prof., chmn. dept. psychology, 1958-67, dean, 1967-69, v.p. acad. affairs, acting dean, 1969-74, prof. emeritus, 1975—; vis. prof. edn. Tchrs. Coll. Columbia U., 1964-65; vis. scholar U. N.C., 1974-76, clin. prof., 1977—; with Florence R. Cobb (weekly radio program Our Children), 1952-53; faculty study fellowship Ford Found., 1953; cons. Peace Corps, Kenya, 1977-78; Mem. Gov.'s Com. on Mental Health, S.D., 1954; mem. S.D. Gov.'s Com. Mental Retardation, 1962; councilor Internat. League Socs. for Mentally Handicapped, 1963- 65, pres., 1966-70; bd. dirs. Joint Commn. on Mental Health of Children, 1966-70; chmn. Joint Commn. Internat. Aspects Mental Retardation, 1970-73; chmn. tech. adv. com. Joint Commn. Accreditation of Hosps., 1971-73; Mem. Pres.'s Com. on Mental Retardation, 1973-79, vice chmn., 1977-79. Author: Man's Way, 1942, Forecast of Fulfillment, 1972; editor, prin. author: Mental Retardation: A Report to the President, 1976, Mental Retardation, Past and Present, 1977; Contbr. articles and revs. to profl. jours. Served with USNR, 1944-45; assigned duty on U.S.S. Wichita. Mem. A.A.A.S., Am. Assn. U. Profs., Am. Philos. Assn., Am. Psychol. Assn., Soc. Religion in Higher Edn., Nat. Assn. Retarded Children (pres. 1964-65), S.D. Assn. Retarded Children (pres. 1954), Am. Assn. Mental Deficiency, Sigma Xi, Phi Beta Kappa. Home: 1 Weiner St Chapel Hill NC 27514

COBB, HUBBARD HANFORD, magazine editor, writer; b. N.Y.C., Aug. 5, 1917; s. Frank I. and Margaret Hubbard (Ayer) C.; m. Elizabeth Youngblood Simon, Feb. 6, 1954. Grad., Avon (Conn.) Prep. Sch., 1936. Bldg. editor Am. Home mag., 1952-61, editor, 1961-69; author syndicated column home problems, 1946-60, condr. radio program home bldg., 1947-54; contbg. editor Woman's Day mag., 1972-84. Author: How to Build Your Dream House, 1948, Home Handyman's Guide, 1949, Homeowners Guide to Remodeling, 1950, Complete Homeowner, 1965, The Dream House Encyclopedia, 1970, How to Buy and Remodel the Older House, 1972, How to Paint Anything, 1972, (with Betsy Cobb) Vacation Houses—All You Should Know Before You Buy or Build, 1973, City People's Guide to Country Living, 1973, Preventive Maintenance for Your House or Apartment, 1975, Improvements That Increase the Value of Your House, 1976, Woman's Day Homeowners Handbook, 1976. Served with USAAF, World War II. Mem. Author's Guild. Home: PO Box 353 Old Saybrook CT 06475

COBB, JAMES RICHARD, banker; b. Little Rock, Feb. 12, 1942; s. James Harvol and Elizabeth (Whitaker) C.; m. Virginia Stuart, July 4, 1965; children: William Claiborne, Cynthia Ruffin. B.S.B.A., U. N.C., 1965. Mgr. Del. Coca—Cola, Wilmington, 1965-73; v.p. Mid-Atlantic Canners Assn., Hamburg, Pa., 1971-73, Comml. Nat. Bank, Little Rock, 1974-77, sr. v.p., 1977-78, exec. v.p., 1978-83; pres. Comml. Bankstock Inc., Little Rock, 1981-83; vice chmn. bd. First Comml. Bank N.A., 1983—. Former pres., dir. Little Rock unit Am. Cancer Soc.; dir. Ark. div. Am. Cancer Soc.; dir. Central Ark. Radiation Therapy Inst., Pulaski Acad. Clubs: Little Rock Country, Little Rock Racquet. Office: Commercial Bankstock Inc 200 Main St Little Rock AR 72203

COBB, JEWEL PLUMMER, college president; b. Chgo., Jan. 17, 1924; (div.)1 child. A.B., Talladega Coll., 1944; M.S., N.Y. U., 1947, Ph.D. in Biology, 1950. Fellow Nat. Cancer Inst., 1950-52; instr. anatomy U. Ill. Coll. Medicine, 1952-54; research surgery Postgrad. Med. Coll., N.Y. U., 1955, asst. prof., 1955-60; Cancer Research Found. prof. biology Sarah Lawrence Coll., 1960-69; prof. zoology, dean Conn. Coll., 1969-76; prof. biology, dean Douglass Coll., Rutgers U., 1976-81; pres. Calif. State U.-Fullerton, 1982—; Dir. Travelers Ins. Co.; Former mem. commn. on acad. affairs Am. Council on Edn.; Bd. dirs. 21st Century Found., Nat. Center Resource Recovery, Nat. Sci. Bd., 1974-80, Nat. Inst. Medicine. Recipient Alumnae Woman of Yr. award N.Y. U., 1979. Fellow N.Y. Acad. Scis., Tissue Culture Assn.; mem. AAUW, Sigma Xi. Spl. research on tissue culture studies human neoplasms, changes produced by promising chemotherapeutic agts., mechanisms normal and abnormal pigment cell metabolism. Office: Calif State U Fullerton CA

COBB, JOHN BOSWELL, JR., educator, clergyman; b. Kobe, Japan, Feb. 9, 1925; s. John Boswell and Theodora Cook (Atkinson) C.; m. Jean Olmstead Loftin, June 18, 1947; children: Theodore, Cliford, Andrew, Richard. M.A., U. Chgo. Div. Sch., 1949, Ph. D., 1952. Ordained to ministry United Meth. Ch., 1950. Pastor Towns County Circuit, N.Ga. Conf., 1950-51; faculty Young Harris Coll., Ga., 1950-53, Candler Sch. Theology and Emory U., 1953-58, Sch. Teology, Claremont, Calif., 1958—; Avery prof. Claremont Grad. Sch., 1973—; mem. commn. on doctrine and doctrinal standard United Meth. Ch., 1968-72. Author: A Christian Natural Theology, 1965, The Structure of Christian Existence, 1967, Christ in a Pluralistic Age, 1975. Dir. Center for Process Studies. Fulbright prof. U. Mainz, 1965-66; fellow Woodrow Wilson Internat. Ctr. for Scholars, 1976. Mem. Am. Acad. Religion, Am. Metaphys. Soc. Home: 1009 N College Ave Claremont CA 91711 Office: Sch Theology Claremont CA 91711

COBB, LESLIE DAVIS, utility executive; b. Beaumont, Tex., Jan. 4, 1935; d. Leslie Lethrage and Willie Sammie (Wiltshire) Davis; (div.)children: Terry W. Ogden, David Bryan Ogden. Student, Lamar U., public utility exec. program U. Mich. With Hall & Hall Ins., Beaumont, 1953-54; with Gulf States Utilities Co., Beaumont, 1955—, sec. to chmn. bd., 1974-79, corp. sec., 1979—. Mem. Am. Soc. Corp. Secs., Beaumont C. of C. Episcopalian. Clubs: Beaumont, Bus. and Profl. Men's. Address: Gulf States Utilities Co 350 Pine St Beaumont TX 77701

COBB, RUTH, artist; b. Boston, Feb. 20, 1914; d. Charles Edward and Bessie (Cohen) C.; m. Lawrence Kupferman, Apr. 29, 1937; children: Nancy Rose, David. Diploma, Mass. Coll. Art, 1935. One-woman shows, Shore Gallery, Boston, 1958, 60, 63, 65, 70, DeCordova Mus., Lincoln, Mass., 1955, Art Unlimited Gallery, San Francisco, 1961, Cober Gallery, N.Y.C., 1962, 65, 67, McNay Mus., San Antonio, 1966, Phila. Art Alliance, 1962, Galerie Moos, Montreal, Que., Can., 1969, Witte Mus., San Antonio, 1967, Harold Ernst Gallery, Boston, 1974, 75, 76, Midtown Gallery, N.Y.C., 1981, 82; represented in permanent collections, Boston Mus. Fine Arts, Brandeis U., Butler Inst. Am. Art, Munson-Williams-Proctor Inst., Addison Gallery Am. Art, Va. Mus. Fine Arts, DeCordova Mus., Tufts U.; featured in TV program Artist At Work, 1981; work featured in Am. Artist mag.,

1979. Recipient awards Pa. Acad. Fine Arts, 1967, Allied Artists N.Y.C., 1966. Mem. Am. Watercolor Soc. (award), Boston Watercolor Soc. (award), Allied Artists Am. (award), NAD (award).

COBB, VINCENT, actor, writer, photographer; b. Los Angeles, Apr. 16, 1943; s. Lee J. and Helen (Beverley) C.; m. Joan; 1 dau. by previous marriage, Jennifer; stepdaus.—Dana, Lauren. Student, U. Calif., Berkeley, UCLA. Freelance actor in all media; writer, photographer, pub. in books, mags., newspapers and brochures, 1963—. Mem. Screen Actors Guild, Actors Equity Assn., AFTRA, Am. Soc. Mag. Photographers. Address: Box 5432 Beverly Hills CA 90210

COBB, VIRGINIA HORTON, artist, educator; b. Oklahoma City, Nov. 23, 1933; d. Wayne and Ruth (Goodale) Horton; m. Bruce L. Cobb, Dec. 30, 1951; children—Bruce Wayne, Juliann, William Stuart. Student, U. Colo., 1966-67, Community Coll., Denver, 1967; student of, William Schimmel, Ariz., 1965-66, Edgar Whitney, N.Y.C., 1966, Chen Chi, N.Y.C., 1974. Comml. artist and designer Ruth Horton Studios, Oklahoma City, 1954-63; instr. seminars, 1974—, including; N.Mex. Watercolor Soc., Albuquerque, 1976, Okla. Mus. Art, Oklahoma City, 1976, Upstairs Gallery Workshops, Arlington, Tex., 1977, 78, 79, 80, St. Louis Art Guild, 1980, Alaska Water Color Soc., Anchorage, 1981, Needham (Mass.) Art Center, 1981, N.C. Watercolor Soc., Charlotte, 1981, San Diego Watercolor Soc., 1981, S.C. Water Color Soc., Florence, 1981; guest instr. Crafton Hills Coll. Master Seminars, Yucaipa, Calif., 1979, 80, 81, U. Alaska, Anchorage, 1981; lectr. Sta. KRDO-TV, 1977, Francis Marion Coll., Florence, 1981, Sta. KAKM, Anchorage, 1981. Contbr. articles to art publs.; one-woman shows of watercolor paintings, Jack Meier Galleries, Houston, 1979-81, Sturh Mus., Grand Island, Nebr., 1982, group shows include, NAD, N.Y.C., 1978, 79-81, San Bernardino (Calif.) County Mus., 1978, Nat. Watercolor Invitational, Rochester, N.Y., 1981, Rocky Mountain Nat. Watermedia Exhbt., Golden, Colo., 1978, 79, 81; represented in permanent collections, NAD, Jefferson County (Colo.) Public Library, Foothills Art Center, Golden, Colo., St. Lawrence U., Canton, N.Y., N.Mex. Watercolor Soc., Albuquerque. Recipient Foothills Art Center award, 1976, Edgar Fox award Watercolor U.S., 1973, Denver award Rocky Mountain Nat. Exhbn., 1981. Mem. NAD (Walter Biggs Meml. award 1978, 81), Nat. Watercolor Soc. (Strathmore Paper Co. award 1975), Am. Watercolor Soc. (Paul B. Remmey Meml. award 1974, Arches Paper Co. award 1977, Edgar Whitney award 1978, Mary Pleisner Meml. award 1980, High Winds medal 1981, Silver Medal of Honor 1983, guest demonstrator 1980, nat. juror 1981, Dolphin fellow 1982), Watercolor Soc. Houston (chairperson profl. standards 1980-81), Rocky Mountain Watermedia Soc. Office: 3507 Roseland Houston TX 77006

COBB, WILLIAM LYMAN, banker; b. Sutherland, Iowa, May 31, 1909; s. Burt L. and Carrie Louise (Dollman) C.; m. Ruth Arlene Mountain, July 14, 1934; children: Carolyn Ann, William Lyman Jr. Student, Des Moines U., 1928-30. Dir., mem. exec. com. Internat. Gen. Industries, Inc., Globe Industries, Inc., Intermediate Credit Corp., Kliklok Corp., Northeastern Ins. Co., Hartford, Hawkeye-Security Ins. Co., United Security Ins. Co., United Services Life Ins. Co., Bankers Security Life Ins. Soc., Internat. Bank Washington; dir. Central Nat. Bank & Trust Co., Des Moines, Nat. Bank of Ga., Atlanta. Served as lt. USNR, 1943-46. Mem. Washington Bd. Trade, Nat. Lawyers Club Washington, Des Moines C. of C., Phi Sigma Chi. Clubs: Congressional Country (Bethesda, Md.); Embassy (Des Moines); Nat. Lawyers. Home: 1200 N Nash St Arlington VA 22209 Office: 1701 Pennsylvania Ave NW Washington DC 20006

COBB, WILLIAM MONTAGUE, anatomist, physical anthropologist, medical editor, emeritus educator; b. Washington, Oct. 12, 1904; s. William Elmer and Alexzine E. (Montague) C.; m. Hilda B. Smith, June 26, 1929 (dec. June 1976); children: Carolyn Cobb Wilkinson, Hilda Amelia Cobb Gray. A.B. (Blodgett scholar), Amherst Coll., 1925, Sc.D., 1955; M.D., Howard U., 1929, L.H.D. (hon.), 1980; Ph.D., Western Res. U., 1932; cert. in embryology, Marine Biol. Lab., Woods Hole, Mass.; student, U.S. Nat. Museum, Washington U.; LL.D., Morgan State Coll., 1964, U. Witwatersrand, South Africa, 1977; Sc.D., Georgetown U., 1978, Med. Coll. Wis., 1979, U. Ark., 1983; D.Med. Sci., Brown U., 1983. Intern Freedmen's Hosp., Washington, 1929-30; instr. embryology Howard U., 1928-29, asst. prof. anatomy, 1932-34, assoc. prof., 1934-42, prof. anatomy, 1942-69, head dept., 1947-69, distinguished prof. anatomy, 1969-73, prof. emeritus, 1973—; vis. prof. anatomy Stanford U., 1972, U. Md., 1974, W.Va. U., 1980; Disting. Univ. prof. U. Ark. Med. Scis. Center, 1979; vis. prof., Danz lectr. U. Wash., 1978; vis. prof. orthopaedic surgery Harvard U., 1981; vis. prof. anatomy Med. Coll. Wis., 1982; dir. Disting. Sr. Scholars Lecture Series U. D.C., 1983; jr. med. officer U.S. Dept. Agr., 1935; mem. Pub. Health Advisory Council of D.C., 1953-61, chmn., 1956-58; chief med. examiner Freedmen's Hosp. Bd., D.C. SSS, 1941; civilian cons. to surgeon gen. U.S. Army, 1945; mem. exec. com. White House Conf. on Health, 1965; Fellow in anatomy Western Res. U., 1933-39, asso. anatomy, 1942-44. Founder: Bull. of Medico-Chirurg. Soc. D.C, 1941; editor, 1945—, Jour. Nat. Med. Assn, 1949-77; author monographs, articles. Rosenwald fellow, 1941-42; recipient citations from Opportunity mag., 1947, Chgo. Defender, 1948, Washington Afro-Am., 1948; Distinguished Service award Medico-Chirurg. Soc. D.C., 1952; D.S.M. Nat. Med. Assn., 1955; Meritorious Service award Med. Soc. of D.C., 1968; Meritorious Pub. Service award Govt. of D.C., 1972; Disting. Public Service award U.S. Navy, 1978, 82. Fellow Am. Anthrop. Assn., Gerontol. Soc., AAAS (mem. 1957-59), Assn. Anatomists (Henry Gray award 1980), Am. Assn. Phys. Anthropologists (v.p. 1948-50, pres. 1957-59), Am. Eugenics Soc. (dir. 1957-68), Anat. Soc. Gt. Brit. and Ireland, Nat. Med. Assn. (state v.p. 1943, editor 1949-77, chmn. council on med. edn. and hosps. 1949-63, nat. pres. 1964-65), Nat. Urban League (health specialist 1945-47), NAACP (chmn. nat. med. com. 1950, dir. 1949—, pres. 1976-82), Am. Soc. Mammalogists, Am. Assn. History of Medicine, Washington Soc. History of Medicine (pres. 1972), Assn. Study of Negro Life and History, Anthrop. Soc. Washington (pres. 1949-51), Medica-Chirurgical Soc. D.C. (rec. sec. 1935-41, pres. 1945-47, 54-56), Omega Psi Phi (chmn. scholarship com. 1939-48), Sigma Xi, Alpha Omega Alpha. Presbyterian. Club: Cosmos (Washington). Home: 1219 Girard St NW Washington DC 20009 Office: Howard U Washington DC 20059

COBBLE, JAMES WIKLE, educator; b. Kansas City, Mo., Mar. 15, 1926; s. Ray and Crystal Edith (Wikle) C.; m. Margaret Ann Zumwalt, June 9, 1949; children—Catherine Ann, Richard James. Student, San Diego State Coll., 1942-44; B.A., No. Ariz. U., 1946; M.S., U. So. Calif., 1949; Ph.D., U. Tenn., 1952. Chemist Oak Ridge Nat. Lab., 1949-52; postdoctoral research assoc. U. Calif., Berkeley, 1952-55, instr. dept. chemistry, 1954; asst. prof. dept. chemistry Purdue U., Lafayette, Ind., 1955-58, asso. prof., 1958-61, prof., 1961-73; prof., dean Grad. div. San Diego State U., 1973—; cons. in field. Contbr. articles to sci. publs. Vice pres. San Diego State U. Found., 1975—. Served to lt. (j.g.) USNR, 1945-46. Recipient E.O. Lawrence award U.S. AEC, 1970; Guggenheim fellow, 1966; Robert A. Welch Found. lectr., 1971. Fellow Am. Inst. Chemists, Am. Phys. Soc.; mem. Am. Chem. Soc., Sigma Xi, Phi Kappa Phi, Alpha Chi Sigma, Phi Lambda Upsilon. Home: 1380 Park Row La Jolla CA 92037 Office: Dept Chemistry San Diego State Univ San Diego CA 92182

COBBOLD, RICHARD SOUTHWELL CHEVALLIER, biomedical engineer, educator; b. Worcester, Eng., Dec. 10, 1931; emigrated to Can., 1956, naturalized, 1968; s. Reynold Chevallier and Betty Joyce (Lindner) C.; m. Margaret Mary St. Aubyn, Aug. 2, 1963; children—Adrian Chevallier, David Chevallier, Christopher Mark. B.Sc. in Physics, Imperial Coll., U. London, 1956; M.Sc. in Biomed. Engring, U. Sask., 1961; Ph.D. in E.E, U. Sask., 1965. Asst. expertl. officer Ministry of Supply, Sevenoaks, Kent, Eng., 1949-53; sci. officer Def. Research Bd. Can., Ottawa, 1956-59; lectr. elec. engring. U. Sask., 1960-61, asst. prof., 1961-65, asso. prof., 1965-66, U. Toronto, 1966-70, prof., 1970—; dir. Inst. Biomed. Engring., 1974-83; acting dir. Biomed. Instrumentation Devel. unit, 1977-78. Author: Theory and Application of Field-Effect Transistors, 1970, Transducers for Biomedical Measurements: Principles and Applications, 1974; Mem. editorial bd.: Ultrasound in Medicine and Biology, 1979, Jour. of Biomedical Engring, 1978, Sensors and Actuators, 1980; Contbr. to profl. jours., numerous articles in field. Fellow Royal Soc. Can.; mem. IEEE, Can. Med. and Biol. Engring. Soc. Roman Catholic. Club: N. Toronto Tennis. Patentee in field. Office: Institute of Biomedical Engineering University of Toronto Toronto ON M5S 1A4 Canada

COBBS, JOHN LEWIS, retired magazine editor; b. Washington, Sept. 10, 1917; s. John Lewis and Jessie (Ware) C.; m. Phyllis Conway White, Dec. 27, 1941; children: John Lewis, Nicholas Hamner. Student, U. N.C., 1935-36; B.A. with great distinction, Stanford U., 1939, M.A., 1940; postgrad., Harvard U., 1940-41. Research asst. Nat. Indsl. Conf. Bd., 1941-42; finance editor Bus. Week mag., N.Y.C., 1942-43, Washington corr., 1943-45, bus. policy editor, 1945-50, asst. mng. editor, 1950-63, mng. editor, 1963-66, editor, 1966-82; Mem. vis. com., econs. dept. Harvard, 1970-76. Contbr. articles mags. Mem. Chappaqua Bd. Edn., 1957-61; Trustee Chappaqua (N.Y.) Pub. Library, 1967-73, Joint Council Econ. Edn., 1972-82. Recipient school bell award N.E.A., 1958, distinguished service award Sigma Delta Chi, 1959; Reporting award Overseas Press Club, 1972; G.M. Loeb Achievement award, 1972. Mem. Phi Beta Kappa, Phi Gamma Delta, Sigma Delta Chi. Republican. Episcopalian. Clubs: Harvard (N.Y.C.); Miles River Yacht (St. Michael's, Md.). Home: Rt 1 Box 613 Saint Michael's MD 21663 Office: 1221 Ave of Americas New York NY 10020

COBEN, WILLIAM ALLEN, lawyer; b. Flushing, N.Y., Mar. 3, 1932; s. David and Stella Rose (Lowenthal) C.; (div.)children—Shelly, Laurel, Marshall. B.A., Antioch Coll., 1955; J.D., UCLA, 1963. Bar: Calif. bar 1963. Sta. mgr. Radio Sta. KFKF, Seattle, 1956-59; resident counsel Selmur Prodns. Inc., TV prodn., Los Angeles, 1963-64; dir. bus. and legal affairs Mirish-Rich TV Prodns., Los Angeles, 1964-65; mng. dir. Mirish TV Prodns., Los Angeles, 1965-66; ptnr. firm Sklar, Coben & Stashower, Inc., 1967—, also dir.; dir. Halsey Internat. Co., Los Angeles, Takoma Prodns., Inc., All Record Service, Inc., Oakland, Calif., Churchill Records, Ltd. Mem. Am., Los Angeles County bar assns., Los Angeles Copyright Soc. Democrat. Home: 21390 Rambla Vista Malibu CA 90265 Office: 6399 Wilshire Blvd Los Angeles CA 90048

COBERLY, CAMDEN ARTHUR, chemical engineering educator; b. Elizabeth, W.Va., Dec. 21, 1922; s. James G. Blaine and Edith Luella (Simpson) C.; m. Lenore McComas, June 14, 1946; children: Catherine Elaine, Elizabeth Ann Coberly Benforado, Charles Owen, Robert Olaf. B.S., W.Va. U., 1944; M.S., Carnegie Inst. Tech., 1947; Ph.D., U. Wis., 1949. Chem. engr. Mallinckrodt Chem. Works, 1949-55, chief engr., 1955-64; prof. chem. engring., asso. dir. Engring. Expt. Sta., U. Wis., 1964-68, chmn. dept. chem. engring., 1968-71, asso. dean Coll. Engring., 1971—; mem. AAU-DOD working group export controls; rep. Am. Assn. Engring. Socs. Served to lt. (j.g.) USNR, 1944-46. Fellow Am. Inst. Chem. Engrs.; mem. Am. Chem. Soc., Am. Soc. Engring. Edn., Nat. Assn. Corr. Engrs., AAAS, AAUP, Wis. Acad. Scis., Arts and Letters, Sigma Xi, Tau Beta Pi, Phi Lambda Upsilon, Sigma Gamma Epsilon. Home: 4114 N Sunset Ct Madison WI 53705

COBERLY, WILLIAM BAYLEY, JR., cotton oil corporation executive; b. Tucson, May 8, 1908; s. William Bayley and Winifred (Wheeler) C.; m. Aileen Dorsey, Dec. 10, 1934 (dec. Nov. 1948); children: Sheryl (Mrs. John S. Griffith, Jr.), Aileen (Mrs. John H. Hadley, Jr.), William 3d; m. Victoria Nebeker Mudd, Sept. 16, 1969. A.B., Stanford, 1930. Asso. Calif. Cotton Oil Corp. (predecessor firms), 1930—, dir., asst. gen. mgr., 1945-51, v.p., gen. mgr., 1951—, pres., 1956—, chmn., 1983—, now Coberly-West Co., 1983—; v.p., dir. Coberly-West Co., Bakersfield, Calif., 1951-57, pres., dir., 1957—, chmn., dir., 1983—; chmn., dir. Coberly Ford, Inc., 1957-82; dir. So. Calif. Edison Co., 1953-81. Trustee Found. Econ. Edn., Irvington, N.Y., 1951-76, Harvey Mudd Coll., Claremont, Calif.; bd. overseers Hoover Instn. on War, Revolution and Peace, Stanford, Calif. Mem. Nat. Cottonseed Products Assn. (pres. 1952-53, dir., hon. mem.), Chi Psi. Republican. Conglist. Clubs: California, Beach, Sunset, Lincoln (Los Angeles). Home: 247 Muirfield Rd Los Angeles CA 90004 Office: 606 N Larchmont Blvd Los Angeles CA 90004

COBEY, JAMES FRANCIS, JR., utility executive; b. New Haven, June 26, 1926; s. James Francis and Marie (Coffey) C.; m. Colette Newman, Oct. 15, 1960; children: Elise, David, Matthew. B.S., Yale U., 1948; M.B.A., Harvard U., 1952. Materials engr. Creole Petroleum Corp., Venezuela, 1948-50; accountant Shell Oil Co., Houston, 1952-55, auditor, New Orleans, 1955-57, accountant, financial analyst, N.Y.C., 1957-64; finance mgr. Shell Chem. Co., N.Y.C., 1964-68; accounting mgr. Shell Oil Co., Houston, 1968-71; exec. asst. to v.p. finance United Illuminating Co., New Haven, 1971-73, sec., treas., 1973-75, v.p. finance and accounting, 1975-76, exec. v.p. fin. and adminstrn., 1976-80, pres., 1981—, dir., 1978—. Served with USNR, 1943-46. Mem. Edison Elec. Inst., Elec. Council New Eng. Roman Catholic. Clubs: Quinnipiack, Mory's, Branford Yacht. Home: 1000 Ridge Rd Hamden CT 06517 Office: 80 Temple St New Haven CT 06506

COBEY, RALPH, industrialist; b. Sycamore, Ohio, Aug. 15, 1909; m. Hortense Kohn, Feb. 28, 1944; children: Minnie, Susanne Yetta. Grad., Carnegie Inst. Tech., 1932; D.Sc. (hon.), Findlay Coll., 1958. With Perfection Steel Body Co., Galion, Ohio, 1945-70; pres. Eagle Crusher Co., 1954—, Philips-Davies Co., 1965-70, Cobey Co., 1950-70, Perfection-Cobey, Co., Galion, 1965-70, Galion Corp., 1972—, Daybrook Hydraulic Co., 1973, Diamond Iron Works, 1975, Austin-Western Crusher Co., 1975, Scoopmobile Co., 1976, Crawford County Land Co., World Wide Investment Co., Marion County Land Co.; pres., chmn. bd. Imco, Inc., Crestline, Ohio; dir. 1st Nat. Bank, Galion.; Aide in preparation of prodn. and design of Army tanks OPM, 1940-42. Mem. contbg. com. NCCJ, 1951-55, now area chmn. spl. gifts com.; founder, pres. Harry Cobey Found.; area chmn. U.S. Savs. Bonds; mem. pres.'s advisory council for devel. Ashland (Ohio) Coll.; mem. Ohio Gov.'s Citizens' Task Force on Environ. Protection, 1971-72, Pres.'s Tax Com., 1962-66; pioneer chaplain services in indsl. plants; mem. Ohio Expns. Commn., 1961-64, Radio Free Europe Com.; chmn. Community Heart Fund Campaign, 1971-72; pres., spl. gifts chmn. Crawford County Heart Fund, 1972-77; mem. Ohio fin. bd. Heart Fund, 1973—; mem. Ohio Rep. Fin. Com.; mounted dep. sheriff, Morrow County (Ohio), 1974—; bd. dirs., chmn. long range planning com. Johnny Appleseed Area council Boy Scouts of Am.; hon. life mem. Galion Community Center; trustee Ohio Med-Center Found., Inc., Galion City Hosp. Found. Bd.; mem. president's council Ohio State U.; chmn., founder Minnie Cobey Meml. Library; founder, chmn. bd. trustees Louis Bromfield Malabar Farm Found.; bd. dirs. Morrow County United Appeals; State of Ohio ambassador of natural resources; numerous other civic activities. Served as capt. USAAF, 1942-46, 51; Korea. Recipient Merit award for contbn. to B-29 bomber World War II Dept. Def.; Alumni Merit award Alumni Assn. Carnegie-Mellon U., 1974; Ohio Conservation Achievement award, 1982. Mem. NAM, Nat. Assn. 4-H Clubs, Future Farmers Am., U.S. C. of C. (mem. taxation, fgn. affairs, labor relations coms.). Jewish. Lodges: Masons (32 deg.); Shriners (pres.). Home: 4270 SR 309 Galion OH 44833 Office: Eagle Crusher Co Inc 4250 SR 309 Galion OH 44833

COBHAM, WILLIAM EMANUEL, JR., musician; b. Republic of Panama, May 16, 1944; s. William Emanuel and Ivy Leotta (Headley) C.; m. Marcia Ann McCarthy; children: Ingrid, Kurry. Grad., High Sch. Music and Arts, N.Y.C., 1962. With, Billy Taylor, 1967;; With, N.Y. Jazz Sextet, 1967, Dreams, 1970, Miles Davis, 1971, Mahavishnu Orch., 1972; formed: group Spectrum, 1975; recs. include Shabazz, Total Eclipse, Crosswinds, Spectrum, Smokin', Observations, Best of Billy Cobham, Inner Conflicts, Simplicity of Expression/Depth of Thought, Magic, Life and Time, A Fanky Thide of Sings, (with Miles Davis) Directions, Circle in the Round, Get Up With It, Big Fun, On the Cover, Live-Evil, Jack Jonson, (with Mohavishnu Orchestra) Birds of Fire, The Inner Mounting Flame, Between Nothingness and Eternity, (with George Benson) Blue Benson, Gible Gravy, (with Ron Carter) Spanish Blue, All Blues, Blues Farm, (with Horace Silver) You've Got to Take a Little Love, Serenade to a Soul Sister; profl. photographer, 1965—. Served with AUS, 1965-68. Office: 20 W 86th St New York NY 10024 *

COBIN, MARTIN THEODORE, educator; b. N.Y.C., Oct. 20, 1920; s. Joseph Bernard and Rose (Lubin) Cohen; m. June Peterson, June 27, 1944; children—Lyn Marie (Mrs. William Gullette), Gail Louise, Karen Thea (Mrs. Garett Warner), Peter Martin. Student, CCNY, 1938-40; B.F.A., Ohio U., 1942; M.A., U. Wis., 1947, Ph.D., 1953. Asst. prof. W.Va. U., 1947-55; asst. prof. to assoc. prof. U. Ill., 1955-61; from assoc. prof. to prof. and chmn. dept. communication and theatre U. Colo., 1961—, chmn. dept. theatre and dance, 1976—; with Am. Friends Service Com., East Asia, 1971-73; Play dir. Colo. Shakespeare Festival, 1965, 67, 69, 74, 78, 81, producing dir., 1982—. Author: Theory and Technique of Interpretation, 1959, (with Thorrel B. Fest) Speech and Theater, 1963, From Convincement to Conversion, 1964. Served with AUS, 1942-46. Mem. Am. Theatre Assn., Soc. of Friends. Research on Japanese theater. Home: 3993 Fuller Ct Boulder CO 80303

COBLE, ROBERT LOUIS, educator; b. Uniontown, Pa., Jan. 22, 1928; s. Gomer Lawrence and Dorothy Marguerite (Phillippi) C.; m. Joan Walker, Apr. 14, 1952; children: David, Eric, Catherine, Stefan, Jan. B.S., Bethany (W.Va.) Coll., 1950; Sc.D., M.I.T., 1955. Research assoc. Gen. Electric Co. Research and Devel. Center, Schenectady, 1955-61; faculty dept. materials sci. and engring. M.I.T., Cambridge, 1961—, now prof. ceramics; cons. govt. adv. coms. Contbr. tech. articles to profl. jours. Recipient Pace award Nat. Inst. Ceramic Engrs., 1970, U.S. Sr. Scientist, von Humboldt award Fed. Republic of Germany, 1984. Fellow Am. Ceramic Soc. (Ross Coffin Purdy award); mem. Nat. Acad. Engring. Pioneer, Lucalox (R). Office: 13-4062 Mass Inst Tech 77 Massachusetts Ave Cambridge MA 02139

COBLENTZ, WILLIAM KRAEMER, lawyer; b. San Francisco, July 28, 1922; s. Zach B. and Fritze (Levy) C.; m. Jean Berlin, Nov. 27, 1952; children: Wendy K., Andrew S. B.A., U. Calif.-Berkeley, 1943; LL.B., Yale U., 1947. Bar: Calif. 1947. Exec. dir. Am. Com. United Europe, 1950-51; spl. asst. to atty. gen., Calif., 1951-53, spl. counsel to gov., 1959-61; mem. firm Jacobs, Sills Coblentz Cohen McCabe and Breyer, San Francisco, 1953—; cons. to sec. state, 1962; dir. Pacific Telephone Co., McClatchy Newspapers, Vidal Sassoon Inc. Chmn. bd. regents U. Calif.; bd. dirs. NAACP Legal Def. Fund, San Francisco Airports Commn. Mem. Am., Calif., San Francisco bar assns., Am. Law Inst., Assn. Bar City N.Y. Home: 10 5th Ave San Francisco CA 94118 Office: 1 Embarcadero Ctr San Francisco CA 94111

COBLEY, GEORGE GORDON, physician; b. Sumas, Wash., Aug. 6, 1919; s. William Henry and Anne (Myers) C.; m. Mildred Overheu, May 16, 1946; children—George Gordon II, Candice Ann (Mrs. Roger Norris Hubbard). B.S., U. Wash., 1941; M.D., Columbia, 1944. Intern King County Hosp., Seattle, 1944-45; resident pediatrics Childrens Hosp., Los Angeles, 1945-47; practice pediatrics, Santa Monica, Calif., 1947—; clin. instr. pediatrics U. Calif. at Los Angeles Sch. Medicine, 1954-62, asst. clin. prof. pediatrics, 1963-66, clin. prof. pediatrics, 1966—; v.p. staff St. Johns Hosp., 1972, pres. staff, 1974-75; Mem. Optimist Internat., 1948—, v.p., 1959-60, internat. pres., 1963-64. Bd. dirs. Boys Clubs, Santa Monica, Santa Monica Community Chest. Served to capt. M.C. AUS, 1951- 53. Named Young Man of Year, Santa Monica, 1954. Fellow Am. Acad. Pediatrics; mem. Los Angeles County Med. Assn. (v.p. Bay Dist. br. 1962), A.M.A., Delta Upsilon. Home: 1334 19th St Apt 5 Santa Monica CA 90404 Office: 2021 Santa Monica Blvd Santa Monica CA 90404

COBURN, D(ONALD) L(EE), playwright; b. Balt., Aug. 4, 1938; s. Guy Dabney and Ruth Margaret (Somers) C.; m. Nazlee Joyce French, Oct. 24, 1966 (div.); children: Donn Christopher, Kimberly; m. Marsha Woodruff Maher, Feb. 22, 1975. Student public schs., Balt. Advt. salesman Balt. Sun, 1961; radio time salesman, Balt., 1962-66; propr. Don Coburn & Assocs., advt., Balt., 1966-70; with Stanford Agy., Dallas, 1970-73; propr. Donald L. Coburn Corp. Cons., Dallas, 1973-75. Playwright: The Gin Game, 1976 (Pulitzer prize 1978), Bluewater Cottage, 1979. Served with USNR, 1958-60. Mem. Dramatists Guild, Authors League Am., Soaring Soc. Am.

COBURN, JAMES, actor; b. Laurel, Nebr., Aug. 31, 1928; children: James IV, Lisa. B.A., Los Angeles City Coll. Owner Panpiper Prodns., Hollywood, Calif. Appeared in: movies Ride Lonesome, 1959, The Magnificent Seven, 1960, The Great Escape, 1963, Charade, 1964, The Americanization of Emily, 1964, Major Dundee, 1965, Our Man Flint, 1966, In Like Flint, 1967, Pat Garrett and Billy the Kid, 1973, The Last of Sheila, 1973, Bite the Bullet, 1975, Hard Times, 1975, Sky Riders, 1976, The Last Hard Men, 1976, Midway, 1976, The Muppet Movie, 1979, Fire Power, 1979, Cross of Iron, 1977, Golden Girl, 1979, Loving Couples, 1980, The Baltimore Bullet, 1980, High Risk, 1981, Looker, 1981; TV mini-series The Dain Curse, 1978; producer: The President's Analyst, 1967, Waterhole No. 3, 1967. Address: care Internat Mgmt 8899 Beverly Blvd Los Angeles CA 90048 *

COBURN, JOHN BOWEN, bishop; b. Danbury, Conn., Sept. 27, 1914; s. Rev. Aaron Cutler and Eugenia Bowen (Woolfolk) C.; m. Ruth Alvord Barnum, May 26, 1941; children: Thomas, Judith, Michael, Sarah. A.B. with high honors, Princeton, 1936, D.D., 1960; B.D. cum laude, Union Theol. Sem., 1942; D.D., Amherst Coll., 1955, Harvard, 1964, Huron Coll., 1964, Middlebury Coll., 1970, Bucknell U., 1971, Trinity Coll., 1980, Hamilton Coll., 1982, Williams Coll., 1982; S.T.D., Berkeley Div. Sch., 1958; D.D., Hobart Coll., William Smith Colls., 1967; D.Canon Law, Kenyon Coll., 1968; D.S.T., Gen. Theol. Sem., 1968; D.C.L., U. Kent, Canterbury, Eng., 1978. Tchr., English and biology Robert Coll., Istanbul, Turkey, 1936-39; ordained to ministry Protestant Episcopal Ch., as deacon, 1943, as priest, 1943; asst. minister Grace Ch., N.Y.C., 1942-44, rector, Amherst, Mass.; chaplain Amherst Coll., 1946-53; dean Trinity Cathedral, Newark, 1953-57, Episcopal Theol. Sch., Cambridge, Mass., 1957-68; tchr. St. Acad., Urban League, Harlem, N.Y.C., 1968-69; rector St. James' Ch., N.Y.C., 1969-75; Episcopal bishop of Mass., 1976—; Dir. Corning Glass Works.; del. Epsicopal Gen. Conv., 1955, 61, 64, 67, 69, 70, 73, pres. house deps., 1967-76. Author: Prayer and Personal Religion, 1957, One Family in Christ, 1958, Minister, Man in the Middle, 1963, Anne and the Sand Dobbies, 1964, Twentieth Century Spiritual Letters, 1967, A Life to Live: A Way to Pray, 1973, A Diary of Prayers: Personal and Private, 1975, The Hope of Glory, 1976, Christ's Life: Our Life, 1978, Feeding the Fire, 1980; editor: (with Norman Pittenger) Viewpoints, 1959. Trustee Princeton, Wooster Sch., Union Theol. Sem. Served to lt. (s.g.), Chaplains Corps USNR, 1944-46. Clubs: Century (N.Y.C.); Somerset, Union (Boston). Address: 1 Joy St Boston MA 02108

COBURN, KATHLEEN, writer; b. Stayner, Ont., Can., Sept. 7, 1905; s. John and Susannah (Emerson) C. B.A., U. Toronto, 1928, M.A. (Imperial Order Daus. of Empire War Meml. scholar), 1930; B.Litt., St. Hugh's Coll., Oxford U., 1932; LL.D. (hon.), Queen's U., Kingston, Ont., 1964; D.H.L., Haverford Coll., 1972; D.Litt. (hon.), Trent U., Ont., 1973, Cambridge U., 1975, U. B.C., 1976, U. Toronto, 1978; D.H.L., Princeton U., 1983. Asst. to dean of women Victoria Coll., Toronto, Ont., 1932-35, faculty, 1932-71, prof. English, 1953-71, prof. emeritus, 1971—. Author: The Grandmothers, 1949, Discourse, Royal Instn, 1972, Riddell Memorial Lectures—The Self Conscious Imagination, 1972, In Pursuit of Coleridge, 1977, Experience into Thought—Some Perspectives on Coleridge from His Notebooks, 1979; Editor: The Philosophical Lectures of S.T. Coleridge, 1949, Inquiring Spirit, 1951, rev. edit., 1979, The Sara Hutchinson Letters, 1954, The Notebooks of Samuel Taylor Coleridge, vol. I, 1957, vol. II, 1961, vol. III, 1973, Coleridge—A Collection of Critical Essays, 1967; gen. editor: The Collected Works of Samuel Taylor Coleridge, 24 vols, 1968—. Internat. Fedn. U. Women sr. fellow, 1947; John Simon Guggenheim Meml. fellow, 1953-54, 57-58; Sr. Commonwealth vis. fellow, 1962-63; recipient Leverhulme award, Eng., 1948, Rosemary Crawshay prize Brit. Acad., 1958; decorated officer Order of Can. Fellow Royal Soc. Can. (Chauveau medal 1979), Brit. Acad. (corr.). Office: Victoria Coll 91 Charles St W Toronto ON M5S 1K7 Canada

COBURN, ROBERT CRAIG, philosopher; b. Mpls., Jan. 25, 1930; s. William Carl and Esther Therice (Rudd) C.; m. Martha Louise Means, July 12, 1974. B.A., Yale U., 1951; B.D., U. Chgo., 1954; M.A., Harvard U., 1958, Ph.D., 1958. Asst. prof. philosophy U. Chgo., 1960-65, assoc. prof., 1965-68, prof., 1968-71; prof. philosophy U. Wash., Seattle, 1971—; vis. assoc. prof. philosophy Cornell U., 1966; condr. NEH summer seminar, 1983; cons. ERDA. Contbr. articles to philos. jours., chpts. to books. Ordained elder Rocky Mountain Conf. United Methodist Ch. Andrew Mellon postdoctoral fellow in philosophy U. Pitts., 1961-62; NSF grantee, 1968-69. Mem. Am. Philos. Assn. (exec. com. Pacific div. 1973-74), AAUP, Soc. Values in Higher Edn., Phi Beta Kappa. Home: 6852 28th Ave NE Seattle WA 98115 Office: Dept of Philosophy University of Washington Seattle WA 98195

COBURN, WARREN B(AXTER), utility company executive; b. Stoneham, Mass., Nov. 28, 1926; s. George Sargent and Alene (Phillips) C.; m. Ellen Fitzpatrick, Feb. 12, 1977; 1 son, James Charles children by previous marriage: Alene Coburn-Dunivan, Bruce W. B.A. in Econs., Brown U., 1951, postgrad., 1952. Cert. internal auditor. Mgr. Gen. Edison Electric Co., Lynn, Mass., 1953-68; v.p. Consol. Edison Co. of N.Y. Inc., N.Y.C., 1969—; adv. council CUNY Tech. Inst., 1980—. Chmn. Boro Hall Restoration Found., Bklyn., Downtown Bklyn. Devel. Assn., 1982—; commr. Bklyn. Bridge Centennial Com., 1982—; trustee Bklyn. Acad. Music, 1979—; bd. dirs. Bklyn. Arts and Cultural Assn., 1979—, Westchester County Assn., White Plains, N.Y., 1973-78, Westchester Coalition, 1976-78; pres. Westchester-Putnam council Boy Scouts Am., 1976-78. Recipient Silver Beaver Disting. Service award Boy Scouts Am., 1978, Medger Evers medal Medger Evers Coll., Bklyn., 1983, Good Scout award Greater N.Y. councils Boy Scouts Am., 1982, Quality of Life award Bklyn.-Caledonian Hosps., 1979—. Mem. Mid-Hudson Constrn. Users Council (chmn. 1974-78), Better Bus. Bur. Westchester (dir. 1973-78), ASME (Outstanding Leadership award N.Y. chpt. 1973), Borough President's Service Cabinet, Bklyn. C. of C. Congregationalist. Office: Consolidated Edison Co of NY Inc 30 Flatbush Ave Brooklyn NY 11217

COCA, IMOGENE, actress, comedienne; b. Phila., Nov. 18; d. Joe and Sadie (Brady) C.; m. Bob Burton, 1935; m. King Donovan, Oct., 1960. Made first appearance as tap dancer in N.Y.C. vaudeville at age of 11; debut as comedienne New Faces of 1934; appeared in: Straw Hat Revue, 1939; played in summer shows, Pa., 1938-42; first appearance on TV in Broadway Revue, 1949; on, Your Show of Shows (Emmy 1952), NBC-TV, 1950-54; TV series Grindl, 1963-64; TV shows Imogene Coca Show, 1954-55, Sid Caesar Invites You; appeared in: stage plays The Four Poster, 1973, Prisoner of Second Avenue, 1973, also, Once Upon a Mattress, Plaza Suite, I Can't Hear You When the Water is Running, Twentieth Century; toured with Sid Caesar, Las Vegas and N.Y.C., 1978-79; films include Under the Yum Yum Tree, 1963, Ten from Your Show of Shows, 1973, Rabbit Test. Address: care Actors Equity Assn 1500 Broadway New York NY 10036 *

COCHNAR, ROBERT JOHN, newspaper executive; b. Hackensack, N.J., Aug. 29, 1939; s. Robert Charles and Marie (Stack) C.; m. Myra Phyllis Krasner, Mar. 6, 1970. Student, Lehigh U., 1957-61, Johns Hopkins U., 1962-63. Editor Leader Newspapers, Lyndhurst, N.J., 1956-57; reporter Call-Chronicle Newspapers, Allentown, Pa., 1958-61; asst. to dep. sec. Pa. Dept. Commerce, 1961-62; staff writer Pa. Democratic State Com., 1962; exec. Thompson Publs., Balt., 1963; news editor, mng. editor, exec. editor, v.p., editorial dir. Newspaper Enterprise Assn., Inc., N.Y.C., 1963-77; asst. to editor, assoc. editor San Jose (Calif.) Mercury and News, 1977-81, dep. exec. editor, 1981—; adj. lectr. dept. communications Stanford U., 1981—. Editor: World Travel and Vacation Almanac, 1970; Collected papers at, Archive Contemporary History, U. Wyo., Casper. Middle Atlantic dir. Students for Kennedy-Johnson, 1959-60; exec. dir. Pa. Young Dem. Clubs, 1961-62; mem. vis. com. English dept. Lehigh U.; trustee, v.p. Scripps-Howard Found. Mem. Lehigh U. Alumni Assn., Am. Soc. Newspaper Editors, Deadline Club (v.p.), Calif. Soc. Newspaper Editors (pres. 1983-84), Am. Assn. Sunday and Feature Editors, Calif. UPI Editors Assn. (dir.), Overseas Press Club, AP Mng. Editors Assn. (dir.), Sigma Delta Chi. Clubs: Union League, Dutch Treat (N.Y.C.). Office: 750 Ridder Park Dr San Jose CA 95190

COCHRAN, DOUGLAS EUGENE, corporate executive; b. Winchester, Va., Apr. 3, 1932; s. John Clayton and Clarice S. (Seltz) C.; m. Constance L. Shull, Dec. 11, 1954; 1 son, Brian Scott. B.S. in Accounting, Strayer Coll., Washington, 1952. C.P.A., W.Va. Office mgr., mgmt. trainee Winchester Knitting Mills, 1954-56; with McDonough Co., Parkersburg, W.Va., 1956—, controller, 1966-71, treas., 1968-74, v.p., 1971-74, pres., chief exec. officer, 1974—, also dir.; chmn. Ames. Co. subs. Hanson Trust, P.L.C., 1982—. Bd. dirs. local United Fund, ARC; trustee, past pres. Henry Logan Children's Home, Parkersburg; pres., trustee Wood County Pub. Library, 1980, 81, 83, pres., 1980; mem. adv. council dept. econs., mgmt. and acctg. Marietta (Ohio) Coll. Served with AUS, 1952-54. Mem. Am. Inst. C.P.A.'s, W.Va. Soc. C.P.A.'s. Home: 1005 49th St Vienna WV 26105 Office: PO Box 1774 Parkersburg WV 26101

COCHRAN, GARLAND PERRY (HANK COCHRAN), songwriter; b. Isola, Miss., Aug. 2, 1935; s. Robert Lee and Earlene (McKool) C.; m. Susan Booth; children: James Lee, Garland Perry, Mark Daniel. Writer, song plugger Pamper Music, Inc., Goodlettsville, Tenn., 1959-67, co-owner, writer, 1967-69; writer, profl. cons. Tree Internat., Inc., Nashville, 1969—. Singer in: movie Honeysuckle Rose; also actor; Composer: songs I Fall to Pieces, 1961, She's Got You, 1962, A Little Bitty Tear, 1962, Funny Way of Laughin', 1962, Tears Broke Out on Me, 1962, Why Can't He Be You, 1962, Don't Touch Me, 1966, Make the World Go Away, 1963 (million airs award 1977, Double Platinum Aware), You Comb Her Hair, 1963, I Want to Go With You, 1966, It's Not Love, 1973, That's All That Matters to Me, 1979. Named to Nashville Songwriters Assn. Hall Fame, 1974; Walkway of Stars Country Music Assn., 1967. Rec. on Elektra/Asylum Records. Home: Route 2 Hunters Ln Hendersonville TN 37075 Office: Tree Pub Co Nashville TN 37202 *Make up your mind what you want to be and what you want to do. Then take every path that might lead in that direction. Let everyone know what you want so they can help you... and they will. Be definite and be determined.*

COCHRAN, GEORGE MOFFETT, judge; b. Staunton, Va., Apr. 20, 1912; s. Peyton and Susie (Robertson) C.; m. Marion Lee Stuart, May 1, 1948; children—George Moffett, Harry Carter Stuart. Grad., Episcopal High Sch., Alexandria, Va., 1930; B.A., U. Va., 1934, LL.B., 1936. Bar: Md. bar 1936, Va. bar 1935. Asso. law firm, Balt., 1936-38; partner firm Peyton Cochran and George M. Cochran, Staunton, 1938-64, Cochran, Lotz & Black, 1964-69; justice Supreme Ct., Va., Richmond, 1969—; Pres. Planters Bank & Trust Co., Staunton, 1963-69. Chmn. Woodrow Wilson Centennial Commn. of Va., 1952-58, Va. Cultural Devel. Study Commn., 1966-68; mem. Va. Commn. on Constl. Revision, 1968-69, Jud. Council of Va., 1963-69; Mem. Va. Ho. of Dels., 1948-66, Va. Senate, 1966-68; Chmn. bd. dirs. Stuart Hall; bd. visitors Va. Poly. Inst., 1960-68; trustee Mary Baldwin Coll., 1967-81. Served to lt. comdr. USNR, 1942-46. Mem. ABA, Va. Bar Assn. (pres. 1965-66), Raven Soc., Soc. of Cin., Phi Beta Kappa, Phi Delta Phi, Beta Theta Pi. Episcopalian. Office: Masonic Temple Bldg Staunton VA 24401 also Supreme Court Bldg Richmond VA 23210

COCHRAN, HANK *See* **COCHRAN, GARLAND PERRY**

COCHRAN, JAMES FRANCIS, III, army officer; b. Tallahassee, Fla., Sept. 4, 1929; s. James F. and Helen (Saxon) C.; m. Faye Cole, Nov. 19, 1955; children—James Francis IV, Lewis Cole, Faye Calhoun. B.S. in Bus. Adminstrn, U. Fla., 1950; grad., Inf. Officer Candidate Sch., 1952, Command and Gen. Staff Coll., 1961, Armed Forces Staff Coll., 1965; M.S. in Fin. Mgmt, George Washington U., 1966, Indsl. Coll. Armed Forces, 1970. Commd. 2d lt. U.S. Army, 1952, advanced through grades to maj. gen., 1977; asst. prof. mil. sci. U. Alaska, 1961-64; assigned to (Directorate of Materiel Readiness, Hdqrs. U.S. Army Materiel Command), Washington, 1965-66, staff officer, Vietnam, 1966-67; comdr. 1st Bn., 28th Inf., 1st Inf. Div., Vietnam, 1967-68; assigned to Office of Asst. Vice Chief of Staff, U.S. Army, Washington, 1968-69; chief tactics group (Brigade and Bn. Ops. Dept. of Inf. Sch.), Ft. Benning, Ga., 1970-72; comdr. 2d Inf. Div., Div. Support Command, Korea, 1972-73; chief staff of 82d Airborne Div., Ft. Bragg, N.C., 1973-74; comdr. (First ROTC Region), 1974-77, dir. force programs and structure, Washington, 1977-79, comdg. gen., 1979—. Decorated Legion of Merit with two oak leaf cluster, D.F.C., Purple Heart, Silver Star with oak leaf cluster, Bronze Star with V device with two oak leaf clusters. Mem. Assn. U.S. Army. Presbyterian. Club: Rotary.

COCHRAN, JOHN, news correspondent; b. Montgomery, Ala. Student, U. Ala.; M.A., U. Iowa, 1967. With Birmingham News, then NBC Sales and Service, N.Y.C.; later free-lance reporter, S.E. Asia; reporter, anchorman Sta. WSOC-TV, Charlotte, N.C.; research fellow Washington Center, 1970; reporter Sta. WRC-TV, Washington; news correspondent NBC News, Washington, 1972-78, London, 1978—, chief London corr., 1983—. Office: care NBC News 30 Rockefeller Plaza New York NY 10020 *

COCHRAN, JOHN ARTHUR, economics educator; b. Des Moines, Sept. 25, 1921; s. Arthur John and Lena (McCowin) C.; m. Mary Leffler, July 10, 1943; children: Jacquelyn Sue, Cynthia Elizabeth,Cstherine Edna. A.B., Drake U., 1943; cert., U. Exeter, Eng., 1945; M.A., Harvard U., 1948, Ph.D., 1949. Teaching asst. MIT, Cambridge, 1947-48; teaching fellow Harvard U. (Cambridge), 1948-49; asst. prof. econs. U. Ill., Urbana, 1949-56; monetary economist Fed. Res. Bank N.Y., 1956-57; assoc. prof. econs. So. Ill. U., Carbondale, 1957-62; prof. econs. Ariz. State U., Tempe, 1962—, chmn. dept. econs., 1962-67; vis. prof. U. Colo., 1965, NYU, 1980. Author: Money, Banking and the Economy, 1967, (5th edit.) Money, Banking and the Economy, 1983; contbr. articles to profl. jours. Mem. Ariz. Acad. sponsors Ariz. Town Halls for Ariz. Leaders, 1962—. Served to 1st lt. AUS, 1943-46, 51-52. Mem. Midwest Econ. Assn. (sec.-treas. 1960-62), Phi Beta Kappa (pres. chpt. 1976-77), Phi Kappa Phi, Beta Gamma Sigma. Presbyterian (trustee 1964-67). Home: 412 Loyola Dr Tempe AZ 85282 Office: Arizona State U Tempe AZ 85287

COCHRAN, JOHN EUELL, JR., aerospace engineering educator, lawyer; b. Dawson, Ala., May 22, 1944; s. John Euell and Beatrice Ann (Raley) C.; m. Gladys Carol Holdbrooks, Dec. 26, 1965; children: Christopher, Jonathan. B.A., Auburn U., 1966, M.A., 1967; Ph.D., U. Tex.-Austin, 1970; J.D., Jones Law Inst., 1976. Registered profl. engr., Ala., Ala. 1977. Asst. prof. Auburn U., Ala., 1970-75, assoc. prof., 1975-78, alumni assoc. prof., 1978-80, alumni prof., 1980-81, prof. aerospace engring., assoc. athletic dir., 1981—; cons. Northrup Services, Huntsville, Ala., 1970-71, U.S. Army Missile Command, Medstone Arsenal, Ala., 1975-82, Cooper & Cooper, Baton Rouge, 1978-82, Accident Prevention, Investigation and Analysis, Daleville, Ala., 1983. Contbr. articles to profl. jours. Tau Beta Pi fellow, 1965; Nat. Coll. Athletic Assn. fellow, 1965; NSF fellow, 1968. Fellow AIAA (assoc.); mem. Am. Helicopter Soc., Ala. Soc. Profl. Engrs. (Young Engr. of Year 1980). Democrat. Methodist. Clubs: War Eagle Lions (dir. 1972), Saugahatchee Country (Auburn, Ala.)). Home: 400 Cross Creek Rd Auburn AL 36830 Office: Auburn U Dept Aerospace Engring Auburn AL 36849

COCHRAN, JOHN THOMAS, II, organization executive; b. Butler, Ga., Sept. 30, 1941; s. Robert T. and Marion (Payne) C.; m. Caroline Mansour, July 31, 1961 (div.); children: John Thomas, III, John Stuart, John Alexander. A.B., U. Ga., 1964, J.D., 1977. Dir. congl. relations Job Corps, 1967, Head Start, 1968; legis. rep. Nat. League Cities/U.S. Conf. Mayors, 1969; dep. exec. dir. U.S. Conf. Mayors, Washington, 1971—; sec. Conf. Mayors Research and Edn. Found., 1974. Recipient Disting. Public Service award Jobs Corps, 1968; urban fellow Nat. Tng. Devel. Service, Aspen, Colo., 1973. Mem. Signa Nu. Democrat. Clubs: Federal City, Polo (Washington); Edgemoor Club (Bethesda). Home: 7115 Exfair Rd Bethesda MD 20014 Office: 1620 I St NW Washington DC 20006

COCHRAN, KENDALL PINNEY, educator; b. Newton, Kans., Oct. 12, 1924; s. William Walter and Enid (Pinney) C.; m. Mona S. Hersh, Dec. 19, 1975; stepchildren—Paula L. Hersh, Susan B. Hersh, Kenneth A. Hersh. B.A. cum laude, U. Tex., 1949, M.A., 1950; Ph.D., Ohio State U., 1955. Instr. econs. Ohio State U., 1953-55, asst. prof., 1955-57; asso. prof. North Tex. State U., 1957-59, prof., 1959—, chmn. dept. econs., 1969-81; vis. research scholar London Sch. Econs., 1981-82, U. York, Eng., 1981-82; dir. NSF Econs. Inst., 1964-69; vis. prof. Bishop Coll., 1969; asso. editor Southwestern Social Sci. Quar., 1962-64; editorial bd. North Tex. Bus. Studies, 1961-67; asso. editor Southwestern Jour. Social Edn., 1970. Pres. Denton Credit Union, 1968-69, dir., 1961-69. Served with USAF, 1942-44. Mem. Am. Econ. Assn., Southwestern Econ. Assn. (pres. 1965), Assn. for Evolutionary Econs. (mem. exec. com. 1964), Assn. for Social Econs. (exec. council 1973—, 1st v.p. 1977—, pres. 1978), Tex. Assn. Coll. Tchrs. (coordinator research 1960-64), AAUP (mem. nat. council 1967-70). Democrat. Address: Box 5172 NT Sta Denton TX 76203

COCHRAN, LES, lawyer; b. Brownwood, Tex., Jan. 16, 1935; s. Lester Douglas and Emma May C. B.A., A. and M. Coll., Tex., 1956; LL.B., U. Tex., 1960. Bar: Tex., U.S. Dist. Ct. (so. and no. dists.) Tex., U.S. Ct. Appeals (5th and 11th cirs.), U.S. Supreme Ct., diplomate: civil trial law Tex. Bd. Legal Specialization. Asst. city atty., Abilene, Tex., 1961-64, city atty., 1964-66; partner firms Wagstaff, Alvis, Alvis, Cochran & Leonard, Abilene, 1966-70, Hicks, Hirsch, Glover & Cochran, Houston, 1970-76; individual practice law, Houston, 1976-81; partner firm Barnhart, Mallia, Cochran & Luther, 1981—. Served with AUS, 1956-57. Mem. Tex. City Attys. Assn., Houston, Am. bar assns., State Bar Tex., Tex. Assn. Def. Counsel., Assn. Trial Lawyers Am., Tex. Trial Lawyers Assn. Home: 4435 Mt Vernon St Houston TX 77006 Office: 16th Floor 806 Main Bldg Houston TX 77002

COCHRAN, LESLIE HERSHEL, university administrator; b. Valparaiso, Ind., Apr. 24, 1939; s. Robert H. and Dellcena (Marquart) C.; m. Linda Stockman, May 20, 1978; children: Troy, Kirt, Leslee. B.S., Western Mich. U., 1961, M.A., 1962; Ed.D., Wayne State U., 1968. Mem. faculty Central Mich. U., Mt. Pleasant, 1968-80, assoc. dean, 1970-75, dean fine and applied arts, 1975-76, vice provost, 1976-80; provost S.E. Mo. State U., Cape Girardeau, 1980—; mem. accreditation team N. Central Assn., Chgo., 1982—; mem. exec. Mo. Council Econ. Edn., 1981—. Author: Advisory Committee in Action, 1980, Innovative Program in Industrial Education, 1970; numerous articles. Univ. coordinator United Way, 1981—; mem. exec. bd. Community Concert Assn., Cape Girardeau, 1980—. Japan Soc. Promotion of Sci. fellow, Tokyo, 1976; recipient Meritorious Teaching award Central Mich. U., 1969-71, Nat. Leadership award Am. Vocat. Assn., 1972. Mem. Nat. Assn. Indsl. and Tech. Tchr. Edn. (pres. 1976), Am. Vocat. Assn. (nat. membership chmn. 1969-72). Lodge: Rotary. Home: 2010 Allen Dr Capr Girardeau MO 63701 Office: SE Mo State U 270 Academic Hall Cape Girardeau MO

COCHRAN, LEWIS W., physicist, university official; b. Perryville, Ky., Oct. 12, 1915; s. Ernest Beeler and Mayme (Martin) C.; m. Carolyn Wilson, Nov. 20, 1940; children: Sue Carol, Phillip. B.S., Morehead (Ky.) State Coll., 1936; M.S., U. Ky., 1939, Ph.D., 1952, D. Sc., 1982. Instr. physics Morehead State Coll., 1939-40, 41, asst. prof., 1946; instr. physics Cumberland U., 1941; radio engr. Lexington Signal Depot, 1942; mem. faculty U. Ky., 1946-81, prof. physics, 1957—, acting head dept., 1956-58, asso. dean, 1963-65, provost, 1965-70, acting dean, 1966-67, dean Grad. Sch., v.p. univ. research, 1967-70, v.p. acad. affairs, 1970-81; exec. v.p. Ky. State U., 1982; research physicist Oak Ridge Nat. Lab., summers 1949, 50, 53, 59-60. Served to maj. AUS, 1942-46. Mem. Am. Phys. Soc., Am. Assn. Physics Tchrs., Sigma Xi, Sigma Pi Sigma, Omicron Delta Kappa. Presbyterian (elder). Spl. research low energy nuclear physics, gaseous electronics, neuron physics. Home: 1581 Beacon Hill Rd Lexington KY 40504

COCHRAN, ROBERT GLENN, educator; b. Indpls., July 12, 1919; s. Lucian Glenn and Daisy P. (Wachstetter) C.; m. Mary Olive Worland, Mar. 1945; 1 son, Robert Glenn. B.A., Ind. U., 1948, M.S., 1950; Ph.D., Pa. State U., 1957. Physicist Ohio State Health Dept., 1950; physicist, group leader Oak Ridge Nat. Lab., 1950-55; dir. research reactor, asso. prof. Pa. State U., 1955-59; prof., head dept. nuclear engrng. Tex. A. and M. U., College Station, 1959—; cons. USAF, U.S. AEC, NRC. Contbr. articles to profl. jours. Served with USNR, 1942-45. Mem. Am. Nuclear Soc., Am. Phys. Soc., Am. Soc. Engring. Edn., Sigma Xi, Phi Kappa Phi. Club: Mason. Home: Route 4 Box 530 College Station TX 77801 Office: Tex A and M U College Station TX 77843

COCHRAN, THAD, Senator; b. Pontotoc, Miss., Dec. 7, 1937; s. William Holmes and Emma Grace (Berry) C.; m. Rose Clayton, June 6, 1964; children—Thaddeus Clayton, Katherine Holmes. B.A., U. Miss., 1959, J.D. cum laude, 1965; postgrad. (Rotary Found. fellow), U. Dublin, Ireland, 1963-64. Bar: Miss. bar 1965. Practiced in, Jackson, 1965-72; asso. firm Watkins & Eager, 1965-72; mem. 93d-95th congresses from, Miss., U.S. Senate from, 1979—. Mem. exec. bd. Andrew Jackson council Boy Scouts Am., 1973—. Served to lt. USNR, 1959-61. Named Outstanding Young Man of Jackson, 1971, One of Three Outstanding Young Men of Miss., 1971. Mem. ABA, Miss. Bar Assn. (pres. young lawyers sect.), Omicron Delta Kappa, Phi Kappa Phi, Pi Kappa Alpha. Republican. Baptist. Club: Rotarian. Office: Senate Office Bldg Washington DC 20510

COCHRAN, THOMAS CUNNINGHAM, JR., lawyer, corp. exec.; b. Mercer, Pa., June 4, 1920; s. Thomas Cunningham and Olive Belle (Pierson) C.; m. Helen L. Kent, June 3, 1950; children—Thomas A., Stephen K., Anne L. A.B., Haverford Coll., 1942; M.B.A., Harvard, 1946; LL.B., U. Mich., 1949. Bar: Pa. bar 1950. Counsel, asst. sec. Koppers Co., Inc., 1956-66, v.p., sec., gen. counsel, 1966-77, sr. v.p., gen. counsel, sec., 1977—; dir. Enserch Corp., Black Mountain Gas Co. Served to lt. (s.g.) USNR, 1943-46. Mem. Am., Pa., Allegheny County bar assns., Am. Judicature Soc. Clubs: Duquesne (Pitts.); South Hills Country. Home: 40 Standish Blvd Pittsburgh PA 15228 Office: Koppers Bldg Pittsburgh PA 15219

COCHRAN, WENDELL, magazine editor; b. Carthage, Mo., Nov. 29, 1929; s. Wendell Albert and Lillian Gladys (Largent) C.; m. Corinne Des Jardins, Aug. 25, 1980. A.B., U. Mo., Columbia, 1953, A.M. in Geology, 1956, B.J., 1960. Geologist ground-water br. U.S. Geol. Survey, 1956-58; reporter, copyeditor Kansas City (Mo.) Star, 1960-63; editor Geotimes and Earth Sci. mags., Geospectrum newsletter, Alexandria, Va., 1963-84; v.p. Geol. Survey Inc., Bethesda, Md., 1984—. Co-author: Into Print: A Practical Guide to Writing, Illustrating, and Publishing, 1977; sr. editor: Geowriting: A Guide to Writing, Editing and Printing in Earth Science, 1973; contbr. articles to profl. jours. and encys. Mem. geol. socs. Washington, London, Assn. Earth Sci. Editors (award Outstanding Contbns. 1982), Soc. Scholarly Pub., Dogs in the Night-time. Home: 4812 30th St S Arlington VA 22206

COCHRANE, ERIC, history educator; b. Oakland, Calif., May 13, 1928; s. Eric and Adelaide (Griffith) C.; m. Lydia Steinway, Dec. 23, 1953; children: John, Nicholas. B.A., Yale U., 1949, Ph.D., 1954. Instr. Stanford U., 1953-54; mem. faculty U. Chgo., 1957—, prof. history, 1966—; guest lectr. U. Perugia, 1969-70; Sec. Renaissance Seminar Chgo., 1961-67. Author: Tradition and Enlightenment in the Tuscan

Academies, 1961, The Late Italian Renaissance, 1970, Florence in the Forgotten Centuries (1527-1800), 1973, Historians and Historiography in the Italian Renaissance, 1981; contbr. articles to profl. jours. Trustee Newberry Library, Chgo.; sec. St. Thomas Apostle Parish Council, 1979-81. Fulbright scholar for study in Italy, 1951-53; Guggenheim fellow, 1960-61; Am. Council Learned Socs. fellow, 1965-66, 77-78. Mem. Soc. for Italian Hist. Studies, Cath. Hist. Assn. (v.p. 1973, pres. 1974), Renaissance Soc. Am., Societa Colombaria, Accademia Arte del Disegno, Deputazione Storia Patria Toscana. Home: 5220 S Greenwood Ave Chicago IL 60615 also Via dell'Anguillara 1 50122 Florence Italy Office: U Chgo 1162 E 59th St Chicago IL 60637

COCHRANE, MICHAEL HENRY, steel company executive, holding company executive; b. Windsor, Ont., Can., Feb. 7, 1937; s. and Neva T. C.; m. Margaret Jane; children: Michael D., Martha L., Melissa J., Mark T., Meredith E. B.A., U. Western Ont., 1960; M.B.A., Northwestern U., 1961. With Ford Motor Co. of Can., 1961-69, Gt. West Life Assurance Co., 1969-70; v.p. fin. and planning Air Can., 1970-76; chmn. bd. Reed Paper Ltd., 1976-78; v.p. planning and bus. devel. Massey-Ferguson Ltd., 1978-80; chmn. bd., chief exec. officer Sydney Steel Corp., Toronto, Ont., 1980—; chmn. Can. Investors Holding Corp.; exec. v.p. No. Telecom Ltd.; dir. Morguard Investment Services Ltd.; pres. Can.-China Trade Council. Bd. dirs. Can. Council Christians and Jews. Mem. Fin. Execs. Inst. Clubs: Halifax, Montreal Amateur Athletics Assn., Mt. Royal, Empire, Cambridge, Granite, Albany, Man., Oriental, Met. Home: 50 Buckingham Ave Toronto ON Canada M4N 1R2 Office: 120 Adelaide St W Suite 1120 Toronto ON Canada M5H 1V1

COCHRANE, THOMAS J., advertising agency executive; b. N.Y.C., July 13, 1930; s. Thomas J. and Marguerite (Daly) C.; m. Marion T. Adams, Nov. 5, 1978; m. Ann T. Joseph, Oct. 8, 1955 (div. Apr. 1978); children: Thomas J., Beth Ann. Asst. product mgr. Lambert & Feasley, N.Y.C., 1956-62; prodn. and traffic mgr. Ellington & Co., N.Y.C., 1962-64; v.p. prodn., traffic mgr. West, Weir & Bartel, N.Y.C., 1965-67, Warwick & Legler, 1967-68—; sr. v.p. J. Walter Thompson, N.Y.C., 1968—. Bd. dirs. Bill Coughland Scholarship Fund, N.Y.C., 1972—. Served with USMC, 1951-53. Named Prodn. Man of Yr Advt. Agy. Prodn. Club N.Y., 1970. Mem. Gravure Advt. Council of Gravure Tech. Assn. (dir. 1982—), Advt. Prodn. Club N.Y. (exec. bd. 1982—). Republican. Roman Catholic. Office: J Walter Thompson 466 Lexington Ave New York NY 10017 *

COCHRANE, WILLARD WESLEY, economist; b. Fresno, Calif., May 15, 1914; s. Willard Wesley and Clara (Chambers) C.; m. Mary Herget, Aug. 23, 1942; children: Willard Wesley, Stephen A., James M., Timothy S. B.S., U. Calif. at Berkeley, 1937; M.S., Mont. State Coll., 1938; M.P.A. (Littauer fellow), Harvard U., 1942, Ph.D., 1945; LL.D., Mont. State U., 1967. Economist Dept. Agr., 1939-41, 43-47, dir. agrl. econs., econ. adv. to sec., 1961-64; with FAO, 1947-48; prof. Pa. State U., 1948-51, U. Minn., 1951-59, prof. agrl. econs., 1964-65, 70-81, dean internat. programs, 1965-70; ret., 1981; adj. prof. agrl. econs. U. Calif., Davis, 1981—; vis. prof. U. Chgo., 1958-59; chmn. Minn. Gov.'s Study Commn. on Agr., 1958; cons. CCC, U.S. Dept. Agr., Ford Found.; mem. Presdl. Commn. on Food and Fiber, 1965. Author: (with W. Wilcox) Economics of American Agriculture, 1951, 3d edit., 1974, Economics of Consumption, 1955, Farm Prices: Myth and Reality, 1958, The City Man's Guide to the Farm Problem, 1965, The World Food Problem: A Guardedly Optimistic View, 1969, Agricultural Development Planning: Economic Concepts, Administrative Procedures, and Political Process, 1974, (with Mary Ryan) American Farm Policy, 1948-1973, 1976, The Development of American Agriculture: A Historical Analysis, 1979. Served as ensign USNR, 1942-43. Fellow Am. Farm Econ. Assn. (past pres.); mem. Am. Agrl. Econs. Assn. Democrat. Presbyterian. Club: Cosmos (Washington). Home: 12860 Shake Ridge Rd. Sutter Creek CA 95685 *I try to live by the Golden Rule, I try always to make some contribution to the society in which I live, and I try to live a full, zestful life.*

COCHRANE, WILLIAM HENRY, business executive; b. Norfolk, Va., Apr. 3, 1912; s. William F. and Gretchen (Schneider) C.; m. Elizabeth J. Ballantine, Aug. 3, 1935 (dec. July 1977); children: William Henry, Elizabeth J., Susan B., Peter B.; m. Deborah E. Collyer, June 14, 1978. Student, Princeton, 1931-32. Successively chemist, salesman, dist. mgr., mgr. market and sales analysis, mgr. detergent project U.S. Indsl. Chems. Co., 1932- 52; gen. mgr. indsl. div. Lever Bros. Co., 1952-57; exec. v.p. Neptune Internat. Corp., 1957-58, pres., 1958-69, chmn., 1966-72; also dir.; dir. Los Angeles Soap Co., Harrower Assos.; v.p. Mountain Lake Corp., 1975-77, pres., 1978—. Mem. Vero Beach (Fla.) City Council, 1980—, vice mayor, 1980-82, mayor, 1982—; Bd. dirs. Lake Wales Hosp., Vero Beach Civic Assn. Served from lt. (j.g.) to lt. USNR, 1944-46. Mem. Am. Waterworks Assn. Nat. Planning Assn., Soc. Chem. Industry, Newcomen Soc., UN Assn., Fla. Columbia Alliance. Clubs: Princeton (N.Y.C.); Nassau; Riomar Bay Yacht, Mountain Lake (Fla.); Riomar Country. Home: 2370 Club Dr Vero Beach FL 32963 Office: City Hall Vero Beach FL 32960

COCKBURN, JOHN F., banker; b. Everett, Wash., Apr. 8, 1928; s. Charles G. and Florence S. C.; m. Lynn F. Pierson, June 29, 1960; children—Steven, Matthew, Teresa, Patrick. B.B.A., U. Wash., Seattle, 1950. With Rainier Nat. Bank, Seattle, 1948—, exec. v.p., 1975—, mgr. world banking div., 1980—; pres. Pacific Coast Banking Sch., 1977-79; bd. dirs. Wash. Council Econ. Edn., 1979-81, fin. chmn., 1980-81. Mem. devel. com. Forest Ridge Sch., Bellevue, Wash. Mem. Assn. Res. City Bankers. Congregationalist. Clubs: Rainier (treas.), Seattle Tennis, Wash. Athletic (Seattle); Broadmoor Golf. Home: 1524 Shenandoah Dr E Seattle WA 98112 Office: PO Box 3966 Seattle WA 98124

COCKE, ERLE, JR., consultant; b. Dawson, Ga., May 10, 1921; s. Erle and Elise (Meadows) C., Sr.; m. Madelyn Alice Grotnes, May 28, 1955; children: Elise Carol, Jennifer Aline, Carolyn Laurine. A.B., U. Ga., 1942; M.B.A., Harvard, 1947; LL.D., Mercer U., 1951; L.H.D., Mo. Valley Coll., 1960; D.B.A., Presbyn. Coll., 1979. Asst. gen. mgr. Cinderella Foods, Dawson, 1946-47; exec. dir. Agrl. and Indsl. Devel. Bd. of the State of Ga., 1947-48; gen. indsl. agt., Central of Ga.; Ry. Co., Atlanta, 1948-50; asst. to pres. Delta Air Lines, Atlanta, 1950-54; v.p. Delta Air Lines, Inc., 1954-61; alt. exec. dir. IBRD, Washington, 1961-64; v.p. Peruvian Airlines, Inc., Washington, 1964-66; now cons.; chmn. bd. Cocke and Phillips Internat.; dir. State Mut. Ins. Co., Rome, Ga., First Gen. Ins. Co., Atlanta.; Toured 39 countries as mem. Def. Dept's Spl. Civilian Adv. Com. on Armed Forces Installations, 1951-52; civilian aide to sec. of Army, 1952-60; Co-chmn. Nat. Conf. Fgn. Aspects of U.S. Nat. Security, 1958; U.S. alt. rep. to 14th gen. assembly UN, 1959-60. Entered U.S. Army as lt., Inf., 1941; disch. as major, Inf., 1946; brig. gen. N.G.; ret. Decorated Silver Star, Bronze Star with cluster; Purple Heart with 3 clusters; Croix de Guerre; Chevalier Legion of honor, France; awarded Medal of Honor Republic of the Philippines; Star of Solidarity; Comdr. Knight of Malta., Italy; Diploma and Medal Cruz Roja Red Cross, Spain; Hon. Comrd. Nationalist Chinese Air Force, 1951; Recipient Ga. Jr. C. of C.; award for Outstanding Young Man of the Year, 1949; U.S. Jr. C. of C. for; one of ten Outstanding Young Men of Year, 1950. Mem. U. Ga. Alumni Soc. (past v.p.), Am. Legion (nat. comdr. 1950-51, hon. pres. Soc. Am. Legion Founders 1983), Sphinx Soc., Kappa Alpha. Baptist. Clubs: Mason, Shriner, Army and Navy, City Tavern (Washington). Wounded 3 times; prisoner of war 3 times (actually "executed" by German firing squad and delivered the coup de grace but survived, 1945). Home: 5116 Cammack Dr Bethesda MD 20816 340 E Johnson Street Dawson GA 31742 Office: 1629 K St NW Washington DC 20006

COCKE, NORMAN ATWATER, III, computer company executive; b. El Paso, Tex., June 25, 1945; s. Norman Atwarter and Barbara Muhs (Smith) C.; m. Susan Mary Musgjerd, Aug. 23, 1980. B.S. in Elec. Engring., Duke U., 1968; M.B.A., U. Utah, 1971. Pricing analyst NCR Corp., Dayton, 1973-77, dir. pricing, 1977-79, exec. asst., 1979-80, treas., 1981—; mktg. rep. NCR Comten, Inc., Washington, 1980-81. Mem. Leadership Dayton, 1983; mem. adv. council U. Dayton Bus. Sch., 1983. Served to capt. USAF, 1968-72. Mem. Fin. Execs. Inst., Nat. Assn. Corp. Treas. Republican. Episcopalian. Home: 6522 Senator Ln Dayton OH 45459 Office: NCR Corp 1700 S Patterson Blvd Dayton OH 45479

COCKE, WILLIAM MARVIN, JR., surgeon; b. Balt., Aug. 2, 1934; s. William M. and Clara E. (Bosley) C.; m. Sue Ann Harris, Apr. 25, 1981; 1 son, Gregory William; children by previous marriage: William Marvin III, Catherine Lynn, Deborah Kay, Brian Thomas. B.S. with honors in Biology, Tex. A&M U., 1956; M.D., Baylor U., 1960. Diplomate: Am. Bd. Plastic Surgery (guest examiner 1978). Intern surgery Vanderbilt U. Hosp., Nashville, 1960-61; fellow gen. surgery Ochsner Clinic and Found. Hosp., New Orleans, 1961-64; chief resident surgery Monroe (La.) Charity Hosp., 1963-64; resident reconstructive surgery Roswell Park Meml. Inst., Buffalo, 1965-66; chief resident plastic surgery VA Hosp., Bronx, N.Y., 1966; practice medicine specializing in plastic surgery, Nashville, 1968-75, Sacramento, 1976-79, Bryan, Tex., 1980—; mem. staff St. Joseph's Hosp., Bryan, Bryan Hosp.; asst. prof. plastic surgery Vanderbilt U. Sch. Medicine, Nashville, 1968-69, asst. clin. prof. plastic surgery, 1969-75; assoc. prof. plastic surgery Ind. U. Sch. Medicine, Indpls., 1975-76; chief plastic surgery service Wishard Meml. Hosp., Ind. U., 1975-76; assoc. prof. surgery U. Calif. Sch. Medicine, Davis, 1976-79, chmn. dept. plastic surgery, 1976-79; prof. surgery, chief div. plastic surgery Tex. Tech. U. Sch. Medicine, Lubbock, 1979-80, dir. Microsurg. Research Lab., 1979-80; clin. prof. surgery Tex. A&M U. Sch. Medicine, 1980—. Author textbooks on plastic surgery; contbr. articles to profl. jours. Served with M.C. USAF, 1966-68. Recipient Dean Echols award Ochsner Hosp. Found., 1963. Mem. Am. Soc. Plastic and Reconstructive Surgery (award 1966), A.C.S., Am. Assn. Plastic Surgeons, Soc. Head and Neck Surgeons, Assn. for Acad. Surgery, Internat. Soc. Aesthetic Plastic Surgery, Am. Burn Assn., Alton Ochsner Surg. Soc., AMA, Pan Am. Med. Soc., Brazos-Robertson County Med. Soc. Republican. Episcopalian. Home: 8615 Rosewood College Station TX 77840 Office: 1737 Briarcrest Dr Suite 18 Bryan TX 77801

COCKELL, WILLIAM ARTHUR, JR., naval officer; b. Oswego, N.Y., Aug. 12, 1929; s. William Arthur and Alice Amelia (Barlow) C. B.A., Ohio State U., 1950; M.A., cert. (Russian Inst. grantee), Columbia U., 1952; J.D. with distinction,, U. Mich., 1959. Bar: Mich. bar 1961. Commd. ensign U.S. Navy, 1953, advanced through grades to rear adm., 1980; exec. asst. to comdr. Allied Forces, So. Europe, 1969-70; comdg. officer U.S.S. Farragut, 1970-71; head, strategic concepts section Office Chief of Naval Ops., Washington, 1972-73; exec. dir. Chief Naval Ops. Exec. Panel, 1974-75; comdr. Destroyer Squadron 13, 1975-77; asst. chief of staff (plans) CINCPACFLT, 1977-78; exec. asst. to chief Naval Ops., Washington, 1978-81; comdr. Cruiser-Destroyer Group Five, 1981-83; comdr. tng. command U.S. Pacific Fleet, 1983—. Decorated D.S.M., Legion of Merit. Mem. U.S. Naval Inst., Soc. Nautical Research, Navy Records Soc., Internat. Inst. Strategic Studies, U.S. Strategic Inst., Am. Mil. Inst., Order of Coif, Phi Beta Kappa, Pi Sigma Alpha. Episcopalian. Home: 3222 Browing St San Diego CA 92106 Office: COMTRAPAC San Diego CA 92147

COCKERHAM, COLUMBUS CLARK, geneticist, educator; b. Mountain Park, N.C., Dec. 12, 1921; s. Corbett C. and Nellie Bruce (McCann) C.; m. Joyce Evelyn Allen, Feb. 26, 1944; children: Columbus Clark Jr., Jean Allen, Bruce Allen. B.S., N.C. State Coll., 1943, M.S., 1949; Ph.D., Iowa State Coll., 1952. Asst. prof. biostats. U. N.C., Chapel Hill, 1952-53; mem. faculty N.C. State U., Raleigh, 1953—, prof. stats., 1959-72, William Neal Reynolds prof. stats. and genetics, 1972—; mem. genetics study sect. NIH, 1965-69; cons. adv. com. protocols for safety evaluation FDA, 1967-69. Author papers population and quantitative genetics, plant and animal breeding.; Editor, assoc. editor: Theoretical Population Biology, 1975—; editorial bd.: Genetics, 1969-72; asso. editor: Am. Jour. Human Genetics, 1978-80. Served with USMCR, 1943-46. Recipient N.C. award in sci., 1976, Oliver Max Gardner award, 1980, D.D. Mason faculty award, 1983; grantee Nat. Inst. Gen. Med. Scis., 1960—. Fellow Am. Soc. Agronomy; mem. Nat. Acad. Scis., AAAS, Am. Soc. Animal Sci., Am. Soc. Naturalists, Biometric Soc., Genetics Soc. Am., Am. Soc. Human Genetics, Sigma Xi, Gamma Sigma Delta (award merit 1964), Phi Kappa Phi. Home: 2110 Coley Forest Pl Raleigh NC 27607 Office: Dept Statistics Box 8203 NC State Univ Raleigh NC 27695

COCKETT, ABRAHAM TIMOTHY KEAWEIWI, physician, acad. surgeon; b. Maui, Hawaii, Sept. 4, 1928; s. J. Patrick and Mary (Kekahu) C.; m. Willia L. Sindahl, Mar. 23, 1951; children—Timothy William, Shannon Adeal, Cathy Mary, John. B.S., Brigham Young U., 1950; M.D., U. Utah, 1954. Diplomate: Am. Bd. Urology. Intern VA Hosp., Los Angeles, 1954-55; resident in urology U. Calif., Los Angeles, 1956-60, asso. prof. urology, 1962-69; chief urology Harbor Gen. Hosp., Los Angeles, 1962-69; prof., chmn. dept. urol. surgery U. Rochester, N.Y., 1969—; urologist-in-chief Strong Meml. Hosp., Rochester, 1969—; cons. urology VA hosps., Batavia and Canadaigua, N.Y., Rochester Gen., Highland hosps.; cons., investigator Office Naval Research; mem. Biosatellite II team NASA, 1964-72; attending staff urologist N.Y. State Mental Hosp. Co-author: Manual of Urologic Surgery, 1980; mem. editorial bd.: Lymphology, 1968-74, Contemporary Surgery, 1973—, Urology, 1976—, Jour. Urology, 1976—, (co-editor) Male Infertility: Workup, Treatment and Research, 1977; contbr. articles in field to profl. jours. Served to capt., M.C. USAF, 1960-62. Recipient grants and contracts NASA, NIH, Reg. Med. Program for Kidney Transplantation. Fellow A.C.S.; mem. Am. Assn. Genito-Urinary Surgeons, Am. Urol. Assn., Soc. Univ. Surgeons, Soc. Univ. Urologists, AMA, Undersea Med. Soc., Am. Fertility Soc., Soc. Pediatric Urology. Club: Country of Rochester. Home: 168 Grosvenor Rd Rochester NY 14610 Office: 601 Elmwood Ave Rochester NY 14642 *Success is never final; failure is not fatal; courage is to endure.*

COCKLE, JOHN ROBINSON, lawyer; b. Omaha, June 2, 1921; s. Albert L. and Eda (Marquardt) C.; m. Barbara York, Feb. 19, 1943; children: Sally Y., John Robert, Laura L., Mary T. A.B., U. Neb., 1942; postgrad., U. Nebr., 1946-47; LL.B., Creighton U., 1947. Bar: Nebr. 1947. Asso. firm Brown, Crossman, West, Barton & Quinlan, Omaha, 1947-50; partner firm Neely, Otis & Cockle, Omaha, 1950-53; with trust dept. Omaha Nat. Bank, 1953-68, v.p., 1960-68; v.p. charge trust dept. Marine Nat. Exchange Bank, Milw., 1968-70, sr. v.p., 1970-76; v.p. Marine Corp., 1970-76, dir., 1972-76; pres., dir. Marine Investment Mgmt., Inc., 1973-76; sr. v.p. Nev. Nat. Bank, Reno, 1976-82, gen. counsel, 1981-82; assoc. firm White, Pearl, Murphy and Anderson,, 1983—; sec. Nev. Nat. Bancorp., 1977-80; Pres. Comprehensive Health Planning Assn. Southeastern Wis., 1972-74; dir. Nev. Med. Liability Ins. Assn., 1979—. Served with USAAF, 1942-46. Mem. Am., Nebr., Wis., Nev. bar assns., Wis. Trustees Assn. (pres. 1973-74), Nev. Bankers Assn. (chmn. trust div.). Clubs: Rotarian., Hidden Valley Country. Home: 3500 San Mateo Ave Reno NV 89509 Office: 50 W Liberty St Suite 940 Reno NV 89501

COCKLIN, ROBERT FRANK, association executive; b. Lincoln, Nebr., Feb. 13, 1919; s. Frank Dietrich and Helen Catherine (Sampson) C.; m. Ruth Elizabeth Castner, June 25, 1942; children: John Andrew, Mary Collison (dec.). Student, U. Nebr., 1938-39, U.S. Army Command and Staff Coll., 1964, Army War Coll., 1969. Asso. editor Field Arty. Jour., Washington, 1946-48; bus. mgr. N.G. Assn., Washington, 1948-50; dir. public affairs Assn. U.S. Army, Arlington, Va., 1950-77, exec. v.p., 1977—; dir. United Services Life Ins. Co. Author: Battery Duties, 1950, also pamphlets and articles. Trustee George C. Marshall Research Found. Served with field arty. U.S. Army, 1941-48; maj. gen. Res. ret. Decorated D.S.M., Bronze Star, Air medal, Purple Heart. Roman Catholic. Club: Army-Navy. Home: 1322 N Lynnbrook Dr Arlington VA 22201 Office: 2425 Wilson Blvd Arlington VA 22201

COCKMAN, JAMES DALE, coffee company executive; b. Kernersville, N.C., Dec. 10, 1932; s. Ulysses Franklin and Mary Helen (Reele) C.; m. Cathy Dumas, June 20, 1977; children: Angela, Kimberly, Stephen. B.A., Alexander Hamilton Inst., 1956; M.B.A., Syracuse U., 1968. Nat. sales mgr. Thomas J. Lipton Co., Englewood Cliffs, N.J., 1956-66; v.p. mktg. Roman Products Corp., Hackensack, N.J., 1966-73, Rudco Industries, Teaneck, N.J., 1973-79; v.p. mktg. and sales Popsicle Industries, Inc., Englewood, pres., chief exec. officer, 1979-84, Superior Coffee Co. div. Consol. Foods Corp., Bensenville, Ill., 1984—; instr. Syracuse U. Grad. Sch. Bus., 1968-72; dir. Midlantic Nat. Bank/North. Chmn. bd. elders Ponds Reform Ch., Oakland, N.J., 1969—; bd. dirs. Grad. Sch. Sales, Syracuse U., 1972—, Nat. Commn. for Prevention of Child Abuse; also mem. Congl. liaison com. Served with USN, 1951-53. Mem. N.J. C. of C. and Industry (dir. 1980, chmn. bd. 1983), Am. Mgmt. Assn., Pres.'s Assn., N.Y. Sales Execs., Sales and Mktg. Execs. Internat., Dairy Foods and Indsl. Supply Assn., Am. Frozen Foods Inst. (past dir.). Office: Superior Coffee Co 990 Supreme Dr Bensenville IL 60106

COCKRELL, ERNEST HARRIS, oil executive, rancher; b. Houston, Sept. 28, 1945; s. Ernest Dashiell and Virginia (Harris) C.; m. Janet Schuster, Aug. 2, 1968; children: Ernest Dashiell, David Allen. B.S. in Engring. Sci., U. Tex.-Austin, 1967, M.B.A. hon., 1970. Petroleum engr. Cockrell Oil Corp., Houston, 1970-72, exec. v.p., 1972-78, pres., 1978—; dir. Pennzoil Co., Houston, Intrepid Drilling Corp., N.W. Crossing Bank. Bd. visitors Salk Inst., 1983; exec. bd. Sam Houston Area council Boy Scouts Am., Houston, 1977; bd. dirs., exec. com. Houston Mus. Natural Sci., 1981; bd. visitors M.D. Anderson Hosp., Houston, 1975; trustee Methodist Hosp., Houston, 1978-80. Named Outstanding Young U. Tex.-Ex-Student, 1980, Disting. Grad. U. Tex. Coll. Engring., 1981. Mem. Young Pres. Orgn., Houston C. of C. (dir. 1980-81, 82-83), Omicron Delta Kappa, Pi Epsilon Tau, Tau Beta Pi. Methodist. Clubs: Houston, Pamada, Houston Country. Home: 3953 Inverness Houston TX 77019 Office: Cockrell Oil Corp 1212 Main St Suite 999 Houston TX 77002

COCKRELL, LILA MAY, civic orgn. exec., former mayor San Antonio; b. Ft. Worth, Jan. 19, 1922; d. Robert Bruce and Velma (Tompkins) Banks; m. Sidney Earl Cockrell, Jr., June 20, 1942; children—Carol Ann (Mrs. Robert Lee Gulley), Cathy Lynn (Mrs. Donald James Garman). B.A. in Speech, So. Methodist U., 1942, L.H.D. (hon.), 1981, D.Sc., Our Lady of Lake U. Mem. San Antonio City Council, 1963-70, 73-81, mayor pro-tem, 1969-75, mayor, 1975-81; exec. dir. United San Antonio, 1981—; mem. Tex. Gov.'s Commn. Status Women, 1970-72, vice chmn., 1970-72; voting rep. City San Antonio on exec. com. Alamo Area Council Govts., 1970-81, vice chmn., 1971, chmn., 1973—; sec. San Antonio charter Revision Com., 1971; dir. community relations Ecumencial Center Religion and Health, San Antonio, 1973-75; mem. Tex. Adv. Commn. on Intergovtl. Relations, 1975—, Mayor's Adv. Com. to Gov. of Tex., 1979—, Local Govt. Policy Adv. Com. to Sec. of Energy, 1979—. Pres. League Women Voters, Dallas, 1953-55 Pres. League Women Voters, San Antonio, 1959-63, Horace Mann Jr. High Sch. PTA, San Antonio, 1959-60; coordinator vol. sers. San Antonio Chest Hosp., 1970-73; pres. Ch. Women United San Antonio, 1971-72; parliamentarian Mil.-Civilian Club, San Antonio, 1972. Served as ensign WAVES USNR, World War II. Named Headliner of Year Theta Sigma Phi, 1964; hon. v.p. Beautify San Antonio Assn.; recipient Beautification award Magnolia Greene Garden Club, 1967, Woman of Achievement award So. Meth. U., 1967, San Antonio Bus. and Profl. Women's Club, 1969, Outstanding Citizen of Year award Council, 1972, One of Ten Outstanding Women of 1972 award San Antonio Express and News, 1972, Politician of Yr. award, 1979; named Politician of Decade San Antonio Light, 1979; hon. life mem. San Antonio Garden Center, Woman's Pavilion '68, 1968, San Antonio Garden Center, Woman's Pavilion '68, Tex. P.T.A, 1969, Zonra Club San Antonio, 1970. Mem. Nat. Assn. Regional Councils (past dir.), Nat. League of Cities (dir. 1975-77, adv. council 1977—), U.S. Conf. Mayors (adv. bd. 1976—), Tex. Mcpl. League (dir. 1973-81, 2d v.p. 1973-74, 1st v.p. 1974-75, pres. 1975-76). Presbyn. Home: 254 E Rosewood San Antonio TX 78212

COCKRUM, WILLIAM MONROE, III, investment banker; b. Indpls., July 18, 1937; s. William Monroe II C. and Katherine J. (Jaqua) Moore; m. Andrea Lee Deering, Mar. 8, 1975; children: Catherine Ann, William Monroe, IV. A.B. with distinction, DePauw U., Greencastle, Ind., 1959, M.B.A., Harvard U., 1961. With A.G. Becker Paribas Inc., 1961—, mgr. nat. corp. fin. div., 1968-71, mgr. pvt. investments, Los Angeles, 1971—, fin. and adminstrv. officer, 1974-80, sr. v.p., 1975-78, vice chmn., 1978—, also dir.; dir. Transcon Lines, Burrows, Inc., Sunlaw Operating Corp., Masti-Kure, Inc., Knapp Communications Corp., Gen. Hydrocarbons Inc. Mem. Delta Kappa Epsilon. Clubs: University (Chgo.); Monterey (Palm Desert, Calif.). Office: 2029 Century Park E Suite 3400 Los Angeles CA 90067 also 55 Water St New York NY 10041

COCKS, FRANKLIN HADLEY, materials scientist; b. S.I., N.Y., Oct. 1, 1941; s. Charles Franklin and Ruth (Hadley) C.; m. Pamela Kay Pfaff, Aug. 6, 1966; children—Elijah Eugene, Josiah Charles. B.S., MIT, 1963, M.S., 1964, Sc.D., 1965; postgrad. (Fulbright fellow), Imperial Coll. Sci. and Tech., London, 1965-66. Registered profl. engr., N.C.; registered patent agt. Staff scientist Tyco Labs., Waltham, Mass., 1966-67, sr. scientist, 1967-70, asst. head materials sci. dept., 1970-72; assoc. prof. Duke U., Durham, N.C., 1972-76, prof. dept. mech. engring. and materials sci., 1976—; cons. Los Alamos Sci. Lab., 1979—. Author: (with M.L. Shepard, J.B. Chaddock, C.M. Harman) Introduction to Energy Technology, 1976, Manual of Industrial Corrosion Standards and Control; Editor ASTM spl. tech. publ., 1973. NSF fellow, 1964-65; recipient NASA award, 1974. Mem. Nat. Assn. Corrosion Engrs., AIME, Instn. Metallurgists (Brit.), Sigma Xi, Tau Beta Pi. Club: London House (life). Patentee in field. Office: Dept Mech Engring and Materials Sci Duke U Durham NC 27706

COCKS, GEORGE GOSSON, chemical microscopy educator; b. Sioux City, Iowa, Mar. 22, 1919; s. George Green and Nellie Patricia (Gosson) C.; m. Marian L. Singer, May 11, 1942; children: Gary, Kathleen (Mrs. Thomas Sadlowski), Francis, Kenneth. B.S. in Chemistry, Iowa State U., 1941; Ph.D. in Chem. Microscopy, Cornell, 1949. Researcher Battelle Meml. Inst., Columbus, Ohio, 1949-64; prof. chem. microscopy Cornell U., 1964-81, prof. emeritus, 1981—; cons. Los Alamos Sci. Lab., 1980-81, staff mem. chem. microscopy dept., 1981—. Scoutmaster Central Ohio council Boy Scouts Am., 1956-64. Served to lt. comdr. USNR, 1942-45. NSF grantee to study crystallization inorganic materials in polymers, 1966-68, to study biomed. uses collagen, 1972—. Fellow Royal Micros. Soc., AAAS (council 1970-75); mem. Am. Optical Soc., Am. Chem. Soc., Electron Microscopy Soc. Am. (exec. sec. 1964-76), Sigma Xi, Phi Kappa Phi. Patentee in field. Home: 549 Todd Loop Los Alamos NM 87544

COCKSHUTT, ERIC PHILIP, research scientist; b. Brantford, Ont., Can., May 30, 1929; s. Eric Morton and Kathleen Isobel (Buck) C.; m. Julia Ann Fink, Sept. 11, 1954; children: Martha Jane, Catherine Margaret, Eric William, Amanda Mary, Paul Edmund. B.A.Sc in Mech. Engring, U. Toronto, 1950; M.S., M.I.T., 1951, Sc.D., 1954. Research officer Engine Lab., NRC, Ottawa, Ont., 1953-67, sect. head, 1967-75, dir. energy research, 1975—; sessional lectr. Carleton U., Ottawa, 1959-73. Ethyl Corp. fellow, 1952-54. Fellow Can. Aero. and Space Inst. (Casey Baldwin award 1960, 64); mem. Can. Soc. Mech. Engring. Anglican. Home: 120 Dorothea Dr Ottawa ON K1V 7C7 Canada Office: Nat Research Council Ottawa ON K1A 0R6 Canada

COCO, ALFRED JOSEPH, law educator, librarian; b. Moreauville, La., Feb. 28, 1933; s. Fulgence Joseph and Velma Marie (Lemoine) C.; m. Joyce Marie Manning, June 13, 1953; children: Paul Dominique, Brandon Joseph. B.A., U. Tex., 1957; J.D., St. Mary's U., 1960; M.Law Librarianship, U. Wash., 1962. Bar: Tex. 1960, Colo. 1973. Individual practice law, San Antonio, 1960-62; asst. prof. law, law librarian St. Mary's U. Sch. Law, San Antonio, 1962-66; prof. law, law librarian U. Houston Coll. Law, 1966-72, U. Denver Coll. Law, 1972—. Book rev. editor: Tex. Bar Jour., 1964-66; contbr. chpts. to textbooks; author: Finding the Law: A Workbook for Laypersons, 1983. Served with USAF, 1951-53. Mem. Am. Assn. Law Libraries (pres. 1977—), Am., Tex., Colo. bar assns. Democrat. Roman Catholic. Home: 800 S Jackson Denver CO 80209 Office: 1900 Olive St Denver CO 80220

COCO, JAMES, actor; b. N.Y.C., Mar. 21, 1930; s. Felice and Ida (Detestes) C. Student, Uta Hagen Bergdorf Studios, 1960. Broadway appearances include Last of the Red Hot Lovers, 1969, The Devils, 1965, Passage to India, 1963, Man of La Mancha, 1967, Arturo Ui, 1968, Everybody Loves Opal, 1966, Little Me, 1982, Wally's Cafe, 1982, You Can't Take It With You, 1983; off-Broadway appearances; appeared in: films Only When I Laugh; TV miniseries The French Atlantic Affair, 1979; TV shows Raquel Welch Special (recipient Obie awards.), St. Elsewhere (Emmy award); author: The James Coco Diet. Address: care Paul H Wolowitz 59 E 54th St New York NY 10022 *If you give it up, it's just as well—you never would have made it anyway.*

CODDING, FREDERICK HAYDEN, lawyer; b. Hopewell, Va., Dec. 13, 1938; s. Francis Chadwick and Ruthcille Sharon (Craven) C.; m. Judith Willis Hawkins, Apr. 30, 1966; children: Forrest Hayden, Judith Chadwick, Cally Willis, Clare Catharine. A.B., Coll. William and Mary, 1962; J.D., Georgetown U., 1966. Bar: Va. 1966, D.C. 1968. Legal asst. VA, Washington, 1963-65; Capitol Hill reporter, editor Congressional Monitor, Washington, 1966; law clk. to chief judge D.C. Ct. Appeals, 1966-68; individual practice law, Va. and Washington; v.p., counsel Nat. Assn. Miscellaneous, Ornamental and Archtl. Products Contractors, Fairfax, Va., 1970—; counsel, dir. Nat. Assn. Reinforcing Steel Contractors, Fairfax, 1970—. Editor pub. legis., adminstrv., bldg. and constrn. industry newsletters, reports. Mem. federally established rev. bds. for constrn. industry, N.Y.C. Bldg. Standards Com. Council; pres. Fairfax County Youth Club. Mem. ABA, D.C. Bar Assn., Va. Bar Assn., Fairfax Bar Assn., Nat. Council Erectors, Fabricators and Riggers, Sigma Nu. Office: 10382 Main St Fairfax VA 22030

CODDING, GEORGE ARTHUR, JR., political science educator; b. Salem, Oreg., June 23, 1923; s. George Arthur and Maude Fern (Corlies) C.; m. Yolanda Celeste Legnini, June 17, 1961; children: Christine Diane, George Arthur III, William Henry, Jennifer Celeste. Student, Willamette U., 1940-42; B.A., U. Wash., 1943, M.A., 1948; D. Polit. Sci, U. Geneva, 1952. Lectr. dept. polit. sci. U. Pa., 1953-55, asst. prof., 1955-61; asso. prof. polit. sci. U. Colo. at Boulder, 1961-65, prof. polit. sci., 1965—, chmn. dept., 1971-73, chmn. B.A. in Internat. Affairs Program, 1977—; vis. prof. Grad. Inst. Internat. Studies, U. Geneva, 1973-74; tech. sec. Internat. Telecommunications Union, 1949, cons. to sec.-gen., 1964-65; cons. UNESCO, 1957-58, 73, Nat. Commn. Causes and Prevention of Violence, 1968-69, Australian Fedn. Comml. Broadcasters, 1973, Office Telecommunications, Dept. Commerce, 1975, Office Telecommunications Policy, Exec. Office of Pres., 1976-77, FCC, 1979, Internat. Inst. Communications, 1982; mem. adv. bd. Gen. Electric Space Broadcast, 1967-70; exec. bd. Radio Colo., 1969-78. Author: The International Telecommunication Union, 1952, Broadcasting Without Barriers, 1959, The Federal Government of Switzerland, 1961, The Universal Postal Union, 1964, Governing the Commune of Veyrier: Politics in Swiss Local Government, 1967, (with William Safran) Ideology and Politics: The Socialist Party of France, 1979, (with Anthony M. Rutkowski) The International Telecommunication Union in a Changing World; editorial bd.: Monograph Series in World Affairs, 1964-78; mem. adv. bd.: Denver Jour. Internat. Law and Policy, 1971—. Exec. bd. Southeastern Pa. chpt. Ams. for Democratic Action. Served with USNR, 1943-46. Guggenheim fellow, 1958-59; Faculty fellow U. Colo., 1965-66, 73-74; Behavioral Scis. Evaluation Panel; NSF grad. fellow, 1969-73; NSF grantee, 1979-80. Mem. Am., Internat. polit. sci. assns., Internat. Studies Assn. (mem. governing council 1972-73, pres. West 1972-73), Am. Soc. Internat. Law, Pi Sigma Alpha. Club: Trout Unlimited (pres. 1976). Home: 6086 Simmons Dr Boulder CO 80303

CODDINGTON, EARL ALEXANDER, mathematician, educator; b. Washington, Dec. 16, 1920; s. Cyrus Alexander and Lillian (Dezarn) C.; m. Susan Klaber, Nov. 17, 1945; children: Alan Alexander, Robert Henry, Claire Helen. Ph.D., Johns Hopkins, 1948. Instr. Johns Hopkins, 1948-49; instr. Mass. Inst. Tech., 1949-50, C.L.E. Moore instr., 1950-52; mem. faculty U. Calif. at Los Angeles, 1952—, prof. math., 1959—, chmn. math. dept., 1968-71; Fulbright lectr. U. Copenhagen, Denmark, 1955-56, vis. prof., 1963-64; vis. asso. prof. Princeton, 1957-58. Author: (with N. Levinson) Theory of Ordinary Differential Equations, 1955, An Introduction to Ordinary Differential Equations, 1961; Cons. editor math., Holden-Day, Inc., 1960—. Mem. Am. Math. Soc. (coop. editor procs. 1952-55, coop. editor trans. 1957-62), Math. Assn. Am., AAUP, Phi Beta Kappa, Sigma Xi. Home: 764 Wildomar St Pacific Palisades CA 90272 Office: Math Dept Univ California Los Angeles CA 90024

CODER, SAMUEL MAXWELL, clergyman, educator; b. Straight, Pa., Mar. 25, 1902; s. Emmanuel Miller and Abbie Mary (Bailey) C.; m. Elizabeth Maria Dieterle, Feb. 20, 1932; children—Margaret Elizabeth (dec.), Maxine Joyce, Donald Maxwell. Student, Evang. Theol. Coll., Dallas, 1932-35; B.S., Temple U., 1938; Th.B., Dallas Theol. Sem., 1938; Th.M., 1940; D.D., Bible Theol. Sem. of Los Angeles, 1949. Bus. exec., 1928-32; ordained to ministry Presbyn. Ch., 1938; pastor Grace Ch, Camden, N.J., 1935-38, Chelsea Ch., Atlantic City, N.J., 1938-43, Evangel Ch., Phila., 1944-45; mem. faculty Moody Bible Inst., Chgo., 1945, v.p. and dean edn., 1947-69, now emeritus. Editor in chief, Moody Press, 1946; gen. editor: The Wycliffe Series of Christian Classics, 1950—; Author: Youth Triumphant, 3 vols., Moody Corr. Course, 1946, Dobbie, Defender of Malta, 1946, God's Will for Your Life, 1950, Jude: the Acts of the Apostates, 1955, Israel's Destiny, 1978, The Moody Christian Worker's New Testament, 1980; editor: Memoirs of McCheyne, 1947, Our Lord Prays for His Own, 1950, The World to Come, 1954, Nave's Topical Bible, 1976; Contbr. articles to religious jours. Republican. Home: 1860 Sherman Ave Evanston IL 60201

CODERE, HELEN FRANCES, anthropologist, educator, univ. dean; b. Winnipeg, Man., Can., Sept. 10, 1917; came to U.S., 1919, naturalized, 1924; d. Charles Francis and Mabelle (Prosser) C. B.A. summa cum laude, U. Minn., 1939; Ph.D., Columbia, 1950. Instr. Vassar Coll, 1946-50, asst. prof., 1951-53, asso. prof., 1955-57, prof., 1958-63; vis. lectr. anthropology U. B.C., 1954-55, Northwestern U., winter 1963; mem. faculty Bennington Coll., 1963-64; prof. anthropology Brandeis U., 1964—, dean, 1975-77; anthrop. fieldwork Kwakiutl Indians of, B.C., 1951-55, Rwanda, Africa, 1959-60; Mem. adv. panel on anthropology Nat. Sci. Found., 1968-71. Author: Fighting with Property: A Study of Kwakiutl Potlatching and Warfare, 1792-1930, 1950, The Biography of an African Society, Rwanda 1900-1960; also articles.; Editor: Kawkiutl Ethnography (Franz Boas), 1966. Faculty fellow Vassar Coll., 1956; Social Sci. Research Council fellow, 1956, 62-63; Guggenheim fellow, 1959-60. Fellow Am. Anthrop. Assn. (exec. council 1966-69); mem. AAAS, African Studies Assn., Am. Ethnol. Soc. (pres. 1972-73), Northeastern Anthrop. Assn. (pres. 1973), Phi Beta Kappa. Office: Dept Anthropology Brandeis U Waltham MA 02154

CODRARO, LAWRENCE FREDERICK, watch company executive;; b. Bklyn., Apr. 27 1926; s. Natale and Frances (Cerasuolo) C. B.S., Fordham U., 1946, J.D., 1950; LL.M., N.Y. U., 1961. Bar: N.Y. state bar 1950, Conn. bar 1978. Atty. N.Y. Ordnance Dist., 1951-56, Mergenthaler Linotype Co., 1956-58; with Bulova Watch Co., Inc., 1958—, asst. counsel, 1958—, corp. sec., 1967—, counsel, 1979—, v.p., 1980—. Served with AUS, 1946-47. Mem. Am. Watch Assn. (dir., exec. com. N.Y.C.), Westchester/Fairfield Corp. Counsel Assn. Home: 290 Overlook Dr Greenwich CT 06830 Office: Bulova Park Flushing NY 11370

CODY, DOUGLAS THANE ROMNEY, otorhinolaryngologist, educator; b. St. John, N.B., Can., June 23, 1932; came to U.S., 1958, naturalized, 1973; s. Douglas F. and Eleanor Mae (Romney) C.; m. Joanne Dae Gerow, 1963; children: Douglas Thane R., Romney Joanne. M.D., C.M., Dalhousie U., Halifax, N.S., 1957; Ph.D., U. Minn., 1963. Intern St. John Gen. Hosp., 1956-57; resident in pathology Provincial Labs., St. John, 1957-58; resident in otolaryngology Mayo Found., Rochester, Minn., 1958-63; mem. faculty Mayo Grad. Sch. Medicine, 1963—, prof. otolaryngology, 1974—; cons. otolaryngology Mayo Clinic, 1963-68, chmn. dept., 1968—, bd. govs., 1977—; trustee Mayo Found., 1977—; Schall lectr. Mass. Eye and Ear Infirmary, 1975. Author: Your Child's Ears, Nose and Throat: A Parent's Medical Guide, 1974, Diseases of the Ears, Nose and Throat: A Guide to Diagnosis and Management, 1980; also numerous articles; editor profl. jours. Recipient John Black award surgery Dalhousie U. Med. Sch., 1955, Edward John Noble award fgn. travel Mayo Found., 1961. Fellow ACS (gov. 1980); mem. Am. Acad. Ophthalmology and Otolaryngology (research award 1961, award merit 1972), Am. Council Otolaryngology (dir. 1980—), Am. Otol. Soc. (trustee research fund 1980—), Am. Acad. Otolaryngology (dir. 1977—, sec. instrn. courses 1977—), Dalhousie U. Med. Alumni Assn. (dir. 1978—), Alumni Assn. Mayo Found. Med. Edn. and Research, Am. Laryngol., Rhinological and Otol. Soc., Am. Otol. Soc., Assn. Acad. Depts. Otolaryngology, Barany Soc. Centurion Club of Deafness Research Found., Otosclerosis Study Group, Soc. Univ. Otolaryngologists, Sigma Xi. Office: 200 1st St SW Rochester MN 55901

CODY, IRON EYES, actor; b. Okla., Apr. 3, 1915; s. Thomas Long Plume and Frances Salpet; m. Bertha Parker, Sept. 15, 1936; children: Robert Francis, Arthur William. Student, Los Angeles City Coll., 1940-41. Hon. rep. Shakespeare Archery Corp. Author: Indian Sign Talk in Pictures, 1952, Little White Chieftain, 1963, Indian Talk, 1970, Brit. edit., 1972; Contbr. articles on Am. Indian to newspapers.; Motion picture appearances include Sitting Bull, 1954, A Man Called Horse, 1968, Cockeyed Cowboys of Calico County, 1969, El Condor, 1969, Greyeagle, 1977, others; appeared on: TV Keep Am. Beautiful series, 1970—; stage appearances include: The American, 1930, My Blossom Bride, 1931, White God, and Red God, 1932; narrator, cons.: films The American Indian-After the White Man Came; narrator: LAPD ednl. films Indian Culture. Master of ceremonies Little Big Horn Indian Assn., Grand Council Am. Indian, Confederated Tribes of Am. Indians, Am. Indian Week, others; pres. Little Big Horn Indian Charitable Assn.; chmn. Nat. Am. Indian Drug Prevention; nat. hon. chmn. We Turn in Pushers; hon. mem. Am. Indian Free Clinic; active Boy Scouts Am.; Bd. dirs. Los Angeles City-County Native Am. Indian Commn., Southwest Museum. Star on Hollywood Walk of Fame, 1983. Mem. Los Angeles Indian Center (life), Los Angeles Library Assn. (dir., photographer), The Westerners (dir., photographer Los Angeles corral), Screen Actors Guild (dir.), AFTRA (dir.), Los Angeles Karate Assn. Office: care Dade/Rosen Associates 999 N Doheny Dr W Suite 102 Los Angeles CA 90069 *Nearly all my life, it has been my policy to help those less fortunate than myself. My foremost endeavors have been, with the help of the Great Spirit, to dignify my people's image through humility and love of my country. It is my sincerest wish to reach the hearts of the people of the world, by my Keep America Beautiful film of the "Crying Indian" so they will be more aware of the dangers of pollution facing the world today.*

CODY, JANE MERRIAM, classicist; b. Chgo., Oct. 20, 1941; d. John Henry and Charlotte (Orr) Merriam; m. Bruce Patrick McNall; children: Erin Elizabeth, Thomas Edan, Katherine Anne McNall. A.B., Randolph-Macom Women's Coll., 1963; M.A., Bryn Mawr Coll., 1964, Ph.D., 1968. Instr. Pomona Coll., 1967-68; asst. prof. classics U. So. Calif., 1968-71, assoc. prof., chmn. dept. classics, 1971-74, 80—. Contbr. articles on Roman coins, history and lit. to profl. jours. Fellow Am. Council Learned Socs., 1975-76. Mem. Am. Philol. Assn., Archaeol. Inst. Am., Royal Numis Soc., Am. Numis Soc. Office: U So Calif Taper Hall 224 Los Angeles CA 90089

CODY, RICHARD JOHN, English educator; b. London, Eng., Jan. 5, 1929; married; 2 children. B.A., London U., 1952; M.A., U. Minn., 1958, Ph.D. in English, 1961; M.A. (hon.), Amherst Coll., 1968. Instr. to asst. prof. English U. Minn., 1960-63; assoc. prof. English Amherst Coll. (Mass.), 1963-68; prof. English Amherst Coll., 1968—; Folger prof. English Amherst Coll. (Mass.), coll. librarian, 1970-74, chmn. dept. English, 1971-73. Author: The Landscapeof the Mind: Pastoralism and Platonic Theory in Tasso's Aminta and Shakespeare's Early Comedies, 1969; editor: (contbr.) Newsletter of Friends of the Amherst Coll. Library, 1972. Office: Dept English Amherst Coll Amherst MA 01002 *

CODY, THOMAS GERALD, architectural engineering and consulting executive; b. Holyoke, Mass., Feb. 18, 1929; s. John Francis and Mary Gertrude (Scanlon) C.; m. Kathleen Mary Maguire, Nov. 17, 1956; children—Kathleen, Joseph. A.B., Coll. of Holy Cross, 1950; postgrad., Boston Coll., 1950-52; M.B.A., Harvard U., 1957. Cert. mgmt. cons. Various corporate mgmt. positions, 1955-62; v.p. Fry Cons., Inc., Chgo., 1962-64, Los Angeles, 1964-70, Washington., 1970-72; exec. dir. U.S. Equal Employment Opportunity Commn., Washington, 1972-74; asst. sec. for adminstrn. HUD, Washington, 1974-76; v.p., Washington mgr. L.B. Knight & Assos., Inc., 1976—; pres. Lester B. Knight Mgmt. Cons. Group, 1979—, Thomas Cody & Assos., Annapolis, Md. and Washington, 1981—; chmn. indsl. adv. com. Anne Arundel County Opportunities Industrialization Center, 1978—. Mem. Archtl. and Transp. Barriers Compliance Bd., 1974—, Anne Arundel Commn. on Women, 1977—; Bd. dirs. Found. for Jr. Blind, Los Angeles, 1968-70. Served as 1st lt. USMCR, 1953-55. Mem. Inst. Mgmt. Consultants (dir. Washington chpt.). Clubs: Harvard (N.Y.C.); Annapolis Yacht. Home: 2659 Queen Anne Circle Annapolis MD 21403

CODY, WALTER JAMES MICHAEL, lawyer; b. Memphis, Mar. 13, 1936; s. Walter James and Bess Lou (Hill) C.; m. Suzanna Marten; children: Jane Barton, Michael. B.A., Southwestern at Memphis, 1958; J.D., U. Va., 1961. Bar: Tenn. 1961. Partner Burch, Porter & Johnson, Memphis, 1961-77, 81—; U.S. atty. Western Dist. Tenn., Memphis, 1977-81; lectr. LeMoyne-Owen Coll., Southwestern at Memphis, Memphis State U. Law Sch. Contbr. to: You Can't Eat Magnolias, 1972. Pres. L.Q.C. Lamar Soc., 1970-71; chmn. Shelby County Democratic Party, 1972-74; mem.-at-large Memphis City Council, 1975-77; trustee, mem. exec. com. Memphis Acad. Arts. Served to 1st lt. U.S. Army Res., 1961-67. Recipient Sam A. Myer Meml. award, 1976. Mem. Am., Tenn., Memphis and Shelby County bar assns., Nat. Assn. Former U.S. Attys., Memphis and Shelby County Legal Services Assn. (dir.). Episcopalian. Office: 130 N Court Memphis TN 38103

CODY, WILMER ST. CLAIR, superintendent schools; b. Mobile, Ala., Jan. 1, 1937; s. Wilmer St. Clair and Madeline (Maygarden) C.; m. Caroline Marie Burns, Aug. 16, 1958; children: David Marshall, Alison Marie. A.B., Harvard Coll., 1959; Ed.M., Harvard U., 1960, Ed.D., 1967. Tchr. Newton (Mass.) Schs., 1960; tchr. Mobile County Schs., 1960-62, prin., 1962-64; dir. tchr. edn. Atlanta Schs., 1966-67; supt. Chapel Hill (N.C.) Schs., 1967-71; sr. research asso. Nat. Inst. Edn., 1971-73; supt. Birmingham (Ala.) City Schs., 1973-83, Montgomery County Schs., Rockville, Md., 1983—. Contbr. articles to ednl. jours. Mem. Nat. Advisory Com. on Juvenile Justice and Delinquency Prevention, 1976-78; bd. dirs. Community Chest, Campfire Girls; trustee Nat. Council Econ. Edn.; mem. Nat. Assessment Edn. Policy Council, 1981—. Named Educator of Year ALA, 1977. Mem. Am. Assn. Sch. Adminstrs., Am. Edn. Research Assn., Phi Delta Kappa. Methodist. Home: 105 E Lenox St Chevy Chase MD 20815 Office: 850 Hungerford Dr Rockville MD 20850

COE, BENJAMIN PLAISTED, state official; b. Long Beach, Calif., Aug. 24, 1930; s. Benjamin and Mary Plaisted (Ricker) C.; m. Margaret Jane Butler, Sept. 5, 1953; children: Benjamin B., Elizabeth C., Mary Susan, Margaret Jane. A.B., Bowdoin Coll., 1953; B.S., Ch.E., MIT, 1953. Lic. profl. engr., N.Y. With silicone products dept. Gen. Electric Co., Waterford, N.Y., 1953-65, process econs. engr., 1963-65; exec. dir. Vols. for Internat. Tech. Assistance, Schenectady, 1965-68, exec. dir. U.S.A. div., 1969-73, v.p., 1971-73; now exec. dir. Temporary State Commn. Tug Hill, N.Y. State Legislature. Mem. vestry Trinity Episcopal Ch., 1978-81, warden, 1981—; bd. dirs. Schenectady Symphony, 1969; chmn. pub. service div. Jefferson County United Way. Named Exec. of Yr. Watertown Profl. Secs. Internat., 1978-79. Mem. Am. Inst. Chem. Engrs. (chmn. N.E. N.Y. sect. 1965), Am. Soc. Pub. Adminstrn., Phi Beta Kappa, Sigma Xi, Tau Beta Pi. Club: Rotary. Home: 314 Paddock St Watertown NY 13601 Office: State Office Bldg Watertown NY 13601 *I have come to think that success should be measured internally, between man and his maker, rather than by external signs. My goals are to involve myself with mankind in a worthwile way and at the same time keep my family fed, healthy, and in a position to work toward their own goals.*

COE, CHARLES NORTON, educator; b. Rahway, N.J., Apr. 29, 1915; s. Maxwell Alanson and Ethel May (Norton) C.; m. Elizabeth Brown, July 11, 1953; children—Timothy Maxwell, Dorothy Elizabeth. B.A. cum laude, Amherst Coll., 1937; M.A., Trinity Coll., Conn., 1940; Ph.D., Yale U., 1950. Instr. English and Latin Williston (Mass.) Acad., 1937-39; asst. English Trinity Coll., 1939-47; headmaster Williston Jr. Sch., 1947-48; asst. prof. English U. Idaho, 1948-51, assoc. prof., 1951-54, prof., head dept. humanities, 1954-59; prof. English, dean Grad. Sch., No. Ill. U., 1959-64; provost Monmouth Coll., West Long Branch, N.J., 1964-66, v.p. academic affairs, 1966-73, dean grad. studies, 1973-77, prof. English, 1964-80, prof. English emeritus, 1980—. Author: Wordsworth and the Literature of Travel, 1953, Shakespeare's Villains, 1957, Demi-devils: The Character of Shakespeare's Villains, 1963. Served with AUS, 1943-46. Mem. Nat., N.J. edn. assns., Modern Lang. Assn., Nat. Council Tchrs. English, Coll. English Assn., Phi Beta Kappa, Alpha Phi Omega, Phi Kappa Psi, Phi Delta Kappa. Episcopalian. Home: 3 Southern Dr Tinton Falls NJ 07724

COE, DONALD KIRK, newspaper editorial writer; b. Tuscaloosa, Ala., Nov. 21, 1934; s. Glen Dale and Hazel Mae (Coley) C.; m. Frances Ellen Truman, May 31, 1958; children—Mark William, Sandra Elizabeth, Bonnie Lee. B.A., U. Ala., 1957. Wire editor Xenia (Ohio) Daily Gazette, 1958-59; reporter, county editor Sharon (Pa.) Herald, 1959-61; asst. wire editor Pitts. Press, 1961-66; in public relations and fund raising Carnegie-Mellon U., Pitts., 1966-70; editorial writer St. Petersburg (Fla.) Times, 1970-75; chief editorial writer Chgo. Sun-Times, 1975—. Served to capt. U.S. Army Res., 1958-68. Recipient Ill. UPI award, 1977. Mem. Sigma Delta Chi (pres. coll. chpt. 1957). Presbyterian. Home: 723 Bonnie Brae River Forest IL 60305 Office: 401 N Wabash Ave Chicago IL 60611

COE, FRED ATKINS, JR., foundation executive; b. Arlington, N.J., Nov. 11, 1916; s. Fred Atkins and Ella M. C.; m. Zita C. McMahon, Apr. 18, 1940; children: Fred Atkins and Walter W. (twins). B.S. in Indsl. Adminstrn., Yale U., 1938; LL.D., Phila. Coll. Pharmacy and Sci., 1980. With W.Va. Pulp & Paper Co., 1933-34, Seth Thomas Clocks div. Gen. Time Instruments, 1938-40, Carnegie-Ill. Steel subs. U.S. Steel Corp., 1940-45; with Burroughs Wellcome Co., Research Triangle Park, N.C., 1945-81, distbn. mgr., 1951-52, v.p. distbn., 1952-60, exec. v.p., 1960-68, pres., chmn. bd., 1968-81; dir. Wellcome Found. Ltd., London, 1973—, Wachovia Corp., 1979-81, Durham Corp., 1979—; pres. Research Triangle Found., 1982—. Mem. Pharm. Mfrs. Assn. (dir. 1968-81), Proprietary Assn. (dir. 1977-81). Episcopalian. Clubs: Yale of N.Y.; Carolina Country (Raleigh, N.C.); MacGregor Downs Country (Cary, N.C.); Pinehurst (N.C.) Country. Home: 1011 Marlowe Rd Raleigh NC 27609 Office: Research Triangle Found PO Box 12255 Research Triangle Park NC 27709

COE, FREDRIC L., physician, educator, researcher; b. Chgo., Dec. 25, 1936; s. Lester J. and Lillian (Chaillen) C.; m. Eleanor Joyce Brodny, May 5, 1965; children: Brian, Laura. A.B., U. Chgo., 1955; M.S., U. Chgo., 1957, M.D., 1961. Am. Bd. Internal Medicine. Intern Michael Reese Hosp., Chgo., 1961-62, resident, 1962-65, U. Tex. S.W.

Med. Sch., 1967-69; chmn. nephrology Michael Reese Hosp., 1972-82; prof. medicine U. Chgo., 1977—, prof. physiology, 1979—; chmn. nephrology A.M. Billings Hosp., Chgo., 1982—. Author: Nephrolithiasis, 1978; editor: Renal Therapeutics, 1978, Nephrolithiasis, 1980, Hypercalciuric States, 1983. Served to capt. USAF, 1961-67. Grantee NIH, 1977—, NIH, 1982—. Fellow ACP; mem. Am. Soc. Clin. Investigation, Am. Physiol. Soc., Assn. Am. Physicians. Jewish. Home: 5490 S Shore Dr Chicago IL 60615 Office: Renal Section Dept Medicine U Chgo 950 E 59th St Chicago IL 60637

COE, (MATCHETT) HERRING, sculptor; b. Loeb, Tex., July 22, 1907; s. Burrell Columbus and Ida Forbes (Herring) C. Student, South Park Coll., (now Lamar U.), 1924-26, Cranbrook Art Acad., 1939-40. Freelance sculptor, 1931—; works include Dick Dowling, Sabine Pass, Tex., 1930's, Battalion Meml, Guadalcanal, also underwater sculpture, Camp Parks, Calif., 1940's; Tenants, Houston Zoo, Twilight Watch, Villa de Matel, Houston, 1950's, The Texan, Vicksburg (Miss.) Nat. Mil. Park, Fantasy, Soc. Medalists, 1960's, Family Group, Magnolia Cemetery, Beamont, Tex., 1970's, Colt; pvt. collection Supplement to Family Group, 1980's. Served with USN, WWII. Recipient Disting. Alumnus award Lamar U., 1983. Mem. Nat. Sculpture Soc. Patentee expression changing doll. Studio: 2554 Gladys Beaumont TX 77702 *My creative efforts have been expressions of theory about reality—finite reaches into the realm of infinity.*

COE, MICHAEL DOUGLAS, anthropologist, educator; b. N.Y.C., May 14, 1929; s. William Rogers and Clover (Simonton) C.; m. Sophie Dobzhansky, June 5, 1955; children—Nicholas, Andrew, Sarah, Peter, Natalie. A.B., Harvard, 1950, Ph.D., 1959. Asst. prof. U. Tenn., 1958-60; mem. faculty Yale, 1960—, prof. anthropology, 1968—; Adviser Robert Woods Bliss Collection Pre-Columbian Art, Dumbarton Oaks, Harvard, 1963-80. Author: La Victoria, An Early Site on the Pacific Coast of Guatemala, 1961, Mexico, 1962, The Jaguar's Children: Pre-Classic Art of Central Mexico, 1965, The Maya, 1966, (with Kent V. Flannery) Early Cultures and Human Ecology in South Coastal Guatemala, 1967, America's First Civilization, 1968, The Maya Scribe and his World, 1973, Classic Maya Pottery at Dumbarton Oaks, 1975, Lords of the Underworld, 1978, (with Richard A. Diehl) In the Land of the Olmec, 1980, Young Lords and Old Gods, 1982; contbr. articles to profl. jours. Fellow Royal Anthrop. Soc., AAAS; mem. Soc. Am. Archaeology, Sociedad Mexicana de Antropologia, Soc. for Hist. Archaeology, Conn. Acad. Arts and Scis., Sigma Xi. Club: Limestone Trout. Home: 376 St Ronan St New Haven CT 06511

COE, PAUL FRANCIS, demographer, economist; b. Horton, Kan., Oct. 29, 1909; s. Clarence Griffin and Laura (Blakely) C.; m. Evelyn Marie Eseman, Sept. 24, 1933; children: Lynn (Mrs. David J. Nordland); Jean (Mrs. Stephen R. Garman), Laura (Mrs. Arthur Coe). Ph.B., U. Chgo., 1932, postgrad., 1933-34; postgrad., Dept. Agr. Grad Sch., No. Va. Coll. Complaint adjuster Mandel Bros., Chgo., 1932; office mgr. pvt. bus., Chgo., 1933-34; research asst. Fed. Emergency Relief Adminstrn., also WPA., Washington, 1934-37; economist FHA, Washington, 1938-39, economist and asst. chief, 1939-42, economist, chief, 1942-47, economist, analytical statistican, demographer, editor, 1947-65; dir. research Population Reference Bur., Washington, 1965-67; pvt. cons., 1967-69; statistician, spl. asst. for text analysis, housing div. Census Bur., Washington, 1969-73; pvt. cons., 1973—; mem. fed. com. standard met. statis. areas Exec. Office of Pres., 1950-65, mem. tech. com. on area definitions, 1960-65; participant interagy, adv. com. population and housing censuses of, 1950, 60; mem. Population and Housing Census Users Conf., 1966. Author: FHA Homes in Metropolitan Districts, 1934-40, 1942; co-author: Ann. FHA Reports to Congress, 1938-47; Author: Tunisia—History and Trends of Economic, Demographic, Labor Force, Production, and Politics, 1969, FHA Techniques of Housing Market Analysis, 1970, Technique for Preparation of Housing Market Analyses, 1974; co-author: Housing Census, Vols. 1, 2, 3, 1970, General Demographic Trends for Metropolitan Areas, 1970, Census Tracts, 1970; Contbr. numerous articles on econs., statistics, housing, demography, mktg. Chmn. U. Chgo. Arlington Alumni Fund dr., 1962, 63. Mem. Population Assn. Am., Lambda Alpha (alumni hon. award in land econs.), Alpha Kappa Psi, Phi Kappa Sigma. Methodist (exec. com. 1960-62). Clubs: Masons, Order Eastern Star. Home: 601 N Buchanan St Arlington VA 22203

COE, ROBERT CAMPBELL, surgeon; b. Seattle, Nov. 14, 1918; s. Herbert Everett and Lucy Jane (Campbell) C.; m. Josephine Austin Weiner, Mar. 24, 1942; children: Bruce Everett, Virginia Austin, Matthew Daniel. B.S., U. Wash., 1940; M.D., Harvard U., 1950. Diplomate: Am. Bd. Thoracic Surgery, Am. Bd. Surgery. Intern Mass. Gen. Hosp., Boston, 1950-51, asst. resident, 1951-54, chief surg. resident, 1955, chief surg. clinics, 1956; instr. surgery Harvard Med. Sch., 1956; practice medicine specializing in thoracic and vascular surgery, Seattle, 1957—; mem. staff Children's Hosp., Harborview Hosp., Seattle Gen. Hosp.; attending surgeon Swedish Hosp.; cons. thoracic surgeon Firland Sanitarium, Seattle, 1957-68, Children's Hosp. Tumor Clinic, 1968—; mng. partner Invex & Inpark med. offices, Seattle, 1970—; clin. prof. U. Wash., 1973—; mem. Wash. State Med. Disciplinary Bd., 1981—; chmn. med. adv. bd. Physio-control. div. Eli Lilly, 1979—; pres. 1st Mercer (Wash.) Corp., 1969-73, 80—, treas., 1973—; owner, operator Hidden Valley Guest Ranch Cle Elum, Wash., 1969—; developer Kula Estate, Maui, Hawaii; treas. 13th Internat. Cancer Congress. Editor: King County Med. Soc. Bull, 1964-70; mem. adv. bd.: Pacific Northwest Mag, 1968—; Contbr. articles to profl. jours. Mem. Mayor's Harbor Adv. Com., 1958-61; chmn. bd. N.W. Seaport Inc., hist. museum, Kirkland, Wash., 1974-75. Served with USNR, 1941-46. Decorated Bronze Star. Fellow ACS; mem. North Pacific Surg. Assn. (sr. mem.), Pacific Coast Surg. Assn. (sr. mem.), King County Med. Soc. (jud. council 1972-78, chmn. 1976-78), Seattle Surg. Soc (pres. 1969), Psi Upsilon. Episcopalian. Clubs: Seattle Yacht, Cruising of Am. Home: 7260 N Mercer Way Mercer Island WA 98040 Office: 1117 Columbia St Seattle WA 98104

COE, ROBERT STANFORD, educator; b. Cin., July 9, 1919; s. Louis Herman and Alma Mary (Jenkins) C.; m. Nancy Jean Ayres, Oct. 28, 1950; children: Carolyn Lee, William Ayres, Jon Bruce. B.S., Miami U., Oxford, Ohio, 1941; M.S., U. Houston, 1948, Ph.D., 1957. Asst. to v.p. Dresser Industries, Dallas, 1956-58; personnel adminstr. Ling-Temco-Vought, Dallas, 1958-64; prof., grad. adviser Stephen F. Austin State U. (Tex.), 1964-69; prof., chmn. dept. mgmt. Angelo State U., San Angelo, Tex., 1969—; lectr. U. Tex.-Arlington, 1960-64; pres. Mgmt. Resources Assocs., San Angelo, 1970—. Contbr. articles to profl. jours. Mem. Gov.'s Com. on Goals for Tex., 1970. Served with USNR, 1941-45. Mem. Am. Psychol. Assn., Acad. Mgmt., AAUP, Am. Inst. Decision Scis., Alpha Kappa Psi, Phi Kappa Phi, Pi Kappa Alpha. Presbyterian. Clubs: San Angelo Country, Rolling Hills Country. Lodge: Rotary. Home: 3223 Trinity St San Angelo TX 76901 Office: Angelo State U San Angelo TX 76901 *Since my high school days, my life has been guided by the principle expressed by the Latin phrase, "Esse Quam Videre", which means,-to be, rather than to appear to be.*

COE, WARD BALDWIN, JR., lawyer; b. Riderwood, Md., Aug. 24, 1913; s. Ward Baldwin and Marguerite Almy (Hall) C.; m. Diana Chittenden, Jan. 18, 1942; children: Diana, Ward III, Henry, Michael. A.B., Princeton U., 1936; LL.B., Harvard U., 1939. Bar: Md. bar 1939. Since practiced in, Balt.; assoc. Ward B. Coe, 1939-41, John R. Norris, 1940; assoc. firm Carman, Anderson & Barnes, 1945-49, Anderson & Barnes, 1949-52; partner firm Anderson, Barnes & Coe, 1952-58, Anderson, Barnes, Coe & King, 1958-63, Anderson, Coe & King, 1963—; mem. Md. State Bd. Law Examiners, 1963-72, sec., 1963-68; asst. atty. gen., State of Md., 1949-52; mem. Gov.'s Commn. to Revise Annotated Code of Md., 1975—. Bd. dirs. Balt. Legal Aid Bur., 1947-53, Balt. League for Crippled Children and Adults, 1952-58, Md. Soc. Crippled Children and Adults, 1955-61; trustee Gilman Sch., 1964-67. Served with AUS, 1941; Served with USNR, 1941-45. Fellow Md. Bar Found. (dir. 1977—, sec. 1979-81); mem. ABA, Md. Bar Assn., Bar Assn. Balt. City, Wednesday Law Club. Home: 9616 Sherwood Rd Owings Mills MD 21117 Office: 800 Fidelity Bldg Charles at Lexington Baltimore MD 21201

COE, WILLIAM CHARLES, psychology educator; b. Hanford, Calif., Oct. 22, 1930; s. Bernard and Bertha (Vaughan) C.; children: Karen Ann, William Vaughan. B.S., U. Calif., Davis, 1958; postgrad., Fresno State Coll., 1960-61; Ph.D. (NSF fellow), U. Calif., Berkeley, 1964. Research helper Fresno State Coll., 1960-61; research asst. U. Calif., Berkeley, 1961-62, 63-64, NSF research fellow, 1963-64; clin. psychology trainee VA Hosp., San Francisco, 1962-63; staff psychologist Langley Porter Neuropsychiat. Inst., San Francisco, 1964-66; pvt. practice psychology, Fresno, Calif., 1965—; asst. clin. prof. med. psychology U. Calif. Sch. Medicine, San Francisco, 1965-66; instr. corr. div. U. Calif., Berkeley, 1967—; asst. prof. psychology Fresno State Coll., 1966-68; assoc. prof. psychology Calif. State U., Fresno, 1968-72, prof., 1972—, chmn. dept. psychology, 1979—; instr. Calif. Sch. Profl. Psychology, Fresno, 1973, Northeastern U., Boston, 1974; research assoc. U. Calif., Santa Cruz, 1975; cons. Tulare and Kings County Mental Health Clinics, Kingsview Corp., 1966-68, Visalia Unified Sch. Dist., 1967-68; Head Start Program, Fresno, 1970-71, Fig Garden Hosp., 1972-73, Concentrated Employment Program, 1973-74, VA Hosp., 1974. Author: (with T.R. Sarbin) The Student Psychologists Handbook: A Guide to Source, 1969, Hypnosis: A Social Psychological Analysis of Influence Communication, 1972, Challenges of Personal Adjustment, 1972, (with L. Gagnon and D. Swiercinsky) instructors Manual for Challenges of Personal Adjustment, 1972, Psychology X118: Psychological Adjustment, 1973; Contbr.: chpts. to Behavior Modification in Rehabiliation Settings, 1975, Helping People Change, 1975, 80, Encyclopedia of Clinical Assessment, 1980; contbr. articles to profl. jours. Served with USAF, 1951-55. Decorated D.F.C., Air medal with oak leaf cluster.; NSF grantee, 1967, 71. Fellow Am. Psychol. Assn.; fellow Soc. for Clin. and Exptl. Hypnosis; mem. Western Psychol Assn., Calif. Psychol Assn., San Francisco Psychol Assn. (editor San Francisco Psychologist 1966), Central Calif. Psychol. Assn. (pres. 1969, dir. 1972-73), Assn. for Advancement Behavior Therapy, Phi Beta Kappa, Sigma Xi, Phi Kappa Phi, Psi Chi. Office: Dept Psychology Calif State U Fresno CA 93740

COELHO, TONY, congressman; b. Los Banos, Calif., June 15, 1942; s. Otto and Alice (Branco) C.; m. Phyllis Butler, June 10, 1967; children: Nicole, Kristin. B.A., Loyola U., Los Angeles, 1964. Agr. asst. to Rep. B.F. Sisk, 1965-70, adminstrv. asst., 1970-78; mem. 96th-98th Congresses from, 15th Calif. Dist.; majority whip-at-large 96th-97th Congresses from; sec.-treas. United Democrats for Congress; chmn. Dem. Congressional Campaign Com.; mem. Dem. Steering and Policy Com. Mem. nat. implementation task force Epilepsy Found. Am. Roman Catholic. Office: 403 Cannon House Office Bldg Washington DC 20515

COEN, ROBERT JOSEPH, advt. agy. exec.; b. Orange, N.J., June 25, 1923; s. John Francis and Mary Elizabeth (Whitford) C.; m. Wanda G. Gonski, Oct. 13, 1956; children—Lisa, Robert, Theodore. B.S., Holy Cross Coll., Worcester, Mass., 1947; M.A., Columbia U., 1948. Dir. applied Sci. div. Interpublic Corp., N.Y.C., 1964-68; mgr. media research McCann-Erickson Co., N.Y.C., 1969-75, sr. v.p., dir. econs. and forecasting, 1975—. Author ann. U.S. advt. Expenditure stats., 1950-80; contbg. editor: Advt. Age. Served with USNR, 1942-46. Mem. Market Research Council, TV/Radio Research Council, Advt. Research Council. Roman Catholic. Home: 255 Gregory Ave West Orange NJ 07052 Office: 485 Lexington Ave New York NY 10017

COERPER, MILO GEORGE, lawyer; b. Milw., May 8, 1925; s. Milo Wilson and Rose (Schubert) C.; m. Lois Hicks, Apr. 11, 1953; children: Milo Wilson, Allison Lee, Lois Paddock. B.S., U.S. Naval Acad., 1946; LL.B., U. Mich., 1954; M.A., Georgetown U., 1957, Ph.D., 1960. Bar: D.C. 1954. Since practiced in, Washington; asso. firm Wilmer & Broun, 1954-60; firm Coudert Bros., 1961-63, mem. firm, 1964—; ordained deacon Episcopal Ch., 1978, priest, 1979, St. Andrews Ch., Clear Spring, Md., 1979—. Contbr. articles to profl. jours. Trustee, vice chmn. Canterbury Cathedral Trust in Am. Served to ensign USN, 1946-49; to lt., 1951-53. Mem. Bar Assn. D.C., Assn. Bar City N.Y., ABA, Md. State Bar Assn., Am. Law Inst., Am. Soc. Internat. Law, Internat. Law Assn. Clubs: Army and Navy, Metropolitan, Chevy Chase; Union League (N.Y.C.). Home: 7315 Brookville Rd Chevy Chase MD 20015 Office: 1 Farragut Sq S Washington DC 20006 also Box 24 Clear Spring MD 21722

COES, KENT DAY, artist; b. Chgo., Feb. 14, 1910; s. Harold Vinton and Agnes Wickfield (Day) C.; m. Helen Elizabeth Stoll, May 29, 1937. Student, Grand Central Sch. Art, N.Y.C., 1928-32, Art Students League, N.Y.C., 1930-34, N.Y. U., 1935-38. Mem. art staff publs. div. McGraw-Hill, Inc., 1947-75; ret., 1975; tchr. Montclair Art Mus., 1955, 60, East Orange (N.J.) High Sch. Adult Edn. div., 1959, Bloomfield Art League, 1971. Numerous group shows galleries and museums, U.S., Can., Mexico, Australia, Hong Kong, and, London; represented watercolors permanent collections, U. Pa., St. Lawrence U., Canton, N.Y., U. Scranton (Pa.), U. Wyo., Montclair (N.J.) Art Mus., Norfolk (Va.) Mus. Arts and Scis., Charles and Emma Frye Mus., Seattle, Holyoke (Mass.) Mus. Art, Nat. Acad. Design, N.Y., also pvt. and indsl. collections. Served with F.A. AUS, 1943-46; ETO. Recipient awards watercolors Am. Watercolor Soc., N.J. Watercolor Soc., Salmagundi Club, Balt. Watercolor Club, Acad. Artists Assn.; Gold medal honor Allied Artists Am., Hudson Valley Art Assn.; Bronze medal Nat. Arts Club; Silver medal N.J. Watercolor Soc. Academician Nat. Acad. Design.; Mem. Am. Watercolor Soc., N.J. Watercolor Soc. (founder-mem., pres. 1947-48), Artists Fellowship, Allied Artists Am., Acad. Artists Assn., Grand Central Galleries, Hudson Valley Art Assn. Republican. Unitarian. Club: Salmagundi (N.Y.C.). Address: 463 Valley Rd Upper Montclair NJ 07043

COETZEE, JOHANNES FRANCOIS, educator; b. Bloemfontein, S. Africa, Nov. 25, 1924; came to U.S., 1951, naturalized, 1974; s. Johannes Frans and Sarah Sophia (Van Der Merwe) C.; m. Mona Luyten, Sept. 1, 1954; 1 son, Pieter Francois. M.Sc., U. Orange Free State, South Africa, 1949; Ph.D., U. Minn., 1956. Lectr. U. Orange Free State, 1949-51, U. Witwatersrand, S. Africa, 1956-57; mem. faculty U. Pitts., 1957—, prof., 1966—; Chmn. commn. electroanalytical chemistry Internat. Union Pure and Applied Chemistry, 1979. Co-editor: monograph Solute-Solvent Interactions, Vol. 1, 1969, Vol. 2, 1976; Contbr. articles to profl. jours. Mem. Am. Chem. Soc. (chmn. chem. edn. group Pitts. sect. 1967, dir. Pitts. sect. 1980), Sigma Xi, Phi Lambda Upsilon. Home: 4233 Parkman Ave Pittsburgh PA 15213

COFER, CHARLES NORVAL, psychologist, educator; b. Cape Girardeau, Mo., June 1, 1916; s. Charles Norval and Ernestine (Osterloh) C.; m. Justine Marie Donnelly, Aug. 3, 1940; children: Thomas Michael, Jonathan Charles; m. Lynette K. Friedrich, July 4, 1976. A.B., S.E. Mo. State Coll., 1937; M.A., U. Iowa, 1937; Ph.D., Brown U., 1940. Mem. faculty George Washington U., 1941-47, asst. prof., 1946-47; mem. faculty U. Md., College Park, 1947-59, prof. psychology, 1951-59; prof., dir. grad. studies in psychology NYU, 1959-63; vis. prof. U. Calif.-Berkeley, 1962-63; prof. Pa. State U., University Park, 1963-67, 68-77, prof. emeritus, 1977—; prof., chmn. dept. psychology U. Md., College Park, 1967-68; prof. U. Houston, 1976-81; research prof. dept. psychology U. N.C., Chapel Hill, 1981—; lectr. Duke U., 1981—. Author: (with M.H. Appley) Motivation: Theory and Research, 1964; also numerous articles.; editor: Psychol. Rev., 1965-70. Mem. Am. Psychol. Assn. (chief editorial adviser 1979-82), D.C. Psychol. Assn. (past pres.), Md. Psychol. Assn. (past pres.) Eastern Psychol. Assn. (past pres., dir. 1965-68), Psychonomic Soc. (bd. govs. 1965-70), AAAS (council 1970, chmn. sect. psychology 1973-74), Sigma Xi. Research on cognitive processess and motivation. Home: 810 Greenwood Rd Chapel Hill NC 27514 Office: Dept Psychology U NC Chapel Hill NC 27514

COFER, HENRY JACKSON, JR., bus. exec.; b. Washington, Ga., Nov. 23, 1926; s. Henry Jackson and Ruby (Ray) C.; m. Allie Padgett, Aug. 25, 1947; children—Jacqueline Carole, Rebecca Gale, Leslie Claire. Student, Clemson U., 1944-45, Draughton's Bus. Sch., Atlanta, 1947-48. Engring. asst. Dupont de Nemours, Inc., Wilmington, Del., 1952-55; with SeaPak Corp., St. Simons Island, Ga., 1955-69; now pres., chief exec. officer Rich-SeaPak Corp.; dir. Rich Products Corp., Buffalo, Coastal Bank of Ga., Brunswick.; Mem. Atlantic States Marine Fisheries Commn.; mem. Nat. Adv. Com. Oceans and Atmosphere. Served with U.S. Mcht. Marine. Mem. Brunswick-Glynn County C. of C., Nat. Frozen Food Assn. (dir.), Nat. Fisheries Inst. (pres. 1971, dir.), Nat. Shrimp Breaders and Processors Assn., Southeastern Fisheries Assn., Jaycees (past pres.). Republican. Episcopalian. Clubs: River (Jacksonville, Fla.); Sea Island Beach and Golf. Home: 4202 12th St East Beach Saint Simons Island GA 31522 Office: PO Box 667 Saint Simons Island GA 31522

COFFEE, JAMES FREDERICK, retired lawyer; b. Decatur, Ind., Mar. 6, 1918; s. Claude M. and Frances N. (Butler) C.; m. Jeanmarie Hackman, Dec. 29, 1945 (dec. 1978); children: James, Carolyn, Susan, Sheila, Kevin, Richard, Elizabeth, Thomas, Claudia; m. Marjorie E. Masterson, Oct. 4, 1980. B.C.E., Purdue U., 1939; J.D., Ind. U., 1947. Bar: Wis. 1947, Ill. 1952. Patent atty. Allis Chalmers Mfg. Co., Milw., 1947-51; mem. firm Anderson, Luedeka, Fitch, Even & Tabin (and predecessors), Chgo., 1951-64, partner, 1956-64; individual practice law, Chgo., 1964-71; partner law firm Coffee & Sweeney, Chgo., 1971-76; partner, gen. counsel design firm Marvin Glass & Assos., Chgo., from 1973, now ret. Served to capt. AUS, 1941-46. Mem. ABA, Ill. Bar Assn., Chgo. Bar Assn. (chmn. com. patents, trademark and unfair trade practices 1967), Am. Patent Law Assn., Patent Law Assn. Chgo. (chmn. com. copyrights 1969), Am. Judicature Soc. Clubs: Tower of Chgo. (bd. govs. 1978—, sec. 1982-83), Tower of Chgo. (treas. 1983—). Home: 320 Earls Ct Deerfield IL 60015

COFFEE, JOSEPH DENIS, JR., college chancellor emeritus; b. Glens Falls, N.Y., Dec. 8, 1918; s. Joseph Denis and Kathryne Grace (Dwyer) C.; m. Margaret Mary Jennings, Oct. 7, 1941; children: John Allan, James Jennings, Mary Joyce Coffee Dies, Barbara Grace Coffee Wolf, Matthew Brian, Margaret Erin Coffee Giovannini, Ann Ellen Coffee Beach. A.B., Columbia U., 1941. Asst. to gen. sec. Columbia U., N.Y.C., 1946-50, dir. devel., 1950-60, assoc. dean, 1959-60, asst. pres. for alumni affairs, 1960-66; v.p. Eisenhower Coll., Seneca Falls, N.Y., 1966-69, exec. v.p., 1969-76, acting pres., 1975-76, pres., 1976-80, chancellor, 1980-81, chancellor emeritus, 1981—; dir. scholarship program Joint Industry Bd., Elec. Industry of N.Y., 1947-81; exec. sec. Com. for Corporate Support Am. Univs., 1962-64. Chmn. March Dimes campaign, Closter, N.J., 1953; active Boy Scouts Am.; former treas., dir. Anglo-Am. Hellenic Bur. Edn.; pres. Seneca County United Way, 1973-75; Chmn. Teaneck Polit. Assembly, 1967-68; Trustee Teaneck Bd. Edn., 1961-64, 65-68, Columbia U., 1978—; bd. dirs. Nat. Women's Hall of Fame. Served from ensign to lt. comdr. USNR, 1941-46. Mem. Seneca Falls Hist. Soc. (former trustee), Psi Upsilon. Roman Catholic. Clubs: Princeton (N.Y.C.); Rotary (Seneca Falls) (past pres.).

COFFELT, JOHN J., university president; b. Neosho, Mo., Dec. 26, 1924; s. Roscoe John and Estella Matilda (Turner) C.; m. Anna Marie Nelson, Feb. 27, 1945; children: Susan Ann (Mrs. Robert Lyon), Margaret Jean (Mrs. Duane Spatar), Janet Lee (Mrs. Robert Bannon), John Byron. B.S., U. Denver, 1948; M.A., Northeastern State U., Greeley, Colo., 1951; Ed.D., U. Colo., 1962. Aircraft mechanic Boeing Aircraft Corp., Seattle, 1942-43; bookkeeper Colo. Nat. Bank, Denver, 1946-48; dir. accounts and records, registrar, instr. State Tchrs. Coll., Dickinson, N.D., 1948-52; dir. research Colo. Dept. Edn., Denver, 1952-56; dir. Colo. Legis. Com. on Edn., Colo. Sch. Bd. Assn., Boulder, 1958-62; coordinator research, Okla., 1962-65; vice chancellor research and planning Okla. State Regents for Higher Edn., Oklahoma City, 1965-68; v.p. adminstrv. affairs Youngstown (Ohio) State U., 1968-73, pres., 1973—. Mem. exec. com. Mahoning Area council Boy Scouts Am.; bd. dirs. McGuffey Centre; trustee Youngstown Hosp. Assn., N.E. Ohio U. Coll. Medicine, N.E. TV of Ohio, Butler Inst. Am. Art. Served with USAAF, 1943-45. Decorated Air medal, D.F.C.; recipient Man of Year award Am. Negro Police Assn., 1980-81, Youngstown C. of C., 1983. Mem. Am. Assn. State Colls. and Univs., Youngstown C. of C., Alpha Kappa Psi, Phi Delta Kappa, Phi Kappa Phi. Clubs: Mason (32 deg.), Lion.). Office: 410 Wick Ave Youngstown OH 44555

COFFEY, DONALD STRALEY, scientist; b. Bristol, Va., Oct. 10, 1932; s. Edwin Douglas and Loula Mayo (Straley) C.; m. Eula Mayme Cosby, Dec. 24, 1953; children—Kathryn Marie, Carol Teresa. B.S., E. Tenn. State U., 1957; Ph.D., Johns Hopkins U., 1964; D.Sc. (hon.), King Coll., 1977. Chemist N.Am. Rayon Corp., Elizabethton, Tenn., 1955-57; chem. engr. Westinghouse Electronic Corp., Balt., 1957-60; mem. faculty Johns Hopkins U. Med. Sch., 1965—, prof. pharmacology, oncology and urology, 1974—; dir. research Brady Urol. Inst., Johns Hopkins Hosp., 1969; mem. USPHS study sect. exptl. therapeutics Nat. Prostatic Cancer project; asst. editor Jour. Molecular Pharmacology. Bd. dirs. Md. div. Am. Cancer Soc. Recipient Research Career and Devel. award USPHS, 1966-72. Mem. Am. Soc. Pharmacology and Exptl. Therapeutics, Am. Soc. Biol. Chemists, Am. Assn. Cancer Research (D. R. Edwards medal 1981). Democrat. Methodist. First isolator of nuclear matrix. Home: 1212 Oak Croft Dr Lutherville MD 21093 Office: Johns Hopkins Hosp 725 N Wolfe St Baltimore MD 21205 *Knowing what you want to do makes the long hours of required work a pleasure.*

COFFEY, JOHN LOUIS, judge; b. Milw., Apr. 15, 1922; s. William Leo and Elizabeth Ann (Walsh) C.; m. Marion Kunzelmann, Feb. 3, 1951; children: Peter Lee, Elizabeth Mary Coffey Robbins. B.A., Marquette U., 1943, LL.B., 1948, LL.D., 1984; M.B.A. (hon.), Spencerian Coll., 1963. Bar: Wis. 1948, U.S. Dist. Ct. 1948, U.S. Supreme Ct. 1948. Asst. city atty., Milw., 1949-54; judge Civil Ct., Milw., 1954-60, Milw. Mcpl. Ct., 1960-62, Circuit Ct., Milw., 1962-72; sr. judge Circuit Ct. (criminal div.), Milwaukee County, 1972-75, chief presiding judge, 1976; circuit ct. judge Circuit Ct. (civil div.), Milwaukee County, 1976-78; justice Wis. Supreme Ct., Madison, 1978-82; circuit judge U.S. Ct. Appeals (7th cir.), Chgo., 1982—; mem. Wis. Bd. Criminal Ct. Judges, 1960-78, Wis. Bd. Circuit Ct. Judges, 1962-78. Chmn. adv. bd. St. Joseph's Home for Children, 1958-65; mem. adv. bd. St. Mary's Hosp., 1964-70; mem. Milwaukee County council Boy Scouts Am.; chmn. St. Eugene's Sch. Bd., 1967-72, St. Eugene's Parish Council, 1974; mem. vol. services adv. com. Milwaukee County Dept. Public Welfare; bd. govs. Marquette U. High Sch. Served with USNR, 1943-46. Recipient Disting. Service award Cudworth Post Am. Legion, 1973; named Law Alumnus of Yr. Marquette U., 1980. Fellow Am. Bar Found.; mem. Alpha Sigma Nu. Roman Catholic. *I have tried to the best of my ability to render justice to all and remembered that "We are a country of laws, not of men"—and while protecting the individual's rights I have not lost sight of the common good of all mankind—and cautioned each and every one who appeared before me that with every right there is a corresponding obligation.*

COFFEY, JOSEPH DANIEL, agricultural economist; b. Martinsville, Ind., Mar. 17, 1938; s. John L. and Mildred E. (Leonard) C.; m. Eloise G. Eskew, June 19, 1960; children: John, Bradley, Mark. B.S., Purdue U., 1960; M.S. (NDEA grad. fellow 1961-63), N.C. State U., 1963, Ph.D., 1966. Vis. prof. U. Agraria, Lima, Peru, 1963-65; asst. prof. agrl. econs. U. Calif., Berkeley, 1965-69; agrl. economist Office Sec., Dept. Agr., 1969-72; prof. agrl. econs. Va. Poly. Inst. and State U., Blacksburg, 1972-81, chmn. dept., 1972-79; dir. econs. and planning So. States Coop., Inc., Richmond, Va., 1981—. Served as 2d lt. U.S. Army, 1960-61. Recipient cert. merit Dept. Agrl., 1971, Presdl. citation, 1972. Mem. Am. Agrl. Econs. Assn. (dir. 1977-80), So. Agrl. Econs. Assn. (pres. 1978). Presbyterian. Home: 3221 Regatta Pointe Ct Midlothian VA 23113 Office: Southern States Coop Inc PO Box 26234 Richmond VA 23260

COFFEY, JOSEPH IRVING, international affairs educator; b. St. Louis, Feb. 13, 1916; s. Joseph Aloysius and Catherine Elizabeth (Burns) C.; m. Maryann Bishop, May 13, 1978; children—John Patrick, Catherine Elizabeth, Judith Ann, Megan Forbes, Susan Fox, James Odell; 1 stepdau., Janet Lynn Bishop. B.S., U.S. Mil. Acad., 1939; postgrad., Columbia U., 1943-45; Ph.D. in Internat. Relations, Georgetown U., 1954. Asst. dir. programs, spl. studies project Rockefeller Bros. Fund, 1956-57; exec. asst. to spl. asst. to Pres. for security ops. coordination, Washington, 1958-60; mem. staff Pres.'s Com. on Info. Activities Abroad, White House, 1960; research analyst Inst. for Def. Analyses, Washington, 1960-63; chief office of nat. security studies Bendix Systems div., Ann Arbor, Mich., 1963-67; prof. public and internat. affairs U. Pitts., 1967-82, dir. Ctr. for Internat. Security Studies, 1975-81, sr. research fellow Ctr. Internat. Security Studies, 1981—; cons. AID, ACDA, Dept. Def., Dept. State, Internat. Communications Agy. Author: books in field including Strategic Power and National Security, 1971, Arms Control and European Security, 1977. Served to col. U.S. Army, 1939-60. Internat. Inst. Strategic Studies research asso., 1972-73; Stockholm Internat. Peace Research Inst. fellow, 1977; NATO research fellow, 1981. Mem. Am. Acad. Polit. and Social Sci., Council Fgn. Relations, Internat. Inst. Strategic Studies, Internat. Studies Assn. Home: 4305 Centre Ave Pittsburgh PA 15213 Office: 4G17 Forbes Quad U Pitts Pittsburgh PA 15260

COFFEY, THOMAS ARTHUR, college president; b. Mpls., Apr. 6, 1936; s. Patrick Joseph and Agnes Bridget (Haley) C.; m. Maureen Ann Sullivan, July 13, 1962; children: Catherine, Mary, Patrick. A.B., St. Ambrose Coll., 1960; M.A., Coll. St. Thomas, 1966, U. S.D., 1967, Ed.D., 1968; postgrad, Harvard U., 1979. Tchr. secondary pub. sch., Mpls., 1962-66; teaching asst. U. S.D., Vermillion, 1966-68; asst. prof. edn. and psychology Hamline U., St. Paul, 1968-71; faculty U. Colo., Boulder, summer 1971; assoc. prof. edn. Mankato Stae U., Minn., 1971-76; mgr. mktg. and sales Waterquip Corp., Sioux Falls, S.D., 1955-62; dir. clin. experiences Hamline U., 1968-71; dir. Urvan tr. Mankato State U., 1971-76; dean div. continuing edn. Am. U., Washington, 1976-82; pres. Thomas More Coll., Crestview Hills, Ky., 1982. Shell grantee; Mankato State U. Urban Ctr. grantee; Am. U. global studies fed. grantee. Mem. Nat. Univ. Continuing Edn. Assn., Assn. Higher Edn., Am. Personnel and Guidance Assn., Am. Assn. Univ. Adminstrs., Assn. Continuing Higher Edn. (sec.-treas. region V), Assn. Supervision and Curriculum Devel., Phi Delta Kappa. Home: 2612 Shaker Rd Lakeside Park KY 41017 Office: Thomas More Coll Crestview Hills KY 41017

COFFEY, THOMAS FRANCIS, JR., editor; b. Walthourville, Ga., Feb. 14, 1923; s. Thomas Francis and Julian (Bacon) C.; m. Mary Corley, Apr. 6, 1946; 1 dau., Mary Cynthia Smith. Grad. high sch.; student, Am. Press Inst., Columbia, 1964, Program for Urban Execs., Mass. Inst. Tech., 1970. Reporter Savannah (Ga.) Eve. Press, 1940-42; civilian pub. relations dir. AUS, Camp Stewart, Ga., 1942; asst. city editor, sports editor Savannah Eve. Press, 1945-55, city editor, 1960-64, mng. editor, 1964-67; news dir. sta. WSAV-TV, Savannah, 1955-57; sports editor Savannah Morning News, 1957-60, mng. editor, 1967-69, asso. editor, 1974—. Asst. city mgr., City of Savannah, 1969-74; Bd. dirs. United Way of Savannah. Served with AUS, 1943-45. Decorated Bronze Star, Purple Heart. Mem. Ga. Heart Assn. (dir. 1st dist.), Ga. A.P. News Council, Greater Savannah Hall Fame Assn. (pres. 1969), Internat. City Mgmt. Assn., Am. Legion, Sigma Delta Chi. Republican. Episcopalian (lay reader). Clubs: Lion., Am. Business (past pres. Savannah chpt.). Home: 209 Kensington Dr Savannah GA 31405 Office: Savannah News Bldg 111 W Bay St Savannah GA 31402 *Dedication to the task at hand/Compassion and concern for others/ Gratitude to those who have built this nation/Faith in God.*

COFFEY, TIMOTHY, physicist; b. Washington, June 27, 1941; s. Timothy and Helen (Stevens) C.; m. Paula Marie Smith, Aug. 24, 1963; children: Timothy, Donna, Marie. B.S. in Elec. Engring. (Cambridge scholar 1958), MIT, 1962; M.S. in Physics, U. Mich., 1963, Evening News Assn. fellow, 1964, Ph.D., 1967. Research physicist Air Force Cambridge Research Lab., 1964; theoretical physicist EGG, Inc., Boston, 1966-71; head plasma dynamics br., then supt. plasma physics div. Naval Research Lab., Washington, 1971-80, asso. dir. research for gen. sci. and tech., 1980-83, dir. research, 1983—. Recipient award Naval Research Lab., 1974, 75. Fellow Am. Phys. Soc.; mem. Am. Inst. Physics, AAAS, N.Y. Acad. Scis., Internat. Union Radio Sci. Office: 4555 Overlook Ave SW Washington DC 20375

COFFIN, DAVID LINWOOD, specialty chemicals and nonwoven materials manufacturing company executive; b. Windsor Locks, Conn., Dec. 15, 1925; s. Dexter Drake and Elizabeth (Dorr) C.; m. Marie Jeanne Cosnard des Closets, Sept. 15, 1973; children by previous marriage: Deborah Lee, David Linwood, Robert George. Student, Trinity Coll., Hartford, Conn., New Eng. Coll. Chmn. bd., exec. officer Dexter Corp., Windsor Locks; dir. Milton Bradley Co., Hartford, Conn., Conn. Bank & Trust Co., Conn. Mut. Life Ins.; mem. adv. bd. Liberty Mut. Ins. Co. Conn. Bd. dirs. Kimball Union Acad., Inst. of Living, Trinity Coll., Greater Hartford chpt. ARC. Served with USNR, World War II. Mem. World Bus. Council. Clubs: Hartford Gun, Hartford; Lake Sunapee Yacht (N.H.); Sky (N.Y.C.). Home: 1177 Prospect Ave West Hartford CT 06105 Office: 1 Elm St Windsor Locks CT 06096

COFFIN, DAVID ROBBINS, art historian, educator; b. N.Y.C., Mar. 20, 1918; s. H. Errol and Lois (Robbins) C.; m. Nancy Merritt Nesbit, June 10, 1947; children—Elizabeth, David Tristram, Lois, Peter. A.B., Princeton, 1940, M.F.A., 1947, Ph.D., 1954; postgrad., Yale, 1940-41. Instr. fine arts U. Mich., 1947-49; lectr. art and archaeology Princeton, 1949-54, asst. prof., 1954-56, asso. prof., 1956-60, prof. art and archaeology, 1960-66, Marquand prof. art and archaeology, 1966-70, Howard Crosby Butler Meml. prof. history architecture, 1970—, chmn. dept. art and archaeology, 1964-70; editor in chief Art Bull., 1959-62. Author: Villa d'Este at Tivoli, 1960, The Villa in the Life of Renaissance Rome, 1979; editor: The Italian Garden, 1st Dumbarton Oaks Colloquium on History of Landscape Architecture, 1972. Recipient Howard R. Marraro book award Am. Cath. Hist. Assn., 1979; Fulbright research award to Italy, 1951-52; McCosh Faculty fellow, also Am. Council of Learned Socs. fellow, 1963-64; Guggenheim Meml. Found. fellow, 1972-73, Alice Davis Hitchcock book award Soc. Archtl. Historians, 1960. Mem. Coll. Art Assn. Am. (dir. 1957-61), Soc. Archtl. Historians (dir. 1968-70, treas. 1970-71), Renaissance Soc., Phi Beta Kappa. Home: 143 McCosh Circle Princeton NJ 08540 Office: Dept Art and Archaeology Princeton U Princeton NJ 08544

COFFIN, FRANK MOREY, judge; b. Lewiston, Maine, May 11, 1919; s. Herbert Rice and Ruth (Morey) C.; m. Ruth Ulrich, Dec. 19, 1942; children: Nancy, Douglas, Meredith, Susan. A.B., Bates Coll., 1940, LL.D., 1959; postgrad. indsl. adminstrn., Harvard U., 1943, LL.B., 1947; LL.D., U. Maine, 1967, Bowdoin Coll., 1969. Bar: Maine 1947. Law clk. to fed. judge Dist. of Maine, 1947-49, engaged in practice, Lewiston, 1947-52; Verrill, Dana, Walker, Philbrick & Whitehouse, Portland, Maine, 1952-56; mem. 85th-86th Congresses from 2d Dist. Maine, House Com. Fgn. Affairs; mng. dir. Devel. Loan Fund, Dept. State, Washington, 1961; dep. adminstr. AID, 1961-64; U.S. rep. devel. assistance com. Orgn. Econ. Coop. and Devel., 1964-65; judge 1st circuit U.S. Ct. Appeals, 1965—, chief judge, 1972-83; chmn. Maine Democratic Com., 1954-56. Author: Witness for Aid, 1964, The Ways of a Judge-Reflections from the Federal Appellate Bench, 1980. Trustee Bates Coll.; mem. Overseas Devel. Council. Served from ensign to lt. USNR, 1943-46. Mem. Am. Acad. Arts and Scis. Office: 156 Federal St Portland ME 04112

COFFIN, JOHN DEVEREUX, financial service company executive; b. Elko, Nev., Apr. 17, 1937; s. J. Reginald and M. Margaret (Thompson) C.; m. Anne Gagnebin, Apr. 7, 1962; children: Samuel D., Thomas H. B.A., Williams Coll., 1959. First v.p. Bache Halsey Stuart, N.Y.C., 1960-72; mng. dir. Bach & Co. Ltd., London, 1972-76; exec. v.p. Drexel Burnham Lambert Group Inc., N.Y.C., 1976—, dir.; vice chmn., dir. mem. exec. com. Commondity Exchange Inc., N.Y.C.; dir. Winchester Diversified Ltd., Bermuda, Winchester Internat. Ltd., Winchester Overseas Ltd. Clubs: Univ. (N.Y.C.); Rumson (N.J.) Country; Hurlingham (London). Home: 1192 Park Ave New York NY 10028 Office: Drexel Burnham Lambert Inc 60 Broad St New York NY 10004

COFFIN, JOSEPH JOHN, insurance company executive, business consultant; b. Indpls., Nov. 26, 1911; s. Joseph H. and Nona V. (Albright) C.; m. Marjorie M. Holcomb, Nov. 16, 1933; children—J. Robert, Joan Louise Coffin Close, William H. Student, DePauw U., 1929-31, Butler U., 1940-41. Sales and sales dist. mgr. J.B. Simpson Inc., Chgo., 1932-36; dist. rep. Alemite Sales Co., Chgo., 1936-38; agt., agy. supr. J.R. Townsend Agy. of Equitable Life Ins. of Iowa, Indpls., 1938-45; agy. mgr. Commonwealth Life Ins. Co. of Louisville, Indpls., 1945-48; sales mgr., v.p., gen. mgr., pres. J.I. Holcomb Mfg. Co., 1948-73; v.p. public relations Top Quality Chems. Co., Indpls., 1975—; chmn. bd. Mut. Hosp. Ins. Co., Inc. (Blue Cross of Ind.), Indpls., 1971—; bus. cons. Mem. adv. council Christian Theol. Sem., 1967—; bd. dirs. Suemma Coleman Home for Unwed Mothers, 1960-71, pres., 1970-71; bd. dirs. Found. for Religious Studies, 1970—. Served with USCG, 1942-45. Recipient Brotherhood citation NCCJ, 1965; honoree City of Hope, 1975. Mem. Chem. Spltys. Mfg. Assn. (bd. govs. 1962-71), Meridian Kessler Neighborhood Assn. Republican. Quaker. Clubs: Rotary (Indpls.) (pres. 1960-61); (dist. gov. 1973-74); Indpls. Athletic, Masons (32°) (Indpls.). Office: 120 W Market St Indianapolis IN 46204

COFFIN, LAURENCE EDMONDSTON, JR., landscape architect, urban planner; b. Toronto, Ont., Can., May 28, 1928; came to U.S., 1930; s. Laurence Edmondston and Josephine (Hewitt) C.; m. Beatriz deWinthuysen, Jan. 4, 1958; children: Thomas Amory, Alisa Winthuysen. B.S. in Hort., Va. Poly. Inst. and State U., 1952; M.L.A., Harvard U., 1957. Ptnr. Coffin & Winthuysen, East Lansing, Mich., 1962-65; asst. prof. Mich. State U., East Lansing, 1960-65; adj. assoc. prof. Cath. U. Am., Washington, 1966-81; ptnr. Coffin & Coffin, Washington, 1966—; mem. A/E select bd. Pa. Ave. Devel. Corp., Washington, 1978—; mem. design adv. panel DHCD, Balt., 1978—; sec. Internat. Inst. Site Planning, Washington, 1980—; lectr. city planning Georgetown U., 1968, George Washington U., 1973, U. Md., 1982; vis. evaluator Landscape Archtl. Accreditation Bd., 1979—. Elder Presbyterian Ch., Washington, 1977—. Fellow Am. Soc. Landscape Architects; mem. Am. Inst. Cert. Planners. Democrat. Home: 6351 31st St NW Washington DC 20015 Office: Coffin & Coffin 914 11th St NW Washington DC 20001

COFFIN, LOUIS FUSSELL, JR., mech. engr.; b. Schenectady, Aug. 30, 1917; s. Louis Fussell and Laura C. (Glen) C.; m. Mary Elizabeth McCarthy, Apr. 24, 1943; children—John, Sarah (Mrs. Joseph Fitzgerald), Laura (Mrs. Thomas Koch), Robert, Patricia (Mrs. Jeffrey Mullen), Deborah (Mrs. Patrick Higgins), Louis Fussell III, Margaret. B.S., Swarthmore (Pa.) Coll., 1939; Sc.D., Mass. Inst. Tech., 1949. From asst. to asst. prof. mech. engring. Mass. Inst. Tech., 1939-49; research asso., then supr. mech. metallurgy Knolls Atomic Power Lab., Gen. Electric Co., 1949-54, mech. engr. corporate research and devel., Schenectady, 1954—; adj. prof. mech. engring. Rensselaer Poly. Inst., Troy, N.Y., 1955-60, Union Coll., Schenectady, 1965—; vis. fellow Clare Hall Cambridge U., 1976. Author. Recipient Alfred E. Hunt award Am. Soc. Lubrication Engrs., 1958; award excellence Carborundum Co., 1974; Clayton lectr. Inst. Mech. Engrs., London, 1974; Coolidge fellow, 1974. Fellow ASME (Nadai award 1979), Am. Soc. Metals (Albert Sauveur Achievement award 1980), ASTM (chmn. E9 com. on fatigue 1974—, Dudley award 1975, award of merit 1978); mem. Nat. Acad. Engring., Am. Inst. Metall. Engrs. (Disting. Career award 1978), Sigma Xi, Pi Tau Sigma, Sigma Tau. Patentee in field. Home: 1178 Lowell Rd Schenectady NY 12308 Office: Corporate Research and Devel Gen Electric Co PO Box 8 Schenectady NY 12301

COFFIN, TRISTRAM, author, editor; b. Hood River, Oreg., July 25, 1912; s. Clarence Eugene and Lenora (Smith) C.; m. Margaret Avery, June 26, 1933; children: Lynne Coffin Cronyn, Stephen Avery. A.B., DePauw U., 1933. Reporter Indpls. Times, 1933-37; asst. to gov. Ind., 1937-41; with Office Facts and Figures, OWI, 1941-44; White House corr. CBS, 1945-47; newspaper columnist, 1948-51, free-lance writer and broadcaster, 1951—. Author: Washington Watch Newsletter, 1968-74; Author: Missouri Compromise, 1947, Your Washington, 1954, Not To The Swift, 1961, The Passion of the Hawks, 1964, Mine Eyes Have Seen the Glory, 1964, The Sex Kick, 1966, Senator Fulbright, 1966; editor: Washington Spectator, 1974—. Mem. P.E.N. Home: 5601 Warwick Pl Chevy Chase MD 20815 Office: P O Box 70023 Washington DC 20088 *The impelling drive of my life has been a thirst for information about man and his political institutions.*

COFFIN, WILLIAM SLOANE, JR., clergyman; b. N.Y.C., June 1, 1924; s. William Sloane and Catherine (Butterfield) C.; m. Eva Anna Rubinstein, Dec. 12, 1956 (div. 1968); children: Amy Elizabeth, Alexander Sloane, David Andrew; m. Harriet Gibney, 1969. Student, Yale Sch. Music, 1942-43, Union Theol. Sem., N.Y.C., 1949-50; B.A., Yale U., 1949, B.D., 1956; D.D. (hon.), Wesleyan U. With CIA, 1950-53; ordained to ministry Presbyn. Ch., 1956; acting chaplain Phillips Acad., 1956-57; chaplain Williams Coll., 1957-58; univ. chaplain Yale U., 1958-75; sr. minister Riverside Ch., N.Y.C., 1977—. Author sermons in books, 1962, Once to Every Man, 1977. Bd. dirs. Pres.'s Adv. Council Peace Corps, Operation Crossroads Africa, Am. Freedom of Residence Fund. Served with AUS, 1943-47. Recipient Conn. Valley B'nai B'rith award for Americanism. Office: Riverside Church Riverside Dr and 122d St New York NY 10027 *

COFFINDAFFER, CLARENCE LEE, librarian; b. Clarksburg, W.Va., Oct. 8, 1941; s. William Easter and Betty Ann (Hawkins) C.; m. Nancy Flynn, Mar. 23, 1966 (div.); children: Tabatha, Mary Margaret, Fritz. B.A. in Speech-English, Salem Coll., 1966; M.L.S., U. Pitts., 1972; postgrad., Wis. Adult Inst., 1973, W.Va. U., 1974. Librarian, asst. prof. Glenville (W.Va.) State Coll., 1975-76; dir., asst. prof. Alderson-Broaddus Coll., Philippi, W.Va., 1976-78; dir. Raleigh County Pub. Library, Beckley, W.Va., 1978-79; coordinator Kaiser Coal Co. Inc., Bellington, W.Va., 1979-81; state librarian S.D. State Library, Pierre, 1981—. Bd. dirs. Bibliographic Center for Research, Denver, 1981—; mem. adv. com. MINITEX, St. Paul, 1981—; v.p. Online Catalog Inc., Minn., N.D., S.D., 1983. Mem. Western Council State Librarians (sec.), ALA, Chief Officers State Library Agencies, Mountain Plains Library Assn., S.D. Library Assn., Alpha Psi Omega, Beta Phi Mu. Republican. Am. Baptist. Club: Pierre Players. Lodge: Elks. Office: 800 N Illinois St Pierre SD 57501

COFFMAN, EDWARD MCKENZIE, historian; b. Hopkinsville, Ky., Jan. 27, 1929; s. Howard Beverly and Mada (Wright) C.; m. Anne Nelson Rouse, June 30, 1955; children: Anne Wright, Lucia Page, Edward McKenzie. A.B., U. Ky., 1951, M.A., 1955, Ph.D. (So. Faculty fellow), 1959. Instr., asst. prof. Memphis State U., 1957-61; research asso. George C. Marshall Research Found., 1960-61; asst. prof., asso. prof., prof. history U. Wis., Madison, 1961—; Dwight D. Eisenhower vis. prof. Kans. State U., 1969-70; vis. prof. mil. history U.S. Mil. Acad., 1977-78; disting. vis. prof. USAF Acad., 1982-83; mem. adv. com. Dept. Army Mil. History Program, 1971-76; mem. Nat. Hist. Publs. and Records Commn., 1972-76. Author: The Hilt of the Sword: The Career of Peyton C. March, 1966, The War to End All Wars: The American Military Experience in World War I, 1968; editorial bd.: Mil. Affairs, 1974-77, Arno Press series The American Military Experience and The Friedrich W. vonSteuben Papers, 1977—. Served with U.S. Army, 1951-53. Recipient Outstanding Civilian Service medal Dept. Army, 1978; Guggenheim fellow, 1973-74; Harmon Lectr. U.S. Air Force Acad., 1976; Am. Philos. Soc. grantee, 1960. Mem. Am. Mil. Inst. (pres. 1983—), U.S. Commn. Mil. History (trustee), Orgn. Am. Historians, So. Hist. Soc., Inter-univ. Seminar on Armed Forces and Soc., Phi Beta Kappa. Democrat. Home: 5802 Anchorage Ave Madison WI 53705 Office: Dept History U Wis Madison WI 53706

COFFMAN, FRANKLIN E(DWARD), government agency administrator; b. Liverpool, Ky., Mar. 6, 1942; m. Elaine Hobbs, Feb. 22, 1963; 1 son, Christopher Michael. B.S. cum laude, Western Ky. U., 1964; M.A., cum laude, Vanderbilt U., 1966; Ph.D. cum laude, Vanderbilt U., 1970. Health physicist U.S. AEC, Oak Ridge, 1966-68; math. prof. Fisk U., 1969-70; dir. Fusion Technology div. Dept. of Energy, Germantown, Md., 1976-78, dir. Office of Coordination of Spl. Nuclear Projects, 1978-80, dep. asst. sec. for waste mgmt., 1980-82; dir. Office Terminal Waste Disposal and Remedial Action, Washington, 1983—. Mem. Am. Nuclear Soc. (v.p.), Sigma Xi. Home: 9412 Bethany Pl Gaithersburg MD 20879 Office: Office of Terminal Waste Disposal and Remedial Action US Dept Engergy Route 118 Germantown MD 20545

COFFMAN, JAY DENTON, physician, educator; b. Quincy, Mass., Nov. 17, 1928; s. Frank David and Etta (Kline) C.; m. Louise G. Peters, June 29, 1955; children: Geoffrey J., Joanne K., Linda J., Robert B. A.B., Harvard U., 1950; M.D., Boston U., 1954. Med. intern Univ. Hosp., Boston, 1954-55, asst. resident in medicine, 1955-56, chief resident in medicine, 1957-58, fellow in cardiovascular disease, 1956-57, sect. head peripheral vascular dept., 1960—; asso. in medicine Boston U. Med. Sch., 1960-65, mem. faculty, 1965—, prof. medicine, 1970—. Co-author: Ischemic Limbs, 1973. Trustee Solomon Carter Fuller Mental Health Center, Boston, 1975-81. Served to capt. M.C. USAR, 1958-60. Diplomate Am. Bd. Internal Medicine.; Mem. Am. Soc. Clin. Investigation, Am. Fedn. Clin. Research, Am. Physiol. Soc., Am. Heart Assn., A.C.P., Begg's Soc., Phi Beta Kappa, Alpha Omega Alpha. Office: 75 E Newton St Boston MA 02118

COFFMAN, PHILLIP HUDSON, university administrator; b. Lincoln, Nebr., Nov. 27, 1936; s. Rowland Francis and Elberta (Hudson) C.; m. Carolyn J. Nimmo, July 23, 1983; children by previous marriage: Phillip C., Catherine L. B.Mus. Edn., U. Nebr., 1958; M.Mus., U. Idaho, 1962; Ph.D., U. Toledo, 1971. Tchr. public schs., Rushville, Nebr., 1958-59; instr. Doane Coll., Crete, Nebr., 1959-60; teaching asst. U. Idaho, Moscow, 1960-62, instr., 1962-65; asso. prof., chmn. dept. music Jamestown (N.D.) Coll., 1965-68; adminstv. intern U. Toledo, 1968-71; asso. prof., head dept. music U. Minn., Duluth, 1971-76; prof., dean Sch. Fine Arts, 1976—; mem. Lincoln Symphony, 1954-60, Toledo Symphony, 1969-71; guest artist Ednl. TV; instr. Internat. Music Camp, 1967-68. Contbr. articles to profl. jours. Pres. Civic Music Assn., 1967, Campus Ministry Bd., 1972-75, Minn. Coll. and Univ. Council for Music, 1976; music adjudicator, interviewer Bush Leadership Fellows Program, 1977—; chmn. bd. Duluth Festival of Arts, 1979-81. F.E. Olds scholar, 1963; Bush Found. fellow, 1973. Mem. Internat. Council Fine Arts Deans, Theta Xi, Phi Mu Alpha, Pi Kappa Lambda, Kappa Kappa Psi. Home: 4601 Woodland Duluth MN 55803 Office: School Fine Arts U Minn Duluth MN 55812

COFFMAN, STANLEY KNIGHT, JR., educator, former college president; b. Huntington, W. Va., Dec. 30, 1916; s. Stanley Knight and Werneth (Brockmeyer) C.; m. Ann Channing Wrentmore, Dec. 27, 1942; children: Ann Channing, Stanley Knight III, Eric Ewing. A.B., Haverford Coll., 1939; M.A., Ohio State U., 1940, Ph.D., 1948. Part-time instr. English Ohio State U., 1946-48; faculty U. Okla., 1948-62, prof. English, 1956-62; asst. dean Univ. Coll., 1954-62; prof. English, chmn. dept. Bowling Green (Ohio) State, 1962-70; acting dean Grad. Sch., 1967-68, v.p. acad. affairs, 1968-70, provost, 1970; pres. SUNY, New Paltz, 1972-79, prof. English, Albany, 1979—. Author: Imagism, 1951; Contbr. articles to profl. jours. Served with AUS, 1942-46; lt. col. Res. Mem. MLA, Phi Beta Kappa, Omicron Delta Kappa. Presbyn. (past elder). Office: State Univ NY Albany NY 12203

COFFMAN, WILLIAM EUGENE, educational psychologist; b. Belington, W.Va., June 13, 1913; s. Walter E. and Mary (Thornhill) C.; m. Eloise Clarke, Dec. 21, 1939; children—Mary Eloise, Judith Ann Coffman Piche. Student, Potomac State Coll., Keyser, W.Va., 1930-32;

B.S. in Edn, Wittenberg U., 1934; M.A., W.Va. U., 1938; Ed.D., Columbia U., 1949. Tchr. Mineral County (W.Va.) Schs., 1934-37, prin., 1937-44; asso. prof. Okla. State U., 1949-52; asst. dir. test devel. div. Ednl. Testing Service, Princeton, N.J., 1952-54, asso. dir., 1954-57, dir., 1957-60; dir. research and devel. CEEB Program, 1960-66, research adviser, 1966-69; E.F; E.F. Lindquist prof. ednl. measurement, dir. Iowa testing program U. Iowa, Iowa City, 1969-81, prof. emeritus, 1981—; Vis. prof. edn. Syracuse U., 1966; vis. lectr. Princeton Theol. Sem., 1964-69; cons. Nat. Assessment Ednl. Progress, Systems Devel. Corp., Ford Found./Calif. Assessment Program. Author: (with Fred Godshalk, Frances Swineford) The Measurement of Writing Ability, 1966, Developing Tests for the Culturally Different, 1965; Editor: Frontiers of Educational Measurement and Information Systems, 1973, (with B. Randhawa) Visual Learning, Thinking and Communication, 1978; Contbr.: Educational Measurement, 2d edit. Served with U.S. Army, 1944-45. Recipient Alumni Achievement award Potomac State Coll. of W.Va. U., 1980. Fellow Am. Psychol. Assn.; mem. Am. Ednl. Research Assn., Nat. Council Measurement in Edn. (pres. 1972-73), Alpha Tau Omega. Home: Apt 406 201 N 1st Ave Iowa City IA 52240

COFFRIN, ALBERT WHEELER, judge; b. Burlington, Vt., Dec. 21, 1919; s. Morris Daniel and Florence Belle (Browe) C.; m. Elizabeth Ann MacCornack, May 14, 1943; children—Peter S., Albert W., III, James W., Nancy (Mrs. Michael G. Furlong). A.B., Middlebury Coll., 1941; LL.B., Cornell U., 1947. Bar: Vt. bar 1948. Mem. firm Black & Wilson, Burlington, 1947-51, 52-56, Black, Wilson, Coffrin & Hoff, 1956-60; partner Coffrin & Pierson, 1962-68, Coffrin, Pierson & Affolter, 1968-72; judge U.S. Dist. Ct., Dist. of Vt., 1972—. Trustee Middlebury Coll. Served with USN, 1942-45, 51-52; to comdr. Res., 1952-66. Fellow Am. Bar Found.; mem. Am., Vt., Chittenden County bar assns., Phi Delta Phi, Kappa Delta Rho. Republican. Unitarian. Club: Burlington Tennis. Office: Box 522 Burlington VT 05402

COGAN, DAVID GLENDENNING, physician, educator; b. Fall River, Mass., Feb. 14, 1908; s. James Joseph and Edith (Ives) C.; m. Frances Capps, July 14, 1934; children—Christy (dec.), Frances, Ann, Priscilla. A.B., Dartmouth, 1929, med. student, 1930-31; M.D., Harvard, 1932, 1937-38. Intern U. Chgo. Clinics, 1931-32; resident Mass. Eye and Ear Infirmary, Boston, 1932-34, asso. surgeon, 1943-54, surgeon, 1954-60, chief ophthalmology, 1963-68; practiced medicine, Boston, 1934-73; dir. Howe Lab. Ophthalmology, Harvard, 1940-74, asso. prof. ophthalmic research, 1943—; prof. ophthalmology Harvard Med. Sch., 1955—, chmn. dept., 1963-68, Henry Willard Williams prof., 1963-70, emeritus, 1974—; now chief neuro-ophthalmic sect. Nat. Eye Inst., 1974—; Mem. council Nat. Inst. Neurologic Diseases and Blindness, Council Nat. Eye Inst., NIH. Author: Neurology of the Ocular Muscles, 1946, rev. edit., 1958, Neurology of the Visual System, 1966, Ophthalmic Manifestations of Systematic Vascular Disease, 1974; Editor-in-chief: Archives of Ophthalmology, 1960-66; cons. editor, 1966-70; mem. editorial bd.: Graefes Archiv für Ophthalmologie, 1972-81. Recipient Warren Triennial prize Mass. Gen. Hosp., 1944; Proctor award, 1954; Knapp prize A.M.A., 1955; Howe medal Am. Ophthal. Soc., 1965; Research to Prevent Blindness award, 1969; Gonin Medal, 1974; Vail award, 1976; Ophthalmic Pathology Labs. named in his honor Mass. Eye and Ear Infirmary, 1983. Mem. Am. Acad. Arts and Sci., Am. Ophthal. Soc., Am. Soc. Clin. Research, Nat. Soc. Prevention Blindness (dir.); hon. mem. Can. Ophthal. Soc., Irish Ophthal. Soc., Japanese Ophthal Soc. Club: Cosmos. Home: 4713 Trent Ct Chevy Chase MD 20815 Office: Bldg 10 Room 6C401 NIH Bethesda MD 20205

COGAN, DAVID HAROLD, corporate executive; b. nr. Barton, Vt., Jan. 10, 1909; s. Bened and Annie (Grant) C.; m. Martha Sharp, 1957; 1 son, Bruce M. Student, Northeastern U., 1926-30. Sales engr. Hytron Corp., Salem, Mass., 1930, sales mgr., 1931; pres., dir. Air King Products Co., Inc., Bklyn., 1946-54, Royal Wood Products Co., Inc., 1946-54, King Assos., Inc., 1946-54, CBS-Columbia, Inc., 1951-54, Seymour Chevrolet Sales, Inc., 1954-67, Continental Discount Fund, Inc., 1955-64, Tri-Continental Realty Corp., 1960-67, Victoreen Instrument Co., 1957-74; pres. treas., dir. D.H. Cogan, Inc., 1952-65, Pathe Radio Corp., 1942-54, Ravac Electronics Corp., 1942-57, Continental Holding Corp., 1954-61; v.p. dir. Hytron Radio & Electronics Corp., 1931-54, CBS, Inc., 1951-54, CBS-Hytron, 1951-54; treas., dir. Atlantic Realty, Inc., 1952-57, Continental Holding Corp., 1954-61; dir. Premier Microwave, 1963-83; chmn. bd. Mirawal Corp., 1955-56, VLN Corp., 1955-74, Phaostron Instrument & Electronic Co., 1966-69, Bohn Bus. Machines, Inc., 1964-68, Colonial Press, Inc., 1967-74, Dreyfus Consumer Bank, 1982—, Dreyfus Life Ins. Co., 1982—; chmn. bd., pres. Nuclear Electronics Ohio, Inc., 1955-59; vice chmn. bd., dir. Sheller-Globe Corp., 1974—; pres., treas., dir. D.H.C. Inc., 1967-79, Natick Corp., 1973—; dir., chmn. exec. com. Estey Organ Co., 1956-64; dir. Dreyfus Tax Exempt Bond Fund, Inc., Dreyfus Tax Exempt Money Market Fund, Inc., The Dreyfus Corp. Vice pres., sec., dir. L. Peter Cogan Found.; pres., treas., dir. David H. Cogan Found.; bd. dirs., trustee Northeastern U.; bd. dirs. Nat. Energy Found.; trustee Nat. Commn. for Coop. Edn.; chmn. bd. Am. Council for Nationalities Service. Mem. N.A.M., Radio Electronic TV Mfrs. Assn. Clubs: Stamford Yacht; Princeton (N.Y.C.). Home: 70 W Hill Rd Stamford CT 06902 Office: 18 E 80th St New York NY 10021 also 1505 Jefferson Ave Toledo OH 43697

COGAN, DAVID JOSEPH, theatrical producer; b. Rumania, July 24, 1923; came to U.S., 1923, naturalized, 1928; s. Morris and Helen (Meyers) C.; m. Ferne Cogan, 1946; children: Sharon Ann, Carol Lynn. B.B.S., St. John's U., 1945. Owner legitimate theatre Biltmore Theatre, N.Y.C., 1960—, Eugene O'Neill Theatre, 1964—, Plaza Theatre, Viking Theatre, Phila., Doric Apts., Union City, N.J., Churchill Apts., White Plains, N.Y.; partner firm Cogan, Bell & Co., N.Y.C., 1955—; pres. David J. Cogan Agy., Inc. (theatrical agy. and mgmt. firm), N.Y.C., 1955-; bus. mgr. numerous theatrical notables, 1956—; tchr. prodn. and theatrical mgmt. New Sch. Social Research Grad. Sch., 1971; pres. Cogan Mgmt., Inc., 1968—. Producer: film Run Across the River, 1954; stage plays A Raisin in the Sun, 1958, Midnight Sun, 1959, In the Counting House, 1961, Does the Tiger Wear a Necktie; co-producer: stage play Odd Couple, 1965; (Recipient Critics award for A Raisin in the Sun, 1959, TV Emmy award 1970); Contbr. articles to mags. Treas., mem. bd. Family Inst., N.Y.C., 1961—; chmn. legitimate theatre sect. N.Y. chpt. A.R.C., 1964—; Bd. dirs. Young Childrens Music Sch. and Dance, N.Y.C., 1959—, Berkshire Theatre Festival, Eugene O'Neill Found. Mem. Nat. Soc. Pub. Accountants, Actors Studio (bd. dirs.), League N.Y. Theatres, N.Y. Theatre Owners Assn. Office: 350 Fifth Ave New York NY 10118

COGAN, EDWARD J., educator, author; b. Milw., Jan. 18, 1925; s. Leo J. and Elizabeth (Berman) C.; m. Frances Bernstein, Aug. 3, 1947; 1 dau., Deborah. B.A., U. Wis., 1946, M.A., 1948; Ph.D., Pa. State U., 1955. Instr. math. Pa. State U., 1948-55, Dartmouth, 1955-57; mathematician IBM Corp., summer 1957; mem. faculty sci. and math. Sarah Lawrence Coll., 1957; dir. Inst. Sci. and Math. Tchrs., 1958-62; co-dir. Upward Bound summer residence program, 1966-70, Office Spl. Programs, 1974-78. Author: A Formalization of the Theory of Sets from the Point of View of Combinatory Logic, 1955, Foundations of Analysis, 1962, also articles. Mem. Math. Assn. Am., Assn. Symbolic Logic, AAUP. Home: 1 Wilgarth Rd Bronxville NY 10708

COGAN, JAMES RICHARD, lawyer; b. Jersey City, Jan. 31, 1928; s. Frank and Lillian (Blankley) C.; m. Arrial Seelye, May 14, 1955; children—Sarah, George, Julia. B.A., Yale U., 1950; LL.B., Columbia U., 1953. Bar: N.Y. bar 1954. Assoc. firm Sullivan & Cromwell, N.Y.C., 1953-57, Alexander & Green, 1957-62, ptnr., 1962—; trustee, treas. Bunbury Co., Inc.; pres., dir. S. Forest Co., Inc. Bd. dirs. The Village Nursing Home, N.Y.C., Am. Friends of Plantin-Moretus Mus., in Antwerp; trustee, pres. Windham Found., Grafton, Vt.; trustee Charlotte Palmer Phillips Found.; bd. dirs. Corp. for Relief of Widows and Children of Clergymen, Aging in Am., Inc.; mem. choir sch. com. St. Thomas Ch. Served with U.S. Army, 1946-47. Assoc. Knight St. John of Jerusalem. Mem. ABA, N.Y. County Lawyers Assn., Am. Coll. Probate Counsel, N.Y.C. Bar Assn. Episcopalian. Clubs: Salmagundi Artists, Yale. Home: 43 Fifth Ave New York NY 10003 Office: 299 Park Ave New York NY 10171

COGAN, JOHN FRANCIS, JR., lawyer; b. Boston, June 13, 1926; s. John Francis and Mary (Galligan) C.; m. Mary T. Hart, May 1, 1951; children: Peter G., Pamela E., Jonathan C., Gregory M. A.B. cum laude, Harvard U., 1949, LL.B., 1952. Bar: Mass. 1953. Since practiced in, Boston; ptnr. firm Hale and Dorr, 1957-80, mng. ptnr., 1976—; pres. Pioneer Fund, Inc., Boston, 1963—, Pioneer Group, Inc., 1963—, Pioneering Mgmt. Corp., 1963, Pioneer II, Inc., 1969—, Pioneer Bond Fund, 1978—, Pioneer Three, Inc., 1983—; dir. Seatrain Lines, Inc., 1959-65; sec. Cabot, Cabot & Forbes Co., 1963-72, Ritz-Carlton Hotel Co., Boston, 1964-79; corporator Boston 5 Savs. Bank, 1961-79; chmn. exec. com., dir. Pioneer Western Corp., 1968-79; sr. v.p., dir. Western Res. Life Assurance Co., Ohio, 1968-79; dir. Scandia Trading Co., Inc. Treas. Lexington (Mass.) Counseling Service, 1964-69; chmn. bd. trustees Univ. Hosp., Boston, 1965—; Treas. Friends of Harvard Track, 1964-66; mem. Lexington Capital Expenditures Com., 1967-73; Mem. Mass. Democratic State Com., 1968-80; Bd. dirs. Wendell P. Clark Meml. Assn., Walker Home for Children, Brigham Surg. Found.; trustee Boston U. Med. Center; bd. govs. Investment Co. Inst., 1971-74, 75, 81, 82, chmn. bd. govs., 1978-80. Served with USNR, 1944-46. Mem. Internat., Am., Inter-Am., Mass., Boston bar assns., Boston Estate and Bus. Planning Council (past pres.), Boston Probate and Estate Planning Forum (sec. 1958-73), Nat. Assn. Security Dealers (gov. 1983—). Home: 29 Patterson Rd Lexington MA 02173 office: 60 State St Boston MA 02109

COGAN, MARSHALL S., textile executive; b. Boston, 1937. Grad., Harvard U., 1959, M.B.A., 1962. With Carter Berlind Weill, 1962-67; vice chmn. Cogan Gerland Weill & Levitt, 1968-71, CBWL Hayden-Stone, 1973; co-founder M C Corp., 1974; chmn. bd. Southwing Mgmt. Corp.; chmn. bd., dir. Gen. Felt Industries, Inc., Saddle Brook, N.J. Address: Gen Felt Industries Inc Park 80 Plaza W One Saddle Brook NJ 07662 *

COGAN, ROBERT DAVID, composer; b. Detroit, Feb. 2, 1930; s. Leon and Merrium (Gottschalk) C.; m. Pozzi Escot, July 1, 1959. B.Mus. with distinction, U. Mich., 1951, M. Mus., 1952; student composition, Berkshire Music Center, 1953; M.F.A., Princeton U., 1956; composition, Staatliche Hochschule für Musik in Hamburg, Germany, 1958-60. Teaching asst. theory and composition U. Mich., 1951-52; teaching asst. music Princeton, 1954-55; participant Salzburg (Austria) Seminar Am. Studies, 1950, European Cultural Found., Copenhagen, Denmark, 1961; lectr., vis. cultural affairs office USIA, Bonn, Germany, 1960-61; pvt. teaching composition, N.Y.C., 1961-63; chmn. theoretical studies New Eng. Conservatory Music, 1963-68, chmn. grad. theoretical studies, 1968—; program head, mem. Eastern regional exec. bd. Inst. for Music in Contemporary Edn., 1966-69; guest composer Berkshire Music Center, 1968; lectr. 1st internat. seminar Composers N. and S. Am., Ind. U., 1965, USIS and Peruvian Ministry of Culture Invitational, Lima, 1972; Mem. Ford Found.-Music Educators Nat. Conf. panel on teaching composition, theory, music history in the univ., 1965; participant Internat. Music Festival and Congress, Yugoslavia, 1972. Composer: Fantasia for Orchestra, 1951, Songs on Texts by Ezra Pound, 1952-54, Two Compositions for String Trio, 1956-59, Sounds, and variations for Piano, 1959-61, Spaces and Cries for Five Brasses, 1962- 64; performed, Jordan Hall, Boston, 1965, Whirl. . .ds I, 1967, Whirl. . .ds II: red allen hock ct, 1969, Whirl. . .ds I & II: no attack of organic metals, 1973, dr. faustroll, thinking, 1975, utterances, 1978, algebra and mornings, 1981; contexts memories, 1982; Author: (with Pozzi Escot) Sonic Design: The Nature of Sound and Music, 1972; author: Sonic Design: Practice and Problems, 1979, New Images of Musical Sound, 1983; Contbr. (with Pozzi Escot) articles to profl. jours. Recipient Young Composers Radio award Broadcast Music, Inc., 1952; Fulbright scholar, Brussels, Belgium, 1952-53; Chopin scholar in composition Kosciuszko Found., 1954; fellow MacDowell Colony, 1958, 62-65; German Govt. grantee for study in Hamburg, 1958-59, 59-60; fellow European Cultural Found., 1960, Reemstsma Found., Hamburg, 1960-61; Paderewski Fund commn. for symphonic work, 1964-65; Guggenheim fellow, 1968-69. Mem. Internat. Soc. Contemporary Music (dir. U.S. sect.), Phi Beta Kappa. Home: 24 Avon Hill St Cambridge MA 02140 Office: 290 Huntington Ave Boston MA 02115

COGBURN, EDMUND LEWIS, lawyer; b. Okeene, Okla., Feb. 28, 1932; s. Beryl L. and Gladys I (Shirley) C.; m. Marilyn Bailey, May 29, 1954; 1 son, Brian Evan. Student, Bartlesville Jr. Coll., 1948-49, Edinburgh Regional Coll., 1949-50; B.B.A. with honors, U. Tex., 1952, LL.B., 1954. Bar: Tex. bar 1954. Practiced in, San Antonio, 1956-58, Houston, 1958—, asst. atty. gen., state of Tex., 1954; mem. firm Remy and Burns, 1956-58; asso. firm Dow and Dow, 1958-62; partner firm Dow, Cogburn and Friedman, 1962—; Adj. prof. law U. Houston, 1966, 71-73; Vice pres. Tex. Bill of Rights Found., Houston, 1972-73. State Democratic committeeman Senatorial Dist. 13, Harris County, Tex., 1974—; chmn. Harris County Delegation to State Dem. Conv., 1966. Served to 1st lt. Mil. Police Corps AUS, 1954-56. Mem. ABA, Tex. Bar Assn., Houston Bar Assn. (mem. continuing legal edn. com. 1972-76), Tex. Assn. Cert. Civil Trial Specialists (pres. Houston chpt.), Houston Jr. C. of C. (chmn. com. on pub. affairs 1959-60), Order of Coif, Phi Delta Phi. Democrat. Mem. Methodist Episcopal Ch. Club: Mason. Home: 5002 Doliver Dr Houston TX 77056 Office: 2300 Coastal Tower Houston TX 77046

COGGAN, FREDERICK DONALD, former archbishop of Canterbury; b. London, Eng., Oct. 9, 1909; s. Cornish Arthur and Fanny Sarah (Chubb) C.; m. Jean Braithwaite Strain, Oct. 17, 1935; children—Dorothy Ann, Ruth Evelyn. B.A., St. John's Coll., Cambridge U., 1931, M.A., 1935; student, Wycliffe Hall, Oxford, 1934; B.D., U. Toronto, 1941; D.D. (hon.), Wycliffe Coll., Toronto, Can., 1944; Lambeth D.D., U. Leeds, 1958, Cambridge (Eng.) U., 1962, U. Aberdeen, Saskatoon, Huron, Tokyo, Hull, 1963, U. Manchester, 1972, Moravian Theol. Sem., 1976; H.H.D., Westminster Choir Coll., Princeton, 1966, D.Litt., 1967; S.T.D., Gen. Theol. Sem., 1967; LL.D., Liverpool U., 1972; D.C.L., Kent U., 1975; D.Univ., U. York, 1975, King's Coll., London, 1975. Ordained to ministry Ch. of Eng., 1934; asst. lectr. Semitic langs. and lit. Manchester U., 1931-34; curate St. Mary, Islington, London, 1934-37; prof. N.T. Wycliffe Coll., Toronto, 1937-44; prin. London Coll. Div., 1944-56, bishop of Bradford, 1956-61, archbishop of York, 1961-74, archbishop of Canterbury, 1974-80; chmn. Coll. of Preachers.; Prelate Order St. John Jerusalem, 1967—. Created baron of Canterbury and Sissinghurst, 1980; Author: A People's Heritage, 1944, The Ministry of the Word, 1945, The Glory of God, 1950, Stewards of Grace, 1958, Five Makers of the New Testament, 1962, Christian Priorities, 1963, The Prayers of the New Testament, 1967, Sinews of Faith, 1969, Word and World, 1971, Convictions, 1975, On Preaching, 1978, Great Words of the Christian Faith, 1978, Sure Foundation, 1981. Address: Kingshead House Sissinghurst Kent England

COGGESHALL, PETER COLLIN, paper products mfg. co. exec.; b. Darlington, S.C., Sept. 22, 1915; s. Robert Werner and Mary Beulah (Walden) C.; m. Rosanne Howard, Jan. 24, 1942; children—Peter Collin, Rosanne Howard. A.B., U. S.C., 1936; M.B.A., Harvard U., 1938. Research staff Harvard U., 1938-39; with Sonoco Products Co., Hartsville, S.C., 1939—, v.p., 1961-76, exec. v.p., 1976—, also dir.; dir. Sonoco Internat. Co. Trustee McLeod Regional Med. Center, Florence, S.C., Coker Coll., Hartsville, S.C. Served as officer AUS, 1943-45. Mem. Phi Beta Kappa, Omicron Delta Kappa, Alpha Tau Omega. Presbyterian. Clubs: Damon Gun, Rotary. Home: 547 Lakeshore Dr Hartville SC 29550 Office: Sonoco Products Co 2d St Hartsville SC 29550

COGGIN, WALTER ARTHUR, clergyman; b. Richmond, Va., Feb. 10, 1916; s. Walter Arthur and Mary Veronica (Moshy) C. Student, Belmont (N.C.) Abbey Jr. Coll., 1934-36, Belmont Abbey Sem., 1939-43; A.B., St. Benedict's Coll., Atchison, Kan., 1939; postgrad, U. N.C., 1942; M.A., Cath. U., 1948, Ph.D., 1954. Became Benedictine monk, 1936; ordained priest Roman Catholic Ch., 1943; vicar Belmont Abbey Monastery, 1956-60; abbot-ordinary of Belmont Abbey Nullius, 1960-70; tchr. philosophy Belmont Abbey Coll., 1970—; Mem. 2d Vatican Council, 1962-65. Mem. N.C. Philos. Soc. (pres. 1955-56), Am. Cath. Philos. Assn. Address: Belmont Abbey Belmont NC 28012

COGGINS, HOMER DALE, hospital administrator; b. Ashdown, Ark., July 19, 1922; s. John Homer and Iola Mae (Turner) C.; m. Dorothy Ann Murrell, Mar. 12, 1944; children: Frank Edward, Carolyn Ruth, Cathy Ann. Student, Southeastern State Coll., Durant, Okla., 1951; B.S., Okla. Bapt. U., 1953, cert. hosp. adminstrn., 1954; LL.D. (hon.), Georgetown Coll., 1980. Partner, Hugo Tobacco & Candy Co., Okla., 1946-50; adminstrv. resident Wesley Hosp., Oklahoma City, 1954, asst. adminstr., 1954-55; adminstr. Central Bapt. Hosp., Lexington, Ky., 1955-65; exec. v.p. Ky. Bapt. Hosp., Louisville, 1965-73; asst. to pres. Bapt. Hosps., Inc., Louisville, 1973-74, pres., 1974—. Pres. Hugo City Council, 1948-50. Served to capt. AUS, World War II. Recipient Outstanding Alumnus award Okla. Bapt. U., 1976. Fellow Am. Coll. Hosp. Adminstrs. (regent from Ky. 1975-77); mem. Lexington Hosp. Council (pres. 1958), Met. Louisville Hosp. Council (pres. 1967), Ky. Hosp. Assn. (pres. 1961-62), Am. Hosp. Assn. (ho. of dels. 1964-76). Republican. Baptist (deacon). Clubs: Rotarian., Filson. Home: 2651 Cherokee Pky Louisville KY 40204 Office: 768 Barret Ave Louisville KY 40204

COGGINS, JACK BANHAM, author, artist; b. London, July 10, 1914; U.S., 1923, naturalized, 1943; s. Sidney George and Ethel May (Dobby) C.; m. Alma Woods, Jan. 15, 1948. Student, Grand Central Sch. Art, 1931-33, Art League, 1933-34. Mem. faculty art dept. Hunter Coll., N.Y.C., 1948-53; instr. fine arts Wyomissing (Pa.) Inst. Fine Arts, 1959—; Mem. adv. bd. Phila. Maritime Mus., 1968—. Free-lance comml. artist doing work for, Life mag., U.S. Steel, Elec. Boat Co., Brown & Bigelow, others, 1940-53; author, illustrator, 1957—; represented in permanent collections, U.S. Navy, U.S. Coast Guard, NOAA, Phila. Maritime Mus., Reading (Pa.) Public Mus. and Art Gallery, Am. Def. Preparedness Assn., banks, corps., also pvt. collections.; Author, illustrator: Illustrated Book of Knights, 1957, Arms and Equipment of Civil War, 1962, Horsemen of World, 1963, Flashes and Flags, 1963, Nets Overboard, 1965, Hydrospace, 1966, Horseman's Bible, 1966, The Fighting Man, 1966, By Star and Compass, 1967, Prepare to Dive, 1971, Boys in Revolution, 1967, Ships and Seamen of American Revolution, 1969, The Campaign for Guadalcanal, 1972, Campaign for North Africa, 1980, Marine Painter's Guide, 1983. Served with AUS, 1943-45; ETO. Recipient Am. Revolution Round Table award for best book on Am. Revolution, 1969. Mem. Am. Def. Preparedness Assn., U.S. Naval Inst. Address: PO Box 57 Boyertown PA 19512 *Having found long ago that no form of endeavor comes easily to me, I have developed a capacity for hard work, preceded by painstaking preparation and research. Despite the widespread acceptance of modern slap-dash methods, I can recommend the above approach to any would-be artist.*

COGGINS, WILMER JESSE, physician, colledge adminstrator; b. Madison, Fla., Feb. 20, 1925; s. Wilmer Jesse and Audrey (Walker) C.; m. Deborah Ferne Reed, Apr. 16, 1949; children: Pamela, Deborah, Wilmer Jesse, Audrey Ann, Christopher. M.D., Duke U., 1951. Intern Georgetown U. Med. Ctr., Washington, 1951-52; resident U. Fla. Coll. Medicine, Gainesville, 1960-62, instr. internal medicine, 1962-63, asst. prof., 1963-67, assoc. prof., 1967-73, prof., 1975-80, U. Md., College Park, 1974-75; dean Coll. Community Health Scis. U. Ala., Tuscaloosa, 1980—. Author: (with W.E. Carter) Cannabis in Costa Rico, 1980. Served to 1st lt. U.S. Army, 1944-46. Recipient Fla. Blue Key, 1971, Hon. Physicians Asst. award U. Fla. Coll. Medicine, 1976. Fellow Am. Coll. Health Assn. (pres. 1974-75, Ruth C. Boynton award 1976); mem. Med. Assn. State Ala., AMA, Tuscaloosa County Med. Soc., Nat. Rural Primary Care Assn. (exec. com. 1978-81). Democrat. Presbyterian. Club: North River Yacht (Tuscaloosa). Home: 28 Edwardian Pl Northport AL 35476 Office: College of Community Health Scis. PO Box 6291 University AL 35486

COGSWELL, ARNOLD, financial management executive; b. Albany, N.Y., Feb. 15, 1924; s. Ledyard, Jr. and Dorothy Treat (Arnold) C.; m. Jessie Batcheller, July 11, 1953; children—Arnold, Jessie Jackson, Elizabeth Ledyard. B.A., Yale, 1950. Treas. Aird Island Inc., Albany, 1949—, pres., 1954—; chmn. bd. Pitts. Tube Co. Trustee, chmn. Albany Med. Center, Inc.; gov., treas. Union U.; trustee Rensselaer Poly. Inst.; chmn., pres., trustee Iroquois Hosp. Consortium; pres., treas. Albany's Hosp. for Incurables; trustee, chmn. Hosp. Trustees of N.Y. State. Served with AUS, 1943-46. Fellow, Calhoun Coll. Home: 99 Old Niskayuna Rd Loudonville NY 12211 Office: 54 State St Room 800 Albany NY 12207

COGSWELL, DOROTHY MCINTOSH, artist, educator; b. Plymouth, Mass., Nov. 13, 1909; d. Clarence H. and Ruth (McIntosh) C. B.F.A., Yale U., 1933, M.F.A., 1939. Instr. Mt. Holyoke Coll., 1939-44, asst. prof., asso. prof., 1947-59, prof., 1959-74, chmn. dept. art, 1960-69, dir. art collection, 1970-74, prof. emeritus, 1974—. One-woman shows, G.W.V. Smith Mus., Springfield, One man shows, Albany Inst. History and Art, U. Mass., Elmira Coll., Rutgers U., others, retrospective exhbn., Mt. Holyoke Art Mus., 1974; exhibited group shows, N.Y. World's Fair, N.Y. Watercolor Soc., Conn. Acad., New Haven Paint and Clay Club; represented in permanent collections, Springfield Mus. Fine Arts, Newport Assn., Holyoke Mus., murals, Mt. Holyoke Coll. Recipient 1st watercolor prize Eastern States, 1941; purchase award Holyoke Bicentennial, 1976; Fulbright lectr. Nat. Art. Sch., Sydney, Australia, 1957-58. Mem. Springfield Art League (pres. 1942-43), Mt. Holyoke Friends of Art (chmn. 1947-60), Art League Manatee County (v.p. 1981-83), Ringling Museums. Congregationalist. Home: 3860 Ironwood Ln Apt 402 Bradenton FL 33529

COGSWELL, FREDERICK WILLIAM, educator, poet, editor; b. East Centreville, N.B., Can., Nov. 8, 1917; s. Walter Scott and Florence (White) C.; m. Margaret Hynes, July 3, 1944; children—Carmen Patricia Cogswell Robinson (dec.), Kathleen Mary Cogswell Forsythe. B.A. with honors, U. N.B., 1949, M.A., 1951; Ph.D. (Imperial Order Daus. Empire fellow), U. Edinburgh, Scotland, 1952; LL.D. (hon.), St. Francis Xavier U., 1982. Instr. to asso. prof. dept. English U. N.B., Fredericton, 1952-64, prof., 1964-83, prof. emeritus, 1983—. Editor: The Fiddlehead, 1952-66, Humanities Assn. Bull, 1967-72; publisher: Fiddlehead Poetry Books, 1956—; Author: poetry The Stunted Strong, 1954, The Haloed Tree, 1957, Descent From Eden, 1959, Lost Dimension, 1960, Star People, 1968, Immortal Plowman, 1969, In Praise of Chastity, 1970, The Chains of Liliput, 1971, The House Without A Door, 1973, Light Bird of Life, 1974, Against Perspectives, 1977; collected poems A Long Apprenticeship, 1980, Selected Poems, 1982, Pearls, 1983; translator: The Testament of Cresseid, 1958, One Hundred Poems of Modern Quebec, 1970, 71, A Second Hundred Poems of Modern Quebec, 1971, The Poetry of Modern Quebec, 1976, Confrontation, 1973; Author: The Complete Poems of Emile Welligan, 1983; translator: anthologies Five New Brunswick Poets, 1961, (with W.S. MacNutt and Robert Tweedie) The Arts in New Brunswick, 1967, (with Thelma Reid Lower) The Enchanted Land, 1968, One Hundred Poems of Modern Quebec, A Second Hundred Poems of Modern Quebec, The Poetry of Modern Quebec; Contbr. poems, articles to profl. jours. Mem. sr. arts fellowship awards com. Can. Council, 1972, mem. centennial poetry awards com., 1968; mem. Leave fellowship awards bd. humanities sect., 1973, 74; mem. poetry sect. Gov. Gen.'s award bd., 1973, chmn., 1974; bd. dirs. Can. Found., 1983—. Served with Canadian Army, 1940-45. Decorated Order of Can.; Recipient Bliss Carman medal for poetry, 1946, 47; Douglas Gold medal, 1949; Gold medal for service to poetry as magazine editor Republic of Philippines, 1965; Gold medal as distinguished poet, 1965; Nuffield fellow, 1959-60; Can. Council Sr. fellow, 1967-68. Mem. League Canadian Poets (regional exec. 1973-80, hon. life mem.), Canadian Authors Assn., Internat. P.E.N., Assn. Can. Pubs. (hon. life), Ind. Pubs. Assn., Atlantic Pubs. Assn. (pres. 1979-80), Assn. Can. and Que. Lits. (pres. 1978-80). Home: 769 Reid St Fredericton NB Canada E3B 3V8 *Anything I have accomplished has come about because it has been very easy for me to work hard at anything in which I have been interested and I have been interested in a good many things.*

COGSWELL, GLENN DALE, lawyer; b. nr. Kingman, Kans., Feb. 1, 1922; s. Carl Clifford and Susie (Schisler) C.; children (by previous marriage): Carolyn, David; m. Judith Hahn; children: Michael Christian, Dia Michelle, Niki Lyn, Shea Lara. Student, U. Kans., 1940; A.B., Washburn U., 1943, LL.B., 1947, J.D., 1969. Bar: Kans. bar 1947. Since practiced in, Topeka; judge Ct. of Topeka, 1949-51, Shawnee County Probate and Juvenile Cts., 1951-57; ptnr. Goodell, Casey Briman & Cogswell, 1965-78, Cogswell, Storey, Green & Chubb, 1979—; State chmn. Kans. Young Republican Fedn., 1955-57; del. Rep. Nat. Conv., 1956; Rep. nominee lt. gov. Kans., 1958. Served to lt. (j.g.) USNR, 1943-46. Recipient Distinguished Service award Kan. Jr. C. of C., 1955, DeMolay Legion of Honor, 1956. Mem. ABA, Kans. Bar Assn., Topeka Bar Assn. (pres. 1981-82), Am. Coll. Probate Counsel, Am. Legion, Native Sons Kans. (past pres.), Kans. Probate Judges Assn. (past pres.), Phi Delta Theta, Delta Theta Phi. Episcopalian. Club: Mason (Shriner). Home: 2929 SW Lagito Dr Topeka KS 66614 Office: Shadow Wood Office Park 5863 SW 29th St Topeka KS 66614

COHAGEN, CHANDLER CARROLL, architect; b. nr. Sioux City, Iowa, Apr. 24, 1889; s. John and Mary Frances (Turner) C.; m. Flora Brown, Sept. 18, 1917. B.S. in Architecture, U. Mich., Ann Arbor, 1915. Pvt. archtl. practice, Billings, Mont., 1915-42, 45—; chief architect U.S. Ordnance Plant, Eau Claire, Wis., 1942-43, Muscatine, Iowa, 1943-45; past pres. Mont. Bd. Archtl. Examiners; pres. Nat. Council Archtl. Registration Bds., 1962. Alderman City of Billings, 1936. Fellow AIA (past pres. Mont. chpt., Scholastic medal 1915), Internat. Inst. Arts and Letters; life mem. Am. Soc. Heating and Ventilating Engrs.; mem. Billings C. of C. (past pres.), Alpha Rho Chi (founder), Delta Phi. Republican. Mem. Christian Ch. (Disciples of Christ). Clubs: Masons (grand master), DeMolay (treas. internat. supreme council). Address: 19 Burlington Ave Billings MT 59101

COHAN, GEORGE SHELDON, advt. and pub. relations exec.; b. Oak Park, Ill., May 30, 1924; s. Charles and Ann (Holt) C.; m. Natalie Holmes, Dec. 14, 1974; children—Barry, Gail, Charles, Victoria. Student, Colo. Sch. Mines, 1941-42, Ind. U., 1942-43; B.S. in Mech. Engring, U. Cin., 1948; postgrad., John Marshall Law Sch., 1954-56. Certified bus. communicator. Field engr. Indsl. Erectors, Inc., Chgo., 1948-50; sales engr. Fairbanks-Morse & Co., Chgo., 1950-56; v.p., account supr. Hoffman & York Advt. Agy., Milw., 1956-62, Tobias & Olendorf, Chgo., 1962-65; sr. v.p., gen. mgr. Bozell & Jacobs, Inc., Chgo., 1965-74; chmn. bd., pres. Cohan & Paul, Inc., Chgo., 1975; dir. Forest Labs., N.Y.C., Universal Gift Cert., Inc. Author: play Black Mutiny, 1948; Contbr. articles to profl. jours. Mem. Central Ind. council Boy Scouts Am., 1965-69; mem. exec. com. March of Dimes, 1965-69, ANTA, 1948-51. Served to 1st lt. C.E. AUS, 1943-45; CBI. Recipient Outstanding Merit award 8th Pan Am. Ry. Congress, 1954; 1st pl. Nat. Lithographic Soc., 1955; 15th ann. G.D. Crain award, 1981; gold award Chgo. Assn. Direct Mktg., 1979, 80; named to Advt. Hall of Fame, 1981. Mem. Am. Legion, ASME, Bus. and Profl. Advertisers Assn. (internat. pres. 1976-77, Best Seller award 1954, Best of Show 1962, Best of Show Indpls. 1966-67, ABP award 1971, Addy Gold award 1979, award for profl. excellence 1978, gold medal 1979, 80), Pub. Relations Soc. Am., Screen Actors Guild, Bus. and Profl. People for Public Interest (dir. 1979—). Unitarian. Home: 3740 N Lake Shore Dr Chicago IL 60613 Office: 625 N Michigan Ave Chicago IL 60611

COHAN, JOHN ROBERT, lawyer; b. Arnhem, Netherlands, Feb. 10, 1931; came to U.S., 1940, naturalized, 1945; s. Max and Ann (deWinter) C.; m. Joan B. Gollob, Sept. 6, 1954; children: Deborah Joyce, Steven Mark, Judson Seth; m. Patricia S. Cohan, Nov. 8, 1970; m. Roberta Cohan, Nov. 23, 1980. B.S. in Bus. Adminstrn, U. Ariz., 1952; LL.B., Stanford U., 1955. Bar: Calif. bar 1956, Cert. specialist in taxation. Assoc. firm Irell & Manella, Los Angeles, 1955-61, ptnr., 1961—; chmn. U.So. Calif. Tax Inst., 1983—; Adj. prof. U. Miami Sch. Law, 1975—; lectr. fed. income taxation U. So. Calif. Sch. Law, 1961-63; lectr., writer Calif. Continuing Edn. Bar Program, 1959—; Practicing Law Inst., 1968—, also various tax and probate insts. Editor: Drafting California Revocable Trusts, 1972, 2d edit., 1984, Drafting California Irrevocable Trusts, 1973, Inter Vivos Trusts, Shephard's Citations, 1975; Contbr. articles on tax, estate planning, probate law to profl. jours. Pres. Portals House, Inc., 1966-69; chmn. Jewish Big Bros., Los Angeles, 1963-65; bd. dirs. Hope for Hearing Research Found., 1965-77, pres., 1972—, trustee, 1978—; chmn. charitable founds. com. Big Bros. Big Sisters Am., 1965-67, chmn. internat. expansion, 1967—, pres. western region, 1977-78; also bd. dirs.; bd. dirs. Jewish Community Found., 1979—, chmn. legal com., 1978—; mem. planning com. U. So. Calif. Tax Inst., 1969—, chmn., 1983—; mem. planning com. U. Miami Estate Planning Inst.; bd. dirs. Los Angeles Campus Hebrew Union Coll., 1974-77. Fellow Am. Coll. Probate Counsel; Mem. ABA (chmn. com. on estate planning for closely held bus. 1979—, vice chmn. estate and gift tax com. of sect. on taxation), Los Angeles Bar Assn. (com. on fed. and Calif. death and gift taxation 1965—, co-chmn. com. on bioethics 1979-80), Beverly Hills Bar Assn. (past chmn., lawyer placement com. and probate com.), Calif. State Bar (probate and trust com. 1971-74), Internat. Acad. Probate and Trust Law (exec. com.), Town Hall of Los Angeles (exec. com., past pres. Western div.), Beta Gamma Sigma, Alpha Kappa Psi, Phi Alpha Delta. Home: 4233 Aleman Dr Tarzana CA 91356 Office: 1800 Ave of Stars Century City Los Angeles CA 90067 *I have tried to make my life a quest for excellence, not only in my career, but in serving others through charitable and educational organizations.*

COHAN, LEON SUMNER, electric company executive, lawyer; b. Detroit, June 24, 1929; s. Maurice and Lillian (Rosenfeld) C.; m. Heidi Ruth Seelmann, Jan. 22, 1956; children: Nicole, Timothy David, Jonathan Daniel. B.A., Wayne State U., 1949, J.D., 1952. Bar: Mich. 1953. Sole practice, Detroit, 1954-58; asst. atty. gen. State of Mich., Lansing, 1958-61, dep. atty. gen., 1961-72; v.p. legal affairs Detroit Edison Co., Detroit, 1973-75, v.p., 1975-79, sr. v.p., 1979—, gen. counsel, 1975—; dir. Union Savs. & Loan Assn., Faygo Beverages, Inc. Mem. State Bd. Ethics; bd. dirs. Mich. Cancer Found., Suburban Detroit Theatres, Inc., Orch. Hall; mem. Mich. Council for Arts; mem. nat. agys. com. Jewish Welfare Fedn.; mem. Arts Commn. adv. com. Detroit Inst. Arts; mem. exec. bd. Friends of Detroit Pub. Library; v.p. Jewish Community Council Met. Detroit. Served in U.S. Army, 1952-54. Recipient Disting. Alumni award Law Sch., Wayne State U., 1972; Disting. Service award Bd. Govs., Wayne State U., 1973. Mem. Am., Detroit bar assns., State Bar Mich., Mich. Gen. Counsel Assn., Am. Arbitration Assn. (mem. comml. panel). Democrat. Jewish. Clubs: Detroit Athletic (Detroit); Detroit. Home: 5324 Forest Way Bloomfield Hills MI 48013 Office: 2000 2d Ave Detroit MI 48226

COHEA, TERRY CLINE, drilling company executive; b. Tulsa, Feb. 11, 1949; s. William Cline C. and Margaret Ann (Gray) Seal; m. Kathryn Darlene Graham, Apr. 28, 1979. B.S. in Petroleum Engring., U. Tulsa, 1971. Petroleum engr. Getty Oil Co., 1971-75; drilling engr. Marion Drilling & Services Co., Mobile, Ala., 1975-77, v.p., 1977-79, pres., 1979—. Home: 700 Cedar Ave Fairhope AL 36532 Office: Marion Drilling & Services Co PO Box 3027 Mobile AL 36652

COHEE, JAMES JOSEPH, hotel exec.; b. Jenkintown, Pa., June 9, 1935; s. George E. and Gertrude (Moranz) C.; m. Barbara Haverman, July 8, 1967; children—Jeffrey Todd, Teri Ann, Michael James, Jennifer Nancy, Steven Joseph. B.S. in Hotel Adminstrn, Cornell U., 1959. Cook/front office Treadway Inns, Williamstown, Mass., 1959-61; asst. mgr. Barclay Hotel, N.Y.C., 1961-63; gen. mgr. Stouffer Inn, Detroit, 1963-65, Ft. Lauderdale, Fla., 1965-67, St. Louis, 1967-71, Denver, 1971-74; v.p. Western region AIRCOA, Denver, 1973-76; v.p., gen. mgr. Boca Raton Hotel and Club, Fla., 1976-80; v.p. Arvida Corp.; gen. mgr. Boca West Resort and Club, 1980—; resort real estate owner, developer The Duck Key Club, 1983—. Advanceman George Romney for Gov. Mich. Campaign, 1964. Served with airborne U.S. Army, 1956-58. Recipient Meritus award Mo. Hotel-Motel Assn., 1971; award Denver Conv. and Tourist Bur., 1974. Mem. Cornell Soc. Hotelmen. Republican. Roman Catholic. Home: 4409 Frances Dr Delray Beach FL 33445 Office: PO Box 225 Boca Raton FL 33432

COHELEACH, GUY JOSEPH, artist; b. N.Y.C.; s. Gaetan Guy and Flavia Marie (Aymong) C.; m. Patricia Arlene McGauley; children: George G., Coleen P., Hugh G., Guy G. (dec.), Elizabeth P. (dec.). Grad., Cooper Union; D.Arts (hon.), Coll. William and Mary, 1975. Bd. dirs. Hawk Mountain Sanctuary, Soc. Animal Artists, Found. for Environ. Edn. One-man shows, A & F Gallery, N.Y.C., Gallery Wildlife Art, Louisville, Am. Mus. Natural History, N.Y.C., numerous others throughout U.S.; group shows include Bird Artists of World, Tryon Gallery, London, Mammal Artists of World, Nairobi, Kenya, Bird Artists of Am., Graham Gallery, N.Y.C., Am. Mus. Natural History, Denver Mus., Corcoran Gallery, Washington; represented in permanent collections, White House, Nat. Gallery, Nat. Wildlife Fedn. Gallery, Am. Mus. Natural History, Nat. Audubon Soc. Gallery. Served with AUS. Recipient Mzuri Safari Internat. Wildlife Artist's Magnum Opus award; Conservation award African Safari Club, 1976; blue ribbon award Printing Industries Am., 1969-81. Fellow Explorers Club; mem. Soc. Animal Artists, Nat. Audubon Soc. (life), Nat. Wildlife Fedn. (life), East African Profl. Hunters Assn. (hon.). Clubs: Adventurers (N.Y.); Boone and Crocket, Campfire, Pres.'s (U. Tenn.). Prints of work American Eagle chosen by Dept. State as gifts for vis. fgn. heads of state. Office: Pandion Art Box 728 Jensen Beach FL 33457 *I believe anyone can attain a very high degree of success in any field as long as he or she loves his chosen field and is not afraid of work.*

COHEN, ABRAHAM J. (AL COHEN), educator; b. Chelsea, Mass., Mar. 19, 1932; s. Samuel and Sarah (Lisofsky) C.; m. Isabel M. Reardon, Aug. 23, 1959; children: David Joseph, Jonathan William, Jennifer Eve. B.S., Salem State Coll., 1959; M.Edn., Boston U., 1960; postgrad., U. Calif. at Santa Barbara, 1968, Fordham U., 1965; Ed.D., Columbia U., 1974; grad., U.S. Army Command and Gen. Staff Coll., 1975, Indsl. Coll. Armed Forces, 1976, Air Force War Coll., 1977. Tchr. social studies jr. high schs., Chelsea, 1959-61; coordinator instructional materials and service North Reading (Mass.) Pub. Schs., 1961-64; supr. instructional materials and sch. libraries White Plains (N.Y.) Pub. Schs., 1964—, coordinator health edn., 1974—; pres. Ednl. Film Library Assn. and Am. Film Festival, N.Y.C., 1971-73; Lectr. sch. continuing edn. NYU, 1965-68, Sch. Library Service Columbia U., 1972—; dir. audio visual center Salem (Mass.) State Coll., 1961-62; mem. adv. bd. Ednl. Products Information Exchange Inst., N.Y.C., 1972—; instr. U.S. Army Command Gen. Staff Coll.; comdt. 1150th USAR Sch., Ft. Hamilton, N.Y., 1983—. Contbr. articles to profl. jours. Scoutmaster, instl. rep. Muscoot-Westchester council Boy Scouts Am., 1971-72; pres. Westchester Library Assn., 1972-74; mem. expansion com. J.C. Hart Library, Yorktown, N.Y., 1969-71; pres. Westchester County Ednl. Communications Assn., 1968-69; Chmn. bd. dirs., pres. Yorktown Jewish Center, 1969-70; bd. dirs. Westchester div. Am. Cancer Soc., chmn. pub. edn., 1981-83. Served with AUS, 1952-54; col. Res. Recipient Gen. John J. Pershing award U.S. Army Command and Gen. Staff Coll., 1975, Educator of Yr. award Am. Cancer Soc., 1983. Mem. Mass. Audio Visual Assn. (dir. 1962-64), Ednl. Media Council (dir. 1971-73, exec. com. 1972-73), N.Y. State Edn. Communications Assn. (dir. 1968-69), Assn. Edn. Communications and Tech., Phi Delta Kappa. Club: Mason. Home: 2601 Darnley Pl Yorktown Heights NY 10598 Office: Education House 5 Homeside Lane White Plains NY 10605

COHEN, ALAN NORMAN, business executive; b. Clifton, N.J., Dec. 19, 1930; s. Samuel and Ida (Phillips) C.; m. Joan Meryl Fields, Nov. 25, 1953; children: Laurie Elizabeth, Gordon Geoffrey. Student, Dartmouth, 1948-49; A.B., Columbia U., 1952, LL.B., 1954. Bar: N.Y. 1954. Asso. firm Cahill, Gordon, Reindel & Ohl, N.Y.C., 1954-55, Paul, Weiss, Goldberg, Rifkind, Wharton & Garrison, 1957-63, partner, 1964-70, 78-80; pres., dir. Andal Corp., N.Y.C., 1980—; exec. v.p., dir., mem. exec. com. Warner Communications, Inc., N.Y.C., 1970-74; pres., chief exec. officer, dir., mem. exec. com. Madison Sq. Garden Corp., N.Y.C., 1974-77; chmn. N.J. Nets, 1978-83; owner, vice chmn. bd. Boston Celtics, 1983—; bd. govs. NBA, 1978—. Bd. overseers Grad. Sch. Mgmt. and Urban Professions, New Sch. Social Research; Bd. dirs. others. Served with AUS, 1955-57. Mem. N.Y. State Bar Assn., Assn. Bar City N.Y. Office: 60 Madison Ave New York NY 10010

COHEN, ALAN SEYMOUR, physician; b. Boston, Apr. 9, 1926; s. George I. and Jennie (Laskin) C.; m. Joan Elizabeth Prince, Sept. 12, 1954; children: Evan, Andrew, Robert. B.A. magna cum laude, Harvard U., 1947, M.D., Boston U., 1952. Intern Harvard Med. Service, Boston City Hosp., 1952-53, resident, 1953-55; exchange registrar in medicine Dundee Royal Infirmary and U. St. Andrews, Scotland, 1975-76; research and clin. fellow in medicine (rheumatology) Mass. Gen. Hosp., Boston, 1956-58; instr. Harvard Med. Sch. and Mass. Gen. Hosp., 1958-60; head arthritis and connective tissue disease sect. Evans dept. clin. research Mass. Meml. Hosp., Boston, 1960-72; Conrad Wesselhoeft prof. medicine Boston U. Sch. Medicine, 1972—, prof. pharmacology, 1974—; dir. Arthritis Center, 1977—; dir. div. medicine Boston City Hosp., 1973—; dir. Thorndike meml. lab., 1973—. Editor: Laboratory Diagnostic Procedures in the Rheumatic Diseases, 1967, rev. edit., 1975, (with others) Symposium on Amyloidosis, 1968, (with R. Friedin and M. Samuels) Medical Emergencies: Diagnostic and Management Procedures from Boston City Hospital, 1977, Rheumatology and Immunology, 1979; contbr. over 400 articles to profl. jours. Trustee Arthritis Found., Atlanta, 1976—, Mass. chpt., 1966—; vice chmn. Mass. chpt., 1971—, pres., 1981—. Served as asst. surgeon; USPHS, 1953-55. Recipient Outstanding Alumnus award Boston U. Sch. Medicine, 1975; Purdue Frederic Arthritis award, 1979; James H. Fairclough, Jr. award for disting. service to Mass. chpt. Arthritis Found., 1981; Alumni award for spl. distinction (silver medal) Boston U., 1981. Fellow A.C.P.; mem. Am. Rheumatism Assn. (pres. 1978-79), Am. Soc. Clin. Investigation, Assn. Am. Physicians, o2Am. Fedn. Clin. Research, Am. Soc. Exptl. Pathology, Interurban Clin. Club, Soc. Exptl. Biology and Medicine, Electron Microscopy Soc. Am., New Eng. Soc. for Electron Microscopy, Am. Soc. Cell Biology, N.Y. Acad. Sci., AMA, Mass. Med. Soc., New Eng. Rheumatism Assn. (past pres.), Italian Rheumatism Soc. (hon.), Spanish Rheumatism Soc. (hon.), Finnish Rheumatism Soc. (hon.), Brazilian Rheumatism Soc. (hon.), Irish Soc. Rheumatism and Rehab. (hon.), Boston U. Sch. Medicine Alumni Assn. (past pres.), Phi Beta Kappa, Alpha Omega Alpha. Jewish. Clubs: Harvard (Boston); Wightman Tennis Center (Weston, Mass.). Office: Thorndike Lab Room 314 Boston City Hosp 818 Harrison Ave Boston MA 02118

COHEN, ALBERT, musician, educator; b. N.Y.C., Nov. 16, 1929; s. Sol A. and Dora C.; m. Betty Joan Berg, Aug. 28, 1952; children—Eva Denise, Stefan Berg. B.S., Juilliard Sch. Music, 1951; M.A., NYU, 1953, Ph.D. (Fulbright fellow), 1959; postgrad., U. Paris, 1956-57. Mem. faculty U. Mich., Ann Arbor, 1960-70, assoc. prof. music, 1964-67, prof., 1967-70; prof. music, chmn. dept. SUNY-Buffalo, 1970-73, Stanford (Calif.) U., 1973—; William H. Bonsall prof. music Stanford (Calif.) U., 1974—; editor Broude Bros. Ltd., N.Y.C., Info. Coordinators, Detroit. Author: Treatise on the Composition of Music, 1962, Elements or Principles of Music, 1965, (with J.D. White) Anthology of Music for Analysis, 1965, (with L.E. Miller) Music in the Paris Academy of Sciences, 1666-1793, An Index, 1979, Music in the French Royal Academy of Sciences, 1981; contbr. articles to profl. jours. Guggenheim fellow, 1968-69; NEH, 1975-76, 82-83. Mem. Internat., Am., French musicol. socs., Galpin Soc. (Eng.), Music Library Assn. Office: Dept Music Stanford U Stanford CA 94305

COHEN, ALBERT DIAMOND, merchandising executive; b. Winnipeg, Man., Can., Jan. 20, 1916; s. Alexander and Rose (Diamond) C.; m. Irena Kankova, Nov. 6, 1953; children: Anthony Jan, James Edward, Anna Lisa. Grad., St. Johns High Sch., Winnipeg, 1930. Pres. Gendis Inc., Winnipeg, 1953—; pres., chief exec. officer Gendis, Inc., 1968—; chmn. exec. com. Met. Stores of Can., Ltd., Winnipeg, 1961—, Greenberg Stores Ltd.; sec., treas., dir. Saan Stores Ltd.; chmn., chief exec. officer Sony of Can. Ltd., 1975—; dir. Pan Can. Petroleum Ltd. Pres. Winnipeg Clin. Research Inst., 1975-80, Paul H.T. Thorlakson Research Found., 1978-80.; hon. chmn. St. John's Ravenscourt Sch., 1984. Served with Royal Can. Navy, 1942-45. Office: 1370 Sony Pl Winnipeg MB Canada R3C 3C3

COHEN, ALEX, publisher; b. N.Y.C., Jan. 1, 1927; s. Henry and Fanny (Menche) C.; m. Audrey Joan Katz, Dec. 23, 1950; children—Elynn Ruth, Laura Susan, Philip Henry. B.B.A. cum laude, Coll. City, N.Y., 1950; J.D., Bklyn. Law Sch., 1958; LL.M., N.Y. U., 1963. Bar: N.Y. State bar 1958; C.P.A., N.Y. Engaged as pub. accountant, 1950-62, pvt. practice as pub. accountant, 1962-75, tax atty., 1958—; lectr. taxation Bernard Baruch Grad. Sch., 1968-69; spl. investigator N.Y. State Elections Frauds Bur., 1958. Pub.: Client's Monthly Alert; founder, publisher: Practical Accountant mag, N.Y.C., 1968—; tech. editor: Jour. Taxation, 1963-68; Author: Accounting Shortcuts and Workpaper Techniques, 1970; Contbr. articles to profl. jours.; Editor: Tulane Tax Institute, 1974, Tactics and Strategies in Handling A Tax Audit, 1973. Founder, treas. North Jersey Operetta Guild, 1968. Served with AUS, 1945-46. Mem. Am. Inst. C.P.A.'s, N.Y. State Soc. C.P.A.'s, N.Y. County Bar Assn. Home: 152 Kakeout Rd Kinnelon NJ 07405 Office: 964 3d Ave New York NY 10022

COHEN, ALEXANDER H., theatrical and television producer; b. N.Y.C., July 24, 1920; s. Alexander H. and Laura (Tarantous) C.; m. Jocelyn Newmark, Jan. 12, 1942; 1 dau., Barbara Ann; m. Hildy Parks, Feb. 24, 1956; children: Gerald Parks, Christopher Alexander. Ed., NYU. Producer plays, 1941—; starting with Angel Street: other prodns. include Words and Music, 1974; Who's Who in Hell, 1974, Good Evening, 1974, Comedians, Hellzapoppin, 1976, Anna Christie, 1977, I Remember Mama, 1979, A Day in Hollywood/A Night in the Ukraine, 1980, 84 Charing Cross Road, 1982, Edmund Kean, Carmen, Play Memory, 1984; also numerous plays presented in, West End of London (Eng.); including Come as You Are, 1776; The Happy Apple, Who Killed Santa Claus?, Applause, Harvey; for television has produced ann. Antoinette Perry (Tony) Awards Show, 1967-84; other TV prodns include A World of Love; CBS-TV Spl. for, UNICEF, 1970, Marlene Dietrich's I Wish You Love, 1972, CBS: On the Air, A Celebration of Fifty Years, 1978, Night of 100 Stars, 1982, Parade of Stars, 1983, The Best of Everything, 1983. Bd. govs., v.p. League N.Y. Theatres and Producers; trustee, v.p. Actors Fund Am. Served with inf. AUS, 1943-44. Clubs: Players, City Athletic. Office: Shubert Theatre 225 W 44th St New York NY 10036

COHEN, ALLAN RICHARD, broadcasting exec.; b. Bklyn., Dec. 27, 1947; s. Ike and Fae C.; m. Roberta Segal, July 12, 1970; children—Evan, Stacie. B.S., Hofstra U., 1970; M.M., Poly. Inst. Bklyn., 1976. Electronics engr. Sperry Systems Mgmt. Div., Gt. Neck, N.Y., 1970-74; with CBS, 1974—; dir. planning and adminstrn. WCBS-TV, 1977-79; v.p., personnel CBS Broadcast Group, 1979-80; v.p., gen. mgr. KMOX-TV, St. Louis, 1980—. Bd. dirs. Boys Town, St. Louis Children's Hosp., St. Louis Psychoanalytic Inst. Mem. Am. Mgmt. Assn., Mo., Ill. broadcasters assn., Nat. Assn. Broadcasters. Office: One Memorial Dr St Louis MO 63102

COHEN, ALLAN RICHARD, lawyer; b. Chgo., Feb. 25, 1923; s. Louis and Ruth (Cohen) C.; m. Audrey Doris Levy, Oct. 14, 1960; children: Joseph, David, Gale. B.A., U. Wis., 1947, J.D., 1949; postgrad., Northwestern U., 1953-54. Bar: Ill. 1950. Since practiced in Chgo. Served with AUS, 1943-45. Decorated Presdl. citation with oak leaf cluster. Mem. Fed. Bar Assn., Ill. Bar Assn. (vice chmn. comml. banking and bankruptcy sect. 1977—), Chgo. Bar Assn. (vice chmn. com. bankruptcy 1972-73, chmn. 1973-74, panelist bankruptcy seminars 1968, 72, 74, 82, 83), Zeta Beta Tau, Tau Epsilon Rho. Club:

Elms Swim Tennis (Highland Park, Ill.). Office: Suite 920 55 W Monroe St Chicago IL 60603

COHEN, ANDREW STUART, architect, landscape architect; b. Waterbury, Conn., Feb. 11, 1930; s. Edward and Edna Louise (Braverman) C.; m. Belle J. Grogins, June 14, 1953; children: Lori, Peter Avery, Jody. B.Arch., Yale U., 1953, M.Arch., 1953. Architect Gordon MacMaster (Architect), Cheshire, Conn., 1957-61; architect, partner Cohen & D'Oliveira, Waterbury, 1967-72; prin. Andrew S. Cohen Architect, Waterbury, 1961—; asst. v.p. property mgmt. Colonial Bank, Waterbury, 1982—; sec. Conn. Archtl. Registration Bd., 1966-79; class agt. Yale Sch. Architecture, Class of 1953, 1978—. Editor: Conn. Architect mag, 1964-65. Fellow AIA; mem. Conn. Soc. Architects. Club: Masons. Home: Westwood Dr Middlebury CT 06762 Office: Colonial Bank Waterbury CT 06702

COHEN, ARTHUR ALLEN, author, publisher; b. N.Y.C., June 25, 1928; s. Isidore Meyer and Bess (Junger) C.; m. Elaine Firstenberg Lustig, Oct. 14, 1956; 1 dau., Tamar Judith. B.A., U. Chgo., 1946; M.A., 1949; M.A. fellow Jewish philosophy, Jewish Theol. Sem. Am., 1951-53. Co-founder Noonday Press, N.Y.C., 1951; founder, pres., exec. editor Meridian Books, Inc., N.Y.C., 1955; (acquired by World Pub. Co., 1960); pres. Meridian Books; v.p. World Pub. Co., 1961; dir. religious pub. Holt, Rinehart, and Winston, Inc., 1961-64, editor-in-chief gen. book div., v.p., 1964-68; cons. editor E.P. Dutton; mng. editor Documents 20th Century Art, Viking Press, 1968-72; pres. Ex Libris, 1974—; cons. project on religion and free soc. Fund for Republic, 1957-61. Author: Martin Buber, 1958, The Natural and the Supernatural Jew: An Historical and Theological Introduction, 1963, The Carpenter Years, 1967, The Myth of the Judeo-Christian Tradition, 1970, A People Apart: Hasidism in America, 1972, In the Days of Simon Stern, 1973, (with Mordecai Kaplan) If Not Now, When?, 1973, Osip Emilevich Mandelstam, 1974, Sonia Delaunay, 1975, A Hero in His Time, 1975, Acts of Theft, 1980, An Admirable Woman, 1983, The Tremendum, 1981; Contbr. to: Am. Catholics: A Protestant-Jewish View, 1959, Christianity: Some Non-Christian Appraisals, 1964, Sacramentum Mundi, 1964; others.; Editor: Anatomy of Faith, 1960, Humanistic Education and Western Civilization, 1964, Arguments and Doctrines: A Reader in Jewish Thinking, 1970, The New Art of Color: The Writings of Robert and Sonia Delaunay, The Jew, 1980; contbr. articles to religious publs. Home: 160 E 70th St New York NY 10021 Office: 160A E 70th St New York NY 10021

COHEN, ARTHUR G., real estate executive; b. Bklyn., Apr. 23, 1930; s. Louis Diamond and Frances (Kostick) C.; m. Karen D. Bassine, June 6, 1954; children: Susan, Lauren, Debra, Rochelle, Katherine. B.A., U. Miami, Fla., 1951; LL.B, N.Y. Law Sch., 1954. Chmn. bd. Arlen Realty and Devel. Corp., N.Y.C., API Trust, 1973-81; trustee John Hancock Mut. Fund, 1972; dir. Citicorp, N.Y.C., 1974-80, Home Title N.Y., 1974-81; guest lectr. Harvard Bus. Sch., 1975-78, Wharton Sch., 1977; mem. real estate adv. commn. Citibank, 1978-80; founder Urban Devel. Corp., 1971. Trustee Brandeis U., 1978—, Albert Einstein Coll. Medicine; mem. Spl. Mission to Israel, 1968—, Pres. Johnson's Pres. Club, 1963-68; chmn. Democratic Party Fundraising for Hubert Humphrey, N.Y.C., 1968; spl. envoy to aid under-privileged nations, 1967—. Clubs: Glen Oaks Country, Palm Beach Country. Office: Arlen Realty and Devel Corp 1501 Broadway New York NY 10036

COHEN, ARTHUR MORRIS, artist; b. N.Y.C., Jan. 2, 1928; s. Morris Aaron and Flora (Hasson) C.; m. Elizabeth Copstein, Jan. 15, 1972; 1 son, Ezekiel. Student, Cooper Union, 1947-49, Art Student's League, N.Y.C., 1951, 60. Exhibitor permanent collections, Met. Mus. Art, N.Y.C., Hirshhorn Mus., Washington, Bklyn. Mus., N.Y.C., Boston Mus., Mus. City N.Y., N.Y. Hist. Soc., Everson Mus., Syracuse, Cooper Hewitt Mus., N.Y.C., group shows, Everson Mus., Syracuse, Nat. Acad. Design, N.Y.C., 1976, 82, 83, David Findlay Gallery, N.Y.C., 1983, Hirshhorn Mus., Washington, 1979-80, group show, Bklyn. Mus., N.Y.C., 1983, group shows, Cooper Hewitt Mus., N.Y.C., 1983, one-man shows, Blue Mountain Gallery, N.Y.C., 1980, 83, Swansborough Gallery, Wellfleet, Mass., 1983, Peter Rose Gallery, N.Y.C., 1982, Munson Gallery, Chatham, Mass., 1981, Swansborough Gallery, 1980, Forum Gallery, N.Y.C., 1976, Roko Gallery, N.Y.C., 1970. Served with U.S. Army, 1946-47. N.Y. State grantee, 1977; Ingram Merill grantee, 1979; Guggenheim grantee, 1981. Mem. Nat. Acad. Design. Jewish. Home: 55 Tiemann Pl New York NY 10027

COHEN, BENJAMIN BERNARD, English educator; b. Balt., May 30, 1922; s. Louis I. and Lillie (Laken) C.; m. Lucian Anderson, July 29, 1952. A.B., U. Md., 1943, M.A., 1944; Ph.D., Ind. U., 1950. Instr. Wayne U., 1948-52; asst. prof. Ga. Inst. Tech., 1953-55, Ind. State Tchrs. Coll., Terre Haute, 1955-57; asso. prof. Jacksonville (Ala.) State Tchrs. Coll., 1957-59, Oglethorpe U., 1959-60; asso. prof., prof. Wichita State U., 1960-68; prof. English, U. Mo., St. Louis, 1968—; Fulbright lectr., Norway, 1973. Author: Writing About Literature, 1963, rev. edit., 1973, Working for Literary Understanding, 1966; Editor: The Recognition of Nathaniel Hawthorne, 1969, Guide to Nathaniel Hawthorne, 1970; Contbr. articles to profl. jours. Recipient Excellence in Teaching award Wichita State U., 1968; Am. Council Learned Socs. research scholar Yale, 1952-53. Mem. Modern Lang. Assn., Nathaniel Hawthorne Soc. Home: 7433 Overbrook Dr Saint Louis MO 63121

COHEN, BERNARD, neurologist, educator; b. Newark, Apr. 30, 1929; s. Samuel and Ruth (Rosenblum) C.; m. Phoebe Ann Freeman, Oct. 30, 1955; children: Margaret, Alexander, Nathaniel. A.B., Middlebury Coll., 1950; M.D., N.Y. U., 1954. Diplomate: Am. Bd. Neurology and Psychiatry. Intern Mt. Sinai Hosp., N.Y.C., 1954-55; resident in neurology N.Y. U., Bellevue Med. Center, N.Y.C., 1955-57; asst. resident psychiatry Hillside Hosp., Queens, N.Y., 1957-58; with Marine Biol. Lab., Woods Hole, Mass., 1960; fellow neurology Columbia, N.Y.C., 1960-62; vis. fellow in otolaryngology U. Tokyo, Japan, 1965; asst. attending neurologist Mt. Sinai Hosp., N.Y.C., 1961-70; asso. prof. neurology Mt. Sinai Sch. Medicine, N.Y.C., 1966—; asso. prof. physiology; expert in neurology FDA, HEW, Washington, 1975-79; adj. prof. Queens Coll., City U., N.Y., 1973—; attending neurologist Elmhurst Gen. Hosp., Queens, N.Y., 1973-80, Mt. Sinai Hosp., N.Y.C., 1970—; prof. neurology Mt. Sinai Sch. Medicine, N.Y.C., 1970—, Dr. Morris B. Bender prof. neurology, 1976—; dir. Neurobiology Grad. Program, 1981—. Contbr. articles on oculomotor and vestibular research to profl. jours.; editorial bd.: Am. Jour. Physiology, 1971-76, Jour. Applied Physiology, 1971-76, Brain Research, 1971—, Brain Research Revs, 1979—, Experimental Brain Research, 1980—. Bd. dirs. Am. Brass Quintet, 1981—. Served with M.C. U.S. Army, 1958-60. Nat. Inst. Neurol. and Communicative Disease and Stroke and predecessor agy. fellow, 1960-62; Devel. award, 1967-73; grantee, 1961—, Neurol. Study Sect. A, 1978—; NSF grantee, 1974-76; N.Y.C. Health Research Council grantee, 1973-75; NIMH Grantee, 1975-79; Nat. Eye Inst. grantee, 1978—. Mem. Am. Acad. Neurology, Am. Neurol. Assn., Am. Physiol. Soc., Barany Soc., Assn. Research in Neurol. and Mental Disorders (sec. treas. 1979—), Assn. Research in Vision and Ophthalmology, Eastern EEG Soc., Harvey Soc., N.Y. Acad. Medicine, N.Y. Acad. Scis., N.Y. Neurol. Soc., Soc. Neurosci. Club: Orient Yacht. Home: 131 Riverside Dr New York NY 10024 Office: Mt Sinai Sch Medicine Dept Neurology Annenberg 21-74 1 Gustave Levy Pl New York NY 10029

COHEN, BERNARD CECIL, polit. scientist, educator; b. Northampton, Mass., Feb. 22, 1926; s. Louis Mark and Lena (Slotnick) C.; m. Laura Mae Propper, Sept. 1, 1947; children—Barbara Ellen, Janie Louise. B.A., Yale, 1948, M.A., 1950, Ph.D., 1952. Research asst. Yale, 1950-51; research asst., then research asso. Princeton, 1951-59, asst. prof., 1957-59; mem. faculty U. Wis., 1959—, prof. polit. sci., 1963-73, Quincy Wright prof. polit. sci., 1973—, chmn. dept., 1966-69; asso. dean Grad. Sch., 1971-75; vis. research scholar Carnegie Endowment Internat. Peace, 1965-66; mng. editor World Politics, 1956-59, mem. bd. editors, 1959-60, 72-78, Internat. Studies Quar., 1966-78. Author: The Political Process and Foreign Policy, 1957, The Press and Foreign Policy, 1963, The Public's Impact on Foreign Policy, 1973; Editor: Foreign Policy in American Government, 1965. Served with AUS, 1944-46. Ford Found. Faculty Research fellow, 1969-70; fellow Center Advanced Study Behavioral Scis., 1961-62, 69-70; Fulbright-Hays research scholar, Netherlands, 1975-76; Guggenheim fellow, 1981-82. Mem. Am., Midwest polit. sci. assns., Internat. Studies Assn. Home: 1034 Seminole Hwy Madison WI 53711

COHEN, BERNARD LEONARD, physicist, educator; b. Pitts., June 14, 1924; s. Samuel and Mollie (Friedman) C.; m. Anna Foner, Mar. 30, 1950; children: Donald, Judith, Frederick, Ernest. B.S., Case Inst. Tech., 1944; M.S., U. Pitts., 1948; D.Sc., Carnegie Inst. Tech., 1950. With Oak Ridge Nat. Lab., 1950-58; prof. physics U. Pitts., 1958—; dir. Sarah Mellon Scaife Nuclear Physics Lab., 1965-78; on leave with Gen. Atomic Lab., San Diego, 1959-60, Inst. for Def. Analysis, Washington, 1962, Brookhaven Nat. Lab., 1965, Los Alamos Sci. Lab., 1969, Inst. Energy Analysis, Oak Ridge, 1974-75, Argonne Nat. Lab., 1978-79; cons. numerous govtl. agys. and pvt. corps. Author: Heart of the Atom, 1967, Concepts of Nuclear Physics, 1971, Nuclear Science and Society, 1974, Before It's Too Late: A Scientist's Case for Nuclear Power; Contbr. numerous articles to profl. jours. Fellow Am. Phys. Soc. (chmn. div. nuclear physics 1974-75, Bonner prize for nuclear physics 1981), AAAS; mem. Am. Assn. Physics Tchrs. (nat. council 1973-78), Am. Nuclear Soc. (chmn. div. environ. scis. 1980-81), Health Phys. Soc. Home: 5414 Albemarle Ave Pittsburgh PA 15217

COHEN, BERTRAM DAVID, psychologist, educator; b. Bklyn., Jan. 16, 1923; s. Irving and Rose (Rabinowitz) C.; m. Helen Elizabeth Swartley, Aug. 8, 1946; children: Philip S., Sarah L., Matthew A., Michael B., Aaron M., Andrew S. B.A., Bklyn. Coll., 1944; M.A., U. Ia., 1945, Ph.D., 1949. Asst. prof. Ind. U., 1949-52; chief psychologist Iowa City VA Hosp., 1952-56; dir. psychology Lafayette Clinic, Detroit, 1956-62; dir. clin. tng. Rutgers U., 1962-69, chmn. grad. psychology, 1970-74, adj. prof. Grad. Sch. Applied and Profl. Psychology, 1974—; prof. psychiatry Coll. Medicine and Dentistry N.J.-Rutgers Med. Sch., 1965—; cons. NIMH, VA, Rutgers Mgmt. Services; mem. certification commn. for psychology state Mich., 1960-62; Mem. bd. profl. advisers Coll. Profl. Psychology, Maplewood, N.J., 1971-74. Assoc. editor: Jour. Exptl. Research in Personality, 1964-72; assoc. editor, 1979-82; adv. editor: Jour. Cons. and Clin. Psychology, 1964-73; cons. editor: Jour. Abnormal Psychology, 1973-79. Trustee Warren Twp. Library Assn., N.J. Acad. Psychology, 1978—. NSF grantee, 1963-74; NIMH grantee, 1963-69; Fulbright scholar, Denmark, 1975-76. Fellow Am. Psychol. Assn. (chmn. sect. 3 div. clin. psychology 1969-70); fellow Am. Coll. Neuropsychopharmacology; mem. N.J. Group Psychotherapy Soc. (pres. 1976-77), Sigma Xi. Home: 9 Rockage Rd Warren NJ 07060

COHEN, BURTON JEROME, financial executive; b. Phila., Dec.8, 1933; s. Alexander David and Esther (Mirrow) C.; m. Jane McDowell, Mar. 16, 1968; children: Paul, Joshua, Douglas, Glen. B.S. in Acctg, Temple U., 1955; student, c. Program, Harvard U. Operations v.p. Cakemasters, Inc., Phila., 1957-61; mgr. IBM, Phila., White Plains, N.Y., N.Y.C., 1961-70; ptnr. Touche & Ross & Co., N.Y.C., 1970-77; ptnr., nat. dir. fin. and adminstrn. Coopers & Lybrand, N.Y.C., 1977-82; exec. dir. Paul, Weiss, Refkind, Wharton & Garrison, N.Y.C., 1982—; adj. prof. Columbia U. Grad. Sch. Bus.; lectr. Am. Mgmt. Assn. seminars.; Mem. adv. bd. Borough Manhattan Community Coll. Author: Cost Effective Information Systems, 1971; contbr. to: Info. Systems Handbook, 1975. Served with Fin. Corps U.S. Army, 1955-57. Mem. Fin. Execs. Inst. Club: Masons. Home: 63 Adams Ln New Canaan CT 06840 Office: 1251 Ave of Americas New York NY 10020

COHEN, CALVIN JAMES, apparel manufacturer; b. Cleve., Aug. 4, 1932; s. Edward Samuel and Mollie (Rubenstein) C.; m. Dolores Gorman, Dec. 27, 1953; children: Nancy Beth, Edward Gerald. B.B.A., Western Res. U., 1954. Asst. controller Bobbie Brooks, Inc., Cleve., 1954-60, asst. treas., 1960-66, corporate treas., divisional v.p., 1966-73, corporate treas., 1973-77, v.p. fin., treas., 1977-79, exec. v.p., treas., 1979-82, treas., 1982—, dir., 1972-82. Office: 3830 Kelley Ave Cleveland OH 44114

COHEN, CHARLES EMIL, art historian, educator; b. N.Y.C., July 11, 1942; s. Philip and Hannah (Abramson) C.; m. Sondra Eileen Cohen, Sept. 27, 1964; children: Joshua K., Jonathan E. B.A., Columbia U., 1963; M.F.A., Princeton U., 1965; Ph.D., Harvard U., 1971. Tutor Harvard U., Cambridge, Mass., 1967-68, head teaching fellow, 1969-70; asst. prof. art U. Chgo., 1970-75, assoc. prof., 1975-80, chmn. art dept., 1976-82, prof. art, 1980—. Author: Drawings of G.A. da Pordenone, 1980, I Disegni di Pomponio Amalteo, 1975; contbr. articles to profl. jours. Guggenheim fellow, 1983; fellow Am. Council Learned Socs., 1980, Gladys Krieble Delmas Found., 1980; summer fellow NEH, 1983. Mem. Coll. Art Assn. Am., Midwest Art History Soc., U. Chgo. Renaissance Seminar. Jewish. Home: 5514 S University Ave Chicago IL 60637 Office: U Chicago Dept Art 5540 S Greenwood Ave Chicago IL 60637

COHEN, DAVID, public affairs specialist, educator; b. Phila., Oct. 10, 1936; s. Joseph and Gertrude (Schwalb) C.; m. Carla Furstenberg, Sept. 7, 1958; children: Aaron, Eve. B.A., Temple U., 1957. Researcher, adminstr. contracts Upholsterers Internat. Union, 1958-63; legis. rep. Ams. for Democratic Action, 1963-67; legis. rep. indsl. union dept. AFL-CIO, 1967-68; assoc. legis. dir. Council for Community Action; program mgr. Center for Community Change, Washington, 1968-71; legis. cons. Common Cause, Washington, 1971, dir. field orgn., 1971-73, v.p. ops., 1973-74, exec. v.p., 1974-75, acting pres., 1975, pres., chief operating officer, 1975-76, pres., chief exec. officer, 1976-81; pres. Social Devel. Corp., 1982—; sr. fellow Roosevelt Ctr. Study Am. Policy, 1982—; lectr. Coe Coll., 1964-71, Wharton Sch., U. Pa., spring 1975; adj. prof. Washington Ctr. Pub. Affairs, U. So. Calif., 1981—. Contbr. articles to jours., newspapers, mags. Mem. Washington Jewish Community Relations Council, 1972-74; mem. legal ethics com. of D.C. Bar, 1977; chmn. Am. Democratic Action exec. com., 1969-71. Fellow Calhoun Coll., Yale U. (1975-78). Jewish. Office: 2010 Massachusetts Ave NW Suite 400 Washington DC 20036

COHEN, DAVID HARRIS, neurobiology educator; b. Springfield, Mass., Aug. 26, 1938; s. Nathan Edward and Sylvia (Golden) C.; m. Arline Wyler, June 17, 1960 (div. Aug. 1980); children: Bonnie, Daniel, Ian; m. Anne Helen Remmes, Jan. 17, 1981. B.A., Harvard U., 1960; Ph.D., U. Calif.-Berkeley, 1963. Postdoctoral fellow UCLA, 1963-64; asst. prof. physiology Western Res. U., Cleve., 1964-68; assoc. prof. to prof. physiology U. Va. Med. Sch., Charlottesville, 1968-79; prof., chmn. neurobiology SUNY, Stony Brook, 1979—. Contbr. articles to profl. jours. Bd. advisors Nat. Coalition for Sci. and Tech., Washington, 1982—. Recipient Research Career Devel. award NIH, 1969-74. Mem. Soc. Neurosci. (pres. 1981-82), Palovian Soc. (pres. 1978-79), Assn. Neurosci. Depts. and Programs (pres. 1981-82), Nat. Soc. Med. Research (bd. dirs. 1981—), Council Acad. Socs. (adminstrv. bd. 1982—). Jewish. Club: Boars Head (Charlottesville, Va.). Home: 246 Christian Ave Stony Brook NY 11790 Office: Dept Neurobiology and Behavior SUNY Stony Brook NY 11794

COHEN, DAVID WALTER, periodontist, educator; b. Phila., Dec. 15, 1926; s. Abram and Goldie (Schlein) C.; m. Betty Axelrod, Dec. 19, 1948; children: Jane Ellen, Amy Sue, Joanne Louise. D.D.S., U. Pa., 1950; D.Sc. (hon.), Boston U., 1975, Ph.D., Hebrew U., Jerusalem, 1977, U. Athens, 1979. Diplomate: Am. Bd. Periodontology (chmn. 1972). Research fellow pathology and periodontia Beth Israel Hosp., Boston, 1950-51; mem. faculty U. Pa. Sch. Dentistry, Phila., 1951—, prof. periodontics, 1962—, chmn. dept., 1962—; dean Sch. Dental Medicine, 1972—; mem. staff Albert Einstein Med. Center, Phila., Children's Hosp.; vis. prof. Boston U. Sch. Grad. Dentistry, 1972—; nat. cons. periodontics USAF, 1965-69; Bd. govs. Hebrew U., Jerusalem. Author: (with H.M. Goldman) Periodontia, 1957, (with others) An Introduction to Periodontia, 1959, Periodontal Therapy, 1960; also numerous chpts.; Contbr. articles to profl. jours. Served with USN, 1944-45. Fellow AAAS, Am. Acad. Oral Pathology, Am. Acad. Periodontology, Inst. of Medicine of Nat. Acad. Scis.; mem. Am. Soc. Periodontists (pres. 1967). Office: 4001 Spruce St Philadelphia PA 19104

COHEN, DONALD SUSSMAN, mathematician, educator; b. Providence, Nov. 30, 1934; s. Leo Sussman and Anne (Mogelever) C.; m. Natalie Shulman, Sept. 7, 1958; children: Julie Elisabeth, Susan Louise. Sc.B. in Physics, Brown U., 1956; M.S. in Statistics, Cornell U., 1962; Ph.D. in Applied Math, Courant Inst., N.Y. U., 1962. Mem. faculty Calif. Inst. Tech., 1965—, prof. applied math., 1971—, chmn. faculty, 1983—; Cons. govt. and industry; chmn. nat. com. applied math. Am. Math. Soc.-Soc. Indsl. and Applied Math., 1974-77; vis. prof. Tech. U. Denmark, 1969; lectr. in field. Contbr. to profl. jours.; editor procs. books; editorial bd.: Applied Math, 1974—. Mem. AAAS (mem.-at-large sect. com. on math. 1979-83), Am. Math. Soc., Soc. Indsl. and Applied Math (editor rev. 1970—). Home: 1725 Homet Rd Pasadena CA 91106 Office: Applied Math 217-50 Calif Inst Tech Pasadena CA 91125

COHEN, DONN ISAAC, lawyer; b. York, Pa., Sept. 20, 1930; s. Herbert Bank and Mildred (Charlap) C.; m. Janet Lee Klaw, Dec. 21, 1953; children—David K., Martha Lee, Paul W., Louise B. A.B., U. Pa., 1951; LL.B. cum laude, Harvard U., 1954. Bar: Pa. bar 1954, U.S. Supreme Ct. bar 1958. Partner firm Cohen, Senft & Rubin, York, 1956-65, Liverant, Senft & Cohen, 1965; asst. dist. atty. York County, 1958-61; Bd. dirs. York Hosp., 1969-79, chmn. bd., 1977-79; bd. dirs. Community Services Pa., 1971-77, v.p., 1973-74. Trustee York Coll. of Pa., 1970—, sec., 1973—; bd. dirs. United Way of, York County, 1962-68, pres., 1963-64; bd. dirs. Strand-Capitol Performing Arts Center, 1980—. Served with U.S. Army, 1954-56. Mem. Am. Law Inst., Am. Bar Assn., Pa. Bar Assn., York County Bar Assn. Jewish. Club: Democrat. Home: Grantley Rd Extended York PA 17403 Office: 15 S Duke St York PA 17405

COHEN, EDWARD, cons. engr.; b. Glastonbury, Conn., Jan. 6, 1921; s. Samuel and Ida (Tanewitz) C.; m. Elizabeth Belle Cohen, Dec. 19, 1948 (dec. June 1979); children—Samuel, Libby, James; m. Carol Suzanne Kaleb, Jan. 11, 1981. B.S. in Engring, Columbia U., 1945, M.S. in Civil Engring, 1954. Registered profl. engr., N.Y., Conn., Fla., Ga., Md., N.J., Pa., D.C., Okla., Va., Wis., Del., Nat. Council Engring. Examiners. Engring. aide Conn. Hwy. Dept., 1940-41; asst. engr. East Hartford Dept. Pub. Works, 1942-44; structural engr. Hardesty & Hanover, N.Y.C., 1945-47, Sanderson & Porter, 1947-49; lectr. architecture Columbia, 1948-51; with Ammann & Whitney (cons. engr.), N.Y.C., 1949—, partner, 1963-74, sr. partner, 1974-76, mng. partner, 1977—; exec. v.p. in charge bldg., transp., communications, mil. projects Ammann & Whitney, Inc., 1963-78, chmn., chief exec. officer, 1978—; v.p. Ammann & Whitney Internat. Ltd., 1963-73; pres. Safeguard Constrn. Mgmt. Corp., 1973—; cons. to govt. and industry.; Stanton Walker lectr. U. Md., 1973; adv. com. Urban and Civil Engring. U. Pa., 1974—; mem. engring. council Columbia U., 1975—; dir. Concrete Industry Bd., 1976—, pres., 1978-79; concrete specialist European Concrete Com. Contbr. manuals to profl. assns., articles to profl. jours.; Co-editor Structural Concrete Handbook, 1981. Bd. dirs. Cejwin Youth Camps, 1972—; trustee Hall of Sci., N.Y.C., 1976—; mem. Bklyn. Bridge Centennial Commn., 1981. Recipient Illig medal Columbia, 1946, Egleston medal Columbia U., 1981; Patriotic Civilian Service award Dept. of Army, 1973. Fellow ASCE (Ridgway award 1946, Civil Engring. State of the Art award 1974, Raymond Reese award 1976, Earnest Howard award 1983, v.p. Met. sect. 1978-79, pres. 1980, chmn. reinforced concrete research council 1980—), N.Y. Acad. Scis. (hon. life, Laskowitz Aerospace research award 1970, vice chmn. engring. sect. 1975-77, chmn. 1977-79), Am. Concrete Inst. (hon. mem., dir. 1966-76, v.p. 1970-72, pres. 1972-73, chmn. bldg. code requirements for reinforced concrete 1963-71, Wason medal 1956, Delmar Bloem award 1973), Am. Cons. Engring. Council; mem. N.Y. Assn. Cons. Engrs. (dir. 1981—), Nat. Acad. Engring., Am. Welding Soc., Am. Nat. Standards Inst. (chmn. minimum design loads for bldgs. and other structures 1968—), ASCE Performance of Structures Research Council (chmn. com. long term observations 1972-76), N.Y. Concrete Constrn. Inst. (pres. tall bldg. council 1975—), Am. Ordnance Assn., Internat. Assn. Bridge and Structural Engrs., Internat. Bridge and Turnpike Assn., Moles, Sigma Xi, Chi Epsilon (hon.), Tau Beta Pi. Jewish religion. Clubs: Engineers (N.Y.C.) (dir. 1974-75); Wings.). Home: 56 Chestnut Hill Roslyn NY 11576 Office: 2 World Trade Center New York NY 10048 *Do not give up personal integrity for any apparent "practical" advantage... Strive successful projects but do not seek personal credit. Make no adverse judgments of people unless it is an active consideration in a necessary decision. Judge people by their actions, not their words.*

COHEN, EDWARD BARON, real estate development and construction company executive; b. Suffolk, Va., July 5, 1918; s. Elias and Rachel (Baron) C.; m. Suzanne Myrna Mendelson, Oct. 27, 1951; children: Andrew Baron, Richard Baron. Student, Coll. William and Mary, 1937-38. Owner, operator men's retail clothing stores, Newport News, Va., 1938-48; owner, operator Oldsmobile dealership, Yonkers, N.Y., 1949-55; vice chmn. Cohen Bros. Realty Corp., N.Y.C., 1955—. Served with Q.M.C. U.S. Army, 1943-46; MTO. Recipient Silver Jubilee Humanitarian Albert Einstein Coll. Medicine, Yeshiva U., N.Y.C., 1981. Mem. Assn. for Better N.Y., Realty Found, N.Y., Real Estate Bd. N.Y., East Side C. of C., Associated Owners and Builders Greater N.Y. Republican. Jewish. Club: Noyac Golf and Country (Sag Harbor, N.Y.). Home: 785 Fifth Ave New York NY 10022 Office: Cohen Bros Realty Corp 805 3d Ave New York NY 10022

COHEN, EDWARD PHILIP, physician, university administrator; b. Glen Ridge, N.J., Sept. 28, 1932; s. Harry and Rae (Berke) C.; m. Toba Joy Gold, Mar. 24, 1963; children—Mark L., Lauren L., Jennifer L., Jonathan M. Tuition scholarship student, U. Miami (Fla.), 1950-53; M.D., Washington U., St. Louis, 1957. Diplomate: Am. Bd. Allergy and Immunology, Nat. Bd. Med. Examiners. Intern. U. Chgo. Hosps., 1957-58; research asso. Nat. Inst. Allergy and Infectious Diseases, NIH, 1958-60; resident in medicine U. Colo. Med. Center,

1960-61, instr. dept. medicine, 1962-74; instr., then asst. prof. microbiology U. Colo., 1963-65; asso. prof. Inst. Microbiology, Rutgers U., 1965-67; asso. prof. microbiology and medicine Rutgers Med. Sch., 1967-68; asso. prof. La Rabida-U. Chgo. Inst. and dept. medicine U. Chgo. Sch. Medicine, 1968-69, asso. prof. depts. medicine and microbiology, 1969-77, prof. microbiology, 1977-79, asst. dean, 1971-73; prof. microbiology and immunology, dean Sch. Basic Med. Scis., Coll. Medicine U. Ill., 1979-82, also prof. Ctr. Edn. and Research in Genetics, 1979-82, dir. Office of Research and Devel., 1982—. Author 135 articles and revs. in field; editor: Immune RNA, 1976, Medicine in Transition: The Centennial of the University of Illinois College of Medicine, 1981; co-editor: Membranes, Receptors and the Immune Response, 1980. Sci. adv. bd. Leukemia Research Found., 1978—; chmn. Biotech. Contact Group City of Chgo., 1982—. Served with USPHS, 1958-60. Spl. postdoctoral fellow USPHS, 1961-63; Research Career Devel. grantee, 1963-65. Mem. Am. Assn. Immunologists, Am. Soc. Cell Biology, Am. Acad. Allergy, Acad. Medicine N.J., Am. Soc. Microbiology, Central Soc. Clin. Research, Chgo. Assn. Immunologists (pres. 1974-75), Chgo. Soc. Allergy, Inst. Medicine Chgo., Reticuloendothelial Soc. Home: 4737 S Kimbark Ave Chicago IL 60615 Office: 1853 W Polk St Chicago IL 60612

COHEN, EDWIN SAMUEL, lawyer, educator; b. Richmond, Va., Sept. 27, 1914; s. LeRoy S. Cohen and Mirian (Rosenheim) C; m. Helen Herz, Aug. 31, 1944; children: Edwin C., Roger, Wendy. B.A., U. Richmond, 1933; J.D., U. Va., 1936. Bar: Va. 1935, N.Y. 1937, D.C. 1973. Asso. firm Sullivan & Cromwell, N.Y.C., 1936-49; partner Root, Barrett, Cohen, Knapp & Smith and (predecessor firm), N.Y.C., 1949-65, counsel, 1965-69; prof. law U. Va., Charlottsville, 1965-68, 73—, Joseph M. Hartfield Prof., 1968-69, 73—, Faculty Center Advanced Studies, 1973-74; asst. sec. treasury for tax policy, 1969-72, under sec. treasury, 1972-73; counsel Covington & Burling, Washington, 1973-77, partner, 1977—; mem. and counsel adv. group on corporate taxes Ways and Means Com. Ho. of Reps., 1956-58; spl. cons. on corps. Am. Law Inst. Fed. Income Tax Project, 1949-54; mem. adv. group Fed. Estate and Gift Tax Project, 1964-68; mem. Va. Income Tax Conformity Study Commn., 1970-71; cons. Va. Income Tax Study Commn., 1966-68; mem. adv. group Commr. Internal Revenue, 1967-68. Recipient Alexander Hamilton award Treasury Dept. Mem. Am. Judicature Soc., ABA (chmn. com. on corporate stockholder relationships 1956-58, mem. council 1958-61, chmn. spl. com. on substantive tax reform 1962-63, chmn. spl. com. on formation tax policy 1977-80), Va. Bar Assn., D.C. Bar Assn., N.Y. State Bar Assn., Va. Tax Conf. (planning com. 1965-68), C. of C. of U.S. (bd. dirs., chmn. taxation com. 1979-84), Assn. Bar City N.Y., N.Y. County Lawyers Assn., Am. Law Inst., Am. Coll. Tax Counsel, Order Coif, Raven Soc., U. Va., Phi Beta Kappa, Omicron Delta Kappa, Pi Delta Epsilon, Phi Epsilon Pi (Nat. Achievement award). Clubs: Broad Street, Colonnade, Boar's Head, Farmington; International (Washington); Capitol Hill, Nat. Lawyers. Home: 104 Stuart Pl Ednam Forest Charlottesville VA 22901

COHEN, ELI EDWARD, educator; b. Chgo., Aug. 3, 1912; s. Kalman and Rose (Sirota) C.; m. Dorothy Hersh, Feb. 17, 1936 (dec. 1959); children: Robert, Ellen, Katey; m. Selma Stein Rosenbaum, May 18, 1969. B.S., U. Ill., 1933; postgrad., Sch. Social Service Adminstrn., U. Chgo., 1934-37. Supr. Marks Nathan Jewish Orphan Home, Chgo., 1933-34; case worker Chgo. Relief Adminstrn., 1934-36; counselor Jewish Vocat. Service, Chgo., 1936-39; dir. Phila. Jewish Vocat. Service, 1939-40; exec. dir. Jewish Occupational Council, N.Y.C., 1940-51; v.p. Exec. Job Counselors, N.Y.C., 1952-57; exec. sec. Nat. Child Labor Com. and div. Nat. Com. Employment Youth, 1958-74, Adv. Council Occupational Edn., 1974-81; instr. New Sch. for Social Research, 1976-82; lectr. N.Y. U., 1951, 64; cons. youth employment Dept. Labor, 1961-64, 66, 69; mem. N.Y. State Adv. Council Vocat. Edn., 1978-81; Dir. Am. Parents Com., 1960-74; dir. Mental Health Film Bd., 1963—, treas., 1976—; dir. Nat. Council Agrl. Life and Labor, 1958-64; mem. U.S. steering com. for World Mental Health Year, 1959-60; nat. panel arbitrators Am. Arbitration Assn., 1953—. Author articles; contbr. books and encys.; Co-editor: Manpower Policies for Youth, 1966. Sec. Nat. Conf. Jewish Social Welfare, 1950-51; mem. N.Y.C. Youth Council, 1977-81; pres. N.Y. Vocat. Guidance Assn., 1949-51; mem. Mayor N.Y.C. Com. Youth and Work, 1960-66; cons. White House Conf. Children and Youth, 1960; mem. Pres.'s Com. Youth Employment, 1961-64; task force youth U.S. Employment Service, 1964; mem. nat. com. Citizens Crusade Against Poverty, 1965-69; cons. anti-poverty task force Nat. Council Chs.; chmn. adv. council for occupational edn. N.Y.C. Bd. Edn., 1968-73; chmn. Council Nat. Orgns. for Children and Youth, 1971-73; vice chmn. Nat. Conf. on Pub. Service Employment, 1971-74; mem. Task Force on Employment Problems of Black Youth, Twentieth Century Fund, 1971-72; mem. adv. com. Nat. Project on Ethnic Am., 1971-74; mem. N.Y. State Manpower Planning Council, 1972-74; Trustee Jobs for Youth, 1974—. Profl. mem. Nat. Vocat. Guidance Assn. of Am. Personnel and Guidance Assn. (past chmn. young workers sect); mem. Nat. Com. for Children and Youth (1968-72); mem. exec. com. N.Y. State com. for 1970 White House Conf. on Children and Youth. Home: 2109 Broadway Apt 7-144 New York NY 10023

COHEN, ELIZABETH G., education and sociology, researcher; b. Worcester, Mass., May 1, 1931; d. Jacob and Anita (Asher) Ginsburg; m. Bernard P. Cohen, Sept. 20, 1953; children: Anita Cohen Williams, Lewis Samuel. B.A., Clark U., Worcester, 1953; M.A., Harvard U., 1955, Ph.D., 1958. Lectr. sociology Boston U., 1957-58; lectr. sociology and edu. Stanford U., 1962-66, asst. prof., 1966-69, assoc. prof., 1969-75, prof., 1975—, dir. Environ. for Teaching, 1970-76, chmn. social sci. in edu., 1970—, dir. program for complex instruction, 1982—. Author: A New Approach to Applied Research, 1970; contbr. chpts. to books and articles in field to profl. jours. Woodrow Wilson fellow, 1954-55; AAUW fellow, 1956-57; Fulbright fellow, 1972. Mem. Ctr. for Research on Women (policy bd. 1975-79), Pacific Sociol. Assn. (v.p. 1981-82), Sociology of Edn. Assn. (v.p. 1982-83), Am. Sociol. Assn. (sect. chmn. 1979-80), Am. Ednl. Research Assn. Democrat. Jewish. Home: 851 Sonoma Terr Stanford CA 94305 Office: Stanford Univ Sch of Edn Stanford CA 94305

COHEN, EUGENE ERWIN, university health institute administrator; b. Johnstown, Pa., Nov. 1, 1917; s. Leroy Samuel and Ann (Aronson) C.; m. Lee Woodard Edmundson, Dec. 31, 1944; children: William Palmer, Margaret Gene, Ann Woodard. B.B.A., U. Miami, Fla., 1941, M.B.A., 1951; postgrad., Wayne State U., 1944-45, U. N.C., 1951-52. Mem. faculty U. Miami, 1945—, asso. prof. accounting, 1954-67, prof. accounting, 1967-79, prof. emeritus, 1979—, treas., 1957-79, v.p., 1958-79, v.p. emeritus, 1979—; also treas. u2Univ. Research Found.; treas. Howard Hughes Med. Inst., 1979—; v.p., dir. Dormitory Housing Assn., Inc.; chmn., pres. Laurel Corp., 1971-73; dir. Fed. Res. br. Bank, Miami, Am. Bankers Ins. Co., Fla., Am. Laser Corp., Garrett & Co., Fla. Fed. Savs. & Loan Assn.; cons. Greyhound Corp., Plastetics, Inc., Reynolds & Co., NSF, NIH; U.S. Office Edn., So. Assn. Colls. and Schs., J.L. Mailman Found., A.L. Mailman Family Found.; stockholders agt. Garrett Trust; rep. Univ. Corp. for Atmospheric Research, 1969-73; mem. com. taxation Am. Council Edn. Cons. editor: Coll. and Univ. Bus. Mag, 1963-68; author articles in field. Bd. dirs. Miami Goodwill Industries, Dade County Citizens Safety Council, Greater Miami Indsl. Commn., Heart Learning Resource Center; pres. Orange Bowl Com., mem., 1950—; chmn. Dade County Higher Edn. Facilities Authority, 1969-81, Jackson Found., 1972—; v.p., dir. Nat. Childrens Cardiac Hosp.; trustee United Way Dade County, White Belt Found.; asso. mem. Internat. Center Coral Gables, 1973—, also, New World Center at, Miami Com.; mem. Health Systems Agy., South Fla.; bd. dirs. Family Services, Miami, 1968-74; mem. Miami Mayor's Spl. Adv. Com. on Interama, 1969-72. Served with AUS, 1941-45. Recipient Distinguished Alumni award U. Miami, 1961, Distinguished Grad. Alumnus award, 1963. Mem. Dade County C. of C., Am. Mgmt. Assn., The Miamians, Nat. Assn. Coll. and Univ. Bus. Officers (dir.), So. Assn. Coll. and Univ. Bus. Officers (pres. 1963), Coll. and Univ. Personnel Assn., Coll. and Univ. Housing Officers Assn., Nat. Assn. Cost Accts., Fin. Execs. Inst. (founder mem. Fla. chpt., chpt. pres. 1963), Fin. Analysts Soc. Miami, Econ. Soc. South Fla., Miami Beach Com. of 100, Hist. Assn. So. Fla. (dir.), Coral Gables Com. of 21, Friends of Univ. Library, Newcomen Soc., Iron Arrow, Omicron Delta Kappa, Alpha Phi Omega, Phi Mu Alpha, Beta Gamma Sigma, Alpha Kappa Psi. Clubs: Univ. Yacht, Miami; Ocean Reef Yacht and Country (Key Largo, Fla.). Home: 6700 SW 117th St Miami FL 33156 Office: Howard Hughes Med Inst PO Box 330837 Coconut Grove FL 33133

COHEN, EZECHIEL GODERT DAVID, physicist, educator; b. Amsterdam, Holland, Jan. 16, 1923; came to U.S., 1963; s. David Ezechiel and Sophie Louise (de Sterke) C.; m. Marina Arnoldina Linnekamp, Apr. 19, 1950; children—Michael Benjamin, Andrea Margaret. B.S. in Math., Physics and Astronomy, U. Amsterdam, 1947, Ph.D., 1957. First asst. U. Amsterdam, 1950-61, asso. prof., 1961-63; research asso. U. Mich., 1957-58, Johns Hopkins, 1958-59; prof., mem. Rockefeller U., 1963—. Editor: Fundamental Problems in Statistical Mechanics, Vol. I, 1961, Vol. II, 1968, Vol. III, 1975, Vol. IV, 1978, Vol. V, 1980, Statistical Mechanics at the Turn of the Decade, 1971, The Boltzmann Equation, Theory and Applications, 1973. Fellow Am. Phys. Soc.; mem. Netherlands Phys. Soc., Royal Dutch Acad. Scis. (corr.). Home: 500 E 63d St New York NY 10021 Office: 1230 York Ave New York NY 10021

COHEN, FELIX ASHER, lawyer; b. Pitts., Aug. 11, 1943; s. Alex Harry and Audrey Gwen (Williams) C.; m. Nancy Ann Wills, July 24, 1971; children: Timothy Asher, Blair Wills Schomaker. A.B., Princeton U., 1965; J.D., U. Pitts., 1971. Bar: Pa. 1972. Systems engr. IBM Corp., Pitts., 1965-68; law clk. U.S. Dist. Ct., Pitts., 1971-72; asso. firm Buchanan Ingersoll Rodewald Kyle & Buerger, Pitts., 1972-75; v.p., sec., counsel, dir. Signal Fin. Corp., Pitts., 1975—. Sec., bd. dirs. Children's Oncology Services of Pitts., Inc., 1977—. Mem. Am. Bar Assn., Pa. Bar Assn., Allegheny County Bar Assn. Home: 131 Ridge Rd Pittsburgh PA 15237 Office: Robinson Plaza Three PO Box 2944 Pittsburgh PA 15230

COHEN, GABRIEL MURREL, editor, publisher; b. Louisville, Aug. 31, 1908; s. Isaac and Jennie (Rosenbaum) C.; m. Helen Aronovitz, Sept. 22, 1939; children: Lawrence, Theodore, Miriam, Debbie, Ben-Zion, Jennie, Hermine, Rena. A.B., U. N.C., 1930. Reporter Louisville Herald-Post, 1927-28, 30-31; founder, editor, pub. Ky. Jewish Chronicle (now Ky. Jewish Post and Opinion), Louisville, 1931—, Ind. Jewish Post (now Ind. Jewish Post and Opinion), Indpls., 1935—, Mo. Jewish Post and Opinion, St. Louis, 1948—, Chgo. Jewish Post and Opinion, Nat. Jewish Post (now Jewish Post and Opinion), Indpls., 1948—. Home: 7984 Lieber Rd Indianapolis IN 46260 Office: 2120 N Meridian St Indianapolis IN 46202

COHEN, GEORGE LEON, lawyer; b. Covington, Ga., June 20, 1930; s. Leon and Callie (Harrison) C.; m. Jacqueline Lanier Edwards, Nov. 17, 1951; children—George Leon, Gardner Edwards. A.B., Va. Mil. Inst., 1951; LL.B., U. Va., 1956. Bar: Va. bar 1956, Ga. bar 1957, D.C. bar 1964. Asso. firm Sutherland, Asbill & Brennan, Atlanta, 1956-62, partner, 1962—. Mem. Am., Atlanta bar assns., Lawyers Club Atlanta, State Bar Ga. (chmn. sect. corp. and banking law 1968-69), Am. Law Inst. Home: 294 Camden Rd NE Atlanta GA 30309 Office: 3100 1st Atlanta Tower Atlanta GA 30383

COHEN, GERSON DAVID, theological seminary chancellor; b. N.Y.C., Aug. 26, 1924; s. Meyer and Nehama (Goldin) C.; m. Naomi Wiener, May 26, 1948; children: Jeremy, Judith. B.A., CCNY, 1944; B.H.L., Jewish Theol. Sem. Am., 1943, M.H.L., 1948; Ph.D., Columbia U., 1958; D.D. (hon.), Princeton U., 1976, Trinity Coll., 1983, D.H.L., NYU, 1978, CUNY, 1979. Rabbi, 1948; librarian Jewish Theol. Sem. Am., N.Y.C., 1950-57; asst. prof. Jewish lit. and instns., 1953-63, prof. history, 1970—, now chancellor; Gustav Gottheil lectr. Semitic langs. Columbia U., 1950-60, asso. prof. history, 1963-67, prof. Jewish history, 1967-70; dir. Center Israel and Jewish Studies, 1968-70, adj. prof. history, seminar asso., 1970—; Bd. visitors Harvard U. Divinity Sch., 1979-83. Author: Story of the Four Captives, 1961, Sefer ha Qabbalah, 1967, Reconstruction of Gaonic History, 1972; contbr. to Great Ages and Ideas of the Jewish People, 1956, Ency. Brit., 1968. Recipient Townsend Harris medal Coll. City N.Y., 1975. Fellow Am. Acad. Jewish Research (editor proc. 1969-72); mem. Alliance Israelite Universelle (dir.), Conf. Jewish Social Studies (dir.), Leo Baeck Inst. (dir.), Jewish Publ. Soc. (dir., chmn. publ. com. 1970-72). Home: 416 W 255th St Bronx NY 10471 Office: Univ of Judaism 15600 Mulholland Drive Los Angeles CA 90024

COHEN, HARLEY, civil engineering educator; b. Winnipeg, Man., Can., May 12, 1933; s. Joseph and Ettie (Gilman) C.; m. Estelle Brodsky, Dec. 25, 1956; children: Brent, Murray, Carla. B.Sc. hons., U. Man., 1956; Sc.M., Brown U., 1958; Ph.D., U. Minn., 1964. Registered profl. engr., Man. Research engr. Boeing Co., Seattle, 1958-60; sr. research scientist Honeywell, Inc., Mpls., 1960-64; asst. prof. civil engring. U. Minn., Mpls., 1964-65; assoc. prof. civil engring. U. Man., Winnipeg, 1965-68, prof., 1968-83, disting. prof., 1983—. Contbr. articles to profl. jours. J.L. Record prof. U. Minn., 1979; Killam scholar, 1982. Mem. Soc. Natural Philosophy, Am. Acad. Mechanics (founder mem.), Soc. Engring. Sci. Home: 55 Tanoak Park Dr Winnipeg MN Canada R2V 2W6 Office: Dept of Civil Engineering University of Manitoba Winnipeg MN Canada R3T 2N2

COHEN, HAROLD LARRY, educator, designer; b. N.Y.C., May 24, 1925; s. Nathan and Fannie (Herman) C.; m. Mary Della Kohn, Nov. 11, 1951; children: Jano Lynn, Lore Devra, David Louis. B.A., Ill. Inst. Tech., 1949. Prof., chmn. dept. design So. Ill. U., Carbondale, 1955-64; assoc. prof. psychiatry and behavioral sci. Johns Hopkins U. Sch. Medicine, Balt., 1967-68; ednl. dir. Inst. Behavioral Research, Silver Spring, Md., 1964-68, exec. dir., 1968-74; pres. The Exptl. Coll., 1970-74; prof., dean Sch. Architecture and Environ Design SUNY, Buffalo, 1974-84. Author: (with others) A Learning Environment, 1971; co-inventor, patentee disposable animal house, 1960; contbr. chpts. to books, articles to profl. jours. Dir.,designer entertainment dist. City of Buffalo, 1976-78; bd. dirs. Mayor's Commn. on Arts and Cultural Affairs, Buffalo, 1978-81, Cambridge Ctr. Behavioral Studies, 1982—; bd. dirs. transit mall task group Niagra Frontier Transit Authority, 1982—; hon. bd. dirs. Albright-Knox Art Gallery, 1982—. Served with USN, 1943-46. Recipient Community Service Faculty award Community Adv. Council SUNY-Buffalo, 1982, Good Design awards Mus. Modern Art, N.Y.C., 1951, 52, 53, Outstanding Faculty award U. Buffalo Found., 1979, Focus award Buffalo Courier Express, 1979. Mem. Assn. for Tropical Biology (dir. 1981-83); assoc. fellow Buffalo Mus. Sci. (1981—). Home: 522 Lafayette Ave Buffalo NY 14222 Office: Sch Architecture and Environ Design 114 Hayes Hall SUNY-Buffalo 3435 Main St Buffalo NY 14214 *Each one of us is part of a total fabric of comprehensive information which grows proportionately to the contributions made by each human being. Two of the most important people in my life have been R. Buckminster Fuller and John E. Walley. I have known and worked with "Bucky" for over thirty years, and with John Walley for over twenty-two. Their contributions live on in their works and in the people they have touched. I consider myself fortunate to have been one of those people.*

COHEN, HENNIG, educator; b. Darlington, S.C., Aug. 26, 1919; s. David A. and Hilda (Hennig) C.; m. Merrie Lou Conaway, June 16, 1946; children—David, Mark, Jonathan. A.B., U. S.C., 1941, M.A., 1948; Ph.D., Tulane U., 1951; M.A. (hon.), U. Pa., 1971. News editor sta. WCOS, Columbia, S.C., 1945-46; dir. pub. relations U. S.C., Columbia, 1946-56; asst. prof. English U. Pa., Phila., 1957-61; asso. prof., 1961-65, prof., 1965-74, John Welsh Centennial prof. history and lit., 1974—; vis. lectr. Bryn Mawr Coll., 1962-63, Swarthmore Coll., 1963-64, 65; vis. prof. Stanford, 1968; Fulbright prof. Am. studies U. London, 1973-74, U. Budapest, 1978. Author: The South Carolina Gazette, 1953; editor: Am. Quar, 1958-70, The Battle Pieces of Herman Melville, 1963, Selected Poems of Herman Melville, 1964, (with William Dillingham) Humor of the Old Southwest, 1964, (with T.P. Coffin) Folklore in America, 1966, The Parade of Heroes, 1978, The American Culture, 1968, The American Experience, 1968, Landmarks in American Writing, 1969, Folklore from the Working Folk of America, 1973, (with James Levernier) The Indians and Their Captives, 1977, (with J. Cahalan) A Concordance of Melville's Moby-Dick, 1978; contbr. articles to profl. jours. Served with USAAF, 1941-45; ETO. Decorated Air medal with five oak leaf clusters.; Guggenheim fellow, 1960; Newberry Library fellow, 1976; Nat. Endowment for Humanities fellow Winterthur Mus., 1980-81. Mem. Melville Soc. (sec. zo41968-74, pres. 1975), Am. Studies Assn. (exec. sec. 1956-61). Jewish religion. Clubs: Franklin Inn; University of Pa. Faculty (Phila.). Home: 37 Amherst Ave Swarthmore PA 19081 Office: Dept English U Pa Philadephia PA 19104

COHEN, HERBERT JAY, publishing company executive; b. N.Y.C., Oct. 12, 1935; s. Nathan and Minnie Rose (Cless) C.; m. Barbara L. Pennet, Apr. 15, 1962 (div. 1981); children: Laura, Neil, Melanie. B.B.A., CCNY, 1956. Fulfillment mgr. Around the World Shoppers Club, Elizabeth, N.J., 1957-60; ops. mgr. Columbia Record Club, N.Y.C., 1960-62; prodn. mgr. Popular Mdse. Co., Passaic, N.J., 1962-66; asst. pub. Xerox Edn. Publs., Middletown, Conn., 1966-72; exec. v.p., dir. Arno Press, N.Y. Times, N.Y.C., 1972-76, pres., 1976-81, Cohen & Co., 1981-84; pres., chief exec. officer Kraus Reprint & Periodicals, Inc., 1984—; lectr. NYU. Contbr. articles to profl. publs. Active Boy Scouts Am., Little League Baseball, Parent Tchrs. Orgn.; trustee, pres. Men's Club; trustee, v.p. Jewish Community Center, Harrison, N.Y. Served to capt. U.S. Army, 1956. Mem. Direct Mail Info. Exchange, Direct Mail Credit Assn. Clubs: Mem. B'nai B'rith. (v.p.), Rye Golf.). Office: Rt 100 Millwood NY 10546

COHEN, HERBERT JESSE, physician, educator; b. N.Y.C., Apr. 27, 1935; s. Barnet and Edith (Lepolstat) C.; m. Marion E. Finger, Aug. 29, 1960; children—Linda Elizabeth, Gerald Daniel, Seth Michael. B.A. (Ford Found. scholar), Columbia, 1955; M.D., State U. N.Y., 1959. Intern Bellevue Hosp., N.Y.C., 1959-60; resident N.Y. Hosp., N.Y.C., 1960-62; asst. instr. Cornell Med. Sch., 1961-62; instr. Tulane Med. Sch., 1962-64; NIH fellow Albert Einstein Coll. Medicine, 1964-66, asst. prof. pediatrics and rehab. medicine, 1966-71, asso. prof., 1971-76, prof., 1976—; dir. Children's Evaluation and Rehab. Clinic, Rose F. Kennedy Center for Mental Retardation and Human Devel., Bronx, N.Y., 1968-74, 78—, Bronx Developmental Services, N.Y. State Dept. Mental Hygiene, 1971-80, Rose F. Kennedy U. Affiliated Facility Tng. Program, 1974—, dir. div. child devel. and devel. disabilities dept. pediatrics, 1981—; vice chmn. Pres.'s Com. on Mental Retardation, 1978-81; mem. study sect. human devel. NIH, 1978-82; mem. profl. adv. bd. various founds. and profl. orgns. Author 2 books; also contbr. articles to profl. pubs. Served with USPHS, 1962-64. Recipient Disting. Humanitarian Research and Devel. awards Mental Retardation Service Orgns.; United Cerebral Palsy Research and Edn. Found. fellow, 1966-68. Fellow Am. Acad. Pediatrics (sec.-treas. child devel. sect. mem. com. on handicapped child), Am. Acad. Cerebral Palsy, Am. Assn. Univ. Affiliated Facilities (pres. 1980-81, dir. 1977—), Am. Assn. Mental Deficiency, AAAS. Office: R F Kennedy Center 1410 Pelham Pkwy S Bronx NY 10461

COHEN, HERMAN, race track executive; b. Balt., Nov. 27, 1894; s. Isaac Meyer and Rosa Marsha (Pondfield) C.; m. Rosa Lebovitz, Jan. 26, 1930 (dec. Apr. 1975); 1 son, Nathan L.; m. Grace Rein, Feb. 11, 1981. Ed. pub. schs. Owner dept. stores, shoe stores and men's wear stores in, Md., Del., W.Va. and N.C., 1912-30, J.G. Valiant Co. (interiors), Balt., 1931-32, Herzog's Men's Store, Washington, 1932-47, Balt. Clothes Mfg. Co. (men's clothes), 1936-38, Louis C. Tiffany Studios (stained glass windows), N.Y.C., 1936-37; engaged in devel. and constrn. on Eastern Seaboard, Fla. to N.J., 1940—; builder, operator, sec., treas. Sta. WAAM-TV, Balt., 1946-57; v.p. J.A. Maurer Co. (cameras and sound equipment), N.Y.C., 1948-63, Precision Film Labs., 1948-63; pres. Fairmount Steel Corp., Phila., 1948-57, Md. Jockey Club; pres., owner, operator Pimlico Race Course, 1952—; sec.-treas. Charlestown (W.Va.) Race Track, 1958-65; pres. Willow Grove (Pa.) Park, amusement center, 1955-65; Bd. dirs. Thoroughbred Racing Assn., 1964—. Pres. Jewish Welfare Fund, Balt., 1962-63; life mem. bd. Asso. Jewish Charities and Welfare Fund, Balt.; trustee Sinai Hosp., Balt., 1952-60; v.p. Balt. chpt. Am. Technion, 1969-78; v.p., treas. Herman and Ben Cohen Charitable Found., 1950-82. Jewish (trustee congregation 1948-65, co-chmn. bldg. com. 1957-62). Office: 1233 Mt Royal Ave Baltimore MD 21217

COHEN, HERMAN JACOB, mathematics educator; b. N.Y.C., Sept. 18, 1922; s. Jacob and Rose (Goldstein) C. B.A., Coll. City N.Y., 1943; M.A., U. Wis., 1946, Ph.D., 1949. Jr. physicist Nat. Bur. Standards, Washington, 1943-44; grad. fellow in applied math. Brown U., Providence, 1944-45; grad. asst. U. Wis., 1945-49; Fulbright scholar U. Paris, 1950-51; mem. math. faculty Coll. City N.Y., 1954—, prof. math., 1970—. Contbr. articles to math. publs. Mem. Am. Math. Soc., Math. Assn. Am., Phi Beta Kappa, Sigma Xi. Home: 90 La Salle St New York NY 10027

COHEN, HERMAN JAY, government official; b. N.Y.C., Feb. 10, 1932; s. Morris and Fannie (Zauzner) C.; m. Suzanne Karpman, Apr. 4, 1957; children: Marc, Alain. B.A. with high honors, CCNY, 1953; postgrad., Am. U., 1959-62. Vice consul Am. Embassy, Paris, 1955-58; cultural exchange officer Dept. State, 1958-62; adminstrv. officer Am. Embassy, Kampala, Uganda, 1962-63; polit. officer Am. consulate gen., Rhodesia, 1963-65; economic officer Am. Embassy, Lusaka, Zambia, 1965-66, dep. chief of mission, Kinshasa, Zaire, 1966-69; dir. central African affairs Dept. State, Washington, 1969-74; polit. counselor Am. Embassy, Paris, 1974-77; U.S. ambassador to Senegal and The Gambia, Dakar, Senegal, 1977-80; dep. asst. sec. for intelligence and research Dept. State, Washington, 1980—; mem. Fed. and Fgn. Service Impasses Panel. Served with U.S. Army, 1953-55. Mem. Am. Fgn. Service Assn., Phi Beta Kappa. Office: Dept State Intelligence and Research Bur 2201 C St Washington DC 20520 *

COHEN, HIRSH JOEL, hospital administrator; b. Montreal, Aug. 26, 1942; U.S., 1978; s. Solly and Mildred (Flanders) C.; m. Aliza Pollack, Aug. 7, 1966; children: Leah, Joshua. B. Commerce, Loyola

Coll., Montreal, 1964, B.A., 1965; M.H.A., U. Montreal, 1971. Planning officer Ont. Hosp., Toronto, 1968-70; adminstr. McMaster U., Hamilton, Ont., Can., 1970-73; asst. dir. Jewish Gen. Hosp., Montreal, 1973-75, dir. hosp. services, 1975-78; adminstr. Holmes div. Univ. Hosp., Cin., 1978—; adv. bd. Hospice, Cin., 1981—; bd. dirs. Greater Cin. Hosp. Council, 1978—. Author: Jour. Hosp. Adminstrs. in Canada, 1977, Dimensions, 1978. Mem. Am. Coll. Hosp. Adminstrs., Can. Coll. Health Care Execs. Home: 3648 Jeffrey Ct Cincinnati OH 45236 Office: Holmes div Univ Hosp Eden and Bethesda Ave Cincinnati OH 45219

COHEN, IRA MYRON, aeronautical engineering educator; b. Chgo., July 18, 1937; d. Harry Nathan and Esther (Lenchner) C.; m. Linda Barbara Einstein, June 12, 1960; children: Susan Ellen, Nancy Beth. B. in Aero. Engring, Poly. Inst., Bklyn., 1958; M.A., Princeton U., 1961, Ph.D. in Aero. Engring, 1963; M.A. (hon.), U. Pa., 1971. Mem. tech. staff Sandia Labs., Albuquerque, summers 1971, 74, 77; asst. prof. engring. Brown U., Providence, 1963-66; asst. prof. mech. engring. U. Pa., Phila., 1966-67, asso. prof. mech. engring., 1967-76, prof. mech. engring., 1976—; guest prof. Technische Hochschule Aachen, W. Ger., 1966; cons. fluid mechanics related problems to industry, 1966—, attys., 1966—; Mem. bd. The Sch. in Rose Valley, Moylan, Pa., 1969-74. Contbr. articles to various publs. Recipient Fulbright Travel grant, 1966. Assoc. Fellow AIAA (sect. sec. 1977-80); Mem. Am. Phys. Soc., AAUP. Office: Dept Mech Engring and Applied Mechanics 111A Towne Bldg D3 U Pa Philadelphia PA 19104

COHEN, IRA STANLEY, psychologist; b. N.Y.C., Sept. 1, 1922; s. Herbert H. and Minnie (Raden) C.; children—Rachel, Sarah. B.A., Queens Coll., 1948; Ph.D., Ind. U., 1953. Asst. prof. psychology State U. N.Y. at Buffalo, 1952-58, asso. prof., 1958-63, prof., 1963—; acting provost Faculty Social Scis. and Adminstrn., 1968-69, provost, 1969-71, chmn. psychology dept., 1978-80; vis. prof. psychiatry Harvard U., 1972-73. Served with AUS, 1942-46. Mem. Am., Eastern psychol. assns., AAUP. Home: 297 Little Robin Rd Buffalo NY 14228 Office: Dept Psychology State U NY at Buffalo Buffalo NY 14226

COHEN, ISADORE T., lawyer; b. Savannah, Ga., Jan. 28, 1908; s. Moses G. and Hannah (Katzoff) C.; m. Sylvia Gold, Sept. 3, 1929; 1 dau., Barbara (Mrs. William Eugene Schatten). LL.B., Atlanta Law Sch., 1927. Bar: Ga. 1927, N.C. 1933. Practice in, Atlanta, 1927-33, Charlotte, N.C., 1933-39; gen. So. counsel A.S.C.A.P., Atlanta, 1939; gen. counsel Tent 21 Variety Club; sr. partner firm Smith, Cohen, Ringel, Kohler & Martin, Atlanta.; Dir. Fulton Industries, Inc., 1956-68; pres. WIIN, Inc., Atlanta. Bd. govs. Israel Bond Com.; mem. nat. joint distbn. com. United Jewish Appeal.; Bd. dirs. Atlanta Jewish Home. Recipient David Ben Gurian Humanities award, 1974. Mem. Am., Ga., N.C. bar assns., Nu Beta. Jewish religion (v.p. temple, 1935-37, supt. Sunday Sch. 1935-37). Clubs: Standard (Atlanta); Charlotte (N.C.). Established Jay and Leslie Cohen chair for judaic studies Emory U. Home: 1371 W Wesley Rd NW Atlanta GA 30327 also Harbour House 2295 S Ocean Blvd Palm Beach FL 33480 Office: First Atlanta Bank Tower Atlanta GA 30383 *I consider reputation and honor the greatest assets a man can have.*

COHEN, ISRAEL, chain store executive; b. 1912; married. With Giant Food Inc., Landover, Md., 1935—, exec. v.p., 1974-75, exec. v.p., chief operating officer, 1975, pres., chief exec. officer, chmn. bd., dir. Office: Giant Food Inc 6300 Sheriff Rd Landover MD 10785 *

COHEN, JEROME, educator; b. Pitts., May 27, 1925; s. Abraham Wolfe and Dorothy (Middleman) C.; m. Florence A. Chanock, Oct. 28, 1945; children—Marcus, Mara, Aaron. B.A., U. Pitts., 1947, Ph.D., 1951; A.A., Princeton, 1943; M.A., Cornell U., 1949. Instr. U. Pitts., 1950-51; asst. prof., asso. prof. Antioch Coll., Yellow Springs, O., 1951-57; prof. Northwestern U. Med. Sch., Chgo., 1957—; dir. Electroencephalogram Lab. Presbyn.-St. Lukes Hosp., Chgo., 1967-72, Cook County Hosp., 1973—; vis. scientist Neurol. Inst., U. London, 1963-64; vis. prof. Hebrew U., 1972—. Served with USNR, 1943-46. Commonwealth Fund fellow, 1963-64. Mem. Am. EEG Soc., Am. Psychol. Assn., Psychophysiol. Research Soc., Internat. Brain Research Soc., AAUP, AAAS, Sigma Xi. Home: 125 Laurel Ave Wilmette IL 60091 Office: 303 E Chicago Ave Chicago IL 60611

COHEN, JEROME ALAN, law educator; b. Elizabeth, N.J., July 1, 1930; s. Philip and Beatrice (Kaufman) C.; m. Joan F. Lebold, June 30, 1954; children: Peter, Seth, Ethan. B.A., Yale U., 1951, LL.B., 1955; postgrad., U. Lyone, France, 1951-52. Bar: Conn. 1955, D.C. 1957. Law sec. to Chief Justice Earl Warren, 1955-56, Justice Felix Frankfurter, 1956-57; assoc. Covington & Burling, Washington, 1957-58; asst. U.S. Atty., Washington, 1958-59; cons. U.S. Senate com. Fgn. Relations, 1959; mem. faculty U. Calif., Berkeley, 1956-65; prof. Harvard Law Sch., 1964—, also assoc. dean and dir. East Asian Legal Studies, mem. exec. com. East Asian Research Ctr., Learned Socs.-Social Sci. Research Council, 1965—; chmn. panel China and world order Soc. Internat. Law, 1967—. Author: The Criminal Process in the Peoples Republic of China, 1949-63, 68; co-author: Taiwan and American Policy, 1971, China Today and Her ancient Treasures, 1974; editor: People's China and International Law, 1974, Contemporary Chinese Law, 1970, The Dynamics of China Foreign Relations, 1970, China's Practice of International Law, 1972; co-editor: Essays on China's Legal Tradition, 1979; editorial bd.: Am. Jour. Internat. Law. Mem. Assn. Asian Studies, Am. Soc. Internat. Law, Council Fgn. Relations, AAUP. Home: 21 Bryant St Cambridge MA 02138 Office: 345 Park Ave New York NY 10154

COHEN, JEROME BERNARD, materials science educator; b. Bklyn., July 16, 1932; s. David I. and Shirley Anne C.; m. Lois Nesson, Sept. 15, 1957; children: Elissa Diane, Andrew Neil. B.S., Mass. Inst. Tech., 1954, Sc.D., 1957. Sr. scientist materials AVCO Corp., Wilmington, Mass., 1958-59; mem. faculty Northwestern U., 1959—, prof. materials sci. and engring., 1965—, chmn. dept. materials sci. and engring., 1973-78, Frank C. Engelhart prof., 1974—, fellow Center Teaching Professions, 1971—, prof. Technol. Inst., 1983—; sci. liaison officer Office Naval Research, London, 1966-67; cons. to govt. and industry. Mem. bd. Author: Diffraction Methods in Materials Science, 1966; co-author: Diffraction from Materials, 1978; Co-editor: Local Atomic Arrangements Studied by X-Ray Diffraction, 1967, Jour. Applied Crystallography, Modulated Structures, 1979. All-Star coach Glencoe (Ill.) Hockey Assn., 1974-77. Served as 1st lt. AUS, 1959. Fulbright fellow U. Paris, 1957-58; recipient Tech. Inst. Teaching award Northwestern U., 1976. Fellow Am. Inst. Metall., Mining and Petroleum Engring. (Hardy Gold medal 1960), Am. Soc. Metals (Henry Marion Howe medal 1981); mem. Am. Soc. Engring. Edn. (George C. Westinghouse award 1976), Am. Ceramic Soc., Am. Crystallographic Assn., Royal Instn. Gt. Britain, AAUP, Sigma Xi, Tau Beta Pi, Alpha Sigma Mu, Phi Lambda Upsilon. Jewish. Patentee in field. Home: 362 Jackson Ave Glencoe IL 60022 Office: 2145 Sheridan Rd Evanston IL 60201

COHEN, JOEL EPHRAIM, scientist; b. Washington, Feb. 10, 1944; s. Hymen Ezra and Alice C.; m. Audrey Jane Biller, June 14, 1970; children: Zoe, Adam. B.A., Harvard U., 1965, M.A., 1967, M.P.H., 1970, Ph.D., 1970, Dr. Public Health, 1973; M.A. (hon.), Cambridge U., 1974. Fellow in math. biology and sociology Soc. of Fellows, Harvard U., 1967-71; asst. prof. biology Harvard U., 1971-72, assoc. prof., 1972-75; prof. populations Rockefeller U., N.Y.C., 1975—; chmn. bd. Siam Inst. Math. and Soc., 1973—. Author: A Model of Simple Competition, 1967, Casual Groups of Monkeys and Men, 1971, Food Webs and Niche Space, 1978. Fellow Center for Advanced Study in Behavioral Scis., Stanford, 1981-82; Recipient Mercer award Ecol. Soc. Am., 1972; John Simon Guggenheim meml. fellow, 1981-82; MacArthur Found. prize fellow, 1981—. Fellow AAAS; Mem. Population Assn. Am., Cambridge Philos. Soc., Math. Assn. Am., Am. Statis. Assn., Am. Soc. Naturalists, Soc. for Indsl. and Applied Math. Jewish. Office: Rockefeller U 1230 York Ave New York NY 10021

COHEN, JOEL ISRAEL, conductor, lutenist, composer; b. Providence, May 23, 1942; s. Jacob Israel and Beatrice (Gross) C.; m. Anne Atema Stabenbordt, Feb. 7, 1983. B.A., Brown U., 1963; M.A., Harvard U., 1965; student of theory and composition with, Nadia Boulanger, Paris, 1965-67. Instr. Brandeis U., Waltham, Mass., 1967-72, U. Mass.-Boston, 1972-74; music dir. The Cambridge Consort, Boston, 1964-70, The Boston Camerata, 1968—; guest lectr. Harvard U., Yale U.; dir. Early Music Acad., Tarn, France, 1972—. Producer: Sta. WGBH, Boston, 1981; condr.-dir.: recording compositions Sacred Service I and II, Dierdre (chamber opera). Chmn. music com. Boston-Strasbourg Sister City Com., 1983; mem. Isham Music Library; com. Harvard U., 1981-82. Danforth fellow, 1963-67; Woodrow Wilson fellow, 1963-64; recipient award in the Arts Signet Soc., Harvard U., 1983. Mem. Phi Beta Kappa. Jewish. Home: 26 Jefferson St Newburyport MA Office: Boston Camerata Inc 25 Huntington Ave Boston MA 02116 *My principal activity as a musician has been the performance of early European music from the Middle Ages, Renaissance, and early Baroque. Closely associated in this enterprise are my colleagues of the Boston Camerata. Our collective goals are to reawaken interest in a neglected musical past, to renew standards of performance and concert programming, and to make early music vital part of contemporary cultural life.*

COHEN, JOSEPH ARTHUR, lawyer; b. N.Y.C., Feb. 28, 1928; s. Benjamin and Frieda (Herman) C.; m. Janice C. Commanday, Aug. 10, 1952; children: Susan Lee, Jonathan Andrew, Nancy Elizabeth. B.B.A., CCNY, 1949; LL.B., Columbia U., 1952; LL.M., NYU, 1958. Bar: N.Y. 1953, U.S. Supreme Ct. 1977. Atty. Armed Services Textile and Apparel Procurement Agy., N.Y.C., 1952-54; assoc. Alexander, Ash, Schwartz & Cohen, N.Y.C., 1954—, partner, 1963—; town judge, Scarsdale, N.Y., 1978—; lectr. Practising Law Inst., N.Y. Treas., Troop 410, Boy Scouts Am., 1970-74; sgt. Scarsdale (N.Y.) Aux. Police, 1971—; mem. Town Club, 1970—, Greenacres Assn., 1965—; mem. parents council Tufts U.; mem. pres.'s roundtable U. Puget Sound. Served with AUS, 1946-47. Mem. Maritime Law Assn., Am., N.Y. State bar assns., Def. Research Inst., Am. Arbitration Assn. Clubs: YMCA Athletic, Merchants. Home: Box 217 Route 31 RD 2 Salem NY 12865 Office: 41 E 42d St New York NY 10017

COHEN, JOZEF, educator, psychophysicist; b. Brookline, Mass., July 21, 1921; s. David J. and Dora A. (Levin) C.; m. Huguette Schachnovitch, July 31, 1958. B.S., U. Chgo., 1942; Ph.D., Cornell U., 1945. Susan Linn Sage fellow Cornell U., 1942-45; mem. research staff Psycho-Acoustic Lab. Harvard, 1945; mem. faculty Cornell U., 1945-48, U. Ill. at, Champaign, 1948—, prof. psychology, 1969—. Author: Eyewitness Series in Psychology, including Personality Assessment, 1969-72; also articles on history of ideas and sci., theory and applications of Euclidean color space including color TV.; co-discoverer: (with Thomas P. Friden) Euclidean color space, 1974. Fellow Am. Psychol. Assn., A.A.A.S.; mem. Midwestern Psychol. Assn., Psychonomic Soc., Sigma Xi. Home: 303 Burkwood Ct W Urbana IL 61801 Office: Psychology Bldg Univ Ill 603 E Daniel St Champaign IL 61820

COHEN, JULES, physician, university dean; b. Bklyn., Aug. 26, 1931; s. Samuel S. and Dora (Goldstein) C.; m. Doris Eidlin, Mar. 25, 1956; children: Stephen E., David E., Sharon E. A.B., U. Rochester, 1953, M.D., 1957. Intern Beth Israel Hosp., Boston, 1957-58; resident, fellow in medicine U. Rochester (N.Y.) Strong Meml. Hosp., 1958-60, mem. faculty, 1963—, prof. medicine, 1973—; NIH research asso., Bethesda, Md., 1960-62; research fellow Postgrad. Med. Sch., London, 1962-63; physician in chief Rochester Gen. Hosp., 1976-82; sr. asso. dean med. edn. U. Rochester Sch. Medicine, 1982—. USPHS research grantee, 1963-69, 74-77; recipient USPHS Research Career Devel. award, 1970-75; Am. Heart Assn. grantee-in-aid, 1969-71. Fellow A.C.P.; mem. Am. Physiol. Soc., Am. Fedn. Clin. Research, Am. Heart Assn. (fellow Council on Clin. Cardiology), Monroe County Med. Soc., N.Y. State Med. Soc., Rochester Acad. Medicine. Jewish. Home: 152 Burkedale Crescent Rochester NY 14625 Office: Sch Medicine and Dentistry U Rochester 601 Elmwood Ave Rochester NY 14642 also

COHEN, JULES SIMON, lawyer; b. Orlando, Fla., Nov. 1, 1937; s. Barney Joseph and Dorothy (Collman) C.; m. Elizabeth Ann Wiese, May 21, 1971; children: Lynda Kaye, Laurel Ann, Richard Wiese, Ronald Herman. B.A., U. Fla., 1959; J.D., Harvard U., 1962. Bar: Fla. 1962. Partner firm Cohen & Cohen, Orlando, Fla., 1962-67; individual practice law, Orlando, 1967—. Contbr. articles to legal jours. Mem. exec. com. Orange County Democratic Exec. Com., 1972-80. Mem. Southeastern Bankruptcy Law Inst. (mem. bd. dirs. 1977—), Fla. Bar (chmn. bankruptcy com. 1973-75, chmn. corp., banking, bus. law sect. 1976-77, lectr. continuing legal edn. com. 1974—, Am. Arbitration Assn.); mem. Orange County Bar Assn., ABA (bus. bankruptcy com. 1978-83), Fed. Bar Assn., Am. Judicature Soc., Comml. Law League Am. Democrat. Jewish. Club: Harvard. Office: 808 N Mills Ave Orlando FL 32803

COHEN, JULIUS, legal educator; b. N.Y.C., Oct. 27, 1910; s. Saul and Mollie (Sidler) C.; m. Lillian Tyson, Dec. 22, 1945. A.B., W.Va. U., 1931; A.M., W. Va. U., 1932; LL.B., W.Va. U., 1937; LL.M., Harvard U., 1938; postgrad., Columbia U. Sch. Law, 1936. Bar: W.Va. 1937, Nebr. 1954. Instr., dept. govt. W.Va. U., 1935-37; asst. prof., 1938-41; legal and adminstrv. aide to gov. State of W.Va., 1940-42; adviser W.Va. Legislative Interim Com., 1939-40; chmn. W.Va. State Election Commn., 1941-43; legal adviser W.Va., Office of Civilian Def., 1941-43; legal div. War Manpower Commn., 1943-44, Alien Property Custodian, 1944-45; prof. law U. Nebr. Coll. Law, 1946-57; vis. prof. Ind. U. Sch. Law, summers 1950, 53, 54, Rutgers Sch. Law, 1956-57, prof. law, 1957—; vis. prof. law Yale U. Law Sch., 1958-59; lectr. Jillin U., China, 1981; vis. disting. prof. law Calif. Western Sch. Law, 1982, 83; legislative aide U.S. Senate, summer 1949, 51. Author: Materials and Problems on Legislation, 1949, rev. 2d edit., 1967, (wih Robson and Bates) Parental Authority: The Community and the Law, 1958; Contbr.: Freedom and Authority in Our Time, 1953, Symbols and Values, 1954, Nomos, 1962, 1968, 1973, (with Haber) The Law School of Tomorrow, 1968; others., to legal and other periodicals. Guggenheim fellow, 1963-64. Mem. Phi Beta Kappa. Home: 16 Clover Ln Princeton NJ 08540

COHEN, KARL PALEY, nuclear energy consultant; b. N.Y.C., Feb. 5, 1913; s. Joseph M. and Ray (Paley) C.; m. Marthe H. Malartre, Sept. 20, 1938; children: Martine-Claude Leboue, Elisabeth M. Brown, Beatrix Josephine Cashmore. A.B., Columbia U., 1933, M.A., 1934, Ph.D., 1937; postgrad., U. Paris, 1936-37. Research asst. to Prof. H. C. Urey Columbia U., 1937-40; dir. theoretical div., SAM Manhattan project, 1940-44; physicist Standard Oil Devel. Co., 1944-48; tech. dir. H.K. Ferguson Co., 1948-52; v.p. Walter Kidde Nuclear Lab., 1952-55; cons. AEC, sr. sci. Columbia U., 1955; mgr. advance engring. atomic power equipment dept. Gen. Electric Co., 1955-65, gen. mgr. breeder reactor devel. dept., 1965-71, mgr. strategic planning, nuclear energy div., 1971-73, chief scientist, nuclear energy group, 1973-78; cons. prof. Stanford U., 1978-81. Author: The Theory of Isotope Separation as Applied to Large Scale Production of U-235, 1951; contbr. articles to profl. jours. Recipient Energy Research prize Alfried Krupp Found., 1977; Chem. Pioneer award Am. Inst. Chemists, 1979. Fellow Am. Nuclear Soc. (pres. 1968-69, dir.), AAAS; mem. Nat. Acad. Engring., Am. Phys. Soc., Cactus and Succulent Soc., Phi Beta Kappa, Sigma Xi, Phi Lambda Upsilon. Office: 928 N California Ave Palo Alto CA 94303

COHEN, LAWRENCE, physician, dentist, educator; b. Leeds, Eng., Nov. 23, 1926; s. Joseph and Millie (Burnstein) C.; m. Gloria Stewart, Dec. 27, 1951; children: Alan Steven, Martin Ian, David Charles. B. Ch.D., L.D.S., Leeds U., 1949, F.D.S.R.C.S., 1951; L.R.C.P., M.R.C.S., Guys Hosp., 1956; Ph.D., U. London, 1966. Clin. instr. U. Birmingham, 1949-50; intern, resident oral surgery Middlesex Hosp., 1956-59; sr. resident plastic unit Stoke Mandeville, 1960-61; sr. resident Univ. Coll., 1961-62, lectr. oral pathology, 1962-63, sr. lectr. oral medicine, 1963-67; prof., head dept. oral diagnosis U. Ill., Chgo., 1967-76; chmn. dept. dentistry, dir. dental edn. Ill. Masonic Med. Center, Chgo., 1976; vis. prof. medicine U. Chgo., 1974-75; cons. oral diagnosis VA West Side Hosp., Chgo. Author: A Synopsis of Medicine in Dentistry, 1972, 77; Editor: Oral Diagnosis and Treatment Planning, 1973. Mem. dental adv. com. Health Edn. Commn., Bd. Higher Edn. State of Ill., 1969-73; chmn. FDA Panel Rev. Oral Cavity Drug Preparations, 1974-80. Served to squadron leader RAF, 1950-52. Recipient Samuel Charles Miller award Am. Acad. Oral Medicine, 1980. Fellow Royal Soc. Medicine, Am. Coll. Dentists; mem. Internat. Assn. Dental Research, Am. Acad. Oral Medicine (pres.-elect 1983), AMA, ADA, Brit. Dental Assn., Sigma Xi. Home: 200 Kilpatrick Ave Wilmette IL 60091 Office: 927 W Wellington Chicago IL 60657 *Never sacrifice others on the altar of expediency.*

COHEN, LAWRENCE JOSEPH, physician, state ofcl.; b. Cheyenne, Wyo., Aug. 19, 1921; s. Hyman R. and Bertha (Silverstein) C.; m. Arline Pasternack, Dec. 19, 1950; children—Craig, Robbin, Brent. B.S., Tulane U., 1943, M.D., 1945, M.P.H., 1966. Diplomate: Am. Bd. Pediatrics. Intern U.S. Naval Hosp., Portsmouth, N.H., 1945-46; sr. resident in pediatrics New Orleans Charity Hosp., 1948-50; practice medicine specializing in pediatrics, Cheyenne, 1950-66; asso. prof. pediatrics U. Colo., 1966—; dir. div. maternal and child health Wyo. Dept. Health, Cheyenne, 1966-68, dir. dept., 1968-69; dir. div. health and med. services Wyo. Dept. Health and Social Services, Cheyenne, 1969—; cons. pediatrics USAF, 1950-66; mem. Gov.'s Select Com. on Med. Edn. Mem. com. United Fund, Cheyenne, 1967-68. Served with USNR, 1945-48. Mem. AMA, Wyo. Med. Soc., Am. Acad. Pediatrics (chmn. Wyo. chpt. 1967-68), Delta Omega. Clubs: Rotary, Young Men's Lit. Home: 3721 McComb St Cheyenne WY 82001 Office: Wyo Dept Health and Social Services Hathaway Bldg Cheyenne WY 82002

COHEN, LAWRENCE SOREL, physician; b. N.Y.C., Mar. 27, 1933; s. Max and Fannie (Cooper) C.; m. Jane Abramson, Aug. 5, 1961; children: Melanie, Wendy. A.B., Harvard U., 1954; M.D., N.Y. U., 1958; M.A. (hon.), Yale U., 1970. Diplomate: Am. Bd. Internal Medicine, Sub Bd. Cardiovascular Diseases. Intern, then resident in medicine Yale-New Haven Hosp., 1958-60, 64-65; asst. in medicine Harvard U. Med. Sch., 1962-64; sr. investigator Nat. Heart, Lung and Blood Inst., 1965-68, mem. task force on arteriosclerosis, 1978-80; asso. prof. medicine U. Tex. Med. Sch., Dallas, 1968-70; prof. medicine Yale U. Med. Sch., 1970-81, Ebenezer K. Hunt prof. medicine, 1981—. Mem. editorial bd.: Circulation, Am. Jour. Cardiology, Am. Heart Jour.; Contbr. over 140 articles to med. jours. Served with USPHS, 1960-62. Mem. Am. Coll. Cardiology (trustee 1978-83, editorial bd. jour.), Am. Heart Assn. (chpt. pres. 1980-81). Address: 333 Cedar St 87 LMP New Haven CT 06510

COHEN, LEONARD, lawyer; b. N.Y.C., Jan. 19, 1925; s. Alexander and Alice (Bloom) C.; m. Jean E. Hide, Nov. 1, 1958; children: Jondy, Jay, Justin, Jennifer. B.S., UCLA, 1948; LL.B., Loyola U., Los Angeles, 1951. Bar: Calif. 1951; C.P.A., Calif. Practiced in, Beverly Hills, 1951—; partner Ervin, Cohen & Jessup, 1952—; pres., vice chmn. bd. Nat. Med. Enterprises, 1969—; lectr. U. So. Calif. Law Sch., 1958—. Author articles in field. Served with USAAF, 1942-46. Mem. Am., Calif., Beverly Hills bar assns., Am. Inst. C.P.A.'s, Phi Alpha Delta, Zeta Beta Tau. Home: PO Box 25980 Los Angeles CA 90025

COHEN, LEONARD (NORMAN COHEN), poet, novelist, musician, songwriter; b. Montreal, Que., Can., Sept. 21, 1934; s. Nathan B. and Marsha (Klinitsky) C. B.A., McGill U., 1955; postgrad., Columbia. With Stranger Music, Inc., N.Y.C. Author: poetry Let Us Compare Mythologies, 1956, The Spice Box of Earth, 1961, Flowers for Hitler, 1964, Parasites of Heaven, 1966; Selected Poems, 1956-68, 1968, The Energy of Slaves, 1973, Death of a Lady's Man, 1979, Choosing to Work, 1979; novels The Favorite Game, 1963, Beautiful Losers, 1966; also articles, songs; recording artist for, Columbia Records. Recipient McGill Lit. award, 1956; Canada Council grant, 1960-61; Quebec Lit. award, 1964; LL.B. (hon.) Dalhousie U., 1971. Address: care Columbia Records 1801 Century Park W Century City CA 90067 *

COHEN, LEONARD ARLIN, physiology educator; b. Bklyn., May 4, 1924; s. Abraham B. and Alice (Spieller) C.; m. Sheila Gold, June 25, 1950; children: Seth David, Jared Ben, Ellyn Beth. B.A., U. Conn., 1948; Ph.D., Yale U., 1952. Instr. to asso. prof. U. Pitts. Sch. Medicine, 1951-61; with Oxford U. Lab. Physiology, 1956-58; head physiology dept. Einstein Med. Ctr., Phila., 1961-70; prof. phys. medicine and rehab. Temple U. Sch. Medicine, 1967-70; prof. physiology Mich. State U., Lansing, 1970—; dir. Regional Med. Program; adminstr., dir. research and devel. Rehab. Center, Inc.; pres., dir. Physiomonitor, Inc., Human Capability Charitable Corp.; cons. Learning Disabilities Clinic. Contbr. articles to profl. jours. Served with AUS, 1942; ETO. Decorated Croix de Guerre; recipient James Hudson Brown award Yale U., 1949; research grants NSF, 1952-53, 59-60, 70-74, NIH, 1954-56, 59-66; Fulbright fellow for advanced research Oxford U., 1956-57; NSF postdoctoral fellow Oxford U., 1957-58; Am. Physiol. Soc. lectr. Meharry Coll., 1969-70. Mem. Jewish War Vets. Home: 15951 Harden Circle Southfield MI 48075 Office: Northland Med Bldg 20905 Greenfield Rd Suite 107A Southfield MI 48075

COHEN, LEWIS ISAAC, lawyer; b. N.Y.C., July 27, 1932; s. Benjamin and Jeannette (Klotzko) C.; m. Sheila Lipman, Sept. 8, 1957; children—Leslie, Bruce, Wendy. B.A., U. Calif. at Los Angeles, 1953; LL.B., Columbia, 1958. Bar: N.Y. State bar 1959, D.C. bar 1964, U.S. Supreme Ct. bar 1966. Atty. FCC, Washington, 1959-64; practiced in Washington, 1964—; partner firm Cohen & Berfield, 1964—. Served with AUS, 1954-56. Mem. Fed., D.C. bar assns., FCC Bar Assn. Home: 6315 Swords Way Bethesda MD 20034 Office: 1129 20th St NW Washington DC 20036

COHEN, LOIS RUTH KUSHNER, government research institute official; b. Phila., May 31, 1938; d. Joseph George and Doris (Bronstein) Kushner. Tchr.'s diploma, Gratz Coll., Phila., 1957; B.A. (Senatorial scholar), U. Pa., 1960; M.S., Purdue U., 1961; Ph.D. (NSF, David Ross fellow), Purdue U., 1963. Research coordinator dept. sociology Purdue U., 1963-64; vis. lectr. Howard U., spring 1964;

social sci. analyst div. dental health USPHS, Washington, 1964-70; chief applied behavioral studies div. dental health USPHS, NIH, Bethesda, Md., 1970-71; chief Office Social and Behavioral Analysis, 1971-74; spl. asst. to dir. Div. Dentistry, 1974-76, Nat. Inst. Dental Research, 1976—; cons. dental health unit WHO, 1970—; co-dir. Internat. Collaborative Study Dental Manpower Systems in Relation to Oral Health Status, 1970; cons. WHO, 1970, 74, 75, Inst. Medicine, Nat. Acad. Sci., 1977-80; vis. lectr. health policy and social medicine Harvard U., Boston, 1981-84. Co-editor: Toward a Sociology of Dentistry, 1971, Social Sciences and Dentistry, Vol. I, 1971, Vol. II, 1984; editorial reviewer: Social Sci. and Medicine, 1975—, Jour. Preventive Dentistry, 1973—, Scandinavian Jour. Dental Research, 1973—; Contbr. numerous articles to profl. jours., books. Recipient Phila. High Sch. for Girls Rowen stipend, 1956. Fellow AAAS (mem. gov. council 1971); mem. Am. Pub. Health Assn., Am. Sociol. Assn., Behavioral Scientists in Dental Research (a founder, pres. 1971-72), D.C. Sociol. Soc., Federation Dentaire Internationale (cons.), Internat. Assn. Dental Research (dir. 1976-77, chmn. internat. relations com. 1979-83), Am. Assn. Dental Research (dir. 1980-81). Office: DHHS USPHS NIH NIDR 9000 Rockville Pike Bethesda MD 20205

COHEN, LOUIS DAVID, emeritus psychology educator; b. Bklyn., Nov. 26, 1912; s. Gutman and Lillie (Kolko) C.; m. Tina Simon, June 28, 1936; children: Myra Cohen Dey, Beth Cohen Shubert. B.S., Bklyn. Coll., 1934; M.A., Columbia U., 1936; postgrad., NYU, 1937-39, Sch. Pub. Health, U. Minn., summer 1969, Cambridge, (Eng.) U., 1970-71; Ph.D., Duke U., 1949. Diplomate: Am. Bd. Profl. Psychology (Southeastern bd. regents 1972-79). Head psychologist N.Y.C. Penitentiary, 1936-38; dir. classification, edn. and welfare Ind. State Farm, Greencastle, 1938-42; assoc. clin. psychology to prof. psychology and med. psychology Duke, 1946-62; prof., chmn. dept. clin. psychology U. Fla., Gainesville, 1962-76, prof. clin. psychology and psychology, 1976-81, prof. emeritus, 1981—; Mem. rev. com. spl. and exptl. tng. br. NIMH, Washington, 1965-69, chmn., 1968-69; mem. Fla. Bd. Examiners Psychology, 1965-67, Commn. on Mental Illness and Retardation, So. Regional Edn. Bd., 1963-68, chmn., 1966-68; cons. field selection office Peace Corps, 1962-68; cons. VA, Washington; mem. adv. com. psychology Fla. Div. Vocat. Rehab., 1969-73, chmn., 1972-73; mem. Council Univ. Dirs. Clin. Psychology, 1975-79, chmn., 1976-78; bd. dirs. Nat. Register Health Service Providers in Psychology, 1974-84. Contbg. editor: Jour. Ednl. and Psychol. Measurement, 1955—; contbr. articles to profl. jours. Bd. dirs. B'nai Israel Synagogue, Gainesville, Fla., pres., 1964-67; bd. dirs. North Central Fla. Community Mental Health Ctr., Gainesville, 1979—, pres., 1980-83, 84—, sec., 1983-84. Served from lt. to lt. col. AUS, 1942-46. Decorated Army Commendation medal. Fellow Am. Psychol. Assn. (edn. and tng. bd. 1974-79, chmn. 1976—, council of reps. 1969-72, 80-84, Disting. Contbn. award 1984), Am. Pub. Health Assn.; mem. N.C. Psychol. Assn. (pres.), Nat. Acads. Practice (Disting. Practitioner), Southeastern Psychol. Assn. (pres. 1964-65), Fla. Psychol. Assn. (pres. 1979-80). Home: 1250 NW 61st Terr Gainesville FL 32605

COHEN, LYNNE GAIL, artist, photographer; b. Racine, Wis., July 3, 1944; d. Lester N. and Sophie (Block) C.; m. Andrew M. Lugg, Mar. 23, 1968. B.S. in Art, U. Wis., 1967; student, University Coll., London, 1964-65; postgrad., U. Mich., 1968; M.A. in Art, Eastern Mich. U., Ypsilanti, 1969. Teaching fellow Eastern Mich. U., 1968, lectr., 1969-70, instr., 1970-73; lectr. U. Ottawa, Ont., 1974-81, 83, asst. prof., 1982-83; assoc. prof. Art Inst. Chgo., 1984. Exhibited one-man show, Space Gallery, Toronto, 1973, U. N.Mex., Albuquerque, 1975, Carpenter Ctr. for Visual Arts, Harvard U., 1978, Yarlow-Salzman Gallery, Toronto, 1979, Floating Gallery, Winnipeg, 1981, Magic Image Gallery, Picering, Ont., 1983, group shows, U. Mich. Photography Show, 1973, Nat. Gallery Can., 1977, Douglas Kenyon Gallery, Chgo., 1980, U. Western Ont., 1981, Eastern Mich. U., 1982; represented permanent collections, Art Inst. Chgo., Nat. Gallery Can., New Orleans Art Mus., Mus. Contemporary Art, Montreal, Bibliotheque Nationale, Paris, others. Recipient Logan award Chgo. Art Inst., 1968; Can. Council grantee, 1978-79, 83. Office: 1100 Laurier U Ottawa ON Canada K1N 6N5

COHEN, MARK HERBERT, broadcasting company executive; b. Boston, Mar. 27, 1932; s. Henry I. and Francis C.; m. Mary Jane Pitman, July 30, 1961; children: Patricia Beth, H. Jonathan, Cathy Ann. B.A. in Bus. Adminstrn., U. Maine, 1954; M.S. in TV Prodn, Syracuse U., 1958. Announcer Sta. WGUY AM-FM, Bangor, Maine, 1954, Sta. WGAN AM-TV, Portland, Maine, 1954-55; various positions in sales, planning and station clearance ABC-TV network, N.Y.C., 1958-68, v.p. sales planning, 1967-70, v.p., asso. dir. planning, bus. and fin. analysis, 1970-76, sr. v.p. fin. and planning, 1976-77, sr. v.p., 1977—; v.p. Am. Broadcasting Cos. Inc., 1981-83, sr. v.p., 1983—. Mem. exec. com. of alumni council U. Maine, 1980—, also mem. art com. Served to 1st lt., inf. U.S. Army, 1955-57. Mem. TV Acad. of Arts and Scis. (v.p. 1983-84), Internat. Radio and TV Soc. (gov. 1980-81). Club: Whippoorwill. Office: 1330 Ave of Americas New York NY 10019

COHEN, MARSHALL HARRIS, radio astronomer, educator; b. Manchester, N.H., July 5, 1926; s. Solomon and Mollie (Epstein) C.; m. Shirley Kekst, Sept. 19, 1948; children—Thelma, Linda, Sara. B.E.E., Ohio State U., 1948, M.S., 1949, Ph.D., 1952. Research asso. Ohio State U., 1950-54; faculty Cornell U., 1954-66; prof. applied electrophysics U. Calif., San Diego, 1966; vis. asso. prof. radio astronomy Calif. Inst. Tech., Pasadena, 1965, prof. radio astronomy, 1968—, exec. officer for astronomy, 1981—. Contbr. articles to profl. jours. Co-recipient Rumford medal Am. Acad. Arts and Sci., 1971; John Simon Guggenheim Meml. Found. fellow, 1960-61, 80-81. Fellow A.A.A.S.; mem. Am. Astron. Soc., Astron. Soc. of Pacific (dir. 1970-73), Internat. Astron. Union, Internat. Sci. Radio Union (U.S. chmn. Commn. V 1969-72). Office: Astronomy Dept Calif Inst of Tech Pasadena CA 91125

COHEN, MARTIN, communications company executive; b. N.Y.C., Jan. 8, 1932; s. I.R. and J.D. C.; m. Nancy L. Young, May 15, 1960; children: Edward M., Jonathan S., George D. A.B., Brown U., 1953; M.B.A., Wharton Sch., U. Pa., 1957. C.P.A., D.C. Tax cons., mgr. price Waterhouse, Washington, 1957-64; tax advisor U.S. Treasury Dept., Washington, 1964-66; various exec. positions The Washington Post Co., 1966-75, v.p. fin., 1975—; dir. Internat. Herald Tribune, S.A., paris, Bowater Mersey Paper Co. Ltd., Liverpool, N.S., Can. Bd. dirs. Childrens Hosp. Nat. Med. Ctr., Washington, 1973—. Served to lst lt. USMC, 1953-55. Recipient Meritorious Service award U.S. Treasury Dept., 1965. Mem. Am. Inst. C.P.A.s, Fin. Execs. Inst. Club: Woodmont Country (Rockville, Md.) (treas. 1982—). Home: 5024 Baltan Rd Bethesda MD 20816 Office: The Washington Post Company 1150 15th St NW Washington DC 20071

COHEN, MARVIN LOU, educator; b. Montreal, Que., Can., Mar. 3, 1935; came to U.S., 1947, naturalized, 1953; s. Elmo and Molly (Zaritsky) C.; m. Merrill L. Gardner, Aug. 31, 1958; children—Mark, Susan. A.B., U. Calif., 1957; M.S., U. Chgo., 1958, Ph.D., 1964. Tech. staff mem. Bell Telephone Labs., Murray Hill, N.J., 1963-64; asst. prof. U. Calif. at Berkeley, 1964-66, asso. prof., 1966-68, prof. physics, 1969—, also; prof. Miller Inst. Basic Research in Sci. of U. Calif., 1969-70, 76-77, chmn., 1977-81; exchange prof. U. Paris, France, 1972-73, summers 1968, 75; U.S. rep. to Semicondr. Commn., Internat. Union Pure and Applied Physics, 1975-81; Alfred P. Sloan fellow Cambridge U., Eng., 1965-67; vis. prof. U. Hawaii, Honolulu, 1978-79. Contbr. articles to tech. jours. Recipient Oliver E. Buckley prize for solid state physics, 1979, award outstanding accomplishment U.S. Dept. Energy, 1981; Guggenheim fellow, 1978-79. Fellow Am. Phys. Soc. (exec. council div. solid state physics 1975-79, chmn. 1977-78); mem. Oliver E. Buckley prize com. (1980-81, chmn. 1981), Nat. Acad. Scis., Sigma Xi. Home: 10 Forest Ln Berkeley CA 94708 Office: Dept Physics U Calif Berkeley CA 94720 *Make decisions only when things go well and stick to them when things go badly.*

COHEN, MARVIN SANFORD, lawyer; b. Akron, Ohio, Oct. 16, 1931; s. Norman J. and Faye (Abramovitz) C.; m. Frances E. Smith, June 19, 1953; children: Samuel David, Jeffrey Lee, Rachel Ann. B.A., U. Ariz., 1953, LL.B., 1957. Bar: Ariz. 1957, D.C. 1980. Practice law, Tucson, 1957—, Washington, 1981—; chief civil dep. Pima County atty., 1958-60; 1st asst. Tucson city atty., 1961; spl. asst. to solicitor Dept. Interior, Washington, 1961-63; mem. firm Bilby, Thompson, Shoenhair & Warnock, 1963-78; mem., chmn. CAB, 1978-81; partner firm Stroock & Stroock & Lavan, Washington, 1981—; Mem. Tucson Fgn. Relations Com., 1968-78; chmn. Ariz. Anti-Defamation League, 1970. Author numerous articles on airline deregulation. Pres. Young Democratic Clubs, Ariz., 1960; del. Dem. Nat. Conv., 1964; chmn. Pima County Dem. Central Com., 1960; pres. Tucson Jewish Community Center, 1972-73, Ariz. Civic Theater, 1975-76; bd. dirs. Ariz. Commn. on Arts and Humanities, 1975-77. Served to 1st lt. USAF, 1953-55. Jewish (bd. dirs. temple). Clubs: Aero, Internat. Ari. Home: 10334 Democracy Ln Potomac MD 20854 Office: 1150 17th St NW Washington DC 20036

COHEN, MAYNARD MANUEL, neurologist, neurochemist, educator; b. Regina, Sask., Can., May 17, 1920; came to U.S., 1920, naturalized, 1925; s. Aleck and Dora (Pinsk) C.; m. Doris Rosenshine; children: Deborah, Elena. A.B., U. Mich., 1941; M.D., Wayne U., 1944; Ph.D., U. Minn., 1953. Intern Woman's Hosp., Detroit, 1944-45, resident pathology, 1945-46, U. Minn. and; Mpls. VA Hosp., 1948-50, resident neurology, 1949-50; faculty U. Minn., 1950-63, prof. neurology, 1959-63; dir. Center Cerebrovascular Research, 1961-63; prof. neurology, head div. U. Ill., 1963-71, prof. pharmacology, 1963—; chmn. dept. neurology Presbyn.-St. Luke's Hosp., Chgo., 1963—; prof., chmn. dept. neurol. scis., prof. biochemistry Rush Med. Coll., 1971—; Mem. med. adv. bd. Ill. Epilepsy League, Epilepsy Found.; mem. neurol. scis. postgrad. tng. grant com. Nat. Inst. Neurol. Diseases and Blindness, 1959-63; mem. biol. scis. tng. grant com. NIMH, 1968-72; adv. com. Council Internat. Exchange Scholars, 1978-81; Fellow Am. Scandinavian Found., Rikshospitalet, Oslo, Norway and; Oslo Community Hosp., 1951-52; NIH fellow dept. biochemistry Inst., Psychiatry, Maudsley Hosp. U. London, Eng., 1957-58; Fulbright-Hays lectr. U. Oslo, 1977. Co-editor: Morphological and Biochemical Correlates of Neural Activity, 1964; Editor: Biochemistry, Ultrastucture and Physiology of Cerebral Anoxia, Hypoxia and Ischemia, 1973, Biochemistry of Neural Disease, 1975; asso. editor: Jour. Neurol. Scis, 1963—; editor: Monographs in Neural Sciences; mem. editorial bd.: Neurology, 1973-76; liaison editor: Jour. Neuroepidemiology, 1982—. Served to capt. M.C. AUS, 1946-47. Recipient Distinguished Service award Wayne State U. Sch. Medicine, 1964, Alumni award Wayne State U., 1970. Mem. Am. Acad. Neurology (v.p. 1967-69, pres.-elect 1979-81, pres. 1981—), Assn. Univ. Profs. Neurology (pres. 1967-68), Biochem. Soc., Am., Norwegian neurol. socs., Am. Assn. Neuropathologists, Assn. Research Nervous and Mental Diseases, Internat., Am. socs. neurochemistry, Norwegian Acad. Scis. and Letters, Sigma Xi, Alpha Omega Alpha. Home: 1000 Chestnut St Wilmette IL 60091 Office: 600 S Paulina Chicago IL 60612

COHEN, MELVIN JOSEPH, neuroscientist; b. Los Angeles, Sept. 28, 1928; s. Samuel and Bessie (Firman) C.; m. Catherine Black, Dec. 27, 1963; children: Frank M., Linn C., Sarah R., Samuel D. B.A., UCLA, 1949, M.A., 1952, Ph.D., 1954; student, U. Calif., Berkeley, 1950-51. Instr. biology Harvard, 1955-57; asst. prof. to prof. biology U. Oreg., 1957-69; prof. biology Yale, 1969—. Contbr. articles to profl. jours. NSF postdoctoral fellow, Stockholm, 1954-55; Guggenheim fellow, Oxford, Eng., 1965. Mem. Nat. Acad. Scis., Internat. Brain Research Orgn., Soc. Gen. Physiologists (pres. 1976-77), Am. Soc. Zoologists, Soc. Neurosci. Home: 15 Salt Meadow Ln Madison CT 06443 Office: Dept Biology Yale New Haven CT 06511

COHEN, MELVIN R., physician; b. Chgo., May 24, 1917; s. Louis M. and Anna S. (Friedman) C.; m. Miriam, May 19, 1946; children—Nancy, Alan. B.S., U. Ill., 1931, M.S. in Pathology, 1933, 1934, A.O.A. (hon.). Diplomate: diplomat Am. Bd. Ob-Gyn. Practice medicine specializing in Ob-Gyn, Chgo.; sr. attending physician Michael Reese Med. Center, Northwestern Meml. Hosp.; founder, since dir. Fertility Inst. Ltd.; prof. Northwestern U. Med. Sch. Author: Laparoscopy, Culdoscopy and Gynecography: Technique and Atlas, 1970. Served with M.C. AUS, 1942-45. Co-recipient Gold medal for exhibit, 1951. Address: 990 N Lake Shore Dr Chicago IL 60611

COHEN, MELVIN STEPHEN, jewelry company executive; b. N.Y.C., July 11, 1919; s. Harry and Sallie (Bodker) C.; m. Frances Mand, Sept. 25, 1942; children: Sallie (Mrs. Michael Goldwyn), Wendie (Mrs. Jerry Sroka). B.S., NYU, 1940; M.B.A., Harvard, 1942. Dir. personnel A. Cohen & Sons Corp. (subsequently Cohen Hatfield Industries Inc., now MacAndrew & Forbes Group Inc.), N.Y.C., 1943-47, dir. sales, 1947-59, pres., 1959-69, chmn. bd., 1969-80, chmn. exec. com., 1980—, also treas.; dir. Maidenform Co. Trustee, vice chmn. Dist. 65 Pension and Welfare Plan, 1979—, vice chmn., 1980. Served to 1st lt. AUS, 1942-46. Mem. Am. Jewelery Distbrs. Assn. (exec. com. 1960—, pres. 1960-62), Jewelry Industry Council (dir. 1970—), Jewelry Security Alliance (dir. 1974—), Internat. Golf Soc. Clubs: Glen Oaks (gov. 1977—, treas. 1980), Glen Oaks (sec. 1981—); 24 Karet (N.Y.C.) (pres. 1975, dir. 1975—); 24 Karet (N.Y.C.) (vice chmn. 1980, chmn. 1983), N.Y.U.). Home: 77 Merrivale Rd Great Neck NY 11020 Office: 36 E 63d St New York NY 10021

COHEN, MICHAEL, physicist; b. N.Y.C., May 9, 1930; s. Joseph George and Emma Naomi (Mabel) C.; m. Regina Anne Buckley, June 8, 1958; children—Adam, Jonathan, Alison. A.B., Cornell U., 1951; Ph.D., Calif. Inst. Tech., 1956. Research asso. Calif. Inst. Tech., 1956-57; mem. Inst. Advanced Study, Princeton, N.J., 1957-58; mem. faculty dept. physics U. Pa., Phila., 1958—, prof., 1975—; cons. Los Alamos Sci. Lab.; co-founder, v.p., hon. trustee Aspen Center for Physics. Fellow Am. Phys. Soc.; mem. Phi Beta Kappa, Sigma Xi. Home: 710 Sussex Rd Wynnewood PA 19096 Office: Dept Physics U of Pa Philadelphia PA 19104

COHEN, MICHAEL I., pediatrician; b. Bklyn., Feb. 9, 1935; s. Nat L. and Fannie (Wechsler) C.; m. Nancy Ann Wood, Oct. 28, 1963; children—Adam Wood, Amy Melissa, Meg Rebecca. B.A., Columbia U., 1956, M.D., 1960. Intern Mary Imogene Bassett Hosp., 1960-61; resident Babies Hosp., N.Y.C., 1961-63; USPHS postdoctoral fellow in gastroenterology Albert Einstein Coll. Medicine, 1965-67, mem. faculty, 1967—, prof. pediatrics, 1976—, chmn. dept., 1980—; dir. div. adolescent medicine Montefiore Hosp., N.Y.C., 1967-80. Author numerous papers in field; contbr. chpts. to books. Served with M.C. USAF, 1963-65. Decorated Air Force Commendation medal. Mem. Am. Acad. Pediatrics (chmn. com. adolescence 1977-80, award sect. adolescence 1980), Soc. Adolescent Medicine, Am. Fedn. Clin. Research, Ambulatory Pediatrics Assn., Soc. Pediatric Research, Am. Psychosomatic Soc., Am. Pediatrics Soc., Am. Gastrointestinal Assn., Alpha Omega Alpha. Office: 111 E 210th St Bronx NY 10467

COHEN, MITCHELL HARRY, U.S. judge; b. Phila., Sept. 11, 1904; s. Harry and Minnie (Rubin) C.; children: Margaret, Fredric. Student, Temple U., 1922-24; LL.B., Dickinson Law Sch., 1928. Bar: N.J. 1930. Practiced in, Camden, 1930-58, city prosecutor, 1936-42, freeholder, Camden County, 1940; judge Camden Mcpl. Ct., 1942-47; county prosecutor, Camden County, 1948-58, county judge, 1958-61; judge Superior Ct. N.J., New Brunswick, 1961-62, U.S. Dist. Ct. N.J., Camden, 1962-73, sr. judge., 1973—. Founder, co-producer Camden County Music Fair, 1955; chmn. Camden County chpt. Sister Kenny Found., Allied Jewish Appeal, Camden.; Leader Camden Republican Com., 1947-58. Served with AUS, World War II. Mem. Am., N.J., Camden County bar assns., Am. Judicature Soc. Office: US Court House and Post Office Bldg 401 Market St Camden NJ 08101 *

COHEN, MORLEY MITCHELL, chain store executive; b. Winnipeg, Man., Can., Jan. 2, 1917; s. Alexander and Rose (Diamond) C.; m. Rita Lillian Stober, Nov. 4, 1957; children—Joanne (Mrs. Barry Goldmeir), Donna Susan (Mrs. Graeme Low). Ed., St. John's Tech. Sch. Pres. Saan Stores, Ltd., Winnipeg, 1954-57; exec. v.p. Gen. Distbrs., Ltd., Montreal, 1958-63, Met. Stores of Can., Ltd., 1964-68, pres., 1969—, chmn., 1979—; dir. Gen. Distbrs., Ltd., Montreal Bd. Trade, 1973-75. Chmn. Combined Jewish Appeal, Montreal, 1970, mem. campaign cabinet, 1980; treas. YMHA and YWHA, Montreal, 1971; chmn. capital fund drive, 1980; treas. United Israel Appeal, 1970-71; chmn. Arthritis Soc., Que., 1981; bd. dirs., v.p. Jewish Community Fund Found., 1980; bd. dirs. Jewish Gen. Hosp., Montreal, Que. Safety League. Served with RCAF, 1940-45. Mem. Internat. Golf Soc. (founder). Clubs: B'nai B'rith, Elmridge Golf and Country (past pres.), Montefiore (Montreal)). Office: PO Box 300 Pointe Claire PQ Canada

COHEN, MORREL HERMAN, physicist, biologist, educator; b. Boston, Sept. 10, 1927; s. David and Rose (Kemler) C.; m. Sylvia Zwein, June 18, 1950; children: Julie, Robert, Daniel, Lisa. B.S. in Physics, Worcester Poly. Inst., 1947, D.Sc. (hon.), 1973; M.A. in Physics, Dartmouth Coll., 1948, Ph.D., U. Calif.-Berkeley, 1952. Mem. faculty U. Chgo., 1952-81, assoc. prof. physics, 1957-60, prof., 1960-81, prof. theoretical biology, 1968—, Louis Block prof. physics and theoretical biology, 1972-81, mem. com. developmental biology, 1973-74, publs. bd., 1969-70; acting dir. James Franck Inst., 1965-66, dir., 1968-71; dir. materials research lab. NSF, 1977-81; sr. sci. advisor corp. research scis. lab. Exxon Research and Engring. Co., 1981—; cons. govt. and industry, 1953—; vis. scientist NRC, Can., 1960, Xerox Corp., 1978; Shrum lectr. Simon Fraser U., 1973; assoc. Clare Hall U. Cambridge, Eng., 1973—; vis. prof. U. Va., 1976, Kyoto U., 1979; mem. adv. panel electrophysics NASA, 1962-66; mem. adv. com. Nat. Magnet Lab., 1963-66; mem. rev. com. solid state sci. and metallurgy div. Argonne Nat. Lab., 1964-67, chmn., 1966, bd. govs., 1982—; chmn. Gordon Conf., 1968, 4th Internat. Conf. Armorphous and Liquid Semicondrs., 1971; mem. adv. com. Inst. Amorphous Studies, 1982—; mem. Army Basic Research Com., 1979—, mem. steering com., 1980—; mem. adv. com. dept. physics U. Tex., Austin, 1982—. Author articles physics of solids, liquids, gases, theoretical and developmental biology.; assoc. editor: Jour. Chem. Physics, 1960-63; mem. editorial bd.: advanced physics monograph series McGraw-Hill Co., 1963-70; editorial bd.: The Physics of Condensed Matter, 1962-74; publs. bd., U. Chgo., 1969-70; bd. editors: Jour. Statis. Physics, 1970-75. AEC fellow, 1951-52; Guggenheim fellow, 1957-58; NSF sr. postdoctoral fellow, Rome, 1964-65; NIH spl. fellow, 1972-73. Fellow Am. Phys. Soc. (council 1978-82, chmn. solid state physics div. 1970, div. councillor 1978-82); mem. AAAS, Am. Inst. Physics, Nat. Acad. Scis., Sigma Xi (nat. lectr. 1966). Home: 1100 Crim Rd Bridgewater NJ 08807 Office: PO Box 45 Linden NJ 07036

COHEN, MORRIS, educator; b. Chelsea, Mass., Nov. 27, 1911; s. Julius Harry and Alice (Ovson) C.; m. Ruth Krentzman, Jan. 24, 1937 (dec.); children—Barbara (Mrs. Willy Nordwind), Joel Alan. S.B., Mass. Inst. Tech., 1933, Sc.D., 1936; D.Tekn. (hon.), Royal Inst. Tech., Stockholm, 1977, D.Tech., Israel Inst. Tech. Asst. prof. Mass. Inst. Tech., 1937-42, asso. prof., 1942-46, prof., 1946-62, Ford prof. materials sci. and engring., 1962-74, Inst. prof., 1974—; hon. prof. Beijing U. Iron and Steel Tech., 1980—, Beijing Inst. Aeros. and Astronautics, 1980—; Metall. cons.; dir. Addison-Wesley Pub. Co., Reading, Mass. Recipient Mathewson Gold medal Am. Inst. Mining, Metall. Engrs., 1953, Inst. Metals Award Am. Inst. Mining, Metall. Engrs., 1952, Robert F. Mehl award, 1953; Clamer medal Franklin Inst., 1959; Gold medal Japan Inst. Metals, 1970; Chevenard medal French Metall. Soc., 1971; Killian faculty achievement award Mass. Inst. Tech., 1974; Procter prize Research Soc. N.Am., 1976; Nat. medal of Sci., 1977; Joseph R. Vilella award ASTM, 1979; Gold medal Acta Metallurgica, 1981. Fellow Metall. Soc. of AIME, Am. Acad. Arts and Scis., N.Y. Acad. Scis., Am. Soc. Metals (past pres., trustee, Howe medal 1945, 49, Gold Medal 1968, Sauveur achievement award 1977, hon. mem.); fgn. fellow Indian Nat. Sci. Acad.; mem. Nat. Acad. Scis., Nat. Acad. Engring., AIME (hon.), Korean Inst. Metals (hon.); hon. mem. Indian Inst. Metals (Kamani Gold medal 1953), Iron and Steel Inst. Japan, Japan Inst. Metals, Metals Soc. London. Home: 491 Puritan Rd Swampscott MA 01907 Office: Mass Inst Tech Cambridge MA 02139

COHEN, MORRIS LEO, librarian; b. N.Y.C., Nov. 2, 1927; s. Emanuel and Anna (Frank) C.; m. Gloria Weitzner, Feb. 1, 1953; children—Havi, Daniel Asher. B.A., U. Chgo., 1947; LL.B., Columbia U., 1951; M.L.S., Pratt Inst., 1959. Bar: N.Y. bar 1951. Pvt. practice, N.Y.C., 1951-58; asst. law librarian Rutgers U. Law Sch., 1958-59, Columbia Law Sch., 1959-61; law librarian, asso. prof. law State U. N.Y. at, Buffalo, 1961-63; Biddle law librarian, prof. law U. Pa. Law Sch., Phila., 1963-71; law librarian, prof. law Harvard U. Law Sch., 1971-81, Yale U. Law Sch., New Haven, 1981—; lectr. Drexel Inst. Sch. Library Sci., 1964-70, Columbia Sch. Library Service, 1965-70; vis. prof. Simmons Coll. Library Sch., 1977-80; Mem. exec. bd. Phila. chpt. ACLU; bd. visitors Columbia U. Law Sch., 1977—. Author: Legal Bibliography Briefed, 1965, Legal Research in a Nutshell, 1968, 3d edit., 1978, How to Find the Law, 8th edit., 1983, Law and Science: A Selected Bibliography, 1980. Nat. Endowment for Humanities grantee. Mem. ALA (chmn. law and polit. sci. sect. 1967-69), AAUP (pres. U. Pa. chpt. 1966-67), Am. Assn. Law Libraries (pres. 1970-71), Am. Bar Assn., Jewish Publs. Soc. (v.p. 1975-80), Bibliog. Soc. Am., Internat. Assn. Law Libraries. Jewish. Home: 84 McKinley Ave New Haven CT 06515

COHEN, MOSES ELIAS, mathematician, educator; b. U.K., Nov. 30, 1937; s. Elias Moses and Katie (Hey) C.; m. Odette Jockel, Sept. 12, 1963; 1 son, Uri Elie. B.S., London U., 1963; Ph.D., U. Wales, 1967. Research fellow French AEC, 1968; asst. prof. Mich. Tech. U., 1968-69; asst. prof. math. Calif. State U., Fresno, 1969-70, asso. prof., 1970-74, prof., 1974—; Asso. fellow Inst. Math. and Applications, U.K. Contbr. articles to profl. jours. Mem. Inst. Physics (U.K), Am. Math. Soc., AAUP. Home: 7131 N Briarwood Fresno CA 93711

COHEN, MYER, former United Nations official; b. Washington, Nov. 9, 1907; s. Myer and Helen (Wolf) C.; m. Elizabeth Elson, Aug.

21, 1933; children: Arthur E., Judith (Mrs. Franz Kretzmann). B.A. with high honors, Swarthmore Coll., 1929; student, Cambridge U., 1929-30, Law Sch. Yale, 1930-31; Ph.D. in Internat. Relations, Law Sch. Yale, 1935. Instr. Sch. Social Studies, San Francisco, 1935-40; asst. regional dir. Farm Security Adminstrn., San Francisco, 1940-44; chief operations UNRRA Displaced Persons Program, 1944-47; asst. dir. gen. Internat. Refugee Orgn., Geneva, Switzerland, 1947-52; resident rep. UN in, Yugoslavia, 1952-56; program dir. UN Tech. Assistance Adminstrn., 1956-58; chief operations UN Spl. Fund, 1959-65; asst. adminstr. UN Devel. Programme, 1965-71, dep. adminstr., 1972-73; sr. cons. Internat. Devel. Research Center, 1974—; asso. Ralph Bunche Inst. on UN.; Bd. dirs. World Rehab. Fund, Inc., N.Y.C. Editor: Selected Supreme Court Decisions, 1937. Decorated Yugoslav Order of Flag with platinum leaf. Mem. Soc. Internat. Devel., UN Assn. (dir. N.Y. chpt.), Phi Beta Kappa. Club: Yale (N.Y.C.). Home: 2 Peter Cooper Rd New York NY 10010 Office: IDRC 708 3d Ave Room 2002 New York NY 10017

COHEN, NORMAN *See* **COHEN, LEONARD**

COHEN, PETER A., security company executive. Pres. Shearson-Am. Express Inc., 1983—. Office: Shearson-Am. Express Inc. 14 Wall St. New York NY 10022

COHEN, PETER ZELIG, manufacturing company executive; b. Montreal, Can., Oct. 4, 1920; s. Harry and Belle (Schleifer) C.; m. Lily Kligma, Jan. 22, 1944; children: Gerald A., Ellen R. B.Eng., McGill U., Montreal, 1943. Cert. profl. engr., Que. Gen. mgr. compressor div. Allis-Chalmers Corp., West Allis, Wis., 1974-76; pres., gen. mgr. Allis-Chalmers Can. Inc., Lachine, Que., 1976-82, pres., chief exec. officer, 1982—; chmn. bd. Sala Machine Works, Mississauga, Ont., 1978—; dir. Stephens-Adamson Can., Belleville, Ont.; v.p., treas. A-C Credit Corp., Toronto, Ont. Mem. Machinery and Equipment Mfrs. Assn. (treas., dir.), Order of Engrs. of Que. Clubs: Hillsdale Golf and Country (St. Therese, Que.); Greystone Curling (Montreal). Lodge: B'nai Brith. Home: 38 Upper Trafalger Pl Montreal PQ Canada H3H 1T3 Office: Allis-Chalmers Can Inc 125 St Joseph Iachine PQ Canada H8S 2I2

COHEN, PHILIP, hydrogeologist; b. N.Y.C., Dec. 13, 1931; s. Isadore and Anna (Katz) C.; m. Barbara Sandler, Dec. 26, 1954; 1 son, Jeffery. B.S. cum laude, CCNY, 1954; M.S., U. Rochester, 1956. With U.S. Geol. Survey, 1956—, asso. chief land info. and analysis office, Reston, Va., 1975-78, asst. chief hydrologist water resources div., Reston, 1978-79, chief hydrologist water resources div., 1979—. Contbr. numerous articles on geology and hydrology to profl. jours. Recipient Ward medal Coll. City, N.Y., 1954; Meritorious Ser. award Dept. Interior, 1975, Disting. Ser. award, 1979. Fellow Geol. Soc. Am.; mem. Am. Water Resources Assn., Am. Geophys. Union, Am. Inst. Profl. Geologists, Sigma Xi. Office: 709 Geol Survey Reston VA 22092

COHEN, PHILIP HERMAN, accountant; b. Bklyn., Dec. 4, 1936; s. David J. and Toby (Jaeger) C.; m. Susan Rudd; 1 dau., Davi Ellen. B.S., NYU, 1957. Acct. Touche Ross & Co., N.Y.C., 1957-64, supr., 1965, mgr., 1966-69, ptnr., 1969-81; exec. v.p. fin., chief fin. officer Integrated Resources, Inc., N.Y.C., 1981—; dir. ALI Equipment Mgmt. Corp., ALI Capitol Corp., ALI Leasing Service; lectr. in field. Bd. dirs. Alpha Epsilon Pi Found., Inc., Nat. Interfrat. Conf., Jewish Bd. Family and Children's Service; bd. dirs. joint purchasing com. Fedn. Jewish Philanthropies. Mem. Found. Acctg. Edn., Am. Inst. C.P.A.s, N.Y. State Soc. C.P.A.s (admissions com. 1968-69, chmn. fin. and leasing com. 1972-74, com. on relations with the bar 1974-76, com. on real estate acctg. 1976-79, com. ins. 1980—, fin. acctg. standards com., dir. 1983—), Fin. Execs. Inst., Am. Acctg. Assn., Nat. Assn. Accts., Soc. Ins. Accts., Alpha Epsilon Pi (supreme gov. 1966-73, nat. pres. 1974-76, mem. fiscal control bd. 1977-81, vice chmn. 1981—), Beta Alpha Psi, Areopagus. Jewish. Club: N.Y. Alumni of Alpha Epsilon Pi. Lodge: Masons. Home: 30 Beekman Pl New York NY 10022 Office: 666 3d Ave New York NY 10017

COHEN, PHILIP PACY, biochemist, educator; b. Derry, N.H., Sept. 26, 1908; s. David Harris and Ada (Cottler) C.; m. Rubye Herzfeld Tepper, June 15, 1935; children: Philip T., David B., Julie A., Milton T. B.S., Tufts Coll., 1930; Ph.D., U. Wis., 1937, M.D., 1938; D.Sc. (hon.), U. Mex., 1979. NRC fellow, Sheffield, Eng., 1938-39, Yale, 1939-40, instr., 1940-41; intern Wis. Gen. Hosp., 1941-42; asst. prof. clin. biochemistry U. Wis., 1942-45, asso. prof. physiol. chemistry, 1945-47, prof., 1947—, chmn. dept. physiol. chemistry, 1948-75, H.C. Bradley prof., 1968—, acting dean, 1961-63; Chmn. com. on growth, mem. exec. com. div. med. scis. NRC, 1954-56; bd. sci. counselors Nat. Cancer Inst., 1957-59, chmn., 1959-61; mem. physiol. chemistry study sect. NIH, 1959-62, nat. adv. cancer council, 1963-67, mem. adv. com. to dir., 1966-70. Mem. Nat. Adv. Arthritis and Metabolic Disease Council, 1970-74; adv. com. biology and medicine AEC, 1963-71; mem. adv. com. on med. research Pan Am. Health Orgn., 1967-75; mem. Nat. Commn. on Research, 1978-80; hon. mem. Med. Sch. Faculty, U. Chile. Commonwealth Fund fellow Oxford U., Eng., 1958. Fellow A.A.A.S.; mem. Nat. Acad. Scis., Am. Soc. Biol. Chemists (treas. 1951-56), Am. Chem. Soc., Biochem. Soc. (Eng.)., Sigma Xi; hon. mem. Harvey Soc., Chiba Med. Soc. (Japan), Argentina Biochem. Soc., Nat. Acad. Med. (Mex.), Japanese Biochem. Soc. Office: 587 Medical Sciences Bldg U Wis Madison WI 53706

COHEN, RALPH, business executive; b. Bridgeport, Conn., Jan. 27, 1919; s. Morris and Dora (Karpilow) C.; m. Florence Golden, Nov. 11, 1951; children—Mark, Doron, Yoav. Student, Mikveh Israel Agrl. Coll., 1936-39, Yale U., 1941-42. With Ampal Am. Israel Corp., N.Y.C., 1950—, exec. v.p., 1969-72, pres., 1972—81, vice chmn. bd., 1982—; co-mng. dir. Indsl. Devel. Bank Ltd., Tel Aviv, 1972—, Israel Ampal Indsl. Devel. Bank Ltd., 1972—82; dir. Bank Hapoalim Ltd., Am. Israeli Bank Ltd., Delek-Israel Fuel Corp. Ltd., Moriah Hotels Ltd. Office: 10 Rockefeller Plaza New York NY 10020 *When finance and industrial development—which has been my life's work—is coupled with a national goal of attaining economic independence for a new and emerging nation, there can be no greater satisfaction.*

COHEN, RAYMOND, educator; b. St. Louis, Nov. 30, 1923; s. Benjamin and Leah (Lewis) C.; m. Katherine Elise Silverman, Feb. 1, 1948; children—Richard Samuel, Deborah, Barbara Beth. B.S., Purdue U., 1947, M.S., 1950, Ph.D., 1955. Instr. mech. engring. Purdue U., 1948-55, asst. prof., 1955-58, asso. prof., 1958-60, prof., 1960—; asst. dir. Ray W. Herrick Labs., 1970-71, dir., 1971—; cons. to industry. Departmental editor of: Ency. Brit, 1957-62; Editorial bd. of: Jour. Sound and Vibration, 1971—. Served as sgt. inf. AUS, 1943-46. NATO sr. fellow in sci., 1971. Fellow ASME, Am. Soc. Heating, Refrigerating and Air Conditioning Engrs.; mem. Am. Soc. Engring. Edn., Soc. Exptl. Stress Analysis, Nat. Soc. Profl. Engrs., Internat. Inst. Refrigeration, Acoustical Soc. Am., Sigma Xi, Pi Tau Sigma, Tau Beta Pi. Home: 316 Leslie Ave West Lafayette IN 47906 Office: RW Herrick Laboratories Purdue Univ West Lafayette IN 47907

COHEN, RICHARD GERARD, lawyer; b. N.Y.C., June 11, 1931; s. Bernhardt and Leah (Cohen) C.; m. Evelyn Streit, June 22, 1952; children: Frances Susan, Andrew Steven, Emilie Streit, Sarah Jane. B.S. in Econs, U. Pa., 1952; LL.B., Columbia U., 1955. Bar: N.Y. 1956. With Office Chief Counsel, IRS, Treasury Dept., 1957-64, tech. asst. to chief counsel, 1961-64; with Lord, Day & Lord, N.Y.C., 1964—. Contbr. articles to profl. jours. Served with Audit Agy. U.S. Army, 1955-57. Mem. ABA, N.Y. State Bar Assn. (chmn. com. on reorgn. problems 1974-76, chmn. com. on incentives 1978-80, com. on partnerships 1981—, 2d vice chmn. tax sect. 1984—), Assn. Bar City N.Y., Am. Law Inst. (cons. Fed. Income Tax Project 1974, reporter 1976-84). Jewish. Club: Wall Street. Office: 25 Broadway New York NY 10004

COHEN, RICHARD MARTIN, journalist; b. N.Y.C., Feb. 6, 1941; s. Harry Louis and Pearl (Rosenberg) C.; m. Barbara Stubbs, May 3, 1969; 1 son, Alexander Prescott. B.S., N.Y. U., 1967; M.S. in Journalism, Columbia U., 1968. With UPI, 1967-68; gen. assignment reporter Washington Post, 1968-76, syndicated columnist, 1976—. Author: A Heartbeat Away, 1973. Office: Washington Post 1150 15th St NW Washington DC 20071

COHEN, RICHARD NORMAN, ins. exec.; b. N.Y.C., Oct. 28, 1923; s. Norman M. and Janet (Goldsmith) C.; m. Ann Robertson, Oct. 25, 1975; children—Daniel Hays, James Matthew, Mark Thompson. Grad., Phillips Exeter Acad., 1941; B.A., Yale, 1947. C.L.U., 1959. Salesman Cohen, Goldman & Co., N.Y.C., 1947-50; mens fashion editor Fawcett Publs., N.Y.C., 1951-52; life ins. broker Mass. Mut. Life Ins. Co., N.Y.C., 1954—; account exec. John M. Riehle, Inc., N.Y.C., 1961-63, v.p., 1963—. Served to 2d lt. USAAF, 1943-45. Mem. Am. Coll. Life Underwriters, Million Dollar Round Table, Beta Theta Pi. Republican. Jewish. Clubs: Yale (N.Y.C.); Century Country (White Plains, N.Y.). Home: 284 Briar Brae Rd Stamford CT 06903 Office: Leonard Newman Agy Inc 199 Main St White Plains NY 10601

COHEN, RICHARD STOCKMAN, U.S. dist. atty.; b. Boston, Apr. 5, 1937; s. Abram I. and Cele (Stockman) C.; m. Suzanne Thomas Burnett, Aug. 29, 1964; children—Andrew Stockman, Meredith Ware. B.B.A., U. Ga., 1958; J.D., Boston U., 1963. Bar: Maine bar 1963. Asst. atty. gen. and counsel Maine Bur. Taxation, Augusta, 1963-65; with Atty. Gen.'s Dept., State of Maine, Augusta, 1963—, chief criminal div., 1966-71, dep. atty. gen. in charge law enforcement and criminal div., 1971-79, atty. gen., 1979-81; U.S. atty. Dist. of Maine, 1981—; chmn. Maine Criminal Justice Planning Assistance Agy., Augusta, 1972-79; mem. Criminal Law Adv. Commn. Mem. Maine-Medico Legal Soc. (pres. 1973). Home: 94 Winthrop St Augusta ME 04330

COHEN, ROBERT ABRAHAM, physician; b. Chgo., Nov. 13, 1909; s. Ezra Harry and Catherine (Kurzon) C.; m. Mabel Jean Blake, Mar. 21, 1933 (dec. Oct. 1972); children—Donald Edward, Margery Jean; m. Alice L. Muth, Mar. 31, 1974. B.S., U. Chgo., 1930, Ph.D., M.D., 1935. Intern Michael Reese Hosp., Chgo., 1937-39, 40-41; resident Johns Hopkins U., Sheppard-Pratt hosps., 1937-41; sr. fellow Inst. Juvenile Research, Chgo, 1939-40; pvt. practice psychiatry, Washington, 1946-48; clin. dir. Chestnut Lodge, Rockville, Md., 1948-53, dir. psychotherapy, 1981—; dir. clin. investigations NIMH, Bethesda, Md., 1953-69, dir. div. clin. and behavioral research, 1969-81, dep. dir. intramural research program, 1969-81; pres. Washington Sch. Psychiatry, 1973—; Bd. dirs. Founds. Fund for Research in Psychiatry, 1960-63, chmn. bd., 1962-63; trustee William Alanson White Psychiat. Found. Served from lt. (j.g.) to comdr. M.C. USNR, 1941-46. Recipient Salmon medal N.Y. Acad. Scis., 1978, Fromm-Reichmann award Am. Acad. Psychoanylsis, 1979, HEW Disting. Service award, 1970. Fellow Am. Psychiat. Assn. (life); mem. Am. Psychoanalytical Assn., Washington Psychoanalytic Soc. (pres. 1951-53), Washington Psychiat. Soc. (pres. 1958-59), Washington Psychoanalytic Inst. (chmn. edn. com. 1953-58, dir. 1959-63), Washington Acad. Medicine. Home: 5216 Elsmere Ave Bethesda MD 20814 Office: 500 W Montgomery Ave Rockville MD 20850

COHEN, ROBERT ALAN, magazine publishing consultant; b. Chgo., July 27, 1953; s. Ronald and Doris (Pannemann) C. B.A. cum laude, Yale U., 1975; M.B.A., Harvard U., 1977. Bus. mgr. Yale Banner Publs., New Haven, 1974-75; comptroller's asst. Time, Inc., N.Y.C., 1977-78; circulation mgr. Sports Illus., N.Y.C., 1978-79; pub. The New Republic, Washington, 1979-81; gen. mgr. Tech. mag., 1981-82; mag. cons., 1982—. Mem. Mag. Pubs. Assn., Direct Mail Mktg. Assn. Club: Yale of N.Y. 250 Fifth Ave New York NY 10001

COHEN, ROBERT ARTHUR, editor; b. Lynn, Mass., Jan. 31, 1930; s. Israel Isadore and Edith Laura (Labrie) C.; m. Bernadette Elizabeth Comeau, June 3, 1950; children: Paula Jean, Regina Marie, Mark Alan, Rachel Anne, Christine Elizabeth. Student, pub. schs., Mass. Asst. book editor U.S. Naval Inst., Annapolis, Md., 1967-68, asst. editor, then mng. editor proc., Washington, 1969-74; pub. relations rep. Am. Legion, 1974-76; editor Naval Affairs mag., 1976-78; mng. editor From the Housetops, Still River, Mass., 1978; publ. services mgr. GTE, Sylvania Systems Group, Needham Heights, Mass., 1980-81. Public relations dir. South Bowie (Md.) Civic Assn., 1969-71, Citizens for Community Schs., Prince George's County, Md., 1972-74. Served with U.S. Navy, 1947-67. Mem. Fleet Res. Assn., Am. Legion, John Birch Soc. Roman Catholic. Club: K.C. Home: Sherry Rd RD 1 Box 600 Harvard MA 01451 Office: RD 3 Box 72 Sherry Rd Harvard MA 01451

COHEN, ROBERT L., corporate executive; b. Sedalia, Colo., Jan. 18, 1929; s. Laurence and Lucile (Draper) C.; m. Lorraine A. Young, Jan. 21, 1962 (dec.); children: Larry, Stanley David, Frank; m. Meryle L. Brooks (dec.); children—Lori, Devra; m. Cynthia D. Peake; 1 son, Sean. B.A., Dartmouth, 1951; M.C.S., Amos Tuck Sch. Bus., 1952. With Witmer Rumsey Ins. Agy., Crystal Lake, Ill., 1951-52; with Navajo Freight Lines, Inc., Denver, 1953-70; exec. v.p. 1958-64, pres., 1964-70; chmn. bd., pres., dir. Hotsy Corp. (name formerly Kanco Tech., Inc.), 1970—; dir. Columbine Nat. Bank, United Bancorp Wyo.; chmn. bd. Denver Nuggets., 1980-82. Trustee Am. Cancer Research Center; trustee Nat. Jewish Hosp. Mem. Am. Trucking Assn. (past v.p.), Colo. Motor Carriers Assn. (past pres.). Home: 3925 S Colorado Blvd Englewood CO 80110 Office: 21 Inveress Way E Englewood CO 80112

COHEN, ROBERT LEONARD, lawyer; b. Newark, June 12, 1937; s. Nat and Sally (Friedman) C.; m. Harriet Posner, Aug. 6, 1963; children—Bruce, Jonathan. B.A., Rutgers U., 1959; LL.B., Columbia, 1962. Bar: N.Y. bar 1962. Atty. SEC, Washington, 1965-70; internat. atty. Westinghouse Corp., N.Y.C., 1970-73; corp. counsel, sec. Microdot Inc., Greenwich, Conn., 1973-75; div. counsel components div. Litton Industries, Passaic, N.J., 1975—. Served as 1st lt. AUS, 1962-64. Mem. Soc. Am. Corp. Secs., Bergenfield Jaycees. Home: 68 Sergent Ct Bergenfield NJ 07621 Office: 270 Passaic Ave Passaic NJ 07055

COHEN, ROBERT SONNÉ, physicist, philosopher, educator; b. N.Y.C., Feb. 18, 1923; m. Robin Gertrude Hirshhorn, June 18, 1944; children: Michael, Daniel, Deborah. B.A., Wesleyan U., Middletown, Conn., 1943; M.S., Yale U., 1943, Ph.D. (NRC fellow), 1948. Instr. physics Yale U., 1943-44, instr. philosophy, 1949-51; sci. staff, war research div. Columbia U. and Communications Bd., U.S. Joint Chiefs Staff, 1944-46; asst. prof. physics and philosophy Wesleyan U., 1949-57; assoc. prof. physics Boston U., 1957-59, prof. physics and philosophy, 1959—, chmn. dept. physics, 1959-73; acting dean Coll. Liberal Arts, 1971-72; chmn. faculty Senate, 1975-76; chmn. Boston U. Center for Philos. and History Sci., 1970—; vis. lectr. humanities and philosophy of sci. Mass. Inst. Tech., 1958-59, 61-62; vis. prof. history of ideas Brandeis U., 1959-60; lectr. history and philosophy of sci. Am. U., Washington, summers 1958-68; vis. fellow Polish and Yugoslav Acad. Sci., 1963, Hungarian Acad. Sci., 1964; vis. prof. philosophy U. Calif. at, San Diego, 1969, Yale U., 1973; research fellow history of sci. Harvard, 1974; Mem., chmn. U.S. Nat. Com. for Internat. Union History and Philosophy of Sci., 1969-75; Trustee Wesleyan U., 1968-84. Author, editor articles, books and jours. in field.; Editor: Boston Studies in Philosophy of Sci. Trustee Bill of Rights Found. Am. Council Learned Soc. fellow philosophy and sci., 1948-49; Ford faculty fellow, Cambridge, Eng., 1955-56; fellow Wissenschafts Rolleg zu Berlin, 1983-84. Fellow AAAS (chmn. sect. L history and philos. sci. 1978-79); mem. Am. Phys. Soc., Am. Assn. Physics Tchrs., Am. Philos. Assn., History Sci. Soc., Philosophy Sci. Assn. (v.p. 1972-75, pres. 1982-84), AAUP, Nat. Emergency Civil Liberties Com. (mem. nat. council), Am. Inst. Marxist Studies (chmn. 1964-82), Fedn. Am. Scientists (nat. council 1967-70), Inst. for Unity of Sci. (exec. com. 1960-74). Home: 44 Adams Ave Watertown MA 02172 Office: Dept Philosophy Boston U Boston MA 02215

COHEN, RONALD, educator; b. Canada, Jan. 22, 1930; came to U.S., 1963; s. Maxwell B. and Pauline (Golant) C.; m. Diana Barbara Williams, June 21, 1955; children—Paul Yerima, Stephen Benjamin. B.A., U. Toronto, 1951; M.Sc., U. Wis., 1955, Ph.D., 1960. Lectr. anthropology U. Toronto, 1958-61; asst. prof. McGill U., 1961-63; mem. faculty Northwestern U., 1963-81, prof. anthropology and polit. sci., 1968-81; prof. anthropology U. Fla., Gainesville, 1981—; vis. prof., head dept. sociology Ahmadu Bello U., Nigeria, 1972-74; fellow Center for Advanced Study in the Behavioral Scis., Palo Alto, Calif., 1976-77; cons. NIMH, 1968-72; Chmn. African Students Found., Can., 1962; Fellow Am. Anthrop. Assn., African Studies Assn. Author: The Kanuri of Bornu, 1967, Dominance and Defiance, 1970; Editor: (with John Middleton) From Tribe to Nation in Africa, 1970, (with Raoul Naroll) Handbook of Method in Cultural Anthropology, 1973, (with Elman Service) Origins of the State, 1978; (with G. Britan), Hierarchy and Society, 1980; asso. editor: Am. Anthropologist, 1970-74, Polit. Anthropology, 1974—. Mem. Assn. Brit. Social Amthropologists. Home: Nanteos Micanopy FL 32667 Office: Dept Anthropology U Fla Gainesville FL 32601 *

COHEN, RONALD ELI, journalist; b. N.Y.C., Jan. 31, 1937; s. Maurice Joseph and Mildred Dolores (Figliuolo) C.; m. Jill M. Greenspan, June 25, 1961; children: Rachel Sue, Jennifer Michelle. B.S. in Journalism and Communications, U. Ill., 1959; M.S. in Journalism (Adolph Ochs scholar), Columbia U., 1966. Reporter Champaign (Ill.) News Gazette, 1960-61, Bridgeport (Conn.) Post-Telegram, 1961; with UPI, 1961—, Hartford, Conn., 1961-62, Montpelier, Vt., 1962-65, gen. news editor, N.Y.C., 1966-72, Washington news editor, 1972-83, Washington bur. chief, mng. editor, 1983—. Served with U.S. Army, 1959-60. Mem. Washington Press Club, Sigma Delta Chi. Club: Gridiron. Home: 8105 Whites Ford Way Potomac MD 20854 Office: 1400 Eye St NW Washington DC 20005

COHEN, SANFORD, educator; b. Cleve., Sept. 8, 1920; s. Louis J. and Celia (Schoenberg) C.; m. Julia Catherine Beach, June 15, 1955; children—Jon, Elizabeth, Melanie. B.A., Ohio State U., 1943, M.A., 1947, Ph.D., 1951. Asst. prof. econs. Western Res. U., 1953-56; asso. prof., prof. econs. Butler U., Indpls., 1957-62; vis. prof. U. Ill., Champaign, 1962-63, U. Mich., 1964-66; prof. econs. U. N.Mex., Albuquerque, 1966—; chmn. dept. econs., 1969-72; vis. prof. Inter-Am. U., San German, P.R., 1969, U. Carabobo, Venezuela, 1976; examiner NLRB, 1948; br. chief WSB, 1951-52; manpower adviser Govt. of Bolivia, 1963-64; faculty dir. Internat. Manpower Inst., U.S. Dept. Labor, summers 1966, 67, 69; manpower adviser, Venezuela, 1970, arbitrator labor-mgmt. disputes. Author: State Labor Legislation, 1937-47, 1948, Labor in the United States, 1960, 5th edit., 1979, Labor Law, 1964, (with others) Management Preparation for Collective Bargaining, 1966; Editor: Issues in Labor Policy, 1977; Contbr. articles to profl. jours. Served with AUS, 1943-45. Mem. Am. Econ. Assn., Indsl. Relations Research Assn., Soc. for Internat. Devel., Nat. Acad. Arbitrators. Home: PO Box 10371 Albuquerque NM 87184

COHEN, SANFORD IRWIN, physician, educator; b. N.Y.C., Sept. 5, 1928; s. George A. and Gertrude (Slater) C.; m. Jean Steinbruecker, Nov. 30, 1952; children—Jeffrey, Debra, John, Robert. A.B. magna cum laude, N.Y. U., 1948; M.B., M.D., Chgo. Med. Sch., 1952. Intern Jackson Meml. Hosp., Miami, Fla., 1952-53; resident psychiatry U. Colo. Med. Center, 1953-54; resident Duke Med. Center, 1954-55, 57-58, mem. faculty, 1956-68, prof. psychiatry, 1964-68, head div. psychosomatic medicine and psychophysiol. research, 1964-68, lectr. psychology, 1960-68; instr. Washington Psychoanalytic Inst., 1964-68; cons. VA Hosp., Durham, N.C., 1957-65, NIMH, 1963-66; prof. psychiatry, chmn. dept. Boston U. Med. Sch., 1970—; Markle scholar med. sci., 1957-62. Contbr. articles to profl. jours., chpts. to books. Recipient Robert Morse award excellence in sci. writing, 1965. Fellow Am. Psychiat. Assn., Am. Coll. Clin. Pharmacology; mem. A.A.A.S., Am. Psychosomatic Soc. Home: 1 Marlborough St Boston MA 02116 Office: Div Psychiatry Med Sch Boston Univ Boston MA 02118

COHEN, SAUL BERNARD, college president, geographer; b. Malden, Mass., July 28, 1925; s. Barnett and Anna (Kaplinsky) C.; m. Miriam Friederman, June 11, 1950; children: Deborah Fae, Louise Esther. A.B., Harvard U., 1947, A.M., 1949, Ph.D., 1955. From instr. to prof. geography Boston U., 1952-65; vis. prof. U.S. Naval War Coll., 1957; prof. geography, dir. Grad. Sch. Geography, Clark U., Worcester, Mass., 1965-78, dean, 1967-70, chmn. faculty, 1973-76, 77-78; pres. Queens Coll., Flushing, N.Y., 1978—; vis. prof. Hebrew U., Jerusalem, 1971, 74, 75; adj. prof. Haifa U., 1977; Cons. social sci. div. NSF, 1966-74, U.S. Office Edn., 1966-77; mem. U.S. nat. delegation Internat. Geog. Union, 1966-69; chmn. com. geography Nat. Acad. of Scis.-NRC, 1966-69. Author: Geography and Politics in a World Divided, 1963, rev. edit., 1973, Problems and Trends in American Geography, 1967, Experiencing the Environment, 1976, Resources and Human Networks, 1977, Jerusalem-Bridging the Four Walls, 1977, Jerusalem Undivided, 1980, Israel's Defensible Borders: A Geopolitical Map; also articles. Jerusalem Undivided; Geog. editor: The Oxford World Atlas, 1973. Fellow AAAS; mem. Consortium Profl. Assns. (chmn. 1965-71), Assn. Am. Geographers (exec. officer 1964-65, del. Am. Council Learned Socs. 1964-66, mem. council 1966-70, chmn. commn. coll. geography 1965-67), Am. Geog. Soc. (council 51970-79). Home: 1008 Shore Rd Douglaston NY 11363 Office: Queens College Flushing NY 11367

COHEN, SAUL G., chemist, educator; b. Boston, May 10 1916; s. Barnet M. and Ida (Levine) C.; m. Doris E. Brewer, Nov. 27, 1941 (dec. July 1971); children—Jonathan Brewer, Elisabeth Jane; m. Anneliese F. Kissinger, June 1, 1973. A.B., Harvard, 1937, M.A., 1938, Ph.D., 1940. Research fellow Harvard, 1939-40, 41-43, instr., 1940-41; NRC fellow, lectr. U. Calif. at Los Angeles, 1943-44; research chemist Pitts. Plate Glass Co., 1944-45, Polaroid Corp., 1945-50, cons., 1950—; with Brandeis U., 1950—, prof. chemistry, 1952—, Univ. prof., 1974—, chmn. Sch. Sci., 1950-55, dean faculty, 1955-59, chmn. dept. chemistry, 1959-66, 68-72; vis. prof. Havard Med. Sch., 1965, Hebrew U., Jerusalem, 1972; dir. Manhattan Fund, Hemisphere Fund, Liberty Fund, C.L. Assets. Bd. overseers Harvard U., 1983—. Fulbright sr.

scholar, 1958-59; Guggenheim fellow, 1958-59. Fellow Am. Acad. Arts and Scis. (council), AAAS; mem. Am. Soc. Biol. Chemists, Am. Chem. Soc. (James F. Norris award 1972, trustee Northeastern sect. 1976—), Chem. Soc. London, AAUP, Fedn. Am. Scientists, Phi Beta Kappa, Sigma Xi. Home: 90 Commonwealth Ave Boston MA 02116 Office: Dept Chemistry Brandeis U Waltham MA 02254

COHEN, SAUL ZELMAN, investment company executive, lawyer; b. Rochester, N.Y., May 5, 1926; s. Max J. and Dora (Cohn) C.; m. Amy Scheuer, Aug. 26, 1956; children: Thomas, Helen, Daniel, Gail, David, Carolyn. B.A., U. Rochester, 1949; LL.B., Harvard U., 1952. Bar: N.Y. 1952. Atty. ABC, N.Y.C.d, 1952-54; mem. Kaye, Scholer, Fierman, Hays & Handler, N.Y.C., 1954-84, ptnr., 1959-84, 61 Assocs., investments, 1984—; dir. Southdown, Inc., Houston, CLC of Am., Inc., St. Louis. Pres. Jewish Bd. Family and Children's Services, Inc., N.Y.C., 1977-81, Vice chmn. bd., N.Y.C., 1981—; trustee Sarah Lawrence Coll., 1973-81; v.p. Fedn. Jewish Philanthropies of Greater N.Y., 1982—. Mem. Assn. Bar City of N.Y., ABA. Democrat. Clubs: Harvard, Harmonie (N.Y.C.); Beach Point (Mamaroneck). Home: 203 Hommocks Rd Larchmont NY 10538 Office: 350 Fifth Ave New York NY 10022

COHEN, SELMA JEANNE, dance historian; b. Chgo., Sept. 18, 1920; d. Frank A. and Minna (Skud) C. A.B., U. Chgo., 1941, M.A., 1942, Ph.D., 1946. Free lance writer, 1949—; editor Dance Perspectives, N.Y.C., 1959-76; founder, dir. Dance Critics Conf., Am. Dance Festival, 1970-72, U. Chgo. Seminars in Dance History, 1974-76; disting. vis. prof. Five Colls., Inc., 1976-77; editor Internat. Ency. Dance, N.Y.C., 1981—. Author: The Modern Dance: Seven Statements of Belief, 1966, Doris Humphrey, An Artist First, 1972, Dance as a Theatre Art, 1974, Next Week, Swan Lake: Reflections on Dance and Dances, 1981. Rockefeller Found. grantee, 1969; Am. Dance Guild award, 1976; Guggenheim fellow, 1980; recipient Profl. Achievement award U. Chgo., 1974; award Dance mag., 1981. Mem. Am. Soc. Aesthetics, Am. Soc. Theatre Research, Dance History Scholars. Office: care Scribner's 597 Fifth Ave New York NY 10017

COHEN, SEYMOUR, lawyer; b. Chgo., Sept. 27, 1917; s. Sol and Sophie (Norinsky) C.; m. Marcia Meltzer, Aug. 10, 1952; children—Susan Ruth, James Burton. B.S., Ind. U., 1939, J.D., 1941. Bar: Ind. bar 1941, Ill. bar 1948, U.S. Supreme Ct. bar 1971. Atty. NLRB, Washington, 1946-47; practiced in, Chgo., 1947—; mem. firm Dorfman, Cohen, Laner & Muchin, Ltd. (and predecessor), 1953—. Mem. Northbrook (Ill.) Library Bd., 1963-69, pres., 1965-67. Served to lt. comdr. USNR, 1941-45. Mem. Chgo. Bar Assn. (chmn. com. labor law 1961-63), ABA. Home: 1201 Wendy Dr Northbrook IL 60062 Office: 1 IBM Plaza Chicago IL 60611 *A belief in one's own abilities is not enough. There must be a need by others for what those abilities can provide. The utilization of those abilities then will produce rewards both for the provider and the receiver.*

COHEN, SEYMOUR STANLEY, biochemist; b. N.Y.C., Apr. 30, 1917; s. Herman and Lena (Tanz) C.; m. Elaine Pear, July 12, 1940; children: Michael, Sara. B.S., CCNY, 1936; Ph.D. in Biol. Chemistry, Columbia U., 1941; Dr.h.c., U. Louvain, Belgium, 1972, U. Kuopio, Finland, 1982. NRC fellow Rockefeller Inst., 1941-42; mem. faculty U. Pa., 1943-71, prof. biochemistry in pediatrics, 1954-71, Charles Hayden-Am. Cancer Soc. prof. biochemistry, 1957-71, Hartzell prof., chmn. dept. therapeutic research Sch. Medicine, 1963-71; Am. Cancer Soc. prof. microbiology U. Colo. Sch. Medicine, Denver, 1971-76; distinguished prof., Am. Cancer Soc. prof. pharm. scis. State U. N.Y., Stony Brook, 1976—; chmn. council analysis and projection Am. Cancer Soc., 1972-74, adviser research, 1974-76; Guggenheim fellow Pasteur Inst., Paris, 1947-48; Jesup lectr. Columbia U., 1967; guest investigator Institut du Radium, Paris, 1967-68; vis. prof. Collège de France, Paris, 1970; vis. fellow Smithsonian Instn., 1973-74; vis. prof. U. Tokyo, 1974, Hadassah Med. Sch., 1974, Zuckerman lectr. tropical disease, 1979; Guggenheim and Lady Davis fellow Faculty Agr., Israel, 1983; fellow Nat. Humanities Ctr., N.C., 1982-83; Trustee Marine Biol. Lab., Woods Hole, Mass.; bd. sci. cons. Sloan-Kettering Inst. Author: Virus-Induced Enzymes, 1968, Introduction to the Polyamines, 1971; editorial bd.: Virology, 1954-59, Jour. Biol. Chemistry, 1959-65, Jour. Cell Physiology, 1966-71, Bacteriological Revs, 1969-73. Recipient certificate war research OSRD, 1945, War Manpower Commn., 1945; War Research medal Columbia U., 1943; Eli Lily award and medal Am. Soc. Bacteriology, Immunology and Pathology, 1951; 1st Mead Johnson award Am. Acad. Pediatrics, 1952; medal Soc. de Chimie Biologique, France, 1964; Borden award Am. Assn. Med. Colls., 1967; Passano award, 1974; Townsend Harris medal CCNY Alumni Assn., 1978; Forster award German Acad. Sci. and Letters, Mainz, 1978; Fogarty scholar NIH, 1973-74. Fellow AAAS (Newcomb Cleveland award 1955); mem. Am. Acad. Arts and Scis., Soc. Gen. Physiologists (councilor, pres. 1967-68), Nat. Acad. Scis., Serbian Acad. Scis. and Art, Inst. Medicine, Am. Assn. Cancer Research (dir. 1974-77). Home: 106 Quaker Path Stony Brook NY 11790 Office: State U NY at Stony Brook Stony Brook NY 11790

COHEN, SHELDON GILBERT, physician; b. Pittston, Pa., Sept. 21, 1918; s. Samuel H. and Dorthy (Goldberg) C. Grad., Wyo. Sem., 1936; student, Syracuse U., 1936-37; B.A., Ohio State U., 1940; M.D., N.Y. U., 1943; D.Sc. (hon.), Wilkes Coll., 1976. Diplomate: Am. Bd. Allergy and Immunology. Intern Bellevue Hosp., N.Y.C., 1944; resident internal medicine VA Hosp., Balt., 1947-48, resident in allergy, Aspinwall, Pa., 1948-49; research fellow U. Pitts. Sch. Medicine, 1949-50; practice medicine specializing in allergy, Wilkes-Barre, Pa., 1951-72; research asso. Addison H. Gibson Lab. Applied Physiology U. Pitts., 1950-51; attending physician Allergy Clinic, Falk Clinics, 1950-51; chief of allergy Mercy Hosp., Wilkes-Barre, 1951-72; attending physician in allergy VA Hosp., Wilkes-Barre, 1951-60, cons. internal medicine, 1960-72; asso. prof. biol. research Wilkes Coll., Wilkes-Barre, 1952-62, prof. biol. research, 1962-68, prof. exptl. biology, 1968-72; cons. extramural programs Nat. Inst. Allergy and Infectious Diseases, 1972-73, chief allergy and immunology br., 1973-76, dir. immunology, allergic and immunologic diseases program, 1977—; regional med. cons. Children's Asthma Research Inst. and Hosp., Denver, 1969-72; mem. medico adv. bd. CARE, 1977—; cons. to Ministry Public Health, State of Kuwait, 1981—; advisor immunology unit WHO, Geneva, Switzerland, 1979—; Bd. dirs. Allergy Found. Am., 1969-81, mem. com. public edn., 1976-81; bd. dirs. Lupus Found. Am., 1978—, exec. v.p., 1981—, mem. med. council, 1978—, mem. research com., 1978—. Contbr. articles to profl. jours.; editorial bd.: Jour. Devel. and Comparative Immunology, 1976-81. Trustee Marywood Coll., Scranton, Pa., 1983—. Served to capt. M.C. USAAF, 1944-46. Recipient Disting. Service award Wyo. Sem., 1978, Clemens von Pirquet award Georgetown U., 1981. Fellow Am. Acad. Allergy (historian 1963-69, v.p. 1979-80, Disting. Service award 1971), A.C.P., Am. Coll. Allergists, Coll. Physicians of Phila.; mem. Am. Assn. Immunologists, Assn. Am. Physicians, Am. Thoracic Soc., Soc. for Investigative Dermatology, Am. Rheumatism Assn., Soc. for Exptl. Biology and Medicine, Collegium Internat. Allergologicum, Am. Fedn. Clin. Research, Sigma Xi. Club: Cosmos. Home: 5500 Friendship Blvd 1927N Chevy Chase MD 20815 Office: Bldg 31 Room 7A52 NIAID Nat Inst Health Bethesda MD 20205

COHEN, SHELDON STANLEY, lawyer; b. Washington, June 28, 1927; s. Herman and Pearl (Jaffe) C.; m. Faye Fram, Feb. 21, 1951; children: Melinda Ann, Laura Eve, Jonathan Adam, Sharon Ruevena. A.B. with spl. honors, George Washington U., 1950, J.D. with highest honors (Charles W. Dorsey scholar), 1952; D.Lit. (hon.), Lincoln Coll. Bar: D.C. 1952, U.S. Supreme Ct. 1956, U.S. Tax Ct. 1956; C.P.A., Md. Accountant, 1950-52; legis. atty. Office Chief Counsel, IRS, Dept. Treasury, 1952-56, chief counsel, 1963-65, commr. internal revenue, 1965-69; assoc. Paul, Weiss, Rifkind, Wharton & Garrison, Washington, 1956-60; ptnr. Arnold, Fortas & Porter, Washington, 1960-63; mem. Cohen & Uretz, Washington, 1969—; lectr. Howard U. Law Sch., 1957-58; professorial lectr. George Washington U. Law Sch., 1958-81; adj. prof. U. Miami (Fla.) Law Sch., 1974—; mem. adv. com. Inst. Estate Planning, U. Miami Law Center, 1969—; Chmn. exec. compensation com. U.S. Pay Bd., 1971-72; mem. Commn. on Founds. and Pvt. Philanthropy, 1969-70; mem. adv. group Commr. IRS, 1969-70; chmn. steering com. Adminstrv. Conf. U.S., 1974—; mem. exec. com. Washington Lawyer's Com. for Civil Rights Under Law, 1975—; pres. Am.-Israel Tax Found.; mem. council Sch. Govt. and Bus. Adminstrn., George Washington U., 1969-79, mem. commn. on governance, 1970, bd. govts. univ., 1980; pres. Law Assn., 1978-79; bd. dirs. Nat. Found. for Jewish Culture; bd. dirs., v.p. United Jewish Appeal of D.C., 1980—; past v.p. Jewish Community Center, Greater Washington; bd. dirs., past v.p. Jewish Community Found. Editorial and bus. sec.: George Washington U. Law Rev, 1952; case notes editor, 1951-52; bd. editors Nat. Law Jour. Past pres. Jewish Social Service Agy., Washington; bd. dirs. Adas Israel Congregation, Jewish Welfare Bd., United Synagogues Am., Common Cause, Nat. Council for a Responsible Firearms Policy, Inc.; bd. regents Omar N. Bradley Found., U.S. Army Hist. Collection, 1970-73; trustee B'nai B'rith Found. of U.S.; spl. tax counsel Democratic Nat. Com., 1969-72, gen. counsel, 1972-77; bd. overseers Jewish Theol. Sem. Am., 1972—; trustee United Jewish Endowment Fund. Served with USNR, 1945-46. Recipient Alumni Achievement award George Washington U., 1965; Arthur Flemming award, 1966; Alexander Hamilton award U.S. Treasury Dept., 1969; Joseph Ottenstein community service award Jewish Social Agy., 1976. Mem. Nat. Acad. Pub. Adminstrn. (chmn. com. on energy 1978—), ABA (chmn. spl. com. on retirement benefits legis. tax sect. 1972-73), Fed. Bar Assn. (council tax sect.), D.C. Bar Assn. (bd. dirs. 1969-72, bd. govs. 1972-75), D.C. Inst. C.P.A.s (hon.), Am.-Israel C. of C. (chmn. tax com. 1980), Order of Coif, Phi Delta Phi, Phi Sigma Delta, Omicron Delta Kappa (hon.), Beta Alpha Psi. (hon.). Clubs: Internat., Cosmos (Washington); B'nai B'rith, Internat. (bd. dirs. 1979—). Lodge: Masons. Home: 5518 Trent St Chevy Chase MD 20815 Office: 1775 K St NW Washington DC 20006

COHEN, SIDNEY, physician; b. N.Y.C., June 7, 1910; s. Adolph and Esther (Gordon) C.; m. Illse Annalouise Franke, Feb. 27, 1934; children—Dorothy Elizabeth, Richard Sidney. Ph.D., Columbia, 1930; postgrad., Coll. City N.Y., 1930-32, Bonn (Germany) U., 1932-38. Diplomate: Am. Bd. Internal Medicine. Intern Jamaica (L.I.) Hosp., 1938-40; resident VA Hosp., Los Angeles, 1946-49; chief research Brentwood Hosp., Los Angeles, 1949-59; chief psychosomatic medicine Wadsworth VA Hosp., Los Angeles, 1959-68; chief Center Studies Narcotics and Drug Abuse NIMH, Chevy Chase, Md., 1968—; asso. clin. prof. medicine U. Calif. at Los Angeles, 1956—; All Univ. lectr. U. Calif., 1965; William Harvey Taylor lectr. Am. Therapeutic Soc., 1964; cons. Suicide Prevention Center, Alcoholism Research Clinic, Central Office Research Psychiatry, Neurology and Psychology.; Mem. sci. adv. bd. Am. Schizophrenia Found.; dir. Los Angeles Med. Research Found. Author: Chemopsychotherapy, 1963, LSD, 1964, The Drug Dilemma, 1968, also numerous articles.; Editor-in-chief: Mind, Psychiatry in Private Practice, 1963-64; editorial bd.: Psychosomatics, 1964—; editor: Jour. Psychopharmacology, 1967. Served to col. M.C. AUS, 1941-46. Mem. Soc. Biol. Psychiatry, Am., Calif., Los Angeles County med. assns., Los Angeles Soc. Neurology and Psychiatry, Calif. Med. Research Assn. Home: 13020 Sky Valley Rd Los Angeles CA 90049 Office: Neuropsychiat Inst Univ of Calif at Los Angeles Los Angeles CA 90024

COHEN, STANLEY, pathologist, educator; b. N.Y.C., June 4, 1937; s. Herman Joseph and Eva (Lapidus) C.; m. Marion Doris Cantor, Aug. 30, 1959; children: Laurie Ellen, Ronald Nelson, Kenneth Stuart. A.B., Columbia U., 1957, M.D., 1961. Intern Albert Einstein Med. Center, Bronx, N.Y., 1961-62; resident Mass. Gen. Hosp., 1962-64; fellow N.Y. U. Med. Center, 1964-66; prof. pathology State U. N.Y., Buffalo, 1968-74; acting dir. Center for Immunology, Buffalo, 1973-74; prof. pathology U. Conn. Health Center, Farmington, 1974—, assoc. chmn., 1976—; mem. study sect. immunological scis. NIH, 1975-79, mem. study sect. allergy and immunology, 1981—; co-chmn. 3d Internat. Lymphokine Workshop, 1982. Contbr. articles in field to profl. jours.; author: Mechanisms of Cell-Mediated Immunity, 1974, Mechanisms of Tumor Immunity, 1976, Mechanics of Immunopathology, 1978, Biology of the Lymphokines, 1979, Interleukins, Lymphokines, and Cytokines, 1983. Served to capt. U.S. Army, 1966-68. Recipient Kinne Award, 1954; Borden award, 1961; Parke-Davis Award in Exptl. Pathology, 1977. Mem. Am. Assn. Pathologists, Am. Assn. Immunologists, Pluto Soc. Home: 11 Glen Hollow St West Hartford CT 06117 Office: U Conn Health Center Farmington CT 06032

COHEN, STANLEY NORMAN, educator, geneticist; b. Perth Amboy, N.J., Feb. 17, 1935; s. Bernard and Ida (Stolz) C.; m. Joanna Lucy Wolter, June 27, 1961; children: Anne, Geoffrey. B.A., Rutgers U., 1956; M.D., U. Pa., 1960. Intern, Mt. Sinai Hosp., N.Y.C., 1960-61; resident Univ. Hosp., Ann Arbor, Mich., 1961-62; clin. asso. arthritis and rheumatism br. Nat. Inst. Arthritis and Metabolic Diseases, Bethesda, Md., 1962-64; sr. resident in medicine Duke U. Hosp., Durham, N.C., 1964-65; Am. Cancer Soc. postdoctoral research fellow Albert Einstin Coll. Medicine, Bronx, 1965-67, asst. prof. devel. biology and cancer, 1967-68; mem. faculty Stanford (Calif.) U., 1968—, prof. medicine, 1975—, prof. genetics, 1977, chmn. dept. genetics, 1978—; mem. com. recombinant DNA molecules Nat. Acad. Sci.-NRC, 1974; mem. com. on genetic experimentation Internat. Council Sci. Unions, 1977—. Mem. editorial bd.: Jour. Bacteriology, 1973-79; asso. editor: Plasmid, 1977—. Served with USPHS, 1962-64. Recipient Burroughs Wellcome Scholar award, 1970; V.D. Mattia award Roche Inst. Molecular Biology, 1977; Albert Lasker basic med. research award, 1980; Wolf prize, 1981; Josiah Macy Jr. Found. faculty scholar, 1975-76; Guggenheim fellow, 1975. Mem. Nat. Acad. Sci., Am. Acad. Arts and Sci., Am. Soc. Biol. Chemists, Genetics Soc. Am., Am. Soc. Microbiology, Am. Soc. Pharmacology and Exptl. Therapeutics, Am. Soc. Clin. Investigation, Phi Beta Kappa, Sigma Xi. Office: Dept Genetics S-337 Stanford U Sch Medicine Stanford CA 94305

COHEN, STEPHEN FRAND, political scientist, educator, author; b. Indpls., Nov. 25, 1938; s. Marvin Stafford and Ruth (Frand) C.; m. Lynn Francis Blair, Aug. 25, 1962; children: Andrew, Alexandra. B.S., Ind. U., 1960, M.A., 1962; Ph.D., Columbia U., 1969; cert., Russian Inst., 1969. Instr. Columbia U., N.Y.C., 1965-68; asst. prof. politics Princeton U., N.J., 1968-73, assoc. prof., 1973-80, prof., 1980—, dir. Russian studies, 1973-80; mem. adv. council U.S. Acad. Scis., Washington, 1979-82. Auhtor: Bukharin and the Bolshevik Revolution, 1973; editor: (with Robert C. Tucker) The Great Purple Trial, 1965, (with Rabinowitch and Sharlet) The Soviet Union Since Stalin, 1980, An End to Silence, 1982; mem.editorial bd.: Slavic Rev., 1977-82; assoc. editor: World Politics, 1972—. Bd. dirs. Am. Com. on East-West Accord, Washington. Fellow Am. Council Learned Socs., 1971, 72-73, John Simon Guggenhiem Found., 1976-77, Rockefeller Found., 1980-81. Mem. Council Fgn. Relations, Am. Polit. Sci. Assn., Am. Hist. Assn., AAAS. Office: Princeton U 204 Corwin Hall Princeton NJ 08544

COHEN, S(TEPHEN) MARSHALL, university dean, philosophy educator; b. N.Y.C., Sept. 27, 1929; s. Harry and Fanny (Marshall) C.; m. Margaret Dennes, Feb. 15, 1964; children: Matthew, Megan. B.A., Dartmouth Coll., Hanover, N.H., 1951; M.A., Harvard U., 1953, Oxford U., Eng., 1977. Jr. fellow, Soc. of Fellows Harvard U., 1955-58, asst. prof. philosophy and gen. edn., 1958-62; asst. prof. U. Chgo., 1962-64, assoc. prof., 1964-67, Rockefeller U., N.Y.C., 1967-70; prof. philosophy CUNY, 1970-83, exec. officer program in philosophy Grad. Sch., 1975-83; prof. philosophy U. So. Calif., Los Angeles, 1983—, dean Div. Humanities, 1983—; lectr. Lowell Inst., Boston, 1957-58; vis. fellow All Souls Coll., Oxford, Eng., 1976-77. Editor: The Philosophy of John Stuart Mill, 1961, (with Gerald Mast) Film Theory and Criticism, 1974, (with Nagel and Scanlan) War and Moral Responsibility, 1974, (with Roger Copeland) What is Dance?, 1983, Philosophy and Public Affairs, 1970—, Philosophy and Society series, 1977-83, Ethical, Legal and Political philosophy Series, 1983—. Fellow Guggenheim Found., 1976-77, Rockefeller Found., 1977. Mem. Am. Philos. Assn., Soc. Ethical and Legal Philosophy. Democrat. Jewish. Office: Univ So Calif Div Humanities Los Angeles CA 90089

COHEN, STEPHEN PHILIP, political science educator; b. Chgo., Mar. 9, 1936; s. Saul and Bess (Passovoy) C.; m. Roberta Sue Brosilow, June 22, 1958; children: Edward, Jeffrey, Peter, Benjamin, Tamara, Susan. B.A., U. Chgo., 1958, M.A., 1959; Ph.D., U. Wis., 1967. Instr., asst. prof. polit. sci. and Asian studies U. Ill., Urbana, 1965-70; assoc. prof. polit. sci. and Asian studies, 1970-80, prof., 1981—; vis. prof. Keio U., Tokyo, 1974, Andhra U., India, 1977-78; co-dir. Office Arms Control, Disarmament and Internat. Security, U. Ill., 1978—; cons. U.S. State Dept. Arms Control Agy., Ford Found., Rockefeller Found., Dept. Def., Asia Soc.; expert witness U.S. Congress, 1981, 83. Author: The Indian Army, 1971, India: Emergent Power?, 1979, (with Richard L. Park) (with C.V. Raghavulu) The Andhra Cyclone of 1977, 1980, The Pakistan Army, 1984; editor: Asian Affairs; contbr. (with Richard L. Park) (with C.V. Raghavulu) articles to profl. jours. Trustee Am. Inst. Indian Studies, 1981—, Am. Inst. Pakistan Studies, 1981—. Ford Found. grantee, 1977-78; Am. Inst. Indian Studies grantee, 1963-65, 67-68, 71-72. Mem. Am. Polit. Sci. Assn., Assn. Asian Studies, Internat. Inst. Strategic Studies, Inter-Univ. Seminar on Armed Forces and Soc., Psi Upsilon. Jewish. Home: 405 S Orchard St Urbana IL 61801 Office: 255 Lincoln Hall 702 S Wright St Urbana IL 61801 *The central challenge facing mankind is a race between self-destructive violence and reasoned restraint. My professional activities as a researcher, teacher, and consultant are devoted to understanding—and ameliorating—the human institutions and forces which have brought us to the edge of catastrophe.*

COHEN, WALLACE M., lawyer; b. Norton, Va., July 11, 1908; s. Jacob Edward and Annie (Hyman) C.; m. Sylvia J. Stone, Sept. 7, 1932; children: Anne E. (Mrs. Steven A. Winkelman), Edward S., David W. Grad., Lake Forest Acad., 1925; S.B., Harvard U., 1929; postgrad., Law Sch., 1930-31; LL.B., Cornell U., 1932. Bar: Mass. 1932, Md. 1952, D.C. 1946, U.S. Supreme Ct 1946. Practice of law, Boston, 1932-38; staff NLRB, Dept. Labor, Shipbldg. Stablzn. Commn., Adv. Commn. Council Nat. Def., OPA, Lend Lease Adminstrn., Fgn. Econ. Assn., 1938-45; dep. administrv. asst. to Pres.; partner Landis, Cohen, Singman & Rauh, Washington, 1951—; Former mem. adv. bd. Clinch Valley Coll. of U. Va.; Fellow Brandeis U. Served with USCGR, 1943-45. Mem. Am., Fed., Fed. Communications, D.C., Mass., Md. bar assns. Clubs: Harvard (Boston and Washington) (former dir. Washington); Lonesome Pine Country (Norton, Va.); Nat. Capital Democratic, Federal City, International, Nat. Press (Washington); Federal Bar. Home: 2444 Massachusetts Ave NW Washington DC 20008 Office: 1019 19th St NW Washington DC 20036 *Neither a procrastinator nor a predator be.*

COHEN, WALTER STANLEY, health services exec.; b. Bklyn., Oct. 24, 1936; s. Harry and Ruth (Spitz) C.; m. Barbara Lee Cooper, June 18, 1960; children—Howard H., Andrea Sue. B.S., U. Buffalo, 1958; student, N.Y. U. Sch. Law, 1960-64. Jr. accountant firm Morris, Sherwood & May (C.P.A.'s), N.Y.C., 1958-59; semi-sr. accountant H. Merdinger & Co. (C.P.A.'s), 1960-61; sr. accountant Skillman & Michaels (C.P.A.'s), N.Y.C., 1961-62; with Blessings Corp., N.Y.C., 1962—, sr. accountant, 1962-66, asst. controller, 1966-69, asst. sec., 1969-70, sec., 1970-79, sec.-treas., 1979. Served with AUS, 1959-60. Mem. Kappa Nu (treas. 1955-56, v.p. 1956-57), B'nai B'rith. Republican. Jewish religion. Home: 1 Bryant Dr Morganville NJ 07751 Office: Brookwood Corp Plaza II 45 Knightsbridge Rd Piscataway NJ 08854

COHEN, WARREN I., history educator; b. Bklyn., June 20, 1934; s. Murray and Fay (Phillips) C.; m. Janice Prichard, June 22, 1957; children: Geoffrey Scott, Anne Leslie. A.B., Columbia U., 1955; A.M., Fletcher Sch. Law and Diplomacy, Tufts U., 1956; Ph.D., U. Wash., 1962. Lectr. U. Calif.-Riverside, 1962-63, asst.l prof., 1963-67, assoc. prof., 1967-71; prof. history Mich. State U., East Lansing, 1971—, dir. Asian Studies Ctr., 1979—; vis. prof. Nat Taiwan U.at, Taipei, 1964-66, Columbia U., 1971; mem. Com. on Am.-East Asian Relations, Cambridge, Mass., 1973—; cons. Nat. Acad. Scis., Washington, 1982—. Author: The American Revisionists, 1967, America's Response to China, 1971, The Chinese Connection, 1978, Dean Rusk, 1980; editor: Diplomatic History, 1979-82, New Frontiers in American-East Asian Relations, 1983. Bd. dirs. Mich. China Council, East Lansing, 1978-83; exec. sec. Gov's Mich. and China Com., Lansing, 1982—; bd. dirs. Japan Council, 1979—. Served to lt. (j.g.) USNR, 1956-59; PTO. Fulbright lectr., Tokyo, 1969-70; research grantee Am. Council Learned Socs., 1968, Ford Found., 1976-77, Henry Luce Found., 1983-84. Mem. Soc. for Historians of Am. Fgn. Relations (v.p. 1983, pres. 1984), Orgn. Am. Historians, Assn. for Asian Studies, ACLU. Democrat. Jewish. Home: 1233 Tanager Ln East Lansing MI 48823 Office: Asian Studies Ctr Mich State U East Lansing MI 48824

COHEN, WILBUR JOSEPH, former government official, public affairs educator; b. Milw., June 10, 1913; s. Aaron and Bessie (Rubenstein) C.; m. Eloise Bittel, Apr. 8, 1938; children: Christopher, Bruce, Stuart. Ph.B., U. Wis., 1934; L.H.D., Adelphi Coll., 1962, Cleve. State U., 1970, Ohio State U., 1970; LL.D., U. Wis., 1966, Yeshiva U., 1967, Brandeis U., 1968, Detroit U., Kenyon Coll., 1969, Mich. State U., 1975, Central Mich. U., 1976; D.S.S., U. Louisville, 1969; D.H., Fla. State U., 1972, Roosevelt U., 1978; D.P.S., Eastern Mich. U., 1982, No. Mich. U., 1983. With Com. Econ. Security, 1934-35; with Social Security Adminstrn., 1935-56; dir. div. research and statistics, 1953-56; prof. pub. welfare adminstrn. U. Mich., 1956-69, 72-83; asst. sec. HEW, 1961-65, undersec., 1965-68, sec., 1968-69; prof. edn. U. Mich., 1969-83, dean, 1969-78; mem. exec. bd. Inst. Social Research, 1969-76; co-chmn. Inst. Gerontology, U. Mich.-Wayne State U., 1969-76; vis. prof. UCLA, 1957; lectr. Catholic U., 1961-62; Sid W. Richardson prof. pub. affairs L.B.J. Sch. Public Affairs, U. Tex., 1980-83, prof. pub. affairs, 1983—; dir. research Pres.'s Com. Universal Tng., 1947; chmn. com. on health and pensions Wage Stablzn. Bd., 1951-52; cons. aging to U.S. Senate Com. Labor and Pub. Welfare, 1956-57, 59, to UN, 1956-57; chmn. Pres.'s Task Force on Health and Social Security, 1960; mem. Adv. Council Pub. Assistance,

1959, Nat. Com. Social Security, 1978-81; chmn. Nat. Com. on Unemployment Compensation, 1978-80, Pres.'s Com. on Mental Retardation, 1968, Pres.'s Com. on Population and Family Planning, 1968; del. Gen. Assembly Internat. Social Security Assn., Turkey, 1961, U.S., 1964, vice chmn. council, 1964; rep. U.S. Govt. at Internat. Confs. Social Security, Internat. Conf. Social Work, Internat. Labor Conf.; chmn. U.S. del. UN Conf. Ministers Responsible Social Welfare, 1968; co-chmn. Health Vols. for Carter-Mondale, 1976. Author: Retirement Policies in Social Security, 1957, (with William Haber) Readings in Social Security, 1948, Social Security, Programs, Problems and Policies, 1960, (with Milton Friedman) Social Security: Universal or Selective?, 1972, (with Charles F. Westoff) Demographic Dynamics in America, 1977; co-author: Income and Welfare in the United States, 1962, Toward a Social Report, 1969, also numerous articles. Trustee J.F. Kennedy Center Performing Arts, 1968; bd. govs. Haifa U., 1971—; chmn. Save Our Security, 1977—. Recipient Distinguished Service award HEW, 1956, Arthur J. Altmeyer award, 1972, award Group Health Assn., 1956, Florina Lasker award, 1961; Blanche Ittelson award, 1962; award Nat. Assn. Mentally Retarded Children, 1965, Assn. Phys. Medicine, 1965; Bronfman Pub. Health prize, 1967; Rockefeller Pub. Service award, 1967; Murray-Green award, 1968; Wilbur award Golden Ring Council Sr. Citizens, 1968; Wis. State U.-Stevens Point award, 1968; Forand award Nat. Council Sr. Citizens, 1969; Jane Addams-Hull House award, 1975; Merrill-Palmer award, 1975; Internat. Assn. Social Security award, 1979. Mem. Am. Pub. Welfare Assn. (Terry Meml. Merit award 1961, dir. 1962-65, pres. 1975-76), Nat. Conf. Social Welfare (Distinguished Service award 1957, pres. 1969), Council Social Work Edn. (ho. of dels. 1959-62, 74-77), Nat. Assn. Social Workers, Indsl. Relations Research Assn. (exec. bd. 1969-72), Am. Econ. Assn., Inst. Medicine of Nat. Acad. Scis. Home: 3700 Stevenson Ave Austin TX 78703 also 9819 Capitol View Ave Silver Spring MD 20910 Office: LBJ Sch Public Affairs U Tex Austin TX 78712

COHEN, WILLIAM, legal educator; b. Scranton, Pa., June 1, 1933; s. Maurice M. and Nellie (Rubin) C.; m. Betty C. Stein, Sept. 13, 1952 (div. 1976); children: Barbara Jean, David Alan, Rebecca Anne; m. Nancy M. Mahoney, Aug. 8, 1976; 1 dau., Margaret Emily. B.A., UCLA, 1953, LL.B., 1956. Bar: Calif. 1961. Law clk. to U.S. Supreme Ct. Justice William O. Douglas, 1956-57; from asst. prof. to asso. prof. U. Minn. Law Sch., 1957-60; vis. asso. prof. UCLA Law Sch., 1959-60, mem. faculty, 1960-70, prof., 1962-70, Stanford (Calif.) Law Sch., 1970—; vis. prof. law European U. Inst., Florence, Italy, fall 1977; Merriam vis. prof. Ariz. State U. Law Sch., Spring 1981. Co-author: The Bill of Rights, a Source Book, 1968, Comparative Constitutional Law, 1978, Constitutional Law Cases and Materials, 1981, Constitutional Law: The Structure of Government, 1981, Constitutional Law: Civil Liberty and Individual Rights, 1982. Home: 698 Maybell Ave Palo Alto CA 94306

COHEN, WILLIAM BENJAMIN, educator, historian; b. Jakobstad, Finland, May 2, 1941; came to U.S., 1957; s. Walter Israel and Rosi (Hirschberg) C.; m. Habiba Suleiman, Oct. 25, 1964; children: Natalie, Leslie. B.A., Pomona Coll., 1962; M.A., Stanford U., 1963, Ph.D., 1968. Vis. lectr. Northwestern U., Evanston, Ill., 1966-67; instr. history Ind. U., Bloomington, 1966-68, asst. prof., 1968-71, assoc. prof., 1971-80, prof., 1980—, chmn. Western European studies, 1978-80, chmn. dept. history, 1980—. Author: Rulers of Empire, 1971, Robert Delavignette, 1977, French Encounter, 1980, European Empire Building, 1980. NEH fellow, 1972. Mem. Am. Hist. Assn. (council for European studies 1981—), Soc. French Hist. Studies (pres. 1980-81, exec. com. 1980-83). Democrat. Home: 529 Hawthorne Dr Bloomington IN 47401 Office: History Dept Ballantine Hall Indiana Univ Bloomington IN 47405

COHEN, WILLIAM MARK, publisher; b. N.Y.C., Aug. 23, 1949; s. Abraham and Florence C. B.A., Columbia U., 1971. Dir. mktg. Human Sci. Press, Inc., N.Y.C., 1972-75; pub., editor The Haworth Press, Inc., N.Y.C., 1975—. Conceptualization, founder numerous profl. jours. in medicine and sci.; editor-in-chief profl. book program. Mem. Am. Soc. Info. Sci., Spl. Libraries Assn., ALA. Democrat. Jewish. Office: The Haworth Press Inc 28 E 22d St New York NY 10010

COHEN, WILLIAM NATHAN, radiologist; b. Balt., Dec. 10, 1935; s. Herbert and Lillian (Goldberg) C.; m. Sylvia Weinstein, Feb. 9, 1964; children: Elaine, Shirah, Jonathan. Student, Johns Hopkins U., 1952-55; M.D., U. Md., 1959. Intern U. Mich. Hosp., Ann Arbor, 1959-60; resident in radiology Mallinckrodt Inst., Washington U., St. Louis, 1960-63; chief radiology sect. Gallup Indian Hosp., USPHS, 1963-65; asst. prof. radiology U. Iowa, Iowa City, 1965-69, asso. prof., 1969-73, prof., 1973-76; prof. radiology SUNY Upstate Med. Ctr., Syracuse, 1976-83, clin. prof. radiology, 1983—; attending radiologist Crouse-Irving Meml. Hosp., Syracuse; vis. prof. radiology Hebrew U., Jerusalem, 1971-72. Contbr. articles in field to med. jours. Fellow Am. Coll. Radiology; mem. Radiol. Soc. N. Am., Am. Roentgen Ray Soc., Am. Inst. Ultrasound in Medicine. Office: Crouse-Irving Meml Hosp 736 Irving Ave Syracuse NY 13210

COHEN, WILLIAM SEBASTIAN, U.S. Senator; b. Bangor, Maine, Aug. 28, 1940; s. Reuben and Clara (Hartley) C.; m. Diane Dunn, Jan. 6, 1962; children—Kevin, Christopher. B.A. cum laude (James Bowdoin scholar, Alumni Fund scholar), Bowdoin Coll., 1962, LL.B., Boston U., 1965; LL.D., St. Joseph's Coll., Windham, Maine, 1974, U. Maine, 1975, Western New Eng. Coll., 1975, Bowdoin Coll., 1975, Nasson Coll., 1975. Bar: Maine bar 1965. Partner Paine, Cohen, Lynch, Weatherbee & Kobritz, Bangor, 1966-72; instr. Husson Coll., 1966, U. Maine, 1968-72; asst. county atty., Penobscot County, Maine, 1968-70; mem. 93d-95th congresses from, Maine; U.S. Senator from, Maine, 1979—; Mem. Zoning Bd. Appeals, 1967-69, Bangor Sch. Com., 1970-71, Bangor City Council, 1969-72, chmn. finance com., 1970-71; mayor, Bangor, 1972; Trustee Unity Coll.; bd. overseers Bowdoin Coll. Author: Of Sons and Seasons, 1978, Roll Call, 1981, Getting the Most Out of Washington, 1982. Recipient Sewall Latin prize, 1961, Emery Latin prize, 1962, Paul Nixon award for leadership; Disting. Service award as outstanding young man Jaycees, 1973; Alumni award for disting. pub. service Boston U., 1976; named to N.E. Hall of Fame Basketball Team, 1962, Outstanding Young Man of Year Nat. Jaycees, 1975; James Bowdoin scholar, 1961-62; Alumni Fund scholar, 1962. Mem. Am. Trial Lawyers Assn. (asst. editor-in-chief Jour. 1965-66, co-editor vols. 32 and 33 Jour.), Maine Trial Lawyers Assn. (v.p. 1970-72). Office: 530 Hart Senate Office Bldg Washington DC 20510

COHEN, YEHUDI ARYEH, anthropology educator; b. N.Y.C., June 7, 1928; s. Meyer Benjamin and Nehama (Goldin) C.; 1 dau., Lisa Ellen. B.A., Bklyn. Coll., 1948; Ph.D., Yale, 1953. Instr. Conn. Coll., 1952-53, Albert Einstein Coll. Medicine, 1955-59; asso. prof. U. Calif. at Davis, 1964-67; prof. anthropology Rutgers U., New Brunswick, N.J., 1967—; lectr. Columbia, 1956-62, U. Chgo. and Northwestern U., 1962-64; vis. prof. U. Pa., 1971. Author: Social Structure and Personality: A Casebook, 1961, The Transition from Childhood to Adolescence, 1964; editor: Man in Adaptation, 3 vols, 1968-71. Served with AUS, 1953-54. Mem. AAAS (Socio-Psychol. award 1955). Address: Douglass Coll Rutgers U Dept Anthropology New Brunswick NJ 08903

COHILL, MAURICE BLANCHARD, JR., judge; b. Pitts., Nov. 26, 1929; s. Maurice Blanchard and Florence (Clarke) C.; m. Suzanne Miller, June 27, 1952; children: Cynthia, Jonathan, Jennifer, Victoria. A.B., Princeton U., 1951; LL.B., U. Pitts., 1956. Bar: Pa. 1957. Judge family div. Common Pleas Ct., Allegheny County, Pitts., 1965-76; now judge U.S. Dist. Ct. for Western Dist., Pa., 1976—; Bd. dirs. Pa. George Jr. Republic, Grove City; bd. visitors Grad. Sch. Social Work, U. Pitts.; chmn. bd. fellows Nat. Center for Juvenile Justice. Served to capt. USMCR, 1951-53. Mem. Am., Pa., Allegheny County bar assns., Nat. Council Juvenile Ct. Judges (v.p.), Pa. Council Juvenile Ct. Judges (past pres.), Pa. Conf. State Trial Judges, Phi Delta Phi. Republican. Presbyterian. Office: Room 803 US Dist Ct US Post Office and Courthouse Courtroom 3 8th Floor Pittsburgh PA 15219

COHLER, BERTRAM JOSEPH, social sciences educator, clinical psychologist; b. Chgo., Dec. 3, 1938; s. Jonas Robert and Betty (Cahn) C.; m. Anne Meyers, June 11, 1962; children: Jonathan Richard, James Joseph. B.A., U. Chgo., 1961; Ph.D., Harvard U., 1967, postgrad., 1967-69; postgrad., Inst. Psychoanalysis, 1975—. Lectr. social relations Harvard U., Cambridge, Mass., 1967-69; assoc. dir. Orthogenic Sch. U. Chgo., 1969-72, dir., 1969-72; asst. prof. U. Chgo., 1969-75, assoc. prof., 1975-81, prof. depts. behavior scis., edn. and psychiatry, 1981—; sci. and profl. staff dept. psychiarty Michael Reese Hosp., Chgo., 1980—; cons. The Thresholds, Chgo., 1972-81, Inst. Psychoanalysis, 1972—, Ill. State Psychiat. Inst., 1977—. Author: (with H. Grunebaum et al) Mentally Ill Mothers and Their Children, 1975, 82, Mothers, Grandmothers, and Daughters, 1981, (with others) Parenthood as an Adult Experience, 1983. Mem. initial rev. group in aging NIMH, Washington, 1982—. Recipient Quantrell prize U. Chgo., 1975, William Rainey Harper Chair, 1978; fellow Inst. Medicine, 1975. Fellow Gerontol. Soc., Soc. Projective Techniques; mem. Am. Orthopsychiat. Assn. (dir. 1981—), Am. Psychol. Assn. (chmn. profl. affairs com. div. 39 1981—), Am. Sociol. Assn., Soc. Research in Child Devel., Chgo. Assn. Psychoanalytic Psychology (pres. 1983—). Home: 5408 S Blackstone Ave Chicago IL 60615 Office: U Chgo 5730 S Woodlawn Ave Chicago IL 60637 *Emphasis on community srevices has been an important tradition in myfamily for several generations. This concern includes making knowledge and skills available to others, providing leadership for organizations, and giving of time where needed. Teaching, writing, and research are all involved in making the world better for my been a part of it. My own goal has been to improve the human condition and to inspire my students to carry on this cocern for the welfare of others.*

COHN, ALVIN GILBERT, musician, jazz composer; b. N.Y.C., Nov. 24, 1925; s. David Emanuel and Gertrude C.; m. Flora Ann Morse, Aug. 23, 1963; children: Michael, Peter, Danna, Lisa, Joseph. Student, public schs., N.Y.C. Saxophonist, Buddy Rich, Woody Herman, Artie Shaw; arranger, orchestrator, Ray Charles, Andy Williams, Tony Bennett; orchestrator: Broadway shows Music! Music!; TV Anne Bancroft Spl; rec. artist Concord Records; tours include, Japan, Eng., S. Am., Can., Senegal, South Africa, France, Holland, Denmark, Sweden, Norway, Switzerland. Mem. Am. Fedn. Musicians, ASCAP. Democrat. Jewish. Office: care Concord Jazz Inc PO Box 845 Concord CA 94522

COHN, AVERN LEVIN, judge; b. Detroit, July 23, 1924; s. Irwin I. and Sadie (Levin) C.; m. Joyce Hochman, Dec. 30, 1954; children: Sheldon, Leslie, Magy, Thomas. Student, John Tarleton Agrl. Coll., 1943, Stanford, 1944; J.D., U. Mich., 1949. Bar: Mich. bar 1949. Practiced in, Detroit, 1949-79; mem. firm Honigman Miller Schwartz & Cohn, Detroit, 1961-79; U.S. dist. judge, 1979—. Mem. Mich. Civil Rights Commn., 1972-75, chmn., 1974-75; Mem. Detroit Bd. Police Commrs., 1975-79, chmn., 1979—; Bd. govs. Jewish Welfare Fedn., Detroit, 1972—. Served with AUS, 1943-46. Mem. Am., Detroit bar assns., State Bar Mich. Jewish. Office: 219 Federal Bldg Detroit MI 48633

COHN, BERNARD SAMUEL, anthropologist, educator; b. Bklyn., May 13, 1928; s. Nathan and Blanche (Herc) C.; m. Rella Israly, Mar. 19, 1950; children: Jenny Miriam, Abigail Catherine, Jacob Israly, Naomi Juliet. B.A., U. Wis., 1949; Ph.D. (Social Sci. Research Council fellow), Cornell U., Ithaca, N.Y., 1954. Research assoc., asst. prof. anthropology U. Chgo., 1956-58, vis. asst. prof. history, 1959-60, prof. anthropology and South Asian history, 1964—; chmn. dept. anthropology, 1969-72; asso. prof., chmn. dept. anthropology U. Rochester, 1960-64; vis. prof. history U. Mich., 1967, 79; research fellow Australian Nat. U., 1979, 82. Assoc. editor: Jour. Asian Studies, 1962-65; editorial bd.: Comparative Studies in Society and History, 1966—, Jour. Peasant Studies. Served with AUS, 1954-56. Rockefeller Found. fellow, 1957-59; Am. Council Learned Socs. fellow, 1962; Guggenheim fellow, 1964; fellow Center Advanced Study Behavioral Scis., 1967-68; Fellow Am. Inst. Indian Studies; NEH fellow, 1982-83. Mem. Assn. Asian Studies (chmn. S. Asia com. 1962-64), Royal (Eng.), Am. anthrop. assns., Am. Soc. Ethnohistory (exec. bd. 1968-70). Home: 5822 S Blackstone Ave Chicago IL 60637

COHN, BERTRAM JOSIAH, investment banker; b. Newark, Sept. 12, 1925; s. Julius Henry and Bessie Ruth (Einson) C.; m. Barbara Biard, June 20, 1956; children: Daniel, Susan, Diana. A.B. cum laude, Harvard, 1949; M.B.A., N.Y. U., 1957. Vice pres. Decatur Iron & Steel Co., Ala., 1951-67; chmn. bd. Schuylkill Lead Corp., Baton Rouge, 1968-70, DPF, Inc., Hartsdale, N.Y., 1970—, Interstate Bakeries Corp., 1970-72; dir. Arrow Electronics Inc., Interstate Brands Corp., Bowne & Co. Inc. Served with AUS, 1943-46. Home: 35 Bonnie Brair Ln Larchmont NY 10538 Office: First Manhattan Co 437 Madison Ave New York NY 10022

COHN, DAVID HERC, association executive, retired foreign service officer; b. Bklyn., July 29, 1923; s. Nathan and Blanche (Herc) C.; m. Verna Elizabeth Peterson, Jan. 29, 1949. A.B., Dickinson Coll., 1948; postgrad., N.Y. U., 1948-49, U. Pa., 1963-64; M.A., U. Miami, 1951. Instr. U. Miami, 1950-51; spl. asst. to div. dir. Dept. Commerce, 1951-56; joined U.S. Fgn. Service, 1956; consul, econ. officer Am. consulate gen., Istanbul, Turkey, 1956-60; 2d sec., economist U.S. Regional Orgn., Paris, 1960-63; economist Office Intelligence Research, Near East and South Asia, Dept. State, 1964-66, economist Bur. Near East and South Asian Affairs, economist Pakistan-Afghanistan Country Directorate, 1966-68; dep. prin. officer Am. consulate gen., Karachi, Pakistan, 1968-70; econ. counselor Am. embassy, Kabul, Afghanistan, 1970-73, comml. counselor, Jakarta, Indonesia, 1973-75, econ.-comml. counselor, 1975-76; econ. and social policy adviser Bur. Internat. Orgn. Affairs Dept. State, 1976-77, dir. Internat. Econ. Policy Office, Bur. Internat. Orgn. Affairs, 1977-78, dir. Office Econ. Research and Analysis, Bur. Intelligence and Research, 1978-80, ret., 1980; asst. v.p. U.S.-USSR Trade & Econ. Council, Inc., N.Y.C., 1981—. Served with AUS, 1943-46. Mem. Am. Fgn. Service Assn., Nat. League Nursing, Omicron Delta Kappa. Clubs: Dacor, Dacor House (Washington). Home: 2500 Johnson Ave Apt 16J Riverdale NY 10463 Office: 805 3d Ave New York NY 10022

COHN, EARL, coffee company executive; b. Chgo., Oct. 16, 1917; s. Harry and Sadie (Silverstone) C.; m. Madelyn Lois Berger, June 29, 1941; children—Steven Jay, Marcia Beth.; m. Dorothy L. Cohn; children: Kerri Lyons, Kip Lyons. B.S., U. Ill., 1939. Salesman Superior Tea and Coffee Co., Chgo., 1939-44, sales supr., 1945-49, sales mgr., 1950-54, sec.-treas., 1955-57, exec. v.p., 1957-59, pres., 1960; chmn. bd.; chmn. bd. Caswell Foods, Inc., San Francisco, 1969—; pres. Mid-Pacific and Mauna Kea Coffee Co., Hawaii, Superior Foods Co., Chgo., Steven Fin. Co.; mem. corp. Culinary Inst. Am.; Mem. exec. com. Israel Bond Orgn.; bd. overseers N.Y. U. Foodservice Mgmt. Mem. Internat. Food Mfrs. Assn., Tau Epsilon Phi. Clubs: Twin Orchard Country; Canyon Country (pres.), Tamarisk Country (Palm Springs)). Home: 3200 Lake Shore Dr Chicago IL 60657 Office: 2278 Elston St Chicago IL 60614 *In selling, goals must be set and all effort must be put forth to achieve them regardless of obstacles. Think of results and money will follow. Never lie; then you don't have to remember what you said previously. Treat others as you want to be treated—success will follow.*

COHN, GERALD L., bus. exec.; b. Easton, Pa., Dec. 9, 1928; s. Samuel A. and Hannah S. (Levine);; s. Samuel A. and Hannah S. (Cohn); m. Marcia Yoffe, Oct. 10, 1954; children—Shelley, Cindy. Student, Pa. State U., 1947-48, Wilkes Coll., 1950-52. Founder, pres. Nautilus Industries, Inc., Freeland, Pa., 1960-70; founder, pres., dir. Refinement Internat. Co. (formerly Ag-Met, Inc.), Hazleton, Pa., 1970—, now vice-chmn.; dir. Hazleton Nat. Bank, Sarama, Inc. Mem. Inst. Scrap Iron Steel, Nat. Assn. Recycling Inst. Jewish. Clubs: B'nai B'rith, Valley Country, Jockey. *

COHN, HARVEY, mathematician; b. N.Y.C., Dec. 27, 1923; s. Morris and Leah (Spielmann) C.; m. Bernice Blaufarb, Mar. 8, 1951; children—Anthony, Susan. B.S., Coll. City N.Y., 1942; M.S., N.Y.U., 1943; Ph.D., Harvard, 1948. Teaching fellow Harvard, 1947-48; asst. prof. Wayne U. (now Wayne State U.), 1948-54, asso. prof., 1955-56; vis. asso. prof. Stanford, 1954-55; asso. prof., then prof., head computer center Washington U., St. Louis, 1956-58; prof. math. U. Ariz., 1958-71; summer lectr. math U. Calif. at Los Angeles, 1960, U. Wis., 1963; Emil Post prof. math. City U. N.Y., 1971-73, distinguished prof., 1973—; cons. Gen. Motors Corp., AEC computing facility at N.Y.U., Nat. Bur. Standards, Argonne Nat. Labs.; Adv. bd. autonomous U. Guadalajara, Mex., 1963—; mem. Inst. for Advanced Study, 1970-71; lektor U. Copenhagen, 1976-77. Author: Second Course in Number Theory, 1962, Conformal Mapping on Riemann Surfaces, 1967, Classical Invitation to Algebraic Numbers and Class Fields. Served with USNR, 1944-46. Recipient William Lowell Putnam prize Harvard, 1946. Mem. Am. Math. Soc., Math. Assn., Am., Assn. Computing Machinery, Phi Beta Kappa, Sigma Xi. Office: Dept Math City U NY 33 W 42d St New York NY 10036

COHN, HASKELL, lawyer; b. Concord, N.H., Dec. 4, 1901; s. Abraham I. and Miriam (Caro) C.; m. Harriet Segal, Mar. 27, 1928; children: Marjorie (Mrs. William H. Wolf), Susan (Mrs. David A. Bensinger). A.B. magna cum laude, Dartmouth Coll., 1922; LL.B., Harvard U., 1925. Bar: Mass. 1926, D.C. 1972. Since practiced in, Boston; sr. partner firm Mintz, Levin, Cohn, Ferris, Glovsky & Popeo (and predecessors), 1933—. Author articles on taxation. Bd. dirs. Greater Boston YMCA, 1956-71. Recipient Alumni award Dartmouth Coll., 1977. Fellow Am. Bar Found., Am. Coll. Probate Counsel; mem. Am. Coll. Tax Counsel, ABA (vice chmn. estate and gift tax com. of tax sect. 1966-68, ho. of dels. 1968-79, com. on specialization 1975-81, task force on lawyer competence 1981-83, consortium on lawyer competency 1983), Nat Conf. Chief Justices (mem. coordinating council), Mass. Bar Assn. (bd. dels. 1969-71), Boston Bar Assn. (chmn. family law 1959-65, pres. 1969-71), Am. Law Inst. (com. on revision estate and gift taxes 1964-67, joint com. continuing profl. edn. 1965—, chmn. adv. com. peer rev. 1978-80, chmn. peer rev. inst.), Harvard Law Sch. Assn. (regional v.p., mem. council 1966-70), Boston Bar Found. (pres. 1969-74), Dartmouth Alumni Assn. (pres. Boston 1954), Phi Beta Kappa. Clubs: Harvard (Boston and N.Y.C.); Union, Curtis, The Law; The Country (Brookline, Mass.). Home: 1010 Memorial Dr. Cambridge MA 02138 Office: One Financial Ctr Boston MA 02111

COHN, HERBERT B., lawyer; b. N.Y.C., Oct. 2, 1912; s. Joseph J. and Lillian (Rosing) C.; m. Kathryn E. Coe, May 24, 1941; 1 dau., Elizabeth (Kark) Kundrat. A.B., Yale U., 1933; LL.B. magna cum laude, Harvard U., 1936. Bar: N.Y. State bar 1936, U.S. Supreme Ct. bar 1940, D.C. bar 1978. Mem. legal staff SEC, 1936-48, dir. op. writ. office, 1942-48; mem. legal staff Am. Electric Power Service Corp., N.Y.C., 1948-67, v.p., dir., chief counsel, 1954-67, exec. v.p. adminstrv. and corporate services, 1967-72, vice chmn. bd., chief adminstrv. officer, 1972-77; dir., mem. exec. com. Am. Electric Power Co., 1966—, vice chmn. bd., 1972-77, chmn. fin. com., 1976—; v.p., dir. Appalachian Power Co., of Ind.; Mich. Electric Co., Ky. Power Co., Ohio Power Co., other subsidiaries, to 1977; of counsel firm Morgan Lewis & Bockius, Washington, 1977—; Chmn. task force on U.S. energy policy study 20th Century Fund, 1976. Editor: Harvard Law Rev, 1934-36. Served from lt. (j.g.) to lt. comdr. USNR, 1942-46. Mem. Am. Bar Assn. (chmn. pub. utility sect. 1968-69), Harvard Law Sch. Assn., Edison Electric Inst. (dir. 1964-67, 70-73, chmn. legal com. 1962-64), Nat. Assn. Electric Cos. (chmn. 1977-78, dir., exec. com. 1975-79, chmn. com. for capital formation through dividend reinvestment 1978—). Clubs: Yale (N.Y.C.); Metropolitan (Washington). Home: Regency at McLean 1800 Old Meadow Rd McLean VA 22102 Office: 1800 M St NW Washington DC 20036

COHN, HOWARD, magazine editor; b. N.Y.C., Nov. 1, 1922; s. Morris and Vivian (Siegel) C.; m. Regina Levy, Apr. 2, 1949; children—Steven B., Robert D. B.A., Am. U., 1947. Assoc. editor Sportfolio mag., 1947-48; assoc. editor, then mng. editor Am. Lawn Tennis mag., 1948-50; assoc. editor Quick mag., 1950-51, Collier's mag., 1951-56; freelance writer, 1957-59; articles editor Pageant mag., 1959, exec. editor, 1959-63; mng. editor True mag., 1964-68, Med. World News mag., 1968, exec. editor, 1968-75, editor, 1975-77; exec. editor McGraw-Hill Newsletter Center, 1977-79; sr. staff editor McGraw-Hill Pub. Co., N.Y.C., 1979-81; editor-in-chief Graduating Engr. mag., 1981—. Served with AUS, 1943-46. Mem. Am. Soc. Mag. Editors. Home: 35 Shirley Ln White Plains NY 10607 Office: 1221 Ave of Americas New York NY 10020

COHN, ISIDORE, JR., surgeon, educator; b. New Orleans, Sept. 25, 1921; s. Isidore and Elsie (Waldhorn) C.; m. Jacqueline Heymann, July 4, 1944 (div. Aug. 1971); children: Ian Jeffrey, Lauren Kerry; m. Marianne Winter Miller, Jan. 3, 1976. M.D., U. Pa., 1945; M.Med. Sci. in Surgery, 1952, D.M.S., 1955. Diplomate: Am. Bd. Surgery. Intern Grad. Hosp. U. Pa., 1945-46; resident in surgery, 1949-52; fellow dept. surg. research U. Pa., 1947-48; vis. surgeon Charity Hosp., New Orleans, 1952-62, sr. vis. surgeon, 1962—; surgeon in chief La. State U. Service, Charity Hosp., 1962—; cons. surgeon VA Hosp., New Orleans, Touro Infirmary; instr. surgery La. State U. Sch. Medicine, New Orleans, 1952-53, asst. prof., 1953-56, asso. prof., 1956-59, prof., 1959—, chmn. dept. surgery, 1962—; mem. surg. research rev. com. VA, Washington, 1967-68; mem. Am. Bd. Surgery, 1969-75; dir. Nat. Pancreatic Cancer Project, 1975—; Mem. editorial bd.: Digestive Diseases and Scis, 1978-82, Am. Surgery, 1963—, Current Surgery, 1964—, Am. Jour. Surgery, 1968—; Mem. editorial board: Surg. Gastroenterology, 1982—. Served to capt. M.C. AUS, 1946-47. Fellow A.C.S.; mem. AMA, Am. Surg. Assn., So. Surg. Assn. (1st v.p. 1979-80, treas.-recorder 1981-82, pres. 1982-83), La. Surg. Assn. (pres. 1968), So. Med. Assn., La., Orleans Parish med. socs., Soc. Univ. Surgeons, Southeastern Surg. Congress (chmn. forum on progress in surgery 1967-69, councillor for La. 1967-73, pres. 1972), Surg. Biology Club II, Assn. Acad. Surgery, James D. Rives Surg. Soc., Internat. Surg. Soc., Am. Gastroenterol. Assn., Bockus Soc. Gastroenterology,

Soc. Surgery Alimentary Tract (trustee 1969-80, recorder 1973-76, pres. 1976-77, chmn. bd. 1977-78), Am. Soc. Microbiologists, Soc. Surg. Oncology, N.Y. Acad. Scis., Soc. Surg. Chairmen, Am. Assn. Cancer Research, Southeastern Cancer Research Assn. (pres. 1975), Collegium Internationale Chirurgiae Digestivae, Am. Cancer Soc. (vice chmn. clin. investigation adv. com. 1969, chmn. clin. investigation adv. com. 1969-73), Sigma Xi, Phi Beta Kappa, Alpha Omega Alpha, Omicron Delta Kappa. Office: Med Sch La State U New Orleans LA 70112

COHN, JESS VICTOR, psychiatrist; b. Cin., Jan. 1, 1908; s. Samuel L. and Hannah (Pritz) C.; m. Norma J. Hana, Sept. 7, 1947; children: Jess Victor, William S., James D. M.D., U. Cin., 1933. Diplomate: Am. Bd. Psychiatry and Neurology. Rotating intern Cin. Gen. Hosp., 1933, resident psychiatry, 1934; resident neurology Bellevue Hosp., N.Y.C., 1935; pres. neuro-psychiat. dept. Broward Gen. Hosp., Ft. Lauderdale, Fla., 1961, mem. active staff, 1955-63; cons. psychiatry Meml. Hosp., Hollywood, Fla., 1957-63, Mt. Sinai Hosp., Miami Beach, Fla., 1956-63; mem. active staff North Broward Provident Hosp., Ft. Lauderdale, 1956-63, Holy Cross Hosp., 1957—, Ft. Lauderdale Beach Hosp., 1957—, Imperial Point Hosp., Boca Raton (Fla.) Community Hosp.; also chief div. psychiatry; cons. psychiatry Social Security Adminstrn., 1963-69, Sinai Hosp., Balt., 1964-69, Carroll County Gen. Hosp., 1965-69; asst. supt. Central State Hosp., Indpls., 1948-50; instr. neuropsychiatry Ind. U. Med. Sch., 1948-50; dir. clerkship in applied practical psychology Butler U., 1949-50; supt. Embreevill (Pa.) State Hosp., 1950-55; asso. psychiatry U. Pa. Med. Sch., 1952-55, 1952-55; asst. prof. psychiatry U. Miami, 1957; supt. Springfield State Hosp., Sykesville, Md., 1963-69; asso. prof. psychiatry Johns Hopkins Med. Sch., 1963-69; psychiatrist Johns Hopkins Hosp., 1963-69; mem. faculty U. Md. Med Sch., 1963-69; clin. asso. prof. psychiatry U. Miami (Fla.) Sch. Medicine, 1979—; psychiatrist Univ. Hosp., 1963-69; regional dir. mental health for Western Md. Founding mem., chmn. med. adv. com. Mental Health Assn. S.E. Fla., 1944-48; chmn. Fla. commn. Internat. Congress Mental Health, 1948. Author articles, bulls. in field. Fellow A.C.P.; mem. A.M.A., Assn. Med. Supts. Mental Hosps. (editor newsletter), Am. Psychiat. Assn. (mem. examining bd. administrv. psychiatry), So. Psychiat. Assn., Pa. Psychiat. Soc., Phila. Psychiat. Soc. (chmn. program com.), Med. Chirurgical Faculty Md., Broward County Med. Assn. (chmn. med. adv. com. to mental health clinic), Broward County Neuropsychiat. Assn. (founding mem., 1st pres.), Fla. Psychiat. Soc., Delaware Valley Group Psychotherapy Soc. (founding mem., chmn. program com., mem. exec. com.), Am. Acad. Psychotherapists, Eastern Psychoanalytic Assn., Am. Coll. Psychiatrists. Address: 501 SW 11th Pl #304 Boca Raton FL 33432

COHN, JUDITH R., lawyer; b. Phila., May 15, 1943; d. Mac and Evelyn (Greenbaum) Rutman; 1 son, Peter Lawrence. B.A., Barnard Coll., 1974; J.D. magna cum laude, U. Pa., 1969. Bar: Pa. 1970, U.S. Supreme Ct. 1974. Law clk. U.S. Ct. Appeals(3d cir.), Phila., 1969-70; assoc. firm Wolf Block Schorr & Solis-cohen, Phila., 1970-77; ptnr. Wolf Block Shorr & Solis-cohen, Phila., 1977—; instr. Law Sch., U. Pa.-Phila., 1978; lectr. in field. Mem. ABA, Pa. Bar Assn., Phila. Bar Assn. Office: 1200 Packard Bldg Philadelphia PA 19102

COHN, LEONARD ALLAN, chemical company executive; b. Oskaloosa, Iowa, May 8, 1929; s. Eli A. and Edna C.; m. Rivalie Sideman, Sept. 2, 1951; children: Sheldon, Sylvia, Elliot. B.S. in Ch.E, Iowa State U., 1951; M.B.A., Washington U., St. Louis, 1955. Registered profl. engr., Iowa. Gen. mgr. Carpet Fiber div. Monsanto Co., Atlanta, 1970-72; gen. mgr. Apparel Fiber div. Monsanto Co., St. Louis, 1973-75, gen. mgr. Plastics div., 1976-78, v.p. energy and material mgmt., 1979—. Mem. Am. Inst. Chem. Engrs., Am. Chem. Soc., Nat. Petroleum Refiners Assn. (dir.). Office: 800 N Lindbergh Blvd Saint Louis MO 63166

COHN, MARCUS, lawyer; b. Omaha, Sept. 20, 1913; s. Sam and Rose (Forman) C.; m. Harryette Evelyn Nightingale, Aug. 20, 1939; children: Lawrence N., Barbara Gale. Student, U. Okla., 1931-34; A.B., U. Chgo., 1935, J.D. cum laude (Bigelow fellow), 1938; LL.M., Harvard U., 1940. Chief field and investigation sect. law dept. FCC, 1940-44; individual practice law, 1944-46; partner Cohn & Marks, Washington; professorial lectr. Grad. Sch. Pub. Law, George Washington U., 1967-78; resource panelist Aspen Inst. Humanistic Studies; participant U. Colo. Conf. World Affairs, 1964-78. Contbr. articles to revs. Mem. council Friends of Folger Library, 1979-83; mem. exec. com. Library of Congress Center for the Book; bd. govs., nat. exec. com. Am. Jewish Com.; mem. Nat. Council for Humanities; chmn. sponsors Cortez A.M. Ewing Found.; bd. visitors, mem. exec. planning com. U. Okla., 1969-76; trustee Arena Stage, Greater Washington Ednl. TV Assn. Recipient Distinguished Service citation U. Okla., 1973. Mem. Fed. Communications Bar Assn. (pres. 1973-74), Am. Bar Assn. (vice chmn. council sci. and tech. sect. 1977-78), Order of Coif, Phi Beta Kappa. Clubs: Internat., Cosmos. Home: 4031 Oliver St Chevy Chase MD 20015 Office: 1333 New Hampshire Ave NW Washington DC 20036

COHN, MICHAEL, publisher; b. N.Y.C., Nov. 14, 1932; s. William and Pauline (Haber) C.; m. Susan Cotton, Aug. 26, 1956; 1 son, Thomas; m. Suzanne Hazen, June 21, 1970; 1 son, Peter. B.S., U. Pa., 1954; LL.B., Harvard U., 1957. Bar: N.Y. bar 1957. With firm Marshall & Vigoda, N.Y.C., 1961-62; with New Am. Library, Inc., N.Y.C., 1962-68, World Pub. Co., 1968-69, Playboy Enterprises, Inc., 1970-79, v.p., dir. book div., 1972-79; pres. Charter Communications, Inc., N.Y.C., 1980—; lectr. Practicing Law Inst., N.Y. U. Contbr. to copyright publs. Mem. Am., N.Y. State bar assns. Club: Harvard (N.Y.C.). Home: 1725 York Ave New York NY 10028 Office: 51 Madison Ave New York NY 10010

COHN, MILDRED, biochemist; b. N.Y.C., July 12, 1913; d. Isidore M. and Bertha (Klein) C.; m. Henry Primakoff, May 31, 1938; children—Nina, Paul, Laura. B.A., Hunter Coll., 1931; M.A., Columbia, 1932, Ph.D., 1938; Sc.D. (hon.), Med. Coll. Pa., 1966, Radcliffe Coll., 1978, Washington U., St. Louis, 1981. Research asst. biochemistry George Washington U. Sch. Medicine, 1937-38; research asso. Cornell U., 1938-46, Washington U., 1946-50, 51-58, asso. prof. biol. chemistry, 1958-60; asso. prof. biophysics and phys. biochemistry U. Pa. Med. Sch., 1960-61, prof., 1961-78, Benjamin Rush prof. physiol. chemistry, 1978-82, prof. emerita, 1982; sr. mem. Inst. Cancer Research U. Pa., 1982—. Editorial bd.: Jour. Biol. Chemistry, 1958-63, 67-72. Established investigator Am. Heart Assn., 1953-59, career investigator, 1964-78. Recipient Garvan medal, Cresson medal., Nat. Medal of Sci. Mem. Am. Philos. Soc., Nat. Acad. Scis., Am. Chem. Soc., Harvey Soc., Am. Soc. Biol. Chemists (pres. 1978), Am. Biophys. Soc., Am. Acad. Arts and Scis., Phi Beta Kappa, Sigma Xi. Office: Inst Cancer Research 7701 Burholme Ave Philadelphia PA 19111

COHN, MILTON SEYMOUR, business executive; b. N.Y.C., Oct. 11, 1920; s. Max B. and Dorothy (Zucker) C.; m. Lucille Sanders, May 20, 1945; children: Bonnie L., Judd M. B.S. cum laude, NYU, 1941, J.D., 1950. Bar: N.Y. 1950. With Cerro Wire & Cable Co., Queens, N.Y., 1945-81, pres., 1955-81, ret., 1981; dir. CCX, Inc., Carle Place, N.Y.; dir., chmn. exec. com. United Aircrafts Products, Inc., Dayton, Ohio; Condec Corp., Old Greenwich, Conn. Bd. dirs. Beth Israel Med. Center, Max B. Cohn Family Found.; trustee Ohr Torah Inst. Mem. Beta Gamma Sigma. Clubs: City Athletic, NYU Fin. Office: 445 Park Ave New York NY 10022

COHN, NATHAN, consultant, former engineering company executive; b. Hartford, Conn., Jan. 2, 1907; s. Harris and Dora Leah (Levin) C.; m. Marjorie Kurtzon, June 30, 1940; children: Theodore Elliot, David Leslie, Anne Harris, Amy Elizabeth, Julie Archer. S.B., M.I.T., 1927; D.Eng. (hon.), Rennsalear Poly. Inst., 1976. With Leeds & Northrup Co., Phila., 1927-72, mgr. market devel. div., 1955-58, v.p. tech. affairs, 1958-65, sr. v.p. tech. affair, 1965-67, exec. v.p. research and corp. devel., 1967-72, dir., 1963-75; cons. mgmt. and tech. of measurement and control, Jenkintown, Pa., 1972—; dir. AEL Industries Inc., Alkco Mfg. Co., Weinschel Engring. Co., Milton Roy Co., Modular Comptar Systems, Parlex Corp.; gen. partner Network Systems Devel. Assos.; pres. Nat. Electronics Conf., 1950; mem. NRC; exec. bd. Found. Instrumentation, Edn. and Research, 1962-64; del. congress Internat. Fedn. Automatic Control, 1960, 63, 66, 69, 72, 75, 78, 81, chmn. tech. com. on applications, 1969-72; chmn. U.S. organizgin com. 1975 World Congress, mem. tech. coms. on computers, systems, mem. com. on social effects of automation, 1975—; mem. vis. com. libraries M.I.T., 1964-69, mem. vis. com. philosophy, 1972-74. Contbr. articles to profl. jours., chpts. to books, textbook. Bd. dirs., v.p. Eagleville (Pa.) Hosp. and Rehab. Center. Fellow IEEE (life, Lamme medal 1968, Edison medal 1982, chmn. fellow com. 1974-76, chmn. awards bd. 1977-78, mem. Centennial com. 1979—); chmn. Intersoc. Hoover Medal (Bd. of Award 1978-81); mem. Instrument Soc. Am. (v.p. industries and scis. 1960-61, sec. 1962, pres. 1963, Sperry medalist 1968, hon. mem. award 1976), AAAS, Franklin Inst. (life, Wetherill medalist 1968, mem. bd. mgrs. 1971—, chmn. bd. mgrs. 1971-75), Nat. Acad. Engring., Engrs. Joint Council (exec. bd. 1975-78, commn. on internat. relations 1978-79), Am. Assn. Engring. Socs. (council for internat. affairs 1980-81), Indsl. Research Inst., Engrs. Council Profl. Devel. (vis. com. curriculum accreditation), Sci. Apparatus Makers Assn. (exec. bd. 1961-62, 66-73, pres. 1969-71, SAMA award 1978), Nat. Soc. Profl. Engrs. (Engr. of Yr. Delaware Valley 1968, State of Pa. 1969), Sigma Xi, Tau Beta Pi, Eta Kappa Nu, Pi Lambda Phi. Jewish. Club: Rydal (Phila.). Patentee electric power systems controls.

COHN, NORMAN STANLEY, educator, university dean; b. Phila., June 26, 1930; s. Jack and Helen Blossom (Burak) C.; m. Margaret Foreman, June 24, 1956; children: Alison, Nicholas, Jason. A.B., U. Pa., 1952; M.S., U. Ky., 1953; Ph.D., Yale, 1957. Research asst. U. Ky., 1952-53; research asst. Yale, 1953, teaching asst., 1953-56; fellow Yale Atypical Growth, summer 1956, Tuttle-U. fellow, 1956-57; research asso. Brookhaven Nat. Lab., summer 1955; postdoctoral fellow Johns Hopkins U., 1957-59; instr. McKoy Coll., 1958-59; asst. prof. botany Ohio U., 1959-64, asso. prof., 1964-68, Distinguished prof. botany, 1968—, head cellular and physiol. bioscis., chmn. dept. botany, 1969-70, dean Grad. Coll., dir. research, 1970-79, mem. Univ. Council, 1975-77, mem. hon. degree com., 1977-79, arts and scis. cabinet, 1967-68, chmn. grad. council, 1970—, mem. faculty senate, 1967-70, 81-84, vice chmn. faculty senate, 1970, chmn. com. on coms., 1971-77; on leave at NSF, Washington, 1979-81; coordinator North Central Self-Study for U., 1973-74; mem. Interagy. Commn. on Plant Scis., 1979-81; participant seminars major univs., colls., U.S., Europe; lectr. U.S. Nat. Acad. Sci.; lectr. research visit, Czechoslovakia, 1968, Yugoslavia, 1973; mem. U.S. Dept. Agr. rev. panel, 1980. Contbr. numerous articles to profl. jours. AEC Contracts Research grantee, 1959-63; Ohio U. Research Com. Research grantee, 1964-65, 67-68, 83-84; NIH research grantee, 1967-70; Fulbright Sr. Research scholar U. Leiden, The Netherlands, 1965-66, 68-69; recipient U.S. Nat. Acad. Sci. award, 1968, 1973. Fellow Ohio Acad. Sci.; mem. Genetics Soc. Am., Am. Inst. Biol. Scis., Am. Soc. Cell Biology, AAAS, AAUP (pres. Ohio U. chpt. 1963-64), N.Y. Acad. Scis., Argonne Univs. Assn., North Central Assn., Research Dirs. Assn., Council Grad. Schs. U.S., Central States Univs. (dir. 1970-73), Midwestern Assn. Grad. Schs. (vice chmn. 1976, chmn. 1977), Phi Beta Kappa (hon.), Sigma Xi. Home: 33 Graham Dr Athens OH 45701 Office: Dept Botany Ohio Univ Athens OH 45701

COHN, ROBERT H., food company executive; b. 1926; married. Entire career with C F S Continental, Chgo., pres., 1968-81, chmn. bd., chief exec. officer, 1981—, also dir. Office: C F S Continental Inc 100 S Wacker Dr Chicago IL 60606 *

COHN, RONALD IRA, advertising agency executive; b. Chgo., Mar. 9, 1936; s. Irving and Claire Ada (Schwartz) C.; children by previous marriage: Lynn, William, Robert; m. Ann Rochelle, Dec. 20, 1970; 1 son, Henry. B.A., U. Ill., 1957. Trainee Chgo. Sun Times, 1956, with dept. real estate, 1957-58; copywriter, TV producer, creative dir. George S. Sandler Advt. agy., 1958-60; chmn., chief exec. Weber, Cohn & Riley, Chgo., 1960—; dir. Euter Mark, Steppenwolf Theater, ImportAnte S.A., Mercados Ltd.; guest lectr. Columbia Coll., Ill. Inst. Tech.; cons. Nat. Co-op. Com. and Ky. Fried Chicken Corp., 1967-71. Editor: Changing Markets of the Sixties, 1961, Chicagoland Homebuilder, 1963, 64. Mem. sch. bd., Deerfield, Ill., 1968. Mem. Am. Advt. Fedn., Chgo. Advt. Club (v.p. 1972-74), Alpha Delta Sigma (pres. 1956), Alpha Epsilon Pi (v.p. 1955-56). Clubs: Mission Hills Country, East Bank, Chgo. Press. Home: 20 E Cedar St Chicago IL 60611 Office: 444 N Michigan Ave Chicago IL 60611

COHN, ROY MARCUS, lawyer; b. N.Y.C., Feb. 20, 1927; s. Albert and Dora (Marcus) C. B.A., Columbia U., 1946, LL.B., 1947. Bar: N.Y. State 1948. With U.S. dist. atty.'s office, N.Y.C., 1947-52, asst. U.S. atty., 1948-50; confidential asst. to U.S. atty., 1950-52; spl. asst. to U.S. atty. gen. McGranery, 1952; chief counsel U.S. Senate Permanent investigations sub-com., 1953-54; asso. firm Saxe, Bacon & Bolan (and predecessor firms), N.Y.C., 1959—; adj. prof. law N.Y. Law Sch., 1957—. Author: Mc Carthy, 1968, A Fool for a Client, 1970, The Answer to Tail Gunner Joe, 1977, How To Stand Up for Your Rights—and Win!, 1981. Pres. Am. Jewish League Against Communism; bd. regents St. Francis Coll., N.Y.C.; chmn. spl. projects Humane Soc.; chmn. bd. Prisoner's Art Program; dir. East Side Conservative Club, N.Y.C., Western Goal's Found.; trustee Roy M. Cohn Found.; Capt. N.Y. State N.G. Recipient ann. award lawyers div. Fedn. Jewish Philanthropies, 1952, Americanism award Am. Legion N.Y. State, 1956, Patriotism award Cath. War Vets., 1970, Leadership award N.Y. County Conservative Party, 1975, Achievement award Jewish Nat. Fund, 1981, City of Peace award B'nai B'rith and State of Israel Bonds, 1983. Mem. Am., Bronx County bar assns. Home: Witherell Dr Rock Ridge Greenwich CT 06830 Office: 39 E 68th New York NY 10021 Office: 24 Hoyt St Stamford CT also Office: 1811 H St Washington DC *Remembrance of parents; unwavering belief in country and its basic ideals; hard work; good friends; the help of God.*

COHN, SAM, motion picture and theartical agent; b. Altoona, Pa., 1929; s. Charles C.; m. Julia Miles; 1 dau.; 1 son by previous marriage. B.A., Princeton U.; degree, Yale U., 1956. With legal dept., bus. affairs dept. CBS, Inc., until 1959; TV producer, 1959-61; counsel Goodson-Todman Prodns., 1961; assoc. ptnr. Marshall, Bratter, Greene, Allison & Tucker, N.Y.C., from 1961; counsel Gen. Artists Corp., from 1965, then co-mgr.; co-mgr. Creative Mgmt. Assn., N.Y.C., 1968-74; agt. Internat. Creative Mgmt., N.Y.C., 1974—; bd. dirs. Josephson Internat. Served with U.S. Army. Office: Internat Creative Mgmt 40 W 5th St New York NY *

COHN, SAMUEL MAURICE, econ. and mgmt. cons.; b. Phila., Nov. 11, 1915; s. Herman and Bessie (Weisberg) C.; m. Alma Cantor, Oct. 2, 1948; children—Anne L., Richard D. B.A., U. Pa., 1936, postgrad., 1936, 38-40. Research asst. Wharton Sch. U. Pa., 1938-39, 41-42; research asst., relocation dir. Phila. Housing Authority, 1939-40; econ. analyst Office War Moblzn. and Reconversion, 1946-47; fiscal economist, chief economist, chief fiscal analysis, dep. asst. dir. for budget rev., asst. dir. for budget rev. Office Mgmt. and Budget and predecessor agy., Exec. Office Pres., Washington, 1947-73; v.p. Robert R. Nathan Assos., Inc., Washington, 1973—. Contbr. articles to profl. jours. Served with AUS; Served with USAAF, 1942-45. Recipient Dir.'s Exceptional Service award Bur. of Budget, 1962; Career Service award Nat. Civil Service League, 1968; Pres.'s award for Distinguished Fed. Civilian Service, 1971; Rockefeller Pub. Service award Princeton U., 1971; Spl. Hon. award Tax Found., Inc., 1976. Mem. Nat. Acad. Pub. Adminstrn., Am. Statis. Assn., Am. Econ. Assn., Nat. Economists Club, Am. Soc. Pub. Adminstrn. Home: 3400 Rose Ln Falls Church VA 22042 Office: 1301 Pennsylvania Ave NW Washington DC 20004

COHN, SHERMAN LOUIS, lawyer, educator; b. Erie, Pa., July 21, 1932; s. Jacob and Bella (Kaufman) C.; m. Tina Aviles, Sept. 24, 1968; children: Ronald Bruce, Jerald Seth, Joshua Daniel, Steven David, Leah Sura. B.S. summa cum laude in Fgn. Service, Georgetown U., 1954, J.D., 1957, LL.M., 1960. Bar: Va. 1957, D.C. 1957, Md. 1978. Law clk. to Judge Burton R. Laub Erie County Ct., Pa., 1955, Walton H. Hamilton, 1957, Judge Charles Fahy, U.S. Ct. of Appeals for D.C. Circuit, 1957-58; staff atty. Appellate sect. Civil div. Dept. Justice, Washington, 1958-62, asst. chief, 1962-65; prof. law Georgetown U. Law Center, Washington, 1965—, dir. continuing legal edn., 1977—; lectr. Catholic U. Law Sch., 1963-65; vis. prof. Am. U. Law Sch., 1969-78; adminstr. Preview of U.S. Supreme Ct. Cases, 1975-79; Cons., litigation counsel Select Com. on Presdl. Campaign Activities U.S. Senate, 1973-74; mem. Jud. Conf. D.C. Circuit, 1965-70, 71-73, 75, 77-78, Jud. Conf. D.C. Ct. Appeals, 1979-81; reporter Nat. Conf. on Appellate Justice, San Diego, 1976. Contbr. articles to profl. jours. Recipient Younger Fed. Lawyer award for outstanding service to U.S., 1964. Mem. Am. Law Inst., Am. Bar Assn., Fed. Bar Assn. (pres. D.C. chpt.), Internat. Assn. Jewish Lawyers and Jurists (pres. Am. sect. 1983—), D.C. Bar Assn., Va. State Bar, Md. Bar Assn., Soc. Am. Law Tchrs., Nat. Assn. Continuing Legal Edn. Adminstrs., Georgetown U. Alumni Assn. (Presdl. citation 1978, John Carroll award 1980). Lodge: B'nai B'rith. Office: 600 New Jersey Ave NW Washington DC 20001

COHN, SIDNEY ELLIOTT, lawyer; b. N.Y.C., Feb. 22, 1908; s. Elias and Dora (Jaffe) C.; m. Vera Boudin, June 21, 1928 (dec.); m. Roberta Seidman Garfield, Sept. 30, 1954; 1 dau., Janet (Mrs. Ronald Neschis); stepchildren: David Garfield, Julie Garfield. Student, U. Pa., 1925-27; LL.B. (mem. Law Rev.), St. John's U., 1931. Bar: N.Y. 1933, U.S. Supreme Ct 1955. Practice in, N.Y.C., 1933—; sr. partner firm Cohn, Glickstein, Lurie, Ostrin, Lubell & Lubell (and predecessor); gen. counsel various trade unions; pres. Highroad Prodns., Inc., Saugatuck Prodns. Enterprises, Inc.; dir. San Juan Racing Assn., Inc. Active United Jewish Appeal, Fedn. Jewish Philanthropies; mem. governing council Am. Jewish Congress; bd. visitors Grad. Sch., CUNY; mem. adv. council Sch. Arts, NYU; mem. Empire State Plaza Arts Commn. Mem. Am., N.Y. State bar assns., N.Y. County Lawyers Assn., Bar Assn. City N.Y. Club: Harmonie (N.Y.C.). Home: 75 Central Park West New York NY 10023 Office: 1370 Ave of Americas New York NY 10019

COHN, STANTON H., medical scientist; b. Chgo., Aug. 25, 1920; s. Harry and Ethel (Goldberg) C.; m. Sylva M. Dushkes, Mar. 20, 1939; children: Avra, Haldan, Holly, Cara, Evan. S.B., U. Chgo., 1946, M.S., 1943; Ph.D., U. Calif.-Berkeley, 1952. Biochemist Argonne Nat. Lab., Chgo., 1946-49; scientist U.S. Naval Radiol. Def. Lab., San Francisco, 1949-58; sr. scientist Brookhaven Med. Research Ctr., Upton, N.Y., 1958—; prof. medicine SUNY, Stony Brook, 1978—. Editor: Non-Invasive Measurement of Bone Mass, 1981; contbr. articles to profl. jours. Served with U.S. Army, 1943-46. Mem. Radiation Research, Am. Physiol. Soc., Sigma Xi. Office: Med Research Ctr Upton NY 11973

COHN, THEODORE, management consultant; b. Newark, June 15, 1923; s. Julius H. and Bessie R. (Einson) C.; m. Dina Berkson, Nov. 28, 1946; children: Don Jonathan, Jordan Ellis, Karen Jane. B.A., Harvard U., 1943; M.A., Columbia U., 1948. With J.H. Cohn & Co. (C.P.A.s), Newark, 1951-74, mng. partner, 1963-74; mgmt. cons., specializing in problems and opportunities of small cos., 1975—. Co-author: Operations Auditing, 1972, How Management Is Different in Small Companies, 1972, Practical Personnel Policies for Small Business, 1973, Survival and Growth: Management Strategies for the Small Firm, 1974, Compensating Key Executives in the Smaller Company, 1979; Mem. editorial adv. bd.: Jour. of Accountancy, 1973; Contbr. articles to profl. jours. Mem. Am. Inst. C.P.A.s (head task force on HRA 1973-74), N.J., N.Y. socs. C.P.A.s, Am. Mgmt. Assn., Nat. Council for Small Bus. Mgmt., Nat. Assn. Accountants. Home: 57 Winding Way West Orange NJ 07052 Office: 57 Winding Way West Orange NJ 07052

COHN, VICTOR EDWARD, journalist; b. Mpls., Aug. 4, 1919; s. Louis and Lillian (Bessler) C.; m. Marcella Rigler, Aug. 30, 1941 (dec. Sept. 1980); children: Jeffrey, Deborah, Phyllis.; m. Ardyce J. Asire, Sept. 4, 1983. A.B., U. Minn., 1941. Editor Minn. Daily, U. Minn., 1940-41; desk man Mpls. Star, 1941-42; copyreader Mpls. Tribune, 1946, reporter, 1946-47, sci. reporter, 1947-67; sci. editor Washington Post, 1968-72, sci.-med. reporter, 1972—; incorporator and dir. Council Advancement Sci. Writing, 1960—; vis. lectr. U. Minn. Sch. Journalism, 1966-67; vis. fellow Harvard U. Sch. Public Health, 1978, 84. Author: 1999 Our Hopeful Future, 1956, Sister Kenny: The Woman who Challenged the Doctors, 1976. Served with USNR, 1942-45. Recipient George Westinghouse award A.A.A.S., 1951, 59; Distinguished Reporting award Sigma Delta Chi, 1952, 56, 59; citations for service to health Minn. Med. Assn., 1955, Minn. Pub. Health Assn., 1966, Mid-Atlantic chpt. Am. Med. Writers Assn., 1976, 80, March of Dimes Birth Defects Found., 1984; Albert Lasker med. journalism award, 1958; Howard W. Blakeslee award Am. Heart Assn., 1963; Distinguished Citizen award Phi Beta Kappa Assn., Minn., 1966; James T. Grady award Am. Chem. Soc., 1971; Nat. Press Club Consumer Reporting award, 1974; Disting. Achievement award U. Minn., 1978; citation for sci. reporting Exploratorium of San Francisco, 1978; Journalism award Am. Acad. Family Physicians, 1982; nat. media award Am. Psychol. Assn., 1983. Fellow AAAS; mem. Nat. Assn. Sci. Writers (pres. 1961-62, Sci.-in-Society reporting award 1973), Am. Newspaper Guild, Phi Beta Kappa. Jewish religion. Office: 1150 15th St NW Washington DC 20071

COHN-HAFT, LOUIS, history educator; b. N.Y.C., Nov. 13, 1919; s. Harry and Goldie (Haft) Cohn-H; m. Betty Jane Schlerman, May 26, 1974; children by previous marriage: Hera, Anthony, Mario. B.A., Columbia U., 1941, M.A., 1949, Ph.D., 1955. Instr. history Columbia U., 1950-53; instr. history Smith Coll., Northampton, Mass., 1953-56, asst. prof., 1956-58, asso. prof., 1958-63, prof., 1963—, chmn. dept. history, 1966-69; dir. NDEA Inst. High Sch. Tchrs. History, summers 1967-68, EPDA, summer 1969; prof. history Hartford Coll. for Women, 1965—. Author: Public Physicians of Ancient Greece, 1956, Source Readings in Ancient History: The Ancient Near East and Greece, 1965. Chmn. Hampshire County (Mass.) chpt. ACLU, 1958-60, mem. exec. com., 1956-66. Served with USAAF, 1942-45. Mem. Am. Hist. Assn., Am. Philol. Assn., History Sci. Soc., Am. Soc.

Papyrology, AAUP, Assn. Ancient Historians. Home: 44 Fairfield Ave Holyoke MA 01040

COHODAS, SAMUEL M., banker. LL.D., No. Mich. U., 1962; Ph.D. hon., Hebrew U. Jerusalem, 1983. Founder Cohodas Bros. fruit and vegetable bus., Mich., 1915; v.p. Ishpeming Hotel Co., Mich.; chmn. bd. First Nat. Bank & Trust Co. Marquette, Mich., First Nat. Bank & Trust Co. Escanaba, Miners' First Nat. Bank of Ishpeming, First Nat. Bank and Trust Menominee, Wis., First Nat. Bank Ironwood, Mich., Iron River Nat. Bank, Gwinn State Savs. Bank, First Nat. Bank Hermansville, Mich., Trenary State Bank, Mich. Fin. Corp., Marquette; mem. Am.-Can. Apple Com.; food cons. OPA, World War II. Treas. Ishpeming Community Chest; active ARC, Boy Scouts Am.; past bd. dirs. Bay Cliff Health Camp; past pres. bd. dirs. Bell Meml. Hosp.; internat. bd. dirs. Boys' Town Jerusalem; bd. dirs. Hebrew U. Jerusalem, Ben Gurion U., Beer Sheba, Israel, CHAI (founders Boys' Town Jerusalem); adv. to pres. to pub. relations No. Mich. U.; mem. exec. com. Operation Action Upper Peninsula; bd. dirs. Child and Family Service Upper Peninsula; trustee No. Mich. U. Devel. Fund; pres. No. Mich. Pres.'s Club; past bd. dirs. Nat. Jewish Hosp. and Research Ctr., Denver; chmn. Marquette County Savs. Bond Com.; mem. Upper Penisula Great Lakes Regional Econ. Devel. Adv. Task Force. Named First Citizen of Ishpeming, 1960. Mem. United Fresh Fruit and Vegetable Assn. (life, past pres., v.p., dir.), Internat. Apple Assn. (life, pres. 1944-46, dir. 1940-43, chmn. bd. 1949-52, treas. 1952-61), Am. Legion (comdr. 1926, 27). Lodges: Rotary; Elks; Masons (33 degree). Office: Mich Fin Corp 101 W Washington St Marquette MI 49855 *

COHODES, ELI AARON, educational consultant, publisher; b. Iron Mountain, Mich., Sept 12, 1927; s. Joseph Harry and Esther Ida (Albert) C.; m. Phyllis Hersh, Jan. 4, 1953; children: Stephen Eliot, David Bruce, Mitchell Joseph, Paul Andrew. B.A., Harvard U., 1950. Assoc. editor Hosp. Mgmt. mag., 1953-54; mng. editor Hospitals (jour. Am. Hosp. Assn.), 1955-59, Trustee mag., 1957-59, Modern Hosp. mag., 1959-63; editor Nation's Schs. mag., Chgo., 1963-68, chmn. editorial adv. bd., columnist, 1968-75; v.p. Instructional Dynamics, Inc., Chgo., 1968-70; pres. Teach'em, Inc., Chgo., 1970—, Pluribus Press, Inc., 1981—; lectr. profl. writing U. Chgo., 1959-63. Co-author: Planning Flexible Learning Places, 1977; Mem. editorial bd.: Coll. and Univ. Bus. mag, 1973-75. Served with AUS, 1945-46. Home: 37 Turnbull Woods Highland Park IL 60035 Office: 160 E Illinois St Chicago IL 60611

COHON, GEORGE ALAN, restaurant company executive; b. Chgo., Il., Apr. 19, 1937; s. Jack Alan and Carolyn (Ellis) C.; m. Susan Silver, Sept. 4, 1960; children: Craig Alan, Mark Steven. B.Sc., Drake U., 1958; J.D., Northwestern U., 1961. Assoc. firm Cohon, Raizes & Regal, Chgo., Il., 1961-67; licensee McDonald's Restaurants, Toronto, Ont., Can., 1967-70; pres., chief exec. officer McDonalds Restaurants, Toronto, Ont., Can., 1970—; adv. dir. McDonald's Corp., Chgo., Il., 1983—. Chmn. bd. govs. Exhibn. Place, Toronto, 1983—; bd. dirs. Can. Post Corp., Ottawa, 1981—; gov. York U., Toronto, 1982—; trustee Drake U., Des Moines, 1983—, Ont. Soc. for Crippled Children, Toronto, 1977—. Recipient Israel Prime Minister's medal, 1981, Humanitarian B'nai B'rith Can., 1983, Alumni Disting. Service Drake U., 1981, Promise of Hope Can. Childrens Found., 1982. Mem. Young Pres. Orgn. Jewish. Home: 112 Forest Hill Rd Toronto Ont. Canada M4V 2L7 Office: McDonalds Restaurants of Can Ltd 20 Eglinton Ave W Toronto ON Canada M4R 2E6

COIGNEY, MARTHA WADSWORTH, theatre organization executive; b. N.Y.C., June 21, 1933; d. Charles and Martha Clay (Hollister) Wadsworth; m. Rodolphe Lucien, Dec. 27, 1969; 3 stepchildren. B.A., Vassar Coll., 1954. Sec. lit. dept. Music Corp. Am., 1956; exec. sec. The Actors Studio, N.Y.C., 1956-59; asst. to pres. Teleprompter Corp., N.Y.C., 1960-61; prodn. asst., sec. to Roger L. Stevens, N.Y.C., 1926-65; asst. dir. Internat. Theatre Inst. U.S., N.Y.C., 1966-69, dir., 1969—, mem. exec. com., 1971—, v.p., 1981—; pres. Nat. Theatre Conf., 1982—; mem. U.S. Nat. Commn., UNESCO, 1976-80; mem. theatre panel N.Y. State Council Arts, 1976-79, chmn., 1978-79; mem. internat. panel Nat. Endowments Arts, 1979-80, qem. small theatre panel, 1981; bd. dirs. Theatre Latin Am., 1973-79. Decorated officer Ordre des Arts et des Lettres, France, 1978. Mem. Nat. Theatre Conf. Club: Cosmopolitan (N.Y.C.). Home: 1200 Fifth Ave New York NY 10029 Office: 1860 Broadway New York NY 10023

COIT, ELISABETH, architect; b. Winchester, Mass.; d. Robert and Eliza Richmond (Atwood) C. Student, Radcliffe Coll., 1909-11, Boston Sch. Mus. Fine Arts, 1911-13; B.Arch., Mass. Inst. Tech.; postgrad., U. Paris, Sorbonne, 1923-24. Designer with Grosvenor Atterbury, architect, 1918-23; pvt. practice of architecture, N.Y.C., 1923-42; architect PHA, Washington, 1942-47; prin. project planner N.Y.C. Housing Authority, 1947-62. Author: Report on Family Living in High Apartment Buildings, 1965; Editor: N.Y. Archtl. Record, 1941-43, Public Housing Design, 1946; Contbr. articles to profl. jours. Cons. N.Y.C. Mayor's Office for Aging, 1969-76; Mem. N.Y.C. Landmarks Preservation Commn., 1970-78. Fellow AIA (Pioneer in Architecture citation N.Y. chpt. 1969); mem. Nat. Assn. Housing and Redevel. Ofcls. (editor Recorder, N.Y.C. met. chpt. 1967—), Citizens' Housing and Planning Council of N.Y.C., NAD (asso.). Home: 330 W 72d St New York NY 10023 also 28 Thatcher Rd Rockport MA 01966

COIT, MARGARET LOUISE, writer; b. Norwich, Conn., 1919; d. Archa Willoughby and Grace Leland (Trow) C.; m. Albert E. Elwell, Jan. 28, 1978. A.B. (Weil scholar), U. N.C., Greensboro, 1941; Litt.D., Woman's Coll., 1959. With Lawrence (Mass.) Daily Eagle, 1941, Newburyport (Mass.) Daily News, 1944, House in the Pines Jr. Coll., Norton, Mass., 1945, Haverhill (Mass.) Gazette, 1946; book reviewer Greensboro Daily News, N.Y. Times, N.Y. Post, others; mem. staff U. N.H. Writers Conf., 1950-61, U. Colo. Writers Conf., 1958—; author-in-residence, Fairleigh Dickinson U., 1955—, prof., 1956-84, Bunker Hill Community Coll., Charlestown, Mass., 1985—. Author: John C. Calhoun: American Portrait, 1950, Mr. Baruch k2(biography), 1957, The Fight for Union, 1961 (Thomas Edison award), The Growing Years, The Sweep Westward, 1963, (with others) Andrew Jackson, 1965, Massachusetts, 1968; Editor: Calhoun: Great Lives Observed, 1970; Contbr. to: Saturday Rev., also others. Moderator W. Newbury Town Meeting. Breadloaf fellow Breadloaf Writers Conf., 1948; Awarded Pulitzer prize for biography, 1951; Book award of Nat. Council of Women U.S., 1958. Vice adm. Confederate Navy of U.S.; Mem. Soc. Am. Historians, Am. Hist. Assn., Phi Beta Kappa. Republican. Episcopalian. *Marriage is the most fascinating, wearing, challenging experience I have had in my life.*

COKE, CHAUNCEY EUGENE, consulting company executive, scientist, educator; b. Toronto, Ont., Can; s. Chauncey Eugene and Edith May (Redman) C.; m. Sally B. Tolmie, June 12, 1941. B.Sc. with honors, U. Man., M.Sc. magna cum laude; M.A., U. Toronto; postgrad., Yale U.; Ph.D., U. Leeds, Eng., 1938. Dir. research Courtaulds (Can.) Ltd., 1939-42; dir. research and devel. Guaranty Dyeing & Finishing Co., 1946-48; various exec. research and devel. positions Courtaulds (Can.) Ltd., Montreal, 1948-59, dir. research and devel.; mem. exec. com. Hart-Fibres Co., 1959-62; tech. dir. textile chem. Drew Chem. Corp., 1962-63; dir. new products fibers div. Am. Cynamid Co., 1963-68, dir. applications devel., 1968-70; pres. Coke & Assoc., Cons., Ormond Beach, Fla., 1970-78, chmn., 1978—; pres. Aqua Vista Corp. Inc., 1971-74; vis. research prof. Stetson U., 1979—. Contbr. articles to profl. jours. Vice chmn. North Peninsula adv. bd. Volusia County Council, 1975-78; bd. dirs. Council of Assns. N. Peninsula, 1972-74, 76-77. Served from 2d lt. to maj. RCAF, 1942-46. Recipient Bronze medal Can. Assn. Textile Colourists and Chemists, 1963. Fellow Royal Soc. Chemistry (Gt. Britain life), Textile Inst. (Gt. Britain), Soc. Dyers and Colourists (Gt. Britain), Inst. Textile Sci. (co-founder, 3d pres.), Chem. Inst. Can. (life), AAAS, N.J. Acad. Sci., Am. Inst. Chemists; mem. Am. Assn. Textile Tech. (life, past pres., Bronze medal 1971), Can. Assn. Textile Colourists and Chemists (hon. life, past pres.), N.Y. Acad. Scis. (life), Fla. Acad. Scis. Clubs: Greater Daytona Beachg Republican Men's (pres. 1972-75), Rep. Pres.'s Forum (pres. 1976-78), Rep. Pres.'s Forum (v.p. 1978—), The Chemist's). Home: 26 Aqua Vista Dr Ormond Beach FL 32074 Office: Ormond by the Sea Ormond Beach FL 32074 *It has been my lifetime experience that one important leadership tool is that of flexibility, the art of being able to adapt to change.*

COKE, FRANK VAN DEREN, museum director; b. Lexington, Ky., July 4, 1921; s. Sterling Dent and Elisabeth (Van Deren) C.; m. Eleanor Barton, 1943 (div. 1980); children: Sterling Van Deren, Eleanor Browning. B.A., U. Ky., 1956; M.F.A., Ind. U., 1958; postgrad., Harvard U. With Van Deren Hardware Co., Lexington, 1946-56, pres., 1953-56; asst. prof. art U. Fla., 1958-61; assoc. prof. art Ariz. State U., 1961-62; prof., dir. art mus. U. N.Mex., 1962-66, chmn. dept., 1963-70, dir. art mus., 1973-79; dep. dir., then dir. Internat. Mus. Photography, Rochester, N.Y., 1970-72; dir. dept. photography San Francisco Mus. Modern Art, 1979—; bd. dirs. Internat. Folk Art Found.; chmn. Albuquerque Fine Arts Adv. Com.; cons. in field. Author: books and catalogues, including Taos and Santa Fe: The Artist's Environment, 1882-1942, 1963, The Painter and the Photograph, 1972, One Hundred Years of Photographic History, 1975, Avant-Garde Photography in Germany, 1919-1939, 1981. Served as officer USNR, 1942-45. Recipient Photography Internat. award, 1955, 56 (2), Modern Photography Internat. award, 1956, U.S. Camera Internat. award, 1957, 58, 60, New Talent USA Art in Am. award, 1960; Guggenheim fellow, 1975. Mem. Coll. Art Assn. (dir. 1973-77), Soc. Photog. Edn. (dir. 1965-70). Office: San Francisco Museum Modern Art McAllister St at Van Ness Ave San Francisco CA 94102

COKER, ELIZABETH BOATWRIGHT (MRS. JAMES LIDE COKER), author; b. Darlington, S.C., Apr. 21, 1909; d. Purves Jenkins and Bessie (Heard) Boatwright; m. James Lide Coker, Sept. 27, 1930; children: Penelope, James Lide. A.B., Converse Coll., 1929; postgrad., Middlebury Coll., 1938. Asso. prof. English Appalachian State U., Boone, N.C., 1971-72. Author: Daughter of Strangers, 1950, The Day of the Peacock, 1952, India Allan, 1953, The Big Drum, 1957, La Belle, 1959, Lady Rich, 1963, The Bees, 1968, Blood Red Roses, 1977, The Grasshopper King, 1981; Contbr. mag. articles, poems. Mem. Hartsville Sch. Bd., 1939-49; sec., dir. Blowing Rock Horse Show Assn., 1943-49; dir. United Cerebral Palsy of S.C.; mem. nat. bd. Med. Coll. Pa.; trustee Converse Coll.; nat. adv. council I.S.S. Mem. Poetry Soc. Ga., AAUW, P.E.N., S.C. Poetry Soc., Authors Guild; mem. Acad. Am. Poets, S.C. Hist. Soc.; Mem. Garden Club Am. Republican. Episcopalian. Clubs: Springdale Hall (Camden, S.C.); Hound Ears (Blowing Rock, N.C.). Home: 620 W Home Ave Hartsville SC 29550

COLADARCI, ARTHUR PAUL, educator; b. Danbury, Conn., Oct. 24, 1917; s. Pietro and Catherine (Bisacca) C.; m. Jane Bottenfield, Mar. 27, 1947; children: Katherine, Theodore. Ed.B., Western Conn. State U., 1940; postgrad., Johns Hopkins, 1941-42; M.A., Yale, 1947, Ph.D., 1950; Sc.D. (hon.), U. Rochester, 1972. Tchr., psychologist Child Study Center, Md., 1940-42; instr. psychology U. Conn., 1947-50; asst. prof. ednl. psychology Ind. U., 1950-52; asso. prof. edn., psychology Stanford, 1952-59, prof. edn. and psychology, 1959—, dean, 1970-79; cons. editor John Wiley & Sons, 1957-75, Wadsworth Pub. Co., 1975-79; cons. Bur. Indian Affairs, 1957-65; partner Charter Assos., Haven Assos., Bel-Moon Assocs., County Assocs.; edn. adviser to Nepal and Spain, 1970—, Iran, 1974-76, Saudi Arabia, 1978, Brazil, 1979—; Bd. dirs. Am. Jour. of Nursing Co., 1973-76, Center for Ednl. Leadership, 1974—, Inter-Am. Improvement Assn., 1975—, Mid-Peninsula Schs., 1980—. Author: Educational Psychology, 1955, (with J.W. Getzels) Theory in Educational Administration, 1955, (with R. Clarke and J. Caffrey) Statistical Reasoning, 1965, (with T. Coladarci) Descriptive Statistics, 1979; mem. editorial bd.: Jour. Exptl. Edn, 1975—, Yearbook on Educational Change, 1976—. Served with AUS, 1942-46. Decorated Purple Heart; Fulbright Sr. Research scholar U. Tokyo, 1957-58. Fellow Am. Psychol. Assn., Am. Ednl. Research Assn.; mem. Internat. Ednl. Research Assn. (exec. com. 1960-70), Internat. Soc. for Gen. Semantics, Cleveland Conf. Office: Stanford U Sch Edn Stanford CA 94305

COLAIANNI, JOSEPH VINCENT, judge; b. Detroit, Mar. 19, 1935; s. P. and Marie D. (Mastrantonio) C.; m. Rita Milena Roll, Oct. 13, 1962; children: Marie Elena, Joseph Vincent, Michael Philip, Vincent Gerard. B.E.E., U. Detroit, 1956; postgrad., Wayne State U., 1956-58; J.D. with honors, George Washington U., 1961. Assoc. firm Fay and Fay, Cleve., until 1965; trial atty. civil div. Dept. Justice, Washington, 1965-70; commr. U.S. Ct. Claims, Washington, 1970-73, trial judge, 1973-82; judge U.S. Ct. Claims D.C., 1982—; mem. sci. liaison com. re Sci. Ct., 1976—; prof. grad. sch. Patent Resources Inst. Chmn. Distric Heights (Md.) Recreation Council, 1969-70; bd. dirs. Henson Valley Montessori Sch.; pres. Tilden PTA, 1979—, Lido Civic Club, 1981; trustee Western Coll. Medicine, 1982-85. Served with USAF. Mem. Am., Fed. bar assns., Patent Office Soc., Mich., Ohio, Washington bars, Phi Delta Phi, Eta Kappa Nu., George Washington U. Law Rev. (1960-61). Office: 717 Madison Pl Washington DC 20005

COLAIZZI, JOHN LOUIS, coll. dean; b. Pitts., May 10, 1938; s. Peter Richard and Lena M. (Sebastian) C.; m. Maria Rose Santoro, Aug. 12, 1967; children—James J., Patricia R., John Louis. B.S., U. Pitts., 1960; M.S., Purdue U., 1962, Ph.D., 1965. Asst. prof. Sch. Pharmacy, W.Va. U., Morgantown, 1964-65; asst. prof., asso. prof. Sch. Pharmacy, U. Pitts., 1965-76, prof., chmn., asso. dean, 1976-78; prof., dean Coll. Pharmacy, Rutgers U., Piscataway, N.J., 1978—; cons. N.J. Dept. Health, Drug Utilization Rev. Panel. Mem. Am. Pharm. Assn., Acad. Pharm. Scis., Am. Soc. Hosp. Pharmacists, Rho Chi, Alpha Zeta Omega. Democrat. Roman Catholic. Home: 117 Connolly Dr Milltown NJ 08850 Office: Rutgers U Coll Pharmacy Piscataway NJ 08854

COLANGELO, JERRY JOHN, profl. sports exec.; b. Chicago Heights, Ill., Nov. 20, 1939; s. Larry and Sue (Drancek) C.; m. Joan E. Helmich, Jan. 20, 1961; children—Kathy, Kristen, Bryan. B.A., U. Ill., 1962. Partner House of Charles, Inc., 1962-63; asso. D.O. Klein & Assos., 1964-65; dir. merchandising Chgo. Bulls basketball club, 1966-68; gen. mgr. Phoenix Suns basketball club, 1968—. Mem. Basketball Congress Am. (exec. v.p., dir.), Phi Kappa Psi. Republican. Baptist. Clubs: University, Phoenix Execs. Office: Phoenix Suns PO Box 1369 Phoenix AZ 85001 *

COLANGELO, TED DONALD, graphic communications executive; b. N.Y.C., Sept. 6, 1935; s. Theodore Baldwin and Jean (Portfolio) C.; m. Katherine Flanagan, Apr. 23, 1968; children: Lynn, Mark, Kate. A.B. with distinction, Brown U., 1957. Account exec. trainee Foote, Cone & Belding, 1957-58; sr. v.p. Colangelo Studios, Inc., White Plains, N.Y., 1958-68; chmn., dir. Ted Colangelo Assos., White Plains, 1968—, The SlideMakers (both cos. subs. Benton & Bowles), N.Y.C., 1974—, 1968—; sr. v.p., dir. Singer & Cole (Advt. Agy.), White Plains, 1972-75. Served with U.S. Army, 1957-58. Recipient numerous awards in graphic competitions including awards N.Y. Art Dirs. Club, Type Dirs. Club, Graphis, CA Mag. Mem. Advt. Club Westchester (founder), Advt. Club Fairfield. Clubs: Weston Field, Weston Racquet (bd. govs.). Home: 7 Ridge Rd Weston CT 06883 Office: 709 Westchester Ave White Plains NY 10604

COLARUSSO, JOSEPH RUTLEY, dept. store exec.; b. N.Y.C., July 2, 1925; s. Joseph N. and Virginia (Diorio) C.; m. Louise Henricks, Apr. 24, 1954; children—Susan, Thomas, Michael, John. Staff asst. Allied Stores Corp., N.Y.C., 1953-56; merchandiser Pomeroys, Levittown, Pa., 1957-62; pres. Muller Co., Lake Charles, La., 1963-69, Pomeroys Central Pa., Harrisburg, 1974—. Served with USN, 1943-46, 50-53. Mem. Nat. Retail Mchts. Assn., Harrisburg C. of C. Club: Berkshire Country. Office: Pomeroys 4th and Market St Harrisburg PA 17105

COLÁS, ANTONIO ESPADA, medical educator; b. Muel, Spain, June 22, 1928; came to U.S., 1962, naturalized, 1968; s. Pedro Lagunas and Antonia Romeo (Espada) C.; m. María Inmaculada Martín, Feb. 24, 1955; children: Antonio de Padua, Juan Bautista, María del Pilar, Santiago. Licentiate, U. Zaragoza, 1951; M.D., U. Madrid, 1953; Ph.D., U. Edinburgh, 1955. Prof. U. Salamanca Med. Sch., Spain, 1955-57; prof., head, grad. div. U. del Valle Med. Sch., Cali, Colombia, 1957-62; prof. U. Oreg. Med. Sch., 1962-68, U. Wis. Med. Sch., Madison, 1968—. Brit. Council scholar, 1953-55; NIH Rockefeller Found.; Ford Found. grantee, 1957—. Mem. Biochem. Soc. Gt. Britain, Sociedad Española de Ciencias Fisiológicas (Spain), A.A.A.S., Am. Chem. Soc., Div. Biol. Chemists, Sociedad Española de Bioquímica (Spain), Endocrine Soc., Am. Soc. Biol. Chemists, Soc. Gynecol. Investigation. Roman Catholic. Research, publs. on studies of biochemistry and mode of action of steroid hormones. Address: U Wis Medical Sch 1300 University Ave Madison WI 53706

COLAS, EMILE JULES, lawyer; b. Montreal, Que., Can., Oct. 3, 1923; s. Emile and Elise (Pila) C.; m. Réjane Laberge, Oct. 25, 1958; children: Bernard, Hubert, Francois. B.Eng., McGill U., 1946, B.C.L., 1949, M.C.L., 1950; B.A., Ottawa U., 1947; LL.D., 1980. Bar: called to Que. bar 1950. Lectr. Faculty Engring. McGill U., 1946-49; del. Carnegie Endowment for Internat. Peace Conf., Ann Arbor, Mich., 1950; since practiced in, Montreal.; Sec., v.p., pres. Jr. Bar Montreal, 1952-56; mem. council Bar of Montreal, 1956-57; 1st v.p., pres., hon. pres. Legal Aid Bur., 1956-61, pres., 1967-72; del. Conf. Commrs. on Uniformity of Legislation in Can., 1956-81, pres., 1969-70; hon. mem., del. Union des Jeunes avocats de France et de la Communaute, Nimes, 1956, Paris, 1959, Bordeaux, 1962; corr. mem. for Can., del. Institut Belge de Droit Internat. et de Droit Compare, Brussels, 1957—. Author: The Judicial Control of Administrative Discretion, 1949, The Concept of Legal Personality and Trade Unions in Canada, 1950, The Labour Tribunals, 1952, The Causes of Divorce, 1976, The Divorce Trial, 1976, The Third Option: A New Constitution for Canada, 1978, Cooperative Law of Quebec, 1980; Contbr. articles to profl. jours. Decorated Knight of Legion of Honor, France; Liberated France medal; Knight Order of Palmes académiques, France; comdr. Order of St. John, Knight of Malta.; Knight Order of St. Gregory the Great. Mem. Corp. Profl. Engrs. Que., Engring. Inst. Can., Bar of Province Que., Canadian Bar Assn. (pres., mem. council Que.), Commonwealth Bar Assn. (past del.), Canadian Inst. Internat. Affairs (past br. sec.), Internat. Law Assn. (pres.), Chambre de Commerce Francaise au Can. (sec., mem. council), Alliance Francaise, Comite France-Amerique, Charity Assn. Bar Montreal (life), Assn. des Anciens du Mont St. Louis (life), Assn. des Anciens de l'Universite d'Ottawa (life), Internat. Union Young Lawyers (past v.p.). Roman Catholic. Club: Touring de France (life). Home: 1 Summerhill Terr Montreal PQ H3H 1B8 Canada Office: Stock Exchange Tower Place Victoria Montreal 3 PQ Canada

COLASURD, RICHARD MICHAEL, lawyer; b. Navarre, Ohio, Apr. 1, 1928; s. Michael and Adeline (Manack) C.; m. Bette Rae Cochrane, Nov. 24, 1956; children: Steven Michael, David Gerard, Cathie Marie. A.B., U. Notre Dame, 1950; J.D., Harvard U., 1953. Bar: Ohio 1953. Practice in, Toledo, 1960—; spl. agt. FBI, 1953-56; asst. U.S. atty. charge, Northwestern Ohio, 1956-60; mem. firm Shumaker, Loop & Kendrick, 1960-64; asst. city law dir., Toledo, 1964; mem. firm Mulholland, Hickey & Lyman, 1964-73; U.S. commr., 1963-67. Mem. Am., Ohio, Toledo bar assns., Soc. Former Spl. Agts. of FBI. Roman Catholic. Clubs: Rotary, Inverness (Toledo). Home: 2520 Edgehill Rd Toledo OH 43615 Office: 1506 Edison Plaza Toledo OH 43604

COLBERG, MARSHALL RUDOLPH, economics educator; b. Chgo., June 11, 1913; s. Rudolph E. and Elvira (Wester) C.; m. Peggy Lou Dean, Nov. 25, 1942 (dec. 1964); children: Marsha, Daniel; m. Grace G. Metz, June 6, 1976; stepchildren: Judith, Barbara, Paul. A.B., U. Chgo., 1934, A.M., 1938; Ph.D., U. Mich., 1950. Economist WPB, 1940-43, Civilian Prodn. Adminstrn., 1945-46; analyst USAF, 1946-50; mem. faculty Fla. State U., 1950—, prof. econs., 1953—, chmn. dept., 1956-67, dir. Ctr. Econ. Edn., 1979-81; assoc. dir. Center for Yugoslav-Am. Studies, Research and Exchanges.; guest lectr. U. Belgrade, 1965-76. Author: (with Allen and Buchanan) Prices, Income and Public Policy, 2d edit, 1959, (with Forbush and Whitaker) Business Economics, 1964, 7th edit., 1984, (with M. Greenhut) Factors in the Location of Florida Industry, 1962, Human Capital in Southern Development, 1939-1963, 1965, Consumer Impact of Repeal of 14-B, 1978, The Social Security Retirement Test: Right or Wrong?, 1978. Mem. Am. Econ. Assn. (com. econ. edn.), So. Econ. Assn. (pres. 1962, chmn. nominating com. 1964), Mont Pelerin Soc. Home: 4509 Andrew Jackson Way Tallahassee FL 32303

COLBERT, CHARLES RALPH, architect; b. Dow, Okla., June 23, 1921; s. James Eden and Alice (Hendon) C.; m. Rosemary Frances Schrafft, Sept. 26, 1946 (dec. May 1954); children—Kathryn H., James Eden III, Thomas M.; m. Frances B. Stern, June 18, 1956 (dec. Apr. 1962). B.Arch., U. Tex., 1943; M.S., Columbia, 1947. Asst. prof. Tulane U., 1947-49; pvt. practice architecture and planning, 1949-50, architecture and city planning, New Orleans, 1953—; supervising architect, dir. Office Planning and Constrn., New Orleans pub. schs., 1951-53; dir. architecture div. Tex. A. and M. Coll., 1956-57; dean Sch. Architecture, Columbia, 1960-63. Mem. La. Bd. Edn., 1970-77. Served to lt. (s.g.) USNR, 1943-45. Fellow AIA; mem. Royal Soc. Arts, Tau Beta Pi. Home and Office: 510 Woodvine Ave Metairie LA 70005

COLBERT, CLAUDETTE (LILY CHAUCHOIN), actress; b. Paris, France; came to U.S., 1910; d. Georges and Jeanne (Loew) Chauchoin; m. Norman Foster, Mar. 13, 1928; m. Joel Pressman, 1935. Grad., Washington Irving High Sch., 1923. Debut as Sibyl Blake in: Wild Westcotts, Frazee Theatre, 1924; later appeared in: plays including The Marionette Man, High Stakes, The Kiss in a Taxi, The Ghost Train, Pearl of Great Price, Tin Pan Alley, See Naples and Die, Eugene O'Neills Dynamo, A Talent for Murder; 1st appearance in London, in the: Barker, 1928; appeared in motion pictures, 1929—, including, The Lady Lies, Manslaughter, The Smiling Lieutenant, Sign of the Cross, Cleopatra, Private Worlds, Maid of Salem, It Happened One Night, The Gilded Lily, I Met Him In Paris, Bluebeard's Eighth Wife, Zaza Midnight, Drums Along the Mohawk, Skylark, Remember the Day, Palm Beach Story, No Time for Love, So Proudly We Hail, Parrish, Since You Went Away, Three Came Home, Bride for Sale, Arise My Love, Sleep My Love; starred in: Broadway plays Marriage-Go-Round, 1958-60, The Irregular Verb To Love, 1963, The Kingfisher, 1978; tour A Community of Two, 1973-74; Chgo. performances Marriage-Go-Round, 1976; appeared in: TV spls. Private Worlds, 1954-56 (Recipient Oscar award for best actress Nat. Acad. Motion Picture Arts and Scis. 1934) *

COLBERT, EDWIN H., paleontologist, museum curator; b. Clarinda, Iowa, Sept. 28, 1905; s. George Harris and Mary (Adamson) C.; m. Margaret Mary Matthew, July 8, 1933; children: George Matthew, David William, Philip Valentine, Daniel Lee, Charles Diller. Student, N.W. Mo. State Tchrs. Coll., 1923-26; B.A., U. Nebr., 1928, Sc.D., 1973; A.M., Columbia U., 1930, Ph.D., 1935; Sc.D., U. Ariz., 1976, Wilmington Coll., 1984. Student asst. Univ. Museum, U. Nebr., 1926-29; univ. fellow Columbia U., 1929-30, lectr. dept. zoology, 1938-39, prof. vertebrate paleontology, 1945-69, prof. emeritus, 1969—; research asst. Am. Museum Natural History, 1930-32, asst. curator, 1933-42, acting curator, 1942, curator, 1943, chmn. dept. amphibians and reptiles, 1943-44, curator of fossil reptiles and amphibians, 1945-70, chmn. dept. geology and paleontology, 1958-60, chmn. dept. vertebrate paleontology, 1960-66, curator emeritus, 1970—; curator vertebrate paleontology Mus. No. Ariz., Flagstaff, 1970—. Author: Evolution of the Vertebrates, 1955, 69, 80, Millions of Years Ago, 1958, Dinosaurs, 1961, (with M. Kay) Stratigraphy and Life History, 1965, The Age of Reptiles, 1965, Men and Dinosaurs, 1968, Wandering Lands and Animals, 1973, The Year of the Dinosaur, 1977, A Fossil Hunter's Notebook, 1980, Dinosaurs: An Illustrated History, 1983; also sci. papers and monographs. Recipient John Strong Newberry prize, Columbia U., 1931; Daniel Giraud Elliot medal Nat. Acad. Sci., 1935; medal Am. Mus. Natural History, 1970. Fellow AAAS, Geol. Soc. Am., Paleontol. Soc. (v.p. 1963), N.Y. Zool. Soc.; mem. Soc. Vertebrate Paleontology (sec.-treas. 1944-46, pres. 1946-47), Soc. Mammalogy, Soc. Ichthyology and Herpetology, Soc. for Study Evolution (editor 1950-52, v.p. 1957, pres. 1958), Nat. Acad. Sci., Sigma Xi. Office: Museum of No Arizona Route 4 Box 720 Flagstaff AZ 86001 *The paramount factor in the development of my scientific career has been a love of original research. Research is creative, and there is true satisfaction in doing creative things.*

COLBERT, LESTER LUM, former automobile co. exec., lawyer; b. Oakwood, Tex., June 13, 1905; s. Lum and Sallie (Driver) C.; m. Daisy Gorman, Nov. 23, 1928 (dec. Aug. 1970); children—Lester Lum, Sarah (Mrs. William C. Cleavenger), Nicholas; m. Robert Ellen Hoke, Oct. 5, 1972. B.B.A., Tex. U., 1925; J.D., Harvard U., 1929; LL.D., Bethany Coll., 1954. Cotton buyer, Tex., 1921-29; practiced law Larkin, Rathbone & Perry, N.Y.C., 1929-33; with Chrysler Corp., 1933-65, mem. operation com., 1933-61, resident atty., 1933-42, v.p., 1935-45, operating mgr., 1942, gen. mgr., 1943-46, pres., 1946-51, v.p., 1949-50, dir., 1949-61, pres., 1950-61, chmn., 1960-61; chmn. bd., dir. Chrysler Corp. of Can., Ltd., 1961-65; trustee Hanover Bank, N.Y.C., 1955-61. Chmn. United Found., Detroit, 1959-60, dir., 1951-62; mem. Nat. Indsl. Conf. Bd., 1958-61; trustee Automotive Safety Found., 1955-61, Com. for Econ. Devel., 1956-61; dir. devel. bd. U. Tex., 1958—; overseers com. to visit Harvard Law Sch., 1952-58. Decorated chevalier Legion of Honor, France, 1959; Texan of Distinction award, 1953; recipient Brother-hood award NCCJ, 1957; award Am. Soc. Tool Engrs., 1958; Distinguished Alumnus award U. Tex., Austin, 1977. Mem. Am. Ordnance Assn. (life), Automobile Old Timers (life), Am., Detroit bar assns., Automobile Mfrs. Assn. (pres. 1958-61), Soc. Automotive Engrs., State Bar Mich., Beta Gamma Sigma. Methodist. Clubs: Detroit Athletic (pres. 1960), Harvard (Detroit); Bloomfield Hills (Mich.) Country; Royal Poinciana, Naples Yacht (Naples, Fla.). Home: 3401 Gulf Shore Blvd N Naples FL 33940 Office: 812 Colonial Ct Birmingham MI 48009

COLBERT, MARVIN JAY, physician; b. Spokane, Nov. 6, 1923; s. John B. and Elizabeth (Peters) C.; m. Eleanor Ruth Rott, June 2, 1951; children—Janet Lynn, James Lee, Lawrence Jay. Student, U. Utah, 1940-43; B.S., Yale, 1943-44; M.D., Boston U., 1949. Diplomate: Am. Bd. Internal Medicine. Intern Presbyn. Hosp., Chgo., 1949-50, resident, 1949-50, VA Hosp., Boston, 1953-54, U. Ill. Research and Ednl. Hosp., 1954-55; practice internal medicine, Belmond, Iowa, 1955-56; mem. faculty U. Ill., 1956—; dir. health service Med. Center, 1959-78, prof. medicine, 1969—; dir. employee health services Evang. Hosp. Assn., Oak Brook, Ill., 1978—; cons. internal medicine, radiol. and environ. research div. Argonne (Ill.) Nat. Lab., 1978—. Pres. Hillcrest P.T.A., Downers Grove, Ill., 1960-62, Parent-Tchrs. Group Chiengmai Co-ednl. Center, Thailand, 1965-66. Served to capt. M.C. AUS, 1943-46, 50-52. Recipient Golden Apple instr. award U. Ill., 1958. Fellow A.C.P.; mem. Am. Assn. Automotive Medicine (dir. 1969-76), Chgo. Soc. Internal Medicine, Am. Fedn. Clin. Research, Sigma Xi. Home: 5600 Plymouth Ct Downers Grove IL 60516 Office: Evangelical Hosp Assn 2025 Windsor Dr Oak Brook IL 60521

COLBERT, ROBERT B., JR., apparel co. exec.; b. Columbus, Ga., Sept. 24, 1921; s. Robert B. and Mae (Hindsman) C.; m. Margaret Moore, Mar. 22, 1942; children—Margaret, Bert, John. Student, Emory U., U. Ga. Chmn. bd., pres., dir. Wayne-Gossard Corp., Chattanooga; chmn. bd., dir. Signal Knitting Mills, Chattanooga, H. W. Gossard Co., Chgo.; dir. Union Planters Nat. Bank, Memphis. Served with USNR, World War II. Office: 701 Market St Suite 922 Chattanooga TN 37401

COLBORN, HARRY WALTER, electrical engineer; b. Pitts., May 27, 1921; s. David Lafayette and Leora Blanche (Lane) C.; m. Mary Ellen Meluch, May 31, 1952; children: David, Kurt. Student, Bliss Elec. Sch., Takoma Park, Md., 1940; B.S. in Elec. Engring., Carnegie Inst. Tech., 1951; postgrad., Oak Ridge Sch. Reactor Tech., 1958. Registered profl. engr., Pa., Md., W.Va. Engr. West Penn Power Co., Pitts. and Greensburg, Pa., 1951-67, system planning mgr., Greensburg, 1967-70; dir. transmission planning Allegheny Power Service Corp., Greensburg, 1970-80; mgr. spl. studies N.Am. Electric Reliability Council, Princeton, N.J., 1980—; mgr. tech. assessment Electric Power Research Inst., Palo Alto, Calif., 1978-79. Contbr. articles to profl. jours. Served with AUS, 1943-46; ETO. Fellow IEEE (chmn. system planning 1976-82). Republican. Presbyterian. Office: NAm Electric Reliability Council Terhune Rd Princeton NJ 08540

COLBOURN, TREVOR, university president, historian; b. Armidale, New South Wales, Australia, Feb. 24, 1927; came to U.S., 1948; s. Harold Arthur and Ella Mary (Henderson) C.; m. Beryl Richards Evans, Jan. 10, 1949; children—Katherine Elizabeth, Lisa Sian Elinor. B.A. with honors, U. London, 1948; M.A., Coll. William and Mary, 1949, Johns Hopkins, 1951, Ph.D., 1953. From instr. to asst. prof. Pa. State U., 1952-59; from asst. prof. to prof. Am. history Ind. U., 1959-67; dean Grad. Sch., prof. history U. N.H., 1967-73; v.p. for acad. affairs San Diego State U., 1973-77, acting pres., 1977-78; pres. U. Central Fla., Orlando, 1978—; mem. com. on grad. studies Am. Assn. State Colls. and Univs. Author: The Lamp of Experience, 1965, The Colonial Experience, 1966, (with others) The Americans: A Brief History, 1972, 3d edit., 1980; Co-editor: The American Past in Perspective, 1970; editor: Fame and the Founding Fathers, 1974. Mem. Am. Hist. Assn., Orgn. Am. Historians. Home: 207 Ranch Rd Maitland FL 32751 Office: U Central Fla PO Box 25000 Orlando FL 32816 *I like to think that I have managed to maintain (and will) my awareness of learning as an ongoing and shared experience, an experience that can be shared in the classroom, in writing and in university administration.*

COLBURN, DANIEL NELSON, II, association executive; b. Mpls., Sept. 17, 1947; s. Daniel William and Marlowe Elaine (Nelson) C. A.B. cum laude, Macalester Coll., 1969. Asst. to gen. mgr. St. Paul Opera Co., 1969-70; devel. asst. Macalester Coll., St. Paul, 1970; project asso. Arts Devel. Assocs., Inc., Mpls., 1970-72; asst. to dir. communications Affiliate Artists, Inc., N.Y.C., 1973-74, dir. info. services, 1974-77, dir. communications, 1977-78; arts program analyst N.Y. State Council on the Arts, 1978-80; exec. dir. Am. Guild Organists, N.Y.C., 1980—. Served with USNR, 1970-72. Mem. Am. Guild Organists, Interfaith Forum on Religion, Art and Arch. Lutheran. Office: 815 Second Ave New York NY 10017

COLBURN, PHILIP WILLIAM, automotive co. exec.; b. Chgo., Jan. 14, 1929; s. Eugene S. and Florence (Lyons) C.; m. Ann Rapport, Apr. 9, 1972; children—Pamela, Michael, Sharon, Elizabeth, Kathryn. B.S. with honors, UCLA, 1950; M.A., U. Denver, 1952. C.P.A., Calif. Pres. Hollywood Accessories, Inc., Los Angeles, 1965-69; chmn. bd., pres., chief exec. officer Orion Industries, Inc., Los Angeles, 1969-74; sr. v.p. Allen Group, Inc., Los Angeles, 1974-75, exec. v.p., dir., 1975—. Trustee Oakwood Sch., Los Angeles, 1973-76; bd. dirs. Westland Sch., Los Angeles, 1970-72. Served with USAF, 1950-54. Mem. Automotive Parts and Accessories Assn. (officer, dir.), Motor and Equipment Mfrs. Assn. (dir., exec. com.). Office: 11611 San Vicente Blvd Suite 660 Los Angeles CA 90049

COLBURN, RICHARD DUNTON, business executive; b. Carpentersville, Ill., June 24, 1911; s. Cary R. and Daisy (Dunton) C.; m. Judith Carol Nash, July 1976; children: Richard Whiting, Carol Dunton, Keith Whiting, Christine Isabel, David Dunton, McKee Dunton. Student, Antioch Coll., 1929-33. Pres. Consol. Foundries Mfg. Corp. (and predecessors), 1944-64; chmn. UK Plant Decco Ltd., U.S. Rentals, Inc.; dir. Consol. Elec. Distbrs., Inc., Cowan, de Groot Ltd., Edmundson Distbn. Ltd., Edmundson Internat., Inc., Hajoca Corp., Fairbanks Co., Frick Co., Edmundson Elec. Ltd., Rolled Alloys, Inc., U.S. Rentals, Inc.; underwriting mem. Lloyds of London. Home and Office: 1120 La Collina Beverly Hills CA 90210 Office: 1 Balfour Pl London England SW1

COLBY, ETHEL, drama and film critic; b. N.Y.C.; d. M. Duckman and (Scharlin) Dallon; m. Julius J. Colby, Sept. 25, 1929; 1 son, Jeffrey Victor. Student, Columbia, 1925-27. Child actress vaudeville, Broadway, 1927-38; featured singing, dancing comedienne: Fabulous Invalid; featured in: others It Shouldn't Happen to a Dog; motion picture actress, 1927-29; radio show Miss Hollywood, 1948-50; drama, film critic, N.Y. Jour. of Commerce and Ridder Papers, N.Y.C., 1938-75; producer, star TV shows, CBS, 1944-46; Broadway Matinee, CBS-TV, Curtain Call, Du-Mont Network TV, 1951-78, also TV programs for stas., WABC, WOR, WNEW, 3 daily radio shows for, Sta. WMCA, Miss Hollywood, Theatre Round-Up, Mr. and Mrs. Go to the Theatre. Mem. Drama Critics Circle (emeritus), Drama Desk (N.Y.C.), Women Broadcasters and Commentators. Am. Club: N.Y. Newspaperwomen's. Home: 10300 West Bay Harbor Dr Bay Harbor Island FL 33154

COLBY, JOY HAKANSON, art critic; b. Detroit; d. Alva Hilliard and Eleanor (Radtke) Hakanson; m. Raymond L. Colby, Apr. 11, 1953; children: Sarah, Katherine, Lisa. Student, Detroit Soc. Arts and Crafts, 1945; B.F.A., Wayne State U., 1946. Art critic Detroit News, 1947—; originator exhibit Arts and Crafts in Detroit, 1906-1976; at Detroit Inst. Arts, 1976; Mem. visual arts adv. panel Mich. Council for Arts, 1974-79; mayor's appointment Detroit Council for Arts, 1974; mem. Bloomfield Hills Arts Council, 1974. Author: Art and A City, 1956, lead essay in Arts and Crafts in Detroit catalog, 1976; Contbr. articles to art periodicals. Recipient Alumni award Wayne State U., 1967, Art Achievement award Wayne State U., 1983. Home: 1145 Lenox St Bloomfield Hills MI 48013 Office: 615 W Lafayette St Detroit MI 48231

COLBY, KENNETH POOLE, insurance company executive; b. Keene, N.H., June 21, 1908; s. Everett Nahum and Grace (Poole) C.; m. Bernece Esther Wilson, July 17, 1933; 1 son, Kenneth P. Student, Clark U., 1927-30. With Nat. Grange Mut. Ins. Co., Keene, 1930—, successively claims adjuster and underwriter, agy. dir., exec. in charge casualty underwriting, 1930-55, v.p., 1955-63, dir., exec. com., 1957—, exec. v.p., 1963-66, pres., 1966-72, chief exec., 1966-73, chmn. bd., 1972-82, hon. chmn. bd., dir., mem. exec., fin. and compensation cons., 1982—; past pres., trustee Keene Savs. Bank.; Past dir. Am. Mut. Ins. Alliance, Nat. Assn. of Mut. Ins. Cos.; past chmn. bd. dirs. N.H. Ins. Guaranty Assn. Del. N.H. Constl. Conv., 1974—; Corporator Mary Hitchcock Hosp., 1974—; former pres., dir. Cheshire Sr. Services Inc. Mem. Nat. Grange., Odd Fellow. Club: Keene Country. Office: 55 West St Keene NH 03431

COLBY, LEWIS JAMES, JR., chem. co. exec.; b. Seattle, Jan. 22, 1934; s. Lewis James and Della (Danielson) C.; m. Harriet Lane Wright Colby, Aug. 23, 1958; children—Cheryl Layne, Steven James. A.A., Santa Rosa Jr. Coll., 1953; B.S., U. Calif., Berkeley, 1955; Ph.D., Purdue U., 1960. Mem. faculty Purdue U., 1959-60; research specialist Atomics Internat., 1960-65; staff phys. chemist AEC, 1966-69; div. dir. Gen. Atomic Co., 1969-75; with Allied Corp., Morristown, N.J., 1975—, pres. nuclear services div., 1976-77, pres. allied chem. nuclear products, 1977, group v.p., 1977-79, sr. v.p., 1979—; Bd. dirs. Atomic Indsl. Forum, Inc., until 1981; bd. dirs., mem. exec. com. Am. Nuclear Energy Council; mem. indsl. adv. com., chemistry dept. Purdue U. Mem. Am. Chem. Soc. Office: Allied Corp Columbia Rd and Park Ave Morristown NJ 07960

COLBY, ROBERT ALAN, library science educator; b. Chgo., Apr. 15, 1920; s. Meyer and Ida (Lewis) C.; m. Vineta Blumoff, May 8, 1947. B.A., U. Chgo., 1941, M.A., 1942, Ph.D., 1949; M.S. in L.S, Columbia U., 1953. Instr. English DePaul U., Chgo., 1946-47; asst. prof. English Lake Forest (Ill.) Coll., 1949-51; lectr. English Hunter Coll., N.Y.C., 1951-53; lang., lit. and arts librarian Queens Coll., Flushing, N.Y., 1953-64, asso. prof. library sci., 1967-69, prof., 1969—; asso. prof. library sci. So. Conn. State Coll., 1964-66; asst. editor Wellesley Index to Victorian Periodicals, 1978. Author: (with Vineta Colby) The Equivocal Virtue: Mrs. Oliphant and the Victorian Literary Marketplace, 1966, Fiction With A Purpose: Major and Minor Nineteenth-Century Novels, 1967, Thackeray's Canvass of Humanity: An Author and His Public, 1979; editor: spl. issue William Makepeace Thackeray, Studies in the Novel, 1981. Served with AUS, 1943-46. Penfield fellow N.Y. U., 1942-43; Guggenheim fellow, 1978-79; Newberry Library fellow, summer 1982. Mem. AAUP, MLA, Bibliog. Soc. Am., ALA, Assn. Am. Library Schs., Victorian Soc. in Am., Research Soc. for Victorian Periodicals, Am. Printing History Assn. Home: 33-24 86th St Jackson Heights NY 11372 Office: Grad Sch Library and Info Studies Dept Queens Coll Flushing NY 11367

COLBY, WILLIAM EGAN, lawyer, former government official; b. St. Paul, Jan. 4, 1920; s. Elbridge and Margaret (Egan) C.; m. Barbara Heinzen, Sept. 15, 1945; children: Jonathan, Catherine (dec.), Carl, Paul, Christine. B.A., Princeton U., 1940; LL.B., Columbia U., 1947. Bar: N.Y. State 1947, D.C. 1976. Atty. firm Donovan Leisure Newton & Irvine, N.Y.C., 1947-49; with NLRB, Washington, 1949-50; attaché Am. Embassy, Stockholm, Sweden, 1951-53, Rome, Italy, 1953-58, 1st sec., Saigon, Vietnam, 1959-62; chief Far East div. CIA, Washington, 1962-68, exec. dir., 1972-73, dep. dir. ops., 1973, dir., 1973-76; ptnr. Colby Miller & Hanes, Washington, 1977-78; now of counsel Reid & Priest, Washington; sr. adv. Internat. Bus.-Govt. Counsellors, Inc., Washington; ambassador, dir. Civil Ops. and Rural Devel. Support, Saigon, 1968-71. Author: Honorable Men—My Life in the CIA. Served to maj. AUS, 1941-45. Decorated Silver Star, Bronze Star; St. Olaf's medal, Norway; Croix de Guerre, France; National Order, Vietnam; mentioned in despatches, Britain; recipient Nat. Security medal; Distinguished Honor award Dept. State; Distinguished Intelligence medal; Intelligence medal of merit; Career Intelligence medal CIA. Mem. Council Fgn. Relations, Phi Beta Kappa. Roman Catholic. Clubs: Cosmos (Washington); Princeton (N.Y.C.); Special Forces (London); Linge Klubben (Oslo). Office: Internat Bus-Govt Counsellors 1625 I St Washington DC 20006

COLBY, WILLIAM GEORGE, JR., banker, economist; b. Northampton, Mass., Mar. 25, 1939; s. William G. and Dorothy (Axford) C.; m. Caroline Yates Foote, June 3, 1961 (div. 1979); children: Caroline Yates, Charlotte Vail, Stewart Fielding McAdie. B.A., Amherst Coll., 1960; M.S., Yale U., 1963, Ph.D., 1970. Security analyst R.W. Pressprich and Co., N.Y.C., 1960-61; economist Fed. Res. Bank, N.Y.C., 1965-69; sr. v.p., treas. First and Mchts. Corp., Richmond, Va., 1969—. Chmn. Va. Council on Econ. Edn., Richmond, 1977; met. chmn. Nat. Alliance of Bus., Richmond, 1977-82; bd. dirs. Richmond Meml. Hosp., 1980—. Mem. ABA (econ. adv. com. Washington chpt. 1977-80), Nat. Economists. Clubs: Country of Va. (Richmond); Adirondack League (Old Forge, N.Y.). Home: 1001 J North Hamilton St Richmond VA 23221 Office: First and Merchants Corp 12th and Main Sts Richmond VA 23261

COLBY-HALL, ALICE MARY, Romance studies educator; b. Portland, Maine, Feb. 25, 1932; d. Frederick Eugene and Angie Fraser (Drown) Colby; m. Robert A. Hall, Jr., May 8, 1976; stepchildren: Philip, Diana Hall Goodall, Carol Hall Erickson. B.A., Colby Coll., 1953; M.A., Middlebury Coll., 1954; Ph.D., Columbia U., 1962. Tchr. French, Latin Orono (Maine) High Sch., 1954-55; tchr. French Gould Acad., Bethel, Maine, 1955-57; lectr. French Columbia U., 1959-60; instr. romance lit. Cornell U., Ithaca, N.Y., 1962-63, asst. prof., 1963-66, assoc. prof., 1966-75, prof. romance studies, 1975—. Author: The Portrait in Twelfth Century French Literature: An Example of the Stylistic Originality of Chretien de Troyes, 1965; Mem. editorial bd.: Speculum, 1976-79, Olifant, 1974—. Fulbright grantee, 1953-54. Mem. Modern Lang. Assn., Medieval Acad. Am. (councillor 1983-86), Internat. Arthurian Soc., Societe Rencesvals, Phi Beta Kappa. Republican. Conglist. Home: 308 Cayuga Heights Rd Ithaca NY 14850 Office: Dept Romance Studies Cornell U Ithaca NY 14853

COLCLASER, H. ALBERTA, lawyer, ret. govt. ofcl.; b. Turtle Creek, Pa., Feb. 19, 1911; d. Levi A. and Bertha M. (Lear) C. A.B., Coll. Wooster, Ohio, 1933, L.L.D., 1965; J.D., Western Res. U., 1936; LL.M., Columbia U., 1939. Asso. editor Banks-Baldwin Law Pub. Co., Cleve., 1936-38; asst. to legal adviser Dept. State, 1939-42, with aviation div., 1942-58, chief air transport sect., 1951-56, asst. chief div., 1956-58; indsl. adviser USRO, 1958-59; chief transp. and communications policy office, civil air attache Am. embassy, Paris, 1959-63; policy officer Office Internat. Aviation, Dept. State, Washington, 1963-65; 1st sec. Am. embassy, Ottawa, Ont., Can., 1965-68; policy officer Office Aviation, Dept. State, Washington, 1968, cons., 1969; specialist transp. products div. Dept. Commerce, 1969-72; exec. asst. to pres. and sec. Coll. of Wooster, 1972-76, counsel, 1976—; mem. U.S. del. Paris Peace Conf., 1946, 3d, 4th, 6th, 7th, 8th, 9th, 10th, 11th, 12th, 14th sessions Legal Com., Internat. Civil Aviation Orgn., ICAO assemblies, 1949, 50, 56, 62; diplomatic conf. pvt. air law Paris Peace Conf. (to 3d, 4th, 6th, 7th, 8th, 9th, 10th, 11th, 12th, 14th sessions Legal Com., Internat. Civil Aviation Orgn., ICAO assemblies), 1952, 55; facilitation div. ICAO, 1948. Recipient Meritorious Service award Dept. State, 1952, Superior Service award Dept. State, Disting. Alumni award Coll. Wooster, 1983. Mem. Am. Soc. Internat. Law, LWV, Phi Beta Kappa, Delta Sigma Rho. Club: Quota. Home: 361 Holmes Blvd Wooster OH 44691 *My career was in a field which offered challenges, a certain degree of pioneering, an opportunity to help develop an activity which was of benefit to mankind, and expanded the communication among people that is necessary to true international friendship. Interest in this work, dedication to its furtherance, and the ability to work with others who shared this dedication made the building of the law of international aviation my life.*

COLDEN, HERBERT, lawyer; b. Chgo., Apr. 7, 1927; s. Hyman and Ety (Strax) Cholodenko; children—David, Deborah, Gregory, Jacqueline. LL.B., Loyola U., Los Angeles, 1951. Bar: Calif. bar 1952. Since practiced in, Los Angeles; partner firm Diamond, Tilem & Colden, 1960-79; lectr. consumer law. Co-chmn. United Jewish Welfare Fund Campaign, Encino, Calif., 1973-78. Served to sgt. USAAF, 1945-47. Mem. Beverly Hills, Los Angeles County bar assns., Am., Calif., Los Angeles trial lawyers assns., Pi Alpha Delta, Tau Delta Phi. Home: 2052 Linnington Ave Los Angeles CA 90025 Office: 1157 S Beverly Dr Los Angeles CA 90035

COLDREN, LARRY ALLEN, electrical engineer, researcher; b. Lewistown, Pa., Jan. 1, 1946; s. Roscoe Calvin and Mary (Hutchison) C.; m. Donna L. Kauffman, Sept. 4, 1966; children: Christopher W., Bret A. B.A., Bucknell U., Lewistown, Pa., 1968, B.S., 1968; M.S., Stanford U., 1969, Ph.D., 1972. Registered profl. engr., N.J. Jr. engr. IBM, Endicott, N.Y., 1966, 67; mem. tech. staff Bell Labs., Holmdel, N.J., 1968-83, supr., 1983—; owner, operator Juniate Retirement Communities Inc., Mifflintown, Pa., 1975-81. Contbr. numerous articles in field to profl. jours.; patentee in field. Active Middletown United Meth. Ch. (N.J.), 1978—; mem. Holmdel Energy Com., 1980-83. Fellow IEEE; mem. Phi Beta Kappa, Pi Mu Epsilon, Tau Beta Pi, Sigma Pi Sigma. Home: 10 Stonehenge Dr Holmdel NJ 07733 Office: Bell Labs Holmdel NJ 07733

COLDWELL, PHILIP EDWARD, financial consultant; b. Champaign, Ill., July 20, 1922; s. Montgomery Ian and Donna Clare (Rose) C.; m. Norma Elaine Abels, June 1, 1947; children: Douglas Michael, Cameron Iliff. B.A., U. Ill., 1946, M.S., 1947; Ph.D., U. Wis., 1952. Teaching asst. U. Ill., at Urbana, 1947; instr. Southwestern La. Inst., Lafayette, 1947-48, asst. prof., 1950-51; instr. Mont. State U., 1949-50; research economist Fed. Res. Bank, Kansas City, 1951-52, economist, officer, Dallas, 1952-62, 1st v.p., 1962-68, pres., 1968-74; mem. bd. govs. Fed. Res. System, Washington, 1974-80; fin. cons., 1980—; lectr. Southwestern Sch. Banking, Dallas, 1962-74; dir. Diamond Shamrock Corp. Contbr. articles to profl. jours. Trustee Austin Coll., Temp Fund, Fed Fund, Muni Fund. Served as pilot USNR, 1942-46. Mem. Am. Econ. Assn., So. Finance Assn., Phi Delta Theta. Presbyn. (elder). Club: Economists (Dallas) (founder, 1st pres.). Home: 2450 Virginia Ave NW Washington DC 20037 Office: 1747 Pennsylvania Ave NW Suite 705 Washington DC 20006

COLE, ALAN Y., lawyer; b. N.Y.C., Oct. 7, 1922; s. Harry I. and Gertrude (Strauchler) C.; m. Gloria H. Glaston, Sept. 18, 1946; children: Charles Glaston, Robert Barry. B.A., Columbia, 1942; LL.B., Yale, 1949. Bar: D.C. bar 1949. Spl. asst. to Atty. Gen. Dept. Justice, Washington, 1949; law sec. to Asso. Justice Robert H. Jackson U.S.

Supreme Ct., 1949-50; asst. gen. counsel Office Def. Mobilization, 1951; practice law, Washington, 1952-64; founder, sr. partner firm Cole & Groner, Washington, 1965—; Mem. nat. panel arbitrators Am. Arbitration Assn., 1954—; mem. Jud. Conf. D.C. Circuit, 1964, 68, 73-76; mem. advisory bd. Fed. Contracts Report, 1971—. Co-author: Moore's Federal Practice, vol. 1A, 2d edit; Editor: Yale Law Jour, 1948-49; sr. contbg. editor and gen. editor: Fed. Bar Jour, 1957-66. Served to warrant officer AUS, 1943-46; ETO, Nuremberg War Trials. Fellow Am. Coll. Trial Lawyers, Internat. Soc. Barristers, Nat. Coll. Criminal Def. Lawyers and Pub. Defenders (vice chmn. bd. regents 1976-77); mem. ABA (ho. of dels. 1974-76, chmn. sect. criminal justice 1976-77), Fed. Bar Assn. (chmn. com. rules of civil procedure 1965-66), Nat. Assn. Criminal Def. Lawyers (pres. elect 1976-77; life), Am. Soc. Writers Legal Subjects. Clubs: Cosmos, Nat. Lawyers (Washington); Yale of N.Y.C. Home: 6808 Marbury Rd Bethesda MD 20817 Office: 1730 K St NW Washington DC 20006

COLE, AUBREY LOUIS, forest products co. exec.; b. Wichita Falls, Tex., Dec. 29, 1923; s. Aubrey Mizell and Lila Ellen (Burge) C.; m. Dorothy Jeanne Willson, Dec. 27, 1944; children—Melissa Ann, Gordon Louis. B.B.A., U. Tex., 1949. Asst. controller Tex. div. Champion Papers Co., Pasadena, 1950-59, corporate controller, Hamilton, Ohio, 1959-65, v.p. mgmt. info. systems, 1966-69; v.p. planning and control U.S. Plywood-Champion Papers, N.Y.C., 1969-73; v.p. mgmt. info. Champion Internat., Stamford, Conn., 1973-74, sr. v.p. control, 1974—; Mem. dirs. assos. U. Tex.; mem. Econ. Policy Council, UN Assn. Served with USNR, 1942-45. Mem. Fin. Execs. Inst., Nat. Assn. Accountants, Alpha Kappa Psi. Home: 237 Newtown Turnpike Wilton CT 06897 Office: 1 Champion Plaza Stamford CT 06921

COLE, BENJAMIN RICHASON, newspaperman; b. Indpls., July 10, 1916; s. Almon Theodore and Maude e6(Richason) C.; m. Alice Louise Porteous, Sept. 11, 1937 (dec. 1982); children: Alan Andrew, Amy (Mrs. George E. Martin, Jr.), Benjamin Richason.; m. Kathleen Gibbs, Feb. 12, 1983. Student, Butler U., 1934-35, Ind. State Tchrs. Coll., 1938, Am. Press Inst. of Columbia, 1948. Reporter Terre Haute Tribune-Star Pub. Co., 1938-40, Terre Haute Star, 1940-44; with Indpls. Star, 1944—, statehouse reporter, 1945-48, asst. city editor, 1948, city editor, 1948-49, Washington Corr., 1949—; corr. Arizona Republic, Phoenix, 1955—. Mem. Sigma Delta Chi. Presbyn. Clubs: Mason., Gridiron, National Press (Washington); Press (Indpls.). Home: 3615 N Glebe Rd Arlington VA 22207 Office: 3615 N Glebe Rd Arlington VA 22207

COLE, BENJAMIN THEODORE, biologist; b. New Brunswick, N.J., May 24, 1921; s. Frederick and Grace King (Trimmer) C.; m. Leona Todd, May 30, 1943; children—Timothy Theodore, Rebecca Joyce. B.S. in Zoology, Duke U., 1949; M.A., 1951; Ph.D. in Physiology, 1954. Instr. physiology Duke U., 1953-54; asst. prof. La. State U., Baton Rouge, 1954-59; research participant biology div. Oak Ridge Nat. Lab., 1959-60, cons., 1960—; asso. prof. biology U. S.C., Columbia, 1960-63, prof., 1963—, head dept., 1964-73. Served with USAAF, 1942-46. Fellow AAAS; mem. Am. Physiol. Soc., Soc. Exptl. Biology, Med. Assn. Southeastern Biologists, S.C. Acad. Sci., Sigma Xi. Home: 3910 Glenfield Rd Columbia SC 29206 *I have always tried to put myself in the other man's place when tempted to be critical of him in any way. I lean heavily on the good Lord for strength and direction at moments of decision.*

COLE, BRUCE HERMAN, advertising executive; b. Chgo., July 22, 1928; s. Leo L. and Kate (Mandelkern) C.; m. Jane Renwick Bagby, June 7, 1953; children: Rosemary Nielsen, Dorothy, Robert Bagby, Frances. Student, U. So. Calif., 1948-50; A.B., Grinnell Coll., 1953. Advt. mgr. Gen. Electric Co., Schenectady, 1953-59; account exec. Reincke, Meyer & Finn, Inc., Chgo., 1959-60; v.p., gen. mgr. Marsteller, Inc., Chgo., 1960-74, exec. v.p., 1974-78; also dir.; sr. v.p., gen. mgr. Glenn, Bozell & Jacobs, Phoenix, 1978-80; pres. Cramer-Krasselt/SW, Phoenix, 1980—, Bruce H. Cole Co., Inc, 1983—; dir., sec. Inertia Dynamics Corp., Chandler, Ariz.; lectr. U. Wis. Mgmt. Center, Ariz. State U.; instr. advt. extension br. Northwestern U. Trustee Marsteller Found., 71976, First Congregational Ch., Western Springs, Ill., United Way Phoenix-Scottsdale, Combined Met. Phoenix Arts; mem. Phoenix adv. bd. Salvation Army; bd. dirs. Health Evaluation and Longevity Planning Found., Inc., Am. Heart Assn., Maricopa County Heart Assn., Phoenix Symphony Assn., Maricopa council Boy Scouts Am. Served with USN, 1946-48. Mem. Am. Mgmt. Assn. (lectr.), Am. Assn. Advt. Agencies (chmn. Chgo. council), Grinnell Coll. Alumni Assn. (chmn. Chgo. chpt.), Sigma Delta Chi. Clubs: Mid-America (dir.), Advt. (dir.), Univ. (dir.), Econ. (Chgo.); Oak Brook (Ill.); Polo, Off-the-Street (v.p., dir.); Meadow (Rolling Meadows, Ill.); Univ., Ariz., Phoenix Country, Plaza, Phoenix Advt. (Phoenix); Univ. of Milw. Home: 4701 E Sparkling Ln Paradise Valley AZ 85253 Office: 3550 N Central Ave Phoenix AZ 85012

COLE, CHARLES CHESTER, JR., educational administrator; b. Altoona, Pa., Sept. 12, 1922; s. Charles Chester and Kathryn Platt (Snyder) C.; m. Mary Elizabeth Ewald, Apr. 20, 1944 (div. 1979); children: Phyllis, Dorothy, Barbara, Elizabeth.; m. Gael Monie O'Brien, Jan. 14, 1983. A.B., Columbia U., 1943, M.A., 1947, Ph.D., 1951; LL.D., Lafayette Coll., 1970. Lectr. history Columbia U., 1946-49; asst. dean Columbia Coll., 1949-57, assoc. dean, 1957-58; instr. history Briarcliff Jr. Coll., 1949; dean Lafayette Coll., 1958-70, provost, 1967-70; pres. Wilson Coll., Chambersburg, Pa., 1970-75; exec. dir. Ohio Humanities Council, Columbus, 1976—; Trustee Ednl. Testing Service, 1968-72, Coll. Entrance Exam. Bd., 1965-68, Cedar Crest Coll., 1972-79; cons. coll. entrance exam. bd. State U. N.Y. Author: The Social Ideas of Northern Evangelists, 1826-1860, 1954, Encouraging Scientific Talent, 1956, Flexibility in the Undergraduate Curriculum, 1962, To Improve Instruction, 1978, Effective Learning, 1980, Improving Instruction, 1982. Served as 1st lt. 8th Air Force USAAF, 1944-45. Recipient Carnegie Corp. adminstrv. travel grant, NSF grant. Mem. Am. Hist. Assn., Assn. Higher Edn. (exec. com. 1955-58), Phi Beta Kappa, Alpha Phi Omega, Phi Alpha Theta. Presbyn. Home: 784 S Cassingham Rd Columbus OH 43209 *Who can really say how successful one's life has been? If there is a secret to success, I believe it is found in the right combination of patience, persistence, humility, high ideals, a sense of humor, a capacity to learn from mistakes, and a willingness to work hard.*

COLE, CHARLES W., JR., bank holding company executive. Pres. First Maryland Bancorp., Baltimore. Office: 25 S Charles St Baltimore MD 21201

COLE, CLARENCE RUSSELL, college dean; b. Crestline, Ohio, Nov. 20, 1918; s. Arthur Leroy and Anita Emma (Stephan) C.; m. Mary Piper, Mar. 15, 1945; children—Carole Ann, Larry Lee, Pamela Sue. Student pre-med., Otterbein Coll., Westerville, Ohio, 1937-39; D.V.M., Ohio State U., 1943, M.S., 1944, Ph.D., 1947. Instr. dept. vet. pathology Ohio State U. Coll. Vet. Med., asst. prof., 1947-49, chmn., 1947-67, assoc. prof., 1949-54, prof., 1954-67, asst. dean, 1960-67, dean, 1967—, prof. vet. pathology, 1952—, prof. comparative pathology, 1954—; Regents prof. Ohio Bd. Regents, 1966—; chmn. Mershon Center Nat. Security, Ohio State U., 1965-67; mem. U. Council Research, 1960-67; adminstr. cons. Vet. Research, Archtl. Engring. Planning, Animal Med. Center, N.Y.C.; cons. nat. adv. research resources council NIH, 1972—, NIH Health Manpower Grants Br; mem. nat. adv. com. Nat. Center for Primate Biology, 1967-70; mem. com. on comparative pathology NRC Nat. Acad. Sci., 1971—; mem. fellowship com. NATO. Recipient Herzfeld lectr. award Auburn U.; 1st award sci. exhibit Ohio State Med. Assn., 1956; 2d award AMA. Mem. Men and Women of Sci., Internat. Acad. Pathologists (exec. council), Internat. Toxoplasmosis Com. (vice-chmn. 1959—), AVMA (Gold award, chmn. adv. bd. vet. med. spltys. 1960-75), Am. Coll. Vet. Pathology (citation 1967, pres. 1967), Assn. Am. Vet. Med. Colls. (sec. treas. 1969—), Ohio Vet. Med. Assn. (trustee), Sigma Xi, Phi Zeta, Omega Tau Sigma. Club: Torch Internat. Address: 1925 Coffey Rd Columbus OH 43210

COLE, CLIFFORD ADAIR, clergyman; b. Lamoni, Iowa, Nov. 16, 1915; s. Fayette V. and Mable F. (Adair) C.; m. Harriett Lucile Hartshorn, June 28, 1936; children—Aletha Rae (Mrs. Justus S. Allen), Beverly Sue (Mrs. Lloyd G. Hilburn, Jr.), Lawrence Dean. Student, Graceland Coll., Lamoni, 1934-35, 41-42, U. Wyo., 1938; B.S. in Edn, Central Mo. State Coll., 1943; postgrad., U. Iowa, 1946, U. Chgo., 1952; M.A. in Edn, U. Mo. at Kansas City, 1957. High Sch. tchr., Lamoni, 1943-46, Bellevue, Ia., 1946- 47; ordained to ministry Reorganized Ch. of Jesus Christ of Latter Day Saints, 1939; minister in, Iowa, 1947-51; dean students Graceland Coll., 1951-53; dir. dept. religious edn. Reorganized Ch. of Jesus Christ of Latter Day Saints, 1955-58, apostle in council twelve, 1958-80, pres. council, 1964-80, cons. to 1st presidency, 1980—. Author: The Prophets Speak, 1954, Working Together in our Families, 1955, Celebrating Together in our Families, 1955, Faith for New Frontier, 1956, The Revelation in Christ, 1963, Modern Women in a Modern World, 1965. Mem. Phi Sigma Pi, Zeta Kappa Epsilon, Kappa Delta Pi. Office: Reorganized Sch of Jesus Christ Latter Day Saints Auditorium Independence MO 64051

COLE, CLYDE CURTIS, JR., assn. exec.; b. Ft. Smith, Ark., May 4, 1932; s. Clyde Curtis and Alta Mae (Lasater) C.; m. Marcia Anne Johnson, Nov. 25, 1953 (div. 1973); children—Clyde Curtis, Deborah Dianne, Douglas Scott, Mark Johnson; m. Joyce L. Ruis, July, 1974. Asso. in Arts and Scis., Northeastern A. and M. Coll., Miami, Okla., 1952; B.A. in History, Econs. and Polit. Sci, Eastern N.Mex. U., Portales, 1954; postgrad., U. N.Mex. Coll. Law, 1954-55; grad., Inst. Organizational Mgmt., U. Colo., 1965. Mgr. Guymon (Okla.) C. of C., 1955-57; asst. dir., exec. dir. Okla. Devel. Council, Oklahoma City, 1957-59; dir. Indsl. Devel. Commn., Columbia, S.C.; and mgr. indsl. dept. Columbia C. of C., 1959-61; exec. dir. Greater Enid (Okla.) C. of C., 1961-65, South Bend-Mishawaka Area C. of C., Ind., 1965-67; exec. v.p. Met. Tulsa C. of C., 1967—; pres. Industries for Tulsa, Inc.; faculty Insts. Orgn. Mgmt., U. Colo., 1964, 65, 69-72, U. Ga., 1971, 75, Tex. Christian U., 1971-72, Santa Clara U., 1971-72, Mich. State U., 1972, So. Meth. U., 1975-76; Mem. Gov.'s Econ. Adv. Council, 1963-65. 1st v.p., bd. dirs. Okla. Good Rds. and Sts. Assn., 1962-65; sec.-treas. So. Indsl. Devel. Council, 1963-64, Econ. Devel. Commn., Tulsa, 1969—; mem. Tulsa Indsl. Authority, 1969—; mem. dean's adv. council Tulsa U., 1972-76; mem. Okla. Citizen's Adv. Council on Goals for Higher Edn.; bd. dirs. Ark. Basin Devel. Assn., Jr. Achievement of Greater Tulsa, Indian Nations Council of Govts.; bd. regents Insts. Orgn. Mgmt. Mem. Am. C. of C. Execs. Assn. (past chmn., mem. bd., sr. counselor), So. Assn. C. of C. Execs. (past pres.), Okla. C. of C. Execs. (past pres.). Home: 4305 S Birmingham Ave Tulsa OK 74105 Office: 616 S Boston Ave Tulsa OK 74119

COLE, DAVID HARRIS, clergyman; b. Lynn, Mass., Apr. 5, 921; s. Milton N. and Lorena (Campbell) C.; m. Isabelle T. Jurasek, July 25, 1963; children—Victoria Stephen, Lynda, Karen, Cynthia, Kevin, Gloria. Student, Northeastern U., 1939-41; A.B., Tufts U., 1947; S.T.B., Crane Theol. Sch., Medford, Mass., 1948; grad., Inst. Pastoral Care, 1950. Ordained to ministry Unitarian Universalist Ch., 1948; pastor, Danvers, Mass., 1944-49, Chgo., 1949-59, Urbana, Ill., 1959-63; Unitarian Ch., Rockville, Md., 1963-69, West Shore Unitarian Ch., Cleve., 1969—; tchr. sociology Montgomery Community Coll., Rockville, 1966-68; Pres. Universalist Youth Fellowship, 1947, Universalist Ministerial Assn., 1956-58, Ill. Universalist Conv., 1952-57, Midwest Universalist Conf., 1958-62; co-pres. Midwest Unitarian-Universalist Conf., 1961-62; pres. Unitarian-Universalist Fellowship for Social Justice, 1965-67, Ohio-Meadville dist. Unitarian-Universalist Assn., 1970-71, 1971-73; sec. Am. Christian Palestine Com., 1950-59; mem. bd. Universalist Service Com., 1949-56, Cleve. Inter Ch. Council, 1975—. Author articles. Pres. Ryder Community Center, Chgo., 1954-59; chmn. Montgomery County Citizens Com. Human Relations, 1965-66, March on Crime., Chgo., 1953, Champaign County (Ill.) Urban League, 1961-63; chmn. bd. Internat. Affairs Inst., Star Island, N.H., 1967; bd. dirs. Meadville Theol. Sch., Chgo., 1962-70; chmn. ch. and Soc. Commn., 1980—. Named Man of the Year Chgo. B'nai B'rith, 1957. Home: 240 Argyle Rd Rocky River OH 44116 Office: 20401 Hilliard Rd Cleveland OH 44116

COLE, DONALD WILLARD, clergyman, cons. psychologist; b. San Diego, Jan. 12, 1920; s. Rolland Ames and Genevieve (Bender) C.; m. Ann Bradford, Sept. 18, 1942; 1 son, Timothy Bradford. Student, U. Redlands; A.B., Stanford, 1942; B.D., Eastern Bapt. Theol. Sem., 1945; Ed.D., Southwestern Bapt. Theol. Sem., 1952; Ph.D., U. London, 1962. Ordained to ministry Bapt. Ch., 1945; pastor Linden Bapt. Ch., Camden, N.J., 1944-46; asso. pastor First Bapt. Ch., San Diego, 1946-48; univ. pastor, dir. Bapt. student work, So. Calif., 1948-52, dean, dir. Bapt. confs., camps, coll. and univ. students, 1948-52; pres. Calif. Bapt. Theol. Sem. and Coll., 1952-59; Brit. Nat. Health Service fellow, 1959-61; dean students, prof. psychology Fuller Theol. Sem., Pasadena, Calif., 1962-70; pvt. practice cons. clin. psychology, psychotherapy, religion, Monrovia, Calif., 1970-74; pastor S. Shores Bapt. Ch., Laguna Niguel, Calif., 1974—. Author: The Role of Religion In The Development of Personality; Contbr. articles to religious publs. Fellow Royal Geog. Soc. London; mem. NEA, Religious Edn. Assn., Am. Group Psychotherapy Assn., Nat. Assn. Mental Health, Acad. Religion and Mental Health, Am. Psychol. Assn., Am. Assn. Schs. Religious Edn., Western, Cal. State, Los Angeles County psychol. assns., Nat. Council Family Relations, Am. Soc. Psychical Research, Am. Acad. Polit. and Social Sci., U.S. Air Force Assn., Alpha Gamma Nu, Alpha Phi Omega. Republican. Home: 245 Via Ballena San Clemente CA 92672 Office: 32712 Crown Valley Pkwy Laguna Niguel CA 92677

COLE, DOUGLAS, English literature educator; b. N.Y.C., July 25, 1934; s. Ronald and Helen Elizabeth (Bladykas) C.; m. Virginia Ann Ford, Nov. 28, 1957; children—David, Stephen, Karen, Kristin. B.A., U. Notre Dame, Ind., 1957; M.A., U. Chgo., 1957; Ph.D. (Woodrow Wilson fellow, Danforth fellow), Princeton U., 1961. Instr. English Yale U., 1960-64, asst. prof., 1964-67, asso. prof., 1967-69; prof. Northwestern U., Evanston, Ill., 1969—, chmn. dept. English, 1974-77; master Humanities Residential Coll., 1981-84. Author: Suffering and Evil in the Plays of Christopher Marlowe, 1962; Editor: 20th Century Views of Romeo and Juliet, 1970, Renaissance Drama XI: Tragedy, 1980; Contbr. numerous articles to profl. jours. Morse fellow, 1966-67. Mem. Modern Lang. Assn., Shakespeare Assn. Am., Soc. Values in Higher Edn. Office: English Dept Northwestern U Evanston IL 60201

COLE, FLOYD CLINTON, utility company executive; b. Middletown, N.Y., Jan. 23, 1926; s. Floyd Emmet and Irene Caroline (Mallory) C.; m. Dorothy Agnes McDonald, June 29, 1946; children: F. Wayne, Sherry L. B.S.M.E., Renssalaer Poly. Inst., 1949. Asst. gas engr. Rockland Light & Power Co., Nyack, N.Y., 1949-52, gas engr., 1952-63; mgr. gas ops. Orange and Rockland Utilities, Inc., Spring Valley, N.Y., 1963-69, dir. ops., 1969-70, v.p. co. and subsidiaries, 1970-73, sr. v.p., Pearl River, N.Y, 1973—. Treas., mem. exec. bd. Harriman Coll., 1979—; mem. Monroe (N.Y.) Planning Bd.; bd. dirs. Arden Hill Hosp., Tri-State United Way; pres. United Way of Rockland County; trustee Arden Hill Hosp. Found., Mus. Village of Orange County. Served with USNR, 1944-47. Mem. Am. Gas Assn., Soc. Gas Lighting, Gas Research Inst., New Eng. Gas Assn. Republican. Methodist. Clubs: Orange County Golf, Elks. Home: Box 599 Monroe NY 10950 Office: 1 Blue Hill Plaza Pearl River NY 10965

COLE, FRANKLIN ALAN, bank holding company executive; b. Park Falls, Wis., May 20, 1926; s. David A. and Elizabeth (Schwid) C.; m. Joan Lauter; children: Todd, Andrew, Robert, Mary, Ellen, Peter. B.A., U. Ill., 1947; J.D., Northwestern U., 1950. Bar: Ill. bar 1950. Practice, in Chgo., 1950-63; asso. Lederer, Livingston, Kahn & Adsit, 1950-55; partner Cole, Wishner, Epstein & Manilow, 1955-63; exec. Ameritin Corp. (formerly Walter E. Heller Internat. Corp.), Chgo., 1963—; pres., chief exec. officer Walter E. Heller Internat. Corp., 1971-73, 79; chmn., chief exec. officer, 1973—; dir. Am. Nat. Bank & Trust Co., Chgo., Mid Con Corp., Oak Industries, Inc., Combined Internat. Corp., Diebel Mfg. Co. Trustee Northwestern U., Evanston, Ill., Michael Reese Hosp. & Med. Center, Chgo.; trustee, exec. com. Chgo. Community Trust; bd. dirs. United Way of Met. Chgo., United Way/Crusade of Mercy, Chgo.; prin. United Chgo. Home: 110 Acorn Ln Highland Park IL 60035 Office: 105 W Adams St Chicago IL 60690

COLE, FRED CARRINGTON, educator; b. Franklin, Tex., Apr. 12, 1912; s. Robert Wiley and Elizabeth (Taylor) C.; m. Lois Ferguson, Aug. 22, 1937; children—Caroline (Mrs. Elmer Cornwell, Jr.), Fred Carrington, Robert Grey, Taylor Morris. A.B., La. State U., 1934, A.M., 1936, Ph.D., 1941; LL.D., Union Coll., 1961, Washington and Lee U., 1968. Editorial asso. Jour. So. History, La. State U., 1936-41; mng. editor, 1941-42; co-editor So. Biography Series, 1938-45; hist. editor. La. State Univ. Press, 1938-42; asso. prof. history Tulane U., 1946-47, prof., 1947-59, dean, 1947-55, acad. v.p., 1954-59; pres. Washington and Lee U., 1959-67, Council on Library Resources, Inc., Washington, 1967-78; asso. editor Mississippi Valley Hist. Rev., 1946-53; Staff asso. edn. Ford Found., 1954-55; cons. med. research and edn. HEW, 1957-58; cons. to Surgeon Gen. on med. manpower, 1958-59; mem. Com. on Internat. Exchange of Persons, 1963-70. Trustee United Negro Coll. Fund, George C. Marshall Found.; bd. dirs. Council Library Resources; chmn. Found. Center, 1973-77; bd. dirs. Ford Motor Co. Fund Scholarship Program, 1965-70; pres. Va. Found. Ind. Colls., 1964-67; chmn adv. com. div. instl. programs NSF, 1957-63; chmn. adv. council coop. research Office Edn., 1965-67; chmn. hist. adv. com. Dept. Army, 1963-67. Served with USNR, 1942-46. Awarded spl. commendation Surgeon Gen. U.S. Navy, 1945; Outstanding Service award Dept. Army, 1967; Centennial citation ALA, 1976; medals Internat. Council Archives, Internat. Fedn. Library Assns., 1977. Mem. ALA (hon.), Am., So., Miss. Valley hist. assns., Am., So. polit. assns., Acad. Polit. Sci., Phi Beta Kappa Assos. (chmn. council nominating com. 1964-67), Sigma Chi, Phi Kappa Phi, Pi Sigma Alpha, Omicron Delta Kappa. Democrat. Baptist. Clubs: Cosmos (Washington); Century (N.Y.C.). Home: 107 Hunter's Ridge Rd Chapel Hill NC 27514

COLE, GEORGE DAVID, physicist; b. Minden, La., June 23, 1925; s. Stephen Peru and Willie Lee (White) C.; m. Ruth Alvera Moore, Mar. 1, 1947; children—Lindy Barry, Karen Cole Wertz, George Marcus. B.S., Northwestern State Coll., La., 1950; M.A., Peabody Coll., 1954; Ph.D. (NSF Sci. Faculty fellow 1961-62), U. Ala., 1963. Tchr. Morgan City (La.) High Sch., 1950-54; asso. prof. Nicholls State Coll. La., Thibodaux, 1954; mem. faculty U. Ala., 1963—, prof. physics, 1972—, head dept. physics and astronomy, 1968—, asst. v.p. acad. affairs, 1980—; cons. Stillman Coll., Tuscaloosa, 1968-69, Insts. Internat. Edn., in Bangladesh and Pakistan, 1967-70. Contbr. articles to profl. jours. Served with USAF, 1943-46. Mem. Am. Phys. Soc., Am. Assn. Physics Tchrs., Sigma Xi (past chpt. pres.), Pi Mu Epsilon, Sigma Pi Sigma. Home: 13 Hickory Hill Tuscaloosa AL 35404 Office: Box 1921 University AL 35486 *

COLE, GORDON HENRY, labor union ofcl., editor; b. Providence, Jan. 11, 1912; s. Albert Jourdan and Margaret Cooper (Ricketts) C.; m. Malvine Gescheidt, Sept. 19. 1939; children—Stephen Adams, Jeremy David; m. Morag Douglas Macintyre, Dec. 19, 1952; children—Gordon Macintyre, Susan Douglas, Margaret Cooper. A.B., Syracuse U., 1934. Newspaper reporter, 1934-37; asso. editor Labor Relations Reporter Bur. Nat. Affairs, 1937-39; labor editor U.S. News, 1939-42, 1942-43; with civilian psychol. warfare br. 12th U.S. Army Group OSS, 1943-45; commr. conciliation U.S. Dept. Labor, 1946-47; cons. Bur. Internat. Labor Affairs, 1978—; editor The Machinist; pub. relations dir. Internat. Assn. Machinists, AFL-CIO, 1947-77; cons. AFL-CIO Labor Studies Center, 1977—. Decorated Medal of Freedom, Croix de Guerre. Mem. Internat. Labor Press Assn. (pres. 1955-57), Am. Newspaper Guild (v.p. 1943-44), Washington Newspaper Guild (pres. 1942), Nat. Press Club, Sigma Delta Chi. Democrat. Presbyterian. Home: 12421 Fairfax Station Rd Clifton VA 22024 Office: George Meany Center for Labor Studies 10000 New Hampshire Ave Silver Spring MD 20903

COLE, HARRY A., judge; b. Washington; m. Doris Freeland; children—Susan, Harriette, Stephanie. A.B. magna cum laude, Morgan State Coll., 1943; LL.D., 1975; LL.B., U. Md., 1949. Apptd. justice of peace, 1951, substitute magistrate, 1952, asst. atty. gen., 1953; asso. judge Md. Circuit Ct., 8th Jud. Circuit, Supreme Bench Balt. City, 1968-77; now asso. judge Md. Ct. Appeals; mem. Md. Senate, 1954-58. Mem. Md. Adv. Com. on Civil Rights to U.S. Civil Rights Commn.; also 1st chmn. Bd. dirs. Balt. Zool. Soc., Union Meml. Hosp., Camp Fire Girls, Balt. Mus. Art; bd. visitors Morgan State Coll.; also chmn.; bd. mgrs. YMCA; mem. exec. com. U.S. Nat. Com. for UNESCO. Served to 1st lt. U.S. Army, 1943-46; ETO. Named Man of Yr. NAACP, Md. Beauticians, A.M.E. Ch. Mem. Am. Judicature Soc., Md. Jud. Conf. (exec. com. 1971), Monumental City Bar Assn., Md. State Bar Assn., Nat. Bar Assn., NAACP (life), U. Md. Law Sch. Alumni Assn. (pres.). Mem. African Methodist Episcopal Ch. Office: Courthouse Baltimore MD 21202 *

COLE, IRA WILLIAM, university dean; b. Mattoon, Ill., Apr. 21, 1924; s. Harry Ellsworth and Carrie Juliet (Connor) C.; m. Sally Ann Savage, Jan. 5, 1944; children: Molly Ann, Timothy William. B.S., U. Ill., 1948, M.S., 1952. Reporter Champaign (Ill.) News-Gazette, 1941-43, 46-47; asst. to dir. U. Ill. Sch. Journalism and Communications, 1948-56; dir. Pa. State U. Sch. Journalism, 1956-57; dean Medill Sch. Journalism Northwestern U., 1957-84; dir. Gannett Urban Journalism Center, 1966—. Trustee Christian Century Found., 1970—, Quill and Scroll Found., 1957—. Served from sgt. to 1st lt., Inf. AUS, 1942-45, 51; pub. informtion specialist, hdqrs. UN Command Far East Command, 1951-52. Mem. Assn. for Edn. Journalism, Am. Med. Writers Assn., A.P. Mng. Editors Assn., Phi Kappa Psi, Sigma Delta Chi, Kappa Tau Alpha. Clubs: Economic, Tavern (Chgo.). Office: Medill School of Journalism Northwestern U 375 E Chicago Ave Evanston IL 60201 also Gannett Urban Journalism Center Two Illinois Center Chicago IL 60601

COLE, JACK WESTLEY, physician; b. Portland, Oreg., Aug. 28, 1920; s. Alva Warren and Louise (Shafer) C.; m. Ruth Adele Kraft, Dec. 22, 1943; children—Deborah, Linda, Douglas, John. A.B., U. Oreg., 1941; M.D., Wash. U., 1944; M.A., Yale, 1966. Mem. faculty Western Res. U. Sch. Medicine, 1952-63; prof., chmn. dept. surgery Hahnemann Med. Coll. and Hosp., 1963-66; Ensign prof. surgery Yale U. Sch. Medicine, 1966—, chmn. dept. surgery, 1966-74, Josiah Macy Jr. faculty scholar, 1974-75, dir. div. oncology and cancer center, 1975—; cons. various hosps. Eleanor Roosevelt Internat. Cancer Research fellow, 1962. Mem. Am. Surg. Assn., Halsted Soc., Soc. Surgery of Alimentary Tract, Am. Soc. Cell Biology, Soc. Cryobiology. Research and publs. on histochemistry, cytochemistry, carcinogenesis; studies dealing with cellular kinetics in normal and abnormal intestinal epithelium. Home: Prospect Ct Woodbridge CT 06525 Office: 333 Cedar St New Haven CT 06510

COLE, JOHN OWEN, banker; b. Forest City, N.C., May 22, 1929; s. Dee Christopher and Faye (Best) C.; m. Katherine Stuart Davidson, June 27, 1953; children: Mark Davidson, D. Matthew, Chapman Stuart, Benjamin Donnell, John Owen II, Jamie Clark, Mary F. B.A., Duke U., 1953. With First Nat. Bank Md., Balt., 1956—, pres., dir., from 1968, now chmn. bd.; mem. fed. adv. council FRS; dir. U.S. Fidelity & Guaranty Co., Balt. Gas & Electric Co. Trustee Goucher Coll. Served with USMCR, 1953-56. Mem. Res. City Bankers Assn. Office: First Nat Bank Md 25 S Charles St Baltimore MD 21201 *

COLE, JOHN POPE, JR., lawyer; b. Washington, Jan. 12, 1930; s. John Pope and Helen (Gorman) C.; m. Patsy Nan Moss, Mar. 20, 1960; children—John Moss, Nina Gorman. B.S., Auburn U., 1953; LL.B., George Washington U., 1956. Bar: D.C. bar 1956, Md. bar 1956, Ga. bar 1961. Atty. FCC, Washington, 1957; partner Smith & Pepper, Washington, 1957-65, Cole, Raywid & Braverman, 1966—. Served with USAF, 1948-49. Home: 5309 Portsmouth Rd Washington DC 20816 Office: 1919 Pennsylvania Ave NW Washington DC 20006

COLE, JONATHAN OTIS, psychiatrist; b. Boston, Aug. 16, 1925; s. Arthur Harrison and Anna (Steckel) C.; m. Kathleen Gleason, July 12, 1952; children: Jonathan Patrick, Joshua Peter. Student, Harvard Coll., 1942-43; M.D., Cornell U., 1947. Intern Peter Bent Brigham Hosp., Boston, 1947-48; resident psychiatry Payne Whitney Clinic, N.Y.C., 1948-51; assoc. prof. Nat. Acad. Scis., Washington, 1953-56; dir. psychopharmacology research br. NIMH, Chevy Chase, Md., 1956-67; supt. Boston State Hosp., 1967-73; prof. psychiatry Tufts Med. Sch., 1967-73; prof., chmn. dept. psychiatry Temple Med. Sch., 1973-74; psychiatrist McLean Hosp., Belmont, Mass., 1974—; lectr. Harvard Med. Sch., Cambridge, Mass. Editor: Psychopharmacology: Problems in Evaluation; Contbr. numerous articles to sci. jours. Served with AUS, 1951-53. Fellow Am. Psychiat. Assn. Am. Coll. Neuropsychopharmacology, Collegium Internationale Neuro-Psychopharmacologicum; mem. Am. Psychopathol. Assn. Home: 78 Powell St Brookline MA 02146 Office: McLean Hosp 115 Mill St Belmont MA 02178

COLE, JOSEPH EDMUND, specialty retail company executive; b. Cleve., Jan. 4, 1915; s. Solomon and Sarah (Miller) C.; m. Marcia Newman, Oct. 31, 1937; children: Jeffrey, Stephan. Student, Ohio State U., 1932, Fenn Coll., Cleve., 1933. Salesman Waldorf Brewing Co., 1933-35; office mgr., then gen. mgr. Nat. Key Shops, Inc., 1935-44; partner, sales dir. Curtis Industries, 1944-50; pres., now chmn. Cole Nat. Corp., Cleve., 1950—; past chmn. Shelter Resources Corp.; past dir. BancOhio Nat. Bank, Cleve. Active Jewish Welfare Fund, Cleve., 1963-64; Chmn. Ohio Citizens for Kennedy, 1960; chmn. Hubert Humphrey for Pres., 1972; mem. Cuyahoga County Democratic Exec. Com., 1960—; chmn. finance com. Dem. Nat. Com., 1973-74; Bd. dirs. Jewish Community Fedn., Cleve., Notre Dame Coll., Cleve.; past trustee Cleve. State U.; past chmn. scholarship fund Ohio State Coll.; life mem. Brandeis U. Mem. Cleve. C. of C. Jewish (trustee temple). Clubs: Masons, (32 deg.), Shriners, Oakwood Country City (Cleve.); Standard (Chgo.); Palm Beach (Fla.) Country. Office: 29001 Cedar Rd Cleveland OH 44124

COLE, KENDALL MARTIN, photographic equipment company executive, lawyer; b. Bangor, Maine, Oct. 25, 1922; s. William Spratt and Alice (Lord) C.; m. Mary Daintry Malloch, Nov. 12, 1949; children: Robert, Jane. A.B. cum laude, Amherst Coll., 1943; J.D., Harvard U., 1948. Bar: Ill. 1949, Pa. 1961, N.Y. 1963. Practiced in, Chgo., 1948-60, Phila., 1960-63, White Plains, N.Y., 1963—; assoc. Carney, Crowell & Leibman, 1948-56, ptnr., 1956-60; asst. gen. counsel Scott Paper Co., 1960-63, Gen. Foods Corp., 1963-64, gen. counsel, 1964-73, v.p., 1967—, 73; asst. gen. counsel Eastman Kodak Co., Rochester, N.Y., 1973-74, v.p., gen. counsel, 1974-78, sr. v.p., 1978—, also dir.; dir. Security N.Y. State Corp.; trustee Monroe Savs. Bank. Served with USNR, 1943-46. Mem. Alpha Delta Phi. Republican. Episcopalian. Clubs: Country (Rochester); Port Royal; Hamilton (Ont.). Office: 343 State St Rochester NY 14650

COLE, KENNETH REESE, JR., business executive; b. N.Y.C., Jan. 27, 1938; s. Kenneth Reese and Laura (Hughes) C.; m. Marilyn Joan Slifer, July 20, 1963; children: Corinne, Megan. B.S. in Bus. Adminstrn, Bucknell U., 1959. Asst. to v.p. operations Elizabethtown Gas Co., Elizabeth, N.J., 1959-61; account rep. J. Walter Thompson Co., N.Y.C., 1965-68; spl. asst. to Pres. Richard M. Nixon, 1969-70, dep. asst. for domestic affairs, 1970-72, dir. domestic council, 1973-74; asst. to Pres. Gerald R. Ford for domestic affairs, 1974-75; sr. v.p. Union Camp Corp., Wayne, N.J., 1975—; dir. Gen. Refractories Co. Trustee Mountainside Hosp., Montclair, N.J., 1976—; Former mem. Pres.'s Commn. on White House Fellowships; mem. Advance Nat. Nixon-Agnew campaign, 1968, Commn. on Intergovtl. Relations, 1973-75. Served to lt. USNR, 1961-65. Republican. Episcopalian. Home: 164 Devon Rd Essex Fells NJ 07021 Office: Union Camp Corp 1600 Valley Rd Wayne NJ 07470

COLE, LEWIS GEORGE, lawyer; b. N.Y.C., Mar. 9, 1931; s. Ralph David and Emma (Balterman) C.; m. Sara Cole Livingston, June 22, 1952; children: Elizabeth, Peter. B.S. in Econs., U. Pa., 1951; LL.B, Yale U., 1954. Bar: N.Y. 1954. Ptnr. Stroock & Stroock & Lavan, N.Y.C., 1958—. Served to 1st lt. U.S. Army, 1954-57. Mem. ABA, Assn. Bar City N.Y., N.Y. State Bar Assn., N.Y. County Lawyers Assn. Office: Stroock & Stroock & Lavan 7 Hanover Sq New York NY 10004

COLE, MAX, artist; b. Hodgeman County, Kans., Feb. 14, 1937; d. Jack Delmont C. and Bertha (Law) Fakes; m. Richard Cole, Sept. 4, 1955 (dec. April 1958); children: Douglas, Janet, Cindy. B.A., Fort Hays State U., 1961; M.F.A., U. Ariz., 1964. Asst. prof. Pasadena (Calif.) City Coll., 1967-78; guest lectr. Claremont (Calif.) Grad. Sch., 1978, Coll. Creative Studies, U. Calif., Santa Barbara, 1977, 79, Contemporary Arts Council, Los Angeles County Mus. Art, 1979, Miami Dade Coll., 1982. Exhibited group shows, Los Angeles County Mus. Art, 1976, Corcoran Gallery Art, Washington, 1977; one-man shows, Louver Gallery, Los Angeles, 1979, 80, Sidney Janis Gallery, N.Y.C., 1977, 80. Home Office: 195 E 3d St New York NY 10009

COLE, NATALIE MARIA, vocalist; b. Los Angeles, Feb. 6, 1950; d. Nathaniel Adam and Maria (Hawkins) C.; m. Marvin J. Yancy, July 30, 1976. B.A. in Psychology, U. Mass., 1972. Rec. singles and albums, 1975— (recipient Grammy for best new artist, best R and B female vocalist 1975, 76, rec. 1 gold single, 3 gold albums., Recipient 2 Image awards NAACP 1976, 77, Am. Music award 1978, other awards.). Mem. AFTRA, Nat. Assn. Recording Arts and Scis., Delta Sigma Delta. Democrat. Baptist. *

COLE, ORLANDO, cellist; b. Phila., Aug. 16, 1908; s. Lucius Sylvanus and Rosalia (Winkler) C.; m. Rosamonde Adams, Jan. 15, 1933; children: Timothy, Deborah, David. Mus.B., Curtis Inst. Music, 1932. Prof. cello New Sch. Music, Phila., from 1942, Curtis Inst. Music, 1952—. Cellist, Curtis String Quartet, 1927-81, concerts, throughout U.S., 1928—, Europe, 1935-37, at, The White House, 1934, in, The White House, London for silver jubilee King George V, 1935. Recipient medal achievement Phila. Art Alliance, 1954. Home: 1017 Keystone Ave Upper Darby PA 19082 Office: Dept of Violincello Curtis Inst of Music Rittenhouse Square Philadelphia PA 19103

COLE, RICHARD, philosopher, educator; b. Evanston, Ill., Oct. 28, 1929; s. Harry and Bertha (Slavitt) C.; m. Marjorie Jean Emerson, May 31, 1958; children—Mark Warren, Wendy Elizabeth, Aletha Jocelyn. B.A. in Math, U. Tex., Austin, 1958; Ph.D., U. Chgo., 1962. Instr. Colo. Coll., 1961-62; asst. prof. Grinnell Coll., 1962-65; asso. prof. philosophy U. Kans., Lawrence, 1965-69, prof., 1969—, acting chmn. philosophy dept., 1969-70, chmn. com. history and philosophy of sci., 1967-69, chmn., 1970-71; visitor Edinburgh U., 1971-72; vis. prof. U. Iowa, 1983. Contbg. author: The Concept of Order, 1968; Editorial bd.: Auslegung; Contbr. articles to profl. jours. Served with Signal Corps and Pub. Information U.S. Army, 1951-53. Mem. Mind Assn., Mountain Plains Philos. Assn. (chmn. exec. com. 1972-73), AAUP (chmn. U. Kans. com. on acad. freedom and tenure 1977-78, exec. com. 1978—, v.p. 1981-82, pres. 1982-83), Am., Internat. metaphys. socs., Philosophy of Sci. Assn., S.W. Philos. Soc. (v.p. 1976-77, pres. 1977-78). Home: 1804 Mississippi St Lawrence KS 66044

COLE, RICHARD JOHN, manufacturing company executive; b. N.Y.C., Oct. 18, 1926; s. Arthur and Anna C.; m. Birgitta Ofling, Aug. 26, 1961; children—Catherine Ann, Richard Arthur, John Eric, Christopher Arne. B.A., Yale U., 1946. Pres. Richard J. Cole, Inc., N.Y.C., 1954-61; gen. mgr. Dynasty of Hong Kong, N.Y.C., 1961-67; pres. M.I. Group div. Manhattan Industries, Inc., 1967—; mng. dir. B. Barclay Internat., Inc. Served with USNR, 1943-46, 52-53. Congregationalist. Club: Fairfield County Hunt. Home: 25 Adams Rd Easton CT 06425 Office: 1466 Broadway New York NY 10018

COLE, RICHARD LOUIS, educational administrator; b. Dallas, Jan. 25, 1946; s. Louis Ray and Mary (Steely) C.; m. Pamela June Jacobs, Nov. 22, 1968; children: Jonathan, Ashley. B.A., North Tex. State U., Denton, 1967, M.A., 1968; Ph.D., Purdue U., 1973. Asst. prof. Geroge Washington U., 1973-78; assoc. Prof. George Washington U., 1978-79; research scholar Yale U., New Haven, Conn., 1979-80; prof. polit. sci., dean urban studies U. Tex.-Arlington, 1980—; cons. Office Revenue Sharing Rand Corp. Author: Introduction to Political Inquiry, 1980, Citizen Participation, 1974, Revenue Sharing, 1976; editorial bd.: Am. Politics Quar., 1977—, Jour. Community Action, 1981—. Mem. Leadership Arlington. Mem. Southwest Polit. Sci. Assn. (v.p. 1983-84), Am. Polit. Sci. Assn. Democrat. Methodist. Home: 704 Tanglewood Ln Arlington TX 76012 Office: Inst Urban Studies U Tex PO Box 19588 Arlington TX 76019

COLE, RICHARD RAY, university dean; b. Forney, Tex., Apr. 20, 1942; s. Richard W. and G. Gladys C.; m. Lynda F. Painter, May 31, 1968. B.J., U. Tex., Austin, 1964, M.A., 1966; Ph.D., U. Minn., 1971. Asst. city editor The News, Mexico City, 1966-67; freelance writer, 1966-67; reporter Harrow Observer, Harrow-on-the -Hill, Eng., 1968; asst. prof. W.Va. U., 1967-68; instr. U. Minn., 1968-71; mem. faculty U. N.C., Chapel Hill, 1971—, prof. journalism, 1979—, dean, 1979—; dir. N.C. Scholastic Press Assn., 1972-79; exec. sec. N.C. Scholastic Press Advisers Assn., 1976-79; mem. nat. scholarship com. Gannett Found., 1980—; judge H.L. Mencken Nat. Writing Award Competition, 1983—; mem. journalism awards program steering com. William Randolph Hearst Found., 1981—; cons. in field. Co-author: Gathering and Writing The News: Selected Readings, 1975; asst. editor: Journalism Quar, 1973—; contbr. articles to profl. publns. Recipient award excellence in undergrad. teaching Amoco Found., 1978; grantee U. Minn., U. N.C., Dept. State, Internat. Communication Agy. Mem. Assn. Edn. Journalism and Mass Communication (exec. com. 1977-79, 81-84, chmn. coms. 1974-75, 77-79, pres. 1982-83, nat. task force on future mass communication of edn. 1983-84), Internat. Assn. Mass Communication Research (council 1980-83), Assn. Schs. of Journalism and Mass Communication (exec. com. 1983—), Inter Am. Press Assn., Sigma Delta Chi, Kappa Tau Alpha. Office: Sch Journalism U NC Chapel Hill NC 27514

COLE, ROBERT BATES, lawyer; b. Scarborough, Eng., Feb. 9, 1911; came to U.S., 1911, naturalized, 1914; s. William and Mary Elizabeth (Bates) C.; m. Frances Lee Arnold, June 23, 1937; children: Charles Robert, George Thomas, Richard Phillip. A.B., U. Fla., 1932, J.D., 1935. Bar: Fla. bar 1935. Since practiced in, Miami; mem. firm Mershon, Sawyer, Johnston, Dunwody & Cole, Miami, Fla., 1946—; sec., dir. Major Appliances, Inc., Miami, 1953—, Lennar Corp., 1969—; sec., treas., dir. Fla. Dairy Producers Coop., Orlando, 1962—. Mem. Com. of 200.; Trustee Bapt. Hosp. Miami, Inc. Mem. Nat. Assn. Coll. and U. Attys., Am., Dade County bar assns., Fla. Bar, Phi Delta Phi, Sigma Chi. Baptist. Clubs: Bankers, Miami; Riviera Country (Coral Gables, Fla.) (past pres.). Home: 2301 Alhambra Circle Coral Gables FL 33134 Office: Southeast First Nat Bank Bldg Miami FL 33131

COLE, ROBERT LEE, corporation executive; b. Rockport, Mo., May 4, 1929; s. Branchie Ray and Mary (Clevenger) C.; children: Brenda Lynn (Mrs. Hill), Bradford Lee. A.A. summa cum laude, Fullerton (Calif.) Jr. Coll., 1949; A.B. cum laude, U. Calif. at Berkeley, 1951. Registered profl. engr., Calif. Asst. to plant mgr., staff indsl. engr. Rheem Mfg. Co., Downey, Calif., 1951-55; asst. to pres., chief prodn. control Longren Aircraft Co., Torrance, Calif., 1955-58; div. mgr. Aerojet-Gen. Corp., Fullerton, 1960-62; mgr. indsl. engring. Downey, 1962-63, exec. asst. to corp. v.p., gen. mgr., El Monte, Calif., 1963-64; corp. mgr. real estate and constrn. dept. Litton Industries, Inc., Beverly Hills, Calif., 1964-67, treas., 1967-69; v.p. Litton Internat., 1967-69; treas. Litton Industries Found., 1967-69; pres. Litton Power Transmission, West Hartford, Conn., from 1969; corporate v.p. Litton Industries; pres. Rust Engring. Co., 1971; group v.p., div. pres. Wheelabrator-Frye, Inc., 1972-73; dir. operations analysis United Techs. Corp. (name formerly United Aircraft Corp.), Hartford, Conn., 1973-74, corp. v.p., pres., 1974-76, corp. v.p., 1974—; sr. v.p., pres. N.Am. elevator ops. Otis Elevator Co. subs., N.Y.C., 1976-81; exec. v.p. Power Group, 1981—; pres. Allied Info. Systems Co., Hartford, Conn.; group v.p. Allied Corp., Morristown, N.J.; dir. Conn. Bank & Trust Co., CBT Corp. Bd. dirs. Inst. Living, Hartford Grad. Center; trustee Wadsworth Atheneum. Clubs: Hartford Gun, Avon (Conn.) Country; Duquesne (Pitts.). Home: One Linden Pl Apt 503 Hartford CT 06106 Allied Info Systems Co Trumbull CT 06609

COLE, ROGER DAVID, biochemist, educator; b. Berkeley, Calif., Nov. 17, 1924; s. Naylor Elmer and Frances (Slankard) C.; m. Thelma Bennett, July 11, 1944; children—David Naylor, Miriam Faith, Janice Joy. B.S., U. Calif. at Berkeley, 1948, Ph.D., 1954. Jr. research biochemist U. Calif. at Berkeley, 1954-55, faculty, 1958—, prof. biochemistry, 1965—, chmn. dept. biochemistry, 1968-73, dir. Electron Microscopy Lab., 1978—; Nat. Found. Infantile Paralysis fellow Nat. Inst. Med. Research, London, Eng., 1955-56; research asso. Rockefeller Inst. Med. Research, N.Y.C., 1956-58; Guggenheim Meml. fellow Lab. for Molecular Biology, Cambridge, Eng., 1966-67; mem. adv. com. Am. Cancer Soc., 1972-75, 79; external examiner Chinese U., Hong Kong, 1974-77; com. mem., sect. chmn., lectr. sci. confs., 1955—, cons. numerous pubs., 1960—. Mem. editorial bd.: Archives Biochemistry and Biophysics, 1965-77, Biochimica Biophysica Acta, 1966-78, Biochemistry, 1971-76, Jour. Biol. Chemistry, 1973-79; Contbr. articles to profl. jours. Mem. AAAS, Am. Soc. Biol. Chemists, Am. Chem. Soc. (nominating com. biol. chemistry div. 1976-77), Sigma Xi (pres. Calif. chpt. 1974-75). Home: 1147 Park Hills Rd Berkeley CA 94708 Office: Biochemistry Bldg U Calif Berkeley CA 94720

COLE, SANDFORD STODDARD, cons. engr.; b. Cuba, N.Y., Nov. 24, 1900; s. John Browning and Inez (Bassett) C.; m. Frances Halderman, July 11, 1925; children—Sandford Stoddard, David Lee, Stephen Hervey. B.S., Alfred (N.Y.) U., 1923, M.S., 1933, Ceramic Engr., 1950, D.Sc. (hon.), 1981; Ph.D., Pa. State U., 1934. Registered profl. engr., N.J., Pa. Fellow Mellon Inst., 1923-32; with titanium div. Nat. Lead Co., 1934-65, asst. mgr. research, 1948-65; cons. engr., 1966—; Trustee Alfred U., 1958-61, Engring. Found, 1962-66, dir. conf., 1966—; dir. Engrs. Joint Council, 1962-65; adv. bd. N.Y. Coll. Ceramics, 1960-65. Editorial bd.: Indsl. Minerals and Rocks, 3d edit, 1960; author tech. papers. Recipient Alumni citation Alfred U., 1952, Recognition award, 1973. Fellow Am. Ceramic Soc., Am. Inst. Chemists; mem. Soc. Mining Engrs. (distinguished mem.; bd. dirs. 1960-66, pres. 1964-65), Am. Inst. Mining Metall. and Petroleum Engrs. (dir. 1963-66, v.p. 1965-66), Am. Chem. Soc., Nat. Inst. Ceramic Engrs., Keramos, Sigma Xi, Phi Kappa Phi. Patentee high temperature phys. chemistry, mineral conversions, smelting titaniferous ores, titanium hydrometallurgy, recovery vanadium values, crystal growth, silica refractories, reactions solid state. Home: 636 S Main St Hightstown NJ 08520 Office: PO Box 121 Hightstown NJ 08520

COLE, SHERWOOD ORISON, psychologist; b. North Scituate, R.I., May 28, 1930; s. Wesley Potter and Ruth Emily (King) C.; m. Dorothy Louise Cole; 2 children. B.A. in Psychology, U. Calif., Santa Barbara, 1958; M.A. in Psychology (USPHS grantee), UCLA, 1961, Ph.D., Claremont Grad. Sch., 1964. Asst. prof. psychology Calif. State Coll., Fullerton, 1964; asso. prof. Whitworth Coll., 1965-66; asst. prof. Rutgers U. Camden Coll. Arts and Scis., 1966-67, asso. prof., 1967-72, prof., 1972—, acting chmn. dept. psychology, 1966-67, chmn., 1967-74; vis. investigator in psychopharmacology Rutgers Research Council; fellow lab. psycho-biology and psychopharmacology Consiglio Nazionale delle Richerche, Rome, 1971-72. Contbr. numerous articles to profl. publs.; reviewer for profl. jours. Served with Med. Service Corps USN, 1951-54. NSF grantee, 1967; USPHS grantee, 1974-75; Rutgers Research Council grantee, 1974-75. Fellow Royal Soc. Health (Eng.); mem. Am., Eastern psychol. assns., AAAS, Psychonomic Soc., N.J. Acad. Sci. (chmn. sect. psychology 1976, 78 meetings), Psi Chi. Office: Rutgers U Psychology Dept Camden NJ 08102

COLE, STEPHEN, sociologist; b. N.Y.C., June 1, 1941; s. Richard and Sylvia (Dym) C.; m. Ann Harriet Brawerman, June 4, 1969; children—Richard, Robert. B.A., Columbia Coll., 1962; Ph.D., Columbia U., 1967. Asst. prof. Columbia U., 1966-68; asst. prof., asso. prof., prof. sociology SUNY at Stony Brook, 1968—; pres. Social Data Analysts, Inc., Setauket, N.Y., 1977—; cons. Nat. Acad. Scis., 1975-80. Author: The Unionization of Teachers, 1969, Social Stratification in Science, 1973, The Sociological Method, 1975, The Sociological Orientation, 1979, Peer Review in the National Science Foundation, 1979, 81. Ford Found. fellow, 1971-72; Guggenheim fellow, 1978-79; fellow Center for Advanced Study in Behavioral Scis., 1978-79; NSF grantee, 1967-78. Mem. Sociol. Research Assn. Office: Dept Sociology State U NY Stony Brook NY 11794

COLE, STERLING, lawyer; b. Painted Post, N.Y., Apr. 18, 1904; s. Ernest Ethelbert and Minnie (Pierce) C.; m. Mary Elizabeth Thomas, July 3, 1929; children—William Sterling, Thomas Ernest, David Aaron. A.B., Colgate U., 1925, LL.D., 1954; LL.B., Albany Law Sch., Union U., 1929; D.Sc., Union Coll.; LL.D., Elmira Coll. Tchr. pub. schs., 1925-26, began practice at, Bath, N.Y., 1930; mem. firm Cole & Cole; mem. 74th to 85th Congresses, 39th and 37th N.Y. Dist.; dir. gen. IAEA, Vienna, Austria, 1957-61; mem. firm Cole and Cole, Washington, 1962—; v.p. Cambridge Nuclear Corp., Mass., Space Research Corp., North Troy, Vt.; Mem. joint com. atomic energy U.S. Congress, 1947-57, chmn., 1953-54; fed. rep. (presdl. appointee) So. Interstate Nuclear Bd., 1969-83; mem. Adv. Council for Internat. Studies, Graz, Austria. Co-author: Atomic Energy Act of 1954. Trustee Colgate U., 1945-50, Woodlawn Found., Elmira Coll.; bd. advisers Robins Awards Am. Served to lt. comdr. USNR, 1939-59. Decorated Order of Merit, Italy; Gt. Golden Decoration of Honor for Merits, Austria; named to Steuben County (N.Y.) Bicentennial Hall of Fame, 1976. Mem. N.Y., Va., D.C. bar assns., Washington Inst. Fgn. Affairs, Phi Beta Kappa, Sigma Nu, Pi Delta Epsilon, Delta Sigma Rho. Republican. Presbyn. (elder). Clubs: Mason., Nat. Lawyers, Sulgrave (Washington). Home: 2201 S Knoll Rd Arlington VA 22202 Office: 1735 Eye St NW Washington DC 20006

COLE, SYLVAN, JR., art dealer; b. N.Y.C., Jan. 10, 1918; s. Sylvan and Dorothy (Stein) C.; m. Vivian Vanderpool, May 1944; children: Nancy, Robert, James; m. Lillyan Wood, Aug. 20, 1953. B.A., Cornell U., 1939. Exec. trainee Sears, Roebuck & Co., 1939-41; with Asso. Am. Artists, Inc., N.Y.C., 1946—, pres., dir., 1958—. Editor: Raphael Soyer: Fifty Years of Printmaking, 1967, Graphic Work of Joseph Hirsch, 1969, Will Barnet Graphics, 1932-1972, 1972, The Lithographs of John Steuart Curry, 1976. Former Pres. N.Y. chpt. Friends of Herbert F. Johnson Mus.; mem. exec. com. Cornell U.; Bd. dirs. Pratt Graphic Art Center. Served to maj. AUS, 1941-46. Mem. Art Dealers Assn. Am. (former dir.). Home: 25 Sutton Pl S New York NY 10022 Office: 20 W 57th St New York NY 10019

COLE, THEODORE MILLER, physiatrist; b. Boston, Dec. 11, 1931; s. William Roswell and Elizabeth (Miller) C.; m. Sandra Lee Shaw, June 20, 1959; children: Eric, Jennifer, Laura and Adam (twins), Leanne. Student, U. N.H., 1952-55; M.D., Tufts U., 1959. Intern New Eng. Med. Center, Boston, 1959-60, resident in medicine, 1960-62, fellow, 1962-63; resident in phys. medicine and rehab. U. Minn., 1963-65, asst. prof. to prof. phys. medicine and rehab., 1965-77; prof., chmn. dept. phys. medicine and rehab. U. Mich. Med. Center, Ann Arbor, 1977—. Contbr. articles on rehab. of physically disabled and sexuality of physically disabled to profl. jours. and books. Chmn. bd. Am. Spinal Injury Found.; Area IV chmn. Democratic Farmer-Labor Party, Minn., 1970. Served with USAF, 1950-52. Named Physician of Year Greater St. Paul Area Council for Handicapped, 1974. Mem. Am. Congress Rehab. Medicine, Am. Acad. Phys. Medicine and Rehab., Am. Spinal Injury Assn., Nat. Rehab. Assn., Assn. Acad. Physiatrists. Democrat. Office: Dept of Physical Medicine and Rehabilitation University Hospital Ann Arbor MI 48109 *As a physiatrist be sensitive, askable, flexible, negotiable, creative, enthusiastic and sincere. Understand your own attitudes, values, limits and strengths in order to help others without imposing upon them. Place a high value on humanness. Acknowledge discomfort and pain, including your own. Carry a low burden of guilt or envy for the circumstances of other people. Lastly, trust people to accept responsibility for themselves.*

COLE, THOMAS WINSTON, JR., college president, chemist; b. Vernon, Tex., Jan. 11, 1941; s. Thomas Winston and Eva Mae (Sharp) C.; m. Brenda S. Hill, June 14, 1964; children: Kelley S., Thomas Winston. B.S., Wiley Coll., Marshall, Tex., 1961; Ph.D., U. Chgo., 1966. Mem. faculty Atlanta U., 1966-82, prof. chemistry, chmn. dept., 1971-82, Fuller E. Callaway prof., 1969-80, project dir. Resource Ctr. Sci. and Engring., 1978-82, univ. provost, v.p. acad. affairs, 1979-82; pres. W.Va. State Coll., Institute, 1982—; vis. prof. U. Ill., summer 1972, MIT, 1973-74; summer chemist Miami Valley Lab. Procter and Gamble co., 1967; Celanese Corp., Charlotte, N.C., 1974, UNCF lectr., 1975-84. Mem. Leadership Atlanta; chmn. environ. protection com. Neighborhood Planning Unit. So. Regional fellow, summer 1961; Woodrow Wilson fellow, 1961-62; Allied Chem. fellow, 1963; Danforth assoc., 1971—. Mem. Am. Chem. Soc., AAAS, Nat. Inst. Sci., Nat. Orgn. Profl. Advancement Black Chemists and Chem. Engrs., Ga. Acad. Sci., Sigma Xi, Sigma Pi Phi, Alpha Phi Alpha. Lodge: Rotary. Home: Upper Washington Ave Institute WV 25112 Office: WVa State Coll PO Box 572 Institute WV 25112

COLE, TODD G., financial company executive; b. Coushatta, La., Mar. 5, 1921; s. Ira and Lucie (Tricke); m. Inez Hamilton, Feb. 9, 1953 (div. 1974); children: Michael H., Diane Cole Janusz; m. Josephine Giovanetti, Oct. 1974; children: Paola Smith, Leda Sanford. Student, La. State U., 1935-37; LL.B., Woodrow Wilson Coll., 1947. C.P.A. With Delta Airlines, 1940-63, dir., exec. v.p. adminstrn., 1959-63; sr. v.p. finance and adminstrn., dir. Eastern Airlines, 1963-67, vice chmn., chmn. finance com., dir., 1967-69; v.p., asst. to pres. C.I.T. Financial Corp., N.Y.C., 1969, v.p. fin., 1969-71, mem. exec. com., 1970—, exec. v.p., 1971-73, pres., chief adminstrv. officer, 1973-80, pres., chief operating officer, 1980—, also dir.; dir. Emery Air Freight. Mem. Ga. Bar Assn. Office: 650 CIT Dr Livingston NJ 07039

COLE, W. STORRS, paleontologist, geomorphologist; b. Albany, N.Y., July 16, 1902; s. Frederick Willard and Edna (Storrs) C.; m. Gladys Florine Watt, June 3, 1926 (dec. 1979). B.S., Cornell U., 1925, M.S., 1928, Ph.D., 1930. Paleontologist Huasteca Petroleum Co., Tampico, Mex., 1926-27, Sun Oil Co., Dallas, 1930-31; research asso. in paleontology Scripps Inst. Oceanography, U. Calif., summers 1931, 35; cons. paleontologist Fla. Geol. Survey, 1929-47; instr. geomorphology Cornell U., 1928-30, Ohio State U., 1931-37, asst. prof., 1937-43, asso. prof., 1943-45, prof., 1945-46; geologist U.S. Geol. Survey, 1947-74; prof. Cornell U., 1946-68, prof. emeritus, 1968—, chmn. geol. dept., 1947-62; mem. geol. and geog. sect. NRC, 1944-47. Contbr. articles to sci. jours. Mem. N.Y. State Museum Adv. Council, 1958-63; bd. dirs. Cushman Found. for Foraminiferal Research, 1951-75, pres., 1953-54, hon. trustee, 1975—, recipient Cushman award, 1983. Fellow Geol. Soc. Am. (3d v.p. 1954), Am. Assn. Geographers, Paleontol. Soc. (pres. 1953), Paleontol. Research Inst., Ohio Acad. Sci. (v.p. 1939), Sigma Xi, Sigma Gamma Epsilon, Gamma Alpha (hon.), Acacia. Lodge: Masons. Home: 310 Fall Creek Dr Ithaca NY 14850 also 10875 Coggins Dr Sun City AZ 85351

COLE, WARD KENNETH, musician; b. Helena, Mont., Jan. 17, 1922; s. Ward B. and Helen H. (Reeves) C.; m. Carolyn Jean Clark, Nov. 14, 1947. B.A., U. Wash., 1948; postgrad., Juilliard Sch. Music, 1951; M.A. (Univ. fellow), Tchrs. Coll. Columbia U., 1952, Ed.D., 1954. Prof. music, chmn. dept. music Frostburg State Coll., 1956-64; asso. prof. U. Toronto, Ont., Can., 1964-68; prof., chmn. dept. music U. Calgary, Alta., Can., 1968-73, prof., 1973-82; sec., treas. Alta. Music Conf., 1971-73; jazz editor Can. Band. Dirs. Jour., 1980—. Trumpeter, Seattle Symphony Orch., 1947-49, Ted Weems Orch., 1949-51, Radio City Music Hall, N.Y.C., 1952-56, Fred Waring Orch., 1954-56; arranger stage band series, Shawnee Press, Delaware Wategap, Pa., 1962-64; Composer: Blues Muse, 1963, Bobcat Rock, 1963, Brazilia, 1964. Served with USAAF, 1943-45. Recipient Deutscher Akademischer Austauschdienst Study award, 1974. Mem. Internat. Trumpet Guild (dir. 1975-77), Phi Delta Kappa, Kappa Delta Pi, Delta Upsilon, Phi Mu Alpha. Clubs: Masons, Shriners, Mont., Calgary Faculty. Home: 2719 17th Ave SW Apt. 326 Calgary AB T3C 6K5 Canada

COLE, WENDELL GORDON, speech and drama educator; b. Chgo., May 15, 1914; s. Herbert F. and Susan (Richards) C.; m. Charlotte Clarice Klein, Dec. 14, 1948. A.B., Albion (Mich.) Coll., 1936; A.M., U. Mich., 1937; Ph.D., Stanford, 1951. Mem. faculty Alma (Mich.) Coll., 1943-45; mem. faculty Stanford U., 1946—, prof. speech and drama, 1963—, exec. head dept., 1956-59, 64-65, 67-69, scene and costume designer, 1945—, acting chmn. dept. drama, 1972-73; chmn. dept. Standford U., 1982-83; scene designer West Bay Opera, 1975-81. Author: The Elements of Scene Design, 1962, Kyoto in the Momoyama Period, 1967, Theatre Architecture, 1970; Editor: The Story of The Meininger, 1963. Mem. Am. Theatre Assn., Soc. Archtl. Historians, U.S. Inst. Theatre Tech., Nat. Trust for Historic Preservation. Home: 853 Esplanada Way Stanford CA 94305

COLE, WILLIAM JAMES, III, state official; b. Jackson, Miss., June 24, 1948; s. William J. and Margaret E. (Moore) C.; m. Deborah Ballard, June 6, 1968. A.A., Hinds Jr. Coll., 1968; B.Public Adminstrn., U. Miss., 1970, J.D., 1974. Bar: Miss. 1974. Mem. staff Miss. State Senate, 1972; legis. asst. to Rep. Charles Griffin, 1972; spl. asst. atty. gen. State of Miss., 1974-77, exec. asst. atty. gen., 1977-79; exec. asst., chief of staff Gov. of Miss., 1979-80; state treas. of Miss., Jackson, 1980—; mem. Miss. State Bond Commn., Public Employees Retirement System Bd. Bd. dirs. Hinds Jr. Coll. Devel. Found., 1979—, pres., 1980; chmn. membership com. Miss. Kidney Found., 1981; bd. dirs. Miss. Soc. Prevention Blindness; mem. Miss. State Democratic Exec. Com., 1980—; del. Miss. Dem. Conv., 1980. Mem. Am. Bar Assn., Miss. Bar Assn., Nat. Assn. State Treas. (v.p.), Hind Jr. Coll. Alumni Assn. (pres. 1980-81). Methodist. Club: Rotary. Home: 906 Madison St Jackson MS 39202 Office: PO Box 138 Jackson MS 39205

COLE, WILLIAM KAUFMAN, lawyer; b. Hartford, Conn., Oct. 5, 1914; s. Francis Watkinson and Grace (Kaufman) C.; m. Julia Emily Kistler, May 29, 1942 (div. 1955); children: David Brockway, Frank Kistler; m. Marion Beach, June 22, 1957. B.A., Yale U., 1936, LL.B., 1939. Bar: Conn. 1939, U.S. Supreme Ct. 1954. Tchr. Laguna Blanca Sch., Santa Barbara, Calif., 1940-42; asso. firm Robinson, Robinson & Cole, Hartford, 1942-48, partner, 1949-79, retired partner, 1980—; dir. Covenant Mut. Ins. Co. Pres. Legal Aid Soc., Hartford County, 1958-62; pres. YMCA of Greater Hartford, 1964-66; trustee McLean Fund, Simsbury, Conn., 1967—, chmn., 1980—; bd. dirs. Hartford Hosp., 1958—, vice chmn., chmn., 1961-76; chmn. bd. trustees Conn. Hosp. Assn., 1977-78; bd. dirs. Westchester and So. Conn. Community Health Plans, chmn., 1980-81. Served with S.C. AUS, 1942-45. Fellow Am. Bar Found. (state chmn.); mem. Am. Law Inst., Am. Bar Assn., Conn. Bar Assn. (pres. 1974-75), Hartford County Bar Assn. (pres. 1963-64). Republican. Congregationalist. Clubs: Hartford, Univ. Hartford; Dauntless (Essex, Conn.); Doolittle (Norfolk, Conn.). Office: 799 Main St Hartford CT 06103

COLE, WILLIAM PORTER, librarian; b. St. Louis, Sept. 11, 1929; s. Saxon and Mary Porter (Moore) C.; m. Alexandra Melpomene Vasos, June 9, 1973; children—Julia Ellen, William Kendall, Heather, Jason Antares. B.A., Washington U., St. Louis, 1952; M.A.L.S., U. Mich., 1962. Pres. Cole Bros. Constrn. Co., Inc., St. Louis County, Mo., 1950-61; adminstrv. asst. Washington U., 1962-63, asso. dir. libraries, 1968-70, dir. libraries, 1970—; mng. editor Library Tech. Reports, ALA, Chgo., 1964-68. Served with USAF, 1948-49. Home: 701 Cherry Tree Ln Olivette MO 63132 Office: Pius XII Meml Library 3655 W Pine Blvd Saint Louis MO 63108

COLECCHIA, FRANCESCA MARIA, educator; b. Pitts.; d. Albert and Ambrosina (Donatelli) C. B.E., Duquesne U.; M.Litt., Ph.D., U. Pitts.; postgrad., Universidad Autonoma Mex.; fellow, Universidad Central del Educador, 1962. Prof. modern langs. Duquesne U., Pitts., chmn. dept., 1977—, dir. lang. lab. programs, 1960-72; asso. editor Duquesne Hispanic Rev., 1961-72, Estudios (Duquesne U.); Fulbright lectr., Colombia, 1963-64; vis. prof. Mt. Mercy Coll., Pitts., spring 1968; lectr. East Carolina U., 1969. Author: Repaso Breve, 1962, Repaso Oral, 1967, Paisajes y Personajes Latinoamericanos, 1971, Selected Latin American One-Act Plays, 1972, Federico Garcia Lorca: An Annotated Bibliography of Criticism, 1979, Federico Garcia Lorca: An Annotated Primary Bibliography, 1981; asso. editor: Garcia Lorca Rev.; contbr. articles to profl. publs. Mem. Atty. Gen.'s Task Force design regional treatment center for women, 1969; bd. dirs., Western regional v.p. Pa. Program for Women and Girl Offenders, Inc., Female Offenders Program. Western Pa. recipient commendation scroll Asociacion Colombiana de Profesores de Ingles, 1964; Amita nat. award for contbns. to edn., 1969; U.S. Office Edn. Inst. grantee, 1971. Mem. AAUW (Pitts. 1st v.p. 1965-67, dir. 1961—, co-chmn. coll. faculty program Pitts. br., pres. br. 1968-70, coll. faculty program com. Pa. div., mem. fellowship com. Pa. div. 1969-70), MLA (v.p. Pitts., mem. Del. Assembly 1978-80), Nat. Assn. Lang. Lab. Dirs. (editor secondary sch. directory), Latin Am. Studies Assn., Am. Assn. Tchrs. Spanish and Portuguese, Inst. Internacional de Literatura Iberoamericana, Asociacion Internacional de Hispanistas, Adminstrv. Women Edn., Delta Kappa Gamma (Pa. profl. affairs com. 1977-79), Sigma Kappa Phi, Phi Kappa Phi, Sigma Tau Delta, Phi Sigma Iota. Club: Zonta (pres. Pitts. 1981-82). Home: 401 Lexington Ave Pittsburgh PA 15215 *If what a man is and the position he occupies depend on the influence of another, rather than on his own merits, he is nowhere and nothing.*

COLEMAN, ALBERT JOHN, mathematics educator; b. Toronto, Ont., Can., May 20, 1918; s. Frank and Phoebe (Gerrard) C.; m. Marie-Jeanne Michele de Haller, July 23, 1953; children: William Frank, Michael Haller. B.A., Univ. Coll., Toronto, 1939; M.A., Princeton U., 1942; Ph.D., U. Toronto, 1943. Dir. Internat. Student Centre, Queen's U., Kingston, Ont., 1962-80; travelling sec. World's Student Christian Fedn., Geneva, 1945-49; successively lectr., asst. prof., asso. prof. U. Toronto, 1949-60; vis. prof. Dublin Inst. Advanced Study, 1952; prof. math. Queen's U., Kingston, 1960—, head dept., 1960-80; cons. alt. energy Fed. Ministry of Energy, Mines and Resources; mem. Sci. Council of Can., 1973-77, Natural Scis. and Engring. Research Council, 1982—. Author: The Task of the Christian in the University, 1947, also math articles and, high sch. textbooks. Lay del. Lambeth Conf., 1978. Mem. Can. Math. Congress (pres. 1973-75), Internat. Math. Union (chmn. exchange commn. 1975-78). Anglican. Home: 185 Ontario St Kingston ON Canada K7L 2V7

COLEMAN, ALMAND ROUSE, educator; b. Smithfield, Va., July 16, 1905; s. Archer Almand and Ruby Booth (Rouse) C.; m. Clare Merryman Whitfield, April 13, 1940 (dec. Jan. 1961); children: Lisa Coleman Rose, William Stephen; m. Louise Hudson Foster, May 21, 1962; stepchildren: Emily (Mrs. John Pickering), Edmund Palmer Foster, George William Foster; 1 son, Charles Almand. A.B., Washington and Lee U., 1926, B.S. in Commerce, 1927, LL.D., 1977; M.B.A., Harvard U., 1934. C.P.A., Va. Asst. to treas. Washington and Lee U., 1926-28; sr. accountant A.M. Pullen & Co., Richmond, Va., 1928-33; acting chief financial analysis and statis. Farm Credit Adminstrn., Washington, 1934-35; asst. trust officer, asst. cashier State Planters Bank and Trust Co., Richmond, 1935-39; asso. prof. Washington and Lee U., 1939-41, prof. accounting, 1941-55; Disting. lectr. accounting, 1979—; vis. prof. accounting Harvard Bus. Sch., 1954-55; prof. bus. adminstrn. U. Va. Grad. Sch. Bus., Charlottesville, 1955-72, Charles C. Abbott prof., 1972-76, prof. emeritus, 1976—; vis. prof. bus. adminstrn. Tenn. Tech. U., 1976-78, Disting. vis. prof., 1978-79. Author: Financial Accounting: A General Management Approach, 1970, (with Brownlee and Smith) Financial Accounting for Management, 1980, Financial Accounting and Statement Analysis: A Manager's Guide, 1982; contbr. to bus. and profl. jours. Served to maj. Ordnance U.S. Army, 1942-45; lt. col. Res., 1950-54. Mem. Am. Inst. C.P.A.'s (accounting procedure com. 1953-56), Am. Accounting Assn. (v.p. 1956), Financial Execs. Inst., Raven Soc., Phi Beta Kappa. Episcopalian. Home: 1867 Field Rd Charlottesville VA 22903

COLEMAN, AMOSS LEE, educator, sociologist; b. Devereaux, Ga., Jan. 3, 1913; s. John Amoss and Magnolia (Lee) C.; m. Alberta Louise Nelson, Dec. 11, 1943; children—Nancy Louise, Martha Lee. B.A., Emory U., 1937; M.A., U. N.C., 1940; Ph.D., Cornell U., 1949. Research analyst Govtl. Research Inst., St. Louis, 1938-39; social sci. analyst, farm population, rural life br. U.S. Dept. Agr., Atlanta, also Freeport, Ill., 1939-42, 45-46; grad. asst. dept. rural sociology Cornell U., 1946-49; asst. prof. U. Ky., 1949-53, asso. prof., 1953-57, prof., 1957—, head, later chmn. dept. sociology, 1959-66; cons. So. Regional Council, State Commn. on Human Rights, Civil Rights div. U.S. Dept. Justice, NSF; state adv. com. U.S. Civil Rights Commn., 1963—. Contbr. profl. jours. Served with AUS, 1942-45. Mem. Am. Sociol. Assn., Rural Sociol. Soc. (pres. 1964-65), So. Sociol. Soc. (pres. 1966-67), North Central Sociol. Soc. Democrat. Home: 316 Cassidy Ave Lexington KY 40502

COLEMAN, BERNELL, physiologist; b. Jefferson County, Miss., Apr. 26, 1929; s. Percy and Julia (Nailor) C.; m. Annie C. Richardson, Jan. 30, 1962; children—Rochelle, Ronald. B.S., Alcorn A. and M. Coll., 1952; Ph.D. (Univ. fellow), Loyola U. Stritch Sch. Medicine, Chgo., 1964. Research asst. in biochemistry U. Chgo., 1956-57; research in cancer Hines (Ill.) VA Hosp., 1957-59; instr. St. Louis U. Sch. Medicine, 1963-65, asst. prof. physiology, 1965-67; asst. prof. Chgo. Med. Sch., 1967-69, asso. prof., 1969-76, prof., 1976, Howard U. Coll. Medicine, Washington, 1976—, chmn. dept. physiology and biophysics, 1979—; lectr. Cook County Grad. Sch. Medicine, U. Ill. Med. Sch.; vis. prof. Rush Med. Coll. Served with U.S. Army, 1953-56; Korea. Recipient research award Chgo. Med. Sch. Bd. Trustees, 1975; NIH research fellow, 1960-61; NIH grantee, 1966-68, 69-74, 74-76, 79—; USPHS fellow, 1961-63; Dept. Def. grantee, 1965-67. Mem. AAUP, Am. Physiol. Soc., Am. Heart Assn., AAAS, Fedn. Am. Socs. Exptl. Biology, Sigma Xi, Phi Rho Sigma. Democrat. Research, numerous publs. in cardiovascular physiology. Home: 14200 Myer Terr Rockville MD 20853 Office: 520 W St NW Washington DC 20059

COLEMAN, BRUCE TAYLOR, computer software company executive; b. Melrose, Mass., Mar. 25, 1939; s. Phillip A. and Elinor (Gay) C.; m. Pamela Morton, Oct. 24, 1970. B.A. in Econs., Trinity Coll., Hartford, Conn., 1961; M.B.A., Harvard U., 1969. Mktg. rep. IBM, 1961-67; dir. mktg., treas. Logic Electronics Inc., 1969-71; pres. Boole & Babbage, Inc., 1971-77; group v.p. Informatics, Inc., 1977-81; exec. v.p. Informatics Gen. Corp., Woodland Hills, Calif., 1981-83, pres., chief operating officer, 1983—, also dir.; dir. Printronix, Inc., Irvine, Calif., 1975. Bd. dirs. Vis. Nurses Assn., Sunnyvale, Calif., 1978—, pres., Sunnyvale, Calif., 1976-77, treas., Sunnyvale, Calif., 1974-75. Served with NG USAF, 1962-68. Baker scholar, 1969. Mem. Young Pres. Orgn., ADAPSO (dir.). Office: Informatic General Corp 21031 Ventura Blvd Woodland Hills CA 91364 *

COLEMAN, CECIL NOBLE, athletic director, university administrator; b. South Bend, Ind., Apr. 12, 1924; s. Cecil Noble and Cleo (Hoover) C.; m. Margaret Foote, June 2, 1945; children: Peggy Ann, Pamela Elizabeth. B.A., Ariz. State U., 1950, M.A., 1953. Coach football North Phoenix High Sch., 1950-55, Long Beach Community Coll., 1955-56, Ariz. State U., 1956-59, Fresno State Coll., 1959-71, dir. athletics, 1964-71, Wichita State U., 1971-72, U. Ill., Champaign, 1972-79, asst. to vice chancellor, 1979—; bd. visitors U.S. Sports Acad. Commr. Midwestern City Conf., 1980—. Served with USMC, 1942-46. Mem. Nat. Assn. Collegiate Dirs. Athletics (pres. 1972-73), Nat. Collegiate Athletic Assn. (mem. council 1976-78), Nat. Phys. Edn. Assn. Republican. Mormon. Home: 509 Park Ln Dr Champaign IL 61820 Office: 1205 W Oregon St Urbana IL 61801

COLEMAN, CHARLES CLYDE, physicist, educator; b. York, Eng., July 31, 1937; came to U.S., 1941; s. Jesse C. and Geraldine (Doherty) C.; m. Sharon R. Slutsky, Aug. 12, 1976; children: Jeffrey Andrew, Matthew Casey. B.A., UCLA, 1959, M.A., 1961, Ph.D., 1968. Asst. prof. physics Calif. State U., Los Angeles, 1968-71, assoc. prof, 1971-76, prof., 1976—; cons. Gen. Dynamics Corp., 1975-77, China Lake Naval Research Labs., 1981; dir. Csula Accelerator Facility; exec. dir. Applied Physics Inst.; sr. research fellow Cambridge (Eng.) U., 1975-76. Contbr. articles to sci. publs. Trustee Calif. State U. Los Angeles Found. NSF grantee, 1976—; NATO Sr. fellow, 1983-84. Fellow Brit. Interplanetary Soc.; mem. Am. Physics Soc., Sigma Xi, Sigma Pi Sigma. Office: Dept Physics Calif State U Los Angeles CA 90032

COLEMAN, CLAIR FLYGARE, gas company executive; b. Ogden, Utah, May 16, 1928; s. Clyde and Jennis (Flygare) C.; m. Kaye Martin, Aug. 26, 1949; children: Rich Flygare, John P., Jolie Coleman Howard. B.S. in Math., U. Utah, 1951; M.S. in Mech. Engring., 1957. Exec. asst. distbn. Mountain Fuel Supply Co., Salt Lake City, 1963-65, gen. mgr. distbg. ops., 1965-68; v.p. distbg. ops. Mountain FuelSupply Co., Salt Lake City, 1968-74; sr. v.p. distbg. ops. Mountain Fuel Supply Co., Salt Lake City, 1974-76, sr. v.p., co. ops., 1976-80; pres. and chief exec. officer transmission div. Mountain Fuel Supply Co. and MF Resources Inc., 1980—, dir., 1975—, Mountain Fuel Resources Inc., 1975—. Mem. adv. council Utah State U., Logan; mem. bus. and econ. adv. council Weber State Coll., Ogden, Utah. Served to 1st lt. with AUS, 1946-48; Korea. Mem. Inst. Gas Tech. (trustee 1983), Am. Gas Assn. (mng. com.), Pacific Coast Gas Assn. (exec. com., Basford Trophy 1974). Club: Alta (Salt Lake City). Office: Mountain Fuel Resources Inc 79 S State St Salt Lake City UT 84147

COLEMAN, CLARENCE, banker; b. Wichita, Kans., Mar. 24, 1909; s. William Coffin and Fanny Lucinda (Sheldon) C.; m. Emry Regester Inghram, Oct. 2, 1935; children—Rochelle, Pamela, Kathryn Sheldon. Student, U. Kans., 1928-32; LL.D., Ottawa U., 1973; D.H.L., Friends U.; D. Laws, Ottawa U. With Coleman Co., Inc., Wichita, 1932—, v.p. charge mfg., 1944, dir., 1935—, asst. gen. mgr., 1951-54; pres. Union Nat. Bank, Wichita, 1957-72, vice chmn. bd., 1972—; chmn. bd., dir. Cherry Creek Inn, Inc., Denver, 1961-69, Kans. Devel. Credit Corp. Bd. dirs. Inst. Logopedics, 1940-74, chmn. bd., 1947-48; bd. dirs. Wichita Symphony Soc.; trustee Wichita Symphony Soc. Found.; bd. dirs. Found. for Study of Cycles, Pitts., Wichita Mental Health Assn., 1956-74, United Fund Wichita and Sedgewick County, 1957-74, Friends U., 1956-74, Wichita Crime Commn., 1953-74; pres. Wichita Crime Commn., 1958; mem. Nat. Budget Com., 1952; chmn. State Mental Health Fund Kans., 1953; Trustee Peddie Sch., Hightstown, N.J., chmn. bd. trustees, 1972-76, chmn. emeritus, 1981. Mem. Mid-Ark. Valley Devel. Assn. (treas.), Wichita C. of C. (pres. 1956, dir. 1947-74), Phi Kappa Psi. Club: Rotarian. Home: 530 Broadmoor Ct Wichita KS 67206 Office: 1005 Union Center Wichita KS 67202

COLEMAN, CY, pianist, composer, producer; b. N.Y.C., June 14, 1929; s. Max and Ida (Prizent) Kaufman. Diploma, N.Y. Coll. Music, 1948; pupil, Rudolph Gruen, Adele Marcus, Bernard Wagenaar, Hall Overton. Pres. Notable Music Co., Notable Records Co. Pianist night clubs, throughout U.S., 1948—; TV appearances on Dumont, 1947-48, Date in Manhattan, 1948-51, Kate Smith Show, 1951-52, Art Ford Greenwich Village Party, 1957-58; contbr.: music John Murray Anderson's Almanac, 1953; background music to Compulsion, 1957; now appearing with, Coleman Collection Milw. Symphony Orch., Syracuse (N.Y.) Symphony Pops Orch., Detroit Symphony Orch., Indpls. Symphony Orch., San Antonio Symphony Orch., Ft. Worth, Edmonton (Can.), New Orleans, Toledo, Tulsa, Hartford Pops, Grand Rapids, Honolulu, Middletown and Spokane symphony orchs.; composer: music for Broadway shows Wildcat, 1960, Little Me, 1962, Sweet Charity, See-Saw, 1973, I Love My Wife, 1977, On the Twentieth Century, 1978, Barnum, 1980, 1966/theme Heartbreak Kid; motion pictures Sweet Charity, N.Y.C., 1965-66; movie version, 1969; rec. artist for, Westminster, Capitol, Columbia, M.G.M., London records; (Recipient Interborough awards Music Edn. League 1934, 35, 36, LaGuardia Meml. award 1961, 2 Emmy awards for TV spl. If They Could See Me Now 1974, Emmy award for Gypsy in My Soul 1975, Drama Desk award for best score I Love My Wife 1977, Cue mag. Golden Apple award for best score I Love My Wife 1977, Tony award Best Score for On the Twentieth Century 1977-78); Composer: popular songs Why Try to Change Me Now, 1952, I'm Gonna Laugh You Out of My Life, 1955, Witchcraft, 1957, Firefly, 1958, It Amazes Me, 1958, You Fascinate Me So, 1958, The Best is Yet to Come, 1959, The Riviera, 1959, Play Boy Theme, 1960, Rules of the Road, 1961, Pass Me By, Pussy Cat, Hey Look Me Over, Big Spender, If My Friends Could See Me Now, Nobody Does It Like Me, I Love My Wife, Hey There Good Times. Mem. ASCAP (dir.), Acad. Motion Picture Arts and Scis., Dramatists Guild (dir.). Office: 161 W 54th St New York NY 10019

COLEMAN, D. JACKSON, ophthalmologist, educator; b. Waverly, N.Y., Dec. 1, 1934; s. Max Elliot and Frances Agnes (Henton) C.; m. Jane Marie Holmes, July 6, 1963; children: Jeffrey, Jonathan, Jeremy. B.S., Union Coll., 1956; M.D., U. Buffalo, 1960. Intern Columbia Med. Div., Bellevue Hosp., N.Y.C., 1960-61; lt. comdr. USPHS Bur. State Services Heart Disease Control Program, Washington, 1961-64; resident in ophthalmology Edward S. Harkness Eye Inst., Columbia Presbyn. Med. Center, N.Y.C., 1964-67, mem. faculty, staff, 1967-79; John Milton McLean prof. Cornell U. Med. Coll., N.Y.C., 1979—; chmn. dept. ophthalmology N.Y. Hosp.-Cornell Med. Center, 1979—, ophthalmologist-in-chief, 1979—. Sr. author: Ultrasonography of Eye and Orbit, 1977; contbr. articles to med. jours. Recipient Wacker award of Club Jules Gonin Internat. Retina Soc., 1976; NIH grantee. Fellow A.C.S., Am. Acad. Ophthalmology; mem. Am. Inst. Ultrasound Medicine (bd. govs. 1970-73), Societas Interationalis de Diagnostic Ultrasonica in Ophthalmology (exec. bd. 1971-81), World Fedn. Ultrasound Medicine and Biology (exec. bd. 1973-82, sec.treas. 1973-77, treas. 1977-82), Am. Intraocular Lens Soc. (sci. advisor 1976-79), Am. Soc. Ophthalmic Ultrasound (bd. govs. 1976—), AMA, N.Y. County Med. Soc., Assn. for Research in Vision and Ophthalmology, Retina Soc., Am. Eye Study Club, Club Jules Gonin. Republican. Methodist. Office: NY Hosp-Cornell Med Center 525 E 68th St New York NY 10021

COLEMAN, DABNEY W., actor; b. Austin, Tex., Jan. 3, 1932; s. Melvin Randolph and Mary (Johns) C.; m. Ann Courney Harrell, Dec.

21, 1957 (div. June 1959); children: Kelly Johns, Randolph, Mary; m. 2d Carol Jean Hale, Dec. 11, 1961 (div.). Student, Va. Mil. Inst., 1949-51, U. Tex., 1951-57, Neighborhood Playhouse Sch. Theatre, 1958-60. Self-employed actor N.Y., Los Angeles, 1960—. Films include This Property is Condemned, The Slender Thread, The Scalp Hunters, The Other Side of the Mountain, The Black Streetfighter, Rolling Thunder, Viva Knievell, North Dallas Forty, Nothing Personal, How to Beat the High Cost of Living, Melvin and Howard, Nine to Five, Tootsie, War Games, Cloak and Dagger; TV includes Mary Hartman, Forever Fernwood, Apple Pie, When She Was Bad, Buffalo Bill; author: two scripts Bright Promise, NBC, 1972. Served with U.S. Army, 1953-55. Recipient Emmy nomination for Buffalo Bill, 1983. Mem. Phi Delta Theta. Episcopalian. Home: 723 Pacific Coast Hwy Los Angeles CA 90402

COLEMAN, D'ALTON CORRY, transportation company executive; b. Edmonton, Alta., Can., Feb. 19, 1936; s. James Alexander and Phillis D. (Rigby) C.; m. Shirley Mae Caruk, Mar. 9, 1957; children: Mitchell James, Kelly Elizabeth. B.A., U. Western Ont., 1968, M.B.A., 1970. Indsl. sales rep. Canadian Johns-Manville Co., Toronto, 1957-69; analyst corp. research Consumers Gas, Toronto, 1969-70; sales mgr. Labatt's Ltd., Toronto, 1970-72; asst. mgr. freight sales CP Rail, Toronto, 1972-73, gen. mgr. mktg. and sales, 1974-76, Montreal, 1976-78, asst. v.p., 1978-81, v.p. eastern region, Toronto, 1981—; v.p., dir. Toronto Ham. & Buffalo Rwy. Co., 1981—; dir. Toronto Terminals Rwy. Co. Officer Brother Order of St. John; mem. Bd. Trade Met. Toronto, Ont. Bus. Devel. Adv. Council, Toronto Redevel. Adv. Council. Clubs: Toronto Traffic, Canadian Rwy., Toronto Squash, U. Western Ont. Alumni. Home: 419 Ontario St Toronto ON Canada Office: CP Rail Rm 354 Union Station Toronto ON Canada M5J 1E8

COLEMAN, DANIEL JOSEPH, II, publisher; b. Clare, Iowa, May 12, 1932; s. Daniel Joseph and Geneva B. (Krebs) C.; children: Daniel, Colin, Dion, Mary Rose, Christina. B.A., U. Notre Dame, 1954. Sales rep. Better Homes and Gardens, Des Moines, 1954-57; mktg. mgr. Popular Mechanics, N.Y.C., 1957-65, Eastern div. sales mgr., 1965-67, dir. advt. sales, 1967-79, assoc. pub., 1979-81, v.p., pub., 1981—. Mem. Automotive Parts and Accessories Assn. (v.p., dir.). Clubs: Nassau Country (Glen Cove, N.Y.); Wings (N.Y.C.). Home: 87-01 Midland Pkwy Jamaica Estates NY 11432 Office: Popular Mechanics 224 W 57th St New York NY 10019

COLEMAN, E. THOMAS, congressman; b. Kansas City, Mo., May 29, 1943; s. Earl T. and Marie (Carlson) C.; m. Marilyn Anderson, June 8, 1968; children: Julie Anne, Emily Catherine, Megan Marie. A.B. in Econs., William Jewell Coll., 1965; M.P.A., NYU, 1969; J.D., Washington U., 1969. Bar: Mo. 1969. Practiced in Gladstone, 1973-76, asst. atty. gen., Mo., 1969-73; mem. Mo. Ho. of Reps., 1973-76, 95th-98th Congresses from 6th Mo. Dist., mem. agr., edn. and labor coms.; chmn. Republican Task Force on Fgn. Policy. Office: 2344 Rayburn House Office Bldg Washington DC 20515

COLEMAN, EARL MAXWELL, publishing company executive; b. N.Y.C., Jan. 9, 1916; s. Samuel Sidney and Rose (Ensleman) C.; m. Frances Louise Allan, Mar. 23, 1942 (div. Mar. 15, 1965); children: Allan Douglass, Dennis Scott; m. Ellen Schneid, Aug. 19, 1973. Student, NYU, 1933-34, CCNY, 1934-35, Columbia U., 1946. Founder, pres. Plenum Pub. Corp. (and predecessors), N.Y.C., 1946-77, chmn. bd. dirs., 1960-77, cons., 1977—; founder Earl M. Coleman Enterprises, Inc. (Pubs.), 1977—. Contbr. poems, short stories to mags. Served with USAAF, 1941-45. Mem. Info. Industry Assn. (dir. 1971—), Assn. Am. Publishers (exec. com. tech.-sci.-med. div. 1970—), Sci. Tech. Med. Publishers (Holland). Home: White Gates W Mt Airy Rd Croton-on-Hudson NY 10520 Office: PO Box T Crugers NY 10521 *Do whatever you do passionately. Never be astonished at the fact that literally all the worldly affairs with which humans busy themselves and into which they pour so much energy, are games, sometimes bloody games, but games. Not only does the passionate player have a greater chance to get ahead in the game, he also enjoys it more than the passive player. Only the person who is willing to be stark naked before his own eyes, which can be the cruelest of mirrors, gets to savor his life to the fullest. Here too, passion serves, for ruthless honesty with self is key to an honest appraisal of anything else.*

COLEMAN, EDMUND BENEDICT, univ. dean; b. Columbia, S.C., Mar. 29, 1926; s. Edmund Benedict and Evelyn (Russell) C.; m. Fumiko Toyoshita, Jan. 1, 1953; children: Meri, John Edmund, Evelyn. B.S., U. S.C., 1958; Ph.D., Johns Hopkins U., 1961. Research scientist Humrro, Ft. Bliss, Tex., 1961-62; asso. prof. Sul Ross State Coll., Alpine, Tex., 1962-64, N.Mex. State U., Las Cruces, 1964-64; prof. psychology, chmn. dept. U. Tex. at El Paso, 1965-67, grad. dean, 1967—. Mem. Nat. Reading Conf., Phi Beta Kappa, Sigma Xi. Spl. research pre-sch. reading. Home: 1001 Baltimore St El Paso TX 79902

COLEMAN, ELIZABETH, college dean; b. N.Y.C., Nov. 23, 1937; d. Lewis and Sophie (Brantman) Ginsburg; m. Aaron Coleman, June 14, 1959; children: Daniel, David. B.A., U. Chgo., 1958; M.A., Cornell U., 1959; Ph.D., Columbia U., 1965. Instr. humanities SUNY, N.Y.C., 1960-65; assoc. dean faculty New Sch. Social Research, N.Y.C., 1966-76, dean Coll. Arts and Scis., 1977—; vis. lectr. Hebrew U., 1972, SUNY-Stony Brook, 1975; curriculum cons. Howard U., 1973; chmn. outside evaluating com. CUNY, 1976. Contbr. articles to profl. pubs. Fellow Ford Found., 1954-58; Woodrow Wilson fellow, 1958-59; F.J.E. Woodbridge fellow Columbia U., 1963-64; Pres.'s fellow Columbia U., 1964-65. Mem. MLA, Nat. Assn. Acad. Deans, Nat. Assn. Women Deans, Am. Assn. Colls (oversight com. 1982—). Office: New Sch Social Research 66 W 12th St New York NY 10011

COLEMAN, FRANCIS CARTER, physician, educator; b. Jackson, Miss., May 14, 1915; s. Francis Marion and Emma (Carter) C.; m. Ruth Yvonne Ellzey, Sept. 2, 1937; children: Nancy Ruth, Stephen Carter, John Timothy, Jeanne Laurie. B.A., Miss. Coll., 1935; M.D., Tulane U., 1941. Diplomate: Am. Bd. Pathology, sec.-treas., 1973, pres., 1973-75, life trustee, 1976—. Intern Touro Infirmary, New Orleans, 1941-42, resident pathology, 1942-45; individual practice medicine, Des Moines, 1946-64; dir. dept. pathology Mercy Hosp., Des Moines, 1946-64; asst. clin. prof. pathology U. Nebr. Coll. Medicine, 1951; clin. prof. pathology U. Iowa Coll. Medicine, 1964-65; pvt. practice, Tampa, Fla., 1964—; dir. Tampa Sch. Med. Tech., 1964—; mem. staff Centro-Asturiano Hosp., Tampa, Centro-Espanol Hosp., Hillsborough Ct. Hosp., Citrus Meml. Hosp., Inverness, Fla., Community Hosp. of New Port Richey, Fla., DeSoto Meml. Hosp., Arcadia, Fla., Tarpon Springs (Fla.) Gen. Hosp., G. Pierce Wood Meml. Hosp., Arcadia, Hardee Meml. Hosp., Wauchula, Fla., Jackson Meml. Hosp., Dade City, Fla.; clin. prof. pathology U. South Fla., 1973—; Dir. Patterson Coleman Labs., Tampa; Mem. Health Services Industry Com., Phase II, 1972-73; mem. nat. manpower adv. com. U.S. Dept. Labor, 1973-74; pres. Drug Abuse Comprehensive Coordination Office, Tampa, 1973-74; mem. spl. com. on nation's health care needs C. of C. of U.S., 1977-79; bd. regents Uniformed Services U. of Health Scis., 1982—. Bd. dirs. Gulf Symphony, pres., 1975-76, chmn. symphony master bd., 1978-79. Recipient Sci. Products award for outstanding service to pathology, 1965, Disting. Service award Am. Soc. Clin. Pathologists and Coll. Am. Pathologists, 1978; Spl. award Am. Pathology Found., 1979. Life Fellow Coll. Am. Pathologists (pres. 1960-61, chmn. council on govt. affairs 1972-78, vice chmn. 3d party reimbursement com. 1979-81, archivist and historian 1979—); Fellow Am. Soc. Clin. Pathologists, A.C.P., Am. Coll. Chest Physicians; mem. AMA (chmn. council legislative activities 1963-64, chmn. polit. action com. 1965-66, chmn. subcom. certification, registration and licensure of council health manpower 1967-73, chmn. council on health manpower 1973-74, Physician's recognition award in continuing med. edn. 1971—), Am. Assn. Blood Banks (pres. 1968-69), AAAS, Soc. Nuclear Medicine, Am. Soc. Cytology, Fla. Med. Assn. (chmn. com. blood 1969-73, alt. del. to AMA 1968—, chmn. council on legislation 1979-80, vice chmn. council 1980—, chmn. com. on nat. legislation 1980—, pres. Fla. med. polit. action com. 1980-83, exec. com. of bd. govs. 1981-82, pres.-elect 1983-84, pres. 1984-85), Hillsborough County Med. Assn. (ex-council 1969-70, pres. 1979-80), Tampa C. of C. (chmn. health care council 1969-74, gov. 1974-77), Tampa World Trade Council (exec. com. 1978-79). Club: Rotarian. Home: 16407 Zurraquin Ct Tampa FL 33612 Office: 4600 N Habana Ave Suite 21 Tampa FL 33614

COLEMAN, GEORGE, tenor and alto saxophonist; b. Memphis, Mar. 8, 1935; s. George and Indiana (Lyle) C.; m. Gloria Bell, Aug. 3, 1959; children—George, Gloria. Ed. pub. schs. Cons. Lenox (Mass.) Jazz Sch. Music, 1958—. Mem., Max Roach Quintet, 1958-59, Miles Davis Quintet, 1963-64, Lionel Hampton Orch., 1965-66, Lee Morgan Quintet, 1969, Elvin Jones Quartet, 1970, George Coleman Quartet, Quintet and Octet, 1974—; (Selected by Internat. Jazz Critics Poll 1958, named Artist of Year, Record World Mag. 1969, Knight of Mark Twain 1972, recipient award for contbns. to music Beale St. Assn. 1977, Tip of the Derby awards 1978, 79, N.Y. Jazz Audience award 1979); Composer, arranger mus. shows. Address: 331 E 14th St New York NY 10003

COLEMAN, GEORGE MELCHIADES, health planner; b. Washington, Apr. 26, 1926; s. George Melchiades and Annie Verdie (Walton) C.; m. Margaret Ann Bakeman, Sept. 24, 1949; children—Heather Lea Coleman Struck, Leslie Beryl Coleman Adkins, Eric Pelham, Sean Kenneth. Student, U. Va., 1943-44; B.A. in Fgn. Affairs, George Washington U., 1950; M.P.H., Johns Hopkins, 1974. Researcher Dept. Navy, Washington, 1950-56, Eastern Conf. Teamsters, 1956; occupational specialist USPHS, Washington, 1956-57; info. officer Pan Am. Health Orgn., Washington, 1957-59; asst. dir. pub. info. OAS, Washington, 1959-61; dir. Peace Corps for Brazil, Rio de Janeiro, 1961-64; spl. asst. to dir. NIMH, Bethesda, Md., 1964-65; adminstr. pub. health and population programs AID, U.S. Dept. State, Washington, 1965-76; dep. dir. Am. Tech. Assistance Center, Gen. Research Corp., McLean, Va., 1976-81; sr. asso. Devel. Assos., Arlington, Va., 1981—. Contbr. articles and trans. on sociology, internat. health programs, and mental health to profl. jours. Mem. Fairfax-Falls Church Mental Health and Mental Retardation Services Bd., 1972-76; chmn. internat. program commn. Unitarian-Universalist Service Com., Boston, 1972—. Served with USNR, 1943-46. Mem. Am. Pub. Health Assn. Unitarian. Club: Nat. Press. Home: 7815 Old Falls Rd McLean VA 22102 Office: Devel Assos 2924 Columbia Pike Arlington VA 22204

COLEMAN, HOWARD S., engineer, physicist; b. Everett, Pa., Jan. 10, 1917; s. Howard Solomon and Amy (Ritchey) C.; children: Michael Howard, Madeline Frances, Thomas Robert, Carl William, Stephen Mitchell Rosenberg; m. Jeannette Eve Dresher, Dec. 27, 1969. B.S., Pa. State U., 1938, M.S. in Physics, 1939, Ph.D., 1942. Registered profl. engr., Va., Ariz., Tex. Faculty Pa. State U., 1934-47, dir. optical inspection lab., 1941-47; dir. optical research lab., asso. prof. physics U. Tex., 1947-51; with Bausch & Lomb, Inc., 1951-62, mgr., v.p. research and engring., 1954-62; head physics research dept., tech. asst. to v.p. charge research Melpar, Inc., Falls Church, Va., 1962-64; dean U. Ariz. Coll. Engring., prof. elec. engring., 1964-68; dir. Spl. Projects Center, Schellenger Research Labs., U. Tex., El Paso, 1968-75, Howard S. Coleman and Assos., 1975—; dep. dir. solar energy div. ERDA, 1976-77; dep. dir. div. solar energy tech. U.S. Dept. Energy, 1977-78, dir. central solar tech. div., 1978-80, dir. tech. and utilization alcohol fuels, 1980-81, prin. dep. asst. sec. for conservation and renewable energy, 1981-84, dir. Div. Solar Thermal Tech., 1984—; cons. to industry, govt., 1941—; spl. research optical inspection devices; mem. Ariz. Bd. Tech. Registration.; Mem. adv. vis. com. electronics U. Rochester, 1952; chmn. vis. com. math. Clarkson Coll. Tech., 1953-63. Recipient Joint Service award, 1942. Fellow Optical Soc. Am.; mem. Am. Phys. Soc., Meteorol. Soc., Inst. Aero. Scis., Am. Assn. Physics Tchrs., Am. Soc. Metals, Internat. Commn. Optics, Am. Geophys. Union, Am. Inst. Physics, Am. Soc. Engring. Edn., Nat. Soc. Profl. Engrs., N.Y. Acad. Scis., Illuminating Engring. Soc., Soc. Photo-Optical Instrumentation Engrs. Patentee in field. Home: PO Box 26368 El Paso TX 79926 *One is not entitled to anything unless it is earned. The greatest satisfaction in life comes from the hard work that leads to a cherished objective.*

COLEMAN, JAMES COVINGTON, educator, author; b. Salem, N.H., Oct. 19, 1914; s. J.C. and Mary (Lillie) C.; m. Azalea Chenault; 1 dau., Ellen. B.A. with highest honors, UCLA, 1938, Ph.D. in Psychology, 1942. Diplomate: Am. Bd. Examiners in Profl. Psychology. Asst. personnel dir., chief psychol. research cons., engring. research div. Douglas Aircraft Co., 1943-45; instr. psychology U. Kans., 1945-47; asst. prof., dir. psychology clinic U. N.Mex., 1946-47; asst. prof. U. So. Calif., 1948-50; dir. psychology clinic sch., asst., asso., then prof. psychology U. Calif. at Los Angeles, 1950-65, prof. psychology, prof. edn., 1964—; pres. Coleman Psychol. Corp.; cons. in field, 1942—; Chmn. research com., statewide acad. senate U. Calif., 1970—; cons. children's div. Camarillo State Hosp., NSF, Am. Psychol. Assn., Scott, Foresman and Co. Author: Personality Dynamics and Effective Behavior, 1960, Psychology and Effective Behavior, 1969, Abnormal Psychology and Modern Life, 1950, 6th edit., 1980, Deep Sea Adventure Series, 3d edit, 1971, Contemporary Psychology and Effective Behavior, 5th edit, 1983; also research articles. Contemporary Psychology and Effective Behavior, 4th edit. Bd. dirs. Christopher Found.; adv. bd. Am. Security Council. Fellow Am. Acad. Polit. Sci., Am. Acad. Polit. and Social Sci., Am. Psychol. Assn., Royal Soc. Health; mem. N.Y. Acad. Scis., AAAS, Calif. Assn. Remedial Tchrs. (dir.), Nat. Council Family Relations, Nat. Council Crime and Delinquency, Day Care and Child Devel. Council Am., Young Pres.'s Orgn. (fac. dir.), Am. Assn. for Higher Edn., AAUP, Western, Calif., Los Angeles psychol. assns., Internat. Platform Assn., Phi Beta Kappa, Sigma Xi, Pi Gamma Mu, Phi Delta Kappa, Delta Chi. Home: 106 Hanapepe Loop Honolulu HI 96825 Office: Dept Psychology Univ California 405 Hilgard Ave Los Angeles CA 90024

COLEMAN, JAMES EDWIN, JR., lawyer; b. Atlanta, May 23, 1923; s. James Edwin and Demis Cecelia (Thrower) C.; m. Margaret Copeland Sutherland, June 24, 1947; children: J. Hamilton, Margaret S., Sarah C., James Edwin III. B.S., Ga. Inst. Tech., 1948; LL.B., U. Va., 1951. Bar: Ga. 1952, Tex. 1954. Mem. firm Carrington, Gowan, Johnson, Bromberg & Leeds, Dallas, 1953-58; partner firm Carrington, Johnson & Stephens, Dallas, 1958-70, Carrington, Coleman, Sloman & Blumenthal, 1970—. Bd. dirs. Research fellow Southwestern Legal Found.; dir. Nat. Inst. for Trial Advocacy, 1981—; Chmn. legal com. Dallas Community Chest, 1957; pres. Dallas Sch. Lunch Assn., 1967. Served to 1st lt. AUS, 1943-46. Decorated Silver Star. Fellow Am., Tex. bar founds., Am. Coll. Trial Lawyers; mem. ABA (council sect. litigation 1973-75, dir. sect. 1975-81), Tex. Bar Assn., Dallas Bar Assn. (v.p. 1965-66), Am. Law Inst., Am. Bd. Trial Advocates (pres. Dallas chpt. 1976-77), Tex., Dallas assns. def. counsel, Sigma Alpha Epsilon, Phi Delta Phi. Methodist (ofcl. bd. 1965-66, 68-71, chmn. trustees 1967). Clubs: City, Tower (Dallas); Metropolitan (Washington). Home: 4420 Fairfax St Dallas TX 75205 Office: 2500 S Tower Plaza of Ams Dallas TX 75201

COLEMAN, JAMES JULIAN, lawyer, businessman; b. New Orleans, May 5, 1915; s. William Ballin and Millie (Davis) C.; m. Dorothy Louise Jurisich, July 30, 1940; children: James Julian, Thomas Blaise, Peter Dee, Dian Judith. B.A., Tulane U., 1934, J.D., 1937; LL.D., Hampdon-Sydney Coll., 1982. Bar: La. 1937. Sr. partner firm Coleman, Dutrey & Thomson, New Orleans; chmn. bd. Internat. MATEX Tank Terminals, Ltd., West Pakistan, Bangladesh, and South Korea, Loving Enterprises; past pres. Internat. Trade Mart, New Orleans Philharmonic Symphony; hon. consul gen. Republic of Korea. Past pres. New Orleans C. of C.; past bd. dirs. U.S. C. of C.; past mem. exec. com., internat. relations com. Miss. Valley World Trade Council; past chmn. New Orleans coordinating com. NASA; past pres. Jr. Achievement New Orleans; founder Peoples League; trustee Principia Coll.; past chmn. bus. council Tulane U.; past pres. Adult Edn. Center; past trustee Cordell Hull Found.; trustee Loving Found.; past bd. dirs. Internat. House, Fed. Relations Assn., La. Civil Service League. Decorated Order Diplomatic Service Merit, Republic Korea; recipient Nat. Achievement award Jr. Achievement, Loving Cup award New Orleans Times-Picayune, 1980, Disting. Alumnus award Tulane U., 1981. Mem. Am., Internat., La., New Orleans bar assns., Am. Judicature Soc. (past dir.), Beta Gamma Sigma (hon.). Christian Scientist (1st reader 1953-56). Home: 10 Audubon Pl New Orleans LA 70118 Office: 321 St Charles Ave New Orleans LA 70130 *The key to success is asking for divine guidance and listening for the answers, then following the divine direction and rejoicing, even though the way may appear to be rugged.*

COLEMAN, JAMES MALCOLM, marine geology educator; b. Vinton, La., Nov. 19, 1935; s. Leo George and Clara (Gaudet) C.; m. Travis Lucille Alexander, July 28, 1958; children: Thomas M., Sarah E. B.S., La. State U., 1958, Ph.D., 1966. Asst. prof. marine geology Coastal Studies Inst., La. State U., Baton Rouge, 1966-69, assoc. prof., 1969-74, asst. dir., 1971-73, prof., acting dir., 1974-75, prof., dir., 1975-80, Boyd prof., dir., 1980—; lectr. Am. Assn. Petroleum Geologists, 1976-78, Shell Oil Co., 1979; mem. devel. council Gulf Univ. Research Council, 1980; cons. numerous oil cos. Cons. editor, Royal Soc. Edinburgh, 1984; contbr. articles to profl. jours. Mem. adminstrv. bd. 1st United Methodist Ch., Baton Rouge, 1981. Named Disting. Research Master La. State U., 1976, Disting. Faculty fellow La. State U. Found., 1976. Mem. Am. Assn. Petroleum Geologists (Leversen medal 1984), Geol. Soc. Am., Soc. Econ. Palentologists and Mineralogists (Shepard medal 1980). Democrat. Lodge: Rotary. Home: 667 Castle Kirk Baton Rouge LA 70808 Office: Coastal Studies Inst La State U Baton Rouge LA 70803

COLEMAN, JAMES PLEMON, U.S. judge; b. Ackerman, Miss., Jan. 9, 1914; s. Thomas A. and Jennie Essie (Worrell) C.; m. Margaret Janet Dennis, May 2, 1937; 1 son, Thomas Allen. Student, U. Miss., 1932-35; LL.B., George Washington U., 1939, LL.D., 1960. Bar: Miss. bar 1937. Sec. to Rep. Aaron Lane Ford, Washington, 1935-39; practiced in, Ackerman; dist. atty. 5th circuit Ct., Dist. of Miss., 1940-46, circuit judge, 1946-50; commr. Supreme Ct. of Miss., Sept. 1 to Oct. 23, 1950; atty. gen., Miss., 1950-56, gov., 1956-60; mem. Miss. Ho. Reps. from Choctaw County, 1960-65; judge U.S. Ct. Appeals 5th Circuit, 1965—, chief judge, 1979—; publisher Choctaw Plaindealer, weekly, 1949-56. Trustee Miss. Coll., 1952-56. Democrat (presdl. elector 1944). Baptist. Club: Mason (Shriner). Office: 115 E Quinn Ave Ackerman MS 39735

COLEMAN, JAMES SAMUEL, educator, sociologist; b. Bedford, Ind., May 12, 1926; s. James Fox and Maurine (Lappin) C.; m. Lucille Richey, Feb. 5, 1949 (div. Aug. 1973); children: Thomas Sedgwick, John Samuel, James Stephen.; m. Zdzislawa Walaszek, 1973; 1 son, Daniel Wlodzimierz. Student, Emory and Henry Coll., 1944-46; B.S., Purdue U., 1949; Ph.D., Columbia U., 1955. Research asso. Bur. Applied Social Research, Columbia U., 1953-55; fellow Center Advanced Study Behavorial Scis., Palo Alto, Calif., 1955-56; asst. prof. sociology U. Chgo., 1956-59, prof., 1973—; asso. prof., prof. social relations Johns Hopkins U., 1959-73. Author: (with Lipset, Trow) Union Democracy, 1956, Community Conflict, 1957, The Adolescent Society, 1961, Introduction to Mathematical Sociology, 1964, Models of Change and Response Uncertainty, 1964, Adolescents and the Schools, 1965, (with others) Equality of Education Opportunity, 1966, Medical Innovation, 1967, Resources for Social Change, 1972, Mathematics of Collective Action, 1973, Power and the Structure of Society, 1973, (with others) Youth: Transition to Adulthood, 1973, Longitudinal Data Analysis, 1981, (with others) High School Achievement, 1982, The Asymmetric Society, 1982. Mem. Am. Sociol. Assn., Nat. Acad. Edn., Am. Acad. Arts and Scis., Nat. Acad. Scis., Am. Philos. Assn., Public Choice Soc. Office: U Chicago Chicago IL 60637

COLEMAN, JOEL CLIFFORD, lawyer; b. Reading, Pa., Dec. 6, 1930; s. Thomas and Lee (Jason) Iscovitz; m. Lois M. Schulman, Feb. 4, 1960; children: Teri, Thomas. B.S. in Econs., U. Pa., 1952, LL.B. cum laude, 1955. Bar: N.Y. 1956. Asso. firm Kaye, Scholer, Fierman, Hays & Handler, N.Y.C., 1955-67; atty. Twentieth-Century Fox Film Corp., N.Y.C., 1967-69; gen. counsel Internat. Playtex, Inc., N.Y.C. and Stamford, Conn., 1969—, sec., 1975—, v.p., 1980—, also dir. Editor: U. Pa. Law Rev., 1953-55; case editor, 1954-55. Trustee Larchmont (N.Y.) Temple, 1973-75. Mem. ABA, N.Y. State Bar Assn., Am. Corp. Counsel Assn., Westchester-Fairfield Corp. Counsel Assn., Order of Coif. Home: 5 Jochum Ave Larchmont NY 10538 Office: 700 Fairfield Ave PO Box 10064 Stamford CT 06904

COLEMAN, JOHN HEWSON, financial consultant; b. Joggins, N.S., Can., Mar. 22, 1912; s. William Bartholomew and Rosalie (Comeau) C.; m. Kathryn Marguerite Mitchell, Sept. 12, 1939; children: Gerald Francis, Kathryn Claire (Mrs. John H. Green). With Royal Bank Can., Toronto, Ont., from 1928, dep. chmn., exec. v.p., 1970-73; pres. J.H.C. Assocs., Ltd., fin. cons., Toronto; chmn. Lehndorff Corp., Maritime Steel and Foundries Ltd., United Group Mut. Funds; dir. Intercity Gas Corp., Colgate-Palmolive Ltd., Gt. Pacific Industries Inc., United Fin. Mgmt. Ltd., Exco Corp. Ltd., Hunter Douglas Can. Ltd., Internat. Minerals & Chem. Corp., Internat. Minerals & Chem. Corp. (Can.) Ltd., Roman Corp., Standard Products (Can.) Ltd., Westburne Internat. Industries Ltd., Thomson Newspapers Ltd. Roman Catholic. Clubs: Knight of Malta., Toronto, Lambton Golf and Country (Toronto). Home: 561 Avenue Rd Suite 603-4 Toronto ON M4V 2J8 Canada Office: Suite 3045 South Tower Royal Bank Plaza PO Box 14 Toronto ON M5J 2J1 Canada

COLEMAN, JOHN MARSHALL, attorney general of Virginia; b. Staunton, Va., June 8, 1942; s. William W. and Marguerite B. C.; m. Nicols Compton Fox, July 9, 1977; children: Sean Kelly, William Philip. B.A. with high honors, U. Va., 1964, J.D., 1970. Bar: Va. bar 1970, U.S. Supreme Ct. bar 1977. Partner firm Lotz, Black, Coleman and Gudal, Staunton, 1970-77; U.S. magistrate Western Dist. Va., 1971-72; mem. Va. Ho. of Dels., 1972-75, Va. Senate, 1975-77; atty. gen., Va., 1977—; mem. Commn. to Study Needs of Elderly, 1973-77; mem. food supply and agr. task force Nat. Conf. State Legislators, 1975-78. Bd. visitors James Madison U., 1972; chmn. Staunton-

Augusta United Fund Dr., 1973. Served as 1st lt. USMC, 1966-69. Named 1 of 5 Outstanding Young Men Va. Jaycees, 1975; nat. winner; Estate Planning Competition, 1970. Mem. Nat. Assn. Attys. Gen., Am. Bar Assn., Phi Beta Kappa, Omicron Delta Kappa. Republican. Episcopalian. Clubs: Raven Soc., Thirteen Soc. Home: 6615 Madison McLean Dr McLean VA

COLEMAN, JOHN ROYSTON, foundation executive, author; b. Copper Cliff, Ont., Can., June 24, 1921; came to U.S., 1946, naturalized, 1954; s. Richard Mowbray and Mary Irene (Lawson) C.; m. Mary N. Irwin, Oct. 1, 1943 (div. 1967); children: John M., Nancy J., Patty A., Paul R., Stephen W. B.A., U. Toronto, 1943; M.A., U. Chgo., 1949, Ph.D., 1950; LL.D., Beaver Coll., 1963, U. Pa., 1968, Gannon Coll., 1975; L.H.D., Manhattanville Coll., 1975, Emory and Henry Coll., 1977, Green Mountain Coll., 1984; D.Litt., Haverford Coll., 1980. Research asso. U. Chgo., 1947-49; instr. econs. Mass. Inst. Tech., 1949-51, asst. prof., 1951-55; asso. prof., asst. head dept. econs. Carnegie Inst. Tech., 1955-60, prof., head dept. econs., 1960-63, dean div. humanities and social sci., 1963-65; asso. dir. econ. devel. and adminstrn. Ford Found., 1965-66, program officer in charge social devel., 1966-67; pres. Haverford (Pa.) Coll., 1967-77, Edna McConnell Clark Found., N.Y.C., 1977—; chmn. bd. dirs. Fed. Res. Bank Phila., 1973-76; dir. Provident Mut. Life Ins. Co., Phila. Savs. Fund Soc., Healthcare Systems Inc.; labor arbitrator, cons., 1953—; cons. indsl. relations research Ford Found. in India, 1960-61; tchr. Am. Economy CBS-TV, 1962-63. Author: Goals and Strategy in Collective Bargaining, 1951, Readings in Economics, 1952, 55, 58, 64, 67, Labor Problems, 1953, 59, Working Harmony, 1955, The Changing American Economy, 1967, Comparative Economic Systems, 1968, Blue Collar Journal, 1974. Lt. N.Y.C. Aux. Police Force; trustee Nat. Jud. Coll.; chmn. bd. advisers Fed. Correctional Inst., Otisville, N.Y. Served with Royal Canadian Navy, 1943-45. Mem. N.Y. Regional Assn. Grantmakers (pres. 1979-81), P.E.N., Soc. of Friends. Office: 250 Park Ave New York NY 10024

COLEMAN, JOHN SHERRARD, orgn. exec.; b. Oahu, Hawaii, Jan. 15, 1914; s. Sherrard and Mary Comstock (Griswold) C.; m. Beverly Reynolds Bridge, Dec. 24, 1944; children—Sherrard, Deborah Reynolds. B.S., Coll. William and Mary, 1935; M.S., Mass. Inst. Tech., 1940. Residential constrn. and design, 1936-38; mem. Nat. Def. Research Com., 1940-43; research asso. Harvard, 1943-44; London rep. OSRD, 1944; div. war research Columbia U., 1945-46; com. underseas warfare NRC, 1947-53; prof. engring. research Pa. State U., 1953; exec. sec. div. phys. scis. Nat. Acad. Scis.-NRC, 1953-65; exec. officer Nat. Acad. Scis., Washington, 1965-79, sr. staff adv., 1979—; dir. Tracor Iitco.; chmn. acoustics panel Research and Devel. Bd., 1952-53; cons. Air Research and Devel. Command, 1952-53, Office Sec. Def., 1953-55; chmn. Pres.'s Com. for Local Action in Sci. and Engring. Mem. naval studies bd. NRC, 1980—; mem. com. on public policy Am. Inst. Physics, 1980—. Recipient Meritorious Pub. Service award, 1958. Club: Fairfax Country. Home: 3010 N Florida St Arlington VA 22207 Office: 2101 Constitution Ave NW Washington DC 20418

COLEMAN, LEONARD STEPHEN, steel company executive; b. Reading, Pa., Aug. 22, 1928; s. Leonard Stephen and Mary Margerite (Vogel) C.; m. Betty R. Reisinger, Nov. 25, 1948; children—Bonita L., Stephan A., Pamela L., Christine A. B.S. in Econs, Albright Coll., Reading, 1952; M.B.A. in Indsl. Mgmt, Temple U., Phila., 1968. Chief accountant Kutztown Foundry & Machine Corp., Pa., 1960-67; with Carpenter Tech. Corp., Reading, 1967—, asst. div. controller, 1972-75, mgr. fin. planning and analysis, 1975-76, treas., 1976-78, asst. v.p.-adminstrn., 1978-80, v.p. adminstrn., 1980-82, v.p. human resources, 1982—; dir. Bank Pa.; part-time instr. Pa. State U. Bd. dirs. Reading Jr. Achievement, St. Joseph's Hosp., Reading. Served with USMCR, 1946-48. Mem. Nat. Assn. Accts. (past nat. dir.), C. of C. Reading and Berks County. Home: 2915 Leisz's Bridge Rd Reading PA 19605 Office: PO Box 662 Reading PA 19603

COLEMAN, LESTER EARL, chemical company executive; b. Akron, Ohio, Nov. 6, 1930; s. Lester Earl and Ethel Angeline (Miller) C.; m. Jean Goudie Moir, Aug. 31, 1951; children: Robert Scott, Kenneth John. B.S., U. Akron, 1952; M.S., U. Ill., 1953, Ph.D., 1955. With Goodyear Tire & Rubber Co., Akron, 1951-52; with Lubrizol Corp., Cleve., 1955—, asst. to pres., 1972, v.p. internat. ops., 1973, exec. v.p., 1974-76, pres., 1976-83, chief exec. officer, 1978—, chmn. bd., 1983—, also dir.; dir. Norfolk So. Corp., Society Nat. Bank, Cleve., Society Corp., S.C. Johnson & Son, Inc., Racine, Wis. Contbr. articles to profl. jours. Vice pres. fin. East Central Region Boy Scouts Am., nat. exec. bd.; trustee Cleve. Mus. Natural History; bd. overseers Dartmouth Med. Sch. Served to capt. USAF, 1955-57. Mem. Am. Chem. Soc. (local chmn. 1973), Chem. Mfrs. Assn., Soc. Chem. Industry, Sigma Xi, Alpha Chi Sigma, Phi Lambda Upsilon, Phi Delta Theta. Methodist. Patentee in field. Office: 29400 Lakeland Blvd Wickliffe OH 44092

COLEMAN, LESTER LAUDY, otolaryngologist; b. N.Y.C., Mar. 11, 1911; s. Auron and Ann (Blum) C.; m. Felicia Slatkin, Sept. 30, 1945; 1 dau., Lisa. B.S., Johns Hopkins U.; M.D., L.I., Coll. Medicine, 1932. Diplomate: Am. Bd. Otolaryngology. Asst. resident in otolaryngology Johns Hopkins Hosp., 1936-38; practice medicine specializing in otolaryngology, N.Y.C., 1940—; med. dir. Morton Prince Center Psychotherapy, N.Y.C.; attending surgeon Manhattan Eye, Ear and Throat Hosp., N.Y. Hosp. Cornell Med. Center; asst. clin. prof. Albert Einstein Sch. Medicine; co-founder Internat. Grad. U. Med. columnist: Speaking of Your Health, King Features, Inc.; producer show, NBC-TV, 1953-56. Served to maj. M.C. AUS, 1942. Fellow Am. Trilogical Soc.; mem. Am. Acad. Psychosomatic Medicine (past v.p.). Home: 1000 Park Ave New York NY 10028 Office: 114 E 72d St New York NY 10021

COLEMAN, LYNN R., lawyer, former government official; b. Vernon, Tex., Aug. 17, 1939. B.A., Abilene Christian Coll., 1961; LL.B., U. Tex., 1964. Bar: Tex. 1964, D.C. 1973. Mem. firm Vinson & Elkins, Houston, 1965-73, Washington, 1973-78; gen. counsel U.S. Dept. Energy, 1978-80, dep. sec., 1980-81; mem. firm Skadden, Arps, Slate, Meagher & Flom, Washington, 1981—; Mem. Adminstrv. Conf. of U.S., 1978-80. Mem. Am. Bar Assn. (spl. com. on energy law 1979-83, coordinating com. on energy law 1983—), Chancellors, Order of Coif, Phi Delta Phi. Office: Skadden Arps Slate Meagher & Flom 919 18th St NW Washington DC 20006

COLEMAN, MARTIN STONE, office furniture company executive; b. N.Y.C., Oct. 22, 1913; s. Adolph H. and Hannah (Stone) C.; m. Janet Mosler, June 30, 1940; children—Ann, John, Nancy. B.S., N.Y. U., 1937. C.P.A., N.Y. Vice pres., treas., dir. Mosler Safe Co., N.Y.C., 1952-61, exec. v.p., treas., 1961-66, pres., dir., 1966-67, chmn. bd., 1968-72; chmn. bd., chief exec. officer Harbor Universal Inc., 1972—, Benedetti Corp., 1974—. Trustee Coleman Found.; Cost insp. Bur. Supplies and Accounts, Navy Dept., 1942-45. Mem. Am. Inst. C.P.A.'s, N.Y. State Soc. C.P.A.'s. Clubs: Sunningdale Country, Harmonie, Tamarisk Country. Home: 740 Park Ave New York NY 10021 Office: 551 Fifth Ave New York NY 10176

COLEMAN, MARY STALLINGS, retired state chief justice; b. Forney, Tex.; d. Leslie C. and Agnes B. (Huther) Stallings; m. Creighton R. Coleman, June 24, 1939; children: Leslie Coleman Hagan, Carol. B.A., U. Md., 1935; J.D., George Washington U., 1939; LL.D., Eastern Mich. U., 1974, Western Mich. U., 1974; L.H.D., Nazareth Coll., 1973; LL.D., Alma Coll., 1973, Olivet Coll., 1973, Detroit Coll. Law, 1975, Adrian Coll., 1976, U. Md., 1978, Saginaw Valley State Coll., 1979, Ferris State Coll., 1981, Hope Coll., 1981, N.Y. Law Sch., 1982; D.P.A., Albion Coll., 1982, U. Detroit, 1983, Grand Valley State Coll., 1984. Bar: D.C. 1940, Mich. 1950. Practiced in, Washington, 1940-46; partner firm Wunsch & Coleman, Battle Creek, Mich., 1950-61; probate and juvenile ct. judge, Calhoun County, Mich., 1961-73; justice Mich. Supreme Ct., 1973-82; dir. K Mart Internat., Nat. Bank Detroit and NBD Bancorp, Biggs/Gilmore. Contbr. articles to profl. publs. Trustee Albion Coll.; mem. Nat. Commn. for Observance of Internat. Women's Year, 1975-76. Recipient Disting. Career award George Washington U., 1973, Disting. Alumni award U. Md., 1973, Distinguished Mem. award Phi Kappa Phi, 1973, award Calhoun County Bd. Edn., 1964, Frat. Order Police, 1967, NAACP Young Adults, 1969, George award Enquirer & News, 1969, Internat. Wyman award Alpha Omicron Pi, 1975, Distinguished Woman award Mich. Bus. and Profl. Womens' Club, 1973; Religious Heritage of Am. award, 1974; named Woman of Year Soroptomists, 1976, Mich. Assn. Professions, 1976; Disting. Citizen award Mich. State U., 1977; joint resolution of commendation Mich. Legislature, 1977; DAR medal of honor, 1978, 1 of 10 Top Michiganians of Yr., 1980; Disting. Service award Mich. Juvenile Detention Assn., 1980; Disting. Alumna award George Washington U., 1980; Award of Merit Am. Judges Assn., 1980; Disting. Vol. Leadership award March of Dimes, 1981; Law Day award Mich. Pines and Dunes council Girl Scouts U.S.A., 1981; Alumni Achievement award, 1983; Mich. Women's Hall of Fame, 1983. Fellow Mich. Bar Found. (Founder); mem. Mich., Am. bar assns., Am. Judicature Soc., Nat. Probate Judges Assn. (life), Am., Mich. assns. women lawyers, Am. Assn. Women Judges, Bus. and Profl. Women's Club, AAUW (Disting. Service award Mich. chpt. 1979), Am. Legion Aux., P.E.O.; hon. mem. Jr. League, Big Sisters-Big Bros., Altrusa Internat., Beta Sigma Phi, Alpha Delta Kappa. Club: Battle Creek Country. Home: 355 E Hamilton Ln Battle Creek MI 49015 *My one overriding thought concerning the achievements and honors listed above is that none are truly mine. They are but reflections of the work and good will of many people — importantly, of an extraordinarily helpful and supportive husband and of our admirable children.*

COLEMAN, ORNETTE, composer, instrumentalist; b. Ft. Worth, Mar. 9, 1930; Randolph and Rosa C.;, 1954; 1 son, Denardo. Player alto and tenor saxophone, trumpet, violin, bassoon; toured with, Clarence Samuels, 1949, with, Pee Wee Crayton, 1950; led quartet with, Don Cherry, Eddie Blackwell and Charlie Haden; appeared in numerous major festivals throughout the world; toured, Japan, Europe and, Africa; recs. for small jazz ensemble include Something Else, 1958, The Shape of Jazz to Come, 1959, Free Jazz, 1960, Chappaque Suite, 1965, At the Golden Circle, Vol. 1, 1965, Empty Foxhole, 1966, Dancing in Your Head, 1976, Fashion Faces, 1979; numerous others; over 100 compositions for small jazz group and larger ensembles including Music of Ornette Coleman containing his works for string quartet and woodwind quintet recorded by, London Symphony Orch. Named to Downbeat Hall of Fame; Guggenheim Found. fellow, 1967, 74. Developer musical theory concept called Harmoldic theory for composers and players. Address: p o box 12 canal street station New York NY 10002 *

COLEMAN, PAUL DARE, educator; b. Stoystown, Pa., June 4, 1918; s. Clyde R. and Catharine (Livengood) C.; m. Betty L. Carter, June 20, 1942; children—Susan Dare, Peter Carter. A.B., Susquehanna U., 1940; M.S., Pa. State U., 1942; Ph.D., Mass. Inst. Tech., 1951, D.Sc. (hon.), 1978. Asst. physics Susquehanna U., 1938-40, Pa. State U., 1940-42; physicist USAF-WADC, Wright Field, Ohio, 1942-46, Cambridge Air Research Center, also; grad. research asso. Mass. Inst. Tech., 1946-51; prof. elec. engring., dir. electro-physics lab. U. Ill. at Urbana, 1951—. Recipient meritorious civilian award USAAF, 1946. Fellow IEEE, Optical Soc. Am.; mem. Am. Phys. Soc., Sigma Xi, Pi Mu Delta, Pi Mu Epsilon, Eta Kappa Nu. Research on millimeter waves, submillimeter waves, relativistic electronics, far infrared molecular lasers, beam wave guides and detectors, chem. lasers, nonlinear optics. Home: 710 Park Ln Champaign IL 61820 Office: Univ Illinois EERL 200 Urbana IL 61801

COLEMAN, PAUL DAVID, anantomy educator; b. N.Y.C., Dec. 2, 1927; s. A. Barnett and Martha L. (Michaels) C.; m. Zinia J. Cereska, Mar. 13, 1955 (div. Sept. 1978); children: Laura A., Paul David; m. 2d Dorothy G. Flood, Feb. 26, 1983. A.B., Tufts U., 1948; Ph.D., U. Rochester, 1953. Asst. prof., research assoc. Tufts U., Medford, Mass., 1956-59; assoc. Computer Ctr. MIT, Cambridge, 1957-59; spl. fellow Johns Hopkins Sch. Medicine, Balt., 1959-62; assoc. prof. Sch. Medicine U. Md., Balt., 1962-67; prof. anatomy Sch. Medicine, U. Rochester, N.Y., 1967—. Contbr. articles to profl. jours. Served to 1st lt. U.S. Army, 1953-56. Recipient research grants NSF, 1958-67, NIH, 1963—; NIH spl. fellow Johns Hopkins U. Sch. Medicine, 1959-62. Mem. Am. Assn. Anatomists, AAAS, Gerontol. Soc., Am. Psychol. Assn. Club: Yacht (Rochester, N.Y.) (bd. dirs. 1971-72). Home: 35 Atkinson St Rochester NY 14608 Office: U Rochester Med Ctr. Box 603 Rochester NY 14642

COLEMAN, PETER TALI, governor American Samoa; b. Pago Pago, Am. Samoa, Dec. 8, 1919; s. William Patrick and Amata (Aumua) C.; m. Nora Stewart, May 31, 1941; children—William Patrick, Peter Talifiliga, Milton John, Amata Catherine Coleman Radewagen, Burton George (dec.), Bruce Joseph, Charles Ulualofaiga, Richard James, Paul Vaelas, Barrett Francis, Alan David, Sina Ellen, Limonmon Mary. B.B.S. in Econs, Georgetown U., 1949, LL.B., 1951; Ph.D. (hon.), U. Guam, 1970. Pacific area analyst Office Ters., Dept. Interior, Washington, 1951-52; pub. defender, planning officer, customs officer Am. Samoa, 1952-55, atty. gen., 1955-56, gov., 1978—; dist. adminstr. Marshall Islands dist. U.S. Trust Ter. Pacific Islands Dept. Interior, 1961-65, dist. adminstr., 1965-69, dep. high commr., 1969-77; alt. U.S. commr. (S. Pacific Commn.), 1959, spl. adviser, 1965, 72. Served with AUS, 1940-45. Named to U.S. Army Hall of Fame, Ft. Benning, Ga., 1982; John Hay Whitney Found. fellow. Office: Office of Governor Pago Pago Tutuila American Samoa 96799 *

COLEMAN, REXFORD LEE, lawyer, educator; b. Hollywood, Calif., June 2, 1930; s. Henry Eugene and Antoinette Christine (Dobry) C.; m. Aiko Takahashi, Aug. 28, 1953 (div.); children: Christine Eugenie, Douglass Craig; m. Sucha Park, June 15, 1978. Student, Claremont McKenna Coll., 1947-49; A.B., Stanford U., 1951, J.D., 1955; M. in Jurisprudence, Tokyo (Japan) U., 1960. Bar: Calif. 1955, Mass. 1969. Mem. faculty Harvard U., 1959-69; mem. firm Baker & McKenzie, San Francisco, 1969-83, income partner, 1971-73, capital ptnr., 1973-83, head Tokyo office, 1971-78; sr. ptnr. Coleman & Gresser (Pacific Law Group), Los Angeles, 1983—; cons. U.S. Treasury Dept., 1961-70; counselor Japanese-Am. Soc. for Legal Studies, 1964—; guest lectr. Ford Seminar on Comparative History, Mass. Inst. Tech., 1968; lectr. Legal Tng. and Research Inst., Supreme Ct., Japan, 1970-73; chmn. fgn. bus. customs consultative com. Bur. Customs, Ministry of Fin., Govt. of Japan, 1971-72; chmn. fgn. bus. consulatative commn. Japanese Ministry of Internat. Trade and Industry, 1973-76. Author: Am. Index to Japanese Law, 1961, Standard Citation of Japanese Legal Materials, 1963, The Legal Aspects Under Japanese Law of an Accident Involving a Nuclear Installation in Japan, 1963, An Index to Japanese Law, 1975; Editor: Taxation in Japan, World Tax Series, 1959—, Japanese Ann. & Internat. Law, 1970—; Chmn. bd. editors: Law in Japan: An Annual, 1964-67. Served to 1st lt., Inf. AUS, 1951-53; now lt. col. Res. Mem. Japanese-Am. Soc. for Legal Studies, Assn. Asian Studies, Am. Polit. Sci. Assn., Internat. Studies Assn., Internat. Fiscal Assn., Acad. Polit. Sci., Am. Acad. Polit. and Social Sci., Am. Soc. Internat. Law, Am. Fgn. Law Assn., Am. Bar Assn., State Bar Calif., Mass. Bar Assn., Mil. Govt. Assn., Res. Officers Assn. (v.p. army dept. Far East 1974-75), U.S. Army Judge Adv. Gen.'s Sch. Alumni Assn., Internat. House Japan (Tokyo), Stanford U. Alumni Assn., Gakushi Kai., Internat. Law Assn. Japan, Japan-Calif. Assn., Pacific Basin Econ. Council, Am. C. of C. in Japan, Nihon Shihō Gakkai, Nihon Kokusai Hō Gakkai, Nihon Kokusai Shihō Gakkai, Sozei Hō Gakkai, Phi Alpha Delta. Episcopalian (vestryman 1966-69; del. Conv. Episcopal Diocese Mass. 1968). Clubs: Tokyo Am.; Harvard (N.Y.C.); Los Angeles Marina City, North Ranch Country. Home: 32314 Blue Rock Ridge Westlake Village CA 91361 Office: Coleman & Gresser (Pacific Law Group) 1900 Ave of Stars Los Angeles CA 90067

COLEMAN, ROBERT E., textile co. exec.; b. Greenville, S.C., 1925. B.S., N.C. State U., 1950. Supr. Graniteville Co. (S.C.), 1950-52; asst. supt. Anchor Rome Mills, Inc., Rome, Ga., 1952-55; with Riegel Textile Corp., 1955—, exec. v.p., 1969-73, pres., 1973—, chief operating officer, 1973-74, chief exec. officer, 1974—, chmn. bd., 1975—, also dir. Address: Suite 800 Green Gate Park 25 Woods Lake Rd Greenville SC 29607

COLEMAN, ROBERT MARSHALL, biology educator; b. Bridgton, Maine, Sept. 27, 1925; s. Louis Elmer and Helen (Marr) C.; m. Patricia Ann Stocum, Dec. 29, 1947; children: Mary Deborah, Kevin Robert. B.S., Bates Coll., 1950; M.S., U. N.H., 1951; Ph.D., U. Notre Dame, 1954. Faculty Russell Sage Coll., Troy, N.Y., 1954-62, asst. prof. biology, 1956-58, asso. prof., 1958-62, Boston Coll., 1962-68; prof. biol. scis. U. Lowell (Mass.), 1968—; Cons. AID, NSF, India, 1965, 68, Lowell Tech. Inst., 1964-67, WHO, Egypt, 1977, Smithsonian Instn., 1976. Contbr. articles profl. jours. Served with AUS, 1943-46. Mem. Am. Soc. Parasitology, Am. Soc. Tropical Medicine and Hygiene, Am. Soc. Microbiology, N.Y. Acad. Scis., Radiation Research Soc., Sigma Xi, Phi Sigma. Home: 25 Eaton Rd W Framingham MA 01701 Office: Univ Lowell Biol Scis Dept Lowell MA 01854

COLEMAN, ROBERT WINSTON, lawyer; b. Oklahoma City, Mar. 1, 1942; s. Clint Sheridan and Genevieve (Ross) C.; m. Judith Moore, Sept. 7, 1963; children: Robert Winston, Jr., Claire Elizabeth. B.A., Abilene Christian Coll., 1964; LL.B., U. Tex., 1968. Bar: Tex. 1968, Ga. 1970. Law clk. to presiding justice U.S. Ct. Appeals (5th cir.), Montgomery, Ala., 1968-69; assoc. Kilpatrick, Cody, Rogers, McClatchey & Regenstein, Atlanta, 1969-75, Stalcup, Johnson, Meyers & Miller, Dallas, 1975-77; ptnr. Meyers, Miller & Middleton, Dallas, 1977-78, Meyers, Miller, Middleton & Weiner, 1978-79, Meyers, Miller, Middleton, Weiner & Warren, 1979-80, Jones, Day, Reavis & Pogue, 1981—. Mem. exec. com. Dallas County Dem. Party. Mem. ABA, Dallas Bar Assn., Tex. Bar Assn., Ga. Bar Assn., Am. Judicature Soc. Baptist. Office: Suite 2700 Bryan Tower Dallas TX 75210

COLEMAN, RON, congressman; b. El Paso, Tex., Nov. 29, 1941; m. Tammy Biel; 1 dau., Kimberly Michelle. B.A., U. Tex.-El Paso, 1963, J.D., 1969; postgrad. in law, Kent U., Canterbury, Eng., 1981. Bar: Tex. 1969. Tchr. El Paso Pub. Schs., 1967; practice law El Paso, 1969; asst. county atty., Tex., 1969-71, 1st asst. county atty., from 1971; mem. Tex. Ho of Reps., 1973-82, 98th Congress from 16th dist. Tex.; majority whip at-large, rep. Democratic Congl. Campaign Com., mem. subcoms. research and devel. and mil. personnel and compensation of armed services com., subcom. commerce, consumer and monetary affairs of govt. ops. com., govt. info., justice and agr. com., govt. activities and transp. com. 98th Congress From 16th dist. Tex.; founder, organizer Border Caucus; mem. Vietmam Vets. Caucus, Congl. Hispanic Caucus, Sunbelt Caucus, Environ. and Energy Study Conf., Arms Control and Fgn. Policy Caucus. Author: Pub. Sch. Fin. Act. Tex. Del. Tex. Constl. Conv., 1974. Named One of 10 Best Legislators Tex. Montly mag.; recipient Adminstrn. Justice award State Bar Tex., 1973, Legis. award State Bar Tex., 1979, Environ. award, 1977, award for edn. Tex. Assn. Sch. Adminstrs. and Sch. Bds., 1977, cert. Tex. Compensatory Edn. Assn., 1979. Office: US House of Reps Washington DC 20515

COLEMAN, SHELDON, business executive; b. Ft. Worth, Nov. 15, 1901; s. William Coffin and Fanny (Sheldon) C.; m. Georgia Cleveland, Dec. 20, 1923 (div. 1949); children—Virginia Lee, Carolyn; m. Galey Dater, May 22, 1951; 1 son, Sheldon. M.E., Cornell U., 1925. Engr. Coleman Co., Wichita, Kans., 1925-32, gen. works mgr., 1932-40, became exec. v.p. and gen. mgr., 1940; later pres., now chmn. bd. Office Chief Exec., Coleman Co., Inc.; dir. 4th Nat. Bank, Wichita. Past vice chmn. bd. govs. ARC.; Mem. Outdoor Recreation Policy Rev. Group. Mem. Gas Appliance Mfrs. Assn. (past pres.), Inst. Appliance Mfrs. (past pres.), N.A.M. Republican. Baptist. Office: Coleman Co Inc 250 N St Francis Ave Wichita KS 67202 *

COLEMAN, SHERMAN SMOOT, orthopedic surgeon; b. Provo, Utah, Dec. 5, 1922; s. Jacob and Allie (Smoot) C.; m. Jane Dalenberg, Dec. 5, 1946; children: Sherman Michael, Don Aubrey, Mary Jennifer. B.S., Brigham Young U., 1946; M.D., M.S., Northwestern U., 1948. Diplomate: Am. Bd. Orthopedic Surgery (pres. 1973-75). Intern Los Angeles County Hosp., 1947-48; resident in orthopedic surgery Northwestern U. Hosps., 1949-55; practice medicine specializing in orthopedic surgery, Chgo., 1955-57, Salt Lake City, 1957—; chief surgeon Shriners Hosp., Salt Lake City, 1957—; prof. orthopedic surgery U. Utah, Salt Lake City, 1968—. Author: Complex Foot Deformities in Children, 1983; Contbg. author: Current Practice Orthopedic Surgery, 1976, Pediatric Orthopedics, 1978; author: Congenital Dysplasia and Dislocation of the Hip, 1978; contbr. chpts. to: Congenital Dislocation of the Hip; contbr. articles to med. jours. Served with USNR, 1943-47, 51-53. Mem. Am. Orthopedic Assn. (traveling fellow 1959, pres. 1977—), Pediatric Orthopaedic Soc. (pres. 1978). Presbyterian. Club: Salt Lake Country. Home: 1469 Wilton Way Salt Lake City UT 84108 Office: 50 N Medical Dr Salt Lake City UT 84132

COLEMAN, SIDNEY RICHARD, physicist, educator; b. Chgo., Mar. 7, 1937; s. Harold Albert and Sadie (Shanas) C. B.S., Ill. Inst. Tech., 1957; Ph.D., Calif. Inst. Tech., 1962. Research fellow dept. physics Harvard U., 1961-63, asst. prof., 1963-66, assoc. prof., 1966-69, prof., 1969—; vis. prof. U. Rome, Italy, 1968, Princeton U., 1973, Stanford U., 1979-80; partner Advent Pubs. Recipient prize for physics lectures Ettore Majorana Centre Sci. Culture; Boris Pregel award N.Y. Acad. Scis. Fellow Am. Phys. Soc., Am. Acad. Arts and Sci., Nat. Acad. Sci.; mem. LILAPA. Home: Unit 12 1 Richdale Ave Cambridge MA 02140 Office: Lyman Lab Harvard U Cambridge MA 02138

COLEMAN, WILLIAM CALDWELL, aviation executive; b. Boston, Sept. 9, 1943; s. William Caldwell and Nancy (Nye) C.; m. Janet Wyman, June 10, 1972; children: Robert B., William C. B.A., Harvard U., 1965, M.B.A., 1972. Mgmt. staff Dept. HEW, Office of Sec., Washington, 1972-74; dir. budget Office Human Services, Commonwealth of Mass., Boston, 1975-77; mgr. clin. service Mass. Gen. Hosp., Boston, 1978-79; dir. adminstrn. and fin. Mass. Port

Authority, Boston, 1979-80, dir. aviation, 1980—. Mem. Gov.s Adv. Com. for Juvenile Justice, Boston, 1976-80. Served to lt. USN, 1966-69. Decorated Bronze Star. Mem. Airport Operators Council Internat. (vice chmn. econs. com.). Democrat. Office: Mass Port Autority 99 High St Boston MA 02110

COLEMAN, WILLIAM THADDEUS, JR., lawyer; b. Germantown, Pa., July 7, 1920; s. William Thaddeus and Laura Beatrice (Mason) C.; m. Lovida Hardin, Feb. 10, 1945; children: William Thaddeus III, Lovida Hardin, Hardin L. A.B. summa cum laude, U. Pa., 1941; LL.B. magna cum laude, Harvard U., 1946. Bar: Pa. bar 1947, D.C. bar 1977. Law sec. Judge Herbert F. Goodrich, U.S. Ct. of Appeals, 3d Circuit, 1947-48, Justice Felix Frankfurter (asso. justice Supreme Ct. U.S.), 1948-49; asso. Paul, Weiss, Rifkind, Wharton & Garrison, N.Y.C., 1949-52, Dilworth, Paxson, Kalish, Levy & Coleman, Phila., 1952-56, partner, 1956-75; sec. Dept. Transp., Washington, 1975-77; sr. partner firm O'Melveny & Myers, Washington, Los Angeles and Paris, 1977—; spl. counsel for transit matters City of Phila., 1952-63; rep. atty. gen. Pa. and Commonwealth of Pa. in litigation to remove racial restrictions at Girard Coll., 1965; dir. IBM, Chase Manhattan Bank, PepsiCo., AMAX, Inc., Pan Am. World Airways, Inc., Phila. Electric Co., Cigna Corp.; bd. govs. Rand Corp.; mem. Pres.'s Com. on Govt. Employment Policy, 1959-61; cons. ACDA, 1963-74; sr. cons., asst. counsel Pres.'s Commn. on Assassination of Pres. Kennedy, 1964; co-chmn. planning sessions White House Conf. to Fulfill These Rights, 1965-66; mem. U.S. del. 24th Session UN Gen. Assembly, 1969; mem. legal adv. com. Council on Environ. Quality, 1970; pub. mem. Pres.'s Nat. Commn. on Productivity, 1970; commr. Price Commn., 1971-72, Phila Fairmount Park Commn., 1967-75; mem. Gov.'s Commn. on Constl. Revision, 1963-65. Contbr. articles to prof. jours. Chmn. bd. NAACP Legal Def. and Ednl. Fund; v.p., trustee, mem. exec. com. Phila. Mus. Art; trustee Brookings Instn.; mem. Trilateral Commn.; mem. exec. com. Lawyers Com. for Civil Rights Under Law; bd. overseers Harvard U., 1975-81, U. Pa. Law Sch., 1978—. Recipient Joseph E. Beale prize, 1946; Langdell fellow, 1946-47. Fellow Am. Coll. Trial Lawyers; mem. Am. Law Inst. (council), ABA (task force on jud. adminstrn.), Phila. Bar Assn. (past chmn. judiciary com.), Am. Arbitration Assn. (gov.), Council Fgn. Relations, Phi Beta Kappa, Pi Gamma Mu. Clubs: Harvard Law Sch., Lawyers, Union League, Socialegal, Junior Legal (Phila.); Arts and Sciences (Germantown); Cosmos, Metropolitan (Washington). Office: O'Melveny & Myers 1800 M St NW Washington DC 20036

COLEN, DONALD JEROME, bus. exec.; b. N.Y.C., Apr. 9, 1917; s. Bernard Daniel and Beth (Shere) C.; m. Marcia Elizabeth Sufrin, Apr. 17, 1943; 1 son, Bernard Daniel. B.S. cum laude, Harvard U., 1938; M.S. in Engring, 1942. Pres. Mardon Mfg. Co., 1946-49; public issues analyst Gen. Electric Co., 1955-60; v.p. Ruder & Finn, N.Y.C., 1960-65; v.p. public affairs Citibank (N.A.), N.Y.C., 1965-80; public affairs cons., 1980—. Author: The Money Movers, 1978. Served with USNR, 1943-46. Mem. Am. Econ. Assn., Soc. Harvard Engrs. and Scientists, Am. Acad. Polit. Sci. Democrat. Club: Harvard of N.Y. Home and Office: 2-D Heritage Crest Southbury CT 06488

COLER, MYRON A(BRAHAM), research engineer, educator; b. N.Y.C., Mar. 30, 1913; s. Marcus and Bertha (Bebarfald) C.; m. Viola Ethel Buchbinder, Nov. 15, 1942; children: Mark D., Sandra Coler Carson. A.B., Columbia U., 1933, B.S., 1934, Ch.E., 1935, Ph.D., 1937; postgrad., N.Y. U., Bklyn. Poly. Inst. With N.Y. U., 1941-75, prof., dir. surface tech. program dir. creative sci. program; supr., research scientist Manhattan Project, 1943-45; cons. numerous cos. and govt. agys.; founder, pres., dir. chmn. bd. Markite Co., Markite Corp., Markite Engring. Co., 1948-69, Coler Engring. Co., 1969—; sponsor-in-residence Franklin Inst. Research Labs., 1975-81. Contbr. numerous articles to profl. jours.; Author: Aircraft Engine Finishes, 1941; Editor, contbg. author: essays on Creativity in the Sciences, 1963; Contbg. author: Invention and Education, 1977. Bd. dirs. Van Weazel Found., Woodward Envicon, Marcus and Bertha Coler Found.; mem. advisory com. Dept. Phys. and Engring. Metallurgy, Polytechnic Inst. N.Y.; mem. pres.'s com. for Sch. Continuing Edn. N.Y. U.; appointee Nat. Inventors Council, 1966-74; mem. state tech. service com. Dept. Commerce; with div. cultural studies UNESCO-Dept. State, 1976—. Named hon. prof. Polytechnic Inst. N.Y.; Weston fellow Electrochem. Mem. Am. Math. Soc., AAAS, N.Y. Acad. Sci., Electrochem. Soc., Am. Ceramic Soc., Am. Chem. Soc., Am. Def. Preparedness Assn., Sigma Xi, Phi Beta Kappa, Phi Lambda Upsilon, Tau Beta Pi, Epsilon Chi. Clubs: Princeton, Kona Kai. Patentee and inventor in field. Home: 56 Secor Rd Scarsdale NY Office: One Washington Square Village New York NY 10012

COLERIDGE, CLARENCE NICHOLAS, bishop; b. Georgetown, Guyana, Nov. 27, 1930; came to U.S., 1950; s. Charles and Ina (DeWeever) C.; m. Euna Jervis, Sept. 8, 1962; children: Cheryl Lisa, Carolyn Bridgett. B.S., Howard U., 1954; M.Div., Drew U., 1960; M.S.W., U. Conn., 1973; D.Min., Andover-Newton Theol. Sch., 1977. Ordained deacon Episcopal Ch., 1961, priest, 1962, consecrated bishop, 1981. Asst. minister St. Philip's Episc. Ch., N.Y.C., 1961; curate, dir. youth St. George's Episc. Ch., Bklyn., 1962-66; chaplain Sea View Hosp., Staten Island, N.Y., 1964-66; rector St. Mark's Episc. Ch., Bridgeport, Conn., 1966-81; counselor, dir. counseling Episc. Social Service, Diocese of Conn., 1974-81; suffragan bishop Diocese of Conn., Hartford, 1981—; dir. Pastoral Devel, of Episc. Ch., 1981—. Dir. Gov.'s Task Force on Racial Justice, 1981—, United Fund Fairfield County, 1967-71; v.p. Bridgeport Day Car, Inc., 1978-81. Recipient cert. of appreciation Afro-Am. Educators Assn., 1978, Outstanding Service award Eldorado Club Inc., 1981; named Citizen of Yr. Omega Psi Phi, 1968, Man of Yr. Nat. Council Negro Women, 1980. Democrat. Home: 29 Indian Rd Trumbull CT 06611 Office: Episcopal Diocese of Conn 1335 Asylum Ave Hartford CT 06105

COLES, ANNA LOUISE BAILEY, nurse adminsr., coll. dean; b. Kansas City, Kans., Jan. 16, 1925; d. Gordon Alonzo and Lillie Mai (Buchanan) Bailey; children—Margot, Michelle, Gina. Diploma, Freedmen's Hosp. Sch. Nursing, 1948; B.S. in Nursing, Avila Coll., Kansas City, Mo., 1960, M.S., Cath. U. Am., 1960; Ph.D. in Higher Edn, Cath. U. Am., 1967. Instr. VA Hosp., Topeka, 1950-52, supr., Kansas City, Mo., 1952-58; asst. dir. in-service edn. Freedmen's Hosp., Washington, 1960-61, adminstrv. asst. to dir. nursing, 1961-66, asso. dir. nursing services, 1966-67, dir. nursing, 1967-69; dean Coll. Nursing, Howard U., Washington, 1968—; cons. Gen. Research Support Program, NIH, 1972-76, VA health care com. NRC-Nat. Acad. Scis., 1975-76, VA Gen. Office continuing edn. com., 1976—; pres. Nurses Examining Bd., 1967-68; mem. Inst. Medicine, Nat. Acad. Scis., 1974—; Mem. D.C. Health Planning Adv. Com., 1968-71, Tri-State Regional Planning Com. for Nursing Edn., 1969, Health Adv. Council, Nat. Urban Coalition, 1971-73. Contbr. articles to profl. jours. Bd. dirs. Iona Whipper Home for Unwed Mothers, 1970-72, Nursing Edn. Opportunities, 1970-72; trustee Community Group Health Found., 1976-77, cons., 1977—; bd. regents State Univ. System Fla., 1977; adv. bd. Am. Assn. Med. Vols., 1970-72. Recipient Sustained Superior Performance award HEW, 1962; Meritorious Public Service award Govt. of D.C., 1968; Avila Coll. medal of honor, 1969. Mem. Nat. League Nursing (dir.), Am. Nurses Assn., Freedman Hosp. Nursing Alumni Assn., Am. Congress Rehab. Medicine, Am. Assn. Colls. of Nursing (sec. 1975-76), Sigma Theta Tau, Alpha Kappa Alpha. Home: 627 G St SW Washington DC 20024 Office: Howard Univ Coll Nursing 2400 6th St NW Washington DC 20059

COLES, DONALD EARL, aeronautics educator; b. St. Paul, Feb. 8, 1924; s. Courtney J. and Lorna (Addison) C.; m. Ellen Searight, Sept. 11, 1947; children: Christopher Lee, Elizabeth Anne, Kenneth Spencer, Janet Jacqueline. B.Aero. Engring., U. Minn., 1947; M.S., Calif. Inst. Tech., 1948, Ph.D., 1953. Research engr. Jet Propulsion Lab., Pasadena, Calif., 1950-53; research fellow Calif. Inst. Tech., 1953-56, mem. faculty, 1953, prof. aeros., 1964—; Cons. to industry, 1954—; mem. Nat. Com. Fluid Mechs. Films, 1960. Producer: ednl. film Channel Flow of a Compressible Fluid, 1966. Served with AUS, 1943-46. Fellow AIAA (Lawrence Sperry award 1953), Am. Phys. Soc.; mem. Sigma Xi. Office: 1201 E California Blvd Pasadena CA 91125

COLES, EMBERT HARVEY, JR., educator; b. Garden City, Kans., Oct. 12, 1923; s. Embert Harvey and Neva (Blanchard) C.; m. Janis Waterman, July 27, 1946; children—Charles David, Kay Ann. D.V.M., Kans. State U., 1945, Ph.D., 1958; M.S., Iowa State U., 1946. Grad. asst., then instr. Iowa State U., 1945-48; practice vet. medicine, Colby, Kans., 1948-54; mem. faculty Kans. State U., 1954—, prof., head dept. pathology parasitology and pub. health, 1964-67, prof. clin. pathology, head dept. infectious diseases, 1968-78, head dept. lab. medicine, 1979—; dean Faculty Vet. Medicine; chief of party U.S. AID program Ahmadu Bello U., Zaria, Nigeria, 1970-72. Author: Veterinary Clinical Pathology, 3d ed, 1979. Mem. Am. Vet. Med. Assn., Am. Soc. Vet. Clin. Pathologists (pres. 1966), Am. Soc. Microbiology, Kans. Vet. Med. Assn., Sigma Xi, Phi Kappa Phi, Gamma Sigma Delta, Phi Zeta. Home: 1612 Denholm St Manhattan KS 66502

COLES, ROBERT, child psychiatrist, educator, author; b. Boston, Oct. 12, 1929; s. Philip and Sandra (Young) C.; m. Jane Hallowell; children—Robert, Daniel, Michael. A.B., Harvard U., 1950; M.D., Columbia U., 1954, Temple U., 1972, Notre Dame U., 1972, Bates Coll., 1972, Wayne State U., 1973, Western Mich. U., 1974, Holy Cross Coll., 1974, Hofstra U., 1975, Coll. William and Mary, 1976, Bard Coll., 1976, U. Lowell, 1976, U. Cin., 1976, Stonehill Coll., 1977, Lesley Coll., 1977, Rutgers U., 1977, Wesleyan U., 1978, Columbia Coll., 1978, Knox Coll., 1978, Cleve. State U., 1978, Wooster Coll., 1978, U. N.C., 1979, Manhattan Coll., 1979, St. Peter's Coll., 1979, Coll. New Rochelle, 1979, Pratt Inst. and Sch. Design, 1979, Berea Coll., 1980, Bklyn. Coll., 1980, Emmanuel Coll., 1980, Colby Coll., 1981. Intern U. Chgo. Clinics, 1954-55; resident in psychiatry Mass. Gen. Hosp., Boston, 1955-56, McLean Hosp., Belmont, Mass., 1956-57, Judge Baker Guidance Center-Children's Hosp., 1957-58; mem. staff children's Unit Met. State Hosp., Waltham, Mass., 1957-58; mem. staff alcoholic clinic Mass. Gen. Hosp.; teaching fellow in psychiatry, mem. psychiat. staff and clin. asst. in psychiatry Harvard Med. Sch., 1955-58; research psychiatrist Harvard U. Health Services, 1963—; lectr. gen. edn. Harvard U., 1966—, prof. psychiatry and med. humanities, 1977—; child psychiat. fellow Judge Baker Guidance Center, Children's Hosp., Boston, 1960-61; mem. Nat. Adv. Com. on Farm Labor, 1965—; cons. Appalachian Vols., 1965—, Rockefeller Found., 1969—, Ford Found., 1969—; mem. Inst. of Medicine, Nat. Acad. Scis., 1973-78; vis. prof. public policy Duke U., 1973—; cons. supr. dept. psychiatry Cambridge (Mass.) Hosp., 1976—; cons. Center for Study of So. Culture, U. Miss., 1979—. Author: Children of Crisis: A Study of Courage and Fear, 1967, Dead End School, 1968, Still Hungry in America, 1969, The Grass Pipe, 1969, The Image is Yours, 1969; Wages of Neglect, 1969, Uprooted Children: The Early Lives of Migrant Farmers, 1970, Teachers and the Children of Poverty, 1970, Erik H. Erikson: The Growth of His Work, 1970, The Middle Americans, 1970, Migrants, Sharecroppers and Mountaineers, 1972, The South Goes North, 1972, Saving Face, 1972, Farewell to the South, 1972, A Spectacle Unto the World, 1973, Riding Free, 1973, The Darkness and the Light, 1974, The Buses Roll, 1974, Irony in the Mind's Life: Essays on Novels by James Agee, Elizabeth Bowen and George Eliot, 1974, Headsparks, 1975, The Mind's Fate, 1975, Eskimos, Chicanos and Indians, 1978, Priviledged Ones: The Well-Off and The Rich in America, 1978, Women of Crisis Lives of Struggle and Hope, (with Jane Hallowell Coles), 1978, Walker Percy: An American Search, 1978, Flannery O'Connor's South, 1980, Women of Crisis; Lives of Work and Dreams, 1980, and other books; contbg. editor: The New Republic, 1966—, Am. Poetry Rev, 1972—, Aperture, 1974—, Lit. and Medicine, 1981—, New Oxford Rev, 1981—; mem. editorial bd.: Integrated Edn, 1967—, Child Psychiatry and Human Devel, 1969—, Rev. of Books and Religion, 1976—, Internat. Jour. Family Therapy, 1977—, Grants mag, 1977—, Learning mag, 1978—, Jour. Am. Culture, 1977—, Jour. Edn, 1979—; bd. editors: Parents' Choice, 1978—; editor: Children and Youth Services Rev, 1978—. Bd. dirs. Field Found., 1968—; trustee Robert F. Kennedy Meml., 1968—, Robert F. Kennedy Action Corps, State of Mass., 1968—, Miss. Inst. Early Childhood Edn., 1968—, Twentieth Century Fund, 1971—; bd. dirs. Reading is Fundamental, Smithsonian Inst., 1968—, Am. Freedom from Hunger Found., 1968—, Am. Parents Com., 1971—; mem. corp. Boston Children's Service, 1970; mem. adv. council Inst. for Nonviolent Social Change of Martin Luther King, Jr. Meml. Center, 1971—, Ams. for Children's Relief, 1972—; mem. nat. com. for Edn. of Young Children, 1972—; mem. nat. adv. council Rural Am., 1976—; trustee Austen Riggs Found., Stockbridge, Mass., 1976—; mem. nat. adv. com. Ala. Citizens for Responsive Public Television, 1976—; mem. adv. com. Nat. Indian Edn. Assn., 1976—; visotor's com. mem. Boston Mus. Fine Arts, 1977; bd. dirs. Boys Club Boston, 1977; vis. com. Boston Coll. Law Sch., 1977; adv. Center for So. Folklore, 1978—; mem. children's com. Edna McConnell Clark Found., 1978—; bd. dirs. Lyndhurst Found., 1978—; mem. nat. adv. bd. Foxfire Fund, Inc., 1979—. Recipient Ralph Waldo Emerson prize Phi Beta Kappa, 1967; Anisfield-Wolf award in race relations Saturday Rev., 1968; Hofheimer award Am. Psychiat. Assn., 1968; Sidney Hillman prize, 1971; Weatherford prize Berea Coll. and Council So. Mountains, 1973; Lilliam Smith Award So. Regional Council, 1973; McAlpin medal Nat. Assn. Mental Health, 1972; Pulitzer prize, 1973 (all received for Children of Crisis, Vols. II, III); disting. scholar medal Hofstra U., 1974; William A. Shonfeld award Am. Soc. Adolescent Psychiatry, 1977; fellow Davenport Coll., Yale U., 1976—. Fellow Am. Acad. Arts and Scis., Inst. Soc., Ethics and the Life Scis.; mem. Am. Psychiat. Assn., Am. Orthopsychiat. Assn. (past dir.), Acad. Psychoanalysis, Nat. Orgn. Migrant Children. Home: 81 Carr Rd Concord MA 01742 Office: 75 Mount Auburn St Cambridge MA 02138

COLES, ROBERT TRAYNHAM, architect; b. Buffalo, Aug. 24, 1929; s. George Edward and Helena Vesta (Traynham) C.; m. Sylvia Rose Meyn, Mar. 28, 1953; children: Marion Brigette, Darcy Eliot. Student, Hampton Inst., 1947-49; B.A., U. Minn., 1951, B. Arch., 1953; M.Arch., M.I.T., 1955; Litt.D. (hon.), Medaille Coll., 1977. Designer Perry, Shaw, Hepburn and Dean (Architects), Boston, 1956-57, Shepley, Bulfinch, Richardson and Abbott (Architects), 1957-58, Carl Koch and Asso., Cambridge, Mass., 1958-59; architect, custom design mgr. Techbuilt, Inc. (housing prefabricators), Cambridge, 1959-60; coordinating architect Deleuw, Cather and Brill, Engrs., Buffalo, 1960-63; prin. Robert Traynham Coles, P.C., Buffalo, 1963—; v.p. Buffalo Archtl. Guidebook Corp., 1979-82; cons. housing research Union Carbide Corp., 1963; vis. prof. State U. N.Y. Coll. at Buffalo, summer 1967, U. Kans., 1969; Vice pres. Eastside Community Orgn. Inc., 1965-68, pres., 1968-77; chmn. Com. for an Urban Univ., 1966-67, Goals for Met. Buffalo, 1967-68; pres. Community Planning Assistance Center Western N.Y., Inc., 1972-74, Archtl. Mus. and Resource Center, 1980—. Editor: newsletter Nat. Orgn. Minority Architects, 1972-75; contbr. to: The Urban Ecosystem: A Holistic Approach, 1974. Bd. dirs. Build a New City, Inc., 1973—; trustee Preservation League N.Y. State, sec., 1978; trustee Western N.Y. Public Broadcasting Assn., 1981—. Recipient Centennial award Medaille Coll., 1975; Edward H. Moeller scholar, 1949-53; Rotch Travelling scholar Boston Soc. Architects, 1955. Fellow AIA (mem. nat. housing com. 1969—, nat. urban design and planning com. 1971—, chmn. social responsibility com. Buffalo-Western N.Y. chpt. 1970-71, dir. 1978—, nat. dep. v.p. minority affairs 1974-75, Whitney E. Young award 1981); mem. Nat. Orgn. Minority Architects (treas. 1976-78, dir. 1978, v.p. 1978), Alpha Kappa Mu. Home: 321 Humboldt Pkwy Buffalo NY 14208 Office: 730 Ellicott Sq Buffalo NY 14203 *Today's architect has a special task which goes beyond simply designing the physical environment. He must be an activist involved in the social and political life of the community. He must address his efforts to change in these areas as well, so that man can make the needed adjustments to an increasingly challenging and rich urban world. He must be an initiator as well as an implementor—a leader more than a follower. He must truly be a revolutionary who sees his architecture as a broad movement to enhance the quality of life of urban man.*

COLESCOTT, ROBERT HUTTON, artist, educator; b. Oakland, Calif., Aug. 26, 1925; s. Warrington Wickham and Lydia Kenner (Hutton) C.; m. Zdenka Falarova, 1950 (div. 1962); children: Alexander, Nicholas; m. Sally Dennett, 1962 (div. 1972); 1 son, Dennett; m. Susan Ables, 1979 (div. 1983); 1 son, Daniel. A.B., U. Calif.-Berkeley, 1949, M.A., 1952; postgrad., Atelier F. Leger, Paris, 1949-50. Assoc. prof. art Portland State Coll, Oreg., 1957-66; vis. prof. art Am. U., Cairo, Egypt, 1966-67; prof. art Calif. State Coll., Stanislaus, 1970-74; vis. lectr. painting and drawing U. Calif.-Berkeley, 1974-79; prof. painting and drawing San Francisco Art Inst., 1976—; vis. artist U. Ariz., Tucson, 1983-84. Exhibited numerous one-man shows, N.Y.C., 1973, 75, 77, 79-82, Albright Coll., Reading, Pa., 1983, group shows, Palm Springs Desert Mus., Calif., 1982, Orgn. Ind. Artists, N.Y.C., Indpls. Mus. Art, Corcoran Mus. Art, Washington, 1983, Whitney Mus. Am. Art, N.Y.C., Fla. Internat. U., Bucknell Coll., Pa., Hamilton Coll., N.Y., Contemporary Arts Mus., Houston, others; represented permanent collections, Seattle Art Mus., San Francisco Mus. Modern Art, Oakland Mus., Calif., Met. Mus. Art, Portland Art Mus., U. Mass., Amherst, U. S. Steel Corp., Pitts, Reed Coll., Oreg., U. Oreg., Columbia Coll., Oreg., pvt. collections; panelist painting selection, Nat. Endowment for Arts, Washington, 1982. Am. Research Center fellow, Egypt, 1965-66; grantee Nat. Endowment Arts, 1976, Nat. Endowment Arts, 1980, 1983. Office: San Francisco Art Inst 800 Chestnut St San Francisco CA 94133 2d Office: Dept Art Univ Ariz Tucson AZ 85721 *Over the years I have tried most diligently not to censor myself.*

COLESCOTT, WARRINGTON WICKHAM, artist, printmaker, educator; b. Oakland, Calif., Mar. 7, 1921; s. Warrington W. and Lydia (Hutton) C.; m. Frances Myers, Mar. 15, 1971; children by previous marriage: Louis Moore, Julian Hutton, Lydia Alice. A.B., U. Calif. at Berkeley, 1942, M.A., 1947; postgrad., Acad. de la Grand Chaumiere, Paris, France, 1950, 53, Slade Sch. Art, U. London (Eng.), 1957. Mem. faculty U. Wis., Madison, 1949—, prof. art, 1957—, Leo Steppat prof., 1979—, chmn. dept., 1958-60; vis. prof. printmaking Tyler Sch. Art, Rome, Italy, 1966, Manhattanville Coll., 1973. One-man shows, Madison Art Center, 1979 and nat. tour, 1978-81, Print Club, Phila., 1983, permanent collections, Mus. Modern Art, Victoria and Alberta Mus., London, Bibliotechque Nat., Paris, N.Y. Pub. Library, Met. Mus., Chgo. Art Inst., Bklyn. Mus., Phila. Mus. Art, Walker Art Center, Mpls., Whitney Mus. Am. Art, invited artist, 8th Brit. Internat. Print Biennale, 1984, 14th Internat. Biennale Graphic Art, Ljubljana, Yugoslavia, 1981, 83. Trustee Elvehjem Mus. Art, U. Wis. Served to 1st lt., inf. AUS, 1942-46. Recipient purchase awards Colorprint USA, 1971, 77, 80, Bklyn. Mus., 1976, Am. Colorprint Soc., 1976, Hawaii Bienial, 1978, 79, award of merit Ill. Regional Print Show, 1978; Fulbright fellow, 1957; Guggenheim fellow, 1965; Nat. Endowment Arts Printmaking fellow, 1975; Artist fellow, 1979, 83-84. Mem. Soc. Am. Graphic Artists (award 1963, 64, 77), Nat. Print Orgn. (bd. dirs. 1979-80), Am. Colorprint Soc., Mid-Am. Coll. Art Assn. Office: Dept Art U Wis Madison WI 53706 *As an artist, I have tried to express ideas in visual form that stem from my experience, intellect and emotional make-up. I feel I have unique qualities that stem from genetic inheritance and, the luck of surviving young adulthood in the forties, manhood in the fifties and maturity in the sixties. It gives one resources and originality and that is the material of my art and, hopefully, my teaching of young artists.*

COLGATE, STIRLING A., physicist; b. N.Y.C., Nov. 14, 1925; m. Rosemary Williamson; children: Henry, Sarah, Arthur. B.A. in Physics, Cornell U., Ithaca, N.Y., 1948, Ph.D., 1952. With Lawrence Radiation Lab., Berkeley, Calif., 1951-52, Livermore, Calif., 1952-64; electron and accelerator physicist; physicist nuclear weapons and tests, 1955; staff Controlled Thermonuclear Fusion project, 1955-64; tech. adviser Conf. Discontinuance Nuclear Weapons Tests, Geneva, 1959; pres. N.Mex. Inst. Mining and Tech., Socorro, 1965-74; sr. fellow, physicist, spl. research on controlled thermonuclear fusion, astrophysics, atmospheric physics Los Alamos Nat. Lab., 1976—; partner Richard M. Colgate (patent devel.), 1958—; Mem. nuclear panel Sci. Adv. Bd., 1959-61; adv. com. fluid mechanics NASA, 1960-62; cons. ballistic missile div. USAF, 1960-62; cons. Def. Atomic Support Agy., 1962-64; mem. adv. com. environ. scis. NSF, 1967; mem. Nat. Acad. Sci. panel on space plasma physics, 1977-79, panel on physics of sun, 1979—; chmn. panel on physics of sun Space Sci. Bd., 1980-81. Trustee-at-large Asso. Univs., 1970-73, Aura-Kitt Peak, 1973-78, Space Sci. Bd., 1976-79. Fellow Am. Phys. Soc.; mem. Am. Astron. Soc., Sigma Xi. Home: 4616 Ridgeway Los Alamos NM 87544 Office: MS 275 Los Alamos Nat Lab Los Alamos NM 87545

COLGRASS, MICHAEL CHARLES, composer; b. Chgo., Apr. 22, 1932; s. Michael Clement and Ann (H) C.; m. Ulla Damgaard, Nov. 25, 1966; 1 son, Neal. Mus.B., U. Ill., 1956; scholar, Tanglewood (Mass.), 1952, 54, Aspen (Colo.), 1953; Pupil, Paul Price, Eugene Weigle, Darius Milhand, Lukas Foss, Wallingford Riegger, Ben Weber. Free-lance solo percussionist maj. N.Y. mus. orgns., 1956—; Narrator, Boston Symphony, 1969, Phila. Orch., 1970; dir.: Virgil's Dream, Brighton Festival; Soloist, Danish Radio Orch., 1965; dir.: opera Nightingale Inc, U. Ill. Contemporary Music Festival, 1975; author, poet own theatre works, 1966—; Composer: Divertimento, 1961, Fantasy Variations, 1961, Wind Quintet, 1962, Light Spirit, 1963, Rhapsody, 1963, Rhapsodic Fantasy, 1965, Sea Shadow, 1966, As Quiet As, 1966, Virgil's Dream, 1967, Three Brothers, 1951, Percussion Music, 1953, Chamber Music for Four Drums and String Quintet, 1954, Chamber Music for Percussion Quintet, 1955, Variations for Four Drums and Viola, 1957, The Earth's a Baked Apple, 1968-69, New People for mezzosoprano, viola, piano, 1969, Nightingale, Inc, Auras for Harp and Orch, 1973, Image of Man, 1974, Concertmasters for 3 violins and orch, 1975, Best Wishes U.S.A. for black and white choruses, folk instruments, jazz band and orch, 1976, Theatre of the Universe for solists, chorus and orch, 1976, Wolf for solo cello, 1976, Letter from Mozart for orch, 1976, Déjà Vu, 1977 (Pulitzer prize 1978), Mystery Flowers of Spring for soprano and piano, 1978, The Tower; for children's musical theatre Something's Gonna Happen, 1978; musical play for 5 brass Flashbacks, 1979; 5 songs for soprano and 4 players Night of the Raccoon, 1979; Delta, for violin, clarinet, percussion and orch, 1979; a mus. drama for solo piano on the writings of Carlos Castaneda Tales of Power, 1980; Metamusic for solo piano, 1981, Momento for 2 pianos and orch., 1982, Demon for amplified piano, tape, radios and orch., 1983, works commd., N.Y. Philharm., CBC, Boston Symphony, Lincoln Center Chamber Mus. Soc., Fromm Found., Corp. for Pub. Broadcasting, Ford Found., Spokane, Detroit, Springfield, Minn. symphony orchs., Musica Aeterna Orch. N.Y., Young Concert Artists, N.Y., Nat. Arts Centre Orch. of Can., New World Festival Arts, works recorded various cos.; Contbr. articles to publs.; columnist: Music Mag. Served with AUS, 1954-56. Guggenheim fellow, 1964-65, 68-69; recipient Fromm award, 1966, Chem. Bank award, 1971, Emmy award for Sta. WGBH-TV film Soundings: The Music of Michael Colgrass for best documentary Nat. Acad. TV Arts and Scis., 1982; Rockefeller grantee, 1967-69. Office: 583 Palmerston Ave Toronto ON Canada M6G 2P6 *I see the composer as a person not separate from life and community but indigenous to it. How to bridge the gap that has developed between the artist and people is the biggest challenge I know, but I find the more I reach out to people the less indifferent they are to the artistic experience.*

COLHOUN, HOWARD POST, investment company executive; b. West Point, N.Y., Nov. 13, 1935; s. Daniel W. and Ella (Speer) C.; m. Patricia Reynolds, June 23, 1962; children—Elizabeth B. Post, Nina R., Alexander H.P., Robin R. B.S.E., Princeton U., 1957; postgrad. (Fulbright scholar), U. Trondheim, Norway, 1957-58; M.B.A., Harvard U., 1961. Engr. Bethlehem Steel Corp., Sparrows Point, Md., 1958-59; staff cons. Arthur D. Little Inc., Cambridge, Mass., 1961-66; v.p. T. Rowe Price Assos. Inc., Balt., 1966—; chmn. bd., dir. Rowe Price New Era Fund Inc., Balt., 1971—; v.p. T. Rowe Price Growth Stock Fund, Rowe Price New Income Fund, Rowe Price Res. Fund, Rowe Price Tax Free Income Fund, Rowe Price New Horizons Fund, T. Rowe Price Tax Exempt Fund, T. Rowe Price Internat. Fund.; founder, mng. ptnr. Emerging Growth Ptnrs., L.P.; dir. Arnold Graphics.; Regular panelist on nat. TV program Wall Street Week, 1970—. Author: Investing in Brooder Technology, 1969, A Fundamentalist's Approach to Growth Stock Investing, 1971. Pres. United Fund of North Shore, Boston, 1965; Trustee, treas. Bryn Mawr Sch.; trustee Investment Mgmt. Workshop, Baltimore County Revenue Authority., Nat. Acquarium Balt., Md. Pension Fund. Mem. Fin. Analysts Fedn.; trustee Balt. Soc. Security Analysts (dir., v.p. 1970-75), Sigma Xi, Tau Beta Pi. Clubs: Green Spring Valley Hunt, Bachelor's Cotillion, Center, Skating of Balt., Harvard Bus. Sch. of Md. (Princeton of Md.) (trustee 1970-71). Home: 211 Green Spring Valley Rd Garrison MD 21055 Office: 400 E Pratt St Baltimore MD 21202

COLI, GUIDO JOHN, JR., chemical company executive; b. Richmond, Va., Sept. 12, 1921; s. Guido and Rena (Pacini) C.; children: Pamela, Patricia, Deborah, Richard. B.S., Va. Poly. Inst., 1941, M.S., 1942, Ph.D., 1949. Registered profl. engr., N.Y., Va. Asst. engr. Va. Health Dept. bur. indsl. hygiene, 1941; asso. chemist Naval Research Lab., 1942-43; instr. chem. engring. Va. Poly. Inst., 1947-48; chem. engr. Mobil Oil Co., Paulsboro, N.J., 1949-50; with Allied Chem. Corp., N.Y.C., 1950-72, group v.p. corp., 1968-72, dir., 1970-72; pres. Am. Enka Co., Enka, N.C., 1979-82; dir. Akzona, Inc., 1979—, pres., chief exec. officer, 1982—; dir. NCNB Nat. Bank of N.C., Brand-Rex Co. Mem. Gov. Va. Commn. to Establish Urban Univ. in Richmond Area, 1966-67; mem. adv. council Coll. of Engring., Va. Poly. Inst.; bd. dirs. St. Joseph's Hosp., Asheville, N.C.; pres. Mountain Health Services, Asheville. Served to lt. USN, 1943-46. Fellow Am. Inst. Chemists; mem. Am. Chem. Soc. (chmn. Va. 1957), Am. Inst. Chem. Engrs., Sigma Xi, Phi Lambda Upsilon, Tau Beta Pi, Phi Kappa Phi, Alpha Kappa Psi. Clubs: University (N.Y.C.); Country of Asheville. Home: Akzona Inc 314 Town Mountain Rd Asheville NC 28804 Office: PO Box 2930 Asheville NC 28802

COLICOS, JOHN, actor; b. Toronto, Ont., Can., Dec. 10, 1928; s. William and Catherine C.; m. Mona McHenry, 1957; children—Edmund, Nicholas. Student, Brae Manor Theatre, Knowlton, Que., Can., 1947-48; drama studies with, Eleanor Stuart, Montreal. Theatre debut in: Book of Job, Montreal, 1944; appeared in numerous plays including roles with, Montreal Repertory Theatre, Can. Repertory Theatre, Ottawa; as Lear in: King Lear at, Old Vic Theatre Co., London, Am. Shakespeare Festival, Stratford, Conn.; specializing in Shakespearean roles; appeared for 4 yrs. at, Stratford (Ont.) Shakespeare Festival; appeared on Broadway as Winston Churchill in: Soldiers, 1969; films include Anne of a Thousand Days, Raid on Rommel, Red Sky at Morning, Doctor's Wives, The Wrath of God, Postman Always Rings Twice, Scorpio, Drum, Breaking Point, Battlestar Galactica, The Changeling, Phobia; also appeared in: numerous radio and TV shows, including General Hospital (Recipient best actor award Dominion Drama Festival 1951)

COLIN, LAWRENCE, space scientist; b. N.Y.C., Jan. 19, 1931; s. Maurice and Celia (Merkin) C.; m. Roberta Miles, June 28, 1953; children: Lee Edward, Lisa Maria. B.E.E., Poly. Inst. Bklyn., 1952; M.E.E., Syracuse U., 1960; Ph.D., Stanford U., 1964. Research engr. USAF Rome Air Devel. Center, Griffiss AFB, N.Y., 1952-64; research scientist NASA Ames Research Center, Moffett Field, Calif., 1964—, chief space sci. div., 1983—; USAF grad. research scholar, 1960. Contbr. sci. articles to profl. jours. Recipient Superior Accomplishment award USAF, 1955, Sustained Performance award, 1966, Spl. Achievement award, 1975, 79, Group Achievement award, 1971, 80, Disting. Service medal, 1980; all NASA). Mem. AIAA, IEEE, Am. Astron. Soc. (div. planetary scis., disting. service medal 1980), Am. Geophys. Union, Sigma Xi. Jewish. Home: 3913 Nelson Dr Palo Alto CA 94306 Office: NASA Ames Research Center MS 245-1 Moffett Field CA 94035

COLIN, RALPH FREDERICK, lawyer; b. N.Y.C., Nov. 18, 1900; s. William and Elizabeth (Benjamin) C.; m. Georgia Talmey, June 2, 1931; children: Ralph Frederick, Pamela Talmey (Lady Harlech). A.B., CCNY, 1918; LL.B., Columbia U., 1921. Bar: N.Y. 1922. Assoc. Rosenberg & Ball, N.Y.C., 1921, mem., 1926, later Rosenberg, Goldmark & Colin; of counsel Rosenman Colin Freund Lewis & Cohen; dir., gen. counsel CBS, 1927-69, Columbia Artists Mgmt., Inc.; adminstrv. v.p., gen. counsel Art Dealers Assn. Am. Cons. editor: Air Law Rev.; contbr. to law reviews and art periodicals. Active early devel. art theatres, N.Y.C.; past dir. Provincetown, Greenwich Village, Actors theatres.; bd. dirs., trustee, v.p. Philharm. Symphony Soc. N.Y., 1942-56; trustee, hon. sec. Baron de Hirsch Fund, 1935-56; trustee, v.p. Mus. Modern Art, N.Y.C., 1954-69, vice chmn. internat. council; trustee Hosp. Joint Diseases, 1932-52, chmn. bd., 1949-51, pres., 1951-52; mem. vis. com. dept. fine arts and Fogg Mus., Harvard U., 1951-73, 75—; bd. visitors Columbia Law Sch., 1961—; bd. dirs. Richard and Dorothy Rodgers Found., Bernheim Found., Woodheath Found., CBS Found., 1953-69; pres. CBS Found., 1956-69; bd. dirs. Am. Fedn. Arts, 1946-56; chmn. radio broadcasting div. Nat. War Fund, 1943-44. Mem. Assn. Bar City N.Y. (exec. com. 1942-46, mem. com. on judiciary 1948-51, com. on grievances 1956-61, chmn. spl. com. on pub. and bar relations 1956-59, v.p. 1960-61, chmn. com. profl. ethics 1961-62), N.Y. County Lawyers Assn., ABA, Fed. Communications, N.Y. State bar assns. Home: 941 Park Ave New York NY 10028 Office: 575 Madison Ave New York NY 10022

COLISH, MARCIA LILLIAN, educator; b. Bklyn., July 27, 1937; d. Samuel and Daisy (Kartch) C. B.A. magna cum laude, Smith Coll., 1958; M.A., Yale U., 1959, Ph.D., 1965. Instr. history Skidmore Coll., Saratoga Springs, N.Y., 1962-63; instr. Oberlin Coll., Ohio, 1963-65, asst. prof., 1965-69; assoc. prof. Oberlin Coll, Ohio, 1969-75; prof. history Oberlin Coll., Ohio, 1975—, chmn. dept. history, 1973-74, 78-81; lectr. history Case Western Res. U., Cleve., 1966-67; editorial cons. W.W. Norton & Co., 1973, John Wiley & Sons, Inc., 1981, SUNY Press, 1983; cons. dept. history Grinnell Coll., 1974, Knox Coll., 1981, St. John's U., 1981, Whitman Coll., 1982; mem. exec. bd. Ohio Program in Humanities, 1976-81, exec. bd., 1978-81, vice chmn., 1979-81. Author: The Mirror of Language: A Study in the Medieval Theory of Knowledge, 2d rev. edit., 1983, The Stoic Tradition from Antiquity to the Early Middle Ages, 1984. Mem. exec. bd. ACLU, 1970-74, chmn., 1972-74, rec. sec., 1976-77, vice chmn., 1979-80; mem. exec. bd. Oberlin YWCA, 1966-70. Recipient Hazel Edgerly prize Smith Coll., 1958; Samuel S. Fels fellow Yale U., 1961-62; younger scholar fellow Nat. Endowment for Humanities, 1968-69; sr. fellow Nat. Endowment for Humanities, 1981-82; vis. scholar Am. Acad. Rome, 1968-69; fellow Inst. for Research in Humanities, U. Wis., 1974-75; Nat. Humanities Ctr. fellow, 1981-82. Mem. Am. Hist. Assn., Medieval Acad. Am., Medieval Assn. Midwest (council 1978-81), Midwest Medieval Conf. (pres. 1978-79), Renaissance Soc. Am., Central Renaissance Conf., Societe Internat. our l'Etude de Philosophie medievale, Phi Beta Kappa. Home: 143 E College St Apt 310 Oberlin OH 44074 Office: Dept History Oberlin Coll Oberlin OH 44074

COLKER, EDWARD, artist, educator; b. Phila., Jan. 5, 1927. Grad., Phila. Coll. Art, 1949; B.S., NYU, 1965. Instr., critic Phila. Coll. Art, Cooper Union, N.Y.C., 1949-66; assoc. prof. Grad. Sch. Fine Arts, U. Pa., 1968-70; dir. Sch. Art and Design, U. Ill., Chgo., 1972-78, research prof. art, 1977-80; dean of visual arts SUNY, Coll. at Purchase, 1980—; cons. in field. One-man shows, Print Club, Phila., 1961, Amel Gallery, N.Y.C., 1965, East Hampton Gallery, N.Y.C., 1969, Douglas Kenyon Gallery, Chgo., 1975, others; represented in permanent collections, Mus. Art, Phila., Library of Congress, Washington, Mus. Modern Art, N.Y.C., Nat. Mus., Stockholm, Rosenwald Collection, N.Y. U., others. Guggenheim Found. fellow, 1961-62; Ill. Arts Council grantee, 1973, 80; Graham Found. grantee, 1977. Mem. Coll. Art Assn. Am. Club: Caxton. Office: SUNY Purchase NY 10577

COLKER, MARVIN LEONARD, classics educator; b. Pitts., Mar. 19, 1927; s. Philip Marcus and Sarah (Grodner) C.; m. Hazel Robinson, Nov. 28, 1959; 1 son, Philip Ian. B.A. summa cum laude, U. Pitts., 1948; Ph.D., Harvard, 1951; postgrad. Sheldon fellow, 1951-52, U. Paris, 1951-52. Instr. classics U. Va., 1953-56, asst. prof., 1956-59, asso. prof., 1959-68, prof., 1967—, chmn. dept. classics, 1963-68; cataloguer Mediaeval manuscripts U. Dublin, Ireland, 1958—, lectr. patristics, Mediaeval Latin, 1962-63; co-dir. Mediaeval manuscripts course standing conf. Nat. and Univ. Librarians, Dublin, 1968. Author: Fulcoii Belvacensis Epistolae, 1954, Henrici Augustensis Planctus Evae, 1956, Richard of S. Victor and the Anonymous of Bridlington, 1962, Analecta Dublinensia: Three Medieval Latin Texts in the Library of Trinity College, Dublin, 1975, Galteri De Castellione Alexandreis, 1978, America Rediscovered in the Thirteenth Century?, 1979; mem. editorial bd.: Medievalia et Humanistica. Grantee Am. Philos. Soc., Trinity Trust, NEH, U. Dublin Fund.; Fellow Am. Council Learned Socs., 1962-63; Sesquicentennial asso. U. Va., 1973-74; Guggenheim fellow, 1973-74. Mem. Am. Philol. Assn., Archaeol. Inst. Am., Mediaeval Acad. Am. (former councillor), Classical Assn. Middle West and South, Phi Beta Kappa. Home: 105 Westminster Rd Charlottesville VA 22901

COLKET, MEREDITH BRIGHT, JR., genealogist, local historian; b. Strafford, Pa., Aug. 18, 1912; s. Meredith Bright and Alberta (Kelsey) C.; m. Julia Beatrice Pelot, June 29, 1945; children: William Currie, Meredith Bright, III, John Pelot. B.A. cum laude, Haverford (Pa.) Coll., 1935, M.A., 1940; Litt.D. (hon.), Baldwin-Wallace Coll., Berea, Ohio, 1974. Asst. in govt. Haverford Coll., 1936; archivist Nat. Archives, Washington, 1937-57; lectr. Am. U., 1950-59; dir., then exec. dir. Western Res. Hist. Soc., Cleve., 1957-80, emeritus, 1980—; founder, dir. Am. Inst. Geneal. Research, 1950-59; mem. Cleveland Heights (Ohio) Landmarks Commn., 1974—, chmn., 1978-82; v.p. Nationalities Services Center, Cleve., 1974-78; lectr. in field, 1944—. Compiler: The Marbury Ancestry, 1936, The Jenks Family of England, 1956; co-compiler: Guide to Genealogical Records in the National Archives, 1964, Founders of Early American Families, 1975; assoc. editor: Am. Genealogist, 1937-50; contbr. articles to profl. jours. Fellow Soc. Am. Archivists, Soc. Genealogists (London), Am. Soc. Genealogists (hon. pres. 1969); mem. Internat. Soc. Brit. Genealogy and Family History (a founder, dir.), Am. Assn. State and Local History (a founder), Columbia Hist. Soc. (hon. mem., past curator, v.p.), New Eng. Historic Geneal. Soc., Nat. Trust Historic Preservation, Nat. Geneal. Soc., Ohio Geneal. Soc., Geneal. Soc. Pa., Hist. Soc. Pa. (life); hon. mem. Acad. Costarricense de Ciencias Genealogicas, Costa Rica. Republican. Methodist. Clubs: Rowfant, Philosophical (Cleve.). Home: 2263 Lamberton Rd Cleveland Heights OH 44118 Office: 10825 East Blvd Cleveland OH 44106

COLL, HELEN F., banker; b. nr. Lovettsville, Va., Dec. 2, 1921; d. Raymond C. and Minnie (Peters) Frye; m. Lee Stanley Sherline, Sept. 1, 1942 (div. Feb. 1955); m. Robert Francis Coll, May 25, 1957. Grad., Washington Sch. Secs., 1940; student, George Washington U., 1945-46; grad., Sch. Financial Pub. Relations, Northwestern U., 1963, Stonier Sch. Banking, Rutgers U., 1966. With Nat. Savs. & Trust Co., Washington, 1940—, bookkeeping clk., note dept. clk., collection teller, sec. trust dept., sec. safe deposit dept., head new accounts dept., sec. to pres., 1948-51, asst. sec., 1951-55, sec., 1955-63, v.p., sec., 1963-66, v.p. sec. bd., 1966-72, sr. v.p., sec. bd., 1972—; sr. v.p., sec. NS & T Bankshares Inc. Mem. Met. Bd. Trade. Mem. Nat. Assn. Bank Women, D.C. Bankers Assn. Presbyterian. Club: City Tavern. Home: 1310 29th St NW Washington DC 20007 also Fantasy Farm Round Hill VA 22141 Office: Nat Savs & Trust Co New York Ave at 15th St NW Washington DC 20005

COLLADAY, MARTIN GRIMES, former air force officer, bus. exec.; b. Hutchinson, Kans., Oct. 5, 1925; s. Glover Stewart and Sarah Ball (Grimes) C.; m. Georgianne Lou Dutton, Jan. 27, 1957; children—Carrie Frances, Amy Lane, Georgianne Lou, Melissa Sarah. B.S., U.S. Mil. Acad., 1946; M.A., George Washington U., 1964. Commd. 2d lt. USAF, 1946, advanced through grades to lt. gen., 1975; ballistic missile programming SAC Hdqrs., 1958-63; asst. for gen. officer matters DCS Personnel USAF Hdqrs., 1966-69; vice comdr. maj. subordinate command Mil. Airlift Command, 1969-70; chief ops. and plans UN Command, Korea, 1970-72; vice dir. joint staff Joint Chiefs of Staff, Washington, 1972-74; chief of staff, hdqrs. SAC, 1974-75; dep. chmn. NATO Mil. Com., Brussels, 1975-77; v.p. public affairs Con Agra, Inc., Omaha, 1980—. Decorated D.S.M., Legion of Merit, Meritorious Service medal, Air Force Commendation medal, Order Nat. Security Merit Republic of Korea. Mem. Am. Legion, Order Daedalian. Presbyn. (elder). Home: 415 Martin Dr N Bellevue NE 68005 Office: Kiewit Plaza Omaha NE 68131

COLLADO, EMILIO GABRIEL, energy company executive; b. Cranford, N.J., Dec. 20, 1910; s. Emilio Gabriel and Carrie (Hansee) C.; m. Janet Gilbert, June 30, 1932 (dec.); children: Emilio Gabriel, Lisa; m. Maria Elvira Tanco de Lopez, Oct. 6, 1972. Student, Phillips Acad., Andover, Mass., 1925-27; S.B., Mass. Inst. Tech., 1931; A.M., Harvard, 1934, Ph.D., 1936. With printing and pub. firm, 1931; econ. analyst U.S. Treasury Dept., 1934-36; economist Fed. Res. Bank N.Y., 1936-38; with Dept. State, 1938-46; asst. chief div. Am. Republics, 1940, spl. asst. to under sec. state, 1941-44; exec. sec. Bd. Econ. Operations, 1941-43, asso. adviser internat. econ. affairs, 1943-44, chief div. financial and monetary affairs, 1944-45; dir. Office Fin. and Devel. Policy, also dep. to asst. sec. for econ. affairs, 1945-46; U.S. exec. dir. Internat. Bank for Reconstrn. and Devel., 1946-47; trustee Export-Import Bank, Washington, 1944-45; with Exxon Corp., 1947-75, asst. treas., 1949-54, treas., 1954-60, dir., 1960-75, v.p., 1962-66, exec. v.p., 1966-75; pres., chief exec. officer Adela Investment Co. S.A., 1976-79; also dir.; chmn., chief exec. officer, dir. Grace Geothermal Corp., 1981-84, dir., cons., 1984—; chmn., dir. Internat. Planning Corp., 1981—; dir. DCNY Corp., Discount Corp. N.Y.; past dir. Morgan Guaranty Trust Co. N.Y.; adv. council Morgan Guaranty Bank Trust Co. N.Y.; past dir. Cold Spring Harbor Lab.; dir. Collado Assos., Otto Wolff U.S. Holding Corp., Boles and Co.; past dir. J.P. Morgan & Co., Inc.; U.S. alt. mem. Inter-Am. Finance and Econ. Adv. Com., 1939-46. Former chmn. com. to visit Sch. Public Health, Harvard; bd. visitors Fletcher Sch. Internat. Diplomacy; trustee Com. Econ. Devel., chmn., 1972-75; trustee Hispanic Soc.; past chmn., now bd. dirs. Center for Inter-Am. Relations; bd. dirs. Work in Am. Inst.; bd. govs., exec. com. Atlantic Inst. Internat. Affairs.; bd. dirs. Am. Soc. Mem. USA/BIAC, bus. and industry adv. com., OECD (former chmn.), Am. Acad. Arts and Scis., Am. Econ. Assn., Internat. C. of C. (mem. exec. com. U.S. council), Atlantic Council U.S. (past vice chmn.), Acad. Polit. Sci. (vice chmn.), Council Fgn. Relations, Phi Mu Delta. Clubs: Metropolitan, Internat. (Washington); Piping Rock, Racquet and Tennis, River. Home: 130 Shu Swamp Rd Locust Valley NY 11560 Office: 1 Rockefeller Plaza New York NY 10020

COLLAS, MICHEL, steel company executive; b. Paris, Nov. 2, 1923; s. Robert and Paulette (Bouchardon) C.; m. Marianne Hubert, Dec. 16, 1950; children: Caroline, Philippe. Grad., Ecole des Mines de Paris, 1984; master law, U. Paris, 1949. With Bur. Mines, 1949-50; with steel div. Ministry of Industry, 1950-51, tech. adviser to minister, 1951-52; supt. tinning, then v.p. ops. Sollac, 1952-59; successively v.p. steel ops., v.p. ops., exec. v.p., dir. gen. CAFL (steel and heavy equipment), 1960-69; dir. gen. Creusot-Loire (steel and heavy equipment), Paris, 1970-78, vice chmn., 1979-82; chmn. bd. Phoenix Steel Corp., Claymont, Del., 1978—, also UCL Securities Inc.; chmn. French Steel Research Inst., 1979—, ARBEL (r.r. cars and auto bodies), 1982—. Decorated chevalier Legion of Honor. Mem. French Mgmt. Assn. (chmn. 1972-74), French Employers Assn. (chmn. edn. tng. and employment com. 1974-79, chmn. internat. trade negotiations com. 1980—), French Steel Producers Assn. (chmn. 1979—). Office: 5 bis Rue de Madrid Paris France

COLLEDGE, CHARLES HOPSON, broadcasting consulting; b. Paterson, N.J., June 3, 1911; s. William Arthur and Mary (Hopson) C.; m. Margaret Whittaker, Sept. 2, 1931; children: Charles Edmund, William Arthur. Student, Newark Coll. Engring., Mass. Inst. Tech., Columbia U. Registered profl. engr., D.C. Engr. NBC, 1933-43, supr. TV operations, Washington, 1947-49; dir. color operations RCA Labs., 1949-50; chief engr. NBC, Washington, 1950-52; dir. spl. events, news operations NBC-TV network, 1952-53, dir. operations and engring., 1953-56, v.p. operations, 1956-59; gen. mgr. broadcasting and TV equipment div. RCA, 1959-60, v.p., gen. mgr., broadcast and TV equipment div., 1960-61, v.p., gen. mgr., 1961-68; mgmt. and engring. cons., 1968—; dir. St. Michaels Bank (Md.). Served from lt. (j.g.) to comdr. USNR, 1943-47. Mem. Nat. Soc. Profl. Engrs., TV Pioneers, Quarter Century Wireless Assn. Clubs: Radio Amateur Old Old Timers; Talbot Country (Easton, Md.); Miles River Yacht, Georgetown (Md.) Racing Fleet, Poplar Island Yacht; Seven Rivers Country, Plantation Golf (Crystal River, Fla.); Masons. Home: Quaker Neck Farm Edgar Cove Bozman MD 21612 Office: Box 175 Bozman MD 21612 *I came to work—to work.*

COLLENETTE, DAVID MICHAEL, member Canadian Parliament, businessman; b. London, June 24, 1946; s. David Henry and Sarah Margaret (Whiteaker) C.; m. Penelope Dorothy Hossack, Oct. 11, 1975; 1 son, Christopher. Student, East York Coll. Inst., Glendon Coll., York U.; postgrad., Carleton U. Client service adminstr. Intern Life Ins., London, 1970-72; exec. dir. Ont. Liberal Party, 1972-74; elected to House of Commons, 1974-80, reselected, 1980—; sec. to Postmaster Gen., London, 1978-79; apptd. sec. to pres. of privy council Postmaster Gen.s, 1980-81; now chmn. com. energy legislation Postmaster Gen.; exec. dir. Toronto and Dist. Liberal Assn.; chmn. Toronto and Dist. Liberal Caucus, 1976-78. Address: 523 Soudan Ave Toronto ON Canada M4S 1X1 *

COLLENS, LEWIS MORTON, legal educator; b. Chgo., Feb. 10, 1938. B.S., U. Ill., Urbana, 1960, M.A., 1963; J.D., U. Chgo., 1966. Bar: Ill. 1966. Assoc. Ross, Hardies, Chgo., 1966-67; spl. asst. to gen. counsel EEOC, Washington, 1967-68; asst. prof. Ill. Inst. Tech., Chgo. Kent Coll. Law, 1970-72, assoc. prof., 1972-74, prof., 1975—, dean Coll. Law, 1974—. Chmn. bd. dirs. Bar Rev. Inst., 1967-74; bd. dirs. Ill. Inst. Continuing Legal Edn., 1974—. Mem. ABA, Ill. Bar Assn., Chgo. Bar Assn., Am. Law Inst., Order of Coif. Office: 77 S Wacker Dr Chicago IL 60606

COLLERY, ARNOLD, economics educator; b. Glen Cove, N.Y., Feb. 1, 1927; s. James Edward and Lillian (Froehlich) C.; m. Helen Odile Cassilly, Feb. 2, 1957; children: Peter Mitchell, Elizabeth Dorsey. B.A. magna cum laude, U. Buffalo, 1950; Ph.D., Princeton U., 1958; M.A. (hon.), Amherst Coll., 1964. Mem. faculty Amherst Coll., 1953-77, prof. econs., 1964-77, chmn. dept., 1957-58, 64-66, 72-73, Clarence Francis prof. social sci., 1974-77, acting dean faculty, 1975-76; prof. econs. Columbia Coll., Columbia U., N.Y.C., 1977—, dean, 1977-82; vis. prof. MIT, summers 1965, 68-74; mem. adv. council dept. econs. Princeton U., 1965-77, chmn., 1972-74; dir. Found. for Teaching Econs., 1979—; cons. to industry; pres. Amherst Inn Co., 1972-74. Author: National Income and Employment Analysis, 1966, rev. edit., 1970, International Adjustment, Open Economies, and the Quantity Theory of Money, 1971. Treas. Hampshire (Mass.) Community Action Commn., 1965-67, mem. bd. dirs., 1965-70; chmn. Town Amherst Rent Control Study Com., 1969-70; asst. dir. for wage and price monitoring Council on Wage and Price Stability, Exec. Office of Pres., 1974-75. Served with AUS, 1945-47. NSF postdoctoral fellow, 1963-64. Mem. Am. Econ. Assn., Phi Beta Kappa. Office: Dept Econs Sch Internat Affairs Columbia Univ New York NY 10027

COLLETT, JOAN, librarian; b. St. Louis; d. Robert and Mary (Hoolan) C.; m. John E. Dustin, Nov. 19, 1983. B.A. magna cum laude, Maryville Coll., 1947; M.A., Washington U., St. Louis, 1950; M.S. in L.S, U. Ill., Urbana, 1954. Regional cons. W.Va. Library Commn., Spencer, W.Va., 1954-56; instr. Rosary Coll., River Forest, Ill., 1956-57; head extension dept. Gary (Ind.) Public Library, 1957-64; librarian Grailville Library, 1965; regional librarian USIA, Latin Am., Africa, 1966-78; exec. dir. librarian St. Louis Public Library, 1978—. Mem. ALA. Office: 1301 Olive St Saint Louis MO 63103

COLLETTE, ALFRED THOMAS, science educator; b. Syracuse, N.Y., Sept. 10, 1922; s. Samuel M. and Pauline (Quint) C. Student, W.Va. Wesleyan Coll., 1940-41, Hamilton Coll., 1943-44; A.B., Syracuse (N.Y.) U., 1947, M.S., 1948, Ph.D., 1952. Asst. prof. Syracuse (N.Y.) U., 1951-54, asso. prof., 1955-59, dual prof. sci. edn. and genetics, 1959—, chmn. dept. sci. teaching, 1954—, prof. bacteriology and botany, 1951—, prof., chmn. zoology dept., 1968-70; dir. acad.

year program NSF, 1958—, dir. fgn. scientist program, 1959-66. Author: Curriculum For The Science Gifted, 1961, Teaching Science in Today's Secondary Schools, 1959, latest edit., 1968, Science Teaching In The Secondary School, A Guide for Modernizing Instruction, 1973, Science Instruction in the Middle and Secondary School, 1984. Served to sgt. USAAF, 1942-46. Grantee NSF, AEC, A.A.A.S.; Mem. Am. Soc. Human Genetics, Nat. Assn. Research Sci. Edn., Am. Genetics Soc., Nat. Sci. Tchrs. Assns., Phi Beta Kappa, Sigma Xi, Kappa Phi Kappa, Phi Kappa Phi, Sigma Pi Sigma, Phi Delta Kappa. Home: 13 Brattle Rd Syracuse NY 13203

COLLEY, JOHN LEONARD, JR., educator, author, management consultant; b. Wilmington, N.C., Feb. 17, 1930; s. John L. and Icie (Hall) C.; m. Tommie Lancaster, Dec. 14, 1950; children: John Lawrence, Claire Ellen, Thomas Michael. B.S., N.C. State U., 1957; M.S., Yale U., 1959; D.B.A., U. So. Calif., 1964. Planning engr. ops. and systems analysis Western Electric Co., 1959-62; chief ops. analysis Hughes Aircraft Co., 1962-65; group leader Research Triangle Inst., Durham, N.C., 1965-67; also lectr. U. So. Calif., 1963-65; adj. prof. indsl. engring. N.C. State U., 1965-67; prof. bus. adminstrn. Darden Grad. Sch. Bus., U. Va., 1967—, Almand R. Coleman prof. bus. adminstrn., 1979—, dir. div. research, 1973-74; Sesquicentennial asso. of Center for Advanced Studies, 1974-75; pres. Southeastern Cons. Group, Ltd., 1969—; dir. J.E. Sirrine Co., Inc., Blue Cross/Blue Shield of Va. Co-author: Operations Planning and Control—Text and Cases, 1977, Operations Planning and Control, 1978. Served with USAF, 1952-56. Mem. Ops. Research Soc. Am., Inst. Mgmt. Sci., Am. Inst. Decision Scis., Sigma Xi, Tau Kappa Epsilon, Tau Beta Pi, Alpha Pi Mu, Beta Gamma Sigma, Phi Kappa Phi. Clubs: Farmington (Charlottesville); Yale (N.Y.C.). Home: 1423 Foxbrook Ln Charlottesville VA 22901 also 8 Pelican Dr Wrightsville Beach NC 28480

COLLEY, NATHANIEL SEXTUS, lawyer; b. Carlowsville, Ala., Nov. 21, 1918; s. Lou Daniel and Fannie F. (Jones) C.; m. Jerlean J. Jackson, May 16, 1942; children—Jerlean E. (Mrs. Jack L. Daniel), Ola Marie (Mrs. Alfred O. Brown), Natalie S. (Mrs. Gary P. Lindsey), Sondra A., Nathaniel Sextus. B.S., Tuskegee Inst., 1941; J.D., Yale, 1948. Bar: Calif. bar 1949. Since practiced in, Sacramento.; Lectr. Calif. Continuing Edn. of Bar; adj. prof. McGeorge Sch. Law, U. of Pacific. Asso. editor: Calif. Trial Lawyers Jour, 1967-74; Contbr. articles to profl. jours. Mem. Calif. Bd. Edn., 1960-63; mem. Pres.'s Commn. on Discrimination in U.S. Armed Services, 1961-63; chmn. Calif. Horse Racing Bd.; Bd. dirs. NAACP, Calif. Jour., Charles F. Kettering Found., Dayton, Ohio; trustee Tuskegee Inst. Served to capt. AUS, World War II; PTO. Mem. Assn. Trial Lawyers of Am., Am., Calif., Sacramento County bar assns., Am. Bd. Trial Advocates, Calif. Trial Lawyers Assn., Yale Law Sch. Assn. (exec. com.), Calif. Jud. Council. Club: Sporgents. Home: 5441 Pleasant Dr Sacramento CA 95822 Office: 1810 S St Sacramento CA 95814

COLLEY, ROGER J., chemical company executive; b. 1938. B.S., U. Pa., 1960. Acct. Lybrand Ross Bros. & Montgomery, 1960-66; with Betz Labs., Inc., Trevose, Pa., 1966—, asst. treas., 1967-70, treas., 1970-75, v.p. fin., 1975-80, exec. v.p., 1980-82, pres., chief operating officer, dir., 1982—. Address: Betz Labs Inc 4636 Somerton Rd Trevose PA 19047 *

COLLIER, ALAN CASWELL, artist; b. Toronto, Mar. 19, 1911; s. Robert Victor and Eliza Frances (Caswell) C.; m. Ruth Isabella Brown, Apr. 7, 1941; 1 son, Ian Munro. Assoc., Ont. coll. Art, 1933; student, Art Students' League, 1937-39. Artist Charles Peters Studio, N.Y.C., 1939-42, various advt. studios, Toronto, 1946-55; trch. Ont. Coll. Art, Toronto, 1955-66. Artist one-man shows, Roberts Gallery, Toronto, 1956, Frye Mus., Seattle, 1964, KensingtonGallery, Calgary, Alta., 1968, Kitcherner-Waterloo Art Gallery, 1969, Culture and Art Ctr., Meml. U., 1970, retrospective exhbn. organized by, Robert McLaughlin Gallery, Oshawa, 1971, numerous Ont. galleries; group shows Biennial of Am. Art, Nat. Gallery, 1955, 61, Kitchener-Waterloo Gallery, 1956, Art Mus. London (Ont.), 1962, Faces of Can., Stratford, Ont., 1964, Can. Artists, 1968, Art Gallery Ont., permanent collections, Nat. Gallery Can., Art Gallery Ont., Art Mus. London, Hamilton Art Gallery, Frye Mus., Seattle, Can. Council Art Bank, others. Served with Can. Army, 1943-46; ETO. Recipient Centennial medal Govt. Can., 1967, Quenn's Jubilee medal Gov. Gen., 1977. Mem. Royal Canadian Acad. Art (academician 1954), Ont. Soc. Artists (pres. 1958-61). Mem. New Democratic Party. Mem. United Ch. Christ. Club: Arts and Letters (Toronto). Home: 115 Brooke Ave Toronto ON Canada M5M 2K3

COLLIER, CLARENCE ROBERT, educator, physician; b. Freeport, Ill., Mar. 25, 1919; s. William Henry and Bertha (Berg) C.; m. Helen Louise Watson, Sept. 3, 1942; children: Roberta, David, Barbara (Mrs. Bob Acquistapace). B.A., Andrews U., 1940; M.D., Loma Linda U., 1949. Intern White Meml. Hosp., Los Angeles, 1948-49, resident, 1949-52; instr. medicine Loma Linda U., 1952-56, asst. prof. medicine, 1956-57, asso. prof. physiology, 1957-64, prof., chmn. dept. physiology and biophysics, 1964-70; asso. prof. medicine U. So. Calif., Los Angeles, 1970-71, prof. medicine and physiology, 1971-83, prof. emeritus, 1983—; cons. in physiology Christian Med. Coll., Vellore, India, 1972—; mem. research screening com. Air Resources Bd. State of Calif., 1983—; chief med. sci. service Rancho Los Amigos Hosp., Downey, Calif., 1962-64. Editorial bd.: Am. Physiol. Soc, 1965-71. Served with AUS, 1941-44. Research fellow Nat. Found. Infantile Paralysis, 1955-56; Sr. research fellow NIH, 1959-62. Fellow ACP; mem. Am. Physiol. Soc., Western Soc. Clin. Research, AAAS, Am. Fedn. Clin. Research, Am. Thoracic Soc. Research in respiratory physiology. Office: 6930 Casa Contenta Somerset CA 95684

COLLIER, DAVID CHARLES, automobile manufacturing company executive; b. Hardisty, Alta., Can., Oct. 28, 1929; came to U.S., 1955, naturalized, 1965; s. William Greaves and Helene Eva (Peterson) C.; m. Eleanor Gwen Beacom, Sept. 1, 1953; children: Carol E., William G., Kimberly E., Catherine M. B.S. in Bus. Adminstrn., Mont. State U., 1956; M.B.A., Harvard U., 1958. Sch. tchr., Eckville, Alta., 1949-50; office mgr. Investors Syndicate Can., 1952-54; mem. comptrollers staff Gen. Motors Corp., Detroit, 1957; asst. comptroller Gen. Motors Can., 1965-67, Gen. Motors Corp., Detroit, 1969, gen. asst. treas., N.Y.C., 1970, treas., 1971-73, v.p., 1973; pres., chief exec. officer, gen. mgr. Gen. Motors Can. Ltd., Ottawa, Ont., 1973-75; v.p. Gen. Motors Corp., 1975-78; gen. mgr. Buick Motor div. Gen. Motors Corp., Flint, Mich., 1975-78; v.p., group exec. in charge fin. group GM, N.Y.C., 1978-80, v.p., group exec. in charge operating staffs, Detroit, 1981—. Office: Gen Motors Corp 3044 W Grand Blvd Detroit MI 48202

COLLIER, EVERETT DOLTON, newspaper executive; b. Long Beach, Miss., Feb. 26, 1914; s. Thomas Lee and Elizabeth Naomi (Cruthirds) C.; m. Mary Margaret Chisholm, Mar. 26, 1950; 1 son, Ervin Cornell. B.A., Rice Inst., 1937. Mem. staff Houston Chronicle, 1934—, polit. editor, 1946-52, editorial writer, 1952-57, asst. editor, 1957-59, mng. editor, 1959-65, v.p., editor, 1965-79, sr. v.p., 1979—, also dir. Bd. dirs. Mus. Med. Sci., Houston, v.p., 1974—; bd. dirs. Tex. Good Rds. Assn., Houston Livestock Show and Rodeo. Mem. Am. Soc. Newspaper Editors, Rice U. Alumni Assn. (pres. 1963), Tex. U.P.I. Editors Assn. (v.p. 1965), Houston C. of C. (dir. 1970), Sons Republic Tex. (hon.). Methodist. Club: Press (Houston). Home: 4622 Ingersoll Ave Houston TX 77027 Office: Houston Chronicle 801 Texas Ave Houston TX 77002

COLLIER, FELTON MORELAND, architect, recreational, zoological consultant; b. Bessemer, Ala., Mar.20, 1924; s. Felton and Grace (Moreland) C.; m. Elizabeth Pettus Buck, Oct. 22, 1955 (div. Dec. 1966); children: Felton Moreland, Marcus Ashby Moreland. Student, Birmingham-So. Coll., 1942-43, Howard Coll., (now Samford U.), 1943; B.A., U. N.C., 1945; postgrad., N.C. State U., 1948-50; B.Arch., Auburn U., 1954; certificate, Nat. War Coll., 1963, Naval War Coll., 1964, Armed Forces Staff Coll., 1966. Archtl. experience with firms in, Birmingham, Ala. and Durham, N.C., 1949-51, 54-57; architect Felton Moreland Collier, Birmingham, 1958—, Felton Moreland Collier and Carroll C. Harmon (Asso. Architects), 1965—; chmn. bd. Harmon, Collier, Bondurant Assos., Inc., Architects/Planners/Designers, 1977-84, Harmon, Collier, Munger Assocs., Inc., 1984—; dir. Stereo Components, Inc., Birmingham, chmn. bd., 1974-84; dir., sec.-treas. Bourgeois, Collier, Harmon & Co., Inc., 1974-84; chmn. bd. Regent Townhomes, Inc., 1979-84; chief lectr. Naval Res. Officers Sch., Birmingham, 1957-69; mem. U.S. Cultural exchange del. architects to, USSR, 1973. Prin. works include McAlpine Community Center; new campus, Daniel Payne Coll., Spain Park, Birmingham Zoo 10 year master plan, entrance bldg. and children's zoo (Magnolia Park), Episc. Cathedral Ch. of Advent Parish House, U. Ala. Diabetes Hosp, (asso. with Carroll C. Harmon), all Birmingham, other recreational, ednl., med. and comml. projects.; Contbr. articles recreational and archtl. jours.; lit. editor: Ala. Architect, 1969-70; editor: AIA/Data, 1976-79. Democratic candidate Ala. Ho. Reps., 1970; Bd. dirs. Ala. Zool. Soc., 1975-78, Advent Episcopal Day Sch., 1977—. Served with USNR, 1945-46; PTO, ETO; to lt., 1951-53; Korea; lt. comdr. Res. Recipient Regional Merit award A.I.A., 1962, Honor award Birmingham chpt. A.I.A., 1965, 81. Mem. A.I.A. (founding mem., sec. Birmingham chpt. 1963-64, v.p. 1966), Birmingham C. of C., Explorers Club, Alpha Tau Omega. Episcopalian (lay reader, vestryman 1969-71, 75-77, 81-83, parish architect 1978—). Home: 2223 20th Ave S Birmingham AL 35223 Office: 1623 S 21st St Birmingham AL 35205 *The architect is in the enviable—and dangerous—position of providing advice to his clients, and also creating something of value for them. He must remember at all times that the creation of something of value is not the architect's work alone, that the process of creation must include people, ideas, means (money), and that the architect will be judged by his skill in melding these components.*

COLLIER, GAYLAN JANE, drama educator; b. Fluvanna, Tex., July 23, 1924; d. Ben V. and Narcis (Smith) C. B.A., Abilene Christian U., 1946; M.A., U. Iowa, 1949; Ph.D., U. Denver, 1957. Instr. speech and drama U. N.C., Greensboro, 1947-48; asst. prof., acting chairperson speech and drama Greensboro Coll., 1949-50; asst. prof. Abilene (Tex.) Christian U., 1950-57, assoc. prof., 1957-60, dir. theatre, 1950-60; assoc. prof., chairperson acting studies Idaho State U., 1960-63; assoc. prof. drama Sam Houston State U., Huntsville, Tex., 1963-65, prof., 1965-67; prof. theatre arts Tex. Christian U., Fort Worth, 1967—, coordinator acting directing program, 1967—. Dir., Scott Actors Repertory Co., 1968, 69, Ft. Worth Repertory Theatre, summer, 1970, 72; over 125 major theatrical prodns. in coll. and community theatres, 1948—, latest being Frings' Look Homeward, Angel, 1979, Harvey, 1980, Our Town, 1981, You Can't Take It With You, 1979, Harvey, 1980, Tartuffe, 1981, Juno and the Paycock, 1982, Vanities, 1982, Morning's at Seven, 1983; judge drama performance, Ft. Worth Community Theatre, 1978, 79; Author: Assignments in Acting, 1966; contbr. articles to profl. jours. Mem. Am. Theatre Assn., Tex. Ednl. Theatre Assn., AAUP. Democrat. Mem. Ch. of Christ. Home: 2616 S University Dr Fort Worth TX 76109 Office: Tex Christian Univ Room 208 Ed Landreth Hall Fort Worth TX 76129

COLLIER, HERMAN EDWARD, JR., college president; b. St. Louis, Aug. 8, 1927; s. Herman E. and Evelyn (Savill) C.; m. Jerline L. Weston, Mar. 25, 1948; children: Herman Edward III, Michael F., Thomas W. B.S., Randolph-Macon Coll., 1950, Sc.D., 1977; M.S., Lehigh U., 1952, Ph.D., 1955, LL.D., 1971; Litt.D., Coll. of Charlestown, 1976. Chmn. dept. chemistry Moravian Coll., 1955-57; research chemist E. I. duPont de Nemours Co., Wilmington, Del., 1957-63; prof. chemistry, chmn. div. natural scis. Moravian Coll., 1963-69, pres., 1969—; cons. sci. adv. bd. Lehigh Regional Consortium, EPA, 1979—; chmn. Commn. Ind. Colls. and Univs. Pa. Mem. Com. to Employ the Handicapped, 1970—; mem. Northampton County Citizens for Regional Progress.; Bd. dirs. United Fund Bethlehem, Historic Bethlehem, Inc.; trustee St. Luke's Hosp., R.K. Laros Found., Moravian Acad. Served with USNR, 1945-46. Mem. Lehigh Valley Assn. Ind. Colls. (dir.), Am. Chem. Soc., AAUP, Am. Inst. Chemists, N.Y. Acad. Scis., Lehigh Valley Automobile Assn. (dir. 1981—), Bethlehem C. of C. (dir. 0—), Phi Beta Kappa, Sigma Xi, Omicron Delta Kappa, Kappa Alpha. Club: Saucon Valley Country (dir.). Patentee mfg. tech. and product quality organo-lead compounds; sodium tetraphenyl boron for potassium detection; periodic table for lecture room, 1953; flame spectra Metallic ions from the H-F Flame, 1957. Office: Moravian Coll Bethlehem PA 18018

COLLIER, JAMES WARREN, lawyer; b. Dallas, July 31, 1940; s. J.W. and Mary Gertrude (Roberts) C.; m. Judith Lane, Dec. 27, 1964; children: Anne Elizabeth, Jennifer Susan. B.A., U. Mich., 1962, J.D., 1965. Bar: N.Y. 1966, Mich. 1968. Assoc. Simpson Thacher & Bartlett, N.Y.C., 1965-66; tax atty. office gen. counsel Ford Motor Co., 1966-67; assoc. Dykema, Gossett, Spencer, Goodnow & Trigg, Detroit, 1967-73, ptnr., 1973—. Contbr. articles to profl. jours. Mem. ABA, Mich. Bar Assn., Detroit Bar Assn. Club: Econ. of Detroit. Home: 743 Pemberton St Grosse Pointe MI 48230 Office: Dykema Gossett Spencer Goodnow & Trigg 35th Floor 400 Renaissance Ctr Detroit MI 48243

COLLIER, OSCAR, literary agent, writer; b. Waco, Tex., Feb. 26, 1924; s. Hosea Oscar and Percy Virginia (Moore) C.; m. Gertrude Barrer, 1942 (div. 1947); 1 dau., Greer (Mrs. Melvin Fitting); m. Gladys Perin Whitridge, 1949 (div. 1970); children: Lisa Whitridge (Mrs. John Cool), Sophia Whitridge; m. Diana Meerwarth, 1970 (div. 1981); 1 son, Christopher. Student, Baylor U., 1941-42, U. Iowa, 1943, Art Students League, 1945-47, New Sch. Social Research, 1947-48. Co-editor Iconograph mag., N.Y.C., 1947-48; N.Y.C. corr. Mediarts mag., 1958; editor, asst. to pres. Fleet Pub. Corp., N.Y.C., 1960-63, pres., editor, 1964-67; v.p. Hobbs, Dormann & Co., Inc., N.Y.C., 1967; partner Collier-Hobbs Agy., 1967-68, Seligmann & Collier, N.Y.C., 1968-75; cons. Collier Assocs., N.Y.C., 1976-78, propr., 1983—; sr. editor Prentice-Hall, Inc., Englewood Cliffs, N.J., 1976-81; writer, book packager, 1981-82. Artist, writer, 1945-59, one man shows, Galerie Neuf, N.Y.C., 1945, Ashby Gallery, N.Y.C.; Contbr. articles stories, poems to various publs. Office: care Collier Assocs 875 Ave of Americas New York NY 10001

COLLIER, ROBERT ARTHUR, lawyer; b. Wichita Falls, Tex., Apr. 3, 1917; s. Robert H. and Lulu (Cross) C.; m. Jeanne Claybrook, Sept. 19, 1942; children: Claybrook, Deborah Leigh. LL.B., U. Tex., 1940. Bar: D.C. bar 1954. Practiced in, Wichita Falls, Tex.; mem. firm McDaniel & Luecke, Wichita Falls, 1940-41; partner firm Collier, Shannon, Rill & Scott (and predecessors), Washington, 1956—; chmn. bd. MacMillan Ring-Free Oil Co., N.Y.C., 1963—. Mem. Pres's. Com. on Mental Retardation, 1972-75, Pres.'s Com. on Employment of Handicapped, 1975-79; mem. nat. adv. com. Jobs for Vets., 1970—. Clubs: Mason (Shriner), Burning Tree (Washington); Metropolitan (Washington and N.Y.C.). Home: 601 Wilkes St Alexandria VA 22314 Office: 1055 Thomas Jefferson St NW Washington DC 20007

COLLIER, ROBERT PERCY, economics educator; b. Pendleton, Oreg., July 18, 1920; s. Percival Meredith and Ruth (Graybill) C.; m. Constance Sayre, Feb. 8, 1943; children: Catherine, Daniel S., Charles S., Hal M., Matthew R. B.A., Reed Coll., 1942; Ph.D., Stanford, 1955. Teaching asst. econs. and accounting Stanford, 1949-51; asst. prof. econs. U. Wash., 1951-52; research coordinator So. Calif. Research Council, 1953-57; asst. prof. econs. Occidental Coll., 1952-57, asso. prof., 1957-58, acting dept. head, chmn. scholarship com., 1953-58; prof. econs. and bus. adminstrn. Utah State U., Logan, 1958-76, head bus. adminstrn. dept., 1958-64, dean Coll. Bus. and Social Scis., 1958-68, dean Coll. Bus., 1968-76; dean Coll. Bus. and Econs., Western Wash. U., Bellingham, 1976-81; pres. Los Lagos Ranch, Inc., 1971—; cons. Joint Council Econ. Edn., 1955-58; chmn. Utah Agr.-Industry Conf., 1959-63; mem. exec. com. Utah Council Econ. Edn., 1961-62, chmn., 1963-65; economist and campus coordinator U.S. AID rural indsl.; tech. assistance project Rio Grande do Norte, Brazil, 1965, acting party chief, summer 1965; visitor faculty econs. and politics U. Cambridge, 1967-68. Author: Purchasing Power Bonds and Other Escalated Contracts, 1969. Mem. Logan City Zoning and Planning Commn., 1962-67. Served with USNR, 1942-46. Recipient Freedom Found. award, 1954; Haynes Found. research fellow, 1957. Mem. Western Econ. Assn. (past mem. exec. com.), Nat. Assn. State Univs. and Land Grant Colls. (commn. on edn. bus. professions, past mem. exec. com.), Midwest Assn. Colls. and Depts. Bus. Adminstrn. (pres. 1973), Am. Assembly Collegiate Schs. Bus. (dir. 1976-80), Western Assn. Collegiate Schs. Bus. (dir. 1977—), Bellingham C. of C. (dir. 1977-83), Cache C. of C. (dir. 1970-74). Presbyn. (trustee). Address: Western Wash Univ Bellingham WA 98225 *I am an economist with a strong commitment to humanistic, individualistic values. From this perspective, I have found education and the discipline of economics to be very compatible. When contemplating the future, I tend to be an optimist, not only because that is the side more often correct, but also because it leaves the viewer in a position to grasp whatever opportunities for improvement do occur.*

COLLIGAN, RICHARD VINCENT, JR., advertising executive; b. Havana, Cuba, Sept. 17, 1951; s. Richard Vincent and Sadie (Fereira) C. (parents Am. Citizens). B.A., NYU, 1974. Account exec. Wunderman, Ricotta & Kline div. Young & Rubicam, N.Y.C., 1974-75, v.p., account supr., 1975-81; pres., chief exec. officer Benton & Bowles Direct Inc., N.Y.C., 1981—. Clubs: University (N.Y.C.); Wee Burn Country (Darien, Conn.). Office: Benton & Bowles Direct Inc 909 3d Ave New York NY 10022

COLLIN, ROBERT EMANUEL, electrical engineering educator; b. Donalda, Alta., Can., Oct. 24, 1928; came to U.S., 1958, naturalized, 1964; s. Knute Emanuel and Hannah (Hanson) C.; m. Kathleen Patricia Smith, Sept. 15, 1952; children: Patricia Ann, Linda Marie, David Robert. B.S. in Engring. Physics, U. Sask., Can., 1951; Ph.D., Imperial Coll., U. London, Eng., 1954. Sci. officer Canadian Def. Research Bd., 1954-58; faculty Case Western Res. U., 1958—, prof. elec. engring., 1965—, chmn. elec. engring. and applied physics dept., 1978-82. Author: Field Theory of Guided Waves, 1960, (with R. Plonsey) Principles and Applications of Electromagnetic Fields, 1961, Foundations for Microwave Engineering, 1966; contbr., editor: (with F.J Zucker) Antenna Theory, 2 vols., 1969. Recipient Jr. Achievement award Cleve. Tech. Socs. Council, 1964. Fellow IEEE (sr. mem., chmn. Que. subsect. 1956-57); mem. Sigma Xi (v.p. Case Inst. Tech. chpt. 1966-67), Eta Kappa Nu. Home: 1041 West Mill Dr Highland Heights OH 44143 Office: 10900 Euclid Ave Cleveland OH 44106

COLLINGS, CHARLES LEROY, supermarket exec.; b. Wewoka, Okla., July 11, 1925; s. Roy B. and Dessie L. C.; m. Frances Jane Flake, June 28, 1947; children—Sandra Jean, Dianna Lynn. Student, So. Methodist U., 1943-44, U. Tex., 1945. Sec., controller, dir. Noble Meat Co., Madera, Calif., 1947-54; chief accountant Montgomery Ward & Co., Oakland, Calif., 1954-56; with Raleys, Sacramento, 1956—, sec., 1958—, pres., 1970—, also dir.; dir. United Grocers Ltd. Bd. dirs. Pro Athlete Outreach, Youth for Christ. Served with USNR, 1943-46. Mem. Calif. Grocers Assn. (dir.). Republican. Baptist. Home: 7465 French Rd Sacramento CA 95828 Office: 1515 20th St Sacramento CA 95814 *My goal is to live my life in such a way that when I leave this earth those who knew me can truthfully say, "He loved his God, and loved and did good toward his fellow man."*

COLLINGWOOD, CHARLES, retired radio, TV commentator; b. Three Rivers, Mich., June 4, 1917; s. George Harris and Jean Grinnell (Cummings) C.; m. Louise Allbritton, May 13, 1946 (dec. 1979). A.B., Cornell U., 1939; student, New Coll., Oxford, Eng., 1939-40. War corr. United Press, London, 1939-41; commentator CBS, 1941-46, United Nations corr., 1946-48, White House corr., 1948-52, radio, TV commentator, 1952-82; chief CBS news bur., London, 1957-60, chief fgn. corr., 1966-75; spl. asst. to dir. Mut. Security Agy., 1952. Author: novel The Defector, 1970. Recipient Headliners award, 1942, 1948; Peabody award for best fgn. reporting, 1943, for tour White House with Mrs. John Kennedy, 1963; Alexander Hadden Medal for promoting world understanding, 1954; Better Understanding award English Speaking Union, 1957; decorated chevalier Legion of Honor, France; comdr. Order Brit. Empire, 1975. Mem. Assn. Radio News Analysts., English Speaking Union (nat. bd. dirs., exec. com. 1976—). Clubs: Century Assn., National Press; Beefsteak, Garrick (London). Office: CBS News 524 W 57th St New York NY 10019

COLLINS, ARTHUR FLETCHER, realty investors corporation executive; b. Chillicothe, Ohio, Nov. 11, 1943; s. Arthur Belmont and Dorothy Kathryn (Pierpont) C.; m. Patricia Ann Munson, Apr. 6, 1966; children: Douglas R., Audrey L., Patrick A. B.B.A., Calif. State U.-Northridge, 1968. C.P.A., Calif.; lic. real estate broker, Calif. Staff auditor Coopers & Lybrand, C.P.A.s, Los Angeles, 1968-72; sr. fin. analyst Angeles Corp., Los Angeles, 1972-74; v.p., treas. UnionAmerica, Los Angeles, 1974-78, United Realty Investors, Inc., Beverly Hills, Calif., 1978—. Mem. Am. Inst. C.P.A.s, Calif C.P.A. Soc., Nat. Assn. Real Estate Investment Trusts, Nat. Assn. Real Estate Cos., Risk and Ins. Mgmt. Soc. Republican. Home: 25620 Cielo Ct Valencia CA 91355 Office: United Realty Investors Inc Suite 700 Wells Fargo Bldg 433 N Camden Dr Beverly Hills CA 90210

COLLINS, ARTHUR STEWART, advertising agency executive; b. Peterborough, Ont., Can., Aug. 4, 1920; s. Frederick L. and Henrietta (Stewart) C.; m. Patricia Mary Holden, Sept. 11, 1948; children: Katherine, Michael, Terrence, Kevin, Brian. Student, Queen's U., 1937-40. Exec. v.p., creative dir. Tandy Advt. Ltd., Toronto, 1946-59; v.p. client services Stanfield Johnson & Hill Ltd., Montreal, 1960-62; v.p., mgr. James Lovick Ltd., Montreal, 1962-63; chmn., chief exec. officer Foster Advt. Ltd., Toronto, 1973—; chmn. Sherwood Communications Group Ltd., Toronto, 1975—; dir. Caledon Advt. Ltd., Toronto, 1976—. Served to flight lt. RCAF, 1940-46. Decorated D.F.C. Mem. Inst. Can. Advt. (chmn.). Progressive Conservative. Anglican. Clubs: Albany (dir. 1978-83); Lambton Golf and Country (Toronto)). Home: 2045 Lakeshore Blvd W Apt 3205 Toronto ON Canada M8V 2L6 Office: Foster Advt Ltd 40 St Clair Ave W Toronto ON Canada M4V 1M6

COLLINS, BEULAH STOWE, columnist; b. Ft. Dodge, Iowa, Mar. 28, 1923; d. Herman Wilmer and Beulah Blanche (Blagden) Stowe; m. Thomas Hightower Collins, Apr. 6, 1946; children—Kent Stowe, Paul Harlan, Todd Stowe. B.A. in Journalism, U. Iowa, 1942; M.A. in Comparative Lit, U. N.C., 1967. Editor: Weekend Chuckles, Los Angeles Times Syndicate, 1955—, Today's Chuckle, 1958—; writer: Golden Years, 1978—, Senior Forum, 1978—; Author: (as Beulah Collins): The Senior Forum, 1964, For Benefit of Clergy, 1966. Served with USNR, 1944-46. Mem. Women in Communications, Inc. Republican. Episcopalian. Home and Office: 15 S Lake Shore Dr Chapel Hill NC 27514

COLLINS, CARDISS ROBERTSON, congresswoman; b. St. Louis; m. George Collins (dec.); 1 son, Kevin. Grad., Northwestern U. Formerly with Ill. Dept. Labor; successively sec. Ill. Dept. Revenue; accountant, revenue auditor; mem. 93d-98th congresses from 7th Ill. Dist.; mem. com. on govt. ops., subcoms. on manpower and housing, energy and commerce com., subcom. on telecommunications; whip-at-large U.S. Ho. of Reps.; mem. House Select Com. Drug Abuse and Control; past chairwoman Mems. of Congress for Peace through Law subcom. on Africa; chairwoman Congressional Black Caucus; Democratic committeewoman 24th Ward, Chicago. Mem. N.A.A.C.P., Chgo. Urban League, Nat. Council Negro Women, Nat. Women's Polit. Caucus, Alpha Kappa Alpha (hon.). Baptist. Address: 2264 Rayburn House Office Bldg Washington DC 20515 *

COLLINS, CHARLES JOSEPH, investment consultant; b. Lake City, Fla., Dec. 7, 1894; s. Thomas Currie and Sarah Frink (Spencer) C.; m. Hazel Beatrice Wharton, Dec. 25, 1919; children: Anne Wharton (Mrs. Henry G. Husted), Josephine Spencer (Mrs. John M. Penberthy). B.A., Va. Mil. Inst., Lexington, 1916, 1926. Investment analyst E.E. MacCrone & Co., Detroit, 1919-23, partner, 1923-63; chmn., dir. Investment Counsel, Inc., 1930-59, mem. adv. bd., 1962—; trustee Investment Co. Am., 1927-32; editor, pub. Investment Letters, Inc., 1934-63; dir. Am. Midland Co., 1930-63, Investment Research Corp., 1927-32, Am. Industries Corp., 1929-33, 55-63, Am. Industries Securities Co., 1930-33; mem. N.Y. Stock Exchange, 1929-30. Author: Fortune's Before You, 1937, The Coming Battle for World Sovereignty, 1971; Contbr. investment articles to financial jours. Trustee Va. Mil. Inst. Found., 1964-78. Entered the CAC U.S. Army, 2d lt., 1917; advanced to maj.; served on front with 8th and 4th French armies, 1st and 2d Am. armies; resigned, Feb. 1919. Mem. Financial Analysts Soc. of Detroit (pres. 1952, dir. 1951-53), Nat. Fedn. Financial Analyst Socs. (dir. 1950- 52), Va. Mil. Inst. Alumni Assn. (dir. 1937-64), Kappa Alpha (Southern). Clubs: Detroit; Country (Grosse Pointe, Mich.). Home: 858 Lochmoor Blvd Grosse Pointe Woods MI 48236

COLLINS, CHARLES ROLAND, lawyer; b. Pitts., Sept. 1, 1931; s. Charles Peyton and Dorothy (Cantley) C.; m. Virginia Anne Wright, Feb. 6, 1955; children: Elizabeth Anne, Charles Edward, Walter Bruce, Richard Allen, Catherine Kaye. B.A., UCLA, 1953; LL.B. cum laude, Harvard U., 1959. Bar: Calif. 1960, Tenn. 1972. Practice, Los Angeles, 1960-68; mem. firm Gibson, Dunn & Crutcher, 1959-68; v.p., gen. counsel, sec. Whittaker Corp., Los Angeles, 1968-71; group exec. pres. Whittaker Community Devel., Inc., Los Angeles, 1970-73; pres. Environ. System Internat., 1973-74; mem. firm Collins Gregory & Rutter Inc., Los Angeles, until 1977; partner firm Hughes Hubbard & Reed, Los Angeles, 1977—; dir. Storage Tech. Corp. Trustee Northrop U. Served to lt. comdr. USNR, 1953-56. Clubs: California, Calif. Yacht, Calabasas Racquet. Home: 23730 Park Antigua Calabasas Park CA 91302 Office: 555 S Flower St Los Angeles CA 90071

COLLINS, COPP, federal consultant; b. Keokuk, Iowa, Dec. 31, 1914; s. Harrie Richards and Elsie (Parsons) C.; m. Frances Cordelia Truax, Sept. 28, 1940; children: Michael Truax, Nicole Elyse, Copp Parsons. B.A., U. Redlands, 1938. Bur. mgr. San Diego bur. UP, asst. Los Angeles bur., 1939-40; flight adminstrn., comml. sales supr. Convair, 1942-47; owner Copp Collins Pub. Relations, San Diego and Beverly Hills, Calif., 1948-51; West Coast rep. pub. relations MBS, 1951-53, mgr. pub. relations, N.Y.C., 1953-55, Bahrain Petroleum Co. Ltd., Bahrain, Persian Gulf, 1955-58; asst. to exec. v.p. Burns & Roe, Inc., N.Y.C., 1958-60; pub. relations cons. Copp Collins Assos., N.Y.C. and Westport, Conn., 1960-61; pres.-cons. Copp Collins Assocs., 1963-67; v.p., dir. pub. relations Chirurg & Cairns, Inc., N.Y.C. and Boston, 1961-62, Friend-Reiss Advt., Inc., 1962-63; pres. Collins & Lynge, Ltd., N.Y.C. and Norwalk, Conn., 1965-67; dir. mktg. merchandising N. Am. Soccer League, 1967-68; dir. info. Nat. Pro Soccer League, 1967-68; asst. to dir. communications Nixon for Pres.; Nixon-Agnew campaign coms.; asst. to dir. communications Office of Pres.-Elect, Washington and N.Y.C., 1968-69; asst. to sec. Dept. Agr., Washington, 1969; cons. public affairs Dept. State, 1969-70; cons. spl. asst. to dir. Peace Corps, 1970-71; asst. to sec., S.W. field rep. Dept. Interior, 1971-73; dir. regional ops. Fed. Energy Office; interagy. coordinator, asst. dir. exec. secretariat FEO-Fed. Energy Adminstrn.; cons. Nat. Energy Info. Center, FEA, 1973-75, Office of Energy Programs, Dept. Commerce, 1975-77; cons. energy and minerals div. GAO, 1977-78, Pres.'s Commn. on Coal, 1978-79, Burns & Roe, Inc., Washington, 1979; cons. to dir. Biomass div., cons. to asst. sec. fossil energy Dept. Energy, Washington, 1979-81; fed. and corporate cons., 1981—. Chmn. public relations adv. council to So. Conn. chpts. ARC, 1955; press aide primary campaign Sen. Clifford Case, 1959-60, Ogden Reid for Congress Com., Westchester County, 1962, 64. Mem. Redlands U. Alumni Assn. (past chpt. chmn.), Pi Kappa Delta, Alpha Phi Gamma, Kappa Sigma Sigma. Republican.

COLLINS, CYRUS STICKNEY, airlines executive; b. Oak Park, Ill., Oct. 31, 1917; s. Frank S. and Margaret (Stickney) C.; m. Madeleine Robertson, Sept. 3, 1941; children: Michael, David, Stephen. A.B., Amherst Coll., 1939. With W.R. Grace & Co., 1939-42; with Pan-Am.-Grace Airways, Inc., 1942-66, asst. to pres., asst. v.p., 1952-56, v.p. sales and traffic, 1956-63, v.p. gen. mgmt., 1963-66; regional v.p. Am. Airlines, 1966-67, v.p. public affairs, 1967-73; v.p. Atlantic/Caribbean, 1973—; pres. Am. Inter-Island (commuter airline), 1978-82. Bd. dirs. Children's Village, Dobbs Ferry, N.Y., pres. bd., 1955-58. Decorated Order Nunez de Balboa (Panama). Mem. Argentine Am. C. of C. (v.p. 1961-63, pres. 1963-65), Beta Theta Pi. Clubs: Sky, Wings (N.Y.C.) (pres. 1970-71); Old Cove Yacht (L.I.)). Home: 20 Sutton Pl S New York NY 10022 Office: 405 Lexington Ave New York NY 10174

COLLINS, DANIEL G., law educator; b. 1930. B.A., Hofstra Coll., 1951; LL.B., NYU, 1954; postgrad. in sociology, New Sch. Social Research, 1957-60. Bar: N.Y. 1955. Assoc. Cravath, Swaine & Moore, 1956-61; now prof. NYU Sch. Law. Past editor-in-chief (NYU Law Rev.). Mem. Nat. Acad. Arbitrators, Order of Coif. Office: NYU Law Sch 40 Washington Sq S New York NY 10012

COLLINS, DANNY EDWARD, union ofcl.; b. Belleville, Ill., Oct. 25, 1927; s. George L. and Lena E. (Yocks) C.; m. Mary Ann Fleischman, May 3, 1953; children—Melinda Sue, David Alan. Student, Belleville Area Coll., 1966-70. Telegraph operator L & N R.R., 1943-45; towerman-operator Terminal R.R. of St. Louis, 1945-54, train dispatcher, 1954-69; acting v.p. Am. Train Dispatchers Assn., 1969-71, internat. sec.-treas., 1971-81, internat. pres., 1981—; sec. bd. dirs. Am. Train Dispatchers Improvement Assn.; chmn. Joint R.R.-Train Dispatcher Com. on Working Conditions; mem. exec. com. Ry. Labor Execs. Assn., also mem. coms. on ry. labor act, internat. affairs, legislation and safety, health and welfare. Served with USN, 1944-46. Mem. Am. Legion. Democrat. Lutheran. Home: 2035 Evergreen Terr Arlington Heights IL 60004 Office: 1401 S Harlem Ave Berwyn IL 60402

COLLINS, DAVID EDMOND, pharmaceutical company executive, lawyer; b. Oak Park, Ill., June 6, 1934; s. Charles Cornelius and Penelope (Jones) C.; m. Judith Elizabeth Thompson, Sept. 16, 1961; children: Patrick, Katherine Ann, Paul, Ann Marie. B.A. magna cum laude, U. Notre Dame, 1956, LL.B., Harvard, 1959. Bar: N.Y. 1961, N.J. 1963. Assoc. Shearman & Sterling, N.Y.C., 1959-62; gen. atty. Johnson & Johnson, New Brunswick, N.J., 1962-64, asst. sec., 1964-70, sec., 1970-75, assoc. gen. counsel, 1973-75, gen. counsel, 1975-78, v.p., dir., 1976-78, co. group chmn., 1981-82, mem. exec. com., 1982—; pres. McNeil Pharm., Spring House, Pa., 1978-81. Frederick Sheldon traveling fellow, 1959-60. Mem. Am. Bar Assn. (mem. sects. antitrust, corps., individual rights), N.J. Bar Assn. Office: Johnson & Johnson 501 George St New Brunswick NJ 08903

COLLINS, EDWARD JAMES, JR., association executive; b. Lawrence, Mass., Mar. 17, 1933; s. Edward James and Mary Elizabeth (Rogers) C.; m. Dorothy Jane McCann, Sept. 19, 1964; 1 son, Edward James; 1 stepdau., Dorothy Lorraine. A.B. in Journalism, U. Calif.-Berkeley, 1959. Mng. editor Brawley Daily News, (Calif.), 1959-62; assoc. exec. dir. Calif. Veterinary Med. Assn., Moraga, Calif., 1962-65; exec. dir. Marin Med. Soc., San Rafael, Calif., 1965-66; asst. dir., prof., pub. relations Calif. Med. Assn., San Francisco, 1966-68; v.p. Assn. Western Hosps., San Francisco, 1968-76; exec. dir. Am. Assn. Med. Soc. Execs., Chgo., 1977-81; pres., chief adminstrv. officer Am. Econ. Devel. Council, Chgo., 1981—. Recipient Agrl. Writers award, 1961, Key Man award Oakland Jaycees, (Calif.), 1964. Mem. Am. Soc. Assn. Execs., No. Calif. Soc. Assn. Execs. (pres. 1973), Chgo. Soc. Assn. Execs. Home: 617 Indian Hill Rd Deerfield IL 60015 Office: 4849 N Scott St Suite 10 Schiller Park IL 60176

COLLINS, FRANK CHARLES, JR., retired naval officer; b. El Paso, Tex., Oct. 29, 1927; s. Frank Charles and Lucile Ellen (Reynolds) C.; m. Esther Frances Shiell, Aug. 16, 1948; children—Lucile F. Collins Silveira, Sue E. Collins Hekman, Francene C. Collins Newman, Virginia A. Collins, Friesen, Melissa Collins Rivera, Laura B. Collins Leach, Frank Charles III. B.A. in Sociology, La. State U., 1949; postgrad., Naval War Coll., 1966, U. So. Calif., 1976, 77. Served as enlisted man USNR, 1945-46; advt. mgr. REA newspaper, Baton Rouge, 1949-50; mgr. drive-in theatre, Lafayette, La., 1950-51; commd. ensign U.S. Navy, 1951, advanced through grades to rear adm., 1978; comdr. (U.S.S. New Orleans), 1953-54, San Diego, 1957-59, 1967-69, ops. officer, Naval Support Activity, Danang, Vietnam, 1966-67; comdr. COMDESRON Nine, San Diego, 1974-76, (Devel. and Tng. Center/Fleet Maintenance Assistance Group, Pacific), 1976-78, chief, Iran, 1978-79, dir. logistics planning, Washington, 1979-81, exec. dir. quality assurance, 1981-83, ret., 1983; corp. v.p.-quality AVCO Corp., Greenwich, Conn., 1983—. Contbr. articles to profl. publs. Decorated Legion of Merit (2), Bronze Star, Navy Commendation medal (all with Combat V), Def. Superior Service medal, Def. Meritorious Service medal., Def. Disting. Service medal. Mem. U.S. Naval Inst., Pi Kappa Alpha. Mem. Christian Reformed Ch. Office: Avco Corp 1400 K St Suite 1100 Washington DC 20006 *In an era now characterized by humanism and relativism, I thank God for having grown up in a society which recognized absolutes-absolutes of morality, self-discipline, individual effort, and national leadership and purpose. I pray we can continue to set an example of concern for others, and as a nation set goals which can bring about a revival of justice, peace, morality and belief in a sovereign God.*

COLLINS, GEORGE JOSEPH, investment counselor. Investment counselor T. Rowe Price Assocs., Inc., Balt. Office: 100 E Pratt St Baltimore MD 21202

COLLINS, GEORGE ROSEBOROUGH, art history educator; b. Springfield, Mass., Sept. 2, 1917; s. Harold Fisher and Lucy Roseborough (Mackay) C.; m. Rosanne Gouverneur Walker, May 17, 1947 (dec. July 1948); 1 son, David Walker; m. Christiane Crasemann, Aug. 30, 1950; children: Nicolas Bernd, Luke Malte. A.B., Princeton U., 1939; M.F.A. with honors, 1942; D.h.c., Universidad Politécnica de Barcelona, 1977. Dep. dir. UNRRA center in, Bremen, Ger., 1945, dir. center in, Kassel-Mattenberg, 1946; mem. faculty Columbia U., N.Y.C., 1946—, prof. art history, 1962—, dir. Coll. Urban Studies, 1980—, Mathews lectr. Sch. Architecture, 1979; dir. Archive of Catalan Art and Architecture, N.Y.C., 1958—; bd. dirs. Spanish Inst., N.Y.C., 1960—; cons. architecture Abbeville Press, Inc., N.Y.C., 1981—; vis. scholar modern city planning Vassar Coll., fall 1967; Hans Vetter Meml. lectr. Carnegie-Mellon U., 1972; vis. prof. program growth and structure of cities Bryn Mawr Coll., 1974, 75; hon. prof. Universidad Nacional Federico Villareal, Lima, Peru and Universidad San Antonio Abad, Cuzco, Peru, 1977; Preston Thomas Meml. lectr. Cornell U., 1978; Shippee Meml. lectr. Wheaton Coll., 1983; interviewed on Gaudí by BBC, 1983. Author: Antonio Gaudí, 1960, also Italian, Spanish and German edits, (with Christiane Crasemann Collins) Camillo Sitte and the Birth of Modern City Planning, 1965, (with Carlos Flores) Arturo Soria y la Ciudad Lineal, 1968, A Bibliography of Antonio Gaudí and the Catalan Movement, 1870-1930, 1973; introduction: Unbuilt America: Forgotten Architecture in the U.S. from Thomas Jefferson to the Space Age, 1976, (with Carlos Flores) The Drawings of Antonio Gaudí, 1977, Visionary Drawings of Architecture and Planning: 20th Century through the 1960's, 1979, Fantastic Architecture: Personal and Eccentric Visions, 1980, (with Juan Bassegoda) The Designs and Drawings of Antonio Gaudí, 1983; also numerous articles.; Editor, translator: (with Christiane Crasemann Collins) Architecture of Fantasy, 1962, Brit. edit., 1963; translator: (with C. C. Collins) City Planning According to Artistic Principles (Camillo Sitte), 1965, The Problem of Building Socialist Cities (N. A. Miliutin), 1975; Contbr. articles to profl. jours. and encys. Bd. dirs. Fine Arts Fedn. N.Y., 1974-75; commr. N.Y.C. Landmarks Preservation Commn., 1976-79. Served in Am. Field Service with Brit. 8th Army; Middle East. Guggenheim fellow, 1962-63; Rockefeller Found. fellow, 1976-77. Mem. N. Am. Catalan Soc. (dir. 1978-82), Hispanic Soc. Am. (corr.), Real Academia de Bellas Artes de San Jorge (corr.) (Barcelona), Internat. Com. Architectural Archtl. Critics, Com. to Preserve Archtl. Records, Coll. Art Assn., Soc. Archtl. Historians, Urban History Group U.S., Planning History Group U.K., Soc. Indsl. Archeology, Soc. Comml. Archeology, Am. Victorian Soc., Brit. Victorian Soc., Phi Beta Kappa (hon. Delta chpt.). Democrat. Home: 448 Riverside Dr New York NY 10027 Office: 702 Casa Italiana Columbia U New York NY 10027

COLLINS, (GEORGE) WILLARD, clergyman, coll. pres.; b. Lewisburg, Tenn., Nov. 12, 1915; s. Walter M. and Maxie (Duncan) C.; m. Ruth Morris, Aug. 7, 1939; children—Carole, Corinne. Jr. coll. diploma, David Lipscomb Coll., 1936; B.A., M.A., Vanderbilt U., 1939; LL.D. (hon.), Pepperdine U., 1965, Harding Coll., 1977. Ordained to ministry Ch. of Christ, 1934; minister Old Hickory (Tenn.) Ch. of Christ, 1939-44; evangelist Collins-Craig Auditorium Meeting, Nashville, 1962, area-wide meetings in, Wichita Falls, Tex., 1960, Tokyo, 1961, Fort Worth, 1962; asso. dir. expansion program David Lipscomb Coll., Nashville, 1944, v.p. coll., 1946-77, pres., 1977—; Sec.-treas. exec. com. Tenn. Ind. Colls. Fund, 1979—. Author: Daily Living for Christ, 1951, A Plea for Christ, 1960, Collins-Craig Auditorium Meeting Sermons, 1962, Great Preachers of Today series, vol. 6, 1964; editorial staff: Gospel Adv, 1955-78, 20th Century Christian, 1944—. Apptd. col. Tenn. Gov.'s Staff, 1960-64. Mem. Am. Coll. Public Relations Assn., Tenn. Council Pvt. Colls. (exec. com. 1979—), David Lipscomb Coll. Nat. Alumni Assn. (past pres.). Office: Office of Pres David Lipscomb Coll Granny White Pike Nashville TN 37203

COLLINS, HARKER, economist, publisher, financial and business consultant; b. Denver, Nov. 24, 1924; s. Clem Wetzel and Marie (Harker) C.; m. Emily Harvey, Aug. 23, 1957; children: Catherine Emily, Cynthia Lee, Constance Marie. B.S., U.S. Naval Acad., 1945. Asst. buyer Montgomery Ward & Co., N.Y.C., 1947-51; prodn. mgr. Diamond Hosiery Mills, High Point, N.C., 1953-55; v.p. Vanette Hosiery Mills, Dallas, 1955-59; v.p., dir. Grote Mfg. Co., Madison, Ind., 1959-71; group v.p., gen. mgr. Bendix Corp., South Bend, Ind., 1971-73; pres., dir. Bandag, Inc., Muscatine, Iowa, 1973-78, chief exec. officer, 1974-78; pres., chief exec. officer Harker Collins & Co., 1978—, also dir.; dir. Mid-Am. Industries, Inc.; pub. newsletter The Economy and You, Update, 1978—; instr. U. Denver, 1948; Bd. dirs. Hwy. Users Fedn., 1970—; chmn. automotive industry liaison com. with Dept. Transp., 1968—, automotive industry excise tax com., 1964-70, automotive industry tariff com., 1964-70, joint operating com. for automotive trade shows, 1969-77. Mem. Pres.'s Com. Hwy. Safety, 1966-68; Bd. dirs. Iowa Ind. Coll. Found., 1976—; bd. fellows Northwood Inst., 1974—; alderman City of Rancho Viejo, Tex., 1980—. Served to ensign USN, 1945-47; to lt. USNR, 1951-53. Recipient Automotive Industry Leadership award, 1965, 74; Fin. World award as chief exec. of yr., 1975, 77. Mem. Automotive Service Industry Assn. (v.p. 1966-67, pres. 1968-69, dir. heavy duty exec. com. 1969-71, chmn. safety and environ. protection com. 1962-67, 70-78), Automotive Sales Council (dir. 1966-67, sec. 1971-72, v.p. 1972-73, pres. 1973-74), Am. Nat. Standards Inst. (chmn. task force on used vehicle standards 1966-74), Home Products Safety Council (pres. 1960-63), Medicine Cabinet Mfg. Council (pres. 1960-63, dir. 1960-68), Truck Safety Equipment Inst. (pres. 1960-63, dir. 1960-68), Internat. Platform Assn., Muscatine C. of C. (dir. 1975-78). Clubs: Rotary, 33 Club (treas. 1977-78). Office: 300 Balboa St Brownsville TX 78520

COLLINS, HAROLD RAY, educational administrator, investment banker; b. Hartford, Ala., Mar. 14, 1919; s. Francis Alex and Vestie (Kinsaul) C.; m. Ruth Bassett, Mar. 1, 1941; children: Harold Ray, Gene Bassett. B.S., Troy State Coll., 1946; M.A., U. Ala., 1953; Ed.D., 1966. Prin. Zion Chapel Sch., Jack, Ala., 1944-48, Goshen (Ala.) High Sch., 1948-66; supt. Pike County Schs., 1966-70, Mobile County (Ala.) Pub. Schs., 1970-76; exec. dir. Springhill Ednl. Lab., Springhill Coll., Mobile, 1976—; v.p. George M. Wood Securities, Mobile; Mem. Ala. State Textbook Commn.; mem. Ala. Jr. Coll. Selection Com. Mem. Nat., Ala. assns. secondary sch. prins., Am., Ala. assns. sch. adminstrs., NEA, Ala. Edn. Assn., Nat. Assn. Sch. Bds., Ala. Assn. Elementary Sch. Prins., Kappa Phi Kappa, Kappa Phi Delta. Baptist. Clubs: Rotarian., Civitan (Mobile). Home: 3251 Rivere du Chien Dr Mobile AL 36606 Office: Springhill Coll Mobile AL 36601

COLLINS, HENRY BASCOM, anthropologist; b. Geneva, Ala., Apr. 9, 1899; s. Henry Bascom and Anna Sophie (Neville) C.; m. Carolyn Walker, Nov. 26, 1931; 1 dau., Judith Ann (Mrs. Mitchell A. Krasny). A.B., Millsaps Coll., 1922, Sc.D. (hon.), 1940; A.M., George Washington U., 1925. Asst. with the Pueblo Bonito expdn. Nat. Geog. Soc., 1922-24; asst. Miss. dept. of Archives and History, 1923; aid, div. ethnology U.S. Nat. Mus., 1924-25, asst. curator, 1925-37, asso. curator, 1938-39; sr. ethnologist Bur. Am. Ethnology, 1939-51; sr. anthropologist, 1951—, acting dir., 1963-65; sr. scientist Smithsonian Office Anthropology, 1965-66, archaeologist emeritus, 1967—; dir. Smithsonian expeditions to, Fla., Miss., La., 1925, 26, 28, 29, Nunivak Island and Bering Sea, 1927, Punuk Island and Bering Strait, 1928, St. Lawrence Island, Norton Sound and Arctic coast, 1929, St. Lawrence Island, 1930, Nat. Geog. Soc.-Smithsonian Expdn., Bering Strait, 1936, Nat. Mus. Canada-Smithsonian expdn. to, Baffin Island, 1948, Cornwallis Island, N.W.T., 1949, 50, 53, Nat. Geog. Soc.-Nat. Mus. Canada-Smithsonian Expedition to, Southampton Island, 1954, 55; Asst. dir. Ethnogeog. Bd., 1943-44, dir., 1944-46; bd. govs. Arctic Inst. N.A., 1944-48, 51-56, 60-65; chmn. bd., 1948; chmn. adv. com. Russian Anthropology Translations Project, 1960—; chmn. directing com. of Arctic Bibliography, 1947-67; v.p. 2d Internat. cong. Ethnol., Anthrop. Scis., Copenhagen, 1938, chmn. Am. delegation, mem. permanent council, 1952—; v.p. 7th Internat. congress, Moscow, 1964; hon. v.p. 32d Internat. Congress Americanists, Copenhagen, 1956. Author: Prehistoric Art of the Alaskan Eskimo, 1929, Archeology of St. Lawrence Island, Alaska, 1937, Outline of Eskimo Prehistory, 1940, Arctic Area (Program of the History of America), 1953, The Aleutian Islands, their People and Natural History, (with A.H. Clark and E.H. Walker), 1946; Editor: Science In Alaska, 1952; Contbr. anthrop., archeol. papers to sci. jours. Served as pvt. U.S. Army, 1918. Recipient gold medal Royal Danish Acad. Sci. and Letters, 1936. Fellow A.A.A.S. (mem. council 1953-60); mem. Am. Anthrop. Assn., Anthrop. Soc. of Washington (pres. 1938, 39), Am. Assn. Phys. Antrhopologists, Soc. Am. Archeology (v.p. 1942, 52), Washington Acad. Scis., Sigma Xi, Pi Kappa Alpha, Sigma Upsilon. Clubs: Explorers (N.Y. C.); Cosmos (Washington). Home: 2557 36th St NW Washington DC 20007 Office: Smithsonian Inst Washington DC 20560

COLLINS, HENRY JAMES, III, insurance company executive; b. Washington, July 9, 1927; s. Henry James and Genevieve (Downey) C.; m. Josephine Ann McDonald, July 13, 1946; children: Jonathan Alexander, Thomas James, Patricia Ann. B.C.S., Strayers Coll., 1951. With Govt. Employees Ins. Co., Washington, 1945, 46-80, treas., 1965-77, comptroller, 1972-80, v.p., 1977-80, Govt. Employees Life Ins. Co., 1980-83; treas. Govt. Employees Corp., Washington, 1966-74, Govt. Employees Fin. Corp., 1966-74; asst. treas. Criterion Ins. Co., 1961-70, treas., 1970-72; dir. Md. Ins. Guaranty Fund.; Mem. auditors and comptrollers adv. com. Nat. Assn. Ins. Commrs. Treas. Oakview Citizens Assn., 1952-53. Served with AUS, 1945-46. 1Mem. Soc. Ins. Accountants, Ins. Accounting and Statis. Assn., Nat. Assn. Ind. Insurers (com. blanks and uniform accounting 1964—, fed. taxes com. 1969-74), Fin. Execs. Inst. (pres. D.C. chpt. 1979-80), Izaak Walton League Am. Home: 204 Bluff Terr Wheaton MD 20902 Office: 1701 Research Bldg Rockville MD 20850

COLLINS, HERSCHEL DOUGLAS, physician; b. Caribou, Maine, Jan. 19, 1928; s. S.W. and Elizabeth (Black) C.; m. Helen Fraser, June 29, 1950; children: Douglas, Gordon, Linda Ann. B.A., U. Maine, 1949; M.D., Harvard U., 1952. Intern Mass. Gen. Hosp., Boston, 1952-53, resident, 1953-55, 72-73; practice medicine specializing in internal medicine, Caribou, 1957-72, 73-75, 80—; dir. Central Maine Family Practice, Augusta, 1975-79, Maine Dartmouth Residency Family Practice, 1979-80. Served with USPHS, 1955-57. Mem. ACP, Inst. Medicine. Office: One Vaughan Pl Caribou ME 04736

COLLINS, J. MICHAEL, educational television executive; b. Buffalo, Feb. 17, 1935; s. John Lloyd and Celestine (Buhrle) C.; m. Marilyn Anne Mercer, Aug. 5, 1961; children: Kevin Michael, Timothy David, Sheila Anne, Jeanne Mary, Julie Lynn. B.S. in Social Scis., Canisius Coll., 1957, L.H.D. (hon.), 1978; postgrad., Mich. State U., 1957-58. Grad. teaching asst. Mich. State U., 1957-58; promotion mgr. WNED-TV, Buffalo, 1959-60, dir. devel., 1961-62, asst. sta. mgr., 1963-65, gen.

mgr., 1966-69, pres., 1970—. Contbg. author: ETV: The Farther Vision, 1967. Trustee United Fund of Buffalo and Erie County, 1967—; trustee Eastern Ednl. Network, 1965—, treas., 1967-70, mem. exec. com., 1967-74, 78-81, chmn. budget and finance com., 1967-70, pres., 1971-72, chmn., 1973-74, v.p., 1980-81; mem. CATV com. Ednl. TV Stas., also mem. devel. adv. com.; exec. bd. Niagara Frontier council Boy Scouts Am., 1971-76; exec. com. Cantalician Center; trustee St. Joseph's Collegiate Inst., 1978—; bd. dirs. Pub. Broadcasting Service, 1972—, vice-chmn., 1974, chmn., 1975; mem. Kenmore-Tonawanda Pub. Schs. Bd. Edn., 1974-81, v.p., 1977, pres., 1978. Mem. N.Y. State Ednl. Radio and TV Assn. (trustee, pres. 1964-65, treas. 1963, editor newsletter 1962), Pub. Relations Assn. Western N.Y. (pres. 1966), Nat. Assn. Ednl. Broadcasters, Canisius Coll. Alumni Assn. (bd. govs. 1960-62, 70-73). Home: 66 Puritan Rd Tonawanda NY 14150 Office: 184 Barton St Buffalo NY 14213

COLLINS, JACK DORR, ret. automobile mfg. co. exec.; b. Mich., Jan. 22, 1921; s. S. Austin and Esther (Dorr) C.; m. H. Mable Webber, Apr. 16, 1944; children—Jeffrey D., Margaret W. B.S. in Mech. Engring, Gen. Motors Inst., 1943. Engr. Gen. Motors Co., 1943-49; asst. chief engr. Borg Warner Corp., 1949-56; with Ford Motor Co., 1956—, chief engr. car elec. systems engring., product devel. group, 1967, exec. dir. powertrain and systems research, engring. and research staff, Dearborn, Mich., 1970-80, exec. dir. engring. staff, 1980-81; dir. product devel. Ford do Brasil, 1968-70, dir., 1968-70; mem. sci. adv. group U.S. Army Tank-Automotive Command; research and tech. adv. council NASA. Author tech. papers. Elder First Presbyn. Ch., Dearborn. Mem. Soc. Automotive Engrs. (certificate appreciation 1976), Engring. Soc. Detroit. Club: Dearborn Exchange (past pres.). Address: 9703 Lindgren Ave Sun City AZ 85373

COLLINS, JAMES ARTHUR, fast food company executive; b. Huntington Park, Calif., Dec. 20, 1926; s. Albert Preston and Lucile Marie (Riglesberger) C.; m. Carol Elizabeth Leonard, July 15, 1950; children: Cathleen E., Kelly L., Michael J., Melissa L. Jr. B.S. in Civil Engring, U. Calif., Los Angeles, 1950. Civil engr. Thiesen Constrn. Co., Pasadena, Calif., 1950-52; owner, operator Airport Village Hamburger Handout, Culver City, Calif., 1952-68; chmn., chief exec. officer Collins Foods Internat., Inc., Los Angeles, 1968—. Bd. dirs. YMCA Met. Los Angeles; past chmn. bd. mgrs. Westside Los Angeles YMCA; chmn., past pres. U. Calif. at Los Angeles Found.; past regent U. Calif. Served with USN, 1944-46. Named Foodservice Operator of Yr. Internat. Foodservice Mfrs. Assn., 1977; recipient Univ. Service award UCLA, 1977, Profl. Achievement award UCLA, 1981, Alumnus of Yr. award, 1982. Mem. Nat. Restaurant Assn., Calif. Restaurant Assn. (dir., past pres.), Bay Area Restaurant Hotel Assn. (past pres.), Chief Execs. Forum, U. Calif. at Los Angeles Alumni Assn. (past pres.), Young Pres. Orgn. (past chmn. Los Angeles chpt.). Republican. Methodist. Club: Rotary (pres. 1962-63). Home: 955 N Bundy Dr Los Angeles CA 90049 Office: PO Box 92092 Los Angeles CA 90009

COLLINS, JAMES DANIEL, educator, philosopher; b. Holyoke, Mass., July 12, 1917; s. Michael Joseph and Mary Magdalen (Rooney) C.; m. Yvonne Marie Stafford, June 6, 1945; 1 son, Michael. A.B., Cath. U. Am., 1941, A.M., 1942, Ph.D., 1944. Leo. Research fellow philosophy Harvard, 1944-45; mem. faculty St. Louis U., 1945—, prof. philosophy, 1956—; Suarez lectr. Fordham U., 1953; Aquinas lectr. Marquette U., 1962; Thomas More lectr. Yale, 1963. Author: The Existentialists, 1952, The Mind of Kierkegaard, 1953, A History of Modern European Philosophy, 1954, God in Modern Philosophy, 1959, The Lure of Wisdom, 1962, Three Paths in Philosophy, 1962, The Emergence of Philosophy of Religion, 1967, Descartes' Philosophy of Nature, 1971, Interpreting Modern Philosophy, 1972, Spinoza on Nature, 1984; Editorial bd.: So. Jour. Philosophy, Am. Philos. Quar., Cross Currents, Internat. Archives for History of Ideas, Internat. Studies in Philosophy, History of Philosophy Quar., Modern Schoolman. Penfield fellow Cath. U. Am., 1944-45; Guggenheim fellow, 1963-64; recipient Cardinal Newman medal Newman Found., 1962; Cath. U. Alumni award, 1962; award for scholarship Nat. Council Cath. Men, 1961; 29th Ann. Christian Culture medal U. Windsor. Mem. Am. Philos. Assn., Am. Cath. Philos. Assn. (pres. 1954, Aquinas medal 1965), Metaphys. Soc. Am. (pres. 1962). Home: 5508 Norway Dr St Louis MO 63121

COLLINS, JAMES FOSTER, government official; b. West Hartford, Conn., Jan. 19, 1922; s. Kenneth Gaston and Mary Elizabeth (Foster) C.; m. Cornelia Agnes Deming, Dec. 30, 1944; children: Lauren Foster, Kenneth Deming, Carole Staley. B.A., Yale U., 1943; postgrad., Columbia U., 1949, Nat. War Coll., 1961-62; M.S., George Washington U., 1971. Research asst. U.S. Senate Atomic Energy Com., 1946; polit. affairs officer UN Secretariat, 1946-49; dep. sec. UN Com. Good Offices in, Indonesia, 1947-48; fgn. affairs officer NSC, 1950-54; 2d sec. Am. embassy, Jakarta, Indonesia, 1954-56; consul Am. consulate, Singapore, 1956-58; assigned State Dept., 1958-61; 1st sec. Am. embassy, Buenos Aires, Argentina, 1962-65, Panama, 1965-69; mem. Bd. Nat. Estimates, Washington, 1969-73; dep. spl. asst. for nat. security Dept. Treasury, 1973-77, spl. asst. to sec. treasury for nat. security, 1977-82; lectr. in field. Author: The United Nations and Indonesia, 1950. Bd. dirs. Panama YMCA, 1966-69, McLean (Va.) Citizens Assn., 1973-77, 79—; mem. Panama C.Z. Coll. Adv. Council, 1966-69. Served with USN, 1942-46. Decorated Bronze Star medal with V.; Recipient Meritorious Service medal Dept. Treasury. Mem. Am. Fgn. Service Assn., Phi Beta Kappa. Home: 6804 Sorrell St McLean VA 22101

COLLINS, JAMES LAWTON, JR., army officer; b. El Paso, Tex., Nov. 5, 1917; s. James Lawton and Virginia Caroline (Stewart) C.; m. Yolande DeMauduit, Oct. 2, 1943; children: Corinne, Sharon, James, Suzanne. B.Sc., U.S. Military Acad., 1939; M.A., U. Va., 1951; postgrad., Naval War Coll., 1948, Armed Forces Staff Coll., 1955, Army War Coll., 1959. Commd. 2d lt. U.S. Army, 1939, advanced through grades to brig. gen., 1965; comdt. U.S. Army Lang. Sch., 1959-62; dir. Def. Lang. Inst., 1962-63; Mil. Assistance Command, Vietnam, 1964-66; dep. asst. chief of staff, intelligence Dept. Army, 1966-67; comdr. V Corps Arty., Germany, 1967-69; chief mil. history Dept. Army, also comdr. Center Mil. History, Washington, 1970—; dir. U.S. Commn. on Mil. History, Am. Mil. Inst., Council on Abandoned Mil. Posts, Am. Com. on History 2d World War; mem. adv. bd. Nat. Armed Forces Mus. Author: The Development and Training of the South Vietnamese Army, 1950-72, 1975, (with others) Allied Participation in Vietnam, 1975; Editor: Memoirs of My Service in the World War (George C. Marshall); Contbr. articles to profl. jours. Decorated D.S.M. with 2 oak leaf clusters, Silver Star, Legion of Merit with oak leaf cluster, Bronze Star, Air medal with oak leaf cluster, Purple Heart, Croix de Guerre, France, others. Mem. Am. Hist. Assn., Am. Mil. Inst., Assn. U.S. Army. Episcopalian. Home: Zulla Vineyards PO Box 1331 Middleburg VA 22117

COLLINS, JAMES MITCHELL, congressman; b. Hallsville, Tex., Apr. 29, 1916; s. Carr P. and Ruth (Woodall) C.; m. Dorothy Dann, Sept. 16, 1942; children: Michael James, Dorothy Colville (Mrs. David R. Weaver), Nancy Miles (Mrs. Richard W. Fisher). B.S.C., So. Meth. U., 1937; M.A., Northwestern U., 1938; C.L.U., Am. U., 1940; M.B.A., Harvard U., 1943. Pres. Consol. Industries, Inc., 1954—, Internat. Industries, Inc., 1954-66, Fidelity Union Life Ins. Co., 1954-65; mem. 90th-97th Congresses from 3d Dist. Tex., mem. Edn. and Labor com., 1967-70, 1970—. Tex. chmn. White House Conf. Youth; bd. dirs. Greater Dallas Planning Council, Salvation Army, YMCA, Dallas Council, Big Bros., Dallas Assembly, United Fund, pres., Dallas Citizens Council World Affairs, Heart Assn.; chmn. Christmas Seal campaign; trustee So. Meth. U.; sr. vice chmn. Nat. Republican Congressional Com., 1974—. Served to capt., C.E. AUS, World War II; ETO. Decorated Medal of Metz; named Man of Yr. Irving Jaycees, 1970, Distinguished Alumnus So. Meth. U., 1971, Man of Year Fedn. Ind. Bus., 1971; 1974 Legislator of Year Mexican-Am. C. of C.; Watchdog of Treasury Nat. Assn. Businessmen. Mem. Am. Legion, Y.P.O., Cycen Fjodr, Mil. Order World Wars, VFW, Blue Key, Phi Delta Theta, Alpha Kappa Psi, Psi Chi. Republican. Baptist. Club: Elk. Office: 2419 Rayburn House Office Bldg Washington DC 20515 Office: 1601 Elm St LB 84 Dallas TX 75201

COLLINS, JAMES PITTENGER, consulting geotechnical engineer; b. Newark, Dec. 22, 1929; s. Roy Charles and Doris Pauline (Rose) C.; m. Jane Tyler Hutchinson, Apr. 16, 1966 (div. Apr. 1978); children: Bradford, Gregory, Susan, Virginia; 1 stepson, Richard Hutchinson. B. Engring., Yale U., 1951; M.S., Columbia U., 1953; S.M., Mass. Inst. Tech., 1959. Prin. engr. Hayden, Harding & Buchana, Boston, 1959-60; v.p. Le Messurier Assos., Inc., Cambridge, Mass., 1960-63; partner James P. Collins & Assos., Pittsford, N.Y., 1963-81; pres. Wagner Assos. (P.C.), Rochester, N.Y., 1981-82, James P. Collins & Assocs., Rochester, 1982—. Served with USN, 1955-58. Fellow ASCE, Am. Cons. Engrs. Council; mem. Nat. Soc. Profl. Engrs., ASTM. Republican. Episcopalian. Home: 161 Branford Rd Rochester NY 14618 Office: 242 Andrews St Rochester NY 14618

COLLINS, JAY WILSON, hospital administrator; b. Cleve., Dec. 30, 1917; s. Charles H. and Alice A. (Murray) C.; m. Ileene J. Lustic, July 11, 1969; 1 son, Grant L. A.B., Fenn Coll., 1940; M.A., Ohio State U., 1941. Regional dir. FSA, Youngstown, Ohio, 1941; mem. faculty Fenn Coll., Cleve., 1942; adminstrv. asst. Univ. Hosp. of Cleve., 1945-46; asst. dir. Samaritan Hosp., Troy, N.Y., 1946-47; pres. Euclid (Ohio) Gen. Hosp., 1947-79; v.p. Regional Health Data Services Inc., 1977-79; pres. Hosp. Fin. Corp., 1974-79; v.p., exec. dir. Euclid Devel. Corp., 1977—. Contbr. articles to profl. jours. Mem. adv. bd. Lakeland Community Coll., 1971-76, Villa Angela Acad., 1975—; councilman City of Euclid, 1971-73; pres. Euclid Community Relations Council, 1968-73; city leader Republican Party, 1975-80; pres. Community Improvement Corp., 1980—; v.p. Fenn Ednl. Commn., 1980—; trustee Euclid YMCA, pres., 1966-68; trustee Fenn Coll., 1954-57, Greater Cleve. Red Cross, 1962-66, Greater Cleve. YMCA, 1970—, Euclid Red Cross, 1961-66, Euclid Civic Orch., 1961-64, Euclid Cultural Council, 1967-68, Early Settlers of Western Res., 1976—; pres. Early Settlers of Western Res., 1983—; trustee Cleve. Area Devel. Fin. Corp., 1982—. Served to capt. M.C., U.S. Army, 1942-45. Recipient Disting. Service award Fenn Coll., 1958, YMCA, 1963, City of Euclid, 1977. Fellow Am. Coll. Hosp. Adminstrs.; mem. Ohio Hosp. Assn. (trustee 1950-58, pres. 1955-56), Greater Cleve. Hosp. Assn. (pres. 1977-79, trustee 1951-79), Am. Hosp. Assn., Internat. Hosp. Fedn., Royal Soc. Health, Soc. Mayflower Descs., SAR (v.p. 1982—), Newcomen Soc. N.Am., Euclid C. of C. (pres. 1978-81), U.S. C. of C. Republican. Presbyterian. Clubs: Mayfield Village Racquet, Riverview Racquet. Lodge: Kiwanis (pres. 1964-65). Office: 333 Babbitt Euclid OH 44123

COLLINS, JERRY ALLAN, assn. exec.; b. Toronto, Ont., Can., Mar. 14, 1936; s. Ralph Gordon and Violet Elizabeth C.; m. Cynthia Mae Connell, Dec. 21, 1963; children—Kimberly Ann, Sean Foster. B.A. in Econs. and Polit. Sci, U. Toronto, 1961. Research asst. Ont. C. of C., Toronto, 1961-62, asst. mgr., 1962-64, gen. mgr., 1964-70; asst. gen. mgr. Bd. of Trade of Met., Toronto, 1970-72, gen. mgr., 1972—. Mem. C. of C. Execs. Can. (past pres.), Am. C. of C. Execs. Clubs: Granite, Empire. Office: PO Box 60 3 First Canadian Pl Toronto ON M5X 1C1 Canada

COLLINS, JOAN HENRIETTA, actress; b. London, May 3, 1936; d. Joseph William and Elsa (Bessant) C.; m. Ronald S. Kass, Mar., 1972; 1 dau., Katie; children from previous marriage: Tara Cynara Newley, Sacha Newley. Films include: I Believe in You, Girl in the Red Velvet Swing, Rally Round the Flag Boys, Island in the Sun, Seven Thieves, Road to Hong Kong, Sunburn, The Stud, Game for Vultures, The Bitch, The Big Sleep; theatre appearance in The Last of Mrs. Cheyney; TV films include: The Man Who Came to Dinner, The Moneychanger, Paper Dolls, The Wild Women of Chastity Gulch; star TV series: Dynasty, 1981—; Author: Past Imperfect, 1978. Office: care William Morris Agy 151 El Camino Beverly Hills CA 90212 *

COLLINS, JOHN WENDLER, consumer products company executive; b. Rutherford, N.J., Nov. 7, 1930; s. Nelson Haley and Agnes Lucinda (Maier) C.; m. Martha E. Raiff, Oct. 26, 1952; children: Bruce, Nancy, Susan; m. Janet Doyle, July 17, 1975. B.A., Dartmouth Coll., 1952. V.p. Procter & Gamble Co., Cin., 1955-76; group v.p. Clorox Co., Oakland, Calif., 1976—, dir., 1983—. Trustee East Oakland Youth Devel. Ctr., Oakland, 1976—; com. mem. United Way, Bay Area, 1976—. Served to lt. USNR, 1952-55. Mem. Phi Beta Kappa. Democrat. Home: 19 Honey Hill Rd Orinda CA 94563 Office: 1221 Broadway Oakland CA 94612

COLLINS, JUDY MARJORIE, singer; b. Seattle, May 1, 1939; d. Charles T. and Marjorie (Byrd) C.; m. Peter A. Taylor, Apr., 1958 (div.); 1 son, Clark Taylor. Pvt. study piano, 1953-56. Debut as profl. folk singer, Boulder, Colo., 1959; has since appeared in numerous clubs, U.S. and, around world; performer concerts including, Newport Folk Festival, ann. concerts, maj. concert halls and summer theatres, throughout U.S. and, Europe; also appeared radio and TV; recording artist, Elektra; profl. acting debut as Solveig in: N.Y. Shakespeare Festival prodn. of Peer Gynt, 1969; producer, dir.: documentary movie A Portrait of the Woman, 1974; recent albums include So Early in the Spring/The First Fifteen Years, 1977, Hard Times for Lovers, 1979, Running for My Life, 1980 (Recipient 6 Gold LPs., Silver medal Atlanta Internat. Film Festival, Blue Ribbon award Am. Film Festival, N.Y.C., Christopher award), Times of Our Lives. Office: care Charles R Rothschild Prodns Inc 330 E 48th St New York NY 10010

COLLINS, LARRY, author, journalist; b. Hartford, Conn., Sept. 14, 1929; s. John Laurence and Helen (Cannon) C.; m. Nadia Hoda Sultan, Sept. 17, 1966; children—John Lawrence III, Michael Kevin. Grad., Loomis Inst., Windsor, Conn., 1947; B.A., Yale U., 1951. With U.P.I., 1956-59, corr., Middle East, 1957-59; Middle East editor Newsweek mag., 1959-61, chief, 1961-64. Author: (with Dominique La Pierre) Is Paris Burning, 1965, Or I'll Dress You in Mourning, 1967, O, Jerusalem!, 1972, Freedom at Midnight, 1975, The Fifth Horseman, 1980, Mountbatten and the Partition of India, 1982. Served with AUS, 1953-55 *

COLLINS, LEROY, lawyer, former governor Florida; b. Tallahassee, Mar. 10, 1909; s. Marvin H. and Mattie (Brandon) C.; m. Mary Call Darby, June 29, 1932; children: LeRoy, Jane, Mary Call, and Darby Collins. LL.B., Cumberland U., 1931. Bar: Fla. 1931, Ark. 1931, Tenn. 1931. Leon County rep. to Fla. Legislature, 1934-40; mem. Senate, 1940-54; gov. Fla., 1955-61; pres. Nat. Assn. Broadcasters, 1961-64; dir. Community Relations Service, 1964-65; undersec. U.S. Dept. Commerce, 1965-66, practiced in Tampa, Fla., 1966-68; of counsel Ervin, Varn, Jacobs, Odom & Kitchen, Tallahassee, 1970—; mem. Fla. Constn. Revision Commn., 1977-78, So. Legal Council, 1977—; former chmn. Nat. Govs. Conf.; Former chmn. So. Govs. Conf.; mem. nat. adv. council Peace Corps. Mem. honor corps NCCJ; chmn. South Regional Edn. Bd., 1955-57; mem. Commn. on Goals for Higher Edn. in South, 1961-62, Commn. on Future of South, 1980-81; trustee Fla. Defenders of Environment, 1981—; bd. dirs. Com. on Constl. System, 1984—. Served as lt. USNR, World War II. Recipient Nelson Poynter award ACLU, 1978, Charles Evans Hughes award NCCJ, 1965, Great Floridian award, 1981. Mem. ABA (chmn. spl. com. legal edn. 1974), Fla. History Assocs. Democrat. Episcopalian. Home: The Grove Tallahassee FL 32303 Office: PO Box 1170 305 S Gadsden St Tallahassee FL 32301

COLLINS, LEROY, JR., Realtor, data processing company executive; b. Tallahassee, Fla., Sept. 3, 1934; s. LeRoy and Mary Call (Darby) C.; m. Jane Sisson; 4 children. B.S., U.S. Naval Acad., 1956. Asst. to pres. Fla. Power and Light Co., 1966-68; salesman IBM, 1968-69; pres. Fin. Transaction Systems, Inc., Tampa, 1969—; pres., dir. Fla. Service Ctr., Inc. (named changed to Telecredit Service Ctr., Inc.), 1974-80; exec. v.p. Telecredit, Inc., 1977-80; pres., dir. Telecredit Service Ctr., Inc., Tampa, 1974-80; pres., broker Dynamic Realty of Tampa, Inc., 1980—; dir. U.S. RESICO, Reistad Corp., Cable Video Communications, Inc., Parker & Parker Cons., Atlantic Nat. Bank Fla. Bd. dirs. Berkeley Prep. Sch., WEDU-Ednl. TV., 1976-83, Bradentonk Hillsborough Community Coll. Served to commodore USNR, 1956—. Mem. Young Presidents Orgn., Golden Triangle Civic Assn., Tampa Com. of 100, Naval Res. Assn., Navy League U.S., Naval Acad. Alumni Assn. Episcopalian. Office: Box 22376 Tampa FL 33622

COLLINS, LESTER ALBERTSON, landscape architect; b. Moorestown, N.J., Apr. 19, 1914; s. Lester and Anne (Albertson) C.; m. Petronella leRoux, July 8, 1947; children—Abigail Anne, Lester Adrian, Oliver Michael. Grad., Choate Sch., 1933; student, Princeton, 1933-35; A.B., Harvard, 1938, M.L.A., 1942. Chmn. dept. landscape architecture Harvard, 1950-53; prin. Collins, Simonds and Simonds, Washington, 1955-70, Lester Collins Assos., 1971—. Pres. Innisfree Found. Bd. dirs., Hubbard Endl. Trust. Served with Am. Field Service, 1942-45. Fulbright scholar, Japan, 1953-54. Fellow Am. Soc. Landscape Architects. Mem. Soc. of Friends. Clubs: Cosmos (Washington); Century Assn. (N.Y.C.). Home: 1415 Thompson St Key West FL 33040

COLLINS, MARIBETH WILSON, foundation executive; b. Portland, Oreg., Oct. 27, 1918; d. Clarence True and Maude (Akin) Wilson; m. Truman Wesley Collins, Mar. 12, 1943; children—Timothy Wilson and Terry Stanton (twins), Cherida Lynne, Truman Wesley. B.A., U. Oreg., 1940. Pres. Collins Found., Lynnridge Investment Co., Portland, Oreg., 1964—; dir. Collins Pine Co., Collins Holding Co., Ostrander Constrn. Co. Bd. trustees, exec. com., mem. campus religious life com. Willamette U., Salem, Oreg. Mem. Gamma Phi Beta. Republican. Methodist. Clubs: Univ., Internat., West Hills Racquet. Home: 2275 SW Mayfield Ave Portland OR 97225 Office: Collins Found 909 Terminal Sales Bldg Portland OR 97205

COLLINS, MARTHA LAYNE, governor Kentucky; b. Shelby County, Ky., Dec. 7, 1936; d. Everett Larkin and Mary Lorena (Taylor) Hall; m. Bill Collins, July 3, 1959; children: Stephen Louis, Marla Ann. Student, Lindenwood Coll.; B.S., U. Ky., 1959. Formerly tchr. Fairdale High Sch., Louisville, Seneca High Sch., Woodford County Jr. High Sch., Versailles; former lt. gov., State of Ky., now gov. Mem. Woodford County (Ky.) Democratic Exec. Com.; mem. Dem. Nat. Com., 1972-76; former coordinator Women's Activities for State Dem. Hdqrs.; del. Dem. Nat. Conv., Miami, 1972, Mid-term charter Conf., Kansas City, 1974; mem. credentials com. Dem. Nat. Com. Vice Presdl. Selection Process Commn.; Ky. chairwoman 51.3 Com. for Carter, 1976; mem. Ky. Dem. Central Exec. Com.; sec. Ky. Dem. Party; elected clk. Ct. of Appeals, 1975; later clk. Supreme Ct. Ky.; past tchr. Sunday sch.; mem. Ky. Commn. on Women; Ky.'s exec. dir. Friendship Force. Mem. Woodford County Jaycee-ettes (past pres.), U. Ky. Alumni Assn., Women's Missionary Union (past pres.), Nat. Conf. Appellate Ct. Clks., Psi Omega Dental Aux. (past pres.). Baptist. Clubs: Bus. and Profl., Women's, Order Eastern Star. Organized first Woodford County Jr. Miss Pageant. Office: Office of Gov State Capitol Frankfort KY 40601 *

COLLINS, MARVA DELOISE NETTLES, educational administrator, educator; b. Monroeville, Ala., Aug. 31, 1936; d. Alex L. and Bessie Maye (Knight) Nettles; m. Clarence Collins, Sept. 2, 1960; children: Patrick, Eric, Cynthia. B.A., Clark Coll., 1957, Howard U., 1980, D.H.L., Wilberforce U., 1980, Chgo. State U., 1981, D.Hum., Dartmouth Coll., 1981. Founder Westside Prep. Sch., 1975, tchr., 1975—. Subject of numerous publs.: including Marva Collins' Way, 1982; subject of: feature film Welcome to Success: The Marva Collins Story, 1981. Mem. Pres.'s Commn. on White House Fellowships, 1981—. Recipient numerous awards, including: Reading Found. Am. award, 1979; Soujourner Truth Nat. award, 1980; Tchr. of Yr. award Phi Delta Kappa, 1980; Am. Public Service award Am. Inst. for Public Service, 1981; Endow a Dream award, 1980; Educator of Yr. award Chgo. Urban League, 1980; Jefferson Nat. award, 1981. Mem. Alpha Kappa Alpha. Baptist. Club: Exec. Was offered and refused position of U.S. Sec. Edn., 1981. Office: 4146 Chicago Ave Chicago IL 60641 *A positive attitude is perhaps one of the richest aspects of my life. I find that I will go out of my way to be surrounded by people who are filled with the art of living, loving, and caring, and not because it is a duty, but because we all feel better when we have made the lives of others better through caring.*

COLLINS, MICHAEL, aerospace official, former astronaut; b. Rome, Oct. 31, 1930; s. James L. and Virginia (Stewart) C. (parents Am. citizens); m. Patricia M. Finnegan, Apr. 28, 1957; children: Kathleen, Ann Stewart, Michael Lawton. B.S., U.S. Mil. Acad., 1952; grad., Advanced Mgmt. Program, Harvard U., 1974; D.Sc., Northeastern U., 1970, Stonehill Coll., 1970; LL.D., St. Michael's Coll., 1970, Southeastern U., 1975. Commd. officer U.S. Air Force, advanced through grades to col., 1970; fighter pilot, flight comdr., U.S., Europe, exptl. flight test officer, Calif.; named astronaut NASA, 1963, pilot, space walker, comdr., Command Module pilot, 1963-69; apptd. asst. sec. state for pub. affairs, Washington, 1970-71; dir. Nat. Air and Space Mus., Smithsonian Instn., Washington, 1971-78, undersec. of Instn., 1978-80; v.p. LTV Aerospace & Def. Co., 1980—; dir. Rand Corp. Author: Carrying the Fire, 1974, Flying to the Moon and Other Strange Places, 1976. Trustee Nat. Geog. Soc. Decorated D.S.M., D.F.C.; recipient Presdl. Medal of Freedom, NASA Distinguished Service and Exceptional Service medals, Hubbard medal, Collier trophy, Goddard Meml. trophy, Harmon trophy, Gen. Thomas D. White USAF Space trophy, gold space medal Fedn. Aeronautique Internat. Fellow Am. Inst. Aeros. and Astronautics, Am. Astronautical Soc.; mem. Washington Inst. Fgn. Affairs, Soc. Exptl. Test Pilots, Order of Daedalians, Washington Nat. Monument Soc. Clubs: Cosmos, Alfalfa, Alibi. Office: LTV Aerospace and Def Co 1725 Jefferson Davis Hwy Suite 900 Arlington VA 22202

COLLINS, MICHAEL JAMES, investment company executive; b. Orange, N.J., July 30, 1944; s. James Mitchel and Dorothy (Dann) C.; m. Wynnell Madison Roach, Nov. 14, 1982; 1 dau. by previous marriage: Catherine Elise. B.A., Stanford U., 1967; M.B.A., Harvard U., 1970; spl. degree program, Inst. Fgn. Trade, 1968. Pres. Intercontinental Prodns., Dallas, 1966-69; v.p. acquisition and new product devel. APC Industries, Austin, Tex., 1969-70, asst. to pres.,

1970-71, v.p. spl. ops., 1971-72; chmn. bd., pres., chief exec. officer, chief operating officer Fidelity Union Life Ins. Co., Dallas, 1972-82; pres. Allianz Investment Corp., Dallas, 1980-82; exec. com. Allianz of Am., 1979-82; pres., chief exec. officer Collins Capital, Dallas, 1982—; vice chmn. The Genra Group, Inc., 1983—; ptnr. Taylor & Taylor Assocs. (venture capital fund), Vent-a-Hood Co.; pres., dir. Collins Diversified, Inc. Trustee KERA-TV Pub. Broadcasting Sta.; trustee, mem. acquisitions com. Dallas Mus. Fine Arts; bd. assocs., found. bd. So. Meth. U.; bd. dirs., v.p. Carr P. Collins Found., Dallas; bd. dirs. Dallas County Community Coll. Dist. Found.; trustee U.S.A. Film Festival., Colo. Outward Bound Sch. Recipient Douglas MacArthur Freedom medal, 1970, Livesaving Rescue Operation spl. citation USCG, 1975; named One of 10 Outstanding Young Men of Am. U.S. Jaycees, 1978. Mem. Young Pres. Orgn. Clubs: Harvard, Stanford, 2Petroleum, City, Willow Bend Polo and Hunt, Preston Trail Golf, Idlewild, Terpsichorean. Address: 5252 Interfirst Two Dallas TX 75270

COLLINS, PAUL JOHN, banker; b. West Bend, Wis., Oct. 26, 1936; s. Curtis Alvin and Adele (Stopenbach) C.; m. Carol Lee Hoffmann, May 8, 1965; children: Ronald Alvin, Julia Downing. B.B.A., U. Wis., 1958; M.B.A., Harvard U., 1961. With Citibank, N.Y.C., 1961—, investment analyst, portfolio mgmt., 1961-70, sr. v.p., chmn. investment policy com., 1970-75, sr. v.p., head dept. corporate planning, 1976-77, sr. v.p., head fin. div., 1977-79, exec. v.p. acctg. and control, 1980-81, exec. v.p. capital markets group, 1982—; dir. Research Corp., Kimberly Clark Corp. Trustee Hosp. for Spl. Surgery, N.Y.C., U. Wis. Found. Republican. Conglist. Club: River (N.Y.C.). Home: 950 Park Ave New York NY 10028 Office: 399 Park Ave New York NY 10043

COLLINS, PHILIP REILLY, lawyer, educator; b. New Orleans, July 26, 1921; s. James Mark and Katherine (Gallaher) C.; m. Mary Catherine O'Leary, Feb. 9, 1946. B.A., Loyola U., New Orleans, 1939, J.D., 1942; M.A. in Govt. and Internat. Law and Relations, Georgetown U., 1948, Ph.D., 1950; LL.M., George Washington U., 1952. Bar: La. 1942, Mass. 1948, D.C. 1953, Md. 1983. Atty. Bur. Land Mgmt., Dept. Interior, Washington, 1946-47; asst. legislative counsel Office of Solicitor, P.O. Dept., 1947-48; individual practice law, Washington, 1954-77, 78—; partner firm MacCracken, Collins & Hawes, 1960-69; chief counsel, staff dir. com. on rules U.S. Ho. of Reps., 1977-78; spl. counsel Fed. Home Loan Bank Bd., 1961-69, Ky. Savs. and Loan League, 1967-68, state of Alaska, 1967-68; vis. prof., spl. asst. to pres. for labor relations Queens Coll., 1969-70; lectr. in pub. adminstrn. sch. social scis. Cath. U. Am., 1954-56; lectr. in law Cath. U. Law Sch., 1954-60. Mem. adv. com. on wills, trusts and other bequests Loyola U., New Orleans, 1966-69; charter mem. bd. visitors Law Sch., 1968—; mem. Pres.'s Council, 1976—. Served to capt. USAAF, 1942-46; PTO; maj. USAF, Korean Conflict; col. Res. Mem. Am., La., Mass., D.C., N.Y.C., Md. bar assns., Delta Theta Phi, Phi Alpha Theta. Democrat. Roman Catholic. Clubs: K.C. (4 deg.); University (Washington)). Home: 1026 16th St NW Washington DC 20036

COLLINS, ROBERT DEVILLE, foreign service officer; b. Oakland, Calif., Dec. 14, 1932; s. Russel Orville and Eugenie Roberta (McIntyre) C.; m. Margaret Carol Snyder, Nov. 22, 1957; children: Robert Russel, Christopher Clement. B.A., U. Calif.-Berkeley, 1954; M.A., Johns Hopkins U., 1956; grad., U.S. Army War Coll., 1980. Intelligence research specialist Dept. State, 1956-59, U.S. vice consul., Hong Kong, 1959-60, Kingston, Jamaica, 1960-62, U.S. consul., Milan, 1966-70, NATO desk staff, 1966-70, 1st sec. Am. Embassy, Rome, 1970-73; 1st sec. U.S. Delegation to NATO, 1973-76; U.S. consul. gen. Dept. State, Palermo, Italy, 1976-79, dir., polit. officer personnel, 1980-82, U.S. consul. gen., Milan, 1982—. Officer sch. bd. Am. Community Sch., Milan, 1965-66. Mem. Am. Fgn. Service Assn. Roman Catholic. Home: Am Embassy APO New York NY 09794 Office: Piazza Repubblica Milano MilanItaly 32 20124

COLLINS, ROBERT EDWARD, pen co. exec.; b. Clyman, Wis., Dec. 26, 1923; s. William J. and Clara S. C.; m. Patricia R. Simonsen, June 25, 1949; children—Judith, Jane, Daniel, David. B.S. in Elec. Engring, U. Wis., 1946, LL.B., 1949. Bar: Wis. bar 1949, Oreg. bar 1950. Practiced in, Evansville, Wis., 1949-50, statute revision counsel, Salem, Oreg., 1950-53, dep. legislative counsel, 1953, practiced in, Janesville, Wis., 1954-57; with legal dept. Parker Pen Co., Janesville, Wis., 1957—, v.p., gen. counsel, sec., 1981—; dir. Omniflight Helicopters, Inc., Janesville. Bd. dirs. YMCA, 1980—, Boys Baseball Janesville, Inc., 1958-80; mem. Janesville Sch. Bd., 1966—, pres., 1968-80. Served with USN, 1944-46. Mem. Am. Bar Assn., Am. Soc. Corporate Secs., Wis. Bar Assn., Rock County Bar Assn., Janesville C. of C. (dir. 1973-76). Office: 1 Parker Pl Janesville WI 53545

COLLINS, ROBERT EMMET, agricultural products company executive; b. Pasadena, Calif., Jan. 24, 1913; s. Lawrence Dennis and Mary Regina (Quinn) C.; m. Gertrude P.; children: Robert Dennis, Michael Boyd, James Patrick, Eileen Mary. Student public schs., Hemet, Calif. Farm worker, Riverside, Calif., 1932-37; field man Agrl. Adjustment Adminstrn., 1938-39; office mgr. Napa Co., 1940, mgr. Sacramento County office, 1941-44; farmer, 1945—; pres. Sacramento County Farm Bur., 1953-54; organizing dir. Calif. Canned Pears Assn., San Francisco, 1953—, pres., 1960-71, chmn. bd. mktg. order, 1970-83; pres. Agrl. Council, Calif., 1963-65; chmn. bd., founder, dir. Pacific Coast Producers, Santa Clara, Calif., 1971—; mem. agrl. adv. bd. U. Calif., Berkeley. Contbr. numerous articles in field to profl. bulls. Mem. Walnut Grove (Calif.) Sch. Bd.; commr. Delta dist. Boy Scouts Am. Recipient Centennial award U. Calif., 1968, Disting. Service to Agr. award; Calif. Farm Bur. Fedn., 1971; Sacramento County Agribus. Man of Yr. Sacramento Met. C. of C., 1972. Mem. Nat. Council Farmer Coops, Calif. Council Agrl. Coops., Sacramento County Farm Bur., Calif. Canning Pear Assn., Tri Valley Growers, Calif. Grain Mktg. Assn. Republican. Clubs: Rotary (pres. club 1956-57, Paul Harris Fellow award Rotary Internat. 1979. Home and Office: PO Box 407 Andrus Island Walnut Grove CA 95690

COLLINS, ROBERT FREDERICK, federal judge; b. New Orleans, Jan. 27, 1931; s. Frederick and Irma V. (Anderson) C.; m. Aloha, Dec. 28, 1957; children: Francesca Collins McManus, Lisa Ann, Nanette C., Robert A. B.A. cum laude, Dillard U., 1951, LL.D. (hon.), 1979; J.D., La. State U., 1954; grad. spl. summer course, Nat. Jud. Coll., U. Nev., 1973. Bar: La. bar 1954. Mem. firm Augustine, Collins, Smith & Warren, New Orleans, 1956-59; instr. law So. U., 1959-61; sr. partner firm Collins, Douglas & Elie, New Orleans, 1960-72; asst. city atty.-legal adv. New Orleans Police Dept., 1967-69; judge ad-hoc Traffic Ct., New Orleans, 1969-72; atty. Housing Authority, New Orleans, 1971-72; judge magistrate sect. Criminal Dist. Ct., Orleans Parish, La., 1971-78; judge U.S. Dist. Ct., Eastern Dist. La., 1978—; asst. bar examiner, State of La., 1970-78. Bd. dirs. New Orleans Housing Council, 1962-64, Social Welfare Planning Council, New Orleans, 1965-67, Dryades St. YMCA, New Orleans, 1963-65, New Orleans Urban League, 1970-72, 75; trustee Loyola U., New Orleans, 1977-83. Served with U.S. Army, 1954-56. Mem. La. Bar Assn., Nat. Bar Assn. (regional dir. 1964-65), Am. Bar Assn., Louis A. Martinet Legal Soc. (pres. 1959-60), Am. Judicature Soc., 5th Circuit Dist. Judges Assn. Democrat. Roman Catholic. Office: 500 Camp St Suite 465 New Orleans LA 70130

COLLINS, ROBERT JOSEPH, journalist; b. Indpls., Jan. 22, 1927; s. Patrick Joseph and Evelyn (Mattingly) C.; m. Sarah Zore, Nov. 28, 1946; children: Kathleen, Carolyn, Cynthia, Mary Louise, Evelyn, Michael, Kevin, Linda. Student, Butler U., 1946-49. With Indpsl. Star, 1948—, columnist, 1960—, sports editor, 1964—. Author: Best of Bob Collins, 1963, Boilermakers: A History of Purdue Football, 1976, (with Mario Andretti) What's It Like Out There, 1970. Served with USNR, World War II. Roman Catholic. Club: Indpls. Press (pres. 1963). Home: 712 N New Jersey Indianapolis IN 46202 Office: 307 N Pennsylvania Indianapolis IN 46206

COLLINS, ROBERT MCVICKAR, medical manufacturing company executive; b. Rhinebeck, N.Y., Dec. 14, 1930; s. Benjamin and Dorothy (McVickar) C.; m. Elaine Johncox, Dec. 11, 1954; children: Susan, Julia, Timothy. B.A. in Polit. Sci., Haverford Coll., 1952; M.B.A. in Mktg., U. Pa., 1958. With market research dept. Parmaseal div. Am. Hosp. Corp., Glendale, Calif., 1958-61, with sales dept., Denver, 1961-63, product mgr., Glendale, 1963-64; pres. COBE Labs. Inc., Glendale, 1964—, Lakewood, Colo., 1964—; dir. Mt. States Employment Council, Denver, NBI, Boulder, Colo. Bd. trustees Denver Art Mus., 1976-83; treas. Inst. for Health, Denver, 1979—; bd. mgrs. Haverford Coll., Pa., 1981—; mem. bus. adv. council U. Denver, 1983—. Served with USN, 1952-56. Named Businessman of Yr. Colo. Small Bus. Adv. Council, 1971. Mem. World Bus. Council, Health Industry Mfrs. Assn. (dir. 1978-81). Club: Trout Unlimited. Office: COBE Labs Inc 1185 Oak St Lakewood CO 80215

COLLINS, ROBERT OAKLEY, history educator; b. Waukegan, Ill., Apr. 1, 1933; s. William George and Louise Van Horsen (Jack) C.; m. Janyce Hutchins Monroe, Oct. 6, 1974; children by previous marriage: Catharine Louise, Randolph Ware, Robert William. B.A., Dartmouth Coll., 1954; A.B. (Marshall scholar 1954-55), Balliol Coll., Oxford U., 1956, M.A., 1960, Yale U., 1958, Ph.D., 1959. Instr. history Williams Coll., Williamstown, Mass., 1959-61; lectr. U. Mass. Extension, Pittsfield, 1960-61; vis. asst. prof. history Columbia U., N.Y.C., 1962-63; asst. prof. history Williams Coll., 1963-65; mem. faculty U. Calif., Santa Barbara, 1965—, prof. history, 1969—, dir., 1967-69, acting vice chancellor for research and grad. affairs, 1970-71, dean grad. div., 1971-80. Author: The Southern Sudan, 1883-1898, 1962, King Leopold, England and the Upper Nile, 1968, Problems in African History, 1968, The Partition of Africa, 1969, Land Beyond the Rivers: The Southern Sudan, 1898-1918, 1971, Europeans in Africa, 1971, An Arabian Diary, 1969, The Southern Sudan in Historical Perspective, 1975, Shadows in the Grass: Britain in the Southern Sudan, 1983. NDEA lang. fellow, 1960-61; Social Sci. Research Council fellow, 1962-63; Rockefeller Found. scholar-in-residence, Bellagio, Italy, 1979; Ford Found. fellow, 1979-81; Fulbright sr. research fellow, 1982; Woodrow Wilson fellow, 1983; recipient Gold class award Order Scis. and Arts Dem. Republic of Sudan, 1980. Mem. Am. Hist. Assn., African Studies Assn., Western River Guides Assn., Explorers Club, Phi Beta Kappa. Home: 735 Calle De Los Amigos Santa Barbara CA 93105 Office: Dept History U Calif Santa Barbara CA 93106

COLLINS, RODNEY STEVEN, historic preservationist, historian; b. Parkersburg, W.Va., Aug. 4, 1946; s. Robert Paul and Mary Virginia (Hathaway) C. A.B., W.Va. U., 1971, M.A., 1972. Tchr. Plesants County Schs., St. Marys, W.Va., 1969-70; instr. history Parkersburg Community Coll., 1974; curator interpretation Ohio Hist. Soc., Columbus-Marietta, 1974-75; project mgr. City of Charleston East End Survey, W.Va., 1975-77; dir., dep. state historic preservation officer, historic preservation unit Dept. Culture and History, Charleston, 1977—, W.Va. capitol historian, 1977—; chmn. bd. Kanawha Valley Hist. and Preservation Soc., Charleston, 1981—; ex-officio mem. W.Va. Archives and History Commn., Charleston, 1981—. Author: (with Pauley and Gioulis) West Virginia Historic Resource Survey Handbook, 1983. Edn. chmn. East Edn. Assn., Charleston, 1976. Recipient Eagle Scout award Boy Scouts Am., 1963. Mem. Nat. Trust Historic Preservation, Soc. Archtl. Historians, Nat. Conf. State Historic Preservation Officers, Preservation Alliance W.Va. Inc., Phi Alpha Theta. Home: 1625 Quarrier St Charleston WV 25311 Office: W Va Dept Culture and History Capitol Complex Charleston WV 25305

COLLINS, ROWLAND LEE, English language educator; b. Bristow, Okla., Sept. 17, 1934; s. John Leland and Velma Grace (Jones) C.; m. Sarah Jo Huff, Apr. 10, 1965; children: Robin Elizabeth, Michael John, Catherine Grace. A.B. in English and Humanities cum laude, Princeton, 1956; M.A. (Woodrow Wilson Found. fellow), Stanford, 1959, Ph.D., 1961. Teaching asso. Stanford, 1958-59; lectr. English Ind. U., 1959-61, instr., 1961-62; asst. prof. English, 1962-65, asso. prof., 1965-67; prof. U. Rochester, 1967—, acting chmn. dept. English, 1970-71, chmn., 1972-81; Council of Humanities fellow Princeton, 1965-66; Woodrow Wilson Found. campus rep. Ind. U., 1963-67, U. Rochester, 1982—. Author: Anglo-Saxon Vernacular Manuscripts In America, 1976; Editor: Fourteen British and American Poets, 1964, Beowulf, 1965; Contbr.: bibliographies to New Cambridge Bibliography of English Lit., vol. III, 1969, vol. I, 1974; Editorial cons.: Victorian Studies, 1963-66; editorial bd.: Your Musical Cue, 1964-69, U. Rochester Library Bull, 1969—; founding editor: Year's Work in Old English Studies, 1968—; asso. editor: Old English Newsletter, 1968—; Author numerous articles, revs. on Old English manuscripts lit. and wills, lexicography, linguistic history, Tennyson, Shakespeare, opera, electronic music, archtl. history, poetry, and lit. history to profl. jours. Trustee Keuka Coll., 1976—; Acad. advisor Montfort Jones and Allie Brown Jones Found., 1961-73, trustee, 1973—, vice chmn., 1974—; mem. Landmark Soc. of Western N.Y., 1968—, trustee, 1970—, sec., 1974-78, pres., 1978-80; mem. Rochester Preservation Bd., 1969-75, vice chmn., 1969-71, chmn., 1971-74; bd. dirs. Hillside Children's Center, 1977-. John Simon Guggenheim Found. fellow, 1965-66. Fellow Rochester Mus. and Sci. Center; mem. Internat. Assn. Univ. Profs. English, Guild of Scholars (sec.-treas. 1975-78), Modern Lang. Assn. Am. (sec. Old English group 1964, chmn. 1964, del. assembly 1977-79), Assn. Depts. English (dir. 1980—), Medieval Acad. Am., Early English Text Soc., Bibliog. Soc. Am., Cambridge (Eng.) Bibliog. Soc., Bibliog. Soc. (London), English Inst., Tennyson Soc. (Am. rep. 1967—), Citizens' Assn. East Ave., Park-Meigs Neighborhood Assn. (pres. 1975-76), Rochester Hist. Soc., Meml. Art Gallery, Rochester Area Ednl. TV Assn., Friends of Rochester Public Library (dir. 1976—), English-Speaking Union (chmn. br. com. scholarship 1969-72). Democrat. Episcopalian (commn. to evaluate seminarians 1974-75). Clubs: Grolier, The Club, Faculty. Home: 16 Arnold Park Rochester NY 14607 Office: Dept of English U of Rochester Rochester NY 14627

COLLINS, ROYAL EUGENE, physicist, petroleum engineering educator; b. Corsicana, Tex., Feb. 25, 1925; s. Royal and Jewell Anna (Truhitte) C.; m. Melissa Good. B.S. in Physics, U. Houston, 1949; M.S., Tex. A&M U., 1950, Ph.D., 1954. Registered profl. engr., Tex. With Magnolia Petroleum Co., Dallas, 1951-52, Stanolind Oil & Gas Co., Tulsa, 1954-55, Humble Oil & Refining Co., Houston, 1955-59; mem. faculty U. Houston, 1959-79, prof. physics, 1967-79; mem. faculty U. Tex., Austin, 1979—, Frank W. Jessen prof. petroleum engring., 1980—; staff cons. med. biophysics Baylor U. Coll. Medicine, 1962-78; cons. to govt. and industry, 1959—. Author: Flow of Fluids Through Porous Materials, 1961, Russian edit., 1965, Japanese edit., 1975, Mathematical Methods for Physicists and Engineers, 1968. Served with USNR, 1942-45. Research grantee Tex. Heart Assn., 1960-62, NSF, 1962, Research Corp. Am., 1969-70, U. Houston, 1970, USAF Office Sci. Research, 1975—, Dept. Energy, 1977-80. Mem. Am. Phys. Soc., Am. Assn. Physics Tchrs., Soc. Petroleum Engrs., Sigma Xi, Sigma Pi Sigma., Phi Epsilon Tau. Home: 2009 Millay Dr Austin TX 78752 Office: Dept Petroleum Engring U Tex Austin TX 78712

COLLINS, SAMUEL CORNETTE, mech. engr.; b. Democrat, Ky., Sept. 28, 1898; s. John Wesley and Rachel Ellen (Caudill) C.; m. Lena Arbragine Masterson, Sept. 4, 1929. B.S., U. Tenn., 1920, M.S., 1924; Ph.D., U. N.C., 1927, D.Sc. (hon.), 1957, LL.D., St. Andrews U., Scotland, 1967. Prof. chemistry Carson-Newman Coll., 1925-26, E.Tenn. State Tchrs. Coll., 1928-30; research asso. Mass. Inst. Tech., 1930-35, asst. prof. chemistry, 1935-42, asso. prof., 1942-46, asso. prof. mech. engring., 1946-49, prof. mech. engring., 1949-64; v.p. Arthur D. Little, Inc. and Cryogenic Tech., Inc., Cambridge, Mass., 1964-71; research chemist Naval Research Lab., Washington, 1971—. Contbr. articles on cryogenic apparatus to profl. jours. Recipient Wetherill medal Franklin Inst., 1951, Kamerlingh Onnes Gold medal Netherlands Refrigeration Soc., 1958, first Samuel C. Collins award Cryogenic Engring. Conf., 1965. Fellow Am. Acad. Arts and Scis. (Rumford medal 1965), ASME (Gold medal 1968); mem. Nat. Acad. Scis. Baptist. Home: 12322 Riverview Rd Fort Washington MD 20744 Office: Code 6430 Naval Research Lab Washington DC 20375

COLLINS, STEPHEN BARKSDALE, hospital administrator; b. Houston, Mar. 14, 1932; s. Ray George and Ruth Ella (Davis) C.; m. Katherine Jane Justice, June 6, 1955; children: Nancy Catherine, Rebecca Jane, Ruth Anne, Stephen Barksdale, Cynthia Marye. B.A., Baylor U., 1954; M.H.A., Washington U., 1956. Asst. adminstr., adminstr. Good Samaritan Hosp., Vincennes, Ind., 1959-65; adminstr. Rosewood Gen. Hosp., Houston, 1965-72; chief exec. officer Lake Charles (La.) Meml. Hosp., 1972—. Bd. dirs. Better Bus. Bur. Served with USAF, 1956-59. Decorated Meritorious Service medal, Commendation medal. Fellow Am. Coll. Hosp. Adminstrs.; mem. C. of C. (dir.), Southeastern Hosp. Conf. (bd. dirs. 1981-82, exec. com. 1983), La. Hosp. Assn. (chmn.-elect 1981, chmn. 1982), Am. Hosp. Assn. Baptist. Club: Rotary. Home: 1602 20th St Lake Charles LA 70601 Office: 1701 Oak Park Blvd Lake Charles LA 70601

COLLINS, TERRANCE ALFRED, food co. exec.; b. Escabana, Mich., Nov. 19, 1941; s. Warren Dale and Dorothy Jean C.; m. Ann Louise Neagle, June 19, 1976; children—Douglas Alan, Eric Alan, Jeaneen Louise, Jeffrey David. Student, Wis. State Coll., 1960-61, Ohio State U., 1962-63. Agent Prudential Ins. Co., Columbus, Ohio, 1962-67; owner Retail Paint Store, Delaware, Ohio, 1967-68; with McDonalds Corp., 1968-77, regional v.p., Los Angeles, 1973-77; pres. Burger Chef Systems, White Plains, N.Y., 1977-81; pres., chief exec. officer Victoria Station, San Francisco, 1981—. Bd. dirs. Indpls. Metro YMCA. Mem. Indpls. C. of C., Internat. Franchise Assn. *High goals, determination and 110 percent effort, along with a belief in one's own self, allows one to be all they can be.*

COLLINS, THEODORE CLYDE, JR., insurance company executive; b. Greensboro, N.C., Dec. 21, 1928; s. Theodore Clyde and Jane Burwell (Matkins) C.; m. Dorothy Anne Buchanan, June 23, 1951; children—Cynthia Leigh, Theodore Clyde III, Laura Anne, John Matkins. A.A., Kings Bus. Coll., 1949. With So. Life Ins. Co., Greensboro, N.C., 1949—; asst. sec. and asst. treas., 1952-61, treas. and asst. sec., 1961-63, v.p. and treas. and asst. sec., 1963-68, v.p. and sec., 1968-71, pres., sr. v.p. and sec., 1971—, dir., 1975—; dir. No. region, mem. trust adv. com. Wachovia Bank & Trust Co., N.C., 1975—. Pres. Greater Greensboro Housing Found., 1974-75; Bd. dirs. Indsl. Counseling Service, 1968—, N.C. United Community Services, 1972-78, Med. Center Bowman Gray Sch. Medicine, Wake Forest U., 1975-81, Greensboro Arts Council, 1980—; bd. dirs. N.C. Bapt. Hosps., 1971-75, 77-80, trustee, 1977-80, also chmn., 1978-80; mem. exec. bd. Gen. Greene council Boy Scouts Am., 1971—; bd. dirs., exec. com. Greater Greensboro Housing Found. Mem. Greensboro C. of C. (pres. 1981-82), Life Office Mgmt. Assn. (bd. dirs. 1980-81), Fin. Execs. Inst. (dir. N.C. chpt. 1972-77), Adminstrv. Mgmt. Soc. (pres. 1962-63, recipient Merit award 1963, Diamond Merit award 1967), Am. Mgmt. Assn. Baptist (deacon, vice chmn. bd. 1975, chmn. 1979). Clubs: Civitan (recipient Man of Year award 1962-63), Greensboro Country, Greensboro City. Office: PO Box 21887 Greensboro NC 27420

COLLINS, THEODORE JOSEPH, lawyer, educator; b. St. Paul, May 3, 1932; s. Theodore Joseph and Clarie (Scanlan) C.; m. Mary Joan Tierney, June 30, 1962 (div.); children: Theodore Joseph, Anthony Joseph. B.A., St. Paul Sem., 1954; J.D. cum alaude, William Mitchell Coll. Law, 1960. Bar: Minn. 1960, U.S. Dist. Ct. Minn. 1960, U.S. Ct. Appeals (8th cir.) 1961, U.S. Supreme Ct. 1963. Asst. gen. counsel 3M Co., 1960-61; asst. corp. counsel gen. city legal work, chief city prosecutor St. Paul, 1963-66; ptnr. Collins and Abramson, St. Paul, 1966-71, Collins, Buckley, Sauntry and Haugh, 1971—; instr. criminal law St. Paul Police Acad., 1963-78; spl. asst. atty. gen., spl. asst. Washington, Ramsey, Dakota and Sherburne countries; mem. adv. bd. LegaL Assistance Ramsey County, So. Minn. Regional Legal Services, Inc. Past pres., chmn. bd. trustees St. Paul-Ramsey Hosp. Med. Edn. and Research Found. Fellow Am. Bar Found.; mem. Ramsey County Bar Assn. (pres. 1976-77), Minn. Bar Assn. (treas. 1978-81, pres. 1982-83), ABA, Am. Judicature Soc. (dir.), Minn. Trial Lawyers Assn., Minn. Def. Lawyers Assn., Minn. Women Lawyers, Washington County Bar Assn. (mem. various coms.). Democrat. Roman Catholic. Lodge: Rotary. Office: W-1100 First Nat Bank Bldg Saint Paul MN 55101

COLLINS, THOMAS ASA, clergyman; b. Rome, Ga., Aug. 31, 1921; s. Earle Strathmore and Hazel (Alverson) C.; m. Anna E. Galloway, Aug. 17, 1944; children—Faye Anne (Mrs. Cullen B. Rivers), Thomas Asa, Robert Earle, William Ray. B.A., Asbury Coll., Wilmore, Ky., 1941, B.D., 1944; M.Div., Emory U., 1944; D.D. (hon.), High Point (N.C.) Coll. Ordained to ministry Methodist Ch., 1944; pastor in, Atlanta, 1942-43, Talbot, Ga., 1943-44, Gatesville, N.C., 1944-49, Raleigh, N.C., 1949-53, exec. dir., 1953-59; 1st pres. N.C. Wesleyan Coll., Rocky Mount, 1959-75; sr. pastor 1st Meth. Ch., Roanoke Rapids, 1976-80, St. Mark's United Meth. Ch., Raleigh, 1980—; prin., tchr. high sch., Gates County, 1944-46; Dir. People's Bank & Trust Co., Rocky Mount, 1966-69; Del. gen. conf. and jurisdictional confs. Meth. Ch., 1960-64, 68, 70; pres. Bd. Global Ministries N.C. United Meth. Conf., 1972-76, N.C. Council Chs., 1967-70; mem. bd. Commn. Christian Edn., Nat. Council Chs., 1959-68; pres. Raleigh Ministerial Assn., 1982-83. Sermon editor: Carolina Cooperator, 1949—; Contbr. articles to religious jours. Pres. Roanoke Rapids United Way, 1976-78, Roanoke Rapids chpt. N.C. Symphony Soc.; chmn. bd. dirs. Life Enrichment Center, 1982-83. Named N.C. Tar Heel of Week, 1959; recipient Distinguished Service award N.C. Council Chs., 1971. Mem. Am. Acad. Religion, Roanoke Rapids Ministerial Assn. (pres. 1977-79), Am. Assn. Colls. and Univs., N.C. Assn. Coll. and Univ. (pres. 1972-74), Omicron Delta Kappa. Democrat. Clubs: Kiwanis (lt. gov. 1972-73), Ruritan (pres. 1947-49). Home: 1200 Manchester Dr Raleigh NC 27609 *The one principle which has clearly dominated all others in my life has been a conviction of the inherent rightness of the life and teachings of Jesus Christ. I have been committed to His service since my early youth and I have tried my best to serve my fellow man, with a particular concern for the youth of my world, as I have believed He would have wanted me to do.*

COLLINS, TRUMAN EDWARD, clergyman; b. Advance, Mo., Aug. 22, 1919; s. Edward and Pearl (Shell) C.; m. Dorothy Virginia Eaker, Dec. 23, 1939; 1 son, Edward Alan. Diploma, Calvary Bible Coll., Kansas City, Mo., 1952. Ordained to ministry Baptist Ch., 1949; pastor Mt. Zion Gen. Bapt. Ch., Granite City, Ill., 1950-64, First Gen. Bapt. Ch., Princeton, Ind., 1964-67, Dover Chapel Gen. Bapt. Ch., Louisville, 1967-69, Southland Bapt. Ch., 1969—; Pres. Nat. Sunday Sch. Bd. Gen. Bapt., 1956-63, moderator nat. conv., 1961-62; pres. Gen. Bapt. Publs. and Edn. Bd., Inc., 1964-66; mem. Liberty Presbyter Gen. Bapt. Assn., Ind., 1965-67, Christian Edn. and Publs. Bd., Inc. of Gen. Baptist Denomination, 1963-66, pres., 1964-65, Illmo Assn. Endowment Corp., 1959-64; dir. Illmo Assn. Youth Camp of Gen. Bapt., 1954-64. Author: Sun Rays In the Sickroom. Pres. Emerson Sch. P.T.A., 1962-63. Mem. Nat. Congress P.T.A., Quad City Ministerial Assn. (treas.), Kentuckana Assn. Gen. Baptist, Greater Louisville Evang. Fellowship (v.p.). Address: 2503 Paddock Ct Louisville KY 40216

COLLINS, VINCENT PATRICK, physician, educator; b. Toronto, Ont., Can., Nov. 11, 1912; came to U.S., 1940, naturalized, 1945; s. John and Laura (Doyle) C.; m. Lois Cowan, Dec. 26, 1942; children: Cowan, Ross, Christopher. M.D., U. Toronto, 1937; J.D., U. Houston, 1964. Diplomate: Am. Bd. Radiology. Intern Toronto Gen. Hosp., 1937-38; demonstrator anatomy, fellow physiology U. Toronto, 1938-39; research fellow Banting Inst., 1939-40; sr. resident pathology N.E. Deaconess Hosp., Boston, 1940-42; resident surg. pathology, instr. surgery Presbyn. Hosp., Columbia, 1942-43, resident radiology, 1945-47, attending radiologist, 1950-52; instr. radiology Columbia U., 1947-49; cons. radiology USPHS Marine Hosp., S.I., 1948-52; asst. prof. Columbia U., 1949-50, assoc. prof. radiology, 1950-52; chief radiotherapy Francis Delafield Hosp., 1950-52; prof. radiology, chmn. dept. Baylor U., 1952-68; radiologist-in-chief Jefferson Davis Hosp., Houston, 1952-68, Ben Taub Gen. Hosp., 1963-68; chief cons. radiology VA Hosp., Houston, 1952-68; attending radiologist Meth. Hosp., Houston, 1955-68; cons. radiology Tex. Children's Hosp., Houston, 1956-68; dir. radiotherapy Rosewood Gen. Hosp., 1969-82, cons., 1982—; cons. radiotherapy Ochsner Clinic, New Orleans, 1968-82, U. Tex. Med. Br., 1969—; prin. cons. radiology Nat. Inst. Gen. Med. Scis., Bethesda, Md., 1966, Lawrence Labs. U. Calif. at Berkeley, 1972-77; med. dir. Houston Inst. for Cancer Research, Detection and Treatment, 1974—; mem. med. adv. com. U.S. Nuclear Regulatory Commn. Served from 1st lt. to capt., M.C. AUS, 1943-45. Decorated Silver Star. Fellow Am. Coll. Radiology, Am. Coll. Legal Medicine; mem. Am. Roentgen Ray Soc., Radiol. Soc. N.Am., Tex. Radiol. Soc., Soc. Surg. Oncology, Am. Radium Soc., N.Y. Acad. Scis., Arthur Purdy Stout Soc., Am. Soc. Therapeutic Radiologists, A.A.A.S., Internat. Acad. Pathology, Sigma Xi. Home: 105 Shasta Dr Houston TX 77024 Office: 9000 Westheimer Rd Suite 53 Houston TX 77063

COLLINS, WALLACE EDMUND JAMES, lawyer, manufacturing company executive; b. Huntington, N.Y., May 16, 1923; s. Wallace E.J. and Cecilia Veronica (Bryne) C.; m. Aldona Helen Barr, May 1, 1954; children—Wallace Edmund James, III, Kevin F., Anne Marie, Paul Vincent. B.A., Fordham U., 1944, J.D., 1946. Bar: N.Y. bar 1946. Asso., then partner firm Palmer, Serles, Delaney, Shaw & Pomeroy (and predecessor), N.Y.C., 1946-64; with N. Am. Philips Corp. (and predecessor), N.Y.C., 1964—, sec., corp. counsel, 1965—, v.p., gen. counsel, 1969—, also v.p., sec. all subsidiaries; dir. Carolina Coach Co., D.C.F. Internat, Inc. Active local Boy Scouts Am., 1960-80; pres. bd. edn. St. Joseph's Sch., Oradell, N.J., 1967-75. Life mem. Nat. Model R.R. Assn., Delta Theta Phi. Roman Catholic. Club: White Beeches Golf and Country. Lodge: K.C. Home: 167 Country Club Dr Oradell NJ 07649 Office: 100 E 42d St New York NY 10017

COLLINS, WESLEY E., furniture company executive. Pres., chief operating officer Broyhill Furniture Industries, Lenoir, N.C. Office: Broyhill Furniture Industries Broyhill Park NC Lenoir 28633§

COLLINS, WILLIAM EDGAR, university official; b. Terra Alta, W.Va., Mar. 31, 1935; s. Lawrence W. and Lela Marie (Jeffers) C.; m. Karen Leah Rymer, Aug. 15, 1959; children: Craig William, David Glenn. B.S. in Agr, W.Va. U., 1957; postgrad., Massey Agrl. Coll., Palmerston North, N.Z., 1958; M.S., U. Wis., 1961, Ph.D., 1965. Part-time instr. U. Wis., 1961-65; program specialist Ford Found. at Inst. Agr., Anand, Gujarat, India, 1965-67; mem. faculty W.Va. U., Morgantown, 1968—, prof. biology, 1974—, dean Coll. Arts and Scis., 1975-81, v.p. acad. affairs and research, 1981—; intern acad. adminstrn. Am. Council Edn., 1971-72. Rotary Found. fellow, 1958; fellow U. Wis. Alumni Research Found., 1959-61. Mem. Endocrine Soc., Soc. Study Fertility, AAAS, Sigma Xi. Methodist. Club: Rotary. Home: 8 Alicia Ave Morgantown WV 26505 Office: 105 Stewart West Va Univ Morgantown WV 26506

COLLINS, WILLIAM FRANCIS, educator, neurosurgeon; b. New Haven, Jan. 20, 1924; s. William F. and Jane (Shanley) C.; m. Gwendolyn Ruth Davis, Dec. 16, 1950; children: William Francis III, Peter Davis, Ruth Ellen. B.S., Yale U., 1944, M.D., 1947. Diplomate: Am. Bd. Neurol. Surgery (mem. 1976-82, chmn. 1980-82, editorial bd. jour. 1979—, chmn. residency rev. com. 1980—). Intern surgery Barnes Hosp., St. Louis, 1947-49, resident neurosurgery, 1951-54; instr. neurosurgery Western Res. U. Sch. Medicine, 1954-57, asso. prof., 1957-63; prof., chmn. dept. neurol. surgery, chmn. dept. Yale Sch. Medicine, 1967—, Cushing prof. surgery, 1970—; fellow Pierson Coll., 1969. Served to capt. M.C. AUS, 1947-49. Mem. Neurosurg. Soc. Am. (pres. 1973-74), Soc. Neurol. Surgeons (sec. 1973-78, pres.-elect 1982-83). Home: 131 Uncas Point Rd Guilford CT 06437

COLLINS, WILLIAM HOWES, marketing and communications company executive; b. East Orange, N.J., Apr. 27, 1908; s. William French and Alice Derfla (Howes) C.; m. Dorothy Jane Walker, Oct. 18, 1932; children—William Walker, Kent Howes, Derfla Jean Collins Patterson. B.A. cum laude, Williams Coll., 1929. Mng. editor, asst. treas. Howes Publ. Co., N.Y.C., 1929-31; dir. univ. service Hapag-Lloyd (Steamship), N.Y.C., 1932-37; asst. advt. mgr. Scott Paper Co., Chester, Pa., 1927-47; dir. advt. Dravo Corp., Pitts., 1947-55; world-wide market exec. Standard-Vacuum Oil Co., White Plains, N.Y., 1955-62; mgr. advt. and marketing research Mobil Petroleum Co., N.Y.C., 1962-64; chmn. bd., pres. Intercontinental Assos., Inc., Essex, Conn., 1964—; Adviser U.S. delegation 5th Internat. Conf. Pub. Affairs, Geneva, 1937; mem. U.S. Trade Devel. Mission to Brazil, 1967, Dept. Commerce Regional Export Expansion Council, 1966—, U.S. Nat. Def. Exec. Res., 1968—. Contbr. articles to profl. jours. Mem. Bd. Edn., Essex, 1967-72; mem. U.S.S. Nathan Hale Com., Conn., 1970—; Bd. dirs. Pitts. YMCA, 1947. Served from lt. (j.g.) to capt. USNR, 1937-68. Mem. Pub. Relations Soc. Am. (pres. Pitts. 1953-55), Assn. Nat. Advertisers (dir. 1953-58), Soc. Mayflower Descendants Pa. (dep. gov. 1948-55), Eastern Indsl. Advertisers Phila. (pres. 1945-47), S.A.R. (auditor Conn., v.p. Nathan Hale br. 1983—), English Speaking Union, Essex Art Assn., Newcomen Soc., Naval Res. Assn., Pa. Soc., Ret. Officers Assn., Massasoit and Essex Hist. Soc., U.S. Naval Inst., Order Founders and Patriots of Am., Phi Beta Kappa, Beta Theta Pi, Delta Phi Epsilon. Conglist. Clubs: Mason., Circumnavigators, Williams (N.Y.C.); Mile Creek (Old Lyme, Conn.); Naval (London). Home: Kentwill Essex CT 06426 Office: PO Box 396 Essex CT 06426

COLLINS, WILLIAM PATRICK, government official; b. Washington, Mar. 16, 1946. Student, Carroll Coll., 1964-67; B.A., U. Mont., 1968. Nat. field dir. Raymond V. Humphreys Assocs., 1971-72; legis. asst. Rep. Alan Steelman of Tex., 1973-76; adminstrv. asst. Rep. Ron Marlenee of Mont., 1976-79; dir. polit. affairs Nat. Assn. Home Builders, 1979-80; asst. to sr. adviser Office Exec. Br Mgmt., Reagan Presdl. Transition Team, Washington, 1980-81; v.p. polit. affairs Nat. Assn. Home Builders, Washington, 1981-83; undersec. Dept. Energy, Washington, 1983—. Office: Dept Energy Room 7B 260 1000 Independence Ave SW Washington DC 20585

COLLINSON, JOHN THEODORE, railroad company executive; b. Pitts., July 29, 1926; s. John Gordon and Katherine (Bichy) C.; m. Patricia Ann Davison, Nov. 15, 1947; children: John G. III, Donald L., Nancy Ann. B.S. in Civil Engring., Cornell U., 1946. Project engr. Dravo Corp., Pitts., 1946; various engring. positions Balt. & Ohio R.R. Co., Pitts., 1946-65, Newark, 1946-65, Akron, Ohio, 1946-65, chief engr., 1965; with Chessie System, Inc., Cleve., 1965—, v.p. ops., 1973-76, exec. v.p., 1976-78; pres., chief exec. officer C & O Ry., Balt. & Ohio R.R., Cleve., 1978—; dir. CSX Corp., Chessie System Railroads, Seaboard System Monumental Corp., Nat. Mine Service, Nat. City Bank. Served to lt. (j.g.) USN; 1943-46. Republican. Presbyterian. Club: Country of Cleve. Lodges: Masons; Shriners. Home: 65 Quail Hollow Dr Moreland Hills OH 44022 Office: PO Box 6419 Cleveland OH 44101

COLLINS-WILLIAMS, CECIL, physician; b. Toronto, Ont., Dec. 31, 1918; s. Ernest and Nell (Hewitt) Collins-W.; m. Jean Hamilton, June 30, 1944; children: Donald, Joan. B.A., U. Toronto, 1941, M.D., 1941. Postgrad. tng. Hosp. Sick Children, Toronto, 1944-45, 1947-50, Children's Hosp., Boston and N.Y.C., 1944-45, 1947-50; practice medicine specilaizing in pediatrics, Toronto, 1950—; head allergy div. Hosp. for Sick Children, Toronto, 1952—, sr. physician, 1960—; prof. pediatrics U. Toronto, 1968—. Conbtr. articles to profl. jours.; author: Pediatric Allergy and Clinic Immunology, 1973. Served with RCNVR, 1945-46. Mem. Can. Soc. Allergy and Clin. Immunology, Am. Acad. Pediatrics, Am. Acad. Allergy, Am. Coll. Allergists, Acad. Medicine Toronto, Brit. Soc. Allergy and Clin. Immunology, Royal Soc. Medicine, Assn. for Care of Asthma, Can. Pediatric Soc., Can. Soc. Immunology. Club: Granite. Office: 555 University Ave Toronto ON Canada M5G 1X8

COLLINSWORTH, EVEN THOMAS, JR., corporation executive; b. Knoxville, Tenn., Oct. 11, 1921; s. E.T. and Lillian (Smith) C.; m. Edith Merory, June 5, 1949; children: Even, Eden, Sean. B.S., U. Tenn., 1943; M.B.A., Harvard U., 1950. Diplomate: registered profl. engr., N.J. Sales mgr. Worthington Corp., Harrison, N.J., 1943-48; dir. bus. research Monsanto Chem. Co., St. Louis, 1950-52; pres., dir. Velsicol Chem Corp., Chgo., 1953-59; chmn. bd. Velsicol Internat. Corp., 1955-59; pres., dir. Fansteel Metall. Corp., North Chgo., 1960-61; v.p. Armour & Co., Chgo., 1963-66, group v.p. indsl. products and grocery products, 1968-69, exec. v.p., dir., 1969-72; chmn., pres., chief exec. officer AXIA Inc., Oak Brook, Ill., 1972—; dir. AXIA Inc., Oak Brook, Ill.; dir. Bucyrus-Erie Co., South Milwaukee, Wis., Nicor Inc., Naperville, Ill. Bd. dirs. Am. Grad. Sch. Internat. Mgmt.; trustee Glenwood Sch. for Boys, Ill. Mem. Chgo. Council Fgn. Relations (dir.), Chgo. Assn. Commerce and Industry (dir.), Conf. Bd. (dir.), Alpha Chi Sigma, Phi Gamma Delta. Clubs: Chicago; Mid-Am. (Chgo.); Waukegan Yacht (Ill.). Home: 33 Briarwood S Oak Brook Il 60521 Office: AXIA Inc 122 W 22d St Oak Brook IL 60521

COLLIS, SIDNEY ROBERT, telephone company executive; b. Oak Park, Ill., Mar. 24, 1924; s. Sidney John and Celia (Steele) C.; m. Lois E. Harding, Feb. 23, 1946; children—Robert H., Elizabeth A., Gail M., April L. Student, Ill. Inst. Tech., 1941-43, U. Santa Clara, 1943-44; B.S. in Elec. Engring, Northwestern U., 1947. Registered profl. engr., Ill. With Ill. Bell Telephone Co., 1947-54, 60-61; with Am. Tel. & Tel. Co., 1954-60, 61-62, asst. v.p., 1968—; asst. v.p. N.Y. Telephone Co., 1962-63, v.p., 1963-68; mem. adv. com. in elec. engring. Newark Coll. Engring. Mem. IEEE, APICS, Nat. Energy Resources Orgn. Home: 70 Fieldstone Dr Basking Ridge NJ 07920 Office: 222 Mount Airy Rd Basking Ridge NJ 07920

COLLMAN, JAMES PADDOCK, educator; b. Beatrice, Nebr., Oct. 31, 1932; (married). B.Sc., U. Nebr., 1954, M.S., 1956; Ph.D. (NSF fellow), U. Ill., 1958. Instr. chemistry U. N.C., Chapel Hill, 1958-59, asst. prof., 1959-62, asso. prof., 1962-67; prof. chemistry, Stanford, 1967—; Frontiers in Chemistry lectr., 1964, Nebr. lectureship, 1968; Venable lectr. U. N.C., 1971; Edward Clark Lee lectr. U. Chgo., 1972; vis. Erskine fellow U. Canterbury, 1972; Plenary lectr. French Chem. Soc., 1974; Dreyfus lectr. U. Kans., 1974; distinguished inorganic lectr. U. Rochester, 1974; Reilley lectr. U. Notre Dame, 1975; William Pyle Philips lectr. Haverford Coll., 1975; Merck lectr. Rutgers U., 1976; FMC lectr. Princeton, 1977; Julius Steiglitz lectr. Chgo. sect. Am. Chem. Soc., 1977; Pres.'s Seminar Series lectr. U. Ariz., 1980; Frank C. Whitmore lectr. Pa. State U., 1980; Plenary lectr. 3d IUPAC Symposium on Organic Synthesis, 1980; Brockman lectr. U. Ga., 1981. Guggenheim fellow, 1977-78. Mem. Am. Chem. Soc. (Calif. Sect. award 1972, soc. award in inorganic chemistry 1975), N.Y. Acad. Sci., Chem. Soc. (London), Nat. Acad. Sci., Am. Acad. Arts and Scis., Phi Beta Kappa, Sigma Xi, Phi Lambda Upsilon, Alpha Chi Sigma. Office: Stanford U Stauffer II Stanford CA 94305

COLLOFF, ROGER DAVID, broadcasting executive; b. Asbury Park, N.J., Feb. 1, 1946; s. Isadore and Shirley Edith (Dessen) C.; m. Margery Ann Bletcher, May 28, 1967; 1 dau., Pamela. A.B. summa cum laude, Brown U., 1967; M.A. (Woodrow Wilson fellow), Yale U., 1972, J.D., 1972. Legis. asst. to Senator Walter Mondale, Washington, 1972-75; dir. govt. affairs CBS Inc., Washington, 1976; sr. staff mem. White House Office of Energy Policy and Planning, Washington, 1977; spl. asst. to sec. of energy, Washington, 1977-78; v.p., asst. to pres. CBS News, N.Y.C., 1979-81, v.p., dir. public affairs broadcasts, 1981-82; v.p. policy and planning Broadcast Group CBS Inc., 1983—. Mem. Phi Beta Kappa. Office: CBS Inc 51 W 52d St New York NY 10019

COLLONS, RODGER DUANE, educator; b. Glenn, Neb., Jan. 8, 1935; s. Rodger Bernard and Ethel Bernice (Littrel) C.; m. Cynthia Carolyn Dyer, May 6, 1961; children: Kevin Rodger, Theresa Rene. B.C.E., U. Tex., El Paso, 1957; J.D., George Washington U., 1961; M.B.A., Ga. State U., 1965, D.B.A., 1967. Bar: Va. 1961, Ga. 1963; registered U.S. patent atty.; C.L.U. Patent examiner U.S. Patent Office, Washington, 1957-60; asso. counsel Strauch, Nolan & Neale, Washington, 1960-61; asso. patent counsel Lockheed Ga. Co., Atlanta, 1961-64; teaching fellow Ga. State U., 1964-65; asst. prof. mgmt. Ga. So. Coll., 1965-66; asst. prof. quantitative analysis Ga. State U., 1966-68; dir. div. adminstrv. scis. Grad. Coll. W.Va., 1969-71; dean. Coll. Bus. and Adminstrn. Drexel U., 1971-76, prof. decision scis., 1976—; James S. Bingay vis. prof. creative leadership Am. Coll., 1979-81. Author: (with Donald Del Mar) Classics in Scientific Management, 1976; editor: Decision Line, 1969-72; contbg. editor: Creative Leadership Rev, 1980-82; bi-monthly series Best's Rev, 1980-83. Bd. dirs. Phila. Civic Ballet, 1974—, pres., 1979-82; bd. dirs. Rosemont-Villanova (Pa.) Civic Assn., 1976—, pres., 1980—. Served to 1st lt. U.S. Army, 1957-58. Recipient certificate of appreciation Allied Social Scis. Assns., 1976. Fellow Am. Inst. Decision Scis. (Distinguished Service award 1971, pres. 1972-73, dir. 1969-76, chmn. fellows 1979—); mem. Middle Atlantic Assn. Colls. Bus. Adminstrn. (pres. 1975-76), Alpha Iota Delta (pres. 1971-72, 73-74, Distinguished Service award 1976, dir. 1972—). Club: Kiwanis (dir. Phila. 1973-76). Patentee container closure, sealing method. Home: 1909 Firethorn Ln Villanova PA 19085 Office: Coll Bus and Adminstrn Drexel U Philadelphia PA 19104

COLLOTON, JOHN WILLIAM, univ. hosp. dir.; b. Mason City, Iowa, Feb. 20, 1931; s. Harold and Miriam (Kelly) C.; m. Mary Ann Hagglund, Oct. 8, 1960; children—Steven, Laura, Ann. B.A. with high honors, Loras Coll., 1953; M.A., U. Iowa, 1957. Hosp. relations rep. Hosp. Service Inc. of Iowa, Des Moines, 1957-58; with U. of Iowa Hosps. and Clinics, Iowa City, 1958—, asso. dir., 1969-71, dir., asst. to univ. pres. for health services, 1971—; dir. Blue Cross, Iowa State Bank & Trust Co.; cons. NIH; pres. adminstrv. bd. Assn. Am. Med. Colls. Council of Teaching Hosps., 1980—. Contbr. articles to profl. publs. Served with Finance Corps U.S. Army, 1953-55. Mem. Am. Coll. Hosp. Adminstrs., Am. Hosp. Assn. (Council Financing 1977), Iowa Hosp. Assn. (chmn. bd. trustees 1977-78, trustee 1978—), Am. Assn. Hosp. Planning, Johnson County (Iowa) Med. Soc., U. Iowa Alumni Assn. Roman Catholic. Club: Rotary. Home: 316 Monroe St Iowa City IA 52240 Office: U of Iowa Hosps and Clinics Newton Rd Iowa City IA 52242

COLLUNGWORTH, LARRY ROSS, residential and commercial real estate developement company executive; b. Toronto, Ont., Can., Sept. 26, 1939; s. Allan Joyce and Ethel Alexandra (David) Cullingworth; m. Betty Kathleen Hughes, July 9, 1966; children: Lisa, Kevin. B.A.Sc., U. Toronto, 1963, P. Eng., 1965; M.B.A., York U., Toronto, 1972. Cons. engr. Proctor & Redfern, Toronto, 1963-68; regional mgr. George Wimpey Can. Ltd., Toronto, 1968-72; mgr. corp. devel. Costain Ltd., Toronto, 1973-74, v.p., fin., sec., 1974-75, sr. v.p., sec., 1975-79, exec. v.p., chief fin. officer, sec., 1979-83, pres., chief operating officer, 1983—, dir. Mem. Assn. Profl. Engrs. Ont., Canadian Inst. Pub. Real Estate Cos. Club: Granite (Toronto). Home: 23 York Valley Crescent Willowdale ON Canada M2P 1A8 Office: Costain Limited Suite 2200 PO Box 428 2 First Canadian Pl Toronto ON Canada M5X 1H9

COLLYER, ROBERT B., b. Decatur, Ill., Oct. 16, 1932; s. Murray Gordon and Frances Mary (Evans) C.; m. Margaret Mary Hebel, Feb. 27, 1960; 1 son, Bryan. B.A., Humbolt Coll., 1956. Cons. DeLeuw Cather & Co., 1957-59; claims and mgr. govt. relations Indsl. Indemnity Co. Calif., San Francisco, San Jose, Sacramento, 1960-73; exec. asst. UBA Inc., Washington, 1974-81; dep. under sec. Employment Standards Adminstrn. U.S. Dept. Labor, Washington, 1981—; co-founder, dir. Nat. Symposium Workers Compensation U. Maine, 1976-80; dir. Western States Self-Ins. Colloquim, Inc., Nat. Employers' Adv. Council on Workers Compensation; cons. Nat. Indsl. Council; mem. Nat. Adv. Commn. on State Workers Compensation Law Compliance U.S. Dept. Labor; mem. Nat. Adv. Commn. on Indsl. Rehab. Research and Tng. Program U. N.C.; mem. steering com. Nat. Workers Compensation Info. Exchange Group; mem. steering com. Permanent Disability Study Adv. Commn. NSF; mem. steering com. U.S. Longshoremen and Harbor Workers' Reform Group. Pres. Marin county Republican Council, (Calif.), 1973; mem. Calif. Rep. Central Com., 1970-73; asst. county chmn. Com. to Re-elect Pres., 1972. Named Republican of Yr. Marin County, 1972. Home: 3112 Trenholm Dr Oakton VA 22124 Office: Employment Standards Administration US Dept Labor 200 Constitution Ave NW Washington DC 20210

COLMAN, JOHN CHARLES, investor, consultant; b. Cleve., Jan. 27, 1927; s. Charles Cecil and Fanny Pauline (Freedman) C.; m. Jane Kate Becker, Feb. 19, 1956; children: James A., David L., Nancy L. B.Chem. Engring., Cornell U., 1949; M.B.A., Harvard U., 1951. With Arthur D. Little, Inc., Cambridge, Mass., 1951-52; Chem. div. Borden Co., Peabody and Leominster, Mass., 1952-56; v.p., dir. A.G. Becker & Co., Chgo., 1956-66; dir. Office Internat. Monetary Affairs, Dept. State, 1966-68; dep. asst. sec. Dept. Treasury, 1968-69; exec. v.p. Continental Ill. Corp., Chgo., 1969-75; pres., chmn. bd. Beeline, Inc., Bensenville, Ill.; dir. Balmorhea Ranches, Inc., Pecos, Tex., DBA Systems, Inc., Melbourne, Fla., Duplex Products Inc., Sycamore, Ill., Corcom, Inc., Libertyville, Ill., Orion Capital Corp., N.Y.C., Premier Indsl. Corp., Cleve.; Vis. faculty mem. Harvard Bus. Sch., Boston, 1966. Bd. dirs. Am. Jewish Joint Distbn. Com., N.Y.C., Jewish Fedn. Met. Chgo.; bd. dirs., pres. Jewish Children's Bur., Chgo., 1979-82; mem. vis. com. Div. Sch., U. Chgo. Served with USNR, 1945-46. Clubs: Mid-day (Chgo.); Lake Shore Country (Glencoe, Ill.). Home: 4 Briar Ln Glencoe IL 60022 Office: 100 Beeline Dr Bensenville IL 60106

COLNON, WILLIAM LYDON, dredging company executive; b. Chgo., Oct. 28, 1928; s. Philip Neemes and Lelia (Lydon) C.; m. Patti Grace Casey, May 3, 1928; children: Jean, Philip, Casey, Patti. B.A., Harvard U., 1949; M.B.A., U. Chgo., 1952; postgrad., MIT, Colo. Sch. Mines. Field engr., estimator Great Lakes Dredge and Dock Co., Chgo., 1950-61, asst. to pres., 1961-63, chief engr., v.p., 1963-71, sr. v.p., 1971-75, exec. v.p., Oak Brook, Ill., 1975-80, pres., chief exec., 1980—; dir. Great Lakes Internat. Mem. Nat. Assn. Dredging Contractors, Internat. Assn. Dredging Contractors (dir. 1966—). Roman Catholic.

COLODNY, EDWIN IRVING, airline executive; b. Burlington, Vt., June 7, 1926; s. Myer and Lena (Yett) C.; m. Nancy Dessoff, Dec. 11, 1965; children: Elizabeth, Mark, David. A.B., U. Rochester, 1948; LL.B., Harvard, 1951. Bar: N.Y. bar 1951, D.C. bar 1958. With Office Gen. Counsel, Gen. Services Adminstrn., 1951-52, CAB, 1954-57, Allegheny Airlines, Inc. (now US Air, Inc.), 1957—, exec. v.p. mktg. and legal affairs, 1969-75; pres., chief exec. officer Allegheny Airlines, Inc. (now US Air Inc.), 1975—, chmn. bd. dirs., 1978—, also dir.; dir. PNC Fin. Corp., Gulf Corp. Trustee U. Rochester; mem. council Internat. Exec. Service Corps. Served to 1st lt. AUS, 1952-54. Recipient James D. McGill Meml. award U. Rochester. Mem. Am. Bar Assn. Home: 8225 Burning Tree Rd Bethesda MD 20817 Office: Hangar 12 Washington Nat Airport Washington DC 20001

COLODNY, ROBERT GARLAND, educator; b. Phoenix, Aug. 5, 1915; s. Isidore Omar and Pauline (Shenberg) C.; m. Dorothy Newman, June 15, 1946; 1 son, Robert Richard. Ph.D., U. Calif., Berkeley, 1950. Research asso. Inst. for Philos. Research, 1953-55; asst. prof. history San Francisco State Coll., 1956; asso. prof. U. Kans., 1957-59; assoc. prof. U. Pitts., 1958-67, prof. history of sci. and European history, 1967—. Author: Struggle for Madrid, 1959, Spain: The Glory and the Tragedy, 1971; Editor: Philosophy of Science Series, U. Pitts., 1961-67, Book Notes, 1971—, In the Labyrinth of Language: The Face of Science, Realms of the Unconscious, 1974-82. Served with AUS, 1941-45. Decorated Army Commendation medal.; Recipient Hans Beimler award, 1970. Mem. Am. Hist. Assn., History of Sci. Soc., N.Y. Acad. Sci., Sigma Xi. Home: 14 Roselawn Terr Pittsburgh PA 15213

COLODZIN, ROBERT S(AMUEL), forest products company executive, communications planning consulting company executive; b. N.Y.C., May 20, 1922; s. Benjamin and Nellie (Schamberg) C.; m. Vienna R. Watkins, Sept. 29, 1978; children by previous marriage: Bonnie, Benjamin. B.A., Queens Coll., 1943; M.A., New Sch. Social Research, 1946; cert. Sorbonne, U. Paris, 1947. TV producer, dir.

Benton & Bowles, N.Y.C., 1954-61; pres. CPI, Inc., N.Y.C., 1961-70; regional dir. and asst. to chmn. Common Cause, Washington and N.Y.C., 1970-72; pres. COMPLAN, Inc., N.Y.C., 1970—; dep. commr. mktg. State of N.Y., Albany, 1975; v.p. pub. affairs Champion Internat. Corp., Stamford, Conn., 1975-81, v.p. external affairs, 1981—; cons. communications. Co-author: Your Career in Television, 1950. Cons. polit. communications to gubernatorial and congl. candidates, presdl. campaign orgn. Served to sgt. USAAF, 1943-45; Aleutian Islands. Mem. Assn. Pub. Policy Analysis and Mgmt., Radio and TV News Dir. Assn., Dirs. Guild Am. Democrat. Jewish. Home: Two Tudor City Pl New York NY 10017 Office: Champion Internat Corp One Champion Plaza Stamford CT 06291

COLOMBO, JOHN ROBERT, poet, editor; b. Kitchener, Ont., Can., Mar. 24, 1936; s. John Anthony and Irene (Nicholson) C.; m. Ruth Florence Brown, May 11, 1959. B.A., U. Toronto, 1959, postgrad., 1959-60. Editorial asst. U. Toronto Press, 1957-59; asst. editor Ryerson Press, Toronto, 1960-63; sr. adv. editor McClelland & Stewart, Toronto, 1964-70; publ. cons., Toronto, 1971—; editor Tamarack Rev., Toronto, 1960-82; Spl. instr. Atkinson Coll., York U., Toronto, 1965-68; mem. adv. arts panel Can. Council, 1968-70; advisor Ont. Council Arts, 1965-68. Author: over 60 books, including Colombo's Canadian Quotations, 1974; (with Nikola Roussanoff) The Balkan Range: A Bulgarian Reader, 1976, Colombo's Canadian References, 1976; anthology The Poets of Canada, 1978; Colombo's Book of Marvels, 1979, Other Canadas: An Anthology of Science Fiction and Fantasy, 1979, Colombo's Hollywood, 1979, 222 Canadian Jokes, 1981, Friendly Aliens, 1981, (with M. Richardson) Not to be Taken at Night, 1981, Selected Poems, 1982, Selected Translations, 1982, Songs of the Indians, 1983, Colombo's Canadiana Quiz Book, 1983, (with George Faludy) Learn This Poem of Mine by Heart, 1983. Recipient Can. Centennial medal, 1967, Order Cyril and Methodius 1st class, Esteemed Knight of Mark Twain. Mem. P.E.N., League Canadian Poets (provisional coordinator 1966-67), Assn. Canadian TV and Radio Artists. Club: Celebrity. Home: 42 Dell Park Ave Toronto ON M6B 2T6 Canada

COLONEY, WAYNE HERNDON, civil engineer; b. Bradenton, Fla., Mar. 15, 1925; s. Herndon Percival and Mary Adore (Cramer) C.; m. Anne Elizabeth Benedict, June 21, 1950; 1 dau., Mary Adore. B.C.E. summa cum laude, Ga. Inst. Tech., 1950. Registered profl. engr. and surveyor, Fla., Ga., Ala., N.C., also Nat. Council Engring. Examiners. Project engr. Constructora Gen. (S.A.), Venezuela, 1948-49, Fla. Rd. Dept., 1950-55; hwy. engr. Gibbs & Hill, Inc., Guatemala, 1955-57, project mgr., Tampa, Fla., 1957-59; project engr., then asso. J.E. Greiner Co., Tampa, 1959-63; partner Barrett, Daffin & Coloney, Tallahassee, 1963-70; pres. Wayne H. Coloney Co., Inc., Tallahassee, 1970-77, chmn. bd. chief exec. officer, 1977—; pres., sec. Tesseract Corp., 1975—; chmn. bd., chief exec. officer Coloney Co. Cons. Engrs., Inc., 1978—; chmn. adv. com. Area Vocat. Tech. Sch., 1965-78. Contbr. profl. jours. Pres. United Fund Leon County, 1971-72; bd. dirs. Springtime Tallahassee, 1970-72, pres., 1981-82; bd. dirs. Heritage Found., 1965-71, pres., 1967; mem. Pres.'s Adv. Council on Indsl. Innovation, 1978-79; bd. dirs. LeMoyne Art Found., 1973, v.p., 1974-75; bd. dirs. Goodwill Industries, 1972-73, Tallahassee-Popoyan Friendship Commn., 1968-73; mem. Adv. Com. for Hist. and Cultural Preservation, 1969-71. Served with AUS, 1943-46. Fellow ASCE; mem. Nat. Soc. Profl. Engrs., Fla. Engring. Soc. (sr.), Am. Water Works Assn., Fla. Inst. Cons. Engrs., Fla. Soc. Profl. Land Surveyors, Tallahassee C. of C., Anak, Koseme Soc., Phi Kappa Phi, Omicron Delta Kappa, Sigma Alpha Epsilon, Tau Beta Pi. Episcopalian. Clubs: Governor's, Killearn Golf and Country, Met. Dinner (past pres.). Patentee roof framing system, tile mounting structure, curler rotating device, bracket system for roof framing. Home: Argyle House 2540 Marston Rd Tallahassee FL 32312 Office: PO Box 5258 Tallahassee FL 32314 *A solid foundation for life and success is the principle that every relationship, personal or business, must and can benefit or profit all parties involved. This combined with the firm belief that anything which man's mind can conceive and in which he can believe can be realized with God's help and guidance, can be a prime factor in building a career which benefits both society and the man.*

COLONNIER, MARC LEOPOLD, neuroanatomist, educator; b. Quebec, Que., Can., May 12, 1930; s. Jean and Enilda (Bourguignon) C.; m. Lise De Gagne, Oct. 24, 1959; 1 son, Jean. B.A., B.Ph., U. Ottawa, 1951, M.D., 1959, M.S., 1960; Ph.D., U. Coll. London, 1963. Asst. prof. anatomy U. Ottawa, 1963-65; asst. prof. dept. physiology U. Montreal, Que., Can., 1965-67; asso. prof., asso. fellow neurol. scis. group Med. Research Council Can., 1967-69; prof., head dept. anatomy U. Ottawa, 1969-76; prof. dept. anatomy Laval U., Quebec City, Que., 1976—. Recipient Lederle Med. Faculty award, 1966, Charles Judson Herrick award Am. Assn. Anatomists, 1967. Fellow Royal Soc. Can.; mem. Am. Assn. Anatomists; Mem. Soc. Neurosci.; mem. Can. Assn. Anatomists (pres. 1973-75). Club: Cajal. Office: Laboratoires de Neurobiologie Pavillon Notre-Dame Hôpital de l'Enfant Jésus Quebec PQ Canada

COLOSIMO, ROBERT, labor relations executive; b. Thunder Bay, Ont., Can., Dec. 25, 1929; s. Henry and Ann Marie (Dolce) C.; m. Marilyn June MacKay, Nov. 3, 1954; children: James Mark, Joy Melanie. Grad., Selkirk High Sch., Thunder Bay. Spl. rep. CP Rail, Montreal, Que., Can., 1961-66, supr. personnel and labor relations, 1966-68, asst. mgr. labor relations, 1968-69, mgr. labor relations, 1969-77, asst. v.p. indsl. relations, 1977-81, v.p. indsl. relations, 1981—. Mem. Ry. Personnel Assn. (exec. com. 1981—, vice chmn.), Am. Mgmt. Assn., C. of C. (employer-employee relations com.). Roman Catholic. Club: Railway (Montreal). Home: 173 King's Rd Pointe Claire PQ Canada H9R 4H6 Office: CP Rail 910 Peel St Po Box 6042 Montreal PQ Canada H3C 3E4

COLOWICK, SIDNEY PAUL, biochemist, educator, editor; b. St. Louis, Jan. 12, 1916; s. Michael and Frieda (Singer) C.; m. Grace Shaffel, 1943; 1 son, Frank Shaffel; m. Maryda Swanstrom, 1951; children: Ann Maryda, Susan, Nancy. B.S., Washington U., 1936, M.S., 1939, Ph.D., 1942. Instr. pharmacology Washington U., 1943-44, asst. prof., 1945-46; asso. Pub. Health Research Inst., N.Y.C., 1946-48; asso. prof. biochemistry U. Ill. Coll. Medicine, Chgo., 1948-49; asso. prof. biology Johns Hopkins U., 1950-54, prof., 1954-59; Am. Cancer Soc. prof. microbiology Vanderbilt U., 1959—, Harvie Branscomb Disting. prof., 1978. Editor: (with Nathan O. Kaplan) Methods in Enzymology, 1955—; exec. editor: Archives Biochemistry and Biophysics, 1970-74. Recipient Eli Lilly award Am. Chem. Soc., 1947. Mem. Am. Soc. Biol. Chemists, Am. Chem. Soc., Internat. Union Biochemistry (enzyme commn.), Nat. Acad. Sci., Am. Acad. Arts and Scis. Home: 709 Crescent Rd Nashville TN 37205

COLQUITT, LANDON AUGUSTUS, mathematics educator; b. Fort Worth, Jan. 25, 1919; s. Fred Augustus and Maude Lena (Pyeatt) C.; m. Betsy Feagan, May 29, 1954; children: Clare E., Catherine A. B.A., Tex. Christian U., 1939; M.A., Ohio State U., 1941, Ph.D., 1948; postgrad., Calif. Inst. Tech., 1942. Asst. instr. math. Ohio State U., 1946-48; mem. faculty Tex. Christian U., 1948—, prof. math., 1955—, chmn. dept., 1962-79; vis. faculty U. Tex., Austin, Spring 1980; sr. nuclear engr. Convair, Fort Worth, summers 1955, 56. Served with USAAF, 1942-46; ETO. Fellow AAAS, Tex. Acad. Scis. (past vice chmn.); mem. Am. Math. Soc., Math. Assn. Am., Soc. Indsl. and Applied Math., Phi Beta Kappa, Sigma Xi, Pi Mu Epsilon. Home: 2601 McPherson Ave Fort Worth TX 76109

COLSON, CHARLES WENDELL, writer, lay minister; b. Boston, Oct. 16, 1931; s. Wendell Ball and Inez (Ducrow) C.; m. Nancy Billings, June 3, 1953; children: Wendell Ball II, Christian B., Emily Ann; m. Patricia Ann Hughes, Apr. 4, 1964. A.B., Brown U., 1953; J.D., George Washington U., 1959; LL.D. hon., Wheaton Coll., 1982, Houghton Coll., 1983, Eastern Coll., 1983. Bar: Mem. D.C. bar 1961-74, mem. Va. bar 1959-75, active mem. Mass. bar 1964-74. Practiced in, Washington, 1961-69; asst. to asst. sec. Navy, 1955-56; adminstrv. asst. Senator Leverett Saltonstall, U.S. Senate, 1956-61; sr. ptnr. Gadsby & Hannah, 1961-69; spl. counsel to Pres. of U.S., 1969-72; ptnr. Colson & Shapiro, Washington, 1973-74; asso. Fellowship House, Washington, 1975—, Prison Fellowship, 1976—. Author: Born Again, 1975, Life Sentence, 1979, Crime and The Responsible Community, 1980, Loving God, 1983. Campaign mgr. Saltonstall campaign, 1960. Served to capt. USMCR, Korean Conflict. Recipient Religious Heritage award, 1977. Mem. Order of Coif, Beta Theta Pi. Baptist. Office: Prison Fellowship PO Box 40562 Washington DC 20016

COLSON, EARL M., lawyer; b. Bklyn., Mar. 8, 1930; s. Abraham and Rebecca (Hecker) C.; m. Helen Theresa Austern, Apr. 24, 1960; children: Adam Thomas, Amy Esther, Deborah Austern. B.S. magna cum laude, Syracuse U., 1950, LL.B., Harvard U., 1957. Bar: N.Y. 1958, D.C. 1960. Assoc. Chadbourne, Parke, Whiteside & Wolff, N.Y.C., 1957-60, Arent, Fox, Kintner, Plotkin & Kahn, Washington, 1960-68, partner, 1968—; adj. prof. law Georgetown U., 1970—; lectr on tax subjects. Author: Capital Gains and Losses, 1975; co-author: Federal Taxation of Estates, Gifts and Trusts, 1975. Bd. dirs. Washington Hebrew Congregation, 1979—, v.p., 1984—; trustee Kingsbury Center, 1978-81. Mem. ABA (chmn. estate and gift tax com. sect. taxation 1972-73), D.C. Bar Assn. (chmn. tax com. 1971-72, treas., bd. govs. 1974-76), Am. Law Inst., City Bar Assn. N.Y. Club: Cosmos/Washington. Office: 1050 Connecticut Ave NW Washington DC 20036

COLSON, ELIZABETH FLORENCE, anthropologist; b. Hewitt, Minn., June 15, 1917; d. Louis H. and Metta (Damon) C. B.A., U. Minn., 1938, M.A., 1940; M.A., Radcliffe Coll., 1941; Ph.D. (A.A.U.W. Traveling fellow), 1945, Brown U., 1978. Asst. social sci. analyst War Relocation Authority, 1942-43; research asst. Harvard, 1944-45; research officer Rhodes-Livingstone Inst., 1946-47, dir., 1948-51; sr. lectr. Manchester U., 1951-53; asso. prof. Goucher Coll., 1954-55; research asso. African Research Program, Boston U., 1955-59, part-time, 1959-63; prof. anthropology Brandeis U., 1959-63, U. Calif. at Berkeley, 1964—; Lewis Henry Morgan lectr. U. Rochester, 1973. Author: The Makah, 1953, Marriage and the Family Among The Plateau Tonga, 1958, Social Organization of the Gwembe Tonga, 1960, The Plateau Tonga, 1962, The Social Consequences of Resettlement, 1971, Tradition and Contract, 1974; Jr. Author (Secondary Education and the Formation of an Elite), 1980; Sr. editor: Seven Tribes of British Central Africa, 1951. Fellow Center Advanced Study Behavioral Scis., 1967-68; Fairchild fellow Calif. Inst. Tech., 1975-76. Fellow Am. Anthrop. Assn., Brit. Assn. Social Anthropologists, Royal Anthrop. Inst. (hon.); mem. Nat. Acad. Sci., Am. Acad. Arts and Scis., Phi Beta Kappa. Office: Dept Anthropology U Calif Berkeley CA 94720

COLSON, STEVEN DOUGLAS, chemistry educator; b. Idaho Falls, Idaho, Aug. 16, 1941; s. Robert William and Ellen Laurine (Pederson) C.; m. Donna Marie Lovell, Sept. 14, 1962; children: Maria, Susan, Douglas, David, Spencer, Steven. B.S., Utah State U., 1963; Ph.D., Calif. Inst. Tech., 1968. Asst. prof. chemistry Yale U., New Haven, 1968-73, assoc. prof., 1973-80, prof. chemistry, 1980—; postdoctoral fellow Nat. Research Council, Ottawa, Ont., Can., 1967-68. Home: 1167 Marion Rd Cheshire CT 06410 Office: Yale Univ 225 Prospect St New Haven CT 06511

COLT, JOHN NICHOLSON, artist, educator; b. Madison, Wis., May 15, 1925; s. Arthur Nicholson and Mary (Niles) C.; m. Ruth Anne Kjaer, Jan. 3, 1981; 1 son, Christopher. B.S., U. Wis., 1949, M.S., 1950. Instr. painting Layton Sch. Arts, Milw., 1956; instr. art Perth (West Australia) Boys Tech, 1957; prof., head art grad. studies U. Wis., Milw., 1957—; vis. prof. U. Sask., Saskatoon, Can., 1959, U. So. Calif., 1965, Am. U., Beirut, 1972. (Recipient Milw. Art Center Medal of Honor 1958, Ford Found. award 1962, 64), One-man shows, Fairweather Hardin Gallery, Chgo., 1964, Milw. Art Mus., 1968, Mpls. Inst. Art, 1970, Neill Gallery, N.Y.C., 1979, 81, Art Acad. Cin., 1980, group shows include, Whitney Mus. Am. Art, N.Y.C., 1958, Walker Art Center, Mpls., 1962-64, 66, Chgo. Art Inst., 1966; represented in permanent collections, Whitney Mus. Am. Art, N.Y.C., Munson Williams Proctor Inst., Utica, N.Y., Milw. Art Mus., Grand Rapids Art Mus. Served with USN, 1943-46. Home: 823 N 2d St Milwaukee WI 53203 Office: Art Dept U Wis Milwaukee WI 53211

COLTER, CYRUS, novelist, lawyer; b. Noblesville, Ind., Jan. 8, 1910; s. James Alexander and Ethel Marietta (Bassett) C.; m. Imogene Mackay, Jan. 1, 1943. J.D., Ill. Inst. Tech. Chgo. Kent Coll. Law, 1940; Litt. D. (hon.), U. Ill., 1977. Bar: Ill. 1940. Practiced in, Chgo., 1946—; agt. IRS, 1940-42; mem. Ill. Commerce Commn., 1950-73; Chester D. Tripp prof. humanities Northwestern U., 1973-78, prof. emeritus, 1978—; cons. AT&T, 1974—. Author: The Beach Umbrella (U. Iowa Sch. Letters award for short fiction 1970); novels The Rivers of Eros, 1972, The Hippodrome, 1973, Night Studies, 1979. Bd. dirs. Sta. WTTW-TV, Chgo., Chgo. Symphony Orch., Ill. Humanities Council, Chgo. Hist. Soc., Chgo. Reporter, Great Books Found.; bd. dirs., treas. Messenger Found., Chgo. Served to capt. F.A. U.S. Army, 1942-46; ETO. Mem. AAUP. Clubs: Commercial (Chgo.); Wayfarers, Cliff Dwellers. Home: 1115 S Plymouth Ct Chicago IL 60605

COLTER, JESSI (JENNINGS) (MIRRIAM JOAN JOHNSON), singer; b. Phoenix, May 25, 1943; d. Arnold Hobson and Helen D. (Perkins) Johnson; m. Waylon Arnold Jennings, Oct. 26, 1969; children—Jennifer Eddy Jennings, Waylon Albright Jennings; stepchildren—Buddy Jennings, Julie Jennings, Terry Jennings. Student public schs., Mesa, Ariz. Rec. artist, Jamie Records, Phila., 1959-68, RCA Records, Nashville, 1968-73, Capitol Records, Los Angeles, 1974—; albums include I'm Jesse Colter, 1975, Jessi, 1975, (with Waylon Jennings, Willie Nelson and Tompall Glaser) Outlaws, 1976, Diamond in the Rough, 1976, Mirriam, 1977, That's the Way a Cowboy Rocks & Rolls, 1978 *

COLTMAN, JOHN WESLEY, physicist; b. Cleve., July 19, 1915; s. Robert White and Louise (Tyroler) C.; m. Charlotte Waters Beard, June 10, 1941; children—Sally Louise, Nancy Jean. B.S. in Physics, Case Inst. Tech., 1937; M.S., U. Ill., 1939, Ph.D. in Physics, 1941. Research scientist Research Labs. Westinghouse Electric Corp., Pitts., 1941-49, mgr. electronics and nuclear physics dept., 1949-60, asso. dir. research labs., 1960-64, research dir. central research labs., 1964-74, dir. research and devel. planning, 1977-80; mem. adv. group on electron devices Dept. Def., 1958-62; mem. Naval Intelligence Sci. Adv. Com., 1971-73, NRC Commn. on Human Resources, 1977-80. Contbr. articles to profl. jours. Recipient Longstreth medal Franklin Inst., 1960; Roentgen medal Remscheid, W. Ger., 1970; Gold medal Radiol. Soc. N.Am., 1982. Fellow Am. Phys. Soc., IEEE; mem. Nat. Acad. Engring., Am. Musical Instrument Soc. Republican. Presbyterian. Inventor x-ray image amplifier, scintillation counter. Home: 3319 Scathelocke Rd Pittsburgh PA 15235

COLTON, ANITA BELLE (ANITA BELLE COLTON), entertainer, singer; b. Chgo., Oct. 18, 1919; d. James and Gladys (Gill) C. Student, Chgo. public schs. Singer and entertainer various Chgo. Music Clubs, 1939-41; singer with, Gene Krupa's Orch., 1941-45, Stan Kenton Orch., 1945-46, Woody Herman Orch., 1946, singing tours with, Quartette in, U.S. and abroad, 1947-81; rec. artist, Polygram, Emily records; appeared in: films Gene Krupa Story, 1956, Zigzag, 1970, Outfit, 1974; TV show 60 Minutes, 1980; Author: High Times, Hard Times, 1981. Mem. AFTRA, Screen Actors Guild, AGVA. Office: care Emily Records PO Box 123 N Haven CT 06473 *From the time I was twelve or thirteen, my life was music. I never thought about being on top. I only wanted to be a part of the scene.*

COLTON, CLARK KENNETH, chemical engineering educator; b. N.Y.C., July 20, 1941; s. Sidney and Goldie (Chases) C.; m. Ellen Ruth Brandner, June 20, 1965; children—Jill Erin, Jason Adam, Michael Ross, Brian Scott. B.Chem. Engring., Cornell U., 1964; Ph.D. (NIH fellow), Mass. Inst. Tech., 1969. Asst. prof. chem. engring. MIT, 1969-73, assoc. prof., 1973-76, prof., 1976—, Bayer prof. chem. engring., 1980—, dep. head dept. chem. engring., 1977; cons. to NIH, FDA, various indsl. orgns.; mem. adv. bd. mil. personnel supplies NRC, 1971-75. Mem. editorial bd.: Jour. Membrane Sci, 1975-81, Jour. Bioengring, 1976-79; contbr. articles to sci. jours. Ford found. fellow, 1969-70; recipient Tchr./Scholar award Camille and Henry Dreyfus Found., 1972. Mem. N.Y. Acad. Scis., Am. Inst. Chem. Engrs. (dir. food, pharm. and bioengring. div. 1978—, recipient Allan P. Colburn award 1977), Am. Soc. Artificial Internal Organs (editorial bd. Jour. 1978—), Am. Diabetes Assn., Am. Soc. for Engring. Edn. (Curtis W. McGraw research award 1980), Biomed. Engring. Soc., AAAS, Sigma Xi, Tau Beta Pi, Phi Lambda Upsilon. Club: Cornell (Boston). Home: 279 Commonwealth Ave Newton MA 02167 Office: Dept Chem Engring Mass Inst Tech Cambridge MA 02139

COLTON, DAVID LEM, mathematician; b. San Francisco, Mar. 14, 1943; s. Ellis and Myrl (Crowder) C.; m. Renate, Dec. 20, 1968; children—Claire, Natasha. B.S., Calif. Inst. Tech., 1964; M.S., U. Wis., 1965; Ph.D., U. Edinburgh, Scotland, 1967, D.Sc., 1977. Asst. prof. math. Ind. U., 1967-71, asso. prof., 1972-74; prof. U. Strathclyde, Glasgow, Scotland, 1975-78, U. Del., Newark, 1978—; vis. prof. McGill U., 1968-69, U. Glasgow, 1971-72, U. Konstanz, 1974-75. Author various research monographs; research, numerous publs. in field; asso. editor: Applicable Analysis, 1974—, Complex Variables and Applications, 1982—. Mem. Soc. Indsl. and Applied Math., Gesellschaft für Angewandte Mathematik und Mechanik. Office: Dept Math U Del Newark DE 19711

COLTON, JOEL, educator; b. N.Y.C., Aug. 23, 1918; s. Philip and Theresa (Cotler) C.; m. Shirley Baron, May 8, 1942; children—Valerie Beth, Kenneth Richard. B.A. magna cum laude, Coll. City N.Y., 1937, M.S., 1938; M.A., Columbia, 1940; Ph.D., 1950. Lectr. history Columbia, 1946-47; successively instr., asst. prof., asso. prof., prof. history Duke, 1947—, chmn. dept. history, 1967-74, chmn. acad. council, 1971-73; dir. for humanities Rockefeller Found., 1974—; cons. Coll. Entrance Exams. Bd., Advanced Placement Program, 1963-68; U.S. mem. Internat. Commn. on History of Social Movements and Social Structures, 1975—, v.p., 1980—. Author: Compulsory Labor Arbitration in France, 1936-39, 1951, (with R.R. Palmer) A History of the Modern World (transl. Arabic, Persian, Swedish, Spanish), 5th edit, 1978, A Study Guide for a History of the Modern World, 5th edit, 1978, Léon Blum: Humanist in Politics, 1966 (French transl. 1968), Twentieth Century: Time-Life Great Ages of Man Series, 1968, rev. edit., 1980; Editor: The Humanities in an International Context, 1976, The Search for a Value Consensus, 1978, Toward the Restoration of the Liberal Arts Curriculum, 1979; bd. editors: Jour. Modern History, 1967-70, Third Republic/Troisième République, 1975—, Hist. Abstracts, 1981—; contbr. articles to profl. jours., encys. and yearbooks. Served to 1st lt., M.I. AUS, 1942-46; ETO. Recipient book award Mayflower Soc., 1967; Townsend Harris medal CCNY Alumni Assn., 1980; Guggenheim fellow, 1957-58; Rockefeller Found. fellow, 1961-62; Nat. Endowment for Humanities sr. fellow, 1970-71. Fellow Am. Acad. Arts and Scis.; mem. Am. Hist. Assn. (Herbert Baxter Adams prize com. 1965-68, com. on internat. hist. activities 1980—), So. Hist. Assn. (council 1971-74, vice-chmn. European sect. 1974-75, chmn. 1975-76), Soc. for French Hist. Studies (v.p. 1972-73), Phi Beta Kappa (pres. Duke chpt. 1956-57). Club: Century Assn. Home: 215 E 68th St New York NY 10021 Office: Rockefeller Found 1133 Ave of Americas New York NY 10036

COLTON, NELSON BURTON, industrial company executive; b. Boston, Sept. 25, 1930; s. Harold Abraham and Pauline Ruth (Leader) C.; m. Barbara Ruth Lowenstein, Oct. 24, 1959 (dec. Apr. 1982); children: Lisa Gail, Julia Lee. B.S. Metall. Engring., Purdue U., 1952; postgrad. indsl. mgmt., Sloan Inst. MIT, 1960-61. Metallurgist N.J. Zinc Co., 1952-55; metall. engr. Union Carbide Metals, Niagra Falls, N.Y., 1955-60; engr.-materials engring. Raytheon Co., Newton, Mass., 1960-61; v.p. mfg. Electronics Metals & Alloys Inc., North Attleboro, Mass., 1961-68; plant mgr. D.E. Makepeace div. Engelhard Minerals & Chems., Attleboro, 1968-71; with Franklin Mint Corp., Franklin Center, Pa., 1971-78, exec. v.p., gen. mgr., 1975-77, exec. v.p. ops., 1977-78; group v.p. metall. ops.industries div. Engelhard Corp., Iselin, N.J., 1978-79, sr. v.p. metall. ops., 1979-81, pres.div., 1981—; dir. Engelhard Corp., Iselin, N.J., Engelhard Industries de Argentina SA, Buenos Aires, Argentina. Named Outstanding Engring. Alumnus Purdue U., 1978. Mem. Internat. Precious Metals Inst. (v.p. Bklyn. 1983—), Silver Users Assn. (exec. com.), Internat. Soc. Hybrid Material. Office: Engelhard Industries Div 70 Wood Ave S Iselin NJ 08830

COLUSSY, DAN ALFRED, airline company executive; b. Pitts., June 3, 1931; s. Dan and Viola E. (Andreis) C.; m. Helene Graham, June 3, 1953; children: Deborah, Jennifer. B.S., 1953; M.B.A., Harvard U., 1965. Applications engr. Jet Propulsion div. Gen. Electric Co., 1956-63; dir. ops. Am. Airlines, N.Y.C., 1965-66; v.p. mktg. N.E. Airlines, Boston, 1966-69; v.p. Wells, Rich, Green Advt. Agy., N.Y.C., 1969-70; v.p. mktg. devel. Pan Am. World Airways, N.Y.C., 1970-72, v.p. passenger mktg., 1972-74, sr. v.p. passenger mktg., 1974, sr. v.p. field ops., 1974-75, sr. v.p. mktg. and services, 1975-76, exec. v.p. mktg. and services, dir., 1976-78, pres., chief operating officer, mem. exec. com., 1978-80, also dir.; chmn., chief exec. officer Columbia Air., Balt., 1980-82; pres., chief exec. officer, dir., mem. exec. com. Can. Pacific Air, Vancouver, B.C., 1982—; dir., mem. exec. com. Can. Pacific Hotels, 1983—. Served to lt. USCG, 1953-56. Clubs: Royal Vancouver Yacht, Larchmond Yacht, Harvard. Office: Can Pacific Air Vancouver Internat Airport Vancouver BC Canada V7B 1V1

COLVARD, DEAN WALLACE, emeritus university chancellor; b. Ashe County, N.C., July 10, 1913; s. W. P. and Mary (Shepherd) C.; m. Martha Lampkin, July 7, 1939; children: Carol Lampkin, Mary Lynda, Dean Wallace. B.S., Berea Coll., 1935; M.A., U. Mo., 1938; Ph.D., Purdue U., 1950, D.Agr., 1961; L.H.D. (hon.), Belmont Abbey Coll., 1978; D. Public Service, U. N.C., Charlotte, 1979. Instr. agr., farm mgr. Brevard Coll., 1935-37; supt. N.C. Mountain Expt. Sta., 1938-46; prof. animal sci. N.C. State Coll., 1947-48, head dept. animal sci., 1948-53; dean agr., 1953-60; pres. Miss. State U., 1960-66; chancellor U. N.C. at Charlotte, 1966-78, chancellor emeritus, 1978—; vis. prof. N.C. State U., 1979—; mng. cons. Sci. Museums of Charlotte, 1980—; dir. Fed. Res. Bank of Richmond, 1955-60, dep. chmn., 1959-60; dir. Mut. Savs. & Loan.; Spl. cons. ICA, Bangkok, Thailand, 1960; chmn. agrl. subcom. Nuclear Energy Adv. Com. for N.C., 1958-60; mem. Gov.'s Research Triangle Devel. Council, 1957-59; co-ordinator Agr. Research Mission in Peru, S. Am., 1954-60; Mem. agr. adv. com. W. K. Kellogg Found., 1954-60; chmn. Miss. Gov.'s Com. on Latin Am. Edn., 1961. Contbr. to publs. in animal sci., agrl. econs., ednl. adminstrn. Chmn. Miss. Rhodes Scholar Com., 1965-66, N.C. Rhodes Scholar Com., 1967, 78; mem. Miss. Jr. Coll. Commn., 1960-66; vice chmn. Dimensions for Charlotte-Mecklenburg, 1973-76; mem. N.C. Council on State Goals and Policy, 1972-76, So. Growth Policies Bd., 1977—, Mecklenburg and Union Counties Health and Hosp. Council, 1967-76; chmn., 1974-76; mem. N.C. Awards Commn., 1969-73; Trustee Cordell Hull Found. for Internat. Edn., 1961-67; bd. dirs., exec. com. U. Research Park, Charlotte, 1967—, vice chmn., 1974-79; trustee Berea Coll., 1956-76, St. Andrews Coll., 1969-76; chmn. bd. trustees N.C. Sch. Sci. and Math., 1978—. Named Man of Year in Agr. in N.C., 1954; recipient Disting. Service award N.C. Farm Bur., 1956, Miss. Farm Bur., 1965, N.C. Grange, 1958; Outstanding Civilian award; U.S. Dept. Army, 1966; Charlotte News Man of Yr. award, 1977. Mem Nat. Assn. State Univs. and Land Grant Colls. (co-chmn. joint com. edn. for govt. service 1961-65, chmn. pres.'s council 1966), Am. Council Edn. (commn. internat. edn. 1966-68, chmn. com. higher adult edn. 1966-68), So. Assn. Colls. and Schs. (commn. colls. 1965-67), Am. Assn. State Colls. and Univs. (dir. 1978), Charlotte C. of C. (dir. 1968-70), Blue Key, Sigma Xi, Omicron Delta Kappa, Phi Kappa Phi, Gamma Alpha, Alpha Gamma Rho, Gamma Sigma Delta, Alpha Zeta. Clubs: Charlotte Country, Charlotte City, Charlotte Rotary (pres. 1978). Home: 1530 Queens Rd Charlotte NC 28207 Office: U NC at Charlotte Charlotte NC 28223

COLVILLE, DAVID ALEXANDER, artist; b. Toronto, Ont., Can., Aug. 24, 1920; s. David Harrower and Florence (Gault) C.; m. Rhoda Wright, Aug. 5, 1942; children: Graham, John, Charles, Ann. B.F.A., Mt. Allison U., 1942. One-man shows, Kestner Gesellschaft, Hanover, W.Ger., 1969, Marlborough Mus. Fine Art, London, 1970, Gemeentmuseum, Arnhem, Netherlands, 1977, Städtische Kuntsthalle, Düsseldorf, W.Ger., Fischer Fine Art, London, Mira Godard Gallery, Toronto and Montreal, 1978, Art Gallery Ont., Toronto, 1983, Staatliche Kunsthalle, Berlin, Mus. Ludwig, Cologne, W.Ger.; represented in permanent collections, Nat. Gallery Can., Mus. Modern Art, N.Y.C., Kestner Gesellschaft, Musee National d'Art Moderne, Paris, Sammlung Ludwig, Aachen, W.Ger., Boymans-Van Beuningen Mus., Rotterdam, Netherlands, Art Gallery Ont.; vis. artist, U. Calif., Santa Cruz, 1967, Berliner Kunstler Programm, 1971. Served with Canadian Army, 1942-46. Decorated companion Order of Can.; recipient Molson prize, 1974. Home and office: 408 Main St Wolfville NS B0P 1X0 Canada

COLVILLE, WILLIAM LYTLE, agronomics educator; b. Oskaloosa, Iowa, Oct. 7, 1925; s. Walter Harold and Florence (Lytle) C.; m. Ethel Joanne Zeinemann, Sept. 3, 1955; children: David Ross, Deborah Cay. B.S., Iowa State U., 1953; M.S., U. Wis., 1954, Ph.D., 1957. Asst. prof. U. Wis., Madison, 1956-57, U. Nebr., Lincoln, 1957-62, assoc. prof., 1962-66, prof., 1966-71, U. Ga., Athens, 1971—, head dept. agronomy, div. chmn., 1971—; instrn. cons. to various univs., 1965—. Contbr. numerous articles to profl. jours. Bd. dirs. Salt-Wahoo Water Shed Dist., Lincoln, 1971. Named Outstanding Tchr. Gamma Sigma Delta, 1965, Outstanding Tchr. Sci. and Tech. U. Nebr., 1966, Prof. of Yr. Agrl. Exec. Bd., 1968. Fellow Am. Soc. Agronomy (exec. com. 1981-84, Agronomic Edn.); mem. Crop Sci. Soc. Am. (pres., exec. com. 1981-84), Soil Sci. Soc. Am., AAAS, Council Agrl. Sci. and Tech. (exec. com.), Ga. Plant Food Ednl. Soc. (hon. life mem.). Presbyterian. Clubs: Agronomy (nat. v.p.) (1952); Cardinal Key). Lodge: Kiwanis. Home: 220 Ponderosa Dr Athens GA 30605 Office: Agronomy Dept Univ of Georgia Athens GA 30602

COLVIN, BURTON HOUSTON, mathematician, government administrator; b. West Warwick, R.I., July 12, 1916; s. Asa Burton and Sara Elsie (Houston) C.; m. Lois Ann Scholes, Dec. 22, 1947; children: Daniel Burton, David Walter, Thomas Alan. A.B., Brown U., 1938, A.M. in Math. (Grand Army of Republic fellow), 1939; Ph.D. in Math. (Univ. fellow), U. Wis., 1943. Instr. math. and mechanics, dept. math. U. Wis., Madison, 1943, instr. math., and asst. prof. math., 1946-51; tech. aide nat. def. research com. Office Sci. Research and Devel., 1944-45; cons. applied mathematician phys. research staff Boeing Co., Seattle, 1951-55, supr. math. analysis group, 1955-58; with Boeing Sci. Research Labs., Seattle, 1958-72, head math. research lab., 1958-70, acting head info. scis. lab., 1966-70, head math. and info. scis. lab., 1970-72; chief div. applied math. Nat. Bur. Standards, Dept. Commerce, Washington, 1972-78; dir. Center for Applied Math., 1978—; NSF lectr., 1957; mem. council Conf. Bd. Math. Scis., 1964, 70-77, chmn., 1975-77; adv. bd. Sch. Math. Study Group, 1963-71, chmn., 1965-66; chmn. computer sci. adv. com. Stanford U., 1970-71. Recipient Silver Medal award Dept. Commerce, 1978, Gold medal award Dept. Commerce, 1981, Presdl. Meritorious Rank award, 1980. Fellow AAAS (council 1965-67, vice-chmn. commn. on sci. edn. 1968-72, chmn. task force on tech. edn. 1968-69); mem. Soc. Indsl. and Applied Math. (vis. scientist lectr. 1962-63, trustee 1962-65, 67-70, 78-80, pres. 1971-72), AAAS (council 1965-67, vice-chmn. commn. on sci. edn. 1968-72, chmn. task force on tech. edn. 1968-69), Math. Assn. Am. (vis. lectr. 1963-65), Am. Math. Soc., NEA, Inst. Math. Stats., Assn. Women in Math., Nat. Council Tchrs. Math, Phi Beta Kappa, Sigma Xi. Office: Nat Bur Standards Center for Applied Math Washington DC 20234

COLVIN, MILTON, political science educator; b. Missoula, Mont., June 20, 1923; s. Howard Milton and Katharine (Ostrander) C.; m. Maria Countess von Kielmansegg, Sept. 1, 1953; children: Christopher, Alexander, Katharine, Maria-Gabriele, Caroline-Leontine (dec.). B.A., Yale U., 1948; Ph.D. cum laude, U. Heidelberg, Germany, 1953. Mem. White House Commn. on Refugees, 1948-50; asst. prof. anthropology U. Mont., 1954-57; asst. prof., then asso. prof. polit. sci. Vanderbilt U., 1957-60; lectr. U. Chgo., 1960-61; asso. prof., prof. politics Washington and Lee U., Lexington, Va., 1961—; vis. prof. Nat. War Coll., Washington, 1965-66, U. Vienna, Austria, 1973-74, Univ. Coll., Oxford, Eng., 1978; NATO fellow, 1981. Contbr. profl. jours. Served with AUS, 1942-45; capt. Res. ret. Decorated. Mem. Am., So. polit. sci. assns., Wilderness Soc., Res. Officers Assn., Zeta Psi. Democrat. Roman Catholic. Home: Honeysuckle Hill Lexington VA 24450

COLVIN, (OTIS) HERBERT, JR., educator, musician; b. El Dorado, Ark., Mar. 18, 1923; s. Otis Herbert and Irene (Hammons) C.; m. Mary Ila Ullom, June 18, 1948; children—Carol Kay (Mrs. James L. Smith), Mary Edith (Mrs. George M. Reitmeier), Susan Elizabeth. B.A., Baylor U., 1944, B.Mus., 1948; M.Mus., U. Colo., 1950; Ph.D., U. Rochester, 1958. Grad. asst. U. Colo., 1948-50; instr. music Tex. Tech. Coll., 1950-55; grad. asst. Eastman Sch. Music, 1955-57; asst. prof. piano Baylor U., 1957-62, chmn. dept., 1958-62, asso. prof. theory, 1962-64, prof., 1964—, chmn. dept., 1962-76, coordinator theory div., 1976—. Concert accompanist; organist, 7th and James Bapt. Ch., 1969—; editor choral compositions.; Composer: Organ Voluntaries Based on Early American Hymn Tunes, 1964, Short Pieces for Organ, 1971, For Sunday; six organ pieces based on modal melodies, 1972, Gloria; anthem for mixed voices and organ, 1974, Nine Hymn Settings for Organ, 1975, For Sunday Volume II; six organ pieces based on modal melodies, 1976, Sheep May Safely Graze; six organ-piano duets on compositions by Bach and Billings, 1977, Surely the Lord Is in This Place; anthem for mixed voices, accompanied, 1977, Four Madrigals; mixed-voice choral settings of A.E. Housman poems, 1978, They That Wait Upon the Lord, 1980, anthem for mixed voices, accompanied; editor choral compositions; contbr. articles to profl. jours. Served with USNR, 1944-46; CBI. Mem. Am. Guild Organists (dean Waco chpt. 1958-60, 68-69, 79-80), Music Tchrs. Nat. Assn., Phi Mu Alpha Sinfonia, Pi Kappa Lambda. Baptist. Club: Mason (32 deg.). Home: 80 Cottonwood St Waco TX 76706 Office: Sch Music Baylor U Waco TX 76703

COLWELL, HOWARD OTIS, advertising executive; b. New Rochelle, N.Y., Sept. 16, 1929; s. Robert Talcott and Louise (Otis) C.; m. Barbara Elaine Hrosenchik, Aug. 14, 1954; children: John Robert, Christian, Mary Louise. A.B., Colgate U., 1953. Copy group head Batten, Barton, Durstine & Osborn, N.Y.C., 1953-59; v.p., creative dir. Tatham-Laird & Kudner, N.Y.C., 1959-68; sr. v.p., creative dir. William Esty Advt., N.Y.C., 1968—; guest lectr. NYU, 1979-81, Pace U., 1980-81, adj. prof., 1982-83. Chmn. YMCA Indian Guides Norwalk-Wilton, 1966; chmn. Wilton Voice on Edn., 1972-75, Wilton Arts Council, 1980-83. Congregationalist. Office: 100 E 42d St New York NY 10017

COLWELL, JOHN AMORY, physician; b. Boston, Nov. 4, 1928; s. Arthur Ralph and Jeane (Haskins) C.; m. Jane Kuebler, June 19, 1954; children: John Clayton, Ann Kimbell, Karen Elizabeth, James Lewis. A.B., Princeton U., 1950; M.D., Northwestern U., 1954, M.S. in Medicine, 1957, Ph.D. in Physiology, 1968. Intern Univ. Hosps., Cleve., 1954-55; resident in internal medicine Passavant Meml. Hosp., Chgo., 1955-57, VA Research Hosp., 1959-60; from instr. to assoc. prof. medicine Northwestern U. Med. Sch., 1960-71; clin. investigator, then chief metabolic sect. VA Research Hosp., 1961-71; prof. medicine Med. U. S.C., Charleston, 1971—, dir. endocrinology-metabolism-nutrition div., dept. medicine, 1972—, research coordinator, 1973-79; assoc. chief staff research and devel. VA Med. Center, Charleston, 1971—; bd. dirs. Am. Diabetes Assn., 1982—, S.C. Diabetes Assn., 1971—. Author: Clinical Recognition and Treatment of Diabetic Vascular Disease, 1975; co-author: Diabetes and Metabolic Disorders, 1975, 82, Diabetes, Endocrinology and Metabolic Disorders, 1981; contbr. articles med. jours. Served to capt. M.C. USAF, 1957-59. Grantee NIH, VA, 1962—. Fellow A.C.P.; mem. AAAS, Am. Diabetes Assn. (fellow 1960-62), Am. Fedn. Clin. Research, Am. Physiol. Soc., Central Soc. Clin. Research, Endocrine Soc., So. Soc. Clin. Investigation. Republican. Episcopalian. Clubs: Skokie Country (Glencoe, Ill.); Carolina Yacht, Kiawah Island (Charleston); Cloister Inn (Princeton U.). Home: 182 Broad St Charleston SC 29401 Office: 171 Ashley Ave Charleston SC 29401

COLWELL, RICHARD JAMES, researcher, educator; b. Sioux Falls, S.D., May 27, 1930; s. George Lionel and Mildred Emma (Muchow) C.; m. Ruth Ann Crockett, June 4, 1960; children—Robert, Catherine, Mary. B.F.A., U. S.D., 1953, Mus.M., 1953; Ed.D., U. Ill., 1961. Tchr. Sioux Falls Pub. Schs., 1955-57; faculty U. Mont., Billings, 1957-61; prof. music and edn. U. Ill., Urbana, 1961—; research cons., editor Bull. Council for Research in Music Edn. Author: The Teaching of Instrumental Music, 1968, Music Achievement Tests, 1-4, 1967-70, The Evaluation of Music Teaching and Learning, 1970, Concepts for a Musical Foundation, 1974, Silver Burdett Competency Tests, 1-18, 1978—; Editorial Bd.: Council Research Music Edn, 1961—, Jour. Research Music Edn, 1976—, Jour. Aesthetic Edn, 1968-76. Served with U.S. Army, 1953-55. Decorated Army Commendation medal.; John Guggenheim fellow, 1975-76; fellow Army War Coll., 1978-79. Mem. Music Educators Nat. Council, NEA, Ill. Music Edn. Assn., Coll. Music Soc., Council Measurement Edn., Am. Ednl. Research Assn., Phi Delta Kappa, Phi Mu Alpha. Home: 406 W Michigan St Urbana IL 61801 Office: U Ill Urbana IL 61801

COLWELL, RITA ROSSI, university official, microbiologist, educator; b. Beverly, Mass., Nov. 23, 1943; d. Louis and Louise (Di Palma) Rossi; m. Jack H. Colwell, May 31, 1956; children: Alison E.L., Stacie A. B.S. with distinction, Purdue U., 1956; Ph.D., U. Wash., 1961. Asst. research prof. U. Wash., Seattle, 1961-64; guest scientist div.applied biology NCR of Can., 1961-63; vis. asst. prof. biology Georgetown U., Washington, 1963-64, asst. prof. biology, 1964-66, assoc. prof., 1966-72; prof. microbiology U. Md., College Park, 1972—, dir. sea grant program, 1977-83, acting dir. Ctr. for Environ. and Estuarine Studies, 1980-81; v.p. acad. affairs U. Md. System, 1983—; cons., adviser to Washington area communications media, Congressman and legislators, 1978; external examiner various univs. abroad, 1964—; mem. coastal resources adv. com. dept. natural resources State of Md., 1979—; mem. numerical data adv. bd. NCR, 1973-76, ocean scis. bd., 1977-80; del. 20th Gen. Assembly, Internat. Union Biol. Scis., Finland, 1979; U.S. del. 16th Assembly, Internat. Council of Sci. Union, Washington, 1976. Author: Collecting the Data (manual numerical taxonomy), 1970, (with M. Zambruski) Rodina-Methods in Aquatic Microbiology, 1972, (with L.H. Stevenson) Estuarine Microbiology Ecology, 1973, (with R.Y. Morita) Effect of the Ocean Environment on Microbial Activities, 1974; contbg. author: Marine and Estuarine Microbiology Laboratory Manual, 1975; contbr. numerous articles on marine microbiology and ecology to sci jours.; editorial bd.: Microbiology Ecology, 1972—, Applied and Environmental Microbiology, 1969-81, Johns Hopkins U. Oceanographic Series, 1981—, Revue de la Fondation Oceanographique Ricard, 1981—, Oil and Petrochem Pollution, 1980—; assoc. editor: Can. Jour. Microbiology, 1972-75; editor-in-chief: Marine Tech. Soc. Jour., 1981—. Mem. Gov's. Sci. Adv. Council, State of Md., 1979-82; bd. dirs. Upper Bay Survey Dept. Natural Resources, State of Md., 1974-75. Recipient Outstanding Women on Campus award U. Md., 1979. Fellow AAAS, Sigma Delta Epsilon, Can. Coll. of Microbiologists, Am. Acad. Microbiology (mem. ad hoc com. on environ. microbiology 1978-79), Washington Acad. Scis. (bd. mgrs. 1976-79); mem. Am. Soc. Microbiology (mem. various sci. coms. 1961—, pres.-elect 1983-84), World Fedn. Culture Collections, U.S. Fedn. Culture Collections (governing bd. 1978—), Am. Inst. Biol. Scis. (bd. govs. 1976-82), Marine Tech. Soc., Am. Oceanic Soc., Classification Soc. of Eng., Soc. for Invertebrate Pathology, Am. Soc. Limnology and Oceanography, Atlantic Estuarine Research Soc., Estuarine and Brackish Water Scis. Assn., Am. Littoral Soc., Soc. for Indsl. Microbiology (bd. govs. 1976-79), Classification Research Group of Eng., Soc. for Gen. Microbiology of Eng., Sigma Xi (ann. achievement award 1981). Home: 5010 River Hill Rd Bethesda MD 20816

COLWILL, JACK MARSHALL, physician, educator; b. Cleve., June 15, 1932; s. Clifford V. and Olive A. (Marshall) C.; m. Winifred Stedman, 1954; children: James F., Elizabeth Ann, Carolyn. B.A., Oberlin Coll., 1953; M.D. (George Whipple scholar), U. Rochester, 1957. Diplomate: Am. Bd. Med. Examiners, Am. Bd. Internal Medicine, Am. Bd. Family Practice. Intern Barnes Hosp., Washington U. Sch. Medicine, St. Louis, 1957-58; resident in medicine U. Washington Affiliated Hosps., Seattle, 1958-60; chief resident U. Hosp., 1960-61; instr. medicine, dir. med. outpatient dept. U. Rochester (N.Y.) Sch. Medicine and Dentistry, 1961-62, sr. instr. medicine, dir. med. outpatient dept., 1962-64; asst. dean, asst. prof. medicine, asst. prof. community health and med. practice U. Mo. Sch. Medicine, Columbia, 1964-67, assoc. dean, asst. prof., 1967-69, assoc. dean for acad. affairs, asst. prof., 1969-70, assoc. dean, assoc. prof., 1970-76, interim chmn. dept. family and community medicine, 1976-77, prof., 1976—, chmn. dept., asso. prof. medicine, 1977—; cons. Office Div. Dir., USPHS, 1977—, Bur. Health Manpower, NIH, 1969-75. Contbr. articles to profl. jours. Mem. AMA, Assn. Med. Am. Colls. (chmn. Midwest-Gt. Plains Group on Student Affairs 1971-73, nat. vice chmn. Group 1973-74, chmn. working group on non-cognitive assessment-adv. to com. on admissions assessment 1974-77), Soc. Tchrs. Family Medicine (bd. dirs. 1978-82, 83-87), Am. Acad. Family Practice, Alpha Omega Alpha. Office: NW 504 Med Scis Bldg Dept Family and Community Medicine U Mo-Columbia Sch Medicine Columbia MO 65212

COLWIN, ARTHUR LENTZ, educator, biologist; b. Sydney, Australia, Jan. 26, 1911; U.S., 1936, naturalized, 1942; m. Laura North Hunter, June 15, 1940. B.Sc., McGill U., 1933, M.Sc., 1934, Ph.D. (NRC Can. fellow), 1935-36; Moyse Travelling fellow, Cambridge (Eng.) U., 1934-35; Seessel fellow, Yale, 1936-37, Royal Soc. Can. fellow, 1937-38. Mem. faculty Queens Coll., 1940-73, prof., 1957-73, emeritus, 1973; adj. prof. Rosenstiel Sch. Marine and Atmospheric Sci., U. Miami, Fla., 1973—; Fulbright research fellow Tokyo (Japan) U., 1953-54; vis. scientist Nat. Inst. Med. Research, London, Eng., 1960. Editor: Jour. Exptl. Zoology, 1964-68, Jour. Morphology, 1964-68; editorial bd.: Biol. Bull, 1969-73, Am. Zoologist, 1970—; Contbr. articles to profl. jours. Trustee Marine Biol. Lab., Woods Hole, Mass., 1962-72. Served to capt. USAAF, 1943-46. Fellow N.Y. Acad. Scis., AAAS; mem. Internat. Inst. Developmental Biology, Internat. Soc. Cell Biology, Am. Soc. Zoologists, Soc. Study Devel. and Growth, Soc. for Study of Reprodn., Electron Microscope Soc. Am. Asso. Spl. research fertilization, devel. biology, cell contacts and assn., membrane structure and behavior. Home: 320 Woodcrest Rd Key Biscayne FL 33149 Office: Rosensteil Sch Marine & Atmospheric Sci U Miami 4600 Rickenbacker Causeway Miami FL 33149

COLYAR, ARDELL BENTON, city health ofcl.; b. Altus, Okla., Mar. 24, 1914; s. Richard N. and Algae (Hughes) C.; m. Florence Benita Morgan, Sept. 1, 1939; children—Ardell Benita (Mrs. John T. Strauss), Paula Cay (Mrs. Larry D. Jackson), Berrie Dee, Melodie Rae. Student, Oklahoma City U., 1935-37; M.D., U. Okla., 1941; M.P.H., Johns Hopkins, 1951; grad., Indsl. Coll. Armed Forces, 1964. Diplomate: Am. Bd. Preventive Medicine. Commd. officer USPHS, 1943-66, med. dir., 1966; rotating intern Broadlawns Gen. Hosp., Des Moines, 1941-42, resident surgery, 1942-43; assigned Okla. Health Dept., 1944-48; div. dir. Venereal Disease Control, 1946-48; clin. investigator Okla. U. Med. Sch., 1945-47; health officer Pittsburg County, Okla., 1949-50; med. cons., 1951-54; dir. Arctic Health Research Center, 1954-65; dep. chief Med. Care Adminstrn., 1966; commr. health, Okla., 1966-71; dir. Anchorage Health Dept., 1971-76; practice preventive and indsl. medicine, Anchorage, 1976—; prof. pub. health adminstrn. U. Okla. Sch. Health. Fellow Am. Coll. Preventive Medicine; mem. AAAS, Am. Pub. Health Assn., AMA, Am. Assn. Pub. Health Physicians. Baptist (deacon). Spl. research epidemiology infections and communicable diseases in Arctic regions. Office: 3550 Stanford Dr Anchorage AK 99504 *Life is a trust given to one for an indefinite period, in momentary units; a stewardship subject only to his will and commitment. He cannot buy life, nor can he pay for it; he can only respond to it by spending his life in gratitude to the Giver of Life and to those who also have received the gift.*

COMAY, AMOS, corp. exec.; b. N.Y.C., Mar. 4, 1915; s. Joseph and Nellie (Schorr) C.; m. Ethel Comay, Dec. 31, 1935; children: Sholom David, Deborah Esther. Partner, F.&B. Woodenware Co., Pitts., 1937-46; v.p. Action Industries, Inc., Pitts., 1946-50, pres., 1950-68, chmn., 1968—, chief exec. officer, 1968-82. Pres., Nat. Found. for Jewish Culture, 1978-82; v.p. United Jewish Fedn. Pitts., 1977-79; bd. dirs., exec. com. Am. Jewish Joint Distbn. Com., 1977—; bd. dirs. Council Jewish Fedns., 1974-78; nat. exec. com. United Jewish Appeal, 1970-77. Served with USNR, 1945-46. Democrat. Office: 460 Nixon Rd Cheswick PA 15024

COMBE, CHARLES JOSEPH, management consultant; b. Winnipeg, Man., Can., July 19, 1922; s. Charles Victor and Jessie Winifred (Cochrane) C.; m. Marnie Verner, Feb. 10, 1945; children: Peter Verner, Jodie Grace, Victoria Jane, Kelly Speirs. B.Commerce, U. Man., 1950; A.M.P., Harvard U., 1978. Mgr. Carma Developers, Ltd., Calgary, Alta., Can., 1958-68, cons., 1968-72; vice chmn. bd., chief exec. officer Carma, Ltd., Calgary, 1972-82, chmn. bd., 1983—; dir. Mainstream Bldgs., Ltd., Christiana Homes, Inc., San Diego, Alta. Gas Chems., Ltd., Edmonton, Petralgas (N.Z.), Wellington, Alta. Gas Chems. Inc., Parsippany, N.J., Carma Developers, Inc., Houston; pres., dir. EBMOC Mgmt., Ltd. Served as flight lt. RCAF, 1941-45. Decorated D.F.C.; T. Eaton Co. scholar, 1949. Mem. Urban Devel. Inst. (pres. Alta. chpt. 1976-77, plaque 1980), Urban Land Inst. Conservative. Mem. United Ch. Can. Clubs: Silver Springs Golf and Country, Edgemore Racquet (Calgary). Home: 2519 Charlebois Dr NW Calgary ABCanada T2L 0T5 Office: Carma Ltd 6715 8th St NE Calgary AB Canada T2E 7H7

COMBE, JOHN CLIFFORD, JR., lawyer; b. New Orleans, Jan. 5, 1939; s. John Clifford and Gladys Ann (Reine) C.; m. Lynne Wendel Watson, July 11, 1964; children: John, Wendy, Holly. B.B.A., Tulane U., 1960, LL.B., 1965. Bar: La. 1965, U.S. Dist. Cts. (ea. and mid. dists.) La. 1965, U.S. Ct. Appeals (5th cir.) 1965, U.S. Supreme Ct. 1971, U.S. Ct. Appeals (11th cir.) 1981. Assoc. Jones, Walker, Waichter, Poitevent, Carrere & Denegre, New Orleans, 1965-70, ptnr., 1970—. Editor: La. Bar Jour., 1975-77; contbr. articles to legal jours. Organizer and mem. Crestmont Park Improvement Assn.; chmn. St. Catherine of Sienna Parish Liturgy Com., 1976-78; organizer Greater New Orleans Law Explorer Program Boy Scouts Am., 1974; mem. St. Catherine of Sienna Parish Sch. Bd., 1976—, Christian Bros. Found., 1975-78, Serra Club of Greater New Orleans. Served to lt. USN, 1960-62. Mem. Internat. Assn. Ins. Counsel, La. Assn. Def. Counsel (speaker 1973), New Orleans Assn. Def. Counsel (bd. dirs. 1969-75), Am. Judicature Soc. (bd. govs. 1982—), Def. Research Inst. (del. 9th ann. meetings local def. groups 1975, 76), Nat. Conf. Bar Pres., So. Regional Conf. Bar Pres., ABA (ho. of dels. 1982—), La. State Bar Assn. (bd. govs. 1973-74, 75-76, 76-77, 78-80, sec.-treas. 1975-77, pres. 1979-80), Kappa Sigma Alumni Assn. (pres. 1973-74), Phi Delta Phi. Republican. Roman Catholic. Clubs: Metairie Country (La.); Bienville, Cactus; Stratford (New Orleans). Home: 133 Hollywood Dr Metairie LA 70005 Office: 18th Floor 225 Baronne St New Orleans LA 70112

COMBES, BURTON, physician, educator; b. N.Y.C., June 30, 1927; s. Nathan and Helen (White) C.; m. Mollie Hart Allensworth, June 3, 1948; children: Burton, Hilary Elizabeth, Rustin Bradley. A.B., Columbia U., 1947, M.D., 1951. Diplomate: Am. Bd. Internal Medicine. Intern, then asst. resident in medicine Presbyn. Hosp., N.Y.C., 1951-53, asst. physician, 1953-56; USPHS postdoctorate research fellow Columbia U. Coll. Phys. and Surg., 1953-55; research fellow Am. Heart Assn., Columbia U. Coll. Phys. and Surg., 1955-56, Univ. Coll. Hosp. Med. Sch., London, 1956-57; mem. faculty U. Tex. Southwestern Med. Sch., Dallas, 1957—, prof. internal medicine, 1967—; cons. VA, 1965—; mem. gastroenterology and tng. com. NIH,

1972; adv. council Nat. Inst. Arthritis, Metabolism and Digestive Diseases, 1975-80; chmn. bd. Am. Liver Found., 1976-80; mem. Nat. Digestive Diseases Adv. Bd., 1981—. Editorial bd.: Am. Jour. Physiology, 1968-71; editor liver physiology and disease sect.: Gastroenterology, 1977-81. Served with USNR, 1945-47. Mem. Am. Assn. Study Liver Diseases (councillor 1967, pres. 1971), Am. Fedn. Clin. Research, Am. Soc. Clin. Investigation, So. Soc. Clin. Investigation, Central Soc. Clin. Research, Am. Gastroenterol. Assn., Internat. Assn. Study Liver, Assn. Am. Physicians, Soc. Exptl. Biology and Medicine, Sigma Xi, Alpha Omega Alpha. Office: 5323 Harry Hines Blvd Dallas TX 75235

COMBS, BERT THOMAS, lawyer; b. Manchester, Ky., Aug. 13, 1911; s. Stephen Gibson and Martha (Jones) C.; m. Mabel Hall, June 15, 1937; children: Lois Ann Combs Weinberg, Thoms George; m. 2d Helen C. Simons Techtin, Aug. 30, 1969. Student, Cumberland Coll., 1929-31; LL.B., U. Ky., 1937. Bar: Ky. 1937. City atty. City of Prestonburg, Ky., 1950; commonwealth's atty. 31st Jud. Dist. Ky., 1950-51; judge Ct. Appeals of Ky., 1951-55; gov. Commonwealth of Ky., 1959-63; judg U.S. Ct. Appeals (6th cir.), 1967-70; ptnr. Wyatt, Tarrant & Combs, Louisville, 1970—; dir. Forum Group, Inc., Cin., New Orleans, and Tex., Pacific R.R. Co.; bd. dirs. Ky. Export Resources Authority, Ky Funeral Dirs. Burial Assn., Inc.; mem. ACDA, 1978-80. Served to capt. AUS, 1941-46. Decorated Bronze Star, Medal of Merit, Philippines; recipient Joseph P. Kennedy Internat. award, 1963; named Ky.'s Outstanding Atty., 1964. Fellow Am. Bar Found.; mem. Order of Coif, Phi Delta Phi. Democrat. Baptist. Lodge: Masons. Office: 2600 Citizens Plaza Louisville KY 40202

COMBS, CLARENCE MURPHY, anatomist, educator; b. Louisville, Apr. 13, 1925; s. C.H. and Mary (Murphy) C.; m. Virginia Lee Thompson, Aug. 24, 1946 (div. Oct. 1964); children: Jeanne Marie, Stephen Murphy, Nancy Clare. A.B., Transylvania U., 1946; M.S., Northwestern U., 1948, Ph.D., 1950. Instr. W.Va. U. Med. Sch., 1948; Ward fellow Northwestern U. Med. Sch., 1946-50, faculty, 1950-66, prof. anatomy, 1963-66, mem. faculty Grad. Sch., 1962-66; prof., chmn. dept. anatomy Chgo. Med. Sch., 1966-76, acting dean Sch. Grad. and Postdoctoral Studies, 1975-76, prof. anatomy, 1966—; asso. prof. U. P.R. Med. Sch., 1958-60; chief sect. perinatal physiology Nat. Inst. Neurol. Disease and Blindness, San Juan, P.R., 1958-60, spl. cons., 1958; Spl. lectr. Ill. State Psychopathic Inst., 1954-58. Editorial bd.: Dorland's Med. Dictionary, 1965; revision of Parr's Med. Ency., 1976; editor: Webster's Illus. Med. Ency., 1980. USPHS Sr. Research fellow, 1959-61; recipient Research Career Devel. award USPHS, 1961-64, Outstanding Basic Sci. Prof. award Chgo. Med. Sch., 1970, 80, 81, 83, 84, Disting. Alumni citation in Sci. Transylvania U., 1970, Alumni Disting. Achievement award, 1980. Mem. Am. Assn. Anatomists, Soc. for Neurosci., Internat. Brain Research Orgn., AAUP, AAAS, Biol. Stain Commn., Sigma Xi. Research, publs. on relationships between cerebellum and other parts of central and peripheral nervous systems, interconnections between cerebral cortex and diencephalon, gross structure of spinal cord segments, neurophysiol. regulation lingual movement. Home: 1706 Washington St Evanston IL 60202 Office: 3333 Green Bay Rd North Chicago IL 60064

COMBS, HARRY BENJAMIN, aircraft company executive; b. Denver, Jan. 27, 1913; s. Albert Henry and Mildred (Berger) C.; m. Virginia Prout, Feb. 28, 1956; children: Harry Benjamin, Anthony, Clara (Mrs. Christopher Moore). B.S., Yale, 1935; postgrad., Colo. U., 1927-38. Salesman Pan Am. Airways, N.Y.C., 1935-37; with Bosworth Chaunte-Loughridge & Co. (investment bankers), Denver, 1937-39; owner, pres. Combs Aircraft, Inc., Denver, 1939-66; chmn. bd., adviser Gates Aviation & Combs Aircraft, Inc., Denver, 1966-72; pres., dir. Gates Learjet Corp., Wichita, Kans., 1972—; dir. Kans. State Bank, Wichita. Author: Kill Devil Hill, Secret of the Wright Brothers (Aviation Writers Assn. writing award for best non-fiction book 1979). Colo. dir. CD, 1951-54; mem. Yale Scholarship Com., 1951, Yale Alumni Bd., 1962, Project Beacon Com., 1961, Colo. Water Pollution Bd., 1965-72, Colo. Game and Fish Commn., 1965-72; chmn. Colo. Game and Fish Commn., 1971. Served to 1st lt. USAAF, 1944-45. Mem. Nat. Air Trade Assn. (Colo. chmn. 1946-49), Gen. Aviation and Mfg. Assn. (dir. 1973—, Aviation Man of Yr. award 1974), Soc. Free Space Floaters, Conquistadores del Cielo, Lafayette Flying Corps (hon.), Delta Psi. Clubs: Denver, Denver Country, Arlberg Ski (Denver); Rollings Hills Country, Wichita Country, Wichita (Wichita, Kans.); Wings, Yale, New York; Nat. Aviation (Washington); Mach II, OX 5. Home: 2552 E Alameda Ave Denver CO 80209 Office: Gates Learjet Corp PO Box 1289 Wichita KS 67201

COMBS, THOMAS NEAL, lawyer; b. Dallas, Nov. 30, 1942; s. Thomas James and Edith (Gibson) C.; m. Dorothy Elaine Bell, Mar. 12, 1965; children—Thomas Neal, James, John. J.D. with honors, So. Meth. U., 1968. Bar: D.C. bar 1968, U.S. Supreme Ct. bar 1975, Mich. bar 1976. Asso. firm Alston, Miller & Gaines, Washington, 1968-70, Marmet & Webster, 1970-73; asso., partner firm Webster, Kilcullen & Chamberlain, Washington, 1973-75; v.p., gen. counsel, sec. Fruehauf Corp., Detroit, 1975—; dir. Fruehauf Fin. Co., Fruehauf Internat. Ltd., Fruehauf Can., Kelsey Hayes Can.; lectr. various tax insts., 1968—. Contbr. articles to profl. publs. Bd. visitors So. Meth. U. Sch. Law. Mem. Am., Mich. bar assns., Bar Assn. D.C., D.C. Bar, Am. Judicature Soc., Am. Soc. Corp. Secs., Order of Coif. Clubs: Metropolitan (Washington); Detroit, Detroit Athletic, Country of Detroit. Home: 30 Elm Ct Grosse Pointe Farms MI 48236 Office: 10900 Harper Ave Detroit MI 48232

COMCHOC, RUDOLPH A., wholesale and retail grocery company executive; b. Ambridge, Pa., 1935; married. B.B.A., U. Cin., 1959. Store mgr., supr. The Kroger Co., 1959-67; supr. Allied Supermarkets Inc., 1967-70; dir. mdse. Giant Food Inc., 1970-74; field rep., dir. mdse. P A & S Small Co., 1974-76, gen. mgr., 1976—; v.p. York div. S.M. Flickinger Co. Inc., Buffalo, 1978-81, exec. v.p. div. ops., 1981—. Served with N.G., 1953-54. Office: SM Flickinger Co Inc 45 Azalea Dr Box 1086 Gardenville Indsl Park Buffalo NY 14240 *

COMDEN, BETTY, writer, dramatist, lyricist, performer; b. Bklyn., May 3, 1919; d. Leo and Rebecca (Sadvoransky) C.; m. Steven Kyle, Jan. 4, 1942; children: Susanna, Alan. Student, Bklyn. Ethical Culture Sch., Erasmus Hall High Sch.; B.S., N.Y. U. Writer, performer nightclub act, Revuers; writer: (with Adolph Green) book and lyrics Broadway shows On the Town, 1944-45, Billion Dollar Baby, Two on the Aisle, Bells are Ringing, Fade-Out—Fade-In, Subways are for Sleeping, A Doll's Life, 1982 (Tony nomination); (with Adolph Green) lyrics for Hallelujah, Baby!; screen plays Auntie Mame; (performed with A. Green in show of their works) screenplay and lyrics for A Party, 1959, 77; co-author: book for Applause, 1970; also appeared in: On the Town, 1944; lyricist, dir.: (with Adolph Green) "Lorelei", 1973; book and lyrics On the 20th Century, 1978 (Recipient Donaldson award and Tony award for Wonderful Town, as co-lyricist best score 1953, Tony award for Hallelujah, Baby, as co-writer best score 1968, Tony award for Applause 1970, Tony award for lyrics and book On the 20th Century, Woman of Achievement award N.Y. U. Alumnae Assn. 1978, N.Y.C. Mayor's award Art and Culture 1978, named to Songwriters Hall of Fame 1980). Recipient Donaldson award and Tony award for Wonderful Town, as co-lyricist best score, 1953. Mem. Dramatists Guild (council). Office: care The Dramatists Guild 234 W 44th St New York NY 10036

COME, ARNOLD BRUCE, emeritus seminary president; b. Lansing, Mich., Mar. 9, 1918; s. Edward Peter and Maude (McAllister) C.; m. Elizabeth Leota McClure, Sept. 9, 1942; children: Arnold Bruce, Lee McClure. A.B., Mich. State U., 1939; Th.B., Princeton Theol. Sem., 1942, Th.D., 1946. Ordained to ministry Presbyterian Ch., 1942; pastor Robert Grand Meml. Presbyn. Ch., Phila., 1942-45; teaching fellow Princeton Theol. Sem., 1945-46; prof. philosophy and religion Centre Coll. of Ky., 1946-52; prof. systematic theology San Francisco Theol. Sem., 1952-82, pres., 1967-82, pres. emeritus, 1982—; sr. assoc. Westminster Coll., Cambridge U., 1982; vis. lectr. United Theol. Coll. and U., Sydney, Australia, 1983; mem. dept. on laity World Council Chs., 1966-68; mem. Theol. Commn.,World Presbyn. Alliance, 1955-65; mem. bd. Christian edn. United Presbyn. Ch. U.S.A., 1968-71; mem. Council on Evangelism, 1967-70, Council Theol. Sems., 1966—, Gen. Assembly Mission Council, 1979—; chief organizer Pacific Basin Theol. Network, 1977. Author: Human Spirit, Holy Spirit, 1959, Agents of Reconciliation, 1960, An Introduction to Barth's Dogmatics for Preachers, 1963, Drinking: A Christian Position, 1964, Reluctant Revolution, 1965. Carnegie research grantee, 1950; Am. Assn. Theol. Schs. fellow, 1959-60. Mem. Phi Kappa Tau, Phi Kappa Phi, Omicron Delta Kappa. Home: 1107 S Eliseo Greenbrae CA 94904

COME, DONALD ROBERT, social scientist; b. Lansing, Mich., Mar. 21, 1921; s. Edward Peter and Maude Fannie (McAllister) C.; m. Mary Frances Bush, Dec. 14, 1952. B.A., Mich. State U., 1942; M.A., Duke U., 1943; Ph.D., Princeton U., 1949; J.D., Thomas M. Cooley Law Sch., 1976. Mem. faculty L.I. U., 1946-47; mem. faculty Mich. State U., East Lansing, 1947—, chmn. dept. social sci., 1975—, asst. dean for acad. affairs Coll. Social Sci., 1980—; mem. com. on devel. of social scis. Coll. Bd., 1978—. Author: (with Paul L. Dressel) Impact of Federal Support of Science on the Publicly Supported Universities and Colleges in Michigan, 1969; Editor, contbg. author: Mich. State U. Social Sci. Series, Vols. 1-4, 1962; contbg. author to: Readings in Social Science, 1958. NSF grantee, 1967-69. Mem. Nat. Assn. Liberal and Gen. Studies, Am. Bar Assn., Phi Kappa Phi, Pi Kappa Phi. Democrat. Presbyterian. Home: 1425 Sunnyside Ave Lansing MI 48910 Office: Coll Social Sci Mich State U East Lansing MI 48824

COMEGYS, WALKER BROCKTON, lawyer; b. Oklahoma City, July 30, 1929; s. Walker B. and Dorcas (McConnell) C.; m. Adelaide M. Eicks, June 19, 1954; children: Elizabeth Lee, Catherine. B.A. with honors, U. Tex., 1951; LL.B., Harvard U., 1954. Bar: Mass. 1955, D.C. 1972, U.S. Supreme Ct. 1970. Asso. Goodwin, Procter & Hoar, Boston, 1954-64, partner, 1964-69; dep. asst. atty. gen. antitrust Dept. Justice, Washington, 1969-72, asst. atty. gen. antitrust, 1972; ptnr. Powers & Hall P.C., Boston, 1975-79, dir., 1979-84; sole practice, Boston, 1984—; lectr. Boston U. Sch. Law, 1984—; U.S. del. OECD, Paris, 1970, 72; chmn. New Eng. Antitrust Conf., 1967, 68, co-chmn., 1983, 84. Adv. bd. editors: Antitrust Bull., 1967-69; contbr.: ABA Antitrust Section Antitrust Law Developments, 2d edit., 1984. Mem. Bd. Zoning Appeals, Town of Wenham (Mass.), 1972—; bd. overseers Met. Center Performing Arts, Boston, 1981-84, Wang Center Performing Arts, 1984—. Mem. ABA (chmn. Sherman act com. antitrust sect. 1966-69, mem. council antitrust sect. 1972-76), Internat. Bar Assn. (com. 1984—), Boston Bar Assn. (chmn. antitrust com. 1968-69), N.Y. State Bar Assn., Fed. Bar Assn. Home: 202 Main St Wenham MA 01984 Office: One Boston Pl Suite 945 Boston MA 02108

COMER, DONALD, III, investment company executive, photographic processing company executive; b. N.Y.C., June 23, 1938; s. Donald and Isabel (Anderson) C.; m. Jane Stephens, May 4, 1962; children: Jason Legare, Luke McDonald, Carrie St. George. B.S., U. Ala., 1962. With Cowikee Mills, Eufaula, Ala., 1962-82, plant mgr., 1965-66, v.p., 1966-68, pres., treas., dir., 1968-82; pres., dir. Aurizon Inc., 1982—, Photocraft Inc., 1982—; past pres., treas., dir. Avondale Mills, Sylacauga, Ala.; dir. Techsonic Industries, Eufaula, Amsouth; adv. dir. Southeast div. Am. Mut. Ins. Cos., Boston. Bd. dirs. Ala. Safety Council; past chmn. Ala. Ethics Commn. Served with USAF, 1961-64. Club: Mountain Brook Country (Birmingham). Home: 3152 Pine Ridge Rd Birmingham AL 35213

COMER, DONALD, JR., textile co. exec.; b. Birmingham, Ala., May 18, 1913; s. Donald and Gertrude (Miller) C.; m. Isabel Anderson, Oct. 29, 1936; children: Donald III, Isabel Anderson. With Avondale Mills, Sylacauga, Ala., 1932—, exec. v.p., 1954-70, pres., chief exec. officer, treas., 1970-75, chmn. bd., chief exec. officer, 1975—, also dir.; with Cowikee Mills, Eufaula, Ala., 1943—, treas., pres., 1956-67, chmn. bd., 1967-75; chmn. 1st Fed. Savs. & Loan Assn., Sylacauga, Home Fed. Savs. & Loan Assn., Birmingham, Am. Mut. Liability Ins. Co., Wakefield, Mass., Associated Industries Ala.; dir. Am. South Bancorp.; adv. bd. Chem. Bank, N.Y.C. Past bd. dirs. Birmingham YMCA; bd. govs. Ala. Assn. Ind. Colls.; past pres. Chocolocco council Boy Scouts Am.; mem. exec. com. Southeastern Region; trustee So. Research Soc., Am. Bible Soc.; dir. Ala. div. Laymen's Nat. Bible Com.; chmn., bd. dirs. Sylacauga Recreation Dept.; bd. visitors U. Ala., mem. pres.'s council, Birmingham. Recipient Silver Beaver award, Silver Antelope award Boy Scouts Am.; Textile award N.Y. Bd. of Trade, 1974; Ala. Acad. of Honor award; Textileer award Ala. Textile Mfrs. Assn. Mem. Am. Textile Mfrs. Inst. (pres. 1973-74, 83-84), Internat. Textile Mfrs. Inst. (1st v.p.), Birmingham C. of C. (past dir.), Ala. C. of C. (pres. 1980, 81). Home: Comer Hill Sylacauga AL 35150 Office: Avondale Mills Avondale Ave Sylacauga AL 35150

COMER, EVAN PHILIP, manufacturing company executive; b. Cumberland Gap, Tenn., May 29, 1927; s. Evan Mitchell and Margaret Nola (Estep) C.; m. Mary Blanc, Aug. 28, 1948; children: Vivian, Jane Comer Beckner. B.A., Carson-Newman Coll., Jefferson City, Tenn., 1948; M.A., Columbia U., 1949. Asst. prof. psychology, dir. student personnel and placement Furman U., Greenville, S.C., 1949-52; self-employed writer, 1952-53; supervisory conf. leader Union Carbide Nuclear Co., Oak Ridge, 1953-55; instr. in-plant tng. U. Tenn., Knoxville, 1955-56; with Foote Mineral Co., 1956-67, 69—, v.p., gen. mgr. chems. and minerals div., 1970-80, pres., chief exec. officer, Exton, Pa., 1980-84, also dir.; pres. Southeastern Community Coll., Whiteville, N.C., 1967-69; mem. Pa. adv. bd. Liberty Mut. Ins. Co.; exec. com. Phila. Mfrs. Mut. Ins. Co.; dir. PMMI.; Mem. adv. bd. Carson-Newman Coll.; mem. bd. Pa. Sci. and Engring. Found.; mem. Pa. Gov.'s Sci. Adv. Com.; mem. adv. council Pa. Tech. Assistance Program, Pa. State U. Contbr. articles to bus. and industry publs. Chmn. bd. Chester County Pvt. Industry Council, 1983-84. Served with USNR, 1945-46. Mem. AIME, Ferroalloys Assn. (Chmn. bd. dirs. 1983—), Am. Mining Congress. Republican. Baptist. Club: Mining (N.Y.C.). Office: Foote Mineral Co Route 100 Exton PA 19341

COMER, JAMES PIERPONT, psychiatrist; b. East Chicago, Ind., Sept. 25, 1934; s. Hugh and Maggie (Nichols) C.; m. Shirley Ann Arnold, June 20, 1959; children—Brian Jay, Dawn Renee. A.B., Ind. U., 1956; M.D., Howard U., 1960; M.P.H., U. Mich., 1964. Served with USPHS, Washington and Chevy Chase, Md., 1961-68; intern St. Catherine's Hosp., East Chicago, 1960-61; resident Yale Sch. Medicine, 1964-67; asst. prof. psychiatry Yale Child Study Center and dept. psychiatry, 1968-70, asso. prof., 1970-75, prof., 1975—, Maurice Falk prof. psychiatry, 1976—; asso. dean Yale Med. Sch., New Haven, 1969—; dir. pupil services Baldwin-King Sch. Project, New Haven; dir. Conn. Energy Corp.; trustee Conn. Savs. Bank; cons. Joint Commn. on Mental Health of Children, Nat. Commn. on Causes and Prevention of Violence, NIMH; mem. nat. adv. mental health council HEW; Henry J. Kaiser Sr. fellow Center for Advanced Study in the Behavioral Scis., Stanford, 1976-77. Author: Beyond Black and White, 1972, Black Child Care, 1975, School Power, 1980; Editorial bd.: Am. Jour. Orthopsychiatry, 1970-76, Youth and Adolescence, Jour. Negro Edn; columnist: Parents mag; Contbr. articles to profl. jours. Bd. dirs. Dixwell Soul Sta. and, Yale Afro-Am. House, Children's TV Workshop; trustee Wesleyan U.; mem. profl. adv. council Nat. Assn. Mental Health; mem. ad hoc adv. com. Conn. Research commn. Recipient Child Study Assn.-Wel-Met Family Life book award, 1975; Howard U. Disting. Alumni award, 1976; John and Mary Markle Found. scholar, 1969—; Rockefeller Public Service award, 1980; Media award NCCJ, 1981. Mem. AMA, Am. Psychiat. Assn., Am. Orthopsychiat. Assn., Am. Acad. Child Psychiatry, NAACP, Black Coalition of New Haven, Alpha Omega Alpha, Alpha Phi Alpha. Home: 21 Kent Dr North Haven CT 06517 Office: 333 Cedar St New Haven CT 06510 *As a black child, I sometimes had doubts about my future opportunities for success in our predominantly white country. My parents counselled me never to let the issue of race stand in my way; that the time of greater opportunity for blacks would come. They advised me to work hard, prepare myself, to strive to be the best or among the best in every undertaking, and at the same time be respectful of all people, regardless of their abilities, race, beliefs, or station in life. I have lived by this advice and it has served me well. I have learned not to strive for top position but to let my work take me where it will in line with my interests.*

COMEY, DALE RAYMOND, insurance company executive; b. Attleboro, Mass., Mar. 26, 1941; s. Charles and Evelyn (Chagot) C.; m. Marilyn A. Phillips, Apr. 8, 1967; children: Adam, Rachel, Zachary. B.S., U. Conn., 1963. Various actuarial positions Hartford Ins. Group, 1965-69; asst. actuary Hartfold Ins. Group, 1970-71, assoc. actuary, 1971-72, actuary, 1972-74, asst. v.p., 1974-76, v.p., 1976-79, sr. v.p., 1980-83; exec. v.p. Hartford Ins. Group, 1983—. Served as capt. U.S. Army, 1963-65. Fellow Casualty Actuarial Soc.; mem. Am. Acad. Actuaries. Office: Hartford Ins Group Hartford Plaza Hartfold CT 06115

COMEY, J. MARTIN, pharmaceutical company executive; b. N.Y.C., Feb. 7, 1934; s. John J. and Anna May (McCann) C.; m. Margaret A. Doyle, Jan. 17, 1957; children—Rita, James, Peter, Deirdre, Louise, Anne, Christopher, Margaret. B.S. in Accounting, Fordham U., 1957; M.B.A. in Corporate Fin, NYU, 1965. Auditor Eckes & Dean (C.P.A.s), N.Y.C., 1957-60; tax acct. Sperry Rand Corp., N.Y.C., 1960-62; tax mgr. Pet, Inc., St. Louis, 1962-66; tax dir. Schering-Plough Corp., Kenilworth, N.J., 1966-75, treas., 1976—, v.p., 1979—; mem. bd. mgrs. Provident Savs. Bank, Jersey City. Trustee Mountainside Hosp., Montclair, N.J. Mem. Am. Inst. C.P.A.s, N.J., N.Y. socs. C.P.A.s, Fin. Execs. Inst. Office: 2000 Galloping Hill Rd Kenilworth NJ 07033

COMFORT, ALEXANDER, medical biologist, author; b. London, Eng., Feb. 10, 1920; came to U.S., 1974; s. Alexander Charles and Daisy Elizabeth (Fenner) C.; m. Jane Tristram Henderson, June 8, 1973; 1 son by previous marriage, Nicholas Alfred Fenner. B.A., Trinity Coll., Cambridge (Eng.) U., 1943, M.B., B.Ch., 1944, M.A., 1945; Ph.D., London U., 1949, D. Sc., 1962, D.C.H., 1946. Licentiate Royal Coll. Physicians. House physician London Hosp., 1944; resident Royal Waterloo Hosp., London, 1945-46; lectr. physiology London Hosp., 1948-51; Nuffield Research fellow Univ. Coll. London, 1951-65; head Med. Research Council Group on Aging, 1965-72, dir. research, 1972-74; sr. fellow Inst. Higher Studies, Santa Barbara, Calif., 1975—; lectr. dept. psychiatry Stanford, 1974-83; prof. dept. pathology U. Calif. Med. Sch., Irvine, 1976-78; adj. prof. Neuropsychiat. Inst., UCLA, 1979—; cons. geriatric psychiatry Brentwood VA Hosp., Los Angeles. Author: (with Jane T. Comfort) The Facts of Love; numerous others.; Editor: Experimental Gerontology, 1965—; Contbr. articles to profl. jours. Recipient Karger Meml. prize in gerontology, 1969. Mem. Royal Coll. Surgeons, Coll. Physicians and Surgeons (Sask.), Royal Soc. Medicine (London), Brit. Soc. Research on Aging (pres. 1969). Office: 683 Oak Grove Dr Santa Barbara CA 93108

COMFORT, CLAYTON LEE, marine corps officer; b. Wells, Kans., Feb. 20, 1930; s. Levi Lawrence and OpalMatilda (Plunkett) C.; m. Ardis June Bruce, Mar. 1, 1960; children: Anne Frances, Lawrence Jay, Rebecca Lee. B.S. in Archtl. Engring., U. Kans., 1953; M.S. in Aero. Engring., U.S. Naval Postgrad. Sch., 1963; postgrad., U.S. Army War Coll., 1974-75. Commd. 2d lt. U.S. Marine Corps, advanced through grades to brig. gen., 1978; comdg. officer Marine Air Base Squadron 11, Danang, Vietnam, 1970-71, All-Weather Attack Squadro 332, Cherry Point, N.C., 1971-72; br. head weapons systems br. Dept. Aviation, Washington, 1975-78; asst. wing comdr. 3D Marine Aircraft Wing, MCAS El Toro, Santa Ana, Calif., 1978-80, comdg. gen., 1982—. Decorated Bronze Star medal with combat V, Meritorious Service medal, Air medal with numeral 2, Navy Commendation medal. Home: Quarters A MCAS El Toro Santa Ana CA 92709 Office: Third Marine Aircraft Wing FMF MCAS El Toro Santa Ana CA 92709

COMFORT, JOHN, headmaster; b. Pelham, N.Y., Nov. 23, 1928; s. Harold Wesley and Lillian (Whitely) C.; m. Sally Bayne Smith, June 19, 1948; children: John, Cynthia Lynn, Jeffrey Wesley, Sally Bayne. Grad., Deerfield Acad., 1946; B.A. cum laude, Williams Coll., 1950; M.A., Columbia U., 1960. Tchr. Greenwich (Conn.) Country Day Sch., 1950-56; head upper sch. Sewickley (Pa.) Acad., 1956-58; founding headmaster Ensworth Sch., Nashville, 1958-64; headmaster Graland Country Day Sch., Denver, 1964-75, St. Martin's P.E. Sch., Metairie, La., 1975-80, St. Anne's Episcopal Sch., Denver, 1980—; Mem. Gov.'s Commn. Status Women in Colo., 1971-73; mem. nat. devel. council George Peabody Coll., Nashville, 1972—. Bd. dirs. Boys Clubs Denver, 1971-75, 80—; trustee Loretto Heights Coll., Denver, 1970-75. Mem. Nat. Assn. Ind. Schs. (dir. 1971-76), Nat. Assn. Episcopal Schs. (dir. 1983—), Country Day Sch. Headmasters Assn., Nat. Assn. Prins. Schs. for Girls, Phi Beta Kappa, Psi Upsilon. Club: South Boulder Park Ecol. Assn. Address: 3086 S Trenton St Denver CO 80231

COMFORT, THOMAS EDWIN, educator; b. Streator, Ill., Apr. 15, 1921; s. Patrick James and Jane (Dickinson) C.; m. Evelyn Lorraine Trotter, Oct. 1, 1945; children—Thomas Edwin, Judith Ann, Patrick James, Kathleen Ann, Michael James. A.B., Northwestern U., 1943; A.M., U. Ill., 1951, Ph.D., 1954. Self-employed as ins. broker, 1945-47; instr. Latin, Greek, French and English St. Ambrose Coll., Davenport, Iowa, 1947-48; instr. French U. Ill., 1949-54; mem. faculty Tex. A. and M. U., 1954-58, 61, 63-65, asso. prof. French, 1957-65; dir. English lang. program, Morocco, 1958-60; dir. Turkish Air Force Lang. Sch., Izmir, 1961-63; prof. French Ill. State U., Normal, 1965—; Vice pres. Tex. Acad. Sci., 1957. Served to lt. (j.g.) USNR, 1943-46; PTO. Bonbright scholar in langs. and lit., 1942-43. Mem. Am. Assn. Tchrs. French, Am. Council Teaching Fgn. Langs., Modern Lang. Assn., Am. Assn. U. Profs., Phi Beta Kappa, Phi Eta Sigma, Eta Sigma Phi. Home: Towanda IL 61776

COMFORT, WILLIAM TWYMAN, JR., banker; b. Ellsworth, Kan., Aug. 3, 1937; s. William Twyman and Leoti Dora (Shackleford) C.; m. Nathalie Pierrepont, June 6, 1964; children: Nathalie Pierrepont, William Twyman III, James Theodore, Stuyvesant Pierrepont. B.A.,

Okla. U., 1959, LL.B., 1961; LL.M., NYU, 1964. With W.E. Hutton & Co., N.Y.C., 1962-73, partner, 1969-73, sr. v.p., 1973-74, Citibank, N.Y.C., 1974—; exec. dir. Citicorp Internat. Bank Ltd., London, 1976-78; chmn. bd. Kirk Corp., Balt., 1972-74; chmn., pres. Citicorp Venture Capital Ltd., Citicorp Capital Investors Ltd.; dir. Pa. Va. Corp., Phila., James River Corp. of Va., Safeguard Bus. Systems, King of Prussia, Pa. Served with U.S. Army, 1961. N.Y. Bar Assn., Okla. Bar Assn. Clubs: Piping Rock (Locust Valley, N.Y.); Racquet and Tennis. Home: Duck Pond Rd Locust Valley NY 11560 Office: 399 Park Ave New York NY 10043

COMFORT, WILLIAM WISTAR, mathematics educator; b. Bryn Mawr, Pa., Apr. 19, 1933; s. Howard and Elizabeth (Webb) C.; m. Mary Constance Lyon, Mar. 30, 1957; children—Martha Wistar, Howard III. B.A., Haverford Coll., 1954; M.S., U. Wash., 1957, Ph.D., 1958; M.A. (hon.), Wesleyan U., Middletown, Conn., 1969. Teaching asst., research asst. U. Wash., 1954-58; B. Peirce instr. Harvard, 1958-61; asst. prof. U. Rochester, 1961-65; asso. prof. U. Mass., 1965-67; prof. math. Wesleyan U., Middletown, 1967—, Edward Burr Van Vleck prof. math., 1982—, chmn. dept., 1969-70, 80-82; vis. prof. U. Ark., 1965, McGill U., Montreal, 1970-71, U. Heidelberg, 1974, Istituto Matematico Leonida Tonelli, Pisa, Italy, 1974, Athens U., 1978, Universidad Nacional Autonome de Mex., 1983; Mem. Internat. Congress Mathematicians, Russia, 1966. Author: (with S. Negrepontis) The Theory of Ultrafilters, 1974, Continuous Pseudometrics, 1975, Chain Conditions in Topology, 1982; Editorial bd.: Procs. Am. Math. Soc, 1972-75; mng. editor, 1974-75; Editorial bd.: Topology Procs., 1976—, Am. Math. Monthly, 1983—; Contbr. articles to profl. jours. Bd. mgrs. Haverford Coll., 1971-74; trustee Ind. Day Sch., Middlefield, Conn., 1972-75. Recipient Excellence-in-teaching award U. Rochester, 1966. Mem. Math. Assn. Am., Am. Math. Soc. (council 1972-75, 83—, assoc. sec. Eastern region 1983—), Assn. Symbolic Logic, N.Y. Acad. Scis., Conn. Acad. Scis. and Engring., Phi Beta Kappa. Mem. Soc. of Friends. Home: 26 Pine St Middletown CT 06457 Office: Wesleyan U Middletown CT 06457

COMINGS, DAVID EDWARD, physician; b. Beacon, N.Y., Mar.8, 1935; s. Edward Walter and Jean (Rice) C.; m. Shirley Nelson, Aug. 9, 1958; children: Mark David, Scott Edward, Karen Jean.; m. Brenda Gursey, Mar. 20, 1982. Student, U. Ill., 1951-54; B.S., Northwestern U., 1955, M.D., 1958. Intern Cook County Hosp., Chgo., 1958-59, resident in internal medicine, 1959-62; fellow in med. genetics U. Wash., Seattle, 1964-66; dir. dept. med. genetics City of Hope Med. Center, Duarte, Calif., 1966—; mem. genetics study sect. NIH, 1974-78; mem. sci. adv. bd. Hereditary Disease Found., 1975—, Nat. Found. March of Dimes, 1978—. Editor: (with others) Molecular Human Cytogenetics, 1977, Am. Jour. Human Genetics, 1979—; editorial bd.: Cytogenetics and Cell genetics, 1979—. Served with U.S. Army, 1962-64. NIH grantee, 1967—. Mem. Assn. Am. Physicians, Am. Soc. Clin. Investigation, AAAS, Am. Soc. Human Genetics (dir. 1974-78), Am. Soc. Cell Biology, Am. Fedn. Clin. Research, Western Soc. Clin. Research, Council Biology Editors. Office: City of Hope Med Center 1500 E Duarte Rd Duarte CA 91010

COMINI, ALESSANDRA, art historian, educator; b. Winona, Minn., Nov. 24, 1934; d. Raiberto and Megan (Laird) C. B.A., Barnard Coll., 1956; M.A., U. Calif., Berkeley, 1964; Ph.D. with distinction, Columbia U., 1969. Teaching asst. U. Calif., Berkeley, 1964, vis. instr., 1967; preceptor Columbia U., 1965-66, 67-68, instr., 1968-69, asst. prof., 1969-74; vis. asst. prof. So. Methodist U., summers 1970, 72, assoc. prof. art history, 1974-75, prof., 1975—, Univ. disting. prof., 1983—; Alfred Hodder resident humanist Princeton U., 1972-73; vis. asst. prof. Yale U., 1973; vis. humanist various univs., lectr. in English, German and Italian at various univs. and museums in, U.S., Eng., Italy, Germany, and Austria; panelist NEH Museums and Public Programs, 1978—. Author: Schiele in Prison, 1973, Egon Schiele's Portraits, 1974 (Nat. Book award nominee 1975), Gustav Klimt, 1975, also German, French and Dutch edits, Egon Schiele, 1976, also German, French and Dutch edits, The Fantastic Art of Vienna, 1978, The Changing Image of Beethoven, 1985; contbr. numerous articles to Arts Mag., also; author various catalogue introductions. Recipient Charles Rufus Morey Book award Coll. Art Assn. Am., 1976, Laural award AAUW, 1979; named Outstanding Prof., 1977, 79, 83; AAUW travel fellow, 1966-67; Nat. Endowment for Humanities grantee, 1975. Mem. ASCAP, Coll. Art Assn. Am. (dir. 1980—), Women's Caucus for Art (dir. 1974—), Tex. Inst. Letters. Democrat. Home: 2900 McFarlin Dallas TX 75205 Office: Dept Art History So Meth U Dallas TX 75255

COMISKEY, EDWARD ALAN, advertising agency executive; b. N.Y.C., Apr. 1, 1942; s. Edward John and Eleanore (Kurtz) C.; m. Nina Knoblauch, July 3, 1965; children: Carolyn, Elisabeth, Kathryn. A.B., Dartmouth Coll., 1963. Sales specialist Campbell Sales Co., Camden, N.J., 1964-66; sr. v.p. Young & Rubicam Inc., N.Y.C., 1966—. Office: Young Rubicam Inc 285 Madison Ave New York NY 10017

COMISKEY, JAMES AUGUST, banker; b. New Orleans, Oct. 16, 1926; s. James Edward and Laura (Arceneaux) C.; m. Blanche Catherine Mouledoux, Aug. 20, 1952; children: Margaret, Marian, James, Laura, Michelle, Jeanne, Eileen, Paula, Louise, Elizabeth, Catherine. B.A., Loyola U., New Orleans, 1948, J.D., 1951. Bar: La. 1951. U.S. judge Eastern Dist. La., 1967-75; pres. Bank La., New Orleans, 1975—, also dir.; dir. Bank of South, Fidelity Bank and Trust Co. Councilman-at-large, New Orleans, also, pres. council, 1961-62; del. La. Democratic nat. convs., 1956, 60, 64; candidate for mayor, New Orleans, 1962; del. La. Constl. Conv., 1956; Mem. pres.'s council, trustee Loyola U., New Orleans. Served with inf. AUS, 1944-46. Mem. La. Bar Assn., St. Thomas More Catholic Lawyers Assn. Home: 1100 City Park Ave New Orleans LA 70119 Office: 321 St Charles Ave New Orleans LA 70130

COMISKY, MARVIN, lawyer; b. Phila., June 5, 1918; m. Goldie Elving; children: Ian M., Hope A., Matthew J. B.S.C. summa cum laude, Temple U., 1938; LL.B., U. Pa., 1941; LL.D., Dickinson Sch. Law, 1970. Bar: Pa. 1942. Law clk. to presiding justice Pa. Superior Ct., 1941-42; law clk. to presiding justice Pa. Supreme Ct., 1946; assoc. Lemuel B. Schofield, Phila., 1946-54; ptnr. Brumblow & Comisky, 1954-59, Blank, Rome, Comisky & McCauley, Phila., 1959—, mng. ptnr., 1968—; mem. Pa. Bd. Law Examiners, 1974-75; chmn. Pa. Law Enforcement Council, 1968; dir. Continental Bank. Assoc. trustee U. Pa. Law Sch.; bd. dirs. Robin Hood Dell Concerts. Inc., Phila. Geriatric Ctr.; professions chmn. Am. Cancer Soc., 1978. Fellow Am. Bar Found., Am. Coll. Trial Lawyers36, Internat. acad. Trail Lawyers; mem. Phila. Bar Assn. (chancellor 1965), Pa. Bar Assn. (past pres.), ABA (del. 1965, 70), Am. Judicature Soc., Nat. Assn. Def. Lawyers in Criminal Cases, Order of Coif, Beta Gamma Sigma. Office: 1200 Four Penn Ctr Philadelphia PA 19103

COMISSIONA, SERGIU, conductor; b. Bucharest, Rumania, June 16, 1928; s. Isaac and Jean L. (Haufrecht) C.; m. Robinne Florin, July 16, 1949. Ed. music conservatoire, Bucharest; Mus.D. (hon.), Peabody Conservatory Music, 1972; L.H.D. (hon.), Towson State U., 1980; D.F.A. (hon.), Washington Coll., Chestertown, Md., 1980, Western Md. Coll., 1977, U. Md., 1981, Johns Hopkins U., 1982. Mus. dir., Rumanian State Ensemble Orch., 1950-55; prin. condr., Rumanian State Opera, 1955-59; musical dir., Haifa (Israel) Symphony, 1959, Israel Chamber Orch., 1960-65, Goteburg (Sweden) Symphony Orch., 1966-69; mus. adviser, condr., Ulster Orch., Belfast, Ireland, 1967-69; mus. dir., Balt. Symphony Orch., 1969-84; musical adviser, Temple U. Music Festival, 1975-76; artistic dir., 1976-80; music dir., prin. condr., Chautauqua Symphony Orch. Summer Festival, 1976-78; music adviser, Am. Symphony Orch., 1978-82; artistic adviser, Houston Symphony Orch., 1980-82; music dir., Houston Symphony Orch., 1983—; permanent guest condr., Radio Philharm. Orch. of Netherlands, 1982-83; chief condr., Radio Philharm. Orch. of Netherlands, 1983—. Decorated Order Merit 2d Class, Rumania; winner internat. competition for young condrs., Besancon, France, 1956; recipient Gold medal award City of Goteborg, 1973; Ditson Condr.'s award Columbia U., 1979. Mem. Royal Swedish Acad. Music (hon.). Office: 615 Louisiana Baltimore MD 77002

COMITO, FRANK JAMES, association executive; b. Reading, Pa., Dec. 8, 1952; s. Frank James and Charlotte Katherine (Landis) C. B.S. in Edn., Temple U., 1976. Tchr. mktg. Norristown Area High Sch., Pa., 1976-80; coordinator spl. projects St. Thomas-St. John C. of C., St. Thomas, V.I., 1980-82; exec. dir. St. Croix C. of C., V.I., 1982—; bd. dirs. Pvt. Industry Council V.I., 1982; mem. adv. bd. Camp Arawak, St. Croix, V.I., 1983—. Editor: Chamber Rev., 1982—. Chmn. spl. events com. United Way St. Thomas, V.I., 1981; media rep. Bahai's of V.I., 1983. Recipient commendation for youth work Pa. Ho. of Reps., 1980, commendation for community service Valley Forge C. of C., 1980, 1st Place Civic Consciousness award Seven-Up Co., 1980, 1st Place Creative Mktg. Project award Sales Mktg. Execs. Internat., North Atlantic Region, 1980. Mem. Pa. Assn. Mktg. Tchrs. (sec. 1978-80), Distributive Edn. Clubs Am. (trustee Pa. 1978-80), Nat. Assn. Exec. Dirs. Office: St Croix C of C 16Aa Church St Christiansted St Croix VI 00820

COMMES, THOMAS ALLEN, manufacturing company executive; b. Aurora, Ill., May 29, 1942; s. Theodore C. and Ada Marie (Bohrer) C.; m. Diane J. Bartlett, June 19, 1965; children: Jennifer, Elizabeth. B.S., St. Thomas Coll., St. Paul, 1964. C.P.A., Minn. Sr. accountant EDP specialist Haskins & Sells, C.P.A.s, Minn., 1964-69; plant mgr., dir. corp. acctg. Gould Inc., 1968-75; v.p., controller, treas., chief fin. officer W.T. Grant Co., 1975-76; v.p., corp. controller Saks Fifth Ave., N.Y.C., 1976-79; sr. v.p. fin., chief fin. officer Sherwin-Williams Co., Cleve., 1979—, also dir. Mem. Minn. Soc. C.P.A.s. Office: 101 Prospect Ave NW Cleveland OH 44115

COMMIRE, ANNE, playwright; b. Wyandotte, Mich.; d. Robert and Shirley (Moore) C. B.S., Eastern Mich. U., 1961; postgrad., Wayne State U., N.Y. U. Author: plays Shay, 1973, Put Them All Together, 1978, Transatlantic Bridge, 1977, Sunday's Red, 1980, Melody Sisters, 1983; teleplay Rebel for God, 1980; teleplays Hayward's, 1980; editor: Something About the Author, 1970—, Yesterdays Authors of Books for Children, 1977-78. Recipient Eugene O'Neill Theatre award, 1973, 78, 83; Creative Artists Program grantee, 1975; Rockefeller grantee for playwriting, 1979. Mem. Dramatists Guild, Writers Guild Am. Home: 81R Oswegatchie Rd Waterford CT 06385 Office: 274 W 95th St New York NY 10025

COMMON, FRANK BREADON, JR., lawyer; b. Montreal, Can., Apr. 16, 1920; s. Frank Breadon and Ruth Louise (Lang) C.; m. Katharine Ruth Laws, Sept. 7, 1946; children: Katharine Ruth, Anne Elizabeth, Frank Breadon (dec.), Diana Melanie, Ruth Elizabeth, Jane Laws, James Lang. Diploma in engring, Royal Mil. Coll., 1940; B.Civil Law, McGill U., 1948. Bar: created Queen's counsel 1959, Called to Canadian bar 1948. Mem. firm Montgomery, McMichael, Common, Howard, Forsyth & Ker (and successor firms), 1948-68; sr. partner firm Ogilvy & Renault; chmn. bd., dir. Common Cents Ltd., Canadian Corps., Ltd., World Intellectual Properties, Ltd. (Bermuda); chmn. bd., dir. PHH Can. Services Inc., Cadbury Schweppes Powell Ltd.; dir. Royal Bank Can., PHH Group Inc., Balt., Selco Mining Co. Ltd., Ralston Purina Co., Can., N. Am. Car (Can.) Ltd., Ciba-Geigy Can. Ltd. Gov., past pres., chmn. Douglas Hosp.; gov. Montreal Gen. Hosp.; Former alderman City of Westmount, Que.; Exec. com. Canadian Red Cross.; Founder pres. Can. Found. for Ednl. Devel. Served as officer Royal Can. Engrs., 1940-45. Mentioned in despatches. Mem. Can. Bar Assn. (past mem. council), Canadian Tax Found., Mil. Engrs. Assn. Can. (past pres. Montreal br.). Clubs: Mount Royal; Mount Bruno, Brook (N.Y.C.); Bayou (La.). Home: 3940 Cote des Neiges Rd Apt B-101 Montreal PQ Canada H3H 1W2 Office: Suite 1100 1981 McGill College Ave Montreal H3A 3C1 PQ Canada

COMMONER, BARRY, biologist, educator; b. Bklyn., May 28, 1917; s. Isidore and Goldie (Yarmolinsky) C.; m. Lisa Feiner, 1980; children by previous marriage: Lucy Alison, Frederic Gordon. A.B. with honors, Columbia, 1937; M.A., Harvard, 1938, Ph.D., 1941; D.Sc., Hahnemann Med. Coll., 1963, U. Calif., 1967, Grinnell Coll., 1968, Lehigh U., 1969, Williams Coll., 1970, Ripon Coll., 1971, Colgate U., 1972, Cleve. State U., 1980; LL.D., Clark U., 1974. Asst. biology Harvard, 1938-40; instr. biology Queens Coll., 1940-42; asso. editor Sci. Illus., 1946-47; asso. prof. plant physiology Washington U., St. Louis, 1947-53, prof., 1953-76, chmn. dept. botany, 1965-69, dir., 1965-81, Univ. prof. environ. sci., 1976-81; prof. earth and environ. scis. Queens Coll., Flushing, N.Y., 1981—, dir. Center for the Biology of Natural Systems, 1981—; vis. prof. community health Albert Einstein Coll. of Medicine, N.Y.C., 1981—; Pres. St. Louis Com. for Nuclear Info., 1965-66, bd. dirs., 1966—; mem. Nat. Tb Commn. on Air Conservation, 1966-68; bd. dirs. Scientists Inst. Pub. Info., from 1963, co-chmn., 1967-69, chmn., 1969-78, chmn. exec. com., from 1978; chmn. spl. cons. group sonic boom Dept. Interior, 1967-68; adv. council on environ. edn. Office Edn. HEW, 1971; internat. sponsoring com. Chaim Weizmann Centenary Celebration, 1974-75; adv. com. Coalition Health Communities, 1975; mem. sec.'s adv. council U.S. Dept. Commerce, 1976. Author: Science and Survival, 1966, The Closing Circle, 1971 (Phi Beta Kappa award, Internat. prize City of Cervia, Italy), La Technologia del Profitto, 1973, The Poverty of Power, 1976 (Premio Iglesias award, Sardinia, Italy 1978), Ecologia e Lotte Sociali, 1976, l'energia alternativa, 1978, The Politics of Energy, 1979; Editorial bd.: World Book Ency, 1968-73, Environment mag, 1977; mem. adv. bd.: Science Year, 1967-72; editorial adv. bd.: Hon. Chemosphere, from 1972; bd. sponsors: In These Times, 1976—. Bd. cons. experts Rachel Carson Trust for Living Environment, 1967—; adv. com. Center for Devel. Policy, 1978; mem. bd. Univs. Nat. Anti-War Fund; adv. bd. Fund for Peace, 1978; Citizens Party candidate for pres. of U.S., 1980. Served to lt. USNR, 1942-46. Recipient Newcomb Cleveland prize AAAS, 1953; 1st Humanist award Internat. Humanist and Ethical Union, 1970; medal AIA, 1979; decorated comdr. Order of Merit, Italy, 1977. Fellow AAAS (chmn. com. sci. in promotion of human welfare 1958-65, dir. 1967-74, chmn. com. on environ. alterations 1969-72), Am. Sch. Health Assn. (hon.); mem. Soc. Biol. Chemists, Soc. Gen. Physiologists, Am. Soc. Plant Physiologists, Sierra Club, Nat. Parks Assn. (trustee 1968-70), Soil Assn. Eng. (hon. life v.p.), Am. Chem. Soc., Am. Soc. Biol. Chemists, Fedn. Am. Scientists, Ecol. Soc. Am., Inst. Environmental Edn. (trustee), Phi Beta Kappa, Sigma Xi. Office: Queens Coll Center for Biology Natural Systems Flushing NY 11367 *

COMMONS, DORMAN L., shipping company executive; b. Denair, Calif., 1918. Student, Stanford U. Staff acct. John F. Forbes & Co., 1943-47; sr. v.p. Douglas Oil Co., 1947-64, also dir.; sr. v.p. fin. Occidental Petroleum Co., 1964-72; cons. fins., 1972-73; pres., chief exec. officer Natomas Co., San Francisco, 1974—, also dir.; chmn. bd., chief exec. officer Am. Pres. Lines subs. Natomas Co., 1977—, also dir. Office: Natomas Co 601 California St San Francisco CA 94108

COMMONS, KIM STEVEN, chess master; b. Lancaster, Calif., July 23, 1951; s. Howell and Shirley Elanor (Kinney) C. B.S., U. Calif. at Los Angeles, 1973. Instr. chess U. Calif. at Los Angeles extension, 1972-73, Pepperdine U., Malibu, Calif., 1971-72. Master title, 1968, sr. master, 1973, internat. master, 1976; tournaments include 2d pl. Am. Open, 1968, 1st pl., 1974, 75, 1st pl. Pacific Southwest Open, 1969, 72, 1st pl. Los Angeles Open, 1970, 72, 1st pl. Calif. Open, 1972, 1st pl. Calif. Invitational Championship, 1972, 1st pl. Paul Masson Open, 1973, 1st pl. Mid South Open, 1971, 74, 6th pl. U.S. Invitational Jr. Championship, 1971, 1st pl. Fedn. Internat. des Eches internat. chess tournaments, Plovdiv, Bulgaria, 1976, Primorsco, Bulgaria, 1976, Varna, Bulgaria, 1976; mem. U.S. Student Olympic Chess Team, Austria, 1972; mem. 1st pl. U.S. Men's Olympic Chess Team, Haifa (Israel) Chess Olympiad, 1976, individual gold medal for 6th bd.; bronze medal 1st bd. Student Olympics, Mexico City, 1977, also capt.; team capt. U.S. World Youth Olympic Team, 1978; 4th place Internat. Chess Tournament, Lublin, Poland, 1978. *

COMO, PERRY, singer; b. Canonsburg, Pa., May 18; s. Pietro and Lucille (Travaglini) C.; m. Roselle Beline; 3 children. Student pub. schs., Canonsburg. With, Carlone Band, later Ted Weems, 1937; singer night clubs, RCA-Victor Records; screen debut Something for the Boys, 20th Century Fox; motion pictures include If I'm Lucky; star: Perry Como show, NBC-TV, also TV spls. (Named best vocalist Motion Picture Daily TV poll 2-53, Emmy, Peabody, Christopher awards 1956, named personality of year Variety Club 1956); Recordings include Love You So. Decorated knight comdr. Equestrian Order Holy Sepulchre Jerusalem. Address: RCA Records 1133 Ave of the Americas New York NY 10036 *

COMO, WILLIAM MICHAEL, editor; b. Williamstown, Mass., Nov. 10, 1925; s. Michael and Janet (Caporale) C. Merit certificate, Am. Acad. Dramatic Arts, 1947. Sales mgr. Dance Mag., N.Y.C., 1954-60, advt. mgr. and asst. to pub., 1961-69, editor in chief, 1970—, After Dark, the Nat. Mag. of Entertainment, N.Y.C., 1968-79; lectr. on dance. Dancer, actor, N.Y., Calif., 1948-53; Editor: Raoul Gelabert's Anatomy for the Dancer, 1964. Served with AUS, 1944-46. Recipient award Dance Tchr's. Club of Boston, 1974; named hon. lt. col. aide-de-camp Gov. of Ala., 1981; Dancing Ambassadors of Friendship, 1977; honoree Dance Masters of Am., Inc., 1979; A Celebration of Men in Dance, 1981. Office: Danad Pub Co Dance Mag 33 W 60th St New York NY 10023

COMPARIN, ROBERT ANTON, mechanical engineering educator; b. Hurley, Wis., July 25, 1928; s. Anton Joseph and Evelyn S. (Ebli) C.; m. Ida Masone, Aug. 4, 1956; children—Robert J., Evelyn, Thomas, James, Nancy. B.S. in Mech. Engring, Purdue U., 1954, M.S., 1958, Ph.D., 1960. Instr. Purdue U., 1954-60; staff engr. IBM Corp., Endicott, N.Y., Zurich, 1960-62; asst. prof. mech. engring. U. Maine, 1962-64; prof. mech. engring. Va. Poly. Inst., Blacksburg, 1964-74; chmn. mech. engring. dept. N.J. Inst. Tech., Newark, 1974-77; dean engring. Fenn Coll. Engring., Cleve. State U., 1977-83; chmn. dept. mech. engring. Va. Poly. Inst., 1983—. Served with USAF, 1946-49, 50-51. Mem. ASME, Am. Soc. Engring. Edn., Sigma Xi. Roman Catholic. Home: 1502 Carlson Dr Blacksburg VA 24060 Office: Va Poly Inst Blacksburg VA 24061

COMPERE, CLINTON LEE, physician; b. Greenville, Tex., Feb. 17, 1911; s. Edward L. and Clara (Davison) C.; m. Katharine Gram, Mar. 31, 1949; children: Clinton Lee, Mary Katherine. B.S., U. Chgo., 1936, M.D., 1937. Diplomate: Am. Bd. Orthopaedic Surgery. Intern Henry Ford Hosp., Detroit, 1938-39; resident Blodgett Meml. Hosp., Grand Rapids, Mich., 1939-40; practice medicine specializing in orthopaedic surgery, Chgo., 1946—; mem. sr. attending staff Chgo. Wesley Meml. Hosp., 1949—, chief staff, 1964-66; acad. dir. Prosthetic Research Center, Chgo., 1955—, Prosthetic-Orthotic Edn., 1958—; dir. Rehab. Engring. Center, 1972—; cons. 5th Army Hdqrs., 1947—; cons. amputee clinics Regional Office VA, 1947—; assoc. prof. orthopaedic surgery Northwestern U. Med. Sch., 1954-65, prof., 1965—, Edwin Ryerson prof., chmn. dept. orthopaedic surgery, 1978-80; vice chmn. bd. Rehab. Inst., Chgo.; mem. med. adv. com. Ill. Div. Vocational Rehab.; sec.-treas. Orthopedic Research and Edn. Found., 1972-78; med. dir. Ill. State Med. Drs. Services, 1980—. Co-author: Fracture Treatment, 1937, also articles. Served to lt. col., M.C. AUS, 1940-46. Recipient citation Pres.'s Com. Employment Physically Handicapped, 1959; Profl. Achievement award U. Chgo., 1979. Mem. Am. Acad. Orthopaedic Surgeons (sec. 1959-62, pres. 1963-64), Ill., Chgo. med. socs., A.M.A., A.C.S., Am., 20th Century orthopaedic assns., Chgo. Orthopaedic Soc., Clin. Orthopaedic Soc., Ill. Soc. Med. Research, Internat. Soc. Orthopaedic Surgery and Traumatology, Alpha Omega Alpha. Home: 2397 Demaret Dr Dunedin FL 33528 Office: 233 E Erie St Chicago IL 60611

COMPTON, ALLEN T., justice state supreme court; b. Kassas City, Mo., Feb. 25, 1938; m. Barbara Comton; 1 child. B.A., U. Kans.; LL.B., U. Colo. Staff atty. legal services office in Colo., later entered pvt. practice; supervising atty. Alaska Legal Services, Juneau, 1970-73; sole practice, Juneau, 1973-76; judge Superior Ct., Alaska, 1976-80; justice Alaska Supreme Ct., Anchorage, 1980—. Mem. 4 bar assns. including Juneau Bar Assn. (past pres.). Office: Alaska Supreme Ct 303 K St Anchorage AK 99502

COMPTON, ANN WOODRUFF, news correspondent; b. Chgo., Jan. 19, 1947; d. Charles Edward and Barbara (Ortlund) C.; m. William Stevenson Hughes, Nov. 25, 1978; children: William Compton, Edward Opie, Ann Woodruff. B.A., Hollins (Va.) Coll., 1969. Reporter, anchorwoman WDBJ-TV (CBS), Roanoke, Va., 1969-70, polit. reporter, state capitol bur. chief, Richmond, Va., 1971-73; fellow Washington Journalism Center, 1970, trustee, 1978—; network radio anchorwoman ABC News, N.Y.C., 1974-79, 81-84, White House corr., Washington, 1979-81, 84—, congl. corr., 1979-81; mem. adv. bd. Gannett Found. Ctr. for Media Studies, Columbia U., 1984—. Mem. White House Corrs. Assn. (dir. 1977-79). Office: ABC News 1717 DeSales St NW Washington DC 20036

COMPTON, ASBURY CHRISTIAN, state justice; b. Portsmouth, Va., Oct. 24, 1929; s. George Pierce and Edyth Gordon (Christian) C.; m. Betty Stephenson, Nov. 17, 1953; children: Leigh Christian, Mary Bryan, Melissa Anne. B.A., Washington and Lee U., 1950, LL.B., 1953, LL.D. (hon.), 1975. Bar: Va. 1957. Mem. firm May, Garrett, Miller, Newman & Compton, Richmond, 1957-66; judge Law and Equity Ct., City of Richmond, 1966-74; justice Supreme Ct. Va., Richmond, 1974—. Trustee Collegiate Schs., Richmond, 1972—, chmn. bd., 1978-80; mem. adminstrv. bd. Trinity United Methodist Ch., Richmond, 1974-78; trustee Washington and Lee U., 1978—. Served as officer USNR, 1953-56. Decorated Letter of Commendation. Mem. Va. Bar Assn., Va. State Bar, Bar Assn. City Richmond, Washington and Lee U. Alumni Assn. (past pres., dir.), Omicron Delta Kappa, Phi Kappa Sigma, Phi Alpha Delta. Club: Country of Va. Home: 5508 Queensbury Rd Richmond VA 23226 Office: PO Box 1315 Richmond VA 23210

COMPTON, CHARLES DANIEL, chemistry educator; b. Elizabeth, N.J., Jan. 8, 1915; s. Charles Daniel and Janie (Little) C.; m. Ida Lightman, Dec. 19, 1953. A.B., Princeton, 1940; Ph.D. in Chemistry, Yale, 1943. Research chemist Calco Chem. Co., 1943; instr. Princeton, 1944-46; research assoc. Manhattan Dist. Project, Princeton, 1943-44; mem. faculty Williams Coll., 1946—, prof., 1957—, chmn. chemistry dept., 1964-74, Halford R. Clark prof. natural sci., 1966-72, Ebenezer Fitch prof. chemistry, 1972-77, Ebenezer Fitch prof. chemistry emeritus, 1977—; lectr. chemistry New Coll., U. South Fla., 1979-81. Author: Introduction to Chemistry, Inside Chemistry, also Japanese transl., 1982; also articles. Fellow AAAS; mem. Am. Chem. Soc., Phi Beta Kappa, Sigma Xi. Home: 216 Sherwood Dr Bradenton FL 33507

COMPTON, FORREST, actor; b. Reading, Pa., Sept. 15, 1925; s. Harry Oswald and Estella Deborah (Noecker) C.; m. Jeanne Adele Sementini, Sept. 28, 1975. B.A., Swarthmore Coll., 1949; M.F.A., Yale U., 1953. N.Y. stage debut as Cassio in Othello, 1953; appeared in: over 100 plays including Spoon River Anthology, Sleuth, Look Homeward Angel, Mr. Roberts; feature films include The Outsider, Inherit the Wind, The Children's Hour, Kings Go Forth; TV appearanced include That Girl; TV appearances include The FBI, Hogan's Heroes, Mannix; TV appernces include The Fugitive; appeared in role of Col. Gray on: Gomer Pyle TV series; appears in role of Mike Karr on: TV daytime drama The Edge of Night, 1970—. Served with U.S. Army, 1943-46. Decorated Purple Heart. Mem. Screen Actors Guild, AFTRA, Actors Equity Assn., Nat. Acad. TV Arts and Scis. Club: Players (West Side Tennis.) *

COMPTON, JAMES RANDOLPH, real estate developer; b. Montclair, N.J., Dec. 12, 1921; s. Randolph Parker and Dorothy (Danforth) C.; m. Beverly Lucille Arnerich, May 29, 1954 (dec. Oct. 1980); children: W. Danforth, Randolph Owen, Marshal James.; m. Patricia Oakes, Sept. 11, 1982. B.A., Princeton U., 1943; M.B.A., U. Chgo., 1948. With Minn. Mining Co., St. Paul, 1948-49, Mpls.-Honeywell Co., Mpls., 1949; personnel supr. Northwest Airlines Inc., St. Paul, 1950-51; contract adminstr. Food Machinery & Chem. Corp., San Jose, Calif., 1951-57; self-employed real estate developer, San Jose, 1957—. Vice chmn. Danforth Found., 1974—; chmn. Santa Clara County chpt. NCCJ, 1969-70; pres. Montalvo Assn., Saratoga, Calif., 1977-83; trustee Expt. in Internat. Living, 1974—, Fund for Peace, 1973—, Music and Arts Found. Santa Clara Valley, 1967—; bd. dirs. Inst. for Med. Research of Santa Clara County, 1974—, Calif. Actors Theater, 1979-82, Calif. League Conservation Voters, 1983—; mem. No. Calif. adv. bd. United Negro Coll. Fund, 1974—; mem. adv. bd. Ctr. for Def. Info. of Fund for Peace. Served with USMCR, 1943-47. Recipient Service award San Jose area Anti-Defamation League, 1974. Episcopalian. Club: University (San Jose). Home: 15040 Oriole Rd Saratoga CA 95070 Office: PO Box 457 Los Gatos CA 95031

COMPTON, JOHN ROBINSON, rake co. exec.; b. Elmira, N.Y., Feb. 24, 1923; s. William Randall and Ada (Viele) C.; m. Jean Elinor York, Apr. 17, 1943; children—John York, Jan Elizabeth (Mrs. Harriss M. Ganey), Julie Ann (Mrs. Michael Lindstrom). B.S. cum laude, Syracuse U., 1950. Accountant, factory mgr. York Modern Corp., Unadilla, N.Y., 1947-51, pres., 1969—; also treas., dir.; accountant Brewer-Titchener Corp., Binghamton, N.Y., 1951-52; div. controller Riegel Paper Corp., Riegelwood, N.C., 1953-65, corporate controller, N.Y.C., 1966-69; pres. York Modern Corp., 1969—, Mail-Print, Inc., 1970—. Served to 2d lt. USAAF, World War II. Methodist. Home: RD 2 Bainbridge NY 13733 Office: York Modern Corp Unadilla NY 13849

COMPTON, NORMA HAYNES, university dean; b. Washington, Nov. 16, 1924; d. Thomas N. and Lillian (Laffin) Haynes; m. William Randall Compton, Mar. 27, 1946; children: William Randall, Anne Elizabeth. A.B., George Washington U., 1950; postgrad., Cath. U., 1954, Am. U., 1954-55, U. Tenn., 1958, Ia. State U., 1960; M.S., U. Md., 1957, Ph.D., 1962. Researcher Julius Garfinckel & Co., Washington, 1955; tchr. Montgomery Blair High Sch., Silver Spring, Md., 1955-57; instr. home econs. U. Md., 1957-60, teaching and research fellow, 1960-61, assoc. prof. home econs., 1962-63; assoc. prof. Utah State U., 1963-64, prof., 1964-68, head dept. clothing and textiles, 1964-67, dir., 1967-68; dean Sch. Home Econs. Auburn (Ala.) U., 1968-73, Sch. Consumer and Family Scis., Purdue U., 1973—; psychology extern St. Elizabeth's Hosp., Washington, 1962-63. Author: (with Olive Hall) Foundations of Home Economics Research: A Human Ecology Approach; author: (with John Touliatos) Approaches to Child Study; Contbr. articles to profl. jours. Bd. dirs. Home Hosp., Lafayette, Inc. Mem. Am., Ind. home econs. assns., Am. Assn. Univ. Adminstrs., Assn. Adminstrs. Home Econs. in State Univs., Land Grant Colls., Am. Soc. Consumer Affairs Profls. in Bus., Assn. Consumer Research, Nat. Council Family Relations, Phi Beta Kappa, Sigma Xi, Phi Upsilon Omicron, Phi Kappa Phi, Gamma Sigma Delta, Omicron Nu, Psi Chi. Presbyterian. Address: Purdue U Dean Sch Consumer and Family Scis Stone Hall West Lafayette IN 47907

COMPTON, RALPH THEODORE, JR., engineering educator; b. St. Louis, July 26, 1935; s. Ralph Theodore and Ethel (Evans) C.; m. Lorraine Fielding, Nov. 9, 1957; children: Diane Marie, Ralph Theodore III, Richard Thomas. S.B., MIT, 1958; M.Sc., Ohio State U., 1961, Ph.D., 1961. Jr. engr. DECO Electronics, Leesburg, Va., 1958-59; sr. engr. Battelle Meml. Inst., Columbus, Ohio, 1959-62; asst. supr. Antenna Lab., Columbus, 1962-65; asst. prof. Case Inst. Tech., Cleve., 1965-67; fellow, guest prof. Tech. Hochschule, Munich, W. Ger., 1967-68; assoc. prof. Ohio State U., Columbus, 1968-78, prof. elec. engring., 1978—; cons. to various orgns., U.S., Europe, Israel, 1969—. Contbr. chpts. to books, articles to profl. jours. Fellow Battelle Meml. Inst., 1961; NSF fellow, 1967; recipient Outstanding Paper awards Ohio State Electro-Sci. Lab., 1978, 80, 82, M. Barry Carlton award IEEE Aerospace and Electric Systems Soc., 1983, Sr. Research award Ohio State U. Engring. Coll., 1983. Fellow IEEE (assoc. editor Jour. Trans. on Antennas Propagation 1970); mem. Antenna and Propagation Soc. (chmn. Columbus chpt. 1971-72), Sigma Xi (sec.-treas. Case Inst. Tech. chpt. 1965-67), Pi Mu Epsilon. Home: 477 Poe Ave Worthington OH 43085 Office: Dept Elec Engring Ohio Stae U 2015 Neal Ave Columbus OH 43210

COMPTON, RANDOLPH PARKER, investment banker; b. Macon, Mo., Mar. 18, 1892; s. William R. and Caroline (Parker) C.; m. Dorothy Danforth, Oct. 11, 1917 (dec.); children: W. Danforth (dec.), James Randolph, Ann Randolph (Mrs. Ellis M. Stephens), John Parker (dec.). Grad., Smith Acad., St. Louis, 1911; LL.B., Princeton, 1915; postgrad., Harvard Bus. Sch., 1943. Vice pres. charge N.Y. office William R. Compton Co., 1919-29; propr. mcpl. bond firm, N.Y.C., 1929-34; v.p. charge mcpl. bond dept. Lazard Freres & Co., N.Y.C., 1934-41, Union Securities Corp., 1941-42; corp. relations mgr. Republic Aviation Co., Ltd., Farmingdale, L.I., N.Y., 1943-44; v.p. Kidder, Peabody & Co., Inc. (Investment bankers), N.Y.C., 1945—. Past treas., trustee Scarsdale (N.Y.) Found.; hon. trustee, mem. bd. Meharry Medical Coll.; chmn. emeritus, trustee Fund for Peace, N.Y.C. Served as ensign USN, World War I. Republican. Conglist. (trustee). Clubs: Recess, Princeton (N.Y.C.); Fox Meadow Tennis; Am. Yacht (Rye, N.Y.). Home: 53 Brookby Rd Scarsdale NY 10583 Office: 10 Hanover Sq New York NY 10005

COMPTON, W. DALE, physicist; b. Chrisman, Ill., Jan. 7, 1929; s. Roy L. and Marcia (Wood) D.; m. Jeanne C. Parker, Oct. 14, 1951; children: Gayle Corinne, Donald Leonard, Duane Arthur. B.A., Wabash Coll., 1949; M.S., U. Okla., 1951; Ph.D., U. Ill., 1955; D.Eng. (hon.), Mich. Technol. U., 1976. Physicist U.S. Naval Ordnance Test Sta., China Lake, Calif., 1951-52, U.S. Naval Research Lab., Washington, 1955-61; prof. physics U. Ill. at Urbana, 1961-70, dir. coordinated sci. lab., 1965-70; dir. chem. and phys. scis., exec. dir. sci. research staff, v.p. research Ford Motor Co., Dearborn, Mich., 1971—; Mem. Presdl. Commn. for Award of Medal of Sci., 1979—; mem. vis. com. Nat. Bur. Standards, 1975—, chmn. vis. com., 1979. Author: (with J.H. Schulman) Color Centers in Solids, 1962; Editor: Interaction of Science and Technology, 1969. Bd. dirs. Mich. Cancer Found. Fellow Am. Phys. Soc., AAAS, Washington Acad. Scis.; mem. Research Soc. Am., Nat. Acad. Engring.

COMRIE, ALLAN, investment co. exec.; b. Enfield, Conn., Sept. 25, 1919; s. James M. and Ruth (Steele) C. B.A., U. Conn., 1943. Security analyst Home Ins. Co. N.Y., 1946-51; with Great Am. Ins. Co., 1951-69, financial sec., 1956-64, v.p., sec., 1964-67, sr. v.p., dir., 1967-69; pres., dir. U.S. & Fgn. Securities Corp., N.Y.C., 1969—; chmn., dir. Keswick Assos.; dir. Atlantic Mut. Ins. Co., Centenial Ins. Co. Served with AUS, 1943-46. Home: 40 Sheridan Dr New Canaan CT 06840 Office: 767 Fifth Ave New York NY 10022

COMROE, JULIUS HIRAM, JR., educator; b. York, Pa., Mar. 13, 1911; s. Julius Hiram and Mollie (Levy) C.; m. Jeanette Wolfson, June 30, 1936; 1 dau., Joan Von Gehr. A.B., U. Pa., 1931, M.D., 1934, D.Sc. (hon.), 1978; Commonwealth Fund fellow, Nat. Inst. Med. Research, London, 1939; M.D. (hon.), Karolinska Inst., Stockholm, 1968; D.Sc., U. Chgo., 1968. Intern Hosp. of U. Pa., 1934-36; instr. in pharmacology U. Pa. Med. Sch., 1936-40, asso., 1940-42, asst. prof., 1942-46; prof. physiology and pharmacology U. Pa. Grad. Sch. Medicine, 1946-57; prof. physiology, dir. Cardiovascular Research Inst., U. Calif. Med. Center, San Francisco, 1957-73, Herzstein prof. biology, 1973-78; chmn. 1st Teaching Inst. Asso. Am. Med. Colls., 1953, also chmn., 1961 Inst; chmn. Physiology Study Section, 1955-58; mem. bd. sci. counselors Nat. Heart Inst., 1957-61; mem. Nat. Adv. Mental Health Council, 1958-62, Nat. Adv. Heart Council, 1963-67, Nat. Adv. Heart and Lung Council, 1970-74, Pres.'s Panel Heart Disease, 1972; mem. adv. com. to dir. NIH, 1976-78; Cons. med. research div. CWS, 1944-46. Author: Physiological Basis for 02 Therapy, 1950, Methods in Medical Research, Vol. 2, 1950, The Lung: Clinical Physiology and Pulmonary Function Tests, 1955, 62, Physiology of Respiration, 1964, 74, Pulmonary and Respiratory Physiology (Dowden), 1976, Retrospectroscope-Insights to Medical Discovery, 1977, Exploring the Heart, 1983; Editor: Physiology for Physicians, 1963-66, Circulation Research, 1966-70, Ann. Rev. Physiology, 1971-75; asso. editor: Am. Rev. Respiratory Disease, 1973-79; mem. editorial bd.: Proc. Nat. Acad. Scis, 1977—. Recipient Am. Physiol. Soc. Travel award, 1938, Research Achievement award Am. Heart Assn., 1968, Coll. medal Am. Coll. Chest Physicians, 1970, Trudeau award, 1974, Wiggers award, 1974, Gold Heart award Am. Heart Assn., 1975; Kovalenko medal Nat. Acad. Scis., 1976; Sci. Contbns. award ACP, 1977; Daggs award Am. Physiol. Soc., 1977; medal U. Calif., San Francisco, 1978; Eugenio Morelli award Accademia dei Lincei, Rome, 1979; Abraham Flexner award in med. edn. Am. Assn. Med. Colls., 1979. Fellow Am. Coll. Cardiology (hon.), Royal Coll. Physcians (London), Royal Soc. Medicine (London); mem. Assn. Am. Physicians, Am. Physiol. Soc. (pres. 1960-61), Am. Soc. for Pharmacology and Exptl. Therapeutics (councilor 1953-56), Nat. Acad. Scis. (mem. bd. medicine 1967-70), Inst. Medicine (exec. com. 1970), Am. Acad. Arts and Scis., Harvey Soc. (hon. mem.), Am. Soc. for Clin. Investigation, Phi Beta Kappa, Sigma Xi, Alpha Omega Alpha. Home: 555 Laurent Rd Hillsborough CA 94010 Office: Cardiovascular Research Inst U Cal Med Center San Francisco CA 94143

COMSTOCK, DALE ROBERT, university dean; b. Frederic, Wis., Jan. 18, 1934; s. Walter and Frances (Lindroth) C.; m. Mary Jo Lien, Aug. 18, 1956; children—Mitchell Scott, Bryan Paul. B.A., Central Wash. State Coll., 1955; M.S., Oreg. State U., 1962, Ph.D., 1966. Tchr. math. Kennewick (Wash.) High Sch., 1955-57, 59-60; instr. Columbia Basin Coll., Pasco, Wash., 1956-57, 59-60; programmer analyst Gen. Electric Co., Hanford Atomic Works, Richland, Wash., 1963; prof. math. Central Wash. U., Ellensburg, 1964—, dean, 1970—; on leave as sr. program mgr. U.S. ERDA, also Presdl. interchange exec., 1976-77; mem. Pres.'s Commn. on Exec. Devel., 1976-77; cons. NSF India program, 1968, 69; mem. grant proposal rev. panels NSF, 1970, 71, 76, 77; pres. Western Assn. Grad. Schs., 1979-80. Served with AUS, 1957-59. NSF fellow, 1960-61; grantee, summer 1964. Mem. Am. Math Soc., Math. Assn. Am., Assn. Computing Machinery (exec. com.), Soc. Indsl. and Applied Math., Northwest Coll. and Univ. Assn. for Sci. (pres. 1980-83). Methodist. Home: 106 N Mount Daniels Dr Ellensburg WA 98926

COMSTOCK, GEORGE WILLS, educator, epidemiologist; b. Niagara Falls, N.Y., Jan. 7, 1915; s. George Frederick and Ella G. (Wills) C.; m. Margaret Karr, Aug. 29, 1939; children—Gordon F., Lloyd K., Martha W. B.S. with honors, Antioch Coll., 1937; M.D., Harvard, 1941; M.P.H., U. Mich., 1951; Dr.P.H., Johns Hopkins, 1956. Diplomate: Am. Bd. Preventive Medicine. Intern U.S. Marine Hosp., Balt., 1941-42; commd. officer USPHS, 1941-62; dir. Muscogee County Tb Study, Columbus, Ga., 1946-55; epidemiologist Tb program USPHS, 1956-62; mem. faculty Johns Hopkins Sch. Hygiene and Pub. Health, 1962—, prof. epidemiology, 1966—; cons. Tb program USPHS, 1962—; disease control study sect. NIH, 1964-67; dir. Tng. Center Pub. Health Research, 1963—. Editor-in-chief: Am. Jour. Epidemiology, 1979—; author articles in field. Named to Hall of Fame Am. Lung Assn., 1980. Fellow Am. Pub. Health Assn.; mem. Am. Thoracic Soc., Am. Epidemiol. Soc., Soc. Epidemiologic Research Washington County Med. Soc., Am. Heart Assn. (fellow council on epidemiology). Home: Route 2 Box 405 Smithsburg MD 21783 Office: Box 2067 Hagerstown MD 21740

COMSTOCK, RALPH J., JR., banker; b. Rexburg, Idaho, Oct. 18, 1917; s. Ralph J. and Gladys (Bassett) C.; m. Bernice Broomfield, July 3, 1942; children—Ralph J. III, Christine, Robert Stephen. Student, U. Idaho, 1935-37; B.S., U. Utah, 1939; grad., Pacific Coast Sch. Banking, U. Wash., 1954. With First Security Bank Idaho, N.A., Boise, 1946—, exec. v.p., 1962-65, pres., 1965-77, chmn., chief exec. officer, 1977—, also dir.; v.p., dir., mem. exec. com. First Security Corp., Salt Lake City; v.p., dir. First Security Co., Salt Lake City; dir. Am. Fine Foods, Inc., Payette.; Mem. regional adv. com. 13th Nat. Bank Region, 1968-69. Treas. Ida. div. Am. Cancer Soc., 1963-68; Bd. dirs. Pacific Coast Sch. Banking, 1966-72, chmn. bd., 1970; trustee St. Luke's Hosp., Boise, Boise State U., Boise Jr. Coll. Dist.; bd. dirs. U. Idaho Found., 1977—. Served to maj. AUS, 1941-46. Recipient Businessman of Year award Alpha Kappa Psi, Idaho State U., 1970; Distinguished Eagle Scout award Boy Scouts Am., 1970; named hon. alumnus U. Idaho, 1978, Exec. of Yr. Profl. Secs. Assn., 1981. Mem. Am. Bankers Assn. (Idaho v.p. 1968), Idaho Bankers Assn. (pres. 1968), Greater Boise C. of C. (pres. 1967), Idaho C. of C. (dir., mem. exec. com., pres. 1970-71), Asso. Taxpayers Idaho (pres. 1963-65), Am. Legion (past post comdr.), 40 and 8, S.A.R., Sigma Chi, Alpha Kappa Psi (hon.). Republican. Clubs: Mason, Rotarian (pres. Pocatello 1956), Elk.; Arid, Hillcrest Country (Boise). Home: 2888 Leisure Dr Boise ID 83704 Office: PO Box 7069 Boise ID 83730

COMSTOCK, ROBERT RAY, newspaper editor; b. N.Y.C., Sept. 17, 1927; s. Kenneth Franklin and Phyllis Abigail (Taylor) C.; m. Barbara Sylvia Corner, June 30, 1956; children: Eric Taylor, Katherine Sylvia. Litt.B. in Journalism, Rutgers U., 1952. Reporter Ridgewood (N.J.) News, 1953; successively reporter, polit. writer, public affairs editor, asst. editor Hackensack (N.J.) Record, 1954-75, v.p., exec. editor, 1977—; talk show moderator sta. WNET-13, Newark, 1970-71; instr. Seton Hall U., S. Orange, N.J., 1974-75; dir. public info. State of N.J., Trenton, 1975-77; mem. N.J. Public Broadcasting Authority, 1978—, chmn., 1979-80. Mem. N.J. Com. for Humanities, 1982—. Served with USNR, 1945-48. Mem. Am. Soc. Newspaper Editors, AP Mng. Editors Assn., N.J. Legis. Corr. Club (pres. 1965-67), Sigma Delta Chi (pres. N.J. chpt. 1969-71). Home: 219 Hope St Ridgewood NJ 07450 Office: 150 River St Hackensack NJ 07602

CONABLE, BARBER B., JR., congressman; b. Warsaw, N.Y., Nov. 2, 1922; s. Barber B. and Agnes G. (Gouinlock) C.; m. Charlotte Williams, Sept. 13, 1952; 4 children. A.B., Cornell U., 1942, LL.B., 1948. Bar: N.Y. 1948. Practice in Buffalo, 1948-50, in Batavia, 1952-64; mem. N.Y. State Senate, 1963-64, 89th-98th congresses from 30th Dist. N.Y.; mem. ways and means com., standards of ofcl. conduct com., joint com. on internal revenue taxation, past chmn. ho. Republican policy com. and rep. research com. Editor: Cornell Law Quar, 1947-48. Mem. sr. adv. com. Kennedy Inst. Politics; trustee U.S. Capitol Hist. Soc., Mus. Am. Indian. Served with USMCR, 1942-46, 50-51. Republican. Club: Rotary (pres. Batavia). Home: 10532 Alexander Rd Alexander NY 14005 Office: 237 Cannon House Office Bldg Washington DC 20515 *

CONABOY, RICHARD PAUL, judge; b. Scranton, Pa., June 12, 1925. Student, U. Scranton, 1945; LL.B., Cath. U. Am., 1950. Bar: Pa. 1951. Ptnr. firm Powell & Conaboy, Scranton, 1951-54; assoc. firm Kennedy O'Brien & O'Brien, Scranton, 1954-62; judge Pa. Ct. Common Pleas, Scranton, 1962-80, U.S. Dist. Ct. Middle Pa., 1980—; pres. Pa. Joint Council on Criminal Justice System; mem. Nat. Conf. Juvenile Justice, Nat. Conf. Corrections. Contbr. articles to legal jours. Bd. dirs. Marywood Coll., U. Scranton. Mem. Pa. Conf. State Trial Judges, ABA, Pa. Bar Assn., Am. Judicature Soc. Office: US Courthouse Washington Ave Scranton PA 18501

CONACHER, DESMOND JOHN, educator; b. Kingston, Ont., Can., Dec. 27, 1918; s. William Morison and Madeline Mary (Cashel) C.; m. Mary Smith, Aug. 2, 1952; children: Hugh Anthony, Susan Mary. B.A., Queen's U., Kingston, 1941, M.A., 1942; Ph.D., U. Chgo., 1950. Master Upper Can. Coll., Toronto, Ont., 1943-46; lectr. classics Dalhousie U., Halifax, N.S., 1946-47; asst. prof. U. Sask., 1947-52, asso. prof., 1952-58, Trinity Coll., U. Toronto, 1958-65, prof., 1965—, head classics dept., 1966-72, chmn. classics dept., 1972-75. Author: Euripidean Drama, 1967, Aeschylus' Prometheus Bound: A Literary Commentary, 1980; Contbr. articles on ancient Greek tragedy to profl. jours. Bd. dirs. Can. Fedn. Humanities, 1981-84. Shorey Research fellow U. Chgo., 1942-43; Nuffield Research fellow Oxford U., 1957-58; Can. Council Leave Research fellow Oxford U., 1971-72; Bonsall vis. prof. classics Stanford U., 1981. Fellow Royal Soc. Can.; mem. Classical Assn. Can. (mem. editorial bd. jour. 1968-73), Am. Philol. Assn. (dir. 1974-77). Home: 126 Manor Rd E Toronto E ON Canada

CONANT, ALLAH B., JR., lawyer; b. Waco, Tex., July 24, 1939; s. Allah B. and Frances Louise (James) C.; m. Sheila Conant; children: Heather Lee, Lisa Lynn, Leslie Marie. B.A., N. Tex. State Coll., Denton, 1961; J.D. cum laude, Baylor U., 1963. Bar: Tex. 1963. Since practiced in, Dallas; partner firm Shank, Irwin & Conant, 1964—. Contbr. to legal jours. Mem. Internat. Bar Assn., Am. Bar Assn. (council gen. practice sect. 1977-80, chmn. 1982-83), Dallas Bar Assn., State Bar Tex., Am. Soc. Internat. Law, Trial Attys. Am., Baylor Law Sch. Counsellors, Baylor Law Alumni Assn. (dir. 1979—), Baylor Law Rev. Ex-Editors Assn., N.Tex. State U. Alumni Assn. (dir., v.p.), Inst. of Dirs. (London), Sigma Phi Epsilon, Omicron Delta Kappa, Phi Delta Phi (historian 1962). Clubs: Lancers (Dallas); Annabel's (London). Home: 8247 Forest Hills Blvd Dallas TX 75218 Office: 4100 Thanksgiving Tower Dallas TX 75201

CONANT, HOWARD ROSSET, steel company executive; b. Chgo., Sept. 30, 1924; s. Louis J. and Fredericka (Rosset) Cohn; m. Doris S. Kaplan, Dec. 14, 1947; children: Alison Sue, Howard R., Meredith Ann. B.S., U. Pa., 1947. Pres., dir. Interstate Steel Co., Des Plaines, Ill., 1947-71, chmn. bd., 1971—; pres., dir. Elliott Paint & Varnish Co., Chgo., 1961-76; dir. Valspar Co., Mpls., Interstate Steel Supply Co., Facets Multimedia, Inc.; chmn. bd. dirs. White Products Corp., 1965-67. Discussion leader Center Study of Continuing Edn., 1955-62; dir. Com. for Sane Nuclear Policy, 1964-69; mem. Bus. Execs. Move for Vietnam Peace, 1965-73. Served with AUS, 1943-46; PTO. Mem. World Bus. Council, Chgo. Pres.'s Orgn. Clubs: Ridge and Valley Tennis (Glenview); Carlton (Chgo.); East Bank. Home: 736 Greenacres Ln Glenview IL 60025 Office: 401 Touhy Ave Des Plaines IL 60018

CONANT, HOWARD SOMERS, educator, artist; b. Beloit, Wis., May 5, 1921; s. Rufus P. and Edith B. (Somers) C.; m. Florence C. Craft, June 18, 1943; children: Judith Lynne Steinbach, Jeffrey Scott. Student, Art Students League of N.Y., 1944-45; B.S., U. Wis.-Milw., 1946; M.S., U. Wis.-Madison, 1947; Ed.D., U. Buffalo, 1950. Instr. art, asst. head housefellow U. Wis., 1946-47; asst. prof. art State Coll. for Tchrs., Buffalo, 1947-50, prof. art, 1950-55; chmn. dept. art edn. also chmn. art collection NYU, 1955-76; head dept. art U. Ariz., Tucson, 1976—; art edn. cons. NBC-TV, also Girl Scouts Am. TV series, 1958-60; field reader, also Title III program cons. U.S. Office of Edn.; adviser N.Y. State Council on Arts, 1962-63, Conn. Commn. on Arts, 1967-68; cons. Ford Found., 1973, Children's Theatre Assn., 1973. Moderator: weekly TV program Fun to Learn About Art, WBEN-TV, Buffalo, 1951-55; exhibited one man shows; also represented maj. group exhbns. and coll. art collections; executed mural, Sperry High Sch., Henrietta, N.Y., 1971, Good Samaritan Med. Ctr., Phoenix, 1982; Author: (with Arne Randall) Art in Education, 1959, 63; Author, editor: Vol. 4, Masterpieces of the Arts, New Wonder World Cultural Library, 1963, Seminar on Elementary and Secondary School Education in the Visual Arts, 1965, Art Education, 1964, Art Workshop Leaders Planning Guide, 1958, Lincoln Library of the Arts (2 vols.), 1973; art editor: Intellect, 1975-78; Art editor: USA: Today, 1978—; asso. editor: Arts mag., 1973-75; contbr. articles profl. publs. Dept. State lectr., India, 1964; Dir. Waukesha County (Wis.) YMCA Art Program, 1946-48, Children's Creative Art Found., 1959-60; mem. adv. com. Coll. of Potomac, 1966. Served as lt. USAAF, 1943-46. Recipient medal Nat. Gallery Art, 1966; Disting. Alumnus award U. Wis.-Milw., 1968. Mem. Coll. Art Assn., Internat. Art Critics Assn., Alliance for Arts in Edn., Nat. Assn. Schs. Art and Design, Nat. Com. Art Edn. (council, chmn. 1962-63), Inst. Study of Art in Edn. (bd. govs. 1965-72, pres. 1965-68). Club: Torch (N.Y.C.) (pres. 1965-66). Office: Dept Art U Ariz Tucson AZ 85721 *I have learned to freely follow my interests from one area of concern or involvement to another without feeling guilty about "putting off until tomorrow what one can do today." I have learned to be an innovator and an enjoyer, rather than a solemn plodder. I have learned how to do three, four, even five things more or less at once, much like an organist handling contrapuntal melodies. As* *a result, I am a happy professor, artist, author, lecturer, administrator, and private human being whose multiple interests seem highly compatible and, indeed, essential to one another.*

CONANT, ROBERT SCOTT, harpsichordist, educator; b. Passaic, N.J., Jan. 6, 1928; s. Frederick B. and Bessie (Scott) C.; m. Nancy Lydia Jackson, Oct. 10, 1959; children—Elizabeth Scott, Andrew Frederick. B.A., Yale U., 1949, Mus. M., 1956. Asst. prof., curator Yale Collection Mus. Instruments Sch. Music, Yale, 1961-66; fellow Silliman Coll., 1961-66, asso. fellow, 1966-71; asso. prof. music history and harpsichord Chgo. Mus. Coll., Roosevelt U., 1967-71, prof., 1971—. Concert harpsichordist, N.Y. Town Hall recital debut, 1953; ann. tours as recitalist, chamber music player, U.S., Europe, 1956—; appeared with, Pitts., Chgo. and Denver Symphonies; soloist, Casals Festival, 1963; lectr., performer numerous colls., univs.; mem., Viola da Gamba Trio of Basel, 1968—; Recorded for, Decca, Columbia, RCA Victor; Author: (with others) Twentieth-Century Harpsichord Music: a Classified Catalog, 1974; Contbr. articles to profl. jours. Founder, pres. Festival of Baroque Music, Greenfield Center, N.Y. Served with AUS, 1951-53. Mem. Coll. Music Soc. (treas. 1971-74), Am. Musicol. Soc., Am. Mus. Instrument Soc. Home: 154 Maple Ave Wilmette IL 60091 Office: 430 S Michigan Ave Chicago IL 60605 also Wilton Rd Greenfield Center NY 12833

CONARD, ALFRED FLETCHER, legal educator; b. Grinnell, Iowa, Nov. 30, 1911; s. Henry S. and Laetitia (Moon) C.; m. Georgia Murray, Aug. 7, 1939; children—Joy L., Deborah J. A.B., Grinnell Coll., 1932, LL.D., 1971; postgrad., U. Iowa, 1932-34; LL.B., U. Pa., 1936; LL.M., Columbia, 1939, J.S.D., 1942. Bar: Pa. 1937, Mich. 1967. Practice in Phila., 1937-38; asst. prof. U. Kansas City (Mo.) Law Sch., 1939-42, acting dean, 1941-42; atty. OPA, 1942-43, Office Alien Property Custodian, 1945-46; asso. prof., then prof. law U. Ill. Law Sch., 1946-54; prof. law U. Mich. Law Sch., 1954—; lectr. U. Istanbul, 1958-59, Luxembourg, 1959, Mexico, 1963, Brussels, 1965, Salzburg, 1971; chmn. editorial adv. bd. Bobbs-Merrill Co., 1962-78; Exec. com. Am. Assn. Law Schs., 1964-65, chmn. research com., 1968-70, pres., 1971, chmn. bus. assns. sect., 1979. Author: Studies in Easements and Licenses, 1942, Cases on Business Organization, 3d edit, 1965, Automobile Accident Costs and Payments: Studies in the Economics of Injury Reparation, 1964, Corporations in Perspective, 1976, Enterprise Organization,, 3d edit., 1982; Editor in chief: Am. Jour. Comparative Law, 1968-71; chief editor bus. and pvt. orgns.: Internat. Ency. Comparative Law; editorial adv. bd.: Am. Bar Found. Research Jour, 1976—. Served OSS AUS, 1943-45. Decorated Purple Heart; Ordre des Chevaliers de la Couronne, Belgium; recipient Kulp Meml. award Am. Risk & Ins. Assn., 1965; Guggenheim fellow, 1975. Mem. AAUP (chpt. pres. 1963-64), NRC, Am. Bar Assn. (exec. com. corp. law sect. 1967-71, com. on corp. laws 1974-80, com. on clin. legal edn. 1981—), Internat. Acad. Comparative Law, State Bar Mich., Am. Law Inst., Law and Soc. Assn. (trustee 1968-75), Council on Law-Related Studies (trustee 1969-74), Phi Beta Kappa, Order of the Coif. Mem. Soc. of Friends. Club: Rotarian (club pres. 1976-77). Home: 16 Heatheridge Ann Arbor MI 48104

CONARD, JOHN JOSEPH, financial official; b. Coolidge, Kans., June 30, 1921; s. Joseph Harvey and Jessie May (Shanstrom) C.; m. Virginia Louise Powell, Sept. 13, 1947; children—Joseph Harvey II (dec.), James Powell, Spencer Dean, John Joseph. B.A., U. Kans., 1943, M.A., 1947; D. Internat. Law, U. Paris, 1951. Instr. polit. sci. U. Kans., 1946-49, asst. to chancellor, 1970-75; spl. asst. U.S. Mut. Security Agy., Paris, France, 1951-54; editor, pub. Kiowa County Signal, Greensburg, Kans., 1955-70; exec. officer bd. regents State of Kans., Topeka, 1976-82; pres. Higher Edn. Loan Program of Kans., Inc., Overland Park, Kans., 1982—; v.p. Higher Edn. Assistance Found., 1982—; dir. Haviland (Kans.) State Bank. Mem. Kans. Ho. of Reps., 1959-69; mem. State Fin. Council, 1961-69; speaker of House, 1967-69; exec. asst. to Gov. Kans., 1975-76; trustee William Allen White Found., 1959—. Served to ensign USNR, 1943-45. Summerfield scholar, 1939-42; Rotary Found. fellow, 1949-50. Mem. VFW, Phi Beta Kappa, Sigma Delta Chi, Pi Sigma Alpha, Tau Kappa Epsilon. Republican. Congregationalist. Clubs: Masons, Rotary. Home: Route 1 Lecompton KS 66050 Office: 10950 Grandview Dr Suite 270 Overland Park KS 66210

CONARROE, JOEL OSBORNE, educator, editor; b. West Orange, N.J., Oct. 23, 1934; s. Elvin Hamn and Elizabeth (Lofland) C. B.S., Davidson Coll., 1956; M.A., Cornell U., 1957; Ph.D., NYU, 1966; Ph.D. (hon.), Southwestern, 1983. Asst. prof. English, U. Pa., 1966-71, asso. prof., 1971-77, prof., 1977—, chmn. dept. English, 1973-77, master Van Pelt Coll. House, 1974-77, univ. ombudsman, 1971-73, dean faculty arts and scis., 1983—; exec. dir. MLA, N.Y.C., 1978-83; editor PMLA, 1978-83; mem. selection com. Commonwealth Award in Lit., 1980-83; v.p. Nat. Book Critics Circle, 1981—. Author: William Carlos Williams' Paterson: Language and Landscape, 1970, John Berryman: An Introduction to the Poetry, 1977; author essays and revs. Served with U.S. Army, 1957-58. Recipient Founders Day award NYU, 1966; Lindback Teaching award U. Pa., 1970; Guggenheim fellow, 1977-78; Yaddo fellow, 1973, 76. Mem. Am. Soc. Assn. Execs., MLA, Phi Beta Kappa. Clubs: Franklin Inn (Phila.); Century Assn., Andalusia (Pa.). Office: 116 College Hall U Pa Philadelphia PA 19104

CONATON, MICHAEL JOSEPH, financial executive; b. Detroit, Aug. 3, 1933; s. John Martin and Margaret Alice (Cleary) C.; m. Margaret Ann Cannon, Sept. 3, 1955; children—Catherine, Macaira, Michael, Margaret, Elizabeth. B.S., Xavier U., 1955. Public accountant Stanley A. Hitter, C.P.A., Cin., 1956-58; controller The Moloney Co., Albia, Iowa, 1958-61; v.p. fin. The Midland Co., Cin., 1961-80, sr. v.p., chief fin. officer, 1980—, also dir.; dir. United Midwest Bancshares, Inc., So. Ohio Bank. City councilman, Albia, 1959-61. Served to lt. USMC, 1955-56. Mem. Fin. Execs. Inst., Cin. Soc. Fin. Analysts. Home: 1016 Paxton Ave Cincinnati OH 45208 Office: 111 E 4th St Cincinnati OH 45202

CONAWAY, ORRIN BRYTE, political scientist; b. Middlebourne, W.Va., Feb. 14, 1918; s. Orrin Bryte and Maude Kramer (Carpenter) C.; m. Lydia Pritsky, July 17, 1965; children—Charles Orrin, Margaret Ann. B.A., W.Va. Wesleyan Coll., 1940; M.A., Am. U., 1944; Ph.D., Syracuse U., 1950. Asst. dir. Grad. Sch. U.S. Dept. Agr., 1951-57; dean Albany Grad. Sch. Public Adminstrn., 1957-62; prof. Syracuse U., 1957-62, N.Y. U., 1957-62; prof., dean Grad. Sch. Public Affairs, SUNY, Albany, 1962-68; Benedum prof. Am. govt., chmn. dept. polit. sci. U. W.Va., 1968-83, Benedum prof. emeritus, 1983—; cons. on public adminstrn. to fgn. govts.; mem. Pres.'s Adv. Council on Intergovtl. Personnel Policy, 1971-74. Author: (with others) More Effective Public Service—A Report to the President and Congress, vols. I, 1973, II, 1974, The Coordination of Federal and State Coal Mine Health and Safety Programs With Special Reference to the Federal Coal Mine Health and Safety Act of 1969, vols. I and II, 1971; editor: Legislative-Executive Relations in the Government of the United States, 1953, Democracy in Public Administration, 1955, Public Administration and Race Relations, 1963; contbr. articles on public adminstrn. to profl. publs. Maxwell fellow Maxwell Sch., Syracuse U., 1946-47. Mem. Am. Polit. Sci. Assn., Am. Soc. Public Adminstrn. Democrat. Methodist. Home: Harewood Box 16 Morgantown WV 26505 Office: 316 Woodburn Hall Dept Polit Sci U WVa Morgantown WV 26506

CONCEPCION, DAVID ISMAEL, baseball player; b. Oeurrare de la Costa, Aragua, Venezuela, June 17, 1948. Student, Augustin Codazi Coll. Shortstop with Cin. Reds, 1970—. Played All-Star Game, 1975, 76, 77, 78, 79, 80, 81, 82. Office: care Cin Reds 100 Riverfront Stadium Cincinnati OH 45202

CONCORDIA, CHARLES, electrical engineer, consultant; b. Schenectady, June 20, 1908; s. Francis G. and Susie Elizabeth (Decker) C.; m. Frances Butler, Dec. 18, 1948. Sc.D. (hon.), Union Coll., 1971. With Gen. Electric Co., Schenectady, 1926-73, in electric utility systems engring., 1936-73, applications engr., 1936-49, in aircraft devel., 1941-45, cons. engr., 1949-73; cons. electric power systems engring., Venice, Fla., 1973—; lectr. various univs. Author: Synchronous Machines, 1951; contbr. 120 articles to profl. jours. Recipient Lamme medal Am. Inst. Elec. Engrs., 1961; Coffin award Gen. Electric Co., 1942; Steinmetz award, 1973; named Engr. of Yr. Profl. Engrs. Soc., 1963. Fellow IEEE, ASME, AAAS; mem. Assn. Computing Machinery (founding mem.), Conf. Internationale des Grands Reseaux Electriques a Haute Tension, Nat. Acad. Engring., Nat. Soc. Profl. Engrs., Sigma Xi, Tau Beta Pi. Republican. Presbyterian. Clubs: Venice Yacht, Mohawk Golf. Patentee in field (6). Home and Office: 702 Bird Bay Dr W Venice FL 33595 *I am told that I tend never to take anything on faith, but that I try to find the truth without fear or favor. If there is a talent that I have, it is the ability to abstract the simple essentials from complex problems; and I have never had an uninteresting job.*

CONDE', MICHAEL HUGO, winery executive; b. Reichenberg, Czechoslovakia, Mar. 13, 1939; emigrated to Can., 1959; s. Walter Paul and Hedi (Simon) Conde'-J.; m. Heike Glade, Apr. 19, 1963; m. 2d Carolyn Zena Ferstman, Aug. 1, 1980; children: Stephane, Natasha. B. Commerce, Hamburg Sch. Econs., W. Ger., 1959; diploma in commerce, Hamburg Bd. Trade, 1959. Sales mgr. Gen. Wire & Cable, Coburg, Ont., 1960-66; sales and mktg. mgr. Gen. Foods, Ltd., Vancouver, Winnipeg and Toronto, 1966-72; sales mgr. gen. mgr. Gen. Electric Co., Montreal and Toronto, 1972-76; v.p. John Labatt Catelli div., Montreal, 1976-80; pres. Ridout div. John Labatt, Toronto, 1980—. Organizer Ont. Progressive Conservative Party, Toronto, 1980. Mem. Toronto Bd. Trade, Can. Wine Inst. (chmn., dir.), Grocery Products Assn. Lutheran. Home: 58 Browning Ave Toronto ON Canada M4K 1V9 Office: Ridout Wines Ltd Suite 405 201 City Centre Dr Mississauga ON Canada L5B 2T4

CONDIT, CARL WILBUR, history educator; b. Cin., Sept. 29, 1914; s. Arthur Thomas and Gertrude (Pletz) C.; m. Isabel Marion Campbell, June 19, 1943; children: Stephen Campbell, Richard Stuart, Kenneth Arthur. B.S. in Mech. Engring., Purdue U., 1936; M.A., U. Cin., 1939, Ph.D., 1941, L.H.D. (hon.), 1967, Knox Coll., 1981, DePaul U., 1983; hon. fellow history sci., U. Wis., 1951-52. Instr. math. and mechanics ordnance tng. div. War Dept., Cin., 1941, War Prodn. Sch., 1941-42, Engring. Coll., U. Cin., 1942-44; asst. designing engr. bldg. dept. N.Y.C. R.R., Cin., 1944-45; asst. prof. Carnegie Inst. Tech., 1946-47; from instr. to asso. prof. Northwestern U., Evanston, Ill., 1945-46, 47-61, prof. history, art history and urban affairs, 1961—; Research asso. Smithsonian Instn., 1966-67, mem. adv. council, 1973—. Author: The Rise of the Skyscraper, 1952, The Port of New York: A History of the Rail and Terminal System from the Grand Central Electrification to the Present, 1981, American Building Art: The 19th Century, 1960, American Building Art: The 20th Century, 1961, The Chicago School of Architecture, 1964, (with others) Technology in Western Civilization, 1967, American Building: Materials and Techniques, 1968, Chicago 1910-29: Building, Planning, and Urban Technology, 1973, Chicago 1930-70: Building, Planning, and Urban Technology, 1974, The Railroad and the City: A Technological and Urbanistic History of Cincinnati, 1977, The Pioneer Stage of Railroad Electrification, 1895-1905, 1977, The Port of New York: A History of the Rail and Terminal System from the Beginning to Pennsylvania Station, 1980; editor: (with Eugene Ferguson) Technology and Culture, 1962-76. Recipient Abbott Payson Usher prize Soc. for History Tech., 1968; Civil Engring. History and Heritage award ASCE, 1971; Disting. Service award Chgo. chpt. AIA, 1980. Mem. AAUP, ACLU, History Sci. Soc., Soc. Archtl. Historians (Disting. Achievement award Chgo. chpt. 1982), Soc. History Tech. (exec. council 1959-63, Leonardo da Vinci medal 1973). Home: 9300 Linder Ave Morton Grove IL 60053 Office: Northwestern U Evanston IL 60201

CONDIT, (ELEANOR) LOUISE, ret. mus. supr.; b. Balt., May 7, 1914; d. George Smith and Bessie Blaine (Madeira) C.; m. Frederic G. M. Lange, Sept. 19, 1946. A.B., Vassar Coll., 1935; A.M., Columbia, 1941. Carnegie grant for study edn. museums of, Brit. Isles, Scandinavia, Germany, France, Netherlands, summer 1939; supr. edn. Bklyn. Children's Mus., 1935-42; supr. Jr. Mus. Met. Mus. Art, 1943-61, asst. dean charge Jr. Mus., 1961-68, asso. in charge Jr. Mus., 1968-72, mus. educator in charge Jr. Mus., 1972-80, dep. vice dir. ednl. affairs, 1974-78, dep. dir. ednl. affairs, 1978-80; active mem. U.S. Nat. Com. for Internat. Council Museums, 1972-78. Incorporator Bergen Community Mus., Hackensack, N.J. Mem. Am. Assn. Museums (council 1957-63, v.p. 1960-63), Museums Council N.Y.C. (sec.-treas. 1960-65, vice chmn. 1977-78), Archaeol. Inst. Am. (dir. N.Y. chpt. 1973-77), N.Y. Film Council, Am. Assn. Youth Museums (pres. 1972-74), Inst. Study Art in Edn. (dir. 1974-78), Phi Beta Kappa. Home: 1203 Emerson Ave Teaneck NJ 07666

CONDON, BREEN O'MALLEY, lawyer; b. Boston, Mar. 24, 1944; s. William Jospeh and Dorothy (Murphy) C.; m. Bernadette Fogel, Dec. 18, 1972 (div.). A.B., Georgetown U., 1966; J.D., Fordham U., 1971. Assoc. White & Case, N.Y.C., 1971-80; v.p. and gen. counsel Hardee's Food Systems, Inc., Rocky Mount, N.C., 1980-82; sr. v.p., gen. counsel, sec. Imasco USA, Inc., Rocky Mount, 1982—. Editor: Fordham Law Rev., 1969-71. Served to 1st lt. USAR, 1966-68. Mem. ABA. Roman Catholic. Clubs: N.Y. Athletic; Benvenue Country (Rocky Mount). Office: Imasco USA Inc 1233 N Church St Rocky Mount NC 27801

CONDON, FRANCIS EDWARD, foundation administrator, retired chemistry educator; b. Abington, Mass., Oct. 12, 1919; s. Maurice Francis and Eva Isabel (Cole) C.; m. Mary Anna Medvetz, Jan. 9, 1943; children: Francis E., Mary Ellen (Mrs. George Laessig III), John M., Arthur T., Dorothy A. (Mrs. Ronald G. Waldt), James M., Rita C. A.B., Harvard, 1941, Ph.D., 1944. Research chemist Phillips Petroleum Co., Bartlesville, Okla., 1944-52; asst. prof. chemistry CCNY, 1952-61, assoc. prof., 1962-66, prof., 1967-82, ret., 1982, Louis J. Curtman prof., 1976-78; founder, chmn. Seven Siblings Found., Ltd., 1977—; vis. prof. Purdue U., 1960. Author: (with H. Meislich) Introduction to Organic Chemistry, 1960, Study Projects in Physical Chemistry, 1963, also articles.; Contbr.: chpt. Catalysis, 1958. Mem. planning bd. Borough of Bogota, N.J., 1963; Trustee, pres. Bogota Swim Club, Inc., 1967-71. Petroleum Research Fund grantee, 1967-70; NSF Sci. Faculty fellow U. So. Calif., 1964-65. Mem. Am. Chem. Soc. (dir. N.Y. sect. 1967-68), U.S. Chess Fedn. (life), Glen Rock (N.J.) Chess Club (pres. 1975-79), St. Joseph Holy Name Soc. (pres. 1974-75), Sigma Xi. Home: 471 Larch Ave Bogota NJ 07603

CONDON, GEORGE EDWARD, journalist; b. Fall River, Mass., Nov. 6, 1916; s. John Joseph and Mary Agnes (O'Malley) C.; m. Marjorie Philona Smith, May 9, 1942; children—Theresa, John, George, Katherine, Mary, Susan. B.Sc., Ohio State U., 1940. Publicity dir. Mt. Union Coll., Alliance, Ohio, 1941; info. dir. Agrl. Adjustment Adminstrn. for Ohio, 1941-42; mem. staff Cleve. Plain Dealer, 1943—, gen. columnist, 1962—. Author: Cleveland-The Best-Kept Secret, 1967, Laughter from the Rafters, 1968, Stars in the Water, 1972, Yesterday's Cleveland, 1976, Yesterday's Columbus, 1977, Cleveland: Prodigy of the Western Reserve, 1979. Recipient Ohioana Library Assn. Lit. award, 1975, Cleve. Women's City Club Lit. award, 1975, Emily Gray Burke Meml. award lit., 1979; also award Cleve. Newspaper Guild; awards for public service, copy editing and column writing Press Club Cleve. Mem. Sigma Delta Chi, Pi Sigma Alpha. Home: 1096 Erie Cliff St Lakewood OH 44107 Office: 1801 Superior Ave Cleveland OH 44114

CONDON, JOSEPH F., engineering company executive; b. N.Y.C., Jan. 22, 1925; s. Joseph Francis and Helen Marie (Carboy) C.; m. Ann Merwin Foote, Jan. 16, 1954; children—Alicia Merwin, Joseph Francis III, Susan Olney, Sarah Avery. B.A., Brown U., 1950; Certificate of Econ. and Diplomatic History, London Sch. Econs. and Polit. Sci., 1951. Econ. and polit. analyst U.S. Dept. State, Washington, 1952-55; sect. chief U.S. Dept. Commerce, Washington, 1955-59; asst. to v.p. Parsons & Whittemore Inc., N.Y.C., 1959-60, comml. mgr., London, 1960-63; mng. dir. Ishikawajima Harima-Parsons & Whittmore, Tokyo, 1963-65; v.p. Parsons & Whittemore, N.Y.C., 1965-72; sr. v.p. Wheelabrator-Frye Inc., N.Y.C., 1972; chief exec. officer Wheelabrator Internat. Inc., Hampton, N.H., 1972-75; v.p. internat. fin. The Lummus Co., Bloomfield, N.J., 1976-78; v.p.-internat. Combustion Engring., Inc., Stamford, Conn., 1978—; dir. Interstate Brands Corp., Kansas City, Mo., Viacom Internat., Inc., N.Y.C., Interstate Bakeries Inc., Kansas City, Mo. Bd. dirs. Internat. Study and Research Inst. Served with USNR, 1943-46; PTO. Rotary fellow; Fulbright grantee. Mem. Council Fgn. Relations, Am. Mgmt. Assn., World Council. Clubs: Metropolitan; Fox Meadow Tennis (Scarsdale, N.Y.). Address: 900 Long Ridge Rd Stamford CT 06902

CONDON, LESTER PATRICK, housing consultant; b. Mt. Vernon, N.Y., Oct. 13, 1922; s. Lester P. and Eileen V. (Malone) P.; m. Vera Crossley, Apr. 21, 1946; children: Thomas J., John K., Leslie Patricia, Marietta, Lisa Ann. B.Sc., Providence Coll., 1943; postgrad., Georgetown U. Law Sch., 1948-51; Ford Found. scholar, U. Chgo., 1957. Spl. agt. FBI, 1947-51; asst. chief security OPS, 1951-53; dir. investigation U.S. Ho. of Reps. Com. on Govt. Operations, 1953-54; spl. asst. to adminstr. HHFA, 1954-55, dir. compliance div., 1955-60; dep. commr. FHA, 1960-61, asst. commr. audit and exam., 1961-62; insp. gen. U.S. Dept. Agr., 1962-69; asst. sec. for adminstrn. HUD, 1969-72; exec. v.p. Fed. Nat. Mortgage Assn., Washington, 1972-82, dir., 1972-78; ret., 1982, housing cons., 1982—; Chmn. bd. dirs. Nat. Center for Housing Mgmt.; dir. Equity Investors Inc., Austin, Tex. Served to lt. (j.g.) USNR, World War II. Decorated Purple Heart; recipient Distinguished Service awards HHFA, HUD. Mem. Soc. Former Spl. Agts. FBI, Inst. Internal Auditors, Am. Legion, Phi Delta Phi. Roman Catholic. Clubs: University (Washington); Army/Navy Country. Home and office: 1306 Janney's Ln Alexandria VA 22302

CONDON, RICHARD, author; b. N.Y.C., Mar. 18, 1915; s. Richard Aloysius and Martha (Pickering) C.; m. Evelyn Rose Hunt, January 14, 1938; children: Deborah Condon Weldon, Wendy Condon Jackson. Ed. pub. schs., N.Y.C. Author: play Men of Distinction, 1953; children's record albums The Horse Stories, 1947; novels pub. 21 langs. The Oldest Confession, 1958, The Manchurian Candidate, 1959, Some Angry Angel, 1960, A Talent for Loving, 1961, An Infinity of Mirrors, 1964, Any God Will Do, 1966, The Ecstasy Business, 1967, Mile High, 1969, Vertical Smile, 1971, Arigato, 1972, And then We Moved to Rossenarra, 1973, The Mexican Stove, 1973, Winter Kills, 1974, The Star Spangled Crunch, 1974, Money is Love, 1975, The Whisper of the Axe, 1976, The Abandoned Woman, 1977, Bandicoot, 1978, Death of a Politician, 1978, The Entwining, 1980, Prizzi's Honor, 1982, A Trembling Upon Rome, 1983; screenplay Prizzi's Honor; contbr. to nat. magazines. Decorated chevalier La Confrérie du Tastevin, 1968, commanderie du Bontemps, 1969, chevalier Chaine des Rotisseurs, 1976. Donor Richard Condon Collection to Boston U. Library, 1965. Office: care Harold Matson Co 276 Fifth Ave New York NY 10001 care Abner Stein 10 Roland Gardens London SW 7 3PH England *Writers must do their best to tell their stories well, to involve people, emotion, place, stress, all the things that will hold an audience. All the things that hold an audience are called "entertainment." A writer may call himself an artist but he cannot just sit down and consciously create art. What is art is not likely to be decided for many decades after the work has been produced - and then is often re-decided. We must not feel badly if we think of literature as entertainment rather than as transcendental enlightenment. That is the kiss of a wish. Readers read to be entertained, not to purchase the awe of the ages which will follow.*

CONDON, ROBERT EDWARD, surgeon, educator; b. Albany, N.Y., Aug. 13, 1929; s. Edward A. and Catherine (Kilmartin) C.; m. Marcia Jane Pagano, June 16, 1951; children: Sean Edward, Brian Robert. A.B., U. Rochester, 1951, M.D. (N.Y. Bd. Regents scholar), 1957; M.S., U. Wash., 1965. Diplomate: Am. Bd. Surgery (examiner), Nat. Bd. Med. Examiners. Intern King County Hosp., Seattle, 1957-58; resident dept. surgery U. Wash. Sch. Medicine (and affiliated hosps.), 1958-65; postdoctoral research fellow Nat. Heart Inst., 1961-63; asst. prof. surgery Baylor Coll. Medicine, Houston, 1965-67; assoc. prof. surgery U. Ill. Coll. Medicine, Chgo., 1967-69, prof., 1969-70; prof., head dept. surgery U. Iowa Coll. Medicine, Iowa City, 1971-72; prof. surgery Med. Coll. Wis., Milw., 1972—, chmn. dept. surgery, 1979—; chief surg. services Wood VA Hosp., Milw., 1972-81; attending surgeon Milw. County Gen. Hosp., Columbia Hosp., 1972—; cons. Deaconess, St. Luke's, Luth., St. Mary, St. Joseph hosps., Milw. Author: (with others) Abdominal Pain: A Guide to Rapid Diagnosis, 1969, Manual of Surgical Therapeutics, 5th edit, 1981, Hernia, 2d edit, 1978, Surgical Care, 1980; Assoc. editor: Rev. of Surgery; editorial bd.: Jour. Clin. Therapeutics, Archives of Surgery, Surgery, Jour. Surg. Oncology. Served with USMCR, 1951-53. Recipient sr. class award as Outstanding Faculty Member Baylor U. Coll. Medicine, 1966, Excellence in Teaching award Phi Chi, 1967, Certificate of Appreciation U. Iowa Coll. Medicine, 1971, Tchr. of Year award, 1972, Med. Coll. Wis., 1983; Guggenheim fellow, 1963-64. Mem. A.C.S., AAAS, AMA, Am., Central, Western surg. assns., Wis., Chgo., Milw. surg. socs., Soc. U. Surgeons, Soc. Clin. Surgery, Med. Research Soc. (London), Milw. Acad. Medicine, Royal Soc. Medicine, N.Y. Acad. Scis., Assn. Am. Med. Colls., Soc. Surgery Alimentary Tract, Am. Assn. Surgery of Trauma, Internat. Soc. Surgery, Collegium Internationale Chirurgiae Digestivae, Milw. Acad. Surgery, Assn. for Acad. Surgery. Home: 2300 E Kensington Blvd Milwaukee WI 53211 Office: 8700 W Wisconsin Ave Milwaukee WI 53226

CONDON, THOMAS J., university administrator, historian; b. New Haven, July 27, 1930; m. Ann Kathleen Gorman, 1962; children: Katherine, Caroline, Gregory. B.A., Yale U., 1952; M.A., Boston Coll., 1953; Ph.D., Harvard U., 1962. Teaching fellow history Harvard U., 1959-62; asst. prof. history U. N.B. (Can.), Fredericton, 1962-66; exec. asso. Am. Council Learned Socs., N.Y.C., 1966-70; vis. asso. prof. history Ind. U., 1967-68, City U. N.Y., 1968-69; prof. history, dean of Arts U. N.B., 1970-77, prof. history, dean and v.p., 1977-79, acting pres., 1979-80, prof. history, v.p., 1980—; hon. research fellow Inst. U.S. Studies, U. London, 1975-76; mem. Humanities Research

Council Can., 1972-73; Chmn. adv. com. on arts in N.B. Minister of Youth, 1973-75; bd. govs. Rothesay Collegiate Sch., 1977—, U. N.B., 1977—; mem. St. John Arts Council, 1978—; chmn. engring. task force Maritime Provinces Higher Edn. Commn., 1977-78, mem., 1982—, Mayor's Policy Com., St. John Human Devel. Project, 1979—, Commn. on Fgn. Students Policy, Can. Bur. Internat. Edn., Ottawa, 1980—; chmn., pres. Bi-Capitol Project, Inc., 1982. Author: New York Beginnings: The Commercial Origins of New Netherland, 1968; Mem. editorial bd.: Computers and the Humanities, 1969-70, Acadiensis, 1970—; contbr. articles to profl. jours. Vice pres. St. John Can. Games, 1980—. Served with USNR, 1953-57. Can. Council grantee, 1964, 65. Mem. Can. Soc. Study of Higher Edn. (exec. council 1978-81), Am. Hist. Assn., Brit. Assn. Am. Studies, Can. Assn. Am. Studies, Can. Conf. Arts, Can. Hist. Assn., Can. Univs. Soc. Gt. Brit., N.B. Hist. Soc., York-Sunbury Hist. Soc. Home: 1 Jersey Ln Rothesay NB E0G 2W0 Canada Office: Box 5050 Saint John NB E2L 4L5 Canada

CONDON, VERNER HOLMES, JR., financial executive; b. Bloomington, Ill., June 26, 1926; s. Verner Holmes and Lucille (Dennis) C.; m. Ann Garman, Sept. 3, 1949; children—Martha, Nancy. B.S., Pa. State U., 1948; M.B.A., Northwestern U., 1949. Securities analyst Harris Trust & Savs. Bank, Chgo., 1949-51; with Ford Motor Co., 1951-68, controller tractor div., 1961-62, marketing mgr., 1962-68; v.p. finance AMBAC Industries, Inc., Carle Place, N.Y., 1968-78; exec. v.p., chief fin. officer Gen. Public Utilities Corp., Parsippany, N.J., 1979—. Served with USNR, 1944-46. Mem. Financial Execs. Inst. Home: Post House Rd Morristown NJ 07960 Office: 100 Interpace Pkwy Parsippany NJ 07054

CONE, CARL BRUCE, history educator; b. Davenport, Iowa, Feb. 22, 1916; s. Carl S. and Lena (Peterson) C.; m. Mary Louise Regan, Dec. 20, 1942; 1 son, Timothy. B.A., U. Iowa, 1936, M.A., 1937, Ph.D., 1940. Instr. history Allegheny Coll., Meadville, Pa., 1940-41; research asst. Iowa Hist. Soc., 1941-42; asst. prof. history La. State U., 1942-47; faculty U. Ky., Lexington, 1947—, prof. history, 1956—, chmn. dept., 1965-70; Summer vis. prof. U. Mo., 1952, La. State U., 1960, Miami U., Oxford, Ohio, 1964; dir. U. Ky. summer seminar Nat. Endowment Humanities, 1975. Author: Torchbearer of Freedom, 1952, Burke and the Nature of Politics: The Age of the American Revolution, 1957, Burke and the Nature of Politics: The Age of the French Revolution, 1964, The English Jacobins, 1968, Hounds in the Morning, 1981; also articles. Mem. Lexington Civil Service Commn., 1958-68; bd. dirs. Lexington Library, 1978-83. Recipient Nat. Book award Phi Alpha Theta, 1965; Sang award U. Ky., 1968; Disting. Citizen award City of Lexington, 1981; Hallam prof. U. Ky.; also Faculty fellow Fund Advancement Teaching, 1951-52; Guggenheim fellow, 1963-64; Am. Council Learned Socs. grantee, 1971. Mem. Am. Hist. Assn., So. Hist. Assn. (exec. council 1977-80, chmn. European sect. 1972), Am. Catholic Hist. Assn. (pres. 1967), So. Conf. Brit. Studies (pres. 1972), Omicron Delta Kappa, Phi Beta Kappa, Phi Alpha Theta (internat. council 1975—). Republican. Roman Catholic. Lodge: Kiwanis. Home: 203 Sycamore Rd Lexington KY 40502

CONE, EDWARD TONER, composer, music educator; b. Greensboro, N.C., May 4, 1917; s. Julius Washington and Laura Barbara (Weill) C. A.B., Princeton U., 1939, M.F.A., 1942; D.Mus. (hon.), U. Rochester, 1973, D.F.A., U. N.C.-Greensboro, 1983. Asst. prof. dept. music Princeton U., 1947-52, assoc. prof., 1952-60, prof., 1960—; Andrew D. White prof.-at-large Cornell U., 1979—; Treas. Am. sect. Internat. Soc. Contemporary Music, 1950-52. Composer numerous compositions, 1 symphony, other works for piano, voice, chorus, orch., chamber combinations, 1939—; Author: Musical Form and Musical Performance, 1968, The Composer's Voice, 1974; Co-editor: Perspectives of New Music, 1965-69; adv. editor, 1969-72. Guggenheim fellow in composition, 1947-48. Mem. AAUP. Club: Century. Home: 18 College Rd W Princeton NJ 08540

CONE, JAMES HAL, theologian, educator, author; b. Fordyce, Ark., Aug. 5, 1938; s. Charlie M. and Lucy (Frost) C. B.A., Philander Smith Coll., 1958; B.D., Garrett Theol. Sem., 1961; M.A., Northwestern U., 1963, Ph.D., 1965. Asst. prof. religion and philosophy Philander Smith Coll., Little Rock, 1964-66; asst. prof. religion Adrian (Mich.) Coll., 1966-69; asst. prof. theology Union Theol. Sem., N.Y.C., 1969-70, asso. prof., 1970-73, prof., 1973-77, Charles A. Briggs prof. systematic theology, 1977—; vis. prof. Afro-Am. history U. of Pacific, Stockton, Calif., summer, 1969; vis. asso. prof. religion Barnard Coll., N.Y.C., 1969-71, 74; vis. prof. theology Drew U., Madison, N.J., 1973; lectr. systematic theology Woodstock Coll., N.Y.C., 1971-73; vis. prof. theology Princeton (N.J.) Theol. Sem., 1976, Notre Dame Sch. Theology, New Orleans, summer, 1977, Howard U. Sch. Religion, Washington, 1980. Author: Black Theology and Black Power, 1969 (transl. into Dutch, 1970, German, 1971, Japanese, 1971, Korean, 1979), A Black Theology of Liberation, 1970 (transl. into Spanish, 1973, Italian, 1973, Japanese, 1974), The Spirituals and the Blues: An Interpretation, 1972 (transl. into German, 1973), God of the Oppressed, 1975 (transl. into Japanese, 1976, Italian), My Soul Looks Back, 1982; contbr. articles to profl. publs.; editorial bd.: Jour. Religious Thought, 1975—, Union Sem. Quar. Rev, 1975—, Renewal, 1970—; contbg. editor: Christianity and Crisis, 1970; co-editor: Black Theology: A Documentary History, 1966-79, 1979. Mem. Nat. Com. Black Churchmen, 1969—; mem. adv. bd. Schomburg Corp., 1975-80. Rockefeller Found. grantee, 1973-74. Mem. Am. Theol. Soc., Am. Acad. Religion, Am. Soc. Christian Ethics, Soc. Study Black Religion, Ecumenical Assn. Third World Theologians. Mem. African Methodist Episcopal Ch. Home: 606 W 122d St New York NY 10027 Office: Union Theological Seminary 3041 Broadway New York NY 10027 *

CONE, SPENCER BURTIS, architect, engr.; b. Garden City, Kans., Jan. 12, 1910; s. Roy Spencer and Gertrude Ella (Burtis) C.; m. Nancy Howard, July 29, 1946; children—Catherine Howard, John Spencer. B.S., Armour Inst. Tech., 1933. Pvt. practice architecture, Vt., N.H., 1934-37; partner Cone/Vogelgesang Architects, Chgo., 1937-41; ptnr. Cone/Dornbusch (Architects/Engrs.), Chgo., 1947-82, Cone and Kalb (Architects), 1943—; pres., dir. Comac, Inc., Chgo. Works include Bryan Jr. High Sch, Elmhurst, Hubbard Woods Fashion Center (archtl. awards), Madison Elementary Sch, Skokie, Ill. (honor awards Chgo. chpt. AIA, Chgo. Assn. Commerce and Industry), Barrington Middle Sch, Forest Elementary Sch, (distinguished bldg. awards Chgo. chpt. AIA), Chgo. Assn. Commerce and Industry.). Pres. Chgo. Fine Arts Music Found., 1966-68; mem. Mayor's Adv. Coms. on Bldg. Code Amendments and Standards and Tests, 1967—. Served with USN, 1941-44; PTO. Fellow AIA (pres. Chgo. chpt. 1969, chmn. nat. com. ednl. facilities planning 1968-69). Clubs: Dunham Wood Riding (Wayne, Ill.); Arts (dir.), Chgo. Farmers, Builders (Chgo.). Home: Taana Farms 39W067 Kaneville Rd Batavia IL 60510 Office: Cone and Kalb Architects 549 W Randolph St Chicago IL 60606

CONE, SYDNEY M., III, lawyer; b. Greensboro, N.Y., Nov. 30, 1930; s. Sydney M. and Isabel (Frank) C.; m. Michele Nadine Calleux, Dec. 22, 1952; children: Timothy, Annabelle. A.B., Haverford Coll., 1952; LL.B., Yale U., 1959. Bar: N.C. 1959, D.C. 1960, N.Y. 1970. Assoc. Cleary, Gottlieb, Steen & Hamilton, Washington, 1959-62, Brussels, 1962-66, Paris, 1966-68, N.Y.C., 1968-69, ptnr., 1969—; spl. asst. to undersec. of state U.S. State Dept., Washington, 1961; lectr. Yale Law Sch., New Haven, 1975-76; mem. Institute d'Etudes Europeennes, (Brussels U.), 1964-66. Editor-in-chief: Yale Law Jour., 1958-59; contbr. articles to profl. jours. Served to lt. (j.g.) USN, 1953-56. Mem. Assn. Bar City N.Y., ABA, Union Internationale des Avocats (exec. com.). Clubs: Sky, University. Home: 1050 Park Ave New York NY 10028 Office: 1 State Street Plaza New York NY 10028

CONERLY, RICHARD PUGH, corporation executive; b. Jackson, Ala., May 6, 1924; s. William L. and Eunice (Pugh) C.; m. Iva Jean Brightwell, Aug. 12, 1956; children: William Edward, Robert Andrew, Christopher Brightwell, Elizabeth Anne. Student, Howard Coll., Birmingham, Ala., 1942; B.J., U. Mo., 1949; LL.B., Harvard U., 1952. Bar: Mo. 1952. Practice in, St. Louis, 1952-65; assoc., partner Thompson & Mitchel, 1952-65; v.p., gen. counsel, exec. v.p. Peabody Coal Co., St. Louis, 1965-69; pres. Pott Industries Inc., St. Louis, 1969—; vice-chmn. Houston Natural Gas Corp., 1979—. Served with USAAF, 1942- 46. Home: 339 Hawthorne St Webster Groves MO 63119 Office: 3010 Mercantile Tower Saint Louis MO 63101

CONESE, EUGENE PAUL, manufacturing company executive; b. Eastchester, N.Y., Aug. 1, 1929; s. Frank P. and Frances (Lisi) C.; m. Anna May R. Savino, Nov. 5, 1955; children: Deborah Ann, Susan Marie, Eugene Paul, Mark Paul. B.B.A., Iona Coll., 1951; postgrad., N.Y. U. Sch. Bus. Adminstrn., 1954-55. Sr. accountant Deloitte Haskins & Sells (C.P.A.s), 1951-53, 55-57; asst. controller B.T. Babbitt Co., 1958-60; v.p. Funk & Wagnalls, 1960-65, v.p., dir. mktg. Reader's Digest Books div., 1966-67; chief fin. officer Black Clawson Co., 1967-69; pres., chief exec. officer, dir. Irvin Industries Inc., Stamford, Conn., 1969-79; founder, pres. Conese Assoc., Inc., 1979-80; pres., chmn. Haskon Corp., Taunton, Mass., 1980—; chmn. The Greenwich Co., Ltd., Stamford, 1984—. Served with AUS, 1953-54. Mem. Fin. Execs. Inst. (chmn. N.Y. chpt. orgn. and mgmt. com. N.Y. chpt. 1956), Machinery and Allied Products, Inst. (accounting prins. bd. 1967-69), Am. Safety Belt Council (dir. 1972-79), Phenolic Brake Piston Council (dir. 1984—), Am. Mgmt. Assn., Planning Execs. Inst., Beta Gamma Sigma. Clubs: American (London, Eng.); Innis Arden Golf (Old Greenwich, Conn.); Segreganset Country (Taunton, Mass.). Home: 16 Stepping Stone Ln Greenwich CT 06830 Office: The Greenwich Co Ltd 2001 W Main St Stamford MA 06902

CONEWAY, PETER RICHARD, investments company executive; b. Cleve., Apr. 13, 1944; s. Albert Earl and Clara Laroux (Durham) C.; m. Marsella Lynn Martin, July 29, 1967; children: Natalie, Cecile. B.B.A., U. Tex., 1966; postgrad., U. Hong Kong, 1967; M.B.A., Stanford U., 1969. In instl. sales Goldman, Sachs & Co., Dallas, 1969-75, v.p., resident mgr., Houston, 1975-78, ptnr., 1978—. Trustee Stanford Bus. Sch., 1983—, Houston Ballet Found., 1983—, Houston Lyric Theatre, 1983—, Mus. Fine Arts, 1983—; bd. dirs. Houston Symphony Soc., 1983—; vice chmn. Houston Bapt. U. President's Council, 1979. Fellow Rotary Found., 1966-67. Allied mem. N.Y. Stock Exchange. Baptist. Clubs: River Oaks, Tejas, Coronado (Houston). Office: Goldman Sachs and Co 1000 Louisiana Suite 2200 Houston TX 77002

CONFER, OGDEN PALMER, feed and flour mill executive; b. Mpls., Nov. 14, 1921; s. Ogden Armour and Ruth (Palmer) C.; m. Elizabeth McElhenny, Dec. 20, 1941; children: Ogden William, Kay, Richard Palmer, Carol. Student, Westminster Coll., Mo., 1939-40; B.B.A., U. Minn., 1943. Mgr. feed div., v.p. Hubbard Milling Co., Mankato, Minn., 1946-59, pres., 1959-70, chmn. bd., chief exec. officer, Mdankato, Minn., 1970—; dir. Northwest Bank, Mankato, Confer Bros., Mpls. Mem. N.W. Feed Mfrs. Assn. (past pres.), Am. Feed Mfrs. Assn. (dir., chmn. bd. 1970—), Millers Nat. Fedn. (past dir.), Mankato C. of C. (past dir.). Presbyterian (trustee, elder). Club: Mankato Golf (past dir.). Lodges: Kiwanis; Elks. Home: Route 6 Mankato MN 56001 Office: Hubbard Milling Co 424 N Front St Mankato MN 56001

CONFORTI, MICHAEL PETER, art historian, museum curator; b. Bradford, Mass., Apr. 3, 1945; s. Sven and Cecile C. B.A., Trinity Coll., Hartford, Conn., 1968; M.A., Harvard U., 1973, Ph.D. (Nat. Endowment Arts Museum fellow 1974-75), 1977; fellow art history, Am. Acad. Rome, 1975-77. Cataloguer Sotheby & Co., London, 1968-69, dir. tng. program, N.Y.C., 1969-71; curator sculpture and decorative arts Fine Arts Mus., San Francisco, 1977-80; chief curator, Bell Meml. curator decorative arts and sculpture Mpls. Inst. Arts, 1980—. Author articles in field. Mem. Decorative Arts Socs., Furniture History Soc., Am. Ceramic Circle, Silver Soc., Psi Upsilon. Clubs: Harvard (N.Y.C.); Travellers (London). Home: 1912 Dupont Ave S Minneapolis MN 55403 Office: Mpls Inst Arts Minneapolis MN 55404

CONGDON, JOHN RHODES, corporate exec.; b. Balt., Feb. 17, 1933; s. Earl Everett and Lillian Francis (Herbert) C.; m. Barbara Natalie Neblett, June 17, 1952; children—Susan Lee, John Rhodes, Jeffrey Whitefield. Student, U. Richmond, 1952-53. Joined Old Dominion Freight Line as driver, 1951; now chmn.; pres., founder Old Dominion Truck Leasing, 1963—; dor. Nat. Truck Leasing System; pres. Va. Hwy. Users Assn., 1976-78. Deacon River Rd. Ch., 1971-81; pres. Dorset Woods Civic Assn., 1973-74. Served with U.S. Army, 1953-55. Mem. Va. Hwy. Users Assn., River Rd. Citizens. Clubs: Willow Oaks Country, Masons, Shrine. Home: 109 Walsing Dr Richmond VA 23229 Office: 7511 White Pine Rd Chesterfield VA 23832

CONGDON, THOMAS B., JR., publisher; b. New London, Conn., Mar. 17, 1931; s. Thomas B. and Lula Hanes (Caffey) C.; m. Constance Michele Bossard, Sept. 20, 1958; children—Pamela Lemle, Elizabeth Caffey. Student, St. George's Sch., 1946-49; B.A., Yale U., 1953; M.S. in Journalism, Columbia U., 1956. Editor Saturday Evening Post, Phila. and N.Y.C., 1956-64, sr. editor, 1964-68; editor Harper & Row, N.Y.C., 1968-71; sr. editor Doubleday & Co., N.Y.C., 1971-74; editor-in-chief E.P. Dutton & Co., N.Y.C., 1974-75; editorial dir. Thomas Congdon Books, 1976-79; pres., pub. Congdon & Weed Inc., N.Y.C., 1979—. Served to lt. (j.g.) USNR, 1950-55. Club: Century Assn. (N.Y.C.). Office: Congdon & Weed Inc 298 Fifth Ave. New York NY 10001

CONGDON, WILLIAM GROSVENOR, artist; b. Providence, Apr. 15, 1912; s. Gilbert Maurice and Caroline (Grosvenor) C. B.A., Yale U., 1939. Author: In My Disc Gold, 1962, Esistenza-Viaggio Diario pittore american, 1975, Heart in the Eye, 1979, America Addio-Lettere a Belle, 1980, Cantiere dell' Artista, 1983; One man exhbns. include, Betty Parsons Gallery, N.Y.C., 1948-68, Jeffress Gallery, London, 1958, Obelisco Gallery, Rome, 1952, 57, Cadario Gallery, Milan, Italy, 1962, 69, Palazzo Reale, Milan, 1962, Palazza dei DiAmanti, Ferrara; represented in permanent collections, Pa. Acad. Fine Arts, Phila., Corcoran Gallery, Washington, Whitney Mus. Am. Art, N.Y.C., Tokyo Art Mus., Met. Mus. Art, N.Y.C., Mus. Modern Art, N.Y.C., numerous others. Served with Brit. 8th Army with Am. Field Service, 1942-45. Recipient Temple gold medal Pa. Acad. Fine Arts, 1951; Clark award Corcoran Gallery, 1953. Roman Catholic.

CONGER, BOB VERNON, plant and soil science educator; b. Greeley, Colo., July 2, 1938; s. Vernon Fred and Florence Violet (Pierce) C.; m. Donna Dee Russell, June 5, 1960; children: Gregory, Rhonda, Stephen, Michael. B.S., Colo. State U., 1963; Ph.D., Wash. State U., 1967. Asst. prof. Wash. State U., Pullman, 1967-68, U. Tenn., Knoxville, Oak Ridge, 1968-73, assoc. prof., 1973-78, prof. dept. plant and soil sci., 1978—; editor CRC Critical Revs. in Plant Scis., 1981—; assoc. editor Environ. and Exptl. Botany, 1979—. Author, editor: Cloning Agricultural Plants Via in Vitro Techniques, 1981; contbr. articles to prof. jours. Predoctorial trainee NASA, 1964-67; research grantee Nat. Soybean Corp. Improvement, 1973-75, U.S. Dept. Agr., 1979-81, 82—. Mem. AAAS, Am. Genetic Assn., Crop Sci. Soc. Am., Tissue Culture Assn., Plant Molecular Biology Assn., Internat. Assn. Plant Tissue Culture, Sigma Xi, Phi Kappa Phi, Alpha Zeta, Beta Beta Beta. Methodist. Home: 723 Robertsville Rd Oak Ridge TN 37830 Office: U Tenn Dept Plant and Soil Sci PO Box 1071 Knoxville TN 37901

CONGER, CLEMENT ELLIS, fgn. service officer, curator; b. Rockingham, Va., Oct. 15, 1912; s. Clement E. and Hallie (Ramsay) C.; m. Lianne Hopkins, May 29, 1948; children—William Ramsay, Jay Alden, Shelley Louise. Grad., Strayer Coll., George Washington U., 1933-34, Adj. Gen. Officer Candidate Sch., Ft. Washington Md., 1943; D.H.L., Coll. William and Mary, 1977. Asst. finance examiner PWA, 1933-34; officer mgr., corr. Chgo. Tribune, Washington, 1934-41; office mgr. U.S. Rubber Co., Washington, 1941-42, pub. relations asst., N.Y.C., 1946-47; staff asst., asst. exec. dir. asst. sec. state for occupied areas Dept. State, 1947-49; staff asst., asst. exec. dir. Bur. German Affairs, 1949-54, asst. chief protocol, 1955-57, dep. chief protocol, 1958-61; spl. asst. to dir., exec. sec. ACDA State Dept., Washington, 1962-69; dep. chief protocol, 1969-70; curator Diplomatic Reception Rooms State Dept., 1961—, White House curator, 1970—; lectr. on diplomatic reception rooms Dept. of State and; White House.; Advisor White House Preservation Fund; mem. Com. for Preservation White House; mem. men's adv. com. Gunston Hall Plantation, Va.; mem. Com. Disting. Ams. for Mt. Vernon; vice chmn. Com. on Gov.'s Mansion, Richmond, Va.; mem. Supreme Ct. Hist. Commn.; chmn. pres.'s house refurbishing com. Coll. William and Mary; former trustee Va. Mus. Fine Arts, Richmond, Woodrow Wilson Birthplace Found.; v.p. Lee-Jackson Found.; chmn. Historic Alexandria Found.; mem. men's adv. com. Gunston Hall Plantation, Va.; pres. Va. Trust for Historic Preservation. Producer color motion picture travel films; Contbr. articles, illustrations to various publs. radio, TV programs. Bd. overseers Sweet Briar Coll.; sr. warden Christ Ch., Alexandria, Va. Served from 2d lt. to maj. AUS, 1942-46; asst. sec. combined civil affairs com. Combined Chiefs Staff. Recipient Eleanor Clay Ford award, 1978; Thomas Jefferson award Am. Soc. Interior Designers, 1978; Gold medal of honor Nat. Arts Club, 1980; Agora award The Marketplace, Phila., 1980; others. Mem. Soc. Cincinnati, Chevaliers de Tastevin. Episcopalian. Clubs: Metropolitan, Chevy Chase, Army-Navy Country (Washington). Home: 320 Mansion Dr Alexandria VA 22302 Office: Dept State Washington DC 20520 Address: The White House Washington DC 20500

CONGER, FRANKLIN BARKER, oil company executive; b. San Francisco, Oct. 20, 1929; s. Franklin Barker and Katherine C.; m. Joan Smith, Sept. 1950; children: Anne M., Lisa W., Donald H., Stephen B. B.A., U. Calif., Berkeley, 1951. With Shell Oil Co., 1951-80, div. exploration mgr., 1965-80; with Ashland Oil, Inc., 1980—; pres. Ashland Exploration, Inc., Houston, 1980—. Fellow Geol. Soc. Am.; mem. Am. Assn. Petroleum Geologists. Republican. Office: PO Box 218330 Houston TX 77218

CONGER, HARRY MILTON, mining co. exec.; b. Seattle, July 22, 1930; s. Harry Milton, Jr. and Caroline (Gunnell) C.; m. Phyllis Nadine Shepherd, Aug. 14, 1949; children: Harry Milton IV, Preston George. E.M., Colo. Sch. Mines, 1955. Registered profl. engr., Ariz., Colo. Shift foreman Asarco, Inc., Silver Bell, Ariz., 1955-64; mgr. Kaiser Steel Corp. Eagle Mountain Mine, 1964-70; v.p., gen. mgr. Kaiser Resources, Ltd., Fernie, B.C., Can., 1970-73, Consolidation Coal Co. (Midwestern div.), Carbondale, Ill., 1973-75; v.p. Homestake Mining Co., San Francisco, 1975-77, pres., 1977-78, pres., chief exec. officer, 1978-82, chmn., pres., chief exec. officer, 1982—, also dir.; dir. Calif. Portland Cement Co., Pacific Gas & Electric Co. Mem. Sch. Bd., Eagle Mountain, Calif., 1968-69; bd. dirs. Bay Area Council. Served with C.E. U.S. Army, 1956. Recipient Disting. Achievement medal Colo. Sch. Mines, 1978. Mem. Am. Inst. Mining Engrs., Mining and Metallurgy Soc. Am., Mining Club, Am. Mining Congress (dir.), Conf. Bd. (dir.). Republican. Episcopalian. Clubs: Commonwealth, Pacific Union, Bankers, World Trade, Diablo Country. Office: 650 California St San Francisco CA 94108

CONGER, JOHN JANEWAY, psychologist, educator; b. New Brunswick, N.J., Feb. 27, 1921; s. John C. and Katharine (Janeway) C.; m. Mayo Trist Kline, Jan. 1, 1944; children: Steven Janeway, David Trist. B.A. magna cum laude, Amherst Coll., 1943; M.S., Yale U., 1947, Ph.D., 1949; D.Sc. (hon.), Ohio U., 1980, D.Sci., Amherst Coll., 1983. Asst. prof. psychology Ind. U., 1949-53; chief staff psychologist U.S. Naval Acad., 1951-52; mem. faculty U. Colo. Sch. Medicine, prof. psychology, 1957—, asso. dean, 1961-63, v.p. for med. affairs, 1963-70, dean, 1963-68; fellow Center for Advanced Study in Behavioral Scis., Stanford, Cal., 1970-71; vis. scholar Inst. Human Devel., U. Calif., Berkeley, 1978; v.p., dir. health program John D. and Catherine T. MacArthur Found., 1980-83, cons., 1983—; cons. to NIH, VA, USPHS.; Vice chmn. Colo. Bd. Psychology Examiners, 1961-64; mem. Gov. Colo. Com. Mental Health, 1957; chmn. mental health adv. council Colo. Dept. Pub. Health, 1957-61; mem. tng. com. Nat. Inst. Mental Health, 1959-62; mem. Western council mental health research and tng. Western Interstate Commn. Higher Edn., 1959-66; chmn. research com. President's Com. Traffic Safety, 1960-63; vice chmn. nat. motor vehicle safety adv. council Dept. Transp., 1967-70; mem. inter-council com. constrn. univ.-affiliated facilities for mentally retarded Dept. Health, Edn. and Welfare, 1967-70, mem. sec.'s adv. com. traffic safety, 1966-69; council research and planning Am. Hosp. Assn., 1965-68; nat. adv. mental health council USPHS, 1965-69; nat. adv. com. John F. Kennedy Center for Research on Edn. and Human Devel., 1965-76, chmn., 1970-74; mem. adv. com. on undergrad med. edn. AMA, 1969-70; adv. com. on casualty ins. Dept. Transp., 1970; mem. Pres.'s Task Force on Hwy. Safety, 1970, President's Commn. on Mental Health, 1977-78; mem. com. study nat. needs for biomed. and behavioral sci. research personnel Nat. Acad. Scis., 1976-80; mem. Inst. Medicine/Nat. Acad. Scis., summer 1983. Author: Child Development and Personality, 6th edit, 1984, Readings in Child Development, 1964, 3d edit., 1984, Personality, Social Class and Delinquency, 1965, Adolescence and Youth: Psychological Development in a Changing World, 3d edit., 1984, Basic and Contemporary Issues in Developmental Psychology, 1975, Contemporary Issues in Adolescent Development, 1975, Psychological Development: A Life-Span Approach, 1979, Adolescence: Generation Under Pressure, 1979, Essentials of Child Development and Personality, 1980, also articles. Served to lt. USNR, 1944-46, 51-52. Recipient Stearns Alumni medal for extraordinary Service U Colo., 1970. Fellow Am. Psychol. Assn. (mem. policy and planning bd. 1967-70, rec. sec., dir. 1974-79, pres.-elect 1980-81, pres. 1980-82, past pres. 1982-83), AAAS, Soc. Research in Child Devel. (program chmn. 1975); mem. Denver Med. Soc. (hon. mem.), Colo. Med. Soc. (Disting. Service award 1970), Phi Beta Kappa, Sigma Xi, Alpha Omega Alpha (hon.). Club: Cosmos. Home: 130 S Birch St Denver CO 80222

CONGER, KYRIL B., urologist; b. Berlin, Germany, Apr. 11, 1913; s. Seymour Beach and Lucile (Bailey) C.; m. Joy Springer, June 1, 1945; children: Steven B., Kyril B. II, James W. and William T. (twins). A.B., U. Mich., 1933, M.D., 1936. Instr. urology U. Mich. Hosp., 1941; urologist; med. group, Honolulu, 1946-47; prof. urology, dept. head Temple U. Med. Sch. and Hosp., Phila., 1947-82; urologist VA Ctr.,

Ft. Meyers, Fla., 1982—; area cons. urology VA Mid-Atlantic State and P.R. Contbr. articles to profl. jours.; Author: Transurethral Prostatic Surgery, 1964. Served from lt. to col. M.C. AUS, 1942-46; urology sect. 298th Gen Hosp. Fellow A.C.S.; mem. Am. Urological Assn., Sigma Xi, Nu Sigma Nu. Home: 920 Iris Ct Marco Island FL 33937 Office: 3401 N Broad St Philadelphia PA 19140

CONGER, WILLIAM FRAME, artist, educator; b. Dixon, Ill., May 29, 1937; s. Robert Allen and Catherine Florence (Kelly) C.; m. Kathleen Marie Onderak, May 23, 1964; children: Sarah Elizabeth, Clarisa Lynn. Student, Art Inst. Chgo., 1954, 56-57, 60, 62; B.F.A., U. N.Mex., 1960; M.F.A., U. Chgo., 1966. Asst. prof. Rock Valley Coll., Rockford, 1966-71; vis. lectr. Beloit Coll., 1969; prof., chmn. dept. art DePaul U., Chgo., 1971—; lectr. U. Chgo., 1976-83, Cornell U., 1980; adj. prof. So. Ill. U., 1984. One man shows, Burpee Mus., Rockford, Ill., 1971, Douglas Kenyon Gallery, Chgo., 1974, 75, Krannert Center for Arts, Urbana, Ill., 1976, Zaks Gallery, Chgo., 1978, 80, 83, Roy Boyd Gallery, Chgo., 1984, group shows include, Art Inst. Chgo., 1963, 71, 73, 78, 80, Mus. Contemporary Art, Chgo., 1976, Krannert Mus., Urbana, Ill. State Mus., 1978, E.B. Crocker Gallery, Sacramento, 1977, Phoenix Mus., Mitchell Mus., 1980, Notre Dame U., 1981, Sonoma State U., 1983, Cowles Mus., Arts Club Chgo.; represented in permanent collections, Art Inst. Chgo., Ill. State Mus., Mus. Contemporary Art, Chgo., No. Ill. U., DePaul U., Jonson Mus., U. N.Mex., others, also pvt. collections U.S. and worldwide.; Revs. and commentary in Arts mag., Art Forum, Art News; others. Bd. dirs. Ox Bow Art Sch. Recipient Bartels award Art Inst. Chgo., 1971; Clusmann award, 1973; Friedman awards U. Chgo., 1965, 66. Mem. Coll. Art Assn. Am., Phi Sigma Tau. Home: 3014 W Hollywood Ave Chicago IL 60659 Office: Dept Art DePaul U 802 W Belden Chicago IL 60614

CONINE, ERNEST, newspaper columnist; b. Dallas, Dec. 31, 1925; s. Ernest and Myrtle Eva (Elkins) C.; m. Phyllis Joan Hoyland, Nov. 28, 1953 (dec.); m. Ulla Fisher, Jan. 10, 1981. B.S., So. Methodist U., 1948. Staff writer UPI, Dallas, 1948-51; Washington corr. Dallas Times Herald, 1952-55; successively Washington corr., Moscow corr., New Eng. mgr. Bus. Week mag., 1955-63; fgn. corr. Los Angeles Times, Vienna, 1963-64, public affairs columnist, mem. editorial bd., Los Angeles, 1964—; mem. adv. bd. Center Internat. and Strategic Affairs, UCLA, 1975—; mem. Calif. Seminar Internat. Security and Fgn. Affairs, 1970—, Los Angeles Com. Fgn. Affairs, 1973—. Contbr. articles to nat. magazines. Served with AUS, 1944-46, 51-52. Mem. Sigma Delta Chi. Club: Nat. Press (Washington). Office: Los Angeles Times Times Mirror Sq Los Angeles CA 90053

CONKIN, PAUL KEITH, history educator; b. Chuckey, Tenn., Oct. 25, 1929; s. Harry Thomas and Dorothy (Staten) C.; m. Dorothy L. Tharp, 1954; 3 children. B.A., Milligan Coll., 1951; M.A., Vanderbilt U., 1953, Ph.D., 1957. Asst. prof. history U. Southwestern La., 1957-59; asst. prof., assoc. prof., prof. U. Md., 1959-67; prof. U. Wis., Madison, 1967-76, Merle Curti prof., 1976-79; disting. prof. history Vanderbilt U., Nashville, 1979—. Author: The New Deal, 1967, F.D.R. and the Origins of the Welfare State, 1967, Puritans and Pragmatists, 1968, Self-Evident Truths, 1974, Prophets of Prosperity, 1980; co-author: The Heritage and Challenge of History, 1971; author: A History of Recent America, 1974; co-editor: New Directions in American Intellectual History, 1979. Guggenheim fellow, 1965-66; sr. fellow Nat. Endowment for Humanities, 1972-73. Mem. Am. Hist. Assn. (Beveridge award 1958), Orgn. Am. Historians. Home: 1003 Tyne Blvd Nashville TN 37220

CONKLIN, CAROL MARIE, transportation company executive; b. Jamaica, N.Y., Dec. 7, 1931; d. Raymond Jerome and Caroline Veronica (Zagora) C. LL.B., U. Detroit, 1955. Bar: Mich. Title officer, atty. Lawyers Title Corp., Detroit, 1955-72; mem. real estate legal staff Gen. Motors Corp., Detroit, 1972-77, 83—, sec., N.Y.C., 1978-83, Gen. Motors Acceptance Corp., 1977-78. Recipient Tribute to Women in Internat. Industry award Nat. Bd. YWCA, 1978. Mem. ABA, Mich. Bar Assn., Am. Soc. Corporate Secs. Inc. Roman Catholic. Office: Gen Motors Corp 767 5th Ave New York NY 10021

CONKLIN, CLARENCE ROBERT, lawyer; b. Arcadia, Kan., Aug. 18, 1899; s. Thomas C. and Elizabeth (Yoos) C.; m. Ellen Gleason Birkhoff, Aug. 20, 1932 (dec. May 1972); children: Robert D. Birkhoff (stepson), Adrienne Diane (Mrs. Russell F. Stephens. Jr.), Thomas William, Ellen Melissa C. (Mrs. David P. Harmon, Jr.). Student, Phillips U., 1919-1921, Okla. State Coll., 1923; A.B., Drake U., 1925; J.D., U. Chgo., 1928. Bar: Ill. 1928. With Nat. Surety Corp., claims atty., 1929-1937; with Toplis & Harding, 1937-1945; partner law firm of Heineke & Conklin, and Heineke Conklin & Schrader, 1945-67; of counsel Conklin & Adler Ltd., Chgo., 1979—; counsel various ins. underwriters. Mem. Internat. Assn. Ins. Counsel, Am., Ill., Chgo. bar assns., Maritime Law Assn. U.S., Beta Theta Pi, Phi Alpha Delta. Clubs: Union League (Chgo.); Hinsdale (Ill.) Golf; Misquamicut (Watch Hill, R.I.); Cypress Lake Country (Ft. Myers, Fla.). Home: Buttonwood Ln Sanibel FL 33957

CONKLIN, EVERETT LAWSON, environmental horticulturist; b. Farmingdale, N.Y., Jan. 11, 1908; s. George and Grace (Williams) C.; m. Ruth Purick, June 20, 1931; children: Everett George, Patricia Conklin Clinton, Betty Jane Conklin Baxter. Student, NYU. Accredited profl. nurseryman, N.J. State Nurserymen's Assn., 1979.; cert. interior horti culturist, 1983. Sales mgr. Bobbink & Atkins, East Rutherford, N.J., 1938-54; div. mgr., dir. Bobbink Nurseries, East Rutherford, 1954-57; pres. Everett Conklin & Co., Inc., Montvale, N.J., 1957-82, chmn., 1982—; pres. Everett Conklin-West, Inc., Tustin, Calif., 1974—; Everett Conklin Canada, Ltd., 1975—; Mem. N.J. Rural Adv. Commn., 1955-60; pres. Bergen County Bd. Agr., 1957-58; chmn. floral decorations com. Pres. Nixon Inaugural Ball, 1969, 73; advisor U.S. Dept. Agr., 1971—; ofcl. horticulture advisor Winter Olympic Games, Lake Placid, N.Y., 1980; Bd. dirs. Internat. Flower Show, N.Y.C., 1958-72; mem. hort. com. Smithsonian Instn., 1979-81. Ann. designer, stager, Hess Internat. Flower Show, Allentown, Pa., 1962-73; designer, stager floral decorations, Four Seasons Restaurant, N.Y.C., 1959-82, Macy New York annual flower shows, 1975-82; planter interior gardens, Ford Found. Bldg, N.Y.C., 1967—, Crown Center Hotel, Kansas City, 1973—, Winter Garden, Rainbow Center, Niagara Falls, 1977-83, Met. Mus. Art, Charles Engelhardt Garden Ct, 1980-82; guest lectr.: Cunard Line, Queen Elizabeth II, 1982; Co-author: Handbook of Speciality Elements in Architecture, 1981; bot. name pronunciation guide, advisor: Am. Horticulturist mag., 1983; author, lectr., in field. Recipient numerous hort. awards including Nat. AAN Landscape award, 1960, 61, 68, 69, 71, 72, 73, 74, 75, 76, 77, 78, 79, 80, 81, Internat. Floral Achievement award, 1965, Florists Transworld Delivery Assn. award, 1971, Florafax award, 1971, Teleflora award, 1971, 75, Golden Flower award, 1971, Asso. Landscape Contractors Am. nat. awards, 1971-81, Am. Inst. Interior Designers ann. award, 1973, Man of the Year award, 1974, 77, First Florist of Land award Mich. State Florists Assn., 1973, also nat. awards Am. Soc. Landscape Architects, 1978, Fla. Nurserymen's Assn., 1978; Participant's medal Winter Olympics, 1980; Nat. Landscape award Mrs. Ronald Reagan, 1981; numerous others; named to Nat. Foliage Hall of Fame, 1979; Nat. Floricultural Hall of Fame, 1980. Mem. Am. Hort. Soc. (dir. 1977—), N.J. Florists Assn. (pres. 1954-55), Nat. Interior Plantscape Assn. (pres.-elect 1979—, awards 1979, 80), Am. Acad. Florists (trustee, awards 1967-72), N.Y. Florists Club (pres. 1968, awards 1969-72), Met. Retail Florists Assn. (pres. 1966), Soc. Am. Florists (pres. 1971-73, trustee Found. 1978—, Endowment Safefounder award 1971, 74, 77), Soc. Archtl. Historians, Am. Forestry Assn., N.J. Agrl. Soc., IPA Acad. Poets, many others. Office: 319 W Passaic Ave Rutherford NJ 07070 *As man cannot live by bread alone, neither can he live without the comfort and solace found in an environment in which trees, plants and flowers are plentiful. The desert peoples seek the oasis, but the oasis peoples seldom seek the desert. This is the philosophy of my business in which mediocrity of purpose or result have never been acceptable.*

CONKLIN, GEORGE MELVILLE, retired food company executive; b. Roselle Park, N.J., Dec. 29, 1921; s. Melville Guy and Anna Elizabeth (McMahon) C.; m. Jean Austin Wiley, Feb. 19, 1944; children: Andrea, Blair. B.S., Clarkson Coll. Tech., 1947; M.S., Newark Coll. Engring., 1951. Draftsman Babcock & Wilcox, N.Y.C., 1939-42; indsl. engr. Johns-Manville Co., Manville, N.J., 1947-48, Western Electric Co., Kearny, N.J., 1948-50, Gen. Ceramics, Keasby, N.J., 1950-51; indsl. engring. supr. Gen Electric Co., Bloomfield, N.J., 1951-52; with M & M/Mars, Hackettstown, N.J., 1952—, pres., 1968-78, chmn., 1980—; group pres. Mars, Inc., 1979-80. Trustee Clarkson Coll. Tech. Served with inf. AUS, 1943-45. Decorated Combat Inf. badge. Mem. Chocolate Mfrs. Am., Nat. Confectioners Assn. Clubs: Roxiticus Golf (Bernardsville, N.J.); Pine Valley Golf (N.J.); Loantaka Skeet (Florham Park, N.J.); Quail Ridge Country (Delray Beach, Fla.); Somerset Hill Golf (Bernardsville, N.J.). Home: 3899 Quail Ridge Dr Boynton Beach FL 33436 *Be a leader that most people do not notice so that when a job is done well, the people believe that they did it themselves.*

CONKLIN, GORDON LEROY, editor; b. Cuba, N.Y., June 8, 1927; s. Clarence Monroe and Mabel Anna (Nottingham) C.; m. Edith Onolee Stapley, Aug. 13, 1949; children: Maureen Kelly, Lance Sherwood. B.S., Cornell U., 1949, M.S., 1950. Farm loan supr. Deleware Nat. Bank, Delhi, N.Y., 1950-52; asst. county agrl. agt., Cayuga County, N.Y., 1954-59; asst. editor Am. Agriculturist, Ithaca, N.Y., 1959-62, editor, 1962—; dir. Am. Agriculturist Found., Inc., 1963—. Mem. Trumansburg Central Sch. Bd., 1966-73. Served with U.S. Army, 1952-54. Recipient Agrl. Cons. award Farm Credit Service, 1967; Distinguished Service to Agr. award N.Y. State Assn. County Agrl. Agts., 1974; Hon. Empire Farmer award Future Farmers Am., 1967; award Freedoms Found., 1964. Mem. Am. Agrl. Editors Assn., N.Y. Forest Owners Assn. (dir.), N.Y. Agrl. Soc., Alpha Zeta. Republican. Methodist. Home: 108 Iradell Rd Ithaca NY 14850 Office: PO Box 370 Ithaca NY 14851 *It has been my observation that each person is a mixture of plus and minus . . . even as the universe is composed of atoms made up of particles bearing positive and negative electronic potential. All I ask of any person is that his or her positives outweigh the negatives, and that a residue of the positive remain in the ledger of life when that person no longer casts a shadow in the sun.*

CONKLIN, HAROLD COLYER, anthropologist, educator; b. Easton, Pa., Apr. 27, 1926; s. Howard S. and May W. (Colyer) C.; m. Jean M. Morisuye, June 11, 1954; children: Bruce Robert, Mark William. A.B., U. Calif.-Berkeley, 1950; Ph.D., Yale U., 1955. From instr. to assoc. prof. anthropology Columbia U., 1954-62; lectr. anthropology Rockefeller Inst., 1961-62; prof. anthropology Yale U., 1962—, chmn. dept., 1964-68; curator of anthropology Yale Peabody Mus. Natural History, 1974—; mem. Inst. for Advanced Study, Princeton U., 1972; fellow Center for Advanced Study in Behavioral Scis., Stanford, Calif., 1978-79; field research in, Philippines, 1945-47, 52-54, 55, 57-58, 61, 62-63, 64, 65, 68-69, 70, 73, 80-81, 82, 83, 84, Malaya and Indonesia, 1948, 57, 83, Calif. and N.Y., 1951, 52, Guatemala, 1959; Dir., com. problems and policy Social Sci. Research Council, 1963-70; spl. cons. Internat. Rice Research Inst., Los Baños, Philippines, 1962—; book rev. editor Am. Anthropologist, 1960-62; mem. Pacific sci. bd. Nat. Acad. Scis.-NRC, 1962-66. Author: Hanunóo Agriculture, 1957, Folk Classification, 1972, Ethnographic Atlas of Ifugao, 1980; other publs. on ethnol., linguistic and ecol. topics. Served with AUS, 1944-46. Guggenheim fellow, 1973; recipient Internat. Sci. prize Fyssen Foundation, 1983. Fellow Am. Anthrop. Assn. (exec. bd. 1965-68), Royal Anthrop. Inst., N.Y. Acad. Scis. (sec. sect. anthropology 1956), Am. Acad. Arts and Scis., Sigma Xi; mem. Am. Ethnol. Soc. (councilor 1960-62, pres. 1978-79), Nat. Acad. Scis., Koninklijk Inst. voor Taal-Land- en Volkenkunde, Linguistic Soc. Am., Soc. Am. Archaeology, Kroeber Anthrop. Soc., Phila. Anthrop. Assn., Am. Geog. Soc., Am. Oriental Soc., Assn. Asian Studies, Classification Soc., La Société de Linguistique de Paris, Far Eastern Prehistory Assn., Soc. Econ. Botany, Internat. Assn. Plant Taxonomy, AAAS, Phi Beta Kappa. Home: 106 York Sq New Haven CT 06511 Office: 51 Hillhouse Ave New Haven CT 06520

CONKLIN, HUGH RANDOLPH, management consultant; b. Battle Creek, Mich., Oct. 20, 1911; s. Hugh William and Ida Charlotte (Maier) C.; m. Mary Alice Kendel, Mar. 12, 1938; children: Hugh Randolph, Drue Kendel. B.S. in Engring, U. Mich., 1933; postgrad. Advanced Mgmt. Program, Harvard U. With Gen. Foods Corp., 1933-57, Eastern regional Sales mgr., 1954-55, nat. sales mgr., 1955-57; with Lever Bros. Co., 1957-71, v.p. sales, 1962-71; v.p. nat. sales Pepsicola Co., Purchase, N.Y., 1971-72; pres. Hugh Conklin Assocs., 1972—; broker-assoc. Century 21 Spinning Wheel Realtors, Tierra Verde, Fla., 1983—; past v.p., dir. Econ. and Market Research Co., Inc. Past trustee Osteo. Hosp. and Clinic of N.Y.; trustee Post Grad. Inst. Osteo. Medicine and Surgery; past bd. dirs. Found. for Research, N.Y. Acad. Osteopathy; past mem. bd. govs. N.Y. Coll. Osteo. Medicine and Surgery; past gov. Clinton Youth Center, N.Y.C.; past chmn. trustees 101 Assn. Served to capt., inf. AUS, 1942-46; CBI. Decorated Bronze Star, Combat Inf. badge. Mem. N.Y. Sales Execs. Club, Delta Kappa Epsilon. Clubs: U.S. Power Squadron; Gulf Beaches Rotary (Treasure Island, Fla.); Pass-A-Grill Yacht, Old Salts Fishing. Office: care Hugh Conklin Assos 108 11th St E Tierra Verde FL 33715

CONKLIN, KENNETH EDWARD, lawyer; b. Keota, Iowa, Aug. 21, 1939; s. Cleo W. and Viola A. (Hammes) C.; children: David S., Steven J. Student, St. Ambrose Coll., 1957-59, Ariz. State U., 1960-61; B.S., N.E. Mo. State U., 1966; J.D., Washington Coll. Law Am. U., 1969. Bar: Md., D.C., U.S. Supreme Ct., U.S. Ct. Appeals, U.S. Ct. Claims. Asst. mgr. Equitable Life Ins. Co., Washington, 1966-69; atty. Pub. Defender Office, 1969-70; partner firm Conklin & Noble, Chevy Chase, Md., 1970-76, Leighton, Conklin, Lemov, Jacobs and Buckley, Washington, 1977-83; chmn. bd. dirs. Amex Internat., Inc.; dir. Eastern Pines Devel. Corp., Gem Bus. Systems Inc., Energy Utilization Lab., Inc., Omex Trading Internat., Inc., Automated Leasing Ltd., Telecommunications Resource, Inc. Adviser, atty. Legal Aid, 1969-75; Mem. Montgomery County (Md.) Republican Club, v.p., 1972-73. Served with spl. forces AUS, 1962-65; Vietnam. Mem. Am., Montgomery County, Md. State, D.C. bar assns., Assn. Trial Lawyers Am. Club: Ski (Washington). Home: 922 24th St NW Washington DC 20037 Office: 10395 Democracy Ln Fairfax VA 22030

CONKLIN, MARIE ECKHARDT, biologist, educator; b. Derby, Conn., Sept. 30, 1908; d. Malcolm Moyer and Elizabeth Nancy (McLean) Eckhardt; m. G. Howard Conklin, June 27, 1931 (dec.); children—Elizabeth Nancy, George William. B.A., Wellesley Coll., 1929; M.S., U. Wis., 1930; Ph.D., Columbia U., 1936. Teaching asst. dept. botany Wellesley Coll., 1930-31; research Bklyn. Botanic Garden, 1935-36; research asso. dept. genetics Carnegie Inst. of Washington at Cold Spring Harbor, 1936-41; instr. to prof. Adelphi U., 1943-72, chmn. dept. biology, 1953-67; research collaborator Brookhaven Nat. Lab., 1959-72; lectr./adj. prof. San Diego State U., 1972—; v.p. for acad. affairs Rancho Bernardo Center for Continuing Edn.; dir. Adelphi Coll., NSF, and AEC summer insts. and in-service programs for high sch. tchrs. sci., 1959-64. Author: Genetic and Biomedical Aspects of the Development of Datura, 1976, (with D.L. Hartl) Genetics Study Guide, 1977. Mem. AAAS, Sigma Xi, Sigma Delta Epsilon. Home: 12062 Caminito Cadena Rancho Bernardo San Diego CA 92128

CONKLIN, RICHARD CHARLES, lawyer; b. Melrose Park, Ill., July 26, 1929; s. Charles I. and Gladys M. (Raedel) C.; m. Lilius Burns Scott, Oct. 18, 1952; children: Christene Conklin Malmquist, Barbara Conklin Funk. B.S. in Acctg., U. Ill., 1951; J.D., Northwestern U., 1958. Bar: Ill. 1958, U.S. Dist. Ct. (no. dist.) Ill. 1958. Ptnr. firm Lord, Bissell & Brook, Chgo., 1970—. Served with USAF, 1951-55. Office: Lord Bissell & Brook 115 S LaSale St Chicago IL 60603

CONKLIN, ROBERT ELLIOT, life ins. co. exec.; b. Goshen, N.Y., Dec. 19, 1936; s. William Roe, Jr. and Evelyn M. C.; m. Ann Brunson, June 25, 1960; children: Robert Elliot, Evann E., Melissa Ann. A.B. in Econs, Bucknell U., 1958. Real estate appraiser J.N. Weems & Co., El Paso, Tex., 1960-61; with N.Y. Life Ins. Co., 1961—, mgr. Chgo. office, 1967-70, asst. v.p., N.Y.C., 1970-72, v.p. real estate and mortgage loan dept., 1972-81, sr. v.p. in charge real estate dept., 1981—; lectr. in field. Mem. adv. bd. NYU Extension. Served as officer U.S. Army, 1958-60. Mem. Am. Inst. Real Estate Appraisers, Urban Land Inst., Sigma Alpha Epsilon. Republican. Presbyterian. Home: 95 Lawrence Dr Berkeley Heights NJ 07922 Office: 51 Madison Ave New York NY 10010

CONKLIN, THOMAS WILLIAM, lawyer; b. Chgo., Mar. 1, 1938; s. Clarence Robert and Ellen Pauline (Gleason) C.; m. Gail Quillman; children: Thomas William, Sarah Adrienne. B.A., Yale, 1960; J.D., U. Chgo., 1963. Bar: Ill. 1964. Partner firm Upton, Conklin & Leahy, Chgo., 1969-72, Conklin, Leahy & Eisenberg, 1972-79, Conklin & Adler Ltd., 1979—. Contbr. numerous articles to legal jours. Served with USAF, 1963-64. Mem. ABA, Chgo. Bar Assn., Fed. Bar Assn., Traffic Club of Chgo., Maritime Law assn., Am. Arbitration Assn., Internat. Assn. Ins. Counsel. Clubs: Yale of N.Y., Union League of Chgo., Attic. Home: 200 S Waiola St LaGrange IL 60525 Office: 100 W Grand Ave Chicago IL 60610

CONKLING, ROGER LINTON, Consultant, retired utility executive; b. Bloomington, Ill., July 12, 1917; s. Robert Edwin and Helen (Ricketts) C.; m. Meta Baskerville, Apr. 4, 1941; children—Mary Beth, Jane Linton, Roger Marc. B.B.A., Northwestern U., 1941; M.A., U. Oreg., 1948; LL.D., U. Portland, 1972. With Public Service Co. of No. Ill., Chgo. and Joliet, 1936-42; economist Bonneville Power Adminstrn., Portland, Oreg., 1945-47, asst. to power mgr., 1948-51, chief system devel., 1952-53, chief customer service, 1954, dir. budget and mgmt., 1955-56, asst. to adminstr., 1957; v.p., asso. H. Zinder & Assos., Inc., Washington, 1958-61; pres. Conkling, Inc. (cons.), Portland, 1962-67; v.p. N.W. Natural Gas Co., Portland, 1967-76, sr. v.p., 1976-82, ret., 1982; Cons., 1982—; former pres., dir. Pacific Western Pipeline Corp., Portland; mem. grad. faculty Oreg. System Higher Edn., Portland, 1946-56. Past pres., chmn. Oreg. United Appeal; pres. Delauney Inst. Mental Health, 1964; mem. Gov.'s Com. Child Care, 1964; bd. dirs. Cath. Charities, Inc., Portland, 1957-58, 61-64; pres. Oreg. State Soc., Washington, 1960; chmn. exec. com. Nat. Found., Washington, 1958-60; chmn. March of Dimes campaign, Portland, 1957; bd. dirs. Mental Health Assn., 1957-58, Cath. Services for Children, 1954-57, Oreg. Symphony Assn., NCCJ, 1980-82, Found. Oreg. Research and Edn., 1967-80; chmn. bd. regents U. Portland; trustee Providence Children's Center; chmn. ann. fund dr. Oreg. Symphony, 1981. Served with USNR, 1942-45. Recipient Distinguished Service award Dept. Interior; Arthur S. Fleming award Jr. C. of C. Mem. Am. Econ. Assn., Western Econ. Assn., Fed. Govt. Accts. Assn., Am. Gas Assn., Pacific Coast Gas Assn., Assn. Wash. Gas Utilities (trustee, past pres.), Beta Gamma Sigma, Delta Mu Delta. Club: Multnomah Athletic (Portland). Home and Office: 2539 SW Hill Crest Dr Portland OR 97201

CONLAN, JOHN BERTRAND, lawyer; b. Oak Park, Ill., Sept. 17, 1930; s. John B. and Ruth S. (Anderson) C.; m. Irene Danielson, Sept. 13, 1968; children: Christopher, Kevin. B.S., Northwestern U., 1951; J.D., Harvard U., 1954; postgrad. (Fulbright scholar), U. Cologne, W. Ger., 1954-55, Hague Acad. Internat. Law, 1958. Bar: Ill. bar 1954, Ariz. bar 1966, D.C. bar 1977. Asst. corp. counsel City of Chgo., 1955-56; individual practice law, Phoenix, 1966—; dir. Gen. Automation, Inc., Anaheim, Calif., 1979—, Telmark, Inc.; mem. faculty U. Md., 1958-59, Ariz. State U., 1962; mem. Ariz. Senate, 1964-72, 93d and 94th Congresses from 4th dist. Ariz. Served with U.S. Army, 1956-59. Named Outstanding Young Man in Ariz. U.S. Jaycees, 1965; recipient George Washington Honor medal Freedoms Found. at Valley Forge, 1957, 1973, Leader in Govt. award Religious Heritage Am., 1975. Mem. ABA, Ariz. Bar Assn., D.C. Bar Assn. Republican. Club: Capitol Hill.

CONLAN, LEO FRANCIS, food company executive; b. Chgo., July 27, 1937; m. Charlene O'Connor, Apr. 29, 1961; children: Suzanne, Paul, Michael, Martin. B.S., Notre Dame U., 1959. Controller Kroger Co., Los Angeles, 1968-71, program mgr., Cin., 1971-75, controller, Memphis, 1975-79; v.p. fin. Bi-O. Inc., Mauldin, S.C., 1979—; dir. Bi-Lo Inc., Mauldin, S.C. Home: 107 Berrywood Ct Greer SC 29651 Office: Bi-Lo Inc Drawer 99 Mauldin SC 29662

CONLAN, RICHARD JOHN, ins. co. exec.; b. Bronx, N.Y., Aug. 2, 1924; s. Richard John and Eleanor (Coveney) C.; m. Jo Ann Kasper, Sept. 4, 1948; children—Thomas, John. Student, Manhattan Coll., 1942; B.S., Mass. Inst. Tech., 1948. With Met. Life Ins. Co., N.Y.C., 1948—, 2d v.p., 1968-71, overall responsibilities for electronics, 1971-72, v.p., 1972-76, sr. v.p., 1976—. Served with USNR, 1943-46. Roman Catholic. Club: Silver Spring Country (Ridgefield, Conn.). Home: 43 Bald Hill Rd Wilton CT 06897 Office: 1 Madison Ave New York City NY 10010

CONLAND, STEPHEN, publishing company executive; b. Hartford, Conn., Apr. 22, 1916; s. Henry Holton and Caroline Mathilde (Henschel) C.; m. Gladys Bett Burton, Mar. 10, 1944; 1 son, Robert Stephen. A.B., Yale U., 1939; M.B.A., Harvard U., 1941. Adminstrv. mgr. Burlington Industries, N.Y.C., 1948-55; with Berkley Pub. Corp., N.Y.C., 1956—, pres., 1959—; asso. Moseley Assos., Inc. (pub. cons.), N.Y.C., 1979. Mem. Commn. on Aging, Granby, Conn.; trustee Granby Homes for Sr. Citizens, Inc. Served to lt. col. Q.M.C., AUS, World War II; Res. ret. Decorated Bronze Star. Mem Assn. Am. Pubs. (sr. adv. com.). Clubs: Yale (N.Y.C.); Harvard Business School of No. Conn.; Hempstead Hill (West Granby, Conn.); Hartford (Conn.). Home: 11 Silkey Rd West Granby CT 06090

CONLEY, CARROLL LOCKARD, physician, emeritus educator; b. Balt., May 14, 1915; s. Harry Lewis and Harriet (Coulbourne) C.; m. Edith DeYoung, Feb. 27, 1943; children: Anne Marie (Mrs. R.J. Weaver), Jean Alice. A.B., Johns Hopkins U., 1935; M.D., Columbia U., 1940. Intern Presbyn. Hosp., N.Y.C., 1940-42; fellow medicine Johns Hopkins, 1946, instr. to assoc. prof. medicine, 1947-56; prof.

medicine Johns Hopkins U., 1956—, Disting. Service prof., 1976-80, emeritus, 1980—; dir. hematology div. Johns Hopkins Hosp., 1947-80, dir. labs., 1956-66; hon. assoc. prof. medicine Guy's Hosp. Med. Sch., London, Eng.; Cons. USPHS, FDA, Army, VA, WHO; mem. com. on blood NRC, 1954-63, chmn. subcom. on thrombosis and hemorrhage, 1962-64; chmn. hematology study section NIH, 1962-65; mem. sickle cell disease adv. com. Dept. HEW, 1971-73; Disting. sr. clinician USPHS, 1980—. Editorial bd.: Archives of Internal Medicine, 1959-65, Blood, the Jour. of Hematology, 1954-67, Bull. of Johns Hopkins Hosp, 1963-70; Contbr. med. textbooks and profl. jours. Served from lt. to maj. M.C. AUS, 1942-45. Recipient Bicentennial medal Coll. Physicians and Surgeons, 1967. Fellow ACP (master 1983, Disting. Tchr. award 1983), Royal Coll. Physicians (London); mem. Assn. Am. Physicians, Am. Soc. Clin. Investigation, AMA, Am. Soc. Hematology (exec. com. v.p. 1973-74, pres. 1975-76), European Soc. Hematology (corr. mem.), Interurban Clin. Club, Phi Beta Kappa, Alpha Omega Alpha. Home: 120 E Lake Ave Baltimore MD 21212 Office: Johns Hopkins Hosp Baltimore MD 21205

CONLEY, CHARLES CAMERON, educator, mathematician; b. Royal Oak, Mich., Sept. 26, 1933; s. Charles Andrew and Bertha Cameron (Cameron) C.; m. Catharine Anastasia Smith, Dec. 28, 1963; children—Charles Henry, Catharine Anastasia, John Alan. B.S., Wayne State U., 1957, M.A., 1959; Ph.D., Mass. Inst. Tech., 1961. Research scientist Courant Inst. Math. Scis., N.Y.C., 1961-63, fellow, 1969-70; asst. prof. U. Wis. at Madison, 1963-65, asso. prof., 1965-68, prof., 1968—; vis. research scientist T.J. Watson Research Center, Yorktown Heights, N.Y., 1971-72; Cons. to NASA, 1963-66. Asso. editor: Jour. Applied Mathematics, 1967-70. Served with USAF, 1951-55. Fellow N.Y. Acad. Scis.; mem. Am. Math. Soc., Phi Beta Kappa. Home: 5101 Lake Mendota Dr Madison WI 53705

CONLEY, CLARE DEAN, magazine editor; b. Caldwell, Idaho, Jan. 22, 1929; s. Claris F. and Gladys (Goodall) C.; m. Mike Ann Packard, Aug. 4, 1951; children: Brent, Kim, Ted. Student, Stanford, 1947-49; B.A., Coll. Idaho, 1951. Newspaper and Freelance writer, 1951-61; mem. staff Field and Stream mag., 1961-72, editor-in-chief, 1970-72, True Mag., 1972-73; marketing dir. Hydro-Catalyst Corp., 1974; editorial dir. Popular Publs. Corp., N.Y.C., 1975-77; dir. mag./book dept. Carl Byoir & Assos., Inc., N.Y.C., 1978-80; editor-in-chief Outdoor Life, Times Mirror Mags. Inc., N.Y.C., 1980—. Author: Guide to Upland Birds, 1966. Named Outstanding Young Alumni of Coll. Ida., 1964, Outstanding Young Man of Am., 1965; recipient Carl Byoir Outstanding Writer of Yr. award, 1980, Internat. Wildlife Found. Conservation award, 1982. Mem. Outdoor Writers Assn. Am., Advt. Sportsmen's Club N.Y., Am. Soc. Mag. Editors, Rod and Gun Editors Assn. Met. N.Y., Aircraft Owners and Pilots Assn. Club: N.Y. Athletic. Home: Hemlock Farms Hawley PA 18428 Office: 380 Madison Ave New York NY 10017 *Most of my life, people who read my name thought I was my wife and that my wife was me. So here for all the world to see I am setting the record straight. I'm me.*

CONLEY, EUGENE ALLEN, ins. co. exec.; b. Nebraska City, Nebr., Oct. 3, 1925; s. Melville Evans and Margaret (Allen) C.; m. Erma Grace Fuller, June 27, 1948; children: Tom, Roger, John, Carol Sue. B.S., U. Nebr., 1949; D.Sc. (hon.), Med. Center. C.L.U. Agt. Am. Mut. Life Ins. Co., Omaha, 1948-54, supr., supt. agts., v.p., dir. agts., dir., Des Moines, 1954-72; exec. v.p., dir. Guarantee Mut. Life Co., Omaha, 1972-76, pres., 1976—; dir. U.S. Nat. Bank of Omaha; Bd. dirs. Am. Council Life Ins., Washington.; Life Ins. Agy. Mgmt. Assn. Hartford, Conn. Bd. dirs. Omaha Zool. Soc.; trustee Nebr. Ind. Coll. Found., So. Methodist U., Clarkson Hosp.; mem. cons. com. SAC; mem. pres.'s adv. council Creighton U.; chmn. bd. govs. Nebr. Wesleyan U.; gov. Knights of Ak-Sar-Ben; co-chmn. fund drive United Way Midlands, 1976-77, pres., 1979-80; past crusade chmn. Am. Cancer Soc.; co-chmn. NCCJ. Served with USNR, 1943-46. Recipient Americanism citation B'Nai B'rith, 1982; named Citizen of Yr. United Way, 1983. Mem. Nat. Assn. Life Underwriters, Coll. Life Underwriters, Life Ins. Agy. Mgmt. Assn., Omaha C. of C. (chmn., dir.), Nebr. Assn. Commerce and Industry (dir.), Phi Kappa Psi. Clubs: Omaha, Omaha Country, Plaza, Masons, Shriners. Home: 9715 Brentwood Rd Omaha NE 68114 Office: 8721 Indian Hills Dr Omaha NE 68114

CONLEY, GERARD P., state senator, railroad clerk; b. Portland, Maine, Jan. 3, 1930; s. Thomas J. and Catherine A. (Murphy) C.; m. Ann Duff, July 18, 1952; 12 children. Student, Portland Jr. Coll., 1954. Mem. Maine Ho. of Reps., Augusta, 1964-68, Maine Senate, 1968—, pres., 1982—, asst. Democratic leader, 1972-74, Democratic leader, 1974-82; mem. Maine CSC, 1968-72; chmn. Portland West Adv. Commn. Model Cities Program, 1972-76; mem. Maine Council on Alcohol and Drug Abuse Prevention, 1976—, Maine Com. on Aging., Augusta, 1978—. Mem. Portland City Council, 1962-72, mayor, 1971-72. Served with U.S. Army, 1947-48. Mem. Brotherhood of R.R., Airline and Steamship Clks. Roman Catholic. Office: Office of President Maine Senate Sta 3 State House Augusta ME 04333 *

CONLEY, GLEN TAYLOR, corporation executive; b. Wanette, Okla., Dec. 28, 1923; s. Taylor and Pearl (Waddle) C.; m. Hazel Carla Sandrini, Oct. 3, 1956; 1 son, Kelly Ugo. Student, Bakersfield Jr. Coll., (Calif.). Foreman Bechtel Corp., San Francisco, 1952-53; supt. Fluor Corp., Los Angeles, 1953-56; v.p. Paul Hardeman, Inc., Los Angeles, 1956-64; pres. Conley Contractors, Montebello, Calif., 1964-66, Fischbach & Moore, Internat., Dallas, 1966-80, Fischbach & Moore, Inc., 1980—; dir. Fischbach Corp., N.Y.C., 1980—. Served to tech. sgt. U.S. Army, 1943-46; Japan. Decorated Presdl. Citation Combat Infantryman's Badge with 6 gold stars. Roman Catholic. Lodges: Beavers; Elks. Office: Fischbach & Moore Inc 11030 Ables Ln Dallas TX 75229

CONLEY, HOWARD HARRY, JR., retired life insurance company executive; b. Little Rock, Oct. 30, 1915; s. Howard Harry and Marie (Cates) C.; m. Katharine Edwards, Apr. 15, 1945; children: Howard III, Alston, Katharine, John. B.S., U. Pa., 1936; certificate, Am. Coll. Chartered Life Underwriters. With N.Y. Life Ins. Co., N.Y.C., 1936-80, 2d v.p. sales adminstrn., 1958-74, v.p. mktg. adminstrn., 1974-80. Mem. Am. Soc. Chartered Life Underwriters. Congregationalist. Club: Riverside Yacht. Home: 7 Druid Ln Riverside CT 06878

CONLEY, JAMES DANIEL, foundation executive; b. Chgo., Oct. 5, 1928; s. Joseph Cornelius and Eleanor Mary (Kenny) C.; m. Jane Harris, Aug. 27, 1955; children: Katharine, Grace, Sean. A.B., U. Notre Dame, 1955; postgrad., Am. U., 1956. With Dept. Def., 1955-57; with USIA, 1957-78; press and cultural officer, Brazil, 1957-59, Yugoslavia, 1960-64, Belgium, 1965-68; fgn. affairs officer USIA, Washington, 1968-70, spl. asst. to dep. dir. policy and plans, 1970-71; 1st sec., then counselor for pub. affairs Am. embassy, Lisbon, Portugal, 1971-75; counselor for pub. affairs, Kinshasa, Zaire, 1975-77; temp. duty Am. embassy, Mogadiscio, Somalia, 1978; dir. no. regional office Hist. Landmarks Found. Ind., South Bend, 1979—. Editorial bd.: Fgn. Service Jour, 1970-71. Mem. Task Force on Diplomacy for 70's; program mgmt. reform for Dept. State, 1970—. 1970—; chmn. Luso-Am. Ednl. Commn. (Fulbright), Lisbon, 1974-75; mem. bd. edn. Am. Sch. Kinshasa, 1976-77; pres. bd. trustees South Bend Art Ctr., 1982-84. Served with U.S. Army, 1951-52. Recipient USIA Dir.'s award outstanding creativity, 1973. Mem. Am. Fgn. Service Assn. Home: 310 W Navarre St South Bend IN 46616 Office: 1016 W Washington St South Bend IN 46601

CONLEY, JAMES EDWARD, surgeon; b. Harrisville, R.I., Aug. 10, 1913; s. Edward James and Emily Rachel (Davies) C.; m. Lillian Brandt Quirk, Sept. 16, 1941; children—Emily, James, Robert, Bruce, Ellen, William Katherine. B.S. cum laude, Providence Coll., 1935, M.D., Harvard U., 1939. Diplomate: Am. Bd. Surgery. Intern, resident Mass. Gen. Hosp., Boston, 1939-43; practice gen. and vascular surgery, Milw., 1946—; mem. staff Columbia, Milw. Children's, County Gen. hosps.; prof. surgery Med. Coll Wis., 1946—. Mem. editorial adv. bd.: Cancer Bull. Cancer Program, 1957-62; contbr. articles to profl. jours. Pres. Quirk Found., 1968—; v.p. Florentine Opera Assn., 1971. Served with USNR, 1943-46. Decorated Bronze Star (2); Recipient Disting. Service award Am. Cancer Soc., 1966. Fellow A.C.S.; mem. Internat. Cardiovascular Soc., Soc. Vascular Surgery, Midwestern Vascular Surgery Soc. (founder mem.), Central Surg. Assn., Milw. Surg. Soc. (pres. 1966-67), Milw. Acad. Medicine (pres. 1959-60), Royal Soc. Medicine. Club: Univ. (Milw.). Home: 1406 E Fox Ln Milwaukee WI 53217 Office: 425 E Wisconsin Ave Milwaukee WI 53202

CONLEY, PHILIP JAMES, JR., air force officer; b. Providence, May 22, 1927; s. Philip James and Lillian Loretta (Burns) C.; m. Shirley Jean Andrews, Jan. 26, 1956; children: Sharon, Kathleen, Anne, James. B.S., U.S. Naval Acad., 1950; M.S., U. Mich., 1956, Rensseler Poly. Inst., 1963. Commd. 2d lt. USAF, 1950, advanced through grades to maj. gen., 1979; dep. chief staff, ops. Air Force Systems Command, Andrews AFB, Washington, 1974-75, chief staff, 1975-78; comdr. Air Force Flight Test Center, Edwards AFB, Calif., 1978-82, Hanscom AFB, Mass., 1983—. Decorated Legion Merit with oakleaf cluster, Air medal (2), D.F.C., D.S.M. Mem. Air Force Assn., Order of Daedalians, U.S. Naval Acad. Alumni Assn., Am. Legion. Roman Catholic. Clubs: Pisces (Washington); Vikings (Los Angeles). Home: 4 Andrews Dr Bedford MA 01730 Office: ESD/CV Hanscom AFB MA 01731

CONLEY, ROBERT FRANCIS, aerospace company executive; b. Beatrice, Nebr., Feb. 7, 1923; s. Albert H. and Frances C. (Cooper) C.; m. Sybil Jane Harder, June 8, 1947 (div. 1957); m. Joline Jordan, June 7, 1959; children: Erin, Patrick, David. B.A., San Diego State Coll., 1950; LL.B., U. Calif.-Berkeley, 1953. C.P.A., Calif. V.p. mktg. Canadair Ltd., Montreal, 1963-66; comml. dir. Gen. Dynamics Corp., N.Y.C., 1966-71; pres. Lockheed Mid-East, Beirut, 1971-79; v.p. internat. mktg. Lockheed Corp., Burbank, Calif., 1979-81, sr. v.p., 1981—; dir. Lockheed Arabia, Riyadh, Saudi Arabia, Gulf Tech. Corp., Kuwait, Lockheed Mid-East, S.A., Geneva. Republican. Methodist. Clubs: Sky (N.Y.C.); Equestrian (Riyadh). Home: PO Box 811641 Amman Jordan Office: Lockheed Corp PO Box 551 Burbank CA 91520

CONLEY, WILLIAM DONALD, corporation public affairs executive; b. Duluth, Minn., Oct. 6, 1927; s. William F. and Emelda (Rouleau) C.; m. Janet M. Knutson, June 7, 1952; children: Kevein, Karin Conley Balgaard, Paul. B.A., U. Minn., 1949. Mgr. compensation Honeywell Inc., Mpls., 1966-70, corp. dir. compensation, 1973-79, v.p. pub. affairs, 1979—; dir. employee relations Honeywell Info. Systems, Boston, 1970-73; bd. dirs., mem. exec. com. Pub. Affairs Council, Washington, 1980—; council mem. Machinery and Allied Products Inst., Washington, 1980—, Conf. Bd.-Pub. Affairs Research Council, N.Y.C., 1980—. Bd. dirs. Minn. Council Econ. Edn., Mpls., 1982—, Eitel Hosp., Mpls., 1983—. Served to sgt. 1st class U.S. Army, 1953-55. Mem. Mpls. C. of C. (dir. 1981—). Roman Catholic. Lodge: Rotary. Office: Honeywell Inc Honeywell Plaza Minneapolis MN 55408

CONLIN, ALFRED THOMAS, food co. exec.; b. Lawrence, Mass., Apr. 18, 1921; s. Alfred A. and Helene (Roy) C.; m. Mary McKee Butler, June 29, 1946; children—Robert Thomas, James Alfred, Nancy Kee. A.B., Harvard, 1942; student, U. Pa., 1946-47, Drexel Inst. Tech., 1947-49. With Campbell Soup Co., 1946-59, supt. can mfg., 1957-59; with Hunt Foods and Industries, Inc., 1959—, v.p. container group, can and glass divs., 1962-64, v.p. indsl. group, container, crushing mill and shellfish divs., 1964—; pres. United Can Co., So. Cotton Oil Co., Inc., 1964-80, So. Shell Fish Co., Inc., 1964-77. Served to lt. USNR, 1942-46. Club: Harvard (So. Calif.). Home: 14857 La Cuarta Whittier CA 90605 Office: 2600 E Nutwood Fullerton CA 92634

CONLIN, ROXANNE BARTON, lawyer; b. Huron, S.D., June 30, 1944; d. Marion William and Alyce Muraine (Madden) Barton; m. James Clyde Conlin, Mar. 21, 1964; children: Jacalyn Rae, James Barton. B.A., Drake U., Des Moines, 1964, J.D., 1966, M.P.A., 1979; LL.D. (hon.), U. Dubuque, 1975. Bar: Iowa bar 1966. Asso. firm Davis, Huebner, Johnson & Burt, Des Moines, 1966-67; dep. indsl. commnr. State of Iowa, 1967-68, asst. atty. gen., 1969-76; U.S. atty. So. Dist. Iowa, 1977-81; adj. prof. law U. Iowa, 1977-79; guest lectr. numerous univs. Chmn. Iowa Women's Polit. Caucus, 1973-75, del. nat. steering com., 1973-77; cons. U.S. Commn. on Internat. Women's Year, 1976-77. Contbr. articles to profl. publs. Nat. committeewoman Iowa Young Democrats; also pres. Polk County Young Dems., 1965-66; del. Iowa Presdl. Conv., 1972; Dem. candidate for gov. of Iowa, 1982; nat. policy chmn. John Glenn for Pres. Com., 1983—; bd. dirs. Riverhills Day Care Center. Recipient award Iowa Civil Liberties Union, 1974; named to Iowa Women's Hall of Fame, 1981; other awards.; Fischer Found. scholar, 1965-66; Readers Digest scholar, 1963-64. Mem. Am., Iowa bar assns., ACLU, NAACP, Common Cause, Assn. Children Learning Disabilities, Internat. Platform Assn., Women's Equity Action League, NOW (dir. 1969), Phi Beta Kappa, Alpha Lambda Delta, Chi Omega (Social Service award). Office: Suite 1 Stephens Bldg Des Moines IA 50309

CONLON, ELLEN CATHERINE, business exec.; b. N.Y.C., Jan. 24, 1940; s. Thomas Francis and Catherine Veronica (Fagan) C. Student, Pace U., Baruch Coll. Advt. mgr. J'ean D'Albret, N.Y.C., 1961-64; adminstrv. asst. Schwerin Research, N.Y.C., 1964-69; corp. sec. John Blair & Co., N.Y.C., 1969—, 1975—. Mem. Am. Soc. Corp. Secs., Risk Ins. Mgmt. Soc. Office: John Blair & Co 1290 Ave of the Americas New York NY 10104

CONLON, EUGENE, artist, adminstrator; b. Boston, Dec. 17, 1925; s. James Edward and Mary Honor (Dalton) C.; m. Marie Elizabeth Hommel, Sept. 1, 1952; children: Michelle, Meridith, Sally, Eugenia. B.F.A., Mass. Coll. Art, 1950. Designer-illustrator Rust Craft Pubs., Boston, 1953-61, MIT, Cambridge, 1961-66; instr. painting Mass. Coll. Art, Boston, 1966-67; artist-designer Avco Research Inc., Everett, Mass., 1967-70; art dir. Donnelly Advt., Boston, 1970-78, Ackerley Communications, Stoneham, Mass., 1978—; commd. 22 paintings Bd. Room Internat. Silver Co., Meriden, Conn., 1976. Served with USN, 1943-46. Recipient Purchase prize S.W. Mo. Mus., 1966, Gold Medal Acad. Artists Asssn., 1978, Purchase prize Wichita Centennial, 1970, 1st prize Cape Cod Art Assn., 1982. Mem. Am. Watercolor Soc., New Eng. Watercolor Soc. (sec., treas.), Guild Boston Artists, N.A.D. (assoc.). Roman Catholic. Clubs: Boston Art Dirs.; South Shore Art Assn. (Cohasset, Mass.). Home: 74 Proctor Rd Braintree MA 02184

CONLON, JACK MARTIN, real estate company executive; b. Parsons, Kans., Oct. 8, 1931; s. John Thomas and Alice M. (MacCaskill) C.; children from previous marriage: Lisa, Catherine, Julia (dec.). B.S., U. Kans., 1957; student, U. So. Calif., 1957-59. C.P.A., Calif. C.P.A. Peat, Marwick, Mitchell & Co., Los Angeles, 1957-59, Kansas City, Mo., 1959-63; pres. Coachella Valley Savs. & Loan Assn., Palm Springs, Calif., 1963-72; exec. v.p. Sunrise Corp., Los Angeles, 1972-75; pres. Conlon Cos., 1975-76, Sunrise Co., Palm Desert, Calif., 1976—. Dir., treas. Palm Springs United Fund, 1966-67; dir., sec.-treas. Palm Springs Conv. and Visitors Bur., 1967—; Dir. Palm Springs Republican Assembly, 1971; Trustee Palm Valley Sch. Served with USN, 1951-54. Mem. Am. Savs. and Loan Inst. (instr.), Soc. Controllers and Finance Officers Savs. Instns. (pres. 1966), Palm Springs C. of C. (pres.), Phi Kappa Psi. Clubs: Rotarian., Palm Springs, Canyon Country, The Lakes Country, Rancho Las Palmas, Monterey. Home: 70-263 Sonora Rd Rancho Mirage CA 92270 Office: 75-005 Country Club Dr Palm Desert CA 92260

CONLON, JAMES JOSEPH, conductor; b. N.Y.C., Mar. 18, 1950; s. Joseph Michael and Angeline (Leibinger) C. Mus.B., Juilliard Sch., 1972. Condr. opera prodn., Juilliard Sch., 1972; mem. orchestral conducting faculty, 1972-75; condr. opera prodn., N.Y. Philharmonic, 1974-75, Met. Opera, N.Y.C., 1976—, major symphony orchs. in U.S. and Can., including, N.Y.C., Phila., Cleve., Chgo., Boston and, Los Angeles, also orchs. and opera cos. in, Gt. Britain, Germany, Italy, France and, The Netherlands; music condr., Cin. May Festival, 1979—; music dir.: Rotterdam Philharm. Orch., 1983. Recipient Samuel Chotzinoff awards Aspen Music Festival, 1968, 69, Nat. Orchestral Assn. award, 1972. Mem. Am. Fedn. Musicians. Office: care Columbia Artists Mgmt Inc 165 W 57th St New York NY 10019

CONLON, LAWRENCE WILLIAM, mathematics educator; b. Decatur, Ill., June 17, 1933; s. Thomas Edward and Edna N. (Bozman) C.; m. Jacquelyn Flatken Hampel, Sept. 8, 1979. B.S., Spring Hill Coll., 1958; A.M., Harvard U., 1959, Ph.D., 1963; S.T.L., Boston Coll., 1967. Vis. asst. prof. math. Washington U., St. Louis, 1967-70, vis. assoc. prof., 1970-73, assoc. prof., 1973-78, prof., 1978—; asst. prof. St. Louis U., 1968-71, assoc. prof., 1971-73; vis. mem. Inst. Advanced Study, Princeton, N.J., summer 1975, summer 1979; vis. assoc. prof Fordham U., 1977-78; professeur associe Universite des Sciences et Techniques de Lille, France, 1978; vis. mem. Institut des Hautes Etudes Scientifiques, Bures-sur-Yvette, France, 1977-78. Contbr. articles to profl. publs. Mem. Am. Math. Soc., Math. Assn. Am. Roman Catholic. Home: 1550 Autumn Leaf Dr Ballwin MO 63011 Office: Washington U Dept Math Saint Louis MO 63130

CONLON, MICHAEL WILLIAM, lawyer; b. Wilkes Barre, Pa., Nov. 9, 1946; s. William Peter and Dorothy (Stone) C.; m. Alice Cario, June 14, 1969; children: Michele, Stacia. A.B., Cath. U., 1968; J.D., Duke U., 1971. Bar: Tex. 1971. Ptnr. Fulbright & Jaworski, Houston, 1978—. Office: Bank of Southwest Bldg Houston TX 77005

CONLON, ROBERT KENNETH, advertising agency executive; b. N.Y.C., Dec. 12, 1937; s. Kenneth Charles and Catherine C.; m. Susan Morris, May 25, 1968; children—Kenneth Hall, Elizabeth. B.A., Adelphi U., Garden City, N.Y., 1960. From jr. copywriter to v.p. BBDO Advt. Inc., N.Y.C., 1967-77; assoc. creative dir. SSC&B Inc., N.Y.C., 1977-80, sr. v.p., creative exec., 1980-82, exec. v.p., 1982—. Served with USAR, 1960-61. Home: 22 Country Club Rd New Canaan CT 06840 Office: 1 Dag Hammarskjold Plaza New York NY 10017

CONLY, JOHN FRANKLIN, engineering educator, researcher; b. Ridley Park, Pa., Sept. 11, 1933; s. Harlan and Mary Jane (Roberts) C.; m. Jeannine Therese McDonough, Apr. 14, 1967; children: J. Paul, Mary Ann. B.S., U. Pa., 1956, M.S., 1958; Ph.D., Columbia U., 1962. Instr. U. Pa., Phila., 1956-58; research asst. Columbia U., N.Y.C., 1959-62; asst. prof. engring. San Diego State U., 1962-65, assoc. prof., 1965-69, prof., 1969—, chmn. dept., 1971-74, 77—, wind tunnel dir., 1978—. D. and F. Guggenheim fellow, 1958. Assoc. fellow AIAA (sect. chmn. 1970, best U.S. sect. 1970). Republican. Episcopalian. Office: San Diego State U Dept Aerospace Engring San Diego CA 92182

CONMY, PETER THOMAS, pub. library exec.; b. San Francisco, July 8, 1901; s. Thomas Cherry and Mary Henrietta (Richter) C.; m. Emiliette Constance Storti, July 11, 1928; children—Constance Louise, Thomas Peter. A.B., U. Calif., 1924, M.A., 1927, Ed.D., 1937, B.L.S., 1947; M.A., Stanford, 1941; LL.B., U. San Francisco, 1952. Tchr. jr. high schs., San Francisco, 1926, tchr., counselor, debate coach, evening sch. tchr. evening high sch. registrar and evening high sch. prin., 2 pub. schs., 1927-43; serving at Horace Mann Fr. High Sch., Mission High Sch., Evening High Sch. of Commerce and; Galileo Evening High Sch.; named city librarian of, Oakland, Calif., 1943; charge Oakland Pub. Library dept. including; Oakland Pub. Mus., Snow Mus., Oakland Art Gallery. Author: History of the Entrance Requirements of the University of California, 1928, Aids to the Study of Government, 1928, History of Public School Finance in California, 1937, Self Determination and the Paris Peace Conference, 1941, Public School-Public Library Relationships, 1945, Studies in English Education during the 18th Century, 1946, The Date of the Founding of San Francisco, 1947, A Centennial Evaluation of the Treaty of Guadalupe Hidalgo, 1848-1948, The Queen of the Avenue, the History of St. Francis Church, 1949, The Public Library and The State, 1962, also numerous articles on Calif. History pub. by, Native Sons of Golden West. Mem. Selective Service Bd. 100., San Francisco, 1943, chmn., 1944—; city historian, Oakland, 1969—. Decorated Knight of Saint Gregory, 1963, Knight of Malta, 1976. Mem. A.L.A., Calif. Library Assn. (pres. 1961), N.E.A., Calif. Tchrs. Assn., Calif. Hist. Soc., Am. Polit. Sci. Assn., Native Sons of Golden West (grand pres. 1949-50, dir. hist. research 1954—), Young Men's Inst., Phi Delta Kappa, Phi Delta Kappa. Clubs: K.C. (4 deg.), Rotarian., Elk., Serra (pres. 1952). Home: 1066 Ardmore Ave Oakland CA 94610 Office: 2101 Telegraph Ave Oakland CA 94612

CONN, ARTHUR LEONARD, energy consultant; b. N.Y.C., Apr. 5, 1913; s. Nathan Avram and Jennie (Harmel) C.; m. Bernice Robbins, Sept. 2, 1937 (dec. May 1970); children: Robert Harmel, Elizabeth (Mrs. J. Geoffrey Magnus), Alex Paul; m. Irene Sekely Farkas, June 10, 1972. S.B. in Chem. Engring., MIT, 1934, S.M., 1935; grad., Inst. Mgmt., Northwestern U., 1959. Asst. to dir. research Blaw-Knox Co., Pitts., 1936; exptl. chemist ALCO Products div. Am. Locomotive Co., 1936-39; with Standard Oil Co. Ind. and Amoco Oil Co. subs., 1939-78; group and sect. leader in charge Boron isotope separation Manhattan Project, 1943-46, div. dir., 1950-59, supt. tech. service, 1959; dir. process devel. Amoco Oil Co., 1960-62, research coordinator, 1962-64, sr. cons. engr., 1964-67, dir. govt. contracts, 1967-78; pres. Arthur L. Conn & Assocs., Ltd., cons. in new energy, 1978—; cons. AEC, 1951-53, Office Coal Research, ERDA, Dept. Energy, 1968-82, Synthetic Fuels Corp., 1983; mem. indsl. adv. com. U. Ill.-Chgo., 1971-78; indsl. com. advising CUNY on coal research, 1972-79; mem. com. on coal liquefaction, chmn. com. on processing coal and shale liquids Nat. Acad. Engring., 1975-80; trustee Engring. Info. Inc., 1982—. Contbr. articles to profl. jours. Thorp fellow, 1935. Fellow AAAS (council 1970-73), Am. Inst. Chem. Engrs. (dir. 1966-71, v.p. 1969, pres. 1970, Founders award 1976); mem. Am. Chem. Soc. Patentee in field. Office: 1469 E Park Pl Chicago IL 60637

CONN, GEORGE ALBERT, government official; b. Evanston, Ill., Apr. 24, 1933; m. Jane Conn, June 29, 1963; children: Tracy Kathryn, Sean Michael, Jamie Lynn. B.S., Northwestern U., 1955. Asst. dir. alumni affairs Northwestern U., Evanston, Ill., 1961-63; asst. dir. pub. relations Morton Salt Co., Chgo., 1963-66; exec. dir. Ill. Gov.'s Com. on Employment of Handicapped, 1966-72; cons. to Nat. Capitol Park

Service for Bicentennial, Washington, 1974; dir. Office Pub. Affairs-Rehab. Services Adminstrn.-HEW, Washington, 1972-75; dir. planning White House Conf. on Handicapped Individuals, Washington, 1975-77; legis. dir. Nat. Vets Orgn., 1979; commr. Rehab. Services Adminstrn.-U.S. Dept. Edn., Washington, 1981—. Bd. dirs. Nat. Paraplegia Found., 1966-72; pres. Nat. Wheelchair Basketball Assn., 1966-76; mem. VA Com. on Comprehensive Rehab., 1981—, Com. for Purchase from the Blind and Other Severely Handicapped, 1982—, Fed. Interagy. Com. on Rehab. Research, 1982—; dir. Handicapped Desk-Reagan-Bush Campaign, Arlington, Va., 1980. Served as 1st lt. USAF, 1955-58. Mem. U.S. Paralympics Team, 1961-64; recipient 17 gold medals U.S. Paralympic Team, 1961-64, VFW award, 1967, Alumni award of merit Northwestern U., 1971, Courage award Courage Rehab. Ctr., Golden Valley, Minn., 1982, Human Goals award Dept. Def., 1982; named Outstanding Handicapped Employee Dept. HEW, 1975; named to Nat. Wheelchair Basketball Hall of Fame, 1977, Outstanding Young Man Jaycees, 1966-67. Office: Rehab Services Adminstrn Dept Edn 400 Maryland Ave SW Washington 20202

CONN, HADLEY LEWIS, JR., physician, educator; b. Danville, Ind., May 6, 1921; s. Hadley L. and Fyrne (Holtsclaw) C.; m. Betty Jean Aubertin, Sept. 18, 1946; children: Eric Hadley, Jeffrey Wood, Thomas Brian, Andrew Randall, Lisabeth Ann. B.A., U. Ind., 1942, M.D., 1944; M.S. (hon.), U. Pa., 1972. Assoc. scientist Brookhaven (N.Y.) Nat. Lab., 1953-55; asst. prof. U. Pa. Sch. Medicine, Phila., 1956-59, assoc. prof., 1959-64, prof. medicine, 1964-72; dir. Clin. Research Center Hosp. of U. Pa. Sch. Medicine, 1970-72; chmn. dept. medicine Presbyn.-U. Pa. Med. Center, Phila., 1964-69; vis. prof. medicine Am. U. Beirut, 1969-70; chmn. dept. medicine Univ. Medicine and Dentistry N.J.-Rutgers Med. Sch., Piscataway, N.J., 1972-83, dir. Cardiovascular Inst., 1982—, disting. prof. medicine, 1984—. Author: Myocardial Cell, 1966, Cardiac and Vascular Disease, 1971. Sec. Nat. Bd. Med. Examiners, 1962-65; bd. govs. Am. Heart Assn., 1969-72; pres. Heart Assn. S.E. Pa., 1967, Detweiler Found. Served to capt. M.C. AUS, 1946-48. Mem. ACP, Am. Coll. Cardiology (dir. 1963-69), AMA, Am. Soc. Clin. Investigation, Am. Clin. and Climatological Soc., Assn. Univ. Cardiologists, Am. Phys. Soc., Assn. Profs. Medicine, Phi Beta Kappa, Alpha Omega Alpha. Republican. Clubs: Rittenhouse; Merion Cricket (Phila.). Home: 253 Wendover St Princeton NJ 08540

CONN, HAROLD O., physician, educator; b. Newark, Nov. 16, 1925; s. Joseph H. and Dora (Kobrin) C.; m. Marilyn Barr, May 2, 1951; children: Chrysanne, Steven A., Dorianne. B.S., U. Mich., 1946, M.D., 1950. Diplomate: Am. Bd. Internal Medicine. Intern Johns Hopkins Hosp., 1950-51; asst. resident Grace New Haven Community Hosp., 1951-52, chief resident, 1955-56; James Hudson Browne research fellow, 1952-53; dir. med. edn. Middlesex Meml. Hosp., 1956-57; clin. investigator VA, 1957-61; chief med. service VA Hosp., West Haven, Conn., 1959-60, chief hepatic research lab., 1961—; instr. Yale Sch. Medicine, 1955-58, asst. prof., 1958-66, asso. prof., 1966-71, prof., 1971—; vis. asso. prof. Washington U. Sch. Medicine, 1968; vis. prof. Stanford U. Sch. Medicine, 1975-76, UCLA Sch. Medicine. Author: The Hepatic Coma Syndromes and Lactulose, 1979; editor: +-Cyanidanol-3 in Diseases of the Liver, 1981; mem. editorial bd.: Viewpoints on Digestive Disease, 1968-73; editorial bd.: Gastroenterology, 1970—; editor for liver disease and physiology, 1973-77; editorial bd.: Jour. Clin. Trials, Italian Jour. Gastroenterology, 1977—; asso. editor: Hepatology, 1980—. Bd. dirs. Am. Liver Found., 1977-80. Served to ensign USNR, 1943-44. Recipient Rorer award Am. Jour. Gastroenterology, 1973, William Beaumont award clin. research, 1974; Conn. paddle tennis mixed doubles champion (asphalt), 1963. Fellow A.C.P.; Mem. Assn. Am. Physicians, Am. Soc. Clin. Investigation, Internat. Assn. Study Liver, Sydenham Soc. (sec. 1968—, mem. med. adv. bd. Seminars and Symposia 1974—), Hepatic Perfusion Soc. (pres. St. Louis chpt.), Am. Assn. Study Liver Disease (v.p. 1971, pres. 1972, dir. postgrad. course on portal hypertension), Am. Fedn. Clin. Research, Am. Gasteroenterol. Assn. (councillor 1974-77), Viral Hepatitis Venereal Transmission Soc. (pres. 1976), Soc. for Clin. Trials (dir. 1978—); hon. mem. Australian Soc. Gastroenterology, Brazilian Assn. for Study of Liver, China Med. Assn. (Shanghai br.). Clubs: Conn. Sunfish (commodore 1967), Westwood Cinema and Sun Soc. (chmn. 1982—). Home: 420 Miles Rd Orange CT 06477 Office: VA Hosp W Spring St West Haven CT 06516 also 333 Cedar St New Haven CT 06608 *It is among my professional goals to apply the principles of the laboratory to the bedside, to enhance and enliven medical writing and to introduce humor into the somber realm of the medical literature.*

CONN, JACK TRAMMELL, banker, lawyer; b. Ada, Okla., Nov. 19, 1909; s. Jared Trammell and Carrie (Chaplin) C. Grad., E. Central Coll., Ada, 1931; LL.B., U. Okla., 1940; hon. doctorate, Oklahoma City U., 1968. Bar: Okla. 1940. Practice in, Ada, 1940-64, Oklahoma City, 1947-64; of counsel Linn & Helms, Oklahoma City, 1984—; pres., chmn. bd. Okla. State Bank, Ada, 1951-64; chmn. bd., chief exec. officer Fidelty Bank N.A., Oklahoma City, 1964—, vice chmn. bd., 1978—; chmn. Fidelity of Okla., Inc. Author: autobiography One Man in His Time, 1979; contbr. to profl. jours. Named to Okla. Hall of Fame. Mem. Am. Bankers Assn. (past pres.), Okla. Bankers Assn. (past pres.), Metro Concourse Assn. (pres.), Okla. Hist. Soc. (pres., chmn. Diamond Jubilee commn.), Order of Coif, Phi Delta Phi, Sigma Nu. Lodges: Masons (33 deg., Jester); Shriners. Home: 7202 Waverly St Oklahoma City OK 73120 Office: PO Box 24128 Oklahoma City OK 73124

CONN, REX BOLAND, JR., physician, educator; b. Marengo, Iowa, Aug. 3, 1927; s. Rex Bol and Helena Dorothea (Schoenfelder) C.; m. Victoria Grace Sellens, Dec. 28, 1950; children: Elizabeth Marian, Victoria Anne, Mary Catherine. B.S., Iowa State U., 1949; M.D., Yale U., 1953; B.Sc., U. Oxford, Eng., 1955; M.S., U. Minn., 1960. Prof. pathology, dir. clin. labs. W.Va. Med. Center, Morgantown, 1960-68; prof. lab. medicine, dir. dept. Johns Hopkins Med. Instns., Balt., 1968-77; prof. pathology and lab. medicine, dir. clin labs. Emory U., Atlanta, 1977—; Mem. pathology tng. com. NIH, 1972-73; cons. Walter Reed Army Med. Center, 1972-77. Co-editor: Current Diagnosis, 1980, 7th edit., 1984, Yearbook of Pathology and Clinical Pathology, 1980. Served with USNR, 1945-46. Mem. Coll. Am. Pathologists, Am. Soc. Clin. Pathologists (dir. 1975-81), Acad. Clin. Lab. Physicians and Scientists (pres. 1972—). Home: 2505 Greenglade Rd Atlanta GA 30345 Office: 1364 Clifton Rd Atlanta GA 30322

CONN, ROBERT HENRY, government official, former naval officer; b. Boonton, N.J., June 8, 1925; s. Henry Hammond and Violet (Doremus) C.; m. Virginia Inness-Brown, July 6, 1946; children: Portia Conn Hirschman, Judith Conn Bell, Robert H., Patricia, Catherine E. B.B.A., U. Miss., 1955; M.S., U. Rochester, 1962; D.B.A., Ind. U., 1965; student, U.S. Naval War Coll., 1963. Commd. ensign U.S. Navy, 1946, advanced through grades to capt., 1967; asst. dir. budgets and reports Office Navy Comptroller (U.S. Navy), Washington, 1969-72, ret., 1972; mgr. fed. liaison div. Arthur Anderson & Co., Washington, 1972-81; comptroller of the navy Dept. Navy, Washington, 1981—; asst. prof. naval sci. U. Rochester, N.Y., 1959-62; lectr. Armed Forces Indsl. Coll., Nat. War Coll., Naval War Coll.; dir. Clipper Belt Lacer Co. Author: Financial Management Systems for Political Campaigns, 1972. Bd. dirs. Navy Mut. Aid Soc., 1970-72. Decorated Legion of Merit, Meritorious Service medal. Fellow Sigma Iota Epsilon; mem. Am. Soc. Mil. Comptrollers. Republican. Episcopalian. Clubs: N.Y. Yacht (N.Y.C.); Army-Navy; Capitol Hill (Washington). Home: 6668 Midhill Pl Falls Church VA 22043 Office: Comptroller of Navy Dept Navy Rm 4E 768 Pentagon Washington DC 20350

CONN, ROBERT WILLIAM, nuclear engineering educator; b. Bklyn., Dec. 1, 1942; s. William Conrad and Rose Marie (Albanese) C.; m. Gloria Trovato, Sept. 21, 1963; children: Carole, William. B.Chem.Engring., Pratt Inst., 1964; M.S., Calif. Inst. Tech., 1965; Ph.D. in Engring. Sci, 1968. NSF postdoctoral fellow Euratom Community Research Center, Ispra, Italy, 1968-69; research asso. Brookhaven Nat. Lab., Upton, N.Y., 1969-70; vis. asso. prof. U. Wis., Madison, 1970-72, mem. faculty, 1972-80, prof. nuclear engring., 1975-80, dir. fusion tech. program, 1974-79; prof. engring. and applied sci. UCLA, 1980—; cons. to govt. and industry. Author papers, chpt. in book. Recipient Curtis McGraw Research award Am. Assn. Engring. Edn., Outstanding Service cert. U.S. Dept. Energy; Predoctoral fellow NSF, 1964-66, AEC, 1966-68; Romnes Faculty fellow, 1977. Mem. Am. Nuclear Soc., Fellow (Outstanding Achievement award for excellence in research, Fusion Div.), Am. Phys. Soc.; Mem. AAAS, Sigma Xi, Tau Beta Pi. Home: 1818 Parnell Ave Los Angeles CA 90025 Office: 6291 Boelter Hall UCLA Los Angeles CA 90025 *It is often so that the more critical a problem appears, the more fun is the resulting challenge.*

CONNABLE, ALFRED BARNES, business director; b. Kalamazoo, Feb. 20, 1904; s. Alfred B. and Frances (Peck) C.; m. Dorothy Jean Malcomson, Apr. 15, 1927 (div. 1972); children: Nancy M., Alfred B. III, John Lee (dec.); m. Tenho S. Hindert, Nov. 11, 1972. Student, Culver Mil. Acad., 1921; A.B., U. of Mich., 1925; M.B.A., Harvard, 1929; H.H.D., Western Mich. U., 1962. Sales asst. Kalamazoo Vegetable Parchment Co., 1925-28; asst. sec. Selected Securities Corp. of Detroit, 1928-30; successively asst. sec., asst. v.p. and dir. of investment analysis dept. Detroit Trust Co., 1930-43; state price adminstr. for Mich. OPA, 1942-43; state mgr. Wendell L. Willkie presdl. campaign, 1943-44; instr. investments and econs Detroit Inst. Tech., 1929-30; chmn., dir. Monroe Calculating Co., 1944-58; chmn. Lafourche Realty Co., Inc., Kalamazoo; dir. Hayes-Albion Co., 1967-74, Albion Malleable Iron Co., 1945-67, Am. Nat. Bank & Trust Co. of Mich., 1946-76, Kalamazoo Sled & Toys Co., Inc., 1944-68, Kalamazoo Ice and Fuel Co., 1945-72, Hayes Industries, Inc., Jackson, Mich., 1947-67, KVP Sutherland Paper Co., 1946-66, Litton Industries, 1958-61; Regent U. Mich., 1942-58, emeritus, 1960. Trustee Douglas Community Assn.; trustee emeritus Western Mich. U.; mem. exec. com. Community Chest; dir., past pres. Kalamazoo Symphony Orch. Soc.; mem. adv. council Assn. Governing Bds. Univs., Colls.; past pres. Assn. of Governing Bds. of State Univs. and Colls., Am. Symphony Orchestra League (dir.); mem. exec. com. Mich. Artrain, Inc.; former mem. Mich. State Council for the Arts. Mem. Pi Delta Epsilon, Alpha Kappa Psi, Delta Kappa Epsilon. Republican. Presbyn. Clubs: Rotarian., U. of Mich. (Detroit and Kalamazoo); Harvard (N.Y.); Univ. (Ann Arbor). Home: 3808 Skyrise Center 525 S Burdick St Kalamazoo MI 49007 Office: 1201 Am Nat Bank Bldg Kalamazoo MI 49007

CONNAL, ALLAN BRUCE, sports television network executive; b. N.Y.C., July 21, 1928; s. Alexander and Catherine (Foligno) C.; m. Mathilde Pfieffer, Apr. 14, 1951; children: Christine, Susan, Bruce, Cathy, Diane, Linda, Allan, Scott. Student, Columbia U., 1948-50. In entertainment and news prodn. WNBC-TV and NBC, N.Y.C., 1947-61; prodn. mgr. news NBC, N.Y.C., 1961-64, adminstr. sports, 1964-70, exec. producer sports, 1970-75, v.p. sports ops., 1975-79; exec. v.p., chief operating officer ESPN, Bristol, Conn., 1979—; mem. adv. bd. Norwich U., Vt., 1983. Served with U.S. Army, 1950-52. Recipient Emmy award for NBC's coverage of World Series Nat. Assn. TV Arts and Scis., 1975, Ace award Nat. Cable TV Assn., 1981, award for Cablecasting Excellence, 1982. Mem. Nat. Assn. TV Arts and Scis., Nat. Cable TV Assn. Office: ESPN 935 Middle St Bristol CT 06010

CONNALLY, JOHN BOWDEN, lawyer; b. Floresville, Tex., Feb. 27, 1917; s. John Bowden and Lela (Wright) C.; m. Idanell Brill, Dec. 21, 1940; children: John Bowden III, Sharon, Mark. LL.B., U. Tex., 1941. Pres., gen. mgr. radio sta. KVET, Austin, Tex., 1946-49; adminstrv. asst. to Senator Lyndon B. Johnson, 1949; mem. firm Powell, Wirtz & Rahaut, Austin, 1949-52; atty. for Sid W. Richardson & Perry R. Bass (ind. oil operators), Fort Worth, 1952-61; sec. U.S. Navy, 1961; gov. of Tex., 1963-69; partner Vinson & Elkins, Houston, 1969-71, 72—; sec. U.S. Treasury, Washington, 1971-72; spl. adviser to the Pres., 1973; spl. counsel to bd. dirs. and exec. com. Am. Gen. Cos., Houston; dir. Justin Industries, Falconbridge Nickel Mines, Ltd., First City Bancorp. Tex., Inc., First City Nat. Bank of Floresville, Continental Airlines, Inc., Dr. Pepper Co.; Mem. U.S. Adv. Council on Exec. Orgn., 1969-70; mem. Pres.'s Fgn. Intelligence Adv. Bd., 1972-74, 76-77, Adv. Com. on Reform Internat. Monetary System. Trustee Andrew W. Mellon Found., 1973—; bd. dirs. Meth. Hosp., Am. Trauma Soc.; adv. com. on law and nat. security Am. Bar Assn.; trustee Southwestern Legal Found., Found. for Bus., Politics and Econs., Houston. Recipient Distinguished Alumnus award U. Tex. Ex-Students Assn., 1961. Mem. Houston C. of C. (dir.), Conf. Bd. Republican. Club: Houston Met. Racquet (dir.). Office: chapman energy inc p o box 45743 dallas TX 75245 *

CONNAR, RICHARD GRIGSBY, surgeon; b. Zanesville, Ohio, Jan. 11, 1920; s. Virgil Norwood and Anna Margaret (Grigsby) C.; m. Elizabeth Dickens, May 18, 1946; children: Cathleen, Elizabeth Ann, Richard Grigsby. B.A., Duke U., 1941, M.D., 1944. Intern, then resident in internal medicine Duke U. Hosp., 1944-46, resident in gen. and thoracic surgery, 1948-53; asst. prof. surgery Duke U. Med. Sch., 1953-55, regional rep., 1956—; practice medicine specializing in thoracic and cardiovascular surgery, Tampa, Fla., 1955—; mem. staff Tampa Gen. Hosp., 1955—, chief surgery, 1962-66, 72—, chief sect. thoracic and cardiovascular surgery, 1969—; clin. prof. surgery U. South Fla. Med. Sch., Tampa, 1972-82, prof., chmn. dept. surgery, 1982—, adv. com., 1972-77; cons. Fla. Crippled Children's Commn., MacDill AFB Hosp., S.W. Fla. Tb Sanitarium; chmn. med. adv. bd. Hillsborough County Hosp. and Welfare Bd., 1962-64; mem. Fla. Tb Bd., 1964-69; adv. com. U. Fla. Coll. Medicine, 1975. Contbr. articles to med. jours. Bd. dirs. U. South Fla. Found.; bd. counselors U. Tampa, 1965-70; chmn. Duke U. Nat. Council, 1970-71. Served to capt. M.C. USAAF, 1946-48. Fellow A.C.S. (pres. Fla. chpt. 1967-68, bd. govs. 1970-76); mem. AMA (ho. dels. 1971—, council med. edn. 1974-82, vice chmn. 1981), Fla. Med. Assn., Hillsborough County Med. Assn. (pres. 1970-71), Fla. Heart Assn. (award 1967, dir. 1962-68), Hillsborough County Heart Assn. (dir. 1957-76, award 1960), So. Surg. Assn., Am. Assn. Thoracic Surgery, So. Thoracic Surg. Assn., Soc. Vascular Surgery, Fla. Thoracic Soc. (pres. 1971-72), Soc. Thoracic Surgeons (governing council 1981—, Am. Coll. Chest Physicians, Internat. Cardiovascular Soc.), So. Assn. Vascular Surgery, Fla. Soc. Thoracic and Cardiovascular Surgeons (pres. 1978-79), Royal Soc. Medicine, Liaison Com. for Grad. Med. Edn., Liaison Com. for Med. Edn., Duke U. Gen. Alumni Assn. (pres. 1973-74), Phi Beta Kappa, Omicron Delta Kappa, Alpha Omega Alpha, Sigma Alpha Epsilon. Clubs: Explorers, University, Tampa Yacht and Country, Ye Mystic Krewe of Gasparilla, Palma Cela Golf and Country. Home: 3305 Jean Circle Tampa FL 33609 Office: Dept Surgery U South Fla Coll Medicine 12901 N 30th St Box 16 Tampa FL 33612

CONNARE, WILLIAM GRAHAM, bishop; b. Pitts., Dec. 11, 1911; s. James J. and Nellie T. (O'Connor) C. B.A., Duquesne U., 1932, Litt.D., 1961; M.A., St. Vincent Coll., Latrobe, Pa., 1934, L.H.D., 1962; LL.D., Seton Hill Coll., 1960. Ordained priest Roman Catholic Ch., 1936; named domestic prelate, 1955; asst. pastor St. Canice, Pitts., 1936-37, St. Paul's Cathedral, 1937-49; adminstr. St. Richard's Ch., Pitts., 1949-55, pastor, 1955-60; chaplain Univ. Cath. Club, Pitts., 1947-60, Cath. Interracial Council Pitts., 1953-60; dir. Soc. Propagation of Faith, 1950-59; vicar for religious as rep. Bishop of Pitts., 1959-60; consecrated bishop of Greensburg, Pa., 1960—. Bd. dirs., chmn. community services com. Urban League Pitts., 1950-60; mem. Pitts. Commn. Human Relations, 1953-60, Allegheny County Council Civil Rights, 1953-60; bd. dirs. Allegheny County Council Civil Rights, 1958-60; bd. dirs. Pitts. br. N.A.A.C.P., 1959-60; Episcopal chmn. Nat. Cath. Com. on Scouting, Boy Scouts Am., 1962-70; Episcopal moderator div. youth activities U.S. Cath. Conf., 1968-70; mem. Bishop's Commn. for Liturgical Apostolate, 1967-72; chmn. commn. on missions Nat. Conf. Cath. Bishops, 1967-71, mem. adminstrv. bd., 1967; mem. Bishop's Com. on Missions, 1971; mem. council Christian Assos. Southwest Pa., 1972; chmn. Am. Bd. Cath. Missions, 1972; mem. Episcopal adv. bd. Word of God Inst., 1974; Episcopal adviser Nat. Cath. Stewardship Council, 1974. Address: 723 E Pittsburgh St Greensburg PA 15601 *

CONNELL, ALASTAIR MCCRAE, physician; b. Glasgow, Scotland, Dec. 21, 1929; came to U.S., 1970; s. Alex McCrae and Maud (Crawford) C.; m. Joyce Dethlefs, 1983; children: Stewart, Fiona, Alison, Iain, Andrew. B.Sc., U. Glasgow, 1951, M.B., Ch.B., 1954, M.D., 1969. Intern Western Infirmary, Glasgow, 1954-55; resident in gastroenterology Central Middlesex and St. Mark's Hosp., London, 1957-60; practice medicine specializing in gastroenterology, 1960—; mem. med. staff Med. Research Council, 1960-64; sr. lectr. clin. sci. Queen's U., Belfast, No. Ireland, 1964-70; Mark Brown prof. medicine Med. Center, U. Cin., 1970-79, dir. div. digestive diseases, 1970-79, prof. physiology, 1972-79, asso. dean, 1975-77; dir. Office Clin. Affairs, 1975-77; dean Coll. Medicine, U. Nebr. Med. Center, 1979—, prof. internal medicine, 1979—; mem. sci. adv. bd. Nat. Found. for Ileitis and Colitis, 1974—, chmn. research devel. com., 1974-78; mem. Personal Health Com. Ohio, 1974-76; trustee Medco Peer Rev., 1974-79. Author: Clinical Tests of Gastric Function, 1973; Asso. editor: Am. Jour. Digestive Diseases; Contbr. articles to profl. jours. Served with M.C. Royal Army, 1955-57. Fellow Royal Coll. Physicians (Edinburgh), A.C.P.; mem. Am. Gastroent. Assn., Brit. Soc. Gastroenterology, Med. Research Soc., Internat. Group for Study Intestinal Motility (past pres.), S.W. Ohio Digestive Diseases Soc. (pres. 1973-76), Cin. Lit. Club. Office: Office of Dean U Nebr Coll Medicine Omaha NE 68105

CONNELL, EVAN SHELBY, JR., author; b. Kansas City, Mo., Aug. 17, 1924; s. Evan Shelby and Elton (Williamson) C. Student, Dartmouth, 1941-43, U. Kans., 1946-47, Stanford U., 1947-48, Columbia U., 1948-49. Editor Contact mag., 1959-65. Author: The Anatomy Lesson and Other Stories, 1957, Mrs. Bridge, 1959, The Patriot, 1960, Notes From a Bottle Found on the Beach at Carmel, 1963, At the Crossroads, 1965, The Diary of a Rapist, 1966, Mr. Bridge, 1969, Points for a Compass Rose, 1973, The Connoisseur, 1974, Double Honeymoon, 1976, A Long Desire, 1979, The White Lantern, 1980, St. Augustine's Pigeon, 1980, Son of the Morning Star: Custer and the Little Bighorn, 1984. Served as naval aviator, 1943-45. Eugene Saxton fellow, 1953; Guggenheim fellow, 1963; Rockefeller Found. grantee, 1967. Address: 487 Sherwood Dr Sausalito CA 94965

CONNELL, GEORGE EDWARD, scientist, univ. pres.; b. Saskatoon, Sask., Can., June 20, 1930; s. James Lorne and Mabel Gertrude (Killins) C.; m. Sheila Harriet Horan, Dec. 27, 1955; children—James, Caroline, Thomas, Margaret. B.A., U. Toronto, Can., 1951, Ph.D. in Biochemistry, 1955. NSF postdoctoral fellow, U.S., 1956-57; asst. prof. biochemistry U. Toronto, Ont., 1957-62, asso. prof., 1962-65, prof., chmn. dept. biochemistry, 1965-70, asso. dean, 1972-74, v.p. research and planning, 1974-77; pres. U. Western Ont., London, 1977—. Fellow Chem. Inst. Can., Royal Soc. Can.; mem. Am. Soc. Biol. Chemists, Biochem. Soc. (U.K.), Can. Biochem. Soc. (pres. 1973-74), Can. Soc. for Immunology. Clubs: Univ. (Toronto); London Hunt. Home: 1836 Richmond St London ON N6A 4B6 Canada Office: Univ of Western Ontario Office of President London ON Canada

CONNELL, GROVER, food co. exec.; b. N.Y.C., Apr. 12, 1918; s. Grover Clevel and Violet Regina (Connell) C.; m. Patricia Day, July 31, 1940; children—Ted, Terry, Toni. B.S. in Bus. Adminstrn, Columbia, 1939. With Connell Rice & Sugar Co., Inc., Westfield, N.J., 1939—, pres., 1950—. Served to lt. USNR, 1942-46. Democrat. Presbyterian. Home: 207 Watchung Fork Westfield NJ 07090 Office: 45 Cardinal Dr Westfield NJ 07090

CONNELL, HUGH P., advertising agency executive, lawyer; b. Bethlehem, Pa., May 7, 1931; s. Joseph B. and Mary (McFadden) C.; m. Susan Richardson Hobbs, July 2, 1965; children: Hugh Richardson, Andrew Warfield, Edward William. A.B., Moravian Coll., 1953; LL.B., U. Pa., 1956; student, Hague Acad. Internat. Law, 1959; LL.M., U. London, Eng., 1960. Bar: Pa. 1956, N.Y. 1963. Lectr. internat. law U. London, Eng., 1960-62; with firm Coudert Bros., N.Y.C., 1962-65; gen. counsel J. Walter Thompson Co., N.Y.C., 1966—, v.p., 1967-73, sec., 1972—, sr. v.p., 1973, exec. v.p., 1974—, dir., 1974—; exec. v.p. JWT Group, Inc., 1980—, also dir.; dir. Hill and Knowlton, Inc., Euro Holding B.V., Simmons Market Research Bur., Inc., Survival Anglia, Ltd., Crosswoods Vineyards, Inc. Trustee Nat. Soc. to Prevent Blindness, Jackson Lab., Bar Harbor, Maine., Moravian Coll. Served with AUS, 1956-58. Mem. Am. Soc. Internat. Law, Soc. Pub. Tchrs. Law (U.K.), Pilgrims of U.S. Clubs: Bedford Golf and Tennis; Union (N.Y.C.); Wadawanuck (Stonington, Conn.). Home: 28 Water St Stonington CT 06378 Office: 466 Lexington Ave New York NY 10017

CONNELL, JOHN GIBBS, JR., former government official; b. Atlanta, Sept. 26, 1914; s. John Gibbs and Vena Estelle (Turner) C.; m. Bernice E. Siewerdsen, Oct. 2, 1941; children: Sharon Elaine, Candace Anne. A.A., George Washington U., 1948, A.B., 1952. With U.S. Civil Service Commn., 1935-38, U.S. Housing Authority, 1938-40; with War Dept. and Army Dept., 1940—; personnel mgr. Office of Sec. Army, 1942-54, asst. for security and personnel, 1954-62, dep. adminstrv. asst. to sec. army, 1962-66, adminstv. asst. to sec. army, 1966-79; Chmn. Army Security Screening Bd., 1953-66; prin. adminstrv. officer Army Loyalty-Security Program, 1950—; mem. Army Bd. Correction Mil. Records, 1947-62; Army Dept. rep. interdepartmental com. to study govt. employee security programs for Pres. Truman, 1951-52; Army rep. Exec. Officers Group, 1968—; mem. Dept. Def. Concessions Com., 1966—; Army rep. Fed. Exec. Bd., 1969—; mem. adv. com. Nat. Archives and Records Service, 1973. Bd. dirs. Army-Air Force Civilian Welfare Fund, Youth Devel. Inst. Served to 2d lt. USAAF, 1943-45; 1st lt. OSS, 1945-46; maj. M.I. Army Res. Recipient Army Exceptional Civilian Service medal, 1973, 75, 79, 40 Year Certificate of Service award, 1975, Meritorious Civilian Service award, 1977. Mem. Fed. Sr. Exec. Service (charter mem.), Nat. Assn. Ret. Fed. Employees, Art League Alexandria, Sigma Nu. Presbyn. (elder). Home: 302 Cloverway Alexandria VA 22314 *I try to govern my life so as to serve others as I would have them serve me. I believe in the inherent dignity of man as an individual.*

CONNELL, JOSEPH EDWARD, insurance executive; b. Niagara Falls, N.Y., Oct. 8, 1930; s. George Kerr and Katharine Elsa (Vodra) C.; m. Patricia Jane Parsons, Aug. 22, 1953; children: Douglas Edward, Marjorie Elsa. B.A., Antioch Coll., 1954; postgrad., George Washington U., 1956-58. C.P.A., Mich., Tex. With Coopers & Lybrand (C.P.A.s), 1958-74, partner, SEC specialist, Detroit, 1958-62, Mpls., 1962-73, Des Moines, 1973-74; sr. v.p., controller, treas. Republic Nat. Life Ins. Co., Dallas, 1974—. Served to lt. USNR, 1955-58. Fellow Life Mgmt. Inst.; mem. Am. Inst. C.P.A.s, Nat. Assn. Accts., Fin. Execs. Inst. Unitarian. Clubs: Canyon Creek Country, White Rock Marathon. Home: 422 Fall Creek Dr Richardson TX 75080 Office: Box 226210 Dallas TX 75266

CONNELL, LAWRENCE, banker; b. N.Y.C., Sept. 30, 1936; s. Lawrence and Miriam (Cunningham) C.; m. Marion Avery Fitch, Oct. 16, 1965; children: Elizabeth, Rachel. B.A., Harvard U., 1958; J.D., Georgetown U., 1966; M.A., Trinity Coll., Hartford, Conn., 1973. Bar: Calif. 1967, D.C. 1979. With Office Comptroller of Currency, U.S. Treasury Dept. (various locations), 1958-68, nat. bank examiner, Washington, 1963-66, dep. regional adminstr. of nat. banks, San Francisco and Boston, 1966-68; v.p., cashier, counsel Hartford Nat. Bank & Trust Co., 1968-71; sec. Hartford Nat. Corp., 1969-75; pres., dir. Hartford Trust Co. N.Y., 1972-75; chmn. Nat. Credit Union Adminstrn., 1979-81; pres., dir. Washington Mut. Savs. Bank, 1982—; vice chmn. Neighborhood Reinvestment Corp., 1979—; chmn. Nat. Consumer Coop. Bank, 1979-81; mem. Depository Instns. Deregulation Com., 1980—; Chmn. Conn. Health and Ednl. Facilities Authority, 1971-75. Mem. Gov.'s Com. on Conn. Uniform Consumer Credit Code, 1969-70, Glastonbury (Conn.) Citizens' Adv. Council of the Community Devel. Action Plan, 1969-71, Conn. Bank Commn., 1975-77; bd. dirs., treas. Hartford Stage Co., 1969-77; bd. dirs. World Affairs Council, Hartford, 1970; trustee Coop. Housing Found., 1981—, Seattle Symphony, 1982—. Served with AUS, 1959. Mem. Am. Bar Assn., State Bar Calif., D.C. bar. Club: Harvard (Washington and N.Y.C.). Home: 500 W Roy St #307 Seattle WA 98119 Office: 1101 2d Ave Seattle WA 98101

CONNELL, PHILIP FRANCIS, food industry executive; b. Hamilton, Ont., Can., Jan. 20, 1924; s. Maurice W. and Kathleen (Richardson) C. B.A., McMaster U., Can., 1946. Chartered accountant, 1950. With Clarkson Gordon & Co., Hamilton and Toronto, 1946-57; comptroller Canadian Westinghouse Co. Ltd., Hamilton, 1957-67; controller Domtar Ltd., Montreal, 1967-68; v.p. finance George Weston Ltd., Toronto, Ont., 1968-75; v.p. fin. Loblaw Cos., Ltd., Toronto, Ont., 1972-75; sr. v.p. fin., dir. Oshawa Group Ltd., 1976—. Fellow Fin. Execs. Inst. (pres. Hamilton chpt. 1966-67), Ont. Inst. Chartered Accountants (gov., treas.). Clubs: Hamilton, National. Home: 400 Walmer Rd Toronto ON Canada Office: 302 East Mall Islington ON M9B 6B8 Canada

CONNELL, WILLIAM FRANCIS, diversified company executive; b. Lynn, Mass., May 12, 1938; s. William J. and Theresa (Keaney) C.; m. Margot C. Gensler, May 29, 1965; children: Monica Cameron, Lisa Terese, Courtenay Erin, William Christopher, Terence Alexander, Timothy Patrick. B.S. magna cum laude, Boston Coll., 1959; M.B.A., Harvard, 1963. Controller Olga Co., Inc., Van Nuys, Calif., 1963-65; asst. treas. Litton Industries, Inc.; also pres. div. Marine Tech., Inc., 1965-68; treas. Ogden Corp., N.Y.C., 1968-69, v.p., treas., 1969-71, sr. v.p., 1971-72, exec. v.p., 1980—; chief exec. officer, chmn. bd. Ogden Leisure, Inc.; chmn. bd., chief exec. officer Ogden Food Service, Inc., Ogden Recreation, Inc., Ogden Security, Inc., Ogden Services Inc.; dir. Ogden Corp., various Ogden subsidaries, 1969—. Active fund raising Boston Coll., trustee, chmn. bd. trustees, 1980—; trustee St. Elizabeth Hosp., Boston, Boston 200 Corp. Served to 1st lt. AUS, 1959-61. Mem. Greater Boston C. of C. (dir.), Beta Gamma Sigma, Alpha Sigma Nu, Alpha Kappa Psi. Roman Catholic. Clubs: Algonquin, Univ. (Boston); Tedesco Country. Home: 111 Ocean Ave Swampscott MA 01907 Office: 111 Waldemar Ave E Boston MA 02128

CONNELLY, ALBERT R., lawyer; b. N.Y.C., Mar. 24, 1908; s. John E. and Julia (Broughey) C.; m. Eleanor Milburn, June 17, 1930; children: Mary, Jean. B.A., Yale, 1929, LL.B., 1932. Bar: N.Y. 1933. Since practiced in, N.Y.C.; partner Cravath Swaine & Moore (and predecessors), from 1941, now ret. ptnr. Trustee emeritus Berkshire Sch.; hon. bd. dirs. Greer-Woodycrest Children's Services. Fellow Am. Bar Found., Am Coll. Trial Lawyers, N.Y. Bar Found.; mem. Am., N.Y. State, N.Y. County bar assns., Assn. Bar City N.Y., Am. Arbitration Assn. (dir.). Clubs: Union, Down Town Assn, Yale (N.Y.C.); St Andrews Golf (Hastings, N.Y.); Metropolitan (Washington). Home: 36 E 72d St New York NY 10021 Office: 1 Chase Manhattan Plaza New York NY 10005

CONNELLY, FRANCIS JOHN, university dean, business administration educator; b. N.Y.C., Jan. 13, 1942; s. Thomas M. and Madeline V. (Devlin) C. B.B.A., CUNY, 1964; M.B.A., Wash. State U., 1966; D.B.A., Ind. U., 1972. Dir. grad. studies Howard U., Washington, 1974-75; assoc. dean Washington U., St. Louis, 1970-79; asst. v.p. Baruch Coll.-CUNY, N.Y.C., 1979-81, dean Sch. Bus. and Pub. Adminstrn., 1981—; pres. Potomac Cons. Group, Fairfax, Va., 1975—; cons. Co-author contract research projects; contbr. writings to profl. pubis.; editor: Am. Assembley Collegiate Schs. Bus. Jour., 1975-78. Advisor pub. adminstrn. U.S. Dept. Treasury, Washington, 1974-75. Fellow Ind. U., 1967-68. Fellow Acad. Mktg. Sci.; mem. Am. Mktg. Assn., Inst. Mgmt. Sci., Beta Gamma Sigma, Phi Kappa Phi. Office: Sch Bus and Pub Adminstrn Baruch Coll-CUNY Lexington Ave New York NY 10010

CONNELLY, JOHN EDWARD, JR., lawyer; b. N.Y.C., Mar. 4, 1904; s. John Edward and Julia (Broughey) C; m. Evelyn R. Weir, Dec. 15, 1972. Grad., Berkshire Sch., Sheffield, Mass., 1922; A.B., Middlebury Coll., 1926; LL.B., Harvard U., 1929. Bar: N.Y. 1930. Since practiced in, N.Y.C.; counsel, former ptnr. Olwine, Connelly, Chase, O'Donnell Weyher (and predecessors), 1952—; pres., dir. Seas Shipping Co., Inc.; dir. McGuire Bros., Inc. Bd. dirs. Life Extension Found., Ada Howe Kent Found. Mem. Am. Bar Assn., N.Y. County Lawyers Assn., Assn. Bar City N.Y., N.Y. State Bar Assn., Am. Judicature Soc., New Eng. Soc., Chi Psi. Clubs: Harvard, Union (N.Y.C.). Home: 799 Park Ave New York NY 10021 Office: 299 Park Ave New York NY 10017

CONNELLY, JOHN FRANCIS, industrialist; b. Phila., Mar. 4, 1905; m. Josephine O'Neill, Apr. 1938; children—Josephine, Emily, John, Thomas, Judith, Christine. LL.D. (hon.), LaSalle Coll., Villanova U., 1958. Dir. Crown Cork & Seal Co., Phila., 1956—, pres., 1957-76, chmn. bd., 1957—, chief exec. officer, 1979—; chmn. bd. Connelly Containers, Inc. Chmn. Archbishop's laity com. Office: Crown Cork & Seal Co 9300 Ashton Rd Philadelphia PA 19136 *

CONNELLY, JOHN MATTHEW, lawyer, insurance company executive; b. Kansas City, Mo., June 10, 1942; s. Matthew Anthony and Helen Madelene (Angremeyer) C.; m. Patricia Gwen Moylan, Nov. 23, 1963; children: Anastasia, Josephine, Kimberly, John, Steven, Erin, Alycia, Kelly, Elizabeth. A.A., Met. Jr. Coll., Kansas City, 1967; B.A., U. Mo., Kansas City, 1972, J.D., 1973. Bar: Mo. 1973. Underwriter Glens Falls Ins. Co., Kansas City, 1966-69, Employers Reins. Corp., 1969-71, staff atty., 1971-76, assoc. gen., counsel, 1976-81, gen. cousel, 1981—. Bd. dirs. Jr. Achievement Greater Kansas City. Served with USN, 1960-63. Mem. Phi Kappa Phi. Office: Employers Reinsurance Corp 2500 Metcalf Overland Park KS 66201

CONNELLY, JOHN PETER, physician, educator; b. Boston, May 12, 1926; s. Thomas J. and Bridget (Finnegan) C.; m. Martha T. Cronin, June 24, 1950; children: Maureen, Martha, Eileen, Marie, Cathleen, John, Michael. B.S., Boston Coll., 1951; M.D., Georgetown U., 1955. Diplomate: Am. Bd. Pediatrics. Intern Royal Victoria Hosp., Montreal, Que., Can., 1955-56; jr. resident children's service Mass. Gen. Hosp., Boston, 1956-57, asst. resident, 1957-58, chief resident, 1961-62; sr. residentin pediatrics Johns Hopkins Hosp., Balt., 1957-58; practice medicine specializing in pediatrics, Boston, 1958-73; asst. pediatrician children's service Mass. Gen. Hosp., 1961-64, chief children's ambulatory clinic, 1963-64, chief ambulatory div., 1964-69, pediatrician, 1967-73, med. dir. pediatric nurse practitioner program, 1964-73; exec. dir. Bunker Hill Health Ctr., 1967-73; vis. physician Lying-In div. Boston Hosp. for Women, 1961-69, cons. maternal and children health, 1968-69; teaching fellow in pediatrics Harvard U., 1957-58, 61-62, instr., 1962-64, assoc. inpediatrics, 1964-67, asst. clin. prof. pediatrics, 1967-69, assoc. prof. pediatrics, 1969-73; chief pediatrics Foster McGaw Hosp., Loyola U., Maywood, Ill., 1972-76; prof., chmn. dept. pediatrics Stritch Sch. Medicine Loyola U., Maywood, Ill.; sr. lectr. Sch. Social Adminstrn. and Policy, U. Chgo., 1979—; chmn. dept. health service devel. Am. Acad. Pediatrics, Evanston, Ill., 1976-83; dep. asst. commr. health City of Boston, 1969-73; cons. Boston Children's Service Assn., 1966-73, Nat. Ctr. for Health Services Research and Devel. HEW, 1970-72, Office Asst Sec. Health and Sci. Affairs, HEW, 1971-73; civilian cons. in pediatrics U.S. Naval Hosp., Chelsea, Mass.; dir. Mass. Dental Service Corp., 1971-73; mem. Mass. Gov.'s Adv. Council, Comprehensive Health Planning Agy., 1971-73, Harvard Ctr. for Community Health and Med. Care, 1968-73; mem. adv. bd. B.S. in Pediatrics program U. Colo., Denver, 1969-70; mem. community resources com. Interinstl. Cardiovascular Ctr., Chgo., 1973-75; mem. Ill. Sudden Infant Death Syndrome Study Commn., 1975-81. Author: (with L. Berlow) You're Too Sweet— A Manual for Juvenile Diabetics, 1969, (with J.D. Stoeckle and R.M. Farrisey) The Nurse Clinician, 1974; contbr. chpts. to books, numerous articles to profl. jours. Bd. dirs. Mass. Soc. for Prevention Cruelty to Children, 1967-73, Orphans of Italy, Inc., 1962-73, Cath. Charitable Bur., Boston, 1968-70; cons. Cath. Charitable Bur., Boston, 1970-73. Served with AUS, 1944-45; served to capt. M.C. USAF, 1958-61; served to rear adm. M.C. USNR, 961. Decorated Knight Order of Malta. Mem. Mass. Med. Soc., Chgo. Med. Soc., New England Pediatric Soc., Chgo. Pediatric Soc., Am. Fedn. Clin. Research, Am. Acad. Pediatrics (council on practice, chmn. liason com. with Am. Nurses Assn. 1970-72), Assn. for Ambulatory Pediatric Services, Logan-Brophy Soc. Oral Surgery (hon.), Am. Diabetes Assn., New Eng. Diabetes Assn., Royal Coll. Medicine (London), Irish and Am. Pediatric Soc. (sec.-treas. 1968-70, exec. council 1970—, pres. 1976-77), U.S. Naval Inst., Am. Legion, Alpha Omega Alpha. Clubs: Union Boat, Appalachian Mountain (Boston); Harvard, Chgo. Athletic. Home: 147 Herrick Rd Riverside IL 60546 Office: Loyola Univ Med Ctr 2160 S 1st Ave Maywood IL 60153

CONNELLY, WILLIAM HOWARD, foundation executive; b. Cambridge, Mass., Aug. 28, 1920; s. Marion Sims and Katherine Belle (Porter) C.; m. Frances Payne Fuller, June 7, 1947; children: Nancy F. Connelly Truesdell, Johnston P., Amy Connelly Natale. Richard S. A.B., Princeton U., 1943; M.B.A., Harvard U., 1950. Agt. to C.L.U. Nat. Life Ins. Co., Hartford, Conn., 1950-68; asst. dir. Hartford Found. Pub. Giving, West Hartford, Conn., 1968-71, dir., 1971-83, dir. devel., 1983—; bd. dirs. Coordinating Council for Founds., Roberts Found. Adv. com.: (Eugene Struckoff) Handbook for Community Foundations, 1977. Chmn. Suffield (Conn.) Bd. Edn., 1967-68. Served with F.A. U.S. Army, 1943-46; M.I., 1951-52; ETO. Decorated Bronze Star; recipient Charter Oak Leadership medal Greater Hartford C. of C., 1978. Mem. Council on Founds. Republican. Baptist. Clubs: Rotary, Hartford, Suffield Country. Home: 272 N Main St Suffield CT 06078 Office: 45 S Main St West Hartford CT 06107

CONNER, BRUCE, artist, film-maker; b. McPherson, Kans., Nov. 18, 1933; s. William Nicholas and Berenice (Matson) C.; m. Jean Marilyn Sandstedt, Sept. 1, 1957; 1 son, Robert Michael. B.F.A., U. Nebr., 1955; student, Bklyn. Mus. Art Sch., 1956. Tchr. Calif. Coll. Arts and Crafts, 1965, San Francisco Art Inst., 1966-67, 72, UCLA Extension, 1973, San Jose State U., 1974, San Francisco State U., 1976; lectr. Mus. Modern Art, N.Y.C., Kongresshalle, Berlin, Fraser Gallery, London, Flaherty Film Seminar, Carnegie Inst., Wadsworth Atheneum, Chgo. Art Inst., Los Angeles Art Mus., U. B.C., Mexico City Film Soc., others. Film-maker: 16 mm films including A Movie, 1958, Cosmic Ray, 1962, Leader, 1964, Vivian, 1965, Ten Second Film, 1965, Breakaway, 1966, Looking for Mushrooms, 1967, Report, 1963-67, The White Rose, 1967, Permian Strata, 1969, 5X Marilyn, 1973, Crossroads, 1976, Take the 5:10 to Dreamland, 1976, Valse Triste, 1977, Mongoloid, 1978, America Is Waiting, 1981; (Brandeis U. Creative award 1979). Recipient Neallie Sullivan award San Francisco Art Assn., 1963, Copley Found. award, 1965, gold medal Sesta Biennale D'Arte Republica di San Marino, 1967, Francis Scott Key award, 1975, citation in film Brandeis U. Creative Awards, 1979; grantee Ford Found., 1964, Nat. Endowment for Arts, 1973, Am. Film Inst., 1974; Guggenheim fellow, 1975. Office: 45 Sussex St San Francisco CA 94131

CONNER, JOHN WAYNE, Romance languages educator; b. Peterson, Utah, Jan. 16, 1919; s. Melville Drader and Gaynell (Rogers) Conners W.; m. Aileen O'Grady, Nov. 7, 1942; children: Alison, Catherine, Johanna, Wayne. B.A. hon., Queen's U., 1941, M.A., 1942; Ph.D., Princeton U., 1948. Instr. Washington U., St. Louis, 1948-49, asst. prof., 1949-55, assoc. prof., 1955-62; prof., chmn. dept. fgn. langs. U. Fla., Gainesville, 1962-68, chmn. dept. Romance langs., 1968-80, chmn. humanities council, 1968-73, acting dir. program in Linguistice, 1982-84, Disting. Service prof., 1977—; mem. Woodrow Wilson Fellowship Selection Com. Region VI, 1964-67. Served to capt. Can. Army, 1942-45; ETO. Research and travel grantee Am. Council Learned Socs., 1958-62, Am. Philos. Soc., 1957-59; fellow Camargo Found., France, 1981. Mem. MLA (del. assembly 1973-75, chmn. French VI 1976), Am. Assn. Tchrs. France, AAUP, South Atlantic MLA (chmn. studies award com. 1975-76). Office: Dept Romance Langs U Fla Gainesville FL 32611

CONNER, TROY BLAINE, JR., lawyer; b. Moundsville, W.Va., Jan. 23, 1926; s. Troy Blaine and Ethel (Barbour) C.; m. Betty Lenore Luzier, Dec. 29, 1953; children: Troy Blaine III, Kimberly Ann, Robert James, David Jefferson. A.B., W.Va. U., 1945, J.D., 1948. Bar: W.Va. 1948, U.S. Supreme Ct 1957, D.C. 1969. Practice in, Morgantown, W.Va., 1948-53; trial atty. criminal and internal security divs. Dept. Justice, 1953-58; the trial counsel AEC, 1958-70; exec. dir. CAB, 1970-71; sr. partner firm Conner & Wetterhahn, P.C., Washington, 1973—; chmn. KMC, Inc., 1976—; mem. adv. council environ. edn. HEW, 1976-77. Trustee Salem Coll., 1975-80; bd. dirs. W.Va. U. Found., 1974—. Fellow Internat. Acad. Law and Sci.; mem. Am. Nuclear Soc., Am., W.Va., D.C., Fed. bar assns., Internat. Nuclear Law Assn., Atomic Indsl. Forum, W.Va. U. Alumni Assn., Nat. Aero. Assn., Phi Sigma Kappa. Republican. Methodist. Clubs: Aero, Circus Saints and Sinners, Lawyers, Capitol Hill (Washington); Lakeview Country (Morgantown, W.Va.); Sea Colony (Bethany Beach, Del.). Home: 9416 Firethorn Ct Potomac MD 20854 Office: 1747 Pennsylvania Ave NW Washington DC 20006

CONNER, WILLIAM CURTIS, judge; b. Wichita Falls, Tex., Mar. 27, 1920; s. D.H. and Mae (Weeks) C.; m. Janice Files, Mar. 22, 1944; children—William Curtis, Stephen, Christopher, Molly. B.B.A., U. Tex., 1941, LL.B., 1942; postgrad., Harvard, 1942-43, Mass. Inst. Tech., 1943. Bar: Tex. bar 1942, N.Y. State bar 1949. Asso., mem. firm Curtis, Morris & Safford (and predecessor firm), N.Y.C., 1946-73; judge U.S. Dist. Ct., So. dist. N.Y., 1973—. Served to lt. USNR, 1942-45; PTO. Recipient Jefferson medal N.J. Patent Law Assn. Mem. N.Y. Patent Law Assn. (pres. 1972-73). Presbyterian (elder). Club: St. Andrews Golf. Office: US Courthouse Foley Sq New York NY 10007

CONNERS, JOHN D., food company executive; b. 1924; married. B.B.A., Coll. Great Falls, 1948. Various sales and mgmt. positions Beatrice Foods Co., Inc., Chgo., 1948-73, mgr. Far West dairy regulation, 1973-75, v.p. Western dairy area, 1975-77, sr. v.p. domestic dairy and agrl. product divs., Chgo., 1977-79, corp. exec. v.p. domestic dairy, soft drink and agrl. products divs., dir., 1979-83, vice chmn. bd., 1983—. Office: Beatrice Foods Co Inc 2 N LaSalle St Chicago IL 60602 *

CONNERY, PAUL JOSEPH, diversified co. exec.; b. Fort Smith, Ark., Jan. 14, 1923; s. Arthur James and Ervema (Wolcott) C.; m. Audrey Dolores Zimmerman, May 14, 1949; 1 son, Brian Arthur. B.S., S.W. Mo. State U., 1943; M.B.A., Northwestern U., 1948. Accountant Arthur Andersen & Co., 1948-50; asst. treas. Iowa Power & Light Co., 1950-53; sec., treas. Ohio Valley Electric Corp., 1953-57; v.p., comptroller New Haven R.R., 1957-60; v.p. fin. Am. Cable & Radio Corp., 1960-62; dir. fin. controls IT&T, 1962—. Served as capt. inf. AUS, 1942-46. Mem. Am. Mgmt. Assn., Nat. Assn. Accountants, Fin. Execs. Inst. Office: ITT 320 Park Ave New York NY 10022

CONNERY, ROBERT HOWE, educator, author; b. St. Paul, Oct. 1, 1907; s. Robert Henry and Nellie Elizabeth (Collins) C. A.B., U. Minn., 1929, A.M., 1930; Ph.D., Columbia, 1935. Instr. U. Minn., 1930-31, Columbia, 1933-38; asso. prof. Cath. U. Am., Washington, 1939-42, Stanford, 1946-48; prof. U. Ill., 1948-49, Duke, 1949-66; prof. govt. Columbia, 1966-76, prof. emeritus pub. law and govt., 1976—; Cons. Hoover Commn. on reorgn. exec. br. govt., 1948, Brookings Instn. Survey Adminstrn. U.S. Fgn. Affairs, 1950, Survey NATO and UN, 1952, Sec. of Def. on NATO, 1951, N.Y. State commn. on govtl. operations of N.Y.C., 1959-60; exec. sec. com. on modern zoning, 1959-60; cons. NIMH, 1961-66; dir. reports Mayor's Office, N.Y.C., 1954-55; dep. city adminstr., N.Y.C., 1965. Author: The Navy and the Industrial Mobilization in World War II, 1951, (with Richard Leach) The Federal Government and Metropolitan Areas, 1960, Forrestal and the Navy, (with Robert Albion), 1962, (with others) The Politics of Mental Health, 1968; Editor: Teaching Political Science, 1965, Urban Riots, 1968, Municipal Income Taxes, 1968, Governing the City, 1969, The Corporation and the Campus, 1970, Unionization of Municipal Employees, 1971, Control or Fate in Economic Affairs, 1971, Governing New York State, 1974, (with Gerald Benjamin) Rockefeller of New York, 1979. Commd. lt. USNR, 1942; advancing to comdr.; on duty Office of Sec. of Navy. Fellow Brookings Instn. Mem. Acad. of Polit. Sci. (pres. 1966—). Roman Catholic. Club: Cosmos (Washington). Home: Mtd Route 210(B) Oyster Bay NY 11771

CONNERY, SEAN, actor; b. Aug. 25, 1930; s. Joseph and Euphamia C.; m. Diane Cilento, 1962 (div.); 1 son, 1 stepdau.; m. Micheline Roquebrune, 1975. Dir., Tantallon Films Ltd., 1972—; films include No Road Back, 1956, The Hill, 1956, Action of the Tiger, 1957, Another Time, Another Place, 1957, Hell Drivers, 1958, Tarzan's Greatest Adventure, 1959, Darby O'Gill and the Little People, 1959, On the Fiddle, 1961, The Longest Day, 1962, The Frightened City, 1962, Woman of Straw, 1964, Marnie, 1964, A Fine Madness, 1966, Shalako, 1968, The Molly Maguires, 1968, The Red Tent, 1969, The Anderson Tapes, 1970, The Offence, 1973, Zardoz, 1973, Ransom, 1974, Murder on the Orient Express, 1974, The Wind and the Lion, 1975, The Man Who Would be King, 1975, Robin and Marian, 1976, A Bridge Too Far, 1977, The Great Train Robbery, 1979; as James Bond: Cuba, 1979; Dir.: Meteor, 1979, Sword of the Valiant, 1982, Wrong is Right, 1982, Five Days One Summer, 1982; as James Bond: Dr No, 1963, From Russia with Love, 1964, Goldfinger, 1965, Thunderball, 1965, You Only Live Twice, 1967, Diamonds are Forever, 1971, Octopussy, Never Say Never Again, 1983. Served with Brit. Royal Navy. Address: care Creative Artists Agy Inc 1888 Century Park E Suite 1400 Los Angeles CA 90067 *

CONNERY, VINCENT LINUS, union official; b. Scranton, Pa., Oct. 1, 1922; s. Vincent Eugene and Mary Catherine (Kelly) C.; m. Rosemary Anne Schwarz, May 26, 1951; 1 son, Vincent Patrick. B.S., U. Scranton, Pa., 1949. Staff acct. Arthur Young & Co., N.Y.C., 1948-50; agt. IRS, Wichita, 1950-67; nat. pres. Nat. Treasury Employees, Washington, 1966—. Served with USAAF, 1942-45. Democrat. Roman Catholic. Clubs: Optimist, Elks. Office: Nat Treasury Employees 1730 K St NW Washington DC 20006 *

CONNICK, CHARLES MILO, clergyman, educator; b. Conneaut Lake Park, Pa., Mar. 23, 1917; s. Walter and Iola Belle (Wintermute) C.; m. Genevieve Shaul, June 7, 1941; children: Joy (Mrs. J. Bruce Parker), Christopher Milo, Nancy (Mrs. David F. Jankowski). Student, Edinboro State Coll., 1935-36; A.B., Allegheny Coll., 1939, D.D., 1960; S.T.B., Boston U., 1942, Ph.D., 1944; Roswell R. Robinson fellow, Harvard U., 1942-43; postgrad., Episcopal Div. Sch., 1942-44. Ordained deacon United Meth. Ch., 1941, elder, 1942; assoc. minister St. Paul's Methodist Ch., Lowell, Mass., 1940-41, Copley Meth. Ch., Boston, 1941-42; dir. Wesley Found., Harvard U.; also minister to students Harvard Epworth Meth. Ch., Cambridge, Mass., summers 1943-44; sr. instr. pub. speaking Curry Coll., Boston, 1942-44; head Bible dept. Northfield Sch., East Northfield, Mass., 1944-46; prof. religion, chmn. dept. philosophy, religion Whittier (Calif.) Coll., 1946-82, prof. religion emeritus, 1982—; chmn. social sci. div., 1950, 60, pres. faculty senate, 1970-71, dir. coll. study tour to Europe, Middle East, around the world, summers 1955-69; pres. I-TAC, 1976—; Danforth assoc., 1959—, Danforth sr. assoc., 1964—; spl. lectr. Bibl. lit. Sch. Religion, First Congl. Ch., Los Angeles, 1947-62; mem. Western Pa. Conf., United Meth. Ch., 1942—; exec. sec. Presdl. Selection Com., 1969-70; cons. for colls. and univs. seeking new presidents, 1971—; adv. council Calif. Christian Com. for Israel, 1974—. Author: Build on The Rock, You and the Sermon on the Mount, 1960, Jesus, the Man, the Mission, and the Message, 1963, 2d edit., 1974, The Message and Meaning of the Bible, 1965, The New Testament: An Introduction to its History, Literature and Thought, 1972, 2d edit., 1978; Editorial adviser to maj. publishers, 1964—; Contbr. articles to religious jours. and mags. Trustee Whittier Coll., 1982—. Recipient Distinguished Alumnus award Boston U., 1971; C. Milo Connick chair in religion established Whittier Coll., 1982. Mem. Consumers Coop. Whittier Inc. (pres. 1949-53), AAUP (Whittier pres. 1970-72), Pacific Coast Assn. for Religious Studies (exec. com. 1947-60), Am. Acad. Religion (pres. Western Region 1953-54), Soc. Bibl. Lit., Am. Oriental Soc., Am. Christian Assn. for Isreal (mem. nat. adv. com. 1964-69), Phi Sigma Tau, Kappa Phi Kappa, Chi Delta Sigma, Omicron Delta Kappa. Home: 6249 Roundhill Dr Whittier CA 90601 Office: 13421 E Philadelphia St Whittier CA 90608

CONNICK, ROBERT ELWELL, educator; b. Eureka, Calif., July 29, 1917; s. Arthur Elwell and Florence (Robertson) C.; m. Frances Spieth, Dec. 19, 1952; children—Mary Catherine, Elizabeth, Arthur, Megan, Sarah, William Beach. B.S., U. Calif. at Berkeley, 1939, Ph.D., 1942. Faculty U. Calif., Berkeley, 1942—, research Manhattan project, 1943-46, asst. prof. then asso. prof. chemistry, 1945-52, prof., 1952—, chmn. dept., 1958-60, dean, 1960-65, vice chancellor acad. affairs, 1965-67, vice chancellor, 1969-71. Contbr. articles profl. jours. Guggenheim fellow, 1949, 59. Mem. Am. Chem. Soc., Nat. Acad. Scis., Phi Beta Kappa, Sigma Xi, Pi Mu Epsilon. Home: 50 Marguerita Rd Berkeley CA 94707

CONNIFF, RAY, conductor, composer, arranger; b. Attleboro, Mass., Nov. 6, 1916; s. John Lawrence and Maude (Angela) C.; m. Emily Jo Ann Imhof, Feb. 14, 1938; children: James Lawrence, Jo Ann Patricia; m. Ann Marie Engberg, Aug. 24, 1947; 1 foster son, Richard J. Bibo.; m. Vela Schmidheiny, Aug. 24, 1968; 1 dau., Tamara Allegra. Student, Juilliard Sch. Music; studied with Tom Timothy, Sol Kaplan, Hugo Friedhofer. Trombone Player, arranger, Bunny Berigan, Bob Crosby, Artie Shaw, Harry James orchestras; arranger, composer, conductor, rec. artist, Columbia Records. Office: PO Box 36 Encino CA 91316 *With each passing year I am more fully convinced of the need to establish contact with and receive guidance from the Father of the Universe.*

CONNOLLY, ARTHUR GUILD, lawyer; b. Boston, Nov. 8, 1905; s. George Augustus and Elizabeth Campbell (Burns) C.; m. Gerardine Laffey, Nov. 25, 1936; children—Arthur Guild, Ronald G., Christopher G., Gerardine L., Mary G., Thomas A. B.S. in Chem. Engring, Mass. Inst. Tech., 1927; LL.B., Harvard, 1930. Bar: Admitted Mass., D.C. bars 1932, Del. bar 1940. With legal dept. Universal Oil Products Co., Chgo., 1930-31; patent dept. duPont Co., Wilmington, Del., exec. asst. dir., 1936-42; pvt. practice law, Wilmington, 1942—; sr. partner Connolly, Bove & Lodge (and predecessor firms), 1944—. Pres. Laffey-McHugh Found., Arguild Found. Fellow Am. Coll. Trial Lawyers; mem. Am., Del. bar assns., Am. Patent Law Assn. Clubs: Harvard of Delaware, M.I.T. of N.Y., Wilmington Country. Home: 2000 S Ocean Ln Fort Lauderdale FL 33316 also 102 School Rd Wilmington DE Office: Farmers Bank Bldg Wilmington DE 19899

CONNOLLY, J. WRAY, food company executive; b. Pitts., Jan. 8, 1934; m. Shirley Betz, Sept. 3, 1955; children: Paul X., Mark L., Christopher I., Claire L., Michael J. A.B., St. Vincent Coll., 1955; J.D., U. Pitts., 1958. Bar: Pa. 1958. Atty. H.J. Heinz Co., 1961-67, treas., 1973-76; pres., chief exec. officer Heinz U.S.A., Pitts., 1980—; v.p. Ore-Ida Foods Inc., 1967-73; pres., chief exec. officer Hubinger Co., Keokuk, Iowa, 1976-79; dir. Murphy Co., Consol. Natural Gas Co. Trustee Keokuk Area Hosp., 1976-79, Univ. Health Ctr., Pitts.; bd. dirs. Eye and Ear Hosp., Pitts., St. Vincent Coll., Latrobe, Pa., Red Cross, Pitts.; mem. bd. visitors U. Pitts. Grad. Sch. Bus. Roman Catholic. Clubs: Duquesne, Sewickley Hts., Allegheny. Office: Heinz USA 1062 Progress St Pittsburgh PA 15212

CONNOLLY, JOHN EARLE, surgeon, educator; b. Omaha, May 21, 1923; s. Earl A. and Gertrude (Eckerman) C.; m. Virginia Hartman, Aug. 12, 1967; children: Peter Hart. John Earle, Sarah. A.B., Harvard U., 1945, M.D., 1948. Diplomate: Am. Bd. Surgery (bd. dirs. 1976-82), Am. Bd. Thoracic and Cardiovascular Surgery, Am. Bd. Vascular Surgery. Intern. in surgery Stanford U. Hosps., San Francisco, 1948-49, surg. research fellow, 1949-50, asst. resident surgeon, 1950-52, chief resident surgeon, 1953-54, surg. pathology fellow, 1954, instr. surgery, 1957-60, John and Mary Markle Scholar in med. scis., 1957-62, from asst. prof. to assoc. prof. surgery, 1960-65; prof., chmn. dept. surgery U. Calif.-Irvine, 1965-78; surg. registrar professional unit St. Bartholomew's Hosp., London, 1952-53; resident in thoracic surgery Bellevue Hosp., N.Y.C., 1955; resident in thoracic and cardiovascular surgery Columbia-Presbyn.Med. Ctr., N.Y.C., 1956; attending surgeon Stanford Med. Ctr., Palo Alto, Calif., 1959-65; chmn. cardiovascular and thoracic surgery U. Calif.-Irvine Med. Ctr., 1968—; attending surgeon St. Joseph's Children's Hosp., Orange, Calif., 1968—, Anaheim Meml. Hosp. (Calif.), 1970—; mem. adv. council Nat. Heart, Lung, and Blood Inst.-NIH, 1981—; cons. Long Beach VA Hosp., Calif., 1965—, Long Beach Naval Hosp. Contbr. articles to profl. jours.; editorial bd.: Jour. Cardiovascular Surgery, 1974—, Western Jour. Medicine, 1975—, Jour. Stroke, 1979—, Jour. Vascular Surgery, 1983—. Bd. dirs. Audio-Digest Found., 1974—, Franklin Martin Found., 1975-80. Served with AUS, 1943-44. Fellow ACS (gov. 1964-70), Royal Coll. Surgeons (hon.), Royal Coll. Surgeons Ireland (hon.), ACS (regent 1973-84, v.p. 1984-85); mem. Am. Surg. Assn., Soc. Univ. Surgeons, Am. Assn. Thoracic Surgery (council 1974-78), Pacific Coast Surg. Assn. (recorder 1972-78), San Francisco Surg. Soc., Los Angeles Surg. Soc., Soc. Vascular Surgery, Western Surg. Assn., Internat. Cardiovascular Soc. (pres. 1977), Soc. Internat. Chirurgie, Soc. Thoracic Surgeons (councillor 1983—), Western Thoracic Surg. Soc. (pres. 1978), Orange County Surg. Soc. (pres. 1984-85). Clubs: California (Los Angeles); San Francisco Golf, Pacific Union, Bohemian (San Francisco); Cypress Point (Pebble Beach, Calif.); Harvard (N.Y.C.). Home: 5135 Altoona Ln Irvine CA 92715 Office: Dept surgery U Calif Irvine CA 92717

CONNOLLY, JOHN JOSEPH, medical college president; b. Worcester, Mass., Feb. 4, 1940; s. Nicholas John and Margaret Anne (Flynn) C.; m. Ingrid Schlemminger, Apr. 11, 1964; children: Sean Timothy, Cheryl Lea. B.S., Worcester State Coll., 1962; M.A., U. Conn., 1963; Ed.D., Tchrs. Coll., Columbia U., 1972; LL.D., Mercy Coll., 1980. Tchr., counselor Worcester public schs., 1963-65; dir. admissions, registrar Sullivan County Community Coll., South Fallsburg, N.Y., 1965-67; asst. dean faculty, dir. community and extension services Mercer County Community Coll., Trenton, N.J., 1967-68; asst. to pres., dir. community and extension services, 1968-70; dean of coll. Hartford Community Coll., Bel Air, Md., 1970-73; pres. Dutchess Community Coll., Poughkeepsie, N.Y., 1973-81; pres., chief exec. officer N.Y. Med. Coll., Valhalla, N.Y., 1981—; cons. in field; dir. First Savs. & Loan Assn., Poughkeepsie. Contbr. articles to profl. jours. Bd. dirs. United Way of Dutchess County, pres., 1978; chmn. bd. trustees St. Francis Hosp., Poughkeepsie, 1976-80; chmn. Dutchess County Indsl. Devel. Agy., 1978-81; trustee N.Y. Med. Coll., chmn. acad. affairs com.; trustee Culinary Inst. Am., Poughkeepsie Area Fund, 1973-78, St. Agnes Hosp., Westchester County Hist. Soc.; bd. dirs. Econ. Devel. Corp. Dutchess County, Westchester County Mental Health Assn.; hon. chmn. Dutchess/Columbia br. Am. Lung Assn., 1979. Recipient Disting. Service award Poughkeepsie Jaycees, 1974; Marie Y. Martin award Assn. Community Coll. Trustees, 1978; named Man of Yr. Dutchess County Legislature, 1980; One of 100 Outstanding Young Leaders in Higher Edn. Change mag., 1979. Mem. Am. Assn. Higher Edn., Assn. Colls. and Univs. State N.Y. (mem. exec. com.), Asso. Colls. Mid-Hudson Area (pres. 1976-79), Internat. Intercultural Consortium (vice chmn.), Phi Delta Kappa. Roman Catholic. Office: Office of Pres NY Med Coll Valhalla NY 10595

CONNOLLY, JOHN MARTIN, publishing executive; b. Phila., May 3, 1952; s. John Martin and Phoebe (Gerber) C.; m. Kathleen Robinson, Jan. 24, 1982. B.A., St. Norbert Coll., 1974; student, Loyola U., Rome, 1972-73. Sales rep. Prentice-Hall Inc., DePere, Wis., 1974-76, Phila., 1976-78, mktg. editor, Englewood Cliffs, NJ, 1978-82; v.p., editorial dir. J.B. Lippincott Co., Phila., 1982—. Capt. Phila. United Way, 1983. Mem. Am. Assn. Pubs. Roman Catholic. Club: Cynwyd (Phila.). Home: 909 Hagysford Rd Penn Valley PA 19072 Office: J B Lippincott Co 227 6th St Philadelphia PA 19104

CONNOLLY, MICHAEL JOSEPH, III, state official; b. West Roxbury, Mass., Apr. 20, 1947; s. Michael Joseph and Florence C.; m. Lynda Murphy, Aug. 14, 1971; children: John Ronan, Justin, Allison, Lauren. A.B., Holy Cross Coll., 1969; J.D., New Eng. Sch. Law, 1976. Tchr. math. Boston Latin Sch., 1972; mem. Mass. Ho. of Reps., 1973-79, chmn. spl. legis. com. on commuter traffic, 1973-79; sec. of state Commonwealth of Mass., 1979—; Chmn. Mass. Hist. Commn.; chmn. Archives Adv. Commn. Mem. Health Planning Council Greater Boston, Marriage Encounter. Mem. Mass. Bar Assn., Nat. Assn. Secs. of State. Club: Holy Cross (Boston). Home: 42 Cerdan Ave Roslindale MA 02131 Office: State House Room 340 Boston MA 02133

CONNOLLY, THOMAS ARTHUR, archbishop; b. San Francisco, Oct. 5, 1899; s. Thomas and Catherine (Gilsenan) C. Ed., St. Patrick's Sem., Menlo Park, Calif., 1915-26, Cath. U., 1930-32; J.C.D. Ordained priest Roman Catholic Ch., 1926; asst. pastor, 1926-30, sec. to archbishop, 1934-39; chancellor Archdiocese San Francisco, 1935-48; named domestic prelate, 1936; pastor Mission Dolores Ch., San Francisco, 1939-48; apptd. aux. bishop, San Francisco, titular bishop, Sila, 1939, consecrated, 1939; apptd. vicar del. Cath. Chaplains U.S. Army and Navy, Pacific Coast, 1941; apptd. coadjutor bishop, Seattle, 1948, bishop, 1950, archbishop, 1951—; apptd. asst. at Pontifical Throne, 1959. Author: Appeals in Canon Law, 1932. Office: 1104 Spring St Seattle WA 98104

CONNOLLY, THOMAS JOSEPH, bishop; b. Tonopah, Nev., July 18, 1922; s. John and Katherine (Hammel) C. Student, St. Joseph Coll. and St. Patrick Sem., Menlo Park, Calif., 1936-47, Catholic U. Am., 1949-51; J.C.D., Lateran Pontifical U., Rome, 1952; D.H.L. (hon.), U. Portland, 1972. Ordained priest Roman Catholic Ch., 1947; asst. St. Thomas Cathedral, Reno, 1947, asst., rector, 1953-55; asst. Little Flower Parish, Reno, 1947-48; sec. to bishop, 1949; asst. St. Albert the Gt., Reno, 1952-53, pastor, 1960-68, St. Joseph Ch., Elko, 1955-60, St. Theresa's Ch., Carson City, Nev., 1968-71; bishop, Baker, Oreg., 1971—; Tchr. Manogue High Sch., Reno, 1948-49; chaplain Serra Club, 1948-49; officialis Diocese of Reno; chmn. bldg. com., dir. Cursillo Movement; moderator Italian Cath. Fedn.; dean, mem. personnel bd. Senate of Priests; mem. Nat. Bishops Liturgy Com., 1973-76; region XII rep. to Nat. Conf. Cath. Bishops, 1973-76, mem. adv. com., 1974-76; bd. dirs. Cath. Communications Northwest, from 1977. Club: K.C. (state chaplain Nev. 1970-71). Home: 3805 N Cedar St Baker OR 97814 Office: 2215 First St PO Box 826 Baker OR 97814 *

CONNOLLY, WALTER JUSTIN, JR., banker; b. Boston, Aug. 3, 1928; s. Walter Justin and Helen Agnes (Cavanagh) C.; m. Paulina Quilty, Apr. 14, 1951; children: Timothy J., Kevin A., Mary-Elise, Walter Justin III, Paulina, Sarah D. B.A. in History, Yale U., 1950. With Hartford Ins. Group, 1955-58, Hornblower & Weeks, Hartford, Conn., 1958-61; chmn., dir., chief exec. officer Conn. Bank & Trust Co., Hartford, 1961—; dir. Conn. Mut. Life Ins. Co., Dexter Corp. Bd. dirs. Greater Hartford Arts Council, St. Francis Hosp., Kingswood/Oxford Sch. Served with USMC, 1952-55. Mem. Am. Bankers Assn., Assn. Res. City Bankers, Conn. Bankers Assn., Greater Hartford C. of C. (dir.). Clubs: Hartford, Hartford Golf, Hyannis Port Yacht. Office: One Constitution Plaza Hartford CT 06115 *

CONNOR, DAVID EDMUND, banker; b. Omaha, Sept. 23, 1925; s. Edward James and Eleanor (McGilton) C.; m. Carroll Luthy, Apr. 15, 1950; children: Susan, Sara. B.A., Yale U., 1947. Vice pres. Connor Co., Peoria, Ill., 1947-52, dir., 1947—; with Comml. Nat. Bank, Peoria, 1952—, pres., 1967—; dir., pres. Comml. Nat. Corp., Peoria, 1980-83; dir. Midwest Fin. Group, Peoria, 1983—,; dir. Central Ill. Light Co., Peoria, TP&W R.R. Pres. bd. dirs. Peoria Devel. Corp., 1964—; trustee Bradley U., 1970—; chmn. Ill. Arts Council, 1981-83. Mem. Ill. State C. of C. (dir. 1970-76), Ill. Bankers Assn. (dir. 1983—), Peoria Area C. of C. (dir. 1976—), Phi Beta Kappa. Clubs: Country Club of Peoria, Racquet, Chicago. Office: Comml Nat Bank 301 SW Adams St Peoria IL 61631

CONNOR, FRANCIS J., manufacturing executive; b. 1930. B.A., Maryknoll Coll., 1952. With Am. Can Co., 1957—; sales engr., supt M & T Chems., Inc., 1960, sales mgr. coatings div., 1966, v.p., gen. sales mgr. corporate sales, 1968, group v.p. ops., 1970, pres., 1972—; sr. v.p., group exec. Am. Can Internat., 1975, sr. v.p., sector exec. packaging bus., 1979, corp. exec. v.p., 1980, pres., 1981—. Address: Am Can Co American Ln Greenwich CT 06830 *

CONNOR, FRANK J(OSEPH), container company executive; b. Yonkers, N.Y., Sept. 11, 1930; s. Nicholas J. and Marie (Fitzsimmons) C.; m. A. Joan Taylor, Jan. 14, 1956; children: Mary Beth, Francis, Kathleen, Richard. B.A. in Liberal Arts, Maryknoll Coll., 1952; student, Newark Coll. Engring., 1957, Wayne State U., 1958. With M&T Chems. subs. Am. Can Co., 1957-75, pres., 1972-75, Am. Can Co., Greenwich, Conn., 1975—; sr. v.p., group exec. Am. Can Internat., 1975-79, exec. v.p., sector exec. packaging and metals, 1980-81, pres., chief operating officer, 1981—, dir. Mem. Southwestern Area Commerce and Industry Assn. (dir. Conn. 1981—), Can. Mfrs. Inst. (dir. 1979—). Clubs: Landmark (Stamford, Conn.); Sky (N.Y.C.); St. James (London). Home: 5 Mayapple Rd Stamford CT 06903 Office: Am Can Co American Ln Greenwich CT 06830

CONNOR, J. ROBERT, editor; b. N.Y.C., Jan. 31, 1927; s. Joseph M. and Ethel May (Ball) C.; m. Marie Louise Zolezzi, Sept. 6, 1952; children: Jeanne Marie, Robert Brian, Ellen Louise. B.A., Hunter Coll., 1951. Copy editor sports desk N.Y. Mirror, N.Y.C., 1950-52; mng. editor Mechanix Illustrated Mag. div. Fawcett Publs., N.Y.C., 1953-70; editor-in-chief CBS Publs., spl. interest publs., N.Y.C., 1970-72; editor-in-chief Motor Mag. div. Hearst Corp., N.Y.C., 1972-77; editor Construction Contracting, 1978-79; editor-in-chief Graduating Engr. McGraw-Hill, Inc., 1979—, 81, Housing mag., 1981—; editor Bus. Week, 1981—, Bus. Week Almanac, 1981—, New Product Devel., 1982—; editor-in-chief Bus. Week's Guide to Careers, 1982—. Author: A Job With A Future in Automotive Mechanics, 1969, (with Heinz Ulrich) The National Job-Finding Guide, 1981; contbr. numerous articles to popular mags. Served with AUS, 1945-46. Mem. Internat. Motor Press Assn. (pres. 1966-67). Home: 8 Woodvale Ln Huntington NY 11743 Office: 1221 Ave of Americas New York NY 10020

CONNOR, JAMES EDWARD, JR., chemical company executive; b. New Haven, Feb. 14, 1924; s. James Edward and Rose Marie (McGovern) C.; m. Margery Hawe, Apr. 7, 1951; children: James, Anne, William, Joan, Margery, Peter. B.A., Harvard U., 1944, M.A., 1948, Ph.D., 1950. Research chemist Atlantic Refining Co., 1949-60, asst. mgr. research, 1960-61, mgr. research, 1961-66, Arco Chem. Co., Glenolden, Pa., 1966-78, mgr. research and devel., 1978-79, v.p. chems. research and devel., 1979-81; v.p. research Arco Chem. Co. div. Atlantic Richfield Co., Newtown Square, Pa., 1981—. Served with USN, 1944-46. Mem. Am. Chem. Soc., Soc. Chem. Industry, N.Y. Acad. Sci. Democrat. Roman Catholic. Patentee in field. Home: 1421 Hillside Rd Wynnewood PA 19096 Office: 3801 W Chester Pike Newtown Square PA 19073

CONNOR, JAMES RICHARD, university administrator; b. Indpls., Oct. 31, 1928; s. Frank Elliott and Edna (Felt) C.; m. Zoe Ezopov, July 7, 1954; children: Janet K., Paul A. B.A., U. Iowa, 1951; M.S., U. Wis., 1954, Ph.D., 1961. Asst. prof. history Washington and Lee U., 1956-57, Va. Mil. Inst., 1958-61; asst. dir. Salzburg Seminar in Am. Studies, 1961-62; joint staff mem. Wis. Coordinating Com. Higher Edn., 1962-63; dir. Inst. Analysis; asst. prof. history U. Va., 1963-66; asso. prof. history, asso. provost No. Ill. U., 1966-69; provost, acad. v.p., prof. history Western Ill. U., 1969-74; chancellor U. Wis.-Whitewater, 1974—; asso. dir. Va. Higher Edn. Study Com., 1964-65; Am. Council Edn. intern acad. adminstrn. Stanford U., 1965-66; staff dir. Study of Governance of Acad. Med. Center, Josiah Macy, Jr., Found., 1968-70; mem. commn. on higher edn. North Central Assn., 1970-75, 79—, cons.-examiner, 1972—. Author: Studies in Higher Education, 1965; contbr., Ency. Brit. Served with AUS, 1946-47, 51-53. Woodrow Wilson fellow, 1953-54; So. fellow, 1957-58. Mem. Am. Hist. Assn., Orgn. Am. Historians, AAUP, Phi Beta Kappa, Phi Eta Sigma, Phi Kappa Phi, Phi Delta Kappa, Beta Gamma Sigma, Phi Alpha Theta, Delta Sigma Pi. Home: Route 2 Linden Dr Whitewater WI 53190 Office: U Wis Whitewater WI 53190

CONNOR, JEROME JOSEPH, civil engineering educator; b. Boston, May 19, 1932; s. Jerome Joseph and Catherine (Brady) C.; m. Barbara Lorraine Masse, Apr. 12, 1958; children: Patricia, Stephen, Brian, Michael, Mark, Tracey. S.B., MIT, 1953, S.M., 1954, Sc.D., 1959. Prof. civil engring. MIT, Cambridge, 1962—; William Lincoln Smith prof. Northeastern U., Boston, 1982—; engr., applied mechanics br. Army Materials and Mechanics Research Ctr., 1957-62; cons. Stone & Webster, VTN Consol., Westinghouse Electric Co. Author: Analysis of Structural Member Systems, 1976, (with C. Brebbia) Finite Element Techniques for Fluid Flow, 1976, Finite Element Techniques for Fluid Flow, Japanese edit., 1976, Finite Element Techniques for Fluid Flow, Italian edit., 1978, Finite Element Techniques for Fluid Flow, Russian edit., 1979, (with C. Chrysostomides) Behavior of Offshore Structrues, 1982; contbr. articles to profl. jours. Chmn. Troop 368 Boy Scouts Am., Arlington, Va., 1974—. Mem. ASCE, AAAS, Boston Soc. Civil Engrs., Sigma Xi, Chi Epsilon. Roman Catholic. Office: Northeastern Univ Huntington Ave Boston MA 02115 *

CONNOR, JOHN ANTHONY, English educator, poet, playwright; b. Manchester, Eng., Mar. 16, 1930; came to U.S., 1967, naturalized, 1982; s. John and Dorothy Mabel (Richings) C.;, June 21, 1961 (div. 1972); children: Samuel, Simon, Rebecca. M.A., U. Manchester, 1967, Wesleyan U., Middletown, Conn., 1972. Textile designer Calico Printers Assn., Manchester, 1944-60; art tchr. Sch. Design, Salford, Eng., 1960-62; lectr. liberal studies Inst. Tech., Bolton, Eng., 1962-64; vis. writer Amherst Coll., 1967-68; prof. lit. Wesleyan U., 1971—. Author: poems With Love Somehow, 1962, Lodgers, 1968, New and Selected Poems, 1982; numerous plays. Served with Brit. Cavalry, 1948-50. Fellow Royal Soc. Lit. Home: 44 Brainerd Ave Middletown CT Office: Dept English Wesleyan University Court St Middletown CT 06457

CONNOR, JOHN THOMAS, business executive; b. Syracuse, N.Y., Nov. 3, 1914; s. Michael J. and Mary (Sullivan) C.; m. Mary O'Boyle, June 22, 1940; children: John Thomas, Geoffrey, Lisa Forrestal. A.B. magna cum laude, Syracuse U., 1936; J.D., Harvard U., 1939; D.Sc., Phila. Coll. Pharmacy, 1959, Hahnemann Med. Coll., 1964; LL.D., Rutgers U., 1964; D.H.L., Ohio No. U., 1965; LL.D., St. Louis U., 1965, Boston Coll., 1965, Syracuse U., 1965, Manhattan Coll., 1967, Mt. Mary Coll., 1967, N.J. Coll. Medicine and Dentistry, 1967, St. Peters Coll., 1968, Pratt Inst., 1969, Fairleigh Dickinson U., 1973; D.E., Stevens Inst., 1976. Bar: N.Y. 1939. Asso. firm Cravath, deGersdorff, Swaine & Wood, 1939-42; gen. counsel OSRD, 1942-44; counsel Office Naval Research, also spl. asst. to sec. navy, 1945-47; gen. atty. Merck & Co., Inc., Rahway, N.J., 1947, sec., 1947-51, counsel, 1947-53, v.p., 1950-55, pres., dir., 1955-65; U.S. sec. commerce, 1965-67; pres. Allied Chem. Corp., 1967-68, dir., 1967-80, chief exec. officer, 1968-79, chmn. bd., 1969-79, Schroders, Inc., N.Y.C.; dir. J. Henry Schroder Bank & Trust Co., 1980—; dir. Gen. Motors Corp., Am. Broadcasting Cos., Schroders Ltd., Merck & Co., Inc.; Mem. Bus. Council, Council Fgn. Relations. Trustee Syracuse U. Served to capt. USMCR, 1944-45. Recipient Presdl. certificate of merit, 1948; N.J. Brotherhood award NCCJ, 1959; Jefferson medal N.J. Patent Law Assn., 1962; Harvard Bus. Club award, 1965; named N.J. Bus. Statesman of Year, 1964; recipient Pub. Services award Advt. Council, 1967. Mem. Phi Beta Kappa. Office: Schroders Inc One State St New York NY 10004

CONNOR, JOSEPH E., accountant; b. N.Y.C., Aug. 23, 1931; s. Joseph E. C.; m. Cornelia B. Camarata, Apr. 17, 1958; children: Anthony, Cornelia, David. A.B. summa cum laude, U. Pitts.; M.S. in Bus., Columbia U. Joined Price Waterhouse & Co., N.Y.C., 1956, ptnr., 1967—, mng. ptnr. Western region, Los Angeles, 1976-78, chmn. policy bd., 1978—; cons. fgn. direct investment program U.S. Dept. Commerce; project adv. research study Am. Inst. C.P.A.s; lectr. in field.; mem. adv. council U. Columbia Grad. Sch. Bus.; bd. visitors U. Pitts. Grad. Sch. Bus., Georgetown U. Sch. Bus., UCLA Grad. Sch. Mgmt.; mem. adv. bd. U. So. Calif. Sch. Acctg.; mem. Pres.'s Mgmt. Adv. Council, Pres.'s Pvt. Sector Survey on Cost Control. Contbr. articles to profl. jours. Trustee YMCA Greater N.Y.; bd. overseers Meml. Sloan Kettering Inst.; bd. dirs. Georgetown U.; bd. govs. corp. fund Kennedy Ctr. Performing Arts. Served to 1st lt. U.S. Army, 1954-56. Mem. Am. Inst. C.P.A.s (council), N.Y. State Soc. C.P.A.s (chmn. internat. ops. com., mem. acctg. and auditing com., real estate acctg. com.), Calif. Soc. C.P.A.s (legis. com.), U.S. C. of C., Internat. C. of C. (dir. U.S. council). Clubs: Met. (Washington); Links, George Town, Board Room, Greenwich Country, Seaview Country. Office: Price Waterhouse & Co 1251 Ave of Americas New York NY 10020 *

CONNOR, LARRY JEAN, agricultural economics educator; b. Northe Platte, Nebr., Nov. 7, 1934; s. John and Ida Belle (Kammerer) C.; m. Dee Ann Stephens, May 22, 1965; children: Noelle, Kevin. B.S., U. Nebr., 1956; M.S., Okla. State U., 1960, Ph.D., 1964. Agrl. economist Agrl. Research Service U.S. Dept. Agr., 1956-61, 64-66; research asst. agrl. econs. Okla. State U., Stillwater, 1961-64; mem. faculty Mich. State U., East Lansing, 1966—, prof. agrl. econs., 1974—; dept. chmn. Mich State U., East Lansing, 1978—. Author: (with S.B. Harsh, G. Schwab) Managing th Farm Business, 1981; contbr. articles to profl. jours. Served as 2d lt. AUS, 1957. Mem. Am. Agrl. Econs. Assn. (outstanding doctoral thesis 1974, 77), Internat. Assn. Agrl. Economists, Mich. Assn. Farm Mgrs. and Rural Appraisers. Lutheran. Home: 3870 Sheldrake St Okemos MI 48864 Office: Mich State U Agrl Hall Rm 202 East Lansing MI 48824

CONNOR, LAWRENCE STANTON, journalist, editor; b. Indpls., Aug. 31, 1925; s. Nicholas John and Agnes (Peelle) C.; m. Patricia Jean Alandt, Nov. 3, 1956; children—Carolyn, Julia, Lawrence Stanton, Maureen, Janet, Michael Connor. Student, Butler U., summers, 1943, 47, U. Ky., 1943, Miss. State U., 1944; A.B., U. Notre Dame, 1949; postgrad., Fordham U., 1949. With Indpls. Star, 1949—, chief copy desk, news editor, city editor, 1963-79, editor, 1979, mng. editor, 1979—. Served with USAAF, 1943-46. Mem. Am. Soc. Newspaper Editors, AP Mng. Editors Assn. Roman Catholic. Club: Indpls. Press. Office: Indianapolis Star 307 N Pennsylvania St Indianapolis IN 46206

CONNOR, RICHARD L., publisher, editor; b. Bangor, Maine, Apr. 22, 1947; s. Hugh G. and Alyce M. C.; m. Marian Buescher; children: Christina, Rory. B.A., Hillsdale Coll., 1970. Reporter Jackson (Mich.) Citizen Patriot, 1968, reporter-photographer, 1971-73; sports editor, mng. editor Hillsdale (Mich.) Daily News, 1968-71; news editor Belleville (Ill.) News Democrat., 1973-74, editor, 1974-77, Oakland Press, Pontiac, Mich., 1977-79; pub., editor, pres. Times Leader, Capital Cities Communications, Inc., Wilkes-Barre, Pa., 1979—; bd. dirs. Capital Cities Communications Minority Intern Program. Bd. dirs. Wilkes-Barre C. of C.; trustee Tilton Sch. Recipient 1st pl. Investigative Reporting award Inland Daily Press Assn., 1975, E.W. Scripps First Amendment award, Alumni Achievement award Hillsdale Coll. Mem. Am. Soc. Newspaper Editors, Am. Newspaper Pubs. Assn. Roman Catholic. Club: Kiwanis. Office: 15 N Main Wilkes-Barre PA 18711

CONNOR, ROBERT DICKSON, educator; b. Edinburgh, Scotland, May 15, 1922; s. Robert and Jane (Dickson) C.; m. Sheila Carmichael Telfer, Dec. 27, 1948; children—David, Graham. B.Sc., U. Edinburgh, 1942, Ph.D., 1949. Asst. lectr. Edinburgh U., 1947-49, lectr., 1949-57; asso. prof. physics U. Man., Can., 1957-60, prof., 1960—, asso. dean arts and sci., 1963-68, acting dean grad. studies, 1968, vice-dean arts and sci., 1968, dean, 1969-70, dean sci., 1970-79; prof. Faculty of Edn., 1979—; Mem. Fisheries Research Bd., 1965-76. Served with RAF, 1942-46. Recipient Centennial award for outstanding contbns. to sci. edn. in high schs., 1967. Fellow Inst. Physics (London). Home: 638 Elm St Winnipeg MB R3M 3P4 Canada

CONNOR, ROGER GEORGE, state justice; b. N.Y.C., Apr. 23, 1926; s. George B. and Frances Wilmarth (Kennan) C.; m. Anabel Simpson, Nov. 14, 1959 (div. Mar. 1970); children—Roger George, Sibella Simpson. Student, U. B.C., Can., 1947-48; B.A. in Polit. Sci, U. Wash., 1951; LL.B., U. Mich., 1954. Bar: Alaska bar 1955. Practice in, Juneau, 1955-56, 61-68; U.S. atty. 1st Jud. Dist. Alaska, Juneau, 1956-59; exec. asst. criminal div. Dept. Justice, Washington, 1959-61; justice Alaska Supreme Ct., Anchorage, 1968—; Mem. fisheries law com. World Peace Through Law Center, 1966—; mem. Alcoholism Adv. Bd. Alaska, 1967-69. Trustee Alaska Legal Services Corp., 1967-68. Served with USNR, 1944-46. Mem. ABA, Alaska Bar Assn. (bd. govs. 1965-68, pres. 1967-68). Office: 303 K St Anchorage AK 99501

CONNOR, SEYMOUR VAUGHAN, historian, author; b. Paris, Tex., Mar. 4, 1923; s. Aikin Beard and Gladys (Vaughan) C.; 1 son, Charles Seymour. B.A., U. Tex., 1948, M.A., 1949, Ph.D., 1952. Archivist W.Tex. State U., 1952-53, Tex. State Library, 1953-55; prof. history, dir. S.W. collection Tex. Tech. U., Lubbock, 1955-63, prof. history, 1965-79, prof. emeritus, 1979—; vis. prof. Angels State Coll., 1964-65. Author: Preliminary Guide to Texas Archives, 1956, Peters Colony of Texas, 1959, A Biggers Chronicle, 1961, Adventure in Glory, 1965, Texas: A History, 1971, (with Odie Faulk) North America Divided: The Mexican War, 1846-48, 1971, (with W.C. Pool) Texas, the 28th State, 1971, (with Odie Faulk) La Guerra de Intervencion, 1846-1848, 1975, Texas in 1776, 1975, (with J.M. Skaggs) Broadcloth and Britches: The Santa Fe Trade, 1976; Editor: Texas Treasury Papers (3 vols.), 1955, The West Is for Us, 1957, Builders of the Southwest, 1959, Saga of Texas (6 vols.), 1965, Dear America, 1971; Contbr. articles to profl. jours. Served with AUS, 1943-45; ETO; Served with USAR, 1946-52. Fellow Tex. Hist. Assn. (exec. council 1957-70, pres. 1967-68); mem. Phi Kappa Tau, Phi Kappa Psi, Phi Alpha Theta. Home: 3503 45th St Lubbock TX 79413 *As a graduate student I feared that well-intentioned "liberalism" could destroy this country from within; as an active historian and educator I have fought against the growing anti-American view of the national character; as a professor emeritus I am now witness to the fiberless fragmentation of a society ruled by a bureaucratic gargantua.*

CONNOR, THOMAS BYRNE, physician, educator; b. Balt., Dec. 21, 1921; s. John Stephen and Ann Loretta (McCabe) C.; m. Eleanor Ann Rulis, Oct. 10, 1957; children: Thomas Byrne, Kathyrn McCabe. A.B., Loyola Coll., Balt., 1943; M.D., U. Md., 1946. Intern Mercy Hosp., Balt., 1946-47, resident medicine, 1949-51; fellow medicine Johns Hopkins Hosp., Balt., 1951-56, asst. physician, 1951-59; asst. prof. medicine Sch. Medicine, U. Md., 1956-59, asso. prof., 1959-67, prof., 1967—, dir. div. endocrinology and metabolism, 1956—; staff physician U. Md. Hosp., Balt., 1956—; dir. Clin. Research Center, 1961—; cons. medicine Balt. VA Hosp., 1966—, Mercy Hosp., Balt., 1965—; trustee Good Samaritan Hosp., Balt., 1979—, Stella Maris Hospice Operating Corp., 1982—. Editorial bd.: Jour., Clin. Endocrinology and Metabolism, 1961-67, Bull. of U. Md. Sch. Medicine, 1982—. Served to lt. (j.g.), M.C. USNR, 1947-49. Fellow A.C.P.; mem. Endocrine Soc., Am. Diabetes Assn., AAAS, Am. Fedn. Clin. Research, Balt. City Med. Soc., Am. Clin. and Climatol. Assn., Md. Soc. Internal Medicine (council), Am. Soc. Bone and Mineral Research, Interurban Clin. Club, U. Md. Sch. Medicine Alumni Assn. (bd. dirs. 1981—), Alpha Omega Alpha. Research and publs. in calcium and bone metabolism, parathyroid disorders. Home: 112 Croydon Rd Baltimore MD 21212 Office: 22 S Greene St Baltimore MD 21201

CONNOR, WILLIAM ELLIOTT, physician, educator; b. Pitts., Sept. 14, 1921; s. Frank E. and Edna S. (Felt) C.; m. Sonja Lee Newcomer, Sept. 19, 1969; children: Rodney William, Catherine Susan Connor Mulford, James Elliott, Christopher French, Peter Malcolm. B.A., U. Iowa, 1942, M.D., 1950. Diplomate: Am. Bd. Internal Medicine, Am. Bd. Nutrition. Intern USPHS Hosp., San Francisco, 1950-51; resident in internal medicine San Joaquin Gen. Hosp., Stockton, Calif., 1951-52; practice medicine specializing in internal medicine, Chico, Calif., 1952-54; resident in internal medicine VA Hosp., Iowa City, 1954-56; cons., 1967-75; mem. faculty U. Iowa Coll. Medicine, 1956-75, prof. internal medicine, 1967-75; acting dir., then dir. Clin. Research Center, 1967-75, dir. lipid-atherosclerosis sect., cardiovascular div., 1974-75; vis. prof. Basic Sci. Med. Inst., Karachi, Pakistan, 1961-62, Baker Med. Research Inst., Melbourne, Australia, 1982; vis. fellow clin. sci. Australian Nat. U., Canberra, 1970; prof. cardiology and metabolism-nutrition, head sect. clin. nutrition, dir. lipid-atherosclerosis lab., assoc. dir. Clin. Research Center, U. Oreg. Health Scis. Center, Portland, 1975—; chmn. heart and lung program project com. Nat. Heart and Lung Inst., NIH, 1974-75, chmn. rev. com. A, 1975-76, chmn. lipid metabolism adv. com., 1971-72, mem. gen. clin. research centers com., 1976-80; mem. arteriosclerosis, lipid metabolism and hypertension com. Natl. Heart and Lung Inst., NIH, 1982—. Contbr. numerous articles to med. jours.; Editor: Jour. Lab. and Clin. Medicine, 1970-73; mem. editorial bds., reviewer profl. jours. Mem. Johnson County (Iowa) Central Democratic Com., 1965-69; mem. nat. council Fellowship Reconciliation; nat., North Central and Pacific Northwest bds. Am. Friends Service Com. Served with AUS, 1943-46. Research fellow Am. Heart Assn., 1956-58; A.C.P. traveling fellow Sir William Dunn Sch. Pathology, Oxford, Eng., 1960; recipient Career Devel. Research award Nat. Heart Inst., 1962-73. Mem. AAAS, A.C.P., Am. Diabetes Assn. (vice chmn. food and nutrition com. 1972-74), Am. Fedn. Clin. Research, Am. Heart Assn. (chmn. council arteriosclerosis 1975-78, exec. com. council epidemiology 1967-70, exec. com. council cerebral vascular disease 1966-68), Am. Soc. Clin. Nutrition (pres. 1978), Am. Inst. Nutrition, AMA, Am. Oil Chemists Soc., Am. Physiol. Soc., Am. Soc. Clin. Investigation, Am. Soc. Study Arteriosclerosis, Assn. Am. Physicians, Central Soc. Clin. Research, Nutrition Soc., Soc. Exptl. Biology and Medicine (council 1971-72, pres. Iowa sect. 1971-72), Western Assn. Physicians, Western Soc. Clin. Research, AAUP (pres. U. Iowa chpt. 1968-69, pres. Oreg. Health Sci. U. chpt. 1978-79), Phi Beta Kappa, Sigma Xi, Alpha Omega Alpha. Research in nutrition, lipid metabolism, blood vessel diseases. Home: 2600 SW Sherwood Pl Portland OR 97201 Office: Oreg Health Scis U Portland OR 97201

CONNORS, CHUCK KEVIN JOSEPH, actor; b. Bklyn., Apr. 10, 1921; m. Betty Jane Riddle (div.); 4 children. Ed., Seton Hall U. Profl. baseball player with Bklyn. Dodgers, 1949, Chgo. Cubs, 1951; later on West Coast. Various TV and motion picture appearances; starred in: The Rifleman series, ABC-TV, 1958; later in: The Thrillseekers; appeared in: Roots, 1977, The Yellow Rose; films include Walk the Dark Street, 1956, Tomahawk Trail, 1957, Designing Woman, 1957, Geronimo, 1962, Move Over Darling, 1963, Synanon, 1965, Ride Beyond Vengeance, 1966, Captain Nemo and the Underwater City, 1969, Pancho Villa, 1971, Support Your Local Gunfighter, 1971, Soylent Green, 1972, Tourist Trap, 1979, Airplane II: The Sequel, 1982, others. Served with U.S. Army. Recipient TV Champion award, 1958; Golden Globe award, 1959 *

CONNORS, DONALD DENNIS, JR., lawyer, arbitrator; b. Warren, Ohio, Apr. 13, 1920; s. Donald Dennis and Ruth Anne (Seeds) C.; m. Mary Jane Hobson, Sept. 18, 1948 (dec. June 1979); children: Anthony Hobson, Matthew Dennis; m. Elizabeth Blake, Sept. 22, 1979. A.B., U. Notre Dame, 1942; LL.B., Georgetown U., 1953. Bar: Calif. 1954, D.C. 1953. Spl. agt. FBI, Seattle, 1946-48, Washington, 1948-50; staff mem. com. on judiciary U.S. Senate, Washington, 1951-53; assoc. Brobeck, Phleger & Harrison, San Francisco, 1953-60, ptnr., 1960—; adj. prof. law U. San Francisco, 1954-55. Mem. Mcpl. Employees Relations Panel, San Francisco, 1975-76. Served to maj. U.S. Army, 1942-46. Mem. Bar. Assn. D.C., Calif. Bar Assn. Republican. Roman Catholic. Clubs: World Trade; Mchts. Exchange (San Francisco). Home: 66 Seacliff Ave San Francisco CA 94121 Office: Brobeck Phleger & Harrison Spear St Tower One Market Plaza San Francisco CA 94105

CONNORS, DORSEY (MRS. JOHN E. FORBES), TV and radio commentator, newspaper columnist; b. Chgo.; d. William J. and Sarah (MacLean) C.; m. John E. Forbes; 1 dau., Stephanie. B.A. cum laude, U. Ill. Floor reporter WGN-TV Republican Nat. Conv., Chgo., Democratic Nat. Conv., Los Angeles, 1960. Appeared on: Personality Profiles, WGN-TV, Chgo., 1948, Dorsey Connors Show, WMAQ-TV, Chgo., 1949-58, 61-63, Armchair Travels, WMAQ-TV, 1952-55, Homeshow, NBC, 1954-57, Haute Couture Fashion Openings, NBC, Paris, France, 1954, 58, Dorsey Connors program, WGN, 1958-61, Tempo Nine, WGN-TV, 1961, Society in Chgo, WMAQ-TV, 1964; writer: column Hi! I'm Dorsey Connors, Chgo. Sun Times, 1965—; Author: Gadgets Galore, 1953, Save Time, Save Money, Save Yourself, 1972. Founder Ill. Epilepsy League; mem. exec. bd. Chgo. Beautiful Com.; mem. woman's bd. Children's Home and Aid Soc.; mem. women's bd. USO. Mem. AFTRA, Screen Actor's Guild, Nat. Acad. TV Arts and Scis., Soc. Midland Authors, Chgo. Hist. Soc. (guild com., costume com.), Chi Omega. Office: Chgo Sun Times 401 N Wabash Chicago IL 60611

CONNORS, EDWARD MICHAEL, clergyman, seminary and college president; b. Bronx, N.Y., Feb. 23, 1921; s. Edward and Mary (O'Loughlin) C. B.A., St. Joseph's Coll., Yonkers, N.Y., 1943; student, St. Joseph's Sem., Yonkers, 1943-47; M.A., Cath. U., 1949, Ph.D., 1951. Ordained priest Roman Cath. Ch., 1947; mem. staff St. Patrick's Cathedral, N.Y.C., 1950-52; prof. Cathedral Coll., 1952-53; tchr. Cardinal Hayes High Sch., Bronx, N.Y., 1953-59; asso. supt. schs. Archdiocese N.Y., 1959-68, supt. schs., 1968-72; ednl. adviser Lincoln Center, 1968-72; chaplain Maria Regina High Sch., Hartsdale, N.Y.; Episcopal vicar Westchester County, 1972-82; Pres. St. Joseph's Sem. and Coll., 1982—. Author: (with Martin J. Quigley) Catholic Action in Practice, 1964. Address: St Joseph's Seminary and College Yonkers NY 10704

CONNORS, EUGENE KENNETH, lawyer; b. Dobbs Ferry, N.Y., Oct. 3, 1946; s. Edward Michael and Eileen (Burke) C.; m. Mary Therese Hannan, Nov. 23, 1968; children: Kevin Patrick, Kathryn Margaret. B.A., Holy Cross Coll., 1968; J.D., Columbia U., 1971. Bar: Pa. 1971. Assoc. Reed Smith Shaw & McClay, Pitts., 1971-76, ptnr., 1977—; adj. prof. St. Francis Coll., Loretto, Pa., 1975—. Bd. dirs. Sch. Vol. Assn. Pitts., 1973—. Mem. ABA, Pa. Bar Assn., Allegheny County Bar Assn. Office: 747 Union Trust Bldg Pittsburgh PA 15219

CONNORS, GERALD ANTHONY, business executive; b. Janesville, Wis., June 13, 1927; s. Anthony G. and V.E. (Cress) C.; m. Lila Elizabeth Ligocki, June 19, 1948; children: Michael, Lynn, Timothy, Kevin. B.S., Marquette U., 1951. With Emery Air Freight, 1951-72, sr. v.p., gen. mgr., 1969-72; pres., chmn. bd. Air Express Internat.-Wings & Wheels Express, Inc., Jamaica, N.Y., 1972-74; pres. Connors Enterprises, St. Germain, Wis., 1974—. Active various civic affairs. Served with inf. AUS, 1944-47; ETO. Office: 8000 Found Lake Rd Germain WI 54558

CONNORS, JAMES SCOTT (JIMMY CONNORS), tennis player; b. East St. Louis, Ill., Sept. 2, 1952; s. James and Gloria (Thompson) C.; m. Patti McGuire; 1 son, Brett David. Student, UCLA. Joined World Championship Tennis, Inc., 1972. Recipient Player of Year award, 1974; named All-Am., 1971; ranked no. 1 male tennis player in U.S. and World, 1976; ranked no. 1 in world, 1978. Winner Australian Men's Singles, 1974, Wimbledon Men's Singles, 1974, 82, Wimbledon Men's Doubles (with Ilie Nastase), 1973, U.S. Pro Championship Men's Singles, 1973, Cologne Cup, 1976, U.S. Clay Ct. Championship-Men's Singles, 1974, 76, 78, 79, U.S. Open Men's Singles, 1974, 76, 78,82, 83, U.S. Indoor Open Men's Singles, 1973, 74, 75, 78, 79,83, Pro Indoor Men's Singles, 1976, 78, 79, 80, U.S. Open Men's Doubles (with Ilie Nastase), 1975, U.S. Indoor Men's Doubles (with Frew McMillan), 1974, (with Ilie Nastase), 1975, U.S. Clay Ct. Men's Doubles (with Ilie Nastase), 1974, S.African Men's Singles, 1973, 74, World Championship Tennis Singles, 1977, Grand Prix Masters Championship, 1978, U.S. Nat. Indoor Men's Singles, 1978, Australian Indoor Men's Singles, 1978; mem. Davis Cup Team, 1976, 81, World Cup Team, 1976.

CONNORS, JEANNE LOUISE, businesswoman; b. La Crosse, Wis., July 17, 1940; d. Frank Joseph and Sylvia Marguerite (Harris) Subera; (div.)children: Christine Marguerite, Corinne Marie, Brian Francis. Secretarial degree, Madison (Wis.) Bus. Coll., 1957; A.A., Madison Area Tech. Coll., 1982; student, U. Wis.-Madison, 1983—. Exec. sec. Pure Oil Co., Madison, 1958-61; editor Solar Tech. Report and Electric Comfort Conditioning News, Elec. Info. Publs., Inc., Madison, 1974-80; asst. to pres. Badgerland Harvestore Systems, Inc., Edgerton, Wis., 1980-81; adminstrv. asst. studies in behavioral disabilities autism project U. Wis.-Madison, 1981—. Bd. dirs. Freedom House, Madison, Wis. Mem. Epsilon Sigma Alpha (past chpt. pres.). Democrat. Home: 1705 Northfield Pl Madison WI 53704 Office: 2132 Fordem Ave Madison WI 53704 *I feel success is the result of constant struggle to increase the boundaries of the mind and an equally constant vigilance against complacency, which is the origin of ignorance.*

CONNORS, JIMMY *See* **CONNORS, JAMES SCOTT**

CONNORS, JOHN MICHAEL, JR., advertising agency executive; b. Boston, June 9, 1942; s. John Michael and Mary (Horrigan) C.; m. Eileen Marie Ahearn; children: John, Timothy, Susanne, Kevin. Grad., Boston Coll., 1963. Mktg. rep. Campbell Soup Co., Boston, 1963-65; account exec. Batten, Barton, Durstine & Osborne, New York and Boston, 1965-68; pres. Hill, Holiday, Connors, Cosmopulos, Inc., Boston, 1968—. Trustee Kennedy Meml. Hosp. Children, 1975—, Boston Coll., 1979—; trustee Boston Community Access and Programming Found.; bd. dirs. Big Brother Assn. Boston, 1976—; chmn. pub. relations adv. com. Boston Coll., 1975—; mem. cabinet United Way of Mass. Bay, 1979. Named one of Boston's Ten Outstanding Young Leaders Jaycees, 1972. Mem. Advt. Club Greater Boston (past pres.), Am. Assn. Advt. Agys. (chmn. Northeast council), New Eng. Broadcasting Assn. (past pres.). Roman Catholic. Clubs: Longwood Cricket, Dennis Yacht, Badminton and Tennis. Home: 175 Ward St Newton MA 02159 Office: John Hancock Tower 200 Clarendon St Boston MA 02116

CONNORS, JOHN STANLEY, publishing company executive; b. Worcester, Mass., July 26, 1925; s. Frank J. and Lucy A. (Kennedy) C.; m. Catherine Lightbourne; children: Susan, Patricia, Kathleen, Richard, Jane, John, Allison White. Student, Mich. State Coll., 1943, 46-49, U.S. Mil. Acad., 1945-46. With advt. dept. N.Y. Daily News, 1949-53; merchandising dir. R.W. Orr Assocs., Inc., 1953-56; with N.Y. World Telegram & Sun, 1956, Am. Weekly, 1956-59, Sat. Evening Post, N.Y.C., 1960-65, N.Y. sales mgr., 1963, nat. sales mgr., 1963-65, advt. dir., 1965; pub. Holiday, 1967-68; v.p. Curtis Pub. Co., 1964-71; v.p., pub. Psychology Today mag., 1968-71; pres., pub. Travel and Leisure mag.; exec. v.p. Am. Express Pub. Corp. (wholly owned subs. Am. Express Co.), dir., mem. exec. com., 1979—; pres., pub. Internat. Rev. of Food and Wine mag. (Am. Express pub. affiliate.); Chmn. adv. bd. masters degree program New Sch. for Social Research. Served with AUS, 1943-45. Mem. Mag. Pubs. Assn. (dir.), Pacific Area Travel Assn., Caribbean Travel Assn., Am. Soc. Travel Agts., World Travel Orgn., Travel Industry Assn. Am., African Travel Assn. (v.p. bd. dirs. 1976—, pres. N.Y. chpt. 1976-79, 1st African individual achievement award), Delta Sigma Phi, Alpha Phi. Roman Catholic. Clubs: N.Y. Atrium, Sky, Netherlands. *Problem-solving remains forever within the realm of possibility if one takes the time to evaluate all the components of the solution. By knowing precisely where one wants to go, one is able to anticipate enough of the pitfalls and extenuating circumstances to guarantee success. And if one can also recognize that success is not a destination, but rather a route, then each attained goal becomes the substance of one's next great achievement.* *

CONNORS, KENNETH ANTONIO, chemist; b. Torrington, Conn., Feb. 19, 1932; s. Peter Francis and Adeline (Gioia) C.; m. Patricia R. Smart, Dec. 30, 1972. B.S., U. Conn., 1954; M.S., U. Wis., 1957, Ph.D., 1959. Research asso. dept. chemistry Ill. Inst. Tech., Chgo., 1959-60, Northwestern U., Evanston, Ill., 1960-61; asst. prof. Sch. Pharmacy, U. Wis., Madison, 1962-65, asso. prof., 1965-72, prof., 1972—. Author: A Textbook of Pharmaceutical Analysis, 3d edit, 1982, Reaction Mechanisms in Organic Analytical Chemistry, 1973. Served with U.S. Army, 1961. Fellow AAAS, Acad. Pharm. Scis.; mem. Am. Chem. Soc., Am. Pharm. Assn., Acad. Pharm. Scis., AAAS, N.Y. Acad. Scis. Office: Sch Pharmacy U Wis Madison WI 53706

CONNORS, LEO GERARD, fin. co. exec.; b. Mahanoy City, Pa., July 2, 1927; s. Leo V. and Jean C. (Klitsch) C.; m. Ann Seydel, Oct. 18, 1952; children—Kevin, Deirdre, Christopher, Carl, Leo, John, Maura, Miriam, Stacey, Matthew. B.S. in Bus. Adminstrn, St. Joseph's U., Phila., 1951. Accountant Bulletin Co., Phila., 1952; sr. accountant Frank Vallei (C.P.A.), Phila., 1952-55, Peat, Marwick, Mitchell & Co. (C.P.A.'s), 1955-61; with Fin. Am. Corp., Allentown, Pa., 1961—, treas., 1977—, sr. v.p., 1977—. Mem. Hanover Twp. (Pa.) Planning Commn., 1977-79. Served with AUS, 1945-47. Mem. Nat. Consumer Fin. Assn., Am. Inst. C.P.A.'s, Nat. Accountants Assn., Fin. Execs. Inst., Pa. Inst. C.P.A.'s. Republican. Roman Catholic. Office: 1105 Hamilton St Allentown PA 18101

CONNORS, MIKE (KREKOR OHANIAN), actor; b. Fresno, Calif., Aug. 15, 1925. Student, U. Calif. at Los Angeles. Appeared in: films Sudden Fear, 1952, Sky Commando, Day of Triumph, Flesh and Spur, The Ten Commandments, 1956, Seed of Violence, Good Neighbor Sam, 1964, Where Love has Gone, 1964, Situation Hopeless but not Serious, Harlow, 1965, Stagecoach, 1966, Kiss the Girls and Make Them Die, 1967, Avalanche Express, 1979; TV appearances include Tightrope, 1959; and the series Mannix, 1967-74; TV movies The Killer Who Wouldn't Die, 1976, Revenge for a Rape, 1976, The Long Journey Back, 1978 (Recipient Golden Globe award for series Mannix.). Office: care Internat Creative Mgmt 8899 Beverly Blvd Los Angeles CA 90048 *

CONNORS, ROBERT MICHAEL, aluminum products mfg. co. exec.; b. Camden, N.J., Dec. 5, 1933; s. William B. and Mary (McGrath) C.; m. June D. Terrel, Oct. 6, 1956; children—Debra Lynn, Patricia Anne, Robert M., Carol June. A.A., U. Fla., 1959, B.S. in Bus. Adminstrn, 1960. Certificate in Accounting, Rutgers U., 1953; C.P.A., Fla. With Ernst & Whinney, Atlanta and Miami, 1960-68, supr. audit staff, 1966, mgr. audit staff, 1968; asst. to pres. Keller Industries, Miami, 1968-69, treas., 1969-77, sec., 1974-77, v.p., 1975, sr. v.p., mem. corp. exec. com., 1977—, dir., 1974—. Adviser Jr. Achievement, Miami, 1967. Served with F.A. AUS, 1954-56; ETO. Mem. Am. Inst. C.P.A.'s, Fla. Inst. C.P.A.'s, Nat. Assn. Accountants, Risk Ins. Mgmt. Soc. Democrat. Roman Catholic. Home: 4700 Pierce St Hollywood FL 33021 Office: 18000 State Rd 9 Miami FL 33162

CONOLE, CLEMENT VINCENT, corporate executive; b. Binghamton, N.Y., Sept. 29, 1908; s. P.J. and Briget (Holleran) C.; m. Marjorie Anable, Sept. 26, 1931; children—Barbara (Mrs. Francis B. McElroy), Marjorie (Mrs. Marjorie A. Hargrave), Richard, Jacalyn (Mrs. John N. Harman III). B.S.C.E., Clarkson Coll. Tech., Potsdam, N.Y., 1931; postgrad., Cornell U., N.Y. U., Yale U.; M.B.A., Fla. Atlantic U. Licensed profl engr. and land surveyor, N.Y., Pa. Engr. City of Binghamton, also N.Y. State, 1930-32; ptnr. Richmeyer, Harding and Conole, 1932-33; engr. Dept. of Interior, 1933-35; dist. dir. Fed. Works Adminstrn.; dist. supt. N.Y. Unemployment Ins. Div., 1936-37; asst. state indsl. commr., N.Y., 1937-39, dep. indsl. commr., 1939-43; dir. indsl. bur. C. of C. Bd. of Trade of Phila., 1943-44, operating mgr., 1945-46, exec. v.p., 1946-52; also editor, pub. Greater Phila. mag., 1945-50; v.p. Bankers Securities corp., 1952-55; pres. Municipal Publs., Inc., 1947-50; pub. relations cons. Phila.-Balt. Stock Exchange, 1947-52; chmn. bd., pres., dir. Hearn Dept. Stores, Inc., N.Y.C., 1952-54; dir., chmn. bd. James McCutcheon & Co., 1956-57; chmn. bd., dir. Bus. Supplies Corp. Am., Skytop, Pa., 1962-65; chmn. bd. dir., pres. Tabulating Card Co., Inc., Princeton, N.J., 1955-62; chmn. bd. dir. Am. Bus. Mgmt. Co., 1955-62, Whiting Paper Co., Inc., 1959-62, Sky Meadow Farms, Inc., 1965-68, Am. Bus. Machines Co., 1958-65, Data Processing Supplies Co., 1959-65, Am. Bus. Execs. Co., 1960-65, Am. Bus. Investment Co., 1958-62, Gen. Bus. Supplies Corp., 1965-70; prof. adminstrn. Fla. Atlantic U., 1972-74; now chmn. bd. trustees, pres. Am. Coll. Adminstrs. Execs. Mgrs., Laguna Hills, Calif.; dean Sch. Adminstrn., Coll. Boca Raton; exec. head. mgmt. engring. div. S.D. Leidesdorf & Co., 1954-55; dir. City Stores Corp., City Stores Merc. Co., Inc., City Splty. Stores Co., Inc., Oppenheim Collins & Co., Franklin Simon Co., N.Y.C., R.H. White Co., Boston, Wise Smith & Co., Hartford, Conn. Mem. Broome County Planning Commn., 1936-

38, Pa. War Manpower Commn.; chmn. War. Emergency Bd. N.Y. State, 1941; industry mem. appeals com. Nat. War Labor Bd., 1943-45; cons. HOLC and FHA, 1936-39; chmn. Armed Forces Regional Council, Pa. and Del., 1950-52; mem. adv. com. 2d Army, 4th Naval Dist.; pres. 175th Anniversary of the Signing of the Declaration of Independence, 1951, Phila. Conv. and Visitors Bur., 1953; chmn. United Com. Fund, Princeton; apptd. mem. State Commn. to reorgn. Govt. City N.Y., 1953, Mayor's Adv. Council; chmn. com. on city mgmt. and adminstrn. Mayor's Adv. Council, 1954, Citizens Com. to Keep N.Y. Clean, 1955, Citizens Com. on Cts., 1955; pres. Quiet City Campaign, 1956; vice chmn., sec. Phila. Parking Authority.; Trustee William Shelton Harrison Found., Hun School, Princeton, N.J., Clarkson Coll. of Tech. Mem. Am. Mgmt. Assn., A.I.M. (president's council, charter mem. adv. bd.), Nat. Retail Research Inst. (dir.), Bronx Bd. Trade (dir. 1954-64), Ave. of Americas Assn. (dir. 1952-55), Soc. for Advancement Mgmt., Nat. Assn. Cost Accountants, Commerce and Industry Assn. N.Y. (treas., dir., mem. exec. com. 1954-58), Lambda Iota (pres.), Delta Upsilon (trustee), Phi Beta Lambda. Clubs: Midday, Philadelphia Country, Lake Placid, Skytop, Merion Cricket, Racquet, Poor Richard, Pen and Pencil (Phila.); Economic, Union League (N.Y.C.); Nat. Golf Links of Am. (Southampton, L.I.); Uptown; Springdale Golf, Rotary, Nassau (Princeton, N.J.); Laguna Hills (Calif.) Golf, Boca Raton, Pinehurst Country, Royal Palm Yacht and Country (gov.), P.G.A. National Golf.). Office: Executive Center PO Box 2704 Laguna Hills CA 92653

CONOVER, HARVEY, publisher; b. New Rochelle, N.Y., Oct. 23, 1925; s. Harvey and Dorothy (Jobson) C.; m. Isabel McIver Toner, Dec. 27, 1980; children: Harvey III, Stephen, Jeffrey, Cynthia. B.S., U.S. Naval Acad., 1949. With Mill & Factory mag., 1953-54, Purchasing mag., 1954-56; dist. mgr. Volume Feeding mag., 1956-57; sales mgr. Volumne Feeding mag., 1958-59; pub. Boating Industry mag., 1959-62; exec. v.p. Conover-Mast Publs., Inc., 1962-64, pres., 1964-68; pres. Conover-Mast div. Cahners Pub. Co., Inc., N.Y.C., 1968-73, v.p., 1974—. Served to lt. (j.g.) USN, 1949-53. Mem. Am. Bus. Press Assn., Bus./Profl. Advt. Assn., Yacht Racing Assn. Club: N.Y. Yacht. Home: 7 Half Moon Way Dolphin Cove Stamford CT 06902 Office: Cahners Pub Co 205 E 42d St New York NY 10017

CONOVER, ROBERT FREMONT, artist; b. Trenton, N.J., July 3, 1920; s. Norman and Emily (Fox) C.; m. Ruth Hagemen, May, 1949 (dec.); 1 dau., Christine. Student, Phila. Mus. Sch. Art, 1938-42, Art Studuents League N.Y., 1945-47, Bklyn. Mus. Sch., 1948-50. Mem. faculty New Sch. Social Research, 1958—, Bklyn. Mus. Art Sch., 1960—, Lenox Sch., 1961-66, Newark Sch. Fine and Indsl. Art, 1966—. One-person shows, Laurel Gallery, N.Y.C., 1949, New Gallery, N.Y.C., 1951-53, Zabriskie Gallery, 1955-61, New Sch. Social Research, 1966-75; exhibited in group shows, Mus. Modern Art, N.Y.C., Met. Mus., N.Y.C., Art Inst., Chgo., Bklyn. Mus., Whitney Mus. Am. Art, Pa. Acad., Carnegie Inst., others; represented in permanent collections, Bklyn. Mus., Met. Mus. Art, N.Y.C., N.Y. Public Library, Detroit Inst. Art, Library Congress, Washington, Nat. Gallery Art, Washington, Smithsonian Inst., Tokyo Mus. Modern Art, Whitney Mus. Am. Art, N.J. State Mus., Mus. Art, Skopje, Yugoslavia, others. Served with AUS, 1942-45. Fellow MacDowell Colony, 1955-58, Yaddo, 1959-60; CAPS grantee N.Y. State, 1976. Mem. Am. Abstract Artists, Soc. Am. Graphic Artists. Home: 162 E 33d St New York NY 10016

CONRAD, CHARLES, JR., former astronaut, business executive; b. Phila., June 2, 1930; s. Charles and Frances V. (Sargent) C.; m. Jane DuBose, June 17, 1953; children: Peter, Thomas, Andrew, Christopher. B.S. in Aero. Engring, Princeton, 1953. Commd. ensign U.S. Navy, 1953, advanced through grades to lt. comdr., 1964; project test pilot, armaments test div. Navy Dept., 1959-60; flight instr., performance engr. U.S. Naval Test Pilot Sch., 1960-61; flight instr. for F4H Naval Air Sta., Miramar, Calif., 1961-62; safety flight officer Fighter Squadron 96, 1963; astronaut Manned Spacecraft Center, NASA, Houston, 1964-74, pilot, 1965, comdg. pilot, 1966, comdr., 1969, 1973; v.p. ops. Am. TV & Communications Corp., Denver, 1974-78; v.p. mktg. Douglas Aircraft Co., Long Beach, Calif., 1978-80, sr. v.p., 1980—. Recipient Congressional medal of Honor, 1978. Fellow Soc. Exptl. Test Pilots; assoc. fellow Am. Inst. Aero. and Astronautics. Office: 3855 Lakewood Blvd Long Beach CA 90846 *

CONRAD, DONALD GLOVER, insurance executive; b. St. Louis, Apr. 23, 1930; s. Harold Armin and Velma Glover (Morris) C.; m. Stephania Sanzone, Feb. 8, 1980; children by previous marriage: Marcy Conrad Morrow, Suzanne, Mark. Student, Wesleyan U., 1948-49; B.S., Northwestern U., 1952; M.B.A., U. Mich., 1957. With Exxon Co., 1957-70, fin. adv., The Hague, Netherlands, 1965-66, treas., London, 1966-70; sr. v.p. Aetna Life & Casualty Co., Hartford, Conn., 1970-72, exec. v.p., 1972—, also dir.; dir. Terra Nova Ins. Co., Ltd., London, Satellite Bus. Systems., Samuel Montagu Holdings, Ltd., London, Federated Investors, Pitts. Bd. govs. Nat. Hockey League; bd. dirs., mem. exec. com. Am. Council for Arts, Greater Hartford Arts Council; chmn. Downtown Council, Hartford; corporator Hartford Hosp.; bd. dirs. Inst. of Living, Hartford; elector Wadsworth Atheneum, Hartford; trustee Trinity Coll. Served to lt. USNR, 1952-55. Club: Hartford (dir.). Office: 151 Farmington Ave Hartford CT 06156

CONRAD, EDWARD EZRA, physicist, nuclear engineer, scientific corporation executive; b. Richmond, Calif., June 11, 1927; s. Milford and Bessie (Kaplan) C.; m. Priscilla Gales, June 17, 1951; children: Pamela Gales, Robin Conrad Sturm, Susan Conrad St. Germain. B.A., U. Calif.-Berkeley, 1950; M.S., U. Md.-College Park, 1955, Ph.D., 1970. Research physicist Harry Diamond Labs., Washington, 1953-70, lab. chief, 1971-73, assoc. tech. dir., 1973-76; asst. to dep. dir. Def. Nuclear Agy., Washington, 1976-79, dep. dir. sci. and technology, 1979-83; v.p. Kaman Scis. Corp., Colorado Springs, 1983—; cons. Def. Nuclear Agy., Washington. Contbr. chpts. to books and articles in field to profl. jours. Served with USN, 1945-46. Recipient Meritorious Civilian Service medal U.S. Army, 1976, Exceptional Civilian Service medal Def. Nuclear Agy., 1980, Disting. Civilian Service medal Sec. Def., 1983; fellow U.S. Army, 1960. Fellow IEEE; mem. Am. Phys. Soc., Sigma Xi. Jewish. Club: Cosmos. Home: 7500 Marbury Rd Bethesda MD 20817 Office: Kaman Scis Corp 1911 Jefferson Davis Hwy Arlington VA 22202

CONRAD, HANS, educator, metall. engr.; b. Konradstahl, Germany, Apr. 19, 1922; came to U.S., 1926, naturalized, 1944; s. Henry K. and Martha Ann (Bader) C.; m. Emma Ann Bort, June 10, 1944; children—Sandra Joy, Roberta Lee, Gary Richard. Student, Washington and Jefferson Coll., 1940-42; B.S. in Metall. Engring, Carnegie Inst. Tech., 1943; M.Eng., Yale, 1951, D.Eng., 1956. Research metallurgist Chase Copper & Brass Co., Waterbury, Conn., 1953-55; supervisory engr. Westinghouse Research Labs., Churchill Boro, Pa., 1955-59; sr. research specialist Atomics Internat., Canoga Park, Calif., 1959-61; head dept. physics Aerospace Corp., El Segundo, Calif., 1961-64; tech. dir. Franklin Inst. Research Labs., Phila., 1964-67; prof., chmn. dept. metall. engring. and materials sci., asso. dir. Inst. Mining and Minerals Research, U. Ky., Lexington, 1967-80; prof., head dept. materials engring., dir. minerals and materials research programs N.C. State U., 1981—. Contbr. articles to profl. jours. and books. Recipient U. Ky. Research award, 1971; U.S. Sr. Scientist award Alexander von Humboldt-Stiftung, 1974; Japan Soc. Promotion Sci. vis. prof., 1976. Fellow Am. Soc. Metallurgy; mem. Am. Inst. M.E., Am. Soc. Metals, Am. Soc. Testing and Materials, Sigma Xi, Tau Beta Pi. Home: 205 Glasgow Rd Cary NC 27511

CONRAD, LARRY ALLYN, lawyer, past secretary state Indiana; b. Laconia, Ind., Feb. 8, 1935; s. Marshall and Ruby (Rooksby) C.; m. Mary Lou Hoover, Dec. 28, 1957; children—Jeb Allyn, Amy Lou, Andrew Birch, Jody McDade. A.B., Ball State U., 1957; LL.B., Ind. U., 1961. Legis. asst. to Senator Birch Bayh of Ind., Washington, 1963-64; chief counsel U.S. Senate Subcom. on Constnl. Amendments, 1964-69; sec. state Ind., 1970-78; ptnr. firm Conrad & Hafsten, Indpls., 1978—. Hon. chmn. Ind. March of Dimes, 1974; bd. dirs. Mus. of Indian Heritage, Indpls., Dance Kaleidscope, Commn. for Downtown, Inc., Indpls., Indpls. Zool. Soc.; pres. Hemophilia of Ind., 1979—; mem. exec. council Indpls. chpt. City of Hope; vice chmn. membership Indpls. Urban League; mem. adv. com. Ind. Spl. Olympics Com.; bd. dirs. Ind. Resource Corp.; hon. chmn. crusade Ind. div. Am. Cancer Soc., 1983; bd. dirs., sec. Downtown Promotion Council; leadership adv. council Ind. Com. Humanities.; Democratic candidate for gov. Ind. Recipient citation of merit Ind. Vocat. Rehab. Services, 1972; recipient Man of Yr. award Indpls. Press Club, 1983. Mem. NAACP (life); mem. ABA, Ind. State Bar Assn., Indpls. C. of C., Indpls. Conv. and Visitors Bur. (bd. dirs.). Home: 7153 N Meridian St Indianapolis IN 46260 Office: 615 Merchants Bank Bldg Indianapolis IN 46204

CONRAD, MARCEL EDWARD, JR., physician, educator; b. N.Y.C., Aug. 15, 1928; s. Marcel Edward and Lulu Marie (Geraghty) C.; m. Patricia Jane Hutchon, Jan. 16, 1948; children—Marcel Edward, III, Mark E., Carol J., Erin E., Julia P. B.S., Georgetown U., 1949, M.D., 1953. Intern Walter Reed Gen. Hosp., Washington, 1953-54, resident, then chief resident in internal medicine, 1955-60; service in, Korea; mem. staff Walter Reed Army Inst. Research, 1961-74, chief dept. hematology, 1965-74; chief clin. investigation service Walter Reed Army Med. Center, 1971-74; clin. asst. prof., then clin. asso. prof. medicine Georgetown U. Med. Sch., 1964-74; ret., 1974; prof. medicine U. Ala. Med. Sch., Birmingham, also dir. div. hematology and oncology, 1974-83; prof. medicine, dir. div. hematology and oncology U. South Ala., 1983—. Contbr. numerous articles med. publns. Commd. 1st lt. M.C. U.S. Army, 1953; advanced through grades to col., 1968. Decorated Legion of Merit with oak leaf cluster; recipient Skinner medal U.S. Army, 1955, Hoff medal, 1962, John Shaw Billings award, 1967, William Beaumont award, 1972, Walter Reed award, 1974. Fellow Internat. Soc. Hematology, A.C.P.; mem. Assn. Am. Physicians, Am. Soc. Clin. Investigation, Am. Physiol. Soc., Internat. Soc. Blood Transfusion, Am. Soc. Hematology, Am. Soc. Clin. Oncology, Soc. Exptl. Biology and Medicine, AAAS, So. Soc. Clin. Investigation, Am. Fed. Clin. Research. Roman Catholic. Office: Div Hematology and Oncology U South Ala Mobile AL 36688

CONRAD, PAUL ERNEST, transportation consultant; b. Hartford, Conn., June 11, 1927; s. Ernest and Agnes Anita (Eis) C.; m. Audrey Grace Lindner, June 17, 1947; children—Cynthia Dale, Robin Sue, Kristen Diane. B.S., U. Conn., 1949. Hwy. engr. Fed. Hwy. Adminstrn., S.E. U.S., Conn. and N.Y., 1949-55; prin. asso. Wilbur Smith & Assocs., Columbia, S.C., 1955-69, sr. v.p., 1969-72, exec. v.p., 1972—, dir., 1960-77, 83—. Bd. dirs. Spring Valley Homeowners Assn., 1976-77. Served with USN, 1945-46. Mem. Nat. Soc. Profl. Engrs., Inst. Transp. Engrs., Am. Inst. Planners, ASCE, Transp. Research Bd., Cons. Engrs. Council. Lutheran. Club: Spring Valley Country. Home: 129 Parkshore Dr E Cola SC 29204 Office: 1301 Gervais St Columbia SC 29202

CONRAD, PAUL FRANCIS, editorial cartoonist; b. Cedar Rapids, Iowa, June 27, 1924; s. Robert H. and Florence G. (Lawler) C.; m. Barbara Kay King, Feb. 27, 1954; children: James, David, Carol, Elizabeth. B.A., U. Iowa, 1950. Editorial cartoonist Denver Post, 1950-64, Los Angeles Times, 1964—; cartoonist Los Angeles Times Syndicate, 1973—; lectr. Cooke-Daniels Lecture Tours, Denver Art Mus., 1964; Richard M. Nixon chair Whittier Coll., 1977-78. Exhibited sculpture and cartoons, Los Angeles County Mus. Art, 1979; (Recipient Editorial Cartoon award Sigma Delta Chi 1963, 69, 71, Pulitzer prize editorial cartooning 1964, 71, 84); Author: The King and Us, 1974, Pro and Conrad, 1979. Served with C.E. AUS, 1942-46; PTO. Journalism award U. So. Calif., 1972; Overseas Press Club award, 1970. Mem. Phi Delta Theta. Democrat. Roman Catholic. Office: Times Mirror Sq Los Angeles CA 90053

CONRAD, ROBERT (CONRAD ROBERT FALK), actor, singer; b. Chgo., Mar. 1, 1935. Ed., Northwestern U. Pres. Robert Conrad Prodns., 1966—. Starred in: TV series Hawaiian Eye, 1959-63, Wild Wild West, 1965-69, The D.A, 1971-72, Baa Baa Black Sheep, 1976, Centennial, 1978, The Duke, 1979, A Man Called Sloane, 1979; appeared in: films Thundering Jets, 1958, Palm Springs Weekend, 1963, Young Dillinger, 1965, Murph, the Surf, 1975, Wild Wild West Revisited, 1979, More Wild Wild West, 1980, Coach of the Year, 1981, Breaking Up Is Hard to Do, 1980; TV series Wrong is Right, 1982 *

CONRAD, WILLIAM, actor, producer, director; b. Louisville, Sept. 27, 1920. Attended, Fullerton Jr. Coll. Radio announcer KMPC, Los Angeles, till 1943. Starred in: radio series Gunsmoke, 1949-60; film debut in: The Killers, 1946; other film appearances include: 30, 1959, Body and Soul, Sorry, Wrong Number, East Side, West Side, The Naked Jungle, Moonshine County Express, 1977; prod. films: Two On a Guillotine, 1965, Brainstorm, 1965, An American Dream, 1966, A Covenant With Death, 1967, First to Fight, 1967, The Cool Ones, 1967, The Assignment; TV credits: Night Cries, 1978; The Brotherhood of the Bell, Conspiracy to Kill; producer, dir.: Klondike; producer: 77 Sunset Strip; dir.: 35 episodes True; star: TV series The D.A, 1971-72, O'Hara, U.S. Treasury, 1971-72, Cannon, 1971-76, Nero Wolfe, from 1981; appeared in: TV movies The Rebels; narrator: TV shows Return of the King; producer: TV movie Turnover Smith. Served with USAAF, 1943-45. Office: care Creative Artists Agy 1888 Century Park E Suite 1400 Los Angeles CA 90067 *

CONRADES, GEORGE HENRY, information systems company executive; b. St. Louis, Feb. 26, 1939; s. Ralph Andrew and Elizabeth (Quermann) C.; m. Patricia Ruth Belt, Feb. 9, 1963; children: Elizabeth, Laura, George, Mary Emma, Anna. B.A., Ohio Wesleyan U., 1961; M.B.A., U. Chgo., 1972. With IBM, 1961—, sales rep., Columbus, Ohio, 1961-69, sr. mktg. mgr., Chgo., 1969-73, asst. to pres. data processing div., White Plains, N.Y., 1973-75, regional mgr., St. Louis, 1975-76, exec. asst. to chmn., Armonk, N.Y., 1976-78; v.p. mktg. gen. systems div., Atlanta, 1978-80; pres. data processing div. IBM, White Plains, N.Y., 1980-82, corp. v.p., pres. nat. accounts div., Armonk, 1982-83, corp. v.p., asst. group exec. Info. Systems and Tech. Group, Harrison, N.Y., 1983-84; corp. v.p., group exec. Asia/Pacific Group, Tokyo, 1984. Trustee Ohio Wesleyan U., Delaware, Ohio; mem. council Grad. Sch. Bus. U. Chgo. Mem. U. Chgo. Grad. Sch. Bus. Alumni Assn. (bd. dirs.). Episcopalian. Office: IBM World Trade A/FE Corp Route 9 North Tarrytown NY 10591

CONRAT, RICHARD FRAENKEL, photographer, solar heating co. exec., educator. Studied at, Reed Coll.; B.A., U. Calif. at Berkeley. Design cons. Dorothea Lange Meml. Exhbn. Mus. Modern Art, 1966. Exhibited, San Francisco Mus. of Art, Oakland (Calif.) Mus., M.H. De Young Mus., U. Calif. at Berkeley Art Mus., Whitney Mus. Art, N.Y.C.; Co-author: The American Farm: A Photography History, 1977, Executive Order 9066, 1971. Guggenheim fellow, 1968-69. Home: 1501 Felta Creek Rd Healdsburg CA 95448

CONRON, JOHN PHELAN, architect; b. Brookline, Mass., Dec. 4, 1921; s. Carl Edward and Katherine (Phelan) C. Student, U. So. Calif., 1940-41; B.Arch., Yale U., 1948. Draftsmn. Whelan & Westman, Boston, 1948-52; owner, prin. John P. Conron (Architect), Santa Fe, N.Mex., 1952-61; partner Conron-Lent Architects, Santa Fe, 1961—, Conron-Muths (restoration architects), Santa Fe and Jackson Hole, Wyo., 1975—; pres. The Centerline, Inc., Santa Fe., 1952—. Projects include Centerline, Inc, Santa Fe, KB Ranch, near Santa Fe; restoration Stephen W. Dorsey Mansion State Monument, Colfax County, N.Mex., Palace of the Govs, Santa Fe, Pipe Spring Nat. Monument, Ariz.; Editor: La Cronica de Nuevo Mexico, 1976—; co-editor: N.Mex. Architecture mag, 1960-66; editor, 1966—. Vice Chmn. N.Mex. Cultural Properties Com., 1968-80; founder v.p. Las Trampas Found., 1967—; trustee Internat. Inst. Iberian Colonial Art, Santa Fe, pres., 1978—; bd. dirs. Preservation Action., 1976-80. Served with USAAF, 1941-45. Recipient Merit award AIA, 1962, Spl. Commendation award, 1970. Fellow AIA, Am. Soc. Interior Designers (pres. N.Mex. chpt. 1966-68, 74-75, regional v.p. 1970-73, Historic Preservation award for restoration Palace of Govs. 1980); mem. N.Mex. Soc. Architects (past pres.), Am. Soc. Man Environ. Relations (dir. 1973—), Hist. Soc. N.Mex. (1st v.p. 1979-80, pres. 1980—). Home: NW of Santa Fe Santa Fe NM 87501 Office: 314 McKenzie St Santa Fe NM 87501

CONROY, DAVID JAMES, chem., diversified mfg. co. exec.; b. Blue Island, Ill., Feb. 12, 1918; s. William Edmund and Ruth Elizabeth (King) C.; m. Lois Elizabeth Hepner, Jan. 12, 1946; children—Susan, Pamela (Mrs. Timothy Williams), Christine (Mrs. Andrew Breslin), William Peter. B.S., Harvard U., 1939, J.D., 1947. Bar: Pa. bar 1947, N.C. bar 1974. Individual practice law, Scranton, Pa., 1947-61; atty., corp. sec. Internat. Salt Co., Clarks Summit, Pa., 1961-70, Akzona Inc., Asheville, N.C., 1971—. Mem. Abington Heights (Pa.) Sch. Bd., 1958-70; pres. United Way Asheville and Buncombe County, 1979-80; trustee Meml. Mission Hosp., Asheville, 1973—, pres., 1980—; bd. dirs. Western Carolina Univ. Found., 1980—. Served with A.C. USNR, 1941-46. Decorated D.F.C. Mem. Am. Bar Assn., Am. Soc. Corp. Secs. (regional pres. 1976, dir. 1980—), Pa. Bar Assn., N.C. Bar Assn., Asheville Area C. of C. (dir. 1976-80). Clubs: Harvard (N.Y.C.); Biltmore Forest, Asheville Downtown. Home: 36 Sunset Summit Asheville NC 28804 Office: PO Box 2930 Asheville NC 28802

CONROY, DONALD PATRICK, writer; b. Atlanta, Oct. 26, 1945; s. Donald and Frances Dorothy (Peek) C.; m. Lenore Guerewitz, Mar. 21, 1945; children—Jessica, Melissa, Megan, Gregory, Emily. B.A. in English, The Citadel, 1967. Author: The Boo, 1970, The Water is Wide, 1972, The Great Santini, 1976, The Lords of Discipline, 1980 (Recipient Lillian Smith award for fiction So. Regional Council 1981, Ga. Gov.'s award for Arts 1978, NEA award for Achievement in Edn. 1974, Anisfield-Wolf award 1972). Ford Found. Leadership Devel. grantee, 1971. Mem. Authors Guild Am., Writers Guild, PEN. Democrat. Home and Office: care The Old New York Book Shop 1069 Juniper St Atlanta GA 30309

CONROY, JACK (JOHN WESLEY CONROY), author, editor; b. Moberly, Mo., Dec. 5, 1899; s. Thomas Edward and Eliza Jane (McCollough) C.; m. Elizabeth Gladys Kelly, June 30, 1922 (dec. Oct. 17, 1982); children: Margaret Jean (Mrs. James Walter Tillery, dec.), Thomas Vernon (dec.), Jack. Student, U. Mo., 1920-21; L.H.D., U. Mo. at Kansas City, 1975. Editor The Rebel Poet, 1931-32, The Anvil, 1933-37, The New Anvil, 1939-41; asso. editor Nelson's Ency. and Universal World Reference Ency., 1943-47; sr. editor New Standard Ency., Chgo., 1947-66; dir. Standard Information Service, 1949-55; lit. editor Chgo. Defender, 1946-47, Chgo. Globe, 1950; instr. fiction writing Columbia Coll., 1962-66. Author: The Disinherited, 1933, reissued 1963, A World To Win, 1935, (with Arna Bontemps) The Fast Sooner Hound, 1942, They Seek A City, 1945, Slappy Hooper, The Wonderful Sign Painter, 1946, Sam Patch, The High, Wide and Handsome Jumper, 1951, Anyplace But Here, 1966, The Jack Conroy Reader, (edited by Jack Salzman and David Ray), 1980; editor: (with Ralph Cheyney) Unrest, 1929-31, Midland Humor: A Harvest of Fun and Folklore, 1947, (with Curt Johnson) Writers in Revolt: The Anvil Anthology, 1973. John Simon Guggenheim fellow for creative writing, 1935; recipient James L. Dow award Soc. Midland Authors, 1966; award Literary Times, 1967; Lit. award Mo. Library Assn., 1977; Mark Twain award Soc. for Study Midwestern Lit., 1980; Louis M. Rabinowitz Found. grantee, 1968; Nat. Endowment of Arts grantee, 1978. Mem. Soc. Midland Authors (v.p. Mo.), Chgo. Council Fgn. Relations, Internat. Platform Assn. Methodist.

CONROY, JOHN WESLEY *See* **CONROY, JACK**

CONROY, SARAH BOOTH, writer, editor; b. Valdosta, Ga., Feb. 16, 1927; d. Weston Anthony and Ruth (Proctor) Booth; m. Richard Timothy Conroy, Dec. 31, 1949; children: Camille Booth, Sarah Claire. B.S., U. Tenn., 1950. Continuity writer Sta. WNOX, 1945-48; commentator, writer Sta. WATO, 1948-49; reporter, architecture columnist Knoxville News Sentinel, 1949-56; asso. editor The Diplomat mag., 1956-58; columnist Washington Post, 1958-68, design editor, columnist, 1970-82, staff writer style, columnist, 1982—; reporter, art critic Washington Daily News, 1968-70; regular contbr. N.Y. Times, 1968-70; mem. adv. bd. Horizon mag. Mem. AIA (hon.), Nat Arts Club. Home: 5016 16th St NW Washington DC 20011 Office: 1150 15th St NW Washington DC 20071

CONROYD, W. DANIEL, university administrator, lawyer; b. Oak Park, Ill., Oct. 1, 1920; s. Walter Earl and Lucille Mary (McCabe) C.; m. Margaret Ann McAuliff, Feb. 13, 1943; children: Colleen Conroyd Strening, Maureen Conroyd Fitzgerald, Michael, Sheila Conroyd Hogan, Alicia Conroyd Smith. B.S. in Commerce, Loyola U., Chgo., 1942; J.D., DePaul U., 1947. Bar: Ill. 1947. Clk. FBI, 1942-44; wage adminstr. Montgomery Ward & Co., 1944-45; with Loyola U., Chgo., 1945—, asst. to pres., 1955-59, v.p. devel. and pub. relations, 1959—. Bd. advisers Cath. Charities. Served with USNR, 1943. Mem. Pub. Relations Soc. Am., Am. Coll. Pub. Relations Assn., Am. Alumni Council, ABA, Ill. Bar Assn., Chgo. Bar Assn., Pub. Relations Clinic, Serra Internat., Delta Theta Phi, Tau Kappa Epsilon. Clubs: Economic, Chgo. Athletic Assn., Whitehall, Execs. (Chgo.); North Shore Country (Glenview, Ill.). Home: 3108 Walden Ln Wilmette IL 60091 Office: 820 N Michigan Ave Chicago IL 60611

CONSAGRA, SOPHIE CHANDLER, academy administrator; b. Radnor, Pa., Apr. 28, 1927; d. Alfred D. and Carol (Ramsay) Chandler; children: Maria, Pierluigi, Francesca, George. B.A., Smith Coll., 1949; M.A., Cambridge (Eng.) U., 1952. Exec. dir. Del. Arts Council, 1972-78; dir. visual arts and architecture N.Y. State Council Arts, 1978-80; dir. Am. Acad. in Rome, 1980-84, pres., 1984—; cons. Nat. Endowment Arts. Address: Am Acad in Rome 41 E 65th St New York NY 10021

CONSELMAN, FRANK BUCKLEY, geologist, educator; b. N.Y.C., Oct. 1, 1910; s. Theophile and Elinor (Lachiver) C.; m. Grace M. Carter, Feb. 17, 1934; children: Thomas T., Margaret E. (Mrs. T.E. Dunn), Charles A. B.S., N.Y. U., 1930, M.S., 1931; postgrad., Columbia, 1930-31, Harvard, summers 1930, 32; Ph.D., U. Mo., 1934.

Geologist Mo. Geol. Survey, 1934; geologist Gypsy Oil Co. and Gulf Oil Corp., 1935-41; dist. geologist Gt. Lakes Carbon Corp., 1946; dist. mgr. Am. Trading & Prodn. Co., 1947; cons. geologist, 1947-69, 76—; dir. Internat. Center for Arid and Semi-Arid Land Studies; prof. geosci. Tex. Tech U., Lubbock, 1969-76, ret., 1976, adj. prof., 1978-83, Weeks prof. petroleum geology, 1983—; Disting. prof. petroleum geology U. N.Mex., 1979; v.p. Associated Nuclear Cons. Am., Ltd., 1979—; exploration mgr., dir. Westico Energy Co., 1980-82; vis. lectr. U. Tex., 1959, 68; mem. U.S. Nat. Com. on Geology, 1970-74, U.S. Nat. Commn. for UNESCO, 1976—; mem. exec. com. Internat. Oil and Gas Ednl. Center. Served to lt. col. AUS, 1941-45. Recipient Alumni Gold medal U. Mo., 1974; N.Y. U. Alumni medal, 1980. Fellow Explorers Club; mem. Am. Assn. Petroleum Geologists (hon. mem., v.p. 1960-61, pres. 1968-69), Am. Inst. Profl. Geologists (editor 1963-65, pres. 1974, Ben H. Parker medal 1977), Am. Geol. Inst. (pres. 1975), Soc. Mining Engrs., Soc. Petroleum Engrs., Assn. Engring. Geologists, Lubbock Geol. Soc. (past pres.), Abilene Geol. Soc. (past pres., hon. mem.), Sigma Xi, Sigma Gamma Epsilon. Home: Ransom St Canyon TX 79366

CONSIDINE, FRANK WILLIAM, container corporation executive; b. Chgo., Aug. 15, 1921; s. Frank Joseph and Minnie (Regan) C.; m. Nancy Scott, Apr. 3, 1948. Ph.B., Loyola U., Chgo., 1943. Owner F. J. Hogan Agy., Chgo., 1945-47; asst. to pres. Graham Glass Co., Chgo., 1947-51; owner F.W. Considine Co., Chgo., 1951-55; v.p. Metro Glass div. Kraftco, Chgo., 1955-60; v.p., dir. Nat. Can Corp., Chgo., 1961-67, exec. v.p., 1967-69, pres., 1969—, chief exec. officer, 1973—, also mem. fin. com., chmn. exec. com., mem. corp. devel. com.; dir. Allis Chalmers Corp., Ency. Brittanica, 1st Chgo. Corp., 1st Nat. Bank Chgo., Internat. Minerals & Chem. Corp., Maytag Co., Tribune Co. Past chmn. U.S. sect. Egypt Bus. Council; trustee Loyola U., Chgo.; trustee, mem. exec. com. Mus. Sci. and Industry Chgo.; bd. dirs. Can Mfrs. Inst., Evanston Hosp., Lyric Opera of Chgo., Field Mus. Natural History, Jr. Achievement Chgo., Econ. Devel. Com. Chgo.; commr. Ill. Indsl. Devel. Authority. Served to lt. USNR, 1943-46. Mem. Econ. Club Chgo., Am. Inst. Food Distbrn. (bd. trustees, chmn.), Chgo. Assn. Commerce and Industry (past pres.). Clubs: Economic, Chicago, Commercial, Mid Am. (Chgo.); Glen View. Office: 8101 Higgins Rd Chicago IL 60631

CONSOLI, MARC-ANTONIO, composer; b. Catania, Italy, May 19, 1941; came to U.S., 1956, naturalized, 1967; s. Francesco Gabriele Settimo and Rosa (Puglisi) C.; m. Elizabeth Jean Szlek, June 19, 1971. B.Mus., N.Y. Coll. Music, 1966; M.Mus., Peabody Conservatory, 1967; M.Mus. Arts, Yale U., 1971, D.Mus. Arts, 1977. Lectr. Bridgeport U.; vis. prof. U. Western Ont., 1975. Composer, 1966—; Composer, works performed by, Balt. Symphony Orch., N.Y. Philharm., Los Angeles Philharm., Louisville Orch.,, Ensemble Kontrapunkte, Vienna, Austria, Monday Evening Concerts, Los Angeles, Berkshire Music Center, Yale Players for New Music, Gaudeamus Festival, Netherlands, Royan Festival, France; Composer commns. for, Graz (Austria) radio sta., Royan Festival, others; performer, dir.-mem., Yale Players for New Music, 1969-71, The Experiment, 1974; Composer: Equinox I, 1967, Equinox II, 1968, Isonic, 1970, Interactions I-IV, 1970-71, Profiles, 1972-73, Music for Chambers, 1974, Canti Trinacriani, 1975, Sciuri Novi I, 1974, Sciuri Novi II, 1975, Tre Canzoni, 1976, Odefonia, 1976, Vuci Siculani, 1979, Naked Masks, 1980, The Last Unicorn, 1981, Afterimages, 1982; string quartet Fantasia Celeste, 1983. Recipient award Nat. Inst.-Am. Acad. Arts and Letters, 1975; Guggenheim Found. fellow, 1971-72, 79-80; Fulbright fellow, Poland, 1972-74; Creative Artists Pub. Service grantee, 1975; Nat. Endowment for Arts grantee, 1979. Mem. Broadcast Music Inc., Am. Composers Alliance, Am. Music Center. Address: 95-27 239th St Bellerose NY 11426

CONSTABLE, ELINOR GREER, diplomat; b. San Diego, Feb. 8, 1934; d. Marshall Raymond and Katherine (French) Greer; m. Peter Dalton Constable, Mar. 8, 1958; children: Robert, Philip, Julia. B.A., Wellesley Coll., 1955. Mem. staff Dept. Interior, 1955-71, Dept. State, 1955-71, OEO, 1955-71; sr. assoc. Transcentury Corp., Washington, 1971-72; with Dept. State, Washington, 1973-77, dir. investment affairs, 1978-80; dep. asst. sec. Internat. Fin. and Devel., 1980-83, dep. asst. sec. for econ. and bus. affairs, 1983—; capital devel. officer US AID, Pakistan, 1977-78. Office: US Dept State 2201 C St NW Washington DC 20520

CONSTABLE, GILES, historian, research library executive; b. London, Eng., June 1, 1929; s. William George and Olivia (Carson-Roberts) C.; m. Esther Van Horne Young, 1959; children: Olivia Renie, John Van Horne. B.A., Harvard U., 1950, Ph.D., 1957; Dr. (hon.), U. Paris (France), 1980. Tutor history Harvard U., Cambridge, Mass., 1954-55, asst. prof. to assoc. prof., 1958-66, Lea Prof. medieval history, 1966-77, prof. history, 1977—; dir. Dumbarton Oaks Research Library and Collection, Washington, 1977—, bd. scholars, 1973-80, sr. fellow, 1980—; lectr. Center Advanced Studies Medieval Civilization, Poitiers, France, 1961; vis. prof. Catholic U. Am., 1978—. Asst. editor: Speculum, 1958-78; editor: Petrus Venerabilis 1156-1956, 1956; author: Monastic Tithes from Their Origins to the Twelfth Century, 1964, The Letters of Peter the Venerable, 1967, Medieval Monasticism: A Select Bibliography, 1976, Letters and Letter Collections, 1976, Religious Life and Thought, 1979; editor: Consuetudines benedictinae variae, 1975. Guggenheim fellow, 1967-68. Fellow Medieval Acad. Am. (v.p. 1978-79, 79-80), Royal Hist. Soc.; mem. Am. Hist. Assn., New Eng. Hist. Assn. (v.p. 1975-76, pres. 1977-78), New Eng. Medieval Conf. (pres. 1976-77). Address: Dumbarton Oaks 1703 32rd St Washington DC 20007 *

CONSTABLE, PETER DALTON, ambassador; b. Syracuse, N.Y., Apr. 10, 1932; s. Robert Dalton and Theckla (Youngblood) C.; m. Elinor Jackson Greer, Mar. 8, 1958; children: Robert Dalton, Philip Sherburne, Julia French. A.B., Hamilton Coll., 1953; M.A., Johns Hopkins U., 1957; student, Nat. War Coll., 1972-73. Research asst. U.S. Senate, Washington, 1956-57; fgn. service officer Dept. State, 1957—, dir. Pakistan, Afghanistan and Bangladesh affairs, Washington, 1972-76, dep. chief of mission, Islamabad, Pakistan, 1976-79, dep. asst. sec., Washington, 1979-82; ambassador to Zaire, Kinshasa, 1982—. Served with U.S. Army, 1953-55. Recipient Disting. Honor award Dept. State, 1981. Mem. Am. Fgn. Service Assn. *

CONSTANCE, THOMAS ERNEST, lawyer; b. Union City, N.J., May 16, 1936; s. James and Effie (Economides) C.; m. Janet Barbara Raynor, Nov. 21, 1970; children: Nicole Susan, Jo Anne Barbara, Patricia Anne. B.S., NYU, 1958; J.D., St. John's U., 1964. Bar: N.Y. 1965. Since practiced in N.Y.C.; partner, mem. exec. com. Shea & Gould, 1971—; dir., mem. audit com. Weldotron Corp., 1979—; dir. U.S. Playing Cards Corp., Repco, Inc.; mem. audit com. Polycast Technology Corp. Served to lt. AUS, 1958-60. Mem. ABA, Bar Assn. City N.Y., Sigma Phi Epsilon, Phi Delta Phi. Clubs: The University (N.Y.C.); Manhasset Bay (N.Y.) Yacht. Home: Longwood Rd Sands Point NY 11050 Office: 330 Madison Ave New York NY 10017

CONSTANTIN, JAMES ALFORD, educator; b. Tulsa, June 15, 1922; s. Jules Joseph and Nelle (Alford) C.; m. Wanda Anita Moyer, May 18, 1941; children—Nina Katherine (Mrs. Robert Dean Beaird), James Alford, Jules Joseph II, Anne C. (Mrs. Gary A. Calinsky). B.B.A., U. Tex., 1943, M.B.A., 1944, Ph.D., 1950. Instr. U. Tex., 1946-47; asst. prof., asso. prof., asst. dir. Bur. Bus. Research, U. Ala., Tuscaloosa, 1947-52; asso. prof. U. Wash., 1952-53; prof. mktg. and transp. U. Okla., Norman, 1953—, David Ross Boyd prof. bus. adminstrn., 1969—. Author: (with W.J. Hudson) Motor Transportation, 1958, Principles of Logistics Management, 1966, (with W.N. Peach) Zimmermann's World Resources and Industries, 3d edit, (with R.E. Evans, M.L. Morris) Marketing Strategy and Management, 1976. Served with USAAF, 1942-43. Mem. Transp. Research Forum, Am. Soc. Traffic and Transp. Home: 520 Merrywood Ln Norman OK 73069

CONSTANTINE, MICHAEL, actor; b. Reading, Pa., May 22, 1927; s. Theoharis and Andromache (Foteadou) Efstration; m. Julianna McCarthy, Oct. 5, 1953 (div. Apr. 1973); children—Thea, Brendan; m. Kathleen Patricia Christopherson, Sept. 29, 1974; stepchildren—Casey and Eric Martin. Grad. high sch. Broadway debut in Inherit The Wind; understudy to: Paul Muni, 1955-57; appeared in: Broadway plays Arturo Ui, The Miracle Worker, Compulsion, The Egg; numerous television prodns., including The Love Tapes, 79 Park Ave., The Pirate; motion pictures include The North Avenue Irregulars, 1979, The Reivers, Justine, The Hustler, If Its Tuesday This Must Be Belgium, Don't Drink the Water, Voyage of the Damned; appeared in numerous TV movies; star: TV series Room 222, 1968-74, Sirotta's Court, 1976 (Recipient Emmy award for best supporting actor in comedy series 1969) *

CONSTON, HENRY SIEGISMUND, lawyer; b. Dresden, Germany, Dec. 18, 1928; came to U.S., 1947, naturalized, 1952. B.S. in Bus. Adminstrn, N.Y. U., 1955, J.D., 1958, LL.M., 1961. Bar: N.Y. State 1959. With Calif. Tex. Oil Corp., N.Y.C., 1947-61; asso. firm Walter Conston & Schurtman, P.C., and predecessors, 1961-62; mem. firm Walter Conston Schurtman & Gumpel (P.C., and predecessors), 1962—; reporter Internat. Fiscal Congress, 1974. Contbr. articles to legal jours. Bd. dirs. Margaret Tietz Center for Nursing Care, N.Y. Found. Nursing Homes, Inc. Mem. N.Y.C. Bar Assn., Internat. Fiscal Assn. Office: 90 Park Ave New York NY 10016

CONTA, BART JOSEPH, educator; b. Rochester, N.Y., Mar. 29, 1914; s. Joseph and Mary (Dalcin) C.; m. Ruth Fletcher, Nov. 26, 1937; childrenFred, Jacquelyn (Mrs. Jefferson Tippett), Susan (Mrs. Steven Kearl). B.S., U. Rochester, 1936; M.S., Cornell U., 1937. Registered profl. engr., N.Y. Instr. Cornell U., Ithaca, N.Y., 1937-40, asst. prof., asso. prof. mech. engring., 1941-47, prof., 1951—; research engr. Texaco Corp., Beacon, N.Y., 1940- 41; prof. mech. engring. Syracuse U., 1947-51; Ford Found. vis. prof. Universidad del Valle, Cali, Colombia, 1964-65. NSF fellow U. Calif. at Berkeley, 1967-68. Mem. AAAS, AAUP, Soc. for History Tech., Phi Beta Kappa, Sigma Xi, Tau Beta Pi, Pi Tau Sigma, Phi Kappa Phi. Clubs: Statler (past pres.), Tower.). Home: 211 White Park Rd Ithaca NY 14850

CONTA, LEWIS DALCIN, mechanical engineer; b. Rochester, N.Y., Sept. 16, 1912; s. Joseph and Mary Elizabeth (Dalcin) C.; m. Hilda Agnes Bowen, Aug. 31, 1935 (div.); children: Jean Patricia Conta Holland, Barbara Ann Conta Boyer, Robert Lewis; m. Carolyn H. Conklin. B.S. with highest distinction, U. Rochester, 1934, M.S., 1935; Ph.D., Cornell U., 1942. Registered profl. engr., N.Y. Instr. U. Rochester, N.Y., 1935-37, prof. mech. engring., chmn. engring. div., 1950-59, asso. dean for grad. studies, 1959-64; on leave as program dir. spl. engring. programs engring. div. NSF, 1967-69; instr. Cornell, Ithaca, N.Y., 1937-42, asst. prof. mech. engring., 1942-46; instr. diesel engine Naval Tng., 1941-42, asst. supr., 1942-45, supr., 1945-46; research engr. and sect. head Air Reduction Research Labs., Murray Hill, N.J., 1946-48, cons., 1948-60; dean engring., dir. div., also prof. U. R.I., Kingston, 1969-77; dir. Univ. Energy Center, dir. div. research and devel., prof. mech. engring., 1977-78, prof. emeritus, 1980—; resident engr. Engring. Socs. Commn. on Energy, Washington, 1978-80; engring. cons., 1980—; adj. prof. aerospace and mech. engring. U. Ariz., 1980—; cons. and research Crucible Steel Co., Marquette Metal Products Co., NRC, Thermoelectron Corp., A.D. Little, Inc., Brookhaven Nat. Lab., others; mem. com. to reorganize Navy Diesel Engine Schs., Washington, Feb.-Apr. 1943; mem. commn. on Edn. for Engring. Professions, Nat. Assn. State Univs. and Land Grant Colls., 1971-74. Author tech. papers and reports. Mem. ASME (v.p. 1966-68, v.p. for research 1981-83, chmn. Rochester sect. 1956-57, chmn. diesel and gas engine power div. 1973-74, mem. policy bd. research 1973-81), Am. Soc. Engring. Edn. (chmn. New Eng. sect. 1970), Nat. Soc. Profl. Engrs., AAUP, Assn. Engring. Colls. N.Y. (pres. 1953-55), Phi Beta Kappa, Sigma Xi, Tau Beta Pi, Phi Kappa Phi, Pi Tau Sigma. Patentee in field. Home: 915 LaHuerta Green Valley AZ 85614

CONTE, RICHARD NICHOLAS, architect; b. Pitts., Sept. 14, 1918; s. Phillip and Margaret (Del Gauido) C.; m. Ida Weinstein, June 18, 1956. B.S., U. Ill., 1947; student, Royal Academia de Bella Arts, Italy, 1945, Roosevelt U., 1948-49. With planning dept. U. Ill. Med. Campus, Chgo., 1941; draftsman Harza Engring Co., Chgo. and Wyo., 1942, Traveleti & Suter, 1946; architect Leickenko & Esser, 1947-50; partner Barancik, Conte & Assos., Chgo., 1950—; archtl. instr. U. Ill., 1946-47. Served with AUS, 1942-45. Mem. A.I.A. Home: 1116 W North Shore Chicago IL 60626 Office: 407 S Dearborn St Chicago IL 60605

CONTE, SAMUEL DANIEL, computer scientist; b. Lackawanna, N.Y., June 5, 1917; s. Samuel and Amelia (Jiuditta) C.; m. Margaret Mary Boyle, Oct. 24, 1970; children—Cheryl, Robert. B.S., Buffalo State Coll., 1939; M.S., U. Buffalo, 1943; Ph.D., U. Mich., 1950. Prof. Wayne State U., 1946-56; mgr. math. dept. Aerospace Corp., Los Angeles, 1956-62; head computer sci. dept. Purdue U., Lafayette, Ind., 1962-79, prof. computer sci., 1979—; cons. NSF. Author: Elementary Numerical Analysis, 3d edit., 1980, Solid State Geometry, 1956, Plasma Dispersion Function, 1961; Contbr. articles profl. jours. Served with AUS, 1943-46. Mem. Am. Math. Soc., Assn. for Computing Machinery, Soc. for Indsl. and Applied Math., Math. Assn. Am. Home: 3746 Capilano Dr West Lafayette IN 47906

CONTE, SILVIO O., congressman; b. Pittsfield, Mass., Nov. 9, 1921; s. Ottavio and Lucia (Lora) C.; m. Corinne L. Duval, Nov. 11, 1947; children: Michele, Sylvia, John, Gayle. LL.B., Boston Coll., 1949; hon. degrees, Williams Coll., 1970, Hampshire Coll., North Adams State Coll., 1972, U. Mass., 1974, Amherst Coll., Boston Coll., Georgetown U., Boston U., 1983, Westfield State Coll., 1983. Bar: Mass. 1949. Since practiced in, Pittsfield; mem. 86th-97th congresses 1st Dist. Mass.; mem. appropriations com., transp. subcom., house select com. on small bus., migratory bird conservation commn.; mem. Mass. Senate, 1950-58; chmn. coms. on ins., constl. law, jud., chmn. legis. research council, chmn. spl. coms. for investigation health and welfare trust funds; co-chmn. New Eng. Congressional Caucus, 1973—. Bd. regents Smithsonian Instn. Named outstanding young man of year Mass. Jr. C. of C., 1954. Republican. Office: 2300 Rayburn House Office Bldg Washington DC 20515 also 78 Center St Arterial Pittsfield MA 01201 also 200 High St Holyoke MA

CONTER, THOMAS MICHAEL, publisher; b. Oak Park, Ill., May 5, 1949; s. Frank Joseph and Marlene Barbara (Dantzeisen) C.; m. Belinda Alice Lawrence, Aug. 4, 1973; 1 dau., Meghann Lorean. B.A., U. Ill.-Chgo., 1971, J.D., 1974. Bar: Ill. 1974, Colo. 1977. Project mgr. Callaghan and Co., Glenview, Ill., 1974-76; sponsoring editor Shepard's/McGraw-Hill, Colorado Spring, 1976-79, editor-in-chief, 1979-81; pub. John Wiley & Sons, Inc., Colorado Spring, 1981—. Editor: Negligence Compensation, Vol. 15, 1975, Negligence Compensation, Vol. 16, 1975, Negligence Compensation, Vol. 17, 1976. Mem. Am. Judicature Soc., Ill. State Bar Assn., Assn. Trial lawyers Am., ABA. Office: John Wiley & Sons Inc 627 N Weber St Colorado Springs CO 80903 *I have always been a positivist. If two different outcomes are likely in any given situation, I will hope and plan on the rosy scenario.*

CONTERATO, BRUNO PAUL, architect; b. Chgo., June 12, 1920; (married); 3 children. B.S., Ill. Inst. Tech., 1948. Registered architect, Ill. Partner Office of Mies Van Der Rohe, Chgo., 1969-75; prin. firm Fujikawa, Conterato, Lohan & Assos., Chgo., 1975—; chmn. bd. FCL Assocs., Chgo., 1983—. Pres. alumni bd. Ill. Inst. Tech., 1984—, trustee, 1984—. Served to capt. USAAF, 1942-45, 51-53. Fellow AIA (dir., v.p., pres. Chgo. chpt. 1970-75, v.p. Ill. council 1974, dir. Ill. council 1973). Home: 225 Country Club Pl Geneva IL 60134 Office: 225 N Michigan Ave Chicago IL 60601

CONTI, JAMES JOSEPH, educator, chem. engr.; b. Coraopolis, Pa., Nov. 2, 1930; s. James Joseph and Mary (Smrekar) C.; m. Concetta Razziano, May 13, 1961; children—Lori Ann, James Robert. B.Chem. Engring., Poly. Inst. Bklyn., 1954, M.Chem. Engring., 1956, D. Chem. Engring., 1959. Sr. engr. Bettis atomic power div. Westinghouse Electric Corp., 1958-59; mem. faculty Poly. Inst. N.Y., 1959—, prof. chem. engring., 1965—, chmn. dept., 1964-70, provost, 1970-78, v.p. ednl. devel., 1978—; cons. to industry and govt., 1960—. Author articles. Trustee Webb Inst. Naval Architecture. Fellow Am. Inst. Chemists; mem. Am. Inst. Chem. Engrs., Am. Soc. Engring. Edn., N.Y. Acad. Scis., AAAS, Sigma Xi, Tau Beta Pi, Phi Lambda Upsilon, Omega Chi Epsilon. Patentee in field. Home: 26 Miami Rd Bethpage NY 11714 Office: Broad Hollow Rd Farmingdale NY 11735

CONTI, SAMUEL, judge; b. Los Angeles, July 16, 1922; s. Fred and Katie C.; m. Dolores Crosby, July 12, 1952; children: Richard, Robert, Cynthia. B.S., U. Santa Clara, 1945; LL.B., Stanford U., 1948, LL.D. Bar: Calif. 1948. Pvt. practice, San Francisco and Contra Costa County, 1948-60, city atty., Concord, Calif., 1960-69; judge Superior Ct. Contra Costa County, 1968-70, U.S. Dist. Ct., No. Dist. Calif., San Francisco, 1970—. Mem. Bd. Edn. Pittsburg Unified Sch. Dist., 1952-58; mem. Sch. Redistricting Com. for Contra Costa County, 1956-58. Served with AUS, 1940-44. Mem. Central Contra Costa Bar Assn. (pres.), Concord C. of C. (pres.), Alpha Sigma Nu. Office: US Dist Court House PO Box 36060 San Francisco CA 94102

CONTI, SAMUEL FRANCIS, university dean; b. Bklyn., Dec. 24, 1931; s. John and Sabina C.; m. Judith Rosenberg, Jan. 27, 1954; children: Deborah, Scott, Suzanne. B.S., Bklyn. Coll., 1952; M.S., U. Conn., 1956; Ph.D., Cornell U., 1959. Research asso. Brookhaven Nat. Lab., Upton, N.Y., 1959-61; instr. Dartmouth Coll. Med. Sch., 1961-62, asst. prof. microbiology, 1962-63, asso. prof., 1963-66; dir. T.H. Morgan Sch. Biol. Scis.; asso. dean arts and sci. U. Ky., Lexington, 1966-80; dean grad. studies and research U. Mass., Amherst, 1980, acting dean engring., 1981-82, acting provost, vice chancellor, 1983-84, vice-chancellor research, 1984—; Found. Microbiology lectr., 1967-68, 79-80; chmn. basic sci. commn. McDowell Cancer Network, 1976-80; mem. nat. adv. council allergy and infectious disease NIH, 1982; chmn. com. govtl. and assn. relations Council Grad. Schs., 1983. Editorial bd.: Jour. Bacteriology, 1965-80, Biology Digest, 1973—. Mem. Ky. Gov.'s Commn. on Endangered Species, 1977-80. Served in U.S. Army, 1953-55. Recipient Career Devel. award NIH, 1963-66; W.B. Sturgill award U. Ky., 1978. Mem. Am. Acad. Microbiology, Am. Soc. Microbiology, Am. Soc. Biol. Chemistry, AAAS, Phi Kappa Phi. Home: 40 Harris Mountain Rd Amherst MA 01002 Office: Grad Research Center U Mass Amherst MA 01003

CONTI, THOMAS ANTONIO, actor, writer, director; b. Paisley, Scotland, Nov. 22, 1941; s. Alfonso and Mary (McGoldrick) C.; m. Kara Drummond Wilson, July 2, 1967; 1 dau., Nina. Appeared in plays on London's West End; Savages, Other People, The Black and White Minstels, Don Juan; Broadway debut in: Whose Life Is It Anyway?, 1979 (Tony award); appeared in: They're Playing Our Song, 1980; dir.: Before the Party, 1980; appeared in films, including: Galileo, Eclipse, Merry Christmas Mr. Lawrence, Reuben, Reuben, American Dreamer, Saving Grace; appeared in TV plays, including: The Beaux Stratagem; appeared in: Brit. TV prodns. Glittering Prizes, Princess and the Pea, Faerie Tale Theatre. Club: Garrick (London). Office: care Chatto and Linnit Globe Theatre Shaftesbury Ave London W1 England

CONTIE, LEROY JOHN, JR., judge; b. Canton, Ohio, Apr. 2, 1920; s. Leroy John and Mary M. (DeSantis) C.; m. Janice M. Zollars, Nov. 28, 1953; children: Ann L., Leroy John III. B.A., U. Mich., 1941, J.D., 1948. Bar: Ohio 1948. Law dir. City of Canton, 1952-60; chmn. Canton City Charter Commn., 1963; mem. Stark County Bd. Elections, Canton, 1964-69; judge Common Pleas Ct., Stark County, 1969-71, U.S. Dist. Ct., No. Dist. Ohio, Cleve., 1971-82, U.S. Ct. Appeals (6th cir.), Cin., 1982—. Trustee Stark County Legal Aid Soc., Canton chpt. ARC; adv. bd. Walsh Coll., Canton, Ohio., U. Akron Law Coll. Served with AUS, 1942-46. Mem. Am., Ohio, Stark County, Summit County, Cuyahoga County, Akron bar assns., Am. Judicature Soc., U.S. Jr. C. of C. (internat. senator), Canton Jr. C. of C. (trustee), Stark County Hist. Soc., Stark County Wilderness Soc., Am. Legion, Sigma Phi Epsilon (Nat. citation award), Phi Alpha Delta., Omicron Delta Kappa. Roman Catholic. Clubs: K.C. (4 deg.), Elks.). Office: US Courthouse Akron OH 44308

CONTNEY, JOHN J., association executive; b. Milw., Oct. 15, 1932; s. Francis Anthony and Rose (Nowicki) C.; m. Dawn Georgette Wintz, Sept. 7, 1963; children: Wade Anthony, Ross Joseph. B.A., Marquette U., 1956, M.B.A., 1965; M.S., Barry U., 1975. Asst. to v.p. Boston Store, Milw., 1950-56; v.p., sales mgr. Records Unlimited, Inc., Milw., 1956-60; exec. v.p. Columbia S.E., Miami, Fla., 1960-63; asst. to pres. Color Corp., Tampa, Fla., 1964-65; mgr. mktg. Textile Rental Services Assn. Am. (formerly Linen Supply Assn. Am.), Miami, 1965-72, asst. exec. dir., 1973, gen. mgr., 1974-75, exec. dir., 1975—; Lectr. various groups.; chmn. edn. com., sponsor Clean '83. Contbr. articles to profl. jours. Served with AUS, 1954-56. Mem. Am. Soc. Assn. Execs., Fla. Soc. Assn. Execs. (past pres., Exec. of Year 1982), World Ednl. Congress Laundering and Dry Cleaning (chmn. laudry cleaning council), South Fla. Assn. Execs., Am. Mktg. Assn., Alpha Delta Sigma. Home: 601 Grand Concourse Miami Shores FL 33138 Office: 1250 E Hallandale Beach Blvd Suite 703 Hallandale FL 33009

CONTOIS, DAVID ELY, coll. dean; b. Battle Creek, Mich., Jan. 18, 1928; s. Ely Joseph and Grace (Gillard) C.; m. Lois Warren Swiggett, Sept. 7, 1952; children—Michael J., Charles D. Student, U. Mich., 1945-47; B.A., U. Cal. at Los Angeles, 1950; M.S., U. Hawaii, 1952; Ph.D., U. Cal. at San Diego, 1957. Asst. research microbiologist Scripps Inst. Oceanography, U. Cal. at San Diego, 1953-58; asst. prof. microbiology U. Hawaii, 1958-64, asso. prof., 1964-68, prof., 1968—, chmn. dept., 1962-64, dir. biology program, 1961-64, asst. dean, 1964-66, asso. dean, 1966-69, dean, 1969—; cons. microbiologist, 1958-64; Chmn. steering com. Foundational Approaches to Sci. Teaching, 1966—; mem. Hawaii Curriculum Council, 1966-68. Served with AUS, 1947-48. NIH grantee, 1958-60; NSF grantee, 1962-64. Mem. AAAS, Am. Soc. Microbiology, Soc. Gen. Microbiology, Sigma Xi, Theta Chi.

Research, publs. on marine microbiology and microbial growth kinetics, 1953. Home: 1599 Kalani Uka Pl Honolulu HI 96821

CONTRERAS, FRANCISCO, airline executive; b. Mexico City, June 16, 1934; s. Francisco and Raquel (Serrano) C.; m. Maria de Lourdes Rodrigues, Sept. 22, 1956; children: Francisco, Javier, Maria de Lourdes, Raquel. B.A., U. So. Calif., 1956; postgrad., Harvard U., 1969. Mgr. pub. relations Coca-Cola Export, Mexico and Central Am., 1966-69, dir. mktg. systems, 1969-72; regional dir. sales and services Eastern Airlines, Mexico City, 1972-76, v.p. sales and services, 1976—; sports commentator Televisa TV, Mexico, 1966—. Adviser Nat. Tourism Council, 1966—. Mem. Skull and Dagger. Clubs: Univ., Skal (Mexico City). Mem. Davis Cup tennis, 1953-65. Nat. collegiate doubles tennis champion, 1956, 57. Home: Antonio Sola 18 Mexico DF Mexico 06600 Office: Eastern Air Lines Inc Plaza de la Reforma 30 Mexico DF Mexico 06600

CONTRERAS, PHILLIP A., lawyer, mfg. co. exec.; b. El Paso, Tex., Oct. 2, 1934; s. Felipe and Margaret (Edgar) C.; m. Carolyn E. Ahnert, Aug. 24, 1962; children—Kimberly, Kelly, Kaysi. B.S. in Civil Engring, Seattle U., 1958; LL.B., So. Meth. U., 1965. Bar: Tex. bar 1966. Engr. trainee Boullion, Griffith & Christofferson, Seattle, 1955-58; hydraulic engr. U.S.C.E., Dallas, 1961-66; mgr. properties for Latin Am. Braniff Internat., Dallas, 1966-68; legal counsel, asst. sec. Mohawk Airlines, Utica, N.Y., 1968-71; v.p. legal internat. White Motor Corp., Eastlake, Ohio, 1971-75, asst. gen. counsel, sec., 1975-79; also dir., pres. WMISA, 1975-79; dir. numerous subs. White Motor Corp.; v.p., gen. counsel Ferro Corp., 1979—. Bd. dirs. Cosmopolitan Community Center, Utica, N.Y., 1968-71. Served to 1st lt. U.S. Army, 1958-61. Mem. Tex., Am. bar assns., Am. Soc. Internat. Law, Am. Soc. Corp. Secs., Tex. Soc. Profl. Engrs., Ohio Fgn. Commerce Assn., Greater Cleve. Internat. Lawyers Club. Roman Catholic. Clubs: Mayfield Village Racquet, Cleve. Soaring. Home: 11419 Snow White Dr Dallas TX 75229 Office: Ferro Corp One Erieview Plaza Cleveland OH 44114

CONVERSE, CHANDLER B., investment company executive; b. Boston, Oct. 18, 1931; s. Roger W. and Rose (Bullock) C.; m. Jean McElroy, June 19, 1954; children: Chandler B., Floyd McElroy. B.A., Yale U., 1954; M.B.A., Stanford U., 1959. With E. F. Hutton, San Francisco, Calif., 1956-59; with Calvin Bullock Ltd., N.Y.C., 1959—, pres., 1979—, also dir.; dir. Nation-Wide Securities; Monthly Income Shares, Money Shares, High Income Shares, Banner Fund, Bullock Tax-Free Shares. Served with U.S. Army, 1954-56. Clubs: River, Siwanoy Country. Office: Calvin Bullock Ltd One Wall St New York NY 10005

CONVERSE, GORDON NOBLE, photo-journalist; b. Medford, Mass., July 16, 1920; s. Stanley C. and Alice (Noble) C.; m. Shirley E. Wixon, Sept. 27, 1947; children—Linda J., Deborah J. Student, Tilton Jr. Coll., 1939-41, N.Y. Inst. Photography, 1941-42. Photo editor Christian Sci. Monitor, Boston, 1946—. Co-author: Come See the Place—The Holy Land Jesus Knew, 1978, Fishers of Men—The Way of the Apostles, 1980; One-man show, Siembab Gallery, Boston, 1963; exhbt. group shows, Principia Coll., Harvard, Boston U., DeCordova Mus., Boston Arts Festival, Boston Mus. Fine Arts Sch. Recipient Brotherhood award Nat. Conf. Christians and Jews, 1955, 60, Newhouse citation Syracuse U. Sch. Journalism, 1961, Nat. Sch. Bell award, 1961, award in photography Freedoms Found., 1964, Yankee Quill award Acad. New Eng. Journalists, 1965. Mem. Nat. Press Photographers Assn. (Newspaper-Mag. Photographer of Year 1959, Picture of Year-1st place Presdl. award 1964, 1st place pictorial picture of year 1965, Graflex award Photographer of Year 1965), Boston Press Photographers Assn. (recipient over 50 awards). Home: 67 Pine St Needham MA 02192 Office: 1 Norway St Boston MA 02115

CONVERSE, PHILIP ERNEST, social science educator; b. Concord, N.H., Nov. 17, 1928; s. Ernest Luther and Evelyn (Eaton) C.; m. Jean Gilmore McDonnell, Aug. 25, 1951; children: Peter Everett, Timothy McDonnell. B.A., Denison U., 1949, D.H.L. (hon.), 1974; M.A., State U. Iowa, 1950; cert., U. Paris, 1954; M.A., U. Mich., 1956, Ph.D., 1958; D.H.L. (hon.), U. Chgo., 1979. Asst. prof. sociology U. Mich., 1960-65, prof. sociology and polit. sci., 1965—, Robert C. Angell Disting. prof., 1975—; asst. study dir. Inst. Social Research U. Mich., 1956-58, study dir., 1958-65, program dir., 1965-82, dir. Ctr. for Polit. Studies, 1982—; trustee Ctr. Advanced Study in Behavioral Scis., 1980—, Russell Sage Found., 1982—. Co-author: The American Voter, 1960, Elections and the Political Order, 1966, The Human Meaning of Social Change, 1972, The Quality of American Life, 1976; contbr. articles to profl. jours. Served with U.S. Army, 1950-52. Recipient Disting. Faculty Achievement award U. Mich., 1973; Fulbright fellow, 1959-60; NSF fellow, 1967-68; Guggenheim fellow, 1975-76; Ctr. Advanced Study in Behavioral Scis. fellow, 1979-80. Mem. AAAS, Am. Sociol. Assn., Am. Polit. Sci. Assn. (pres. 1983—), Internat. Soc. Polit. Psychology (pres. 1980-81), Internat. Studies Assn., Nat. Acad. Scis., Am. Acad. Arts and Scis. Home: 1212 Cambridge Rd Ann Arbor MI 48104 Office: Institute for Social Research The Univ of Mich Ann Arbor MI 48104

CONVERTI, VINCENZO, computer services manager; b. Roseto, Italy, Nov. 11, 1925; came to U.S., 1949; s. Rocco and Maria Antoinette (Russo) C.; m. Marjorie Ruth Pefley, Sept. 12, 1951; children: Mark, David, Paul, Cathy. B.S. in E.E., U. Ariz.-Tucson, 1952, M.S., 1956. Research engr. Ariz. Computer Research, Phoenix, 1955-59; systems engring. supr. Ariz. Pub. Service, Phoenix, 1959-67, systems engring. mgr., 1967-75, computer service mgr., 1975—. Contbr. in field. Fellow IEEE (chmn. power system engring. com. 1980-81). Republican. Home: 7039 N 14th St Phoenix AZ 85020 Office: Ariz Pub Service PO Box 21666 Phoenix AZ 85020

CONVERY, FRANK WRAY, communications comnpany executive; b. Peterborough, Ont., Can., Aug. 2, 1925; s. Frank Ernest and Iris (Wray) C.; m. Marilyn Joyce Hebb, Sept. 11, 1954; children: Mark, Steven, Michael, Lynn. B.A., U. Western Ont., 1948. Account exec. F.H. Hayhurst Co. Ltd. (advt. agy.), Toronto, Ont., 1950-60, v.p., 1960-70, dir. account services, 1965-70, pres., 1970-81, chmn., pres., 1982; chmn. Hedwyn Communications Inc., Toronto, 1983—; dir. Willhurst Communications Ltd., Caledon Advt. Ltd. Bd. govs. North York Gen. Hosp. Served with RCAF, 1943-45; Served with Royal Naval Vol. Res., 1945. Mem. Inst. Canadian Advt. (dir. 1971—), Kappa Alpha. Club: Donalda (Toronto). Office: Hedwyn Communications Inc 55 Eglinton Ave Suite 500 East Toronto ON Canada M4P 1G9

CONVY, BERT, actor; b. St. Louis, June 23, 1939; s. Bert and Monica Convy; m. Anne; children—Jennifer, Joshua, Jona. Game show host, actor, singer; host: TV prodns. Tattletales, 1974, The Late Summer, Early Fall Bert Convy Show, 1976; appeared in: motion pictures Semi-Tough, 1978, Hero At Large, 1980 (Recipient Emmy award as best game show host Nat. Acad. TV Arts and Scis. 1977). Address: care Creative Artists Agy 1888 Century Park E Suite 1400 Los Angeles CA 90067 *

CONWAY, ALVIN JAMES, hospital administrator; b. N.Y.C., Aug. 18, 1925; s. James and Florence (Farbman) C.; children: James, John, Susan, Christopher. B.A. in Mgmt., CCNY, 1952; M.S. in Hosp. Adminstrn., Columbia U., 1954. Exec. dir. Knickerbocker Hosp., N.Y.C., 1960-70; dir. div. health and hosps. Roman Catholic Charities Diocese Bklyn., 1970—; pres. Cath. Med. Ctr. Bklyn. and Queens, Jamaica, N.Y., 1970—; lectr. preceptor Columbia U. Sch. Pub. Health, Cornell U. Sloan Inst. Hosp. Adminstrn., 1960—. Contbr. articles to profl. jours. Served with AUS, 1943-46. Fellow Am. Coll. Hosp. Adminstrs., Royal Soc. Health, Am. Pub. Health Assn.; mem. N.Y. Hosp. Assn., Greater N.Y. Hosp. Assn. (gov. 1970-80), Queensboro Council Social Welfare (dir. 1973—). Roman Catholic. Home: 219 Martling Ave Tarrytown NY 10591 Office: 88-25 153d St Jamaica NY 11432

CONWAY, DWIGHT COLBUR, educator; b. Long Beach, Calif., Nov. 14, 1930; s. Dee A. and Ruth (Mills) C.; m. Diane Faye Coulter, Aug. 25, 1962; children—Kathleen Coulter, Karyn Mills, Michael Dwight, Patrick Hugh. B.S., U. Calif. at Berkeley, 1952; M.S., U. Chgo., 1953, Ph.D., 1956. Postdoctoral student Purdue U., West Lafayette, Ind., 1956-57, asst. prof., 1957-63; asso. prof. chemistry Tex. A. and M. U., College Station, 1963-67, prof., 1967—. U.S. Rubber Co. fellow, 1953-54; DuPont teaching fellow, 1954-55; recipient Excellence in Teaching award Standard Oil Co. of Ind., 1969. Mem. Am. Chem. Soc. (chmn.), Am. Phys. Soc., Am. Soc. Mass Spectrometry, Phi Beta Kappa, Sigma Xi, Alpha Chi Sigma. Home: 1909 Bee Creek Dr College Station TX 77840 Office: Dept Chemistry Tex A and M U College Station TX 77843

CONWAY, E. VIRGIL, banker, lawyer; b. Southhampton, N.Y., Aug. 2, 1929; m. Elaine Wingate, June 28, 1969; children: Allison, Sarah (by previous marriage). B.A. magna cum laude in Philosophy and Religion, Colgate U., 1951; LL.B. cum laude, Yale U., 1956. Bar: N.Y. 1956. Asso. firm Debevoice, Plimpton, Lyons and Gates, N.Y.C., 1956-64; 1st. dept. supt. Banks of State N.Y., 1964-67; sec. N.Y. State Banking Bd., 1964-67; exec. v.p. Manhattan Savs. Bank, N.Y.C., 1967-68; pres., chmn., trustee The Seamen's Bank for Savs., 1969—; dir. Union Pacific Corp.; chmn. exec. compensation com., mem. exec. and fin. coms.; dir. J.P. Stevens & Co., Inc., chmn. investment com., mem. audit and exec. compensation coms.; dir. Nat. Securities and Research Corp.; trustee, mem. exec. com. Atlantic Mut. Ins. Co.; trustee, chmn. fin. com., mem. exec., exec. compensation, nominating, budget and contracts coms. Consol. Edison Co. of N.Y.; N.Y. rep. Conf. of State Bank Suprs., 1970-77, mem. adv. council, 1973-74; mem. adv. com. to N.Y. State Supt. Banks, 1967-70. Editor: Yale Law Jour. Chmn. Temporary State Commn. on Water Supply Needs of Southeastern N.Y., 1970-75; mem. Audit Com. N.Y.C., Mayor's Mgmt. Adv. Bd., N.Y.C., 1975-77; del. Republican State Conv. N.Y., 1962, 66; pres. N.Y. Young Rep. Club, 1962-63; bd. mgrs. Seaman's Ch. Inst. N.Y. and N.J.; mem. adv. bd. N.Y. U. Real Estate Inst.; bd. dirs. Realty Found. N.Y.; bd. dirs., mem. audit, fin., exec. coms. Josiah Macy, Jr. Found.; trustee, vice chmn. Citizens Budget Commn.; trustee N.Y.C. Police Found., Pace U., N.Y.C., Colgate U., 1970-76; trustee N.Y. council Boy Scouts Am., N.Y. State Maritime Mus.; trustee, treas. South Street Seaport Mus.; bd. govs., pres. Federal Hall Meml. Assos., Inc.; bd. dirs., treas., mem. policy com. N.Y.C. Partnership, Inc. Served with USAF, 1951-53; capt. Res. Recipient Humanitarian award Jewish Hosp. and Research Center, Denver, 1977; Man of Year award Realty Found. N.Y., 1978; Good Scout award Greater N.Y. councils Boy Scouts Am., 1980; Spl. Recognition award NAACP, 1980; Disting. Service to Higher Edn. medal Brandeis U., 1976; Urban Leadership award N.Y. U., 1981. Mem. Nat. Assn. Mut. Savs. Banks (dir.), Savs. Banks Assn. N.Y. State (dir.; pres. 1978-79, former chmn. legis.), N.Y. C. of C. and Industry (dir.), Real Estate Bd. N.Y. (bd. govs. 1976-79), Assn. Bar City N.Y., Am. Bar Assn., N.Y. State Bar Assn., Newcomen Soc., Econ. Club N.Y., Econ. Devel. Council N.Y.C. (dir.), Phi Beta Kappa. Clubs: Union League, Links, Down Town Assn. (N.Y.C.); Fort Orange (Albany, N.Y.); Siwanoy Country. Office: 30 Wall St New York NY 10005

CONWAY, HARRY DONALD, research engr., educator; b. Chatham, Eng., Dec. 3, 1917; came to U.S., 1947, naturalized, 1956; s. John and Ada Frances (Young) C.; m. Dorothy Daphne Adams, Aug. 24, 1946 (dec. 1976); children—Geoffrey, Peter. B.Sc., London U., 1942, Ph.D., 1945, D.Sc., 1949; M.A., Cambridge (Eng.) U., 1946, Sc.D., 1972. Sci. officer, research on high temperature properties of metals Nat. Phys. Lab., Teddington, Eng., 1942-45; univ. demonstrator engring. Cambridge (Eng.) U. and dir. studies St. Catharine's Coll., 1946-47; asso. prof. engring. mechanics Cornell U., Ithaca, N.Y., 1947-48, prof. engring. mechanics, 1948—. Author: Aircraft Strength of Materials, 1947, Mechanics of Materials, 1950; Contbr. articles on theoretical analyses of plates and shells, elastic vibrations, lubrication to profl. jours. John Simon Guggenheim fellow and vis. prof. Imperial Coll., London U., 1953-54; NSF sr. postdoctoral fellow, 1961-62; Julius F. Stone vis. prof. Ohio State U., 1958-59; Sir Joseph Whitworth scholar, 1941; Sir John Johnson scholar London U., 1941. Address: Thurston Hall Cornell University Ithaca NY 14853

CONWAY, HOBART MCKINLEY, JR., geo-economist; b. Hackleburg, Ala., Nov. 1, 1920; s. Hobart McKinley and Eva (Kelly) C.; m. Rebecca Warner Kellam, Sept. 17, 1942; children—Linda, Laura. B.S., Ga. Inst. Tech., 1940, B.A. in Engring., 1941. Research engr. NASA, 1941-44, 46-47; dir. So. Assn. Sci. and Industry, Atlanta, 1948-53; pres. Conway Research, Inc., Atlanta, 1954—; dir. Sitenet, 1983—; mem. U.S. Devel. Mission to S.E. Asia, 1962; cons. AID, 1963-68; chmn. Ga. Sci. and Tech. Commn., 1965-66, Caracas Interam. Devel. Seminar; indsl. devel. cons., 15 countries. Editor: Industrial Development mag, 1954-64, Site Selection Handbook, 1954-64, Weather Handbook, 1974, Industrial Facility Planning, 1976, Industrial Park Growth, 1979; Author: The Airport City, 1977, Pitfalls in Development, 1978, Marketing Industrial Buildings and Sites, 1980, Disaster Survival, 1981, The Good Life Index, 1981. Mem. Ga. Senate from 41st Dist., 1963-64, 67-68. Served with USNR, 1944-46. Recipient medal Time mag., 1953. Fellow AAAS; mem. Indsl. Devel. Research Council (founder, dir., recipient award 1979), Aircraft Owners and Pilots Assn. Presbyterian. Also research reports on facilities planning. Home: 3272 Inman Dr NE Atlanta GA 30319 Office: 1954 Airport Rd NE Atlanta GA 30341

CONWAY, JAMES VALENTINE PATRICK, forensic document examiner, former postal service executive; b. Scottdale, Pa., July 16, 1917; s. James Aloysius and Mary Margaret (Yahner) C.; m. Mildred E. Garypie, Aug. 6, 1936; children: James W., Ruth A. Conway Masonek, Colleen L. Conway Weyland, Judith Conway Henderson. Student, St. Vincent Coll., Latrobe, Pa., 1931-34, Cambria-Rowe Bus. Coll., Greensburg, Pa., 1935-36. Diplomate: Am. Bd. Forensic Document Examiners. With U.S. Postal Service, 1939-80, regional chief insp., San Francisco, 1971-73; exec. asst. to Postmaster Gen., Washington, 1973-75, sr. asst. Postmaster Gen. for employee and labor relations, 1975-78, dep. postmaster gen., 1978-80, bd. govs., 1978-80. Fellow Am. Acad. Forensic Scis.; mem. Internat. Assn. Chiefs Police, Internat. Assn. Identification, Am. Soc. Questioned Document Examiners. Democrat. Roman Catholic. Club: Elks.

CONWAY, JILL KATHRYN KER, college president; b. Hillston, New South Wales, Australia, Oct. 9, 1934; d. William Innis and Evelyn Mary (Adames) Ker; m. John James Conway, Dec. 22, 1962. B.A., U. Sydney, Australia, 1958; Ph.D., Harvard, 1969; hon. degrees, St. Thomas (N.B.) U., 1974, Mt. Holyoke Coll., 1975, Amherst Coll., 1976, York U., Toronto, 1977, U. N.H., 1977, Westfield State Coll., 1979, Mt. St. Vincent U., Halifax, N.S., 1980, Wesleyan U., 1980, U. Mass., 1981, Williams Coll., 1982. Lectr. history U. Toronto, Ont., Can., 1964-68, asst. prof., 1968-70, assoc. prof., 1970-75, v.p., 1973-75; pres. Smith Coll., Northampton, Mass., 1975—, Sophia Smith prof., 1975—; dir. IBM World Trade Ams./Far East, Merrill Lynch Co., Arthur D. Little, Inc. Author: The Female Experience in Eighteenth- and Nineteenth-Century America: A Guide to the History of American Women, 1982. Trustee Hampshire Coll., Clarke Sch. for Deaf, Coll. Retirement Equities Fund, Acad. of Music, Northampton; bd. dirs. Ctr. Communications, Council for Fin. Aid to Edn., Inc., Ind. Sector, Washington; 2d v.p. New Eng. Colls. Fund, Inc.; mem. Nat. Resource Center of Girls Clubs Am. Mem. Am., Can. hist. assns., Assn. Ind. Colls. and Univs. in Mass. (vice chmn.), Am. Antiquarian Soc. Research, numerous publs. on Am. social and intellectual history, history of family life and sex roles, history of edn. Home: 8 Paradise Rd Northampton MA 01063 Office: Office of the President Smith Coll Northampton MA 01063

CONWAY, JOHN THOMAS, utility company executive, lawyer; b. N.Y.C., May 10, 1924; s. John Joseph and Johannah (Stanley) C.; m. Priscilla Harris, Sept. 13, 1947 (div. 1978); children: John, Daniel, Sean, Thomas, Christopher, Johannah. B.N.S., Tufts U., 1945, B.S. in engring., 1947; J.D., Columbia U., 1949. Bar: N.Y. 1949, U.S. Supreme Ct. 1952. Spl. agt. FBI, Washington, 1950-56; asst. dir. U.S. Congress Joint Com. on Atomic Energy, Washington, 1956-62, exec. dir., 1962-68; exec. asst. to chmn. Consol. Edison, N.Y.C., 1968-78, exec. v.p., 1982—; pres. Am. Nuclear Energy Council, Washington, 1978-82, chmn. bd., 1983—; bd. dirs. Empire State Energy Research Com., N.Y., 1970-76, Atomic Indsl. Forum, 1976-78; mem. overiste com. U.S. Com. Energy Awareness, Washington, 1982—. Bd. dirs. Youth for Energy Independence, Washington, 1982—; mem. N.Y.C. Mayor's Com. for Sci., 1969-76. Served to lt. j.g. USN, 1943-46. Mem. Fed. Bar Assn., Bar Assn. City N.Y., Am. Nuclear Soc. Democrat. Roman Catholic. Clubs: University, Democratic (Washington). Office: Consol Edison Co 4 Irving Pl New York NY 10003

CONWAY, JOSEPH G., banker; b. Grand Rapids, Mich., 1920. B.B.S., U. Mich., 1949. Accounting clk. Internat. Harvester Co., 1940-41; clk. FBI, Dept. Justice, 1941-47; with Nat. Bank Detroit, 1949—, credit analyst, 1951-53, asst. cashier, 1953-68, sr. v.p., exec. officer, 1968-72, exec. v.p., 1972-79, vice chmn. bd., 1979—; dir. MasterCard Internat. Inc., Reichhold Chems., Inc., NBD Bancorp Inc. Served to 1st lt. AUS, 1943-46. Office: Woodward and Fort Detroit MI 48232 *

CONWAY, KEVIN, actor, director; b. N.Y.C., May 29, 1942; s. James John C. and Margaret (Sanders) O'Brien; m. Mila Quiros, Apr. 5, 1966. Broadway and Off-Broadway appearances include Elephant Man, Of Mice and Men, Moonchildren; Broadway and Off-Broadway appearances Red Ryder; Broadway and Off-Broadway appearances include One Flew Over the Cuckoo's Nest, Life Class, Other Places; films include Slaughterhouse Five, Portnoy's Complaint, FIST, Paradise Alley, The Funhouse, Flashpoint; TV appearances include Rage of Angels, The Scarlet Letter, The Deadliest Season, The Lathe of Heaven, Elephant Man, Something About Amelia; dir.: plays Off-Broadway and Lincoln Ctr. Mecca, Old Flames. Bd. dirs. Second Stage Co. Served with USN, 1960-62. Recipeint Village Voice Obie award, 1973; recipient Drama Desk award, 1973-74. Mem. Screen Actors Guild (bd. dirs. 1979-81), Nat. Acad. TV Arts and Scis. Clubs: Players, Friars (N.Y.C.). The true relevance of one's life and work is, to me, embodied in the aggressive pursuit of the elusive trinity of caring, candor and curiosity. Home and Office: 25 Central Park W New York NY 10023

CONWAY, LYNN ANN, government official; b. Mount Vernon, N.Y., Jan. 2, 1938. B.S., Columbia U., 1962, M.S. in Elec. Engring., 1963. Mem. research staff IBM Corp., Yorktown Heights, N.Y., 1964-68; sr. staff engr. Memorex Corp., Santa Clara, Calif., 1969-73; mem. research staff Xerox Corp., Palo Alto, Calif., 1973-78, research fellow, mgr. vlsi systems area, Paolo Alto, Calif., 1978-82, research fellow, mgr. knowledge systems area, Palo Alto, Calif., 1982-83; asst. dir. for strategic compusing Def. Advanced Research Projects Agy., Arlington, Va., 1983—; vis. assoc. prof. elec. engring. and computer sci. MIT, Cambridge, Mass., 1978-79. Co-author: textbook Introduction to VLSI Systems, 1980. Recipient Ann. Achievement award Electronics mag., 1981. Mem. IEEE, Am. Assn. for Artificial Intelligence, AAAS, Assn. Computing Machinery. Home: 1200 N Nash St Arlington VA 22209 Office: Def Advanced Research Projects Agy 1400 Wilson Blvd Arlington VA 22209

CONWAY, MARY ELIZABETH, nursing educator, university dean; b. Albany, N.Y., Nov. 4, 1923; d. Paul H. and Elizabeth J. (Miller) C. Student, Syracuse U., 1941-43; B.S. in Nursing, Columbia U., 1947; M.Nursing Adminstrn., U. Minn., 1958; Ph.D. in Sociology, Boston U., 1972. Supr. surg. services Mass. Gen. Hosp., Boston, 1953-57; asst. dir. nursing Albany (N.Y.) Med. Center, 1958-63; dir. nursing Monroe Community Hosp., Rochester, N.Y., 1963-65; cons. nurse Bur. Hosp. Nursing, N.Y. State Health Dept., Albany, 1965-68; asso. prof. Boston U. Sch. Nursing, 1972-76, chmn., 1972-76; dean Sch. Nursing, U. Wis., Milw., 1976-80, Med. Coll. Ga., Augusta, 1980—; cons. Sch. Nursing, SUNY, Albany, 1975-76, Russell Sage Coll., Troy, N.Y., 1973-77; chmn. nurse adv. council to SSS, N.Y. State, 1966-68. Editorial bd.: Jour. Research in Nursing and Health, 1977. Mem. N.Y. Gov.'s Adv. Council on Vocat. Rehab., 1966-68; bd. dirs. Health Services Rensselaer Area, Troy, 1966-68, United Way Greater Milw. Allocations Bd., 1976-80. Recipient citation Pres. U.S., 1965-68; HEW grantee, 1979-80. Fellow Am. Acad. Nursing (pres. 1980-81); mem. Sigma Xi, Sigma Theta Tau. Home: 1308 Jamaica Ct Augusta GA 30909 Office: Sch Nursing Med Coll Ga Augusta GA 30912

CONWAY, ROBERT JOSEPH, recreation equipment manufacturing company executive; b. Belle Harbor, N.Y., May 13, 1935; s. James Joseph and Margretta (Loures) C.; m. Ruth Ann Pickard, Oct. 4, 1958; children: Donna Ann, Karen Ann, Lynne Patricia, Nancy Ruth. B.S., Georgetown U., 1957; A.M.P., Harvard Bus. Sch., 1983. With AMF Inc., Westbury, N.Y., 1958—, div. v.p. sales, bowling products group, 1967-77, pres. bowling div., 1977, dep. group exec., 1977-79, corp. v.p., group exec., 1979—. Served with N.G., 1957-58. Office: AMF Inc Jericho Turnpike Westbury NY 11590

CONWAY, STEPHEN S., JR., manufacturing company executive; b. Chgo., July 6, 1926; s. Stephen S. and Helen (Moran) C.; m. Eleanor O'Toole, Jan. 24, 1950; children—Stephen, Bernard, James, John, Catherine. B.S., Toledo U., 1951. With Abex Corp., N.Y.C., 1950—, pres. friction products div., Troy, Mich., 1976-78, corp. group v.p. automotive, 1978-79, corp. exec. v.p., 1979-80, pres., chief exec. officer, 1980—, also dir.; dir. Sharp Die & Mold Co. Served with USNT, 1944-46. Mem. Soc. Automotive Engrs. Republican. Roman Catholic. Clubs: Apawamis (Rye, N.Y.); Sky, University, River (N.Y.C.); University (Chgo.). Office: 530 Fifth Ave New York NY 10036

CONWAY, THOMAS JAMES, lawyer; b. Kansas City, July 20, 1913; s. Thomas James and Nell M. (O'Sullivan) C.; m. Eleanor M. Nolan, June 4, 1938; children—Terry N., Brian J., Diana S. LL.B., Washington U., St. Louis, 1935. Bar: Mo. bar 1935. Atty. Kansas City Park Dept., 1936-42; asst. city counselor, Kansas City, 1942-50; chief trial atty. City Counselor's Office, 1950-59; partner firm Popham, Conway, Sweeny, Fremont & Bundschu, Kansas City, 1959—. Decorated knight Holy Sepulchre. Mem. Am., Mo., Kansas City bar assns., Internat. Soc. Barristers, Pi Epsilon Delta, Kappa Alpha. Roman Catholic. Clubs: K.C., Carriage, Kansas City Racquet. Home: 1227 W 64th Terr Kansas City MO 64113 Office: Commerce Bank Bldg Kansas City MO 64106

CONWAY, TIM, comedian; b. Willoughby, Ohio, Dec. 15, 1933; m. Mary Anne, 1961; children: Kelly Ann, Timothy, Patrick, Jaimie, Corey, Seann. Student, Bowling Green (Ohio) State U. Writer/dir., occasional performer, Sta. KWY-TV, Cleve.; regular: TV series McHale's Navy, 1962-66, Rango, 1967, The Tim Conway Show, 1970, The Tim Conway Comedy Hour, 1970, The Carol Burnett Show, CBS, 1975-78, The Tim Conway Show, 1980-83; other TV appearances include Hollywood Palace, Steve Allen Show, Garry Moore Show, That's Life; film appearances include McHale's Navy, 1964, McHale's Navy Joins the Air Force, 1965, The World's Greatest Athlete, 1973, The Apple Dumpling Gang, 1975, Gus, 1976, Billion Dollar Hobo (also writer), 1978, They Went That-a-way and that-a-way (also writer), 1978; also numerous nightclub appearances, TV commls.; TV movie Roll, Freddy, Roll, 1974. Served in U.S. Army. Recipient Emmy awards. Mem. AFTRA. Office: 425 S Beverly Dr Beverly Hills CA 90212 *

CONWAY, WILLIAM GAYLORD, zoologist; b. St. Louis, Nov. 20, 1929; s. Frederick Eldridge and Alice Harriet (Gaylord) C. A.B., Washington U., 1951. Curator birds St. Louis Zool. Park, 1950-56; curator birds N.Y. Zool. Soc., N.Y.C., 1956-72; asso. dir., 1960-61, gen. dir., 1966—; Bd. dirs. Internat. Council for Bird Protection (Am. sect.). Contbr. articles to profl. jours. Fellow N.Y. Zool. Soc.; mem. Brit. Avicultural Soc. (hon.; v.p.), Am. Ornithologists Union (elective), Cooper Ornithol Soc., Internat. Wild Waterfowl Assn. (dir.), Wilson Ornithol. Club, World Wildlife Fund, Am. Appeal (dir.), Internat. Union Conservation of Nature (dir.), Cultural Instns. Group (past pres.), Am. Conservation Assn. (dir.), Lab. Ornithology (dir.), Am. Assn. Zool. Parks and Aquariums (past pres., dir.), Internat. Survival Service Commn. Expdns. to Trinidad, Argentina, Bolivia. Office: NY Zool Park New York NY 10460

CONWELL, ESTHER MARLY, physicist; b. N.Y.C., May 23, 1922; d. Charles and Ida (Korn) C.; m. Abraham A. Rothberg, Sept. 30, 1945; 1 son, Lewis J. B.A., Bklyn. Coll., 1942; M.S., U. Rochester, N.Y., 1945; Ph.D., U. Chgo., 1948. Lectr. Bklyn. Coll., 1946-51; mem. tech. staff Bell Telephone Labs., 1951-52; physicist GTE Labs., Bayside, N.Y., 1952-61, mgr. physics dept., 1961-72; vis. prof. U. Paris, 1962-63; Abby Rockefeller Mauze prof. M.I.T., 1972; prin. scientist Xerox Corp., Webster, N.Y., 1972-80, research fellow, 1981—; cons., mem. adv. com. engring. NSF, 1978—. Author: High Field Transport in Semiconductors, 1967, also research papers; editorial bd.: Jour. Applied Physics; proc.: IEEE. Fellow IEEE, Am. Phys. Soc. (sec.-treas. div. condensed matter physics 1977—); mem. Soc. Women Engrs. (Achievement award 1960), Nat. Acad. Engring. Patentee in field. Office: 800 Phillips Rd Webster NY 14580

CONY, EDWARD ROGER, newspaperman; b. Augusta, Maine, Mar. 15, 1923; s. Daniel William and Mary (Doyle) C.; m. Susan Wheat, June 12, 1954; children—Ann, Daniel, Elizabeth, Katharine, Marilyn, Lauren. B.A. in Polit. Sci, Reed Coll., 1948; M.A., Stanford, 1951. Reporter The Oregonian, Portland, 1951-52; with The Wall Street Jour., 1953-70, successively mem. staff San Francisco office, news bur. mgr., Los Angeles, Southeastern news bur. mgr., Jacksonville, Fla., 1953-60, news editor, N.Y.C., 1960-64, asst. mng. editor, 1964-65, mng. editor, 1965-70; exec. editor Dow Jones Publs., N.Y.C., 1970—, now v.p. news. Trustee Reed Coll., 1974—. Recipient Pulitzer prize for nat. reporting, 1961. Home: 7 Gull's Cove Manhasset NY 11030 Office: 22 Cortlandt St New York City NY 10007

CONYERS, JOHN, JR., congressman; b. Detroit, May 16, 1929; s. John and Lucille (Simpson) C. B.A., Wayne State U., 1957, J.D., 1958; LL.D., Wilberforce U., 1969. Bar: Mich. 1959. Legis. asst. to Congressman John Dingell, 1959-61; sr. partner firm Conyers, Bell & Townsend, 1959-61; referee Mich. Workmen's Compensation Dept., 1961-64; mem. (89th-98th congresses from 1st Dist. Mich.); sr. mem. Judiciary Com., chmn. subcom. on criminal justice, mem. subcom. on civil and constl. rights; mem. Govt. Ops. Com., mem. subcom. on commerce, consumer and monetary affairs, mem. subcom. on intergovtl. relations; Past dir. edn. Local 900, U.A.W.; mem. adv. council Mich. Liberties Union; gen. counsel Detroit Trade Union Leadership Council; vice chmn. nat. bd. Ams. for Democratic Action; vice chmn. adv. council ACLU; an organizer Mems. Congress for Peace through Law; bd. dirs. numerous other orgns. including African-Am. Inst., Commn. Racial Justice, Detroit Inst. Arts, Nat. Alliance Against Racist and Polit. Repression, Nat. League Cities. Sponsor, contbg. author: Am. Militarism, 1970, War Crimes and the American Conscience, 1970, Anatomy of an Undeclared War, 1972; contbr. articles to profl. jours. Trustee Martin Luther King Jr. Center for Non-Violent Social Change. Served to 2d lt. AUS, 1950-54; Korea. Recipient Rosa Parks award SCLC. Mem. NAACP (exec. bd. Detroit), Kappa Alpha Psi. Democrat. Baptist. Office: 2313 Rayburn House Office Bldg Washington DC 20515

CONYERS, NATHAN GEORGE, auto dealer, lawyer; b. Detroit, July 3, 1932; s. John James and Lucille (Simpson) C.; m. Diana Callie Howze, Aug. 25, 1956; children—Nancy, Steven, Susan, Ellen, Peter. LL.B., Wayne State U., 1959. Bar: Mich. bar 1959. Mem. firm Colven, Snowden, Smith & Keith, Detroit, 1960-63; partner Keith, Conyers & Anderson, 1964-67; sr. partner Conyers, Anderson, Brown & Wahls, Detroit, 1967-70; pres. Conyers Ford, Inc., Detroit, 1970—; Spl. asst. atty. gen. State of Mich., 1967-70. Mem. Mich. Bd. State Canvassers, 1967—, chmn., 1971. Served with AUS, 1953-55. Mem. Nat. Black Auto Dealers Assn. (pres.). Office: 2475 W Grand Blvd Detroit MI 48208

COODER, RY, recording artist, guitarist; b. Los Angeles, Mar. 15, 1947. Played with, Jackie DeShannon, 1963, Taj Mahal, 1966, Capt. Beefheart, 1967; performed studio session work, through late 1960's; recorded with, Rolling Stones, Randy Newman, Maria Muldaur; co-writer: movie scores Candy, 1968, Performance, 1970, The Long Riders, 1980; albums include Borderline. Office: care Press Relations Warner Bros Records 3300 Warner Blvd Burbank CA 91510

COOGAN, PETER FRANCIS, lawyer; b. Watertown, Wis., Dec. 3, 1904; s. William and Eleanor (McFarland) C.; m. Barbara Tracy, June 4, 1942; children: Eleanor Coogan Merrill, Rosalind Coogan Anderson, Peter Weston, Matthew Allen. Student, Marquette U., 1923-26; LL.B., Case Western Res. U., 1939; M.A., Boston U., 1941; LL.M., Harvard U., 1942. Bar: Mass. 1942, U.S. Dist. Ct. Mass. 1942, U.S. Ct. Appeals (1st cir.) 1942. Assoc. Ropes & Gray, Boston, 1942-50, ptnr., 1950-77, of counsel, 1977—; lectr. Yale U. Law Sch., Harvard U. Law Sch.; practitioner-in-residence Duke U.; disting. vis. prof. U. Va., U. Ga., U. So. Calif., U. Houston, Vt. Law Sch.; scholar-in-residence Murphy, Weir & Butler, San Francisco, 1980—; mem. permanent editorial bd. Uniform Comml. Code, 1953—; mem. Nat. Bankruptcy Conf., 1955—; del. U.S. State Dept. Conf. on Internat. Leasing, 1977; lectr. continuing legal edn. program Am. Law Inst.-ABA. Prin. author: (with Hogan and Vagts) Secured Transactions Under the Uniform Commercial Code, 4 vols., 1963—; bd. overseers (Case Western Res. U.), 1969-72. Chmn. vis. com. Case Western Res, U. Law Sch., 1965-71; bd. overseers Case Western Res. U., 1969-72. Mem. Boston Bar Assn., N.Y. Bar Assn., ABA, Am. Law Inst., ABA Soc. Fellows, Fellows Mass. Bar, Soc. Benchers (Case Western Res. U.). Club: Harvard (Boston and N.Y.C.). Address: Box E Quechee VT 05059

COOGAN, PHILIP SHIELDS, pathologist; b. Peoria, Ill., Feb. 13, 1938; s. Paul Mathew and Elizabeth Ann (Shields) C.; m. Carol Jean Gerlach, June 18, 1960; children: Mary Brighid, Philip Gerlach, Joseph Baker, Clare Ann. Student. U. Notre Dame, 1955-58; M.D., St. Louis U., 1962. Diplomate: Am. Bd. Pathology. USPHS summer research trainee pathology St. Louis U. Med. Sch., 1959-61; intern Presbyn.-St. Luke's Hosp., Chgo., 1962-63, resident, 1963-67; research pathologist, chief histopathology U.S. Air Force Sch. Aerospace Medicine, 1967-69; asst. prof. pathology Rush Med. Coll., Chgo., 1971-73, assoc. prof., 1972-75; assoc. prof. pathology Northwestern U., Chgo., 1974-78; dir. anatomic pathology Northwestern Meml. Hosp., Chgo., 1974-78; prof., chmn. dept. pathology Quillen-Dishner Coll. Medicine, East Tenn. State U., Johnson City, 1978—; cons. FDA, 1972-81, USPHS, 1962-67. Assoc. editor: Year Book Pathology and Clinical Pathology, 1978-80. Served with USAF, 1967-69. Recipient Hektoen award Chgo. Path. Soc., 1969; named Outstanding Tchr. East Tenn. State U. Coll. Medicine, 1980, 81, 83. Mem. Internat. Acad. Pathology, Am. Soc. Exptl. Pathology, Am. Soc. Pathologists, AAAS, AMA., Alpha Omega Alpha. Roman Catholic. Office: Dept Pathology East Tenn State U Johnson City TN 37601

COOGLE, JOSEPH MOORE, JR., advertising agency executive; b. Louisville, Jan. 13, 1933; s. Joseph Moore and Dorothy Virginia (Miller) C.; m. Maryhelen Doty, Jan. 27, 1957; children: Suzanne Grace, Virginia Louise. B.S., U. Ky., 1957; M.B.A., U. Chgo., 1958. Grocery products salesman Pillsbury Co., Mpls., 1958-59, marketing research up to sr. research analyst, 1959-62, up to marketing mgr., grocery products marketing dept., 1962-65; account exec. Ketchum, MacLeod & Grove, Pitts., 1965-66, account supr., 1966-68, v.p., account mgr., 1968-70, v.p., dir. marketing, research and media planning, 1970-72, sr. v.p., 1972—, dir. ops. planning, 1975-77, dir. mktg., N.Y.C., 1977-79, exec. v.p., 1978-79; pres. Ketchum Internat., Inc., Pitts., 1979—. Former chmn. Pitts. chpt. Am. Assn. Advt. Agys.; Trustee Pressley Ridge Sch., Pitts. Council Internat. Visitors; bd. dirs. Three Rivers Shakespeare Festival, Pitts. Dance Council. Served with AUS, 1953-55. Mem. Am. Mktg. Assn., Am. Mgmt. Assn., Sales Execs. Club N.Y., Beta Gamma Sigma. Lutheran. Clubs: Edgeworth (Sewickley, Pa.); Erie Yacht (Pa.). Home: Sewickley PA 15143 Office: 4 Gateway Center Pittsburgh PA 15222

COOK, ADDISON GILBERT, educator; b. Caracas, Venezuela, Apr. 1, 1933; s. Harold Reed and Florence (Hosie) C.; m. Nancy Lois Spriggs, Aug. 18, 1956; children—Virginia Lynn, Shirley June, Diane Joyce. B.S., Wheaton Coll., 1955; Ph.D., U. Ill., 1959. Research asso. Cornell U., 1959-60; prof. chemistry Valparaiso U., 1960, chmn. dept., 1970—; cons. chemistry div. Argonne (Ill.) Nat. Lab. Editor, contbr.: Enamines: Synthesis, Structure, and Reactions, 1969; Contbr. articles profl. jours. Recipient Research Corp. grant, 1960-61; Petroleum Research Fund grant, 1963-69. Mem. Am. Chem. Sco., Chem. Soc. (London), Ind. Acad. Sci., Sigma Xi, Phi Lambda Upsilon, Pi Mu Epsilon. Mem. Evangel. Free Ch. Am. Home: 2308 Shannon Dr Valparaiso IN 46383

COOK, ALBERT SPAULDING, comparative literature and classics educator, writer; b. Exeter, N.H., Oct. 28, 1925; s. Albert Spaulding and Adele (Farrington) Cook V.; m. Carol Rubin, June 19, 1948; children: David, Daniel, Jonathan. A.B., Harvard U., 1946, M.A., 1947, postgrad., 1947-48. Asst. prof. U. Calif., Berkeley, 1953-56; assoc. prof., then prof. Western Res. U., Cleve., 1957-63; prof., chmn. SUNY, Buffalo, 1963-66, prof., dir. comparative lit., 1964-71; prof. English and comparative lit. Brown U., Providence, 1971-78, prof. comparative lit., 1978—, prof. comparative lit. and classics, 1980—; Fulbright prof. U. Munich, W. Ger., 1956-57, U. Vienna, Australia, 1960-61; sr. fellow Center for Advanced Study Behavioral Scis., 1966-67. Author: criticism The Dark Voyage and the Golden Mean, 1949, 66, The Meaning of Fiction, 1960, The Classic Line, 1966, Prisms, 1967, The Root of the Thing: Job and the Song of Songs, 1968, Enactment: Greek Tragedy, 1971, Shakespeare's Enactment, 1976, Myth and Language, 1980, French Tragedy: The Power of Enactment, 1981, Changing the Signs: The Fifteenth Century Breakthrough, 1984; poetry Progressions, 1963, The Charges, 1970, 72, Adapt the Living, 1981; author, producer: plays Double Exposure, 1958, Night Guard, 1962, Big Blow, 1964, Check, 1966, The Death of Trotsky, 1971; translator: Oedipus Rex, 1957, 60, The Odyssey of Homer, 1967; author: Oedipus Rex: A Mirror for Greek Drama, 1963, 82, Plays for the Greek Theatre, 1972, 83, The Odyssey: A Critical Edition, 1972; contbr. articles in field to profl. jours., poems to various periodicals. Harvard U. jr. fellow, 1948-51; Fulbright fellow, U. Paris, 1952-53; Guggenheim fellow, Parris, 1969-70; fellow classical studies Found. Hardt, Geneva, 1968,75; sr. fellow Soviet Ministry Edn., Internat. Research and Exchange Bd., 1972; Camargo Found. fellow, 1977; fellow Clare Hall, Cambridge U., 1982. Mem. Am. Soc. Aesthetics, MLA, Am. Comparative Lit. Assn. Episcopalian. Home: 92 Elmgrove Ave Providence RI 02906 Office: Brown U Box E Providence RI 02912

COOK, ANN JENNALIE, English educator, association executive; b. Wewoka, Okla., Oct. 19, 1934; d. Arthur Holly and Bertha Mabelle (Stafford) C.; children: Lee Ann Harrod, Amy Ceil Harrod; m. John Donelson Whalley, Sept. 10, 1975. B.A., U. Okla., 1956, M.A., 1959; Ph.D. (Danforth Grad. fellow for women), Vanderbilt U., 1972. Instr. English U. Okla., 1956-57; tchr. English, N.C. and Conn., 1958-61; instr. So. Conn. State Coll., 1962-64; asst. prof. U. S.C., 1972-74; adj. asst. prof. Vanderbilt U., 1976—, assoc. prof., 1982—; exec. sec. Shakespeare Assn. Am., Nashville, 1975—. Author: Privileged Playgoers of Shakespeare's London, 1981; asso. editor: Shakespeare Studies, 1973-80; mem. editorial bd.: Medieval and Renaissance Drama in Eng, Shakespeare Quar., Shakespeare Studies; contbr. articles to profl. publs. Trustee Council for Research in the Renaissance. Recipient Letseizer award, 1956, Nat. Leadership award Delta, Delta, Delta, 1956; Folger summer fellow, 1973; Donelson fellow, 1974-75. Mem. Internat. Shakespeare Assn., Shakespeare Assn. Am., Modern Lang. Assn., AAUP, Shakespeare Inst., Soc. Values in Higher Edn., Renaissance Soc. Am., Southeastern Renaissance Soc., Phi Beta Kappa. Episcopalian. Home: 91 Valley Forge Nashville TN 37205 Office: Shakespeare Assn Am 6328 Vanderbilt Sta Nashville TN 37235

COOK, BART R., dancer; b. Ogden, Utah, June 7, 1950; s. Dell W. and DeLila (Robinson) C. Prin. dancer, asst. ballet master, N.Y.C. Ballet. Office: NYC Ballet NY State Theater Lincoln Center Plaza New York NY 10023

COOK, BENJAMIN HOPSON, manufacturing company executive; b. Shreveport, La., Apr. 7, 1926; s. Tom and Eva (Hopson) C.; m. Irene Owen, Aug. 20, 1948; children: Lura Haden Cook Norman, Terry Ellen Cook Slater, Paul Stuart. B.S. in Bus. Adminstrn, La. State U., 1948. Co-founder Stemco Mfg. Co., Longview, Tex., 1951; (merged into Garlock Inc, Rochester, N.Y. 1964), v.p. oil seal group, 1969-72, pres., parent co., 1972-76, chmn., chief exec. officer, 1976—, also dir.; exec. v.p. Colt Industries, N.Y.C., 1976—; dir. Tex. Commerce Bank-Longview, Schlegel Corp., Rochester. Bd. dirs. Tex. Mfrs. Assn., 1969-71, Longview YMCA, 1966-69, United Fund, Longview, 1970-72. Mem. Indsl. Mgmt. Council (dir. 1976—), Soc. Automotive Engrs., La. State U. Alumni Assn. Methodist. Home: Route 2 Box 209N Longview TX 75605 Office: PO Box 8090 Longview TX 75601

COOK, CAMILLE WRIGHT, legal educator; b. Tuscaloosa, Ala.; d. Reuben Hall and Camille Tunstall (Searcy) Wright; children: Sydney, Reuben, Cade, Camille. A.B., U. Ala., 1945, J.D., 1948. Bar: Ala. 1948. Asst. prof. law Auburn (Ala.) U. Law Sch., 1968; mem. faculty Sch. Law, U. Ala., 1968—, assoc. dean, dir. continuing legal edn., prof. law, 1975—; mem. expedited arbitration panel Steel Industry; bd. dirs. U. Ala. Law Sch. Found., 1975—. Mem. Smithsonian Council, Washington, 1972-78, Ala. Air Pollution Commn., 1971-81. Mem. Am., Ala. bar assns., Farrah Law Soc. (trustee 1972—). Episcopalian. Home: 32 Ridgeland Tuscaloosa AL 35406 Office: Box CL University AL 35486

COOK, CHARLES DAVENPORT, pediatrician, educator; b. Mpls., Nov. 30, 1919; s. Henry W. and Ellen (Davenport) C.; m. Carolyn Crowther, June 12, 1976; 1 dau., Deborah McC.; children by previous marriage: Andrew D., Sheila D., Peter G., Charles Davenport II. A.B., Princeton U., 1941; M.D., Harvard U., 1944; M.A. (hon.), Yale U., 1964. Intern U. Minn. Hosp., 1944-45; fellow Mayo Clinic, 1945-46; resident Mass. Gen. Hosp., 1948-49; chief resident Children's Hosp., Boston, 1949-51; assoc. clin. prof. pediatrics Harvard Med. Sch., 1963-64; prof., chmn. dept. pediatrics Yale Sch. Medicine, 1964-74; vis. prof. U. Conn. Health Center, 1974-75; prof. pediatrics Downstate Med. Center, State U. N.Y., Bklyn., 1975-81, chmn. dept., 1975-81; Edward H. Townsend, Jr. prof. pediatrics U. Rochester, N.Y., 1981—; chief pediatrics Rochester Gen. Hosp., 1981—; vis. scholar Japan Soc. Promotion Sci., Nagoya, 1974; vis. prof. Ben Gurion U. Negev, Beersheva, Israel, 1976. Served with M.C. AUS, 1945-47. Mem. Am. Pediatric Soc. (sec., treas. 1964-75). Research med. care, med. edn. Address: 1425 Portland Rochester NY 14621 *On the basis of training as an academic pediatrician, my work for the past several decades has been directed to the development of techniques for the evaluation of physicians and for the assurance of quality care for children. While quality care for all is still a distant goal, third party payors and consumers are beginning to demand accountability and computers are beginning to facilitate the quality assurance programs we have developed.*

COOK, CHARLES DAVID, lawyer, bus. exec.; b. Saginaw, Mich., Apr. 5, 1924; s. Charles Christian and Grace (Robins) C.; m. Bobette Ringland, Oct. 30, 1947; children: Ian Ainsworth, Kendra. A.B., U. Mich., 1947; LL.B., Columbia U., 1950, M.A. in Internat. Affairs, 1950. Bar: N.Y. 1951, D.C. 1965, Fed. Dist. Ct. So. N.Y 1965, Supreme Ct. U.S 1967. Asso. dir. Inst. World Affairs seminar, Twin Lakes, Conn., summer 1950; mem. U.S. Mission to UN, 1950-62, dep. counselor, chief polit. sect., 1956-60, counselor, 1960-62; partner firm Barco, Cook, Patton & Blow, 1962-67; sr. counsel Gen. Tel. & Electronics Internat., 1967-72; v.p., gen. counsel, sec., dir. GTE Internat., 1972-78; gen. counsel, cons. Copadco Ltd., 1978-81; of counsel Patton, Boggs & Blow, Washington, 1981—; affiliate Law Offices Ismail S. Nazer, Al-Khobar, Saudi Arabia, 1981—; adj. prof. internat. bus. transactions Bklyn. Law Sch., 1980; lectr. in field. Counselor U.S. delegations UN Gen. Assemblies, 1958-61; accompanied Ambassador Adlai Stevenson on Presdl. mission to S.Am., 1961; mem. U.S. delegation disarmament com., Geneva, Switzerland, 1962; adviser U.S. delegation WHO, Geneva, 1962; spl. cons. Pres. Nixon's Commn. for Observance of 25th Anniversary of UN. Exec. bd. Westchester-Putnam council Boy Scouts Am. Served to ensign USNR, 1943-46. Univ. seminar asso. Columbia, 1961-73. Mem. Am. Bar Assn. (anti-trust, corp. banking and bus., internat. law sects.), Assn. Bar City N.Y. (past com. on lawyers role in search for peace), Internat. Law Assn. (Am. br.), Am. Soc. Internat. Law, Westchester-Fairfield Counties Corporate Counsel Assn. (1st chmn. internat. com.), Am. Arbitration Assn. (past arbitrator). Clubs: Bronxville Field Club.; American (London). Home: One Legget Rd Bronxville NY 10708 Office: Law Offices of IS Nazer PO Box 154 Al-Khobar Saudi Arabia

COOK, CHARLES LOUIS, curator; b. Lakeland, Fla., Feb. 19, 1949; s. Louis Calvin and Lauris Naomi (Wilson) C.; m. Angela Adair Askew, Aug. 29, 1981; 1 dau., Rachel Adair. A.A. in Bus. Adminstrn., Polk Community Coll., 1969; student, Lee Coll., 1970-71, U. Central Fla., 1979-80. Curator wildlife Walt Disney World Co., Lake Buena Vista, Fla., 1976—, animal keeper, 1972-76; co-dir., adv. com. Dusky Seaside Sparrow, Maitland, Fla., 1982—. Recipient accreditation Discovery Island Zool. Park by Am. Assn. Zool. Parks and Aquariums, 1981. Fellow Am. Assn. Zool. Parks and Aquariums; mem. Fla. Audubon So. Democrat. Office: Walt Disney World Co PO Box 40 Lake Buena Vista FL 32830 *

COOK, CHARLES WILKERSON, JR., banker; b. Nashville, Sept. 10, 1934; s. Charles Wilkerson and Virginia (Jones) C.; m. Sally Randolph Frierson, June 24, 1961; children: Charles Wilkerson III, John Stephenson Frierson. B.S., Yale U., 1956; postgrad., Stonier Grad. Sch. Banking, Rutgers U., 1964-66. With Third Nat. Bank, Nashville, 1959—, exec. v.p., head funds mgmt. and planning div., 1976-79, pres., 1979—, also dir.; dir. Third Lease Corp., Third Nat. Corp., Empire Pencil Corp. Author: History of a Bank Merger, 1969. Mem. Nashville-Davidson County Govt. Social Services Commn., 1970—; sr. warden Christ Episcopal Ch., Nashville, 1970-71; pres. Episc. Churchmen of Tenn., 1974; mem. bishop and council Episc. Diocese of Tenn., 1979-81; bd. dirs. United Way Nashville, Jr. Achievement of Nashville, Bill Wilkerson Hearing and Speech Center, Nashville, 1970-80, Ensworth Sch., Nashville, 1978-81, Better Bus. Bur. Nashville, Nashville Meml. Hosp.; mem. adv. bd. Salvation Army, Nashville, 1976-79. Served with USN, 1956-59; capt. Res., 1977—. Mem. Res. City Bankers Assn., Am. Bankers Assn. (edn. devel. and policy council), Robert Morris Assos., Am. Inst. Banking., Nashville C. of C. (bd. govs. 1982—). Clubs: Yale of N.Y.C., Belle Meade Country; Exchange (Nashville); Army-Navy (Washington). Office: Third Nat Bank Nashville TN 37244

COOK, CHARLES WILLIAM, government official; b. Yankton, S.D., Sept. 27, 1927; s. William O. and Kathryn S. (Eymer) C.; m. Virginia M. Fosness, May 30, 1950; children: Jennifer Cook Clark, William O. II, Amy E. A.B. summa cum laude; Dean Akeley fellow, U. S.D., 1951; M.S., Calif. Inst. Tech., 1954, Ph.D., 1957. Head nuclear physics Convair Corp., San Diego, 1957-60; chief Ballistic Missile Def. br. Advanced Research Project Agy., Washington, 1961; corp. dir. elec. research and devel. No. Am. Aviation Inc., El Segundo, Calif., 1961-67; dep. div. chief CIA, Washington, 1967-71; asst. dir. def. research and engring. Dept. Def., Washington, 1971-74; dep. under sec. for space systems Air Force, 1974-79, dep. asst. sec. for space plans and policy, 1979—; cons. McGraw Hill, Inc., N.Y.C., 1962—. Contbr. articles to profl. jours. Served with A.C. AUS, 1944-47. Fellow AIAA (asso.); mem. IEEE (sr.), Am. Phys. Soc., Am. Inst. Physics, Sigma Xi, Phi Beta Kappa, Sigma Pi Sigma. Home: 1180 Daleview Dr McLean VA 22102 Office: SAFALS Room 4D 939 Pentagon Washington DC 20330

COOK, CHAUNCEY WILLIAM WALLACE, corporate executive; b. Hugo, Okla., June 22, 1909; s. Chauncey William and Minnie Malona (Cherry) C.; m. Ethel Frances Crain, Dec. 27, 1934; children: David William, Frances Ann (Mrs. John A. Cole). B.S., U. Tex., 1930; postgrad., Columbia U., 1930-31; LL.D., C.W. Post Coll., L.I. U., 1967, Babson Inst. Bus. Adminstrn., 1967, Iona Coll., 1968; L.H.D.,

Pace Coll., 1969; D.Eng., Mich. Tech. U., 1969. Prodn. engr. Procter & Gamble Co., 1931-37, plant engr., 1937-42; chief engr. Gen. Foods Corp., 1942-44, div. mgr. mfg. and engring., 1944-46, div. prodn. mgr., 1946-51, div. product mgr., 1951-52, div. sales and advt. mgr., 1952-53, asst. div. gen. mgr., 1953-55, v.p. corp., gen. mgr., Hoboken, N.J., 1955-59, exec. v.p., 1959-62, dir. corp., 1960—, pres., 1962-65, pres., chief exec. officer, 1965-66, chmn., chief exec., 1966-72, chmn., pres., chief exec., 1972, chmn., chief exec., 1972-73, chmn., 1973-74, chmn. exec. com., 1974-80; dir. Tex. Commerce Bank of Austin, Tex., 1973—; Mem. The Bus. Council, 1966—; chmn. food sub-council Nat. Indsl. Pollution Control Council, 1970-73. Trustee Com. for Econ. Devel., 1965-74, Council of Americas, 1965-74; trustee The Conf. Bd., 1964-76, chmn., 1972-73; bd. dirs. Council Better Bus. Burs., 1970-73; mem. devel. bd. U. Tex., 1969—, chmn. devel. bd., 1981-83. Recipient Distinguished Engring. grad. award U. Tex., 1963; Distinguished Achievement award U. Tex. Ex-Students Assn. N.Y., 1963; Distinguished Alumnus award Ex-Students Assn. U. Tex., 1965; Alumni medal Columbia U. Alumni Assn., 1969; C. Walter Nichols award N.Y. U. Grad. Sch. Bus. Adminstrn., 1972; Herbert Hoover award Am. Wholesale Grocers Assn., 1979. Mem. Pi Sigma Epsilon (hon.), Tau Beta Pi, Beta Gamma Sigma, Eta Kappa Nu, Delta Chi. Clubs: Capital, Lakeway Yacht, Headliners (Austin, Tex.); World of Tennis (Lakeway, Tex.). Office: 1801 Lavaca St Suite 15E Austin TX 78701

COOK, CHRISTOPHER CAPEN, artist, museum director; b. Boston, May 28, 1932; s. Warren Foster and Katherine Ellis (Capen) C.; m. Julia Shears Nichols, Dec. 21, 1953; children: Brett Warren, Ethan Christopher, Esther Shears, Silas Baldwin, Katharine. B.A., Wesleyan U., 1954; M.F.A., U. Ill., 1959. Instr. art Colby Jr. Coll., Waterville, Maine, 1956, U. N.H., Durham, 1959-63, asst. prof., 1963-64; asst. dir. Addison Gallery Am. Art, Phillips Acad., Andover, Mass., 1964-69, dir., Andover, Maine, 1969—; dir. I.C.A., Boston, 1971-72, also dir. exhbn. program; vis. prof. Lesley Coll., Cambridge, Mass., 1974-77; vis. artist-tchr. Sch. Mus. Fine Arts, Boston, 1977-78. Author: Possibles, 1969, Book of Instnats, 1970, Poem-System Anytime, 1971; exhibited one-man shows, Colby Jr. Coll., Waterville, Maine, 1963, Phillips Exeter Acad., Andover, Mass., 1966, Eleanor Rigelhaupt Gallery, Boston, 1967, U.N.H., Durham, 1969, Bradford Jr. Coll., 1970, Jack Wendler Gallery, London, 1973, Inst. Contemporary Art, Boston, group shows, DeCordova Mus., Lincoln, Mass., 1964, Boston Art Festival, Smith Coll. Mus. Art, Northeastern Regional Mead Corp., 1965, Mus. Modern Art, N.Y.C., 1970, Center Art and Communications, Buenos Aires, Argentina, Center Art and Communications, Kyoto, Japan, 1971. Mem. Council on Museums and Edn. in Visual Arts (1973—); bd. advisers Archives of Am. Art (1972—). Home: Lee NH Office: Addison Gallery of Am Art Phillips Acad Andover MA 01810

COOK, CLARENCE SHARP, physics educator; b. St. Louis Crossing, Ind., Aug. 18, 1918; s. Clarence C. and Musa Gladys (Sharp) C.; m. Marian Norma Waring, June 19, 1943; children: Sherma Louise, Wayne William. A.B., DePauw U., 1940; M.A. in Physics, Ind. U., 1942, Ph.D., 1948. Asst. prof. physics Washington U., St. Louis, 1948-53; head nuclear radiation br. U.S. Naval Radiol. Def. Lab., San Francisco, 1953-60, head nucleonics div., 1960-62, physics cons. to sci. dir., 1962-65, head radiation physics div., 1965-69; lectr. U. Santa Clara, Calif., 1969-70; prof. physics U. Tex. at El Paso, 1970—, chmn. dept., 1970-72, 80-83. Author: Modern Atomic and Nuclear Physics, 1961, Structure of Atomic Nuclei, 1964; Contbg. author: (Reinhold) Ency. of Physics; Contbr. articles to profl. jours. Mem. bd. Civil Service Examiners for Scientists and Engrs., Pasadena, Calif., 1955-58, chmn., 1957-58; bd. dirs., exec. bd. El Paso Radiation Center Found., 1971-80; bd. dirs. El Paso Public TV Found., 1972-81; mem. univ. coordinating com. Tex. Energy Adv. Council, 1975-79. Served to capt. AUS, 1942-46. Fulbright research scholar Aarhus (Denmark) U., 1961-62. Fellow Am. Phys. Soc., Calif. Acad. Scis., AAAS; mem. Am. Assn. Physics Tchrs., Am. Geophys. Union, Meteoritical Soc., Health Physics Soc., Phi Beta Kappa, Sigma Xi. Club: Explorers (fellow). Home: 285 Maricopa El Paso TX 79912 Office: U Tex at El Paso El Paso TX 79968

COOK, DAVID ALASTAIR, pharmacology educator; b. Haslemere, Surrey, Eng., May 19, 1942; emigrated to Can., 1967; s. James W. and Monica (Reekes) C.; m. Barbara Waller, Sept. 8, 1967. M.A., Oriel Coll., Oxford U., D.Phil. Postdoctoral fellow U. Alta., Edmonton, 1967-70, asst. prof., 1970-74, assoc. prof., 1974-79, prof., 1979—, chmn. dept. pharmacology, 1981—. Contbr. articles to profl jours.; course designer, Canadian Equestrian Fedn., 1981. Named Tchr. of Yr. Med. Students Assn., 1974, 79, 81, 83; recipient Pharm. Soc. Jour. award, 1977. Mem. Pharm. Soc. Can., Western Pharm. Soc., Soc. Toxicology of Can., Canadian History Club. Office: Dept Pharmacology U Alberta Edmonton AB Canada T6G 2H7

COOK, DAVID CHARLES, III, publisher and editor; b. Elgin, Ill., June 11, 1912; s. David Charles, Jr. and Frances Lois (Kerr) C.; children: Margaret Anne, Martha L., Bruce L., Gregory D., Rebecca. Student, Occidental Coll., 1930-32; Ph.B., U. Chgo., 1934; Lit.D., Judson Coll., 1965. Chmn. bd. David C. Cook Pub. Co. (founded by grandfather 1875), Elgin, Ill., 1934, editor-in-chief of its 35 curriculum publs. Author: Walk the High Places, 1964, Invisible Halos, 1975. Dir. youth study tour Cultural Travel Found., 1955; v.p. Elgin Council Chs., 1954, pres., 1956-57; governing bd. Elgin Community Chest; pres. David C. Cook Found.; trustee Conf. Point Camp, Judson Coll., Elgin, Laubach Literacy, 1st Methodist Ch. Mem. Phi Kappa Psi. Office: David C Cook Pub Co 850 N Grove Ave Elgin IL 60120

COOK, DON, foreign correspondent; b. Bridgeport, Conn., Aug. 8, 1920; s. Paul J. and Nelle Brown (Reed) C.; m. Cherry Mitchell, Oct. 31, 1943 (dec. 1983); children: Christopher, Jennifer, Adrienne, Deborah, Caron, Danielle, Dominique. Student pub. schs., Abington, Pa. With St. Petersburg (Fla.) Times, 1938-40, Jenkintown (Pa.) Times-Chronicle, 1940-41; with Phila. bur. Trans-radio Press Service, 1941, Washington bur., 1941-43; with N.Y. Herald Tribune, Washington, 1943-45, London, 1945-49, corr., West Germany, 1949-52, roving European corr., Paris, 1952-55, chief London bur., 1956-60, chief European corr., Paris, 1960-65; Paris corr. Los Angeles Times, 1965—. Author: Floodtide in Europe, 1965, The War Lords: Eisenhower, 1975, Ten Men and History, 1981, Charles de Gaulle, a biography, 1983; contbr. to popular mags. Trustee Am. Sch. Paris, 1972-80. Recipient William the Silent award for journalism, 1956; English Speaking Union award for better understanding, 1957; citation Overseas Press, 1966. Mem. Assn. Am. Corrs. in London (past pres.), Authors Guild, Anglo-Am. Press Assn. Paris, Internat. Inst. Strategic Studies (London). Clubs: Garrick (London); Century (N.Y.C.). Office: Los Angeles Times 73 Champs-Elysees Paris 75008 France

COOK, DONALD JACK, educator, chemist; b. Rock Island, Ill., Feb. 12, 1915; s. Herbert Edgar and Daisy (Strupp) C.; m. Marion McCauley, Sept. 9, 1939; children: Christine Margaret, Hope Ann. A.B., Augustana (Ill.) Coll., 1937; M.A., U. Ill., 1938; Ph.D., Ind. U., 1944. With Am. Container Corp., Rock Island, 1939-40; mem. faculty Augustana Coll., 1940-41; with Tex. Co., 1941-42, Lubrizol Corp., 1944-45; mem. faculty DePauw U., 1945—, prof. chemistry, 1954-80, prof. emeritus, 1980—, head dept., 1964-80; with div. sci. personnel and edn. NSF, 1961-62; spl. research nitrogen heterocyclics. Contbr. profl. jours. Purdue U., postdoctoral fellow, 1952-53. Mem. Am. Chem. Soc. Republican. Methodist. Lodges: Rotary; Masons. Home: 625 E Washington St Greencastle IN 46135

COOK, DORIS MARIE, accounting educator; b. Fayetteville, Ark., June 11, 1924; d. Ira and Mettie Jewel (Dorman) C. B.S. in Bus. Adminstrn., U. Ark., 1946, M.S., 1949; Ph.D., U. Tex., Austin, 1969. C.P.A., Okla., Ark. Jr. acct. Haskins & Sells, C.P.A.s, Tulsa, 1946-47; instr. acctg. U. Ark., 1947-52, asst. prof., 1952-62, asso. prof., 1962-69, prof., 1969—. Contbr. articles to profl. jours. Named Woman of Yr., Fayetteville Bus. and Profl. Women's Club, 1977. Mem. Fayetteville Bus and Profl. Women's Club (pres. 1973-74, 75-76), Ozarks Econ. Assn. (editor newsletter 1982—), Ark. Fedn. Bus. and Profl. Women's Clubs (treas. 1979-80), Ark. Soc. C.P.A.s (v.p. 1975-76, sec. Student Loan Found. 1981—, pres. chpt. 1980-81), Am. Acctg. Assn. (nat. membership chmn. 1982-83, chmn. Arthur Carter Scholarship com. 1984-85), Am. Inst. C.P.A.s, Am. Woman's Soc. C.P.A.s, Mortar Bd., Beta Gamma Sigma, Beta Alpha Psi (nat. pres. 1977-78, nat. newsletter editor 1973-77), Phi Gamma Nu, Alpha Lambda Delta, Delta Kappa Gamma (sec. 1976-78, pres. 1978-80), Phi Kappa Phi. Home: 1115 Leverett St Fayetteville AR 72701 Office: U Ark Dept Acctg Fayetteville AR 72701

COOK, DOUGLAS NEILSON, theatre educator; b. Phoenix, Sept. 22, 1929; s. Neil Estes and Louise Y. (Wood) C.; m. Joan Stafford Buechner, Aug. 11, 1956; children: John Richard, Peter Neilson, Stephen Barton. Student, Phoenix Coll., 1948-49, U. Chgo., 1949-50, UCLA, 1950-52, Los Angeles Art Inst., 1948; B.F.A., U. Ariz., 1953; M.A., Stanford U., 1955; postgrad., Lester Polakov Studio Stage Design, 1966-67. Instr. San Mateo (Calif.) Coll., 1955-57, Nat. Music Camp, Interlochen, Mich., 1961; asst. prof. drama U. Calif., Riverside, 1957-66, asso. prof., 1967-70; prof. theatre and film Pa. State U., University Park, 1970—. Actor, Corral Theatre, Tucson, 1952-53, Orleans (Mass.) Arena Theatre, 1953; dir., designer, Palo Alto (Calif.) Community Theatre, 1954, Millbrae Community Theatre, 1955-57, Peninsula Children's Theatre, 1956-57; assoc. producer: Utah Shakespearean Festival, Cedar City, 1966—; producer, Pa. State Festival Theatre, State College, 1970—. Instl. rep. Juniata Valley council Boy Scouts Am., 1973-77; bd. dirs. Central Pa. Festival Arts, 1970-75. Humanities grantee U. Calif., 1964-65; Arts fellow U. Calif., 1966-67. Mem. Am. Theatre Assn. (dir. 1977—, exec. com. 1979-80, pres.-elect 1984-85), U.S. Inst. Theatre Tech., AAUP, Am. Soc. Theatre Research, Am. Nat. Theatre Assn., Univ. Resident Theatre Assn. (dir. 1971—, v.p. 1973-77, pres. 1977-82), Theatre Assn. Pa. (dir. 1972-76), Nat. Theatre Conf. (v.p. 1983—). Home: 526 Westview Ave State College PA 16803 Office: Pa State U University Park PA 16802

COOK, EDWARD JOSEPH, college president; b. N.Y.C., July 8, 1925; s. Clinton J. and Catherine A. (Cullen) C.; m. Dorothy A. Collins, July 21, 1951; children: Barbara A., Thomas E., Patricia M. B.S. summa cum laude, Fordham U., 1949, Ph.D., 1958; M.A., Columbia U., 1950. Assoc. prof., chmn. dept. econs. Sch. Bus., Fordham U., N.Y.C., 1950-62; asst. dean Sch. Bus., chmn. econs. dept. St. John's U., N.Y.C., 1962-64; prof. econs., dir. div. bus. C.W. Post Coll., Greenvale, N.Y., 1964-69, exec. dean Sch. Bus. Adminstrn., 1969-73; pres. C. W. Post Center, L.I. U., Greenvale, 1973—; mgmt. cons. to U.S. Navy and pvt. industry, 1969-73. Author: Causes of Commercial Bank Failures in New York State, 1958, (with R. Vizza) The Marketing Concept, 1968, (with A.F. Chapman) Peter Drucker, Contributions to Business Enterprises, 1970. Served with U.S. Army, 1943-45. Decorated Purple Heart. Mem. L.I. Regional Adv. Council Higher Edn. (trustee), Commn. Ind. Colls. and Univs. (exec. com.), Am. Econ. Assn. Roman Catholic. Office: C W Post Center of Long Island University Greenvale NY 11548

COOK, EDWARD WILLINGHAM, diversified industry executive; b. Memphis, June 19, 1922; s. Everett Richard and Phoebe (Willingham) C.; m. Patricia Long, Mar. 17, 1973; children: Patricia Kendall, Mark W.; children by previous marriage: Edward Willingham, Everett Richard II, Barbera Moore Cook Brooks. A.B., Yale U., 1944. Chmn. bd., chief exec. officer Cook Internat., Inc., Palm Beach, Fla. and Memphis; dir. First Tenn. Corp., Memphis; mem. Cotton Adv. Com., 1964-68; mem. exec. com. Nat. Council for U.S.-China Trade, 1973-78; mem. President's Export Council, 1973-79; dir. Chgo. Bd. Trade, 1974-76. Chmn. Memphis-Shelby County Airport Authority, 1968-81, Squire, Shelby County Ct., 1948-66. Served to maj. USAAF, 1943-45; MTO. Decorated D.F.C., Bronze Star, Air medal with six oak leaf clusters. Mem. So. Cotton Assn. (past pres.), Cotton Council Am. (dir. 1962-65), Cotton Council Internat. (dir. 1964-65), Am. Cotton Shippers Assn. (past pres.). Episcopalian. Clubs: Memphis Country, Memphis Hunt and Polo; Links (N.Y.C.); Everglades, Bath and Tennis (Palm Beach, Fla.). Office: 855 Ridge Lake Blvd Memphis TN 38117 also 322 Royal Poinciana Plaza Palm Beach FL 33480

COOK, ELTON STRAUS, chemist; b. Oberlin, Ohio, Dec. 24, 1909; s. Edward Monroe and Bertha (Straus) C.; m. Elizabeth Luck, June 1, 1935; children—Edward Mark, David Charles. B.A. summa cum laude, Oberlin Coll., 1930; Ph.D., Yale, 1933, postdoctoral fellow chemistry, 1933-34. Head dept. organic prodn. Wm. S. Merrell Co., Cin., 1934-37; research prof., head div. chemistry and biochemistry St. Thomas Inst. (formerly Institutum Divi Thomae), Cin., 1937—, dean, 1945—, v.p., dir., 1955-70, mem., 1970—; formerly dir. Internat. Hormones, Inc., Rookwood Pottery; sec. sci. adv. council Sperti Drug Products Corp., 1966-72. Contbr. numerous publs. to tech. jours. Del. 3d-11th Internat. Cancer Congresses; mem. Cin. Mayor's Com. Atomic Engergy, 1948; Dir. Mariemont Town Meeting, 1955-58; Alumni bd. Oberlin Coll., 1958-59. Recipient diploma of honor 1st Pan Am. Cancer Cytology Congress, 1957; Ann. Chemist award Cin. sect. Am. Chem. Soc., 1964. Fellow Am. Inst. Chemists (dist. dir. hon. mem. 1969), AAAS, Chem. Soc. London, Ohio Acad. Sci.; mem. Am. Chem. Soc. (chmn. Cin. 1958), Am. Pharm. Assn., Biochem. Soc. Gt. Britain, History Sci. Soc., Soc. Exptl. Biology and Medicine, Am. Assn. Cancer Research, N.Y. Acad. Sci., Ohio Inst. Chemists (pres. 1973-75), Phi Beta Kappa, Sigma Xi (v.p. Cin. 1955-57). Home: 6503 Park Ln Mariemont Cincinnati OH 45227 Office: 1842 Madison Rd Cincinnati OH 45206

COOK, FIELDER, producer-director; b. Atlanta, Mar. 9, 1923; s. George Lindsey and Marion (Fielder) C.; m. Sarah Eden Chamberlin, Apr. 1, 1950; children: Rebecca Eden, Lindsey Fielder. B.A. cum laude in English Lit, Washington and Lee U., 1947; postgrad. Elizabethan drama, U. Birmingham, Eng., 1948; D.Fine Arts, Washington and Lee U., 1973. Exec. J. Walter Thompson (advt.), 1950-56; partner Unit Four. Dir.: Lux Video Theatre, 1950-53; producer-dir.: Kraft TV Theatre, 1953-56, Kaiser Aluminum Hour, 1956-57; TV producer-dir.: Am. Jewish Com, 1961-62; freelance dir., Studio One, Philco-Goodyear Playhouse, U.S. Steel-Goodyear Playhouse, Playhouse 90, 1957-62; pres., Eden Prodns., Inc.; producers-dir.: Du Pont Show of Week, 1962-64; TV pilot films for series Beacon Hill; dir.: motion pictures Patterns, 1956, Home is the Hero, 1958, A Big Hand for the Little Lady, 1966, How to Save a Marriage and Ruin Your Life, 1966, Prudence and the Pill, London, 1967, Eagle in a Cage, Yugoslavia, 1969, The Hideaways, 1973; theatrical prodn. A Cook for Mr. General, 1961; author: original TV plays Zone Four, 1950, The Moment of the Rose, 1953, Throw Me a Rope, 1957; (Recipient TV awards for Patterns 1955); dir.: Snapfinger Creek, A Profile in Courage, 1956; Throw me a Rope, 1957, Project Immortality, 1959, A Big Deal in Lorado, 1962, Brigadoon, 1965, Teacher, Teacher, 1968, The Price, 1970, The Homecoming, 1971, The Hands of Cormac Joyce, 1972, Beacon Hill, 1975, Judge Horton and the Scottsboro Boys, 1976, Too Far to Go, 1979. Served to ensign USNR, 1944-46. Mem. Acad. TV Arts and Scis. (bd. govs.), Dirs. Guild Am. (v.p., mem. nat. bd.). Clubs: Players, N.Y. Athletic (N.Y.C.); Riviera Country (Los Angeles). Home: NY Athletic Club 180 Central Park S New York NY 10019

COOK, FRANCES D., diplomat; b. Charleston, W.Va., Sept. 7, 1945; d. Nash and Vivian C. B.A., Mary Washington Coll. of U. Va., 1967; M.P.A., Harvard U., 1978. Certificats d'Etudes, Université d'Aix-Marseille (France), 1966. Commd. fgn. service officer Dept. State, 1967; spl. asst. to R.S. Shriver, ambassador to France, 1968-69; mem. U.S. Del. Paris Peace Talks on Viet-Nam, 1970-71; cultural affairs officer, consul Am. Consul Gen., Sydney, Australia, 1971-73; cultural affairs officer, first sec. Am. Embassy, Dakar, Senegal, 1973-75; personnel officer for Africa USIA, Washington, 1975-77; dir. office public affairs African Bur. Dept. State, Washington, 1978-80; ambassador to Republic of Burundi, 1980-83; consul gen., Alexandria, Egypt, 1983—. Bd. dirs. Leopold Senghor Found., Washington. Recipient various honor awards Dept. State. Mem. Am. Fgn. Service Assn., Council on Fgn. Relations. Clubs: Harvard (N.Y.C.); International (Washington). Office: Am Consulate Gen 110 Ave Horreya Alexandria Egypt

COOK, FRED JAMES, journalist, author; b. Point Pleasant, N.J., Mar. 8, 1911; s. Frederick P. and Huldah (Compton) C.; m. Julia Barbara Simpson, June 5, 1936 (dec. 1974); children—Frederick P. II, Barbara J. (Mrs. Michael F. Gallagher); m. Irene H. Line, 1976. Litt.B., Rutgers U., 1932. Reporter Asbury Park Press, N.J., 1933-36, desk man, city editor, 1938-44; editor N.J. Courier, Toms River, 1936-37; rewriteman, feature writer N.Y. World Telegram and Sun, 1944-59; free-lance writer, 1959—. Author of: numerous books including The FBI Nobody Knows, 1964, The Corrupted Land, 1966, The Secret Rulers, 1966, The Plot Against the Patient, 1967, What So Proudly We Hailed, 1968, The Nightmare Decade, The Life and Times of Senator Joe McCarthy, 1971, Julia's Story, The Tragedy of an Unnecessary Death, 1976; Author: The Great Energy Scam: Private Billions vs. Public Good, 1983. Mem. adv. council on med. licensure and profl. conduct N.Y. State Legislature. Recipient Page One award N.Y. Newspaper Guild, 1958, 59, 60, spl. award for crusading journalism, 1980; Sidney Hillman Found. award, 1960. Mem. Authors League Am. *A writer, I believe, should have a dedication to truth; and once his research and intelligence convince him that he has found a kernel of that truth, he should write it as forcefully as he can, regardless of personal cost. If he is to be solely concerned with the pursuit of the larger dollar, he is not going to remain for long a writer whose words carry to his readers a sense of his own integrity.*

COOK, FRED S., educator; b. Lima, Ohio, July 17, 1920; s. J. Fred and Ruth (Greenawalt) C.; m. Betty Jean Samsal, Apr. 6, 1941; children: Linda Jean Cook Hickman, Marcia Diane. Student, Bluffton Coll., 1938-41; B.Sc., Ohio No. U., 1946; M.A., U. Mich., 1948, Ph.D., 1953. Instr. bus. adminstrn. Ohio No. U., 1947-48; teaching fellow, lectr. edn. U. Mich., 1948-52, vis. prof., summers 1953-54; head bus. edn. dept. Coe Coll., Cedar Rapids, Iowa, 1952-55; asst. prof. edn. in charge bus. and audio-visual edn. Stanford U., 1955-60; asso. prof. bus. and distbn. edn. Wayne State U., 1960-63, prof., 1963-83, chmn. dept., 1960-71, dir. div. vocat. and applied arts edn., 1971-72, asso. head div. tchr. edn., 1972-83; dir. research and edn. Nat. Secs. Assn. Internat., 1960-69; dir. Inst. Research and Devel. Competency Based Tchr. Edn. Programs, 1973-83; lectr. Indsl. Edn. Inst.; chmn. bd. govs. Fund Advancement Bus. Edn., 1959-60; bd. govs. Research and Devel. in Bus. Edn., 1st v.p., 1967—; pres. Research and Devel. in Edn., Ltd., 1976—. Sr. author: Gregg Junior High Typing, 3d edit., 1978, (with Lenore S. Forti) Professional Secretary's Handbook, 1971, 2d edit., 1981; editor: Secretarial Study Guide, 2d edit, 1970, Secretaries on the Spot, 2d edit., 1967, Secretarial Techniques Manual, 1963; contbr. numerous articles to profl. jours. Served with AUS, 1944-45. Recipient award of merit as Outstanding Bus. Educator of Year, Am. Vocat. Assn., 1976. Mem. Calif. Bus. Edn. Assn. (state pres. 1959-60), Nat. Office Mgmt. Assn. (nat. dir. 1959, past chpt. pres.), North Central Bus. Edn. Assn. (2d v.p. 1964-65), Delta Pi Epsilon. Researcher, dir. numerous research and devel. projects. Home: 19944 Doyle Pl E Grosse Pointe Woods MI 48236

COOK, FREDERICK HAROLD, transportation services company executive; b. Bloomington, Ind, Sept. 23, 1915; s. Frederick Raymond and Frances Irene (Allen) C.; m. Beryl A. Anderson, Feb. 25, 1939; children: Susan C. Murray, Nancy A. B.S., Ind. U., 1936, LL.D. hon., 1965. Chmn., pres. Congoleum-Nairn, Inc., Kearny, N.J., 1955-68; mng. dir. Dillon, Read & Co., Inc., N.Y.C., 1968-76; vice-chmn. bd. Purolator, Inc., Piscataway, N.J., 1981, pres., chief exec. officer, 1981-82, chmn., pres., chief exec. officer, 1982, chmn. bd., 1983—; dir. Englehard Corp., Menlo Park, N.J., 1970—, Nat. Gypsum Co., Dallas, 1972—, Nat. Newark & Essex Bank, 1964-68. Served to lt. USNR, 1942-45. Republican. Episcopalian. Home: Young's Rd New Vernon NJ 07976 Office: Purolator Inc 255 Old New Brunswick Rd Piscataway NJ 08854

COOK, GEORGE THOMAS, newspaper exec.; b. Indpls., Apr. 12, 1921; s. James Merkle and Mary (Harp) C.; m. Mary Frances Berry, May 3, 1952; children—Frances Ellen, Christopher Alan. A.B. in Journalism, U. Ala., 1949. Reporter Birmingham (Ala.) Post-Herald, 1949-62, state editor, 1962-65, city editor, 1965-66, mng. editor, 1966-80, asso. editor, 1980—. Served to 1st lt., inf., Military Police, Transp. Corps AUS, 1940-46. Methodist. Office: 2200 4th Ave Birmingham AL 35202

COOK, GEORGE VALENTINE, lawyer, electronics company executive; b. Glendale, N.Y., Feb. 14, 1927; s. Walter Preston and Ida Ruth (Smith) C.; m. Edith Wengler, Sept. 4, 1948; children: George V., James, Robert, Laura, Barbara, Mary, Walter, Elizabeth. B.A., Columbia U., 1949, LL.B., 1952. Bar: N.Y. 1953, U.S. Dist. Ct. (so. dist.) N.Y. 1955, U.S. Dist. Ct. (ea. dist.) N.Y. 1955, U.S. Ct. Appeals (2d cir.) 1955, U.S. Ct. Appeals (3d cir.) 1982. Assoc. Dewey, Ballantine, Bushby, Palmer & Wood, N.Y.C., 1952-56; mem. legal staff N.Y. Telephone Co., N.Y.C., 1956-59, 60-61; atty. AT&T, N.Y.C., 1959-60, 61-65, v.p., 1973-76; v.p. regulatory matters Western Electric Co., Inc., N.Y.C., 1966-72, v.p. gen. counsel, 1976-83, also dir.; exec. v.p., gen. counsel AT&T Technologies, Inc., N.Y.C., 1984—; dir. Teletype Corp., Sandia Corp., Western Electric Ltd. Contbr. articles to profl. jours. Active alumni activities Columbia U. Served to 2d lt. U.S. Army, 1945-47. Fellow Am. Bar Found.; mem. ABA, N.Y. State Bar Assn., Assn. Gen. Counsel, Nat. Legal Aid and Defender Assn. (dir.). Home: 127 Somerset Ave Garden City NY 11530 Office: 222 Broadway New York NY 10038

COOK, GEORGE WALLACE FOSTER, lawyer, tree farmer; b. Shrewsbury, Vt., May 20, 1919; s. Edward Jay C. and Helen M. (Cook) Foster; m. Laicita Warburton Gregg, Sept. 21, 1947; children: Constance Cook Whitmer, David Welling, Jonathan Foster, Timothy George, Heather Tiffany. A.B., Middlebury Coll., 1940; LL.B., Columbia U., 1948; LL.M., Georgetown U., 1952. Bar: D.C. 1949, Vt. 1955. Counsel Dept. of Navy, Washington, 1948-55; practice, Rutland, Vt., 1955-69; mem. Kinney & Cook, Rutland, Vt., 1955-63; U.S. atty. Dept. Justice, Rutland, Vt., 1969-78; U.S. magistrate Adminstrv.

Office U.S., Rutland, Vt., 1978-81; tree farmer. Mem. Vt. Senate, Montpelier, 1959-69 chmn. jud. com. 1963-69, pres. pro team 1965-69; mem. platform com. Republican Nat. Conv., 1964; chmn. Vt. Constl. Revision Commn., 1967-69. Served to 2d lt. USAF, 1943-46. Mem. ABA, Vt. Bar Assn., Rutland County Bar Assn. Home: 70 Litchfield Ave Rutland VT 05701 Office: US Atty Dept Justice Rutland VT 05701

COOK, HAROLD DALE, fed. judge; b. Guthrie, Okla., Apr. 14, 1924; s. Harold Payton and Mildred Arvesta (Swanson) C.; (div.)children—Harold Dale II, Caren Irene, Randall Swanson. B.S. in Bus, U. Okla., 1950, LL.B., 1950, J.D., 1970. Bar: Okla. bar 1950. Individual practice law, Guthrie, Okla., 1950, county atty., Logan County, Okla., 1951-54, asst. U.S. atty., Oklahoma City, 1954-58; asso. firm Butler, Rinehart and Morrison, Oklahoma City, 1958-61; partner Rinehart, Morrison and Cook, 1961-63; legal counsel and adviser to Gov. State of Okla., 1963-65; partner firm Cook and Ming, Oklahoma City, 1965, Cook, O'Toole, Ming and Tourtellotte, 1966-68, Cook, O'Toole and Tourtellotte, 1969-70, Cook and O'Toole, 1971; gen. counsel Shepherd Mall State Bank, Oklahoma City, 1967-71, pres., 1969-71, chmn. bd., 1969-71; dir. Bur. of Hearings and Appeals, Social Security Adminstrn., HEW, 1971-74; judge U.S. Dist. Ct., Tulsa, 1974-79; chief judge No. Dist. Okla., 1979—; mem. legal adv. council Okla. Hwy. Patrol, 1969-70; mem. magistrates com. Jud. Conf. U.S., 1980—; mem. indsl. adv. council Bur. Bus. and Econ. Research, U. Okla., 1970-71. First v.p. PTA, Sunset Elementary Sch., 1959-60; v.p. Parent-Tchrs. & Students Assn., John Marshall High Sch., Oklahoma City, 1970-71, pres., 1971; mem. Econ. Opportunity Com., Okla., 1963-65; tchr. Sunday sch. classes for coll., high sch. and adult ages Village Methodist Ch., Oklahoma City, 1959-65; mem. bd. of stewards First Meth. Ch., Guthrie, Okla., 1951-54. Served with USAAF, 1943-45. Recipient Secretary's Spl. Citation HEW, 1973. Fellow Am. Bar Found.; mem. ABA, Fed. Bar Assn., Okla. Bar Assn. (del. to state bar convs.), Oklahoma City C. of C. Republican. Clubs: So. Hills Country, Shriners, Masons, Tulsa, Order Eastern Star (past worthy patron Okla.), Scottish Rite (hon. insp. gen.). Office: United States Court House Tulsa OK 74103

COOK, HARRY CLAYTON, JR., lawyer; b. Washington, Mar. 25, 1935; s. Harry Clayton and Lillian June (A'harrah) C.; children—Christianne, Nicole, Harry Clayton III. B.S. in Chem. Enging, Princeton U., 1956; LL.B., U. Va., 1960. Bar: Colo. 1960, N.Y. 1961, Pa. 1966, D.C. 1973. Asso. firm Sullivan & Cromwell, N.Y.C., 1960-63, Holme Roberts & Owen, Denver, 1964, Pepper Hamilton & Scheetz, Phila., 1965-69, partner, 1969-70, 73; on assignment as sr. tax counsel Sun Oil Co., Phila., 1970; partner firm Cadwalader Wickersham & Taft, Washington, 1974—; gen. counsel Maritime Adminstrn.; mem. Maritime Subs. Bd., U.S. Dept. Commerce, Washington, 1970-73; U.S. del. to Soviet Union for Maritime Agreement between U.S. and USSR, 1971-73; mem. citizens adv. panel U.S. Office of Tech. Assessment, 1982-83; mem. presdl. transition team Fed. Maritime Commn., 1980-81. Contbr. articles to profl. jours. Bd. dirs. Inst. for Fgn. Policy Analysis, Inc., 1980—, Com. on the Present Danger. Mem. ABA (tax sect. 1965—), tax sect. (adminstr. practice sect. 1974—), D.C. Bar Assn., Fed. Bar Assn. (com. gen. counsels 1970—), Am. Law Inst., Adminstrv. Conf. U.S. (chmn. com. on judicial rev. 1982—), Maritime Law Assn. U.S. (marine fin. com. 1981—), Order of Coif, Phi Delta Phi. Clubs: Racquet of Phila.; Univ. (N.Y.C.). Office: 1333 New Hampshire Ave Suite 700 Washington DC 20036

COOK, HOWARD CARL, lawyer, former state senator; b. Toledo, Feb. 20, 1918; s. Henry D. and Caroline (Ackerman) C.; m. Elizabeth M. Ruch, Nov. 13, 1943; children: Susan E. Cook Thompson, Howard Carl. B.A., Wittenberg Coll., 1939; LL.B., Harvard U., 1942, J.D., 1969. Bar: Ohio 1942. Since practiced in Toledo; mem. firm Cline, Bischoff and Cook, 1946—; pres. Cline, Cook, Weisenburger & Drescher Co., LPA, 1980—; civil service commr., Toledo, 1948-52, vice mayor, 1952-53, councilman, 1952-53, 59-67; mem. Ohio Senate, 1967-74; dir. Nat. Cement Products Co., Centre Super Market Inc. Pres. bd. trustees Riverside Hosp., 1961-67; bd. govs. Ohio Fair Plan; past pres. Brotherhood Am. Luth. Ch. Served with USNR, 1942-45. Mem. Am., Ohio, Toledo bar assns., Amvets (past state vice comdr.), Toledo Area C. of C. (past trustee), Am. Legion, Phi Gamma Delta, Tau Kappa Alpha, Theta Alpha Phi, Alpha Kappa Psi. Home: 3818 Beechway Blvd Toledo OH 43614 Office: One Library Sq 911 Madison Ave Toledo OH 43604

COOK, JAMES, editor, writer; b. Schenectady, N.Y., Nov. 9, 1926; s. Harold James and Ruth May (Turner) C.; m. Claire Rose Kehrwald, Sept. 12, 1953; children—Karen Louise, Cassandra Claire. A.B., Bowdoin Coll., 1947; A.M., Columbia U., 1948. Instr. English Yankton (S.D.) Coll., 1948-49, Ohio U., 1949-52; editor Popular Publs., N.Y.C., 1952-53; mng. editor Railroad mag., 1953-55; asso., sr. editor Forbes mag., N.Y.C., 1955-76, exec. editor, 1976—; reviewer Forbes Restaurant Guide, 1970-71; editor Forbes in Arabic, 1975-76. Home: 200 W 16th St New York NY 10011 Office: 60 Fifth Ave New York NY 10011

COOK, JAMES IVAN, clergyman, religious educator; b. Grand Rapids, Mich., Mar. 8, 1925; s. Cornelius Peter and Cornelia (Dornbos) C.; m. Jean Rivenburgh, July 8, 1950; children: Mark James, Carol Jean, Timothy Scott, Paul Brian (dec.). B.A., Hope Coll., 1948; M.A., Mich. State U., 1949; B.D., Western Theol. Sem., 1952; Th.D., Princeton Theol. Sem., 1964. Ordained to ministry Reformed Ch. America, 1953. Pastor Blawenburg Reformed Ch., N.J., 1953-63; instr. bibl. langs. Western Theol. Sem., Holland, Mich., 1963-65, asst. prof. bibl. langs., 1965-67, prof. bibl. langs. and lit., 1967-77, Anton Biemont prof. N.T., 1977—; chmn. Theol. Commn., Reformed Ch. Am. N.Y.C., 1980—; pres. Gen. Synod-Reformed Ch. Am., N.Y.C., 1982-83. Author: Edgar Johnson Goodspeed, 1981; contbg. editor: Grace Upon Grace, 1975; contbg.: Saved by Hope, 1978, The Church Speaks. Served with U.S. Army, 1943-45; ETO. Mem. Soc. Bibl. Lit. Home: 1004 Shore Dr Holland MI 49423 Office: Western Theol Sem 86 E 12th St Holland MI 49423

COOK, JAMES SAMUEL, jewelry manufacturing company executive; b. Needham, Mass., Sept. 12, 1928; s. William A. and Frances (Cohoon) C.; m. Phyllis Towne, Sept. 12, 1953; children: Allison, James, Deborah, Jonathan, Susan. B.A., Brown U., 1950. Personnel asst., fgn. market analyst First Nat. Bank of Boston, 1952-56; with W.R. Grace & Co., 1956-74; pres., chief exec. officer L.G. Balfour Co., Attleboro, Mass., 1974—; chmn. bd. L.G. Balfour Co. of Can. Ltd.; dir. McCormick Co.; trustee Attleborough Savs. Bank. Trustee Sturdy Meml. Hosp., Attleboro. Served to capt. USMC, 1951-56. Mem. NAM (dir., regional vice chmn.), Mfg. Jewelers and Silversmiths Am. (dir.), Asso. Industries Mass. (dir.), Conf. Bd. (mem. N.E. regional council). Office: 25 County St Attleboro MA 02703

COOK, JEAN LOUISE, soprano; b. Phoenix, Mar. 6, 1937; d. Cecil Clifford and Nadine Mary (Larimer) C.; m. David Kreitzer. B.A. cum laude in Speech Arts, U. Calif., Santa Barbara, 1958; postgrad., Music Acad. of West, Santa Barbara, 1958-60. Debut as Pamina in: Mozart's Die Zauberflote at, Opernhaus Zurich, 1960; appeared with, Opernhaus Zurich, 1960-63, Opernhaus Koln, Germany, 1965-66, Opernhaus Koln, Duesseldorf, 1966-67, Opernhaus Koln, Essen, Germany, 1967-70, major opera cos. of, Geneva, Munich, Berlin, Hamburg, Barcelona, Palermo, Trieste, San Francisco; freelance concert and opera singer in, Geneva, Barcelona, Met. Opera, N.Y.C., Seattle Opera, Houston Opera, Ariz. Opera, Manila Opera; vocal coach. Named Outstanding Alumna in Performing Arts U. Calif., Santa Barbara, 1975; Martha Baird Rockefeller grantee, 1960, 64. Mem. Am. Guild Mus. Artists. Home and Office: 1442 12th St Los Osos CA 93402

COOK, JOHN CHRISTOPHER, association executive; b. Mayfield, Ky., Jan. 28, 1953; s. John Ellis and Betty Elaine (Humphries) C. B.A., U. Ky., 1976. Ptnr., mgr. Humphries Tobacco, Mayfield, Ky., 1976-80; dir. pub. relations U.S. Congressman Carroll Hubbard, Jr., Washington, 1980; chief fin. officer Greenplace U.S.A., Washington, 1981, adminstrv. dir., chief exec. officer, 1981—; treas. Antarctic Project, Washington, 1982—; bd. dirs. Greenplace Internat. Inc., Lewes, Eng., 1983—. Democrat. Baptist. Home: 3940 Livingston St NW Washington DC 20015 Office: Greenplace USA 2007 R St NW Washington DC 20009

COOK, JOHN ROWLAND, coal co. exec.; b. N.Y.C., May 20, 19- 41; s. Rowland B. and Carmalyn C.; m. Erika Kostick, Aug. 23, 1969; children—Dana, Karen. B.A. in Econs, Rutgers U., 1963; M.B.A., Harvard U., 1969. With Bankers Trust Co., N.Y.C., 1966-67; v.p. fin., treas., sec., chief fin. officer Molycorp., Inc., White Plains, N.Y., 1969-79; v.p. fin. and adminstrn., chief fin. officer N. Am. Coal Corp., Cleve., 1979—. Served to 1st lt. USAR, 1963-65. Mem. Fin. Execs. Inst. Address: N Am Coal Corp 12800 Shaker Blvd Cleveland OH 44120

COOK, JULIAN ABELE, JR., federal judge; b. Washington, June 22, 1930; s. Julian Abele and Ruth Elizabeth (McNeill) C.; m. Carol Annette Dibble, Dec. 22, 1957; children: Julian Abele III, Peter Dibble, Susan Annette. B.A., Pa. State U., 1952; J.D., Georgetown U., 1957. Bar: Mich. 1957. Law clk. to judge, Pontiac, Mich., 1957-58; asso. firm Bledsoe, Ford & Bledsoe, Detroit, 1958-60, Taylor, Patrick, Bailer & Lee, 1960-61; assoc. firm Cook & Hooe, Pontiac, 1961-65; ptnr. firm Hempstead, Houston, McGrath & Cook, Pontiac, 1965-68; individual practice law, Pontiac, 1968-74; assoc. firm Cook, Wittenberg, Curry & Magid, Pontiac, 1975, Cook & Curry, 1976-78; judge U.S. Dist. Ct. Eastern Dist. Mich., Detroit, 1978—; adj. prof. law U. Detroit Sch. Law, 1971-74; gen. counsel Sta. WTVS (Public TV), 1973-78; labor arbitrator Am. Arbitration Assn. and Mich. Employment Relations Commn., 1975-78; mem. Mich. Law and the Media Com., 1978—, Mich. State Bd. Ethics, 1977-78; dir. HGH Univ. Health Systems. Contbr. articles to legal jours. Mem. exec. bd. dirs., past pres. Child and Family Services Mich.; bd. dirs. Todd-Phillips Children's Home, Inc., Detroit Urban League, Mich. Heart Assn.; mem. adv. council Ashland Theol. Sem. Served with Signal Corps U.S. Army, 1952-54. Recipient merit citation Pontiac Area Urban League, 1971; resolution Mich. Ho. of Reps., 1971; named Boss of Yr. Oakland County Legal Secs. Assn., 1973-74; Pathfinders award Oakland U., 1977; Service award Todd-Phillips Home, Inc., 1978. Fellow Am. Bar Found.; mem. NAACP (Disting. Citizen of Yr. 1970, mem. state constl. revision and legal redress com. 1963), Mich. Bar Assn. (chmn. constl. law com. 1969, vice-chmn. civil liberties com. 1970), Oakland County Bar Assn. (chmn. continuing legal edn. com. 1968-69, jud. liaison Dist. Ct. com. 1977, continuing legal edn. com. 1977, unauthorized practice law com. 1977), Am. Bar Assn., Nat. Bar Assn., Fed. Bar Assn. (dir. Detroit chpt.), Wolverine Bar Assn., Georgetown U. Alumni Assn. (bd. dirs.). Office: 277 US Courthouse Detroit MI 48226

COOK, LEONARD CLARENCE, manufacturing company executive; b. Gay's River, N.S., Can., July 20, 1936; came to U.S., 1966; s. Clarence Ralph and Bertha L. (Webster) C.; m. Florence Joyce Bousfield, Sept. 23, 1961; children: Douglas, L. Scott, Heath, Tamara. B.Sc., Royal Mil. Coll., Kingston., Ont., 1959. Prodn. mgr. Eaton Corp., 1966-77, dir. purchases, Cleve., 1977-78, v.p. materials mgmt., 1978-82, ops. gen. mgr., Aurora, Ohio, 1982—. Trustee Rainey Inst., Cleve., Hiram House, Cleve.; loaned exec. Pres.' Hire Program, Cleve., 1977-78. Served to capt. Can. Armed Forces, 1959-66. Mem. Soc. Automotive Engrs., Machinery and Allied Products Inst., Nat. Assn.Purchasing Mgmt., Ohio C. of C. (dir.). Republican. Episcopalian. Clubs: Country (Pepper Pike, Ohil); Pine Lake Trout (Chagrin Falls, Ohio). Home: 180 Sterncrest Dr Moreland Hills OH 44022

COOK, LEROY FRANKLIN, JR., educator, physicist; b. Ashland, Ky., Dec. 12, 1931; s. LeRoy Franklin and Dorothy (Williams) C.; m. Arrelle Janet Rapp, June 16, 1957; children: Nancy Grace, Laura Arrelle, Andrew LeRoy. B.A., U. Calif.-Berkeley, 1953, M.A., 1957, Ph.D., 1959. Instr. Princeton U., 1959-62, asst. prof., 1962-65; asso. prof. U. Mass., Amherst, 1965-68, prof. physics, 1968—, acting head physics dept., 1969-71, head physics and astronomy dept., 1971-75, 79—; cons. Inst. Def. Analyses, Arlington, Va., 1963-67; vis. fellow Clare Hall, Cambridge U., spring 1972. Contbr. articles profl. jours. Mem. exec. com. Gt. Trails council Boy Scouts Am. Served with AUS, 1953-55. Fellow Am. Phys. Soc.; mem. AAAS, AAUP, Sigma Xi. Home: 48 Morgan Circle Amherst MA 01002

COOK, LOWDRICK M., petroleum company executive; b. 1928; married. B.S., La. State U., 1950, 1955; M.B.A., So. Meth. U., 1965. Petroleum engr. Union Producing Co., 1955-56; with sales dept. Nabors Trailers, 1956; with Atlantic Richfield Co., Inc., Los Angeles, 1956—, enging. trainee, 1956-61, adminstrv. asst., 1961-64, sr. personnel dept., then personnel mgr., Los Angeles, 1964-67, labor reins. con., 1967-69, mgr. labor reins. dept., 1969-70, v.p., gen. mgr. product div. Western area, 1970-72, v.p. mktg. products div., 1972-73, v.p. corp. planning div., 1973-74, v.p. products div., 1974-75, v.p. transp. div., 1975-77, sr. v.p. transp. div., 1977-80, exec. v.p., dir., 1980—; dir. Domtar, Inc. Served to 1st. U.S. Army, 1950-53. Office: Atlantic Richfield Co Inc 515 S Flowers St Los Angeles CA 90071 *

COOK, LYLE EDWARDS, fund-raising executive; b. Astoria, Oreg., Aug. 19, 1918; s. Courtney Carson and Fanchon (Edwards) C.; m. Olive Freeman, Dec. 28, 1940; children: James Michael, Ellen Anita Cook Otto, Mary Lucinda Cook Vaage, Jane Victoria. A.B. in History, Stanford U., 1940, postgrad., 1940-41. Instr. history Yuba Jr. Coll., Marysville, Calif., 1941-42; methods analyst Lockheed Aircraft Corp., 1942-45; investment broker Quincy Cass Assos., Los Angeles, 1945-49; mem. staff Stanford U., 1949-66, asso. dean Sch. Medicine, 1958-65; sr. staff mem. Lester Gorsline Assos., Belvedere, Calif., 1966-72, v.p., 1967-70, exec. v.p., 1970-72; v.p. univ. relations U. San Francisco, 1973-75; fund-raising and planning cons., 1975; dir. fund devel. Children's Home Soc. Calif., 1976-78; exec. dir. That Man May See, Inc., San Francisco, 1978—; trustee, chmn. bd. The Fund Raising Sch.; spl. cons. NIH, 1960-62. Mem. Nat. Soc. Fund Raising Execs. (bd. dirs. Inst.), Stanford Assos., Theta Delta Chi. Episcopalian. Club: Belvedere Tennis. Home: 1750 Lagoon View Dr Tiburon CA 94920 Office: 374 Parnassus Ave Suite 312 San Francisco CA 94143

COOK, M(ELVIN) GARFIELD, chemical company executive; b. Woodbury, N.J., June 17, 1940; s. Melvin Alonzo and Wanda (Garfield) C.; m. Margo Dawn Taylor, Aug. 24, 1965; children: Dawn Ann, Melvin, Katherine, JoAnn, Carol, Mary, Taylor, Stephen, Michael. B.S. in Physics, U. Utah, 1966. Research assoc. IRECO Chems., Salt Lake City, 1966-67; gen. mgr. Mesabi Blasting, Inc., Biwabik, Minn., 1967-69; v.p. ops. IRECO Chems., 1969-71, exec. v.p., 1971-72, pres., chief exec. officer, 1972—; dir. Def. Systems, Inc., Salt Lake City; advisor on explosives and propellants Dept. Def., Washington, 1979—; bd. govs. Inst. of Makers of Explosives, Washington, 1972—. Author: Everlasting Burnings, 1981, Ency. Modern Explosives, 1972—, (with M.A. Cook) Science and Mormonism, 1967. Vice pres. N.E. Bench Region Council, Salt Lake City, 1974; chmn. voting dist. Republican Party, 1973. Served with USAR, 1958-66. Mem. Mayflower Soc. Republican. Mormon. Lodge: Rotary. Office: IRECO Chemicals 11th Floor Crossroads Tower 50 S Main St Salt Lake City UT 84144

COOK, MICHAEL, playwright; b. London, Feb. 14, 1933; s. George William C.; m. Madonna Decker, Dec. 28, 1973; children: Michael, Diane, Graham, Elaine, Adrian, Etain, Rowena, Christopher, Sarah, Sebastian, Fergus. Grad. in drama with distinction, Nottingham U. Coll. Edn., 1966. Profl. soldier with REME, Intelligence, 1949-61; primary tchr., 1961-63; drama specialist Meml. U. Nfld. (Can.), St. John's, 1966-69, lectr. in English, 1969-72, asst. prof. English, 1972-78, asso. prof., 1978—; free-lance journalist, 1967—; artistic dir. St. John's Festival of Arts, 1969-76; gov. Can. Conf. of Arts, 1975-79; chmn. arts grants/awards com. Govt. Ndlf./Labrador, 1978-79; mem. Nfld. Arts Council, 1979-82. Author: plays The Head, Guts and Sound Bone Dance, 1974, Jacob's Wake, 1975, Tiln and Other Plays, 1976, Three Plays, 1977, Not As A Dream, 1978, The Fisherman's Revenge, 1978, The Gayden Chronicles, 1979, A Special Providence, 1980, The Deserts of Bohemia, 1981, The Painful Education of Patrick Brown, 1983; also author numerous radio and TV plays. Decorated Queen's Jubilee medal; Can. Council sr. arts grantee, 1973-74, 1979-80. Mem. Playwrights Can., Assn. Can. Radio and TV Actors, Guild Can. Playwrights (v.p.). Home and Office: Box 327 Rural Route 1 Petley Random Island NF A0E 1J0 Canada

COOK, MICHAEL COLEMAN, utility executive; b. N.Y.C., Sept. 28, 1939; s. Joseph and Nancy (Fellerman) C.; m. Carole Hare, Feb. 3, 1962; children: Allison, Roberta, Andrew. B.Chem. Enging., CCNY, 1960; M.B.A., Baruch Coll., 1969. Project engr. AEC, N.Y.C., 1960-65; sr. engr. Mobil Oil Corp., N.Y.C., 1965-67; investment banker Sartorius & Co., N.Y.C., 1967-70; v.p. Earl Bronsteen & Co., N.Y.C., 1970-71; sr. cons. Auerbach Assos., N.Y.C., 1971-72; treas. Fla. Power & Light Co., Miami, 1972-77, v.p., 1977-84, group v.p., 1984—. Bd. dirs. Jr. Achievement of Greater Miami, 1972—, pres., 1976, chmn. bd., 1977. Mem. Am. Inst. Chem. Engrs., Fin. Execs. Inst. Office: PO Box 029100 Miami FL 33102

COOK, MICHAEL LEWIS, lawyer; b. Rochester, N.H., Mar. 5, 1944; s. Israel J. and Molly L. C.; m. Stephanie L. Cook, Apr. 11, 1976. A.B., 1965; J.D., NYU, 1968. Bar: N.Y. 1968. Assoc. Weil, Gotshal & Manges, N.Y.C., 1970-75, ptnr., 1975-80, Skadden, Arps, Slate, Meagher & Flom, 1980—; adj. prof. law NYU Sch. Law, 1975—. Co-author: A Practical Guide to the Bankruptcy Reform Act, 1979; contbr.: Collier on Bankruptcy, 1979, Collier Bankruptcy Guide, 1981. Mem. ABA, Assn. Bar City N.Y., Fed. Bar Council. Home: 101 W 12th St Apt 9P-R New York NY 10011 Office: Skadden Arps Slate Meagher & Flom 919 3d Ave New York NY 10022

COOK, MILTON OLIN, educator; b. Preston, Miss., Jan. 21, 1933; s. Milton Chester and Rosie Mae (Fulton) C.; m. Millicent Corean King, July 28, 1957; children—Kimberly Suzanne, Leslie Corean. A.A., E. Miss. Jr. Coll., 1953; postgrad, Millsaps Coll., 1957; M.Ed., Emory U., 1960; Ed.D., Auburn U., 1963. Tchr. math. Avondale High Sch., Decatur, Ga., 1957-61; research asso. Office of Instl Research, Auburn U., 1961-63; psychologist DeKalb County Sch., Decatur, Ga., 1963-64; asst. dir. Commn. on Coordination of Higher Ednl. Fin., Little Rock, 1964-69; dir. Ark. Dept. Higher Edn., Little Rock, 1969-79; exec. v.p. Ark. Tech. U., 1979—. Contbr. numerous articles to profl. jours. Active 1st United Methodist Ch., Russellville, Ark.; bd. dirs North Hills Sch., N. Little Rock, 1978—. Served with U.S. Army, 1954-56. Mem. State Higher Edn. Exec. Officers (mem. exec. com. 1976-79, past pres.), Assn. Governing Bds. of Colls. and Univs., Phi Delta Kappa, Phi Kappa Phi. Democrat. Office: Ark Tech U Russellville AR 72801

COOK, PAUL M., manufacturing company executive; b. Ridgewood, N.J. B.S. in Chem. Enging, M.I.T., 1947. With Stanford Research Inst., Palo Alto, Calif., 1949-53, Sequoia Process Corp., 1953-56; with Raychem Corp., Menlo Park, Calif., 1957—, former pres., chief exec. officer, dir., now chmn., chief exec. officer, dir. Office: Raychen Corp 300 Constitution Dr Menlo Park CA 94025 *

COOK, PAUL WENTWORTH, mfg. co. exec.; b. New Bedford, Mass., July 17, 1921; s. Louis deLaittre and Helena (Lindsay) C.; m. Marjory Louise Biggart, Dec. 12, 1944; children—Billie Louise, Paul Wentworth, Elizabeth Stanton, James Rowland. Grad., Phillips Acad., Andover, Mass., 1939; A.B., Harvard, 1943, Advanced Mgmt. Program, 1972; M.B.A., J.D., U. Mich., 1950; LL.M., N.Y. U., 1962. Bar: N.Y. bar 1952; C.P.A., N.Y. Tax specialist Lybrand, Ross Bros., and Montgomery, C.P.A.'s, N.Y.C., 1950-55; sr. tax accountant ACF Industries, Inc., 1955-57; sr. analyst Mobil Oil Corp., 1957-58; asst. controller Mobil Oil of Can. Ltd., 1958-60, div. controller, 1960-62, mgr. tax adminstrn., 1962-66; with Lever Bros. Co., 1966—, treas., 1968—. Bd. dirs., past pres. N.J. Taxpayers Assn.; former mem. exec. bd. Union council Boy Scouts Am.; bd. dirs. Cranford United Fund. Served to 1st lt. AUS, World War II. Recipient Silver Beaver award, 1975. Mem. Am. Bar Assn. (past chmn. com. excise and employment taxes), N.A.M., Am. Inst. C.P.A.'s, Financial Execs. Inst., Am. Mgmt. Assn., Phi Kappa Phi, Beta Gamma Sigma. Episcopalian. Club: University (N.Y.C.). Home: 105 Cranford Ave Cranford NJ 07016 Office: 390 Park Ave New York NY 10022

COOK, RAMONA GRAHAM (RAMONA GRAHAM), author; b. San Miguel, Calif., Jan. 3, 1892; d. Oswell M. and Florence (Mead) Graham; m. William R. Cook, Sept. 17, 1924; 1 son, William R. Student pub. schs., Cornell Coll., Thomas Normal Tng. Sch. Lit. chmn. Mass. State Fedn., 1948-50; pres. Boston chpt. then pres. Mass. chpt Nat. League Am. Pen Women, nat. v.p., Washington, 1966-68, nat. pres., 1968-70. Author: book of poems From Boston, 1936, Hills of New England, 1946, What the Heart Craves, 1956, Aeolus Drives, 1969; non fiction With Uncle Thomas, 1967; poems Ballads From A Cart, 1970; numerous poems pub. in popular mags. and newspapers, including, Sat. Evening Post, Am. Scholar, Yankee mag., N.Y. Times, Advance; author short fiction. Life mem. N.E. Women's Press Assn.; mem. Boston Authors Club. Home: 109 Main St Box 394 Rockport MA 01966

COOK, RICHARD KELSEY, aerospace industry executive; b. White Plains, N.Y., Nov. 14, 1931; s. Albert James and Frances Elizabeth (Butler) C.; m. Marjorie S. Schellabarger, Sept. 10, 1959 (div.); children: Geoffrey, Patrick, Sarah, Catherine. Postgrad., Stanford U., 1979; A.B., George Washington U., 1958. Legis staff Am. Trucking Assn., 1959-61; adminstrv. asst. Rep. Edwin B. Dooley, 1961; legis. asst. Rep. Oliver P. Bolton, 1963-65; profl. staff mem. Banking and Currency Com., U.S. Ho. of Reps., Washington, 1965-69; spl. asst. to Pres. of U.S., Washington, 1969-73; v.p. Lockheed Corp., Washington, 1973—. Served with USAF, 1949-53. Mem. Tau Kappa Epsilon. Clubs: Aero. (pres. 1979), Met.; Burning Tree (Washington). Office: Lockheed Corp 1825 I St NW Suite 1100 Washington DC 20006

COOK, RICHARD WALLACE, engineer; b. Muskegon, Mich., Aug. 8, 1907; s. Harry James and Rose (Van Dame) C.; m. Helen L. Benson, Dec. 25, 1934. B.S., Mich. State U., 1933. Registered profl. engr., Wis. Marine constrn. Gt. Lakes area, 1933-35; resident engr. in charge constrn. Consoer, Townsend & Quinlan (cons. engrs.), 1935-40; dep. mgr. Oak Ridge operations AEC, 1947-49, mgr., 1949-51, dir. prodn., Washington, 1951, asst. gen. mgr. mfg., 1954, dep. gen. mgr., 1954-58; dir. adminstrn. govt. products group Am. Machine and Foundry Co., 1958-59; divisional v.p., dep. group exec., also group exec. Atomic Energy Group, AMF, 1959-61, v.p., dep. group exec. Titan program and govt. products group; dir. AMF Atomics Can., Ltd., 1959-61, dir. atomics and adminstrv. divs., 1962; corporate v.p. spl. products Advance Products Group AMF, 1962-64; asst. dir. research and devel. operations, dep. dir. operations, sci. and engring. Marshall Space Flight Center, NASA, Huntsville, Ala., 1964-69, dep. dir. mgmt., 1969-73; mng. partner Pines Assocs., Southern Pines, N.C., 1973—; chmn. bd. F.R. Lawrence & Co. (investments.), People's Advantage Corp.; Bd. dirs. Seven Lakes Land Owners Assn., 1979-83. Served from 1st lt. to col., Q.M.C., C.E. AUS, 1940-47. Decorations include Legion of Merit, Army Commendation ribbon, Meritorious Service Unit Star; recipient Mich. State U. Centennial award, 1955; AEC Distinguished Service award, 1956; Exceptional Service medal NASA, 1969; Distinguished Service medal NASA, 1973. Mem. ASCE, Phi Kappa Tau, Blue Key, Scabbard and Blade. Club: Elks. Home and office: Seven Lakes Box 550 West End NC 27376

COOK, ROBERT ANDREW, college president; b. Santa Clara, Calif., June 7, 1912; s. Charles Alfred and Daisy (Gray) C.; m. Coreen Nilsen, Sept. 24, 1935; children: Carolyn (Mrs. Wendell Borrink), Marilyn (Mrs. John Parry), Lois (Mrs. Michael Gillern). Grad. pastor's course, Moody Bible Inst., Chgo., 1930; B.A., Wheaton (Ill.) Coll., 1934; B.D., Eastern Bapt. Sem., 1939; LL.D., Northwestern Schs., Mpls., 1950; L.H.D. (hon.), Bob Jones U., 1945; Ped.D., Houghton Coll., 1965. Ordained to ministry Baptist Ch., 1931; pastor in, Phila., 1934-39, LaSalle, Ill., 1939-44, Chgo., 1944-48; pres. Youth for Christ Internat., 1948-57; v.p. Scripture Press, Wheaton, 1957-61; pres. King's Coll., Briarcliff Manor, N.Y., 1962—; Daily broadcaster radio stas. throughout East and Midwest, 1963—. Author: Reaching Youth for Christ, 1944, Now That I Believe, 1949, It's Tough to be a Teenager, 1955, How to Get Along with Christians, 1956, Just Between Us, 1960, Leveling with God, 1966, Walk with the King Today, 1978; also articles. Pres. Nat. Assn. Evangelicals, 1962-64. Mem. NEA, Nat. Religious Broadcasters (1st v.p.), Evang. Theol. Soc., Am. Assn. Higher Edn., Ministerial Assn. Evang. Free Ch. Am. Home: 224 Central Dr Briarcliff Manor NY 10510

COOK, ROBERT DONALD, business executive; b. Chicago Heights, Ill., Nov. 1, 1929; s. Webster Warren and Gladys (Miner) C.; m. Maxine Jensen, Nov. 11, 1950; children: Carolyn Jean, Robert Donald II. B.S. in Bus, U. Md., 1956; grad. advanced mgmt. program, Harvard U., 1973. C.P.A., Md. Audit mgr. Arthur Andersen & Co. (C.P.A.'s), Washington, 1956-63; comptroller Peoples Drug Stores, Washington, 1963-68; v.p., controller Booz, Allen & Hamilton, Inc., Chgo., 1968-72; pres. Cookemper Rentals, Inc., Barrington, Ill., 1971-73; controller Esmark, Inc., Chgo., 1973-77; sr. exec. v.p., pres. foods Castle & Cooke, Inc., San Francisco, 1977—. Served with USNR, 1948-52. Mem. Inst. C.P.A.s, Fin. Execs. Inst., Beta Alpha Psi. Clubs: Masons (32 deg.), Shriners.). Home: 75 Rolling Hills Rd Tiburon CA 94920 Office: 50 California St San Francisco CA 94111

COOK, ROBERT HOWARD, sculptor; b. Boston, Apr. 8, 1921; s. Robert Howard and Elizabeth (King) C.; m. Joan Marble, Mar. 10, 1951; children: Jennifer, Henry Marble. Student, Demetrios Sch. Sculpture, Boston, 1938-42, Beaux Arts, Paris, France, 1945. Sculptor, Rome, Italy, 1948—; Hon. trustee Sculpture Center, N.Y.C. Author, designer: Family Album in Bronze, 1976, Twelve Commissions, 1978, In Motion, 1979; subject of: documentary film World of Robert Cook, 1979; major commns. include Thespis, Canberra (Australia) Theater Center, 1965, Dinoceras, 345 Park Ave., N.Y.C., 1971, Achievement, Sun Co., Radnor, Pa., 1978, Camel, Jeddah, Saudi Arabia, 1982, Horserace, Jeddah, Saudi Arabia, 1983, Sun Co., Radnor, Pa., 1978, others in, Dallas, Johnson City, Tenn., Boston, San Diego, Racine, Wis. Served with C.E. AUS, 1942-46. Recipient 2d prize Prix de Rome Competition, 1943, Nat. Acad. Arts and Letters award, 1948, Tiffany Found. award, 1948; Fulbright fellow, 1949. Mem. Sculptors Guild N.Y.C. Home: 91 Piazza Borghese Rome Italy 00186 Office: 51 A Via Margutta Rome Italy 00187

COOK, SAM B., banker; b. Jefferson City, Mo., Apr. 20, 1922; s. Howard and Gertrude (Shuman) C.; children: Sam Bryan, Cynthia Ann Grumney, Sarah McAdam Tryhus, Julia. Student, U. Mo., 1941-43; B.A., Yale U., 1948. With Chase-Manhattan Bank, N.Y.C., 1948-50; with Central Trust Bank, Jefferson City, 1950—, v.p., dir., 1953-61, pres., 1961-80, chmn. bd., 1980—, dir., 1961—; chmn. bd. First Nat. Bank of Clayton, 1970—; pres. Central Bancompany, 1971-77, chmn., 1977—; dir. M.P.R.R., 1964-82, Union Electric Co. Campaign chmn. Jefferson City United Community Fund, 1954; Mo. treas. Crusade for Freedom, 1957; mem. Gov.'s Task Force on Higher Edn., Mo. Hwy. Commn., 1963; chmn. Jefferson City Commn. on Environ. Quality, 1972-74, co-chmn., 1980-81; dean's adv. council bus. and pub. adminstrn. U. Mo., Columbia, 1978—; chmn. exec. com. Greater Jefferson City Com.; chmn. Jefferson City Housing Authority, 1981—; treas. Mo. Council on Econ. Edn., mem. exec. com., 1980—; Trustee, treas. William Woods Coll.; trustee St. Louis Art Mus.; campaign chmn. YMCA, 1977; trustee Washington U., 1974—. Served to capt. F.A. AUS, 1943-46. Named outstanding young man Jefferson City, 1958. Mem. Mo. Bankers Assn. (pres. 1958-59), Mo. C. of C. (pres. bd. dirs. 1977-79), Phi Beta Kappa, Phi Delta Theta. Home: 3308 Country Club Dr Jefferson City MO 65101 Office: Central Bank 238 Madison St Jefferson City MO 65101

COOK, SAMUEL DUBOIS, university president, political scientist; b. Griffin, Ga., Nov. 21, 1928; s. Manuel and Mary Beatrice (Daniel) C.; m. Sylvia Merelene Fields, Mar. 18, 1960; children: Samuel DuBois, Karen Jarcelyn. A.B., Morehouse Coll., 1948, LL.D., 1972; M.A., Ohio State U., 1950, Ph.D., 1954, L.H.D., 1977; LL.D., Duke U., 1979, Ill. Coll., 1979. Asso. prof. polit. sci. So. U., 1955-56; prof., chmn. dept. polit. sci. Atlanta U., 1956-66; asso. prof. Duke U., Durham, N.C., 1966-71, prof., 1971-74; pres. Dillard U., New Orleans, 1975—; vis. prof. U. Ill., 1962-63, UCLA, summer 1966; program officer higher edn. and research Ford Found., 1969-71; cons. in field. Contbr. articles to profl. jours. and anthologies. Mem. So. Growth Policies Bd., 1972-73, N.C. Council on Goals and Policies, 1971-74; mem. exec. com. So. Regional Council, 1967-69; trustee Martin Luther King Jr. Center for Social Change, 1968—; bd. dirs. Council for Library Resources, 1976—; mem. advisory council Jt. Center for Polit. Studies, 1972-75; trustee Duke U. Served with U.S. Army, 1953-55. Fellow Rockefeller Found., Ford Found., Social Sci. Research Council, So. Edn. Found., Omega Psi Phi Nat.; Mem. Am. Polit. Sci. Assn. (past mem. exec. council, v.p. 1978-79), Conf. Black Polit. Scientists, Assn. for Study Afro-Am. Life and History (mem. exec. council), So. Polit. Sci. Assn. (past pres.), Nat. Council for Humanities, Pi Sigma Alpha, Phi Beta Kappa, Omicron Delta Phi, Omega Psi Phi, Sigma Pi Phi. Democrat. Baptist. Home: 2601 Gentilly Blvd New Orleans LA 70122 Office: Dillard U 2601 Gentilly Blvd New Orleans LA 70122 *Perhaps the most difficult and precious of all achievements is that of being a decent human being.*

COOK, STANTON R., newspaper publisher; b. Chgo., July 3, 1925; s. Rufus Merrill and Thelma Marie (Bogerson) C.; m. Barbara Wilson. B.S. in Mech. Engring, Northwestern U., 1949. Dist. sales rep. Shell Oil Co., 1949-51; prodn. engr. Chgo. Tribune, 1951-60, asst. prodn. mgr., 1960-65, prodn. mgr., 1965-67, prodn. dir., 1967-70, dir. ops., 1970, gen. mgr., 1970-73, pub., 1973—; v.p. Chgo. Tribune Co., 1967-70, exec. v.p., 1970-73, chief officer, 1974-76, chmn., 1974—; v.p., dir. Tribune Co., Chgo., 1967-70, exec. v.p., 1970-73, chief officer, 1974—; 2d vice chmn., dir. AP; former dep. chmn. and dir. Fed. Res. Bank of Chgo., chmn., 1984. Trustee, chmn. citizens bd. U. Chgo., Mus. Sci. and Industry, Field Mus. Natural History, all Chgo., Robert R. McCormick Trusts and Founds., MacArthur Meml. Found. Mem. Am. Newspaper Pubs. Assn. (trustee, dir.), Chgo. Council Fgn. Relations (dir.), Chgo United (exec. com.). Office: 435 N Michigan Ave Chicago IL 60611 *

COOK, STEPHEN ARTHUR, mathematics and computer science educator; b. Buffalo, Dec. 14, 1939; s. Gerhard Albert and Lura (Lincoln) C.; m. Linda Marie Craddock, May 4, 1968; 1 son, Gordon. B.S. in math., U. Mich., 1961, S.M., Harvard U., 1962, Ph.D., 1966. Asst. prof. U. Calif.-Berkeley, 1966-70; assoc. prof. U. Toronto, 1970-75, prof., 1975—. Contbr. articles to profl. jours. E.W.R. Staecie Meml. fellow, 1977-78; Killam research fellow Can. Council, 1982-83; recipient ACM Turing award Assn. Computing Machinery, 1982. Home: 6 Indian Valley Crescent Toronto ON Canada M6R 1Y6 Office: Dept Computer Sci U Toronto Toronto ON Canada M5S 1A4

COOK, STUART DONALD, physician, educator; b. Boston, Oct. 23, 1936; s. Martius and Nina (Schwartzman) C.; m. Josepha Emdin, June 26, 1960; children—Andrew, Peter, Jonathan. A.B., Brandeis U., 1957; M.S., U. Vt., 1959, M.D., 1962. Diplomate: Am. Bd. Psychiatry and Neurology. Intern Upstate Med. Center, Syracuse, N.Y., 1962-63, resident in neurology, 1965-67, chief resident, 1967-68; instr. dept. neurology Albert Einstein Coll. Medicine, Bronx, N.Y., 1968-69; asst. prof. neurology Coll. Physician and Surgeons, Columbia U., 1969-71; prof. medicine N.J. Med. Sch., Newark, 1971—, chmn. dept. neuroscis., 1972—; chief neurology service VA Med. Center, East Orange, N.J., 1971—; vis. scientist div. virology Nat. Inst. Med. Research, London, 1977-78; cons. HEW. Contbr. articles to profl. jours. Served with USN, 1963-65. Mem. Am. Acad. Neurology (S. Weir Mitchell award 1968), Am. Assn. Neuropathologists, AAUP, Am. Fedn. Clin. Research, Assn. Univ Profs. Neurology, Harvey Soc., N.Y. Acad. Sci., Sigma Xi, Alpha Omega Alpha. Home: 26 Dogwood Dr Morristown NJ 07960 Office: VA Med Center East Orange NJ 07019

COOK, WALLACE LAWRENCE, lawyer, consumer products company executive; b. N.Y.C., Sept. 10, 1939; m. Daphne Prout; children: Lawrence, Randolph. A.B. cum laude, Harvard U., 1961, A.M.P., 1980; LL.B., U. Va., 1964. Bar: N.Y. 1965. Assoc. firm Burlingham, Underwood & Lord, N.Y.C., 1965-68; asst. counsel Gen. Signal Corp., N.Y.C., 1968-70; counsel Norton Simon Inc., N.Y.C., 1970-75, assoc. gen. counsel, 1975-78, asst. to chmn., 1978-80, v.p. human resources, 1980-82, sr. v.p., 1982—. Bd. dirs. Charles A. Dana Found. Mem. ABA, N.Y. State Bar Assn., N.Y.C. Bar Assn. Clubs: Tokeneke (Darien, Conn.); Sky (N.Y.C.). Office: Norton Simon Inc 277 Park Ave New York NY 10017

COOK, WAYNE MICHAEL, public transportation executive; b. Springfield, Vt., Mar. 25, 1943; s. Howard Cutter and Constance Ann (Wolski) C.; m. Margaret Ann Wood, Jan. 29, 1966; children—Patrick Howard, Stephen Michael. Student, Tex. A & I U., 1961-62, St. Mary's U., San Antonio, 1965-67. Chief police, dir. safety City of Bishop, Tex., 1970-72; mgr. dept. loss control San Antonio Transit System, 1973-78, asst. gen. mgr., 1977-78; gen. mgr. VIA Met. Transit, San Antonio, 1978—; vis. prof. Northeastern U. Center for Continuing Edn. Named Transit Gen. Mgr. of Yr. Nat. Transit Inst., Northeastern U., 1981. Mem. Greater San Antonio C. of C., Am. Public Transit Assn., S.W. Transit Assn. (pres. 1980-82). Club: Rotary. Home: 900 Tuxedo St San Antonio TX 78209 Office: 800 W Myrtle St San Antonio TX 78212

COOK, WILLIAM BOYD, college dean, chemist; b. Dallas, July 20, 1918; s. James Monroe and Lucile (Holl) C.; m. Romerta Marie Fox, Sept. 4, 1942 (dec. May 24, 1980); 1 son, Kem Holland; m. Roberta H. Crews, June 6, 1981. B.A., U. Tex., 1940; M.S., U. Colo., 1942; Ph.D., U. Wyo., 1950. Chemist, analyst Monsanto Chem. Co., 1942-43, research asso., 1943-47; instr., then asst. prof. chemistry U. Wyo., 1949-52; research asso. U. Calif., 1952; vis. prof. Princeton, 1953; asso. prof. Baylor U., 1953-57; prof. chemistry, head dept. Mont. State Coll., 1958-67; dean Coll. Natural Scis., Colo. State U., Fort Collins, 1967-84; vis. prof. Cambridge U., 1962-63; vis. scholar Stanford U., 1965-67; program dir. summer insts. NSF, 1957; cons. U.S.-Indo Conf. Chem. Edn. and Research, 1969; exec. dir. Adv. Council Coll. Chemistry, 1965-67; corr. com. teaching chemistry Internat. Union Pure and Applied Chemistry, 1970—; mem. adv. com. grants Research Corp., 1969-75; cons. sci. teaching div. UNESCO, 1969. Mem. bd. publ.: Jour. Chem. Edn., 1959-62, 67-70, 75; chmn. bd. publ., 1977—. Recipient Gold Medal award Colo. sect. Am. Chem. Soc., 1972. Fellow AAAS, Chem. Soc. London; mem. Am. Chem. Soc. (sec. div. chem. edn. 1959-62, chmn. 1969, gov. internat. conf. edn. chemistry 1969), Sigma Xi. Home: 1615 Miramont Dr Fort Collins CO 80524

COOK, WILLIAM HOLMES, fed. judge; b. Carbondale, Ill., June 2, 1920; s. Rex Holmes and Dola Mary (Carter) C. Student, So. Ill. U., 1938-40; LL.B., Washington U., St. Louis, 1947. Bar: Ill. bar 1947, U.S. Supreme Ct. bar 1956. Practice law, Charleston, Ill., 1949-52; atty. FTC, Washington, 1954-59, asst. to chmn., 1957-59; asso. chief counsel for property and spl. matters Bur. Naval Weapons, Navy Dept., 1959-63; counsel Armed Services Com., Ho. of Reps., 1964-74; judge U.S. Ct. Mil. Appeals, Washington, 1974—. Served to 1st lt. AUS, 1942-46. Home: 2501 Calvert St Washington DC 20008 Office: US Ct Mil Appeals Washington DC 20442

COOK, WILLIAM HOWARD, architect; s. Clare Cyril and Matilda Hermine (Schuldt) C.; m. Nancy Ann Dean, Feb. 1, 1949; children—Robert, Cynthia, James. B.A., U. Cal. at Los Angeles, 1947; B.Arch., U. Mich., 1952. Chief designer Fabrica de Muebles Camacho-Roldan, Bogota, Colombia, S.Am., 1949-52; asso. architect Orus Eash, Traverse City, Mich., Ft. Wayne, Ind., 1952-60; partner Cook & Swaim (architects), Tucson, 1961-68; project specialist in urban devel. Banco Interamericano de Desarrollo, Buenos Aires, Argentina, 1968-69; pres. Cain, Nelson, Wares, Cook and Assos., architects, Tucson, 1969—. Bd. dirs. Campus Christian Center of U. Ariz. Served to lt. (j.g.) USNR, 1943-46. Mem. AIA (pres. So. Ariz. 1967), Ariz. Soc. Architects (pres. 1970), Ariz. Soc. of AIA (Architect's medal 1981). Presbyterian. Club: Rotarian. Home: 7065 Mesa Grande Ct Tucson AZ 85715 Office: CNWC Architects 2552 N Alvernon Tucson AZ 85712

COOK, WILLIAM SUTTON, transportation company executive; b. Duluth, Minn., Sept. 6, 1922; s. Ellis Ray and Marjorie Sutton C.; m. Jacqueline Chambers Simmons, Nov. 29, 1980; children by previous marriage—Virginia Ann, William Sutton, James J., Andrew J. B.B.A., U. Minn., 1948. Various fin. positions Gen. Electric Co., 1948-62; comptroller, then v.p., comptroller Pa. R.R./Pa. Central Co., 1962-68; v.p., comptroller Ebasco Industries, Inc., 1968-69; v.p. fin., then exec. v.p. Union Pacific Corp., N.Y.C., 1969-77, pres., 1977—, chief exec. officer, 1983—, also dir.; dir. Stauffer Chem. Co., Fed. Res. Bank of N.Y., Boise Cascade Corp., Royal Group, Inc. Served to capt. AUS, 1943-46. Mem. Fin. Execs. Inst., Bus. Roundtable. Clubs: Links, Brook, Econ., Board Room (N.Y.C.); Blind Brook (Purchase, N.Y.); Quail Creek Country (Naples, Fla.). Home: 55 Fox Run Ln Greenwich CT 06830 Office: 345 Park Ave New York NY 10154

COOKE, ALFRED ALISTAIR, journalist, broadcaster; b. Manchester, Eng., Nov. 20, 1908; naturalized, 1941; s. Samuel and Mary Elizabeth (Byrne) C.; m. Ruth Emerson; 1 son, John Byrne; m. Jane White Hawkes; 1 dau., Susan Byrne. Scholar, Jesus Coll., Cambridge, 1st class English Tripos, 1929, B.A., 1930; Commonwealth Fund fellow, Yale, 1932-33, Harvard, 1933-34; LL.D. (hon.), U. Edinburgh, 1969, U. Manchester, 1973, Litt.D., St. Andrew's U., 1976. Film critic BBC, 1934-37, commentator on Am. affairs, 1938—; London corr. NBC, 1936-37; spl. corr. Am. affairs London Times, 1938- 42; Am. feature writer London Daily Herald, 1941-43; UN corr. (Manchester) Guardian, 1945-48, chief U.S. corr., 1948-72. TV emcee: Omnibus, 1952-61; host: TV Masterpiece Theatre, 1971—; writer, narrator: TV series America: A Personal History of the U.S, 1972-73; (4 Emmy awards 1973); Author: Douglas Fairbanks, 1940, A Generation On Trial, 1950, One Man's America, 1952, Christmas Eve, 1952, A Commencement Address, 1954, Talk About America, 1968, Alistair Cooke's America, 1973, Six Men, 1977, The Americans: Fifty Letters from America on our life and times, 1979, Masterpieces, 1981; co-author: Above London, 1980; Editor: Garbo and the Night Watchmen, 1937, The Vintage Mencken, 1955, The Granta, 1931-32. Recipient Peabody award for internat. news reporting, 1952, 73; Benjamin Franklin medal Royal Soc. Arts, 1973; Howland medal Yale U., 1977; Spl. Peabody award, 1983; decorated knight comdr. Brit. Empire, 1973. Clubs: Nat. Press (Washington); Royal and Ancient G.C. (St. Andrews); San Francisco Golf; Athenaeum (London). Address: 1150 Fifth Ave New York NY *

COOKE, BRIAN A., airline company executive; b. Belfast, Ireland, 1919. Grad., U. Hawaii, 1945. Acct. Los Angeles Baseball Club, 1941-42; v.p., fin., dir. Hawaiian Airlines Inc., 1945-64; v.p., asst. to pres. World Airways Inc., 1964-68, sr. v.p., 1968-82, pres., chief exec. officer, 1982—. Office: World Airways Inc Bldg 601 Earhart Rd Oakland CA 94614 *

COOKE, CONSTANCE BLANDY, librarian; b. Woodbury, N.J., Mar. 7, 1935; d. John Chase and Josephine Spond (Black) Blandy; m. Len B. Cooke, Jr., Jan. 7, 1978. B.A., U. Pa., 1956; M.A., U. Denver, 1957. Adult cons. Onondaga Library System, Syracuse, N.Y., 1965-66; asst. dir. Mt. Vernon (N.Y.) Public Library, 1966-75; dep. dir. Queens Borough Public Library, Jamaica, N.Y., 1975-79, dir., 1980—; founder pres. Literacy Vols. Mt. Vernon, 1972-74. Mem. ALA, Am. Mgmt. Assn., Soc. Advancement Mgmt., N.Y. Library Assn. Republican. Episcopalian. Home: 8 Pennsylvania Blvd Village of Bellerose Floral Park NY 11001 Office: 89-11 Merrick Blvd Jamaica NY 11432

COOKE, DAVID OHLMER, government official; b. Buffalo, Aug. 31, 1920; s. Lot Howell and Thekla Thusnelda (Ohlmer) C.; m. Marion Louise McDonald, Nov. 21, 1947; children: Michele C., Lot H., David O. B.S., SUNY, Buffalo, 1941, M.S., 1942; LL.B., George Washington U., 1950. Bar: D.C. 1950. Mem. faculty U.S. Sch. Naval Justice, 1951-54; mem. staff JAG, Office of Navy, 1957-61; mem. Reorgn. Task Force, Dept. Def., 1958; mem. staff Office of Organizational and Mgmt. Planning, OSD, 1961-64, dir., 1964-69; dep. asst. sec. for adminstrn. Dept. Def., Washington, 1969—; dir. Washington Hdqrs. Services, 1977—. Recipient Disting. Service medal Dep. Navy, 1967; Disting. Civilian Service medal Dept. Def., 1972; medal with bronze palm, 1973; medal with silver palm, 1975; Sec. Def. medal for outstanding public service, 1977; medal for disting. public service, 1981; Meritorious Exec. award, 1980; Roger W. Jones award for Exec. Leadership Am. U., 1983. Mem. ABA, Fed. Bar Assn., Maritime Law Assn., Am. Soc. Public Adminstrn. Club: Army-Navy Country. Home: 1412 23d Rd S Arlington VA 22202 Office: Office Dep Asst Sec Def Room 3E843 The Pentagon Washington DC 20301

COOKE, EDWARD WILLIAM, business executive, former naval officer; b. Fonda, Iowa, 1921; s. Edward William and Mary Ann (Mackey) C.; m. Dorothea Lou Greaves, May 7, 1949; children: Edward, Bruce, Teresa, Ann, Patrice, David. B.S. in Engring., U.S. Naval Acad., 1945; M.S. in Internat. Affairs, George Washington U., 1967; postgrad., Harvard Grad. Sch. Bus., 1969. Commd. ensign U.S. Navy, 1945, advanced through grades to vice adm., 1975; various sea and shore assignments, 1945-55, comdg. officer Navy Nuclear Power Tng. Unit, Idaho Falls, 1956-58, comdg. officer U.S.S. Harder, 1958-59; comdg. officer U.S.S. Skate, 1960-61, U.S.S. George Washington, 1962-66; exec. asst. to asst. sec. navy, Washington, 1967-68, comdr. Submarine Squadron Five, 1970-71, comdr. Submarine Flotilla One, 1971-72; dir. budget and reports Dept. Navy, Washington, 1972-75, dep. chief naval ops. (logistics), 1975-78; ret., 1978; gen. mgr. coal gassification W.R. Grace & Co., Memphis, 1978—, exec. v.p. agrl. chems. group, 1979—. Decorated Legion of Merit with 2 oak leaf clusters, D.S.M. Home: 2571 Countrywood Pkwy Cordova TN 38018 Office: WR Grace & Co Agrl Chems Group 100 N Main St Memphis TN 38103

COOKE, EILEEN DELORES, librarian, association executive; b. Mpls., Dec. 7, 1928; d. Walter William and Mary Frances C. B.S. in L.S, Coll. St. Catherine, 1952; extension courses, U. Minn. Bookmobile librarian Mpls. Pub. Library, 1952-57; br. asst. Queensborough Pub. Library, 1957-58; br. asst., hosp. librarian, pub. relations specialist Mpls. Pub. Library, 1958-63; asst. dir. Washington office ALA, 1964-68, asso. dir., 1968-69, dep. dir., 1969-72, dir., 1972—; lectr. U. Mich., Ann Arbor; cons. to fed. relations commn. Am. Council on Edn. Contbr. articles to profl. jours. Bd. visitors Sch. Library and Info. Sci., Cath. U. Mem. ALA, Minn., D.C. library assns., Women's Joint Congressional Com., Joint Council on Ednl. Telecommunications (past pres.), Higher Edn. Group Washington, Pub. Service Satellite Consortium, World Future Soc., Women's Nat. Book Assn. (treas. Washington/Balt. chpt.). Office: American Library Assn 110 Maryland Ave NE Washington DC 20002

COOKE, HERBERT BASIL SUTTON, geologist, educator; b. Johannesburg, S.Africa, Oct. 17, 1915; s. Herbert Sutton and Edith Mary (Sutton) C.; m. Dorothea Winifred Hughes, Oct. 23, 1943; children: Christopher, Patrick. B.A., Cambridge (Eng.) U., 1936, M.A., 1940; M.Sc., U. Witwatersrand, 1940, D.Sc., 1947; LL.D. hon., Dalhousie U., 1982. Geologist Central Mining & Investment Corp., Johannesburg, 1936-38; lectr. geology U. Witwatersrand, 1938-47, sr. lectr., 1953-57, reader, 1957-61; pvt. cons. geologist, Johannesburg, 1947-53; assoc. prof. geology Dalhousie U., Halifax, N.S., Can., 1961-63, prof., dean arts and sci., 1963-68, Carnegie prof. geology, 1968-81, prof. emeritus, 1981—; geol. cons., 1981—; Chmn. Bernard Price Inst. for Paleontol. Research, Johannesburg, 1958-61. Author: Geology for South African Students, 1939, rev. edits., 1948, 54, 60, 65, Science in South Africa, 1949; editor: (with V.J. Maglio) Evolution of African Mammals, 1978; Contbr. articles to profl. jours. Served with S.African Air Force, 1941-45. Recipient Canadian Centennial medal, 1967. Fellow Royal Soc. S.Africa (life), Geol. Soc. London, Am. Philos. Soc., Royal Meteorol. Soc., Geol. Soc. Am.; mem. Geol. Soc. S.Africa (du Toit Meml. lectr. 1957), S.African Geog. Soc. (pres. 1949-50), S.African Archeol. Soc. (pres. 1950-51), S.African Assn. for

Advancement Sci. (v.p. 1959-60, sect. pres. 1952-54), N.S. Inst. Sci. (pres. 1967-68). Home: 2133 154th St White Rock BC Canada V4A 4S5

COOKE, JACK KENT, business executive, publisher; b. Hamilton, Ont., Can., Oct. 25, 1912; s. Ralph Ercil and Nancy (Jacobs) C.; m. Jeanne Maxwell Williams, Oct. 31, 1980 (div.); 1 son by previous marriage, John Kent. Student, Malvern Collegiate. Joined No. Broadcasting and Pub. Ltd., Can., 1937; partner Thomson Cooke Newspapers, 1937-52; pres. Sta. CKEY, Toronto, Ont., 1944-61, Liberty of Can., Ltd., 1947-61, Toronto Maple Leaf Baseball Club Ltd., 1951-64, Micro Plastics, Ltd., Acton, Ont., 1955-60, Robinson Indsl. Crafts, Ltd., London, Ont., 1957-63, Precision Die Casting Ltd., Toronto, 1955-60, Consol. Frybrook Industries, Ltd., 1952-61, Aubyn Investments, Ltd., 1961-68, Continental Cable Television, 1965-68; chmn. Jack Kent Cooke Inc.; chmn. bd. Transam. Microwave, Inc., 1965-69; chmn., chief operating officer, chief exec. officer Pro-Football, Inc. (Washington Redskins, Nat. Football League), Washington; pres. Calif. Sports, Inc. (Los Angeles Lakers, Nat. Basketball Assn., Los Angeles Kings, Nat. Hockey League), 1965-79, The Forum of Inglewood, Inc., 1966-79; dir., chmn. exec. com. H & B Am. Corp., 1969-70; chmn., chief exec. officer Teleprompter Corp., 1974—; chmn. Group W. Cable Inc. (formerly TPT Corp.), 1974-81; chmn. bd., pres. The Raljon Corp., Nev., The Ercil Corp., The JKC Corp.; chmn. bd. pres. One Two, Corp., Nev., 1976—, Video Tape Enterprises, 1976—, JKC Realty, Inc., N.Y.C., 1979—, Kent Farms, 1979—, Rosenzweig Center, Phoenix, 1983—. Trustee Little League Found., City of Hope; bd. govs. Arthritis Found.; bd. dirs. Nat. Athletic Inst.

COOKE, JACK KENT, diversified company executive; b. Hamilton, Ont., Can., Oct. 25, 1912; s. Ralph Ercil and Nancy (Jacobs) C.; m. Jeanne Maxwell Williams, Oct. 31, 1980 (div.); 1 son by previous marriage, John Kent. Student, Malvern Collegiate. Joined No. Broadcasting and Pub. Ltd.,, Can., 1937; ptnr. Thomas Cooke Newspapers, 1937-52; pres. Sta. CKEY, Toronto, Ont., Can., 1944-61, Liberty of Can. Ltd., 1947-61, Toronto Maple Leaf Baseball Club Ltd., 1951-64, Micro Plastics, Ltd., Acton, Ont., Can., 1955-60, Robinson Indsl. Crafts, Ltd., London, Ont., Can., 1957-63, Precision Die Casting Ltd., Toronto, Ont., Can., 1955-60, Consol. Frybook Industries, Ltd., 1952-61, Aubyn Investments, Ltd., 1961-68, Continental Cablevision Inc., 1965-68; chmn. Jack Kent Cooke Inc.; chmn. bd. Transamerica Microwave, Inc., 1965-69; chmn., chief operating officer, chief exec. officer Pro-Football Inc. Washington Redskins, Nat. Football League, Washington, 1960; pres. Calif. Sports, Inc (Los Angeles Lakers, Nat. Basketball Assn., Los Angeles Kings, Nat. Hockey League), 1965-79, The Forum of Inglewood, Inc., 1966-79; dir., chmn. exec. com. H & B Am. Corp, 1969-70; chmn., chief exec. officer Teleprompter Corp., 1974-81; chmn. Group W Cable Inc. (formerly Teleprompter Corp.), 1981—; chmn. bd., pres. The Raljon Corp., Nev., 1976—, The Ercil Corp., 1976—, JKC Corp., 1976—, One Two Corp., 1976—, Video Tape Enterprises, 1976—, JKC Realty, Inc. (Chrysler and Kent Bldgs.), N.Y.C., 1979—, Kent Farms, 1979—, Rozenzweig Ctr., Phoenix, 1983—. Trustee Little League Found., City of Hope; bd. govs. Arthritis Found. Mem. Nat. Athletic Inst. (bd. dirs.).

COOKE, JACOB ERNEST, history educator, author; b. Aulander, N.C., Sept. 23, 1924; s. Jacob E. and Myrtle (Basemore) C.; m. Jean Gordon, Nov. 3, 1956; children: Jacob Ernest III. A.B., U. N.C., 1947; Ph.D., Columbia U., 1955. Instr., then asst. prof. Columbia U., 1953-61; asso. editor Papers of Alexander Hamilton, 1955-70; prof. history, head dept. Carnegie Inst. Tech., 1961-62; John Henry MacCracken prof. history Lafayette Coll., 1962—; vis. prof. Columbia, 1969; resident scholar Rockefeller Study and Conf. Ctr., Bellagio, Italy, spring 1982. Author: Frederick Bancroft, 1956, The March of Democracy, vols. VI and VII, 1965, The Age of Responsibility, 1965, The Kennedy Years, 1966, Tench Coxe and the Early American Republic, 1978, Alexander Hamilton: A Biography, 1982; Editor: The Federalist, 1961, Reports of Alexander Hamilton, 1964, The Challenge of History, 1965, A History of the American Colonies, 13 vols, 1974—, Dictionary of American History, 7 vols, 1967, Tench Coxe and the Early Republic, 1978. Served with USAAF, 1941-45. Guggenheim fellow, 1968-69; NIH fellow, 1972-73; Nat. Humanities Center fellow, 1981. Mem. Am. Hist. Assn., Orgn. Am. Historians, Soc. Am. Historians, Phi Beta Kappa, Phi Alpha Theta. Home: 172 Shawnee Ave Easton PA 18042

COOKE, KENNETH, newspaper executive; b. Providence, Feb. 18, 1932; s. and Gladys Isabel Edlund; m. Catherine Della Coble, May 20, 1970; 1 dau., Jennifer. Profl. Photography degree, N.Y. Inst. Photography, 1953. With R.I. Photo Lab., 1954-55, N.C. News & Observer, Raleigh, 1955-73; chief photographer, picture editor Fayetteville (N.C.) Observer-Times, 1973—. Served with AUS, 1952-53. Decorated Combat Med. Badge.; Recipient Sprague award. Mem. Nat. Press Photographers Assn. (pres. 1979), N.C. Press Photographers Assn. (pres. 1961). Office: Fayetteville Observer-Times PO Box 849 Fayetteville NC 28302

COOKE, KENNETH LLOYD, educator, mathematician; b. Kansas City, Mo., Aug. 13, 1925; s. Sidney Kenneth and Mildred Blanche (Brown) C.; m. Margaret Sarah Burgess, Aug. 18, 1950; children: Catherine Sarah, Robert K., Susan E. B.A., Pomona Coll., 1947; M.S., Stanford, 1949, Ph.D., 1952. Instr., then asst. prof. math. State Coll. Wash., Pullman, 1950-57; mem. faculty Pomona Coll., 1957—, Joseph N. Fiske prof. math., 1963—, chmn. dept., 1961-71; cons. RAND Corp., 1956-65; mathematician Research Inst. Advanced Studies, Balt., 1963-64; NSF sci. faculty fellow Stanford, 1966-67; Fulbright research scholar U. Florence, Italy, 1971-72; vis. prof. Brown U., 1978-79, Inst. Math. Applications, U. Minn., 1983. Author: (with Richard Bellman) Differential- Difference Equations, 1963, Modern Elementary Differential Equations, 2d edit, 1971, (with Richard Bellman and J.A. Lockett) Algorithms, Graphs and Computers, 1970, (with Donald Bentley) Linear Algebra with Differential Equations, 1973, (with Colin Renfrew) Transformations: Mathematical Approaches to Cultural Change, 1979. Served with USNR, 1944-46. Mem. Am. Math. Soc., Math. Assn. Am., Soc. Indsl. and Applied Math., AAUP, AAAS, Phi Beta Kappa, Sigma Xi. Mem. United Ch. Christ. Home: 654 Northwestern Dr Claremont CA 91711

COOKE, LAWRENCE HENRY, judge; b. Monticello, N.Y., Oct. 15, 1914; s. George L. and Mary (Pond) C.; m. Alice McCormack, Nov. 25, 1939; children—Edward M., George L., II, Mary L. Cooke Opie. B.S. cum laude, Georgetown U., 1935; LL.B., Albany Law Sch., Union U., 1938, LL.D. (hon.), 1975, Siena Coll., 1964, N.Y. Law Sch., 1979, Bklyn. Law Sch., 1980, Pace U., 1980. Bar: N.Y. bar 1939. Individual practice law, Monticello, 1939-53, Sullivan County judge, 1954-61; Supreme Ct. justice 3d Jud. Dist., 1962-68; asso. justice Appellate div. 3d Dept., Albany, 1969-74; asso. judge N.Y. State Ct. Appeals, Albany, 1975-78, chief judge, 1979—; 1st vice chmn. and mem. exec. council Conf. Chief Justices, 1979—; pres.-elect, bd. dirs. Nat. Center for State Cts., 1979—; chmn. N.Y. Fair Trial, Free Press Conf., 1979—; John F. Sonnett Meml. lectr. Fordham U. Law Sch., 1981; Charles Evans Hughes Meml. lectr. New York County Lawyers Assn., 1981. Supr. Town of Thompson, N.Y., 1946-49; chmn. Sullivan County Bd. Suprs., 1947-48. Recipient Torch of Liberty award B'nai B'rith, 1967. Mem. ABA, N.Y. State Bar Assn. (past chmn. young lawyers sect.), Sullivan County Bar Assn. (pres.). Democrat. Roman Catholic. Home: 415 Broadway Monticello NY 12701 Office: Ct of Appeals Hall Eagle St Albany NY 12207 also Courthouse Monticello NY 12701

COOKE, LLOYD MILLER, former organization executive; b. LaSalle, Ill., June 7, 1916; s. William Wilson and Anna (Miller) C.; m. Vera E. Schlegel, June 29, 1957; children: Barbara Anne, William E. B.S., U. Wis., 1937; Ph.D., McGill U., 1941; LL.D. (hon.), Coll. of Ganado. Lectr. McGill U., 1941-42; sect. leader Corn Products Refining Co., Argo, Ill., 1942-46; group leader Films Packaging div. Union Carbide Corp., Chgo., 1946-49, dept. mgr., 1950-54, asst. to mgr. tech. div., 1954-57, asst. dir. research, 1957-65, mgr. market research, 1965-67, mgr. planning, 1967-70, dir. urban affairs, N.Y.C., 1970-78, corp. dir. univ. relations, 1973-76, corp. dir. community affairs, 1976-77, sr. cons., 1978-81; mem. Nat. Sci. Bd., 1970-82; cons. Office of Tech. Assessment, U.S. Congress, 1972-79; vice chmn. Econ. Devel. Council of N.Y., 1978-81; pres. Nat. Action Council on Minorities in Engring., 1981-83, pres. emeritus, 1983—. Contbr. articles to profl. jours. Mem. Community Conf. Bd., Downers Grove, Ill., 1968-70; trustee McCormick Theol. Sem., 1976-80. Recipient Proctor prize sci. Sci. Research Soc. Am., 1970. Fellow Am. Inst. Chemists (honor scroll Chgo.), N.Y. Acad. Scis.; mem. Am. Chem. Soc., AAAS, Sigma Xi, Phi Kappa Phi, Beta Kappa Chi. Clubs: Chicago Chemists, N.Y. Chemists. Home: 1 Beaufort Rd White Plains NY 10607 Office: 3 W 35th St New York NY 10001

COOKE, MERRITT TODD, banker; b. Phila., Mar. 20, 1920; s Merritt Todd and Beatrice (Crawford) C.; m. Mary T. Cooke, Sept. 24, 1949 (dec.); children—Mary Marshall, Merritt Todd; m. Margaret S. Groome, Dec. 4, 1965. B.A., Princeton, 1942; M.C.P., Mass. Inst. Tech., 1947. Exec. dir. Del. County Planning Commn., Media, Pa., 1951-55; v.p. W.A. Clarke Mortgage Co., Phila., 1956-60; asst. v.p. First Pa. Bank, Phila., 1961-65; with The Phila. Saving Fund Soc., 1966—, pres., 1971—, chmn., chief exec. officer, 1979—, also trustee; trustee Mut. Assurance Co., Phila.; dir. Provident Mut. Ins. Co. Pres. United Fund Phila., 1974-76; bd. dirs. Pa. Hosp., Phila., chmn., 1969-75; v.p. United Way Phila., 1976—; bd. dirs. Greater Phila. Partnership, Phila. Urban Coalition, Old Phila. Devel. Corp., Market Street East Devel. Corp., Penn's Landing Corp., Phila. Orch. Assn.; trustee Phila. Mus. Art. Served with AUS, 1942-46. Mem. Phi Beta Kappa, Lambda Alpha. Home: Greenlands Newtown St Rd Media PA 19063 Office: 1212 Market St Philadelphia PA 19107

COOKE, PAUL DENVIR, advt. agy. exec.; b. Phila., Jan. 26, 1920; s. Charles J. and Katharine (Freer) C.; m. Marian K. Spiegel, Oct. 17, 1943; 1 dau., Katharine M. B.A., Yale, 1942. Account exec. Compton Advt., Inc., N.Y.C., 1948, v.p., 1953-63, sr. v.p., 1963-67, exec. v.p., 1967-70, vice chmn. bd., 1970-76. Served to lt. USNR, 1942-48. Mem. Newcomen Soc. N.Am., Navy League U.S. Clubs: Univ., Yale (N.Y.C.); Hackensack Golf (Oradell, N.J.). Home: 282 Schley Pl Teaneck NJ 07666

COOKE, ROBERT EDMOND, physician, former college president; b. Attleboro, Mass., Nov. 13, 1920; s. Ronald Melbourne and Renee Jeanne (Wuillumier) C.; m. Sharon Riley, Nov. 20, 1978; 1 dau., Susan; children by previous marriage—Robyn (dec.), Christopher, Wendy, W. Robert, Kim. B.S., Sheffield Sci. Sch., Yale U., 1941, M.D., 1944; postgrad. (NIH postdoctorate fellow), Sch. Medicine, 1948-50, John and Mary R. Markle scholar, 1951-55. Intern, asst. resident dept. pediatrics New Haven Hosp., 1944-46; instr. pediatrics Yale, 1950-51, asst. prof. pediatrics, physiology, 1951-54, asso. prof., 1954-56; resident to asso. pediatrician Grace-New Haven Community Hosp., 1951-56; pediatrician-in-chief Johns Hopkins Hosp., 1956-73; chmn. dept. Johns Hopkins Sch. Medicine, 1956-73; Grover Powers prof. pediatrics Nat. Assn. Retarded Children, 1957-59, Given Found. prof. pediatrics, 1962-73; vis. prof. Harvard U., 1972-73; vice chancellor for health scis., prof. pediatrics U. Wis., 1973-77; pres. Med. Coll. Pa., 1977-80; A. Conger Goodyear prof. pediatrics, med. dir. Children's Rehab. Center SUNY-Buffalo, 1982—; cons. Mass. Dept. Mental Health, 1980-82, Office Tech. Assessment, 1974—; Mem. nat. adv. bd. mental health Jr. C. of C.; sci. adv. council Children's Hosp. Research Found.; chmn. med. adv. bd. Kennedy Found.; mem. med. adv. bd. Balt. chpt. Cystic Fibrosis, United Cerebral Palsy Greater Balt., Md. Soc. Mentally Retarded Children, Children's Guild; mem. adv. council Yale U. Sch. Medicine, Colo. Allergy Research Inst.; mem. nat. commn. for protection human subjects of biomed. and behavioral research Office Asst. Sec. Health, 1974—; mem. health manpower rev. com. VA, Washington, 1974—. Editor, contbr. to pediatric textbooks, profl. jours. Trustee Children's Rehab. Inst., Nat. Commn. Protection Human Subjects. Served from lt. to capt. M.C. AUS, 1946-48. Recipient Mead Johnson award in pediatrics, 1954; Kennedy Internat. award for distinguished service in field mental retardation, 1968. Fellow Am. Acad. Pediatrics; Distinguished fellow Am. Psychiat. Assn.; mem. Am. Pediatric Soc., Soc. for Pediatric Research (pres. 1965-66), Am. Soc. for Clin. Investigation, Md. Med. Soc., AMA, Am. Pub. Health Assn., Am. Fedn. Clin. Research, Inst. of Medicine, Aurelian Hon. Soc., Phi Beta Kappa, Sigma Xi, Alpha Omega Alpha. Office: 54 Knob Hill Rd Orchard Park NY 14127 *My goal has been to enjoy socially useful achievement. To achieve that has required periods of self renewal to adapt to a rapidly changing world.*

COOKE, ROBERT JOHN, emeritus history educator; b. Kingston, N.Y., Apr. 12, 1923; s. Harry and Anna (Hyl) C.; m. Barbara Dexter, 1951 (div. 1973); children: Kathleen Anne, Christian Seán, Kevin Michéal, Deborah Gaye, Brian Patrick; 1 dau., Siobhán Bríghid. B.S. in Social Sci., SUNY, 1949; A.M. in History, Columbia U., 1950; Ph.D. in Am. Studies, Maxwell Grad. Sch. Pub. Affairs, Syracuse U., 1964. Asst. in Am. civilization Columbia U., 1949-50; tchr. social studies and English Goshen (N.Y.) High Sch., 1950-54; staff Citizens Edn. Project, Carnegie Found., 1950-54; asst. prof. social sci. Ball State U., Muncie, Ind., 1954-59; instr. Am. studies Maxwell Grad. Sch. Pub. Affairs, Syracuse U., 1960-65, dir. Chautauqua Center, 1960-62; assoc. Inter-Univ. Project I, Ford Found., 1962-65; prof. Am. studies and history Southampton Coll., L.I. U., 1965-83, prof. emeritus, 1983—, chmn. history dept., 1966-70, 73-83, chmn. Am. studies program, 1968-83, dir. humanities div., 1970-73, chmn. exec. com. faculty council, 1977-79; vis. lectr. Trinity Coll., Dublin, Ireland, 1974. Contbr. articles to profl. jours., chpts. to books. Mem. legis. affairs com. N.Y. State Democratic Com., 1973-75. Served to lt. USMC, 1942-46; PTO. Mem. Am. Hist. Assn., Am. Studies Assn. (chmn. and editor bibliography com. 1964-65), Nat. Council for Social Studies (book rev. editor jour. 1964-68, chmn. standing com. on research 1961-63, bd. dirs. 1966-69), Am.-Irish Hist. Soc., Am. Com. for Irish Studies, Irish Nat. Caucus, Orgn. Am. Historians, Sinn Féin (provo). Home: PO Box 1002 Riverhead NY 11901

COOKE, ROBERT WILLIAM, science journalist; b. Alhambra, Calif., Mar. 26, 1935; s. Loren Elvin and Edith (Mason) C.; m. Sue B. Cato, Sept. 10, 1960; children: Gregory, Karen, Emily. B.S. in English, Calif. State Poly. Coll., 1961; M.S. in Journalism, UCLA, 1962; postgrad. in advanced sci. writing (Univ. fellow), Columbia U., 1969-70. Reporter-photographer Pomona (Calif.) Progress-Bull., 1962-63; newsman AP, Los Angeles, 1963-67; sci. writer Calif. Inst. Tech., 1967-69, Pasadena (Calif.) Star-News, 1970-73; sci. editor Boston Globe, 1973—. Author: Improving on Nature, The Brave New World of Genetic Engineering, 1977, Earthfire; the Eruption of Mt. St. Helens, 1982. Served with USCG, 1954-58. Recipient James T. Grady award Am. Chem. Soc., 1981. Mem. Nat. Assn. Sci. Writers, Kappa Tau Alpha. Democrat. Methodist. Office: Boston Globe Boston MA 02107

COOKE, WILLIAM BRIDGE, mycologist; b. Foster, Ohio, July 16, 1908; s. William Thomas Hunter and Katharine May (Bridge) C.; m. Vivian Greenwald, June 12, 1942. B.A., U. Cin., 1937; M.S., Oreg. State U., 1939; Ph.D., Wash. State U., 1950. Research asso. dept. plant pathology Wash. State U., Pullman, 1950-51; mycologist charge fungus studies Robert A. Taft Water Research Center, U.S. Dept. Health, Edn. and Welfare, Cin., 1952-65; mycologist Advanced Waste Treatment Research Lab., Fed. Water Pollution Control Adminstrn., Dept. Health Edn. Welfare, 1965-66, Dept. Interior, Cin., 1966-69; research asso. botany dept. Miami U., Oxford, Ohio, 1968-70; sr. research asso. Miami Valley Project, U. Cin., asso. with dept. biol. scis., 1970—; vis. prof. aquatic microbiology Flathead Lake Biol. Sta., U. Mont., Bigfork, summer 1974; Cons. Bur. Solid Waste Mgmt., EPA.; Attended 1st Internat. Mycol. Symposium on Taxonomy Fungi U. Madras, India; chmn. Joint Task Group of Fungi, Standard Methods for Exam. of Water and Wastewater. Author: A Laboratory Guide to Culture and Identification of Sewage Fungi, 1963, Our Mouldy Earth, 1970; chpt. in Recent Advances in Aquatic Mycology, 1975, Ecology of Fungi, 1979; contbr.: 2 chpts. to Edward Stuhl's Wildflowers of Mount Shasta. Served Q.M.C. AUS, 1945-46. Recipient Superior Service award HEW, 1960; Excellence award Fed. Water Pollution Control Adminstrn. U.S. Dept. Interior, 1971. Fellow A.A.A.S., Ohio Acad. Sci., Am. Acad. Microbiology (charter); mem. Mycol. Soc. Am. (chmn. foray com.), Ecol. Soc. Am., Am. Inst. Biol. Scis., Bot. Soc. Am., Am. Soc. Plant Taxonomy, Internat. Assn. Plant Taxonomists, Cal. Bot. Soc., Brit. Mycol. Soc., Internat. Soc. Human and Animal Mycology, Sierra Club (life), Calif. Acad. Scis. (life), Explorers Club. Research and publs. list of flora and fungi of Mt. Shasta, Calif. Developed techniques demonstrating presence of fungus populations in sewage and polluted waters. Home: 1135 Wilshire Ct Cincinnati OH 45230

COOKE, WILLIAM DONALD, university administrator, chemistry educator; b. Phila., May 15, 1918; s. William Donald and Gertrude (Raith) C.; m. June Marie Orr, Oct. 5, 1946; children: W. Donald, Peter K., Christopher A., Catherine A., M. Timothy, Antonia. B.S., St. Joseph's Coll., Phila., 1940; student, Mass. Inst. Tech., 1941-42; M.S., U. Pa., 1947, Ph.D., 1949; fellow, Princeton, 1949- 51. Mem. faculty Cornell U., Ithaca, N.Y., 1951—, prof. chemistry, 1957—, acting chmn. dept. chemistry, 1984, dean Grad. Sch., 1964-73, v.p. research, 1969-83, dir. occupational health and safety programs, 1983—; Mem. Nat. Bd. Grad. Edn., 1972-75; trustee Fordham U., 1970-78; chmn. bd. Associated Univs. Inc., 1978-81; mem. exec. com. LeMoyne Coll., 1978-82, Boyce Thompson Inst. Plant Research, 1977-83, Tompkins County Area Devel. Corp., 1978-83. Contbr. to profl. jours. Served to maj. USAAF, 1942-46; ETO. Mem. Am. Chem. Soc. (chmn. analytical div. 1964-65), Assn. Grad. Schs. (pres. 1971). Home: 38 Deerhaven Dr Ithaca NY 14850

COOKSON, ALAN HOWARD, electrical engineer, researcher; b. London, July 3, 1939; U.S., 1968; s. Joseph and Rachel (Wiseman) C.; m. Elizabeth Rosamond Ritblat, Oct. 24, 1965; children: Richard Jonathan, Simon Charles. B.Sc. in Engring. with 1st class honors, Queen Mary Coll., London U., 1961, Ph.D. in Elec. Engring., 1965. Chartered engr., Gt. Brit. Research fellow Queen Mary Coll., London, 1964-65; research officer Central Elec. Research Labs., Leatherhead, Eng., 1965-68; sr. engr. Westinghouse Research & Devel. Ctr., Pitts., 1968-75, mgr. gas cable research, power cir. breaker, Westborough, Mass., 1975-80, Pitts., Mass.; mgr. insulation Westinghouse Research & Devel., Mass., 1980—; U.S. tech. expert on insulating materials Internat. Conf. Large Elec. Systems, 1982—; convener Working Group on Gas Insulated Cables, Internat. Conf. Large Elec. Systems, 1980—. Editor: Digest of Literature on Dielectrics, 1970; contbr. articles to profl. jours.; patentee in field. Mem. adv. com. Miss. State U., 1983. Fellow IEEE, Instn. Elec. Engrs. London; mem. Inst. Physics London. Home: 30 Holland Rd Pittsburgh PA 195235 Office: Westinghouse Research and Devel Ctr 1310 Beulah Rd Pittsburgh PA 195235

COOKSON, ALBERT ERNEST, tel. and tel. co. exec.; b. Needham, Mass., Oct. 30, 1921; s. Willard B. and Sarah Jane (Jack) C.; m. Constance J. Buckley, Sept. 10, 1949; children—Constance J., William B. B.E.E., Northeastern U., 1943; M.E.E., Mass. Inst. Tech., 1951; Sc.D., Gordon Coll., 1974. Group leader Research Lab. Electronics, Mass. Inst. Tech., 1947-51; lab. dir. ITT Fed. Labs., Nutley, N.J., 1951-59, v.p., dir. operations, Paramus, N.J., 1959-62; pres. ITT Intelcom, Falls Church, Va., 1962-65; dep. gen. tech. dir. Internat. Tel. and Tel. Corp., N.Y.C., 1965-66, v.p., tech. dir., 1966-68, sr. v.p., gen. tech. dir., 1968—; chmn. bd. ITT Interplan; dir. Internat. Standard Electric, ITT Industries.; Mem. Def. Communications Satellite Panel; adviser research and engring. on def. communications satellite systems Dept. Def.; mem. indsl. panel sci. and tech. NSF.; Mem. Fairfax County Econ. and Indsl. Devel. Com., 1962-65; mem. nat. council Northeastern U.; mem. pride com. U. Hartford, 1973-76; elec. engring./computer adv. bd. Mass. Inst. Tech., 1977—. Served with USNR, 1943-46. Fellow IEEE; mem. Armed Forces Communications and Electronics Assn., Am. Mgmt. Assn., Am. Inst. Aeros. and Astronautics, Electronic Industries Assn., Sigma Xi, Tau Beta Pi. Patentee frequency search and track system. Home: 2 Baywater Dr Darien CT 06820 Office: 320 Park Ave New York NY 10022

COOL, RODNEY LEE, physicist, educator; b. Platte, S.D., Mar. 8, 1920; s. George E. and Muriel (Post) C.; m. Margaret E. MacMillan, June 21, 1949; children: Ellen, John, Mary Lee, Adrienne. B.S., U. S.D., 1942; M.A., Harvard U., 1947, Ph.D., 1949. Research physicist Brookhaven Nat. Lab., Upton, L.I., N.Y., 1949-59, dep. chmn. high energy physics, 1960-64, asst. dir. high energy physics, 1964-66, asso. dir., 1966-70, sec. high energy adv. com., 1960-67, chmn., 1967-70; prof. exptl. high energy physics Rockefeller U., N.Y.C., 1970—; Mem. policy com. Stanford Linear Accelerator Center, 1962-67, 76-80; mem. Asso. Univs. High Energy Panel, Asso. Univs., Inc., 1963-70; mem. Walker panel, com. on sci. and pub. policy Nat. Acad. Sci., 1964; mem. Princeton-Pa. Accelerator Sci. Com., 1966-68; mem. high energy physics adv. panel AEC, 1967-70; chmn. physics adv. com. Nat. Accelerator Lab., 1967-70; mem. adv. panel for physics NSF, 1970-73; sci. asso. European Center Nuclear Research, 1973—; trustee Univs. Research Assn., 1977-83; mem. rev. com. Argonne Univs. Assn., 1978-80. Co-editor: Advances in Particle Physics, vols. I and II, 1968; contbr. articles to profl. jours. Served to maj., Signal Corps AUS, 1942-46. Decorated Bronze Star medal. Fellow Am. Phys. Soc. (program cons. div. particles and fields 1968-70); mem. Nat. Acad. Scis., Phi Beta Kappa, Sigma Xi. Home: 450 E 63d St New York NY 10021 Office: Rockefeller University New York NY 10021

COOLBAUGH, FRANK, mining exec., cons.; b. Rapid City, S.D., Dec. 21, 1908; s. Melville Fuller and Osie (Smith) C.; m. Dallos Inez Davies, Aug. 17, 1947; 1 son, Melville James. E.M., Colo. Sch. Mines, 1933; grad., Advanced Mgmt. Program, Harvard, 1947. Coal miner U.S. Fuel Co., Mohrland, Utah, 1928-30; from mine helper to asst. mill supt. Climax Molybdenum Co., Climax, Colo., 1933- 42, planning dir., asst. gen. supt., resident mgr., gen. mgr., v.p., 1946-59, pres., 1959-60, dir., 1955-58; pres., dir. Climax Uranium Co.; v.p. Am. Metal Climax, Inc., 1958-60, pres., 1960-65, chmn., chief exec. officer, 1966-67, cons., 1967-68, dir., 1958-68; pres., dir. Coolbaugh Mining Corp., 1969—; mine developer, cons. industry, 1968—; dir. Newmont Mining

Corp., Ranchers Exploration & Devel. Corp., Lakewood Colo. Nat. Bank.; Trustee Colo. Sch. Mines Research Inst. Served to capt., C.E. AUS, 1942-46. Mem. Am. Inst. Mining and Metall. Engrs., Mining and Metall. Soc. Am., Am. Mining Congress. Presbyn. Home: 1700 Maple St Golden CO 80401 Office: 8700 W 14th Ave Lakewood CO 80215

COOLEY, ANDREW LYMAN, army officer; b. St. Louis, Oct. 14, 1934; s. Andrew L. and Algretta R. (Carr) C.; m. Joan Lynn Wheatley, Jan. 9, 1958; children: Cathleen Wheatley, Caroline Carr. B.A., George Washington U., 1964, M.A., 1967; M.S., U.S. Army Command and Gen. Staff Coll., 1966; postgrad., U.S. Army War Coll., 1972-73. Commd. 2d lt. U.S. Army, 1955, advanced through grades to maj. gen.; stationed in, Continental U.S. and Hawaii, 1955-64; bn. adv., Vietnam, 1964-65; aide to chief of staff SHAPE, Belgium, 1967-69; tank bn. comdr., Germany, 1969-70; mem. staff Dept. Army, Pentagon, 1970-72; brigade comdr. and div. chief of staff, Korea, 1975-77, exec. to comdr. in chief Pacific, Hawaii, 1978-79; asst. div. comdr. 101st Airborne Div., 1979-81; asst. dep. dir. for politico-mil. affairs, plans and policy directorate Joint Chiefs of Staff, Washington, 1981-83; mil. adviser Habib-Draper Mission, Lebanon, 1982-83; dir. strategy, plans and policy Dept. Army, 1983—. Author: Diplomatic Significances of the Great White Fleet, 1966, Realistic Deterrence in NATO, 1973. Decorated Legion of Merit, Bronze Star, Air medal, D.S.M., Def. D.S.M., others; Fed. Exec. fellow Brookings Instn., 1977-78; named to Officer Candidate Sch. Hall of Fame, 1979. Mem. Assn. U.S. Army, Armor Assn. Episcopalian. Home: 4504 Dolphin Ln Alexandria VA 22309 Office: Dir Strategy and Planning Dept Army Washington DC 20301

COOLEY, DENTON, surgeon, educator; b. Houston, Aug. 22, 1920; s. Ralph C. and Mary (Fraley) C.; m. Louise Goldsborough Thomas, Jan. 15, 1949; children: Mary, Susan, Louise, Florence, Helen. B.A., U. Tex., 1941; M.D., Johns Hopkins U., 1944; Doctorem Medicinae (hon.), U. Turin, Italy, 1969. Diplomate: Am. Bd. Surgery, Am. Bd. Thoracic Surgery (bd. 1965—). Intern Johns Hopkins Sch. Medicine, Balt., 1944-45, resident surgery, 1945-50; sr. surg. registrar thoracic surgery Brompton Hosp. for Chest Diseases, London, Eng., 1950-51; asso. prof. surgery Baylor U. Coll. Medicine, Houston, 1954-62, prof. surgery, 1962-69; chief surg. div., founder Tex. Heart Inst., Houston. Served as capt., M.C. AUS, 1946-48. Decorated Condeacoracion Al Merito, Ecuador; Knight Order Vasco Nunez de Balboa, Panama; recipient Grande Medaille U. Ghent, Belgium, 1963; Humanitarian award Variety Clubs Internat., 1963; Coronat medal St. Edwards U., 1963; named Kappa Sigma Man of Year award, 1964, Distinguished Citizen award Rotary Club Houston, 1965; Rene Leriche prize Internat. Surg. Soc., 1965-67; Billings Gold medal A.M.A., 1967; Vishnevsky medal Vishnevsky Inst., USSR, 1971; Theodore Roosevelt award Nat. Collegiate Athletic Assn., 1980; Presdl. Medal of Freedom, 1984; named one of ten outstanding Young Men in U.S. U.S. Jr. C. of C., 1955. Fellow A.C.S. (gov. 1965-68); mem. Soc. Thoracic Surgeons, Thoracic Soc., So. Med. Assn., Am. Assn. Thoracic Surgery, Soc. Univ. Surgeons, Am. Coll. Cardiology, Am. Coll. Chest Physicians, Am., Pan-Pacific, Western, So. surg. assns., Tex. Acad. Sci., Soc. Clin. Surgery, Internat. Cardiovascular Soc., Internat. Coll. Surgeons, Soc. Vascular Surgery, Halsted Soc., Tex. Surg. Soc., Internat. Soc. Surgery. Performed numerous heart transplants; implanted 1st artificial heart, 1969. Office: Tex Heart Inst 6720 Bertner Houston TX 77030 *As a person progresses along the path of life, he may achieve certain goals he set for himself as a youth. But to reach a more complete fulfillment he must forever extend and improve his goals to utilize more fully his talents and accomplishments. Too often, a man receives recognition for his deeds early in life and contents himself prematurely with living in peace and self satisfaction.* *

COOLEY, JAMES WILLIAM, researcher; b. N.Y.C., Sept. 18, 1926; s. William F. and Anna (Fanning) C.; m. Ingrid Uddholm, May 1, 1957; children: William, Anna-Carin, Lars. B.A., Manhattan Coll., Riverdale, N.Y., 1949; M.A., Columbia U., 1951, Ph.D., 1951. Programmer Inst. Advanced Study, Princeton, N.J., 1953-56; research staff Courant Inst., NYU, 1956-62; research staff mem. IBM Watson Research Ctr., Yorktown Heights, N.Y., 1962—. Patentee fast fourier transform. Served with USAAF, 1945-46. Fellow IEEE. Office: IBM Watson Research Ctr Yorktown Heights NY 10598

COOLEY, NANCY COLVER (MRS. ROME G. ARNOLD, II), marketing company executive; b. Carlinville, Ill.; d. John Raymond and Gladys Irwin (Jones) Colver; m. Rome G. Arnold II, 1954; children: Rome G. III, Gregory, Christopher. Student, Colo. Coll.; B.S. with honors, Northwestern U., postgrad., U. Chgo. Psychologist Skokie Sch., Winnetka, Ill.; founder, pres. Nat. Cert. Interviews, Inc.; founder RAM Services, Inc., Chgo., 1968, pres., 1974—; editor The RAM Report (monthly mag.), 1977-82; pres. RAM Data Corp. div. IMS Internat., 1980-82, Fashion Insights Internat., Ltd., N.Y.C., 1983—; cons. State Dept., N.Y. Times; lectr. Am. Mgmt. Assn. Bd. dirs. Chgo. Hearing Soc., Lyric Opera Guild of Chgo.; mem. women's bd. Boy Scouts Am. Mem. Am. Mktg. Assn. (com. chmn.), Am. Assn. for Pub. Opinion Research (com. chmn.), Am. Apparel Mfg. Assn. (com. chmn.), Nat. Retail Mchts. Assn. (steering com.), Kappa Alpha Theta. Clubs: Saddle and Cycle (Chgo.); Overseas Press (N.Y.C.). Home: 5940 Sheridan Rd Chicago IL 60660 also 19 E 37th St New York NY 10016 Office: Fashion Insights Internat Ltd 1466 Broadway New York NY 10036 Office: 1127 Thorndale Ave Chicago IL 60660

COOLEY, NORMAN VALE, JR., naval officer, surgeon; b. Santa Monica, Calif., Jan. 9, 1927; s. Norman Vale and Edna Fern (James) C.; m. Martha Ann Hoover, Aug. 14, 1949; children: Camille Rosso, Candace, Noel, Norman Vale. B.A., Occidental Coll., 1947; M.D., U. So. Calif., 1951. Diplomate: Am. Bd. Surgery. Commd. officer U.S. Navy, advanced through grades to rear adm., 1981; comdg. officer U.S. Naval Regional Med. Ctr., Naples, Italy, 1977-81, Naval Regional Med. Ctr., Portsmouth, Va., 1981-83; comdr. Naval Med. Command, Mid-Atlantic Region, Norfolk, Va., 1983—. Decorated Legion of Merit. Fellow ACS (gov. 1982—); mem. Assn. Mil. Surgeons U.S. Office: Naval Med Command Mid-Atlantic Region 6500 Hampton Blvd Norfolk VA 23508 *

COOLEY, RICHARD PIERCE, banker; b. Dallas, Nov. 25, 1923; s. Victor E. and Helen (Pierce) C. B.S., Yale, 1944. With Wells Fargo Bank, San Francisco, 1949-82, exec. v.p., 1965-66, pres., chief exec. officer, 1966-79, chmn. bd., chief exec. officer, 1979-82, also dir.; chmn., chief exec. officer, pres. Seattle-1st Nat. Bank, 1983—; chmn. bd., chief exec. officer, dir. Wells Fargo & Co., 1968-83; dir. UAL, Inc., Howmett Turbine Components Corp., Pechiney Ugine Kuhlmann Corp. Trustee Children's Hosp., San Francisco, Rand Corp., Calif. Inst. Tech., Pasadena. Served to 1st lt. Armed Services. Decorated Air medal. Mem. Assn. Res. City Bankers, Smithsonian Instn. Nat. Assn. (bd. dirs.), Calif. C. of C. (bd. dirs.). Office: Sea First Corp 1001 4th Ave Seattle WA 98124

COOLEY, ROBERT NELSON, radiologist, educator; b. Woodlawn, Va., Mar. 12, 1911; s. Elmer Jackson and Elizabeth Lee (Clark) C.; m. Eula Grace Jarnagin, July 1, 1948; children—Helen Hope, Caroline, Robert Nelson. M.D., U. Va., 1934. Diplomate: Am. Bd. Radiology (trustee, pres. 1974). Intern Bellevue Hosp., N.Y.C., 1934-36, Mary McClelland Hosp., Cambridge, N.Y., 1936; resident Johns Hopkins Hosp., Balt., 1941-42, 46-48; practice medicine, specializing in radiology, Balt., 1948-53, Galveston, Tex., 1953—; mem. staffs U. Tex. Med. Br. Hosps., Galveston; asst. prof., radiology Johns Hopkins U. Sch. Medicine, Balt., 1948-50, asso. prof., 1950-53; prof. U. Tex. Med. Br., 1953—, chmn. dept. radiology, 1953-76. Author: (with R.D. Sloan, M.H. Schreiber) Radiology of Heart and Great Vessels, 1956, 2d edit., 1966, 3d edit., 1979; contbr. articles to profl. jours. Served from 1st lt. to maj. M.C. AUS, 1942-46. Fellow Am. Coll. Radiology (Gold medal); mem. AAUP, Am. Heart Assn., Am. Roentgen Ray Soc., AMA, Assn. U. Radiologists (Gold medal), Galveston County Med. Soc., Tex. Med. Assn., Tex. Radiol. Soc., Radiol. Soc. N.Am. Presbyn. (elder). Home: 1913 Oaklawn Dr LaMarque TX 77568 Office: 915 Strand St Galveston TX 77550

COOLEY, THOMAS MCINTYRE, II, lawyer, educator; b. Detroit, Mar. 5, 1910; s. Thomas Benton and Abigail (Hubbard) C.; m. Helen Stringham, June 24, 1938; children—Abigail Jane, Harriet Stringham, Hilary Elizabeth. Grad., Phillips Exeter Acad., 1928; A.B., U. Mich., 1932; LL.B., Harvard, 1935, 1935-36. Bar: Mich. bar 1936, D.C. bar, Va. bar 1947, Pa. bar 1958. Asso. firms Dykema, Jones & Wheat, Detroit, 1937-38, Barbour, Garnett, Pickett, Keith & Glassie, Washington, 1948-50, Weaver & Glassie, 1950-58; instr., asst. prof. law Western Res. U., 1938-41; mem. Bd. Immigration Appeals, Dept. Justice, 1941, asso. dir. alien enemy control, chief alien enemy litigation, 1941-44, 46-47; dep. dir. displaced persons UNRRA, 1944-45; counsel immigration com. U.S. Ho. of Reps., 1945-46, subcom. on labor mgmt. relations U.S. Senate, 1949-50; asso. counsel com. on govt. ops. U.S. Ho. of Reps., 1950; prof. Ohio State U. Law Sch., summer 1949; dean U. Pitts. Law Sch., 1958-65, prof. law, 1966-80, prof. emeritus, 1981—, pres. univ. faculty senate, 1967, chief research div. Health Law Center, 1966-68; prof. law U. Ill. Law Sch., 1965-66; Counsel Citizens Com. on Displaced Persons, 1947-48; counsel Central Blood Bank Pitts., 1960-76; arbitrator numerous labor relations matters, 1960—. Contbr. articles and revs. to legal periodicals. Mem. Pa., D.C., Va., Allegheny County bar assns., Am. Arbitration Assn., Nat. Acad. Arbitrators, Soc. Profls. in Dispute Resolution. Home and office: 4644 Filmore St Pittsburgh PA 15213

COOLIDGE, EDWIN CHANNING, chemistry educator; b. Mt. Vernon, Ohio, Jan. 30, 1925; s. Walter Hatheral and Sarah Helen (Fay) C.; m. Bonita Mae Warner, May 1, 1953; 1 son, Edwin Channing. A.B. in Chemistry, Kenyon Coll., 1944; Ph.D., Johns Hopkins, 1949. Research chemist Procter & Gamble Co., Cin., 1949-54; asst. prof. chemistry Hamilton Coll., Clinton, N.Y., 1954-58; asst. prof. N.Mex. Inst. Mining and Tech., Socorro, 1958-61; asso. prof. Stetson U., Deland, Fla., 1961-64, prof. chemistry, 1965—; dir. NSF Undergrad. Research Program, Stetson U., 1964-67; dir. Mid-Fla. Colls. Year Abroad Program, Inc., 1968-69, German dir., 1969-70; Fulbright lectr. Paedagogische Hochschule, Freiburg, Germany, 1982-83. Contbr. articles to profl. jours. Served with AUS, 1950-52. Mem. Am. Chem. Soc., Chem. Soc. London, Phi Beta Kappa, Sigma Xi, Gamma Sigma Epsilon, Omicron Delta Kappa. Episcopalian. Home: 2446 E New York Ave Deland FL 32724

COOLIDGE, HAMILTON, life insurance company executive; b. Boston, Nov. 11, 1924; s. John Gardner and Mary Louise (Hill) C.; m. Barbara F. Bowles, Oct. 16, 1948; children: John H., Linda B., Hope McL., Malcolm H. B.A., Harvard U., 1946, M.P.A., 1952. With New Eng. Mut. Ins. Co., Boston, 1947—, sr. v.p., 1977—; dir. Brookline (Mass.) Trust Co. Chmn. tree planting com. Town of Brookline, 1962—, mem. planning bd., 1966-76; bd. dirs. New Eng. Forestry Found., 1950—, Children's Mus. Boston, 1950—. Served with USAAF, 1941-44. Mem. Mortgage Bankers Assn. (gov. 1978-81, exec. com. 1980), Mass. Audubon Soc. (dir. 1964—). Episcopalian. Office: 501 Boylston St Boston MA 02117

COOLIDGE, HAROLD JEFFERSON, international conservationist; b. Boston, Jan. 15, 1904; s. Harold and Edith (Lawrence) C.; m. Helen Carpenter Isaacs, Apr. 25, 1931 (div. 1972); children: Nicholas, Thomas, Isabella; m. Martha Thayer Henderson, May 26, 1972. Grad., Milton Acad., 1922; student, U. Ariz., 1922-23; B.S., Harvard, 1927, Cambridge (Eng.) U., 1927-28; D.Sc., George Washington U., 1959, Seoul Nat. U., 1965, Brandeis U., 1970. Asst. mammalogist Harvard African Expdn. to Liberia, Belgian Congo, 1926-27; leader Indo-China div. Kelley-Roosevelt's Field Mus. Expdn., 1928-29; asst. curator mammals Mus. Comparative Zoology, Harvard, 1929-46, asso. mammalogy, 1946-70; leader Asiatic Primate Expedition, 1937; exec. dir. Coolidge Found., 1946-51; exec. dir. Pacific sci. bd. Nat. Acad. Scis.-NRC, 1946-70; collaborator U.S. Nat. Park Service, 1948—; Sec. Am. Com. Internat. Wild Life Protection (now Am. Com. Internat. Conservation), 1930-51, chmn., 1951-71, hon. chmn., 1971—; hon. cons. Bernice P. Bishop Mus., 1953—; cons. OBOR, U.S. and Indonesia; adviser Pacific Studies Peabody Mus. Salem, 1974—; pres. Internat. Union for Conservation Nature and Natural Resources, 1966-72, hon. pres., 1972—, v.p. internat. commn. nat. parks, 1948-54, 63-66, chmn., 1958-63, mem., 1963-76, hon. mem., 1976—, chmn. species survival service commn., 1949-58, mem., 1958-76, hon. mem., 1976—; sec. gen. 10th Pacific Sci. Congress, Honolulu, 1961; chmn. 1st World Conf. on Nat. Parks, Seattle, 1962; Bd. dirs. L.S.B. Leakey Found., U.S. World Wildlife Fund, 1962—; bd. dirs. Internat. World Wildlife Fund, 1966-78, mem. of honor, 1979—; bd. dirs. Inst. Nat. Pour la conservation de la Nature de Zaire (hon.), Charles Darwin Found. for Galapagos Islands, Research Ranch, Inc.; hon. mem. bd. dirs. Island Resources Found.; v.p. Fauna Preservation Soc., U.K.; bd. dirs. emeritus Hawaii Pacific Tropical Botanic Gardens, African Wildlife Leadership Found.; trustee William P. Wharton Conservation Trust, Sci. and Aeros. Adv. Com., Lindbergh Fund; chmn. Lindbergh Fund; corp. Boston Mus. Sci.; adv. bd. Cultural Survival Inc., 1975—; mem. adv. council Internat. Crane Found., 1977—; hon. pres. H. J. Coolidge Ctr. for Environ. Leadership; hon. mem. NRC, Philippines.; hon. dir. Bat Conservation Soc. Author: (with Theodore Roosevelt) Three Kingdoms of Indo-China, 1933; sci. publs. on primates, internat. conservation. Served to maj. AUS, 1943-45. Decorated Mil. Legion of Merit, U.S.; decorations from Ecuadorian, French, Laotian, Annamite, Cambodian, Belgian govts., Prince of Netherlands; recipient 75th Anniversary medal of merit U. Ariz., 1960; Hutchinson medal Garden Club Am., 1963; Albright medal Am. Scenic and Historic Preservation Soc., 1969; Silver medal Internat. Achievement award U.S. Nat. Parks Centennial Commn., 1972; Browning award Smithsonian Instn., 1978; Phillips medal Internat. Union Conservation of Nature and Natural Resources, 1978; J. Paul Getty Wildlife Conservation prize, 1979. Fellow N.Y. Zool. Soc. (gold medal 1969), Pacific Sci. Assn. (hon. life); mem. Am. Soc. Mammalogists (life), Common Cause, Caribbean Cons. Assn., Inst. Nat. Parks Belgian Congo (dir. 1955-60), Nat. Parks and Conservation Assn. (sec. 1946-59, dir. 1959-74), Pacific Sci. Assn. (U.S. mem. Pacific sci. council 1962-72), Monticello Assn., Chgo. Mus. Natural History (life), Internat. Inst. Differing Civilizations (Brussels), Cercle Zoologique Congolaise (hon., Belgium), Zool. Soc. London (corr.), Sigma Xi. Episcopalian. Clubs: Harvard Travellers, Tavern (Boston); Cosmos (Washington); Harvard, Boone and Crockett, Explorers (N.Y.C.) (chmn. edn. com. 1976). Home: 38 Standley St Beverly MA 01915

COOLIDGE, RITA, singer; b. Nashville, 1944; m. Kris Kristofferson, Aug. 19, 1973 (div. June 1980); 1 dau., Casey. Student, Fla. State U. Singer with, Delaney & Bonnie Bramlett, Joe Cocker, Leon Russell, Kris Kristofferson; also soloist; film appearance: Pat Garrett and Billy the Kid, 1973, A Star is Born, 1980; recordings include Love Me Again (Recipient Grammy awards.); performed: title song All Time High in Octopussy. Office: care Ron Rainey Mgmt Inc 9454 Wilshire Blvd Suite 206 Beverly Hills CA 90212 *

COOLIDGE, THOMAS RICHARDS, insurance company executive; b. Boston, Jan. 29, 1934; s. Harold Jefferson and Helen Carpenter (Isaacs) C.; m. Susan Lane Freiberg, May 8, 1965; children: Laura Jefferson, Anne Richards, Thomas Lawrence. A.B. cum laude, Harvard U., 1955, J.D., 1960. Bar: N.Y. 1963. Assoc. firm Carter, Ledyard & Milburn, N.Y.C., 1960-68, partner, 1968-74; pres. Diebold Groups, Inc. (cons.), N.Y.C., 1974-75; sr. v.p. Parsons & Whittemore, Inc., N.Y.C., 1975-82; v.p., dir. Stenbeck Reassurance Co., Inc., N.Y.C., 1982—; pres. Coolidge & Co., Inc., 1982—; dir. Millidyne Inc., Sandvik, Inc., 1972-82. Bd. dirs., vice chmn. Neighborhood Com. on Asphalt Green, 1969—; trustee Vincent Astor Found., 1972—, Sala, Inc., 1974-77. Served as lt. Armored F.A. U.S. Army, 1955-57. Mem. Am. Bar Assn., N.Y. State Bar Assn., Assn. Bar City N.Y. Republican. Episcopalian. Clubs: Brook, River. Office: Coolidge & Co Inc Beebe Hill Rd Falls Village CT 06031

COOMBE, V. ANDERSON, valve mfg. co. exec.; b. Cin., Mar. 5, 1926; s. Harry Elijah and Mary (Anderson) C.; m. Eva Jane Romaine, Sept. 26, 1957; children—James, Michael, Peter. B.E., Yale, 1948. Asst. to pres. Wm. Powell Co., Cin., 1953-57, v.p., 1957-63, exec. v.p., 1963-69, pres., treas., 1969—, also dir.; dir. First Nat. Bank Cin., Union Central Life Ins., Lodge & Shipley Co., Eagle-Picher Industries. Clubs: Camargo, Queen City, Cincinnati Country (Cin.). Home: 6 Corbin Ln Cincinnati OH 45208 Office: 2503 Spring Grove Ave Cincinnati OH 45214

COOMBES, JAMES ARTHUR, mgmt. cons.; b. Hamilton, Ont., Can., Apr. 12, 1921; came to U.S., 1924, naturalized, 1931; s. James Arthur and Jane (DePledge) C.; m. Margaret Dorothy Ann Fallon, Oct. 12, 1946; children—James A., Thomas P., Robert W., Richard A., Ronald C., Janet A. B.B.A., Western Res. U., (now Case-Western Res. U.), 1949. Accounting mgr. Indsl. Rayon Corp., Cleve., 1949-51; controller The S-P Mfg. Corp., Cleve., 1952-58; cons. Robert Heller & Assos., Cleve., 1959-62; controller Union Switch and Signal Co., Pitts., 1963-64; v.p. finance Andy Gard Corp., Pitts., 1965-66; acquisition specialist Baerwald, Porco & DeBoer, Pitts., 1967; v.p. Amerofina, Inc., Pitts., 1968; pres. Argus, Inc., Columbia, S.C., 1969; dir.; chmn. bd. Interphoto Corp., Long Island City, N.Y.; dir. Noma-Worldwide Inc., Chgo., Oxford Speaker Co., Uranya Hellas, Athens, Greece, 1970-73; pres. Accura Group Ltd., Tokyo, 1972-74; mgmt. cons. James Coombes Assos., Pitts., 1974—; chmn. bd. Michiana Lumber & Supply Inc., Edwardsburg, Mich., 1976—; pres. Winchester Corp., Pitts., 1976—. Served with USMCR, 1942-45. Home: 1318 Washington Rd Pittsburgh PA 15228 Office: PO Box 11806 Pittsburgh PA 15228

COOMBS, CLYDE HAMILTON, psychologist, educator; b. Paterson, N.J., July 22, 1912; s. Clyde and Mildred (Horandt) C.; m. Lolagene Convis, Sept. 1, 1939; children: Steven, Douglas. A.B., U. Calif., Berkeley, 1935, M.A., 1937; Ph.D., U. Chgo., 1941; D.S.S. (hon.), U. Leiden, Netherlands, 1975. Instr. psychology U. Chgo., 1939-41, research asso. biophysics, 1939-41; research psychologist Adj. Gen.'s Office, War Dept., 1941-43; mem. faculty dept. psychology U. Mich., Ann Arbor, 1947—, Disting. Univ. prof., 1978—; vis. prof. Harvard U., Boston, 1948-49; vis. research prof. U. Amsterdam, Netherlands, 1955-56; cons. Dept. Army, 1957-59; lecture tour various univs. in, Europe, 1964-65; vis. prof. U. Colo., Boulder, 1965, U. Wash., Seattle, 1967; cons. VA Hosp., Ann Arbor, 1968-69; vis. prof. U. Western Australia, 1969, Central U. Venezuela, 1970, Inst. Psychology, Academia Sinica, Beijing, China, 1981; mem. U.S.-USSR Interacad. seminar math. psychology, Tbilisi, Russia, 1979; vis. research scholar U. London, 1978; mem. com. biometry and epidemiology NIH, 1971. Author: (with R.M. Thrall and R.C. Davis) Decision Processes, 1954, (with R.C. Kao) Nonmetric Factor Analysis, 1955, A Theory of Data, 1964, (with R.M. Dawes and A. Tversky) Mathematical Psychology: An Elementary Introduction, 1970; cons. editor: Psychol. Rev, 1953-58; book rev. editor: Psychometrics, 1951-54. Served from capt. to maj. U.S. Army, 1943-46. Decorated Legion of Merit; recipient Fulbright award, 1955-56, Fulbright-Hayes award, 1975; named Disting. Sr. Faculty lectr. U. Mich., 1980. Fellow Am. Psychol. Assn. (pres. div. 5 1958-59, chmn. bd. sci. affairs 1960-62), Am. Acad. Arts and Scis., Am. Statis. Assn. (hon.); mem. Soc. Math. Psychology (pres. 1977-78), Psychometric Soc. (pres. 1955-56), Nat. Acad. Scis., Psychol. Assn. Spain (hon.). Home: 3419 Daleview Dr Ann Arbor MI 48103 Office: 580 Union Dr Dept Psychology Univ Mich Ann Arbor MI 48109

COOMBS, JOHN WENDELL, business executive; b. Salt Lake City, Jan. 29, 1905; s. John Hardy and Merle (Halliday) C.; m. Norma Druke, June 7, 1929; 1 son, John Wendell. A.B., U. Utah, 1926; LL.B., George Washington U., 1934. Examiner R.F.C., Washington, 1935-42, asst. to dir., 1945-46; pres. Aeronautical Tng. Soc., Washington, 1943-45; asst. to pres. Transam. Corp., San Francisco, 1946-51, v.p., 1952-57; v.p., sec., dir. Gen. Metals Corp., Oakland, Calif., 1957-63; v.p. Transam. Fin. Corp. (formerly Pacific Fin. Corp.), 1963-69, dir., 1969-71; v.p., dir. Transam. Comml. Corp. (formerly Transam. Fin. Corp.), 1963-65, pres., dir., 1965-69; chmn. Bankers Mortgage Co., San Francisco, 1967-70, dir., 1966-72; pres. Transam. Devel. Co., 1968-69, chmn., 1969-70, dir., 1966-80; pres., dir. Transam. Land Capital, Inc., 1968-83; pres. Mortgage Trust of Am., 1969-72, chmn., 1972-81; also chmn. Transam. Mtg. Adv., Inc., 1969-70, cons., 1981—, dir., 1969-72; chmn. Transinternat. Hotel Co., 1969—; v.p. Transam. Corp., 1968-70, cons., 1970—. Office: 1150 S Olive St Los Angeles CA 90015

COOMBS, ROBERT HOLMAN, sociologist, educator, author; b. Salt Lake City, Sept. 16, 1934; s. Morgan Scott and Vivian (Holman) C.; m. Carol Jean Cook, May 29, 1958; children: Robert Scott, Kathryn, Lorraine, Karen Youn Jung, Holly Ann, Krista Ho Jung, David Jeremy. B.S., U. Utah, 1958, M.S., 1959; Ph.D., Wash. State U., 1964. Asst. prof. sociology Iowa State U., 1963-66; postdoctoral fellow Behavioral Sci. Center, Bowman Gray Sch. Medicine, Wake Forest U., 1966, asst. prof., 1966-68, asso. prof., 1968-70; career research specialist Calif. Dept. Mental Hygiene, Camarillo, 1970-73; asso. research sociologist UCLA, 1970-77, adj. asso. prof. biobehavioral scis. Sch. Medicine, 1977-78, adj. prof., 1978-81, prof. med. sociology, 1981—; chief Camarillo Neuropsychiat. Inst., 1970-78; asst. dir. research UCLA Neuropsychiat. Inst., Center for Health Scis., 1978-81; dir. Office Edn. of Neuropsychiat. Inst., 1980—, UCLA Family Learning Center, Oxnard, Calif., 1977—. Author: Psychosocial Aspects of Medical Training, 1971, Junkies and Straights: The Camarillo Experience, 1975, Socialization in Drug Abuse, 1976, Mastering Medicine: Professional Socialization in Medical School, 1978, Making it in Medical School, 1979; also numerous chpts. and articles; asso. editor: Family Relations: Jour. Applied Family and Child Studies, 1970—, Clin. Sociology Rev., Jour. Clin. Sociology, Jour. Marriage and the Family; contbg. editor: Jour. Drug Issues, 1977—. Bishop, Winston-Salem (N.C.) Ward, Ch. Jesus Christ of Latter-day Saints, 1969-70, Camarillo (Calif.) Ward, 1972-77. Served with U.S. Army, 1958. Grantee NIMH, 1968-73, Nat. Fund Med. Edn., 1969-71, Law Enforcement Assistance Adminstrn., 1971-76, Nat. Inst. Drug Abuse, 1977-80, Calif. Dept. Alcohol and Drug Programs, 1977—, Father Flanagan's Boys Home, 1977—, CETA, Ventura County, Calif., 1978. Mem. Am., Internat. sociol. assns., Nat. Council

Family Relations, Assn. Am. Med. Colls., Soc. for Study Social Problems, Assn. Behavioral Scis. and Med. Edn., Conf. Social Sci. and Health, Clin. Sociology Assn., AAAS, Sigma Xi, Phi Kappa Phi. Democrat. Home: 1612 Hobart Dr Camarillo CA 93010 Office: Dept Psychiatry and Biobehavioral Scis UCLA Sch Medicine 760 Westwood Plaza Los Angeles CA 90024 *I have surrounded myself with superior people, those whose specialized talents have enriched my thinking and productivity. I actively pursue the association and assistance of those whose skills exceed my own.*

COOMBS, WALTER PAUL, lawyer, social science educator; b. Missoula, Mont., Aug. 20, 1920; s. Walter Omar and Wilhelmina (Gerlach) C. A.B., U. Mont., 1939, J.D., 1941. Bar: Mont. 1941. Sec. to gov., Mont., 1941-43; chmn. Mont. Indsl. Accident Bd., 1943-46; spl. atty. U.S. Dept. Justice, 1946-49; cons. U.S. Dept. State, 1949-53; exec. dir. Los Angeles World Affairs Council, 1953-67; gen. sec. Calif. State Univs. and Colls., 1967-70; prof., chmn. dept. social scis. Calif. State Poly. U., Pomona, 1970—; labor arbitrator, 1950—, cons. internat. programs to mayor of Los Angeles, 1973—. Trustee Pan Pacific Center; chmn. Mayor's Council on Internat. Visitors. Decorated Order Brit. Empire; comdr. Order of Lion (Finland); Order of Merit (W. Ger.); Order of Crown (Belgium); Recipient award Air Force Assn. Arts and Scis., 1963; Disting. Service award Govt. of Philippines, 1956; Order of White Elephant (Thailand). Mem. Nat. Acad. Arbitrators, ABA, AAUP, English Speaking Union (dir.), Los Angeles Town Hall, World Affairs Council (dir.), Am. Com. on East-West Accord (dir.), Los Angeles Com. on Fgn. Relations, Chevalier du Tastevin, Sierra Club. Republican. Lutheran. Club: Masons. Home: 23519 Silver Spring Ln Diamond Bar CA 97165 Office: 3801 W Temple Ave Pomona CA 91768

COON, CARLETON STEVENS, JR., foreign service officer; b. Paris, France, Apr. 27, 1927; s. Carleton Stevens and Mary (Goodale) C.; m. Janet January Wulsin, June 14, 1949 (dec. 1967); children: William, Howard, Katharine, Elizabeth, Ellen, Richard; m. Jane S. Abell, Jan. 2, 1968. B.A. cum laude, Harvard, 1949. Joined U.S. Fgn. Service, 1949, Kreis resident officer, Germany, 1950-52; 2d sec. embassy, Damascus, Syria, 1952-56, New Delhi, India, 1956-59; served on Cyprus, later India desks State Dept., 1959- 63; consul, prin. officer, Tabriz, Iran, 1963-65, India desk, 1965-68; assigned Nat. War Coll., Ft. McNair, Washington, 1968-69; dir. Presdl. appointments staff, 1969-70; counselor, dep. chief mission Am. embassy, Kathmandu, Nepal, 1970-73; diplomat-in-residence Carleton Coll., 1973-74; minister-counselor, dep. chief mission Am. Embassy, Rabat, Morocco, 1974-76; dep. dir. Fgn. Service Inst., Washington, 1976-79; dir. Office North African Affairs, 1979-81; ambassador to Nepal, Kathmandu, 1981—. Office: Kathmandu Dept State Washington DC 20520

COON, JANE ABELL, ambassador; b. Dover, N.H., May 9, 1929; d. Max F. and Virginia (Bennett) Abell; m. Carleton Stevens Conn, Jr., Jan. 2, 1968; step children: William, Howard, Katharine, Elizabeth, Ellen, Richard. B.A., Coll. of Wooster, Ohio, 1951, LL.D (hon.), 1983. Commd. fgn. service officer Dept. State, 1956, 2d sec., Karachi, Pakistan, 1957-59, consul, Bombay, India, 1960-64, 1st sec., New Delhi, India, 1965-67, country dir., for Pakistan, Afghanistan, Bangladesh, Washington, 1977-79, dep. asst. sec. Near East and South Asia, 1979-81, ambassador to Bangladesh, Dacca, 1981—. Mem. Soc. Woman Geographers, Council Fgn. Relations. Office: Dacca Dept State Washington DC 20520

COON, MINOR JESSER, biological chemistry educator; b. Englewood, Colo., July 29, 1921; s. Minor Dillon and Mary (Jesser) C.; m. Mary Louise Newburn, June 27, 1948; children: Lawrence R., Susan L. B.A., U. Colo., 1943; Ph.D., U. Ill., 1946; D.Sc. (hon.), Northwestern U., 1983. Postdoctoral research asst. in biochemistry U. Ill., 1946-47; instr. dept. physiol. chemistry U. Pa., 1947-49, asst. prof., 1949-53; asso. prof., 1953-55; prof. dept. biol. chemistry U. Mich. Med. Sch., 1955—, chmn. dept., 1970—; research fellow dept. pharmacology N.Y. U., 1952-53; research fellow Fed. Poly. Inst., Zürich, Switzerland, 1961-62; cons. Oak Ridge Inst. Nuclear Studies, 1956-58; mem. adv. council Life Ins. Med. Research Fund, 1960-65; mem. biochem. study sect. NIH, 1963-66, research career award com., 1966-70. Editor-in-chief: Biochemical Preparations, 1962, Microsomes, Drug Oxidations and Chemical Carcinogenesis, 1980; mem. editorial bds.: Biochemistry, 1971-74, Molecular Pharmacology, 1972—, Jour. Biol. Chemistry, 1976—, Proc. Sci. Conf. on Cytochrome P-450: Structural and Functional Aspects, 1980; Contbr. articles to profl. jours. Recipient Distinguished Faculty achievement award U. Mich., 1976; William C. Rose award in biochemistry and nutrition, 1978; Bernard B. Brodie award in drug metabolism, 1980; Disting. Faculty lectureship award in biomed. research U. Mich., 1980. Fellow N.Y. Acad. Scis.; mem. Am. Chem. Soc. (award in enzyme chemistry 1959), Am. Soc. Biol. Chemists (sec. 1981—), Am. Soc. Pharmacology and Exptl. Therapeutics, Biophys. Soc., AAAS, Assn. Med. Sch. Depts. Biochemistry (pres. 1974-75), Internat. Union Biochemistry (chmn. oxygenases interest group 1981—), Am. Inst. Biol. Scis., Am. Soc. Microbiology, Am. Oil Chemists Soc., Nat. Acad. Scis., Phi Beta Kappa, Sigma Xi, Phi Kappa Phi, Alpha Chi Sigma, Phi Lambda Upsilon. Home: 1901 Austin Ave Ann Arbor MI 48104 Office: Dept Biol Chemistry U Mich Ann Arbor MI 48109

COONEY, BARBARA, illustrator, author; b. Bklyn., Aug. 6, 1917; d. Russell Schenck and Mae Evelyn (Bossert) C.; m. Guy Murchie, Dec. 1942 (div. Mar. 1947); children: Gretel, Barnaby; m. Charles T. Porter, July 16, 1949; children: Charles Talbot, Phoebe. B.A., Smith Coll., 1938; student, Art Students League, 1940. Author, illustrator: Miss Rumphius. Recipient Caldecott medal for Chanticleer and the Fox, 1958, U. So. Miss. medal, 1975, Smith Coll. medal, 1976, Caldecott medal, 1980, Am. Book award, 1983. Home: Pepperell MA 01463

COONEY, DAVID MARTIN, orgn. exec.; b. Los Angeles, Aug. 5, 1930; s. Arthur B. and Margaret M. (Metcalf) C.; m. Beverly Satchwell, Feb. 22, 1952; children—Kathleen Cooney Lambert, David M., Karen L., Kacy L. B.A., U. So. Calif., 1951; M.S., George Washington U., 1965; grad., Naval War Coll., 1965. Commd. ensign U.S. Navy, 1951, advanced through grades to rear adm., 1976; pub. affairs officer (6th Fleet), pub. affairs officer comdr. in chief, 1967-71, asst. chief of info., Washington, 1971-73, dep. chief of info., 1973-75, chief of info., 1975-80, asst. to sec. of Navy for mgmt., 1980-81, ret., 1981; pres. Goodwill Industries of Am., Washington, 1981—. Mem. nat. council Boy Scouts Am., 1978—. Decorated Disting. Service medal, Legion of Merit with gold star, others; Alumni Merit award U. So. Calif., 1979. Home: 6203 Larstan Dr Alexandria VA 22312 Office: Goodwill Industries America 9200 Wisconsin Ave Washington DC 20024

COONEY, GEORGE AUGUSTIN, lawyer; b. Detroit, July 12, 1909; s. Augustin W. and Mary (McBride) C.; m. Julia Grace Starrs, Oct. 26, 1940; children: George Augustin Jr., Michael Edward, Timothy John. A.B., U. Detroit, 1932, J.D., 1935. Bar: Mich. 1935, Fed. 1935. Since practiced in, Detroit; mem. firm Cooney & Cooney (P.C.), Detroit, 1969—; lectr. in field. Editor news and comment sect.: Probate and Trust Law Jour. Served with USAAF, World War II. Recipient Tower award U. Detroit, 1973. Fellow Am. Coll. Probate Counsel; mem. Am., Detroit, Fed. bar assns., State Bar Mich., Cath. Lawyers Soc. Detroit (dir.), Soc. Irish-Am. Lawyers, Am. Judicature Soc., Selden Soc., Mich. Assn. Professions, Am. Philatelic Soc., Royal Can. Philatelic Soc., Detroit Zool. Soc. Clubs: K.C. (4 deg.), Stoney Point (Ont.) Sportsmans, Detroit Golf; Nat. Lawyers (Washington); Lawyers (Detroit). Home: 1725 Van Dyke Ave Detroit MI 48214 Office: 2329 One Kennedy Sq Detroit MI 48226

COONEY, JAMES PATRICK, physician; b. Parnell, Iowa, Mar. 17, 1903; s. James Francis and Catherine Agnes (Kennedy) C.; m. Irene Kelly, Aug. 4, 1928; 1 son, James P. B.S., U. Iowa, 1925, M.D., 1927; grad., Army Med. Sch., Army Med. Field Service Sch., 1929. Diplomate: Am. Bd. Radiology. Entered U.S. Army, 1927, advanced through grades to maj. gen., 1955; intern Fitzsimons Army Hosp., Denver; staff Sternberg Hosp., Manila, Letterman Army Hosp., San Francisco, Mil. Acad. Sta. Hosp., West Point, N.Y., Walter Reed Army Hosp., Washington; chief radiologist Gorgas Gen. Hosp., C.Z., 1940-43; exec. officer, asst. comdt. England Gen. Hosp., Atlantic City, 1943-45; mem. group to study med. and hospitalization methods, Sweden, 1945; rep. Army Surgeon Gen., Manhattan Engring. Dist., 1946; later med. dir.; mem. spl. mission to Japan to study A-bomb survivors at Hiroshima; cons. Armed Forces Spl. Weapons Project; dir. spl. projects div. Office Army Surgeon Gen.; radiol. safety officer Eniwetok tests, 1949, 51; chief radiol. br. div. mil. application AEC, 1951; surgeon Japanese Logistical Command, Yokohama, 1951-53; spl. asst. to comdg. gen. Walter Reed Army Med. Center, 1953; comdt. Med. Field Service Sch., Brooke Army Med. Ctr., Ft. Sam Houston, Texas, 1953-55; dep. surgeon gen. Army, 1955-58; chief surgeon European Command, Ger., 1959-60; ret., 1960; v.p. med. affairs Am. Cancer Soc., 1960-69; dir. 3d Nat. Cancer Survey Atlanta Area, Ga. Regional Med. Program, 1969—. Decorated Legion of Merit with oak leaf cluster, Bronze Star, D.S.M.; hon. mem. Class of 1941, U.S. Mil. Acad. Fellow Am. Coll. Chest Physicians, Am. Coll. Radiology, Am. Coll. Gastroenterology (hon.); mem. Radiol. Soc. N.Am., Nat. Tb Assn., Radioation Research Soc., AMA, Am. Roentgen Ray Soc. (emeritus). Home: 3653 N Stradford Rd NE Atlanta GA 30342 Office: 938 Peachtree St NE Atlanta GA 30309

COONEY, JAMES PATRICK, JR., health services management educator, researcher; b. West Point, N.Y., Nov. 9, 1933; s. James Patrick and Lillian Irene (Kelly) C.; m. Sondra Sue Cooper, Dec. 1, 1956; children: James Patrick, Christopher, Andrew, Amy. B.S., U. Iowa, 1955, M.A., 1957; Ph.D., U. Minn., 1968. Assoc. dir. research Nat. Blue Cross Assn., Chgo., 1963-65; dir. research Am. Hosp. Assn., Chgo., 1965-69; assoc. dean, assoc. prof. Sch. Pub. Health, UCLA, 1969-71; dir. health service research center Northwestern U., Am. Hosp. Assn., Chgo., 1971-75; chief exec. officer R.I. Health Services Research Inc., Providence, 1975-79; assoc. dir. health research stats. and tech. Office Asst. Sec. Health, Washington, 1979-81; chmn., prof. dept. health adminstrn. Duke U., Durham, N.C., 1981—; mem. U.S. Nat. Com. on Vital and Health Stats., Washington, 1975-79; cons. Office Tech. Assessment, Washington, 1976-78, Nat. Ctr. Health Stats., 1965-79, Nat. Ctr. Health Service Research, 1968-79, Social Security Adminstrn., 1969-79. Author: The Large Urban Public Hospital, 1972, Use of Clinical Data for Hospital Management, 1974, Multi-Hospital Systems, 1975, Effect of Inflation-Recession on Hospital Use, 1980. Served to capt. Med. Service Corps, U.S. Army, 1956-61; ETO. Fellow W.K. Kellogg Found., Sch. Pub. Health, U. Minn.-Mpls., 1961-64; recipient cert. disting. performance HHS, 1979-80. Mem. Internat. Epidemiol. Assn., Am. Hosp. Assn., Am. Pub. Health Assn., Omicron Delta Kappa. Home: 502 Constitution Dr Durham NC 27705 Office: Duke U Med Ctr Box 3018 Durham NC 27710

COONEY, JOAN GANZ, TV executive; b. Phoenix, Nov. 30, 1929; d. Sylvan C. and Pauline (Reardan) Ganz; m. Peter G. Peterson, 1980. B.A., U. Ariz., 1951. Reporter Ariz. Republic, Phoenix, 1953-54; publicist NBC, 1954-55, U.S. Steel Hour, 1955-62; producer Channel 13/WNET, pub. affairs documentaries, N.Y.C., 1962-67; TV cons. Carnegie Corp. N.Y., N.Y.C., 1967-68; exec. dir. Children's TV Workshop (producers Sesame Street, Electric Company, also others), N.Y.C., 1968-70, pres., trustee, 1970—; trustee Channel 13/Ednl. Broadcasting Corp.; dir. Xerox Corp., May Dept. Stores Co., Johnson & Johnson, Chase Manhattan Corp., Chase Manhattan Bank N.A., Met. Life Ins. Co. (Recipient numerous awards for Sesame St. and other TV programs including, Nat. Sch. Pub. Relations Assn. Gold Key 1971). Mem. Pres.'s Commn. on Marihuana and Drug Abuse, 1971-73, Nat. News Council, 1973-81, Council Fgn. Relations, 1974—, Pres.'s Commn. for Agenda for 80's, 1980-81, Adv. Com. for Trade Negotiations, 1978-80; mem. Gov.'s Commn. on Internat. Yr. of the Child, 1979, Carnegie Found. Nat. Panel on High Sch., 1980-82. Disting. Service medal Columbia Tchrs. Coll., 1971; Soc. Family Man award, 1971; Nat. Inst. Social Scis. Gold medal, 1971; Frederick Douglass award N.Y. Urban League, 1972; Silver Satellite award Am. Women in Radio and TV; Woman of Yr. in Edn. award Ladies Home Jour., 1975; Woman of Decade award, 1979; NEA Friends of Edn. award; Kiwanis Decency award; NAEB Disting. Service award; 5th Women's Achiever award Girl Scouts U.S.A.; Stephen S. Wise award, 1981; Harris Found. award, 1982. Mem. NOW, Nat. Acad. TV Arts and Scis., Nat. Inst. Social Scis., Internat. Radio and TV Soc., Am. Women in Radio and TV. Office: Children's TV Workshop 1 Lincoln Plaza New York NY 10023

COONEY, JOHN GORDON, lawyer; b. Bklyn., Jan. 21, 1930; s. John Philip and Josephine (Gordon) C.; m. Patricia Ruth McEwen, June 8, 1957; 1 son, J. Gordon. A.B., St. John's U., 1951, LL.B., 1953. Bar: N.Y. 1953, Pa. 1962, D.C. 1970. Asso. Patterson, Belknap & Webb, N.Y.C., 1953-55; staff counsel U.S. Industries, N.Y., 1956-57; atty. SEC, Washington, 1957-59, FTC, 1959-61; partner Schnader, Harrison, Segal & Lewis, Phila., 1963—; dir. Delta Data Systems Corp.; arbitrator Am. Arbitration Assn., 1964—; public mem. nat. com. on arbitration Nat. Assn. Securities Dealers, 1977-83; dir. Attys. Liability Assurance Soc., 1979—. Dir., pres. Strafford Village Assn., 1969-70; bd. govs. N.Y.C. Young Republican Club, 1957. Recipient Superior Service award FTC, 1961. Mem. Am. Law Inst., ABA (council sect. corp., banking and bus. law 1980—), N.Y. Bar Assn., Phila. Bar Assn. Roman Catholic. Clubs: Union League (Phila.); Overbrook Golf, Merion Cricket. Home: 320 Gatcombe Ln Bryn Mawr PA 19010 Office: Packard Bldg Philadelphia PA 19102

COONEY, JOSEPH PATRICK, lawyer; b. Hartford, Conn., Aug. 30, 1906; s. Jeremiah and Margaret (Dwyer) C.; m. Mary M. Malliet, June 28, 1933 (dec. Jan. 1974); children—Jane (Mrs. V.J. Dowling), Edwina (Mrs. H.T. Gillis), Margaret (Mrs. B.J. Coughlin), Anne, Joseph Patrick, Mary Alice (Mrs. Edgar A. Belden), Barbara (Mrs. Robert G. Oliver); m. Marion Cobden, May 29, 1976. LL.B., Georgetown U., 1929. Mem. Conn. State Senate (2d Senatorial dist.), 1931-33, 1937, 1941; mem. Hartford Co. Commn., 1933-39, Hartford Aviation Commn., 1930-31; asst. U.S. dist. atty., 1941-43; Mem. Hartford County Grievance Com., 1961-65; chmn. Conn. Gov.'s Ad Hoc Com. Jud. Nominees, 1975-77. Trustee of Catholic Family Services St. Agnes Home, St. Joseph Coll.; bd. dirs. St. Francis Hosp., Conn. Hosp. Assn.; pres., 1961-62, Mt. St. Benedict Cemetery, Conn. Inst. for Blind, Hosp. Council Greater Hartford,, 1962-63; bd. incorporators Inst. Living, Mt. Sinai Hosp. Recipient John Carroll award Georgetown U., 1965. Fellow Am. Coll. Trial Lawyers; mem. Internat. Soc. Barristers, ABA. (ho. dels. 1966-67), Conn. Bar Assn. (pres. 1965-66, chmn. com. on jud. selection), Hartford County Bar Assn. (pres. 1946-48). Roman Catholic. Club: Knight St. Gregory. Home: 795 Prospect Ave B-1 West Hartford CT 06105 Office: 266 Pearl St Hartford CT 06103

COONEY, LLOYD EVERETT, broadcasting executive; b. Council Bluffs, Iowa, June 3, 1923; s. Cecil E. and Vera E. (Williams) C.; m. Betty Lou Packard, Mar. 4, 1946; children: Shauna, Kevin and Kim (twins). B.S., U. Utah, 1949, postgrad., 1949-50. Sales rep. Paul Revere Ins. Co., Salt Lake City, 1949-51; dir. pub. relations Intermountain Hosp. Service (Blue Cross), Salt Lake City, 1951-54; v.p., gen. mgr. sta. KSL-TV, Salt Lake City, 1954-64; pres., gen. mgr. KIRO radio and TV stas., Seattle, 1964-80; mem.-at-large CBS Radio Affiliates Adv. Bd., 1979-80; broadcast cons., 1980—; dir. broadcasting Seattle Supersonics, 1980—; v.p., dir. Bonneville Internat. Corp., Salt Lake City, 1968-80; chmn. Seattle br. Fed. Res. Bank of San Francisco, 1975-80. Trustee Seattle Salvation Army, Am. Heart Assn. of Wash.; chmn. Seattle-King County Conv. and Visitors Bur., 1973-75. Served with 82d Airborne Div. AUS, 1943-46. Named Man of Year Seattle Variety Club, 1968, Seattle's Salesman of Year Sales and Marketing Execs., 1969, Media Man of Year Wash. Assn. Realtors, 1969; recipient TV journalism award Sigma Delta Chi, 1970, 1st and 3d place for TV commentary and analysis-editorial, 1973, 3d place, 1976, 2d and 3d place, 1977; Americanism medal Am. Legion, 1971; 2 George Washington Honor medals, 1971; Honor certificate, 1972; prin. award pub. address category, 1974; all Freedoms Found.; Abe Lincoln award, 1978; Emmy award for editorials Nat. Assn. TV Arts and Scis., 1968; citation Variety Club Internat., 1978; Gavel award Am. Bar Assn., 1978; Tightrope award Seattle/Opportunities Industrialization Center, 1978; Key Man award Wash. State Council of League of United Latin Am. Citizens, 1979. Mem. Wash. State Assn. Broadcasters, Downtown Seattle Devel. Assn. (v.p. 1970—), Seattle C. of C., Alpha Kappa Psi (hon., award 1972). Clubs: Rainier (bd. dirs.), Variety, Broadmoor Golf (Seattle). Home: Bellevue WA 98004 Office: 1111 3d Ave Bldg Suite 2888 Seattle WA 98101

COONEY, RAY HOWARD, manufacturing company executive; b. Akron, Ohio, Dec. 14, 1921; s. Frederick B and Myrtle A. (Young) C.; m. June H. Hawkins, June 13, 1947; children: Pamela J., Cooney Trent, Robbie L. Cooney Johansson, Mark R. B.A.E., U. Fla., 1943; postgrad., Georgetown U., 1946, Syracuse U., 1973-74. Asst. sales and advt. mgr. Adams Packaging Assn., Auburdale, Fla., 1946-48; v.p. Flag Sulphur & Chem. Co., Tampa, Fla., 1960-63, pres., 1963-67; sales mgr. Niagara Chem. div. Food Machinery, Tampa, 1967-68; mktg. dir. Scotty's Inc., Winter Haven, Fla., 1968-69, v.p., 1969-73, pres., chief exec. officer, 1973—; dir. Christian Towers, Fla. Guarantee & Trust Co., St. Petersburgh, Fla. Pres. Fla. Agrl. Research Inst., 1967-68; bd. govs. Lake Region YMCA. Served to sgt. inf. AUS, World War II. Decorated Purple Heart. Republican. Mem. Christian Ch. (Disciples of Christ). Lodges: Cypress Gardens Rotary (pres.); Masons; Shriners. Home: 5 Lake Link Dr SE Winter Haven FL 33880 Office: Scotty's Inc PO Box 939 Winter Haven FL 33880

COONROD, RICHARD ALLEN, internat. food co. exec.; b. Mahaska, Kans., Mar. 30, 1931; m. Phyllis Clark, Jan. 7, 1960; children—Amy, Wade, Paul. B.S., Kans. State U., 1953. With Pillsbury Co., 1956—, v.p., gen. mgr. commodity merchandising, 1975-77, v.p., gen. mgr. agri-products div., 1977-78, group v.p., gen. mgr., 1978-79, exec. v.p., 1979—, pres. agri-products, 1981—; dir. Northwestern Nat. Bank, Mpls. Campaign chmn. Minn. United Negro Coll. Fund, 1979; bd. dirs. Mpls. Jr. Achievement, Urban Coalition, Art Inst. Mpls.; trustee Minn. 4-H Found., 1981—. Served to capt. USAF, 1954-56. Mem. Millers Nat. Fedn. (exec. com.), St. Louis Grain Exchange (pres. 1973-74), Chgo. Bd. Trade. Clubs: Mpls.; Interlaken Country (Edina, Minn.). Office: 608 2d Ave S Minneapolis MN 55402

COONS, JOHN E., legal educator, lawyer; b. 1929. B.A., U. Minn., 1950; J.D., Northwestern U., 1953. Bar: D.C. 1953, Ill. 1953. Trial atty. Army Panel Bd. Contract Appeals, 1953-55; asst. prof. Northwestern U., 1955-58, assoc. prof., 1958-62, prof., 1962-68, asst. dean Sch. Law, 1955-60; vis. prof. U. Calif.-Berkeley Sch. Law, 1967-68; prof., 1968—. Author: (with Clune and Sugarman) Private Wealth and Public Education, 1970, (with Sugarman) Education by Choice, 1978; past mng. editor: Northwestern U. Law Rev. Served with U.S. Army, 1953-55. Mem. Cleve. Conf., Order of Coif. Office: U Calif Law Sch 225 Boalt Hall Berkeley CA 94720

COONS, MARION MCDOWELL, supermarket chain exec.; b. Macedonia, Iowa, Apr. 11, 1915; s. Lindsey D. and Luella May (McDowell) C.; m. Margaret Lorrene McReynolds, June 23, 1940; children—Kenton Richard, Kenneth Lee. B.S.C., State U. Iowa, 1938. With Hy-Vee Food Stores, Inc., 1940—, sec.-treas., 1943-75, v.p., treas., 1975-80, sr. v.p., chief fin. officer, 1980—; chmn. bd. dirs. Nat. Bank and Trust Co. of Chariton, Iowa; sec.-treas., dir. Chariton Storage Co.; treas., dir. Iamo Realty Co., Hy-Vee Found., Inc. Chmn. Lucas County Republican Central Com.; pres., dir. Chariton Community Sch. Bd., 1961-70; mem. Chariton City Council, 1955-61. Recipient Silver Beaver award Boy Scouts Am., 1974. Mem. Fin. Execs. Inst. Methodist. Clubs: Rotary, Masons, Shriners. Office: 1801 Osceola Ave Chariton IA 50049

COONS, RONALD EDWARD, historian, educator; b. Elmhurst, Ill., July 24, 1936; s. William A. and Madeline Louise (Theisen) C. B.A., DePauw U., Greencastle, Ind., 1958; A.M., Harvard U., 1959, Ph.D., 1966. Teaching fellow history Harvard U., 1961-62, 63-66; research fellow Inst. Europäische Geschichte, Mainz, W.Ger., 1962-63; mem. faculty U. Conn., Storrs, 1966—, prof. history, 1979—. Author: Steamships, Statesmen and Bureaucrats: Austrian Policy Towards the Steam Navigation Company of the Austrian Lloyd, 1836-1848, 1975, I primi anni del Lloyd Austriaco, 1983; also articles. Mem. exec. com. St. Mark's Episcopal Chapel, Storrs, 1976-77. Nat. Endowment Humanities summer fellow, 1969; Am. Council Learned Socs.-Am. Philos. Soc. grantee, 1974; NIH grantee, 1979; Gladys K. Delmas Found. grantee, 1983-84. Mem. Am. Hist. Assn., Conf. Group Central European History, AAUP, New Eng. Hist. Assn., Verein Geschichte der Stadt Wien, Phi Beta Kappa (chpt. sec. 1977—), Phi Alpha Theta, Phi Mu Alpha. Democrat. Home: 476 Prospect St Willimantic CT 06226 Office: Dept History Univ Conn Storrs CT 06268

COONTZ, GUSTAF, assn. exec.; b. Vienna, Austria, Nov. 7, 1919; emigrated to U.S., 1937; s. Max and Friedericke (Wechsberg) Kuntz; m. Clare Elliot McSheehy, Nov. 19, 1942; children—Robert, Otto, Eric, Raymond, Clare. Student, Worcester Poly. Inst., 1937-38; B.A., Clark U., 1941. Supr. order dept. Coppus Engring. Corp., Worcester, Mass., 1946-48, sales engr., 1949-55, dir. indsl. relations, 1956-60, treas., 1961-69, dir., 1956-69; consul, sr. econ.-comml. officer, dir. Trade Center, Am. consulate, Frankfurt, Germany, 1970-74; counselor of embassy for comml. affairs, Bonn, Germany, 1974-79; gen. mgr. Am. Embassy Assn., 1979—. Mem. Worcester City Council, 1962-69, vice mayor, 1962-65, 68-69; Bd. dirs. St. Vincent Research Found., 1967-70; trustee Clark U., 1967-70. Served to 1st lt. AUS, 1941-46. Recipient Disting. Service award Clark U. Alumni Assn., 1970; Superior Honor award Dept. State, 1979; Cert. of Appreciation Dept. Commerce, 1979. Mem. Adminstrv. Mgmt. Soc. (pres. Worcester chpt. 1959), Clark U. Alumni Assn. (pres. 1960). Clubs: Rotary, University (Worcester). Home: Steubenring 11 5300 Bonn 2 Germany Office: Am Embassy Box 270 APO New York NY 09080

COOP, FREDERICK ROBERT, govt. ofcl.; b. San Diego, Mar. 1, 1914; s. Ernest Frederick and Hazel (Angier) C.; m. Jean Haven, Feb. 11, 1939; children—Susan, Robert, Thomas, Elizabeth. A.B., U. Calif. at Berkeley, 1935; M.S. in Pub. Adminstrn, U. So. Calif., 1937.

Personnel technician Calif. Personnel Bd., 1937-41; personnel dir., Pasadena, Calif., 1941-49; personnel cons. UN, 1947; city mgr., Inglewood, Calif., 1949-56, Fremont, Calif., 1956-58; chief pub. services div. U.S. Ops. Mission to Yugoslavia, 1958-61; city mgr., Newport Beach, Cal., 1961-64, Phoenix, 1964-69; regional dir. HEW, San Francisco, 1969-71; dir. pub. adminstrn. services Arthur D. Little, Inc., San Francisco, 1972-78; pres. Robert Coop Assos., Moraga, Calif., 1978—, Coop Mgmt. Services Inc., 1981—. Served to lt. comdr. USNR, World War II. Named Young Man of Year, 1947, Pasadena Jr. C. of C. Mem. Pub. Personnel Assn., Internat. City Mgmt. Assn. (pres. Calif. 1956, regional v.p.), Am. Soc. Pub. Adminstrn. (bd. dirs.), Nat. Acad. Pub. Adminstrn.

COOP, WILLIAM ALFRED, publisher, editor; b. Kansas City, Mo., Apr. 4, 1923; s. Alfred M. and Ernestine H. (Vickers) C.; m. Pauline Johnson, Sept. 24, 1940. Student, Baylor U., 1938, U. Mo., 1939. Reporter Springfield (Mo.) News Leader and Press, Dallas Times Herald; copy chief Burnet Kuhn Advt., Chgo.; dir. corp. communications Anderson Co., Gary, Ind.; copy writer D'Arcy Advt. Co., Chgo.; founder, pub. William A. Coop, Inc., Chgo., 1968—. Pub.: others publs. Road King mag. Office: 23060 S Cicero Richton Park IL 60471

COOPER, ARNOLD MICHAEL, psychiatrist; b. N.Y.C., Mar. 9, 1923; s. Morris and Clara (Aronow) C.; m. Madge Huntington, June 28, 1973; children by previous marriage: Andrew, Melissa, Thomas. A.B., Columbia U., 1943, cert. psychoanalytic medicine, 1956; M.D., U. Utah, 1947. Research fellow in medicine Harvard U., 1947-48; asst. in medicine Thorndike Meml. Lab., Boston City Hosp., 1947-48; intern internal medicine Presbyn. Hosp., N.Y.C., 1948-50; psychiat. resident Bellevue Hosp., N.Y.C., 1950-53; mem. faculty Columbia U. Coll. Physicians and Surgeons, 1968—, clin. prof. psychiatry, 1971-74; lectr. Columbia U. Div. Humanities and Contemporary Civilization, 1964-79; prof. psychiatry, dir. tng. N.Y. Hosp.-Cornell U. Med. Center-Payne Whitney Clinic, 1974—; supr., tng. psychoanalyst Psychoanalytic Clinic Tng. and Research, 1961—. Editor: Literature and Psychology; Psychoanalysis and Contemporary Thought; Contbr. articles on masochism, narcissism, applied psychoanalysis, psychoanalytic and psychiat. edn. to profl. jours. Mem. Am. Psychoanalytic Assn. (pres. 1980-82), Am. Assn. Dirs. Psychiat. Residency Tng., Am. Coll. Psychiatry, Am. Psychiat. Assn., N.Y. Psychiat. Soc., Assn. Dirs. Med. Student Edn., Assn. Psychoanalytic Medicine (pres. 1975-77), Am. Coll. Psychoanalysis, Vidonian Soc., Alpha Omega Alpha. Club: Century Assn. (N.Y.C.). Office: 525 E 68th St New York NY 10021

COOPER, ARTHUR IRVING, association executive; b. Providence, Mar. 23, 1922; s. Irving and Ellen Christina (Skog) C.; m. Margaret V. Heck, Aug. 20, 1943; children: James, Jeffrey, Jennifer. B.A., Johns Hopkins U., 1943; M.B.A., Am. U., 1959. C.P.A., Md. With Am. Automobile Assn., Falls Church, Va., 1953—, exec. v.p., treas., 1978—; dir. Automobile Club Ins. Co. of Ohio.; treas. AAA Found. Traffic Safety. Served with USAAF, 1943-45. Decorated Air medal. Mem. Am. Inst. C.P.A.s, Md. Assn. C.P.A.s, Fin. Execs. Inst. Lutheran. Clubs: Westwood Country (Vienna, Va.); Pinehurst (N.C.) Country, Country of N.C. Lodge: Elks. Home: 2352 Mallory Ct Falls Church VA 22043 Office: 8111 Gatehouse Rd Falls Church VA 22047

COOPER, ARTHUR MARTIN, magazine editor; b. N.Y.C., Oct. 15, 1937; s. Benjamin Albert and Elizabeth (Sadock) C.; m. LaRee Hamlett, May 6, 1967 (dec. Dec. 1976); m. Amy Levin, June 9, 1979. B.A., Pa. State U., 1959. Writer, reporter Harrisburg Patriot (Pa.), 1964-66; corr. Timemag., N.Y.C., 1966-67; assoc. editor Newsweek, N.Y.C., 1967-76; editor Penthouse mag., N.Y.C., 1976-77, CBS Family Weekly, 1978-83; editor-in-chief Gentlemen's Quar., Conde-Nast Publs., N.Y.C., 1983—. Served to lt. (j.g.) USN, 1960-63. Profl. journalism fellow Stanford U., 1970-71. Mem. Am. Soc. Mag. Editors. Home: 20 W 64th St Apt 34L New York NY 10023 Office: Conde Nast Publications Gentlemen's Quarterly 350 Madison Ave New York NY 10017

COOPER, ARTHUR WELLS, ecologist; b. Washington, Aug. 15, 1931; s. Gustav Arthur and Josephine (Wells) C.; m. Jean Farnsworth, Aug. 30, 1953; children: Paul Arthur, Roy Alan. B.A., Colgate U., 1953, M.A., 1955; Ph.D., U. Mich., 1958. Asst. prof. botany N.C. State U., Raleigh, 1958-63, assoc. prof., 1963-68, prof., 1968-71, prof. forestry, 1976-80, head dept. forestry, 1980—; asst. sec. N.C. Dept. Natural and Econ. Resources, Raleigh, 1971-76. Trustee N.C. Nature Conservancy, Chapel Hill, N.C., 1977—; mem. N.C. Coastal Resources Commn., Raleigh, 1976—; chmn. Com. of Scientists for Nat. Forest Mgmt. Act, Washington, 1977-79,82. Recipient Sol Feinstone award SUNY Coll. Environ. Sci. and Forestry, Syracuse, 1982. Mem. Ecol. Soc. Am. (v.p. 1974, pres. 1981, cert. sr. ecologist), N.C. Acad. Sci. (pres. 1979), AAAS, Soc. Am. Foresters (chmn. N.C. div. 1984), Assn. Southeastern Biologists. Democrat. Home: 719 Runnymede Rd Raleigh NC 27607 Office: Dept Forestry NC State U Raleigh NC 27695

COOPER, B.D., corporate executive. Exec. Internat. Ore & Fertilizer Corp. Office: Internat Ore & Fertilizer Corp 1230 Ave of Americas New York NY 10020§

COOPER, BENJAMIN F., univ. dean; b. Warsaw, N.C., Nov. 22, 1924; s. Ben F. and Macy (Jones) C.; m. Hazel May Strickland, Sept. 17, 1947; children—Ben F., Caran S., Cana S. A.B., U. N.C., 1947, B.S., 1950, M.S., 1951, Ph.D., 1956. Asst. prof. U. N.C., 1956-57; asso. prof. Ore. State U., 1957-61, U. Ga., 1961-65, prof., 1965-66; dean Coll. Pharmacy and Allied Health Professions, N.E. La. U., 1966-73, prof., 1966-73; dean Sch. Pharmacy, Auburn U., 1973—; cons. USPHS, NSF. Served with USNR, 1944-46, 51-53. Mem. Am., Ala. pharm. assns., Sigma Xi, Rho Chi, Phi Delta Chi, Pi Kappa Alpha. Clubs: Masons, Elks, Lions, Rotary, Toastmasters (pres.). Office: Sch Pharmacy Auburn U Auburn AL 36830

COOPER, BERNARD RICHARD, physicist; b. Everett, Mass., Apr. 15, 1936; s. Edward and Florence (Solomon) C.; m. Sylvia Lenore Birman, Jan. 21, 1962; children—Jean Alane, David Jacob, Marilyn Clyta. B.S. in Physics, MIT, 1957; Ph.D. (NSF fellow), U. Calif.-Berkeley, 1961. Research asso. Atomic Energy Research Establishment, Harwell, Eng., 1962-63; research fellow Harvard U., 1963-64; physicist Gen. Electric Research and Devel. Center, Schenectady, 1964-74; Claude Worthington Benedum prof. physics W.Va. U., Morgantown, 1974—; cons. Argonne Nat. Lab., Mass. Inst. Tech. Nat. Magnet Lab.; vis. staff mem. Los Alamos Sci. Lab. Editor: Scientific Problems of Coal Utilization, 1978, Chemistry and Physics of Coal Utilization, 1981, The Science and Technology of Coal and Coal Utilization, 1983; contbr. articles to profl. jours. NSF research grantee, 1977—; Dept. Energy grantee, 1980—. Fellow Am. Phys. Soc. (chmn. study on research planning for coal utilization and synthetic fuel prodn. 1980-81); mem. IEEE, Am. Vacuum Soc., Sigma Xi. Democrat. Jewish. Club: B'nai B'rith (pres. W.Va. council 1978-79). Office: Dept Physics WVa U Morgantown WV 26506

COOPER, CHARLES BYRON, life insurance company executive; b. Seattle, Mat 5, 1938; s. Byron Soren and Helen Geraldine (Lamb) C.; m. Judith Lorain Whitver, Mar. 18, 1961 (div. 1982); children: Cathleen, Charles. B.A. in Econs., U. Wash., 1960, J.D., 1963. Bar: Wash. 1963, Pa. 1967. Asst. sec. Koppers Co. Inc., Pitts., 1966-70; v.p. Commonwealth Life, Louisville, 1970-73; exec. v.p. Ga.Internat. Life, Atlanta, 1973-75; sr. v.p. Am. Income Life Ins. Co., Waco, Tex., 1975-76, exec. v.p., 1976-77; pres. Am. Income LIfe Ins. Co., Waco, Tex., 1977—; dir. Action Industries, Inc., Pitts. Pres. United Way, Waco, 1981, Contbrs. Rev. com., 1983. Fellow Life Mgmt. Inst. Office: Am Income Life Ins Co 1200 Wooded Acres Dr Waco TX 76710

COOPER, CHARLES EDWARD, management consultant; b. North Wildwood, N.J., Jan. 31, 1933; s. Bernard and Esther (Worobe) C.; m. Judith Glijansky, Aug. 11, 1956; children: Ann, Robert, Bernard. B.S., Temple U., 1958; postgrad in law, Universidad de Santa Maria, Caracas, Venezuela, 1961. Cons. Corp. Venozolana de Formento, Caracas, 1958-60; gen. mgr. El Avila, Barquisimeto, Venezuela, 1960-62; cons. Distbr. Venozolana de Azucars, S.R.I., Caracas, 1961; owner, pres. Procesamiento Electrico de Datos, C.A., Caracas, 1962-65; rep. IBM World Trade, Caracas, 1965-66; dir. Texfin C.A., Caracas, 1966-68; v.p., dir. Computer Systems Tech., Inc., Jenkintown, Pa., 1968-70; v.p. Nat. Computer Analysts, Snc., Princeton, N.J., 1970-74; prin. Coopers & Lybrand, Phila, 1974—; dir. Princeton Transport. Bd. dirs. Children's Aid Soc., Pa. Served with USN, 1951-53. Recipient cert. Pres. Carter, 1978. Mem. Nat. Assn. Accts., Inst. Mgmt. Cons., Bank Adminstrn. Inst. Clubs: Philmont Country; Union League (Phila.). Office: First Internat Plaza 1100 Louisana St Suite 4100 Houston TX 77002

COOPER, CHARLES G., toiletries and cosmetics company executive; b. Chgo., Apr. 4, 1928; s. Benjamin and Gertrude C.; m. Miriam Meyer, Feb. 11, 1951 (dec. Oct. 17, 1984); children: Debra, Ruth, Janet, Benjamin. B.S. in Journalism, U. Ill., 1949. With sales promotion dept. Maidenform Co., N.Y.C., 1949-51; with circulation promotion dept. Esquire mag., Chgo., 1951-52; with Helene Curtis Industries Inc., Chgo., 1953—, pres. salon div., 1971-75, pres. consumer products div., 1975-82, corp. exec. v.p., 1982—. Served with AUS, 1952-53. Mem. Nat. Wholesale Druggists Assn., Nat. Assn. Chain Drug Stores. Club: Mid-Am. (Chgo.). Office: 4401 W North Ave Chicago IL 60639

COOPER, CHARLES GORDON, insurance company executive; b. Providence, May 31, 1927; s. Irving and Helen Christina (Skog) C.; m. Barbara Caroline Termohlen, June 17, 1950; 1 dau., Marie Suzanne. B.A., Ohio Wesleyan U., 1949. C.L.U. Group rep. Washington Nat. Ins. Co., 1949-53, asst. mgr., 1953-58, mgr., 1958-63, dir. assn. field services, 1963-65, asst. sec., 1965-67, 3d v.p., 1967-72, 2d v.p., 1972-77, v.p., 1977-79, sr. v.p., 1979-83, exec. v.p., Evanston, Ill., 1983—, dir., mem. exec. com., 1979—; sr. v.p.-mktg. Washington Nat. Corp., Parent Co. Washington Nat. Ins. Co., Evanston, 1983—; dir. Washington Nat. Trust Co., 1974—, chmn. exec. com., 1979—; chmn., dir. Washington Nat. Fin. Services, Inc., 1979—; pres., dir. Washington Nat. Equity Co., 1973-83, chmn. bd., 1983—. Bd. dirs. North Shore Assn. for Retarded, Evanston, 1983—. Served with USNR, 1945-46; PTO. Mem. Am. Coll. Life Underwriters, Chartered Life Underwriters, Nat. Assn. Life Underwriters, Chgo. Life Underwriters Assn., Nat. Assn. Health Underwriters, Chgo. Health Underwriters. Republican. Club: Thorngate Country (Deerfield, Ill.). Lodge: Masons. Office: Washington Nat Ins Co 1630 Chicago Ave Evanston IL 60201

COOPER, CHARLES HOWARD, photo-journalist, newspaper publishing company executive; b. Clinton, N.C., July 17, 1920; s. John Howard and Ella Jane (Bass) C.; m. Nell Elizabeth Slaughter, Jan. 2, 1943; children: Charles Howard, John Philip. Grad., U.S. Air Force Sch. Photography, 1943. Chief photographer, mgr. photo dept. Durham Herald Co. (N.C.), 1945—; pub. Durham Morning Herald, 1945, Durham Morning Sun, 1945—; chmn. Miss Nat. Press Photographer Pageant, 1952, 53, 55. Mem. Citizens Safety Com., Durham, 1961-71. Served with USAAF, 1942-45; ETO. Mem. Nat. Press Photographers Assn. (exec. dir. 1963—, Fellowship award 1958, Joseph A. Sprague award 1961, Pres.'s medal 1964, 67, Merit award 1965, Joseph Costa award 1977, life mem.), Carolinas Press Photographers Assn. (pres. 1952-54). Democrat. Am. Baptist. Office: Nat Press Photographers Assn PO Box 1146 Durham NC 27702

COOPER, DANIEL LEANDER, naval officer; b. East Liverpool, Ohio, May 21, 1934; s. William Brooks and Rowena Amelia (Smila) C.; m. Betty Jane Ogilvie, June 18, 1958; children: Amy Louise, Cynthia Jane. Student, Washington and Jefferson Coll., 1952-53; B.S., U.S. Naval Acad., 1957; M.P.A., Harvard U., 1963. Commd. ensign U.S. Navy, 1957, advanced through grades to rear adm., 1980; mil. aide to (Vice Chief Naval. Ops.), Washington, 1968-71, comdg. officer, Pearl Harbor, Hawaii, 1972-74, exec. asst. to, Washington, 1974-76, comdr., New London, Conn., 1976-79, dep. dir., Washington, 1979-80, dep. comdr., comptroller, 1980-83, dir. navy budget and reports, 1983—. Decorated Meritorious Service medal (4). Mem. U.S. Naval Inst. Methodist. Home: 4824 King Richard Dr Annandale VA 22003 Office: Dept Navy Washington DC 20390

COOPER, DONALD LEE, physician; b. Columbus, Kans., Aug. 11, 1928; s. Calvin M. and J. Pearl (Mullen) C.; m. Dona Faye Maddux, June 4, 1950; children—Donald Lee, Catherine Susan, Cheryl Lyn, Tad Houston. A.B., Kans. State Coll., 1949; M.D., U. Kans., 1953. Intern St. Mary's and Childrens Mercy hosps., Kansas City, Mo., 1953-54; pvt. practice medicine, Manhattan, Kans., 1956-57; team physician, asst. dir. Health Center Kans. State U., 1957-60; dir. health service, team physician Okla. State U. Hosp. and Clinic, Stillwater, 1960—; vis. lectr. div. sportsmedicine, dept. orthopedic surgery Coll. Medicine U. Okla. Health Scis. Center, 1974—; liaison officer Am. Coll. Health Assn. to Nat. Athletic Trainers Assn., 1963—; Am. chmn. 1st Am.-Soviet Conf. on Student Health, Moscow, Russia, 1967; team physician U.S. Olympic Team, 1967-68. Author: (with others) Standard Nomenclature of Athletic Injuries, 1966; Contbr. articles med. jours. Served to capt. USAF, 1954-56. Recipient Pres.'s Challenge Sportsmedicine award Nat. Athletic Trainers Assn., 1974; Bill Coltrin Meml. award Western Athletic Conf. Sports Writers Assn., 1974; Edward Hitchcock award Am. Coll. Health Assn., 1975. Mem. AMA (chmn. com. med. aspects sports 1976—, mem. council sci. affairs 1976—), Nat. Collegiate Athletic Assn. (med. cons. to football rules com. 1969—), Am. Coll. Health Assn. (past pres., mem. exec. com.), Southwestern Coll. Health Assn. (past pres.), Nat. Athletic Trainers Assn., Alpha Omega Alpha, Nu Sigma Nu. Presbyterian (elder 1971—). Club: Lion. Home: 1001 Liberty Ln Stillwater OK 74074 Office: Okla State U Hosp and Clinic Stillwater OK 74074 *We must realize and accept that life is neither fair nor unfair; one must accept it as a unique journey composed of all types of experiences. It is not so much what happens to us as we go along in life, it is how we react to what happens that is so very important.*

COOPER, E. CAMRON, oil company executive; b. Redlands, Calif., Apr. 14, 1939; d. Jack and Ekla (Scott) C. B.A., Stanford U., 1960. Research asst., registered rep. Smith, Barney & Co., Inc., N.Y.C., 1960-62; investment analyst Bank of Am., Los Angeles, 1962-63; asst. mgr. research dept. Lester, Ryons & Co., Los Angeles, 1963-67, dir. sales tng. program, sales analyst for spl. situations, asst. to sales ptnr., 1967-68, dir. research, 1968-69; sr. investment analyst Hornblower & Weeks-Hemphill, Noyes, 1969-72; registered rep. Loeb, Rhoades & Co., Los Angeles, 1972-74; mgr. investor relations Atlantic Richfield Co., Los Angeles, 1974-75, investment officer, 1975-78, treas., 1978—, v.p., 1983—. Trustee Scripps Coll., Children's Hosp. Los Angeles, Seaver Inst. Mem. Stanford U. Alumni Assn., Cap and Gown. Republican. Home: 620 Busch Garden Ln Pasadena CA 91105 Office: Atlantic Richfield Company 515 S Flower St Los Angeles CA 90071

COOPER, EDWARD HAYES, lawyer, educator; b. Highland Park, Mich., Oct. 13, 1941; s. Frank Edward and Margaret Ellen (Hayes) C.; m. Nancy Carol Wybo, June 29, 1963; children: Lisa, Chandra. A.B., Dartmouth Coll., 1961; LL.B., Harvard U., 1964. Bar: Mich. bar 1965. Law clk. Hon. Clifford O'Sullivan, U.S. Ct. of Appeals, 1964-65; individual practice law, Detroit, 1965-67; adj. prof. Wayne State U. Law Sch., 1965-67; asso. prof. U. Minn. Law Sch., 1967-72; prof. law U. Mich. Law Sch., Ann Arbor, 1972—; adv. Restatement of the Law, 2d, Judgements, 1976-80. Author: (with C.A. Wright and A.R. Miller) Federal Practice and Procedure: Jurisdiction, Vols. 13-19, 1975-81; Contbr. articles to law revs. Mem. Am. Bar Assn., Mich. Bar Assn., Am. Law Inst. Office: 320 Hutchins Hall Law Sch U Mich Ann Arbor 48105 Office: MI 48109

COOPER, EDWIN LOWELL, educator; b. Oakland, Tex., Dec. 23, 1936; s. Edwin Ellis and Ruthesther (Porchè) C.; m. Helene Marie Antoinette Tournaire, Sept. 13, 1969; children—Astrid Madeleine, Amaury Tournaire. B.S., Tex. So. U., 1957; M.S., Atlanta, 1959; Ph.D., Brown U., 1963. UHPHS postdoctoral fellow U. Calif. at Los Angeles, 1962-64, asst. prof. anatomy, 1964-69; asso. prof., 1969-73, prof., 1973—; vis. prof. Instituto Politecnico Nacional, Mexico City, 1966; Mem. adv. com. Office Sci. Personnel, NRC, 1972-73; mem. bd. sci. counselors Nat. Inst. Dental Research, 1973—. Author: Comparative Immunology; Editor: Phylogeny of Transplantation Reactions, 1970, Invertebrate Immunology, 1974; founding editor: Internat. Jour. Developmental and Comparative Immunology, 1977—. Guggenheim fellow, 1970; Fulbright scholar, 1970; Eleanor Roosevelt fellow Internat. Union Against Cancer, 1977-78. Fellow AAAS (council 1971, chmn. sect. 1976); mem. Soc. Invertebrate Pathology (founding), Pan Am. Congress Anatomy (founding), Am. Assn. Anatomy, Transplantation Soc., Am. Assn. Immunologists, Am. Soc. Zoologists (program officer 1974—, founder div. comparative immunology 1975), Brit. Soc. Immunology, Societe d'Immunologie Francaise, Sigma Xi. Office: Dept Anatomy School Medicine Univ Calif Los Angeles CA 90024 *Aims must always be high, so that when fate is cruel, there is somewhere to fall. Aiming for the bottom leaves nowhere to fall.*

COOPER, EUGENE BRUCE, speech pathology educator; b. Utica, N.Y., Dec. 20, 1933; s. Clements Everett and Beulah (Wetzel) C.; m. Crystal Silverman, Sept. 12, 1965; children: Philip Adam, Ivan Bruce. B.S., SUNY, Geneseo, 1955; M.Ed., Pa. State U., 1957, D.Ed., 1962. Speech-lang. pathologist Franklin County schs., Chambersburg, Pa., 1957-59; asst. prof. Ohio U., 1962-64, Pa. State U., 1964-66; program specialist U.S. Office Edn., 1966; exec. sec. sensory study sect., research and demonstrations Rehab. Services Adminstrn., HEW, 1966-67; mem. faculty U. Ala., 1967—, prof. speech-lang. pathology, 1969—, chmn. dept. communicative disorders, 1967—, dir. speech and hearing center, 1967; chmn. Ala. Bd. Examiners Speech Pathology and Audiology, 1979; cons.-at-large Nat. Student Speech-Lang.-Hearing Assn., 1983-85. Author: Personalized Fluency Control Therapy, 1976, Understanding Stuttering: Information for Parents, 1979, (with Crystal Cooper) The Cooper Personalized Fluency Control Therapy Program, 1984; also articles. Fellow Am. Speech, Lang. and Hearing Assn. (legis. council 1971-72, 85-87); mem. Council Exceptional Children (pres. div. children communication disorders 1975-76), Nat. Council Grad. Programs in Speech, Lang. Pathology and Audiology (pres. 1978-80), Nat. Council State Bds. Examiners Speech-Lang. Pathology and Audiology (pres. 1980), Nat. Council Communication Disorders (chmn. 1982), Nat. Alliance Prevention and Treatment Stuttering (chmn. 1984), Nat. Rehab. Assn., Sigma Xi. Office: PO Box 1903 University AL 35486

COOPER, FRANCIS LOREN, advertising executive; b. Dodge Center, Minn., Nov. 30, 1919; s. Harold U. and Grace (Miller) C.; m. Shirley Edith Garniss, Jan. 27, 1945; children: Donald R., Lynne A. Cooper Lichtermann. B.A., U. Minn., 1941. Newspaper reporter, Mpls., Rochester, Minn., Waseca, Minn., 1932-41; with N.Y. Life Ins. Co., N.Y.C., 1946—, asst. v.p., 1961-65, 2d v.p., 1965-67, v.p., 1967-79; mktg. cons. Media Networks, Inc., Dunedin, Fla., 1980—, Standard Rate & Data Service, Inc., 1980—. Chmn. Wilton (Conn.) Charter Revision Commn., 1972-73; chmn. Wilton Republican Com., 1962-70; ofcl. Little League Baseball, 1954-79; chmn. pub. relations adv. com. City of Dunedin (Fla.). Served in USMC, 1941-45, 50-52; lt. Col. Res. ret. Recipient Meritorious Service award Life Ins. Advertisers Assn., 1980. Mem. Pub. Relations Soc. Am. (accredited), Life Ins. Advertisers Assn. (pres. 1971-72), Am. Legion. Presbyterian. Clubs: Masons, Dunedin Country.

COOPER, FRANK EVANS, banker; b. Seattle, Nov. 28, 1928; s. Frank Homer and Marguerite Caroline (Madison) C.; m. Erlene Rose Johnson, June 30, 1951; children—Dawn Rene, Frank Evans. B.B.A., U. Wash., 1950; M.B.A., Pacific Coast Grad. Sch. Banking, 1958-61. Br. mgr. Comml. Credit Corp., Eugene, Oreg., 1951-58; v.p. Puget Sound Nat. Bank, Tacoma, 1958-64; pres., chief exec. officer, dir. Bank of Tacoma, 1965-68; supr. banking State of Wash., Olympia, 1968-70; sr. v.p. Bank of Hawaii, Honolulu, 1970-72; pres., chief exec. officer, dir. Bank Honolulu, 1972-76; owner Frank Cooper & Assos., 1976-80; pres., chief exec. officer Equitable Savs. & Loan, Huntington Beach, Calif., 1980—; dir. Security & Gen. Bank, Ltd., Vila, New Hebrides, World Finance, Honolulu, Guardian Finance, Mahalo Acceptance, Hula Records, Ltd., Keehi Drydock Corp.; internat. fin. and mgmt. cons. Chmn. Western States Commrs. Banking, 1970; dir. Nat. Assn. Bank Commrs., 1970. Mem. bd. Tacoma Community Coll., 1967-69; mem. adv. bd. Nat. Consumer Finance Assn., 1969; Del. Wash. Republican convs., 1958-68; precinct committeeman, Tacoma, 1950-69; del. Rep. Nat. Conv., 1964, 68; mem. Wash. Ho. of Reps., 1963-64; chmn. Hawaii Rep. Com., 1979—; bd. dirs. Jessie Dslyn Boys' Ranch, Tacoma, Mary Bridge Children's Hosp., Tacoma; trustee Annie Wright Girls' Acad., Tacoma, U. Wash. Grad. Sch. Banking. Mem. C. of C. Hawaii (chmn. visitor industry com.), Hawaii Bankers Assn. (exec. com.), Navy League, Sales and Mktg. Execs. Honolulu. Clubs: Oahu Country, Outrigger Canoe, Honolulu Press, Plaza, Univ. Union (pres.), Pacific, Waikiki Yacht (Hawaii); Masons, Shriners, Jesters, Elks, Rotary, Lions. Home: 1039 Waiiki St Honolulu HI 96821 Office: PO Box 2700 Huntington Beach CA 92647

COOPER, FRANKLIN SEANEY, speech scientist; b. Robinson, Ill., Apr. 29, 1908; s. Frank A. and Myrtle Alma (Seaney) C.; m. Frances Edith Clem, Feb. 14, 1935; children: Robert Craig, Alan Kent. B.S. in Engring. Physics, U. Ill., 1931; Ph.D. in Physics, Mass. Inst. Tech., 1936; D.Sc. (hon.), Yale U., 1976. Teaching and research asst. U. Ill., 1931-34, Mass. Inst. Tech., 1934-36; research engr. Gen. Electric Research Labs., 1936-39; asso. research dir. Haskins Labs., New Haven, 1939-55, 75—, pres., research dir., 1955-75; liaison officer, then sr. liaison officer OSRD, 1941-46; vis. com. dept. modern langs. Mass. Inst. Tech., 1949-65; adv. com. research div. Coll. Engring., N.Y. U., 1949-65; bd. dirs. Center Applied Linguistics, 1968-74; adj. prof. phonetics Columbia U., 1955-65; adj. prof. linguistics U. Conn., 1969-80, vis. prof., 1980—; sr. research asso. linguistics Yale U., 1970-76; fellow Calhoun Coll., 1971-80, asso. fellow, 1980—; adv. panel on White House tapes U.S. Dist. Ct. D.C., 1973-74; chmn. communicative scis. interdisciplinary cluster President's Biomed. Research Panel, 1975; mem. adv. council Nat. Inst. for Neurol. and Communicative Disorders and Stroke, NIH, 1978-81. Author papers, book chpts. speech processing, perception and prodn., aids for blind and deaf, biophysics, high-voltage/high vacuum engring. Recipient Presdl. Certificate of Merit, 1948; honors of assn. Am. Speech and Hearing Assn., 1966; Warren medal Soc. Exptl. Psychology, 1975; Fletcher-Stevens award Brigham Young U., 1977. Fellow IEEE (Pioneer award speech communication 1972), Acoustical Soc. Am. (Silver medal speech communication 1975); mem. Nat. Acad. Engring., Sigma Xi. Congregationalist. Club: Cosmos (Washington). Home: 5 Parsell Ln Westport CT 06880 Office: 270 Crown St New Haven CT 06511

COOPER, FRED, distributing company executive; b. Chgo., July 10, 1936; s. Abraham and Ida (Schulman) C. B.A., Carleton Coll., 1958. With Continental Distbg. Co., Inc., Rosemont, Ill., 1959—, pres., chief exec. officer, 1979—. Active Michael Reese Hosp. Aux., Jewish United Fund, State of Israel Bonds. Served with U.S. Army, 1958-59. Recipient Disting. Wholesaler of Yr. award Time Mag., 1983. Mem. Wine and Spirits Wholesalers Am. (dir.), Wine and Sprits Shippers Assn. (treas. 1978), Ill. Wholesale Liquor Dealers Assn. (v.p.). Republican. Jewish. Clubs: Standard, Mchts. and Mfrs., Green Acres Country. Home: 1110 N Lake Shore Dr Apt 20N Chicago IL 60611 Office: Continental Distributing Co Inc 9800 W Balmoral Ave Rosemont IL 60018

COOPER, FREDERICK EANSOR, lawyer; b. Thomasville, Ga., Jan. 18, 1942; s. Martin Milner and Margeret (Philips) C.; m. Helen Dykes, Dec. 10, 1966; children: Frederick Eansor, Johnson Joseph. B.A., Washington and Lee U., 1964; J.D., U. Ga., 1967. Bar: Ga. Partner firm Herndon & Cooper, Thomasville, 1972-73; gen. counsel Flowers Industries, Inc., Thomasville, 1973-74, gen. counsel, sec., 1974—, corp. v.p., 1978-83, exec. v.p., 1983-84, pres., 1984—, dir., 1975—. Chmn. Ga. Republican Com., 1981—. Served with JAGC AUS, 1967-72; mem. Res. Presbyterian. Club: Rotary. Home: 203 Junius St Thomasville GA 31792 Office: PO Box 1338 Thomasville GA 31792

COOPER, GEORGE BRINTON, educator; b. Phila., Apr. 14, 1916; s. Lloyd W. and Esther L. (Cooper) C. B.A. in Social Scis. with highest honors, Swarthmore Coll., 1938, Univ. Coll., London, Eng., 1938-39; M.A., Yale U., 1942, Ph.D., 1948; Lit.D. hon., Trinity Coll., 1983. Mem. faculty Trinity Coll., Hartford, Conn., 1941—, prof. history, 1958—, Northam prof., 1964-83, chmn. dept., 1964-74, sec. of Coll., 1974-83; mng. editor Jour. Brit. Studies, 1961-79; Sir Arnold Lunn Meml. lectr. London, 1982; Am. vice consul, London, 1944-46; mem. adv. com. Yale edit. Horace Walpole Correspondence, 1972—; Mem. Hartford Bd. Edn., 1959-65, pres., 1961-62. Chmn. Gov. Conn. Bi-Partisan Com. Redistricting Conn. Senate, 1960; nat. adv. cancer council USPHS, 1961-64; Bd. dirs. Hartford Pub. Library, 1964-71, corporator, 1962—; corporator St. Francis Hosp., 1982—; trustee Lewis-Walpole Library of Yale U., Farmington, Conn., 1979—; trustees Cesare Barbieri Found., 1970—, chmn., 1976-82; trustee Historic Deerfield, Inc., 1976—. Served with USNR, 1943-44. Mem. Conf. Brit. Studies, Am. Hist. Assn., Phi Beta Kappa, Pi Gamma Mu, Delta Upsilon. Democrat. Clubs: Yale, Grolier (N.Y.C.); Hop Meadow Country (Simsbury, Conn.); Sloane, Ski of Gt. Brit. (London); University, Monday Evening, Twilight (Hartford). Home: Box 38 West Simsbury CT 06092 Office: Trinity Coll Hartford CT 06106

COOPER, GEORGE ROBERT, electrical engineer, educator; b. Connersville, Ind., Nov. 29, 1921; s. William Russell and Margaret (Frederick) C.; m. Helen Elizabeth Conder, Nov. 23, 1949 (div. 1982); children: George Michael, David Russell, Susan Rachael, Ann Elizabeth, Steven Robert, Thomas Jonathan.; m. Elizabeth Jane Heald, Jan. 30, 1982. B.S., Purdue U., 1943, M.S., 1945, Ph.D., 1949. Instr. elec. engring. Purdue U., 1943-49, asst. prof., 1949-51, asso. prof., 1951-55, prof., 1955—; cons. elec. engring. Fellow IEEE; mem. Am. Soc. Elec. Engrs., Sigma Xi, Eta Kappa Nu, Tau Beta Pi, Sigma Pi Sigma. Patentee in field. Home: PO Box 2273 West Lafayette IN 47906 Office: Sch Elec Engring Purdue U Lafayette IN 47907

COOPER, GRANT BURR, lawyer; b. N.Y.C., Apr. 1, 1903; s. Louis Baxter and Josephine (Christensen) C.; m. Edna Reynolds, Nov. 21, 1929 (dec. 1934); children—Judith Ann (Mrs. Cooper Hunt), Natalie Caroline (Mrs. Rollin D. Wallace); m. Phyllis A. Norton, Apr. 3, 1935; children—Meredith Jane (Mrs. Robert K. Worrell), Grant Burr, John Norton. Student, Pace Coll., N.Y.C., 1921; LL.B., Southwestern U., 1926. Bar: Calif. bar 1927. With Office Dist. Atty., Los Angeles, 1929-35, 40-42, chief dep. dist. atty., 1940-43; dep. city atty., Los Angeles, 1935-38, pvt. practice, 1946—; spl. prosecutor, State of Hawaii, 1976-78, spl. dep. atty. gen., 1976-78, Chief asst. ins. commr., Calif., 1943; pres. Los Angeles Health Commn., 1944; Mem. bd. councilors U. So. Calif. Law Center, 1969—. Fellow Am. Bar Found., Am. Coll. Trial Lawyers (past bd. regents, pres. 1962-63); mem. Los Angeles County Bar Assn. (pres. 1960-61, trustee 1951-52, 56- 62), State Bar Calif. (bd. govs. 1953-56, v.p. 1956). Clubs: Mason (Shriner), Chancery, Century City Rotary, Legion Lex (Los Angeles); Tuna (Catalina, Calif.). Home: 3447 Wrightview Dr North Hollywood CA 91604 Office: One Century Plaza 2029 Century Park E Suite 3910 Los Angeles CA 90067

COOPER, HAL, television director; b. N.Y.C., Feb. 23, 1923; s. Benjamin and Adeline (Raichman) C.; m. Marta Lucille Salcido, June 26, 1971; 1 son, James Benjamin; children by previous marriage: Bethami, Pamela. B.A., U. Mich., 1946. Performer, Big Bro.'s Rainbow House, Mut. Network, 1936-41; asst. dir., Dock Street Theatre, Charleston, S.C., 1946-48; writer, producer: TV Babysitter, DuMont TV Network, 1948-52, The Magic Cottage, 1950-56; dir., producer: various daytime TV shows including Kitty Foyle; and others, 1950-57; producer: stage play The Troublemakers, London, 1952; dir.: TV shows including All in the Family, 1960—; dir., exec. producer: Maude, CBS, Hollywood, Calif., 1972-78. Served to lt. (j.g.) USNR, 1943-46. Mem. Writers Guild Am., ASCAP, Screen Actors Guild, AFTRA, Actors Equity, Dirs. Guild Am. (trustee 1964-75, mem. benevolent and edn. com. 1963-75, trustee pension plan 1964-75). Address: 2651 Hutton Dr Beverly Hills CA 90210

COOPER, HAL DEAN, lawyer; b. Marshall County, Iowa, Dec. 8, 1934; s. Truman B. and Golda F. (Chadwick) C.; m. Constance B. Simms, Dec. 31, 1960; children: Shannon, Charles, Ellen. Student, Neb. U., 1952-54; B.S. in Mech. Engring., Iowa State U., 1957; J.D. with honors, George Washington U., 1962. Bar: Iowa 1963, Ohio 1963, U.S. Supreme Ct. 1971. Assoc., ptnr. Fay & Fay, Cleve., 1962-67; ptnr. Meyer, Tilberry & Body, Cleve., 1967-69, Yount, Tarolli, Weinshenker & Cooper, 1969-72; trial judge U.S. Ct. Claims, Washington, 1972-75; ptnr. Jones, Day, Reavis & Pogue, Cleve., 1975—. Served with AUS, 1957-59. Mem. ABA, Cleve. Pat. Law Assn. Episcopalian. Clubs: Rowfant, Clifton. Lodge: Masons. Home: 16924 Edgewater Dr Lakewood OH 44107 Office: Jones Day Reavis & Pogue 7100 Huntington Bldg Cleveland OH 44115

COOPER, HARRIS, foods company executive; b. Trenton, N.J., Nov. 17, 1937; s. Victor and Dora (Popkin) C.; m. Patricia A. Schulte (div. Feb. 1978); children: Christine Mary, Theodore Victor; m. Patrice A. Dilly, Nov. 4, 1978. Student, St. Louis U., 1955-58, S.J.D., 1962. Bar: Mo. 1962, U.S. Supreme Ct. 1963. Ptnr. Bild & Cooper, St. Louis, 1962-66; dist. ops. mgr. Avis Rent A Car, St. Louis, 1966-67; v.p. licensee div. Nat. Car Rental System, Mpls., 1967-70; pres., chief exec. officer Internat. Dairy Queen, Inc., Mpls., 1970—; adj. prof. NYU, 1980-83, bd. overseers Ctr. Foodservice Mgmt., 1978-83; mem. adv. bd. Internat. Foodservice Mfrs. Assn., 1978-83. Bd. dirs. Squatennial, 1982, 83, Fund for Legal Aid Soc., Mpls., 1982—; mem. adv. bd. Salvation Army, Mpls., 1978—; bd. dirs. Nat. Kidney Found. Upper Midwest, 1978—. Mem. ABA, Mo. Bar Assn., Minn. Bar Assn., Hennepin County Bar Assn., St. Louis Bar Assn. Republican. Clubs: Olympic Hill Golf (Eden Prairie, Minn.); Hazeltine Golf (Chaska, Minn.). Office: Internat Dairy Queen Inc PO Box 35286 Minneapolis MN 55435

COOPER, IRVING BEN, U.S. judge; b. London, Eng., Feb. 7, 1902; came to U.S., 1912, naturalized, 1921; s. Max and Rachel (Shimansky) C.; m. Anita Bennett, Mar. 28, 1929; children—Richard Bennett, Benita H. (Mrs. Theodore Lee Marks). LL.B., Washington U., 1925. Bar: N.Y. bar 1927. Gen. practice civil law, N.Y.C., 1927-38; asso. counsel ambulance chasing investigation Appellate div. N.Y. Supreme Ct., 1928; asso. counsel bar assns. disciplinary proc., 1928-30, spl. dep. atty. gen. to investigate improper med. practices, 1929, asso. counsel investigation Magistrates courts, 1930-31; asso. counsel to Judge Samuel Seabury in investigation N.Y.C. Govt., 1932-33; spl. counsel Dept. Investigation, N.Y.C., 1934-37; city magistrate, 1938-39; asso. justice Ct. Spl. Sessions, 1939-51, chief justice, 1951-60; U.S. dist. judge So. Dist. N.Y., 1961—, now sr. judge; lectr., cons. program of law and psychiatry Menninger Found., 1960; lectr. criminal law, 1960-61; Hon. pres. Univ. Settlement, N.Y.C.; trustee Nat. Council Crime and Delinquency, chmn. criminal courts sect., adv. counsel of judges, 1954-69. Trustee Reconstructionist Found. Recipient Silver Buffalo award Boy Scouts Am., 1965. Mem. Am. Judicature Soc., Assn. Bar City N.Y., N.Y. County Lawyers Assn., Am. Bar Assn. (chmn. com. on sentencing, probation and parole 1957-61). Office: US Courthouse Foley Sq New York NY 10007

COOPER, IRVING S., neurosurgeon; b. Atlantic City, July 15, 1922; s. Louis and Eleanor Lillian (Cooper) C.; m. Mary Dan Frost, Dec. 15, 1944; children—Daniel Alan, Douglas Paul, Lisa Frost; m. Sissel Holm, Jan. 31, 1970; children—David Louis, Erik Holm, Charles Spencer. B.A., George Washington U., 1942, M.D., 1945; M.S., Ph.D., U. Minn., 1951; D.Sc. (hon.), Trinity Coll., Hartford, Conn., 1974, Fordham U., 1974. Diplomate: neurology Am. Bd. Neurology and Psychiatry, Am. Bd. Neurol. Surgery. Intern U.S. Naval Hosp., St. Albans, N.Y., 1945-46; fellow neurosurgery Mayo Found., 1948-51; mem. faculty N.Y.U. Med. Sch., 1961-64, prof. clin. neurosurgery, 1954-64; research prof. neuroanatomy N.Y. Med. Coll.; research prof. neurosurgery N.Y. U.; dir. Inst. Neurosci., St. Barnabas Hosp., N.Y.C., 1954-78; prof., dir. Center for Physiol. Neurosurgery, Westchester County-N.Y. Coll. Med. Center, Valhalla, N.Y., 1978—; pres. Naples (Fla.) Inst. for Advanced Studies in Medicine and Humanities; spl. research devel., practice, teaching specialized brain operations for treatment Parkinsonism, related diseases, devel. cryogenic surgery; Eliza Savage vis. prof., Australia, 1962; vis. prof. Mayo Found., 1974, Nat. Hosp., U. London, Eng., 1974. Author: The Neurosurgical Alleviation of Parkinsonism, 1956, Parkinsonism: Its Medical and Surgical Therapy, 1961, Involuntary Movement Disorders, 1968, The Victim is Always the Same, 1973, The Pulvinar-LP Complex, 1973, The Cerebellum, Epilepsy and Behavior, 1973, Living with Chronic Neurologic Disease, 1976, It's Hard to Leave While the Music's Playing, 1977, Cerebellor Stimulation. Served to lt. (j.g.), M.C. USNR, 1946-48. Recipient Lewis Harvey Taylor award Am. Therapeutic Soc., 1957, St. Barnabas Hosp. award, 1959, Modern Medicine award, 1960, Alumni Achievement award George Washington U., 1960, award in medicine N.Y. Philanthropic League, 1960, Civic award in medicine Bronx Bd. Trade, 1961, Humanitarian award Nat. Cystic Fibrosis Found., 1962, Gold medal Worshipful Soc. Apothecaries, London, 1967, Bronze award Am. Congress Rehab. Med., 1967; Comenius medal U. Bratislava, Czechoslovakia; Alumni Achievement award U. Minn., 1965. Fellow A.C.S., Am. Geriatric Soc., N.Y. Acad. Medicine, N.Y. Acad. Sci.; mem. Harvey Cushing Neurosurg. Soc., AMA (Hektoen Bronze medal 1957, 58, Certificate of Merit 1961), Neurosurg. Soc. Am., Am. Acad. Neurology, Soc. Cryobiology (gov.), Soc. Cryosurgery (pres.), Am. Fedn. Clin. Research, Pan Am. Soc. U.S., Am. Congress Phys. Medicine and Rehab., Amyotrophic Lateral Sclerosis Soc. Am. (trustee), Scandinavian Neurosurg. Soc., Brit. Soc. Neurol. Surg. (hon.), Med. Honor Soc., Czechoslovak Neurosurg. Soc., Sigma Xi (hon.), Alpha Omega Alpha; hon. mem. Neurol. and Neurosurg. Soc. Argentina, Egyptian Neurosurg. Soc., Soc. Neurology and Neurosurgery Cuba, Neurol. Soc. Czechoslovakia, Luther Rice Soc., Authors Guild. Home: 3753 Fort Charles Dr Naples FL 33940 Office: Center Physiologic Neurosurgery Westchester County Med Center Valhalla NY 10570

COOPER, JACK ROSS, pharmacology educator, researcher; b. Ottawa, Ont., Can., July 26, 1924; came to U.S., 1948; s. Harry and Jean (Levine) C.; m. Helen Achbar, Aug. 14, 1951; children: Marilyn, Sheila, Nancy. B.A., Queen's U. Kingston, Ont., 1948; M.A., George Washington U., 1952, Ph.D., 1954; M.A. hon., Yale U., 1971. Asst. prof. pharmacology Yale U., New Haven, 1953-63, assoc. prof., 1963-71, prof., 1971—. Author: The Biochemical Basis of Neuropharmacology, 4th edit., 1982; editorial bd.: Biochem. Pharmacology: Jour. Neurochemistry. Served with RCAF, 1944. Smith, Kline and French research fellow, 1950-52; USPHS predoctoral fellow, 1952-54; postdoctoral fellow USPHS, 1954-56; spl. fellow USPHS, London, 1965-66. Mem. Am. Soc. Neurochemistry, Internat. Soc. Neurochemistry, Am. Soc. Pharmacology and Exptl. Therapeutics, Soc. Neurosci. Democrat. Jewish. Home: 11 Jenick Ln Woodbridge CT 06525 Office: Yale U Sch Medicine 333 Cedar St New Haven CT 06510

COOPER, JACKIE, actor, director, producer; b. Los Angeles, Sept. 15, 1922. V.p. in charge West Coast Screen Gems, Inc., 1963-69. Actor, beginning at age three: motion pictures include The Love Machine, 1970; The Chosen Survivors, 1973, Superman, 1978, Superman II, 1981, Superman III, 1983; Broadway plays include King of Hearts; star: TV series People's Choice, NBC-TV, 1955-58, Hennessey, CBS-TV, 1959-62, Mobile One, ABC-TV, 1975; numerous TV appearances include Ironside; TV films Mobile Two, 1975, Operation Petticoat, 1977; dir.: film Stand Up and Be Counted, 1972; dir. and producer: numerous TV spls. including Zenith Salutes 25 Years of Television, 1973; dir. over 12 TV movies, 1977—; (recipient Emmy award for best comedy dir. for program M, also best dramatic dir. Nat. Acad. TV Arts and Scis. 1974). Served with USNR, World War II; capt. Res. ret. Decorated Navy Commendation medal, Legion of Merit. Address: care Creative Artists Agy 1888 Century Park E Suite 1400 Los Angeles CA 90067

COOPER, JAMES HAYES SHOFNER, congressman, lawyer; b. Nashville, June 19, 1954; s. William Prentice Jr. and Horetense (Powell) C. B.A., U. N.C., 1975, Oxford U., 1977; J.D., Harvard U., 1980. Atty. Waller, Lansden, Dortch & Davis, Nashville, 1980-82; mem. 98th Congress from 4th Tenn. dist. Rhodes Scholar, 1975; Morehead scholar, 1972. Mem. Phi Beta Kappa. Democrat. Episcopalian. Home: 413 E Lane St Shelbyville TN 37160 Office: US Ho of Reps Washington DC 20515

COOPER, JAMES RICHARD, psychiatrist; b. Pitts., Jan. 19, 1943; s. Frederic Price and Ruth Lawrence (Stalder) C.; m. Margaret O'Neill, Sept. 22, 1979; 1 son, James Niall. B.S., Geneva Coll., Beaver Falls, Pa., 1965; M.D., Jefferson Med. Coll., 1969. Diplomate: Am. Bd. Psychiatry and Neurology. Dir. div. med. and profl. affairs Nat. Inst. Drug Abuse, Rockville, MD, 1973-82, asst. dir. med. affairs, 1982—; practice medicine specializing in psychiatry, Washington, DC, 1973—. Editor: Research on the Treatment of Narcotic Addiction, 1983; author editor monographs. Mem. Am. Psychiat. Assn., Washington Psychiat. Soc. Home: 3932 Military Rd NW Washington DC 20015 Office: Nat Inst Drug Abuse 5600 Fishers Ln Rockville MD 20857

COOPER, JAMES ROBERT, manufacturing company executive; b. St. Louis, Aug. 19, 1939; s. Charles Alva and Cora Imogene (Shifley) Copper; m. Patricia Leeper, Aug. 12, 1961; children: Susan, Robin, Julie. A.B., Culver-Stockton Coll., 1961; M.S., U. Tenn.-Knoxville, 1969. Tchr. Mo. Mil. Acad., Mexico, 1961-63; mgr. applications analysis Nuclear div. Union Carbide, Oak Ridge, Tenn., 1963-69; mgr. corp. mgmt. scis. Coca-Cola Co., Atlanta, 1969-76; v.p. strategic planning and analysis Pillsbury Co., Mpls., 1976-80; v.p. strategic planning IC Industries, Inc., Chgo., Il., 1980—; council mem., v.p. Inst. Mgmt. Scis., Providence, 1970—. Mem. Mgmt. Sci. Roundtable, Chgo. Council Fgn. Relations. Club: Optimist. Office: 111 E Wacker Dr Chgo. IL. 60601

COOPER, JAMES WAYNE, lawyer; b. New Britain, Conn., May 22, 1904; s. James E. and Elizabeth C. (Wayne) C.; m. Louise B. Field, June 26, 1929; children: Field McIntyre, James Nicoll, Peter Brintnall. Grad., Choate Sch., 1922; B.A., Yale, 1926, LL.B., 1929. Bar: Conn. 1929. Law clk. to Judges T.W. Swan, Learned Hand, N.Y.C., 1929-30; instr. Yale Law Sch., 1930-32; asso. Watrous, Hewitt, Gumbart & Corbin, New Haven, 1932-35; partner Tyler, Cooper & Alcorn (and predecessor firms), 1935—; Counsel Anna Fuller Fund, 1938-79. Pres. Foote Sch. Assn., Inc., 1947-49; sec. New Haven Found., 1947-67; mem. Yale Council, 1954-59, exec. com., 1956-59, pres., 1958-59. Fellow Saybrook Coll., Am. Bar Assn.; mem. Conn. Bar Assn. (pres. 1957-58), New Haven County Bar Assn. (pres. 1948-49), Conn. Bar Found. (pres. 1973-75). Clubs: Graduate, Quinnipack (New Haven). Home: 21 Clark Rd Woodbridge CT 06525 Office: 205 Church St New Haven CT 06509

COOPER, JAY LESLIE, lawyer; b. Chgo., Jan. 15, 1929; s. Julius Jerome and Grayce (Wolkenheim) C.; m. Darice Richman, July 30, 1970; children: Todd, Leslie, Keith. J.D., De Paul U., 1951. Bar: Ill. 1951, Calif. 1953, U.S. Supreme Ct. 1965. Partner firm Cooper, Epstein & Hurewitz (and predecessors), Beverly Hills, Calif., 1955—; guest lectr. Advanced Profl. Program Legal Aspects of Music and Rec. Industry, U. So. Calif., 1968, 70, 75, Entertainment Industry Conf., 1971; instr. practical aspects of music and rec. industry U. So. Calif., 1970-72; guest lectr. Calif. Copyright Conf., 1967, 71, 73, 75, 77, v.p., 1975, pres., 1976-77; co-chmn. ann. program The Rec. Contract, UCLA, 1977—; lectr. Midem, 1977—; adj. prof. entertainment law Loyola U. Law Sch., Los Angeles, 1978—. Profl. musician with, Les Brown, Charlie Barnet, Frank Sinatra, Los Angeles Philharmonic, others, 1945-55; Editor: (with Irwin O. Spiegel) Record and Music Publishing Forms of Agreement in Current Use, 1971, Annual Program on Legal Aspects of Entertainment Industry, Syllabus, 1966-70; Contbr.: articles to profl. jours. Annual Program on Legal Aspects of Entertainment Industry, Syllabus. Named Entertainment Lawyer of Yr. Billboard mag., 1975. Mem. ABA (chmn. music and personal appearances div., forum com. on entertainment and sports industries 1983-84), Beverly Hills Bar Assn. (chmn. entertainment law com. 1972-75), Calif. Copyright Soc. (pres. 1976), Los Angeles County Bar Assn., Calif. Bar Assn., Ill. Bar Assn., Los Angeles Copyright Soc., Nat. Acad. Rec. Arts and Scis. (chpt. pres. 1973-75, nat. pres. 1975-77), Internat. Assn. Entertainment Lawyers (exec. com.). Office: 9465 Wilshire Blvd Beverly Hills CA 90212

COOPER, JEAN SARALEE, judge; b. Huntington, N.Y., Mar. 7, 1946; d. Ralph and Henrietta (Halbreich) C.; m. Bert Morse Concklin, Aug. 26, 1978; children: Mitzi Jo, John Todd. B.A., Sophie Newcomb Coll. of Tulane U., 1968; J.D., Emory U., 1970. Bar: La. 1970, Ga. 1970, U.S. Dist. Ct. (ea. dist.) La. 1970, U.S. Ct. Appeals (5th cir.) 1972, U.S. Ct. Appeals (2d cir.) 1976, U.S. Ct. Appeals (4th cir.) 1979, U.S. Ct. Appeals (fed. cir.) 1982, U.S. Supreme Ct. 1974. Trial atty. Office of Solicitor, U.S. Dept. Labor, Washington, 1970-73, spl. projects asst., 1973, sr. trial atty., 1973-77; adminstrv. judge Bd. Conract Appeals, HUD, Washington, 1977—; acting chmn. and chief judge Bd. Contract Appeals, HUD, Washington, 1980-81, vice chmn., 1983; bd. govs. Straight, Inc.; cons., lectr. Contbr. articles to profl. jours. Recipient Moot Court award Tulane Law Sch., 1968. Mem. ABA, Am. Law Inst., La. Bar Assn., Am. Judicature Soc., Inst. Jud. Adminstrs., Nat. Conf. Bds. of Contracts Appeals Mems., Nat. Assn. Women Judges, Exec. Women in Govt. Republican. Address: 451 7th St SW Suite 2158 Washington DC 20410

COOPER, JEROME A., lawyer; b. Brookwood, Ala., Jan. 15, 1913; s. Marks Benjamin and Etta (Temerson) C.; m. Lois Harriet McMillen, Aug. 16, 1938; children: Ellen (Mrs. Benjamin L. Erdreich), Carol (Mrs. James D. Sokol). A.B. Cum laude, Harvard, 1933, LL.B., 1936. Bar: Ala. bar 1936. Practice in, Birmingham, 1946—; law clk. U.S. Dist. Judge Davis, 1936-37, U.S. Supreme Ct. Justice Hugo L. Black, 1937-40; regional atty. Solicitors Office, Dept. Labor, 1940-41; partner firm Cooper, Mitch & Crawford, 1950—; mem. Pres. Kennedy's Lawyers' Com. for Civil Rights Under Law, 1963; pres. adv. council Public Radio Sta. WBHM, 1980—. Mem. editorial adv. bd.: The Ala. Lawyer. Mem. Birmingham area Manpower Resource Devel. Planning Bd., 1969—; chmn. community devel. com. Operation New Birmingham; mem. Jefferson County Drug Abuse Coordinating Com., 1970-76; Pres. Jefferson County Assn. Mental Health, Birmingham Jewish Community Center, United Jewish Fund; mem. Southeastern regional adv. bd. Anti-Defamation League, 1981; exec. bd. Birmingham Concentrated Employment Program; pres. Positive Maturity; sec., exec. bd. Jefferson County Com. Econ. Opportunity; pres. Crisis Center, 1976; mem. Gov.'s Task Force on Unemployment, 1983; Democratic candidate for Ala. Senate, 1966; bd. dirs. Birmingham Symphony Assn. Served to lt. comdr. USNR, 1942-45. Fellow Internat. Soc. Barristers; Mem. Ala. Law Inst., Adminstrv. Conf. U.S. Jewish (trustee temple). Home: 42 Fairway Dr Birmingham AL 35213 Office: 409 N 21st St Suite 201 Birmingham AL 35203

COOPER, JEROME MAURICE, architect; b. Memphis, Jan. 24, 1930; s. Samuel and Bessie (Phillips) C.; m. Jean Kanter, Dec. 29, 1957; children: David Franklin, Samuel Randolph, Beth Lauren. B.S., Ga. Inst. Tech., 1952, B.Arch., 1955; postgrad., U. Rome, Italy, 1956-57. Draftsman Willner & Millkey, Atlanta, 1955-56; Fulbright fellow, Rome, 1956-57; designer Abreu & Robeson, Atlanta, 1957-59, Heery & Heery, 1959-60; pres. Cooper, Carry & Assos., Inc., Atlanta, 1960—. Prin. works include Coll of Architecture bldg, Ga. Inst. Tech., Hickory Hollow Mall (AIA Design award), United Am. Plaza, Crawford & Co. Corp. Hdqrs, Gen. Motors Regional Hdqrs (AIA Design award); Prin. works include: Green Hill Mall (AIA Design award); Prin. works include Heritage Village at Sea Pines. Served to lt. (j.g.) USN, 1952-54. Fellow AIA (pres. chpt., nat. dir.). Home: 1070 Judith Way NE Atlanta GA 30324 Office: 3520 Piedmont Rd NE Atlanta GA 30305

COOPER, JOHN ALFRED, JR., realtor; b. Memphis, Sept. 13, 1938; s. John Alfred and Mildred (Borum) C.; m. Pat McInnis, Oct. 23, 1965; children: Mary Virginia, John Alfred III, Borum. Student, U.

Ark., 1961. With Cherokee Village Devel. Co., Inc., 1962—, exec. v.p., 1967—; pres. John A. Cooper Co., 1968—, Cooper Communities Inc., 1972—; dir. Land Devel. Assn., Wal-Mart Stores, Inc., Ark. Power and Light Co. Bd. dirs. Ark. Nature Conservancy. Clubs: Memphis Country, Little Rock Country. Home: Bella Vista AR 72712 Office: Bentonville AR 72712

COOPER, JOHN ALLEN DICKS, med. educator; b. El Paso, Tex., Dec. 22, 1918; s. John Allen Dicks and Cora (Walker) C.; m. Mary Jane Stratton, June 17, 1944; children—Margaret Ann, John Allen Dicks, Patricia Alison, Randolph Arend Stratton. B.S. in Chemistry, N.Mex.State U., 1939, LL.D. (hon.), 1971; Ph.D. in Biochemistry, Northwestern U., 1943, M.D., 1951, D.Sc. (hon.), 1972; D.Honoris Causa, U. Brasil, 1958; D.Sc. (hon.), Duke U., 1973, Med. Coll. Ohio, Toledo, 1974, Med. Coll. Wis., 1978, N.Y. Med. Coll., 1981, D.Med. Sci, Med. Coll. Pa., 1973. Intern Passavant Meml. Hosp., Chgo., 1951, mem. attending staff, 1955-69; mem. faculty Northwestern U., 1943-69, prof. biochemistry, 1957-69, asso. dean, 1959-63, dean scis., 1963-69, mem. faculty, 1955-69, Georgetown U., 1970—; prof. practice of health policy Duke, 1973-78; vis. prof. U. Brasil, 1956, U. Buenos Aires, 1958; dir. radioisotope service VA Research Hosp., Chgo., 1954-65, cons. in research, 1954-69; adviser to adminstr. AID, U.S. Dept. State, 1966-71; Mem. bd. of pub. health advisers State of Ill., 1962-69; mem. Ill. Legis. Com. Atomic Energy, 1964-69; mem. policy adv. bd. Argonne Nat. Lab., 1957-63, mem. review com. divs. biol. and med. research and radiol. physics, 1958-63, chmn. review com., 1958-62; mem. com. on licensure AEC, 1956-69, cons. div. edn. and tng., 1963; mem. adv. council on health research facilities NIH, 1965-69; organizing com. Pan Am. Fedn. of Assn. Med. Colls., 1962-64, treas., 1963-76; adv. com. personnel for research Am. Cancer Soc., 1962-66; cons. commr. food and drugs FDA, 1965-70; spl. cons. to dir. NIH, 1968-70; cons. to div. physician and health professions edn. Bur. Health Manpower Edn. NIH, 1970-73; mem. adv. com. instnl. relations NSF, 1967-71; cons. edn. and tng. surgeon gen. U.S. Navy, 1972-73; mem. Inst. Medicine, Nat. Acad. Scis., 1972—; chmn. Fedn. Assns. Schs. Health Professions, 1972; mem. spl. med. adv. group VA, 1981—; Mem. alumni council Northwestern U.; Mem. bd. higher edn., Ill., 1964-69; chmn. Gov.'s Sci. Adv. Council, State Ill., 1967-69; mem. council Asso. Midwest Univs., 1963-68, v.p., bd. dirs., 1964-65, pres., bd. dirs., 1965-66; v.p., bd. trustees Argonne Univs. Assn., 1965-68; bd. dirs. Nat. Fund Med. Edn., 1970-79. Editor: Jour. Med. Edn, 1962-71. Served to 1st lt., San. Corps AUS, 1945-47. Recipient Outstanding Alumni award N.Mex. State U., 1960; Alumni medal Northwestern U., 1976; John and Mary R. Markle scholar in acad. medicine, 1951-56. Mem. Am. Soc. Biol. Chemists, Assn. Am. Med. Colls. (del. numerous confs., mem. various coms., pres. 1969—), AMA, AAAS, Central Soc. Clin. Research, Chgo. Inst. Medicine, Am. Hosp. Assn. (hon.), Asociación Venezolana Para el Avance de la Ciencia (hon.), Sigma Xi, Alpha Omega Alpha. Clubs: Cosmos (Washington); Tavern (Chgo.). Home: 4118 N River St Arlington VA 22207 Office: No 1 DuPont Circle NW Washington DC 20036

COOPER, JOHN JOSEPH, lawyer; b. Vincennes, Ind., Oct. 20, 1924; s. Homer O. and Ruth (House) C.; m. Nathalie Brooke, 1945. A.B., Stanford, 1950, LL.B., 1951; LL.M., U. So. Calif., 1964. Bar: Calif. 1952. Practice in, San Francisco, 1951-54, Los Angeles, 1954-61, Palo Alto, 1961—; gen. counsel, v.p. Varian Assos., 1970—; lectr. Am. Law Inst.-Am. Bar Assn., Seattle, 1964, Kansas City, 1965, 66; moderator Trademark and Copyright Inst., George Washington U., 1968; participant Tokyo Conf., U.S.-Japanese Patent Licensing Symposium, U. Wash.-Japanese Inst. Internat. Bus. Law, 1968; speaker Mid-Am. World Trade Conf., Chgo., 1971. Contbr.: chpt. to Patent and Know-How Licensing in Japan and the United States; also law rev. articles and profl. jours. Served with USNR, 1942-45. Mem. ABA, Calif. Bar Assn. (speaker Conf. Corp. Counsel 1969), Am. Corp. Counsel Assn. (bd. dirs. San Francisco chpt.), Santa Clara Bar Assn. Republican. Home: 191 Ramoso Rd Portola Valley CA 94025 Office: 611 Hansen Way Palo Alto CA 94303

COOPER, JOHN SHEPHERD, utility company executive, lawyer; b. San Francisco, Mar. 10, 1931; s. John B. and Lucy B. (Shepherd) C.; m. Ann Phillips, Apr. 22, 1951; children: Kenneith, Joyce, Ellen, Thomas. A.B. in History with honors, U. Calif.-Berkeley, 1952, LL.B., 1957; grad. exec. program, Stanford U., 1971. Bar: Calif., U.S. Supreme Ct. With Pacific Gas and Electric Co., 1957—, mgr. comml. dept., San Francisco, 1971-76, mgr. energy conservation and services, 1976-79, v.p. customer ops., 1979-81, sr. v.p. personnel, 1981—; speaker, witness on conservation of electric and gas energy as econ. energy resources, early 1970s; participant Dunbarton Oaks Energy Symposoium, 1979; bd. dirs. Pvt. Industry Council, San Francisco. Served with inf. U.S. Army, 1952-54. Recipient Energy Conservation award Dept. Energy Region IX, 1980, Cal-Neva Community Action Conservation award, 1980. Mem. Pacific Coast Elec. Assn., Pacific Coast Gas Assn., Bay Area Jr. Achievement, State Bar Calif. Republican. Presbyterian. Club: Engrs. (San Francsico). Office: 245 Market St San Francisco CA 94106 *

COOPER, JOHN SHERMAN, lawyer, former diplomat; b. Somerset, Ky., Aug. 23, 1901; s. John Sherman and Helen Gertrude (Tartar) C.; m. Lorraine Rowan Shevlin, Mar. 17, 1955. Student, Centre Coll., Ky., 1918-19; A.B., Yale U., 1923; postgrad., Harvard Law Sch., 1923-25, U. Ky., U. Pitts., Yale U., Georgetown Coll., Berea Coll., Eastern Ky. State U., Lincoln Meml. U., Nasson Coll., Centre Coll., Thomas More Coll., Pikeville Coll., Morehead State U., Georgetown U., U. Louisville. Bar: Ky. 1928. Mem. lower ho. Ky. Legislature, 1928-30; judge, Pulaski County, Ky., 1930-38; circuit judge 28th Jud. Dist. Ky., 1946; mem. U.S. Senate from Ky., 1947-1948, 52-55, 57-73; mem. com. fgn. relations, pub. works and environment, com. rules and adminstrn., mem. select com. on standards and conduct; apptd. adviser to Sec. State Acheson, NATO meetings, 1950-51; U.S. del. Gen. Assembly, UN, 1949-51, 68, 81; U.S. ambassador to India, Nepal, 1955-56, German Democratic Republic, 1974-76; mem. law firm Gardner, Morrison & Rogers, Washington, 1949-51; of counsel Covington & Burling (attys.), Washington, 1973-74, 76—; adj. prof. George Washington U., 1973-74; mem. Pres.'s Commn. to Investigate Assassination of Pres. Kennedy, 1964. Trustee Centre Coll., John F. Kennedy Sch. Govt., Harvard. Served from pvt. to capt. AUS, 1942-45; ETO. Decorated Bronze Star. Mem. Am., Ky., D.C. bar assns., Am. Acad. Polit. Sci., Am. Legion, VFW, Beta Theta Pi. Republican. Baptist. Club: Rotarian. Headed reorgn. German jud. system, Bavaria, after hostilities ceased, 1945. *

COOPER, JOSEPH, political scientist, dean; b. Boston, Sept. 10, 1933; s. Charles and Esther (Balder) C.; m. Frances Lorna Wollin, Aug. 24, 1965; children: Samuel Wollin, Meryl Charlotte. A.B. summa cum laude, Harvard U., 1955, A.M., 1959, Ph.D. (Brookings research fellow 1959-60), 1961. Asst. prof. govt. Harvard U., 1963-67; mem. faculty Rice U., Houston, 1967—, prof. polit. sci., 1970—, chmn. dept., 1967-72, Lena Gohlman Fox prof., 1978—, dean, 1979—; staff dir. commn. adminstrv. rev. U.S. Ho. of Reps., 1976-78; bd. dirs. Project 87, Am. Polit. Sci. Assn.-Am. Hist. Assn., 1978-81, S.W. Center Urban Research, 1967-73, 74-76, 78-82, sec.-treas., 1970-71, sec., 1979-82. Author: The Origins of the Standing Committees and the Development of the Modern House, 1970; also articles.; Co-editor: Sage Yearbook on Electoral Studies, 1975—; bd. editors: Congress and the Presidency. Sr. fellow NEH, 1973. Mem. Am. Polit. Sci. Assn. (sec. 1979), Southwestern Polit. Sci. Assn. (pres. 1977), So. Polit. Sci. Assn., Midwest Polit. Sci. Assn., Jefferson Davis Assn. (dir. 1980—), Houston Philos. Soc., Houston Com. Fgn. Relations, Phi Beta Kappa., Sigma Xi. Club: Harvard (Houston). Office: Sch Social Scis Rice U PO Box 1892 Houston TX 77251

COOPER, KATHLEEN MARIE, economist; b. Dallas, Feb. 3, 1945; d. Patrick Joseph and Ferne Elizabeth (McDougle) Bell; m. Ronald James Cooper, Feb. 6, 1965; children—Michael, Christopher. B.A. in Math. with honors, U. Tex., Arlington, 1970, M.A. in Econs, 1971, Ph.D., U. Colo., 1980. Research asst. econs. dept. U. Tex., Arlington, 1970-71; corp. economist United Banks of Colo., Denver, 1971-80, chief economist, 1980-81; v.p., sr. fin. economist Security Pacific Nat. Bank, Los Angeles, 1981—. Mem. Nat. Assn. Bus. Economists (past mem. exec. council), Am. Bankers Assn. (past mem. econ. adv. com.), Am. Econ. Assn. Office: Econs Dept H8-12 PO Box 2097 Terminal Annex Los Angeles CA 90071

COOPER, KEN ERROL, agribusiness company executive, university administrator; b. Bryan, Ohio, Mar. 10, 1939; s. George Wayne and Agnes Anibel (Fisher) C.; m. Karen Cremean, June 17, 1961; children: Kristin, Andrew. B.S., Bowling Green State U., 1961; M.B.A., Miami U., Oxford, Ohio, 1962; Ph.D., U. Minn., 1984. Instr. Miami U., 1962-63; lectr. U. Minn., 1965-67; group v.p. Land O'Lakes, Inc., Mpls., 1967-82; v.p. fin. and adminstrn. Hamline U., 1981—; vis. prof. (on leave) Coll. of St. Thomas, St. Paul, 1981-82; dir. Group Health, Inc.; Trustee Westmar Coll.; mem. Iowa Supreme Ct. Adv. Council, 1972-75, North Central Devel. Found. Republican. Methodist. Office: Hamline U Saint Paul MN 55104

COOPER, KENNETH BANKS, business executive, former army officer; b. Ft. Leavenworth, Kans., Nov. 12, 1923; s. Avery John and Ona Carey (Gibson) C.; m. Virginia Leah Adkins, Dec. 29, 1979; children by previous marriage: Kenneth, Robert. B.S., U.S. Mil. Acad., 1944; M.S., Mass. Inst. Tech., 1951. Commd. 2d lt. U.S. Army, 1944, advanced through grades to lt. gen.; World War II service in South Pacific, Philippines, Japan, 1944-46; assigned to Manhattan Project-Armed Forces Spl. Weapon Project, N.Mex., Eniwetok, and Washington, 1946-48; mem. nuclear weapons staff AEC, Washington, 1951-55; nuclear weapons planning officer SHAPE, Paris, 1955-58; project mgr., ballistic missile def. research Advanced Research Projects Agy., Washington, 1959-63; bn. comdr., Korea, 1963-64; dir. Army Nuclear Power Program, 1965-66; with Def. Com. Planning Group, 1966-68; exec. to Sec. of Army, 1968-70; brigade comdr., Vietnam, 1970-71; dep. dir. civil works Office Chief of Engrs., Washington, 1971-72, asst. chief engrs., 1972-75; dep. comdr. in chief U.S. Army, Europe, Heidelberg, W.Ger., 1975-77; dep. adviser to Sec. of Def., 1977-78; ret., 1978; group gen. mgr. Service and Constrn. Group, ITT, Nutley, N.J., 1978-79; dep. asst. sec. def. for plans and resources Office of Asst Sec. Def., Washington, 1980-81; pres. SPC Internat., Arlington, Va., 1981—. Decorated Legion of Merit, D.S.M. Mem. Soc. Mil. Engrs., Sigma Xi. Club: Army Navy Country. Office: 1500 Wilson Blvd Arlington VA 22209

COOPER, LEON MELVIN, lawyer; b. Los Angeles, July 24, 1924; s. Harry and Edith (Goldman) C.; m. Shirley Abbey, July 9, 1978; children: Katharine Lee, Victoria Lee, Wendy Elizabeth, Christopher Knopf. A.B., UCLA, 1944; LL.B., Harvard U., 1949; LL.M., U. S.C., 1965. Bar: Mass. 1949, Calif. 1950. Since practiced in, Los Angeles; mem. firm Pacht, Ross, Warne, Bernhard & Sears, Inc. Mem. Alcoholic Beverage Control Appeals Bd., Calif., 1965-67; chmn. Alcoholic Beverage Control Bd., Los Angeles, 1966-67; So. chmn. Calif. Democratic Central Com., 1968-71. Served to lt. comdr. USNR, World War II; Korea. Decorated medal of Commendation with battle clasp. Mem. Los Angeles Bar Assn., ABA, State Bar Calif., State Bar Mass. Clubs: Los Angeles Yacht, St. Francis Yacht, Univ. Office: 1800 Ave of Stars Fifth Floor Los Angeles CA 90067

COOPER, LEON N., physicist, educator; b. N.Y.C., Feb. 28, 1930; s. Irving and Anna (Zola) C.; m. Kay Anne Allard, May 18, 1969; children: Kathleen Ann, Coralie Lauren. A.B., Columbia U., 1951, A.M., 1953, Ph.D., 1954, D.Sc., 1973; D.Sc. hon. degrees, U. Sussex, Eng., 1973, U. Ill., 1974, Brown U., 1974, Gustavus Adolphus Coll., 1975, Ohio State U., 1976, U. Pierre et Marie Curie, Paris, 1977. NSF postdoctoral fellow, mem. Inst. for Advanced Study, 1954-55; research assoc. U. Ill., 1955-57; asst. prof. Ohio State U., 1957-58; assoc. prof. Brown U., Providence, 1958-62, prof., 1962-66, Henry Ledyard Goddard U. prof., 1966-74, Thomas J. Watson Sr. prof. sci., 1974—; co-dir. Center for Neural Sci.; lectr. Summer Sch., Varenna, Italy, 1955; vis. prof. Brandeis Summer Inst., 1959, Bergen Internat. Sch. Physics, Norway, 1961, Scuola Internatzionali Di Fisica, Erice, Italy, 1965, L'Ecole Normal Supèrieure, Centre Universitaire Internationale, Paris, 1966, Cargèse Summer Sch., 1966; cons. indsl., ednl. orgns. Author: Introduction to The Meaning and Structure of Phsyics, 1968; Contbr. articles to profl. jours. Alfred P. Sloan Found. research fellow, 1959-66; John Simon Guggenheim Meml. Found. fellow, 1965-66; Recipient Comstock prize Nat. Acad. Scis., 1968, Nobel prize, 1972. Fellow Am. Phys. Soc., Am. Acad. Arts and Scis.; mem. Am. Philos. Soc., Nat. Acad. Scis., Phi Beta Kappa, Sigma Xi. *

COOPER, LEROY GORDON, JR., former astronaut, bus. exec.; b. Shawnee, Okla., Mar. 6, 1927; s. Leroy Gordon and Hattie Lee (Herd) C.; m. Trudy B. Olson, Aug. 29, 1947 (div.); children—Camala Keoki, Janita Lee; m. Susan Taylor, May 6, 1972; children—Elizabeth Jo, Colleen Taylor. Student, U. Hawaii, 1946-49, European extension U. Md., 1951-53; B.S. in Aero. Engring, Air Force Inst. Tech., 1956; grad., Exptl. Test Pilot Sch., USAF, 1957. Commd. lt. USAF, 1949, advanced through grades to col., 1965; jet fighter pilot, 1950-54, pilot exptl. flight test engring., 1957-59; astronaut with Project Mercury, NASA, 1959-70; made 22 orbit flight in Faith 7, 1963; worked with Gemini program of Astronaut Office, made 122 Orbit flight in Gemini V, 1965; worked with Apollo lunar program; v.p. research and devel. W.E.D. Enterprises, 1974-80; pres. Gordon Cooper Cons., 1975—. Recipient Harmon trophy; Colliers trophy. Mem. Am. Inst. Aero. and Astronautics, Soc. Exptl. Test Pilots, Am. Astronautical Soc. Club: Mason (Shriner, Jester). Office: 5011 Woodley Ave Encino CA 91436 *

COOPER, LESTER IRVING, TV producer; b. N.Y.C., Jan. 20, 1919; s. Samuel and Clara (Levine) C.; m. Audrey Rosemary Levey, July 1, 1949; children: Kim, Elizabeth, Matthew. Student, NYU, 1936, Columbia U. extension, 1936. Writer, Warner Bros., Hollywood, Calif., 1937-41; screenwriter, J. Arthur Rank-Brit. Nat. Pictures, London, 1945-49; chief copy editor, Esquire mag., 1949-50; with, Lester Cooper Prodns., films, 1953-55, CBS, 1953-55, NBC, 1955-58; supervising producer, head writer: PM, Westinghouse Broadcasting Co., 1959-61; producer: Exploring the Universe, 1962-64; with: ABC News, 1965—; creator, writer, dir., exec. producer: Animals Animals Animals (Emmy award, Peabody award, Action for Children's TV award), 1976-81 (Ohio State U. award); (Recipient Journalism TV award AMA 1967, Albert Lasker Med. Journalism award 1970); Writer-producer: Hemingway's Spain, 1968 (Peabody award), Can You Hear Me?, 1967, Heart Attack, 1969, This Land is Mine, 1970; creator: Make a Wish (Peabody award 1971), 1971 (Emmy award 1974). Served with AUS, 1941-45. Mem. Dirs. Guild Am., Writers Guild Am. Office: ABC News 7 W 66th St New York NY 10023 *If I have discovered anything over the years, it is that inspiration is no substitute for sitting down and doing it.* *

COOPER, LOUISE FIELD, author; b. Hartford, Conn., Mar. 8, 1905; d. Francis Elliott and Anna (Dunning) Field; m. James Wayne Cooper, June 26, 1929; children—Field (Mrs. Colin McIntyre), James Nicoll, Peter Brintnal. Student, Miss Porter's Sch., Farmington, 1921-24. Author: The Lighted Box, 1942, The Deer on the Stairs, Love and Admiration, Summer Stranger, 1947, The Boys from Sharon, 1950, The Cheerful Captive, 1954, The Windfall Child, 1963, Widows and Admirals, 1964, A Week at the Most, 1967, One Dragon Too Many, 1971, large print edit., 1978, Breakaway, 1977, 5 pub. works issued in paperback 1973, also large print edit. 1978; Contbr. short stories to New Yorker mag. Home: 21 Clark Rd Woodbridge New Haven CT 06525

COOPER, MARIO, educator, artist; b. Mexico City, Mexico, Nov. 26, 1905; U.S., 1915; s. Luis and Maria (Garfias) C.; m. Aileen Whetstine, Feb. 26, 1927 (div. Apr. 1964); children—Vincent, Patricia; m. G. Dale Meyers, Oct. 1964. Student, Otis Art Inst., Los Angeles, 1924, Chouinard Art Sch., Los Angeles, 1925, Grand Central Art Sch., N.Y.C., 1927-37; pupil, F. Tolles Chamberlin, Louis Treviso, Pruett Carter, Harvey Dunn. Staff artist Tracey Locke & Dawson, Dallas, 1925, Honig Cooper Advt., San Francisco, 1926; freelance artist, Los Angeles, San Francisco, N.Y.C., 1926-27; visualizer and layout man Batten, Barton, Durstine & Osborne, N.Y.C., 1927-28; art dir. Lord Thomas, 1929-31; instr. illustration, advt. art Columbia, 1937-41, Grand Central Art Sch., 1941-45, Art Students League, 1945, Vets. Class, Soc. Illustrators, 1945-50, Pratt Inst., 1950-57; tchr. watercolor Art Students League, N.Y., 1957—; instr. watercolor Nat. Acad. Sch. Fine Arts, 1959; guest instr. Municipal Mus. Art, Springfield, Mo., 1961, Laguna Beach Art Assn., 1962; lectr. Coll. City N.Y., 1962—; art cons. USAF, 1959; pres. U.S. Com. Internat. Assn. Plastic Arts, UNESCO, 1976-77. (Recipient various gold and 1st awards for sculpture, watercolor awards include, Harriet Sanford Stuart purchase prize Am. Watercolor Soc. 1955, awards in soc.'s anns. 1961-63, Emily Lowe award 1956, Herb Olsen award 1959, achievement award 1967, Famous Artists award, Watercolor USA award 1968, awards 1969, 70, 71, Bklyn. Soc. Artists award 1955, Grumbacher award Allied Artists Am. 1956, 1st award NAD 1956, Samuel F.B. Morse medal 1967, medal of Achievement Inst. Art Mexico 1970, Greathouse medal 1978, Audubon Artists Silver medal 1979); Author: Flower Painting in Watercolor, 1962, Drawing and Painting the City, 1967, Painting with Watercolor, Mario Cooper, 1972, Watercolor by Design, Mario Cooper, 1980; paintings in collection, USAF Acad., 1931—; illustrator stories by, P.G. Woodhouse, Alfred Noyes, Gouverneur Morris, Quentin Reynolds, Clarence Budington Kelland, Agatha Christie, Eric Maria Remarque; represented in permanent collections, Met. Mus. Art, N.Y.C., Library of Congress, Library Royal Soc. Arts, London, NAD, Butler Inst. Am. Art., Reading (Pa.) Public Mus., Adelphi Coll.; represented at, St. Luke's Hosp., Denver, Madonna and Child; exhibited sculpture, Third Internat. Sculpture Phila., 1949, Pa. Acad., 1948-51, Nat. Acad., 1947, 49, 50, 51, others, water colors various acads. and soc. shows, Exchange Exhbn. Royal Painters in Watercolour, London, 1962, Ichiban Gallery, Tokyo, Fuji Daimaru Gallery, Kyoto. On temporary duty for USAF in the, 1954; Far East; on temporary duty for USAF in the, 1956; to Hokkaido, Korea, Formosa, Alaska. Fellow Royal Soc. Arts (London); mem. Royal Watercolor Soc. (London) (hon.), Audubon Artists (hon. pres. 1954-58, Gold medal of honor 1974, Silver medal 1979, Ralph Fabri medal 1978), NAD, Soc. Illustrators (life), Nat. Sculptors Soc., Artists Guild (v.p. N.Y. 1936), Am. Watercolor Soc. (pres. 1959—, Gold medal of honor 1974, High Winds medal 1979, Silver medal 1980, High Winds medal 1981), Calif. Watercolor Soc., Tex. Watercolor Soc., Casein Painters Soc., Knickerbocker Artists, N.J. Painters and Sculptors, Allied Artists Am., Nat. Acad. (council 1973-76), Watercolor Soc. Mexico (hon.), Canadian Soc. Painters in Water Colour (hon.). Clubs: Officers (hon.), Salmagundi (hon., Medal of Honor for disting. contbn. to arts 1980). Commd. by NASA to document Apollo 10 and Apollo 11 flights to moon at Cape Kennedy, 1969; commd. by EPA to document the environment. Address: 1 W 67th St New York NY 10023

COOPER, MARSH ALEXANDER, mining company executive; b. Toronto, Ont., Can., Oct. 8, 1912; s. Frederick W. and Gertrude (Marsh) C.; m. Doris Elsie Roos, Sept. 13, 1941. B.Sc., M.Sc., U. Toronto, 1935; postgrad., Harvard, 1938-39; D.Sc. (hon.), St. Francis Xavier U., 1974. Partner James, Buffam & Cooper, 1937-67; pres., chief exec. officer McIntyre Mines, Ltd., 1967-69, Falconbridge Ltd., Toronto, 1969-80, also dir.; pres. M.A. Cooper Cons., Inc., 1980—; dir. Falconbridge Dominicana C. Por A., Corp. Falconbridge Copper, Crown Life Ins. Co., Extendicare Ltd., McIntyre Mines Ltd., Superior Oil Co., Burns Food Ltd. Mem. Soc. Econ. Geologists, Assn. Profl. Engrs. Provinces of Ont. and B.C., Am. Inst. Mining, Metall. and Petroleum Engrs., Can. Inst. Mining and Metallurgy, Engring. Inst. Can. Office: PO Box 40 Commerce Ct W Toronto ON Canada M5L 1B4

COOPER, MARTIN, electronics company executive; b. Chgo., Dec. 26, 1928; s. Arthur and Mary C.; children: Scott David, Lisa Ellen. B.S.E.E., Ill. Inst. Tech., 1950, M.S.E.E., 1957. Research engr. Teletype Corp., Chgo., 1953-54; with Motorola, Inc., Schaumburg, Ill., 1954-83, ops. dir., 1967-76, div. mgr., 1977-78, v.p., corp. dir. research and devel., 1978-83; chmn., chief exec. officer Cellular Bus. Systems, Inc., 1983—; Mem. computer-telecommunications bd. Nat. Research Council, 1979—; mem. indsl. adv. bd. U. Ill.-Chgo., 1980—. Served with USNR, 1950-54. Fellow IEEE (pres. vehicular tech. soc. 1973-74, telecommunications policy bd. 1976—, award for contbns. to radiotelephony, Centennial medal awardee), Radio Club of Am. Patentee in field. Home: 235 W. Menomonee Chicago IL 60614 Office: 450 E Ohio St Chicago IL 60611 *It is essential that we conduct ourselves as though each of our fellow humans is honest, values his or her word, is ethical and moral. They will rise to our honorable expectations just as they can sink to our base suspicions.*

COOPER, MICHAEL ANTHONY, lawyer; b. Passaic, N.J., Mar. 29, 1936. B.A., Harvard U., 1957, LL.B., 1960. Bar: N.Y. State 1961, U.S. Supreme Ct. 1969. With firm Sullivan & Cromwell, N.Y.C., 1960—, partner, 1968—; Bd. dirs. Legal Aid Soc., pres., 1981-83; Bd. dirs. Lawyers Com. for Civil Rights Under Law. Fellow Am. Coll. Trial Lawyers; mem. Am., N.Y. bar assns., Assn. Bar City N.Y., Am. Law Inst., N.Y. County Lawyers Assn., Am. Judicature Soc. Office: 125 Broad St New York NY 10004

COOPER, MILTON, real estate development executive; b. N.Y.C., Mar. 15, 1929; s. Aaron and Fannie (Liebowitz) C.; m. Shirley Mandelker, Sept. 9, 1950; children: Clifford, David, Matthew, Todd. B.B.A., CCNY, 1949; LL.B., Bklyn. Law Sch., 1952. Bar: N.Y. 1952. Ptnr. Jaffin, Schneider, Kimmel & Galpeer, N.Y.C., 1952-66, Galpeer & Cooper, 1966-70; pres. Kimco Corp., Roslyn, N.Y., from 1966; chmn. bd. Alpha Portland Industries, Easton, Pa.; dir. Power Test Corp., Westbury, N.Y. Office: Alpha Portland Industris Inc 15 S 3d St Easton PA 18042

COOPER, NORTON J., liquor and wine company executive; b. Phila., Aug. 16, 1931; s. Maurice J. and Elsie (Goldstein) C.; (div.)children: Moss, Robin. B.A., Cornell U., 1953. With Charles Jacquin et Cie Inc., Phila., 1955—, pres., chief exec. officer, prin. owner, 1979—. Author: off-Broadway prodn. Ballad of Jazz Street,

1959. Served to 1st lt. AUS, 1953-55. Decorated Ordre de Chevalier de Provence.

COOPER, PAUL, musician, educator; b. Victoria, Ill., May 19, 1926; s. Charles Frederick and Jessie Anne (Tullgren) C.; m. Christiane Ebert, Apr. 30, 1953; children: Claudia Renée, Ian Paul. B.A., U. So. Calif., 1950, M.A., 1953, D.Mus.Arts, 1956; student (Fulbright fellow), Nat. Conservatory Paris and Sorbonne, 1953. Minister music St. Matthew's Luth. Ch., North Hollywood, Calif., 1954-55; faculty U. Mich. Ann Arbor, 1955-68, prof. music, 1965-68, chmn. theory dept., 1966-68; prof. music, composer in residence, head acad. div. U. Cin., 1968-74; prof. music, composer in residence, chmn. scholar faculty Shepherd Sch. Music, Rice U., Houston, 1974—, Lynette Autrey prof. music, 1982—; State Dept. cultural rep. Internat. Exhbn., Zagreb, Yugoslavia, 1965; guest lectr. colls., univs., 1968—. Performer, 1953—; music critic, Los Angeles Mirror, 1952-55, Ann Arbor News, 1959-65; composer, author, 1967—; Author: Workbooks for Perspectives in Music, 1973-75, Perspectives in Music Theory, 1973, 2d edit., 1981, Dimensions of Sight Singing, 1981; Contbr. revs. and articles to profl. jours., catalogue of original compositions contains 5 symphonies, 6 string quartets, 6 concertis, 4 oratorios for double chorus and orch., diverse instrumental and vocal chamber music. Served from pvt. to 1st lt., inf. AUS, 1944-47, 50-52. Horace H. Rackham research grantee, 1960, 68; Ford Found. research grantee, 1967; rec. grantee, 1975; Rockefeller Found. performance grantee, 1967; Nat. Endowment for Arts grantee, 1973, 79; Guggenheim Found. fellow, 1965, 72; recipient Ann. Standard award ASCAP, 1968—, Am. Acad. and Inst. Arts and Letters award, 1977; Rice U. Pres.'s Fund grantee, 1977. Mem. Music Tchrs. Nat. Assn. (v.p. 1975-77, exec. bd. 1977—). Office: Shepherd Sch Music Rice U PO Box 1892 Houston TX 77001 *For a composer whose roots are found in rural Illinois and who now lives and works in a dynamic Houston the idea of contributing to a great American culture is a source of pride, energy, and enthusiasm. I think in musical, rather than verbal or oral, terms. My guides and constant inspirations on this exhilarating journey have been Nadia Boulanger, Ross Lee Finney, and the perfectionist poet, C.E. Cooper.*

COOPER, PAULA, art dealer; b. Mass., Mar. 14, 1938. Student, Pierce Coll., Athens, Greece, Sorbonne, Paris, Goucher Coll. Asst. World House Galleries, N.Y.C., 1959-61; pvt. dealer, 1962-63; with Paula Johnson Gallery, N.Y.C., 1964-65; dir. Park Place Gallery, N.Y.C., 1965-67, Paula Cooper Gallery, 1968—. Office: Paula Cooper Gallery 155 Wooster St New York NY 10012 *

COOPER, REGINALD RUDYARD, orthopaedic surgeon, educator; b. Elkins, W.Va., Jan. 6, 1932; s. Eston H. and Kathryn (Wyatt) C.; m. Jacqueline Smith, Aug. 22, 1954; children—Pamela Ann, Douglas Mark, Christopher Scott, Jeffrey Michael. B.A. with honors, W.Va. U., 1952, B.S., 1953; M.D., Med. Coll. Va., 1955; M.S., U. Iowa, 1960. Diplomate: Am. Bd. Orthopedic Surgeons (examiner 1968—). Orthopedic surgeon U.S. Naval Hosp., Pensacola, Fla., 1960-62; asso. in orthopedics U. Iowa Coll. Medicine, Iowa City, 1962-65, asst. prof. orthopaedics, 1965-68, asso. prof. orthopedics, 1968-71, prof. orthopedics, 1971—, chmn. orthopedics, 1973—; research fellow orthopedic surgery Johns Hopkins Hosp., Balt., 1964-65; exchange fellow to Britain for Am. Orthopedic Assn., 1969. Trustee Nat. Easter Seals Research Found., 1977-81, chmn., 1979-81. Served to lt. comdr. USNR, 1960-62. Mem. Iowa, Johnson County med. socs., Orthopedic Research Soc. (sec.-treas. 1970-73, pres. 1974-75), Am. Acad. Orthopedic Surgeons (Kappa Delta award for outstanding research in orthopedics 1971), Canadian, Am. Orthopedic assns., Am. Acad. Orthopedic Surgeons (dir. 1973-74), N.Y. Acad. Sci., Assn. Bone and Joint Surgeons, AMA, Am. Rheumatism Assn., Am. Fedn. Clin. Research, Am. Acad. Cerebral Palsy, Am. Acad. Orthopedic Surgeons (chmn. exams. com. 1978-82, sec. 1982). Home: 201 Ridgeview Ave Iowa City IA 52240

COOPER, RICHARD ALAN, hematologist; b. Milw., Sept. 23, 1936; s. Peter and Annabelle (Schlomovitz) C.; m. Jaclyn Koppel, June 22, 1958; children: Stephanie, Jonathan. B.S., U. Wis., 1957; M.D., Washington U., St. Louis, 1961. Intern Harvard U. Med. Services, Boston City Hosp., 1961-63, resident in medicine, 1965-66; fellow in hematology Thorndike Meml. Lab., Boston City Hosp., 1966-69; asst. prof. medicine Harvard Med. Sch., 1969-71; chief hematology div. Thorndike Meml. Lab. and Harvard Med. Services, Boston City Hosp., 1969-71; prof. medicine, dir. Cancer Center, chief hematology-oncology sect. U. Pa., Phila., 1971—. Mem. editorial bd.: Blood, 1979—, Lipid Research, 1983—. Served with USPHS, 1963-65. NIH grantee. Mem. Am. Soc. Hematology, Am. Soc. Clin. Oncology, Am. Fedn. Clin. Research, Am. Soc. Clin. Investigation, Assn. Am. Physicians, Phi Beta Kappa, Alpha Omega Alpha. Office: 3400 Spruce St Philadelphia PA 19104

COOPER, RICHARD FOSS, lawyer; b. Strafford, N.H., Aug. 12, 1915; s. Burt Randall and Emily Lillian (Foss) C.; m. Elizabeth Hall Wentworth, Oct. 19, 1940; children: Candace Wentworth, Randall Foss. Student, Phillips Exeter Acad.; A.B., Dartmouth Coll., 1937; LL.B., Harvard U., 1940. Bar: N.H. bar, fed. dist. cts 1940. Pres. Cooper, Hall, Whittum & Shillaber P.C., since 1946; city solicitor, 1946-50; justice Rochester Dist. Ct.; dir. BankEast Savs. Bank and Trust, Grange Mut. Ins. Co., Loan Mountain Recreation Corp.; Chmn. N.H. Bd. of Probation, 1961-74; dep. chmn. Gov.'s Com. on Crime and Delinquency, 1968-73. Served as lt. USNR, 1942-46; capt. Res. Mem. Am., N.H., Strafford County bar assns., Newcomen Soc. N. Am., N.H. Assn. Municipal and Dist. Ct. Judges (pres. 1971-72), N.H. Dept. Res. Officers Assn. (pres. 1970-71), Gamma Delta Chi. Republican (chmn. state com. 1947-52, 54; mem. nat. com. 1952-60; chmn. finance com. 1953-57). Club: Mason. Home: 1 Dartmouth Ln Rochester NH 03867 Office: 76 Wakefield St Rochester NH 03867

COOPER, RICHARD LEE, journalist; b. Grand Rapids, Mich., Dec. 8, 1946; s. Harold Ralph and Elizabeth (DeSchipper) C.; m. Carol Jean Bonjernoor, Sept. 5, 1968; children—Jason Adam, Jessica Lynne. Student, Grand Rapids Jr. Coll., 1965-67; B.A., Mich. State U., 1969. Reporter Rochester (N.Y.) Times-Union, 1969-77, Phila. Inquirer, 1977—; instr. journalism Temple U., 1980—. Mem. Chesapeake Bay Triton Fleet. Recipient N.Y. State Asso. Press Spot News First Place award, 1972, 76; Pulitzer prize for gen. local reporting, 1972; Distinguished Alumni award Grand Rapids Jr. Coll., 1974; Outstanding Contbn. in Pub. Info. award N.Y. State Bar Assn., 1977; 1st prize for investigative reporting Gannett News, 1977. Mem. Phila. Newspaper Guild, Pen and Pencil Club, Sigma Delta Chi. Presbyn. Office: 400 N Broad St Philadelphia PA 19101

COOPER, RICHARD NEWELL, educator, economist; b. Seattle, June 14, 1934; s. Richard Warren and Lucile (Newell) C.; m. Carolyn Jane Cahalan, June 5, 1956 (div. 1980); children: Laura Katherine, Mark Daniel.; m. Ann Lorraine Hollick, Jan. 1, 1982. A.B., Oberlin Coll., 1956, LL.D. (hon.), 1978; M.Sc. (Econs.), London Sch. Econs., 1958; Ph.D., Harvard U., 1962; M.A. (hon.), Yale U., 1966. Sr. staff economist Council Econ. Advisers, 1961-63; asst. prof. econs. Yale U., 1963-65, prof., 1966-77, provost, 1972-74; dep. asst. sec. state internat. monetary affairs Dept. State, 1965-66, undersec. for econ. affairs, 1977-81; prof. econs. Harvard U., Cambridge, Mass., 1981—; mem. Trilateral Commn.; dir. Phoenix Mut. Life Ins. Co., Wards Co.; Bd. dirs. Inst. Internat. Econs., Ctr. European Policy Studies. Author: Economics of Interdependence, 1968, Currency Devaluation in Developing Countries, 1971, Economic Mobility and National Economic Policy, 1974; editor, contbr.: A Reordered World, 1973, The International Monetary System under Flexible Exchange Rates, 1982; contbr. articles to profl. jours. Fellow Am. Acad. Arts and Scis.; mem. Am. Econ. Assn., Royal Econ. Soc., Council Fgn. Relations. Office: 1737 Cambridge St Cambridge MA 02138

COOPER, ROBERT ARTHUR, JR., pathologist, educator; b. St. Paul, Aug. 27, 1932; s. Robert Arthur and Theodora (Yarborough) C.; m. June Lorraine Spalty, Aug. 29, 1969; children: Robert Arthur, III, Timothy Rychner, Theodore Thomas. A.B., U. Pa., 1954; M.D., Jefferson Med. Coll., Phila., 1958. Intern Moffitt Hosp., U. Calif., 1958-59, resident in pathology, 1959-62; chief resident in pathology Women's Free Hosp. and Boston Lying-in Hosp., Harvard, 1962-63; teaching fellow Harvard Med. Sch., 1962-63; from asst. prof. to prof. pathology U. Oreg. Med. Sch., 1963-69; mem. faculty U. Rochester (N.Y.) Med. Sch., 1969—, assoc. dean curricular affairs, assoc. prof. pathology, 1969-72, prof. pathology, dir. surg. pathology, 1972-75, prof. oncology in pathology, dir. cancer center, 1974—; cons. subcom. on comprehensive cancer centers Nat. Cancer Adv. Bd., Nat. Cancer Inst., 1976-78, mem. breast cancer treatment com. (breast cancer task force), div. cancer biology, 1974-77, mem. cancer center support grant rev. com., 1978-82, chmn., 1981-82; bd. sci. counsellors div. resources ctr. and community activities Nat. Cancer Inst., 1983—; mem. spl. study sect. cancer epidemiology NIH, 1972; bd. dirs. United Cancer Council, Inc., v.p., 1981—; bd. dirs. Monroe County unit Am. Cancer Soc., 1976-80, mem. profl. edn. com. N.Y. State div., 1974-78; cons. Population Council, Rockefeller U., 1972—; mem. Lasker award jury Lasker Found., 1977. Author articles, chpts. in books.; Asso. editor: Internat. Jour. Radiation Oncology, Biology and Physics, 1974—; mem. editorial bd.: Cancer Clin. Trials, 1977—. Bd. dirs. Brighton Little League, 1973-77, vice commnr., 1975-76; bd. dirs. Wilnot Found., 1981—. Recipient Allan J. Hill Teaching award U. Oreg. Med. Sch., 1966, 67, 69; named 2d Year Tchr. of Year U. Rochester Med. Sch., 1973; Lester P. Slade civic achievement award Real Estate Bd. of Rochester, 1980; research fellow Am. Cancer Soc., 1960-61; grantee Nat. Cancer Inst., 1975—. Mem. Eastern Ski Assn., Alpha Omega Alpha. Clubs: Hunt Hollow Ski (Naples, N.Y.); Genesee Valley (Rochester, N.Y.). Home: 555 Clover Hills Dr Rochester NY 14618 Office: U Rochester Cancer Center 601 Elmwood Ave Box 704 Rochester NY 14642

COOPER, ROBERT ELBERT, state supreme court justice; b. Chattanooga, Oct. 14, 1920; s. John Thurman and Susie Inez (Hollingsworth) C.; m. Catherine Pauline Kelly, Nov. 24, 1949; children: Susan Florence Cooper Hodges, Bobbie Cooper Martin, Kelly Ann, Robert E. B.A., U. N.C., 1946; J.D., Vanderbilt U., 1949. Bar: Tenn. 1948. Asso. Kolwyck and Clark, 1949-51; partner Cooper and Barger, 1951-53; asst. atty. gen. 6th Jud. Ct. Tenn., 1951-53; judge 6th Jud. Circuit Tenn., 1953-60, Tenn. Ct. Appeals, 1960-70, presiding judge Eastern div., 1970-74; justice Tenn. Supreme Ct., 1974—, chief justice, 1976, 84; chmn. Tenn. Jud. Council, 1967—; mem. Tenn. Jud. Standards Commn., 1971—. Mem. exec. bd. Cherokee council Boy Scouts Am., 1960-64; bd. dirs. Met. YMCA, 1956-65, St. Barnabas Nursing Home and Apts. for Aged, 1966-69. Served with USNR, 1941-46. Mem. Am., Tenn., Chattanooga bar assns., Conf. Chief Justices, Phi Beta Kappa, Order of Coif, Kappa Sigma, Phi Alpha Delta. Democrat. Presbyterian. Clubs: Signal Mountain Golf and Country, Masons (33 deg.), Shriners). Home: 196 Woodcliff Circle Signal Mountain TN 37377 Office: Hamilton County Justice Bldg Chattanooga TN 37402

COOPER, ROBERT SHANKLIN, govt. ofcl.; b. Kansas City, Mo., Feb. 8, 1932; s. Robert S. and Edna A. (Pobanz) C.; m. Margaret Niven Shipman, Apr. 15, 1956; children—Jonathan A., James G. B.S. in Elec. Engring, U. Iowa, 1954; M.S., Ohio State U., 1958; Sc.D., Mass. Inst. Tech., 1963, 1963-65. Mem. staff elec. engring. dept. Mass. Inst. Tech., 1958-65; mem. staff Lincoln Lab., 1965-72; asst. dir. def. research and engring. Dept. Def., 1972-75; dep. dir. Goddard Space Flight Center, Greenbelt, Md., 1975-76, dir., 1976-79; v.p. engring. Satellite Bus. Systems, McLean, Va., 1979-81; dir. Def. Adv. Research Projects Agy., Arlington, Va., 1981—. Served with USAF, 1954-56. Westinghouse fellow, 1958; recipient Sec. Def. Meritorious Civilian Service award, 1975. Mem. AAAS, IEEE, Sigma Xi, Tau Beta Pi, Eta Kappa Nu. Office: 1400 Wilson Blvd Arlington VA 22209

COOPER, STEPHEN, microbiology educator; b. N.Y.C., Aug. 6, 1937; s. Haskell and Florence (Leshen) C.; m. Alexandra Lee Winer, Aug. 21, 1960; children: Eric, Michael. B.A., Union Coll., 1959; Ph.D., Rockefeller Inst., 1963. NSF fellow Univ. Microbiology Inst., Copenhagen, 1963-64, Hammersmith Hosp., London, 1964-65; research assoc. Tufts Med. Sch., Boston, 1965-66; asst. research prof. SUNY-Buffalo, 1966-70; assoc. prof. U. Mich. Med. Sch., Ann Arbor, 1970-78, prof. microbiology, 1978—; Fogarty Internat. fellow Imperial Cancer Research Fund, London, 1976; sec.-treas. Complete Cuisine Ltd., Ann Arbor, 1978—. Mem. Am. Microbiology Soc., AAAS. Home: 1407 Lincoln St Ann Arbor MI 48104 Office: Dept Microbiology and Immunology U Mich Med Sch Ann Arbor MI 48109

COOPER, STEPHEN HERBERT, lawyer; b. N.Y.C., Mar. 29, 1939; s. Walter S. and Selma (Herbert) C.; m. Linda Cohen, Aug. 29, 1965 (dec.); m. 2d Karen Gross, Sept. 6, 1981; 1 son, Zachary Noel. A.B., Columbia U., 1960, J.D. cum laude, 1965. Bar: N.Y. 1965. Assoc. Breed, Abbott & Morgan, N.Y.C., 1965-66, Weil, Gotshal & Manges, 1966-73, ptnr., 1973—. Served to lt. USNR, 1960-62. Mem. ABA. Democrat. Jewish. Club: City Athletic (N.Y.C.). Home: 1125 Park Ave New York NY 10128 Office: Weil Gotshal & Manges 767 Fifth Ave New York NY 10153

COOPER, STUART LEONARD, chemical engineering educator, researcher, consultant; b. N.Y.C., Aug. 28, 1941; s. Jacob and Anna (Bloom) C.; m. Marilyn Portnoy, Aug. 29, 1966; children: Gary, Stacey. B.S., MIT, 1963; Ph.D., Princeton U., 1967. Asst. prof. chem. engring. U. Wis., Madison, 1967-71, assoc. prof., 1971-74, prof., 1974—, chmn. dept., 1983—; vis. assoc. prof. U. Calif.-Berkeley, 1974; vis. prof. Technion, Haifa, Israel, 1977; cons. in field; trustee Argonne Univs. Assn., Argonne Nat. Lab., 1975-81. Editor: Multiphase Polymers, 1979, Biomaterials: Interfacial Phenomena and Applications, 1982; contbr. numerous articles in field to profl. jours. Lady Davis fellow, 1977. Fellow Am. Phys. Soc.; mem. Am. Chm. Soc. (Best Paper award 1976), Am. Inst. Chem. Engrs., Am. Soc. Artificial Internal Organs, Soc. Biomaterials. Office: Univ Wis Dept Chem Engring Madison WI 53706

COOPER, SUSAN MARY, author; b. Burnham, Bucks, Eng., May 23, 1935; came to U.S., 1963; d. John Richard and Ethel May (Field) C.; m. Nicholas John Grant, Aug. 3, 1963 (div. 1983); children: Jonathan Roderick, Katharine Mary. M.A., Oxford (Eng.) U., 1956. Staff writer The Sunday Times, London, 1956-63; columnist Western Mail, Cardiff, Wales, 1963-72. Author: Mandrake, 1964, Behind the Golden Curtain: A View of the U.S.A, 1965, Over Sea, Under Stone, 1965, J.B. Priestley: Portrait of an Author, 1970, Dawn of Fear, 1970, The Dark is Rising (Boston Globe/Horn Book award), 1973 (Newbery Honor Book), Greenwitch, 1974, The Grey King, 1975 (Newbery medal), Silver on the Tree, 1977, Jethro and the Jumbie, 1979, The Silver Cow, 1983, Seaward, 1983, (with Hume Cronyn) Foxfire, a play with songs, 1983; Editor: Essays of Five Decades (J.B. Priestley), 1968; Contbr. articles to newspapers, mags., anthologies. Mem. Authors Guild, Soc. Authors, Writers Guild Am., ASCAP. Address: care Atheneum Publishers 597 Fifth Ave New York NY 10017

COOPER, THEODORE, pharmaceutical company executive, physician; b. Trenton, N.J., Dec. 28, 1928; s. Victor and Dora (Popkin) C.; m. Vivian Cecilia Evans, June 16, 1956; children—Michael Harris, Mary Katherine, Victoria Susan, Frank Victor. B.S., Georgetown U., 1949; M.D., St. Louis U., 1954, Ph.D., 1956. USPHS fellow St. Louis U. Dept. Physiology, 1955-56; clin. asso. surgery br. Nat. Heart Inst., Bethesda, Md., 1956-58; faculty St. Louis U., 1960-66, prof. surgery, 1964-66; prof., chmn. dept. pharmacology U. N.Mex., Albuquerque, 1966-68, on leave, 1967-69; assoc. dir. artificial heart, myocardial infarction programs Nat. Heart Inst., Bethesda, 1967-68; dir. Nat. Heart and Lung Inst., 1968-74; dep. asst. sec. for health HEW, 1974-75, asst. sec. health, 1975-77; dean Med. Coll., Cornell U., N.Y.C., 1977-80; provost for med. affairs Cornell U., 1977-80; exec. v.p. Upjohn Co., Kalamazoo, 1980—; mem. USPHS Pharmacology and Exptl. Therapeutics Study Sect., 1964-67; Bd. overseers Meml. Sloan-Kettering Cancer Center. Author: (with others) Nervous Control of the Heart, 1965, Heart Substitutes, 1966, The Baboon in Medical Research, Vol. II, 1967, Factors Influencing Myocardial Contractility, 1967, Acute Myocardial Infarction, 1968, Advance in Transplantation, Prosthetic Heart Valves, 1969, Depressed Metabolism, 1969; Editorial bd.: Jour. Pharmacology and Exptl. Therapeutics, 1965-68, 77—, Circulation Research, 1966-71; editor: Supplements to Circulation, 1966-71; sect. co-editor for: Jour. Applied Physiology, 1967-70; Contbr. numerous articles med. jours. Recipient Borden award, 1954; Albert Lasker Spl. Public Service award, 1978; Ellen Browning Scripps medal, 1980. Mem. Am. Soc. Pharmacology and Exptl. Therapeutics, Am. Physiol. Soc., Soc. Exptl. Biology and Medicine, Am. Soc. Clin. Investigation, Am. Fedn. Clin. Research, Am. Soc. Artificial Internal Organs, Internat. Cardiovascular Soc., Am. Coll. Chest Physicians, AAUP, Am. Coll. Cardiology, AAAS, Sigma Xi. Discoverer new techniques of denervating heart which have helped delineate role of nerves in heart, on its ability to function under a wide variety of circumstances, and on its ability to respond to drugs. Home: 3656 Woodcliff Dr Kalamazoo MI 49008 Office: Upjohn Co 7000 Portage Rd Kalamazoo MI 49001

COOPER, THEODORE GLESTON, drama educator; b. Miami, Fla., Aug. 14, 1939; s. Theodore Gladstone and Ruth T. (Greene) C.; m. Valerie W. Mills, Dec. 23, 1981; 1 dau. byprevious marriage, Maria Teresa; 1 dau., Irene Ruth. B.F.A., Howard U., 1971; M.A., U. Miami, 1972; doctoral candidate, Laurence U. Acct. exec. Fin. Programs of Denver, 1961-63; info. officer, then career devel. officer OEO, Washington, 1965-70; acct. exec. New Wave Communications, Washington, 1968-70; dir. pub. relations Dr. Martin Luther King Devel. Corp., Miami, 1971-72; prof. drama Howard U., Washington, 1973—, chmn. dept., 1972-78; founder Homecoming Dinner Theatre; founder, dir. M. Ensemble Co., Miami, 1971-74; dir. Colonial Players, Annapolis, Md., 1982—; founder, pres., artistic dir. Reminicense Inc., Washington, 1975—; bd. dirs., pres. EBO Arts, Annapolis, 1979—; bd. dirs. Danfort Assocs., 1980—; mem. adv. bd. (Ctr. for Ethnic Music, Coll. Fine Arts), 1981—; nat. cons. Ctr. for Study So. Culture, U. Miss., Oxford, 1981—. Author: novel Obeah, God od Voodoo, 1978; play Queen's Chillun; auhtor: A Town Called Tobyville; author: Chocolate Boy, Have You Seen Mommy Lately, Portrait of a Woman, Chickenbone Special, Goodnight Mary Beck; co-author: Onstage in America, 1984; assoc. editor: Afro-Am. Jour. Philosophy; editor-in-chief: Dascin Lit. Soc. Drama Jazz House Inc. Recipient letters of appreciation Coalition of One Hundred Black Women of D.C. Inc., Pennsylvania Ave. Devel. Corp., cert. for disting. service U. Without Walls, Howard U., 1980, U. D.C., 1982. Mem. Am. Theatre Assn., Capitol Hills Arts Workshop, Nat. Soc. Lit. and Arts, Internat. Platform Assn., Smithsonian Assocs., Am. Film Inst., Cultural Alliance D.C. Home: 33 Heritage Ct Annapolis MD 21401 Office: 2455 6th St Washington DC 20055

COOPER, THOMAS A., banker; b. Phila., July 19, 1936; m. June Danenberger; children: Aleta, Anita, Alane, Allison, Anne, Thomas. B.A., Haverford (Pa.) Coll., 1957; B.D., Drew U., 1960; postgrad., U. Pa.; P.M.D., Harvard U., 1973. Bd. dirs. S.E. chpt. ARC; trustee Haverford Coll., Thomas Jefferson U., Thomas Jefferson Hosp. Club: Brant Beach Yacht (vice commodore 1983). Office: Girard Bank Girard Plaza Philadelphia PA 19101

COOPER, THOMAS EDWARD, government official; b. Lindsey, Calif., May 31, 1943; s. James W. C. and Carmen (Kemper) Lewelling; m. Helen Schildknecht, June 15, 1968; 1 dau., Nichole. B.S.M.E., U. Calif.-Berkeley, 1966, M.S.M.E., 1967, Ph.D., 1970. Acting asst. prof. mech. engring. U. Calif.-Berkeley, 1970-71; asst. prof. mech. engring. Naval Postgrad. Sch., Monterey, Calif., 1971-74, assoc. prof., 1974-75; mem. profl. staff Com. on Armed services U.S. Ho. of Reps., Washington, 1976-83; asst. sec. of air force for research, devel. and logistics, Washington, 1983—; cons. Lawrence Radiation Lab., Livermore, Calif., Naval Weapons Ctr., China Lake, Calif., Naval Weapons Lab., Dahlgren, Va. Contbr. articles in heat transfer and bio-engring. to profl. jours. Recipient John Schieffelin medal Naval Postgrad. Sch., 1975. Mem. ASME, N.Am. Research Soc., Sigma Xi, Tau Beta Pi. Home: 827 Elaine Ct Alexandria VA 22308 Office: Hdqrs US Air Force The Pentagon Washington DC 20330

COOPER, THOMAS LUTHER, printing co. exec.; b. Statham, Ga., Sept. 30, 1917; s. William Henry and Ovelia Jane (Arnold) C.; m. Helen Brown, Aug. 30, 1941; 1 son, Thomas Luther. Student, Ga. State U., 1938-39, High Mus. Art, Atlanta, 1946. With Constn. Pub. Co., Atlanta, 1936-50, head photoengraving dept., 1947-50; pres. So. Engraving Co., Atlanta, 1950—, Photo Process Engraving Co., 1954—; pres., gen. mgr. So. Photo Process Engraving Co., Atlanta, 1955-76; v.p. Perry Communications, 1976—; v.p., dir. Beck Engraving Co., Inc., Phila., 1968-76; dir. J.M. Tull Metals Co., Inc. Exec. bd. Atlanta Area council Boy Scouts Am.; Trustee Shorter Coll., Rome, Ga.; mem. adv. council Ga. State U.; chmn. bd. Ga. State U. Found. Served to capt. USAAF, 1942-45. Recipient Craftsman of Year award Inland Printer and Am. Lithographer mag., 1961. Mem. Internat. Assn. Printing House Craftsmen (pres. 1959-60), Am. Photoengravers Assn. (exec. com. 1952-54), Southeastern Photoengravers Assn. (pres. 1951-52), Nat. Soc. Art Dirs., Printing Industry Atlanta, Advt. Club Atlanta, Mil. Order World Wars, Am. Legion. Baptist. Clubs: Mason (Shriner), Rotarian (pres. 1975), Rotarian (gov. dist. 690 of Ga. 1981-82), Commerce, Capital City (Atlanta). Home: 77 E Andrews Dr NW 211 Atlanta GA 30305 Office: 2181 Sylvan Rd SW Atlanta GA 30344

COOPER, WARREN STANLEY, manufacturing executive; b. N.J., Jan. 18, 1922; s. Edwin and Louise (Hartje) C.; children: Susan, Edwin, Scott. B.S., Drexel U., 1947, M.B.A., 1954. C.P.A., Mass. Indsl. engr., then office mgr. Container Corp. Am., 1947-50; asst. treas. Pioneer Folding Box Co., 1950- 54; partner Hitchcock & Co. (C.P.A.'s), Springfield, Mass., 1954-64; exec. v.p. Standex Internat. Corp., Salem, N.H., 1964-75, pres., chief operating officer, 1975—, also dir.; dir. Dentsply Inc., Doxey Mfg. Co., Dresher, Inc., Bingo King Inc. Served to 1st lt. USAAF, 1942-45. Mem. Am. Inst. C.P.A.s, Fin. Execs. Inst., Lambda Chi Alpha. Home: 64 Worcester Rd Hollis NH 03049 Office: Standex Internat Corp Manor Pkwy Salem NH 03079

COOPER, WESLEY PAUL, metalworking machines and equipment company executive; b. Lakewood, Ohio, Apr. 12, 1918; s. Andrew L. and Claudia J. (Nelson) C.; m. Cecil R. Meyer, Aug. 23, 1939; children: Douglas O., Kenneth C., Donald A., Karen Cooper Paytosh, Jennifer J., Paul L. Attended, Case Western Res. U., 1939, Advanced Mgmt. Program, Harvard U. Bus. Sch., 1963. With Acme-Cleveland Corp., Cleve., 1936—, pres., 1972—, chief exec. officer, 1975—, chmn. bd., 1981—, chmn. exec. com., 1983—; dir. Hayes-Albion Corp., AmeriTrust Corp., SIFCO Industries, Inc.; Trustee Codrington Found., State Troopers of Ohio; vice chmn., sec. Ednl. Research Council Am.; past pres. Associated Industries Cleve. Mem. Nat. Machine Tool Builders Assn. (dir.), Machinery and Allied Products Inst., Greater Cleve. Growth Assn. Mem. United Ch. of Christ. Clubs: Union, University, Avon Oaks Country, Pepper Pike. Office: Acme-Cleveland Corp 30195 Chagrin Blvd Suite 300 Cleveland OH 44124

COOPER, WILLIAM EUGENE, consulting engineer; b. Erie, Pa., Jan. 11, 1924; s. William Hall and Ruth E. (Dunn) C.; m. Louise I. Ferguson, June 23, 1946; children: Margaret, Glenn, Keith, Joyce, Carol. Student, Stevens Inst. Tech., 1941-43; B.S., Oreg. State Coll., 1947, M.S., 1948; Ph.D., Purdue U., 1951. Instr. Purdue U., 1948-52; cons. engr. Knolls Atomic Power Lab., Gen. Electric Co., 1952-63; engring. mgr. Lessells and Assos., Waltham, Mass., 1963-68; sr. v.p., tech. dir. Teledyne Materials Research, Waltham, 1968-76; cons. engr. Teledyne Engring. Services, Waltham, 1976—. Contbr. articles to tech. jours. Served with AUS, 1943-46. Named Distinguished Engring. Alumnus Purdue U., 1974. Fellow ASME (B.F. Langer Nuclear Codes and Standards award 1978, hon. mem. boiler and pressure vessel com. 1980, v.p. codes and standards and mem. exec. com. of council 1980-81, v.p. codes and standards 1981-84, Pressure Vessel and Piping medal 1983); mem. Soc. Exptl. Stress Analysis (Murray lectr. 1977), Am. Nat. Standards Inst. (dir. 1981-84), Sigma Xi, Pi Tau Sigma, Sigma Pi Sigma. Home: 83 Fifer Ln Lexington MA 02173 Office: 130 2d Ave Waltham MA 02254

COOPER, WILLIAM JAMES, JR., history educator; b. Kingstree, S.C., Oct. 22, 1940; s. William James and Mamie (Mayes) C.; m. Patricia Holmes, Sept. 1, 1962; children: William James III, Michael Holmes. A.B., Princeton U., 1962; Ph.D., Johns Hopkins U., 1966. Asst. prof. history La. State U., Baton Rouge, 1968-70, assoc. prof., 1970-78, prof., 1978—, dean Grad. Sch., 1982—. Author: The Conservative Regime: South Carolina 1877-1890, 1968, The South and the Politcs of Slavery 1828-1856, 1978, Liberty and Slavery: Southern Politics to 1860, 1983; editor: Social Relations in Our Southern States (Daniel Hundley), 1979, So. Biography Series, 1979—. Served to capt. U.S. Army, 1966-68. Sr. fellow Inst. So. History, Johns Hopkins U., 1971-72; research fellow Charles Warren Ctr. Studies in Am History, Harvard U., 1975-76; Guggenheim fellow, 1980-81; named Disting. Research Master La. State U., 1980. Mem. Am. Hist. Assn., Orgn. Am. Historians, So. Hist. Assn., Soc. Historians of Early Republic. Presbyterian. Home: 250 Amherst Ave Baton Rouge LA 70808 Office: Dept History La State U Baton Rouge LA 70803

COOPER, WILLIAM MARION, physician; b. Pitts., Jan. 12, 1919; s. Lardin Monroe and Sophia Antoinette (Swartz) C.; m. Sara Georgia Thomas, Jan. 19, 1942; children—Mikell Lee Cooper Schenck, William Marion, Thomas L., George Robert. B.S., Pa. State U., 1939; M.D., Hahnemann Med. Coll., 1943. Diplomate: Am. Bd. Internal Medicine, Am. Bd. Hematology. Intern Shadyside Hosp., Pitts., 1943; resident U. Pitts. Sch. Medicine, 1946-48, Cleve. Clin. Found., 1948; practice medicine specializing in internal medicine and hematology, Pitts., 1948—; mem. staff Presbyn.-Univ., Shadyside, Western Pa., Magee Woman's Hosps.; chief dept. medicine Shadyside Hosp., 1980; mem. med. faculty U. Pitts., 1948—, clin. prof. medicine, 1958—, dir. div. continuing edn., 1970-80, asso. dean continuing edn., 1974-80; dir. continuing edn. Univ. Health Center, Pitts., 1975-80; Med. dir. Central Blood Bank, Pitts., 1951-60, Pitts. Skin and Cancer Found., 1958-65. Contbr. articles to med. jours. Served with M.C. U.S. Army, 1944-45. Mem. AMA, Pa., Allegheny County med. socs., Am., Internat. socs. hematology, A.C.P. (bd. govs. 1965-71), Am. Assn. Med. Colls., Am. Soc. Internal Medicine, AAAS. Clubs: Oakmont (Pa.) Country; Univ. (Pitts.). Home: 813 W Waldheim St Pittsburgh PA 15215 Office: 4815 Liberty Ave Pittsburgh PA 15224

COOPER, WILLIAM WAGER, educator; b. Birmingham, Ala., July 23, 1914; s. William Wager and Rae (Rossman) C.; m. Ruth Fay West, Sept. 11, 1944. A.B., U. Chgo., 1938; postgrad., Columbia U., 1940-42; D.Sc. (hon.), Ohio State U., 1969, M.A., Harvard U., 1976, D.Sc., Carnegie-Mellon U., 1982. Asst. to comptroller TVA, 1938-40; prin. economist Bur. Budget, 1942-44; asst. prof. econs. U. Chgo., 1944-46; asst. prof. to prof. Carnegie-Mellon U., 1946-68, dean, 1968-75, Univ. prof. mgmt. sci. and pub. affairs, 1975-76, research prof. mgmt. sci. and pub. policy, 1976—; Arthur Lowes Dickinson prof. accounting Grad. Sch. Bus. Adminstrn., Harvard U., 1976-80; Foster Parker prof. fin. mgmt. and acctg. Grad. Sch. Bus. Adminstrn. U. Tex., Austin, 1980—. Author: (with A. Charnes) Management Models and Industrial Applications of Linear Programming, (with H. Leavitt, M.W. Shelly) New Perspectives in Organization Research, (with others) Studies in Budgeting, (with A. Charnes and R. Niehaus) Studies in Manpower Planning, (with Y. Ijiri) Eric Louis Kohler: Accounting's Man of Principles; Editorial bd.: Auditing: A Jour. Practice and Theory; contbr. articles to profl. jours. Co-recipient John Von Neumann Theory prize, 1982. Fellow Econometric Soc., AAAS, Inst. Constructive Capitalism; mem. Inst. Mgmt. Sci. (past pres.), Ops. Research Soc. Am. (editorial bd. 1957-68). Home: 4 Hillside Ct Austin TX 78746

COOPERMAN, BARRY S., educational administrator, educator, scientist; b. N.Y.C., Dec. 11, 1941; m., 1963; 2 children. B.A., Columbia U., 1962; Ph.D. in Chemistry, Harvard U., 1968. NATO fellow biochemistry Pasteur Inst., 1967-68; from asst. prof. to assoc. prof. dept. chemitry U. Pa., 1968-77, prof. bioorganic chemistry, 1977—, v.p. for research, 1982—. Trustee Assoc. Univs., Inc., 1983—. Mem. Am. Soc. Biol. Chemists, Am. Chem. Soc. Research in field mechanism of phosphoryl transfer enzymes; photoaffinity labels for ribosome and adenylic acid receptor sites. Office: Dept Chemistry 358 Chemistry Univ Pa Philadelphia PA 19104 *

COOPERMAN, LEON G., investment company executive; b. N.Y.C., Apr. 25, 1943; s. Harry and Martha (Rosenstein) C.; m. Toby F.; children: Wayne M., Michael S. B.A., CUNY-Hunter Coll., 1964; M.B.A., Columbia U., 1967. Cert. fin. analyst. Quality control engr. Xerox Corp., Webster, N.Y., 1965-67; ptnr. Goldman, Sachs & Co., N.Y.C., 1967—. Trustee United Jewish Appeal, N.J., 1980. Mem. Fin. Analyst Fedn. (dir. 1980—), N.Y. Soc. Security Analysts (pres. 1980). Club: Atlantis Yacht (Monmouth Beach, N.J.). Home: 45 Watchung Rd Short Hills NJ 07078 Office: Goldman Sachs and Co 55 Broad St New York NY 10004 *

COOPERRIDER, LUKE K., law educator; b. 1918. B.S., Harvard U., 1940; J.D., U. Mich., 1948. Bar: Ohio 1949. Assoc. Squire, Sanders and Dempsey, Cleve., 1948-52; asst. prof. U. Mich., Ann Arbor, 1952-55, assoc. prof., 1955-58, prof., 1958-83, prof. emeritus, 1983—; vis. prof. U. Ga., 1979. Past mem. editorial bd. (Mich. Law Rev.). Served with U.S. Army, 1941-46. Mem. Order of Coif. Address: 12424 Firebird Dr Sun City West AZ 85375

COOPERRIDER, TOM SMITH, botanist; b. Newark, Ohio, Apr. 15, 1927; s. Oscar Harold and Ruth Evelyn (Smith) C.; m. Miwako Kunimura, June 13, 1953; children: Julie Ann, John Andrew. B.A., Denison U., 1950; M.S., U. Iowa, 1955, Ph.D. (NSF fellow), 1958. Instr. biol. scis. Kent (Ohio) State U., 1958-61, asst. prof., 1961-65, asso. prof., 1965-69, prof., 1969—, dir. exptl. programs, 1972-73, curator herbarium, 1968—; dir. Bot. Gardens and Arboretum, 1972—; mem. editorial bd. Univ. Press, 1976-79; on leave as asst. prof. dept. botany U. Hawaii, 1962-63; NSF researcher Mountain Lake Biol. Sta., U. Va., summer 1958; faculty mem. Iowa Lakeside Lab., U. Iowa, summer 1965; cons. endangered and threatened species U.S. Fish and Wildlife Service, Dept. Interior, 1976—; cons. Davey Tree Expert Co., 1979—, Ohio Natural Areas Council, 1983—. Author: Ferns and Other Pteridophytes of Iowa, 1959, Vascular Plants of Clinton, Jackson and Jones Counties, Iowa, 1962; editor: Endangered and Threatened Plants of Ohio, 1983. Served with U.S. Army, 1945-46. NSF predoctoral fellow, 1957-58; NSF research grantee, 1965-72. Fellow Ohio Acad. Scis. (v.p. 1967), Explorers Club; mem. Am. Soc. Plant Taxonomists, Internat. Assn. Plant Taxonomists, AAAS, Bot. Soc. Am., Nature Conservancy, Wilderness Soc., Blue Key, Sigma Xi. Home: 548 Bowman Dr Kent OH 44240

COOPERSTEIN, SHERWIN JEROME, medical educator; b. N.Y.C., Sept. 14, 1923; s. Joseph and Bessie (Berger) C.; m. Alice Ruth Peskin, June 1, 1947; children—Rhonda Ann, Lawrence Alan. B.S., Coll. City N.Y., 1943; D.D.S., N.Y. U., 1948; Ph.D. in Anatomy, Western Res. U., 1951. Instr. biology Coll. City N.Y., 1943, 46-48; research asso. physiology N.Y. U., 1946-48; instr. anatomy Western Res. U., 1948-49, fellow anatomy, 1949-51, sr. instr., 1951-52, asst. prof. anatomy, 1952-55, asso. prof., 1955-64, asst. dean, 1957-64; prof., head dept. anatomy U. Conn. Schs. Medicine and Dental Medicine, Farmington, 1964—; Mem. adv. panel on med. student research NSF, 1960-61; mem. anatomical scis. tng. com. Nat. Inst. Gen. Med. Scis., 1966-70; mem. spl. study sect. on diabetes centers NIH, 1973-75, mem. ad hoc study sect. on research tng. grants in systems and integrative biology, 1977; mem. adv. panel on research personnel needs in basic biomed. sci. Nat. Acad. Scis./NRC, 1976—. Contbr. articles profl. jours.; editorial adviser: Diabetes Lit. Index, 1966-79. Served with AUS, 1943-44. Mem. AAAS, Am. Chem. Soc., Marine Biol. Lab., Am. Assn. Anatomists, Assn. Anatomy Chairmen, Assn. Am. Med. Colls., Am. Soc. Biol. Chemists, Am. Diabetes Assn., Sigma Xi. Home: 10 Hillsboro Dr West Hartford CT 06107 Office: U Conn Health Center Farmington Ave Farmington CT 06032

COOR, LATTIE FINCH, university president; b. Phoenix, Sept. 26, 1936; s. Lattie F. and Elnora (Witten) C.; m. Ina Fitzhenry, Jan. 18, 1964; children: William Kendall, Colin Fitzhenry, Farryl MacKenna Witten. A.B. with high honors (Phelps Dodge scholar), No. Ariz. U., 1958; M.A. with honors (Univ. scholar, Universal Match Found. fellow, Carnegie Corp. fellow), Washington U., St. Louis, 1960, Ph.D., 1964; LL.D. (hon.), Marlboro Coll., 1977, Am. Coll. Greece, 1982. Adminstrv. asst. to Gov. Mich., 1961-62; asst. to chancellor Washington U., St. Louis, 1963-67, asst. dean Grad. Sch. Arts and Scis., 1967-69, dir. internat. studies, 1967-69, asst. prof. polit. sci., 1967-76, vice chancellor, 1969-74, univ. vice chancellor, 1974-76; pres. U. Vt., Burlington, 1976—; cons. HEW; spl. cons. U.S. Commr. Edn., 1971-74; chmn. commn. on govtl. relations Am. Council on Edn., 1976-80; dir. New Eng. Bd. Higher Edn., 1976—; Co-chmn. joint com. on health policy Assn. Am. Univs. and Nat. Assn. State Univs. and Land Grant Colls., 1976—. Mem. Nat. Assn. State Univs. and Land Grant Colls. (exec. com.), New Eng. Assn. Schs. and Colls. (pres. 1981-82), New Eng. State Univ. Assn. Office: Office of Pres Univ Vt Waterman Bldg Burlington VT 05401

COORS, JOSEPH, brewery executive; b. 1917. With Adolph Coors Co., Golden, Colo., v.p., 1947, vice chmn., 1975, pres., 1977—, vice chmn., chief operating officer, 1982—. Office: Adolph Coors Co East of Town Golden CO 80401 *

COORS, PETER HANSON, beverage company executive; b. Denver, Sept. 20, 1946; s. Joseph and Holly (Hanson) C.; m. Marilyn Gross, Aug. 23, 1969; children: Melissa, Christien, Carrie Ann, Ashley, Peter, David. B.S. in Idsl. Engring., Cornell U., 1969; M.B.A., U. Denver, 1970. Prodn. trainee, specialist Adolph Coors Co., Golden, Colo., 1970-71, dir. fin. planning, 1971-75, dir. market research, 1975-76, v.p. self distbn., 1976-77, v.p. sales and mktg., 1977-78, sr. v.p. sales and mktg., 1978-82, div. pres. sales, mktg. and adminstrn., 1982—; pres. Coors Distbn. Co., 1976-82, 1976-81, chmn., 1981—, dir., Adolph Coors Co., 1973—, asst. sec.-treas., 1974-76; dir. CADGO, 1975—; pres., chmn., dir. Adolph Coors Co., 1977—. Bd. dirs. Nat. Wildlife Fedn., 1978-81; hon. bd. dirs. Colo. Spl. Olympics Inc., 1978—; trustee Colo. Outward Bound Sch., 1978—, Adolph Coors Found., Regis Edn. Corp., Pres.'s Leadership Com., U. Colo., 1978—; chmn. Nat. Commn. on the Future of Regis Coll., 1981-82; chmn. devel. com. Regis Coll., 1983—; mem. Colo. State Fair Commn., 1982—. Mem. Mountain Bicyclist Assn. (dir. 1978—), Ducks Unlimited (nat. trustee 1979, sr. v.p., mem. mgmt. com., exec. com. 1982—, dir. Can. 1982—). Clubs: Met. Denver Exec. (dir 1979, pres. 1981—. Office: Adolph Coors Co Mail 339 Golden Co 80401

COORS, WILLIAM K., brewery executive; b. Golden, Colo., 1916. Chmn. bd., chief exec. officer Adolph Coors Co., Golden. Office: Adolph Coors Co Golden CO 80401 *

COORTS, GERALD DUANE, horticulturist; b. Emden, Ill., Feb. 3, 1932; s. Ralph Albert and Hannah Tena (Wubben) C.; m. Annette Bosman, Sept. 14, 1957; children—David Jonathan, Charles Frederick, Cynthia Anne. B.S. (Danforth fellow), U. Mo., 1954, M.S., 1958; Ph.D., U. Ill., 1964. Instr. horticulture Purdue U., 1959-61; asst. prof. horticulture U. R.I., 1964-68; asso. prof. plant and soil sci. So. Ill. U., Carbondale, 1968-72, prof., 1972—, chmn. dept., 1973—. Bd. dirs. Jackson County YMCA, 1975-81, Green Earth, Inc. Served to 1st lt. Chem. Corps AUS, 1954-56. Recipient Obelisk award for outstanding teaching, 1972. Mem. U.S. Jr. C. of C. (chpt. v.p. 1966-67), Am. Soc. Hort. Sci., Am. Soc. Agronomy, Am. Hort. Soc., Council Agr. Sci. and Tech., Plant Growth Regulator Soc. Am., Soc. Am. Florists, Sigma Xi (chpt. pres. 1982-83), Alpha Zeta, Gamma Sigma Delta, Pi Alpha Xi, Phi Mu Alpha, Phi Sigma, Phi Kappa Phi, FarmHouse. Club: Kiwanis (dir. chpt. 1983-84). Home: 1714 Colonial Dr Carbondale IL 62901 *I attribute whatever success I have attained to having been raised on the farm and learning first-hand about "the world of work." My father was a task master who demanded and received high standards of performance from his sons.*

COOVER, HARRY WESLEY, mfg. co. exec.; b. Newark, Del., Mar. 6, 1919; s. Harry Wesley and Anna (Rohm) C.; m. Muriel Zumbach, Sept. 17, 1941; children—Harry Wesley, Stephen R., Melinda Coover Paul. B.S. in Chemistry (Southerland prize 1941), Hobart Coll., Geneva, N.Y., 1941; M.S., Cornell U., 1942, Ph.D., 1944. Research chemist Eastman Kodak Co., Rochester, N.Y., 1944-49; sr. research chemist Tenn. Eastman Co., Kingsport, 1949-54, research asso., 1954-63, head polymers div., 1963-65, dir. research, 1965-73, v.p., 1970-73, exec. v.p., 1973-81; v.p. Eastman Kodak Co., Kingsport, 1981—. Author. Mem. Internat. Union Pure and Applied Chemistry, Am. Chem. Soc. (So. Chemist award 1960, Speaker of Year award N.E. Tenn. sect. 1962), AAAS, Am. Assn. Textile Tech., Am. Inst. Chemists, Assn. Research Dirs., Dirs. Indsl. Research, Indsl. Research Inst. (pres. 1981-82), Soc. Chem. Industry, Soc. Plastics Industry, Textile Research Inst. (trustee), N.Y. Acad. Scis. Presbyterian. Clubs: Lions, Masons. Patentee in field. Office: 1101 Eastman Rd PO Box 3866 Kingsport TN 37664

COOVER, ROBERT LOWELL, author; b. Charles City, Iowa, Feb. 4, 1932; s. Grant Marion and Maxine (Sweet) C.; m. Maria del Pilar Sans-Mallafre, June 3, 1959; children—Diana Nin, Sara Chapin, Roderick Luis. B.A., Ind. U., 1953; M.A., U. Chgo., 1965. Instr. Bard Coll., 1966 67, U. Iowa, 1967-69, Columbia U., 1972, Princeton U., 1972-73, Va. Mil. Inst., 1976, Brown U., 1980-81, Brandeis U., 1981. (Recipient William Faulkner award for best first novel 1966, citation in Fiction, Brandeis U. 1970); Author: The Origin of the Brunists, 1966, The Universal Baseball Association, J. Henry Waugh, Prop, 1968, Pricksongs and Descants, 1969; plays A Theological Position, 1972, The Water Pourer, 1972; film On a Confrontation in Iowa City, 1969, The Public Burning, 1977, Hair O' the Chine, 1979, After Lazarus, 1980, Charlie in the House of Rue, 1980, A Political Fable (The Cat in the Hat for President), 1980, Spanking the Maid, 1981. Served with USNR, 1953-57. Rockefeller grantee, 1969; Guggenheim fellow, 1971, 74; Acad. Arts and Letters awardee, 1976. Address: care Georges Borchardt 136 E 57th St New York NY 10022

COPE, DAVID HOWELL, composer, author, educator; b. San Francisco, May 17, 1941; s. Howell Nicolson and Charlotte Evelyn (Schleicher) C.; m. Mary Jane Stluka, Aug. 12, 1967; children: Tim, Steve, Brian, Gregory. Mus.B., Ariz. State U., 1963; Mus.M., U. So. Calif., 1965. Lectr. music Kans. State Coll., 1966-68, Calif. Luth. Coll., 1969; lectr. Cleve. Inst. Music, 1970-73; asst. prof., resident composer Miami U., Oxford, Ohio, 1973-78; prof. U. Calif. at Santa Cruz, 1978—; lectr. in field; vis. composer numerous univs. Author: New Directions In Music, 1971, 2d edit., 1976, New Music Notation, 1976, New Music Composition, 1976; editor: Composer Mag, 1967-80; contbr. numerous articles to profl. jours.; Composer numerous compositions, including; orch. Streams; band Re-birth; chamber ensemble Margins; brass choir and percussion Requiem for Bosque Redondo; cello and tape Arena; orch. Threshold and Visions; flute and piano Triplum; piano, wind orch. Variations; Recorded: Iceberg Meadow, 1968, K, Weeds, 1970, Variations for Piano and Wind Orch, 1973, Re-birth, 1975, Cycles, 1975, Bright Angel, 1976, Threshold and Visions, 1979. Miami U. Faculty Research fellow, 1973-74; NEA fellow, 1976; at McDowell Colony, 1979. Mem. ASCAP (Standard Panel award 1971-83), Am. Soc. Univ. Composers, Phi Mu Alpha Sinfonia, Pi Kappa Lambda. Home: 317 Nobel Dr Santa Cruz CA 95060 *I venture to touch the symbiotic relationships between the sonic spectrum of the cultural and personal guts of humankind.*

COPE, HAROLD CARY, former university president; b. Westown, Pa., Aug. 9, 1918; s. Joshua A. and Edith (Cary) C.; m. Ann Elizabeth Reeves, Apr. 17, 1943; children: David Harold, Sarah Ann, Elizabeth R., Hannah Sue. B.S., Cornell U., 1941; postgrad., U. Omaha, 1953-54, U. Mich., 1959. Supr. student union cafeteria Cornell U., 1941-42; dietician Earlham Coll., 1946-49, mgr. resident halls, 1949-52, mgr. resident halls, accountant, 1952-55, asst. comptroller, 1955-58, bus. mgr., 1958-67, v.p. bus. affairs, 1967-72; pres. Friends U., Wichita, Kans., 1972-79, pres. emeritus, 1979—, cons., staff worker deferred giving, 1979-82, chmn. fin. com., 1980-82; mem. Kans. State adv. bd. Title I Funds, 1974-79. Active Cub Scouts Am., 1947-51; chmn. stewardship and fin. bd. 5 Years Meeting, Soc. of Friends, 1960-66, mem. exec. council, 1960-70, nat. bd. com., 1966-72; pres. Friends Extension Corp., 1963-72; bd. dirs., treas. Friends Fellowship Retirement Home, 1964-70; clk. White Water Monthly Meeting of Friends, 1963-66, Ind. Yearly Meeting, 1965-71, Univ. Friends Ch., 1980-82; mem. nat. bd. dirs. Am. Friends Service Com., 1968-74, 79—, mem. exec. com., 1970-74; Chmn. Richmond (Ind.) Housing Authority, 1968-72; mem. Sedgwick County Zoo Adv. Bd., 1973-79, Wichita Alcoholism Task Force, 1972-74; sec. Kans. Found. Pvt. Coll.-Secondary Schs., 1973-75; Bd. dirs., sec. Quaker Hill Found., 1969-72; treas., bd. dirs. Partnership for Productivity Found., 1969-72; bd. dirs., mem. exec. com. Richmond YMCA, 1969-72; bd. dirs. Sunflowers Ednl. TV Corp., 1972-74, Salvation Army, 1976-82, Wichita United Way, 1977-82; chmn. planning div. Wichita United Way, 1979-82; trustee Friends United Meeting, 1971—, chmn., 1975—; chmn. bd. advs. Earlham Sch. Religion Sem., 1979—. Mem. Ind. Assn. Bus. Officers (pres. 1960-61), Central Assn. Bus. Officers (mem. exec. com. 1970-71), Am. Assn. Pres.'s Ind. Colls. and Univs. (sec. 1974-76, v.p. 1976—), Wichita C. of C. Clubs: Kiwanian (dir. 1967-72), Rotarian., Y's Mens (pres. 1959-60), Y's Mens (dist. gov. 1960-61). Home: Pendle Hill Wallingford PA 19086

COPE, JACKSON IRVING, English language educator; b. Muncie, Ind., Sept. 1, 1925; s. Raymond M. and Helen (Jackson) C.; m. Paula Maureen Doss, 1979; children by previous marriage: Dryden, Tami, Cameron. B.A., U. Ill., 1950; Ph.D., Johns Hopkins U., 1952. Instr. Ohio State U., 1952-54; asst. prof. Washington U., 1954-58; assoc. prof., then prof. Rice U., 1958-62; mem. faculty Johns Hopkins, 1962-72, prof. English, 1963-72; Leo S. Bing prof. English U. So. Calif., 1972—; vis. Butler prof. SUNY, Buffalo, 1978; resident scholar Rockefeller Found., Bellagio, 1981; mem. exec. com. Humanities Inst., 1981—, exec. sec., 1982—. Author: Joseph Glanvill, Anglican Apologist, 1956, The Metaphoric Structure of Paradise Lost, 1962, The Theater and the Dream, 1973, Joyce's Cities, 1981; editor (Thomas Sprat): History of the Royal Soc, 1958; (Joseph Glanvill), Plus Ultra, 1958, Novel vs. Fiction: The Contemporary Reformation, 1981. Served to 2d lt. USAAF, 1943-45. Bissing fellow, 1954-55; Folger Library fellow, 1954, 60; Guggenheim fellow, 1958-59; Am. Council Learned Socs. fellow, 1963-64. Mem. MLA, Renaissance Soc. Am., Malone Soc., James Joyce Found., Am. Soc. for 18th Century Studies, Phi Beta Kappa, Phi Kappa Phi. Office: English Dept Univ So Calif Los Angeles CA 90089-0354

COPE, KENNETH WAYNE, chain store executive; b. Rifle, Colo., May 31, 1924; s. William Grant and Mary (Park) C.; m. Patricia Miller, Feb. 1, 1946; children: Kimberly Ann, Bradley Mark. B.A., La Sierra Coll., Arlington, Calif., 1948; postgrad., U. Wash., 1948-50. C.P.A., Calif. From staff accountant to mgr. Price Waterhouse & Co., C.P.A.s, Los Angeles, 1950-58, resident mgr., Phoenix, 1959-63; regional controller Lucky Stores, Inc., San Leandro, Calif., 1963-68, v.p., corp. controller, 1968—. Served with AUS, 1943-46. Mem. Am. Inst. C.P.A.s, Calif. Soc. C.P.A.s, Fin. Execs. Inst. Republican. Episcopalian. Home: 1683 Graff Ave San Leandro CA 94577 Office: 6300 Clark Ave Dublin CA 94566

COPE, LEWIS, newspaper reporter; b. Sweetwater, Tex., June 24, 1934; s. Millard L. and Margaret Wallace (Kilgore) C.; m. Betty Joan Ball, June 28, 1958; children—Margaret, Elizabeth, Mary Amelia. B.A., Washington and Lee U., Lexington, Va., 1955, Columbia U. Grad. Sch. Journalism, 1963-64. Reporter Greenville (Tex.) Herald-Banner, 1957-60; copy editor Richmond (Va.) Times Dispatch, 1960-62; copy editor, news editor San Antonio Express, 1962-66; sci. reporter Mpls. Tribune, 1966—; Council Advancement Sci. Writing writer-in-residence Nat. Cancer Inst., 1976. Author: Save Your Life, 1979. Served as officer AUS, 1955-57. Recipient award merit Am. Assn. Blood Banks, 1974, Journalism award Am. Acad. Family Physicians, 1976, 79, Penney award lifestyle reporting U. Mo., 1977, Nat. Media award Am. Cancer Soc., 1977, Blakeslee award Am. Heart Assn., 1979, Cecil award Arthritis Found., 1982. Mem. Nat. Assn. Sci.

Writers (exec. com. 1982—), Sigma Delta Chi (pres. Minn. chpt. 1973-74, dep. regional dir. 1974—). Episcopalian. Home: 5217 W 91st St Bloomington MN 55437 Office: 425 Portland Ave Minneapolis MN 55488

COPELAND, DARRYL WADE, engineering and technical services company executive; b. Uhricsville, Ohio, Oct. 30, 1936; s. Carl Henry and Emma Belva (Guilder) C.; m. Shirley Ann Bradley, Dec. 28, 1957; children: Darryl Wade, Carl Bradley, Thomas Brian. B.S.E.E., Duke U., 1958; M.S., Johns Hopkins U., 1965; spl. grad., MIT, 1959. Engr. Westinghouse Electric Corp., Balt., 1961-64; v.p. H.L. Yoh Co., Phila., 1964-70, sr. v.p., 1970-75; pres. Cole-Layer-Trumble Co., Dayton, Ohio, 1975-80; exec. v.p. Day & Zimmermann Inc., Phila., 1980—. Served to capt. USAF, 1958-61. Mem. Am. Def. Preparedness Assn., Internat. Assn. Assessing Officers. Republican. Methodist. Clubs: Tavistock Country, Seaview Country, Peale, Vesper. Lodges: Masons; Shriners. Home: 1241 Charleston Rd Cherry Hill NJ 08034 Office: 1818 Market St Philadelphia PA 19103

COPELAND, DONALD EUGENE, research marine biologist; b. Mendon, Ohio, Feb. 6, 1912; s. Arland Murlin and Chloe (Severns) C.; m. Marjorie Groves, June 20, 1941; children: Sandra Kay, Jane Hance, Diana Sue. A.B., Rochester U., 1935; M.A., Amherst Coll., 1937; Ph.D., Harvard U., 1941. Instr. zoology U. N.C., 1941-42; asst. then assoc. prof. zoology Brown U., 1946-51; chief aviation physiologist Office Surgeon Gen., USAF, 1951-53; profl. assoc. Nat. Acad. Scis.-NRC, 1953-56; exec. sec. NIH, 1956-59; prof. zoology Tulane U., 1959-77, prof. emeritus, 1977—, chmn. dept., 1959-65; mem. (Marine Biol. Lab.), Woods Hole, Mass., 1948—, ind. investigator, 1977—; Mem. morphology and genetics study sect., physiology study sect. NIH, 1952-53. Served to capt. USAAF, 1942-46. Mem. Am. Assn. Anatomists, Am. Soc. Zoologists, Soc. Study Devel. and Growth, Am. Soc. Cell Biologists, Am. Physiol. Soc. Research histophysiology and ultra structure salt secreting mechanisms, gas secretion in swim bladders, oxygen elevation in fish eye, secretion of aqueous humor in fish eye. Home: 41 Fern Ln Woods Hole MA 02543

COPELAND, GEORGE FREDERICK, bearing company executive; b. St. Thomas, Ont., Can., May 15, 1923; came to U.S., 1950; s. Harley Anon and Irene Grace (Hepburn) C. (Sinclair); m. Lillian Marie Roden, Dec. 8, 1945; children: Stephen George, Susan Irene, Richard Harley. Sr. matriculator, London (Ont., Can.) Seuth Collegiate, 1942; student, Queens U., Kingston, Ont., Can., 1943, Am. Inst. for Fgn. Trade, Phoenix, 1959, Harvard Bus. Sch., 1967. Div. indsl. engr. Timken Co., Canton, Ohio, 1957-58; pres. Timken Co. Brazil, Sao Paulo, 1959-66, Can. Timken Ltd., St. Thomas, 1966-73, Tyson Bearing Co., Glasgow, Ky., 1973-79; pres., chief exec. officer Brenco Inc., Petersburg, Va., 1980—. Pres. St. Thomas Bd. Trade, St. Thomas Art Gallery. Recipient City of St. Thomas Dedicated Service to Community award, 1973, award Soc. Advancement Mgmt., 1973. Mem. Am. Inst. Indsl. Engrs. (v.p. 1959-60, contbn. to indsl. engrig. award 1967). Republican. Presbyterian. Clubs: Country of Petersberg, Jordan Point Country; Downtown (Richmond, Va.). Home: 3007 Riverside Ave Hopewell VA 23860 Office: Branco Inc Petersburg Indsl Park Petersburg VA 23804

COPELAND, HUNTER ARMSTRONG, real estate financial executive; b. Birmingham, Ala., Oct. 22, 1918; s. Miles Axe and Leonora (Armstrong) C.; m. Courteney Bass, May 27, 1978; children: Susan Diane Copeland Locke, Hunter Armstrong, John McGregor, Miles, Ann Armstrong. Student, U. Ala., 1936-37; grad. advanced mgmt. course, Harvard U., 1952. Mortgage appraiser Prudential Ins. Co. Am., Birmingham, 1946-54; mortgage broker Huntoon-Paige, N.Y.C., 1954-57; pres. Huntoon Copeland & Hedin, N.Y.C., 1958-70; exec. dir. Hunter Copeland and Assos., N.Y.C., 1970-75; v.p. Colwell Co., N.Y.C., 1970-75; pres. Copeland-Tresnan & Hornblower Inc., N.Y.C., 1975-78, Hunter Copeland and Assos., Birmingham, Ala., 1978—; trustee Md. Realty Trust, Balt.; organizer, dir. New Canaan Bank & Trust Co., Conn.; mem. Ala. Cert. Bd. Alcoholism and Drug Counselors. Bd. dirs. Nat. Council on Alcoholism; exec. dir. Alcoholism Council of Central Ala.; pres. Brookwood Lodge Found., Inc., Birmingham; mem. Republican Nat. Com. Served with inf. AUS, 1941-45; to col. USAF, 1952-54. Decorated Silver Star, Bronze Star with 4 oak leaf clusters, Purple Heart with oak leaf cluster.; named to Inf. Officers Hall of Fame, Ft. Benning, Ga., 1982. Mem. Mortgage Bankers Assn. Am., Mortgage Bankers Assn. N.Y. (gov.), Am. Pub. Health Assn., Nat. Assn. Alcoholism and Drug Abuse Counselors, Internat. Council Alcohol and Addictions, Nat. Assn. Children of Alcoholics, Jellinek Med. Assn., Nat. Rifle Assn., Nat. Skeet Assn., Ducks Unltd., Newcomen Soc., USAF Assn., Mil. Order World Wars, Oceanic Soc., Smithsonian Inst., Def. Orientation Conf. Assn., U.S. Senatorial Club, Am. Mus. Natural History, Nat. Trust Hist. Preservation, Met. Mus. Art, Birmingham Mus. Art, Birmingham Bot. Soc., Birmingham Hist. Soc., Better Bus. Bur. Birmingham, Birmingham C. of C., Commerce Exec. Soc. of U. Ala., Nat. Security Council (nat. adv. bd.), Chi Phi. Clubs: Kiwanis; Union League, Met. (N.Y.C.); New Canaan Field, Monday Morning Quarterback; Country of Birmingham, The Club, Birmingham, Relay House (Birmingham). Office: Suite 401 Med Towers Bldg Birmingham AL 35203 also 14E 52d St New York NY 10022

COPELAND, JAMES WILLIAM, state supreme ct. justice; b. Woodland, N.C., June 16, 1914; s. Luther Clifton and Nora Lucille (Benthall) C.; m. Nancy Hill Sawyer, Oct. 11, 1941; children—Emily Robinson, James William, Buxton Sawyer. A.B., Guilford Coll., 1934; J.D. with honors, U. N.C., 1937; grad., Nat. Coll. State Trial Judges, Reno, 1968, 72, Sr. Appellate Judges Conf., N.Y. U., 1977. Bar: N.C. bar 1936. Practiced in, Woodland, 1937-41, Murfreesboro, 1946-61; chmn. Bd. Elections Northampton and Hertford Counties; legis. counsel to Gov. N.C., 1961; judge Superior Ct., N.C., 1961-75; asso. justice N.C. Supreme Ct., 1975—; mem. N.C. Adv. Budget Commn., 1957-61, N.C. Bar Council, 1954-57; pres. N.C. Trial Judges Conf., 1973-74; Mem. N.C. Senate, 1951-61, chmn. judiciary and appropriations coms., 1957, 59; del. Democratic Conv., 1956. Served as lt. USNR, 1942-46. Recipient Disting. Alumni award Guilford Coll., 1980. Mem. Am. Bar Assn. (del. trial judges conf. 1968-75, appellate judges conf. 1975—). Democrat. Methodist. Clubs: Masons, Shriners. Home: 407 E High St Murfreesboro NC 27855 also Raleigh Towne Apt 21 521 Wade Ave Raleigh NC 27605 Office: PO Box 157 Murfreesboro NC 27855 also PO Box 1841 NC Supreme Ct Raleigh NC 27602

COPELAND, JOAN MILLER, actress; b. N.Y.C.; d. Isidore and Augusta (Barnett) Miller; m. George Kupchik; 1 son, Eric. Student, Bklyn. Coll. Appeared: on Broadway Sundown Beach, 1949, Detective Story, 1950, Handful of Fire, Tovarich, Two By Two, 1970, Pal Joey (nominated outstanding actress in a musical Drama Desk 1976), The American Clock (Drama Desk award for leading actress in play 1981); off Broadway plays Conversation Piece, End of Summer, Candida; off Broadway The Price; actress: nat. tour Brighton Beach Memoirs; films The Goddess, Middle of the Night, Roseland, A Little Sex; TV shows Love of Life, Search For Tomorrow, How to Survive a Marriage, One Life to Live, (playing Greta) As the World Turns; playing Greta All in the Family, Nurse, Cagney & Lacey. Mem. The Actors Studio. Home: 88 Central Park W New York NY 10023

COPELAND, JOHN ALEXANDER, III, physicist; b. Atlanta, Feb. 6, 1941; s. John Alexander and Gay Elise (Stafford) C.; m. Sandra Jeanne Chandler, June 18, 1960; children: Brian Christopher, Trudi Kathleen. B.S., Ga. Inst. Tech., 1962, M.S., 1963, Ph.D., 1965. Research physicist Ga. Inst. Tech., 1965; mem. tech. staff Bell Telephone Labs., 1965-82, supr., 1967-76, head repeater research dept., Holmdel, N.J., 1976-82; v.p. engrng. tech. Sangamo Weston/ Schlumberger, Atlanta, 1982—. Recipient Distinguished Service award Atlanta Civil Def., 1965; Best Paper award Internat. Solid States Circuits Conf., 1967. Fellow IEEE (editor trans. electron devices 1971-73, Morris N. Liebmann award 1970); mem. Am. Phys. Soc. Club: Sea Bright Lawn. Patentee gallium arsenide microwave devices, magnetic-bubble computer memories, silicon integrated circuits. Home: 1070 Green Way Atlanta GA 30338 Office: Sangamo Weston Inc. PO Box 48400 Atlanta GA 30362

COPELAND, JOHN ALLEN, food packing company executive; b. Converse, La., Aug. 9, 1923; s. Robert S. and Lou (Leysath) C.; m. Lois A. Hansen, Sept. 24, 1945; children: John A., Wade K., Victor G. B.S. in Bus. Adminstrn., La. State U., 1948. With beef dept. Swift & Co., Sioux City, Iowa, 1948-53, with operating and corp. mgmt., various locations, 1953-66, v.p., Chgo., 1966-73, pres. Fresh Meats div., 1973-80; pres., chief exec. officer Swift Ind. Packing Co., Chgo., 1980, Swift Ind. Corp., 1981—; chmn. bd. Nat. Live Stock and Meat Bd., Chgo., 1972-74, Am. Meat Inst., Washington, 1981-83; industry rep. Dept. Agr. Task Force, Washington, 1979. Served to capt. U.S. Army, 1943-45; Europe. Republican. Lutheran. Office: Swift Ind Corp 115 W Jackson Blvd Chicago IL 60604

COPELAND, JOHN WESLEY, textile company executive; b. Greenville, N.C., Aug. 19, 1935; s. Wade Dunlap and Gladys (Brigman) C.; m. Ann Frost, Sept. 28, 1935; children: Ann Shelton, John Wesley. B.S., N.C. State U., 1957; M.B.A., U. N.C., 1960. Mktg. mgr. Carlton Inc., Cerryville-Salisbury, N.C., 1960-64; exec. v.p. Delta Thread div. (Carlton Inc.), Salisbury, 1964-70, pres., 1970-77; chmn. Piedmont Mill Supply, Salisbury, 1978-79; exec. v.p. Am. and Efird Mills Inc., Mt. Holly, N.C., 1979—, dir., 1979—; dir. Cym Corp., Salisbury, 1964—, Piedmont Mill Supply, 1978—, Copeland Bus. Service Inc., Gastonia, N.C., 1979—. Chmn., fund raising com. N.C. Heart Assn., Chapel Hill, 1966; pres. Salisbury Rowan YMCA, 1977; chmn. Rowan Republican Com., Salisbury, 1964-65, Thread Inst., 1977. Served to 1st lt. U.S. Army, 1957-59. Recipient Gold Medalion N.C. Heart Assn., 1967. Methodist. Clubs: Gaston (Gastonia);. Home: 3320 Lincoln Ln Gastonia NC 28052 Office: Am and Efird Mills Inc PO Box 507 Holly NC 28120

COPELAND, JOHN WILSON, educator; b. New Castle, Pa., Sept. 13, 1922; s. Samuel Bruce and Margaret (Wilson) C.; m. Alice Dorthea Tear, Aug. 27, 1949; children—Mary Alice, Ann Wilson, Susan Teare. Student, Muskingum Coll., 1940-42, Oberlin Coll., 1942-43, A.B., 1947; M.A. (Telluride scholar), Cornell U., 1949, Ph.D., 1953. Instr. philosophy Boston U., 1951-55; asst. prof. U.Pitts., 1955-60, asso. prof., 1960-65, Drew U., 1965-71, prof. philosophy, 1971—. Contbr. articles to profl. jours. Served with USNR, 1943-46. Merrill Found. Faculty Research fellow, 1962. Mem. Am. Philos. Assn., Am. Soc. for Polit. and Legal Philosophy, Conf. Study Polit. Thought. Democrat. Home: 6 Forest Rd Madison NJ 07940

COPELAND, LEE GORDON, architect, urban designer, educator; b. Spokane, Wash., Mar. 26, 1937; s. Sidney Z. and Sylvia G. C.; m. Rolaine Vines, Aug. 19, 1961; children—Lene, Michael. B.Arch., U. Wash., 1960; M.Arch., M.City Planning, U. Pa., 1963. Urban designer Phila. City Planning Commn., 1962-63; urban designer, architect Geddes, Brecher, Qualls & Cunningham, Phila., 1963-64; asst. prof., asso. prof. Coll. Arch. and Urban Planning, U. Wash., 1964-72, prof., dean, 1972-78; prin. Joyce, Copeland, Vaughan & Nordfors (Architects and Urban Designers), Seattle, 1966-77; prof. architecture and planning, dean Grad. Sch. Fine Arts, U. Pa., Phila., 1979—. Served as 2d lt., inf. U.S. Army, 1960-61. Fellow AIA. Office: Grad Sch Fine Arts U Pa Philadelphia PA 19104

COPELAND, LILA, artist; b. N.Y.C., Apr. 29, 1922; d. Abraham and Fannie (Richlin) C.; m. John C. Nichols, 1942. Student, Art Students League, N.Y.C., 1940, Pratt Graphic Art Center, 1963. One-woman exhbns. include, Ward Eggleston Galleries, N.Y.C., 1958, d'Alassio Gallery, N.Y.C., 1962, Okla. Mus. Art, 1963, Jasper Rared Mus., Mass., 1964, Albany (Ga.) Mus., Arwin Galleries, Detroit, 1972, Paul Kessler Gallery, Provincetown, Mass., 1974, group shows include, Brandeis U., DePauw U., Wichita Falls Art Mus., Provincetown Artists Assn., State Capitol Mus., Wash., Community Sch., Rowayton, Conn., Woodmere (L.I., N.Y.) Acad.; represented in permanent collections, Nat. Collection of Fine Arts, Smithsonian Instn., Phila. Mus. Fine Arts, Boston Mus. Fine Arts, Bibliotheque Nationale, Paris, Brit. Mus., London, Musee Cantonal des Beaux Arts, Lausanne, France, Museo de arts Contomporanea, Madrid, N.Y. Pub. Library, N.Y.C., Israel Mus., Jerusalem, Bibliotheque Nationale, Brussels, Everson Mus. Art, Syracuse, N.Y., Art Students League, N.Y.C. (Recipient Norman Waite Harris bronze medal Art Inst. Chgo.). Mem. Provincetown Artists Assn.

COPELAND, MORRIS ALBERT, economist; b. Rochester, N.Y., Aug. 6, 1895; s. Albert Edwards and Jenny (Morris) C.; m. Mary Phelps Enders, Dec. 21, 1929; children—Helen (Mrs. R.E. Grattidge), Robert Enders. A.B., Amherst Coll., 1917, L.H.D., 1957; Ph.D., U. Chgo., 1921. Instr. econs. Cornell U., 1921-25, asst. prof., 1925-28, prof., 1928-30, leave of absence, 1927-29; served successively with Brookings Grad. Sch., Nat. Bur. Econ. Research, U. Wis. Exptl. Coll. and; Fed. Res. Bd.; prof. econs. U. Mich., 1930-36, leave of absence, 1933-35; exec. sec. Central Statis. Bd., Washington, 1933-39; dir. research Bur. of Budget, Washington, 1939-40; chief munitions br. WPB, 1940-44; with Nat. Bur. Econ. Research, 1944-59; prof. econs. Cornell U., 1949-65, Robert J. Thorne prof. econs., 1957-65; vis. prof. econs. U. Mo., 1966-67, State U. N.Y. at Albany, 1967-71; Fulbright lectr. Delhi (India) Sch. Econs., 1950-51. Author: A Study of Moneyflows in the U.S, 1951, Fact and Theory in Economics, 1958, Trends in Government Financing, 1961, Our Free Enterprise Economy, 1964, Toward Full Employment, 1966, Essays in Socioeconomic Evolution, 1980; contbr. to econ. publs. Fellow Am. Statis. Assn. (past v.p.); mem. Am. Econ. Assn. (past pres.), Phi Beta Kappa, Phi Delta Theta. Home: Bay Village 8400 Vamo Rd Apt 762 Sarasota FL 33581

COPELAND, RONALD MAX, business administration educator. B.B.A., U. Mass., 1961; M.S., Pa. State U., 1962; Ph.D., Mich. State U., 1966. Asst. prof. Elizabethtown Coll., 1962-64; assoc. prof. Pa. State U., 1966-72; prof. U. S.C., 1972-81; Cowan research prof. acctg. Northeastern U., Boston, 1981—. Author: (with G.E. Philips) Financial Statements: Problems from Current Practice, 1969, (with D.L. Crumbley, J.F. Mojdak) Advanced Accounting, 1971, (with P. Dascher) Managerial Accounting, 2d edit., 1978, (with R. Ingram, R. Baker) Local Government Finances in South Carolina, 1979, (with P. Dascher, D. Davidson) Financial Accounting, 1980, (with R. Ingram) Municipal Financial Reporting and Disclosure Quality, 1983; contbr. rev. and articles to profl. jours., 1983. Mem. Am. Acctg. Assn. (chmn. com. on fin. standards 1979-80, chmn. Southeastern regional exec. com. 1980), Nat. Acctg. Assn., Fin. Exec. Inst. (dir. So. Carolinas chpt. 1978-80), Beta Alpha Psi. Home: 35 Knollwood Ln Mayland MA 01778 Office: College of Business Administration Northeastern University 360 Huntington Ave Boston MA 02115

COPELAND, WILLIAM JOHN, banker; b. Uniontown, Pa., July 4, 1918; s. Thomas Alva and Jean (Hawthorne) C.; m. Joan Engelsen, Jan. 20, 1981; children—Thomas A., Jean Clare M. B.A., Pa. State U., 1940; J.D., U. Pitts., 1947. With Pitts. Nat. Bank (formerly Peoples First Nat. Bank & Co.), 1947—, head bus. devel. dept., trust div., 1959-64, asst. to exec. officer charge trust div., 1964-68, exec. v.p. charge trust div., 1968, vice chmn. bd., 1972—; dir. Ryan Homes, Inc. Bd. dirs. Hosp. Council Western Pa., St. Clair Meml. Hosp., Nat. Flag Found.; chmn. Health Systems Agy. Southwestern Pa.; mem. exec. bd. Allegheny Trails council Boy Scouts Am.; trustee Robert Morris Coll., Carlow Coll., Allegheny County Med. Soc. Found., Westinghouse Ednl. Found., Westinghouse Electric Fund, Henry C. Frick Ednl. Commn.; pres. Civic Light Opera Assn. Served with USAAF, 1941-46. Clubs: Duquesne, St. Clair Country, Concordia (Pitts.); Catawba Island (Port Clinton, Ohio). Home: 22 Mission Dr Pittsburgh PA 15228 Office: 5th Ave and Wood St Pittsburgh PA 15265

COPELAND, WILLIAM MACK, hospital administrator, lawyer; b. Harriman, Tenn., Jan. 21, 1937; s. John Hyder and Margaret Elizabeth (Gardner) C.; m. Barbara Ann Leurck, 1980; children: Elizabeth, William, Brian, George, Carolyn. B.A., So. Colo. State U., 1965; M.S., U. Colo., 1969; J.D., No. Ky. State U., 1977. Bar: Ohio 1978, U.S. Dist. Ct. (so. dist.) Ohio 1978. Commd. 2d lt. U.S. Air Force, 1954, advanced through grades to capt., 1968, ret., 1975; assoc. adminstr. St. George Hosp., Cin., 1976-77, adminstr., 1977-78; pres. St Francis-St. George Hosp., Inc., Cin., 1978—, St. Francis-St. George Health Services, Inc., 1983—; lectr. Patients Rights Inst.; chmn. Greater Cin. Hosp. Council; charter pres. Dayton Area Adminstrs. Group; adj. faculty Xavier U., InterAm. U. Contbr. articles to profl. jours. Vice chmn. dept. health affairs Ohio Catholic Conf., chmn. strategic plan com. and mem. legis. com. Decorated Meritorious Service medal, Air Force Commendation medal with oak leaf cluster; recipient Monsignor Griffin award Ohio Hosp. Assn., 1979. Fellow Am. Coll. Hosp. Adminstrs., Nat. Health Lawyers Assn., Am. Acad. Hosp. Attys., Soc. Ohio Hosp. Attys. (chmn. pub. relations com., mem. govt. liaison com.), Ohio Hosp. Assn., Am. Hosp. Assn. (rep. Health Industry Bar Code Council), Cath. Health Assn. U.S. (govt. relations com., health planning com.), Am. Soc. Law and Medicine, ABA, Ohio Bar Assn., Cin. Bar Assn. Lodge: Kiwanis. Office: 3131 Queen City Ave Cincinnati OH 45238

COPENHAVER, JOHN THOMAS, JR., federal judge; b. Charleston, W.Va., Sept. 29, 1925; s. John Thomas and Ruth Cherrington (Roberts) C.; m. Camille Ruth Smith, Oct. 7, 1950; children—John Thomas III, James Smith, Brent Paul. A.B., W.Va. U., 1947, LL.B., 1950. Bar: Law clk. to U.S. dist. judge Ben Moore, So. Dist. of W.Va., 1950-51; mem. firm Copenhaver & Copenhaver, Charleston, 1951-58; U.S. bankruptcy judge So. Dist. W.Va., Charleston, 1958-76, U.S. dist. judge, 1976—; adj. prof. law W.Va. U. Coll. Law, 1970-76; mem. faculty Fed. Jud. Center, 1972-76; Pres. Legal Aid. Soc. Charleston, 1954; Chmn. Mcpl. Planning Commn. City of Charleston, 1964; chmn., pres. W.Va. Housing Devel. Fund, 1969-72; chmn. vis. com. W.Va. U. Coll. Law, 1980-83; mem. adv. com. on bankruptcy rules Jud. Conf. U.S. Contbr.: articles in fields of bankruptcy and comml. law to Bus. Lawyer, Am. Bankruptcy Law Jour., Personal Fin. Law Quar., W. Va. Law Rev., others. Served with U.S. Army, 1944-46. Recipient Gavel award W.Va. U. Coll. Law, 1971, Outstanding Judge award W. Va. Trial Lawyers Assn., 1983. Mem. Am., W.Va., Kanawha County bar assns., Nat. Bankruptcy Conf., Nat. Conf. Bankruptcy Judges (past pres.), Phi Delta Phi, Beta Theta Pi. Republican. Presbyterian. Office: US Courthouse Charleston WV 25329

COPENHAVER, WILLIAM PIERCE, chemical company executive; b. Tazewell, Va., Oct. 15, 1924; s. Henry Baker and Fern (Spencer) C.; m. Jane Foote Farrier, Mar. 1, 1946; children: Andrew, Paula, John, Elisabeth, David. B.S., Va. Poly. Inst. and State U., Blacksburg, 1948; grad. Advanced Mgmt. Program, Harvard U., 1966. Dir. planning, then plant mgr. Celanese Co. U.S., 1962-67; v.p., ops. mgr., then v.p., gen. mgr. Celanese Co. Can., Montreal, 1969-72; chmn. bd., pres., dir. Columbia Nitrogen Corp., also; Nipro Inc., Augusta, Ga., 1972—; dir. Synres Chem. Co., Ga. R.R. Bank, Augusta, So. area of Arkwright Co., Boston. Vice pres. Augusta United Way; exec. bd. local Boy Scouts Am.; bd. dirs. St. John's United Methodist Ch., Augusta. Served with USAAF, 1942-45. Decorated Air medal. Mem. Augusta C. of C., Nat. Alliance Bus. (dir.), Mfg. Chemists Assn., Am. Mgmt. Assn., Fertilizer Inst., Petrochem. Energy Group. Clubs: West Lake Country, Augusta Country, Pinnacle. Office: Nipro Inc PO Box 1483 Augusta GA 30913 *

COPI, IRVING MARMER, philosophy educator; b. Duluth, Minn., July 28, 1917; s. Samuel Bernard and Rose (Marmer) C.; m. Amelia Glaser, Mar. 20, 1941; children: David Marmer, Thomas Russell, William Arthur, Margaret Ruth. B.A., U. Mich., 1938, M.S., 1940, M.A. (Univ. fellow 1946-47), 1947, Ph.D., 1948; postgrad., U. Chgo., 1938-39. Instr. philosophy U. Ill., 1947-48; faculty U. Mich., 1948-69, prof. philosophy, 1958-69, research asso., 1951-52, Engring. Research Inst., 1954-59; research logician Inst. Sci. and Tech., 1960-61; prof. philosophy U. Hawaii, Honolulu, 1969—; research asso. U. Calif. at Berkeley, 1954; vis. lectr. Air Force U., 1958-66, Georgetown U. Logic Inst., 1960; vis. prof. Princeton, 1959-60, U. Hawaii, 1967; acad. visitor London Sch. Econs., 1975; Cons. Office Naval Research, 1952. Author: Introduction to Logic, 6th edit, 1982, Symbolic Logic, 5th edit, 1979, Introduccion a la Logica, 1962, Introduzione alla Logica, 1965, Theory of Logical Types, 1971, Li-tse Hsueh, 1972, Tarkasastra Ka Paricaya, 1973, Lo-chi-Kai-lun, 1973, Introducao a Logica, 1974, Mavo Lelogika, 1977, Lógica Simbólica, 1979; also numerous essays.; Editor: (Plato): Theaetetus, 1949, (with J.A. Gould) Readings in Logic, 1964, 2d edit., 1972, (with R.W. Beard) Essays on Wittgenstein's Tractatus, 1966, (with J.A. Gould) Contemporary Readings in Logical Theory, 1967, Contemporary Philosophical Logic, 1978. Faculty fellow Fund Advancement Edn., 1953-54; Guggenheim fellow, 1955-56; Fulbright sr. fellow, 1975. Mem. Am. Philos. Assn., Assn. Symbolic Logic, Mich. Acad. Letters, Arts and Scis., AAUP (chpt. pres. 1968-69), Phi Beta Kappa, Phi Kappa Phi. Democrat. Jewish (pres. congregation 1962-63). Home: 1618 Kamole St Honolulu HI 96821

COPLAN, ALFRED IRVING, retail company executive; b. Balt., Jan. 20, 1925; s. Maxwell L. and Rose (Sirasky) C.; m. Helen J. Friedman, Aug. 21, 1945; childrenD: Jan Coplan Rivitz, Lee. B.S., U. Va., 1944. C.P.A., Md., 1946. Pub. acct. Harry B. Gorfine & Co., Balt., 1944-50; asst. controller, sec., controller Reliable Stores Corp., Columbia, Md., 1950-59, v.p., treas. fin., 1959-80, pres., 1980—, also dir. Officer, trustee Aaron Straus and Lillie Straus Found., Balt., 1959—; pres., bd. dirs. Assoc. Jewish Charities of Balt., 1982—; bd. dirs. Assoc. Jewish Charities and Welfare Fund Balt., 1960—; bd. dirs., past pres. Levindale Geriatric Home and Hosp., Balt., 1968—, Balt. Hebrew Congregation, 1963—; bd. dirs. Balt. Symphony Orch., 1979—. Served to sgt. U.S. Army, 1946-47. Office: Reliable Stores Corp 6301 Stevens Forest Rd Columbia MD 21045

COPLAN, NORMAN ALLAN, lawyer; b. New Rochelle, N.Y., Apr. 23, 1919; s. Louis I. and Jeanette (Loevin) C.; m. Joan E. Shapiro, July 11, 1954; children: Jeffrey, Neil, Jennifer. B.A., Columbia, 1940, J.D., 1942. Bar: N.Y. 1942. Practiced in, N.Y.C., 1942—; mem. firm

Bernstein, Weiss, Coplan, Weinstein & Lake, 1942—; mem. faculty Sch. Architecture, Pratt Inst., 1965-70; adj. prof. City U. N.Y., 1979—; cons. N.Y. State U. Constrn. Fund, 1968; Mem. nat. council arbitrators Am. Arbitration Assn., 1956—. Author: Architectural and Engineering Law, 1967; column It's The Law in Progressive Architecture mag, 1958—; co-author: Avoiding Liability in Architecture, Design and Construction, 1983; Editor: column It's The Law, 1951. Served with USAAF, 1942-46. Mem. N.Y. State Bar Assn., Bar Assn. City N.Y., AIA (hon.). Home: 33 Maplewood Rd Hartsdale NY 10530 Office: 120 E 41st St New York NY 10017

COPLAND, AARON, composer; b. Bklyn., Nov. 14, 1900; s. Harris Morris and Sarah (Mittenthal) C. Grad., Boys High Sch. Bklyn., 1918; studied music privately; pupil piano, Victor Wittgenstein and Clarence Adler; composition, Rubin Goldmark and Nadia Boulanger; H.H.D., Brandeis U., 1957, Ill. Wesleyan U., 1958; Mus. D., Princeton U., 1956, Oberlin Coll., 1958, Temple U., 1959, U. Hartford, 1959, Harvard U., 1961, Syracuse U., U. R.I., U. Mich., 1964, Kalamazoo Coll., 1965, U. Utah, 1966, Jacksonville U., 1967, Rutgers U., 1967, Fairfield U., 1968, Ohio State U., 1970, N.Y. U., 1970, Columbia U., 1971, York U., Eng., 1971, U. Fla., 1972, L.I. U., 1974, Bklyn. Coll., 1975, U. Portland, Oreg., 1975, Ottawa (Kans.) U., 1976, U. Rochester, N.Y., 1976, U. Leeds, Eng., 1976, Tulane U., New Orleans, 1976. Lectr. music New Sch. for Social Research, N.Y.C., 1927-37, Harvard U., spring 1935, 44; instr., then asst. dir. Berkshire Music Center, 1940; Charles Eliot Norton prof. poetry Harvard U., 1951-52; dir. Am. Music Center; treas. Arrow Music Press.; Dir. Koussevitsky Music Found.; v.p. Edward MacDowell Assn., Walter W. Naumberg Found. Composer music, 1920—; Founder: (with Roger Sessions) Copland-Sessions Concerts, 1928-31; founder: Am. Music Festivals at Yaddo, Saratoga Springs, N.Y., 1932; (N.Y. Music Critics Circle award 1945 (for Appalachian Spring), Oscar for The Heiress film score Acad. Motion Picture Arts and Sci. 1950, gold medal for music Am. Acad. Arts and Letters 1956); Works: (orchestra) Orchestral Variations, 1957, First Symphony, 1928, Music for the Theatre, 1925, A Dance Symphony, 1925, Concerto for Piano and Orchestra, 1926, Symphonic Ode, 1929, 55, Short Symphony, 1933, Statements, 1935, El Salon Mexico, 1936, Music for Radio, 1937, An Outdoor Overture, 1938, Quiet City, 1940, Lincoln Portrait, 1942; ballet Grohg, 1925, Hear Ye, Hear Ye, 1934, Billy the Kid, 1938, Rodeo, 1942, Appalachian Spring, 1944; opera for high schs. The Second Hurricane, 1937; motion pictures The City, 1939, Of Mice and Men, 1939, Our Town, 1940, North Star, 1943, The Red Pony, 1948, The Heiress, 1949, Something Wild, 1961; chamber music Two Pieces for String Quartet, 1928, Vitebsk, 1929, Piano Variations, 1930, Piano Sonata, 1941, Violin Sonata, 1943, Third Symphony, 1946, In the Beginning; mixed chorus, 1947, Clarinet Concerto, 1948, Music for a Great City, 1964; Author: What to Listen for in Music, 1939, revised edit., 1957, Our New Music, rev. edit., 41, 68, Twelve Poems of Emily Dickinson, 1950, Quartet for Piano and Strings, 1950, Music and Imagination, 1952, The Tender Land; opera, 1954, Piano Fantasy, 1957, Nonet for strings, 1960, Connotations for Orch., 1962, Emblems for Band, 1965, Inscape for orch., 1967, Duo for flute and piano, 1971, Three Latin America Sketches for orch, 1971, Night Thoughts for piano, 1972, Threnody I: Igor Stravinsky, In Memoriam, 1971, Threnody II: Beatrice Cunningham, In Memoriam; author: Copeland on Music, 1960; contbr. to: Modern Music. Guggenheim fellow, 1925-26; Recipient RCA Victor award $5,000, 1930; Pulitzer prize for music, 1944; Presdl. medal of Freedom, 1964; Howland Meml. prize Yale U., 1970; decorated comdr.'s cross Order Merit, West Germany).; Hon. mem. Accademia Santa Cecilia, Rome, Academia Nacional de Bellas Arts, Buenos Aires, Argentina, Royal Philharmonic Soc., London, N.Y. Philharmonic Soc., Internat. Soc. for Contemporary Music, Royal Acad. Music, London. Mem. Am. Acad. Arts and Scis., League Composers (chmn. bd. dirs.), ASCAP, Nat. Inst. Arts and Letters, Am. Acad. Arts and Letters (past pres.), Royal Soc. Arts London, Academie de Beaux Arts of Academie Francaise. Address: care Boosey & Hawkes Inc 24 W 57th St New York NY 10019 *

COPLANS, JOHN RIVERS, artist; b. London, June 24, 1920; U.S., 1960; s. Joseph Moses and Celia (Taneborne) C.; (div.)children: Barbara Ann, Joseph John. Student, L'academie de la grande chaumiere Paris, 1947-49. Sr. lectr. Maidstone Coll. Art, Eng., 1956-60; vis. prof. U. Calif., Berkeley, 1960-61; dir. art gallery U. Calif. at Irvine, 1965-70; sr. curator Pasadena (Calif.) Mus. Modern Art, 1967-71; founding editor ARTFORUM Mag., San Francisco, 1962, editor-in-chief, N.Y.C., 1971-76; dir. Akron (Ohio) Art Inst., 1978-80; pub., editor Dialogue mag., Ohio, 1978-80; disting. vis. prof. Am. U., Cairo, 1983. Exhibited paintings, photographs and prints in one-man and group shows, U.K., Europe, U.S., 1950-63; represented in collections, Met. Mus., N.Y.C., Mus. Modern Art, N.Y.C., Cleve. Mus., Art Inst. Chgo., Bezalel Nat. Mus., Israel, Municipal Mus., Amsterdam, Netherlands, Biblioteque Nationale, Paris; Author: Cezanne Watercolors, 1967, Serial Imagery, 1968, Andy Warhol, 1970, Roy Lichtenstein, 1972, Ellsworth Kelly, 1973, Decisions, Decisions, 1976, Weegee The Famous, 1968; Organized numerous mus. exhbns. and, articles for art mags. Served with RAF, 1938-40; served to capt. King's African Rifles, 1940-46. Recipient Frank Jewitt Mather award, 1974; Guggenheim fellow, 1969; Nat. Endowment for Arts fellow, 1975, 80.

COPLEY, DAVID RONALD, engineering and construction company executive; b. Los Angeles, Apr. 26, 1940; s. John Edward and Ruth Louise (Smith) C.; m. Elizabeth Alyce Phelan, May 16, 1970. B.S. with distinction, U.S. Naval Acad., 1962, M.B.A., Harvard U., 1972. Asso. corp. fin. Kuhn, Loeb & Co. (investment bankers), N.Y.C., 1972-75; mgr. project fin. Fluor Corp., Los Angeles, 1975-77, treas., Irvine, Calif., 1977-81; pres. Power div. Fluor Engrs., Inc., Chgo., 1981—. Served to lt. comdr. U.S. Navy, 1962-70. Clubs: Harvard (N.Y.C.); Huntington Harbour Yacht. Address: 200 W Monroe St Chicago IL 60606

COPLEY, HELEN KINNEY, newspaper publisher; b. Cedar Rapids, Iowa, Nov. 28, 1922; d. Fred Everett and Margaret (Casey) Kinney; m. James S. Copley, Aug. 16, 1965 (dec.); 1 son, David Casey. Attended, Hunter Coll., N.Y.C., 1945. Assoc. The Copley Press, Inc., 1952—, chmn. exec. com., chmn. corp., dir., 1973—, chief exec. officer, sr. mgmt. bd., 1974—; chmn. bd. Copley News Service, San Diego, 1973—; chmn. editorial bd. Union-Tribune Pub. Co., 1973—; pub. San Diego Union and The Tribune, 1973—. Chmn. bd., trustee James S. Copley Found., 1973—; mem. Friends of Internat. Center, La Jolla, La Jolla Mus. Contemporary Art, La Jolla Town Council, Inc.; life patroness Makua Aux.; charter mem. San Diego Women's Council, Navy League; Life mem. San Diego Hall of Sci.; mem. San Diego Soc. Natural History; mem. women's com. San Diego Symphony Assn., Scripps Meml. Hosp. Aux., Social Service League of La Jolla; Life mem. Star of India Aux., Zool. Soc. San Diego; mem. YWCA; hon. chmn., bd. dirs. Washington Crossing Found.; trustee, bd. dirs. Freedoms Found. at Valley Forge; trustee, trustee devel. com. Scripps Clinic and Research Found.; trustee U. San Diego. Mem. Inter Am. Press Assn. (dir.), Calif. Press Assn., Am. Soc. Newspaper Editors, Am. Press Inst., Calif. Newspaper Pubs. Assn., Greater Los Angeles, Nat., San Diego, San Francisco press clubs, Nat. Newspaper Assn., Western Newspaper Found., Sigma Delta Chi. Republican. Roman Catholic. Clubs: Aurora (Ill.) Country; Cuyamaca, San Diego Yacht, Univ., U. San Diego Presidents (San Diego); De Anza Country (Borrego Springs, Calif.); La Jolla Beach and Tennis, La Jolla Country. Office: PO Box 1530 La Jolla CA 92038

COPLEY, PATRICK O'NEIL, college president; b. Seneca, Mo., Feb. 4, 1933; s. Charles Milton and Lorraine Lida (McCoy) C.; m. Elizabeth Ann Wheeler, Nov. 8, 1953; children: Chazell, Charlene, Patrice. B.A., Grand Canyon Coll., Phoenix, 1958; M.A., Ariz. State U., 1959, Ed.D., 1967. Dir. edn. and music Parkview Baptist Ch., Phoenix, 1955-59; tchr. Central High Sch., Phoenix, 1959-65; asst. dean Sch. Edn., U. Mo., St. Louis, 1965-67; dean Sch. Edn., S.W. Mo. State U., Springfield, 1967-82; pres. Mo. Bapt. Coll., St. Louis, 1982—. Author articles in field. Bd. dirs. Springfield United Cerebral Palsy, Mo. Bapt. Children's Home, St. Louis. Served with USAF, 1951-55. HEW grantee, 1977-81. Mem. Am. Assn. Colls. Tchrs. Edn. (council state reps.), Mo. Assn. Colls. Tchrs. Edn. (pres. 1977-79), Tchr. Edn. Council of State Colls. and Univs. (pres. 1980-81), Mo. State Tchrs. Assn., Phi Delta Kappa, Kappa Delta Phi, Alpha Phi Omega. Office: 12542 Conway Rd Saint Louis MO 63141

COPLEY, STEPHEN MICHAEL, metallurgical engineering educator; b. Urbana, Ill., Apr. 29, 1936; s. Michael Joseph and Marion Elizabeth (Partlow) C.; m. Marcia Elizabeth Thornton, Nov. 28, 1957; children: Michael Thornton, Sara Marie, Philip Stephen, Paul Ellis, Peter Leland, Susan Elizabeth, Stephen Joseph. A.A., U. Calif. at Berkeley, 1956, B.A., 1959, M.S., 1961, Ph.D., 1964. Research asso., sr. research asso., group leader, sect. supr. Advanced Materials Research and Devel. Lab., Pratt & Whitney Aircraft Co., Middletown, Conn., 1964-70; asso. prof. materials sci. and mech. engring. U. So. Calif., Los Angeles, 1970-76, Kenneth T. Norris prof. metall. engring., 1972—, chmn. dept. materials sci., 1975-81; prof. materials sci. and mech. engring., 1976—; Mem. materials sci. and engring. adv. bd. McGraw-Hill. Subject editor: Ency. of Materials Sci.; Contbr. articles to profl. jours.; Patentee in field. Recipient Region VII Edn. Achievement award Soc. Mfg. Engrs., 1978. Fellow Am. Soc. Metals (exec. com. 1973—, program chmn. Westec Conf. 1976, chmn. Los Angeles chpt. 1980-81); fellow Inst. Advancement Engring.; Mem. Metall. Soc., Am. Inst. Mining and Metall. Engrs. (phys. metallurgy com., high temperature alloys com.), Am. Ceramic Soc., ASME., Soc. Mfg. Engrs., Sigma Xi. Home: 4029 Via Nivel Palos Verdes Estates CA 90274 Office: Dept Materials Sci U So Calif Los Angeles CA 90007

COPP, DOUGLAS HAROLD, physiologist, educator; b. Toronto, Ont., Can., Jan. 16, 1915; s. Charles Joseph and Edith Mable (O'Hara) C.; m. Winnifred A. Thompson, July 15, 1939; children: Mary Louise Copp Macdonald, Carolyn Ann, Patricia Jane Copp Montpellier. B.A., U. Toronto, 1936, M.D., 1939, LL.D., 1970; Ph.D., U. Calif., Berkeley, 1943; LL.D., Queen's U., 1970; D.Sc., U. Ottawa, 1973, Acadia U., 1975, U. B.C., 1980. Instr., asst. prof. physiology U. Calif., Berkeley, 1943-50; prof., head dept. physiology U. B.C., Vancouver, 1950-80; Pres. Nat. Cancer Inst. Can., 1968-70. Decorated officer Order of Can., 1971, companion, 1980; recipient Gairdner Found. ann. award, 1967; Nicolas Andry award, 1968; Steindler award, 1974; Gold medal in sci. and engring. B.C. Research Council, 1980; William F. Neuman award Am. Soc. Bone and Mineral Research, 1983. Fellow Royal Soc. Can. (Flavelle gold medal 1972, council 1973-75, 77—, pres. acad. sci. 1978—), Royal Soc. (London), Royal Coll. Physicians (Can.); mem. Can. Physiol. Soc. (pres. 1963-64), Faculty Assn. U. B.C. (pres. 1965-66). Research in bone metabolism, phosphate depletion, calcium regulation in vertebrates. Discovered calcitonin, teleocalcin. Home: 4755 Belmont Ave Vancouver BC Canada V6T 1A8

COPP, JAMES HARRIS, sociologist, educator; b. Thief River Falls, Minn., Apr. 28, 1925; s. Vivian Emery and Irene (Sorenson) C.; m. Veronica Fliegel, Sept. 12, 1953; children—Christine, John, Karen, Sarah, Martha. B.A., U. Minn., 1949, M.A., 1951; Ph.D., U. Wis.-Madison, 1954. Research dir. 4-H Club Wis., Madison, 1953-54; asst. prof. rural sociology Kans. State U., 1954-55, U. Wis.-Madison, 1955-56; asst. prof. Pa. State U., 1956-62, assoc. prof., 1962-66, prof., 1966-67; chief br. human resources Econ. Research Service U.S. Dept. Agr., Washington, 1967-72; prof., head dept. sociology and anthropology Tex. A&M U., 1972-81, prof., head dept. rural sociology, 1972-80, prof. dept. sociology and rural sociology, 1981—; vis. prof. Mich. State U., 1960, U. Wis.-Madison, 1966; cons. Office Tech. Assessment U.S. Congress, Nat. Inst. on Aging, HEW, Bd. Agrl. and Renewable Resources NRC. Editor: Our Changing Rural Society, 1964; editor: Rural Sociology, 1976-79. Recipient State 4-H Alumni award Minn. 4-H, 1964. Mem. Am. Sociol. Assn., AAAS, Rural Sociol. Soc. (pres. 1972), Southwestern Sociol. Assn., So. Sociol. Soc., So. Assn. Agrl. Scientists, Phi Beta Kappa. Home: 1101 Pershing Dr College Station TX 77843 Office: Dept Sociology Tex A and M U College Station TX 77843

COPPEL, ALFRED, author; b. Oakland, Calif., Nov. 9, 1921; s. Alfredo Jose and Ana Roumalda y Coppel deMarini; m. Elisabeth Schorr, 1943; children—Elisabeth Ann, Alfred III. Student, Stanford U., 1943. Books include Hero Driver, 1952, Dark December, 1960, The Gate of Hell, 1968, the Rebel of Rhada, 1968, The Navigator of Rhada, 1969, A Storm of Spears, 1970, The Starkham of Rhada, 1971, The Landlocked Man, 1972, The Dragon, 1977. Served to 1st lt. USAAF, WW II. *

COPPEL, HARRY CHARLES, educator, entomologist; b. Galt, Ont., Can., Jan. 2, 1918; came to U.S., 1957, naturalized, 1964; s. Archibald Aaron and Bertha (Siegal) C.; m. Joyce Lucille Vineberg, Sept. 3, 1950; children—David Brian, Ann Gail. B.S.A., Ont. Agrl. Coll., 1943; M.S., U. Wis., 1946; Ph.D., N.Y. State Coll. Forestry, Syracuse U., 1949. Research scientist, div. entomology Can. Dept. Agr., Belleville, Ont., 1943-57; faculty U. Wis., 1957—, prof. entomology, 1965—. Author: (with McLeod and McGugan) A Review of the Biological Control Attempts Against Insects and Weeds in Canada, 1962, (with J.W. Mertins) Biological Insect Pest Suppression, 1977. Mem. Entomol. Soc. Am. (editorial bd. 1961-66, gov. bd. 1965-67), entomol. socs. Can., Ont. (dir. 1952), Wis. Entomol. Soc. (pres. 1973), Wis. Phenological Soc., Wis. Acad. Arts, Sci. and Letters, Internat. Orgn. for Biol. Control (bd. govs. Western Hemisphere Regional Sect. 1975—), Sigma Xi, Phi Sigma, Alpha Xi Sigma, Gamma Sigma Delta. Home: 4313 Bagley Pkwy Madison WI 53705

COPPENS, PHILIP, chemist; b. Amersfoort, Holland, Oct. 24, 1930; s. Alexander and Sophie (Berkeley) C.; m. Marguerite Louise Anholt, Aug. 6, 1957; children—Alon, Eldad, Daniel David. Ph.D., U. Amsterdam, Netherlands, 1960. Chemist Weizmann Inst. Sch., Rehoboth, Israel, 1957-60, 62-65; chemist Brookhaven Nat. Lab., Upton, L.I., N.Y., 1960-62, 65-68; prof. chemistry SUNY, Buffalo, 1968—; adj. prof. applied physics and engring. sci. Cornell U., 1982—; vis. prof. Fordham U., 1966-67, Aarhus U., Denmark, 1973, U. Grenoble, France, 1974-75; mem. materials research adv. com. NSF, 1980-82; mem. Nat. Synchotron Light Source User Exec. Com., 1983—. Mem. Am. Crystallographic Assn. (v.p. 1977, pres. 1978), Am. Chem. Soc., AAAS, Royal Dutch Acad. Scis. (corr.). Office: Dept Chemistry State U NY Buffalo NY 14214

COPPERMAN, STUART MORTON, pediatrician, 334; b. Bklyn., June 5, 1935; s. Irving and Anne (Reisfeld) C.; m. Renee Stein, Aug. 17, 1958; children: Beth, Allan. Cara. B.A. cum laude, Bklyn. Coll., 1956; M.D., SUNY-Bklyn., 1960. Diplomate: Am. Bd. Pediatrics. Rotating intern. L.I. Jewish Hosp., New Hyde Park, N.Y., 1960-61, resident in pediatrics, 1961-63; practice medicine specializing in pediatrics, Merrick, N.Y., 1965—; mem. staff L.I. Jewish Hillside Med. Ctr., Schneider Children's Hosp., New Hyde Park Ctr., East Meadow Ctr., Hempstead (N.Y.) Gen. Hosp.; clin. asst. prof. pediatrics SUNY Med. Sch.-Stony Brook, 1972—; assoc. prof. clin. health studies Sch. Allied Health, 1977—; clin. instr. physicians asst. program Stony Brook Med. Ctr., 1972—; prof. pediatrics St. George's Med. Coll., St. Vincent, W.I., acting chmn. pediatrics, 1979-80; med. adviser Assn. Children with Downs Syndrome, 1971—; mem. com. for handicapped Bellmore Sch. Dist., 1976—; mem. ad hoc com. on community as sch. Merrick-Bellmore Schs., 1976—; preceptor in pediatrics Physicians Asst. Program; lectr. in field, cons. in field; mem. doctor's adv. com. Shaare Zedek Hosp., Jerusalem, 1974—. Appearance TV shows on Downs Syndrome, learning disabilities, CPR, first aid, TV's effect on children, infectious disease, prevention of cigarette smoking among children, 1972—; contbr. articles to profl. jours.; researcher on hetacillin, 1966, pyridoxine effect on serotonin level and performance in children with Down's Syndrome, 1970-75, Alice in Wonderland syndrome as presenting symptom of infectious mononucleosis, 1966-77, on transmission of group A Beta hemolytic strep infection from pet reservoirs to children, 1963-81. Mem. sch. bd. Temple Beth Am., Merrick, 1972-78, mem. exec. com., Merrick, 1973-74, chmn. com. Israel and World Affairs, Merrick, 1976-78, mem. sch. com., Merrick, 1976-78, mem. ritual com., Merrick, 1976—, mem. temple bd., Merrick, 1976-77; mem. legis adv. com. 8th Senatorial Dist., N.Y., 1975—; mem. profl. adv. bd. So. Shore div. YM-YWHA. Served with U.S. Army, 1963-65. Recipient Physicians Recognition award AMA, 1966-69, 69-72, 72-75, 75-78, 79-81, 82—, testimonial dinner and plaque Assn. Children with Down's Syndrome, 1972, Best Clin. Tchr. of Pediatrics award Nassau County Med. Ctr., 1981-82. Fellow Am. Acad. Pediatrics (chmn. com. TV effects on children 1976—), Internat. Coll. Pediatrics; mem. N.Y. State Med. Soc., Nassau County Med. Soc., AMA, Nassau Pediatric Soc. (mem. exec. bd. 1972—, chmn. com. on mental health 1972—), A Non-Smoking Generation Internat. (organizer, med. dir. Am. div.), Am. Lung Assn., Nassau-Suffolk Lung Assn. (life mem.) (dir. 1982-84), Am. Physicians Fellowship for Israel Med. Assn., Assn. Children with Learning Disabilities (mem. profl. adv. bd.), La Leche League, Latin Am. Parents Assn., Alpha Epsilon Pi (chancellor Phi Theta chpt. 1955-56), Phi Delta Epsilon (consul Zeta chpt. 1960). Club: B'nai B'rith. Office: 3137 Hewlett Ave Merrick NY 11566

COPPINGER, RAYMOND PARKE, biologist, educator; b. Boston, Feb. 7, 1937; s. John Raymond and Frances (Sheppard) C.; m. Lorna L. Baxter, Dec. 27, 1958; children: Karyn D., Timothy L. A.B., Boston U., 1959; M.A., U. Mass., 1965; four-coll. Ph.D., U. Mass., Amherst Coll., Smith Coll., Mt. Holyoke Coll., 1968. Postdoctoral research assoc. Amherst assoc., Mass., 1968-70; prof. biology Hampshire Coll., Amherst, 1970—; lectr. on animal behavior, human and canine behavior; cons. UN Devel. Program, Chad, Africa, Caribbean Area. Co-author 13 week TV series on human adaptation; contbr. articles to publs. Mem. adv. bds. various local instns. Recipient various pvt. and fed. grants for predator control research. Mem. Explorers Club, Am. Soc. Mammalogists, Sigma Xi. Home: Chestnut Hill RDF Montague MA 01351 Office: Hampshire Coll. Box SS Amherst MA 01002

COPPLE, WILLIAM PERRY, judge; b. Holtville, Calif., Oct. 3, 1916; s. Perry and Euphie (Williams) C.; m. Rowena Tucker, Nov. 14, 1936; children: Virginia (Mrs. Richard Schilke), Leonard W., Steven D. A.B., U. Calif. at Berkeley, 1949, LL.B., 1951. Bar: Ariz. 1952. Various positions with U.S. Govt., also pvt. employers, 1936-48; practice in, Yuma, Ariz., 1952-65; U.S. dist. atty. Dist. Ariz., Phoenix, 1965-66; judge U.S. Dist. Ct. Dist. Ariz., 1966—; Mem. Ariz. Hwy. Commn., 1955-58, Gov. Ariz. Com Fourteen for Colo. River, 1963-65; chmn. Yuma County Democratic Central Com., 1953-54, 59-60. Mem. Am. Bar Assn., Am. Judicature Soc. Office: Room 7025 US Courthouse Phoenix AZ 85025 *

COPPOLA, ANTHONY, supervisory electronic engineer; b. Bklyn., July 14, 1935; s. Frank and Barbara (Tambasco) C.; m. Joan Elizabeth Garvey, Nov. 12, 1966; children: Stephen, Paul, Dominic, Jane. B.A. in Physics, Syracuse U., 1956; M.S. in Engring. Adminstrn., 1966; cert. of completion, Air War Coll., Griffiss AFB, N.Y., 1981. Lic. pvt. pilot. Electronic engr. Rome Ari Devel Ctr., U.S. Air Force, Griffiss AFB, N.Y., 1956-60; group leader Rome Air Devel Ctr., U.S. Air Force, Griffiss AFB, N.Y., 1960-72, sect. chief, 1972—; guest instr. Air Force Inst. Tech., 1964-78, George Washington U., 1969-70, Air Force Acad., 1973. Contbr. articles in field to profl. jours. Advisor Mohawk Valley Engrs. Exec. Council, Utica, N.Y., 1978-82. N.Y. state scholar, 1952; recipient Superior Performance award U.S. Air Force, 1965, 81, Cert. of Merit U.S. Air Force Systems Command, 1979. Fellow IEEE (editor Reliability Soc. newsletter 1981, sect. chmn. 1982-83, Centennial medal 1984); mem. AIAA, Armed Forces Mgmt. Assn., Pi Delta Epsilon, U.S. Chess Fedn. Club: Ft. Stanwix Pistol (Rome, N.Y.). Home: 18 Melrose Ave Utica NY 13502 Office: Rome Air Devel Ctr RADC-RBET Griffiss Air Force Base NY 13502

COPPOLA, CARMINE, composer, condr.; b. N.Y.C., June 11, 1910; s. August and Maria (Zasa) C.; m. Italia Pennino, Apr. 30, 1934; children—August, Francis, Talia. Diploma, Juilliard Sch. Music, 1933; Mus.M., Manhattan Sch. Music, 1950. Mem. music staff, WTIC, Hartford, Conn., Radio City Music Hall; 1st flutist, Detroit Symphony, NBC Orch.; music dir., Merrick Prodns., Los Angeles Civic Opera; composer: numerous scores for film including Napoleon, The Godfather, Parts I and II, Apocalypse Now, The Black Stallion; opera Escorial, 1979; (recipient Oscar for musical score The Godfather Part II, Acad. Motion Pictures Arts and Scis.). Calif. Arts Council grantee. Mem. ASCAP, Acad. Motion Pictures, Arts and Scis., Beta Gamma. *

COPPOLA, FRANCIS FORD, director, producer, film writer; b. Detroit, Apr. 7, 1939; s. Carmine C.; m. Eleanor Neil; 3 children. B.A., Hofstra U., 1958; Master of Cinema, UCLA, 1968. Artistic dir., Zoetrope Studios.; Dir.: motion pictures Dementia 13, 1964, You're a Big Boy Now, 1967, Finian's Rainbow, 1968, The Rain People, 1969, One from the Heart, 1981; writer: This Property Is Condemned, 1966, Reflections In a Golden Eye, 1967, The Rain People, 1969, Is Paris Burning, 1966, Patton, 1970, The Great Gatsby, 1974; writer, producer and dir.: The Godfather (Acad. awards for Best Screenplay and Best Picture, nominee for Best Dir., Film Dir.'s award Dirs. Guild Am. 1972), The Godfather, Part II, 1974 (Acad. awards for Best Screenplay, Best Dir. and Best Picture), The Conversation, 1974, Apocalypse Now, 1979; producer: TV movie The People; co-writer, producer, dir.: motion picture The Outsiders, 1983, Rumble Fish, 1983; producer: motion pictures THX 1138, 1971; exec. producer: Black Stallion, 1979; producer: motion picture The Black Stallion Returns, 1983; co-writer, producer, dir.: The Escape Artist, 1982; exec. producer: motion pictures Hammett. Mem. Dirs. Guild Am. Inc. Office: Zoetrope Studios 916 Kearny St San Francisco CA 94133

COPPS, DONALD WILLIAM, food industry co. exec.; b. Stevens Point, Wis., May 10, 1914; s. Clinton William and Jeanette (Wilson) C.; m. Mary Jane Krembs, Oct. 12, 1935; children—Sally (Mrs. Richard Jensen), Michael, Mary Jane (Mrs. Tom Windels), Donald, Elizabeth (Mrs. John Stange). Ph.B., Carroll Coll., 1937. Pres. Copps Corp., Stevens Point, 1946-73, chmn. bd., 1973-80, chief exec. officer, 1976-80, chmn. exec. com., 1980—; also dir. Copps Distbg. Co., Copps Realty Corp., D-C Corp., Saving Stamp Corp.; dir. Citizens Nat. Bank. Bd. dirs. Viterbo Coll., 1970—; chmn. Citizens Youth Com., 1952-56; co-chmn. Marquette U. Civic Com., 1959-63; pres. Youth

Baseball Assn., 1951-53; chmn. spl. gifts com. bldg. funds Cath. High Schs.; fund-raising drive chmn. Stevens Point Municipal Swimming Pool, 1956; Bd. dirs. U. Wis./Stevens Point Found., Goodwill Industries of North Central Wis., 1976—; pres. bd. trustees Stevens Point Area YMCA. Recipient Distinguished Citizen award Stevens Point, 1958. Mem. Wis. Food and Tobacco Inst. (treas., dir. 1961-63), Super Market Inst. (dir. at large 1963-65), Ind. Grocers Alliance (dir. 1968-80), President's Assn. Inc., Stevens Point C. of C. (pres. 1943), St. De LaSalle Aux., Notre Dame of the Lake Assos. Roman Catholic. Clubs: Elks, Serra (past pres.); K.C., Kiwanis (Stevens Point); Carroll Coll. C. Home: 1124 Soo Marie Ave Stevens Point WI 54481 Office: 2828 Wayne St Stevens Point WI 54481

COPPS, TIMOTHY JAMES, food co. exec.; b. Stevens Point, Wis., May 17, 1942; s. Gordon F. and Marguerite H. (Meyer) C. B.S., Marquette U., 1965. C.P.A., Wis. Sr. accountant Haskins & Sells, Milw., 1965-71; controller The Copps Corp., Stevens Point, 1971-77, treas., 1974-77, exec. v.p.-retail, 1977-79, pres., 1979—, also dir. Mem. Am. Inst. C.P.A.'s, Wis. Soc. C.P.A.'s. Office: 2828 Wayne St Stevens Point WI 54481

COQUILLARD, GEORGE CLARKE, insurance company executive; b. South Bend, Ind., Sept. 23, 1919; s. Alexis E. and Mary (Clarke) C.; m. Mary Theresa Voll, Jan. 21, 1950. A.B., Harvard U., 1941, M.B.A., 1943. Sr. v.p. Nat. Life Ins. Co. Vt., Montpelier, 1975-77, exec. v.p., 1977-83; vice chmn. bd. Nat. LIfe Ins. Co., Montpelier, 1983—; chmn. bd. Sentinel Advisors, Inc.; pres. Sentinel Group Funds, Inc. Trustee Central Vt. Med. Ctr., Montpelier, 1983—. Served to lt. USN, 1943-46; PTO. ETO. Home: Rural Route 1 Murray Rd Montpelier VT 05602 Office: Nat Life Ins Co National Life Dr Montpelier VT 05602

COQUILLETTE, DANIEL ROBERT, lawyer, legal educator; b. Boston, May 23, 1944; s. Robert McTavish and Dagmar Alvida (Bistrup) C.; m. Judith Courtney Rogers, July 5, 1969; children: Anna, Sophia, Julia. A.B., Williams Coll., 1966; M.A. Juris., Univ. Coll., Oxford U., Eng., 1969; J.D., Harvard U., 1971. Bar: Mass. 1974, U.S. Dist. Ct. Mass. 1974, U.S. Ct. Appeals (1st cir.) 1974. Law clk. to presiding justice Mass. Supreme Ct., 1971-72; to Warren E. Burger, chief justice U.S. Supreme Ct., 1972-73; assoc. Palmer & Dodge, Boston, 1973-75, ptnr., 1980—; assoc. prof. law Boston U., 1975-78; vis. assoc. prof. law Cornell U., Ithaca, N.Y., 1977-78; vis. prof. law Harvard Law Sch., 1978-79, 83—. Contbr. articles to legal jours. Trustee, sec.-treas. Ames Found.; treas. Byron Meml Fund; propr. Boston Athenaeum. Recipient Kaufman prize in English Williams Coll., 1966, Sentinel of the Republic prize in polit. sci. Williams Coll., 1965; Hutchins scholar, 1966-67; Fulbright scholar, 1966-68. Mem. Am. Law Inst., ABA, Mass Bar Assn. (chmn. task force on model rules of profl. conduct), Boston Bar Assn. (chmn. law sch. liaison com.), Am. Soc. Legal History, Selden Soc. (state corr.), Colonial Soc. Mass. (mem. council), Phi Beta Kappa. Democrat. Quaker. Clubs: Curtis, Tavern, Club of Old Volumes. Home: 12 Rutland St Cambridge MA 02138

COQUILLETTE, ROBERT MCTAVISH, retired chemical company executive; b. Ft. Wayne, Ind., Oct. 31, 1918; s. Leon and Ruby (McTavish) C.; m. Dagmar Alvilda Bistrup, May 4, 1940; children—Daniel Robert, William Hollis. B.S., Harvard, 1939. Mem. mfg. dept. Procter and Gamble Co., 1939-44; mfg. supt. Dewey and Almy Chem. Co. div. W.R. Grace Co., 1946-50, mgr. rubber spltys. div., 1950-53, asst. to pres., 1953-55, gen. mgr. overseas chem. div., 1955-57, v.p., 1957—; pres. Ohio Rubber Co. div., also dir. Eagle-Picher Co., 1962-65; v.p. corp. adminstrn. group W.R. Grace & Co., 1965-67, corp. v.p. chem. group ops., 1967-72, exec. v.p. corp. adminstrn., 1972-76, exec. v.p., chief tech. officer, 1976-78, sector exec., 1978-83, ret., 1983. Served to lt. (j.g.) USNR, 1944-46. Clubs: Harvard, N.Y. Yacht (N.Y.C.). Office: W R Grace & Co 1114 Ave of Americas New York NY 10036

CORAN, ARNOLD GERALD, pediatric surgeon, educator; b. Boston, Apr. 16, 1938; s. Charles and Anne (Cohen) C.; m. Susan Williams, Nov. 17, 1960; children: Michael, David, Randi Beth. B.A. cum laude, Harvard U., 1959, M.D., 1963. Diplomate: Am. Bd. Surgery, Am. Bd. Thoracic Surgery. Intern Peter Bent Brigham Hosp., Boston, 1963-64, resident in surgery, 1964-68, chief surg. resident, 1969; resident in surgery Children's Hosp. Med. Center, Boston, 1965-66, sr. surg. resident, 1966, chief surg. resident, 1968; instr. surgery Harvard, Cambridge, Mass., 1967-69; asst. clin. prof. surgery George Washington U., 1970-72; head physician pediatric surgery Los Angeles County-U. So. Calif. Med. Center, 1972-74; asst. prof. surgery U. So. Calif., 1972-73, assoc. prof., 1973-74; prof. surgery U. Mich., Ann Arbor, 1974—; head sect. pediatric surgery U. Mich. Hosp., 1974—; Surgeon-in-chief Mott Children's Hosp. Contbr. numerous articles in field to profl. jours. Served to lt. comdr. MC AUS. Fellow ACS; mem. Am. Acad. Pediatrics, Am. Surg. Assn., Soc. Univ. Surgeons, Am. Pediatric Surg. Assn., Western, Central surg. assns. Home: 3450 Vintage Valley Rd Ann Arbor MI 48105 Office: Mott Children's Hosp Room F7516 Box 66 Ann Arbor MI 48109

CORBALLY, JOHN EDWARD, educator; b. South Bend, Wash., Oct. 14, 1924; s. John Edward and Grace (Williams) C.; m. Marguerite B. Walker, Mar. 12, 1946; children—Jan Elizabeth, David William. B.S., U. Wash., 1947, M.A., 1950; Ph.D., U. Calif.-Berkeley, 1955; LL.D., U. Md., 1971, Blackburn Coll., 1972, Ill. State U., 1977, Ohio State U., 1980; Litt.D., U. Akron, 1979. Tchr. Clover Park High Sch., Tacoma, 1947-50; prin. Twin City High Sch., Stanwood, Wash., 1950-53; asst. prof. edn., assoc. prof. Ohio State U., Columbus, 1955-60, prof., 1960-69, dir. personnel budget and exec. asst. to pres., 1960-64, v.p. adminstrn., 1964-66, provost, v.p. acad. affairs, 1966-69; chancellor, pres. Syracuse (N.Y.) U., 1969-71; pres. U. Ill., Chgo. and, Urbana-Champaign, 1971-79, pres. emeritus, 1979—, disting. prof. higher edn., Urbana-Champaign, 1979-82, disting. prof. emeritus, 1982—; pres., dir. John D. and Catherine T. MacArthur Found., 1979—; dir. Ill. Bell Telephone Co., Bankers Life and Casualty Co., 1st Nat. Bank in Champaign., Midwest Fin. Group, Peoria,-, Ill., Borg-Warner Corp.; Mem. Commn. on Govt. Relations, Am. Council on Edn., 1972-76; bd. visitors Air U., 1974-80; mem. governing bd. Ill. Council Econ. Edn., 1972-80; bd. dirs. Ill. Ednl. Consortium, 1973-78; chmn. Nat. Council on Ednl. Research, Nat. Inst. Edn., 1973-79; bd. dirs. Council for Fin. Aid to Edn., 1973-79, Found. for Teaching Econs., 1978—. Author: Introduction to Educational Adminstration, 6th edit, 1983, Educational Administration: The Secondary School, 2d edit, 1965, School Finance, 1962. Trustee Joint Council on Econ. Edn., Lincoln Acad. Ill., 1971-83, Mus. Sci. and Industry, 1971-79. Served to lt. (j.g.) USNR, 1943-46. Recipient Centennial medal U. Calif. Alumni Assn. and Sch. Edn. Alumni Soc., 1976; Disting. Eagle award Boy Scouts Am. Mem. Phi Beta Kappa, Phi Kappa Sigma, Phi Kappa Phi, Omicron Delta Kappa, Chi Gamma Iota, Beta Gamma Sigma, Alpha Phi Omega. Clubs: Tavern, Wayfarers, Chgo., Econ., Mid-Day (Chgo.); Glen View, Useless Bay (Wash.) Country. Office: 140 S Dearborn #700 Chicago IL 60603

CORBATO, CHARLES EDWARD, geology educator; b. Los Angeles, July 12, 1932; s. Hermenegildo and Charlotte Carella (Jensen) C.; m. Patricia Jeanne Ferg, May 18, 1957; children: Steven, Barbara, Susan. B.A., UCLA, 1954, Ph.D., 1960. Instr. geology U. Calif., Riverside, 1959, Los Angeles, 1959-60, asst. prof., 1960-66; asso. prof. Ohio State U., Columbus, 1966-69, prof., 1969—, chmn. dept. geology and mineralogy, 1972-80; Geophysicist U.S. Geol. Survey, 1966-74. Fellow Geol. Soc. Am.; mem. Am. Geophys. Union, Soc. Exploration Geophysics, Am. Inst. Profl. Geologists, Internat. Assn. Mathematical Geology, Delta Tau Delta. Home: 2400 Buckley Rd Columbus OH 43220 Office: 125 S Oval Mall Columbus OH 43210

CORBATÓ, FERNANDO JOSÉ, educator; b. Oakland, Calif., July 1, 1926; s. Hermenegildo and Charlotte (Jensen) C.; m. Isabel Blandford, Nov. 24, 1962 (dec. July 1973); children: Carolyn Suzanne, Nancy Patricia; m. Emily S. Gish, Dec. 6, 1975; stepchildren: David Lawrence Gish, Jason Charles Gish. Student, UCLA, 1943-44; B.S. in Physics, Calif. Inst. Tech., 1950, Ph.D., Mass. Inst. Tech., 1956. With Computation Center, Mass. Inst. Tech., 1956-66, dep. dir., 1963-66; head computer systems research group of project MAC Mass. Inst. Tech., 1963-72, co-head div., 1972-73, co-head automatic programming div., 1972-73, mem. faculty, 1962—, prof. computer sci. and engring., 1965—, asso. dept. head for computer sci. and engring., 1974-78, 83—, Cecil H. Green prof. computer sci. and engring., 1978-80, dir. computing and telecommunication resources, 1980-83; Mem. computer sci. and engring. bd. Nat. Acad. Sci., 1971-73. Co-author: The Compatible Time Sharing System, 1963, Advanced Computer Programming, 1963. Served with USNR, 1944-46. Fellow IEEE (W.W. McDowell award 1966, Computer Pioneer award 1982), AAAS, Am. Acad. Arts and Sci., Nat. Acad. Engring.; mem. Assn. Computing Machinery (council 1964- 66), Am. Fedn. Info. Processing Socs. (Harry Goode Meml. award 1980), Am. Phys. Soc., Sierra Club, Sigma Xi. Home: 88 Temple St West Newton MA 02165 Office: 545 Technology Sq Cambridge MA 02139

CORBELL, WILLARD JASON, food company executive; b. Pearl City, Ill., Oct. 29, 1912; s. William and Margaret (Schasker) Corbett; m. Alice Carman, Aug. 12, 1936; children: Ann, John. B.S., U. Ill., 1934, Ph.D., 1942; M.S., U. Wis., 1935. Research asst. U. Ill., Urbana, 1935-41; dir. lab. Nat. Dairy Products, Cleve., 1941-42; tech. dir. Dean Foods, Rockford, Ill., 1943-70, dir., 1947-80, v.p., 1957-70, sr. v.p., 1980—. Mem. Sigma Xi. Lodge: Kiwanis (pres.). Home: 2020 Greenfield Ln Rockford IL 61107 Office: 1126 Kilburn St Rockford IL 61107

CORBEN, HERBERT CHARLES, physicist; b. Portland, Dorset, Eng., Apr. 18, 1914; came to U.S., 1946, naturalized, 1950; s. Harold Frederick and Margaret (Hart) C.; m. Beverly Balkum, Oct. 25, 1957; children: Deirdre (Mrs. John W. DeGroote), Sharon, Gregory. B.A., U. Melbourne, 1933, B.Sc., 1934, M.A., 1936, M.Sc., 1936; Ph.D., Cambridge U., 1939. Lectr. math. and physics New England U. Coll., Armidale, Australia, 1941; lectr. math., physics U. Melbourne, Australia, 1942-46; acting dean Trinity Coll., Melbourne, 1942-46; asso. prof. Carnegie Inst. Tech., 1946-51, prof., 1951-56; part-time lectr. physics U. Pitts., 1947; Fulbright vis. prof. U. Genoa, Milan, and Bologna, 1951-53; part-time lectr. physics U. So. Calif., 1957-58; asso. dir. Research Lab. Ramo-Wooldridge Corp. and Space Tech. Labs, Inc., Los Angeles, 1956-60; dir. Quantum Physics Lab., 1961-68; chief scientist Phys. Research Center, 1966-68; distinguished vis. prof. physics Queens Coll., 1968; acting dean faculties Cleve. State U., 1968-69, dean faculties, 1969-70, v.p. acad. affairs, 1970-72, dean Coll. Grad. Studies, prof. physics, 1968-72; prof. physics Scarborough Coll., U. Toronto, 1972—, vis. prof., 1980-82, chmn. phys. scis. group, 1972-76; faculty Harvey Mudd Coll., Claremont, Calif., 1978-80, scholar-in-residence, 1982—; Commonwealth Fund fellow U. Calif. and; Princeton U., 1939-41. Author: Classical and Quantum Theories of Spinning Particles, 1968; co-author: Classical Mechanics, 1950, 2d edit., 1960, internat. edit., 1964; Contbr. to: International Dictionary of Physics and Electronics, 1956. Mem. Am. Phys. Soc., Am. Soc. Physics Tchrs. Home: 4249 La Junta Dr Claremont CA 91711 Office: Dept Physics Harvey Mudd Coll Claremont CA 91711 *Faith in the order of nature is a source of both certainty and wonder. This certainty is my foundation; the wonder is my religion. Together, they form the quest for truth that influences every area of my life. I am fascinated by the unsolved problems both of science and mankind, and I am dedicated to finding accurate solutions. In sharing knowledge through research and teaching, I believe that the certainty is reinforced, the wonder multiplied, and truth interpreted and carried forward.*

CORBER, ROBERT JACK, lawyer; b. Topeka, June 29, 1926; s. Alva Forrest and Katherine (Salzer) C.; m. Joan Irene Tennal, July 16, 1949; children—Janet, Suzanne, Wesley Sean, Robert Jack II. B.S. in Aero. Engring, U. Kans., 1946; J.D. cum laude, Washburn U., 1950; postgrad., U. Mich., 1950-51. Bar: Kans. bar 1950, D.C. bar 1951, U.S. Supreme Ct. bar 1964. Asso. firm Steptoe & Johnson, Washington, 1951-57, partner, 1957-75, 80—; commr. ICC, Washington, 1975-76; partner firm Conner, Moore & Corber, Washington, 1977-80. Author: Motor Carrier Leasing and Interchange Under the Interstate Commerce Act, 1977; contbr. legal and polit. articles to various publs. Chmn. Arlington (Va.) Republican Com., 1960-62; chmn. Va. 10th Congl. Dist. Rep. Com., 1962-64; state chmn. Rep. Party of Va., 1964-68. Served to lt. (j.g.) USNR, 1944-47. Mem. Am. Bar Assn., Bar Assn. D.C. (chmn. adminstrv. law sect. 1978-79, chmn. continuing legal edn. com. 1979—), Motor Carrier Lawyers Assn., ICC Practitioners Assn. Methodist. Clubs: Met., Internat., Capitol Hill, Washington Golf and Country (Washington). Home: 3701 N Harrison St Arlington VA 22207 Office: Steptoe & Johnson 1250 Connecticut Ave NW Washington DC 20036

CORBETT, BRADFORD GARY, plastics and chemicals company executive; b. N.Y.C., Oct. 15, 1937; s. Arthur and Luetta J. (Smith) C.; m. Gunhild Grunde, Oct. 29, 1960; children: Bradford Gary, Pamela, Todd. B.A., Wagner Coll., N.Y.C., 1960. Sales serviceman Barrett div. Allied Chem. Corp., 1960-65, dir. sales plastics and bldg. products, 1965-66; pres. Universal Pipe & Plastics, Inc., 1966-70, Robintech, Inc., Ft. Worth, 1970-74, chmn. bd., chief exec. officer, 1974—; chmn. bd. Plastiline, Inc.; mem. Internat. Trade Conf. of S.W. Active Southwestern Expn. and Fat Stock Show; mem. adv. council Big Brothers Am. Recipient Spirit of Achievement award Jr. Achievement of Tarrant County, 1976; Humanitarian award, 1977; Salesman of Yr. award, 1978. Mem. Am. League Prof. Baseball Clubs (exec. mem.), Young Pres.'s Orgn. Clubs: Petroleum; Metropolitan (N.Y.C.); Aardvark Soc., Shady Oaks Country, River Crest Country. Office: PO Box 2342 Fort Worth TX 76113

CORBETT, CLETUS JOHN, lawyer, shoe company executive; b. Columbus, Ohio, June 18, 1907; s. Patrick J. and Mary (Byrne) C.; m. Margaret P. Burns, Aug. 26, 1946. Student, Ohio State U., 1924-29; LL.B., Franklin U., 1941; J.D., Capital U., 1966. Bar: Ohio 1941. Acct. Proctor-Gamble Co., Jackson, Miss., Memphis, 1929-33; with SCOA Industries, Inc., Columbus, 1934—, counsel, v.p., 1957-66, sec., 1966-72, emeritus dir., 1983—; practiced in, Columbus; counsel firm Porter, Stanley, Platt & Arthur, Columbus, until 1976; with firm Iverson, Yoakum, Papiano & Hatch, Los Angeles, 1976; counsel firm Postlewaite, O'Brien & Mann, Columbus, 1976; individual practice law, Columbus, 1976—. Served with USAAF, 1942-45. Decorated Air medal with nine oak leaf clusters. Mem. Am., Ohio, Columbus bar assns., Am. Judicature Soc., Phi Kappa, Iota Lambda Pi. Clubs: Columbus Athletic, Univ. Home: 4223 Clairmont Rd Columbus OH 43220 Office: Suite 702 33 N High St Columbus OH 43215

CORBETT, ELIZABETH MARIE, librarian; b. Paterson, N.J., Mar. 23, 1926; d. Alfred and Freda (Hartung) Crew; m. Edward Richard Corbett, Oct. 9, 1954. B.A., Wellesley Coll., 1947; M.L.S., Simmons Coll., 1969. Various positions in treasury depts. Bell System Cos., N.Y.C., San Francisco, Boston, 1947-68; circulation librarian Barnard Coll., N.Y.C., 1969-80, dir. library, 1980—; cons. Silliman U. Library, Dumaguete City, Philippines, 1977; mem. com. and chmn. United Bd. for Christian Higher Edn. in Asia, N.Y.C., 1978—. Contbr. articles to library jours. Mem. ALA, N.Y. Library Assn. (pres. acad. and spl. library sect. 1979-80). Home: 59 Delo Dr Tappan NY 10983 Office: Barnard Coll Library Broadway at 117th St New York NY 10027

CORBETT, FRANK JOSEPH, advertising executive; b. N.Y.C., July 5, 1917; s. Daniel and Frances (Manson) C.; m. Dolores Pierce, May 23, 1959; children: Kenneth, Beverly. Ph.G., Columbia U., 1938; postgrad., U. So. Calif., 1947, UCLA, 1947, NYU, 1945-46. Dist. sales mgr., mgr. market research dept. William R. Warner Co., N.Y.C., 1944-46; dir. product devel. and market research, advt. mgr., also asst. to dir. sales Harrower Lab., Inc., Glendale, Calif. and; Jersey City, 1946-51; account exec. Jordan-Sieber Advt. Agy., Chgo., 1951-55; partner, v.p. Jordan, Sieber & Corbett (advt.), 1955-60; cons. pharm. field, 1960-61; founder, pres. Frank J. Corbett, Inc. (advt.), 1961-78, chmn. bd., 1978—, BBDO Healthcare Internat., 1978—. Mem. Midwest Pharm. Advt. Club, Am. Pharm. Assn., Pharm. Mfrs. Assn., Am. Med. Writers Assn. Home: 1320 N State Pkwy Chicago IL 60610 Office: 211 E Chicago Ave Chicago IL 60611

CORBETT, GARY EDWARD, insurance company executive; b. Victoria, C., Can., Jan. 23, 1936; came to U.S., 1963, naturalized, 1969; s. William Oliphant and Bertha Emily (Castley) C.; m. Dorothy Consuelo Forster, Aug. 22, 1958; children: Marilyn, Daryl. B.Commerce, U. B.C., 1958. From actuarial student to asst. actuary Mfrs. Life Ins. Co., Toronto, Ont., 1958-63; from actuary to chief exec. officer Safeco Life Ins. Co., Seattle, 1963-71; sr. v.p. strategic planning and research Safeco Corp., Seattle, 1981-83; v.p., corp. actuary Mfrs. Life, Toronto, 1983—. Bd. dirs. Wash. Spl. Olympic, 1981—. Fellow Soc. Actuaries (gov. 1973-76, 81—); mem. Am. Acad. Actuaries, Can. Inst. Actuaries. Republican. Clubs: Rotary, Seattle Tennis. Home: 8910 Inverness Dr NE Seattle WA 98115 Office: 200 Bloor St E Toronto ON Canada M4W 1E5

CORBETT, J. RALPH, foundation executive; b. Flushing, L.I., N.Y., Dec. 5, 1900; s. Burnett Lewis and Pearl C.; m. Patricia Barry, July 23, 1930; children: Gail Barry, Thomas R. LL.B., N.Y. Law Sch., 1923; D.H.L., U. Cin., 1967; LL.D., Xavier U., 1974, Edgecliff Coll., 1975. Began career in, N.Y.C., serving as marktg. cons. and adviser to Eastern mfg. and fin. orgns.; owner advt. agy.; cons. to early radio broadcasting stas.; adviser Sta. WLW, 1932-37; founder NuTone, Inc., Cin., 1936, pres., then chmn. bd., until 1967; pres. Corbett Found., Cin., 1967—; Spl. adviser Coll.-Conservatory Music, U. Cin., 7 years; head publicity com., spl. adviser fund drive Cin. Inst. Fine Arts, 1973; cons. Nat. Endowment for Arts, Washington. Author: In Spite of All. Donated funds for constrn. Corbett Auditorium and Patricia Corbett Pavilion at Corbett Center for Performing Arts at U. Cin.; active (through found.) in support 7 Cin. hosps., 24 U.S. opera orgns., Royal Opera House, Covent Garden, Eng., Glyndebourne Opera, Eng., Cin. Symphony Orch., teaching studio for young Am. opera singers in, Zurich, Switzerland, Montessori Sch. at, Mercy Center, Cin.; apptd. 1st chmn. Ohio Arts Council, 1965; mem. U.S. Govt. businessmen's team conducting seminars in, Belgium, 1954 mem. U.S. Govt. businessmen's team conducting seminars in, Jamaica, 1960; Pres. May Festival Assn., 1971, now mem. bd.; former chmn. bd. trustees Cin. Symphony Orch.; now mem. exec. com.; mem. bd. Cin. Opera Assn., Cin. Ballet Co., Cin. Inst. Fine Arts; chmn. bd. Cin. Music Hall Assn.; established Corbett Lecture Series at U. Cin. Recipient Great Living Cincinnatian award Cin. C. of C., 1970; (with wife) Ohio's first Cultural Honor award, 1971; recipient Founders of Chgo. Province of Soc. of Jesus award Jesuit Community of Xavier U.; inducted into Housing Hall of Fame, 1982. Mem. MacDowell Soc. Cin., Cin. Hist. Soc. Presbyn. Clubs: Commercial, Queen City, Bankers (Cin.). Office: 1501 Madison Rd Cincinnati OH 45206

CORBETT, JAMES WILLIAM, physicist, educator; b. N.Y.C., Aug. 25, 1928; s. Amos Bryant and Julia (Holmes) C.; m. M.E. Grenander, May 5, 1972. B.S., U. Mo.-Columbia, 1951, M.A., 1952; Ph.D., Yale U., 1955; D.Sc., King Meml. Coll., 1979. Research assoc. Yale U., New Haven, 1955; physicist Gen. Electric Research and Devel. Ctr., Schenectady, 1955-68; mem. faculty physics dept. SUNY, Albany, 1968—, prof., 1968-81, Disting. Service prof., 1981—, chmn. dept. physics, 1969-70, lectr. oncology and turology Coll. Gen. Studies, 1972-78,80, dir. Inst. Study of Defects in Solids, 1973—; adj. prof. Rensselaer Poly. Inst., 1964-68; Disting. vis. prof. Am. U., Cairo, 1973; vis. prof. Ecole Normale Superieure, 1976, U. Paris VII, 1976; sr. Fulbright prof. Tbilisi State U. (U.S.S.R.), 1979; active internat. confs. (U.S.S.R.), 1979. Editorial adv. bd.: Radiation Effects, Crystal Lattice Defects, Radiation Effects Letters; assoc. editor: Materials Letters; author: Electron Radiation Damage in Semiconductors and Metals, 1966, Radiation Effects in Semiconductors, 1971, Radiation-Induced Voids in Metals, 1972, Lattice Defects in Semiconductors, 1976,77; contbr. articles to sci. jours. Democratic Committeeman, 1960-63. Served to 2d lt. Signal Corps U.S. Army, 1946-48..M. Stewart fellow, 1951-52; Charles Coffin fellow, 1954-55; recipient Ivanne Javakinshvili medal, 1977; Guggenheim fellow, 1979; Wissenschaftlichen Mitglieder, Kaiserlich-Konigliche Bobmisch Physikalische Gessellschaft, 1982; named Citizen Laureate Univ. Found.-Albany, 1982. Fellow N.Y. Acad. Scis., Am. Phys. Soc. (vice chmn. N.Y. State sect. 1975-77, chmn. sect. 1977-79); mem. IEEE (sr.), Am. Assn. Physics Tchrs., Materials Research Soc., Electrochem. Soc., AAAS, Am. Cryptogram Assn., Am. Physicists Assn., Soc. Wine Educators (charter), Phi Beta Kappa (chpt. pres. 1978-79), Sigma Xi. Home: 269 Brookhaven Dr East Berne NY 12059 Office: SUNY-Albany Albany NY 12222

CORBETT, JOHN DUDLEY, chemistry educator; b. Yakima, Wash., Mar. 23, 1926; s. Alexander Hazen and Elizabeth (Dudley) C.; m. Irene Lienkaemper, Aug. 7, 1948; children: John Scott, Julia Barton, James Dudley. B.S. cum laude, U. Wash., 1948, Ph.D. (duPont research fellow), 1952. Asst. prof., asso. chemist Iowa State U. dept. chemistry and Ames Lab. AEC (now Dept. of Energy), 1952-58; asso. prof., chemist Iowa State U. and Ames Lab. AEC, 1958-63, prof., sr. chemist, 1963—, disting. prof. scis. and humanities, 1983—, chmn., div. chief, 1968-73, program dir., materials chemistry, 1974-79; chmn. molten salts Gordon Research Confs., 1963, mem. council, 1964-67; cons. E.I. duPont de Nemours & Co., 1956-63, 73-79, Oak Ridge Nat. Lab., 1969-72, Monsanto, 1977-79. Contbr. articles to profl. jours. Served with USNR, 1944-46. Mem. Am. Chem. Soc. (councilor, past chmn. Ames sect.), AAUP, Sigma Xi, Phi Lambda Upsilon, Phi Kappa Phi, Pi Mu Epsilon, Delta Tau Delta. Episcopalian. Home: Route 5 Ames IA 50010

CORBETT, LEO JOSEPH, investment banker; b. Winthrop, Mass., May 29, 1948; s. John Keats and D. Ann C. B.A., Harvard U., 1970, M.B.A., 1975. Mem. staff Congl. Budget Office, Washington, 1975-77; exec. asst. to under sec. HEW, Washington, 1977-78, asso. commr. social security for govtl. affairs, 1979, asso. commr. social security for mgmt., budget and personnel, 1979-80; v.p. Salomon Bros., N.Y.C., 1980—. Mem. Associated Harvard Alumni. Democrat.

CORBETT, LEON H., JR., university dean, lawyer; b. Burgaw, N.C., July 21, 1937; s. Leon H. and Evie (Williams) C.; m. Rachel Stevens,

Dec. 23, 1960; children: Lauren E., Leon H., III. B.A., Wake Forest U., 1959, J.D., 1961. Bar: N.C. 1961. Gen. practice, Burgaw, 1964-65, Wallace, N.C., 1967-68; revisor of statutes Office Atty. Gen. N.C., 1965-67; mem. faculty Wake Forest U. Law Sch., 1968—, prof. law, 1974—, asso. dean, 1979—, asso. gen. counsel, 1979—, corp. sec., 1983—; cons. in field, 1970—. Contbr. articles to legal publs. Deacon, Reynolda Presbyn. Ch., Winston-Salem, 1972, elder, 1977-80. Served as officer U.S. Army, 1961-64. Decorated Army Commendation medal; recipient Appreciation award N.C. Acad. Trial Lawyers, 1979; Outstanding Alumnus award Wake Forest U. Sch. Law, 1981. Mem. ABA, N.C. Bar Assn., N.C. State Bar, Forsyth County Bar Assn., N.C. Criminal Code Commn. Democrat. Home: 405 Archer Rd Winston-Salem NC 27106 Office: Wake Forest U Sch Law PO Box 7206 Reynolda Station Winston-Salem NC 27109

CORBETT, (WINFIELD) SCOTT, author; b. Kansas City, Mo., July 27, 1913; s. Edward Roy and Hazel Marie (Emanuelson) C.; m. Elizabeth Grosvenor Pierce, May 11, 1940; 1 dau., Jane Florence. B.J., U. Mo., 1934. Tchr. of English (part-time) Moses Brown Sch., Providence, R.I., 1957-65. Author: over 60 books, latest being The Case of the Silver Skull, 1974, The Great Custard Pie Panic, 1974, The Case of the Burgled Blessing Box, 1975, The Boy Who Walked on Air, 1975, The Great McGoniggle's Gray Ghost, 1975, Captain Butcher's Body, 1976, The Black Mask Trick, 1976, The Hockey Girls, 1976, The Great McGoniggle's Key Play, 1976, The Hangman's Ghost Trick, 1977, Bridges, 1978, The Discontented Ghost, 1978, The Mysterious Zetabet, 1979, The Donkey Planet, 1979, Home Computers, 1980, The Deadly Hoax, 1981, Grave Doubts, 1982. Served with inf. U.S. Army, 1943-46. Recipient Edgar Allan Poe award Mystery Writers of Am., 1962, Mark Twain award, 1975, Golden Archer award, 1979. Mem. Authors League Am., Providence Preservation Soc. Address: 149 Benefit St Providence RI 02903

CORBIN, ALBERT CHARLES, shipbuilding company executive; b. Barbados, W.I., Apr. 11, 1913; came to U.S., 1915, naturalized, 1924; s. Charles Alexander and Miriam Grace (King) C.; m. Helen Rowe, Jan. 21, 1939. B.S., Wagner Coll., S.I., 1935; postgrad., N.Y. U. Grad. Sch. Bus. Adminstrn., 1935-37. With bur. accounts and deposits Treasury Dept., 1935-41; comptroller Todd-Bath Iron Shipbldg. Corp., New Eng. Shipbldg. Corp., 1942-46; with Todd Shipyards Corp., 1946—, treas., 1966-68, v.p. contracts and procurement, 1968-69; v.p. finance, treas., 1970-75, sr. v.p. adminstrn., 1975-78, internat. marine cons., arbitrator marine and indsl. disputes, 1978—. Chmn. bd. Wagner Coll., 1958-60, chmn. devel. council, 1960-63, chmn. capital fund campaign, 1963-66. Mem. Am. Soc. Naval Architects and Marine Engrs. Clubs: Whitehall (N.Y.C.); Richmond Country Yacht. Home: 1101 Todt Hill Rd Staten Island NY 10304 Office: 1 State St Plaza New York NY 10004

CORBIN, ARNOLD, educator; b. Bklyn., Feb. 16, 1911; s. Harris and Sonia (Kadish) Kowarsky; m. Claire Rothenberg, Aug. 22, 1937; children—Lee Harrison, Karen Sue. B.S. summa cum laude, Harvard U., 1931, M.B.A. with distinction, 1934; Ph.D., N.Y. U., 1954. Research specialist, buyer R.H. Macy & Co., N.Y.C., 1934-39; buyer, merchandiser L. Bamberger & Co., Newark, 1939-40; pres., owner Corbin Foods, N.Y.C., 1946-47; chief technologist U.S. Army Q.M.C., Inspection Service, N.Y.C., 1947-49; lectr., asst. prof. Baruch Sch. Bus. and Pub. Adminstrn., City U., N.Y.C., 1947-54; partner Corbin Assos. (mktg. and mgmt. cons.), Delray Beach, Fla., 1949—; asso. prof. N.Y. U. Sch. Commerce, Accounts and Finance, 1954-55, asso. prof. Grad. Sch. Bus. Adminstrn., 1954-57, prof., 1957-76, prof. emeritus, 1976—; dir. Yardley of London, Inc., 1972-74; co-founder, dir. L.I. Comml. Rev., 1954-57; Mem. Brit. Exports Mktg. Adv. Com., 1965-68; mem. nat. mktg. adv. com. U.S. Dept. Commerce, 1967-72. Author: (with John W. Wingate) Changing Patterns in Retailing, 1956, Bibliography of Graduate Theses in Marketing, 1957, (with Hector Lazo) Management in Marketing, 1961, (with George Blagowidow and Claire Corbin) Decision Exercises in Marketing, 1964, (with Claire Corbin) Implementing the Marketing Concept, 1973; Contbr. chpts. to handbooks, textbooks, articles to encys. and profl. jours. Served with AUS, 1940-46. Ford Found. fellow, 1960. Mem. Am. Mktg. Assn. (dir. N.Y. chpt. 1960-63, nat. dir. 1963-65, v.p. mktg. edn. 1966-67, pres. 1975-76), N.Y. U. Grad. Sch. Bus. Alumni Assn. (dir. 1961-67), Am. Arbitration Assn., Phi Beta Kappa, Beta Gamma Sigma, Eta Mu Pi, Mu Kappa Tau, Alpha Delta Sigma. Club: N.Y. University. Home and office: 177 Waterford Crescent Delray Beach FL 33446 2 Margarita St Toms River NJ 08757

CORBIN, CLAIRE (MRS. ARNOLD CORBIN), educator; b. N.Y.C., July 16, 1913; d. Herman and Anna (Kessler) Rothenberg; m. Arnold Corbin, Aug. 22, 1937; children: Lee Harrison, Karen Sue. B.S., NYU, 1933, M.S., 1941, Ph.D., 1956, postdoctoral, 1957-60; postdoctoral, Yeshiva U., 1957-60. Sales trainee Namm Store, N.Y.C., 1929-30; mdsg. trainee Macys, N.Y.C., 1930-32, Gimbels, 1932-33; buyer Macys, 1939-40; owner The Guildery gifts, N.Y.C., 1944-45; dir. sales tng. Loft Candy, N.Y.C., 1945-46; partner Corbin Assos., Delray Beach, Fla., 1949—; dir. promotion and tng. Decorative Fabrics Inst., N.Y.C., 1948-57; dir. Women's group activities MBS, WOR-TV, N.Y.C., 1948-58; prof. mktg. emeritus Coll. Bus. Adminstrn., Fordham U., Bronx, 1957—; mem. faculty Hofstra U., 1949-57, L.I. U., 1939-44, Baruch Sch., CUNY, 1946-49, Hunter Coll., 1946-47. Editor: Haire Publ., N.Y.C., 1933-39, Two to Six, N.Y.C., 1946-47, Today's Women, N.Y.C., 1947-48; co-author: Principles of Retailing, 1955; Co-author: Principles of Advertising, 1963, Decisions Exercises in Marketing, 1964, New Trends In American Marketing, 1965, Implementing the Marketing Concept, 1973; contbr. to: Handbook of Marketing Management, 1973. Namm scholar, 1929-33; N.Y. State Regents scholar, 1929-33. Mem. AAUP (sec.-treas. 1961-71), AAUW (chmn. mass media 1967-68), Am. Mktg. Assn. (sec.-treas. 1970-73), Am. Acad. Advt. (nat. fin. com. chmn. 1966-67), Advt. Women N.Y., Am. Soc. Interior Designers, Publ. Club N.Y., Nat. Home Fashions League (v.p. 1955-56), Beta Gamma Sigma, Eta Mu Pi, Kappa Delta Pi, Pi Lambda Theta, Gamma Alpha Chi. Home and Office: 177 Waterford Crescent Delray Beach FL 33446 Home and Office: 2 Margarita St Toms River NJ 08757

CORBIN, KENDALL BROOKS, physician, scientist; b. Oak Park, Ill., Dec. 31, 1907; s. William Sherman and Emma (Heacock) C.; m. Eryl Portia Wallace, Jan. 2, 1932; children: Kendall Wallace, Edwin Malcolm. A.B., Stanford, 1931, M.D., 1935. Diplomate: Am. Bd. Psychiatry and Neurology. Instr. anatomy Stanford, 1935-38; NRC fellow in medicine Neurology Inst., Northwestern U., 1937-38; assoc. prof. anatomy Tenn. U., then prof. and chief div. anatomy, 1938-46, in charge neurology, 1943-46; prof. neurology Mayo Found., Minn. U., and; cons. in neurology Mayo Clinic, 1946-72, head sect. neurology, 1956-63, sr. cons. neurology, 1963-72, pres. staff, 1968; asso. dir. Mayo Found. for Med. Edn. and Research, Grad. Sch. of U. Minn., 1950-54; chmn. bd. devel. Mayo Found., 1969-73, emeritus, 1973—; mem. residency rev. com., neurology and psychiatry, 1952-56. Contbr. articles on nervous system to med. jours. Chmn. Rochester Com. Higher Edn., 1955-60; bd. dirs. United Fund Rochester, 1962-68; chmn. Island Assn., 1975-76. Mem. Am. Neurol. Assn., Am. Acad. Neurology, A.M.A., Am. Assn. Anatomists, Am. Physiol. Soc., Soc. Exptl. Biology and Medicine, Minn. Med. Assn., Central Neuropsychiat. Assn., Minn. Soc. Neurology and Psychiatry, Siesta Key Assn. (dir. 1981—), Phi Beta Kappa, Sigma Xi, Alpha Omega Alpha. Club: Sanderling (dir. 1975-78). Home: 645 16th St SW Rochester MN 55901 Office: Mayo Clinic Rochester MN 55901 *Avoid succumbing to the Peter Principle: 1. Obtain the best, most complete training in your field of specialization. Do not use short-cuts. 2. Avoid tempting promotions or job offers, especially involving administrative duties, which will interfere with your progression in your chosen field. 3. Similarly, avoid offers which appear to enhance your power, prestige or financial status, if such interfere with your growth and experience in your field of knowledge.*

CORBIN, ROBERT K., state attorney general; b. 1928; (m); 3 daus. B.S., Ind. U., 1952, J.D., 1956. Bar: Ariz. 1956. County atty., Maricopa County, 1965-69; chmn. Maricopa County Bd. Suprs., 1974-77; atty. gen. State of Ariz., Phoenix, 1979—; mem. stats. adv. bd. U.S. Bur. Justice; chmn. Ariz. Criminal Justice Commn. Served with USN, 1946-48. Mem. Ariz. State Bar Assn. (past mem. ethics com.), Maricopa County Bar Assn., Ariz. County Attys. Assn., NRA, Nat. Assn. Attys. Gen. (chmn. antitrust com. 1981-83), Americans for Effective Law Enforcement (pres. 1974), Conf. Western Attys. Gen. (chmn. 1982). Republican. Club: Masons. Home: 1275 W Washington Phoenix AZ 85007 Office: Office of Atty Gen Dept of Law State Capitol Phoenix AZ 85007

CORBIN, SOL NEIL, lawyer; b. Bklyn., Apr. 16, 1927; s. Nathan I. and Sarah (Kaiser) C.; m. Tanya Jacobs, Aug. 7, 1963; 1 son, David J. B.S., Columbia, 1948; LL.B. cum laude, Harvard, 1951. Bar: N.Y. 1952. Practiced in, N.Y.C., 1952—; law clk. Judge Charles D. Breitel, 1954-56; counsel Gov. of N.Y., 1962-65; partner Corbin, Silverman, Sanseverino & Taylor, N.Y.C., 1970—; Mem. N.Y. State Banking Bd., 1969-76; Chmn. N.Y. State Commn. Constl. Conv., 1966-67; mem. N.Y. State Commn. Local Govt. Powers, 1971-73; chmn. N.Y. State Crime Control Planning Bd., 1974-75; mem. Chief Judge's Com. to Recruit State Ct. Adminstr., 1973; trustee in bankruptcy Franklin N.Y. Corp., 1974—; spl. counsel Vice Pres. U.S., 1975. Trustee N.Y. Pub. Library, League Sch. Served with USNR, 1945-46. Mem. Am., N.Y.C., N.Y. State bar assns., Am. Arbitration Assn. (chmn. comml. sect. law com.), Am. Law Inst. Home: 1100 Park Ave New York NY 10028 Office: 280 Park Ave New York NY 10017

CORBOY, PHILIP HARNETT, lawyer; b. Chgo., Aug. 12, 1924; s. Harold Francis and Marie (Harnett) C.; m. Doris Marie Conway, Nov. 26, 1949; children—Philip Harnett, Joan Marie, John, Thomas. Student, St. Ambrose Coll., 1942-43, U. Notre Dame, 1945; J.D., Loyola U., 1948. Bar: Ill. bar 1949. Asst. corp. counsel City Chgo., 1949-50; individual practice, 1950—. Contbr. articles to profl. jours. Trustee Roscoe Pound Found. Served with AUS, 1943-45. Fellow Am. Coll. Trial Lawyers; mem. ABA. (chmn. litigation sect. 1979-80), Ill. Bar Assn., Chgo. Bar Assn. (pres. 1972-73), Law Sci. Acad., Am. Judicature Soc., Am., Ill. trial lawyers assns., Nat. Inst. Trial Advocacy (vice chmn. 1971-72), Internat. Acad. Trial Lawyers, Internat. Soc. Barristers, Inner Circle Advs. Clubs: Evanston Golf, Chgo. Athletic Assn. Home: 9519 N Monticello Evanston IL 60203 Office: Suite 630 33 N Dearborn St Chicago IL 60602

CORBY, FRANCIS MICHAEL, JR., manufacturing executive; b. Chgo., Feb. 2, 1944; s. Francis M. and Jean (Wolf) C.; m. Diane S. Orselli, Aug. 5, 1972; children: Francis Michael III, Brian A., Christopher S. B.A., St. Mary of the Lake, 1966; M.B.A., Columbia U., 1969. Treasury mgr. Chrysler Peru S.A., Lima, 1973-74; fin. dir. Chrysler Wholesale Ltd., London, 1974-76; mng. dir. Chrysler Comml. S.A. de C.V., Mexico City, 1976-77; v.p., treas. Chrysler Fin. Corp., Troy, Mich., 1977-80; treas. Joy Mfg. Co., Pitts., 1980—; dir. Joy Fin. Co. Bd. dirs. Vocat. Rehab. Ctr., St. Scholastica Parent Tchrs. Guild. Mem. Fin. Execs. Inst. Clubs: Duquesne, Pitts. Field.

CORCORAN, BARBARA ASENATH, author; b. Hamilton, Mass., Apr. 12, 1911; d. John Gilbert and Anna (Tuck) C. B.A., Wellesley Coll., 1933; M.A., U. Mont., 1955. Instr. English, U. Ky., No. Center, 1956-57; with story dept. CBS-TV, Hollywood, Calif., 1957-58; tchr. English, Marlborough Sch., Hollywood, 1958-59; instr. English, U. Colo., 1960-65; instr. Corr. Sch. Creative Writing, 1964-72; instr. English, Palomar Coll., San Marcos, Calif., 1965-69. Author: numerous children's books including Make No Sound, 1977, Hey, That's My Soul You're Stomping On, 1977, Me and You and a Dog Named Blue, 1979, Rising Damp, 1979, Strike!, 1983; also adult books Abigail; also writes under pen names Paige Dixon and Gail Hamilton; contbr. stories to popular mags. Recipient William Allen White award, 1972, Nat. Sci. Tchrs.-Children's Book Council award, 1974, 77. Mem. Authors League Am. Democrat. Episcopalian. Home and Office: PO Box 4394 Missoula MT

CORCORAN, DAVID, newspaper editor; b. N.Y.C., July 22, 1947; s. William and Ruth (Brody) Diebold; m. Karrie Olick; 1 son, Thomas. B.A., Amherst Coll., 1969; fellow journalism, Stanford U., 1976-77. Tchr. Rockland Country Day Sch., Congers, N.Y., 1969-70; reporter Hackensack (N.J.) Record, 1969-73, editorial writer, then asst. editor, 1973-77, editor editorial page, 1977—; instr. journalism Seton Hall U., S. Orange, N.J., 1977-78. Mem. Am. Soc. Newspaper Editors, Nat. Conf. Editorial Writers, Sigma Delta Chi (dir. N.J. chpt. 1980—, pres. N.J. chpt. 1983—). Home: 437 Wildwood Rd Northvale NJ 07647 Office: 150 River St Hackensack NJ 07602

CORCORAN, EILEEN LYNCH, educator; b. Newark, Mar. 12, 1917. A.B. in English, Montclair (N.J.) State Coll., 1938, Litt.D. (hon.), 1976; M.S. in Elem. Edn, SUNY, Brockport, 1953; spl. edn. cert., U. Rochester, 1958; Ed.D., SUNY, Buffalo, 1970. High sch. tchr. spl. edn., 1957-65; coordinator spl. edn. Bd. Coop. Ednl. Services, 2d Supervisory Dist., Monroe County, N.Y., 1965-67; asst. prof. to asso. prof. D'Youville Coll., Buffalo, 1967-72, dir. spl. edn., 1969-72; dir. edn. Children's Psychiat. Centre, N.Y. State Dept. Mental Hygiene, 1970-71; mem. faculty SUNY, Brockport, 1972-81, prof. curriculum and instrn., 1977-81, prof. emeritus, 1981—; bd. visitors Monroe Devel. Center, Rochester; mem. adv. council Commn. on Quality of Care for Mentally Disabled, State of N.Y.; cons. in field. Author curriculum materials, articles. Fellow Am. Assn. Mental Deficiency; mem. Council Exceptional Children (pres. N.Y. State 1971, Disting. Service award), AAUW, AAUP, Assn. Children with Learning Disabilities, Delta Kappa Gamma. Address: 17442 105th Ave Sun City AZ 85373 *As an educator concerned with the developmentally disabled, I look on the years from 1960 to 1980 as the Golden Years in the education of the handicapped. To have lived a professional life during those years was most challenging. To see the education of those children move from the institution to an open society, from no public school classes in most areas to a multitude of special classes, and then to see those children move back into the mainstream of education with programs designed to meet their individual needs was most gratifying.*

CORCORAN, HOWARD FRANCIS, U.S. judge; b. Pawtucket, R.I., Jan. 25, 1906; s. Thomas Patrick and Mary Josephine (O'Keefe) C.; m. Esther Pierce, May 31, 1952. Grad., Phillips Exeter Acad., 1924; A.B., Princeton, 1928; LL.B., Harvard, 1931. Bar: N.Y. bar 1935, D.C. bar 1956. With Dept. Agr., 1933-34, TVA, 1934-35; legal asso. SEC, 1935-38; asst. Office U.S. Atty. for So. Dist. of N.Y., 1938-43; U.S. atty. So. Dist. N.Y., 1943; partner firm Corcoran, Kostelanetz & Gladstone, N.Y.C., 1946-54, Corcoran, Foley, Youngman & Rowe, Washington, 1954-65; U.S. dist. judge for D.C., Washington, 1965—. Served to lt. col. AUS, 1943-45. Decorated Bronze Star, Croix de Guerre with star, France). Mem. Am., Fed. bar assns., Bar Assn. of D.C., Assn. Bar City N.Y., Phi Delta Phi. Roman Catholic. Clubs: Princeton, Army-Navy, Congressional Country (Washington). Home: 2801 New Mexico Ave NW Washington DC 20007 Office: US Courthouse Washington DC 20001

CORCORAN, JAMES MARTIN, JR., lawyer; b. Evanston, Ill., Nov. 12, 1932; s. James M. and Ethel M. (Fitzgerald) C.; m. Catherine F. Howland, Aug. 6, 1955; children: Mary Carol, John Kevin, Lawrence T., Rosemary C., Pauline M., Moira E., Daniel P. A.B., U. Notre Dame, 1955, J.D., 1956. Bar: Ill. 1956. Practiced in, Evanston, 1956-78; partner Corcoran & Corcoran (attys.), Evanston, 1957-63, sr. partner, 1964-72; pres. Corcoran & Corcoran, P.C., Evanston, 1973-78, Chgo., 1983—; partner firm D'Ancona & Pflaum, 1979-83; lectr. in field. Author: Alternatives to Probate, 1972, Suggested Will and Trust Clauses, 1973, In the Office-A Form Book For Lawyers, 1974, Probate Forms for Estates of Minors, Incompetents and Decedents, 1977, Estate and Gift Taxation for the General Practitioner, 1979, (with others) Drafting Wills and Trust Agreements, rev., 1983; Contbr. chpts. to continuing legal edn. books, articles to profl. jours.; sect. editor: Ill. Bar Jour., 1965—. Mem. sch. bd. St. Mary's Sch., 1969-72. Recipient Harrison Tweed award Assn. Continuing Legal Edn. Adminstrs., 1975; Distinguished Service award Chgo. Estate Planning Council, 1975. Fellow Am. Coll. Probate Counsel (editorial bd. Probate Notes 1975-78); mem. ABA, Ill. Bar Assn. (bd. govs. 1972-75), Chgo. Bar Assn. Roman Catholic. Home: 929 Sheridan Rd Evanston IL 60202 Office: 221 N LaSalle St Suite 2230 Chicago IL 60601

CORCORAN, JOHN, marine animal center executive. V.p., gen. mgr. Marineland, Rancho Palos Verdes, Calif. Office: Marineland PO Box 937 Rancho Palos Verdes CA 90274§

CORCORAN, JOHN JOSEPH, judge; b. N.Y.C., Aug. 12, 1920; s. John Joseph and Ellen (Fitzgerald) C.; m. Evelyn Dynan Madden, Apr. 29, 1943; children: Patricia Corcoran Holt, Joanne, John, Maureen, Mary. B.S., Georgetown U., 1948, J.D., 1951. Bar: D.C. 1952. Legal cons. Am. Legion, 1952-56; atty. adviser Nat. Security Agy., 1957; dir. Am. Legion Nat. Rehab. Commn., 1958-67; asst. to gen. counsel VA, 1968-69, gen. counsel, 1969-77; adminstrv. judge Contract Appeals Bd., 1977—. Served to capt. USAAF, 1942-45; col. Res.; ret. Decorated Legion of Merit, D.F.C., Air medal with three oak leaf clusters, N.Y. State Conspicuous Service Cross. Mem. ABA, Fed., D.C. bar assns. Home: 9513 Cable Dr Kensington MD 20895 Office: 810 Vermont Ave Washington DC 20420

CORCORAN, MARY BARBARA, educator; b. Pasadena, Calif., May 22, 1924; d. George Ernest and Ina Pearl (Thomas) Morrison; m. James Leonard Corcoran, Dec. 22, 1956; children: Ann Morrison, Elizabeth Phippen. B.A., Wellesley Coll., 1946; M.A., Radcliffe Coll., 1949; postgrad., U. Munchen, 1949-50; Ph.D., Bryn Mawr Coll., 1958. Translator U.S. War Dept. (Nuremberg), Germany, 1946-47; instr. German Wellesley Coll., Mass., 1947-48; faculty Vassar Coll., Poughkeepsie, N.Y., 1953—, prof. German, 1977—. Mem. Am. Assn. Tchrs. German, AAUP, MLA. Mem. United Ch. of Christ. Office: Dept German Vassar Coll Poughkeepsie NY 12601

CORCORAN, PAUL JOHN, physician; b. Washburn, Wis., June 8, 1934. B.S., Georgetown U., 1955; M.D., 1959; M.S. in Phys. Medicine and Rehab., U. Wash., 1968. Diplomate: Am. Bd. Phys. Medicine and Rehab. Intern U. Oreg. Hosps., 1959-60; resident in rehab. medicine NYU, 1963-66; postdoctoral fellow HEW-Social and Rehab. Services; Acad. Career trainee dept. rehab. medicine U. Wash. Med. Center, 1966-68; asst. attending physiatrist Presbyn. Hosp. City N.Y.; asst. prof. rehab. medicine Columbia U., 1968-72; dir. residency tng. in rehab. medicine Columbia-Presbyn. Med. Center, N.Y.C., 1969-72; asso. prof. rehab. medicine Boston U., 1972-76; adj. asso. prof. Sargent Coll. Allied Health Professions, 1974—; asso. prof. Tufts U., 1976-78, prof., 1978—, acting chmn. dept. rehab. medicine, 1977-78, chmn. dept., 1978-81; physiatrist-in-chief Rehab. Inst., New Eng. Med. Center Hosp., Boston, 1978-81; chief rehab. medicine service Boston City Hosp., 1975-77, Boston VA Med. Center, 1980—; cons. in field; instr. NYU Grad. Sch. Prosthetics and Orthotics, 1970-77; vis. physician rehab. medicine Univ. Hosp., Boston, 1972-76; project dir. New Eng. Regional Rehab. Research and Tng. Center, 1977-81. Contbr. chpts. to books, articles to profl. publs.; editorial bd. Archives Phys. Med. and Rehab., 1971-77. Trustee Easter Seal Research Found., 1975-78; chmn. profl. adv. com. Mass. Easter Seal Soc., 1976; trustee Carroll Rehab. Center for Blind, 1975-78; mem. rehab. services nat. adv. com. HEW, 1976-77; chmn. Mass. Interagy. Council on Ind. Living, 1977-79. Served to lt. M.C., USN, 1960-63. Mem. Am. Assn. Acad. Physiatrists (pres. 1981-83). Home: 92 Appleton St Boston MA 02116 Office: Rehab Medicine Service Boston VA Med Center 150 S Huntington Ave Boston MA 02130

CORCORAN, THOMAS JOSEPH, writer/cons., former ambassador; b. N.Y.C., Sept. 6, 1920; s. John T. and Mary A. (Carroll) C. B.S.S., St. John's U., 1940; student S.E. Asia lang. and area, Georgetown U., 1953. Mem. U.S. Fgn. Service, 1948—; vice consul, Barcelona, Spain, 1948-50, Hong Kong, 1950-51, sec. embassy, Saigon, Viet-Nam, 1951-53, charge d'affaires ad interim, Vientiane, Laos, 1951-52, Phnom Penh, Cambodia, 1952, consul, Hanoi, N. Viet-Nam, 1954-55; officer in charge Viet-Nam affairs Dept. of State, 1956-58, 1958-59; assigned (Armed Forces Staff Coll.), 1959-60, dep. polit. adv. to comdr. in chief Pacific, 1960-62, dep. chief mission, counselor, Ouagadougou, Upper Volta, 1962-64, dir. working group, Vietnam, 1964-65, 1st sec., Saigon, 1965, consul gen., Danang, Vietnam, 1966; grad. Nat. War Coll., 1968; country dir., Laos and Cambodia, 1968-73, dep. chief mission, counselor, Port-au-Prince, Haiti, from 1973, prin. officer, Quebec, Que., Can., 1974-75; minister-counselor Am. embassy, Vientiane, Laos, 1975-77; ambassador to, Burundi, 1977-80, now writer/cons. Served to lt. (s.g.) USNR, World War II. Home: 2725 29th St NW Washington DC 20008

CORCORAN, TOM, congressman; b. Ottawa, Ill., May 23, 1939; m. Helenmarie Anderson, 1962; children: Camilla, Evan, Philip, Steven, Monica. B.A., Notre Dame U., 1961; postgrad., U. Ill., 1962, U. Chgo., 1963, Northwestern U., 1967. Vice pres. Chgo.-North Western Transp. Co., 1974-76; adminstrv. asst. to leaders Ill. State Senate, 1966-69; dir. State of Ill. office, Washington, 1969-72; mem. 95th-98th congresses from 15th Ill. Dist. Served in U.S. Army, 1963-65. Republican. Office: 2447 Rayburn House Office Bldg Washington DC 20515 *

CORD, ALEX (ALEXANDER VIESPI), actor; b. N.Y.C., Aug. 3, 1931; m. Joanna Pettet, 1968. Studied at, Shakespeare Acad., Stratford, Ont., Can., Actors Studio, N.Y.C. Acted two years in summer stock; toured with, Stratford Shakespeare Co., 1961; appeared in: films Synanon, 1965, Stagecoach, 1966, The Scorpio Letters, The Prodigal Gun, The Brotherhood, 1968, Stiletto, 1969, The Dead Are Alive, 1972, Chosen Survivors, 1974, Sidewinder 1, 1977, Grayeagle, 1978; TV films: Hunter's Man, Genesis II, Beggarman Thief, The Girl Who Saved Our America; numerous guest appearances on TV series *

CORDARO, MATTHEW CHARLES, utility executive, nuclear engineer; b. N.Y.C., July 25, 1943; s. Matteo C. and Josephine (Picone) C.; m. Janet Chick, June 24, 1967; children: Anne Marie, Allison. B.S., C.W. Post Coll., 1965; M.S. in Nuclear Engring., NYU, 1967; Ph.D. in Applied Nuclear Physics, Cooper Union, 1970. Asst. engr. L.I. Lighting Co., Hicksville, N.Y., from 1966, successively assoc. engr., nuclear physicist, sr. environ. engr., mgr. environ. engring., v.p. engring., 1978—; guest research assoc. Brookhaven Nat. Lab., 1968-

71; adj. assoc. prof. nuclear engring. Poly. Inst. N.Y., 1979-80; adj. asst. prof. engring. C.W. Post Coll., 1968-72. Contbr. articles to profl. jours. Council overseers C.W. Post Coll.; bd. dirs. Adelphi U. Energy Ctr.; mem. community adv. bd. Sta. WLIW pub. TV, Garden City, N.Y. AEC fellow, 1965-66. Mem. Am. Nuclear Soc., Heatlh Physics Soc. Club: Huntington Crescent (N.Y.). Office: LI Lighting Co 175 E Old Country Rd Hicksville NY 11801

CORDASCO, FRANCESCO, sociologist, educator; b. N.Y.C., Nov. 2, 1920; s. Giovanni and Carmela (Madorma) C.; m. Edna Vaughn, Oct. 22, 1946; children—Michael, Carmela. B.A., Columbia, 1942; M.A., N.Y. U., 1945, Ph.D., 1959; student, U. London, U. Salamanca. Prof. English L.I.U., 1946-53; prof. edn. Fairleigh Dickinson U., then; Seton Hall U., 1953-63; prof. edn. Montclair (N.J.) State Coll., 1963—; vis. prof. N.Y. U., City U. N.Y., U. London, U. P.R.; cons. migration div. Commonwealth P.R., U.S. Office Edn., also municipal, county, state and fed. anti-poverty programs; cons. com. edn. and labor com. U.S. Ho. of Reps., labor and welfare com. U.S. Senate; mem. N.J. adv. council Elementary and Secondary Edn. Act Title III Programs; mem. N.J. Adv. Council Vocat. Edn.; mem. com. on racism and social justice Nat. Council for Social Studies. Author: Research, 1948, 15th edit., 1974, Junius Bibliography, 1949, rev. edit., 1974, 18th Century Bibliographies, 1950, Adam Smith: A Bibliographical Checklist, 1950, Bohn Libraries, 1951, Daniel Coit Gilman and the Protean Ph.D.: The Shaping of American Graduate Education, 1960, A Brief History of Education, 1963, 5th edit., 1981, Educational Sociology, 1965, Education in the Urban Community, 1969, School in the Social Order, 1970, Puerto Rican Community and its Children, 1968, 3d edit., 1982, Jacob Riis Revisited: Poverty and the Slum in Another Era, 1968, Minorities in the American City, 1970, Teacher Education in the United States: A Guide for Foreign Students, 1971, Puerto Ricans on the U.S. Mainland, 1972, Italians in the United States, 1972, Puerto Rican Experience, 1973, Italian American Experience, 1974, Equality of Educational Opportunity, 1973, The Puerto Ricans, 1973, The Italians: Social Backgrounds of an American Group, 1974, Studies in Italian American Social History, 1975, Bibliography of American Educational History, 1975, Bilingual Schooling in the United States, 1976, Immigrant Children in American Schools, 1976, Spanish for Hospital and Medical Personnel, 1977, Tobias G. Smollett, M.D, 1978, Sociology of Education, 1978, Bilingual Education in American Schools, 1979, Medical Education in the U.S, 1979, American Ethnic Groups, 1980, The White Slave Trade and the Immigrants, 1981, American Medical Imprints, 1820-1910: A Bibliography, 1983; also numerous articles.; Editor: Social History of Poverty, 15 vols, 1968-70, Puerto Rican Experience, 33 vols, 1975, Italian American Experience, 39 vols, 1975, Bilingual Education in the U.S., 40 vols, 1978, American Ethnic Groups: The European Heritage, 47 vols, 1981. Mem. bd. edn. Newark Archdiocese; mem. exec. bd. Mt. Carmel Guild; trustee Christ Hosp., Jersey City. Served with AUS, World War II. Recipient Brotherhood award NCCJ, Order Merit Republic Italy. Fellow Am., Brit. sociol. assns.; mem. Soc. Advancement Edn. (trustee). Home: 6606 Jackson St West New York NJ 07093 Office: Montclair State Coll Upper Montclair NJ 07043

CORDAY, ELIOT, physician, med. researcher; b. Prince Rupert, C., Can., June 29, 1913; came to U.S., 1946, naturalized, 1951; s. David and Katie (Goldberg) C.; m. Marian Lipkind, Aug. 20, 1940; children—Joanne Corday Kozberg, Stephen R. M.D., U. Alta., Can., 1940. Diplomate: Am. Bd. Internal Medicine. Intern in medicine U. Alta. Hosp., 1939; then resident in medicine; resident in cardiology Bellevue Hosp., N.Y.C., 1946, Mt. Sinai Hosp., 1946-47; practice medicine specializing in cardiology, Los Angeles; chief cardiology Cedars-Sinai Med. Center, Los Angeles, 1950-61, sr. attending physician, 1961—, sr. research scientist, 1961—; nat. cons. cardiology to Surg. Gen., USAF, 1967-77; med. adv. panel on heart disease to President of U.S., 1972; mem. joint council subcom. on cerebrovascular disease to NIH, 1969-77; clin. prof. medicine UCLA; hon. prof. medicine U. Santo Tomas, Philippines, U. Chile; Del Amo vis. pro univs. Barcelona and Madrid, Spain, 1957, 59; John F. Kennedy Meml. lectr., Concord, Mass., 1968, Ricardo D. Molina lectr., Manila, 1968, David Flett DuPont Meml. lectr., Wilmington, Del., 1968; Luis Guerrero Meml. lectr. U. Santo Tomas, 1971; James Sherwood Taylor lectr. Ark. Heart Assn., 1974, Ernst Simonson Meml. lectr., 1974; vis. disting. prof. cardiology Swedish Soc. Cardiology, 1979; Dvorkin Meml. lectr. U. Alta., 1981; mem. nat. adv. com. Jules Stein Eye Inst.; Mem. Citizens for Treatment of High Blood Pressure, Washington. Author: The Auricular Arrhythmias, 1951, Accelerated Conduction, 1952, Disturbances in Heart Rate, Rhythm and Conduction, 1962, Myocardial Infarction, 1971, Controversies in Cardiology, 1977, Clinical Strategies in Ischemic Heart Disease, 1979; contbr. numerous articles on cardiology to med. jours.; asso. editor: Am. Jour. Cardiology, 1960-75, Jour. Electrocardiology, 1964-77, Coeur et Medecine Interne, 1974—; editorial bd.: Drug Therapy; editor sect. cardiology: Contemporary Therapy. Served in RCAF, 1941-45. Decorated Order of Merit, Philippines, 1971; comdr. Nat. Order So. Cross, Brazil, 1979; comdr. Order of Liberator San Martin, Argentina, 1977; recipient numerous awards, latest being; Gold medal of Merit Ministry of Health Argentina, 1974; Myrtle Wreath award So. Pacific Coast Region Hadassah, 1977; Purkynje medal Czechoslovakian Soc. Cardiology, 1978. Fellow A.C.P., Am. Coll. Cardiology (pres. 1965-66, Disting. Fellowship award 1968, Cummings Humanitarian award 1963-65, 71, 74, 76, mem. internat. edn. com. 1961—), Am. Coll. Chest Physicians (regent 1964-73), Am. Coll. Nuclear Medicine, Am. Heart Assn. (dir. 1965-66, mem. council cerebrovascular disease), Brazilian Soc. Cardiology (hon.); mem. Los Angeles Acad. Medicine, AMA (cert. Merit 1962, 70, 77, chmn. sect. diseases of chest 1971-75), Los Angeles County Med. Assn. (mem. adv. com. to city council Beverly Hills dist. 1978-79, chmn. com. med. schs., editorial com. 1977-78, rep. to Am. Heart Assn. Greater Los Angeles 1977), Calif. Med. Assn., Interam. Soc. Cardiology (dir. 1968-72). Republican. Jewish. Club: Hillcrest Country (Los Angeles). Originator concepts of cerebrovascular and mesenteric vascular insufficiency. Home: 810 N Roxbury Dr Beverly Hills CA 90210 Office: 436 N Roxbury Dr Beverly Hills CA 90210

CORDELL, JOE B., diversified corporation executive; b. Daytona Beach, Fla., Aug. 4, 1927; s. Joe Wynne and Ada Ruth (Wood) C.; m. Joyce Hinton, June 16, 1951; children: Joe B., Coleman Wynn, Lauren. Student, Yale U., 1945-46, Fla. So. Coll., 1946-47; B.S. in Bus. Adminstrn, U. Fla., 1949. C.P.A. Intern Price Waterhouse Corp., N.Y.C., 1948-49, staff acct., 1949-50, audit mgr., Atlanta, 1950-58; v.p. Jim Walter Corp., Tampa, Fla., 1958-70, sr. v.p., treas., 1970-74, pres., chief operating officer, dir., 1974—; dir. Royal Trust Bank of Tampa, Gen. Instrument Corp., Fla. Steel Corp., from 1978. Past pres., trustee U. Fla. Found.; trustee bus. adv. council U. Fla. Served with USNR, 1945-46. Mem. Am. Inst. C.P.A.s, Ga. Inst. C.P.A.s, Fla. Inst. C.P.A.s, Greater Tampa C. of C., Com. of 100, Alpha Kappa Psi, Alpha Tau Omega. Methodist. Clubs: Tower of Tampa, Tampa Yacht and Country, Palma Ceia Golf and Country, Wildcat Cliffs Country, University of Tampa, Ye Mystic Krewe of Gasparilla. Office: Jim Walter Corp 1500 N Dale Mabry Hwy Tampa FL 33607 *

CORDER, DUANE RALPH, television engineer; b. Milw., Dec. 6, 1925; s. Ralph and Olive Jeanette (Palmer) C.; m. Joyce M. Ponschock, Oct. 8, 1949; children: Donna, Jeffrey, John. B.S. in TV Engring, Am. TV Lab., 1950. TV engr. ABC, Chgo., 1950-71, 82—; treas. local 41 Nat. Assn. Broadcast Employees and Technicians, Chgo., 1967-71, internat. sec.-treas., 1971-82; trustee ABC-Nat. Assn. Broadcast Employees and Technicians, 1971—. Mng. editor: Nabet News, 1971-82. Served with USMC, 1943-46. Home: 704 Pinecroft Dr Roselle IL 60172 Office: Nat Assn Broadcast Employees and Technicians 343 S Dearborn St Chicago IL 60604

CORDER, JIM W., educator; b. Jayton, Tex., Sept. 25, 1929; s. Nolan John and Ina Ruth (Durham) C.; m. Patsy Ruth Akey, Apr. 1, 1951; children—David Harold, Catherine Elaine, Melinda Sue. B.A., Tex. Christian U., 1953, M.A., 1954; Ph.D., U. Okla., 1958. Mem. faculty Tex. Christian U., Fort Worth, 1958—, prof. English, chmn. dept., 1966-77, dean arts and scis., 1978-81, asso. vice chancellor, 1981—. Author: A College Rhetoric, 1962, Rhetoric a Reader, 1965, A Handbook of Current English, 1968, 75, 78, 81, Uses of Rhetoric, 1971, Finding a Voice, 1973, Contemporary Writing, 1979. Served with AUS, 1950-52. Mem. Nat. Council Tchrs. English, S. Central Modern Lang. Assn., Modern Lang. Assn., Am. Assn. Higher Edn., Coll. English Assn., Phi Beta Kappa, Phi Eta Sigma. Presbyterian (elder). Home: 3137 Stadium Dr Fort Worth TX 76109

CORDERO, ANGEL T., JR., jockey; b. San Juan, P.R., Nov. 8, 1942; s. Angel T. and Mercedes (Hernandez) C.; m. Santa Cordero, Sept. 26, 1962; children: Angel Thomas, Merly Suzette. Student, Inst. P.R. Winner Ky. Derby, 1974, 76, Preakness Stakes, 1980, Belmont Stakes, 1976; recipient Jockey of Yr. award Turf Riders of Nation, 1982, Seagrams, 1982, George Wolf award Turf Riders of Nation; honored Angel Cordero Jr. Day, P.R. Office: NY Racing Assn PO Box 90 Jamaica NY

CORDES, ALEXANDER CHARLES, lawyer; b. Buffalo, Aug. 14, 1925; s. Alexander J. and Margaret (Markens) C.; m. Jane Wells, Feb. 9, 1976; children by previous marriage: John J., Ann T., Susan A. B.A., Yale, 1947; LL.B., U. Buffalo, 1950. Bar: N.Y. 1950. Assoc. firm Kenefick, Bass, Letchworth, Baldy & Phillips, 1950-54; asst. U.S. atty. Western Dist. N.Y., 1954-56; partner firm Phillips, Lytle, Hitchcock, Blaine & Huber, Buffalo, 1956—; Mem. Erie County Bd. Suprs., 1960-61. Served with USNR, 1943-46. Fellow Am. Coll. Trial Lawyers, N.Y. Bar Found.; mem. Am., N.Y. State, Erie County bar assns., Fellows of Am. Bar Found. Presbyterian. Clubs: Tennis and Squash, Pundit (Buffalo); Cherry Hill (Ridgeway, Ont., Can.). Home: 121 Norwood Ave Rear Buffalo NY 14222 Office: Marine Midland Center Buffalo NY 14203

CORDES, DONALD WESLEY, hospital administration consultant; b. Stephenson County, Ill., Dec. 31, 1917; s. Theodore J. and Fannie (Van Osterloo) C.; m. Harriet Davies, Oct. 11, 1947; children: Beverly Ann, Karen Sue. A.B. cum laude, Hope Coll., Holland, Mich., 1940; M.A., U. Mich., 1941; postgrad. hosp. adminstrn, Columbia U., 1945-46. Adminstrv. asst. St. Luke's Hosp., N.Y.C., 1944-47; exec. v.p., then pres. Iowa Methodist Med. Center, Des Moines, 1947-83; cons. Cordes and Assoc., Des Moines, 1983—; Bd. dirs. Nat. Health Council, 1969-75, Iowa Mental Health Assn. Mem. Am. Hosp. Assn. (trustee 1960-63, Disting. Service award 1980), Iowa Hosp. Assn. (trustee 1950-62, pres. 1952-53), Upper Midwest Hosp. Conf. (trustee 1952-61, pres. 1957-58), Nat. Assn. Meth. Hosps. and Homes (pres. 1963-64), Am. Coll. Hosp. Adminstrs. (regent 1963-64, gov. 1964-66, pres. 1967-68, Gold medal 1975), Am. Assn. Hosp. Planning (dir. 1975). Methodist. Clubs: Des Moines, Wakonda. Home: 5715 Woodland Rd Des Moines IA 50312 Office: Cordes and Assocs 1221 Center St Des Moines IA 50309

CORDES, EDWARD JOHN, food company executive; b. St. Louis, Jan. 13, 1925; s. Edward Carl and Mary Florence (Goller) G.; m. Ruth May Haupter, Aug. 8, 1945; children: Nancy Ellen, David Edward. B.A., St. Louis U., 1950. With Ralston Purina Co., St. Louis, 1949—, corp. v.p. soybean div. and corp. transp., 1973-79, sr. v.p., 1979—. Served with inf. U.S. Army, 1944-46. Decorated Gold Star. Mem. Nat. Soybean Processors Assn. (vice chmn.), Chgo. Bd. Trade, St. Louis Grain Exchange, Nat. Inst. Oilseed Products. Methodist. Clubs: Missouri Athletic, Algonquin Country (St. Louis). Office: 835 S 8th St Saint Louis MO 63164

CORDES, EUGENE HAROLD, biochemist; b. York, Nebr., Apr. 7, 1936; s. Elmer Henry and Ruby Mae (Hofeldt) C.; m. Shirley Ann Morton, Nov. 9, 1957; children: Jennifer Eve, Matthew Henry James. B.S., Calif. Inst. Tech., 1958; Ph.D., Brandeis U., 1962. Instr. chemistry Ind. U., Bloomington, 1962-64, asst. prof., 1964-66, asso. prof., 1966-68, prof., 1968-79, chmn., 1972-78; exec. dir. biochemistry Merck, Sharp and Dohme Research Labs., Rahway, N.J., 1979—, v.p. biochemistry, 1982—. Author: (with Henry Mahler) Biological Chemistry, 1966, 2d. edit., 1971, Basic Biological Chemistry, 1969, (with Riley Schaeffer) Chemistry, 1973; also articles. NIH Career Devel. award, 1966; Alfred P. Sloan Found. fellow, 1968. Mem. Am. Chem. Soc., AAAS, Am. Soc. Biol. Chemists. Home: 649 Nottingham Pl Westfield NJ 07090

CORDES, LOVERNE CHRISTIAN, interior designer; b. Cleve., Feb. 13, 1927; d. Frank Andrew and Loverne Louise (Brown) Christian; m. William Peter Cordes, Nov. 14, 1959; children: Christian Peter, Carey Pomeroy. B.S., Purdue U., 1949. Owner, mgr. Loverne Christian Cordes, Chagrin Falls, Ohio, 1967—; tchr. John Carroll U., Cleve., 1976-77. Interior designer, Fred Epple Co., Cleve., 1949-67. Fellow Am. Soc. Interior Designers, AIA, Nat. Home Fashion League (past pres. Ohio chpt.), Am. Inst. Interior Designers (past pres. Ohio chpt., nat. bd. dirs. 1969-75, nat. v.p. East Central region 1972-75, nat. exec. bd. 1972-75, recipient 1st Presdl. citation 1973, 74, 75); mem. Soc. Collectors Dunham Tavern Mus. (bd. dirs. 1961-62), Dunham Dames (past pres.), Western Reserve Hist. Soc., Cleve. Mus. Art, Cleve. Garden Center, Chagrin Falls Hist. Soc., Nat. Trust for Historic Preservation, Internat. Platform Assn., Arcadian, Kappa Kappa Gamma. Republican. Congregationalist. Clubs: Chagrin Valley Country., Dogwood Garden. Address: 60 S Franklin St Chagrin Falls OH 44022

CORDIER, HUBERT VICTOR, educator; b. North Canton, Ohio, Apr. 27, 1917; s. Emery Andrew and Minnie (Lahr) C.; m. Ruth Virginia Roop, Aug. 3, 1940; 1 son, Gary Michael. B.A., Manchester Coll., Ind., 1939; M.A., Mich. State U., 1942; Ph.D., U. Ill., 1955. Tchr., coach Columbia (Ind.) City High Sch., 1939-40; teaching fellow Mich. State U., 1940-42; asst. prof. speech Allegheny Coll., Meadville, Pa., 1946-49; head dept. radio and TV U. Ill. at Urbana, 1949-68; dir. broadcasting, prof. speech U. Iowa, Iowa City, 1968—, also head. div. broadcasting and film.; Bd. dirs., chmn. Nat. Ednl. Radio, Assn. Pub. Radio Stas. Served with USAAF, 1944-46. Mem. Assn. Profl. Broadcasting Edn. (pres., bd. dirs.), Nat. Assn. Ednl. Broadcasters (chmn. publs. com.), Am. Assn. U. Profs., Speech Assn. Am., Radio and TV News Dirs. Assn. Methodist. Home: 306 Stewart Rd RR6 Iowa City IA 52240

CORDING, RICHARD ARNOLD, college dean; b. Pinehurst, N.C., June 23, 1936; s. Melvin C. and Helen (Rhudy) C.; m. Frances Scott Watson, Apr. 21, 1957; children: Susan, Lisa, Sheri, Jennifer. A.B., U. N.C., Chapel Hill, 1960; M.A., U. Mo.-Columbia, 1963, Ph.D., 1968. Instr, philosophy U. Mo., Columbia, 1961-68; asst. prof. Bradley U., Peoria, Ill., 1969-70; mem. faculty Sam Houston State U., Huntsville, Tex., 1970—, prof. philosophy, 1970—, chmn. dept., 1980-81, dean Coll. Arts and Scis., 1979—. Contbr. articles to profl. jours. Bd. dirs. United Way, 1977-80. Mem. Coll. Council Arts and Scis. Deans, Am. Philos. Soc. Methodist. Lodge: Rotary. Office: Office Dean Coll Arts and Scis Sam Houston State U Huntsville TX 77341

CORDINGLEY, WILLIAM ANDREW, newspaper publisher; b. Des Moines, Aug. 24, 1917; s. William Andrew and Louise (Cookerly) C.; m. Mary Jeannette Bowles, Mar. 17, 1942; children: William Andrew, Thomas Kent, Constance Louise. Grad., Phillips Exeter Acad., 1936; B.S., Harvard U., 1940. With Mpls. Star and Tribune, 1940-65, nat. advt. mgr., 1949-65; pub., pres. Great Falls (Mont.) Tribune, 1965—; pres. South Idaho Newspapers, Inc., 1977-82, chmn., 1982—; dir. Mont. Mag., Northwestern Nat. Bank, Great Falls.; Vice chmn. Helena br. Mpls. Fed. Res. Bank, 1970, 72, chmn., 1971, 73, 74, 75. Trustee Breck Sch., Mpls., 1962-65; bd. dirs. Great Falls Symphony, 1965-70, Russell Gallery, Great Falls, 1965-76, Mpls. Curative Workshop, 1952-65; mem. council of 50, U. Mont., 1966-70; mem. U. Mont. Citizens Council, 1979-83; mem. pres.'s council Coll. Great Falls, 1971—, trustee, 1979—, vice chmn. bd. trustees, 1981-83; bd. dirs. Endowment and Research Found., Mont. State U., 1968-73; Mem. regional adv. group Mountain State Regional Med. Programs, 1967-71. Served to lt. col. AUS, 1941-46; ETO, MTO and NATOUSA. Mem. Am. Newspaper Pubs. Assn., Mpls Sales and Mktg. Execs. (v.p. 1963-65), Great Falls C. of C. (dir. 1967-70), Sigma Delta Chi. Episcopalian. Clubs: Hazeltine Nat. (Mpls.) (bd. govs. 1962-65); Meadowlark Country (Great Falls) (bd. dirs. 1966-69); Harvard Varsity.). Lodge: Rotary. Home: 42 Prospect Dr Great Falls MT 59405 Office: Great Falls Tribune Great Falls MT 59405

CORDOVA, VALDEMAR A., judge; b. Phoenix, Dec. 6, 1922; s. Louis H. and Carmen A. C.; m. Gloria Orduno, July 18, 1945; children: Kenneth, Valerie, Lexia. J.D., U. Ariz., 1950. Bar: Ariz. 1950. Practiced in, Phoenix, 1950-65, 67-76; partner firm Renaud, Cook, Miller & Cordova, 1967-76; judge Superior Ct. Ariz., Phoenix, 1965-67, 76-79, U.S. Dist. Ct., 1979—. Mem. Phoenix City Council, 1956-59, Phoenix Civil Service Bd., 1962-65, Phoenix Adjustment Bd., 1954-56. Served with USAAF, 1940-45. Decorated Air medal, Purple Heart. Mem. Am., Ariz., Maricopa County bar assns., Ariz. Judges Assn., Am. Legion. Democrat. Roman Catholic. Club: Vesta. Address: US Dist Ct 7418 US Courthouse Phoenix AZ 85025

CORDTZ, HOWARD DAN, TV correspondent; b. Gary, Ind., May 1, 1927; s. Edmund Richard and Edna B. (Cox) C.; m. Mildred R. Peck, 1947 (div. 1970); children: Wendy, Kay, Richard, Jeffrey; m. Ann L. Woodfield, 1975. B.A., Stanford U., 1949. News editor Hanford (Calif.) Daily Sentinel, 1950-52; reporter, sports writer Cleve. Plain Daler, 1952-55; reporter, Detroit bur. mgr., Paris corr., Senate corr. The Wall St. Jour., 1955-66; Washington editor, asso. editor Fortune mag., 1966-74; econs. editor ABC News, N.Y.C., 1974—. Mem. selection com. Carnegie-Mellon Profl. Fellows. Served with USN, 1945-46. Recipient Christopher award, 1975; Janus awards, 1975, 76, 77, 78; Media award for Econ. Understanding, 1978, 80; Martin Gainsbrugh award, 1979. Mem. Econ. News Broadcasters Assn. (founding pres. 1977), Assn. Radio and TV News Analysts. Office: ABC News 7 W 66th St New York NY 10023

CORDTZ, RICHARD W., labor union official; b. Chgo., Dec. 20, 1921; s. Raymond and Grace C.; m. June, 1949. Student, Ripon Coll., 1946-47, San Diego State Coll., 1947-48. Mem. Service Employees Internat. Union, Washington, 1947—; organizer local 102, Service Employees Internat. Union, Detroit, 1947-50; internat. rep. Service Employees Internat. Union, 1951-68; pres. local 79, Service Employees internat. Union, Detroit, 1955-80; internat. v.p. Service Employees Internat. Union, 1972-80, sec.-treas., 1980—. Mem. Wayne County Tax Allocation Commn., Mich. Wage Deviation Bd.; bd. dirs. Detroit Urban League, 1975-80; commr. Dept. transp., City Detroit, 1974-80. Office: Service Employees Internat Union 2020 K St NW Washington DC 20006 *

COREA, (ARMANDO) CHICK, pianist, composer; b. Chelsea, Mass., June 12, 1941; s. Armando John and Anna (Zaccone) C.; children—Thaddeus, Liana. Student, Columbia, 1960, Juilliard Sch. Music, 1961. Pianist with, Mongo Santamaria, 1962; pianist, composer with, Blue Mitchell, 1965, Stan Getz, 1966-68; pianist with, Miles Davis, 1969-71; with, Sarah Vaughan, 1970; founder, leader and pianist: group Return to Forever, 1971—; over 100 recs. including Return to Forever, Piano Improvisations 1 & 2, Leprechaun, My Spanish Heart, Mad Hatter, Delphi 1, 2, & 3, Light as a Feather, Romantic Warrior, Hymn of the Seventh Galaxy, Music magic (Recipient Grammy awards 1975, 76, 78, 79); founder, leader and (Playboy Music Poll awards 1973, 77, 79, 80, Downbeat awards 1973, 74, 75, 76, 78, 79, 80, named Jazz Musician of World, Jazz Forum Music Poll (Europe) 1974, Jazzman of Yr., Swing Jour. (Japan) 1978, Swing Jour. Critics Poll 1980); Author: The Jazz Style of Chick Corea, 1972. Mem. Ch. of Scientology. Address: 2635 Griffith Park Blvd Los Angeles CA 90039 *I always knew that music would be my life's work, but learning to live life itself has been a constant search for the right way. I searched through rebellion, drugs, diets, mysticism, religions, intellectualism, and much more only to begin to find, with the help of the incredible teachings of L. Ron Hubbard, that truth is basically simple and feels good, clean, and right. And that learning to know myself and communicate with my surroundings with an honest and unafraid intention to really look and be willing to see what's there is the surest way to success.*

COREA, LUIS FELIPE, banker, cons.; b. Washington, May 23, 1910; s. Luis Felipe and India Bell (Fleming) C.; m. Ann Margot Helring, Sept. 12, 1939. Student, George Washington U., 1932-36; certificate, Stonier Grad. Sch. Banking, Rutgers U., 1948. With Riggs Nat. Bank, Washington, 1926-75, v.p., mgr. fgn. dept., 1950-63, sr. v.p., 1963-75, cons., 1975—; dir. Dynalectron Corp., 1957-79; mem. adv. com. Export-Import Bank U.S., 1963-64; Mem. Def. Industry Adv. Council subcom. mil. exports Def. Dept., 1963-72; vice-chmn. Md. Regional Export Expansion Council, 1967-75; Mem. adv. council Sch. Langs. and Linguistics, Georgetown U., 1964-75; council advisers Edmund A. Walsh Sch. Fgn. Service, Georgetown U., 1965-75; bd. dirs., exec. com. Internat. Student House, 1964-69. Trustee, treas. Meridian House Found., 1967-69; chmn. Meridian House Internat., 1975-79; trustee Consortium of Univs., Washington, 1975—. Served to lt. comdr. USNR, 1942-45. Decorated chevalier Nat. Order Merit, France; commendatore Ordine al Merito della Repubblica Italiana; knight Sovereign Mil. Order Malta; knight Holy Sepulchre. Mem. Acad. Polit. Sci., Am. Inst. Banking, Bankers Assn. for Fgn. Trade (dir. 1958-60, 61-63, pres. 1963-64), Met. Washington Bd. Trade (World Trade award 1964), Am. Legion (comdr. post), Confrerie des Chevaliers du Tastevin (grand officier honoraire), Japan Am. Soc. Washington, Washington Inst. Fgn. Affairs. Clubs: Chevy Chase (Md.); Internat. (Washington) (pres. 1971-77). Home: 1701 N Kent St Arlington VA 22209

CORELL, ROBERT WALDEN, educator; b. Detroit, Nov. 4, 1934; s. George W. and Grace R. (Hagl) C.; m. Billie Jo Proctor, June 16, 1956; children—Robert Walden, David Richard, Beth Anne. B.S. in Mech. Engring, Case Inst. Tech., 1956, Ph.D., 1964; M.S., Mass. Inst. Tech., 1959. Engr. Gen. Electric Co., Cleve., 1955, program engr., Lynn, Mass., 1956-57; instr. U. N.H., 1957-58, asst. prof., 1959-60, asso. prof., 1964-66, prof., 1966—, chmn. dept. mech. engring., 1964-72, dir. marine program, 1975—, dir. sea grant program, 1975—; dir. Marine Systems Engring. Lab., 1976—; research engr. Huggins Hosp.,

Wolfeboro, N.H., 1957-60, Highland View Hosp., Cleve., 1960-64; vis. investigator Woods Hole Oceanographic Inst., 1965; research asso., vis. prof. Scripps Instn. Oceanography, 1971-72; Cons. U.S. Navy Oceanographic Programs, USCG, Gen. Motors Corp., Ford Motor Co., Corning Glass, Wood Products, Inc., Apasco Products, Huggins Hosp., Honeywell, Raytheon Co., IBM. Contbr. articles in medicine, med. engring., ocean sci. and tech. to profl. jours. Dist. commr. Boy Scouts Am., 1957-58. Mem. AAAS, Am. Soc. Engring. Edn., IEEE, Marine Tech. Soc., Sea Grant Assn. (pres. 1979-80), Sigma Xi, Tau Beta Pi, Sigma Alpha Epsilon. Home: Durham Point Rd Durham NH 03824

CORELLI, FRANCO, tenor; b. Ancona, Italy, Aug. 4, 1923; m. Moretta Di Lelio, 1958. Student naval engring., U. Bologna, Italy, Pesaro Conservatory of Music. Made: operatic debut as Don Jose in Carmen, Spoleto (Italy) Festival, 1952; made: Met. Opera debut as Manrico in Il Trovatore, 1961; performed at major opera houses in, Vienna, Paris, Hamburg, Bologna, Florence, Genoa, Milan, Naples, Rome, Venice, Lisbon, Barcelona, London, Chgo., Miami, Phila., San Francisco; has sung: major parts in Boris Godunov, Andrea Chenier, Turandot, Tosca, Ernani, Aida, Don Carlos, Forza del Destino, Cavalleria Rusticana, I Pagliacci, Romeo and Juliet. Winner vocal competition Florence (Italy) Music Festival, 1951. Office: care Columbia Artists Mgmt 165 W 57th St New York NY 10019 *

CORELLI, JOHN CHARLES, physicist, educator; b. Providence, Aug. 6, 1930; s. John and Immacolata (Caldarelli) C.; m. Evelyn L. Hostetter, June 20, 1959; children: Carolyn Margaret, John Joseph. B.Sc., Providence Coll., 1952; M.S., Brown U., 1954; Ph.D., Purdue U., 1958. Physicist Knolls Atomic Power Lab., Gen. Electric Co., 1958-61; mem. faculty Rensselaer Poly. Inst., 1962—, prof. nuclear engring. and sci., 1962—; cons. NASA, summer 1962, Gen. Electric Co. Contbr. articles to profl. jours. NIH Fellow U. Rochester, 1971. Mem. Am. Phys. Soc., Am. Nuclear Soc., Rensselaer Newman Found., Sigma Xi. Roman Catholic. Research on radiation and ion beam effects in metals, ceramics and semiconductors, radiation chemistry of polymers. Home: 33 Belle Ave Troy NY 12180 *The sun expends energy, gives us warmth and light, and keeps the world and mankind going by feeding the necessary life cycle for our survival. I in turn feel I can make a minuscule contribution by also expending energy, by hard work, and by becoming like a "sun" and continuing the process of creation, culminating as a Son of God.*

CORENA, FERNANDO, bass; b. Geneva, Switzerland, Dec. 22, 1916; emigrated to U.S., 1954; s. Dimitri and Ugolina (Albertini) C. Bacalaurea, U. Frybourg, Switzerland. Operatic debut in Arena of Verona, La Scala, Milan; leading bass with, Metropolitan Opera, at Theatro Colon, Buenos Aires, Stattsoper, Berlin, Covent Garden, London, Lyric Opera, Chgo., San Francisco Opera, Vienna Staatsoper, Grand Theatre, Geneva, Rome Opera, Vienna Staatsoper, Florence Maggio Musicale et Comunale; also appeared in, Brussels, Nice, Paris, Lisbon, Barcelona, Hartford, Houston, Miami, New Orleans, Phila., Washington., festival appearances include, Salzburg, Edinburgh, Holland, Athens. Home: Via San Giorgio 18 6976 Castagnola Switzerland Office: Metropolitan Opera House New York NY 10023

CORETTE, JOHN E., lawyer, utilities executive; b. Butte, Mont., Apr. 20, 1908; s. John E. and Mary Taaffe (Driscoll) C.; m. Elsie Charlotte Pauly, Jan. 2, 1932 (dec.); children: Joan Elise Corette Hanley, John E., III, William Pauly, Diane Corette Simperman; m. Sallie Sheridan, Jan. 3, 1972. Student, U. Mont., 1926; J.D., U. Va., 1930; LL.D., Coll. Great Falls, 1958, Carroll Coll., Helena, Mont., 1970. Bar: Mont. 1929, Va. 1929. Practiced law, Missoula, 1930-34; partner Corette, Smith & Dean, Butte, 1934-79; counsel Mont. Power Co., 1934-44, v.p., asst. gen. mgr., 1944-52, pres., chief exec. officer, 1952-67, chmn., chief exec. officer, 1967-73, chmn. bd., 1973-78, chmn. emeritus, 1978—, dir., 1948-80, Pacific Gas Transmission Co., 1959—, Canadian-Mont. Pipe Line Co., 1951-79, Fed. Res. Bank Mpls., Helena br., 1950-53, Canadian-Mont. Gas Co., Ltd., 1950-79, Fed. Res. Bank Mpls., 1954-61, Altana Exploration Co., 1948-80, First Bank System, 1961-76, Burlington No. Ry., 1970-72, Western Energy Co., 1951-80, Northwestern Resources Co., 1971-80; U.S. del., com. electric power UN Econ. Commn. for Europe, 1957, 58; dir. U.S. nat. com. World Energy Conf., 1971-74; mem. energy fin. adv. com. Fed. Energy Adminstrn., 1971-76; mem. exec. adv. com. Nat. Power Survey, 1974-77, FPC; trustee Freedoms Found. Valley Forge, 1966-73, Thomas Alva Edison Found., 1969-73; mem. Stanford Research Inst. Council, bd. dirs., 1961-78, Nat. Indsl. Conf., 1964-72; mem. pres.'s council Carroll Coll., 1964-75, trustee, 1975—. Mem. Edison Electric Inst. (pres. 1958-59), Nat. Assn. Electric Cos., NAM (dir. 1966-73), Bus. Council, U.S., Polson (Mont.) chambers commerce, Am., Mont., Silver Bow County bar assns. Clubs: Rotary (pres. 1938-39), Country (Butte); Desert Island Country (Rancho Mirage, Calif.). Home: East Shore Polson MT 59860 899 Island Dr Rancho Mirage CA 92270 Office: 40 E Broadway Butte MT 59701

COREY, ELIAS JAMES, chemistry educator; b. Methuen, Mass., July 12, 1928; s. Elias and Tina (Hashem) C.; m. Claire highham, Sept. 14, 1961; children: David, John, Susan. S.B., MIT, 1948, Ph.D., 1951; A.M. (hon.), Harvard U., 1959, D.Sc., U. Chgo., 1968, Hofstra U., 1974, contd., Colby Coll., 1977. From instr. to asst. prof. U. Ill., Champaign-Urbana, 1951-55, prof., 1955-59; prof. chemistry Harvard U., Cambridge, Mass., 1959—, Sheldon Emory prof., 1968—. Contbr. articles to profl. jours. Bd. dirs. phys. sci. Alfred P. Sloan Found., 1967-72; mem. sci. adv. bd. dirs. Robert A. Welch Found. Recipient Intrasci. Found. award, 1968, Ernest Guenther award in chemistry of essentials oils and related products, 1968, Harrison Howe award, 1971, Ciba Found. medal, 1972, Evans award Ohio State U., 1972, Linus Pauling award, 1973, Dickson prize in sci. Carnegie Mellon U., 1973, George Ledlie prize in sci. Harvard U., 1973, Nichols medal, 1977, Buchman award Calif. Inst. Tech., 1978, Franklin medal in sci. Franklin Inst., 1978, Sci. Achievement award CCNY, 1979; fellow Swiss-Am. exchange, 1957, Guggenheim Found., 1957-58, 68-69, Alfred P. Sloan Found., 1956-59. Mem. Am. Acad. Arts and Scis., AAAS, Am. Chem. Soc. (award in synthetic chemistry 1971, Pure Chemistry award 1960, Fritzche award 1968, Md. sect. Remsen award 1974, Arthur C. Cope award 1976), Nat. Acad. Sci., Sigma Xi. Home: Avon Hill St Cambridge MA 02140 Office: Dept Chemistry Harvard U Cambridge MA 02138

COREY, GORDON RICHARD, financial advisor, former utilities executive; b. Osceola, Wis., Sept. 27, 1914; s. Ralph Watson and Bessie Mabel (Simpson) C.; m. Margarete Moeller Grenn, 1967; children by prev. marriage: Eleanor (Mrs. George Tatge), Margaret (Mrs. Ross Amundson), Ralph, Martha. B.A., U. Wis., 1936; M.B.A., Northwestern, 1940. C.P.A., Ill. Vice pres. Commonwealth Edison Co., 1953-62, exec. v.p., 1962-64, chmn. finance com., 1964-73, vice chmn., from 1973, now ret., also div.; now pvt. fin. adv.; dir. Nukem, Inc., Inland Steel Co., Chgo., Perkins & Will, Inc. Clubs: Commercial, Wayfarers. Home: 2511 Park Pl Evanston IL 60201

COREY, JEFF, actor, director, educator; b. N.Y.C., Aug. 10, 1914; s. Nathan and Mary (Peskin) C.; m. Hope Victorson, Feb. 26, 1938; children: Eve, Jane, Emily. Student, Feagin Sch. Drama, 1930-32, UCLA, 1955. Prof. drama Calif. State U.-Northridge, 1966-71, Chapman Coll.'s World Campus Afloat, 1973—; founder creative drama workshop Los Angeles Juvenile Hall, 1968; Bd. dirs. Ojai Music Festivals Inc. Stage actor, N.Y.C., 1932-40; actor numerous motion pictures, Hollywood, Calif., 1940—; dir. TV films, various firms, 1970—, profl. actors workshop, Hollywood, 1951—; Contbr. articles on film, stage acting to profl., popular publs. Served with USNR, 1943-45. Mem. Acad. Motion Picture Arts and Scis., Screen Actors Guild (dir.).

COREY, KENNETH EDWARD, geography and urban planning educator; b. Cin., Nov. 11, 1938; s. Kenneth and Helen Ann (Beckman) C.; m. Marie Joanne Fye, Aug. 26, 1961; children: Jeffrey Allen, Jennifer Marie. B.A. with honors, U. Cin., 1961, M.A., 1962, M.C.P., 1964, Ph.D., 1969. Instr. U. Cin., 1962-65, asst. prof. community planning, 1965-69, assoc. prof., 1969-74, prof., 1974-79, head grad. community planning and geography, 1969-78; assoc. prof. community planning and geography U. R.I., 1966-67; prof. geography, planning, chmn. dept. geography, dir. urban studies U. Md., 1979—; vis. prof. geography Univ. Coll. Wales, Aberystyth, 1974-75; chmn. Cin. Model Cities Bd., 1974; trustee Met. Washington Housing Planning Assn., 1980-82. Author: The Local Community, 1968, Community Internships for Undergraduate Geography Students, 1973, The Planning of Change, 3d edit., 1976. Bd. dirs. Potomac River Basin Consortium, Washington, 1982—. Recipient Service award Community Chest and Council Cin., 1979, Planning Div., 1979, Coalition of Neighborhoods, Cin., 1979, 83, medal of city Mayor of Seoul, South Korea, 1980. Mem. Am. Inst. Cert. Planners, Am. Planning Assn., Assn. Am. Geographers, Assn. Asian Studies, Asia Soc., World Future Soc. Democrat. Home: 10412 Kinloch Rd Silver Spring MD 20903 Office: U Md 1113 LeFrak Hall CollegePark MD 20742

COREY, PAUL FREDERICK, author; b. Shelby County, Iowa, July 8, 1903; s. Edwin and Margaret Morgan (Brown) C.; m. Ruth Lechlitner, 1928; 1 dau., Anne Margaret. A.B. in Journalism, U. Ia., 1925. On staff The Economist, Chgo., 1925-26; with Retail Credit Co., N.Y.C., 1926; later with Ency. Brit.; with Real Estate Record and Builders Guide, N.Y.C., 1929-30, Nat. Ency., 1930-31. Ret. to a farm, Putnam County, N.Y., to write, 1931; furniture designer, Cavedale Craftsman.; Author books, 1936-46; teen-age novel Five Acre Hill, 1946; novel Acres of Antaeus, 1946; juvenile The Little Jeep, 1946; Shad Haul, 1947, Corn Gold Farm, 1948, Homemade Homes, 1951, Milk Flood, 1956, Home Workshop Furniture Projects, 1957, Holiday Homes: A Build-it-yourself Handbook, How to Build Country Homes on a Budget; novel The Planet of the Blind; biography Bachelor Bess: My Sister; Do Cats Think? Notes of a Cat-Watcher, Are Cats People?, 1979; also short stories. Mem. Sci. Fiction Writers Am., Authors Guild. Guerrilla warfare specialist; did work on the subject in connection with First Service Command Tactical Sch., Sturbridge, Mass., 1942. Home: 267 Cavedale Rd Sonoma CA 95476 *Somewhere in my growing up I became conditioned with a stubborn determination to accomplish what I set out to do. All of my accomplishments have been abetted by fortuitous circumstances which were outside of my control, and without which I could not have succeeded.*

CORFMAN, PHILIP ALBERT, obstetrician-gynecologist, government research administrator; b. Berea, Ohio, July 19, 1926; s. Stanley Albert and Anita (Tritschler) C.; m. Eunice Ruth Luccock, Jan. 29, 1950; children: Stanley, Caris, Timothy, Lewis. B.A., Oberlin Coll., 1950; M.D., Harvard U., 1954. Diplomate: Am. Bd. Ob-Gyn. Intern and resident in surgery Boston City Hosp., 1954-56; resident in Ob-Gyn Boston Hosp. for Women, 1956-59; obstetrician, gynecologist Rip Van Winkle Clinic, Hudson, N.Y., 1959-63; Josiah Macy Jr. Found. fellow in Ob-Gyn Columbia U., 1963-64; cons. in Ob-Gyn, asst. to dir. for population research Nat. Inst. Child Health and Human Devel., Bethesda, Md., 1964-68; dir. Center for Population Research, 1968—; teaching fellow in Ob-Gyn Harvard U., 1956-59; mem. adv. com. on Ob-Gyn FDA; mem. adv. group to expanded programme of research devel. and research tng. in human reprodn., mem. steering com. on instl. strengthening WHO. Contbr. articles in population research, contraception and gynecol. cancer to profl. jours. Served with USN, 1944-46. Recipient Superior Service award HEW, 1975. Mem. Am. Coll. Obstetricians and Gynecologists, Soc. Study Fertility, Assn. Profs. Gynecology and Obstetrics. Office: NIH Landow Bldg 7910 Woodmont Ave Bethesda MD 20205

CORI, CARL FERDINAND, educator, biochemist; b. Prague, Czechoslovakia, Dec. 5, 1896; came to U.S., 1922, naturalized, 1928; s. Carl I. and Maria (Lippich) C.; m. Gerty Theresa Radnitz, Aug. 5, 1920 (dec. 1957); 1 son, Carl Thomas; m. Anne FitzGerald Jones, Mar. 23, 1960. Student, Gymnasium, Austria, 1906-14; M.D., German U. Prague, 1920, U. Trieste, Italy, 1974; Sc.D., Yale, Western Res. U., 1947, Boston U., 1948, Cambridge U., Eng., 1949, U. Granada, Spain, 1966, Brandeis U., 1965, Monash U., Melbourne, Australia, 1966, Washington U., St. Louis, 1967, St. Louis U., 1967, Gustavus Adolphus Coll., 1963. Asst. in pharmacology U. Graz, Austria, 1920-21; biochemist State Inst. for Study Malignant Disease, Buffalo, 1922-31; prof. pharmacology and biochemistry Washington U. Sch. Medicine, 1931-66; cons. biochemistry, vis. lectr. Mass. Gen. Hosp., Harvard U. Med. Sch., Boston, 1966—, dir. Enzyme Research Lab., 1966—; mem. faculty Harvard Med. Sch., 1966—. Contbr. articles, chiefly on carbohydrate metabolism and enzymes of animal tissues to Am. sci. jours.; Mem. editorial bd.: Biochimica et Biophysica Acta. Recipient Nobel Prize in medicine and physiology, 1947; Willard Gibbs medal Am. Chem. Soc., 1948; Sugar Research Found. award, 1947, 50; Lasker award, 1946; Squibb award, 1947; St. Louis award. Mem. Nat. Acad. Scis.; hon. mem. Harvey Soc.; mem. Am. Soc. Biol. Chemists, Am. Chem. Soc. (Mid-West award 1946), A.A.A.S., Royal Soc. London, Am. Philos. Soc., Sigma Xi.

CORI, GREGORY SALVATORE, mgmt. cons.; b. Bklyn., May 22, 1925; s. Domenick and Catherine (Ruggiero) C.; m. Theresa M. Priolo, Oct. 29, 1949; children—Janice-Cathy, Joyce-Terri. Student, Juilliard Sch. Music, 1942; B.S., Columbia, 1949, M.S., 1950; postgrad., City Coll. N.Y., 1952-53, N.Y. U., 1954. Sales promotion work with Am. Tobacco Co., 1949-50; mktg. and mktg. research work Willmark Research Co., N.Y.C., 1950-51; advt. mgr. Miehle-Goss-Dexter Co., N.Y.C., 1951-55; mgr. mktg. div. Sel-Rex Corp., Nutley, N.J., 1955-62; founder, pres. Mktg. Communications, Inc., Wayne, N.J., 1962—; officer, dir. Summit Sci. Corp., Fairfield, N.J., 1974—; dir. Platronics, Inc., Linden, N.J., 1967—; asso. prof. mktg. studies Rutgers U., 1957—, 1974—; mktg. cons. Am. Motors Co., 1964-65, Battelle Research Inst., Geneva, 1968-69; guest.speaker, lectr. in field. Contbr. profl. jours. Served with USMCR, 1943-46. Named Advt. Man of Yr. Nat. Indsl. Advertisers Assn., 1960. Mem. Nat. Assn. Indsl. Advertisers (pres. N.J. chpt. 1961-62). Inventor TEA charter (Total Environment Analysis) applying sci. method graphically for exposition of bus. problems and devel. and implementation of responsive solutions. Home: 60 Pine Lake Dr NE Wayne NJ 07470 Office: 31 Dwight Pl Fairfield NJ 07006

CORIDEN, GUY EDWARD, govt. ofcl.; b. Syracuse, N.Y., May 31, 1921; s. Guy Edward and Lucy (Lamb) C.; m. Mary Louise Winbigler, Apr. 21, 1956. B.S., Ind. U., 1942; M.A., Marquette U., 1950, Fletcher Sch. Law and Diplomacy, 1951. Security analyst Paul H. Davis & Co., Chgo., 1946-48; reins. underwriter AMRICO, Chgo., 1948-49; adminstrv. positions with U.S. Govt., 1951-60; staff adminstr. Pres.'s Commn. Nat. Goals, 1960-61; dir. Office European Programs, Bur. Ednl. and Cultural Affairs, State Dept., 1962-73, Office Internat. Arts Affairs, 1973-76; mem. U.S. del. Conf. Security and Cooperation in Europe, 1973-75; dep. staff dir. Congl. Commn. on Security and Cooperation in Europe, 1976-79; asso. dir. Office Mgmt. Ops., Dept. State, 1979—; Mem. nat. adv. com. Wayne State U. Urban Affairs Inst., 1968-72. V.p. N.W. council Big Bros. Nat. Capital Area, 1971-73; mem. nat. adv. com. Center for Met. Planning, Johns Hopkins U., 1975—; trustee Nat. Children's Island, 1975-78. Served with AUS, 1942-45; ETO. Decorated Star medal. Mem. Urban League, Left Bank Jazz Soc., Les Cent Chevaliers du Vin, Les Amis du Vin. Club: Lakewood Country (Rockville, Md.). Home: 2204 Wyoming Washington DC 20008

CORIGLIANO, JOHN PAUL, composer; b. N.Y.C., Feb. 16, 1938; s. John Corigliana and Rose (Buzen) C. B.A. cum laude, Columbia U., 1955. Composer: Concerto for Piano and Orch., 1968, A Dylan Thomas Trilogy: A Choral Symphony, 1961-76, Concerto for Oboe and Orch., 1975, Concerto for Clarinet and Orchestra, 1977, Pied Piper Fantasy: Concerto for Flute and Orch., 1981; film score Altered States, 1980. Guggenheim fellow, 1968. Mem. ASCAP, Assn. Classical Music (dir.), Bohemians. Home: 365 West End Ave New York NY 10024 Office: care G. Schirmer Inc 866 3d Ave New York 10022

CORIN, HAROLD SEYMORE, retail department store executive; b. Chgo., Dec. 17, 1926; s. Edwin Michael and Sophie (Radis) C.; m. Dolores Lillian Bassin, Sept. 7, 1947; 1 son, Edward Michael. B.S., Roosevelt U., Chgo. Div. mdse. mgr. Fair Store, Chgo., 1954-63; v.p., gen. mdse. mgr. Richards, Miami, Fla., 1963-65, Evans Fur Co., Chgo., 1965-67; gen. mdse. mgr. soft lines Lit Bros., Phila., 1967-70; pres., chief exec. officer Bergner Weise, Rockford, Ill., 1970-82; pres. P.A. Bergner, Peoria, Ill., 1982—. Pres. bd. dirs. Children's Devel. Center, Rockford; v.p. Winnebago County Heart Assn.; bd. dirs. Ill. Heart Assn.; chmn. Winnebago County Heart Fund. Served with USNR, 1944-46; PTO. Decorated Purple Heart. Mem. Nat. Retail Mchts. Assn., Rockford C. of C. (bd. dirs.), Am. Mgmt. Assn. Jewish. Home: 9052 Locust Ln Peoria IL 61615 Office: 200 SW Adams St Peoria IL 61626

CORINALDI, AUSTIN, hospital administrator; b. N.Y.C., Mar. 31, 1921; s. Oswald and Claris (A.) C.; m. Dorothy Newby, June 24, 1944; children: Dyhann Dorothy, Greg Austin. B.A., N.Y. U., 1949; M.P.H., Columbia U., 1964, M.S., 1969. Joined as pvt. USAAF, 1943, served, to 1946; as acting staff sgt.; Pub. Health Sanitarian N.Y.C. Dept. of Health, 1950-69; tchr. health edn. N.Y.C. Bd. of Edn., 1955-67; dep. asst. commr. Harlem Hosp. Center, N.Y.C., 1969-70, asso. exec. dir., 1970-74, acting exec. dir., 1974-77; dep. exec. dir. Bird S. Coler Hosp., N.Y.C., 1977—; adj. asst. prof. pub. health Columbia U.; guest lectr. St. Joseph Coll., Bkly. Mem. Am. Coll. Hosp. Adminstrs., Am. Hosp. Assn., Am. Pub. Health Assn., Royal Soc. Health (Eng.), Nat. Environ. Health Assn. Home: 2600-7 Netherland Ave Riverdale NY 10463 Office: Coler Meml Hosp Franklin D Roosevelt Island New York NY 10044

CORK, EDWIN KENDALL, mining company executive; b. Toronto, Ont., Can.; Stepson Stephen M. DuBrul and C.; m. Eve Slater, Dec. 31, 1960; children: Sarah, John, Peter, Mary. B.Commerce, U. Toronto, 1954. Economist Gilbert Jackson & Assocs., Toronto, 1954-59; with Noranda Mines Ltd., Toronto, 1959—, sr. v.p., treas., since 1980—; dir. Bank of N.S., E-L Fin. Corp.; governing council U. Toronto, 1979—; mem. Can. Inst. Internat. Affairs, 1975—. Christian Scientist. Clubs: National, Caledon Ski, Hart House. Office: PO Box 45 Commerce Ct W Toronto ON Canada M5L 1B6

CORKER, CHARLES EDWARD, lawyer; b. Boise, Idaho, Jan. 16, 1917; s. Charles Edward and Alma Bruce (Gill) C.; m. Betty Holman, Oct. 12, 1943; children—Bruce D., Carolyn Corker-Free, Edward Holman. A.B., Stanford U., 1941; LL.B., Harvard U., 1946. Bar: Calif. bar 1947, U.S. Supreme Ct 1954. Asst. sec. to Senator William E. Borah, 1937-40; asst. prof. law Stanford U., 1946-48, asso. prof., 1948-52, prof., 1952-53; dep. atty. gen. State of Calif., Los Angeles, 1954-59, asst. atty. gen., 1959-65; prof. U. Wash., 1965—. Served to lt. USNR, 1943-46. Mem. Am. Law Inst., Am. Bar Assn. Democrat. Home: 4128 55th Ave NE Seattle WA 98105 Office: U Wash Sch Law Seattle WA 98105

CORKLE, FRANCESCA THERESE, ballet dancer; b. Seattle, Aug. 2, 1952; d. Robert Francis and Claire Virginia (Ryan) C. Student pvt. schs., Forest Ridge, Wash., Virginia Ryan, Edna McRae, Robert Joffrey. Performing debut with, N.W. Ballet Guild, Seattle, 1957; with, Seattle Symphony, 1960, 67; mem.: dance troupe Aida, Seattle, 1962; with, Joffrey Ballet Co., N.Y.C., 1969-79, Pitts. Ballet, 1979—; mem. dance panel, N.Y. State Council on the Arts, 1975-76. Recipient First prize Victoria (B.C.) Dance Festival, 1962; Vancouver (B.C.) Festival Certificate and Trophy, 1963. Office: care Pittsburgh Ballet Theatre 244 Blvd of the Allies Pittsburgh PA 15222 *

CORLESS, HARRY, chemical executive; b. Coppull, Eng., Oct. 6, 1928; s. Albert and Edith (Cheetham) C.; m. Jean Houghton, Jan. 24, 1953; children: John Timothy, Victoria Elizabeth, James Anthony. B.Eng., U. Liverpool, 1949. With Imperial Chem. Industries, Ltd. (various locations), 1953—; sr. v.p. ICI Americas Inc., Wilmington, Del.; 1976-79, exec. v.p., 1979-82, pres., chief exec. officer, 1982—, also dir.; dir. Del. Trust Co. Trustee, bd. dirs. Wilmington Med. Center, 1980—. Served to 2d lt. Brit. Army, 1951-53. Mem. Soc. Chem. Industry. Office: ICI Americas Inc New Murphy and Concord Pike Wilmington DE 19897

CORLEY, DONALD EARL, legal educator, lawyer; b. Linden, Ala., June 22, 1932; s. Lavander Price and Jessie (Mayton) C.; m. Myra Jeanette Glenn, Aug. 23, 1958; children: Katherine, Mark, Susan. B.S., Auburn U., 1953, postgrad., 1955-56; J.D., Samford U., 1969. Bar: Ala. bar 1969. Accountant Am. Cast Iron Pipe Co., Birmingham, Ala., 1956-67, tax accountant, 1967-69; asst. prof. law U. Ala. Coll. Commerce and Bus. Adminstrn., 1969-71, Cumberland Sch. Law, Samford U., 1971-73, asso. prof., 1973, prof., 1974—, acting dean, 1972, dean, 1974-84. Author: Estate Planning: A Conceptual Approach, 1971. Served with USAF, 1953-55. Mem. Birmingham Bar Assn., Ala. Bar Assn., Am. Bar Assn., Am. Law Inst., Phi Kappa Phi, Theta Xi, Phi Alpha Delta, Delta Sigma Pi. Baptist. Club: Rotary (Birmingham). Home: 1438 Lantana Dr Birmingham AL 35226 Office: 800 Lakeshore Dr Birmingham AL 35229

CORLEY, ELLEN, university dean; b. Bloomington, Ill., Oct. 1, 1942; d. Gale Cosart and Lillian (Myers) C. A.A., Cottey Coll., 1962; A.B., Coll. of Wooster, 1964; M.S. in Edn. (fellow), Ind. U., 1969, Ed.D., 1972. Field dir. No. Ind. council Girl Scouts U.S.A., Michigan City, Ind., 1964-67; assoc. instr. Ind. U., Bloomington, 1970-72; asst. dean evening divs. Northwestern U., Chgo. and Evanston, Ill., 1972-75, dean div. continuing edn., 1975-83, dean Coll. Continuing Propl. Edn., 1983—, asst. prof. Sch. Edn., 1973-78, assoc. prof. Sch. Edn., 1978—. Bd. dirs. YWCA of Met. Chgo., 1983—. Mem. Am. Assn. Adult and Continuing Edn., Assn. Continuing Higher Edn., Women's Equity Action League, Ill. Adult and Continuing Educators Assn., Ill. Council Continuing Higher Edn. (exec. com. 1981-83, sec.-treas. 1983—), Cottey Coll. Alumnae Assn. (dir. 1980-82, v.p. 1982—), NOW. Club: P.E.O. (cert. of appreciation 1975). Office: 339 E Chicago Ave Chicago IL 60611

CORLISS, JOHN OZRO, zoology educator; b. Coats, Kans., Feb. 23, 1922; s. Clark L. and Catharine (Smith) C.; m. Anna Jane Lea, Mar. 16, 1968; children: Susan Elizabeth, Joan Alison, Kimberley Ann, Jennifer Sara Corliss and Margaret L. Swenson. B.S., U. Chgo., 1944; B.A., U. Vt., 1947; Ph.D., NYU, 1951; D.Sci. (hon.), Universite de Clermont, France, 1973. Postdoctoral fellow AEC, Coll. de France, Paris, 1951-52; instr. zoology Yale, 1952-54; asst. prof. to prof. zoology U. Ill., Urbana, 1954-64, prof., head dept. biol. scis., Chgo. Circle, 1964-69; dir. systematic zoology NSF, 1969-70; prof., chmn. dept. zoology U. Md., College Park, 1970—; hon. research asso. zoology U. Coll., London, Eng., 1960-61; vis. prof. zoology U. Exeter, Eng., 1961-62; vis. prof. protozoology, Shanghai, China, 1980, Geneva, Switzerland, 1980; Mem. NSF panel systematic biology, 1966-69; mem. Nat. Com. Internat. Biol. Program, 1966-68; commr. Internat. Commn. on Zool. Nomenclature, 1972—; mem. corp. Biol. Lab., Woods Hole, Mass. Author: The Ciliate Protozoa, 1961; 2d edit., 1979; contbr. numerous articles on protozoology to profl. jours. Served to capt. USAAF, 1943-46. Fellow AAAS, Am. Inst. Biol. Scis.; mem. Soc. Protozoologists (past pres; mem. editorial bd., past editor), Am. Micros. Soc. (past editor, past pres.), Council Biology Editors (past chmn., CBE Meritorious award 1982), Am. Soc. Zoologists (past pres.), Soc. Systematic Zoology (past pres.), Am. Soc. Parasitologists, Internat. Congress Systematic and Evolutionary Biology (convenor 1970-74, 76-80), Internat. Union Biol. Scis. (chmn. U.S. nat. com. 1971-73), numerous other socs., Phi Beta Kappa. Home: 9512 E Stanhope Rd Kensington MD 20895 Office: Dept Zoology University of Md College Park MD 20742

CORMACK, ALLAN MACLEOD, physicist, educator; b. Johannesburg, South Africa, Feb. 23, 1924; came to U.S., 1957, naturalized, 1966; s. George and Amelia (MacLeod) C.; m. Barbara Jeanne Seavey, Jan. 6, 1950; children: Margaret, Jean, Robert. B.Sc., U. Cape Town, South Africa, 1944, M.Sc., 1945; research student, Cambridge (Eng.) U., 1947-50. Lectr. U. Cape Town, 1946-47, 1950-56; research fellow Harvard U., 1956-57; asst. prof. physics Tufts U., Medford, Mass., 1957-60, assoc. prof., 1960-64, prof., 1964-80, University prof., 1980—. Recipient Ballou medal Tufts U., 1978; Nobel prize in medicine and physiology, 1979; Medal of Merit U. Cape Town, 1980. Fellow Am. Phys. Soc., Am. Acad. Arts and Sci., Royal Soc. South Africa (fgn.); mem. South African Phys. Soc., Nat. Acad. Scis., Sigma Xi. Research on nuclear and particle physics; computed tomography and related math. topics. Office: Physics Dept Tufts U Medford MA 02155

CORMAN, AVERY, author; b. N.Y.C., Nov. 28, 1935; s. Maurice and Ruth (Brody) C.; m. Judy Lishinsky, Nov. 5, 1967; children: Matthew, Nicholas. B.S., NYU, 1956. Author: novels Oh, God!, 1971, The Bust-Out King, 1977, Kramer Versus Kramer, 1977, The Old Neighborhood, 1980; contbr. articles to nat. mags.; screenwriter for ednl. films. Mem. Authors Guild, Writers Guild Am., PEN. Office: care Arlene Donovan ICM 40 W 57th St New York NY 10019

CORMAN, CID, poet, editor; b. Boston, June 29, 1924; s. Abraham and Celia (Kravitz) C.; m. Shizumi Konishi, Feb. 14, 1965. A.B., Tufts U., 1945; postgrad., U. Mich., 1946-47, U. N.C., 1947, U. Paris, 1954-55. Tchr. USIS; pvt. tchr. in, Bari/Matera, Italy, 1956-57, Kyoto Joshidai, Japan, 1958-60, Ryukoku U., 1962-64, Doshisha U., Kyoto, 1965-66, CC's dessert shop, 1974-79; owner, operator Sister City Tea House, Boston, 1981, tchr. poetry, 1981; lectr. in field worldwide. Author: numerous poetry books, including In Good Time, 1964, Sun Rock Man, 1962, Words for Each Other, 1967, And Without End, 1968, Plight, 1969, Living Dying, 1970, Out and Out, 1972, 0/1, 1974, 'S, 1976, Antics, 1977, Auspices, 1978, Tabernacle, 1980, Aegis: Selected Poems 1970-80, 1983; editor: Word for Word: Essays on the Art of Language, 1977, At Their Word: Essays on the Art of Language, 1978, Origin (Japan), from 1951; appeared on: Sta. WMEX, Boston, 1949-51; numerous poetry readings. Recipient awards, including; Chapelbrook Found. award, 1965, 66, 67; Fulbright grantee, 1954; Coordinating Council of Little Mags. grantee, 1970-71, 78-79. Mem. Phi Beta Kappa. Office: care Station Hill Press Station Hill Rd Barrytown NY 12507 *If I have nothing to offer you in the face of death—the ache behind every ache, the instant man knows, I have no claim as poet. My song must sing into you a little moment, stay in you what presence can muster—of sense more than meaning, of love more than sense, of giving the life given one with the same fulness that brought each forth, each to each from each, nothing left but the life that is going on.* *

CORMAN, EUGENE HAROLD, motion picture producer; b. Detroit, Sept. 24, 1927; s. William and Anne (High) C.; m. Nan Chandler Morris, Sept. 4, 1955; children: Todd William, Craig Allan. B.A., Stanford U., 1948. Vice-pres. Music Corp. Am., Beverly Hills, Calif., 1950-57; owner, operator Corman Co. (motion pictures), Beverly Hills, 1957—; pres. Penelope Prodn. Inc., Los Angeles, 1965—, Chateau Prodn. Inc., 1972—; v.p. 20th Century Fox TV, Beverly Hills. Producer: The Big Red One, 1978-79, F.I.S.T, 1977-78. Recipient Emmy award for A Woman Called Golda, Cath. Christopher award for A Woman Called Golda. Mem. Acad. Motion Picture Arts and Scis., TV Acad. Arts and Scis., Los Angeles County Mus. Art (patron), Beverly Hills Tennis Club, Theta Delta Chi. Roman Catholic. Office: 20th Century Fox TV Box 900 Beverly Hills CA 90213

CORMAN, JAMES CHARLES, former congressman; b. Galena, Kans., Oct. 20, 1920; s. Ransford Darwin and Edna (Love) C.; m. Virginia Little, 1946 (dec. May 1966); children—Mary Anne, James Charles; m. Nancy Malone, 1978; 1 son, Adam Ransford. B.A., UCLA, 1942; J.D., U. So. Calif., 1948; LL.D. (hon.), San Fernando Valley Sch. Law, 1968. Bar: Calif. bar 1949. Practiced in, Van Nuys, Calif., 1949-50, 52-57; mem. 87th-93d congresses from 22d Calif. Dist., 94th-96th congresses from 21st Calif. Dist., chmn. Democratic nat. congl. com., com. on ways and means, chmn. subcom. on public assistance and unemployment compensation, mem. com. on small bus.; mem. Nat. Adv. Commn. on Civil Disorders, 1967; Mem. Los Angeles City Council, 1957-60. Trustee Kennedy Center for Performing Arts, Internat. Orphans, Inc., Child Guidance Clinic of San Fernando Valley. Served to col. USMCR, 1942-46, 50-52; col. Res.; ret.). Mem. Calif., Los Angeles, San Fernando Valley bar assns., Am. Legion, VFW, NAACP (life). Democrat. Methodist. Club: Lion.

CORMAN, ROGER WILLIAM, motion picture producer-director; b. Detroit, Apr. 5, 1926. A.B., Stanford, 1947; postgrad., Oxford (Eng.) U., 1950. Founder, pres. New World Pictures, 1970-83, New Horizons Prodn. Co., 1983—. Producer: Monster from the Ocean Floor, 1953, Grand Theft Auto, I Never Promised You a Rose Garden, Thunder and Lightning, Avalanche, Deathsport, Piranha; dir.: Five Guns West, 1955; producer, dir.: films, including Battle Beyond the Stars, 1980, Cannonball, 1980, The Bees, 1980, Galaxy of Terror, 1980, Forbidden World, 1980; others, 1980; dir., Von Richthofen and Brown; distbr.: films including Small Change; Films shown at numerous film festivals. Mem. Producers Guild Am., Dirs. Guild Am. Office: New Horizons Prodn Co 11600 San Vicente Blvd Los Angeles CA 90049 *

CORMIER, RAMONA THERESA, philosophy educator; b. Breaux Bridge, La., Jan. 21, 1923; d. Arthur Joseph and Florence (Breaux) C. B.A., U. Southwestern La., 1943; M.A., U. So. Calif., 1948; Ph.D., Tulane U., 1960. Music tchr. St. Martin Parish, La., 1948-49; vocal music tchr. Ouachita Parish High Sch., Monroe, La., 1949-58; instr. philosophy Newcomb Coll., New Orleans, 1960-61, U. Tenn., Knoxville, 1961-63, asst. prof., 1963-65; asst. prof. philosophy Bowling Green (Ohio) State U., 1965-68, assoc. prof., 1969-72, prof., 1972—, assoc. provost, 1979—, dean continuing edn. and summer programs, 1984—; asso. dir. Philosophy Documentation Center, 1967-73; v.p. Philosophy Information Center, 1967-73. Author: (with Pallister) Waiting for Death, 1979; asso. editor: (with Lineback) The Philosopher's Index: An Internat. Index to Philosophical Periodicals, 1967-73; Co-editor: Internat. Directory of Philosophy and Philosophers, 1972-73; editor, 1974-75; Editor: (with Lineback and Chinn) Encounter: An Introduction to Philosophy, 1970. Served as ensign USNR, 1943-46. Mem. Am. Philos. Assn., Am. Soc. Aesthetics, So. Soc. Philosophy and Psychology, Ohio Philos. Assn. (program chmn. 1971-72, pres. 1973-76), AAAS. Home: 149 Baldwin Ave Bowling Green OH 43402

CORMIER, ROBERT EDMUND, writer; b. Leominster, Mass., Jan. 17, 1925; s. Lucien Joseph and Irma Margaret (Collins) C.; m. Constance B. Senay, Nov. 6, 1948; children:Roberta Susan, Peter Jude, Christine Judith, Renee Elizabeth. Student, Fitchburg (Mass.) State Coll., 1943-44, Litt.D. (hon.), 1977. Script/comml. writer Radio Sta. WTAG, Worcester, Mass., 1946-48; reporter, columnist Worcester Telegram & Gazette, 1948-55; reporter, columnist, asso. editor Fitchburg Sentinel & Enterprise, 1955-78; writing coach, cons. Worcester Telegram & Gazette. Author: Now And At the Hour, 1960, A Little Raw on Monday Mornings, 1963, Take Me Where the Good Times Are, 1965, The Chocolate War, 1974, I Am the Cheese, 1977, After the First Death, 1979, Eight Plus One, 1980, The Bumblebee Flies Anyway, 1983; contbr. short stories to, Redbook, McCalls, Saturday Evening Post, Sign, St. Anthony Messenger. Trustee Leominster Public Library, 1977—. Recipient Best News Story in New Eng. award AP, 1959, 74; K. R. Thomson Prize Thomson Newspapers, Inc., 1974; Bread Loaf Writers' Conf. fellow, 1968. Roman Catholic. Club: L'Union St. Jean Baptiste d'Amerique. Home: 1177 Main St Leominster MA 01453 *To write with clarity, the simple telling word or phrase, omitting unnecessary adjectives or adverbs; to write the truth, however it sears or burns or perhaps soars; to select words that move and dance and sing upon the page; to make the reader say: My God, that's how it is.*

CORN, ALFRED DEWITT, poet, educator; b. Bainbridge, Ga., Aug. 14, 1943; s. A.D. and Grace (Lahey) C.; m. Ann Rosalind Jones, July 24, 1967 (div. 1971). B.A., Emory U., 1965; M.A., Columbia U., 1970. Preceptor Columbia Coll., N.Y.C., 1968-70; free-lance writer, N.Y.C., 1971-77; vis. lectr. Yale U., New Haven, 1977-79; assoc. prof. Conn. Coll., New London, 1978-81; lectr. Columbia U., N.Y.C., 1983, CUNY, 1983-84. Author: All Roads at Once, 1976, A Call in the Midst of the Crowd, 1978, The Various Light, 1980, Notes from a Child of Paradise, 1984. Recipient award Nat. Endowment for Arts, 1979, Levinson prize Poetry mag., 1982, Spl. award Am. Acad. and Inst. Arts and Letters, 1983; fellow Ingram Merrill Found., 1974. Mem. PEN, Nat. Book Critics Circle, Poetry Soc. Am. Home: 54 W 16th St New York NY 10011

CORN, JOSEPH EDWARD, JR., arts administrator; b. St. Louis, Oct. 20, 1932; s. Joseph Edward and Melba (Goldberg) C. A.B., Yale U., 1954. Gen. mgr. August Opera Festival, St. Louis, 1960-64; pres. Theatrical Assocs., St. Louis, 1960-68; mgr. Western Opera Theater, San Francisco, 1969-74, San Francisco Opera, 1972-75; spl. asst. to exec. dir. Met. Opera, N.Y.C., 1975, dir. planning and pub. affairs, 1976-77; mgr. Opera Co. of Phila., 1977-80; dir. Opera-Mus. Theatre Program, Nat. Endowment Arts, Washington, 1980-81; exec. v.p., gen. dir. Wolf Trap Found. for Performing Arts, Vienna, Va., 1981-82; gen. dir. Minn. Opera Co., St. Paul, 1982—; producer Gateway Theater, St. Louis, 1963-66; dir. Performing Arts Office, Washington U., St. Louis, 1964-67; dir. publicity and pub. relations St. Louis Municipal Opera and Entertainment Enterprises, St. Louis, 1967; Cons. for OPERA Am., 1972-80, bd. dirs., mem. exec. com., 1977-80; mem. music adv. panel Nat. Endowment for Arts, 1972-76, mem. fed.-state reassessment steering com., 1976-77, mem. opera/musical theater adv. panel, 1978-80; also cons.; mem. performing arts and music adv. panels Calif. Arts Commn., 1973-75; pres. Am. Arts Alliance, 1977-79; trustee Nat. Opera Inst., 1977-80, 82—; chmn. music adv. com., mem. council Yale U., 1978-80; v.p. Greater Phila. Cultural Alliance, 1979-80. Bd. dirs. Nat. Com. on U.S.-China Relations, 1982—, Midwest China Ctr., 1983—, First All-Children's Theater of N.Y., 1983—; bd. dirs. Music Theater Group Lenox Art Ctr., 1983—.

CORN, MERTON, banker; b. Bklyn., Sept. 15, 1934; s. Abraham and Rose (Stamm) C.; m. Jacqueline A. Desjardins Wexler, 1983; children: Steven, Dara; stepchildren: Karen and Danniel Wexler. A.B., Bklyn. Coll., 1958. With N.Y. State Banking Dept., 1958-63, Bankers Trust Co., N.Y.C., 1963-66; with First Jersey Nat. Bank, Jersey City, 1966-71, sr. v.p., 1969-71, Trust Co. N.Y., 1971-72; 1st v.p. Exchange Nat. Bank Chgo., 1972-73; pres., dir. Central State Bank, N.Y.C., 1973-75, Chelsea Nat. Bank, 1975-76; exec. v.p. Union Chelsea Nat. Bank, N.Y.C., 1977; pres., dir. Gateway State Bank, S.I., N.Y., 1977—; dir. Chyron Corp. Served with USNR, 1952-55. Mem. Robert Morris Assos., Staten Island C. of C. (dir.). Home: 109 Belmont St Englewood NJ 07631 Office: 1630 Richmond Rd Staten Island NY 10304

CORN, MORTON, environmental engineer, educator; b. N.Y.C., Oct. 18, 1933; s. Julius and Sophie (Haber) C.; m. Jacqueline Karnell, Aug. 21, 1955; children—Matthew Irwin, Frederick Eliot. B.S. in Chem. Engring, Cooper Union, 1955; M.S., Harvard, 1956, Ph.D., 1961. Asst. san. engr. USPHS, Cin., 1956-58; research asso. Harvard, 1960-61; asst. prof. U. Pitts., 1962-65, assoc. prof., 1965-66, prof. Grad. Sch. Pub. Health and Sch. Engring., 1967-79; prof. and div. head environ. health engring. Sch. Hygiene and Public Health, Johns Hopkins U., Balt., 1980—; pres. Morton Corn; Assocs., Cons. Engrs., 1977—; cons. div. biology and medicine AEC, 1965—; chmn. air pollution research grants com. EPA, 1968-71, mem. sci. adv. bd., 1978-81; mem. com. on biol. effects air pollution Nat. Acad. Scis., 1971, mem. com. risk assessment, 1982-83; mem. expert panel occupational health WHO, 1973—; asst. sec. labor for occupational safety and health U.S. Dept. Labor, 1975-77; mem. Allegheny County Air Pollution Adv. Com., 1967-72; mem. nat. adv. com. health vital stats. Dept. Health and Human Services, 1979—. Translation editor: Adhesion of Dusts and Powders by A.D. Zimon, 1970; Mem. editorial bd.: Excerpta Medica, 1965; Contbr. articles to profl. jours. NSF postdoctoral fellow U. London, 1961-62; WHO fellow, 1970; Guggenheim fellow, 1972. Fellow Am. Pub. Health Assn.; mem. Am. Inst. Chem. Engrs., Air Pollution Control Assn., Am. Indsl. Hygiene Assn., AAAS, Am. Conf. Govt. Indsl. Hygienists (chmn. 1983-84), Sigma Xi. Home: 1714 Eutaw Pl Baltimore MD 21217 Office: Johns Hopkins U 615 N Wolfe St Baltimore MD 21217

CORNATZER, WILLIAM EUGENE, biochemist, educator; b. Mocksville, N.C., Sept. 23, 1918; s. William Pinkston and Stella Augusta (Vogler) C.; m. Margaret Virginia Freeman, Mar. 30, 1946; children—Nancy Freeman, William Eugene. Student, Mars Hill Coll., 1935-37; B.S., Wake Forest Coll., 1939; M.S., U. N.C., 1941, Ph.D., 1944; postgrad., Oak Ridge Inst. Nuclear Studies, 1948; M.D., Bowman Gray Sch. Medicine, 1951. Student asst. zoology Wake Forest Coll., 1937-38, 1938-39; grad. and student asst. biol. and food chemistry U. N.C., 1939-41, Fels Research fellow, 1941-45; asst. prof. biochemistry Bowman Gray Sch. Medicine, 1946-51; prof., head dept. biochemistry med. sch. U. N.D., Grand Forks, 1951—, Chester Fritz distinguished prof., 1973—; also dir. Ireland Research Lab.; Mem. biochem. test com. Nat. Bd. Med. Examiners; mem. White Ho. Com. for Orgn. Conf. on Food, Nutrition and Health, 1969. Mem. bd. editors: Jour. Clin. Chemistry, 1971—; mem. editorial bd.: Jour. Nutrition, 1975—; Author articles sci. jours. Recipient Frank Billing award for original investigation; Silver medal AMA, 1951; Nat. Scis. Travel award to Internat. Congress Biochemistry, Paris, 1952, Tokyo, 1967; travel award Internat. Congress Cancer, London, Eng., Am. Assn. for Cancer Research, 1958; travel award to 1st Internat. Congress Pharmacology, Stockholm, 1961, Internat. Union Physiol. Sci.; NSF Travel award to 7th Internat. Congress Biochemistry, Tokyo, 1967; travel award 8th Internat. Congress Nutrition, Am. Inst. Nutrition, Prague, 1969, 9th Congress, Mex., 1972; Distinguished Service award U. N.C., 1970; Outstanding Sci. Research award U. N.D. chpt. Sigma Xi, 1970; Distinguished Alumnus award Bowman Gray Med. Sch., 1976. Fellow A.C.P., N.Y. Acad. Scis., Am. Inst. Chemists, AAAS; mem. Am. Assn. Oil Chemists, Nat. Acad. Clin. Chemistry, Am. Bd. Clin. Chemistry (dir.), Am. Assn. Clin. Chemists (nat. exec. com. 1957), Am. Assn. for Study of Liver Disease, Central Soc. for Clin. Research, Radiation Research Soc., Am. Chem. Soc., Am. Soc. Biol. Chemistry, So. Soc. for Clin. Research, Am. Fedn. for Clin. Research, Soc. Exptl. Biology and Medicine, AAUP, Am. Inst. Nutrition, Elisha Mitchell Sci. Soc., N.D. Acad. Scis. (pres. 1956), N.D. Diabetic Assn., Royal Soc. Medicine. Methodist. Research in properties of proteins, quinine metabolism, anti-malarial testing, phospholipide metabolism, radioactive isotopes, biol. effects of radiation. Address: University of ND Med Sch Grand Forks ND 58201 *Faith in yourself and your Creator/Positive thinking/High Objectives/Hard work*

CORNBLATH, MARVIN, pediatrician, educator; b. St. Louis, June 18, 1925; s. David and Sophia (Kornblett) C.; m. Joan Senturia, Aug. 29, 1948; children—Nancy Moshe, Polly Cornblath Manin, Ben S. Student, Washington U., St. Louis, 1944, M.D. cum laude, 1947. Diplomate: Am. Bd. Pediatrics. Rotating intern St. Louis Jewish Hosp., 1947-48; resident pediatrics St. Louis Children's Hosp., 1948-50; asst. pediatrics Washington U. Sch. Medicine, 1948-50; instr., then asst. prof. pediatrics Johns Hopkins Sch. Medicine, 1953-59; lectr. John Hopkins Sch. Medicine, 1975—; research asso., adj. attending pediatrician Sinai Hosp., Balt., 1953-59; pediatrician out-patient dept. Johns Hopkins Hosp., 1956-59; asst. prof., then asso. prof. Northwestern U. Med. Sch., 1959-61; asst. chmn. div. pediatrics Michael Reese Hosp., Chgo., 1959-61; asso. prof., then prof. pediatrics U. Ill. Coll. Medicine, 1961-68; attending physician, physician-in-charge neonatal service Research and Ednl. Hosps., Chgo., 1961-68; attending physician Cook County Hosp., Chgo., 1963-68; prof. pediatrics U. Md. Sch. Medicine, 1968—, chmn. dept., 1968-78; spl. asst. to sci. dir. Nat. Inst. Child Health and Human Devel., NIH, 1978-82; med. cons. Nordisk-U.S.A., 1982—. Author numerous articles in field. Served to 1st lt. M.C. AUS, 1951-53. Mem. Soc. Pediatric Research, Am. Acad. Pediatrics, AAAS, Am. Pediatric Soc., Brit. Biochem. Soc., Am. Soc. Biol. Chemists, Endocrine Soc., Am. Physiol. Soc., Am. Diabetes Assn., Sigma Xi, Alpha Omega Alpha. Home: 3809 St Paul St Baltimore MD 21218

CORNBLATT, MAX, automotive batteries manufacturing company executive; b. Boston, Feb. 10, 1906; s. Samuel and Sarah C.; m. Celia Zalkin, July 5, 1941; children: Barbara Ann, Gail, Marcia. Sales mgr. Beacon Battery Co., Boston, 1926-36; pres., chief exec. officer Eastern Battery Co, Boston, 1936-66; dir., v.p. adminstrn. Gen. Battery Corp., Reading, Pa., 1966-71, sr. v.p. corp., 1971-82, cons., 1983—; dir. Gen. Battery Corp., Reading, Pa., 1966-73. Home: 2030 S Ocean Blvd Hallandale FL 33009

CORNELIO, ALBERT CARMEN, insurance executive; b. Winsted, Conn., Feb. 9, 1930; s. Carmine E. and Mary (Petrunti) C.; m. Elizabeth Ann Lach, June 2, 1956; children: Charles C., Catherine M., Michael J., Julia A. Student, Washington-Jefferson Coll., 1947-50; LL.B., Boston U., 1957. Bar: Mass. 1957. Atty. Berkshire Life Ins. Co., Pittsfield, Mass., 1957-60, counsel, 1960-65, asso. gen. counsel, 1965-68, v.p. and gen. counsel, 1968-70, sr. v.p., 1970-71, sr. v.p. mktg. and ins. services, 1971-76, exec. v.p.-mktg., 1977-82, pres., chief exec. officer, 1982—; sec., dir. Berkshire Equity Sales Inc.; dir. Berkshire Life Ins. Co., First Agrl. Bank. Bd. dirs. Mass. Taxpayers Found., Mass. Bus. Roundtable. Served with USNR, 1950-54. Mem. Am., Mass., Berkshire bar assns., Am. Soc. C.L.U.s, Life Mgmt. Inst. Home: 84 Spadina Pkwy Pittsfield MA 01201 Office: 700 South St Pittsfield MA 01201

CORNELISON, FLOYD SHOVINGTON, JR., educator, psychiatrist; b. San Angelo, Tex., Apr. 30, 1918; s. Floyd Shovington and Nannie Lee (Brewer) C.; m. Erwina Ladelle Bode, Aug. 30, 1940 (div. 1966); 1 dau., Ann Brewer; m. Ruth Reeder Williams, Sept. 17, 1966. B.A., Baylor U., 1939; postgrad., Northwestern U., 1939-40, Columbia, 1943-45; M.D., Cornell U., 1950; M.S., Boston U., 1958. Diplomate: Am. Bd. Psychiatry and Neurology. Intern Grasslands Hosp., Valhalla, N.Y., 1950-51; resident psychiatry Mass. Meml. Hosp., Boston U. Sch. Medicine, also Boston State Hosp., 1951-54; from asst. psychiatry to instr. Boston U. Sch. Medicine, 1951-58; lectr. psychology Tufts Coll., 1954-56; successively asst. prof., asso. prof., cons. prof. psychiatry U. Okla. Sch. Medicine, 1958-64; prof. psychiatry Jefferson Med. Coll., Thomas Jefferson U., Phila., 1962—, chmn. dept., 1962-74; past mem. staff numerous hosps.; med. staff Wilmington Med Center; cons. area hosps., 1962—; med. dir. Freedom From Fear, Inc., 1980-83; Mem. Mental Health Film Bd., N.Y.C., 1961—; dir. Marka T. du Pont Inst. Human Behavior, Wilmington, Del., 1971-75. Author articles; producer films in field. Fellow psychiat. films Med. Audio-Visual Inst., Assn. Am. Med. Colls., 1951-53; candidate Boston Psychoanalytic Inst., 1954-58. Fellow Am. Coll. Psychiatrists, Am. Psychiat. Assn.; fellow Royal Australian and New Zealand Coll. Psychiatrists; mem. AMA, Del. Psychiat. Soc., Del., New Castle County med. socs., Sigma Xi. Initiated self-image experience, photographic confrontation technique in psychiat. research. Home: 16 Stone Hill Rd Wilmington DE 19803 Office: Profl Bldg Augustine Cut-Off Wilmington DE 19803

CORNELIUS, CHARLES EDWARD, educator; b. Huntington Park, Calif., Dec. 19, 1927; s. Samuel Paul and Alberta (Johnson) C.; m. Bette Jean Watt, Sept. 2, 1948; children—Steven, Clifford, John, Aimee. B.S. in Animal Sci, U. Calif., 1949, 1951, D.V.M., 1953, Ph.D., 1957. Asst. prof., then asso. prof. U. Calif., Davis, 1957-66; chmn. dept. physiology, 1965-66; prof., dean Coll. Vet. Medicine, Kans. State U., Manhattan, 1966-71; dean Coll. Vet. Medicine, U. Fla., Gainesville, 1971-80; dir. Calif. Primate Research Center, U. Calif., Davis, 1980—; Mem. study sect. gen. medicine NIH, 1965-69, mem. nat. adv. council to health research facilities, 1969-73; nat. civilian cons. for vet. medicine USAF, 1970-71; mem. panel on new drug regulations HEW, 1976-77. Author: Clinical Biochemistry of Domestic Animals, 1963, 70; Editor: (with Simpson) Advances in Veterinary Science, 1966—. Chmn. funding com. Vet. Sch. in Israel. Named Fla. Vet. of Year, 1979. Mem. Am. Physiol. Soc., Soc. Exptl. Biology and Medicine, Am. Vet. Med. Assn., Am. Gastroenterol. Assn., Nat. Soc. Med. Research (dir. 1971-76). Home: 117 C St Apt C Davis CA 95616

CORNELIUS, HELEN LORENE, singer, song writer; b. Hannibal, Mo., Dec. 6, 1941; d. Joseph Clifton and LuElsie Elizabeth Johnson;

children: Joseph Ross, Christina Gail, Dennis Wayne. Student public schs., Monroe City, Mo. Appeared on: Ted Mack Amateur Hour, 1969, 70 (winner each time); song writer, Columbia Screen-Gems, Nashville, 1970-72; staff writer, Duchess Music div. MCA Music Co., Nashville, 1972-76; rec. artist, RCA Records, 1975-80; regular mem.: TV show Nashville On The Road, 1976-80; prin. artist The Helen Cornelius Show, 1976—; (with former singing partner Jim Ed Brown) recs. include (three 1 records and 11 Top Ten Records.). Mem. Broadcast Music Inc., AFTRA, Country Music Assn. (Vocal Duo of Yr. 1977), Nat. Assn. Songwriters Internat., West Coast Acad. Country Music. Baptist. Office: PO Box 746 Brentwood TN 37027 *I have always believed in God, and the power of positive thinking. One can really achieve anything they desire, provided they believe and the desire be strong enough. God did not create failures—he gave each of us talent—talent that is only stifled by disbelief in oneself.*

CORNELIUS, WILLIAM EDWARD, utilities company executive; b. Salt Lake City, Sept. 6, 1931; s. Edward Vernon and Gladys (Bray) C.; m. Mary Virginia Bunker, June 13, 1953; children: Mary Jean, Linda Anne. B.S., U. Mo., 1953; M. Liberal Arts, Washington U., St. Louis, 1983. C.P.A., Mo. Mgr. Price Waterhouse & Co., St. Louis, 1955-62; asst. comptroller Union Electric Co., St. Louis, 1962-64, dir. corporate planning, 1964-67, exec. v.p., 1968-80, pres., 1980—, chief exec. officer, 1984—, also dir.; dir. Centerre Bank N.A., Centerre Bancorp. Bd. dirs. William Woods Coll., St. Louis Children's Hosp., Mercantile Library; trustee Washington U. Served to 1st lt. AUS, 1953-55. Mem. Beta Theta Pi. Clubs: Bellerive Country, Noonday, St. Louis, Log Cabin. Home: 2 Dunlora Ln Saint Louis MO 63131 Office: PO Box 149 Saint Louis MO 63166

CORNELL, GEORGE WADE, univ. adminstr.; b. Ashtabula, Ohio, Jan. 7, 1920; s. Robert Blee and Blanche Olive (Bortz) C.; m. Barbara Esther Greene, Dec. 21, 1942; children—Sarah Jean, Deborah Ann, David Wade. B.S., Kent State U., 1947; M.S. in L.S, Western Res. U., 1949; Ph.D., Ohio State U., 1968. Tchr. English Warren Twp. Schs., Leavittsburg, Ohio, 1947-48; catalog librarian Antioch Coll., Yellow Springs, Ohio, 1949-50, tech. services librarian, 1953-69; head catalog librarian Kent (Ohio) State U., 1950-53; dir. library services State U. N.Y. at Brockport, 1969—; Mem. adv. council Rochester Regional Resources Library Council, 1969—; mem. library adv. council SUNY, 1980-82. Served to capt. 63d Inf. Div. AUS, 1942-46. Decorated Bronze Star. Mem. ALA. Methodist. Home: 20 Havenwood Dr Brockport NY 14420

CORNELL, GEORGE WASHINGTON, II, journalist; b. Weatherford, Okla., July 24, 1920; s. Charles H. and Gladys (Cameron) C.; m. Jo Ann Reeves, Apr. 1, 1944 (div. June 1981); children: Marion Emma, Harrison Reeves. A.B., U. Okla., 1943; L.H.D., Defiance Coll., 1962. Reporter Daily Oklahoman, Oklahoma City, 1943-44; newsman A.P., N.Y.C., 1947-51, religion columnist, 1951—. Author: They Knew Jesus, 1957, The Way and its Ways, 1963, Voyage of Faith, 1964, (with Douglas Johnson) Punctured Preconceptions, 1972, Behold the Man, 1974, The Untamed God, 1975, Ballad of the Lord, 1984. Served to 2d lt., inf. AUS, 1944-47. Redipient Nat. Religious Pub. Relations Council award, 1953, Religion Heritage in Am. Faith and Freedom award, 1960, Religion Newswriters Assn. Supple Meml. award, 1961, Jim Merrell Religious Liberty Meml. award, 1977, William E. Leidt award, 1978. Mem. Am. Newspaper Guild, Religious Newswriters Assn. Episcopalian. Home: 250 1st Ave New York NY 11050 Office: 50 Rockefeller Plaza New York NY 10020

CORNELL, HARRY M., JR., mattress company executive. Chmn., pres. chief exec. officer Leggett & Platt, Inc., Carthage, Mo. Office: Leggett & Platt Inc One Leggett Rd Carthage MO 64836§

CORNELL, JOHN PAUL, utilities executive; b. Clendenin, W.Va., Mar. 4, 1924; s. Isaac Harry and Carrie Ernestine (Rawson) C.; m. Frances Louise Glover, Sept. 26, 1944; 1 dau., Patricia Ann. Student, Marshall U., 1947-48, Morris Harvey Coll., 1949-51. Sr. v.p., dir. Columbia Gas System, Inc., 1962-72, v.p. finance, accounting, Wilmington, Del., 1972-74, sr. v.p., 1974-81, chief fin. officer, 1974—, exec. v.p., 1981—, also dir.; dir. Columbia Alaskan Gas Transmission Corp., Columbia Coal Gasification Corp., Columbia Gas Devel. Corp., Columbia Gas System Service Corp., Columbia Gulf Transmission Corp., Columbia Hydrocarbon Corp., Columbia LNG Corp., Inland Gas Co., Inc., Bank of Del., Wilmington, Associated Electric & Gas Ins. Services, Ltd., Bermuda; bd. dirs. Utilities Publ. Com. Served to lt., naval aviator USNR, 1942-45. Mem. Am. Gas Assn., Kennett Pike Assn., Port of Wilmington Maritime Soc. Republican. Methodist. Clubs: Mason. Clubs, Wilmington Country, Univ. and Whist. Home: 909 Barley Dr Wilmington DE 19807 Office: 20 Montchanin Rd Wilmington DE 19807

CORNELL, PAUL GRANT, educator; b. Toronto, Ont., Can., Sept. 13, 1918; s. Beaumont Sandfield and Margaret (Wilson) C.; m. Christina Mary Suckling, Dec. 6, 1941; children—John Grant, Virginia Susan, Benjamin William, Jennifer Margaret. B.A. in History, U. Toronto, 1940, M.A., 1948, Ph.D., 1956. Mem. faculty dept. history Acadia U., Wolfville, N.S., Can., 1949-60; prof., chmn. dept. U. Waterloo, Ont., Can., 1960-69, dean of arts, 1970-74, v.p. acad., 1972, prof. history, 1973—. Editor: Ontario History, 1962-78; Author: The Alignment of Political Groups in Canada, 1962, (with others) Canada: Unity in Diversity, 1967, Canada: Unitè et Diversitè, 1968; Contbr. to profl. jours. Served with Canadian Army, 1940-46; also with Canadian Militia. Awarded Efficiency Decoration for service in armed forces. Fellow Royal Hist. Soc.; mem. Can. Hist. Soc. (editor jour. 1952-56), Ont. Hist. Soc. (pres. 1973-74), N.S. Hist. Soc., Inst. Pub. Adminstrn. Can. Anglican (lay asst.). Home: 202 Laurier Pl Waterloo ON N2L 1K8 Canada Office: Dept History U Waterloo Waterloo ON N2L 3G1 Canada

CORNELL, RICHARD GARTH, biostatistics educator; b. Cleve., Nov. 18, 1930; s. Russell Gervas and Grace (Garlick) C.; m. Valma Yvonne Edwards, June 3, 1961; children: Sharon Yvonne, Russell Glenn, Carol Elizabeth. B.A., U. Rochester, 1952; M.S., Va. Poly. Inst., 1954, Ph.D., 1956. Statistician, Nat. Communicable Disease Center, Atlanta, 1956-58, chief lab. and field sta. stats. unit, 1958-60; asso. prof. stats. Fla. State U., 1960-68, prof. stats., 1968-71; prof., biostats. U. Mich., Ann Arbor, 1971—, chmn. dept., 1971-84; asso. editor for biostats. Marcel Dekker, Inc.; cons. to govt. and industry. Served with USPHS, 1956-58. Mem. Biometric Soc. (program chmn. 1968, 71, pres. Eastern N.Am. region 1975, council 1978—), Am. Statist. Assn. (chmn. biometrics sect. 1973, program chmn. ann. meeting 1981), Am. Scientific Affiliation, Phi Beta Kappa, Sigma Xi., Phi Kappa Phi, Pi Mu Epsilon. Baptist (deacon 1962—). Research, publs. in biometrics to sci. jours. Home: 6149 Saline Waterworks Rd Saline MI 48176

CORNELL, ROBERT ARTHUR, government official; b. Mineola, N.Y., Sept. 8, 1936; s. Herbert and Clara (Lange) C.; m. Nadine E. Dittmer, May 4, 1962; children: Robert Arthur, James E., Suzanne N. A.B., Columbia U., 1958, postgrad., 1965-66; postgrad., Pacific Luth. U., 1960-61, Am. U., 1964-65; M.B.A., NYU, 1963. With Grace Nat. Bank, N.Y.C., 1961-63, U.S. Govt., Washington, 1963-69, IBM World Trade Corp., 1970, S.J. Rundt & Assocs., N.Y.C., 1970-71, cons., 1970-71; dep. dir. Office Econ. Research U.S. Internat. Trade Commn., Washington, 1971-76, dir. Office Trade and Industry, 1976-77, dep. dir. ops., 1977-79; asst. dir. for stockpile trans. GSA, Washington, 1979-80; dep. asst. sec. for internat. trade and investment policy U.S. Treasury Dept., Washington, 1980—; mem. faculty U. Md., 1968; pvt. cons. in econs. and fin. Contbr. articles to profl. jours. Served with USN, 1958-61. Recipient Arthur S. Flemming award, 1974. Mem. Am. Econ. Assn., Western Econ. Assn., Nat. Economists Club, Nat. Assn. Bus. Economists. Lutheran. Home: 705 Winhall Way Silver Spring MD 20904 Office: U S Treasury Dept 15th and Pennsylvania Ave NW Washington DC 20220

CORNELL, THOMAS BROWNE, artist, educator; b. Cleve., Mar. 1, 1937; s. Norman Monrod and Betty (Browne) C.; m. Christa Vaughan Kinkel, May 1, 1976; children: Anna Olivia, Nicolas Browne. B.A., Amherst Coll., 1959; postgrad., Yale U. Sch. Art and Architecture, 1959-60. Faculty U. Calif. at Santa Barbara, 1960-62; prof. art Bowdoin Coll., 1962—; mem. visual arts program Princeton U., 1969-70. Author: The Monkey with 11 etchings, 1959, The Defense of Gracchus Babeuf with 21 etchings, 1964; one-man shows, Yale U. Art Gallery, Williams Coll. Art Mus., Santa Barbara Mus. Art, 1965, Wesleyan U., Conn., 1967, Bowdoin Coll., Maine, Princeton U., 1971, Muhlenberg Coll., 1976, Barridoff Galleries, Maine, U. Bridgeport, Conn., 1977, U. Redlands, Calif., 1979, A. M. Sachs Gallery, N.Y.C., 1979, 81, Santa Barbara (Calif.) Mus. Art, 1980, group shows include, DeCordova Mus., Lincoln, Mass., 1963, Mus. Modern Art, N.Y.C., 1966, Pa. State U., 1974, Maine State Mus., Bklyn. Mus., 1976, Cleve. Mus. Art, USIA, 1977, U. Va. Art Mus., 1978, Tatistcheff & Co., N.Y.C., 1979, Nat. Portrait Gallery, Washington, Artists Choice Mus., N.Y.C., Weatherspoon Art Gallery, N.C., Pratt Graphic Center, N.Y.C., 1980, Brit. Internat. Print Biennele, West Yorkshire, 1982, Robert Schoelkopf Gallery Ltd., N.Y.C., Helmsly-Spear, N.Y.C., 1983. Recipient Louis Comfort Tiffany award, 1961, Nat. Inst. Arts and Letters award, 1964; Nat. Found. on Arts and Humanities fellow, 1966-67; Fulbright grantee Inst. for Internat. Edn., 1966; Ford Found. grantee, 1969-70. Mem. Coll. Art Assn., Figurative Alliance N.Y., NAD. 475 Dean St Brooklyn NY 11217

CORNELSEN, PAUL FREDERICK, manufacturing and engineering company executive; b. Wellington, Kans., Dec. 23, 1923; s. John S. and Theresa Albertine (von Klatt) C.; m. Floy Lila Brown, Dec. 11, 1943; 1 son, John Floyd. Student, U. Wichita, 1939-41, 45-46; B.S. in Mech. Engrng, U. Denver, 1949. With Boeing Airplane Co., 1940-41, Ralston Purina Co., St. Louis, 1946—, v.p. internat. div., 1961-63, adminstrv. v.p., gen. mgr. internat. div., 1963-64, v.p., 1964-68, dir., 1966—, exec. v.p., 1968-78, vice chmn. bd., chief operating officer, 1978-81, pres. internat. group, 1964-77; pres., chief exec. officer Moehlenpah Industries Inc., St. Louis, 1981—; dir. Boatmen's Nat. Bank, St. Louis, Boatmen's Bancshares, Inc., Petrolite Corp.; founding mem. Latin Am. Agribusiness Investment Corp., 1970—; Founding mem. industry coop. program UN Agys., Rome, Italy. Mem. Nat. 4-H Council Adv. Com.; trustee Ill. Coll., Jacksonville. Served to 1st lt. AUS, World War II; Served to 1st lt. AUS, also Korean War. Decorated Silver Star. Home: 506 Fox Ridge Rd Saint Louis MO 63131 Office: 700 Office Pkwy Creve Couer MO 63177

CORNELSEN, RUFUS, clergyman; b. Colony, Okla., Jan. 29, 1914; s. Isaac and Anna (Boese) C.; m. Frances Louise Deen, Aug. 4, 1946; children: Susan Kathleen Cornelsen France, David Alan, Sara Ann Cornelsen Kaminski. A.B., Southwestern State Tchrs. Coll., Weatherford, Okla., 1935; Th.B., So. Bapt. Theol. Sem., 1937; B.D., Union Theol. sem., 1939; postgrad., Columbia U., 1939-40, Lutheran Theol. Sem., 1941-42, Princeton Theol. Sem., 1948-49; Litt.D., Gettysburg Coll., 1964. Ordained to ministry United Lutheran Ch., 1942; pastor Emanuel Luth. Ch., New Brunswick, N.J., 1942-57, Luth. Student Assn., Rutgers U., 1942-57; asso. dir. social action United Luth. Ch. Am., 1957-58, dir. social action, 1958-62; sec. for civil and econ. life Luth. Ch. in Am., 1962-65; rep. to UN, 1964-65; asso. gen. sec. for planning and program Nat. Council Chs. of Christ in U.S., 1965-68; exec. dir. Met. Christian Council Phila., 1968-79; dir. Office of Christian-Jewish Relations, Nat. Council Chs., 1980-82; chmn. Nat. Inst. on the Holocaust, 1982—; exec. sec. New Brunswick Council Chs., 1945-46; mem. social missions com. Luth. Synod N.Y., 1947-50; exec. bd. Luth. Synod N.J., 1950-52, mem. bd. social missions, 1950-56, pres., 1955-56; mem. commn. social responsibility United Luth. Ch., 1952-57; Luth. World Fedn. fellow study laymen's insts., Europe, 1958; mem. bd. social ministry Luth. Ch. Am., 1966-72, cons. div. mission to, N.Am., 1973-76; bd. dirs. Union Theol. Sem., 1958-76, Phila. Fellowship Commn., 1968—; past trustee Protestant Found. Students, Rutgers U. Contbr. articles, chpts. to religious publs. Mem. nat. council, nat. bd. YMCA, 1967-72, mem. armed services com., 1967-72; bd. govs. USO. Mem. Urban League New Brunswick (dir. 1944-68, pres. 1946- 48), Nat. Council Chs. (rep. Latin Am. Conf. Ch. and Soc. 1962), World Council Chs. Home: 415 S Chester Rd Swarthmore PA 19081

CORNELSON, GEORGE HENRY, textile company executive; b. Spartanburg, S.C., July 12, 1931; s. George Henry III and Elizabeth Miller (Woodward) C.; m. An Martin Shaw, Oct. 6, 1956; children: George Henry V, Martin Shaw,Scott Montgomery, Elizabeth Woodward. Student, Davidson Coll., 1949-51; B.S. in Textiles, N.C. State U., 1953; postgrad., Harvard U. Grad. Sch. Bus. Adminstrn., 1953-54. With indsl. engring. dept. Clinton Mills, Inc., (S.C.), 1954-55, 57-58, v.p., 1958-70; exec. v.p. CLinton Mills, Inc., (S.C.), 1970-79; pres. Clinton Mills, Inc., (S.C.), 1979—, dir.; v.p. Clinton Mills Sales Corp., 1958-70; dir. M.S. Bailey & Son, bankers, Clinton, Mid-Am. Yarn Mills, Pryor, Okla., Elastic Fabrics of Am., Greensboro, N.C.; pres., dir. Clinton Mills of Geneva, (Ala.); mem. S.C. Gov.'s Trade Mission to Far East, Hong Kong, Singapore, Kuala Lumpur, Mayaysia, Taiwan, 1980; bd. dirs. N.C. Textile Found., 1982-83. Trustee Presbyn. Coll., Clinton, 1959-68, S.C. Found. Ind. Colls., 1971-82, Thornwell Home for Children, Clinton, 1968-76; mem. exec. com. Thornwell Home for Children, CLinton, 1973-74, sec. bd. trustees, Clinton, 1974; organizing chmn. Greater Clinton Planning Commn., 1967; pres. Clinton Community Chest and United Fund, 1963-64; chmn. Laurens County dist. Boy Scouts Am., 1973, mem. exec. bd. Blue Ridge Council, 1974; deacon 1st Presbyn. Ch., Clinton, 1959-67, elder, Clinton, 1967-73, 76-81; mem. adv. com. Bailey Found., Clinton. Served with USAF, 1955-57. Recipient Disting. Service award Clinton Jr. C. of C., 1962, Outstanding Young Alumnus award N.C. State U., 1965. Mem. Am. Textiles Mfrs. Inst. (research and tech. service com. 1964-71), Am. Textile Mfrs. Inst. (vice chmn. edn. com. 1975-76, mem. cotton com. 1981-82, safety and health com. 1981-82), S.C. Textile Mfrs. Assn. (dir. 1973-82, pres. 1979-80), S.C. C. of C. (dir., exec. com. 1975-79), Clinton C. of C. (dir. 1959-61, 66), CLinton C. of C. (v.p. 1968, pres. 1969), Phi Psi, Kappa Alpha. Lodge: Clinton Lions. Home: Merrie Oaks Clinton SC 29325 Office: Clinton Mills Drawer 1215 Clinton SC 29325

CORNELY, PAUL BERTAU, educator, physician; b. Guadeloupe, French W.I., Mar. 9, 1906; U.S., 1921, naturalized, 1934; s. Eleodore and Adrienne (Mellon) C.; m. Mae Stewart, June 23, 1934; 1 son, Paul Bertau. A.B., U. Mich., 1928, M.D., 1931, Dr. P.H., 1934, D.Sc. (hon.), 1968, D. Pub. Service, U. of Pacific, 1972. Diplomate: Bd. Preventive Medicine and Pub. Health. Intern Lincoln Hosp., Durham, N.C., 1931-32; mem. faculty Howard U. Coll. Medicine, Washington, 1934—, chief div. phys. medicine and rehab., 1959-64, prof., chmn. dept. preventive medicine and pub. health, 1955-73, prof. emeritus, 1973—; pres. Tech. Assos., Inc., 1977—; med. dir. Freedmen's Hosp., Washington, 1947-58; chmn. bd. dirs. Profl. Exam. Service, 1978—; cons. AID, 1960-74; asst. to exec. med. officer United Mine Workers Welfare and Retirement Fund, Inc., 1971-74; sr. med. cons. System Scis. Inc., Bethesda, Md.; mem. Pres.'s Commn. on Population and Am.'s Future, 1970-72; mem. com. of cons. on cancer Senate Com. on Labor and Pub. Welfare, 1970-72; mem. exec. com. Pres.'s Com. on Employment of Handicapped, 1971—; bd. dirs. Physicians Forum, 1947-67, pres., 1960-61, Community-Group Health Found., 1968-73. Recipient Sesquicentennial award U. Mich., 1967; Nat. Merit award Delta Omega Soc., 1979; Disting. U.S. Immigrant award Citizens Com. Immigration Reform, 1982. Fellow Am. Coll. Preventive Medicine, Am. Coll. Hosp. Adminstrs. (hon.); mem. Med. Soc. D.C. (Community Service award 1964), Am. Cancer Soc. (v.p. 1962- 63), Am. Pub. Health Assn. (exec. com. 1964—, pres. 1969-70, chmn. exec. bd. 1970-71, Sedgwick Meml. award 1972), D.C. Pub. Health Assn. (pres. 1963-65, Disting. Service award 1971). Home: 1338 Geranium St NW Washington DC 20012 Office: Howard U Sch Med 520 W St NW Washington DC 20059

CORNETT, JOHN ANTHONY, business executive; b. Shedd, Oreg., Dec. 26, 1924; s. John Anthony and Lena (Powers) C.; m. N. Joyce Hill, Oct. 4, 1943; children: Michael John, Ronald Allen, Cheryl Rae. B.S., Oreg. State U., 1949, M.S., 1952; grad., Internat. Mktg. Inst., Harvard U., 1962. Vice pres. mfg. Kroger Co., Cin., 1965-74, corp. v.p., 1974-77, sr. v.p., 1977-82, vice chmn., 1982—, dir. Trustee Bethesda Hosp., Cin., 1978—; vice chmn. Cin. Council on World Affairs, Cin., 1980—; bd. dirs. Cin. Mus. Natural History, 1983—. Served with USAAC, 1943-46. Clubs: Hyde Park Country (dir. 1982—), Queen City; Bankers (Cin.). Office: The Kroger Co 1014 Vine St Cincinnati OH 45201

CORNETT, LLOYD HARVEY, JR., historian; b. Seminole, Okla., Aug. 29, 1930; s. Lloyd Harvey and Edna Lee (Walker) C.; m. Rosemary Lou Arkett, Nov. 10, 1951; children: Lloyd Harvey, III, Rosemary Lynne, Carlton Wayne, Curtis Lee. B.A., U. Okla., 1951, M.A., 1954; postgrad., U. N.Mex., 1965, Auburn U., 1977. Asst. dir. command history 2d Air Force, U.S. Air Force, 1955-57; historian Air Def. Command, 1957-58, asst. dir. command history Continental Air Def. Command, 1958-59, asst. dir. command history N.Am. Air Def. Command, 1959-61, center historian Air Force Missile Devel. Center, 1961-70, historian Air Force Spl. Weapons Center, 1970-72, command historian Aerospace Def. Command, 1972-73, command historian Air Tng. Command, 1973-74; dir. U.S. Air Force Hist. Research Center, Maxwell AFB, Ala., 1974—; Mem. Gov.'s Com. for Ala. Conf. on Library and Info. Services; bd. advisors Ala. Hist. Commn. Committeeman Boy Scouts Am., 1963-70, 75-79; mem. at large adminstrv. bd. Meth. Ch., 1978-81. Served with USMCR, 1951-53. Mem. AIAA (tech. com. on history), Western History Assn., N.Mex. Public Records Commn. (alt. chmn.). Democrat. Home: 3751 Marie Cook Dr Montgomery AL 36109 Office: HQ AFSHRC/CC Maxwell AFB AL 36112

CORNETT, RICHARD ORIN, educator and consultant; b. Driftwood, Okla., Nov. 14, 1913; s. Grover Cleveland and Essie (Richardson) C.; m. Lorene Huston, May 26, 1943; children: Linda, Robert, Stanley. B.S., Okla. Baptist U., 1934; M.S., U. Okla., 1937; postgrad., U. Ill., 1938-39; Ph.D., U. Tex., 1940; D.Sc., Hardin-Simmons U., 1954; Litt.D., Jacksonville U., 1964; LL.D., Belknap Coll., 1967. Instr. physics Okla. Bapt. U., 1935-37, asso. prof., 1940-41, prof., 1941; asst. supr. physics Pa. State Engring., Sci., Mgmt., Def. Tng. Program, 1941-42; lectr. electronics Harvard U., 1942-45; spl. research asso. OSRD, 1945; asst. to pres. Okla. Baptist U., 1945-46, v.p., 1946-47, exec. v.p., 1947-51; exec. sec. Edn. Commn., So. Bapt. Conv., 1951-58, So. Assn. Bapt. Colls. and Schs., 1951-58; editor So. Bapt. Educator, 1951-58; specialist for coll. and univ. orgn. and adminstrn. U.S. Office Edn., 1959, exec. asst. to dir. div. higher edn., 1959-61, acting asst. commr., dir., 1961-64, dir. div. ednl. orgn. and adminstrn., 1964-65; v.p. Gallaudet Coll., Washington, 1965-75, research prof., dir. cued speech programs, 1976—; mem. U.S. del. UNESCO Conf. on Devel. Higher Edn. in Africa, 1962; dir. Ann. Inst. on Coll. and Univ. Planning, Soc. for Coll. and Univ. Planning, 1975-77. Author: (with White, Weber, Manning) Practical Physics, 1943, Algebra, A Second Course, 1945, (with others) Electron Tubes and Circuits, 1947, Cued Speech Manual for Teachers, 1983; cued speech lessons in 28 langs.; co-author: Cued Speech Handbook for Parents, 1971. Republican. Baptist. Originator of Cued Speech communication method for deaf; originator, co-developer electronic lipreading aid for deaf; patentee in field. Home: 8702 Royal Ridge Ln Laurel MD 20708 Office: Gallaudet Coll Florida Ave and 7th St NE Washington DC 20002 *If one is to be included in the company of those who give their very best, he must be able to create within himself a vision of success and have the courage to follow that vision. Two kinds of men follow visions: those who are fools and those who do great things. The man who sees a vision and has the impulse to follow it is not permitted to know in advance which he will turn out to be.*

CORNETT, WILLIAM FORREST, JR., management consultant; b. Denver, Oct. 2, 1919; s. William Forrest and Julia Condit (Smith) C.; m. Lois Jean Carr, Mar. 7, 1943; children: William F., James W., Gina J. Cornett Jacobsen. B.S., U. So. Calif., 1948, M.S., 1964. Adminstrv. analyst, City of San Diego, 1948-51; mgmt. cons. assoc. Louis J. Koreger & Assocs., San Francisco, 1951-53; asst. city mgr., San Mateo, Calif., 1953-56, city mgr., La Verne, Calif., 1956-59, City of South Gate, Calif., 1959-66; city adminstr., Fullerton, Calif., 1966-76, city mgr., Riverside, Calif., 1976-80; exec. v.p. Riverside Bd. Realtors, 1980-81; So. Calif. mgr. Pub. Service Skills, Inc., 1982—; mem. Calif. Intergovtl. Bd.; mem. exec. bd. city mgrs. div. League Calif. Cities. Contbr. articles to profl. jours. Pres., Girls Club, N. Orange County.; mem. Riverside County Grand Jury, 1982—. Served to comdr. USNR, 1941-46. Mem. Am. Soc. Pub. Adminstrn., Internat. City Mgmt. Assn., Western Govtl. Research Assn. (council mem.). Lutheran (council). Club: Rotary. Home: 2645 Horace St Riverside CA 92506

CORNFELD, DAVE LOUIS, lawyer; b. St. Louis, Dec. 24, 1921; s. Abraham and Rebecca (David) C.; m. Martha Herrmann, May 30, 1943; children: Richard Steven, James Allen, Lawrence Joseph. A.B., Washington U., St. Louis, 1942, LL.B. (editor Law Quar. 1943), 1943. Bar: Mo. 1943. Practice law, St. Louis; partner Husch, Eppenberger, Donohue, Elson & Cornfeld (and predecessor), 1954—; adj. prof. Washington U., 1966—. Bd. dirs. Jewish Fedn., St. Louis, 1977-80, 83—, Jewish Ctr. for Aged, 1981—. Served with AUS, 1945-46. Mem. ABA (past chmn. com. taxation income estates and trusts, vice chmn. sect. taxation 1977-80, editor-in-chief Tax Lawyer 1977-80), St. Louis Bar Assn. (past chmn. taxation com), Am. Law Inst., Am. Coll. Probate Counsel (regent 1984—), Am. Coll. Tax Counsel (regent 1980—), Order of Coif. Jewish (trustee temple 1967—). Club: Masons. Home: 834 Oakbrook Ln University City MO 63132 Office: 100 N Broadway Saint Louis MO 63102

CORNFIELD, MELVIN, lawyer, electronics company executive; b. Chgo., June 5, 1927; s. Harry and Annabelle (Maltz) C.; m. Edith Pauline Haas, June 24, 1951; children: Daniel Benjamin, Deborah S. (Mrs. David N. Alexander). A.B., U. Chgo., 1948, J.D., 1951. Bar: D.C. 1951, N.Y. 1958. Atty. durable goods div. Office Price Stblzn., Washington, 1951-53; atty.-advisor Chief Counsel's Office IRS, Washington, 1953-58; asso. firm Willkie, Farr, Gallagher, Walton &

FitzGibbon, N.Y.C., 1958-63; dir. taxes NBC, Inc., 1963-66; staff v.p. tax affairs RCA Corp., N.Y.C., 1966-76, v.p., treas., 1976-82, v.p. tax affairs, 1982—. Served with USAAF, 1946-47. Home: 4703 Iselin Ave Riverdale NY 10471 Office: RCA Corp 30 Rockefeller Plaza New York NY 10020

CORNGOLD, STANLEY ALAN, German and comparative literature educator, writer; b. Bklyn., June 11, 1934; s Herman and Estelle (Bramson) C.; m. Marie Josephine Brettle, July 29, 1961 (div. May 1969); 1 dau., Isabel Anna; m. Laina Savory, Nov. 1, 1979 (div. July 1982). A.B., Columbia U., 1957; postgrad., Sch. Oriental and African Studies-U. London, 1957-58; M.A., Cornell U., 1963, Ph.D., 1969; postgrad., U. Basel (Switzerland), 1965-66. Instr. English U. Md. European div., 1959-62; teaching asst. English Cornell U., 1963-64; teaching asst. French Cornell U, 1964-65; asst. prof. German Princeton U., 1966-72, assoc. prof., 1972-79, assoc. prof. German and comparative lit., 1979-81, prof., 1981—, dir. grad. studies dept. German, 1978-82. Author: The Commentators' Despair 1973; editor: Aspekte der Goethezeit 1977, Thomas Mann, 1875-1975 1975; translator The Metamorphosis 1972. Served with U.S. Army, 1955-57. Am. Council Learned Socs. fellow, 1965-66; Nat. Endowment for Humanities fellow, 1973-74; Guggenheim Found. fellow, 1977-78. Mem. PEN, Acad. Lit. Studies, Kafka Soc. Am., N.Am. Nietzsche Soc. Democrat. Jewish. Home: 20 Erdman Ave Princeton NJ 08540 Office: Dept German Princeton U 224 E Pyne Bldg Princeton NJ 08544

CORNISH, DUDLEY TAYLOR, historian, educator; b. Carmel, N.Y., Jan. 11, 1915; s. Stanley Dyckman and Jane (Taylor) C.; m. Maxine Fisher, Sept. 10, 1946; 1 son, Dudley Taylor. A.B., U. Rochester, 1938; M.A., U. Colo., 1947, Ph.D. in History, 1949. Asst. prof., then asso. prof. Kans. State Tchrs. Coll., Pittsburg, 1949-58; prof. history Pittsburg State U., 1958—, chmn. dept. social sci., 1959-61, chmn. dept. history, 1966-78; John F. Morrison prof. mil. history U.S. Army Command and Gen. Staff Coll., Ft. Leavenworth, Kans., 1978-79; mem. Kans. Am. Revolution Bicentennial Commn., 1974-76; mem. selection com. Ft. Leavenworth Hall of Fame, 1977-83. Author: The Sable Arm: Negro Troops in the Union Army, 1861-1865, 1956, chpt. in The Embattled Confederacy, Vol. III of the Image of War: 1861-1865, 1982; compiler: The Negro in Civil War Books, A Critical Bibliography, 1967; editor in chief: Midwest Quar., 1959-67; asso. editor, 1967-77. Served to capt. AUS, 1942-46. Asso. fellow Truman Library; mem. Am. Mil. Inst., U.S. Naval Inst., Kans. History Tchrs. Assn. (pres. 1957), So. Hist. Assn., Kans. Hist. Soc. (pres. 1973), Orgn. Am. Historians, Alpha Delta Phi, Omicron Delta Kappa, Phi Alpha Theta. Office: Pittsburg State University Pittsburg KS 66762

CORNISH, EDWARD SEYMOUR, editor; b. N.Y.C., Aug. 31, 1927; s. George Anthony and Elizabeth Furniss (McLeod) C.; m. Sally Woodhull, Oct. 12, 1957; children: George Anthony, Jefferson Richard Woodhull, Blake McLeod. Diplome d'etudes, U. Paris, France, 1948; A.B., Harvard U., 1950. Copy boy, cub reporter Evening Star, Washington, 1950-51; staff corr. U.P. Assn., Richmond, Va., 1951-52, Raleigh, N.C., 1952-53, London, 1953-54, Paris, 1954-55, Rome, 1956; staff writer Nat. Geog. Soc., 1957-69; founder, pres. World Future Soc., Washington, 1966—; creator, editor The Futurist Mag., 1966—; editor World Future Soc. Bull., 1968-77; cons. to govt., bus. and ednl. orgns. Author: The Study of the Future, 1977; editor: Resources Directory for America's Third Century, 1977, The Future: A Guide to Information Sources, 1977, 1999: The World of Tomorrow, 1978, Communications Tomorrow, 1982, Careers Tomorrow, 1983, Global Solutions, 1984; editorial cons.: Nat. Goals Research Staff, 1970, White House report Toward Balanced Growth, 1970. Bd. dirs. World Watch Inst., 1974—; adv. bd. Inst. for Alternative Futures. Mem. Internat. Sci. Writers Assn. Home: 5501 Lincoln St Bethesda MD 20817 Office: World Future Soc 4916 St Elmo Ave Washington DC 20814

CORNUELLE, HERBERT CUMMING, business executive; b. Cin., Mar. 25, 1920; s. Herbert Cumming and Gertrude (Schleitzer) C.; m. Jean Bradbeer, Dec. 20, 1942; children: John, Richard, Bruce, Ann. A.B., Occidental Coll., 1941; postgrad., U. Denver, 1942. With Dole Corp., Honolulu, 1953-63, v.p., 1955-58, pres., dir., 1958-63; exec. v.p., dir. United Fruit Co., Boston, 1963-67, pres., 1967-69; exec. v.p. Dillingham Corp., Honolulu, 1969-70, pres., 1970-81; trustee Campbell Estate, Honolulu, 1982—. Served to lt. USNR, 1942-45. Mem. Phi Beta Kappa. Clubs: Pacific, Oahu Country (Honolulu); Pacific Union (San Francisco). Office: 900 Fort St #1450 Honolulu HI 96813

CORNWALL, JOHN MICHAEL, savings and loan executive; b. Dallas, Oct. 5, 1935; s. John Vincent and Mattie Lee (Parks) C.; m. Sharon Lynne Holloway, June 21, 1958; children: Deborah Lynne, Michele Elaine. B.B.A., Tex. A. and M. U., 1957; student, Savs. and Loan Sch., U. Ga., 1962-63, Ind. U., 1968-70. Sr. v.p. Oak Cliff Savs., Dallas, 1959-70; pres. Ft. Worth Savs. & Loan, 1970-71; exec. v.p. 8.8 Corp., Dallas, 1971-72, First Tex. Fin. Corp., 1972-77; exec. v.p., chief operating officer First Tex. Savs., Dallas, 1978-79, pres., chief operating officer, 1979-81, pres., 1981-82, chief exec. officer, 1981—, chmn., 1982—. Mem. adv. bd. Leadership Dallas; vice chmn. bd. dirs. Crossroads Community Center, Dallas, 1968-70; mem. Urban Rehab. Standards Bd., Dallas, 1972-73; bd. dirs., mem. exec. com. Longhorn council Boy Scouts Am., 1970-71; treas., bd. dirs. Dallas Center for Ch. Renewal, 1978-79; mem. bd. elders Fellowship Bible Ch., Dallas, 1976—. Served to 2d lt. U.S. Army, 1957-58. Mem. Nat. Savs. and Loan League, U.S. League of Savs. Assn. (mem. capital stock com.), others. Office: First Tex Savs Assn 14951 Dallas Pkwy Dallas TX 75240

CORNWALL, RICHARD S., finance company executive; b. N.Y.C., Jan. 22, 1932; s. Samuel C. and Nora Adele (Fitzgerald) C.; m. Nancy Lee Ness, June 30, 1956; children: S. Christopher, Richard Stephen, Brian Robert, David Andrew. B.A. in Econs, Wesleyan U., Middletown, Conn., 1954; grad., Rutgers U. Grad. Sch. Banking, 1964; grad. mgmt. course, Am. Mgmt. Assn. Sch., N.Y.C., 1965; student, Wharton Sch. Finance, U. Pa., 1957-58. Spl. agt., trainee Indemnity Ins. Co. N.Am., 1954-55; spl. agt. Resolute Ins. Co., 1955-56; v.p. Phila. Nat. Bank, 1956-67; exec. v.p. Bank of Commonwealth, Detroit, 1967-70; v.p., gen. ops. mgr. comml. indsl. and real estate financing operations Ford Motor Credit Co., Dearborn, Mich., 1970-72; pres., chief exec. officer Aetna Bus. Credit, Inc., East Hartford, 1973-80, Barclays Am./Bus. Credit, Inc., 1980—; exec. v.p., dir. Barclays Am. Corp., Charlotte, N.C. Home: Ray Hill Rd East Haddam CT 06423 Office: Barclays Am/Bus Credit Inc PO Box 118 Hartford CT 06101

CORNWELL, CHARLES DANIEL, phys. chemist, educator; b. Williamsport, Pa., Dec. 27, 1924; s. John G. and Anna (Moul) C.; m. Blanche M. Haskins, Sept. 1, 1951. A.B. with distinction, Cornell U., 1947; Ph.D. in Chem. Physics, Harvard, 1951. Research asso. State U. Iowa, 1950-52; mem. faculty U. Wis., 1952—, prof. chemistry, 1962—. Served with USNR, 1944-46. Mem. Am. Phys. Soc., Am. Chem. Soc., Phi Beta Kappa, Phi Kappa Phi. Spl. research nuclear magnetic resonance, microwave spectroscopy. Home: 3108-6 Creek View Dr Middleton WI 53562

CORNWELL, DAVID GEORGE, educator, biochemist; b. San Rafael, Calif., Oct. 8, 1927; s. John Nevius and Nora (Jonasen) C.; m. Normagene Coon, Mar. 14, 1959; children: Karen Sue, David Andrew. B.A. with honors, Coll. Wooster, 1950; M.A., Ohio State U., 1952; Ph.D., Stanford U., 1955. NRC fellow Harvard U., 1954-56; faculty Ohio State U., 1956—, prof. physiol. chemistry, 1963—, chmn. dept. physiol. chemistry, 1965-80, asso. dean acad. affairs Coll. Medicine, 1979—; mem. nutrition study sect. NIH, 1966-70, nutrition sci. tng. rev. sect., 1970-73. Contbr. articles chemistry lipids and lipoproteins to profl. jours.; editorial bd.: Jour. Lipid Research, 1962-66, adv. bd., 1974-78, Jour. Nutrition, 1969-72; editorial adv. bd.: Chem. Abstracts, 1979—. Served with AUS, 1946-47. Co-recipient hon. mention for research 6th Internat. Congress Hematology, 1956. Mem. Am. Chem. Soc., Biophys. Soc., Am. Soc. Biol. Chemists, Am. Oil Chemists Soc., Am. Inst. Nutrition, Alpha Omega Alpha, Sigma Xi. Presbyterian (elder). Home: 2290 Middlesex Rd Columbus OH 43220

CORNWELL, DAVID JOHN MOORE (JOHN LE CARRÉ), author; b. Poole, Dorset, Eng., Oct. 19, 1931; s. Ronald Thomas Archibald and Olive (Glassy) C.; m. Alison Ann Sharp, Nov. 27, 1954 (div. dissolved 1972); children: Simon, Stephen, Timothy; m. Valerie Jane Eustace, 1972; 1 son, Nicholas. Student, Bern (Switzerland) U., 1948-49; B.A. in Modern Langs, Lincoln Coll., Oxford (Eng.) U., 1956. Tutor Eton Coll., 1956-58; mem. Brit. Fgn. Service, 1959-64, 2d sec. embassy, Bonn, Germany, 1961-63, consul, Hamburg, Germany, 1963-64. Author: Call for the Dead, 1961, Murder of Quality, 1962, The Spy Who Came in From the Cold (Mystery Writers of Am. Novel of Yr.), 1963 (Brit. Crime Novel of Yr. award, Somerset Maugham award), The Looking-Glass War, 1965, A Small Town in Germany, 1968, The Naive and Sentimental Lover, 1971, Tinker Tailor Soldier Spy, 1973, The Honorable Schoolboy, 1977 (James Tait Black Meml. prize, Crime Writers Assn. gold dagger), Smiley's People, 1980, The Little Drummer Girl, 1983. Recipient Edgar Allen Poe award, 1965. Address: care John Farquharson Ltd Bell House Bell Yard London WC2A 2JU England *

CORONA, ALFONSO VARGAS, advertising agency executive; b. Mexico City, Nov. 22, 1948; s. Alfonso Blake and Bertha (Vargas) C.; m. Coti Corona Del Paso, Dec. 4, 1971; children: Alfonso, Paola, Santiago. Student, Universidad La Salle, 1964-66, Escuela Tecnica de Publicidad, 1966-69, U. Tex., 1970, Council Internat. Relations, 1970. Acct. exec. Camacho Orvananos, Mexico City, 1971-72, Davo Y L.M. Publicidad, 1972-73, Publicidad Ferrer, 1973-75, Publicidad D'Arcy, 1975-78; acct. supr. Doyle Dane Bernbach, Mexico City, 1978-80; pres. Foote Cone & Belding de Mex, Mexico City, 1980—. Roman Catholic. Club: Golf Mex. (Tlalpan). Home: Av San Jeronimo No 10200 Mexico DF Mexico Office: Foote Cone Belding Mex SA Salamanca No 102-10 Piso Mexico DF Mexico 06700

CORONITI, FERDINAND VINCENT, physics educator, consultant; b. Boston, June 14, 1943; s. Samuel Charles and Ethel Marie (Havlik) C.; m. Patricia Ann Smith, Aug. 30, 1969; children: Evelyn Marie, Samuel Thomas. A.B., Harvard U., 1965; Ph.D., U. Calif.-Berkeley, 1969. Research physicist UCLA, 1967-70, asst. prof. physics, 1970-74, assoc. prof., 1974-78, prof. physics and astronomy, 1978—; cons. TRW Systems. Contbr. articles to sci. jours. NASA grantee, 1974; NSF grantee, 1974. Mem. Am. Geophys. Union, Am. Astron. Soc., Internat. Union Radiol. Sci. Home: 10475 Almayo Ave Los Angeles CA 90064 Office: Dept Physics 401 Hilgard Ave Los Angeles CA 90024

CORONTZOS, ROBERT, lawyer; b. Great Falls, Mont., Oct. 27, 1937; s. Thomas T. and Dena C. B.S. magna cum laude, Coll. of Great Falls, 1959; J.D. with high honors, U. Mont., 1962. Bar: Mont. 1962, U.S. Dist. Ct. Mont. 1962. Mng. ptnr. Jardine, Stephenson, Blewett & Weaver, Great Falls, 1963—; dir. Walker Lumber Co., Western Office Equipment. Fellow Am. Bar Found., Am. Coll. Probate Counsel; mem. ABA (ho. of dels., state bar del.), State Bar Mont., Cascade County Bar Assn., Am. Judicature Soc. Office: PO Box 2269 Great Falls MT 59403

CORPE, WILLIAM ALBERT, microbiologist; b. Walworth, Wis., Jan. 11, 1924; s. John and Doris (Healy) C.; m. Mary Elinor Milham, Aug. 27, 1949; children: Linda Elizabeth, Richard Milham. B.S., U. Wis., 1948, M.S., 1950; Ph.D., Pa. State U., 1956. Asst. prof. Western Ky. State Coll., Bowling Green, 1950-53; asst. prof. Barnard Coll. and Columbia U., N.Y.C., 1956-60; USPHS spl. research fellow U. New South Wales, Australia, 1963-64; research collaborator Brookhaven Nat. Lab., Upton, N.Y., 1965-71; assoc. prof. grad. faculty Columbia U., 1960-67, prof. biol. scis., 1967—; cons. industry and govt. Contbr. articles to profl. jours., chpts. to books. Mem. Closter (N.J.) Environ. Commn., 1975-82. Served with USMC, 1942-46. NIH and NSF grantee. Mem. Am. Soc. Microbiology, Can. Soc. Microbiology, Soc. Indsl. Microbiology, N.Y. Acad. Sci., Sigma Xi (sec. chpt. 1970-79). Home: 49 Alpine Dr Closter NJ 07624 Office: 606 W 120 St New York NY 10027

CORR, EDWIN GHARST, ambassador; b. Edmond, Okla., Aug. 6, 1934; s. E.L. and Rowena C.; m. Susanne Springer, Nov. 24, 1957; children: Michelle Ruth, Jennifer Jean, Phoebe Rowena. B.S., U. Okla., 1957, M.A., 1961; postgrad., U. Tex., 1968-69. Fgn. service officer Dept. State, Washington, 1961-72, dep. asst. sec. internat. narcotics matters, 1978-80; polit. officer, exec. asst. to ambassador Am. Embassy, Bangkok, Thailand, 1972-75, counselor polit. affairs, Quito, Ecuador, 1975-76, dep. chief of mission, 1976-78, ambassador to Peru, Lima, 1980-81, ambassador to Bolivia, La Paz, 1981—. Author: The Political Process in Colombia, 1971. Served to capt. USMC, 1957-60. Mem. Am. Fgn. Service Assn. Home: 1617 Jenkins St Norman OK 73069 Office: Am Embassy La Paz APO Miami FL 34032

CORRADA DEL RIO, BALTASAR, Congressman; b. Morovis, P.R., Apr. 10, 1935; s. Romulo and Ana Maria (del Rio) Corrada Del R.; m. Beatriz Betances, Dec. 24, 1959; children—Ana Isabel, Francisco Javier, Juan Carlos, Jose Baltasar. B.A. in Social Scis, U. P.R., 1956, J.D., 1959. Bar: P.R. bar 1959. Practiced in, San Juan, from 1959; atty., chmn. Civil Rights Commn. P.R., 1970-72; pres. editorial bd. P.R. Human Rights Rev., 1971-72; mem. 95th-98th Congresses as resident commr. from P.R. Founder, dir. P.R. Teleradial Inst. Ethics; mem. Dem. Nat. Com. Mem. Am., Fed., P.R. bar assns. New Progressive Democrat. Roman Catholic. Club: Exchange. Home: 7813 Carrleigh Pkwy Springfield VA 22152 Office: US House of Representatives Washington DC 20515

CORRADI, PETER, construction and engineering consultant;; b. Bklyn., Nov. 24, 1910; s. Manlis and Mary (Bosco) C.; m. Helena Olive Corley, Jan. 23, 1937; children—Peter R., Patricia, Carol. B.S. in Civil Engring, N.Y.U., 1936, Sc.D., 1956. Design engr. Port of N.Y. Authority, 1934-39; commd. lt. (j.g.) USN, 1940, advanced through grades to rear adm., 1961; dep. chief Bur. Yards and Docks; also dep. chief civil engr. U.S. Navy, Washington, 1958-62, chief bur., chief civil engrs., 1962-65; ret.; v.p., gen. mgr. Gibbs & Hill, Inc. (cons. engrs.), 1965-66, pres., chief exec. officer, 1966-69; exec. v.p., dir. Raymond Internat., Inc., N.Y.C., 1969-72, chmn. bd., Houston, 1972-76, chmn. fin. com., 1976; consultant, Naples, Fla., 1976—; dir. Daniel, Mann, Johnson, Mendenhall Inc., Los Angeles.; Bd. govs. N.Y. Bldg. Congress; bd. dirs. Engrs. Joint Council. Decorated Bronze Star medal, D.S.M. Fellow ASCE; mem. Nat. Soc. Profl. Engrs., Soc. Am. Mil. Engrs. (past pres.), Moles (past pres., mem. exec. com. award for outstanding achievement in constrn. industry 1976). Clubs: Seaview Country (Absecon, N.J.); Imperial Golf (Naples, Fla.); Army Navy (Arlington, Va.). Home: 2905 Gulf Shore Blvd N Naples FL 33940

CORRADO, FRED, food company executive; b. Mt. Vernon, N.Y.; s. Anthony Edward and Rose (Capone) C.; m. Josephine Ann Gonda, July 4, 1962; children: David, Paul, Christopher. B.B.A. in Acctg, Manhattan Coll., 1961; grad. Advanced Mgmt. Program, Harvard U., 1983. C.P.A., N.Y. Sr. auditor Arthur Andersen & Co. (C.P.A.'s), N.Y.C., 1961-65; controller Romney Cosmetics Co. div. Pfizer Co., Stamford, Conn., 1966-68; with ITT Corp., 1968-69, Kenton Corp., 1969-73, Nabisco Brands USA (name formerly Standard Brands Inc.), 1973—; pres. Planters div. Nabisco Brands USA, East Hanover, N.J., 1980-84; exec. v.p., chief operating officer Nabisco Brands Ltd., Toronto, 1984—. Mem. Fin. Execs. Inst., Am. Inst. C.P.A.s, Planning Execs. Inst. Home: 9 Coventry Ct Croton-on-Hudson NY 10520 Office: Nabisco Brands USA East Hanover NJ 07936

CORRALES, PATRICK, professional baseball manager; b. Los Angeles, Mar. 20, 1941; s. David and Josephine (Rivera) C.; m. Sharon Ann Grimes, Sept. 23, 1960 (div. July 22, 1969); children: Rena M., Michele D., Patricia A.; m. 2d Donna Ardene Myers, Mar. 7, 1983; 1 son, Patrick David Parker. Grad., Fresno High Sch., Calif., 1959. Signed with Phila. Phillies, 1959, profl. baseball player, 1959-78; mgr. Tex. Rangers, Arlington, 1978-80, Phila. Phillies, 1982-83, Cleve. Indians, 1983—; coach Am. League All-Stars, Seattle, 1979, Nat. League All-Stars, Chgo., 1983. Holder Am. Karate Acad. Brown Belt. Democrat. Roman Catholic. Office: Cleveland Indians Boudreau Blvd Cleveland OH 44114

CORREA, GUSTAVO, educator; b. Colombia, Sept. 20, 1914; came to U.S., 1941, naturalized, 1956; s. Urbano and María (Forero) C.; m. Inés, Aug. 20, 1947; children: Amanda, Albert, Patricia. Licenciado, Escuela Normal Superior, Bogota, 1941; Ph.D., Johns Hopkins U., 1947. Nat. dir. secondary edn., Bogota, 1948-50; vis. prof. Spanish, U. Oreg., 1950-51; asso. prof. Spanish, Tulane U., 1951-54, U. Chgo., 1954-56, U. Pa., 1956-59; prof. Spanish, Yale U., 1959—; Co-editor Hispanic Rev., 1958-60, adv. editor, 1960—. Author: El espíritu del mal en Guatemala; ensayo de semántica cultural, 1955, La Poesía mítica de Federico García Lorca, 1957, El simbolismo religioso en las novelas de Pérez Galdós, 1962, Realidad, Ficcion y símbolo en las novelas de Pérez Galdós, 1966, Poesía espanola del siglo Veinte, Antología, 1972, Antología de la poesía española, 1900-1980 (2 vols.), 1980. Mem. Modern Lang. Assn. Am., Am. Assn. Tchrs. Spanish and Portuguese; mem. Hispanic Soc. Am. Home: 84 Crooked Tree Ln #106 Vero Beach FL 32960 Dept Spanish Yale U New Haven CT 06520

CORREA, HENRY A., manufacturing executive; b. N.Y.C., Mar. 9, 1917; s. Enrique A. and Maria (Helm) C.; m. Elizabeth Winchester, Dec. 9, 1944. B.S. in Bus. Adminstrn., St. Louis U., 1937. With Robertson Aircraft Corp., St. Louis, 1937-38; chief pilot, sales mgr. Atlantic Aviation Service, Wilmington, Del., 1938-41; fgn. sales mgr. Bendix Internat. div. Bendix Corp., 1945-57; v.p. fgn. ops. ACF Industries, Inc., N.Y.C., 1958, v.p. mktg., 1959-63, v.p. exec. dept., 1964-65, exec. v.p., dir., 1965-67, pres., 1967-81, vice chmn., 1981—; dir. Petroleum & Resources Corp., Nat. Starch & Chem. Corp., Fischbach Corp., Petroleum and Resources Corp. Mem. Met. Opera Assn.; hon. trustee Children's Aid Soc. Served from 1st lt. to maj. AUS, 1943-45. Decorated Army Commendation medal; recipient hon. pilot wings Colombia Air Force, 1945; Andrew Wellington Cordier fellow Columbia U. Mem. Quiet Birdmen. Clubs: Sky, Union, N.Y. Yacht (N.Y.C.); Riomar Bay Yacht (Vero Beach, Fla.); Fishers Island (N.Y.) Golf, Fishers Island Yacht; John's Island (Vero Beach, Fla.); Niantic Bay Yacht (Niantic, Conn.). Office: care ACF Industries Inc 750 3d Ave New York NY 10017

CORRELL, ALSTON DAYTON, forest products company executive; b. Brunswick, Ga., Apr. 28, 1941; s. Alston Dayton and Elizabeth (Flippo) C.; m. Ada Lee Fulford, June 23, 1963; children: Alston Dayton, Elizabeth Lee. B.S.B.A., U. Ga., 1963; M.S. in Pulp and Paper Tech., U. Maine, 1966, U. Maine, 1967. Pres. paperboard div. Mead Corp., Dayton, Ohio, 1977-80, pres. paperboard group, 1980, group v.p. paperboard, 1980, group v.p. paper, 1980-81, group v.p. forest products, 1981-83, sr. v.p. forest products, 1983—; dir. Ga. Kraft Co., Rome, Brunswick Pulp & Paper Co., Ga., Northwood Pulp & Timber Ltd., Prince George, B.C., Can., B.C. Forest Products Ltd., Vancouver. Republican. Presbyterian. Office: Mead Corp Courthouse Plaza NE Dayton OH 45463 *

CORRELL, JAMES WILLIAM, physician, educator; b. Bklyn., Dec. 6, 1919; s. Charles Daniel and Florence Olive (Ritter) C.; m. Cynthia Cannon Hewitt, Aug. 7, 1948; children—Catherine Hewitt, James William. B.A., Brown U., 1941; M.D., Cornell U., 1944. Diplomate: Nat. Bd. Med. Examiners, Am. Bd. Neurol. Surgeons. Intern in surgery New Haven Hosp.; asst. in surgery Yale U. Sch. Medicine, 1944-45; intern in pathology N.Y. Hosp., N.Y.C., 1946; asst. resident pathologist, 1947-48; asst. pathology Cornell U. Med. Coll., N.Y.C., 1947-48, instr. pathology, 1948-49; research fellow neurosurgery Coll. Phys. & Surg., Columbia, 1949, instr. neurol. surgery, 1955-60, asso., 1960-61, asst. prof. clin. neurol. surgery, 1961-64, asso. prof., 1964-76, prof., 1976—; asst. resident neurologist Neurol. Inst. N.Y. Columbia-Presbyn. Med. Center, 1950, asst. resident neurosurgeon, 1951-53; resident neurosurgeon Francis Delafield Hosp., N.Y.C., 1952, clin. asst. vis. neurosurgeon, 1955—; asst. neurosurgeon Valley Hosp., Ridgewood, N.J., 1956-60, neurosurgeon, 1960—; mem. staff Bergen Pines County (N.J.) Hosp., 1957-59, Paterson (N.J.) Gen. Hosp., 1958—, St. Francis Hosp., N.Y.C., 1957-62, N.Y. Psychiat. Inst., N.Y.C., 1955; cons. Englewood (N.J.) Hosp., 1956—. Contbr. articles to med. jours. and textbooks. Served with M.C. USN, 1953-55. Mgm. Am., Pan Am. med. assns., Med. Soc. County N.Y., Bergen County Med. Soc., Am. Acad. Neurology and Neurol. Surgery, A.C.S., Am. Assn. Neurol. Surgeons, Congress Neurol. Surgeons, Assn. Research Nervous and Mental Disorders, Am. Epilepsy Soc., N.Y. Acad. Scis., Soc. Italiana Per Lo Studio Dell'Arteriosclerosi, Soc. Exptl. Biology and Medicine, West Side Clin. Soc., Soc. Neurosci., Am. Heart Assn. (stroke council). Home: 46 Glenwood Rd Upper Saddle River NJ 07458 Office: 710 W 168th St New York NY 10032

CORRES, ALONSO V., physician; b. Copacabana, Colombia, Feb. 12, 1939; came to U.S., 1964, naturalized, 1968; s. Bernardo and Bertha (Velez) C.; children: Sonya, Yvonne. M.D., Javeriana U., (S.Am.), 1963. Diplomate: Am. Bd. Neurol. Surgery. Intern Maimonides Hosp., Bklyn., 1964-65, resident in gen. surgery, 1965; resident Flower and Fifth Ave. Hosp., N.Y.C., 1967-68; resident in neurology VA Hosp., Bronx, 1968-69; resident in neurosurgery Mt. Sinai Hosp., N.Y.C., 1969-74; practice neurosurgery, Bklyn., 1975—; dir. neurosurgery USPHS, S.I., 1975—; cons. neurosurgeon Bronx VA Hosp., 1976—; clin. instr. neurosurgery Mt. Sinai Sch. Medicine, N.Y.C., 1974—; attending neurosurgeon Beth Isreal Med. Ctr., N.Y.C., Queens Hosp. Ctr., Jamaica, N.Y., Bklyn. Jewish Hosp., Luth. Med. Ctr. Meth. Hosp., Bklyn.; commd. USPHS, 1975, advanced through grades to capt., 1978—. Served with U.S. Army, 1965-67. Home and Office: 63 Essex Ave Montclair NJ 07042

CORRICK, ANN MARJORIE, communications executive; b. Grosse Pointe, Mich; d. John A. and Mary (Nickell) C. B.J., U. Tex., 1943. Reporter Transradio Press Service, Washington, 1943-51; producer

Am. Forum of the Air, also; Youth Wants to Know, NBC, Washington, 1951-52; Washington corr. and broadcaster WDSU-TV, New Orleans, 1954-58; asst. chief Washington News Bur.; also reporter-broadcaster Westinghouse Broadcasting Co., Washington, 1958-66; USIA congl. liason officer Expo '67, Montreal, Can., 1967; info. officer USIA Fgn. Service, Saigon, Vietnam, 1968-70; dir. promotion and communication Corrick Internat., Santa Cruz, Calif., 1980—. Recipient Sylvania citation for producing and moderating TV film Dateline Washington for WDSU-TV, 1955, Theta Sigma Phi Nat. Headliner award, 1962. Mem. Radio-TV Corrs. Assn. (pres. 1961-62, Women in Communications.). Club: Washington Press (sec. 1966-67). Home and Office: 113 Felix St Apt 6 Santa Cruz CA 95060

CORRICK, RICHARD MAYNARD, football team executive; b. Ottumwa, Iowa, Apr. 22, 1934; s. Maynard Wesley and Dorothy (Boyd) C.; m. Bonnie Jane Brown, June 16, 1980; children: Traci, Richard. B.S., Oreg. State U., 1957. Asst. football coach Notre Del Rio High Sch., North Sacramento, Calif., 1957-68, Riverside City Coll., Calif., 1958-59, Iowa State U., Ames, 1959-64, Ariz. State U., Tempe, 1964-65, U. Calif-Berkeley, 1965-72; dir. player personnel Green Bay Packers, Wis., 1972. Home: 1939 Wood Ln Green Bay WI 54303 Office: Green Bay Packers Football Club 1265 Lombardi St Green Bay WI 54303

CORRIGAN, DANIEL, clergyman; b. Pontiac, Mich., Oct. 25, 1900; s. Herbert James and Katherine (Burns) C.; m. Elizabeth Waters, Sept. 21, 1926. B.D., Nashotah (Wis.) Theol. Sem., 1926, S.T.M., 1943, D.D., 1955. Ordained to ministry P.E. Ch., 1924; pastor in, Portage, Wis., 1925-31, Oconomowoc, Wis., 1931-43, Balt., 1944-48, St. Paul, 1948-58; chaplain St.Francis House, U. Wis., 1944; suffragan bishop, Colo., 1958-60; dir. home dept. Nat. Council P.E. Ch., 1960-68; minister to coll. Amherst (Mass.) Coll., 1968-69; dean Bexley Hall, Rochester (N.Y.) Centre for theol. studies, 1969-71; assisting bishop of, Los Angeles, 1972—. Chmn. dept. Christian social relations Diocese of Minn., 1952-58; pres. Am. Ch. Inst. for Negroes, 1960—; mem. joint commn. P.E. Gen. Conv. Edn. Holy Orders, 1958—; Vice pres. Minn. Indian Commn., 1955-58; pres. St. Paul Council Human Relations, 1954-58; mem. Gov. of Minn. Commn. on Resettlement, 1955-58; Trustee Nashotah Theol. Sem. Recipient Bishop William Scarlett award, 1979; John Nevin Sayre award, 1979. Fellow Am. Soc. Religion and Culture. Home: 131 Hermosillo Santa Barbara CA 93108

CORRIGAN, E. GERALD, banker; b. Waterbury, Conn., 1941. Student, Fairfield U., Fordham U. Vice-pres. Fed. Res. Bank of N.Y., until 1980, sr. v.p., 1980; spl. assignment to chmn. bd. govs. Fed. Res., 1979-80; pres. Fed. Res. Bank of Mpls., 1980—. Trustee, Macalester Coll., 1981—, Joint Council Econ. Edn., 1981—. Office: Fed Res Bank of Mpls 250 Marquette Ave Minneapolis MN 55480

CORRIGAN, FREDRIC H., corporate executive; b. Grand Forks, N.D., Dec. 2, 1914; s. Thomas S. and Bertha (Wolff) C.; m. Mary Leslie, Dec. 30, 1939; children: Leslie (Mrs. John G. Turner), Fredric Wolff, Nancy (Mrs. Kenneth B. Woodrow). Student, U. Minn., 1933-36. Grain merchandiser Peavey Co., Mpls., 1936-43, Duluth, Minn., 1946-55, Mpls., 1955-77, exec. v.p., 1959-65, pres., 1965-77, chief exec. officer, 1968-77, chmn. bd., 1975-77; dir. Camel Bank, Phoenix; Pres. Duluth Bd. Trade, 1954-55, Mpls. Grain Exchange, 1967-68. Bd. dirs. United Fund Mpls., 1967-72, Mpls. YMCA, 1970-78, Mpls. Urban Coalition, 1971-74, Greater Mpls. C. of C., 1972-75, U. Minn. Found., 1976—, Minn. Orch., 1974-80, also Western, Minn. golf assns.; bd. dirs. Northwestern Hosp., 1975—, chmn., 1977-79; trustee Evans Scholars Found., 1968-72. Served with USNR, 1942-46. Mem. Sigma Chi. Methodist (trustee). Clubs: Minneapolis, Minikahda; Desert Forest (Carefree, Ariz.). Home: 3150 W Calhoun Pkwy Minneapolis MN 55416 Office: 405 Peavey Bldg 730 2d Ave S Minneapolis MN 55402

CORRIGAN, HAROLD CAULDWELL, accountant, metals company executive; b. Montreal, Que., Can., Mar. 3, 1927; s. Harold Willard and Dorothy Margaret (Cauldwell) C.; m. Eve Ellwood, June 14, 1952; children—Susan, Ann. B.Comm., McGill U., Montreal, 1950, Licentiate of Acctg., 1953; Diploma; Centre D'Etudes Industrielles, 1959. Chartered acct. With Alcan Aluminium, 1950—, now v.p. corp. relations, Montreal; dir. Mortgage Ins. Co. Can., Simpsons-Sears Acceptance Co. Ltd., MICC Investments Ltd., IAC Ltd., Continental Bank of Can., Simpson-Sears Ltd. Served with Royal Can. Naval Res., 1945. Mem. Can. Mfrs'. Assn. (pres. 1975-76). Anglican. Clubs: Toronto, University of N.Y.C., B&R, Mt. Royal. Home: 3011 Barat Rd Montreal PQ H3Y 2H4 Canada Office: 1188 Sherbrooke St W Montreal PQ H3A 3G2 Canada

CORRIGAN, JAMES HENRY, JR., business executive; b. Buffalo, Mar. 15, 1926; s. James Henry and Mary Cleta (Frainie) C.; m. Barbara Ann Cronk, Mar. 31, 1951; children: Barbara Ann, Jim, Mike. B.S., Duke U., 1947. Vice pres., gen. sales mgr. Keller Industries, 1961-63; v.p., div. mgr. Maule Industries, Miami, Fla., 1963-66; sales mgr. metals div. RJR Archer, Inc., Winston-Salem, N.C., 1967-70, v.p., gen. mgr. metals div., 1970-72, pres., chief exec. officer, 1972-76; pres. RJR Foods, Inc., Winston-Salem, 1976-78; asst. to chmn. and chief exec. officer R.J. Reynolds Industries, Inc., 1978-80; pres., chief exec. officer Mebane (N.C.) Packaging Corp., 1980—; dir. Rex Plastics, Thomasville, N.C., Northwestern Bank, North Wilkesboro, N.C. Trustee Winston Salem Arts Council; mem. exec. com. N.C. Citizens Assn. Served with USNR, 1944-46. Mem. Winston-Salem C. of C. (dir.). Republican. Roman Catholic. Club: Forsyth Country. Home: 830 Glen Echo Trail Winston-Salem NC 27106 Office: PO Box 408 Mebane NC 27302 *The time has come, in my life, when it is not only appropriate, but necessary, that a higher priority be assigned to participation in public issues and the political process in support of our economic and political system.*

CORRIGAN, JAMES JOHN, JR., pediatrician; b. Pitts., Aug. 28, 1935; s. James John and Rita Mary (Grimes) C.; m. Carolyn Virginia Long, July 2, 1960; children—Jeffrey James, Nancy Carolyn. B.S., Juniata Coll., Huntingdon, Pa., 1957; M.D. with honors, U. Pitts., 1961. Diplomate: Am. Bd. Pediatrics (hematology-oncology). Intern, then resident in pediatrics U. Colo. Med. Center, 1961-64; trainee in pediatric hematology-oncology U. Ill. Med. Center, 1964-66; asso. in pediatrics Emory U. Med. Sch., 1966-67, asst. prof., Atlanta, 1967-71; mem. faculty U. Ariz. Coll. Medicine, Tucson, 1971—, prof. pediatrics, 1974—; chief sect. pediatric hematology-ongology, also dir. Mountain States Regional Hemophilia Center, U. Ariz., Tucson, 1978—. Assoc. editor: Am. Jour. Diseases of Children, 1982—; Contbr. numerous papers med. jours. Grantee NIH, Mountain States Regional Hemophilia Center, Ga. Heart Assn., Gen. Electric Co., Am. Cancer Soc., CIBA Pharm. Co. Mem. Am. Acad. Pediatrics, Am. Soc. Hematology, Soc. Pediatric Research, Western Soc. Pediatric Research, Internat. Soc. Toxinology, Western Soc. Pediatric Research (Ross award Pediatric research 1975), Am. Heart Assn. (council thrombosis), Internat. Soc. Thrombosis and Haemostasis, Am. Pediatric Soc., World Fedn. Hemophilia, Ariz. Med. Assn., Pima County Med. Assn., Alpha Omega Alpha. Republican. Roman Catholic. Office: Dept Pediatrics U Ariz Health Scis Center 1501 N Campbell Ave Tucson AZ 85724

CORRIGAN, JOHN EDWARD, JR., banker, lawyer; b. Chgo., Sept. 26 1922; s. John Edward and Veronica (Mulvey) C.; m. Eileen Williams, Nov. 4, 1950 (div. 1979). B.A., Harvard, 1943, J.D., 1949. Bar: Ill. bar 1950. With First Nat. Bank Chgo., 1949-79, asst. v.p., 1960-61, v.p., 1961-72, sr. v.p., 1972-79; partner firm Hedberg, Tobin, Corrigan & Wolf, Chgo., 1980—. Served with AUS, 1943-46, 51-52. Home: 560 Greenwood Ave KenilWorth IL 60043 Office: 1 First Nat Plaza Chicago IL 60603

CORRIGAN, PAUL JAMES, JR., hospital administrator; b. Cleve., Nov. 11, 1933; s. Paul James and Lucille (Ryan) C.; m. Dyann Robertson, Nov. 27, 1976; children by previous marriage: Michael Shaun, Patricia Colette. B.S., U. Nebr., 1962; M.H.A., Baylor U., 1969; J.D., Nashville Night Law Sch., 1983. Entered USAF, 1952, advanced through grades to maj., 1972; adminstr. health services Med. Service Corps, Calif., Tex., Germany, 1952-72; hosp. adminstr. Western State Psychiat. Hosp., Bolivar, Tenn., 1972-76; asso. dir. Vanderbilt U. Hosp., Nashville, 1976—; mem. faculty div. med. adminstrn. Vanderbilt U. Sch. Medicine, 1977—; dir. Mid-south Med. Center Council; preceptor grad. program hosp. adminstrn. Med. Coll. Va. Decorated Meritorious Service medal.; recipient Service Testimonial Chief Chaplains USAF. Mem. Tenn. Hosp. Assn. (council on profl. practice and edn.), Assn. Mental Health Adminstrs., Am. Coll. Hosp. Adminstrs., Ret. Officers Assn., Assn. Mil. Surgeons U.S., VFW. Clubs: Masons (32 deg.), Shriners). Address: 806 Fountainhead Ct Brentwood TN 37027 *To demand of others no more than I demand of myself. In my dedication to health care, to continuously strive to insure ethical professional practices and look for means to improve that portion of the U.S. health care delivery system for which I am responsible.*

CORRIGAN, ROBERT ANTHONY, university chancellor; b. New London, Conn., Apr. 21, 1935; s. Anthony John and Rose Mary (Jengo) C.; m. Joyce D. Mobley, Jan. 12, 1975; children by previous marriage: Kathleen Marie, Anthony John, Robert Anthony; 1 stepdau., Erika Mobley. A.B., Brown U., 1957; M.A., U. Pa., 1959, Ph.D., 1967. Researcher Phila. Hist. Commn., 1957-59; lectr. Am. civilization U. Gothenburg, Sweden, 1959-62, Bryn Mawr Coll., 1962-63, U. Pa., 1963-64; prof. U. Iowa, 1964-73; dean U. Mo., Kansas City, 1973-74; provost U. Md., 1974-79; chancellor U. Mass., Boston, 1979—. Author: American Fiction and Verse, 1962, 2d edit., 1970, also articles, revs.; editor: Uncle Tom's Cabin, 1968. Vice chmn. Iowa City Human Relations Commn., 1970-72; mem. Iowa City Charter Commn., 1972-73; chmn. Md. Com. Humanities, 1976-78; mem. Howard County (Md.) Commn. Arts, 1976-79; Chmn. bd. trustees Boston Com. Inc.; Bd. dirs. John F. Kennedy Library, Thompsons Island Edn. Found.; Founding mem. Alden Seminar. Smith-Mundt prof., 1959-60; Fulbright lectr., 1960-62; grantee Standard Oil Co. Found., 1968, Nat. Endowment Humanities, 1969-74, Ford Found., 1969, Rockefeller Found., 72-75, Dept. State., 1977. Mem. Am. Studies Assn., Assn. Study Afro-Am. Life and History, Popular Culture Assn., Boston C. of C. (dir.), World Affairs Council (dir.), Fulbright Alumni Assn. (dir. 1978-80). Democrat. Office: Harbor Campus Univ Mass Boston MA 02125

CORRIGAN, ROBERT WILLOUGHBY, university dean; b. Portage, Wis., Sept. 23, 1927; s. Daniel and Elizabeth (Waters) C.; m. Mary Kathryn Kolling, Dec. 18, 1953 (div. Sept. 1960); children: Michael Edward, Timothy Patrick; m. Elizabeth Trevor Seneff, June 15, 1963 (div. June 1969); m. Jane Langley, Aug. 1, 1969 (div. Feb. 1979); m. Jo Ann Johnson, Aug. 19, 1979. B.A., Cornell U., 1950; M.A., Johns Hopkins, 1952; Ph.D., U. Minn., 1955. Instr. drama Johns Hopkins, 1950-52; instr. theatre, classics U. Minn., 1952-54; asst. prof., dir. drama Carleton Coll., 1954-57; asso. prof. theatre Tulane U., 1957-61; founder, editor Tulane Drama Rev. (now The Drama Rev.), 1957-62; Andrew Mellon prof., head drama dept. Carnegie Inst. Tech., 1961-64; prof. dramatic lit. NYU, 1964-68, dean Sch. Arts, 1965-68; pres. Calif. Inst. Arts, 1968-72; prof. English and theater U. Mich., 1973-74; dean Sch. Fine Arts, U. Wis., Milw., 1974—; cons. to Chandler Pub. Co., Dell Pub. Co., Houghton Mifflin.; Adviser in theatre in Greece for State Dept., 1962, USIA lectr. in, Europe, 1976, 82, 83; Sr. Fulbright lectr. U. Innsbruck, Austria, 1980-81; chmn. Internat. Council Fine Arts Deans, 1970-71. Translator: Chekhov: Six Plays, 1962, Appia: Music and the Art of the Theatre, 1962; Author or editor: New Theatre of Europe, Vol. 1, 1962, Vol. 2, 1964, Vol. 3, 1967, Theatre in the Twentieth Century, 1963, The Modern Theatre, 1964, The Art of the Theatre, 1964, The Context and Craft of Drama, 1964, Masterpieces of the Modern Theatre, 1966, The Theatre in Search of a Fix, 1973, Tragedy: Vision and Form, 1965, 2d edit., 1981, Comedy: Meaning and Form, 1965, 2d edit., 1981, Laurel Classical Drama Series, 1964-65, Laurel British Drama Series, 1965, Arthur Miller: 20th Century Views, 1969, The World of the Theatre, 1979, The Making of Theatre: From Drama to Performance, 1981; many others. Trustee Simon's Rock Early Coll., 1976-79, Milw. Art Mus., 1976—. Recipient Citation of Merit Niagara U., 1967, Ill. Theatre Assn., 1979, Ky. Theatre Assn., 1979. Fellow Am. Theatre Assn. (v.p. publs. 1983); Mem. Nat. Theatre Conf., Nat. Council Arts Edn., Sigma Delta Chi, Sigma Phi. Episcopalian. Home: 1037 E Ogden Ave Milwaukee WI 53202

CORRIGAN, WILLIAM THOMAS, former news executive; b. Bridgeport, Conn., Sept. 18, 1921; s. Thomas F. and Anna M. (Callan) C.; m. Harriett Bell, Sept. 1, 1951; children: Kevin, Brian. A.A., U. Bridgeport, 1940; B.S., Am. U., 1948. Reporter Bridgeport Herald, sports broadcaster sta. WUST, Washington, 1947; writer, producer NBC News, 1948-51; mng. editor NBC-TV (newsreel), 1951-52; assignment editor NBC-TV News, 1952-53; Washington mgr. CBS Syndication, Washington bur. chief, 1953-59; dir. news and pub. affairs KNXT, West Coast bur. chief CBS Newsfilm, 1959-61; Am. editor Eichman Trial, Jerusalem, Israel, 1961; mgr. Washington bur. NBC News, N.Y.C., 1962; producer Huntley Brinkley Report, Wash., 1963-65; dir. operations NBC, N.Y.C., 1965-68; gen. mgr. operations NBC News, N.Y.C., 1968-73, gen. mgr. news, 1973-79, dir. broadcast service, 1979-81. Served as sgt. USAAF, World War II. Decorated D.F.C., Air medal. Mem. Radio-TV News Dirs. Assn., White House Photographers Assn., Radio-TV Corrs. Assn., Phi Sigma Kappa, Sigma Delta Chi. Clubs: Nat. Press (Washington); Darien Boat, Venice Yacht, Bird Bay Golf. Home: 609 White Pine Tree Rd Venice FL 33595

CORRIN, BROWNLEE SANDS, educator, political scientist; b. Bellevue, Pa., Mar. 25, 1922; s. John Grimshaw and Alice (Turkington) C.; m. Mary Elizabeth Dyer, May 18, 1946; children: Adaline Elizabeth, Rebecca Sands, David Montgomery, John Brownlee. A.B., Stanford, 1947, M.A., 1950, Ph.D., 1959. Teaching asst. Stanford, 1949-52; mem. faculty Goucher Coll., Towson, Md., 1952—, prof. polit. sci., 1965-76, prof. communication, 1976—, chmn. dept. polit. sci., 1958-73, chmn. dept. internat. relations, 1958-69, 73-77, dir. communication program, 1976, chmn. faculty history and social scis., 1966-69; dir Field Politics Ctr., 1954-76; Elections analyst ABC, 1964-76; producer Politics of Laughter, WCVT-FM, Balt., 1976-78; issue analyst WJZ-TV, Balt., 1975-78; vis. lectr. Johns Hopkins, 1962, U. Md., 1962-68; cons. Md. Constl. Conv. Common., 1965-67; dir. edn. WTOW FM-AM Balt., 1968-70; dir. BSCR&D (public affairs and communication); Chmn. working com. New Eng. Conf. Teaching Fgn. Langs., 1966. Contbr. articles to profl. jours. Mem. Baltimore County Council Charter Revision Com., 1961-62, Md. Legislative Com. Campaign Costs, 1964; bd. govs. WJHU-FM, Balt., 1979—; mem. bd. Library Trustees of Baltimore County, 1968-80, v.p. bd., 1973, pres., 1974-77; Precinct leader, chmn. Baltimore County Republican Dist. Exec. Com., 1952-63; chmn. Md. Rep. Arts and Scis. Com., 1962; treas. for candidate to Md. Constl. Conv., 1967; mem. Rep. Nat. Arts and Scis. Com.; also cons. Rep. House Conf. Com., 1963-64; Bd. dirs. UN Assn. Md., 1956-66. Served to maj. AUS, 1942-47; CBI. Mem. Am. Humor Studies Assn., Biofeedback Soc. Am., Eastern Communications Assn., Am. Polit. Sci. Assn., AFTRA, Am. Soc. Internat. Law, Am. Soc. Pub. Adminstrn., Speech Communication Assn., Internat. Communications Assn., Internat. Inst. Space Law, Internat. Studies Assn., Popular Culture Soc., Nat. Council Social Studies, Nat. Fedn. Local Cable Programmers, World Future Soc., Pi Sigma Alpha, Sigma Alpha Epsilon. Episcopalian. Club: Army and Navy (Washington). Home: 201 Dunbeath Ct Lutherville MD 21093 Office: Goucher Coll Towson MD 21204 *To move, search, discover, and act on the frontiers of human learning and beyond. To understand that human learning is in inter-relationship and not best perceived or grasped from within the artificial boxes of academic/professional disciplines. To recognize that advancement of the human condition interweaves with the use-understanding of human communication.*

CORRINGTON, LOUIS EARLE, JR., banker; b. Chgo., Nov. 8, 1916; s. Louis Earle and Katrina (Oller) C.; m. Marjorie E. Hayn, Dec. 31, 1955; 1 dau., Margo Louise. Clerical positions various banks, 1934-40; asst. cashier Am. Nat. Bank & Trust Co., Chgo., 1940-54; v.p. S.E. Nat. Bank, Chgo., 1955-56; pres. Guaranty Bank & Trust Co., Chgo., 1956-62; pres., dir. Merc. Nat. Bank of Chgo., 1962-67; pres. Coran, Inc., Chgo., 1967—. Served to capt. USAAF, 1942-46. Clubs: Chicago Athletic Assn., Bankers, Executives (Chgo.); Barrington Hills Country. Home: 362 Bateman Circle Barrington Hills IL 60010 Office: 600 N LaSalle St Chicago IL 60610

CORRIPIO AHUMADA, ERNESTO, archbishop; b. Tampico, Mex., June 29, 1919. Ordained priest Roman Cath. Ch., 1942; aux. bishop, Zapara, Mex., 1953, named bishop of, Tampico, 1956, bishop of, Artequera, 1967, Puebla de los Angeles, 1976, now archibishop of, Mexico City, primate of, Mex, tchr. sem., Tampico, 1945-50. Address: Apartado Postal 24-433 Mexico 7 DF Mexico *

CORROON, ROBERT FRANCIS, insurance company executive; b. Bklyn., June 30, 1922; s. James Francis and Katherine V. (Larkin) C.; m. Helen Van Voorhis Maitland, Feb. 4, 1956; children: Helen, Robert, Richard, Andree, Christopher, Peter. B.A., Williams Coll., 1944; B.S., U. Ariz., 1945. Chmn., chief exec. officer Corroon & Black Corp., N.Y.C., 1972—; dir. Coll. of Ins., N.Y.C., Project Orbis, Internat. Ins. Seminars. Recipient award Indsl. Home for Blind, N.Y.C., 1983. Mem. Jansen Green Syndicate-Lloyds of London (underwriting mem.). Republican. Roman Catholic. Clubs: Turf and Field, Lawrence Beach (N.Y.C.); Mill Reef (Antigua) (mem. governing body). Home: Khakum wood Greenwich CT 06830 Office: Coroon & Black Corp Wall St Plaza New York NY 10005

CORRY, JOHN ADAMS, lawyer; b. Springfield, Ohio, Nov. 17, 1931; s. Homer C. and Cornelia B. (Adams) C.; m. Emily McKnight, Apr. 20, 1963; 1 dau., Anne McKnight Corry. A.B., Princeton U., 1953; LL.B., Harvard U., 1956; LL.M., NYU, 1961. Bar: N.Y. Assoc. firm Davis Polk & Wardwell, N.Y.C., 1956-67, ptnr., 1967—; mem. Fed. Income Tax Project Tax Adv. Group, Am. Law Inst., 1978-83. Elder Reformed Ch. of Bronxville. Mem. ABA, N.Y. State Bar Assn. (chmn. com. on fin. instns.), Bar Assn. City N.Y. Republican. Club: Siwancy (Bronxville). Office: Davis Polk & Wardwell 1 Chase Manhattan Plaza New York NY 10005

CORRY, MARTHA LUCILLE, geographer, educator; b. Springfield, Ohio, Feb. 27, 1919; d. Thomas Elden and Cecilia Colette (Kilcoyne) C. B.A., B.Sc. in Edn, Ohio State U., 1941; certificate, McGill U. Geography Summer Sch., 1948; M.A., U. Ia., 1947, Ph.D. in Geography, 1953. Tchr. social studies high schs., Hartford, Ohio, 1941-42, Centerville, Ohio, 1942-44; critic tchr. social studies Univ. High Sch., U. Iowa, Iowa City, 1944-48, research asst. dept. geography, 1948-49, instr. social sci., 1949-51; faculty geography dept. State U. Coll., Oneonta, N.Y., 1951—, asso. prof., 1953-59, prof., 1959—, chmn. dept. geography, 1970-83; Cons. social studies Ia. Secondary Curriculum Revision Program, 1946-47; comparative edn. soc. field study, USSR, 1958; State U. N.Y. Faculty senator State U. Coll., Oneonta, 1960-63; participant USSR for Geographer, A Traveling Colloquium in USSR, 1967; participant seminar in Yugoslavian lit. State Edn. Dept., 1969-70; seminar U. Belgrade, Yugoslavia, 1972. Fulbright travel grantee; Danforth summer grantee Osmania U., Hyderabad, India, 1962. Mem. Assn. Am. Geographers (chmn. middle states div. 1977), Am. Geog. Soc., Nat. Council for Geog. Edn., AAUP (past pres. local chpt.), AAUW, Phi Beta Kappa, Pi Lambda Theta, Pi Sigma Alpha, Kappa Delta Pi. Presbyterian. Club: Oneonta Country. Home: 36 College Terr Oneonta NY 13820

CORRY, ROBERT JOHN, surgeon; b. Cleve., Dec. 3, 1934; s. Robert Milton and Isabel Catherine (Gledhill) C.; m. Linda Sally Selin, June 5, 1965; children: Robert, Sara, Catherine. Student, Univ. Sch., 1951-53; A.B. magna cum laude, Yale U., 1957; M.D., Johns Hopkins U., 1961. Diplomate: Am. Bd. Surgery. Intern Johns Hopkins U. Hosp., 1961-63; surg. asst. resident Mass. Gen. Hosp., Boston, 1965-67, chief resident, 1968-69, asst. surgery, 1969-73; teaching fellow Harvard Med. Sch., 1968-69, instr., 1969-72, asst. prof. surgery, 1972-73; attending surgeon, asso. prof. surgery U. Iowa Coll. Medicine, Iowa City, 1973-76, prof. surgery, 1976—, chmn. dept. surgery, 1982—, dir. transplantation, 1973—; cons. Iowa City VA Hosp., 1973—; Bd. dirs., med. advisory com. Kidney Found. Iowa, 1973—, chmn., 1978-79. Contbr. articles to profl. jours. Mem. AMA, A.C.S., Am. Surg. Assn., Transplantation Soc., Am. Soc. Transplant Surgeons, Soc. U. Surgeons, Assn. Acad. Surgery, Soc. Surgery of Alimentary Tract, Mass., Iowa, Johnson County med. socs., Iowa Acad. Surgery (pres. 1983), Iowa Clin. Surg. Soc., Internat. Coll. Surgeons, Collegium Internationale Chirurgiae Digestivae, Central Surg. Assn., Am. Assn. Tissue Banks. Home: 319 Hutchinson Ave Iowa City IA 52240 Office: Univ Hosps Iowa City IA 52242 *I believe that one's full potential should be utilized in all endeavors. One should pursue a program of excellence constantly striving to improve his performance.*

CORSA, HELEN STORM, educator; b. Amherst, Mass., Sept. 27, 1915; d. John and Mary (Thomas) C. B.A., Mt. Holyoke Coll., 1938; M.A., Bryn Mawr Coll., 1939, Ph.D., 1942. Instr. English Hartwick Coll., Oneonta, N.Y., 1942-43; instr., asst. prof. English Russell Sage Coll., Troy, N.Y., 1943-48; instr., asst. prof., asso. prof., prof. English Wellesley (Mass.) Coll., 1948—, Martha Hale Shackford prof. English, 1971-81. Author: Chaucer: Poet of Mirth and Morality, 1964, also articles.; Mem. com. to produce: Variorum Edit. Works of Chaucer. Roman Catholic. Home: 1990 Old Kings Hwy Box 245 West Barnstable MA 02668-0245

CORSARO, FRANK ANDREW, theater, musical theater, opera theater and TV dir.; b. N.Y.C., Dec. 22, 1924; s. Joseph and Marie (Quarino) C.; m. Mary Cross Bonnie Lueders, May 30, 1971; 1 son, Andrew. Grad. in Drama, Yale, 1947. Tchr. pvt. acting class for singers.; Trustee Nat. Opera Inst. Dir.: Broadway prodn. A Hatful of Rain, 1955-56; dir.: plays The Night of the Iguana, 1961-62, Treemonisha, 1975, Cold Storage, 1978, Whoopee, 1979, Knockout, 1979, N.Y.C. Opera, 1958—, Washington Opera Soc., 1970-74, St. Paul Opera, 1971, Houston Grand Opera, 1973-77; asso. artistic dir., 1977—; appeared in: Broadway prodn. Mrs. McThing, 1951; film

Rachel, Rachel, 1967; Author: adaptation L'Histoire du Soldat, 1974, Memoir Maverik, 1978. Mem. Dirs. Guild Am., Soc. Stage Dirs., Choreographers, Am. Guild Mus. Artists. Home: 33 Riverside Dr New York NY 10023 Office: New York City Opera Lincoln Center Plaza New York NY 10023

CORSE, JOHN DOGGETT, lawyer; b. Jacksonville, Fla., Mar. 16, 1924; s. Herbert Montgomery and Carita Ann (Doggett) C.; m. Margaret Murchison, Aug. 4, 1951; children: Carita Doggett, John Doggett, Margaret Murchison. B.S., U.S. Naval Acad., 1946; LL.B., U. Va., 1957. Bar: Fla. 1957, Ga. 1974. Commd. ensign U.S. Navy, 1946, advanced through grades; resigned, 1954; partner firm Ulmer, Murchison, Ashby & Ball, Jacksonville, 1957-75, Powell, Goldstein, Frazer & Murphy, Atlanta, 1975—; pres. Gt. Am. Mgmt. Corp., Atlanta, 1972-75, chmn. bd., 1975; sr. v.p., dir. UniCapital Corp., Atlanta, 1972-75; mng. trustee Gt. Am. Mortgage Investors, 1972-75. Editor-in-chief: Va. Law Rev, 1956-57. Mem. Am. Bar Assn., Fla. Bar Assn., D.C. Bar Assn., Va. Bar Assn., Ga. Bar Assn. Clubs: Timuquana Country, Fla. Yacht (Jacksonville); Piedmont Driving (Atlanta). Home: 2790 Habersham Rd NW Atlanta GA 30305 Office: 1100 Citizens and So Nat Bank Bldg 35 Broad St Atlanta GA 30335

CORSINI, ANDREW CAMERON, accountant; b. Middleboro, Mass., July 29, 1935; s. Leon Henry and Margaret Sarah (Cameron) C.; m. Yvonne Loraine Grenier, Nov. 3, 1957; children—Lynn, Andrew Cameron, Bryan, David, Stephen. B.S., Providence Coll., 1957. C.P.A., Mass. Audit supr. Coopers & Lybrand, Boston, 1960-67; with Swank Inc., Attleboro, Mass., 1967—, treas., 1973—; dir. First Bristol County Nat. Bank, Attleboro. Campaign chmn. Attleboro United Way, 1979, pres., 1980. Served with USN, 1957-60. Mem. Am. Inst. C.P.A.'s, Mass. Soc. C.P.A.'s. Roman Catholic. Clubs: Serra (Attleboro); K.C. Office: Swank Inc 6 Hazel St Attleboro MA 02703

CORSINI, RAYMOND JOSEPH, psychologist; b. Rutland, Vt., June 1, 1914; s. Joseph August and Evelyn Carolyn (Lavaggi) C.; m. Kleona Rigney, Oct. 10, 1965; 1 dau., Evelyn Anne. B.S., CCNY, 1939, M.S. in Edn, 1941; Ph.D., U. Chgo., 1955. Prison psychologist Auburn (N.Y.) Prison, 1941-45, San Quentin Prison, 1945-47, Wis. Prison System, 1947-50; research asso. U. Chgo., 1955-57; pvt. practice indsl. psychology Alfred Adler Inst., Chgo., 1957-63; asso. prof. Ill. Inst. Tech., 1964-65, U. Calif. at Berkeley, 1965-66; pvt. practice psychology, Honolulu, 1965—; faculty research affiliate Sch. Pub. Health, U. Hawaii, 1970—; affiliate grad. faculty dept. psychology, U. Hawaii; founder, sr. counselor Family Edn. Centers Hawaii, 1966—. Author: Methods of Group Psychotherapy, 1957, Roleplaying in Business and Industry, 1961, Roleplaying in Psychotherapy, 1966, The Family Council, 1974, The Practical Parent, 1975, Role Playing, 1980, Give In or Give Up, 1981, Individual Psychology: Theory and Practice; Editor: Critical Incidents in Psychotherapy, 1959, Adlerian Family Counseling, 1959, Critical Incidents in Teaching, 1965, Critical Incidents in School Counseling, 1972, Critical Incidents in Nursing, 1973, Current Psychotherapies, 1973, Current Personality Theories, 1977, Readings in Current Personality Theories, 1978, Great Cases in Psychotherapy, 1979, Alternative Educational Systems, 1979, Theories of Learning, 1980, Comparative Educational Systems, 1981, Handbook of Innovative Psychotherapies, 1981, Adolescence: The Challenge, Encyclopedia of Psychology, 1984, Jour. Individual Psychology, 1974, 76. Bd. dirs. Hawaii chpt. John Howard Assn., 1966-68. Recipient James McKeen Cattell award psychology Psychol. Corp., 1944; Sertoma award, 1980. Mem. Am. Psychol. Assn., Am. Soc. Adlerian Psychology. Club: Waikiki Yacht (Honolulu). Address: 140 Niuiki Circle Honolulu HI 96821

CORSO, GREGORY NUNZIO, poet; b. N.Y.C., Mar. 26, 1930; s. Fortunato and Michelina (Colonna) C.; m. Sally November, May 7, 1963 (div.); 1 dau., Mirandia; m. Belle Carpenter, 1968; 1 dau., Cybelle Nuncia; 1 son, Max-Orphé. Manual laborer, N.Y.C., 1950-51; with Los Angeles Examiner, 1951-52; mcht. seaman Norwegian vessels, 1952-53. Began appearing in poetry readings in, East and Midwest, mid-1950's; Author: poems The Vestal Lady on Brattle, 1955, Gasoline, 1958, Bomb, 1958, Marriage, 1959 (Longview Found. award), The Happy Birthday of Death, 1960, Long Live Man, 1962, Selected Poems, 1962, Elegiac Feelings American, 1970; novel The American Express, 1961, The Mutation of the Spirit, 1964, There is Yet Time to Run Back Through Life and Expiate All That's Been Sadly Done, 1965, 10 Times a Poem, 1967; play This Hung-Up Age, 1955, The Little Black Door on the Left, 1968, Poesy: Heirlooms from the Future, 1978; Co-editor: Young American Poetry, 1961. Recipient Poetry Found. award. Address: care Phoenix Bookshop 18 Cornelia St New York NY 10014 *

CORSON, DALE RAYMOND, univ. pres. emeritus, physicist; b. Pittsburg, Kans., Apr. 5, 1914; s. Harry Raymond and Alta (Hill) C.; m. Nellie Elizabeth Griswold, June 17, 1938; children—David, Bruce, Richard, Janet. A.B., Coll. Emporia, Kans., 1934, L.H.D., 1970; M.A., U. Kans., 1935; student, Ohio State U., 1935-36; Ph.D., U. Calif., 1938; Sc.D., U. Rochester, 1975, Elmira Coll., 1977; LL.D., Hamilton Coll., 1973, Columbia, 1972. Instr., research fellow U. Calif., 1938-40; asst. prof. U. Mo., 1940-43, asso. prof., 1943-45; staff Radiation Lab., Mass. Inst. Tech., 1941-43; tech. adviser War Dept., 1943-45; staff Los Alamos Sci. Lab., 1945-46; asst. prof. Cornell U., 1946-47, asso. prof., 1947-52, prof., 1952—, chmn. dept. physics, 1956-59, dean, 1959-63, provost, 1963-69, pres., 1969-77, chancellor, 1977-79, pres. emeritus, 1979—; dir. K Mart Corp., Internat. Minerals & Chems. Corp. Recipient Presdl. cert. of Merit, 1948. Fellow Am. Phys. Soc., Am. Acad. Arts and Scis., N.Y. Acad. Scis.; mem. Nat. Acad. Engring., Phi Beta Kappa, Sigma Xi, Tau Beta Pi. Clubs: Cosmos, Cornell. Home: 144 Northview Rd Ithaca NY 14850 Office: Cornell U 615 Clark Hall Ithaca NY 14853

CORSON, FRED PIERCE, bishop; b. Millville, N.J., Apr. 11, 1896; s. Jeremiah and Mary E. (Payne) C.; m. Frances Beaman, Mar. 22, 1922; 1 son, Hampton Payne. A.B., Dickinson Coll., Carlisle, Pa., 1917, A.M., 1920, D.D., 1931, L.H.D., 1944; B.D., Drew U., 1920; also; L.H.D. numerous hon. degrees including, St. Charles Borromeo Cath. Sem., 1981. Ordained to ministry Methodist Episcopal Ch., 1920, consecrated bishop, 1944; pastor, Jackson Heights, N.Y., New Haven, Port Washington, N.Y., Simpson Ch., Bklyn., until 1929; supt. Bklyn. So. Dist., N.Y. East Conf., 1930-34; pres. Dickinson Coll., 1934-44, also trustee; permanent chaplain Faith of Our Fathers Chapel, Freedoms Found., 1968—; titular pastor Old St. George's Ch., 1968—; bishop-in-residence Christ United Meth. Ch., St. Petersburg, Fla.; mem. ecumenical theol. symposium 41st Eucharistic Congress.; trustee Wyoming Sem., Pennington Sch. for Boys, Drew U., Westminster Theol. Sem., Lycoming Coll.; hon. pres. trustee Temple U.; pres. Council Bishops, 1952-53; fraternal messenger to Gen. Conf. Brazil, 1950; v.p. Meth. World Council, 1956-61, pres., 1961-66, now sr. presiding bishop; ofcl. Meth. rep. Kirchentag Assembly, Stuttgart, Ger., 1952; mem. Bishops Commn. for Meth.-Catholic Conversations, 1968—; sr. cons. to schs. and colls. United Meth. Ch., 1968—; civilian dir. 32d Coll. Tng.; spl. lectr. various colls. and univs., 1945—, del. to gen. conf., 1932, 40, 44; mem. univ. senate, mem. book com., world peace commn. Detachment (air crew), 1943-44; mem. Nat. Council Chs. of Christ, Com. on Internat. Goodwill, Pa. Gov.'s Com. for Revision State Constn.; chmn. Sec. of War's Clergy Commn. To Inspect Occupied Countries of Europe, 1948; ofcl. rep. Meth. Ch. to Centennial Celebration of Methodism in China, 1948; ofcl. Meth. rep. to Army and Navy Chaplains, Japan, 1948; del. World Council Chs., 1954; religious cons. Armed Forces in Far East Command, 1954; chaplain Republican and Democratic nat. convs., 1948, 52; del., observer 2d Vatican Council, Rome, 1962, 63, 64, 65; pres. Gen. Bd. Edn., Meth. Ch., 1948-60. Author: (with others) Augustin Cardinal Bea; editor: Bridges To Unity; contbr.: Documents of Vatican II. Bd. dirs. Freedoms Found., Valley Forge, Pa. Recipient Yorktown medal Soc. of Cin.; Kappa Sigma Man of Year, 1950; St. Olav medal, Norway, 1964; Gourgas medal (Masonic decoration), 1964; Royal Order of Scotland; Phila. Pub. Relations award, 1965; decorated knight Royal Order Scotland, 1977; Meritorious Leadership award World Meth. Ch., 1979; named to Football Found. Hall of Fame; named Ark. Traveler, 1983. Mem. Newcomen Soc., Phi Beta Kappa (Bicentennial fellow 1976), Phi Beta Kappa Assos., Kappa Sigma, Omicron Delta Kappa, Tau Kappa Alpha. Clubs: Masons (N.Y.C., Phila.) (33 deg.); KT; Kiwanis, Union League (N.Y.C., Phila.).

CORSON, JOHN JAY, consultant, trustee; b. Washington, Dec. 8, 1905; s. Eben White and Ellen (Pawling) C.; m. Mary Turner Tilman, Nov. 15, 1930 (dec. July 1975); children: John Jay, Nancy Tilman. B.S., U. Va., 1926, M.S., 1929, Ph.D., 1932. Editorial asso. Richmond (Va.) News Leader, 1929-33; prof. econs. U. Richmond, 1933-38; asst. exec. dir. Social Security Bd., 1936-38; dir. Bur. Old Age and Survivors Ins., 1938-41, 43-44, U.S. Employment Service, 1941-42; dep. dir. gen. UNRRA, 1944-45; exec. Washington Post, 1945-50; mgmt. cons. McKinsey & Co., 1951-66; prof. pub. internat. affairs Princeton, 1962-66; pres. Am. Blood Commn., 1975-78; cons. to dir. gen. UNESCO, 1963-64, OAS, 1960, ILO, 1962; govts. of, Tanzania, 1974, San Salvador, 1975, Panama, 1976-78, Iran, 1976-77, Turkey, 1978, Argentina, 1979, Sri Lanka, 1980, Pakistan, 1980, Thailand, 1982, 83; Bd. overseers Sweet Briar Coll., 1960-70; trustee Marymount Coll. Va., 1970—, Chgo. Med. Sch., 1971-75, George Mason U., 1972-80, Salzburg (Austria) Seminar Am. Studies, 1966-80, Ednl. Testing Service, 1964-68. Author: Manpower for Victory, 1943, Executives for the Federal Service, 1952, Economic Needs of Older People, (with John W. McConnell), 1955, The Governance of Colleges and Universities, 1960, rev. edit., 1975, (with Joseph P. Harris) Public Administration in Modern Society, 1964, (with Shale Paul) Men Near the Top, 1966, Business in the Humane Society, 1971, (with Harry V. Hodson) Philanthropy in the 70's, 1973, (with George A. Steiner) Measuring Business Social Performance: The Corporate Social Audit, 1974. Mem. Am. Soc. Pub. Adminstrn. (pres. 1948-49), Phi Beta Kappa. Home: McLean House Apt 402 6800 Fleetwood Rd McLean VA 22101

CORSON, KEITH D., corporation executive; b. Granger, Ind., 1935. Student, Wichita State U., 1958-59. Dir. Coachmen Industries, Inc., Middlebury, Ind.; chief exec. officer Koszegi Products, Inc., South Bend, Ind.; dir. Medallion Plastics, Inc. Office: 702 S Chapin St. South Bend IN 46624

CORSON, THOMAS HAROLD, recreational vehicle manufacturing company executive; b. Elkhart, Ind., Oct. 15, 1927; s. Carl W. and Charlotte (Keyser) C.; m. Dorthy Claire Scheide, July 11, 1948; children: Benjamin Thomas, Claire Elaine. Student, Purdue U., 1945-46, Rennsselaer Poly. Inst., 1946-47, So. Meth. U., 1948-49. Chmn. bd. Coachmen Industries, Inc., Middlebury, Ind., 1965—, past pres., also pres. and/or chmn. bd.; dir. First State Bank Middlebury, Robertson's Dept. Stores, Canton Drop Forge Co. (Ohio), Midwest Commerce Bank, Elkhart.; chmn., sec. Greenfield Corp., Middlebury. Chmn. Elkhart County Republican Fin. Com., 1971—; trustee Ball State U.; mem. adv. bd. Goshen (Ind.) Coll.; trustee Interlochen (Mich.) Arts Acad. and Nat. Music Camp. Served with USNR, 1945-47. Mem. Ind. Mfrs. Assn. (dir.), Elkhart C. of C. (past dir.). Methodist. Clubs: Masons, Shriners, Elcona (past dir.); Capitol Hill (Washington); Imperial Golf (Naples, Fla.). Home: PO Box 504 Middlebury IN 46540 Office: Coachmen Dr PO Box 30 Middlebury IN 46540 *I am thankful that pride, confidence, and determination were instilled in me as a youngster. I was determined to utilize my God-given talents completely in my quest for success. I realized success was not measured by monetary gains alone, but by contributions to mankind.*

CORT, BUD, actor; b. Rye, N.Y., Mar. 29, 1951; s. Joseph Parker and Alma Mary (Court) Cox. Student, N.Y. U.; studied with, Bill Hickey, Joan Darling, David Craig. Latest films The Secret Diary of Sigmund Freud, Electric Dreams; Broadway debut in Wise Child; toured U.S., Europe with cabaret act. Recipient Crystal Star award for best actor in Harold and Maude. Mem. Acad. Motion Picture Arts and Scis., Cinematheque du Paris, Actor's Studio-Dirs. Unit. Office: care M Silverman and Co 9021 Melrose Ave Los Angeles CA 90069 *I've been asked by many young people just how one becomes an actor. I personally think you are either born that way or not. However, whether the fire to perform is all consuming, as it was in my case or merely a means of expression and communication as it has been with various people I've worked with, I truly think the key is to be found in serious study of the technique of acting. I studied for 14 years with many acting teachers, each one of whom shed some light in his own unique way on a complex and exhilarating world. Study is essential.*

CORTADA, JAMES N., former diplomat; b. N.Y.C., May 10, 1914; s. James A. and America D. (Colas) C.; m. Shirley E. Barlow, Nov. 25, 1944; children: James William, Vera Christina, Monica Elodia. B.S., Havana (Cuba) Bus. Coll., 1948. Pvt. bus., 1932-42; fgn. service officer Dept. State, 1942-70; assigned successively, Havana, Dept. Commerce, Washington, Barcelona, Spain, Dept. of State, Basra, Iraq, Cairo, Egypt; dep. dir., then dir. Office Near East and South Asia Regional Affairs, Dept. State, Washington, 1960- 62; charge d'affaires, Taiz, Yemen, 1963-64; Dept. State sr. fellow UCLA, 1964-65; dean Sch. Profl. Studies, Fgn. Service Inst., 1965-67; Am. consul gen., Barcelona, 1967-70, mayor, Town of Orange, Va., 1978-82. Mem. Town of Orange Council, Town of Orange Planning Commn., 1983—; Bd. dirs. Orange County Econ. Devel. Corp. Mem. Orange County C. of C. (dir.), Orange County Hist. Soc. (v.p.), Royal Acad. Belles Lettres (corr., Barcelona). Clubs: Rotarian (dir. Orange Club), Dacor House (Washington)). Home: 127 Peliso Ave Orange VA 22960 *Whether policy matters in which I had a hand contributed to the security and welfare of our nation, or not, was the basic principle which guided my judgment.*

CORTELYOU, JOHN R., university chancellor; b. Chgo., July 21, 1914; s. B.W. and Margaret (Cuddy) C. B.A., St. Mary's Sem., M.A., 1940; M.S., DePaul U., 1943; Ph.D., Northwestern U., 1949. Instr. dept. biol. scis. DePaul U., Chgo., 1943-46, asst. prof., 1946-50, prof., chmn. dept., 1950, then pres. univ., chancellor, 1981—, also trustee. Mem. Am. Soc. Zoologists, AAAS, Sigma Xi. Office: DePaul U 25 E Jackson Blvd Chicago IL 60604 *

CORTEWAY, ROBERT C., banker; b. Milw., Mar. 28, 1944; children: Nelson T., Robert C. B.S., Calif. State U., 1966; M.B.A., UCLA, 1967. With Security Pacific Nat. Bank, 1967—, chief credit and mktg. officer London br., sr. corp. account officer, N.Y.C., credit adminstr. internat. banking, Los Angeles, chief mgr. subs., Hong Kong, sr. v.p. and adminstr. Asia-Australasia hdqrs., now adminstr. corp. banking group. Office: Security Pacific Nat Bank 333 S Hope St Los Angeles CA 90071

CORTISSOZ, PAUL, English educator; b. N.Y.C., Nov. 9, 1924; s. Alfred and Helen (O'Brien) C.; m. Geraldine Smith, Aug. 27, 1949; children: Anne, Celia Jo, Marie. B.A., Manhattan Coll., 1947; M.A., Columbia, 1949; Ph.D., N.Y.U., 1955. Instr. Manhattan Coll., Bronx, N.Y., 1947-53, asst. prof., 1953-58, asso. prof., 1958-64, prof., 1964—, head English and world lit. dept., 1963-67, 70-78. Author: (with Francis Davy) Perspectives for College, 1963. Served with USAAF, 1942-45. Recipient Founders Day award N.Y.U., 1955. Mem. Modern Lang. Assn., AAUP. Home: 12 Hazelton Circle Briarcliff Manor NY 10510 Office: Manhattan Coll Pkwy Bronx NY 10471

CORTOR, ELDZIER, painter; b. Richmond, Va., Jan. 10, 1916; s. John and Ophelia (Twisdale) C.; m. Sophia Schmidt, Aug. 20, 1951; children: Michael, Mercedes. Student, Art Inst. Chgo., 1936-41, Inst. Design, 1942, 43, 47, Columbia U., 1946. Painting instr. Centre D'Art, Port au Prince, Haiti, 1949-51; printmaker Pratt Inst., Bklyn., 1972-74. Exhibited: one man shows Le Husee' de Peuple Haitien, Port-au-Prince, Haiti, 1950, Centre d'Art, Port-au-Prince, 1950, Elizabeth Nelson Gallery, Chgo., 1951, James Whyte Gallery, Washington, 1953, group shows, Met. Mus. Art, N.Y.C., 1950, Studio Mus. Harlem, N.Y.C., 1973, 82, Boston Mus. Fine Arts, 1975, Museo de Arte Moderno La Pertulia, Cali, Colombia, 1976, Columbia Mus. Art, S.C., 1980; represented permanemt collections, Smithsonian Inst., Washington, permanent collections, Am. Fedn. Art, N.Y.C., Mus. Modern Art, N.Y.C., IBM Corp., N.Y.C. Recipient Bertha A. Florsheim award Art Inst. Chgo., 1945, William H. Bartels award, 1946, Carnegie Inst. award, 1947. Home: 35 Montgomery St Apt 19E New York NY 10002

CORUM, B.H., hospital official; b. Hillsboro, Ala., Nov. 12, 1933; s. Buford Hubert and Novia Pearl (Terry) C.; m. Carol Hill, Mar. 21, 1954; 1 dau., Renee. B.S., Auburn U., 1955; postgrad., U. Ala.-Mobile, 1960; M.H.A., Baylor U., 1962; postgrad., U. Md.-Chateauroux, (France), 1963-64, Air Force Inst. Tech., U. Fla., 1969-72; Ph.D., U. Fla., 1975. Commd. 2d lt. Med. Service Corps, U.S. Air Force, 1956, advanced through grades to col., 1977; pharmacy officer, asst. adminstr. 2789th Air Force Hosp., Brookley AFB, Mobile, Ala., 1956-60; asst. adminstr. Air Force Hosp., Chateauroux, 1962-65, Wilford Hall U.S. Air Force Med. Ctr., San Antonio, 1965-67; adminstr. U.S. Air Force Hosp., Cannon AFB, Clovis, N. Mex., 1967-69; chief med. personnel programs and analysis Air Force Personnel Ctr., Randolph AFB, San Antonio, 1972-77; dir. personnel Hdqrts. Aerospace Med. Div., Brooks AFB, San Antonio, 1977-79; chief exec. officer, adminstr. Wilford Hall USAF Med. Ctr., San Antonio, 1979-81, ret., 1981; exec. dir. Bexar County Hosp. Dist., San Antonio, 1981—; adj. faculty mem. St. Mary's U., San Antonio, 1977—, Our Lady of Lake U., Webster Coll., St. Louis, Trinity U., San Antonio, Baylor U., Waco, Tex., 1979—; assoc. dean hosp. services U. Tex. Health Sci. Ctr., San Antonio, 1982—. Decorated Legion of Merit (2). Fellow Am. Coll. Hosp. Adminstrs., Am. Acad. Med. Adminstrs.; mem. Tex. Hosp. Assn. (ho of dels. 1981—, chmn.-elect dist. adv. bd. 1983-84), Alamo Hosp. Assn. (chmn. 1983-84), Acad. Mgmt., Greater San Antonio C. of C., San Antonio-Mex.-North C. of C., Fed. Execs. Assn. Democrat. Baptist. Club: Journal (San Antonio). Lodge: Rotary. Home: 546 Crestway St San Antonio TX 78239 Officer: Bexar County Hosp Dist 4502 Medical Dr San Antonio TX 78284

CORWIN, NORMAN, writer, director, producer; b. Boston, May 3, 1910; s. Samuel H. and Rose (Ober) C.; m. Katherine Locke, Mar. 1947; children: Anthony, Diane. Student pub. schs., Boston, also Winthrop, Mass.; Litt.D., Columbia Coll., 1967, L.H.D., 1978. Writer, producer, dir. CBS; lectr. various univs.; disting. vis. lectr. San Diego State U., 1977-78; vis. prof. U. So. Calif., 1981—; Patten Meml. lectr. Ind. U., 1981; dir. creative writing U. So. Calif. Sch. Music and Art, Idyllwild, 1970—; Mem. LaGuardia One World Meml. Commn. to Europe, 1948; Trustee Los Angeles Internat. Film Expn.; mem. film adv. bd. Los Angeles County Mus. Art; mem. adv. bd. Inst. for Readers Theatre, Poetry Therapy Inst. Wrote, produced radio broadcasts; chief spl. projects, UN Radio; wrote films for, RKO, MGM, 20th-Century Fox, UN; writer, dir., prod.: 26 By Corwin, 1941, This is War, 1942, An American in England, 1942, Columbia Presents Corwin, 1944-45; writer, dir.: stage play The Hyphen; writer for: films Scandal at Scourie, Lust for Life (Oscar nominee), The Blue Veil, The Story of Ruth; creator, host: TV series Norman Corwin Presents for Westinghouse Group W, 1971; author: TV spl. The Ct. Martial of the Tiger of Malaya, 1974; writer, host: TV series Academy Leaders, 1979; Author: They Fly Through the Air With the Greatest of Ease, 1940, Thirteen by Corwin, 1942, More by Corwin, 1944, On a Note of Triumph, 1945, Untitled and Other Works, 1947, Dog in the Sky, 1952, The Plot to Overthrow Christmas, 1952, The World of Carl Sandburg, 1961, Overkill and Megalove, 1963, Prayer For the 70s, 1969, Holes in a Stained Glass Window, 1978, Greater than the Bomb, 1981, A Date with Sandburg, 1981, Trivializing America, 1983; plays Cervantes, 1973, Together Tonight, 1975; Contbr. articles to mags.; Writer: text of Human Rights Cantata, Yes Speak Out Yes (commd. by UN). Recipient Page One award Am. Newspaper Guild, 1944-45, Distinguished Merit award NCCJ, 1945; Unity award Interracial Film and Radio Guild, 1945; citation Nat. Council Tchrs. English, 1945, Assn. Tchrs. Social Studies of N.Y., 1945; award Am. Schs. and Colls. Assn., 1946; first place in nat. poll radio editors Billboard mag., for On a Note of Triumph, 1946; co-winner 1st prize Met. Opera awards for new Am. opera, The Warrior, produced Jan. 1947; Freedom award telecast Between Americans, 1951; hon. grant Am. Acad. Arts and Letters; Valentine Davies award Writers Guild Am., 1972; Artists award U. Judaism, 1972; Pacific Pioneer Broadcasters' Carbon Mike award, 1974; Preceptor's award San Francisco State U., 1979. Fellow Radio Hall of Fame; mem. Acad. of Motion Picture Arts and Scis. (chmn. documentary awards com., co-chmn. scholarship com., bd. govs. 1980—), Aspen Film Conf. (steering com.), Authors League Am., Dramatists Guild, Writers Guild Am. (dir.), Dirs. Guild Am. Wendell Willkie One World and (flew around world, recording speeches leaders of state, artists and scientists, June-Oct. 1946), first award Inst. for Edn. by Radio, 1946; prod. and narrated One World Flight, 1947. Home: 1840 Fairburn Ave Los Angeles CA 90025

CORWIN, STANLEY JOEL, book publisher; b. N.Y.C., Nov. 6, 1938; s. Seymour and Faye (Agress) C.; children—Donna, Ellen. A.B., Syracuse U., 1960. Dir. subsidiary rights, v.p. mktg. Prentice-Hall, Inc., Englewood Cliffs, N.J., 1960-68; v.p. internat. Grosset & Dunlap, Inc., N.Y.C., 1968-75; founder, pres. Corwin Books, N.Y.C., 1975; pres., pub. Pinnacle Books, Inc., Los Angeles, 1976-79; pres. Stan Corwin Prodns. Ltd., media co., and Dana/Corwin Enterprises, 1980—; lectr. Conf. World Affairs, U. Colo., 1976, U. So. Calif., 1978, U. Denver, 1978, Calif. State U., Northridge, 1980; participant Pubmart Seminar, N.Y.C., 1977. Author: Where Words Were Born, 1977; Contbr.: articles to Los Angeles Times; short stories to Signature Mag. Mem. Pres. Carter's U.S. Com. on the UN, 1977. Served with AUS, 1960. Nat. prize winner short story contest Writers' Digest, 1966. Mem. Assn. Am. Pubs.

CORWIN, SWIFT CHURCHILL, lawyer; b. N.Y.C., Feb. 16, 1916; s. Charles L. and Gladys (Barnes) C.; m. Elizabeth Lyon, Nov. 29, 1947; children—Joan B., Robert L., Swift Churchill. A.B., U. Mich., 1937; LL.B., Harvard, 1940. Bar: Ohio bar 1940. Since practiced in, Toledo; mem. firm Shumaker, Loop and Kendrick, 1947—; Mem. Ohio Bd. Uniform Laws, 1960-72. Bd. dirs. Boys Club, Toledo, 1947—, pres., 1973-75. Served to capt. AUS, 1942-46. Mem. Am., Ohio, Toledo bar assns., Am. Judicature Soc., Delta Kappa Epsilon. Republican. Episcopalian. Clubs: Toledo, Caranor Hunt and Polo. Home: 553 Willow Ln Perrysburg OH 43551 Office: 1000 Jackson St Toledo OH 43624

CORY, ELEANOR THAYER, composer, educator; b. Englewood, N.J., Sept. 8, 1943; d. David Clevel and Constance (Thayer) C.; m. Joel William Gressel, June 17, 1973; 1 dau., Katherine Cory. B.A., Sarah Lawrence Coll., 1965; M.A.T., Harvard U., 1966; Mus.M., New Eng. Conservatory, 1970; D.Musical Arts, Columbia U., 1975. Preceptor Columbia U., 1970-72; adj. lectr. Bklyn. Coll., 1971-72; asst. prof. Baruch Coll., City U. N.Y., 1973-78, Yale U., New Haven, 1978—; Bd. dirs. Am. Composers Alliance, 1975-81, 2nd v.p., 1977-81. Composer: for soprano and 10 instruments Waking, 1974, Octagons; for flute, clarinet, bassoon, piano, vibraphone, guitar, violin and cello, 1976, Counterbrass; for French horn, trumpet, trombone, piano and percussion, 1978, Designs; for piano trio, 1979, Suite à la Brecque; solo piano, 1979, Surroundings; for mezzo-soprano and piano, 1981; recs. Octagons, 1981, Epithalamium, 1981, Designs, 1982. Recipient Composer/Librettist award Nat. Endowment for Arts, 1976; Creative Artist Public Service grantee N.Y. State Council on Arts, 1976; Am. Composers Alliance Rec. award, 1981; MacDowell Colony fellow, 1977. Office: Dept of Music Yale Univ 143 Elm St New Haven CT 06520

CORY, JOSEPH GABRIEL, biochemist; b. Tampa, Fla., Jan. 27, 1937; s. Fred and Amelia (Alchediak) C.; m. Ann Henderson, Aug. 31, 1963; children—Fred, John, Sarah. B.S., U. Tampa, 1958; Ph.D. (USPHS fellow), Fla. State U., Tallahassee, 1963. Asst. mem. dept. biochemistry Albert Einstein Med. Center, Bronx, N.Y., 1964-65; mem. faculty U. South Fla., Tampa, 1965—, prof. biochemistry, chmn. dept., 1974—. Recipient USPHS Career Devel. award, 1969-73. Mem. Am. Soc. Biol. Chemists, Am. Assn. Cancer Research, Am. Chem. Soc., Soc. Exptl. Biology and Medicine, S.E. Cancer Research Assn., Sigma Xi. Roman Catholic. Office: 12901 N 30th St Tampa FL 33612

CORY, WILLIAM EUGENE, research company executive; b. Dallas, Apr. 5, 1927; s. William Leroy and Maude (Cole) C.; m. Doris Garlington, Jan. 1, 1947; children: William E., II, Madeline K. B.S. in Elec. Engring, Tex. A&M U., 1950; M.S., UCLA, 1959. Registered profl. engr., Tex. Elec. engr., supervisory elec. engr. USAF Security Service, San Antonio, 1950-57; electronic systems engr., aircraft devel. engr. specialist Lockheed Aircraft Co., Burbank, Calif., Marietta, Ga., 1957-59; sr. research engr. Southwest Research Inst., San Antonio, 1959-61, mgr. communications, 1961-65, dir., 1965-72, v.p. electronic systems research dept., 1972—; bd. dirs. MIDCON, Chgo., 1977—. Contbr. articles to various publs. Served with USN, 1945-46; served with USAF, 1951-52. Decorated Air Force Res. medal, Nat. Def. Service medal, Am. Campaign medal. Mem. IEEE (dir. 1972-73), Bioelectromagnetic Soc., Old Crows Assn. Patentee in field. Home: 4135 High Sierra San Antonio TX 78228 Office: 6220 Culebra Rd San Antonio TX 78284

CORYELL, DONALD DAVID, professional football coach; b. Seattle, Oct. 17, 1924. B.A., U. Wash., 1950, M.A., 1951. Asst. coach U. Wash., 1953-54; coach Wenatchee Valley Jr. Coll., 1955, Whittier Coll., 1957-59; asst. coach U. So. Calif., 1960; head coach San Diego State U., 1961-72, St. Louis Cardinals, 1973-77, San Diego Chargers, 1978—. Office: San Diego Chargers San Diego Stadium PO Box 20666 San Diego CA 92120 *

CORYELL, GLYNN HEATH, corporate executive; b. Lexington, Ky., May 8, 1929; s. Glynn Lawrence and Allie May (Heath) C.; m. Diane Garnett Dobyns, Dec. 27, 1955 (div. Aug. 1981); children: Heather Diane, Holly. A.B., Harvard U., 1951; student, Law Sch., 1951-52, 54-55; M.B.A., Northwestern U., 1957. Supr. cost accounting Proctor & Gamble Co., Cin., 1957-60; sr. financial analyst Socony Mobil Oil Corp., N.Y.C., 1961-62; dir. corp. profit planning, corp. economist Libby, McNeill & Libby, Chgo., 1962-67; treas. Lyntex Corp., N.Y.C., 1968-69; asst. treas. Standard Brands, Inc., N.Y.C., 1969-71; v.p. adminstr. and ops. Standard Brands Foods Co., N.Y.C., 1971-73; financial v.p. Grand Union Co., Elmwood Park, N.J., 1973-76; exec. v.p., chief fin. officer, dir. Cramer Electronics, Inc., Newton, Mass., 1976-79; sr. v.p., chief fin. officer, dir. Kuhn's-Big K Stores Corp., Nashville, 1979-81; v.p. fin. and adminstrn., sec. Sunmark, Inc., St. Louis, 1981—. Served with Intelligence U.S. Army, 1953-54. Mem. Am. Statis. Assn., Nat. Assn. Bus. Economists, Fin. Execs. Inst., Nat. Assn. Accountants. Republican. Baptist. Club: Harvard of St. Louis. Home: 11361 Le Monaco Way Apt 23B Saint Louis MO 63126 Office: Sunmark Cos 10795 Watson Rd Saint Louis MO 63127

CORYELL, ROGER CHARLES, newspaper executive; b. Alliance, Nebr., May 21, 1916; s. Rex Laverne and Evangeline (Richardson) C.; m. Julia Lewis Hornady, Sept. 21, 1956; children: Coreen Coryell Haydon, Roger Charles, Julia Lewis, Elizabeth Eve. Student, St. Ambrose Coll., Davenport, Iowa, 1937-41; spl. studies, UCLA, NYU. Advt. exec. Lee Syndicate, Davenport, Iowa, 1938-46, Miami News (Fla.), 1947-56; gen. mgr. Met. Asso. Services, N.Y.C., 1957-58; asst. pub. Capitol Newspapers Albany, N.Y., 1959-69; v.p., gen. mgr. Hartford (Conn.) Times, 1970-71, pres., pub., 1971-73; gen. mgr. Fresno (Calif.) Bee, 1974-83; dir. journalism adv. bd. and bus. adv. council Sch. Bus., Calif. State U., Fresno. Past bd. dirs. Albany (N.Y.) area ARC, Hartford (Conn.) area ARC, Conn. Opera Assn.; pres. Fresno Philharm. Assn. Served with U.S. Army, 1944-45. Decorated Army Commendation medal; recipient Silver Medal award Printers Ink, 1966. Mem. Am. Newspaper Pubs. Assn., Fresno C. of C. (past dir.). Republican. Congregationalist. Clubs: Academy, Fig Garden Swim and Racket. Home: 504 N Bethel St Sanger CA 93637

CORZINE, JON STEVENS, investment banker; b. Taylorville, Ill., Jan. 1, 1947; s. Roy Allen and Nancy June (Hedrick) C.; m. Joanne Dougherty, Sept. 8, 1968; children: Jennifer, Jeffrey Dougherty. B.A., U. Ill., 1969; M.B.A., U. Chgo., 1973. Bond officer Continental Ill. Nat. Bank, Chgo., 1970-73; asst. v.p. BancOhio Corp., Columbus, 1974-75; gen. ptnr. Goldman, Sachs & Co., N.Y.C., 1975—. Served USMC, 1969-70. Democrat. Office: Goldman Sachs & Co 85 Broad St New York NY 10004

COSAND, JOSEPH PARKER, JR., educator; b. Albuquerque, Nov. 18, 1914; s. J. P. and Minnie Lillian (Floyd) C.; m. Kathleen Marie Miller, Sept. 10, 1937; children: Sylvia Marie (dec.), Norman Parker. A.B. in Chemistry, Whittier Coll., 1936, LL.D., 1962; M.A. in Chemistry, U. So. Calif., 1937; postgrad. in Chemistry and Ednl. Adminstrn, U. Calif. at Berkeley, 1950-53; LL.D., St. Louis U., 1972; L.H.D. (hon.), U. Mo., 1967, Washington U., St. Louis, 1973, Dr. Pub. Service, Central Mich. U., 1973. Tchr. Ft. Bragg (Calif.) Jr. High Sch., 1939-41, Taft (Calif.) High Sch., 1941-43; tchr. Taft Jr. Coll., then chief adminstrv. officer, 1946-50; chief adminstrv. officer Contra Costa Coll., Richmond, Calif., 1950-58, Santa Barbara (Calif.) City Coll., 1958-62; pres. Jr. Coll. Dist. of St. Louis, 1962-71; prof. edn. U. Mich., Ann Arbor, 1971-80, emeritus prof. higher edn., 1980—, also dir., 1971-76; dep. commr. for higher edn. U.S. Office of Edn., Washington, 1972-73; Cons. to various colls., univs. and state ednl. orgns. in U.S., 1960—; vis. prof. U. Calif. at Santa Barbara, summers 1959, 61, 62; mem. Higher Edn. Coordinating Council for Met. St. Louis, 1963-71, Coll. Entrance Exam. Bd. Council on Coll. Level Exams., 1965-71, Commn. on Non-Traditional Study, 1971-73, Commn. on Acad. Tenure, 1971-72, Nat. Commn. on Financing Postsecondary Edn., 1972-73; mem. governance com. Edn. Commn. for the States, 1972-74; mem. tech. adv. council Ednl. Testing Service's Univ. Year for Action, 1973-74; mem. adv. council New Career Program Empire State Coll., 1973-75; mem. nat. adv. council U. Mid-Am., 1974-78; mem. nat. adv. bd. Community Coll. Air Force, 1977—. Cons. editor: Jour. for Higher Edn, 1974-80, Community Coll. Research Quar, 1977—. Bd. dirs. Calif. League for Nursing, 1952-55, St. Joseph's Hosp., St. Louis, 1968-71, St. Louis Ednl. TV Commn., 1963-71, Am. Coll. Testing Program, 1973-79, EDUCOM, 1974-76. Served with USNR, 1943-46. Danforth grantee, 1960-61. Mem. Calif. Jr. Coll. Assn. (1961-62), Coordinating Council for Higher Edn. (charter mem. 1960-62), Am. Council on Edn. (dir. 1969-72, chmn. bd. trustees 1970-71), Am. Assn. for Higher Edn. (dir. 1965-68), Am. Assn. of Jr. Colls. (dir. 1969-72, 81-84), N. Central Assn. Colls. and Secondary Schs. (exec. com. 1969-71). Home: 557 A West Side Rd Friday Harbor WA 98250 *Philosophy for an educator: Far better than sharing our riches with others is to reveal their riches to themselves.*

COSBY, BILL, actor, entertainer; b. Phila., July 12, 1937; s. William Henry and Anna C.; m. Camille Hanks, Jan. 25, 1964; children—Erika Ranee, Erinn Charlene, Ennis William, Ensa Camille, Evin Harrah. Student, Temple U.; Ph.D. in Edn, U. Mass. Pres. Rhythm and Blues Hall of Fame, 1968—. Appeared in numerous night clubs, including, The Gaslight, N.Y.C., Hungry I, San Francisco, Shoreham Hotel, Washington, Basin St. East, N.Y.C., Hilton, Las Vegas, Nev., Harrah's Lake Tahoe; guest appearances on numerous TV shows, including The Electric Co, 1972; co-star: TV show I Spy; star: The Bill Cosby Show, 1969, 72-73; recs. include Revenge (Grammy award Nat. Acad. Performing Arts and Scis. 1967); To Russell, My Brother, With Whom I Slept, 200 M.P.H, Why Is There Air, Wonderfulness, It's True, It's True, Bill Cosby is a Very Funny Fellow—Right, I Started Out as a Child, 8:15, 12:15; films include Hickey and Boggs, 1972, Man and Boy, 1972, Uptown Saturday Night, 1974, Let's Do It Again, 1975, Mother, Jugs and Speed, 1976, A Piece of the Action, 1977, California Suite, 1978, Devil and Max Devlin, 1979; (Recipient 4 Emmy awards 1966, 67, 68, 69, 8 Grammy awards, named number 1 in comedy field Top Artists on Campus Poll (album sales) 1968); Author: The Wit and Wisdom of Fat Albert, 1973, Bill Cosby's Personal Guide to Power Tennis. Served with USNR, 1956-60

COSE, ELLIS JONATHAN, educational administrator, editorial writer, columnist; b. Chgo., Feb. 20, 1951; s. Raney and Jetta (Cameron) C. B.A. in Psychology, U. Ill., Chgo., 1972; M.A. in Sci., Tech. and Public Policy, George Washington U., 1978. Columnist, reporter Chgo. Sun-Times, 1970-77; sr. fellow and dir. energy policy studies Joint Center for Polit. Studies, Washington, 1977-79; editorial writer, columnist Detroit Free Press, 1979-81; resident fellow Nat. Acad. Scis./NRC, 1981-82; spl. writer USA TODAY, 1982-83; pres. Inst. Journalism Edn., 1983—; mem. environ. adv. com. Dept. Energy, 1978-79, Nat. Urban League Energy Project, 1979-80. Author: Energy and Equity: Some Social Concerns, 1978, Energy and the Urban Crisis, 1978. Named Outstanding Young Citizen Chgo. Jaycees, 1977; recipient 1st place newswriting award Ill. UPI, 1973; Stick-o-Type award Chgo. Newspaper Guild, 1975; numerous others. Office: North Gate Hall U Calif-Berkeley Berkeley CA 94720

COSELL, HOWARD (HOWARD WILLIAM COHEN), sportscaster; b. Winston-Salem, N.C., Mar. 25, 1920; s. Isadore and Nellie Cohen; m. Mary Edith Abrams, 1944; children: Jill, Hillary. Grad., N.Y. U., 1940. Practiced law, until 1956; sportscaster ABC, 1956—. Appeared in: films The World's Greatest Athlete; TV appearances include Sonny & Cher Show; guest host: Tonight and Dick Cavett shows; host: TV shows Saturday Night Live with Howard Cosell; Author: Cosell, 1973, Like It Is, 1974; Editor: N.Y. U. Law Rev. Nat. chmn. Multiple Sclerosis, 1976. Served to maj. AUS, World War II. Mem. Phi Beta Kappa. Office: ABC-TV 1330 Ave of Americas New York NY 10019 *

COSENZA, ARTHUR GEORGE, opera dir.; b. Phila., Oct. 16, 1924; s. Luigi and Maria (Piccolo) C.; m. Marietta Muhs, Sept. 16, 1950; children—Louis John, Arthur William, Maria. Student, Ornstein Sch. Music, Phila., 1946-48, Berkshire Music Festival, 1947, Am. Theater Wing, N.Y.C., 1948-50. Asso. prof. Coll. Music, Loyola U. of South, 1954—, dir. opera workshop, 1954—; dir. Opera Program for City of New Orleans, 1955-73. Performed leading baritone roles with opera cos. throughout, U.S., Can., 1947-70; baritone, New Orleans Opera, 1954-70; producer operas, 1960—; resident stage dir., 1965-70; gen. dir., 1970—. Served with AUS, 1943-45. Decorated Purple Heart medal; cavaliere Order Star Italian Solidarity; cavaliere Ufficiale dell' Ordine al Merito, Italy; officier Ordre des Arts et des Lettres. Mem. Am. Guild Mus. Artists (hon. life), Blue Key. Home: 1720 Soniat St New Orleans LA 70115 Office: 333 St Charles Ave New Orleans LA 70130

COSER, LEWIS ALFRED, sociology educator; b. Berlin, Germany, Nov. 27, 1913; came to U.S., 1941, naturalized, 1948; s. Martin and Margarete (Fehlow) C.; m. Rose Laub, Aug. 25, 1942; children: Ellen, Steven. Student, Sorbonne, Paris, France, 1935-38; Ph.D. in Sociology, Columbia U., 1954. Instr. U. Chgo., 1948-50; mem. faculty Brandeis U., 1951-68, prof. sociology, 1960-68; distinguished prof. State U. N.Y., Stony Brook, 1969—; fellow Center for Advanced Study Behavorial Scis., Stanford, Calif., 1968-69, 79-80; vis. prof. U. Calif. at Berkeley, 1957-58. Author: The Functions of Social Conflict, 1956, (with B. Rosenberg) Sociological Theory, 1957, 5th edit., 1982, (with Irving Howe) The American Communist Party, 1957, 2d edit., 1962, Sociology Through Literature, 1963, rev. edit., 1971, Men of Ideas, 1965, Georg Simmel, 1965, Political Sociology, 1967, Continuities in the Study of Social Conflict, 1967, Masters of Sociological Thought, 1971, enlarged edit., 1977, Greedy Institutions, 1974, (with Kadushin and Powell) The Culture and Commerce of Publishing, 1982. Mem. Am. Sociol. Assn. (pres. 1975-76), Eastern Sociol. Soc. (pres. 1964-65), ACLU, AAUP. Home: 52 Erland Rd Stony Brook NY 11790

COSGRIFF, STUART WORCESTER, physician; b. Pittsfield, Mass., May 8, 1917; s. Thomas F. and Frances Deford (Worcester) C.; m. Mary Shaw, Jan. 23, 1943; children: Mary, Thomas, Stuart, Richard, Robert. B.A., Holy Cross Coll., 1938; M.D., Columbia U., 1942, D.Med. Sci., 1948. Diplomate: Am. Bd. Internal Medicine. Intern Presbyterian Hosp., N.Y.C., 1942-43; asst. resident in medicine, 1943, 46-47, chief resident, 1947-48; instr. in medicine Columbia U., N.Y.C., 1948-50, clin. asst. prof. medicine, 1951-63, clin. assoc. prof., 1963-73, clin. prof. medicine, 1973-83, clin. prof. emeritus, 1983—; attending physician Presbyn. Hosp., N.Y.C., 1948-83; individual practice medicine, specializing in internal medicine and vascular diseases, N.Y.C., 1948—; cons. internal medicine Dir. Selective Service, N.Y.C., 1957-73; dir. thrombo-embolic clinic Vanderbilt Clinic, N.Y.C., 1948-83. Contbr. articles to med. jours. Served to capt. M.C., U.S. Army, 1943-45; PTO. Fellow ACP, Pan Am. Med. Assn.; mem. AMA, Am. Heart Assn., Alpha Omega Alpha. Roman Catholic. Club: Knickerbocker Country (Tenafly, N.J.). Home: 11 Park St Tenafly NJ 07670 Office: 161 Fort Washington Ave New York NY 10032

COSGROVE, FRANK DENNIS, orgn. exec.; b. Paterson, N.J., Oct. 19, 1926; s. Frank J. and Elizabeth Marie (McSherry) C.; m. Jean C. Drake, Dec. 28, 1948; children: Jeanne, Timothy. B.S. in Phys. Edn., Health and Recreation, St. Bonaventure U., 1951. Dir. recreation, Clifton, N.J., 1951-56, dir. parks and recreation, Warren, Mich., 1956-64; exec. dir. Am. Youth Hostels, Inc., 1964-75; with Nat. Recreation and Park Assn., Colorado Springs, Colo., 1975—; U.S. del. Internat. Youth Hostel Fedn. Confs., Poland, 1965, Austria, 1966, Japan, 1968, Finland, 1970, Eng., 1972, Zurich, 1974; mem. White House Conf. on Internat. Coop., 1964, White House Conf. on Nat. Beautification, 1965, White House Conf. on Children, 1970, Pres. Johnson's Spl. Taskforce on Travel, 1968. Bd. dirs. Macomb County Assn. Retarded Children, 1959-64; trustee Macomb County Community Coll., 1964—. Served with USNR, 1944-46. Named Most Outstanding Recreation Dir. in N.J., 1955. Mem. Nat. Recreation and Parks Assn., Am. Recreation Soc., Am. Soc. Assn. Execs., N.Y. Soc. Assn. Execs. Clubs: Lion, Elk. Office: Nat Recreation and Park Assn 3500 Ridge Rd PO Box 6900 Colorado Springs CO 80934

COSGROVE, HOWARD EDWARD, JR., utility exec.; b. Phila., Apr. 12, 1943; s. Howard Edward and Margaret (May) C.; m. Roberta Joyce Olewine, Apr. 19, 1965; children—Pamela Joyce, Susan Ann. B.S. in Mech. Engring, U. Va., 1966; M.B.A., U. Del., 1970. Registered profl. engr., Del. With Delmarva Power Co., Wilmington, Del., 1966—, mgr. fin., 1979, v.p., chief fin. officer, 1979—. Mem. Nat. Soc. Profl. Engrs., Fin. Execs. Inst. Home: 212 Wilshire Ln Newark DE 19711 Office: 800 King St Wilmington DE 19899

COSGROVE, JOHN EDWARD, labor union official, consultant; b. Keokuk, Iowa, Mar. 26, 1923; s. H. Edward and Alleyne (Keefe) C.; m. Katherine Marv Mines, Jan. 27, 1951; children—Kathleen Cyr, Patricia Stille, Edward, Eileen, Gregg, Margaret Speake, Ceclia, Maureen, Alice Morcan, Thomas. Student, St. Ambrose Coll., 1940-43; J.D., U. Notre Dame, 1948; postgrad., Drake U., 1950. Bar: Iowa bar 1948, also U.S. Supreme Ct 1948. Atty. office solicitor U.S. Dept. Labor, 1949-50; dir. edn. Iowa Fedn. Labor, 1951-54; asst. dir. edn. AFL-CIO, 1955; asst. dir. Office Emergency Planning Exec., Office of President, 1961-67; dir. Office Regional Devel. Planning, Econ. Devel. Adminstrn., U.S. Dept. Commerce, 1967-69; dir. dept. social devel.-urban affairs U.S. Cath. Conf., 1969-74; dir. legislation pub. employee dept. AFL-CIO, 1975—; lectr. Drake U., Des Moines, 1952-53, Sch. Fgn. Service, Georgetown U., 1957-60; rep. U.S. at Labor Edn. Cong. European Productivity Agy., France, 1958; to indsl. planning com., sr. civil emergency planning com. NATO, 1962; chmn. bd. dirs., pres. Fund for Assuring an Ind. Retirement, 1979-83. Contbr. to assn. law jours. Served with A.C. AUS, 1943-46; capt. USAF, 1952. Decorated knight Papal Order St. Gregory, 1975. Mem. Am. Fedn. Govt. Employees. Democrat. Catholic. Home: 3953 Lantern Dr Silver Spring MD 20902

COSGROVE, JOHN PATRICK, editor; b. Pittston, Pa., Sept. 25, 1918; s. Raymond Patrick and Alice (Gilroy) C.; m. Patricia Ellen O'Hara, Mar. 26, 1951. Ed. pub. schs., Pa. Reporter, Wilkes-Barre (Pa.) Record, 1936-37, AP, Washington, 1938-40; writer, research Nat. Republican Congl. Com., Washington, 1940; exec. asst. U.S. Senator Hiram W. Johnson, 1941-42; free lance writer, 1946-48; dir. publs. Broadcasting Publs., Inc. (pubs. Broadcasting Businessweekly, Television monthly, Broadcasting Yearbook), Washington, 1948-68; cons. editor Acropolis Books, Ltd., 1969—, bd. editorial advs. and contbrs. Acropolis Bus. History and Heritage Series, 1980—. Author: The Gendreau Story: War History of DE 639; editor: SHRDLU-An Affectionate Chronicle of the first fifty years of the Nat. Press Club, 1959. Publicity dir. Honor Am. Day Celebration, 1970; exec. dir. Am. Historic and Cultural Soc., Inc., 1970—; sec. Nat. Christmas Pageant of Peace, 1974—, mem. com. to light nat. Christmas tree; Washington rep. Nat. Com. Neurol. Disorders and Stroke, 1972-78, R.R. Task Force for Northeast Region, 1973-75; adv. council Celtic cultural program Georgetown U., Washington, 1980—; bd. dirs. Am. Irish Found., 1967—, pres., 1971-73; bd. dirs. Washington chpt. Nat. Multiple Sclerosis Soc., 1962-70. Served with USNR, 1942-46; assigned Office Censorship, Washington, 1942; U.S.S. Gendreau, 1943-46. Mem. Destroyer Escort Sailors Assn. (life; dir. 1981—), Am. Legion, Soc. Friendly Sons of St. Patrick (dir. 1976-82), Sigma Delta Chi. Roman Catholic. Clubs: Nat. Press (Washington) (bd. govs. 1956-59, v.p. 1960); Nat. Press (Washington) (pres. 1961, chmn. awards com. 1974); Nat. Press (Washington) (chmn. election com. 1978); Nat. Headliners (Atlantic City); Circus Saints and Sinners (1st v.p., dir., dir. P.T. Barnum tent 1973). Home: 9512 Persimmon Tree Rd Potomac MD 20854 Office: 520 Pennsylvania Bldg Washington DC 20004

COSINDAS, MARIE, photographer; b. b., Boston, 1925. Student, Modern Sch. Fashion Design, Boston, Boston Mus. Sch.; student photography under Ansel Adams, 1961; student photographer under Minor White, 1963, 64; D.F.A., Moore Coll. Art, 1967. Illustrator, designer, 1945-60, freelance, photographer, Boston, 1960—; instr. Colo. Coll. Summer Photog. Workshops, Colorado Springs, 1972-78; artist-in-residence Dartmouth Coll., Hanover, N.H., 1976; vis. lectr. visual and environ. studies Harvard U., Cambridge, Mass., 1977-78. One-woman shows, U. N.H., Durham, 1962, one-man shows, Harvard U., 1963, Internat. Mus. Photography, George Eastman House, Rochester, N.Y., 1964, Mus. Fine Arts, Boston, 1966, Mus. Modern Art, N.Y.C., U. N.C., Chapel Hill, 1967, Art Inst. Chgo., 1967, 80, 10th Festival of Two Worlds, Spoleto, Italy, 1967, Currier Gallery Art, Manchester, N.H., 1968, Kenyon and Eckhardt, N.Y.C., U. Wis., Madison, 1969, Dartmouth Coll., 1976, Inst. Contemporary Art, Boston, Kunstlerhaus, Vienna, Austria, 1977; exhibited in group shows including, Nat. Gallery Can., Ottawa, Ont. (toured Can. and U.S.), 1967-73, Friends of Photography, Carmel, Calif., 1968, Internat. Ctr. Photography, N.Y.C., 1975, Boston Atheneum, 1977, Mus. Modern Art, N.Y.C., 1978, Corcoran Gallery, Washington, 1979, Art Inst. Chgo., 1982; represented in permanent collections, Mus. Modern Art, N.Y.C., Met. Mus. Art, N.Y.C., Met. Mus. Art, N.Y.C., Visual Studies Workshop, Rochester, Addison Gallery Am. Art, Andover, Mass., Polaroid Corp., Cambridge, Art Inst. Chgo.; author: (with text by Tom Wolfe) Marie Cosindas: Color Photographs, 1978. Recipient Artist-in TV Sta. WGBH-Rockefeller Found., 1967, award Nat. Acad. TV Arts and Scis., 1976; Guggenheim fellow, 1967.

COSPER, RUSSELL A., educator; b. Lansing, Mich., May 30, 1910; s. J. D. Lincoln and Grace Alice (Bond) C.; m. Vera M. Lucas, Aug. 22, 1936; children—Ronald Lee, David Russell, Sylvia Margot. A.B., Western Mich. U., 1933; A.M., U. Mich., 1937, Ph.D., 1947. High sch. tchr., East Detroit, Mich., 1934-37; asst. prof. English Eastern Mich. U., 1937-46; mem. faculty Purdue U., Lafayette, Ind., 1946—, prof. English, 1956-76, prof. emeritus, 1976—, head dept., 1961-69. Author: This Is Your Language, 1940, Toward Better Reading Skill, 1959. Served to lt. USNR, 1943-46. Mem. Am. Dialect Soc., Modern Lang. Assn., Nat. Council Tchrs. English. Home: 1325 Sunset Ln West Lafayette IN 47906 Office: English Dept Purdue Univ Lafayette IN 47907

COSSA, DOMINIC FRANK, baritone; b. Jessup, Pa., May 13, 1935; s. Dominic and Pauline (Stella) C.; m. Janet Edgerton, Dec. 26, 1956; children: Francine, Gian. B.S. in Psychology, U. Scranton, Pa., 1959; M.A., U. Detroit, 1961; postgrad., Detroit Inst. Mus. Arts, 1960-61, Phila. Acad. Vocal Arts, 1961-63; L.H.D., U. Scranton, 1982. Debut, N.Y.C. Opera, 1961, Met. Opera, N.Y.C., 1970, San Francisco Opera; rec. artist for, London Records, Elixir of Love, Le Huguenots, RCA Victor, Julius Caesar; appeared in title role in: world premiere of Gian Carlo Menotti's The Hero, 1976; now leading baritone, N.Y.C. Opera and; leading baritone, Met. Opera. Recipient Liederkrantz award; Met. Nat. Council 1st place prize; winner Am. Opera Auditions, WGN

Auditions; Rockefeller grantee. Mem. Am. Guild Mus. Artists (dir.). Roman Catholic. Office: c/o Colbert Artists Mgmt Inc 111 W 57th St New York NY 10019 *One must keep a sense of balance and proportion. Whenever thoughts of success and career become foremost in my mind, I try to place it in a larger perspective. There are certainly issues of greater importance in life than my success or failure. In a word, I try to be honest with myself even if it's painful.*

COSSOTTO, FIORENZA, mezzo-soprano; b. Crescentino, Italy, Apr. 22; m. Ivo Vinco. Student, Turin (Italy) Conservatory, La Scala Sch., Milan, Italy. Opera debut as Sister Mathilde in: world premier of Dialogue of Carmelites, La Scala Opera, 1957; played first major role at La Scala as Leonora in: La Favorita, 1962; Covent Garden debut as Neris in: Medea, 1959; Am. debut as Leonora in: La Favorita at, Chgo. Lyric Opera, 1964; Met. Opera debut as Amneris in: La Gioconda, 1968; Paris Opera debut as Adalgisa in: Samson et Dalila, 1965, other appearances include, Vienna Staatsoper, Teatro Colon, Easter and Salzburg festivals, numerous opera cos., Europe, Mex., U.S.; also recital and concert artist. Office: care Columbia Artists Mgmt Inc 165 W 57th St New York NY 10019

COSSUTTA, ARALDO ALFRED, architect; b. Island of Krk, Yugoslavia, Jan. 11, 1925; came to U.S., 1950, naturalized, 1951; s. Martin K. and Marija (Korosec) C.; m. Thelma Claire Bouchet, Sept. 16, 1950; children: Louis Michel, Renée Claire. Student, U. Belgrade, 1945-46, Ecole des Beaux Arts, Paris, 1947-50; M.Arch., Harvard, 1952. With Atelier of LeCorbusier, France, 1949; with Michael Hare & Assos., N.Y.C., 1952-55, I.M. Pei & Partners, 1955-73, asso., 1959-63, partner, 1963-73, Cossutta & Ponte, N.Y.C., 1973-77; prin. Cossutta & Assos., Architects P.C., N.Y.C., 1978—. Important works include Hyde Park Apts, Chgo., Green Center for Earth Scis, Cambridge, Mass., L'Enfant Plaza, Washington, Christian Sci. Ch. Center, Boston; Master plan for Tête de la Défense, Paris, Credit Lyonnais Tower, Lyon, France, Long Wharf Hotel, Boston, The Greenhouse, Boston, Harbor Tower Apts, Portsmouth, Va. Fellow AIA. Home: RFD Middle Rd Chilmark MA 02535 Office: Cossutta & Assocs 600 Madison Ave New York NY 10022 also 39 av du Roule/92200 Neuilly-sur-Seine France also Blvd de Waterloo 33 1000 Brussels Belgium

COST, JAMES PETER, artist; b. Phila., Mar. 3, 1923; s. Peter and Rose (Perry) C.; m. Betty Jo Root, Apr. 17, 1957; children: Curtis, Shelley, Janet, Nancy. B.A., U. Calif. at Los Angeles, 1950; M.S., U. So. Calif., 1959. Tchr. art Los Angeles City Sch. Dist., 14 years; lectr. art Northwood Insts., Midland, Mich., Dallas, 1971; mem. faculty of art Principia Coll., 1975. One-man shows, Northwood Inst., Midland, 1971, R.W. Norton Gallery, Shreveport, La.; exhibited in group shows at, Artists Guild Gallery Am., Carmel, 1961-63, James Peter Cost Gallery, (1964), Mus. Fine Arts, Springfield, Mass., 1965, 73, Nat. Arts Club, N.Y.C., 1966; represented in permanent collection, R.W. Norton Mus., Shreveport, also numerous pvt. collections. Pres. Carmel Bus. Assn., 1970; Republican candidate for La. State Assembly, 1982. Served with USCGR, 1942-45. Recipient gold medal Franklin Mint, 1973. Republican. Christian Scientist. Office: PO Box 3638 Carmel CA 93921 *Briefly and in reverse order of importance, the ideas, goals and standards necessary to ones success are: an over-all plan, a time line, religion, talent, hard work, self discipline and—most important—an understanding, enthusiastic, and sympathetic wife.*

COSTA, ERNEST FIORENZO, graphic designer; b. Bklyn., July 3, 1926; s. Eugene and Mary (Peveri) C.; m. Judith Ann Petrella, Dec. 26, 1953; children: Deirdre Ann, Christopher Robert. Student, Black Mountain Coll., Ashville, N.C., 1944; A.A., Pratt Inst., 1946. Art dir. Conde Nast Publs., Irving Serwer Advt. Agy., Carl Reimer Advt. Agy., Morey, Humm & Johnstone Advt. Agy., Dowd Redfield & Johnstone Advt. Agy., 1946-56; art and copy group supr. Grey Advt., 1956-66; v.p. Richard K. Manoff Advt., 1966-69; propr. Ernest Costa Photography, Inc., 1969-73; pub. Creative Foods Inc., 1973; art editor House & Garden Mag., N.Y.C., 1973-76, Interiors and Residential Interiors Mag., 1976-79; advt. mgr. Americana Center, 1979—; instr. advt. design N.Y.C. Community Coll. Exhibited, Pa. Acad. Fine Arts, Bklyn. Mus., Nat. Art League, Grace Gallery; represented in permanent collections, Mus. Modern Art, Library of Congress. Active Bridges Inc. Hot Line, Little Neck, N.Y., Little Neck Beautification Com.; chmn. Prospect Ave. Block Assn.; mem. media com. Marriage Encounter; chmn. cultural com. Ams. of Italian Heritage Inc.; co-chmn. Welcome home com. St. Anastasia, 1979. Recipient awards Type Dirs. Club, Am. TV Commls. Festival, Am. Inst. Graphic Arts, Internat. Film and TV Festival. Mem. Art Dir.'s Club N.Y. (award), Nat. Acad. TV Arts and Scis., United Fedn. Coll. Tchrs. Roman Catholic (communications com. ch.). Home: 109 Prospect Ave Douglaston NY 11363

COSTA, JOSEPH, press photographer; b. Caltabelotta, Sicily, Italy, Jan. 3, 1904; s. Giuseppi and Francesca (Stravalli) C.; m. Marguerite Macdonell, Oct. 18, 1930 (dec.); 1 dau., Frances Joyce; m. Margaret H. King, Nov. 22, 1967. Ed. pub. schs., N.Y.C. Staff photographer N.Y. Morning World, 1920-27, N.Y. News, 1927-46; photo supr., King Features Syndicate; chief photographer Sunday Mirror Mag., 1946-63; exec. editor Nat. Press Photographer mag., N.Y.C., 1946-67, editor emeritus, 1967—; illustrations editor World Book Ency. Sci. Service, Inc., Houston, 1967-69; guiding faculty Famous Photographers Sch., Westport, Conn.; vis. prof. Sch. Journalism and Graphic Arts, E. Tex. State U., Commerce, 1974-75; lectr. journalism Ball State U., Muncie, Ind. Author weekly photo feature for newspapers, 1968-70; now head, Photography for Publ.; also cons.; Host: weekly TV show Photog. Horizons, Dumont Network, N.Y.C., (1946-47); Author: Beginner's Guide to Color Photography, 1955; Editor: Complete Book of Press Photography, 1950. Recipient Merit award Press Photographers Assn. N.Y., 1947; asso. Photog. Soc. Am., 1949; fellow, 1956; Fellowship award and Sprague award Nat. Press Photographers Assn., 1949; Robin G. Garland educator award Nat. Press Photographers Assn., 1980; citation Kent State U., 1949; Germain G award, 1952; U. Mo. Honor medal, 1954; spl. citation in journalism Ball State U., 1980; Quill and Scroll award Internat. Hon. Soc. High Sch. Journalists, 1983; Photog. Adminstrs. award for Edu. in Photography, 1983; Ind AP Broadcasters Assn. award, 1984. Mem. Press Photographers Assn. N.Y., Nat. Press Photographers Assn. (founder, 1st pres., chmn. bd. dirs. 1948-64), Soc. Profl. Journalists, Sigma Delta Chi. Home: 25301 Outlook Dr Carmel CA 93923 *Throughout my lifetime, both in business and in my social contacts, it has always been my aim to give the best that was in me to the limit of my ability, to do what is right as God gave me the light to understand right from wrong, to share my professional knowledge with students, beginners, and those less experienced, and to work unstintingly for the advancement of my profession.*

COSTA, MARY, soprano; b. Knoxville, Tenn. Student, Los Angeles Conservatory of Music. V.p. Hawaiian Fragrances, Honolulu, 1972; Vice pres. Calif. Inst. Arts. Film voice of Sleeping Beauty by Walt Disney; appeared TV commls., 1955-57, debut, Los Angeles Opera, 1958; in: La Boheme, San Francisco Opera, 1959; as Violetta in: La Traviata at, Met. Opera, N.Y.C., 1964; appeared, Glyndebourne Opera House, Royal Opera House Covent Garden, Teatro Nacional de San Carlos, Grand Theatre de Geneve, Vancouver, Lisbon, Kiev, Leningrad, Tbilisi, Boston, Cin., Hartford, Newark, Phila., San Antonio, Seattle; toured U.S. with: Bernstein's Candide; appeared: English prodn. Candide; revival Bernstein's Candide at John F. Kennedy Center for Performing Arts, 1971; tour, Soviet Union, 1970; Bolshoi debut in La Traviatta, 1970; starring role: motion picture The Great Waltz, 1972; appeared internat. recitals, orchs. Named Woman of Year, Los Angeles, 1959; recipient DAR Honor medal, 1974; Mary Costa Scholarship established at U. Tenn., 1979. Address: care Calif Artists Mgmt 23 Liberty St San Francisco CA 94110

COSTA, PAT VINCENT, corporate executive; b. Cambridge, Mass., Sept. 4, 1943; s. Vincent James and Mary Florence (Mercurio) C.; m. Kathleen Ann Valachovic, Aug. 9, 1975; 1 dau., Jessica Kate Ward. B.S. in Elec. Engring., Northeastern U.; M.S., MIT; M.B.A., Harvard U. Tech. dir. H.F. Livermore Co., Boston, 1970-72; pub. Telecommunications mag. Horizon House Pub., Dedham, Mass., 1972-74; asst. to v.p. Am. Sci. and Engring., Cambridge, 1974-76;; v.p. ops. div. GCA (Vacuum Industries), Somerville, Mass., 1978-79, asst. gen. mgr., 1979-80, gen. mgr., Chgo., Il, 1980-82, v.p., group v.p., 1982-83;. Mem. Am. Mgmt. Assn., Soc. Mfg. Engrs. Robotics Internat., Sci. Apparatus Makers Assn., Eta Kappa Nu, Tau Beta Pi, Phi Kappa Phi. Club: Harvard Bus. Sch. (Boston). Office: GCA Corp 209 Burlington rd Bedford MA 01730

COSTA, ROBERT RICHARD, educator, aquatic ecologist; b. Youngstown, Ohio, May 9, 1928; s. Robert A. and Lottie (Milanowsk) C. B.S., Youngstown U., 1950; M.S., Iowa State U., 1951; Ph.D., U. Pitts., 1967. Fishery biologist Fla. Game and Fish Commn. (Okeechobee), 1951-52; tchr. Liberty High Sch., Youngstown, Ohio, 1953-61, head sci. dept., 1955-61; Fulbright tchr., Yorkshire, Eng., 1957-58; asst. to assoc. prof. biology Youngstown U., Ohio, 1961-68; assoc. prof. biology SUNY-Brockport, 1968-73; research limnologist, dir. Fancher Biol. Sta., N.Y., 1970-73; prof., dir. biology dept. Clarkson Coll., Potsdam, N.Y., 1973-76, prof., chmn. biology dept., 1976—; ecol. resource adviser State N.Y., 1974—; research participant NSF, 1963. NSF fellow, 1960-62. Mem. AAAS, Am. Inst. Biol. Scis., Ecol. Soc. Am., Am. Soc. Limnology and Oceanography, Brit. Freshwater Assn., Nat. Sci. tchrs. Assn., Nat. Assn. Biology Tchrs. Am., Ohio Acad. Sci., Rochester Acad. Sci. Home: Bagdad Rd PO Box 208 Potsdam NY 13676 Office: Dept Biology Clarkson Coll Potsdam NY 13676

COSTA, SEQUERIA, pianist, educator; b. Luanda, Angola, July 18, 1929; s. Antonio and Emma (Sequeria) C.; m. Tania Achot; children: Svetlana, Marina; m. Vera Couto; children: Carlos Manuel, Vera. Cordelia Brown Murphy Disting. Prof. piano U. Kans. Sch. Fine Arts, Lawrence, 1977; jurist Tchaikowsky Internat. Piano Competitions, Moscow; founder Vianna da Motta Competition, Lisbon. Soloist, Moscow and Leningrad Philharm. Orchs., Alice Tully Hall, N.Y.C., 1980, Carnegie Hall, N.Y.C., 1981, Music Festivals, Iran, France, Yugoslavia, Bath (Eng.); touring soloist, Gulbenkian Orch., Far East, mainland China. Recipient Grand Prix Marquerite Long-Jacques Thibaud Piano Competition, 1951, Harriet Cohen Beethoven medal, 1960. Address: PO Box 2296 Lawrence KS 66044

COSTA, VICTOR CHARLES, fashion designer; b. Houston, Dec. 17, 1935; s. Russell and Mary (Candelari) C.; m. Mary Therese Tschumy, June 28, 1958; children: Kevin, Adrienne. B.A., U. Houston, 1958; cert., Ecole Chambre Syndicale de la Couture Parisienne, 1958. Designer Murray Hamburger, 1959, Pandora, N.Y.C., 1960-64; designer, v.p. Suzy Perette, N.Y.C., 1965-73; pres. designer Victor Costa, Inc., Dallas, 1973—; dir. Tex. Commerce Bank, Casa Linda. Bd. dirs. Dallas Civic Opera. Recipient Am. Designer award May Co. Calif.; Stix, Baer, Fuller Golden Fashion award; Dallas Flying Colors Fashion award, 1980; recipient Tommy, 1983, Cert. Merit City of Atlanta, 1983. Mem. Council Fashion Designers Am., Am. Fashion Assn. Roman Catholic. Office: 3000 Irving Blvd Dallas TX 75247

COSTA, WALTER HENRY, architect; b. Oakland, Calif., July 2, 1924; s. Walter H.F. and Mamie R. (Dunkle) C.; m. Jane Elisabeth Ledwich, Aug. 28, 1948; 1 dau., Laura. B.A., U. Calif., Berkeley, 1948, M.A., 1949. Designer Mario Corbett (architect), San Francisco, 1947-48, Ernst Born (Architect), 1949; draftsman Milton Pflueger, San Francisco, 1950-51; designer Skidmore, Owings & Merrill, San Francisco, 1951-57, participating asso., then asso. partner, 1957-69, gen. partner, 1969—. Bd. dirs. East Bay Regional Park Dist., 1977; trustee Cogswell Coll., San Francisco; mem. city council, Lafayette, Calif., 1972-76, mayor, 1973. Served with USSNR, 1943-46. Fellow AIA. Clubs: Olympic, Univ. (San Francisco). Home: 1264 Redwood Ln Lafayette CA 94549 Office: 1 Maritime Plaza San Francisco CA 94111

COSTA-GAVRAS, (HENRI) KOSTANTINOS, film dir., writer; b. Athens, Greece, 1933; m. Michele Ray, 1968; children—Alexandre, Helene. Student, Hautes Etudes Cinematographiques, Sorbonne, Paris. Ballet dancer, Greece; asst. to film dirs. Yves Allegret, Jacques Demy, Rene Clair, Rene Clement. Dir., writer: film The Sleeping Car Murders; dir., co-writer: Z; dir. films: Un Homme de Trop, L'Aveu (The Confession), 1970, State of Siege, 1973, Madame Rosa (also actor), 1978, Clair de Femme, 1979 (Recipient prize for Un Homme de Trop, Moscow Film Festival 1966, Acad. award for Best Fgn. Lang. Film for Z 1969, named best dir. Cannes Film Festival 1975) *

COSTAIN, CECIL CLIFFORD, physicist; b. Ponoka, Alta., Can., June 16, 1922; s. Henry Hudson and Elida Mary (Eakin) C.; m. Cynthia Hazell Ewing, July 26, 1949; children: Linda Carol, Charles Gordon. B.A. with hons, U. Sask. (Can.), 1941, M.A., 1947; Ph.D., Cambridge (Eng.) U., 1951. With spectroscopy sect. div. physics NRC Can., Ottawa, Ont., 1951-71, time and frequency sect. div. physics, 1972—, now head sect. time and frequency; prin. research officer NRC Can. Contbr. numerous articles to profl. jours. Served to lt. comdr. RCNVR, 1942-45. Decorated D.S.C.; Exhbn. of 1851 scholar, 1947. Fellow Royal Soc. Can., IEEE; mem. Can. Assn. Physicists (pres. 1980). Home: 49 Cedar Rd Ottawa ON K1J 6L5 Canada Office: Div Physics NRC Can Ottawa ON K1A 0S1 Canada

COSTANTINO, JAMES, business executive; b. Braintree, Mass., Mar. 20, 1930; s. John and Susan C.; m. Dolores Ann Billek, Aug. 23, 1966; children: Christopher, Jeffrey. B.S. Mech. Engring., U. Mass., 1958; M.E.A., George Washington U., 1961; Ph.D., Am. U., 1971. Diplomate: registered profl. engr., Mass. Mech. engr. FAA, Washington, 1958-63; dir. tech. mgmt. and support NASA, Washington, 1963-71; secretarial rep. Dept. Transp., Phila., 1971-73; exec. asst. Dep. Sec. Transp., Washington, 1974-76; dir. Transp. Systems Ctr., Cambridge, Mass., 1976-84; exec. v.p., chief operating officer Jaycor, Alexandria, Va., 1984—; mem. Boston Fed. Exec. Bd., 1976—. Recipient Apollo Achievement award NASA, 1970, Meritorious Achievement medal U.S. Dept. Transp., 1974, Disting. Engring. Alumnus award U. Mass., 1980; decorated Presdl. Rank (Meritorious) Sr. Exec. Service, Washington, 1981. Mem. Am. Astron. Soc. (sr. bd. dirs. 1982—, Eagle award sci. and tech. 1980), AIAA, Soc. Automotive Engrs., AAAS, Nat. Soc. Profl. Engrs., Mass. Soc. Profl. Engrs. Home: 96 Sagamore Rd Wellesley Hills MA 02181 Office: Jaycor 205 S Whiting St Alexandria VA 20234

COSTANZO, HENRY JOHN, govt. ofcl.; b. Edgewater, Ala., June 20, 1925; s. Joseph and Mary (De Falco) C.; m. Maxine Kruse, Mar. 11, 1955; children—Maria Cristina, Luisa Francesca. Student, Birmingham-So. Coll., 1941-42, George Washington U., 1942-44; M.A., Columbia, 1949. Economist ECA/spl. mission to Italy, 1949-51; asst. Treasury rep., Rome, 1952-53, Treasury rep., Seoul, Korea, 1954-55; financial adviser, chief program planning div. UN Command, Office Econ. Coordinator, Seoul, 1955-57; adviser Middle Eastern dept. Internat. Monetary Fund., 1958-61; chief South Asia and Near East div. Office Internat. Finance, Treasury Dept., 1961-62; dir. Office Latin Am., 1962-67, AID mission to Korea, 1967-69; dir./counselor econ. affairs embassy., Seoul, 1968-69; mem. bd., exec. dir. Inter-Am. Devel. Bank, Washington, 1970-71, exec. v.p., 1972-74, exec. sec. joint ministerial com. bd. govts. World Bank and IMF on transfer real resources to developing countries, 1974-76, fin. mgr., Washington, 1976—. Served with AUS, 1944-46. Address: 414 N Lee St Alexandria VA 22314

COSTAR, JAMES WILLIAM, educator; b. Hawarden, Iowa, Feb. 19, 1925; s. Ward William and Beulah Marie (McNaughton) C.; m. Joy LaVonne Olson, June 2, 1951; children: Deborah, David. B.S., U. S.D., 1950, M.A., 1952; Ed.D., Mich. State U., 1958. Tchr.-counselor Canton (S.D.) High Sch., 1950-52; dir. guidance services Canton Public Schs., 1952-54; grad. asst. Coll. Edn., Mich. State U., E. Lansing, 1954-55, instr., asst. prof., assoc. prof., prof., chmn. dept. counseling and ednl. psychology, 1955-81, prof. adminstrn. and higher edn., 1981—; cons. 13 countries; instr. various univs. Author: The Follow-up Study: an Evaluation System for Improvement of Schools, 1976; co-author: Guidance Services in the Elementary Sch, 1961, Guidance Services in the Secondary School, 1963; contbr. chpts. to books, booklets, pamphlets, articles to profl. publs. Served with AC, USN, 1944-46. Mem. Am. Personnel and Guidance Assn., Mich. Personnel and Guidance Assn. (outstanding counselor/educator 1976), Nat. Vocat. Guidance Assn., Assn. Counselor Edn. and Supervision, Am. Sch. Counselors Assn., Phi Delta Kappa. Home: 1988 Yuma Trail Okemos MI 48864 Office: 410 Erickson Hall Michigan State Univ East Lansing MI 48824

COSTELLO, ALBERT JOSEPH, business executive; b. N.Y.C., Sept. 4, 1935; s. John and Lena (Compiani) C.; m. Barbara Theresa Antolotti, May 31, 1958; children: Gregory A., Peter M., Albert Joseph. B.S., Fordham U., 1957; M.S., NYU, 1964. With Am. Cyanamid Co., 1957—, asst. mng., mng. dir., Mexico City, Madrid, Spain, 1974-77, div. v.p., Wayne, N.J., 1977-82, pres. agrl. div., 1982, group v.p., 1982-83, exec. v.p., 1983—. Patentee in field. Served with U.S. Army, 1959-61. Mem. Nat. Agrl. Chems. Assn. (dir. 1982—). Office: Am Cyanamid Co 1 Cyanamid Plaza Wayne NJ 07470 *

COSTELLO, EDWARD JOSEPH, JR., lawyer, venture capitalist; b. N.Y.C., Apr. 18, 1939; s. Edward Joseph and Madeleine Catherine Carroi C.; m. Karin Bergstrom; 1 dau. by previous marriage, Catharine Alison. A.B., Fordham Coll., 1961; J.D. (Root-Tilden scholar), N.Y. U., 1964. Bar: Fla. 1965, N.Y. State 1967, Calif. 1969. Asso. firm Donovan, Leisure, Newton & Irvine, N.Y.C., 1964; spl. agt. FBI, Washington, 1964-67; asso. firm O'Melveny & Myers, Los Angeles, 1967-72; partner firm Costello & Walcher, Los Angeles, 1972—; lectr. in field. Contbr. articles profl. publs. Judge pro tempore Los Angeles Municipal Ct., 1972—. Mem. Friends of Chinese People (founder, chmn. 1968-73), Am., Fla., N.Y. State, Los Angeles County bar assns. Home: 11060 Cashmere St Los Angeles CA 90049 Office: 10850 Wilshire Blvd Suite 1000 Los Angeles CA 90024

COSTELLO, ELVIS (DECLAN PATRICK MCMANUS), musician, songwriter; b. London, 1954; (married). Albums include My Aim is True, 1977, This Year's Model, 1978, Armed Forces, 1979, Get Happy, 1980, Trust, 1980; appears in concert, U.S. and Eng., 1978—. Office: care Columbia Records 51 W 52d St New York NY 10019 *

COSTELLO, JAMES JOSEPH, electrical manufacturing company executive; b. Boston, Feb. 15, 1930; s. James Joseph and Jennie Theresa (Boyle) C.; m. Mary Virginia Bird, May 7, 1960; children: James, Susan, Maureen, Thomas, Daniel. B.S. in Bus. Adminstrn, Northeastern U., 1953. With Gen. Electric Co. (various locations), 1956—, div. fin. mgr., Schenectady, 1971-76, group fin. mgr., Pittsfield, Mass., 1976-77, staff exec., Fairfield, Conn., 1977-79, v.p., comptroller, 1979—; Dir. nat. council Northeastern U., 1980-81. Served as officer U.S. Navy, 1953-56. Mem. Fin. Execs. Inst., Fin. Acctg. Standards Bd. (subcom. on measurements). Office: 3135 Easton Turnpike Fairfield CT 06431

COSTELLO, JOHN FRANCIS (JACK), JR., lawyer; b. Lindsay, Okla., Mar. 5, 1935; s. John Francis and Pauline (Bohanon) C.; m. Rinda Regent, Feb. 20, 1965 (div. June 1978); children: Wade B., Kelsie D. B.B.A., U. Okla., 1957, J.D., 1964. Bar: Okla. bar 1964, Tex. bar 1965. With Ft. Worth Nat. Bank, 1964-79, sec. to bd., 1971-79; v.p., sec. Tex. Am. Bancshares Inc., 1972-79. Past pres., dir. Tarrant County Easter Seal Soc.; past bd. dirs., mem. adv. bd. Tarrant County Jr. Achievement; bd. dirs. Ft. Worth Zool. Assn., Van Cliburn Internat. Quadrennial Piano Competition; past bd. dirs., past treas. Van Cliburn Found.; bd. dirs., past mem. exec. com. Edna Gladney Home. Served to capt. AUS, 1957-66. Decorated Commendation medal. Mem. ABA, Tex. Bar Assn., Okla. Bar Assn., Ft. Worth-Tarrant County Bar Assn., Ft. Worth Art Assn., Confrerie des Chevaliers du Tastevin, Sigma Chi, Phi Alpha Delta. Clubs: Ft. Worth, Ridgler Country, Steeplechase. Home: 5102 Sealands Ln Fort Worth TX 76116 Office: PO Box 9002 Fort Worth TX 76107

COSTELLO, JOSEPH MARK, III, broadcasting and motion picture executive; b. New Orleans, Nov. 8, 1940; s. Joseph Mark and Josephine Antoinette (Cortese) C. Ed., Loyola U., New Orleans, 1959-61; L.H.D. (hon.), London Inst. Applied Research, 1973; postgrad., Harvard Grad. Sch. Bus., 1977-78. Program dir. Dixie Stas., 1961-63; pres., dir. Broadcasting Inst. Am., 1963—; pres., owner, gen. mgr. Sta. WRNO-FM and Shortwave, Gulf South Broadcasters, Ltd., New Orleans, 1967—, Sta. KXOR, Thibodaux, La., 1973—; owner, dir. Sta. KSMI, Donaldsonville, La., 1973—, Sta. KKAY, White Castle, La., 1976—; partner Sta. KGLA, Gretna, La., 1969—; owner, operator movie theatres Abalon, Oakridge Plaza Cinema 5, Chalmette Cinema 6, LaPlace Twin Cinema, Uptown Sq. Cinema, GSB Screening Studio, all New Orleans; owner, operator GSB Booking Service; cons. in field; dir. Broadcasting Inst.; chmn. affiliates advisory bd., govt. relations com. ABC Radio Network; mem. select adv. com. U.S. Congress. Active Ann. Earth Day Celebrations; mem. Republican Nat. Com. Recipient Service award UPI, 1965; Abe Lincoln award for establishment of new prison, 1973; award for Sta. WRNO Esquire Mag., 1974. Mem. Acad. TV Arts and Scis., La. Assn. Broadcasters (pres.), Nat. Assn. Broadcasters (legis. liaison dir. for La.), Greater New Orleans Assn. Broadcasters (pres.), Soc. Broadcast Engrs., Nat. Radio Broadcasters Assn. (v.p., regional dir.). Roman Catholic. Clubs: Diamondhead Yacht, Diamondhead Country, K.C. Home: 4042 S Pin Oak Ave New Orleans LA 70114 Office: 4539 1-10 Service Rd Metairie LA 70002

COSTELLO, RICHARD NEUMANN, advt. agy. exec.; b. Phila., Sept. 2, 1943; s. Joseph Neumann and Katherine Cash (Birkhead) C.; m. Ann M. Dodds, Oct. 24, 1970; children—Brian Stuart, Gregory Scott. B.A. in English, U. Pa., 1965, M.B.A. in Mktg, 1967. Account mgr. Ogilvy & Mather, Inc., N.Y.C., 1967-71; v.p. Rosenfeld, Sirowitz & Lawson, Inc., N.Y.C., 1971-73; pres. Baron, Costello & Fine, Inc., N.Y.C., 1973-77, TBWA Advt., Inc., 1977—. Home: 50 Shadow Brook Rd Chappaqua NY 10514 Office: 292 Madison Ave New York NY 10017

COSTELLO, RUSSELL HILL, newspaper executive; b. Lewiston, Maine, Oct. 22, 1904; s. Louis B. and Sadie (Brackett) C.; m. Jane H. Cassidy, May 5, 1928; children: Alice Ann (Mrs. Robert E. Dillingham), James Russell, Jane Mary (Mrs. Daniel J. Wellehan, Jr.). Student, Bates Coll., 1924-26, Mass. Inst. Tech., 1927-30. With Lewiston Daily Sun, 1930—, treas., 1955—, pres., 1959—, also dir. Former mem. Gov.'s Council on Art and Culture; devel. council U. Maine. Served to maj. Maine State Guard, 1943-46. Mem. Maine Publishers Assn. (past pres.), New Eng. Publishers Assn., Am. Publishers Assn., New Eng. Council (dir.), Lewiston C. of C. (dir., past pres.), New Eng. Mech. Assn. (past pres.). Home: 97 Bardwell St Lewiston ME 04240 Office: 104 Park St Lewiston ME 04240

COSTELLO, THOMAS JOSEPH, clergyman; b. Camden, N.Y., Feb. 23, 1929; s. James G. and Ethel A. (Dupont) C. S.T.L., Cath. U. Am., 1954, J.C.B., 1960. Ordained priest Roman Cath. Ch., 1954; sec. Diocesan Tribunal, Diocese of Syracuse, 1958; supt. schs. Cath. Diocese of Syracuse, 1960-75; pastor Our Lady Lourdes Ch., Syracuse, N.Y., 1975-78; aux. bishop, Syracuse, 1978—. Home: 1515 Midland Ave Syracuse NY 13205 Office: 240 E Onondaga St Syracuse NY 13202

COSTES, NICHOLAS CONSTANTINE, aerospace technologist, government official; b. Athens, Greece, Sept. 20, 1926; came to U.S., 1948, naturalized, 1959; s. Constantine Nicholas and Anna (Papadopoulou) C.; m. Polytime Andros, Nov. 22, 1958; children: Constantine Nicholas, Anna, Christina Smaragtha. Diploma, Sci. Sch., Athens Coll., 1945; student, Athens Nat. Tech. U, 1945-48; A.B., Darthmouth Coll., 1950; M.S.C.E. (George W. Davis scholar), Athens Nat. Tech. U., 1951; A.M., Harvard U., 1962, M.E., 1962; M.S., N.C. State U., 1955, Ph.D. (Ford Found. fellow), 1965. Registered profl. engr., N.C., Ill. Teaching fellow dept. civil engring. N.C. State U., Raleigh, 1951-53, instr., 1962-63; materials engr. N.C. State Hwy. and Pub. Works Commn., Raleigh, 1953-56; research civil engr. U.S. Army Cold Regions Research and Engring. Lab., Hanover, N.H., 1956-62; sr. research scientist systems dynamics lab Marshall Space Flight Center, NASA, Huntsville, Ala., 1965—; team leader soil mechanics investigation sci. team Apollo 14-17; cons. geotech. engring., 1965—. Contbr. articles and tech. reports to profl. jours. Recipient Dartmouth Soc. Engrs. prize, 1951, cert. of appreciation NASA, 1970, Group Achievement award Lunar Roving Vehicle Team, NASA, 1971, invention award NASA, 1971, Astronauts' Silver Snoopy award, 1972, commendation achievement, 1973, Norman medal ASCE, 1972. Fellow ASCE (Chmn. program com. aerospace council 1973-75, exec. com. aerospace div. 1976-82, chmn. 1980-81, profl. coordination com. 1982—); mem. Nat. Soc. Profl. Engrs., AAAS, Soc. Am. Mil. Engrs., AIAA (dir. Ala. sect. 1976-79, Outstanding Aerospace Engr. award 1976, Martin Schilling award 1979), Am. Geophys. Union, Soc. Engring. Sci., Dartmouth Soc. Engrs., Soc. Harvard Engrs. and Scientists, Assn. Civil Engrs. Greece (hon.), Am. Men and Women of Sci., Sigma Xi, Phi Kappa Phi, Chi Epsilon. Greek Orthodox. Home: 4216 Huntington Rd SE Huntsville AL 35802 Office: Space Scis Lab GC Marshall Space Flight Center Huntsville AL 35812

COSTIGAN, CONSTANCE FRANCES, artist, educator; b. Hoboken, N.J., July 3, 1935; d. Charles Francis and Joan Aletta (Visser) C.; m. John Francis Christian, June 6, 1959 (div. 1972); m. Michael Krausz, May 14, 1976. B.S., Simmons Coll. and Boston Mus. Sch. Fine Arts, 1957; M.A., Am. U., 1965; postgrad., U. Calif.-Berkeley, 1972, U. Va.-Fairfax, 1968-69, U. D.C., 1973-74. Tchr. Va. Designer Smithsonian Instn., Washington, 1957-59; cons. design Smithsonian Inst., Washington, 1962-68; drawing and design instr. Smithsonian Instr., Washington, 1971-76; asst. prof. design George Washington U., Washington, 1976—; curator Arlington Art Ctr., Va., 1980; jurist and judge art show D.C. area, 1975, 76, 80, 82; disting. vis. prof. Am. U., Cairo, Dec. 1980, Jan. 1981. Author: Leonardo, 1982, Elements of Art: Line, 1980; one-woman shows No. Va. Community Coll., Alexandria, 1983, Barbara Fiedler Gallery, Washington, 1979-82, Phillips Collection, Washington, 1977, Gulbenkian Gallery, U. Kent, Canterbury, Eng., 1975, Talbot Rice Arts Ctr., Edinburgh, Scotland, 1974, Design Ctr. Gallery, Cleve., Annenburg Arts Ctr., Phila., 1973, numerous group shows; represented pub. collections, Hirschborn Mus. and Sculpture Garden, Washington, Phillips Collection, Washington, U. Iowa Mus., Iowa City, pub. collection, Dimock Gallery, George Washington U., numerous pvt. collections. Fellow Macdowell Colony, 1977, Ossabaw Island project, 1980; grantee Lester Hereward Cooke Found., 1978-79. Fellow Royal Soc. Arts; mem. Coll. Art Assn. Home: 603 S Carolina Ave SE Washington DC 20003 Office: George Washington U Art Dept Washington DC 20052

COSTIGAN, EDWARD JOHN, investment banker; b. St. Louis, 1914. A.B., St. Louis U., 1935; M.B.A., Stanford U., 1937. Past pres., past vice-chmn. Stifel Nicolaus & Co., Inc.; dir. Fin. Corp., 1962-64, NASD, 1967-69; bd. govs. Midwest Stock Exchange. Trustee Calvary Cemetery Assn. Mem. Securities Industry Assn. (gov. 1968-69). Home: 9056 Saranac Dr Saint Louis MO 63117 Office: 500 N Broadway Saint Louis MO 63102

COSTIGAN, GIOVANNI, educator; b. Kingston-on-Thames, Eng., Feb. 15, 1905; s. John Francis and Helen Anne (Warren) C.; m. Amne MacMillan Johnson. B.A., U. Oxford, 1926, M.A., 1930, M.Litt., 1941; M.A., U. Wis., 1928, Ph.D., 1930; D.Litt., Lewis and Clark Coll., Portland, Oreg., 1967. Faculty dept. history U. Idaho, 1930-34; mem. faculty dept. history U. Wash., Seattle, 1934—, prof., 1948—; Mem. nat. com. ACLU. Author: Sir Robert Wilson: A Soldier of Fortune in the Napoleonic Wars, 1932, Life of Sigmund Freud, 1965, Makers of Modern England, 1967, History of Modern Ireland, 1969. Served from 1st lt. to capt. USAAF, 1943-45. Mem. Phi Beta Kappa. Office: Dept History U Wash Seattle WA 98105 *In his love of truth and deep concern for humanity, Albert Einstein, a true humanist, may well serve as an inspiration to all who live in this troubled twentieth century. I have tried to remember the example which he set.*

COSTIKYAN, EDWARD NAZAR, lawyer; b. Weehawken, N.J., Sept. 14, 1924; s. Mihran Nazar and Berthe (Muller) C.; m. Barbara Fatt, Mar. 5, 1977; children: Gregory John, Emilie Berthe. A.B., Columbia U., 1947, LL.B., 1949. Bar: N.Y. 1949, U.S. Supreme Ct. 1964. Law sec. to judge Harold R. Medina U.S. Dist. Ct., N.Y.C., 1949-51; ptnr. firm Paul, Weiss, Rifkind, Wharton & Garrison, N.Y.C., 1960—; lectr. New Sch. Social Research. Author: Behind Closed Doors: Politics in the Public Interest, 1966, How to Win Votes: The Politics of 1980, 1980; co-author: Re-Structuring the Government of New York City, 1972, New Strategies for Regional Cooperation, 1973; research editor: Columbia Law Rev.; bd. editors: N.Y. Law Jour., 1976—; contbr. articles of legal, polit. subjects to periodicals and profl. jours.; permanent condr., Oratorio and Orchestral Soc., N.Y.C. Chmn. N.Y. State Task Force on N.Y.C. Jurisdiction and Structure, 1971-72; vice-chmn. State Charter Revision for N.Y.C., 1972-77; mem. com. character and fitness 1st Jud. Dept. Democratic dist. leader, 1955-65; county leader Dem. County Com. N.Y. County, 1962-64; presdl. elector Dem. Party, 1964; trustee Columbia U.; bd. dirs., vice-chmn. Fund City N.Y.; bd. dirs. 42d St Redevel. Corp. Served to lt. AUS, 1942-46. Fellow Am. Coll. Trial Lawyers; mem. Assn. Bar City N.Y., ABA, N.Y. State Bar Assn., Columbia Law Alumni. Unitarian. Club: Century. Home: 50 Sutton Pl S New York NY 10022 Office: Paul Weiss Rifkind Wharton & Garrison 345 Park Ave New York NY 10154

COSTIN, FRANK, psychologist, educator; b. Louisville, Jan. 15, 1914; s. Samuel and Jennie (Ressnier) C.; m. Lela Madeline Brown, Nov. 22, 1950; children: Julia Jane, Jeanne Adeline. A.B., U. Louisville, 1936; A.M., U. Chgo., 1941, Ph.D., 1948. Tchr., Louisville Pub. Schs., 1936-42; asst. prof. to prof. psychology U. Ill., Urbana-Champaign, 1948—; Vis. prof. psychology and edn. U. Oreg., 1950, 54, 56; vis. scholar U. London, Eng., 1968, 75; vis. prof. U. Coll. Dublin, Ireland, U. Bradford, Eng.; research dir., cons. Champaign (Ill.) Human Relations Commn., 1961-65; chmn. psychologist exam. com. Ill. Dept. Registration and Edn., 1976-78. Author: Abnormal Psychology, 1976; cons. and contbg. editor: Teaching of Psychology; contbr. articles to profl. jours. Served with USAAF, 1942-46. Fellow Am. Psychol. Assn. (pres. div. teaching psychology 1983-84); mem. AAUP. Home: 701 W Healey Street Champaign IL 61820 Office: 731 Psychology Bldg U Ill 603 E Daniel Champaign IL 61820

COSTLE, DOUGLAS M., educator; b. Long Beach, Calif., July 27, 1939; m. Elizabeth Rowe; 1 son, 1 dau. A.B., Harvard U., 1961; J.D., U. Chgo., 1964. Trial atty. civil rights div. U.S. Dept. Justice, 1964-65; atty. Econ. Devel. Adminstrn., U.S. Dept. Commerce, 1965-67; asso. firm Marshall Kaplan Gans & Kahn, San Francisco, 1968-69; sr. staff asso. Pres.'s Adv. Council on Exec. Orgn., 1969-70; fellow Woodrow Wilson Internat. Center for Scholars of Smithsonian Instn., 1971; dep. commr. Conn. EPA, 1972-73, commr., 1973-75; asst. dir. Congressional Budget Office, 1975-77; adminstr. EPA, 1977; adj. lectr. Kennedy Sch. Govt., Harvard U., Cambridge, Mass., 1981—; vis. scholar Sch. Public Health, 1981—; chmn. U.S. Fed. Regulatory Council, 1978-81, Radiation Policy Council, 1980-81

COSTLEY, GARY EDARD, food company executive; b. Caldwell, Idaho, Oct. 26, 1943; s. Donald Clifford and Verna C.; m. Cheryl J. Zesiger, Dec. 21, 1963; children: Angela I., Chad D. B.S., Oreg. State U., M.S., Ph.D. in Nutrition-Biochemistry. With Kellogg Co., Battle Creek, Mich., formerly dir. nutrition, dir. public affairs, v.p. public affairs, v.p. and asst. to pres., sr. v.p. corp. devel., now sr. v.p. sci. Trustee Miller Found., Battle Creek. Mem. Am. Inst. Nutrition. Democrat. Lutheran. Office: 235 Porter St Battle Creek MI 49015 *

COSTLOW, JOHN DEFOREST, zoology educator; b. Brookville, Pa., Jan. 28, 1927; s. John DeForest and Kathryn (Scott) C.; m. Ann O'Rourk, May 31, 1952 (div. May 1980); children: Jane T., Beth S.; m. Virginia Mason Herrman, Feb. 27, 1982. B.S., Western Md. Coll., 1950; Ph.D., Duke U., 1956. Research assoc. Duke U. Marine Lab., Beaufort, N.C., 1954-59, prof., dir., 1968—; asst. prof. zoology Duke U., Beaufort, 1959-65, assoc. prof., 1965-67; liaison scientist Office Naval Research, London, 1966-68; on leave Cambridge U., Eng. Contbr. numerous articles to sci. publs. Mayor Town of Beaufort, 1963-66; pres. Beaufort Hist. Assn., 1962-66, 68-70. Recipient numerous grants NSF, Dept. Energy, NIH, UNESCO, Rockefeller Found. Republican. Episcopalian. Office: Duke U Marine Lab Pivers Island Beaufort NC 28516 *

COSTON, NICHOLAS GREGORY, corporation executive; b. Providence, Mar. 10, 1942. B.S., U.S. Mil. Acad., 1962; M.S., U. San Francisco, 1964; J.D., Indiana U., 1969. Bar: Ind. 1969. With NL Industries, M.Y.C., 1969—, regional mgr., 1970-74, sr. v.p., 1974-78, exec. v.p., M.Y.C., 1978—; dir. Coal Creek Minning Co. Bd. dirs. Goodman Theatre; trustees Williams Coll. Mem. Ind. Bar Assn., ABA, Young Pres.'s Orgn. Club: University. Address: Werik BLdg 1 Salvati Way Providence RI 02909

COSTONIS, JOHN J., law educator, lawyer; b. 1937. A.B., Harvard U., 1959; LL.B., Columbia U. Bar: D.C. 1967, Ill. 1968. Asst. prof. U. Pa., 1965-69; assoc. Ross, Hardies, O'Keefe, Babcock & Parsons, Chgo., 1968-70; vis. assoc. prof. U. Ill.-Chgo., 1970, prof., 1972-77, NYU, 1978—; vis. lectr. internat. law U. Chgo., 1968; vis. prof. U. Calif.-Berkeley, 1975-76; advisor to pres. Adv. Council of Hist. Preservation, to Nat. Endowment for Arts, NSF, Sec. Interior, and Nat. Trust for Hist. Preservation. Past articles editor: Columbia Law Rev. Served to 1st lt. I.C. U.S. Army, 1960-62. Mem. Am. Law Inst., Am. Planning Assn. Office: NYU Law Sch 40 Washington Sq S New York NY 10012

COSTRELL, LOUIS, government administrator; b. Bangor, Maine, June 26, 1915; s. Solomon Nathan and Annie (Cohen) C.; m. Esther Klaiman, Apr. 11, 1942; children: James A., Daniel N., Robert M. B.S., U. Maine, 1939; postgrad., U. Pitts., 1940-41; M.S., U. Md., 1949. With Elliot Co., Ridgeway, Pa., 1940, Westinghouse Corp., East Pittsburgh, 1940-41, Bur. Ships, Dept. Navy, Washington, 1941-46; with Nat. Bur. Standards, Dept. Commerce, Washington, 1946—, chief radiation instrumentation sect., 1952—; Tech. adviser to U.S. Nat. Com. for Internat. Electrotech. Commn., 1962—; chmn. AEC Nuclear Instrument Modules Com. (now Dept. Energy Nat. Instrumentation Methods), 1964—. Recipient Meritorious Service award Dept. Commerce, 1955, Disting. Service award, 1968, Spl. Service award, 1963; Edward Bennett Rosa award, 1979. Fellow IEEE (chmn. profl. group on nuclear sci. 1960-61, H. Diamond meml. award 1975, nuclear and plasma sci. merit award 1975), Washington Acad. Sci.; mem. Am. Phys. Soc., Am. Philos. Soc., Am. Nat. Standards Inst. (chmn. com. on radiation instruments 1960—), Tau Beta Pi, Phi Kappa Phi. Home: 10614 Cavalier Dr Silver Spring MD 20901 Office: Radiation Instrumentation Sect Bur Standards Washington DC 20234

COSWAY, RICHARD, legal educator; b. Newark, Ohio, Oct. 20, 1917; s. Paul Taunton and Edith Harriet (Crawford) C.; m. Serena Boland, June 8, 1957; children: Robert Gordon, Paul Richard. A.B., Denison U., 1939; J.D., U. Cin., 1942. Bar: Ohio 1942. Prof. law U. Cin., 1946-58, U. Wash., Seattle, 1958—, disting. prof., 1980—; atty. Dept. Justice, Washington, 1952-53; vis. prof. law So. Meth. U., Dallas, 1954, 67-68, U. Puget Sound, Tacoma, Wash., 1965, 66; vis. prof. Hasting's Coll. Law, 1981-82; commr. on uniform state laws State of Wash. Author: (with Warren Shattuck) Washington Practice, vols. 7 and 8, 1967, (with Warren Shattuck and Herbert Ma) Trade and Investment in Taiwan, 1973. Served with U.S. Army, 1942-46. Recipient Disting. teaching award U. Wash., 1980. Mem. Am. Bar Assn., Seattle-King County Bar Assn. Clubs: Rainier, Swedish, Elks, Masons. Office: Law Sch U Wash Seattle WA 98195

COTA, JOHN FRANCIS, utility co. exec.; b. Mason City, Iowa, Oct. 28, 1924; s. Sylvester D. and Ina (McAlpine) C.; m. Margaret Louise Allen, Oct. 22, 1945; children—David J., Julie A., Daniel A., Kim F. Student, Drake U., 1942; B.S., Iowa State U., 1947. Cadet engr. Iowa Power & Light Co., Des Moines, 1948, project mgr., 1949, chief gas engr., 1954-57; v.p., gen. mgr. Winnebago Natural Gas Corp., Kaukauna, Wis., 1957-58; pres., dir. Natural Gas Distbrs., Inc., Madison, Wis., 1958; asst. v.p. Wis. Gas Co., Milw., 1960-64, v.p. ops., 1964-69, exec. v.p., 1969-75; dir., 1968-75; v.p., asst. to chmn. Am. Natural Resources, Detroit, 1975-78; v.p. engring. and constrn. Mich. Wis. Pipe Line Co., Detroit, 1978—. Served with USNR, 1942-45. Mem. Am., Midwest gas assns., Mich. Utilities Assn. Clubs: Detroit Athletic, Country of Detroit, Rotary; Riverbend Country (Tequesta, Fla.); Rancho Bernardo Swim and Tennis (San Diego). Home: 680 Bedford Ln Grosse Pointe MI 48230 Office: One Woodward Ave Detroit MI 48226

COTA-ROBLES, EUGENE HENRY, biologist, educator; b. Nogales, Ariz., July 13, 1926; s. Amado and Feliciana Cota-R.; m. Rut Lill-Gun Engberg, Dec. 7, 1957; children: Peter, Erik, Feliciana. B.S., U. Ariz., 1950; M.A., U. Calif., Davis, 1954, Ph.D. in Microbiology, 1956. Mem. faculty U. Calif., Riverside, 1956-70, prof. biology, 1969-70; prof. microbiology, head dept. Pa. State U., 1970-73; acad. vice chancellor U. Calif.-Santa Cruz, 1973-79, prof. biology, mem. biology bd. studies, 1973—, provost Crown Coll.; mem. Nat. Sci. Bd., 1978-84; mem. nat. adv. council devel. instns. HEW, 1979-80; founding mem., sec. Nat. Chicano Council Higher Edn., 1978-80; mem. biomed. research support com., div. research resources NIH, 1978-80; mem. task force disproportionate Rep. Blacks and Hispanics in State Correctional Instns. Calif. Dept. Health and Welfare, 1979—; grad. fellowship adv. com. Calif. Student Aid Commn., 1978-80. Author papers in field. Postdoctoral fellow; USPHS, 1957-58. Mem. Am. Assn. Higher Edn., AAAS, Am. Soc. Microbiology, Electron Micrscope Soc. Am., Soc. Advancement Chicanos and Native Americans in Sci. (pres. 1973-75), Sigma Xi. Democrat. Address: Crown Provost House U Calif-Santa Cruz Santa Cruz CA 95064

COTE, EVA, member Canadian Parliament; b. Rimouski, Que., Can., Jan. 1, 1934; d. Leonidas and Marie-Anna (Belanger) Lachance; m. Robert Cote, Aug. 30, 1955; children: Elaine, Bruno, Ann. Student, Soeurs du Saint-Rosaire Convent. Elected to House of Commons, 1980—; chmn. com. on agr., 1980—. Trustee La Neigette and Bas St.-Laurent Sch. Bds.; mem. exec. Centres de Services Sociaux du Bas du Fleuve, 1975-79, v.p., 1977-78. Mem. Rimouski C. of C. Liberal. Roman Catholic. Address: 30 Leonidas St Rimouski PQ Canada G5L 2S7 *

CÔTÉ, JEAN-PIERRE, lt. gov. Quebec; b. Montreal, Jan. 9, 1926; s. Joseph Emile and Cédia (Roy) C.; m. Germaine Tremblay, July 31, 1948; children: Andrée, Gilbert, Danielle, Robert, Paul, Hélène, Jocelyne, Isabelle. Student, Longueuil Coll. Tech. Sch. and Sch. Dental Tech. Elected mem. Ho. of Commons from constituency of Longueuil, Que., 1963, 65, 68, postmaster gen., 1965-68, 70-72, minister of nat. revenue, 1968-70; mem. Senate, 1972-78; lt. gov. of, Que., 1978—. Mem. Longueuil Sch. Bd., 1960-63, chmn., 1961-63; Can. rep. meeting of Internat. Labor Orgn., Geneva, Switzerland; former commr. Diocese of St. Jean Boy Scouts. Liberal. Roman Catholic. Office: 1050 rue St Augustin Cité Parlementaire Quebec PQ G1A 1A1 Canada

CÔTÉ, ROGER ALBERT, physician, educator; b. Manchester, N.H., Aug. 28, 1928; s. Joseph Emile and Lilian (Delisle) C.; m. Mariette Lucienne Brodeur, Dec. 21, 1952; children—Denis, Suzanne, Jeannette, David, Daniel. B.A., Assumption Coll., Worcester, Mass., 1950; M.D., U. Montreal, Que., Can., 1955; M.Sc. in Pathology, Marquette U., 1964. Diplomate: Nat. Bd. Med. Examiners, Am. Bd. Pathology. Intern U. Montreal affiliated hosps., 1954-55; resident anatomic pathology Mt. Auburn Hosp., Cambridge, Mass., 1955-56, New Eng. Med. Center, Boston, 1956-57; resident clin. pathology VA Hosp., Wood, Wis., 1959-60, staff, 1960-64; asst. prof. pathology Marquette U. Sch. Medicine, Milw., 1962-64; asst. prof. Tufts U. Sch. Medicine, Boston, 1964-68, asso. prof., 1968-69; prof. pathology, 1969—; chmn. dept. pathology Faculty Medicine, 1969-77; dir. clin. labs. Med. Center, U. Sherbrooke, Que., Can., 1969-73; chief lab. service VA Hosp., Boston, 1964-69, dir., 1967-69; Mem. corp. U. Hosp., Sherbrooke, Que., 1971-74; Canadian mem. sci. adv. bd. Institut de Recherche d'Informatique et d'Automatique; mem. pathology and lab. medicine research eval. com. VA, Washington, 1967-69. Author: (with Ross C. Kory, Agnes L. Korthy) Atlas of Lung Diseases as Demonstrated by New Techniques, 1964; also articles.; Editor-in-chief: Systematized Nomenclature of Medicine, 1976, 2d edit., 2 vols., 1979. Served as capt. USAF, 1957-59. Fellow Coll. Am. Pathologists (chmn. com. nomenclature); mem. Internat. Acad. Pathology, Am. Soc. Clin. Pathologists, N.Y. Acad. Scis., Royal Coll. Phys. and Surg. Can., Canadian Assn. Pathologists. Home: 1229 Jogues Sherbrooke PQ J1H 2Y2 Canada

COTELLESSA, ROBERT FRANCIS, electrical engineering educator, former university official; b. Passaic, N.J., June 7, 1923; s. Joseph Cornelius and Helen (Dodds) C.; m. Violette Babette Foeller, Sept. 11, 1948; children: Joseph Arthur, Anne Louise, Diane Frances. M.E., Stevens Inst. Tech., 1944, M.S., 1949; Ph.D., Columbia U., 1962. Prof. elec. engring., dir. Lab. for Electroscience Research, Sch. Engring. and Sci., N.Y.U., 1962-68; prof., chmn. elec. and computer engring. Sch. Engring., Clarkson Coll. Tech., Potsdam, N.Y., 1968-80; provost, prof. elec. engring. and computer sci. Stevens Inst. Tech., Hoboken, N.J., 1980-83, sr. v.p. for acad. affairs, dean engineering, 1983-84; prof. elec. and computer engring. Clarkson U., Potsdam, N.Y., 1984—; dir. Engring. Info. Inc.; cons. Bridgeport (Conn.) Engring. Inst., 1962—, David W. Taylor Naval Ship Research-Devel. Center Annapolis, 1965-79; mem. adv. panel elec. scis. sect. NSF, Washington, 1975-78; mem. research adv. council Research Corp., Pub. Service Electric and Gas Co., 1981—; dir. N.J. Energy Research Inst., 1981-84; mem. Engring. Socs. Library Bd., 1980—. Contbr. articles to profl. jours. Mem. Bd. Edn., Glen Rock, N.J., 1966-68; v.p. Ridgewood-Glen Rock council Boy Scouts Am., 1967-68. Served to lt. (j.g.) USNR, 1943-46. Recipient Tau Beta Pi Faculty award Clarkson Coll. Tech., 1969. Fellow AAAS (council del. Sect. M 1979-82), IEEE (v.p. publ. activities 1973, v.p. tech. activities 1974-75, exec. v.p. 1976, U.S. Activities Bd. citation of honor 1979, Centennial medal 1984); mem. Am. Phys. Soc., Am. Soc. Engring. Edn., Sigma Xi, Chi Psi, Tau Beta Pi, Eta Kappa Nu, Pi Delta Epsilon. Patentee in field. Home: 901 Hudson St Hoboken NJ 07030 Office: Stevens Inst Tech Castle Point Station Hoboken NJ 07030

COTHEN, GRADY COULTER, clergyman; b. Poplarville, Miss., Aug. 2, 1920; s. Joseph H. and Mamie (Coulter) C.; m. Bettye Major, June 11, 1941; children: Carole Lorraine Cothen Shields, Grady Coulter. B.A., Miss. Coll., 1941, D.D. (hon.), 1964; M.C.T., New Orleans Bapt. Theol. Sem., 1944,; D.D., Calif. Bapt. Coll., 1962, Miss. Coll., 1964; LL.D., William Jewell Coll., 1971; D.Hum., U. Richmond, 1975; L.H.D., Okla. Bapt. U., 1975, Campbell Coll., 1978. Ordained to ministry Bapt. Ch.; pastor chs. in Chattanooga, Oklahoma City, and Birmingham, Ala., 1946-61; exec. sec.-treas. So. Bapt. Gen. Conv. Calif., 1961-66; pres. Okla. Bapt. U., 1966-70, New Orleans Bapt. Theol. Sem., 1970-74, Bapt. Sunday Sch. Bd., 1975—; mem. exec. com. Bapt. World Alliance, 1965—, also chmn. com. on edn. and evangelism; also chmn. com. on acad. and theol. edn.; mem. exec. com. Am. Assn. Theol. Schs., 1972-74; 1st v.p. So. Bapt. Conv., 1963; trustee Fgn. Mission Bd., 1949-55, Okla. Bapt. U., 1955-59, New Orleans Bapt. Theol. Sem., 1955-60. Author: Unto All the World: Bold Mission, The God of the Beginning, Faith and Higher Education. Met. bd. dirs. YMCA. Served with USN, 1944-46. Recipient E.Y. Mullins award So. Bapt. Theol. Sem., 1981, Disting. Alumnus award New Orleans Bapt. Theol. Sem., Miss. Coll. Democrat. Home: Box 264 Hermitage TN 37076 Office: 127 9th Ave N Nashville TN 37234

COTHRAN, TILMAN CHRISTOPHER, sociology educator; b. Hope, Ark., Nov. 17, 1918; s. Thomas C. and Willie (McClellan) C.; m. Gladys Vivian Williams, Aug. 18, 1940; children: Brenda Faye, Tilman Christopher. A.B., U. Ark. at Pine Bluff, 1939; M.A., Ind. U., 1942; Ph.D. (Gen. Edn. Bd. fellow 1945-47; Henderson award scholarship 1947), U. Chgo., 1949. Registrar, cashier U. Ark. at Pine Bluff, 1939-42, prof. sociology, chmn. dept. social sci., 1942-47, prof., chmn. div. social sci., 1949-59; prof. sociology, chmn. div. social sci.

Dillard U., 1947-49; Ware prof. sociology, chmn. dept. Atlanta U., 1959-70; dir. U.S. Office Econ. Opportunity Multi-Purpose Tng. Center for Southeastern Region, 1968-70; v.p. acad. affairs Governors State U., Park Forest South, Ill., 1970-72; asso. dean (Coll. Arts and Scis.); chmn. social scis. Western Mich. U., Kalamazoo, 1972-79, dir. internat. edn., 1975-79, Fiscal Yr. prof. sociology and gerontology, 1979—; vis. prof. sociology, acting head dept. Tex. So. U., summer 1949; vis. prof. Western Mich. Coll. Edn., summer 1950; vis. prof. gerontology U. Ala.-Birmingham, fall 1982; vis. scholar dept. sociology U. Chgo., spring 1979. Editor: Phylon mag, 1959-70. Research analyst Dept. Army, Japan and Korea, 1951; leader Operation Crossroads Africa for Am. students in Kenya, 1961; mem. Kalamazoo County Commn. on Human Services, 1975-82, Kalamazoo County Commn. on Aging, 1982—, South Central Mich. Commn. on Aging, 1982—; chmn. Atlanta Com. Coop. Action, Ga. adv. com. U.S. Commn. Civil Rights.; Bd. govs. Governors Gen. Hosp., 1970-72. Fellow Am. Sociol. Assn.; mem. Nat. Council on New Careers (exec. com.), Ga. Sociol. Soc. (pres.), Assn. Behavioral Scis., Soc. Study Social Problems; AAUP Alpha Kappa Mu, Alpha Kappa Delta, Delta Tau Kappa (hon.). Address: Dept Sociology Western Mich Univ Kalamazoo MI 49008

COTLAR, MORTON, organizational scientist, educator; b. Phila., Feb. 19, 1928; s. Joseph and Henrietta B. (Klaits) C.; m. Gayle Epstein, Aug. 20, 1954; children: Geri Lynda, Gary Michael. B.S. in Mech. Engring, Drexel U., 1950, M.S. in Aero. Engring, 1955; Ph.D., U. Ga., 1969. Registered profl. engr. Chief engr. Sunshine Sci. Instruments, Phila., 1953-56; sr. mgmt. engr. Sperry Rand, Gt. Neck, N.Y., 1956-67; adj. prof. systems mgmt. Poly. Inst. N.Y., N.Y.C., 1964-67; asst. prof. mgmt. U. Ga., Athens, 1967-70; prof. mgmt. U. Hawaii, Honolulu, 1970—, L. J. Buchan Disting. prof., 1977-78; vis. prof. Colo. State U., Ft. Collins, 1974-75, 77-78, Boston U., 1982; founder, exec. dir. Videodocumentary Clearinghouse; cons. comml. and instl. orgns.; lectr. mgmt. devel. programs. Author books jour. articles, monographs, films, videotapes in field. Mem. Acad. of Mgmt. (nat. officer 1975-76), Mensa, Beta Gamma Sigma (Nat. Disting. Prof. award), Phi Delta Kappa, Pi Tau Sigma. Home: Suite 2201 Harbor Sq 700 Richards St Honolulu HI 96813

COTLOW, LEWIS NATHANIEL, explorer; b. Bklyn., Feb. 5, 1898; s. Nathaniel and Lena (Greene) C.; m. Charlotte Faith Messenheimer, Dec. 18, 1966. Student, George Washington U., NYU. Traveling rep. U.S. Shipping Bd., vis. and reporting on important harbors in, Far East, Near East and S. Am., 1919-21, extensive travels throughout world gathering lecture material, 1930-35; Lecturer. Author: Passport to Adventure, 1942, Amazon Head-hunters, 1953, Zanzabuku, 1956, In Search of the Primitive, 1966, The Twilight of the Primitive, 1971. Served with U.S. Army, World War I; Served with U.S. Naval Intelligence, World War II. Recipient gold medal Adventures Club, N.Y.C., 1937; Spl. Recognition award Explorers Club, 1975. Fellow Royal Geog. Soc. Gt. Britain. Clubs: Ends of the Earth; Explorers (gold medal 1977), Adventurers (past pres.), Circumnavigators (past pres., Magellan award 1977), Dutch Treat (N.Y.C.); Adventurers (Chgo.); Bohemian (San Francisco); Palm Beach Round Table (dir.); Old Port Yacht (North Palm Beach) (dir.). Conducted expdn. Belgian Congo and Tanganyika, pioneering in color film of big game and primitive tribes, 1937; comdr. expdn. to Upper Amazon, making pioneer color film of primitive tribes, including Yaguas (2000 miles up river) and Jivaro head-hunters (2800 miles up River), 1940; condr. 2d expdn. to Amazon, studying and filming primitive life, 1945; co-condr. Armand Denis-Lewis Cotlow African expdn. to make authentic adventure-exploration technicolor feature film of big game and primitive tribes of Belgian Congo, Uganda, etc., entitled Savage Splendor, 1946-47; condr. 3d Amazon expdn. to Ecuador, Peru, Brazil, making authentic technicolor feature film, Jungle Headhunters, collected enthnol. specimens for Am. Mus. of Natural History, 1949; condr. Lewis Cotlow 3d African expdn. to Tanganyika, Belgian Congo. producing Trucolor feature film of big game and tribes entitled Zanzabuku (Dangerous Safari), 1954-55; condr. expdn. to New Guinea, prod. color documentary film of inhabitants Primitive Paradise, 1958-59, expdn. to Ellesmere Island making documentary film Eskimo traditional life High Arctic, 1962; expeditions to revisit tribes of Upper Xingu River, Brazil, 1963, Pygmy tribe, Congo, 1964; fifth Amazon expdn., 1968, fifth African expdn., 1969; mem. goodwill mission to China, 1977, photog. and research missions to Outer Mongolia, Gobi and Siberia, 1977, Antarctica, 1978, China, 1980. Home: 132 Lakeshore Dr North Palm Beach FL 33408

COTRUBAS, ILEANA, opera singer, lyric soprano; b. Galati, Romania; m. Manfred Ramin. Student, Scoala speciala de Musica, Bucharest, Ciprian Porumbescu Conservatory, Bucharest, Musikakademie, Vienna, Austria. Debut as Yniold in: Pelleas et Melisande, Bucharest Opera, 1964; appeared with, Frankfurt (W. Ger.) Opera, 1968-71, Staatsoper, Vienna, 1970—, Covent Garden, London, 1971—, Saatsoper, Munich, W. Ger., 1973—, Lyric Opera Chgo., 1973-75, 83—, Opera Paris, 1974—, La Scala, Milan, Italy, 1975—, Met. Opera, N.Y.C., 1977—, San Francisco Opera, 1978; major roles include Zerlina in: Don Giovanni; Norina in: Don Pasquale; Mimi in: La Boheme; also Susanna, Pamina, Gilda, Violetta, Tatyana, Micaela, Manon, Antonia, Melisande. Recipient 1st prize Internat. Singing Competition, Hertogenbusch, Netherlands, 1965, Munich Radio Competition, 1966; Kammersängerin Vienna Staatsoper, 1981. Office: Columbia Artists Mgmt 165 W 57th St New York NY 10019 *

COTSONAS, NICHOLAS JOHN, JR., physician, medical educator; b. Boston, Jan. 28, 1919; s. Nicholas John and Louise Catherine (Lapham) C.; m. Betty Borge, Nov. 21, 1970; children by previous marriage: Nicholas III, Bruce, Elena. A.B., Harvard, 1940; M.D. cum laude, Georgetown U., 1943. Intern D.C. Gen. Hosp., Washington, 1944, resident in chest diseases, 1946-47, asst. med. resident, 1947-48, chief med. resident, 1948-49; asst. prof. medicine Georgetown U. Sch. Medicine, 1949-53; chief med. officer, med. div. D.C. Gen. Hosp., 1951-53; asst. prof. medicine U. Ill. Coll. Medicine, Chgo., 1953-57, assoc. prof., 1957-62, prof., 1962-70; dean, prof. medicine Peoria Sch. Medicine, U. Ill., 1970-79; prof. medicine U. Ill.-Chgo., 1979—, assoc. vice chancellor for acad. affairs, Chgo., 1979-82; mem. Bradley Assocs., 1972-79; bd. dirs. Ill. Heart Assn., 1972-79, pres., 1976-77; bd. dirs. Ill. Central Health Systems Agy., 1976-79, Planned Parenthood Assn. Greater Peoria Area, 1971-79; mem. Statewide Health Coordinating Council, 1978-79; bd. dirs. Chgo. Heart Assn., 1980-82, Inst. Religion and Medicine, 1980. Asst. editor: Disease-A-Month, 1960-77; asso. editor, 1977-80; editor, 1980—. Served to capt. AUS, 1944-46. Recipient Raymond Allen award U. Ill. Coll. Medicine, 1955, Faculty of Yr. award, 1978. Fellow A.C.P., Am. Heart Assn. (council clin. cardiology 1963), Am. Coll. Cardiology, Inst. Medicine Chgo.; mem. Am. Fedn. Clin. Research, AMA, Ill., Chgo. med. socs., Chgo. Soc. Internal Medicine, Harvard Soc. Chemists, Sigma Xi, Alpha Omega Alpha. Office: U Ill-Chgo PO Box 6998 Chicago IL 60680

COTTAM, GRANT, botany educator; b. Sandy, Utah, Aug. 26, 1918; s. Walter Pace and Effie (Frei) C.; m. Diana McQuarrie, Apr. 5, 1942; children: Cynthia, Richard McQuarrie, Daniel Grant, Margaret Effie, Liatris. B.A., U. Utah, 1939; Ph.D., U. Wis., 1948. Tchr. Roosevelt Jr. High Sch., Salt Lake City, 1939-40; fellow U. Wis., 1946-48; asst. prof. U. Hawaii, 1948-49; mem. faculty U. Wis., 1949—, prof. botany, 1960—, chmn. dept., 1970-73, 79-82; dir. Center for Biotic Systems, 1978-79. Asso. editor: Ecology, 1955-57, 63-65; contbr. articles to profl. jours. Served to capt. AUS, 1941-46; PTO. Decorated Silver Star, Bronze Star; Guggenheim fellow, 1954-55. Fellow AAAS; mem. Ecol. Soc. Am., British Ecol. Soc., Wis. Acad. Sci., Arts and Letters. Home: 2021 Kendall Ave Madison WI 53705

COTTAM, HOWARD REX, former ambassador, educator, ofcl.; b. St. George, Utah, July 27, 1910; s. Heber and Edith (Brooks) C.; m. Katherine Stokes, Aug. 30, 1934; 1 dau., Lillian Meredith. A.B., Brigham Young U., 1932; Ph.B., U. Wis., 1938, Ph.D., 1941; student, Nat. War Coll., 1952. Asst. prof. Pa. State Coll., 1940-42; chief rent examiner OPA, Pitts., 1942; prin. agrl. economist U.S. Dept. Agr. and chief program appraisal War Food Adminstrn., N.E. region, N.Y.C., 1942-44; agrl. economist U.S. embassy, Paris, France, 1944-46, agrl. attache U.S. embassy, Rome, 1946-47, 1st sec. and consul, 1947-50, counselor embassy and chief food and agrl. div. E.C.A. spl. mission to Italy, 1950-52; U.S. resident liaison officer to FAO of U.N., 1951-52; also U.S. mem. on commodity problems, com. on relations with internat. orgns., del. 6th conf.; chmn. appeals com. UN FAO; assigned to Nat. War Coll., Washington, 1952-53; counselor of embassy for econ. affairs, The Hague, dep. dir. of U.S. operation missions to Netherlands, 1953-55, counselor of embassy and ICA rep., The Netherlands, 1955-56, counselor of embassy, dir. U.S. operations mission to Brazil, 1956-57, minister for econ. affairs, dir. mission, 1957-60; dep. asst. sec. Bur. Nr. Eastern and South Asian Affairs, U.S. Dept. State, 1960-63; Am. ambassador, Kuwait, 1963-69; N. Am. rep. of FAO/UN, 1969-74, cons., 1974; chmn. adv. com. Am.-Arab Assn. for Commerce and Industry, 1978-79; vis. prof. Am. U., Washington, 1974—; adviser to U.S. delegate FAO Council, Rome, 1950, 51, 52, Internat. Cotton Adv. Council, 1952; U.S. observer Internat. Fedn. Agrl. Technicians, Geneva, 1947, at Internat. Conf. Proposed David Lubin Acad., Rome, 1949; Alternate U.S. mem. permanent com. Internat. Inst. Agrl., Rome, 1947; alternate agrl. mem. U.S. Trade Agreements Com., Annecy, France, 1949; treas., bd. mem. Netherlands-U.S. Ednl. Found., 1953-56; alternate U.S. mem. Internat. Tin Study Group, The Hague, 1955-56; Hon. pres. Internat. Sch. of Kuwait, 1963-69; trustee Near East Found., 1969-78; bd. advisers Airline Passengers Assn., 1969-76; ex officio trustee Am. Freedom from Hunger Found., 1969-72; mem. adv. panel World Population Soc., 1973—; bd. dirs. Am. Near East Relief Agy., 1972-75; mem. external adv. com. World Food Inst., Ames, Iowa, 1973-74. Mem. Soc. Internat. Devel. (dir. Washington chpt. 1972-73), Washington Fgn. Affairs Inst., UN Assn. (mem. bd., v.p. Capitol Area div. 1973—, 3d v.p. 1976-78), Am. Agrl. Econs. Assn., AAAS. Clubs: Cosmos, DACOR House (Washington). Home: 2245 46th St NW Washington DC 20007 Office: American University Washington DC 20016

COTTEN, JOSEPH, actor; b. Petersburg, Va.; s. Joseph and Sally (Wilson) C.; m. Lenore Kip (dec.); m. Patricia Medina, 1960. Student, Robert Nugent Hickman Dramatic Sch., Washington. Pres. Mercury Theatre, 1944. Actor in: David Belasco prodns. Dancing Partners, Tonight or Never, 1930-31; in stock, Copley Theater, Boston, 1931-32; actor in popular stage plays, 1932-40, including, The Philadelphia Story, 1939-40, Calculated Risk, 1962; writer and appeared as actor in: Mercury Theatre of Air, 1938-39; radio actor: Lockheed Aircraft weekly radio program America Ceiling Unlimited, 1943-44; actor in motion pictures, 1940—, the first being, Citizen Kane, Lydia; later films include The Third Man, 1948, September Affair, Half-Angel, 1951, Special Delivery, 1955; other films Caravans; stage plays Sabrina Fair, N.Y.C., 1953-54, Once More With Feeling, N.Y.C., 1958-59, Hush, Hush, Sweet Charlotte, 1964; nat. road tour Seven Ways of Love, 1964; host, narrator: 20th Century-Fox TV Hour, 1955-56; narrator: TV show Hollywood and the Stars, 1963-64; appeared in: TV series On Trial, 1957-58, Angel Wore Red, 1959, Gun in Hand, 1960. Home: Los Angeles CA Office: 6363 Wilshire Blvd Los Angeles CA 90048

COTTER, BERCHMANS PAUL, JR., judge; b. Narberth, Pa., Sept. 9, 1937; s. Berchmans Paul and Mary Regina (McShane) C.; m. Mary Anna Jordan, May 2, 1964; children: Mary Amelia, Berchmans Paul, Sarah Elizabeth, Ruth Anne, David Matthew. A.B., Princeton U., 1959; J.D., Georgetown U., 1968. Bar: Va. 1968, D.C. 1968, Pa. 1969, U.S. Ct. Appeals (D.C. cir.) 1968, U.S. Ct. Appeals (3d cir.) 1969, U.S. Supreme Ct. 1972, U.S. Ct. Claims 1973. Law clk. to judge U.S. Dist. Ct., Washington, 1966-68; atty. Dechert, Price & Rhoads, Phila., 1968-70, Kaler, Worsley, Daniel & Hollman, Washington, 1970-74; adminstrv. judge HUD, Washington, 1976-78; chief adminstrv. judge Bd. Contract Appeals, Washington, 1979-80, Nuclear Regulatory Commn., 1980—; staff mem. Commn. on Govt. Procurement, Washington, 1971-72; lectr. Am. Law Inst.-ABA, Washington, 1981; mem. faculty Nat. Jud. Coll., Reno, 1983—; mem D.C. Circuit Jud. Conf., 1984—. Bd. dirs. Fairfax Opportunities Unltd., Annandale, Va., 1980-81. Acad. scholar Princeton U., 1955-57; recipient Outstanding Performance award HUD, 1977. Mem. ABA (jud. adminstrv. div. and pub. contracts sect.), Fed. Bar Assn., Nat. Conf. Bd. Contract Appeals (treas., bd. dirs. 1980-81), Nat. Conf. Adminstrv. Law Judges (exec. com. adminstrv. law sect. 1983—), D.C. Bar Assn., Va. Bar Assn., Pa. Bar Assn., Princeton U. Alumni Assn. (exec. com. 1980-82, pres. Class of 1959 1978-83). Republican. Roman Catholic. Clubs: Capitol Hill, Princeton (Washington). Office: Atomic Safety and Licensing Bd Panel-Nuclear Regulatory Commn Washington DC 20555

COTTER, DANIEL A., diversified company executive. B.A., Marquette U., 1957; M.B.A., Northwestern U., 1960. With Cotter & Co., Chgo., 1959—, pres., chief operating officer. Office: Cotter & Co. 2740-52 N. Clyborne Ave Chgo IL 60614

COTTER, FRANCIS PATRICK, electrical manufacturing company executive; b. N.Y.C., June 12, 1922; s. Patrick and Mary (Condron) C.; children: John, Mary Alice, Catherine, Frank; m. Malinda Ann DuBose, Apr. 10, 1965; 1 son, Patrick. B.S., N.Y. U., 1943; LL.B., Cath. U. Am., 1955. Bar: D.C. 1955. Spl. agt. FBI, 1947-52; profl. staff mem. Joint Com. Atomic Energy, 1952- 56, cons., 1956—; exec. asst. to v.p. atomic power div. Westinghouse Electric Corp., 1956-62, v.p. atomic, def. and space group, Washington, 1963-73, v.p. govt. affairs, 1972—; dep. insp. gen. fgn. assistance State Dept., 1962-63; spl. cons. select com. astronautics and space exploration U.S. Ho. of Reps.; cons. State Dept., AEC; mem. nat. energy study Dept. Interior.; mem. bd. Am. Nuclear Energy Council. Bd. dirs. Nat. Epilepsy Found. Served to capt. USMCR, 1943-46. Mem. D.C. Bar Assn. Democrat. Roman Catholic. Clubs: University, Congressional Country (Washington). Home: 3626 Quesada Street NW Washington DC 20015 Office: 1801 K St NW 9th Floor Washington DC 20006

COTTER, GEORGE EDWARD, airline co. exec.; b. Wuchang, China, May 14, 1918; s. Francis James Meadows and Ida Miller (Taylor) C.; m. Ruth Margaret Ellen O'Hare, May 18, 1950; children—Christopher Lamont, Ellen Douglas, Carol Hollister. Grad., Hotchkiss Sch., 1937; A.B., Wesleyan U., Middletown, Conn., 1941; J.D., Cornell U., 1946. Bar: Conn. bar 1946, N.Y. bar 1947. Asso. firm Davis Polk Wardwell Sunderland & Kiendl, N.Y.C., 1946-54; with Freeport Sulphur Co., 1954-65, sec., 1964-65; exec. v.p., gen. counsel, sec., dir. Continental Air Lines, Inc., Los Angeles, 1965—; pres., dir. Continental Hotels, Inc., 1970—, Continental Air Serivces, Inc., 1970—; dir. Inter Island Resorts, Ltd. Contbr. articles to legal jours. Served to lt. USNR, World War II. Mem. Am., N.Y. State, Litchfield County (Conn.) bar assns., Am. Judicature Soc. Home: 1033 Chantilly Rd Los Angeles CA 90024 Office: 7300 World Way West Los Angeles CA 90009

COTTER, JOHN M., diversified company executive; b. 1904. With Dayton's Bluff Hardware Co., 1916-23; salesman Raymer Hardware Co., 1923-28; gen. ptnr. Kohloop Hardware, 1928-31; gen. mdse. mgr. Kelly-How-Thompson Co., 1933-42; v.p., gen. mgr. Oakes & Co., 1942-48; with Cotter & Co., Chgo., 1948—, chmn. bd., chief exec. officer, dir. Officer: Cotter & Co 2740-52 N Clybourn Ave Chicago IL 60614 *

COTTER, JOSEPH FRANCIS, hotel chain executive; b. Brockton, Mass., May 18, 1927; s. Joseph and Sarah (Thornell) C.; m. Catherine Sullivan, Sept. 16, 1950; children: Robert, Michael, Richard, Mary, Kathleen, Ann, Christine, Peter. B.S. cum laude, Boston Coll., 1949. C.P.A., Mass., N.Y. Accountant Price Waterhouse & Co., N.Y.C., 1949-67; v.p., controller Howard Johnson Co., Braintree, Mass., 1967-70; exec. v.p., comptroller, dir. Sheraton Corp., Boston, 1970—; corporator Charlestown Savs. Bank. Former vice chmn. bd. trustees Boston Coll.; chmn. bd. dirs. Greater Boston YMCA.; bd. dirs. United Way of Massachusetts Bay. Mem. Am. Inst. C.P.A.s, N.Y. Soc. C.P.A.s, Mass. Soc. C.P.A.s, Fin. Execs. Inst., Am. Hotel and Motel Assn., Greater Boston C. of C. (dir.), Boston Coll. Alumni Assn. (past pres.). Club: Executives (v.p.). Home: 312 Forest Ave Cohasset MA 02025 Office: 60 State St Boston MA 02109

COTTER, PATRICK WILLIAM, lawyer; b. Merrill, Wis., Apr. 11, 1916; s. William Bernard and Clara (Ament) C.; m. Lois Katherine Schaus, July 11, 1942; children: Michael William, Patrick Sanford, Timothy John. B.A., U. Wis., 1938, LL.B., 1940, LL.M., 1946. Bar: Wis. 1940. Asso. firm Loomis, Roswell & Chembers, Mauston, 1940-41; partner firm Quarles & Brady (and predecessors), Milw., 1946—; dir., sec. bd. Sivyer Steel Corp., Milw.; Mem. Spl. Com. for Wis. Income Tax Simplification. Vice chmn. com. on needs of handicapped children United Way Greater Milw., Inc., 1957-61, corp. mem., 1960—, chmn. bd., mem. exec. com., program and allocations coms., bd. dirs., 1975-81; mem. bd. Whitefish Bay Pub. Library, 1963-65; corp. mem. Children's Service Soc. Wis.; sec., treas., dir. Stackner Family Found., Inc., Milw.; bd. govs., bd. dirs. Mt. Mary Coll.; bd. dirs., exec. com. Milw. Symphony; bd. dirs., devel. and endowment coms. Milw. Art Mus.; bd. dirs. Bucyrus Erie Found., South Milw.; sec., treas., bd. dirs. Ralph Evinrude Found., Inc.; bd. dirs. U. Wis. Found., Vis. Nurse Assn. (corp. mem.), Milw., U.S.O., Milw., Ole Evinrude Found., Inc., United Performing Arts Fund; co-chmn. fund drive United Performing Arts Fund, 1973, mem. exec. com., pres., 1975-76; bd. dirs. Children's Outing Assn., Kearney and Trecker Found.; mem. adv. com. planned giving Marquette U., 1975—; trustee Milw. Symphony Orch. Endowment Trust; mem. nat. com. Advocates for Arts; bd. dirs. Planning Council for Mental Health and Social Services; mem. Milwaukee County Council; mem. devel. com. Boy Scouts Am.; mem. pres.'s council Cardinal Stritch Coll.; exec. com., bd. dirs. Goals for Milw. 2000; co. chmn. Action for Goals 2000; mem. Greater Milw. Com.; mem. council Med. Coll. Wis. Served from 2d lt. to maj. AUS, 1941-46. Decorated Silver Star, Bronze Star with oak leaf cluster; recipient Pro Urbe award Mt. Mary Coll., 1977, Disting. Service award Alonzo Cudworth Post, Am. Legion, 1977; Mrs. Walter H. Stiemke award United Performing Arts Fund, 1980; Disting. Service award U. Wis. Alumni Club of Milw., 1981; award for community service NCCJ, 1982; Disting. Service award Met. Milw. Civic Alliance, 1983. Mem. ABA (ho. of dels.), Milw. Bar Assn. (chmn. exec. com., pres. 1963-64), Wis. Bar Assn. (gov. 1955-56, chmn. taxation sect. 1961-63), Am. Law Inst., Milw. Bar Found., Ripon Coll. Assos., Benchers Soc. (charter), Am. Judicature Soc., Am. Legion (judge adv. Wis. dept. 1977), U. Wis. Law Alumni Assn. (pres. 1958-59, 70-71), Res. Officers Assn. (pres. Wis. dept. 1957-58). Clubs: Milw. Athletic (dir.), Milwaukee.). Home: 8217 N Lake Dr Milwaukee WI 53217 Office: 780 N Water St Milwaukee WI 53202

COTTER, WILLIAM DONALD, state official, former newspaper editor; b. Hartford, Conn., June 5, 1921; s. William Joseph and Alice I. (Murphy) C.; m. Alice K. Liller, Jan. 22, 1944; children: Carol A., Mary L., Alice E., William J., James D., Donald W. B.A., Fordham U., 1943; postgrad. polit. Sci., St. John U., 1956-57, Syracuse U., 1958. Reporter L.I. Star-Jour., Long Island City, 1947-51; night city editor Nassau Rev., Rockville Centre, N.Y., 1952-53; night editor Jersey Jour., Jersey City, 1954; mag., Sunday editor L.I. Press, Jamaica, N.Y., 1955-58; city editor Syracuse Herald-Jour./Am., 1958-66, editor, 1966-83; chmn. N.Y. State Energy Research and Devel. Authority, 1983—; commr. N.Y. State Energy Commn., 1983—; chmn. N.Y. State Energy Planning Bd., 1983—; instr. journalism Syracuse U., 1960-66. Former bd. dirs. Community Gen. Hosp., Boys Town of Italy, Erie Canal Mus.; past chmn. communications com. LeMoyne Coll.; chmn. Onondaga County Energy Com., 1975-83. Served with USNR, 1943-46. Mem. Am. Soc. Newspaper Editors, N.Y. State Soc. Newspaper Editors (pres.). Roman Cath. Clubs: Syracuse Press (pres. 1964), Auburn Golf and Country (dir.). Home: RD 2 Box 82 Skaneateles NY 13152 Office: NY State Energy Office 2 Rockefeller Plaza Albany NY 12223

COTTER, WILLIAM JOSEPH, grain co. exec.; b. Bayonne, N.J., Jan. 24, 1921; s. Michael and Nora Agnes (Sullivan) C.; m. Virginia Alicia McMahon, 1949 (dec. 1962); children—William Joseph, Alicia Ann Cotter Wilson; m. Almedia Jo Ford, June 28, 1966; children—Kathleen Jo, Christopher Michael. B.B.A., Coll. City N.Y., 1947; LL.B., N.Y. U., 1955. Spl. agt. FBI, 1947-51; with CIA, 1951-69; chief postal insp. U.S. Postal Service, 1969-75; v.p., chief compliance officer Bunge Corp., N.Y.C., 1975—. Served to capt. USAAF, 1942-46. Mem. Soc. Former Spl. Agts. FBI. Home: 3731 Acosta Rd Fairfax VA 22031 Office: 1 Chase Manhattan Plaza New York NY 10005

COTTER, WILLIAM RECKLING, college president; b. Detroit, Mar. 9, 1936; s. Fred Joseph and Esther Jean (Reckling) C.; m. Linda Jane Kester, June 14, 1959; children—David Andrew, Deborah Anne, Elizabeth Anne. B.A. in Polit. Sci. magna cum laude, Harvard U., 1958, J.D. cum laude, 1961. Bar: N.Y. State bar 1962, U.S. Supreme Ct. bar 1965. Law clk. to U.S. Fed. Judge, N.Y.C., 1961-62; M.I.T. fellow in Africa, Nigeria, 1962-63; asso. firm Cahill, Gordon, Sonnett, Reindell & Ohl, N.Y.C., 1964-65; White House fellow assigned to Sec. of Commerce, Washington, 1965-66; Ford Found. rep. to, Colombia and Venezuela, 1966-70; pres. African-Am. Inst., N.Y.C., 1970-79, Colby Coll., 1979—. Contbr. articles on fgn. policy and edn. to profl. jours. Bd. dirs. Pvt. Agys. Collaborating Together, 1975-81; Chmn. bd. trustees Oyster Bay, East Norwich (N.Y.) Public Library, 1975-79; trustee African-Am. Inst., 1970—; bd. dirs. Sta.-WCBB-TV, Lewiston, Maine., Waterville Red Cross, Kennebec Valley Regional Health Agy.; chmn. bd. visitors Baxter Sch. for the Deaf. Mem. Council Fgn. Relations. Club: Univ. (N.Y.C.). Office: Office of Pres Colby Coll Waterville ME 04901

COTTING, JAMES CHARLES, manufacturing company executive; b. Winchester, Mass., Oct. 15, 1933; s. Edward L. and Mary Ellen (Worrell) C.; m. Marjorie A. Kirsch, Feb. 8, 1963; children: James Charles, Steven Robert, Brenda Ann-Marie. B.A., Ohio State U., 1955. Acctg. supr. U.S. Steel Corp., Pitts., 1959-61; mgr. profit analysis Ford Motor Co., Dearborn, Mich., 1961-63; mgr. devel. planning A. O. Smith Corp., Milw., 1963-66; asst. controller Gen. Foods Corp., White Plains, N.Y., 1966-71; v.p. planning Internat. Paper Co., N.Y.C., 1971-

76, v.p., controller, 1976-79; sr. v.p.-fin. and planning and chief fin. officer Internat. Harvester Co., Chgo., 1979-82, exec. v.p./fin., 1982-83, vice chmn., chief fin. officer, 1983—; dir. IH Credit Corp., IH Finanz AG Switzerland; bd. govs. Adela Investment Co.; Mem. The Mid-Am. Com., Chgo. Com., MAPI Fin. Council, Conf. Bd., Council Fin. Execs., Officer's Conf. Group. Served to lt. USN, 1955-58. Mem. Phi Beta Kappa, Alpha Tau Omega. Clubs: Econ. Chgo., Montclair Golf, Barrington Hills Country, Mid-Am. Office: 401 N Michigan Ave Chicago IL 60611

COTTINGHAM, ROBERT, artist; b. Bklyn., Sept. 26, 1935; s. James G. and Aurelia Ann C.; m. Jane Marie Weismann, Dec. 23, 1967; children: Reid Ann, Molly Jane, Kyle Annie Bliss. A.A., Pratt Inst., 1963. Art dir. Young & Rubicam Advt., Inc., N.Y.C., 1959-64, Los Angeles, 1964-68; tchr. Art Center Coll. Design, Los Angeles, 1969-70. One man shows include, Aldrich Mus., Ridgefield Conn., 1979, Galerie de Gestlo, Cologne, W. Ger., Delta Gallery, Rotterdam, Netherlands, Getler-Pall Gallery, N.Y.C., Thomas Segal Gallery, Boston, 1980, Ball State U., U. Bridgeport (Conn.), Fendrick Gallery, Washington, 1981, Mattatuck Mus., Waterbury, Conn., Swain Sch. Design, New Bedford, Mass., CoeKerr Gallery, N.Y.C., 1982, Signet Arts, St. Louis, 1983, Wichita Art Mus., Kans., numerous group shows specializing in realism, contemporary art; represented in numerous permanent collections including, Whitney Mus. Am. Art, N.Y.C., Cleve. Art Mus., Detroit Mus. Art, Phila. Mus. Art, Harvard, Honolulu Acad. Art, Carnegie Inst., Pitts., U. Iowa, Long Beach (Calif.) Mus. Art, Indpls. Mus. Art, Dartmouth Coll., Mus. Modern Art, N.Y.C., Guggenheim Mus., N.Y.C., Hirshhorn Mus. and Sculpture Garden, Washington, Nat. Mus. Am. Art, Washington, Princeton U., Yale U., others, including numerous European museums. Served with U.S. Army, 1955-58. Nat. Endowment Arts grantee, 1974-75. Address: Blackman Rd Newtown CT 06470

COTTINGHAM, WILLIAM BROOKS, university administrator; b. Chgo., Dec. 1, 1933; s. Ellis Brooks and Lillian Beverly (Nixon) C.; m. Gloria Dawn Smith, Sept. 12, 1975; children by previous marriage: Cynthia Mae, Cheryl Ann, Karen Jo. B.S.M.E., Purdue U., 1955, M.S.M.E., 1956, Ph.D., 1960. Mem. tech. staff Bell Telephone Labs., Whippany, N.J., 1960-63; asso. prof. Sch. of Mech. Engring. Purdue U., West Lafayette, Ind., 1963-66, prof., 1966-75; head sch. Sch. of Mech. Engring., Purdue U. (Mech. engring.), 1970-75; dean acad. affairs Gen. Motors Inst. (name changed to GMI Engring. and Mgmt. Inst. 1982), Flint, Mich., 1975-76; pres., 1976—; founding partner, pres. TecTran, Inc., Lafayette, Ind., 1968-72; guest researcher Medisch Fysisch Inst., Utrecht, Netherlands, 1970. Author: (with P.W. McFadden) Physical Design of Electronic Systems, Vol. 4, 1970. Pres. bd. dirs. Lafayette Symphony Orchestra, 1969-70, bd. dirs., 1969-75; bd. dirs. Flint Inst. Music, 1975—. Mem. ASME, Soc. Automotive Engrs., Am. Phys. Soc. Am. Soc. Engring. Edn., Pi Tau Sigma, Sigma Xi, Tau Beta Pi. Club: Mason. Patentee in field. Home: 2142 Briar Hill Flint MI 48503 Office: 1700 W 3d Ave Flint MI 48502

COTTLE, OWEN BOOTH, manufacturing company executive; b. St. Louis, Nov. 17, 1923; s. Barnard H. and Evelyn (Davis) C.; m. Florence J. Godfrey, Sept. 1, 1946; children: Diane, Owen, Kathleen, Donald; m. Elizabeth M. Ahearn, Oct. 22, 1960. Student, Pa. State U., 1941-43, Pace U., 1945-47. Treas. Abex Corp., N.Y.C., 1965—. Served with AUS, 1943-45. Mem. Fin. Execs. Inst. Clubs: Princeton Club N.Y., Masons. Home: 252 Marietta Ave Hawthorne NY 10532 Office: Abex Corp 530 5th Ave New York NY 10036

COTTON, AYLETT BOREL, lawyer; b. San Francisco, Apr. 10, 1913; s. Aylett Rains and Alice (Borel) C.; m. Martha Jane Knecht, June 29, 1940; children—Kristi (Mrs. Robert L. Spence), Gail (Mrs. Kenneth G. High, Jr.), A. Lindley. A.B., Stanford, 1935, J.D., 1938. Bar: Calif. bar 1938. Practice in, San Mateo, 1939, 80—, Burlingame, 1952-59, San Francisco, 1940-42, 45-52, 59-80; partner Cotton, Seligman and Ray (and predecessor firms), 1959-80; adminstrv. officer, real estate div. U.S. Army C.E., San Francisco and Salt Lake City, 1942-45; Developer Borel Pl. Office Center, San Mateo, 1961—. A founder Guardsmen, San Francisco, 1947; a founder Crystal Springs and Uplands Sch. Hillsborough, Calif., 1952, pres. trustees, 1952-57, life mem. bd., 1957—; Alt. del. Republican Nat. Conv., 1956, 60. Mem. ABA, Calif. Bar Assn., San Mateo Bar Assn., San Francisco Bar Assn. (chmn. com. judiciary 1969), Stanford Law Soc. San Francisco (pres. 1974-75), Soc. Calif. Pioneers, Atlantic Union, Delta Kappa Epsilon, Phi Delta Phi. Conglist. Clubs: Bohemian, Commonwealth, Guardsmen (San Francisco); Burlingame Country. Office: 1611 Borel Pl San Mateo CA 94402

COTTON, DANA MESERVE, ednl. cons.; b. Wolfeboro, N.H., Oct. 17, 1905; s. Jacob Henry and Sarah Frances (Meserve) C.; m. Margaret Fenner Berry, Dec., 1972; children by previous marriage—John Pierce, Rebecca. A.B., U. N.H., 1928, LL.D., 1968; Ed.M., Harvard U., 1943; postgrad., Columbia Tchrs. Coll., Oxford (Eng.) U.; LL.D., Am. Internat. Coll., 1953, U. N.H., 1970; Ed.D., Tufts U., 1955; L.H.D., New Eng. Coll., 1959; D.Sc., Nasson Coll., 1972. Dir. guidance Maine Dept. Edn., Augusta, 1940-44; asst. to dean admissions, mem. bd. freshman advisers Harvard, 1944-72, sec. faculty edn., 1957-72, acting dean, 1971-72; cons. edn. and industry, 1972—; Rec. sec. New Eng. Sch. Devel. Council, 1950-72; mem. edn. com. New Eng. Council, 1954-72, New Eng. Council Econ. Devel., 1949-72; exec. sec.-treas. New Eng. Assn. Colls. and Secondary Sch., 1947-70. Mem. New Eng. Citizens Crime Commn., 1966-72. Episcopalian. Club: Mason. Home: 6 Occom Ridge Hanover NH 03755

COTTON, DONALD ROBERT, hardware supply company executive; b. Elmira, N.Y., Dec. 20, 1929; s. Robert E. and Edith (Beechey) C.; m. Lola Jean Snelling, Mar. 30, 1960; children: Gina Sue, Lori Jayne, Susie Kiki. B.S. in Sci., Ithaca Coll., 1952. Registered phys. therapist. Sales mgr. consumer products div. Corning Glass Works, N.Y., 1963-70; dealer, membership mgr. Am. Hardware-Servistar Co., East Butler, Pa., 1970-75; mktg. mgr. Am Hardware-Servistar Co., East Butler, Pa., 1975-79; sr. v.p. mktg. Am. Hardware-Servistar Co., East Butler, Pa., 1979—; v.p., dir. Cayman Kai Resort Ltd., Grand Cayman, B.W.I., 1975—; dir. Home Center Show, Chgo., 1979-82. Mem. Republican Eagles, Washington, 1982—; bd. dirs. Butler Chamber of Congress, 1975, Brussell Mueller Found., 1972-75. Served to 2d lt. U.S. Army, 1952-55. Named Hardware Merchandiser of Yr. Hardware Mdse. Mag., Chgo., 1972. Mem. Am. Mgmt. Assn., Hardware Gold Assn., So. Wholesale Hardware Assn. (exec. bd. dirs. 1983—). Clubs: Butler Country (gold com.) (1970); Cayman Kai Yacht (social dir.) (1975—). Home: 1205 Oakirdge Dr Butler PA 16001 Office: Am Hardware Servistar Grant St East Butler PA 16029

COTTON, DOYLE WHITE, JR., oil company executive, real estate development company executive; b. Enid, Okla., July 17, 1931; s. Doyle White and Alice Marie (Champlain) C.; m. Priscilla Jane Carter, Feb. 19, 1955; children: Allison Marie, Elizabeth Leigh. Student, pvt. sch., Andover, N.H. Vice pres. Mercury Drilling, Tulsa, to 1965; pres. Cotton Petroleum Corp., Tulsa, 1965-76, chmn. bd., 1965—; pres. Cotton Properties, Tulsa, 1978—; dir. United Energy Resources, Inc., Houston, Lawrence Mgmt., N.Y.C., Burkhart Petroleum Corp., Tulsa, First Nat. Bank, Oklahoma City. Trustee Mt. Vernon Coll., Washington, 1982-83. Served to cpl. U.S. Army, 1952-53. Republican. Episcopalian. Office: Cotton Properties Inc 4660 One Williams Ctr Tulsa OK 74172

COTTON, EUGENE, lawyer; b. N.Y.C., May 20, 1914; s. Jacob and Ida (Fundler) C.; m. Sylvia Glickstein, Jan. 21, 1940; children: Richard, Stephen Eric. B.S.S., Coll. City N.Y., 1933; LL.B., Columbia U., 1936. Bar: N.Y. 1936, Ill. 1948. Asso. firm Szold & Brandwen, N.Y.C., 1936-37; atty. N.Y. Labor Relations Bd., N.Y.C., 1937-41; spl. counsel FCC, Washington, 1941-42; asst. gen. counsel CIO, Washington, 1942-48; partner firm Elson & Cotton, Chgo., 1948-50, Cotton, Watt, Jones & King, 1951—; Gen. counsel United Packinghouse Workers Am., 1948-68; gen. counsel packinghouse dept. Amalgamated Meat Cutters, Butcher Workmen Am., 1968-79. Served with USNR, 1943-45. Mem. Ill., Chgo. bar assns., Chgo. Council Lawyers. Club: City of Chgo. (gov., pres. 1966-68). Home: 935 E 49th St Chicago IL 60615 Office: 1 IBM Plaza Chicago IL 60611

COTTON, FRANK ALBERT, chemist, educator; b. Phila., Apr. 9, 1930; s. Albert and Helen (Taylor) C.; m. Diane Dornacher, June 13, 1959; children: Jennifer Helen, Jane Myrna. Student, Drexel Inst. Tech., 1947-49; A.B., Temple U., 1951, D.Sc. (hon.), 1963; Ph.D., Harvard U., 1955; Dr. rer. Nat. (hon.), Bielefeld U., 1979, D.Sc., Columbia U., 1980, Northwestern U., 1981, U. Bordeaux, 1981, St. Joseph's U., 1982, U. Louis Pasteur, 1982, U. Valencia, 1983, Kenyon Coll., 1983, Technion-Israel Inst. Tech., 1983. Instr. chemistry M.I.T., 1955-57, asst. prof., 1957-60, assoc. prof., 1960-61, prof., 1961-71; Robert A. Welch Distinguished prof. chemistry Tex. A&M U., 1971—; Cons. Am. Cyanamid, Stamford, Conn., 1958-67, Union Carbide, N.Y.C., 1964—. Author: (with G. Wilkinson) Advanced Inorganic Chemistry, 4th edit, 1980, Basic Inorganic Chemistry, 1976, Chemical Applications of Group Theory, 2d edit, 1970, (with L. Lynch and C. Darlington) Chemistry, An Investigative Approach; Editor: Progress in Inorganic Chemistry, Vols. 1-10, 1959-68, Inorganic Syntheses, Vol. 13, 1971, (with L.M. Jackman) Dynamic Nuclear Magnetic Resonance Spectroscopy, (with R.A. Walton) Multiple Bonds between Metal Atoms. Recipient Michelson-Morley award Case Western Res. U., 1980, Nat. Medal of Sci., 1982. Mem. Nat Acad. Scis., Am. Soc. Biol. Chemists, Am. Chem. Soc. (awards 1962, 74, Baekeand medal N.J. sect. 1963, Nichols medal N.Y. sect. 1975, Pauling medal Oreg. and Puget Sound sect. 1976, Kirkwood medal N.Y. sect. 1978, Gibbs medal Chgo. sect. 1980), Am. Acad. Arts and Scis., Royal Danish Acad. Scis. and Letters (hon.), N.Y. Acad. Scis. (hon. life), Göttingen Acad. Scis. (corr.), Royal Soc. Chemistry (hon.), Societa Chimica Italiana (hon.). Home: Route 2 Box 285 Bryan TX 77801 Office: Tex A and M U College Station TX 77843

COTTON, JOHN, Realtor; b. San Diego, Mar. 23, 1913; s. Oscar W. and Violet (Savage) C.; m. Margaret Georgia McNeil, Sept. 26, 1936; children: Lawrence M., Margaret (Mrs. John B. Harris), Joan (Mrs. Larry Cairncross). Student, Calif. State U. at San Diego, 1931, 33, Stanford, 1931, 32, 34. Salesman O.W. Cotton, Realtor, San Diego, 1934-46; partner O.W. Cotton Co., San Diego, 1946—; pres. Cotton Property Mgmt. Co. (name changed to Cotton-Ritchie Corp.), Realtors), San Diego, 1977—; real estate broker, appraiser, counselor, property mgr.; lectr. in field. Mem. Calif. Real Estate Commn., 1968-76; chmn. San Diego Housing Adv. and Appeals Bd., 1962-69; mem. pres.'s real estate adv. com. U. Calif., 1954-56, 65-72. Recipient Bronze medal City of Paris, 1975. Mem. San Diego Bd. Realtors (pres. 1951), Calif. Assn. Realtors (pres. 1956), Nat. Assn. Realtors (pres. 1969), Internat. Real Estate Fedn. (pres. Am. chpt. 1973, dep. world pres. 1977-79, Distinguished Service award 1968), Inst. Real Estate Mgmt. (pres. San Diego 1948), Am. Inst. Real Estate Appraisers (nat. v.p. 1966, pres. San Diego 1962), Am. Soc. Real Estate Counselors, San Diego Apt. and Rental Owners Assn. (pres. 1944-46), Calif. Apt. Owners Assn. (pres. 1948-49), Nat. Apt. Owners Assn. (v.p. 1953), San Diego Downtown Assn. (pres. 1961), Am. Arbitration Assn. (nat. panel arbitrators 1967-83), San Diego C. of C. (dir. 1970-74, v.p. planning 1974), Am. Right of Way Assn. Presbyterian (elder). Club: Lion. Office: 233 A Street San Diego CA 92101

COTTON, JOHN PIERCE, headmaster; b. Winchester, Mass., Nov. 25, 1937; s. Dana Meserve and Gereldine Pierce;; s. Dana Meserve and Gereldine C.; m. Deborah Elliott, Sept. 18, 1960; children—John Elliott, Sarah Pierce, Nathaniel Curtis Hasty, Ethan Sprague. Grad., Phillips Exeter Acad., 1956; A.B., Harvard, 1960; M.A., U. Colo., 1967. Trust asso. First Nat. Bank Boston, 1962-64; sr. master upper school Colo. Acad., Englewood, 1964-68; headmaster Kimball Union Acad., Meriden, N.H., 1968-74, St. Andrew's Sch., Boca Raton, Fla., 1974—; bd. dirs. Fla. Council Ind. Schs., 1976—. Pres. N.H. Pub. Broadcasting Council, Durham, 1971-74, Gold Coast Acad. Council, 1975—; coordinator Common Cause, 2d Congl. Dist. N.H., 1970-72; Bd. dirs. N.H. Council on World Affairs, 1968-74; trustee Gulf Stream Sch., Council for Religion in Ind. Schs., 1977—; incorporator N.H. Charitable Found., 1972-74; corp. mem. Mary Hitchcock Meml. Hosp., Hanover, N.H., 1971-74. Mem. Ind. Schs. Assn. No. New Eng. (pres. 1972-74), Episcopal Sch. Assn. S.E. Fla. (v.p. 1976—), Headmasters Assn. Episcopalian. Club: Harvard (Boston). Home: St Andrews Rd Boca Raton FL 33434 Office: St Andrew's Sch Boca Raton FL 33434

COTTON, WILLIAM DAVIS, lawyer, banker; b. Jonesville, La., Feb. 9, 1904; s. George Spencer and Lizzie (Davis) C.; m. Anna Mae Puddin Allen, Nov. 25, 1927; children—Carole, Jean Ann, Stephen Wayne. Student, La. State U., 1922-27, LL.B., 1927, J.D., 1968. Bar: La. bar 1928. Practice in, Rayville, La., 1929—; sr. mem. firm Cotton, Bolton, Roberts & Hoychick, 1946—; chmn. bd. 1st Republic Bank Rayville, 1952—, pres., 1952-68; research fellow Southwestern Legal Found.; Mem. council La. Law Inst., 1959—. Del. gen. confs. Methodist Ch., 1960, 64, 66, 68, 72, 76, 80, chancellor La. conf., 1970—; mem. La. Commn. on Constnl. Revision, 1970-72; Mem. La. Senate from 32d Dist., 1940-44; chmn. Richland Parish Democratic Exec. Com., 1961-76; Trustee Glenwood Hosp., West Monroe, La., 1962-78. Served to lt. col. AUS, 1941-46; ETO. Decorated Bronze Star; named Outstanding Layman La. Miss. W. Tenn. Dist. Kiwanis, 1970, Meth. Man of Yr., La., 1965. Fellow Am. Coll. Probate Counsel, Am. Bar Found.; mem. Am. Bar Assn., La. Bar Assn. (bd. govs. 1946-48, pres. 1965), Am. Judicature Soc. Clubs: Mason (32 deg.), Kiwanian (internat. trustee 1941-42, 46-48). Home: 219 Julia St Rayville LA 71269 Office: 307 Madeline St Rayville LA 71269

COTTONE, BENEDICT PETER, lawyer; b. N.Y.C., Apr. 26, 1909; s. Pellegrino and Pina (Grisafi) C.; m. Louise Cleverdon, Apr. 25, 1941 (div. May 1983); children: Michael Benedict, Vincent William.; m. Rosemary Medeiros, June 9, 1983 (div. Mar. 1984). A.B., Cornell U., 1930; LL.B., Yale U., 1933. Bar: N.Y. 1934. Pvt. practice, 1934-35; entered Fed. Govt. service, 1935; with SEC as atty. in Protective Com. Study, 1935-36; atty. with spl. telephone investigation of FCC, 1936-37; legal staff Fed. Power Commn., 1937-38; spl. asst. to atty. gen. assigned to Temp. Nat. Econ. Com. in Congl. hearings on patent practices, 1938; sr. atty. CAA, 1938-39, chief litigation sect., 1939, asst. gen. counsel, 1941-46; gen. counsel FCC, 1946-53; U.S. del. Anglo-Am. Telecommunications Conf., Bermuda, 1945, ITT Conf., Paris, 1949. Mem. Atty. Gen.'s Com. on Organized Crime, 1950. Mem. bars N.Y., D.C., D.C., Am., Fed. Communications bar assns., Acad. Polit. Sci., Am. Judicature Soc., Phi Beta Kappa, Phi Kappa Phi., Alpha Phi Delta. Democrat. Clubs: Ivy League (Sarasota, Fla.); Cornell (N.Y.C. and Sarasota); Broadcast Pioneers. Home: 443 Meadowlark Dr Bird Key Sarasota FL 33577

COUCH, GEORGE ROBERT, metals company executive; b. St. Louis, Oct. 9, 1919; s. George W. and Ruth N. C.; m. Roberta Nielsen, Apr. 29, 1950. B.S.Ch.E., Mo. Sch. Mines and Metallurgy, 1941; M.S.Ch.E., Newark Coll. Engring., 1952; grad., Advanced Mgmt. Program, Harvard U., 1979. Engr. U.S. Steel Corp., Chgo., 1941-42, Magnesium Reduction Co., Lucky, Ohio, 1942-45, Nat. Lead Co., Sayreville, N.J., 1946-56, Am. Metal Ltd., 1956-62; v.p. Molybdenum Corp. Am., N.Y.C., 1962-64; asst. to gen. mgr. Western Mining div. Kennecott Copper Corp., Salt Lake City, 1965-69; pres. Amax Splty. Metals Corp., Greenwich, Conn., 1968—; v.p. Amax, Inc., Greenwich, 1976-82. Served with U.S. Army, 1945-46. Mem. AIME (pres. Metall. Soc. 1979, dir. 1978-80), Am. Soc. Metals, Mining Club N.Y. Republican. Home: 108 Goldfinch Allamuchy NJ 07840

COUCH, JAMES FITTON, JR., judge; b. Des Moines, May 30, 1917; s. James Fitton and Mildred (Angel) C.; m. Evelyn Brodie, Feb. 28, 1941; 1 son, James Fitton III. Student, George Washington U., 1935-37; LL.B., Washington Coll. Law, 1941. Bar: D.C. 1942, Md. 1950. Practice law, Brentwood and Mt. Rainier, Md., 1950-71; judge Md. Dist. Ct., Upper Marlboro, 1971-72, Md. Circuit Ct., 1972-77, Md. Ct. Spl. Appeals, Annapolis, 1977-82, Md. Ct. Appeals, 1982—. Served to maj. U.S. Army, 1942-47; ETO. Recipient award for prof. excellence Washington Coll. Law, 1983. Fellow Md. Bar Found.; mem. Prince George's County Bar Assn., Md. Bar Assn. Home: 10105 Towhee Ave Adelphi MD 20783 Office: Court of Appeals Md PO Box 416 Upper Marlboro MD 20772

COUCH, JESSE WADSWORTH, insurance company executive; b. Atlanta, Mar. 2, 1921; s. Jesse Newton and Laura (Day) W.; m. Charlotte Lucretia Collins, Jan. 13, 1945; children: Robert Collins (dec.), Laura W. A.B., Princeton, 1947. With 1st Nat. Bank Houston, 1947-51; asso. Wray Assos., Houston, 1951-60; partner Wray, Couch & Elder, Houston, 1960-69; v.p. Marsh & McLennan, Inc., 1969—. Mem. exec. bd. Episcopal Diocese of Tex., 1965-67, 68-71; Bd. dirs. Houston-Harris County YMCA, 1969-74, Houston Soc. Prevention Cruelty to Animals, 1974—, Tex. div. Am. Cancer Soc.; mem. exec. com. Tex. div. Am. Cancer Soc., 1982—; chmn. Cancer Crusade Greater Houston, 1981-83; trustee Mus. Fine Arts, Houston, 1970-74, Houston Arboretum and Nature Ctr., 1978—. Served to capt. USAAF, 1943-46. Mem. Houston C. of C. (aviation com. 1965-75). Clubs: Eagle Lake (Tex.) Rod & Gun; Houston Country, Bayou, Allegro, Tejas, Athletic, Rotary (Houston). Home: 6015 Pine Forest Houston TX 77057 Office: 1100 Milam Bldg Houston TX 77002

COUCH, J.O. TERRELL, lawyer, former oil company executive; b. San Antonio, Mar. 3, 1920; s. Quest C. and Mattie H. (Terrell) C.; m. Willynn Miles Brooks, July 31, 1943; children: J.O. Terrell, Jr., Leland Brooks, Nancy Miles. Student, San Antonio Jr. Coll., 1937-38; LL.B., U. Tex., 1942; grad., Advanced Mgmt. Program, Harvard, 1968. Bar: Tex. 1942, Ohio 1967. Partner firm Lattimore & Couch, Ft. Worth, 1946-49, Lattimore, Couch & Lattimore, 1949-51; asso. firm McGown, McGown, Godfrey & Logan, Ft. Worth, 1951-52; atty. Marathon Oil Co., Houston, 1952-61, div. atty., 1961-67, gen. counsel, Findlay, Ohio, 1967-74, dir., 1969-74; sole practice, Houston, 1975; partner firm Hutcheson & Grundy, Houston, 1976—; Mem. adv. bd. Internat. and Comparative Law Center; mem. adv. bd. Internat. Oil & Gas Ednl. Center of Southwestern Legal Found., 1967—, vice chmn., 1973-77. Served with CIC AUS, 1942-46; ETO, PTO. Mem. ABA (mem. natural resources law sect. council 1972-76, vice chmn. 1976, chmn.-elect 1977-78, chmn. 1978-79), Houston Bar Assn. (chmn. mineral com. 1966), State Bar Tex. (chmn. mineral law sect. 1961-62, mem. internat. law sect. council 1976-79), Tex. Mid-Continent Oil and Gas Assn., N.Mex. Oil and Gas Assn. (exec. com. 1965-66, adv. com. 1965-67), Alpha Tau Omega. Presbyn. Clubs: Houston Country, Ramada, Allegro. Home: 4930 Post Oak Timber Houston TX 77056 also 712 Mariner Lakeway Austin TX 78746 Office: 3300 Citicorp Ctr Houston TX 77002

COUCH, JOHN NATHANIEL, botanist; b. Prince Edward County, Va., Oct. 12, 1896; s. John Henry and Sallie Love (Terry) C.; m. Else Dorothy Ruprecht, May 28, 1927; children—John Philip, Sally Louise Couch Gooder. Student, Trinity Coll. (Duke U.), 1914-17; A.B., U. N.C., 1919, A.M., 1922, Ph.D., 1924, U. Nancy (France), spring 1919, U. Wis., summer, 1923. Instr. botany U. N.C., 1917-18; sci. tchr. high sch., Chapel Hill, N.C., 1919-20, Charlotte, N.C., 1920-21; instr. botany U. N.C., Chapel Hill, 1922-25, asst. prof., 1927-28, asso. prof., 1928-32, prof., 1932-45, Kenan prof. botany, 1945-67, Kenan prof. botany emeritus, 1967—; NRC fellow in botany Carnegie Instn., Cold Spring Harbor, N.Y., 1925-26, Mo. Bot. Garden, 1926-27; with Johns Hopkins Bot. Exploration, Jamaica, B.W.I., summer, 1926; vis. prof. Johns Hopkins, winters, 1933-35, U. Va., summer, 1933; cultural exchange specialist U.S. Dept. State, India, 1961; mem. N.C. Gov.'s Sci. Adv. Com., 1961-64; v.p. XI Internat. Bot. Congress, Seattle, 1969; Spl. adviser to chmn. OSRD, 1944. Author: (with W.C. Coker) The Gasteromycetes of the Eastern United States and Canada, 1928, The Genus Septobasidium, 1938; Asso. editor: Mycologia, 1937-39; editor: Jour. Elisha Mitchell Sci. Soc, 1946-60; Contbr. articles on bot. subjects to profl. jours. Served with U.S. Army, 1918-19. Recipient Walker grand prize Boston Soc. Natural History, 1939; Meritorious Tchrs. award Assn. Southeastern Biologists, 1954; certificate of merit Bot. Soc. Am., 1956; first N.C. award in sci., 1964. Fellow A.A.A.S. (v.p.; chmn. botany sect. 1962); mem. Nat. Acad. Sci. India (hon. fgn. mem.), Bot. Soc. Am. (chmn. Southeastern section 1951), Am. Mycol. Soc. (pres. 1943), Nat. Acad. Sci. (U.S.A.), Am. Mosquito Control Assn., N.C. Acad. Sci. (pres. 1946-47, Jefferson award, Poteat medal 1937), Indian Phytopath. Soc., Elisha Mitchell Sci. Soc. (pres. 1937-38), Sigma Xi. Democrat. Baptist. Research on sexuality, culture and ciliary structure of water fungi; symbiosis between scale insects and fungi; fungi parasitic in mosquitoes; discovered Actinoplanaceae (Actinomycetales). Home: 1109 Carol Woods Chapel Hill NC 27514

COUCH, ROBERT BARNARD, physician; b. Guntersville, Ala., Sept. 25, 1930; s. Ezekiel Harvey and Frances Jane (Barnard) C.; m. Katherine Frances Klein, Apr. 23, 1955; children—Robert Steven, Leslie Ann, Colleen Frances, Elizabeth Lee. B.A., Vanderbilt U., 1952, M.D., 1956. Diplomate: Am. Bd. Internal Medicine. Intern Vanderbilt U. Hosp., Nashville, 1956-57, resident in medicine, 1959-61; clin. asso. NIH, Washington, 1957-59, sr. investigator, 1961-65, head clin. virology sect., 1965-66; asso. prof. Baylor Coll. Medicine, Houston, 1966-71, dir. influenza research center, 1974—, prof. microbiology and immunology and medicine, 1971—; mem. research rev. panels infectious diseases VA; cons. NIH, Dept. Def. Contbr. articles to med. jours. Served to sr. surgeon USPHS, 1957-66. Mem. Soc. Exptl. Biology and Medicine, Am. Soc. Microbiology, Infectious Diseases Soc. Am., AAAS, Am. Assn. Immunologists, A.C.P., Am. Fedn. Clin. Research, So. Soc. Clin. Investigation, Am. Soc. Clin. Investigation, Am. Assn. Physicians, Am. Soc. Epidemiology. Office: 1200 Moursund Ave Houston TX 77030

COUCH, VIRGIL LEE, govt. ofcl.; b. Princeton, Ky., Nov. 12, 1907; s. John and Malta Ann (Duke) C.; m. Martha Pence Duncan, Dec. 24, 1931 (dec. Mar. 14, 1949); 1 son, John Lee; m. Violet Mae Showers, Aug. 29, 1952. B.S., U. Ky., 1930. Personnel officer several govtl. agys., 1935-51; dep. asst. adminstr., dir. personnel, dir. Nat. Civil Def. Staff Coll. and Tng. Center; exec. officer for tng. and edn., dir. field exercises Atomic Test Operations; dir. warden div., dir. industry office FCDA, OCDM; also asst. dir. civil def. Office Civil Def. and Def. Civil Preparedness Agy., Dept. Def., Washington, 1951—. Author articles and booklets in field. Chmn. Arlington County (Va.) Civil Service Commn., 1951-54; mem. Arlington County Merit System Review Bd., 1950- 51. Recipient award for greatest contbn. to nat. def.; Distinguished Service citation Am. Soc. Indsl. Security, 1972; Distinguished Alumni award U. Ky., 1961; named to Ky. Hall of Fame, 1970. Mem. Soc. Personnel Adminstrn. (nat. pres. 1949-50), Soc. Advancement Mgmt. (v.p. 1949-50), Am. Soc. Indsl. Security (hon. mem.), Alpha Delta Sigma, Delta Sigma Pi, Alpha Tau Omega, and others. Democrat. Methodist. Clubs: Mason (32, Shriner), University of Kentucky (Washington); Pyramid (Lexington, Ky.); Optimist. Home: 4906 N 28th St Arlington VA 22207

COUDERT, FERDINAND WILMERDING, lawyer; b. N.Y.C., Feb. 9, 1909; s. Frederic Rene and Alice Tracy (Wilmerding) C.; m. Helen F. Carey, Oct. 14, 1942; dec. Oct. 1971. A.B. magna cum laude, Harvard, 1930, A.M., 1933; LL.B., Columbia, 1937. Bar: N.Y. 1938. Practiced in N.Y.C., 1938—; mem. firm Coudert Bros., 1938-64. Past pres. bd. Brez Found.; bd. dirs., past v.p. Humanities Fund; past sec., bd. dirs. C.T. Loo Chinese Ednl. Fund. Served from 1st lt. to maj. AUS, 1942-46. Fellow Frick Collection.; Mem. France Am. Soc. (dir.), Soc. Colonial Wars. Clubs: Paris American (past pres.); Century, University, Sky (N.Y.C.); Union Interalliee (Paris). Home: Rural Route 2 Joshuatown Rd Box 294 Old Lyme CT 06371

COUEY, DUANE EMERSON, church administrator; b. Milw., Sept. 13, 1924; s. Ralph Emerson and Hazel Viola (Lindsey) C.; m. Edith Rosalyn Griswold, Sept. 6, 1947 (dec. Sept. 1982); children: Patricia Louise, Ralph Floyd. Student, U. Wis., 1946-47; B.A. in Religious Studies, Park Coll., 1978. Lithographer, Moebious Printing Co., Milw., 1942; fabricator Product Miniature Co., Inc., Milw., 1946-54, supt. mfg., 1947-54; ch. adminstr. Memphis dist. Reorganized Ch. Jesus Christ of Latter-Day Saints, 1954-57, asst. to first presidency, 1958, pres. Los Angeles Stake, 1959-60, mem. council Twelve Apostles, 1960, mem. first presidency, 1966-82, presiding patriarch, 1982—. Contbr. articles to religious jours. Mem. Citizens' Adv. Com. Selection Chief of Police, Independence, Mo., 1968; bd. corporators Independence Sanitarium and Hosp., trustee, 1966-72. Served with USNR, 1943-46. Office: The Auditorium PO Box 1059 Independence MO 64051

COUGHANOWR, DONALD RAY, educator; b. Brazil, Ind., Mar. 11, 1928; s. Ray L. and Anna (Burdon) C.; m. Effie Natsis, Mar. 6, 1955; children—Corinne Ann, Christine Ann, David Donald. B.S., Rose Poly. Inst., 1949; M.S., U. Pa., 1951; Ph.D. in Chem. Engring, U. Ill., 1956. Process engr. Standard Oil Co. Ind., Whiting, 1951-53; prof. chem. engring. Purdue U., 1956-67; prof., head dept. chem. engring. Drexel U., 1967—; cons. Dow Chem. Co., Electronic Assos., Inc. Author: Process Systems Analysis and Control, 1965. Mem. Am. Inst. Chem. Engrs., Instrument Soc. Am., Am. Soc. Engring. Edn., Tau Beta Pi. Home: 504 Midland Circle St Davids PA 19087 Office: Drexel University 32nd and Chestnut Sts Philadelphia PA 19104

COUGHLAN, GARY PATRICK, food corporation executive; b. Fresno, Calif., Feb. 14, 1944; s. Edward Patrick and Elizabeth Claire (Ryan) C.; m. Mary Cary Kelley, Dec. 21, 1967; children: Christopher, Sarah, Laura, Claire, Moira. B.A., St. Mary's Coll., 1966; M.A. in Econs., UCLA, 1967; M.B.A., Wayne State U., 1971. Sr. fin. analyst Burroughs Corp., Detroit, 1969-72; group v.p. field service Dart Industries, Los Angeles, 1972-78, v.p. ops. services, 1978-81, Dart & Kraft Inc., Northbrook, Ill., 1981-82; v.p. fin. retail food group Kraft Inc., Glenview, Ill., 1982—; instr., prof. fin. Extension Program UCLA, 1974-80. Mem. Fin. Execs. Inst.(Chgo.). Republican. Roman Catholic. Home: 1135 Central Rd Glenview IL 60025 Office: Kraft Inc Kraft Court Glenview IL 60025

COUGHLAN, JOHN APPLEBY, economics educator; b. Silver Spring, Md., Feb. 16, 1929; s. Paul Mackin and Frances (Appleby) C. Student, U. Md., 1947-49; B.A., Villanova U., 1952; M.A., Catholic U. Am., 1958, Ph.D., 1965; post-doctoral research, London Sch. Econs., 1981-82. Entered Order of St. Augustine, 1949, ordained priest, 1955; tchr. math. and econs., social studies dir. Archbishop Carroll High Sch., 1956-63; prof. econs. Villanova U., 1964-68, 81—, chmn. econs. dept., 1964-68; v.p. acad. affairs, dean of coll. Merrimack Coll., 1968-75, exec. v.p., 1975-76, pres., 1976-81; Trustee Villanova U., 1974-82. Mem. Am. Econ. Assn. Address: Dept Econs Villanova U Villanova PA 19085

COUGHLAN, (JOHN) ROBERT, author, journalist; b. Kokomo, Ind., July 7, 1914; s. William Henry and Lucile DeNevers (Ernsperger) C.; m. Patricia Ann Collins, June 30, 1939; children—John Robert, Brian Christopher, Kevin Brooks, Cynthia Davis. B.S., Northwestern U., 1936. Mem. staff Fortune mag., 1937-43, asso. editor, 1938-43; text editor Life mag., 1943-49, mem. editorial staff as writer-editor, 1943-70; editorial asso. Kennedy Found., 1971-73. Now contbr. to various jours. and publs.; Author: The Wine of Genius, 1951, The Private World of William Faulkner, 1954, Tropical Africa, 1962, The World of Michelangelo, 1966, Elizabeth and Catherine, 1974, (collaborated with Rose Kennedy on memoirs) Times to Remember, 1974; contbr. anthologies, newspapers, mags. Recipient Benjamin Franklin award, 1953; Lasker award for med. journalism, 1954, 59; Benjamin Franklin citation, 1954; citation for excellence Overseas Press Club, 1957; Sigma Delta Chi award for Distinguished Service to Journalism, 1959; merit citation Nat. Edn. Writers Assn., 1961; award of recognition Northwestern U., 1962; Heywood Broun citation Am. Newspaper Guild, 1963; Ann. Book award Nat. Assn. Ind. Schs., 1967; Putnam award, 1974. Club: Century Assn. Address: Madison St Sag Harbor NY 11963

COUGHLAN, PATRICK CAMPBELL, lawyer; b. Orange, N.J., May 28, 1940; s. Gerald Noel and Carten (Van Schuick) C.; m. Marlee Turner, Aug. 9, 1974; children—Kimberly Campbell, Devon Gerald, Carter Turner. B.A., Duke U., 1962, J.D., 1965. Bar: Fla. 1965, U.S. Supreme Ct. 1968, Calif. 1974. Asso. firm Alley, Maass, Rogers, Lindsay & Chauncey, Palm Beach, Fla., 1969-72, partner, 1972-74; judge Municipal Ct., Ocean Ridge, Fla., 1970-72; asso. firm Richards, Watson, Dreyfuss & Gershon, Los Angeles, 1974-75, partner, 1975—; atty. City of Rancho Palos Verdes (Calif.), 1975-82, City of San Fernando (Calif.), 1977-82, City of Rancho Palos Verdes, Seal Beach, Calif., 1978—, La Habra Heights, Calif., 1979—, Avalon, Calif., 1981—, Rolling Hills, Calif., 1981—, Westlake Village, Calif., 1981—. Pres. No. Pines, Inc.; Trustee, sec. Gulf Stream Sch. Found., Inc.; bd. dirs. Mountains Restoration Trust., 1981-82. Served to capt. USAF, 1965-68. Mem. Am. Bar Assn., State Bar Calif., Fla. Bar, Los Angeles County Bar Assn. Roman Catholic. Club: Los Angeles Athletic. Home and Office: RR Box 279 RT 285 Raymond ME 04071

COUGHLIN, BARRING, lawyer; b. Wilkes-Barre, Pa., Dec. 19, 1913; s. Clarence Dennis and Helen Verner (Barring) C.; m. Harriet Stager Curtiss, Nov. 15, 1941; children: Barring, Curtis, Dennis, Constance Coughlin Howe. A.B., Princeton U., 1935; J.D. magna cum laude, Harvard U., 1938. Bar: D.C. 1939, Ohio 1940. Law clk. to presiding justice U.S. Ct. Appeals, Washington, 1938-39; assoc. Thompson, Hine & Flory, Cleve., 1939-53; ptnr. Thompson. Hine & Flory, Cleve., 1953—. Trustee Citizens League, 1958-66, Cuyahoga County Hosp. Found., 1964-66, Cleve. Homemakers Service Assn., 1966-68, Medusa Found., 1969—, Cyrus Eaton Found., 1968—. Served to lt. USCG, 1942-45. Mem. ABA, Am. Law Inst., Ohio Bar Assn., Cleve. Bar Assn. Republican. Presbyterian. Clubs: Adirondack League (Old Forge, N.Y.); Chagrin Valley Hunt (Gates Mills, Ohio); City (Cleve.); Edgewater Yacht; Mid-Day (Cleve.); Princeton (N.Y.C.); Union (Cleve.). Home: 2290 Ardleigh Dr Cleveland Heights OH 44106 Office: 629 Euclid Ave 1100 Nat City Bank Bldg Cleveland OH 44114

COUGHLIN, BERNARD JOHN, university president; b. Galveston, Tex., Dec. 7, 1922; s. Eugene J. and Celeste M. (Ott) C. A.B., St. Louis U., 1946, Ph.L., 1949, S.T.L., 1956; M.S.W., U. So. Calif., 1959; Ph.D., Brandeis U., 1963. Joined S.J., Roman Cath. Ch., 1942, ordained priest, 1955; tchr., counselor chs. in, Wis. and Kans., 1949-54; research asst. Los Angeles Juvenile Probation Project, 1959; social work ednl. cons., Guatemala City, summer 1960; mem. faculty St. Louis U., 1961-74; prof. Sch. Social Service, 1970-74, dean, 1964-74; pres. Gonzaga U., Spokane, Wash., 1974—; mem. program com. Nat. Conf. Cath. Charities, 1964-68, mem. com. legislation social justice, 1973—, bd. dirs., 1973—, mem. com. study and study cadre, 1970-72; mem. adv. com. social welfare service Model Cities, St. Louis, 1967-68; council social work edn. Commn. Internat. Social Work Edn., 1968-81, adv. com. project on integrative teaching and learning, 1968-69, adv. com. population dynamics and family planning, 1969-71, structure rev. com., 1970-71; bd. dirs. Health and Welfare Council Met. St. Louis, 1968-74; chmn. task force community planning Child Welfare League Am., 1967-69; chmn. Conf. Deans Schs. Social Work, 1972-73; chmn. nominating com. U.S. com. Internat. Council Social Work, 1973—; cons. in field, del. internat. confs.; mem. Assn. Governing Bds., 1980-81, Council for Postsecondary Edn., 1979—. Author: Church and State in Social Welfare, 1965, also articles, revs., chpts. in books. Bd. dirs. United Way Spokane County, 1982—; mem. Inland Empire council Boy Scouts Am., 1982—; mem. Nat. Conf. Cath. Charities. Fulbright lectr. Colombia, 1970, 71; Grantee NIMH, 1963-68. Mem. Nat. Assn. Social Workers (chmn. cabinet div. profl. standards 1970-73), Internat. Assn. Schs. Social Work, Internat. Council Social Welfare, Nat. Conf. Social Welfare., Internat. Assn. Univ. Pres. (vice chmn. U.S. western regional council 1982—, mem. steering com. 1982—), Council Social Work Edn., Mo. Assn. for Social Welfare. Address: Gonzaga U Spokane WA 99258

COUGHLIN, EDMOND, insurance company executive; b. Annapolis, Md., June 24, 1924; s. William C. and Helen (Johnson) C.; s. Betty Ann Heise, June 28, 1947; children: John Allen, Mary Carol, Janice Ann, Mark Edmond, Daniel. B.S. in Bus., U. Balt., 1952. With Nationwide Ins. Co., Columbus, Ohio, 1953—, sr. v.p. ops., 1981—; dir. Colonial Ins. Co., Anaheim, Calif., Scottsdale Ins. Co., Ariz. Past pres. Ohio Soc. to Prevent Blindness. Served with AUS, 1943-46; ETO. Recipient Exec. of Year award Columbus chpt. Profl. Secs. Internat., 1972, Young Man of Year award Anne Arundel County Jr. C. of C., (Md.), 1959. Mem. Nat. Assn. Life Underwriters, Columbus Life Underwriters Assn, Life Ins. Mktg. Research Assn. (mem. research council). Roman Catholic. Office: Nationwide Ins Co One Nationwide Plaza Columbus OH 43216

COUGHLIN, JACK, printmaker, sculptor, art educator; b. Greenwich, Conn., Feb. 19, 1932; s. John J. and Gabrielle S. (Jones) C.; m. Joan M. Hopkins, July 5, 1958; children: Maura, Molly. Student, Art Students League, N.Y.C., 1950-52; B.F.A., R.I. Sch. Design, 1954, M.S., 1961. Asst. prof. art U. Mass., Amherst, 1964-68, asso. prof., 1968-73, prof., 1973—. One-man shows, Hendriks Gallery, Dublin, Ireland, 1971, 74, 76, 78, 80, 83, Harvard U., 1974, Associated Am. Artists, N.Y.C., 1977, group shows include, 17th Biennial Am. Printmaking, Bklyn., 1970, Davidson Nat. Print Show, 1973, NAD, 1974-79, numerous others; represented in permanent collections, Met. Museum Art, N.Y.C., Mus. Modern Art, N.Y.C., Nat. Collection Arts, Washington. Served with U.S. Army, 1954-56. Recipient numerous awards, prizes for work, including; Am. Drawing Biennial award, 1965; Nat. Inst. Arts and Letters award, 1969. Mem. NAD (asso.), Soc. Am. Graphic Artists (Madson award for etching 1977), Boston Printmakers. Home: N Leverett Rd Montague MA 01351

COUGHLIN, LAWRENCE, Congressman; b. Wilkes-Barre, Pa.; s. R. Lawrence and Evelyn (Wich) C.; m. Susan MacGregor; 4 children. A.B., Yale U.; M.B.A., Harvard U.; LL.B., Temple U. Former mem. Pa. Senate, Pa. Ho. of Reps.; mem. 91-98th Congresses from 13th Pa. Dist., mem. appropriations com., ranking mem. trans. subcom. Bd. dirs. Easter Seal Soc., Big Bros. Assn., Montgomery County Opportunities Industrialization Ctr., Med. Coll. Pa. Served to capt. USMC; Korea. Recipient first human rights award Interreligious Task Force on Soviet Jewry, Montgomery County Opportunities Industrialization Ctr.; named outstanding young man Main Line C. of C. Mem. Am. Legion, Mil. Order of Fgn. Wars, Marine Corps League. Office: Room 2467 Rayburn House Office Bldg Washington DC 20515

COUGHLIN, RICHARD JOHN, construction company executive,, educator; b. Montclair, N.J., Aug. 22, 1931; s. Jeremiah A. and Caroline (Landwehr) C.; m. Eileen Crann, Dec. 29, 1956; children—Anne, Richard, Mary Beth, Carolyn. B.S. in Acctg., Seton Hall U., 1953; M.B.A., Rutgers U., 1959. C.P.A., N.J. Staff acct. Peat, Marwick, Mitchell & Co. (C.P.A.'s), Newark, 1956-60; asst. gen. mgr. Tiffany & Co., Newark, 1960-64; with Frank Briscoe Co., Inc., Newark, 1964-81, treas., controller, 1966-70, exec. v.p., 1970-79, pres., 1979-81; exec. v.p. T.J. McGlone, Edison, N.J., 1981-82; chmn. bus. div. Mt. St. Mary Coll., Newburgh, N.Y., 1982—; dir. Carteret Savs. and Loan Assn. Served with USNR, 1953-56; capt. Res. Mem. Nat. Assn. Accts., Fin. Execs. Inst., N.J. Soc. C.P.A.s. Home: 29 Fairview Pl Upper Montclair NJ 07043 Office: Mt St Mary Coll Bus Div Newburgh NY 12550

COULLING, SIDNEY BAXTER, educator; b. Bluefield, W.Va., Feb. 13, 1924; s. Louis Roberdeau and Eva (Steger) C.; m. Mary Price Stirling, June 23, 1958; children—Margaret Howard, Anne Baxter, Philip Price. A.B., Washington and Lee U., 1948; M.A., U. N.C., 1949, Ph.D., 1957. Engaged as instr. of English Fla. State U., 1949-52, U. Md., 1955-56; mem. faculty Washington and Lee U., 1956—, prof. English, 1965—. Author: Matthew Arnold and His Critics, 1974. Served with AUS, 1943-46. Mem. Modern Lang. Assn. Am., Phi Beta Kappa. Home: 604 Marshall St Lexington VA 24450

COULMAN, GEORGE ALBERT, chemical engineer, educator; b. Detroit, June 29, 1930; s. William John Thompson and Mary (Coulman); m. Annette Marie Felder, Sept. 1, 1956; children: Karl, Paula. B.S., Case Inst. Tech., 1952, Ph.D. (Ford Found. fellow), 1962; M.S., U. Mich., 1958. Process devel. engr. Dow Corning Corp., Midland, Mich., 1954-57; mgr. devel. Am. Metal Products Co., Ann Arbor, Mich., 1958-60; asst. prof. chem. engring. U. Waterloo (Ont., Can.), 1961-64; mem. faculty Mich. State U., East Lansing, 1964-76, prof. chem. engring., 1974-76; prof. chem. engring., chmn. dept. Cleve. State U., 1976—; cons. in field. Author numerous papers in field. Served with AUS, 1952-54. Mem. Am. Inst. Chem. Engrs., Combustion Inst., Am. Chem. Soc., Am. Soc. Engring. Edn., Cleve. Engring. Soc. Office: 1963 E 24th St Cleveland OH 44115

COULSON, JOHN SELDEN, marketing consultant; b. Chgo., Aug. 14, 1915; s. Leonard Ward and Mabel (Selden) C.; m. Jane Eleanor Rinder, Nov. 28, 1943; children: Jane Greer, Nancy Allen Coulson Hobor, Ann Selden Coulson Hubbard, Sara Rinder Coulson Ellis. B.A., U. Chgo., 1936; M.B.A., Harvard, 1938. With Montgomery Ward & Co., Chgo., 1938-41, 45-48; sr. asso. Joseph White & Assos., Chgo., 1948-50; research supr. Leo Burnett Co., Inc., Chgo., 1950-55, mgr. research dept., 1955-58, v.p. charge research, 1958-77; dir. Leo Burnett USA, 1973-77; partner Communications Workshop, Inc., 1977—; lectr. U. Chgo., 1955, 78, Northwestern U., 1960-71, Columbia Coll., 1974-76, U. Ill., 1977. Mktg. Issues editor: Jour. Mktg. 1960-81; editorial bd.: Jour. Advt, 1971—; mem. policy bd.: Jour. Consumer Research, 1972-79; Contbr.: chpts. to On Knowing the Consumer, 1966, Handbook of Modern Marketing, 1970. Mem. citizens bd. U. Chgo., 1969—; bd. mgrs. Lawson YMCA, Chgo., 1970—; bd. govs. Chgo. Heart Assn., 1980—. Served to lt. comdr. USNR, 1941-45. Mem. Am. Statis. Assn. (past pres. Chgo. chpt.), Am. Marketing Assn. (past pres. Chgo. chpt., nat. v.p.), Am. Assn. for Pub. Opinion Research (exec. council 1969-72, 78-81), U. Chgo. Alumni Assn. (pres. 1969-73), Psi Upsilon, Alpha Kappa Psi. Clubs: Univ., Plaza (Chgo.); Harvard Bus. Sch. of Chgo. (bd. dirs. 1976-82). Home: 175 E Delaware Pl Apt 9009 Chicago IL 60611 Office: 168 N Michigan Ave Chicago IL 60601

COULSON, KINSELL LEROY, meteorologist; b. Hatfield, Mo., Oct. 7, 1916; s. Charles Samuel and Nora Madge (Swank) C.; m. Vera Vivien Vainer, Mar. 23, 1947. B.S., Northwest Mo. State Tchrs. Coll., 1942; M.A., UCLA, 1952, Ph.D., 1959. Jr. meteorologist U.S. Weather Bur., Chgo., 1942; meteorologist UN, Shanghai, China, 1946-47, Naval Civil Service, China Lake, Calif., 1950-51; assoc. research meteorologist UCLA, 1951-59; meteorologist Stanford Research Inst., Menlo Park, Calif., 1959-60; mgr. geophysics Gen. Electric Space Scis. Lab., Phila., 1960-65; prof. meteorology U. Calif.-Davis, 1965-79; dir. Mauna Loa Obs., Hilo, Hawaii, 1979—; cons., lectr. Author: Solar and Terrestrial Radiation: Methods and Measurements, 1975, (with J.V. Dave and Z. Sekera) Tables Related to Radiation Emerging, From a Planetary Atmosphere with Rayleigh Scattering, 1960; contbr. articles to profl. jours.; patentee atmospheric density calulator. Served with USN, 1943-46. Recipient numerous research grants. Mem. Am. Meteorol. Soc., Am. Geophys. Union, Am. Solar Energy Soc., AAAS, No. Calif. Energy Assn., Planetary Soc., Mauna Kea Astron. Soc., Sigma Xi. Home: 2405 Kalanianaole PH-11 Hilo HI 96720 Office: Mauna Loa Obs Rm 202 Fed Bldg Hilo HI 96720

COULSON, ROBERT, association executive; b. New Rochelle, N.Y., July 24, 1924; s. Robert Earl and Abby (Stewart) C.; m. Cynthia Cunningham, Oct. 15, 1960; children: Cotton Richard, Dierdre, Crocker, Robert Cromwell, Christopher. B.A., Yale, 1950; LL.B., Harvard U., 1953. Bar: N.Y. and Mass. 1954. Assoc. Whitman, Ransom & Coulson, N.Y.C., 1954-61; partner Littlefield, Miller & Cleaves, N.Y.C., 1961-63; exec. v.p. Am. Arbitration Assn., N.Y.C., 1963-72, pres., 1972—; Cons. N.Y. State Div. Youth, 1961-63; pres. Youth Consultation Service of N.Y., 1970. Author: How to Stay Out of Court, 1968, Labor Arbitration: What You Need to Know, 1973, Business Arbitration: What You Need to Know, 1980, The Termination Handbook, 1981, Fighting Fair, 1983; Editor: Racing at Sea, 1958; Contbr. articles profl. jours. Bd. dirs. Fedn. Protestant Welfare Agys., pres., 1982-84; Bd. dirs. Internat. Council for Comml. Arbitration, Ctr. for Community Justice, Edmund Gould Found. for Children. Mem. Am., N.Y. State bar assns., Assn. Bar City N.Y. (sec. 1960-62). Clubs: New York Yacht, Riverside (Conn.) Yacht. Home: 9 Reginald Rd Riverside CT 06878 Office: 140 W 51st St New York NY 10020

COULTER, ELIZABETH JACKSON, biostatistician; b. Balt., Nov. 2, 1919; d. Waddie Pennington and Bessie (Gills) Jackson; m. Norman Arthur Coulter Jr., June 23, 1951; 1 son, Robert Jackson. A.B., Swarthmore Coll., 1941; A.M., Radcliffe Coll., 1946, Ph.D., 1948. Asst. dir. health study Bur. Labor Statss., San Juan, P.R., 1946; research asst. Milbank Meml. Fund, N.Y.C., 1948-51; economist Office Def. Prodn., 1951-52; research analyst Children's Bur.-HEW, 1952-53; statistician, then chief statistician Ohio Dept. Health, 1954-65; lectr. econs., then clin. asst. prof. preventive medicine Ohio State U., 1964-65; asst. clin. prof. biostats. U. Pitts. Sch. Pub. Health, 1958-62; assoc. prof. biostats. U. N.C., Chapel Hill, 1965-72, prof., 1972—, assoc. dean undergrad. pub. health studies, 1979—, assoc. prof. econs., 1965-78; adj. assoc. prof. hosp. adminstrn. Duke U., 1972-79. Contbr. articles to profl. jours. Mem. Am. Pub. Health Assn. (govering council 1970-72), Am. Econ. Assn., Am. Statis. Assn., Am. Acad. Polit. and Social Sci., AAAS, Biometric Soc., Sigma Xi, Delta Omega. Methodist. Home: 1825 N Lake Shore Dr Chapel Hill NC 27514 Office: Sch Pub Health U NC Chapel Hill NC 27514

COULTER, JAMES BENNETT, state ofcl.; b. Vinita, Okla., Aug. 2, 1920; s. Robert Leslie and Louise (Robinson) C.; m. Norma R. Brink, June 1, 1942; children—Linda Coulter Prandoni, James Bennett. B.S. in Civil Engring, U. Kans., 1950; M.S., Harvard U., 1954; D.Sc. (hon.), Washington Coll., 1979. Registered profl. engr., Md., Kans. Commd. officer USPHS, 1950-66; asst. commr. environ. health Md. Dept. Health, Balt., 1966-69; sec. Md. Dept. Natural Resources, Annapolis, 1969—; mem. vis. com. Sch. Engring. and Applied Physics, Harvard. Bd. dirs. Blue Shield Md.; trustee Chesapeake Research Consortium. Served with C.E. AUS, 1940-45. Decorated Bronze Star. Mem. Am. Acad. Environ. Engrs. (Gordon M. Fair award 1971, pres. 1978), ASCE, Am. Public Health Assn., Nat. Soc. Profl. Engrs., Am. Water Works Assn., Tau Beta Pi, Sigma Tau. Home: 1069 Double Gate Rd Davidsonville MD 21035 Office: Tawes Office Bldg Annapolis MD 21404

COULTER, MYRON LEE, university president; b. Albany, Ind., Mar. 21, 1929; s. Mark Earl and Thelma Violet (Marks) C.; m. Barbara Bolinger, July 21, 1951; children: Nan and Benjamin (twins). B.S., Indiana State Tchrs. Coll., 1951; M.S., Ind. U., 1956, Ed.D., 1959; H.L.D. (hon.), Coll. Idaho, 1982. Tchr. English, Reading Mich.) Pub. Schs., 1951-52; tchr. elementary grades Bloomington (Ind.) Pub. Schs., 1954-56; instr. edn. Ind. U., Bloomington, 1958-59; asst. prof. Pa. State U., 1959-64, asso. prof., 1964-66; vis. prof. U. Alaska, Fairbanks, 1965; asso. dean edn., prof. edn. Western Mich. U., Kalamazoo, 1966-68, v.p. for adminstrn., prof. edn., 1968-76, interim pres., 1974; pres. Idaho State U., Pocatello, 1976—; del. Israeli Univs., 1976, Am. Assn. State Colls. and Univs. to People's Republic of China, 1981; cons. in fields. Author school textbooks. Bd. dirs. Kalamazoo C. of C., 1975-76; lay leader Kalamazoo Meth. Ch., 1971-74; trustee Bronson Hosp., Kalamazoo, 1975-76; bd. dirs. Pocatello Jr. Achievement. Served with U.S. Army, 1952-54. Named Disting. Alumnus Ind. State U., 1975; recipient award Western Mich. U. Alumni Assn., 1974, resolution of tribute Mich. State Legislature, 1976. Mem. Internat. Reading Assn., Am. Assn. State Colls. and Univs. (bd. dirs. 1981—), Nat. Soc. for Study Edn., Western Coll. Assn. (exec. com. 1981—), Pocatello C. of C. (dir. 1977-80), Phi Delta Kappa, Omicron Delta Kappa. Clubs: Pocatello Country., Rotary. Home: 341 S 7th Ave Pocatello ID 83201 Office: Campus Box 8310 Idaho State U Pocatello ID 83209

COULTER, NORMAN ARTHUR, JR., university administrator; b. Atlanta, Jan. 9, 1920; s. Norman Arthur and Carabelle (Clark) C.; m. Elizabeth Harwell Jackson, June 23, 1951; 1 son, Robert Jackson. B.S., Va. Poly. Inst., 1941; M.D., Harvard U., 1950; postgrad. fellow, Johns Hopkins U., 1950-52. Instr. math. dept. Va. Poly. Inst., 1946; asst. to assoc. prof. physiology dept. Ohio State U., 1952-65; dir. biophysics div., physiology dept., 1962-65; assoc. prof. depts. surgery and physiology U. N.C., Chapel Hill, 1965-67, prof., 1967—, chmn. bioengrng.-biomath. program, 1969-82, dir. grad. studies, 1982—. Author: Synergetics: An Adventure in Human Development, 1976; also articles in profl. jours. Symergetics: An Adventure in Human

Development. Served to maj. A.A.A. AUS, 1941-46. Mem. Biophys. Soc., Am. Physiol. Soc., Biomed. Engring. Soc., Soc. Neurosci., IEEE, Soc. Gen. Systems Research, Assn. Computing Machinery, Physicians for Social Responsibility, Sigma Xi. Home: 1825 N Lake Shore Dr Chapel Hill NC 27514

COUNCE, SHIELA JEAN, anatomy educator; b. Hayes Center, Nebr., Mar. 18, 1927; d. Hardy Melva and Florence Ruth (Enyeart) C.; m. R. Bruce Nicklas, Sept. 17, 1960. B.A., U. Colo., 1948, M.A., 1950; Ph.D., Edinburgh U., (Scotland), 1954, postgrad., 1955-56; postgrad. (NSF fellow), U. Zurich, 1956-57. Research assoc. (Jackson Lab.), Bar Harbor, Maine, 1954-55, Yale U., New Haven, 1957-65; asst. prof. dept. anatomy Duke U., Durham, N.C., 1965-72, assoc. prof., 1972-78, prof., 1978—; mem. cell biology panel NIH, 1977-79. Author, editor: Developmental Systems: Insects, vol. 1, 1972; author: Development Systems: Insects, vol. 2, 1973. Fulbright scholar, 1950, 51; Atkinson fellow AAUW, 1952; MacCauley fellow, 1955-56; vis. sci. fellow Max-Planck Inst., Tubingen, Ger., 1972-73; vis. prof. Zool. Inst., Siena, Italy, 1979; NSF grantee, 1957-81. Fellow AAAS; mem. Am. soc. Cell Biology, Soc. Development Biology, Am. Soc. Naturalists, Am. Zoologists, Genetics Soc. Am. Democrat. Office: Duke U Dept Anatomy Durham NC 27710

COUNCE-NICKLAS, SHEILA JEAN, biologist; b. Hayes Center, Nebr., Mar. 18, 1927; d. Hardy Melva and Florence Ruth (Enyeart) Counce; m. (Robert) Bruce Nicklas, Sept. 17, 1960. B.A., U. Colo., 1948, M.A., 1950; Ph.D., Edinburgh (Scotland) U., 1953. Mem. staff Jackson Lab., Bar Harbor, Maine, 1954; NSF postdoctoral fellow U. Zurich, 1955-56; research assoc. Yale U., 1956-65; mem. faculty Duke U., 1965—, prof. anatomy, 1978—; mem. panel NIH, 1978-80. Contbr. articles to profl. jours.; co-editor: Development Systems, Insects, 2 vols., 1972-73. Fulbright fellow, 1950-52; AAUW fellow, 1952-53; Macauley fellow, 1954-55; NSF grantee, 1956-81. Fellow AAAS; mem. Genetics Soc., Soc. Devel. Biology, Am. Soc. Naturalists, Am. Soc. Zoologists, Am. Soc. Cell Biology, AAUP, N.C. Acad. Sci., S.E. Assn. Biologists, Sigma Xi. Democrat. Office: Dept Anatomy Duke U Med Ctr Durham NC 27710

COUNSELL, RAYMOND ERNEST, educator; b. Vancouver, C., Can., Aug. 20, 1930; s. Ernest and Florence Rose (Church) C.; m. Elizabeth Ann Short, Sept. 28, 1957; children—Steven Raymond, Ronald Lloyd, Catherine Ann. B.S.P., U. B.C., 1953; Ph.D., U. Minn., 1957. Sr. research chemist G.D. Searle & Co., Skokie, Ill., 1957-64; prof. medicinal chemistry and pharmacology U. Mich., Ann Arbor, 1964—; Cons. to pharm. industry and NIH. Contbr. articles to profl. jours. Recipient Gold medal for pharmacy Horner Labs., 1953; Am. Cancer Soc. research award, 1964; Czerniak prize for nuclear medicine, 1974; Eleanor Roosevelt Internat. fellow, 1972. Fellow Acad. Pharm. Scis. (chmn. sect. on medicinal chemistry 1971), AAAS; mem. Am. Chem. Soc. (chmn. div. medicinal chemistry 1971), Soc. Nuclear Medicine, Am. Soc. for Pharmacology and Exptl. Therapeutics. Patentee in field. Home: 2257 Delaware Dr Ann Arbor MI 48103

COUNSIL, WILLIAM GLENN, electric utility executive; b. Detroit, Dec. 13, 1937; s. Glenn Dempsey and Jean Beverly (Rzepecki) C.; m. Donna Elizabeth Robinson, Sept. 10, 1960; children: Glenn, Craig. Student, U. Mich., 1955-56; B.S., U.S. Naval Acad., 1960. Ops. supr., asst. plant supt. sta. supt. N.E. Nuclear Energy Co., Waterford, Conn., 1967-76; project mgr., v.p. nuclear engring. and ops. N.E. Utilities, Hartford, Conn., 1976-80, sr. v.p. nuclear engring. and ops., 1980—; dir. Conn. Yankee Atomic Power Co., Haddam Heck. Served with USN, 1956-67. Mem. Atomics Indsl. Forum (policy com.), Inst. Nuclear Power Ops. (chmn. industry rev. com.), Conn. Am. Nuclear Soc. Republican. Presbyterian. Home: 212 Natchaug Dr Glastonbury CT 06033 Office: PO Box 270 Hartford CT 06101 *My goal has been to improve our quality of life first through service in the United States Navy and second by ensuring an adequate and safe energy supply for our country.*

COUNSILMAN, JAMES EDWARD, educator; b. Birmingham, Ala., Dec. 28, 1920; s. Joseph Walter and Ottilia Lena (Schamburg) C.; m. Marjorie E. Scrafford, June 15, 1943; children: Cathy, James (dec.), Jill, Brian. B.S., Ohio State U., 1947; M.S., U. Ill., 1948; Ph.D., U. Iowa, 1951. Mem. phys. edn. faculty, swim coach Cortland (N.Y.) State U., 1952-57; mem. faculty Ind. U., Bloomington, 1957—, prof. phys. edn., 1966—, swim coach, 1957—; pres. Counsilman Co., Inc. (film producers and publishers), 1971—, Counsilman and Assos. (swimming pool constrn. cons.), 1971—. Author: The Science of Swimming, 1969, The Complete Book of Swimming, 1977, Competitive Swimming Manual, 1977. U.S. Olympic Men's Team coach, 1964, 76; founding pres. Internat. Swimming Hall of Fame, 1963. Served as bomber pilot USAAF, 1943-45. Decorated Air medal with cluster, D.F.C. Ind. swim teams have won 20 consecutive Big Ten Swimming championships, 1961-80, 83; 6 consecutive NCAA championships, 1968-73. Fellow Am. Coll. Sports Medicine; mem. AAHPER, Am. Swim Coaches Assn. (past pres.), Coll. Swim Coaches Assn., English Channel Swim Assn. (oldest person to successfully swim channel 1979). Home: 3806 Cameron Dr Bloomington IN 47401 Office: Assembly Hall Ind U Bloomington IN 47405

COUNTRYMAN, DAYTON WENDELL, lawyer; b. Sioux City, Iowa, Mar. 31, 1918; s. Cleve and Susie (Schaeffer) C.; m. Ruth Hazen, Feb. 2, 1941; children—Karen, Joan, James, Kay. B.S., Iowa State Coll., 1940; LL.B., State U. Iowa, 1948, J.D., 1969. Bar: Iowa bar 1948. Since practiced in, Nevada; ptnr. Hadley & Countryman, Nevada, Iowa, 1949-64; now ptnr. Countryman & Zaffarano P.C.; county atty. Story County (Iowa), 1950- 54; atty. gen. Iowa, 1954-56; Candidate for U.S. Senate, 1956, 1960, 68. Air Force Res. pilot USAAF, 1941-46. Mem. VFW, Am. Judicature Soc., Am. Legion, Iowa State U. Alumni Assn. (pres. 1970-71), Am., Iowa, Story County bar assns., Iowa 2B Jud. Dist. Assn. Methodist. Clubs: Masons, Lions (pres. 1975-76). Home: Route 1 PO Box 28 Nevada IA 50201 Office: 505 J Ave Nevada IA 50201

COUNTRYMAN, EDWARD FRANCIS, historian, educator; b. Glens Falls, N.Y., July 31, 1944; s. Edward Francis and Agnes (Alford) C.; 1 son, Samuel Robert. B.A., Manhattan Coll., 1966; M.A., Cornell U., Ithaca, N.Y., 1969, Ph.D., 1971. Lectr. in histroy U. Canterbury (N.Z.), 1970-74; lectr. U. Warwick (Eng.), 1975-83, sr. lectr., 1983—; vis. lectr. U. Cambridge (Eng.), 1979-80, NYU, N.Y.C., 1980-81. Cons. editor: Radical History Rev., 1982—; author: A People in Revolution, 1981 (Bancroft prize 1982). Active civil rights movement, U.S., 1965-68; spokesperson Anti-War Movement, N.Z., 1970-73; active Campaign for Nuclear Disarmament, Eng., 1981—. Woodrow Wilson fellow, 1966-67; Danforth fellow, 1966-71; Samuel Foster Haven fellow, 1983. Mem. Brit. Assn. Am. Studies. Home: 1 Beauchamp Ave Leamington Spa Warwicks England CV32 5RE Office: Comparative Am. Studies U Warwick Conventry England CV4 7AL

COUNTRYMAN, GARY LEE, insurance company executive; b. South Bend, Wash., July 30, 1939; s. William T. and Vernela K. (Stewart) C.; m. Sally Ann Mathews, Aug. 16, 1958; children: Christopher John, Susan Michelle, Sherry LeeAnn, Stefanie May. B.S., U. Oreg., 1961, M.S., 1963. With Liberty Mut. Ins. Co., Boston, 1963—, pres., 1981—; dir. Liberty Mut. Ins. Group, Bank of Boston Corp., 1st Nat. Bank of Boston. H.T. Miner fellow, 1962-63. Mem. Am. Inst. Property and Liability Underwriters. Club: Algonquin (Boston). Office: Liberty Mut Ins Co 175 Berdeley St Boston MA 02117

COUNTRYMAN, JOHN RUSSELL, ambassador; b. Bklyn., Jan. 25, 1933; s. H. Russell and Lucille Ida (Pliska) C.; m. Illona Zwolski Vachon, May 20, 1973; 1 dau., Vanessa Ann. B.S., Fordham U., 1954; student Fulbright scholar, U. Berlin, Germany, 1954-55; M.A., U. Miami-Fla., 1961; student, Army War Coll., 1975-76. Commd. fgn. service officer Dept. State, 1962, vice consul, Istanbul, 1963-65, staff aide to ambassador-at-large Harriman, 1965-66, chief econ. sect. U.S. Consul, Dhahran, 1968-70, dept. prin. officer U.S. Consul, 1970-71, chief econ. sect. Am. Embassy, Tripoli, Libya, 1971-73, dep. chief of mission Am. Embassy, Libreville, Gabon, 1973-75, dep. dir. Arabian Peninsula Affairs, Washington, 1976-78, dep., acting dir. Near Eastern Regional Affairs, 1978-79, dir. Arabian Peninsula Affairs, 1979-81, ambassador to the Sultanate of Oman, 1981—. Served with USAF, 1956-58. Mem. Middle East Inst., Phi Kappa Phi. Republican. Roman Catholic. Home: 4505 Macomb St NW Washington DC 20016 Office: American Embassy Muscat Dept. State Washington DC 20520

COUNTRYMAN, VERN, educator; b. Roundup, Mont., May 13, 1917; s. Alexander and Carrie (Harriman) C.; m. Vera Pound, Nov. 9, 1940; children—Kay, Debra. B.A., U. Wash., 1939, LL.B., 1942; student, Yale Law Sch., 1947-48. Bar: Wash. State bar 1942, Md. bar 1955, D.C. bar 1956, Mass. bar 1965. Law clk. to Justice William O. Douglas, 1942- 43; asst. atty. general Wash. State, 1946; instr. U. Wash. Sch. Law, 1946-47; asst., then asso. prof. law Yale Law Sch., 1948-55; practice law with firm Shea, Greenman & Gardner, Washington, 1955-59; dean U. N.Mex. Sch. Law, 1959-64; prof. law Harvard, 1964—. Served with USAAF, 1943-46. Mem. Am. Bar Assn., Order of Coif, Phi Beta Kappa. Home: 98 Adams St Lexington MA 02173

COUNTS, JAMES CURTIS, management consultant; b. Goldfield, Colo., Aug. 2, 1915; s. James Henry and Georgine (Niesley) C.; m. Virginia Lee Shugart, Oct. 10, 1940; children: Carol Lee Counts Hooper, Janis Lee Counts Ocean, Jay Curtis. A.B. in Polit. Sci., UCLA, 1937; postgrad., U. So. Calif., 1937-39, Southwestern Law Sch., 1939-41. With Douglas Aircraft Co., Inc., 1941-69, dir. employee relations, 1962-64, v.p. employee relations, 1964-69; mem. Nat. Labor Mgmt. Panel, 1963-68, Pacific Coast Regional Manpower Adv. Com., 1964-68; pub. mem. Constrn. Industry Collective Bargaining Commn., 1969—; dir. Fed. Mediation and Conciliation Service, 1969-73, mem. collective bargaining com. in constrn., 1974—; pres. Contractors Mut. Assn., 1973-77, Trucking Mgmt. Inc., 1978-81; mgmt. cons., 1981—. Mem. Citizens Adv. Council on Status of Women, 1967-69; chmn. bd. mgrs. Los Angeles YMCA, 1947—; bd. dirs. UCLA Alumni Bd., 1962-64; nat. trustee NCCJ, 1974—, Amyotrophic Lateral Sclerosis Soc. Am., 1982—. Mem. Westwood (Calif.) Jaycees (pres. 1950-51), Blue Key, Zeta Psi. Presbyterian (trustee). Home: 3105 Haddington Dr Los Angeles CA 90064

COUNTS, STANLEY THOMAS, electronics company executive, retired naval officer; b. Okfuskee County, Okla., July 3, 1926; s. Claud Curtley and Thelma (Thomas) C.; m. Bettejan Heft, Nov. 18, 1949; 1 dau., Ashlie Heft. B.S., U.S. Naval Acad., 1949, U.S. Naval Postgrad. Sch., 1954, M.S., 1955. Commd. ensign U.S. Navy, 1949, advanced through grades to rear adm., 1972; comdg. officer USS Bronstein, 1963-64, comdg. officer USS Towers, 1966-68, project mgr. NATO Seasparrow Surface Missile System, 1968-70, comdg. officer USS Chgo., 1970-71, dir. ships, weapons, electronics and asso. systems Office Asst. Sec. Def. for Installations and Logistics, Washington, 1971-73, dep. comdr. Naval Ordnance Systems Command, 1973-74, comdr., 1974, vice comdr. Naval Sea Systems Command, 1974-76, comdr. Cruiser-Destroyer Group 5, San Diego, 1976-78, ret., 1978; exec. Hughes Aircraft Co., Fullerton, Calif., 1979—. Decorated Legion of Merit with 3 oak leaf clusters, Bronze Star. Home: 856 La Jolla Rancho Rd LaJolla CA 92037 Office: Hughes Aircraft Co Fullerton CA 92634

COUPE, IRENE FAY, publishing company executive; b. Rapid City, S.D., Mar. 31, 1928; d. John and Dorothy Alberta (Barr) Drips; m. Lawrence Edgar Coupe, June 25, 1951; children—Cecil John, Larry Douglas. Student, Coll. of Idaho, 1945-47. Tchr. pub. schs., Glenns Ferry, Castleford and Twin Falls, Idaho, 1947-51; reporter, copy reader, women's editor Statesman Newspapers, Boise, Idaho, 1961-64; editor Leisure Publs., Los Angeles, 1964-81; ret., 1981. Recipient Meritorious Service award Nat. Swimming Pool Inst., 1970. Office: 5625 Kearny Villa Rd San Diego CA 92123

COUPE, JOHN DONALD, university official, economics educator; b. Holyoke, Mass., Aug. 29, 1931; s. Alfred and Erna (Hohenberger) C.; m. V. Sylvia Kajander, Aug. 23, 1958; children: Jeffrey A., Stephen R., Cynthia E. B.S., Worcester Poly. Inst., 1953; M.A., Clark U., 1957, Ph.D., 1960. Mem. faculty U. Maine, Orono, 1958-61, asst. prof., 1962-66, prof. econs., 1966—, chmn. dept., 1969-76, v.p. fin. and adminstrn., 1979—; asst. prof. econs. Kent State U., 1961-62; cons. Casco Bank & Trust Co., 1966-68, State Credit Research Com., 1964, 69; Chmn. Maine Manpower Adv. Com., 1964-72, vice chmn., 1972-73; mem. Woodlands Taxation Study Com., 1970, Maine Adv. Council on Vocat. Edn., 1971-72. Author: (with A. Raphaelson and T. Siedlik) A Study of the Vacation Industry in Maine, 1961, (with David Clark) The Bangor Area Economy: Its Present and Future, 1967, (with D. Savage and others) The Economics of Environmental Improvement, 1974; contbr. articles to profl. jours. Chmn. Forest Lands Taxation Rev. Com., 1971-72, Forest Land Valuation Adv. Council, 1974-77; mem. Joint Select Com. on State Valuation, Maine, 1976-77; adv. council Maine Dept. Manpower Affairs, 1974-78; cons. New Eng. Regional Commn., 1971-73, Growth Center Project. Served with AUS, 1953-55. Mem. Am. Econ. Assn., AAUP, Phi Kappa Phi. Home: 100 Forest Ave Orono ME 04473

COUPER, RICHARD WATROUS, educator, foundation executive; b. Binghamton, N.Y., Dec. 16, 1922; s. Edgar W. and Esther (Watrous) C.; m. Patricia Pogue, Sept. 24, 1946,; children: Frederick Pogue, Barrett Williams, Thomas Hayes, Margaret Channing. A.B., Hamilton Coll., Clinton, N.Y., 1944, LL.D., 1969; A.M. in Am. History, Harvard U., 1948; L.H.D., N.Y. U., 1974; LL.D., St. Joseph's Coll., 1982. With Couper-Ackerman-Sampson, Inc. (and predecessor), Binghamton, 1948-62, treas., 1957-60, dir., 1957-63, v.p., 1960-63; adminstrv. v.p. Hamilton Coll., 1962-65, v.p., 1965-66, acting pres., 1966-68, v.p., provost, 1968-69, charter trustee, 1967—; dep. commr. higher edn. N.Y. State Edn. Dept., 1969-71; pres., chief exec. officer N.Y. Pub. Library, N.Y.C., 1971-81, pres. emeritus, 1981—; pres. Woodrow Wilson Nat. Fellowship Found., Princeton, N.J., 1981—, also trustee, 1981—; dir Security Mut. Life Ins. Co., Binghamton, Equitable Money Market Account, Inc., Security Equity Life Ins. Co., Equitable Govt. Securities Account, Inc., Equitable Tax-Free Account, Inc. Trustee Link Found., 1970—; trustee John Simon Guggenheim Meml. Found., N.Y.C., 1978—, Carl and Lily Pforzheimer Found., Inc., 1983—. Served to capt. U.S. Army, 1942-46. Mem. Orgn. Am. Historians, Am. Hist. Assn., New York State Hist. Assn. (trustee 1979—, v.p.), Phi Beta Kappa.). Clubs: Harvard, Century Assn., Lotos (N.Y.C.); Sadaquada Golf, Ft. Schuyler (Utica, N.Y.). Home: 51 Cleveland Ln Princeton NJ 08540 Office: Woodrow Wilson Nat Fellowship Found 16 John St Box 642 Princeton NJ 08542

COUPLAND, DON, former air force officer; b. Warsaw, Ind., July 11, 1915; s. Alfred Augustus and Abbie (Bennett) C.; m. Jean Barringer, Dec. 27, 1941 (dec. Nov. 1969); children: Gail B. Coupland Wardley, Jack B., Judy B.; m. Maxine Evans; stepchildren: Edwin Evans, Sherry Evans. B.S. in Aero. Engring., Purdue U., 1936; grad., Advanced Flying Sch., 1938, Mil. Officer Tng. Sch., 1940, USAAF Engring. Sch., 1941, USAAF Inst. Tech., 1947, Air War Coll., 1951. Commd. 2d lt. F.A. Res., 1936, apptd. aviation cadet, 1937; advanced through grades to maj. gen. USAF, 1957; airplane comdr., engring. officer 35th Pursuit Squadron, 1938-39, procurement and prodn. project officer USAAF Material Div., 1939-42, chief engine sect., maintenance div. USAAF Material Div., 1942-44, officer-in-charge operational engring. Hdqrs. 20th Air Force, Guam, 1944-45, exec. to dep. comdr. engring Air Tech. Services Command, 1945-46, chief prodn. planning office Directoriate Procurement and Indsl. Planning, 1947-50, asst. chief staff supply, also dep. comdr. Air Material Forces, Europe, 1951-54, asst. dir., then dir. materiel programs, dep. chief staff/materiel Hdqrs. USAF, 1954-58, 1st dep. comdr. ballistic missiles, then dep. comdr. San Bernardino Air Materiel Area, Norton AFB, Calif., 1958-60, comdr. ballistic missiles center Air Material Command, Los Angeles, 1960-61, vice comdr. ballistic systems div. Air Force Systems Command, 1961, comdr. Ogden Air Material Area, Air Force Logistics Command, Hill AFB, Utah, 1961-64; auditor gen. U.S. Air Force, Washington, 1964-67; ret.; pres. NGS, Inc., 1967—. Decorated Legion of Merit with four oak leaf clusters. Mem. Order Daedalians, AIAA, Air Force Assn. (hon. life), Nat. Rifle Assn., Air Force Acad. Athletic Assn. (life charter), Nat. Def. Transp. Assn., Am. Ordnance Assn., Ogden C. of C. Clubs: Ogden Golf and Country, Weber (Ogden); AFB Golf, AFB Rod and Gun, Administrative (Hill AFB); Arrowhead Country. Home: 3705 Hemlock Dr San Bernardino CA 92404

COURANT, ERNEST DAVID, physicist; b. Goettingen, Germany, Mar. 26, 1920; came to U.S., 1934, naturalized, 1940; s. Richard and Nina (Runge) C.; m. Sara Paul, Dec. 9, 1944; children: Paul N., Carl R. B.A., Swarthmore Coll., 1940; M.S., U. Rochester, 1942, Ph.D., 1943; M.A. (hon.), Yale U., 1962. Scientist Atomic Energy Project, Montreal, Que., Can., 1943-46; research asso. physics Cornell U., 1946-48; mem. staff Brookhaven Nat. Lab., 1947—, sr. physicist, 1960—; Brookhaven prof. physics Yale U., 1962-67; vis. prof. Yale, 1961-62; prof. physics and engring. State U. N.Y. at Stony Brook, 1967—; vis. asst. prof. Princeton, 1950-51; cons. Gen. Atomic div. Gen. Dynamics Corp., 1958-59; vis. physicist Nat. Accelerator Lab., 1968-69. Fulbright research fellow Cambridge (Eng.) U., 1956. Fellow Am. Phys. Soc., AAAS; mem. Nat. Acad. Scis., N.Y. Acad. Scis. (Boris Pregel prize 1979). Co-originator strong-focusing particle accelerators. Home: 109 Bay Ave Bayport NY 11705

COURNAND, ANDRE F., physiologist; b. Paris, France, Sept. 24, 1895; came to U.S., 1930, naturalized, 1941; s. Jules and Marguerite (Weber) C.; m. Sibylle Blumer (dec. 1959); children: Muriel, Marie-Eve, Marie Claire; m. Ruth Fabian, 1963 (dec. 1973); m. Beatrice Bishop Berle, 1975. B.A., Sorbonne U., Paris, 1913, P.C.B. in Sci, 1914; M.D., U. Paris, 1930; Dr. h.c., U. Strasbourg, 1957, U. Lyon, 1958, U. Brussels, 1959, U. Pisa, 1960, Columbia U., 1965, U. Brazil, 1965, U. Nancy, 1969; D.Sc., U. Birmingham, 1961, Gustavus Adolphus Coll., 1963. Prof. emeritus medicine Coll. Phys. & Surg., Columbia. Served with French Army, 1915-19. Decorated Croix de Guerre (France); recipient Laureate (silver medal), faculty medicine U. Paris; Andrea Retzius silver medal Swedish Soc. Internal Medicine; Lasker award USPHS; winner (with Dr. Dickinson W. Richards and Dr. Werner Forssman) of 1956 Nobel Prize in medicine and physiology; recipient Jiminez Diaz prize, 1970. Fellow Royal Soc. Medicine; mem. Nat. Acad. Scis. U.S.A., de l'Academie Nationale de Medecine (fgn.) (France), Academie Royale de Medecine de Belgique, Am. Physiol. Soc., Assn. Am. Physicians, Brit. Cardiac Soc., Swedish Soc., Internal Medicine, Soc. Medicale Hopitaux de Paris, Academie des Sciences, Institut de France (fgn. mem.). Clubs: Century Assn., Am. Alpine. Home: 142 E 19th St New York NY 10003

COURT, KATHRYN DIANA, editor; b. London, Dec. 23, 1948; U.S., 1976; d. Ian Howard and Elizabeth Irene (Freeman) Onslow; m. David Court, Mar. 25, 1972; m. Jonathan Coleman, July 8, 1978. B.A. in English with honors, U. Leicester, 1970. Editor William Heinemann Ltd., London, 1971-76; editor Penguin Books, N.Y.C., 1977-79, editorial dir., 1979—. Home: 16 Park Ave New York NY 10016 Office: 625 Madison Ave New York NY 10022

COURTEMANCHE, A(LBERT) DOUGLAS, plastic surgeon, educator; b. Gravenhurst, Ont., Canada, Nov. 16, 1929; s. Melville Albert C. and Margaret (Simpson) LaRonde; m. Anne Constance Douse, Mar. 20, 1950; children: Douglas John, David Michael, Peter, Nancy Anne. M.D., U. Toronto, 1955. Intern Toronto Gen. Hosp., 1955-56, Shaughnessy Hosp., Vancouver, B.C., Can., 1956-57, resident, 1956-57, Bangour Gen. Hosp., Edinburgh, Scotland, 1958-59; sr. house surgeon Hosp. for Sick Children, London, 1959; sr. registrar Stoke Mandeville Hosp., Aylesbury, Eng., 1959-60; research fellow U. B.C., Vancouver, 1962-63, clin. instr. plastic surgery, 1963-71, clin. asst. prof., 1971-73, clin. assoc. prof., 1973-79, clin. prof., 1979—, head div. plastic surgery, 1975—; active surg. staff Vancouver Gen. Hosp., 1962—, head div. plastic surgery, 1975—; active surg. staff Children's Hosp., Vancouver, 1962—; cons. surg. staff Univ. Hosp., Vancouver, 1976—. Contbr. articles to profl. jours. Chmn. med. exec. com. and med. bd. Vancouver Gen. Hosp., 1982. Fellow Royal Coll. Physicians and Surgeons Can.; mem. Can. Soc. Plastic Surgeons (pres. 1982-83), Am. Soc. Plastic and Reconstructive Surgeons, Am. Burn Assn., Am. Cleft Palate Assn. Club: Royal Vancouver Yacht. Home: 1163 W 29th Ave Vancouver BCCanada V6H 2E6 Office: 306-888 W 8th Ave Vancouver BCCanada V5Z 3Y1

COURTENAYE, RICHARD HUBERT, former foreign service officer; b. Pomona, Cal., Mar. 27, 1923; s. John and Juanita (Case) C.; m. Norma Jean Drew, July 22, 1953; children: Mary Ann, Catherine. Student, U. Calif.-Berkeley, 1940; A.B., UCLA, 1944; postgrad., U. Mich., 1944-45; M.P.A., Harvard U., 1956. Press, radio work War Dept., Osaka, Japan, 1946-47; joined U.S. Fgn. Service, 1947; vice consul, Barcelona, Spain, 1947-48, 3d sec. embassy, Mexico City, Mexico, 1949-50, 2d sec. embassy, Quito, Ecuador, 1951-53, vice consul, Kobe-Osaka, Japan, 1953-55, 2d sec., consul embassy, Madrid, Spain, 1956-58; chief middle Am. br. State Dept., 1959-61, chief inter-Am. polit. div., 1961-62; dir. Office Research and Analysis for Am. Republics, 1962; consul gen., Que., Can., 1962-64, Windsor, Ont., Can., 1964-68, Tijuana, Baja Calif., Mexico, 1968-71, fed. regional council rep., Denver, 1971-73, consul gen., Tangier, Morocco, from 1973, internat. student exchange cons., 1982—; Dir. Pacific Intercultural Exchange, 1979-82, chmn. bd. dirs., 1980-82. Served to capt. AUS, 1943-46; PTO. Mem. Natural Resources Def. Council, Nat. Assn. Fgn. Student Affairs, Am. Fgn. Service Assn. Conglist. Home: 9167 Grossmont Blvd La Mesa CA 92041

COURTER, JAMES A., congressman; b. Montclair, N.J., Oct. 14, 1941; s. Joseph A. and Madeleine C.; m. Carmen McCalmen, Dec. 5, 1970; children: Donica, Katrina. B.A., Colgate U., 1963; J.D., Duke U., 1966. Vol. U.S. Peace Corps, Venezuela, 1967-69; asst. corp. counsel City of Washington, 1969-70; atty. Union County Legal

Services, Plainfield, N.J., 1970-71; 1st asst. Warren County prosecutor, 1973-77; mem. 96th and 98th Congresses from 13th N.J. Dist. Mem. Civic adv. council Hackettstown Community Hosp.; bd. dirs. Warren County Legal Services. Mem. Nat. Dist. Atty.'s Assn., County Prosecutors N.J. Assn., N.J. Fedn. Planning Ofcls., N.J. Inst. Mcpl. Attys., N.J. Trial Attys. Assn., N.J. Bar Assn., Am. Bar Assn., Warren County Bar Assn., Washington Bar Assn. Club: Hackettstown Rotary (past pres.). Home: 19 Reese Ave Hackettstown NJ 07840 Office: 325 Cannon House Office Bldg Washington DC 20515

COURTNEY, CHARLES EDWARD, government official; b. Modesto, Calif., June 11, 1936; s. Samuel Ernest and Mary Christine (Rasmussen) C.; m. Donna Lee Speight, Mar. 23, 1957; children: Christine Marie, Katherine Anne, Aaron Charles. B.A., Stanford U., 1958; M.A., Calif. State U., San Francisco, 1960. Tchr. in, Calif., 1960-62; student affairs officer USIS, Istanbul, Turkey, 1963-64, cultural affairs officer, 1964-67; center programs officer Near East/South Asia USIA, Washington, 1967-70; dir. USIS Eastern India, Calcutta, 1970-72, Bangladesh, Dacca, 1972; dep. asst. dir. for South Asia USIA, Washington, 1972-75; counselor for pub. affairs Am. Embassy, Islamabad, Pakistan, 1975-76, Ankara, Turkey, 1977-80; dir. communication services Nat. Center for Productivity and Quality of Working Life, Washington, 1976-77; prin. sr. insp. ICA, Washington, 1980-81; dep. dir. Voice of Am., Washington, 1981-82; dir. North African, near Eastern and South Asian affairs USIA, Washington, 1982-83, dir. European affairs, 1983—; Mem. Fulbright Ednl. Exchanges Selection Com., Turkey, 1964-67, India, 1970-72; mem. exec. com. English Speaking Union, Calcutta, 1970-72; vice chmn. Commn. for Ednl. Exchange between U.S. and Turkey, 1977-80; bd. dirs. Turkish Am. Univ. Assn., Istanbul, 1965-67, Indo-Am. Soc., Calcutta, 1970-72. Mem. Am. Fgn. Service Assn. Home: 985 N Quintana St Arlington VA 22205

COURTNEY, GLADYS (ATKINS), university dean; b. Erwin, Tenn., June 10, 1930; d. James Berry and Martha Jane (Fender) Atkins; m. John Harold Courtney, July 10, 1967; children—Jonathan David, Martha Elizabeth. Diploma, Baroness Erlanger Hosp. Sch. Nursing, 1951; B.S., La. Coll., 1956; M.S., La. State U., 1958; Ph.D., U. Ill., 1964. Nurse in sevaral hosps., 1951-60; mem. faculty Malone Coll., Canton, Ohio, 1965-68; mem. faculty, dir. nurse scientist program U. Ill., Chgo., 1969-76, mem. faculty, head dept. gen. nursing, 1971-76; dean Sch. Nursing, U. Mo., Columbia, 1976-80, mem. faculty, 1976-81; dean Coll. Nursing, Mich. State U., East Lansing, 1981—; cons. in field. Contbr. articles to profl. jours. NIH predoctoral fellow, 1963-64; recipient other grants. Mem. Am. Nurses Assn., Nat. League for Nursing, Sigma Xi, Sigma Theta Tau. Republican. Club: Zonta Internat. Home: 1016 Killdeer Dr Mason MI 48854 Office: Coll Nursing Life Scis Bldg East Lansing MI 48824 *Education which prepares us to learn how to learn should assist us in advancing society. Common, as well as difficult, problems should be addressed more objectively and productively by truly educated people. I keep striving to be educated.*

COURTNEY, HOWARD PERRY, clergyman; b. Frederick, Okla., Dec. 20, 1911; s. Columbus C. and Dotty Lee (Whelchel) C.; m. Vaneda Harper, Mar. 21, 1932; 1 son, Howard Perry. Grad., L.I.F.E. Bible Coll., 1932, D.D., 1944. Ordained to ministry Internat. Ch. of the Foursquare Gospel, 1933; pastor chs., Racine, Wis., 1932-34, Terre Haute, Ind., 1934, Portland, Ore., 1935-36, Riverside, Calif., 1936-39, Urbana, Ill., 1939; dist. supr. Great Lakes dist., Internat. Ch. of the Foursquare Gospel, 1940-44, gen. supr., v.p., 1950; gen. supr., dir. fgn. missions, 1944-50, v.p., 1953-80, gen. supr., 1953-74; pastor Angelus Temple, Los Angeles, 1950-53, 77-81; mem. faculty L.I.F.E. Bible Coll., 1937-39, 44-74; Chmn. adv. com. Pentecostal World Conf., 1958-61. Mem. Pentecostal Fellowship North Am. (chmn. 1953, 54, 65-66), Nat. Assn. Evangelicals (bd. mem. 1953-54, 59-60, 66-67, 69—). Office: 1100 Glendale Blvd Los Angeles CA 90026

COURTNEY, JACQUELINE DIANNA, actress; b. East Orange, N.J.; d. Russell Kenneth and Florence Ann C.; (div.)1 dau., Jennifer Desiderio. Grad., Profl. Children's Sch., N.Y.C. Voted Best Actress of Yr. Daytime TV Mag., 1971; Best Actress Afternoon TV, 1973, Daytime TV Mag., 1974; 1st in Top 10, 100 times. Office: Press Relations ABC Entertainment 1330 Ave of Americas New York NY 10019 *

COURTNEY, JAMES EDMOND, mining company executive; b. Meadville, Pa., Dec. 28, 1931; s. Alexis James and Marian (Winans) C.; m. Eileen Patricia Alman, Nov. 2, 1970; children: Alison M., David E., Jotham C. A.B., Dartmouth Coll., 1953; M.B.A., Amos Tuck Sch. Bus. Adminstrn., 1954; LL.B., Harvard U., 1959. Ptnr. firm Jones Day Reavis & Pogue, Cleve., 1959-74; v.p. Hanna Mining Co., Cleve., 1974-78, sr. v.p., 1978-79, exec. v.p., 1979—, dir., 1981—; dir. Iron Ore Co Can., St. John del Rey Mining Co., p.l.c., Midland S.W. Corp. Trustee Western Res. Hist. Soc., Cleve., 1980; mem. adv. bd. Council of Ams. Served to lt. USN, 1954-56. Mem. Am. Iron and Steel Inst., Am. Mining Congress, Am. Iron Ore Assn., Internat. Econ. Policy Assn. (dir.). Clubs: Union, Clevelander, Westwood; Rolling Rock (Ligonier, Pa.); International (Washington). Home: 13834 Lake Ave Lakewood OH 44107 Office: 100 Erieview Plaza Cleveland OH 44114

COURTNEY, WILLIAM FRANCIS, food and vending service co. exec.; b. Altoona, Pa., July 3, 1914; s. W. Francis and Mary Edith (Hopkins) C.; m. Mary Jane Kelley, June 5, 1946; children—Sarah Ann, William Francis, Thomas Gerard, Richard Christopher. Mgmt. staff W.T. Grant Co., 1933-37; sales mgr. Coca-Cola Co., 1937- 48; partner Automatic Refreshment Service, 1948-60; pres. Servomation Youngstown, Ohio, 1960—; v.p. Servomation Corp., 1963-71; pres. Serex Corp., 1971—; dir. Mahoning Nat. Bank, Youngstown. Served to capt., inf. AUS, 1945; PTO. Decorated Bronze Star. Mem. Nat. Automatic Merchandising Assn., Ohio Automatic Merchandising Assn. (past pres., dir.). Republican. Club: Youngstown. Home: 725 Blueberry Hill Canfield OH 44406 Office: 5211 Mahoning Ave Youngstown OH 44515

COURTOIS, EDMOND JACQUES, lawyer; b. Montreal, Que., Can., July 4, 1920; s. Edmond and Cleophee (Lefebvre) C.; m. Joan Miller, Oct. 23, 1943; children: Nicole, Jacques, Marc. B.A., Coll. de Montreal, 1940; LL.B., U. Montreal, 1943. Bar: Que. 1946, created Queen's counsel 1963. Partner Stikeman Elliott Tamaki Mercier & Robb, 1953—; chmn. bd., dir. United N.Am. Holdings Ltd.; pres., dir. La Compagnie Foncière du Man. (1967) Ltée., CIIT, Inc., Elican Devel. Co. Ltd.; v.p., dir. Bank N.S., Can. Life Assurance Co.; dir. Trizec Corp. Ltd., Rolland Inc., QIT-Fer et Titáne Inc., Norcen Energy Resources Ltd., Phoenix Steel Corp., Ritz-Carlton Hotel Co. of Montreal, Ltd., McGraw-Hill Ryerson Ltd., Brinco Ltd., CAE Industries Ltd., Eaton/Bay Dividend Fund Ltd., Eaton/Bay Income Fund, Eaton/Bay Viking Fund Ltd., Eaton/Bay Commonwealth Fund Ltd., Eaton/Bay Internat. Fund Ltd., Eaton/Bay Leverage Fund Ltd., Eaton/Bay Growth Fund Ltd., Eaton/Bay Venture Fund Ltd., Abitibi Asbestos Mining Co. Ltd. Bd. dirs. Montreal Symphony Orch. Served to lt. Royal Can. Navy, 1943-45. Mem. Can. Bar Assn., bars Montreal, Que. Office: 38th Floor 1155 Dorchester Blvd W Montreal PQ H3B 3V2 Canada

COURTSAL, DONALD PRESTON, manufacturing company executive; b. New Haven, Dec. 30, 1929; s. Frederick Joseph and Viola (Schiffel) C.; m. Frances L. Chase, May 22, 1954; children: Lyle Donald, Charles Francis. B.S. in Mech. Engring, U.S. Coast Guard Acad., 1951; M.S. in Naval Architecture and Marine Engring, M.I.T., 1956. With shipbldg. div. Bethlehem Steel Co., Quincy, Mass., 1956-64; with Dravo Corp., 1965—, gen. mgr. engring. works div., corp. v.p., Pitts., 1976-82, treas., corp. v.p., 1982—; pres. Dravo Wellman Co.; mem. ship research com. Nat. Acad. Scis., 1979-81. Author papers in field. Served with USCG, 1951-54. Mem. Soc. Naval Architects and Marine Engrs. (v.p. 1979—, exec. com. 1974-77, 80—, mem. council 1974—, chmn. adv. public service com. 1978—), Am. Waterways Operators. Unitarian. Clubs: Pymatuning Yacht; Duquesne (Pitts.). Office: Neville Island Pittsburgh PA 15225

COUSINS, JANE CAMPBELL, Realtor; b. Camden, S.C., June 29, 1924; d. Herbert Allison and Mabel Henning Campbell; m. James Lee Cousins, Dec. 19, 1949; children: Charles Henning, James Lee, Julie Elizabeth, Mary Allison. Student, Catherine Gibbs Sch., N.Y.C., 1945. Sec. to adj. Shaw Field Army Airfeld, 1942-44; field rep. ARC, 1944-47; stewardess Pan Am. Airways, from 1947; real estate asso., from 1964; founder, pres., chief exec. officer Cousins Assos., Miami, Fla., 1967—; pres., chief exec. officer Merrill Lynch Realty/Cousins; dir. Fed. Res. Bank Atlanta, 1982—. Bd. dirs. Jr. Achievement, Boy Scouts Am.; trustee Fairchild Tropical Gardens, South Miami Hosp., Fla. Meml. Coll.; dir. Dade County Devel. Authority; mem., past pres. Beaux Arts of Lowe Gallery, U. Miami.; visitors com. U. Miami. Recipient Marketer of Yr. award Acad. Mktg. Sci., 1981. Mem. Miami Dade County C. of C. (dir.), Fla. State C. of C. (dir.), Nat. Assn. Real Estate Bds. Republican. Episcopalian. Club: Jr. League Miami. Home: 5445 SW 105th St Miami FL 33156 Office: 5830 SW 73d St Miami FL 33143

COUSINS, MARGARET, author, editor; b. Munday, Tex., Jan. 26, 1905; d. Walter Henry and Sue Margaret (Reeves) C. A.B., U. Tex., 1926; Litt.D. (hon.), Williams Woods Coll., 1980. Asso. editor So. Pharm. Jour., Dallas, 1927-32, editor, 1932-37; asso. editor Pictorial Rev., 1937-38; copy writer, gen. promotion dept. Hearst Mags., 1938-42; asso. editor Good Housekeeping, 1942-45, mng. editor, 1945-58, McCall's mag., 1958-61; sr. editor Doubleday & Co., N.Y.C., 1961-70; spl. assignment Holt, Rinehart & Winston, 1970; fiction and book editor Ladies Home Jour., 1971-73. Author: Uncle Edgar and the Reluctant Saint, 1948; juvenile Ben Franklin of Old Philadelphia, 1952; short story collection Christmas Gift, 1952; We Were There at the Battle of the Alamo, 1958; collaborator: (with Margaret Truman) Souvenir, 1955; author: anthology Stories of Love and Marriage, 1961; (pseudonym Avery Johns) Traffic with Evil, 1962; juvenile Thomas Alva Edison, 1965. Mem. San Antonio River Walk Commn.; bd. dirs. Arts Council San Antonio. Recipient Achievement medal Alpha Chi Omega, 1955; Award of Achievement Tex. Ex-Student's Assn., 1956; J.C. Penney-Mo. Sch. Journalism award for mag. writing, 1969; George Washington medal Freedoms Found. at Valley Forge, 1969; Distinguished Alumna award U. Tex., 1973; Arts and Letters award Friends of San Antonio Pub. Library, 1982. Mem. Authors League (council), Authors Guild (council), Tex. Inst. Letters, Philos. Soc. Tex., Theta Sigma Phi (Headliner award 1946), Alpha Chi Omega. Clubs: Cosmopolitan, St. Anthony, Giraud. Home: Box 1626 San Antonio TX 78296 *I was a prairie child and early in life began to depend on magazines and books. They enhanced my world and it became my ambition to work with such media and enhance the world of others. In that period and remote place, my mother found the women's service magazines a cultural life-line. I suppose it was for this reason that I sought employment in that genre. Those magazines celebrated the home, and I came from a happy one, which had profited by them.*

COUSINS, NORMAN, author, lectr.; b. Union Hill, N.J., June 24, 1915; s. Samuel and Sara (Miller) C.; m. Ellen Kopf, June 23, 1939; children—Andrea, Amy Loveman, Candis Hitzig, Sara Kit. Litt.D., Am. U., 1948; L.H.D., Boston U., Colby Coll., 1953, Denison U., 1954, Colgate U., 1958; Litt.D., Elmira Coll., Franklin and Marshall Coll., Ripon Coll., Wilmington Coll., 1957, U. Vt., 1957, Newark State Coll., 1958, Drake U., 1961, Mich. State U., 1967, Maryville Coll., 1975, U. Ala., 1975; LL.D., Washington and Jefferson Coll., 1956, Syracuse U., 1956, Albright Coll., 1957, Chapman Coll., U. R.I., 1965, Temple U., 1958, Duquesne U., 1964; Ed.D., R.I. Coll. Edn., 1958; Litt.D., Western Mich. State U., Ripon Coll., U. Bridgeport (Conn.), U. Ariz., Brandeis U., Coll. Notre Dame, 1965; D.H.L., Lafayette Coll., 1965; D.L., U. N.C., 1969, U. Denver, 1971. Lit. editor, mng. editor Current History mag., 1935-40; editor Saturday Rev., 1940-71, 73-77, chmn. bd. editors, 1978, editor emeritus, 1980—; adj. prof. Sch. Medicine, UCLA.; Chmn. bd. dirs. Nat. Ednl. TV, 1969-70; chmn. Nat. Programming Council for Pub. TV, 1970—; Editor U.S.A.; mem. editorial bd. Overseas bur. O.W.I., World War II; U.S. Govt. lectr. (Smith Mundt) in, India, Pakistan, Ceylon, 1951, Japan-Am. Exchange lectr., Japan, 1953; Chmn. Conn. Fact Finding Commn. on Edn., 1948-52; co-chmn. Citizens' Com. for Nuclear Test Ban Treaty; mem. Commn. to Study Orgn. Peace; hon. pres. United World Federalists; chmn. Com. Culture and Intellectual Exchange, Internat. Cooperation Yr., 1965, Mayor's Task Force Air Pollution, N.Y.C., 1966—. Author: The Democratic Chance, 1942, Modern Man Is Obsolete, 1945, Talks with Nehru, 1951, Who Speaks for Man?, 1952, In God We Trust; The Religious Beliefs of the Founding Fathers, 1958; Editor: A Treasury of Democracy, 1941, (with William Rose Benét) and) Anthology of the Poetry of Freedom, 1943, Writing for Love or Money, 1949, Doctor Schweitzer of Lambarene, 1960, In Place of Folly, 1961, Present Tense, 1967, The Improbable Triumvirate, 1972, The Celebration of Life, 1975, Anatomy of An Illness, 1979, The Human Option, 1981, The Physician in Literature, 1981; Editorial supr.: March's Dictionary-Thesaurus, 1980. Mem. Hiroshima Peace Center Assos.; trustee Charles F. Kettering Found., Menninger Found., Ruth Mott Found. Recipient Thomas Jefferson award for Advancement of Democracy in Journalism, 1948; Tuition Plan award for outstanding service to Am. Edn., 1951; Benjamin Franklin citation in mag. journalism, 1956; Wayne U. award for nat. service to edn., 1956; Lane Bryant citation for pub. service, 1958; John Dewey award for service to edn., 1958; N.Y. State Citizens Edn. Commn. award, 1959; Publius award N.Y. met. com. United World Federalists, 1964; Eleanor Roosevelt Peace award, 1963; Overseas Press Club award, 1965; Distinguished Citizen award Conn. Bar Assn., 1965; N.Y. Acad. Pub. Edn. award, 1966; Family of Man award, 1968; Aquinas Coll. Ann. award, 1968; nat. mag. award Assn. Deans Journalism Schs., 1969; Peace medal UN, 1971; Carr Van Anda award for contbns. to journalism Ohio U., 1971; Gold medal for lit. Nat. Arts Club, 1972; Journalism Honor award U. Mo. Sch. Journalism, 1972; Irita Van Doren Book award, 1972; award for service to environment Govt. of Can.; Henry Johnson Fisher award as mag. pub. of yr. Mag. Pubs. Assn., 1973; Human Resources award, 1977; Convocation medal Am. Coll. Cardiology, 1978; Author of Yr. award Am. Soc. Journalists and Authors, 1981. Mem. World Assn. World Federalists (pres.), P.E.N., UN Assn. (dir. U.S.), Council Fgn. Relations, Nat. Acad. Scis. (commn. on internat. relations). Clubs: Coffee House, Nat. Press, Overseas Press, Century Assn., Pilgrims Am. Home: 2644 Eden Pl Beverly Hills CA 90210 Office: Room 2859 Slichter Hall Sch Medicine UCLA Los Angeles CA 90024

COUSINS, ROBERT DACEY, corporation executive; b. Mobile, Ala., Sept. 7, 1921; s. Reuben and Ruby (Dacey) C.; m. Ruth Brady, Apr. 9, 1948; children: Nancy Andrews, Robert Dacey, Daivd Bruce. Student, The Citadel; B.S., U.S. Naval Acad., 1942. Sales rep. Procter & Gamble Co., Montgomery, Ala., 1947-51; sales and sales mgmt. positions Curtis 1000, New Orleans, Dallas, St. Paul, 1953-64, gen. mgmt. positions, Louisville, 1964-75, pres., Smyrna, Ga., 1975—. Served to comdr. USN, 1942-49, 52-54. Recipient Silver Beaver award Boy Scouts Am., 1974; named Ky. Col., 1969. Mem. Ga. Bus. and Industry Assn. (bd. govs. 1976-83). Republican. Methodist. Lodge: Kiwanis. Office: Curtis 1000 1000 Curtis Dr Smyrna GA 30080 *

COUSINS, ROBERT JOHN, nutritional biochemist; b. N.Y.C., Apr. 5, 1941; s. Charles Robert and Doris Elizabeth (Sifferlen) C.; m. Elizabeth Anne Ward, Jan. 25, 1969; children: Sarah, Jonathan, Allison. B.A., U. Vt., 1963; Ph.D., U. Conn., 1968. NIH postdoctoral fellow biochemistry U. Wis., 1968-70; asst. prof. nutrition Rutgers U., 1971-74, assoc. prof., 1974-77, prof. nutritional biochemistry, 1977-79, prof. II (Distng. Prof.), 1979-82, dir. grad. program in nutrition, 1976-82; Boston family prof. human nutrition and biochemistry U. Fla., Gainesville, 1982—; mem. nutrition study sect. NIH; mem. numerous editorial bds/. Contbr. articles in nutritional biochemistry to profl. jours. Future Leader grantee Nutrition Found., Inc., 1972; recipient Mead Johnson award in nutrition, 1979; NIH grantee, 1972—. Mem. Am. Soc. Biol. Chemists, Am. Inst. Nutrition, Biochem. Soc., Soc. Exptl. Biology and Medicine, Am. Chem. Soc., AAAS, Soc. Toxicology, Sigma Xi. Home: 4510 NW 20th Pl Gainesville FL 32605 Office: Dept Food Sci and Human Nutrition U Fla Gainesville FL 32611

COUSINS, THOMAS GRADY, real estate developer; b. Atlanta, Dec. 7, 1931; s. Isaac William and Lillian Adelade C.; m. Ann Draughon, Mar. 17, 1956; children: Caroline, Lillian, Thomas Grady. B.S., U. Ga., 1952. Vice pres. sales Knox Homes Corp., Atlanta, 1959—; chmn. bd. Cousins Properties, Inc. (and related cos. Atlanta Coliseum, Inc.); pres. Internat. City Corp. Elder North Ave. Presbyn. Ch., 1970—; bd. dirs. Central Atlanta Progress, Atlanta Music Festival Found.; trustee Rockefeller U., U. Ga. Found. Served with USAF, 1952-54. Recipient Charles M. Watt, Jr. award, 1973, award of merit U. Ga., 1965; named Outstanding Young Man of Yr. Atlanta Jr. C. of C., 1974. Mem. Atlanta C. of C. (life, bd. dirs.), Blue Key. Clubs: Peachtree Golf, Piedmont Driving, Capital City. Address: 800 N Omni Internat Atlanta GA 30335

COUSLAND, WALTER CORNELIUS, army officer; b. Washington, Feb. 23, 1932; s. Cornelius Walter and Roma Lucille (McTaggart) C.; m. Carol Fore Mason, June 12, 1965; children: Julia Kim Andrews, Scott Wilson Andrews, Beth Anne. B.S., U.S. Mil. Acad., 1953; M.A., U. Pa., 1962. Commd. 2d lt. U.S. Army, 1953, advanced through grades to brig. gen.; dep. comdr. Adj. Gen. Ctr., 1978-79; asst. div. comdr. 25th Inf. Div., 1979-80; staff officer Tng. and Doctrine Command, 1980; now with office of dep. sec. of def. for pub. affairs. Decorated Silver Star with oak leaf cluster, Legion of Merit with 2 oak leaf clusters, D.F.C, Bronze Star, Purple Heart, others. Mem. Assn. U.S. Army, Assn. Grads. U.S. Mil. Acad., Alumni Assn. U.S. War Coll. Episcopalian. Home: 151 Bernard Rd Fort Monroe VA 23651 Office: Office of Dep Asst Sec of Def for Pub Affairs Dept Def Washington DC

COUSTEAU, JACQUES YVES, marine explorer, film producer, writer; b. St. Andre-de-Cubzac, France, June 11, 1910; s. Daniel P. and Elizabeth (Duranthon) C.; m. Simone Melchior, July 11, 1937; children: Jean-Michel, Philippe (dec.). Bachelier, Stanislas Acad., Paris, 1927; midshipman, Brest Naval Acad., 1930; D.Sc., U. Calif., Berkeley, 1970, Brandeis U., 1970. Founder Groupe d'etudes et de recherches sous-marines, Toulon, France, 1946; founder, pres. Campagnes oceanographiques francaises, Marseille, 1950, Centre d'etudes marines avancees (formerly Office Francais de recherche sous marine), 1952; leader Calypso Oceanographic Expdns.; dir. Oceanographic Mus., Monaco, 1957—; promoted Conshelf saturation dive program, 1962; gen. sec. I.C.S.E.M., 1966. (Recipient numerous awards, including: Motion Picture Acad. Arts and Scis. award (Oscar) for best documentary feature, The Silent World, also for The World Without Sun, 1965, for best short film The Golden Fish 1960, Grand Prix, Gold Palm, Festival Cannes for The Silent World 1956); author and producer documentary films which received awards at Paris, Cannes and Venice film festivals.; Author: Par 18 metres de fonds, 1946, La Plongee en scaphandre, 1950, The Silent World, 1952, (editor with James Dugan) Captain Cousteau's Underwater Treasury, 1959, (with James Dugan) The Living Sea, 1962, World Without Sun, 1965, (with Philippe Cousteau) The Shark: Splendid Savage of the Sea, 1970, (with Ph. Diole) Life and Death in a Coral Sea, 1971, Diving for Sunken Treasure, 1971, The Whale: Mighty Monarch of the Sea, 1972, Octopus and Squid, 1973, Galapagos, Titicaca, the Blue Holes: Three Adventures, 1973, Diving Companions, 1974, Dolphins, 1975, Jacques Cousteau: The Ocean World, 1979, A Bill of Rights for Future Generations, 1980, The Cousteau Almanac of the Environment, 1981; contbr. (with Ph. Diole) articles to, Nat. Geographic Mag. Served as lt. de vaisseau French Navy, World War II. Decorated comdr. Legion of Honor, Croix de Guerre with palm, Merite Agricole, Merite Maritime, officer Arts and Lettres; Potts medal Franklin Inst., 1970; Gold medal Grand Prix d'oceanographie Albert I, 1971. Fgn. asso. Nat. Acad. Scis. U.S.A. Partly responsible for invention of aqualung, 1943; leader sci. cruise around world, 1967, basis for television series The Undersea World of Jacques-Yves Cousteau; leader expdn. to Antaratic and Chilian coast, 1972. Address: care Cousteau Soc 777 3 Ave New York NY 10017 *

COUSY, BOB JOSEPH, sports commentator; b. N.Y.C., Aug. 9, 1928; s. Joseph and Juliette (Corlet) e7C.); m. Marie A. Ritterbusch, Dec. 9, 1950; children—Marie Collette, Mary Patricia. B.S. in Bus, Coll. of Holy Cross, 1950. Basketball player Boston Celtics, 1950-63; basketball coach Boston Coll., Chestnut Hill, Mass., from 1963; chmn. phys. fitness program H.P. Hood & Sons, Boston, from 1963; head coach Cin. Royals, Kansas City-Omaha Kings, to 1973; formerly commr. Am. Soccer League; now color commentator Boston Celtics. Author: Basketball is My Life, 1956, Last Loud Roar, 1965, Basketball Principles, 1971, The Killer Instinct, 1976. Chmn. Mass. Cystic Fibrosis Found., from 1956; nat. dir. Big Brothers, 1964-65. Named to Basketball Hall of Fame, 1971. Address: care Press Relations Boston Celtics Boston Garden North Sta Boston MA 02114 *

COUTTS, JAMES ALLAN, former Canadian government official, consultant; b. High River, Alta., Can., May 16, 1938; s. Ewart E. and Alberta (Allan) C. B.A. in Econs, U. Alta., 1960, LL.B., 1961; M.B.A., Harvard U., 1968. Bar: Called to bar 1962. Barrister and solicitor McLaws & Co., Calgary, Alta., 1961-63; appointment sec. to Prime Minister of Can. Lester B. Pearson, 1963-66; cons. McKinsey & Co., N.Y.C., Zurich and Toronto, 1968-70; founding ptnr. Can. Cons. Group, Toronto, 1970-75; prin. sec. to Right Honorable P.E. Trudeau, 1975-81; pres. Louther Cons. Co. Bd. govs. L.B. Pearson Coll. of Pacific, Victoria, B.C.; bd. govs. Hosp. Sick Children, Niagara Inst.; Federal Liberal candidate, 1962. Mem. United Ch. Can. Club: Rideau (Ottawa). Home: 31 Lowther Ave Toronto ON M5R 1C5 Canada Office: 609 Bloor St W Suite 202 Toronto ON Canada M6G 1K5

COUTTS, JOHN WALLACE, chemist, educator; b. Neepawa, Man., Can., Feb. 2, 1923; came to U.S., 1946, naturalized, 1956; s. John Wallace and Lavina (Murray) C.; m. Blanche A. Muris, Dec. 22, 1959; 1 son, J. Blayd Ott. B.Sc., U. Man., 1945, M.Sc., 1947; Ph.D., Purdue U., 1950. Asst. prof. chemistry Mt. Union Coll., Alliance, Ohio, 1950-55; asso. prof. Lake Forest (Ill.) Coll., 1955-62, prof., chmn. dept.,

1962—; vis. prof. Purdue U., summers 1955, 56, 57, Northwestern U., 1958, 60, 61, 78, U. Calif. at Berkeley, 1967-68, Rensselaer Poly. Inst., 1974-75. Author: (with Dwight E. Gray) Man and His Physical World, 2d edit, 1966. Fulbright lectr. U. Peshawar, Pakistan, 1958-59. Home: 106 E Sheridan Rd Lake Bluff IL 60044 Office: Lake Forest College Lake Forest IL 60045

COUTTS, RONALD THOMSON, pharmaceutical sciences educator; b. Glasgow, Scotland, June 19, 1931; emigrated to Can., 1963, naturalized, 1971; s. Ronald Miller and Helen Alexandrina (Crombie) C.; m. Sheenah Kirk Black, Sept. 4, 1957; children: Marin, Alan, Kathryn. B.S. in Pharmacy, Glasgow U., 1955, Ph.D. in Chemistry, 1959; D.S. In Medicinal Chemistry, U. Strathclyde, Glasgow, 1976. Lectr. medicinal chemistry Sunderland Tech. Coll., Eng., 1959-63; asst. prof., assoc. prof. medicinal chemistry U. Sask., Can., 1963-66; assoc. prof., prof. medicinal chemistry U. Alta., Edmonton, Can., 1966—, asst. dean Faculty Pharmacy and Pharm. Scis., 1979—; vis. prof. Chelsea Coll., U. London, 1972-73; pres. Xenotex Service Ltd. Author: (with G.A. Smail) Polysaccharides, Peptides and Proteins, 1966; contbr. chpts. to textbooks, articles to research publs.; editorial bd.: Asian Jour. Pharm. Scis., 1978—; sci. editor: Can. Jour. Pharm. Scis., 1967-72; patentee in field. Recipient various research grants. Fellow Chem. Inst. Can., Royal Soc. Chemists U.K., Pharm. Soc. Gt. Britain, Royal Soc. Can.; mem. Chem. Soc. Gt. Britain, Pharmacol. Soc. Can., Western Pharmacology Soc. (U.S.), Am. Chem. Soc., Soc. Toxicology Can., Can. Coll. Neuropsychopharmacology, Assn. Acad. Staff U. Alta. (pres. 1978-79). Clubs: Windermere Golf and Country, Faculty Club U. Alta. Office: Faculty Pharmancy and Pharm Scis Univ Alta Edmonton AB Canada T6G 2N8 *

COUTURE, JEAN GUY, bishop; b. Quebec, Que., Can., May 6, 1929; s. Odilon and Eva (Drolet) C. B.A., Laval U., Quebec, 1949, B.Ph., 1949, L.Theol., 1953, L.Sc.Phys., 1959. Ordained priest Roman Cath. Ch., 1953; prof. math. and scis. St. Georges High Sch. and Coll., Beauce, Que., 1953-65, adminstr. coll., 1961-68; mem. adminstrn. Roman Cath. Diocese Quebec, 1968-75; bishop of Hauterive, Que., 1975-79, of Chicoutimi, 1979—. Home and Office: 602 est Racine Chicoutimi PQ G7H 5C3 Canada

COUTURE, RONALD DAVID, art administrator, design consultant; b. Ware, Mass., Dec. 1, 1944; s. Roy and Thelma Mary (Ledger) C.; m. Sandra Elaine Sharpe, Sept. 28, 1968; children: David, Meredith. Diploma, Butera Sch. Art, Boston, 1966. Graphic designer Sta. WGBH-TV Ednl. Found., Cambridge, Mass., 1970-73; promotion art dir. The Boston Globe, 1973-74, editorial design dir., 1974-77; asst. mng. art dir. N.Y. Times, 1977-78, assoc. mng. art dir., 1978-79, mng. art dir., 1979—; design cons. Met. Cultural Alliance, Boston, 1972-77; guest lectr. Boston U. Sch. Communications, 1977; judge 62d Ann Exhibit, The Art Dirs. Club of N.Y., 1983; internat. editorial design Internat. Editorial Design Forum, N.Y.C., 1983. Contbr. articles in field to profl. jours. Mem. Westborough Planning Bd., Mass., 1977; aptd. regional rep. Central Mass. Regional Planning Bd., Westborough, 1977; aptd. chmn. Archtl. Rev. Bd., Mount Kisco, N.Y., 1977, 80, 83; mem. task force Labor Market Info. Network of N.Y. Labor Dept. and N.Y.C. Dept. Employment, 1979. Recipient Gold medal set design New England Theater Conf., 1974, Gold medal newspaper design Soc. Newspaper Design, 1980, Gold medal chart design, 1981. Mem. Art Dirs. Club N.Y., Am. Inst. Graphic Artist, Art Dirs. Club Boston, Nat. Computer Graphics Assn., Soc. Publ. Design. Roman Catholic. Home: 43 Prospect St Mount Kisco NY 10549 Office: The New York Times 229 W 43rd St New York NY 10036

COUZENS, FRANK, JR., banker; b. Detroit, Jan. 18, 1924; s. Frank and Margaret (Lang) C.; m. Joan Marie Ulrich, Aug. 9, 1947; children: Joan Marie (Mrs. Thomas V. Cliff), Margaret Mary (Mrs. Michael W. Crandall) Ann Marie, Mary Carol (Mrs. Lawrence R. Marantette), Frank III, William Ulrich, John Manning. B.S., U. Detroit, 1948. With Mfrs. Nat. Bank Detroit, 1951—, officer, 1955, 2d v.p., 1956-60, v.p., 1960-64, v.p. adminstr., 1964-67, sr. v.p., 1967-71, sr. v.p., sr. trust officer, 1971-77, exec. v.p., 1977—; pres., trustee Oakland Housing Inc., Birmingham, Mich.; v.p., dir. Wabeek Corp., Birmingham; dir. Jacobson Stores Inc., Mich. Trustee Children's Hosp. Mich., 1973—, chmn. fin., 1976—; trustee United Community Services, 1971, v.p., 1974, pres., 1975, chmn. bd., 1977-81; mem. exec. com. Greater Detroit Area Health Council, 1974—, mem. budget and fin. com., 1980—, chmn. Project Health Care, 1982—; mem. Citizens' Com. Higher Edn. Served with USNR, 1942-46. Recipient Ser. Recognition Citizens Com. Higher Edn.; Silver Beaver award Detroit area council Boy Scouts Am. Mem. Greater Detroit C. of C. Roman Catholic. Clubs: Economic, Detroit Athletic, Country, Hundred, Cardinal (Detroit); Otsego Ski. Home: 66 Lothrop Rd Grosse Pointe Farms MI 48236 Office: 100 Renaissance Center Detroit MI 48243

COVAL-APEL, NAOMI MILLER, dentist; b. Bayonne, N.Y.; d. Jacob Paul and Bertha Miller; m. Robert Simon Apel; children: Payson Rodney, Mark Lawrence, Ilya Sandra. Attended, U. Chgo., 1933-36; B.S., N.Y. U., 1939; D.D.S., Columbia, 1943. Practice dentistry specializing in temporomandibular joint dysfunctions, practice ltd. to orthodontics, Glen Cove, L.I., N.Y., 1946—; instr. postgrad. courses in orthodontics for local and nat. dental socs. extension refresher groups;; past instr. N.Y. Dental Sch.; lectr. U.S. and fgn. countries, S. Am. univs., 1969; attending Peninsula Gen. Hosp., 1959-82; attending dentist N.Y. Infirmary., 1943-51; Chmn. Nassau County for Fluoridation, L.I. Fluoridation Com., 1960; del. Oral Hygiene Com. N.Y. Editor Internat. Jour. Orthodontics.; Contbr. numerous articles to profl. publs. Past pres. 5 Towns Aux. Peninsula Gen. Hosp.; patron, sponsor Island Concert Hall; active Hull House; leader Girl Scouts U.S.A., 8 yrs; pres. Lawrence High Sch. P.T.A., 1966, 5 Towns Am. Jewish Congress; bd. dirs. Am. Cancer Soc. Scholar, Art Inst.; v.p. sisterhood Temple Israel, 13Lawrence. Recipient award William Jarvie Soc. Dental Research, 1942. Fellow Soc. Oral Physiology and Occulsion; mem. Am. Dental Assn., 10th Dist Dental Soc., Assn. Dental Editors (1st woman dental editor), Columbia Alumni (exec. bd.), N.Y. State Assn. Professions (charter), Am. Soc. for Study Orthodontics, William Jarvie Soc. for Dental Research, Fedn. Dentaire Internat., Brit. Soc. Orthodontics, Pan Am. Med. Assn., Acad. Dental Medicine, Assn. Women Dentists (editor-in-chief bull., v.p., dir. postgrad. courses), Internat. Acad. Orthodontics (editor jour., v.p. Eastern sect., sec.), Fedn. Orthodontic Socs., Rockaway Dental Soc., AAAS, Nat. Council Jewish Women (life), Am. Jewish Congress (mem. bd., pres. Five Towns chpt.), Fedn. Am. Orthodontists, Am. Assn. Study Psychoanalysis, Am. Acad. Oral Medicine, N.Y. Acad. Scis., Nat. Geog. Soc., Am. Mus. Natural History, Assn. for Women Sci., Internat. Soc. Artists, Internat. Platform Assn. (charter mem.), Am. Red Mogen David Assn., Rapa Nui Soc. Easter Islands, Fellowship of Reconciliation, Nat. Women's Polit. Caucus, Nat. Orgn. Women, Pulse of Women (v.p.), Wildlife Soc. Kenya.; Mem. B'nai B'rith (v.p.), Hadassah. Clubs: Wayfarers, National Travel. Research on thyroidectimized rats to determine tooth growth; developed original technique for repositioning mandible. Mem. numerous pvt. anthrop. expdns. *All the vicissitudes of youth, all the stresses of building a career, all the agonies of rearing children are worth the journey, when one sails toward the finishing line with a magnificent spouse who is one's best friend.*

COVALT, ROBERT BYRON, chemical executive; b. Chgo., Nov. 8, 1931; s. Byron L. and Thelma A. (Adams) C.; m. Virginia, Aug. 17, 1952; children: Karen Elizabeth, David Byron. B.S. in Chem. Engring., Purdue U., 1953; M.B.A., U. Chgo., 1967. Devel. engr. B.F. Goodrich Chem. Co., Avon Lake, Ohio, 1953-54; with Morton Chem. Co., 1956—, v.p. engring. and mfg., Chgo., 1973-78, group v.p., 1978-79, pres., 1979—. Served as 1st lt. USAF, 1954-56. Recipient Disting. Engring. Alumnus award Purdue U. Mem. Am. Inst. Chem. Engrs., Am. Chem. Soc., Soc. Chem. Industry. Office: 2 N Riverside Plaza Chicago IL 60606

COVAULT, LLOYD R., JR., hospital administrator; b. Troy, Ohio, Feb. 3, 1928; s. Lloyd R. and Anne Marie (Grisez) C.; m. Janet Eileen Davidson, June 12, 1951; children: Sheryl Ann, Jane Helen, Michael Lee, Roger Ken. B.A., Miami U., Oxford, Ohio, 1950; M.D., Ohio State U., 1954. Extern Orient (Ohio) State Inst., 1953-54, staff physician, 1954-57, clin. dir., until 1966, asst. supt., 1968-70; psychiat. tng. Central Ohio Psychiat. Hosp., Columbus, 1966-68, psychiatrist, 1982—; supt. Columbus State Inst., 1970-74; med. dir. North Central Community Mental Health Center, 1974-79; dir. Southeast Mental Health Center, Columbus, 1979—; psychiatrist Southwest Mental Health Ctr. (part-time), Columbus, 1982—; Med. dir. Madison County Mental Health Center, London, Ohio, 1984—; practice psychiatry, part-time, Columbus, 1968-75; Mem. Franklin County Mental Health and Retardardation Bd., 1970-74. Fellow Am. Assn. Mental Deficiency; mem. Am. Psychiat. Assn., Ohio Psychiat. Assn. (mem. council 1975—), Neuropsychiat. Soc. Central Ohio (pres. 1973-74), Mental Health Supts. Assn. (pres. Ohio dept. 1973-74). Home: 11096 Darby Creek Rd Orient OH 43146 Office: Southwest Mental Health Center 199 S Central Ave Columbus OH 43223 Office: Madison County Hosp 210 N Main St London OH 43140

COVER, FRANKLIN EDWARD, actor; b. Cleve., Nov. 20, 1928; s. Franklin Held and Britta (Schreck) C.; m. Mary Bradford Stone, Jan. 30, 1965; children: Bradford Franklin, Susan Henderson. B.A., Denison U., 1951; M.A., Western Res. U., 1954, M.F.A., 1955. Debut at, Cain Park Theatre, Cleve., 1945; mem. acting staff, Cleve. Playhouse, 1954-58; appeared at, New York Theatre in, Julius Caesar, 1959, Phoenix Theatre (under Ford grant) in, Henry IV, She Stoops to Conquer, Plough and the Stars, The Octoroon, Hamlet, 1960-61; Broadway plays include Giants Sons of Giants, 1961-62, Calculated Risk, 1962-63, Abraham Cochrane, 1964, Any Wednesday, 1965-66, The Investigation, 1966, A Warm Body, 1967, The Freaking Out of Stephanie Blake, 1967, Forty Carats, 1968-70, Applause, 1972, The Killdeer, 1974; appeared in: motion pictures Mirage, 1964, What's So Bad About Feeling Good?, 1966, Such Good Friends, 1969, The Great Gatsby, 1978, The Stepford Wives, 1973, The Day the Bubble Burst, 1980, A Woman Called Golda, 1981; appeared on: television shows Jackie Gleason Show, 1960's, The Investigation, 1967, Play of the Week, 1960, Edge of Night, 1967, Love of Life, 1960, Trials of O'Brien, 1962, Naked City, 1959, Defenders, 1960, Armstrong Circle Theatre, 1960, The Doctors, 1966, What Makes Sammy Run, 1959, The Secret Storm, 1969, All My Children, 1970, Change at 125th St, 1973; appeared in: television movies Shortwalk to Daylight, 1972, Connection, 1973; star in: television show The Jeffersons, 1974—; performed title role in: Macbeth at White House state dinner for Pres. Kennedy, 1961. Vestryman Ch. of the Resurrection, 1970s, warden, 1983; hon. trustee Cleve. Playhouse. Served to lt. USAF, 1951-53. Mem. Screen Actors Guild (dir.), AFTRA, Equity, Players Club New York, English Speaking Union, Blue Key, Kappa Sigma, Omicron Delta Kappa.

COVER, ROBERT M., law educator; b. Boston, July 30, 1943; s. Jacob L. and Martha (White) C.; m. Diane Bornstein, Oct. 29, 1967; children: Avidan, Leah. B.A., Princeton U., 1965; LL.B., Columbia U., 1968. Asst. prof. law Columbia U., N.Y.C., 1968-71; vis. sr. lectr. law and Am. studies Hebrew U., Jerusalem, 1971-72, vis. prof. law, 1975; assoc. prof. law Yale U., New Haven, 1973—, Chancellor Kent prof. law and legal history, dir. Law and Humanities Inst., 1981—. Author: (with Owen Fiss) Structure of Procedure, 1979. Pres. Yale Friends of Hillel, New Haven, 1980—. Fellow Guggenheim Found., 1981-82. Democrat. Jewish. Office: Yale Univ Law Sch 127 Wall St New Haven CT 06520

COVER, THOMAS MERRILL, electrical engineering and statistics educator; b. San Bernardino, Calif., Aug. 7, 1938; s. William Llewellyn and Carolyn Loraine (Merrill) C.; m. Sandran Detert (div. 1972); 1 son, William Detert. B.S. in Physics, M.I.T., 1960; M.S.E.E., Stanford U., 1961, Ph.D., 1964; postgrad., Harvard U., 1971-72. Asst. prof. elec. engring. Stanford U., Calif., 1964-67, assoc. prof., 1967-72, assoc. prof. elec. engring. and statistics, 1972, prof., 1973—; vis. assoc. prof. elec. engring. M.I.T., Cambridge, 1971; cons. SRI, Palo Alto, Calif., 1973—, Bell Labs., Murray Hill, N.J., 1973. Vinton Hayes fellow, 1971-72. Fellow IEEE; mem. Inst. Math. Statistics, Info. Theory Soc. (pres. 1972, outstanding paper award 1972). Home: 906 Addison St Palo Alto CA 94301 Office: Stanford Univ Durand Bldg 121 Stanford CA 94305

COVERDALE, GLEN EUGENE, life insurance company executive; b. Trafalgar, Ind., Jan. 9, 1930; m. Laurel Larson, Mar. 21, 1951; children—Beth Karen, Anne Christine. A.B. cum laude, Franklin (Ind.) Coll., 1951; M.B.A., Ind. U., 1952. With Met. Life Ins. Co., 1954—, exec. v.p. charge real estate investments, chief exec. officer, N.Y.C., 1978-83; dir. Doubletree Inns, Inc; mem. adv. bd. Real Estate Inst. NYU. Trustee Urban Land Inst. Served with AUS, 1952-54. Decorated Commendation medal. Fellow Life Office Mgmt. Assn.; mem. Real Estate Bd. N.Y. (bd. govs.), Sigma Alpha Epsilon, Beta Gamma Sigma, Phi Alpha Theta. Home: 355 Heights Rd Ridgewood NJ 07450 Office: 1 Madison Ave New York NY 10010

COVERDALE, ROBERT FREDERICK, air force officer; b. Amherst, Ohio, Sept. 24, 1930; s. Frederick John and Odelia Martha (Henes) C.; m. Norma Jean Tate, June 9, 1957; children: Lisa, Amy, Tate. B.A., Ohio Wesleyan U., 1952; postgrad., Armed Forces Staff Coll., Norfolk, Va., 1967. Commd. 2d lt. U.S. Air Force, 1952, advanced through grades to lt. gen., 1981; chief, employment test br. 2 Employment Test Div., Directorate Operational Test and Evaluation Dep. Chief of Staff, Plans and Ops., Hdqrs. U.S. Air Force, Washington, 1968-71; vice comdr. 516th Tactical Airlift Wing, Tactical Air Command, Dyess AFB, Tex., 1971-72; comdr. 463d Tactical Airlift Wing, Tactical Air Command, Dyess AFB, Tex., 1972-73, 314th Tactical Airlift Wing, Little Rock AFB, 1973-74; 834th Airlift Div., 1974-75, Operating Location A, 21st Air Force Mil. Airlift Command, Pope AFB, N.C., 1975; comdr. 317th Tactical Airlift Wing and U.S. Air Force Airlift Center, Pope AFB, 1975-77; dep. chief of staff-plans, then chief of staff Hdqrs. Mil. Airlift Command, Scott AFB, Ill., 1977-80; comdr. 22d Air Force, Travis AFB, Calif., 1980-81; vice comdr.-in-chief Mil. Airlift Command, Scott AFB, 1981—. Decorated D.S.M., Legion of Merit with oak leaf cluster, Meritorious Service medal with oak leaf cluster, Air Force Commendation medal with oak leaf cluster, Republic of Vietnam Cross of Gallantry with palm, Republic of Korea Order Nat. Security Merit. Mem. Air Force Assn., Airlift Assn., Armed Forces Mut. Benefit Assn. (bd. govs.), Order Daedalians, Phi Gamma Delta. Club: Masons. Home: 200 E Losey St Scott AFB IL 62225 Office: Mil Airlift Command Vice Comdr in Chief Scott AFB IL 62225

COVERT, EUGENE EDZARDS, educator, engineer; b. Rapid City, S.D., Feb. 6, 1926; s. Perry and Eda (Edzards) C.; m. Mary Solveig Rutford, Feb. 22, 1946; children: David H., Christine J., Pamela M., Steven P. B.S., U. Minn., 1946, M.S., 1948; Sc.D., MIT, 1958. Registered profl. engr., Mass.; chartered engr., U.K. Preliminary design group USNADS, Johnsville, Pa., 1948-52; mem. staff MIT Aerophysics Lab., 1952—, asso. dir. aerophysics lab., 1963—, asso. prof. aeronautics and astronautics, 1963-68, prof., 1968—; cons. Bolt, Beranek & Newman, Inc., Hercules, Inc., MIT Lincoln Lab., U.S. Army Research Office; chief scientist USAF, 1972-73; mem. panel Naval Aeroballistic Adv. Com., 1965-75; mem., chmn. USAF Sci. Adv. Bd.; chmn. Power, Energetics and Propulsion panel Adv. Group for Aerospace Research and Devel. NATO; dir. Megatech Inc., Billerica, Mass., Sverdrup ARO Inc., Tullahoma, Tenn. Served with USNR, 1943-47. Recipient Exceptional Civilian Service award USAF, 1973, Univ. Educator of Yr. award Am. Soc. Aerospace Edn., 1980, Pub. Service award NASA, 1980. Fellow AIAA, Royal Aero. Soc.; mem. AAAS, N.Y. Acad. Sci., Nat. Acad. Engring., Sigma Xi. Office: Mass Inst Tech 77 Massachusetts Ave Cambridge MA 02139

COVERT, FRANK MANNING, lawyer, corporate executive; b. Canning, N.S., Can., Jan. 13, 1908; s. Archibald Menzies and Minnie Alma (Clarke) C.; m. Mary Louise Covert, Aug. 25, 1934; children: Michael, Susan, Peter, Sally. B.A., Dalhousie U., 1927, LL.B., 1929. Bar: Called to N.S. bar 1930. Practice in, Halifax, N.S., 1930-40, 45—; sr. partner Stewart, MacKeen & Covert, 1963—; asst. gen. counsel Dept. Munitions and Supply, 1940-42; Pres. Ben's Holdings, Ltd., 1956—; chmn. bd. Maritime Paper Products Ltd., 1959—; dir. Bowater Mersey Paper Co. Ltd., Eastern Tel. & Tel. Co., Minas Basin Pulp & Power Co. Ltd., Can. Keyes Fibre Co. Ltd., Nat. Sea Products Ltd. Served as navigator RCAF, 1942-45. Decorated D.F.C., Order Brit. Empire, officer Order of Cordoba. Home: 5885 Spring Garden Rd Halifax NS Canada Office: PO Box 997 Halifax NS Canada B3J 2X2 *1) In anything you do, you ask: "Is this what I would want someone to do if they were doing it for me?" 2) Forget yesterday, work today, and plan tomorrow.*

COVEY, CHARLES WILLIAM, editor; b. Middlesboro, Ky., Sept. 29, 1918; s. Charles G. and Bertha (Bowman) C.; m. Mary Ruth Gibson, Sept. 16, 1943; children: Charles C., Catherine A. B.A. in Chemistry and Physics, Lincoln Meml. U., 1940. Instr. army aviation course Lincoln Meml. U., 1942-43; instr. naval meteorology Auburn Poly. Inst., 1943-44; instr. instrument engr. Union Carbide Nuclear Co., Oak Ridge, 1944-49, head instrument engring. dept., Paducah, Ky., 1952-54; head customer and sales tng. Taylor Instrument Co., Rochester, N.Y., 1949-52; editor ISA Jour., Instrument Soc. Am., Pitts., 1954-62; v.p., editorial dir. Compass Publs., Inc., Arlington, Va., 1962-74; program analyst Nat. Ocean Service, NOAA, Washington, 1974—. Served with USNR, 1943-44. Fellow Instrument Soc. Am. (pres. Oak Ridge 1944, Paducah 1953, nat. v.p., mem. exec. bd. 1953, chmn. nat. publs. com. 1951-52); founding mem. Marine Tech. Soc. Home: 1820 Dalmation Dr McLean VA 22101 Office: Herbert C Hoover Bldg Room 4018 NOAA Washington DC 20230

COVEY, CYCLONE, history educator; b. Guthrie, Okla., May 21, 1922; s. Cyclone Davis and Lola (Best) C.; m. Bonnie Mae Bagby Hansen, June 12, 1949; children: Christopher Cyclone, Mark Nicholas, Julie Kristiana, Jonathan Baldridge, Timothy Nathaniel. B.A., Stanford U., 1944, Ph.D., 1949; postgrad., U. Chgo., 1944-45, U. Okla., 1945-46; postdoctoral, Harvard U., 1953-54. Instr. history, humanities Reed Coll., Portland, Oreg., 1947-50; instr. humanities, music Okla. A. and M., Stillwater, 1950-51; prof. govt., history, fgn. langs. McKendree Coll., Lebanon, Ill., 1951-53, 54-56; faculty fellow Harvard U., Cambridge, Mass., 1953-54; vis. asst. prof. Am. studies Amherst (Mass.) Coll., 1956-57; from asst. prof. to prof. Okla. State U., Stillwater, 1957-68; prof. history Wake Forest U., Winston-Salem, N.C., 1968—; Ford postdoctoral fellow, 1953, Carnegie vis. asst. prof., 1956, Oak Ridge seminarian, 1964, Danforth asso., 1962; dir. Wake Forest in Venice, 1972. Author: The Wow Boys, 1957, The American Pilgrimage, 1960, Cabeza de Vaca's Adventures in the Unknown Interior of America, 1961, A Cyclical Return to the Timeless Three-Clock Revolution, 1966, The Gentle Radical, 1966, Calalus, 1975; composer: Aburst with Song, 1970; windquintet Birdsong Woods, 1980; piano trio Whether My Bark Went Down, 1980. Democrat. Home: 4071 Tangle Ln Winston-Salem NC 27106

COVEY, F. DON, energy company executive; b. Lubbock, Tex., June 19, 1934; s. Foy Wallace and Letha Beatrice (Dumas) C.; m. Mary Helen Key, Nov. 5, 1955; children: Frank P., Don W. B.S. in Petroleum Engring., Tex. Tech. U., 1955. Various engring. positions Shell Oil Co., Tex., Okla. and La., 1955-64, div. petroleum engr., Houston and Bakersfield, Calif., 1964-68, chief petroleum engr., New Orleans, 1968-70, div. prodn. mgr., 1970-76; sr. v.p. prodn. Mitchell Energy Corp., Houston, 1976-79; pres. exploration and prodn. div. Mitchell Energy & Devel. Corp., The Woodlands, Tex., 1979—. Mem. Soc. Petroleum Engrs., Am. Petroleum Inst., Tex. Mid-Continent Oil and Gas Assn. Republican. Mem. Ch. of Christ. Club: Woodlands Country. Office: Mitchell Energy & Devel Corp PO Box 4000 The Woodlands TX 77380

COVEY, FRANK MICHAEL, JR., lawyer; b. Chgo., Oct. 24, 1932; s. Frank M. and Marie B. (Lorinz) C.; m. Patricia Ann McGill, Oct. 7, 1961; children: Geralyn F., Michael III, Hegis Patrick. B.S. with honors, Loyola U., Chgo., 1954, J.D. cum laude, 1957; S.J.D., U. Wis., 1960. Bar: Ill. 1957, U.S. Sup. Ct. 1965. Research assoc. Wis. Gov.'s Com. on Revision Law of Eminent Domaine, 1958; law clk. Ill. Appellate Ct., 1959; assoc. firm Belnap, Spencer, Hardy & Freeman, Chgo., 1959-60, McDermott, Will & Emery, 1960-64, ptnr., 1965—, mem. exec. com., 1979-81, mgmt. com., 1979-82, inc. ptnr., 1981—; instr. Northwestern U. Sch. Law, 1958-59, Loyola Univ. Coll., 1958-69, 79-80; assoc. gen. counsel Union League Civic and Arts Found., 1967-69, v.p., 1972-75, pres., 1972-73, mng. dir., 1975-80; co-dir. Grand Park study team Nat. Commn. on Causes and Prevention of Violence, 1968. Author: Roadside Protection Through Access Control, 1960, (with others) Federal Civic Practice in Illinois, 1974, 78, Business Litigation I - Competition and Its Limits, 1978, Class Actions, 1979; contbr. articles in field to profl. jours. Mem. bd. athletics Loyola U., 1970-72, mem. estate planning com., 1969-81, mem. com. on the future of the law sch., 1975-76, trustee, 1979—, mem. citizens bd., 1979—; bd. dirs. Chgo. Bldg. Congress, 1978-82, sec., 1982—; mem. revenue adv. com. Chgo City Council, 1983—. Recipient award Conf. on Personal Fin. Law, 1955, Founders Day award Loyola U., 1976, Distings Service award, 1980, medal of Excellence Loyola U. Law Sch., 1979. Mem. ABA, Ill. State Bar Assn. (Lincoln award 1963), Chgo. Bar Assn., Fed. 7th Circuit Lawyers, Catholic Lawyers Guild, Chgo. Council Lawyers, Am. Judicature Soc., North Shore Bd. Realtors (assoc.), Internat. Assn. Ins. Counsel, Def. Research Inst., Ill. Hist. Soc., Air Force Assn., Loyola U. Alumni Assn. (pres. 1965-66), Loyola U. Law Sch. Alumni Assn. (chmn. alumni fund campaign 1967-68, v.p. alumni 1968-69, pres. 1969-70, chmn. Thomas More Club 1973-75), Blue Key, Phi Alpha Delta, Alpha Sigma Nu, Pi Gamma Mu, Delta Sigma Rho. Clubs: Union League (Chgo.) (bd. dirs. 1977-80, chmn. house com. 1977-80); Legal, Law (Chgo.). Home: 1104 W Lonnquist Blvd Mount Prospect IL 60056 Office: McDermott Will & Emery 111 W Monroe St Chicago IL 60603

COVEY, HAROLD DEAN, insurance company executive; b. Clinton, Ill., Sept. 8, 1930; s. Elmer Lloyd and Nora (Fittro) C.; m. Margaret F. Thompson, Mar. 25, 1951; children: Cheryl Covey Ramsey, Philip H.

B.S. in Bus. Adminstrn., Ill. Wesleyan U., Bloomington, 1956. Various underwriter positions State Farm Mut. Auto. Ins. Co., Bloomington, 1950-64, div. mgr., Greeley, Colo., 1964-69, exec. asst., Bloomington, 1969-71, dep. regional v.p., Santa Ana, Calif., 1971-72; v.p. underwriting, Bloomington, 1972—; dir. Nat. Industry Com., N.Y.C., 1974-78, chmn., 1976; bd. govs. S.C. Reins. Facility, Columbia, 1973-79; trustee Md. Auto Ins. Fund, Annapolis, 1976—; dir. Conf. Casualty Ins Cos., Indpls., 1978—, pres., 1981-82; dir. N.J. Auto Ins. Assn., Trenton, 1983—. Bd. dirs. United Way of McLean County, Bloomington, 1973—, pres., Bloomington, 1980-81; bd. dirs. Ill. Wesleyan U. Assocs., 1975-80. Served with USN, 1952-54. Mem. Soc. C.P.C.U.s, Soc. C.L.U.s. Republican. Presbyterian. Lodges: Kiwanis (dir. 1973-74); Masons; Shriners. Home: 4 Lucille Lane Normal IL 61761 Office: State Farm Mut Auto Ins Co One State Farm Plaza Bloomington IL 61701

COVEY, MOODY, oil company executive; b. Bristow, Okla., Oct. 7, 1929; s. Cyclone Davis and Lola Effie (Best) C.; m. Betty Lou Gilbert, Aug. 20, 1949; 1 son, Brent Roger. B.S., Okla. State U., 1949. With Getty Oil Co. and affiliated cos., 1950—, various assignments, Drumright, Okla., Tulsa, Houston, San Francisco, Los Angeles, Tokyo, 1950-71, corp. employee and pub. relations mgr., 1971, v.p., rep. dir. Mitsubishi Oil Co. Ltd., Tokyo, 1972-76; v.p. adminstrn. Skelly Oil Co., 1976; v.p. corp. adminstrn. Getty Oil Co., 1977—. Bd. dirs. Getty Oil Co. Found. Mem. Am. Petroleum Inst. Republican. Presbyterian. Clubs: Jonathan, Los Angeles. Lodge: Masons. Office: 3810 Wilshire Blvd Los Angeles CA 90010

COVEY, RONALD HARRY, insurance company executive; b. Nashua, N.H., Apr. 30, 1932; s. Harry Raymond and Lucille A. (Bourassa) C.; m. Elaine R. Guerette, Sept. 25, 1954; children: Ronald Harry, Dana M., LuAnn L., Bryan D. Student public schs., Manchester, N.H. Mgr. methods and procedures dept. N.H. Ins. Co., Manchester, 1966-74, asst. sec., 1968-72, sec., from 1972, now officer in charge duplicating and supply depts. Served with U.S. Army, 1952-54, 61-62. Mem. Assn. Systems Mgmt., In-Plant Mgmt. Assn., N.H. Graphic Arts Assn. Office: 1750 Elm St Manchester NY 03107 *

COVEY, VICTOR CHARLES BAMERT, art conservator; b. Morehead City, N.C., Nov. 28, 1916; s. Floyd E. and Wilhelmina (Bamert) C.; m. Lucia Elizabeth D'Antoni, Aug. 11, 1941 (div. 1980); children: Victor Lance, Laurence Colt. Diploma, Balt. City Coll., 1938; student jewelry design and execution, Alvin Schmidt, jeweler, Balt., 1938-39, Corcoran Gallery, 1953-59, Brussels, 1963, 1968. Master tool maker Glenn L. Martin Aircraft Co., Balt., 1940-49; art technician Balt. Mus. Art, 1949-53, chief conservator of art, 1953-72; chief art conservation Nat. Gallery of Art, Washington, 1972-83, chief art conservation, emeritus-sr. conservator for spl. projects, 1983—; former conservator Wurzburger Collections of Pre-Columbian African, Oceanic and Modern Sculpture (Balt. Mus. Art), 1954-74, Collections of African sculpture and contemporary paintings Mr. and Mrs. Robert Meyerhoff, Balt., 1954-74, Dr. and Mrs. Israel Rosen, Roland Gibson Art Found.; collaborator in testing Rhikon Corp., Covey Solid-State Hygrometer invention., Cleve., 1980-83. Apptd. conservator: Archaeol. Finds. of People's Republic of China, Dept. State exhbn., U.S., 1975, Peking, 1975, Holy Crown of St. Stephen and Hungarian Coronation Regalia, Ft. Knox, Ky., 1977-78, Budapest. Mem. N.E. Community Orgn., Balt., 1969-72. Fellow Am. Inst. for Conservation (dir. 1975-76), Internat. Inst. Conservation; mem. Washington Conservation Guild (pres. 1974-75), Nat. Conservation Adv. Council (v.p. 1976-77). Democrat. Lutheran. Home: 3717 Rexmere Rd Baltimore MD 21218 Office: Nat Gallery of Art 6th and Constitution Aves Washington DC 20565

COVI, DARIO ALESSANDRO, art historian, educator; b. Livingston, Ill., Dec. 26, 1920; s. Joe J. and Cecilia (Menghini) C.; m. Anna Madeline Cundiff, Sept. 7, 1960. B.Ed., Eastern Ill. U., 1943; M.A., State U. Iowa, 1948; postgrad., U. London, 1949, U. Florence, 1950; Ph.D., NYU, 1958. Instr., U. Louisville, 1956-58, asst. prof., 1958-61, asso. prof., 1961-64, prof., 1964-70; curator Art Collection, 1958-63, 79—, acting head dept. fine arts, 1960-63, chmn. dept., 1963-67, 76-79, vis. prof., 1974-75, Allen R. Hite prof. art history, 1975—; prof., chmn. dept. Duke, 1970-75. Author: Prints from the Allen R. Hite Art Institute Collection, 1963; Contbr. articles profl. jours. Mem. exec. com. Ky. Arts Commn., 1965-70; Ky. chmn. Com. to Rescue Italian Art, 1966-67; Bd. dirs. Art Center Assn. Louisville, 1960-68, Print Collectors Club, Louisville. Served with AUS, 1943-46. Recipient Disting. Alumnus award Eastern Ill. U., 1979; hon. mem. Amici di Brera e dei Musei Milanesi, 1967. Fellow Am. Council Learned Socs., I Tatti; mem. Coll. Art Assn. Am., Southeastern Coll. Art Conf., Renaissance Soc. Am., Midwest Art History Soc., AAUP. Home: 2019 Grasmere Dr Louisville KY 40205

COVINGTON, CLARENCE ALLEN, JR., lawyer; b. Chattanooga, Feb. 19, 1916; s. Clarence Allen and Mabel (Nelson) C.; m. Mary Ellen Moore, Dec. 28, 1940; children: Constance Anne (Mrs. Richard Stevens), Mary Katherine (Mrs. Thomas E. Lichak), Clarence Allen III, Richard M. A.B., Ohio U., 1938; J.D., Ohio State U., 1940. Bar: Ohio 1940. Practice in, Youngstown, 1946—; sr. partner Henderson, Covington, Stein, Donchess & Messenger, 1947—; cóunsel, sec., dir. Ajax Magnethermic Corp., Powell Essco Products Co., Hynes Industries, Inc., J & S Aluminum Products Co., A.H. Buehrle Co., Aluminum Billets, Inc., Powell Pressed Steel Co., Renner Co., Benada Aluminum Co., Superior Industries, Inc., Dental Prosthetic Systems, Inc., Med-Dent Realty, Inc.; gen. counsel, dir. Calex Corp., Control Transformer Corp., Clayton Heating; dir. Dollar Savs. & Trust Co. Regional, OPA, 1940-43. Chmn. Zoning Commn., 1948—; pres. Local Sch. Bd., 1951-59; chmn. local SSS bd., 1953—. Served to lt. USNR, 1943-46. Mem. ABA, Ohio Bar Assn., Mahoning County Bar Assn. (past pres.), Youngstown Bar Assn., Am. Arbitration Assn. (arbitrator), Am. Judicature Soc., Youngstown Hosp. Assn. (chmn. bd. 1977—). Home: 4123 Windsor Rd Youngstown OH 44512 Office: Wick Bldg Youngstown OH 44503

COVINGTON, HAROLD DOUGLAS, university chancellor; b. Winston-Salem, N.C., Mar. 7, 1935; s. Henry and Fannie C.; m. Beatrice Mitchell, June 14, 1958; children—Anthony Douglas, Jeffrey Steven. B.S., Central State U., Wilberforce, Ohio, 1957; M.S., Ohio State U., 1958, Ph.D., 1966. Formerly psychologist Dayton (Ohio) Public Schs.; supr. testing and research Gary (Ind.) Public Schs., asst. supt. for curriculum public schs., Saginaw, Mich., dep. supt. schs., public schs., Montclair, N.J.; v.p. devel. affairs Tuskegee Inst.; now chancellor Winston-Salem (N.C.) State U.; adj. prof. and lectr. various univs., colls. Bd. dirs. ARC, N.C. Theater Arts; trustee Nat. Council Econ. Edn.; mem. N.C. Med. Care Commrs.; mem. adv. bd. Office for Advancement of Public Negro Colls.; mem. adv. com., dept. tng. and devel. United Negro Coll. Fund.; vice chairperson public services area United Way Campaign. Recipient awards from various orgns., including NAACP, Nat. Council Negro Women, Alpha Phi Alpha, Phi Delta Kappa, Nat. Council Exceptional Children, Saginaw Model Cities Policies Bd. Mem. Winston-Salem C. of C. (dir.), Am. Assn. State Colls. and Univs. (bd. dirs.). Club: Rotary (Winston-Salem). Office: Office of Chancellor Winston-Salem State U Winston-Salem NC 27102

COVINGTON, ROBERT NEWMAN, lawyer, educator; b. Evansville, Ind., Sept. 9, 1936; s. George Milburn and Roberta (Newman) C.; m. Paula Anne Hattox, July 29, 1972. B.A., Yale U., 1958; J.D., Vanderbilt U., 1961. Bar: Tenn. 1961. Asst. prof. law Vanderbilt U., Nashville, 1961-64, assoc. prof., 1964-69, prof., 1969—; vis. prof. U. Mich., 1971, U. Calif., Davis, 1975-76, U. Tex., 1983; Adminstrv. law officer Calif. Agrl. Labor Relations Bd., 1975-76; cons. Tenn. Dept. Labor, 1972, Tenn. Law Library Commn., 1965-75. Author works in field. Mem. Am. Bar Assn., Tenn. Bar Assn., Am. Arbitration Assn., Order of Coif, Phi Beta Kappa. Democrat. Episcopalian. Club: Univ. (Nashville). Home: 907 Estes Rd Nashville TN 37215 Office: Vanderbilt Law Sch Nashville TN 37240

COVINO, BENJAMIN GENE, anesthesiologist, educator; b. Lawrence, Mass., Sept. 12, 1930; s. Nicholas and Mary (Zannini) C.; m. Lorraine Gallagher, Aug. 22, 1953; children: Paul, Brian. A.B., Holy Cross Coll, 1951; M.S., Boston Coll. Grad. Sch., 1953; Ph.D. (Life Ins. fellow), Boston U. Grad. Sch., 1955; M.D., U. Buffalo, 1962. Teaching fellow Boston U., 1954-55; asst. prof. pharm. Tufts U. Sch. Med., Boston, 1957-59; asst. prof. physiology U. Buffalo Sch. Med., 1959-62; med. dir. Astra Pharm. Products, Worcester, 1962-66, v.p. sci. affairs, 1967-78; prof. anesthesiology U. Mass. Med. Sch., 1976-79; cons. physiologist St. Vincent's Hosp., Worcester, 1963-79; chmn. anesthesiology Brigham and Women's Hosp. and prof. anesthesia Harvard U. Med. Sch., Boston, 1979—. Contbr. articles to profl. jours. Bd. dirs. St. Vincent's Research Found.; trustee Assumption Coll., Worcester, Mass. Served to 1st lt. USAF, 1955-57. Mem. Am. Physiol. Soc., Am. Heart Assn., Am. Fedn. Clin. Research, Am. Soc. Pharmacology and Exptl. Therapeutics, Am. Soc. Anesthesiology, Alpha Omega Alpha. Office: 75 Francis St Boston MA 02115 *

COWAN, DWAINE OLIVER, chemist, educator; b. Fresno, Calif., Nov. 25, 1935; s. Oliver F. and Eva Belle (Parsons) C.; m. LaVon H. Adams, Feb. 2, 1963. B.S., Fresno State Coll., 1958; Ph.D., Stanford U., 1962. Research fellow Calif. Inst. Tech., 1962-63; mem. faculty Johns Hopkins U., 1963—, prof. chemistry, 1972—; mem. chemistry research evaluation panel, directorate chem. scis. Air Force Office Sci. Research, 1976-80. Author: (with R.L. Drisko) Elements of Organic Photochemistry, 1976; also over 125 articles. Sloan fellow, 1968-70; Guggenheim fellow, 1970-71. Mem. Am. Chem. Soc., Chem. Soc. Eng., Am. Phys. Soc., AAAS, Inter-Am. Photochem. Soc., Sigma Xi, Phi Lambda Upsilon. Address: Johns Hopkins Univ Baltimore MD 21218

COWAN, EDWARD, journalist; b. Bklyn., Nov. 14, 1933; s. Marcy Hamilton and Jennie (Taleisnik) C.; m. Ann Louise Wrubel, July 1, 1962; children: Jeffrey Wrubel, Emily Martha, Rachel Jennifer. B.A., Columbia Coll., 1954; M.A. in Econs., Johns Hopkins U., 1960. With U.P.I., 1957-62; with N.Y. Times, 1962—, banking reporter, 1963-65, Benelux corr., Brussels, Belgium, 1965-66, corr. London bur., 1966-67, corr. Toronto (Can.) Bur., 1967-72, Washington corr., 1972-83; Washington econs. editor, 1983—; instr. econs. Johns Hopkins, 1956-57; cons. U.S. Bur. Budget, 1963; co-founder Chronicle, Barton, Vt., 1974. Author: Oil and Water: The Torrey Canyon Disaster, 1968; contbr. to: The Economist, 1977—. Served with AUS, 1954-56. Recipient Chanler Hist. Essay prize Columbia, 1954. Home: 3924 Harrison St NW Washington DC 20015 Office: NY Times 1000 Connecticut Ave NW Washington DC 20036

COWAN, FAIRMAN CHAFFEE, lawyer; b. Wellesley Hills, Mass., Apr. 22, 1915; s. James Franklin and Hortense Victoria (Fairman) C.; m. Martha Logan Allis, Apr. 24, 1943; children: Douglas Fairman, Frederick Allis, Leonard Chaffee. A.B., Amherst Coll., 1937; LL.B., Harvard U., 1940; grad. 44th advanced mgmt. program, Harvard Bus. Sch. Bar: Mass. 1940. Assoc. Goodwin, Procter & Hoar, Boston, 1940-41, 46-52, partner, 1952-54; gen. counsel, clk., sec., v.p., dir. Norton Co., 1955-79; of counsel Bowditch & Dewey, Worcester, Mass., 1979—; dir. Mechanics Bank, Worcester. Vice chmn. Worcester Civic Center Commn., 1977-79; chmn. Pvt. Industry Council, Worcester Area CETA Consortium; bd. dirs. Legal Assistance Corp. of Central Mass., Social Service Planning Corp. Worcester, Worcester Area Career Edn. Consortium; trustee Clark U., 1964-76, 79—, Meml. Hosp., Worcester. Served to lt. USNR, 1942-45. Mem. Am., Mass., Worcester County, bar assns., Mass. Civic League (past v.p.), Citizen Plan E Assn. Worcester (past v.p.), Worcester Fire Soc., Phi Beta Kappa, Alpha Delta Phi. Republican. Home: 48 Berwick St Worcester MA 01602 Office: 311 Main St Worcester MA 01608

COWAN, FINIS EWING, federal judge; b. Dallas, Oct. 16, 1929; s. Finis E. and Kathleen (Hardwicke) C.; m. Juliet Delcambre, May 28, 1951; children: Eleanor Marie, Kathleen J., Virginia, Finis E., Lionel. B.A., Rice U., 1951; LL.B., U. Tex., 1956. Bar: Tex. 1956. Assoc. Baker & Botts, Houston, 1956-66, ptnr., 1966-77; U.S. dist. judge for So. Dist. Tex., Houston, 1977—. Served with USMC, 1951-53. Mem. Am. Coll. Trial Lawyers. Office: 613 US Post Office Bldg Galveston TX 77550

COWAN, FRANK, photographer; b. N.Y.C., Sept. 26, 1934; s. Maurice and Susan (Romain) C.; m. Elizabeth Langley, May 18, 1968. Student, Coll. City N.Y. Independent creative photographer, 1955—; photog. illustrations using real people; pres. Frank Cowan Studio, Inc., 1962—, Cowan Realty Corp., 1963—, Cowan Antique Co., 1979—. Recipient numerous awards and gold medals. Home: Birch Hill Rd Patterson NY 12563 Office: 5 E 16th St New York NY 10003

COWAN, GARY LAWRENCE, lawyer; b. Livingston, Mont., Oct. 19, 1934; s. R. Lee and Marjorie (Hughes) C.; m. Dorothy Roberts, Nov. 25, 1960; children: Laura Anne, William Roberts. B.A., U. Mont., 1956, M.A., 1957; J.D., U. Chgo., 1960. Bar: Ill. bar 1960, D.C. bar 1965, Mich. bar 1970. Asso. firm Sidley & Austin, Chgo., 1960-68, partner, 1969—; gen. counsel Mich. Consol. Gas Co., 1973-81, Wis. Pipeline Co., 1982—, Am. Natural Resources Co., 1983—. Clubs: Detroit, Grosse Pointe Hunt. Office: One Woodward Ave Detroit MI 48226

COWAN, IAN MCTAGGART, univ. chancellor; b. Edinburgh, Scotland, June 25, 1919; s. Ian McTaggart and Laura (Mackenzie) C.; m. Joyce Stewart Racey, Apr. 21, 1936; children—Garry Ian McTaggart, Ann McTaggart (Mrs. Mikkel Schau). B.A., U. B.C., 1932, D.Sc., 1977; Ph.D., U. Calif., Berkeley, 1935; LL.D., U. Alta., 1971, Simon Fraser U., 1981; D.Environ. Sci., Waterloo U., 1976. Head teaching fellow U. Calif., Berkeley, 1932-35; asst. biologist B.C. Provincial Mus., Victoria, 1935-38, asst. dir., 1938-40; with U. B.C., Vancouver, 1940-79, asst. prof. zoology, 1940-45, prof. zoology, 1945-53, prof., head zoology dept., 1953-64, dean faculty grad. studies, 1964-75, dean emeritus, 1975—, mem. senate, 1952-75; mem. acad. bd. Province B.C., 1964—, chmn., 1969-75, chmn. acad. council, 1978—; chancellor U. Victoria, 1979—. Mem. Environ. Council Can., 1971-74, chmn., 1974—; Bd. govs. Arctic Inst., 1950-56; mem. select com. nat. parks U.S. Sec. Interior, 1966-67. Decorated officer Order of Can.; recipient Leopold medal, 1970; Canadian Centennial medal, 1964; Fry medal, 1976; Queen Elizabeth Jubilee medal, 1977. Fellow Royal Soc. Can., Calif. Acad. Sci., A.A.A.S., Pacific Sci. Assn. (hon. life). Home: 3919 Woodhaven Terr Victoria BC Canada

COWAN, IRVING, hotel exec.; b. Irvington, N.J., Apr. 27, 1932; s. Joseph and Adele (Goldman) Cohen; m. Marjorie Friedland, Dec. 29, 1956; children—Debra Jean, Cynthia Ann, Jonathan David. Student, U. Miami, 1949-50. Pres. Diplomat Hotel and Country Clubs, Hollywood, Fla., 1960—; dir. City Nat. Bank Hallandale, Fla.; v.p. Hasam Realty Corp., Hasam Farms, Inc. Mem. Founders Club Mt. Sinai Hosp., Miami; bd. dirs. Hwy. Safety Found. Served with USCGR, 1950-53. Mem. Hollywood C. of C. (dir.), Com. of 100. Jewish religion (v.p.). Clubs: Jockey, Palm Bay, Le International, Ocean Reef, Cricket, Capitol, 200 of Greater Miami. Home: 1615 Diplomat Pky Hollywood FL 33020 Office: 3515 S Ocean Dr Hollywood FL 33022

COWAN, J MILTON, linguist; b. Salt Lake City, Feb. 22, 1907; s. James Brimley and Mabel Vickers (Brown) C.; m. Theodora Mary Ronayne, Sept. 1, 1934; children—J Ronayne, Bruce Milton, Julia. A.B., U. Utah, 1931, A.M., 1932; fellow, U. Calif. at Berkeley, 1932-33; Ph.D., U. Iowa, 1935; student, Univ. of Leipzig, Germany, 1929-30. Research asso. U. Iowa, 1935-38; asst. prof. German, 1938-41, asso. prof., 1942; dir. intensive lang. program Am. Council Learned Socs., 1942-46; also spl. cons. War Dept. in charge of lang. phase of Army Specialized Tng. Program and other such tng. programs in war and state depts. and other govt. agys.; prof. linguistics and dir. div. modern langs. Cornell U., 1946-72; pres. Spoken Lang. Services, Inc., 1972—; asso. with Linguistic Inst. sponsored by Linguistic Soc. as prof. or lectr. U. Mich., 1938, 40, U. N.C., 1941, U. Wis., 1944, U. Mich., summer 1948. Author: Pitch and Intensity Characteristics of American Stage Speech; Co-author: Conversational Arabic; Editor: A Dictionary of Modern Written Arabic. Fellow Acoustical Soc. Am.; mem. Am. Council Learned Socs. (dir. 1956-60), Linguistic Soc. Am. (sec.-treas., bus. mgr. pubs. 1939-50, pres. 1966), Sigma Xi. Home: 107 Hanshaw Rd Ithaca NY 14850

COWAN, JAMES DOUGLAS, architect; b. Yakima, Wash., June 19, 1920; s. James and Alma Louise (Shuster) C.; m. Ruth Weeden Moulton, Feb. 16, 1943; children: Laurie, Janet, Deborah. M.Arch., Yale U., 1947. Mgr., Maloney & Whitney, Yakima, 1953-56; partner Cowan & Paddock, Yakima, 1956-66; exec. dir. Wash. State Council AIA, Seattle, 1967; sr. asso. The Richardson Assos. (TRA), Seattle, 1968-78; v.p., mgr. planning and design dept. Seattle-First Nat. Bank, 1978-79; ind. profl. cons. project adminstrn., 1979—. Pres. Community Concert Assn., Yakima, 1960-66; chmn. Planning Commn., Yakima, 1961-65. Served to lt. comdr. USNR, 1941-45. Fellow AIA (pres. Wash. State council 1966). Episcopalian. Club: Rotary (Seattle).

COWAN, MARK DOUGLAS, government official, lawyer; b. Kankakee, Ill., Dec. 4, 1949; s. George Morterud and Esther (Shusterman) C.; m. Laura Macomber, June 26, 1981. B.A., U. Minn., 1971; J.D., Cath. U. Am., 1976. Desk chief ops. officer CIA, Washington, 1975-78, asst. legislative counsel, 1978-80; com. counsel Com. on Standards Ofcl. Conduct U.S. Ho. of Reps., Washington, 1980-81; dep. asst. sec. U.S. Dept. Labor, Washington, 1981-82, chief of staff, 1982—. Editor: Environ. Econ. Jour., 1982—. Mem. Old Presbyn. Meeting House, Alexandria, Va., 1981—. Served to capt. USAF, 1971-73. Mem. ABA, Assn. Former Intelligence Officers, Va. State Bar, D.C. Bar, Minn. Alumni Assn. (pres. 1979-81, bd. dirs. 1978—), Phi Sigma Kappa. Republican. Presbyterian. Clubs: Capitol Hill (Washington); Skyline Racquet (Arlington, Va.). Office: US Dept Labor 200 Constitution Ave Washington DC 20210 *In achieving success in any endeavor, there is no substitute for long hours and perseverance. Added to that is the basic belief that honesty must bea foundation for all one's dealings and that the maintenance of faith can help overcome any difficulty. The goal to return in small measure to this nation what it has given to me in ample quantity is what has motivated me in my governmentservice.*

COWAN, MICHAEL HEATH, dean; b. Kansas City, Mo., July 26, 1937; s. Heath Hal and Dora Lewellyn (Bolen) C. B.A., Yale U., 1959, Ph.D., 1964; postgrad., Cambridge (Eng.) U., 1962-63. From instr. to asst. prof. English and Am. studies Yale U., 1963-69; dean Branford Coll., 1964-66; asso. prof. lit. and community studies U. Calif., Santa Cruz, 1969-73, prof. lit., 1973—; provost Merrill Coll., 1979-79, chmn. Am. studies com., 1978—, also dean humanities and arts. Author: City of the West: Emerson, America and Urban Metaphor, 1967, Twentieth Century Interpretation of the Sound and the Fury, 1968. Woodrow Wilson fellow, 1959; Danforth fellow, 1959-64; Morse fellow, 1967-68; Nat. Humanities fellow, 1975-76; Nat. Endowment for Humanities demonstration grantee, 1977-78. Mem. MLA, Am. Studies Assn. (v.p. Calif. chpt. 1982—, nat. council 1983—). Office: Humanities Div Univ Calif Santa Cruz CA 95064 *

COWAN, RICHARD SUMNER, systematic botanist; b. Crawfordsville, Ind., Jan. 23, 1921; s. Walter Harrison and Eura B. (Walker) C.; m. Mary Frances Minnich, June 28, 1941; children: Richard A., Diedra Anne, Charles Ian. A.B., Wabash Coll., 1942; M.S., U. Hawaii, 1948; Ph.D., Columbia U., 1952. Teaching asst. U. Hawaii, 1946-48; tech. asst. N.Y. Bot. Garden, N.Y.C., 1948-52, asst. curator, 1952-57; asso. curator Smithsonian Instn., Washington, 1957-62; asst. dir. Mus. Natural History, 1962-65, dir., 1965-73, sr. botanist, 1973—; Sec. nat. com. XI Internat. Bot. Congress; mem. nat. com. Internat. Biol. Program. Co-author 6 vol. reference work on systematic botany.; Contbr. articles profl. jours. Served with USNR, 1943-45. NSF fellow, 1952-53. Mem. Am. Inst. Biol. Scis., AAAS, Am. Soc. Plant Taxonomists, Internat. Assn. Plant Taxonomy. Methodist. Home: 1301 S Scott St Arlington VA 22204 Office: Smithsonian Instn Washington DC 20560

COWAN, ROBERT GEORGE, retired banker; b. Lake Linden, Mich., Feb. 25, 1905; s. William Robert and May Agnes (Harrison) C.; m. Hazel Witherall Damon, May 29, 1930. Student, Phillips Exeter Acad., Mass. Inst. Tech.; B.S., NYU, 1930; grad., Grad. Sch. Banking, Am. Bankers Assn., 1940; LL.D., Upsala Coll., 1955. Statistician research dept., bank examiner, chief analysis div. of bank exams. div. Fed. Res. Bank N.Y., 1927-38; cashier Nat. Newark & Essex Banking Co., Newark, 1938-40, pres., dir., from 1940, now ret.; chmn. Nat. Newark & Essex Bank, 1962-70; former mgr. Howard Savs. Inst. Past pres. Greater Newark Devel. Council; past trustee Marcus L. Ward Home, Newark Mus., Victoria Found. Mem. N.J. C. of C. (past dir.). Clubs: Essex (Newark); Somerset Hills Country. Home: Boxwood Hollow Bernardsville NJ 07924

COWAN, ROBERT JENKINS, radiologist, educator; b. Greensboro, N.C., Apr. 22, 1937; s. John Columbus and Edith (Jenkins) C.; m. Leila Caroline Sikes, June 18, 1960; children: Caroline Martin, Barbara Haynes. A.B., U. N.C., 1959, M.D., 1963. Diplomate: Am. Bd. Radiology (guest examiner), Am. Bd. Nuclear Medicine. Intern in medicine Presbyn. Hosp., Columbia-Presbyn. Med. Center, N.Y.C., 1963-64, resident, 1966-67; resident in radiology N.C. Bapt. Hosp., Winston-Salem, 1967-70; instr. radiology Bowman Gray Sch. Medicine, Wake Forest U., Winston-Salem, 1970-71, asst. prof., 1971-74, asso. prof., 1974-79, prof., 1979—; dir. nuclear medicine N.C. Bapt. Hosp., Winston-Salem, 1977—; med. dir. nuclear med. tech. tng. program Forsyth Tech. Inst., Winston-Salem, 1977—. Contbr. articles to profl. jours. Served to capt., M.C. U.S. Army, 1964-66. Decorated Bronze Star medal; Am. Cancer Soc. fellow, 1969-70; James Picker scholar, 1970-73. Mem. Soc. Nuclear Medicine (council Southeastern chpt. 1972—, pres. Southeastern chpt. 1978, trustee 1983—), Radiol. Soc. N. Am., Am. Coll. Radiology, Am. Coll. Nuclear Physicians, AMA, Eastern Radiol. Soc., N.C. Radiol. Soc., Med. Soc. N.C., Alpha Omega Alpha. Methodist. Office: Bowman Gray Sch Medicine Winston-Salem NC 27103

COWAN, STUART DUBOIS, publisher, consultant, writer; b. Tarrytown, N.Y., Apr. 30, 1917; s. Stuart DuBois and Lucy D. (Coffey) C.; m. Pauline Horn, Nov. 2, 1940 (dec. Dec. 1974); children: Stuart A., Robert B.; m. Grace R. Lombardi, Dec. 1976; stepchildren: Jan and Candace Lombardi. B.A., Princeton U., 1939. With Raytheon Co., Lexington, Mass., 1959-63, v.p. comml. marketing, 1960-63; pres., chief exec. officer United Research, Inc., Cambridge, Mass., 1963-69; exec. v.p. Radio Publs., Inc., 1970—, also dir.; dir. Greenwood Union Cemetery Corp. Co-author: Vigor-How to Get in Shape for Life, 1968, Better Shortwave Reception, 1970, The Truth About Citizens Band Antennas, 1971, The Radio Amateur Antenna Handbook, 1978, (with Edward J. Beattie, Jr., M.D.) Toward the Conquest of Cancer, 1980. Served with USNR, 1941-46. Mem. IEEE, U.S. Naval Inst. Clubs: Stage Harbor Yacht; Princeton (N.Y.C.). Home: North St Box 596 Rye NY 10580

COWAN, WALLACE EDGAR, lawyer; b. Jersey City, Jan. 28, 1924; s. Benjamin and Dorothy (Zunz) C.; m. Ruth Daitzman, June 8, 1947; children: Laurie, Paul, Judith. J.D. cum laude, Harvard U., 1950; B.S. magna cum laude, N.Y.U., 1947. Partner firm Stroock, Stroock & Lavan (attys.), N.Y.C., 1950—; sec., dir. Ametek, Inc.; sec. The Whitlock Corp., Marshall Cavendish Corp. Mem. Teaneck (N.J.) Adv. Bd. on Parks, Playgrounds and Recreation, 1966—, chmn., 1974—; pres. No. Valley Commuters Assn.; v.p., trustee Congregation Beth Sholom, Teaneck. Served to 1st lt. USAF, 1942-45. Decorated Air medal with Silver cluster. Mem. Am. Bar Assn., N.Y. State Bar Assn., Beta Gamma Sigma. Home: 499 Emerson Ave Teaneck NJ 07666 Office: 7 Hanover Sq New York NY 10004

COWAN, WALTER GREAVES, newspaper editor; b. Bond, Miss., Mar. 24, 1912; s. Decatur Douglas and Mary Hermina (Jonte) C.; m. Margaret Martinez, Sept. 28, 1940; children: Walter Greaves, William Douglas. Grad., Gulf Coast Jr. Coll., 1932; B. Journalism, U. Mo., 1936. Reporter New Orleans Item, 1936-39, asst. city editor, 1939-40; pub. relations and advt. rep. G., M. & O. R.R., 1941-45; reporter New Orleans States, 1945-46, city editor, 1946-64; mng. editor New Orleans States-Item, 1964-69, editor, 1969-79; also v.p. Times-Picayune Pub. Corp.; asst. prof. journalism U. New Orleans, 1980—. Trustee New Orleans Mus. Art.; chmn. vis. com. Loyola U. Sch. Communications, 1983—; bd. dirs. Friends of Tulane U. Library, 1983—. Recipient Hall of Fame award Gulf Coast Jr. Coll., 1980. Mem. A.P. Mng. Editors Assn. (pres. La.-Miss. 1971-72). Home: 7715 Nelson St New Orleans LA 70125 Office: New Orleans States-Item 3800 Howard Ave New Orleans LA 70140

COWAN, WARREN J., public relations firm executive; b. N.Y.C., Mar. 13, 1924; s. Rubey J. and Grace (Andriesse) C.; m. Josette Banzet, Apr. 8, 1973; children: Linda, Bonnie, Claudia. B.A., UCLA. With Alan Gordon & Assocs., pub. relations, 1941-42, Henry C. Rogers (became Rogers & Cowan, Inc. 1960), Beverly Hills, Calif., 1945-49, ptnr, 1949-64, pres., 1964—. Served with USAAF, 1942-45. Mem. Motion Picture Acad. Arts and Scis., TV Acad. Arts and Scis. Club: Friars. Office: Rogers & Cowan Inc. 9665 Wilshire Blvd Beverly Hills CA 90212 *

COWAN, WILLIAM MAXWELL, neurobiologist; b. Johannesburg, South Africa, Sept. 27, 1931; s. Adam and Jessie Sloan (Maxwell) C.; m. Margaret Sherlock, Mar. 31, 1956; children: Ruth Cowan Eadon, Stephen Maxwell, David Maxwell. B.Sc., Witwatersrand U., Johannesburg, 1951, B.Sc. (Hons.), 1952; D.Phil., Oxford U., 1956, B.M., B.Ch., 1958, M.A., 1959. From demonstrator to lectr. anatomy Oxford U., 1953-66; fellow Pembroke Coll., 1958-66; vis. prof. anatomy Washington U. Med. Sch., St. Louis, 1965-66, prof., chmn. dept., 1968-80; asso. prof. U. Wis. Med. Sch., Madison, 1966-68; research prof., dir. Weingart Lab. Devel. Neurobiology, Salk Inst. Biol. Studies, La Jolla, Calif., 1980; mem. Inst. Medicine, Nat. Acad. Scis., 1978; fgn. asso. Nat. Acad. Scis., 1981. Editor-in-chief: Jour. Neurosci.; editor: Am. Revs. Neurosci. Fellow Am. Acad. Arts and Scis., Royal Soc. (London); mem. Internat. Brain Research Orgn. (exec. council), AAAS, Anat. Soc. Gt. Britain and Ireland, Royal Micros. Soc., Am. Assn. Anatomists, Soc. Neurosci. (pres. 1977-78), Sigma Xi, Alpha Omega Alpha. Home: 1230 Avocet Ct Cardiff CA 92007 Office: Salk Inst PO Box 85800 San Diego CA 92138

COWARD, HAROLD GEORGE, educator; b. n. Calgary, Alta., Can., Dec. 13, 1936; s. George L. and Hazel I. (Rogers) C.; m. Rachel Maiklem, Sept. 10, 1960; children: David, Kenneth, Susan. B.A., U. Alta., 1958, B.D. (George R. Holbrook scholar 1963, G.J. Welbourn scholar 1964, 65, univ. grantee 1964, St. Stephen's Coll. prize 1965), 1967, M.A. (univ. grantee 1969), 1969; Ph.D. (grad. fellow 1970-72), McMaster U., 1973. Research fellow Centre Advanced Studies in Theoretical Psychology, U. Alta., 1969-71; vis. research scholar Centre Advanced Study Philosophy, Banaras Hindu U., Varanasi, India, 1972; mem. faculty U. Calgary, 1973—, prof. religious studies, 1980—, head dept., 1976—; dir. Calgary Inst. Humanities, 1980—; chmn. Shastri Indo-Can. Inst. com., 1977—. Author: Bhartrhari, 1976, Sphota Theory of Language, 1980; editor: (with T.M. Penelhum) Mystics and Scholars, 1977, (with Krishna Sivaraman) Revelation in Indian Thought, 1977, Language in Indian Philosophy and Religion, 1978, (with L.S. Kawamura) Religion and Ethnicity, 1978, (with John Woods) Humanities in the Present Day, 1980, Scholarly Communication, 1980, (with Egar, Royce, Kessel and Moss) Psychological Epistemology: A Critical Review of the Empirical Literature and Theoretical Issues, 1978; (with George Williams) Jung and India, 1981; Calgary's Growth: Bane or Boon?, 1981, (with Larsen) Ethical Issues in the Allocation of Health Care Resources, 1982, Studies in Indian Thought: The Collected Papers of Professor T.R.V. Murti, 1983, Religious Pluralism and the World Religions, 1983, (with Slater, Wiebe and Boutior) Traditions in Contact and Change, 1983, (with Svilpis) The Use and Abuse of Language, 1983, (with Raja) The Philosophy of Language, 1984. St. Stephen's Coll. travelling scholar, 1970; grantee Can. Council, 1975-76, 76, 77, 78, U. Calgary, 1975-76, 76, 77, 78. Mem. Can. Soc. Study Religion (exec. com. 1975-78, chmn. nominating com. 1975-76, chmn. Indian philosophy and religion sect. 1975-77, pres. 1982-84), Can. Corp. Studies in Religion (chmn. publs. com. 1979—, bd. dirs. 1980—, v.p. 1981—), Am. Acad. Religion.; mem. Internat. Assn. of the History of Religions (sec. planning com., XIVth Internat. Congress 1980, Chmn. program com. 1980, section coordinator, psychology of religion section 1980, assoc. editor proceedings, XIVth Internat. Congress 1981). Office: 2500 University Ave NW Calgary AB T2N 1N4 Canada

COWARD, JAMES KENDERDINE, chemist; b. Buffalo, Oct. 13, 1938; s. Harold Wilbur and Ethel Rae (Hand) C.; m. Maria Adelaide Durso, June 7, 1975; 1 son, Robert. A.B., Middlebury Coll., 1960; M.A., Duke U., 1964; Ph.D., SUNY-Buffalo, 1967. Asst. prof. pharmacology Yale U., 1969-74, assoc. prof., 1974-79; assoc. prof. chemistry Rensselaer Poly. Inst., 1979-82, prof., 1982—; vis. prof. Salk Inst., 1977-78. Contbr. articles to profl. jours. NIH fellow, 1966-68; recipient various grants. Mem. Am. Chem. Soc., Chem. Soc. (London), Am. Soc. Biol. Chemists, AAAS, Sigma Xi. Home: 10 24th St Troy NY 12180 Office: Dept Chemistry Rensselaer Poly Inst Troy NY 12181

COWART, ELGIN COURTLAND, JR., naval medical officer; b. Dothan, Ala., July 9, 1923; s. Elgin Courtl and Annie Susie (McAllister) C.; m. Madeleine M. Hoffman, Oct. 31, 1976; children by previous marriage—Susan, Stephen Courtland. B.S., Tulane U., 1944, M.D., 1946. Diplomate: Am. Bd. Pathology. Intern Touro Infirmary, New Orleans, 1946-47; commd. lt. (j.g.) M.C. USNR, 1947; assigned Trust Ter. Pacific and Guam; resigned USNR, 1950; gen. practice medicine, Brookhaven, Miss., 1950-55; rejoined M.C. USN, 1956, advanced through grades to capt., 1962; resident in pathology Naval Med. Sch., Bethesda, Md., 1956-60; service in, Egypt and Vietnam; comdg. officer Naval Hosp. in U.S.S. Sanctuary, 1970-71, Naval Hosp., Port Hueneme, Calif., 1971-75; dep. dir. Armed Forces Inst. Pathology, Washington, 1975-76, dir., 1976—; exec. dir. Am. Registry of Pathology, 1981—. Co-author: Billings Microscope Collection, 1967. Decorated Legion of Merit, Army Commendation medal, Def. Superior Service medal; recipient Physicians Recognition award AMA, 1983-86. Mem. Am. Soc. Clin. Pathologists, AMA, Assn. Mil. Surgeons, Coll. Am. Pathologists, Washington Soc. Pathology, Internat. Acad. Pathology, Assn. Clin. Scientists. Home: 8104 Lakenheath Way Potomac MD 20854 Office: Armed Forces Inst Pathology Washington DC 20306

COWART, WILLIAM SLATER, JR., utility exec.; b. Cowart, Va., Oct. 31, 1917; s. William Slater and Alice (Sherman) C.; m. Pauline Sara Cox, Aug. 3, 1944; children—William S. III, Paula Alyce, Zilla Virginia (Mrs. David Forsythe), Bryan Charles. B.S. in Engring, Va. Poly. Inst., 1940; postgrad., Harvard, 1941, Mass. Inst. Tech., 1942; M.S. in Nuclear Physics, Ohio State U., 1947, George Washington U., 1949. Commd. 2d lt. USAAF, 1940; advanced through grades to col. USAF, 1949; dir. operations joint Task force armed forces and AEC, Eniwetok and Bikini atolls, 1951-54; comdr. Tactical Strike Force, Langley AFB, Va., 1955-56; chief air research and devel. Tactical Systems Div., 1957-58; dir. Nat. Aviation Facilities Exptl. Center, Atlantic City, 1958-60; ret., 1960; with Atlantic Electric Co., 1960—, sr. v.p. prodn., operations, sales, 1966-68, sr. v.p. customer and employee relations, sales, 1968—; pres. Atlantic Housing, Inc., Atlantic City, 1969—; v.p. Overland Realty, Inc., Atlantic City, 1971—. Chmn. West Jersey Bicentennial Corp., 1970—, Mayor's Airport Com., 1962—; pres. Atlantic County chpt. Am. Cancer Soc., 1965-69, Miss Am. Pageant, 1968-72; now bd. dirs. Miss Am. Pageant; mem. air-land service com., bd. dirs. N.J. Citizens' Transp. Council, 1971—; pres. Transfair, N.J. Transp. Expns.; Bd. dirs. Atlantic Area council Boy Scouts Am., 1960-68, Atlantic-Cape May council Girl Scouts U.S., 1962-68; bd. dirs. Del. Valley council, 1969—, v.p., 1974—; trustee So. N.J. Devel. Council; chmn. Atlantic County Pvt. Industry Council, 1979—; met. chmn. Nat. Alliance of Bus., 1978—; v.p., sec. Atlantic City TV Corp., 1978—; regional adv. Nat. Community Bank. Mem. Atlantic City C. of C. (pres., dir.), S. Jersey C. of C. (dir.), Edison Electric Inst. (hon. mem. sale's exec. conf.). Club: Rotarian. Discoverer Radioactive Selenium 73, 1947. Home: Still Meadows Absecon NJ 08201 Office: Atlantic Electric Co 1600 Pacific Ave Atlantic City NJ 08404

COWDEN, ROBERT LAUGHLIN, educator; b. Warren, Ohio, Apr. 11, 1933; s. Harry L. and Martha E. (McGregor) C.; m. Corinne Lucille Leister, June 7, 1954; children: Chris, Craig, Clark. B.Music Edn., Muskingum Coll., 1954; M.Ed., Kent State U., 1957; Ph.D., Ohio State U., 1969. Coordinator instrumental music Parma Pub. Schs., Ohio, 1954-69; assoc. prof. U. Cin. Coll.-Conservatory of Music, 1969-76; prof. music Ind. State U., Terre Haute, 1976—, chmn. dept., 1976—. Author: Curriculum for Orchestra, 1969, Bowing for Better Sound, 1971; contbr. articles to profl. jours. Mem., officer Terre Haute Symhony Orch. Bd., 1976—. Recipient Master Tchr. Martha Holden Jennings Found., 1967; named Man of Yr. Parma Area Fine Arts Council, 1968; John Hay fellow, 1964; Ind. State U. grantee, 1983. Mem. Ohio Music Edn. Assn. (pres. 1976), Nat. Sch. Orch. Assn. (dir.), Music Educators Jour., Phi Delta Kappa, Phi Kappa Phi, Pi Kappa Lambda. Lodge: Kiwanis. Home: 3839 Riley Ave Terre Haute IN 47803 Office: Dept Music Ltd Univ Terre Haute IN 47809

COWDEN, WILLIAM BRUCE, clothing company executive; b. Salina, Kans., Dec. 10, 1917; s. Jay Rahl and Lelah (Lyter) C.; m. Barbara Rehm, July 15, 1951; children: Paul David, William Bruce, Jay Norman, Roger Rehm. B.A., William Coll., 1940. V.p. Cowden Mfg. Co., Lexington, Ky., 1949-64, exec. v.p., 1964-73, pres., 1973-80, chmn. bd., 1980-83; dir. 2d Nat. Bancorp, Lexington, 2d Nat. Bank & Trust Co. Chmn. bd. Sayre Sch., Lexington, 1982; trustee St. Joseph Hosp., Lexington, 1983, Cardinal Hill Hosp., Lexington, 1983; mem. exec. bd. Blue Grass Council, Boy Scouts Am., Lexington, 1983; mem. devel. council U. Ky., Lexington, 1983; bd. dirs. Am. Heart Assn., Ky. affiliate. Served to 1st lt. U.S. Army, 1942-46. Recipient Satre Sch. Medallion, 1983, Army Commendation medal, Silver Beaver award Boy Scouts Am., 1981. Democrat. Presbyterian. Clubs: Idle Hour Country, The Lexington. Home: 407 Adair Rd Lexington KY 40502

COWEE, JOHN WIDMER, univ. chancellor; b. Wausau, Wis., Aug. 1, 1918; s. Charles Arthur and Hattie L. (Widmer) C.; m. Nancy Lee Pendleton, Dec. 22, 1973; children—John Widmer, Jeffrey Deane. B.A., U. Wis., Madison, 1947, M.B.A., 1948, Ph.D., 1950, LL.B., 1956. Bar: Wis. bar. Mem. faculty U. Calif., Berkeley, 1954-66, prof. bus. adminstrn., 1960-66, chmn. dept., 1961-66, prof. law, 1954-66, dean, 1961-66; provost Marquette U., Milw., 1967-74, v.p. bus. and fin., 1966-67, prof. law, prof. bus. adminstrn., 1966-76; exec. v.p. Marquette U. Med. Sch., 1967-69; prof. bus. adminstrn., prof. law U. Colo., Boulder, 1976—, chancellor health affairs, 1976—; trustee, asst. sec. Calif. Physicians Service, 1959-66; bd. govs. Internat. Ins. Seminars; dir. Calif.-Western States Life Ins. Co., Nordberg Mfg. Co., Milw., Marine Nat. Exchange Bank, Sta-Rite Industries; chmn. policyowners exam. com. Northwestern Mut. Life Ins. Co., Milw. Author studies, reports. Trustee Am. Conservatory Theatre Found., San Francisco, Univ. Sch., Milw., Davis Inst. Care and Study of Aging, Denver; bd. dirs. Marquette U. Sch. Medicine, Wis. Heart Assn.; adv. com. Lingnan Inst. Bus. Adminstrn., Chinese U., Hong Kong. Served with AUS, 1942-46. Decorated Bronze Star. Mem. Am., Wis. bar assns., Internat. Assn. Ins. Law (co-founder Am. sect.), Internat. Ins. Seminars, Am. Assn. U. Adminstrs., Phi Alpha Delta. Clubs: University (Milw.); Denver. Home: 260 S Eudora St Denver CO 80222 Office: 4200 E 9th Ave Denver CO 80262

COWELL, FRED J., hospital administrator; b. Louisville, May 22, 1939; s. and Nora C. C.; m. Jean Shafer, Nov. 23, 1972. B.S., W.Va. U., 1967. Asst. adminstr. Monongalia Gen. Hosp., Morgantown, W.Va., 1963-67; with Jackson Meml. Hosp., Miami, Fla., 1967—, dep. exec. dir., 1972, dir. hosp. ops., 1974—, exec. dir., 1976—; pres. Public Health Trust of Dade County, 1977—; bd. dirs. Health Systems Agy. South Fla., Inc. Mem. Fla. Hosp. Cost Containment Bd., 1979—, Fla. Task Force on Competition and Consumer Choices in Health Care, 1983. Mem. Am. Hosp. Assn., South Fla. Hosp. Assn. (dir.), Fla. Hosp. Assn., Council Teaching Hosps. (adminstrv. bd. 1980-82), Greater Miami C. of C. (trustee). Methodist. Home: 15920 Kingsmoor Way Miami Lakes FL 33014 Office: 1611 NW 12th Ave Miami FL 33136

COWELL, MARION AUBREY, JR., lawyer; b. Wilmington, N.C., Dec. 25, 1934; s. Marion Aubrey and Alice Saunders (Hargett) C.; children: Lindsay G., Mark P. B.S. B.A., U. N.C., 1958, LL.B., 1964. Bar: N.C. 1964. Pvt. practice law, Durham, N.C., 1964-72; asso. law firm Bryant, Lipton, Bryant and Batte, 1964-69, partner, 1971-72; pvt. practice law, Durham, 1969-70; gen. counsel Cameron Brown Co., Raleigh, N.C., 1972-78; sr. v.p., gen. counsel, sec. First Union Corp., Charlotte, N.C., 1978—. Office: First Union Corp One First Union Plaza Charlotte NC 28288

COWEN, DONNA RUTH, actress, dancer; b. Birmingham, Ala., May 2, 1949; d. Robert Virgil and Theda Mayo (Pearson) C. Student, Am. Ballet Center Sch., 1969. Prin. dancer, Joffrey Ballet, N.Y.C., 1969-77; prin. dancer, Dennis Wayne Dancers, 1977-78, Nureyev and the Joffrey Ballet on Broadway, 1979; actress appearing in: films Soup For One. Recipient Obelisk award City of Birmingham, 1976. Mem. Screen Actors Guild, Actors Equity Assn. Republican. Episcopalian. Office: 125 Worth Ave Palm Beach FL 33480

COWEN, EUGENE SHERMAN, broadcasting executive; b. N.Y.C., May 2, 1925; s. Jacob M. and Shirley (Sherman) C.; m. Phyllis L. Wallach, Jan. 29, 1948; children: James Sherman, Stephanie Jane. B.A. magna cum laude, Syracuse U., 1949, M.A., 1954. Reporter Syracuse Herald-Jour., 1948-52; reporter Newhouse News Bur., Washington, 1952-53; press sec. Rep. Frances P. Bolton, Washington, 1953-56; info. officer HEW, Washington, 1956-58; v.p. Standard Public Relations, Washington, 1958-59; asst. to Senator Hugh Scott, 1959-69; spl. asst., dep. asst. to Pres., White House, 1969-71; v.p.-Washington ABC, 1971—. Mem. public relations com. Washington Hebrew Congregation.; bd. dirs. United Cerebral Palsy, Washington. Served with U.S. Army, 1943-46. Decorated Air medal. Mem. Nat. Assn. Broadcasters (dir.), Phi Beta Kappa. Clubs: Internat. Broadcasters, Pisces. Home: 2759 Unicorn Ln NW Washington DC 20015 Office: 1150 17th St NW Washington DC 20036

COWEN, MARTIN LINDSEY, univ. dean; b. Wheeling, W.Va., Aug. 26, 1920; s. Martin Lindsey and Agnes (Troll) C.; m. Eleanor Boaz, Dec. 29, 1949; children—Martin Lindsey III, Velma Merrifield, William Boaz, Carolyn Troll, Eleanor Lee. B.A., U. Va., 1942, J.D., 1947; LL.M., Harvard, 1965. Bar: Ohio bar 1947, Va. bar 1955, Ga. bar 1965. Pvt. practice, Bridgeport, Ohio, 1947-51; mem. faculty U. Va. Law Sch., 1951-64, prof. law, 1956-64, asso. dean, 1960-64; prof. law, dean U. Ga. Sch. Law, 1964-72, Case Western Res. U. Sch. Law, Cleve., 1972—; Mem. Ohio Commn. on Uniform State Laws. Served to lt. comdr. USNR, 1942-46. Fellow Am. Bar Found.; mem. Am. Law Inst., Order of Coif, Raven Soc., Phi Beta Kappa, Delta Tau Delta, Phi Delta Phi, Omicron Delta Kappa.

COWEN, ROBERT HENRY, lawyer; b. Williamston, N.C., Jan. 16, 1915; s. Henry Herbert and Jenette (Mobley) C.; m. Sue Henderson, Aug. 6, 1953; children—Robert H., Susan Carol, Sarah Cantrell. J.D., Wake Forest Coll., 1942. Bar: N.C. bar 1942, U.S. Supreme Ct. bar 1942. Practiced in, Williamston, 1975—; atty. U.S. Dept. Labor, Richmond, 1945-46; counsel to com. on mcht. marine and fisheries U.S. Ho. of Reps.; U.S. atty. Eastern dist. N.C., 1961-69; counsel, joint com. on printing U.S. Senate, 1969-75. Mayor, Town of Williamston, 1947-57, 75—; mem. N.C. Senate, 1957-58; Bd. dirs. N.C. League Municipalities, 1976—. Served with USNR, World War II. Mem. Am., N.C. bar assns., Jr. C. of C., Am. Legion. Baptist. Clubs: Rotary, Roanoke Country. Home: 103 Woodlawn Dr Williamston NC 27892

COWEN, ROY CHADWELL, JR., German educator; b. Kansas City, Mo., Aug. 2, 1930; s. Roy Chadwell and Mildred Frances (Schuetz) C.; m. Hildegard Bredemeier, Oct. 6, 1956; 1 son, Ernst Werner (dec.). B.A., Yale U., 1952; Ph.D., U. Gottingen, W.Ger., 1960. Instr. U. Mich., Ann Arbor, 1960-64, asst. prof., 1964-67, assoc. prof., 1967-71, prof., 1971—, chmn. dept. Germanic langs., 1979—. Author: Christian Dietrich Grabbe, 1972, Naturalismus Kommentar zu einer Epoche, 1973, Hauptmann Kommentar zum dramatischen Werk, 1980, Hauptmann Kommentar zum nichtdramatischen Werk, 1981. Served with USN, 1952-56. Recipient Williams Teaching award U. Mich., 1967; sr. fellow NEH, 1972-73. Mem. MLA, Internationale Vereinigung fur Germanistik. Democrat. Methodist. Home: 2874 Baylis Dr Ann Arbor MI 48104 Office: Dept Germanic Langs and Lits U Mich Ann Arbor MI 48109

COWEN, WILSON, judge; b. nr. Clifton, Tex., Dec. 20, 1905; s. John Rentz and Florence Juno (McFadden) C.; m. Florence Elizabeth Walker, Apr. 18, 1930; children—W. Walker, John E. LL.B., U. Tex., 1928. Bar: Tex. bar 1928. Pvt. practice, Dalhart, Tex., 1928-34, judge, Dallam County, Tex., 1935-38; Tex. dir. for Farm Security Adminstrn., 1938-40, regional dir., 1940-42; commr. U.S. Ct. Claims, 1942-43, 45-59, chief commr., 1959-64, chief judge, 1964-77, sr. judge, 1977—; asst. adminstr. War Food Adminstrn., 1943-45; spl. asst. to sec. agr., 1945. Past chmn., past trustee Landon Sch. for Boys, Bethesda. Mem. State Bar Tex., Fed., Am. bar assns., Order of Coif, Delta Theta Phi. Presbyterian. Clubs: Cosmos, Nat. Lawyers (Washington); Masons. Home: 2500 Virginia Ave NW Washington DC 20037 Office: US Court Appeals Fed Circuit Washington DC 20439

COWEN, WILSON WALKER, publisher; b. Dalhart, Tex., June 5, 1934; s. Wilson and Florence Elizabeth (Walker) C.; m. Claudine LaHaye, Aug. 25, 1971; 1 son, Charles Wilson. A.B., Harvard, 1956, Ph.D., 1965. Advt. and promotion Little Brown & Co., 1958-59; partner Walker-deBerry Pubs., Cambridge, Mass., 1959-64; with U. Press of Va., Charlottesville, 1965—, asso. dir., 1968-69, dir., 1969—; teaching fellow Harvard, 1959-64; lectr. English U. Va., 1965-71, prof., 1971—. Mem. bd.: Papers of George Washington. Woodrow Wilson fellow, 1960; Timothy Dexter fellow, 1964. Mem. Bibliog. Soc. U. Va. (dir.), Charlottesville Civic League (dir.), Phi Beta Kappa. Democrat. Clubs: Grolier (N.Y.C.); Cosmos (Washington); Farmington Hunt (Charlottesville). Home: 1844 Winston Rd Charlottesville VA 22903 Office: Box 3608 University Sta Charlottesville VA 22903

COWGILL, CAROL ANN, lawyer; b. Plainfield, N.J., Apr. 21, 1946; d. Daniel E. and Winifred M. (MacQuillan) C. B.A., Duke U., 1968; J.D., U. Chgo., 1971. Bar: D.C. 1967, Ill. 1971, U.S. Supreme Ct. 1974. Staff atty. EPA, Washington, 1971-73; atty. Washington office Consumers Union, 1973-75; dir. Washington office Am. Acad. Family Physicians, 1975-79; atty. adv. Office of Gen. Counsel, Dept. Energy, Washington, 1979—. Vice pres., exec. bd. S.W. Neighborhood Assembly, Washington, 1979-80; sec. Potomac Valley AAU Tae Kwon Do Com., 1977-78; sec.-treas. Nat. AAU Tae Kwon Do Com., 1978; mem. D.C. Bd. Appeals and Rev., 1979—. Mem. Bar Assn. D.C. (chmn. consumer affairs com. 1979-80), Fed. Bar. Assn. (chmn. com. health and welfare 1978-79), ABA, Washington Council Lawyers, ACLU. Democrat. Clubs: Potomac, Pedalers Touring, YMCA Tae Kwon Do. Home: 2369 G St SW Washington DC 20024 Office: Office of Gen Counsel Dept Energy 475 L'Enfant Plaza W SW Suite 2970 Washington DC 20024

COWGILL, DONALD OLEN, sociologist, educator; b. Wood River, Nebr., May 10, 1911; s. Olen and Gertrude (Quisenberry) C.; m. Mary Catherine Strain, Sept. 1, 1935; children—Martha Jane (Mrs. Paul Burns), Donald Franklin, Catha Jean. A.B. with high honors in spl. field, Park Coll., 1933; A.M. (Van Blarcom scholar 1934-35, U. fellow 1935-36), Washington U., 1935; Ph.D. (George Leib Harrison fellow), U. Pa., 1940; postgrad., U. Minn., summer 1941, U. Mo., 1942-43. Asst. prof. sociology Drury Coll., 1937-40, asso. prof., head dept. sociology, 1940-42, dean men, dir. counseling, 1941-42; sr. research analyst Mo. Social Security Commn., 1942-43; research asst. to v.p. Studebaker Corp., 1943-45; prof., head dept. sociology Drake U., 1945-46, Wichita State U., 1946-67; prof. U. Mo., Columbia, 1967—, chmn. depts. sociology and rural sociology, 1970-72; vis. prof. U. Mo., summers 1948, 66; lectr. Mindolo Ecumenical Centre, Kitwe, Zambia, summer 1962; Fulbright lectr. Chiengmai U., Thailand, 1964-65; resident cons. Mahidol U., Thailand, 1968-69; research cons. Wichita Community Planning Council, 1946-1967. Author: Residential Mobility of An Urban Population, 1935, Mobile Homes: A Study of Trailer Life, 1941, Methodology of Planning Census Tracts, 1949, Wichita Street Index for Census Tracts, 1951, Religious Preferences of the Families of Wichita, 1958, People of Wichita, 1960, Aging and Modernization, 1972; articles on population, urban sociology, social gerontology. Inter-Univ. Council on Aging fellow, summer 1959; Midwest Council on Aging fellow, summer 1961. Fellow Am. Sociol. Assn., Gerontol. Soc., AAUP; mem. Population Assn. Am., Midwest Sociol. Soc. (pres. 1952-53), Midwest Council for Social Research on Aging (pres. 1962-64), Pi Kappa Delta, Alpha Kappa Delta. Home: 819 Greenwood Ct Columbia MO 65201

COWGILL, F(RANK) BROOKS, insurance company executive; b. Hungtington Park, Calif., Mar. 16, 1932; s. Frank H. and Henriette J. (Dickey) C.; m. Mary Lucena Hanna, Dec. 22, 1954; children: David B., Ann M. A.B., Stanford U., 1954, M.B.A., 1956. Analyst treas.'s dept. Exxon Corp., N.Y.C., 1958-61; sr. analyst treas.'s dept. WR Grace Co., Cambridge, Mass., 1961-62; with New England Mut. Life Ins. Co., Boston, 1962—, v.p., treas., 1979—. Served to 1st lt. U.S. Army, 1956-58. Mem. Inst. Chartered Fin. Analysts, Boston Security Analysts Soc. Conglist. Clubs: Boston Econ., Treasurers (Boston). Office: 501 Boylston St Boston MA 02117

COWGILL, URSULA MOSER, biologist, educator; b. Bern, Switzerland, Nov. 9, 1927; came to U.S., 1943, naturalized, 1945; d. John W. and Mara (Siegrist) Moser. A.B., Hunter Coll., 1948; M.S., Kans. State U., 1952; Ph.D., Iowa State U., 1956. Staff Mass. Inst. Tech., Lincoln Lab., Lexington, Mass., 1957-58; field work Doherty Found., Guatemala, 1958-60; research asso. dept. biology Yale, New Haven, 1960-68; prof. biology and anthropology U. Pitts., 1968-81; environ. scientist Dow Chem. Co., Midland, Mich., 1981—; mem. environ. measurements adv. com. EPA, 1976-80. Contbr. numerous articles on ecology, biology and minerology to sci. publs. Trustee Carnegie Mus., Pitts., 1971-75. NSF grantee, 1960-78; Wenner Gren Found. grantee, 1965-66; Penrose fund Am. Philos. Soc. grantee, 1978; Sigma Xi grant-in-aid, 1965-66. Mem. Soc. Am. Naturalists, Geochem. Soc., Soc. Environ. Geochemistry and Health, Soc. Study of Fertility, Mineral Soc. Gt. Britain and Am., Soc. Applied Spectroscopy, Internat. Soc. Theoretical and Applied Limnology, N.Y. Acad. Sci. Office: Dow Chemical Co 1702 Bldg Midland MI 48640

COWHILL, WILLIAM JOSEPH, naval officer; b. Bklyn., May 29, 1928; s. Joseph Henry and Lucy Rose (Foppiano) C.; m. Shirley F. Smith, Feb. 3, 1984; children: Robin, Joseph, Michael, Douglas. B.S., Northwestern U., 1950. Commd. ensign U.S. Navy, 1950, advanced through grades to vice adm., 1979; comdg. officer U.S.S. Dace and U.S.S. Will Rogers, 1965-68, PCO instr. Div. Naval Reactors, AEC, 1968-70, comdg. officer U.S.S. Holland, Rota, Spain, 1970-72, nuclear power program mgr. Bur. Naval Personnel, 1972, comdr. Tng. Command, U.S. Atlantic Fleet, 1973-75, asst. dep. chief naval ops. for submarine warfare Office of Chief Naval Ops., Washington, 1975-77, comdr. Submarine Force, U.S. Pacific Fleet, 1977-79, dep. chief naval ops. for logistics Office of Chief Naval Ops., Washington, 1979-83, dir. logistics Joint Chiefs Staff, 1983—. Decorated Legion of Merit, Disting. Service medal. Mem. Naval Inst. Home: 1336 Elsinore Ave McLean VA 22102 Office: Director Logistics Orgn Joint Chiefs Staff The Pentagon Rm 2E828 Washington DC 20301 *

COWIE, BRUCE EDGAR, communications exec.; b. Prince Albert, Sask., Can., Mar. 6, 1938; s. Louis Leroy and Janet Louise (Anderson) C.; m. Marlene Lehman, July 28, 1958; children—Cameron, Robert, Caron-Dawn. Student pub. schs., Prince Albert. Announcer Sta. CKOM, Saskatoon, Sask., 1956-59; with Sta. CKCK-TV (and subsidiaries), Regina, Sask., 1959—, gen. mgr. sta., 1972-77; v.p., gen. mgr. Harvard Communications, 1977—; pres. Braeloch Cons. Ltd. (communications cons.), Braeside Holdings; dir. Western Surety Co., Can. TV Network; mem. program com. CTVTV Network; founding chmn. Canpro, 1974. Alderman, City of Regina, 1963-67; pres. Sask. Roughrider Football Club, 1976, Western Football Conf., 1980; bd. dirs. Can. Football League Exec. Com. Served to 2d lt. Regina Rifle Regiment Res., 1965. Mem. Western Assn. Broadcasters (pres. 1976-77), Canadian Assn. Broadcasters (dir.), Nat. Assn. TV Program Execs., Broadcast Promotion Assn., Regina C. of C., United Services Inst. Club: Assinabdia. Home: 113 Tibbitts Rd Regina SK Canada Office: PO Box 2000 Regina SK S4P 3E5 Canada

COWIE, WILLIAM HENRY, JR., banker; b. Bridgeport, Conn., Jan. 24, 1931; s. William Henry and Jane A. (Callahan) C.; m. Theresa Lois Baldwin Kirkwood, Feb. 9, 1952 (div. 1973); children: William John, Karen Sue, Kathleen Ellen, Nancy Carol, Christopher Paul. B.S. in Econs., U. Pa., 1952. Regional credit mgr. U.S. Steel Corp., N.Y.C., 1954-57; regional v.p. nat. div. Irving Trust Co., N.Y.C., 1957-71; exec. v.p. Union Trust Bancorp/Union Trust Co. Md., Balt., 1971-72, pres., 1972—; dir. A.J. Buck & Son, Inc., Balt. Bd. dirs. Balt. Symphony Orch., 1980—; exec. com. S. Balt. Gen. Hosp.; bd. regents Morgan State U., Balt. Served to capt. USMC, 1952-54. Democrat. Episcopalian. Clubs: Baltimore Country, Center (bd. govs.), Maryland, Merchants (dir.). Office: Union Trust Bancorp/Union Trust Co Md Baltimore and St Paul Sts Baltimore MD 21202 *

COWING, WALTER LISHMAN, publishing executive; b. London, Eng., Feb. 14, 1926; emigrated to Can., 1929; s. Walter and Clara Emma C.; m. Beverley Doreen Hay, Aug. 24, 1946; children: Paula Doris, Richard Walter, Glen Arthur. Student schs., East York, Ont., 1938-41. With Can. Law Book, Ltd., Agincourt, Ont., 1941—, asst. gen. mgr., 1959-67, v.p., 1967-68, pres., 1968—, Western Legal Publs., Ltd., 1983; pres., dir. Walbev Holdings Ltd.; v.p., dir. Jobborn Mfg. (1975) Ltd., 1975—, Garden City Press Ltd., 1976—; sec. Can. Lawyer Mag. Ltd., Emond Montgomery Publs. Ltd.; dir. Aurland Holdings Ltd. Served in Can. Inf., 1944-45. Mem. Council of Printing Industries, Can. Aquanats. Anglican. Clubs: National, Bayview Country (pres. 1977). Home: 24 Vintage Ln Thornhill ON L3T 1X6 Canada Office: 240 Edward St Aurora ON L4G 3S9 Canada

COWLES, ARTHUR WOODRUFF, business executive; b. Crawfordsville, Ind., Nov. 2, 1918; s. Frank Hewitt and Mary Anne (Eby) C.; m. Luella Grassbaugh, Dec. 31, 1941 (div.); children—Kathleen, Arthur Woodruff III, Shelley Ann; m. Helen P. Date, Mar. 5, 1976; children—Kirby, John, Matthew, Julia, Jennifer. B.A., Wooster Coll., 1940; grad., Advanced Mgmt. Program, Harvard, 1966. With Gen. Electric Co., 1945-50, Carborundum Co., 1950-54; with Marsteller, Inc., Chgo. and Pitts., 1955-66, exec. v.p., 1960-66; v.p. exec. dept. Koppers Co., Pitts., 1966—; dir. McCreary Tire and Rubber Co. Served with inf., 1941-45. Mem. Pub. Affairs Council Washington (past chmn.). Clubs: Fox Chapel Racquet, Duquesne, Laurel Valley. Home: 6901 N Montezuma Dr Tucson AZ 85718 Office: Koppers Bldg Pittsburgh PA 15219

COWLES, CHARLES, art dealer; b. Santa Monica, Calif., Feb. 7, 1941; s. Gardner and Jan (Streate) C. Student, Stanford, 1959-65. Assoc. pub. Artforum mag., San Francisco, 1964-65, pres., 1965-79; pub., pres. Artforum, Inc., Los Angeles, 1965-67, pub., pres., chmn., N.Y.C., 1967-79; chmn. Collegiate Press, N.Y.C., 1968-71; curator modern art Seattle Art Mus., 1975-79; pres., dir. Charles Cowles Gallery, N.Y.C., 1980—; Mem. Fine Arts Council Fla., 1972-75; Trustee Studio Mus. in Harlem, N.Y.C., 1967-75, Miami Art Ctr., 1973-75, San Francisco Art Inst., 1978-80, Cowles Charitable Trust, 1983—; mem. internat. council Mus. Modern Art, N.Y.C., 1967-79; chmn. bd. Jennifer Miller Dance Co., 1981—. Served with USCGR, 1962-70. Office: 420 W Broadway New York NY 10012

COWLES, FLEUR FENTON (MRS. TOM M. MEYER), author, artist; m. Gardner Cowles, Dec. 27, 1946 (div. 1955); m. Tom Montague Meyer, Nov. 18, 1955. LL.D., Elmira (N.Y.) Coll., 1954. Spl. cons. Famine Emergency Com., White House, Washington, 1946; asso. editor, dir. spl. editorial depts. Look mag., 1947, fgn. corr., 1955-58; asso. editor Quick mag., 1949; editor Flair mag., 1950-51, Flair Annual, 1952; fgn. dir. Cowles Mags., Inc.; cons. to chief of staff Hdqrs. USAF, 1950; mem. nat. adv. com. on women's participation Fed. Civil Def. Adminstrn., 1953-55; Spl. rep. Pres. Eisenhower (with rank of spl. ambassador) at coronation of Queen Elizabeth II of Eng.; mem. Lord Mayor's Adv. Com., Mermaid Theatre Trust, London. Author: Bloody Precedent, 1952, The Case of Salvator Dali, 1959, The Hidden World of Hadhramoutt, 1963, Tiger Flower, 1968, Treasures of the British Museum, 1970, Lion and Blue, 1974, Friends and Memories, 1975, Flower, 1980, All Too True, 1981, The Flower Game, 1983; exhibited paintings, London, 1959, 63, 66, 75, N.Y.C., 1960, 62, 64, 67, 73, Rome, 1961, Paris, 1962, Athens, 1966, Los Angeles, 1967, Madrid, Rio de Janeiro, 1966, 68, Dallas, 1969, 71, São Paulo, 1965, 66, 72, Seattle, 1970, San Francisco, 1973, Detroit, 1974, Kans., 1975, Dusseldorf, 1976, Singer Mus., Holland, 1977, Cheekwood Mus., Nashville, 1978, Hammer Galleries, Partridge Gallery, London, Gregg Juarez Gallery, 1980, Roelant Gallery, Amsterdam, S. L. Gallery, Dallas, Partridge Galleries, Boston, others. Mem. Conn. Commn. to Study Potentials of Aging; chmn., pres. Louis E.K. Leakey Found., Europe; trustee Elmira Coll., Leakey Fund U.S.A., Soc. Rehab. Facially Disfigured; internat. trustee World Wildlife Fund; mem. council Am. Museum in Bath (Eng.). Decorated chevalier Legion of Honor (France), 1951; Queen's medal, Gt. Britain; cavalier Order So. Cross (Brazil), 1953, comdr., 1973; comdr. Order of Bienfasence (Greece), 1955; La dama de Isobel Catolica (Spain), 1976. Mem. Women's Nat. Press Club, Royal Geog. Soc., Royal Soc. Arts. Home: A5 Albany Picadilly London England

COWLES, GARDNER, publisher; b. Algona, Iowa, Jan. 31, 1903; s. Gardner and Florence M. (Call) C.; m. Lois Thornburg, May 17, 1933 (div. 1946); children: Lois Cowles Harrison, Gardner, III, Kate Cowles Nichols; m. Jan Streate Cox, May 1, 1956; 1 dau., Virginia. Grad., Phillips Exeter Acad., 1921; A.B., Harvard U., 1925; LL.D. (hon.), Drake U., 1942, Coe Coll., 1948, L.I. U., 1955, Grinnell Coll., 1957, Colls. Hobart and William Smith, 1968; L.H.D., Bard Coll., 1950, Cornell Coll., 1951, Mundelein Coll., 1968; Sc.D., Simpson Coll., 1955; Litt.D., Iowa Wesleyan Coll., 1955, Morningside Coll., 1958. City editor Des Moines Register, 1925, news editor, 1926-27; asso. mng. editor Des Moines Register and Tribune, 1927, mng. editor, 1927-31, exec. editor, 1931-39, asso. pub., 1939-43, pres., 1943-71; chmn. bd., editor in chief Cowles Communications, Inc., N.Y.C., 1937-71, hon. chmn. bd., 1971-83, Cowles Broadcasting, Inc., 1983—; dir. emeritus United Air Lines, UAL, Inc.; domestic dir. Office of War Information, Wash., 1942-43; resigned; with Wendell Willkie, round world flight, 1942. Trustee U. Miami, Drake U., Tchrs. Coll., Columbia U.; Trustee emeritus Mus. Modern Art. Mem. Am. Soc. Newspaper Editors (former mem. bd.), Des Moines C. of C. (dir. 1930-47), Greater Des Moines Com. Harvard Class of 1925 (treas.), Phi Beta Kappa (hon.), Delta Sigma Pi, Alpha Delta Sigma. Clubs: Des Moines; Blind Brook (Purchase, N.Y.); Harvard, Links, Economic, Knickerbocker (N.Y.C.); Indian Creek Country, The Bath (Miami Beach, Fla.); Nat. Golf Links Am.; Shinnecock Hills Golf (Southampton, N.Y.). Home: 12 Indian Creek Island Surfside FL 33154 Office: Cowles Charitable Trust 630 Fifth Ave New York NY 10111

COWLES, JOHN, JR., publisher; b. Des Moines, May 27, 1929; s. John and Elizabeth (Bates) C.; m. Jane Sage Fuller, Aug. 23, 1952; children: Tessa Sage Flores, John, Jane Sage, Charles Fuller. Grad., Phillips Exeter Acad., 1947; A.B., Harvard U., 1951; Litt.D. (hon.), Simpson Coll., 1965. With Cowles Media Co. (formerly Mpls. Star and Tribune Co.), 1953-83; v.p. Cowles Medicine Co. (formerly Mpls. Star and Tribune Co.), 1957-68; editor Cowles Media Co. (formerly Mpls. Star and Tribune Co.), 1961-69, pres., 1968-73, 79-83, editorial chmn., 1969-73, chmn., 1973-79, dir., 1956—; pres. Harper's Mag., Inc., 1965-68, chmn. bd., 1968-72; dir. Harper & Row, Pubs., Inc., N.Y.C., 1965-81, chmn., 1968-79; dir. Des Moines Register & Tribune Co., 1960—, Farmers & Mechanics Savs. Bank, Mpls., 1960-65, Cowles Communications, Inc., N.Y.C., 1960-65, Equitable Life Ins. Co. Iowa, Des Moines, 1964-66, 1st Bank Systems, Inc., Mpls., 1964-68, A.P., N.Y.C., 1966-75, Midwest Radio-TV, Inc., Mpls., 1967-76. Mem. adv. bd. on Pulitzer Prizes, Columbia U., 1970-83; campaign chmn. Mpls. United Fund, 1967; bd. dirs. Guthrie Theatre Found., 1960-71, pres., 1960-63, chmn., 1964-65; trustee Phillips Exeter Acad., 1960-65; bd. dirs. Walker Art Center, 1960-69, Minn. Civil Liberties Union, 1956-61, Urban Coalition Mpls., 1968-70, Mpls. Found., 1970-75, German Marshall Fund U.S., 1975-78, Am. Newspaper Pubs. Assn., 1975-77; mem. govt. affairs com. Am. Newspaper Pubs. Assn., 1976-79. Served from pvt. to 2d lt. AUS, 1951-53. Named one of ten outstanding men of year U.S. Jr. C. of C., 1964. Mem. Greater Mpls. C. of C. (dir. 1978-81, chmn. stadium site task force 1977-82), Council on Fgn. Relations, Atlantic Inst., Sigma Delta Chi. Clubs: Minneapolis, Woodhill (Mpls.); Century Assn. (N.Y.C.). Home: 1225 La Salle Ave Minneapolis MN 55403 Office: 430 1st Ave N Minneapolis MN 55401

COWLES, MILLY, educator; b. Ramer, Ala., May 29, 1932; d. Russell Fail and Sara (Mills) C. B.S., Troy State U., 1952; M.A., U. Ala., 1958, Ph.D. (grad. fellow), 1962. Tchr. pub. schs., Montgomery, Ala., 1952-59; asst., then asso. prof. Grad. Sch. Edn. Rutgers U., 1962-66; asso. prof. U. Ga., 1966-67; prof., dir. early childhood devel. and edn. Sch. Edn., U. S.C., Columbia, 1967-73; asso. dean, prof. Sch. Edn., Foundla., Birmingham, 1973-80, dean, prof., 1980—; Dir. Williamsburg County Schs. Career Opportunity Program, 1970-73; cons. So. Edn. Found., Atlanta, Ga. Inst. Higher Edn. U. Ga., also numerous sch. systems throughout Northeast and South. Editor, contbg. author: Perspectives in the Education of Disadvantaged Children, 1967. Pres. bd. dirs. 2d Reformed Ch. Nursery Sch., New Brunswick, N.U., 1963-66; bd. dirs. S.C. Assn. on Children Under Six, 1969-73. Recipient Outstanding Public Educator award Capstone Coll. Edn. Soc. U. Ala., 1977. Mem. Am. Ednl. Research Assn., Soc. for Research Child Devel., AAAS, AAUP, Nat. Council Tchrs. English, Internat. Reading Assn., Assn. for Supervision and Curriculum Devel. (mem. council on early childhood edn. 1969—, dir. 1978-82), Nat. Assn. for Edn. Young Children, Assn. for Childhood Devel. Internat., N.Y. Acad. Scis., Kappa Delta Pi (chpt. treas. 1964-66), Kelta Kappa Gamma. Research and publs. on psycholinguistic behaviors of rural children. Home: 4000 Rock Ridge Rd Birmingham AL 35210

COWLES, WILLIAM HUTCHINSON, 3D, newspaper publisher; b. Spokane, Wash., Mar. 4, 1932; s. William Hutchinson and Margaret (Paine) C.; m. Allison Stacey, Mar. 28, 1959; children: William Stacey, Elizabeth Allison. B.A., Yale U., 1953; J.D., Harvard U., 1959. Bar: Wash. 1959. Pres., pub. Cowles Pub. Co. (pubs. The Spokesman-Rev., Spokane Chronicle), N.W. Farmer-Stockman, Inc. (pubs. Wash. Farmer-Stockman, Oreg. Farmer-Stockman, Idaho Farmer-Stockman, Utah Farmer-Stockman), Spokane, 1970—, Mont. Farmer-Stockman, Inc. (pubs. Mont. Farmer-Stockman), Billings, 1970—; v.p., dir. Inland Empire Paper Co., Millwood, Wash., 1964—; dir. Allied Daily Newspapers, 1970-71, pres., 1972-74; dir. AP, 1974-83, 1st vice-chmn., 1982-83. Bd. dirs. Inland Empire council Boy Scouts Am., 1960—, Spokane Symphony Soc., 1961-78; bd. dirs. United Crusade Spokane County, 1963-74, pres., 1970; bd. overseers Whitman Coll., 1966—. Served to lt. USNR, 1953-56. Mem. Am. Soc. Newspaper Editors, Am. Newspaper Pubs. Assn. (dir. 1980—), Newspaper Advt. Bur. (dir. 1968—, chmn. 1978-80), Beta Theta Pi, Sigma Delta Chi. Club: Spokane. Office: The Spokesman-Review and Spokane Chronicle W 999 Riverside Ave Spokane WA 99210

COWLEY, ALAN HERBERT, chemist, educator; b. Manchester, Eng., Jan. 29, 1934; came to U.S., 1958; s. Herbert and Dora (Smalley) C.; m. Deborah Elaine Cole, Jan. 26, 1977; 1 dau., Emily Margaret McLaughlin; children by previous marriage: Peter, David, Alison Jane. B.Sc., U. Manchester, 1955, M.Sc., 1956, Ph.D., 1958. Postdoctoral fellow, instr. U. Fla., 1958-60; tech. officer Imperial Chem. Industries, Ltd., Eng., 1960-62; mem. faculty U. Tex., Austin, 1962—, prof. chemistry, 1969—. Author: Compounds Containing Phosphorus-Phosphorus Bonds, 1973; also tech. papers; editorial bd.: Inorganic Chemistry, Chem. Revs. Dalton Chem. scholar, 1955-58; Guggenheim fellow, 1976-77. Mem. Am. Chem. Soc., Royal Soc. Chemistry (award 1980). Home: 2501 Woodmont Austin TX 78703 Office: Welch 4-334 Univ Texas Austin TX 78712

COWLEY, JOHN MAXWELL, educator; b. Peterborough, South Australia, Feb. 18, 1923; came to U.S., 1970; s. Alfred Ernest and Doris (Milway) C.; m. Roberta Joan Beckett, Dec. 15, 1951; children—Deborah Suzanne, Jillian Patricia. B.Sc., U. Adelaide, Australia, 1942, M.Sc., 1945, D.Sc., 1957; Ph.D., Mass. Inst. Tech., 1949. Research officer Commonwealth Sci. and Indsl. Research Orgn., Melbourne, Australia, 1945-62, chief research officer, head crystallography sect., 1960-62; prof. physics U. Melbourne, Australia, 1962-70; Galvin prof. physics Ariz. State U., Tempe, 1970—; Mem. U.S. Nat. Com. for Crystallography, 1973-78. Author: Diffraction Physics, 1975; Editor: (with others) Acta Crystallographica, 1971-80; Contbr. articles to profl. jours. Fellow Australian Acad. Sci., Inst. Physics (London), Australian Inst. Physics, Royal Soc. (London); mem. Internat. Union Crystallography (mem. exec. com. 1963-69), Am. Inst. Physics, Am. Crystallographic Assn., Electron Microscope Soc. Am. (dir. 1971-75). Home: 1718 E Gaylon Dr Tempe AZ 85282

COWLEY, LUIS M., psychiatrist; b. Havana, Cuba, June 22, 1921; came to U.S., 1960, naturalized, 1967; s. Luis M. and Guillermina (Morales) C.; m. Yolanda M. Perez, Aug. 29, 1948; children: Ana, Margarita, Luis, Maria, Yolanda, Felipe. M.D., Havana U., 1944. Student house officer Havana (Cuba) U. Hosp., 1940-44, intern, 1944-45; resident psychiatry San Juan de Dios Psychiat. Sanatorium, Havana, 1945-47, psychiatrist, vice dir., 1947-49, psychiatrist, 1949-60; psychiatrist, clin. dir. Perez Vento Psychiat. Sanatorium, Havana, 1957-60; asso. psychiatry Havana U. Hosp., 1946-50; instr., adjoined prof. clin. therapeutic Havana U. Sch. Medicine, 1946-50; asso. in psychiatry Elizabeths Hosp., Washington, 1947; staff, physician charge intensive treatment Terrell (Tex.) State Hosp., 1961, staff physician, supr. psychiat. residency tng. and white female acute treatment program, 1961-62, clin. dir., 1963-64, supt., 1967-81; psychiat. resident Parkland Meml. Hosp., Dallas, 1962-63; clin. prof. psychiatry U. Tex. Southwestern Med. Sch., 1965—. Recipient ann. award Tex. Assn. Mental Health, 1967; hon. mem. Psychology Club, East Tex. State U., 1969. Fellow Am. Psychiat. Assn.; mem. Pan Am., Am., Tex. med. assns., Kaufman County Med. Soc., Tex., Dallas neuropsychiat. assns., Guild Catholic Psychiatrists, N.Y. Acad. Scis. Address: 1800 Hanover Dr Richardson TX 75081

COWLEY, MALCOLM, writer; b. Belsano, Pa., Aug. 24, 1898; s. William and Josephine (Hutmacher) C.; m. Muriel Maurer, June 18, 1932; 1 son, Robert William. A.B., Harvard, 1920; postgrad., U. Montpellier, France, 1921-22; Litt.D. (hon.), Franklin and Marshall Coll., 1961, Colby Coll., 1962, U. Warwick, Eng., 1975, U. New Haven, 1976, Monmouth Coll., 1978, U. Conn., 1983. Free lance writer and translator, 1925-29; asso. editor The New Republic, 1929-44; lit. adviser Viking Press, 1948—; vis. prof. U. Wash., 1950, Stanford, 1956, 59, 60-61, 65, U. Mich., 1957, U. Calif., 1962, Cornell, 1964, U. Minn., 1971, U. Warwick, Eng., 1973; Lectr. Author: Blue Juniata, 1929, Exile's Return, 1934, rev. edit., 1951, (with others) After the Genteel Tradition, 1937, rev. edit., 1964, The Dry Season, 1941, The Literary Situation, 1954, (with Daniel P. Mannix) Black Cargoes, 1962, The Faulkner-Cowley File, 1966, Think Back on Us, 1967, Blue Juniata: Collected Poems, 1968, A Many Windowed House, 1970, (with Howard E. Hugo) The Lesson of the Masters, 1971, A Second Flowering, 1973, -And I Worked at the Writer's Trade, 1978, The Dream of the Golden Mountains, 1980, The View from 80, 1980; translator (from the French): Variety (Paul Valéry), 1926, The Sacred Hill (Maurice Barres), 1929, Imaginary Interviews (André Gide), 1944, etc; Editor: Adventures of an African Slaver, Captain Canot, 1927, Books That Changed Our Minds, 1939, The Portable Hemingway, 1944, The Portable Faulkner, 1946, The Portable Hawthorne, 1948, The Complete Whitman, 1948, The Stories of F. Scott Fitzgerald, 1950, Writers at Work, 1958, Leaves of Grass: The First Edition, 1959, (with Robert Cowley) Fitzgerald and the Jazz Age, 1966; Contbr. to mags. Recipient award Nat. Endowment for Arts, 1967; Signet Soc. medal, 1976; Hubbell medal MLA, 1979; Gold medal Am. Acad. and Inst., 1981. Mem. Nat. Inst. Arts and Letters (pres. 1956-59, 62-65), Am. Acad. Arts and Letters (chancellor 1967-77, Gold medal 1981), Phi Beta Kappa. Clubs: Harvard, Century (N.Y.C.); Bibliophages. Home: Church Rd. Sherman CT 06784

COWLEY, R ADAMS, physician; b. Layton, Utah, July 25, 1917; s. William Wallace and Alta Louise (Adams) C.; (div.)1 dau., Kaye Cowley Pace. Student, U. Utah, 1938-40; M.D., U. Md., 1944. Intern U. Md. Hosp., 1944-45, resident in surgery, 1945-46, 48-49; fellow exptl. surgery U. Md. Med. Sch., 1947-48; jr. clin. instr., then sr. clin. instr. thoracic surgery U. Mich. Hosp., 1949-51; dir. cardiopulmonary lab. U. Md. Med. Sch., 1951-62, asso. dept. surgery, 1953-55, mem. faculty, 1955—, prof. thoracic and cardiovascular surgery, 1961—, chmn. div. thoracic surgery, 1961-70; dir. Md. Inst. Emergency Med. Services Systems, 1973—; past mem. coms. NRC; mem. Nat. Hwy. Safety Adv. Com., 1978-81; Md. Hwy. Safety Coordinating Com., 1978—. Contbr. numerous articles profl. publs. Served as officer M.C. AUS, 1946-57. Recipient Disting. Alumni award U. Utah, 1979, Balt.'s Best award, 1980, Congl. Cert. Merit, 1980; also various service and appreciation awards. Fellow A.C.S.; mem. Am. Surg. Assn., So. Surg. Assn., Soc. Vascular Surgery, Am. Assn. Automotive Medicine, Am. Assn. Thoracic Surgery, Soc. Thoracic Surgeons (a founder), AMA, Balt. Med. Soc., Med. and Chirurgical Soc. Md., John Alexander Soc., Am. Trauma Soc. (a founder; William S. Stone lectr. 1978), AAAS, Internat. Cardiovascular Soc., So. Thoracic Surg. Assn., Am. Assn. Surgery Trauma, Shock Soc., Societe Internationale de Chirurgie, Soc. Med. Cons. Armed Forces, So. Surg. Congress, Soc. Critical Care Medicine, Am. Coll. Emergency Room Physicians (citation Md. chpt. 1980), Underseas Med. Soc., U. Md. Surg. Soc. (pres. 1974), Md. Thoracic Soc. (pres. 1960), U. Assn. Emergency Med. Services.

COWLING, ELLIS BREVIER, plant physiologist, university official; b. Waukeegan, Ill., Dec. 11, 1932; s. Ellis and Marion (Brevier) C.; m. Evelyn Betts Wright, Aug. 25, 1956; children: Evelyn, Emily. B.S., State U. Coll. Forestry, Syracuse, N.Y., 1954, M.S., 1956; Ph.D., U. Wis., 1959; Fil. Doktor, U. Uppsala, Sweden, 1970. Pathologist U.S. Forest Products Lab., Madison, Wis., 1956-59; asst. prof. forest pathology Sch. Forestry, Yale U., New Haven, 1960-65, assoc. prof., 1965-68; prof. plant pathology and forest resources N.C. State U., Raleigh, 1968—, assoc. dean for research Sch. Forest Resources, 1978—; docent U. Uppsala, Sweden, 1970—; Vice chmn. bd. on agrl. and renewable resources Nat. Acad. Scis., 1976-80; chmn. Nat. Atmospheric Deposition Program, 1977-83. Editor: (with James G. Horsfall) Plant Disease: an Advanced Treatise, 1977-80; assoc. editor: Ann. Rev. of Plant Pathology, 1971—. Recipient Research award Sigma Xi, 1968; N.C. award for Achievement in Sci., 1973; Oliver Max Gardner award Consol. U. N.C., 1981. Fellow Internat. Acad. Wood Sci. (Vienna), Am. Phytopathol. Soc.; mem. Nat. Acad. Scis., AAAS. Democrat. Presbyterian. Home: 2310 Weymouth Ct Raleigh NC 27612 Office: Sch Forest Resources NC State U Raleigh NC 27650

COWLING, WILLIAM, textile fiber company executive; b. Coventry, Eng., Aug. 26, 1925; emigrated to Can., 1964; s. William Thomas and Rose (Hopkins) C.; m. Rhoda Muriel Bushnell, Aug. 6, 1949; children: William David, Anne Helena. Grad., Tech. Coll. Coventry, 1945; M.I.Chem.E., Technol. Inst. Gr. Brit., 1956. Chartered chemist, profl. engr. Ont. Research chemist Courtaulds Ltd., Coventry, Eng., 1945-59, chief chemist, Preston, Eng., 1959-64; tech. mgr. Courtaulds Can. Inc., Cornwall, Ont., 1964-70, plant mgr., 1970-73, gen. mgr., 1973—, pres., chief exec. officer, 1981—, dir.; dir. BCL Canada Inc., Cornwall, Can. Textiles Inst., Ottawa. Fellow Royal Soc. Chemistry; mem. Inst. Chem. Engrs. Anglican. Home: Rural Route 2 Williamstown ON Canada K0C 2J0 Office: Courtaulds Inc 1150 Montreal Rd Cornwall ON Canada K5H 5S2

COWPERTHWAITE, LOWERY LEROY, educator; b. Princeton, Kans., Mar. 22, 1917; s. Lowery Isaac and Lynne Bondell (Fish) C.; m. Margaret Elizabeth Farmer, Aug. 11, 1949; children—Thomas, Joseph. B.A., Ottawa (Kans.) U., 1939; M.A., U. Iowa, 1946, Ph.D., 1950. Tchr. high schs., Kans., 1939-42; instr. speech U. Iowa, 1948-49; asso. prof. speech Richmond Area U. Center, 1949-54; prof. speech, dir. Sch. Speech, Kent (Ohio) State U., 1954—; Co-founder Va. Speech and Drama Assn., 1950, pres., 1953. Contbr. articles in field, also to books. Served with USAAF, World War II. Mem. Speech Communication Assn., Assn. for Communication Adminstrn., Central States Speech Assn., Speech Communication Assn. Ohio, Sigma Chi, Pi Kappa Delta, Delta Sigma Rho, Tau Kappa Alpha, Alpha Psi Omega, Omicron Delta Kappa. Episcopalian. Club: Mason. Home: 615 Pioneer Ave Kent OH 44240

COX, AINSLEE, musician; b. Big Spring, Tex., June 22, 1936; s. William Arthur and Mardilla (Taylor) C. Student, Westminster Choir Coll., 1953-57; B. Mus., U. Tex., 1959, M. Music in Composition, 1960. Condr. ch. choirs, choral festivals, Tex., N.J., 1950-62; guest condr. Goldman Band, N.Y.C., 1968, asst. condr., 1969, asso. condr., 1970-74, co-condr., 1975-79; orchestral, opera condr. Spoleto Festival, 1965; asst. condr. Am. Symphony Orch., 1967-68, asso. condr., 1968-72; guest condr., rec. artist, U.S., Europe, 1970—; asst. condr. N.Y. Philharm. Orch., 1973-75; music. dir., condr. Okla. Symphony Orch., Oklahoma City, 1974-78; music dir. Guggenheim Concerts, 1979—, Chamber Opera Theatre of N.Y., 1980-82; lectr. in field, also cons. Mem. adv. panel Okla. Arts and Humanities Council, 1975-78. Composer choral, organ works.; contbg. editor: Music Jour. mag., 1963—. Recipient ASCAP award for service to contemporary music, 1975, 76, 77, 78. Mem. Nat. Assn. Composers U.S.A., Pi Kappa Lambda. Home: 404 W 22d St New York NY 10011 Office: Guggenheim Concert Band 300 Madison Ave New York NY 10017

COX, ALBERT HARRINGTON, JR., economist; b. St. Louis, Oct. 13, 1932; s. Albert Harrington and Hildegarde (Raab) C.; m. Frances Marie French, Apr. 12, 1960; children: Cynthia, Bruce Harrington. B.B.A., U. Tex., 1954, M.B.A., 1956; Ph.D., U. Mich., 1965. Asst. prof. finance So. Meth. U., Dallas, 1959; economist First Nat. City Bank, N.Y.C., 1960-61; sec. research com. Am. Bankers Assn., N.Y.C., 1962-64; v.p., economist First Nat. Bank, Dallas, 1965-68; spl. asst. to chmn. Pres.'s Council Econ. Advs., Washington, 1969-70; exec. v.p., chief economist, dir. Lionel D. Edie & Co., N.Y.C., 1970-75; sr. econ. adv. Merrill Lynch, Pierce, Fenner & Smith, Inc., N.Y.C., 1970-75; pres. Merrill Lynch Econs., Inc., N.Y.C., 1976-81, chmn., 1982—; chief economist Merrill Lynch & Co., 1976-81; mng. dir. Merrill Lynch White Weld Capital Markets Group; dir. Merrill Lynch Capital Fund; mem. econ. adv. bd. Dept. Commerce, 1974-76; Mem. inflation policy task force Pres.-elect Ronald Reagan, 1980. Author: Regulation of Interest Rates on Bank Deposits, 1966; Contbg. economist: Bankers Monthly mag., 1970—; Contbr. articles to profl. jours. Mem. Nat. Assn. Bus. Economists (dir.), Securities Industries Assn. (chmn. econ. adv. com. 1979-80), Am. Econ. Assn., Beta Gamma Sigma, Beta Theta Pi, Phi Eta Sigma. Republican. Mem. Reformed Ch. Clubs: Bronxville Field, Siwanoy Country (Bronxville). Home: 80 Tanglewylde Ave Bronxville NY 10708 Office: One Liberty Plaza 165 Broadway New York NY 10080

COX, ALBERT REGINALD, physician; b. Victoria, C., Can., Apr. 18, 1928; s. Reginald Herbert and Marie Christina (Fraser) C.; m. Margaret Dobson, May, 1954; children—Susan, David John, Steven Fraser. B.A., U. B.C., 1950, M.D., 1954. Intern Vancouver Gen. Hosp., 1954-55, resident, 1955-59; fellow in cardiology U. Wash., 1959-61; asst. prof. medicine U. B.C., 1962-65, asso. prof., 1966-69; prof., chmn. medicine Meml. U., St. John's, Nfld., Can., 1969-74, dean medicine, 1974—; Bd. dirs. Internat. Grenfell Assn., Gen. Hosp. Corp. Fellow Royal Coll. Physicians Can., A.C.P., Am. Coll. Cardiology; mem. Nfld. Med. Assn., Canadian Med. Assn., Can. Soc. Clin. Investigation, Assn. Can. Med. Colls. (pres. 1980-81), Alpha Omega Alpha. Presbyterian. Home: 144 Waterford Bridge St John's NF A1E 1C9 Canada Office: Faculty Medicine Memorial U St John's NF Canada

COX, ALLAN J., management consultant; b. Berwyn, Ill., June 13, 1937; s. Brack C. and Ruby D. C.; m. Jeanne Begalke, 1961 (div. 1966); 1 dau., Heather; m. Bonnie Lynne Welden, 1966; 1 dau., Laura. B.A., No. Ill. U., 1961, M.A., 1962. Instr. Wheaton (Ill.) Coll., 1963-65; asso. Case and Co., Inc., Chgo., 1965-66, Spencer Stuart & Assos., Inc., 1966-68; v.p. Westcott Assos., Inc., Chgo., 1968-69; founder, pres. Allan Cox & Assocs., Inc., 1969—. Author: Confessions of a Corporate Headhunter, 1973, Work, Love and Friendship, 1974, The Cox Report on the American Corporation, 1982; also articles. Bd. dirs. Chgo. Crime Commn. Mem. Am. Sociol. Assn., Am. Soc. Adlerian Psychology; mem. Art Inst. Chgo.; Mem. Alpha Kappa Delta. Presbyterian. Clubs: Chgo., Tavern; University (N.Y.C.). Home: 1515 Astor St Chicago IL 60610 Office: 400 N Michigan Ave Chicago IL 60611

COX, ALLAN V., geophysicist, educator, university dean; b. Santa Ana, Calif., Dec. 17, 1926; s. Vernon D. and Hilda (Schultz) C. B.S., U. Calif., 1955, M.A., 1957, Ph.D., 1959. Geol. field asst. U.S. Geol. Survey, Alaska, 1950, 51,54, geophysicist, Menlo Park, Calif., 1959—; research assoc. Stanford, 1962-67, prof. geophysics, 1967—, dean, 1979—. Mem. Nat. Acad. Sci., Am. Acad. Arts and Scis., Geol. Soc. Am., Am. Geophys. Union, Am. Assn. Petroleum Geologists, AAAS, Sigma Xi. Office: Sch Earth Sci Stanford U Stanford CA 94305

COX, ALVIN EARL, shipbuilding executive; b. Norfolk, Va., May 25, 1918; s. Lucian Baum and Mabel Earl (Oliver) C.; m. Barbara Marshall Fuller, Mar. 15, 1947; children: Susan Riedel, Catherine Baum. B.S., Webb Inst. Naval Architects, 1941; postgrad., Oak Ridge Sch. Reactor Tech., 1953-54, Carnegie Inst. Tech., 1958. Certified profl. engr., Va. With Newport News Shipbldg. & Dry Dock Co., Va., 1941—, LHA project dir., 1966-68, DLGN 36 and 37 program mgr., 1968, sr. program mgr., 1969-73, gen. mgr., 1973-75; v.p. J.J. Henry Co., Inc., N.Y.C., 1975—; Mem. naval architecture com. Am. Bur. Shipping; mem. ship research com. Nat. Acad. Scis.-Nat. Research Council; mem. subcom. Navy/Industry Adv. Com.; mem. prodn. panel Navy Marine Corps Acquisition Rev. Com., 1975. Contbr. to: Reactor Shielding Design Manual, 1956. Vice pres. Family Service-Travelers Aid, 1964, Peninsula United Fund, 1965. Served to lt. USNR, 1944-46. Mem. Soc. Naval Architects and Marine Engrs. (sect. chmn., council mem., v.p.), Am. Soc. Naval Engrs., Propeller Club Am. Clubs: Warwick Lions (v.p. 1948); James River Country (Newport News)). Home: 407 Quantuck Ln Westfield NJ 07090 Office: Suite 9528 Two World Trade Center New York NY 10048

COX, ALVIN JOSEPH, JR., pathologist; b. Manila, P.I., Mar. 6, 1907; s. Alvin Joseph and Mary Amelia (Barnett) C.; m. Helen Files Pollard, Feb. 2, 1947; children: Roger Allen, Barbara Anna, Carolyn Frances. A.B., Stanford U., 1927, M.D., 1931. Instr. pathology Stanford U., 1933-35, asst. and asso. prof. pathology, 1936-41, prof., 1941—, head dept., 1941-64, prof. pathology in dermatology, 1964—; exchange asst. Pathol. Inst., U. Freiburg, Germany, 1935-36. Mem. Am. Assn. Pathologists and Bacteriologists, Soc. for Exptl. Biology and Medicine, A.M.A., Am. Soc. Exptl. Pathology, Internat. Acad. Pathology, Am. Acad. Dermatology, Soc. Investigative Dermatology, Am. Soc. Dermatopathology, Alpha Omega Alpha, Alpha Kappa Kappa. Home: 1400 Geary Blvd Apt 1509 San Francisco CA 94109 Office: 300 Pasteur Dr Stanford CA 94305

COX, ARCHIBALD, lawyer, educator; b. Plainfield, N.J., May 17, 1912; s. Archibald and Frances Bruen (Perkins) C.; m. Phyllis Ames, June 12, 1937; children—Sarah, Archibald, Phyllis. A.B., Harvard, 1934, LL.B., 1937, LL.D. (hon.), 1975; hon. degrees; LL.D., Loyola U., Chgo., 1964, U. Cin., 1967, U. Denver, 1974, Amherst Coll., 1974, Rutgers U., 1974, Mich. State U., 1976, Wheaton Coll., 1977, Northeastern U., 1978, Clark U., 1980; L.H.D., Hahnemann Med. Coll., 1980, U. Mass., 1981. Bar: Mass. bar 1937. In gen. practice with Ropes, Gray, Best, Coolidge & Rugg, Boston, 1938-41; atty. Office of Solicitor Gen., U.S. Dept. Justice, 1941-43, solicitor gen., 1961-65; asso. solicitor Dept. Labor, 1943-45; lectr. law Harvard, 1945-46, prof. law, 1946-61, Williston prof. law, 1965-76, Carl M. Loeb U. prof., 1976—; solicitor gen., U.S., 1966; spl. investigator cases Mass. Legislature, 1972; dir. Office Watergate Spl. Prosecution Force, Washington, 1973; Co-chmn. constrn. Industry Stablzn. Com., 1951-52; chmn. Wage Stablzn. Bd., 1952. Author: (with Derek C. Bok) Cases on Labor Law, 1948, 8th edit., 1976, 9th edit. (with Bok and Robert Gorman), 1981, Law and the National Labor Policy, 1960, (with Mark DeWolfe Howe, J.R. Wiggins) Civil Rights, the Constitution and the Courts, 1967, The Warren Court, 1968, The Role of the Supreme Court in American Government, 1976, Freedom of Expression, 1981. Mem. bd. overseers Harvard, 1962-65. Mem. Am. Bar Assn., Am. Acad. Arts and Scis., Common Cause (chmn. 1980—). Home: Glezen Ln Wayland MA 01778 Office: Harvard Law Sch Cambridge MA 02138

COX, BRUCE BALDWIN, advertising executive; b. Amboy, Ind., Sept. 5, 1931; s. Ralph H. and Thelma A. (Baldwin) C.; m. Judith Brown, June 10, 1953; children: Christopher, Jennifer, Wendy. B.S., Ind. U., 1953, M.A., 1954. Producer-dir. (WTTV-TV), Bloomington, Ind., 1952-54, WLWT-TV, Cin., 1954-57; asst. gen. mgr. WLWI-TV, Indpls., 1957-64; program dir. WLOS-TV, Asheville, N.C., 1964-65; broadcast exec. Compton Advt., N.Y.C., 1965-72, sr. v.p., dir. programming, 1972—, dir., 1982—; lectr. UCLA Network Programming, 1979—; exec. supr. TV series Search for Tomorrow, 1980, TV series Guiding Light, 1972, TV series As the World Turns, 1980, various pilots, movies. Recipient 18 achievement awards in broadcasting. Mem. Nat. Assn. TV Program Execs., Internat. Acad. TV Arts and Scis. Home: 14 Highland Ave Darien CT 06820 Office: 625 Madison Ave New York NY 10022

COX, CHAPMAN BEECHER, government official, lawyer; b. Dayton, Ohio, July 31, 1940; s. Charles Benjamin and Jewel Lorene (Nicholson) C.; m. Jeannette Gail Korody, Aug. 28, 1964; children: Charles Benjamin, Andrew David. B.A., U. So. Calif., 1962; J.D., Harvard U., 1965. Bar: Calif., Colo., U.S. Ct. Mil. Appeals. Assoc. Adams, Duque & Hazeltine, Los Angeles, 1968-72, Sherman & Howard, Denver, 1972-74, ptnr., 1974-80, mng. dir., 1980-81; dep. asst. sec. U.S. Dept. Navy, Washington, 1981-83, asst. sec., 1983—; vis. lectr. U. Colo. Sch. Law, Boulder, 1977-78. Contbr. articles to legal jours. Gen. counsel Colo. Republican party, Denver, 1977-81; del. U.S. Dept. State cultural exchange mission to Syria and Jordan, 1979; ruling elder Wellshire Presbyterian Ch., Denver, 1977-80. Served to lt. col. USMCR, 1965-68. Fellow Am. Coll. Probate Counsel; mem. ABA, Calif. Bar Assn., Colo. Bar Assn. (bd. govs 1977-79, chmn. probate and trust law sect. 1978-79), Denver Estate Planning Council, Harvard Law Sch. Assn. (sec.-treas. Denver 1978-81). Clubs: University (Denver); Army-Navy (Washington). Office: Dept Navy Pentagon Washington DC 20350 *

COX, CLAIR EDWARD, II, educator, physician; b. Lawrenceville, Ill., Sept. 2, 1933; s. Clair Edward and May E. (Judy) C.; m. Clarice Wicks, Aug. 23, 1958; children—Clair Edward III, Daniel Paul, Kevin Christopher, Kenneth Harold. Student, U. Mich., 1951-54, M.D., 1958. Diplomate: Am. Bd. Urology. Intern U. Colo. Med. Center, Denver, 1958-59, surg. resident, 1959-60; resident urology U. Cal. Med. Center at San Francisco, 1960-63; mem. faculty Bowman Gray Sch. Medicine, Wake Forest U., Winston Salem, N.C., 1963-72, asso. prof., 1967-70, prof. urology, 1970-72; prof., chmn. dept. urology U. Tenn. Med. Sch., Memphis, 1972—; Active nat. bladder cancer project, 1970—. Contbr. profl. jours. Fellow A.C.S., mem., Am. Assn. Genito-Urinary Surgeons, Am. Urological Assn., Internat. Soc. Nephrology, Am. Soc. Nephrology, A.M.A., N.Y. Acad. Scis., Infectious Disease Soc. Am., Soc. Univ. Urologists, Am. Assn. Med. Colls., Am. Soc. Microbiology. Research kidney and bladder cancer. Home: 6011 Sweetbriar Cove Memphis TN 38138

COX, CLAUDE RUSSELL, telecommunications equipment company executive; b. Chgo., Mar. 18, 1916; s. Claude Ernest and Mary Ella (Veazey) C.; m. Florence Mildred Freiberger, June 21, 1941; children: Nancy Cox Gassman, Peggy Jean. B.S., U. Chgo., 1937, M.S., 1939, M.B.A., 1950. Dir. sales and engring. Andrew Corp., Orland Park, Ill., 1940-50, gen. mgr., 1950-58, exec. v.p., 1958-67, pres., 1967-71, pres., chief exec. officer, 1971-82, chmn. dir., 1982—. Bd. dirs. Palos Community Hosp., 1974—; mem. vis. com. phys. scis. U. Chgo.; mem. Orland Park Elem. Sch. Dist. Bd., 1963-69. Fellow IEEE; mem. Electronics Industries Assn. (past v.p., dir.), Ill. Mfrs. Assn. (dir. 1980—), Phi Beta Kappa, Beta Gamma Sigma, Sigma Xi. Presbyterian. Office: 10500 W 153rd St Orland Park IL 60462

COX, DAVID JACKSON, biochemistry educator; b. N.Y.C., Dec. 22, 1934; s. Reavis and Rachel (Dunaway) C.; m. Joan M. Narbeth, Sept. 6, 1958 (dec. Oct. 8, 1982); children: Andrew Reavis, Matthew Bruce, Thomas Jackson. B.A., Wesleyan U., 1956; Ph.D., U. Pa., 1960. Instr. biochemistry U. Wash., 1960-63; asst. prof. chemistry U. Tex., 1963-67, assoc. prof., 1967-73; prof., head dept. biochemistry Kans. State U., 1973—; vis. prof. U. Va., 1970-71. NSF predoctoral fellow, 1956-59; NSF sr. postdoctoral fellow, 1970-71. Mem. Am. Soc. Biol. Chemists, Am. Chem. Soc., AAAS, N.Y. Acad. Scis., Phi Beta Kappa, Sigma Xi. Democrat. Presbyterian. Home: 2846 Oregon Ln Manhattan KS 66502 Office: Dept of Biochemistry Kansas State University Manhattan KS 66506

COX, DONALD MORGAN, oil company executive; b. Huntington, W.Va., Aug. 31, 1922; s. Gordon L. and Evelyn (Bearden) C.; m. Maria A. Radoslovich, Dec. 17, 1977. B.S. in Chem. Engring., Va. Poly. Inst., 1943. With Exxon Corp. and affiliates, 1943—; exec. v.p., then pres. Esso Internat. Co., 1967-71; sr. v.p., dir. Exxon Corp., N.Y.C., 1971—; trustee Emigrant Savs. Bank. Bd. dirs. Bus. Council Internat. Understanding, Nat. Fgn. Trade Council; mem. Am. Council on Ger., Brit., N.Am. Com.; trustee Bluefield Coll., W.Va.; bd. dirs. Minority Engring. Edn. Effort. Served with USNR, 1944-46. Mem. Am. Chem. Soc. Roman Catholic. Clubs: Winged Foot, Lotos. Home: 200 E 66th St New York NY 10021 Office: Exxon Corp 1251 Ave of the Americas New York NY 10021

COX, DONALD WILLIAM, physician; b. Carrollton, Ohio, Aug. 20., 1931; m. Jane Louise Teets, June 7, 1953; children: Donald Jeffrey, Gary Alan, Steven Lewis, Suzanne Louise. B.S., Mt. Union Coll., Alliance, Ohio, 1953; M.D., Geroge Washington U., 1957. Diplomate: Am. Bd. Obstetrics and Gynecology. Intern George Washington U., 1957-58; resident Walter Reed Army Med. Ctr., 1961-64; commd. capt. U.S. Army, 1958, advanced through grades to col., 1972; asst. chief obstetrics and gynecology, Ft. Belvoir, Va., 1964-65, chief, 1965-66; asst. cheif obstetrics and gynecology Gorgas Hosp., Canal Zone, Republic Panama, 1966-70; sr. research fellow reproductive endocrinology U. Wash., Seattle, 1970-72; asst. chief Madigan Army Med. Ctr., Tacoma, 1972-74, chief, 1974-77; ret., 1977; assoc. prof. ob-gyn W. Va. U., Morgantown, 1977-80, acting chmn. dept., 1980, chmn., 1980—. Co-chmn. Monongolians Against Sexual Assault, 1982-83. Fellow Am. Coll. Ob-Gyn, Am. Fertility Soc.; mem. Central Assn. Obstetrics and Gynecologists, Assn. Profs. Gynecology and Obstetrics. Home: 2 Ridge Pl Morgantown WV 26505 Office: West Virginia University Medical School Dept of Obstetrics and Gynecology Morgantown WV 26506

COX, EARL GLENN, construction company executive; b. Paonia, Colo., Apr. 12, 1922; s. Edward Earl and Frederica Ernestine (Zorn) C.; m. Sylvia Dorothy Rishavy, Mar. 20, 1943; 1 dau., Marilyn Jean Cox Richin. B.S. in Accounting, U. Denver, 1948. Mgr. fin. Gen. Electric Co., various locations, 1948-68; controller, treas., dir. Baker Perkins, Inc., Saginaw, Mich., 1968-73; v.p. fin., treas., dir. Darin & Armstrong, Inc., Detroit, 1973-83; with Gen. Semicondr. Industries, Tempe, Ariz., 1982—. Served with AUS, 1943-46. Mem. Nat. Assn. Accountants, Fin. Execs. Inst. Republican. Home: 13682 110th Ave Sun City AZ 85351 Office: 2001 W 10th Pl Tempe AZ 85281

COX, EBBIE LEE, insurance company executive; b. Kevil, Ky., Jan. 10, 1927; s. Guy and Myra (Tucker) C.; m. Betty Jacks, June 17, 1950; children: Terry, Michael, Janice. Student, U. Miami, Fla., 1946-47, Wayne State U., 1947-50. With Mich. Mut. Ins. Co., 1952—, br. mgr., Kalamazoo, Saginaw and Grand Rapids, 1953-68, asst. v.p., Detroit, 1968-70, resident v.p., Grand Rapids, 1970-78, exec. v.p., Detroit, 1978-79, pres., 1979-81, pres. and chief exec. officer, 1981—; dir. Alliance Am. Insurers, Chgo., Mut Reins. Bur., Cherry Valley, Ill., Improved Risk Mutuals, White Plains, N.Y. Bd. dirs. Downtown Detroit Br. YMCA, 1978—; exec. bd. Greater Detroit Area council Boy Scouts Am., 1981—. Served with U.S. Army, 1945-46. Mem. Mich. Assn. Ins. Cos. (dir. Lansing 1981—), Mich. State C. of C. (dir. Lansing 1982—). Republican. Presbyterian. Clubs: Detroit Athletic, Detroit Golf, Renaissance. Lodge: Masons. Office: Mich Mut Ins Co 28 W Adams Ave Detroit MI 48226 *

COX, EXUM MORRIS, investment manager; b. Santa Rosa, Calif., Feb. 5, 1903; s. Exum Morris and Mary Eleanor (Anderson) C.; m. Elsie Margaret Storke, Sept. 6, 1934; children—Cynthia Morris Huntting, Susana More (Mrs. James T. Fousekis), Thomas Storke. A.B., U. Calif., 1924; M.B.A., Harvard U., 1928. With Dodge & Cox, 1933—, ptnr., 1933-59, pres., 1959-72, chmn. bd., 1972-77, hon. chmn., 1977—; chmn. bd. Dodge & Cox Balanced Fund, 1933-79, trustee, 1979—; dir. Dodge & Cox Stock Fund. Bd. dirs., v.p. San Francisco, Community Chest, 1946-48; bd. dirs. San Francisco Tb Assn., 1948-52, Bay Area Ednl. TV Assn., 1961-70; trustee San Francisco Mus. Modern Art, pres., 1955-60; trustee Katherine Branson Sch., 1950-57; vice chmn. Citizens Adv. Com. to Atty. Gen. Calif. on Crime Prevention, 1954-58; mem. Calif. Delinquency Prevention Commn., 1963-67, San Francisco Library Commn., 1963-64; trustee U. Calif. Hastings Law Center Found., 1974—, pres., 1980—; trustee U. Calif. at Berkeley Found., 1972—, v.p., 1974-77, pres., 1977-79. Mem. Investment Counsel Assn. Am. (gov. 1955-58, 61-67), Calif. Acad. Scis. (trustee, chmn. bd. trustees 1967-73, treas. 1963-67), Sigma Chi. Clubs: Anglers (N.Y.C.); Bankers, Pacific Union, Bohemian. Home: 2361 Broadway San Francisco CA 94115 Office: 35th Floor Crocker Plaza 1 Post St San Francisco CA 94104

COX, FREDERICK MORELAND, social worker, university dean; b. Los Angeles, Dec. 8, 1928; s. Frederick Alfred Edward and Ethel (Moreland) C.; m. Gay Campbell, June, 1951; children: Lawrence, Elizabeth, Sherman. B.A., UCLA, 1950, M.S.W., 1954; D.S.W., U. Calif., Berkeley, 1968. Caseworker child welfare Los Angeles Bur. Public Assistance, 1952-53; mental health counselor Los Angeles Superior Ct., 1953; caseworker Family Service Bur., Oakland, Calif., 1954-57; program dir. Easter Seal Soc., Oakland, 1957-60; asst. prof. to prof. social work U. Mich., Ann Arbor, 1964-76; prof., dir. Sch. Social Work, Mich. State U., East Lansing, 1976-80; prof., dean Sch. Social Welfare, U. Wis., Milw., 1980—; instr. Contra Costa Coll., San Pablo, Calif., 1956-57. Sr. co-editor: collections of readings on community orgn. practice Community-Action Planning Development, A Casebook, 1974, Tactics and Techniques of Community Practice, 1977, 2d edit., 1984, Strategies of Community Organization, 3d edit, 1979. Chmn. Ann Arbor Housing Commn., 1970-71; pres. non-profit housing devel. corp., 1970-75. NIMH spl. research fellow, 1960-63. Mem. Council on Social Work Edn., Nat. Assn. Social Workers, Acad. Cert. Social Workers, Am. Sociol. Assn. Office: 1099 Enderis Hall Milwaukee WI 53201

COX, GARDNER, artist; b. Holyoke, Mass., Jan. 22, 1906; s. Allen Howard and Katherine Gilbert (Abbot) C.; m. Phyllis Moyra Byrne, Dec. 3, 1937; children: Benjamin, Katherine Gilbert Abbot, James Byrne, Phyllis Byrne. Student, Art Students League, N.Y.C., 1924, Harvard U., 1924-27, Boston Mus. Sch., 1928-30, MIT, 1929-31. Head dept. painting Boston Mus. Fine Arts Sch., 1954-55; artist-in-residence Am. Acad. in Rome, 1961; chmn. Blanche Colman Award Jury, 1961—; exec. com. Boston Arts Festival, 1959-67; mem. Mass. Fine Arts Commn., 1965—. Work exhibited, Carnegie Mus., 1941, Va. Mus. Fine Arts, 1946, 1948, Art Inst. Chgo., 1948, 49, 51, Met. Mus. Art, 1950, U. Ill., 1950-51, Inst. Contemporary Art, Boston, 1953, one-man shows, Farnsworth Mus., Rockland, Maine, 1956, Newport (R.I.) Art Assn., 1966, Corcoran Gallery, Washington, 1975, Boston Athenaeum, 1981; represented permanent collections, Boston Mus. Fine Arts, Fogg Mus., Harvard U., Addison Gallery, Andover, Mass., Wadsworth Atheneum, Hartford, Conn., Yale U., Wellesley Coll., Wabash Coll., MIT, Mt. Holyoke Coll., Boston Athenaeum, Santa Barbara (Calif.) Art Mus., Dept. State, Dept. Army, Dept. Def., Dept. Labor, Dept. Air Force, Dept. Transp., FAA, Middlebury Coll., Nat. Gallery Washington, Nat. Portrait Gallery, Collection of U.S. Supreme Ct., Brandeis U., Princeton U., U.S. Ct. Appeals, Boston, State House, Boston, permanent collections, Clark Art Inst., Williamstown, Mass., others. Trustee Am. Acad. in Rome, 1962—, St. Gaudens Meml., Cornish, N.H., 1959—. Served with AUS, 1942-45. Recipient M.V. Kohnstamm prize Am. Exhibit Water Colors, Art Inst. Chgo., 1949, Norman Walt Harris Bronze medal 60th Ann. Am. Exhibit, 1951. Mem. Am. Acad. Arts and Scis., Nat. Inst. Arts and Letters, NAD (academician), Phi Beta Kappa (hon.). Clubs: Tavern, St. Botolph (Boston); Century (N.Y.C.). Home: 88 Garden St Cambridge MA 02138 Office: 30 Ipswich St Boston MA 02215

COX, GENE SPRACHER, forestry educator; b. Norton, Va., Mar. 21, 1921; s. Dewitt Cam and Kathleen (Spracher) C.; m. Neil Ruth Jones, Jan. 19, 1946; children: Thomas, Alan. B.S., Duke U., 1947, M.S., 1948, Ph.D., 1953. Asst. prof. Stephen F. Austin State U., Nacogdoches, Tex., 1951-53; from asst. prof. to assoc. prof. U. Mont., Missoula, 1953-60; from assoc. prof. to prof. forestry U. Mo., Columbia, 1960—; vis. scientist NSF, 1969-71. Served with U.S. Army, 1942-45. Recipient Superior Teaching Gamma Sigma Delta, 1966, Outstanding Teaching Standard Oil Found., 1969, Faculty Alumni U. Mo. Alumni Assn., 1981. Mem. Soc. Am. Foresters, Soil Sci. Soc. Am., Ecol. Soc. Am., Am. Soc. Agronomy, AAAS, Sigma Xi, Xi Sigma Phi, Gamma Sigma Delta. Unitarian. Home: 1800 Princeton Dr Columbia MO 65201

COX, GILBERT EDWIN, lawyer, diversified industry exec.; b. 1917; (married). B.B.A., U. Tex., 1938, LL.B., 1940. Bar: Hawaii bar, Tex. bar. Formerly mem. firm Cades, Cox, Schutte, Fleming & Wright, Honolulu; exec. v.p. Amfac Inc., 1969-74, pres., chief operating officer, 1974-78; pres., chief exec. officer Alexander & Baldwin, Inc., 1978-80; of counsel firm Cades, Schutte, Fleming & Wright, Honolulu, 1980—; dir. Bishop Ins. Co., Honolulu, Itel Corp., San Francisco, Pacific Guardian Life Ins. Co., Honolulu. Served to maj. USAF, 1940-46. Clubs: Silverado Country (Napa, Calif.); Oahu Country, Pacific (Honolulu); Pacific Union (San Francisco). Office: 1000 Bishop St PO Box 939 Honolulu HI 96808

COX, GLENN ANDREW, JR., petroleum executive; b. Sedalia, Mo., Aug. 6, 1929; s. Glenn Andrew and Ruth Lonsdale (Atkinson) C.; m. Veronica Cecelia Martin, Jan. 3, 1953; children: Martin Stuart, Grant Andrew, Cecelia Ruth. B.B.A., So. Methodist U., 1951. With Phillips Petroleum Co., Bartlesville, Okla., 1956—, asst. to chmn. operating com., 1973-74, v.p. mgmt. info. and control, 1974-80, exec. v.p., 1980—, dir., 1982—; dir. First Nat. Bank, Bartlesville; exec. bd. Center Internat. Bus., Dallas. Pres. Cherokee Area council Boy Scouts Am., 1977-82. Served as pilot USAF, 1951-55. Mem. Am. Petroleum Inst. (dir.), Bartlesville Area C. of C. (pres. 1978). Methodist. Club: Hillcrest Country. Office: 18 Phillips Bldg Bartlesville OK 74004

COX, HARRY SEYMOUR, financial executive; b. Covington, Ky., Mar. 23, 1923; s. Harry S. and Rebecca E. (Wolfe) C.; m. Sally I. Stoneburner, Aug. 31, 1946; children: Inga Cox Walker, Sally Cox Sattler, Christopher. B.A., Ohio Wesleyan U., 1947. Acct., Barrow, Wade, Guthrie & Co., Cleve., 1947-55; acct. White Consol. Industries Inc., Cleve., 1956-68, v.p., treas., 1973—; chief fin. officer Commodore Corp., Syracuse, Ind., 1981—; chmn. bd. Laub Baking Co., Cleve., 1968-72. Served to lt. USNR, 1942-46. Mem. Sigma Alpha Epsilon. Methodist. Clubs: Westwood Country (Rocky River, Ohio); Country of Ashland; Clifton (Lakewood, Ohio); Union (Cleve.). Office: RR2 Box 172 Leesburg IN 46538

COX, HARVEY GALLAGHER, theologian; b. Phoenixville, Pa., May 19, 1929; s. Harvey Gallagher and Dorothea (Dunwoody) C.; m. Nancy Nieburger, May 10, 1957; children—Rachel Lianelly, Martin Stephen, Sarah Irene. A.B. with honors in history, U. Pa., 1951; B.D. cum laude, Yale, 1955; Ph.D., Harvard, 1963. Dir. religious activities Oberlin Coll., 1955-58; program asso. Am. Baptist Home Mission Soc., 1958-62; fraternal worker Gossner Mission, East Berlin, 1962-63; asst. prof. Andover Newton Theol. Sch., 1963-65; asso. prof. church and soc. Harvard, 1965-70, Victor Thomas prof. divinity, 1970—; Cons. Third Assembly World Council Chs., New Delhi, India, 1961. Author: The Secular City, 1965, God's Revolution and Man's Responsibility, 1965, The Feast of Fools, 1969, The Seduction of the Spirit: The Use and Misuse of People's Religion, 1973, Turning East: The Promise and Peril of the New Orientalism, 1977; Editorial bd.: Christianity and Crisis. Chmn. bd. Blue Hill Christian Center, 1963-66; chmn. Boston Indsl. Mission. Office: Divinity Sch Harvard Univ Cambridge MA 02140 *

COX, HEADLEY MORRIS, JR., educator; b. Mt. Olive, N.C., July 25, 1916; s. Headley Morris and Frank (English) C.; m. Irene Todd, June 26, 1940; children—John Morris, Deborah English (Mrs. Kenneth Gunnels), Thomas Headley. A.B., Duke, 1937, A.M., 1939; postgrad., U. Colo., 1944-45; Ph.D., U. Pa., 1958. Successively instr., asst. prof., asso. prof., prof. English Clemson (S.C.) U., 1939—, head dept., 1950-69, dean, 1969-80; Sr. Fulbright lectr. in Am. lit. Universitat Graz, Austria, 1958-59. Served with USNR, 1944-46. Mem. MLA, Am. Dialect Soc., Phi Beta Kappa. Methodist. Home: 213 Riggs Dr Clemson SC 29631 Office: 204 Strode Tower Clemson U Clemson SC 29631

COX, HENRY, research company executive, research engineer; b. Phila., Mar. 7, 1935; s. Henry Robert and Helen (Kane) C.; m. Mary Ann Shaw, Sept. 3, 1960; children: James, Daniel, Michael, Diane. B.S., Coll. Holy Cross, 1956; Sc.D., MIT, 1963. Analyst Office Sec. of Def., 1970-72; research assoc. Scripps Instn. Oceanography, LaJolla, Calif., 1972-73; officer in charge Naval Underwater Systems Ctr., New London, Conn., 1973-76; div. dir. Def. Advanced Research Projects Agy., 1976-78; project mgr. Naval Electronic Systems Command, Arlington, Va., 1978-81; divisional v.p. Bolt Beranek & Newman, Inc., Arlington, 1981—. Contbr. articles to tech. jours. Served to capt. USN, 1956-81. Decorated Legion of Merit, Meritorious Service medal, Navy Commendation medal; recipient Def. Superior Service medal Dept. Def., 1978. Fellow Acoustical Soc. Am., IEEE; mem. Am. Soc. Naval Engrs. (hon., Gold medal 1980), Soc. Indsl. and Applied Math., U.S. Naval Inst. Roman Catholic. Home: 8112 Saxony Dr Annadale VA 22003 Office: Bolt Beranek & Newman Inc 1300 N 17th St Arlington VA 22209

COX, JAMES CHARLES, librarian; b. Chgo., July 8, 1927; s. Ora Clay and Maude Emily (White) C.; m. Dorothy Jean Watters, Aug. 22, 1953. Ph.B., Loyola U., Chgo., 1950, postgrad., 1952-53; M.A. in L.S, Rosary Coll., River Forest, Ill., 1956, U. Chgo., 1971-72. Mem. faculty Loyola U., Chgo., 1952—, asst. librarian, 1953-55, librarian, 1955-56, asst. librarian univ., 1956-58, asso. librarian univ. libraries, 1958-59, dir. libraries, 1959-71; asst. librarian Lewis Towers Library, Loyola U., Chgo., 1972-74; chief librarian Loyola U. Med. Center, 1974—. Contbr. articles to profl. jours. Served with USNR, 1945-46, 50-52. Mem. ALA, Cath. Library Assn. (chmn. Ill. 1962-63, program chmn. 1961-63, chmn. cataloging and classification sect. 1965-67, mem. exec. bd. 1967-73, pres. 1975-77), Ill. Library Assn., Med. Library Assn., Bibliog. Soc. Am., Bibliog. Soc. (London). Roman Catholic. Home: 5926 N Bernard St Chicago IL 60659 Office: 2160 S 1st Ave Maywood IL 60153

COX, JAMES D., legal educator; b. 1943. J.D., U. Calif. Hastings Sch. Law, 1969; LL.M., Harvard U., 1971. Bar: Calif. 1970. Atty.-adv. Office Gen. Counsel FTC, Washington, 1969-70; teaching fellow Boston U., 1970-71; asst. prof. U. San Francisco, 1971-74; assoc. prof. U. Calif. Hastings Sch. Law, 1974-75; vis. assoc. prof. Stanford U., 1976-77; prof. U. Calif. Hastings Sch. Law, 1977-79; vis. prof. Duke U. Sch. Law, spring 1979, prof., 1979—; mem. com. on corps. State Bar Calif.; E.T. Bost research prof., fall 1980. Author: Sum and Substance of Corporations, 3d edit., 1975, Financial Information, Accounting and the Law, 1980. Mem. Am. Law Inst., Order of Coif, Phi Kappa Phi. Office: Duke U Sch Law Durham NC 27706

COX, JAMES DAVID, art gallery executive; b. South Bend, Ind., Aug. 18, 1945; m. Mary Anna Goetz. Dir. Grand Central Art Galleries, N.Y.C., 1977—. Exec. editor: Illuminator, 1977. Mem. N.Y. Acad Art (bd. dirs. 1983—), Am. Art Dealers Assn., Nat. Arts Club. Clubs: Salmagundi; Dutch Treat (N.Y.C.). Office: Grand Central Art Galleries Inc 24 W 57th St New York NY 10019

COX, JAMES TALLEY, lawyer; b. Temple, Tex., Sept. 22, 1921; s. George Allan and Jane (Talley) C.; m. Alice Tarver, Jan. 12, 1945; children: Martha (Mrs. John S. Daniels), Louise, Anne, Allan. B.B.A., U. Tex., 1943; LL.B., 1947. Bar: Tex. 1947, U.S. Supreme Ct. 1951. Spl. atty. Justice Dept., Washington, 1947-48; staff atty. Tax Ct. U.S., Washington, 1948-50; trial atty. Treasury Dept., Phila., 1950-51; tax counsel Schlumberger Well Services, Houston, 1951-65; mem. firm Hoover, Cox & Shearer, Houston, 1965—; Partner Agy. Mgmt. Assocs., 1969-78; v.p., dir. Westchase Travels, Inc., 1972—; dir. Western Bank. Contbr. articles to profl. publs. Bd. dirs. Houston Met. YMCA, 1972-78, Pin Oak Charity Horse Show Assn., 1972—, Retina Research Found., 1977—. Served to lt. USNR, 1943-46. Mem. Am., Tex., Houston bar assns., Tax Research Assn. (exec. com. 1950-67), Delta Theta Phi, Phi Kappa Psi. Republican. Presbyn. Home: 11701 Forest Glen Houston TX 77024 Office: 700 Western Bank Bldg 5433 Westheimer Houston TX 77056

COX, JAMES WILLIAM, newspaper executive; b. Waldron, Ark., Oct. 18, 1937; s. George T. and Louise M. (Harris) C.; m. Nichola F. Goudreau, Mar. 20, 1969; 1 son, James William. B.B.A., U. Tex., Arlington, 1974. With Donrey Media group, 1958-65; bus. mgr. Las Vegas (Nev.) Rev.-Jour., also chief accountant Western Corp. acctg. Dept., 1960-65; controller Palmer Media Group, 1965-69; with A.H. Belo Corp. (publisher Dallas Morning News), 1969—, internal auditor, then treas., 1969-79; sr. v.p., controller (Dallas Morning News), 1969—. Mem. budget com. Dallas County chpt. ARC, 1973-74; mem. planning com. Goals for Dallas, 1981—. Mem. Inst. Newspaper Controller and Fin. Officers, Fin. Execs. Inst., Sigma Alpha Epsilon. Clubs: Las Colinas Country, Chaparral. Home: 3609 Hidalgo St Irving TX 75062 Office: Dallas Morning News Communications Center Dallas TX 75265

COX, JEROME ROCKHOLD, JR., elec. engr.; b. Washington, May 24, 1925; s. Jerome R. and Jane (Mills) C.; m. Barbara Jane Lueders, Sept. 2,1951; children—Nancy Jane Cox Battersby, Jerome Mills, Randall Allen. S.B., Mass. Inst. Tech., 1947, S.M., 1949, Sc.D., 1954. Mem. faculty Washington U., St. Louis, 1955—, prof. elec. engring., 1961—, prof. biomed. engring. in physiology and biophysics, 1965—, dir., 1964-75, chmn. computer labs., 1967—, program dir. tng. program tech. in health care, 1970-78, chmn. dept. computer sci., 1975—, sr. research asso., 1975—; co-chmn. computers in cardiology conf. Inst. Medicine, Nat. Acad. Scis., 1974—; cardiology adv. com. Nat. Heart and Lung Inst., 1975-78; mem. epidemiology biostatistics and bioengring. cluster President's Biomed. Research Panel, 1975. Editorial bd.: Computers and Biomed. Research, 1967—; asso. editor, IEEE, trans. biomed. engring., 1969-71. Served with U.S. Army, 1943-44. Fellow Acoustical Soc. Am., IEEE; mem. Biomed. Engring. Soc., Biophys. Soc., Assn. Computing Machinery, Sigma Xi, Eta Kappa Nu, Tau Beta Pi. Author, patentee air traffic control, computerized tomography. Office: Dept Computer Sci Box 1045 Washington Univ St Louis MO 63130

COX, JOHN PAUL, educator, astrophysicist; b. Ft. Myers, Fla., Nov. 4, 1926; s. James B. and Bess L. (Tollette) C.; m. Jane B. Blizard-Cox, July 1972. A.B., Ind. U., 1949, M.S., 1950, Ph.D., 1954. Mem. faculty Cornell U., 1954-62; vis. scientist Courant Inst. Math. Scis., NYU, 1962-63; vis. fellow Joint Inst. Lab. Astrophysics, Boulder, Colo., 1963; asso. prof. astrophysics U. Colo., Boulder, 1963-65, prof. astrophysics, 1965—; vis. prof. dept. math. Monash U., Melbourne, Australia, 1972; cons. Smithsonian Astrophys. Obs., Cambridge, Mass., 1957, 59, 60, Los Alamos Sci. Lab., 1960—; asst. engr. Pratt & Whitney Aircraft Corp., East Hartford, Conn., 1958. Mem. Am. Phys. Soc., Am. Astron. Soc., N.Y. Acad. Scis., Colo.-Wyo. Acad. Scis., Internat. Astron. Union, Royal Astron. Soc., Astron. Soc. Pacific, Sigma Xi, Phi Eta Sigma. Home: 827 16th St Boulder CO 80302

COX, JOHN WILLIAM, physician, naval officer; b. St., Aug. 31, 1928; s. William Elbert and Evelyn Ann (Schenck) C.; m. Anne Maczewsk, June 11, 1949; 1 son, William. M.D., St. Louis U., 1952, Ph.D. (USPHS fellow), 1953. Diplomate: Am. Bd. Internal Medicine. Asso. physiology St. Louis U., 1949-53; dir. research labs. VA Hosps., St. Louis, 1953-54; intern Naval Hosp., San Diego, 1954, resident internal medicine, 1956-59; commd. lt. (j.g.) M.C. U.S. Navy, 1954, advanced through grades to vice adm., 1980; chief of medicine, dir. clin. services U.S. Naval Hosp., Subic Bay, Philippines, 1961-63, chief cardiovascular and respiratory disease div., Phila., 1963-65, chmn. dept. medicine, dir. research, 1965-69; asst. head. edn. and tng. Bur. Medicine and Surgery, Washington, 1969-71, head, 1971-72, asst. chief for human resources and profl. ops., 1976-78; comdg. officer Naval Regional Med. Center, San Diego, 1978-80; surgeon gen. of Navy, chief Bur. Medicine and Surgery, Navy Dept., Washington, 1980—; comdg. officer Med. Tng. Inst., Bethesda, Md., 1973-74, Health Scis. Edn. and Tng., Bethesda, 1974-77; asst. prof. Thomas Jefferson U., Phila., 1963-65, asso. prof., 1965-73; mem. Nat. Bd. Med. Examiners, 1969—; mem. bd. regents Nat. Library Medicine, 1972—; bd. regents Uniformed Services U. of Health Scis, 1980—; bd. govs. Armed Forces Inst. Pathology, 1980—. Contbr. articles to med. jours. Decorated Legion of Merit, Navy Meritorious Service medal (2). Fellow A.C.P., Am. Coll. Cardiology (trustee 1972-79, treas. 1975-79), AMA (mem. Ho. of Dels. and chmn. council on fed. and mil. medicine 1971—), Am. Coll. Chest Physicians; mem. Nat. Med. Vets. Soc. (dir. 1976—), Am. Heart Assn., Soc. Med. Consultants to Armed Forces, Assn. Mil. Surgeons (mem. exec. council 1971—), Mil. Order of Carabo. Office: Office Surgeon Gen BUMED Navy Dept Washington DC 20372

COX, JOSEPH WILLIAM, univ. adminstr.; b. Hagerstown, Md., May 26, 1937; s. Joseph F. and Ruth E. C.; m. Regina M. Bollinger, Aug. 17, 1963; children—Matthew, Andrew, Abigail. B.A., U. Md., 1959, Ph.D., 1967. Teaching asst. dept. history U. Md., 1960-64; successively instr., asst. prof., asso. prof., prof. history Towson (Md.) State U., 1964—, dean evening, summer and minimester programs, 1972-75, acting pres., 1978-79, v.p. acad. affairs and dean of univ., 1979—. Author: Champion of Southern Federalism: Robert Goodloe Harper of South Carolina, 1972, The Early National Experience: The Army Corps of Engineers, 1783-1812, 1979; mem. bd. editors: Md. Hist. Mag. Chmn. Md. Com. for Humanities, 1979—; Mem. adv. council Md. Gen. Hosp. Sch. Nursing. Recipient Outstanding Graduating Sr. award U. Md. Men's League, 1959. Mem. AAUP, Am. Assn. Higher Edn., Am. Assn. State Colls. and Univs., Phi Kappa Phi, Omicron Delta Kappa. Lutheran. Office: Towson State Univ Towson MD 21204 *

COX, JOSH CURTIS, JR., banker, consultant; b. New Orleans, Oct. 20, 1941; s. Josh Curtis and Catherine (Harrison) C.; m. Carol Joyce Busto, Oct. 1983; 1 son, David. B.A., U. Richmond, 1969; Cert. in comml. banking, Am. Inst. Banking, Richmond, 1970, Rutgers U., 1974, U. Va., 1968. Sr. v.p. Comml. and Indsl. Bank, Memphis, 1976-78; pres., chief exec. officer Trust Co., Columbus, Ga., 1978-81; sr. v.p. First Okla. Bancorp., Okalhoma City, 1981—; pres., chief exec. officer First Okla. Trust Co., 1981—; chmn., pres., chief exec. officer Okla. Nat. Bank, Oklahoma City, 1982—; cons. in banking, 1976—. Bd. dirs. South Oklahoma City YMCA, 1983; campaign chmn., bd. dirs. United Way, Columbus, Ga., 1981. Clubs: Quail Creek Country (Oklahoma City); Green Island Country (pres. 1979-80). Office: First Okla Bancorp 210 Park Ave Oklahoma City OK 73102 *A well-run financial institution is like a pyramid. Those bricks at the top give it final shape and direction, but they are not what make it strong.*

COX, KENNETH ALLEN, lawyer, communications exec.; b. Topeka, Dec. 7, 1916; s. Seth Leroy and Jean (Sears) C.; m. Nona Beth Fumerton, Jan. 1, 1943; children—Gregory Allen, Jeffrey Neal, Douglas Randall. B.A., U. Wash., 1938, LL.B., 1940; LL.M., U. Mich., 1941; LL.D., Chgo. Theol. Sem., 1969. Bar: Wash. bar 1941. Law clk. Wash. Supreme Ct., 1941-42; asst. prof. U. Mich. Law Sch., 1946-48; with firm Little, Palmer, Scott & Slemmons (and predecessor), Seattle, 1948-61, partner, 1953-61; spl. counsel com. interstate and fgn. commerce charge TV inquiry U.S. Senate, 1956-57; chief broadcast bur. FCC, Washington, 1961-63, commr., 1963-70; counsel to communications law firm Haley, Bader & Potts, 1970—; sr. v.p. MCI Communications Corp., 1970—; Lectr. U. Washington Law Sch., part-time 1954, 60; adj. prof. Georgetown U. Law Center, 1971, 72. Vice pres. Municipal League Seattle and King County, 1960, Seattle World Affairs Council, 1960; pres. Seattle chpt. Am. Assn. UN, 1957; chmn. one of five citizen subcoms. Legis. Interim Com. Edn., 1960; Bd. dirs. Nat. Pub. Radio, 1971-80; bd. dirs. Nat. Advt. Rev. Bd., 1971-74, chmn. bd., 1976—. Served to capt. Q.M.C. AUS, 1943-46, 51-52. Recipient Alfred I. duPont award in broadcast journalism Columbia U., 1970. Mem. Am., Fed. Communications, Wash. State, D.C. bar assns., Order of Coif, Phi Beta Kappa, Phi Delta Phi. Democrat. Conglist. Home: 5836 Marbury Rd Bethesda MD 20817 Office: 1133 19th St NW Washington DC 20036

COX, KENNETH VICTOR, telephone company executive; b. Allison, N.B., Can., May 14, 1922; s. Charles Hilton and Hattie May (Mollins) C.; m. Mary McNeill Dow, June 3, 1944; children: David R., Rodney A., Marilyn L., Kenneth H. B.Sc. in Elec. Engring., U. N.B., 1942, D.Sc. (hon.), 1979, D.B.A., U. Moncton, 1973, LL.D., St. Thomas U., 1982. With N.B. Telephone Co., Ltd., St. John, 1942—, chief engr., 1956-58, gen. mgr., 1958-59, exec. v.p., 1959-65, pres., chief exec. officer, 1965-77, chmn. bd., 1977—, pres., 1980—, dir., mem. exec. com., 1959—, chmn. exec. com., 1977; pres., chief exec. officer Bruntel Holdings Ltd.; dir. Eastern Tel. & Tel. Co., N.Am. Life Assurance Co., Maritime Electric Co. Ltd., Fraser Inc., Bank of N.S., SDL/Datacrown Inc.; Datacrown Inc.; mem. bd. mgmt. Trans-Can Tel. System; chmn. N.B. Research and Productivity Council, 1971. Hon. bd. govs. Can. Assn. Mentally Retarded. Fellow Engring. Inst. Can.; mem. Assn. Profl. Engrs. N.B. (past pres.), Conf. bd. Can., Can. Atlantic Council C.E.O.s. Clubs: Rotary (hon.), Westfield Golf and Country, Riverside Golf and Country, Union. Home: 216 Roderick Row St John NB E2M 4J8 Canada Office: One Brunswick Sq St John NB E2L 4K2 Canada

COX, LESTER LEE, broadcasting executive; b. Springfield, Mo., Nov. 6, 1922; s. Lester Edmund and Mildred Belle (Lee) C.; m. Claudine Viola Barrett, Jan. 19, 1946; 1 son, Lester Barrett. A.B. in Econs., Westminster Coll., 1944, LL.D., 1974; postgrad., U.S. Mil. Acad., 1944-46; M.B.A., Drury Coll., 1965. Pres., Springfield TV, Inc. (KYTV), 1958-79, K.C. Air Conditioning, North Kansas City, 1968—, Mid-Continent Telecasting, Inc. (KOAM-TV), Pittsburg, Kans., Pittsburg Broadcasting Co. (KOAM); Pres., Ozark Motor & Supply Co., Springfield, Modern Tractor & Supply Co.; chmn. bd., dir. Ozark Air Lines, St. Louis; dir. Commerceshares, Inc., Kansas City, Mo., Fed. Home Loan Bank, Des Moines, 1967-71. Mem. Mo. Bd. Health, 1968-73, past chmn.; mem. Commn. on Higher Edn. for Mo., 1977-83; pres. Ozark Empire council Boy Scouts Am., 1960; chmn. bd. Lester E. Cox Med. Center; bd. dirs. Westminster Coll., 1949-79, Drury Coll., 1965-79, Midwest Research Inst., Kansas City. Served with AUS, 1943-46, to; capt., 1951-53. Recipient Silver Beaver award Boy Scouts Am., 1961; named Hon. col. Gov. of Mo., 1960-64, 68-72. Mem. Central States Shrine Assn. (pres. 1970). Clubs: Masons, Shriners, Hickory Hills Country. Home: RFD 9 Box 401 Springfield MO 65804 Office: 440 E Tampa St Springfield MO 65806

COX, MARSHALL, lawyer; b. Cleve., Nov. 17, 1932; s. Marshall H. C. and Mary (Bateman) Mills; m. Nancy Huntley, Aug. 3, 1957; 1 dau., Vanessa. B.A., Vanderbilt U., 1954; J.D., Ohio State U., 1958. Bar: N.Y. 1959. Assoc. Cahill, Gordon & Reindel, N.Y.C., 1959-67, ptnr., 1968—. Served to 1st. lt. U.S. Army, 1955-57; Korea. Mem. N.Y. County Lawyers Assn. (dir.). Republican. Unitarian. Clubs: Down Town Assn. (N.Y.C.); Nantucket Yacht (Mass.). Home: 13 Vandam St New York NY 10013 Office: Cahill Gordon & Reindel 80 Pine St New York NY 10005

COX, MAURICE R., bank holding company executive; b. Louisville, Oct. 30, 1944; s. Frank D. and Margaret A. C.; children—Tavner R., M. Tyler. B.A., U. Ky., 1967; J.D., U. Louisville, 1971. Bar: Ky. bar 1971. With comml. lending dept. First Nat. Bank Louisville, 1967-71; pvt. practice, Louisville, 1971-72; with comml. lending dept. Ariz. Bank, Phoenix, 1972-77; v.p. comml. lending AmSouth Bancorp., also First Nat. Bank Birmingham, Ala., 1977-78; sr. v.p. AmSouth Bancorp., 1978, exec. v.p., 1979—. Mem. ABA, Ky. Bar Assn. Methodist. Home: 3302 Boxwood Dr Montgomery AL 36111 Office: 32 Commerce St Montgomery AL 36111

COX, OWEN DEVOL, judge; b. Joplin, Mo., Mar. 20, 1910; s. George B. and Agnes (Swartz) C.; m. Geraldine Martin, Nov. 18, 1939; children—Cornelia Fay Cox Cole, Courtney Quinn Cox Gibson, George Martin. B.A., U. Kans., 1931, LL.B., 1933. Bar: Kans. bar 1933, Tex. bar 1934. Practiced in, Raymondville and Corpus Christi, 1934-70; asst. atty. gen. State of Tex., Austin, 1942; city atty., Corpus Christi, 1943-47; asso. firms S.L. Gill, Raymondville, 1934-37, Boone, Davis & Cox, Corpus Christi, 1948-52, Boone, Davis, Cox & Hale, 1952-70; judge U.S. Dist. Ct., So. dist. Tex., Corpus Christi, 1970—. Mem. Corpus Christi Charter Commn., 1953; alt. del. Republican Nat. Conv., 1964, del., 1968; mem. Tex. Rep. Exec. Com., 1966-70. Mem. ABA, Nueces County Bar Assn. (pres. 1948), State Bar Tex., Am. Judicature Soc. Episcopalian. Club: Kiwanian. Office: PO Box 2567 Corpus Christi TX 78403 *

COX, RALPH F., petrochemical corporat on executive; b. 1932; married. B.S., Tex. A&M U., 1954. Reservior engr. Atlantic Richfield Co., 1956-60, dist. reservior engr., 1960-61, supr. offshore La. dist., 1961-66, supr. offshore Tex., 1966-68, north slope coordinator, Alaska, 1969-70, resident mgr. Alaska dist., 1970-72, regional mgr. Alaska, 1972-73, v.p., gen. mgr. internat. div. Los Angeles, 1973-77, sr. v.p., 1977-78, exec. v.p., dir., 1978—. Office: Atlantic Richfield Co Inc 515 S Flower St Los Angeles CA 90071 *

COX, RICHARD JOSEPH, broadcasting executive; b. Bklyn., Aug. 21, 1929; s. Harry Joseph and Rosemary Magdelene (Broderick) C.; m. Ray Louise Bradley, Oct. 2, 1954; children: Christopher Bradley, Cynthia Anne, John Anthony, Claudia Claire. Student, Fordham U., 1947-49. With Young & Rubicam Inc. (advt. agy.), N.Y.C., 1949-66, v.p. in charge radio and TV, 1963-66, Doyle Dane Bernbach (advt. agy.), 1966-71; v.p. in charge program devel. Tomorrow Entertainment Inc. (TV and motion picture prodns.), 1971-73; pres. Y&R Ventures, Inc. (radio and TV distbn. and consultation), N.Y.C., 1974-78; pres. subs. DCA Prodns. Inc. (radio and TV program prodn.), N.Y.C., 1974-78; owner, pres., exec. producer DCA TV, Inc., 1978-81; pres. CBS Cable div. CBS Inc., 1981—. Co-producer: off-Broadway play Orlando Furioso, 1970; (Recipient spl. Obie award for off-Broadway excellence 1971). Mem. Pres.'s Com. on Drug Abuse, 1969-70. Served with Psychol. Warfare Group, 1951-53. Mem. Nat. Cable TV Assn., Cable Advt. Bur. (dir.), Acad. TV Arts and Scis., Radio and TV Execs. Soc., Nat. Assn. TV Program Execs., Dirs. Guild Am. Republican. Roman Catholic. Clubs: Players, Burke Hollow, Vets of 7th Regt. Home: 135 Westport-Easton Turnpike Fairfield CT 06430 Office: 51 W 52d St New York NY 10019

COX, ROBERT GENE, consultant; b. Liberal, Kans., June 3, 1929; s. Clarice Elden and Margaret Verene (Jones) C.; m. Eileen Frances Hinshaw, July 10, 1953; children: Ann Rebecca, Allan Robert. B.A. with honors, U. N.Mex., 1951, J.D., 1955; grad., Fgn. Service Inst., 1956, Harvard Bus. Sch., 1978, 79. Joined fgn. service, 1956; 3d to 2d sec. Am. embassy, Panama, 1956-58; Am. vice-consul, Caracas, Venezuela, 1959-61; Korea desk officer Dept. State, Washington, 1961-62, chief of staff mgmt. planning, 1963-65, officer in charge mission to, Israel, 1965; staff asst. to Pres., The White House, 1966-68; partner William H. Clark Assos., N.Y.C. and Chgo., 1968-71; sr. staff officer UN Secretariat, Vienna and N.Y.C., 1971-72; pres. Hennes & Cox, Inc., N.Y.C., Washington and Los Angeles, 1972-75; prin., nat. dir. human resource systems Ernst & Ernst, Cleve., 1975-78; ptnr., mng. dir. Arthur Young & Co., N.Y.C., 1979-83; div. pres. PA Cons. Group, N.Y.C., 1983—; dir. Sloane & Hinshaw, Inc., 1979-80; mem. history faculty Fla. State U., 1958; cons. Commn. U.S.-Latin Am. Relations, 1974; sr. advisor Commn. Orgn. of Govt. for Conduct of Fgn. Policy, 1974-75; expert witness on mil. value of Panama Canal U.S. Ho. of Reps., 1977; ITT lectr. Georgetown U., 1981. Author: Defense Department Diplomacy in Latin America, 1964, Choices for Partnership or Bloodshed in Panama, 1975, The Canal Zone: New Focal Point in U.S.-Latin American Relations, 1977, The Chief Executive, 1980, Planning for Immigration: A Business Perspective, 1981, Selection of the Chief Executive Officer, 1982. Bd. dirs. community drug control program, Glen Ridge, N.J., 1971-72; dep. to county chmn. Albuquerque Democratic Party, 1954; adviser on exec. selection to transition staff of Pres.-elect Carter, 1976-77; treas. Caribbeana Council, 1977-78; trustee Unitarian Ch. of All Souls, N.Y.C., 1981—, sec., 1979-80, pres., 1983—. Served to capt. USMC, 1951-55; Korea. Mem. Jonesville (Mich.) Heritage Assn., Council Fgn. Relations (chmn. study group on immigration and U.S. fgn. policy 1978), Royal Econ. Soc. (Eng.), Am. Soc. Internat. Law, Unitarian Hist. Soc. Eng., Internat. Assn. Religious Freedom, Center for Study of Presidency, SAR. Unitarian. Clubs: Harvard Bus., Union League (N.Y.C.). Home: 225 Central Park W Apt 1207 New York NY 10024 Office: 200 Park Ave New York NY 10166

COX, ROBERT JOE, professional baseball team manager; b. Tulsa, May 21, 1941; m. Pamela C.; children: Kami, Keisha. Student, Reedley Jr. Coll. (Calif.). Baseball player Calif. League, Reno, 1960, Northwest League, Salem, 1961-62, Tex. League, Albuquerque, 1963-64, Pacific Coast League, Salt Lake City, 1965, Tacoma, 1966, Internat. League, Richmond, 1967, New York Yankees, Am. League, 1968-69, Internat. League, Syracuse, 1970; mgr. Ft. Lauderdale, Fla. State League, 1971, West Haven, Eastern League, 1972, Syracuse, Internat. League, 1973-76, Atlanta Braves, Nat. League, 1978-81, Toronto Blue Jays, Am. League, 1982—. Office: c/o Toronto Blue Jays PO Box 7777 Adelaide St PO Toronto Ont Canada M5C 2K7 *

COX, RONALD BAKER, management consultant, educator; b. Chattanooga, Sept. 27, 1943; s. Fred T. and Mary A. (Baker) C.; m. Nancy C. Barger; children: Kathy, David, Sherry. B.S. in Mech. Engring, U. Tenn., 1965, M.S., 1968; M.B.A., Vanderbilt U., 1980; Ph.D., Rice U., Houston, 1970. Registered profl. engr., Tenn. Design engr. duPont Co., 1965-66; dir. engring. Ind. Boiler Co., 1966-68; dir. engring. research U. Tenn., Chattanooga, 1972-74, dean engring., 1979—; dir. motor vehicle diagnostic demonstration program Dept. Transp., 1974-76; pres. Internat. Engring. and Mgmt. (mgmt. and engring. cons.), 1968—. Author articles, reports, columns in field. Deacon Signal Mountain (Tenn.) Bapt. Ch., 1972—. Named Engr. of Yr. Greater Chattanooga Area, 1982. Mem. ASME (chpt. pres. 1979-80), Am. Soc. Engring. Edn., Tex. Soc. Profl. Engrs., Order Engring., Chattanooga C. of C. (com. chmn. 1976-77), Sigma Xi, Tau Beta Pi. Club: Clug: Chattanooga Engrs. (pres. 1980). Office: Sch Engring U Tenn Chattanooga TN 37401

COX, THOMAS RICHARD, historian, educator; b. Portland, Oreg., Jan. 16, 1933; s. James Louis and Helen Melissa (Case) C.; m. Mary Margaret MacGillivray, Nov. 24, 1954; children: Dianne Lynne, James Kimberly, Cynthia Ann, Michael William. Student, Whitman Coll., 1951-52; B.S., Oreg. State Coll., 1955; postgrad., U. Hawaii, 1963-64; M.S., U. Oreg., 1959, Ph.D., 1969. Tchr. public high schs., Sisters, Oreg., 1956-59, Tulelake, Calif., 1959-63; teaching asst. U. Oreg., 1964-67; asst. prof. history San Diego State U., 1967-70, asso. prof., 1970-74, prof., 1975—; Tchr. Interchange fellow East-West Center, 1963-64; Fulbright prof., Japan, 1975-76, Forest History Soc. fellow, 1979-80, Huntington Library fellow, 1981, U. Tokyo research fellow, 1984. Author: Mills and Markets, 1974 (Emil and Kathleen Sick Lecture book award 1975); Bd. editors: Jour. Forest History, 1973—; Contbr. articles to hist. jours. Mem. Sisters City Council, 1958-59. Recipient Max Savelle prize Phi Alpha Theta, 1965, Theodore Blegen award Forest History Soc., 1974, 82; Nat. Endowment for Humanities grantee, 1976-77. Mem. Orgn. Am. Historians, Forest. History Soc. (dir. 1974-82), Forest. History Assn. (pres. 1978-80), Agrl. History Soc., Western History Assn., Assn. Asian Studies. Home: 8615 Hudson Dr San Diego CA 92119 Office: History Dept San Diego State U San Diego CA 92182

COX, THOMAS RIGGS, JR., business cons.; b. N.Y.C., Sept. 23, 1918; s. Thomas Riggs and Marian Dunlop (Buckley) C.; m. Joan Buckley, June 22, 1973; children—Thomas R., III, Christopher M., Marian B., Elizabeth B. Grad., Middlesex Sch.; A.B., Williams Coll., 1940. With Young & Rubicam, N.Y.C., 1948-61, sr. v.p., 1958-61; exec. v.p. Wilson, Haight & Welch, Inc., Hartford, Conn., 1961-65, pres., chief exec. officer, 1965—, chmn., 1975-78, also dir.; dir. Conval Inc., Somers, Conn., Info. Systems Inc., Bristol, Conn. Bd. dirs. Wadsworth Atheneum, pres., 1974; bd. dirs. Hartford Symphony, 1966-72, Watkinson Library, 1975—; corporator Hartford Hosp., Mt. Sinai Hosp., St. Francis Hosp., Inst. for Living; trustee Hartford Art Sch., 1964-68, Hartford Coll. for Women. Served with USNR, 1943-45. Mem. Am. Assn. Advt. Agys. (dir. 1972-74), New Eng. Council (dir. 1966—), St. Nicholas Soc. of N.Y., Soc. Colonial Wars. Clubs: Hartford, Hartford Golf (Conn.). Home: Boxwood Berkshire Rd Bloomfield CT 06002

COX, WARREN JACOB, architect; b. N.Y.C., Aug. 28, 1935; s. Oscar Sydney and Louise Bryson (Black) C.; m. Claire Christie-Miller, July 1, 1975; children: Alexandra Louise, Samuel Oscar. B.A. magna cum laude, Yale, 1957, M.Arch., 1961. Partner Hartman-Cox Architects, Washington, 1965—; vis. archtl. critic Yale, 1966, Cath. U. Am., 1967, U. Va., 1976; lectr. Works include master plan, dormitory and chapel, Mt. Vernon Coll., EURAM bldg. Nat. Perm. Bldg, Folger Library remodeling, Washington, Immanuel Presbyn. Ch., Nat. Humanities Center, Van Ness Ctr., Am. Embassy, Malaysia. Mem. Georgetown Commn. Fine Arts, 1971-75; dir. Center for Palladian Studies in Am., 1982—. Recipient Nat. Honor awards AIA, 1970, 71, 81, 83, AIA-AAJC awards, 1970-71, 75, also; first Louis Sullivan award, 1972; Biennial awards Potomac Valley chpt. AIA, 1968, 70, 72, 74, 76; AIA Homes for Better Living award, 1976, 81; D.C. AIA preservation awards, 1977, 78, 80, 81, 83; Met. Washington Bd. Trade awards, 1967, 69, 71; Washington chpt. AIA awards, 1979, 81, 82, 83; other nat. and regional awards. Fellow AIA. Home: 3111 N St NW Washington DC 20007 Home: also Kennersley Church Hill Md 21623 Office: 1071 Thomas Jefferson St NW Washington DC 20007

COX, WILLIAM HAROLD, judge; b. Indianola, Miss., June 23, 1901; s. Adam Charles and Lillie Emma (Ray) C.; m. Edwina Berry, June 30, 1927; children—William Harold, Joanne Cox Bellenger. B.S., LL.B., U. Miss., 1924. Bar: Miss. bar 1924. Practiced in, Jackson, 1924-61; U.S. dist. judge So. Dist. Miss., 1961—, chief judge, 1962-71; mem. Miss. Bd. Bar Admissions, 1932-36. Chmn. Hinds County Democratic Exec. Com., 1950-61; presdl. elector, 1952. Office: PO Drawer 2447 Jackson MS 39205 *

COX, WILLIAM PLUMMER, architect; b. Savannah, Ga., Aug. 17, 1915; s. Charles Howard and Hannah (Plummer) C. B.Arch., U. Pa., 1937. Pvt. archtl. practice, Memphis, 1946—; lectr. U. Tenn.; faculty State Tech. Inst., Memphis; lectr. State Tech. Inst., Memphis State U., 1975—. Works include hosps. and schs. Pres. Memphis Little Theater, 1952-53; bd. dirs. Memphis YMCA, 1955-74, hon. life bd. dirs., 1974—. Served to lt. comdr. USNR, 1941-50. Fellow AIA (pres. Memphis chpt. 1951); mem. Constrn. Specifications Inst. (pres. Memphis chpt. 1961-62), Tenn. Soc. Architects (pres. 1953-54, dir. 1969-73), ASTM. Clubs: Memphis Yacht (commodore 1967), Memphis Kiwanis (dir. 1965-75). Home: 393 Colonial Rd Memphis TN 38117 Office: 22 N Front St 808 Memphis TN 38103

COXE, LOUIS OSBORNE, educator, poet; b. Manchester, N.H., Apr. 15, 1918; s. Charles Shearman and Helen Eyre (Osborne) C.; m. Edith Winsor, June 28, 1946; children: Robert Winsor, Louis Osborne, Charles Shearman, Helen Eyre. A.B., Princeton U., 1940. Instr., Princeton U., 1946; Briggs-Copeland fellow Harvard U., 1948-49; asst., then asso. prof. U. Minn., 1949-55; prof. English, Bowdoin Coll., 1955—, Pierce prof. English, 1956-65. Author: The Sea Faring, 1947, The Second Man, 1955, The Wilderness, 1958, The Middle Passage, 1960, The Last Hero, 1965; (with Robert Chapman) (play) Billy Budd, 1952, Nikal Seyn and Decoration Day, 1966; Edwin Arlington Robinson: The Life of Poetry, 1969, Enabling Acts: Selected Essays in Criticism, 1976, Passage: Selected Poems, 1979. Past trustee N.Y. Sch. Interior Design. Served with USNR, 1942-46. Recipient Creative Arts award Brandeis U., 1961; Sewanee Rev. fellow, 1955; Fulbright fellow, 1959-60, 71-72. Mem. P.E.N., Dramatists Guild. Home: RD 2 Adams Rd Brunswick ME 04011

COXETER, HAROLD SCOTT MACDONALD, mathematician; b. London, Feb. 9, 1907; s. Harold Samuel and Lucy (Gee) C.; m. Hendrina J. Brouwer, Aug. 20, 1936; children—Edgar, Susan Coxeter Thomas. B.A., Trinity Coll., Cambridge (Eng.) U., 1929, Ph.D., 1931, postgrad. (fellow), 1931-35; hon. degrees, U. Alta., Arcadia U., U. Waterloo, Trent U., U. Toronto. Rockefeller Found. fellow Princeton U., 1932-33, Procter fellow, 1934-35; asst. prof. math. U. Toronto, 1936-44, asso. prof., 1944-48, prof., 1948—; vis. prof. numerous univs. including Columbia U., 1949, U. Amsterdam, 1966, Calif. Inst. Tech., 1977, U. Bologna, 1978. Author: Non-Euclidean Geometry, 1942, Regular Polytopes, 1948, The Real Projective Plane, 1949, Introduction to Geometry, 1961, Projective Geometry, 1964, Twelve Geometric Essays, 1968, Regular Complex Polytopes, 1974. Fellow Royal Soc. London and Can.; mem. K. Nederlandse Akademie Wetensch. (fgn.); hon. mem. Mathematische Gesellschaft, Wiskundig Genootschap, London Math. Soc. Home: 67 Roxborough Dr Toronto ON M4W 1X2 Canada Office: U Toronto Toronto ON M5S 1A1 Canada

COYLE, DONALD WALTON, broadcasting executive; b. London, Ont., Can., June 17, 1922; emigrated to U.S., 1924, naturalized, 1950; s. Lorne S. and Pearle A. (Walton) C.; m. Patricia Robinson, June 6, 1946; children: D. Lorne, Deborah A., Sharon R. B.A., Amherst Coll., 1948; student, Am. Inst. Banking, 1948-49. Indsl. analyst Comml. Nat. Bank & Trust Co., N.Y.C., 1947-50; with ABC, N.Y.C., 1950-70, beginning as writer, successively mgr. radio and TV network research, dir. TV network research, dir. radio and TV network research, dir. TV sales devel. and research, 1950-57, v.p. TV network sales devel. and research, 1957-58; v.p., gen. sales mgr. ABC-TV network; v.p. charge ABC Internat. div., Am. Broadcasting-Paramount Theaters, Inc., 1959-61; pres. A.B.C. Internat. Television, Inc., 1961-70; founder, chmn. Intercontinental Communications, Inc., N.Y.C., 1970—; pres. Adtel, Ltd., Toronto. Co-author: Recommended Standards for Radio and Television Program Audience Size Measurements, 1954. Served as pilot RCAF, 1942-45. Mem. Chi Psi. Episcopalian. Office: First Canadian Pl Suite 3800 Toronto ON Canada M5X 1A4

COYLE, MARTIN ADOLPHUS, JR., lawyer, electronic and engring. co. exec.; b. Hamilton, Ohio, June 3, 1941; s. Martin Adolphus and Lucille Baird C.; m. Sharon Sullivan, Mar. 29, 1969; children—Cynthia Ann, David Martin, Jennifer Ann. B.A., Ohio Wesleyan U., 1963; J.D. summa cum laude, Ohio State U., 1966. Bar: N.Y. bar 1967. Asso. firm Cravath, Swaine & Moore, N.Y.C., 1966-72; chief counsel securities and fin. TRW Inc., Cleve., 1972-73, sr. counsel, asst. sec., 1973-75, asst. gen. counsel, asst. sec., 1976, asst. gen. counsel, sec., 1976-80, v.p., gen. counsel, sec., 1980—; sec. TRW Found., 1975-80, trustee, 1980—. Vice pres., trustee Christian Residences Found.-Wade Park Manor; chmn., sec. Martin A. Coyle Found. Mem. Am. Bar Assn., Am. Soc. Corporate Secs. (pres. Ohio regional group 1979-80), Assn. Gen. Counsel, Ohio Bar Assn., Bar Assn. Greater Cleve. Clubs: Clevelander, Mayfield Country. Co-inventor voting machine. Home: 23175 Laureldale Rd Shaker Heights OH 44122 Office: TRW Inc 23555 Euclid Ave Cleveland OH 44117

COYLE, PHILIP WAIDLER, lawyer; b. Binghamton, N.Y., Oct. 17, 1929; s. Leo Vincent and Cecelia Marie (Hourihan) C.; m. Gwendolyn, May 11, 1957; children: Philip Waidler Jr., Matthew R., Andrew B., Howard N., Mary G., Kevin H., Ann M. A.B., Colgate U., 1951; J.D., Harvard U., 1956. Bar: N.Y., Calif. Assoc. Chamberlain & Willi, N.Y.C., 1956-59, Brobeck, Phleger & Harrison, San Francisco, 1959-65, ptnr., 1965—. Office: Brobeck Phleger & Harrison Spear Tower 1 Market Plaza San Francisco CA 94105 *

COYLE, WILLIAM, educator; b. Edinboro, Pa., Nov. 8, 1917; s. William and Vere (Steadman) C.; m. Charlotte Bliley, July 27, 1940; children—Mary Jo, Daniel, Barbara. B.S., Edinboro State Coll., 1938; M.Litt., U. Pitts., 1940, M.A., 1942; Ph.D., Western Res. U., 1948. Instr. English U. Pitts., 1939-42, 45-46, Western Res. U., 1946-48; mem. faculty Wittenberg Coll., 1948-68, prof. English, 1956-68, chmn. dept., 1964-68; prof. English Fla. Atlantic U., Boca Raton, 1968—, chmn. dept., 1969-79; Fulbright lectr., Sao Paulo, Brazil, 1962-63. Author: Research Papers, 1959, Ohio Authors and Their Books, 1960, The The Young Man in American Literature, 1969, others; also articles, revs. Served with USMCR, 1942-45. Mem. Modern Lang. Assn., Popular Culture Assn., Coll. English Assn. Democrat. Home: 3121 Lowson Blvd Delray Beach FL 33444

COYNE, FRANK HOLDER, corporation executive; b. N.Y.C., Oct. 13, 1925; s. Frank and Pauline (Newman) C.; m. Shirley Donohue, July 23, 1949. A.B., Harvard U., 1947, M.B.A., 1951. Fin. analyst So. Pacific Co., N.Y.C., Houston and San Francisco, 1951-67; v.p. mgmt. services Burlington No. Inc., St. Paul, 1967-70, v.p. fin., 1971-75, exec. v.p. fin. and adminstrn., 1976-82; exec. v.p. Miami Corp., Chgo., 1982—; dir. St. Paul Cos., 1976—. Served with USN, 1944-46. Republican. Roman Catholic. Clubs: Chicago; Minnesota (St. Paul); Harvard (N.Y.C.). Home: 10 E Schiller Chicago IL 60610 Office: 410 N Michigan Ave Chicago IL 60611

COYNE, JAMES KITCHENMAN, presidential assistant, former congressman; b. Farmville, Va., Nov. 17, 1946; s. James K. and Pearl (Black) C.; m. Helen Mercer, Nov. 24, 1970; children: Alexander Black, Katherine Mercer, Michael Atkinson. B.S. in Econs. and Adminstrv. Scis., Yale U., 1968; M.B.A., Harvard U., 1970. Pres. Coyne Chem. Corp., Phila., 1970-81; founder, chmn. Energy Mgmt. Assos., Phila., 1977-78, Rechem Corp., 1976-80; mem. 97th Congress from 8th Pa. Dist.; now spl. asst. to U.S. pres. The White House; lectr. Wharton Sch. Fin., U. Pa., 1975-78. Author: Alternative Fuels for Energy Transportation, 1975. Supr. Upper Makefield Twp., Bucks County, Pa., 1979; active fundraising activities Republican Party. Named Outstanding Faculty Mem. Wharton Sch. Mem. Com. of 70, Lower Bucks C. of C., Nat. Assn. Chem. Distbrs., Yale Engring. Assn., Aircraft Owners and Pilots Assn. Presbyterian. Club: Harvard Bus. Sch. (pres. 1974-76). Office: 1600 Pennsylvania Ave NW Washington DC 20900

COYNE, JOSEPH GILLICK, government official; b. Aberdeen, S.D., Oct. 29, 1934; s. A. Earl and Ann Elizabeth (Gillick) C.; m. Joyce Ann Satterfield, Mar. 31, 1962. Student, Grad. Sch. Bus. Adminstrn., Harvard U., 1976. Dir. office product and program devel. Nat. Tech. Info. Service, U.S. Dept. Commerce, Springfield, Va., 1970-78; mgr. tech. info. center U.S. Dept. Energy, Oak Ridge, 1978—; treas. abstracting bd. Internat. Council Sci. Unions., Paris, 1983—; mem. tech. info. panel NATO Adv. Group for Aerospace Research and Devel., Paris, 1976—. Mem. Planning Commn. Anderson County, Tenn., 1982—. Recipient Gold medal U.S. Dept. Commerce, 1972, Exceptional Service award U.S. Dept. Energy, 1983. Mem. AAAS, Am. Soc. Info. Sci. Club: Optimists (v.p. 1982-83). Lodge: Elks. Home: 620 Riverbend Rd Clinton TN 37716 Office: US Dept Energy PO Box 62 Oak Ridge TN 37831

COYNE, M. JEANNE, state supreme court justice; b. Mpls., Dec. 7, 1926; d. Vincent Mathias and Mae Lucille (Steinmetz) C. B.S. in Law, U. Minn., 1955, J.D., 1957. Bar: Minn. 1957, U.S. Dist. Ct. Minn. 1957, U.S. Ct. Appeals (8th cir.) 1958, U.S. Supreme Ct. 1964. Law clk. Minn. Supreme Ct., St. Paul, 1956-57; assoc. Meagher, Geer & Markham, Mpls., 1957-70, ptnr., 1970-82; assoc. justice Minn. Supreme Ct., St. Paul; mem. Am. Arbitration Assn., 1967-82; mem. bd. conciliation Archdiocese St. Paul and Mpls., 1981-82; instr. U. Minn. Law Sch., Mpls., 1964-68; mem. Lawyers Profl. Responsibility Bd., St. Paul, 1982; chmn. com. rules of civil appellate procedure Minn. Supreme Ct., St. Paul, 1982-83. Editor: Women Lawyers Jour., 1971-72. Mem. ABA, Minn. State Bar Assn., Nat. Assn. Women Lawyers, Nat. Assn. Women Judges, Minn. Women Lawyers Assn. (dir.), U. Minn. Law Alumni Assn. Office: Minn Supreme Ct 230 State Capitol Saint Paul MN 55155

COYNE, WILLIAM JOSEPH, congressman; b. Pitts., Aug. 24, 1936; s. Phillip and Mary (Ridge) C. B.S., Robert Morris Coll., 1965. Mem. Pa. Ho. of Reps., 1970-72; mem. Pitts. City Council, 1973-80, 96th-98th Congresses from 14th Dist. Pa. Served with AUS, 1955-57. Democrat. Roman Catholic. Office: 424 Cannon House Office Bldg Washington DC 20515 *

COZAN, LEE, clinical psychologist; m. June 1, 1947. B.A., Am. U., 1948; M.A., George Washington U., 1951, Ph.D., 1964. Research psychologist U.S. Govt., Washington, 1954-64; pvt. practice psychology, N.J., 1964-74; regional dir. Fla. Div. Mental Health, Ft. Lauderdale, 1974-76; mental hosp. adminstr. So. Fla. State Hosp., Hollywood, 1976-79; pres. Inst. Mental Health, Hollywood, 1979-81; dir. mental health program Fla. Dept. Health and Rehab. Services, Ft. Lauderdale, 1979-82; clin. psychologist Assocs. in Psychiatry, 1983—; pres. Applied Psychology Corp., 1983—; adj. prof. Fla. Atlantic U., 1974-79, Nova U., 1979-80. Editor: Jour. Indsl. Psychology, 1961-65, Jour. Engring. Psychology, 1963-68; cons. editor: Jour. Schizophrenia, 1970-71. Mem. Broward County (Fla.) Republican Exec. Com., 1976-80. Served with U.S. Army, 1941-46. Mem. Am. Psychol. Assn., AAAS, Nat. Geog. Soc., Human Factors Soc., Fla. Psychol. Assn. Greek Orthodox. Research, publs. in psychology. Office: 1219 SE 4th Ave Fort Lauderdale FL 33316

CRABB, BARBARA BRANDRIFF, U.S. dist. judge; b. Green Bay, Wis., Mar. 17, 1939; d. Charles Edward and Mary (Forrest) Brandriff; m. Theodore E. Crabb, Jr., Aug. 29, 1959; children—Julia Forrest, Philip Elliott. A.B., U. Wis., 1960, J.D., 1962. Bar: Wis. bar 1963. Asso. firm Roberts, Broadman, Suhr and Curry, Madison, 1968-70; research asst. U. Wus. Law Sch., 1968-70, Am. Bar Assn., Madison, 1970-71; U.S. magistrate, Madison, 1971-79; U.S. dist. judge Western Dist. Wis., 1979—, chief judge, 1980—; mem. Gov. Wis. Task Force Prison Reform, 1971-73. Membership chmn., v.p. Milw. LWV, 1966-68; mem. Milw. Jr. League, 1967-68. Mem. Am. Bar Assn., Nat. Council Fed. Magistrates, Nat. Assn. Women Judges, State Bar Wis., Dane County Bar Assn., U. Wis. Law Alumni Assn. Home: 741 Seneca Pl Madison WI 53711 Office: Box 1724 Madison WI 53701

CRABB, FREDERICK HUGH WRIGHT, archbishop; b. England, Apr. 30, 1915; emigrated to Can., 1957, naturalized, 1977; s. William Samuel and Florence Mary (Wright) C.; m. Margery Coombs, Sept. 26, 1946; children: John, Alison, Elizabeth, Peter. B.D. with 1st class honours, U. London, 1939; D.D. (hon.), Wycliffe Coll., Toronto, 1958, St. Andrew U., Saskatoon, Sask., 1963, Coll. of Emmanuel and St. Chad, Saskatoon, 1979. Engaged in farming, 1935; ordained to ministry Ch. of Eng., 1939; asst. priest, Teignmouth and Phymouth, Eng., 1939-42, dist. missionary, Akot, So. Sudan, 1942-45; prin. Bishop Gwynne Coll., Mundri, So. Sudan, 1945-51; vice prin. London Coll. Div., 1951-57; prin. Coll. Emmanuel and St. Chad, Saskatoon, 1957-67; asst. Christ Ch., Calgary, Alta., 1967-69; rector St. Stephen's Ch., Calgary, 1969-75; bishop of Athabasca, Alta., 1975-77, archbishop of

Athabasca, met. of Ruperts Land, 1977-83; assoc. rector St. Cyprian's Ch., Calgary, 1983—; mem. gen. synod and coms. Anglican Ch. Can.; dir. Anglican Sch. of Lay Ministry; chaplain Calgary Dist. RCMP Vets. Assn. Author articles in field. Club: Rotary. Home: 3438 Chippingdale Dr NW Calgary AB Canada T2L 0W7

CRABBE, JOHN CROZIER, telecommunications cons.; b. Pomona, Calif., July 3, 1914; s. Arthur and Louise A. (Wiley) C.; m. Bobbin Gay Peck, June 17, 1940; children—John Crozier, William Charles, Barbara Gay. Student, Modesto (Calif.) Coll., 1931-34, Fresno (Calif.) State Coll., 1934-36; B.A., Coll. Pacific, 1937, M.A., 1940; postgrad., U. Iowa, 1938, N.Y. U., 1940, Stanford, 1951, Ohio State U., 1951-52. Dir. broadcasting activities Coll. of Pacific, 1937-58; lectr. radio edn. Stanford, summer 1951; asst., office radio-TV edn. Ohio State U., 1951-52; exec. sec. Delta-Sierra Ednl. TV Corp., 1953; dir. radio and TV Nat. Music Camp, Interlochen, Mich., 1954-55; program asso. Ednl. TV and Radio Center, Ann Arbor, Mich., 1955-56; exec. sec. Central Calif. Ednl. TV, 1955-58; gen. mgr. Sta. KVIE, 1958-69; spl. cons. radio edn., schs. central Calif.; chmn. TV Adv. Com. State Calif., 1967-69; cons. in broadcasting (East Africa) RTV Internat., N.Y., 1964; pres. Western Ednl. TV Network, 1967-69; mem. interim mgmt. group Corp. for Pub. Broadcasting Network Operation, 1969; cons. in pub. broadcasting, 1969-73; cons. Joint Com. on Telecommunications Calif. Legislature, 1973-74; asso. Arthur Bolton Assos., 1972-73; gen. mgr. Tel-Vue Stockton, Inc., Calif., 1972; dir. telecommunications, gen. mgr. KTSC-TV-FM, U. So. Colo., Pueblo, 1976-81; cons., 1981—; Bd. dirs. Rocky Mountain Corp. for Public Broadcasting; bd. govs. Pacific Mountain Network. Contbr. articles to profl. publs. Served as lt. USNR, 1943-46. Mem. Assn. for Ednl. Radio-TV (pres. 1950-53), Western Radio TV Conf. Home: 1031 LaSierra Dr Sacramento CA 95825 *I have always cherished a commitment to a concept that change is exciting and good. Keeping abreast of and adjusting to change - change in goals, thoughts, ideas, principles of conduct - keeps one flexible and demands continuing accommodation to new developments. Forecasting benchmarks of human conduct and, by indirection, leading others toward predictable behaviour makes me an active participant in the process of change. This preoccupation makes it impossible to become sedentary - physically or intellectually.*

CRABBE, JOHN ROTH, lawyer; b. London, Ohio, Mar. 29, 1906; s. Charles C. and Isa M. (Roth) C.; m. Eleanor S. Hommon, Dec. 20, 1933; children—Constance (Mrs. Michael A. Dehlendorf), Benjamin R. (dec.). B.A., Ohio State U., 1927, M.A., J.D., 1931; LL.M., Harvard, 1932. Bar: Ohio bar 1931. Asst. atty. gen., Ohio, 1933-37; partner firm Crabbe & Tootle, London, Ohio, 1937-39; dep. supt. ins., Ohio, 1939-43, supt. ins., 1943-45; asso. firm Ballard & Dresbach, Columbus, Ohio, 1945-51; partner Crabbe, Brown, Jones, Potts & Schmidt (and predecessor firms), Columbus, 1951-78, of counsel, 1978—. Pres. Bexley Area Art Guild, 1967; Mem. Bexley (Ohio) City Council, 1955-72, pres., 1966-72. Fellow ABA Found., Ohio Bar Assn. Found. (trustee 1970-76); mem. ABA (chmn. sect. ins., negligence and compensation law 1962-63, chmn. standing com. unemployment and social security 1965-66), Ohio Bar Assn., Columbus Bar Assn., Am. Judicature Soc., Assn. Life Ins. Counsel, Pi Kappa Alpha, Phi Delta Phi. Republican. Methodist (past chmn. ofcl. bd., trustee). Clubs: Mason., Columbus Country, University, Crichton (Columbus). Home: 2877 E Broad St B14 Columbus OH 43209 Office: One Nationwide Plaza 25th Floor Columbus OH 43215

CRABBE, ORVAL ROBERT, distillery executive; b. Chapleau, Ont., Can., Apr. 18, 1923; s. Harold Isaac and Susan (Maclellan) C.; children: Gregory, Kevin, Denise. Ed., U. Detroit. With Hiram Walker-Gooderham & Worts Ltd., 1941—, mktg. mgr. Internat. div., 1970-71; exec. v.p. Hiram Walker Internat. Co., 1971, pres., 1971-77; v.p. Hiram Walker & Sons Ltd., Windsor, Ont., 1977-80; pres. Hiram Walker Inc., Farmington Hills, Mich., 1980—. Pres. Can. Red Cross, Windsor, Ont.; chmn. bd. govs. Met. Gen. Hosp., Windsor, United Way, Windsor, 1979. Home: 5704 N Pinnacle West Bloomfield MI 48033 Office: 31275 Northwestern Hwy Suite 221 Farmington Hills MI 48018

CRABBÉ, PIERRE, chemist, educator; b. Brussels, Dec. 29, 1928; s. Francois and Simone (Doutreligne) C.; m. Lucie de Guchteneere, Apr. 25, 1956; children: Emmanuel, Marie-Noelle, Veronique. Tech. Chem. Engr., Institut Meurice-Chimie, Brussels, 1952; D.Chimie, U. Paris, 1954; D.Sc., U. Strasbourg, 1967. Instr. Inst. Meurice-Chimie, Brussels, 1959-60; dir. chem. research Syntex S.A., Mexico City, 1964-73; prof. U. Iberoamericana, Mexico City, 1962-73, U. Nacional Autonoma Mex., 1965-74; hon. prof. Inst. Tech. Monterrey, Mex., 1968—; vis. prof. Ga. Inst. Tech., Atlanta, 1968; prof. U. Grenoble, France, 1973-79; prof., chmn. dept. chemistry U. Mo., Columbia, 1979—; cons. WHO, UNESCO.; sec. gen. Internat. Orgn. for Chem. Scis. in Devel., 1981—. Author: (with G. Ourisson, O. Rodig) Tetracyclic Triterpenes, 1964, Optical Rotatory Dispersion and Circular Dichroism, 1965, Introduction to Chiroptical Methods, 1972, Prostaglandin Research, 1977; contbr.: articles to profl. jours. Prostaglandin Research. Mem. Mexican Acad. Sci., N.Y. Acad. Scis., Am. Chem. Soc., Belgian Chem. Soc., Chem. Soc. (London). Office: Dept Chemistry U Mo Columbia MO 65211

CRABILL, KENNETH KAYE, savings and loan association executive; b. Allen, Okla., Aug. 11, 1932; s. John Victor and Emma Gladys (Loving) C.; m. Margaret Ruth Glassey, Aug. 25, 1962; children: Carl Gordon, Sheryl Ann. B.S. in Accounting and Fin, UCLA, 1959. C.P.A., Calif. Treas. Financial Savs. and Loan Assn., Culver City, Calif., 1963-67; controller Community Savs. and Loan Assn., Long Beach, Calif., 1967-68; dir. fin. planning Financial Facts, Inc., Los Angeles, 1968-70, dir., 1970—; sr. v.p. fin., treas. Financial Fedn., Inc., Los Angeles, 1970—; dir. United Savs. and Loan Assn. Served with USAF, 1951-54. Mem. Am. Inst. C.P.A.s, Calif. Soc. C.P.A.s, Fin. Execs. Inst. Republican. Address: Financial Fedn Inc 9801 Washington Blvd Culver City CA 90230

CRABTREE, BEVERLY JUNE, college dean; b. Lincoln, Nebr., June 22, 1937; d. Wayne Uniack and Frances Margaret (Wibbels) Deles Dernier; m. Robert Jewell Crabtree, June 1, 1958; children: Gregory, Karen. B.S. in Edn., U. Mo., 1959, M.Ed., 1962; Ph.D., Iowa State U., 1965. Tchr. home econs. public schs., Pierce City and Sarcoxie, Mo., 1959-61; faculty home econs. Mich. State U., E. Lansing, 1964-67; asso. prof., coordinator home econs. edn. U. Mo., Columbia, 1967-72, prof., coordinator home econs. edn., 1972-73, asso. dean home econs. and dir. home econs. extension programs, 1973-75; dean Coll. Home Econs., Okla. State U., Stillwater, 1975—; faculty Family Impact Seminar Inst. Ednl. Leadership George Washington U., 1976-82, Cath. U. Am., 1982—; mem. nat. panel of cons. for Vocat. Ednl. Personnel Devel., 1969-70; mem. nat. com. on future of coop. ext. USDA and Nat. Assn. State Univs. and Land Grant Colls., 1982. Contbr. articles in field to profl. jours. Recipient U. Mo. Faculty Alumni award, 1977, Profl. Achievement award Iowa State U. Coll. Home Econs., 1983; Gen. Foods fellow, 1963-64; Iowa State U. Coll. Home Econs. Centennial Alumni award, 1971; U. Mo. Coll. Home Econs. Alumni Citation of Merit, 1976. Mem. Am. Home Econs. Assn. (pres. 1977-78, chmn. Ctr. for Family Adv. Council 1982-83, mem. council profl. devel. 1980-83), Okla. Home Econs. Assn., Nat. Assn. State Univs. and Land Grant Colls. (mem. commn. home econs. 1981-84), Assn. Tchr. Educators, Home Econs. Edn. Assn., Nat. Council of Adminstrs. of Home Econs., Am. Ednl. Research Assn., Am. Assn. Higher Edn., Nat. Assn. Tchr. Educators for Home Econs. (pres. 1969), Nat. Council on Family Relations, Omicron Nu, Phi Upsilon Omicron, Phi Delta Kappa, Omicron Delta Kappa, Pi Lambda Theta, Phi Kappa Phi, Gamma Sigma Delta. Republican. Methodist. Home: 1007 W Eskridge Ave Stillwater OK 74075 Office: Home Econs West Okla State U Stillwater OK 74078

CRABTREE, BRUCE ISBESTER, JR., architect; b. Chattanooga, Sept. 1, 1923; s. Bruce Isbester and Anna Hunter (Kirkpatrick) C.; m. Dolly Nance Fischer, Mar. 31, 1948; children: Ann Hunter, Burce Isbester III, Drucilla, Raymond, Thomas. Student, Vanderbilt U., 1942-43, Clemson Coll., 1943-44; B.S., Va. Poly. Inst., 1948. Registered architect, Tenn. Architect, designer Hart & McBryde, Nashville, 1948-52; ptnr. Taylor & Crabtree, Nashville, 1952-81; v.p. Taylor & Crabtree-Wiley & Wilson, Nashville, 1981—. Architect works include, James K. Polk Performing Arts Ct., 1980, Andrew Jackson State Office Bldg, 1974, Athletic and Convocation Ctr., Middle Tenn. State U., 1975, residence of Mr. and Mrs. Marshall Trammell, Jr. (AIA award 1961). Bd. dirs. Nashville YMCA, 1968; pub. adv. panel GSA, Atlanta, 1973-74. Served to tech. sgt. AUS, 1943-45; PTO. Fellow AIA (pres. Middle Tenn. chpt. 1966); mem. Tenn. Soc. Architects (pres. 1967, Medal of Merit 1969), Tau Beta Pi, Omicron Delta Kappa, Sigma Chi. Roman Catholic. Clubs: Belle Meade Country, Cumberland, Exchange (Nashville). Home: 424 Sunnyside Dr Nashville TN 37205 Office: Taylor & Crabtree-Wiley & Wilson 1812 Broadway Nashville TN 37203

CRABTREE, JOHN HENRY, JR., educator, university administrator; b. Raleigh, N.C., Nov. 11, 1925; s. John Henry and Ruth (Jones) C.; m. Anne Brown, Aug. 28, 1948; children: John Henry III, Roy Eugene, Cynthia Anne, Ralph Newton. B.A., U. N.C., 1950, M.A., 1951, Ph.D. (Carnegie fellow), 1957. Asso. prof. Presbyn. Jr. Coll., Maxton, N.C., 1951-54; prof. English, Furman U., Greenville, S.C., 1957—, asso. dean acad. affairs, 1965-68, dean students, 1968-73, chmn. dept. English, 1973—, acad. dean, 1978-82, v.p. acad. affairs and dean, 1982—. Served with USNR, 1944-46. So. fellow U. N.C., 1959; Danforth asso. Mem. South Atlantic MLA, Coll. English Assn., Southeastern Renaissance Conf., Shakespeare Assn. Am., Internat. Shakespeare Assn., Phi Beta Kappa. Baptist. Home: Route 7 Hathaway Circle Greenville SC 29609

CRACRAFT, BRUCE NOEL, lawyer; b. Indpls., Dec. 24, 1921. Student, Ind. U., 1942, Butler U., 1946; LL.B., Stetson U., 1949. Bar: Fla., Ind. 1949. Assoc. Slaymaker, Locke & Reynolds, Inpls., 1949-54, ptnr., 1955; atty. Ind. Bell Telephone Co., Indpls., 1955-59, gen. atty., 1959-72, v.p., gen. counsel, 1972—; dir. Statesman Ins. Co. Bd. dirs. Child Guidance Clinic, Marion County, Ind., 1957-65, pres., Marion County, Ind., 1960-61; bd. dirs. Ind. Legal Found.; mem. Gov.'s Task Force on Bus. Tax, 1983—; mem. bd. visitors Ind. U. Sch. Law, Indpls.; mem. Ind. Jud. Council on Legal Edn. and Competence at the Bar. Served to 1st lt. USAAF, 1942-45. Fellow Am. Bar Found., Ind. Bar Found. (vice chmn. 1983—); mem. ABA, Ind. Bar Assn. (chmn. adminstrv. law com., del. 1969-73), Indpls. Bar Assn., Am. Judicature Soc., Nat. Tax Assn.-Tax Inst. Am. (dir.), Lawyers Assn. Indpls. (pres. 1960), Lawyers Club (pres. 1981), Am. Right of Way Assn. (pres. 1965), Ind. Taxpayers Assn. (pres., dir.), Ind. C. of C. (chmn. taxation com.), Sigma Delta Kappa, Phi Kappa Psi. Clubs: Columbia, Skyline. Home: 5253 Shorewood Dr Indianapolis IN 46220 Office: 240 N Meridian St Suite 1800 Indianapolis IN 46204

CRADDOCK, BILLY WAYNE (CRASH CRADDOCK), entertainer; b. Greensboro, N.C., June 16, 1940; s. William Frank and Grace (Hodge) C.; m. Mae Lanning, June 22, 1959; children: Billy Wayne, Steve, April. Student pub. schs. Rock and roll performer, U.S. and Australia, 1950-70; appeared on: TV Arthur Godfrey Show, 1959, Dick Clark's Am. Bandstand, 1959; country/western rec. artist, ABC Records, 1970—; known as Mr. Country Rock; mem. group, The Dream Lovers, from 1974; recent recs. include Laughing and Crying, Living and Dying (Named Country Comeback Artist, Billboard Mag. 1971, Up and Coming Country Artist, Cashbox Mag. 1971, Most Promising Male Vocalist, Music City News 1972, recipient Encore award Record World 1971). Mem. Country Music Assn., Am. Fedn. Musicians, Screen Actors Guild. Baptist. Office: PO Box 6798 Greensboro NC 27405 also care IHT 816 19th Ave S Nashville TN 37203 *

CRADDOCK, CAMPBELL, geologist, educator; b. Chgo., Apr. 3, 1930; s. John and Bernice (Campbell) C.; m. Dorothy Dunkelberg, June 13, 1953; children—Susan Elizabeth, John Paul, Carol Jean. B.A., DePauw U., 1951; M.A., Columbia U., 1953, Ph.D., 1954. Geologist Shell Oil Co., N.Mex., Tex., Colo., Wyo., 1954-56; asst. prof. U. Minn., Mpls., 1956-60, asso. prof., 1960-67; prof. geology U. Wis., Madison, 1967—, chmn. dept., 1977-80; leader Antarctic geologic field research programs, 1959-69, 80, Alaskan geologic field research programs, 1968-81, Svalbard field programs, 1977—; cons. C.E., AUS, 1957-58, N. Star Research Inst., 1965-68, Dept. State, 1976; vis. scientist N.Z. Geol. Survey, 1962-63; lectr. Nanjing and Beijing univs., China, 1981; chmn. panel geology and geophysics NRC, 1967-71, mem. polar research bd., 1978—; U.S. mem. working group on geology Sci. Com. on Antarctic Research, 1967—, chmn. group, 1973-80; co-chief scientist Leg 35, Deep Sea Drilling Project, Antarctica, 1974; chmn. Antarctic panel Circum-Pacific Map Project, 1979—; cons. Phillips Petroleum Co., 1980. Editor: Antarctic Geoscience, 1982; Co-editor: Geologic Maps of Antarctica, Folio 12, Antarctic Map Folio Series, Am. Geog. Soc., 1970, Initial Reports of the Deep Sea Drilling Project, Vol. 35, 1976; Contbr. articles sci. jours. Higgins fellow, 1951-52; NSF fellow, 1952-53; research grantee, 1957—; recipient U.S. Antarctic Service medal, 1968; Bellingshausen-Lazarev medal Soviet Acad. Scis., 1970; Alumni citation DePauw U., 1976. Fellow Geol. Soc. Am. (chmn. sect. 1982-83, books editor 1982—); mem. Internat. Union Geol. Scis. (mem. commn. on structural geology 1968-76, mem. com. on tectonics 1976—, del. Sci. Com. on Antarctic Research 1974—, mem. com. on geologic map of world 1974—), Polar Research Bd. (1978-82), Internat. Union Geol. Scis. (v.p. for Antarctica 1979—), Am. Geophys. Union, Am. Assn. Petroleum Geologists, Phi Beta Kappa, Sigma Xi. Mailing Address: 1109 Winston Dr Madison WI 53711 Office: Dept Geology and Geophysics U Wis Madison WI 53706

CRADDOCK, CRASH *See* **CRADDOCK, BILLY WAYNE**

CRAFT, DOUGLAS DURWOOD, artist; b. Greene, N.Y., Oct. 20, 1924; s. Harry Benjamin and Phoebe (Hotchkiss) C.; m. Elizabeth Louise Harms, Sept. 8, 1951. B.F.A., U. Chgo. and Art Inst. Chgo., 1950; M.A. in Painting, U. N.Mex., 1953. Prof. fine arts Coll. New Rochelle, N.Y., 1970—; vis. artist in residence U. Ky., 1964; exchange prof., artist in residence Royal Coll. Art, London, 1964-65; guest artist curator Selected Women, Painters Castle Gallery, Coll. New Rochelle (NY), 1982. One-man shows include, Kasha Heman Gallery, Chgo., 1963, 61, U. N.Mex., 1964, 52, U. Ky., 1964, Travers Festival Gallery, Edinburgh, Scotland, 1965, Royal Coll. Art, London, 1964, Carnegie Mellon U., 1968, Mus. Art, Carnegie Inst., Pitts., 1968, Fischbach Gallery, N.Y.C., 1973, Jersey City Mus., 1978, 55 Mercer Gallery, N.Y.C., 1980; represented in permanent collections, Newark Mus., Art Inst. Chgo., U. Ky., Mus. Modern Art, N.Y.C., Whitney Mus. Am. Art, N.Y.C., U. N.Mex.; represented by, Condeso/Lawler Gallery, N.Y.C. Served with USNR, 1943-46. Recipient Logan Bronze medal and prize Art Inst. Chgo., 1966; Harry Allison Logan Meml. award Chautauqua Art Assn., 1963; Jury award in painting Carnegie Inst., 1968. Home: 240 Ogden Ave Jersey City NJ 07307

CRAFT, EDWARD OLIVER, lawyer; b. Kingsbury, Ind., Nov. 13, 1916; s. John Allen and Olive May (Canfield) C.; m. Wilma Clare Williams, Oct. 26, 1940; children: Elizabeth, Alice, John. A.B., Ind. U., 1938, J.D. with high distinction, 1940. Bar: Ind. 1940, D.C. 1977, U.S. Tax Ct. 1978, U.S. Supreme Ct. 1979, U.S. Ct. Appeals for 9th circuit 1983. Practice in, Evansville, 1940-41; mem. legal staff Office Legis. Counsel, U.S. Ho. of Reps., 1941-72, legis. counsel, 1962-72; partner firm Wickham & Craft, Washington, Chgo., Bloomington, Ind., 1977-81, Piper & Marbury, Bloomington and Washington, 1981—. Student editor: Ind. Law Rev, 1938-39; student chmn., 1939-40. Served with AUS, 1943-45. Mem. Am., Fed., Ind. bar assns., Am. Judicature Soc., Nat. Lawyers Club, Phi Delta Phi, Order of Coif. Office: 703 S Rose Ave Bloomington IN 47401 also 888 16th St NW Washington DC 20006

CRAFT, HAROLD DUMONT, JR., radio astronomer; b. Newark, May 28, 1938; s. Harold Dumont and Mavena Patricia (Brierley) C.; m. Carole Judith Gaebel, June 9, 1962; children—Adam Brierley, David Josiah. B.E.E., Cornell U., 1961, Ph.D., 1970; M.E.E., N.Y. U., 1963. Mem. tech. staff Bell Telephone Labs., Murray Hill, N.J., 1961-65; grad. research asst. Cornell U., 1965-69, tech. coordinator, 1971-73; mem. tech. staff Comsat Labs., Clarksburg, Md., 1969-71; dir. ops. Arecibo (P.R.) Obs., Nat. Astronomy and Inosphere Center, 1973-81; acting dir. Nat. Astronomy and Ionosphere Center, 1981-82; dir. telecommunications Cornell U., Ithaca, NY, 1982—. Author research articles. Mem. Am. Astron. Soc., AAAS, Internat. Sci. Radio Union, Am. Geophys. Union, IEEE, Tau Beta Pi, Eta Kappa Nu. Address: Cornell U 104 Maple Ave Ithaca NY 14850

CRAFT, LOREN ROBERT, journalist; b. Milw., Nov. 7, 1928; s. Loren Alvin and Jennie Mae (McClintock) C.; m. Sylvia Barbara Fine, June 22, 1957; children: Susan, Laura, Diana. Student, Temple U., Phila., CCNY, Hunter Coll., N.Y.C. Writer, reporter Phila. Bull., 1948-52; writer N.Y. Post, 1954-55, N.Y. Daily News, 1955-63; news editor Sta. WNEW, N.Y.C., 1963-66; editor, news producer Sta. WABC-TV, N.Y.C., 1966-69; news producer Sta. WCBS-TV, N.Y.C., 1969-70; arts and entertainment editor N.Y. News, 1977—. Author: Hoodlums, Los Angeles, 1957. Served with CIC AUS, 1952-54. Home: 220 E 42d St Hastings-on-Hudson NY 10706 Office: 270 E 42d St New York NY 10017

CRAFT, ROBERT, musician, writer; b. Kingston, N.Y., Oct. 20, 1923; s. Raymond and Arpha (Lawson) C. B.A., Juilliard Sch. Music, 1946. Spl. seminar lectr., Dartington, Eng., 1957, Princeton U., 1959; Lucas lectr. Carleton Coll., 1981-82. Condr. orchs. in, Europe, Am. and Japan, 1952—; made world tour, 1961-62; condr. recs. including complete music Arnold Schoenberg, Alban Berg, Anton Webern, Edgar Varese; Co-author: Conversations with Stravinsky, 1959, Memories and Commentaries, 1960, Expositions and Developments, 1962, Dialogues and a Diary, 1963, Table Talk, 1965, Themes and Episodes, 1966, (with Arnold Newman) Bravo Stravinsky, 1967, Retrospections and Conclusions, 1970, Stravinsky: The Chronicle of a Friendship, 1972, Themes and Conclusions, 1972, Current Convictions: Views and Reviews, 1977, Stravinsky: Selected Correspondence, Vol. 1 1981, Vol. 2, 1984. Served with AUS, 1943. Office: care Alfred Knopf Inc 201 E 50 St New York City NY 10022 *

CRAFT, ROBERT HOMAN, banker, corporate executive; b. L.I., N.Y., Feb. 9, 1906; s. George Wallace and Nellie A. (Homan) C.; m. Janet M. Sullivan, Feb. 5, 1938; children: Robert Homan, Carol Ann (Mrs. C. Barry Schaefer), George Sullivan. B.S., U. Pa., 1929. Asst. treas. Guaranty Trust Co. of N.Y., 1937-40, 2d v.p., 1940-43, v.p., treas., 1943-52; exec. v.p., dir. Am. Securities Corp., N.Y.C., 1953-56; pres., vice chmn. Chase Internat. Investment Corp., 1956-60; pres., chmn. exec. com. Paribas Corp., 1960-64; chmn. finance com., dir. Miss. River Corp., 1965—, financial v.p., 1965-70, chmn. bd., 1971-73; chmn. finance com., dir., mem. exec. com. M.P. R.R. Co., 1965-76; dir., chmn. finance com. Miss. River Transmission Corp.; trustee, exec. com., chmn. investment policy com. N.Y. Bank Savs., 1944—; chmn. finance com., dir. Tex. & Pacific Ry. Co., 1965-76; dir., chmn. finance com., mem. exec. com. Mo. Improvement Co., C. & E.I. R.R., 1965-76, Mo.-Ill. R.R. Co., 1965-76; dir., mem. exec. com. Mass. Mut. Corporate Investors, Mass. Mortgage Income Investors; mem. exec. com. Merc. Trust Co., St. Louis, 1965-71; now adviser, dir.; mem. Lower Manhattan adv. bd. Chem. Bank N.Y. Trust Co.; dir. Sentinal Funds, Mich. Chem. Corp., Modern Am. Mortgage Co., 1st Beehive Co., Intertel Corp.; chmn. A.B.S. Industries; dir., mem. exec. com., investment policy com. Mass. Mut. Life Ins. Co.; dir., chmn. finance com. Combined Communications Corp.; Cons. Fed. Res. Bd., 1952. Bd. dirs., treas. N.Y. Heart Assn., 1941-66; vice chmn. Youth Consultation Service, 1967, gen. chmn., 1968—. Mem. Investment Bankers Assn. Am. (pres. 1956-57), Pilgrims of U.S. Clubs: University, Bond, Wall Street (past pres., gov.), Fox Meadow Tennis, Scarsdale (N.Y.) Golf, Blind Brook, Shenorock Shore, Rockefeller Center Luncheon, Augusta Nat. Golf; Colony (Springfield, Mass.); Desert Forest Golf (Carefree, Ariz.); Ponte Vedra (Fla.); Ranch. Home: 2 Rectory Ln S Scarsdale NY 10583

CRAFTS, ROGER CONANT, anatomist, educator; b. Lewiston, Maine, Jan. 26, 1911; s. Seldon T. and Alice (Conant) C.; m. Margaret Dean Findley, Aug. 10, 1938; children—Roger Conant, Susan. B.S., Bates Coll., 1933; Ph.D., Columbia, 1941. Teaching asst. dept. biology Bates Coll., 1931-33; research asst. dept. anatomy Columbia Coll. Medicine, 1934-39, instr. anatomy, 1939-40, Boston U. Sch. Medicine, 1941-43, asst. prof., 1943-49, asso. prof., 1949-50; Francis Brunning prof. anatomy, head dept. U. Cin. Coll. Medicine, 1950-79, prof. anatomy, 1979-81, Francis Brunning prof. emeritus, 1981—; fellow Grad. Sch. U. Cin., 1961—; Cons. div. fellowships, NIH, 1960-63, health facilities div., 1962-63; chmn. council faculties Midwest-Gt. Plains region Assn. Am. Med. Colls., 1969-70. Author: A Guide to a Regional Dissection and Study of the Human Body, revised edit, 1979, A Textbook of Human Anatomy, 2d edit, 1979; Contbr. articles to profl. publs. Bd. mgmt. YMCA, Cin., 1955-57; mem. Citizens Sch. Com., 1967-78, exec. com., 1967-70, chmn., 1968-70. Recipient silver medallion Columbia U., 1967. Fellow AAAS; mem. Am. Assn. Anatomists (chmn. nominating com. 1965-66, mem. nominating com. 1978-79), Midwest Anatomists Assn. (pres. 1968-69), Assn. Am. Med. Colls., Cincinnatus Assn., Phi Beta Kappa, Sigma Xi (pres. U. Cin. chpt. 1965-67). Home: 3230 Daytona Ave Cincinnati OH 45211

CRAGER, JAY CECIL, JR., banker; b. Beaumont, Tex., Nov. 3, 1928; s. Jay Cecil and Alice (Beckett) C. B.A., U. Tex., 1948, B.B.A., 1949, M.B.A., 1951; postgrad., Grad. Sch. Banking of South, La. State U., 1957. C.P.A., Tex. Asst. v.p. Am. Nat. Bank of Beaumont, 1951-59; with Allied Bank of Tex., Houston, 1959—; now exec. v.p., dir.; exec. v.p., chief fin. officer dir. Allied Bancshares, Inc.; dir. Mchts. Bank of Port Arthur, Tex. Mem. Tex. Soc. C.P.A.'s, Houston Clearing House Assn. (dir.), Southwestern Automated Clearing House Assn. (dir.). Clubs: Houston, Houston Athletic. Home: 1400 Hermann Dr Apt 17E Houston TX 77004 Office: Allied Bancshares Inc Suite 210 Esperson Bldg Houston TX 77002

CRAGG, JOHN GORDON, economist, educator; b. Toronto, Ont., Can., May 3, 1937; m. Olga Browzin, Sept. 8, 1962; children: Michael,

Philip. B.A., McGill U., 1958, Cambridge U., Eng., 1960; Ph.D., Princeton U., 1965. Asst. prof. econs. U. Chgo., 1964-67; asst. prof. econs. U. B.C., Vancouver, 1967-68, assoc. prof., 1968, prof., 1971—, head dept. econs., 1976—; staff mem., dir. research Prices and Incomes Commn., 1969-71. Co-author: Expectations and the Structure of Prices, 1982; Contbr. articles to profl. jours. Bd. dirs. St. George's Sch., Vancouver. Home: 6 Semana Crescent Vancouver BC V6N 2E2 Canada Office: Dept Econs U BC 997 1873 East Mall Vancouver BC V6T 1Y2 Canada

CRAGG, LAURENCE HAROLD, former university president, chemist; b. Lethbridge, Alta., Can., Sept. 7, 1912; s. Harry Humphries and Louise (Howson) C.; m. Jean Irvine Dowling, Dec. 27, 1938; children: Elizabeth Cragg Sutherland, Ronald, James. B.A., U. Toronto, 1934, M.A., 1935, Ph.D., 1937; D.C.L., Acadia U., 1963; D.Sc., U. N.B., 1964, McMaster U., 1973, Brandon U., 1976; LL.D., St. Thomas U., 1973, Mt. Allison U., 1976. Lectr., prof. chemistry Brandon Coll., 1937-43, dean residence, 1937-38; lectr. chemistry McMaster U., 1943-44, asst. prof., 1944-47, asso. prof., 1947-53, prof., 1953-59, chmn. dept. chemistry, 1958-59; vis. lectr. U. Mich., summer 1954, 55; v.p., prof. chemistry U. Alta., 1959-63; pres.-elect Mt. Allison U., Sackville, N.B., Can., 1962-63, pres., vice-chancellor, 1963-75, pres. emeritus, prof. chemistry emeritus, 1975—; part-time lectr. McMaster U., 1976-79; mem. panel shock and plasma expanders Def. Research Bd. Can., 1955-63; mem. Alta. Research Council, 1960-63, NRC Can., 1965-68, chmn. scholarship com., 1967-68, chmn. com. on support of new and smaller univs., 1967, chmn. research com. on high polymer research, 1947-50, mem. adv. com. on regional devel. program, 1971-75; mem. N.B. Research and Productivity Council, 1963-70; pres. Can. Nat. Commn. for UNESCO, 1972-78, mem. exec. com., 1968—; mem. Can. del. 17th-19th Gen. Confs., Paris, 1972, 74, Nairobi, 1976, vice-chmn. Can. del., 1974, 76; mem. Can. Sci. del. to Czechoslovakia, 1966, Can. higher edn. del. to People's Republic China, 1974. Co-author: (with R.P. Graham) An Introduction to the Principles of Chemistry, 1954, The Essentials of Chemistry, 1956, (with G.S. Motherwell, V.E. Bullock and R.P. Graham) The Essentials of Chemistry in the Laboratory, 1957, (with R.P. Graham and J.V. Young) The Elements of Chemistry, 1959. Bd. dirs. Can. Univs. Found., 1963-65, Assn. Can. Univs. and Colls., 1965-67; bd. dirs. Family Services Hamilton-Wentworth, 1981—, v.p., 1983—. Recipient Montreal medal Chem. Inst. Can., Chem. Edn. award, 1966, Centennial medal Can., 1967. Fellow Chem. Inst. Can. (councillor 1950-53, 55-58, dir. profl. affairs 1957-59, v.p. 1961, pres. 1962), Royal Soc. Arts; mem. Sci. Council Can. (mem. com. on support of research in univs. 1967-69), Assn. Univ. and Colls. Can. (dir. 1965-67), Assn. Atlantic Univs. (exec. council 1965-75, vice chmn. 1973-75), Am. Chem. Soc., Hamilton Assn. for Advancement of Lit., Sci. and Art (pres. 1955-56, 80-81). Mem. United Ch. Can. (chmn. bd. men 1954-62, mem. exec. gen. council 1956-60, del. to World Council Chs., New Delhi, 1961, commr. gen. council 1948-56, 71, mem. gen. commn. on union 1967-73, mem. com. on union and joint mission 1973-76, chmn. standing com. on sci., tech. and ethics 1974-80, mem. com. theol. edn. for ministry 1977-80, mem. joint nat. com. on union negotiations 1977—). Research the chemistry of the sour taste; chem. warfare defense, phys. chemistry of high polymers; blood plasma substitutes. Home: 3252 Robert St Burlington ON L7N 1E7 Canada

CRAGON, HARVEY GEORGE, computer engineer; b. Ruston, La., Apr. 21, 1929; s. Miller M. and Lou Willie (Bond) C.; m. Henrietta Herbert, Sept. 2, 1950. B.S., La. Poly. Inst., Ruston, 1950. Engr. So. Bell Telephone, New Orleans, 1950-53, Hughes Aircraft, Los Angeles, 1953-57; mem. ARO Inc, Tullahoma, Tenn., 1957-58; sr. fellow Tex. Instruments Inc., Dallas, 1958—. Patentee in field. Trustee The Computer Mus., Boston, 1982—. Served with U.S. Army, 1951-52. Fellow IEEE (Emmanuel R. Piore award 1984); mem. Nat. Acad. Engring., Assn. Computing Machinery, Charles Babbage Inst, IEEE Computer Soc. Office: Tex Instruments PO Box 226015 M-S 238 Dallas TX 75266

CRAHAN, JACK BERTSCH, mfg. co. exec.; b. Peoria, Ill., Aug. 24, 1923; s. John F. and Ann B. (Bertsch) C.; m. Peggy Furey, Sept. 9, 1944; children—Patrick Michael, Colleen Mary, Kevin Furey. B.S., U. Minn., 1948; J.D. in Bus., Loyola U., Chgo., 1954; B.S. in Acctg., Loyola U., 1959. With Flexsteel Industries, Inc., Dubuque, Iowa, 1948—, plant mgr., 1950-54, gen. mgr., v.p., 1955-70, exec. v.p., 1970—, dir., 1970—, Dubuque Bank and Trust, 1978—. Bd. regents Loras Coll., 1967-80, 81—; bd. dirs. Xavier Hosp., 1969—, Boys Club Am., 1981—. Served with USNR, 1942-43; Served with USMC, 1943-46, 51-52. Decorated D.F.C. (2), Air medal (6). Republican. Roman Catholic. Home: 1195 Arrowhead Dubuque IA 52001 Office: PO Box 847 Dubuque IA 52001

CRAHAN, MARGARET ELLEN, historian, educator; b. Catskill, N.Y., June 2, 1939; d. Thomas Joseph and Mary Elizabeth (Fitzgerald) C. A.B., Coll. New Rochelle, 1960; M.A., Georgetown U., 1963; Ph.D., Columbia U., 1967. Instr. Lehman Coll., Bronx, N.Y., 1967-68, asst. prof., 1969-74, assoc. prof. history, 1974—; vis. prof. Johns Hopkins U., Washington, 1981-82; Luce prof. Occidental Coll., Los Angeles, 1982—; dir. human rights project Woodstock Theol. Ctr., Washington, 1980-82; bd. dirs. Washington Office on Latin Am., 1978-82. Editor: (with Franklin W. Knight) Africa and the Caribbean, 1979; author, editor: Human Rights and Basic Needs in the Americas, 1982. Fellow Fulbright Found., 1963-64, Social Sci. Research council-Am. Council Learned Socs., 1974-76; John Courtney Murray fellow Woodstock Theol. Ctr., 1977-79. Mem. Latin Am. Studies Assn. (exec. council 1973-75), Conf. Latin Am. Historians. Home: 825 West End Ave New York NY 10025 Office: Occidental Coll 1600 Campus Rd Los Angeles CA 90041

CRAIB, DONALD FORSYTH, JR., insurance company executive; b. Seattle, May 4, 1925; s. Donald Forsyth and Rubye (Drysdale) C.; m. Evelyn L. Poyer, Dec. 21, 1947; children: John L., Donald Forsyth, Laura L., Janet R. B.S. cum laude, UCLA, 1949. Regional mgr. Allstate Ins. Co., Sacramento, 1950-64, asst. sec., 1966-68, regional v.p., 1968-70, v.p. investments, 1971-73, group v.p. investments, 1974-76, exec. v.p., treas., 1977-78, vice chmn. bd., 1979-80, chmn. bd., chief exec. officer, 1982—, also dir.; vice chmn. bd. Sears Roebuck & Co., Chgo., 1980-82; pres., chmn. bd. Met. Savs. and Loan Assn., Los Angeles, 1964-68, also dir. Trustee UCLA Found. Served with USMCR, 1943-46; PTO. Mem. Phi Kappa Sigma. Republican. Congregationalist. Clubs: Pauma Valley Country; Onwentsia (Lake Forest, Ill.). Home: 1871 Mission Hills Ln Northbrook IL 60062 also Office: Allstate Plaza Northbrook IL 60062

CRAIB, RALPH GRANT, newspaperman; b. Oakland, Calif., Jan. 31, 1925; s. Alexander Leslie and Martha O.C. (Clerk) C.; m. Karola Maria Saekel, Dec. 4, 1962; children: Lisa Maria, Betsy Anne. B.A. with honors, San Francisco State U., 1950. Copy boy, then reporter and feature writer Oakland Tribune, 1942- 59; mem. staff San Francisco Chronicle, 1959—, editorial writer, 1968-70, mem. editorial bd., 1978—; information officer, mem. staff gov. Am. Samoa, 1965-66. Bd. dirs. No. Calif. chpt. Americans for Democratic Action, 1967-68. Served with AUS, World War II; ETO. Decorated Bronze Star, Combat Inf. badge; recipient Joseph R. Knowland newswriting award, 1952; Edward McQuade journalism award, 1977; Reid Found. fellow, 1955. Mem. San Francisco-Oakland Newspaper Guild (exec. com. 1976-78). Democrat. Club: Explorers (N.Y.C.). Home: 638 The Alameda Berkeley CA 94707 also 1145 Lokoya Rd Napa CA 94576 Office: San Francisco Chronicle San Francisco CA 94119

CRAIG, ALBERT MORTON, educator; b. Chgo., Dec. 9, 1927; s. Albert Morton and Adda (Clendenin) C.; m. Teruko Ugaya, July 10, 1953; children—John, Paul, Sarah. B.S., Northwestern U., 1949; postgrad., Universite de Strasbourg, 1949-50, Kyoto U., 1951-53, Tokyo U., 1955-56; Ph.D., Harvard, 1959. Instr. U. Mass., 1957-59; instr. Harvard, Cambridge, Mass., 1959-60, asst. prof., 1960-63, asso. prof., 1963-67, prof., 1967—; dir. Harvard-Yenching Inst., 1976—. Author: Choshu in the Meiji Restoration, 1961, (with others) East Asia: The Modern Transformation, 1965, East Asia: Tradition and Transformation, 1973; Co-editor: Personality in Japanese History, 1970; editor: Japan, A Comparative View, 1979. Served with AUS, 1946-47. Mem. Assn. Asian Studies. Home: 172 Goden St Belmont MA 02178 Office: 2 Divinity Ave Cambridge MA 02138

CRAIG, ALLEN BRUCE, restaurant chain executive; b. Miami, Fla., May 25, 1942; s. Raymond Mershon and Rosalena (Murphy) C.; m. Diane Ferrell, Apr. 25, 1964; children: Christopher, Scott. B.S., Fla. State U., 1964. Asst. store mgr. Richards, Miami, 1964-68; exec. v.p. Burger King, Englewood, Colo., 1968—. Served with U.S. Army, 1965-71. Republican. Office: 6200 S Syracuse Way Suite 415 Engelwood CO 80111

CRAIG, CORNELIUS ABERNATHY, II, insurance company executive; b. Nashville, Jan. 27, 1929; s. Edwin Wilson and Elizabeth (Wade) C.; m. Virginia Hubble Tipton, Apr. 24, 1954. B.A., Vanderbilt U., 1951. With Nat. Life and Accident Ins. Co., Nashville, 1951-83, sr. v.p. sales and mktg., 1971-74, exec. v.p. mktg., 1974-77, sr. exec. v.p., 1977-80, chmn. bd., chief operating officer, 1980-82, pres., chief exec. officer, 1982-83, also dir.; chmn. bd., pres., chief operating officer, dir. Nat. Property Owners Ins. Co.; chmn. bd., chief operating officer, dir. NLT Mktg. Services, Inc., 1982-83; dir. NLT Corp., Third Nat. Bank Nashville. Mem. Nat. council Boy Scouts Am., 1968—; past pres. Middle Tenn. council, past pres. Area II.; trustee Episcopal High Sch., Alexandria, Va. Recipient Silver Beaver award Boy Scouts Am., 1970, Silver Antelope award, 1980. Mem. Life Ins. Mktg. and Research Assn. (dir.; former chmn. combination companies com., former chmn. agy. officer round table; past chmn. ann. meeting com.), Underwriters Tng. Council (past mem. bd.), Life Insurers Conf. (past chmn.), Nashville C. of C. (past bd. govs. and exec. com.), Phi Delta Theta. Methodist. Clubs: Belle Meade Country (Nashville); Ponte Vedra (Fla.). Home: 4411 Truxton Pl Nashville TN 37205 Office: Am Gen Center Nashville TN 37250

CRAIG, DAVID JEOFFREY, manufacturing company executive; b. Wyandotte, Mich., Sept. 29, 1925; s. Geoffrey F. and Catherine R. C.; m. Shirley M. Lemhagen, Mar. 3, 1945; children: Susan Craig Noyes, Janice Craig, Sandra Craig Blum, Jeffrey Allan. B.S. in Physics, U. Detroit, 1950, M.S. summa cum laude, 1951; postgrad., U. Mich., 1952-53. With The BOC Group, 1956—, dir. corp. planning and devel., 1970-71, group v.p., 1971—; dep. group mng. dir. BOC Group plc, London, 1979-83; mng. dir. engring. and tech. BOCI Ltd., London, 1983—; dir. The BOC Group, Canox, BOC Group plc. Mem. Am. Iron and Steel Inst., Compressed Gas Assn. Club: Ridgewood Country. Home: Box 527 Saddle River NJ 07458 Office: BOC Group plc Hammersmith House London W6 England and BOC Group Inc 85 Chestnut Ridge Rd Montvale NJ 07645

CRAIG, DAVID W., judge, educator; b. Pitts., Feb. 17, 1925; s. David and Ella (Williamson) C.; m. Ella Van Kirk, July 15, 1945; children—Linda Marie Craig Mooser, Muriel Jean Craig Lagnese. A.B., U. Pitts., 1948, J.D., 1950. Bar: Pa. bar 1950. Research asst. U. Pitts. Law Sch., 1950-51; law clk. Ct. Common Pleas Allegheny County, 1951-52; partner firm Moorhead & Knox, Pitts., 1952-61; city solicitor, Pitts., 1961-65, dir. pub. safety, 1965-69; partner firm Baskin, Sachs & Craig, 1962-78; judge Commonwealth Ct. Pa., 1978—; Adj. prof. Carnegie-Mellon U., 1969—. Author: Pennsylvania Building and Zoning Laws, 1951. Chmn. City Planning Commn., Pitts., 1960-61; mem. nat. adv. council FPC, 1962-65. Served to 1st lt. USAAF, 1943-45; ETO. Decorated D.F.C. Mem. Am. Planning Assn. (pres. 1963-64). Democrat. Presbyterian. (elder). Home: 1812 Foxcroft Ln Allison Park PA 15101 Office: 101 Fort Pitt Commons Pittsburgh PA 15219

CRAIG, EUGENE W., retired editorial cartoonist; b. Ft. Wayne, Ind., Sept. 5, 1916; s. James S. and Katherine (Dahl) C.; m. Joyce C. Ayers, Nov. 21, 1951; children: Sandra (Mrs. David E. Miller), Pamela, (Mrs. Stephen A. Mitchell), Mark, Steve. Student pub. schs. Artist, editorial cartoonist, Ft. Wayne News-Sentinel, 1934-51; editorial cartoonist, Bklyn. Eagle, 1951-55, Columbus (Ohio) Dispatch, 1955-81; Creator: Quick Quotes. Mem. Am. Assn. Editorial Cartoonists. Home: 73 E Kramer St Canal Winchester OH 43110 Office: 34 S 3d St Columbus OH 43215

CRAIG, GEORGE ARMOUR, humanities educator; b. Cleve., Nov. 15, 1914; s. George Lochead and Theresa Joyce (Cusick) C.; m. Margaret Adele Ball, June 24, 1939; children—James Ball, Sara Margaret. A.B., Amherst Coll., 1937; A.M., Harvard U., 1938, Ph.D., 1947. Instr. Harvard U., 1939-40; mem. faculty Amherst (Mass.) Coll., 1940—; prof. English Amhest (Mass.) Coll., 1954—, Williston prof., 1975—, Kenan prof., 1979—, acting pres., 1983—; vis. lectr. Harvard U., 1956-57. Contbr. articles to profl. jours.; editor anthologies. Mem. MLA, English Inst. Club: Century Assn. N.Y. Office: Office of Pres Amherst Coll Amherst MA 01002

CRAIG, GEORGE ARTHUR, marketing and sales executive; b. Buffalo, July 22, 1923; s. Roy Vincent and Margaret (Connors) C.; m. Rittchell Marion Peterson, Aug. 27, 1949; children: Rittchell Anne, Scott Roy, Sandra Lynn. B.A., Knox Coll., 1949; A.M.P., Harvard U., 1959. Commerce agt., gen. agt., dir. indsl. devel. Chgo. & Eastern Ill. R.R., Chgo., 1951-58, v.p. traffic, 1958-61; v.p. mktg. Tex. & Pacific R.R., Dallas, 1961-65; asst. v.p. sales Mo. Pacific R.R., St. Louis, 1965-77, v.p., Houston, 1977-82, sr. v.p. mktg., 1982-83; sr. v.p. mktg. and sales Union Pacific-Mo. Pacific R.R., Omaha, 1983—. Served with USAAF, 1942-45. Mem. Nat. Freight Transp. Assn., Nat. Def. Transp. Assn. Republican. Presbyterian. Home: 11122 William Plaza Omaha NE 68144 Office: Union Pacific-Mo Pacific RR 1416 Dodge St Omaha NE 68179

CRAIG, GEORGE BROWNLEE, JR., entomologist; b. Chgo., July 8, 1930; s. George Brownlee and Alice Madeline (McManus) C.; m. Elizabeth Ann Pflum, Aug. 7, 1954; children: James Francis, Mary Catherine (dec.), Patricia Ann, Sarah Lynn. B.A., Ind. U., 1951; M.S., U. Ill., 1952, Ph.D., 1956. Research asst. entomology U. Ill., 1951-53; entomologist Mosquito Abatement Dist., summers 1951-53; research entomologist Chem. Corps Med. Labs., Army Chem. Center, Md., 1953-57; asst. prof. biology dept. U. Notre Dame, Ind., 1957-61, assoc. prof., 1961-64, prof., 1964-74, George and Winifred Clark distinguished prof. biology, 1974—; dir. WHO Internat. Reference Centre for Aedes, U. Notre Dame; vis. research dir. Internat. Centre for Insect Physiology and Ecology, Nairobi, Kenya, 1968-76. Contbr. articles on Aedes mosquitoes to profl. publs. Chmn. Ind. Vector Control Adv. Council, 1975—. Served as 1st lt., Med. Service Corps U.S. Army, 1954-55. Research grantee NIH, AEC, WHO, NSF, Dept. Def., Nat. Acad. Sci. Fellow Am. Acad. Arts and Scis., Nat. Acad. Sci., Ind. Acad. Scis.; mem. Entomol. Soc. Am. (bd. govs. 1969-75, medal for distinguished teaching 1975), Am. Mosquito Control Assn. (Outstanding Research award 1976), Am. Soc. Tropical Medicine and Hygiene (councilor 1978-83), Sigma Xi. Home: 19645 Glendale Ave South Bend IN 46637 Office: Biology Dept U Notre Dame Notre Dame IN 46556

CRAIG, GLENDON BROOKS, state official; b. Lindsay, Calif., Jan. 8, 1933; s. Alton Brooks and Henrietta (Chamblee) C.; m. Dorothy Jackson, Mar. 29, 1952; children—Kevin, Craig, Deborah Ann. A.A. in Police Sci, Coll. Sequoias, Visalia, Calif., 1952; postgrad., Calif. Lutheran Coll., Calif. State U., Los Angeles; grad., Exec. Inst., U. Calif., Davis, 1980, FBI Nat. Exec. Inst., 1980. Mem. Visalia Police Dept., 1955-56; mem. Calif. Hwy. Patrol, 1956-83, dep. chief, 1972, commr., 1975-83; dir. Div. Law Enforcement, Dept. Justice State of Calif., 1983—; mem. President's Nat. Hwy. Safety Adv. Com., 1976-79. Author articles in field. Chmn. for Calif. United Way, 1979; exec. com. Sacramento chpt. United Cerebral Palsy Assn., 1980-81, hon. chmn. telethon, 1980. Served with AUS, 1953-55. Recipient award public safety Nat. Traffic Safety Adminstrn., 1976, dist. Communications and Leadership award Toastmasters Internat., 1976, Disting. Alumni award Calif. Community Coll. Assn., 1980; named Safety Citizen of Yr. Sacramento Safety Council, 1979, Pub. Safety Officer of Yr. Dictograph/Internat. Assn. Chiefs of Police, 1982. Mem. Nat. Safety Council (exec. bd. Sacramento), Calif. Peace Officers Assn. (dir.). Republican. Methodist. Office: 2555 1st Ave PO Box 898 Sacramento CA 95804 *The wise leader recognizes the achievements of those who work with and for him; it is the accomplishments of others that ultimately make any leader successful. Those fortunate enough to hold posts of responsibility sometimes mistakenly take for themselves the respect intended for the position.*

CRAIG, GORDON ALEXANDER, historian, educator; b. Glasgow, Scotland, Nov. 26, 1913; came to U.S., 1925; s. Frank Mansfield and Jane (Bissell) C.; m. Phyllis Halcomb, June 16, 1939; children: Susan, Deborah, Gordon, Martha Jane, Charles Grant. B.A., Princeton U., 1936, M.A., 1939, Ph.D., 1941, D.Litt. hon., 1970; B.Litt., Oxford U., Eng., 1938; D.Phil. hon., Free U. Berlin, 1983. Instr. history Yale U., New Haven, 1939-41; instr. to prof. history Princeton U., N.J., 1941-61; prof. history Stanford U., Calif., 1961—, J.E. Wallace Sterling prof. humanities, 1959-79, J.E. Wallace Sterling prof. humanities emeritus, 1979—; prof. history Free U. Berlin, 1962—. Assoc. editor, contbr.: Makers of Modern Strategy, 1943; joint editor, contbr.: The Diplomats, 1919-1939, 1953; author: The Politics of the Prussian Army, 1640-1945, 1955, From Bismarck to Adenauer: Aspects of German Statecraft, 1958, Europe Since 1815, 1961, Europe Since 1815, 6th edit, 1983, The Battle of Koniggratz, 1964, War, Politics and Diplomacy: Selected Essays, 1966, Treitschke's History of Modern Germany, 1975, Economic Interest, Militarism and Foreign Policy: Essays of Eckart Kehr, 1977, Germany, 1866-1945, 1978, The Germans, 1982, Force and Statecraft: Diplomatic Problems of Our Times, 1983, The End of Prussia, 1984. Hon. mem. Berlin Hist. Commn., 1975—; political analyst Office Strategic Services, Dept. State, Washington, 1941-43; pub. mem. Fgn. Service Selection Bd., 1948-49; cons. U.S. Arms Control and Disarmament Agy., 1964-68; adv. bd. U.S. Marine Corps Hist. Sect., Washington, 1972-74. Served to capt. USMC, 1944-46. Guggenheim fellow, 1969-70, 82-83. Fellow Center for Advanced Study in the Behavioral Scis.; mem. Inst. for Advanced Study, Am. Acad. Arts and Scis., Am. Philos. Soc. (council mem.), Am. Hist. Assn. (pres. 1983), Internat. Com. of Hist. Scis. (1st v.p. 1975—), Phi Beta Kappa. Democrat. Presbyterian. Home: 451 Oak Grove Ave Melo Park CA 94025 Office: Dept History Stanford Univ Stanford CA 94035

CRAIG, GRACE J., developmental psychologist, educator; b. Newton, Mass., July 9, 1937; d. Charles Edgar and Lucille (Burnham) Johnson; m. Ralph P. Craig, June 20, 1959; 1 dau., Talli Lynn. B.A., U. Mass., 1959, M.S., 1962, Ph.D., 1967. Sch. psychologist Dalton (Mass.) Public Schs., 1962-64; lectr. Smith Coll., Northampton, Mass., 1966-70; asst. prof. human devel. U. Mass., Amherst, 1970-74, asso. dean, 1975-79, prof., chmn. dept. human devel. and edn., 1979—. Author: Human Development, 1975, 3d edit., 1983, Child Development, 1979, (with Riva Sprecht) Human Development: a social work perspective, 1982. Mem. Nat. Assn. for Edn. Young Children, Am. Psychol. Assn., Soc. for Research Child Devel. Office: U Mass 365 Hills South Amherst MA 01003

CRAIG, HARALD FRANKLIN, lawyer; b. Lima, Ohio, Oct. 27, 1930; s. Harald F. and Bessie M. (Rose) C.; m. Kaarina M. Craig; children: Harald Franklin III, Anne Marie. B.A., Bowling Green State U., 1952; J.D., Ohio State U., 1955. Bar: Ohio 1955. Since practiced in, Toledo; sr. partner firm Brown, Baker, Schlageter & Craig, 1957—; dir. Bernard Engraving Co., Electra Mfg. Corp., Reichert Stamping Co. Served to 1st lt. JAG Office USMCR, 1955-57. Mem. Am., Ohio, Toledo bar assns., Am. Judicature Soc., Trial Lawyers Assn. Home: 3773 Hillandale Rd Toledo OH 43606 Office: 711 Adams St First Federal Plaza Toledo OH 43624

CRAIG, HARMON, geochemist, oceanographer; b. N.Y.C., Mar. 15, 1926; s. John Richard and Virginia (Stanley) C.; m. Valerie Kopecky, Sept. 27, 1947; children—Claudia Campbell, Cynthia Camilla, Karen Constance. M.S., U. Chgo., 1950, Ph.D., 1951. Research asso. Enrico Fermi Inst. Nuclear Studies, U. Chgo., 1951-55; with Scripps Instn. Oceanography, U. Calif., San Diego, 1955—; now prof. geochemistry and oceanography; Guggenheim fellow U. Pisa, 1962-63; chief scientist on 12 oceanographic expdns.; expdn. leader UN (FAO) Lake Tanganyika Expdns., 1973, 75; chief scientist on 16 oceanographic expdns.; expdn. leader UNDP Phase-2 Geothermal Survey of Ethiopia, 1976; mem. Haicheng earthquake study del., China, 1976, Yangbajain geothermal field study, Tibet, 1980. Contbr. numerous articles to profl. publs.; editor: Earth and Planetary Sci. Letters, 1971—. Served with USN, 1944-46. Recipient V. M. Goldschmidt medal Geochem.Soc., 1979, A.L. Day medal Geol. Soc. Am., 1983. Mem. Nat. Acad. Scis., Am. Acad. Arts and Scis., Am. Geophys. Union., Explorers Club. Home: 8553 La Jolla Shores La Jolla CA 92037 Office: Scripps Instn Oceanography A-020 U Calif San Diego La Jolla CA 92093

CRAIG, JAMES LYNN, consumer products company executive, physician; b. Columbia, Tenn., Aug. 7, 1933; s. Clifford Paul and Maple (Harris) C.; m. Suzanne Anderson, July 20, 1957; children: James Lynn, Margaret; m. Roberta Anne, May 17, 1980. Pre-med., Middle Tenn. State U., 1953; M.D., U. Tenn., 1956; M.P.H., U. Pitts., 1963. Diplomate: Am. Bd. Preventive Medicine, Am. Bd. Family Practice. Intern U. Tenn. Meml. Hosp., Knoxville, 1957; resident in occupational medicine U. Pitts., 1962-64, TVA, Chattanooga, 1964-65, physician, 1966-69, chief med. officer, Chattanooga, 1969-74; corp. med. dir. Gen. Mills Corp., Mpls., 1974-76, v.p. corp. med. dir., 1976-80, v.p. dir. health and safety, 1980—; clin. instr. U. Tenn., Memphis, 1970-74, Mcharry Med. Sch., Nashville, 1972-74; clin. prof. U. Minn., Mpls., 1979—. Contbr. articles to profl. jours. Bd. dirs. Mpls. Blood bank, 1976—, Minn. Bible coll., Rochester, 1978-83, Minn. Heart Assn., Mpls., 1976—, Children's Heart Fund, Mpls., 1976—. Served to capt. USAF, 1958-61. Recipient Physician Recognition award AMA, 1975, 78, 81. Fellow Am. Occupational Medicine Assn. (dir. 1974-78), Am. Acad. Occupational Medicine (treas. 1982-83, sec. 1983-84), Am. Acad. Family Practice; mem. Occupational Health Inst. (chmn. 1983-84), N. Central Occupational Medicine Assn. (pres. 1977). Home:

10008 S Shore Dr Minneapolis MN 55441 Office: Gen Mills Corp 9200 Wayzata Blvd Minneapolis MN 55426 *The activities of my life are based on a balance between quality and acceptance.*

CRAIG, JAMES WILLIAM, physician; b. West Liberty, Ohio, Jan. 23, 1921; s. J. Frank and Helen Clara (Scarborough) C.; m. Helen Catherine Lang, Sept. 18, 1948 (dec.); children—Maribeth, Jon, William, Barbara; m. Wendy Burnip Johnson, June 23, 1972; stepchildren—Steven, Barbara, Philip, Laura Johnson. B.S., Western Res. U., 1943, M.D., 1945. Intern, asst. resident in medicine Presbyn. Hosp., N.Y.C., 1945-46, 48-50; fellow in medicine Western Res. U. Sch. Medicine, Cleve., 1950-52, from instr. to asso. prof. medicine, 1952-72; prof. medicine, asso. dean Sch. Medicine U. Va., Charlottesville, 1972—. Condr. research; contbr. articles on diabetes mellitus and intermediary metabolism to publs. Served with AUS, 1946-48. Recipient Lederle med. faculty award, 1962-64. Mem. Am. Diabetes Assn., Am. Inst. Nutrition, Soc. for Exptl. Biology and Medicine, Am. Fedn. Clin. Research, Central Soc. for Clin. Research, Med. Soc. Va., Phi Beta Kappa, Sigma Xi, Alpha Omega Alpha. Home: 101 Indian Spring Rd Charlottesville VA 22901 Office: Box 458 Univ Virginia School of Medicine Charlottesville VA 22908

CRAIG, JOHN GILBERT, JR., newspaper editor; b. Wilmington, Del., Apr. 13, 1933; s. John Gilbert and Ruth (Veasey) C.; m. Candace Best, June 27, 1981; children: Eliza, Landon, Peter, Emily Dutton. B.A., Trinity Coll., Hartford, Conn., 1954; M.A., Fletcher Sch. Internat. Law and Diplomacy, Medford, Mass., 1957. Mem. staff News-Jour. Co., Wilmington, Del., 1968-75, exec. editor, v.p., 1970-75; asst. to pubs. Pitts. Post-Gazette, 1976-77, editor, 1977—; founding ptnr. Arts Devel. Advisors (preservationists), 1975-76. Chmn. First Amendment Coalition of Pa., 1982—; trustee Va. Theol. Sem., 1980—. Served with AUS, 1954-56. Named Editor of Year Nat. News Press Photographers Assn., 1973. Mem. Am. Soc. Newspaper Editors, Alpha Delta Phi. Democrat. Episcopalian. Club: Wilmington Country. Home: 1234 Resaca Pl Pittsburgh PA 15212 Office: 50 Blvd of Allies Pittsburgh PA 15222

CRAIG, LARRY EDWIN, congressman; b. Council, Idaho, July 20, 1945; s. Elvin and Dorothy C. B.A., U. Idaho; postgrad, George Washington U. Farmer, rancher, Midvale area, Idaho; mem. Idaho Senate, 1974-80, 97th-98th Congresses from 1st Dist. Idaho; mem. select com. on aging, com. on edn. and labor, com. on interior and insular affairs. 97th Congress from 1st Dist. Idaho; Chmn. Idaho Republican State Senate Races, 1976-78. Pres. Young Rep. League Idaho, 1976-77; mem. Idaho Rep. Exec. Com., 1976-78; chmn. Rep. Central Com. Washington County, 1971-72; advisor vocat. edn. in public schs. HEW, 1971-73; mem. Idaho Farm Bur., 1965-79. Served with U.S. Army N.G., 1970-74. Methodist. Home: Midvale ID 83645 Office: 1318 Longworth Cannon House Office Bldg Washington DC 20515

CRAIG, LILLIAN *See* **REED, KIT**

CRAIG, MACK WAYNE, college executive; b. Obion, Tenn., May 13, 1925; s. Guy and Katherine (Andrews) C.; m. Dorothy Discher, Aug. 28, 1946 (dec. Nov. 1959); children—Larry, David, Marnie. B.A., Vanderbilt U., 1946; M.A., George Peabody Coll., 1948, Ph.D., 1958. Ordained to ministry Ch. of Christ, 1942; minister in, Fla. and Tenn., 1942—; instr. David Lipscomb High Sch., Nashville, 1945-49, prin., 1949-57; minister Vultee Ch. Christ, Nashville, 1968-78; dean David Lipscomb Coll., 1957—, now dir. nat. devel. bd. Author articles. Past bd. govs. Belle Meade Mansion; exec. com. Historic Nashville Inc. Mem. Nat., Tenn. edn. assns., Assn. Deans Am. Colls., Assn. Higher Edn., Phi Beta Kappa. Home: 1919 Tyne Blvd Nashville TN 37215

CRAIG, MARY FRANCIS SHURA, writer, educator; b. Pratt, Kans., Feb. 27, 1923; d. Jack Fant and Mary Francis (Milstead) Young; m. Daniel Charles Shura, Oct. 24, 1943 (div. Oct. 24, 1943); children: Marianne Francis Shura Sprague, Daniel Charles, Alice Barrett, Craig Stout; m. Raymond C. Craig, Dec. 8, 1961; 1 dau., Mary Forsha. Creative writing tchr., summer conf. U. Kans., Lawrence, 1961—; tchr. adult edn. Coll. St. Teresa's, Kansas City, Mo., 1960-61; tchr. creative writing Avila Coll., U. N.D., Calif. State U., U. Kans., Central Mo. State U., N.E. Mo. State U.; lectr. confs., v.p., dir., 1950—. Writer: adult and children's books as Mary Grancis Sura, Mary Craig, M.S. Craig Simple Spigott, 1960 (on 100 Best list World Book Ency. 1960), Garrett of Greta McGraw, 1967, Mary's Marvelous Mouse, 1962, Nearsighted Knight, 1963 (on Best list NY. Times 1963), Run Away Home, 1964, Backwards for Luck, 1968, Shoeful of Shamrock, 1965, A Tale of Middle Length, 1967, Pornada, 1969, The Valley of the Frost Giants, 1971, Topcat of Tam, 1972, The Shop on Threnody Street, 1972, A Candle for the Dragon, 1973, Ten Thousand Serveral Doors, 1973, The Cranes of Ibycus, 1974, The Riddle of Ravens Gulch, 1975, The Season of Silence, 1976, Gray Ghosts of Taylor Ridge, 1978, Mister Wolf and Me, 1979, The Barkley Street Six-Pack, 1979, Chester, 1980 (Pinetree award 1983), Happles and Cinnamunger, 1981, Eleanor, 1983, The Chicagoans, Dust to Diamonds, 1981, Were He a Stranger, 1978, To Play the Fox, 1982; Writer: adult and children's books as Mary Francis Shura, Mary Craig, M.S.Craig Lyon's Pride, 1983, Pirate's Landing, 1983, Gilliam's Chain, 1983; contbr. fiction to popular mags., 1969—, poetry to popular mags., 1960—; weekly columnist: Scrapbook from Shuranuff Farm, 1960-64. Mem. Authors Guild., Authors League Am., Soc. Children's Bookwriters, Mystery Writers Am. (regional pres.), Childrens Reading Round Table, Crime Writers Great Britain. Home and Office: 301 Lake Hinsdale Dr Apt 112 Clarendon Hills Il 60514

CRAIG, NANCY ELLEN, painter; b. Bronxville, N.Y.; d. Victor Irving and Julia (Hill) C.; m. Preston Carter, May 10, 1963. Student, Sweetbriar Coll., Bennington Coll., Art Student's League, Academie Julien, Paris, Hans Hofmann Sch. Art, Taubes Sch. Art. One-man exhbns., Graham Gallery, N.Y.C., 1966, Lyford Cay Gallery, Nassau, Bahamas, 1971, Merradin Gallery, London, 1972, Wellfleet (Mass.) Art Gallery, 1973, Galería Bética, Madrid, 1975, Galería Los Canos Sotogrande, Spain, 1978; represented, Balt. Mus. Art, Met. Mus., N.Y.C., New Britain Mus. (Conn.); Author: Portrait Painting in Oil. Recipient Julien F. Detmer award for best oil Hudson Valley Show; Mary E. Karasick award Nat. Assn. Women Artists; S. Karasick prize Nat. Assn. Women Artists; Patron's prize Audubon Artists; Gold Medal Honor Allied Artists; 1st Benjamin Altman prize NAD; Henry Ward Ranger purchase prize NAD. Address: Box 57 Truro MA 02666

CRAIG, PAUL MAX, JR., lawyer; b. Munich, Ger., Aug. 8, 1921; came to U.S., 1941, naturalized, 1944; s. Paul Max and Helen A. C.; m. Leonie R. Hildebrand, June 26, 1962; children: Anthony P., Claudine A., Stephen P. B.S. in Elec. Engring, Worcester (Mass.) Poly. Inst., 1946; LL.B., Georgetown U., 1950, LL.M., 1952. Bar: D.C. bar 1950. Patent examiner U.S. Patent Office, 1946-50; patent adviser Office Chief Ordnance, Dept. Army, 1950-52; pvt. practice, Washington, 1952—; partner firm Craig & Antonelli (and predecessor firm), 1967—. Served with USNR, 1944-46. Mem. Am., Inter-Am. bar assns., Am. Patent Law Assn., Assn. Internat. Pour La Protection de la Propriete Indsl., Licensing Execs. Soc., Am. Soc. Internat. Law, Assn. Trial Lawyers Am. Home: 207 Quaint Acres Dr Silver Spring MD 20904 Office: 1825 L St NW Washington DC 20006

CRAIG, ROBERT CHARLES, educator; b. Sault Sainte Marie, Mich., Mar. 9, 1921; s. Frank Lyle and Sylva (Crowell) C.; m. Rosalie Esther DeBoer, Sept. 2, 1950; children: Bruce R., Stephen F., Jeffrey A., Barbara Anne. B.S., Mich. State U., 1943, M.A., 1948; Ph.D., Tchrs. Coll., Columbia U., 1952. Research assoc. Columbia U. Tchrs. Coll., 1950-52; asst. prof. State U. Wash., Pullman, 1952-55; research scientist Am. Insts. for Research, Pitts., 1955-58, cons. for ednl. research, 1958-70; assoc. prof. Marquette U., Milw., 1958-62, prof., 1962-66; prof. ednl. psychology Mich. State U., East Lansing, 1966—, chmn. dept. counseling and ednl. psychology, 1966-81; dir. U.S. Office Edn. Grad. research tng. program, 1966-72; Lectr. psychology U. Pitts., 1956-57; dir. Project TALENT, 1957-58. Author: Transfer Value of Guided Learning, 1953, (with A.M. Dupuis) American Education, Origins and Issues, 1963, Psychology of Learning in the Classroom, 1966, (with H. Clarizio, William Mehrens) Contemporary Issues in Educational Psychology, 1969, 74, 77, 81, Contemporary Educational Psychology, 1975, (with V.H. Noll and D.P. Scannell) Introduction to Educational Measurement, 1979. Served to lt. (j.g.) USNR, 1943-46. Fellow AAAS, Am. Psychol. Assn.; mem. Am. Ednl. Research Assn., Nat. Council Measurement in Edn., Sigma Xi, Phi Delta Kappa, Phi Kappa Phi. Research on discovery versus reception learning. Home: 185 Maplewood Dr East Lansing MI 48823

CRAIG, ROBERT GEORGE, dental science educator; b. Charlevoix, Mich., Sept. 8, 1923; s. Harry Allen and Marion Ione (Swinton) C.; m. Luella Georgine Dean, Sept. 29, 1945; children: Susan Georgine, Barbara Dean, Katherine Ann. B.A., U. Mich., 1944, M.S., 1951, Ph.D. (E.I. du Pont research fellow 1952-53), 1955. Research chemist Linde Air Products Co., 1944-50, Texaco, Inc., Beacon, N.Y., 1954-55; research assoc. U. Mich. Engring. Research Inst., 1955-57; faculty dept. dental materials Sch. Dentistry, U. Mich., Ann Arbor, 1957—, asst. prof., 1957-60, assoc. prof., 1960-64, prof., 1964—, chmn. dept., 1969—; mem. exec. com. U. Mich. Sch. Dentistry, 1972-75, mem. budget priorities com., 1978-81, chmn., 1979-81; mem. sci. adv. com. (Dental Research Inst.), 1980—; cons. Walter Reed Army Hosp., 1969-75. Author: Restorative Dental Materials, 6th edit, 1980, (with K.A. Easlick, S.I. Seger and A.L. Russell) Communicating in Dentistry, 1973, (with W.J. O'Brien, J.M. Powers) Dental Materials-Properties and Manipulation, 2d edit, 1979, (with J.M. Powers) Workbook for Dental Materials, 1979; Editor, contbr.: Dental Materials Review, 1977, Dental Materials-A Problem Oriented Approach, 1978; asst. editor: Jour. Biomed. Materials Research, 1983—; cons. editor: Jour. Dental Research, 1971-73, 77—, Jour. Dental Edn, 1971-76, Jour. Oral Rehab, 1974—, Mich. State Dental Jour, 1973-77; Contbr. (with J.M. Powers) articles to profl. jours. Research grantee Nat. Inst. Dental Research, 1965-76; Nat. Sci. Service Tng. grantee, 1976—. Mem. Am. Nat. Standards Inst. (chmn. spl. com. 1968-77), Internat. Assn. Dental Research (pres.-elect dental materials group 1972-73, pres. 1973-74, Wilmer Souder award 1975), Am. Assn. Dental Schs. (chmn. biomaterials sect. 1977-79), Am. Chem. Soc., ADA, Soc. Biomaterials (Clemson award for basic research in biomaterials 1978, program chmn. 1983—), Phi Kappa Phi, Phi Lambda Upsilon, Sigma Xi (sec. U. Mich. chpt. 1978-81), Omicron Kappa Upsilon. Home: 1503 Wells St Ann Arbor MI 48104

CRAIG, STEPHEN WRIGHT, lawyer; b. N.Y.C., Aug. 28, 1932; s. Herbert Stanley and Dorothy (Simmons) C.; m. Margaret M. Baker, June 10, 1958; children: Amelia Audrey, Janet Elizabeth, Peter Baker. A.B., Harvard, 1954, J.D., 1959. Reporter Daily Kennebec Jour., Augusta, Maine, 1956; engaged in pub. relations with Am. Savoyards, 1957; atty. IRS, San Francisco, 1959-61; atty.-adviser U.S. Tax Ct., 1961-63; ptnr. Snell & Wilmer, Phoenix, 1963-78, Winston & Strawn (formerly Craig, Greenfield & Irwin), 1978; guest lectr. Amos Tuck Sch. Bus., Dartmouth, 1962; lectr. Ariz. and N.Mex. Tax Insts., 1966-67. Chmn. Jane Wayland Child Guidance Center, 1968-70; mem. Maricopa County Health Planning Council, chmn. mental health task force.; Mem. Ariz. Republican Com., 1967-72; Bd. dirs. Combined Met. Phoenix Arts, 1968, adv. bd., 1968-69; adv. bd. Ariz. State U. Tax Insts., 1968-70; bd. dirs. Phoenix Community Council, 1970-73, Ariz. Kidney Found., Ariz. Acad. Served with AUS, 1954-56. Mem. Am., County bar assns., state bars Ariz., Calif., Maine, Hasty Pudding Inst., Sigma Alpha Epsilon. Episcopalian (sr. warden, diocesan council). Office: 3101 N Central Ave, Ste 1500 Phoenix AZ 85012

CRAIG, WALTER EARLY, U.S. district judge; b. Oakland, Calif., May 26, 1909; s. Jubal Early and Marie (Craig) C.; m. Meta Elizabeth Jury, Oct. 25, 1935; children: William Early, Meta Lucille. A.B., Stanford U., 1931, LL.B., 1934; LL.D., Ariz. State U., 1963, U. San Diego, 1964; S.J.D., Suffolk U., 1964. Bar: Calif. 1934, Ariz. 1936. Legal dept. regional office HOLC, 1934-36; ptnr. Fennemore, Craig, Allen & Bledsoe, Phoenix, 1936-55, Fennemore, Craig, Allen & McClennen, 1955-63; U.S. judge Ariz. dist., 1963—, chief judge, 1972-79; Mem. Ariz. Code Commn., 1951-56; appeal agt. Maricopa County Selective Service, 1945-64; mem. Ariz. Jud. Council, 1950-63; spl. counsel Pres.'s Commn. on Assassination of Pres. Kennedy, 1963-64; chmn. Nat. Conf. Fed. Trial Judges, 1972-73. Bd. dirs. Sun Angel Found.; exec. com. planning county hosp., 1952-60; bd. visitors Stanford U. Sch. Law, 1958-63; bd. dirs. Maricopa County Hosp. Devel. Assn., 1955-62, Am. Bar Endowment; pres., 1979-81, Ariz. State U. Found., Ariz. Community Found.; chmn. bd. visitors Ariz. State U. Coll. Law; trustee Forensic Scis. Found., 1972-75, Harry S. Truman Ednl. Found., 1975-79. Served with USN, World War II. Decorated Order So. Cross, Brazil). Fellow Am. Bar Found.; mem. Am. Law Inst., ABA (state chmn. jr. bar conf., ho. dels. 1947—, bd. govs. 1958-61, pres. 1963-64), Ariz. Bar Assn. (pres. 1951-52), Maricopa County Bar Assn. (pres. 1941), Am. Judicature Soc. (dir. 1951-61), Inter-Am. Bar Assn. (council), Internat. Bar Assn. (council), Can. Bar Assn. (hon. mem.), Assn. Bar of City N.Y., Am. Acad. Forensic Scis., Ariz. Acad., Ariz. State U. Law Soc. (pres. 1972-74), Ninth Circuit Dist. Judges Assn. (pres. 1973-75), El Ilustre y Nacional Colegio de Abogados de Mexico (hon.), Barra Mexicana (hon.), El Colegio de Abogados de la Ciudad de Buenos Aires (hon.), Colegio de Abogados del Uruguay (hon.), Western States Bar Council (pres. 1956-57), Am. Legion, Phi Gamma Delta, Phi Delta Phi. Clubs: Arizona, Phoenix Country, Kiva, Stanford (past pres.), Thunderbirds (Phoenix) (past pres.). Lodges: Elks (Phoenix); Rotary (Phoenix). Office: US Court House Phoenix AZ 85025

CRAIG, WILLIAM FRANCIS, banker; b. Phila., 1931; married. B.S. in Econs., Villanova U., 1953; M.B.A., Drexel U., 1959. Tax acct. Phila. Electric Co., 1956-60, head energy and minerals dept., asst. div. head nat. div., 1960-76; exec. v.p. Shawmut Bank of Boston, 1976—, pres., dir., Pittston Co.; vice chmn. bd. Shawmut Corp. Office: Shawmut Bank of Boston One Federal St Boston MA 02211 *

CRAIGE, ERNEST, physician, educator; b. El Paso, Tex., June 3, 1918; s. Branch and Else (Kohlberg) C. B.A., U. N.C., 1939; M.D., Harvard U., 1943. Intern in medicine Mass. Gen. Hosp., Boston, 1943, asst. resident, 1946-47, resident, 1947-48, clin. and research fellow in medicine and resident in cardiology, 1949-50, asst. in medicine, 1950-52; teaching fellow in medicine Harvard U. Med. Sch., Boston, 1949-50; asst. prof. medicine U. N.C., Chapel Hill, 1952-55, asso. prof., 1955-62, prof., 1962—, Henry A. Foscue disting. prof., 1971—; chief cardiology N.C. Meml. Hosp., Chapel Hill, 1952-78. Served with U.S. Army, 1944-46; ETO. Rhodes scholar Oxford U., 1939. Fellow Am. Coll. Cardiology, Philippine Coll. Cardiology; mem. Am. Heart Assn., Am. Clin. and Climatological Assn., Am. Soc. Echocardiography, Assn. Univ. Cardiologists, Argentina Soc. Cardiology, Alpha Omega Alpha. Office: Div Cardiology U NC Med Sch 338 Clin Sci Bldg 229H Chapel Hill NC 27514

CRAIGHEAD, FRANK COOPER, JR., ecologist; b. Washington, Aug. 14, 1916; s. Frank Cooper and Carolyn (Johnson) C.; m. Esther Melvin Stevens, Nov. 9, 1943 (dec. 1980); children: Frank Lance, Charles Stevens, Jana Catherine. A.B., Pa. State U., 1939; M.S., U. Mich., 1940, Ph.D., 1950. Sr. reearch assoc. Atmospheric Scis. Ctr., N.Y., 1967-77; wildlife biologist, cons. U.S. Dept. Interior, Washington, 1959-66; wildlife biologist U.S. Forest Service, Washington, 1957-59; mgr. desert game range U.S. Dept. Interior, Las Vegas, 1955-57; cons. survival tng. Dept. Def., Washington, 1950-55; pres. Craighead Environ. Research Inst., Moose, Wyo., 1955—; research assoc. U. Mont., Missoula, 1959—, Nat. Geographic Soc., Washington, 1959—; lectr. in field. Author: Track of the Grizzly, 1979, A Field Guide to Rocky Mountain Flowers, 1963, Hawks, Owls and Wildlife, 1956, How to Survive on Land and Sea, 1943, Hawks in the Hand, 1937. Mem. Pryor Mountain Wild Horse Adv. Com., Dept. Interior, 1968; mem. Horizons adv. group Am. Revolution Bicentennial Commn., 1972. Recipient citation Sec. of Navy, 1947, letter of commendation U.S. Dept. Interior, 1963, Disting. Alumnus award Pa. State U., 1970; alumni fellow Pa. State U., 1973; recipient John Oliver LaGorce Gold medal Nat. Geog. Soc., 1979. Mem. Wilderness Soc., AAAS, Wildlife Soc., Explorers Club, Phi Beta Kappa, Sigma Xi, Phi Sigma, Phi Kappa Phi. Home: PO Box 156 Moose WY 83012 Office: Craighead Environ Research Inst PO Box 156 Moose WY 83012

CRAIGHEAD, GEORGE PALMER, management consultant; b. Indpls., Oct. 22, 1929; s. George Vankirk and Janet Louise (Palmer) C.; m. Peggy Ann Walters, Aug. 16, 1958; children: Scott, Bradford, Catherine. A.B., Yale U., 1952; M.B.A., Harvard U., 1956. Sales rep. Gen. Electric Co., Bridgeport, Conn., 1956-59; dir. mktg. research C.H. Masland & Sons, N.Y.C., 1959-61; dir. mktg. cons. services Touche Ross & Co., Detroit, 1961-66; exec. v.p. William H. Clark Assos., Inc., N.Y.C., 1967-77; pres. Egon Zehnder Internat., Inc. (U.S.A.), N.Y.C., 1977-83; prin. Craighead Assocs. Inc., Stamford, Conn., 1983—; Pres. Assn. Exec. Recruiting Consultants, 1974-76. Served with M.I. U.S. Army, 1953-55. Clubs: Woodway Country (Darien, Conn.); Landmark (Stamford); Univ., Yale (N.Y.C.). Home: 6 Fox Hill Ln Darien CT 06820 Office: 645 Fifth Ave New York NY 10022

CRAIGHEAD, RODKEY, banker; b. Pitts., July 24, 1916; s. Ernest S. and Florence L. (Rodkey) C.; m. Carol M. Price, June 26, 1943 (dec. June 1978); children: Rodkey, Virginia, Corinne; m. La Verne Hastings, Mar. 1979. B.S., U. Pitts., 1942; postgrad., Grad. Sch. Banking, U. Wis., 1959-61. With Mellon Nat. Bank, Pitts., 1936-41; with Detroit Bank & Trust Co., 1946—, v.p., 1961-67, sr. v.p., 1967-69, exec. v.p., 1969-73, dir., 1971—, pres., 1974—, chmn., chief exec. officer, 1977—; pres., dir. Detroitbank Corp., 1974-81, chmn., chief exec. officer, 1977-81; dir. Winkelman Stores, Inc., Detroit. Bd. dirs. Detroit Symphony Orch; bd. dirs. New Detroit, Inc., Alma Coll. Served to capt. AUS, 1942-46. Mem. Greater Detroit C. of C. (dir.). Presbyterian. Clubs: Detroit Athletic (dir.), Detroit, Economic (Detroit) (dir.); Bloomfield Hills Country.). Home: 3912 Maple Hill E West Bloomfield MI 48033

CRAIGHILL, FRANCIS HOPKINSON, III, lawyer; b. Richmond, Va., May 20, 1939; s. Francis Hopkinson and Catherine Ruteledge (Willink) C.; m. Marcee Martha Fareed, 1978; 1 dau., Amara Katherine. B.A., U. N.C., Chapel Hill, 1961; LL.B., U. Va., 1964. Bar: N.C. bar, D.C. bar 1966. Ford Found. fellow, legal adviser Govt. of Lesotho, 1964-66; freelance corr., Vietnam, fall 1967; law clk. to judge U.S. Dist. Ct. for D.C., 1966-67; assoc. firm Zuckert, Scoutt & Rasenberger, Washington, 1968-70; ptnr. firm Dell, Craighill, Fentress & Benton, Washington, 1970-83, Craighill & Fentress, 1983—; Mng. dir. Advantage Internat., Washington, 1983—. Co-author: Ballots or Bullets: What the 1967 Elections Could Mean, 1968. Trustee Va. Episcopal Sch., Lynchburg. Mem. Am., N.C. bar assns., Bar Assn. D.C., Descs. Signers Declaration of Independence. Clubs: Metropolitan, 1925 F St. (Washington). Home: 1350 Ballantrae Ln McLean VA 22101 Office: 1575 Eye St NW Washington DC 20005

CRAIGIE, PETER CAMPBELL, religion educator; b. Lancaster, Eng., Aug. 18, 1938; s. Hugh Brechin and Lilia Campbell (Murray) C.; m. Elizabeth Alexander, Sept. 5, 1964; children: Cregor John, Gillian. M.A. with honors, U. Edinburgh, Scotland, 1965; M.Th., U. Aberdeen, Scotland, 1968; Ph.D., McMaster U., 1970. Asst. prof. dept. religion Carleton U., Ottawa, Ont., Can., 1970-71, McMaster U., 1971-74; assoc. prof. dept. religious studies U. Calgary, Alta., Can., 1974—, chmn. dept. religious studies, 1977—. Author: Commentary on the Book of Deuteronomy, 1976; contbr. articles to profl. jours. Mem. Am. Acad. Religion, Soc. Bibl. Lit., Canadian Soc. Bibl. Studies (sec.-treas. 1971-72, exec. sec. 1975-78). Home: 3605 6th St SW Calgary AB Canada Office: Dept Religion Univ Calgary 2500 University Dr Calgary AB Canada T2N 1N4

CRAIGIE, WALTER WILLIAMS, SR., investment broker-dealer; b. Richmond, Va., Nov. 7, 1904; s. Frank John and Mary Hooper (Williams) C.; m. Helen Pendleton Walker, June 19, 1926; children: Harriet Craigie Van Houten, Walter Willson, Carter W. Student pub. schs., Richmond; hon. doctorate, Randolph Macon Coll. Lic. securities dealer, Va., W.Va., N.Y., N.C., Calif. Clk. Nat. State & City Bank, Richmond, 1917-18; jr. dept. head Fed. Res. Bank, Richmond, 1918-22; gen. mgr. Richmond Car Works, 1922-27; sr. partner F. W. Craigie & Co. (Municipal bonds), Richmond, 1932-65; pres. Craigie Inc. (stocks and bonds), Richmond, 1965-72, chmn. bd., 1972-80, chmn. exec. com., 1980—. Former pres. Episcopal Churchmen Diocese Va., mem. diocesan task force; v.p., trustee St. John's Ch. Found., Richmond; trustee and hon. alumnus Randolph-Macon Coll.; hon. trustee Va. Union U.; trustee Richmond Meml. Hosp.; mem. advisory com. YWCA, Richmond. Mem. Richmond Soc. Fin. Analysts (former pres.), Investment Bankers Assn. Am. (former v.p.), Richmond C. of C. Clubs: Deep Run Hunt (Richmond) (former pres.); Commonwealth, Downtown, Bull and Bear. Office: 814 E Main St Richmond VA 23219

CRAIGMILE, DAVID FRANCIS, manufacturing company executive; b. Oak Park, Ill., June 6, 1928; s. Charles S. and Nellie M. (Truby) C.; m. Carol A. Maurer, Apr. 21, 1956; children: Deborah, Jennifer, Catherine, David, Charles, Nancy. B.C.S., Drake U., 1950; M.B.A., U. Pa., 1951. Ops. mgr. Bell & Howell Co., Chgo., 1961-65, mgr. camera prodn., 1965-66; v.p. mfg. Jostens, Inc., Mpls., 1966-70, Bell & Howell, Chgo., 1970-73; exec. v.p. ops. Skil Corp., Chgo., 1973-77, pres. U.S. Power Tool Group, 1977-80, exec. v.p., 1980-82, Elkay Mfg. Co., Oak Brook, Ill., 1982—. Vice chmn. DuPage Young Republicans, 1954-55; charter officer, dir. Hinsdale Jaycees, 1954-56; mem. Drake U. Alumni Fund Bd., 1972-76. Served with AUS, 1951-53. Mem. Midwest Indsl. Mgmt. Assn. (dir. 1971-73, 78—), Work-Factor Assos. Midwest. Roman Catholic. Club: Exmoor Country (Highland Park, Ill.). Home: 312 E Cherokee Ln Lake Forest IL 60045 Office: 2222 Camden Ct Oak Brook IL 60521

CRAIGMYLE, RONALD M., investment banker; b. Toronto, Ont., Can., June 19, 1896; s. James M. and Jessie (Gregory) C.; m. Louise de

Rochemont, Apr. 10, 1923; children—Ronald M., Mary Louise Magee, Robert de Rochemont. A.B., Columbia, 1920, B.S. in Bus, 1921. With Minsch, Monell & Co., 1920-24; partner Burley, Peabody & Craigmyle, N.Y.C., 1924-26, Craigmyle & Co. (later Craigmyle, Pinney & Co., then Fahnestock & Co., mems. N.Y. Stock Exchange), 1926—; ret. chmn. Giant Portland & Masonry Cement Co.; Vice pres. Intercollegiate Flying Assn., 1919-21. Mayor Village of Matinecock, N.Y., 1954-67; Trustee Columbia U., 1957-63. Mem. Psi Upsilon. Republican. Episcopalian. Clubs: Piping Rock; Met., Univ., N.Y. Stock Exchange Luncheon, Pilgrims Soc., St. Andrews Soc. (N.Y.C.); Beach (Palm Beach, Fla.); Creek, Everglades, Bath and Tennis. Home: Piping Rock Rd Box 321 Locust Valley NY 11560 Office: 110 Wall St New York NY 10005

CRAIN, BLUFORD WALTER, JR., architect; b. Longview, Tex., Jan. 31, 1914; s. Bluford Walter and Ethel (Smith) C.; m. Ann Lacy, Dec. 28, 1946; children: Lacy Crain, Bluford Walter III, Rogers Lacy. B.Arch., U. Tex., 1937; M.Arch., Harvard U., 1939. Partner Crain/Anderson, Inc., Houston and Longview, 1946—; exec. v.p. Rogers Lacy, Inc., Longview, 1947—; dir. Longview Nat. Bank. Mem. devel. bd. U. Tex., Austin; mem. adv. council Sch. Architecture Found. Served to lt. USNR, 1941-45. Fellow AIA (pres. NE Tex. chpt. 1957); mem. Tex. Soc. Architects (dir. 1966), Kappa Sigma. Presbyterian. Home: PO Box 2146 Longview TX 75601 Office: PO Box 352 Longview TX 75601

CRAIN, CULLEN MALONE, elec. engr.; b. Goodnight, Tex., Sept. 10, 1920; s. John Malone and Margaret Elizabeth (Gunn) C.; m. Virginia Raftery, Jan. 16, 1943; children—Michael Malone, Karen Elizabeth. B.S. in Elec. Engring, U. Tex., Austin, 1942, M.S., 1947, Ph.D., 1952. From instr. to asso. prof. elec. engring. U. Tex., 1943-57; group leader communications and electronics Rand Corp., Santa Monica, Calif., 1957-69, asso. head engring. and applied scis., 1969—; cons. to govt., 1958—. Author numerous papers in field. Pres. Austin chpt. Nat. Exchange Club, 1954, Santa Monica chpt., 1975. Served with USNR, 1944-46. Fellow IEEE; mem. Nat. Acad. Engring. Inventor microwave atmospheric refractometer. Home: 463 17th St Santa Monica CA 90402 Office: 1700 Main St Santa Monica CA 90406

CRAIN, MRS. G.D., publishing company executive; m. G.D. Crain Jr. (dec. Dec. 15, 1973). Asst. treas. Crain Communications Inc., Chgo., 1941-61, sec., 1943-74, treas., 1961-74, chmn. bd., 1974—. Office: Crain Communications Inc 740 N Rush St Chicago IL 60611

CRAIN, JAMES FRANCIS, telephone company executive; b. Leominster, Mass., Apr. 29, 1931; s. John Harold and Mary Adeline (McCann) C.; m. Marylin Elizabeth Premezzi, Sept. 19, 1954; children: Karen, Susan, Kevin. A.B., Columbia Coll., N.Y.C., 1953; certificate, Carlton Coll., Minn., 1967. Dir. placement Columbia Coll., 1955-68; gen. accounting mgr. New Eng. Tel. & Tel., Boston, 1968, gen. plant mgr., 1969-71, asst. v.p. personnel, 1972-75, treas., 1976-83, v.p. fin., 1983—. Bd. overseers Wellesley Inst.; bd. advs. grad. bus. program Simmons Coll.; trustee U. Mass., Cary Meml. Library, Lexington, Mass.; bd. dirs. Mass. Com. to Improve Quality of Work, Children's Hosp., Boston, Harvard Community Health Plan. Served with AUS, 1954-55. Recipient Bjorkwell prize Columbia Coll., 1953, prize for profl. bus. excellence Simmons Coll., 1976. Mem. Fin. Execs. Inst., Columbia Coll. Alumni, Macom Honor Soc. Democrat. Roman Catholic. Clubs: Treasurer's, Economic, Newcomer (Boston). Home: 68 Asbury St Lexington MA 02173 Office: Room 1801 185 Franklin St Boston MA 02107

CRAIN, JAMES LARRY, university president; b. Franklinton, La., July 16, 1935; s. Henry and Birdie Von (Blackwell) C.; m. Jean Etta Lott, Oct. 15, 1955; children: Ricky Lynn, Rita Ann, Randall Henry. B.S. in Biology, U. So. Miss., 1957, Ph.D. in Zoology, 1966; M.A., Stpehen F. Austin State U., 1963. Tchr. sci. Varnado High Sch., (La.), 1957-64; asst. prof., assoc. prof. Southeastern La. U., Hammond, 1966-72, 72-76, cons., biologist, 1972-74, pres., 1980—; asst. sec. La. Dept. Culture, Baton Rouge, 1976-78; sec. La. Dept. Culture, Recreation and Tourism, 1978-80; genetic counsel Sickle Cell Anemia Program, Hammond, 1974-75; dir. Natural Sci. Mus., Hammond, 1967-76. Mem. Arts Council, Hammond, 1982, Cultural Found., 1982, Friends of Cabildo, New Orleans, 1982, La. Hist. Assn., Baton Rouge, Old State Capitol Assocs. Named Citizen of Yr. Kiwanis, 1982; recipient award of merit for preservation of material culture S.E. La. Hist. Assn., 1981. Mem. Am. Assn. State Colls. and Univs., Northlake Mus. and Nature Ctr.; mem./ Am. Soc. Arms Collectors, Hammond C. of C. Democrat. Presbyterian. Club: Rotary. Home: 408 W Dakota St Hammond LA 70401 Office: Southeastern La U PO Box 784 Hammond LA 70402

CRAIN, JOHN WALTER, historian; b. Amarillo, Tex., July 11, 1944; s. John Clyde and Roma (McDowell) C.; m. Mary Hemingway, Aug. 18, 1973; 1 son, John Matthew. B.A., U. Tex., Austin, 1966; M.A., S.W. Tex. State U., 1970; cert. arts adminstrn., Harvard U., 1975; cert. mus. mgmt., U. Calif.-Berkeley, 1979. Dir. Star of the Republic Museum, Washington-on-the-Brazos, Tex., 1971-76, Dallas Hist. Soc., 1976—; cons. in field, 1971—. Mem. Am. Assn. Museums, Am. Assn. State and Local History, Tex. Assn. Museums, Tex. State Hist. Soc. Methodist. Club: Commerce. Office: PO Box 26038 Dallas TX 75226

CRAIN, RANCE, publisher, editor. Pres., editor-in-chief Crain's Chicago Bus., Chgo. Office: Crain's Chicago Business 740 Rush St Chicago IL 60611§

CRAM, DONALD JAMES, chemistry educator; b. Chester, Vt., April 22, 1919; s. William Moffet and Joanna (Shelley) C.; m. Jane Maxwell, Nov. 25, 1969. B.S., Rollins Coll., 1941; M.S., U. Nebr., 1942; Ph.D. (Nat. Research fellow), Harvard, 1947, U. Uppsala, 1977, D.Sci., U. So. Calif., 1983. Research chemist Merck and Co., 1942-45; asst. prof. chemistry UCLA, 1947-50, asso. prof., 1950-56, prof., 1956—; chem. cons. Upjohn Co., 1952—, Union Carbide Co., 1960-81, Eastman Kodak Co., 1981—; State Dept. exchange fellow to Inst. de Quimica, Nat. U. Mex., summer 1956; guest prof. U. Heidelberg, Germany, summer 1958; guest lectr., South Africa, 1967; Centenary lectr. Chem. Soc. London, 1976. Author: (with S.H. Pine, J.B. Hendrickson and G.S. Hammond) Organic Chemistry, 1960, 4th edit., 1980, Fundamentals of Carbanion Chemistry, 1965, (with John H. Richards and G.S. Hammond) Elements of Organic Chemistry, 1967, (with J.M. Cram) Essence of Organic Chemistry, 1977; Contbr.: chpts. to Applications of Biochemical Systems in Organic Chemistry; also articles in field of host-guest complexation chemistry, carbonium ions, stereochemistry, mold metabolites, large ring chemistry. Named Young Man of Yr. Calif. Jr. C. of C., 1954, Calif. Scientist of Yr., 1974; recipient award for creative work in synthetic organic chemistry Am. Chem. Soc., 1965, Arthur C. Cope award, 1974; Herbert Newby McCoy award, 1965, 75; award for creative research organic chemistry Synthetic Organic Chem. Mfrs. Assn., 1965; Am. Chem. Soc. fellow, 1947-48; Guggenheim fellow, 1954-55. Mem. Am. Chem. Soc., Nat. Acad. Scis., Am. Acad. Arts and Scis., Royal Soc. Chemistry, Sigma Xi, Lambda Chi Alpha. Club: San Onofre Surfing. Home: 1250 Roscomare Rd Los Angeles CA 90077

CRAM, REGINALD MAURICE, retired Air Force officer; b. Northfield, Vt., Apr. 29, 1914; s. Archie Rice and Beatrice (Cleveland) C.; m. Kathryn E. Mosher, June 29, 1937; children: Robin (Mrs. Paul Lualdi), Marilyn Jane (Mrs. Vcevold Strekalovsky). B.S., Norwich U., 1936, D.Mil. Sci. (hon.), 1974; postgrad., Boston U. Law Sch., 1937-38, Air Force Intelligence Sch., 1943, U.S. Army Command and Gen. Staff Coll., 1944, Nat. Art Sch., 1949, Armed Forces Staff Coll., 1951, State Dept. Fgn. Service Inst., 1961; M.A., U. Md., 1963. With Office Adj. Gen. Vt., 1938-41; asst. U.S. property and disbursing officer, State of Vt., 1946-47, commd. 2d lt. Cav., 1936; advanced through grades to maj. gen. USAF, 1968; with anti-submarine campaign USAAF, 1941-42; Asiatic-Pacific Theatre with USMC, 1943-45; plans and operations officer Hdqrs. USAF, 1947-51; sec. Can./U.S. Regional Planning Group, NATO, 1951-54; dir. plans 3d USAF, Eng., 1954-55; with Supreme Hdqrs. Allied Powers, Europe, 1955-57; comdr. Orientation Group USAF, 1957-61; with Orgn. Joint Chiefs of Staff, 1961-64; ret., 1964; dep. adj. gen. Vt., 1964-66, adj. gen., 1967-81. Past pres. Long Trail council Boy Scouts Am.; nat. dir. Am. Cancer Soc.; trustee Norwich U. Decorated Legion of Merit, Air medals D.S.M. Air Force, Joint Commendation medal, Air Force Commendation medal, Army Commendation medal; recipient Vt. Distinguished Service medal. Mem. N.G. Assn. U.S. (Disting. Service medal), N.G. Assn. Vt., Soc. Colonial Wars (dep. gov.-gen.), Ret. Officers Assn. (dir.), Am. Legion, VFW, Vt. Hist. Soc., Vt. Archeol. Soc., Theta Chi, Pi Sigma Alpha. Conglist. Clubs: Mason, Rotarian (past dist. gov.). Home: 936 S Prospect St Burlington VT 05401

CRAMBLETT, HENRY GAYLORD, pediatrician, virologist, educator; b. Scio, Ohio, Feb. 8, 1929; s. Carl Smith and Olive (Fulton) C.; m. Donna Jean Reese, June 16, 1960; children: Deborah Kaye, Betsy Diane. B.S., Mt. Union Coll., 1950; M.D., U. Cin., 1953. Diplomate: Am. Bd. Pediatrics, Am. Bd. Microbiology. Clin. research asso. Nat. Inst. Allergy and Infectious Diseases, Clin. Center, Bethesda, Md., 1955-57; faculty State U. Iowa, 1957-60, asst. prof., 1958-60; faculty Bowman Gray Sch. Medicine, 1960-64, prof. pediatrics, 1963-64, dir. virology lab., 1960-64; prof. pediatrics Ohio State U., Columbus, 1964—, prof. med. microbiology, 1966—, exec. dir. Children's Hosp. Research Found., 1964-73, chmn. dept. med. microbiology, 1966-73, dean Coll. Medicine, 1973-80, acting v.p. for med. affairs, 1974-80, v.p. health scis., 1980-83, Warner M. and Lora Kays Pomerene chair in medicine, 1982—; Mem. Ohio Med. Bd.; chmn. com. on cert., subcert. and recert. Am. Bd. Med. Specialists; mem. coms. on written exam., comprehensive qualifying evaluation program Nat. Bd. Med. Examiners; chmn. Accreditation Council Continuing Med. Edn.; mem. adv. com. on undergrad. med. evaluation; pres. Fedn. State Med. Bds.; bd. dirs. Ohio State U. Hosp., 1979-80. Recipient Hoffheimer prize U. Cin., 1953, Eben J. Carey award in anatomy, 1950. Fellow Am. Acad. Microbiology, AAAS; mem. Infectious Diseases Soc. Am., So. Soc. Pediatric Research (past pres.), Soc. Pediatric Research, Am. Pediatric Soc., Am. Acad. Pediatrics, Midwest Soc. Pediatric Research, Soc. Exptl. Biology and Medicine, Am. Soc. Microbiology, Alpha Omega Alpha. Research, publs. on etiologic assn. virus infections in illnesses of infants and children, estimation of importance of various viruses in morbidity and mortality in pediatric age group. Home: 2480 Sheringham Rd Columbus OH 43220 Office: 200 Adminstrn Center 370 W 9th Ave Ohio State U Columbus OH 43210

CRAMER, CHARLES LEONARD, economics educator; b. Chamois, Mo., Oct. 30, 1928; s. Charles C. and Matilda (Wenger) C.; m. Julia M. Koch, June 11, 1955; children: Christine, Keith, Caroline. B.S., U. Mo.-Columbia, 1950, M.S., 1954, Ph.D., 1960. Mem. faculty dept. agrl. econs. U. Mo., Columbia, 1960-71, chmn. dept., 1971-82, prof. agrl. econs., 1982—. Served with U.S. Army, 1950-52. Mem. Am. Agrl. Econs. Assn. Presbyterian. Lodge: Kiwanis. Home: 309 Defoe Dr Columbia MO 65201 Office: Univ Mo 200 Memford Hall Columbia MO

CRAMER, DALE LEWIS, economics educator; b. Dixon, Ill., June 25, 1924; s. Ray C. and Rebecca (Levan) C.; m. Hula Jean Bond, Aug. 30, 1946; children: Becky Cramer Oyler, Craig Alan, Randall Scott. B.S., Bradley U., 1949, M.A., 1951; Ph.D., La. State U., 1958. Asst. prof. econs. La. State U., 1953-54, U. Tex. at El Paso, 1955-57, asso. prof., 1957-58; asso. prof. econs. U. Ala., 1958-63, prof., 1963—, head dept., 1968-72, acting head dept., 1981-82. Contbr. articles to profl. jours. Served with AUS, 1943-46. Earhart Found. fellow, 1954-55. Mem. Am., So. econ. assns., AAUP, Omicron Delta Epsilon, Beta Gamma Sigma. Home: 103 Riverdale Tuscaloosa AL 35406 Office: Univ Alabama University AL 35486

CRAMER, DOUGLAS SCHOOLFIELD, broadcasting executive; b. Louisville, Aug. 22; s. Douglas Schoolfield and Pauline (Compton) C.; m. Joyce Haber, Sept. 25, 1966 (div. 1973); children: Douglas Schoolfield, III, Courtney Sanford. Student, Northwestern U., 1949-50, Sorbonne, Paris, 1951; B.A., U. Cin., 1953; M.F.A., Columbia U., 1954. Prodn. asst. Radio City Music Hall, N.Y.C., 1950-51; with script dept. Metro-Goldwyn-Mayer, 1952; mng. dir. Cin. Playhouse, 1953-54; instr. Carnegie Inst. Tech., 1955-56; TV supr. Procter & Gamble, 1956-59; broadcast supr. Ogilvy, Benson & Mather, 1959-62; v.p. program devel. ABC, 1962-66, 20th Century-Fox-TV, Los Angeles, 1966-68; exec. v.p. in charge prodn. Paramount TV, 1968-71; ind. producer, pres. Douglas S. Cramer Co., 1971—; exec. v.p. Aaron Spelling Prodns., 1976—. Exec. producer: Bridget Loves Bernie, CBS-TV, 1972-73, QB VII, 1973-74, Dawn: Portrait of a Teenage Runaway, NBC-TV, 1976; co-exec. producer: Love Boat, ABC, 1977-84, Vegas, ABC, 1978-81, Wonder Woman, ABC, 1975-77, CBS, 1977-78; Co-exec. producer: Dynasty, 1981-84, Matt Huston, 1982-84, Hotel, 1983-84; co-exec. producer, ABC, 1981; Author: plays Call of Duty, 1953, Love Is A Smoke, 1957, Whose Baby Are You, 1963. Bd. dirs. dance presentations Los Angeles Music Center; trustee MOCA, Los Angeles. Served with U.S. Army, 1954. Mem. Beta Theta Pi. Club: Univ. (N.Y.C.). Office: Warner Hollywood Studios 1041 N Formosa Ave Los Angeles CA 90046

CRAMER, EDWARD M., lawyer, performing rights licensing organization executive; b. N.Y.C., May 27, 1925; s. Israel and Elsie (Neuman) C.; m. Robin Metzger, June 13, 1982; children by previous marriage: Evin Joyce, Marjorie Sue Cramer Thistle, Charles Harris. A.B., Columbia U., 1947; LL.B. with distinction, Cornell U., Ithaca, N.Y., 1950; LL.M., NYU, 1953; H.H.D. (hon.), Lincoln Coll. (Ill.), 1982. Bar: N.Y. 1950, U.S. Supreme Ct 1950. Teaching fellow NYU Sch. Law, 1950-51; with firm Rosenman, Colin, Kaye, Petshek, Freund & Emil, N.Y.C., 1951-60; pvt. practice law, also mem. firm Cramer & Hoffinger, N.Y.C., 1960-68; pres., chief exec. officer Broadcast Music, Inc., 1968—; Treas. Copyright Soc. U.S., 1963-68, 78-79, bd. editors bull., 1953-63. Pres. Urban League N.J., 1955; v.p. Congregation Adas Emuno. Served with USNR, 1943-46. Recipient Man of Year award B'nai B'rith, 1978. Mem. Nat. Music Council (v.p.), Broadcast Pioneers (pres. 1984), Order of Coif. Jewish. Home: 254 Chestnut St Englewood NJ 07631 Office: 320 W 57th St New York NY 10019

CRAMER, HAROLD, lawyer; b. Phila., June 16, 1927; s. Aaron Harry and Blanche (Greenberg) C.; m. Geraldine Hassuk, July 14, 1954; 1 dau., Patricia Gail. A.B., Temple U., 1948; LL.B. cum laude, U. Pa., 1951. Bar: Pa. bar 1951. Law clk. to judge Common Pleas Ct. No. 2, 1953; mem. law faculty U. Pa., 1954; asso. firm Shapiro, Rosenfeld, Stalberg & Cook, 1955-56, partner, 1956-67; partner firm Mesirov, Gelman, Jaffe & Cramer, Phila., 1974-77, Mesirov, Gelman, Jaffee, Cramer & Jamieson, 1977—; instr. Nat. Inst. Trial Advocacy, 1970—. Co-author: Trial Advocacy, 1968; contbr. articles to profl. jours. Chmn. bd. Eastern Pa. Psychiat. Hosp., 1974-81, Grad. Hosp., 1975—; trustee Fedn. Jewish Agys., Jewish Publ. Soc. Served to 1st lt. U.S. Army, 1951-53. Decorated Bronze Star. Fellow Am. Bar Found.; mem. Phila. Bar Found. (trustee), ABA, Pa. Bar Assn. (ho. of dels. 1966-75, 78—, bd. govs. 1975-78), Phila. Bar Assn. (bd. govs. 1967-69, chmn. 1969, vice chancellor 1970, chancellor 1972, editor The Shingle 1970—), Am. Law Inst., U. Pa. Law Alumni Soc. (bd. mgrs. 1959-64, pres. 1968-70), Order of Coif (past chpt. pres., nat. exec. com. 1973-76), Tau Epsilon Rho (chancellor Phila. grad. chpt. 1960-62). Clubs: Locust, Philmont Country. Home: 728 Pine St Philadelphia PA 19106 Office: Fidelity Bldg 123 S Broad St Philadelphia PA 19109

CRAMER, HERBERT, transportation service company executive; b. Mt. Vernon, N.Y., Sept. 27, 1932; s. Herbert and Mary (Arterburn) C.; m. Adrienne Joan Henry, Nov. 9, 1957; children: Thomas, Patricia, Stephen, Kathleen, David. B.B.A., Iona Coll., New Rochelle, N.Y., 1956. Accountant Peat, Marwick, Mitchell & Co., C.P.A.s, N.Y.C., 1956-62; controller United Artists Records,Inc., N.Y.C., 1962-65; v.p. Hudson Gen. Corp., Gt. Neck, N.Y., 1965-79, pres., 1979—. Address: Hudson Gen Corp 111 Great Neck Rd Great Neck NY 11022

CRAMER, JOHN GLEASON, JR., physics educator, experimental physicist; b. Houston, Oct. 24, 1934; s. John Gleason and Frances Ann (Sakwitz) C.; m. Pauline Ruth Bond, June 2, 1961; children: Kathryn Elizabeth, John Gleason III, Karen Melissa. B.A., Rice U., 1957, M.A., 1959, Ph.D. in Physics, 1961. Postdoctoral fellow Ind. U., Bloomington, 1961-63, asst. prof., 1963-64; asst. prof. physics U. Wash., Seattle, 1964-68, assoc. prof., 1968-74, prof., 1974—, dir. nuclear physics lab., 1983—; W. Ger. Bundesministerium guest prof. U. Munich, 1971-72; mem. program adv. com. Los Alamos Meson Physics Facility, Los Alamos Nat. Lab., 1976-77; program adviser-cons. Lawrence Berkeley Lab., Calif., 1979-82. Contbr. articles to tech. and popular publs. Fellow Am. Phys. Soc. (exec. com. div. nuclear physics 1981-83). Home: 7002 51st Ave NE Seattle WA 98115 Office: Dept Physics FM-15 U Wash Seattle WA 98195 *When I was in about the eighth grade of junior high school I made the most important discovery of my life. I discovered that, for some reason, society was willing to pay respectable salaries to a certain group of people for doing what I would gladly do for free. These people were research scientists, and what they did was to discover how the universe really worked. From that point on I channeled all my effort into joining this select group, and I have been having a wonderful time ever since.*

CRAMER, JOHN MCNAIGHT, lawyer; b. Lewistown, Pa., Sept. 23, 1941; s. John Mumma and Elaine Elizabeth (McNaight) C.; m. Susan Oakman, Nov. 26, 1966; children: Natalie, Daniel, Melinda. A.B., Junista Coll., 1963, 1963. Bar: Pa. 1968. Law clk. U.S. Dist. Ct. So. Dist. N.Y., 1966-67; assoc. Reed Smith Shaw & McClay, Pitts., 1967-76, ptnr., 1976—. Mem. editorial staff: Harvard Law Rev. Trustee Junista Coll., Huntington, Pa., 1981—. Mem. ABA, Pa. Bar Assn., Fed. Bar Assn., Allegheny County Bar Assn., Acad. Trial Lawyers Allegheny County. Democrat. Presbyterian. Club: Harvard-Yale-Princeton (Pitts.). Home: 8 Robin Rd Pittsburgh PA 15217 Office: 747 Union Trust Bldg Pittsburgh PA 15230

CRAMER, JOHN SCOTT, banker; b. Charlotte, N.C., Dec. 10, 1930; s. Stuart Warren, Jr. and Julia (Scott) C.; m. Nancy Arnott, Aug. 9, 1952; children: Julia Baxter, Alice Arnott. A.B., U. N.C., 1953. With Wachovia Bank & Trust Co., 1955—, asst. v.p., Charlotte, 1958-61, v.p., 1961-64, sr. v.p., bd. mgrs., 1964-71, exec. v.p., head banking div., Winston-Salem, N.C., 1971-74, vice chmn. bd., head fiduciary div., 1974—, also dir.; vice chmn. bd., dir. The Wachovia Corp.; dir. John M. Scott & Co., Shadowline, Inc., Chatham Mfg. Co., Linville Resorts, Inc., Cramer Realty Co. Trustee Campbell Coll. Trust Edn. Found., Inc.; vice-chmn. bd. N.C. Sch. Arts; mem. central selection com. J. Motley Morehead Found.; active numerous civic, ednl. and service orgns. Served to 1st lt. USAF, 1953-55. Mem. Am. Bankers Assn., Res. City Bankers Assn., Necomen Soc. Am. (chmn. N.C. com.), Sigma Alpha Epsilon. Clubs: Linville (N.C.) Golf; Old Town (Winston-Salem). Home: 2700 Reynolds Dr Winston-Salem NC 27104 Office: Wachovia Bank & Trust Co 3d and Main Sts Winston-Salem NC 27101 also PO Box 3099 Winston-Salem NC 27102

CRAMER, MORGAN JOSEPH, JR., internat. mgmt. exec.; b. Monessen, Pa., Oct. 6, 1906; s. Morgan J. and Cecilia (Michaels) C.; m. Miriam Fuchs, Jan. 28, 1933; 1 dau., Cynthia Jeanette. Student mech. engring., Lehigh U., 1924-27. Various positions export and govt. sales operations P. Lorillard Co., 1931-46, export mgr., 1946-49, export and govt. sales mgr., 1949-54, dir. govt. operations, 1954-60, v.p., dir. internat. operations, 1960-61, dir., exec. com., pres., chief exec. officer, 1962-65; pres., chief exec. officer Royal Crown Cola Internat., Ltd., 1966-69, chmn. bd., chief exec. officer, 1969-70; v.p. internat. operations Royal Crown Cola Co., 1966-70; pres. Morgan J. Cramer Assos., Inc., N.Y.C., 1970—. Trustee N.Y. Polyclinic Hosp., 1960—, Lehigh U., 1973—; bd. dirs. Greater N.Y. Fund, 1960—. Served as 1st lt. Q.M.C. AUS, 1943-46. Recipient commendation medal OQMG, 1946. Mem. Def. Supply Assn., Advt. Council, Nat. Fgn. Trade Council, Lehigh U. Alumni Assn. (pres. 1972-73). Clubs: Marco Polo, Sky, Lehigh U. (N.Y.C.); Pelham (N.Y.) Country; Saucon Valley (Bethlehem, Pa.). Home and Office: PO Box 18075 Fountain Hills AZ 85268

CRAMER, RICHARD CHARLES, artist, educator; b. Appleton, Wis., Aug. 14, 1932; s. Joseph S. and Mildred (Kuck) C.; m. Carol Markel, Apr. 4, 1970. B.F.A., Layton Sch. Art, 1954; B.S., U. Wis.-Milw., 1960, M.S., 1961, M.F.A., 1962. Art instr. U.S. Army Spl. Services, Ft. Huachuca, Ariz., 1955-57; grad. instr. U. Wis., Madison, 1960-62; asst. prof. art Elmira Coll., N.Y., 1962-66; prof. painting Tyler Sch. Art, Temple U., Phila., 1966—; vis. artist SUNY-Oswego, 1982, U. Wis.-Milw., 1982. Exhibited one-man shows, Arnot Art Mus., Elmira, N.Y., 1964, Pa. Acad. Fine Arts, Phila., 1978, New Gallery Contemporary Art, Cleve., 1980, Eric Makler Gallery, Phila., 1981, GHJ, N.Y.C., 1983; group shows Contemporary Drawings, Phila. Mus. Art, 1979, Smithsonian Inst. traveling exhibit, 1979, Phila. Coll. Art, 1980, Inst. Contemporary Art, Boston, 1981, Cranbrook Acad. Art Mus. Recipient McGraw Rock award Elmira Coll., 1963; redipient Prize Munson-Williams Proctor Inst., 1965; recipient research awards Temple U., 1972, 74, 75, 78. Mem. AAUP, Coll. Art Assn. Home: 723 Chestnut St Philadelphia PA 19106 Office: Tyler Sch Art Temple U Beech and Penrose Aves Philadelphia PA 19126

CRAMER, RICHARD LOUIS, editor; b. Los Angeles, Apr. 5, 1947; s. Martin Michael and Charlotte Sonia (Kessel) C.; m. Arlene Renee Jacobs, June 15, 1969; children: Matthew Hunter, Brandon Lloyd. B.S.B.A., Calif. State U., 1969. Editor-in-chief Environ. Quality mag., Los Angeles, 1970-73; editor East/West Network, Los Angeles, 1973-75; editor-in-chief Denver mag., 1975-76; sr. editor Los Angeles mag., 1976-77; West coast editor Playboy mag., Los Angeles, 1977; editor-in-chief, asst. pub. Oui mag., Los Angeles, 1977-80; pres. FourWay Communications, West Los Angeles, Calif., 1981—. Served with USAFR, 1966-70. Mem. Am. Soc. Journalists and Authors. Office: 2052 Cotner Ave West Los Angeles CA 90025

CRAMER, ROBERT ELI, geography educator; b. Washington, June 19, 1919; s. John W. and Minnie (Smith) C.; m. Margery Fay Reeser, Dec. 31, 1941; children: Judith Fay, Barbara E., Timothy R. A.B., Ohio U., 1943; S.M., U. Chgo., 1947, Ph.D., 1952. Cartographic engr.

Aero Chart and Info. Center, St. Louis, 1942, 45-46, cartography cons., summer 1956; instr. geography J.S. Morton Jr. Coll., Cicero, Ill., 1947-50; asst. prof. Memphis State Coll., 1950-51; sr. indsl. research analyst Directorate of Intelligence USAF, Washington, 1951-54; prof. geography East Carolina Coll., Greenville, 1954—, chmn. dept., 1962-76; dir. East Carolina U. semester in Costa Rica, 1977, 79, 80, 81, East Carolina U. semester in Morocco, 1982. Author: Manufacturing Structure of the Cicero District, Metropolitan Chicago, 1952, A Work Book in Essentials of Cartography and Mapping, 1963, rev. edit., 1976, A Work Book in Earth and Man, 1967, Work book in Essentials of Map Reading and Interpretation, 1969, North Carolina-A Geographical Survey, 1976, 2d edit., 1980, Map Reading, 1980; Contbr. articles to profl. jours. Mem. tech. adv. com. area devel. Gov. N.C. Spl. Adv. Com., 1960—; mem. N.C. Adv. Bd. on Peace Corps, Spl. Adv. Com. Gov. N.C., 1962. Served with USAAF, 1943-44. Japan Soc. for Promotion of Scis. research scholar, 1977-78. Mem. Assn. Am. Geographers, Nat. Council Geog. Edn. (N.C. coordinator geography, mem. exec. bd. 1962—), N.C. Geog. Soc. (chmn. 1971-73), Gamma Theta Upsilon (internat. pres. 1971-73). Home: 1408 Evergreen Dr Greenville NC 27834

CRAMER, ROBERT VERN, college president; b. Fayetteville, Ark., Jan. 6, 1933; s. Paul and Fern (Way); m. Joan Sullivan, Sept. 6, 1953; children: Paula Jo, Melinda Kay, John Aaron. A.B., Monmouth (Ill.) Coll., 1954; M.A., U. Conn., 1964, Ph.D., 1965. Tchr. Monmouth Jr. High Sch., 1954-56; prin. Vandalia (Ill.) Elementary Sch., 1956-57; dir. publicity and publs. Monmouth Coll., 1957-59; dir. publs. and pub. information, also instr. journalism Millikin U., Decatur, Ill., 1959-61; v.p. Old Sturbridge (Mass.) Village, 1961-64; asst. dean, instr. Sch. Edn., U. Conn., 1964-65; v.p. Hanover (Ind.) Coll., 1965-68; pres. Northland Coll., Ashland, Wis., 1968-71, Carroll Coll., Waukesha, Wis., 1971—; Dir. Aeroshade Inc., Waukesha., Heritage Bank, Milw.; Vice pres. Wis. Found. Ind. Colls., 1969-71, pres., 1971-73, treas., 1973-76, sec., 1979-83; commr. Commn. Instns. Higher Edn., North Central Assn., 1972-76; Bd. dirs. Wis. Assn. Ind. Colls. and Univs., 1974-82, v.p., 1973-75; bd. dirs. Council of Ind. Colls., 1977—, chmn. bd. dirs., 1983—; sec. Council Advancement Ind. Colls., 1979-81, vice chmn., 1981—; bd. dirs. Central States Coll. Assn., pres., 1975-77. Contbr. articles to profl. jours. Bd. dirs. Waukesha United Way, 1975-78, Waukesha Symphony, 1972-76, Waukesha Meml. Hosp., 1973-82, Lad Lake Residential Treatment Center for Emotionally Disturbed Boys, 1974-78, Wis. Council on Econ. Edn., 1976-79, Milw. chpt. ARC, 1973-81; vice chmn. Milw. chpt. ARC, 1978-80; mem. nexus com. Presbyn. Coll. Union, 1973-83; bd. dirs. Am. Council Edn., 1983—; sec. Presbyn. Coll. Union, 1977-79, pres., 1979-81. Recipient Outstanding Young Alumnus award Monmouth Coll., 1968, Disting. Alumni award, 1980. Mem. Wis. Assn. Higher Edn. (exec. com., sec. 1972-73, pres. 1973-74), Delta Sigma Nu, Phi Delta Kappa, Theta Chi. Clubs: University (Milw.); Merrill Hills Country (Waukesha). Home: 115 S East Ave Waukesha WI 53186

CRAMER, WILLIAM ANTHONY, biophysics educator; b. N.Y.C., June 11, 1938; s. Robert and Sylvia (Blumstein) C.; m. Hanni Aebersold, June 11, 1964; children: Rebecca, Jean-Marc, Gabrielle, Nicholas. B.S., M.I.T., 1959; M.S., U. Chgo., 1960, Ph.D., 1965. NSF post doctoral fellow U. Calif., San Diego, 1965-67, research asso., 1967-68; asst. prof. dept. biol. scis. Purdue U., West Lafayette, Ind., 1968-73, asso. prof., 1973-78, prof., 1978—; mem. molecular biology panel NSF, 1978-80, head panel predoctoral fellowships in biophysics and biochemistry, 1979; mem. panel competitive grants USDA, 1983. Editor: Archives Biochemistry and Biophysics, 1979—; Contbr. articles to profl. jours. Research career devel. award NIH, 1970-75; EMBO fellow U. Amsterdam, 1974-75. Mem. Am. Soc. Biol. Chemists, Biophysical Soc. Office: Dept Biol Sci Purdue U West Lafayette IN 47907

CRAMER, WILLIAM F., capitol good executive; b. Oak Park, Ill., Aug. 9, 1923; s. Alfred W. and Flora M. (Countier) C.; m. Nancy Elizabeth Ward, Nov. 18, 1944; children: William F., Kenneth A. B.S.M.E., U. Tex., 1950. Pres., chief exec. officer Ozone Industries, Inc., N.Y.C., 1972-75; group v.p. Joy Mfg. Co., Pitts., 1975-76, sr. v.p., 1976-78, exec. v.p., 1978; pres., chief operating officer Joy Indsl. Equipment Co., Pitts., 1978—; v.p., gen. mgr., various tech. divs., dir. Service Tech. Corp. and LTV Aerospace Co., Dallas, 1967-72, Wheeling Machine Products Co., W.Va., 1977—. Served to 1st lt. U.S. Army, 1940-46; PTO. Republican. Club: Optimist (pres. 1957-60). Office: Joy Industrial Equipment Co 301 Grant St Pittsburgh PA 15219 *

CRAMER, WILLIAM SMITH, physicist; b. Frederick, Md., Aug. 25, 1914; s. John William and Minnie Agnes (Smith) C.; m. Patricia Ann Parker, Nov. 27, 1947; children: Marian Patricia Cramer Wood, Ann Roberta Cramer Sills. B.S., Ursinus Coll., 1937; ScM., Brown U., 1938, Ph.D., 1948. Instr. math. U. Md., 1938-39; instr. Pikeville (Ky.) Coll., 1939-40; physicist Naval Ordnance Lab., Silver Spring, Md., 1942-56, Office Naval Research, Washington, 1956-66, David W. Taylor Naval Ship Research and Devel. Center, Bethesda, Md., 1966-76; v.p. Mar Assocs., Inc., Rockville, Md., 1976-83. Assoc. editor: Jour. Acoustical Soc. Am, 1959-62, 72-83; Contbr. articles profl. jours. Fellow Acoustical Soc. Am. (mem. exec. council 1966-69, v.p. 1975-76); mem. Phys. Soc. Am., Sigma Xi. Home: 11512 Colt Terr Silver Spring MD 20902

CRAMP, DONALD ARTHUR, hospital administrator; b. Meaford, Ont., Can., Dec. 23, 1936; s. Reginald Graham and Sarah Agnus (Robinson) C.; m. Lynda Maria D'Acunto, Feb. 14, 1970; 1 son, Donald Arthur. B.A., U. Western Ont., 1960; M.Sc., Columbia U., 1962. With Bank of Am., San Francisco, 1962-64; with Gen. Motors Corp., Oshawa, Ont., 1964-66; asst. adminstr. South Nassau Communities Hosp., Oceanside, N.Y., 1966-70; dir. Highland View Hosp., Cleve., 1970-71; sr. v.p. Cuyahoga County Hosp. Systems, 1971-76; exec. dir. Univ. Hosp., U. Louisville, 1976-80; asst. v.p. Ohio State U. Hosps., Columbus, 1980-84; exec. dir. Univ. Hosps., Columbus, 1980-84; pres. U. Alta. Hosps., Edmonton, Can., 1984—; asst. prof. Sch. Medicine, Case Western Res. U., Cleve., 1970-76, Sch. Allied Med. Professions, Ohio State U., 1981—; guest lectr. N.Y. Sch. Adminstrv. Medicine, Columbia U., 1966-70. Contbr. to profl. publs. Bd. dirs. Nassau Heart Assn., 1967-70. Fellow Am. Public Health Assn., Am. Coll. Hosp. Adminstrs.; mem. Am. Hosp. Assn. (chmn. research and publ., public gen. sect. 1971—), Beta Theta Pi. Club: Nat. Exchange (dir. 1967-70). Home: 171 Wolf Willow Crescent Edmonton ABCanada T5T 1T3

CRAMPTON, BRUCE SIDNEY, professional golfer; b. Sydney, Australia, Sept. 28, 1935; s. Hector Arnold and Beatrice Any (Foster) C.; m. Joan Mary Findlay, Dec. 21, 1963; children—Jay Arnold, Roger Bruce. Certificate, Canterbury (N.S.W.) Boy's High Sch., 1952. Amateur golfer in, Australia, 1949-53, rep. Australia against New Zealand, 1953, profl. golfer, 1953—, Am. Golf Classic, 1973, Houston Open, 1975; represented Australia in Can. Cuo Matches, 1957, 63, 64, 72; mem. All-Am. Golf Team, 1970, 72, 73. Mem. profl. golfers assns. Am., Australia. Winner Australian Open Championship, 1956, Far East Open Championship, 1959, Milw. Open Championship 1961, Motor City Open Championship, 1962, Tex. Open Championship, 1964, Bing Crosby Nat. Pro-Amateur Tournament, 1965; Colonial National Invitational, 1965, 500 Festival Open, 1965, West End Classic, 1968, Hawaiian Open, 1969, Westchester Classic, 1970, Western Open, 1971, Phoenix Open, 1973, Dean Martin Tucson Open, 1973, Houston Open, 1973. Home: 7107 Spanky Branch Dr Dallas TX 75248 Office: 14110 Dallas North Pkwy Suite 100 Dallas TX 75240

CRAMPTON, CHARLES GREGORY, history educator; b. Kankakee, Ill., Mar. 22, 1911; s. Charles C. and Carrie (Beecher) C.; m. Mary Helen Patrick Walters, 1978; children: Patricia, Juanita. A.B., U. Calif. at Berkeley, 1935, M.A., 1936, Ph.D., 1941. Teaching asst. history U. Calif. at Berkeley, 1937-40; spl. agt. FBI, 1943-45; depot historian Calif. Q.M. Depot, Oakland, 1944-45; prof. history U. Utah, 1945-79, Duke research prof., 1972-76, dir. Western History Center, 1966-68; Rockefeller Found. travelling fellow Latin Am., 1941-42, 48-49; vis. prof. U. Panama, 1955. Author: Outline History of the Glen Canyon Region 1776-1922, 1959, Standing Up Country, The Canyon Lands of Utah and Arizona, 1964, Land of Living Rock: The Grand Canyon and the High Plateaus, Arizona, Utah, Nevada, 1972, The Zunis of Cibola, 1977; Editor: Yosemite and the High Sierra, 1957; also articles. Mem. Phi Alpha Theta (pres. 1949-50). Home: 1342 Hogan Circle Saint George UT 84770

CRAMPTON, SCOTT PAUL, lawyer; b. Cleve., Sept. 1, 1913; s. Paul Scott and Mary Runnells (Fayram) C.; m. Harriet Yenne, Jan. 12, 1963; children: Don Paul, Scott Charles, Susan Runnells; stepchildren—Lucinda Ann Lommasson, Louis Harlan Lommasson. B.A. cum laude, Am. U., 1935; LL.B., George Washington U., 1939. Bar: D.C. 1938. Practiced with firm George E.H. Goodner, Washington, 1939-51; ptnr. firm Prince, Taylor & Crampton, Washington, 1951-61, Worth & Crampton, 1961-71; asst. atty. gen. tax div. U.S. Dept. Justice, Washington, 1971-76; ptnr. firm Hamel, Park, McCabe & Saunders, Washington, 1976-79; of counsel firm Bogan & Freeland, Washington, 1979-83; ptnr. Macdonald, McInerny, Guandolo, Jordan & Crampton, Washington, 1983—. Mem. Am. Bar Assn. (past chmn. sect. taxation 1969-70), Phi Alpha Delta. Clubs: Kiwanian., Metropolitan, Nat. Lawyers (Washington). Home: 11701 River Dr Lorton VA 22079 Office: 1090 Vermont Ave NW Washington DC 20005

CRAMPTON, STUART JESSUP BIGELOW, physicist, educator; b. N.Y.C., Nov. 3, 1936; s. Henry Edward and Harriet Elizabeth (Jessup) C.; m. Susan Harris, Dec. 29, 1961; children: David Stuart Jessup, Rebecca Lynn, Alexandra Lee. B.A., Williams Coll., 1958, Worcester Coll., Oxford (Eng.) U., 1960, M.A., 1965; Ph.D., Harvard U., 1964. NSF postdoctoral fellow Harvard U., 1964-65; mem. faculty Williams Coll., 1965—, prof. physics, 1975—, Barclay Jermain prof. natural philosophy, 1979—, chmn. dept. physics, 1970-77, chmn. dept. physics and astronomy, 1977-80; vis. prof. U. Paris VI, 1982-83; mem. grants adv. com. Research Corp.; cons. Hughes Research Labs. Author papers in field. Recipient NSF Faculty Profl. Devel. award, 1977-78; NATO sr. postdoctoral research fellow, 1975; grantee Nat. bur. Standards, NSF, Office Naval Research, NASA. Fellow Am. Phys. Soc.; mem. Am. Assn. Physics Tchrs., Sigma Xi, Sigma Phi. Episcopalian. Home: 54 Grandview Dr Williamstown MA 01267 Office: Bronfman Sci Center Williams Coll Williamstown MA 02167

CRAMTON, ROGER CONANT, lawyer, legal educator; b. Pittsfield, Mass., May 18, 1929; s. Edward Allen and Dorothy Stewart (Conant) C.; m. Harriet Cutter Haseltine, June 29, 1952; children: Ann, Charles, Peter, Cutter. A.B., Harvard U., 1950; J.D., U. Chgo., 1955. Bar: Vt. 1956, Mich. 1964, N.Y. State 1979. Law clk. to S.R. Waterman, U.S. Ct. of Appeals for 2d Circuit, 1955-56; to Harold H. Burton, U.S. Supreme Ct., 1956-57; asst. prof. U. Chgo., 1957-61; assoc. prof. U. Mich. Law Sch., 1961-64, prof., 1964-70; chmn. Adminstrv. Conf. of U.S., 1970-72; asst. atty. gen. Justice Dept., 1972-73; dean Cornell U. Law Sch., Ithaca, N.Y., 1973-80; Robert S. Stevens prof., 1973—; Mem. U.S. Commn. on Revision Fed. Ct. Appellate System, 1973-75; bd. dirs. U.S. Legal Services Corp., 1975-79, chmn. bd., 1975-78. Author: (with others) Conflict of Laws, 3d edit, 1981; also articles.; editor: Jour. Legal Edn., 1981—. Mem. Am. Bar Assn., Am. Law Inst., Assn. Am. Law Schs. (1985), Am. Acad. Arts and Scis., Order of Coif, Phi Beta Kappa. Republican. Conglist. Club: Ithaca Yacht. Home: 49 Highgate Circle Ithaca NY 14850

CRANCH, EDWARD TITUS, college dean, engineer; b. Bklyn., Nov. 15, 1922; s. Clarence E. and Mary Emily (Smith) C.; m. Virginia Mae Harrison, Mar. 8, 1945; children: Virginia, Edmund, Timothy. Student, Newark Coll. Engring., 1941-43; B.S. in Mech. Engring., Cornell U., 1945, Ph.D., 1951. Asst. prof. Cornell U., Ithaca, N.Y., 1951-54, assoc. prof., 1954-56, prof. and head mechanics dept., 1956-64, prof. and head theoretical and applied mechanics dept., 1966-68, assoc. dean, 1967-72, dean engring., 1972-78; pres. Worcester Poly. Inst., Mass., 1978—; dir. Xtek Corp., Cin., Tompkins County Trust Co., Ithaca. Contbr. articles on applied mechanics to tech. jours. Bd. dirs. Albany Med. Ctr., N.Y., Latin Am. scholarship program of Am. Univs. NSF fellow, 1958-59, 64-65. Fellow ASME; mem. ASTM, Am. Soc. Engring. Edn., Soc. Exptl. Stress Analysis, Sigma Xi, Tau Beta Phi, Phi Kappa Phi. Office: Office of Pres Worcester Poly Inst West of Inst Worcester MA 01609

CRANDALL, DELMAR WESLEY (DEL), professional baseball manager; b. Ont., Can., Mar. 5, 1950. Player Boston Braves, Nat. League, 1949-50, Milw. Braves, Nat. League, 1953-63, San Francisco Giants, Nat. League, 1964, Pitts. Pirates, Nat. League, 1965, Cleve. Indians, Am. League, 1966; in pvt. bus., 1967-68, mgr., 1969-70, Evansville, Am. Assn., 1971-72, Milw. Brewers, Am. League, 1972-75, Salinas, Calif. League, 1976-77; coach Calif. Angeles, Am. League, 1977; mgr. Albuquerque, Pacific Coast League, 1978-83, Seattle Mariners, Am. League, 1983—; played World Series, 1957, 58; mem. World Series winning team, 1957. Office: Seattle Mariners PO Box 4100 100 S King St Suite 300 Seattle WA 98104 *

CRANDALL, KENNETH HARTLEY, cons. geologist; b. Spencer, Iowa, Feb. 10, 1904; s. Walter Gove and Gertrude (Robbins) C.; m. Claire Wofford, Oct. 17, 1929 (dec. Nov. 1974); children—Kenneth Hartley, William Wofford; m. Frances Lamar Lund, Sept. 5, 1977. A.B., Stanford, 1924. Vice pres. exploration, dir. Standard Oil Co. Calif., San Francisco, 1950-69; cons. geologist; cons. prof. Stanford, 1969-79; dir. Callahan Mining Corp., Phoenix. Fellow Geol. Soc. Am.; mem. Am. Inst. Profl. Geologists, Am. Assn. Petroleum Geologists (pres. 1969-70, hon. mem. 1973—, Sidney Powers Meml. award), Calif. Acad. Sci., Phi Beta Kappa, Sigma Xi. Clubs: Pacific Union, Stock Exchange (San Francisco); Claremont Country (Oakland); San Francisco. Home: 209 Crocker Ave Piedmont CA 94610

CRANDALL, LEE WALTER, civil and structural engr.; b. Hartford, Wis., July 26, 1913; s. Walter R. and Kathryn (Canar) C.; m. Gladys Lucile Wells, Dec. 31, 1938; 1 son, Gordon Lee. B.S., U. Wis., 1936, M.S., 1937; Ph.D., Stanford U., 1952. Instr. civil engring. U. Colo., 1937-38, asst. prof., 1943-46, asso. prof., 1947-48; asst. structural engr. U.S. Bur. Reclamation, Denver, 1939-42; asso. prof. civil engring. U. Wis.-Madison, 1948-57, prof., 1957-80, prof. emeritus civil and environ. engring., 1980—; cons. engr. in field. Fulbright research scholar State Inst. Tech. Research, Helsinki, Finland, 1953-54. Mem. ASCE, Nat. Soc. Profl. Engrs., Am. Soc. Engring. Edn., Forest Products Research Soc., Am. Forestry Assn., Sigma Xi. Club: Tech. (pres. Madison, Wis. 1976-77). Home: 1008 Beloit Ct Madison WI 53705 Office: 2228 Engring Bldg U Wis Madison WI 53706

CRANDALL, MICHAEL GRAIN, mathematician, educator; b. Baton Rouge, La., Nov. 29, 1940; s. Bruce Elbridge and Irene (Anderson) C.; m. Sharon Lee Metcalf, Sept. 8, 1962; children: Elizabeth Catherine, Brady Neil, Ian Michael. B.S., U. Calif., Berkeley, 1962, M.A., 1964, Ph.D., 1965. Instr. U. Calif., Berkeley, 1965-66; asst. prof. Stanford U., 1966-69, UCLA, 1969-70, asso. prof., 1970-73, prof., 1973-76; prof. dept. math. and Math. Research Center, U. Wis., Madison, 1974—. Editor: Nonlinear Evolution Equations, 1978; Assoc. editor: Nonlinear Analysis: Theory, Methods and Application, Annales de l'institut Henri Poincare Analyse nonlineaire. Mem. Am. Math. Soc. (council), Soc. for Indsl. and Applied Math. Home: 5614 Lake Mendota Dr Madison WI 53705 Office: Univ Wis Math Research Center 610 Walnut St Madison WI 53706

CRANDALL, ROBERT LLOYD, airline executive; b. Westerly, R.I., Dec. 6, 1935; s. Lloyd Evans and Virginia (Beard) C.; m. Margaret Jan Schmults, July 6, 1957; children: Mark William, Martha Conway, Stephen Michael. Student, Coll. William and Mary, 1953-55; B.S., U. R.I., 1957; M.B.A., U. Pa., 1960. With Eastman Kodak Co., Rochester, 1960-62, Hallmark Cards, Kansas City, Mo., 1962-66; asst. treas. TWA Inc., N.Y.C., 1966-70, v.p. systems and data services, 1970-71, v.p., controller, 1971-72; sr. v.p., treas. Bloomingdale Bros., N.Y.C., 1972-73; sr. v.p. fin. Am. Airlines, Inc., N.Y.C., 1973-74, sr. v.p. mktg., 1974-80, pres., 1980—, also dir. Served with Inf. U.S. Army, 1957. Office: Am Airlines Inc PO Box 619616 Dallas/Ft Worth Airport TX 75261

CRANDALL, STEPHEN HARRY, engineering educator; b. Cebu, Philippines, Dec. 2, 1920; s. William Harry and Julia Josephine (Kuenemann) C.; m. Patricia Estelle Stickel, Jan. 21, 1949; children: Jane S., William S. M.E., Stevens Inst. Tech., 1942; Ph.D., MIT, 1946. Registered profl. engr. Mem. staff radiation lab MIT, Cambridge, 1942-43, instr. math, Cambrige, 1944-46, asst. prof. mech. engring., Cambridge, 1947-51, assoc. prof., 1951-58, prof., 1958—, Ford prof. engring., 1975—, head div. applied mechanics, 1957-59, 61-67, head. div. mechanics and materials, 1968-71; vis. prof., Marseille, France, 1960, U. Mex., 1967, Ecole Nationale Superieure de Mecanique, Nantes, France, 1978. Author: Engineering Analysis, 1956, Random Vibration in Mechanical Systems, 1963, (with others) Dynamics of Mechanical and Electronmechanical Systems, 1968; editor: Random Vibration vol. 1, 1958, Random Vibration vol. 2, 1963, (with others) Mechanics of Solids, 1959; author, 3d edit., 1978; contbr. artcles to profl. jours. Fulbright fellow, exchange prof. Inperial Coll., London, 1949; NSF sci. faculty fellow, vis. scholar U. Calif.-Berkeley, 1964-65; hon. research assoc. Harvard U., 1971-72. Fellow Am. Acad. Arts and Scis., ASME (Worcester Reed Warner medal 1971, Worcester Reed Warner medal 1978-80), Am. Acoustical Soc. (Trent-Crede medal 1978), Am. Acad. Mechanics, AAAS; mem. Soc. Indsl. and Applied Math., Am. Math. Soc., Am. Soc. for Engring. Edn., Internat. Union Theoretical and Applied Mechanics (chmn. U.S. del. 1974), Nat. Acad. Engring. Home: Tabor Hill Rd Lincoln MA 01773 Office: Dept. Mech Engring MIT Cambridge MA 02139

CRANDALL, WALTER ELLIS, physicist; b. Norwich, Conn., Dec. 18, 1916; s. Louis M. and Bessie (Smith) C.; m. Ellen Delaney, May 22, 1944; children—Jacqueline Louise, Thomas Philip. B.S. in Physics, Worcester (Mass.) Poly. Inst., 1940; Royal Vector fellow, Stanford U., 1940-41; Ph.D., U. Calif., Berkeley, 1951. Civilian with Naval Bur. Ordnance, 1941-43; physicist Berkeley Lab., U. Calif. Radiation Lab., 1948-54, Lawrence Livermore (Calif.) Lab., 1954-62; with Northrop Corp., 1962—, chief scientist research and tech. center, Palos Verdes, Calif., 1978—, corp. v.p., 1973—; cons. Boeing Corp. Served with USNR, 1943-45. Mem. Sigma Xi, Phi Gamma Delta. Club: Malibu LaCosta Beach (v.p. 1973-75). Research in electronic, magnetic, neutronic and optical devices, theory vision and audition. Home: 21930 Carbon Mesa Rd Malibu CA 90265 Office: 1 Research Park Palos Verdes CA 90274

CRANDELL, DWIGHT SAMUEL, museum director; b. Parke County, Ind., Nov. 30, 1943; s. Terence Wesley and Alice Ruth (Cox) C.; m. Rachel Louise Wentworth, June 14, 1965; children: Jeremy, Abigail, Joanna, Joshua. B.A., Principia Coll., 1965; M.A., SUNY-Oneonta, 1974. Asst. in research and adminstrn. Mt. Vernon (Va.) Ladies Assn. of the Union, 1965-66; exhibits coordinator, ednl. docent Children's Mus., Indpls., 1972-73, curator exhibits research and planning, 1973-77, collections dir., 1977-81; dir. devel., asst. dir. St. Louis Mus. Sci. and Natural History, 1981-82, exec. dir., 1982—. Served to capt. USAF, 1966-71. Nat. Mus. Act travel grantee, 1973. Mem. Am. Assn. Museums, Assn. Sic. Mus. Dirs., Midwest Museums Conf., Mo. Museums Assocs. (v.p. 1983-84), Assn. Sci-Tech. Ctrs. (bd. dirs. 1983—). Christian Scientist. Club: Rotary. Office: St Louis Science Center 5050 Oakland Ave St Louis MO 63110

CRANDLES, GEORGE MARSHAL, insurance company executive; b. Yonkers, N.Y., Apr. 9, 1917; s. George and Beatrice (MacVitty) C.; m. Mary Genevieve McInerney; children: Mary, Joan, Barbara, Sheila, George. Student, CCNY, 1937-40, N.Y. U., 1947-49. With Met. Life Ins. Co., 1936-82, asst. v.p., then v.p., 1963-80, sr. v.p. in charge regional corp. investment ops., N.Y.C., 1980-82; dir. Bard Mfg. Co., Am. Retirement Corp., Reeves Bros., Inc. Served with AUS, 1942-45. Mem. N.Y. Soc. Security Analysts. Republican. Roman Catholic.

CRANDON, JOHN HOWLAND, surgeon; b. Boston, Apr. 28, 1912; s. LeRoiGoddard and Mina Marguerite (Stinson) C.; m. Dorothy Katherine Tebbe, July 14, 1940; children: Alan Tebbe, Mary Elizabeth. A.B., Harvard U., 1933, M.D., 1937. Diplomate: AM. Bd. Surgery. Intern Harvard U. service Boston City Hosp., 1937-39, resident in surgery, 1937-39,1939-41; asst. prof. surgery Tufts U. Med. Sch., 1947-62, assoc. prof., 1962—; chief of surgery Little Co. of Mary Hosp., Cambridge, Mass., 1957-62, Winthrop Hosp., 1971—; past vis. surgeon Boston City Hosp.; mem. courtesy staff Mt. Auburn Hosp., Univ. Hosp., Brooks Hosp. Contbr. chpts. to books and articles to med. jours. Trustee Winthrop Hosp. Served to comdr. M.C., USNR, 1941-45. USPHS gantee, 1957-62. Mem. ACS, New Eng. Surg. Soc., Am. Soc. Surgery Hand, Mass. Med. Soc., N.Y. Acad. Sci. Clubs: Harvard, Cottage Park Yacht. Home: 47 Hilltop Rd Chestnut Hill Brookline MA 02167 Office: Bentley MedCtr Winthrop MA 02152 *The practice of medicine has been challenging, worrisome, and generally satisfying; however the ever increasing cost of medical care and the proliferating governmental regulations to attack this problem are producing a decrease in the quality of patient care and a deteriotating relationships between doctor and patient, doctor and doctor, doctor and hospital boards.*

CRANE, `BARBARA BACHMANN, photographer, educator; b. Chgo., Mar. 19, 1928; d. Burton Stanley and Della (Kreeger) Bachmann; children—Elizabeth, Jennifer, Bruce. Student, Mills Coll., 1945-48; B.A. in Art History, N.Y. U., 1950; M.S. in Photography, Inst. Design, Ill. Inst. Tech., 1966. Chmn. photography dept. New Trier High Sch., Winnetka, Ill., 1964-67; prof. photography Sch. Art Inst. Chgo., 1967—; vis. prof. Phila. Coll. Art, 1977, Sch. Mus. Fine Arts, Boston, 1979, Cornell U., Ithaca, N.Y., 1983; panelist Ill. Arts Council, 1981. Author: retrospective monograph Barbara Crane: The Evolution of a Vision, 1948-1980, 1980, 83; traveling exhbn. Barbara Crane, 1948-80. Photography fellow Nat. Endowment for Arts, 1975; Guggenheim Meml. fellow in photography, 1979-80; Polaroid Corp. grantee, 1979—. Mem. Soc. Photog. Edn., Friends of Photography

(Carmel, Calif.) (trustee 1974—), Chgo. Network. Home: 3164 N Hudson Chicago IL 60657 *My work is my life's keel bringing enrichments discovered in the process. Many of my photographic ideas have grown from chance or accident, both visually and technically, or from a gift of the subject matter itself. I welcome an unaccountable occurrence stemming from combinations of shutter speed, subject changes, technical happenings, my mistakes, and whatever. When such unpredictable pictures appear, I try to harness the visual episode by taking pictures that will allow the new experience to happen with intent. Fortunately, this way of working seems to expand my ideas and to continuously generate new visual experiences.*

CRANE, BARBARA JOYCE, publishing company executive, author; b. Trenton, N.J., June 2, 1934; d. Herman and Elizabeth (Stein) Cohen; m. Stuart G. Crane, Aug. 27, 1956; children: Susan Jill, Patricia Lynne. B.A., Vassar Coll., 1956. Tchr. Trenton Pub. Schs., 1956-58; prin. Little People's Sch., Yardley, Pa., 1964-66; reading cons. Newtown Friends Sch., Pa., 1967-68, Trenton State Coll., 1968-69; dir. Demonstration Sch., Trenton State Coll., 1969-70; pres. Crane Pub. Co., Trenton, 1968—; mem. social, polit. concerns com. Nat. Assn. Bilingual Edn., Washington, 1980. Author: reading systems Categorical Sound System, 1977, Crane Reading System: PACER Program, Spanish Crane Reading System, 1982; test Crane Oral Dominance Test, 1976; contbr. articles to various publs. Bd. dirs. Inst. New World Archaeology, Chgo., 1981—. Grantee Vassar Coll., 1967-68, Trenton State Coll., 1968-69, State N.J., 1968. Mem. Internat. Reading Assn., Nat. Assn. Bilingual Edn. Clubs: Vassar College, Metedeconk River Yacht. Home: 1909 Yardley Rd Yardley PA 19067 Office: Crane Pub Co 1301 Hamilton Ave Trenton NJ 08629

CRANE, BARRY, director, producer; b. Detroit; m. Shirlee Roseberg; m. Arline Anderson; children: Ben, Shari. Student, U. Mich. Formerly with, Pasadena Playhouse; then prodn. asst., King Bros.; then from 2d asst. dir. to prodn. mgr., 4 Star TV; then assoc. producer-dir., Paramount Co.; then producer: Mission Impossible, all from 1960-79; now dir.: TV shows Trapper John. Mem. Dirs. Guild Am., Producers Guild Am., Writers Guild, Am. Contract Bridge League (6-time winner McKenny trophy, World Mixed Pair champion). Office: care Brad Marer & Assos 9201 Wilshire Blvd Suite 203 Beverly Hills CA 90210

CRANE, BENJAMIN FIELD, lawyer; b. Holden, Mass., May 5, 1929; s. Frederick Turner and Gertrude (Stange) C.; m. Sarah Anne Molloy, Feb. 8, 1959; children: Michael Turner, Elizabeth Loring, Susan Field. B.A., State U. Iowa, 1951; LL.B., NYU, 1954. Bar: N.Y. 1955. Assoc. Cravath, Swaine & Moore, N.Y.C., 1954-63, ptnr., 1963—. Served with U.S. Army, 1946-47. Mem. ABA, Assn. Bar City N.Y., N.Y. State Bar Assn. Clubs: Wall Street (N.Y.C.); Travellers (Paris). Office: Cravath Swaine & Moore 1 Chase Manhattan Plaza New York NY 10005

CRANE, DANIEL B., congressman; b. Chgo., Jan. 10, 1936; m. Judy Van Brunt, 1970; children: Nathan, Joshua, Kimberly, Elizabeth, Emily, Heidi. A.B., Hillsdale (Mich.) Coll., 1958; D.D.S., Ind. U., 1963; postgrad., U. Mich., 1964-65. Practice dentistry; dir. Crane Clinic, 1963-67; mem. 96th and 98th Congresses from Ill. 19th Dist. Served to capt. U.S. Army. Mem. Assn. Am. Dentists, C. of C. Republican. Office: Room 115 Cannon House Office Bldg Washington DC 20515

CRANE, DWIGHT BURDICK, business educator; b. West Palm Beach, Fla., Nov. 24, 1937; s. Leslie Burdick and Abigail (Boydston) C.; m. Loretto Anne Ford, Oct. 24, 1964; children: Catherine, Elizabeth, Paul. S.B., MIT, 1959; M.B.A., U. Mich., 1961; M.S., Carnegie-Mellon U., 1964, Ph.D., 1965; M.A. (hon.), Harvard U., 1976. Asso. economist Mellon Bank, Pitts., 1964-67, dir. mgmt. scis., 1967-69; lectr. Harvard U. Grad. Sch. Bus. Adminstrn., 1969-72, asso. prof., 1972-76, prof., 1976—; dir. Cash Res. Mgmt., Inc.; cons. in field. Author: (with Michael J. Riley) NOW Accounts: Strategies for Financial Institutions, 1977, (with Stephen P. Bradley) Management of Bank Portfolios, 1975, Managing Credit Lines and Commitments, 1973, (with R. Kimball and W. Gregor) The Effects of Banking Deregulation, 1983; mem. editorial adv. bd.: (with Stephen P. Bradley) Jour. Bank Research; editor: Financial Management, 1983. Alfred P. Sloan scholar, 1955-59; Marvin Bower Faculty Research fellow, 1974-75. Mem. Am. Fin. Assn., Western Fin. Assn. Office: Harvard Univ Sch Bus Adminstrn Boston MA 02163

CRANE, EDWARD J., airline executive; b. 1928; m. Margaret Struif; children: Steven, Edward J., Mary Ann, John. Grad., St. Louis U. Sch. Commerce and Fin., 1951. Accounting dept. comptroller Ozark Air Lines, Inc., St. Louis, 1951-60, v.p., comptroller, 1960-65, v.p., treas., 1965-68, exec. v.p., treas., 1968-71, pres., chief exec. officer, 1971-; dir. Bank of St. Louis, Valley Industries, Gen. Bancshares Corp. Mem. pres.'s council, trustee St. Louis U.; bd. dirs. United Way, 1977-83, Regional Commerce and Growth Assn. St. Louis, St. Louis Council Boy Scouts Am.; trustee Incarnate Word Hosp. Served with USMC, World War II. Mem. Assn. Local Transport Airlines (past chmn., bd. dirs.), Air Transport Assn. (bd. dirs.), Air Conf. (bd. dirs.). Home: St Louis County MO Office: Ozark Airlines PO Box 10007 Lambert Field St Louis MO 63145

CRANE, EDWARD MATTHEWS, JR., publishing consultant; s. Edward M. and Margaret (Atha) C.; m. Mary Cordelia Thompson, Mar. 23, 1945; children: Edward Matthews III, Cordelia Houghton; m. Jean Drummond Ijams, July 20, 1966. A.B., Princeton U., 1945. Coll. salesman D. Van Nostrand Co., Inc., 1945-49, asso. editor, 1949-54, mgr. coll. dept., 1954, sec., 1954-58, sec., v.p., 1958-63, pres., 1963-68, Van Nostrand Reinhold Co. div. Litton Ednl. Pub., Inc., 1969-70; dir., pres. Van Nostrand Reinhold Co., Ltd., chmn., London; cons., 1968-69; pres. Litton Internat. Pub., Inc., 1969-70, Boutwell, Crane, Moseley Assos., 1971-73; chmn. Crane Russak & Co., 1972—; pres. Pitman Pub. Co., N.Y., 1973-75. V.p. Council for Fin. Aid to Edn., 1977—; Trustee Curran Found., Wilmington, Del.; bd. dirs. Aerospace Found., N.J. Hist. Soc. Office: 680 Fifth Ave New York NY 10019

CRANE, FENWICK JAMES, insurance company executive; b. Cleve., July 9, 1923; s. Reginald J. and Ellie (Combs) C.; m. Vivian Muskatt, Oct. 21, 1947; children: Patricia, Susan. B.A., U. Mich., 1947. C.L.U. With N.Y. Life Ins. Co., 1950-69; with Family Life Ins. Co., 1969—, pres., chmn. bd., Seattle, 1969—; dir. Merrill Lynch & Co. Inc., Prudential Bank, Seattle, Pay and Save Corp. Served with USMCR, 1942-45. Clubs: Rainier, Wash. Athletic, Seattle Golf, Broadmoor Golf. Address: Park Place Bldg Seattle WA 98101

CRANE, FRANK S., hospital administrator; b. Wilkes Barre, Pa., Aug. 16, 1938; m. Mary Crane; children: Steven, Abigail, Sarah. B.A., U. Colo., 1957-61, M.B.A., 1966; diploma hosp. adminstrn., U. Toronto, 1969. Adminstrv. asst. Millard Fillmore Hosp., Buffalo, 1969-71; adminstr. Lafayette Gen. Hosp., Buffalo, 1972-73; assoc. adminstr. Millard Fillmore Hosp., Buffalo, 1973, adminstr., 1974-80; pres. Bridgeport Hosp., (Conn.), 1980—; exec. v.p. corp. ops. United Health Care, Bridgeport, 1982—. Recipient Norman Leeds Meml. Trophy United Way Eastern Fairfield County, 1982. Mem. Am. Coll. Hosp. Adminstrs., Conn. Hosp. Assn. (dir., sec.). Club: Rotary (Bridgeport). Office: Bridgeport Hosp 267 Grant St Bridgeport CT 06610 *

CRANE, HORACE RICHARD, educator, physicist; b. Turlock, Calif., Nov. 4, 1907; s. Horace Stephen and Mary Alice (Roselle) C.; m. Florence Rohmer LeBaron, Dec. 30, 1934; children—Carol Ann, Janet (dec.), George Richard. B.S., Calif. Inst. Tech., 1930, Ph.D., 1934. Research fellow Calif. Inst. Tech., 1934-35; mem. faculty U. Mich., Ann Arbor, 1935—, prof. physics, 1946—, chmn. dept. physics, 1965-72, George P. Williams Univ. prof., 1972-78, emeritus, 1978—; Research asso. (radar) Mass. Inst. Tech., 1940-41; physicist Carnegie Inst. Washington, 1941; project dir., proximity fuze project U. Mich., 1941-43, atomic energy project, 1943-45; cons. NDRC, 1941-45; mem. standing com. on controlled thermonuclear research AEC, 1969-72; Vice pres. Midwestern Univs. Research Assn., 1956-57, pres., 1957-60; mem. policy bd. Argonne Nat. Lab., 1957-67; Bd. govs. Am. Inst. Physics, 1964-71, chmn., 1971-75; mem. Commn. on Human Resources, 1977-80, Council for Internat. Exchange of Scholars, 1977-80. Contbr. sci. articles to profl. mags. Recipient Davisson-Germer prize, 1967; Henry Russel lectr., 1967; Distinguished Alumni medal Cal. Inst. Tech., 1968; Distinguished Service award U. Mich., 1957. Fellow Am. Phys. Soc., AAAS, Am. Acad. Arts and Scis.; mem. Nat. Acad. Scis., Am. Assn. Physics Tchrs. (pres. 1965, Oersted medal 1977), Sigma Xi. Clubs: Research Univ. of Mich. (pres. 1956-57); Science Research (U. Mich.) (v.p. 1946-47, pres. 1947-48. Inventor of Race Track, a modified form of synchrotron for nuclear studies, 1946; made early discoveries in field of artificially produced radioactive atoms, 1934-39; measurements of magnetic moment of free electron, 1950. Home: 830 Avon Rd Ann Arbor MI 48104

CRANE, IRVING DONALD, pocket billiards player; b. Livonia, N.Y., Nov. 13, 1913; s. Scott W. and Laura (Stark) C.; m. Althea H. Sleight, Oct. 23, 1937; children—Irving Donald, Sandra. Student, Lima Jr. Coll., 1931, Hobart Coll., 1932. Cons., exhbn. player A.M.F., 1963-64; exhbn. player for U.S. Army Brunswick Co., 1944-47. Author: (with George Sullivan) The Young Sportsman's Guide to Pocket Billiards, 1964; contbg. author: Sportsman's Ency, 1971; Short subject films Cue Men, 1942, Cue Tricks, 1946. Named Athlete of Year Rochester Press and Radio Club, 1970; recipient Pepsi-Cola Sports award Rochester (N.Y.) Profl. Salesman Assn., 1973; named to Hall of Fame Profl. Pool Players Assn., 1976, Billiard Congress Am., 1978. Winner pocket billiards championships: World or Internat., 1942, 46, 55, 68, 69, 70, 72, U.S. Nat., 1950, 55, Eastern States Regional 3 Cushion, 1952, Tournament of Champions, 1963, U.S. Masters, 1964, Schaeffer Pocket Billiard Classic, 1965, Ballantine Invitational, 1965, U.S. Open, 1966, Salt City Open, 1970, U.S. Masters Classic, 1975, World Series of Pocket Billiards, 1978. Address: 270 Yarmouth Rd Rochester NY 14610

CRANE, JOHN BEVER, economics educator; b. Chgo., July 20, 1903; s. George Washington and Eliza (Bever) C.; m. Catherine Dickson, Jan. 31, 1925 (div.); children: Marilyn Elsbeth, Robert Dickson; m. Joan Elizabeth Stauffer, Sept. 11, 1938. A.B., Northwestern U., 1924; M.A., Harvard, 1926, Ph.D., 1932; student, London (Eng.) U., 1934-35. Instr. econs. Harvard, 1928-37; asst. prof. econs. Northwestern U., 1937-42; dir. econ. history Ill. Cities Project, 1938-41; sr. economist ICC, Washington, 1942-43; prin. economist, chief transp. sect. Dept. Commerce, 1943-44; dir. econ. research Glenn L. Martin Co., Balt., 1944-45; pres. Transp. Analysts, Inc., Washington, 1945-46; dir. spl. U.S. Senate Com. on Econ. Resources, also adminstrv. asst. to U.S. Senator George W. Malone, Washington, 1947-50; dir. overseas operations, also author syndicated daily newspaper column Europe Day by Day Hopkins Syndicate, 1950-59; prof. econs. Kans. State U., 1960-61; v.p. Ind. Inst. Tech., 1961-62; holder Musser endowed chair, prof. econs., chmn. dept. Iowa Wesleyan Coll., 1962-72, chmn. social sci. div., 1963-68, dir., 1963-68, 1963-72, prof. emeritus, 1972-; internat. trade analyst BKW Assos., Inc., 1975, Bus. Analysis & Systems Info. Corp., 1977—; Dir. air mail investigation U.S. House Com. on Post Office and Post Rds., 1932-33; cons. various cos., govt. agys., 1937—; lectr. Council Fgn. Relations, 1961; Sch. Advanced Internat. Studies, Johns Hopkins, 1944-46. Author: Europe Day by Day, 1952, (with Joan S. Crane) The Story of the Soviet Union, 1969, History of American Aviation to 1917, 1974, also articles in periodicals, profl. jours., govt. pubs. Sheldon fellow, 1931; Social Sci. Research Council fellow, 1934-35. Mem. Am. Econ. Assn., Assn. Evolutionary Econs., Alpha Delta Phi, Sigma Delta Rho, Order of Artus. Club: Rotarian. Home: PO Box 210 Washington VA 22747

CRANE, JOHN C., insurance broker; b. 1934. B.S., U. Colo., 1959. Ptnr. Haskins & Sells, C.P.A.'s, 1959-70; controller Great Western Sugar Co., 1970-72; exec. v.p., sec., treas. Centurex Corp., 1972-74; v.p. fin. Fred S. James & Co. Inc., N.Y.C., 1974-75, sr. v.p. fin. and adminstrn., then exec. v.p. fin. and adminstrn., 1975—, dir. Office: James & Co Inc 55 Water St New York NY 10041 *

CRANE, KEITH, consumer products manufacturing company executive; b. 1921. With Colgate Palmolive Co., N.Y.C., 1937—, gen. mgr., Australia, 1965-72, v.p. and gen. mgr., 1972-74; corporate v.p., mgr. The Kendall Co., 1974-75, pres., chief operating officer, dir., 1975—, chief exec. officer, 1979—, chmn. bd., 1980—. Served with Armed Forces, 1941-45. Office: Colgate Palmolive Co 300 Park Ave New York NY 10022

CRANE, LOUIS ARTHUR, labor arbitrator; b. Cleve., Apr. 15, 1922; m. Eleanor Darling, May 1979; children by previous marriage: Kevin A., Kathryn E., Julie E. B.B.A., U. Mich., 1945, M.B.A., 1947; LL.B., Wayne State U., 1950. Arbitrator, U.S. Rubber Co. and United Rubber, Cork, Linoleum and Plastic Workers Am., 1961-67; chmn. bd. arbitration Jones & Laughlin Steel Corp. and United Steelworkers Am., 1967-74; arbitrator Continental, Am. can cos. and United Steelworkers Am., 1968-74; mem. system bd. adjustment Eastern Airlines Inc. and Internat. Assn. Machinists, 1967—, Eastern Airlines Inc. and Air Line Pilots Assn., 1969—; permanent arbitrator Gt. Lakes Steel Corp. and United Steelworkers Am., 1974—; arbitrator Penn-Dixie Steel Corp. and United Steelworkers Am., 1973-83, Internat. Harvester Co. and United Automobile Aerospace and Agrl. Implement Workers, 1976-79; umpire Rockwell Internat. Corp. and U.A.W., 1976—, Rockwell Internat. Corp. and United Steelworkers Am., 1976-82; mem. system bd. adjustment T.W.A. and Internat. Assn. Machinists, 1975—, TWA and Airline Pilots Assn., 1977—, United Airlines and Airline Pilots Assn., 1975-82, Continental Airlines and Airlines Pilots Assn., 1976—; arbitrator Budd Co. and UAW, 1976—, Youngstown Sheet & Tube and United Steelworkers Am., 1977-84, Crucible Steel (Colt Industries) and United Steelworkers Am., 1984—; permanent arbitrator Nat. Can Corp. and United Steelworkers Am., 1982—; mem. Presdl. Emergency Bd. 164, 1964. Author: articles The Arbitrator and the Parties, 1958, Labor Arbitration and Industrial Changes, 1963, Labor Arbitration at the Quarter-Century Mark, 1972. Served to capt. AUS, 1943-46. Mem. State Bar Mich. (chmn. labor relations law sect. 1960-61), Nat. Acad. Arbitrators (gov. 1964-67), Phi Kappa Phi, Beta Gamma Sigma. Clubs: Univ. Detroit, Hidden Valley. Home: 3076 Glouchester Troy MI 48084 Office: 2153 Penobscot Bldg Detroit MI 48226

CRANE, MICHAEL PATRICK, arts administrator; b. St. Louis, Dec. 24, 1948; s. Donald Francis and Doris Virginia (Jennings) C.; m. Toni M. Vezeau, July 7, 1979; children: Benjamin Harris, William. M.F.A., Sch. Art Inst., Chgo., 1976. Co-founder N.A.M.E. Gallery, Chgo., 1973-74; adminstr. All the Ch'go Fog Performance Gallery, Chgo., 1974-76; founder, editor Running Dog Press, Chgo., 1975—; resident fellow Inst. Advanced Studies in Contemporary Art, San Diego, 1977-78; dir. art galleries Calif. State U., Sacramento, 1978-79, San Jose State U., 1979-83; gallery/mus. dir. Arvada Ctr. for Arts and Humanities, Colo., 1983—; lectr. Calif. State U., Sacramento, San Jose, 1978-83. Author: Fill in this Space, 1975, Landscapes, 1976; co-editor: Correspondence Art, 1981. Home: 9105 Brooks Dr Arvada CO 80004 Office: Arvada Center 6901 Wadsworth Arvada CO 80003

CRANE, NEAL DAHLBERG, manufacturing company executive; b. Stanley, Wis., Oct. 28, 1916; s. and (Dahlberg) C.; m. Elizabeth Henery, 1954. A.B., Ripon (Wis.) Coll., 1938; student, U. Wis., 1938-40. Grad. asst., research asst. physics dept. U. Wis., 1938-40; staff Radiation Lab., Mass. Inst. Tech., 1941; dir. operations div. (Office Tech. Services, Dept. Commerce), 1946-47; staff mem., later dir. resources div. Research and Devel. Bd., Office Asst. Sec. Def. for Research and Devel., 1947-56; cons. asst. sec. def. research and engring., 1956-62; spl. asst. to sci. dir. research labs Gen. Motors Corp., 1956-61; dir. applied devel. dept., research and devel. div. Am. Machine & Foundry Co., 1961-62, dept. dir. research and devel. div., 1962-64, v.p. research and devel. div., 1964-66; v.p., asst. group exec. process equipment group, 1966-67; pres. Ben Hogan, 1967-70; v.p., dep. group exec. sports products group AMF, Inc., 1970; pres. Jacobsen Mfg. Co., 1971-74, chmn., 1974-76; v.p. ALI, Inc., 1974-77; dir. Modine Mfg. Co. Served to lt. col., Signal Corps AUS, 1941-46. Decorated Legion of Merit, Bronze Star, U.S.; Order Brit. Empire. Mem. AAAS. Clubs: Duquesne (Pitts.); Fort Worth. Home: 5805 Boca Raton Fort Worth TX 76112

CRANE, PHILIP MILLER, congressman; b. Chgo., Nov. 3, 1930; s. George Washington and Cora (Miller) C.; m. Arlene Catherine Johnson, Feb. 14, 1959; children: Catherine Anne, Susanna Marie, Jennifer Elizabeth, Rebekah Caroline, George Washington V, Rachel Ellen, Sarah Emma, Carrie Esther. Student, DePauw U., 1948-50; B.A., Hillsdale Coll., 1952; postgrad., U. Mich., 1952-54, U. Vienna, Austria, 1953, 56; M.A.; Ind. U., 1961; Ph.D., 1963; LL.D., Grove City Coll., 1975; Doctor en Ciencias Politicas, Francisco Marroquin U., 1979. Advt. mgr. Hopkins Syndicate, Inc., Chgo., 1956-58; teaching asst. Ind. U., Bloomington, 1959-62; asst. prof. history Bradley U., Peoria, Ill., 1963-67; dir. schs. Westminster Acad., Northbrook, Ill., 1967-68; mem. 91st-97th congresses, 12th Ill. Dist., 91st-98th congresses, 12th Ill. Dist. (Ways and Means Com.). Author: Democrat's Dilemma, 1964, The Sum of Good Government, 1976, Surrender In Panama: The Case Against the Treaty, 1977; Contbr.: Continuity in Crisis, 1974, Crisis in Confidence, 1974, Case Against the Reckless Congress, 1976, Can You Afford This House?, 1978, View from the Capitol Dome (Looking Right), 1980. Pub. relations dir. Vigo County (Ind.) Republican Orgn., 1962; dir. research Ill. Goldwater Orgn., 1964; mem. nat. adv. bd. Young Ams. for Freedom, 1965—; Bd. dirs., chmn. Am. Conservative Union, 1965-81, Intercollegiate Studies Inst.; trustee Hillsdale Coll. Served with AUS, 1954-56. Recipient Distinguished Alumnus award Hillsdale Coll., 1968, Independence award, 1974; William McGovern award Chgo. Soc., 1969; Freedoms Found. award, 1973. Mem. Am. Hist. Assn., Orgn. Am. Historians, Acad. Polit. Sci., Am. Acad. Polit. and Social Scis., Phila. Soc., ASCAP, Phi Alpha Theta, Pi Gamma Mu. Methodist. Office: 1035 Longworth House Office Bldg Washington DC 20515 *

CRANE, RICHARD A., savs. and loan assn. exec.; b. San Francisco, Jan. 25, 1943; s. Alvin J. Crane and Harriett A. (Stith) Brown; m. Donna A. Kokorudz, May 13, 1967; 1 son, James J. With Golden West Fin. Corp. and World Savs. and Loan Assn., Oakland, Calif., 1963—, treas., 1972-74, sec., treas., 1974-76, v.p., sec., 1979—. Mem. Am. Soc. Corp. Secs. Office: 1970 Broadway Oakland CA 94612

CRANE, ROBERT KELLOGG, biochemist, educator; b. Palmyra, N.J., Dec. 20, 1919; s. Wilbur Fiske and Mary Elizabeth (McHale) C.; m. Mildred Ellen Price, July 19, 1941 (div. Apr. 1962); children—Barbara Joan, Jonathan Townley; m. Laura Jane Scott, Apr. 13, 1972. B.S., Washington Coll., Chestertown, Md., 1942; Ph.D., Harvard U., 1950; Sc.D. (h.c.), Washington Coll., 1982. Chemist Atlas Powder Co., 1942-43; instr. chemistry N.E. Mo. State Tchrs. Coll., Kirksville, 1943-44; asst. biochemist Mass. Gen. Hosp., Boston, 1949-50; mem. faculty Washington U. Med. Sch., St. Louis, 1950-62; prof. biochemistry, chmn. dept. Chgo. Med. Sch., 1962-66; prof., chmn. dept. physiology Rutgers Med. Sch., New Brunswick, N.J., 1966—; Mem. biochemistry test com. Nat. Bd. Med. Examiners; mem. sponsoring com. Internat. Conf. on Biol. Membranes. Editorial com. sect. alimentary canal: Handbook of Physiology; editorial bd.: Archives of Biochemistry and Biophysics; editor: Gastrointestinal Physiology; Contbr. numerous articles in field. Served with USNR, 1944-46. Recipient Distinguished Achievement award Am. Gastroenterology Assn., 1969; Alumni citation Washington Coll., 1963; Community Service award St. Andrews Sch., 1963; Dr. Harold Lamport award N.Y. Acad. Scis., 1979; Sir Arthur Hurst Meml. lectr. Brit. Soc. for Gastroenterology, 1969; Fellow AEC, 1947-49. Fellow Am. Inst. Chemists, N.Y. Acad. Sci.; mem. Am. Soc. Biol. Chemists, Am. Soc. Cell Biology, Corp. Marine Biol. Lab., Am. Chem. Soc., A.A.A.S., Am. Gastroent. Assn., Biophys. Soc., Soc. Gen. Physiologists, Am. Physiol. Soc. (chmn. pub. affairs com.), Fedn. Am. Soc. Exptl. Biology (chmn. pub. info. com.), Internat. Union Physiol. Scis. (sci. program com.), Sigma Xi. Home: 70 W Valley Brook Rd Long Valley NJ 07853 Office: CMDNJ-Rutgers Med Sch Piscataway NJ 08854

CRANE, ROBERT Q., state treasurer; b. Providence, Mar. 21, 1926; married; 5 children. Student, Boston Coll. Sch. Bus. Adminstrn. Food broker, sales mgr., 15 yrs., ins. broker, 8 yrs.; treas., receiver gen. State of Mass., Boston, 1964, 65—. Mem. Mass. Ho. of Reps., 1957-64, asst. majority leader, 2 yrs.; chmn. Mass. Democratic Com., 1971-73, Mass. State Lottery Commn., 1972—. Served with USMC. Mem. Am. Legion, DAV, VFW. Democrat. Lodges: K.C.; Elks. Office: Office of the Treasurer 227 State House Boston MA 02133 *

CRANE, STEPHEN ANDREW, holding company executive; b. Bklyn., June 12, 1945; s. Andrew Joseph and Judith Rebecca C. A.B., Princeton U., 1967; M.B.A., Harvard U., 1971. With Orion Capital Corp., N.Y.C., 1976-82, treas., 1978-82, v.p. fin., chief fin. officer, 1981-82; sr. v.p., chief fin. officer Corroon & Black Corp., N.Y.C., 1982—. Republican. Clubs: University, N.Y. Athletic., Down Town Assn. Home: 115 Central Park W New York NY 10023 Office: Wall Street Plaza New York NY 10005

CRANE, STUART, investment banker; b. Nassau County, N.Y., July 22, 1930; s. Ben and Sacy (Louis) C.; m. Barbara Cohen, Aug. 27, 1956; children: Susan, Patty. B.A., N.Y. U., 1952. Chartered fin. analyst. Chmn. MLP Pub. Co., Trenton, N.J., 1971—; gen. ptnr. Fahnestock & Co., N.Y.C. Mem. N.Y. Soc. Security Analysts. Clubs: Metedeconk River Yacht, Greenacres Country. Address: Yardley Rd Yardley PA 19067

CRANEFIELD, PAUL FREDERIC, educator, physician; b. Madison, Wis., Apr. 28, 1925; s. Paul Frederic and Edna (Rothnick) C. Ph.B., U. Wis., 1946, Ph.D., 1951; M.D., Albert Einstein Coll. Medicine, 1964. Fellow biophysics Johns Hopkins U., 1951-53; from instr. to assoc. prof. physiology State U. N.Y. Downstate Med. Center, N.Y.C., 1953-62; research fellow psychiatry Albert Einstein Coll. Medicine, 1960-64; exec. sec. com. publs. and med. information, editor bull. N.Y. Acad.

Medicine, 1963-66; adj. assoc. prof. pharmacology Columbia Coll. Physicians and Surgeons, 1964-75, adj. prof., 1975—; assoc. prof. Rockefeller U., 1966-75, prof., 1975—. Author: (with Hoffman) The Electrophysiology of the Heart, 1960, Paired Pulse Stimulation of the Heart, 1968, (with C. McC. Brooks) The Historical Development of Physiological Thought, 1959, The Way In and the Way Out, 1974, The Conduction of the Cardiac Impulse, 1975, Claude Bernard's Revised Edition of his Introduction a L'Etude de la Médicine Expérimentale, 1976; also numerous articles.; Editor: Jour. Gen. Physiology, 1966—; mem. editorial bd.: Circulation Research Spl. Collections; cons. editor: Internat. Microform Jour. Legal Medicine, 1969-77. Chmn. bd. dirs. LaMama Exptl. Theatre Club, 1965-69; chmn. bd. dirs. Circle Repertory Co., 1970-76, The Working Theatre; trustee Milton Helpern Library Legal Medicine. Recipient Einthoven medal U. Leiden, 1983. Fellow N.Y. Acad. Medicine, Internat. Acad. History of Medicine; mem. Am. Physiol. Soc., Biophys. Soc., Am. Assn. History Medicine, Episcopal Actors Guild. Clubs: Century, Players (N.Y.C.); Nat. Arts; Coffee House (N.Y.C.); Cosmos (Washington); Savile (London). Home: 310 E 9th St New York NY 10003 Office: 1230 York Ave New York NY 10021

CRANSTON, ALAN, U.S. senator; b. Palo Alto, Calif., June 19, 1914; s. William MacGregor and Carol (Dixon) C.; m. Norma Weintraub, May 19, 1978; children: Robin MacGregor (dec.), Kim MacGregor. Student, Pomona Coll., 1932-33, U. Mexico, 1933; A.B., Stanford, 1936. Fgn. corr. Internat. News Service, Eng., Italy, Ethiopia, Germany, 1936-38; Washington rep. Common Council Am. Unity, Washington, 1940-41; chief fgn. lang. div. O.W.I., Washington, 1942-44; exec. sec. Council for Am.-Italian Affairs, Inc., Washington, 1945-46; partner bldg. and real estate firm Ames-Cranston Co., Palo Alto, Calif., 1947-58; controller State of Calif., 1959-67; pres. Homes for a Better America Inc., 1967-68; v.p. Carlsberg Financial Corp., Los Angeles, 1968; mem. U.S. Senate from Calif., 1969—; Democratic whip U.S. Senate, 1977—; mem. com. on banking, housing and urban affairs, mem. com. on fgn. relations, ranking Dem. mem. com. on vets. affairs, mem. Dem. steering com., Dem. policy com. Author: The Big Story, 1940, The Killing of the Peace, 1945. Mem. exec. com. Calif. Democratic Central Com., 1954-60; pres. Calif. Dem. Council, 1953-57; mem. Dem. steering com., Dem. policy com. Served with AUS, 1944-45. Mem. United World Federalists (nat. pres. 1949-52). Club: Overseas Press Am. Office: 112 Hart Office Bldg Washington DC 20510

CRANSTON, JOHN MONTGOMERY, lawyer; b. Denver, Oct. 5, 1909; s. Earl Montgomery and Florence Terry (Pitkin) C.; m. Pearl M. Kreps, June 21, 1934; children—Theodore J., Jacqueline G., Harold D. A.B., Stanford U., 1929, J.D., 1932; LL.D., Calif. Western Law Sch., 1977; D.H.L., U.S. Internat. U., 1980. Bar: Calif. bar 1932, U.S. Supreme Ct 1970. Asso. firm Gray, Cary, Ames and Driscoll, San Diego, 1932-45; partner Gray, Cary, Ames & Frye, 1945—; lectr. Stanford U. Law Sch., 1946; Spl. Master U.S. Dist. Ct., 1958-61. Dir. San Diego County Water Authority, 1965—, chmn., 1978-80; dir. Met. Water Dist. So. Calif., 1975—; mem. Colo. River Bd. Calif., 1977—; bd. trustees U.S. Internat. U., 1965—. Mem. ABA (state del. 1968-74), Internat. Bar Assn., San Diego County Bar Assn. (past treas., dir.), State Bar Calif. (exec. com. Conf. State Bar Dels. 1961-64, mem. commn. on jud. qualifications 1968-73, bd. govs. 1964-67), World Assn. Lawyers, Am. Law Inst., Am. Coll. Probate Counsel, Am. Judicature Soc., Am. Bar Found., Order of Coif, Phi Alpha Delta. Republican. Methodist. Club: English-Speaking Union (dir., v.p.). Home: 337 Pacific Ave Solana Beach CA 92075 Office: 2100 Union Bank Bldg San Diego CA 92101

CRASEMANN, BERND, physicist, educator; b. Hamburg, Germany, Jan. 23, 1922; came to U.S., 1946, naturalized, 1955; s. Pablo Joaquin and Hildegard Carlota (Vorwerk) C.; m. Jean Millicent McEown, June 7, 1952. A.B., U. Calif. at Los Angeles, 1948; Ph.D., U. Calif. at Berkeley, 1953. With Lavadora de Lanas S.A., Viña del Mar, Chile, 1941-46; asst. prof. physics U. Oreg., Eugene, 1953-58, asso. prof., 1958-63, prof., 1963—, chmn. dept., 1976—; Guest asso. physicist Brookhaven Nat. Lab., Upton, N.Y., 1961-62; vis. prof. U. Calif. at Berkeley, 1968-69, Université Pierre et Marie Curie, Paris, 1977; cons. Lawrence Radiation Lab., 1954-68, physicist, 1968-69; mem. com. on atomic and molecular sci. NRC/Nat. Acad. Scis., 1976—; vis. scientist NASA Ames Research Center, 1975-76. Author: (with J.L. Powell) Quantum Mechanics, 1961; Editor: Atomic Inner-Shell Processes, 1975; mem. editorial bd.: Phys. Rev. C, 1978; Contbr. articles to sci. jours. Mem. region XIV selection com. Woodrow Wilson Nat. Fellowship Found., 1959-61, 62-68. Recipient Ersted award for distinguished teaching U. Oreg., 1959; NSF research grantee, 1954-64; U.S. AEC grantee, 1964-72; NASA grantee, 1972-79; AFOSR grantee, 1979—. Fellow Am. Phys. Soc. (chmn. div. electron and atomic physics 1981-82, councillor 1983-86); mem. Am. Assn. Physics Tchrs. (pres. Oreg. sect. 1956-57), Sierra Club, ACLU, Phi Beta Kappa. Office: Dept Physics U Oreg Eugene OR 97403

CRAVEN, C. ROY, JR., museum director, art educator; b. Cherokee Bluffs, Ark., July 29, 1924; s. Roy and Edna (Morris) C.; m. Lorna Elizabeth Andreae, Sept. 19, 1948; children: Curtis Andreae, Hillary Yvonne. B.A., U. Chattanooga, 1949; postgrad., Art Students League, N.Y.C., 1949-50; M.F.A., U. Fla., 1956. Chmn. dept. art Stratford Coll., Danville, Va., 1950-52; graphic designer Purse Advt., Chattanooga, 1952-54; instr. art U. Chattanooga, 1953-54; mem. faculty U. Fla., 1954—; prof. art, dir. univ. gallery, 1967—; past bd. dirs. Southeastern Museums Conf.; cons. on art of India, 1957—. Freelance artist/photographer, N.Y.C., 1949-50; Author: Indian Sculpture in the Ringling Museum of Art, 1961, Ceremonial Centers of the Maya, 1975, A Concise History of Indian Art, 1976, also articles, exhbn. catalogues.; exhbn. of paintings and photographs, Met. Mus. Art, 1952, other museums in, U.S. and abroad, archtl. relief executed for, Jacksonville (Fla.) Civic Auditorium, 1962, Med. Bldg. at Wesley Retirement Village, Orangedale, Fla., 1964. Served with USAAF; Served with 1942-45; CBI. Fulbright scholar, India, 1962-63; grantee Dept. Edn., 1968—, U. Fla., 1974, Am. Philos. Assn., 1977. Fellow Royal Soc. Arts; mem. Am. Assn. Museums, Internat. Council Museums, Asia Soc., Southeastern Coll. Arts Conf., Fla. Art Museums Dirs. Assn. (charter), Phi Beta Kappa, Phi Kappa Phi. Home: 6818 NW 65th Ave Gainesville FL 32606 Office: Univ Gallery Univ Fla Gainesville FL 32611

CRAVEN, CLIFFORD JOHN, college president; b. Huntington, Mass., Jan. 4, 1920; s. John and Marjorie (Perkins) C.; m. Marion McCarthy, Jan. 8, 1943; children—Marion (Mrs. David L. Payne), Dean, Carolyn (Mrs. David J. Hersh), Nancy (Mrs. Ronald M. Bullock), Constance. A.B., Syracuse U., 1942, Ed.D., 1951; M.A., Columbia, 1946; LL.D., Seinan Gakuin U. Japan, 1977. Instr. polit. sci., asst. dean Syracuse U., 1946-52; dean students N.Y. State Tchrs. Coll., Oneonta, 1952-56; dean acad. affairs SUNY Coll., Oneonta, 1964-71, pres., 1971—; dean student affairs U. Okla., 1956-64; Fulbright lectr. U. Würzburg (W. Ger.), 1982. Served to capt. USAAF, 1942-45; ETO; col. USAF Ret. Vis. fellow Cambridge U., 1977. Mem. Am. Polit. Sci. Assn., Comparative Edn. Soc. Club: Rotarian. Home: 166 East St Oneonta NY 13820

CRAVEN, DONALD NEIL, former finance company executive; b. Springfield, Mass., Aug. 18, 1924; s. C.S. and Edna B. (Blanchard) C.; m. Betty L. Rodda, July 16, 1947; 1 dau., Patricia Craven Matheson. Student, Williams Coll., 1942-43, Grad. Sch. Bus., Columbia U., 1967. Advt. sales staff Springfield Newspapers, 1946-51; fin. br. mgr. Assos. Investment Co., South Bend, Ind., 1951-62; br. mgr. Ford Motor Credit Co., Boston, 1962-64; br. mgr., then regional mgr. Chrysler Fin. Corp., 1964-69; v.p. Eastern U.S., 1969-80; dir. Indsl. Components Corp., Wilbraham, Mass. Bd. dirs., mem. fin. com. Springfield chpt. ARC.; treas. Springfield chpt. S.C.O.R.E. Served with USMC, 1943-46, 50-51. Clubs: Landmark (Stamford, Conn.); Dennis (Mass.) Yacht, Masons, Shriners. Home: 18 Manchester Terr Springfield MA 01108

CRAVEN, JAMES BRAXTON, III, lawyer, educator; b. Portsmouth, Va., Dec. 8, 1942; s. James Braxton and Mary Wilson (Kristler) C.; m. Sara Ann Harris, Aug. 22, 1964; children: James, Joseph, William. Midshipman, U.S. Naval Acad., 1960-61; A.B., U. N.C., 1964; J.D., Duke U., 1967, M.Div., 1981. Bar: N.C. 1967. Law clk. to presiding justice U.S. Dist. Ct., Alexandria, Va., 1967-68; trail atty. civil rights div. Dept. Justice, 1968-69; ptnr. Everett, Everett, Creech & Craven, Durham, N.C., 1969-80; sole practice, Durham, 1980—; vis. prof. U. N.C., Chapel Hill, 1971-81; clin. assoc. in law Duke U., 1973—. Contbr. articles to legal jours. Served to lt. comdr. USNR. Mem. ABA, N.C. State Bar, N.C. Bar Assn., Am. Law Inst., Jud. Conf. 4th Cir. (permanent mem.). Democrat. Episcopalian. Club: Army-Navy (Washington). Home: 1015 Watts St Durham NC 27701 Office: PO Box 1366 Durham NC 27702

CRAVEN, JOHN HOWARD, economist, banker; b. Eureka, Utah, Feb. 7, 1921; s. Percy H. and Anna (Mathisen) C.; m. Lucile Hess, Apr. 26, 1943; children: Michael, David, Kathryn, Christopher. A.B., Brigham Young U., 1942; M. Pub. Adminstrn., Harvard, 1946, M.A., 1947, Ph.D., 1951. Intern Nat. Inst. Pub. Affairs, 1942-43; economist State Dept., 1945-46; asst. prof. econs. U. Wyo., 1947-50; economist program staff Dept. Interior, 1951-52; program officer Inst. Interam. Affairs, Bolivia, 1952-53; asso. economist Bank of Am., San Francisco, 1954-60, chief economist, 1960-65, v.p., 1963-65, Fed. Res. Bank San Francisco, 1965-68, sr. v.p., 1968-73; sr. v.p., economist Union Bank, Los Angeles, 1973—; mem. mission to Burma to study investment climate, 1961; mem. World Bank mission to Spain, 1961. Pres. Union Bank Found., 1981-82; trustee Calif. NHS Found., 1982—. Mem. Am. Econ. Assn., Western Econ. Assn., Nat. Assn. Bus. Economists, Nat. Economists Club, Am. Statis. Assn., Internat. Assn. Energy Economists, Am. Bankers Assn. (econ. adv. com. 1978-81), Calif. Bankers Assn. (dir. research div.), U.S. C. of C. (banking, monetary and fiscal policy com. 1978-81). Home: 3626 Malibu Vista Dr Malibu CA 90265 Office: Union Bank 445 S Figueroa St Los Angeles CA 90071

CRAVEN, JOHN PINNA, civil engineering educator; b. Bklyn., Oct. 30, 1924; s. James McDougal and Mabel (Pinna) C.; m. Dorothy Drakesmith, Feb. 4, 1951; children: David John, Sarah Johannah. B.S. in Civil Engring, Cornell U., 1946, M.S., Calif. Inst. Tech., 1947; Ph.D., U. Ia., 1951; J.D., George Washington U., 1959. Hydrodynamicist David Taylor Model Basin, 1951-59; chief scientist U.S. Navy Spl. Projects Office, 1959-71, project mgr. deep submergence systems project, 1965-67, chief scientist project, 1967-70; vis. prof. polit. sci. and naval architecture Mass. Inst. Tech., 1969-70; dean marine programs U. Hawaii, Honolulu, 1970-81; marine affairs coordinator State Hawaii, 1970-76, 77—; dir. Law of Sea Inst., 1977—; adj. prof. Herbert M. Humphrey Inst., 1983—. Served with USNR, 1943-46. Recipient Meritorious Civilian Service award Navy Dept., 1953, Distinguished Civilian Service award, 1960; Fleming award U.S. C. of C., 1960; William S. Parsons award Navy League, 1966; Distinguished Civilian Service award Dept. Def., 1969; Lockheed award Menne Tech. Soc., 1982. Mem. Nat. Acad. Engrs. Presbyterian. Home: 4921 Waa St Honolulu HI 96821 Office: Univ of Hawaii Honolulu HI 96822 *Adaptation to opportunity and adversity with the goal of increasing mankind's rewards and reducing his catastrophes—with malice toward none and compassion for all.*

CRAVEN, ROY CURTIS, JR., educator, art gallery director; b. Cherokee Bluffs, Ala., July 29, 1924; s. Roy Curtis and Edna (Morris) C.; m. Lorna Elizabeth Andreae, Sept. 19, 1948; children: Curtis A., Hillary Y. B.A., U. Tenn.-Chattanooga, 1949; student, Art Students League N.Y., 1949-50; M.F.A., U. Fla., 1956. Photographer Chattanooga Times, 1946-47; head dept. art Stratford Coll., Danville, Va., 1950-51; instr. art U. Chattanooga, 1952-53; graphic designer Purse Advt., Chattanooga, 1952-54; mem. faculty U. Fla., Gainesville, 1954—, prof. art, 1967—, dir. univ. art gallery, 1966—; past mem. bd. Southeastern Mus. Conf., Fla. Arts Council. Exhibited one man shows, various U.S. mus. and galleries; represented Paintings in pub. and pvt. collections; author: Ceremonial Centers of the Maya, 1974, Concise History of Indian Art, 1976. Served with USAAF, 1942-46. Sr. Fulbright research scholar, 1962-63; grantee U.S. Dept. Edn., 1968-73, Am. Philos. Soc., 1977. Fellow Royal Soc. Arts; mem. Asia Soc., Assn. Asian Studies, Am. Assn. Mus., Fla. Art Mus. Dirs. Assn., Phi Beta Kappa. Home: 6818 NW 65th Ave Gainesville FL 32606 Office: Univ Gallery Univ Fla Gainesville FL 32611

CRAVENS, RAYMOND LEWIS, university administrator; b. St. Bernard, Ohio, Dec. 5, 1930; s. R.L. and Ethel (Hammonds) C.; m. Ann Powell, Aug. 11, 1956; children—Andrea Lee, Alicia. A.B., Western Ky. State Coll., 1952, M.A., 1955; Haggin scholar, U. Ky., 1955-57, Ky. Research Found. fellow, 1957, Ph.D., 1958. Prof. govt. Western Ky. U., 1958—, dean of coll., 1959-64, dean of faculty, 1964-66, v.p. acad. affairs, dean faculties, 1966-77, dean pub. service and internat. programs, 1977-80, dir. Coop. Ctr. for Study in Britain, 1982—; chmn. Ky. Council Acad. Vice Presidents; pres. Ky. Council on Internat. Edn., 1973-81; mem. adv. com. on tchr. edn. Ky. Council on Pub. Higher Edn. Served as 1st lt. USAF, 1952-54. Named one of 3 outstanding young men in state Ky. Jr. C. of C., 1964. Mem. So. Acad. Deans, Am. Soc. Pub. Adminstrn., So. Assn. Colls. (commn. on colls.; chmn. com. admissions to membership). Baptist. Club: Mason. Home: 610 E Main St Bowling Green KY 42101

CRAVER, JAMES B., lawyer, diversified manufacturing company executive; b. Morristown, N.J., July 20, 1943; s. Herbert Seward and Anne (Brady) C.; m. Elinor Ladd, Aug. 27, 1966; children: Elisabeth Ladd, Amy Richmond. A.B. cum laude, Harvard U., 1965; J.D., U. Pa., 1970. Bar: N.Y. 1970, Mass. 1974, Ohio 1980. Assoc. firm Sullivan & Cromwell, N.Y.C., 1970-73; asst. counsel, asst. sec. Mass. Fin. Services Co., Boston, 1973-76; gen. counsel, sec. Anchor Corp., Elizabeth, N.J., 1976-79; sec., sr. corp. counsel B.F. Goodrich Co., Akron, Ohio, 1979—. Mem. N.Y. Bar Assn., Mass. Bar Assn. Clubs: Sakonnet Golf (Little Compton, R.I.); Mendham (N.J.) Golf and Tennis; Harvard (Boston and Akron); University (Akron). Home: 2963 Hudson-Aurora Rd Hudson OH 44236 Office: 500 S Main St Akron OH 44318

CRAVIT, DAVID, advertising agency executive; b. Toronto, Ont., Can., Apr. 19, 1945; s. Harry and Ruth (Lappin) C.; children: Matthew Brian, Joanna Ruth. B.A., U. Toronto, 1971. Copywriter Lawrence Wolf Advt., Toronto, 1969-71; v.p., creative dir. Saffer Cravit & Freedman Advt., Toronto, 1971—. Ghost writer: Divorced Parenting, 1982. Jewish. Home: 607 Spadina Rd Toronto ONCanada M5P 2X1 Office: Saffer Cravit & Freedman Advt Inc 180 Duncan Mill Rd Toronto ONCanada M3B 1Z6

CRAWFORD, ALBERT BENJAMIN, JR., manufacturing company executive; b. Tucson, Feb. 3, 1928; s. Albert Benjamin and Ethel Maude (Duniven) C.; m. Bettie Nan Houston, June 23, 1950; children: Richard, Christine, Kenneth, Melinda, Jennifer. B.S. in Mil. Sci., U.S. Mil. Acad., 1950; M.S. in Elec. Engring., Stanford U., 1955, M.S. Indsl. Engring., 1956. Commd. 2d lt. U.S. Army, 1950, advanced through grades to maj. gen., 1974; comdr. (12th Signal Group), Vietnam, 1969, dep. dir., 1970-71, project mgr., Ft. Monmouth, N.J., 1971-75, comdg. gen., 1975-76, ret., 1976; corp. mgr. info. services, dir. corp. planning Digital Equipment Corp., Maynard, Mass., 1976—. Decorated D.S.M., Legion of Merit with oak leaf cluster, Bronze Star, Meritorious Service medal. Mem. Soc. Mgmt. Info. Systems. Republican. Home: 11 Munnings Dr Sudbury MA 01776 Office: 146 Main St. Maynard MA 01754

CRAWFORD, BRODERICK, motion picture actor; b. Phila., Dec. 9 1911; s. Helen Broderick and;; s. Lester C.; m. Joan Tabor (div.); children: Lauren, Kim, Kelly. Head of Broderick Crawford Enterprises, 1952—. Began on stage; screen debut The Woman's Touch, 1937; Pictures include Eternally Yours, 1940, I Can't Give You Anything But Love, Baby, Slightly Honorable, When the Daltons Rode, 1942, Sin Town, Broadway, Butch Minds the Baby, 1946, The Runaround, Black Angel, 1947, Slave Girl, 1948, The Time of Your Life, 1949, All the King's Men, 1950, Born Yesterday, 1951, Night People, 1954, Not as a Stranger, 1955, Convicts 4, 1962, Fastest Gun Alive, 1956, Between Heaven and Hell, 1956, The Oscar, 1966, Gregoria and His Angels, The Texican, 1966, The Tattered Web, 1971, Look What's Happened to Rosemary's Baby, 1976, Hell's Bloody Devils, Won Ton Ton, The Dog Who Saved Hollywood, 1976, A Little Romance, 1979, There Goes The Bride, 1980, Liar's Moon, 1982; appeared in: TV movie Hunter, 1976; Star: TV series Highway Patrol, 1955-59, King of Diamonds, 1961, The Interns, 1971; numerous TV appearances, including Saturday Night Live, G.E. Theatre, Ford Theatre, Bat Masterson, Burke's Law, U.S. Steel Hour, Name of the Game, Playhouse 90, Love American Style, Alias Smith and Jones, Banacek, Jigsaw, Harry O, Medical Story, City of Angels, Merv Griffin Show; stage play That Championship Season, 1974. Recipient Acad. Award for Best Actor, 1950. Address: care Contemporary-Korman Artists Ltd 132 Lasker Dr Beverly Hills CA 90212 *

CRAWFORD, BRUCE EDGAR, advertising executive; b. West Bridgewater, Mass., Mar. 16, 1929; s. Harry Ellsworth and Nancy (Morrison) C.; m. Christine Ameling, Feb. 1, 1958; 1 son, Robert Bosworth. B.S. in Econs, U. Pa., 1952. With Benton & Bowles, Inc., N.Y.C., 1954-58; v.p. Ted Bates & Co., N.Y.C., 1958-61; advt. dir. Chesebrough Ponds Inc., N.Y.C., 1961-63; with Batten, Barton, Durstine & Osborn, Inc., N.Y.C., 1963—, pres., from 1978, BBDO Internat., N.Y.C., 1975—, chief exec. officer, 1977—. Bd. dirs. Met. Opera Assn. Served with U.S. Army, 1947-48. Mem. Assn. Advt. Agencies Am. Republican. Clubs: Racquet and Tennis (N.Y.C.); Turf and Field. Office: BBDO Internat 383 Madison Ave New York NY 10017 *

CRAWFORD, BRYCE LOW, JR., chemist, educator; b. New Orleans, Nov. 27, 1914; s. Bryce Low and Clara Hall (Crawford) C.; m. Ruth Raney, Dec. 21, 1940; children: Bryce, Craig, Sherry Ann. A.B., Stanford U., 1934, M.A., 1935, Ph.D., 1937; Nat. Research fellow, Harvard U., 1937-39. Instr. chemistry Yale U., 1939-40; asst. prof. U. Minn., Mpls., 1940-43, assoc. prof., 1943-46, prof. phys. chemistry, 1946-82, Regents' prof. chemistry, 1982—, chmn. dept., 1955-60, dean grad. sch., 1960-72; Mem. Grad. Record Exam. Bd., 1968-72; chmn. Council Grad Schs. in U.S., 1962-63; pres. Assn. Grad. Schs., 1970; dir. research on rocket propellants under Div. 3 Nat. Def. Research Com., 1942-45. Editor: Jour. Phys. Chemistry, 1970-80. Trustee Midwest Research Inst., 1963—. Guggenheim fellow, 1950-51, 72-73; Fulbright grantee Oxford, 1951, Oxford, Tokyo, 1966; recipient Presdl. Cert. of Merit. Mem. Am. Chem. Soc. (dir. 1969-77, Priestley medal 1982, Pitts. Spectroscopy award, Ellis Lippincott award), Optical Soc. Am., AAAS, AAUP, Am. Phys. Soc., Nat. Acad. Scis. (council 1975-78, home. sec. 1979—), Coblentz Soc., Am. Philos. Soc., Am. Acad. Arts and Scis., Phi Beta Kappa, Sigma Xi, Phi Lambda Upsilon, Alpha Chi Sigma. Episcopalian. Clubs: Campus, Cosmos. Specialist in molecular structure and molecular spectra. Home: 1545 Branston St Saint Paul MN 55108 Office: Molecular Spectroscopy Lab U Minn 207 Pleasant St SE Minneapolis MN 55455

CRAWFORD, CARL BENSON, civil engineer, Canadian government research administrator; b. Dauphin, Man., Can., Oct. 2, 1923; s. Arthur Benson and Eileen Agnes (Einarson) C.; m. Adah May Shanks, Sept. 6, 1948; children: Nora, Henry, Margaret, Blair. B.Sc.C.E., Queen's U., Kingston, Ont., Can., 1949; M.Sc. in Soil Engring, Northwestern U., 1951, D.I.C., U. London, 1957. Machine operator Otis-Fensom Elevator Co., Hamilton, Ont., 1941-42; personnel expeditor B.C. Bridge & Dredging Co. (Can.), Prince Rupert, 1942-43; research officer soil mechanics sect. Bldg. Research div. Nat. Research Council Can., Ottawa, Ont., 1949-53, head soil mechanics sect., 1953-69, asst. dir., 1969-74, dir., 1974—; Bd. dirs. Conseil International du Batiment pour la Recherche l'Etude et la Documentation; mem. adv. bd. Centre for Bldg. Studies, Concordia U., Montreal, Que., Can.; mem. Constrn. Industry Devel. Council of Can. Contbr. articles to tech. publs. Served with RCAF, 1943-45. Recipient Robert F. Legget award Can. Geotech. Soc., 1977. Mem. Assn. Profl. Engrs. Ont., ASTM (Hogentogler award 1961, Spl. Service award 1968, hon. mem. 1977—, dir.), ASCE, Can. Constrn. Assn., Can. Research Mgmt. Assn., Engring. Inst. Can. (v.p. 1981—), Internat. Soc. Soil Mechanics and Found. Engring. (v.p. N.Am.). Home: 198 Cluny St Ottawa ON K1G 0K2 Canada Office: DBR/NRC Montreal Rd Ottawa ON K1A 0R6 Canada

CRAWFORD, CAROL TALLMAN, government executive; b. Mt. Holly, N.J., Feb. 25, 1943; m. Ronald Crawford; children: Timothy, Jeffrey, Richard. B.A., Mt. Holyoke Coll., 1965; J.D. magna cum laude, Washington Coll. Law, Am. U., 1978. Bar: Va. 1978, D.C. 1979. Legis. asst. to Senator Bob Packwood, Washington, 1969-75; assoc. firm Collier, Shannon, Rill & Scott, Washington, 1979-81; exec. asst. to chmn. FTC, Washington, 1981-83, acting exec. dir., 1982, dir. bur. consumer protection, 1983—; sr. advisor Reagan-Bush Transition Team, 1981. Trustee Barry Goldwater Chair of Am. Instns., Ariz. State U., Phoenix, 1983—. Mem. ABA, D.C. Bar Assn., Va. Bar Assn., Phi Delta Phi. Republican. Office: FTC 6th & Pennsylvania Ave NW Washington DC 20580

CRAWFORD, CHARLES MCNEIL, winery executive; b. Antioch, Calif., Sept. 23, 1918; s. Robert Elmer and Alice (Hust) C.; m. Sarah Katherine Glover, Aug. 19, 1940; children: Robert McNeil, Judith Lee. B.S., U. Calif. at Berkeley, 1940; M.S., Cornell U., 1941. Trainee Great Western Electro-Chem. Co., Pittsburg, Calif., 1939; research asst. N.Y. State Agrl. Expt. Sta., Geneva, N.Y., 1940; winemaker-chemist Urbana Wine Co., Hammonsport, N.Y., 1941; v.p., sec. E & J Gallo Winery, Modesto, Calif., 1942-; mem. Am. Found. for Viticulture and Enology. Recipient Merit award Am. Soc. Quality Control, 1972; Cornell U. Research fellow, 1940-41. Mem. Am. Soc. Enologists (Merit award 1966), Am. Chem. Soc., Inst. Food Tech., Wine Inst. (tech. com.), Nat., Calif. socs. profl. engrs., N.Y. Acad. Sci., Calif. Acad. Sci., AAAS, Modesto Engring. Club, Alpha Zeta. Clubs: Modesto Swim and Racquet, F.W. Ski Assn., Tahoe Yacht. Home:

2752 Sherwood Ave Modesto CA 95350 Office: PO Box 1130 Modesto CA 95353

CRAWFORD, CHARLES MERLE, educator; b. Kirksville, Mo., Oct. 5, 1924; s. Charles Samuel and Malinda (Lockhart) C.; m. Mary Ann Swope, June 12, 1948; children: Roger Steven, Guy Alan, Sarah Jane, Laura Beth. Student, U. Pa., 1943-44; B.S., U. Ill., 1948, M.S., 1949, Ph.D., 1953. Instr. U. Fla., 1949-51, asst. prof., 1953-55; mktg. dir. Mead Johnson & Co., Evansville, Ind., 1955-65; prof. Grad. Sch. Bus. Adminstrn., U. Mich., Ann Arbor, 1965—, mem. exec. com., 1970-74, chmn. dept. mktg., 1979-81; prof. new products mgmt. Grad. Sch. Bus. Adminstrn., U-Mich., 1983—. Author: The Future Environment for Marketing, 1968, New Products Management, 1983. Served with AUS, 1943-45. Mem. Ann Arbor C. of C. (exec. com. 1972), Am. Mktg. Assn. (v.p. 1965-66), Product Devel. Assn. (internat. pres. 1976-78), Sales Mktg. Execs., Alpha Kappa Psi, Phi Kappa Phi, Beta Gamma Sigma. Republican. Conglist. Club: Kiwanian (pres. 1975). Home: 2151 S 7th St Ann Arbor MI 48103

CRAWFORD, CHERYL, theatrical producer; b. Akron, Ohio, Sept. 24, 1902; d. Robert K. and Luella Elizabeth (Parker) C. Student, Buchtel Coll., 1 year; A.B. cum laude, Smith Coll., 1925, Litt.D., 1966. Produced plays while at, Smith Coll.; casting dir., Theatre Guild, N.Y.C., 1926-30; one of founders and dirs., The Group Theatre, 1930-37; produced: Awake and Sing by Clifford Odets; produced independently: (with Judith Anderson) Oh, Men, Oh, Women, 1954, Comes a Day, Camino Real, Shadow of a Gunman, Rivalry, Sweet Bird of Youth, Period of Adjustment, 1960, Andorra, Jennie, Brecht on Courage, 1962, Mother Courage and Her Children, 1963, Double Talk, 1964, Celebration, 1969, Colette, 1970, Yentl by Isaac Basheviz Singer. Named Woman of Yr., 1959; recipient Achievement medal Brandeis U., 1964. Home and Office: 400 E 52d St New York City NY 10022

CRAWFORD, DAVID COLEMAN, diversified mfg. co. exec.; b. Dixon, Ill., Mar. 7, 1930; s. and Grace F. (Coleman) C.; m. Carolyn J. Morrow, Nov. 11, 1958; children—Eugene, Richard, Grace. B.S., Norwich U., 1952; M.S., U. Ill., 1954. Design engr. Freeport Sulphur Co., New Orleans, 1956-62; sr. engr. ETCO Engrs. & Assos., New Orleans, 1962-64; mgr. constrn. Offshore Co., Houston, 1964-70; asst. gen. mgr. Far East Levingston Shipbldg. Co., Singapore, 1970-71; with Marathon Mfg. Co., Houston and, Singapore, 1971—, sr. v.p., 1973-74, exec. v.p., 1974—, also dir.; dir. several subs. cos. Trustee Norwich U. Served with C.E. U.S. Army, 1954-56. Mem. ASCE, Am. Welding Soc., Sigma Xi, Chi Epsilon, Tau Beta Pi. Republican. Baptist. Clubs: Lakeside Country, Petroleum of Houston, Houston Engring. Research on brazed copper joints, 1952-54. Home: 611 Durley Rd Houston TX 77079 Office: 600 Jefferson St Houston TX 77002

CRAWFORD, EARL BOYD, former govt. ofcl.; b. Washington, Apr. 13, 1906; s. James Albert and Olla Lola (Nigh) C.; m. Gertrude Galloway, June 15, 1927; 1 son, Christopher Paul. Student, Strayer Bus. Coll., 1924; grad., Mt. Pleasant Sch. for Secs., 1929. Sec. to mem. of Congress, 1932-36; sec., chief staff to dir. gen. U.S. Constn. Sesquicentennial Commn., 1936-39; staff adminstr., clk. Com. Fgn. Affairs Ho. of Reps., 1939-70; mem. U.S. del. UN Conf. Internat. Orgn., San Francisco, 1945, UN Gen. Assembly, London, 1946, N.Y., 1946, 49, 50, 53, Paris, 1951; sec. UN com. UNRRA, 1946, mem. U.S. del., 1946; staff mem. U.S. del. Consultative Assembly Europe, Strasbourg, France, 1965, 66, 67; Mem. adv. com. inst. position U.S. world affairs Am. U., lectr. U.S. fgn. policy, 1949, 50; served with spl. Congl. study mission, Alaska, 1947, Europe, 1951, Far East, South Asia, Middle East, 1954, Mediterranean, 1956, Guatemala, Mex., 1957, Japan, Vietnam, Thailand, 1965, Colombia, 1968; congl. del. 6th-8th NATO Parliamentarian's Conf., Paris; mem. del. Brit.-Am. Parliamentary Conf., Bermuda, 1961, 63, 64, 66, 68, staff mem., 1966, 68; U.S. del. Commonwealth Parliamentary Conf., Wellington, New Zealand, 1965, Consultative Assembly Council Europe, 1968; staff mem. U.S. del. North Atlantic Assembly, The Hague, Netherlands, 1970; ofcl. observer 22d ann. session North Atlantic Assembly, Colonial Williamsburg, Va., 1976. Author: ofcl. report U.S. Constn. Sesquicentennial Commn. contained in History of the Formation of the Union Under the Constitution, 1941. Mem. Am. Polit. Sci. Assn., Am. Acad. Polit. and Social Sci., Am. Soc. Internat. Law. Home: 8235 The Midway Annandale VA 22003

CRAWFORD, EDWARD HAMON, insurance company executive; b. Truro, N.S., Can., Aug. 14, 1925; s. Edward Smith and Marie Eva (Hamon) C.; m. Barbara Mary Smith, June 25, 1955; children: Douglas Edward Smith Crawford, Robert Gordon Smith Crawford. B.A. in Polit. Sci. and Econs., U. Toronto, 1948. With Can. Life Assurance Co., Can. Life Investment div., 1948—, investment rep., Brit. Isles, 1952, asst. treas., Toronto, Ont., Can., 1957, asso. treas., 1963, treas., 1964, v.p., treas., 1967, exec. v.p., 1970, dir., 1971, pres., 1973—; dir. Canadian Imperial Bank of Commerce, Gulf Can. Ltd., Moore Corp. Ltd., Interprovisional Pipe Line Ltd.; chmn. Can. Enterprise Devel. Corp. Ltd., Can. Life and Health Ins. Assn., Inc.; Bd. dirs. Am. Council Life Ins. Trustee Hosp. for Sick Children, Toronto; bd. govs. St. Andrew's Coll. Served with RCAF, 1943-45. Clubs: Toronto Golf, Toronto, Granite, York. Home: 47 Daneswood Rd Toronto ON M4N 3J7 Canada Office: 330 University Ave Toronto ON M5G 1R8 Canada

CRAWFORD, EUGENE BENSON, JR., health adminstr.; b. Tuskegee, Ala., Apr. 18, 1925; s. Eugene B. and Madge (Abercrombie) C.; m. Elizabeth Virginia Wilson, Oct. 2, 1948; children—Elizabeth Kenyon Walkinshaw, Madge Lane Hurdle, Virginia Wilson. B.S., U. N.C., 1948, grad. exec. program, 1966; certificate, N.C. Bapt. Hosp., 1949. Adminstrv. resident N.C. Bapt. Hosp., Winston-Salem, 1948-49; asst. adminstr. Moore Meml. Hosp., Pinehurst, N.C., 1949-51; asso. dir. to dir., asst. prof. N.C. Meml. Hosp. of U. N.C., 1951-66; v.p. adminstrn. Wilmington (Del.) Med. Center, 1966—. Served with USNR, 1942-46. Fellow Am. Coll. Hosp. Adminstrs.; mem. Assn. Del. Hosps. (pres. 1970, 79), Am. Hosp. Assn., Am. Assn. Med. Colls., Md., Del., Va., D.C. Hosp. Assn. (pres. 1973). Home: 1022 Warwick Ln Barley Mill Cts Greenville DE 19807 Office: PO Box 1668 Wilmington DE 19899

CRAWFORD, FRANK STEVENS, educator; b. Scranton, Pa., Oct. 25, 1923; s. Frank Stevens and Louise (Kindl) C.; m. Bevalyn D. Bunker, June 29, 1962; children—Sarah T., Matthew B. Ph.D., U. Calif., Berkeley, 1953. Research asso. Lawrence Radiation Lab., 1953-58; asst. prof. physics U. Calif., Berkeley, 1958-60, asso. prof., 1960-65, prof., 1965—. Author: Waves, 1968. Served with USAAF, 1943-45. Mem. Am. Phys. Soc., Am. Assn. Physics Tchrs. Home: 2826 Garber St Berkeley CA 94705

CRAWFORD, FRANKLIN DAVID, publishing co. exec.; b. Denver, Aug. 9, 1928; s. Clifford Theodore and Sarah Ann (Fergeson) C.; m. Ruth Emilia Dallenbach, Oct. 19, 1957; children—Mark Franklin, Grant Robert. B.A., Alma White Coll., 1953. Retail exec. Saks Fifth Av., N.Y.C., 1954-56, Federated Dept. Stores, 1956-58, Allied Stores Corp., 1958-61, J.C. Penney Corp., 1961-63; owner, pres. Princeton (N.J.) Microfilm Corp., 1963—; pres. Nat. Library Service Co., Princeton, 1974—, V.P. Realty, Inc., 1967—. Chmn. bd. U.S. Hist. Documents Inst., Washington, 1970—; cons. Alma White Coll., Zarephath, N.J.; Vice pres., bd. dirs. Weaver Found., St. Louis, 1966—. Served with USAF, 1946-49, 53-54. Republican. Clubs: Nassau, Beadensbrook, West Side Tennis. Home: 231 Lambert Dr Princeton NJ 08540 Office: 707 Alexander Rd Princeton NJ 08540

CRAWFORD, H(AZLE) R(EID), city ofcl., housing mgmt. exec.; b. Winston-Salem, N.C., Jan. 18, 1939; s. Hazle and Mary (Reid) C.; m. Eleanora Braxton, Oct. 8, 1956; children—Leslie, Hazle, George, Gregory, Lynne. Student, Howard U., 1961-63, D.C. Tchrs. Coll., 1963-65, Am. U., 1967; B.A., Chgo. State U. Cert. property mgr. Mgr. Frederick W. Berens Sales, Inc., Washington, 1964-66, property mgr., 1966-68, Polinger Co., 1968-69; v.p. Polinger-Crawford Corp., 1969-73; pres. H.R. Crawford, Inc., 1972-73; v.p. Kaufman & Broad Asset Mgmt., Inc., 1971-73; asst. sec. housing mgmt. HUD, Washington, 1973-76; with Edgewood Mgmt. Corp., Chevy Chase, Md., 1976—; Faculty Howard U., 1971-73; cons. Dept. Def., States of Mich. and N.Y. Chmn. Area Neighborhood Planning Council, 1967-68; council of chairmen Programs for Children and Youth, 20 neighborhood planning councils, 1968-69, 11th Police Precinct Citizens Adv. Council, 1968-69, 6th Dist. Police-Citizens Adv. Council, 1970-71; treas. Congress Heights Assn. for Service and Edn., Inc., 1970-71; pres. Urban Rehab. Corp., Archdiocese of Washington, 1971-72; mem. Archdiocese of Washington, 1970—, Nat. Urban League, 1973—, Council Black Presdl. Appointees, 1973—, D.C. City Council, 1980—; Bd. dirs. Bonabond, Inc., Washington Adv. Bd. Recreation, Anacosta Econ. Devel. Corp., Frederick Douglas Community Center, Congress Heights Assn. for Services and Edn., Am. Cancer Soc., Jr. Citizens Corp., Inc., Goodwill Industries, SCLC, NAACP; mem. exec. com. Far East Community Services; mem. D.C. Bd. Equalization and Rev. Served with USAF, 1957-65. Recipient Presdl. citation, 1970; Life fellow award Kiwanis Internat., 1973; Outstanding Achievement award Nat. Assn. Real Estate Brokers, 1974; Joint Minority Contractors award Nat. Assn. Minority Architects, Nat. Assn. Minority Contractors, Nat. Assn. Housing Specialists and United Mortgage Bankers, 1974; Career Excellence award People United to Save Humanity, 1974; award of recognition of contbn. to local housing authorities in U.S. Mayor of Las Vegas, 1974, Nat. Capitol Housing Authority, 1976, So. Conf. Black Mayors, 1976; also numerous pub. service awards and keys to cities. Mem. Inst. Real Estate Mgmt. (J. Wallace Paletou award 1974, Mgr. of Year award 1973), Builders, Owners and Mgrs. Assn., Nat. Assn. Housing and Redevel. Ofcls. (hon. life mem. So. regional council), Profl. Property Mgrs. Assn., Washington Bd. Realtors, Washington Real Estate Brokers, Nat. Assn. Home Builders. Democrat. Home: 3195 Westover Dr SE Washington DC 20020 Office: 1443 Pennsylvania Ave Washington DC 20003 *Notwithstanding the many years in the field of housing management, I find that I am still fascinated by the ever changing facets of the industry. Being able to assist in the resolution of the problems encountered by the less fortunate has been most rewarding. During my years in the business, I am honored to be acquainted with so many associates of such high integrity and sensitivity towards resolving the problems of the low and moderate income families in the United States.*

CRAWFORD, IRVING POPE, microbiologist; b. Cleve., Nov. 20, 1930; s. Merwin William and Mildred (Pope) C.; m. Edna May Barstow, July 2, 1955; children—William Wilder, James Leon. A.B., Stanford U., 1951, M.D., 1955. NSF fellow Washington U., St. Louis, 1954-55; NSF postdoctoral fellow Stanford U., 1958-59; asst. prof., then asso. prof. microbiology Western Res. U. Med. Sch., 1959-65; mem. dept. microbiology Scripps Clinic and Research Found., La Jolla, Calif., 1965-77; prof. microbiology, chmn. dept. U. Iowa, Iowa City, 1977—. Served as officer M.C. U.S. Army, 1955-57. Mem. Am. Soc. Microbiology, Am. Soc. Biol. Chemists, Genetics Soc. Am., AAAS. Office: Dept Microbiology U Iowa Iowa City IA 52242

CRAWFORD, JAMES DOUGLAS, lawyer; b. Phila., May 31, 1932; s. James A. and Katharine M. (Eavenson) C.; m. Judith N. Dean, Apr. 29, 1977; 1 dau., Christopher Anne Crawford Samson. A.B., Haverford Coll., 1954; LL.B., U. Pa., 1962. Bar: Pa. 1963, D.C. 1979, U.S. Supreme Ct. 1968. Assoc. Montgomery, McCracken, Walker & Rhoads, Phila., 1962-66; asst. dist. atty., Phila., 1966-68, dep. dist. atty., chief appeals div., 1968-72; gen. counsel Redevel. Authority of City of Phila., 1972-74; partner Schnader, Harrison, Segal & Lewis, Phila., 1974—; lectr. in law U. Pa., 1971-73; bd. dirs. Defender Assn., Phila., 1975—, Nat. Assn. Law Placement, 1978-79. Bd. dirs. ACLU, 1978—; bd. dirs. ACLU of Pa., 1969—, v.p., 1980—; bd. dirs., mem. exec. com. ACLU of Greater Phila., 1972—, v.p., 1983—; mem. exec. com. Friends of Phila. Mus. Art, 1980—, fin. sec., 1981-82, co-chmn., 1982—. Served with U.S. Army, 1955-57. Mem. Am. Bar Assn., Pa. Bar Assn., Phila. Bar Assn. (gov. 1973-75, chmn. com. of censors 1972), Fed. Bar Assn., Am. Law Inst., Order of Coif, Phi Beta Kappa. Republican. Presbyterian. Club: Peale. Home: 3811 The Oak Rd Philadelphia PA 19129 Office: 1600 Market St Suite 3600 Philadelphia PA 19103

CRAWFORD, JOHN EDWARD, scientist; b. Richmond, Va., June 6, 1924; s. James Henry and Loretta Ellen (Bankerd) C.; m. Mary Elizabeth Ayres, May 15, 1948; children: Michelle Lorraine, Caprice Lizette. B.A., Johns Hopkins, 1947. Geologist uranium exploration program U.S. Geol. Survey, 1948-51; nat. stockpile materials specialist Munitions Bd., Office Sec. Def., 1951-53; prodn. engr. uranium in Tenn. and Fla. AEC, 1953-54; specialist on source, feed, fissionable materials Bur. Mines, 1954-57, nuclear tech. adviser to dir., 1957-60, chief nuclear engr. for atomic research programs, 1960-63; dir. Marine Mineral Tech. Center, Tiburon, Calif., 1963-66; pres., founder Crawford Marine Specialists, Inc., San Rafael, Calif., 1966-76; pres. Earth Tech. Corp., San Rafael, 1973-77; mgr. geothermal and small hydro research programs U.S. Dept. Energy, San Francisco, 1977—. Author: Facts Concerning Uranium Exploration and Production, 1956; Contbr articles to govt. and profl. jours. Mem. Calif. Gov.'s Commn. Ocean Resources, 1966-67, Calif. Gov.'s Small Hydro Task Force, 1981-82. Served with AUS, 1943-46. Mem. Geol. Soc. Am., Am. Soc. Oceanography, Marine Tech. Soc. (past chmn. marine mineral resources com.), Delta Upsilon. Home: 261 Parque Fuente Rohnert Park CA 94928 Office: 1333 Broadway Oakland CA 94612

CRAWFORD, KENNETH CHARLES, govt. ofcl.; b. Nokomis, Ill., Oct. 31, 1918; s. Charles Bryant and Blanche Dora (Gates) C.; m. Madge Marie Douglas, Aug. 23, 1942; 1 son, James Douglas. B.A., Ill. Coll., 1946, S.J.D. (hon.), 1970; J.D., U. Va., 1951; grad., Command and Gen. Staff Coll., 1957, Army War Coll., 1962; M.A., George Washington U., 1962. Bar: Va. bar 1951, Ga. bar 1967, Korean bar 1965, U.S. Supreme Ct. bar 1970, D.C. bar 1977. Commd. 2d lt. U.S. Army, 1942, advanced through grades to col., 1962; served in (F.A. and JAG Corps); tchr. legal subjects U. Md., U. Ga., Ga. State U., Nat. U., Washington, 1957-67; comdr. JAG Sch., 1967-70; ret., 1970. Editor: Laws of the Republic of Korea, 1964. Asso. dir. edn. Southwestern Legal Found., Dallas, 1970-71; dir. edn. and tng. Fed. Judicial Center, Washington, 1971—. Decorated Legion of Merit with 2 oak leaf clusters, Soldiers medal, Bronze Star medal, Army Commendation medal with 2 oak leaf clusters; Belgian Fourragere. Mem. State Bar Va., State Bar Ga., D.C. Bar, Korean Bar, Order of Coif. Home: 2827 29th St NW Washington DC 20008 Office: 1520 H St NW Washington DC 20005

CRAWFORD, LESTER MILLS, JR., veterinarian; b. Demopolis, Ala., Mar. 13, 1938; s. Lester Mills and Susan Doris (Mitchell) C.; m. Catherine Walker, July 27, 1963; children: Catherine Leigh, Mary Stuart. D.V.M., Auburn U., 1963; Ph.D., U. Ga., 1969. Pvt. practice vet. medicine, Meridian, Miss. and Birmingham, Ala., 1963-64; research and devel. staff Agrl. div. Am. Cyanamid Co., Princeton, N.J., 1964-66, also cons.; assoc. prof. pharmacology, assoc. dean Coll. Vet. Medicine, U. Ga., 1970-75; dir. Bur. Vet. Medicine, FDA, HEW, Rockville, Md., 1978-80, 82—; head dept. physiology-pharmacology U. Ga., 1981-82; cons. pharm. industry, agribus. FDA. Contbr. sci. articles to profl. jours. Lay speaker Methodist Ch., 1970—; bd. dirs.; Ga. div. Am. Cancer Soc. U. Ga. Faculty Club, Athens Acad. Recipient Alpha Psi Nat. Council award Am. Coll. Vet. Pharmacology and Therapeutics, 1977; A.M. Mills award; K.F. Meyer award; named Outstanding Sr. Auburn U. Sch. Vet. Medicine, 1963; Commr.'s spl. citation FDA. Mem. AVMA (Aux. award), Ga. Vet. Med. Assn., D.C. Vet. Med. Assn., AAAS, Sigma Xi, Phi Zeta, Phi Kappa Phi. Republican. Club: Athens (Ga.) Country. Home: 11925 Gainsborough Rd Potomac MD 20854 Office: Bur Vet Medicine FDA 5600 Fishers Ln Rockville MD 20857 *I have always predicated my own life on the certain knowledge that God is still at work in the world. I believe that every person carries a divine spark, and that the function of leadership is to ignite that spark. I furthermore believe that a Franciscan love of and respect for animals is a prerequisite for membership in the human race. And I believe that the true rewards in life are to be found in communion with family, friends and colleagues.*

CRAWFORD, LEWIS CLEAVER, consulting engineer; b. Salina, Kans., Dec. 7, 1925; s. Percival Wallace and Viva Estelle (Beichle) C.; m. Helen Aleyne Henry, May 28, 1950; children: Dorothy Caroline, Lewis Henry. B.Engring., Yale U., 1946. Registered profl. engr., Kans. Engr. Cemenstone Corp., Pitts., 1946-47; engr., then asso. Wilson & Co. (engrs. and architects), Salina, 1947-67, partner, 1967—; dir. Saltec, Inc.; bd. dirs. Kans. Builders Forum, Kans. U. Center for Research; mem. adv. com. Am. Gas Assn. Served with USNR, 1943-46. Fellow ASCE; mem. Nat. Soc. Profl. Engrs., Am. Concrete Inst., Kans. Cons. Engrs. (chmn.), Kans. Engring. Soc. (dir.), SAR. Republican. Methodist. Club: Salina Country. office: 631 E Crawford St Salina KS 67401

CRAWFORD, MARIA LUISA, geology educator; b. Beverly, Mass., July 18, 1939; d. William Theodore Buse and Barbara (Kidder) Aldana; m. William A. Crawford, Aug. 29, 1963. B.A., Bryn Mawr Coll., 1960; postgrad., U. Oslo, 1960-61; Ph.D., U. Calif., 1965. Asst. prof. Bryn Mawr Coll., Pa., 1965-73, assoc. prof., 1973-79, PROF., 1979—; chmn. dept. geology Bryn Mawr. Coll., Pa., 1976—; chmn. women geoscientists com. Am. Geol. Inst., 1976-77; mem. U.S. Nat. Com. Geochemistry, 1980-82. NASA grantee, 1973-76; NSF grantee, 1967—. Fellow Geol. Soc. Am. (councillor 1982—), Mineral Soc. Am.; mem. Mineral Assn. Can., Am. Geophys. Union, Norwegian Geol. Soc., Phila. Geol. Soc., Assn. Women in Sci. Office: Dept Geology Bryn Mawr Coll Bryn Mawr PA 19010

CRAWFORD, MEREDITH PULLEN, research psychologist; b. Sweetbriar, Va., Oct. 13, 1910; s. Leonidas Wakefield and Helen May (Meredith) C.; m. Helen Cartwright Grizzard, Aug. 20, 1936 (dec. Mar. 1978); children: Meredith P. (dec.), Ann C., Susan B.; m. Celia Deese Knox, Aug. 7, 1982. A.B., Vanderbilt U., 1931; A.M., Columbia, h61932, Ph.D., 1935. Univ. fellow in psychology Columbia, 1933-34; research asst. Lab. Primate Biology, Yale, 1934-39; Instr. psychology Barnard Coll., Columbia, 1939-40; asst. prof., then prof. psychology Vanderbilt U., Nashville, 1940-51, dean Jr. Coll., 1945-49, dean instrn. Coll. Arts and Sci., 1949-51; dir. George Washington U. Human Resources Research Office, 1951-69; pres. Human Resources Research Orgn., 1969-76; research engr. George Washington U., 1976-78. Adminstrv. officer for accreditation Am. Psychol. Assn., 1978-82. Served as officer USAAF aviation psychology program, 1942-45. Recipient Distinguished Civilian Service award Sec. Army, 1961. Fellow AAAS (sec. sect. J 1978-82), Am. Psychol. Assn. (treas. 1958-67, award for outstanding sci. and profl. contbn. div. mil. psychology 1976); mem. Am. Ednl. Research Assn. (fin. adviser 1970-73), Phi Beta Kappa, Sigma Xi, Delta Kappa Epsilon. Methodist. Club: Cosmos. Home: 3563 Hamlet Pl Chevy Chase MD 20815

CRAWFORD, MORRIS DECAMP, JR., banker; b. Nyack, N.Y., Sept. 11 1915; s. Morris DeCamp and Grace (Blauvelt) C.; m. Dorothy Duncan Babcock, May 2, 1942; children: Duncan, Gordon, Linda. S.B. magna cum laude, Harvard U., 1937, LL.B., 1940. Bar: N.Y. 1940. With firm Cadwalader, Wickersham, Taft, N.Y.C., 1940-53; with Bowery Savs. Bank, N.Y.C., 1953—, exec. v.p., 1959-62, pres., 1962-66, chmn. bd., chief exec. officer, 1966-80; trustee Tchrs. Ins. & Annuity Assn.; dir. Adams Express. Former mem. Pres. Nixon's Commn. on Fin. Structure and Regulation; bd. dirs. Regional Plan Assn.; past bd. dirs. USO of Met. N.Y.; past bd. dir. United Way of N.Y.; former chmn. bd. 42d St. Redevel. Corp.; former mem. adv. com. Joint Center Urban Studies, M.I.T. and Harvard U.; formerly trustee Russell Sage Found., W.T. Grant Found.; trustee Cathedral Ch. St. John the Divine, N.Y.C., 1976—, N.Y. Pub. Library. Served to maj. AUS, 1942-46; PTO. Mem. Savs. Bank Assn. N.Y. State (former dir.), Nat. Assn. Mut. Savs. Banks (pres. 1964-65, former dir.). Mem. P.E. Ch. Clubs: Harvard (N.Y.C.); Greenwich (Conn.) Country. Home: 71 Gilliam Ln Riverside CT 06878

CRAWFORD, NEIL STANLEY, Canadian provincial official; b. Prince Albert, Sask., Can., May 26, 1931; d. William Francis and Hannah (Hoehn) C.; m. Catherine May Hughes, Sept. 3, 1951; children: Scot, Teresa, Ian, Elaine, Sandra, Robert. Bar: Alta. 1955. Created Queen's Counsel, 1972; practice law, Alta., 1955-61, 63-71, exec. asst. to Prime Minister of Can., 1961-63; mem. Alta. Legis. Assembly, 1971—; apptd. Provincial Cabinet as Minister of Health and Social Devel., 1971, apptd. Minister of Labor, 1975, apptd. Atty. Gen. and Govt. House Leader, 1979—. Alderman City of Edmonton, 1966-71. Served to lt/ Can. Arty., 1950-51. Mem. Can. Bar Assn., Law Soc. Alta. Progressive Conservative. Office: 227 Legislature Bldg Edmonton AB Canada T5K 2B6

CRAWFORD, NORMAN CRANE, JR., college president; b. Newark, Oct. 30, 1930; s. Norman Crane and Anna (Wares) C.; m. Garnette Bell, June 25, 1955; children: Sally Jean, Ellen Ann. B.S. in Edn, Rutgers U., 1951, M.Ed., 1957; Ph.D., Northwestern U., 1966. Scholarship dir. Nat. Merit Scholarship Corp., Evanston, Ill., 1957-62; asst. dean arts and sci., asst. to provost U. Del., 1962-66, 67-70; lectr. in edn., 1967-70; acting dir. exams. Coll. Entrance Exam. Bd., N.Y.C., 1966-67; pres. Salisbury (Md.) State Coll., 1970-80, Drury Coll., Springfield, Mo., 1981-83. Served to lt. j.g. USN, 1951-55. Joint recipient Higher Edn. Leadership award Gov. Del., Gov. Md., Gov. Va., 1974; named hon. trustee Ward Found. Wildfowl Art Museum, 1977. Mem. Phi Delta Kappa. Episcopalian. Home: 227 Pinehurst Ave Salisbury MD 21801

CRAWFORD, OLGA ELVERA ANDERSON (MRS. WILLIAM JOHN CRAWFORD), retired publishing company executive; b. Boston, Apr. 13, 1909; d. Carl Axel and Elsa Maria (Dahlgren) Anderson; m. William John Crawford, June 15, 1929; children—James Clarke, William John. Grad. high sch. Sec. Frost & Adams Co., Boston, 1926-30; sec. to v.p. Spaulding-Moss Co., Boston, 1931-32, supr. tech. typing dept., 1932-42; with Addison-Wesley Pub. Co., Reading, Mass., 1942-81, supr. copy-editing, 1942-64, corp. sec., clk., 1947-81, v.p., 1949-65, sr. v.p., 1965—; dir. Crawford Marine

Electronics, Gloucester, Mass. Republican. Congregationalist. Home: 132 1/2 Wheeler St Gloucester MA 01930

CRAWFORD, RAYMOND MAXWELL, JR., nuclear engineer; b. Charleston, S.C., July 28, 1933; s. Raymond Maxwell and Mary Elizabeth (Bates) C.; m. J. Denise LeDuc, Mar. 10, 1951; children: Denis, Michael, Deborah, Peter, Elizabeth. B.S., Wayne State U., 1958, M.S., 1960; Ph.D., UCLA, 1969. Instr. Wayne State U., 1960-63; asst. prof. Calif. State U., Northridge, 1963-66; mem. tech. staff Atomics Internat., 1969-71; nuclear engr. Argonne Nat. Lab., Ill., 1971-74; assoc. and asst. head nuclear safeguards and licensing div. Sargent & Lundy, Chgo., 1974-80; v.p. Sci. Applications, Inc., Oak Brook, Ill., 1980-83; engring. dir. Nutech, Chgo., 1983—; tech. cons. Atomic Power Devel. Assn., 1962-63; summer fellow NASA Lewis Research Ctr., 1965-66. Contbr. articles to profl. jours. Scoutmaster, counsellor Boy Scouts Am., 1963-66; active YMCA, 1966-69, Recs. for Blind, 1964-65. Recipient numerous awards. Mem. Western Soc. Engrs., Am. Nuclear Soc., Am. Inst. Chem. Engrs., Am. Chem. Soc., Nat. Soc. Profl. Engrs., Am. Sci. Affiliation, N.Y. Acad. Sci., AAAS, Sigma Xi, Tau Beta Pi, Phi Lambda Upsilon. Home: 1005 E Kennebec Ln Naperville IL 60540 Office: 225 N Michigan Ave Chicago IL 60601

CRAWFORD, RICHARD (ARTHUR CRAWFORD), musicology educator; b. Detroit, May 12, 1935; s. Arthur Richard and Mary Elizabeth (Forshar) C.; m. Sophie Shambes, Dec. 27, 1958 (div. 1965); children: Lynn E., William J.; m. Penelope Marie Ball, Apr. 26, 1967; children: Amy E., Anne L. Mus.B., U. Mich., 1958, Mus.M., 1959, Ph.D., 1965. Instr. musicology U. Mich., Ann Arbor, 1962-66, asst. prof., 1966-69, asso. prof., 1969-75, prof., 1975—; vis. prof. Bklyn. Coll., City U. N.Y., 1973-74. Author: Andrew Law, American Psalmodist, 1968, American Studies and American Musicology, 1975, Civil War Songbook, 1977, (with David P. McKay) William Billings of Boston: 18th-century Composer, 1975; contbr. articles and revs. to profl. jours., New Grove Dictionary Music, New Oxford Companion to Music, liner notes for recs. Mem. editorial bd. New World Records, N.Y.C.; cons. NEH. U. Mich. Rackham postdoctoral fellow, summer 1967, 69-70; Inst. for Studies in Am. Music sr. research fellow, 1973-74; Guggenheim fellow, 1977-78. Mem. Am. Musicological Soc. (pres. 1982-84), Soc. for Ethnomusicology, Music Library Assn., Am. Antiquarian Soc. (fellow summers 1972, 73), Sonneck Soc., Internat. Assn. for Study Popular Music. Home: 1158 Baldwin St Ann Arbor MI 48104 Office: Burton Tower U Mich Ann Arbor MI 48109

CRAWFORD, RICHARD BRADWAY, biologist, psychology educator; b. Kalamazoo, Feb. 16, 1933; s. Kenneth and Alma (Smith) C.; m. Betty J. Jacobs, Jan. 30, 1954; children: Kathleen, Christine, Kevin, Nancy. A.B., Kalamazoo Coll., 1954; Ph.D. in Biochemistry, U. Rochester, 1959. Postdoctoral fellow U. Rochester, N.Y., 1959; instr. to assoc. prof. U. Pa., 1959-67; assoc. prof. to prof. biology Trinity Coll., Hartford, Conn., from 1967, chmn. dept., from 1978; now mem. psychology faculty West Chester State Coll., Pa.; asst. dir., trustee Mt. Desert Island Biol. Lab., Salsbury Cove, Maine, 1966—. Contbr. articles to profl. jours. Mem. Inlands, Wetlands and Water Courses Commn., Wethersfield, Conn., 1976-81. Mem. AAAS, Am. Soc. Zoology. Democrat. Baptist. Office: Dept Psychology West Chester State Coll West Chester PA 19380

CRAWFORD, R(OBERT) GEORGE, lawyer; b. Mpls., Oct. 30, 1943; s. Robert John and Agnes C.; m. M. Holly, May 17, 1980; 1 dau., Katherine Barnes. B.A., Harvard U., 1965, J.D., 1968. Bar: Ohio 1969, D.C. 1971, Calif. 1972. Law clk. to Justice Bryon R. White, U.S. Supreme Ct., 1968-69; assoc. Jones, Day, Reavis, & Pogue, Cleve., 1969-70; staff asst. to Pres., White House, Washington, 1970-72; gen. counsel. v.p. Archon Inc., Beverly Hills, Calif., 1972-75; gen. ptnr. Jones, Day, Reavis & Pogue, Los Angeles, 1976—. Pres., Harvard U. Law Rev., 1966-68. Mem. ABA, Calif. Bar Assn., Los Angeles Bar Assn., Phi Beta Kappa. Episcopalian. Club: Harvard (N.Y.C.). Home: 13417 Java Dr Beverly Hills CA 90210

CRAWFORD, ROBERT J., chemistry educator; b. Edmonton, Alta., Can., July 8, 1929; s. Robert J. and Margaret (Pickles) C.; m. Agnes Joan, Oct. 10, 1956; children: Maureen, Anne, Linda, Eric. B.S., U. Alta., 1952, M.S., 1954; Ph.D., U. Ill., 1956. Asst. prof. U. Alta., Edmonton, 1956-62, assoc. prof., 1962-67, prof., 1967—, chmn. dept. chemistry, 1979—. Contbr. articles to profl. jours. Bd. govs. U. Alta., 1979-82; bd. dirs. Unitarian Ch., 1959-62. Fellow Chem. Inst. Can., Chem. Soc. London. Office: U Alta Edmonton AB Canada T60 1W2 *

CRAWFORD, ROY EDGINGTON, lawyer; b. Topeka, Dec. 23, 1938; s. Roy E. and Ethel Trula (Senne) C.; m. Kristy S. Pigeon, June 27, 1981; children: Michael, Jennifer. B.S., U. Pa., 1960; LL.B., Stanford U., 1963. Bar: Calif. 1964, U.S. Ct. Mil. Appeals 1964, U.S. Tax Ct. 1969, U.S. Dist. Ct. (no. dist.) Calif. 1971, U.S. Ct. Claims 1974, U.S. Supreme Ct. 1979. Contbr. chpts. to books; bd. editors: Stanford U. Law Rev., 1962-63. Served to capt. AUS, 1964-67. Recipient award of merit U.S. Ski Assn., 1980. Mem. ABA (chmn. com. on state and local taxes 1979-81), Calif. State Bar Assn., San Francisco Bar Assn., Calif. Trout (bd. dirs. 1970—, v.p. 1975—), Beta Gamma Sigma. Office: Brobeck Phleger & Harrison 1 Market Plaza San Francisco CA 94105

CRAWFORD, STANLEY EVERETT, physician, educator; b. Dallas, Nov. 9, 1924; s. Sam and Nina (Harris) C.; m. Saradell David, Feb. 7, 1948; children—Stanley E., Jr., John David, Samuel Harris. B.A., h4U. Tex., 1945; M.D., 1948. Intern Billings Hosp., Chgo., 1948-49; resident pediatrics U. Tex. Med. Br., Galveston, 1949-50, U. Minn., 1952-54; practice medicine specializing in pediatrics, Jackson, Tenn., 1954-61; asso. prof. pediatrics U. Tenn., Memphis, 1961-68; prof., chmn. pediatrics U. Tex. Med. Sch., San Antonio, 1968-72, dean, 1972-80; dean, v.p. for med. affairs U. South Ala., Mobile, 1980—; cons. Wilford Hall USAF Hosp., 1969—. Examiner Am. Bd. Pediatrics, 1967—, mem. exec. com., 1974—; Mem. adv. com. Foster Grandparent Project, 1970—; mem. exec. com. Children's Hosp. Found., 1968—. Served with USNR, 1950-52. Mem. AMA (vice chmn. pediatric sect. 1967-68), Sigma Xi, Alpha Omega Alpha. Club: Rotary. Home: 206 Ridgewood Pl Mobile AL 36608 Office: U South Ala Coll Medicine Med Sci Bldg Mobile AL 36688

CRAWFORD, SUSAN N. YOUNG, library director, educator; b. Vancouver, B.C., Can.; d. James Y. and S. Young; m. James Weldon Crawford, July 5, 1955; 1 son, Robert James. B.A., U. B.C., 1948; M.A., U. Toronto, 1950, U. Chgo., 1954, Ph.D., 1970. With bur. library and indexing service ADA, 1954-56; with office exec. v.p. AMA, Chgo., 1956-60, dir. div. library and archival services, 1960-81; asso. prof. Sch. Library Sci., Columbia U., N.Y.C., 1972-75; prof., dir. Sch. Medicine Library, Washington U., 1981—. Author books and sci. papers; mem. editorial bd.: Med. Socioecon. Research Sources; asso. editor: Jour. Am. Soc. Info. Sci.; editor-in-chief: Bull. of Med. Library Assn., 1982—. Bd. regents Nat. Library Medicine, NIH, 1971-75. Janet Doe hon. lectr., 1983. Fellow AAAS; mem. ALA, Med. Library Assn. (Eliot award 1976, chmn. com. on surveys and stats. 1966-75, publs. panel 1977-80), Soc. Social Studies of Sci., Am. Soc. Info. Sci., Sigma Xi (mem./chmn. numerous coms.). Home: 2418 Lincoln St Evanston IL 60201 Office: 4580 Scott Ave Saint Louis MO 63110

CRAWFORD, VERNON D'ORSAY, ednl. adminstr.; b. Amherst, N.S., Can., Feb. 13, 1919; came to U.S., 1947, naturalized, 1953; s. Roy David and Lydia (Edgett) C.; m. Helen Dell Avison, May 15, 1943; children—Lynn Kathleen (Mrs. David Hood), Dell Marie (Mrs. Ronald Byrd). B.A., Mt. Allison U., Sackville, N.B., 1939, LL.D., 1975; M.S., Dalhousie U., Halifax, N.S., 1943; Ph.D., U. Va., 1949. Physicist Naval Research Establishment of Can., Halifax, 1943-45; lectr. Dalhousie U., 1944-47; asso. prof. physics Ga. Inst. Tech., Atlanta, 1949-55, prof., 1955-64, dir., 1964-68, prof. physics, dean, 1968, acting pres., 1969, v.p. acad. affairs, 1969—; acting chancellor Univ. System of Ga., 1979—, chancellor, 1980—. Mem. Sigma Xi, Phi Kappa Phi, Sigma Pi Sigma, Omicron Delta Kappa, Phi Kappa Sigma. Home: 2875 Habersham Rd NW Atlanta GA 30305

CRAWFORD, WALTER HAMILTON, community developer; b. Hattiesburg, Miss., Aug. 16, 1906; s. Walter and Ada (Richardson) C.; m. Lillian Marie Williams, July 22, 1927; children—Carolyn, Catherine. Student, Gulf Coast Mil. Acad., 1922-23, U. Ala., 1924-26. Bus. mgr., supt. South Miss. Infirmary, Hattiesburg, 1926-33; founder Crawford Corp., New Orleans, 1934, pres., 1934-74; self employed, 1974—; pres. Crofton Corp., Md. Mem. Regional Vol. Credit Ext. Com., 1954-59; community builders council Urban Land Inst., 1949-51; mem. Nat. Housing Center Bd., 1955-57, chmn., 1955; Pres. United Givers Fund, 1958. Recipient citation for overseas housing U.S. Army Engrs., 1940; ann. award for excellence in merchandising Practical Builder mag., 1951, 53; named to Nat. Housing Hall of Fame, 1978. Mem. Nat. Assn. Home Builders, Home Mfrs. Assn., Miss. Hosp. Assn. (organizer 1931), New Orleans, Annapolis, Jackson, Baton Rouge chambers commerce, Sigma Chi. Baptist. Clubs: Mason (32 deg.), Shriner., Union League (Chgo.); New Orleans Athletic, Baton Rouge Country, City (pres. 1959), City (dir. 1980-81). Home: 1855 Country Club Dr Baton Rouge LA 70808 Office: Box 66183 Baton Rouge LA 70896

CRAWFORD, WILLIAM AVERY, retired U.S. ambassador; b. N.Y.C., Jan. 14, 1915; s. John Raymond and Pauline Marguerite (Avery) C.; m. Barbara Gardner, Oct. 19, 1940; children: Barbara, Pauline, William, John, Elizabeth; m. Gudrun Elisabet Hådell, Apr. 19, 1980. A.B., Haverford Coll., 1936; student, U. Madrid, summer 1936; diploma, Ecole Libre des Sciences Politiques, 1938; postgrad., Harvard, 1944-45, Russian Inst., Columbia, 1949-50. Apptd. fgn. service officer, vice consul of career, sec. diplomatic service, 1941, 3d sec., vice consul, Havana, Cuba, 1941-44; mem. U.S. del. Allied Commn. on Reparations, Moscow, 1945; 3d sec., vice consul, Moscow, 1945-47, 2d sec., 1947; USSR desk officer Dept. State, 1947; polit. adviser U.S. delegation UN Gen. Assembly, 1949; 2d sec., consul, Paris, 1950-52, 1st sec., 1952-54; dep. dir. Office Eastern European Affairs, Dept. of State, 1954-56; assigned to Nat. War Coll., 1956-57; counselor, dep. chief of mission, Prague, 1957- 59; dir. Office Research and Analysis for Sino-Soviet Bloc, Dept. State, 1959-61; E.E. and M.P. to Rumania, 1961-64, A.E. and P., Rumania, 1964-65; spl. asst. internat. affairs to Supreme Allied Comdr. Europe, Paris, 1965-67; sr. fgn. service insp., 1967-70; dir. WJS, Inc., Washington, Fgn. Bondholders Protective Council, Inc. Mem. Washington Inst. Fgn. Affairs. Clubs: Metropolitan, Chevy Chase (Washington). Home: 4402 Boxwood Rd Bethesda MD 20816

CRAWFORD, WILLIAM BASIL, JR., journalist; b. Waukegan, Ill., June 22, 1941; s. William Basil and Jane Elinore (Murray) C.; 1 dau., Kirsten Jane. B.History, U. Chgo., 1963. Fiscal officer Chgo. Truck Drivers Union, 1964-68; writer, editor City News Bur. Chgo., 1968-72; writer Chgo. Tribune, 1972—; tchr. basic writing and advanced reporting Northwestern U. Recipient Pulitzer prize for spl. local reporting, 1976; Sweepstakes award Ill. AP, 1976; award for best investigative story, 1976; 3d place award for investigative story, 1976; best investigative story, 1975; 2d place award for investigative story UPI, 1976; 3d place, 1976; honorable mention, 1974, Steward Mott Found., 1977; Jacob Schur award, 1978. Mem. U. Chgo. Alumni Assn., Chgo. Reporters Assn., Chgo. Press Club. Office: Chgo Tribune 435 N Michigan Ave Chicago IL 60611

CRAWFORD, WILLIAM DONHAM, retired utilities executive; b. Little Rock, June 22, 1923; s. Sidney Robert and Blanche (Donham) C.; m. Colene King, June 6, 1947; children: Carol, Bruce Donham, Philip King. Student, U. Ark., 1941-43; B.S., U.S. Naval Acad., 1947; M.S., Calif. Inst. Tech., 1948. Chief Office Sci. and Tech., Pan Am. Union, Washington, 1949-50; staff AEC, 1951-54; with Middle South Utilities, Inc., N.Y.C., 1955-63, asst. sec., asst. treas., 1956-59, v.p., 1959-63, Consol. Edison Co., N.Y., 1963-69, adminstrv. v.p., 1966-69; mng. dir. Edison Electric Inst., N.Y.C., 1969-70, pres., 1971-78; now dir.; chmn., chief exec. officer Gulf States Utilities Co., Beaumont, Tex., from 1978, now ret., hon. chmn. bd.; dir. First City Bank Beaumont; adv. dir. Comml. Nat. Bank, Little Rock. Trustee Thomas A. Edison Found.; bd. dirs. Am. Nuclear Energy Council. Served with USN, 1947-49. Club: Baltusrol Golf (Springfield, N.J.). Home: 104 W Caldwood Beaumont TX 77707

CRAWFORD, WILLIAM F., corp. exec., cons.; b. Chgo., Apr. 11, 1911; s. William Wilberforce and Mona (Richards) C.; m. Ruth M. Fellinger, May 4, 1935; children: Judith Crawford Smith, Susan (dec.), Constance Crawford Dry, Barbara Crawford Boger, William Edwin. Student, Northwestern Mil. and Naval Acad., 1925-29, U. Chgo., 1929-31. Sec., Edward Valves, Inc. (formerly Edward Valve & Mfg. Co., Inc.), East Chicago, Ind., 1931-37, v.p., 1937-41, pres., dir., 1941-63; pres. dir. Republic Flow Meters Co., Chgo., 1957-61, Valve Products, Inc., Knox, Ind., 1950-63, W.E. Bowler Co., Phila., 1954-63; v.p., dir. Rockwell Mfg. Co., Pitts., 1945-72, chmn. fin. com., 1963-73; adv. dir. Rockwell Internat. Corp., Pitts., 1973-79; v.p., dir. Chgo. Fittings Corp.; chmn. W.F. Crawford & Assos., Chgo.; dir. Flex-Weld, Inc., Chgo., Keflex, Inc., Tec-Line Products, Inc., Atlantic India Rubber Works, Inc., Mogul Rubber Corp., Goshen, Ind., Rubbernek Fittings Ltd., Birmingham, Eng., U.S. Flexible Metallic Tubing Co., San Francisco, Kelco Industries, Woodstock, Ill. Contbr. articles to profl. jours. Trustee Crawford Found., Chgo., IIT Research Inst., Ill. Inst. Tech.; Mem. valve industry adv. com. WPB, 1941-45, 50-52. Mem. Valve Mfrs. Assn. (pres. 1959-61, 64-65, Silver Gavel award 1972), ASME, Newcomen Soc. N.Am., Art Inst. Chgo., Field Mus. Natural History (Chgo.), Delta Upsilon. Republican. Congregationalist. Clubs: Union League, Adventurers, Econ., Tavern (Chgo.); Duquesne (Pitts.). Home: 4950 Chicago Beach Dr Chicago IL 60615 also PO Box 1800 Sun Valley ID 83353 Office: 185 N Wabash Ave Chicago IL 60601

CRAWFORD, WILLIAM HOWARD, JR., dentist, university dean; b. Montclair, N.J., Apr. 14, 1937; s. William Howard and Emma Marian (Morton) C.; m. Lynn Nadine Ross, Sept. 6, 1958; children: Kimberly Joan, John William. A.B. in Zoology, U. So. Calif., 1958, D.D.S., 1962; M.S. in Pathology, 1964. Asst. prof. pathology U. So. Calif. Sch. Dentistry, 1966-69, assoc. prof., 1969—, asst. dean, 1969-70, assoc. dean, 1970-77, interim dean, 1972-75, dean, 1977—; cons. Commn. Dental Accreditation. Contbr. articles on uncommon oral lesions to profl. jours. Served with Dental Corps U.S. Army, 1964-66. Recipient Mayor's Service citation City Los Angeles, 1974; So. Calif. Acad. Oral Pathology fellow, 1967. Fellow Am. Coll. Dentists, Internat. Coll. Dentists, Am. Acad. Oral Pathology; mem. ADA, Calif. Dental Assn., Los Angeles Dental Soc., Am. Assn. Dental Schs., Western Conf. Deans, Dental Examiners, Pierre Fauchard Acad., Sigma Xi, Omicron Kappa Upsilon. Office: U So Calif Sch Dentistry Room 203 Los Angeles CA 90089

CRAWFORD, WILLIAM REX, JR., former U.S. ambassador; b. Phila., Apr. 22, 1928; s. William Rex and Dorothy (Buckley) C.; m. Virginia Vollrath Lowry, Sept. 12, 1950; 1 dau., Sarah Lowry. B.A. cum laude, Harvard, 1948; M.A., U. Pa., 1950. Joined U.S. Fgn. Service, 1951-79; fgn. service officer, Jidda, 1951-53, Venice, 1954, Arabic lang. tng., 1955-57, consul in Aden, charge d'affaires Yemen, 1957-59; officer charge Arab-Israeli affairs State Dept., 1959-64, Morocco, 1964-67, Cyprus, 1968-72; ambassador to Yemen Arab Republic, 1972-74, Cyprus, 1974-78; dep. asst. sec. state for Near Eastern and South Asian affairs, 1978-79; exec. dir. Nat. Com. to Honor 14th Centennial of Islam, 1979. Served with USNR, 1948-49. Recipient Dept. State Meritorious Service award, 1959; William A. Jump award for Dintinguished Fed. Service, 1964; Woodrow Wilson fellow Princeton, 1967-68; Pres. Eisenhower exchange fellow, 1982. Mem. Middle East Inst. Club: Hasty Pudding Inst. Home: 4520 Jamestown Rd Bethesda MD 20016 Office: 256 S 16th St Philadelphia PA 19102

CRAWFORD, WILLIAM WALSH, consumer products company executive; b. Clearwater, Fla., Oct. 7, 1927; s. Francis Marion and Frances Marie (Walsh) C. B.S., Georgetown U., 1950; LL.B., Harvard, 1954. Bar: N.Y. 1955, Ill. 1972. Assoc. firm Sullivan & Cromwell, N.Y.C., 1954-58; counsel Esso Standard Oil, N.Y.C., 1958-60; partner Alexander & Green, N.Y.C., 1960-71; v.p. Internat. Harvester Co., Chgo., 1971-76; v.p., gen. counsel, sec., 1976-80; sr. v.p. gen. counsel Dart & Kraft, Inc., 1980-81, sr. v.p., gen. counsel, sec., 1981—. Mem. ABA, Ill. Bar Assn., Assn. Bar City N.Y., Am. Soc. Corp. Secs., Assn. Gen. Counsel. Clubs: Saddle and Cycle, Chgo. Address: 2211 Sanders Rd Northbrook IL 60062

CRAWFORD-MASON, CLARE WOOTTEN, television producer; b. Durham, N.C., July 22, 1936; d. Charles Thomas and Clare (Erly) Wootten; m. Robert Watts Mason; children: Victor Lawrence Crawford Jr., Charlene Elizabeth Crawford; stepchildren—John Mason, Robert Mason 3d. B.A., U. Md., 1958. Reporter, columnist Washington Daily News, 1961-72; columnist Washington Star News, 1972-74; Washington bur. chief People mag., 1974-82; reporter, sr. producer NBC-TV, 1969-80; pres. CC-M Prodns. Inc., Washington, 1981—; East Coast producer Newscope, 1983—. Producer: If Japan Can, Why Can't We, 1980 (Dupont award Columbia Sch. Journalism). Recipient Bill Pryor Meml. award, 1st prize Washington Newspaper Guild, 1966; Distinguished Pub. Affairs Reporting award Am. Polit. Sci. Assn., 1967; Nat. Assn. Broadcasters award, 1971; two Emmy awards Nat. Acad. TV Arts and Scis., 1972; award for broadcast investigative reporting AAUW, 1972; award for investigative reporting Chesapeake Press Assn., 1971; Douglas Southall Freeman award for pub. service Va. Assn. Press Broadcasters, 1972; Washington Newspaper Guild award, 1974; Blue Ribbon Am. Film Festival, 1977. Mem. AFTRA. Democrat. Roman Catholic. Club: Washington Press. Home: 7755 16th St NW Washington DC 20012 Office: People Mag 888 16th St NW Washington DC

CRAWLEY, JUDITH ROSEMARY (MRS. F. RADFORD CRAWLEY), writer, director; b. Ottawa, Ont., Can., Apr. 21, 1914; d. Roderick Percy and Rheba (Fraser) Sparks; m. F. Radford Crawley, Oct. 1, 1938; children: Michal Crawley Crosley, Patrick, Roderick, Alexander, Jennifer, Mariah. B.A., McGill U., 1936. Pres. Can. Film Inst., 1980-81. Cameraman, editor, dir., writer, Ottawa, 1938-75; films include The Loon's Necklace, 1949; series Ages and Stages, 1947-54; Child Devel. series, 1952-62, The Man Who Skied Down Everest, 1975 (Acad. award). Recipient awards Edinburgh Festival, 1949, Venice Bienale, 1949, Golden Reel award Chgo. Scholastic, 1949-60. Home and Office: 200 Rideau Terr Ottawa ON K1M 0Z3 Canada

CRAWLEY, THOMAS EDWARD, educator; b. Prospect, Va., Mar. 7, 1920; s. Charles William and Camilla Virginia (Taylor) C.; m. William Roberta Armistead, June 3, 1952. B.A., Hampden-Sydney Coll., 1941; M.A., U. N.C., 1953, Ph.D., 1965. Mem. faculty Hampden-Sydney (Va.) Coll., 1946—, prof. English, 1965—, dir. music, 1946-76, dean students, 1956-64, Hurt prof. English, 1968—. Author: The Structure of Leaves of Grass, 1970, also articles on Whitman and Poe.; Editor: Four Makers of the American Mind, 1976. Served to lt. USNR, 1941-46. Decorated Bronze Star.; Recipient Cabell Distinguished Prof. award Hampden-Sydney Coll., 1968, Bicentennial research grant, 1973. Mem. Modern Lang. Assn., Phi Beta Kappa, Omicron Delta Kappa, Kappa Alpha Order. Democrat. Presbyterian. Clubs: Briery Country, Commonwealth. Home: Thornton Pl Hampden-Sydney VA 23943 *I learned early that life for me without good music and good books would prove waterish and thin. Later I learned that these two blessings were most meaningful when shared freely with others. It seemed natural, therefore, that my life's goal should be that of study in order to serve in the offices of literary scholar and teacher.*

CRAWSHAW, RALPH, psychiatrist; b. N.Y.C., July 3, 1921. A.B., Middlebury (Vt.) Coll., 1943; M.D., N.Y. U., 1947. Diplomate: Nat. Bd. Med. Examiners, Am. Bd. Psychiatry and Neurology. Intern Lenox Hill Hosp., N.Y.C., 1947-48; resident Menninger Sch. Psychiatry, Topeka, 1948-50, Oreg. State Hosp., Salem, 1950-51; practice medicine specializing in psychiatry, Washington, 1954; staff psychiatrist C.F. Menninger Meml. Hosp., Topeka, 1954-57; asst. chief VA Mental Hygiene Clinic, Topeka, 1957-60; staff psychiatrist Community Child Guidance Clinic, Portland, Oreg., 1960-63; founder, clinic dir. Tualatin Valley Guidance Clinic, Beaverton, Oreg., 1961-67; pvt. practice medicine, specializing in psychiatry, Portland, 1960—; mem. staff Holladay Park Hosp., 1961—; lectr. dept. child psychiatry U. Oreg. Med. Sch., 1961-63, clin. prof. dept. psychiatry, 1976; lectr. Sch. Social Work, Portland State U., 1964-67; founder Benjamin Rush Found., 1968, pres., 1968—; founder Friends of Medicine, 1969, Ct. of Man, 1970, Club of Kos, 1974. Contbr. editor: AMA Jour. of Socio-Econs, 1972-75; Columnist: Prism mag, 1972-76, The Pharos, 1972—, Portland Physician, 1975; Contbr. articles to med. jours. Cons. Bur. Hearings and Appeals, HEW, 1964—, Albina Child Devel. Center, Portland, 1965-75, HEW Region 8 Health Planning, 1979; mem. Inst. Medicine, Nat. Acad. Sci., 1978, Oreg. Health Coordinating Council, 1979; Mem. Gov.'s Adv. Com. on Mental Health, 1966-72; ad hoc com. Nat. Leadership Conf. on Am. Health Policy, 1976, Gov.'s Adv. Com. on Med. Care to Indigent, 1976—; trustee Millicent Found., 1964-67, Multnomah Found. for Med. Care, 1977; vis. scholar Center for Study Democratic Instns., 1969, Jack Murdock Charitable Trust, 1977; U.S.-USSR exchange scholar, 1973. Served with AUS, 1943-46; to lt., M.C. USN, 1951-54. Named Oreg. Dr./Citizen of Yr., 1978; U.S.-USSR exchange scholar, 1973, 79. Fellow Am. Psychiat. Assn.; mem. AMA, Nat. Med. Assn., Oreg. Med. Assn. (trustee 1972—), Multnomah County Med. Soc. (pres. 1975), Royal Soc. Medicine, Inst. of Medicine of Nat. Acad. Sci., Am. Psychol. Assn., N.Pacific Soc. Neurology and Psychiatry, Soc. for Psychol. Study Social Issues, Western European Assn. Aviation Psychology, Am. Med. Writers Assn., AAAS, Portland Psychiatrists in Pvt. Practice (pres. 1971), Alpha Omega. Address: 2525 NW Lovejoy St Suite 404 Portland OR 97210

CRAY, SEYMOUR R., computer designer; b. Chippewa Falls, Wis., 1925. Grad., U. Minn., 1950. Begin career with UNIVAC; participant in founding Control Data Corp., 1957; sr. v.p., designerCDC 6600 and CDC 7600 (now called Cyber 76), 1957; founder Cray Research Inc.,

Mendota Heights, Minn., 1972, designer Cray-1 computer. Office: Cray Research Inc 1440 Northland Dr Mendota Heights MN 55120 *

CREAGER, JOE SCOTT, geology educator; b. Vernon, Tex., Aug. 30, 1929; s. Earl Litton and Irene Eugenia (Keller) C.; m. Barbara Clark, Aug. 30, 1951; children: Kenneth Clark, Vanessa Irene. B.S., Colo. Coll., 1951; postgrad., Columbia, 1952-53; M.S., Tex. A. and M. U., 1953, Ph.D., 1958. Asst. prof. dept. oceanography U. Wash., Seattle, 1958-61, assoc. prof., 1962-66, asst. chmn., 1964-65, prof. geol. scis., 1966—, asso. dean arts and scis. for earth and planetary scis., also asso. dean for research, 1966—; program dir. for oceanography NSF, 1965-66; chief scientist numerous oceanographic expdns. to Arctic and Sub-arctic including Leg XIX of Deep Sea Drilling project, 1959—; vis. geol. scientist Am. Geol. Inst., 1962, 63, 65; U.S. Nat. coordinator Internat. Indian Ocean Expedition, 1965-66; vis. scientist program lectr. Am. Geophys. Union, 1965-72; Battelle cons., advanced waste mgmt., 1974; cons. to U.S. Army C.E., 1976, U.S. Depts. Interior and Commerce, 1975; exec. sec., exec. com., chmn. planning com. Joint Oceanographic Insts. Deep Earth Sampling, 1970-72, 76-78. Editorial bd.: Internat. Jour. Marine Geology, 1964—; assoc. editor: Jour. Sedimentary Petrology, 1963-76; asst. editor: Quaternary Research, 1970-79; contbr. articles to profl. jours. Skipper Sea Scout Ship, Boy Scouts Am., Bryan, Tex., 1957; coach Little League Baseball, Seattle, 1964-71, sec., 1971; cons. sci. curriculum Northshore Sch. Dist., 1970; mem. Seattle Citizens Shoreline Com., 1973-74, King County Shoreline Com., 1980. Served with U.S. Army, 1953-55. Colo. Coll. scholar, 1949-51; NSF grantee, 1962—; ERDA grantee, 1962-64; U.S. Army C.E. grantee, 1975—; Office of Naval Research grantee; U.S. Dept. Commerce grantee; U.S. Geol. Survey grantee. Fellow Geol. Soc. Am., AAAS; mem. Internat. Assn. Quaternary Research, Am. Geophys. Union, Internat. Assn. Sedimentology, Internat. Assn. Math. Geologists, Soc. Econ. Paleontologists and Mineralists, Marine Tech. Soc. (sec.-treas. 1972-75), Sigma Xi, Beta Theta Pi, Delta Epsilon. Club: Explorers. Home: 6320 NE 157th St Bothell WA 98011 Office: Dept Oceanography WB-10 U of Wash Seattle WA 98195

CREAMER, THOMAS FISHBACK, former banker; b. Bklyn., Sept. 29, 1917; s. William G. and Blanche (Fishback) C.; m. Phoebe Johnson, Feb. 1, 1955; children: Elizabeth, Thomas C., George, Jane, Deane. S.B., Mass. Inst. Tech., 1940. Asst. to pres. Mass. Inst. Tech., Cambridge, 1940-42; exec. asst. to Dr. Karl T. Compton, head Office Field Service OSRD, 1942-46; with Citibank (formerly First Nat. City Bank of N.Y.), N.Y.C., 1946-76, asst. v.p., 1950-56, v.p., 1956-66, sr. v.p., 1966-69, exec. v.p., 1969-76; vice chmn. Econ. Devel. Council, N.Y.C., 1976-80; cons. Nat. Exec. Service Corps, 1981-83; trustee Property Capital Trust, Boston; dir. Anglo Co. Ltd., N.Y.C., St. Joseph Light & Power Co., Mo., U.S. Life Ins. Co., N.Y.C., Affiliated Fund, Lord Abbett Mut. Funds. Bd. govs. White Plains (N.Y.) Hosp. Med. Center; mem. M.I.T. Corp., 1974-79; trustee United Presbyterian Found., 1975-81; trustee local Presbyn. Ch., 1973-76, 79—. Clubs: Univ., Mass. Inst. Tech. (N.Y.C.); Golf, Fox Meadow Tennis (Scarsdale, N.Y.); Mid-Ocean (Bermuda); Ausable (Keene Valley, N.Y.); Pine Valley Golf (N.J.); Royal and Ancient Golf of St. Andrews (Scotland); Honorable Company of Edinburgh Golfers (Muirfield, Scotland). Home: 45 Tisdale Rd Scarsdale NY 10583 Office: 200 Madison Ave New York NY 10016

CREAMER, WILLIAM HENRY, III, insurance company executive; b. Narberth, Pa., Mar. 24, 1927; s. William Henry and Stella Elizabeth (McShane) C.; m. Anne Tyson Greer, Sept. 20, 1952; children—William Henry IV, Anne McSherry Creamer Gregg, Mary Greer. B.S. in Econs, Villanova U., 1951. C.L.U. With N.Y. Life Ins. Co., 1951—, gen. mgr., Towson, Md., 1957-60, regional supt. tng., 1960-62, gen. mgr., Scranton, Pa., 1962-66, Arlington, Va., 1966-69, supt. agencies, N.Y.C., 1969-70, regional v.p., Mpls., 1970-74, v.p., N.Y.C., 1974—. Served with USN, 1945-46. Mem. Nat. Assn. Life Underwriters, Am. Soc. C.L.U.s, U.S. Power Squadron (exec. officer Shrewsbury squadron), Estate Planning Council (past dir.). Republican. Roman Catholic. Clubs: Shrewsbury River Yacht, Kiwanis (past pres. Scranton chpt., past dir.). Home: 3 Wardell Ave Rumson NJ 07760 Office: 51 Madison Ave New York NY 10010

CREAN, JOHN GALE, hat manufacturer; b. Toronto, Ont., Can., Nov. 4, 1910; s. Adam G. C. and Lauda (Gale) C.; m. Margaret Dobbie, Dec. 2, 1939; children: John F.M., Jennie S., Susan M., Patricia L. B.Commerce, U. Toronto, 1932. With Robert Crean & Co., Ltd. (hat mfrs.), Toronto, 1932—, pres., 1947—, Adam Hats Can., Ltd., 1955-70; dir. Kelsey Wheel Co. Ltd., Scythes & Co. Ltd.; Chmn. Ont. regional com. Canadian C. of C., 1952-53, vice chmn. exec. council, 1952-53, mem. Can.-U.S. com., 1950-53, 61-65, chmn., 1961-62, immigration com., 1949, pres., 1955-56; dir. Canadian council Internat. C. of C., 1962—, pres. Canadian council, 1970-72, 74-75, v.p., 1970-72, 74-75, pres., 1975-76, Can. Bus. and Industry Adv. Com., 1981-83; dir. Internat. Bus. Council Can.; pres. Wilton Park Assos. Chmn. council Bishop Strachan Sch., 1954-65; pres. Canadian bus. and industry adv. com. OECD, 1972-74; bd. govs. Hillcrest Hosp.; chmn. bd. Ont. Sci. Centre, 1964-69; exec. com. Trinity Coll., U. Toronto, 1968-74; chmn. Canadian Bus. Group for Multilateral Trade Negotiations, 1973-79, Can. BIAC Com. on Transnat. Corp.; Canadian adviser Internat. Mgmt. and Devel. Inst., Washington. Mem. Canadian Inst. Internat. Affairs (exec. com. 1963, chmn. finance com. 1972, chmn. exec. com., pres. 1981—), Canadian Orgn. for Simplification of Trade Procedures (chmn. bd. 1978-80), Canadian Centenary Council (dir. 1964-69), Kappa Sigma. Clubs: Univ., Badminton and Racquet (Toronto); Royal Canadian Yacht, Queens, Champlain Soc. Address: 161 Forest Hill Rd Toronto 7 ON Canada M5P 2N3 *There are two essential factors. First, there is no substitute for an ability to judge men, to which there follows the corollary that it is important to know from whom to seek advice and then to have the courage to follow it. Secondly, an ability to fit the particular into the whole, which in our complicated society, means being able to see how its cultural, economic, political and strategic elements can influence a given situation.*

CREASMAN, WILLIAM THOMAS, obstetrician and gynecologist, educator; b. Miami, Ariz., Sept. 3, 1934; s. George Dewey and Pauline (Cate) C.; m. Erble Jeannie Garrett, Aug. 29, 1958; children: Valrie Kay, William Scott. B.A., Baylor U., 1956, M.D., 1960. Intern Jefferson Davis Hosp., Houston, 1960-61; resident U. Rochester, N.Y., 1963-67; asst. prof. M.D. Anderson Hosp., Houston, 1969-70; asst. prof.dept. ob-gyn Duke Med. Ctr., Durham, N.C., 1970-74, assoc. prof., 1974-78, prof., 1978—, James Ingram prof., 1982—; trustee N.C. Cancer Inst., Lumberton, 1976—; key investigator Duke Comprehensive Cancer Ctr., 1971—. Author: Gynecologic Oncology, 1981; contbr. articles to profl. jours. Recipient Pres's award Am. Coll. Obstetricians and Gynecologists, 1973, First Prize paper Am. Coll. Obstetricians and Gynecologists, 1980; Robertson Meml. lectr., Dundee, Scotland, 1976. Fellow Am. Coll. Obstetricians and Gynecologists, Am. Gynecol. and Obstetrical Soc.; mem. Soc. Gynecologic Oncologists (sec-treas. 1975-78), Am. Radium Soc., Soc. Pelvic Surgeons. Republican. Baptist. Home: 2944 Friendship Rd Durham NC 27710 Office: Dept Ob-Gyn Duke Med Ctr. Durham NC 27705

CREAVEN, PATRICK JOSEPH, physician, research oncologist; b. Eng., Jan. 31, 1933. B.S., St. Mary's Hosp. Med. Sch., U. London, 1956, Ph.D., 1964. House surgeon Bedford Gen. Hosp.; also house physician Barnet Gen. Hosp., Eng., 1956-57; asst. lectr. biochemistry U. London, St. Mary's Hosp. Med. Sch., 1963-64, lectr., 1964-66; chief, biochemistry Tex. Research Inst. Mental Sci., 1966-69; chief, oncological pharmacology Nat. Cancer Inst., VA Med. Oncology Br., 1969-75; assoc. chief Cancer Research Clinic, Roswell Park Meml. Inst., Buffalo, 1975-79, chief dept. clin. pharmacology and therapeutics, 1979—; assoc. research prof. pharmacology Roswell Park div. Grad. Sch. SUNY-Buffalo, 1975—. Contbr. articles to profl. jours. Fellow Am. Coll. Clin. Pharmacology, Royal Soc. Health; mem. Am. Assn. Cancer Research, Am. Soc. Clin. Oncology, Eastern Coop. Oncology Group. Office: Roswell Park Meml Inst 666 Elm St Buffalo NY 14263

CRECINE, JOHN PATRICK, political science educator, university official; b. Detroit, Aug. 22, 1939; s. Jess and Janet K. (Hull) C.; m. Barbara Paltnavich, Aug. 17, 1968; children: Robert Patrick, Kathryn Alicia. B.S. in Indsl. Mgmt., Carnegie-Mellon U., 1961, M.S., 1963, Ph.D., 1966. Asst. prof. polit. sci. and sociology U. Mich., 1965-67, prof., dir. Inst. Pub. Policy Studies, 1968-75; economist Rand Corp., Santa Monica, Calif., 1967-68; fellow Ctr. for Advanced Study Behavioral Scis., 1973-74; prof. polit. economy Carnegie-Mellon U., Pitts., 1976—, dean Coll. Humanities and Social Scis., 1976-83, sr. v.p. for acad. affairs, 1983—; pres. BPT, Inc., 1963—. Author: A Dynamic Model of Urban Structure, 1968, Governmental Problem Solving: A Computer Simulation of Municipal Budgeting, 1969, Defense Budgeting: Organizational Adaptation of External Constraints, 1970; editor: Financing the Metropolis: The Role of Public Policy in Urban Economics, 1970. Sec., commr. Ann Arbor Planning Commn., Mich., 1969-73. Mem. Am. Econ. Assn., Am. Soc. Pub. Adminstrs., Am. Polit. Sci. Assn., Inst. Mgmt. Scis., Am. Coll. Swimming Coaches Assn. Office: Carnegie-Mellon U 610 Warner Hall Pittsburgh PA 15213 *

CREDE, ROBERT HENRY, educator, physician; b. Chgo., Aug. 11, 1915; s. William H. and Ethel (Starke) C.; m. Marjorie L. Lorain, Aug. 29, 1947; children: William, Victoria, Christina. A.B., U. Calif., Berkeley, 1937, M.D., 1941. Diplomate: Am. Bd. Internal Medicine. Commonwealth fellow, instr. medicine U. Cin. Coll. Medicine, 1947-49; intern San Francisco City and County Hosp., 1941-42; asst. resident medicine U. Calif. Hosp., San Francisco, 1945-46, chief resident medicine, 1946-47; mem. faculty U. Calif. Sch. Medicine, San Francisco, 1949—, prof. medicine, 1960—, vice chmn. dept., 1965-80, asso. dean, 1960-73, 79—, chmn. div. ambulatory and community medicine, 1965-80. Author articles in field. Served to capt., M.C. AUS, 1942-46. Recipient Guy K. Woodward prize internal medicine U. Calif. Sch. Medicine, 1941, Gold Headed Cane award, 1941. Fellow Am. Coll. Preventive Medicine, Am. Geriatrics Soc.; mem. Am. Fedn. Clin. Research, Soc. for Research and Edn. in Primary Care Internal Medicine, Am. Psychosomatic Soc., Am., Calif. med. assns., San Francisco Med. Soc., Soc. Tchrs. Preventive Medicine. Office: Univ Calif Med Center San Francisco CA 94143

CREECH, FULTON HUNTER, shipbldg. exec.; b. Washington, July 8, 1929; s. Fulton Hunter and Pauline MacKay (Bryan) C.; m. Betty Frost Baldwin; children—Kathryn, Leslie, Nancy, Rone, Carol, Clark, Hunter III. B.A., U. Va., 1951, LL.B., 1957; student, Advanced Mgmt. Program, Harvard U., 1971. Bar: Va. bar 1957. Atty. Navy Dept., 1957-61; contract adminstr. Kaman Aircraft, Bloomfield, Conn., 1961-62; atty. Ingalls Shipbldg., 1962-64; asst. to gen. counsel Newport News Shipbldg. and Dry Dock Co., Va., 1964-66, asst. personnel mgr., 1966, asst. gen. counsel, 1966-67, asst. sec., asst. gen. counsel, 1967-70, sec., gen. counsel, 1970-74, v.p., 1974-77, 80—, spl. counsel, 1979-80; dir. United Va. Bank/Peninsula, Peninsula Meml. Park. Trustee Hampton Roads Acad.; chmn. Indsl. Devel. Authority, Yorktown, Va.; mem. bd. visitors Christopher Newport Coll. Served to lt. (j.g.) USNR, 1951-54. Mem. Va., Fed. bar assns., Sigma Nu. Presbyterian (elder). Clubs: Mason., Propeller, James River (Va.) Country, Chesapeake. Home: 124 Land Grant Rd Yorktown VA 23692 Office: 4101 Washington Ave Newport News VA 23607

CREECH, GLENWOOD LEWIS, university president; b. Middleburg, Ky., Dec. 31, 1920; s. Chester B. and Tennie (Estes) C.; m. Martha Josephine Brooks, Apr. 4, 1942; children: Carolyn Ann, Walton Brooks. Student, Centre Coll., 1937-38; B.S., U. Ky., 1941, M.S., 1950; Ph.D. (W.K. Kellogg Found. fellow), U. Wis., 1957. Tchr. Stanford (Ky.) High Sch., 1946-49; research specialist U. Ky., Lexington, 1951-54, editor., 1954-56, prof., v.p., 1965-73; prof. U. Wis. at Madison, 1957-59; dir. div. agr. W.K. Kellogg Found., Battle Creek, Mich., 1959-65; prof. adminstrn., pres. Fla. Atlantic U., Boca Raton, 1973—; Vis. prof. Cornell U., 1958; cons. U.S. Dept. State, U.S. Dept. Agr. Bd. dirs. U. Ky. Devel. Council, 1965-73, U. Ky. Athletics Assn., 1965-73, Spindletop Hall, Inc., Lexington, 1965-73, Children's Theatre, 1966-73, Living Arts and Sci. Center of Central Ky., 1966-73, Boca Raton YMCA, 1975—, Fla. Endowment for Humanities, 1977-79; trustee St. Andrew's Sch., Boca Raton, 1975-77, Boca Raton Community Hosp., 1981—; public trustee Miami Ednl. TV Sta., 1974-79; mem. Historic Boca Raton Preservation Bd. Commrs., 1975-78; bd. dirs., pres. United Way of Greater Boca Raton, 1979-80; pres. Fla. Assn. of Colls. and Univs., 1980-81, Econ. Council of Palm Beach County. Served with AUS, 1941-46. Recipient Disting. Service award U. Ky. Alumni Assn., 1967; named to Hall of Disting. Alumni U. Ky., 1975. Mem. Greater Boca Raton C. of C., Blue Key., Phi Delta Kappa, Omicron Delta Kappa, Delta Sigma Pi, Phi Kappa Phi, Phi Theta Kappa, Beta Gamma Sigma. Club: Rotary (Boca Raton) (hon.). Home: 700 S Ocean Blvd 605 Boca Raton FL 33432

CREECH, HUGH JOHN, chemist; b. Exeter, Ont., Can., June 27 1910; came to U.S., 1938, naturalized, 1945; s. Richard Newton and Edith (Sanders) C.; m. E. Marie Hearne, July 10, 1937; children: Richard Hearne, Joan Marie. B.A., U. Western Ont., 1933, M.A., 1935; Ph.D. (research fellow), U. Toronto, 1938; postgrad., Harvard U., 1938-41. Asst. prof. U. Md., 1941-43, asso. prof., 1943-45; lectr. Bryn Mawr (Pa.) Coll., 1945-47; immunochemist Inst. for Cancer Research and Lankenau Hosp. Research Inst., Phila., 1945-47, head dept. chemotherapy, 1947-57, chmn. div. chemotherapy, 1957-70, sr. mem., 1949—; chmn. adminstrv. com. Inst. Cancer Research, 1947-54; mem. U.S. nat. com. Internat. Union Against Cancer, 1957-60, 80—; antimalarial research U. Md. with OSRD, Washington, 1943-45; expert cons. to Surgeon Gen. U.S. Army, 1947-49. Recipient numerous awards for research NIH, Am. Cancer Soc. Mem. Am. Assn. Cancer Research (sec.-treas. 1952-77, v.p. 1977-78, pres. 1978-79, archivist 1983—), Sigma Xi. Home: 702 Preston Rd Erdenheim Philadelphia PA 19118 Office: Inst for Cancer Research Fox Chase Cancer Center Philadelphia PA 19111

CREECH, WILBUR LYMAN, air force officer; b. Argyle, Mo., Mar. 30, 1927; s. Paul and Marie (Maloney) C.; m. Carol Ann DiDomenico, Nov. 20, 1969; 1 son, William L. Student, U. Mo., 1946-48; B.S., U. Md., 1960; M.S., George Washington U., 1966; postgrad., Nat. War Coll., 1966. Commd. 2d lt. U.S. Air Force, 1949; advanced through grades to gen.; fighter pilot 103 combat missions USAF, North Korea, 1950-51; pilot USAF Thunderbirds, 1953-56; comdr., leader Skyblazers, Europe aerial demo team USAF, 1956-60; dir. Fighter Weapons Sch., Nellis AFB, Nev., 1960-61; advisor to comdr. Argentine Air Force, 1962; exec., aide to comdr. Tactical Air Command, 1962-65; dep. officer fighter wing, 177 combat missions in F-100 fighters and asst. dep. chief staff for ops. 7th Air Force, Vietnam, 1968-69; comdr. fighter wings USAF in Europe, Spain and W.Ger., 1969-71; dep. for ops. and intelligence Air Forces Europe, 1971-74; comdr. Electronic Systems Div., Hanscom AFB, Mass., 1974-77, asst. vice chief of staff, Washington, 1977-78; comdr. Tactical Air Command, Langley AFB, Va., 1978—. Decorated D.S.M. with oak leaf cluster, Silver Star medal, Legion of Merit with 2 oak leaf clusters, D.F.C. with 3 oak leaf clusters, Air medal with 14 oak leaf clusters, Air Force Commendation medal with 2 oak leaf clusters, Army Commendation medal, Spanish Grand Cross Aero. Merit with white ribbon. Mem. Air Force Assn., Order of Daedallans. Office: Tactical Air Command Langley AFB VA 23665

CREED, ROBERT PAYSON, SR., literature educator; b. Phila., Apr. 22, 1925; s. Edward E. and Blanche H. (Southerland) C.; children: Mary Louise, Robert Payson. B.A., Swarthmore Coll., 1948; M.A., Harvard U., 1949, Ph.D., 1956. Instr. Smith Coll., Northampton, Mass., 1952-56; asst. prof. Brown U., Providence, 1956-61; assoc. prof. Brwon U., Providence, 1961-65, SUNY-Stony Brook, 1965-67, prof., 1967-69; prof. English U. Mass., Amherst, 1969—, dir. grad. studies in English, 1969-72, prof., chmn. dept. comparative lit., 1980—; cons. G&C Merriam Co., Springfield, Mass., 1955-56. Writer, chief performer: Beowulf, Sta. WNYC, pub. radio, 1979 (awards Corp. Pub. Broadcasting); editor: Old English Poetry: 15 Essays, 1967. Served to 1st lt. (j.g.) USNR, 1943-46. Guggenheim fellow, 1962-63; Nat. Endowment Humanities fellow, Yugoslavia, 1976; Inst. Advanced Studies in Humanities fellow Edinburg U., 1976; Am. Council Learned Socs. grantee, 1978. Mem. MLA, AAAS, Internat. Assn. Univ. Profs. English. Home: Star Route Lakeview Shutesbury MA 01072 Office: U Mass Dept Comparative Lit Amherst MA 01003 *Though a professor of literature, I have become more and more deeply concerned with oral traditions. Behind surviving traditions — indeed, behind literature and language itself — lie tens of thousands of years of what we may call Memorable Speech, spoken capsules of cultural informations. Back of Memorable Speech lies the origin of human lanuage. Through the study of (sound-) patterned Memorable Speech, I am trying to work back towards the beginning of lanuage, our most adaptive and humanizing mechanism.*

CREEDON, JOHN J., insurance company executive; b. N.Y.C., Aug. 1, 1924; s. Bartholomew and Emma (Glynn) C.; m. Vivian Elser, Aug. 17, 1947 (dec. 1981); children: Juliette, Michele, John, David.; m. Diane Ardouin, 1983; children: Jean Phillippe, Genevieve. B.S. magna cum laude, N.Y. U., 1952; LL.B. cum laude, N.Y. U., 1955; LL.M., N.Y. U., 1962. Bar: N.Y. State 1955, U.S. Supreme Ct. 1960. With Met. Life Ins. Co., N.Y.C., 1942—, v.p., asso. gen. counsel, 1970-73, sr. v.p., gen. counsel, 1973-76, exec. v.p., 1976-80, pres., dir., 1980-83, pres., chief exec. officer, 1983—; chmn. bd. Met. Property & Liability Ins. Co., 1979-80, dir., 1980-81, Melville Corp., NYNEX; adj. prof. law N.Y. U. Law Sch., 1962-72; bd. dirs., pres. Am. Bar Found., 1980-82; chmn. bd. Met. Life Found.; trustee Practising Law Inst., 1968-81, N.Y. U., N.Y. U. Law Center Found., Am. Coll.; mem. legal adv. com. N.Y. Stock Exchange; chmn. Life Ins. Council N.Y., 1977-78. Editor: The Bus. Lawyer, 1973-74; contbr. articles to profl. jours. Served with USNR, 1943-46. Mem. ABA (assembly del. 1972-75, chmn. sect. corp. banking and bus. law 1975-76), N.Y. State Bar Assn., Assn. Bar City N.Y., Assn. Life Ins. Counsel (pres. 1977-78), Am. Law Inst., N.Y. State C. of C. and Industry, Alliance for Free Enterprise, S.S. Huebner Found. Office: 1 Madison Ave New York NY 10010

CREEGAN, ROBERT FRANCIS, philosophy educator; b. Battle Creek, Mich., Mar. 27, 1915; s. Charles Cole and Harriet (Stephenson) C.; m. Doris Ryan, Dec. 27, 1940; 1 son, Charles Louis. Student, Oberlin Coll., 1932-34; A.B., Marietta Coll., 1936; M.A., Duke, 1937, Ph.D., 1939. Asst. Coll. of William and Mary, 1939-40; asst. prof. Cumberland U., 1940-43, U. Miss., 1943-44, Bucknell U., 1944-45, Whitman Coll., 1945-47, Carleton Coll., 1947-48, Ohio U., 1948-52; prof. philosophy dept. State U. N.Y. at Albany, 1952—; vis. prof. No. Ill. U., summer 1948, No. Iowa U., summer 1952, Central Wash. State Coll., 1955, U. Ariz., summer 1970; mem. founding com. Am. Anomalous Phenomena Soc., 1978—; lectr. Nat. sponsor Univs. Com. on Problems of War and Peace.; cons. in philosophy Aerial Phenomena Research Orgn. Abstractor Psychol. Abstracts.; Author: The Shock of Existence, 1954, The Magic of Truth, 1980; also articles in profl. jours., ednl. reports. Mem. Internat. Platform Assn., N.Y. Acad. Scis., AAAS, Am. Philos. Assn., Am. Psychol. Assn., AAUP, Internat. Phenomenological Soc., Soc. Advancement Edn., World UFO Reports Panel, Fedn. Am. Scientists. Presbyterian (elder). Home: 28 Wellington Rd Delmar NY 12054 Office: State U NY at Albany Albany NY 12222

CREEKMORE, MARION VIRGIL, JR., diplomat; b. Memphis, Jan. 8, 1939; s. Marion Virgil and Grace (Blalock) C.; m. Linda Rae Burlingame, June 6, 1961; children—Mary Catherine, Debra Lynn. B.A., Vanderbilt U., 1961; M.A., Tulane U., 1963, Ph.D., 1968. With Dept. State, 1965-77, 79—; officer in charge producer countries Office Fuels and Energy, 1975-77; dir. office devel. fin. Dept. State, 1977; dep. asst. sec. of state Internat. Orgns. Bur., 1979-81; dep. chief of mission U.S. Embassy, New Delhi, 1981—; dir. Office Internat. Energy Policy, Dept. Energy, Washington, 1978-79; asst. prof. history Memphis State U., 1968-70. Recipient Superior Honor award Dept. State, 1977, 81. Office: US Embassy New Delhi care Dept State Washington DC 20520

CREEL, AUSTIN BOWMAN, educator; b. Alexandria, Va., Nov. 8, 1929; s. Benjamin Kemper and Bertha A. (Naff) C.; m. Patricia Ann Harrison, June 23, 1954; children: Stephen, Kathryn. B.S., Northwestern U., 1950; B.D., Colgate Rochester Div. Sch., 1954; M.A., Yale U., 1957, Ph.D., 1959. Ordained to ministry Am. Baptist Conv., 1952; asst. chaplain U. Rochester Coll. for Men, 1950-52; del. ecumenical confs. in India, travel in Asia, 1952-53; student minister Calvary Presbyn. Ch., Rochester, N.Y., 1953-54; asst. prof. religion U. Fla., Gainesville, 1957-64, assoc. prof., 1964-77, prof., 1977—, dir. Asian studies, 1973-75, chmn. dept. religion, 1977—. Author: Dharma in Hindu Ethics, 1977; editor: A Larger View: Delton L. Scudder's Prayers and Addresses, 1973. Trustee Alachua Gen. Hosp., Gainesville, 1969-72, vice chmn., Gainesville, 1970-71. Recipient Sigmund Livington Interfaith prize Northwestern U., 1949; postdoctoral fellow in Asian religions, Poona, India, 1965. Mem. Am. Acad. Religion, Am. Inst. Indian Studies (trustee 1974—, exec. com. 1980-82), Assn. Asian Studies (pres. S.E. conf. 1978-79), Soc. Asian and Comparative Philosophy, Am. Oriental Soc., Soc. Sci. Study of Religion. Home: 1228 NW 36th Dr Gainesville FL 32605 Office: Dept Religion Univ Fla Gainesville FL 32611

CREEL, DANA SHANNON, foundation executive; b. College Park, Ga., May 24, 1912; s. Dana Anderson and Mary Virginia (Shannon) C.; m. Jane Rebecca Haislip, June 11, 1955. LL.B., Emory U., 1934; M.B.A., Harvard U., 1936; LL.D., Cornell Coll., 1962. Bar: Ga. Bar 1934, N.Y. bar 1939. With Irving Trust Co., 1936-39, Prentice Hall Co., 1939-40; asso. philanthropy John D. Rockefeller, Jr., 1940-42, 46-60; sec. Rockefeller Bros. Fund, 1947-51, dir., 1951-68, pres., 1968-75, vice chmn., 1975-78, trustee, 1968-81; sec. Sealantic Fund, 1947-51, dir., trustee, 1951-73; pres., trustee Sleepy Hollow Restorations, 1951—; trustee Seamen's Bank for Savs., 1961—; dir. Morningside Area Alliance, 1960-76. Mem. sr. execs. council Conf. Bd., 1969-76; trustee African-Am. Inst., 1957-83, chmn. bd., 1964-79; trustee, v.p. Interchurch Center, 1958-83; trustee Inst. Coll. and Univ. Adminstrs., 1960-67, Am. Conservation Assn., 1963-83; pres., trustee Martha Baird Rockefeller Fund for Music, 1962-71, chmn., 1971—; dir. Rockefeller

Family Fund, 1967-72; governing council Rockefeller Archive Center Rockefeller U., 1974—, chmn., 1978—. Served with AUS, 1942-46. Mem. Council Fgn. Relations. Clubs: Century Assn., Univ. Home: Sharon CT 06069

CREEL, LUTHER EDWARD, III, lawyer; b. Huntsville, Ala., Sept. 23, 1937; s. Luther Edward and June (Oldacre) C.; m. Nan Dee McHalek, Apr. 11, 1974; children by previous marriage: Scott Mitchell, Todd Oldacre. A.B. in Psychology, George Washington U., 1959; J.D., So. Methodist U., 1963. Bar: Tex. 1963. Since practice in, Dallas; partner firm Creel and Atwood (and predecessors), 1971—; pres. Am. Bankruptcy Inst.; lectr. in field of bankruptcy and reorgn. law. Contbr. articles to legal jours. Mem. ABA (bus. bankruptcy com., internat. bankruptcy law subcom.), Tex. Bar Assn., Dallas Bar Assn. (chmn. bankruptcy sect. 1972), State Bar Tex. (chmn. bankruptcy com. 1979-81). Republican. Baptist. Clubs: City, Lancers. Home: 7155 Elmridge St Dallas TX 75240 Office: 3100 LTV Tower Dallas TX 75201

CREELEY, ROBERT WHITE, author, English language educator; b. Arlington, Mass., May 21, 1926; s. Oscar Slade and Genevieve (Jules) C.; m. Ann MacKinnon, 1946 (div. 1956); children: David, Thomas, Charlotte; m. Bobbie Louise Hall, Jan. 27, 1957 (div. 1976); children: Kirsten, Sarah, Katherine; m. Penelope Highton, 1977; children: William, Hannah. B.A., Black Mountain Coll., 1954; M.A., U. N.Mex., 1960. Instr. Black Mountain Coll., 1954-55; vis. lectr. English U. N.Mex., Albuquerque, 1961-62, lectr., 1963-66, vis. prof., 1968-69, 78-80, SUNY, Buffalo, 1966-67, prof. English, 1967—, Gray prof. poetry and letters, 1978—; lectr. U. B.C., Vancouver, 1962-63; lectr. creative writing San Francisco State Coll., 1970-71. Author: Le Fou, 1952, The Immoral Proposition, 1953, The Kind of Act of, 1953, The Gold Diggers, rev. edit, 1965, All That is Lovely in Men, 1955, If You, 1956, The Whip, 1957, A Form of Women, 1959, For Love, Poems, 1950-60, 1962, The Island, 1963, Poems, 1950-65, 1966, Words, 1967, The Finger, rev. edit, 1970, The Charm, 1968, Numbers, 1968, Pieces, 1969, A Quick Graph, 1970, A Day Book, 1972, Listen, 1973, A Sense of Measure, 1973, Contexts of Poetry, 1973, Thirty Things, 1974, Backward, 1975, (with Marisol) Presences, 1976, Selected Poems, 1976, Mabel: A Story, 1976, Myself, 1977, Hello, 1978, Was That a Real Poem & Other Essays, 1979, Later, 1979, Robert Creeley and Charles Olson: The Complete Correspondence, Vols. 1 and 2, 1980, Vol. 3, 1981, Vol. 4, 1982, Vol. 5, 1983, Mother's Voice, 1981, Echoes, 1982, Collected Poems, 1945-1975, 1983, Mirrors, 1983, Collected Prose, 1984; editor: (with Marisol) Black Mountain Rev, 1954-57, (with Donald M. Allen) New American Story, 1965, The New Writing in the U.S.A, 1967, Selected Writings of Charles Olson, 1967, Whitman: Selected Poems, 1973. Served with Am. Field Service, 1944-45; CBI. Recipient Levinson prize Poetry mag., 1960, Blumenthal-Leviton award, 1965, Union League Civic and Arts Found. prize Poetry mag., 1967; D. H. Lawrence fellow, 1969; Guggenheim fellow, 1964, 71; Rockefeller grantee, 1965; Shelley Meml. award Poetry Soc. Am., 1981; Nat. Endowment Arts Grantee, 1982; DAAD grantee, 1983. Home: Box 384 Waldoboro ME 04572 Office: SUNY 306 Clemens Buffalo NY 14260

CREER, PHILIP DOUGLAS, architect, educator; b. Phila., Aug. 31, 1903; s. Robert C. and Ada L. (Skinner) C.; m. Esther B. Allen, Dec. 1, 1933; children: Philip Douglas, Robert Craine; m. Cleon Adair Kerr, Oct. 25, 1951. B.Arch., U. Pa., 1927. Instr. architecture U. Pa., 1928-31; head dept. architecture Wanamaker Inst., 1927-32, R.I. Sch. Design, Providence, 1933-56; dir. Sch. Architecture U. Tex., Austin, 1956-67; practice architecture; sr. partner Creer, Kent, Cruise & Aldrich, Providence, 1946-61; partner Creer & Roessner, Austin, 1958-63, P.D. Creer, 1963—; cons., 1984—; exec. dir. Tex. Bd. Archtl. Examiners, 1974-84. Archtl. works include schs., hosps., pub. housing, overseas army bases, comml., indsl. and instl. bldgs. R.I. dist. officer Historic Am. Bldgs. Survey. Mem. architects adv. com. Providence Bldg. Code, 1952-54; mem. Mayor Providence adv. com. to write minimum housing standards code, 1953-56, mem. exec. com., chmn. subcom. screening, 1953-56; sec-treas. Tex. Archtl. Found., 1957-63; architects adv. com. Tex. Bldg. Commn., 1958- 60; mem. Austin Parks and Recreation Bd., 1966-70, chmn., 1969; chmn. Austin Historic Landmarks Commn., 1974-80; Past pres. R.I. Soc. Crippled Children and Adults. Recipient award for Hartford Park Pub. Housing Project, Providence; selected one of 10 best in U.S. by architects adv. com. Pub. Housing Authority, 1951; honor award Heritage Soc. Austin, 1976; Disting. Service award City of Austin, 1981. Fellow AIA (past pres. R.I. chpt.; pres. N.E. regional council 1952-55, nat. dir. 1952-55, nat. judiciary com. 1952-59, chmn. 1954-55, 58-59, centennial subcom. Commemorative stamp 1956, pres. Central Tex. chpt. 1960, recipient Edward C. Kemper award 1960, chmn. honor awards com. 1966-67); mem. Tex. Soc. Architects (chmn. fellowship nominating com., mem. profl. devel. com., Llewellyn Pitts award 1975), R.I. Hist. Soc., Soc. Colonial Wars, Shakespear's Head Assn., Phi Sigma Kappa. Clubs: Art (past gov.), University (Providence); Austin, Headliners (Austin). Home: 1605 Gaston Ave Austin TX 78703

CREESE, WALTER LITTLEFIELD, educator; b. Danvers, Mass., Dec. 19, 1919; s. Guy Talbot and Avis (Littlefield) C.; m. Eleanor Roberts, June 16, 1945; 1 son, Guy. A.B. magna cum laude, Brown U., 1941; M.A., Harvard U., 1945, Ph.D., 1950. Tutor, teaching fellow Harvard, 1944-45; instr. Wellesley Coll., 1945; from instr. to prof. Hite Art Inst., U. Louisville, 1946-58, acting head, 1953-54, 56-57; prof. architecture U. Ill., 1958-63; dean Sch. Architecture and Allied Arts, U. Oreg., 1963-68; prof., chmn. div. archtl. history and preservation U. Ill., Urbana, 1968—; vis. summer prof. Harvard U., 1961; cons. hist. sites and bldgs. Nat. Park Service, 1972-79. Author: The Search for Environment, 1966, The Legacy of Raymond Unwin, 1967. Chmn. Louisville and Jefferson County Planning and Zoning Commn., 1952-55. Recipient Spl. award for teaching Gargoyle Soc., 1978; Cultural Achievement award U.S. Dept. Interior, 1979; Fulbright postdoctoral research fellow U. Liverpool, Eng., 1955-56; Smithsonian fellow, 1969-70; Guggenheim fellow, 1972-73; Rockefeller fellow, 1976-77. Hon. mem. AIA; mem. Soc. Archtl. Historians (editor jour. 1950-53, pres. 1958-60), Coll. Art Assn. (dir. 1951-55), Phi Beta Kappa, Phi Kappa Phi, Sphinx Soc. Home: 1817 Moraine Dr Champaign IL 61821

CREGAN, JOHN BARRY, insurance company executive; b. Phila., Jan. 17, 1930; s. Cornelius and Elizabeth (McErnery) C.; m. Mary T. DeCourcey, Sept. 26, 1953; children: John, Mary, Kathleen, Thomas, Nora, Michael. B.S. in Bus. Adminstrn., LaSalle Coll., Phila., 1951; M.A. in Econs., U. Pa., 1962. Investment analyst Provident Mut. Life Ins. Co., Phila., 1954-59, asst. fin. sec., 1960-65, assoc. fin. sec., 1966-68; asst. v.p. Gen. Reins. Corp., N.Y.C., 1968-75, v.p., 1975—. Mem. N.Y. Soc. Security Analysts, Inst. Chartered Fin. Analysts. Home: 6 Delaware Rim Dr Yardley PA 19067 Office: Gen Reins Corp 430 Park Ave New York NY 10022

CREHAN, JOSEPH EDWARD, lawyer; b. Detroit, Dec. 8, 1938; s. Owen Thomas and Marguerite (Dunn) C.; m. Sheila Anderson, Nov. 6, 1965; children: Kerry Marie, Christa Ellen. A.B., Wayne State U., Detroit, 1961; J.D., Ind. U., 1965. Bar: Ind. 1965, Mich. 1966, U.S. Supreme Ct. 1984. Practice in Detroit, 1966—; asso. Louisell & Barris (P.C.), 1967-73; partner Fenton, Nederlander, Dodge, Barris & Crehan (P.C.), 1973-75, firm Barris & Crehan (P.C.), 1975-77; sole practice, 1977—. Mem. Am. Trial Lawyers Assn. Roman Catholic. Home: 1232 Oakwood Ct Fairwood Villas Rochester MI 48063 Office: 10 W Square Lake Rd Bloomfield Hills MI 48013

CREIGER, EDWARD, plastics company executive; b. Boston, Apr. 21, 1908; s. Joseph and Jennie (Bornstein) C.; m. Minna E. Croll, June 12, 1933; 1 son, Ernest L. B.C.S. cum laude, Northeastern U., 1929. Agent IRS, 1935-44; partner Creiger, Singer and Lusardi, C.P.A.s, Worcester, Mass., 1944-68; pres., chmn. bd. Foster Grant Co., Inc., Leominster, Mass., 1968-77; chmn. bd. Quaker Fabric Corp., Fall River, Mass. Bd. dirs. Joseph C. and Esther Foster Found., Inc.; corporator, pres.'s council Northeastern U., former chmn. pres.'s council. Recipient Citation for Disting. Attainment Northeastern U. Club: Boca West Country. Home: 20100 Boca West Dr Boca Raton FL 33434

CREIGH, THOMAS, JR., utility executive; b. Evanston, Ill., Jan. 3, 1912; s. Thomas and Frances (Connor) C.; m. Dorothy Claire Weyer, July 17, 1948; children: Mary Elizabeth, Thomas III, John, James. Grad., Mercersburg (Pa.) Acad., 1929; A.B., Wabash Coll., 1933. With No. Natural Gas Co., 1933-36; with KN Energy, Inc. (formerly Kans.-Nebr. Natural Gas Co., Inc.), 1936—, v.p., 1951-61, pres., 1961-78, chmn. bd., 1978—, also dir.; v.p., dir. Excelsior Oil Corp., 1955-68, pres., 1968-84; pres., dir. Western Gas Corp., 1967—; v.p., dir. Helium, Inc., 1960—; sec., dir. Western Plastics Corp., 1953-69; dir. Dunne Gardner Drilling Co., City Nat. Bank, Hastings, Western Alfalfa Corp., Cap-Con Internat Inc., Cape Constrn. Co., Energy Transmission System, Inc., Advanced Fuel Systems, Inc., Slurry Transport Assos., Nebr. Art Collection.; Trustee Hastings Coll., Inst. Gas Tech. Mem. Nebr. Gov.'s Task Force for Govt. Improvement, 1980-82. Mem. Am. (dir. 1969-73), Midwest (dir. 1965-68) gas assns), Interstate Natural Gas Assn. (dir. 1967-71, 74-82), Nebr. Assn. Commerce and Industry (past pres.), Nebr. Council Econ. Edn. (chmn. 1967-70). Presbyterian (trustee). Home: 1950 N Elm St Hastings NE 68901 Office: KN Energy Inc Hastings NE 68901

CREIGHTON, JOHN DOUGLAS, newspaper publisher; b. Toronto, Ont., Can., Nov. 27, 1929; s. Stanley Dixon and Ethel Grace (Armstrong) C.; m. Marilyn June Chamberlain, June 20, 1953; children: Scott, Bruce, Donald. Grad., Humberside Collegiate, Can., 1948. With Toronto Stock Exchange, 1948; reporter Toronto Telegram, 1948-62, asst. city editor, 1962-65, sports editor, 1965-67, city editor, 1967-69, mng. editor, 1969-72, pub., from 1972; now pub. Toronto Sun.; mem. Nat. Newspaper Awards Com.; dir. McDonald's Restaurant of Can. Ltd., CAE Industries Ltd., Colonia Life Ins. Co. Contbg. editor: Almanac of Can, 1968-69. Active Big Bros. of Can., 1969—. Mem. Toronto Men's Press Club (pres. 1959). Anglican. Club: Lambton Golf and Country (Toronto). Office: Toronto Sun 333 King St E Toronto ON M5A 3X5 Canada *

CREIGHTON, JOHN WALLIS, JR., management educator; b. Yeung Kong, China, Apr. 7, 1916; s. John Wallis and Lois (Jameson) C.; m. Harriet Harrington, June 30, 1940; children: Carol (Mrs. Brian LeNeve), Joan (Mrs. Christopher B. Martin). Student, Wooster Coll., 1933-36; B.S., U. Mich., 1938; A.B., Hastings Coll., 1939; Ph.D. in Wood Tech. and Indsl. Engring., U. Mich., 1954. Operator, sawmill, Cayahoga Falls, Ohio, 1939-41; mem. stall U.S. Bd. Econ. Warfare, Ecuador, 1941-43; asst. gen. mgr. R.S. Bacon Veneer Co., Chgo., 1943-44; gen. mgr., v.p. Bacon Lumber Co., Sunman, Ind., 1943-45; mem. faculty Mich. State U., Lansing, 1945-54, prof. wood tech., 1945-54; asst. to gen. mgr., v.p. Baker Furniture Inc., Grand Rapids, Mich., 1954-58; pres. Creighton Bldg. Co., Santa Barbara, Calif., 1958-65; prof. mgmt. Colo. State U., Fort Collins, 1965-67, U.S. Naval Postgrad. Sch., Monterey, Calif., 1967—, chmn. dept., 1967-71; cons. to govt. Assoc. editor: Jour. Tech. Transfer; author papers in field. Recipient various research grants in lumber mfg., research and orgn. studies for U.S. Navy and U.S. Forest Service. Mem. Soc. Advanced Learning Tech., Am. Arbitration Assn., Def. Preparedness Assn. Presbyterian. Home: 8065 Lake Pl Carmel CA 93923

CREIGHTON, NEAL, army officer; b. Ft. Sill, Okla., July 11, 1930; s. Neal and Charlotte (Gilliam) C.; m. Joan Hicks, Aug. 1, 1958; children: Linda, Lisa, Neal. B.S., U.S. Mil. Acad., 1953; student, U. Madrid, 1959-60; M.A., Middlebury Coll., 1961; grad., U.S. Army Command and Staff Coll., 1967, U.S. Army War Coll., 1970. Commd. 2d lt. U.S. Army, 1953, advanced through grades to maj. gen.; troop assignments, U.S., Germany, 1953-59; from instr. to asst. prof. fgn. lang. U.S. Mil. Acad., 1960-63, staff officer So. Command, Panama, 1964-66, squadron comdr., Vietnam, 1967-68, mil. asst. Office of Sec. Army, Washington, 1970-72, comdr. Combined Arms Tng. Center, Germany, 1973-74, brigade comdr., 1974-76; dep. dir. Ops. and Readiness Directorate, Dept. Army, 1977-78; comdr. 1st Inf. Div., Germany, 1978-80, dep. chief of staff Allied Forces Central Europe, Brunssum, Netherlands, 1980, comdg. gen. 1st Inf. Div., Ft. Riley, Kans., 1980—. Decorated Silver Star medal, Bronze Star medal, Air medal. Mem. Assn. U.S. Army, U.S. Armor Assn. Episcopalian. Office: Comdg Gen 1st Inf Div M Fort Riley KS 66442

CREIGHTON, THOMAS HAWK, architect; b. Phila., May 19, 1904; s. Frank W. and Maude (Hawk) C.; m. Gwen Lux, 1959; children by previous marriage—Thomas Hawk, Anne Genung. A.B., Harvard, 1926; grad., Beaux Arts Inst. Design, 1929. Archtl. designer Shultze & Weaver, Charles B. Meyers, N.Y.C., Freeman, French, Freeman, Burlington, Vt., 1926-38; sr. architect, dept. hosps., N.Y.C., 1938-40; asso. Alfred Hopkins & Assos., 1940-46; editor Progressive Architecture, 1946-63, editorial dir., 1963-64; partner, v.p. John Carl Warnecke & Assos. (architects), San Francisco, 1963- 66; architect and planner, Honolulu, 1966; Adj. prof. architecture, Columbia; 962-63; vis. lectr. U. Hawaii, 1968-69, univ. architect, 1970; spl. columnist Honolulu Advertiser, 1968—. Author: Planning To Build, 1945, Houses, 1947, Building for Modern Man, 1949, The American House Today, 1951, Quality Budget Houses, 1954, Designs for Living, 1955, (with Katherine Morrow Ford) Contemporary Houses, 1961, The Architecture of Monuments, 1962, American Architecture, 1964, The Lands of Hawaii: Their Use and Misuse, 1977. Mem. Honolulu Planning Commn., 1971-74. Fellow AIA; mem. Constrn. Specifications Inst. (hon.). Home and Office: 4340 Pahoa Ave Honolulu HI 96816

CRELIN, EDMUND SLOCUM, educator, anatomist; b. Red Bank, N.J., Apr. 26, 1923; s. Edmund Slocum and Agatha (Bublin) C.; m. Marjorie Joyce McCain, Sept. 11, 1948; children—Sheryl, Edmund Slocum III, Robert, Carole. B.A. cum laude, Central Coll., Iowa, 1947, D.Sc. (hon.), 1969; Ph.D., Yale, 1951. USPHS fellow Yale, 1949-51, instr. anatomy, 1951-55, asst. prof., 1955-61, asso. prof., 1961-68, prof., 1968—; chmn. Human Growth and Devel. study unit Yale-New Haven Med. Center, 1971—; chief sect. human anatomy and devel., dept. surgery Yale U. Sch. Medicine, 1978—; asso. editor Anatomical Record; cons. CIBA-GEIGY Pharm. Co., Summit, N.J. Author: Anatomy of the Newborn, 1969, Functional Anatomy of the Newborn, 1973; Contbr. articles profl. jours. Recipient Yale U. Sch. Medicine F.G. Blake award, 1961; Kappa Delta Research award Am. Acad. Orthopaedic Surgeons, 1976. Mem. AMA, Am. Assn. Anatomists, AAAS, Sigma Xi. Home: 124 Sunset Hill Dr Branford CT 06405 Office: Yale Univ Sch Medicine 333 Cedar St New Haven CT 06510

CREMERS, CLIFFORD JOHN, engineering educator; b. Mpls., Mar. 27, 1933; s. Christian Joseph and Marie Hildegard C.; m. Claudette May Humble, Sept. 25, 1954; children: Carla Ann, Rachel Beth, Emily Therese, Eric John, Melissa Joan. B.S.M.E., U. Minn., 1957, M.S.M.E. (Trane Co. fellow), 1961, Ph.D., 1964. Research fellow mech. engring. U. Minn., 1959-61, instr., 1961-64; asst. prof. mech. engring. Ga. Inst. Tech., Atlanta, 1964-66; asso. prof. U. Ky., Lexington, 1966-71, prof. mech. engring., 1971—, chmn. dept., 1975—; cons. to industry, UNESCO. Contbr. articles on heat transfer to profl. jours. Served with USNR, 1953-55. NSF grantee; NASA grantee. Fellow ASME; mem. AIAA, Am. Soc. Engring. Edn., AAAS, Sigma Xi. Roman Catholic. Home: 3181 Lamar Dr Lexington KY 40502 Office: Dept Mech. Engineering U Ky Lexington KY 40506

CREMIN, LAWRENCE ARTHUR, educator; b. N.Y.C., Oct. 31, 1925; s. Arthur T. and Theresa (Borowick) C.; m. Charlotte Raup, Sept. 19, 1956; children: Joanne Laura, David Lawrence. B.S. in Social Scis., CCNY, 1946; A.M., Columbia U., 1947, Ph.D., 1949, Litt.D., 1975; L.H.D., Ohio State U., 1975, Kalamazoo Coll., 1976; LL.D., U. Bridgeport, 1975, U. Rochester, 1980. Mem. faculty Columbia Tchrs. Coll., N.Y.C., 1948—, Frederick A.P. Barnard prof. edn., 1961—, pres., 1974—; Guggenheim fellow, 1957-58; fellow Center for Advanced Study in Behavioral Scis., 1964-65, 71-72. Author: The American Common School, 1951, The Transformation of the School (Bancroft prize Am. history), 1961, The Genius of American Education, 1965, The Wonderful World of Ellwood Patterson Cubberley, 1965, American Education: The Colonial Experience, 1970, Public Education, 1976, Traditions of American Education, 1977, American Education: The National Experience, 1980 (Pulitzer prize); gen. editor: Classics in Education. Trustee Spencer Found., Children's TV Workshop, Carnegie Found. Advancement of Teaching, Charles F. Kettering Found. Served with USAAF, 1944-45. Recipient research award Am. Ednl. Research Assn., 1969; Butler medal Columbia U., 1972. Mem. Hist. Edn. Soc. (pres. 1959-60), Nat. Soc. Coll. Tchrs. Edn. (pres. 1961-62), Nat. Acad. Edn. (pres. 1969-73), Am. Acad. Arts and Scis., Council Fgn. Relations. Office: Teachers Coll Columbia New York NY 10027

CRENNA, RICHARD, actor; b. Los Angeles. Ed., U. So. Calif. Owner Pendick Enterprises, 1966—. Actor: radio programs including Our Miss Brooks, Boy Scout Jamboree, A Date with Judy, The Great Gildersleeve; TV series Slattery's People, Our Miss Brooks, The Real McCoy's; films Red Sky at Morning, Doctor's Wives, Catlow, Un Flic, The Man Called Noon, Dirty Money, Wait Until Dark, 1967, Pride of St. Louis, It Grows on Trees, Red Skies Over Montana, John Goldfarb, Please Come Home, Star, 1968, The Sand Pebbles, The Deserter, Marooned, 1969, Five Against Texas, Made in Paris, Breakheart Pass, 1976, Death Ship; appeared in: TV series All's Fair, 1976-77; also; TV movies. Mem. Dirs. Guild Am. Address: care William Morris Agy 151 El Camino Beverly Hills CA 90620 *

CRENNER, JAMES JOSEPH, credit services co. exec.; b. Pitts., June 22, 1922; s. Michael J. and Edna T. (Schleich) C.; m. Julia Rossell, Nov. 10, 1945; children: Patricia, Constance. Student, U. Pitts., 1946-54. With Dun & Bradstreet, Inc., 1945-82, mgr. offices, Erie, Pa. and; Winston-Salem, N.C., 1955-58, dist. mgr., Rochester, N.Y., Indpls. and Chgo., 1959-69; pres. Nat. Credit Office subs. Dun & Bradstreet, Inc., N.Y.C., 1969, regional mgr., then v.p., Chgo., 1969-71, sr. v.p. ops., N.Y.C., 1972-75, exec. v.p. ops., 1975-76, pres., 1976—, chmn. bd., 1978-82; exec. v.p. parent co. Dun & Bradstreet Corp., 1982—; lectr. in field. Contbr. articles to newspapers and trade jours. Mem. nat. adv. bd. Am. U., Washington. Served with USMC, 1942-45. Mem. Nat. Assn. Credit Mgmt., Sales Exec. Club, Nat. Sales Mgmt. Assn. (accredited speaker). Clubs: Spring Brook Country (Morristown, N.J.); Board Room (N.Y.C.); Seaview Country (Absecon, N.J.); Rotary. Home: 20 Fieldstone Dr Morristown NJ 07960 Office: 299 Park Ave New York NY 10171 *To be successful is truly the American dream; it is equally true that most citizens are content to just dream about success rather than pay the price for its attainment. For those relatively few "price payers" it is indeed a delight to learn, early in life, that talent deficiencies can be overcome by hard work. Application of that knowledge is responsible for most successful and satisfying careers.*

CRENSHAW, BEN, profl. golfer; b. Austin, Tex., Jan. 11, 1952; m. Polly. Grad., U. Tex. Mem. U.S. World Amateur Cup Team, 1972; prof. golfer, 1973—. Mem. Profl. Golfers Assn. Am. Winner San Antonio-Tex. Open, 1973, Bing Crosby Nat. Pro-Am, Ohio Kings Island Open, Hawaiian Open, 1976, Colonial Nat. Invitational, 1977, NCAA Championship, 1971, 72, 73, Irish Open, 1976, Phoenix Open, 1979, Walt Disney World Team Championship, 1980, Anheuser-Busch Classic, 1980, Masters tournament, 1984. Office: care Profl Golfers Assn Am 5101 River Rd Washington DC 20016 *

CRENSHAW, FRANCIS NELSON, lawyer; b. Washington, Dec. 9, 1922; s. Russell Sydnor and Sally Nelson (Robins) C.; m. Jane Elizabeth Treadwell, Aug. 20, 1949; children—Elizabeth, Page, Marian. Grad., St. George's Sch., 1939; B.A., U. Va., 1943, LL.B., 1948. Bar: Va. bar 1948. Partner Baird, White & Lanning, Norfolk, 1952-55, Baird, Crenshaw & Lanning, 1955-60, Baird, Crenshaw & Ware, 1960-68, Crenshaw, Ware & Johnson, 1968—; mem. Va. Bd. Bar Examiners, 1973—; Mem. Norfolk City Sch. Bd., 1955-64, chmn., 1962-64; Bd. visitors Old Dominion U., 1968-76, rector, 1972-76; mem. bd. commrs., Eastern Va. Med. Authority, 1978-80. Served with USNR, 1943-46. Bronze Star. Fellow Am. Bar Assn.; mem. Va. Bar Assn., Va. State Bar, Norfolk-Portsmouth Bar, Maritime Law Assn. Home: 1001 Graydon Ave Norfolk VA 23507 Office: 1640 Virginia National Bldg Norfolk VA 23510

CRENSHAW, MARION CARLYLE, JR., obstetrician, educator; b. Lancaster, S.C., Apr. 15, 1931; s. Marion Carlyle and Mabel (Byrd) C.; m. Lillian Ruth Blackmon, Nov. 27, 1979; children—Marion Carlyle III, William, Hugh, Faith. B.S. cum laude, Davidson Coll., 1952; M.D., Duke U., 1956. Intern Duke U. Med. Center, Durham, N.C., 1956-57, resident, 1957-62, instr. obstetrics and gynecology, 1961-62, asso., 1964-65, asst. prof., 1965-70, asso. prof., 1970-71, E.C. Hamblen prof. reproductive biology and family planning, 1971-80, asst. prof. pediatrics, 1971-80, asso. physiology, 1965-75; prof., chmn. dept. obstetrics and gynecology U. Md. Sch. Medicine, Balt., 1980—; vis. scholar Physiol.-Lab. Cambridge (Eng.) U., 1978-79. Contbr. articles and chpts. to profl. jours. and books. Served with USAF, 1962-64. Mead Johnson fellow, 1960-61; Macy Faculty fellow, 1966-69. Fellow Howard K. Kane-A.F.A. King Obstet. Soc., Am. Coll. Obstetricians and Gynecologists; mem. Am. Gynecol. Soc., F. Bayard Carter Soc. Obstetricians and Gynecologists (treas. 1970-77, v.p. 1977-79), No Name Soc., Soc. Gynecol. Investigation, N.C. Obstetric and Gynecology Soc., N.Y. Acad. Socs., Perinatal Research Soc., So. Perinatal Assn., Soc. Perinatal Obstetricians (dir. 1977-80), Md. Ob-Gyn Soc. (exec. com. 1981-84), Med. and Chirurg. Faculty of Md. (ho. of dels. 1983-84), Balt. City Med. Soc., Western Ob-Gyn Soc. (hon.), South Atlantic Assn. Obstetricians and Gynecologists (hon.), Splint Soc., N.Am. Travel Club, Phi Beta Kappa., Alpha Omega Alpha. Home: 4312 St Paul St Baltimore MD 21218

CRENSON, MATTHEW ALLEN, political science educator; b. Balt., Apr. 28, 1943; s. Gus Arthur and Charlotte Eugenie (Pasche) C.; m. Alene Louise Childs, Dec. 30, 1964; children: Matthew MacGregor, Ethan Jones. B.A., Johns Hopkins U., 1963; M.A., U. Chgo., 1965, Ph.D., 1969. Research fellow Brookings Instn., 1968; instr. polit. sci. M.I.T., 1968-69; asst. prof. Johns Hopkins U., 1969-73, asso. prof.,

1973-76, prof., 1976—; Vice pres. Balt. Neighborhoods Inst., 1979-80, bd. dirs., 1979—. Author: The Unpolitics of Air Pollution, 1971, The Federal Machine, 1975, (with others) Models in the Policy Process, 1976, Neighborhood Politics, 1983. Woodrow Wilson fellow, 1963-64; Nat. Opinion Research Center tng. fellow, 1964-67. Home: 718 Morningside Dr Towson MD 21204 Office: Dept Polit Sci Johns Hopkins U Baltimore MD 21218

CRÉPEAU, PAUL-ANDRÉ, lawyer; b. Gravelbourg, Que., Can., May 20, 1926; s. Jean-Baptiste and Blanche (Provencher) C.; m. Nicole Thomas, June 26, 1959; children—Francois, Marie-Geneviève, Philippe. Bacheler dès arts, U. Ottawa, Ont., 1946, Lic. en Philosophie, 1947; Lic. en Droit, U. Montreal, Que., 1950; B.C.L., U. Oxford, Eng., 1952; Docteur de Droit, U. Paris, 1955; diplôme supérieur de droit comparé, Faculté internat. de droit comparé, U. Strasbourg, France, 1959. Bar: bar. Asst. prof. U. Montreal Faculty Law; prof. law McGill U. Faculty Law, Montreal, now also Wainwright prof. civil law; pres., 1965-77. Club: McGill U. Faculty. Home: 5 Pl du Vesinet Montreal PQ H2V 2L6 Canada Office: 3690 Peel St Montreal PQ H3A 1W9 Canada

CREPET, WILLIAM LOUIS, botanist; b. N.Y.C., Aug. 10, 1946; s. Louis Henry and Adaire Elaine (Richardson) C.; m. Laura Marie Stewart, July 29, 1972 (div. 1978); m. Ruth Chadab, July 27, 1980. B.A. (N.Y. State Regents scholar), State U. N.Y. at Binghamton, 1969; M.Ph. (Wadsworth fellow), Yale, 1972; Ph.D. (Cullman fellow), Yale, 1973. Cons. to Grad. Sch., U. Tex., Austin, 1972-73; lectr. Ind. U., 1973-75; asst. prof. U. Conn., 1975-78, asso. prof., 1979—. Fellow Explorers Club; mem. Bot. Soc. Am. (chmn. paleobotany sect. 1979-80, Paleobot. award 1972), Am. Inst. Biol. Scis., Beta Chi Sigma. Research on Mesozoic and Tertiary genera. Office: Biol Scis Group U-42 U Conn Storrs CT 06268

CRERAR, DAVID ALEXANDER, geochemistry educator, consultant; b. Toronto, Ont., Can., July 23, 1945; came to U.S., 1969; s. Louis Alexander and Dorothy Mary (Biehl) C.; m. Scotia Wendell MacRae, Aug. 14, 1971. B.Sc., U. Toronto, 1967, M.Sc., 1969; Ph.D., Pa. State U., 1974. Research asst. Can. Geol. Survey, Ottawa, Ont., 1964-66, Halifax, N.S., 1964-66, U. Toronto, 1967-69, Pa. State U. (State College), 1969-74; asst. prof. dept. geology Princeton U., 1974-80, assoc. prof., 1980-83, prof. geochemistry, 1983—; cons. geochemist McCombs-Knutson Assocs. Inc., Mpls., 1982—. Contbr. articles to profl. jours. Recipient Gov. Gen. medal U. Toronto, 1967, Shell disting. term chair in geochemistry Shell Found., Princeton U., 1980, Lindgren award Soc. Econ. Geologists, 1982. Mem. Soc. Econ. Geologists, Geochem. Soc. Home: 50 Patton Ave Princeton NJ 08540 Office: Dept Geology Princeton U. Princeton NJ 08544

CRESON, WILLIAM T., corporation executive; b. 1929. B.S., Purdue U., 1950; M.A., Wharton Sch. Bus. Adminstrn., U. Pa., 1954. With Packaging Corp. of Am., prior to 1968; sr. v.p., gen. mgr. Brown Co., 1968-75; with Crown Zellerbach Corp., San Francisco, 1976—, exec. v.p., mem. exec. com., now pres., chmn., chief exec. officer, dir. Office: Crown Zellerbach Corp 1 Bush St Box 3475 San Francisco CA 94119 *

CRESPI, IRVING, public opinion and market research consultant; b. Bklyn., May 8, 1926; s. Joseph and Esther (Crespi) C.; m. Joan Striefling, Aug. 4, 1968; children: Robert Joseph, Judith Shoshana. B.S.S., CCNY, 1945; M.A., State U. Ia., 1946; Ph.D., New Sch. for Social Research, 1955. Instr. sociology Triple Cities Coll., Endicott, N.Y., 1948-50; asst. prof. sociology Harpur Coll., State U. N.Y., 1950-51, 53-56; v.p. Gallup Orgn., Inc., Princeton, N.J., 1958-70, exec. v.p., 1970-76; v.p. Mathematica Policy Research, 1976-77, sr. v.p., 1977-78, sr. fellow, 1978-79; v.p. Roper Orgn., 1979-81; owner Irving Crespi & Assos., Princeton, 1981—. Author: (with H. Mendelsohn) Polls, Television and New Politics, 1971; also articles on pub. opinion, marketing research. Trustee Paul F. Lazarsfeld Fund, 1977-79. Served with USAF, 1951-53. Mem. Am. Assn. Pub. Opinion Research (v.p. 1975-76), pres. (1976-77, chmn. standards com. 1966-68, conf. chmn. 1970), Am. Sociol. Assn., Am. Mktg. Assn. (dir. 1970-72), World Assn. for Pub. Opinion Research (v.p. 1974-76, pres. 1976-78), Market Research Council. Jewish. Home: 9 Orchard Circle Princeton NJ 08540 Office: 9 Orchard Circle Princeton NJ 08540

CRESPIN, REGINE, soprano; b. Marseilles, France; d. Henri and Margherite (DiMeirone) C. Student, Lycée Français, Conservatoire de Paris. Appeared in: numerous operas including Lohengrin, Mulhouse, France, 1950, Paris, 1951, N.Y.C., 1964, Tosca, Il Trovatore, Otello, Die Walkuere, Oberon, Fidelio, Der Rosenkavalier, Marseilles, Le Nozze di Figaro, Paris, 1956, Dialogues of the Carmelites, 1957, Parsifal, 1958, Ballo in Maschera, 1958, Fedra, Milan, Italy, 1959, Die Walkuere, Vienna, 1959, Der Rosenkavalier, Berlin, 1960; as the Marshallin, London, 1961, Les Troyens, Paris, 1961, Penelope, Buenos Aires, 1961, Otello, Ballo in Maschera, Die Walkuere, Der Rosenkavalier, Vienna, also Rosenkavalier, N.Y.C., 1962, Flying Dutchman, N.Y.C., 1962, Ballo in Maschera, N.Y.C., 1962, La Vestale, N.Y.C., 1962, Herodiade, N.Y.C., 1963, Fidelio, Ballo in Maschera, Tannhauser, Fidelio, Chgo., 1963, Carnegie Hall, 1973, Met. Opera, 1973, Carmen, Met. Opera, 1975, Cavalleria Rusticana, San Francisco Opera, 1976, Dialogues of the Carmelites, Met. Opera, 1977, 78; soloist, N.Y. Philharmonic, 1964-65; appeared in recital, Hunter Coll., 1965. Office: Herbert H Breslin 119 W 57th St New York NY 10019 *

CRESS, GEORGE AYERS, artist, educator; b. Anniston, Ala., Apr. 7, 1921; s. Glen Herbert and Lola Idell (King) C. Student, Emory U., 1938-40, Am. U., 1947-48; B.F.A., U. Ga., 1942, M.F.A., 1949. Instr. art Judson Coll., 1945-46, Mary Baldwin Coll., 1946-47, U. Md., 1947-48; prof., head art dept. U. Chattanooga, 1951-69, U. Tenn. at Chattanooga, 1969—, Guerry prof. art, 1974—; vis. artist Ont. Dept. Edn., 1962, U. Ga., 1965, 69, East Tenn. State U., 1966, U. S.C., 1967. 20 year Retrospective Exhbn., Hunter Mus. and various Southeastern museums, 1971-72; exhibited in one man shows at, Grand Central Moderns, N.Y.C., 1956, Addison Gallery Am. Art, 1972, Bampton Arts Centre, Oxford, Eng., 1976, Hunter Mus., 1978, Columbus (Ga.) Mus., 1980, Agnes Scott Coll. Galleries, 1981, Visual Arts Gallery, U. Ga., 1982, McIntosh Gallery, Atlanta, group shows at, USIA Far East Traveling Show, 1959, First Provincetown Ann., 1958, Pa. Acad., 1960, 62, Butler Inst. Am. Art, 1963, 64, 69, 70, 74, Springfield Art Mus., 1965, 67, Chataugua Ann., 1960, Soc. of Four Arts, Palm Beach, 1961, 62, 63. Bd. dirs. Southeastern Coll. Art Conf., 1974—. Served to 1st lt. USAAF, 1942-45. Mem. Southeastern Coll. Art Conf. (pres. 1956, 66, 83), Tenn. Coll. Art Council (chmn. 1966-67), E.Tenn. Art Edn. Assn. (chmn. 1969), Blue Key, Phi Kappa Phi. Home: 414 East View Dr Chattanooga TN 37404 *The act of painting, for me, is both exhausting and exhilarating, frustrating and stimulating. It is both intellectual and emotional. The artist is involved in a continual process of destroying the illusions of the visual world, and in an attempt to reconstruct them into something new and personal. It is through this very process that he comes nearer to a reality for himself and the viewer.*

CRESSEY, DONALD RAY, educator, sociologist; b. Fergus Falls, Minn., Apr. 27, 1919; s. Raymond Wilbert and Myrtle Athelma (Prentiss) C.; m. Elaine Smythe, Dec. 16, 1943; children: Martha J. Lind, Ann K. Colomy, Mary. B.S., Iowa State U., 1943; Ph.D., Ind. U., 1950. Sociologist Ill. State Penitentiary, Joliet, 1949, U.S. Penitentiary, Terre Haute, Ind., 1951; from lectr. to prof. sociology U. Calif. at Los Angeles, 1949-59, vice chmn. dept. anthropology and sociology, 1957-58, chmn. dept., 1958-61, dean div. social sci., 1960-61; vis. prof. Trinity Coll., Cambridge U., 1961-62, U. Oslo, 1965, U. Washington, summer, 1968, U. Minn., summer 1969, Churchill Coll., Cambridge U., 1970-71, Australian Nat. U., 1973, U. Minn. Law Sch., 1974; dean Coll. Letters and Sci., U. Calif. at Santa Barbara, 1962-67, prof. sociology, 1962—, faculty research lectr., 1978—; Mem. mental health tng. com. NIMH, 1963-67, chmn., 1966-67, mem. policy and planning bd., tng. and manpower resources br., 1964-67; mem. Am. Bar Assn. Commn. on Juvenile Justice Standards, 1972-76; cons. Pres.'s Commn. on Law Enforcement and Adminstrn. Justice, 1965-66, Nat. Commn. Causes and Prevention Violence, 1968, Nat. Inst. Criminal Justice, 1969-79, Calif. Council on Criminal Justice, 1969-72, (also others). Author: Other People's Money, a Study in the Social Psychology of Embezzlement, 1953, (with Edwin H. Sutherland) Principles of Criminology, 5th edit, 1955, 10th 1978, (with Richard A. Cloward, others) Theoretical Studies in Social Organization of the Prison, 1960, Delinquency, Crime and Differential Association, 1964, Functions and Structure of Confederated Crime, 1967, Theft of the Nation, 1969, (with David A. Ward) Delinquency, Crime and Social Process, 1969, Criminal Organization: Its Elementary Forms, 1972, (with Arthur Rosett) Justice by Consent: Plea Bargains in the American Courthouse, 1976, (with James W. Coleman) Social Problems, 1980, 2d edit., 1984, (with Charles A. Moore) Corporation Codes of Ethical Conduct, 1980; editor: The Prison, Studies in Institutional Organization and Change, 1961, Crime and Criminal Justice, 1971; asso. editor: Am. Sociol. Rev, 1953-56, Am. Jour. Sociology, 1958-61, 80-83, Transaction: Soc. Sci. and the Community, 1963-69, Harper and Row Social Problems Series, 1965-75, Social Problems, 1968-74; Contbr. articles to profl. jours. Served with USAAF, 1943-45. Recipient Research prizes Ill. Acad. Criminology, 1964, Am. Soc. Criminology, 1967, 80, Sociol. Research Assn., 1972, U. Calif.-Santa Barbara, 1978, Distinguished Alumnus award Ind. U., 1974; Citation of Merit Iowa State U., 1977; others.; Russell Sage Found. research grantee, 1955-56; travel grantee Am. Council Learned Socs., 1960; research grantee Ford Found., 1960, Peat, Marwick, Mitchell Found., 1979; also others. Fellow Am. Sociol. Assn. (council 1961-63, vis. scientist 1963-65, chmn. criminology sect. 1966-67), AAAS; mem. Law and Soc. Assn., Am. Soc. Criminology, Pacific Sociol. Assn. (pres. 1959-60), Sociol. Research Assn., Am. Correctional Assn., Soc. for Study Social Problems. Club: Earl of Derby (Cambridge, Eng.) (pres. 1962-63). Home: Hope Ranch 4310 Via Esperanza Santa Barbara CA 93110

CRESSMAN, GEORGE PARMLEY, research meteorologist; b. West Chester, Pa., Oct. 7, 1919; s. George R. and Martha S. (Parmley) 8C.; m. Nelia M. Hazard, Feb. 28, 1942 (dec.); children: Ruth, George, Catherine, Florence; m. Frances S. Ankeny, June 29, 1975. B.Sc., Pa. State Coll., 1941; M.Sc., N.Y.U., 1942; Ph.D., U. Chgo., 1949. Engaged in research, teaching U. Chgo., 1946-49; cons. USAF Weather Service, 1949-54; dir. joint weather bur. Navy-Air Force Numerical Weather Prediction Unit, Suitland, Md., 1954—, Nat. Meteorol. Center, 1958-64; dir. Nat. Meteorol. Service, 1964-65, U.S. Weather Bur., Silver Spring, 1965-70, Nat. Weather Service, 1970-79, sr. research meteorologist, 1979—. Served to capt. AUS, 1942-45. Recipient Exceptional Civilian Service award USAF, 1956; Exceptional Service award Dept. Commerce, 1961; IMO prize World Meteorol. Orgn., 1977. Fellow Am. Meteorol. Soc. (councilor 1956-59, 69-72, pres. 1978, asso. editor jour. 1954-65), Am. Geophys. Union, AAAS. Home: 11 Old Stage Ct Rockville MD 20852 Office: National Weather Service 5200 Auth Rd Camps Springs MD 20233

CRESSMAN, RALPH DWIGHT, educator, surgeon; b. Oglesby, Ill., Jan. 17, 1909; s. Ralph Gates and Emily (Blackmore) C.; m. Bernice Moore Klein, Aug. 16, 1935; children—Russell R., Ann Cressman Anderson. A.B., U. Calif. at Berkeley, 1929, M.A., 1931, M.D., 1934. Intern Alameda County Hosp., Oakland, Calif., 1935; postgrad. surg. tng. U. Calif., Vanderbilt U. and San Francisco Gen. hosps., 1935-41; practice surgery Palo Alto (Calif.) Med. Clinic, 1946-78, head sect. gen. surgery, 1960-74; clin. prof. surgery Stanford Med. Sch., 1970-74, emeritus, 1974—. Author articles in field. Served with M.C. AUS, 1942-45. Mem. A.C.S. (gov. 1962- 68, sec. bd. govs. 1967-68), San Francisco Surg. Soc., Pacific Coast Surg. Assn. (sec.-treas. 1964-68, pres. 1975). Home: 360 Everett Ave Palo Alto CA 94301

CRESTON, PAUL, composer; b. N.Y.C., Oct. 10, 1906; s. Gaspare and Carmela (Collura) Guttoveggio; m. Louise Gotto, July 1, 1927; children—Joel Anthony, Timothy William. Student pub. schs., N.Y.C. Organist St. Malachy's Ch., N.Y.C., 1934-67; faculty N.Y. Coll. Music, 1964-68; distinguished vis. prof. Central Wash. State Coll., Ellensburg, 1967, composer-in-residence, prof. music, 1968-75. Made concert tour as pianist and accompanist, 1936; mus. dir.: The Hour of Faith Program, ABC, 1944-50; Author: Rational Metric Notation. Guggenheim fellow in composition, 1938, 39; Recipient citation of merit Nat. Assn. Am. Composers and Condrs., 1941, 43; music award Nat. Inst. Arts and Letters, 1943; N.Y. Music Critics award for Symphony No. 1, 1943; Alice M. Ditson award for Poem for Harp and Orch., 1945; Fedn. Music Clubs award for Symphony No. 2, 1947; Music Library Assn. award for Two Choric Dances, 1948; 1st prize for Symphony No. 1 Paris Referendum Concert, 1952; State Dept. grant as Am. specialist for, Israel and Turkey, 1960; gold medal Nat. Arts Club, 1963; Composer award Lancaster Symphony, 1970. Life fellow Internat. Inst. Arts and Letters; mem. Nat. Assn. Am. Composers and Condrs. (pres. 1956-60, life mem.), ASCAP (dir. 1960-68), Bohemians (gov. 1950-68), Nat. Music Council (exec. com. 1950-68), Kappa Kappa Psi, Phi Kappa Lambda, Pi Mu Alpha Sinfonia. Home: PO Box 28511 San Diego CA 92128

CREUTZ, EDWARD CHESTER, physicist, museum official; b. Beaver Dam, Wis., Jan. 23, 1913; s. Lester Raymond and Grace (Smith) C.; m. Lela Rolefson, Sept. 13, 1937 (dec. Feb. 1972); children: Michael John, Carl Eugene, Ann Jo Carmel Creutz Cosgrove; M. 2d. Elisabeth B. Cordle, Oct. 5, 1974. B.S., U. Wis., 1936, Ph.D., 1939. Research assoc. Princeton U., 1939-40, instr. physics, 1940-41; physicist NDRC, 1941-42, Metall. Lab., U. Chgo., 1942-44, Manhattan Project, Los Alamos, 1944-46; assoc. prof. Carnegie Inst. Tech., Pitts., 1946-49, prof., head dept. physics, dir. Nuclear Research Ctr., 1948-55; dir. John Jay Hopkins Lab. for Pure and Applied Sci., 1955-59; dir. research Gen. Atomic Div. Gen. Dynamics Corp., San Diego, 1955-59; v.p. research and devel. Gen. Atomic div. Gen. Dynamics Corp., San Diego, 1959-67; v.p. research and devel Gulf Gen. Atomic, San Diego, 1967-70; asst. dir. NSF, Washington, 1970-77, acting dep. dir., 1976-77; dir. Bernice Pauahi Bishop Mus., Honolulu, 1977—; mem. adv. council Water Resources Ctr., U. Calif.-Berkeley, 1958-65; mem. sea water conversion com. Water resources Ctr., U. Calif.-Berkeley, 1958-68; adv. com. office Sci. Personnel NRC, 1960-63; mem. exec. council Argonne Nat. Lab. (1946-51); cons. NSF, 1950-68; scientist-at-large Project Sherwood div. research AEC, 1955-56; mem. com. sr. reviewers Dept. Energy, 1972-79, fusion power coordinating com., 1971-79; cons. Oak Ridge Nat. Lab., 1946-58; adv. panel gen. scis. Dept. Def., 1959-63; research adv. com. electrophysics NASA, 1964, tech. adv. com., 1971-77; adj. prof. physics and astronomy U. Hawaii, 1977—. Co-editor: Handbuch der Physik, vols. 14, 15; mem. editorial bd.: Ann. Rev. Nuclear Sci., 1961-66, 72-75; mem.: Handbook of Chemistry and Physics, 1961—; mem. editorial bd.: Interdisciplinary Science Reviews, London, 1976—; editorial adv. com.: Nuclear Sci. nd Engring., 1959-72. Bd. dirs. San Diego Hall Sci. and Planetarium, v.p., 1956-70; v.p. San Diego Industry-Edn. Council, 1956-65; mem. adv. council Dept. Edn. San Diego County. Fellow Am. Phys. Soc. (NRC rep. 1956-57), Am. Nuclear Soc., AAAS, Explorers Club; mem. Nat. Acad. Scis., Social Sci. Assn. Honolulu, Am. Assn. Physics Tchrs., Internat. Platform Assn., ASCAP, Phys. Soc. Pitts. (pres. 1949), Am. Soc. Engring. Edn., ASME, AAUP, IEEE, Am. Inst. Physics (dir.-at-large bd. govs. 1965-68). Home: 3964-D Old Pali Rd Honolulu HI 96817 Office: Bernice Pauahi Bishop Museum PO Box 19000-A Honolulu HI 96819

CREVISTON, RICHARD LEROY, banker; b. North Canton, Ohio, Feb. 19, 1925; s. Forrest John and Dortha Ruth (Shaub) C.; m. Carol Ruth Musson, May 5, 1956; children: Jane Louise, John Richard. B.S., U. Pa., 1948; postgrad., William McKinley Sch. Law, 1948-51, Harvard U., 1945, Ind. U., 1966. Banking and budget officer U.S. Mil. Govt., Ryukyu Islands, 1945-46; adminstrv. asst. Central Nat. Bank Cleve., 1953-56; asst. v.p. Lake County Nat. Bank, Painesville, Ohio, 1956-59; sr. v.p., dir. First Fed. Savs. and Loan Assn., Willoughby, Ohio, 1959-69; exec. v.p. New Eng. Savs. Bank, New London, Conn., 1969-71, chmn., pres., 1971—, dir., 1969—; pres., dir. Savs. Bank Life Ins. Co., Hartford, 1970-76; pres. Savs. Bank Housing Corp., Hartford, 1973-76. Bd. dirs. Conn. Pub. Expenditure Council, 1976-79, 83—, United Way, 1981—; corporator, trustee, bd. mgrs., asst. treas. Lawrence and Meml. hosps., New London; treas. Friends of Mitchell Coll., 1970—, Mitchell Coll., 1976; trustee Mitchell Coll., 1976—; adv. council Lyman Allyn Mus., 1977; trustee Shea Fund, 1977. Served to lt. comdr. USNR, 1943-46, 52-53. Mem. Nat. Assn. Mut. Savs. Banks (exec. com.), Savs. Banks Assn. (exec. com. Conn. 1977—), Savs. Bank Assn. Conn. (exec. com.), Alpha Phi Omega. Club: Thames. Lodges: Masons (32 deg.); Rotary. Home: 254 Great Neck Rd Waterford CT 06385 Office: 63 Eugene O'Neill Dr New London CT 06320

CREW, LOUIE, educator; b. Anniston, Ala., Dec. 9, 1936; s. Erman and Lula (Hagin) C.; m. Ernest Clay, Feb. 2, 1974. B.A., Baylor U., 1958; M.A., Auburn U., 1959; Ph.D., U. Ala., 1971. Teaching fellow Auburn U., 1958-59; master English and sacred studies Darlington Sch., 1959-62, St. Andrew's, Del., 1962-65; master of English and English history Penge Secondary Modern, London, Eng., 1965-66; instr. English U. Ala., 1966-70; dir. Independent Study Program of Experiment in Internat. Living, Eng., 1970-71; prof. English Claflin Coll., Orangeburg, S.C., 1971-73; assoc. prof. Fort Valley (Ga.) State Coll., 1973-79; asso. prof. U. Wis., Stevens Point, 1979—; cons. in field. Author: Sunspots, 1976, The Gay Academic, 1978; Guest editor: College English, 1974, Margins, 1975; editorial bd.: Jour. Homosexuality, 1977—, Notes on Teaching English, 1973—. Alt. del. Wis. Democratic Conv., 1983; Founder INTEGRITY Nat. Orgn. Gay Episcopalians, 1974; bd. dirs. Nat. Gay Task Force, 1976-78; mem. Wis. Gov.'s Council Lesbian and Gay Issues, 1983-85. Nat. Endowment for Humanities fellow, 1974, 77, 81; Fulbright grantee, 1974; recipient INTEGRITY award for Outstanding Contbns. to Christian Understanding of Human Sexuality, 1975. Mem. Conf. Coll. Composition and Communication, Nat. Coalition Black and Third World Gays, Internat. Assn. Black and White Men Together, Gay Acad. Union, Wis. Lesbian/Gay Network, Nat. Council Tchrs. English (dir. 1976-80, co-chmn. com. on lesbians and gay males in the profession 1976-80), Midwest MLA, Stevens Point Osborne User Troop, Assn. Tchrs. Advanced Composition, Assn. U. Wis. Faculties, Inst. Study of Human Resources (nat. adv. trustee 1979—), Phi Kappa Phi, Alpha Psi Omega, Sigma Tau Delta, Lambda Iota Tau. Democrat. Clubs: Campus Gay People's Union, Episcopal Peace Fellowship, Lambda Nat. Book (advisor), SAR.). Office: PO Box 754 Stevens Point WI 54481 *I would never have chosen to face the difficulties that life has thrust upon me as a sexual outsider; but I choose to respect my survival, so initimately does our character integrate with the obstacles which shape us. Folks have us sexual reformers all wrong: we are less about the business of sensuality than is the neighborhood gossip; ours is the task of all others fed on locusts and wild honey: to make way for the truth.*

CREWE, ALBERT VICTOR, physicist, research adminstr.; b. Bradford, Yorkshire, Eng., Feb. 18, 1927; came to U.S., 1955, naturalized, 1961; s. Wilfred and Edith Fish (Lawrence) C.; m. Doreen Blunsdon, Apr. 9, 1949; children—Jennifer, Sarah, Elizabeth, David. B.S. in Physics, U. Liverpool, Eng., 1947, Ph.D., 1951; hon. degrees, Lake Forest Coll., 1972, U. Mo., 1972, Elmhurst Coll., 1972. Asst. lectr. U. Liverpool, Eng., 1950-52, lectr., 1952-55; research asso. U. Chgo., 1955-56, asst. prof., 1956-58, asso. prof., 1958-63; prof. dept. physics and Enrico Fermi Inst., 1963-71, dean phys. scis. div., 1971-81; also William Rather Disting. Service prof. physics and biophysics; dir. particle accelerator div. Argonne Nat. Lab., 1958-61, dir., 1961-66. Chmn. Chgo. Area Research and Devel. Council. Recipient Outstanding Local Citizen in Field of Sci. award Chgo. Jr. Assn. Commerce and Industry, 1961; Outstanding New Citizen of Year award Citizenship Council Chgo., 1962; award for outstanding achievement in field of sci. Immigrant's Service League, 1962; Man of Year in Research award Indsl. Research, Inc., 1970; Michelson medal Franklin Inst., 1977; Duddell medal Inst. of Physics, 1980. Fellow Am. Phys. Soc.; Am. Nuclear Soc.; mem. Sci. Research Soc. Am., Electron Microscopy Soc. Am. (Disting. Service award 1976), N.Y. Microscope Soc. (Abbe award 1979), Am. Acad. Arts and Scis., Nat. Acad. Scis. Nuclear physics research using particle accelerators. Devel. particle accelerator, external beams from cyclotrons and synchrotron design, devel. electron microscopes. Home: 63 Old Creek Rd Palos Park IL 60464

CREWS, FREDERICK CAMPBELL, humanities educator, writer; b. Phila., Feb. 20, 1933; s. Maurice Augustus and Robina (Gaudet) C.; m. Betty Claire Peterson, Sept. 9, 1959; children: Gretchen Elizabeth, Ingrid Anna. A.B., Yale, 1955; Ph.D., Princeton, 1958. Faculty U. Calif., Berkeley, 1958—, instr. in English, 1958-60, asst. prof., 1960-62, assoc. prof., 1962-66, prof., 1966—; mem. study fellowship selection com. Am. Council Learned Socs., 1971-73; mem. selection com. summer seminars Nat. Endowment for Humanities, 1976-77. Author: The Tragedy of Manners, 1957, E.M. Forster: The Perils of Humanism, 1962, The Pooh Perplex, 1963, The Sins of the Fathers, 1966, The Patch Commission, 1968, The Random House Handbook, 1974, 4th edit., 1984, Out of My System, 1975; editor: Red Badge of Courage (Crane), 1964, Great Short Works of Nathaniel Hawthorne, 1967, Starting Over, 1970, Psychoanalysis and Literary Process, 1970, The Random House Reader, 1981. Fulbright lectr., Turin, Italy, 1961-62; Am. Council Learned Socs. fellow, 1965-66; Center for Advanced Study in Behavioral Scis. fellow, 1965-66; Guggenheim fellow, 1970-71; Recipient Essay prize Nat. Endowment for Arts, 1968. Mem. Modern Lang. Assn., Nat. Council Tchrs. of English. Home: 636 Vincente Ave Berkeley CA 94707 Office: Dept English U Calif Berkeley CA 94720

CREWS, HARRY EUGENE, author; b. Alma, Ga., June 6, 1935; s. Ray and Myrtice (Haselden) C.; m. Sally Thornton Ellis, Jan. 22, 1960; children: Patrick Scott, Byron Jason. B.A., U. Fla., 1960, M.Ed., 1962. Mem. faculty Broward Jr. Coll., Ft. Lauderdale, Fla., 1962-68; asso. prof. English U. Fla. at Gainesville, 1968-74, prof. English, 1974—. Author: novels The Gospel Singer, 1968, Naked in Garden Hills, 1969, Karate is a Thing of the Spirit, 1971, This Thing Don't Lead to Heaven, 1970, Car, 1972, The Hawk is Dying, 1973, The Gypsy's Curse, 1974, A Feast of Snakes, 1976, A Childhood: the Biography of a Place, 1978, Blood and Grits, 1979, Florida Frenzy, 1982; columnist: Esquire mag. Served with USMC, 1953-56. Recipient

Am. Acad. Arts and Scis. award, 1972; Nat. Endowment for the Arts grantee, 1974. Home: 1800 NW 8th Ave Gainsville FL 32601

CREWS, RUTHELLEN, education educator; b. McCaysville, Ga., July 3, 1927; d. Robert Harvey and Della P. (Mason) C. B.A., Maryville Coll., 1949; M.S., U. Tenn., 1959; Ed.D., Columbia U., 1966. Tchr. English and speech Cradock High Sch., Portsmouth, Va., 1949-50; elem. tchr. Rose Sch., Morristown, Tenn., 1951-54; tchr. English and speech Morristown High Sch., 1954-58; elem. sch. librarian Knox County Schs. Materials Ctr., Knoxville, Tenn., 1958-60; supr. instrn. Knox County Schs., Knoxville, 1960-65; prof. edn. U. Fla., Gainesville, 1966—; cons. curriculum devel. in pub. schs., lectr. in field. Author: (with others) The World Language textbook series, 1978; contbr. articles in field of edn. to profl. jours. Mem. Nat. Council Tchrs. English, Assn. for Supervision and Curriculum Devel., Internat. Reading Assn., Delta Kappa Gamma. Home: 1719-48 NW 23d Ave Gainesville FL 32605 Office: Coll of Edn U Fla Gainesville FL 32611

CRIBARI, SAMUEL LEWIS, cement mfg. co. exec.; b. Keezer, Colo., June 27, 1905; s. Angelo and Josephine (Leo) C.; m. Angela Marie Guizzetti, June 19, 1928; 1 son, Samuel Lewis. Student, DePaul U., 1931. With Marquette Cement Mfg. Co., Chgo., 1920—, beginning as office boy, successively So. credit mgr., gen. credit mgr., asst. treas., asst. to pres., 1920-50, v.p., dir. marketing, 1950—. Mem. Chgo. Bldg. Congress (dir. 1967—), Chgo. Sales Execs. Club. Clubs: Executives, Builders, Svithiod, Tower (Chgo.); Evanston (Ill.) Country. Home: 1560 N Sandburg Terr Apt 1102 Chicago IL 60610 Office: 20 N Wacker Dr Chicago IL 60606

CRIBB, T. KENNETH, JR., presidential counselor; b. Spartanburg, S.C., 1949. B.A., Washington and Lee U., 1970; J.D., U. Va., 1980. Nat. dir. Intercollegiate Studies Inst., 1971-77; dep. to chief counsel Reagan-Bush Com.; and dep. dir. Transistion Team's Legal and Adminstrv. Agys. Group, Office of Exec. Br. Mgmt., 1980; staff asst. to Pres. U.S.; asst. dir. Office of Cabinet Adminstrn., The White House, 1981, asst. counsellor to Pres., 1982—; council mem. Adminstrv. Conf. U.S., 1983—. Trustee Phila. Soc. Office: The White House 1600 Pennsylvania Ave NW Washington DC 20500 *

CRIBBET, JOHN EDWARD, university chancellor, lawyer; b. Findlay, Ill., Feb. 21, 1918; s. Howard H. and Ruth (Wright) C.; m. Betty Jane Smith, Dec. 24, 1941; children: Carol Ann, Pamela Lee. B.A., Ill. Wesleyan U., 1940, LL.D., 1971; J.D., U. Ill., 1947. Bar: Ill. 1947. Practiced law, bloomington, Ill., 1947—; prof. law U. Ill., Urbana, 1947-67, dean. Coll. Law, 1967-79; chancellor Urbana-Champaign ampus, U. Ill., 1979—; dir. Blommington Fed. Savs. & Loan Assn., State Farm Ins. Co. Author: Cases and Materials on Judicial Remedies, 1954, Cases on Property, 4th edit., 1984, Principles of the Law of Property, 1962, (2d edit.) Principles of the Law of Property, 1975; editor: U. Ill. Law Forum, 1947-55; contbr. articles to legal jours. Chmn. com. on jud. ethics Il. Supreme Ct.; pres. United Fund Champaign County, (Ill.), 1962-63; trustee Ill. Wesleyan U.; mem. exec. com. Assn. Am. Law Schs., 1973-75, pres., 1979. Served to maj. AUS, 1941-45. Decorated Bronze Star, Croix de Guerre. Mem. ABA, Ill. State Bar Assn., Champaign County Bar Assn., Order of Coif. Lodge: Rotary. Home: 23 Sherwin Circle Urbana IL 61820 Office: Office of Chancellor 601 E John Champaign IL 61820

CRICHTON, ANNE OLIVIA JANET, health care and epidemiology educator; b. Edinburgh, Scotland, June 12, 1920; d. John Pringle and Anne (Sprunt) C.; B.A., U. Liverpool, Eng., 1941; cert. in Social Sci., Eng., 1942, M.A., Eng., 1951; postgrad., Bus. Sch., Columbia U., 1954-55; Ph.D., U. Wales, 1969. Personnel mgmt. wartime industry, U.K., 1942-47; tng. officer Inst. Personnel Mgmt., London, 1947-49; lectr. in social sci. Univ. Coll., Cardiff, 1949, sr. lectr., 1959, reader, 1969, head social adminstrn. sect., dept. econs. and dept. sociology, 1959-69; mem. faculty U. B.C., Vancouver, Can., 1969—, assoc., 1969-75; prof. health care and epidemioligy Faculty Medicine, U. B.C., Vancouver, Can., 1975—, program coordinator healt services planning, Vancouver, B.C., 1972-78, head div. health services planning, Vanouver, Can., 1972-75, 77-78, acting dir. health services planning, Vancouver, Can., 1981-82; vis. acad. U. Southampton, Eng., U. New South Wales, Sydney, 1976-77, London Sch. Econs., 1982-83, others; part-time research coordinator Community Health Centres Project, 1971-72; cons. Welsh Regional Hosp. Bd., 1960-69, B.C. Health Security Program Project, 1972-73, Can. Coll. Health Service Execs., 1973, 77, 79. Author: Personnel Management in Context, 1968, (with D.O. Anderson) Industrial Relations and the Personnel Specialists, 1969, What Price Group Practice? and Group Practice in the system, 1973, The Community Health Centre in Canaca, vol. III, 1973, Health Policy, the Fundamental Issues, 1981, Case Studies in the Canadian Health Care System, 5 vols., 1984; contbr. articles to profl. publs. Smith-Mundt grantee U.S. Govt., 1954-55; Tyerman Taylor scholar County Borough of Bootle, Lancs., U.K., 1938-41; WHOfellow, 1974; companion Inst. Personnel Mgmt., 1959; Josiah Macy, Jr., Found. fellow, 1976-77. Home: 4557 Langara Vancouver BC Canada V6R 1C9 Office: Dept Health Care and Epidemiology U B C 5804 Fairview Crescent Vancouver BC Canada V6T 1W5

CRICHTON, JOHN MICHAEL, author, film director; b. Chgo., Oct. 23, 1942; s. John Henderson and Zula (Miller) C. A.B. summa cum laude, Harvard U., 1964, M.D., 1969. Postdoctoral fellow Salk Inst., La Jolla, Calif., 1969-70. Writer, dir. film: Westworld, 1973, Coma, 1978, The Great Train Robbery, 1979, Looker, 1981; Author: The Andromeda Strain, 1969, Five Patients, 1970, The Terminal Man, 1972, The Great Train Robbery, 1975, Eaters of the Dead, 1976, Jasper Johns, 1977, Congo, 1980, Electronic Life, 1983. Recipient Edgar award Mystery Writers Am., 1968, 80; named med. writer of year Assn. Am. Med. Writers, 1970. Mem. Authors Guild, Writers Guild Am. West, Dirs. Guild Am., P.E.N. Am. Center, Acad. Motion Picture Arts and Scis., Phi Beta Kappa. Club: Aesculaepian (Boston). Office: 9348 Santa Monica Blvd Beverly Hills CA 90210

CRICK, FRANCIS HARRY COMPTON, biologist, educator; b. June 8, 1916; s. Harry and Annie Elizabeth (Wilkins) C.; m. Ruth Doreen Dodd, 1940 (div. 1947); 1 son; m. Odile Speed, 1949; 2 daus. B.Sc., Univ. Coll., London; Ph.D, Cambridge U., Eng. Scientist Brit. Admiralty, 1940-47, Strangeways Lab., Cambridge, Eng., 1947-49; biologist Med. Research Council Lab. of Molecular Biology, Cambridge, 1949-77; Kieckhefer Disting. prof. Salk Inst. for Biol. Studies, San Diego, 1977—, non-resident fellow, 1962-73; vis. lectr. Rockefeller Inst., N.Y.C., 1959; vis. prof. chemistry dept. Harvard U., 1959, vis. prof. biophysics, 1962; fellow Churchill Coll., Cambridge, 1960-61, UCLA, 1962; Warren Triennial prize lectr. (with J.D. Watson), Boston, 1959; Korkes Meml. lectr. Duke U., 1960; Henry Sedgewick Meml. lectr. Cambridge U., 1963; Graham Young lectr., Glasgow, 1963; Robert Boyle lectr. Oxford U., 1963; Vanuxem lectr. Princeton U., 1964; Willaim T. Sedgwick Meml. lectr. MIT, 1965; Cherwell-Simon Meml. lectr. Oxford U., 1966; Shell lectr. Stanford U., 1969; Paul Lund lectr. Northwestern U., 1977; Dupont lectr. Harvard U., 1979. Author: Of Molecules and Men, 1966, Life Itself, 1981; contbr. papers and articles on molecular and cell biology to sci. jours. Recipient Prix Charles Leopold Mayer French Academies des Sciences, 1961; recipient (with J.D. Watson) Research Corp. award, 1961, Nobel Prize for medicine, 1962, Gairdner Found. award, 1962, Royal Medal Royal Soc., 1972, Copley Medal, 1976, Michelson-Morley award, 1981. Fellow AAAS, Royal Soc.; mem. Am. Acad. Arts and Scis. (fgn hon.), Am. Soc. Biol. Chemistry (hon.), U.S. Nat. Acad. Scis. (fgn. assoc.), German Acad. Sci., Am. Philos. Soc. (fgn. mem.), French Acad. Scis. (assoc. fgn. mem.). Office: Salk Inst Biol Studies PO Box 85800 San Diego CA 92138 Home: 17409 Gibralter Ct Rancho Bernardo CA 92128 Office: Oak Industries 16516 Via Esprillo Rancho Bernardo CA 92127

CRIGLER, T.P., finance executive; b. Newark, Ark., Mar. 31, 1933; s. Edward Ray and Kate (McDaniel) C.; m. Majieh R. Marandi, Jan. 7 1972; 1 child, Neda T.; children by previous marriage: Kathy J., Robert C., Brian S. B.S., Ark. State U., 1952; M.S., Cornell U., 1955; Ph.D., Okla. State U., 1957. With E.I. DuPont De Nemours & Co., Inc., Wilmington, Del., 1957-61, Armour & Co., Chgo., 1961-70; controller Armour Food Service Co., Phoenix, 1970-72; v.p. Bliss & Laughlin Industries, Inc., Oak Brook, Ill., 1973-83; exec. v.p. Axia Inc., Oak Brook, Ill., 1983—. D. dirs., treas. United Way, Hinsdale-Oak Brook, 1975-78; bd. dirs. Ill. council on Econ. Edn., Chgo., 1982—. Served to 1st lt. U.S. Army, 1952-54. Home: 851 S County Line Rd Hinsdale IL 60521 Office: Axia Inc 122 W 22d St Oak Brook IL 60521

CRIHFIELD, BREVARD EWING, retired association executive; b. Bloomington, Ill., Feb. 10, 1916; s. Roy Horace and Helen Louise (Stevenson) C.; m. Mary Elizabeth Owens, Feb. 12, 1949; children: Mary Elizabeth, John Brevard, Owen Stevenson. Student, Ill. Wesleyan U., 1933-35; A.B., U. Chgo., 1937; M.S., Syracuse U., 1942. Office asst. to chmn. bd. Marshall Field & Co., 1937, credit man, 1938-39; loan officer Indsl. Nat. Bank, Chgo., 1939-41; mng. dir. Schenectady Bur. Mcpl. Research, 1942-44; Washington rep. Council State Govts., 1944-46, research assoc., 1947, Eastern regional rep., 1948-58, exec. dir., 1958-77, spl. services assoc., 1977-78; sec. Nat. Govs.' Conf., 1958-75. Author articles on govt. Mem. Pres.'s Citizen Adv. Com. Fitness of Am. Youth, 1958, Pres.'s Com. on Employment Physically Handicapped, 1959; mem. Census Adv. Com. on State and Local Govt. Statistics, 1963—, Nat. Area Devel. Inst. Council, 1970-74; chmn. State-County-City Service Center, 1974-75; chmn. bd. Nat. Tng. and Devel. Service for State and Local Govts, 1972-73; mem. Nat. Def. Exec. Res., 1963—; Bd. dirs. Nat. Safety Council, 1961-64, Govt. Affairs Inst., 1969-72; chmn. bd. trustees Pub. Adminstrn. Service, 1963-66; trustee Spindletop Found., 1973—, vice chmn., 1974—; chmn. Kentuckians for Gov. Nunn Com., 1979. Mem. Conn. Prison Assn. (v.p. 1957-58), Am. Fedn. State, County and Municipal Employees (pub. service adv. bd., govt. affairs cons.), Sigma Chi. Home: 306 Mariemont Dr Lexington KY 40505 *In retrospect, based on 35 years of governmental public service, I am increasingly convinced that strong states, counties and cities—working in tandem with one another and in cooperation with the national government—provided the best foundation for democracy yet conceived.*

CRILE, GEORGE, JR., surgeon; b. Cleve., Nov. 3, 1907; s. George and Grace (McBride) C.; m. Jane Halle, Dec. 5, 1935 (dec.); children—Ann, Joan, Susan, George; m. Helga Sandburg, Nov. 9, 1963. Ph.B., Yale, 1929; M.D., Harvard, 1933. Intern Barnes Hosp., 1933-34; resident surgeon Cleve. Clinic, 1934-37, mem. surg. staff, 1937—, head dept. gen. surgery, 1956-69, sr. cons. dept. surgery, 1969-72, emeritus cons., 1972; Hon. civilian cons. to surgeon gen. USN, 1951-55. Author: (with Frank Shively) Hospital Care of the Surgical Patient, 1943, Practical Aspects of Thyroid Disease, 1949, Cancer and Common Sense, 1955, (with Jane Crile) Treasure Diving Holidays, 1954, More than Booty, 1966, A Biological Consideration of the Treatment of Breast Cancer, 1967, A Naturalistic View of Man, 1969, To Act as a Unit (The Story of Cleveland Clinic with A.T. Bunts), 1970, (with H. Sandburg) Above and Below, 1970, What Women Should Know about the Breast Cancer Controversy, 1973, Surgery—Your Choices, Your Alternatives; The Crile Cornball Collection, 1979. Served from 1st lt. to comdr. USNR, 1942-45. Fellow A.C.S., Royal Coll. Surgeons (hon.); mem. Am., Central, So. surg. assns., Am. Thyroid Assn. 2060 Kent Rd Cleveland OH 44106 Office: Cleveland Clinic Cleveland OH 44106 *To simplify treatment so that with minimum discomfort and deformity patients can be given the maximum chance of cure.*

CRILE, SUSAN, artist; b. Cleve., Aug. 12, 1942; d. George and Jane Murphy (Halle) C. Student, N.Y. U., 1963-64; B.A., Bennington Coll., 1961-63, 65; postgrad., Hunter Coll., 1971-72. Mem. faculty Fairleigh Dickinson U., 1972, Fordham U., 1972-76, Princeton U., 1973-76, Sarah Lawrence Coll., 1976-79, Sch. Visual Arts, N.Y.C., 1976-82, Barnard Coll., 1983, Hunter Coll., 1983; vis. critic U. Pa., 1980. One-person shows, Kornblee Gallery, N.Y.C., 1971, 72, 73, Fischbach Gallery, N.Y.C., 1974, 75, Brooke Alexander Gallery, N.Y.C., 1975, Phillips Collection, Washington, Fischbach Gallery, 1977, New Gallery, Cleve., Center Gallery Bucknell U., Lewisburg, Pa., 1978, Droll Kolbert Gallery, N.Y.C., 1978, 80, Nina Freudenheim Gallery, Buffalo, 1980, Ivory Kimpton Gallery, San Francisco, 1981, Van Straaten Gallery, Chgo., 1983; exhibited in group shows at, Whitney Mus. Am. Art, N.Y.C., 1972, 82, Corcoran Gallery Art, Washington, 1973, Indpls. Mus. Art, 1974, Lowe Art Gallery, Syracuse, N.Y., 1977, Grey Art Gallery, N.Y.C., 1979, Carnegie Inst., Pitts., 1981, Bklyn. Mus., 1980, 81, 83, Am. Acad., Inst. Arts and Letters, N.Y.C., 1983; poster commn.: Live from Lincoln Center, N.Y.C., 1980; represented in permanent collections, Albright-Knox Art Gallery, Buffalo, Blkyn. Mus., Mus. Art of Carnegie Inst., Pitts., Hirshhorn Mus., Washington, Met. Mus. Art, N.Y.C., Phillips Collection, Washington. Trustee Bennington Coll., 1978-80; Travelling rep. with exhbn. American Paintings in the Eighties, Internat. Communication Agy., Washington, 1981. Recipient resident grant Yaddo, 1970, 71, 74-75, 78, Ingram Mertill Found. grant, 1972, MacDowell Colony resident grant, 1972; NEH fellow, 1982. Home: 168 W 86th St New York NY 10024

CRILLY, WILLIAM MICHAEL, instrument company executive; b. Chgo., Aug. 12, 1924; s. William Michael and Frances (Tuteur) C.; m. Karin Hays, Apr. 17, 1982; children—Jo Ann, Thomas Michael. B.S., Notre Dame U., 1946; M.B.A., Stanford, 1950. Market analyst preliminary design Douglas Aircraft Co., Santa Monica, Calif., 1946-48, exec. asst., 1950-52; dir. marketing, transp. research Planning Research Corp., Los Angeles, 1954-57; asst. to pres. Hawaiian Airlines, Honolulu, 1957-58, v.p. planning and devel., 1959-61, v.p. maintenance and engring., 1961-63; v.p. Eastern Airlines, 1964-66, sr. v.p., 1966-69; v.p., gen. mgr. forest products and real estate div. Riegel Paper Corp., Greenwich, Conn., 1969-71; sr. v.p. planning Pan Am World Airways, N.Y.C., 1971-72, sr. v.p. fin., 1972, exec. v.p. adminstrn., 1972, exec. v.p. fin. and adminstrn. and ops., 1972-75; also dir.; pres., chief exec. officer, dir. Bowmar Instrument Corp., Newbury Park, Calif., 1975—. Served to lt. USNR, 1943-46. Home: 1675 Ryder Cup Dr Westlake Village CA 91362 Office: 850 Lawrence Dr Newbury Park CA 91320

CRIM, ALONZO A., supt. schs.; b. Chgo., Oct. 1, 1928; s. George and Hazel (Howard) C.; m. Gwendolyn Motley, June 11, 1949; children—Timothy, Susan and Sharon (twins). B.A., Roosevelt Coll., 1950; postgrad., Chgo. Tchrs. Coll., 1953-54; M.A., U. Chgo., 1958; Ed.D., Harvard, 1969. Tchr. pub. schs., Chgo., 1954-63; prin. Whittier Elementary Sch., Chgo., 1963-65, Adult Edn. Center, 1965, Wendell Phillips High Sch., 1965-68; supt. dist. 27, Chgo. pub. schs., 1968-69, Compton (Calif.) Union High Sch. Dist., 1969-70, Compton Union Sch. Dist., 1970-73; supt. schs., Atlanta, 1973—; adj. prof. Atlanta U., 1973—, U. Ga., Athens, 1974—. Bd. dirs. Fulton County Bd. Health, Jr. Achievement Greater Atlanta, YMCA Met. Atlanta; adv. bd. Close Up; trustee Ga. Council Econ. Edn. Served with USNR, 1945-46. Recipient Vincent Conray award Harvard Grad. Sch. Edn., 1970, Eleanor Roosevelt Key award Roosevelt U., 1974. Mem. Am. Assn. Sch. Adminstrs., Nat. Alliance Black Sch. Educators, So. Council Internat. and Pub. Affairs, Ednl. Program Assn. Am., Ga. Assn. Sch. Supts. Club: Rotarian. Home: 575 Cativo Dr SW Atlanta GA 30311 Office: 224 Central Ave SW Atlanta GA 30303

CRIM, JACK C., diversified industry executive; b. 1930. B.S., Purdue U., 1954. With Economy Regulator, 1956-62; v.p. ops. Textron Inc., 1962-68; pres. Cuno div. AMF Inc., 1968-73, group v.p. exec. recreation vehicles, 1970-73; group v.p. Textron Inc., 1982-83; pres. Townsend div. AMF Inc., 1981-82; exec. v.p., chief operating officer Talley Industries Inc., 1982-83, pres., chief operating officer, 1983—, dir. Office: Talley Industries Inc 2702 N 44th St Phoenix AZ 85008 *

CRIMI, ALFRED DIGIORGIO, artist; b. Italy, Dec. 1, 1900; s. Filadelfio and Maria (DiGiorgio) C.; m. Mary Timpano, Apr. 11, 1935. Student, NAD, Beaux Arts Inst. Design, both N.Y.C., Scuola Preparatoria a le Arti Ornamentali, Rome. Tchr., CCNY, 1947-53, Pratt Inst., 1948-51, Pa. State U., 1963, now privately; lectr. Columbia U., Pratt Inst., CCNY, Fordham U., others. Featured in art mags.; one-man shows, Babcock Galleries, N.Y.C., 1928, Portland (Oreg.) Mus. Art, 1933, DeYoung Mus., San Francisco, Holyoke (Mass.) Mus., 1962, Fordham U., N.Y.C., 1966, Ringwood Manor Mus., N.J., 1971, Wichita (Kans.) State U., 1980, St. Lawrence U., Canton, N.Y., 1981, group shows include, Whitney Mus. Am. Art, N.Y.C., Met. Mus. Art, N.Y.C., 1952-53, Mus. Modern Art, N.Y.C., 1936, Chgo. Art Inst., Bklyn. Mus., Smithsonian Instn., Washington, Internat. Littoriale, Bologna, Italy, First Internat. Liturgical Arts Exhbn., Trieste, Italy, 1961, Butler Inst. Am. Art, Youngstown, Ohio, DeYoung Meml. Mus., 1933, S.I. Mus, 1956, NAD, Am. Watercolor Soc., Audubon Artists, Mainstreams Internat., Marietta, Ohio, 1968, 69, 72, 74, Am. Artists in Paris Exhbn., 1975-76, numerous others, mosaic and fresco commns. include, Open Air Aquarium, Key West, Fla., Harlem Hosp., N.Y.C., Washington (D.C.) Post Office Dept. Bldg., Rutgers Presbyn. Ch., N.Y.C., Christian Herald Bldg., N.Y.C., various public schs. in N.Y.C.; represented in permanent collections, Holyoke Mus., Columbia (S.C.) Mus., Mus. Fine Arts, Springfield, Mass., U. Md., Springfield (Mo.) Art Mus., Library of Congress, Nat. Mus. Am. Art, Smithsonian Instn.,, Washington, S.I. Mus., Norfolk (Va.) Mus., Butler Inst. Am. Art; represented in, St. Lawrence U., Syracuse U., Wichita State U., Mus. City of N.Y., Bronx Bot. Garden Mus., others; author: A Look Back-A Step Forward, 1984. Recipient awards and prizes; including Allied Artists Am., 1947, N.Y. State Fair, 1951, Art League L.I., 1954, 55, 56, 61, 62, Allied Artists Am., 1956, 60, 64, 74, 75, Grumbacher award Knickerbocker Ann., 1957, Am. Watercolor Soc., 1968, Butler Inst. Am. Art, 1969, Nat. Arts Club, 1969; cert. of merit City of Northampton, Mass., 1980. Mem. Nat. Soc. Mural Painters (v.p. 1937-41), Louis Comfort Tiffany Found., Am. Watercolor Soc., Audubon Artists (pres. 1951-52), Coll. Art Assn., Artists Fellowship (officer), Allied Artists Am., Painters and Sculptors Assn. N.J., Internat. Platform Assn., Fedn. Modern Painters and Sculptors. Home: 615 Pelham Pkwy N Bronx NY 10467 *No matter what I paint, my point of view shall be free and universal. My art shall encompass any school of thought which will enable me to achieve the utmost within my inherent powers of expression. I believe that anything that is constricted into the framework of a rigid plan is bound to be limited in growth and scope.*

CRIMINALE, WILLIAM OLIVER, JR., mathematics educator; b. Mobile, Ala., Nov. 29, 1933; s. William Oliver and Vivian Gertrude (Sketoe) C.; m. Ulrike Irmgard Wegner, June 7, 1962; children: Martin Oliver, Lucca. B.S., U. Ala., 1955; Ph.D., Johns Hopkins U., 1960. Asst. prof. Princeton (N.J.) U., 1962-68; asso. prof. U. Wash., Seattle, 1968-73, prof. oceanography, geophysics, applied math., 1973—, chmn. dept. applied math., 1976—; cons. Aerospace Corp., 1962-65, Boeing Corp., 1968-72, AGARD, 1967-68, Lennox Hill Hosp., 1967-68; guest prof., Can., 1965, France, 1967-68, Germany, 1973-74, Sweden, 1973-74, Nat. Acad. exchange scientist, USSR, 1969, 72. Author: Stability of Parallel Flows, 1967; Contbr. articles to profl. jours. Served with U.S. Army, 1961-62. Boris A. Bakmeteff Meml. fellow, 1957-58; NATO Postdoctoral fellow, 1960-61; Alexander von Humboldt Sr. fellow, 1973-74. Mem. AAAS, Am. Phys. Soc., Am. Geophys. Union, Fedn. Am. Scientists, Soc. Indsl. and Applied Math. Home: 1635 Peach Court E Seattle WA 98712 Office: Applied Math FS-20 U Wash Seattle WA 98195

CRIMMINS, ALFRED STEPHEN, JR., manufacturing company executive; b. Bayonne, N.J., Dec. 6, 1934; s. Alfred Stephen and Agnes Veronica (Corcoran) C.; m. Catherine Lechner, June 11, 1960; children: Karen, Douglas, Jennifer, Michael. B.B.A. cum laude, CCNY, 1960. C.P.A., N.Y. With Price Waterhouse & Co. (C.P.A.'s), 1960-65; mgr. profit analysis Trans World Airlines, Inc., 1965-68; v.p. fin. Bairnco Corp., N.Y.C., 1968-80; exec. v.p. fin., dir. Collins & Aikman Corp., N.Y.C., 1980—. Served with USNR, 1955-56. Mem. Fin. Execs. Inst., Am. Inst. C.P.A.s, N.Y. State Soc. C.P.A.s, Beta Gamma Sigma. Clubs: Union League, Upper Ridgewood Tennis., Charlotte City. Home: 703 Belmont Rd Ridgewood NJ 07450 Office: 210 Madison Ave New York NY 10016

CRIMMINS, JOHN MICHAEL, lawyer; b. Chattanooga, Aug. 31, 1910; s. Patrick Joseph and Mary (Costello) C.; m. Catherine Lucile O'Malley, Aug. 26, 1939; childrenPatrick, Michael, Timothy, Sean, Constance, Martin, Thomas, Kevin, Terrance. Student, Columbus Coll., Dubuque, Iowa, 1926-28; A.B., St. Gregory's Sem., Cin., 1930; J.D., Notre Dame U., 1933. Bar: Ind. bar 1932, Ill. bar 1936, Pa. bar 1944. Counsel RFC, 1935-40, Def. Plant Corp., Washington, 1941-42; with Koppers Co., Pitts., 1942-66, asst. chief counsel, 1950-60, v.p., gen. counsel, 1960-66; pvt. practice law, Pitts., from 1966; mem. firm Titus, Marcus & Shapira. Mem. Am., Pa., Allegheny County bar assns. Office: Oliver Bldg Pittsburgh PA 15222 *

CRIMMINS, PHILIP PATRICK, metallurgical engineer, lawyer; b. Poughkeepsie, N.Y., Aug. 1, 1930; s. Philip Patrick and Eva (Booth) C.; m. Janet E. Ballou, Feb. 14, 1953; children: Lisa Jane, Philip Patrick, Michael Mathew. B.S., MIT, 1952; M.S., Wayne State U., 1959; J.D., U. Pacific, 1972. Registered profl. metall. engr. Metall. engr. Ford Motor Co., Livonia, Mich., 1954-58; dir. high energy ops. Aerojet Tactical Systems Co., Sacramento, 1958—. Served with AUS, 1952-54. Recipient William Sparagen award Am. Welding Soc., 1968. Calif. Fellow Am. Inst. Chemists; mem. Am. Soc. Metals, Fed., Am., Calif. bar assns. Home: 9113 Rosewood Dr Sacramento CA 95826 Office: PO Box 13400 Sacramento CA 95813

CRIMMINS, ROBERT JOHN, life insurance company executive; b. Bklyn., July 7, 1938; s. Joseph Peter and Kathleen Theresa (Chalinoir) C.; m. Judy Anne Mulligan, Sept. 27, 1958; children: Kathleen, Maureen, Robert, Daniel, Margaret, Kevin, Noreen, Patricia, Brian. B.A., St. Johns's U., Jamaica, N.Y. With Met. Life Ins. Co., N.Y.C., 1956—, v.p., 1977-78, sr. v.p. central head office, Tulsa, 1978—. Address: Met Life Ins Co PO Box 500 12902 E 51st St Tulsa OK 74121

CRINELLA, FRANCIS MICHAEL, neuropsychologist; b. Petaluma, Calif., Dec. 22, 1936; s. Marino Peter and Marian Eleanor (Zurlo) C.; m. Terrie Kay Lynd, Sept. 19, 1959; children—Ramona, Gina, Peter,

Andrew, Christina. B.A., U. NotreDame, 1958; M.S., San Francisco State Coll., 1962; Ph.D., La. State U., 1969. Psychology intern Alameda County (Calif.) Guidance Clinic, 1961-62; staff psychologist David Grant USAF Hosp., 1962-66; research asso. spl. edn. La. State U., Baton Rouge, 1966-69; psychology intern, New Orleans, 1968-69; staff psychologist Sonoma (Calif.) State Hosp., 1969-71, sr. psychologist, 1971-72, cons. program rev., Eldridge, Calif., 1972-77; dir. Petaluma Hosp. Dist., 1971-76, treas., 1975; exec. dir. Fairview State Hosp., Costa Mesa, Calif., 1977—; exec. v.p. Westland Devel. Corp., Santa Rosa, Calif., 1962—; asso. clin. prof. psychiatry U. Calif., Irvine, 1978—. Served to capt. USAF, 1962-66. Mem. Soc. Air Force Psychologists, Am., Western psychol. assns., Redwood Psychol. Soc. Clubs: Sonoma Torch (dir. 1973), Sonoma Men's Golf (pres. 1972-73). Contbr. articles to profl. jours). Home: 2501 Harbor Blvd Costa Mesa CA 92626 Office: Fairview State Hosp 2501 Harbor Blvd Costa Mesa CA 92626

CRINKLEY, RICHMOND DILLARD, theatre and TV producer, author; b. Richmond, Va., Jan. 20, 1940; s. James Epes and Sarah Elizabeth (Beck) C. B.A. with honors, U. Va., 1961, M.A., 1962, Ph.D., 1966; postgrad., Oxford U., 1965-67. Asst. prof. English lit. U. N.C., 1967-69; exec. dir. Am. Nat. Theatre and Acad., N.Y.C., 1976-78; exec. dir. Vivian Beaumont Theater, 1978—; trustee Stage II, London, Sta. WETA-TV, Washington, 1969-73; mem. bd. Shakespeare Quar., 1971-73; pres. Cerberus Enterprises, 1982—. Dir. programs, Folger Shakespeare Library; producer, Folger Theatre Group, 1969-73; theatre producer, asst. to chmn., John F. Kennedy Center for Performing Arts, Washington, 1973-76; trustee, 1981—; producer: numerous Broadway plays including The Skin of Our Teeth, 1975, Summer Brave, 1975, The Royal Family, 1975, Sweet Bird of Youth, 1975, Out of Our Father's House (for PBS), 1978, The Elephant Man, 1979, ABC-TV, 1981 (Tony award), The Philadelphia Story, Tintypes, 1980, Macbeth, The Floating Light Bulb, 1981, Passion, 1983; Author: Walter Pater: Humanist, 1971. Fulbright fellow, 1965-67. Mem. Raven Soc., Phi Beta Kappa. Presbyterian. Home: 59 W 71st St New York NY 10023 Office: 1995 Broadway Suite 1200 New York NY 10023

CRIPE, NICHOLAS MCKINNEY, educator; b. Goshen, Ind., Jan. 25, 1913; s. Nicholas M. and Eva Letitia (McKinney) C.; m. Dorothy Mae Dunivan, Jan. 19, 1945. A.B., Goshen Coll., 1949; M.A., Northwestern U., 1949, Ph.D., 1953. With Goshen Rubber Co., 1935-42; instr. speech U. Vt., 1949-50; grad. asst. Northwestern U., 1950-52; lectr. speech Grinnell Coll., 1952-53; head dept. speech Butler U., Indpls., 1953—, prof. speech, 1954-83, prof. emeritus, 1983—; pub. speaker, 1946—. Contbr. articles profl. jours. Candidate for state rep., Ind., 1956; chmn. Marion County (Ind.) Citizens for Kennedy, 1960. Served with inf. AUS, 1942-46. Recipient Baxter award for outstanding teaching Butler U., 1954, Outstanding Prof. award, 1962, Butler medal, 1977. Mem. Am. Forensic Assn. (pres. 1961-63), Midwest Forensic Assn. (Ind. pres. 1969-71), Central States Speech Assn., Speech Assn. Am. (legislative assembly 1965-66), Ind. Speech Assn. (pres. 1970-72), Tau Kappa Alpha, Delta Sigma Rho (nat. council 1970-77, nat. sec. 1966-69, nat. pres. 1972-75), Phi Kappa Phi. Home: 142 E 48th St Indianapolis IN 46205

CRIPPEN, ROBERT LAUREL, naval officer, astronaut; b. Beaumont, Tex., Sept. 11, 1937; s. Herbert W. and Ruth C. (Andress) C.; m. Virginia E. Hill, Sept. 8, 1959; children: Ellen Marie, Susan Lynn, Linda Ruth. B.S. in Aerospace Engring, U. Tex., 1960; grad., USAF Aerospace Research Pilot Sch., 1965. Commd. ensign U.S. Navy, 1960, advanced through grades to capt., 1980; assigned to flight tng., Whiting Field, Fla., 1961, Chase Field, Beeville, Tex., 1961, attack pilot, 1962-64; instr. USAF Aerospace Research Pilot Sch., Edwards AFB, Calif., 1965-66; research pilot USAF Manned Orbiting Lab. Program, Los Angeles, 1966-69; NASA astronaut Johnson Space Center, Houston, 1969—; crew mem. Skylab Med. Experiments Altitude Test, 1972; mem. astronaut support crew Skylab 2, 3 and 4 missions, 1973-74; pilot Space Shuttle Columbia STSI, 1981; head Astronaut Office ascent/entry group Lyndon B. Johnson Space Center, Houston, 1981—; comdr. Space Shuttle Columbia, 1984. Recipient Exceptional Service medal NASA, 1972, Disting. Service medal, 1981; Disting. Service medal Dept. Def., 1981. Mem. Soc. Exptl. Test Pilots. Office: Lyndon B Johnson Space Center Houston TX 77058 *

CRIPPIN, BYRON MILES, JR., lawyer, religious organization executive; b. Topeka, Oct. 19, 1928; s. Byron M. and Grace M. (Smith) C.; m. Marie A. Bradbury, Oct. 29, 1955; children: Patricia, David, Linda. Asso. Liberal Arts, 1948; B.S. in Law, 1950; J.D., 1952. Bar: Minn. 1952. Research asst. Calif. law revision project Stanford U., Palo Alto, Calif., 1954-55; law clk. U.S. Dist. Ct., Mpls., 1955-56; corp. atty. law dept. George A. Hormel & Co., Austin, Minn., 1956-68, gen. atty., head law dept., 1968-74, gen. counsel, 1974-81, corp. officer, 1978-81; gen. counsel, dir. devel., exec. mgr. Willman office Lowell Lundstrom Ministries, 1981—. Past mem. Austin City Charter Commn.; chmn. Mower County Young Republican League, 1956-57; vice chmn. Mower County Rep. Com., 1959-61; chmn. Christian Bus. Men's Com., 1963-64, regional chmn., 1975-81; past mem. adv. bd. Salvation Army; chmn. conf. adminstrv. bd. Free Methodist Ch., 1979-81; bd. dirs. Christian Stewardship Council. Served to 1st lt. U.S. Army, 1952-54. Mem. Am. Bar Assn., Bar Assn. Minn., Kandiyohi Bar Assn. (pres. 1961-62), Minn. Corp. Counsel Assn., U. Minn. Alumni Assn., Order of Coif, Scabbard and Blade, Delta Sigma Rho. Home: 1705 15th Ave SW Willmar MN 56201

CRIQUI, WILLIAM EDMUND, lighting company executive; b. Irvington, N.J., June 25, 1922; s. William Valentine and Josephine Anna (Dotterweich) C.; m. Margaret Elizabeth Burke, Apr. 22, 1950 (dec. Feb. 1976); children: William John, Robert Joseph; m. Joyce Morse McLaughlin, Aug. 14, 1980. B.S. in Accounting, Rutgers U., 1955; certificate machine accounting, N.Y. U., 1958; M.B.A., Seton Hall U., 1966. Certified internal auditor. Sr. auditor Worthington Corp., Harrison, N.J., 1958-62, dir. internal auditing, 1962-67, asst. treas., 1967-69, Studebaker-Worthington, Inc.; also treas. Worthington Corp., N.Y.C., 1969-72; v.p., treas. Worthington Pump Internat., 1971-74; asst. sec., gen. auditor Novo Corp., 1974-75; mgr. fin. services U.S. Radium Corp., Morristown, N.J., 1976-78, asst. treas., 1978-81, USR Lighting, Inc., Parsippany, N.J., 1981—. Treas. Nutley (N.J.) County Com., 1969-77; pres. Nutley Republican Club, 1972; committeeman Essex County, 1968-77; bd. dirs., v.p. Nutley Family Service Bur. Served with AUS, 1942-46. Decorated Purple Heart, Bronze Star medal, Combat Inf. badge. Mem. Inst. Internal Auditors (pres. 1962-63, bd. govs. 1964-66), Holy Name Soc. Elk (mem. crippled childrens com. 1969-71). Home: 91 Deerfield Rd West Caldwell NJ 07006 Office: 661 Myrtle Ave Boonton NJ 07005

CRISCI, MATHEW GERARD, marketing executive; b. N.Y.C., Nov. 3, 1941; s. Mathew Anthony and Frances (Coscia) C.; m. Mary Ann, Nov. 14, 1964; children: Mathew Joseph, Mark Davis, Mitchell Justin. B.S., Iona Coll., 1963. Newspaper reporter Gannett, White Plains, N.Y., 1964-66; life ins. agt. Fidelity Mut. Life, Phila., 1966-68; account exec., v.p., account supr. Young & Rubicam, Inc., N.Y.C., 1969-82; sr. v.p., mgmt. supr., exec. v.p., treas. Integrated Barter Internat., N.Y.C., 1983—, dir., 1983; dir. Young & Rubicam, Sydney, Australia, 1974-76, mem. corp. strategy rev. bd., Sydney and N.Y.C., 1978-82, mem. new products adv. com., 1979-82. Office: Young & Rubicam Internat 285 Madison Ave New York NY 10017 *

CRISER, MARSHALL, lawyer; b. Rumson, N.J., Sept. 4, 1928; s. Marshall and Louise (Johnson) C.; m. Paula Porcher, Apr. 27, 1957; children: Marshall III, Edward, Mary, Glenn, Kimberly, Mark. B.S. in Bus. Adminstrn, U. Fla., 1951, LL.B., 1951 (replaced by J.D., 1967). Bar: Fla. 1951. Practiced in, Palm Beach, 1953—; ptnr. Gunster, Yoakley, Criser & Stewart, 1955—; atty. Palm Beach County Sch. Bd., 1958-64; Dir. Bell South Corp., Flagler System, Inc.; Chmn. Installment Land Sales Bd., 1963-64. Bd. govs. Good Samaritan Hosp., West Palm Beach, pres., 1979—; Mem. Fla. Bd. Regents, 1965, 71—, chmn., 1974-77; pres. designate U. Fla. Served with AUS, 1951-53. Fellow Am. Bar Found.; mem. Fla. Council 100 (chmn. 1979-80), Am. Bar Assn. (ho. dels. 1968-72), Fla. Bar (gov. 1960-68, pres. 1968-69), Fla. State C. of C. (dir.), Fla. Blue Key, Phi Delta Phi, Sigma Nu. Home: 11922 Lost Tree Way Lost Tree Village North Palm Beach FL 33408 Office: univ of florida office of the president gainesville FL 32611

CRISLEY, FRANCIS DANIEL, microbiologist; b. Braddock, Pa., Aug. 19, 1926; s. Frank and Julia (Andrascik) C.; m. Margaretta Schmitt, May 28, 1960; children—Faith, John, Kathleen. B.S., U. Pitts., 1950, M.S., 1952, Ph.D., 1959. Instr. Miami U., Oxford, Ohio, 1952-54, U. Pitts., 1954-58, NSF sci. faculty fellow, 1958-59, research asso., 1959-61; research microbiologist USPHS, 1961-67; prof. biology Northeastern U., Boston, 1967—, chmn. dept. biology, 1967-75; vis. scientist U.S. Army Research and Devel. Command, Natick (Mass.) Labs., 1978—. Author.; Contbr. articles to profl. jours. Served with AUS, 1944-46. Mem. Am. Soc. Microbiology, Soc. Indsl. Microbiology, Sigma Xi, Phi Sigma. Home: 26 Grosvenor Rd Needham MA 02192 Office: Northeastern University 360 Huntington Ave Boston MA 02115

CRISMAN, THOMAS LYNN, lawyer; b. Marlow, Okla., Aug. 10, 1941; s. George Thomas and Mattie Ruth (Wolfe) C.; married; children: Courtney, Hilary. B.S.E.E. with honors, So. Meth. U., 1965; J.D., Georgetown U., 1969. Bar: Tex. 1969. Elec. engr. Western Electric Co., Washington, 1965-69; practiced in, Dallas, 1969—; partner firm Crisman & Moore, 1975—; adj. prof. So. Meth. U. Law Sch., 1970—; dir. Sundance Prodns., Inc., Acmecartoon Co., Inc. Editor: Georgetown U. Law Jour, 1967-69; Contbr. articles to legal jours. Bd. dirs. Sayagyi U Ba Khin Vipassana Found.; adminstrv. assoc., meditation student Vipassana Internat. Acad., Igatpuri, India. Recipient Nathan Burkan Article prize ASCAP, 1968. Mem. Tex., Va. bar assns., Am. Patent Law Assn. (Robert C. Watson article award 1969), Blue Key, Eta Kappa Nu, Sigma Tau, Kappa Mu Epsilon, Phi Delta Phi. Home: 3936 Travis St Dallas TX 75204 Office: 5001 LBJ Freeway Suite 705 Dallas TX 75234

CRISMOND, LINDA FRY, county librarian; b. Burbank, Calif., Mar. 1, 1943; d. Billy Chapin and Lois (Harding) Fry; m. Donald Burleigh Crismond, 1965 (div. Sept. 1980). B.S., U. Calif.-Santa Barbara, 1964; M.L.S., U. Calif.-Berkeley, 1965. Cert. county librarian, Calif. Reference librarian, EDP coordinator San Francisco Pub. Library, 1965-72, head acquisition, 1972-74; asst. univ. librarian U. So. Calif., Los Angeles, 1974-80; chief dep. county librarian Los Angeles County Pub. Library, Los Angeles, 1980-81, county librarian, Downey, 1981—; Western rep. quality control council Ohio Coll.l Library Ctr., Columbus, 1977-80; mem. Am. Nat. Standards Inst., N.Y.C., 1978-80; bd. councillors U. So. Calif. Sch. Library and Info. Mgmt., 1980-83; adv. bd. mem. UCLA Library Sch., 1981—; chmn. bd. dirs. Los Angeles Pub. Library Found., 1982—. Author: Directory of San Francisco Bay Area, 1968. Named Staff Mem. of Year San Francisco Pub. Library, 1968. Mem. ALA (chmn. Percy Jury 1976-78, chmn. Gale Jury 1982-84, exec. com. resources and tech. services div. resources sect. 1980-82), Calif. Library assn. (council 1980-82), Calif. County Librarians Assn. (v.p., pres.-elect. 1984—). Home: 15985 Alcima Ave Pacific Palisades CA 90272 Office: Los Angeles County Pub Library 7400 E Imperial Hwy Downey CA 90241

CRISONA, JAMES JOSEPH, lawyer; b. N.Y.C., Aug. 30, 1907; s. Frank and Rachel (Fantino) C.; m. Claire Peysson, July 8, 1934; children: Claire Mary, Cynthia. B.C.S., N.Y.U., 1928, LL.B., 1931. Sr. partner Crisona Bros., N.Y.C., 1945-57; gen. counsel, dir. Hudson & Manhattan R.R., 1948-54; v.p., gen. counsel, dir. Phoenix-Campbell Corp., 1951-57; pres. Boro of Queens, N.Y.C., 1957-59; supreme ct. justice State N.Y., 1959-76. Former assemblyman and state senator, N.Y. Mem. Am., N.Y. State, Queens County bar assns. Clubs: K.C., Wheatley Hills Country. Home: 118 E 60th St New York NY 10022 Office: 750 3d Ave New York NY 10017

CRISP, PORTER LEE, newspaper editor; b. Asheville, N.C., Nov. 29, 1927. Reporter The Asheville Times, 1949-57; with Greensboro (N.C.) Record, 1957—, mng. editor, 1964-68; exec. news editor Greensboro Daily News and Record, 1968-78, v.p., 1976-78; pres. Greensboro Adventure, 1979. Recipient Freedoms Found. award, also; honor medal, 1950. Office: 1600 E Wendover Ave Greensboro NC 27405

CRISPELL, KENNETH RAYMOND, physician, univ. ofcl.; b. Ithaca, N.Y., Oct. 30, 1916; s. Leslie and Pauline (Wichell) C.; m. Marjorie Risk, Apr. 11, 1942; children—Ann (Mrs. Barth Barnhart), Kathleen (Mrs. Charles Blackmer), Barbara (Mrs. Richard Johnson), Majorie (Mrs. Robert Rourke), Constance, John (dec.). B.S., Phila. Coll. Pharmacy, 1938; postgrad., Cornell U., 1938-39; M.D., U. Mich., 1943. Intern Robert Packer Hosp., Sayre, Pa., 1943-44, resident internal medicine, 1944; resident Ochsner Clinic, New Orleans, 1947-48; fellow biophysics Tulane U., New Orleans, 1948-49; pvt. practice, Ithaca, N.Y., 1946-47; Commonwealth fellow, instr. medicine U. Va., Charlottesville, 1949-51, mem. faculty, 1951-58, 60—, prof. medicine, 1960—, dean, 1962-71, v.p. health scis., 1971-76, univ. prof. law and medicine, 1976—; prof. medicine, chmn. dept. N.Y. Med. Coll., 1958-60. Author numerous articles, monograph in field. Fellow A.C.P.; mem. Am. Soc. Clin. Investigation, Am. Fedn. Clin. Research, So. Soc. Clin. Research (pres. 1963), Am. Goiter Assn., Endocrine Soc., Assn. Am. Physicians, Sigma Xi, Alpha Omega Alpha. Home: Pavilion I West Lawn Charlottesville VA 22901

CRISPO, ANDREW J(OHN), art dealer; b. Phila., Apr. 21, 1945. Ed., St. Joseph's Coll. Pres. Andrew Crispo Gallery, Inc., N.Y.C., 1973—. Editor, contbg. author: Pioneers of American Abstraction, 1973, Ten Americans: Masters of Watercolor, 1974, Twelve Americans: Masters of Collage, 1977; specialist in Am. and European paintings of 18th, 19th and 20th centuries, antiquities of English and French origin of 17th, 18th, 19th and 20th centuries. Forbes fellow Fogg Art Mus. Office: Andrew Crispo Gallery Inc 41 E 57th St New York NY 10022

CRISPO, LAWRENCE WALTER, lawyer; b. N.Y.C., Mar. 23, 1934; s. Charles A. and Elda Beatrice (D'Orazi) C.; m. Wilhelmina Moore, June 11, 1955; children: Susan, Patricia, Christopher, Therese, Marianne, Thomas. B.S. in Polit. Sci, Loyola U., Los Angeles, 1956, J.D., 1961. Bar: Calif. 1961, U.S. Supreme Ct. 1970. Pros. atty. City of Los Angeles, 1961-62; partner firm Breidenbach, Swainston, Yokaitis & Crispo, Los Angeles, 1967—; judge pro tem Los Angeles-Alhambra Mcpl. Ct., 1966—; lectr., mem. faculty U. So. Calif. Law Ctr., Calif. Continuing Edn. of Bar, Calif. Inst. Trial Advocacy, 1978, 79, 80, 82, 83; mem. bench and bar council Los Angeles Superior Ct., 1976—; civil service commr. City of San Gabriel, Calif., 1974—; pres. bd. govs. Loyola U. Law Sch., 1980-81, sec. bd. govs. student bar, 1958-59; speaker on juvenile delinquency, 1961—. Profl. chmn. United Crusade, Alhambra, 1967; mem. solicitation fund Los Angeles YMCA, 1969; precinct chmn. San Gabriel Republican Com., 1968, 70, 72, 74; alt. del. Rep. County Central Com., 1973-76; past pres. Archdiocesan Holy Name Union. Mem. Am. Judicature Soc., Am. Bd. Trial Advocates (exec. com. 1974-77, 81—), Am. Arbitration Assn. (arbitrator 1966—), Los Angeles County Bar Assn. (chmn. jud. com. 1977-78, mem. law office mgmt. exec. com. 1979-82), Wilshire Bar Assn. (pres. 1980-81), State Bar Calif. (ethical practices examiner 1971-72, chmn. adminstrv. com. 1972-76, vice chmn. ct. rules and procedures com. 1980-81, mem. Commn. on Jud. Nominee Evaluation 1982-83), San Gabriel C. of C. (dir. 1975—, pres. 1979-80). Clubs: Elks (past state v.p., past dist. dep.), K.C. (past grand knight). Address: 611 W 6th St Suite 1300 Los Angeles CA 90017

CRIST, GEORGE BRAINARD, marine corps officer; b. Hartford, Conn., Jan. 23, 1931; s. Marion Edward and Ethel Mae (Brainard) C.; m. Barbara Clay, May 25, 1957; children: William, David. B.A. cum laude, Villanova (Pa.) U., 1952; M.A. in Polit. Sci, Auburn (Ala.) U., 1971. Commd. 2d lt. USMCR, 1952, advanced through grades to maj. gen.; service in Korea, Haiti, Vietnam and Europe; dep. dir. ops. (J-3) U.S. European Command, 1978-80; dep. chief staff res. affairs Hdqrs. USMC, 1980-82; vice dir. joint staff Joint Chiefs Staff, 1982—. Decorated Def. Superior Service medal, Legion of Merit with combat V, Bronze Star with combat V, Meritorious Service medal, Air medal (2), Joint Service Commendation medal, Combat Action ribbon; Cross of Galantry with silver and bronze stars; Honor medal, Vietnam). Mem. Marine Corps Assn., Marine Corps Res. Officers Assn., Nat. Assn. Uniformed Services, Phi Sigma Alpha. Episcopalian. Office: Hdqrs USMC (RES) Washington DC 20380

CRIST, JUDITH (KLEIN CRIST), film, drama critic; b. N.Y.C., May 22, 1922; d. Solomon and Helen (Schoenberg) Klein; m. William B. Crist, July 3, 1947; 1 son, Steven Gordon. A.B., Hunter Coll., 1941; teaching fellow, State Coll. Wash., 1942-43; M.Sc. in Journalism, Columbia, 1945. Civilian instr. 3081st AAFBU, 1943-44; reporter N.Y. Herald Tribune, 1945-60, editor arts, 1960-63, theater critic, 1958-63, film critic, 1963-66; film, theater critic NBC-TV Today Show, 1963-73; film critic World Jour. Tribune, 1966-67; critic-at-large Ladies Home Jour., 1966-67; film critic TV Guide, 1965—, N.Y. mag., 1968-75, The Washingtonian, 1970-72, Palm Springs Life, 1971-75; contbg. editor, film critic Saturday Rev., 1975-77, 80—, N.Y. Post, 1977-78, MD/Mrs., 1977—, 50 Plus, 1978-83; instr. journalism Hunter Coll., 1947, Sarah Lawrence Coll., 1958-59; asso. journalism Columbia Grad. Sch. Journalism, 1959-62, lectr. journalism, 1962-64, adj. prof., 1964—. Author: The Cowboy and the Very Naked Girl, 1968, Judith Crist's TV Guide to the Movies, 1974; Contbr. articles to nat. mags. Trustee Anne O'Hara McCormick Scholarship Fund. Recipient Page One award N.Y. Newspaper Guild, 1955; George Polk award, 1951; N.Y. Newspaper Women's Club award, 1955, 59, 63, 65, 67; Edn. Writers Assn. award, 1952; Columbia Grad. Sch. Journalism Alumni award, 1961; named to 50th Anniversary Honors List, 1963; Centennial Pres.'s medal Hunter Coll., 1970, Hunter Alumni Hall of Fame, 1973. Mem. Columbia Journalism Alumni (pres. 1967-70), N.Y. Film Critics, Nat. Soc. Film Critics., Sigma Tau Delta. Office: 180 Riverside Dr New York NY 10024

CRISTOFALO, VINCENT JOSEPH, biochemist, educator; b. Phila., Mar. 19, 1933; s. Charles P. and Adeline A. (Molluro) C.; m. Margaret J. Follet, May 30, 1964; children: Margaret, Jean, Elizabeth, Carolyn, Catherine, Helen. B.S. in Biology and Chemistry, St. Joseph's Coll., 1955; M.A. in Physiology, Temple U., 1958; Ph.D. in Biochemistry (NSF fellow), U. Del., 1962; M.A. hon., U. Pa., 1982. Asst. instr. in gen. biology Temple U., 1957-58, postdoctoral fellow and research assoc., 1961-63, instr. dept. chemistry, 1962-71; grad. research asst. dept. biol. scis. U. Del., 1958-59, grad. research fellow, 1959-60; asst. prof. biochemistry div. animal biology Sch. Vet. Medicine, U. Pa., 1967-69, asso. prof., 1969-74, prof., 1974—; assoc. Wistar Inst., Phila., 1963-69, assoc. prof., 1969-76, prof., 1976—; research assoc. Phila. Geriatric Ctr., 1975—; dir. U. Pa. Ctr. for Study of Aging, 1978—; mem. U. Pa. Faculty Arts and Scis., 1977-80; chmn. Gordon Conf. on Biology of Aging, 1977; mem. com. on med. edn. and geriatrics Nat. Acad. Scis. Inst. Medicine, 1977-78. Contbr. numerous articles to profl. jours.; editor: (with others) Growth, Nutrition, and Metabolism of Cells in Culture, vol. 1, 1972, vol. 2, 1972, vol. 3, 1977, Pharmacological Interventions of the Aging Process, 1978; editorial bd.: Mechanism of Ageing and Development, 1972—, In Vitro, 1975—, Gerontologist, 1976—, Cell Biology Internat. Reports, 1976—, Ann. Rev. Gerontology and Geriatrics, 1978—; interim editor: Jour. Gerontology, 1976; bd. biol. scis. editor, 1976—; editorial cons.: (with others) Exptl. Aging Research, 1979—. USPHS postdoctoral fellow; NIH grantee, 1972-79. Fellow Gerontol. Soc. Am. (chmn. research/edn. com., sect. biology 1974, Kleemeier award 1982); mem. AAAS, Tissue Culture Assn. (exec. bd. 1978—, chmn. publs. com. 1978-80), Internat. Assn. Gerontology (N.Am. regional com.), Am. Physiol. Soc., Am. Soc. Cell Biology, John Morgan Soc., Soc. Exptl. Biology and Medicine, Sigma Xi. Home: 444 Haverford Ave Narberth PA 19072 Office: Wistar Inst 36th St at Spruce Philadelphia PA 19104

CRISTOFER, MICHAEL, actor, author; b. Trenton, N.J., Jan. 22, 1945; s. Joseph Peter and Mary (Muccioli) Procaccino. Student, Catholic U. Am., 1962-65, Am. U., Beirut, 1968-69. Repertory actor, Arena Stage, Washington, 1967-68, Theatre of Living Arts, Phila., 1968, Beirut Repertory Co., 1968-69, N.Y. Shakespeare Festival, 1970, Mark Taper Forum, Los Angeles, 1972-75; stage performance in Chinchilla, 1979; TV appearances in The Entertainer, 1975, The Last of Mrs. Lincoln, 1975, Knuckle, 1976; film appearance in Enemy of The People, 1976; author: plays The Mandala, 1967, Rienzi, 1968, Dorian, 1969, Plot Counter Plot, 1971, Americomedia, 1972, The Shadow Box (Pulitzer prize drama 1977, Antoiette Perry award play 1977), 1972 (Los Angeles Drama Critic award best play 1975), Ice, 1974, Black Angel, 1976, The Lady and the Clarinet, 1980. Recipient Theatre World award for performance, 1977, Los Angeles Drama Critics award for acting, 1973 *

CRISTOL, STANLEY JEROME, chemistry educator; b. Chgo., June 14, 1916; s. Myer J. and Lillian (Young) C.; m. Barbara Wright Swingle, June 1957; children: Marjorie Jo, Jeffrey Tod. B.S., Northwestern U., 1937; M.A., UCLA, 1939, Ph.D., 1943. Research chemist Standard Oil Co., Calif., 1938-41; research fellow U. Ill., 1943-44; research chemist U.S. Dept. Agr., 1944-46; asst. prof., then asso. prof. U. Colo., 1946-55, prof., 1955—, Joseph Sewall disting. prof., 1979—, chmn. dept. chemistry, 1960-62, grad. dean, 1980-81; vis. prof. Stanford U., summer 1961, U. Geneva, 1975, U. Lausanne, Switzerland; with OSRD, 1944-46; adv. panels NSF, 1957-63, 69-73, NIH, 1969-72. Author: (with L.O. Smith, Jr.) Organic Chemistry, 1966; editorial bd., Chem. Revs., 1957-59, Jour. Organic Chemistry, 1964-68; contbr. research articles to sci. jours. Guggenheim fellow, 1955-56, 81, 82; recipient James Flack Norris award in phys.-organic chemistry, 1972. Fellow AAAS, Chem. Soc. London; mem. Am. Chem. Soc. (chmn. organic chemistry div. 1961-62, adv. bd. petroleum research fund 1963-66, council policy com. 1968-73), AAUP, Colo.-Wyo. Acad. Sci., Nat. Acad. Scis., Phi Beta Kappa, Sigma Xi, Phi Lambda Upsilon. Home: 2918 3d St Boulder CO 80302 Office: U Colo Boulder CO 80309

CRITCHLOW, B. VAUGHN, anatomist, educator; b. Hotchkiss, Colo., Mar. 5, 1927; s. Arthur Burtis and Nancy Gertrude (Lynch) C.;

children: Christopher, Eric, Jan, Carey. B.A., Occidental Coll., 1951; Ph.D., UCLA, 1957. Instr. to prof. anatomy Coll. Medicine Baylor U., Houston, 1957-72; prof., chmn. anatomy U. Oreg. Health Scis. Center, Portland, 1972-82; dir. DRPRC, Beaverton, Oreg., 1982—. Served with USN, 1945-46. NIH research career devel. awardee, 1959-69; NIH research grantee, 1958-83. Mem. Am. Assn. Anatomists, Endocrine Soc., Am. Physiol. Soc., Soc. for Neurosci., Internat. Soc. Neuroendocrinology, Internat. Brain Research Orgn. Office: Oregon Regional Primate Research Center 505 NW 185th Ave Beaverton OR 97006

CRITOPH, EUGENE, nuclear research company executive; b. Vancouver, B.C., Can., Mar. 29, 1929; s. Dennis Basil and Lillian Sarah (Stanton) C.; m. Mary Elizabeth Ivens, Feb. 9, 1952; children: Christopher Michael, Stephen Bard, Eugene Mark, Boyd. B.A.Sc., U. B.C., 1951, M.A.Sc., 1957. Physicist AECL Research Co., Chalk River Nuclear Labs., (Ont.), Can., 1953-67, br. head reactor physics, 1967-75, dir. fuels and materials div., 1975-76, dir. advanced projects and reactor physics div., 1976-79, v.p., gen. mgr., 1979—; mem., sec., chmn. European-Am. Com. on Reactor Physics OECD, 1962-69. Mem. Can. Assn. Physicist, Am. Nuclear Soc., Can. Nuclear Soc. Home: 4 Darwin Deep River ON Canada K0J 1P0 Office: Atomic Energy of Can Ltd Chalk River Nuclear Labs Chalk River ON Canada K0J 1J0

CRITTENDEN, JAMES NIXON, food company executive; b. Roseburg, Oreg., May 18, 1931; s. Floyd L. and Frances Gray (Hunt) C.; m. Elizabeth Pflueger, Jan. 16, 1960; children: Lindsey Elizabeth, Blake Stuart. B.A., U. Oreg., 1953; LL.B., Golden Gate U., San Francisco, 1960. Bar: Calif. Asst. cashier Crocker Nat. Bank, San Francisco, 1955-63; atty. firm Pillsbury, Madison & Sutro, San Francisco, 1962-71; with Del Monte Corp., San Francisco, 1972—, now v.p., gen. counsel., sec. Served with AUS, 1953-55. Mem. Am. Bar Assn., State Bar Calif. Office: PO Box 3575 San Francisco CA 94119

CRITZ, RICHARD LAURENS, mag. editor, archtl. cons.; b. Starkville, Miss., June 6, 1922; s. Harry Turner and Ethelyn Lucile (Ferguson) C.; m. Carolyn Anne Herrick, Jan. 17, 1948; children—Martha Carolyn (Mrs. Henry Pearce), Carl Herrick. Student, Northwestern U., 1939-41, Miss. State U., 1941; B.Arch., Yale, 1949; M.Div., Drew Theol. Sem., 1959. Draftsman Wilson, Morris, Crain & Anderson (Architects), Houston, 1949-52; staff architect William B. Tabler, Asso., N.Y.C., 1952-55; pastor Califon Methodist Ch., Califon, N.J., 1958-60; cons. architect dept. architecture Bd. Missions, Methodist Ch., Phila., 1960-68; archtl. cons. to chs., Phila., 1968-73; editor Your Church mag., King of Prussia, Pa., 1973-77; dir. design cons. architect Total Design Inc., King of Prussia, 1978—; organizer, pres., pub., co-editor Vine Life Publs., Inc., King of Prussia, 1978—. Served with USAAF, 1941-45. Mem. AIA, Am. Soc. Ch. Architecture (treas. 1970-73, bd. dirs. 1972-75), Assn. Creative Change, Am. Rock Garden Soc., Phi Mu Alpha. Methodist. Home: 1236 Wendover Ave Rosemont PA 19010 Office: PO Box 27 King of Prussia PA 19406

CRITZER, WILLIAM ERNEST, truck manufacturing company executive; b. Cleve., Aug. 11, 1934; s. Ernest H. and Gertrude (Bell) C.; m. Patricia Suzanne Hawk, Aug. 16, 1957; children—Stephen, David. B.B.A. cum laude, U. Miami, Fla., 1960. Asst. to gen. auditor W.P. R.R., 1960-63; with Consol. Freightways, Inc., San Francisco, 1963—, treas., 1967-72, v.p., treas., 1972-75; pres. Freightliner Corp., Portland, Oreg., 1975—, chief exec. officer, 1977—; exec. v.p. fin. Envirotech Corp., Menlo Park, Calif., 1981—. Served with USAF, 1954-58. Home: 13385 Country Way Los Altos Hills CA 94022 Office: Envirotech Corp 3000 Sand Hill Rd Menlo Park CA 94025

CRIVARO, PETE FRANK, mayor; b. Des Moines, Aug. 6, 1913; John B. and and Anita (Perri) C.; m. Louise J. Abruzzese, Apr. 6, 1936; children: John A., Carmella Crivaro Pigneri. Student, Am. Inst. Bus., Drake U. Community Coll., Des Moines. Legal sec., 1933-36; sec. to mayor of Des Moines, 1936-38; with Des Moines Dept. Public Works, 1938-56; asst. city mgr., then acting city mgr., Des Moines, 1956-64, city mgr., Marion, Iowa, 1964-68; dir. Des Moines Public Housing Authority, 1969-77; community investment dir. Fed. Home Loan Bank, Des Moines, 1978-79; mayor of Des Moines, 1979—; past pres. Des Moines Housing Council; dir.; Homes of Oakridge. Served with USNR, 1948-50. Mem. Internat. City Mgrs. Assn., U.S. Conf. Mayors, Nat. League Cities, Am. Legion (past post comdr., Humanitarian award). Roman Catholic. Club: Southtown Kiwanis (past pres.). Office: City Hall E 1st and Locust Sts Des Moines IA 50307 *

CROCCHIOLO, ANDREW JOHN, hotel executive; b. Bronx, N.Y., June 7, 1935; s. Paul Andrew and Marion Veronica (Hickey) C. B.S., Loyola U., New Orleans, 1956; diploma, Am. Hotel and Motel Assn., 1969. With LaFitte Guiest House, New Orleans, 1964-70, Griswold Inn, Essex, Conn., 1970-74, Waldorf-Astoria, N.Y.C., 1974-75; gen. mgr. Holiday Inn Coliseum, N.Y.C., 1975—. Served with Security Agy. U.S. Army, 1957-60. Recipient cert. Assn. for Retarded Children Inc., 1966. Mem. Internat. Orgn. Hotel Mgrs., Hotel Sales Mgmt. Assn., N.Y. State Hotel Motel Assn., Hotel Assn. N.Y.C. Republican. Roman Catholic. Clubs: Hotel Execs., Waldorf Astoria Alumni. Home: 1200 Humboldt St Denver CO 80218 Office: Bronco Inn 104th Ave Denver CO 80234

CROCE, ARLENE LOUISE, writer; b. Providence, May 5, 1934; d. Michael Daniel and Louise Natalie (Pensa) C. Student, Woman's Coll., U. N.C., 1951-53; B.A., Barnard Coll., 1955. Founder, editor Ballet Rev., 1965-78; dance critic New Yorker mag., 1973—; Hodder fellow Princeton U., 1971; dance panelist Nat. Endowment for Arts, 1977-80. Author books: The Fred Astaire & Ginger Rogers Book, 1972, Afterimages, 1977, Going to the Dance, 1982; (Am. Acad. and Inst. of Arts and Letters award 1979, award of honor for arts and culture N.Y.C. Mayor 1979). Recipient Janeway prize Barnard Coll., 1955; John Simon Guggenheim fellow, 1972. Office: New Yorker 25 W 43d St New York NY 10036

CROCHIERE, RONALD E(LDON), electrical engineer. B.S., Milw. Sch. Engirng., 1967; M.S., MIT, 1968, Ph.D., 1974. Elec. engr. Raytheon, Wayland, Mass., 1968-70, Bell Labs., Murray Hill, N.J., 1974—. Fellow IEEE; mem. Acoustics, Speech and Signal Processing Soc. (pres. 1985). Home: 46 Stewart Ln Berkeley Heights NJ 07922 Office: AT&T Bell Labs 600 Mountain Ave Murray Hill NJ 07974

CROCKER, CHESTER ARTHUR, diplomat; b. N.Y.C., Oct. 29, 1941; s. Arthur M. and Clara C.; m. Saone Baron, Dec. 18, 1965; children—Bathsheba, Karena, Rebecca. B.A., Ohio State U., 1963; M.A. in Internat. Studies, Johns Hopkins U., 1965, Ph.D., 1969. Editorial asst. Africa Report, 1965-66, news editor, 1968-69; lectr. Am. U., 1969-70; staff officer Nat. Security Council, 1970-72; dir. M.S. in Fgn. Service program Georgetown U., 1972-78, dir. African studies, 1976-81; asst. sec. state African affairs, 1981—; cons. in field. Mem., coordinator for Africa Republican Nat. Com.; mem. adv. council Nat. Security and Internat. Affairs; chmn. Africa working group Reagan campaign, 1980. Author: South Africa Defense Posture, 1981, others; editorial bd.: Strategic Rev; contbr. articles to profl. jours. Mem. Council Fgn. Relations, African Studies Assn., Internat. Studies Assn., U.S. Strategic Inst. Clubs: Cosmos, Tahawus. Office: Bur African Affairs Dept State Washington DC 20520

CROCKER, DIANE W., physician, pathologist; b. Cambridge, Mass., 1926; d. Richard and Rose (Fisher) Winston; m. Benjamin Ballard Crocker, Aug. 20, 1949 (div. 1975); children—Deborah Bliss, Kimberly, Anne. Student pvt. schs., Boston and Switzerland; B.A., Wellesley Coll., 1946; M.S., Brown U., 1948; M.D., Boston U., 1952. Diplomate: Nat. Bd. Med. Examiners, Am. Bd. Pathology. Intern Mallory Inst. Pathology, 1952-53; asst. resident New Eng. Deaconess Hosp., Boston, 1953-54; resident, research fellow Heart Assn. Los Angeles Children's Hosp., 1955-56; resident, Am. Cancer Soc. fellow Columbia-Presbyn. Med. Center, N.Y.C., 1956-58; asst. in pathology U. So. Calif., 1955-56, Columbia Coll. Phys. and Surgs., N.Y.C., 1957-58; asso. pathologist Peter Bent Brigham Hosp., Boston, 1958-70, sr. asso. pathologist, 1970, chief cytology, 1969-70, attending staff, 1970-71, cons. computer and data processing in pathology, 1970-71; attending W. Roxbury VA Hosp., Boston, 1960-70; instr. Harvard Med. Sch., 1958-65, asso. in pathology, 1965-68, asst. clin. prof., 1968-69, asst. prof., 1969-70; prof. pathology Temple U. Sch. Medicine, Phila., 1970-73; chief pathology Temple U. Hosp., 1970-72; prof. pathology U. So. Calif. Sch. Medicine, 1973-77; surg. pathologist, chief anatomic pathology data processing Los Angeles County Gen. Hosp., 1973-77; prof., chmn. dept. pathology U. Tenn. Sch. Medicine, 1977—; bus. mgr. Sci. Investment Research, 1966-70; securities broker and financial cons. Hogan-Harry & Co. Inc., 1967-70. Editor: UP Report, 1967-73, New Sci. Investor, 1967-74, Computer PV Charts, 1969-74, Crocker Reports, 1973-74; Contbr. articles med. jours. Bd. dirs. Phila. div. Am. Cancer Soc., 1972-73; bd. dirs., mem. exec. com., v.p. for fund devel. N.E. Los Angeles unit, 1973-77, crusade chmn., 1976-77, bd. dirs., Memphis, 1977—. Fellow Royal Soc. Medicine (London), Internat. Coll. Surgeons in Pathology; mem. So. Calif., Memphis socs. pathologists, AMA, Am. Soc. Clin. Pathologists, Am. Soc. Cytology, Am. Heart Assn. (council on kidney, mem. Cabinet Los Angeles affiliate 1975-77), Internat. Acad. Pathology, Am. Assn. Pathologists, Los Angeles Soc. Pathologists, Los Angeles Acad. Medicine, Memphis Med. Soc., Phi Beta Kappa, Sigma Xi. Clubs: Phila. Medical, Phila. Country, Lake Placid (N.Y.). Home: 285 Waring Rd Memphis TN 38117 Office: Inst Pathology 858 Madison Ave Memphis TN 38163

CROCKER, FREDERICK GREELEY, JR., manufacturing company executive; b. Boston, June 26, 1937; s. Frederick Greeley and Mary Jane (Bigelow) C.; m. Rebecca B. Bennett, Jan. 19, 1980; children: Frederick G., Sephen C., Marian D. B.A. cum laude, Harvard U., 1959; M.B.A., Columbia U., 1964. With Norton Co., Worcester, Mass., 1964—, controller grinding wheel div., 1970-73, v.p., gen. mgr. parent co., 1973-82, v.p., controller parent co., 1982—; trustee Consumers Savs. Bank, Worcester. Pres. trustee Bancroft Sch., Worcester, 1979—; treas. Holden (Mass.) Dist. Hosp., 1967-70; trustee Worcester Found. Exptl. Biology, 1973-75. Served to lt. (j.g.) USNR, 1959-62. Mem. Beta Gamma Sigma. Republican. Home: 10 Surrey Ln Worcester MA 01609 Office: 1 New Bond St Worcester MA 01606

CROCKER, LESTER GILBERT, emeritus foreign language educator; b. N.Y.C., Apr. 23, 1912; m. Billie Danziger, Feb. 16, 1934; children: Roger, Leslie Joyce. B.A., N.Y.U., 1932, M.A., 1934; certificat de littérature française, U. Paris, 1933; Ph.D., U. Calif., 1936; Litt.D. (hon.), U. So. Calif., 1980. Asst. prof. romance langs. Wittenberg Coll., 1937-39, Queens Coll., 1939-44; dir. prodn. Eastern Sound Studios, 1944-48; assoc. prof. Sweet Briar Coll., 1948-50; prof., chmn. dept. modern langs. Goucher Coll., 1950-60; distinguished prof., chmn. dept. romance langs. Case Western Res. U., Cleve., 1960-67, dean humanities, 1967-71, grad. dean, 1963-67; Kenan prof. French U. Va., 1971-80, chmn. French and gen. linguistics, 1971-77, prof. emeritus, 1980—; Guggenheim fellow, Fulbright research scholar U. Paris, 1954-55; vis. prof. Sorbonne, 1975-76; mem. Inst. Advanced Study, Princeton, 1958-59; vis. lectr. U. London, spring 1963; Distinguished visitor U. Australia, U. New Zealand, 1973. Author: La Correspondance de Diderot, 1939, Two Diderot Studies, 1952, The Embattled Philosopher, 1954, rev. edit., 1966, An Age of Crisis: Man and World in Eighteenth Century French Thought, 1959, Nature and Culture, Ethical Thought in the French Enlightenment, 1963, Jean-Jacques Rousseau, The Quest (1712-1758), 1968, Rousseau's Social Contract, an Interpretive Essay, 1968, Jean-Jacques Rousseau: The Prophetic Voice (1758-1778), 1973, Diderot's Chaotic Order: Approach to Synthesis, 1974; Editor: Candide; Diderot's Selected Writings, 1966, The Age of Enlightenment, 1969, Anthologie de la Litterature du Dix-Huitieme Siecle, 1972, others.; Cons. editor: Larousse-Pocket Book French Dictionary, 1955; Contbr. articles to profl. jours. Decorated chevalier dans l'ordre des Palmes academiques, chevalier de la Légion d'honneur; recipient silver medal City of Paris, 1978; Benjamin Franklin fellow Royal Soc. Arts; festschrift, 1979. Mem. Internat. Soc. for Study of 18th Century (pres. 1971-75), Am. Soc. for 18th Century Studies (pres. 1969-71), MLA (chmn. philos. approaches to lit. 1977), AAUP, Société d'Histoire Littéraire (hon. mem.), Phi Beta Kappa. Club: Athenaeum (London). Address: 930 Fifth Ave New York NY 10021 *Fortunately, it is not necessary to be a great man in order to have a good life. Even with limited potentialities, we can look back with satisfaction if we have the feeling that we have done our best to maximize them. Such a feeling enables us to live with our faults and our failures, our shortcomings and our disappointments.*

CROCKER, MALCOLM JOHN, mechanical engineer, noise control engineer, educator; b. Portsmouth, Eng., Sept. 10, 1938; came to U.S., 1963, naturalized, 1975; s. William Edwin and Alice Dorothy (Mintram) C.; m. Ruth Catherine, July 25, 1964; children: Anne Catherine, Elizabeth Claire. B.Sc. in Aeros. with hons, Southampton (Eng.) U., 1961, M.Sc. in Noise and Vibration, 1963; Ph.D. in Acoustics, Liverpool (Eng.) U., 1969. Co-op. apprentice, Vickers scholar Brit. Aerospace Co., Weybridge, Surrey, Eng., 1957-62; research asst. Southampton U., 1962-63, vis. research fellow, 1976; scientist Wyle Labs. Research, Huntsville, Ala., 1963-66; research fellow U. Liverpool, 1967-69; asso. prof. mech. engring. Purdue U., West Lafayette, Ind., 1969-73, prof., 1973-83; asst. dir. acoustics and noise control Herrick labs., 1977-83; prof., chmn. dept. mech. engring. Auburn U. (Ala.), 1983—; vis. prof. U. Sydney, Australia, 1976; cons. to industry, speaker in field; gen. chmn. acoustics confs., including Inter-Noise 72, Washington, 1972, Noise-Con 79 Nat. Conf. Noise Control Engring., West Lafayette, 1979; cons. to industry; speaker in field; gen. chmn. acoustics confs., including Inter-Noise 72, Washington, 1972. Author: Noise and Noise Control, 2 vols, 1975, 82, Benchmark Papers on Noise, 1984; contbr. numerous articles to profl. jours.; editor: books, including Noise and Vibration Control Engineering, 1972, Reduction of Machinery Noise, 1974, rev. edit., 1975; editor-in-chief: Noise Control Engineering, 1973—; editorial bd.: Archives Acoustical, Warsaw, Poland, 1979—. Grantee NSF, 1972-74, 75-77, U.S. Dept. Transp., 1972-73, 79-81, EPA, 1976-80; others. Fellow Acoustical Soc. Am.; mem. Inst. Noise Control Engring./U.S.A. (dir., v.p. for communications, pres. 1981), Inst. Acoustics (London) (asso.). Home: 454 Pinedale Dr Auburn AL 36830 Office: Dept Mech Engring Auburn U Auburn AL 36849

CROCKER, MYRON DONOVAN, judge; b. Pasadena, Calif., Sept. 4, 1915; s. Myron William and Ethel (Shoemaker) C.; m. Elaine Jensen, Apr. 26, 1941; children—Glenn, Holly. A.B., Fresno State Coll., 1937; LL.B., U. Calif. at Berkeley, 1940. Bar: Calif. bar 1940. Spl. agt. FBI, 1940-46; practiced law, Chowchilla, Calif., 1946-58, asst. dist. atty., Madera County, Calif., 1946-51; judge Chowchilla Justice Ct., 1952-58, Superior Ct. Madera County, 1958-59; U.S. judge Eastern Dist. Calif., Sacramento, 1959—. Mem. Madera County Republican Central Com., 1950—. Named Outstanding Citizen Chowchilla, 1960. Mem. Chowchilla C. of C. (sec.). Lutheran. Club: Lion. Office: US Dist Courthouse 1130 O St Fresno CA 93721 *

CROCKETT, CAMPBELL, univ. dean; b. Nicholasville, Ky., Apr. 25, 1918; s. O.B. and Catherine (Campbell) C.; m. Genevieve Kuntz, Oct. 22, 1942 (div.); children—Peter Campbell, Catherine Kuntz. A.B., U. Cin., 1940; A.M., 1941; Ph.D., 1949. From instr. to prof. U. Cin., 1949-60, dean, fellow, 1959-67; dir. Inst. Research, Tng. Higher Edn., 1967-71, acting dean, 1970-71, dean, 1971-76; dir. edn. Palm Beach (Fla.) Inst. Found., 1977—; lectr. Conservatory Music, 1949-54, Art Acad. Cin., 1958-60. Contbr. articles to profl. publs. Fellow Nat. Tng. Labs.; Bd. dirs. Cin. Playhouse in the Park; adv. bd. Inquiry. Served with USAAF, 1942-46. Ford faculty fellow U. Mich. and Harvard, 1951-52; Fulbright research scholar U. Oslo, 1953-54. Mem. Am. Soc. Aesthetics, Am. Philos. Assn., ACLU, AAUP, Am. Assn. Humanistic Psychology. Home: 1600 E Thompson Dr Cincinnati OH 45223

CROCKETT, CLYLL WEBB, lawyer; b. Preston, Idaho, Feb. 16, 1934; s. Frank Lee and Alta (Webb) C.; m. Nan Marie Mattice, June 27, 1958; children—Jeffrey Webb, Nicole, Karen, Cynthia. B.S., Brigham Young U., 1958; M.B.A. Northwestern U, 1959; LL.B., U. Ariz., 1962. Bar: Ariz. bar 1962. Clk. Ariz. Supreme Ct., 1962-63; partner firm Fennemore, Craig, von Ammon & Udall, Phoenix, 1968—; Instr. eve. div. Mesa (Ariz.) Community Coll. Mem. editorial bd.: Ariz. Law Rev, 1961. Mem. charter rev. com., Scottsdale, Ariz., 1966-67, bd. adjustment, Scottsdale, 1968-73, chmn., 1971-73; bd. dirs. Maricopa Mental Health Assn., 1976-78; mem. City of Mesa Crime Commn., 1980—. Mem. Am., Maricopa County bar assns., State Bar Ariz., Phoenix C. of C., Ariz. Acad. Republican. Mem. Ch. of Jesus Christ of Latter-day Saints. Club: Kiwanian. Home: 1510 N Gentry Circle Mesa AZ 85203 Office: 100 W Washington St Phoenix AZ 85003

CROCKETT, ETHEL STACY, librarian; b. Mt. Vernon, N.Y., Jan. 19, 1915; d. Henry Pomeroy and Marian (Putnam) Stacy; m. Clement Wirt Crockett, Aug. 17, 1936 (div. July 1969); children: Patricia Crockett Johnson, Richard; m. Jack Howard Aldridge, June 22, 1973. B.A., Vassar Coll., 1936; M.A., San Jose State Coll., 1962; postgrad., U. Calif.-Berkeley, 1964-65, San Francisco State Coll., 1966. Children's librarian Corning (N.Y.) Meml. Library, 1958; catalog librarian Sequoia Union High Sch., Redwood City, Calif., 1960-61; gen. reference librarian, instr. San Jose (Calif.) City Coll., 1962-68; dir. library services City Coll. San Francisco, 1968-72; dir. Inst. Effective Use of Paraprofls. in Libraries, summer 1971; Calif. State librarian, Sacramento, 1972-80; chmn. Chief Officers of State Library Agencies, 1974-75; mem. Nat. Council on Ednl. Stats., 1975-78; mem. adv. group on the Library to Librarian of Congress, mem. adv. council Ctr. for the Book, 1980—; mem. vis. com. Stanford U. Libraries, 1975-82; mem. adv. council Stanford Library Assos., 1978—. Vice pres. Sir Francis Drake Commn., 1974-80; bd. dirs., treas. Seadrift Property Owners Assn., Stinson Beach, Calif.; bd. dirs. Strybing Arboretum Found., San Francisco, Pacific Horticulture Found.; spl. events chmn. Pacific Horticulture Found., 1982—; bd. dirs. San Francisco Mus. Art, Marin Income Property Owners Assn.; mem. vis. council Living History Centre. Mem. ALA, Book Club of Calif. (dir., v.p. 1983—), Calif. Library Assn., Calif. Inst. Libraries (pres. 1973—). Club: Colophon. Home: PO Box 457 Stinson Beach CA 94970 *My interest as state librarian is to provide excellent library service to all Californians. By aiding and encouraging all libraries to open their collections to patrons beyond their boundaries, I hope to see the great resources of California libraries available to all. My goal is to enable all kinds of libraries to work together cooperatively so that a book need be catalogued only once for all libraries, and so materials can be shared to avoid expensive, duplicative purchases. Thus, the library user will be better served while the cost of service stays within a reasonable limit.*

CROCKETT, GEORGE WILLIAM, JR., congressman; b. Jacksonville, Fla., Aug. 10, 1909; s. George William and Minnie A. (Jenkins) C.; m. Ethelene Jones (dec.); children: Elizabeth Ann Crockett Hicks, George William III, Ethelene C.; m. Harriette Clark, Aug. 1980. A.B., Morehouse Coll., 1931, LL.D., 1972; J.D., U. Mich., 1934; LL.D., Shaw Coll., 1973. Bar: Fla. 1934, W.Va. 1935, Mich. 1944, U.S. Supreme Ct. 1940. Practiced law, Jacksonville, 1934-35, Fairmont, W.Va., 1935-39; sr. atty. Dept. Labor, 1939-43; hearings officer Fed. Fair Employment Practices Commn., Washington, 1943; founder, dir. Internat. UAW Fair Employment Practices Dept.; adminstrv. asst. to internat. sec-treas. UAW; assoc. gen. counsel Internat. UAW, 1944-46; sr. mem. firm Goodman, Crockett, Eden and Robb, Detroit, 1946-66; judge Recorder's Ct., Detroit, 1966-78, presiding judge, 1974-79; vis. judge Mich. Ct. Appeals, 1979; acting corp. counsel City Detroit, 1980; mem. 97th-98th Congresses from Mich.; mem. com. fgn. affairs, com. judiciary, select com. on aging. Mem. exec. bd. Democratic Study Group, U.S. Congress; mem. Congl. Black Caucus, Congl. Auto Caucus, Congl. Arts Caucus; hon. mem. Congl. Hispanic Caucus. Trustee Morehouse Coll. Mem. Nat. Bar Assn. (founder and 1st chmn. Jud. Council), Nat. Lawyers Guild, N.E.-Midwest Econ. Coalition, Congress For Peace Through Law, Phi Beta Kappa, Kappa Alpha Psi. Democrat. Baptist. Office: 1531 Longworth House Office Bldg Washington DC 20515

CROCKETT, GIBSON M., editorial cartoonist; b. Washington, Sept. 18, 1912; s. Hal Gibson and Gertrude Virginia (Lentz) C.; m. Florence E. Abbott, July 4, 1937; children—Gary A. (dec.), Sandra Lea, David (dec.). Grad., Dobyns Bennett High Sch., Kingsport, Tenn., 1929. Mem. staff Washington Evening Star, 1933-75, editorial cartoonist, 1947-75, sport cartoonist, 1940-46, ret., 1975; art dir. Am. Pub. Co., Washington, 1945—. Free lance illustrator mag., 1943—; portrait painter exhibited landscape paintings in local and nat. exhbns. Mem. Editorial Cartoonists Assn., Washington Landscape Painter's Club, Olney (Md.) Art Assn., Balt. Watercolor Soc. Presbyn. Club: Manor Country (Norbeck, Md.). Home and studio: 4713 Great Oak Rd Rockville MD 20853

CROCKETT, JAMES GROVER, III, publisher, musician; b. San Francisco, Feb. 13, 1937; s. James Grover and Virginia (Adams) C.; married; children: Chenoa Denelle, Doya Laurenne, Cordell Miller, Kessel Robinson. B.A. in Communications, Coll. of Pacific, 1958, M.A., 1960. Various positions radio and TV stas., Stockton, Calif., Sacramento, Grants Pass, Oreg., Spokane, Wash., 1952-62; instr. radio-TV dept. U. Idaho, Moscow, 1961-63; concert producer, freelance writer, 1963-70; owner/mgr. Books Universal, Livermore, Calif., 1963-70; arts editor, columnist, writer Livermore Ind., 1968-70; asst. editor Guitar Player mag., Los Gatos, Calif., 1970-71, editor, 1971, pub., editor, 1971—; v.p. GPI Corp., 1971-82, pres., 1982—; also pub. Keyboard mag., Frets mag.; speaker various trade confs. Freelance musician; writer, 1955—; Pub. 1st non-objective coloring book for children, guitar repair manual. Active Music Educators' Nat. Conf., Music Industry Council. Mem. Fretted Instrument Guild Am., Nat. Assn. Music Mchts., Nat. Assn. Rec. Arts and Scis., Alpha Epsilon Rho, Phi Mu Alpha. Office: 20605 Lazaneo Dr Cupertino CA 95014

CROCKETT, JEAN ANDRUS, finance educator; b. Tucson, Apr. 20, 1919; d. Dexter Eli and Hazel Alberta (Thompson) Andrus; m. Martin Bronfenbrenner, June 6, 1940 (div. 1949); m. Robert Oscar Crockett,

Jr., Aug. 1, 1953; children: Jennifer Lynn, Elizabeth Jean, Robert Dexter. B.A. in Econs., U. Chgo., 1939, M.A., 1948, Ph.D., 1950; M.A. in Math., U. Colo., 1946. Statis. analyst U.S. Dept. Commerce, Washington, 1949-50, 52-53; asst. prof. econs. U. Ill., Urbana, 1951; assoc. prof. fin. U. Pa., Phila., 1959-66, prof., 1966—, chmn. dept. fin., 1977-82; past dir. Fed. Res. Bank Phila., chmn., 1982—; dir. Pennwalt Corp., Phila., Nat. Bur. Econ. Res., Cambridge, Mass. Author: Consumer Expenditures and Incomes in Greece, 1967; co-author: Mutual Funds and Other Institutional Investors, 1970; co-editor: Economic Activity and Finance, 1982. Mem. consumer adv. council Fed. Res. Bd., Washington, 1983. Mem. Am. Fin. Assn., Am. Statis. Assn., AAUP, Sigma Xi. Democrat. *

CROCKETT, JERRY BRUCE, lawyer; b. Miami, Fla., Dec. 3, 1930; s. Howard Bruce and Annelise Henrietta (Petersen) C.; m. Anne Howe O'Quinn, Aug. 15, 1953; children: Jeffrey, Gregory, Paul, Whitney, Lisa. A.B., U. Fla., 1952, J.D., 1956. Bar: Fla. 1956. Ptnr. firm Steel, Hector & Davis (and predecessor firm), Miami, 1960—; dir. S.E. Mortgage Co.; chmn. Fla. Bd. Bar Examiners, 1978; lectr. Practicing Law Inst., 1976-80. Editor: U. Fla. Law Rev, 1956. Chmn. YMCA Camp Fla., 1974-75. Served to 1st lt., Transp. Corps U.S. Army, 1952-54. Mem. Am. Law Inst., Am. Bar Assn., Fla. Bar, Dade County Bar Assn., Order of Coif, Phi Beta Kappa. Democrat. Baptist. Home: 701 SW 27th Rd Miami FL 33129 Office: 1400 SE First Nat Bank Bldg Miami FL 33131

CROFT, HARRY ALLEN, psychiatrist; b. Houston, July 2, 1943; s. Louis and Ida (Kaplan) C.; m. Benay Bleacher, Dec. 27, 1964; children—Jamie Sue, Bradley Lane, Chasen Ashley. B.S., So. Meth. U., 1964; M.D., U. Tex. at Galveston, 1968. Intern Brackenridge Hosp., Austin, 1968-69; resident in obstetrics and gynecology U. Tex. Med. Br., 1969-70, resident in psychiatry, 1970-73; dir. methadone program, Galveston County, Tex.; dir. sex therapy program U. Tex., Galveston, 1972-73; commd. capt. U.S. Army, 1973, advanced through grades to maj., 1975; chief (Mental Hygiene Service, Brooke Army Med. Center), Houston, 1973-76, pvt. practice, 1976—; Clin. asst. prof. psychiatry and obstetrics and gynecology Med. Sch. San Antonio, 1973-75; columnist San Antonio Express-News, 1975—. Contbr. articles to profl. jours. Recipient Physician's Recognition award A.M.A., 1974; Meritorious Service medal U.S. Army, 1976; Ware 1st Place Audio-Visual award Dept. Army, 1976. Mem. Am. Psychiat. Assn., Tex. Med. Assn., Am. Assn. Sex Educators and Counselors. Home: 12738 Hunters Chase San Antonio TX 78230 Office: Oak Hills Med Bldg Suite 509 7711 Louis Pasteur San Antonio TX 78229

CROFT, WILLIAM CROSSWELL, corp. exec.; b. Greenville, S.C., Jan. 8, 1918; s. Edward S. and Mary (Crosswell) C.; m. Helen Barbara Engh, Mar. 7, 1942; children—William Crosswell, Mary Barbara, Douglas E., Helen W., Jean Ann. Student, The Citadel, 1935-36; B.S., U.S. Naval Acad., 1940. Tech. supr. Anaconda Wire & Cable Co., Orange, Calif., 1946-48; gen. mgr. William J. Moran Co., Alhambra, Calif., 1948-50; works mgr. Pyle-Nat. Co., Chgo., 1950-52, v.p., 1953-54, exec. v.p., 1955, pres., 1955-76; chmn. Clements Nat. Co., Chgo., 1976—; dir. Paxall, Inc., Chgo., First Nat. Bank & Trust Co., Evanston, Ill., Methode Electronics, Inc., Chgo., Central Ill. Light Co., Peoria. Served from ensign to lt. comdr. USN, 1940-46. Mem. Chgo. President's Orgn., Ill. Mfrs. Assn. (past pres., dir.). Clubs: Union League, Chicago, Glen View, Mid-America (Chgo.). Home: 1145 Central Rd Glenview IL 60025 Office: 2150 W 16th St Broadview IL 60153

CROGHAN, HAROLD HEENAN, corporate executive, lawyer; b. Sioux City, Iowa, May 28, 1924; s. Edmund Harold and Marie Agnes (Heenan) C.; m. Gertrude Anna Murphy, Feb. 4, 1948; children: Catherine, John, Loretto, Margaret. A.B. cum laude, Lawrence U., 1947; Dexter Perkins fellow, U. Rochester, 1947-48; J.D., Cornell U., 1953. Bar: Mo. 1953, Ohio 1967. With firm Stinson, Mag, Thomson, McEvers & Fizzell, Kansas City, Mo., 1953-54, Margolin & Kirwin, Kansas City, 1954-56; atty. Gas Service Co., 1956-66; house counsel Philips Industries, Inc., Dayton, Ohio, 1966-67, asst. sec.-corp. counsel, 1967, v.p., sec., corp. counsel, 1968-74, treas., 1974-77, sec., 1975-77, gen. counsel, 1975—, exec. v.p. adminstrn., 1977—. Served to capt. USMCR, 1943-46, 50-52. Decorated Navy Cross, Silver Star. Mem. Phi Beta Kappa, Phi Delta Theta, Phi Delta Phi. Republican. Roman Catholic. Clubs: Chancery, Vanguard, Rockhill, Hollinger, Tennis, Dayton City Racquet (Dayton). Home: 609 Garden Rd Dayton OH 45419 Office: 4801 Springfield St Dayton OH 45401

CROHN, MAX HENRY, JR., lawyer; b. Asheville, N.C., Feb. 4, 1934; s. Max Henry and Edith Pearl (Hoffman) C.; m. Barbara Jean Morris, Jan. 28, 1960; children: David Michael, Edith Ann, Randal Morris. B.A. in Polit. Sci, U. N.C., 1955; LL.B., Georgetown U., 1961. Bar: D.C. 1961, N.C. 1977. Practiced in, D.C., 1961-68; trial atty. Bur. Restraint of Trade, 1963-65; atty. adviser to chmn. FTC, 1965-66; asso. mem. firm Arnold & Porter, Washington, 1966-68; asso. counsel R.J. Reynolds Industries, Inc., Winston-Salem, N.C., 1968-75, asst. gen. counsel, 1975-78; sec. R.J. Reynolds Tobacco Co., 1971-81, gen. counsel, 1978-81; ptnr. Jacob, Medinger & Finnegan, 1981—; Former chmn. bd. dirs. Forsyth County Econ. Devel. Corp.; bd. dirs. Winston-Salem State U. Found., 1975—. Served to lt. (j.g.) USNR, 1955-58. Mem. Am. Bar Assn., Greater Winston-Salem C. of C. Club: Kiwanian. Home: 440 Archer Rd Winston-Salem NC 27106 Office: 2111 Wachovia Bldg Winston-Salem NC 27101

CROISANT, EUGENE R., banker; b. Chgo., Aug. 2, 1937; s. Edward H. and Alice R. C.; m. Barbara Byczek; children: Thomas D., Cynthia. B.S.C., Loyola U., Chgo., 1959, M.S., 1966; postgrad., Nat. Assn. Bank Audit Control Sch. U. Wis., summers 1964-66. With Continental Ill. Nat. Bank and Trust Co., 1959—, electronics officer, 1966-67, 2d v.p., 1967-69, operating rep., 1969-70, v.p., 1970-71; sr. v.p., 1974-81, exec. v.p., 1981—; dir. Republic Realty; lectr. in field. Mem. com. cabinet selection Ill. Gov., 1977; mem. Ill. Commn. to Investigate Welfare Fraud; trustee George Williams Coll.; trustee, chmn. fin. and devel. coms. Loyola U.; asso. Chgo. Rehab. Inst.; chmn. Human Resources Policy Inst., Boston U. Served to 1st lt. U.S. Army, 1959-61. Mem. Am. Mgmt. Assn. (v.p.), Am. Bankers Assn. Address: 231 S La Salle St Chicago IL 60693

CROM, JAMES OLIVER, educator; b. Alliance, Nebr., July 31, 1933; s. James Harvey and Evalyn Grace (Robinson) C.; m. Rosemary Vanderpool, Jan. 30, 1953; children—Michael Alexander, Marie Celeste, Brenda Leigh. B.S., U. Wyo., 1955. Sales rep. Investors Diversified Services, 1955-57; dist. supr. King Merritt and Co., 1957-59; field sales trainer Dale Carnegie and Assos., Inc., Garden City, N.Y., 1959-60, asst. to v.p. ops. dept., 1960-62, dir. ops. sales course, 1962-64, dir. ops. all courses, 1964-67, v.p. field ops., 1967-74, exec. v.p., gen. mgr., 1974-78, pres., 1978—. Pres. L.I. Ednl. T.V. Council, Inc., 1977-79; former trustee Lincoln Meml. U., Harrogate, Tenn.; v.p. Dorothy Carnegie Found.; mem. Action Com. for L.I. Served with Air N.G., 1951-52; Korea. Mem. L.I. Assn. Commerce and Industry, U.S. C. of C. Republican. Methodist. Home: 14 The Hamlet 96 Estate Dr Jericho NY 11753 Office: 1475 Franklin Ave Garden City NY 11530

CROMARTIE, WILLIAM JAMES, medical educator, researcher; b. Garland, N.C., May 19, 1913; s. Robert Samuel and Mary Blanche (Jester) C.; m. Josephine Colter Rule, Nov. 19, 1945; children: William James, Robert Colter, Mary Blanche, John Benjamin, Martha Anne. Student, Presbyn. Jr. Coll., 1929-30, U. N.C., 1931, U. Ala, 1931-33; M.D., Emory U., 1937. Am. Bd. Internal Medicine. Intern Emory U. div. Grady Hosp., Atlanta, 1937-38; resident Vanderbilt U. Hosp., Nashville, 1938-40; instr. pathology Vanderbilt U., 1939-41; asst, prof. bacteriology and medicine U. Minn., Mpls., 1949-50, assoc. prof., 1950-51; assoc. prof. bacteriology and medicine U. N.C., Chapel Hill, 1951-59, prof. microbiology-immunology-medicine, 1959—; mem. adv. panel microgiology Office Naval Research, Washington, 1950-55; mem. Nat. Bd. Med. Examiners, Phila., 1966-68; mem. infectious disease adv. com. NIH, Bethesda, Md., 1971-75. Bd. govs. Capital Health Planning Agy., Durham, N.C.; mem. exec. com., Reguonal Med. Program N.C., 1972-76. Served to maj. U.S. Army, 1942-46; ETO. Decorated Legion of Merit; named Alumni Disting. Prof. U. N.C., 1980. Fellow Am. Acad. Microbiology (chmn. bd. govs. 1974-75), ACP; mem. Soc. Am. Microbiologists (mem. council 1974-75), Am. Assn. Pathologists, Infectious Disease Soc. Am. Democrat. Home: 204 Weaver Rd Glendale Chapel Hill NC 27514 Office: Sch Medicine U NC 125 MacNider Bldg 202H Chapel Hill NC 27514

CROMBIE, DAVID EDWARD, Canadian govt. ofcl.; b. Toronto, Ont., Can., Apr. 24, 1936; s. Norman and Vera (Beamish) C.; m. Shirley Bowden, May 28, 1960; children—Carrie, Robin, Jonathan. Lectr. in econs. and polit. sci. Ryerson Poly. Inst.; also dir. student services; alderman City of Toronto, 1969-72, mayor, 1972-78; mem. Can. House of Commons, 1978—; minister nat. health and welfare, 1979-80. Conservative. Office: 809 Eastbourne Ave Ottawa ON K1K 0H8 Canada *

CROMBIE, DOUGLASS DARNILL, govt. ofcl.; b. Alexandra, N.Z., Sept. 14, 1924; came to U.S., 1962, naturalized, 1967; s. Colin Lindsay and Ruth (Datnill) C.; m. Pa uline L.A. Morrison, Mar. 3, 1952. B.Sc., Otago U., Dunedin, N.Z., 1947, M.Sc., 1949. N.Z. nat. research fellow Cavendish Lab., Cambridge, Eng., 1958-59; head radio physics div. N.Z. Dept. Sci. and Industry Research, 1961-62; chief spectrum utilization div., chief low frequency group Inst. Telecommunications Scis., Dept. Commerce, Boulder, Colo., 1962-71, dir. inst., 1971-76; dir. Inst. Telecommunication Scis., Nat. Telecommunications and Info. Adminstrn., 1976-80; chief scientist Nat. Telecommunication and Info. Agy., 1980—. Served with N.Z. Air Force, 1943-44. Recipient Gold medal Dept. Commerce, 1970, citation, 1972. Mem. IEEE, Nat. Acad Engring., Union Radio Sci. Internat. Home: 1441 Mariposa Ave Boulder CO 80302 Office: 325 S Broadway Boulder CO 80302

CROMIE, ROBERT ALLEN, author, journalist; b. Detroit, Feb. 28, 1909; s. Robert and Annie Gertrude (Crosby) C.; m. Alice Hamilton, May 22, 1937; children—Michael, Richard, Barbara, James. A.B., Oberlin Coll., 1930, postgrad., 1931-33. Reporter Pontiac (Mich.) Daily Press, 1934-35; reporter Chgo. Tribune, 1936-42, war corr., 1942-46, news reporter, 1946-48, sportswriter, 1948-60, book editor, 1960-69, daily columnist, 1969-74. Host: syndicated Nat. Ednl. TV Book Beat, 1964—, Cromie Circle, WGN-TV, Chgo., 1969—; Author: The Great Chicago Fire, 1958, New Angles on Putting and Chip Shots, 1960, Dillinger, A Short and Violent Life, (with Joe Pinkston), 1962, Par for the Course; anthology, 1964, Golf for Boys and Girls, 1965, Where Steel Winds Blow; poetry anthology, 1968, Chicago in Color, (with Archie Lieberman), 1969, The Great Fire: Chicago 1871, (with Herman Kogan), 1971; Contbr.: other mags. Esquire. Recipient Peabody award for Book Beat, 1969; Irita Van Doren award Am. Booksellers Assn., 1968; named to Chgo. Press Club's Journalism Hall of Fame, 1980. Mem. Chgo. Hist. Soc., Soc. Midland Authors, Authors Guild, A.F.T.R.A., Friends of Lit. Clubs: Arts, Press (Chgo.). Office: care WTTW 5400 N Saint Louis Chicago IL 60625 *

CROMILLER, HAROLD LEE, retired banker, consultant; b. New Orleans, Nov. 3, 1920; s. Harold William and Nell (Lee) C.; m. Ellen Patricia Sutton, Oct. 3, 1953; children: Suzanne Marie, Cynthia Ann, Diane Patricia, Pamela Paige, Renee Magdelaine. Student, Tulane U., 1944; grad., Am. Inst. Banking, 1956. Certified internal auditor. With Hibernia Nat. Bank, New Orleans, from 1938, v.p., comptroller, 1966-72, sr. v.p., comptroller, 1972-73; treas., dir. Hibernia Bldg. Corp., 1966-73; comptroller First Met. Bank Metairie, La., 1973-75, sr. v.p., from 1973; now asst. to pres. Brinson Co., Inc., Haraham, La.; bank specialist Stonier Grad. Sch. Banking. Adv. bd.: Banking Mag. Mem. Am. Inst. Banking (pres. New Orleans 1961), Am. Bankers Assn. (ins. and protection div. exec. com.), Bank Adminstrn. Inst. (pres. New Orleans 1962), Fin. Execs. Inst., Assn. Internal Auditors (pres. New Orleans 1973). Clubs: Metairie (La.); Country. Home: 5016 Purdue Dr Metairie LA 70003 Office: 116 Laitram Ln Haraham LA

CROMLEY, ALLAN WRAY, journalist; b. Topeka, Apr. 11, 1922; s. Frank George and Elsie May (Leedom) C.; m. Marian Minor, Jan. 30, 1949; children: Kathleen, Janet, Carter. B.S. in Journalism (Summerfield scholar 1940-43, 46), U. Kans., 1948. Reporter Kansas City Kansan, 1948-49, Oklahoma City Times, 1949-53; Washington bur. chief Daily Oklahoman and Oklahoma City Times, 1953-77, Colorado Springs Sun, 1977—; dir. Nat. Pres. Bldg. Corp. Sec. standing com. corr. House and Senate Press Galleries, 1961; Bd. visitors U. Okla., 1970-72; trustee William Allen White Found., U. Kans., 1978—. Served as 1st lt. AUS, 1943-45; ETO. Mem. Sigma Delta Chi (dir. Washington chpt. 1984—), Omicron Delta Kappa. Clubs: Nat. Press (Washington) (gov. 1964-68, vice chmn. bd. 1966); Nat. Press (Washington) (v.p. 1967, pres. 1968); Nat. Gridiron (Washington) (v.p. 1977, pres. 1978); Nat. Gridiron (Washington) (treas. 1981). Home: 3320 Stoneybrae Dr Falls Church VA 22044 Office: Nat Press Bldg Washington DC 20045

CROMLEY, RAYMOND AVOLON, syndicated columnist; b. Tulare, Calif., Aug. 23, 1910; s. William James and Grace Violet (Bailey) C.; m. Masuyo Marjorie Suto (dec. Apr. 1946); m. Helen Sue Holcomb (dec. July 1967); children—Donald Stowe, Helen Sue Cromley Shisler, Jessica Lynn, Linda Grace, William Holcomb, Mary Ann, John Austin. B.S., Calif. Inst. Tech., 1933; student, Japanese Lang. Inst., Tokyo, 1936-39, Strategic Intelligence Sch., Washington, 1954. Reporter Pasadena (Calif.) Post, 1928-34, Honolulu Advertiser, 1934-35, Flintridge Sch., Pasadena, 1935-36; reporter, then financial editor Japan Advertiser, Tokyo, 1936-40; editor Trans Pacific (econ. and financial weekly), 1938-40; with Wall St. Jour., 1938-55; far Eastern corr., 1938-47, Washington corr., 1947-55; sci. editor radio program Monitor, 1955-56; econ. and financial commentator NBC radio, 1956-57; asst. producer CBS Radio, 1957-58; mil. analyst Newspaper Enterprise Assn., 1958-64; pres. Cromley News-Features, 1976—; syndicated columnist, 1964—; Asst. logic, freshman English Calif. Inst. Tech., 1928-30; lectr. Air War Coll., 1952, 54, Dept. State Fgn. Service Inst., 1955, 65-67; cons. guerilla war, Asian politics, 1952—. Author: Veterans Benefits, 1966, 2d edit., 1970, 3d edit., 1973, rev. edit., 1975, Educational Benefits, 1968. Chmn. dist. bds. charter rev. Boy Scouts Am., 1956-60; sec. bishop's com. pastoral benefits Va. Conf. Meth. Ch., 1967-68; organizer com. establishment Martha Washington Library, Mt. Vernon, Va., 1954; chmn. Inter-ch. Council Teen Activities and Teen Clubs, Mt. Vernon, 1955-57, World Council Youth, 1932-35. Served to col. AUS, 1943-46; comdg. officer U.S. Mil. and Dept. State Mission to Mao Tse-tung's hdqrs., 1944-45; Yenan) Communist China. Decorated Legion of Merit, Bronze Star medal. Mem. Nat. Trust for Historic Preservation, Asiatic Soc. Japan, State Dept. Corrs. Assn. (pres. 1954-55), White House Corrs. Assn., Ret. Officers Assn., Smithsonian Assos., Nat. Archives Assn., Am. Fgn. Service Assn., Assn. Corcoran Gallery Art, Sigma Delta Chi, Pi Kappa Delta. Republican. Methodist (lay speaker, Sunday sch. tchr.). Clubs: Tokyo Correspondents (exec. com. 1947); Overseas Writers (Washington). Imprisoned by Japanese, 1941-42. Home: 1912 Martha's Rd Hollin Hills Alexandria VA 22307 Office: 12th Floor Wyatt Bldg 777 14th St NW Washington DC 20005

CROMPTON, LOUIS WILLIAM, educator; b. Port Colborne, Ont., Can., Apr. 5, 1925; came to U.S., 1955, naturalized, 1961; s. Clarence Lee and Mabel Elsie (Weber) C. B.A., U. Toronto, 1947, M.A., 1948; A.M., U. Chgo., 1950, Ph.D., 1954. Lectr. math. U. B.C., 1948-49; lectr. English U. Toronto, 1953-55; asst. prof. U. Nebr., 1955-60, asso. prof., 1960-64, prof. English, 1964—; vis. asst. prof. U. Chgo., 1959, U. Calif., Berkeley, 1961. Mem. editorial bd.: Shaw Rev, 1970—; editor: Shaw Series in Bobbs-Merrill Library of Lit. Shaw the Dramatist, 1969, Great Expectations (Dickens), 1964, Arms and the Man (Shaw), 1969, The Road to Equality (Shaw), 1971, The Great Composers (Shaw), 1978; editorial bd. series on homosexuality in lit., Arno Press, 1975, Jour. Homosexuality, 1977—. Recipient Christian Gauss award in lit. criticism Phi Beta Kappa, 1969. Home: 5840 Locust St Lincoln NE 68516

CROMWELL, EDWIN BOYKIN, architect; b. Manila, P.I., Nov. 13, 1909; s. James Ellis and Ada (Henley) C.; m. Henrietta Thompson, May 22, 1937; children: Gertrude Cromwell Levy, Mildred Cromwell Cooper, Patricia Ellis. A.B., Princeton U., 1931, postgrad., 1931-32. Archtl. planner Resettlement Adminstrn., Washington and Ark., 1935-36; chmn. emeritus Cromwell Truemper Levy Parker & Woodsmall, Little Rock, 1941—; pres. Historic Ventures, Inc. Projects include U. Ark. at Little Rock, Ark. Arts Center, Little Rock, Master Plan Ark. State Capitol, Ark. Children's Colony, Winrock Farms, Morrilton, Ark., Consul Gen. resident, Madras, India, Embassy Housing, New Delhi, Maumelle New Town, U. Ark., Little Rock; restoration of residential bldgs. Quapaw Quarter and historic Capital Hotel, Little Rock. Mem. Ark. Sesquicentennial Commn., 1967-70; advisor Nat. Trust for Historic Preservation, 1974-80; dir. Lighthouse for Blind, 1966—; trustee U. of South, Princeton Alumni Council, Ark. Arts Center; mem. Ark. Territorial Restoration Commn.; mem. adv. council U. Ark.-Little Rock, 1978—. Fellow AIA. Episcopalian. Home: 1720 Beechwood Rd Little Rock AR 72207 Office: 101 Spring St Little Rock AR 72201

CROMWELL, FLORENCE STEVENS, educator; b. Lewistown, Pa., May 14, 1922; d. William Andrew and Florence (Stevens) C. B.S. in Edn. (Kappa Kappa Gamma scholar), Miami U., 1943, Washington U., St. Louis, 1949; M.A., U. So. Calif., 1952; certificate in Health Facility Adminstrn, UCLA, 1978. Mem. staff, then supervising therapist Los Angeles County Gen. Hosp., 1949-53; occupational therapist Goodwill Industries, Los Angeles, 1954-55; staff therapist Vis. Nurse Assn., Phila., 1955-56; research therapist United Cerebral Palsy Assn., Los Angeles, 1956-60; dir. occupational therapy Orthopaedic Hosp., Los Angeles, 1961-67; part-time instr., cons. U. So. Calif. (occupational therapy dept.), 1952-53, 58-60, 65-67, asso. prof., 1970-76, acting chmn. dept., 1973-76; occupational coordinator Research and Tng. Center, 1967-70; mem. adv. bd. Project SEARCH, Sch. Medicine, 1969-72; asso. dir. Los Angeles Job Corps Center, 1977-78, cons. in edn. and program devel., 1976—. Author: Manual for Basic Skills Assessment, 1960; editor: Occupational Therapy in Health Care, 1984—; also articles. Mem. scholarship com. Los Angeles March of Dimes, 1963-70; Bd. dirs. Am. Occupational Therapy Found., 1965-69, v.p., 1966-69; bd. dirs. Nat. Health Council, 1975-78. Served to lt. (j.g.) WAVES, 1943-46. Recipient Disting. Alumni award Washington U., 1978. Fellow Am. Occupational Therapy Assn. (pres. 1967-73); mem. Inst. Medicine of Nat. Acad. Scis., So. Calif. Occupational Therapy Assn. (pres. 1950-51), Coalition Ind. Health Professions (chmn. 1973-74), Assn. Schs. Allied Health Professions (dir. 1973-74), World Fedn. Occupational Therapists, Cwen, Mortar Bd., Kappa Delta Pi, Kappa Kappa Gamma. Home: 1179 Yocum St Pasadena CA 91103

CROMWELL, LESLIE, educator, electrical engineer; b. Manchester, Eng., Apr. 2, 1924; came to U.S., 1948, naturalized, 1954; s. Bernard and Lily (Robinson) C.; m. Pamela Goddard, 1944 (div. 1956); children—Russell Norman, Martin Frank, Carol Anne; m. Irina Malkin, June 2, 1956. B.Sc. Tech. in Elec. Engring, U. Manchester, 1943, M.Sc. Tech., 1961; M.S., U. Calif. at Los Angeles, 1951, Ph.D., 1967. Registered profl. elec. engr., Calif. Research engr. Salford Elec. Instruments, Heywood, Eng., 1943-44; aircraft elec. design engr. English Electric Co., Bradford, Eng., 1944-46; elec. engr., mgr. B. Cromwell & Co., Ltd., Manchester, 1946-48; lectr. engring. U. Calif. at Los Angeles, 1948-53, cons., 1961—; asst. prof. engring. Calif. State U., Los Angeles, 1953-56, acting head engring. dept., asso. prof., 1956-57, head engring. dept., 1957-64, prof., 1957—, chmn. interdisciplinary engring. dept., 1968-73, dean engring., 1973-80; cons. Gray & Huleguard, Inc., Los Angeles, 1954-57, Port Hueneme, Calif., 1957-58, Pacific Telephone, 1959, 61—. Author: textbooks Basic Electric Circuits, 1957, Biomedical Instrumentation and Measurements, 2d edit, 1980, Medical Instrumentation for Health Care, 1976; co-author: Social Consequences of Engineering, 1979. Research asso. Cedars-Sinai Med. Research Inst.; v.p. Los Angeles Council Engrs. and Scientists, 1976-77; pres. Inst. Advancement Engring., 1977-78; Mem. engring. liaison com. State Calif., 1959-63, 75-78. NSF sci. faculty fellow, 1965-68; recipient Distinguished Service award U.S. Jr. C. of C., 1961; Eminent engineer Tau Beta Pi, 1968; Distinguished Prof. award Calif. State Coll., 1968. Mem. Am. Soc. E.E. (vice chmn. Pacific S.W. sect. 1959-60), IEEE (sr., chmn. Los Angeles group, engring. in medicine and biology 1968-69, chmn. region 6 council 1970-72), Blue Key, Phi Kappa Phi, Eta Kappa Nu. Clubs: Optimist (pres. 1955-56, v.p. 1959-60), Optimist (pres. 1965-66), Optimist (zone lt. gov. 1966-67), Optimist (dist. leadership tng. chmn. 1968-69), Optimist (dist. awards chmn. 1970-71). Home: 27661 Via Guanados Mission Viejo CA 92692 *I believe that success is due to an optimistic attitude towards life's goals wherein mistakes and misfortunes are not allowed to detract from the greater achievements of the future.*

CROMWELL, NOLAN NEIL, professional football player; b. Smith Center, Kans., Jan. 30, 1955; m. Ellen Cromwell. Ed., U. Kans. Safety Los Angeles Rams, NFL, 1977—. Player NFL Pro Bowl, 1980-82, NFL Championship Game, 1979. Address: care Los Angeles Rams 2327 W Lincoln Ave Anaheim CA 92801 *

CROMWELL, NORMAN HENRY, chemist, educator; b. Terre Haute, Ind., Nov. 22, 1913; s. Henry and Ethel Lee (Harkelroad) C.; m. Grace N. Newell, Jan. 29, 1955; children: Christopher Newell, Richard Earl. B.S. with honors (Rea scholar 1932-35), Rose-Hulman Inst., 1935; Ph.D., U. Minn., 1939. Teaching asst. U. Minn., 1935-39; instr. organic chemistry U. Nebr., Lincoln, 1939-42, asst. prof., 1942-45, assoc. prof., 1945-48, prof., 1948—, Howard S. Wilson regents prof., 1960-70, chmn. dept. chemistry, 1964-70, exec. dean for grad. studies and research, 1970-72, v.p., dean, 1972-73, Regents prof. chemistry Grad. Coll., 1973—; interim dir. Eppley Inst. for Cancer Research, Med. Center, Omaha, 1979-80, dir., 1981-83; guest dept. chemistry MIT, 1967; hon. research asso. Univ. Coll., London, 1950-51, 58-59; hon. research assoc. Calif. Inst. Tech., 1958; Am. Chem. Soc. tour lectr., 1952-70; frontiers of chemistry lectr. Wayne State U., 1958; research lectr. U. Coll., Dublin, Ireland, 1958; vis. prof. U. Calif. Med. Center, 1961; Gordon Research Conf. lectr., 1961, conf. discussion leader, 1970, 77; Hungarian Chem. Soc. lectr., 1962, Sigma

Xi nat. lectr., 1964; Keynote speaker Nat. Com. Adminstrn. Research Conf., 1970; cons. Parke Davis & Co., 1943-46, Smith, Kline & French Labs., 1946-51, Am. Cancer Soc., 1956-58, Philip Morris, Inc., 1964-79, USPHS, 1952-64, chmn. medicinal chem. study sect., 1960-64; Nat. Cancer Inst., 1964-70; pres. 2d Internat. Congress Heterocyclic Chemistry, Montpellier, France, 1969; plenary lectr. 5th Internat. Congress, Ljubljana, Yugoslavia, 1975; U.S.-India exchange scientist, 1977; dir. coop. coll. tchr. devel. program for Nebr. NSF, 1960-63. Asst. editor: Jour. Heterocyclic Chemistry, 1967—; Contbr. articles to research publs. Mem. bd. Lincoln Bryan Hosp. Fulbright advanced research scholar, 1950-51; Guggenheim Meml. fellow, 1950, 58; recipient Outstanding Alumnus Achievement award U. Minn., 1975; Outstanding Research and Creativity award U. Nebr., 1978. Mem. Am. Chem. Soc. (plenary lectr. nat. meeting 1983), Chem. Soc. London, Nebr. Art Assn. (trustee 1958—, v.p. 1971), Sigma Xi, Phi Lambda Upsilon, Sigma Tau, Gamma Alpha, Tau Nu Tau, Alpha Chi Sigma, Alpha Tau Omega. Home: 6600 Shamrock Rd Lincoln NE 68506 Office: Dept Chemistry U Nebr Lincoln NE 68588

CROMWELL, RUE LEVELLE, clinical psychologist, educator; b. Linton, Ind., Nov. 17, 1928; s. George Harrison and Mary Iona (Taylor) C.; m. Evelyn Florence Steiner, Aug. 26, 1950; children: Donna Lisa, Lita Lorraine Cromwell Ferdinand, Joseph Dean, Lincoln Harrison. A.B., Ind. U., 1950; M.A., Ohio State U., 1952, Ph.D., 1955. Asst. instr. psychology Ohio State U., Columbus, 1954-55; mem. faculty George Peabody Coll., Nashville, 1955-63; prof. Vanderbilt U., Nashville, 1963-69; chief psychology div. Lafayette Clinic; prof. Wayne State U., Detroit, 1969-72, U. Rochester, N.Y., 1972—. Served as 2d lt. USAF, 1950. Fellow Am. Psychol. Assn. Home: 56 Clintwood Court D Rochester NY 14620 Office: Dept Psychiatry U Rochester Rochester NY 14642

CRONBACH, LEE JOSEPH, educator, psychologist; b. Fresno, Calif., Apr. 22, 1916; s. Emil George and Cora Mae (Wise) C.; m. Helen Claresta Bower, Dec. 31, 1938; children: Richard, Barbara (dec.), Robert, Joyce, Janet. A.B., Fresno State Coll., 1934; M.A., U. Calif. at Berkeley, 1937; Ph.D., U. Chgo., 1940; L.H.D. (hon.), Yeshiva U., 1967, U. Chgo., 1979, U. Ill., 1982; Ph.D. (hon.), U. Gothenburg, 1977. Tchr. high sch., Fresno, 1936-38; from instr. to asso. prof. State Coll. Wash., 1940-46; asso. psychologist U. Cal. Div. War Research, 1944-45; asst. prof. U. Chgo., 1946-48; asso. prof., then prof. edn., psychology U. Ill., 1948-64; prof. edn. Stanford U., 1964-66, Vida Jacks prof. edn., 1966-80, emeritus, 1980—; mem. Inst. for Advanced Study, Princeton, 1960-61; sci. liaison officer Office Naval Research, London, 1955-56; fellow Center for Advanced Study in Behavioral Scis., Stanford, Calif., 1963-64; Fulbright lectr. U. Tokyo, 1967-68. Author: Essentials of Psychological Testing, 1949, 4th edit., 1983, Educational Psychology, 1954, 3d edit., 1977, Designing Evaluations, 1982, (with Goldine C. Gleser) Psychological Tests and Personnel Decisions, 2d edit, 1965, (with Patrick C. Suppes) Research for Tomorrow's Schools, 1969, (with others) Dependability of Behavioral Measurements, 1972, Toward Reform of Educational Evaluation, 1980, (with Richard E. Snow) Aptitudes and Instructional Methods, 1977; Editor: (with Drenth) Mental Tests and Cultural Adaptation, 1972. Trustee Am. Psychol. Found., 1956-63, pres., 1961-63. Guggenheim fellow, 1971-72; recipient award Ednl. Testing Service, 1971, Tchrs. Coll., Columbia, 1975, Evaluation Research Soc., 1979. Fellow Am. Psychol. Assn. (pres. 1956-57, distinguished sci. contbn. award 1973); mem. Am. Ednl. Research Assn. (pres. 1964-65, distinguished contbn. award 1977), Social Sci. Research Council (chmn. com. learning and edn. process 1962-66, dir. 1964-71), Psychometric Soc. (pres. 1953-54), Nat. Acad. Sci. (mem. com. ability testing 1978-81, mem. com. sci. and public policy 1978-81), Am. Philos. Soc., Am. Acad. Arts and Scis., Nat. Acad. Edn., Sigma Xi, Phi Delta Kappa, Pi Kappa Phi. Home: 16 Laburnum Atherton CA 94025 Office: Stanford U Stanford CA 94305

CRONBACH, ROBERT M., sculptor; b. St. Louis, Feb. 10, 1908; s. Lee and Ruby (Lowenhaupt) C.; m. Maxine Judd Silver, Oct. 12, 1934; children: Paula, Michael Theodore, Lee. Student, St. Louis Sch. Fine Arts, 1925-26, Pa. Acad. Fine Arts, 1927-30; European travel, Cresson scholarship, 1929-30. Exhibited sculpture, Mus. Modern Art, N.Y. C., Nat. Inst. Arts and Letters, Bertha Schaefer Gallery, Whitney Mus., Phila. and, St. Louis art mus., other mus., galleries, one man shows, Bertha Schaefer Galleries, N.Y., 1956, 67, 70, 74; exhbn. group show, Hemisfair, San Antonio, 1968; sculptor decorations lime stone, St. Louis Municipal Auditorium, 1932, tamped concrete decorations, Willerts Park Housing Project, Buffalo, 1939, two bronze statues, Social Security Bldg., Washington, 1940, 120 foot bronze screen, Dorr-Oliver Bldg., Stamford, and bronze wall sculpture for, UN Gen. Assembly Bldg., 1960, Reynolds Metal Corp. Ann. Award Trophy, 1961; Fifteen-foot fountain, St. Louis Fed. Bldg., 1963, fountain for plaza, Charleston (W.Va.) Pub. Library, 1967, Stainless Steel Sculpture, L.I. Assn. Hall of Fame, 1972, sculpture, Fashion Inst. Tech., N.Y.C., 1976, sculpture fountain, James Madison Meml. Library, Library of Congress, Washington, 1973-79, 13 foot outdoor hwy. sculpture, East Hills, N.Y., 1981, decorations pub. and pvt. bldgs., fountains. Mem. Nat. Council on Arts and Govt.; Chmn. bd. govs. Skowhegan Sch. Painting and Sculpture., until 1982. Served with Mcht. Marine, World War II. Mem. Sculptors Guild, Inc., Fedn. Modern Painters and Sculptors, Century Assn. Address: 420 E 86th St New York NY 10028

CRONE, JOHN PORTER, financial consultant; b. Belfast, Northern Ireland; s. Robert and Anna Frances (Porter) C.; m. Christine Evans, Apr. 3, 1954; children: Judith, Michael, Jennifer, Jacqueline, Wendy. Ed., Royal Belfast Acad. Instn., 1942-47; F.C.A., Belfast Coll. Tech., 1951. Mng. dir. Home Oil (U.K.) Ltd., London, 1972-75; v.p. internat. ops., 1975-77, group v.p., Calgary, Alta., Can., 1977-80; pres. Quintet Resources, Ltd., Calgary, 1980—; dir. Can. N.W. Land Ltd., San Antonio Expln. Ltd., Atlantic Energy Corp. Fellow Inst. Chartered Accts. Ireland; mem. Inst. Chartered Accts. Alta. Clubs: Ranchmen's, Calgary Petroleum (Calgary); Uplands Golf (Victoria). Home: 5025 Locke Haven Dr Victoria BC V8N 4J6 Canada Office: 2800 One Calgary Pl Calgary AB T2P 0L4 Canada

CRONE, RICHARD IRVING, physician, ret. army officer; b. Salt Lake City, June 6, 1909; s. Maurice B. and Mildred (Rheinstrom) C.; m. Alla M. Ernst, Mar. 26, 1946; children—Richard A., William E. Student, U. Calif. at Los Angeles, 1927-30; A.B., U. Calif. at San Francisco, 1931, M.D., 1935. Diplomate: Am. Bd. Internal Medicine. Rotating intern Alameda County Hosp., Oakland, Calif., 1934-35; med. resident U. Calif. Hosp., San Francisco, 1935-36, surg. resident, 1937-38; practice medicine specializing in internal medicine, San Francisco, 1936-37; clin. instr. medicine U. Calif. Med. Sch., 1936-37; commd. 1st lt. M.C. U.S. Army, advanced through grades to brig. gen., 1965; contract surgeon Letterman Gen. Hosp., San Francisco, 1939; resident internal medicine Madigan Gen. Hosp., Tacoma, 1947-48, asst. chief med. service, 1948-49, chief dept. medicine, 1961-63, chief dept. medicine, dir. med. edn., 1962-63, comdg. gen., 1965-69; chief med. service 130th Sta. Hosp., Heidelberg, Germany, 1949-51, 51-52, comdg. officer, 1951; med. cons. Hdqrs. U.S. Army in Europe, Heidelberg, 1952-53, 58-61; asst. chief dept. medicine, asst. dir. med. edn. Letterman Gen. Hosp., San Francisco, 1953-56, chief dept. medicine, asst. dir. med. edn., 1956-57; chief med. service, chief profl. services, dir. med. edn. 2d Gen. Hosp., Landstuhl, Germany, 1957-58; chief dept. medicine, cons. to surgeon gen. on internal medicine Walter Reed Gen. Hosp., Washington, 1963-65, ret., 1969; dir. edn. Group Health Coop., Puget Sound, 1969-71; med. cons. State of Calif. Dept. Health, 1972-79. Decorated D.S.M., Legion of Merit with oak leaf cluster, Bronze Star medal, Air medal; Order Yun Hui Nationalist China). Fellow A.C.P.; mem. Tacoma Acad. Internal Medicine (hon.), Phi Beta Pi. Home: 141 Oak Shadow Dr Santa Rosa CA 95405

CRONEBERGER, ROBERT BRUCE, JR., librarian; b. Pottsville, Pa., Jan. 19, 1937; s. Robert Bruce and Ethel Elizabeth (Palmer) C.; m. Carolyn Ann Luck, Jan. 18, 1975; children by previous marriage: Lynn, Marie, Robert Bruce. B.A., Lehigh U., 1958; M.A., U. Pa., 1961; M.L.S., Drexel U., 1962. With Library of Congress, Washington, 1962-69; dep. dir. Detroit Pub. Library, 1969-75, Shelby County Pub. Library and Info. Ctr., 1975-80, dir., 1980—; cons. Info. and Referral, Memphis, 1975—. Pres. Leadership Memphis Alumni Assn., 1983—; chmn. Nat. Commn on Libraries and Info. Sci., Washington, 1980-83; edn. chmn. Memphis Jobs Conf., 1983; div. chmn. United Way of Greater Memphis, 1983; bd. dirs. Memphis Literacy Council, 1980-83. Recipient Dean's Service Lehigh U., 1958, Meritorious Service Library of Congress, 1965. Mem. ALA, Tenn. Library Assn., Southeastern Library Assn., Alliance of Info. Referral Service, Phi Beta Kappa. Democrat. Home: 1945 Cowden St Memphis TN 38104 Office: 1850 Peabody Ave Memphis TN 38104

CRONEMILLER, PHILIP DOUGLAS, physician; b. Altoona, Pa., Aug. 19, 1918; s. Carl Frederich and Marion (Smith) C.; m. Virginia Sones, Nov. 9, 1942; children: Pamela Joan, Philip Douglas, Suzanne Virginia, David Erich. B.S., Juniata Coll., 1939; M.D., U. Pa., 1943. Diplomate: Am. Bd. Surgery. Intern U.S. Naval Hosp., Phila., 1943-44, resident in surgery, 1946-48, staff surgeon, 1952-54, Guantanamo Bay, Cuba, 1949-51, Jacksonville, Fla., 1954, San Diego, 1958-61, chief surgery, dir. research, 1961-63; practice medicine specializing in surgery, Arcadia, Calif., 1963—; attending surgeon Los Angeles County Hosp., City Hope Nat. Med. Center; assoc. clin. prof. surgery U. So. Calif., 1963-77, clin. prof., 1977—. Contbr. articles to profl. jours. Active various community activities. Served to capt. M.C. USN, 1943-63. Fellow ACS, Pan Am. Med. Assn.; mem. Los Angeles County Med. Assn., AMA, Calif. Med. Assn., Los Angeles Surg. Soc., Royal Soc. Medicine (London), San Diego Soc. Gen. Surgeon (hon.). Republican. Methodist. Club: Masons. Home: 217 Sharon Rd Arcadia CA 91006 Office: 1108 S Baldwin St Arcadia CA 91006

CRONENWORTH, CHARLES DOUGLAS, manufacturing company executive; b. Mohawk, Mich., Aug. 7, 1921; s. Jacob and Margaret (Therien) C.; m. Lorraine Evelyn DeBruyne, May 18, 1946; children: Carol, Linda, Mary, Charles. B.S. in Mech. Engring., Mich. Tech. U., 1944. Registered profl. engr., Mich. Design engr. Chrysler Corp., Detroit, 1946-47; project engr. Gen. Foods, St. Clair, Mich., 1947-50; plant mgr. Diamond Crystal Salt Co., St. Clair, Mich., 1950-68, gen. mgr. prodn., 1968-75, pres., chief exec. officer, 1975—; dir. Comml. & Savs. Bank, St. Clair, Maritek Corp., Corpus Christy, Tex., Worldwide Protein Bahamas, Nassau. Mem. chmn. Mich. Mineral Well Adv., Lansing, Mich., 1970-78; major City of St. Clair, 1962-63, councilman, 1955-58. Recipient Silver medal Mich. Tech. U., 1976. Mem. Mich. Soc. Profl. Engrs. (alt. dir. 1958-62), Nat. Soc. Profl. Engrs., Nat. Assn. Mfrs. (dir. 1980—). Republican. Roman Catholic. Lodges: Rotary Internat. (St. Clair pres. 1979-80, St. Clair dir. 1976-82). Home: 129 E Meldrum Circle St. Clair MI 48079 Office: Diamond Crystal Salt Co 916 S Riverside St Clair MI 48079

CRONER, RICHARD, banker, farmer; b. Berlin, Pa., Apr. 3, 1919; s. Joe and Erma C.; m. Helen Schmucker, Jan. 4, 1941; 1 son, Tommy. B.S., Pa. State U., 1940. Engaged in farming, Berlin, 1940—; pres. Philson Nat. Bank, Berlin, 1971—, T. Rich Inc., 1979—; past chmn. bd. Curtice-Burns Inc., Rochester, N.Y., now dir.; chmn. bd. Agway Inc., Syracuse, N.Y., 1980—, dir., 1957—, Pro-Fac Coop, Rochester, Telmark Inc., Agway Ins., Curlice Burns. Mem. Gamma Sigma Delta. Mem. United Ch. Christ. Club: Lions. Address: 310 Dimond St Berlin PA 15530

CRONIN, BONNIE KATHRYN LAMB, state official; b. Mpls., Mar. 11, 1941; d. Edwin Rector and Maude Kathryn (MacPherson) Lamb; m. Barry Jay Cronin, Jan. 23, 1963 (div. Feb. 1972); 1 son, Philip Scott. B.A., U. Mo., 1963, B.S., 1964; M.S., Ill. State U., 1970. Copywriter Neds & Wardlow Advt., Columbia, Mo., 1962-64; tchr. Columbia Sch. System, 1964-68, Normal (Ill.) Sch. System, 1968-69; asst. gen. mgr. WGLT, Normal, 1969-70; dir. devel. Radio Sta. WBUR, Boston, 1970-71, program dir., 1971-75, gen. mgr., 1975-78; dir. public relations Joy of Movement Center, 1978-80; dep. scheduler Anderson for Pres., 1980; scheduler Spaulding for Gov., 1980-81; dir. scheduling John Kerry Campaign, 1982; dir. of scheduling Conn. Lt. Gov.'s Office, dir. ops., 1983-84; dep. campaign mgr. Kerry for Senate Com. Mem. NOW, Nat. Pub. Radio (dir. 1974-77, chairperson devel. com.), Mass. Broadcasters Assn. (dir. 1973-78, chairperson scholarship com., pub. service com., adminstrv. oversight com.). Office: 5 Doane St 6th Floor Boston MA 02109

CRONIN, DANIEL ANTHONY, bishop; b. Newton, Mass., Nov. 14, 1927; s. Daniel George and Emily Frances (Joyce) C. S.T.L., Gregorian U., 1953, S.T.D. summa cum laude, 1956; LL.D., Suffolk U., Boston, 1969, Stonehill Coll., North Easton, 1971. Ordained priest Roman Catholic Ch., 1952; attache Apostolic Internunicature, Addis Ababa, Ethiopia, 1957-61, Secretariat of State, Vatican City, 1961-68; named Monsignor by His Holiness Pope John XXIII, 1962; named titular bishop of Egnatia and aux. bishop of Boston, 1968; Episcopal ordination from Richard Cardinal Cushing (archbishop of Boston), 1968; pastor St. Raphael Ch., Medford, Mass., 1968-70; bishop of, Fall River, Mass., 1970—. Club: K.C. (4). Address: 47 Underwood St PO Box 2577 Fall River MA 02722

CRONIN, GILBERT FRANCIS, insurance company executive; b. Rosetown, Sask., Can., Feb. 16, 1923; came to U.S., 1925, naturalized, 1943; s. Michael E. and Mary A. (Dawson) C.; m. Dorothy M. Fahey, Feb. 5, 1949; children: Michael, Timothy, Patricia, Vincent. A.B., Loyola U., Los Angeles, 1947. With Sears Roebuck and Co., Los Angeles, 1947-48, Prudential Ins. Co. Am., 1948-53, Scott-Hindenach Cons., Los Angeles, 1953-54; with Occidental Life Ins. Co. of Calif., Los Angeles, 1954—; now sr. v.p.; pres., chief exec. officer Transamerica Life Ins. and Annuity Co., Los Angeles, 1977—; dir. TransLife & Annuity Co., Transam. Occidental Life Ins. Co., Transam. Fin. Services. Trustee Southwestern U. Sch. Law. Served with inf. U.S. Army, 1943-46, 50-52. Decorated Silver Star, Bronze Star. Mem. Western Pension Conf. (past pres. Los Angeles chpt.), Am. Council Life Ins., Internat. Found. of Health, Welfare and Pension Plans, Assn. Pvt. Pension and Welfare Plans. Republican. Roman Catholic. Office: Transamerica Life Ins and Annuity Co 1150 S Olive St Los Angeles CA 90015

CRONIN, JAMES WATSON, educator, physicist; b. Chgo., Sept. 29, 1931; s. James Farley and Dorothy (Watson) C.; m. Annette Martin, Sept. 11, 1954; children: Cathryn, Emily, Daniel Watson. A.B., So. Methodist U., (1951); Ph.D., U. Chgo., 1955. Asso. Brookhaven Nat. Lab., 1955-58; mem. faculty Princeton, 1958-71, prof. physics, 1965-71, U. Chgo., 1971—; Loeb lectr. physics Harvard U., 1967. Recipient Research Corp. Am. award, 1967; John Price Wetherill medal Franklin Inst., 1976; E.O. Lawrence award ERDA, 1977; Nobel prize for physics, 1980; Sloan fellow, 1964-66; Guggenheim fellow, 1970-71, 82-83. Mem. Am. Acad. Arts and Scis., Nat. Acad. Sci. Participant early devel. spark chambers; co-discover CP-violation, 1964. Home: 5825 S Dorchester St Chicago IL 60637

CRONIN, JEREMIAH PATRICK, financial executive; b. N.Y.C., Dec. 29, 1943; s. Patrick C. and Nora Mullin Cronin; m. Jane M. Antonaccio, Oct. 2, 1966; children: Jeffrey, Brian. B.B.A., Iona Coll., New Rochelle, N.Y., 1965; M.B.A., Columbia U., 1966. Budget mgr. Merck & Co. Inc., Rahway, N.J., 1966-70; sr. v.p. fin. Research-Cottrell Inc., Somerville, N.J., 1970—. Mem. Fin. Execs. Inst. Roman Catholic. Office: Research-Cottrell Inc PO Box 1500 Somerville NJ 08876

CRONIN, JOSEPH, baseball executive; b. San Francisco, Oct. 12, 1906; s. Jeremiah and Mary (Carolin) C.; m. Mildred June Robertson, Sept. 1934; 3 sons, 1 dau. Grad. high sch. Profl. baseball player in Am. League, 1928; mgr. Washington Senators, 1933-34, Boston Red Sox, 1935-47, gen. mgr. of club, 1948-58; past pres. Am. League Profl. Baseball Clubs, from 1958, now chmn. Co-founder, dir. Mass. Com. Catholics, Protestants and Jews. Named to Baseball Hall Fame, 1956; Knight of Malta. Club: Variety (recipient Great Heart award for work in Jimmy Fund, Boston). Winner Am. League pennant, 1933, 46. Office: 280 Park Ave New York NY 10017

CRONIN, PAUL WILLIAM, energy company executive, former congressman; b. Boston, Mar. 14, 1938; s. William Joseph and Anna (Murphy) C.; m. Kathleen Sears, 1957; children—Kevin P., Kimberley A. Student, Merrimack Coll., Andover, Mass., 1956-58; B.A. in Govt. and Econs, Boston U., 1962; M.P.A., Harvard U., 1969. Chief asst. to Congressman F. Bradford Morse, 1963-67; mem. 93d Congress from Mass.; mem. com. sci. and astronautics, interior and insular affairs subcoms. on energy, sci. and tech., mines, nat. parks; founder, pres., chief exec. officer Sunsav Inc. (mfrs. solar energy systems); a founder Solar Rating and Cert. Corp., 1980; chmn. Highline Products Corp., Old Saybrook, Conn., Polycrete Products Corp.; mem. adv. bd. Solar Energy Research Inst. and Western Sun; nat. pres. Solar Energy Industries Assn.; trustee Solar Energy Research Found.; mem. Internat. Energy Conf., Paris, France, 1976; del. UN Conf. on New and Renewable Sources of Energy, Nairobi, Kenya, 1981. Pres., exec. com., precinct capt. Andover Republican Town Com., 1960; del. Rep. State Convs., 1962, 64, 66, 70, 74, 78, Rep. Nat. Conv., 1968, 72, 76; N.E. regional dir. Rep. Congressional Campaign Com., 1969-70; selectman, Town of Andover, 1963-66; mem. Mass. Ho. of Reps., 1967-69; chmn. Mass. Multiple Sclerosis Soc., Bon Secours Hosp. Guild, Men of Merrimack Coll.; mem. Info. Seminar for Am. Opinion Leaders, Hamburg and Berlin, W.Ger., 1983. Recipient Outstanding Young Man award Jr. C. of C., 1964, Fgn. Policy Assn.; Future Leader award; Paul Revere Leadership medal; Young Rep. Outstanding Citizen award; DAV Distinguished Service award; VFW Silver Star for involvement with a rescue.; named to Hall of Fame Lawrence Boys' Club, 1982. Mem. Mass. Selectmans Assn. (life), Mass. Legis. Assn. (life), Nat. Assn. State Legislators, Solar Energy Industries Assn. (pres.); mem. Former Mems. Congress (life). Clubs: K.C., Hibernians. Home: 8 Punchard Ave Andover MA 01810 Office: 640 S Union St Lawrence MA 01843

CRONIN, PHILIP MARK, lawyer; b. Boston, July 21, 1932; s. Herbert Joseph and Elizabeth Ann (Sullivan) C.; m. Paula Cook Budlong, June 8, 1957; children—Thomas B., Philip S. A.B., Harvard U., 1953, LL.B., 1956. Bar: Mass. bar 1956. Sr. partner firm Withington, Cross, Park & Groden, Boston, 1956—; pres., pub. Harvard mag., 1971-78; city solicitor, Cambridge, Mass., 1968-72. Mng. editor: Mass. Law Rev, 1976-81; editor-in-chief, 1981—. Home: 3 Lincoln Ln Cambridge MA 02138 Office: 73 Tremont St Boston MA 02108

CRONIN, RAYMOND VALENTINE, financial executive; b. Yonkers, N.Y., Feb. 17, 1924; s. Raymond Valentine and Virginia Dolores (Lee) C.; m. Gwendoline Mary Tigar, Sept. 21, 1957; children: Kevin, Peter, Brian, Tracie, Courtney. B.S., NYU, 1949, postgrad., 1949-52. Asst. to comptroller Alexander Smith, Inc., Yonkers, 1949-54; comptroller E.R. Squibb & Son, N.Y.C., 1954-60; v.p. Penick & Ford, Ltd., Cedar Rapids, Iowa, 1960-65, pres., 1965-70; v.p. St. Joe Minerals Corp., N.Y.C., 1971-81; v.p. fin. Miseiricordia Hosp., N.Y.C., 1981-82, YMCA Greater N.Y., 1982—. Republican. Roman Catholic. Clubs: Metropolitan, Canadian, Elks. Home: 5 Whippoorwill Rd Chappaqua NY 10514 also 9 Ancona Ave Ocean Park ME 04063

CRONIN, ROBERT FRANCIS PATRICK, physician, educator; b. London, Eng., Sept. 1, 1926; s. Archibald Joseph and Agnes Mary (Gibson) C.; m. Shirley-Gian Robertson, June 19, 1954; children: David Robert, Diana Christine, Daphne Gian. Student, Princeton U., 1943-44, 46-49; M.D., McGill U., 1954, M.Sc., 1960. Intern Montreal Gen. Hosp., 1953-54; resident Royal Postgrad. Hosp., London, 1954-56; practice medicine, Montreal, 1958-80; prof. medicine, dean Faculty Medicine, McGill U., 1972-77; med. cons. Aga Khan Found., 1980—; sr. physician Montreal Gen. Hosp.; cons. physician Dept. Vets. Affairs. Contbr. articles to profl. jours. Served with RCAF and Brit. Army, 1944-46. Fellow Royal Coll. Physicians London, Royal Coll. Physicians and Surgeons (Can.), A.C.P. Clubs: University (Montreal); Lausanne Golf. Home: En Champ Riond 1815 Baugy Montreux Switzerland

CRONIN, ROBERT LAWRENCE, sculptor, painter; b. Lexington, Mass., Aug. 10, 1936; s. Daniel Augustus and Eileen Ursula (Keating) C.; m. Constance Marie Nelson, June 27, 1964 (div. 1974). B.F.A., R.I. Sch. Design, 1959; M.F.A., Cornell U., 1962. Tchr. Mich. State U., East Lansing, 1965-66, Bennington(Vt.) Coll., 1967-68, Brown U., Providence, 1969-71; tchrs. Sch. Worcester (Mass.) Art Mus., 1972-80. Exhibited one man shows, Mus. Art Carnegie Inst., Pitts., 1981, Sculpture Ctr. Gallery, N.Y.C., Gimpel Fils Gallery, London, 1982, Gimpel & Weitzenhoffer Gallery, N.Y.C.; represented permanent collections, Bklyn. Mus., Worcester Art Mus., Mus. Art Carnegie Inst., Boston Mus. Fine Arts, Mus. Art R.I. Sch. Design. Recipient first prize for painting Boston Fine Arts Festival, 1963, awards Mass. Artists Found., 1975, 79. Mem. College Art Assn. Am., N.Y. Artists Equity Assn. Home and Office: 325 W 16th St Apt 4W New York NY 10011

CRONIN, THOMAS DILLON, physician; b. Houston, Apr. 8, 1906; s. Phillip H. and Julia K. (Dillon) C.; m. Anne C. Heyck, Nov. 6, 1935; children: Thomas Dillon, Robert Hillsman, Anne Frances. Student, Rice Inst., 1924-28; M.D., U. Tex.-Galveston, 1932. Diplomate: Am. Bd. Plastic Surgery (mem. bd. 1961-67). Intern Kansas City (Mo.) Gen. Hosp., 1932-33; resident surgery St. Joseph Hosp., Houston, 1933-34; fellow plastic and oral surgery Mayo Found., Rochester, Minn., 1937-39; now clin. prof. plastic surgery Baylor U.; chief plastic surgery St. Joseph Hosp., 1946-70, dir. plastic surgery residency tng. program, 1970-79; chief plastic surgery Herman Hosp., 1941-69, St. Luke's Episcopal Hosp., 1954-78, Tex. Children's Hosp., 1954-79. Contbr. numerous papers in field plastic surgery. Served from maj. to lt. col., MC AUS, 1943-46. Fellow Am. Assn. Plastic Surgeons (hon.; pres. 1963-64, Mem., Clinician of Yr. 1979), Am. Soc. Plastic and Reconstructive Surgeons (spl. hon. citation 1975), ACS, Am. Assn. Physicians and Surgeons, AMA, Southwestern Surg. Congress, Tex. Surg. Soc. (v.p. 1960), Houston Surg. Soc. (pres. 1971-72). Clubs: Country, Yacht, Doctors (Houston). Home: 2121 Brentwood Dr

Houston TX 77019 Office: 7000 Fannin St Suite 2400 Houston TX 77030

CRONKHITE, LEONARD WOLSEY, JR., physician, college president; b. Newton, Mass., May 4, 1919; s. Leonard Wolsey and Orpah Glencor (Brewster) C.; m. Linda M. Marchky, Aug. 14, 1976; children: Judith, Marcia, Janice, Wendy. B.S., Bowdoin Coll., 1941, LL.D., 1979; M.D., Harvard U., 1950; LL.D., Northeastern U., 1970; L.H.D. (hon.), Curry Coll., 1977. Intern Mass. Gen. Hosp., Boston, 1950-51, resident, 1951-54; practice medicine, Boston; mem. staff Children's Hosp. Med. Center, 1962-77, exec. v.p., 1971-73, pres., 1973-77; cons. staff Mass. Gen. Hosp., 1955-77, Boston Hosp. for Women, 1967-77; lectr. Harvard Med. Sch., 1953-77; pres. Med. Coll. Wis., Milw., 1977—; trustee Northwestern Mut. Life Ins. Co.; dir. Universal Health Services, Inc. Contbr. articles to profl. publs. Trustee Bowdoin Coll.; mem. Wis. Med. Edn. Rev. Com.; bd. dirs. Milw. Regional Med. Center.; Mem. Greater Milw. Com., 1978—. Served with U.S. Army, 1940-45, 61-62. Decorated Legion of Merit with oak leaf cluster, Army Commendation medal, D.S.M.; recipient Bowdoin prize, 1973. Mem. Soc. Med. Adminstrs. (pres.), Assn. Am. Med. Colls. (chmn. 1975-76), Council Teaching Hosps. (chmn. 1972-73), Children's Hosps. Execs. Council, Nat. Acad. Scis. (Inst. Medicine). Clubs: Univ. (Milw.); Harvard (Boston); Army and Navy (Washington). Office: 8701 Watertown Plank Rd Milwaukee WI 53226

CRONKITE, EUGENE PITCHER, physician; b. Los Angeles, Dec. 11, 1914; s. Clarence Edgar and Anita (Pitcher) C.; m. Elizabeth Erna Kaitschuk, Aug. 17, 1940; 1 dau., Christina Elizabeth. A.B., Stanford U., 1936, M.D., 1940; D.Sc. (hon.), L.I. U., 1962. Intern Stanford U. Hosps., San Francisco, 1939-40, resident in medicine, 1941-42; commd. lt. (s.g.) U.S. Navy, 1942, advanced through grades to rear adm., 1969, ret., 1954; head hematology Naval Med. Research Inst., Bethesda, Md., 1945-54; sr. scientist med. dept. Brookhaven Nat. Lab., 1954—, chmn., 1967-79; prof. medicine Health Sci. Center, SUNY, Stony Brook, 1979—. Contbr. articles to med. jours. Recipient Alfred Benzon award, Denmark, 1969; Ludwig Heilmeyer medal, W.Ger., 1974; Semmelwiess award, Hungary, 1975; Alexander von Humboldt sr. scientist award, W.Ger., 1977. Mem. Am. Soc. Hematology (pres. 1970), Internat. Soc. Exptl. Hematology (pres. 1976), U.S. Nat. Acad. Scis., Am. Soc. Clin. Investigation, Assn. Am. Physicians, Am. Soc. Hematology, Am. Assn. Physiologists. Office: Med Dept Brookhaven Nat Lab Upton NY 11973

CRONKITE, WALTER, radio-TV news correspondent; b. St. Joseph, Mo., Nov. 4, 1916; s. Walter Lel and Helen Lena C.; m. Mary Elizabeth Maxwell, Mar. 30, 1940; children: Nancy, Mary, Walter Leland III. Student, U. Tex., 1933-35; LL.D., Rollins Coll., 1966, Bucknell U., Syracuse U.; L.H.D., Ohio State U.; hon. degree, Am. Internat. Coll., Harvard U. News writer, editor Scripps-Howard, also UP, Houston, Kansas City, Dallas, Austin, El Paso, Tex., N.Y.C.; UP war corr., 1942-45, fgn. corr., reopening burs. in Amsterdam, Brussels, chief corr. Nuremberg war crimes trials, bur. mgr., Moscow, 1946-48, lectr., mag. contbr., 1948-49, CBS-News corr., 1950-81, spl. corr., 1981—; mng. editor CBS Evening News with Walter Cronkite, 1962-81. Host spl.: Universe, CBS; anchor for: TV news spls. Vietnam: A War That Is Finished, 1975, In Celebration of US, 1976, Our Happiest Birthday, 1977, The President in China, 1975, Solzhenitsyn; 1984 Revisited; Author: Challenges of Change, 1971. Recipient Peabody award, 1962, 81, several Emmy awards; William A. White award for journalistic merit, 1969; George Polk Journalism award, 1971; Gold medal Internat. Radio and TV Soc., 1974; Alfred I. DuPont-Columbia U. award in Broadcast Journalism, 1978, 81; Presdl. medal of Freedom, 1981. Mem. Acad. TV Arts and Scis. (pres. nat. acad. N.Y. chpt. 1959, Govs. award 1979), Assn. Radio News Analysts, Chi Phi. Clubs: Nat. Press, Overseas, Writers, N.Y. Yacht, Players. Office: CBS News 524 W 57th St New York NY 10019

CRONON, EDMUND DAVID, JR., educator, historian; b. Mpls., Mar. 11, 1924; s. Edmund David and Florence Ann (Meyer) C.; m. Mary Jean Hotmar, May 13, 1950; children: William John, Robert David. Student, Macalester Coll., 1942-43; A.B., Oberlin Coll., 1948; A.M., U. Wis., 1949, Ph.D., 1953; postgrad., Manchester (Eng.) U., 1950-51. Instr., then asst. prof. history Yale U., 1953-59; asso. prof., then prof. history U. Nebr., 1959-62; prof. history U. Wis., Madison, 1962—, dean Coll. Letters and Sci., 1974—, chmn. dept., 1966-69, dir. Inst. Research in Humanities, 1969-74; lectr. for State Dept., Europe and Near East, 1966; Fulbright-Hays lectr. Moscow State U., 1974. Author: Black Moses: The Story of Marcus Garvey and the Universal Negro Improvement Association, 1955, Josephus Daniels in Mexico, 1960, Government and the Economy: Some Nineteenth Century Views, 1960, Contemporary Labor-Management Relations, 1960, The Cabinet Diaries of Josephus Daniels, 1913-1921, 1963, Labor and the New Deal, 1963, Twentieth Century America; Selected Readings, 2 vols, 1965-66, The Political Thought of Woodrow Wilson, 1965, Marcus Garvey, 1973. Mem. exec. com. Wis. Am. Revolution Bicentennial Commn.; adv. bd. Franklin D. Roosevelt Library, 1971-76, Wis. Humanities Com., 1973-77, Council for Internat. Exchange Scholars, 1977-80, Commn. Instns. Higher Edn. N. Central Assn. Colls. and Schs.; bd. dirs., pres. Council of Colls. of Arts and Scis.; trustee Ripon Coll. Served to 1st lt., inf. AUS, 1943-46. Fulbright fellow, 1950-51; Stimson fellow, 1958-59. Fellow Soc. Am. Historians; mem. Am. Hist. Assn., Orgn. Am. Historians (exec. bd.), Wis. Hist. Soc. (bd. curators, pres.), So. Hist. Assn. (exec. council, bd. editors), Phi Beta Kappa. Unitarian. Home: 5601 Varsity Hill Madison WI 53705

CRONQUIST, ARTHUR JOHN (FRANKLIN ARTHUR BEERS), botanist; b. San Jose, Calif., Mar. 19, 1919; s. Frank and Edith Marguerite (Cronquist) Beers; m. Mabel Allred, Dec. 25, 1940; children: John, Elizabeth Lynne. Student, U. Idaho, 1934-36; B.S., Utah State Coll., 1938, M.S., 1940; Ph.D., U. Minn., 1944. Mem. staff N.Y. Bot. Garden, 1943-46, 52—, sr. scientist, 1974—; asst. prof. U. Ga., 1946-48, State Coll. Wash., 1948-51, research asso., 1953—; tech. adviser Belgian Govt., 1951-52. Author: Introductory Botany, 1961, 2d edit., 1971, The Evolution and Classification of Flowering Plants, 1968, Basic Botany, 1973, Asteraceae of Southeastern United States, 1980, An Integrated System of Classification of Flowering Plants, 1981; also numerous articles.; Co-author: Manual of the Vascular Plants of Northeastern U.S. and Adjacent Canada, 1963, Vascular Plants of the Pacific Northwest, 5 vols, 1955-69, Natural Geography of Plants, 1964, Intermountain Flora3 vols., 1972-83. Mem. Internat. Assn. Plant Taxonomists, Bot. Soc. Am. (pres. 1973), Am. Soc. Plant Taxonomists (pres. 1962), Torrey, Bot. Club; mem. New Eng. Bot. Club; Mem. AAAS, Am. Inst. Biol. Scis., Ecol. Soc. Am., Calif. Bot. Soc. Home: 29 Dunderave Rd White Plains NY 10603 Office: NY Botanical Garden Bronx NY 10458

CRONSON, ROBERT GRANVILLE, state auditor; b. Chgo., Dec. 23, 1924; s. Berthold A. and Ethel (Larson) C.; m. Sonjo D. Zollars (div.); children: Karen, Christopher, Keelyn, Morgan, Seth. A.B. in Econs, Dartmouth, 1947; J.D., U. Chgo., 1950. Bar: Ill. 1950. Atty. Daily, Dines, Ross & O'Keefe, Chgo., 1951-53; partner DeBoice, Greening, Ackerman & Cronson, Springfield, Ill., 1957-60; asst. sec. of state of Ill., Springfield, 1958-64; sr. vp., sec. The Chgo. Corp., Chgo., 1965-73; assoc. prof. pub. adminstrn. Roosevelt U., 1973-74; adj. prof. adminstrn. Sangamon State U.; auditor gen., State of Ill., 1974—; Mem. exec. com. post audit sect. Nat. Conf. State Legislatures, Nat. Assn. State Auditors, comptrollers and Treasurers and Nat. Intergovtl. Audit Forum, 1978-80; mem. State Auditor Coordinating Council, Midwest Intergovtl. Audit Forum. Chmn. Midwest Vehicle Proration Compact, 1959-61, Ill. Securities Adv. Com., 1964-73; chmn. William H. Chamberlain Scholarship Fund, Sangamon State U., 1972—. Served to cpl. USMCR, 1942-46. Recipient Fin. Mgmt. Improvement award U.S. Govt., 1980. Mem. Midwest Securities Commrs. Assn. (chmn. 1959-64), Securities Industry Assn. Am. (chmn. state legislation com. 1970-72), Nat. State Auditors Assn. (pres. 1980-81), Phi Kappa Psi. Club: Mason (Chgo.) (Shriner). Home: 57 Country Place Springfield IL 62703 Office: 509 S 6th St Springfield IL 62706

CRONYN, HUME, actor, writer, director; b. London, Ont., Can., July 18, 1911; came to U.S., 1932; s. Hume Blake and Frances Amelia (Labatt) C.; m. Jessica Tandy, Sept. 27, 1942; children: Susan Cronyn Tettemer, Christopher, Tandy. Grad., Ridley Coll., 1930; student, McGill U., 1930-31; grad., Am. Acad. Dramatic Art, 1934; LL.D. (hon.), U. Western Ont., 1974. Lectr. drama Am. Acad. Dramatic Arts, N.Y.C., 1938-39, Actors' Lab., Los Angeles, 1945-46; bd. govs. Stratford Festival, Can. (Recipient Comoedia Matinee Club award for Fourposter 1952, Barter Theatre award for outstanding contbn. to theatre 1961, Delia Austria medal N.Y. Drama League for Big Fish, Little Fish 1961, Antoinette Perry (Tony) award, also Variety N.Y. Drama critics poll of performance as Polonius 1964, 9th ann. award Am. Acad. Dramatic Art 1964, Straw Hat award for best dir. 1972, Obie award for outstanding achievement, disting. performance Krapp's Last Tape 1973, Brandeis U. Creative Arts award 1978, nominee Tony award for The Gin Game 1979, winner Los Angeles Critics award 1979, named to Theatre Hall of Fame 1979); Author: Rope (screen version), 1947, Under Capricorn (screen version), 1948, also various short stories and mag. articles.; First profl. theatre appearance, Nat. Theatre Stock Co., Washington, 1931; appeared in: 1st appearance Hippers Holiday, N.Y.C., 1934, various plays, N.Y.C., including, High Tor, Room Service, The Three Sisters, The Weak Link, Retreat to Pleasure, The Survivors (star); motion pictures include Shadow Of A Doubt, 1943, Life Boat, 1944, The Seventh Cross, 1944, The Postman Always Rings Twice, 1946, The Green Years, 1946, A Letter for Evie (star), 1945, Brute Force (star), 1947, Top O' The Morning; star, 1949, People Will Talk, 1951; starred in: ANTA touring prodn. of Hamlet, 1949; co-starred with Jessica Tandy in: The Little Blue Light, Brattle Theatre, Cambridge, Mass., 1950, The Fourposter, 1951-53, Madame Will You Walk, 1953-54, The Honeys; A Day by the Sea, 1955, The Man in the Dog Suit, 1958; dir.: Portrait Of A Madonna, Los Angeles, 1946, Now I Lay Me Down To Sleep, 1949-50, Hilda Crane, 1950, The Egghead, 1957, all N.Y.C.; appears: major network dramatic shows TV, including Show of the Week; appeared in: films Sunrise at Campobello, 1960, Cleopatra, 1963, Gaily Gaily, 1968, The Arrangement, 1968, There Was a Crooked Man, 1969, Conrack, 1974, Parallax View, 1974, Honky Tonk Freeway, 1980, Garp, 1981, Roll Over, 1981, Impulse, 1981; appeared in the: comedy prodn. Big Fish, Little Fish, 1961; with, Tyrone Guthrie Prodns., Mpls., 1963; played Polonius: Hamlet, N.Y.C., 1964; producer: Slow Dance on the Killing Ground, 1964; produced and starred: (with Jessica Tandy) The Marriage (a dramatic series), 1954, Triple Play, 1958, 59; appeared title role: Richard III, 1965; in: Cherry Orchard, 1965; as Harpagon in: The Miser, Mpls., 1965; as Tobias in: A Delicate Balance, 1966, 67; as Harpagon in: revival The Miser, Mark Taper Forum, Los Angeles, 1968; as Frederick William Rolfe in: Hadrian VII, Stratford Nat. Theatre Co., Can., 1969, tour, 1969-70; as Capt. Queeg in: Caine Mutiny Court Martial, Los Angeles, 1971-72; appeared in: Promenade All, N.Y.C., 1972; dir., appeared in tour, 1972-73; appeared in: (with Jessica Tandy) Samuel Beckett Festival, Lincoln Center, N.Y.C., 1972; and tour Krapp's Last Tape in Samuel Beckett Festival, Toronto, Washington, other cities, 1973, (with Jessica Tandy) Noel Coward in Two Keys, 1974, tour, 1975, Many Faces of Love, 1974, 75, 76; appeared as Shylock in: Merchant of Venice; as Bottom in: A Midsummer Night's Dream, Stratford (Ont., Can.) Festival, 1976; co-producer: (with Mike Nichols and star) The Gin Game (Pulitzer prize 1978), Golden Theatre, N.Y.C., 1977; tour The Gin Game, U.S., Can., Eng., USSR, 1978-79; co-author, star: (with Susan Cooper) Foxfire, Stratford (Ont.) Festival, 1980, Guthrie Theatre, Minn., 1981. Mem. AFTRA, Screen Actors Guild, Writers Guild Am., Actors Equity Assn., Soc. Stage Dirs. and Choreographers, Dramatists Guild. Office: 63-23 Carlton St Rego Park NY 11374

CRONYN, MARSHALL WILLIAM, chemistry educator; b. Oakland, Calif., June 22, 1919; s. George William and Lura (Miller) C.; m. Vesta Elizabeth Wetterborg, Feb. 27, 1942; children: Evan, Gail, Lori. B.A., Reed Coll., 1940; Ph.D. in Chemistry, U. Mich., 1944. Research asso. penicillin project OSRD-Com. on Med. Research, U. Mich., Ann Arbor, 1944-46; Am. Chem. Soc. post-doctoral fellow U. Calif. at Berkeley, 1946-48, instr., 1948-49, asst. prof., 1949-52, Reed Coll., Portland, Oreg., 1952-56, asso. prof., 1956-60, prof., 1960—, chmn. dept. chemistry, 1966-73, v.p., provost, 1982—; mem., cons. Medicinal Chemistry Panel, USPHS, 1961-66. NIH research fellow Cambridge, Eng., 1960-61. Fellow AAAS, Am. Chem. Soc., Soc. Automotive Engring., N.Y. Acad. Sci., Sigma Xi. Club: Portland City. Research and publs. in field. Home: 3232 NW Luray Terr Portland OR 97210

CROOK, DOROTHY (MRS. C. SPRAGUE HAZARD), economist; b. N.Y.C., June 21, 1911; d. Samuel and Mary (Beekman) C.; m. C. Sprague Hazard, Jan. 22, 1947; children: Jonathan Sprague, Neil Livingstone. B.A., Barnard Coll., 1933; M.A., Columbia U., 1938. Editorial asst. div. press intelligence White House, 1933-35; jr. economist Treasury Dept., 1935-37; asst. to economist Chase Nat. Bank, N.Y.C., 1937-39; dir. pub. affairs and legis. Nat. Fedn. Bus. and Profl. Women, 1939-42; pub. affairs officer OWI, London, 1942-45; econ. analyst Voice of Am., N.Y.C., 1945-52, chief talks and features br., 1952-54, econ. editor, 1963-72; press and pub. affairs officer U.S. Mission to UN, 1954-60; exec. dir. U.S. Com. for UN, 1960-63; sr. editor Econ. Impact mag. USIA, 1972-76, editor-in-chief, 1976-81. Mem. Am. Econ. Assn., UN Assn. (area pres. 1980), Phi Beta Kappa. Clubs: Washington Nat. Press, Nat. Economists. Home: 4710 Langdrum Ln Chevy Chase MD 20815

CROOK, ROBERT WAYNE, mutual funds executive; b. Hartford, Conn., Apr. 6, 1936; s. William Gregor and Laura Foster (Keenan) C.; m. Ruth DiSciullo, Nov. 23, 1977; children by previous marriage: Robert Wayne, Laura Sigrid. A.B., Harvard U., 1959; postgrad., U. Va. Sch. Law, 1962. With White, Weld & Co., Inc., Boston, 1961-78, v.p., 1971-75, 1st v.p., 1975-78; pres., dir. White Weld Money Market Fund, Boston, 1974-78, White Weld Govt. Fund, 1977-78; with Merrill Lynch Asset Mgmt., Inc., Boston, 1978—, V.P., 1981—; v.p. Merrill Lynch Funds Distbr., Inc., 1978—; pres., dir. Merrill Lynch Institutional Fund, Inc., Boston, 1978—, Merrill Lynch Govt. Fund, Inc., 1978—; pres. T TEE Merrill Lynch Instutional Tax-Exempt Fund, 1983—. Served with U.S. Army, 1960. Home: 49 May St Everett MA 02149 Office: 125 High St Boston MA 02110

CROOKE, EDWARD AUSTIN, utility executive; b. Washington, July 6, 1938; s. Bernard Davis and Anne Patricia C.; m. Lois Ann McDaniel, Mar. 1, 1969; 1 stepdau., Angela Y. McClanahan. B.S., U. Md., 1968; M.B.A., Loyola Coll., Balt., 1971. With Balt. Gas & Electric Co., 1968—, asst. sec., asst. treas., 1978, v.p. fin. and acctg., sec., 1978—; dir. Resource & Property Mgmt., Inc.; dir. Safe Harbor Water Power Corp., Blue Cross Md. Trustee, mem. exec. com. Council on Econ. Edn. Md.; bd. dirs. YMCA; mem. fin. and audit coms. United Way. Served with U.S. Army, 1956-64. Mem. Edison Electric Inst., Am. Soc. Corp. Secs., Fin. Execs. Inst. Office: PO Box 1475 Baltimore MD 21203

CROOKER, ARTHUR MERVYN, physics educator; b. Cayuga, Ont., Can., Sept. 19, 1909; s. Mervyn Arthur and Evelyn Agnes (Crull) C.; m. Helen Mae MacVicar, June 3, 1939 (dec. 1980); 1 son, Mervyn John Arthur. B.A., McMaster U., 1930; M.A., U. Toronto, 1931, Ph.D., 1935. Research asst. U. Toronto, Ont., Can., 1930-35; 1851 research student U. London, 1935-37; prof. U. B.C., Vancouver, Can., 1937-75, 1975—; spectroscopist Argonne Nat. Lab., Ill., summers 1962-64, NASA, Greenbelt, Md., 1972-76. Served to maj. Can. Army, 1945. Recipient medal Can. Astron. Soc. Fellow AAAS. Conservative. Mem. United Ch. of Canada. Club: Faculty (Vancouver). Home: 1670 Wesbrook Crescent Vancouver BCCanada V6T 1W1 Office: Dept Physics U BC Vancouver BCCanada V6T 1W4

CROOKER, JOHN H., JR., lawyer; b. Houston, Oct. 26, 1914; s. John H. and Marguerite (Malsch) C.; m. Kay Berry; children: Carolyn (Mrs. W.E. Schwing), John H. III, Linda (Mrs. Barry Hunsaker, Jr.), Tara (Mrs. Alec Mize), Allison. B.A. with distinction, Rice U., 1935; LL.B. with highest honors, U. Tex., 1937. Bar: Tex. 1937, D.C. 1953. Practice law, Houston and Washington, 1937-67, 70—; chmn. CAB, 1968-69. Chmn. bd. dirs. U. St. Thomas, Tex., 1974-78. Served to lt. comdr. USNR, 1941-45. Decorated Bronze Star. Mem. State Bar. Tex. (past chmn. corp. sect.), ABA, Am. Law Inst., Houston Bar Found. (chmn. bd. dirs. 1984), Houston C. of C. (chmn. bd. 1978-79). Home: 5457 Holly Springs Houston TX 77056 Office: Bank of Southwest Bldg Houston TX 77002

CROOKS, EDWIN WILLIAM, educator; b. Parkersburg, W.Va, July 29, 1919; s. Edwin William and Rebecca (Dils) C.; m. Joan Schleuniger, Setp. 13, 1952; children: Edwin William III, Ann, Alice. B.S., W.Va. U., 1941, M.A., 1942; M.B.A., Harvard U., 1947; D.B.A., Ind. U., 1959. Mdse. controller Halle Bros. Co., Cleve., 1947-54; prof. mktg., asst. dean W.Va. U., Morgantown, 1954-56, 58-66; chancellor, prof. bus. adminstrn. Ind. U. S.E., New Albany, 1966—; dir. Dils Bros. & Co. Author: Buying Practices of Independent Retailers in W.Va., 1963, Retail Policies in W.Va., 1965; contbr. articles to profl. jours. Vice chmn. Kentuckiana Metroversity, 1969-83; bd. dirs. Leadership Clark County, 1981-83. Served to lt. comdr. USNR, 1942-46. Ford Found. fellow, 1956-58. Mem. Am. Mktg. Assn., Clark County C. of C. (pres. 1983), Phi Beta Kappa, Beta Theta Pi, Beta Gamma Sigma. Methodist. Lodge: Rotary. Home: 1807 Utica Pike Jeffersonville IN 47130 Office: Ind U SE Campus 4201 Grant Line Rd New Albany IN 47150

CROOKS, GLENNA MARIE, government executive; b. Hammond, Ind., Mar. 10, 1950; d. Glenn and LaVergne Joan (Bonneau) C. A.B., Ind. U., 1972, M.S., 1972, Ph.D., 1978. Sch. psychologist Washington Community Schs., Ind., 1972-75; assoc. instr. Ind. U., Bloomington, 1975-76, research and devel. asst., 1976-77; adj. prof. psychology, edn. U. Evansville, Ind., 1977-78; lectr. family practice residency program Desconess Hosp., Evansville, 1978-81; dir. inquiry and evaluation S.W. Ind. Med. Rev. Orgn., Evansville, 1978-79, exec. dir., 1979-81; dep. asst. sec. for health planning and evaluation USPHS/HHS, Washington, 1981—; cons. in field. Author, editor: Sensory-Motor Theory & Activities, 1975; author program guide book. Mem. adv. bd. Sch. Psychol. Services Ind. Dept. Pub. Instruction, Indpls., 1973-75, Daviess County Assn. Retarded Citizens, Ind., 1973-75; mentor Advocacy Ctr. for Talent, Bloomington, 1975-77; cons. Family Birth Ctr., Bloomington, 1976-77; mem., instr. YWCA, Evansville, 1980-81. Grantee in field. Mem. Am. Assn. Profl. Standards REv. Orgns., Cesarean Assn. for Resources and Edn., Internat. Childbirth Assn., Am. Pub. Health Assn. Republican. Club: Petroleum (Evansville). Home: 7728 Groton Rd Bethesda MD 20817 Office: US Public Health Service Dept Health and Human Services Room 703H Humphrey Bldg 200 Independence Ave SW Washington DC 20201

CROOKSTON, J. IAN, financial consultant; b. Ayr, Scotland, 1910. Former trustee Can. Realty Investors. Home: 187 Cottingham St Toronto ON Canada Office: PO Box 35 Toronto Dominion Centre Toronto ON Canada M5K 1C4

CROOM, JOHN HENRY, 111, utility executive; b. Fayetteville, N.C., Dec. 12, 1932; s. John Henry and Mary Dalice (Howard) C.; m. Verna Arlene Willetts, June 21, 1953; children: Mary, Karen, Elizabeth, John. B.S.M.E., N.C. State Coll., 1954. Engr. United Fuel Gas Co., Charleston, W.Va., 1954-69; indsl. sales mgr. Charleston Group Cos., 1969-73; indsl. utilization mgr. Columbia Distbn. Cos., Columbus, Ohio, 1973-74, v.p. engring. and planning, 1974-79; sr. v.p. Columbia Gas System, Wilmington, Del., 1979-80, exec. v.p., dir., 1981-82, pres., dir., 1982—. Bd. dirs. Opportunities Ctr. Inc., Wilmington. Served with AUS, 1954-56. Mem. Nat. Soc. Profl. Engrs. Presbyterian. Home: PO Box 4175 Greenville DE 19807 Office: 20 Montchanin Rd Wilmington DE 19807

CROSBIE, JOHN CARNELL, Canadian government official; b. St. John's, Nfld., Can., Jan. 30, 1931; s. Chesley Arthur and Jessie (Carnell) C.; m. Jane Furneaux, Sept. 8, 1952; children: Chesley, Michael, Beth. B.A. in Polit. Sci. and Econs, Queen's U., Kingston, Ont.; LL.B., Dalhousie U.; postgrad., London Sch. Econs. Bar: Called to Nfld. bar 1957. Practice in, St. John's, 1957-66; mem. St. John's City Council, 1965-66, dep. mayor, 1966; minister Nfld. Dept. Mcpl. Affairs and Housing, 1966-67, Dept. Health, 1967-68; rep. Nfld. Ho. of Assembly from St. John's West, as Liberal, 1966-68; as Progressive Conservative, after 1971, govt. house leader, 1974-75; minister of fin., pres. Treasury Bd., also minister econ. devel. Nfld., 1972-74; minister fisheries, also minister intergovtl. affairs Nfld., 1974-75, minister mines and energy, also minister intergovtl. affairs Nfld., 1975-76; mem. Canadian Ho. of Commons for St. John's West, 1976—, chmn. Progressive Conservative caucus on energy, after 1977, also parliamentary critic for industry, trade and commerce; minister of fin. for Can., 1979-80. Address: House of Commons Ottawa ON K1A 0A6 Canada

CROSBIE, STANLEY BLANDFORD, physician; b. Mpls., May 12, 1906; s. William and Eva (Blandford) C.; m. Helen Blair, Dec. 20, 1937; 1 dau., Joan. Student, Carleton Coll., 1924-26; B.A., U. Minn., 1936, M.D., 1941. Intern, Jersey City Med. Center, 1941-42; resident psychiatry Hudson River State Hosp., Poughkeepsie, N.Y., 1942-43; resident medicine VA Hosp., Mpls., 1946-47; practice medicine, specializing in gastroenterology, Alburquerque, 1947- 49, Grand Junction, Colo., 1949-59, Mpls., 1959-62, Dearborn, Mich., 1962-65; chief gastro-intestinal service VA Hosp., Albuquerque, 1947-49, chief med. service, Grand Junction, 1949-59, dir. profl. services, Mpls., 1959-62, dir., Dearborn, 1962-65, Denver, 1965-70, Phoenix, 1970-72; clinician Maricopa County Dept. Health Services, Phoenix, 1973-83; asst. prof. medicine U. Minn., 1959-62, asst. dean Med. Sch., 1979-62; asso. prof. Wayne State U., 1963-65; asso. prof. medicine U. Colo., 1966-70. Served to maj. M.C., AUS, 1943-46. Fellow ACP; mem. Am. Hosp. Assn., AMA, Chi Psi. Home: 1919 E Claremont St Phoenix AZ 85016 *If I had known I was going to live so long I would have lived more dangerously.*

CROSBY, ALFRED WORCESTER, educator; b. Boston, Jan. 15, 1931; s. Alfred Worcester and Ruth (Coleman) C.; m. Frances E.

Karttunen, May 20, 1983; children by previous marriage: Kevin, Carolyn; stepchildren: Jaana, Suvi. A.B., Harvard U., 1952, A.M.T., 1956; Ph.D., Boston U., 1961. Instr. Albion (Mich.) Coll., 1960-61, Ohio State U., Columbus, 1961-65; asst. prof. San Fernando Valley State Coll., Los Angeles, 1965-66; prof. history Wash. State U., Pullman, 1966-77; prof. U. Tex., Austin, 1977—. Author: America, Russia, Hemp and Napolean, 1965, Columbian Exchange, 1972, Epidemic and Peace, 1918, 1976 (recipient Med. Writer's Assn. award for best book 1976). Served with U.S. Army, 1952-55. NIH fellow, 1971-73; Nat. Humanities Inst. fellow, 1975-76; Fulbright fellow, 1979; Cardozo Furst Professorship Yale U., 1977. Mem. Am. Assn. Environ. History. Home: 2506 Bowman St Austin TX 78703 Office: Dept American Studies U Tex 303 Garrison Hall Austin TX 78712

CROSBY, DAVID, musician; b. Los Angeles, Aug. 14, 1941. With rock group, The Byrds, 1964-68; solo performer, 1969—, (with Graham Nash, Stephen Stills and Neil Young) various recs. and performances, 1969—; film appearance Woodstock, 1970; composer: numerous songs, including Déja Vu, Eight Miles High, Long Time Coming, Wooden Ships *

CROSBY, FRED MCCLELLAN, retail home and office furnishings executive; b. Cleve., May 17, 1928; s. Fred Douglas and Marion Grace (Naylor) C.; m. Phendalyne D. Tazewell, Dec. 23, 1958; children: Fred, James, Llionicia. Grad. high sch. Vice pres. Seaway Flooring & Paving Co., Cleve., 1959-63; pres., chief exec. officer Crosby Furniture Co., Inc., Cleve., 1963-; dir. First Bank Nat. Dir. adv. council Ohio Bd. Workmen's Compensation, 1974-82; chmn. Minority Econ. Devel. Corp., 1972-83; bd. dirs. Council Smaller Enterprise, 1973-80, Goodwill Industries, 1973-80, Woodruff Hosp., 1975-82, Cleve. Devel. Found., Greater Cleve. Growth Assn.; chmn. bd. dirs. Glenville YMCA, 1973-76; trustee Cleve. Play House, Eiza Bryant Ctr.; bd. dirs., treas. Urban League Cleve., 1971-78; mem. adv. council Small Bus. Assn.; trustee Salvation Army, 1980; bd. dirs. Forest City Hosp. Found., Cleve. State U. Found. Served with AUS, 1950-52. Recipient award bus. excellence Dept. Commerce, 1972; Presdl. award YMCA, 1974; Gov. Ohio award community action, 1973; named Family of Yr. Cleve. Urban League, 1971. Mem. Growth Assn. Cleve. (dir.), NAACP (v.p. Cleve. 1969-78), Ohio Council Retail Mchts. (dir.), Ohio Home Furnishing and Appliance Assn. (pres.), Exec. Order Ohio Commodore. Clubs: Mid-Day, Cleve. Play House, Harvard Bus. Sch., Rotary, Clevelander (Cleve.). Home: 2530 Richmond Rd Beachwood OH 44122 Office: 12435 St Clair Ave Cleveland OH 44108

CROSBY, GARY EVAN, actor; b. Los Angeles, June 27; s. Harry Lillis and Dixie Lee (Wyatt) C.; m. Barbara Cosentino, Sept. 6, 1960 (div. 1979); 1 son, Steven Christopher. Grad., Stanford, 1954. Actor on radio, TV and films, 1954—; film appearances include Girl Happy, Operation Bikini, others; TV appearances include Rockford Files, Project UFO, Adam-12, Emergency!, Chase; summer stock and stage appearances in The Odd Couple, What Makes Sammy Run. Served with AUS, 1956-58. Roman Catholic. *

CROSBY, GORDON EUGENE, JR., insurance company executive; b. Remsen, Iowa, Nov. 14, 1920; s. Gordon E. and Florence (Plummer) C.; m. Betty Jo Hubbard, May 2, 1942; children: Gordon Eugene III, Douglas H. Grad., Kemper Mil. Sch., 1938; student, U. Mo., 1938-40. Agt. New Eng. Mut. Life Ins. Co., Knoxville, Tenn., 1945-47, supr., Oakland, Calif., 1946, agy. mgr., Seattle, 1947, gen. agt., 1948-59; v.p., dir. agys. U.S. Life Ins. Co., N.Y.C., 1959-62, sr. v.p., dir. agys., 1962-64, exec. v.p., 1964-66, pres., chief exec. officer, 1966-67; pres., dir., mem. exec. com. USLIFE Corp., 1966, chmn., chief exec. officer, 1967—; chmn. United States Life Ins. Co. in City N.Y., USLIFE Life Ins. of Calif., Pasadena, USLIFE Credit Life Co., Ill., Great Nat. Life Ins. Co., Tex., All Am. Life & Casualty Co., Chgo., USLIFE Credit Corp., Shaumburg, Ill., USLIFE Equity Sales Corp., N.Y.C., USLIFE Savs. & Loan Assn. in Cal., USLIFE Realty Corp., N.Y., USLIFE Title Ins. Co., Dallas, USLIFE Title Ins. Co. N.Y., USLIFE Advisers, Inc., N.Y., Old Line Life Ins. Co. Am., Milw., USLIFE Systems Corp., N.Y., USLIFE Income Fund, Inc., Gen. United Life Ins. Co., Des Moines, USLIFE Fin. & Ins. Services, Inc., Calif., USLIFE Real Estate Services Corp., Dallas, Lincoln Liberty Life Ins. Co., Nebr., Sooner Life Ins. Co., Ponca City, Okla.; Mem. public relations and econ. policy com. Am. Council Life Ins. Bd. dirs. N.Y. chpt. Nat. Multiple Sclerosis Soc., U. Mo.-Columbia Devel. Fund; trustee Coll. of Ins. Served to lt. USNR, World War II; PTO. Decorated Bronze Star medal. Mem. Economic Club N.Y., Newcomen Soc. U. Mo. Alumni Assn., Sigma Chi. Presbyterian. Clubs: Anglers, Brook, India House (N.Y.C.); Long Island (N.Y.). Office: USLIFE Corp 125 Maiden Ln New York NY 10038 *

CROSBY, HARRY HERBERT, rhetoric educator; b. New England, N.D., Apr. 18, 1919; s. Guy L. and Eva (McClellan) C.; m. Jean E. Boehner, Apr. 11, 1943 (dec. 1980); children: Stephen, April, Jeffrey, Rebecca.; m. Mary Alice Brennan, June 26, 1982; stepchildren: Haley, Maura, John. B.A., U. Iowa, 1941, M.A., 1947; Ph.D., Stanford U., 1953. Instr. U. Iowa, 1946-47, 50-51, asst. prof., 1951-58, writing supr., 1956-58; asst. instr. Stanford, 1947-50; instr. San Jose State Coll., 1950; asso. prof. Boston U., 1958-59, prof. rhetoric, 1959—, chmn. div. communications, 1958-65, chmn. div. rhetoric, 1966—; dir. studies Pakistan Air Force Acad., Risalpur, West Pakistan, 1960-62; cons. U.S. Air Force Acad., 1953-60. Co-author: The McLuhan Explosion, 1968, College Writing, 1968, 2d edit., 1974, Just Rhetoric, 1971, The Shape of Thought, 1978, College Spelling, 1980. Mem. bd. aldermen, Newton, Mass., 1970-73; pres. Newton Arts Center, 1979—. Served to lt. col. USAAF, 1942-45. Decorated Air medal, D.F.C. with 2 oak leaf clusters, Bronze Star medal, U.S., Croix de Guerre, France). Mem. Modern Lang. Assn., Nat. Council Tchrs. English, Phi Eta Sigma (hon.). Episcopalian (sr. warden 1971-73). Home: 6 Buckingham Pl Cambridge MA 02138 Office: Boston U Coll Basic Studies Boston MA 02215

CROSBY, JOHN CAMPBELL, author; b. Milw., May 18, 1912; s. Fred G. and Edna (Campbell) C.; m. Mary B. Wolferth, Dec. 7, 1946 (div.); children: Michael Wolferth, Margaret; m. Katharine J. B. Wood, Dec. 1, 1964; children: Alexander, Victoria. Student, Yale U., 1931-33. Reporter Milw. Sentinel, 1933, N.Y. Herald Tribune, 1935-41; syndicated columnist, 1946-65; columnist The Observer, London, Eng., 1965-75. (George Foster Peabody Award, George K. Polk Meml. Award.); Author: Out of the Blue, 1952, With Love and Loathing, 1963, Sappho In Absence, 1969, The Literary Obsession, 1973, Contract on the President, 1973, An Affair of Strangers, 1975, Nightfall, 1976, Company of Friends, 1977, Dear Judgment, 1978, Party of the Year, 1979, Penelope Now, 1981, Men in Arms, 1983. Served with AUS, 1941-46. Home: Esmont VA 22937

CROSBY, JOHN O'HEA, conductor, opera mgr.; b. N.Y.C., July 12, 1926; s. Laurence Alden and Aileen Mary (O'Hea) C. Grad., Hotchkiss Sch., 1944; B.A., Yale, 1950; Litt.D. (hon.), U.N.Mex., 1967, Mus. D., Coll. of Santa Fe, N.Mex., 1968, Mus.D., Cleve. Inst. Music, 1974, L.H.D., U. Denver, 1977. Pres. Manhattan Sch. Music, 1976—. Accompanist, opera coach, condr., N.Y.C., 1951-56; gen. dir., mem. conducting staff, Santa Fe Opera, 1957—; guest condr. various opera cos. in, U.S. and Can., 1967—; condr.: U.S. stage premiere Daphne, 1964; world premiere Wuthering Heights, 1958. Served with inf. AUS, 1945-46; ETO. Roman Catholic. Clubs: Metropolitan Opera, Century Assn., University (N.Y.C.). Office: PO Box 2408 Santa Fe NM 87501

CROSBY, KATHRYN GRANDSTAFF (GRANT CROSBY), actress; b. Houston, Nov. 25; d. Delbert Emery and Olive Catherine (Stokely) Grandstaff; m. Harry L. (Bing) Crosby, Jr., Oct. 24, 1957 (dec. Oct. 1977); children—Harry Lillis III, Mary Frances, Nathaniel Patrick. B.F.A., U. Tex., 1955; R.N., Queens of Angles Sch. Nursing, Los Angeles, 1964; teaching credential, Immaculate Heart Coll., Los Angeles, 1965. Actress: in plays including Sunday in New York, 1963, Pygmalion, Sabrina Fair, 1964, Peter Pan, 1965, Arms and the Man, 1965, Mary, Mary, 1966, The Guardsman, 1967, The Prime of Miss Jean Brodie, 1969, Same Time Next Year, 1977-78; hostess daily TV talk show, sta. KPIX, San Francisco; T.V. appearances Bing Crosby Christmas Specials, Suspense Theater, Ben Casey; Author: Bing and Other Things, 1967; also column Texas Gal in Hollywood, 1952-54. Mem. advisory com. arts State Dept.; Co-chmn. bd. trustees Immaculate Heart Coll.; trustee Eisenhower Med. Center. Named Distinguised Alumae U. Tex., 1969, Rodeo Queen Houston Fatstock Show, 1950. Mem. Am. Conservatory Theatre. Roman Catholic. *

CROSBY, KENNETH MCCORKLE, security and commodity brokerage exec.; b. Greeneville, Tenn., Jan. 31, 1916; s. William H. and Floy (McCorkle) C.; m. Eleanor Stuart Littlejohn, July 7, 1945 (dec. 1977); children—Valerie, Cynthia; m. Margaret A. Griffith, Aug. 16, 1979. A.B., U. Miss., 1937, LL.B., 1939. Spl. agt. FBI, 1939-42; with Merrill Lynch, Pierce, Fenner & Beane Inc., 1943-44; civil attache U.S. Dept. State, Mexico City, Mexico, 1945, legal attache, Montevideo, Uruguay, 1946; mgr. Merrill Lynch, Pierce, Fenner & Smith Inc., Havana, Cuba, 1947-60, Madrid, Spain, 1961-64, Paris, France, 1965, Washington, 1966-78; v.p. internat. and govt. bus., dir. Merrill Lynch Internat., 1978-80; dir. Met. Washington Bd. Trade.; Mem. Mayor's Econ. Devel. Com., 1970; Vice-chmn. Presdl. Inaugural, Washington, 1973. Mem. adv. bd. Salvation Army, 1969; gen. chmn. United Fund Drive; adv. com. Fed. Nat. Mortgage Assn.; pres. Washington Performing Arts Soc.; chmn. Inter. Am. Music Festival; trustee Invest in Am., Meridian House Found., Ford Theatre Soc., Center Strategic and Internat. Studies Georgetown U., Washington Fed. City Council, Pan Am. Devel. Found.; bd. dirs. Spanish Inst., N.Y.C. Decorated Order Civil Merit, Spain, Order Merit, Argentina). Mem. Inter-Am. Soc. (adv. com.), Blue Key, Delta Kappa Epsilon, Phi Alpha Delta, Omicron Delta Kappa, Tau Kappa Alpha. Home: 5001 Upton St NW Washington DC 20016 Office: 1800 K St NW Suite 1121 Washington DC 20006

CROSBY, NORM, comedian; b. Boston, Sept. 15; m. Joan Foley, 1966; children—Daniel, Andrew. Attended, Mass. Sch. Art. Nat. spokesman Anheuser-Busch Natural Light Beer. Began work as comedian in New Eng. clubs, at fraternity and polit. dinners, at numerous civic and charity functions N.Y.C. debut at, Latin Quarter; opening act for Robert Goulet, for 3 years; including appearances at, Diplomat Hotel, Miami, Fla., Sahara, Las Vegas; appeared with, Tom Jones, for four years, including several appearances at, London Palladium, regular appearances at all major hotels in Las Vegas, numerous other appearances, night clubs, concert halls, theaters, TV variety and panel shows; host of: syndicated comedy TV series Norm Crosby's Comedy Shop; numerous plaques, citations for civic work. Nat. hon. chmn. Better Hearing Inst., Washington; trustee Hope for Hearing Found., UCLA; sponsor Norm Crosby Ann. Celebrity Golf Tournament benefiting City of Hope. Served with USCG. Recipient. Office: care Shefrin Co PO Box 48559 Los Angeles CA 90048

CROSBY, PETER MURRAY, company executive; b. Lackawanna, N.Y., July 6, 1934; s. Willis Murray and Ruth Dorothy (Osborne) C.; m. Carol Ann Little, July 20, 1957; children: Philip Murray, Catherine Ann, Christopher Willis, Michael James. B.A. in Chemistry, Coll. of Wooster, 1956; grad. advanced mgmt. program, Harvard U., 1979. With Allied Corp., 1956—, dir.-chems. Allied Chem. Corp. subs., Morristown, N.J., 1976-77, v.p., gen. mgr.-performance chems., 1977-82, exec. v.p. Allied Co. subs., 1982-83, pres. indsl. chems. div. Allied Corp. Chem. Sector, 1983—. Bd. dirs. Butterworth Civic Assn., Morristown, 1970-75, pres., Morristown, 1974-75; bd. mgrs. Jr. Achievement, Inc., Morris, Essex, Hudson Counties, N.J., 1976-81; corp. chmn. United Way, Morristown, 1977, 80; mem. corp. gift com. United Negro Coll. Fund, Newark, 1981-83; bd. dirs. N.J. Gov.'s Mgmt. Improvement Program, Trenton, 1982-83. Mem. Am. Chem. Soc., Synthetic Organic Chem. Mfrs. Am. (dir. 1976-77), Am. Mgmt. Assn. Repbulican. Presbyterian. Club: Springbrook Country (Morristown) (trustee 1983—). Home: 19 Fieldstone Dr Morristown NJ 07960 Office: Allied Corp Indsl Chems Div Columbia Rd and Park Ave Morristown NJ 07960 *The most important aspects in my life have always been people. My family, my friends, and my business associates have all contributed immeasurably to what success I have achieved. I believe that persistence, positive thinking and actions will always overcome whatever obstacles lie in the way of success. And that the greatest force in world are positively reinforced people. Tell people what they have done well and they will search for more challenge. Tell them they have failed and they will avoid challenge.*

CROSBY, ROBERT C., health care company executive; b. 1939; m. B.S. in Acctg., Northwestern State U., 1960. Corp. sr. v.p. Hosp. Corp. Am., Nashville, Tenn., 1976-80, corp. exec. v.p., 1980—, pres. Hosp. Corp. Internat., 1976—. Office: Hosp Corp Am Box 550 Nashville TN 37202 *

CROSLAND, EDWARD BURTON, former telephone company executive, lawyer; b. Montgomery, Ala., Jan. 6, 1912; s. David Woolley and Virginia (Burton) C.; m. Helen Burns, Oct. 21, 1939; children: Edward Burton, Lucien Burns. Student, U. of South, 1930-32; J.D., U. Ala., 1935. Bar: Ala. 1935. Practiced in Montgomery, 1935-38, asst. atty. gen., chief div. local finance, State of Ala., 1938-42; atty. So. Bell Tel. & Tel. Co., Atlanta, 1946, gen. atty., 1949; asst. v.p., atty. AT&T, Washington, 1952-55, asst. to pres., N.Y.C., 1955-58, v.p., 1958-74, sr. v.p., 1974-77; former chmn. bd. Fed. Home Loan Bank of N.Y.; dir. Am. Security Bank N.A. Former trustee Overlook Hosp., Summit, N.J.; trustee U. South. Served as lt. col. JAGC, U.S. Army, 1942-46. Decorated Legion of Merit. Mem. Am., Ala., Ga., D.C. bar assns., Kappa Sigma, Phi Delta Phi, Omicron Delta Kappa. Clubs: Burning Tree, Metropolitan (Washington); Chevy Chase (Md.). Home: 4412 Chalfont Pl Bethesda MD 20816 Office: 1722 Eye St NW Washington DC 20006 also 550 Madison Ave New York NY 10022

CROSS, AUREAL THEOPHILUS, educator; b. Findlay, Ohio, June 4, 1916; s. Raymond Willard and Myra Jane (Coon) C.; m. Christina Aleen Teyssier, Mar. 11, 1945; children—Timothy Aureal, Christina Avonne (Mrs. Stephen Dolen), Jonathan Ariel, Cheryl Aleen (Mrs. Richard M. Bowman), Christopher Charles. B.A., Coe Coll., Cedar Rapids, Ia., 1939; M.S. in Botany, U. Cin., 1941; Ph.D. in Botany and Paleontology, U. Cin., 1943. Instr. to asst. prof. U. Notre Dame, 1943-46; NRC fellow in geology, 1943-44; paleobotanist, Central Expt. Sta., U.S. Bur. Mines, Pitts., 1945; asst. prof. dept. geology U. Cin., 1946-49, asst. prof. dept. botany, 1948-49; part-time geologist Geol. Survey Ohio, 1946-51; coal geologist and paleobotanist W.Va. Geol. and Econ. Survey, 1949-57; asso. prof. to prof. dept. geology U. W.Va., 1949-57; sr. research engr. Pan Am. Petroleum Corp. Research Center, Tulsa, 1957-61, supr. tech. group and research group, 1959-61; prof. dept. geology Mich. State U., East Lansing, 1961—, prof. dept. botany and plant pathology, 1961—; prof. ecology U. Alaska, 1971; research palynologist U. So. Calif., 1972. Editor: Palynology in Oil Exploration, 1964; co-editor: Coal Resources and Research in Latin America, 1978; asso. editor: Fossil Spores and Pollen, 39 vols, 1956-76; Contbr. numerous articles, abstracts and revs. to profl. jours. Chmn. citywide rally Fellowship Christian Athletes, Tulsa, 1960; mem. nat. council U.P. Men, 1966-68, 74—; active Boy Scouts Am., YMCA, others. Bot. Soc. Am. grantee, 1954; Geol. Soc. Am. grantee, 1951; Distinguished lectr. Am. Assn. Petroleum Geologists, 1964. Mem. Bot. Soc. Am. (chmn. paleobot. sect. 1953, 77), Geol. Soc. Am. (chmn. coal geology div. 1966, chmn. N.Central sect. 1969-70, exec. sec. sect. 1971-80), Soc. Econ. Paleontologists and Mineralogists (chmn. research com. 1961-62, councillor in paleontology 1971-73), numerous other internat., nat. and regional profl. assns. Presbyn. Home: 529 N Harrison Rd East Lansing MI 48823 Office: Dept Geology Mich State U East Lansing MI 48824

CROSS, CHRISTOPHER, recording artist, songwriter, singer; b. San Antonio, May 3, 1951; s. Leo Joseph and Edith Ann (Guderman) Geppert; m. Roseann Harrison, Oct. 19, 1971 (div. 1982); 1 son, Justin. Recording artist Warner Bros. Records, Burbank, Calif., 1979—. Composer, performer: album Christopher Cross, 1979, Another Page, 1983; co-writer, performer: Arthur's Theme, 1981 (Acad. award); producer: Alessi Bros. Words and Music, 1979. Recipient Gold Album for Christopher Cross Recording Industry Assn. Am., 1980, Platinum Album for Christopher Cross Recording Industry Assn. Am., 1980, Gold Album for Another Page, 1983, Gold Album for Arthur's Theme, 1982, Globe award for Arthur's Theme, 1982. Office: Front Line Management 9044 Melrose 3d Floor Los Angeles CA 91335

CROSS, CLYDE CLEVELAND, lawyer; b. Brownsville, Tenn., Aug. 17, 1918; s. Clyde C. and Jessie (Mann) C.; m. Helen Cross, June 21, 1941; children: Ann, Clyde, Richard, Jane, Frank, Katherine. B.A., U. Wis., 1940, J.D., 1942. Bar: Wis. 1941, U.S. Supreme Ct. 1960. Ptnr. Langer and Cross, Baraboo, Wis., 1945-80, Cross, Mercer and Maffei, Baraboo, 1980—; instr. trail advocacy U. Wis., 1973-80; bd. dirs., mem. faculty Ct. Practice Inst., 1981—. Contbr. articles to legal jours. Served to lt. USN, 1943-45. Fellow Am. Coll. Trial Lawyers, Am. Bar Found.; mem. State Bar Wis. (pres. 1971-72), Sauk County Bar Assn. (pres. 1960-61), U. Wis. Law Alumni Assn. (pres. 1965-66). Office: PO Box 141 Baraboo WI 53913

CROSS, EASON, JR., architect; b. Bisbee, Ariz., Nov. 14, 1925; s. Eason and Olive (Hardwick) C.; m. Diana Johnson, June 17, 1950,; children—Ben, Becca, Amy, Susan. B.A., Harvard, 1949, M.Arch., 1951. With Prentiss Huddleston & Assos., Tallahassee, Fla., 1950-51, W.D. Compton, Cambridge, Mass., 1951-52, Deigert & Yerkes, Washington, 1952; asso. Charles M. Goodman, Washington, 1952-59, Keyes, Lethbridge & Condon, 1959-61; partner Cross & Adreon, Arlington, Va., 1961—; spl. instr. George Washington U., 1964-65. Pres. Hollin Hills Community Assn., 1978; chmn. Fairfax County Appeals Bd., 1970-80. Served with USNR, World War II. Recipient Ware prize, 1950, Washington Bd. Trade design award, 1965, Bethesda-Chevy Chase C. of C. design awards, 1966, 67; House and Home awards A.I.A., 1965-66; Mid-Atlantic Region design awards, 1967, 69; nat. honor award, 1968; Nat. honor award Am. Inst. Steel Constrn., 1967; 4 awards H.U.D.-Washington Center Urban Studies furniture competition, 1971. Fellow AIA (pres. N. Va. chpt., mem. com. on design, Va. Soc. energy award 1980); Mem. Fairfax County C. of C., Am. Arbitration Assn. (panelist). Democrat. Unitarian. Clubs: Harvard, Fox; Arts (Washington); Hasty Pudding-Institute of 1770 (Harvard). Patentee fastenings and furniture. Home: 2309 Glasgow Rd Alexandria VA 22307 Office: 950 N Glebe Rd Arlington VA 22203

CROSS, FRANK MOORE, JR., educator, semitist; b. Ross, Calif., July 13, 1921; s. Frank Moore and Mary (Ellison) C.; m. Elizabeth A. Showalter, June 20, 1947; children: Susan E., Ellen M., Priscilla Rachel. A.B., Maryville Coll., 1942, Litt.D., 1968; B.D., McCormick Theol. Sem., 1946; Ph.D., Johns Hopkins, 1950; M.A. (hon.), Harvard, 1957. Nettie McCormick fellow Johns Hopkins, 1946-48, Rayner fellow in semitics, jr. instr., 1949-50; vis. instr. McCormick Theol. Sem., 1948-49; Kent fellow Nat. Council Religion in Higher Edn. Johns Hopkins, 1949-50; instr. bibl. history Wellesley Coll., 1950-51; instr. McCormick Theol. Sem., 1951-53, asst. prof., 1954-55, asso. prof., 1955-57; asso. prof. O.T. Harvard Div. Sch., 1957-58; Hancock prof. Hebrew and other Oriental langs. Coll. Arts and Scis., Harvard, 1957—; also curator Semitic Mus., 1958-61, dir., 1974—, chmn. dept. neareastern langs., 1958-65; ann. prof. Am. Sh. Oriental Research, Jerusalem, 1953-54; Albright lectr. Johns Hopkins U., 1980; Mem. Internat. staff for editing Dead Sea Scrolls, 1953—; co-dir. archaeol. expdn. to Judaean Buqeiah, 1955; prin. investigator Am. Schs. Oriental Research-Harvard U.-U. Mich. expdn. to Carthage, 1975-80; archaeol. dir. Hebrew Union Coll., Jerusalem, 1963-64; v.p. Albright Inst. Archaeol. Research, 1970-74. Author: (with David N. Freedman) Early Hebrew Orthography, 1952, The Ancient Library of Qumran, 1958, (with D.N. Freedman) Studies in Ancient Yahwistic Poetry, 1964, Canaanite Myth and Hebrew Epic, 1973; Editor: Scrolls from the Wilderness of the Dead Sea, 1965, (with S. Talmon) Qumran and the History of the Biblical Text, 1975, Magnalia Dei, 1976; editor: Harvard Semitic Monographs; assoc. editor: Harvard Theol. Rev, 1963-74, Bull. of Am. Schs. Oriental Research, 1969—; Contbr. articles for profl. jours. Trustee Am. Schs. Oriental Research, 1973—, pres., 1974-76. Recipient Percia Schimmel award Israel Mus., 1980; Fellow Inst. for Advanced Studies, Hebrew U., Jerusalem, 1978-79. Fellow Am. Acad. Arts and Scis.; mem. Am. Philos. Soc., Am. Oriental Soc., Soc. Bibl. Lit. (pres. 1973-74, William Foxwell Albright award 1980), Bibl. Colloquium, Phi Beta Kappa. Home: 31 Woodland Rd Lexington MA 02173 Office: Harvard Semitic Museum 6 Divinity Ave Cambridge MA 02138

CROSS, GEORGE LYNN, foundation administrator, former university president; b. Woonsocket, S.D., May 12, 1905; s. George and Jemima (Dawson) C.; m. Cleo Sikkink, Oct. 28, 1926; children: Mary-Lynn, George W., Braden Riehl. B.S., S.D. State Coll., 1926, M.S., 1927, D.Sc., 1960; Ph.D., U. Chgo., 1929; LL.D., Oberlin Coll., 1960, Okla. Christian Coll., 1975. Instr. botany U. S.D., 1930-34; prof. botany U. Okla., 1934-38, head dept. botany, 1938-42; acting dean Grad. Coll., 1942-44; acting dir. Research Inst., 1942-44, pres. univ., 1944-68, emeritus, 1968—; pres. Okla. Health Scis. Found., 1968—; Chmn. Fed. Home Loan Bank, Topeka, 1960-68; chmn. bd. Am. Exchange Bank, Norman, Okla.; dir. Friendly Nat. Bank, Oklahoma City., Central Nat. Bank. Public panel mem. 8th Dist. War Labor Bd., 1942; Mem. bd. of univ. presidents William Rockhill Nelson Trust, Kansas City, Mo.; exec. council U. Okla. Research Inst.; Elector N.Y.U. Hall of Fame For Great Ams. Fellow AAAS; mem. Fed. Home Loan Bank Bd. (mem. fed. savs. and loan adv. council 1959), Nat. Assn. State Univs. (pres. 1959-60), Assn. Sci. U. Profs., Torrey Bot. Club, Bot. Soc. Am., NEA, Okla. Acad. Sci., Nat. Geog. Soc., Am. Soc. Naturalists, Okla. Hist. Soc., Norman C. of C., Newcomen Soc., Phi Beta Kappa, Phi Sigma, Alpha Phi Omega. Presbyterian. Home: 812 Mockingbird Ln Norman OK 73071

CROSS, GEORGE R., insurance company executive; b. N.Y.C., May 9, 1923; s. George W. and Mae E. (Fish) C.; m. Shirley Jean Williams, June 24, 1950; children: Stephen, Pamela, Jeffrey, Mark. A.B., Syracuse U., 1947; J.D., Bklyn. Law Sch., 1951; C.P.C.U., 1960. Bar:

N.Y. 1952, U.S. Supreme Ct. 1958. With Atlantic Mut. Ins. Co., 1947-49, adjuster, 1949-52; asst. gen. counsel Nat. Assn. Ins. Agts., 1952-59; with Gt. Am. Ins. Co., N.Y.C., 1959-70, gen. atty., 1963-68, v.p., 1967-70, gen. counsel, 1968-70, sec., 1963-67, 68-70; v.p., asso. gen. counsel, sec. Crum & Forster Ins. Cos., N.Y.C., 1970-73, v.p. govt. affairs, 1973-79; also dir.; v.p. govt. affairs Crum & Forster Corp., N.Y.C., 1979—; chmn. bd. N.J. Property-Liability Ins. Guaranty Assn., 1975—; chmn. N.J. Med. Malpractice Reins. Assn., 1979—; Dir. Va. Ins. Guaranty Assn., N.Y. Ins. Exchange Security Fund; chmn. Fla. Med. Malpractice Ins. Assn.; bd. dirs. Nat. Com. on Ins. Guaranty Funds; chmn. bd. N.Y. Med. Malpractice Ins. Plan, 1976—. Mem. Nanuet (N.Y.) Sch. Bd., 1962-65. Served to 1st lt. USAAF, 1943-45; ETO. Mem. Am. Arbitration Assn., N.Y. Bar Assn., New York County Lawyers Assn., Drug and Chem. Club, Fla. Med. Malpractice Ins. Assn. (chmn.). Club: Masons. Home: 23 Terrace Ave Nanuet NY 10954 Office: 305 Madison Ave Morristown NJ 07960

CROSS, HARRY MAYBURY, law educator; b. Ritzville, Wash., Aug. 23, 1913; s. James Leman and Mary Rosella (Maybury) C.; m. Mylinn A. Gould, Dec. 25, 1935; children: Harry Maybury, BruceMichael, Kim Judson. B.A., Wash. State U., 1936; J.D., U. Wash., 1940. Bar: Wash. 1941. Reporter Yakima (Wash.) Morning Herald, 1937; abstracter, title examiner Wash. Title Ins. Co., Seattle, 1937-40; Sterling fellow in law Yale U., 1940-41; atty. U.S. Treasury Dept., Washington, 1941-42, TVA, Chattanooga, 1942-43; asst. prof. law U. Wash., Seattle, 1943-45, asso. prof., 1945-49, prof., 1949—, asso. dean, 1975-78, acting dean, 1978, 79; vis. prof. Columbia U., 1956-57, NYU, 1964, U. Mich., 1972. Mem. Wash. State Bar Assn., ABA, Nat. Collegiate Athletic Assn. (pres. 1969-70), Order of Coif, Crimson Circle, Phi Beta Kappa, Phi Kappa Phi, Sigma Delta Chi, Phi Alpha Delta, Kappa Sigma. Club: Oval. Home: 12454 100th Ave NE Kirkland WA 98034 Office: U Wash Law Sch JB 20 Seattle WA 98105

CROSS, IRVIE KEIL, religious organization executive; b. Huntington, Ark., Mar. 21, 1917; s. William Earl and Bertha Frances (Harris) C.; m. Johnnie Maxine Sharpe, June 9, 1939; children: Johnnie Keilene Cross Barnes, Maxine Irviene Cross McCombs. Th.M., Missionary Baptist Sem., 1938, Th.D., 1944; D.D., Orthdox Bapt. Inst., 1946, Eastern Bapt. Inst., 1959, Internat. Free Protestant Episcopal U. of London, Eng., 1964. Ordained to ministry Am. Baptist Assn., 1936. Pastor Pauline Bapt. Ch., Monticello, Ark., 1939-41, County Ave Bapt. Ch., Texarkana, Ark., 1941-50, Langdon St. Bapt. Ch., Somerset, Ky., 1950-59; founder, pres. Eastern Bapt. Inst., 1953-67; pres. Eastern Bapt. Assn., 1958-62; founder, dir. office of publicity Am. Bapt. Assn., Texarkana, Ark.-Tex., 1952-67, dir. office of promotion and pub. relations, Texarkana, 1967-74, v.p., 1974-79, pres., 1978-79, mem. history and archives com., 1974—, mem. chaplains commn., 1964—; adminstrv. v.p. Calif. Missionary Bapt. Inst. and Sem., Bellflower, Calif., 1974—; condr. study tours to, Europe and Middle East. Author: Truth About Conventionism, 1955, The Church Covenant, 1955, Paul's Lectures, 1956, Non-Denominational Denomination, 1956, I Believe God, 1966, Tongues, 1973, Baptism Holy Spirit, 1973, Great Commission, 1974, Divine Healing, 1974, Lectures on Israel in Prophecy, 1974, Baptist Heritage Abandoned, 1981, The Universal Church, 1983, A Look at Landmarkism, 1984, The Work of a Deacon, 1984; editor: Sword, 1944-49, Am. Bapt. Digest, 1949-50, Missionary, 1953-67, Bapt. Sentinel, 1974—. Mem. adv. bd. Salvation Army, 1947-50; pres. Kidco, Inc., 1962-74, Lake Cumberland-Dale Hollow Tourist and Travel, 1965; mem. Ky. Devel. Council, 1962. Mem. Four States Aviation Assn. (pres. 1946-47), Somerset-Pulaski County (Ky.) C. of C. (pres. 1962), Somerset Ministerial Assn. (pres. 1954), Ky. Guild Artists and Craftsmen (pres. 1963-67). Club: Masons. Home: 9649 Foster Rd Downey CA 90242 Office: PO Box 848 Bellflower CA 90706 *I have lived by the concept that honesty, truthfulness and moral cleanliness form the foundation of character. I prefer to pursue my own ideas, and am not satisfied short of the top in any endeavor undertaken.*

CROSS, JAMES *See* **PARRY, HUGH JONES**

CROSS, JAMES E., lawyer; b. Fort Dodge, Iowa, Aug. 18, 1921; s. Jim B. and Glady F. (Bird) C.; m. Jean Steigerwald, Sept. 4, 1945; children: Richard Alan, Susan Lynn, Diane Louise, William James. B.S., State U. Iowa, 1942; LL.B., U. So. Calif., 1949. Assoc. O'Melveny & Myers, Los Angeles, 1949-59, ptnr., 1960—; dir. Earle M. Jorgensen Co., Source Capital Inc., Others. Trustee Claremont McKenna Coll., Calif. Mus. Found., Nat. Multiple Sclerosis Soc., Los Angeles World Affairs Council. Mem. State Bar Calif., ABA, Los Angeles C. of C. (dir.). Clubs: Calif.; Regency (Los Angeles). Office: O'Melveny & Myers 400 S Hope St Los Angeles CA 90071 *

CROSS, JENNIFER MARY (MRS. ELLIS M. GANS), author; b. London, Eng., May 10, 1932; d. Thomas Reginald and Ruth Neil (Hodgson) C.; m. Ellis Myron Gans, July 12, 1965; 1 son, Jason David Mycroft. B.A. with honors in History, Kings Coll. U. London, 1953. Sec. to book pub., London, 1953-56; personal asst. to editor Brit. Med. Jour., 1957-58; pub. relations Napper, Stinton, Woolley, London, 1958-63; mem. staff Consumer Action, San Francisco, 1975-76; tchr. and lectr. on consumer affairs. Free-lance writer, 1963—; contbr. to: The Times, London, Punch, Economist, Sunday Times, London, New Statesman; Author: The Supermarket Trap, 1970, rev. edit., 1976, Justice Denied, A History of the Japanese in the United States (for Children), 1974, (with Eli Djeddah) Now I know which side is up, 1976, The Cavity Connection, 1979; Editor: Consumer Action's Guide to Automobile Insurance, 1976. Pub. mem. Calif. Bd. Dental Examiners.; Mem. Coalition for Med. Rights of Women, 1979—, Consumer Fedn. Calif., 1972—; exec. dir. Safe Food Inst., 1977-79; participant White House Conf. on Food, Nutrition and Health, 1969, Nat. Nutrition Policy Study, 1974; consumer rep. Gen. Med. Devices Panel FDA, 1979—; mem. Dept. Agr. panel on meat and poultry inspections, 1979; pub. affairs officer Kaiser Health Plan, Inc., Hayward, Calif., 1982—. Home: 301 Surrey St San Francisco CA 94131

CROSS, JOHN HENRY AARON, retired advertising executive; b. Monticello, Iowa, Jan. 22, 1920; s. Henry A. and Pearl (Heisey) C.; m. Alice Sheehan, Apr. 7, 1951; children: H. Andrew, David McN. B.A., U. Calif.-Berkeley, 1941. With Compton Advt., 1950-69, exec. v.p., 1967-69, also dir.; partner, dir. Jack Tinker & Partners, 1969-70; N.Y.C., 1969-71; exec. v.p. Lennen & Newell, N.Y.C., 1970—; sr. v.p. SSC&B Lintas Worldwide, N.Y.C., 1971-83, ret., 1983; adj. prof. mktg. Pace U., 1980-81. Served with AUS, 1942-48. Clubs: Sleepy Hollow Country (Scarborough); North River Assn., Torch, Chapel Hill Country. Home: 111 Fieldstone Ct Chapel Hill NC 27514

CROSS, LENORA ROUTON, assn. exec.; b. Hope, Ark., Jan. 5, 1920; d. William Ralph and Lillian Lenora (Carrigan) Routon; m. James Calvin Cross, Jan. 17, 1942; children—James Calvin, Ralph William. B.A. in Journalism, La. State U., 1939. City editor Shreveport (La.) Times, 1939-42; br. chief U.S. Army Office Info., 1942; research asso. Time-Life mag., 1942-43; independent research-writer, 1943-67; exec. dir. Bus. and Profl. Women's Found., Washington, 1967-76; bus. mgr. Nat. Bus. Forms Assn., Alexandria, Va., 1977-80. Home: 127 Quay St Alexandria VA 22314

CROSS, LESLIE ERIC, electrical engineering educator; b. Leeds, Eng., Aug. 14, 1923; came to U.S., 1961; s. Charles Eric and Alice Emily (Plant) C.; m. Lorna Lucilla Fish, Apr. 1, 1950; children: Peter Charles, Matthew John, Daniel Eric, Rebecca Lorna, Rachel Jean, Elizabeth Mary. B.Sc., Ph.D., Leeds U., ICI fellow, 1951-54. Research scientist Elec. Research Assn., Eng., 1954-61; assoc. prof. Pa. State U., University Park, 1961-65, prof. elec. engring., 1965—. Fellow Am. Inst. Physics, Am. Ceramics Soc. (electronics award 1968); sr. mem. IEEE; mem. Japan Phys. Soc., Optical Soc. Am. Office: Materials Research Lab Room 251A Pa State U University Park PA 16802 *

CROSS, RALPH EMERSON, mechanical engineer; b. Detroit, June 3, 1910; s. Milton Osgood and Helen (Heim) C.; m. Eloise Florence Fountain, June 18, 1932; children: Ralph Emerson, Carol (Mrs. Peter G. Wodtke), Dennis W. Student, MIT, 1933; D.Eng. (hon.), Lawrence Inst. Tech., 1977. Vice pres. Cross Co., Fraser, Mich., 1932-67, pres., gen. mgr., 1967-79, chmn., 1979-82; chmn. bd. Cross & Trecker, Bloomfield Hills, Mich., 1979-82, chmn. emeritus, dir., 1982—; chmn. bd., chief exec. officer Intelitec Corp., Bloomfield Hills, Mich., 1982—; chmn. bd., pres. Cross Internat. A.G., Fribourg, Switzerland, 1965-68; pres. Cross Export Corp., 1972-80; dir. Axiomatic Inc., Peter G. Wodtke Inc.; spl. cons. to asst. sec. Air Force for Material, 1955-59; Mem. corp. Econ. Devel. Corp. Greater Detroit, 1968-73, Mich. Blue Shield, 1969-74; mem. corp. devel. com. Mass. Inst. Tech., 1970—; mem. Am. Iranian Joint Bus. Council, 1975-76; trustee Lawrence Inst. Tech., 1979—; pres. SME Edn. Found., 1979—. Recipient Engring. citation Am. Soc. Tool Engrs., 1956; Corp. Leadership award Mass. Inst. Tech., 1976. Mem. Nat. Acad. Engring., Nat. Machine Tool Builders Assn. (pres. 1975), Soc. Automotive Engrs., Soc. Mfg. Engrs. (hon.), Engring. Soc. Detroit. Clubs: Detroit Athletic, Lochmoor. Home: 50 N Deeplands Rd Grosse Pointe Shores MI 48236 Home: 4120 Shelldrake Ln Boynton Beach FL 33426 Office: 505 N Woodward Ave Bloomfield Hills MI 48013

CROSS, RICHARD EUGENE, lawyer; b. Madison, Wis., Sept. 20, 1910; s. Frank L. and Josephine Anne (Loranger) C.; m. Mary Caroline Stirling, Aug. 5, 1939; children—Caroline, Virginia, Richard, Martha. A.B., U. Mich., 1935, LL.B., 1938; L.H.D., Lawrence Inst. Tech., 1962—; LL.D., Eastern Mich. U., 1973—. Bar: Mich. 1938. Legal counsel Cross, Wrock, Miller & Vieson.; Dir. Am. Motors Corp., 1954-83, chmn., 1962-66; dir. Mfrs. Life Ins. Co., Toronto, Mountain States Pipe & Supply Co., Packer Corp., Hiram Walker Resources Ltd. Bd. dirs. Woodlawn Assn. Fellow Am. Bar Found.; mem. Detroit Bar Assn., State Bar Mich., Am. Judicature Soc. Office: 400 Renaissance Center Suite 1900 Detroit MI 48243

CROSS, RICHARD JAMES, physician; b. N.Y.C., Mar. 31, 1915; educator;; s. W. Redmond and Julia A. (Newbold) C.; m. Margaret W. Lee, June 28, 1939; children—Richard James, Margaret Lee, Alan Whittemore, Anne Redmond, Jane Randolph. Grad., Groton Sch., 1933; B.A., Yale, 1937; M.D., Columbia, 1941, Med. Sc.D., 1949. Intern Presbyn. Hosp., N.Y.C., 1941-42, asst. resident, 1946-48; instr. medicine Columbia, 1947-49, asso. medicine, 1951-57, asst. prof., 1957-59, asst. dean, 1957-59; asso. dean, asst. prof. medicine U. Pitts. Sch. Medicine, 1959-63; dean faculty medicine U. Ghana, West Africa, 1963; asso. prof. medicine Temple U., 1963-64; asst. to exec. dir. Assn. Am. Med. Colls., 1964-65; lectr. Northwestern U. Sch. Medicine, 1965; prof. medicine Rutgers Med. Sch., Coll. Medicine and Dentistry of N.J., 1965—, asso. dean, 1965-70, prof. community medicine, 1970—, chmn. dept., 1970-80; NRC fellow Pub. Health Research Inst., N.Y.C., 1949-51. Mem. Fair Lawn (N.J.) Bd. Edn., 1951-54. Served to capt., M.C. AUS, 1942-46. Decorated Bronze Star, Purple Heart. Mem. AMA, Assn. Am. Med. Colls., AAAS, Am. Public Health Assn., Am. Coll. Preventive Medicine. Home: 210 Elm Rd Princeton NJ 08540 Office: Rutgers Medical School Box 101 Piscataway NJ 08854

CROSS, RICHARD JOHN, banker; b. Denver, May 22, 1929; s. Arthur Chester and Gertrude Eva (Ryan) C.; m. Mildred Louise Mouton, Jan. 19, 1957; children: John Charles, Carolyn Louise, Paul Arthur. B.S., U. Colo., 1950; M.B.A, Wharton Sch. Finance U. Pa., 1955. Asst. v.p. First Nat. Bank, Boulder, Colo., 1955-60; exec. v.p. Arapahoe Nat. Bank, Boulder, 1960-62; with Lloyds Bank Calif., 1962-81, exec. v.p., 1974-81; sr. v.p. Fidelity Fed. Savs. & Loan, Glendale, Calif., 1981—; vice chmn. Fidelity Nat. Trust, Glendale, Calif., 1981—. Mem. regents council Mt. St. Mary's Coll., Los Angeles; regional bd. Cath. Social Service; councilman, Boulder, 1959-62; bd. dirs. Glendale Symphony Assn.; trustee Flintridge Prep. Sch. Served with USN, 1950-53. Fellow Royal Soc. Arts; mem. Calif. Bankers Assn., So. Calif. Trust Officers Assn., Delta Tau Delta, Phi Epsilon Phi. Democrat. Roman Catholic. Clubs: Sutter (Sacramento); Jonathan (Los Angeles); Oakmont Country (Glendale, Calif.). Home: 1430 Greenbriar Rd Glendale CA 91207 Office: 600 N Brand Blvd Glendale CA 91209

CROSS, ROBERT BRANDT, educator; b. Stockton, Calif., Dec. 9, 1914; s. LaRue Ackley and Theresa (Brandt) C. A.B. in Greek, UCLA, 1937, M.A., U. Calif.-Berkeley, 1939; Ph.D. in Greek-Latin, U. So. Calif., 1948. Asst. prof. classical langs. U. So. Calif., Los Angeles, 1948-57; prof. fgn. langs. U. Ark., Fayetteville, 1957-80, emeritus prof., 1980—. Translator: Milo Rigaud, 1970; writings of E. Yale Dawson in marine biology. Served with USAAF, 1942-45. Mem. Am. Guild Organists, Organ Hist. Soc., Classical Assn. Middle West, Classical Assn. South (v.p. for Ark. 1957-80), Sociedade Brasileira De Romanistas, Desert Tortoise Council, Gopher Tortoise Council. Democrat. Greek Orthodox. Home: Box 1312 Little Rock AR 72203

CROSS, ROBERT CLARK, journalist; b. Cheboygan, Mich., May 12, 1939; s. Warren Clark and Meryle M. (Allaire) C.; m. JuJu Lien; children: Gabriel Francis, Amy Lien. B.A. in Journalism, Wayne State U., 1962. Writer, researcher Newsweek mag., 1962; reporter, editor Chgo. Tribune, 1962-66, 67-82, assoc. editor mag., 1973-82, writer, 1982—; reporter Newsday, 1966-67. Mem. Chgo. Headline Club chpt., Sigma Delta Chi. Office: 435 N Michigan Ave Chicago IL 60611

CROSS, ROBERT T., food company executive; b. 1930. With Scot Lad Foods, Inc., Lansing, Ill., 1959—, pres. Chgo. Grocery, dir., 1968—, corp. v.p., 1971-81, exec. v.p., 1981-82, pres., chief exec. officer, 1982—, dir., 1974—. Office: Scot Lad Foods Inc 1 Scot Lad Ln Lansing IL 60438 *

CROSS, STUART GREEN, hotel executive; b. Palo Alto, Calif., June 28, 1918; s. Robert William and Helen (Green) C.; m. Darlene Winvick, Sept. 19, 1970; children—Robert H., Thomas W. A.B., Stanford U., 1947, M.A., 1950. Instr. history Stanford U., 1950-52; in various managerial positions Yosemite Park and Curry Co., 1952-67, pres., chmn. bd., 1967-72, dir., 1959-72; pres. Nat. Park Found., Washington, 1972-73; exec. v.p. Utah Hotel Co., Salt Lake City, 1973-82, pres., 1982—. Served with U.S. Army, 1940-45. Mem. Calif. State Hotel Assn. (pres. 1969-70), Am. Hotel Assn. (chmn. resort com. 1970-71, chmn. com. on quality environ. 1965-66), Conf. Nat. Park Concessioners (chmn. 1966-72, hon.), Preferred Hotels Assn. (pres.), Nat. Parks and Conservation Assn. (dir.). Home and Office: Hotel Utah Main and S Temple Sts Salt Lake City UT 84111

CROSS, THEODORE LAMONT, lawyer, editor; b. Newton, Mass., Feb. 12, 1924; s. Gorham Lamont and Margaret Moore (Warren) C.; m. Sheilah Burr Ross, Sept. 16, 1950 (div. 1972); children: Amanda Burr, Lisa Warren; m. Mary Warner, 1974. Grad., Deerfield Acad., 1942; A.B., Amherst Coll., 1946; LL.B. (editor law rev. 1948-50), Harvard, 1950. Bar: Mass. bar 1950, N.Y. bar 1953. With firm Hale and Dorr, Boston, 1950-52; treas., sec., v.p. legal affairs, mem. fin. com. bd. dirs. Sheraton Corp. Am., 1963-68; chmn. bd., chief exec. officer, dir. Warren, Gorham & Lamont, Inc.; dir. Mgmt. Reports, Inc., Record Pub. Co., Internat. Thomson Orgn. Inc., Internat. Thomson Holdings, Inc.; editor-in-chief Bankers mag., 1962—, Bus. and Soc. Rev., 1971—; cons. HEW, Fed. Office Econ. Opportunity, 1964-69; Co-founder Banking Law Inst., 1965, chmn., 1965—; dir. Bank Tax Inst., 1964; pub. gov. Am. Stock Exchange, 1972-77; dir. Interracial Council for Bus. Opportunity, Council on Econ. Priorities; lectr. on inner city econs. and minority econ. devel. Harvard, Cornell U., U. Va. Author: Black Capitalism: Strategy for Business in the Ghetto (McKinsey Found. book award 1969), (with wife) Behind the Great Wall, 1979; Founder: Atomic Energy Law Jour., 1959. Trustee Amherst Coll. Served to ensign USNR, 1945-46. Home: 233 Carter Rd Princeton NJ 08540 Office: 870 7th Ave New York NY 10019 also 210 South St Boston MA 02111

CROSS, WILLIAM JOHN, publishing company executive; b. Canandaigua, N.Y., Feb. 26, 1928; s. William Tiffany and Anne Estelle (Monaghan) C.; m. Judith Margaret Haslam, Oct. 23, 1953; children—John Cummings, Martha Tiffany, Alexandra Haslam. A.B., Dartmouth Coll., 1950; M.C.S., Amos Tuck Sch., 1951. With W.R. Grace & Co., 1951-54, Time Inc., 1954-61; with Readers Digest Assn., Inc., Pleasantville, N.Y., 1961—, asst. treas., 1963-72, v.p., 1968-84, treas., 1972-84, pres., chief operating officer, 1984—, also dir., mem. exec. com.; dir. CML Group Inc. Trustee, treas. Kent (Conn.) Sch., 1975-81; warden St. Luke's Episcopal Ch., Somers, N.Y., 1965-66. Served with U.S. Army, 1945-47. Mem. Pilgrims of U.S., Republican. Club: Waccabuc Country. Home: PO Box 182 Somers NY 10589 Office: Readers Digest Assn Pleasantville NY 10570

CROSS, WILLIAM REDMOND, JR., corporate director, foundation executive; b. N.Y.C., Apr. 26, 1917; s. William Redmond and Julia (Newbold) C.; m. Sally Curtiss Smith, June 14, 1958; children: William Redmond III, Pauline Curtiss, Frederic Newbold. Grad., Groton (Mass.) Sch., 1937; B.A., Yale, 1941. With Hanover Bank, N.Y.C., 1941-43, N.Y. Trust Co., 1946-59, v.p., 1951-59, Safe Deposit Co. N.Y. Trust Co., 1952-59, Morgan Guaranty Trust Co., N.Y.C., 1959-64; head Midtown offices, 1962-65, sr. v.p., 1964-73, head met. div. gen. banking dept., 1967-71, sr. credit officer gen. banking div., 1971-72, sr. v.p., head corp. fin. div., 1972-73, exec. v.p.; 1973-78, vice chmn. credit policy com., 1978-79; ret., 1979—; dir. Crompton Co., Inc., N.Y. Times Co., Amax Inc. Bd. dirs. Jacob and Valeria Langeloth Found., 1955—; pres. Jacob and Valerie Langeloth Found., 1979—; bd. dirs. Caramoor Center for Music and Arts, 1976-79; trustee Childrens Aid Soc., 1962-75, Chapin Sch., 1969-75, Citizens Budget Com., 1963-79, Rippowam-Cisqua Sch., Bedford, N.Y., 1974-77. Served to lt. (j.g.) USNR, 1943-46. Clubs: Yale (past dir., past treas.), Racquet and Tennis (N.Y.C.)). Home: RD 2 Box 299 South Bedford Rd Mount Kisco NY 10549 Office: 1 E 42d St New York NY 10017

CROSSAN, ALEXANDER, oil company executive; b. Sacramento, Aug. 7, 1925; s. Alexander and Virginia (Hyden) G.; m. Jasna Thaller, Oct. 6, 1975; children: Karen, Alexander, Christophe, Colleen, Peter, Alexandra. Student, U. of Pacific, 1943-44; B.S. in Chemistry, U. Wash., 1947; B.D., Princeton Theol. Sem., 1952, Th.D. candidate, 1952-55. Product mktg. mgr. Dow Chem. Co., Midland, Mich., 1956-59; mgr. advt. and public relations Dow Chem. Internat., 1959-62; mgr. advt. and pub. relations Dow Chem., Europe, Zurich, Switzerland, 1963-64, gen. mgr. Eastern region, Europe, Vienna, Austria, 1965-78, comml. dir. Eastern region, Zurich, 1979-80, v.p. Eastern region, 1981; pres. Dow Italy, Milan, 1981; exec. v.p. Occidental Petroleum Corp., Los Angeles, 1981—; pres., chief exec. officer Enoxy Chem., S.A., Zurich, 1981-82. Served in USN, 1943-46. Republican. Presbyterian. Office: Occidental Petroleum Corp 10889 Wilshire Blvd Los Angeles CA 90024 *

CROSSEN, CYNTHIA MELINE, journalist; b. Battle Creek, Mich., Nov. 15, 1951; d. John Edward and Katherine Virginia (Peters) C.; m. James Gleick, June 16, 1979. B.A., Macalester Coll., 1973. Reporter Metropolis, Mpls., 1976-77; copy chief Essence, N.Y.C., 1977; assoc. editor N.J. Monthly (Princeton), 1978; mng. editor Am. Lawyer, N.Y.C., 1979-80, exec. editor, 1980-81; mng. editor Village Voice, N.Y.C., 1981—; editorial cons. Jane Mag., N.Y.C., 1982—. Office: Village Voice 842 Broadway New York NY 10003

CROSSEN, FRANK M., construction products manufacturing company executive. Chmn., co-chief exec. officer Centex Corp., Dallas. Office: Centex Corp Republic Nat Bank Tower Dallas TX 75201

CROSSETTE, GEORGE, research geographer; b. Chgo., July 12, 1910; s. Louis Faulkner and Marie (Pearce) C.; m. Elizabeth Uhle Ferg, July 1, 1933; 1 dau., Anne. B.A., George Washington U., 1935; Sc.D., Nat. Inst. Urbiculture, 1960. Supr. wanted criminals sect. FBI, 1934-38; chief geog. research div. Nat. Geog. Soc., 1939-72; ret. Vice pres. Montogomery County Workshop, 1951-54. Author: Founders of the Cosmos Club of Washington, 1966, John Wesley Powell, 1969; The Oceans, 1969, Herbert Wendell Gleason, 1972, also articles. Mayor, Chevy Chase View, Md., 1942-43, dep. sheriff, Hamilton County, N.Y.; Bd. dirs. Ding Darling Found., 1969—. Recipient Meritorious Wartime award Nat. Rifle Assn., 1944. Mem. Defenders of Wildlife (bd. dirs. 1967), D.C. Wildlife Fedn. (sec. treas. 1954-64), U.S. Flag Library Assn. (1st v.p. 1963), Lake George (N.Y.) Hist. Soc. (trustee), Md., Wash. acads. sci., AAAS, U.S. Mil. Engrs., Am. Assn. Geographers.; mem. Explorers (editorial bd. 1970—). Clubs: Cosmos (Washington) (chmn. admissions com. 1967-69, history com. 1968—); Cosmos (Washington) (bd. mgmt. 1970-73, v.p. 1976); pres. (1977, Ann. Disting. Service award), Nat. Press (Washington); Cliff Dwellers (Chgo). Home: 4217 Glenrose St Kensington MD 20895

CROSSFIELD, ALBERT SCOTT, aeronautical science consultant, pilot; b. Berkeley, Calif., Oct. 2, 1921; s. Albert Scott and Lucia (Dwyer) C.; m. Alice Virginia Knoph, Apr. 21, 1943; children: Becky Lee, Thomas Scott, Paul Stanley, Anthony Scott, Sally Virginia, Robert Scott. B.S. in Aero. Engring., U. Wash., 1949, M.S. in Aero. Sci., 1950; D.Sc. (hon.), Fla. Inst. Tech., 1982. Mem. U. Wash. staff charge wind tunnel operation, 1946-50; aerodynamicist, project engr., also pilot research airplanes X-1, X-4, X-5, D-558-I and II, X-F-92, F-102, F-100, F-86, NACA, 1950-55; participation proposal, design, 1st pilot X-15 research aircraft, design specialist, also chief engring. test pilot Los Angeles div. N.Am. Aviation, Inc., 1955-61, dir. test and quality assurance, space and info. systems div., 1961-66, tech. dir. research and engring., space and info. systems div., 1966-67; v.p. flight research and devel. div. Eastern Air Lines, Miami, Fla., 1967-71, staff v.p. transp. systems devel., Washington, 1971-74; sr. v.p. Hawker Siddeley Aviation Inc., Washington, 1974; tech. cons. House Com. on Sci. and Tech., Washington, 1977—; spl. work on the WS-131b Apollo, Saturn S-II, Paraglider programs. Author: Always Another Dawn, 1960; also articles. Served to lt., fighter pilot USNR, 1942-46. Recipient Lawrence Sperry award Inst. Aero. Scis., 1954, Octave Chanute award Inst. Aero. Scis., 1958; Achievement award Am. Astron. Soc., 1959; Calif. wing Air Force Assn., 1959; David C. Shilling award, 1961; Astronautics award Am. Rocket Soc., 1960; Ivan C. Kincheloe award Soc. Exptl. Test Pilots, 1960; Achievement award Nat. Aviation Club, 1961; Godfrey Cabot award Aero Club New Eng., 1961; Internat. Harmon trophy, 1961; Collier trophy, 1962; John J.

Montgomery award Nat. Soc. Aerospace Profls., 1962; Kitty Hawk Meml. award Los Angeles C. of C., 1969; Al J. Engel award Western Res. Hist. Soc. Aviation Hall of Fame, 1983; Ira C. Eaker Hist. fellow AFA, 1982; subject of portrait First Flight Soc., Kitty Hawk, N.C., 1982; named to Nat. Aviation Hall of Fame, 1983. Fellow Soc. Exptl. Pilots (co-founder; chmn. East Coast sect. 1976-77, Ray E. Tenhoff award 1978), Inst. Aerospace Scis., AIAA (chmn. flight test tech. com. 1963-64), Aerospace Med. Assn. (hon); mem. Am. Soc. Quality Control (sect. chmn. Los Angeles 1964-66, Outstanding Contbn. to Quality Control award 1967), Flying Physician Assn. (Man of Yr. 1961), Exptl. Aircraft Assn. (Service to Sport Aviation 1979), Nat. Aviation Club (pres. 1983), Sigma Xi, Tau Beta Pi. Republican. Episcopalian. Home: 12100 Thoroughbred Rd Herndon VA 22071 Office: 2321 Rayburn House Office Bldg Washington DC 20515

CROSSLEY, FRANK ALPHONSO, metallurgical engineer; b. Chgo., Feb. 19, 1925; s. Joseph Buddie and Rosa Lee (Brefford) C.; m. Elaine J. Sherman, Nov. 23, 1950; 1 dau., Desne Adrienne. B.S. in Chem. Engring, Ill. Inst. Tech., 1945, M.S. in Metall. Engring, 1947, Ph.D., 1950. Instr. Ill. Inst. Tech., Chgo., 1948-49; sr. scientist Ill. Inst. Tech. Research Inst., 1952-66; prof. foundry engring., head dept. foundry engring. Tenn. Agrl. and Indsl. State U., 1950-52; sr. mem. research lab. Lockheed Missiles & Space Co., Palo Alto, Calif., 1966-74, mgr. dept. producibility and standards, 1974-78, mgr. dept. missile body mech. engring., 1978-79, cons. engr. missile systems div., 1979—. Contbr. articles to metall. jours. and symposia, 1952-83. Served to ensign USNR, 1944-46; PTO. Fellow Am. Soc. for Metals; mem. Metall. Soc. of AIME, AIAA, SAMPE, Sigma Xi. Congregationlist. Patentee Transage titanium alloys. Office: Lockheed Missiles & Space Co 1111 Lockheed Way Sunnyvale CA 94086 *Choose well how your time is spent. Time spent doing one thing is time that cannot be spent doing something else.*

CROSSLEY, RANDOLPH ALLIN, ret. corp. exec.; b. Cupertino, Calif., July 10, 1904; s. John P. and Elizabeth (Hall) C.; m. Florence Pepperdine, July 23, 1928; 1 dau., Meredith (Mrs. Jack E. Young). Student, A. to Zed Coll. Prep. Sch., 1921-23, U. Calif., 1923-25. Founder Crossley Advt., Honolulu, 1929; pres. Hawaiian Tuna Packers, Ltd., Honolulu, 1930-34, Hawaiian Fruit Packers, Ltd., 1936-54, Aloha Stamp Co., Ltd., 1954-64, Nonou Devel. Co., Ltd., Honolulu; pres., exec. officer Crossley Contracting Co., 1954-63, Crossco, Ltd., from 1964; pres., chief exec. officer Am. Pacific Group, Inc., 1967-69, chmn., chief exec. officer, 1969-72; pres. Am. Pacific Life Ins. Co. Ltd., 1967-69; chmn. Hawaii Corp., 1968-76; pres., dir. Pacific Savs. and Loan Assn., 1962-65; chmn. Medi-Fund Corp., San Francisco, 1969-76; Mem. Public Utilities Commn., 1945-47. Mem. Hawaii Ho. of Reps.; 1943-45 Constl. Conv., 1950, Hawaii Senate, 1959-64; chmn. Rep. party Hawaii, 1950-52; Rep. candidate for gov., 1966, 74, Rep. nat. committeeman from, Hawaii, 1967-69, Presdl. elector, 1972. Mem. NAM (dir. 1970-76), C. of C. Hawaii (dir. 1954-59, 71-74), Newcomen Soc., N. Am. (hon. trustee), Rancheros Visitadores (Calif.). Past trustee, treas. Kawaiahao Ch. Clubs: Outrigger Canoe (Honolulu); Bohemian (San Francisco). Home: PO Box 1518 Pebble Beach CA 93953

CROSSMAN, WILLIAM WHITTARD, business exec.; b. Mineola, N.Y., Aug. 10, 1927; s. Homer Danforth and Emily May (Whittard) C.; m. Mary DeJesu, Dec. 6, 1952; children—William Whittard, Lindsay Maria, Michael DeJesu. B.S. in Engring. Scis, U. Miami, Fla., 1949. West coast mgr., gen. mgr. HiTemp Wires div. Simplex Wire & Cable Co., 1955-69; pres. ITT Surprenant Div., 1969-74, ITT Royal Electric Div., Pawtucket, R.I., 1974-77; group gen. mgr. ITT Corp., N.Y.C., 1977—, v.p., 1979—. Served with USNR, 1945-46; Served with USAF, 1951. Mem. IEEE, Soc. Plastic Engrs., Wire Assn. Republican. Episcopalian. Clubs: Internat. Golf, Owls Head Harbor, San Remo. Home: 24 White Oak Shade Rd New Canaan CT 06840 Office: 320 Park Ave New York NY 10022

CROSSON, FREDERICK JAMES, university dean; b. Belmar, N.J., Apr. 27, 1926; s. George Leon and Emily (Bennett) C.; m. Mary Patricia Burns, Sept. 5, 1953; ldren—Jessica, Christopher, Veronica, Benedict, Jennifer. B.A., Cath. U. Am., 1949, M.A., 1950; postgrad., U. Paris, France, 1951-52; Ph.D., U. Notre Dame, 1956. Instr. U. Notre Dame, 1953-56; asst. prof., 1956-62, assoc. prof., 1962-66, prof., 1966—; dean Coll. Arts and Letters, 1968-76, O'Hara Distinguished prof. philosophy, 1976—. Author: The Modeling of Mind, 1963, Philosophy and Cybernetics, 1967, Science and Contemporary Society, 1967; Editor: Review of Politics, 1976-83. Served with USNR, 1943-46. Mem. AAUP;, Am. Philos. Assn., Phi Beta Kappa. Home: 1307 E Jefferson Blvd South Bend IN 46617 Office: Coll Arts and Letters Notre Dame IN 46556

CROSTHWAIT, JOHN EDWARD, aerospace company executive; b. Willimantic, Conn., Nov. 10, 1932; s. Franklin Samuel and Gertrude Madd (Best) C.; 1 dau., Patricia Ann. B.S., St. Lawrence U., 1954. Test pilot Republic Aviation Corp., Farmingdale, N.Y., 1958-62; engr., mgr. Douglas Aircraft Co., Long Beach, Calif., 1962-68, v.p., 1972-77; program mgr. McDonnell Aircraft Co., St. Louis, 1969-72; pres. McDonnell Douglas Japan Ltd., Tokyo, 1978-82; corp. v.p. McDonnell Douglas Corp., Washington, 1982—; mem. U.S. Del. NATO Indsl. Adv. Group, Brussels, 1982—. Bd. govs. Japan-Am. Soc., Washington, 1983. Served to 1st lt. USMC, 1954-58. Mem. Nat. Aeronautic Assn. (bd. govs. 1982—), Air Force Assn., Tailhook Assn. (charter), Navy League U.S. (life), Assn. of Navy Aviation (charter). Clubs: City Tavern (Washington); National Aviation (bd. govs.); Wings (N.Y.C.). Office: McDonnell Douglas Corp 1225 Jefferson Davis Hwy Arlington VA 22202

CROTHERS, BENJAMIN SHERMAN (SCATMAN), actor; b. Terre Haute, Ind., May 23, 1910; m. Helen Sullivan, 1937; 1 dau., Donna. Began career as nightclub musician; film debut in Meet Me at the Fair, 1949; other films include Hello Dolly, 1969, The Great White Hope, 1970, Lady Sings the Blues, 1972, The King of Marvin Garden, 1972, One Flew Over the Cuckoo's Nest, 1975, The Fortune, 1975, The Shootist, 1976, Silver Streak, 1977, Scavenger Hunt, 1979, Bronco Billy, 1980, The Shining, 1980, Zapped!, 1982, The Rats, 1982; appeared in: TV series Chico and the Man, 1974-78, Roots, 1977; other TV appearances include Beulah, One of the Boys, 1982; voice on cartoon voiceovers. Office: care Don Schwartz & Assos 8721 Sunset Blvd Los Angeles CA 90069 *

CROTHERS, DONALD MORRIS, biochemist, educator; b. Fatehgarh, India, Jan. 28, 1937; came to U.S., 1939, naturalized, 1937; s. Morris K. and Eunice F. C.; m. Leena Kareoja, June 24, 1960; children—Nina H., Kristina A. B.S., Yale U., 1958; B.A., Cambridge U., 1960; Ph.D., U. Calif.-, San Diego, 1963. NSF postdoctoral fellow Max Planck Inst., Gottingen, Germany, 1963-64; asst. prof. Yale U., New Haven, 1964-68, asso. prof., 1968-71, prof. chemistry and molecular biophysics and biochemistry, 1971—, chmn. dept. chemistry, 1975-81; chmn. biophysics, biophysical chemistry B study sect. NIH, 1972-76; co-chmn. nucleic acids Gordon Conf., 1975. Author: Physical Chemistry of Nucleic Acids, 1974, Physical Chemistry with Application to the Life Sciences, 1979; Mem. editorial bd.: Jour. Molecular Biology, 1971-75, Nucleic Acids Research, 1973-82, Biochemistry, 1975-78, Biopolymers, 1977—; Contbr. articles to profl. jours. Recipient Sci. and Engring. award Yale U., 1977; Alexander von Humboldt Sr. Scientist award, 1981; Mellon fellow Clare Coll. Cambridge U., 1958-60; Guggenheim fellow, 1978. Mem. Biophys. Soc. (council 1979-82), Am. Soc. Biol. Chemists. Office: Dept Chemistry Yale U New Haven CT 06520

CROTTY, LEO ALAN, drugstore chain exec.; b. Chgo., Nov. 2, 1929; s. Michael Leo and Helen Marie (Toole) C.; m. Frances Mary Tauscheck, Sept. 1, 1956; children—Robert, Daniel, Kimberly, Lisa, Matthew. B.S., U. Ill., 1958. C.P.A., Ill. Mem. firm Arthur Young & Co. (C.P.A.'s), Chgo., 1958-63, Comml. Trades Inst., 1964-66; with Walgreen Co., Chgo., 1966—, controller, 1971-78, v.p. adminstrn., 1978—. Served with USAF, 1950-54. Mem. Chgo. Retail Fin. Execs. Assn. (dir. 1974—), Ill. Soc. C.P.A.'s, Am. Inst. C.P.A.'s. Office: Walgreen Co 200 Wilmot Rd Deerfield IL 60015

CROTTY, WILLIAM, political science educator; b. Somerville, Mass., Apr. 14, 1936. A.B. with honors, U. Mass., 1958; M.A., U. N.C., 1960, Ph.D., 1964. Asst. prof. polit. sci. U. Ga., Athens, 1963-66, Northwestern U., Evanston, Ill., 1966-69, assoc. prof., 1970-73, prof., 1974—; co-dir. task force on polit. assassination Nat. Commn. on Causes and Prevention Violence, Washington, 1968-70; project dir. Am. polit. parties project Nat. Mcpl. League, 1972-74; guest scholar Woodrow Wilson Internat. Ctr. for Scholars, summer 1971; prin. on broadcast Bill Moyers' Jour. Pub. TV Network, 1980, CBS-TV Spl. Program, 1980; cons. permanent community sample and community action program study Nat. Opinion Research Ctr. Author: books, including: Political Reform and American Experiment, 1977; Decision for the Democrats, 1978, Party Reform, 1983; co-author: books, including: American Parties in Decline, 1980; author monographs; editor, contbg. author: books, including: The Party Symbol, 1980; editor: for electoral politics Policy Studies Jour., 1972-74; contbr. articles to profl. publs. Exec. dir. Freedom To Vote Task Force, Washington, 1969-70, Task Force on Campaign Financing, Washington, 1970; mem. Ams. for Democratic Action 1972 Conv. Reform Task Force, Democratic Party Accountability Commn., 1980—, Com. To Observe Honduran Election, 1981, Com. to Observe Argentine Elections, 1983; mem. exec. bd. com. on party accountability Dem. Party, 1981—. Fellow Ctr. for Higher Edn. U. Oreg., 1965-66; Am. Polit. Sci. Assn. fellow Dem. Nat. Com., 1969-70. Mem. Am. Polit. Sci. Assn. (exec. com. polit. orgns./parties subfield 1982—), Midwest Polit. Sci. Assn., Soc. Polit. Sci. Assn., Am. Assn. Pub. Opinion Analysts, Midwest Assn. Pub. Opinion Research.

CROUCH, ANDRAE, singer, composer, musician; b. Los Angeles, July 1, 1942; s. Benjamin Jerome and Catherine Dorthea (Hodnett) C. Student, Life Bible Coll., Los Angeles. Organizer, leader, The Disciples, gospel group, 1968—; rec. artist 10 albums including Just Andrae (Nat. Acad. Rec. Arts and Scis. Grammy nominee), At Carnegie Hall, Take Me Back, (Grammy award 1976), This Is Another Day, (Dove award 1978), Life in London, (Grammy award 1978, also Dove award); appeared at, White House, 1979; also on numerous TV spls. and talk shows.; Producer record albums. (Recipient Gold Record for song Jesus Is the Answer, named Soul Gospel Artist of 1975 and 1977, Billboard mag., Grammy award for I'll Be Thinking of You 1979, Daviticus awards 1979); Author: Through It All, 1974; Composer numerous songs. Office: care Eubanks-Leopold Mgmt 5525 Oakdale Suite 110 Woodland Hills CA 91364

CROUCH, FORDYCE WILLIAM, lawyer; b. Curlew, Iowa, Feb. 12, 1914; s. Alfred William and Ida Mae (Nicholson) C.; m. Alice Welch, July 2, 1938; children—Ford William, John Steven, Thomas Nicholson. Student, Ft. Dodge Jr. Coll., 1931-33; B.S., U. Minn., 1935, LL.B., 1937. Bar: Iowa bar 1937, Minn. bar 1938. Practice of law, Mpls., 1938—; with M., St. P. & S.S. Ry., Mpls., 1938—, gen. counsel 1957—; v.p., gen. counsel Soo Line R.R. Co., until 1979; ret., 1979. Mem. Am., Minn. bar assns. Republican. Conglist. Club: Mpls. Athletic. Home: 4849 James Ave S Minneapolis MN 55409

CROUCH, JAMES ENSIGN, educator, zoologist; b. Urbana, Ill., Jan. 28, 1908; s. Harry Ensign and Mary Jane (Pierce) C.; m. Mary Vrooman Page, Nov. 28, 1931; children: Jeanette Elnor (Mrs. Alex Rigopoulos), James Page. B.S., Cornell U., 1930, M.S., 1931; Ph.D., U. So. Calif., 1939. Mem. faculty San Diego State Coll., 1932—, prof. zoology, 1940-73, chmn. div. life scis., 1962-69, emeritus, 1973—. Author: Introduction to Human Anatomy, 1958, Functional Human Anatomy, 1965, 3d edit., 1978, Atlas of Cat Anatomy, 1969, (with Dr. J. Robert McClintic) Human Anatomy and Physiology, 1971, 2d edit., 1976, (with Micheline H. Carr) A Laboratory Manual, Anatomy and Physiology, 1977, Essential Human Anatomy: A Text-Atlas, 1982. Fellow San Diego Zool. Soc., San Diego Mus. Natural History (trustee 1971-76); mem. Nat. Audubon Soc., Phi Beta Kappa (hon.), Sigma Xi, Phi Kappa Phi, Phi Sigma. Democrat. Unitarian. Home: 10430 Russel Rd La Mesa CA 92041 *I believe in the use of reason and scientific methods in the pursuit of knowledge and understanding. I believe that human beings are the source, the definers and the arbiters of values and ethics. I am now aware that values change in response to the continuing experience of humans.*

CROUCH, JORDAN JONES, bankers assn. exec.; b. Johnson City, Tenn., July 10, 1909; s. Adam Bowman and Agnes (Jones) C.; m. Elizabeth Wright, June 22, 1933; 1 son, William Wright. A.B., Milligan Coll., 1931; LL.D., 1970; postgrad., Northwestern, 1931-32, Vanderbilt U., 1933. Mgr. Chapman Park Hotel, Los Angeles, 1934-40; asst. to works mgr., mfg. div. Lockheed Aircraft Co., 1940-45; credit analyst Bank of Am. (Los Angeles hdqrs.), 1945-49; v.p. First Nat. Bank of Nev., Reno, 1949-63, sr. v.p., 1963-70, exec. v.p., 1971-74, Nev. Bankers Assn., 1974—. Past pres. Reno-Sparks United Way; exec. bd. Nev. Area council Boy Scouts of Am.; mem. Nev. 4-H Adv. Council; trustee Milligan Coll.; mem. Nev. Exec. Council Econ. Edn.; mem. bd. Coll. Med. Sci., U. Nev.; bd. dirs. Nat. Jud. Coll., Nev. Jr. Achievement. Recipient Silver medal Printers' Ink mag., 1967; Nev. award Christians and Jews Assn., 1965. Mem. Am. Bankers Assn. (past mem. exec. council), Nev. Bankers Assn. (past pres.), Bank Mktg. Assn. (past pres.), Reno C. of C. (past dir.), Nev. Press Assn., Nev. Mining Assn., Colo. River Water Users Assn., Beta Gamma, Kappa Sigma. Clubs: Rotary (past pres.), Execs. (Reno) (past pres.); Prospectors (dir.). Home: 140 Crestview Pl Reno NV 89509 Office: 1 E Liberty St: Reno NV 80505

CROUCH, PAUL FRANKLIN, minister, ch. ofcl.; b. St. Joseph, Mo., Mar. 30, 1914; s. Andrew Franklin and Sarah Matilda (Swingle) C.; m. Janice Wendell Bethany, Aug. 25, 1957; children—Paul F., Matthew W. B.Th., Central Bible Coll. and Sem., Springfield, Mo., 1955. Ordained to ministry, 1955; dir. fgn. missions film and audio visual dept. Assemblies of God, 1955-58; asso. pastor 1st Assembly of God, Rapid City, S.D., 1958-60, Central Assembly of God, Muskegon, Mich., 1960-62; gen. mgr. TV and film prodn. center Assemblies of God, Burbank, Calif., 1962-65; gen. mgr. Sta. KREL, Cornona, Calif., 1965-71, Sta. KHOF, KHOF-TV, Glendale, Calif., 1971-73; founder, pres. Sta. KLXA-TV, Trinity Broadcasting Network, Los Angeles, 1973—. Recipient Best Religious film award Winona Lake Film Festival, 1956. Mem. Nat. Assn. Religious Broadcasters, Western Religious Broadcasters Assn., Assn. Christian TV Stas. (founder). Office: Box A Santa Ana CA 92711 *

CROUCH, THOMAS GENE, lawyer; b. Ft. Worth, June 29, 1933; s. Lloyd Thomas and Vesta (Hardin) C.; m. Sandra Prock; children: Kelly Annette, Kippie Adams, Thomas Michie. B.S., Abilene Christian Coll., 1954; J.D., So. Methodist U., 1957. Bar: Tex. 1957; Lic. auctioneer. With firm Turner, White, Atwood, McLane & Francis, Dallas, 1957-59; with legal dept. Hunt Oil Co., Dallas, 1959-64; pvt. practice with Robert B. Payne, Dallas, 1964-66; pres. firm Crouch & Jones, Dallas, 1966—; dir. Tex. Am. Bank, Prestonwood, Plano; staff asst. to Pres. U.S., 1973. Republican candidate for Tex. Senate, 1966, for, Congress, 1972; chmn. Dallas County Rep. Party, 1969-72; regional dir. Com. to Re-Elect the Pres., 1972; mem. Presdl. Inaugural Com., 1973; bd. dirs. Dallas Assembly, 1970-73, v.p., 1971-72; bd. dirs. Dallas United Way, 1977-83. Served with AUS, 1957-58, 61-62. Mem. ABA; mem. Tex. Bar Assn., Dallas Bar Assn., Fed. Power Bar Assn.; Mem. Nat. Auctioneers Assn., Tex. Auctioneers Assn. (dir. 1977-81), Phi Alpha Delta. Home: 2105 Winding Hollow Plano TX 75075 Office: 2920 Republic Bank Tower Dallas TX 75201

CROUGH, DANIEL FRANCIS, insurance company executive, lawyer; b. Syracuse, N.Y., Feb. 2, 1936; s. Vincent Leo and Sarah Jane (McMahon) C.; m. Domenica Dolores Cappadozy, July 27, 1957; children: Sara, Deborah, Maura, Deanne, Daniel. B.A., LeMoyne Coll., 1957; J.D., Syracuse U., 1960. Bar: N.Y. 1961, Pa. 1969, U.S. Supreme Ct. 1981. Sole practice Syracuse, 1961-63; staff atty. Reliance Ins. Co., Canandaigua, N.Y., 1963-71, Phila., 1963-71, sec., assoc. gen. counsel, 1971-72; v.p., gen. counsel Colonial Penn Ins. Co., Phila., 1972-74, v.p., corp. counsel, 1978-82, sr. v.p., sec., gen. counsel, 1982-83, pres., 1983—; dir. Colonial Penn Ins. Co., Colonial Penn Life Ins. Co., Colonial Penn Franklin Ins. Co., Phila., Intram. Life Ins. Co., N.Y.C. Major gifts chmn. United Fund, Canandaigua, 1966; vice-chmn. E. Whiteland Twp. Govt. Study Commn., Malvern Pa., 1973; dir., pres. Community Services for Human Growth, Paoli, Pa., 1983; dir., 1st v.p. Citizens Crime Commn., Phila., 1983. Mem. ABA, Internat. Assn. Ins. Counsel, N.Y. State Bar Assn., Pa. Bar Assn., Phila. Bar Assn. Republican. Roman Catholic. Clubs: Aronimink Golf (Newton Square, Pa.); Racquet (Phila.). Home: 9 Anthony Dr Frazer PA 19355 Office: Colonial Penn Group Inc 5 Penn Center Plaza Philadelphia PA 19181

CROUSE, FARRELL RONDALL, physician; b. N.C., Sept. 20, 1932; s. Claude Swanson and Zora Maye (Irwin) C.; m. Grace Alice Kenworthy, June 18, 1955; 1 son, Farrell Rondall. B.A. in Chemistry, U. N.C., 1953; M.D., Jefferson Med. Coll., 1958. Diplomate: Am. Bd. Psychiatry and Neurology. Intern Germantown Hosp., Pa., 1958-59; resident in psychiatry Jefferson Hosp., Friends Hosp., Pa., 1959-62; staff psychiatrist U.S. Naval Hosp., Portsmouth, Va., 1962-64; attending psychiatrist Reading Hosp., West Reading, Pa., 1964-65; practice psychiatry, Wyomissing, Pa., 1964-65; clin. psychiatrist II Ancora Psychiat. Hosp., Hammonton, N.J., 1965-67, clin. psychiatrist I, 1967-70, med. dir., chief exec. officer, 1970-76; pvt. practice, Woodstown, N.J., 1977—; cons. prison system, State of N.J. Served to lt. comdr. USNR, 1962-64. Mem. Am. Psychiat. Assn., AMA, N.J. Med. Soc. (council on mental health), Salem County Med. Soc., N.J. Neuropsychiat. Assn., Phi Beta Kappa, Phi Eta Sigma, Delta Phi Alpha, Phi Chi, Sigma Phi Epsilon. Home: Cedar Ln RD 3 Box 255 Laurel Hills Woodstown NJ 08098 Office: 101 N Main St PO Box 280 Woodstown NJ 08098

CROUT, J(OHN) RICHARD, physician, pharmaceutical researcher; b. Portland, Oreg., Dec. 30, 1929; s. John Shaw and Georgia (Jacobs) C.; m. Carol Jean Keith, June 19, 1954; children: Linda Jane, Keith Richard, Andrew Richard. A.B., Oberlin Coll., 1951; M.D., Northwestern U., 1955, M.S., 1956; D.Med. (hon.), U. Uppsala, Sweden, 1977. Intern Passavant Meml. Hosp., Chgo., 1955-56; asst. resident in internal medicine VA Research Hosp., Chgo., 1956-57; clin. asso. Nat. Heart Inst., Bethesda, Md., 1957-60; asst. resident in Medicine N.Y. U.-Bellevue Med. Center, N.Y.C., 1960-61; USPHS fellow, instr. pharmacology Harvard U., 1961-63; asst. prof. pharmacology and internal medicine U. Tex. Southwestern Med. Sch., Dallas, 1963-65, asso. prof., 1965-70; prof. pharmacology and medicine Mich. State U., 1970-71; dep. dir. Bur. Drugs FDA, Rockville, Md., 1971-72, dir. office sci. evaluation, 1972-73; dir. Bur. Drugs, 1973-82; dir. Office of Med. Applications of Research NIH, 1982-84; v.p. med. and sci. affairs Boehringer Mannheim Corp., 1984—; mem. drug research bd. Nat. Acad. Scis-NRC.; chmn. Task Force II, Nat. High Blood Pressure Edn. Program HEW, 1972-73; cons. WHO, 1974—. Contbr. articles to profl. jours. Served to sr. asst. surgeon USPHS, 1957-60; asst. surgeon gen., 1976-84. Recipient Distinguished Service award USPHS, 1977, Spl. Citation Commr. of FDA, 1981, 82; Burroughs Wellcome scholar in clin. pharmacology, 1965-70. Fellow ACP; mem. Am. Fedn. Clin. Research, Am. Soc. Pharmacology and Exptl. Therapeutics, Am. Soc. Clin. Investigation, Am. Soc. Clin. Pharmacology and Therapeutics, Heart Assn., Phi Beta Kappa, Alpha Omega Alpha. Home: 5300 Alta Vista Rd Bethesda MD 20814 Office: 1700 Rockville Pike Suite 400 Rockville MD 20852

CROW, BROWNING, cons. engr.; b. Kansas City, Mo., May 25, 1923; s. Weldon D. and Elizabeth (Browning) C.; m. Helen Gene Veach, Sept. 3, 1946; children—Cathleen, Robert, Nancy. B.A., U. Kansas City, 1944; B.S., U. Mo., 1948. Civil engr. Howard, Needles, Tammen & Bergendoff, Kansas City, 1948-50, asst. project engr., Colo., 1950-52, project engr., Ravenna, Ohio, 1952-56, Cleve., 1956-68, partner, 1968—; Industry adv. bd. Cleve. State U., 1976—. Served with USN, 1943-46. Mem. Nat. Soc. Profl. Engrs., Ohio Soc. Profl. Engrs., Am. Soc. C.E., Am. Pub. Works Assn. Republican. Episcopalian. Clubs: Lakewood Country, Cleve. Athletic, Rotary. Home: 31315 Carlton Dr Bay Village OH 44140 Office: 1 Erieview Plaza Cleveland OH 44114

CROW, ELIZABETH SMITH, editor; b. N.Y.C., July 29, 1946; d. Harrison Venture and Marlis (deGreve) Smith; m. Charles P. Crow, Mar. 2, 1974; children: Samuel Harrison, Rachel Venture. B.A., Mills Coll., 1968; postgrad., Brown U., 1969-70. Editorial asst. New Yorker mag., N.Y.C., 1968-69; exec. editor New York mag., N.Y.C., 1970-78; editor-in-chief Parents mag., N.Y.C., 1978—; free-lance book reviewer Washington Post Book World; v.p. Editors' Organizing Com., 1982—; screener Nat. Mag. Awards, 1982—. Video and software reviewer, Video Rev. mag. Mem. Am. Soc. Mag. Editors (exec. com.), Womens Media Group. Democrat. Club: Cosmopolitan. Office: 685 3d Ave New York NY 10017

CROW, HAROLD EUGENE, family medicine educator, physician; b. Farber, Mo., Jan. 17, 1933; s. Leslie J. and Laura Leone (Sparks) C.; m. Barbara Carol Carlson, June 26, 1954 (div. June 1974); children: Janet L., Jason P.; m. Mary Kay Krenke, July 5, 1974. M.D., U. Mo., 1963. Diplomate: Am. Bd. Family Practice, Am. Bd. Med. Examiners. Intern E.W. Sparrow Hosp., Lansing, Mich., 1963-64; practice medicine specializing in family practice, Lansing, Mich., 1964-70; dir. family practice residency E.W. Sparrow Hosp., Lansing, Mich., 1970-82; chmn. dept. family medicine U. Nev. Sch. Medicine, Reno, 1982—. Bd. dirs. Drug Edn. Ctr., East Lansing, Mich., 1974, med. dir., 1974; mem. bd. health Ingham County, Lansing, Mich., 1978; chmn. Mayor's Adv. Com. Parks, Lansing, 1979. Served with U.S. Army, 1955-57. Mem. Soc. Tchrs. Family Medicine, Mich. Acad. Family Physicians (bd. dirs. 1975-77 1980, pres. elect 1981-82). Presbyterian. Home: 645 College Dr Reno NV 89503 Office: Family Medicine U Nev 410 Mill St Reno NV 89502

CROW, JAMES SYLVESTER, retired banker, railway executive; b. Mobile, Ala., June 23, 1915; s. James S. and Elizabeth (Jackson) C.; m.

Dorothy Farwell, Sept. 21, 1974; children: Michele Marie, Denise Anne, Marcia Lynn, Deborah Jane. Student, U. Ala., 1946-48; grad., Rutgers Sch. Banking, 1959. Clk. First Nat. Bank Mobile, 1932-41, 45-48, mgr. bond dept., 1949-50, asst. cashier, 1951, asst. v.p., 1952; sales mgr. Hendrix & Mayes Investment Bankers, Birmingham, Ala.; asst. cashier First Nat. Bank Birmingham, 1954-55, asst. v.p., 1955-56, v.p., 1957-60, sr. v.p., 1961-66, exec. v.p., 1966-67; v.p. finance So. Ry. Co., Washington, 1967-70; exec. v.p. First Nat. Bank Mobile, 1970-71, pres., 1971-74, chmn. bd., 1974-79; chmn. bd., pres. First Bancgroup Ala., Inc., 1973-79; dir. Ala. Gt. So. R.R., La. So. R.R., Ala. Dry Dock and Shipbldg. Co., Mobile, Lerio Corp., Mobile. Chmn. Am. Cancer Soc., Ala., 1971; Chmn., trustee Ala. Assn. Ind. Colls., 1979-80; trustee So. Research Inst., Birmingham. Mem. Ala. Security Dealers Assn. (pres. 1955), Ala. Bankers Assn. (v.p. 1966-67), Newcomen Soc. N. Am. Episcopalian. Clubs: Country (Birmingham); Athelstan, Country, Lakewood (Mobile); Metropolitan (N.Y.); (Washington). Home: PO Box 69 Montrose AL 36559

CROW, JOHN ARMSTRONG, writer, educator; b. Wilmington, N.C., Dec. 18, 1906; s. George Davis and Olive Lois (Armstrong) C.; m. Josephine Gorden, 1956; children: Diane O., John Armstrong. A.B., U. of N.C., 1927; M.A., Columbia, 1930; Ph. D., Litt.D., U. of Madrid, Spain, 1933. Instr. U. N.C., 1926-27, Davidson Coll., N.C., 1927-28, N.Y.U., 1928-37; instr. U. Calif., Los Angeles, 1937—, chmn. Spanish dept., 1949-54; Helped organize Internat. Inst. of Ibero-Am. Literature, Mexico City, 1938, sec., 1938-40; chmn. Sect. of Cultural Exchange, 1940—. Co-editor: Jour. Revista Iberoamericana; pub.: Mexico City, 1940-42; editor: Latin Am. entries and revisions to Ency. Americana, 1942; Author: books, latest Panorama de las Americas, 1949, 80, Epic of Latin America, 1952, 80, California As a Place to Live, 1953, Mexico Today, 1957, 72, Spanish American Life, 1963, Spain—The Root and the Flower, 1963, 75, Italy: a Journey Through Time, 1965, Greece: the Magic Spring, 1970, An Anthology of Spanish Poetry, 1979; Contbr. articles on lit., history, art, dancing to leading mags. U.S. and Latin Am. also encys. Mem. Soc. Mayflower, Authors League Am., Desc. Knights of Garter, Order of Don Quixote, Phi Beta Kappa. Home: 218 N Bundy Dr Los Angeles CA 90049

CROW, NEIL EDWARD, radiologist; b. Belton, Tex., July 12, 1926; s. Floyd Charles and Mary Virginia (Martin) C.; m. Mary Katherine Claxton, Sept. 11, 1948; children: Neil E., Katherine Lee. B.S., U. Tex., 1946; M.D., U. Ark., 1951. Diplomate: Am. Bd. Radiology. Intern U. Ark. Coll. Medicine, Little Rock, 1951-52, resident in radiology, 1953-56; practice medicine, Hope, Ark., 1952-53; radiologist Holt-Krock Clinic and Sparks Regional Med. Center, Fort Smith, Ark., 1960—; chief staff Sparks Regional Med. Center, 1973; pres. Radiology Services, P.A., Fort Smith, 1976—; cons. radiologist area hosps.; clin. prof. radiology U. Ark., 1961—; dir. Fairfield Communities, Inc., First Nat. Bank. Contbr. articles to profl. jours. Trustee Ark. Tech. U., 1972-77, Sparks Regional Med. Center, 1974—; mem. Fort Smith Sch. Bd., 1969-72, pres., 1972. Served to lt. USNR, 1944-47; col. USAF Res.; ret. Recipient Disting. Alumnus award U. Ark. Coll. Medicine, 1975. Fellow Am. Coll. Radiology; mem. Am. Fedn. Clin. Research, AMA, Air Force Assn., Am. Roentgen Ray Soc., Radiol. Soc. N. Am., U. Ark. Coll. Med. Alumni Assn. (pres. 1972-74), Alpha Omega Alpha. Democrat. Presbyterian. Home: 19 Berry Hill Fort Smith AR 72903 Office: 1500 Dodson Ave Fort Smith AR 72901

CROW, PAUL ABERNATHY, JR., clergyman, religious council exec., educator; b. Birmingham, Ala., Nov. 17, 1931; s. Paul Abernathy and Beulah Elizabeth (Parker) C.; m. Mary Evelyn Matthews, Sept. 11, 1955; children—Carol Ann, Stephen Paul, Susan Margaret. B.S., U. Ala., 1954; B.D., Lexington Theol. Sem., 1957; S.T.M. (Jacobus fellow), Hartford Sem. Found., 1958, Ph.D., 1962; postgrad., Oxford (Eng.) U., 1967-68. Campus minister U. Ala., 1953-54; minister congregations, Ala., Ky., 1955-57; ordained to ministry Christian Ch., 1957; minister First Congl. Ch., Hadley, Mass., 1957-61; asso. prof. ch. history Lexington Theol. Sem., 1961-66, prof., 1966-68; Am. Assn. Theol. Schs. vis. fellow Oxford U., 1967-68; gen. sec. Consultation on Ch. Union, Princeton, 1968-74; pres. Council on Christian Unity, Indpls., 1974—; Mem. central com. World Council Chs., exec. com., plenary faith and order commn., moderator bd. govs. ecumenical inst. Bossey; del. faith and order confs., St. Andrews, Scotland, 1960, Montreal, Que., Can., 1963, Bristol, Eng., 1967, Louvain, Belgium, 1971, Accra, Ghana, 1974, Bangalore, India, 1978; del. assembly, Uppsala, Sweden, 1968, Nairobi, Kenya, 1975, del. ch. union confs., Limuru, Kenya, 1970, Toronto, Ont., Can., 1975; mem. exec. com. Consultation on Ch. Union; chmn. Disciples of Christ del.; mem. exec. com., mem. governing bd. Nat. Council Chs.; co-chmn. Disciples-Roman Cath. Internat. Bilaterals; vis. lectr. Princeton Theol. Sem., 1968—; affiliate prof. Christian Theol. Sem., 1974—; gen. sec. Disciples Ecumenical Consultative Council. Author: Where We Are In Church Union, 1965, The Ecumenical Movement in Bibliographical Outline, 1965, No Greater Love: The Gospel and Its Imperatives, 1967, Church Union at Mid-Point, 1972, Christian Unity: Matrix for Mission, 1982; Editor: Mid-Stream; An Ecumenical Jour, 1974—. Trustee Disiples of Christ Hist. Soc. Mem. Am. Soc. Ch. History, North Am. Acad. Ecumenists, Omicron Delta Kappa, Theta Phi. Democrat. Clubs: Nassau (Princeton, N.J.); Indianapolis Athletic. Home: 7215 Vauxhall Rd Indianapolis IN 46250 Office: 222 S Downey Ave PO Box 1986 Indianapolis IN 46206

CROW, WALTER, JR., security products manufacturing company executive; b. Canton, Ohio, Nov. 6, 1936; s. Walter Lester and Ann Elizabeth (Croxall) C.; m. Joan Elizabeth Campbell, July 2, 1974; children by previous mariage: Catherine, David stepchildren: David, Dan, Darcy, Doug Keener. B.S. in Mech. Engring., U. Cin., 1959. Coop engring. student Diebold, Inc., Canton, Ohio, 1955-59, sales engr., N.Y.C., 1959-64, regional sales mgr., 1964-68, nat. mktg. dir., Canton, 1968-69, v.p. sales Lamson Div., Syracuse, N.Y., 1969-73, v.p. mktg., Canton, 1973-76, v.p. mktg., product mgmt., 1976-82, sr. v.p., 1982—. Mem. Underwriters Labs. security adv. com., Chgo., 1977—, United Arts, Canton, 1976. Mem. Newcomen Soc. N.Am., Am. Mgmt. Assn. Clubs: Brookside Country, Stark County Bluecoats, Lake Cable Sportsmen's, Firestone Country. Office: 818 Mulberry Rd SE Canton OH 44711

CROW, WILLIAM LANGSTAFF, constuction company executive; b. N.Y.C., Mar. 15, 1910; s. Ralph L. and Ella (McClenahan) C.; m. Barbara Baker, Sept. 14, 1936; children—William Langstaff III, Margo B. Crow Reis, Sandra B. (Mrs. Edward Luneburg), Barbara, Ella McClenahan. Grad., Hotchkiss Sch., 1929; A.B., Princeton, 1933. With Wm. L. Crow Constrn. Co., N.Y.C., 1934—, chmn., dir., 1935—; dir. U.S. Trust Corp.; hon. trustee U.S. Trust Co., N.Y., 1951—, United Mutual Savs. Bank, N.Y.C., 1957-. Chmn. Rye (N.Y.) Housing Authority, 1964; mem. Princeton Grad. Council, 1950—; trustee St. Luke's Hosp., N.Y.C. Served to maj. C.E. AUS, 1942-45; ETO. Decorated Bronze Star. Mem. N.Y. Bldg. Congress (bd. govs. 1941-42, 50-54, 62-66, v.p. 1946-50), Princeton Engring. Assn. (pres. 1962-63, exec. com. 1956—), Princeton Alumni Council (exec. com. 1960—). Clubs: Princeton (bd. govs. 1957-66); Am. Yacht (Rye) (commodore 1951-52); Cruising of Am.; Cap and Gown (Princeton). Home: 1316 Casey Key Rd Nokomis FL 33555

CROWDER, MONCURE GRAVATT, banker; b. Richmond, Va., Feb. 7, 1940; s. William Herbert, Jr. and Frances Epes (Gravatt) C.; m. Jo Ann Avery, Aug. 8, 1964; children—Anne York, Caroline Moncure, Moncure Gravatt. B.S. in Fin, U. Va., 1962. With First Nat. Bank Atlanta, 1964—, v.p., 1970-74, sr. v.p., 1974-78, exec. v.p., 1978—; corp. v.p., treas. First Atlanta Corp.; instr. Sch. Banking of South, 1973-80. Bd. dirs. First Montessori Sch., Atlanta, 1972-75, Atlanta Bot. Garden, 1977-80, Atlanta Met. chpt. ARC, 1975-81. Nat. Merit scholar, 1958-62. Mem. Public Securities Assn. (dir. 1977-79), U.S. C. of C., Dealer Bank Assn., Ga. Security Dealers Assn., Atlanta Econs. Club. Republican. Episcopalian. Clubs: Cherokee Townand Country, Atlanta Track. Office: 2 Peachtree St NW Atlanta GA 30383

CROWDUS, GARY ALAN, film distributor, magazine editor; b. Lexington, Ky., Jan. 2, 1945; s. Charles Dallas and Bess May (Rice) C. B.F.A., N.Y.U. Inst. Film and TV, 1969. Founding editor Cineaste Mag., N.Y.C., 1967—; assoc. editor Film Soc. Rev., N.Y.C., 1968-72; v.p. Tricontinental Film Ctr., N.Y.C., 1972-79, Unifilm Inc., 1979-80; gen. mgr. The Cinema Guild, N.Y.C., 1981—; dir. Ctr. Ednl. Prodns., N.Y.C., 1979—; organizing com. U.S. Conf. Alternative Cinema, N.Y.C., 1978-79. Editor, author: The Political Companion to Film; contbr. The Cineaste Interviews, 1983. Home: 116 Saint Marks Pl Apt 8 New York NY 10009 Office: The Cinema Guild 1697 Broadway Rm 802 New York NY 10019

CROWE, ARTHUR LEE, JR., retail store chain executive; b. Los Angeles, July 7, 1923; s. Arthur Lee and Mildred Theresa (Frudden) C.; m. Mary Louise Strub, Feb. 4, 1950; children: Susan, Arthur Lawrence, Charles Edward. B.A., Stanford U.; M.B.A., Harvard U. Vice pres., gen. mdse. mgr. Broadway Dept. Stores; chmn., chief exec. officer Weinstock's; now exec. v.p., dir. Carter Hawley Hale Stores, Inc., Los Angeles; dir. Santa Anita Consol., Hibernia Bank, San Francisco. Served with USN, 1943-46. Republican. Episcopalian. Clubs: River (N.Y.C.); Calif., Los Angeles Turf (dir.), Valley Hunt, Annandale Golf, Stock Exchange (Los Angeles); Pacific Union (San Francisco). Office: Carter Hawley Hale Stores Inc 550 S Flower St Los Angeles CA 90071

CROWE, CAMERON MACMILLAN, chemical engineering educator; b. Montreal, Que., Can., Oct. 6, 1931; s. Ernest Watson and Marianne (Macmillan) C.; m. Jean Margaret Gilbertson, Feb. 15, 1969. Student, Royal Mil. Coll., 1948-52; B.Eng., McGill U., 1953; Ph.D., Cambridge (Eng.) U., 1957. Sr. devel. engr. DuPont of Can., Maitland, Ont., 1957-59; mem. faculty dept. chem. engring. McMaster U., Hamilton, Ont., 1959—, asso. prof., 1964-70, prof., 1970—, chmn. dept., 1971-74. Author: (with others) Chemical Plant Simulation, 1971; Assoc. editor: Canadian Jour. Chem. Engring, 1975-81. C.D. Howe Meml. fellow Rice U., Houston, 1967-68; Athlone fellow, 1953-55. Mem. Am. Inst. Chem. Engrs., Can. Soc. Chem. Engring. Home: 821 Glenwood Ave Burlington ON Canada Office: McMaster Univ Hamilton ON Canada

CROWE, CHARLES LAWSON, educator; b. Chattanooga, Sept. 2, 1928; s. Charles V. and Reita L. (Lawson) C.; m. Harriet Vincent Barker, June 22, 1970; children—Charles Glenn, Thaddeus Lawson. B.A., Duke, 1950; M.A., Columbia, 1955, Ph.D., 1961. Asst. dir. grad. admissions Columbia, 1955-56; instr. to asso. prof. philosophy Sweet Briar Coll., Va., 1956-64; nat. rep., dir. Dissertation Fellowship Program, Woodrow Wilson Found., Princeton, N.J., 1964-67; asso. dean Grad. Sch., asso. prof. philosophy U. Colo., Boulder, 1967, acting dean, asso. prof., 1968, dean, asso. prof., 1969-71, v.p. research, dean, asso. prof., 1971, provost, v.p. research, prof. philosophy, 1971-74, chancellor, 1974-76, prof., 1971-; mem. nat. bd. cons. Nat. Endowment Humanities, 1976—. Contbr. articles to profl. jours. Served with U.S. Army, 1951-53. Fellow Inst. Behavioral Genetics; mem. Am. Philos. Assn., Univ. Corp. for Atmospheric Research (mem.'s rep. 1971-76). Home: 2505 Cragmoor Dr Boulder CO 80303

CROWE, EDWARD WHEELER, pipeline construction executive; b. Tulsa, Aug. 20, 1941; s. Raymond H. and Donna (Wheeler) C.; m. Sharon Kay Weaver, May 7, 1982; children: Kellie, David, Traci. B.B.A., U. Houston, 1965. Project engr. Assoc. Pipe Line Contractors, Inc., Houston, 1966-70; asst. to pres. Assoc. Pipe Line Constractors, Inc., Houston, 1971-73; exec. v.p. Panhandle Constrn. Co., Lubbock, Tex., 1974-76, Assoc. Pipe Line Contractors, Inc., Houston, 1976-77; pres. successor firm Reading & Bates Constrn. Co., Houston, 1977—; dir. Green Holdings, Inc., Des Moines, Wescan Ltd., Edmonton, Alta., Can., TAF-RAB, Dammon, Saudi Arabia. Inventor automatic device for testing pipelines, 1968. Mem. Pipe Line Contractors Assn. (dir., pres. 1983). Office: Reading & Bates Construction Co 3657 Briarpark St Houston TX 77042

CROWE, EUGENE BERTRAND, investment counselor; b. Wadley, Ala., Nov. 2, 1916; s. Will Mack and Eudoxie (Bonner) C.; children: Ray, Robert, Harold, Julie. B.S. in Pub. Adminstrn., Am. U., 1945. With SEC, 1938-40, VA, 1946-48; mgmt. and budget analyst CAA, 1948-50; analyst State Dept., 1950-51; budget examiner Exec. Office Pres., 1951-54; asst. controller Bur. Ordnance, 1954-58; prof. polit. sci. Bir Zeit (Jordan) Coll., 1960-61; pub. adminstrn. adviser to King Hussein of Jordan, 1959-61; dep. asst. postmaster gen., controller Post Office Dept., 1963-66, exec. asst. to dep. postmaster gen., 1967-68; mgmt. cons., Tallahassee, 1968-69; planning and program cons. Fla. Office State Planning, 1969-72; investment counselor, Santa Cruz, Calif., 1972-78, Palm Beach, Fla., 1978—. Author: (with Sir Eric Franklin) Economic Development in Jordan, 1961. Served to maj. USAAF, 1942-46. Cited by King Hussein, 1961. Mem. Am. Soc. Pub. Adminstrn., Soc. Internat. Devel., Fed. Govt. Accountants Assn., Pi Kappa Alpha. Episcopalian. Home: 5420 N Ocean Dr Singer Island FL 33404

CROWE, JAMES JOSEPH, shoe company executive; b. New Castle, Pa., June 9, 1935; s. William J. and Anna M. (Dickson) C.; m. Joan D. Verba, Dec. 26, 1959. B.A., Youngstown State U., 1958; J.D., Georgetown U., 1963. Bar: Va. bar 1963, Ohio bar 1966. Atty. SEC, Washington, 1964-65, Gen. Tire & Rubber Co., Akron, Ohio, 1965-68; sr. atty. Eaton Corp., Cleve., 1968-72; sec., gen. counsel U.S. Shoe Corp., Cin., 1972—, v.p., 1975—. Div. chmn. Fine Arts Fund, 1976; trustee Springer Ednl. Found., 1978—, Cin. Music Festival Assn., 1980—, Invest in Neighborhood Inc., 1982—; group chmn. United Appeal, 1980. Served to 2d lt. U.S. Army, 1958-59. Mem. Ohio, Va., Cin. bar assns., Am. Soc. Corporate Secs., Cin. C. of C., Cincinnatus Assn. Clubs: Cin. Country, Queen City (Cin.). Home: 1285 Crestwood Ave Cincinnati OH 45226 Office: One Eastwood Dr Cincinnati OH 45227

CROWE, MARSHALL ALEXANDER, consultant, former Canadian government official; b. Rossburn, Man., Can., Apr. 14, 1921; s. William Johnston and Georgina Gertrude (Gammon) C.; m. Doris Mary Scanes, Dec. 5, 1942; children: Thomas, Alison, Helen, Sheila, Abigail. B.A., U. Man., 1942. Fgn. service officer Can. Dept. External Affairs, 1947-60; econ. adviser Can. Imperial Bank Commerce, 1960-67; dep. sec. to cabinet Govt. of Can., 1967-71; pres., chmn. Can. Devel. Corp., 1971-73; chmn. Nat. Energy Bd., Ottawa, Can., 1973-77; pres. M.A. Crowe Cons., Inc., 1978—; dir. Assoc.-Kellogg Ltd., Dome Petroleum Ltd., Energy Ventures, Inc., Gulf Interstate Co., Sulpetro Ltd., Pension fund Energy Resources Ltd. Served with Can. Army, 1942-46. Home: Rural Route 2 Portland ON K0G 1V0 Canada Office: 350 Sparks St Suite 408 Ottawa ON K1R 7S8 Canada

CROWE, ROBERT WILLIAM, pub. co. exec., lawyer; b. Chgo., Aug. 20, 1924; s. Harry James and Miriam (McCune) C.; m. Virginia C. Kelley, Mar. 25, 1955 (dec. Feb. 1976); children—Robert Kelley, William Park; m. Elizabeth F. Roenisch, Oct. 22, 1977. A.B., U. Chgo., 1948, J.D., 1949. Bar: Ill. bar 1949. Practice in, Chgo., 1949-57; with R.R. Donnelley & Sons Co., Chgo., 1957—, sec., 1965—, v.p., 1970—; dir. Peoria Jour. Star, Inc., Mobium Corp. for Design and Communication. Bd. dirs. Chgo. Child Care Soc., 1963—; chmn. bd. trustees Christian Century Found., 1966—. Served to 1st lt. USAAF, 1943-45. Decorated Air medal with 5 oak leaf clusters. Mem. Am., Ill., Chgo. bar assns. Republican. Presbyterian. Clubs: Law, Legal, Econ., Univ. (Chgo.). Home: 830 Hill Rd Winnetka IL 60093 Office: 2223 King Dr Chicago IL 60616

CROWE, WILLIAM JAMES, JR., naval officer; b. La Grange, Ky., Jan. 2, 1925; s. William James and Eula (Russell) C.; m. Shirley Mary Grennell, Feb. 14, 1954; children: William Blake, James Brent, Mary Russell. B.S., U.S. Naval Acad., 1946; M.A. in Edn, Stanford U., 1956; Ph.D. in Politics (Harold W. Dodds fellow), Princeton U., 1965. Commd. ensign U.S. Navy, 1946, advanced through grades to adm.; comdg. officer U.S.S. Trout, 1960-62; comdr. Submarine Div. 31, San Diego, 1966-67, sr. adviser Vietnamese Navy Riverine Force, 1970-71, dep. to Pres.'s Spl. Rep. for Micronesian Status Negotiations, 1971-73, dir. East Asia and Pacific region Office of Sec. of Def., Washington, until 1976, comdr. Middle East Force, Bahrain, 1976-77, dep. chief of naval ops. Dept. Navy, Washington, 1977-80, comdr.-in-chief Allied Forces So. Europe, 1980—, comdr.-in-chief Pacific, 1983—. Author supr. ops plan for repatriation of U.S.S. Pueblo crew. Decorated D.S.M., D.D.S.M., Legion of Merit, Bronze Star, Air medal with 6 oak leaf clusters. Mem. U.S. Naval Inst., Am. Polit. Sci. Assn., Internat. Studies Assn., Phi Gamma Delta, Phi Delta Phi. Office: Commander-in-Chief Pacific Camp H M Smith HI 96861 *

CROWELL, ALBERT DARY, physicist, educator; b. Dover, N.H., Feb. 12, 1925; s. Milton Frederick and Esther Ann (Dary) C.; m. Janet Louise Wright, June 21, 1947; children: Judith Ann, Susan Wright, Cynthia Dary. B.S. in Engring. summa cum laude, Brown U., 1946, Ph.D. in Physics, 1950; M.S. in Applied Physics, Harvard, 1947. Instr., then asst. prof. Amherst Coll., 1950-55; mem. faculty U. Vt., Burlington, 1955—, prof. physics, 1961—, chmn. dept., 1961-75; Regional counselor physics State of Vt., 1963-67; vis. prof. phys. chemistry U. Bristol, Eng., 1968; vis. prof. physics U. Southampton, Eng., 1976. Author: (with D.M. Young) Physical Adsorption of Gases, 1962. Trustee Brownell Pub. Library, Essex Junction, Vt. Served with USNR, 1943-46. Mem. AAAS, Am. Phys. Soc., Am. Assn. Physics Tchrs., Am. Vacuum Soc., Sigma Xi. Spl. research adsorption gases on solids. Home: 30 Warner Ave Essex Junction VT 05452 Office: U Vt Burlington VT 05405

CROWELL, CHARLES MONROE, lawyer; b. Lancaster, Pa., Apr. 23, 1910; s. Charles M. and Mabelle (Hagans) C.; m. Peggy Johnson, June 26, 1937; children—Betsy, Susan. A.B., Yale, 1933, LL.B., 1936. Bar: Wyo. bar 1936. Since practiced in, Casper, municipal judge, 1945-47; faculty law Casper Coll., 1945-60. Pres. Wyo. Bd. Bar Examiners, 1958-62; mem. Commn. Uniform State Laws, 1955-57; pres. Wyo. Game and Fish Commn., 1969-71, mem., 1967-75; chmn. legislative-exec. commn. on reorgn. of Wyo. Govt., 1969-71; Mem. Casper Civil Service Commn., 1948-51; mem. distbn. com. Casper Found., 1948-51; drive chmn. Casper Community Chest.; Mem. Wyo. Ho. of Reps., 1945-49; mem. Wyo Republican Com., 1951-57; chmn. Wyo. Rep. Conv., 1956; Trustee Casper Meml. Hosp., 1952-57, pres., 1956-57. Mem. ABA, Wyo. Bar Assn. (pres. 1959-60), Natrona County Bar Assn. (pres. 1945-46), Alpha Sigma Phi. Episcopalian (sr. warden 1947). Clubs: Elk, Kiwanian (lt. gov. 1951), Mason.). Home: 1133 S Wolcott Casper WY 82601 *The gift of life carries with it an obligation beyond providing the necessities for ourselves and our family. That obligation is to our fellow man. Its performance is the true measure of a man.*

CROWELL, EDWARD PRINCE, retired association executive; b. Chillicothe, Ohio, Sept. 17, 1926; s. Harrison P. and Jeannette (Sturtevant) C.; m. Elaine Kittelberger, Apr. 14, 1956. Student, U. Maine, 1946-48; D.O., Kirksville (Mo.) Coll. Osteopathy and Surgery, 1952, D. Osteo. Edn. (hon.), 1983; LL.D. (hon.), Phila. Coll. Osteo. Medicine, 1982. Diplomate: Am. Osteo. Bd. Internal Medicine. Intern Waterville (Maine) Osteo. Hosp., 1952-53; chief resident physician hosps. Phila. Coll. Osteo. Medicine, 1953-56; sr. attending internist Waterville Osteo. Hosp., 1956-63, chmn. dept. medicine, med. dir., 1958-63; asst. exec. dir. Am. Osteo. Assn., Chgo., 1964-66, asso. exec. dir., 1966-68, exec. dir., 1968-82, bur. convs., 1968—, chmn. dept. bus. affairs, 1968—; Mem. adv. council Maine Hosp. Constrn. Com., 1959-64. Served with USNR, 1944-46. Recipient Disting. Service award Am. Osteo. Assn., 1982, Pub. Health award Bd. Regents Okla. U. Coll. Osteo. Medicine, 1982, Phillips medal Ohio U. Coll. Osteo. Medicine, 1982. Fellow Am. Coll. Osteo. Internists. Home: 3245 Prestwick Ln Northbrook IL 60062 Office: 212 E Ohio St Chicago IL 60611

CROWELL, GENTRY, former state official; b. Chestnut Mound, Tenn., Dec. 10, 1932; (married). Mem. 86th-89th Tenn. gen. assemblies; sec. state, Tenn., 1977-81; past pres. Nat. Assn. Secs. State. Mem. Jaycees. Democrat. Methodist. Lodges: Masons; Lions. Office: Office of Sec State State Capitol Nashville TN 37219

CROWELL, HOWARD GARDNER, JR., army officer; b. New Bedford, Mass., Sept. 2, 1932; s. Howard Gardner and Elizabeth (Bullis) C.; m. Sarah Jane Mason, Feb. 19, 1955; children: Judith Anne, David Mason. B.A. in Econs., St. Lawrence U., 1954; M.S. in Personnel Adminstrn., George Washington U., 1969. Commd. officer U.S. Army, advanced through grades to maj. gen.; comdg. officer Div. Support Command, 3d Inf. Div., USAREUR, 1973-75; asst. exec. SACEUR, SHAPE, CINCUSEUCOM, 1975-76; dep. chief combat readiness br. SHAPE, EUCOM, 1976-77; asst. dep. chief of staff and tng. TRADOC, Ft. Monroe, Va., 1977-80, dep. chief staff and tng., 1980-81; comdg. gen. U.S. Army Recruiting Command, Ft. Sheridan, Ill., 1981-83, 3d Inf. Div., USAREUR, 1983—. Decorated Silver Star, Legion of Merit, Bronze Star, Meritorious Service medal. Office: Hdqrs and Hdqrs Co Third Inf Div APO NY 09036 *

CROWELL, JOHN B., JR., govt. ofcl., lawyer; b. Elizabeth, N.J., Mar. 18, 1930; s. John B. and Anna B. (Trull) C.; m. Rebecca Margaret McCue, Feb. 13, 1954; children—John P., Patrick E., Ann M. A.B., Dartmouth Coll., 1952; LL.B., Harvard U., 1957. Bar: N.J. bar 1958, Oreg. bar 1959. Law clk. to Judge Gerald McLaughlin U.S. Ct. Appeals, Newark, 1957-59; atty. Ga.-Pacific Corp., Portland, Oreg., 1959-72; gen. counsel La.-Pacific Corp., Portland, 1972-81; asst. sec. for natural resources and environment Dept. Agr., Washington, 1981—. Served with USN, 1952-54. Mem. Am. Bar Assn., Am. Ornithologists Union, Wilson Ornithol. Soc., Cooper Ornithol. Soc. Republican. Presbyterian. Club: Univ. (Portland). Home: 1185 Hallinan Circle Lake Oswego OR 97034 Office: Office of Sec US Dept Agr Washington DC 20250

CROWELL, LUCIUS, artist; b. Chgo., Jan. 22, 1911; s. Lucius Alfred and Grace (Gapen) C.; m. Priscilla Anne Bromley, Dec. 22, 1936; children—Brigit, Geoffrey, Nicholas, Christopher. Student, Williams Coll., 1928-30, Pa. Acad. Fine Arts, 1930-33. Exhbns. include, Art Inst. Chgo., 1931, Boston Mus. Art, 1949, Phila. Mus. Art, Pa. Acad. Fine

Arts, U. Mich., Calif. Palace of Legion of Honor, 1951, Concord Mus., 1955, Worcester Mus., Boston Soc. Ind. Artists, 1956, Columbus Mus., Widener U.; represented in permanent collections, Boston Mus., Phila. Mus. Art, U. Pa., U. Del., Temple U., Northfield Mus., Pa. Acad. Fine Arts. Served with AUS, 1944-46. Recipient May Audubon Post prize Pa. Acad. Fine Arts, 1983. Mem. Phila. Art Alliance, Coll. Art Assn., Phila. Water Color Club, Chester County Art Assn., Artists Equity. Clubs: Williams (N.Y.C.); Peale (Phila.); Edgemere (Dingman's Ferry, Pa.). Home: 119 Charlestown Rd Phoenixville PA 19460 Office: 59 N Mascher St Philadelphia PA 19106 *I have tried in my painting to avoid being influenced by fad or style and to express myself according to my response to natural phenomena.*

CROWELL, OHMER OREAL, insurance company executive; b. Pulaski, Va., Oct. 2, 1924; s. Ohmer Oreal and Thelma Irene (Repass) C.; m. Patsy Helen Miller, June 12, 1948; children: James Douglas, Susan Patricia, Katherina Ann. B.S., Va. Poly. Inst., 1949. With Nationwide Ins. Co., 1949—, field underwriter, Farmville, Va., 1949-50, audit supr., Columbus, Ohio, 1950-52, underwriting service mgr., Canton, Ohio, 1952-54, regional underwriting mgr., Lynchburg, Va., 1954-59, regional underwriting mgr., regional adminstrn. mgr., Lynchburg, 1959-60, dir. appraisals, Columbus, 1960-62, regional mgr., Trenton, 1962-66, 2d v.p. Medicare, Columbus, 1966-68, v.p. Medicare, 1968-69, v.p. personnel, 1969-77, v.p. central bus. ops., 1977-81, sr. v.p. bus. ops., 1981-82, sr. v.p. mktg., 1983—. Bd. dirs. Met. YMCA, Better Bus. Bur., Central Ohio, Inc.; bd. dir., mem. exec. com. Columbus Cancer Clinic; adv. bd. Nat. Alliance Businessmen. Served with U.S. Army, 1943-45; to 1st lt. U.S. Army, 1950-52. Mem. Am. Soc. C.L.U.s, Soc. Chartered Property and Casualty Underwriters. Lutheran. Lodges: Kiwanis; Masons; Elks. Home: 3430 Sunningdale Way Columbus OH 43221 Office: 1 Nationwide Plaza Columbus OH 43216

CROWELL, RICHARD HENRY, mathematician, educator; b. Northeast, Pa., Apr. 6, 1928; s. Milton Frederick and Esther (Dary) C.; m. Marilyn Nelson, Apr. 2, 1955; children—Philip Nelson, Peter Dary. A.B., Harvard, 1949; postgrad., U. Amsterdam, Netherlands, 1950-51; M.A., Princeton, 1953, Ph.D., 1955; M.A. (hon.), Dartmouth, 1968. Research asst. Princeton, 1955-56; lectr. Mass. Inst. Tech., 1956-58; asst. prof. Dartmouth, 1958-63, asso. prof., 1963-67, prof., 1967—, chmn. math. dept., 1973-79. Author: (with R.H. Fox) Introduction to Knot Theory, 1963, (with R.E. Williamson and H.F. Trotter) Calculus of Vector Functions, 1968, (with W.E. Slesnick) Calculus with Analytic Geometry, 1968. Mem. Am. Math. Soc., Math Assn. Am., Phi Beta Kappa. Mem. United Ch. of Christ. Home: 16 Rayton Rd Hanover NH 03755

CROWELL, ROBERT LELAND, publishing company executive; b. Montclair, N.J., May 11, 1909; s. Thomas Irving and Minnie Helen (Lel) C.; m. Ruth Brown Shurtleff, Dec. 23, 1938 (div.); children: John Leland, Timothy Adams, Benjamin Shurtleff (dec.); m. Muriel B. Hutchinson, Dec. 19, 1967. Student, Phillips Acad., Andover, Mass., 1923-27; A.B., Yale U., 1931. With Thomas Y. Crowell Co., N.Y.C., 1931—, became pres., 1937, treas., 1937-60, chmn. bd., 1960-68, 72-74, pres., prin. exec. officer, 1968-72, also dir.; dir. Franklin Pubs., Inc., 1952-63, treas., 1958-63; dir. Dun-Donnelley Corp., 1972-74; Cons. U.S. Dept. State, 1951-63; adv. com. on books abroad USIA, Dept. State, 1952-63. Author: The Lore and Legends of Flowers, 1982. Bd. govs. Yale U. Press, 1952-67; past trustee Archaeol. Inst. Am., Brattleboro Mus. and Art Center; trustee Am. Schs. Oriental Research, until 1979, Marlboro Coll., until 1980, So. Vt. chpt. Nat. Multiple Sclerosis Soc., until 1980, Moore Free Library Assn.; mem. alumni council Phillips Andover Acad., until 1980; bd. dirs. ACLU, until 1981. Dept. State grantee, lectr., India, 1957. Mem. Alpha Sigma Phi. Mem. Soc. of Friends. Club: Century Assn. (N.Y.C.). Home: Newfane VT 05345

CROWELL, WARREN H., investment banker; b. Los Angeles, 1905. Ed., UCLA, 1927. Partner Crowell, Weedon & Co., Los Angeles. Bd. dirs. Hollywood Presbyn. Hosp., John Tracy Clinic, Los Angeles; bd. dirs., chmn. emeritus Los Angeles Met. YMCA. Home: 801 Bel Air Rd Los Angeles CA 90077 Office: 1 Wilshire Blvd Los Angeles CA 90017

CROWFOOT, JAMES S., university dean. Dean U. Mich. Sch. Natural Resources, Ann Arbor. Office: Office of Dean Sch Natural Resources U Mich Ann Arbor MI 48104§

CROWL, JOHN ALLEN, publishing company executive; b. Winchester, Va., Aug. 10, 1935; s. John Decatur and Cora Elizabeth (LLoyd) C.; m. Dana Jane Bernasek, Aug. 27, 1960; 1 son, Patrick Joseph. B.A., U. Md., 1957, M.A., 1961. Instr. Staunton (Va.) Mil. Acad., 1958-59; asst. dir. public relations Johns Hopkins U., Balt., 1961-64; asso. dir. Editorial Projects for Edn., Inc., Balt. and Washington, 1964-75, v.p., 1975-78; asso. editor Chronicle of Higher Edn., Washington, 1966-72, mng. editor, 1972-79, v.p., pub., 1979—. Served with U.S. Army, 1958. Recipient Edn. Writers award AAUP, 1971. Mem. Edn. Writers Assn. Home: 1819 Corcoran St NW Washington DC 20009 Office: 1333 New Hampshire Ave NW Washington DC 20036

CROWL, PHILIP AXTELL, emeritus educator, historian; b. Dayton, Ohio, Dec. 17, 1914; s. Frank Denton and Clementine (Axtell) C.; m. Mary Ellen Wood, Sept. 9, 1943; children: Ellen Wood (Mrs. Ellen C. O'Neil), Catherine Pauline, Margaret Axtell. A.B., Swarthmore Coll., 1936; postgrad., Yale Law Sch., 1936-37; M.A., U. Iowa, 1939; Ph.D., Johns Hopkins, 1942. Instr. Princeton, 1941-42, asst. prof. history, 1945-49, research asso., 1964; historian Dept. Army, 1949-55; intelligence officer State Dept., 1957-67; dir., cons. John Foster Dulles Oral History Project, Princeton, 1964-66; prof., chmn. dept. history U. Nebr., 1967-73; chmn. dept. strategy Naval War Coll., 1973-80, prof. emeritus, 1980—; Harmon meml. lectr. U.S. Air Force Acad., 1978; lectr. Nat. War Coll., 1981; pres. adv. bd. archival affairs Nat. Archives region 6, Kansas City, Mo., 1968-71; bd. dirs. Harry S. Truman Library Inst., 1968-73; mem. hist. adv. bd. USMC, 1969-71, USAF, 1983—; mem. Nat. Hist. Publs. Commn., 1969-72. Author: Maryland During and After the American Revolution, 1943, (with J.A. Isely) The U.S. Marines and Amphibious Warfare, 1951, (with E.G. Love) Seizure of the Gilberts and Marshalls, 1955, Campaign in the Mariannas, 1960, The Intelligent Traveller's Guide to Historic Britain, 1983; Editor: Prince George's County Maryland Court Records, 1696-1699, 1964; Editorial bd.: (with J. Smith) Mil. Affairs, 1970-73. Served to lt. comr. USNR, 1942-45. Decorated Silver Star medal. Mem. Am. Hist. Soc., Am. Mil. Inst. (trustee 1976-80), U.S. Naval Inst., Marine Corps History Assn. (bd. dirs. 1982—), Phi Beta Kappa, Delta Upsilon. Presbyn. Clubs: Cosmos (Washington); Nassau (Princeton, N.J.). Office: 7 Spindrift Way Annapolis MD 21403

CROWL, R(ICHARD), aluminum company executive; b. New Brunswick, N.J., Aug. 10, 1931; s. Richard Bernard and Ella Marie (Hermann) Crowl C.; m. Lydia Canonico, Aug. 15, 1953 (div. June 1981); children: Joan, Barbara, Robert; m. 2d Katherine Alice Sparks, Dec. 11, 1981; stepchildren: Lauren Albrecht, Beth Albrecht. Student, U. Notre Dame, 1950-51, Am. U., 1952-53; B.S.B.A., Rutgers U., 1955. With Amax, Inc., Greenwich, Conn., 1955-83, exec. v.p., chief fin. officer, 1981-83; exec. v.p. Reynolds Metals Co., Richmond, Va., 1983—. Served with USAF, 1951-52. Roman Catholic. Office: Reynolds Metals Co 6601 W Broad St Richmond VA 23261

CROWLEY, DANIEL FRANCIS, publishing company executive; b. Yonkers, N.Y., Nov. 23, 1915; s. Cornelius Daniel and Elizabeth M. (Treacy) C.; m. Margaret M. Murphy, June 8, 1946; children: Margaret Mary, Daniel Francis. A.B., Columbia, 1936, M.S., 1937. Mem. staff Haskings & Sells, C.P.A.s, N.Y.C., 1937-42, 46-47; with McGraw-Hill, Inc., 1947-80, corporate controller, v.p., controller publs. div., 1961-63, corporate v.p., controller, 1963-68, sr. v.p., finance, data processing, 1968, exec. v.p. finance, 1970-80, also dir., chmn. fin. policy com., until 1981. Mem. adv. com. athletics Columbia U., 1966—; mem. Columbia-Presbyn. Hosp. Joint-Adminstrv. Bd., 1970-81; treas. Columbia-Presbyn. Med. Center Fund, Inc., 1971-81; Alumni trustee Columbia; trustee Financial Accounting Found., 1976-79. Served to comdr. USNR, World War 11. Mem. Financial Execs. Inst. (pres. N.Y.C. chpt. 1967-68, Eastern area v.p. 1972, vice chmn. bd 1975-76, chmn. bd. 1976-77, dir.-at-large 1977—), Am. Inst. C.P.A.'s, Alumni Assn., Columbia Grad. Sch. Bus. (past pres.), Columbia Alumni Fedn. (past sec.-treas.), Am. Legion, Friendly Sons St. Patrick. Clubs: St. Andrews Golf (Hastings-on-Hudson, N.Y.); Columbia Varsity C (past pres.), Knight of Malta.). Home: 41 Euclid Ave Hastings-on-Hudson NY 10706 Office: 1221 Ave of The Americas New York City NY 10020

CROWLEY, JAMES WORTHINGTON, lawyer; b. Cookville, Tenn., Feb. 18, 1930; s. Worth and Jessie (Officer) C.; m. Laura June Bauserman, Jan. 27, 1951; children—James Kenneth, Laura Cynthia; m. Carol Golden, Sept. 4, 1981; m. Joyce A. Goode, Jan. 15, 1966; children—John Worthington, Noelle Virginia. B.A., George Washington U., 1950, LL.B., 1953. Bar: D.C. bar 1954. Underwriter, spl. agt. Am. Surety Co. of N.Y., Washington, 1953-56; adminstrv. asst., contract adminstr. Atlantic Research Corp., Alexandria, Va., 1956-59, mgr. legal dept., asst. sec., counsel, 1959-65, sec., legal mgr., counsel, 1965-67, Susquehanna Corp. (merger with Atlantic Research Corp.), 1967-70; pres., dir. Gen. Communication Co., Boston, 1962-70; v.p., gen. counsel E-Systems, Inc., 1970-, sec., 1976—; v.p., asst. sec., dir. Air Asia Co. Ltd., Tainan, Taiwan, Republic China, 1975—; dir. Cemco, Inc., Continental Electronic Systems, Inc.; v.p., dir. TAI, Inc., Serv-air, Inc., Houston; mem. adv. bd. Internat. and Comparative Law Center, Southwestern Legal Found. Mem. Am. Soc. Corp. Secs., Inf. Mus. Assn., Am. Bar Assn., Nat. Security Indsl. Assn., Omicron Delta Kappa, Alpha Chi Sigma, Phi Sigma Kappa. Republican. Methodist. Home: 16203 Spring Creek Rd Dallas TX 75248 Office: PO Box 226030 Dallas TX 75266

CROWLEY, JEROME JOSEPH, JR., manufacturing company executive; b. South Bend, Ind., Sept. 18, 1939; s. Jerome J. and Rosaleen (Giblin) C.; m. Carol Ann Ellithorn, June 23, 1962; children: Michael, Karen, Brian, Colleen. B.S., U. Notre Dame, 1961; M.B.A., U. Chgo., 1967. With O'Brien Corp., South San Francisco, Calif., 1965—, now pres. Served with USMC, 1961-65. Roman Catholic. Office: 450 E Grand Ave South San Francisco CA 94080

CROWLEY, JOHN JOSEPH, JR., U.S. ambassador; b. Albuquerque, Feb. 10, 1928; s. John Joseph and Myrtis (Duffield) C.; m. Ileana Rivera Cintron, June 12, 1953; children: Gail Marie, Ileana Marie. A.B., W.Va. U., 1949; M.A., Columbia U., 1950; grad., Nat. War Coll., 1970. Instr. U. P.R., 1950-52; joined U.S. Foreign Service, 1952; vice-consul, Maracaibo, 1952-55, vice-consul, 3d sec., Lima, Peru, 1955-59; 1st sec. Am. embassy, Brussels, Belgium, 1960-64; officer charge Venezuelan affairs Dept. of State, 1964-66; counselor, dep. chief of mission, Quito, Ecuador, 1966-69, charge d'affairs, 1967-68, counselor, dep. chief of mission, Santo Domingo, Dominican Republic, 1970-74; dir. Office No. European Affairs, Bur. European Affairs Dept. State, 1974-77; dep. chief of mission U.S. Embassy, Caracas, Venezuela, 1977-80; U.S. ambassador to Suriname, 1980-82; sr. insp. Dept. State, 1982—. Served with AUS, 1946-48. Decorated Order of Merit Ecuador Govt., 1969. Mem. Am. Fgn. Service Assn. Roman Catholic. Office: Dept State Washington DC 20520

CROWLEY, JOHN POWERS, judge; b. Chgo., Oct. 5, 1936; s. William Beaudry and Mary (Powers) C.; m. Elizabeth Gwenellian Davies, Jan. 12, 1963; children—Helen Mary, Margaret Jane, Catherine Anne. Student, U. Notre Dame, 1954-57; LL.B., DePaul U., Chgo., 1960; LL.M., N.Y. U., 1961. Bar: Ill. bar 1960. Asst. U.S. atty. No. Dist. Ill., 1961-65; pvt. practice, Chgo., 1965-70; partner firm Crowley, Burke, Nash & Shea, 1970-76; judge U.S. Dist. Ct., No. Dist. Ill., Chgo., 1976—; instr. DePaul U. Coll. Law, 1962-63, adj. prof., 1976—. Mem. ABA, Ill. Bar Assn., Chgo. Bar Assn. (chmn. criminal law com. 1974-75, bd. mgrs. 1976-78), Nat. Assn. Criminal Def. Lawyers (dir. 1968-70), Blue Circle Soc., Blue Key. Democrat. Roman Cath. Home: 2416 Central Park Evanston IL 60201 Office: 219 S Dearborn Chicago IL 60604

CROWLEY, JOHN ROBERT, real estate devel. co. exec.; b. Niagara Falls, N.Y., July 31, 1929; s. John David and Elizabeth (MacDougal) C.; m. Louette Heydinger, Jan. 23, 1954; children—Jonette, John Robert II, Coleen, Erin, Christopher, Maureen. Student, Niagara U., 1947-51; B.S. in Bus. Adminstrn, Regis Coll., 1952; postgrad., U. Colo., 1955-57. Chief planner Harman, O'Donnell & Henninger, Denver, 1956-63; dir. economic devel. Denver C. of C., 1963-64; staff mgr. Forward Metro, Denver, 1964-66; v.p., dir. G.M. Wallace & Co., Englewood, Colo., 1967-70; exec. v.p. Denver Technol. Center, Inc., Englewood, 1970-74, dir., 1970-77; pres. John R. Crowley & Assos. Inc., Englewood, 1974—; dir. Columbia Savs. & Loan Assn. Chmn. pro tem Regional Transp. Dist., 1969-74, chmn., 1974-80; chmn. Colo. Land Use Commn., 1970-75; mem. Rockefeller Task Force Land Use and Urban Growth, 1972-73. Served in USAF, 1951-55. Mem. Am. Pub. Transit Assn. (dir. 1975—, v.p. 1980-81), Urban LandInst., Denver C. of C. Roman Catholic. Clubs: Univ., Echo Hills Country, Paradise Valley Country, Rotary of Denver. Home: 1645 E Noble Pl Littleton CO 80121 Office: 5967 S Willow Way Englewood CO 80110

CROWLEY, JOHN WILLIAM, English educator; b. New Haven, Dec. 27, 1945; s. John Adam and Mary T. (McKenna) C.; m. Sheila A. Myers, Mar. 17, 1967 (div. 1977); children: Matthew, Anne Marie; m. Susan Wolstenholme, May 27, 1978; 1 son, Raphael. B.A., Yale U., 1967; M.A., Ind. U., 1969, Ph.D., 1970. Asst. prof. English Syracuse (N.Y.) U., 1970-74, assoc. prof., 1974-79, prof., 1979—. Author: George Cabot Lodge, 1976; co-editor: The Haunted Dusk, 1983. Hon. Woodrow Wilson fellow, 1967; NDEA fellow, 1967-70; Nat. Endowment for Humanities summer stipend, 1975. Mem. MLA, Phi Beta Kappa. Democrat. Roman Catholic. Home: 33 Easterly Ave Auburn NY 13021 Office: Syracuse U Syracuse NY 13210

CROWLEY, JOSEPH B., lawyer; b. Chgo., July 15, 1905. Ed., Crane Jr. Coll., Northwestern U.; J.D., Chgo.-Kent Coll. Law, 1926. Bar: Ill. bar 1926. Former master in chancery Superior Ct., Cook County, Ill.; now mem. firm Boodell, Sears, Sugrue, Giambalvo & Crowley, Chgo. Mem. Am., Ill., Chgo. bar assns. Office: Boodell Sears Sugrue Giambalvo & Crowley 69 W Washington St Chicago IL 60602

CROWLEY, JOSEPH FRANCIS, advertising agency executive; b. Boston, Sept. 17, 1932; s. Joseph Francis and Alice Clare (Cherbuy) C.; m. Ruth Jeanette Campbell, June 23, 1956; children: Patricia, Elizabeth. B.S. in Bus. Adminstrn., Northeastern U., 1956. Sr. v.p. Batten, Barton, Durstine & Osborn Inc., N.Y.C., 1956—. Chmn. bd. trustees Stuart Country Day Sch. of Sacred Heart, Princeton, N.J., 1976—. Served to 1st lt. U.S. Army, 1956-58. Republican. Roman Catholic. Office: Batten Barton Durstine Osborn Inc 383 Madison Ave New York NY 10017

CROWLEY, JOSEPH MICHAEL, electrical engineer, educator; b. Phila., Sept. 9, 1940; s. Joseph Edward and Mary Veronica (McCall) C.; m. Barbara Ann Sauerwald, June 22, 1963; children: Joseph W., Kevin, James, Michael, Daniel. B.S., MIT, 1962, M.S., 1963, Ph.D., 1965. Vis. scientist Max Planck Inst., Goettingen, W.Ger, 1965-66; asst. prof. elec. engring. U. Ill., Urbana, 1966-69, assoc. prof., 1969-78, prof., dir. Applied Electrostats. Research Lab., 1978—; pres. JMC Inc., 1981—; cons. to several corps. Contbr. articles to profl. jours.; patentee ink jet printers. Pres. Champaign-Urbana Bd. Cath. Edn., 1978-80. Recipient Gen. Motors scholarship, 1958-62; AEC fellow, 1962-65; NATO fellow, 1965-66. Mem. IEEE (sr.), Electrostats. Soc. Am., Am. Phys. Soc., Soc. Inf. Display, Mensa. Roman Catholic. Home: 506 Elm St Champaign IL 61820 Office: Dept Elec Engring Univ Ill Urbana IL 61801

CROWLEY, JOSEPH NEIL, univ. pres.; b. Oelwein, Iowa, July 9, 1933; s. James Bernard and Nina Mary (Neil) C.; m. Johanna Lois Reitz, Sept. 9, 1961; children—Theresa, Neil, Margaret, Timothy. B.A., U. Iowa, 1959; M.A., Calif. State U., Fresno, 1963; Ph.D. (Univ. fellow), U. Wash., 1967. Reporter Fresno Bee, 1961-62; asst. prof. polit. sci. U. Nev., Reno, 1966-71, asso. prof., 1971-79, prof., 1979—, chmn. dept. polit. sci., 1976-78, pres., 1978—; Policy formulation officer EPA, Washington, 1973-74; dir. instl. studies Nat. Commn. on Water Quality, Washington, 1974-75; cons. in field. Author: Democrats, Delegates and Politics in Nevada: A Grassroots Chronicle of 1972, 1976; editor: (with Robert Roelofs and Donald Hardesty) Environment and Society, 1973. Bd. dirs. Thursday Evening Forum, Center for Religion and Life, Reno, 1970-73, Nev. Ednl. Seminar, 1976—; del. Democratic Nat. Conv., 1972. Served with USAF, 1954-57. Recipient Thornton Peace prize U. Nev., 1971; Nat. Assn. Schs. Public Affairs and Adminstrn. fellow, 1973-74. Mem. Am. Polit. Sci. Assn., Western Polit. Sci. Assn., No. Calif. Polit. Sci. Assn. Roman Catholic. Club: Rotary. Home: 1265 Muir Dr Reno NV 89503 Office: Pres's Office U Nev Reno NV 89557

CROWLEY, LEONARD JAMES, auxiliary bishop; b. Montreal, Que., Can., Dec. 28, 1921; s. James and Agnes (Wheeler) C. B.A., U. Montreal, 1941, Licentiate in Theology, 1947; Licentiate in Canon Law, U. Ottawa, Ont., Can., 1950. Ordained priest Roman Catholic Ch., 1947, bishop, 1971. Aux. bishop Diocese Montreal, 1971—, dir. Office for English Lang. Affairs. Home: 1071 rue de la Cathédrale Montreal PQ Canada H3B 2V4 Office: Archeveche de Montreal 2000 Sherbrooke St W Montreal PQ Canada H3H 1G4

CROWLEY, MART, playwright, producer; b. Vicksburg, Miss., Aug. 21, 1925; s. Edward Joseph and Pauline C. B.A., Catholic U. Am., 1957. Author: plays The Boys in the Band, 1968, Remote Asylum, 1970, A Breeze From the Gulf, 1973; adaptor, producer: screen version The Boys in the Band, 1970; producer: TV series Hart to Hart, 1979—. Address: care Internat Creative Mgmt 740 W 57th St New York NY 10019

CROWLEY, PAT, actress; b. Olyphant, Pa., Sept. 17, 1938; d. Vincent and Helen C.; m. E. Gregory Hookstratten, Feb. 2, 1958; children: Jon, Ann. Appeared in: Broadway plays Tovarich; TV series Please Don't Eat the Daisies; TV Family Upside Down; Appeared in 150 TV shows, 4 TV series, 3 Broadway plays. Vice-pres. Share, Inc.; Bd. dirs. West Lake Sch., Good Shepherd Sch.

CROWLEY, THOMAS H(ENRY), software systems executive; b. Bowling Green, Ohio, June 7, 1924; s. Thomas M. and Esther (Murlin) C.; m. Rita E. Feeney, Aug. 30, 1947; children: Linda, Patricia, Steven, James, Susan, Mary, David, Cynthia, Brian, Terrence, Karen, Elizabeth, Christopher, Thomas. B.E.E., Ohio State U., 1948, M.S., 1950, Ph.D., 1954. With Bell Telephone Labs., Murray Hill, N.J., 1954-67, dir. NIKE-X programming lab., Whippany, N.J., 1967-68, exec. dir. Safeguard design div., Whippany, 1968-75, exec. dir. bus. systems and tech. div., Piscataway, N.J., 1975-79, exec. dir. computing tech. and design engring., Murray Hill, 1979-82, exec. dir. systems software div., 1982-83; v.p. software systems Western Electric Co., 1983—. Author: Understanding Computers, 1967, Modern Communications, 1962. Served with U.S. Army, 1943-46. Named Outstanding Alumnus Ohio State U., 1970; recipient Outstanding Civilian Service award U.S. Army, 1975. Mem. IEEE. Home: 50 Whittredge Rd Summit NJ 07901

CROWN, DAVID ALLAN, criminologist, educator; b. Long Beach, N.Y., Sept. 13, 1928; s. John and Florence (Coe) C.; m. Maria Braml, Feb. 13, 1954; children: Ingrid, Eric. B.S., Union Coll., 1948; M.Criminology, U. Calif., 1960, D.Criminology, 1969. Spl. agt. CIC, 1951-53; asst. dir. San Francisco Indentification Lab., U.S. Postal Inspection Service, 1957-67; dir. Questioned Document Lab., Records Analysis Group, Dept. Army, Washington, 1967-72, Questioned Documents Staff, INR/DDC, U.S. Dept. State, 1972-77; chief Questioned Documents Lab., Office of Tech. Services, 1977-82; Lectr. Chabot Coll., Hayward, Calif., 1966-67, Georgetown U., Washington, 1973; adj. prof. Am. U., Washington, 1971—; professorial lectr. George Washington U., 1973-77, Antioch Sch. Law, 1977—; pres. Crown Forensic Labs., Inc.; chmn. bd. Inst. for Forensic Edn., Inc.; chmn. recert. com. Am. Bd. Forensic Document Examiners. Author: The Forensic Examination of Paints and Pigments, 1968; co-author: Forensic Science, 1982; Contbr. articles to profl. pubs.; Editorial bd.: Jour. Forensic Scis, 1971-73; book rev. editor, 1973-74; asso. editor, 1974—. Mem. Am. Acad. Forensic Scis. (chmn. questioned document sect. 1969-70, exec. com. 1970-74, pres. 1974-75), Am. Soc. Questioned Document Examiners (chmn. accreditation com. 1969-70, sec.-treas. 1976-78, pres. 1980-82), ASTM (chmn. questioned document com. 1970-71, vice chmn. 1972), Forensic Sci. Found. (dir. 1971-72, trustee 1973-75), Am. Coll. Document Examiners (dir. 1970—). Club: Arlington Hall Officers. Home: 3103 Jessie Ct Fairfax VA 22030

CROWN, HENRY, business exececutive; b. Chgo., June 13, 1896; s. Arie and Ida (Gordon) C.; m. Rebecca Kranz, Aug. 12, 1920 (dec. Oct. 1943); children: Robert (dec. July 1969), Lester, John Jacob; m. Gladys Kay, Mar. 1946. Student public schs., Chgo.; LL.D. (hon.), Syracuse U., Barat Coll., DePaul U., DePauw U., Loras Coll., Brown U., D.Engring., Tri State Coll., L.H.D., Jewish Theol. Sem. Am. Clk. Chgo. Fire Brick Co., 1910-12; traffic mgr. Union Drop Forge Co., 1912-16; partner S.R. Crown & Co., 1916-19; treas. Material Service Corp. (bldg. materials), 1919-21, pres., 1921-41, chmn. bd., 1941-59; dir., chmn. exec. com. Gen. Dynamics Corp., 1959-66, 70—; chmn. bd. Henry Crown & Co., 1967; past dir. Hilton Hotels, Waldorf Astoria Corp. Mem. Chgo. CD Corps.; trustee Chgo. Boys' Clubs; adv. mem. bd. trustees DePaul U.; mem. U. Ill. Citizens Com., Loyola U. Citizens Bd., Northwestern U. Assos.; fellow St. Joseph's Coll., Rensselaer, Ind.; asso., fellow Brandeis U.; hon. v.p. N.E. Ill. council Boy Scouts Am. Served as col., C.E. AUS, World War II. Decorated Legion of Merit, U.S.; chevalier Legion d'Honneur, France; Gold Cross Royal Order Phoenix, Greece; Order Ruben Dario, Nicaragua; recipient Horatio Alger award Am. Schs. and Colls. Assn.; Damen award Loyola U., Chgo.; Humanitarian Service award for industry Eleanor Roosevelt Cancer Research Found.; Julius Rosenwald Meml. award Jewish Fedn. and Welfare Fund, Chgo.; Edn. for Freedom award Roosevelt U., Chgo.; Meritorious Public Service award U.S. Navy. Mem. Mil. Order World Wars. Clubs: Masons, Shriners (33 deg.),

Execs., Mid-Day, Standard, Tavern (Chgo.); St. Louis (Mo.); Tamarask (Palm Beach, Fla.); Hillcrest Country (Los Angeles); Westview Country (Miami Beach, Fla.). Home: 900 Edgemere Ct Evanston IL 60202 Office: 300 W Washington St Chicago IL 60606

CROWN, LESTER, corporation executive; b. Chgo., June 7, 1925; s. Henry and Rebecca (Kranz) C.; m. Renee Schine, Dec. 28, 1950; children: Arie, James, Patricia, Daniel, Susan, Sara, Janet. B.S. in Chem. Engring, Northwestern U., 1947; M.B.A., Harvard, 1949. Instr. math. Northwestern U., 1946-47; v.p., dir., chem. engr. Marblehead Lime Co., 1950-56, pres., 1956-66; v.p., dir. Material Service Corp. div. Gen. Dynamics Corp., Chgo., 1953-66, pres., 1970—, chmn., 1983—, also dir.; exec. v.p. Gen. Dyanamics Corp., 1960-66, 77—, dir., 1974—, mem. exec. com., 1982—; also dir.; pres. Henry Crown & Co., Chgo., 1969—; exec. v.p. Gen. Dyanamics Corp., 1960-66; dir. Trans World Corp., Trans World Airlines, Inc., Esmark, Inc., Chgo. Profl. Sports Corp., Oils, Inc., Chgo.; partner N.Y. Yankees Partnership, 1973—. Trustee Northwestern U., Michael Reese Hosp. and Med. Center; bd. dirs. John Crerar Library, Lyric Opera Chgo., Cradle Soc., Children's Meml. Hosp.; bd. advisors Chgo. Zool. Soc.; chmn. bd. overseers Jewish Theol. Sem. Mem. Harvard Bus. Sch. Alumni Assn., Tau Beta Pi, Pi Mu Epsilon, Phi Eta Sigma. Clubs: Lake Shore Country, Northmoor Country, Standard, Economic (dir. 1972), Chicago, Commercial, Mid-America (Chgo.); Carleton; Marco Polo (N.Y.C.); John Evans (Northwestern U.). Home: 1155 Mohawk Rd Wilmette IL 60091 Office: 300 W Washington St Chicago IL 60606

CROWTHER, CLARENCE EDWARD, bishop; b. Bradford, Eng., Mar. 4, 1929; came to U.S., 1959, naturalized, 1964; s. Joseph Austin and Margaret Edith Ellen (Simm) C.; m. Margaret Hird, Apr. 1, 1955; children: Paul, Alison, Deborah; m. Ingrid Schunemann, Dec. 5, 1982. B.A., U. Leeds, Eng., 1950, LL.B., 1952, LL.M., 1953; Ph.D, U. Calif., 1975. Diplomate: ordained to ministry, Episcopal Ch., 1956. Tutor law Exeter Coll., Oxford U., 1952-54; curate Sts. Philip and James Ch. Oxford, Eng., 1956-58; sr. chaplain UCLA, 1958-64; dean St. Cyprian's Cathedral, Kimberly, South Africa, 1964-65; bishop of Kimberly, South Africa, 1965-67, asst. bishop Calif., San Francisco, 1971—; hon. canon Grace Cathedral, San Francisco; lectr. black studies U. Calif.- Santa Barbara, 1970-75; exec. dir. Operation Connection (N.Y.C. and Santa Barbara), 1970-72. Author: Where Religion Gets Lost in the Church, 1969, The Face of Apartheid, 1971; contbr. articles to religious jours. Vis. fellow Ctr. for Study Democratic Instns., Santa Barbara, Calif., 1968-70. Mem. Am. Assn. Pastoral Counselors (diplomate); hon. mem. Am. Assn. Applied Psyhoanalysis. Home: 2050Garden St SantaBarbara CA 93105

CROWTHER, H. DAVID, aerospace company corporate communications executive; b. Long Beach, Calif., Mar. 7, 1930; s. Harry H. Crother and Florabell R. (Reader) C.; m. Helen Jeanette Custer, May 22, 1960; children: John Newton, Kimberly Ann. B.A., Calif. State U.-Long Beach, 1957. Pub. relations coordinator Lockheed-Calif. Co., Burbank, 1959-64, pub. affairs mgr., 1967-72, dir. pub. relations, 1975-81; asst. to v.p. pub. relations Lockheed Corp., Burbank, 1964-67, v.p. corp. communications, 1981—; dir. pub. affairs U.S. Dept. Transp., Washington, 1972-75. Bd. dirs. John Tracy Clinic, Los Angeles, Econ. Literacy Council, Long Beach. Served to lt. U.S. Army, 1951-53; Korea. Decorated Silver Star, Purple Heart; recipient Sec's award U.S. Dept. Transp., 1975. Mem. Calif. Mfrs. Assn. (dir.), Pub. Relations Soc. Am., Pub. Affairs Council, Pub. Affairs Officers Assn. Club: Lakeside Golf (Toluca Lake, Calif.). Home: 10459 Camarillo St Toluca Lake CA 91620 Office: Lockheed Corporation PO Box 551 Burbank CA 91520

CROWTHER, JAMES EARL, radio and TV executive; b. Cleve., Jan. 2, 1930; s. Byron Scott and Leota Belle (Frye) C.; m. Nancy Louise Swanner, Nov. 28, 1953; children: Richard Scott, Robert Phillip, Paul William. B.A., Ohio Wesleyan U., 1956; J.D., U. Mich., 1958. Bar: Tex. 1959. Asso. firm Butler, Binion, Rice, Cook & Knapp, Houston, 1959-67; v.p. Channel Five TV Co., Nashville, 1975—, Channel Two TV Co., Houston, 1970—; v.p., gen. counsel Houston Post Co., 1967-76, exec. v.p., gen. counsel, 1976-83; v.p. Channel Four TV Co., Tucson, 1982—, Channel Eleven TV Co., Meridian, Miss., 1981—, KPRC Radio Co., Houston, 1983—; sec. H & C Communications, Inc., Houston, 1979-83, pres., 1983—; adj. prof. law S. Tex. Law Sch., Houston, 1974-75. Pres. Briargrove Park Property Owners, Inc., 1969-70. Served with USAF, 1951-55. Mem. Am. Bar Assn., Tex. Bar Assn., Houston Bar Assn. Methodist.

CROWTHER, RICHARD LAYTON, architect, consultant, researcher, author, lecturer; b. Newark, Dec. 10, 1910; s. William George and Grace (Layton) C.; m. Emma Jane Hubbard, 1935 (div. 1949); children: Bethe Crowther Allison, Warren Winfield, Vivian Crowther Tuggle; m. 2d Pearl Marie Tesch, Sept. 16, 1950. Student, Newark Sch. Fine and Indsl. Arts, 1928-31, San Diego State Coll., 1932, U. Colo., 1956. Registered architect, Colo. Prin. Crowther & Marshall, San Diego, 1946-50, Richard L. Crowther, Denver, 1951-66, Crowther, Kruse, Landin, 1966-70, Crowther, Kruse, McWilliams, 1970-75, Crowther Solar Group, 1975-82, Richard L. Crowther FAIA, 1982—; lectr. U. Wis., Madison, 1974, U. Ky., Shakertown, 1977, Smithsonian Inst., Washington, 1977, U. Nebr., Lincoln, 1981; judge solar archtl. competition State Ill., Chgo., 1977. Author: Sun/Earth, 1975 (Progressive Architecture award 1975), Sun/Earth, rev. edit., 1983, Affordable Passive Solar Homes, 1983, Paradox of Smoking, 1983. NSF grantee, 1974-75. Fellow AIA (commr. research, edn. and environ. Colo. Central chpt. 1972-75, bd. dirs. chpt. 1973-74, AIA Research Corp. Solar Monnitoring Program award 1978). *Inner awareness, relevancy, persistence and adaptiveness are all that we have in a world of vanity, variety and change*

CROXTON, FRED(ERICK) E(MORY), JR., information specialist, consultant; b. Columbus, Ohio, Oct. 14, 1923; s. Frederick Emory and Rosetta Ruth (Harpster) C.; m. Dorothy Duboise, Apr. 18, 1948 (div. 1978); m. Arlene Beekman Bilbrough, Dec. 1, 1978; children—Elizabeth, Helen. B.A., Oberlin Coll., 1944; M.A., Columbia, 1960. Tech. insp. Kellex Corp., 1944-45; sr. chem. and tech. engr. Union Carbide Nuclear Co., 1946-49; various positions Tech. Info. Service, U.S. AEC, Oak Ridge, 1949-53; supt. info. and records Goodyear Atomic Corp., Piketon, Ohio, 1953-62; dir. Redstone Sci. Info. Center, U.S. Army Missile Command, Huntsville, Ala., 1962-68; exec. v.p. Informatics Tisco, College Park, Md., 1968-70; dir. adminstrv. dept. Library of Congress, Washington, 1970-76, dir. reader services dept., 1976-78, dir. automated systems office, 1978—; cons. in info. system design and mgmt., 1971—. Contbr. articles profl. jours. Chmn. Pike County chpt. ARC, 1959-60; Chmn. bd. Pike County Free Public Library, 1957-62. Served with AUS, 1945-46. Mem. AAAS, Am. Chem. Soc., Spl. Libraries Assn., Assn. U.S. Army. Clubs: Greencastle Country (Burtonsville, Md.); Imperial Lakes Country (Mulberry, Fla.). Office: Library of Congress Washington DC 20540

CROZIER, WILLIAM MARSHALL, JR., bank holding company executive; b. N.Y.C., Oct. 2, 1932; s. William Marshall and Alice (Parsons) C.; m. Prudence van Zandt Slitor, June 20, 1964; children: Matthew Eaton, Abigail Parsons, Patience Wells. B.A. in Econs., Yale U., 1954; M.B.A. with distinction, Harvard U., 1963. With Hanover Bank, N.Y.C., 1954-61, asst. sec., 1959; with BayBanks, Inc., Boston, 1964—, asst. treas., 1965, asst. v.p., 1968, v.p., sec., 1969, sr. v.p., sec., 1973, chmn. bd., chief exec. officer, 1974—, pres., 1977—, dir., 1974—. Trustee Babson Coll., Commonwealth Energy System; incorporator Winsor Sch. and Advent Sch., Boston; overseer Boston Symphony Orch., Boston Mus. Fine Arts, New Eng. Aquarium. Served with U.S. Army, 1955-57. Mem. Boston Econ. Club. Episcopalian. Clubs: Comml.-Mchts., Union, Harvard (Boston); Yale (N.Y.C.). Home: Ridge Hill Farm Rd Wellesley MA 02181 Office: 175 Federal St Boston MA 02110

CRUESS, RICHARD LEIGH, surgeon, university dean; b. London, Ont., Can., Dec. 17, 1929; s. Leigh S. and Martha A. (Peever) C.; m. Sylvia Crane Robinson, May 30, 1953; children: Leigh S., Andrew C. B.A., Princeton U., 1951; M.D., Columbia U., 1955. Diplomate: Am. Bd. Orthopedic Surgery. Intern Royal Victoria Hosp., Montreal, Que., 1955-56, resident surgery, 1956-57, N.Y. Orthopedic Hosp., 1959-60, asst. resident orthopedic surgery, 1960-61, resident orthopedic surgery, 1961-62, Annie C. Kane fellow orthopedic surgery, 1961-62; research asso. depts. orthopedic surgery and biochemistry Columbia U., N.Y.C., 1962-63; John Armour Travelling fellow, 1962-63, Am.-Brit.-Can. Travelling fellow, 1967, practice medicine specializing in orthopedic surgery, Montreal, 1963—; orthopedic surgeon Royal Victoria Hosp., orthopedic surgeon-in-charge, 1968-81, asst. surgeon-in-chief, 1970-81; chief surgeon Shriner's Hosp. for Crippled Children, Montreal, 1970-82; prof. surgery McGill U., Montreal, 1970—, chmn. div. orthopedic surgery, 1976-81, dean faculty medicine, 1981—; hon. cons. orthopedic surgery Queen Elizabeth Hosp., 1972—; mem. clin. grants com. Med. Research Council, 1972-75. Contbr. articles on surgery to profl. jours.; editorial bd.: Jour. Internat. Orthopedics, 1976—, Jour. Bone and Joint Surgery, 1977—, Current Problems in Orthopedics, 1977—. Served to lt. M.C., USN, 1957-59. Fellow Royal Coll. Physicians and Surgeons Can. (chief examiner orthopedic surgery 1970-72), ACS, Am. Acad. Orthopedic Surgeons; mem. Can. Orthopedic Assn. (sec. 1971-76, pres. 1977-78), Can. Orthopedic Research Soc. (pres. 1971-72), Am. Orthopedic Research Soc. (pres. 1975-76), Am. Orthopedic Assn., Assn. Orthopedic Surgeons Province Que. (treas. 1971-72), Société Française de Chirurgie Orthopedique, McGill Osler Reporting Soc. Home: 526 Mount Pleasant Ave Montreal PQ H3Y 3H5 Canada Office: 3655 Drummond St Montreal PQ H3G 1Y6 Canada

CRUICKSHANK, ALEXANDER MIDDLETON, chemistry educator; b. Marlborough, N.H., Dec. 13, 1919; s. George and Edith (Coutts) C.; m. Irene Bromley, Jan. 13, 1945; children: Elaine, Gary Alexander. B.S., R.I. State Coll., 1943, M.S., 1945; Ph.D., U. Mass., 1954. Instr. U. Mass., 1948-52; asst. prof. U. R.I., Kingston, 1953-59, asso. prof., 1959-69, prof. chemistry, 1969-82, prof. emeritus, 1982—, chmn. dept. chemistry, 1976-82; asst. dir. Gordon Research Confs., 1947-68, dir., 1968—. Pres. Town Council, South Kingston, 1961-65, mem., 1975-77; mem. Selective Service Bd., 1969—. Mem. Am. Chem. Soc., Am. Inst. Chemists, AAAS. Lodge: Lions. Home: 1235 Kingstown Rd Kingston RI 02881

CRUICKSHANK, BRUCE, physician, educator; b. Edinburgh, Scotland, May 27, 1920; s. George Bruce and Florence Mary (Hicks) C.; m. Dorothy Harper, May 13, 1944; children—Frances Mary, John Bruce. Ed., U. Edinburgh, 1938-43. Lectr. U. Edinburgh, 1951-56; sr. lectr. U. Glasgow, Scotland, 1956-63; prof. pathology U. Coll. of Rhodesia, 1964-68; prof. U. Toronto, Ont., Can., 1968—. Co-author: Human Histology, 1964, Atlas of Haematology, 1965, 68, 70, 78. Served with RAF, 1944-46. Nuffield Research fellow, 1949-51. Mem. Internat. Acad. Pathology, Path. Soc. Gt. Britain and Ireland, Heberden Soc. Office: Sunnybrook Medical Centre 2075 Bayview Ave Toronto ON M4N 3M5 Canada

CRUICKSHANK, DONALD JAMES, utility company executive, mechanical engineer; b. Edinburgh, Scotland, Nov. 5, 1931; emigrated to Can., 1955; s. John Cecil and Mabel Elizabeth (Harvey) C.; m. Lesley Joan Rowell, 1974; children: Colin, Wendy, Sally, Paula, Jeffrey. A.M.I. in Mech. Engring., Royal Naval Engring. Coll., Plymouth, Eng., 1952; M.Sc., Cranfield Inst. Tech., Eng., 1958. Registered profl. engr., Ont. Commd. cadet Royal Navy, 1945, advanced through grades to lt., 1955, served aboard cruisers and aircraft carriers; commd. lt. Can. Navy, 1955; advanced through grades to lt. comdr. Royal Navy, 1963; served at sea and at Can. Naval Hdqrs. Can. Navy, Ottawa, Ont., ret., 1963; dir. govt. programs Bristol Aerospace Ltd., Winnipeg, Man., Can., 1963-71; v.p., gen mgr. Rolls Royce (Can.) Ltd., Montreal, Que., 1971-74, pres., 1974-79, Can. Telecommunications Carriers Assn., Ottawa, 1979-81; v.p. Bell Can., Ottawa, 1981—; cons. engring. and mgmt., Montreal, 1973. Mem. Can. Aeros. and Space Inst., Assn. Profl. Engrs. (Ont.). Anglican. Clubs: Canada (exec. com. 1979—), Cercle Universiatiare (Ottawa)). Home: 5 Ryeburn Dr Ottawa ON Canada Office: Bell Canada 160 Elgin St Room 890 Ottawa ON Canada K1G 3J4

CRUICKSHANK, WILLIAM MELLON, educator; b. Detroit, Mar. 25, 1915; s. Ward and Alice (Shanor) C.; m. Dorothy Jane Wager, Dec. 26, 1940; children: Alice Ann (Mrs. Roger Johanson), Dorothy Patricia (Mrs. David Crosson), Carol Jean (Mrs. Frederick Adler). A.B., Eastern Mich. U., 1936, Sc.D. (hon.), 1962; M.A., U. Chgo., 1938; Ph.D., U. Mich., 1945; D.H.L. (hon.), Central Mich. U., 1982; J.D. (hon.), Cardinal Stritch Coll., 1982; D.Ped. (hon.), Syracuse U., 1982. Margaret O. Slocum disting. prof. edn., psychology; dir. div. spl. edn. and rehab. Syracuse U., 1946-67, dean summer sessions, 1953-66; prof. psychology, prof. edn., prof. child and family health U. Mich., Ann Arbor, 1966—, chmn. dept. spl. edn., hearing and speech scis., 1977-79; dir. Inst. for Study Mental Retardation and Related Disabilities, 1966-80, dir. emeritus, 1980—; Fulbright lectr., 1968; asso. dir. Inst. San Gabriel Arcangel, Lima, Peru, 1962-63; author, lectr.; Priorsfield research fellow U. Birmingham, Eng., 1973; former cons. N.Y. State Assn. Crippled Children; mem. profl. adv. com. Nat. Soc. Crippled Children and Adults, Nat. Soc. for Prevention Blindness; sr. cons. Teaching Resources Corp., Boston, 1966—; cons. health and ednl. instns., Japan, Eng., France, Netherlands, Denmark, Sweden, Peru, Germany, India; former chmn. Canadian-U.S. Study Group on Mental Retardation, 1968-74; cons. Havern Sch., Colo., 1970-77, Neuro-Edn. Ctr., William Beaumont Coll.; mem. bd. consultants Center for Research on Exceptional Children. U. N.C., 1969-75; mem. adv. com. dept. edn. Govt. Am. Samoa, 1969-71; past mem. profl. adv. bd. Pathway Sch., Norristown, Pa., 1966-70. Author, editor; co-editor books on cerebral palsy, learning disability, perception, exceptional children.; Editorial cons., Syracuse U. Press, 1966—; editorial adviser, Prentice-Hall, Inc., 1966-78; mem. adv. bd. various jours. Bd. dirs. Detroit League for Handicapped, Goodwill, Inc., 1978-80; former adviser Ednl. Policies Commn.; mem. N.Y. State Regents' Council Physically Handicapped; adv. com. tchr. edn. Am. Found. for Blind; ednl. adv. com. Fed. Epilepsy League, 1955-64, United Cerebral Palsy Assn.; mem. Mich. State Planning Adv. Com. on Devel. Disabilities and Constrn. Facilities, 1971—; mem. tech. research adv. com. Mich. Dept. Mental Health, 1975-79; mem. profl. adv. com. Detroit Orthopaedic Center, 1975-79, chmn., 1977-79; mem. profl. adv. com. Bancroft Sch., Atlanta, 1978—; Past trustee Cove Schs., Racine, Wis., 1948-60. Served to capt., adj. gen. dept. AUS, 1942-45. Recipient Catedratico Honorario Universidad Nacional Mayor de San Marcos, Lima, Peru, 1962; J.E. Wallace Wallin award Nat. Council for Exceptional Children, 1965; Outstanding Profl. award Assn. for Children with Learning Disabilities, 1970; Honor award Internat. Fedn. Learning Disabilities, 1976; Newell C. Kephart award Purdue U., 1977; others. Fellow Am. Psychol. Assn. (life, pres. Div. 22, psychol. aspects phys. disability 1969-70), Am. Assn. Mental Deficiency (Outstanding Educator award 1975), Am. Acad. Mental Retardation, Am. Acad. Cerebral Palsy; mem. Internat. Council Exceptional Children (pres. 1952-53), Internat. Neuropsychology Soc., Assn. for Children with Learning Disabilities (profl. adv. com. 1969-75), Internat. Acad. for Research on Learning Disabilities (founder, pres. 1979—), Mich. Assn. for Children with Learning Disabilities (profl. adv. com. 1969-74, 79—), N.Y. State Psychol. Assn., Nat., Mich., Washtenaw County assns. for retarded children. Home: 2855 Whippoorwill Ln Ann Arbor MI 48103

CRUIKSHANK, NELSON HALE, labor economist; b. Bradner, Ohio, June 21, 1902; s. Jesse Lincoln and Jessie Margaret (Wright) C.; m. Florence Crane, Aug. 30, 1928 (dec.); 1 dau., Alice-Marie Cruikshank Hoffman. Student, Oberlin Coll., 1920-21; A.B., Ohio Wesleyan U., 1925, LL.D., 1972; M.Div., Union Theol. Sem., N.Y.C., 1929. Dir. social service dept. Bklyn. Fedn. Chs., 1931-33; labor edn. services, govt. adviser, 1933-42; exec. asst. to labor mem. at. Mgmt.-Labor Policy Com., War Manpower Commn. and dep. vice chmn. in charge of labor relations War Manpower Commn., 1943-44; dir. European Labor div. ECA, 1950-52; mem. A.F. of L. advisers to President's Council of Econ. Advisers, 1948-50; mem. adv. com. on safety in industry Bur. Labor Standards, Dept. Labor, 1947-50; mem. U.S. del. to First Gen. Assembly WHO, Geneva, 1948; rep. A.F. of L. at Econ. and Social Council of UN, Geneva, 1948; mem. nat. hosp. adv. council USPHS, 1946-50; dir. Social ins. activities AFL, 1953-55; dir. dept. social security AFL-CIO, 1955-65; mem. Fed. Adv. Council Dept. Labor, 1953-60, 62-65; mem. statuory adv. council Social Security Financing, 1957-58; mem. Health Ins. Benefits Advisory Council, 1965-72; vis. prof. Sch. Labor and Indsl. Relations Mich. State U., 1966; lectr. Sch. Social Work U. Mich., 1967; vis. prof. social sci. Pa. State U., 1969. Contbr. to labor and religious periodicals. Mem. U.S. Nat. Commn. for UNESCO (exec. com.), 1946-50, Nat. Planning Assn. (labor com.); Mem. com. on experts on social security ILO, 1962-70; pres. Nat. Council Sr. Citizens, 1969-77; chmn. Fed. Council on Aging, 1977-80; councillor to Pres. on Aging, 1977-80; mem. U.S. del. 1st gen. conf. UNESCO, Paris, 1946; mem. cons. group to Sec. HEW; active in, Nat. Council Chs. of Christ in U.S., 1952-68; Bd. visitors Div. Sch., Duke, 1966-71. Recipient Merit award Group Health Assn. Am., 1965. Fellow Am. Coll. Hosp. Adminstrs. (hon.); mem. Seafarer's Internat. Union Democrat. Methodist. Home: 3001 Veazey Terr NW Washington DC 20008 *The men I have known who have had a part in moving our society and our nation forward seem to me to have done it the way the sailors moved their ship through the locks. While putting our strong lines far forward of the vessel for the progressive pull, they maintained a hold astern, bearing in mind that while progress was their purpose, there were enduring values from past experiences.*

CRUIKSHANK, ROBERT LANE, investment company executive; b. Sharon, Pa., Oct. 5, 1936; s. John Wesley and Jeannette Sprague (Lane) C.; m. Marianne Johnson, Nov. 17, 1962; children: Douglas, Christina. B.A. cum laude, Princeton, 1958. With Blyth Eastman Dillon & Co. Inc., N.Y.C., 1958-78, gen. partner, 1966, nat. retail sales partner, 1967, partner in charge br. office, 1970-74, exec. v.p. security div., 1974-77, exec. v.p., mem. exec. com., chief plan officer, 1977-78; gen. partner Neild, Cruikshank & Co., 1979—; vice chmn. Chgo. Bd. Options Exchange. Bd. dirs. United Fund, Bronxville, N.Y., Am.-Scottish Found.; deacon Reformed Presbyterian Ch., Bronxville. Served to 1st lt. U.S. Army, 1959-60. Clubs: Univ., Bronxville Field (N.Y.C.); Quadrangle (Princeton); Stratton Mt. Country (Vt.) (trustee); Racquet, Saddle and Cycle, Attic (Chgo.). Home: 1500 Lake Shore Dr Chicago IL 60610 Office: 141 W Jackson Chicago IL 60604

CRUIKSHANK, THOMAS HENRY, corporation executive; b. Lake Charles, La., Nov. 3, 1931; s. Louis James and Helene L. (Little) C.; m. Ann Coe, Nov. 17, 1955; children: Thomas Henry, Kate Martin, Stuart Coe. B.A., Rice U., 1952; postgrad., U. Tex. Law Sch., 1952-53, U. Houston Law Sch., 1953-55. Bar: Tex.; C.P.A., Tex. Accountant Arthur Andersen & Co., Houston, 1953-55, 58-60; mem. firm Vinson & Elkins, Houston, 1961-69; v.p. Halliburton Co., Dallas, 1969-72, sr. v.p., 1972-80, exec. v.p., 1980, pres., chief exec. officer subs. Otis Engring. Corp., 1980-81, pres., 1981-83, pres., chief exec. officer, 1983—, dir., 1977—; dir. InterFirst Bank Dallas, N.A. Pres. Jr. Achievement, Dallas, 1974-76, chmn., 1976-78, mem. nat. bd., 1976—. Served to lt. (j.g.) USNR, 1955-58. Mem. Am., Tex. socs. C.P.A.s, Am., Tex. bar assns. Clubs: Dallas Petroleum; River Oaks Country (Houston); Dallas Country (gov., 1977-79. Home: 3508 Marquette Dallas TX 75205 Office: 400 N Olive LB 263 Dallas TX 75201

CRUIKSHANK, WARREN LOTT, Realtor; b. Bklyn., Dec. 19, 1916; s. Russell Vernon and Anita Livingston (Lott) C.; m. Kathleen R. Holmes, Oct. 10, 1947; children: Gail Warren, Jeffrey Lloyd, Peter Lott. B.A., Princeton, 1938. Real estate broker, salesman Cruikshank Co., N.Y.C., 1938-69,; pres., chmn. bd., chief exec. officer Ely-Cruikshank Co., Inc., N.Y.C., 1974-80, chmn., 1980-82; former trustee Greenwich Savs. Bank. Author: (with John Burke) Real Estate, Sales and Brokerage, 1975. Past bd. dirs. Downtown-Lower Manhattan Assn.; bd. govs. Hundred Year Assn. N.Y.; mem. Econ. Devel. Commn., Maplewood (N.J.). Mem. N.Y. State Assn. Realtors (past dir.), Am. Inst. Real Estate Appraisers (past pres. chpt. 4), 7th Regt. Vets. Assn., St. Andrews Soc., St. Nicholas Soc., Huguenot Soc. Am. Methodist. Clubs: Princeton of N.Y. (bd. govs.), Princeton Elm (bd. govs.), Princeton Charter, Orange Lawn Tennis. Home: 36 Euclid Ave Maplewood NJ 07040 Office: 2 Wall St New York NY 10005

CRUISE, JAMES EDWIN, museum director, botany educator; b. Port Dover, Ont., Can., June 26, 1925; s. William Edward and Annie Gertrude (Walker) C. B.A., Toronto (Ont.) U., 1950; M.S., Cornell U., 1951, Ph.D. (Henry Strong Denison fellow 1951-52, 52-53), NSF fellow 1952-54, 1954; LL.D. (hon.), Guelph (Ont.) U., 1982. Teaching asst. Cornell U., 1951-54; postdoctoral fellow, instr. in botany Phila. Acad. Sci., 1954-56; asst. prof. botany State U. N.J., 1956-58, asso. prof., 1958-60, prof., 1960-63; asso. prof. botany U. Toronto, 1963-69, prof., 1969—, curator Phanerogamic Herbarium, 1969-75, asso. dean Faculty Arts, Sci., 1972-75; dir. Royal Ont. Mus., Toronto, 1975—; cons. NSF, 1959-63. Contbr. numerous articles to profl. publs., 1954—; editor cons. in systematics and exptl. taxonomy, Am. Jour. Botany, 1963-75, Am. Midland Naturalist. Served with RCAF, 1943-46. Recipient Dominion Skyways Proficiency award RCAF, 1944, G.A. Cox Gold medal in Sci. U. Toronto, 1950; Ont. Research Council scholar, 1950-51. Mem. Ont. Soc. Biologists (pres. 1970-71), Can. Bot. Assn. (sec. 1970-72), Am. Inst. Biol. Scis., Bot. Soc. Am., Am. Soc. Plant Taxonomists, Internat. Soc. Plant Taxonomists, Sigma Xi, Phi Kappa Phi. Mem. United Ch. Canada. Home: 55 Maitland St Apt 1704 Toronto ON M4Y 1C9 Canada Office: Royal Ont Museum 100 Queen's Park Toronto ON M5S 2C6 Canada

CRULL, TIMM F., food company executive; b. 1931; married. B.A., Mich. State U., 1955. Chief operating officer, dir. Norton Simon Inc., 1977-79; with Carnation Co., 1955-77, 80—, exec. v.p., 1980-83, pres., 1983—, also dir. Office: Carnation Bldg 5045 Wilshire Blvd Los Angeles CA 90036

CRUM, DENNY EDWIN (DENZEL CRUM), univ. basketball coach; b. San Fernando, Calif., Mar. 2, 1937; s. Alwin Denzel and June (Turner) C.; m. Joyce Ellaine Lunsford, Sept. 15, 1951; children—Cynthia Lynne, Steven Scott, Robert Scott. B.A., UCLA, 1959;

secondary teaching cert., San Fernando Valley State Coll., 1960. Asst., then head basketball coach Pierce Coll., Los Angeles, 1962-67; asst. coach UCLA, 1968-70; head basketball coach U. Louisville, 1971—. Author articles in field. Named Mo. Valley Conf. Coach of Year, 1973, 75, Coll. Coach of Year, 1974, Metro Conf. Coach of Year, 1979; winner NCAA Championship, 1980. Mem. Nat. Assn. Basketball Coaches. Office: 2301 S 3d St Louisville KY 40292

CRUM, GEORGE FRANCIS, JR., conductor, pianist; b. Providence, R.I., Oct. 26, 1926; s. George Francis and Florence Muriel (Campbell) C.; m. Alice Patricia Snell, Sept. 20, 1951; children: Jennifer, Angela. Student, St. Andrews Coll., 1935-38, Trinity Coll. Sch., 1938-42, Royal Conservatory of Music, Toronto, 1942-46. Coach, asst. condr. Royal Conservatory Opera, Toronto, 1946-51; asst. condr. Can. Broadcasting Corp. Opera Co., 1948-51, condr., 1952-56, Can. Opera, 1948-51; asst. condr. chorusmaster Opera Nacional de Centro-Am., 1949-50; coach opera Salzburg Festival, 1952; founding mem., mus. dir., prin. Condr. Nat. Ballet of Can., Toronto, from 1951; guest condr. major orchs., Can., U.S., Europe, 1951—. Recipient Queen Elizabeth medal, 1977. Mem. Am. Fedn. Musicians. Office: care Nat Ballet Can 157 King St E Toronto ON Canada M5C 1G9 *In return for the joy and privilege of making music, I have always tried my utmost to make each performance better than the one before.* *

CRUM, JAMES MERRILL, lawyer; b. Virginia, Ill., Oct. 14, 1912; s. Elton M. and Anna C. (Freitag) C.; m. Thelma Mae Williams, June 28, 1941; children—Suzanne, Deborah, James Frederick. A.B. with honors, Ind. U., (1937), J.D. with distinction, 1939. Bar: Ind. bar 1939, Fla. bar 1947. Practiced in, Evansville, 1939-40, Indpls., 1941-47, Ft. Lauderdale, Fla., 1947—; assoc. firm Kahn & Dees, 1939-40; law clk. U.S. Dist. Ct., Indpls., 1941, 46; agt., acting agt. charge U.S. Secret Service, 1941-45; ptnr. firm McCune, Hiaasen, Crum, Ferris & Gardner, 1947—; city atty., Hallandale, Fla., 1949-53, 57-63, Plantation, Fla., 1953-59, Miramar, Fla., 1955-59; Supr. Old Plantation Water Control Dist., 1952-74; mem. Broward County Law Library Com., 1955-65. Mem. City Council, Miramar, 1955-59. Mem. Fedn. Ins. Counsel, Am., Fla., Broward County bar assns., Order of Colf. Clubs: The Drummers, One Hundred of Broward County (Ft. Lauderdale). Home: 441 Holly Ln Plantation FL 33313 Office: PO Box 14636 Fort Lauderdale FL 33302

CRUM, JOHN KISTLER, association executive; b. Brownsville, Tex., July 28, 1936; s. John Mears and Mary Louise (Kistler) C. B.S., U. Tex., 1960, Ph.D., 1964; postgrad., Harvard U., 1970. Research fellow Robert A. Welch Found., 1962-64; asst. editor Analytical Chemistry, Am. Chem. Soc., Washington, 1964-65, asso. editor, 1966-68, mng. editor, 1969-70, group mgr. jours., 1970, dir. books and jours. div., 1971-75, treas., chief fin. officer, 1975-80, dep. exec. dir. and chief operating officer, 1981-82, exec. dir., 1982—; chmn. bd. Centcom, Ltd. Contbr. articles to profl. jours. Mem. Chem. Soc. (London), N.Y. Acad. Scis., Am. Chem. Soc., Council Engring. and Sci. Soc. Execs., Assn. Sci. Soc. Editors, Nat. Press Club, Sigma Xi, Phi Theta Kappa. Republican. Clubs: Internat., Cosmos (Washington). Home: 1701 N Kent St Arlington VA 22209 Office: 1155 16th St NW Washington DC 20036

CRUM, LAWRENCE LEE, banking educator; b. Brownsville, Tex., July 25, 1933; s. John Mears and Mary Louise (Kistler) C. B.B.A. with highest honors (Alpha Kappa Psi scholar 1954), U. Tex., Austin, 1954, M.B.A., 1956, Ph.D., 1961; postgrad., Carnegie-Mellon U., 1962, Harvard U., 1965. Ayres fellow Am. Bankers Assn., 1966; Asst. prof., then asso. prof. U. Fla., 1959-65; mem. faculty U. Tex., Austin, 1965—, prof. fin., 1969-82, Tex. Commerce Bancshares Centennial prof. comml. banking, 1982—, chmn. dept., 1969-76, dir. banking program, 1980—; chmn. bd. dirs. San Antonio br. Fed. Res. Bank, Dallas; cons. in comml. banking field. Mem. loan com. Franklin Lindsay Student Loan Fund, 1980—. Author: Time Deposits in Present Day Commercial Banking, 1964, Transition in the Texas Commercial Banking Industry, 1970; co-author: The Development of State-Chartered Banking in Texas, 1978; contbr. articles to profl. jours. Ford Found. fellow, 1963-64. Mem. Am. Fin. Assn., Am. Econ. Assn., Fin. Mgmt. Assn., Beta Gamma Sigma, Phi Kappa Phi. Republican. Home: 3920 Sierra Dr Austin TX 78731 Office: BEB 113 U Tex Austin TX 78712

CRUMB, GEORGE HENRY, composer, educator; b. Charleston, W.Va., Oct. 24, 1929; s. George Henry and Vivian (Reed) C.; m. Elizabeth May Brown, May 21, 1949; children: Elizabeth Ann, David Reed, Peter Stanley. B.Mus., Mason Coll., 1950; M.Mus., U. Ill., 1952; postgrad. (Fulbright fellow), Hochschule fuer Musik, Berlin, Germany, 1955-56, Berkshire Music Center, Tanglewood, Mass., summer 1955; D.Mus. Arts, U. Mich., 1959. Instr. theory Hollins Coll., Va., 1958-59; asst. prof. composition and piano U. Colo., 1959-64; creative asso. composition State U. N.Y. at Buffalo, 1964-65; asst. prof. composition U. Pa., Phila., 1965-66, asso. prof., 1966-71, prof., 1971—, Annenberg prof., 1983—. Composer: String Quartet, 1954, Sonata; for solo violincello, 1955; Variazioni; for large orch., 1959; Five Pieces; for piano, 1962, Night Music I; for soprano, keyboard and percussion, 1963; Four Nocturnes Night Music II; for violin and piano, 1964; Madrigals, Books I and II; for solo voice and instruments, 1965; Eleven Echoes of Autumn; for violin, alto flute, clarinet and piano, 1966; Echoes of Time and the River, 1967 (Pulitzer prize 1968); for orch. Songs, Drones and Refrains of Death for baritone and electric instruments; U. Iowa commn., 1968, Madrigals, Books III and IV; for soprano and instruments, 1969; Night of the Four Moons; for alto and instruments, 1969; Black Angels (Thirteen Images from the Dark Land); for electric string quartet, U. Mich. commn., 1970; Ancient Voices of Children; for soprano and instruments, Coolidge Found. commn., 1970; Vox Balaenae; for electric flute, electric cello and electric piano, 1971; Lux Aeterna; for soprano, sitar, bass flute and two percussionists, 1971; for amplified piano Makrokosmos, Vol. I, 1972, Vol. II, 1973; Makrokosmos, Vol. I Music for a Summer Evening; for 2 amplified pianos and percussion, Fromm Found. commn., 1974; Dream Sequence; for violin, cello, piano, percussion and glass-harmonica, 1976; Star-Child: A Parable; for Solo Soprano, Antiphonal Children's Voices, Bell Ringers and Large Orch., Ford Found. Commn., 1977; Celestial Mechanics, Cosmic Dances; for Amplified Piano, 4-Hands, 1979; Apparition; elegiac songs and vocalises for soprano and amplified piano, 1979; A Little Suite for Christmas, A.D. 1979, 1980, Gnomic Variations for Piano, 1981, Pastoral Drone for Organ, 1982, Processional for piano, 1983, A Haunted Landscape for Orchestra, 1984. Recipient composition prize Broadcast Music Inc., 1957, Koussevitzky Internat. rec. award, 1971, also commns. Koussevitzky Found., 1964, Bowdoin Coll., 1965, U. Chgo., 1966; Creative Arts gold award medal in music Brandeis U., 1979; Rockefeller Found. grantee, 1964; Guggenheim fellow, 1967. Mem. B.M.I., Nat. Inst. Arts and Letters, German Acad. Arts (hon.), Pi Kappa Lambda, Phi Mu Alpha. Office: Music Bldg U Pa Philadelphia PA 19104

CRUMB, OWEN JOSEPH, public relations exec.; b. Stamford, N.Y., Aug. 9, 1925; s. Charles S. and Bretta June (Moore) C.; m. Agatha Cupido, Sept. 30, 1950; children—Michael, Elizabeth Crumb Nestorowycz, Charles, Joseph, John. B.A. in Journalism, Syracuse U., 1949. Corr./editor Asso. Press, Buffalo and Syracuse, N.Y., 1950-56; dir. public relations Eastern Milk Producers Co-op., Syracuse, 1956-59; v.p. Chapman-Nowak, advt. agy., Syracuse, 1959-63; with public relations div. Rumrill-Hoyt, Inc., Rochester, 1963-77, pres., 1972-77; v.p. for corp. communications Hutchins/Young & Rubicam, Inc., Rochester, 1977—. Served with U.S. Army, 1944-46. Mem. Public Relations Soc. Am., Soc. Profl. Journalists, Women in Communications, Advt. Council Rochester. Democrat. Roman Catholic. Club: Univ. (Rochester). Home: 50 Highwood Rd Rochester NY 14609

CRUMBAUGH, LEE FORREST, editor; b. Chgo., Dec. 22, 1947; s. John Howard and Edna Elizabeth (Oberndorfer) C.; m. Sherrill Hawthorne Monroe, June 21, 1969; children: Andrew Monroe, Carroll Virginia. Student, Colo. State U., 1965-67; B.S. in Journalism, U. Ill., 1969; M.B.A., U. Chgo., 1971. Reporter, Hinsdale (Ill.) Doings, 1967; editorial intern Chgo. Daily News, 1968; public relations intern Chgo. Title and Trust Co., 1969; editorial intern U.S. League of Savings Assns., Chgo., 1970; research analyst Savings & Loan News, 1971-72, mktg. dir., 1973-80, editor, 1980—, v.p., 1982—; instr. journalism George Williams Coll., Downers Grove, 1981—. Chmn. Glen Ellyn Fine Arts Festival, 1974, 76; bd. dirs. United Way of Glen Ellyn, 1978-80, community needs survey chmn., 1980-81, pres., 1982-83; chmn. Village of Glen Ellyn Environ. Protection Commn., 1979-81; mem. plan com. Village of Glen Ellyn, 1981-83; mem. Village of Glen Ellyn Bd. of Trustees, 1983—. Mem. Glen Ellyn Jaycees (dir. 1977), Am. Mktg. Assn., Sigma Delta Chi, Phi Kappa Tau. Republican. Mem. United Ch. of Christ. Home: 303 Hawthorne St Glen Ellyn IL 60137 Office: 111 E Wacker Dr Chicago IL 60601

CRUMLEY, JAMES ROBERT, JR., clergyman; b. Bluff City, Tenn., Mar. 30, 1925; s. James Robert and Ida Frances (Fine) C.; m. Sara Annette Bodie, May 26, 1950; children: Frances Crumley Holman, James Robert, Jeanne. B.A., Roanoke Coll., Salem, Va., 1948, D.D. (hon.), 1973; M.Div., Lutheran Theol. So. Sem., Columbia, S.C., 1951; D.D. (hon.), Newberry (S.C.) Coll., 1971, Augustana Coll., Ill., 1982, Muhlenberg Coll., Allentown, Pa., 1983, LL.D., Susquehanna U., Selinsgrove, Pa., 1977, L.H.D., Lenoir-Rhyne Coll., Hickory, N.C., 1979, Litt.D., Bethany Coll., Lindsborg, Kans., 1981, L.H.D., Manhattan Coll., Riverdale, N.Y., 1984. Ordained to ministry Luth. Ch. in Am., 1951; pastor chs. in, Greenville and Oak Ridge, Tenn., Savannah, Ga., 1951-74; sec. Luth. Ch. in Am., N.Y.C., 1974-78, bishop, 1978—; mem. governing bd. Nat. Council Chs. of Christ in USA; mem. central com. World Council Chs.; mem. exec. com. Luth. World Fedn. Author: God and Science, 1965. Bd. commr. Luth. World Ministries; bd. dirs. Luth. Council in USA. Home: 2 Drew Ln East Windsor NJ 08520 Office: 231 Madison Ave New York NY 10016

CRUMMY, ANDREW BERNARD, physician; b. Newark, N.J., Jan. 30, 1930; s. Andrew Bernard and Kathleen (Higgins) C.; m. Elsa Esser, Dec. 27, 1958; children—Colleen, Kevin, Timothy. Student, Georgetown U., 1947-49; B.A., Bowdoin Coll., 1951; M.D., Boston U., 1955. Intern U. Wis., Madison, 1955-56, resident in radiology, 1958-61; fellow in radiology Mt. Auburn Hosp., Cambridge, Mass., 1961-62; fellow in cardiovascular radiology Yale U., 1962-63; asst. prof. radiology U. Colo., 1963-64; mem. faculty dept. radiology U. Wis., Madison, 1964—, prof., dir. cardiovascular radiology. Contbr. articles to med. jours. Served with U.S. Navy, 1956-58. Fellow Am. Heart Assn., Am. Coll. Radiology; mem. Wis. Radiol. Soc. (pres. 1972-73), Soc. Cardiovascular Radiology (pres. 1981-82), Assn. Univ. Radiologists, AMA, Dane County Med. Soc., Wis. Med. Soc., Radiol. Soc. N.Am., Am. Roentgen Ray Soc. Home: 3535 Lake Mendota Dr Madison WI 53705 Office: 600 Highland Ave Madison WI 53792

CRUMP, GIVENS LINDSAY, property management executive; b. DeKalb, Tex., Mar. 25, 1922; s. Andrew Givens and Georgia Berry (Lindsay) C.; m. Elza Murl Hutchinson, Jan. 31, 1943; children: Leslie, Georgia Nell. Student, Paris Jr. Coll., 1939-40, North Tex. State U., 1941-42; B.B.A., U. Tex., 1947. Owner, mgr. dept. stores, DeKalb and New Boston, Tex., 1947-56; with Am. Machine & Foundry Co., 1954-70, div. v.p., 1963-66; chmn. bd. dirs. AMF Australia, 1966-69; asst. group exec., indsl. products group AMF, Inc., 1969-70; v.p. Nat. Corp. for Housing Partnerships, Washington, 1971-72, 75-78, sr. v.p., 1978-79, exec. v.p. property mgmt., 1980—; exec. v.p. Coordinated Bldg. Systems, Inc., Cin.; and pres. CBC Concrete Products, Inc., Cin., 1973-74; pres. NCHP Property Mgmt., Inc., Washington, 1978—, dir., mem. exec. com., 1978—. Mem. adv. council Nat. Rental Housing Council, Nat. Ctr. Housing Mgmt., Multifamily Housing Com.; mem. Fed. Housing Liaison Com. Served with USAAF, 1942-45; served with U.S. Army, 1951-52. Mem. Inst. Real Estate Mgmt. Republican. Club: N.Y. Athletic (N.Y.C.). Home: 1513 Snughill Ct Vienna VA 22180 Office: Nat Corp for Housing Partnerships 1133 15th St NW Washington DC 20005

CRUMP, HAROLD CRAFT, broadcasting executive; b. Amory, Miss., Sept. 28, 1931; s. Harold W. and Eva Elizabeth (Craft) C.; m. Margaret Leigh Glenn, June 28, 1980; children by previous marriage: Harold T., William L., Laurie M. Crump Porter. B.B.A. in Advt, U. Miss., 1953. Asst. advt. mgr. Blythville (Ark.) Courier News Jour., 1955-56; with sta. WTVF (and predecessor), Nashville, 1956—, v.p., dir. sales, 1966-75, sta. mgr., 1969-75, exec. v.p., gen. mgr., 1975-81, 21st Century Prodns. (producers Hee Haw, Candid Camera and Hee Haw Honeys), Nashville, 1975-81; exec. v.p and gen. mgr. Sta. KPRC-TV, Houston, 1981—; mem. govt. relations com. CBS-TV, 1980-81. Bd. dirs. Nashville Jr. Achievement, 1965-71, Jr. Pro Football League, 1967-69, Nashville Drug Treatment Center, 1977, Nashville Salvation Army, 1978-80; vice chmn. Nashville Better Bus. Bur., 1974, chmn. adv. rev. com., 1967; TV chmn. fin. campaign United Givers Fund, 1963; exec. com. Nashville chpt. Muscular Dystrophy Assn., 1972-79; now mem. corp. nat. orgn. trustee Nashville Meml. Hosp., 1979-81. Served to 1st lt. USAF, 1953-55. Recipient Silver medal Am. Advt. Fedn.; named Man of Year in Advt. for Nashville Advt. Fedn., 1971. Mem. Sales and Mktg. Execs. Club Nashville (past dir.), Tenn. Assn. Broadcasters (past pres.), Nat. Assn. Broadcasters, Nat. Assn. TV Program Execs., Alpha Delta Sigma, Delta Kappa Epsilon. Presbyterian. Clubs: Houstonian, Rotary. Home: 303 N Wilcrest Houston TX 77079 Office: KPRC-TV 8181 Southwest Freeway Houston TX 77001

CRUMP, J(AMES) I(RVING), Chinese language and literature educator; b. Newark, Mar. 8, 1921; s. J. Irving and Reta W. (Whitney) C.; children: Christine, J. Jonathan. B.A., Columbia U., 1947; Ph.D., Yale U., 1950. From instr. to prof. Chinese U. Mich., Ann Arbor, 1949—. Author: (with Irving Crump) Dragon Bones in the Yellow Earth, 1963, Intrigues: Studies of the Chan-kuo Ts'e, 1964, Chan-kuo Ts'e, 1970, Ballad of the Hidden Dragon, 1972, Chinese Theater in the Days of Kublai Khan, 1980, Songs from Xanadu, 1983. Served with U.S. Army, 1941-47. Guggenheim fellow, 1955; Fulbright fellow, 1974. Mem. Am. Oriental Soc., Assn. Asian Studies. Office: 3098 Frieze Bldg U Mich Ann Arbor MI 48109

CRUMP, SPENCER, publisher, business executive; b. San Jose, Calif., Nov. 25; s. Spencer M. and Jessie (Person) C.; children by previous marriage: John Spencer, Victoria Elizabeth Margaret. B.A., U. So. Calif., 1960, M.S. in Edn, 1962, M.A. in Journalism, 1969. Reporter Long Beach (Calif.) Ind., 1945-49; free-lance writer, Long Beach, 1950-51; travel columnist, picture editor Long Beach Ind.-Press-Telegram, 1952-56; pres. Crest Industries Corp., Long Beach, 1957-58; editor suburban sects. Los Angeles Times, 1959-62; editorial dir. Trans-Anglo Books, Los Angeles, 1962-73, pub., 1973-81; cons. Interurban Press/Trans Anglo Books, 1981—; pub. Zeta Pubs. Co., 1981—; dir. Trans-Anglo Britain, Trans-Anglo Industries Internat.; chmn. bd. Zeta Internat., 1976—; cons. Queen Beach Press, 1974—, Flying Spur Press, 1976—; mng. dir. Person Properties Co. (now Person-Crump Devel. Co.), Lubbock, Tex., 1951—; dir., Briarwood East, Dallas, Cottonwood Sq., Grand Prairie, Tex.; cons. So. Pacific Transp. Co., 1979—; chmn. journalism dept. Orange Coast Coll., 1966-82. Author: Ride the Big Red Cars, 1962, Redwoods, Iron Horses and the Pacific, 1963, Western Pacific-The Railroad That was Built Too Late, 1963, California's Spanish Missions Yesterday and Today, 1964, Black Riot in Los Angeles, 1966, Henry Huntington and the Pacific Electric, 1970, Fundamentals of Journalism, 1974, California's Spanish Missions — An Album, 1975, Suggestions for Teaching the Fundamentals of Journalism in College, 1976, The Stylebook for Newswriting, 1979, Newsgathering an Newswriting for the 1980s and Beyond, 1981. Mem. Los Angeles County Democratic Central Com., 1961-62. Mem. Book Pubs. Assn. So. Calif., Orange County Press Club, A.C.L.U., Fellowship Reconciliation, Soc. Profl. Journalists. Unitarian-Universalist. Club: Mason. Office: Zeta Pubs Co PO Box 38 Corona del Mar CA 92625

CRUSE, JULIUS MAJOR, JR., pathologist; b. New Albany, Miss., Feb. 15, 1937; s. Julius Major and Effie (Davis) C. B.A., B.S. with honors, U. Miss., 1958; D.Microbiology with honors (Fulbright fellow), U. Graz, Austria, 1960; M.D., U. Tenn., 1964; Ph.D. in Pathology (USPHS fellow), U. Tenn., 1966, USPHS postdoctoral fellow, 1964-67. Mem. faculty U. Miss. Med. Sch., 1967—; prof. immunology Grad. Sch., 1967-74, prof. pathology, 1974—, asso. prof. microbiology, 1974—, dir. grad. studies program in pathology, 1974—, dir. clin. immunopathology, 1978—, dir. immunopathology sect., 1978—, dir. tissue typing lab., 1980—; lectr. pathology U. Tenn. Coll. Medicine, 1967—; adj. prof. immunology Miss. Coll., 1977—. Author: Immunology Examination Review Book, rev. edit, 1975, Introduction to Immunology, 1977, Principles of Immuno-pathology, 1979; editor-in-chief: Survey of Immunologic Research, Survey and Synthesis of Pathology Research, Concepts in Immunopathology; Author also articles. Recipient Pathologists award in continuing edn. Coll. Am. Pathologists-Am. Soc. Clin. Pathologists, 1976; Julius M. Cruse collection in immunology established in his honor Middleton Med. Library U. Wis., Madison, 1979. Fellow AAAS, Royal Soc. Promotion Health, Am. Acad. Microbiology, Intercontinental Biog. Assn.; mem. Am. Assn. Pathologists and Bacteriologists, Am. Soc. Exptl. Pathology, Am. Chem. Soc., Brit. Soc. Immunology, Canadian Soc. Immunology, Am. Soc. Microbiology, Internat. Acad. Pathology, Am. Assn. Immunologists, AMA (Physicians Recognition award 1969-75), Am. Inst. Biol. Scis., Am. Soc. Clin. Pathologists, Canadian Soc. Microbiologists, N.Y. Acad. Scis., Soc. Exptl. Biology and Medicine, Soc. Francaise d'Immunologie, Reticuloendothelial Soc., Transplantation Soc., Electron Microscopy Soc. Am., Am. Assn. History Medicine, Sigma Xi, Phi Kappa Phi, Phi Eta Sigma, Alpha Epsilon Delta, Gamma Sigma Epsilon, Beta Beta Beta. Episcopalian. Office: Dept Pathology Univ Miss Med Center 2500 N State St Jackson MS 39216 *

CRUTCHFIELD, CHARLES HARVEY, broadcasting co. exec.; b. Hope, Ark., July 27, 1912; s. Charles Harvey and Fannie (Lowrance) C.; m. Jacquelin Williams, Nov. 10, 1931; children—Richard Dale, Leslie Crutchfield Tompkins. Student, Wofford Coll., 1929-30; mgmt. devel. seminar, Harvard U., 1959; L.H.D. (hon.), Appalachian State U., 1974. Announcer with various radio stas., N.C., S.C., 1929-33; announcer Sta. WBT, Charlotte, N.C., 1933-35, program mgr., 1935-45; with Jefferson-Standard Broadcasting Co. (named changed to Jefferson-Pilot Broadcasting Co. 1972), Charlotte, 1945—, exec. v.p., 1952-63, pres., 1963—, also dir.; guest lectr. Appalachian State U.; dir. CBS-TV Dist.; sec.-tres. CBS-TV Affiliates Adv. Bd.; speaker in field. Mem. Nat. Population Commn., Nat. Mental Health Bd. Named Man of Year Charlotte Bar Assn., 1968; Charter Mem. N.C. Broadcasting Hall of Fame, 1970; recipient Distinguished Service award N.C. Civitan, 1971, Broadcast Preceptor award San Francisco State Coll., 1967, Abe Lincoln Railsplitter award Radi-TV Commn. So. Bapt. Conv., 1975, Silver Medal award Charlotte Advt. Club, 1968, N.C. Distinguished Citizens award, 1977. Mem. Assn. Maximum Service Telecasters (charter), Nat. Assn. Broadcasters (research com.), N.C. Assn. Broadcasters, Charlotte C. of C. (pres. 1971), U.S. C. of C. (dir. 1974—), Newcomen Soc. N.Am. Democrat. Presbyterian. Clubs: Charlotte City, Charlotte Country, Quail Hollow Country, London Dinner. Home: 2633 Richardson Dr Charlotte NC 28211 Office: Jefferson-Pilot Broadcasting Co One Julian Price Pl Charlotte NC 28208 *The manager must understand this truth: that every human being has an instinctive need to have his worth... his uniqueness... the very fact that he exists recognized. Some call this "stroking," and it is an absolutely essential tool for today's manager.*

CRUTCHFIELD, EDWARD ELLIOTT, JR., banker; b. Detroit, July 14, 1941; s. Edward Elliott and Katherine (Sikes) C.; m. Nancy Glass Kizer, July 27, 1963; children: Edward Elliott, III, Sarah Palmer. B.A., Davidson Coll., 1963; M.B.A., U. Pa., 1965. With First Union Nat. Bank, Charlotte, N.C., 1965—, head retail bank services group, 1970-72, exec. v.p. gen. adminstrn., 1972-73, pres., 1973—; dir. First Union Corp., Bernhardt Industries, Inc. Bd. deacons Myers Park Presbyn. Ch.; bd. dirs. United Community Services, Salvation Army, Charlotte Bd., Charlotte Latin Sch.; trustee Mint Mus. Art, N.C. Nature Conservancy; bd. mgrs. Charlotte Meml. Hosp.; bd. visitors Davidson Coll. Mem. Charlotte C. of C., Assn. Res. City Bankers, Am., N.C. bankers assns., Am. Textile Mfrs. Assn., Young Pres.'s Orgn. Clubs: Charlotte City, Charlotte Country, Linville (N.C.) Golf. Office: Jefferson-First Union Tower Charlotte NC 28288 *

CRUTCHFIELD, FINIS ALONZO, JR., bishop; b. Henrietta, Tex., Aug. 22, 1916; s. Finis Alonzo and Callie (Blair) C.; m. Benja Lee Bell, Jan. 21, 1941; 1 son, Charles Newton. B.A., So. Meth. U., 1937; B.D., M.Div., Duke U.; D.D., Oklahoma City U.; Litt.D., U. Tulsa. Ordained to ministry Methodist Ch.; pastor in, Goodwell, Okla., Elk City, Okla., Muskogee, Okla., McFarlin Meml. United Meth. Ch., Norman, Okla., Boston Ave. United Meth. Ch., Tulsa, 1960-72; bishop La. area United Meth. Ch., New Orleans, 1972-76; bishop Tex. Conf., 1976—; Pres. bd. edn. Okla. Conf. United Meth. Ch.; pres. bd. evangelism, pres. S. Central Jurisdictional Council; mem. gen. bd. edn., mem. gen. commn. on ecumenical affairs; mem. World Meth. Council; del. Assembly on Faith and Order, World Council Chs., New Delhi, 1961. Former mem. Okla., Nat. coms. to employ handicapped; former mem. Okla. Com. on Religion and Medicine.; Former pres. bd. trustees Oklahoma City U., Meth. Home for Children, Tahlequah, Okla., Frances Willard Home, Tulsa; former mem. vis. com. U. Okla. Recipient Distinguished Alumnus award So. Meth. U.; citation NCCJ. Clubs: Masons, K.T. Address: 5215 S Main St Houston TX 77002 *

CRUTCHFIELD, SAM SHAW, JR., lawyer, association executive; b. Nashville, July 15, 1934; s. Sam Shaw and Alfreda (Whitworth) C.; m. Sylvia Ann Dinneen, May 14, 1958; children: Catherine Anne Crutchfield Sprinkle, Firmadge Whitworth, Elizabeth Victoria. B.A., George Washington U., 1960, J.D., 1963. Bar: D.C. 1963. Jud. law clk. to judge D.C. Ct. of Appeals, 1963-64; exec. dir. Va. Commn. Constl. Govt., 1964-67; assoc. counsel Am. Enterprise Inst. Public Policy Research, Washington, 1967-70, asst. to pres., 1970-73, dir. legal studies, 1973; gen. counsel U.S. Postal Rate Commn., 1973-74; exec. dir. Phi Delta Phi Internat. Legal Frat., Washington, 1974—, Phi Delta

Phi Legal Inst., 1976—; confidential advisor presdl. search com. Legal Services Corp., 1982; cons. Nat. Inst. Law Enforcement and Criminal Justice. Contbr. articles to profl. jours.; Editor: D.C. Young Lawyers, 1968-69, The Headnoter, 1978—. Mem. Jud. Conf. for D.C. Circuit, 1969; Vice-pres. Young Republican Club, Arlington, Va., 1968-69; mem. Arlington County Rep. Com., 1968-70, 74-76; exec. dir. Young Rep. Fedn. Va., 1968-69; trustee Del. Law Sch., 1972-74; bd. dirs. Hale Found., 1980—, Nathan Hale Inst., 1983—; co-capt. Reagan Transition Team on U.S. Postal Service and PRC, 1980-81. Served with U.S. Army, 1953-56. Mem. Interam. Bar Assn., Am. Bar Assn., D.C. Bar Assn. (asst. editor jour. 1971-73, editor D.C. Bar Report 1973-74), George Washington U. Law Assn. (dir. 1977-80, exec. council), Am. Judicature Soc., Inst. of Dirs. (assoc.), Assn. Former Intelligence Officers, Phila. Soc., Nat. Rifle Assn. (life), Amateur Trapshooting Assn. (life), N. Am. Hunting Club (charter), Clan Buchanan Soc. Am., Phi Delta Phi. Home: 3528 Gallows Rd Annandale VA 22003 Office: 1750 N St NW Washington DC 20036

CRUTCHFIELD, WILLIAM RICHARD, artist, educator; b. Indpls., June 21, 1923; s. William C. and Vera Eleanor (Wiggam) Neidlinger; m. Barbara Jean Seaman, June 14, 1964. B.F.A., Herron Sch. Art, Ind. U., 1956; M.F.A., Tulane U., 1960. Instr. Herron Sch. Art, Ind. U., Indpls., 1963-65; asst. prof. Mpls. Coll. Art and Design, 1966-67, chmn. found. studies, 1966-67. Author: Owl Feathers, 1975, (film) William Cruthchfield, Sage of Machine Wit, 1973, Crutchfield, A Recollection of the Future, 1977. Served with U.S. Army, 1957-59. Recipient Mary Milliken award Herron Sch. Art, 1956; Fulbright scholar, 1961; named Disting. Artist of Los Angeles 100 Club, Music Center, 1982. Home: PO Box 591 San Pedro CA 90733

CRUZ, JOSE BEJAR, engineering educator; b. Bacolod City, Philippines, Sept. 17, 1932; came to U.S., 1954, naturalized, 1969; s. Jose P. and Felicidad (Bejar) C.; m. Patria Cunanan, June 23, 1953; children: Fe E., Ricardo A., Rene L., Sylvia C., Loretta C. B.S. in Elec. Engring. summa cum laude, U. Philippines, 1953; M.S., MIT, 1956; Ph.D., U. Ill., 1959. Registered profl. engr., Ill. Instr. elec. engring. U. Philippines, Quezon City, 1953-54; research asst. MIT, 1954-56, vis. prof., 1973; instr. U. Ill., Urbana-Champaign, 1956-59, asst. prof., 1959-61, assoc. prof., 1961-65, prof. elec. engring., 1965—; research prof. Coordinated Sci. Lab., 1965—; asso. mem. Center Advanced Study, 1967-68; vis. asso. prof. U. Calif. at Berkeley, 1964-65; vis. prof. Harvard, 1973; pres. Dynamic Systems; mem. theory com. Am. Automatic Control Council, 1967; gen. chmn. Conf. on Decision and Control, 1975. Author: (with M.E. Van Valkenburg) Introductory Signals and Circuits, 1967, (with W.R. Perkins) Engineering of Dynamic Systems, 1969, Feedback Systems, 1972, System Sensitivity Analysis, 1973, (with M.E. Van Valkenburg) Signals in Linear Circuits, 1974; Assoc. editor: Jour. Franklin Inst, 1976-82, Jour. Optimization Theory and Applications, 1981; series editor: Advances in Large Scale Systems Theory and Applications; Contbr. articles fields network theory, automatic control systems, system theory, sensitivity theory of dynamical systems, large scale systems and dynamic games to sci., tech. jours. Recipient Purple Tower award Beta Epsilon U., Philippines, 1969, Curtis W. McGraw Research award Am. Soc. for Engring. Edn., 1972, Halliburton Engring. Edn. Leadership award, 1981. Fellow IEEE (chmn. linear systems com., group on automatic control 1966-68, assoc. editor Trans. on Circuit Theory 1962-64); mem. Control Systems Soc. (adminstrv. com. 1966-75, 78-80, pres. 1979, chmn. awards com. 1973-75, ednl. activities bd. 1973-75, editor Trans. on Automatic Control 1971-73, mem. tech. activities bd. 1979-81, chmn., v.p. tech. activities 1982-83, edn. med. com. 1977-79, v.p. fin. and adminstrv. activities 1976-77, dir. 1980—, vice-chmn. publs. bd. 1981, chmn. panel of tech. editors 1981, chmn. TAB periodicals com. 1981, chmn. PUB Soc. publs. com. 1981), Philippine Engrs. and Scientists Orgn. (pres. 1982), Soc. Indsl. and Applied Math., AAUP, AAAS, U.S. Nat. Acad. Engring., Philippine-Am. Acad. Sci. and Engring. (founding), Internat. Fedn. Automatic Control (theory com. 1981-84), Sigma Xi, Phi Kappa Phi, Eta Kappa Nu. Home: 2014 Silver Ct W Urbana IL 61801 Office: Coordinated Sci Lab U Ill Urbana IL 61801

CRUZ, RAMON A., university president. Pres. Inter Am. U. of Puerto Rico, San Juan. Office: Office of the President Inter Am U. of Puerto Rico GPO Box 3255 San Juan PR 00936

CRUZ-APONTE, RAMON ARISTIDES, educator; b. Barranquitas, P.R., Aug. 31, 1927; s. Demetrio and Juana (Aponte) Cruz; m. Abigail Negron, July 26, 1950; children—Ramon, Luis Roberto, Edgardo, Jorge Ivan. B.A., U. P.R., 1954; M.A., U. Fla., 1957; D.Ed., U. N.C., Chapel Hill, 1964; D.H.L. (hon.), U. Bridgeport, 1977. Tchr. P.R. Dept. Edn., 1945-48, prin., 1948-51, asst. supt. schs., 1954-56, supt. schs., 1957-64, dir. regional office, 1964-66; dean adminstrn. InterAm. U., 1967-69, v.p., 1969-72; now pres.; undersec. of edn. Commonwealth of P.R., 1973, sec. of edn., 1973-76; prof. edn. U. P.R., 1977; pres. Inter-Am. U. P.R., 1977—; mem. Task Force Higher Edn. Planning, 1968-70, Council State Sch. Officers, 1973-76; cons. Inter-Am. U., 1977, P.R. Dept. Edn., 1967-68; mem. Higher Edn. Council, 1973-77; chmn. P.R. Bd. Vocational Edn.; mem. Edn. Commn. of the States, 1973-76; mem. adv. bd. Ednl. Record, Am. Council on Edn., 1980. Exec. com. P.R. chpt. ARC, Jr. Achievement P.R., Boy Scouts Am.; mem. P.R. Bldgs. Authority, 1973-76, P.R. Commn. Human Resources, P.R. Mental Health Commn., 1973-76; chmn. bd. dirs. P.R. Easter Seal Soc., 1978-80. Served with AUS, 1951-53. Named Exec. of Year in Edn. Nat. Secs. Assn., 1976. Mem. P.R. Tchrs. Assn. (v.p. 1970-73), NEA, Am. Assn. Sch. Adminstrs., Am. Assn. Higher Edn., Phi Delta Kappa. Mem. Popular Democratic Party. Roman Catholic. Clubs: Lions (past pres.), Rotary.). Research on pub. sch. personnel policies and procedures, promotion policies. Home: 23 Amatista Bucare Rio Piedras PR 00927 Office: InterAm U PR GPO Box 3255 San Juan PR 00936 *I fully believe that true professional success and personal satisfaction will not come when you overestimate yourself or when you fight for promotion or honors. People will recognize your merits if you really have them.*

CRUZ-ROMO, GILDA, soprano; b. Guadalajara, Jalisco, Mexico; came to U.S., 1967; d. Feliciano and Maria del Rosario (Diaz) Cruz; m. Robert B. Romo, June 10, 1967. Grad., Colegio Nueva Galicia, Guadalajara, 1958; student, Nat. Conservatory of Music of Mexico, Mexico City, 1962-64. With, Nat. and Internat. Opera, Mexico City, 1962-67; toured, Australia, N.Z., S.Am.; with, Dallas Civic Opera, 1966-68, N.Y.C. Opera, 1969-72, Lyric Opera Chgo., 1975; Met. Opera debut as Madama Butterfly, 1970; leading soprano, 1970—; appeared in U.S. and abroad including, Covent Garden, La Scala, Vienna State Opera, Rome Opera, Paris Opera, Florence Opera, Torino Opera, Verona Opera, Portugal, Buenos Aires, others, concert appearances in, U.S., Can., Mexico; U.S. rep., World-Wide Madama Butterfly Competition, Tokyo, 1970; La Scala rep. in: Aida, USSR, 1974; appeared on radio, TV; filmed and recorded: Aida, with Orange Festival, France, 1976; roles include Aida, Madama Butterfly, Suor Angelica, Tosca, Odabella in: Attila; Manon Lescaut, Leonora in: Il Trovatore; Norma; Maddelena in: Andrea Chenier; Desdemona in: Otello; Elisabeth in: others. Don Carlo. Winner Met. Opera Nat. Auditions, 1970; recipient Critics award Union Mexicana de Cronistas de Teatro y Musica, 1973; named Best Singer, 1976-77; season Cronistas de Santiago de Chile, 1976. Home: 397 Warwick Ave Teaneck NJ 07666

CRYDERMAN, WILLIAM DALE, clergyman; b. Detroit, July 4, 1916; s. William Wallace and Mary Belle (McPhee) C.; m. Dorothy C. Gates, Oct. 19, 1935; children—William Leon, Dale Leroy, Lyn Dean, Richard Burton. Ed., Spring Arbor Coll. Photographer Detroit Times, 1935-40; ordained to ministry Free Methodist Ch., 1943; pastor, Albion, Mich., 1940-42; regional dir. Young People's Missionary Soc. Free Meth. Ch. N.Am., 1943-46; field dir. Spring Arbor Coll., 1947-48; pastor, Winona Lake, Ind., 1949-52; dir. Youth for Christ Internat., Japan, Korea, 1953-55; supt. So. Mich. Conf., 1956-68; bishop, 1969—; chmn., organizer Commn. Evangelism and Spiritual Life Nat. Assn. Evangelicals; mem. adv. council Am. Bible Soc., 1969-76; bd. dirs. Free Meth. Ch. N. Am., 1972—, pres., 1977—, pres. bd. adminstrn., 1979—; chmn. World Fellowship Free Meth. Chs. Mem. Gov.'s Com. Food for the Hungry, 1958-60; Trustee Spring Arbor Coll., sec. exec. com., 1960-75. Mem. Nat. Assn. Evangelicals, Christian Holiness Assn. Clubs: Rotarian, Kiwanian. Home: 518 Lincoln St Warsaw IN 46580 Office: 901 College Ave Winona Lake IN 46590 *As a young minister, serving my first church I read in my Bible "I have set before thee an open door" (Rev. 3:8). My lifelong goal has been to enter the doors that God opened. Thus, each opportunity for service in civic, social, community, and church life has been subjected to the question: "Is this one of God's open doors?" Obedience to this simple procedure coupled with a sensitivity to recognize an "open door" has made life a thrilling adventure.*

CRYNES, BILLY LEE, b. Worthington, Ind., Mar. 16, 1938; m. Mary Elizabeth Bildilli, Sept. 22, 1957; children: Lawrence, Stephen, David. B.S. in Chem. Engring., Rose-Hulman Inst. Tech., 1963, M.S., Purdue U., 1966, Ph.D., 1968. Pres. chem. engring. Okla. State U., Stillwater, 1967—, head dept., 1967—; research engr. Nalco Chem. Co., 1969-70, Standard Oil, 1968, E.I. duPont, 1968-70; cons. Oak Ridge Nat. Lab., Arco Corp., Gen. Mills, Global Engring., ERPI. Contbg. author: Chemistry of Coal Utilization, 1981, (with L.F. Albright and W.H. Corcoran) Pyrolysis: Theory and Industrial Practice, 1983, (with L.F. Albright) Pyrolysis: Theory & Practice, 1983. Coach Little League Baseball and Soccer, Stillwater, 1970, 73-76; project chmn. PTA, Stillwater, 1971-72; troop committeeman Will Rogers council Boy Scouts Am., 1974-76, 79. Served with USMC, 1956-58. Recipient Young Engr. of Yr. award Okla. Soc. Profl. Engrs., 1972; MASUA vis. scholar, 1976-77. Mem. Am. Chem. Soc. (nat. treas. 1975-83), am. Chem. Soc. (chmn. elect indsl. and engring. chemistry div. 1983), Am. Inst. Chem. Engrs. Methodist. Office: Department of Chemical Engineering Oklahoma State University Stillwater OK 74078

CRYSTAL, BILLY, actor; b. Long Beach, N.Y., Mar. 14; s. Jack and Helen C.; m. Janice Crystal; children: Jennifer, Linsay. Student, Marshall U., Nassau Community Coll; grad., N.Y. U. House mgr.: for play You're a Good Man Charlie Brown; mem.: group 3's Company; later solo appearances as stand-up comedian; appears on: TV series Soap, 1977-81; other TV appearances include: The Love Boat, The Tonight Show, Saturday Night Live; television films include: Breaking Up is Hard to Do, Death Flight; films include: The Rabbit Test. Office: care ABC Press Relations 1330 Ave of the Americas New York NY 10019 *

CRYSTAL, BORIS, painter; b. nr. Warsaw, Poland, Dec. 25, 1931; came to U.S., 1968, naturalized, 1974; s. Shea and Bronislawa (Blumenfeld) C.; m. Dalia Gilad, Oct. 6, 1961; children—Julius S., Byron R. Student, Plocer's Sch. Fine Arts, 1962-63, Acad. Fine Arts Israel, 1963-64. One-man exhbns. include, Katz Art Gallery, Tel Aviv, 1964, Art Gallery 97, Tel Aviv, 1965-66, Journalist House Art Gallery, Tel Aviv, 1967, Lerner Art Gallery, N.Y.C., 1968, Herzl Inst., N.Y.C., 1969, Roerich Mus., N.Y.C., 1970, Crystal Art Gallery, N.Y.C., 1972-76, group exhbns. include, Katz Art Gallery, 1964-68, Mus. Israel, Tel Aviv, Lerner Art Gallery, 1968-76, Roerich Mus., 1968-76, Jewish Mus., N.Y.C., 1968-76, Mus. Modern Art, N.Y.C., LaGalerie Mouffe, Paris; represented in permanent collections, Katz Art Gallery, Mus. Israel, Art Gallery 97, Journalist House, Continental Gallery, Crown Art Gallery, Herzl Inst., Lerner Art Gallery, Roerich Mus., Jewish Mus., Mus. Modern Art. Recipient Gold medal Accademia Italia delle Arti e del Lavoro, 1980; Contbns. to Arts award Am. Biog. Inst., 1981. Mem. Artists Equity Assn. Address: 65-10 108th St Forest Hills NY 11375

CRYSTAL, LESTER MARTIN, TV producer; b. Duluth, Minn., Sept. 13, 1934; s. Isadore S. and Sara (T.) C.; m. Tania Lee Wilson, June 22, 1958; children: Bradley, Alan, Elizabeth. B.S.J., Northwestern U. Medill Sch. Journalism, 1956, M.S.J., 1957. With NBC-TV, 1963—; exec. producer Nightly News, N.Y.C., 1973-76, v.p., 1976, exec. v.p., 1976-77, pres., 1977-79, sr. exec. producer politics and spl. broadcasts, 1979—; exec. producer MacNeil-Lehrer News Hour, 1983—. Served with U.S. Army, 1957-58. Recipient Emmy awards, 1969, 73. Mem. Radio and TV News Dirs. Assn., Council Fgn. Relations, Sigma Delta Chi. Office: NBC News 30 Rockefeller Plaza New York NY 10020

CSANADY, GABRIEL TIBOR, oceanographer, meteorologist, environmental engineer; b. Budapest, Hungary, Dec. 10, 1925; s. Arpad Kalman and Elizabeth (Marosi) C.; m. Ada Luige, Sept. 3, 1954 (div. 1968); 1 son, Andrew John; m. Joyce Eva Stever, Jan. 19, 1969. Diploma Ing., Technische Hochschule, Munich, W.Ger., 1948; Ph.D., U. New South Wales, Sydney, Australia, 1958. Engr. State Electric Co., Victoria, Melbourne, 1952-54; sr. lectr. U. New South Wales, Sydney, 1954-61; assoc. prof. mech. engring. U. Windsor, Ont., Can., 1961-63; prof. mech. engring. U. Waterloo, Ont., Can., 1963-73; sr. scientist Woods Hole Oceanographic Instn., Mass., 1972—. Author: Theory of Turbomachines, 1964, Turbulent Diffusion in the Environment, 1973, Circulation in the Coastal Ocean, 1982. Recipient Pres.'s prize Can. Meteorol. Soc., 1970, Chandler-Misener award Internat. Assn. Great Lakes Research, 1977; Sherman Fairchild disting. scholar Calif. Inst. Tech., 1982. Fellow Royal Meteorol. Soc. London; mem. Am. Meteorol. Soc. (Editor's award 1975), Am. Geophys. Union, ASME. Office: Woods Hole Oceanographic Instn Woods Hole MA 02543

CSAPLAR, RICHARD CHARLESTON, JR., lawyer; b. N.Y.C., May 18, 1931; m. Joan Androvett, 1953; children: Richard, Kenneth, Robert. B.A., Carleton Coll., Northfield, Minn., 1953; J.D., U. Pa., 1959. Bar: N.Y. 1960, Mass. 1965. Asso. Dewey, Ballantine, Bushby, Palmer & Wood, N.Y.C., 1959-65; founder,1965, since sr. partner Csaplar & Bok (and predecessor), Boston and San Francisco; instr. Boston Coll. Law Sch., 1972-77; adv. Supreme Ct. Afghanistan, 1974-75; sr. Fulbright lectr., Afghanistan, 1974-75. Author: The Afghan Judiciary, 1975; editor: A Collection of Afghan Judician Decisions, 1975. Chancellor to United Meth. Ch. in New Eng., 1972-74. Fellow Am. Bar Found.; mem. ABA, Boston Bar Assn. (council 1980-83). Home: 41 Dawson Dr Needham MA 02192 Office: 1 Winthrop Sq Boston MA 02110

CSAVINSZKY, PETER JOHN, physicist, educator; b. Budapest, Hungary, July 10, 1931; came to U.S., 1959, naturalized, 1964; s. Lajos and Ida (Kiss) C.; m. Barbara J. Fraser, Oct. 1976. Diplom Ing. Chem., Tech. U. Budapest, 1954; Ph.D. in Physics, U. Ottawa, Ont., Can., 1959. Research physicist Hughes Aircraft Co., Newport Beach, Calif., 1959-60, Gen. Dynamics Corp., Rochester, N.Y., 1960-62, Tex. Instruments Inc., Dallas, 1962-65, TRW Systems, Redondo Beach, Calif., 1965-70; asso. prof. physics U. Maine, Orono, 1970-74, prof., 1974—; vis. lectr. U. Calif., Berkeley, summer 1971, UCLA, summers 1972, 73, 74, 75, 76, 77; vis. prof. U. So. Calif., 1977-78. Contbr. articles to profl. jours. Recipient Presdl. Research Achievement award U. Maine, Orono, 1978. Fellow Am. Phys. Soc.; mem. AAAS, Soaring Soc. Am., Sigma Xi. Address: Dept Physics U Maine Orono ME 04469

CSERR, ROBERT, physician, hospital administrator; b. Perth Amboy, N.J., May 29, 1936; s. Frank Joseph and Helen (Bodzany) C.; m. Helen Fitzgerald, May 28, 1962; 1 dau., Ruth. A.B. magna cum laude, Harvard, 1958, M.D., 1962. Med. intern U. Va. Hosp., 1962-63; resident, fellow in psychiatry Mass. Gen. Hosp., Harvard Med. Sch., 1963-66; alcohol coordinator Mass. Gen. Hosp., 1967-68, clin. asso. psychiatry, 1968—; asst. supt. Medfield State Hosp., Harding, Mass., 1968-70, supt., 1970-74, area program dir., 1970-74; dir. Outlook psychiat. facility, Hampstead, N.H., 1974-76; med. dir. Charles River Hosp., Wellesley, Mass., 1976-80, psychiatrist-in-chief, 1980—, Hahnemann Hosp., Boston, 1982—; v.p. clin. affairs Community Care Systems Inc.; asst. clin. prof. psychiatry Boston U. Sch. Medicine, 1968-74, asso. clin. prof., 1979—; asst. psychiatrist Beth Israel Hosp., 1970—; lectr. in psychiatry Harvard Med. Sch., 1972—. Served with AUS, 1966-68. Mem. Am. Psychiat. Assn., Mass. Med. Soc., Mass. Psychiat. Soc. Home: Green Acres North Dighton MA 02764 Office: Charles River Hospital 203 Grove St Wellesley MA 02181 also Community Care Systems Inc 210 Lincoln St Boston MA 02111

CSICSERY-RONAY, ISTVAN, editor, author, publisher; b. Budapest, Hungary, Dec. 13, 1917; came to U.S., 1949; s. Stephen A. and Maria Alexandra (Zichy) Csicsery-R.; m. Elizabeth Tariska, July 27, 1945; children: Elizabeth M., Istvan. Diploma, Diplomatische Akademie, Vienna, Austria, 1939; Ph.D. in Polit. Sci., Royal Hungarian U., Budapest, 1940; cert. in Agronomy, Tech. U. Budapest, 1943, Sch. Diplomacy, Budapest, 1944; M.S.L.S., Catholic U. Am., 1957. Ministerial sec. Fgn. Ministry Hungary, Budapest, 1944-47; polit. analyst Free Europe Com. Inc. of N.Y. at U.S. Library Congress, 1949-56; owner, editor-in chief Occidental Press, Washington, 1953—; sr. cataloger U. Md., 1956-79; dir. external relations Democracy Internat., Washington, 1983—; organizer, dir., lectr. Hungarian fgn. policy between two wars Sch. Fgn. Affairs, Budapest, 1945-46; scriptwriter Voice of Am., 1954—, Radio Free Europe, 1956—; organizer lecture tours in U.S. for Sandor Veress, 1965, Transylvanian writers, 1973. Author: Russian Cultural Penetration in Hurgary, 1951, Szamuzottek Naptara, 1954 (Calendar of Exiles), (with Ferenc Nagy) Appeal to the Governments of the Free Nations, 1955, First Book of Hungary, 1967; drama Salata Kalman, 1984; editor and contbg. author: Koltok Forradalma, 1957 (Poets' Revolution); author numberous publs. of Free Europe Com., 1949-56; TV script Stephen I: His Life and His Reign, 1969; contbr.: Collier's Ency, 1962—, Ency. of Poetry and Poetics, 1965, East Central Europe, A Guide to Basic Publications, 1969, Lands and Peoples, 1972; co-editor: anti-Nazi underground weekly Eb Ura Fako, 1944; editor: Hirunk A. Vilagban, 1951-64 (Our Reputation in the World), Bibliografia, 1957-64, (others); exhibited one-man shows in color photography, U. Md., 1974, Fairfax County Library, Falls Church, Va., 1975. Acting pres. Teleki Pal Munkakozosseg (Paul Teleki movement), anti-Nazi orgn., Budapest, 1943-47; head div. fgn. affairs Smallholders' Party, Budapest, 1945-47. Served to 1st lt. arty. Hungarian Army, 1936-37, 39; Russian front, 1942-43. Cited for work in Resistance, 1945; recipient Silver medal Nat. Color Slides Competition, Hungarian Assn. Amateur Photographers, 1943; grantee Am. Council Learned Socs., 1961-62. Mem. P.E.N., Am. Acad. Polit. and Social Sci., Acad. Polit. Sci., Am. Liszt Soc., Liszt Soc. Eng., Phi Kappa Phi. Club: Klub der Absolventen Und Freunde der Diplomatischen Akademie (Vienna). Home: PO Box 1005 Washington DC 20013

CSOKA, STEPHEN, painter, etcher; b. Gardony, Hungary, Jan. 2, 1897; came to U.S., 1934, naturalized, 1941; s. Istvan and Julianna (Nagy) C.; m. Margaret Muller, Mar. 18, 1934; children—Clara Eve, Frank Stephen. Student, Royal Acad. Art, Budapest, 1922-27. Author: Pastel Painting, 1962; Work shown at internat. exhbns., also, Corcoran Gallery, Washington, 1945, 47, one-man shows, Contemporary Arts, N.Y.C., 1940, 43, 45, 56, Phila. Art Alliance, 1943, Minn. State Fair, Merrill Gallery, N.Y.C., 1963, Galerie Paula Insel, N.Y.C., 1976, Ponce (P.R.) Mus. Art, one-man retrospective, Fashion Inst. Tech., N.Y.C., 1979, Odin Gallery, Port Washington, N.Y., 1981; represented in several museums, including, Library of Congress. Recipient numerous awards and prizes, the later of which are La Tausca Pearl Co. award, 1945; 1,000 purchase prize-etching nat. Print Competition Assn. Am. Artists, 1947; 1,000 Grant Am. Acad. of Arts and Letters, 1948; First in oil Bklyn. Artists, 1949; John Taylor Arms Prize, etching Soc. Am. Etchers, 1952; Gold Medal award Arpad Acad., 1972; several hon. mentions. Mem. Soc. Am. Graphic Artists, Pastel Soc. Am., NAD, Audubon Soc. Home: 85-80 87th St Woodhaven NY 11421

CUA, ANTONIO S., philosophy educator; b. Manila, Philippines, July 23, 1932; came to U.S., 1953, naturalized, 1971; s. Oh and Chio (So) C.; m. Shoke-Hwee Khaw, June 11, 1956; 1 dau., Athene K. B.A., Far Eastern U., Manila, 1952; M.A., U. Calif.-Berkeley, 1954; Ph.D., 1958. Instr., asst. prof. Ohio U., 1958-62; prof., chmn. dept. philosophy SUNY Coll. at Oswego, 1962-69; prof. philosophy Catholic U. Am., Washington, 1969-; vis. prof. U. Mo.-Columbia, spring 1974-75, U. Hawaii, fall 1976-77. Author: Reason and Virtue: A Study in the Ethics of Richard Price, 1966, Dimensions of Moral Creativity: Paradigms, Principles, and Ideals, 1978, The Unity of Knowledge and Action: A Study in Wang Yang-ming's Moral Psychology, 1982; Co-editor: Jour. Chinese Philosophy; Contbr. articles to profl. jours. Mem. Am. Philos. Assn., Internat. Soc. for Chinese Philosophy, Soc. for Asian and Comparative Philosophy (pres. 1978—). Office: Sch Philosophy Cath U Am Washington DC 20017

CUADRA, CARLOS ALBERT, information scientist, management consultant; b. San Francisco, Dec. 21, 1925; s. Gregorio and Amanda (Mendoza) C.; m. Gloria Nathalie Adams, May 3, 1947; children: Mary Susan Cuadra Nielsen, Neil Gregory, Dean Arthur. A.B. with highest honors in Psychology, U. Calif., Berkeley, 1949, Ph.D. in Psychology, 1953. Staff psychologist VA, Downey, Ill., 1953-56; with System Devel. Corp., Santa Monica, Calif., 1957-78, mgr. library and documentation systems dept., 1968-70, mgr. edn. and library systems dept., 1971-74; gen. mgr. SDC Search Service, 1974-78; founder Cuadra Assos., Santa Monica, 1978—. Contbr. articles to profl. jours.; Editor: Ann. Rev. of Info. Sci. and Tech, 1964-75. Mem. Nat. Commn. Libraries and Info. Sci., 1971—. Served with USN, 1944-46. Recipient Merit award Am. Soc. Info. Sci., 1968, Best Info. Sci. Book award, 1969; named Disting. Lectr. of Year, 1970; received Miles Conrad award Nat. Fedn. Abstracting and Indexing Services, 1980. Mem. Info. Industry Assn. (bd. dirs., Hall of Fame award 1980). Home: 13213 Warren Ave Los Angeles CA 90066 Office: 2001 Wilshire Blvd Suite 305 Santa Monica CA 90403

CUATRECASAS, PEDRO MARTIN, research pharmacologist; b. Madrid, Sept. 27, 1936; U.S., 1947, naturalized, 1955; s. Jose and Martha C.; m. Carol Zies, Aug. 15, 1959; children: Paul, Lisa, Diane, Julia. A.B., Washington U., St. Louis, 1958, M.D., 1962. Intern, then resident in internal medicine Osler Service, Johns Hopkins Hosp., 1962-64, asst. physician, 1972-75; clin. asso., clin. endocrinology br. Nat. Inst. Arthritis and Metabolic Diseases, NIH, 1964-66; spl. USPHS postdoctoral fellow Lab. Chem. Biology, 1966-67, med. officer, 1967-70; professorial lectr. biochemistry George Washington U. Med.

Sch., 1967-70; asso. prof. pharmacology and exptl. therapeutics, asso. prof. medicine, dir. div. clin. pharmacology, Burroughs Wellcome prof. clin. pharmacology Johns Hopkins U. Med. Sch., 1970-72, prof. pharmacology and exptl. therapeutics, asso. prof. medicine, 1972-75; v.p. research, devel. and med. Wellcome Research Labs.; dir. Burroughs Wellcome Co., Research Triangle Park, N.C., 1975—; adj. prof. Duke U. Med. Sch., 1975—; adj. prof., mem. adv. com. cancer research program U. N.C. Med. Sch., 1975—; bd. dirs. Burroughs Wellcome Fund. Editor: Receptors and Recognition Series, 1975, Jour. Solid-Phase Biochemistry, 1975-80; editorial bd.: Jour. Membrane Biology, 1973, Internat. Jour. Biochemistry, 1973, Molecular and Cellular Endocrinology, 1973-77, Biochimica Biophysica Acta, 1973-79, Life Scis., 1978—, Neuropeptides, 1979—, Jour. Applied Biochemistry, 1978—, Cancer Research, 1980-81, Jour. Applied Biochemistry and Biotech., 1980—, Toxin Revs., 1981—, Biochem. Biophys. Research Communications, 1981—; contbr. articles to profl. jours. Recipient John Jacob Abel prize in pharmacology, 1972, Laude prize Pharm. World, 1975. Mem. Am. Soc. Biol. Chemists, Nat. Acad. Scis., Inst. Medicine of Nat. Acad. Scis., Am. Soc. Pharmacology and Exptl. Therapeutics (Goodman and Gilman award 1981), Am. Soc. Clin. Investigation, Am. Soc. Clin. Research, Spanish Biochem. Soc., Md. Acad. Scis. (Outstanding Young Scientist of Year 1970), Am. Cancer Soc., Endocrine Soc., Am. Chem. Soc., Am. Diabetes Assn. (Eli Lilly award 1975), Sigma Xi. Home: 626 Kensington Dr Chapel Hill NC 27514 Office: 3030 Cornwallis Rd Research Triangle Park NC 27709

CUBETA, PAUL MARSDEN, educator; b. Middletown, Conn., Mar. 12, 1925; s. Salvatore T. and Marion (Bacon) C.; m. Elizabeth Bransfield Brown, Aug. 25, 1948; children: Philip, David, James. B.A., Williams Coll., 1947; Ph.D., Yale U., 1954. Instr. English, Williams Coll., 1947-49; Carnegie fellow gen. edn. Harvard U., 1956-57; mem. faculty Middlebury (Vt.) Coll., 1952—, prof. English, 1964—, chmn. div. humanities, 1963-67, dean faculty, 1967-70, acad. v.p., 1970-76, v.p., 1976-79, Coll. prof. humanities, 1979—; Asst. dir. Bread Loaf Writers Conf., 1955-64; dir. Bread Loaf Sch. English, 1964—; mem. advanced placement com. English Coll. Entrance Exam. Bd., 1964-68. Editor: Modern Drama for Analysis, 3d. edit., 1962, Twentieth Century Interpretations of Richard II. Served to lt. (j.g.) USNR, 1943-46. Mem. MLA (mem. dels. assembly 1974-77, elections com. 1979-81), Phi Beta Kappa. Home: 39 Seminary St Middlebury VT 05753

CUCCI, CESARE ELEUTERIO, pediatric cardiologist; b. Spoleto, Italy, Dec. 22, 1925; came to U.S., 1954, naturalized, 1958; s. Otto and Anna (Morelli) C.; m. Gilda Morillo, Oct. 22, 1966; children: Susanna, Gardenia, Otto. Diploma in Classics, Coll. St. Maria, Rome, 1943; M.D., State U. Perugia (Italy), 1949. Diplomate: Am. Bd. Pediatrics, Am. Bd. Pediatric Cardiology. Chief, pediatric cardiology service Lenox Hill Hosp., N.Y.C., 1963-81; cons. pediatric cardiologist, 1981—; cons. pediatric cardiology Flushing Hosp., Queens, N.Y., 1970—, Methodist Hosp., Bklyn., 1966—, Booth Meml Hosp., Queens, 1964—, Wyckoff Heights Hosp., Bklyn., 1968—; prof. clin. pediatrics N.Y.U. Hosp., 1976—. Contbr. articles to med. jours. Fellow ACP, Am. Acad. Pediatrics, Am. Coll. Cardiology, Am. Coll. Chest Physicians. Roman Catholic. Club: 7th Regt. Rifle (N.Y.C.). Home: 45 E 62d St New York NY 10021

CUDAHY, RICHARD D., judge; b. Milw., Feb. 2, 1926; s. Michael F. and Alice (Dickson) C.; m. Ann Featherson, July 14, 1956; children: Richard Dickson, Norma Kathleen, Theresa Ellen, Daniel Michael, Michaela Alice. B.S., U.S. Mil. Acad., 1948; LL.B., Yale U., 1955. Commd. 2d. lt. U.S. Army, 1948, advanced through grades to 1st lt., 1950; asst. to legal adv. Dept. State, 1956-57; asso. Isham, Lincoln & Beale, Chgo., 1957-61; pres. Patrick Cudahy, Inc., Wis., from 1961, also dir., Patrick Cudahy Family Co., from 1969; now judge U.S. Ct. Appeals 7th Circuit, Chgo.; lectr. law Marquette U. Law Sch., 1961-66; vis. prof. law U. Wis., 1966-67; chmn. Wis. Regional Export Expansion Council, 1962-64; commr. Milw. Harbor, 1964-66; pres. Milw. Urban League, 1965-66; bus. adv. council Office Econ. Opportunity, 1966—; pres. Gambrinus Soc., 1969; bd. dirs. Nat. Inst. Polit. Communication, 1969—. Chmn. Wis. Democratic party, 1967-68; Dem. candidate for Wis. atty. gen., 1968; bd. dirs. United Community Services, Milw., 1965-66. Mem. Am., Wis., Milw., Chgo. bar assns., Am. Meat Inst. (dir.). Roman Catholic. Office: US Courthouse and Fed Office Bldg 219 S Dearborn St Chicago IL 60604 *

CUDDY, DANIEL HON, banker; b. Valdez, Alaska, Feb. 8, 1921; s. Warren N. and Lucy C.; m. Betty Puckett, Oct. 6, 1947; children: Roxanna, David, Gretchen, Jane, Lucy, Laurel. B.A., Stanford U., 1946. Bar: Alaska bar 1948. Practice in, Anchorage, 1948-53; pres. First Nat. Bank Anchorage, 1951—, now chmn. bd. Office: First Nat Bank 4th Ave and G St Anchorage AK 99501

CUDLIP, WILLIAM BYRNES, lawyer; b. Iron Mountain, Mich., Mar. 4, 1904; s. William John and Luella (Byrnes) C.; m. Lynwood Rockwell Bope, Jan. 5, 1929; children: Mary Luella (Mrs. John S. Jenkins), William John II, David Rockwell, Lynwood Jean (Mrs. John P. Ryan), Charles Thomas. Student, Swarthmore Coll., class 1925; J.D., U. Mich., 1926. Bar: Mich. 1926. Since practiced in, Detroit; cons. partner firm Dickinson, Wright, Van Dusen & Freeman, and predecessor, 1933—; Mem. commn. recodification Mich. laws on financial instns., 1936-37; Commn. for Compilation Mich. Statutes, 1948; mem. Mich. Constl. Conv., 1961-62; mem. nat. adv. council Small Bus. Adminstrn., 1959. Bd. regents U. Mich., 1963-72. Fellow Am. Bar. Found.; mem. Am., Detroit bar assns., Mich. State Bar, Phi Kappa Psi, Phi Delta Phi. Republican. Roman Catholic. Clubs: Little Harbor (Harbor Springs, Mich.); Birchwood Country. Home: Dellwood 5175 S Shore Dr Harbor Springs MI 49740 Office: 1st Nat Bldg Detroit MI 48236

CUDWORTH, ALLEN L., insurance company executive, researcher; b. Tuscaloosa, Ala., Jan. 2, 1929; s. James Rowland and Emily (Latham) C.; m. Cynthia Leach, Dec. 11, 1954; children: Ann, Lindsay, James. B.S. in E.E., U. ALa.-Tuscaloosa, 1949, M.S., MIT, 1952; Sc.D. in Environ. Health, Harvard U., 1967. Cert. Am. Bd. Indsl. Hygiene; registered profl. engr., Mass. Mem. research staff MIT, 1949-55; acoustical engr. Liberty Mut. Ins. Co., Hopkinton, Mass., 1955-62, dir. research, 1967-72, v.p., dir. research, 1972—; dir. Ins. Inst. Hwy. Safety, Washington, 1980—. Author: Industrial Noise Control, 1974. Fellow Acoustical Soc. Am.; mem. Am. Indsl. Hygiene Assn. (dir. 1975-78), Am. Acad. Indsl. Hygiene (chmn. accreditation com. 1980—), Tau Beta Pi. Presbyterian. Club: Wellesley Country (Mass.). Office: Liberty Mutual Insurance Co 175 Berkeley St Boston MA 02117 *

CUEVAS, JOSE LUIS, painter, illustrator; b. Mexico City, Feb. 26, 1934; s. Alberto and Maria Regia (Novelo) Cuevas G.; m. Bertha Riestra, Feb. 17, 1961; children: Mariana, Zimena, Maria-Jose. Exhibited one-man shows, Prisse Gallery, Mexico City, 1953, Pam-Am. Union, Washington, 1954, Pam-Am. Union, N.Y.C., Pam-Am. Union, Paris, Pam-Am. Union, Rome, Pam-Am. Union, Los Angeles, Pam-Am. Union, Buenos Aires, Pam-Am. Union, numerous other cities; Exhibited group exhbns. throughout, N.Am., S.Am., Europe, India, Japan; represented in permanent collections, Mus. Modern Art, N.Y.C., Solomon R. Guggenheim Mus., N.Y.C., Bklyn. Mus., Art Inst. Chgo., Phillips Collection, Washington; represented in other leading collections.; Illustrator: The Worlds of Kafka and Cuevas, 1959, Recollections of Childhood, 1962, Cuevas-Charenton, 1965, Crime by Cuevas, 1968, Homage to Quevedo, 1969, Cuevas Comedies, 1971, Cuaderno de Paris, 1977; Author: Cuevas by Cuevas, 1964, Cuevario, 1973, Confesiones de Jose Luis Cuevas, 1975. Recipient 1st Internat. Drawing award Sao Paulo (Brazil) Bienal, 1959; 1st Internat. award Mostra Internazionale di Bianco e Nero de Lugano, Zurich, Switzerland, 1962; 1st prize Bienal de Grabado, Santiago, Chile, 1964; 1st Internat. award 1st Triennale New Delhi, India, 1968; 1st prize Bienal de Grabado, San Juan, P.R., 1974. Address: Calle Galeana 109/ San Angel Inn Mexico DF Mexico also 28 rue da Condamine Paris France *Far from boring me, the world is to me a constant source of fascination. This does not, to be sure, prevent me from looking at it in my own way. What I see is a sweat-stained mass of businessmen, priests, clerks, prostitutes, bank cashiers, and pregnant women, who go their way, without realizing what they are, seeking oblivion.*

CULBERT, TAYLOR, coll. dean; b. Bklyn., Sept. 15, 1917; s. Isaac Taylor and Fannie (Blauvelt) C.; m. Anne Clark, Aug. 25, 1949; children—Jane Lindsay, John Taylor, Robert Alan. A.B., Yale, 1939; M.A., U. Mich., 1947, Ph.D., 1957. Mem. faculty Ohio U., 1953—, prof. English, 1965—, dean, 1965-70, v.p., dean faculties, 1969-73, exec. v.p., dean faculties, 1973-75, provost, 1975-76, Trustee prof. English, 1976—; pres. Ohio Univ. Press, 1964—. Served to maj. AUS, 1940-46. Home: Rt 3 Box 293 Strouds Run Rd Athens OH 45701

CULBERTSON, HORACE COE, insurance executive; b. Los Angeles, Apr. 24, 1924; s. Henry Coe and Irene A. (Blood) C.; m. Janet Ann Fadley, Dec. 27, 1949; children: Timothy Coe, Gary Dan, William Craig. A.B., Occidental Coll., 1949; student, U. So. Calif., 1948. With Fidelity and Deposit Co. Md., 1949—, exec. v.p., 1966-74, pres., chief exec. officer, 1974-80, chmn., chief exec. officer, 1981-84, chmn. bd., 1984—, also dir., mem. exec. com.; dir., mem. exec. com. Union Bancorp Md., 1968-74, Title Guarantee Co. Md., 1972-78; pres., dir. SwissRe Holding N.Am. Inc., N.Y.C.; dir. Md. Nat. Corp., 1975—, SwissRe Advs. Inc., SwissRe Corp., SwissRe Mgmt. Co., N.Am. Reins. Corp., N.Am. Reassurance Co., Gen. Surety & Guarantee Co., Ltd.; instr. UCLA, 1953-54. First v.p. Wakefield Home Improvement Assn., 1972; mem. Greater Balt. Commn., 1974—; trustee, mem. exec. com. Community Chest Balt., 1968-73; bd. dirs. Balt. United Appeal, 1972, Balt. Area Council Alcoholism, 1969-78, ARC Balt., 1970-76; solicitor Balt. Symphony, 1968-69; trustee St. Joseph Hosp., 1980—. Served with USNR, 1943-46. Mem. Nat. Assn. Casualty and Surety Execs., Surety Assn. Am. (rep. exec. com. 1969-79), Am. Ins. Assn. Am. (rep. exec. com. 1968), Surety Underwriters Assn. So. Calif. (pres. 1964), Ins. Info. Inst. (alt. dir. 1970-71), Beavers Heavy Engring. Contractors Assn. (dir. 1970-75), Met. Balt. C. of C. (v.p. 1972, dir.), Am. Legion, Newcomen Soc., Alpha Tau Omega. Republican. Presbyterian. Clubs: Balt. Country, Center (dir. 1978—), Maryland (Balt.); Towson Golf and Country. Office: Fidelity Bldg Baltimore MD 21201

CULBERTSON, JANET LYNN, artist; b. Greensburg, Pa., Mar. 15, 1932; d. Joseph F. and Helen C. (Moore) C.; m. Douglas I. Kaften, Sept. 30, 1964. B.F.A., Carnegie Inst. Tech., 1953; M.A., N.Y. U., 1963. Instr. art Pace Coll., N.Y.C., 1964-68, Pratt Art Inst., Bklyn., 1973; asso. prof. Southampton Coll., 1976; drawing instr. Parrish Art Mus., 1979. Exhibited in one-woman shows at, 20th Century West Gallery, N.Y.C., 1967, Molly Barnes Gallery, Los Angeles, 1970, Midtown Gallery, Atlanta, 1971, Lerner-Misrachi Gallery, N.Y.C., Lerner Heller Gallery, N.Y.C., 1973, 75, 77, Tower Gallery, Southampton, N.Y., 1976, Benson Gallery, Bridgehampton, N.Y., 1978, 81, 82, 83, Interart Gallery, N.Y.C., 1979, Harriman Coll., N.Y.C., 1980, Nardin Gallery, N.Y.C., 1981, two-woman show, Women's Art Center, San Francisco, 1975, one-woman shows at, Aronson Gallery, Atlanta, 1982, two-woman show, Heckscher Mus., N.Y.C., 1980, four-woman show, Heckscher Mus., N.Y.C.; exhibited in group shows at, Carnegie Mus., Pitts., 1953, Bucknell U. Ann. Drawing, 1966-68, Palos Verdes (Calif.) Mus., 1970, 16th Ann. All Calif. Purchase, Los Angeles Art Assn., 1969-70, Nat. Drawing Ann., San Francisco Mus., 1970, Princeton Gallery Fine Arts, 1972, Ruth White Gallery, N.Y.C., Heckscher Mus., Huntington, N.Y., 1975, 78, Drawing Show, Fleisher Meml., Phila., 1974, Am. Acad. Arts and Letters, N.Y.C., 1975, Kingpitcher Gallery, Pitts., West Broadway Gallery, N.Y.C., 1976, Bronx Mus., Guild Hall, East Hampton, N.Y., 1976, 79, 82, Orgn. Ind. Artists, Animals, N.Y.C., 1978, Parrish Mus., Southampton, N.Y., Meml. Art Gallery, Rochester, N.Y., 1979, Western Carolina U., Cullowhee, N.C., Phoenix Mus., Tucson Mus., 1980, Animals at the Arsenal, N.Y.C., 1981, 50 Nat. Women Artists, Edison Coll. Art Gallery, Ft. Myers, Fla., 1982, others; Contbr. collage to, Attica Book, 1972, Heresies Issue 5, Issue 13. Recipient Guild Hall abstract award, 1979; Creative Artists Public Service grantee, 1979. Home: 525 E 82d St New York NY 10028 Office: PO Box 455 Shelter Island Heights NY 11965

CULBERTSON, JOHN HARRISON, engineer; b. Lansdowne, Pa., Dec. 3, 1905; s. Walter Edwards and Katherine (Evans) C.; m. Grace Jessie Kirby, Sept. 6, 1941; children: Marian Grace Culbertson Hvolbeck, Katherine Kirby Culbertson Prentice, John Harrison. Student, Lehigh U., 1924-28. Plant mgr. Schering Corp., Bloomfield, N.J., 1940-42, Heyden Pennicillin Plant, Princeton, N.J., 1946-47; prodn. mgr. Unexcelled Chem. Corp., N.Y.C., 1947-49; v.p. Drum Co., Bristol, Pa., 1949-50; project dir. Port of N.Y. Authority Harbor Radar Tests, N.Y.C., 1951-52; pres. Nat. Ceramic Co., Trenton, N.J., 1954-55, Culbertson Enterprises, Morristown, N.J., 1956—, also dir.; Ex-officio trustee Assn. N.J. Environ. Commns., 1969—, pres., 1969-73. Bd. mgrs. Morristown Neighborhood House, 1960—, pres., 1969-73; Formerly trustee Wilson Coll., Chambersburg, Pa.; trustee Kirby Episcopal Conf. Center, Glen Summit, Pa., pres., 1974-77; trustee Speedwell Village, 1979—. Served from lt. to comdr. USNR, 1942-45. Recipient Harding Township (N.J.) Outstanding Citizenship award, 1970. Mem. Psi Upsilon. Republican. Presbyn. Clubs: Morristown (N.J.) Field (pres. 1959-65), Chemists (N.Y.C.)). Home: Blue Mill Rd Morristown NJ 07960 Office: 12 Flagler St Morristown NJ 07960

CULBERTSON, JOHN MATHEW, economist, educator; b. Detroit, Aug. 25, 1921; s. Glen A. and Lydia (Hawley) C.; m. Frances Mitchell, Aug. 27, 1947; children—John, Joanne, Lyndall, Amy. B.A., U. Mich., 1946, M.A., 1947, Ph.D., 1956. Economist to bd. govs. Fed. Res. System, 1950-57; mem. faculty U. Wis., Madison, 1957—, prof. econs., 1962—. Author: Full Employment or Stagnation, 1964, Macroeconomic Theory and Stabilization Policy, 1968, Economic Development: An Ecological Approach, 1971, Money and Banking, 1972, 2d edit, 1977; also articles. Served with USAAF, 1943-46. Decorated Air medal. Mem. Am. Econ. Assn. Home: 5305 Burnett Dr Madison WI 53705

CULBERTSON, KATHERYN CAMPBELL, lawyer; b. Tom's Creek, Va., Aug. 14, 1920; d. Robert Fugate and Mary Campbell (Leonard) C. B.S., East Tenn. State U., (1940), George Peabody Library Sch., 1942; J.D., YMCA Night Law Sch., Nashville, 1968. Bar: Tenn. bar 1969. Librarian Bur. Ships Tech. Library, U.S. Navy Dept., Washington, 1945-49, 51-53; librarian Lincoln Elementary Sch., Kingsport, Tenn., 1949-50, 51, Regional Library, Tenn. State Library and Archives, Johnson City, 1953-61; dir. extension services library Met. Govt. Nashville and Davidson County, Tenn, 1961-71; state librarian and archivist State of Tenn., Nashville, 1972-82; practice of law, Nashville; mem. library com. Pres.'s Com. on Employment of Handicapped, 1966—; Nat. Bus. and Profl. Women's Found., 1968-70; pres. Tenn. Fedn. Bus. and Profl. Women's Clubs, 1974-75. Contbg. author: Encyclopedia of Education, 1966; Editor: YMCA Alumni Assn. Bull, 1970-71. Named One of Five Women of Yr. Nashville Banner-Davidson County Bus. and Profl. Women's Club, 1979. Mem. ABA, Tenn. Bar Assn., ALA, Southeastern Library Assn., Tenn. Library Assn., D.A.R. Republican. Clubs: Zonta, Nashville Bus. and Profl. Women's (past pres.). Home: 800 Glen Leven Dr Nashville TN 37204 Office: 1506 Church St Suite 4 Nashville TN 37203

CULBERTSON, PHILIP E., government official; b. Colfax, Wash., Aug. 19, 1925; s. Julian L. and Lucia C.; m. Shirley E. Coskey, Aug. 19, 1950; children: Camden E., Philip E. B.S. in Aero. Engring., Ga. Inst. Tech., 1946; M.S., U. Mich., 1949. Mem. research staff U. Mich., 1948-52; aerodynamicist Convair div. Gen. Dynamics Corp., 1952-56; chief project engr. Atlas space launch vehicles, 1958-65; head aerodynamics and propulsion Bendix Systems Co., 1956-57; with NASA, 1965—; dir. payload integration and mission analysis Office Manned Space Flight, 1973-76, asst. adminstr. planning and program integration, from, 1976-78, asst. adminstr. space transp. systems, 1979-81; assoc. dep. adminstr. NASA, 1981—; exec. dir. President's Com. Sci. and Tech., 1976—; lectr. in field. Served with USNR, World War II. Office: NASA Hdqrs Washington DC 20546 *

CULBREATH, HUGH LEE, JR., electric utility exec.; b. Tampa, Fla., May 11, 1921; s. Hugh Lee and Daphne (Jackson) C.; m. Betty King, June 8, 1944; children: Betty Kay, Hugh Lee III. B.S., U.S. Naval Acad., 1944. Commd. officer USN, 1944, resigned, 1954; with Tampa Electric Co., 1957—, v.p. finance, sec. treas., 1966-71, exec. v.p., sec., treas., 1971, pres., 1971—, chief exec. officer, 1972—; dir. Transco Energy Co., Houston., NCNB Nat. Bank of Fla. Mem. Greater Tampa C. of C. (pres. 1972-73), Sigma Alpha Epsilon. Episcopalian (vestryman 1963-65, 67-69, treas. 1967). Clubs: Tampa Yacht and Country (commodore 1963), University, Exchange (pres. 1961), Palma Ceia Golf and Country, Ye Mystic Krewe of Gasparilla (Tampa). Home: 52 Bahama Circle Tampa FL 33606 Office: PO Box 111 Tampa FL 33601

CULHANE, JOHN JOSEPH, lawyer; b. Yonkers, N.Y., Apr. 24, 1945; s. John Joseph and Anna Rita (Merrins) C. B.S., St. Peters Coll., 1968; J.D., Fordham U., 1973. Bar: N.J. 1973, Wis. 1975. Assoc., ptnr. firm Howard, Peterman & Eisenberg, S.C., Milw., 1975-80; sr. atty., asst. sec. Joseph Schlitz Brewing Co., Milw., 1981-82; assoc. gen. counsel, asst. sec. Stroh Brewing Co., Detroit, 1982-83; v.p., gen. counsel Pabst Brewing Co., Milw., 1983—; dir. Future of Milw., 1983—. Mem. ABA, N.J. Bar Assn., Wis. Bar Assn., Milw. Bar Assn., U.S. Brewers Assn. (Pabst rep.), Wis. Brewers Assn. (Pabst rep.). Roman Catholic. Clubs: University (Milw.); Pewaukee Yacht. Home: N22 W28684 Louis Ave Pewaukee WI 53072 Office: Pabst Brewing Co PO box 766 1000 N Market St Milwaukee WI 53201

CULICK, FRED ELLSWORTH CLOW, educator; b. Wolfeboro, N.H., Oct. 25, 1933; s. Joseph Frank and Mildred Beliss (Clow) C.; m. Frederica Mills, June 11, 1960; children—Liza Hall, Alexander Joseph, Mariette Huxham. Student, U. Glasgow, Scotland, 1957-58; S.B., Mass. Inst. Tech., 1957, Ph.D., 1961. Research fellow Calif. Inst. Tech., Pasadena, 1961-63, asst. prof., 1963-66, asso. prof., 1966-70, prof. engring. and applied physics, 1970—; Cons. to govt. agys. and indsl. orgns. Mem. Am. Phys. Soc., Am. Inst. Aeros. and Astronautics. Home: 1375 E Hull Ln Altadena CA 91001 Office: Calif Inst Tech 301-46 Pasadena CA 91125

CULL, ROBERT ROBINETTE, elec. products mfg. co. exec.; b. Cleve., Sept. 24, 1912; s. Louis David and Wilma Penn (Robinette) C.; m. Alice Jane Harcus, Mar. 29, 1941. B.S. in Physics, M.I.T., 1934. Supr. Eastman Kodak Co., Rochester, N.Y., 1934-39; asst. to gen. mgr. Cleve. Chain & Mfg. Co., 1940-45; partner Tenna Mfg. Co., Cleve., 1945-56; pres. Tenatronics Ltd., Newmarket, Ont., Can., 1956—, Sterling Mfg. Co., Cleve., 1960—. Trustee Garden Center Greater Cleve., 1975-80, pres., 1979-80; trustee Musical Arts Assn. of Cleve. Orch., 1976—. Mem. IEEE, Cleve. Engring. Soc., Sigma Psi. Clubs: Cleve. Yacht, Hermit, Union. Office: 1845 E 30 St Cleveland OH 44114 *

CULLEN, JACK SYDNEY GEORGE BUD, Canadian government official; b. Creighton Mine, Ont., Can., Apr. 20, 1927; s. Chaffey Roi and Margaret Evelyn (Leck) C. B.A., U. Toronto, 1950; LL.B., Osgoode Hall Law Sch., Toronto, 1956. Bar: Called to bar 1956. Barrister-at-law, Sarnia, Ont., 1956-68; mem. parliament for Sarnia-Lambton, 1968—; mem. privy council, 1975—, minister of nat. revenue, 1975-76, of employment and immigration, 1976-79. First pres. Sarnia Edn. Authority, 1962; mem. Sarnia Sch. Bd., 1959. Mem. Lambton Law Assn. (past pres.), Sarnia and Dist. Assn. Mentally Retarded. Liberal. Mem. United Ch. Can. Club: Sarnia Kinsmen (life). Address: Room 330-CB House of Commons Ottawa ON K1A 0A6 Canada

CULLEN, JOHN DARBY, chemical company executive; b. Buffalo, Jan. 11, 1925; s. Robert E. and Anna C. (Darby) C.; m. Ann Lloyd Woodman, Apr. 28, 1951; children: Robert, Andrew, Charles. B.A., B.S., Lehigh U., Bethlehem, Pa., 1948; M.S., Va. Poly. Inst., 1950. With E.I. duPont de Nemours & Co., Wilmington, Del., 1950—, plant mgr., Orange, Tex., 1966-69, various mgmt. positions, Wilmington, 1969-79, v.p. engring., 1979-83, sr. v.p. engring., 1983—. Trustee, mem. bldg. com. Wilmington Med. Center, 1978—; trustee Lehigh U., 1981—. Served with USAAF, 1943-46. Mem. Am. Inst. Chem. Engrs., Nat. Soc. Profl. Engrs., Phi Gamma Delta. Presbyterian. Home: 301 Center Meeting Rd Wilmington DE 19807 Office: Engring Dept Louviers Bldg Wilmington DE 19899

CULLEN, JOHN T., corporation executive; b. 1925; married. B.B.A., St. John's U., 1950. Asst. to pres. Abraham & Straus, N.Y.C., 1943-71, with Allied Stores Corp., 1971—; pres. Donaldson's, 1971-72; div. group mgr. 5 units, then also corp. v.p. Allied Stores Corp., N.Y.C., 1972-74, sr. v.p., 1974-77, exec. v.p., dir., 1977—. Served with USMC, 1943-46. Office: Allied Stores Corp 1114 Ave of Americas New York NY 10036 *

CULLENBINE, CLAIR STEPHENS, lawyer; b. Beardstown, Ill., Nov. 29, 1905; s. Robin James and Victoria (Stephens) C.; m. Jean Williams, Aug. 23, 1930; children—Carol Ann (Mrs. Neal B. Wineman), Robert Stephens. LL.B., Washington U., St. Louis, 1928. Bar: Mo. bar 1928. Practice law, St. Louis, 1928-33; local counsel Md. Casualty Co., 1933-35; spl. counsel Asso. Industries of Mo., 1935-36; dir. research, dir. indsl. relations, 1937-43; indsl. relations mgr. Gaylord Container Corp., 1943-48, counsel, 1948-56; dir. Crown Zellerbach Corp. Industry mem. regional, nat. War Labor Bds., World War II. Mem. Calif. Mfrs. Assn. (dir.), Am. Arbitration Assn. (dir.). Club: Burlingame Country. Home: 50 Mounds Rd Apt 601 San Mateo CA 94402 Office: 1 Bush St San Francisco CA 94119

CULLENS, WILLIAM S., company executive. Pres., chief exec. officer Canron Inc. Office: First Can Pl Suite 6300 PO Box 134 Toronto ON Canada M5X 1A4§

CULLER, ARTHUR DWIGHT, English language educator; b. McPherson, Kans., July 25, 1917; s. Arthur Jerome and Susanna (Stover) C.; m. Helen Lucile Simpson, Sept. 14, 1941; children: Jonathan Dwight, Helen Elizabeth. B.A., Oberlin Coll., 1938; Ph.D., Yale U., 1941. Instr. English Cornell U., 1941-42; instr., then asst. Yale U., 1946-55; prof. English, 1958-, chmn. English dept., 1971-75; assoc. prof. English U. Ill., 1955-58. Author: The Imperial Intellect; A Study of Newman's Educational Ideal, 1955; Editor: (J.H. Newman) Apologia pro Vita Sua, 1956, (with G.P. Clark) Student and Society, 1959, Poetry and Criticism of Matthew Arnold, 1961, Imaginative Reason: The Poetry of Matthew Arnold, 1966, The Poetry of Tennyson, 1977. Fulbright fellow in Eng., 1950-51; Guggenheim fellow, 1961-62, 76; NEH fellow, 1979-80. Mem. MLA, Phi Beta Kappa. Home: 80 Tokeneke Dr North Haven CT 06518 Office: Dept English Yale U New Haven CT 06520

CULLER, FLOYD LEROY, JR., chemical engineer; b. Washington, Jan. 5, 1923; s. Floyd LeRoy Culler; m. Della Hopper, 1946; 1 son, Floyd LeRoy III. B. Chem. Engring. cum laude, Johns Hopkins, 1943. With Eastman Kodak and Tenn. Eastman at Y-12, Oak Ridge, 1943-47; design engr. Oak Ridge Nat. Lab., 1947-53, dir. chem. tech. div., 1953-64, asst. lab. dir., 1965-70, dep. dir., 1970-77; pres. Electric Power Research Inst., Palo Alto, Calif., 1978—; research design chem. engring. applied to atomic energy program, chem. processing nuclear reactor plants, energy research. Mem. sci. adv. com. Internat. Atomic Energy Agy., 1974—; mem. energy research adv. com. Dept. Energy, 1981—. Recipient Ernest Orlando Lawrence award, 1964; Atoms for Peace award, 1969; Robert E. Wilson award in nuclear chem. engring., 1972; Engring. Achievement award E. Tenn. Engrs. Joint Council, 1974. Fellow Am. Nuclear Soc. (dir. 1973-80, spl. award 1977), Am. Inst. Chemists, AAAS, Inst. Chem. Engrs.; mem. Am. Chem. Soc., Nat. Acad. Engring. Home: 1385 Corinne Ln Menlo Park CA 94025 Office: 3412 Hillview Ave Palo Alto CA 94303

CULLER, JOHN RUTLEDGE, architect; b. Lucas, Ohio, Feb. 23, 1911; s. Aaron Andrew and Edna (Rutledge) C.; m. Miriam G. Huntsinger, Feb. 6, 1943; children: Mary Ann, Deborah, Christine, Susan. A.B., Wittenberg U., 1933; B.S. in Architecture, Carnegie Mellon U., 1938. Draftsman archtl. firms, Pitts., 1935-40; chief draftsman Hunting Davis & Dunnels, Pitts., 1940-43; archtl. draftsman govt. projects, Front Royal, Va., El Dorado, Ark., Colorado Springs, Colo., 1943-45, Whitehouse & Price, Spokane, Wash., 1946-50; architect G.A. Pehrson & Assos., Spokane, 1945-46; owner Culler, Gale, Martell, Ericson, Spokane, 1950—; chmn. Spokane County Bldg. Code Bd. Appeals, 1954-62. Architect: Kellogg High Sch., 1956, Shadle Park High Sch., 1958, Spokane Falls Community Coll., 1968, Elma (Wash.) Elem. Sch., 1970, Goldendale High Sch., 1976, Samaritan Hosp., Moses Lake, Wash., 1980. Civic chmn. Spokane Beautification Com., 1966-70; mem. adv. bd. archtl. services GSA, 1967-68; mem. Spokane County Plan Commn., 1978-82, chmn., 1981-82; mem. Spokane Regional Planning Conf., 1982; pres. adv. bd. Vols. Am., Spokane, 1968-70. Mem. AIA (pres. local chpt. 1958-59), Am. Planning Assn., Council Ednl. Facility Planners, Spokane Execs. Assn. (pres. 1959), C. of C. (trustee 1967-68), Phi Kappa Psi. Republican. Lutheran. Clubs: Lions (dist. gov. 1967-68), Athletic Round Table, Univ. Spokane (pres. 1972-73), Spokane Knife and Fork (pres. 1971-72). Home: 5515 W 5th St Rt 14 Box 86 Spokane WA 99204 Office: 707 Peyton Bldg Spokane WA 99201

CULLER, JONATHAN DWIGHT, educator; b. Cleve., Oct. 1, 1944; s. Arthur Dwight and Helen Lucille (Simpson) C.; m. Cynthia Chase, Dec. 27, 1976. Fellow, dir. studies in modern langs. Selwyn Coll., Cambridge U., 1969-74; vis. prof. French and comparative lit. Yale U., 1975; fellow Brasenose Coll. and univ. lectr. French, Oxford U., 1974-77; prof. English and comparative lit. Cornell U., Ithaca, N.Y., 1977—. Author: Flaubert: The Uses of Uncertainty, 1974, Structuralist Poetics: Structuralism, Linguistics and the Study of Literature, 1975, Saussure, 1976, The Pursuit of Signs: Semiotics, Literature, Deconstruction, 1981; author: On Deconstruction: Theory and Criticism after Structuralism, 1982; Advisory editor: New Literary History, 1972—, PTL, 1976-79, Structuralist Review, 1978—; mem. advisory bd., Publs. Modern Lang. Assn., 1978—; mem. editorial bd.: Diacritics, 1974—, Poetics Today, 1979—. Recipient James Russell Lowell prize MLA, 1975; Rhodes scholar, 1966-69; Guggenheim fellow, 1979-80. Home: 643 Jacksonville Rd Jacksonville NY 14854 Office: Dept English Cornell U Ithaca NY 14853

CULLEY, PERRY HAGER, foundation executive; b. Los Angeles, Dec. 19, 1918; s. Perry Mohler and Anne Marie (Hager) C.; m. Patricia Elizabeth Sewell, Sept. 14, 1976; children: Catherine Elizabeth, Victoria Alexandra. Ed., Pasadena Jr. Coll., George Washington U., Georgetown U.; advanced mgmt. program, Harvard U., 1955. News editor OWI, 1941-42; radio news editor UP Bur., Washington, 1942; Washington corr. March of Time and Time Views the News, 1942-45; news editor ABC Radio Network, sta. WMAL, 1945; with fgn. service, 1945-72; successively info. officer Am. Embassy, Paris; info. specialist Dept. State; spl. asst. to ambassador Am. Embassy, Montevideo, asst. to dir. exec. secretariat, 1954, counselor, dep. chief mission, Quito, Ecuador; detailed to, 1959-60; session U.S. Naval War Coll.; then; sr. fgn. service insp.; later consul gen. Am. Embassy, Paris; dep. insp. gen. U.S. Fgn. Service; minister-counselor, dep. chief mission Am. Embassy, Paris.; Pres., exec. gov. Am. Hosp. of Paris, 1972-76; pres. Am. Hosp. of Paris Found., Washington, 1976-77; regional dir. Africa and Mideast programs Project Hope, 1977-82, dir. strategic planning, 1982—. Contbr. articles to mags. Served as ambulance driver Am. Field Service Brit. 8th Army, 1943-44; NATOUSA. Decorated Bronze Cross of Merit; with crossed swords Poland; comdr. Order Nat. Merit Ecuador). Episcopalian. Clubs: St. Cloud Golf and Country (Paris); Knickerbocker (N.Y.C.); Nat. Press. Office: care Project Hope Millwood VA 22646

CULLIGAN, JOHN WILLIAM, corporate executive; b. Newark, Nov. 22, 1916; s. John J. and Elizabeth (Kearns) C.; m. Rita McBride, Feb. 19, 1944; children: Nancy, Mary Carol, Elizabeth, Sheila, Jack, Neil. Student, U. Utah, U. Chi, Philippine U. With Am. Home Products Corp., 1937—, now chmn. bd., chief exec. officer, dir. Bd. dirs., v.p. Council on Family Health; bd. dirs. Am. Found. for Pharm. Edn., Valley Hosp. Found., Ridgewood, N.J.; trustee Seton Hall U., South Orange, N.J.; adv. bd. St. Benedict's Prep. Sch., Newark; co-chmn. Archbishop's Com. of Laity, Newark. Served with AUS, 1943-46. Mem. Proprietary Assn. (v.p., dir.), Bus. Roundtable, Friendly Sons St. Patrick., Knight of Malta, Knight of St. Gregory. Clubs: N.Y. Athletic, Pinnacle (bd. govs.), Hackensack Golf.; Economic (N.Y.C.). Office: 685 3d Ave New York NY 10017

CULLINA, WILLIAM MICHAEL, lawyer; b. Hartford, Conn., July 22, 1921; s. Michael Stephen and Margaret (Carroll) C.; m. Gertrude Evelyn Blasig, Apr. 29, 1961; children: William Gregory, Kevin Michael, John Stephen, Susan Margaret. A.B., Catholic U. Am., 1942; LL.B., Yale, 1948. Bar: Conn. bar 1948. Since practiced in, Hartford; with firm Murtha, Cullina, Richter & Pinney, 1948—, partner, 1952—. Bd. dirs. St. Francis Hosp. and Med. Center, St. Mary Home. Served with USNR, 1942-46. Mem. Am., Conn., Hartford County bar assns., Phi Beta Kappa. Roman Catholic. Clubs: Hartford Tennis, University (Hartford); Hartford. Home: 255 Westmont West Hartford CT 06117 Office: 101 Pearl St Hartford CT 06103

CULLINAN, ELIZABETH, writer; b. N.Y.C., June 7, 1933; d. Cornelius G. and Irene (O'Connell) C. B.A., Marymount Coll., N.Y.C., 1954. Author: House of Gold, 1970, The Time of Adam, 1971, Yellow Roses, 1977, A Change of Scene, 1982; also short stories pub., New Yorker mag. Recipient new writer's award Great Lakes Colls. Assn., 1970; Houghton Mifflin literary fellow, 1970; Nat. Endowment Arts grantee, 1974; Carnegie Fund grantee, 1978. Address: 34 E 68th St New York NY 10021

CULLINAN, VINCENT, lawyer; b. San Francisco, Jan. 22, 1911; s. Eustace and Katherine (Lawler) C.; m. Elizaberh Erlin, Oct. 16, 1937; children—Terrence, Kathleen Cullinan Merchant, Sheila Cullinan Wheeler. A.B. magna cum laude, U. Santa Clara, 1933; LL.D., Stanford U., 1936. Bar: Calif. bar, U.S. Supreme Ct. bar, Fed. Ct. bars of Calif. Partner firm Cushing, Cullinan, Duniway & Gorrill, San Francisco, 1936-41, Cullinan, Hancock, Rothert and Burns, 1946-71, Cullinan Brown and Helmer (and predecessor), San Francisco, 1971—; dir. Schlage Lock Co. Served with Intelligence USN, 1941-45. Mem. San Francisco Bar Assn. (pres. 1968), Am. Law Inst., State Bar Calif. (v.p. 1969), Am. Bar Assn. Republican. Roman Catholic. Clubs: Bohemian (San Francisco); Burlingame Country. Office: 100 Bush St Suite 1100 San Francisco CA 94104

CULLITON, EDWARD MILTON, retired Canadian justice; b. Grand Forks, Minn., Apr. 9, 1906; s. John Joseph and Katherine M. (Kelly) C.; m. Katherine M. Hector, Sept. 9, 1939. B.A., U. Sask., 1926, LL.B., 1928, D.C.L., 1962. Bar: Sask. 1930. Practice in, Gravelbourg, 1930-51; mem. Sask. Legislature, 1935-44, 48-51; provincial sec. Patterson Govt., 1938-41; minister without portfolio, 1941-44; judge Ct. Appeal Sask., 1951-62; chief justice, Sask., Regina, 1962-81; vice chmn. Can. Jud. Council, 1973-81; chancellor U. Sask., 1963-69. Served with Can. Army, 1941-46. Decorated knight comdr. Order of St. Gregory (Vatican), 1963, companion Order of Can., 1981. Home: 1303-1830 College Ave Regina SK S4P 1C2 Canada

CULLMAN, EDGAR MEYER, diversified consumer products co. exec.; b. N.Y.C., Jan. 7, 1918; s. Joseph F., Jr. and Frances Nathan (Wolff) C.; m. Louise Bloomingdale, Aug. 28, 1938; children—Lucy B. (Mrs. Frederick M. Danziger), Edgar Meyer, Susan R. (Mrs. Lawrence A. Kudlow). Student, Hotchkiss Sch., Lakeville, Conn., 1932-36; B.A., Yale, 1940. With Underwriters Trust Co., N.Y.C., 1940-42; with Office Alien Property Custodian, Washington and N.Y.C., 1942-44; partner Cullman Bros. (mems. N.Y. Stock Exchange), N.Y.C., 1946-65; sr. v.p. Cullman Bros., Inc. (tobacco and investments), 1944-62; v.p., dir. Bloomingdale Properties; chmn., chief exec. officer, dir. Culbro Corp.; dir. Companion Life Ins. Co., M. Lowenstein Corp. Vice chmn. Yale Devel. Bd.; Bd. dirs. Mt. Sinai Hosp. Sch. Nursing; bd. dirs., treas. Mt. Sinai Med. Center. Mem. Cigar Assn. Am. (hon. dir.). Clubs: India House (Century Country); Yale (N.Y.C.); Turf and Field, Steeplechase and Hunt Assn., Doubles, Pinnacle. Office: 605 3d Ave New York NY 10158

CULLMAN, HUGH, tobacco company executive; b. N.Y.C., Jan. 27, 1923; s. Howard S. and Elsie (Gottheil) C.; m. Nan Alva Ogburn, May 12, 1951; children: Katherine Victoria, Hugh, Alexandra Miriam. B.S., U.S. Naval Acad., 1945. With Benson & Hedges, 1948-54, mgr. research, 1952-54; with Philip Morris Inc., 1954—, treas., 1959-60, v.p., asst. chief ops., 1960-64, exec. v.p. ops., 1966—, also dir.; exec. v.p. Philip Morris Internat., 1965, pres., 1967-78, also dir.; group exec. v.p. Philip Morris Inc., 1978—; chmn., chief exec. officer Philip Morris U.S.A., 1978—; dir. United Va. Bankshares, Inc., Richmond. Trustee and mem. exec. com. U.S. Council for Internat. Bus.; trustee Colgate Darden Bus. Sch.; bd. sponsors U. Va.; bd. dirs. United Negro Coll. Fund., Inc. Served to lt. USN, 1945-47; PTO. Office: Philip Morris Inc 120 Park Ave New York NY 10017

CULLOM, WILLIAM OTIS, truck leasing co. exec.; b. Huntsville, Ala., Mar. 20, 1932; s. Otis McKinley and Elna (Reese) C.; m. Caryl James, May 26, 1956; children—Cheryl Ann, Jennifer James. B.S., Fla. State U., 1958. Finger-print expert FBI, 1950-52; asst. bus. mgr. Fla. State U., 1954-64; with Ryder Truck Rental Inc., Miami, Fla., 1964-79, exec. v.p. mktg., to, 1979; pres., chief operating officer Jartran, Inc., Coral Gables, Fla., 1979—. Mem. cabinet United Way, Miami, 1974-80; trustee Bethune-Cookman Coll., Daytona Beach, Fla.; chmn. trustees Fla. State U.; mem. pres.'s adv. com. Fla. Meml. Coll., Miami. Served with airborne inf. U.S. Army, 1952-54; Korea. Mem. Am. Trucking Assn., Truck Leasing and Renting Assn. (pres. Fla. chpt. 1972-73), Fla. State U. Nat. Alumni Assn. (pres.), Miami Hist. Assn. Democrat. Methodist. Clubs: Univ., Riviera Country (Miami); Ocean Reef Yacht, Rotary; Winewood Country, Killearn Country (Tallahassee, Fla.). William O. Cullom chair of fin. established at Fla. State U., 1979. Home: 8445 SW 151st St Miami FL 33158 Office: Jartran Inc 3001 Ponce de Leon Blvd Coral Gables FL 33134

CULLUM, JOHN, actor, singer; b. Knoxville, Tenn., Mar. 2, 1930; m. Emily Frankel; 1 son, John David. B.A., U. Tenn. Former tennis player and real estate salesman. N.Y. debut with, Shakespearewrights, 1957; joined, N.Y. Shakespeare Festival, 1960; Broadway debut in: Camelot, 1962; played Laertes in: Hamlet, 1964; other Broadway appearances include: On A Clear Day You Can See Forever, 1965 (Theatre World award 1965), Man of La Mancha, 1966, "1776", 1969, Vivat! Vivat Regina, 1972, Shenendoah, 1975 (Tony award as best actor 1975), The Trip Back Down, 1977, On the Twentieth Century, 1978 (Tony award as best actor in musical 1978), Deathtrap, 1979; other leading roles include plays Hamlet; film appearances include: All the Way Home, 1963, Hawaii, 1966, "1776", 1972; TV movie: A Man Without a Country, The Day After, 1984; public TV movies: Summer, 1980, Carl Sandburg, 1981. Served with U.S. Army. Office: care Internat Creative Mgmt 40 W 57th St New York NY 10019

CULMER, MARJORIE MEHNE, organization executive; b. Duluth, Minn., Mar. 4, 1912; d. John H. and Nettie (Morey) Mehne; m. Charles U. Culmer, Sept. 4, 1936. B.A., Lawrence Coll., 1933; J.D., Northwestern U., 1947; LL.D., Elmhurst Coll., 1962. Mem. profl. staff Girl Scouts of U.S.A., 1934-40, mem. nat. staff, 1943-44, field com. nat. orgn., 1948-56, vice chmn. orgn. and mgmt. com., 1954-57, chmn. Blue Book (policies) com., 1955-57, dir., 1955—, exec. com., 1956-63, pres. nat. orgn., 1957-63, 1st v.p., chmn. field com., Chgo. orgn., 1953-55, mem. bd., 1952-59, 61—, pres., 1955-57, chmn. pub. issues com., 1972-75, mem., 1975-78, chmn. Macy steering com., 1976-78; del. World Conf. Girl Guides and Girl Scouts, Brazil, 1957, Greece, 1960, vice chmn., mem. planning com., Denmark, 1963, mem. planning com., Japan, 1966, Finland, 1969; Can., 1972; hon. assoc. World Conf. Girl Guides and Girl Scouts, Eng., 1975, 1975-1984; tech. cons. Ill. Activities for 1970 White House Conf. for Children and Youth, 1968-70; Trustee, mem. Nat. Assembly for Social Policy and Devel., 1967-74, Com. Internat. Social Devel., 1969-74; Specialist with Bur. Edn. and Cultural Affairs, Dept. State, India, 1964; Mem. com. pub. welfare Welfare Council Met. Chgo., 1964-69; mem. com. Camp Algonquin, 1951—; forum leader White House Conf. Children and Youth, 1960, mem. nat. com., 1958-60; rep. Internat. Women's Year, 1975. Bd. dirs. United Charities Chgo., 1953—, Family Service com., 1960-63; mem. Legal Aid Com., 1956-64; bd. dirs. World Found. Girl Guides and Girl Scouts, 1971—, v.p., 1976—; trustee Lawrence U., 1962—, chmn. acad. affairs com., 1984—; mem. service rev. panel Chgo. Community Fund, 1976—. Recipient Distinguished Service award Lawrence Coll., 1959; Merit award Northwestern U., 1960. Mem. Am., Ill., Chgo. bar assns., Women's Bar Assn. Ill., World Assn. Girl Guides and Girl Scouts (world com. 1963-72, vice chmn. 1966-69, chmn. 1969-72, hon. Assoc. 1972—), Order of Coif, Mortar Bd., Phi Beta Kappa Assos., Phi Beta Kappa. Home: 900 W Lake St PO Box 548 Libertyville IL 60048

CULP, CHARLES ALLEN, insurance company executive; b. Birmingham, Ala., Oct. 23, 1930; s. William Newton and Winifred Evelyn (Orr) C.; m. Elsie Gayle Trechsel Hall, Oct. 1, 1960; children: Charles Allen, Stephen Andrew; stepchildren: John C., Edward P., David G. B.S., U. Ala., 1952; M.B.A., Samford U., Birmingham, 1969. C.L.U. With So. Life & Health Ins. Co., 1950-52, 54-72, v.p., dir., 1965-72; sr. v.p., dir. Investors Fidelity Ins. Co., Birmingham, 1972-74; dir. agys. Gulf Life Ins. Co., Jacksonville, Fla., 1975—, pres., 1980—; also dir.; exec. v.p. Interstate Life Ins. Co., Chattanooga, 1976-80, pres., dir., 1976-80; also dir.; pres., dir. Interstate Fire Ins. Co., 1976-80, dir., 1976—; dir. Gulf United Corp., Gulf Group Services, REDC Co., Invesco Co., Equitable Life Ins. Co., Utility Tool Co., Fin. Computer Services; exec. com. Life Insurers Conf. Area chmn. March of Dimes, Birmingham, 1961, Southside YMCA, Birmingham, 1959-60; bd. dirs. Valley Theatre, Birmingham, 1960, Met. YMCA, Birmingham, 1965-72, United Fund Greater Chattanooga, 1979-80. Served to 1st lt. USAF, 1952-54. Fellow Life Office Mgmt. Assn.; Mem. Am. Soc. C.L.U.s, Phi Eta Sigma, Sigma Alpha Epsilon. Republican. Episcopalian. Clubs: Deerwood Country, University, Sawgrass., Ponte Vedra. Home: 8203 Holly Ridge Rd Jacksonville FL 32216 Office: 1301 Gulf Life Dr Jacksonville FL 32207

CULP, DAVID ALBERT, urologist; b. Sunbury, Pa., Oct. 19, 1919; s. Harry Conrad and Elsie Kathryn (Geiser) C.; m. Anna Elizabeth Keiser, Dec. 25, 1943; children—Roberta Ann, Marylin Elizabeth, David Albert, Matthew Allen, Thomas Edward. B.S., Bucknell U., 1941; M.D., Jefferson Med. Coll., Phila., 1944. Intern Geisinger Meml. Hosp., Danville, Pa.; resident in urology Watts Hosp., Durham, N.C.; mem. faculty dept. urology U. Iowa Coll. Medicine, Iowa City, 1950—, prof., 1961—, head dept. urology, 1974—. Author: (with R.H. Flocks) Surgical Urology, 4th edit, 1975, (with R.H. Flocks, Charles C. Thomas) Radiation Therapy of Early Prostatic Cancer, 1960, (with J.R. Thornbury) The Urinary Tract—A Handbook of Roentgen Diagnosis, 1967; contbr. articles to med. jours. Served with M.C. U.S. Army, 1946-48. Mem. Am. Urol. Assn. (exec. com., pres.-elect, pres., past pres. N. Central sect.), A.C.S., Iowa Urol. Soc., Soc. Pediatric Urology, Am. Assn. Genitourinary Surgeons, Clin. Soc. Genitourinary Surgeons, Societe Internationale D'Urologie, AMA. Home: 4 High View River Heights Iowa City IA 52240 Office: Dept Urology University Hosps Iowa City IA 52242

CULP, RALPH BORDEN, speech and drama educator; b. Monroe, La., Nov. 13, 1929; s. Bertram Winter and Josephine Borden (Buckingham) C.; m. Betty Thomas O'Bannon, Mar. 31, 1956; children—Helen Borden, Elizabeth Winter, Richard Bertram, Jeffrey O'Bannon. Student, Catholic U. Am., 1948-50; B.A., So. Methodist U., 1957, M.A., 1957; Ph.D., Cornell U., 1962. Faculty Rutgers U., 1959-65; faculty, chmn. speech and drama U. Tex. at El Paso, 1965-71, prof., until 1971; prof. speech communication and drama North Tex. State U., Denton, 1971—, dir. drama, 1971-73; Cons. in speech N.J. 4H Clubs, 1962-65. Author: Basic Types of Speech, 1968, The Theatre and Its Drama, 1971, also articles.; Drama editor: So. Speech Communication Jour, 1972-75. Served to 1st lt. USAF, 1950-55. Mem. Speech Communication Assn., Am. Theatre Assn., Southwest Theatre Conf., Tex. Ednl. Theatre Assn. Home: 424 Magnolia Denton TX 76201

CULP, ROBERT, actor, writer, director; b. Oakland, Calif., Aug. 16, 1930; m. Nancy Wilner (div. 1967); 4 children; m. France Nuyen (div. 1969). Student, Coll of Pacific, Washington U., St. Louis, San Francisco State Coll. Play appearances include A Clearing In the Woods; film appearances include PT 109, 1963, Sammy, 1963, The Raiders, 1964, Sunday in New York, 1964, Rhino, 1964, The Hanged Man, Bob & Carol & Ted & Alice, 1969, The Grove, Hannie Caulder, 1972, Hickey and Boggs, 1972, Sky Riders, 1976, The Great Scout and Cathouse Thursday, 1976, Breaking Point, 1976, Inside Out, 1976; acted in TV series Trackdown, 1957, I Spy, 1965-68, The Greatest American Hero, 1981-83; appeared in TV movies Cry for Help, 1975, Strange Homecoming, 1974, Flood!, 1976, A Cold Night's Death, 1973, Outrage, 1973, Houston, We've Got a Problem, 1974, Her Life As a Man, 1984; appeared in 7-part TV series From Sea to Shining Sea, 1974-75; numerous other TV appearances. Office: William Morris Agy 151 El Camino Beverly Hills CA 90212 *

CULP, ROBERT MAX, insurance executive; b. Nelsonville, Ohio, Nov. 19, 1919; s. Samuel H. and Bessie (Auflick) C.; m. Bertha E. Buttler, June 10, 1941; children: Robert, Joseph, Nancy Culp Baumann, Joan Culp Hove. Grad., high sch. C.P.C.U., 1962. Mgr. control br. U.S. Dept. Engrs., Cin., 1942-46; regional underwriting mgr. Nationwide Ins. Co., Columbus, Ohio, 1947-57, reins. v.p., 1957-70, comml. ins. v.p., 1970-80, pres., chief exec. officer, 1980—; also pres. Colonial Ins. Co. Calif. subs., Anaheim; chmn. bd. Scottsdale Ins. Co., Ariz., 1981—. Mem. Soc. C.P.C.U.s. Republican. Roman Catholic. Office: Nationwide Ins Co One Nationwide Plaza Columbus OH 43216 *

CULP, WILLIAM NEWTON, insurance executive; b. Birmingham, Ala., Dec. 25, 1923; s. William Newton and Lilian Winifred (Orr) C.; m. Margaret Shackfield; children: Margaret, William, Carol. B.S.E.E., U.S. Naval Acad., 1945. Agt. So. Life & Health Ins. Co., Birmingham, from 1947, successively sales mgr., asst. v.p., agy. v.p., pres. and dir.; dir. Gen. Capital Corp., Stamford, Conn. Served as ensign USN, 1945-47; PTO. Mem. Life Insurors Conf. (chmn. 1981). Office: 2102 Highland Ave Birmingham AL 35205 *

CULPEPPER, JAMES WILLIAM, government official; b. DuQuoin, Ill., Oct. 27, 1935; s. William Stanley and Juanita Dorothy (Luster) C.; m. Mabel Claire Bondurant, Dec. 24, 1957; children: Julie Ann Thompson, James Jeffrey, John William. B.S., U. Mo., 1957, M.S., 1962; postgrad., Harvard U., 1981. Research assoc. Govtl. Research Inst., St. Louis, 1962-63; mgmt. intern, budget analyst Oak Ridge, 1963-65, budget examiner, Washington, 1965-71, dept. asst. controller for budget, 1971-75; asst. controller for budget U.S. Energy Research and Devel. Adminstrn., Washington, 1975-77; dir. budget U.S. Dept. Energy, 1977-78, assoc. dir. Mil. Application, 1978-79, dep. dir., 1979-81, dep. asst. sec. for security affairs, 1981—. Served to 1st lt. U.S. Army, 1957-61. Recipient Spl. Achievement cert. AEC, 1974, Spl. Achievement awards Energy Research and Devel. Adminstrn., 1976, 77, 79, Presdl. Rank of Meritorious Exec. Pres. of U.S., 1980. Home: 10820 Longmeadow Dr Damascus MD 20872 Office: US Dept Energy Defense Programs Washington DC 20545

CULVER, ARTHUR ALAN, publishing company executive; b. Rose, Kans., Dec. 4, 1906; s. Willard Arthur and Emma Alice (Hutchison) C.; m. Barbara Joy Hammond, Aug. 1, 1935 (dec. Apr. 20, 1970); children: Deborah Susan Culver Lawlor, Arthur Anthony; m. Joan Westfall Caulk, Mar. 1, 1975. Student, Kans. State Coll. Advt. mgr. Baxter Springs (Kans.) Citizen, 1928-39; br. office mgr. William R. Staats Co., 1930-37; advt. mgr., asst. to pub., then v.p., gen. mgr. Press-Enterprise Co., Riverside, Calif.; now pres., dir. Rubidoux Printing Co. Chmn. United Fund Drive, 1960, dir., 1961, pres., 1964. Mem. Am. Newspaper Pubs. Assn., Internat. Press Inst., Inter Am. Press

Assn., Calif. Newspaper Pubs. Assn., LWV (mem. fin. adv. com.), C. of C. (pres. 1949). Republican. Clubs: Victoria (Riverside, Calif.); Wine and Food Soc. Home: 2556 Carlton Pl Riverside CA 92507 Office: 3512 14th St Riverside CA 92501

CULVER, BARBARA GREEN, judge; b. Dallas, Feb. 9, 1926; d. Lawrence F. and Alice (Bryson) Green; m. John R. Culver, Aug. 15, 1947; children: Lawrence L., J. Bryson. B.A. in Journalism, Tex. Tech U., 1947; LL.B., So. Meth. U., 1951. Bar: Tex. 1951. Practiced in Midland, 1951-63; county judge Midland County, Midland, 1963-78; judge 318th State Dist. Ct., 1978—. Mem. Tex. Constl. Revision Commn., 1973; mem. Nat. Adv. Council on Edn. of Disadvantaged Children, 1971-74, Council on Alcoholism, 1978—; bd. dirs. Rape Crisis Center, 1981-83, Tex. Ctr. for Judiciary, 1983-85; mem. Tex. Jud. Budget Bd., 1983—. Mem. ABA (family law sect., adminstrn. of justice sect.), Midland County Bar Assn., State Bar Tex. (chmn. women and law sect. 1980-81, mem. council jud. sect. 1979—, family law council 1980—, cameras in courtroom com. 1981), Nat. Assn. Regional Councils (pres. 1976-77), West Tex. County Judges and Commrs. Assn. (pres. 1975-76), Altrusa. Club: Law Wives of Midland (pres. 1984-85). Home: 1007 Neely St Midland TX 79701 Office: County Courthouse Midland TX 79701

CULVER, CHARLES DAVID, energy company executive; b. Hobbs, N.Mex., July 27, 1935; s. Charles V. and Cleo (Powers) C.; m. Eunice Elaine Cash, Apr. 20, 1963; 1 dau., Catherine Elaine. B.S. in Petroleum Engring, U. Tex., 1958. Engr. Pioneer Natural Gas Co., 1960-62, mgr. gas supply, Amarillo, Tex., 1971-73, v.p. gas supply, 1973-76; asst. supr. drilling and prodn. Amarillo Oil Co., 1962-65; v.p. Cons. Services, Inc., Amarillo, 1965-71; v.p., exec. asst. to pres. Pioneer Corp., Amarillo, 1976-79, exec. v.p., 1979-82, pres., 1982, pres., chief exec. officer, 1983—, also dir.; dir. Sharp Drilling Co., Inc., Tascosa Nat. Bank, Amarillo, Plains Machinery Co., Internat. Tool & Supply Co. Pres. Amarillo YMCA, 1975-76; bd. dirs. Panhandle Area Cancer Council, 1981. Served with AUS, 1959-60. Recipient Harry Mays Meml. award YMCA, 1979. Mem. Am. Assn. Petroleum Geologists, Soc. Petroleum Engrs., So. Gas Assn., Panhandle Geol. Soc., Panhandle Assn. Petroleum Landmen, Natural Gas Men Permian Basin, Natural Gas Men Okla., Natural Gas Men Houston, Tex., Soc. Profl. Engrs., U. Tex., Ex-Students Assn. (pres. Amarillo 1978), Ducks Unlimited (chmn. Tex. Panhandle chpt. 1975). Methodist. Clubs: Amarillo (pres. 1978), Amarillo Kiwanis (dir. 1972-74). Home: 3203 Hawthorne St Amarillo TX 79109 Office: 301 Taylor St Amarillo TX 79163

CULVER, DAVID M., aluminum company executive; b. Winnipeg, Man., Can., Dec. 5, 1924; s. Albert Ferguson and Fern Elizabeth (Smith) C.; m. Mary Cecile Powell, Sept. 20, 1949; children: Michael, Andrew, Mark, Diane. B.Sc., McGill U., 1947; M.B.A., Harvard U., 1949; cert., Centre d'Etudes Industrielles, Geneva, Switzerland, 1950. With Alcan Group, 1949—; v.p. Alcan Internat. Ltd., 1956-62, pres., 1962—, exec. v.p. fabricating and sales, 1968-75, regional exec. v.p. N.Am. and Caribbean, 1975; also dir.; pres. Alcan Aluminium Ltd., 1975—, chief exec. officer, 1979—; dir. Aluminum Co. Can., Ltd., Canadair, MacMillan Bloedel Ltd., Am. Express Co. Served with Can. Inf. Corps, World War II. Mem. Alpha Delta Phi. Office: 1188 Sherbrooke St W Montreal PQ H3A 3G2 Canada

CULVER, DWIGHT WENDELL, educator; b. New Haven, Feb. 15, 1921; s. Mearl Peter and Louisa (Collier) C.; m. Margaret Louise Augustine, June 7, 1943; children—Enid Louise Layden, Timothy Dwight, Jane Christine Barnes, Laura Bernice. B.A., Carleton Coll., 1941; B.D., Yale, 1944, Ph.D., 1948. Asst. prof. sociology Purdue U., 1947-52, asso. prof., 1952-61; asso. dir. Lilly Endowment Study of Pre-Sem. Edn., Mpls., 1961-63; prof. sociology, dept. chmn. St. Olaf Coll., 1963-68; dean Coll. St. Catherine, 1968-71, prof. sociology, 1971—; examiner-cons. North Central Assn. Colls. and Secondary Schs., 1970—. Author: Negro Segregation in the Methodist Church, 1953, We Can and We Will, 1961, (with Keith Bridston) The Making of Ministers, 1964, Pre-Seminary Education: Report of the Lilly Endowment Study, 1965. Trustee United Theol. Sem. Twin Cities, 1975-81. Mem. Am., Midwest sociol. socs., Religious Research Assn., Soc. Sci. Study Religion, Am. Soc. Christian Ethics, Religious Edn. Assn., Phi Beta Kappa. Methodist. Home: 1831 Bayard Ave Saint Paul MN 55116

CULVER, EDWARD HOLLAND, marketing executive; b. Mount Vernon, N.Y., Jan. 14, 1918; s. Ralph Farnsworth and Elizabeth (McMillin) C.; m. Mary Lee Oliver, July 15, 1942; children: Lee F., Edward Holland, Anne A. B.S. in Indsl. Adminstrn, Sheffield Sci. Sch. Yale, 1940. Exec. v.p. Cory Snow, Inc. (advt. agy.), Boston, 1946-50; co-owner, v.p., treas. Meissner & Culver, Inc., Boston, 1950-56; founder, pres., treas. Culver Advt., Inc., Boston, 1956-75; chmn. Culver Marketing Services, Boston, 1969-75; pres. Culver Internat., Inc., Boston, Tokyo, Japan, Seoul, Korea, 1970—; dir. Graham & Gillies & Culver, Ltd., London, Eng., 1971-80; pres. Monadnock Co., 1980—; mng. ptnr. E. H. Culver & Assocs., 1982—. Mem. N. Woods Camp; com. Boston YMCA, chmn., 1965-67; Trustee Children's Mus. Boston, 1966-71. Served to maj. F.A. AUS, 1941-46. Decorated Bronze Star medal. Mem. Bus./Profl. Advt. Assn., Am. Assn. Advt. Agys. (gov. Eastern region 1962-63, 68-70, chmn. New Eng. council 1962-63, nat. dir. 1968-69), Internat. Advt. Assn., Advt. Club Boston, Yale Engring. Assn. Episcopalian. Clubs: University of Boston, Yale, Downtown (Boston); Yale of New York City; Dedham (Mass.); Country and Polo. Home: 1 Wampatuck Rd Dedham MA 02026 Office: PO Box 189 Dedham MA 02026

CULVER, JOHN C., lawyer, former U.S. senator; b. Rochester, Minn., Aug. 8, 1932; m. Ann Cooper; children: Christina, Rebecca, Catherine, Chester John. A.B. cum laude, Harvard U., 1954, LL.B., 1962; postgrad. (Lionel de Jersey Harvard scholar), Emmanuel Coll., Cambridge U. Dean of men Harvard Summer Sch., 1960; legis. asst. to Sen. Edward Kennedy, 1962-63; mem. 89th to 93d Congresses from 2d Dist., Iowa; chmn. Democratic Study Group; U.S. senator from Iowa, 1975-81; mem. firm Arent, Fox, Kintner, Plotkin & Kahn, Washington, 1981—. Served to capt. USMCR. Mem. Iowa, County bar assns. Democrat. Presbyterian. Office: Arent Fox Kintner Plotkin & Kahn 1050 Connecticut Ave NW Washington DC 20036 *

CULVER, ROBERT JOSEPH, union ofcl.; b. Pittston, Pa., Oct. 14, 1920; s. Lyman Joseph and Helen Bernadette (Moffitt) C.; m. Anna Marie Egan, June 10, 1944; children—Mary Ellen, Ann, Jane. Student, St. Michael's Coll., Toronto, 1938-39, Wilkes Coll., 1947-48. With Lehigh Valley R.R. Co., 1942, 46-68, yardmaster, 1950-68; grand sec.-treas. R.R. Yardmasters of Am., Park Ridge, Ill., 1968—. Editor: R.R. Yardmaster Ofcl. Jour, 1968—. Served with USAF, 1942-46. Club: K.C. Home: 1199 Anthony Wheeling IL 60090 Office: 1411 Peterson Park Ridge IL 60068

CULVER, VIRGINIA PRICE, association executive; b. Pitts.; d. John I. and Cecelia (Kinzler) Price; m. John Howard Culver, Oct. 14, 1946; children: Catherine, Raymond Benjamin. B.A., Denison U., 1943. Treas. Token and Medal Soc., D.C., 1961-63, v.p., 1963-64, pres., 1964-66; bd. govs. Am. Numismatic Assn., 1965—, v.p., 1971-73, pres., 1973—; exec. dir. Medallic Commemorative Soc. Internat., 1976—, Numismatic Literary Guild, 1977—; Presdl. appointment to Assay Commn., 1968; numismatic cons. Franklin Mint. Author: (with Chester Krause) Guidebook Franklin Mint Issues; yearly catalog, since, 1974—; Columnist: Coins mag, 1965-72; Contbr. articles to profl. publs. Recipient Best of Show award Calif. State, 1965. Mem. Am. Numismatic Assn. (B.P. Wright 1st award 1962, 63), Gt. Eastern Numismatic Assn. (hon. life mem., named Woman of Year 1974), Blue Ridge Numismatic Assn. (hon. life mem.), So. Calif. Numismatic Assn., Calif. Numismatic Assn., Am. Numismatic Soc., San Gabriel Coin Club (hon. life mem.), Calumet Coin Club (hon. life mem.), Token and Medal Soc. (charter life, medal of merit 1965, Gold Segel lit. award 1966), Numismatic Lit. Guild (charter life, Best Columnist award 1970), Calif. Exonumist Soc. (charter life), Civil War Token Soc. (charter life), Soc. for Internat. Numismatics (charter life), Numismatists of Wis., Orgn. Internat. Numismatists (charter life), Delta Delta Delta. Baptist. Club: Ozaukee Country. First white woman made hon. Seminole Princess, Miami Beach, 1974. Address: 15933 Sierra Pass Way Hacienda Heights CA 91745

CULVERHOUSE, HUGH FRANKLIN, lawyer, football team owner; b. Birmingham, Ala., Feb. 20, 1919; s. Harry Georg and Grace Mae (Daniel) C.; m. Joy McCann, Nov. 14, 1942; children: Gay Culverhouse Gold, Hugh Franklin. B.S., U. Ala., 1941, LL.B., 1947; LL.D. (hon.), Jacksonville U. Bar: Fla. 1955, Ala. 1947. Asst. atty. gen. State of Ala., Montgomery, 1947-49; spl. atty., asst. regional counsel Office of Chief Counsel IRS, Atlanta and Jacksonville, Fla., 1949-56; mem. firm Culverhouse, Botts, Mills & Cone, and predecessors, Jacksonville, Tampa and Miami, Fla., 1956—; mem. adv. com. to commr. internal revenue, 1961-62; pres., owner Tampa Bay Buccaneers, NFL, Tampa, Fla., 1974—; v.p., dir. Port Everglades Steel Corp.; owner Mode, Inc.; dir. Am. Fin. Corp., Host Internat., Inc., Tampa Electric Co., Housing Investment Corp., Gator Distbrs., Inc., Barnett-Winston Co., Major Realty Corp., Gator Trailers Corp., George Washington Corp., McMillen Corp., Barnett Banks of Fla., Inc., Peninsular Life Ins. Co.; partner, owner, developer various real estate projects, Fla., Ind., Ohio; co-owner, pres., dir. Miami Mdse. Mart, Inc. Contbr. articles to legal jours. Mem. faculty U. Ala. Sch. Bus. Adminstrn.; Co-founder, 1st pres. Family Consultation Service, Jacksonville; vice chmn. bd. trustees Jacksonville U.; bd. visitors Coll. Commerce and Bus. Adminstrn., U. Ala.; bd. overseers Stetson U. Coll. Law; del., U.S. Ambassador 1976 Winter Olympics, Innsbruck, Austria; active United Fund of Jacksonville. Served with USAAF, 1941-46; Served with USAF, 1951-53. Recipient Top Mgmt. award Sales and Mktg. Execs. of Jacksonville, Chief award Ind. Colls. and Univs. in Fla. Mem. Am. Judicature Soc., ABA, Ala. Bar Assn., Fla. Bar Assn., Dade County Bar Assn., Birmingham Bar Assn., Miami Bar Assn., Jacksonville Bar Assn. (chmn. tax sect. 1957-59), Am. Acad. Achievement, Knights of Malta. Republican. Episcopalian. Clubs: Timuquana, Fla. Yacht, River, Univ. (Jacksonville); Indian Creek Country, LaGorce Country, Surf, Palm Bay (Miami); Ponte Vedra (Ponte Vedra Beach, Fla.); Univ., Palm Ceia Golf and Country (Tampa). Endowed chair in bus. adminstrn. Jacksonville U. Home: 3301 Bayshore Blvd Tampa FL 33609 1408 North West Shore Tampa FL 33607

CULVERHOUSE, JOY MCCANN, professional football team executive; b. Chgo., Mar. 6, 1920; married, Nov. 14, 1942; children: Gay Culverhouse Gold, Hugh. Student, La. State U., U. Ala. Formerly amateur golfer; v.p. Tampa Bay Buccanners, NFL, Fla., 1981—. Bd. dirs. Found. for Eye Research, U. South Fla. Mem. Delta Delta Delta. State amateur golf champion, Ala., 1941, Fla., 1961. Office: c/o Tampa Bay Buccaneers One Buccaneer Pl Tampa FL 33607 *

CULVERWELL, ALBERT HENRY, historian; b. Portland, Oreg., Jan. 28, 1913; s. John Albert and Nettie L. (Kingery) C.; m. Ethel E. Klein, Aug. 17, 1941 (dec.); children: Cheryl Evelyn, John Albert. Scholarship student in stagecraft, color and design, Cornish Sch., Seattle, 1935-36; B.A., U. Wash., Seattle, 1936, M.A., 1941; postgrad., Am. U., Wash. State U. Mem. faculty Whitworth Coll., Spokane, Wash., 1941-42, 46-50; civilian U.S. Naval Air Sta., Seattle, 1942-45; safety engr., asst. dir. personnel Pacific Car & Foundry Co., Renton, Wash., 1945-46; instr. social sci. Wash. State U., Pullman, 1949-50; asst. prof. history Western Wash. State Coll., Bellingham, 1950-53; historian, supr. interpretation Wash. State Parks, Olympia, 1953-62; chief br. interpretive services Region 4, U.S. Forest Service, Ogden, Utah, 1962-68; dir. Eastern Wash. State Hist. Soc., Spokane, 1968-82; pres. Wash. Art Consortium, 1979—; mem. Wash. Archives Adv. Bd., 1977—; Adv. Council Preservation of Historic Sites and Bldgs., 1968-78, 80—. Author articles in field, also, film and TV scripts. Elder United Presbyn. Ch. U.S.A., 1942—; adminstrv. adv. com. Sheldon Jackson Jr. Coll., Sitka, Alaska, 1961-63; bd. dirs. Westminster Found., 1961-62; mem. Woodway (Wash.) Planning Commn., 1961-63, Wash. Gov.'s Adv. Council on Observance Civil War Centennial, 1961; Gov. Wash. Council Boundary Survey Centennial, 1961. Recipient cert. of commendation Am. Assn. State and Local History, 1965. Mem. Am. Assn. Museums (pres. Western regional conf. 1969-71), Orgn. Am. Historians, Pacific N.W. Hist. Soc., Idaho Hist. Soc., Utah Hist. Soc., Westerners, Phi Sigma Kappa, Pi Sigma Alpha. Club: Rotary. Office: W 2316 1st Ave Spokane WA 99204 *In my life I have striven to achieve something positive in whatever I have done. Success, depends on faith in myself as well as in someone greater than I, and, to an extent, with those with whom I have worked. This has brought a measure of patience to me which has made it possible to accept setbacks which make achievement slow. But when one has gained confidence and patience, success is often achieved.*

CULWELL, CHARLES LOUIS, manufacturing company executive; b. Putnam, Tex., Apr. 26, 1927; s. Willie and Ila Alberta (Crosby) C.; m. Virginia Green, June 10, 1949; children—Andrew Scott, Perry Neal, Curtis Austin, Travis Lee. B.S. in Elec. Engring, U.S. Naval Acad., 1949; M.S. in Mgmt, U.S. Naval Postgrad. Sch., 1969. Commd. ensign U.S. Navy, 1949, advanced through grades to capt., 1969; services in Korea and Vietnam, comdg. officer, Oakland, Calif., 1975-76, ret., 1976; asst. to pres., then v.p. Purex Corp., 1976-79, group v.p., gen. mgr. indsl., instl. and comml. products, Lakewood, Calif., 1979—. Decorated Legion of Merit, Bronze Star with combat V, Meritorious Service medal. Mem. U.S. Naval Acad. Alumni Assn. Republican. Presbyterian. Office: 5101 Clark Ave Lakewood CA 90712

CUMBEY, JAMES CRAIG, government official; b. Danville, Va., June 4, 1928; s. Lacy Thomas and Louise Elizabeth (Amos) C.; m. Shirley Maye Lawrence, Feb. 19, 1954; children: Susan Gayle, Alison Lee. A.A., Longwood Coll., Farmville, Va., 1948. Asst. personnel officer Mallory AF Sta., Memphis, 1958-61; chief personnel mgmt. Hdqrs. USAF, Washington, 1961-67, chief career programs and plans, 1968-74; dep. dir. civilian personnel USAF, Washington, 1975-76, dir. civilian personnel, 1977-79; dep. asst. sec. Air Force, Washington, 1979—; bd. dirs. Grad. Sch. Dept. Agr., 1980-83. Recipient Sustained Superior Performance award U.S. Air Force, 1959, Meritorious Civilian Service award U.S. Air Force, 1967, Outstanding Performance award, 1980-81, Meritorious Exec. Rank Pres. of U.S., 1982. Mem. Internat. Personnel Mgmt. Assn. (pres. 1982). Home: 413 Jackson St Falls Church VA 22046 Office: Dept of Air Force The Pentagon Washington DC 20330

CUMERFORD, WILLIAM RICHARD, fund raising and public relations executive; b. Stroudsburg, Pa., Dec. 3, 1916; s. Reginald Read and Helen (Ryall) C.; m. Rosemary Fisher, Nov. 21, 1939; 1 dau., Helen Diane Cumerford Dorney. B.A., U. Maine, 1937; postgrad. journalism, Columbia U., 1937; H.H.D. (hon.), Salem (W.Va.) Coll., 1976; B.A. in Bus. Adminstrn, Barry Coll., Miami, Fla., 1977. Profl. fund raising exec. Boy Scouts Am., 1937-45; campaign dir. Marts & Lundy Co., N.Y.C., 1945; founder, 1949; since pres. Cumerford Corp. (fund raising cons.), Kansas City, Mo.; founder, 1962; since pres. Ryall Corp. (public relations), Kansas City, Mo.; founder, 1970; since pres. Cumerford Service Corp. (deferred gift cons.), Ft. Lauderdale, Fla.; v.p. Tulsa U., 1950; acting pres. Mo. Valley Coll., Marshall, Mo., 1952-53; lectr. Barry Coll. Author: Planned Giving, Vol. 1, 1957, Vol. 11, 1960, Fund Raising—A Professional Guide, 1977, also articles. Bd. dirs. So. Fla. council Boy Scouts Am., also nat. adviser fin. service; bd. dirs. Ft. Lauderdale Jr. Achievement; fin. chmn. Greater Kansas City Council Chs., 1950-52; fin. adviser Ky. and Mo. Republican Party, 1952-55. Recipient Disting. Eagle award Miami council Boy Scouts Am., 1974; also various service awards. Mem. Am. Assn. Fund-Raising Counsel (exec. com., dir.), Nat. Soc. Fund Raising Counsel (chpt. dir.), Public Relations Soc. Am., Fla. Public Relations Soc., Ft. Lauderdale C. of C., Council Advancement and Support Edn., Navy League. Roman Catholic. Clubs: Kansas City, Rotary, Elks, Coral Ridge Yacht, Internat. Address: 4010 Galt Ocean Dr Apt 1604 Fort Lauderdale FL 33308 also PO Box 2121 Boone NC 28607

CUMING, GEORGE SCOTT, retired lawyer, retired gas company official; b. Lakewood, Ohio, Apr. 10, 1915; s. George Scott and Josephine (MacInnes) C.; m. Dorothy Jane Herbst, May 12, 1943; children: Holiday (Mrs. Jason Baker Tuttle), Noelle (Mrs. John David Brock), George Scott, IV, Reid MacInnes. A.B. cum laude, Western Res. U., 1937; postgrad., Harvard Law Sch., 1941-42, 45-46; J.D., Northwestern U., 1948. Bar: Ill. 1948, Mich. 1950. Auditor Gen. Electric Co., Cleve., 1937-41; asst. sec., asst. gen. atty. Mich-Wis. Pipeline Co., Detroit, 1948-52, Pacific N.W. Pipeline Corp., Salt Lake City, 1955-59; tax acct. Arthur Andersen & Co., Chgo., 1952-55; asst. sec. El Paso Natural Gas Co., Tex., 1960-65, Rocky Mountain regional counsel, 1960-64, Washington counsel, 1964-65, gen. counsel, 1965-80, v.p., 1969-75; also dir.; sr. v.p., gen. counsel, dir. El Paso Co., 1975-80. Served to lt. USNR, 1942-45. Mem. ABA, Ill. Bar Assn., State Bar Mich., Delta Phi Alpha, Delta Sigma Rho, Sigma Delta Psi, Phi Delta Phi. Episcopalian. Home: PO Box 8176 Northfield IL 60093-0724

CUMMIN, ALFRED S(AMUEL), chemist; b. London, Sept. 5, 1924; U.S., 1940, naturalized, 1948; s. Jack and Lottie (Hainesdorff) C.; m. Sylvia E. Smolok, Mar. 24, 1945; 1 dau., Cynthia Katherine. B.S., Poly. Inst. Bklyn., 1943, Ph.D. in Chemistry, 1946; M.B.A., U. Buffalo, 1959. Research chemist S.A.M. labs, Manhattan Project, Columbia U., 1943-44; plant supr. Metal & Plastic Processing Co., Bklyn., 1946-51; research chemist Gen. Chem. div. Allied Chem. & Dye Corp., N.Y.C., 1951-53; sr. chemist Congoleum Nairn, Kearny, N.J., 1953-54; supr. dielecs-advance devel. Gen. Elec. Co., Hudson Falls, N.Y., 1954-56; mgr. indsl. products research dept. Spencer Kellogg & Sons, Inc. (Textron), Buffalo, 1956-59; mgr. plastics div. Trancoa Chem. Corp., Reading, Mass., 1959-62; asso. dir. product devel. service labs. chem. div. Merck & Co., Inc., Rahway, N.J., 1962-69; dir. product devel. Borden Chem. div. Borden Inc., N.Y.C., 1969-72, tech. dir., 1972-73, Borden Inc., 1973-78, v.p. product safety and quality, 1978-81, v.p. sci. and tech., 1981—; mem. exec. com. Food Safety Council, 1976-81, trustee, chmn. membership com., 1976—; bd. dirs. Formaldehyde Inst., 1977—, vice chmn., 1982—, mem. exec. com., 1981—, mem. med. com., 1977—, steering com., 1977—; instr. Poly. Inst. Bklyn., 1946-47; asst. prof. Adelphi Coll., 1952-54; prof. math. sci. U.S. Merchant Marine Acad., 1954; seminar leader Am. Mgmt. Assn.; prof. mgmt. N.Y. U. Sch. Mgmt., 1968—. Contbr. articles to profl. jours. Recipient cert. award Fedn. Socs. Paint Tech., 1965. Mem. Am. Chem. Soc. Fedn. Coatings Tech., Inst. Food Tech., ASTM, Synthetic Organic Chems. Mfg. Assn. (dir. 1977—), Paint Research Inst., Delta Sigma Pi, Gamma Sigma Epsilon, Beta Gamma Sigma, Phi Lamda Upsilon. Research in polymers, electrochemistry, food packaging. Patentee in field. Office: 960 Kings Mill Pkwy Columbus OH 43229

CUMMING, DOUGLAS G(RAHAM), corporation executive; b. Edmonton, Alta, Can., Aug. 21, 1938; s. Maurice Malcolm and Olga Sophie (Berg) C.; m. Margaret Ann Roddick, Aug. 27, 1966; 1 son, Thomas Alexander. Student, Harvard U., 1980-81. With Acklands Ltd., Edmonton, Alta., Can., 1957—, sr. v.p. ops., 1980—. Home: 7727 155th St Edmonton AB Canada T5R 1V9 Office: Acklands Ltd 11905 111th Ave Edmonton AB Canada T5J 2K9

CUMMING, GLEN EDWARD, art museum director; b. Calgary, Alta., Can., July 2, 1936; s. Alexander Edward Brown and Johanna Maria Christina (Van Der Doorn) C. Diploma fine arts, Alta. Coll. Art, 1963. Asst. to dir. Edmonton (Alta.) Art Gallery, 1963-64; dir. expressive arts City of Edmonton Parks and Recreation Dept., 1965-67; curator Regina (Sask.) Public Library Art Gallery, 1967-69; dir. Kitchener-Waterloo Art Gallery, Kitchener, Ont., 1969-72, Robert McLaughlin Art Gallery, Oshawa, Ont., 1972-73, Art Gallery of Hamilton, Ont., 1973—; bd. dirs. Hamilton and Region Arts Council, 1974-75, Art Mag., Toronto, 1977-80; chmn. art adv. com. Mohawk Coll. Applied Arts and Tech., 1979-81; adv. Ont. Coll. Art, 1979-83; Mem. adv. bd. Sir Sandford Fleming Coll., 1973. Editor of: Town Talk, 1965-66. Mem. Ont. Assn. Art Galleries (pres. 1974), Assn. Art Mus. Dirs., Canadian Art Museums Dirs. Orgn. (pres. 1981-83), Internat. Council Museums, Canadian Museums Assn., Am. Assn. Museums, Hamilton C. of C. Clubs: Hamilton., Canadian. Home: Apt 1502 222 Jackson St W Hamilton ON L8P 4S5 Canada Office: Art Gallery of Hamilton 123 King St W Hamilton ON L8P 4S8 Canada

CUMMING, GORDON ROBERTSON, state official; b. Carmangay, Alta., Can., July 31, 1911; came to U.S., 1925, naturalized, 1932; s. William R. and Ivy (Parkinson) C.; m. Helen Stanford, Dec. 24, 1935; children: Douglas Stanford, Janice Dorothy. A.B., U. Calif.-Berkeley, 1933, M.A., 1935. Student investigator bur. efficiency County Los Angeles, 1934-35; adminstrv. asst., then asst. dir. Los Angeles County Hosp., 1935-48; chief bur. hosps. Calif. Dept. Public Health, 1948-63; adminstr. Sacramento Med. Center, 1963-72; dir. research Calif. Hosp. Assn., 1972-76; hosp. cons., 1976-77; acting exec. dir. Calif. Health Facilities Commn., 1977-78, 79-80, mem., 1981-82; exec. dir. Assn. Calif. Health Systems Agys., 1978-79; dir., pres. Calif. Health Data Corp.; cons. Calif. Senate, 1981; trustee Blue Cross, 1969-72, chmn. bd., 1970-72. Mem. joint com. areawide planning hosps. and related health facilities Am. Hosp. Assn.-USPHS, 1961, joint com. planning facilities long-term treatment and care, 1962; mem. hosp. research study sect. NIH, 1955-59, mem. council on regional medical programs, 1964-65; mem. Calif. Health Rev. and Program Council, 1966-70, Commn. for Adminstrv. Services in Hosps., 1969-71. Served to maj. AUS, 1942-46. Mem. Am. Assn. Hosp. Planning (past pres.), Am. Hosp. Assn. (life mem.; chmn. council legis. 1970, spl. com. provision health services 1970-71, award of honor 1971), Calif. Hosp. Assn. (life mem.; pres. 1967—, trustee 1965-68, award of Merit 1955). Home: 6416 Fordham Way Sacramento CA 95831 Office: 827 7th St Sacramento CA 95814

CUMMING, HUGH SMITH, JR., retired diplomat; b. Richmond, Va., Mar. 10, 1900; s. Hugh Smith and Lucy A. (Booth) C.; m. Winifred Burney West, Sept. 21, 1935 (dec. Jan. 1978). Student, Va. Mil. Inst., 1917-20, U. Va., 1920-24. Bar: Va. Banker, London, Bombay, Singapore, Peking, 1924-27; tech. adviser Dept. State, 1928; asst. to U.S. delegation Internat. Econ. Conf., London, and 7th Pan-

Am. Conf., Montevideo, 1933, exec. asst. to sec. of state, 1934, detailed to U.S. consulate, Geneva, in connection Italo-Ethiopian affairs, 1935-36, spl. mission to, Scandinavia and Netherlands, 1939, mem. exec. com. U.S. Antarctic Service, 1939-41, spl. mission, Greenland, 1941, mem. Econ. Warfare Mission, also U.S. del. Internat. Whaling Conf., London, 1943, spl. mission to, Sweden, 1943, 45, rep. State Dept. on Anglo-Swedish-Am. Commn., and chief div. No. European Affairs, 1944, polit. liaison officer U.S. delegation UN Conf. on Internat. Orgn., San Francisco, 1945, spl. mission, Iceland, 1946, counselor Am. embassy Stockholm, 1947-50, counselor Am. embassy with personal rank of minister, Moscow, 1950-52, dep. sec. gen. for polit. affairs NATO, Paris, 1952-53, ambassador to, Indonesia, 1953-57; spl. asst. to sec. of state, dir. intelligence Dept. State, 1957-61, spl. asst. to sec. of state, 1961, cons., 1961-64; Chmn. John Foster Dulles oral history project Princeton. Past mem. bd. dirs. Columbia Hosp. for Women, Washington; trustee Meridian House Found., Family and Child Services Washington, Washington Inst. Fgn. Affairs, Washington Cathedral; chmn. bd., pres. Bath County Community Hosp., Hot Springs, Va.; bd. dirs. Historic Georgetown, Inc., Garth Newel Music Center Found., Hot Springs; past pres. Nat. Cathedral Assn. Served as 2d lt. U.S. Army, 1918. Recipient Raven award U. Va., 1984. Mem. U. Va. Law Sch. Assn., Mil. Order World Wars, S.A.R., Raven Soc., Diplomatic and Consular Officers Ret. (past pres.), Zeta Psi. Episcopalian. Clubs: Metropolitan (past pres.), Cosmos, Alibi, Sulgrave (Washington); Chevy Chase (Md.); Farmington (Charlottesville, Va.); Old Capitol (Monterey, Calif.); Royal Swedish Yacht; Sallskapet (Stockholm). Home: 2811 O St NW Washington DC 20007

CUMMING, ROBERT EMIL, editor; b. Lincoln, Nebr., June 2, 1933; s. Eugene Earl and Christiana (Jensen) C. Student, U. Nebr., 1955; Music Ed. (Presser Found. scholar), Nebr. Wesleyan U., 1956. With Music Jour. mag., N.Y.C., 1958-75, editor-in-chief, 1964-75; with Xerox Edn. Publs., 1977—, librarian, 1976—; Pres. Urban Fedn. Music Therapists. Critic, conductor, singer, stage dir., Village Light Opera Group, Hunter Coll., N.Y.C., Community Opera, Little Orch. Soc.; founder-mem., Singing Editors, nationally concertized, 1970—; toured U.S. and Can. as: stage dir. Naughty Marietta, New Little Orch. Concerts, 1976; Compiler, editor: The Power of Music by Dmitri Shostakovich, 1968, They Talk About Music, 1971-72; Composer: children's operettas Rumplestiltskin, 1952, Song of Andorra, 1953, God is My Salvation, 1954, How Sly, 1954, Ya Gotta Have Love, 1955, The Hills of Sand, 1969; Author: The Revolutionary Mr. Hopkinson, 1973; ann. music report for Living History of the World, 1967-68; Contbr. profl. jours. Mem. N.Y. Gilbert and Sullivan Soc. (pres. 1967-69), Nat. Arts Club, Nat. Fedn. Music Clubs, ASCAP. Episcopalian. Home: Box 196 East Haddam CT 06423 Office: Douglass Assos 17 Haynes St Hartford CT 06103 *I have developed an awareness of the need for: enough strength to overcome loneliness; enough ego to communicate well; enough vision to perceive the need; enough ambition to overcome laziness; enough drive to complete what is begun; enough compassion to wish to help; enough insight to grow humility; enough talent to be grateful; enough intelligence to remain practical; enough wisdom to be open; enough sensitivity to be myself; enough pain to keep in balance; enough pleasure to retain my humor; enough culture to be knowing; enough honesty to admit ignorance; enough love to appreciate symbols; enough religion to sense God.*

CUMMING, ROBERT HUGH, artist, educator, photographer; b. Worcester, Mass., Oct. 7, 1943; s. Robert H. and Evelyn (Schold) C.; m. Sandra S. Staples, Oct. 14, 1972; 1 dau., Avonell. B.F.A., Mass. Coll. Art, 1965; M.F.A., U. Ill., 1967. Lectr. UCLA Extension, 1974-77, Otis Art Inst., Los Angeles, 1975-76, Calif. Inst. Arts, Valencia, 1976-77; asst. prof. U. Calif.-Irvine, 1977-78; assoc. prof. U. Hartford, West Hartford, Conn., 1978—; juror, cons. U.S. Eye Exhibit Winter Olympics, Lake Placid, N.Y., 1979; vis. artist Polaroid Corp., Cambridge, Mass., 1979, Australian Gallery Dirs. Council, Sydney, Australia, 1979. Exhibited retrospective show, Friends of Photography, Carmel, Calif., 1979, Travelling retrospective show, Brisbane, Sydney, Melbourne, Adelaide, and Burney, Australia, 1979, one man shows, Castelli Gallery, N.Y.C., 1982, Werkstatt fur Photographie, Berlin. Grantee Nat. Endowment for Arts, 1972, 75; John S. Guggenheim fellow, 1980; fellow Japan-U.S. Freindship Commn., 1981.

CUMMINGS, BARTON A., advertising agency executive; b. Rockford, Ill., Feb. 4, 1914; s. Earl M. and Myrle (Smith) C. B.S. in Journalism, U. Ill., 1935. Trainee Swift & Co., Argentina, 1935-36; with Benton & Bowles, N.Y.C., 1936-41, Maxon Agy., 1945-47, Compton Advt., Inc., N.Y.C., 1947—, v.p., account supr., 1947-55, pres., 1955-56, chief exec. officer, 1956-70, chmn. bd., 1963-70, chmn. exec. com., 1970—. Bd. dirs. U. Ill. Found.; dir. council of Better Bus. Bur.; chmn. advt. div. N.Y. Heart Assn., 1963-74; bd. dirs. Better Bus. Bur. of Met. N.Y. Inc., 1960-78; chmn. Advt. Ednl. Found., Advt. Council,, 1979-81; dir. Nat. Advt. Rev. Council, 1971—, pres., 1974-79. Served to lt. comdr. USN, 1943-45. Recipient Illini Achievement award U. Ill. Alumni Assn., 1972, I Man of Year, 1972; 1st ann. Big Apple award Advt. Club N.Y., 1981; named to Advt. Hall of Fame, 1978. Mem. Am. Assn. Advt. Agys. (chmn. 1969-70, adv. council), Am. Acad. Advt. (Disting. Service award 1980), Phi Delta Theta, Pi Alpha Mu. Clubs: Adirondack League; President's (U. Ill.). Office: 625 Madison Ave New York NY 10022

CUMMINGS, BOB (ROBERT ORVILLE CUMMINGS, motion picture, stage, TV performer; b. Joplin, Mo., June 9, 1910; s. Charles C. and Ruth A. (Kraft) C.; m. Regina Young; children: Robert Richard, Mary Melinda, Sharon Patricia, Laurel Ann, Anthony Bob, Charles Clarence, Michelle Helene. Student, Drury Coll., Carnegie Inst. Tech., Am. Acad. Dramatic Arts. Lectr. in field. Comml. airplane pilot, instr. Actor in starring roles motion pictures, 1936—, including, Kings Row, Princess O'Rourke, Saboteur, You Came Along, Lost Moment, Dial M for Murder, The Carpetbaggers, What a Way to Go; others; star, dir. TV series: on tour in My Daughter's Rated X, 1975-79, Harvey, Dad's Dilemma, Fun and Games, Marriage-Go-Round, Never Too Late, Love Boat 79; Author: Stay Young and Vital, 1960. Founding mem. Ecology Found. U.S., Washington. Recipient Emmy award as best actor, 12 Angry Men, 1954, award as best actor in comedy Billboard, 1955, best comedy series award for Bob Cummings Show, Billboard, 1955; Emmy nominations for dir. and actor, 1955-59. Office: care Harry C Wilson Caldwell-King Bldg 11117 NE 2d St Bellevue WA 98004 *You can accomplish anything by acting with all your heart as if it's already accomplished. Whether life wears you down or polishes you up is dependent on the stuff you're made of*

CUMMINGS, CHARLES WILLIAM, physician, educator; b. Boston, Nov. 16, 1935; s. Harry Blanchard and Madge (Frey) C.; m. Macon Lee Howard, Dec. 20, 1958; children—Charles William, Lee Blanchard, Evelyn Howard. A.B., Dartmouth Coll., 1957; M.D., U. Va., 1961. Intern Mary Hitchcock Meml. Hosp., Hanover, N.H., 1961-62; resident otolaryngology Harvard U. Med. Sch., 1965-68; practice medicine specializing in otolaryngology, Seattle, 1978—; asso. prof. otolaryngology Upstate Med. Sch., SUNY, Syracuse, 1976-78; prof., chmn. dept. otolaryngology U. Wash. Med. Sch., Seattle, 1978—. Contbr. sci. articles to profl. jours. Served to capt., M.C. USAF, 1963-65. Mem. A.C.S., Soc. Head and Neck Surgeons, Am. Soc. for Head and Neck Surgery, Soc. U. Otolaryngologists, Assn. Acad. Depts. Otolaryngology, Triological Soc., Laryngological Soc., Bronchoesophagological Soc. Episcopalian. Office: RL-30 Dept Otolaryngology U Wash Med Sch Seattle WA 98195

CUMMINGS, CONSTANCE, actress; b. Seattle; d. Dallas Vernon and Kate Logan (Cummings) Halverstadt; m. Benn Wolfe Levy, 1933; children: Jonathan, Jemina. Chmn., Young People's Theatre Panel; mem. Arts Council, 1963-69. Broadway debut Treasure Girl, 1928; London debut Sour Grapes, Repertory Players, 1934; film debut Movie Crazy, 1932; appeared on radio, TV, films, theatre; joined Nat. Theatre Co., 1971; appeared in London stage prodns.: Madame Bovary, 1937; Romeo and Juliet, 1939, Saint Joan, 1939, The Petrified Forest, 1942, Return to Tyass, 1950, Lysistrata, 1957, The Rape of the Belt, 1957, Who's Afraid of Virginia Woolf?, 1964, Justice is a Woman, 1966, Fallen Angel, 1967, Nat. Theatre Co., A Long Day's Journey Into Night, 1972, The Cherry Orchard, 1973, The Circle, 1975, Mrs. Warren's Profession, Vienna, 1976, Wings, U.S., 1978, London, 1979, Hay Fever, 1980, The Golden Age, 1981, The Chalk Garden, N.Y.C., 1982; appeared in others; performed in: Claudel-Honnegar oratorio St. Joan at the Stake, Albert Hall, London, 1949, Peter and the Wolf, Albert Hall, 1955, Wings on Am. pub. TV; dir., Royal Ct. Theatre. Recipient Tony award for Wings, 1979, Obie award, 1979, Drama Desk award, 1979; decorated comdr. Order Brit. Empire. Mem. Brit. Actors Equity (mem. council), Royal Soc. for Encouragement of Arts and Commerce. Mem. Labour Party. Club: Chelsea Arts. Office: 68 Old Church St London SW 3 England

CUMMINGS, DAVID WILLIAM, artist; b. Okmulgee, Okla., July 15, 1937; s. Harold Raymond and Mildred Deloris (Smith) C. B.F.A., Kansas City Art Inst., 1963; M.F.A., U. Nebr., 1967. Prof. SUNY, New Paltz, 1967-70, CUNY, 1971-77, N.Y. U., 1980-81. Exhibited in one-man shows including, Katz Galleries, N.Y.C., 1970, Henri Gallery, Washington, 1969-70, Allan Stone Gallery, N.Y.C., 1974-77, Gallery Alexandra Monett, Brussels, 1975, 77, 79, Sebastian/Moore Gallery, Denver, 1978, Ericson Gallery, N.Y.C., 1981, Shahin Requicha Gallery, Rochester, N.Y., 1983, exhibited in group shows including, St. Louis Mus., 1976, Bronx Mus. Art, 1978, Max Hutchinson Gallery, 1979, Gallery Noire, Paris, Internat. Cultural Center, Antwerp, Belgium, 1980, represented in permanent collections, Whitney Mus. Am. Art, N.Y.C., Los Angeles County Mus., Aldrich Mus. Contemporary Art, Ridgefield, Conn., Phoenix Mus. Art, Jeugd en Plastische Kunst, Ghent, Belgium. Served with U.S. Army, 1957-59. Woods Found. fellow, 1966-67.

CUMMINGS, EDWARD MCLEAN, banker; b. Chgo., Sept. 10, 1921; s. Walter J. and Lillian G. C.; m. Helene de Marcellus, Feb. 26, 1949; children: Henry, Amory, Lawrence, Lillian Ogden, Rose, Alexander, McLean. B.A. in Econs., Yale U., 1942. Asst. v.p. Chem. Bank, N.Y.C., 1946-48; 2d v.p. city groups Continental Ill. Nat. Bank, Chgo., 1948-51, v.p., 1951-62, head city groups, 1962-69, sr. v.p. met. div., 1969-71, exec. v.p., 1971-74, assigned to comml. banking dept., 1974-77, multinat. banking services, 1977-80, sr. area corp. officer, Europe, 1980-82, exec. v.p., head gen. banking services, Chgo., 1982—. Served to lt. USNR, 1942-46; PTO. Clubs: Casino, Onwentsia, Chicago, Racquet, Commercial, Bankers. Office: Continental Ill Nat Bank 231 S LaSalle St Chicago IL 60697

CUMMINGS, FREDERICK JAMES, museum official; b. Floydayda, Tex., Aug. 19, 1933; s. James Sidney and Dollie (Clark) C.; m. Judith Church, July 30, 1955; children: Elihu Clark, Eleanor Louise, Leslie Elizabeth, Fred J. Church, Diana Margaret. B.A., Willamette U., 1954; M.A., Harvard U., 1956; Ph.D., U. Chgo., 1966. Instr. U. Mo., 1961-64; acting dir. Mus. Art and Archeology, 1963-64; curator European art Detroit Inst. Arts, 1964-66, asst. dir., 1966-73, dir., 1973—; adj. prof. history of art Wayne State U., Detroit, 1965—; Bd. dirs. Detroit Artists Market, Center for Creative Studies; mem. adv. com. Archives Am. Art. Author: Art in Italy, 1600-1700, 1965, American Decorative Arts, from the Pilgrims to the Revolution, 1967; co-author, organizer: Romantic Art in Britain: Paintings and Drawings, 1760-1860, 1967; co-organizer: Twilight of the Medici, Late Baroque Art in Florence 1670-1743, 1974; co-organizer, author: Painting in France 1774-1830: The Age of Revolution, 1974-75; editor: (with Charles H. Elam) The Detroit Institute of Arts Illustrated Handbook, 1971; contbr. articles to profl. jours. Decorated Order Merit (2), Italy, France; recipient Silver medal Mich. Acad. Sci., Arts and Letters, 1972. Mem. Am. Soc. for Eighteenth Century Studies, Coll. Art Assn. Am. (exec. com. 1972), Assn. Art Mus. Dirs. Home: 18652 Fairway Dr Detroit MI 48221 Office: 5200 Woodward Ave Detroit MI 48202

CUMMINGS, GEORGE CLARK, lawyer; b. Gloversville, N.Y., Mar. 4, 1916; s. Albert Edward and Effa Cecile (Clark) C.; m. Ruth Zimmer, Aug. 29, 1940; children: Elizabeth Judson (Mrs. Edward Snell), Martha Clark. A.B., Union Coll., 1937; LL.B. cum laude, Harvard U., 1940. Bar: N.Y. bar 1941, Fla. bar 1971. Asso. firm Dorr, Hand, Whittaker & Peet and (predecessor firms), N.Y.C., 1940-49, partner, 1950-59; partner firm Kelley, Drye & Warren and (predecessor firms), N.Y.C., 1959—; instr. Yale U. Law Sch., 1946-47; vis. lectr. Cornell U. Law Sch., 1964, U. Va. Law Sch., 1968, Yale U. Law Sch., 1972-79; Arbitrator small claims part Civil Ct., City of New York, 1959; master spl. term, Part 1A N.Y. Supreme Ct., 1977; mem. com. on local candidates Citizens Union, 1964; N.Y.C. panel Criminal Law Counsel for Indigent Defendants, 1974. Contbr. articles to profl. publs. Mem. N.Y. State Bar Assn., Fla. Bar Assn., Assn. Bar City N.Y., New York County Lawyers Assn., Am. Arbitration Assn. (panel arbitrators). Club: Board Room. Office: 101 New York NY 10178

CUMMINGS, KEALEY CHARLES, union executive; b. Timmins, Ont., Canada, Jan. 24, 1926; s. Charles Gilbert and Ellen (Kealey) C.; m. Lucille Clusieau, July 2, 1949; children: Michael, Charlene, Ellen. Pres. local Can. Union Pub. Employees, Toronto, Ont., Canada, 1956-69; spl. assoc. officer Can. Union Pub. Employee, Toronto, Ont., Canada, 1972-75; nat. sec. treas. Can. Union Pub. Employees, Ottawa, Ont., Canada, 1975—. Candidate New Democratic Party, Toronto, 1967, 71, v.p., Ont., 1966-76. Served with Can. Navy, 1944-46. Roman Catholic. Club: Chaudiere (Aylmer). Lodge: K.C. Home: 42 Florence St Ottawa Ont Canada K2P 0W7 Office: 21 Florence St Ottawa Ont. Canada K2P 0W6

CUMMINGS, LARRY LEE, psychologist, educator; b. Indpls., Oct. 28, 1937; s. Garland R. and Lillian P. (Smith) C.; children—Lee Anne, Glenn Nelson. A.B. summa cum laude, Wabash (Ind.) Coll., 1959; M.B.A., Ind. U., 1961, D.B.A., 1964. Asst. prof., then asso. prof. Grad. Sch. Bus., Ind. U., Bloomington, 1964-67; vis. asso. prof. Grad. Sch. Bus., Columbia U., 1967-68; mem. faculty U. Wis., Madison, 1968-81; prof. Grad. Sch. Bus. and Indsl. Relations Research Inst., lectr. univ. dept. psychology, 1970-81; dir. Center Study Organizational Performance, 1973-81, H.I. Romnes faculty fellow, 1975-81, Slichter research prof., 1980-81, asso. dean social scis., 1975-78; Kellogg disting. research prof. orgnl. behavior Kellogg Grad. Sch. Mgmt., Northwestern U., Evanston, Ill., 1981—; Ford. Found. sr. research fellow, Brussels, Belgium, 1969-70; vis. prof. Faculty Commerce and Bus. Adminstrn., U., B.C., Vancouver, 1971-72. Co-author: Organizational Decision Making, 1970, Performance in Organizations, 1973, Introduction to Organizational Behavior, 1980; co-editor: Readings in Organizational Behavior and Human Performance, rev. edit, 1973, Research in Organizational Behavior, Vol 2, 1980, Vol. 3, 1981, Vol. 4, 1982; cons. editor: Irwin series in mgmt. and behavioral scis; contbr. profl. publs. Woodrow Wilson fellow, 1959-60; fellow Ford Found., 1961-62, summer 1965, grantee; Richard D. Irwin Dissertation fellow, 1963-64; co-recipient McKinsey Found. Mgmt. Research Design award, 1968-69; grantee Richardson Found., 1968-71, Am. Soc. Personnel Adminstrn., 1974-75. Fellow Acad. Mgmt. (editor jour., mem. bd. govs., v.p., nat. programs chmn., pres.), Am. Psychol. Assn., Am. Inst. Decision Scis. (v.p., exec. bd.); mem. Midwestern Psychol. Assn., Indsl. Relations Research Assn., Am. Sociol. Assn., Soc. Personnel Adminstrn., Phi Beta Kappa, Sigma Xi, Beta Gamma Sigma, Tau Kappa Alpha, Delta Phi Alpha, Sigma Chi. Home: 505 N Lake Shore Dr Chicago IL 60611 Office: Kellogg Grad Sch Mgmt Northwestern U Evanston IL 60201

CUMMINGS, MARTIN MARC, physician, scientific administrator; b. Camden, N.J., Sept. 7, 1920; s. Samuel and Cecelia (Silverman) C.; m. Arlene Sally Avrutine, Sept. 27, 1942; children: Marc Steven, Lee Bernard, Stuart Lewis. B.S., Bucknell U., 1941, D.Sc., 1969; M.D., Duke U., 1944; D.Sc., U. Nebr., Emory U.; L.H.D., Georgetown U., 1971; M.D. (hon.), Karolinska Inst., 1972. Diplomate: Am. Bd. Microbiology. Intern, resident Boston Marine Hosp., 1944-46; resident Tb Grasslands Hosp., Valhalla, N.Y., 1946-47; dir. Tb evaluation lab. Communicable Disease Center, USPHS, Atlanta, 1947-49; instr. medicine Emory U. Sch. Medicine, 1948-50, assoc. medicine, 1950-52, asst. prof., 1953; chief Tb sect., also dir. Tb research lab. VA Hosp., Atlanta, 1949-53; dir. research services VA Central Office, Washington, 1953-59; spl. lectr. microbiology George Washington U. Sch. Medicine, 1953-59; prof. microbiology, chmn. dept. Okla. U. Sch. Medicine, 1959-61; chief Office Internat. Research, NIH, USPHS, 1961-63; dir. Nat. Library of Medicine, 1964-84, dir. emeritus, 1984—; assoc. dir. for research grants NIH, 1963-64; chmn. com. med. research Nat. Tb Assn., 1958-59; chmn. panel Sarcoidosis NRC-Nat. Acad. Scis., 1958-60. Author: (with Dr. H.S. Willis) Diagnostic and Experimental Methods in Tuberculosis, 1952; Contbr. chpt. on: Tubercle Bacilli, Diagnostic Procedures and Reagents, 1950. Served with AUS, 1943-44. Recipient Exceptional Service award VA, 1959; Distinguished Service award HEW, 1968; Rockefeller Pub. Service award, 1973; Disting. Achievement award Modern Medicine, 1976; Disting. Service award Am. Coll. Cardiology, 1978; John C. Leonard award Assn. Hosp. Med. Edn., 1979. Fellow AAAS (dir.); Sr. mem. Am. Soc. Clin. Investigation, Am. Fedn. Clin. Research; mem. Am. Clin. and Climatol. Assn. Home: 11317 Rolling House Rd Rockville MD 20852 Office: Nat Library Medicine Bethesda MD 20209

CUMMINGS, MELBOURNE WESLEY, publishing company executive; b. Beverly, Mass., Aug. 15, 1906; s. Edgar Raymond and Alberta Maud (Rines) C.; m. Barbara Lamson, June 2, 1934; 1 dau., Diane. Student (Benjamin Thompson award), U. N.H., 1929, LL.D., 1962. Sales mgr. Record Press, Rochester, N.H., 1929-30; salesman Spaulding-Moss Co., Boston, 1930-35; sales mgr. Lew A. Cummings Co., Manchester, N.H., 1935-46; founder Addison-Wesley Pub. Co., Inc., Reading, Mass., 1942—, pres., 1947-69, chmn. bd., 1947—, chief exec. officer, 1969-78; pres. Benjamin/Cummings Pub. Co., Inc., Menlo Park, Calif.; chmn. bd. Fondo Educativo Interamericano, S.A., Panama, 1967—. Home: 55 Mooreland Rd Melrose MA 02176 also 1 Olde Penzance Rd Rockport MA 01966 Office: Jacob Way Reading MA 01867

CUMMINGS, NANCY BOUCOT, nephrologist, health science administrator; b. Phila., Feb. 21, 1927; d. Joseph Ronald and Katharine (Rosenbaum) Boucot; m. Milton Curtis Cummings, Jr., July 31, 1959; children: Christopher Ronald, Jonathan Benton, Susan Sturgis. B.A., Oberlin Coll., 1947; postgrad., Radcliffe Coll., 1947; M.D., U. Pa., 1951. Rotating intern Pa. Hosp., Phila., 1951-52; resident in internal medicine Hosp. of U. Pa., Phila., 1952-54; research and clin. asst., med. professorial unit Royal Hosp., St. Bartholomew, London, 1954-55, Manchester (Eng.) Infirmary, summer, 1955; research fellow Harvard Med. Sch., 1955-59; asst. in medicine Peter Bent Brigham Hosp., Boston, 1955-58; guest worker Lab. Intermediary Metabolism, Nat. Inst. Arthritis and Metabolic Diseases, Bethesda, Md., 1959-62; research med. officer Walter Reed Army Inst. Pathology, Washington, 1962-66; research med. officer, exptl. medicine div. U.S. Naval Med. Research Inst., Bethesda, 1966-72; with NIH, Bethesda, 1972—; asso. dir. for kidney, urologic and hematologic diseases Nat. Inst. Arthritis, Diabetes, Digestive and Kidney Diseases, 1976—; cons. nephrology/medicine Clin. Center, NIH, 1976—; clin. instr. medicine Georgetown U. Sch. Medicine, Washington, 1960-70, clin. asst. prof., 1970-81, clin. asso. prof., 1981—. Co-editor several books; contbr. articles to profl. jours. Bd. dirs. Nat. Capital Area chpt. Am. Heart Assn., 1975—, chmn. research com., 1976-78; trustee-at-large Nat. Kidney Found., 1975-83; treas. Exec. Women in Govt., 1978-79; mem. vestry St. Albans Episcopal Ch., Washington, 1974-78; lay leader Cathedral St. Peter and St. Paul, 1976—. Recipient Decennial medal Georgetown U. Sch. Medicine, 1980, Disting. Service award Nat. Kidney Found., 1981; named to Hall of Fame, Cheltenham High Sch., 1984; Nat. Found. for Infantile Paralysis fellow, 1954-55; Am. Heart Assn. fellow, 1955-57, 57-62. Mem. Am. Soc. Nephrology, Internat. Soc. Nephrology, Am. Soc. Pediatric Nephrology, Am. Soc. for Artificial Internal Organs, So. Salt, Water and Kidney Club, Am. Fedn. for Clin. Research, Biophys. Soc., AAAS, Soc. Univ. Urologists, Am. Urol. Assn., Am. Soc. Hematology, Coll. Physicians Phila. Home: 4301 Massachusetts Ave NW Washington DC 20016 Office: Room 9A18 Bldg 31 NIADDK NIH Bethesda MD 20205

CUMMINGS, NATHAN, industrialist; b. St. John, N.B., Can., Oct. 14, 1896; s. David and Esther (Saxe) C.; m. Ruth Lillian Kellert, Dec. 30, 1919 (dec. Mar. 1952); children: Beatrice Violet Mayer, Herbert Kellert, Alan Harris. Ed., Economist Tng. Sch., N.Y.C.; hon. degree, Catholic U. Am., Kenyon Coll., The Citadel, U.N.B. (Can.), Tel Aviv U., Israel. Shoe bus., 1914-17, wholesale shoe bus., 1917-24, shoe mfg., 1924-30, importing gen. mdse., 1930-34, mfg. buscuits and candy, all in Can., 1934-38; pres. C.D. Kenny Co., Balt., 1939—; acquired Sprague Warner & Co., Chgo., 1942, Western Grocer Co. and; Marshall Canning Co. of, Marshalltown, Iowa, 1944; acquired Reid, Murdoch & Co., Chgo., 1945; chm. bd. Consol. Grocers Corp., Chgo., 1947-68, 1954, since which time more than 50 cos. have been acquired, now hon. chmn.; mem. exec. com.; dir. Gen. Dynamics Corp. Governing life mem. Art Inst. Chgo.; hon. trustee Met. Mus. of Art; patron Montreal Mus. Fine Arts; patron, governing mem. Mpls. Soc. Fine Arts; mem. citizens bd. U. Chgo.; hon. trustee Mt. Sinai Sch. Medicine; life gov. Jewish Gen. Hosp., Montreal; patron Lincoln Center Performing Arts. Decorated officier French Legion of Honor; commendatore Order of Merit, Italy; commandador Order of Merit, Peru). Clubs: Chicago; Canadian, Board Room (N.Y.C.). Home: Waldorf Towers 100 E 50th St New York NY 10022 Office: 375 Park Ave New York NY 10152

CUMMINGS, NICHOLAS ANDREW, psychologist, coll. pres.; b. Salinas, Calif., July 25, 1924; s. Andrew and Urania (Sims) C.; m. Dorothy Mills, Feb. 5, 1948; children—Janet Lynn, Andrew Mark. A.B., U. Calif. at Berkeley, 1948; M.A., Claremont Grad. Sch., 1954; Ph.D., Adelphi U., 1958. Chief psychologist Kaiser Permanente No. Calif., San Francisco, 1959-76; clin. dir. Biodyne Inst., 1976—; co-dir. Golden Gate Mental Health Center, San Francisco, 1959-75; pres. Calif. Sch. Profl. Psychology, Los Angeles, San Francisco, San Diego, Fresno campuses, 1969-76; chmn. bd. Calif. Community Mental Health Centers, Inc., Los Angeles, San Diego, San Francisco, 1975-77; pres. Blue Psi, Inc., San Francisco, 1972-80, Inst. for Psychosocial Interaction, 1980—; Mental health adv. bd., City and County San

Francisco, 1968-75; bd. dirs. San Francisco Assn. Mental Health, 1965-75; pres., chmn. bd. Psycho-Social Inst., 1972-80; dir. Mental Research Inst., Palo Alto, Calif., 1979—. Served with U.S. Army, 1944-46. Fellow Am. Psychol. Assn. (dir. 1975-81, pres. 1979); mem. Calif. Psychol. Assn. (pres. 1968). Pioneer prepaid mental health plans, profl. schs. psychology. Office: 2150 Judah St San Francisco CA 94122

CUMMINGS, PARKE, writer; b. West Medford, Mass., Oct. 8, 1902; s. Henry Irving and DeVoo P.; m. Mary Virginia Obear, Apr. 6, 1935; children—John Obear, Patricia Ann. Grad., Mercersburg Acad.; B.S., Harvard, 1925. Free-lance writer humor, sports articles, 1925—. Author: The Whimsey Report, 1948, The Dictionary of Sports, 1949, The Dictionary of Baseball, 1950, I'm Telling You Kids for the Last Time, 1951, American Tennis, 1957, Baseball Stories, 1959, The Fly in the Martini, 1961, Fairfield County, An Insiders Guide, 1975; Contbr. articles and verse to popular mags. Home: 178 Compo Rd S Westport CT 06880

CUMMINGS, RICHARD HOWE, banker; b. Springfield, Mass., Nov. 20, 1921; s. Charles H. and Gladys (Howe) C.; m. Cynthia Holt, May 31, 1947; 1 son, Roger Holt. B.A. cum laude, Amherst Coll., 1943; M.B.A. with high distinction, Harvard, 1948. With Nat. Bank Detroit, 1948—, exec. v.p., 1972-78, vice chmn., 1979—; pres., dir. Internat. Bank Detroit, 1969—; vice chmn., dir. NBD Bancorp., 1979—; dir. Braun Engring. Co., Energy Conversion Devices, Inc., Handleman Co., Howell Industries, Hoover Universal, Inc. Served to capt. USAAF, 1942-46. Clubs: Detroit, Detroit Athletic, Bloomfield Hills (Mich.) Country, Birmingham (Mich.) Country. Home: 6927 Pebble Creek Woods Dr West Bloomfield MI 48033 Office: Nat Bank Detroit Detroit MI 48232

CUMMINGS, VICTOR, rehabilitation medical educator; b. Bklyn., Mar. 14, 1925; s. Harry A. and Doris (Cohen) C.; m. Jacqueline Jehman, Nov. 8, 1950; children: David M., Nina. Student, U. Va., 1942-45; M.D., NYU, 1949. Diplomate: Am. Bd. Phys. Medicine and Rehab. Intern Bellevue Hosp., N.Y.C., 1949-50; resident in internal medicine Montefiore Hosp., 1953-54, fellow in phys. medicine and rehab., 1955-57, NYU Med. Ctr., 1955-57; med. dir. Beth Abraham Hosp., Bronx, N.Y., 1963-66; dir. dept. rehab. medicine Lincoln Hosp., Bronx, 1966-70; prof. rehab. medicine Albert Einstein Coll. Medicine, N.Y.C., 1977-82; Eleanor Coghlin chmn., prof. rehab. medicine Med. Coll. Ohio, Toledo, 1982—; dir. Am. Bd. Phys. Medicine and Rehab., Rochester, Minn., 1976—; pres. Am. Congress Rehab. Medicine, Chgo., 1981-82; chmn. sect. on phys. medicine and rehab. N.Y.C. Acad. Medicine, N.Y.C., 1975-76. Served to lt. M.C. USNR, 1950-52; Korea. Fellow ACP; mem. Am. Acad. Phys. Medicine and Rehab. Club: Belmont Country (Perrysburg, Ohio). Office: Med Coll Ohio C 510008 Toledo OH 43699

CUMMINGS, WALTER E., stock exchange executive; b. Everett, Mass.; s. Eli C. and Meariam Hudson; m. Elizabeth C. Williamson, Apr. 21, 1956; children: Mary, David, Scott. Asst. to exec. sec. Boston Stock Exchange, Inc., 1955-64, asst. sec., 1964-68, exec. sec., 1968—, v.p., 1981—; exec. sec. Boston Stock Exchange Clearing Copr., 1980—, Boston Stock Exchange Service Corp., 1980—. Served with USAF, 1951-55; Alaska. Republican. Office: Boston Stock Exchange Inc 1 Boston Pl Boston MA 02108 *

CUMMINGS, WALTER J., U.S. circuit judge; b. Chgo., Sept. 29, 1916; s. Walter J. and Lillian (Garvy) C.; m. Therese Farrell Murray, May 18, 1946 (dec. Nov. 1968); children: Walter J. III, Keith M., Mark F.; m. Marie Campbell Krane, Sept. 6, 1975. A.B., Yale U., 1937; LL.B., Harvard U., 1940. Bar: Ill. 1940. Mem. staff U.S. solicitor gen., Washington, 1940-46; spl. asst. to U.S. atty. gen., 1944-46; partner firm Sidley, Austin, Burgess & Smith, Chgo., 1946-66; solicitor gen., U.S., 1952-53; judge 7th circuit U.S. Ct. Appeals, Chgo., 1966-81, chief judge, 1981—; former mem. Joint Coms. Jud. Articles and Uniform Comml. Code; former grievance commr. Ill. Supreme Ct.; former mem. U.S. Jud. Conf.; also subcom. judicial improvements, chmn. ad hoc com. on disposition of ct. records. Former mem. vis. com. Harvard Law Sch.; former mem. bd. visitors Stanford Law Sch.; mem. vis. com. Northwestern U. Law Sch.; past mem. vis. com. U. Chgo. Law Sch. Past nat. bd. dirs., vice chmn. Ill. div. Am. Cancer Soc.; trustee Loyola U., Chgo.; bd. govs. Citizens Greater Chgo.; governing life mem. Art Inst. Chgo. Named knight of Malta, knight of Holy Sepulchre. Mem. ABA (past chmn. spl. com. fed. rules procedure, past chmn. com. jud. center, mem. com. consumer credit, nat. ct. assistance com., Ross essay contest, mem. ad hoc com. on award of litigation costs), Ill. Bar Assn. (past chmn. internat. law sect., past chmn. antitrust sect., comml. and bankruptcy law com., com. jud. ethics), Chgo. Bar Assn. (past chmn. com. constl. revision, grievance com. div. III A, bd. mgrs., past chmn. com. founds.), Bar Assn. 7th Fed. Circuit (past pres.), Am., Chgo. bar founds., Harvard Soc. Ill. (past dir.), Thomas More Assn. (dir.), Am. Law Inst., Am. Judicature Soc., Appellate Lawyers Assn., Fed. Judges Assn. (bd. dirs.). Roman Catholic. Clubs: Law, Legal, Racquet, Tavern, Standard, Union League, Covenant, Saddle and Cycle (Chgo.); Metropolitan (Washington); Yale (N.Y.C.). Office: Dirksen Fed Bldg 219 S Dearborn St Chicago IL 60604

CUMMINS, ALFRED BYRON, management engineer, educator; b. Ute, Iowa, Mar. 19, 1905; s. Daniel Byron and Myrtle (Chase) C.; m. Maxine Ellen Price, Dec. 23, 1934; children: Mary Alice (Mrs. Wilson), Judith Maxine Cummins Morrison. B.S. cum laude, State U. Iowa, 1931, J.D., M.S., 1938; postgrad., Mass. Inst. Tech., 1931-32, U. Minn., 1938-41, U. Pa., 1941-42. Registered profl. mgmt. engr. Prodn. civilian specialist Armed Services, Phila., 1942- 46; chief indsl. engr. Wilkening Mfg. Co., Phila., 1943-46; cons. mgmt. engr., 1946—; prodn. cons. Armed Services, War Labor Bd., WPB, Engring. Sci. Mgmt. War Tng. Program, U. Pa., War Labor Bd., WPB, Engring. Sci. Mgmt. War Tng. Program, U. Pa., 1941-45; prof. mgmt. dept. Case Western Res. U. Sch. Mgmt., 1947—; organizer, dir. Hough Mfg. Co.; chmn. L-C-L, Inc., Cleve.; Cons. OEEC-EPA, Paris; mgmt. cons. VA hosps.; dir. research pub. health mgmt. systems; mem. nat. panel arbitrators Fed. Mediation and Conciliation Service. Author: Managing Human Resources; Contbr. tech. articles to profl. jours. Mem. Iowa Bar, Soc. for Advancement Mgmt. (past pres. Phila.), Am. Arbitration Assn. (nat. panel arbitrators), Sigma Xi, Tau Beta Pi, Beta Gamma Sigma, Delta Sigma Pi. Patentee office equipment, athletic tng. equipment. Home: N Miles Rd Chagrin Falls OH 44022 Office: Case Western Reserve U Cleveland OH 44106

CUMMINS, BOBBY DEAN, tobacco co. exec.; b. English, Ind., Sept. 29, 1926; s. Densil Highfill and Rue (Nash) C.; m. Gladys Gonzalez, June 24, 1950; children—John Raymond, Dean Robert. B.S., Ind. U., 1949; grad., advanced mgmt. program Harvard, 1963. C.P.A., Ind. Controller Shirley Corp., Indpls., 1948-53; audit supr. Ernst & Ernst, Indpls., 1953-59; v.p., controller Huffman Mfg. Co., 1959-66; v.p.-finance Brown & Williamson Tobacco Corp., Louisville, 1966-80, sr. v.p., 1980—. Mem. Fin. Execs. Inst. (pres. Louisville chpt. 1973), Am. Inst. C.P.A.'s, Ind. Soc. C.P.A.'s, Indpls. Jr. C. of C. (1st v.p. 1958). Club: Rotary. Home: 509 Jarvis Ln Louisville KY 40207 Office: 1600 W Hill St Louisville KY 40232

CUMMINS, DELMER DUANE, historian; b. Dawson, Nebr., June 4, 1935; s. Delmer H. and Ina Z. (Arnold) C.; m. Darla Sue Beard, Oct. 6, 1957; children: Stephen Duane, Cristi Sue, Caroline Renee. B.A., Phillips U., Enid, Okla., 1957; M.A., U. Denver, 1965; Ph.D., U. Okla., 1974; LL.D., Williams Woods Coll., 1979; Hum.D., Phillips U., 1983. Tchr., Jefferson County Public Schs., Denver, 1956-67; mem. faculty Oklahoma City U., 1967-77, Darbeth-Whitten prof. history, 1974-77, curator George Shirk Collection, 1977; chmn. dept. history Oklahoma City U., 1969-72; dir. Robert A. Taft Inst. Govt., 1970-77; pres. div. higher edn. Christian Ch., 1977—; cons. Okla. Heritage Center, 1974-77. Author: (with W.G. White) The American Frontier, 1968, Origins of the Civil War, 1971, The American Revolution, 1968, Contrasting Decades: 1920's and 1930's, 1972, Consensus and Turmoil, 1972, William R. Leigh: Biography of a Western Artist, 1980, A Handbook for Today's Disciples, 1981, (with D. Hohweiler) An Enlisted Soldier's View of the Civil War, 1981; contbr. articles to profl. jours. Trustee Culver-Stockton Coll., 1978—, Tougaloo Coll., 1978—, United Bd. Coll. Devel., 1978-83; Danforth asso., 1976—. Mem. Okla. Assn. History Prof. (v.p. 1970), Okla. Council Humanities (grantee 1974), Phillips U. Alumni Assn. (pres. 1975-76), Nat. Assn. Ind. Colls. and Univs. (secretariat). Mem. Christian Ch. (chmn. bd. 1971-73, nat. gov. bd. 1975—, adminstrv. com. 1976—). Home: 12760 Shady Creek Ln Saint Louis MO 63141 Office: 11780 Borman Dr Saint Louis MO 63146

CUMMINS, HERMAN ZACHARY, physicist; b. Rochester, N.Y., Apr. 23, 1933; s. Louis H. and Rhoda Edith (Kitay) C.; m. Marsha Z. Hirsch, Aug. 18, 1963. B.S., M.S., Ohio State U., 1956; Diplome d'Etudes Superieures (Fulbright fellow), U. Paris, 1957; Ph.D., Columbia U., 1963. Research asso. Columbia U., N.Y.C., 1963-64; asst. prof. physics Johns Hopkins U., Balt, 1964-67, asso. prof., 1967-69, prof., 1969-71; prof. physics N.Y.U., 1971-73; distinguished prof. physics City Coll., City U. N.Y., 1973—. Fellow Am. Phys. Soc., N.Y. Acad. Scis. Research in laser light scattering physics, phase transititions and critical phenomena, solid state and biophysics. Office: Dept Physics City Coll City U NY New York NY 10031

CUMMINS, JOHN STEPHEN, bishop; b. Oakland, Calif., Mar. 3, 1928; s. Michael and Mary (Connolly) C. A.B., St. Patrick's Coll., 1949. Ordained priest Roman Catholic Ch., 1953; asst. pastor Mission Dolores Ch., San Francisco, 1953-57; mem. faculty Bishop O'Dowd High Sch., Oakland, 1957-62; chancellor Diocese of Oakland, 1962-71; rev. monsignor, 1962, domestic prelate, 1967; exec. dir. Calif. Cath. Conf., Sacramento, 1971-77; consecrated bishop, 1974, aux. bishop of, Sacramento, 1974-77, bishop of, Oakland, 1977—; Campus minister San Francisco State Coll., 1953-57, Mills Coll., Oakland, 1957-71; Trustee St. Mary's Coll., 1968-79. Home: 634 21st St Oakland CA 94612 Office: 2900 Lake Shore Ave Oakland CA 94610

CUMMINS, JOSEPH HERVEY, lawyer; b. Winchester, Ind., June 19, 1916; s. George Frederich and Teresa Elsie (Brown) C.; m. Susie Van Sickle, Oct. 19, 1945; children—Karen (Mrs. Steven Freeburg), Scott, Fred, Lynn (Mrs. John Dannhausen). A.B., De Pauw U., 1937; J.D., Northwestern U., 1940; postgrad., Grad. Inst. Bus. Econs., U. So. Calif., 1957. Bar: Ill. 1940, Colo. 1941, Calif. 1946. Trial lawyer Burlington R.R., Chgo., 1940-41, Denver, 1941-42, Santa Fe R.R., Los Angeles, 1946-51, 53-62; partner firm Garibaldi & Cummins, Los Angeles, 1951-53, Cummins, White & Breidenbach, 1962-78, Cummins, White, Robinson & Robinson, 1978-80, Cummins & White, 1980—; mem. State Bar Disciplinary Bd., Los Angeles, 1972—, chmn., 1974. Served to lt. USNR, 1942-46. Mem. Am. Bd. Trial Advs. (nat. pres. 1972—, dir), Am., Ill., Colo., Los Angeles County, Pasadena bar assns., Calif. State Bar (bd. govs. 1974-77, v.p. 1977, commn. on jud. nominees evaluation 1978-80, chmn. 1980-82), So. Calif. Def. Council, Am. Coll. Trial Lawyers (chmn. So. Calif. state com. 1980-81), Internat. Assn. Ins. Counsel, Internat. Soc. Barristers, Chancery Club, Phi Alpha Delta. Clubs: Mason., Jonathan, San Gabriel Country. Home: 2141 N Villa Heights Rd Pasadena CA 91107 Office: 888 W 6th St Los Angeles CA 90017

CUMMINS, KENNETH BURDETTE, educator; b. New Washington, Ohio, July 27, 1911; s. Royal Clinton and Pearl (Rittenour) C. A.B., Ohio Wesleyan U., 1933; M.A., Bowling Green State U., 1939; Ph.D., Ohio State U., 1958. Tchr. sci. and math. Sulphur Springs (Ohio) High Sch., 1933-40, New Washington High Sch., 1941-57; asst. prof. math. Kent State U., 1957-59, asso. prof., 1959-64, prof., 1964-81, emeritus prof., 1981—; chmn. dept., 1964-65; Dir. Math. Inst., NSF. Author: Teaching of Mathematics, 1970; Contbr. articles to profl. jours. Recipient alumni award for distinguished teaching Kent State U., 1968, 76, President's medal, 1981; Christofferson-Fawcett Math. Edn. award, Ohio, 1981. Mem. Math. Assn. Am., Nat. Council Tchrs. Math., Central Assn. Sci. and Math. Tchrs., Ohio Acad. Sci., Phi Beta Kappa, Sigma Xi, Sigma Pi Sigma, Pi Mu Epsilon, Kappa Delta Pi. Home: 421 Center St New Washington OH 44854 Office: Kent State University Kent OH 44242

CUMMIS, CLIVE SANFORD, lawyer; b. Newark, Nov. 21, 1928; s. Joseph Jack and Lee (Berkie) C.; m. Ann Denburg, Mar. 24, 1956; children: Andrea, Deborah, Cynthia, Jessica. A.B., Tulane U., 1949; J.D., U. Pa., 1952; LL.M., N.Y. U., 1959. Bar: N.J. 1952. Law sec. Hon. Walter Freund, Appellate Div., Superior Ct., 1955-56; partner firm Cummis & Kroner, Newark, 1956-60; chief counsel County and Mcpl. Law Revision Commn., State of N.J., Newark, 1959-62; partner firm Schiff, Cummis & Kent, Newark, 1962-67, Cummis, Kent, Radin & Tischman, 1967-70; sr. v.p., dir. Cadence Industries, N.Y.C., 1967-70; dir. Plume & Atwood Industries, Stamford, Conn., 1969-71; pres. Sills, Beck, Cummis, Radin & Tischman, P.A., Newark, 1970—; dir. Essex County State Bank, Financial Resources Group; instr. Practising Law Inst. Chief counsel County and Mcpl. Revision Commn., 1959-62, N.J. Pub. Market Commn., 1961-63; counsel Bd. Edn. of South Orange and Maplewood, 1964-74, Town of Cedar Grove, 1966-70, Bd. Edn. of Dumont, 1968-72; mem. com. on rules and civil practice N.J. Supreme Ct., 1975-78. Bd. editors: N.J. Law Jour, 1964—. Trustee Newark Beth Israel Med. Center, 1965-75, Northfield YM-YWHA, 1968-70, Coll. Medicine and Dentistry N.J., 1980—, Newark Mus.; bd. govs. Daus. of Israel Home for Aged, 1968-70; mem. N.J. Commn. on Statue of Liberty. Served with Adj. Gen. Corps U.S. Army, 1953-55. Fellow Am. Bar Found.; mem. Am. Law Inst., Am. Judicature Soc., Am. Bar Assn., N.J. Bar Assn., Essex County Bar Assn. Democrat. Jewish. Clubs: City Athletic (N.Y.C.); Greenbrook Country (Fairfield, N.J.). Office: 33 Washington St Newark NJ 07102

CUMMISKEY, CHARLES JOSEPH, educator, univ. dean; b. St. Louis, Feb. 12, 1924; s. Charles Joseph and Sarah (Hickey) C. B.S., U. Dayton, 1943; M.S., Northwestern U., 1952; Ph.D., U. Notre Dame, 1956. Joined Soc. of Mary, 1941; tchr. math. and sci. secondary schs., 1943-52; mem. staff dept. chemistry St. Mary's U., San Antonio, 1955—, prof., 1965—, chmn. dept., 1957-66, 78—, v.p., dean faculties, 1966-75; research asso. AEC radiation project U. Notre Dame, 1953-55; Vis. scientist secondary schs. Am. Chem. Soc., 1962-65; dir. NSF undergrad. research participation program, 1959-60. Robert A. Welch Found. grantee, 1962-74. Mem. Am. Chem. Soc. (past pres. San Antonio sect.), Albertus Magnus Guild, Tex. Acad. Sci., Sigma Xi. Research on properties of complex anionic species. Address: One Camino Santa Maria San Antonio TX 78284

CUMMISKEY, J. KENNETH, former college president; b. Boston, Nov. 18, 1928; s. Joseph K. and Helen F. (Penney) C.; m. Joan Lydia Ross, Aug. 13, 1953; children: Lynn Anne, David Ross. B.S., Springfield Coll., 1952; M.Ed., Oreg. State U., 1953; Ph.D., Stanford U., 1963. Tchr., coach Sweet Home (Oreg.) High Sch., 1953-55; asso. prof. edn. phys. edn., coach Oreg. Coll. Edn., 1955-65; asso. dir. Peace Corps, Morocco, 1965-66; supr. edn. programs Tng. Corp. Am.; dir. headstart tng. programs Territory of Guam, Islands of Trust Territories, 1966-68; dir. community services project Am. Assn. Jr. Colls., 1968-71; exec. dir. Nat. Council Community Services, 1970-72; v.p. acad. affairs New Eng. Coll., Henniker, N.H., 1971-73, pres., 1973-81, pres. emeritus, counsel to bd. trustees, 1981—; mem. N.H. Postsecondary Edn. Commn., 1978—; Auditor Henniker, 1977-80; mediator N.H. Public Employee Labor Relations Bd., 1977—; steering com. N.H. Common Cause, 1975-81; bd. advisers Merrimack Valley Coll., 1981—; mem. N.H. Commn. to Study Impact of Tax-Exempt Non-Fed. Instl. Property on Localities, 1979-81; mem. exec. com. New Eng.-China Consortium, 1981—. Author works in field.; Mem. adv. bd.: Community Edn. Jour, 1970-73; editorial bd.: Jour. Edn, 1971-73. Served with U.S. Army, 1946-48, 51-54. Fellow Royal Soc. Arts; Mem. NEA, Am. Psychol. Assn., Nat. Council Community Services and Continuing Edn., Am. Assn. Higher Edn., N.H. Coll. and Univ. Council (pres. 1979-81), Phi Delta Kappa. Unitarian. Clubs: Univ. (N.Y.C.); Arundel Yacht. Office: New England Coll Henniker NH 03242

CUNDALL, DONALD ROGER, rancher, state senator; b. Glendo, Wyo., May 30, 1925; s. Edwin Paul and Ruth Frances (Troupe) C.; m. Doris Moran, May 18, 1946; children—Jerry, Ronald, Tyler, Michael. Student, Mont. Sch. Mines, Colo. Coll. Rancher; mem. Wyo. Senate, 1972—, chmn. health, edn. and welfare com., 1976-80, pres., 1981—. Served with U.S. Navy, 1944-48. Republican. Office: Wendover Rt Guernsey WY 82214

CUNDIFF, EDWARD WILLIAM, marketing educator; b. Long Beach, Calif., Sept. 28, 1919; s. Harry Thomas and Martha Magdalene (Koltes) C.; m. Margaret Wallace Stroud, Sept. 8, 1956; children: Richard Wallace, Gregory Edward, Geoffrey William. B.A., Stanford, 1940, M.B.A., 1942; Ed.D., 1952; Ed.D. Ford fellow, Harvard Sch. Bus. Adminstrn., 1956. Retailing exec., 1946-48; instr. mktg. San Jose State Coll., 1949-52; asst. prof., later asso. prof. mktg. Syracuse U., 1952-58, asst. dean, 1954-58; prof. mktg., chmn. dept. mktg. adminstrn. U. Tex., 1958-73, asso. dean, 1973-76; L.J. Buchan distinguished vis. prof. U. Tex. at San Antonio, 1976-77; Charles C. Kellstadt prof. mktg. Emory U., 1977—; vis. prof. mktg., Fontainebleau, France, Palmermo, Sicily, 1960-61. Author: (with R.R. Still) Sales Management: Decisions, Policies and Cases, 4th edit, 1981, Basic Marketing: Concepts, Environment, and Decisions, 1964, rev. edit., 1970, Essentials of Marketing, 1966, (with R.R. Still and N.A.P. Govoni) Fundamentals of Modern Marketing, 3d edit, 1980; editor: Jour. Mktg, 1973-76. Served to lt. (s.g.) USNR, World War II. Mem. Am. Mktg. Assn. (v.p. 1980—), So. Mktg. Assn. (pres. 1967-68), Beta Gamma Sigma, Delta Sigma Pi, Theta Chi. Home: 1657 Mason Mill Rd Atlanta GA 30329

CUNDIFF, PAUL ARTHUR, English language educator; b. Ferguson, Ky., Nov. 14, 1909; s. William Gilbert and Cynthia Isbelle (Haney) C.; m. Mary Christine Fritsche, Aug. 7, 1948. A.B., Georgetown (Ky.) Coll., 1933; A.M., U. Ky., 1935; Ph.D., Cornell, 1940. Instr. English U. Ky., 1934-36, Cornell, 1937-40; tchr. English Wright Jr. Coll., Chgo., 1940-42; instr. English Northwestern U., 1945-46; chmn. English dept. Sampson Coll., N.Y., 1946-47; prof. and head English Dept. Butler U., 1947-53, prof. English, 1947-61, dean coll. liberal arts and scis., 1953-59; chmn. dept. English U. Del., 1961-66, H. Rodney Sharp prof. English, 1966—. Author: Browing's Ring Metaphor and Truth, 1972, Robert Browning: A Shelley Promethean, 1977, Robert Browning: Compiler of the Shelley Concordance, 1982; Contbr. articles to profl. jours. Served to lt. AUS, 1942-45; ETO; historian 8th Corps, writing history of Battle of the Bulge for Corps. Decorated Bronze star. Mem. Am. Assn. Acad. Deans (sec.), Modern Lang. Assn. Am., AAUP, Coll. English Assn., Phi Kappa Phi, Sigma Tau Delta, Pi Kappa Delta, Lambda Chi. Club: Literary (Indpls.). Home: 7010 B Santa Ana Dr Tampa FL 33617

CUNDY, KENNETH RAYMOND, scientist; b. Spearfish, S.D., Dec. 22, 1929; s. Raymond and Letitia (Johnston) C.; m. Elsie Marie Schlachter, Nov. 30, 1957. B.A., Stanford U., 1950; postgrad., Sch. Medicine, 1950-52; M.S. in Microbiology, U. Wash., 1953, U. Calif., Berkeley, 1957-60, Ph.D., 1965. Diplomate: Am. Bd. Med. Microbiology. Research microbiologist U. Calif., Berkeley, 1957-60; bacteriologist Gerber Products Co., Oakland, Calif., 1960-61; research microbiologist U. Calif., Davis, 1961-65; postdoctoral fellow med. microbiology Temple U. Sch. Medicine, Phila., 1965-67, instr. microbiology, 1966-67, asst. prof., 1967-71, asso. prof. microbiology and immunology, 1971-77, prof., 1977—, pres. med. faculty senate, 1977-78; pres. univ. faculty senate Temple U., 1979-80; dir. clin. microbiology Temple U. Hosp., 1970-84, epidemiologist, 1984—; asso. dir. bacteriology St. Christopher's Hosp., Phila., 1967-68, dir. diagnostic microbiology lab., 1968-70. Served with USNR, 1954-57. Fellow Am. Acad. Microbiology; mem. Am. Soc. Microbiology, AAAS, N.Y. Acad. Scis., Coll. Physicians Phila., Sigma Xi. Episcopalian. Clubs: Phila. Sketch, Commonwealth of Calif. (San Francisco); Pa. Soc. Lodge: Masons. Research in infectious disease process, mechanisms of pathogenicity, anaerobic microbiology, bacterial pathogenesis in cystic fibrosis. Home: 513 Delancey St Philadelphia PA 19106 Office: Temple U Sch Medicine Broad & Ontario Sts Philadelphia PA 19140

CUNEO, ERNEST L., lawyer, journalist, author; m. Margaret Watson (dec. 1976); children: Sandra, Jonathan. B.A., Columbia U., LL.B., LL.D., D.H.L. Bar: N.Y., D.C., U.S. Supreme Ct. Past law sec. Fiorello H. La Guardia; past asso. counsel Dem. Nat. Com.; past dir. Freedom House, Woodrow Wilson Inst. Internat. Scholars; pres., chmn. bd. N.Am. Newspaper Alliance; exec. editor-at-large Sat. Eve. Post. Author: Dynamics of World History. Served to maj. USMCR; ret.; OSS liaison officer to White House, British Security, State Dept., FBI, World War II. Decorated by Italy, Britain and; City of Genoa. Clubs: Varsity, National Press, Overseas Press, Silurians, University, OSS Veterans. Office: 1511 K St NW Washington DC 20005

CUNERD, EARL H., charitable association executive; b. Phila., Jan. 26, 1918; s. Lewis Earl and Helen Elizabeth (Phy) C.; m. Vivian Carter Gaines, Jan. 4, 1941; 1 son, Earl Stephen. Certificate of proficiency with honors, U. Pa., 1940; postgrad., Rutgers U. Grad. Sch. Banking, 1956. From messenger to asst. v.p. First Nat. Bank of Phila., 1936-55; asst. v.p. First Pa. Co., Phila., 1955-56; asst. v.p. to divisional v.p. Girard Trust Bank, Phila., 1956-67; exec. dir. United Cerebral Palsy Assns., Inc., N.Y.C., 1967—, asst. treas., 1967; founder, dir. Nat. Industries for Severely Handicapped, 1974—, chmn. bd., 1978-80; Vice pres. Nat. Health Council, 1973, pres. elect, 1974, pres., 1975, chmn. continuing edn. com., 1974; treas. Rehab. Internat.-U.S.A., 1975-77, mem. assembly, 1976—. Chmn. Youth for Eisenhower Com. of Phila., 1952; co-chmn. Phila. chpt. NCCJ, 1959-62; chmn. United Negro Coll. Fund. of Phila., 1960-61; v.p. Crime Commn. of Phila., 1964-67; mem. Cheltenham Twp. Sch. Bd., 1955-61, v.p., 1960-61; commr. Cheltenham Twp., 1962-66, chmn. fin. com., 1962-66; pres. United Cerebral Palsy of Phila. and Vicinity, 1962-66; v.p. United Cerebral Palsy of Pa., 1965-67; mem. adv. com. Goodwill Industries of Am., Vols. in Rehab. Project, 1971-74, Nat. Council on Vol. Action, 1969-71; Asst. treas. Republican Com. of Pa., 1952-58. Served to lt. U.S. Maritime Service, 1942-45. Named Outstanding Young Man of

Phila., 1952. Mem. Am. Inst. Banking (nat. championship debating team 1948), Phila. Jr. C. of C. (pres. 1951-52), Phila. Council of Chs. (pres. 1957-59). Presbyterian (elder). Clubs: Union League (Phila.); Seaview Country (Absecon, N.J.). Home: Nixon Dr and Lois Ln Moorestown NJ 08057 Office: 66 E 34th St New York NY 10016

CUNHA, TONY JOSEPH, animal scientist, emeritus dean; b. Los Banos, Calif., Aug. 22, 1916; s. Anthony August and Maria (Silvera) C.; m. Gwen Smith, Sept. 1, 1941; children: Becky Jane, Sharon Marie, Susan Ann. Student, Calif. Poly Coll., 1936-39; B.S., Utah State U., 1940, M.S., 1941; Ph.D., U. Wis., 1944. Instr. Wash. State U., 1944, asst. prof., 1945, assoc. prof., 1946-48; assoc. prof. dept. animal sci. U. Fla., 1948-50, prof., head dept., 1950-75, Distinguished Service prof., 1972-75, emeritus, 1975—; dean Sch. Agr., Calif. State Poly. U., Pomona, 1975-80, emeritus, 1980—, univ. cons. in agr., 1980—. Author: Swine Feeding and Nutrition, 1957, rev. edit., 1977, Horse Feeding and Nutrition, 1980; co-editor: Crossbreeding Beef Cattle, 1963, Factors Affecting Calf Crop, 1967, Crossbreeding Beef Cattle, series 2, 1973; editor: Animal Feeding and Nutrition Series; contbr. articles to profl. publs. Named Alumnus of Yr. Calif. Poly. Coll., 1956; Sr. Faculty award Fla. chpt. Gamma Sigma Delta, 1959; Man of Yr. award in Fla. agr. Progressive Farmer mag., 1966; Morrison award for $2000 for distinguished research Am. Soc. Animal Sci., 1968; Internat. award for distinguished service to agr. Gamma Sigma Delta, 1976. Fellow AAAS; mem. Am. Soc. Animal Sci. (v.p. 1961, pres. 1962), Am. Inst. Nutrition, AAUP, Newcomen Soc. Am., Fla. Acad. Sci., Soc. Exptl. Biology and Medicine, Sigma Xi, Gamma Sigma Delta (Fla. pres. 1958), Alpha Zeta, Gamma Alpha, Phi Sigma, Alpha Gamma Rho, Phi Kappa Phi. Roman Catholic. Lodge: Rotary. Home: 1220 Charmont Rd La Verne CA 91750 Office: Sch of Agr Calif State Polytechnic U Pomona CA 91768

CUNIN, JOHN RAYMOND, industrial distributing company executive; b. Akron, Ohio, Sept. 11, 1924; s. Earl Augusta and Mary Elizabeth (McAlonan) C.; m. Marilyn Ann McGuigan, Aug. 30, 1952; children: John M., Mary Catherine, Thomas K., Jane D., William E. Student, John Carroll U., Cleve., 1946-47, Akron U., 1947-48, Gen. Motors Inst., 1967. With Bearings, Inc., Cleve., 1948—, dist. mgr., then gen. sales mgr., 1972-80, pres., chief operating officer, after 1980, chmn., chief exec. officer, 1980—, also dir. Mem. adv. bd. Our Lady of the Wayside Homes for the Handicapped, Avon, Ohio, 1968. Served with USAAF, 1942-45; ETO. Decorated D.F.C., Air medal. Mem. Power Transmission Distbrs. Assn. Democrat. Clubs: Rotary, Univ., Caterpillar. Office: Bearings Inc 3600 Euclid Ave Cleveland OH 44115

CUNLIFFE, SYDNEY JOSEPH, civil engineer, consultant; b. Port Haney, C., Can., Oct. 28, 1919; s. Sydney Alred and Catherine Euphemia (Jones) C.; m. Doris Ethel Beaulne, Sept. 2, 1946; children: Robert, Douglas, Raymond, Edward. B.A.Sc., U. B.C., Vancouver, 1950, P.Eng., 1952; LL.D., U. Victoria. Field engr. B.C. Dept. Hwys., Vancouver Island, 1950-51, asst. surfacing engr., B.C., 1951-56; chmn. bd. Willis, Cunliffe, Tait and Co., Victoria, B.C., 1956—, DeLeuw Cather (Can.) Ltd., 1979—; mem. Victoria adv. bd. Royal Trust Co.; Mem. Constrn. Industry Devel. Council, 1980—; chmn. Consultative Com. on Cons. Engring.; vice-chmn. Victoria Art Gallery, 1963-67, Victoria Planning Commn., 1965-75, chmn., 1970-75. Pres. Victoria YM-YWCA, 1963-65; chmn. bd. U. Victoria Found.; mem. Univs. Council of B.C. Served to capt. Royal Can. Arty., 1940-46. Named Hon. Citizen City of Victoria, 1971, Citizen of Year, 1978; decorated Order of Can. Fellow Engring. Inst. Can., Can. Soc. Civil Engring.; mem. Assn. Cons. Engrs. Can. (pres.), Victoria Downtown Bus. Assn. (v.p.), Can. Tech. Asphalt Assn. (pres. 1962), Assn. Profl. Engrs. B.C. (pres. Victoria br. 1961-62, R.A. McLachlan award 1966), Rds. and Transp. Assn. Can. Clubs: Union of B.C. (pres. 1970-72), Rotary., Victoria Golf, Faculty of U. Victoria. Home: 1530 Despard Ave Victoria BC V8S 1T3 Canada Office: 827 Fort St Victoria BC V8W 1H6 Canada

CUNNIFF, PATRICK FRANCIS, mechanical engineer; b. N.Y.C., Oct. 25, 1933; s. Martin and Della (McDonald) C.; m. Patricia McCann, June 18, 1960; children: Brian, John, Elizabeth, Christopher. B.C.E., Manhattan Coll., 1955; M.S., Va. Tech. U., 1957, Ph.D., 1962. Research mech. engr. U.S. Naval Research Lab., 1960-63; mem. dept. mech. engring. U. Md., 1963—, prof., 1969—; cons. vibration and noise control. Author: (with D. Anand) Engineering Mechanics—Statics and Dynamics, 1973, Environmental Noise Pollution, 1977. Served with USPHS, 1956-59. U.S. Steel Found. fellow, 1959-60. Mem. ASME, Am. Soc. Engring. Edn. Democrat. Roman Catholic. Lodge: Rotary. Office: Dept Mech Engring Univ of Md College Park MD 20742

CUNNINGHAM, ARTHUR FRANCIS, educator, univ. dean, business cons.; b. Bklyn., Mar. 23, 1922; s. John Michael and Alice (Heggerty) C.; m. Maureen Reidy, Feb. 13, 1970; 1 dau. by previous marriage, Linda June. Student, Am. U., 1946-47; B.S., L.I. U., 1950; LL.B., Bklyn. Law Sch., 1953, J.D., 1967; postgrad., N.Y.U. Grad. Sch., 1954-56; M.B.A., U. Detroit, 1958. Bar: N.Y. bar 1954. With Fairbanks, Co., N.Y.C., 1950-51, Lever Bros. Co., 1951-55; sr. financial analyst Ford Motor Co., 1955-56; gen. sales mgr. DWG Cigar Corp., Detroit, 1956-60; asst. to pres. Nalley's, Inc., Tacoma, 1960-61, exec. v.p., dir., 1961-62; exec. v.p. Seeman Bros., Inc., Carlstadt, N.J., 1962-65; dir.; v.p., gen. mgr. food div. Leslie Salt Co., San Francisco, 1965-67; past pres., dir. Koratron Co., Inc., San Francisco, Koratec, Inc.; past v.p., dir. Koracorp Industries, Inc.; prof. mktg. San Francisco State U., 1975—, dean, 1975—; dir. Infomedia Corp., Palo Alto, Calif., Torrent Corp., Lake Geneva, Wis., Industry/Edn. Council Calif.; pres., dir. Western Assn. Collegiate Schs. Bus.; bus. cons., 1975—. Food chmn. United Good Neighbors Campaign, Tacoma, 1962; bd. dirs. Resource Center for Women, Palo Alto. Served with USAAF, 1942-45. Clubs: Rotary, Commonwealth (San Francisco); N.Y. Athletic. Home: 230 Paseo Bernal Moraga CA 94556 Office: 1600 Holloway Ave San Francisco CA 94132 also 235 Montgomery St Suite 965 San Francisco CA 94104

CUNNINGHAM, BILLY, basketball coach; b. Bklyn., June 3, 1943; m. Sondra Cunningham, 1966; children: Stephanie, Heather. Grad., U. N.C. Profl. basketball player Phila. 76ers, 1965-72, 74-76, Carolina Cougars, 1972-74; coach Phila. 76ers, 1977—. Named Most Valuable Player Am. Basketball Assn., 1973. Appeared in Nat. Basketball Assn. All Star Game, 1969, 70, 71, 72; coached team to NBA Championship, 1983. Office: Phila 76ers Veterans Stadium PO Box 25040 Philadelphia PA 19147 *

CUNNINGHAM, BRUCE ARTHUR, biochemist; b. Winnebago, Ill., Jan. 18, 1940; s. Wallace Calvin and Margaret Wright (Clinite) C.; m. Katrina Sue Susdorf, Feb. 27, 1965; children—Jennifer Ruth, Douglas James. B.S., U. Dubuque, 1962; Ph.D., Yale U., 1966. NSF postdoctoral fellow Rockefeller U., N.Y.C., 1966-68, asst. prof. biochemistry, 1968-71, assoc. prof., 1971-77, prof. molecular and devel. biology, 1978—. Editorial bd.: Jour. Biol. Chemistry, 1978-83. Camille and Henry Dreyfus Found. grantee, 1970-75; recipient Career Scientist award Irma T. Hirschl Trust, 1975. Mem. Am. Soc. Biol. Chemists, Am. Assn. Immunologists, Am. Chem. Soc., Harvey Soc. Democrat. Lutheran. Research on structure and function of molecules on cell surfaces. Office: 1230 York Ave New York NY 10021

CUNNINGHAM, CARL ROBERT, music critic, educator; b. Los Angeles, Oct. 21, 1931; s. William Clement and Ruth (George) C. Mus.B., U. Notre Dame, 1952; M.A., U. So. Calif., 1965. Instr. piano and theory Punahou Sch., Honolulu, 1960-63; lectr. music theory U. Hawaii, 1962-63; choir dir. Sacred Heart Cath. Ch., Honolulu, 1959-63; music critic San Francisco Chronicle, 1965-66; music editor Houston Post, 1966—; spl. lectr. music U. St. Thomas, Houston, 1968-70, chmn. dept., 1970-76, asso. prof. music, 1976—. Served with USN, 1952-56. Rockefeller Found. fellow, 1964-66. Address: 4747 Southwest Freeway Houston TX 77001

CUNNINGHAM, SISTER CATHARINE JULIE, college president; b. San Francisco, Oct. 22, 1910; d. John Francis and Mary Cecilia (McCarthy) C. B.A., U. Calif.-Berkeley, 1932; M.A., Catholic U. Am., 1954; L.H.D. (hon.), U. San Francisco, 1978. Mem. Sisters of Notre Dame de Namur, 1932—; prin. high sch., 1942-56; pres. Coll. of Notre Dame, Belmont, Calif., 1956-80, chancellor, 1981—, also trustee. Trustee, Roman Catholic Seminary Corp., San Francisco. Address: 1500 Ralston Ave Belmont CA 94002

CUNNINGHAM, CHARLES BANKER, III, manufacturing company executive; b. St. Louis, Oct. 1, 1941; s. Charles Baker C. and Mary Blythe (Cunningham); m. Georganne Rose, Sept. 17, 1966; children: Margaret B., Charles B. IV. B.S., Washington U., St. Louis, 1964; M.S., Ga. Inst. Tech., 1966; M.B.A., Harvard U., 1970. Dir. fin. The Cooper Group, Raleigh, N.C., 1972-75, v.p. adminstrn., 1975-77; v.p. devel. Cooper Industries Inc., Houston, 1977-79, v.p. ops., 1980-82, exec. v.p., 1982—; pres. Indsl. Equipment Group, 1979-80. Dir. Sam Houston council Boy Scouts Am., Houston, 1981—. Served to 1st lt. U.S. Army, 1966-68; Iran. Decorated Army Commendation medal. Office: Cooper Industries Inc PO Box 4446 Houston TX 77210

CUNNINGHAM, CLARK EDWARD, anthropology educator; b. Kansas City, Mo., Mar. 13, 1934; s. John Stephen and Mary Elizabeth (Brown) C.; m. Ritva Aulikki Kokko, June 2, 1969; children: Nathalie Noëlle, Eric Stephen. B.A., Yale, 1957; B.Litt. (Rhodes scholar), U. Oxford, Eng., 1959, D.Phil., 1963. Research asso., vis. lectr. anthropology Yale, New Haven, Conn., 1963, 65-68; vis. asst. prof. U. Ill., Urbana, 1963-64, asso. prof., 1968-72, prof., 1972—; vis. asso. prof. Chiang Mai U., Thailand, 1968-70; project specialist Ford Found., Ujung Pandang, Indonesia, 1975-76. Author: The Postwar Migration of the Toba-Batak to East Sumatra, 1958; Co-editor: Studies of Health Problems and Health Behavior in Saraphi, North Thailand, 1970, Symbolism and Cognition, 1981; contbr. articles to profl. jours. Mem. state, regional selection coms. Rhodes Scholarship, 1973-75, 77-79. Recipient Hatch prize Yale, 1957; Am. Council of Learned Socs. grantee; Population Council grantee; Ford Found. grantee; Wenner-Gren Found. grantee; Midwest Univs. Consortium Internat. Activities grantee; Smithsonian Instn. grantee. Fellow Am. Anthrop. Assn., Koninklijk Inst. voor Taal, Land- en Volkenkunde, AAAS, Royal Anthrop. Inst.; mem. Assn. Social Anthropologists of U.K. and Commonwealth, Assn. Asian Studies. Home: 602 Eliot Dr Urbana IL 61801

CUNNINGHAM, DOROTHY JANE, educator; b. Jersey City, Nov. 7, 1927; d. John Henry and Alice Geraldine (McCabe) C. A.B., Caldwell Coll., 1949; M.S., Cath. U., 1951; Ph.D., Yale U., 1966. Asst. prof. dept. biol. scis. Montclair (N.J.) State Coll., 1958-62; postdoctoral research fellow Yale U. Sch. Medicine, New Haven, 1966-67, lectr. environ. physiology, 1967-79, asst. prof. epidemiology (environ. physiology), 1969-70; asso. prof. physiology Sch. Health Scis., Hunter Coll., City U. N.Y., 1970-75, prof., 1975—; lectr. div. environ. medicine, dept. community medicine Mt. Sinai Sch. Medicine, 1971-82; adj. prof. environ. medicine Inst. Environ. Medicine, N.Y. U. Med. Center, 1981—; Trustee Caldwell Coll., 1971-77; chmn. com. on Grad. Sch., Yale U. Council, 1981—; vis. fellow environ. health Yale U. Sch. Medicine and John B. Pierce Found. Lab., 1982-83. Editorial bd.: The Sciences, 1978—. Fellow N.Y. Acad. Scis. (v.p. 1977-81), N.Y. Acad. Medicine (asso.); mem. Am. Physiol. Soc., Harvey Soc., Am. Fedn. for Clin. Research, AAAS, Soc. for Occupational and Environ. Health, Yale Sci. and Engring. Assn. (exec. bd. 1975-82, v.p. met. dist. 1982—), Assn. of Yale Alumni (gov. 1979-82), Sigma Xi (pres. Hunter Coll. chpt. 1980-82, grants-in-aid of research com. 1979—). Office: Sch Health Scis Hunter Coll City U NY 440 E 26th St New York NY 10010

CUNNINGHAM, EMORY O., publishing company executive; b. Kansas, Ala., Mar. 17, 1921; s. Emory O. and Belle (Kelly) C.; m. Jeanne Loftis, Dec. 21, 1951; children: James Emory, David Lee, Sara Jeanne, Mary Lou. B.S. in Agrl. Sci, Auburn U., 1948, D.Sc. (hon.), 1981, L.H.D., U. Ala., 1980. Pres. So. Progress Corp. (formerly Progressive Farmer Co.), pubs. Progressive Farmer, So. Living, Decorating & Craft Ideas mags., Oxmoor House books, 1968—; dir. SouthTrust, Ala. Gas Corp., SouthTrust Corp., Saunders Leasing System. Adv. bd. Boy Scouts Am.; trustee Birmingham Symphony, Ida Cason Callaway Found., Ala. Assn. Ind. Colls., So. Research Inst.; bd. dirs. Birmingham Met. Devel. Bd., Ala. 4-H Club Found.; chmn. press adv. com. U. Ala.; mem. adv. com. Auburn U. Sch. Agr.; mem. adv. bd. Salvation Army.; mem. sponsors adv. bd. Future Farmers Am. Found. Recipient Man of Yr. award Birmingham Advt. Club, 1971; Hall of Fame award Miss. Gulf Coast Jr. Coll., 1973; Man of Yr. in Service to Agr. award Birmingham C. of C., 1975; Ala. Acad. Honor, 1977; Man of Yr. in So. Advt. award, 1976; Communicator of Yr. award Internat. Sales and Mktg. Execs., 1978; Ala. Free Enterprise award Nat. Farm-City Week Com., 1979; Holly Mitchell award Ala. chpt. Am. Soc. Landscape Architects, 1980; Man of South award Dixie Bus. Mag., 1980; Discover Am. travel award; Emory Cunningham Day named in his honor Birmingham Audubon Soc. Mem. Agrl. Pubs. Assn. (past pres., dir.), Mag. Pubs. Assn. (dir., sec. exec. com., vice chmn., Henry Johnson Fisher award 1975), Newcomen Soc. N.Am. (chmn. Ala. 1977), Birmingham C. of C. (dir.). Office: 820 Shades Creek Pkwy Birmingham AL 35209 also PO Box 2581 Birmingham AL 35202

CUNNINGHAM, GEORGE CHRISTOPHER, pediatrician, public health administrator; b. San Francisco, July 25, 1930; s. George C. and Frances (Watt) C.; m. Judith Ann Little, Dec. 28, 1958 (dec. Sept. 1980); childrn: Michael, Eric, Kerry Ann. B.S. in Biology, U. San Francisco, 1952; postgrad., U. So. Calif., 1952-53; M.D., UCLA, 1959; M.P.H., U. Calif.-Berkeley, 1968. Diplomate: Am. Bd. Pediatrics. Peidatrics intern UCLA, 1959-60; resident in pediatrics Children's Hosp. of East Bay, 1960-62, research staff fellow, 1962-65; practice medicine specializing in pediatrics, Oakland, Calif., 1962-65, practice medicine specializing in preventive medicine, 1965—; chief hereditary defects unit Bur. Maternal and Child Health, Calif. Dept. Pub. Health, Berkeley, 1966-68, chief maternal and child health br., Sacramento, 1969-77, chief genetic disease sect., 1977—; assoc. pediatrician U. Calif. Med. Ctr., San Francisco, 1970—; cons. NRC, Office Tech. Assessment, U.S. Senate, Children's Def. Fund. Contbr. articles on pediatrics to profl. jours. Nat. adv. com. Allan Gutmacher Inst., N.Y.C., 1972-81; bd. dirs. Calif. Interagy. Council on Family Planning, 1970-85, Am. Parents Com., 1970-76. Recipient Outstanding Services award Calif. Rural Indian Health Bd., 1971, Outstanding Human Services award Calif. Human Services Orgn., 1975, Calif. Dietitians award, 1978. Fellow Am. Acad. Pediatrics; mem. Am. Assn. Maternal and Child Health (dir. 1972-73), East Bay Pediatric Soc., Calif. Assn. Maternal and Child Health (pres. 1972-73, Leadership award 1974), Nat. Assn. Interns and Residents, Am. Pub. Health Assn., AAAS, Assn. State Maternal and Child Health and Crippled Children Dirs. (pres. 1973-76), Oakland Mus. Assn., East Bay Bot. and Zool. Soc., Sigma Chi. Democrat.

CUNNINGHAM, GEORGE WOODY, business exec.; b. Union City, Tenn., Dec. 3, 1930; s. Mose Marshall and Zula Ethel (Easterwood) C.; m. Patricia G. Pate, Dec. 31, 1954; children—John, Ann. B.S. in Chem. Engring, U. Tenn., 1954, M.S. in Metallurgy, 1955; Ph.D. in Metall. Engring, Ohio State U., 1960. Prin. metall. engr. Battelle Meml. Inst., Columbus, Ohio, 1955-58, project leader, 1958-60, asst. div. cons., 1960-62, research asso., 1962-64, chief materials thermodynamics div., 1965-66; mem. fuels and materials br. div. reactor devel. and tech. AEC, Washington, 1966-68, dep. chief fuels and materials br., 1969-70, chief liquid metal projects br., 1970-73, asst. dir. engring. and tech., 1973-75; dep. dir. tech. ERDA, Washington, 1975-76; dir. div. waste mgmt., program dir. for nuclear energy Dept. Energy, 1977-78; counselor atomic energy U.S. Mission to IAEA, Vienna, 1978-79; asst. sec. for nuclear energy Dept. of Energy, 1980-81; dir. nuclear studies Mitre Corp., McLean, Va., 1981—; mem. Am. del. Internat. Working Group on Fast Reactors, 1976; chmn. U.S.-U.K. Libby-Cockcroft Exchange on Ceramic Fuels, 1967, AEC High Temperature Fuels Working Group, 1967, U.S. Fast Breeder Reactor Team Visit Japan, 1971, U.S.-USSR Coordinating Com. on Fast Reactors, 1976. Contbr. articles to profl. jours. Mem. Am. Soc. Metals, Sigma Xi, Tau Beta Pi, Lambda Chi Upsilon., Alpha Chi Sigma. Home: 7025 Sulky Ln Rockville MD 20852 Office: The Mitre Corp 1820 Dolley Madison Blvd McLean VA 22102

CUNNINGHAM, GLENN CLARENCE, govt. ofcl.; b. Omaha, Sept. 10, 1912; s. George Warner and Emma (Seefus) C.; m. Janis Thelen, July 25, 1941; children—Glenn Clarence, Judith, Mary, James Robert, David George, Ann Melissa. A.B., U. Omaha, 1935. Mgr. Jr. C. of C., Omaha, 1937-40, pres., 1945-46; mgr. Convention Bur., Omaha C. of C., 1941, Omaha Safety Council, 1941-47; Mem. 85th-91st Congresses, 2d Nebr. dist.; asst. to dir. Bur. Outdoor Recreation, Dept. Interior, Washington, 1971—; Fire commr., also mem. bd. edn., City of Omaha, 1947-48, mayor, 1948-54; del. Republican Nat. Conv., 1948, 52; Nebr. dir. U.S. Savs. Bond div. U.S. Treasury, 1954-56; bd. govs. Met. Tech. Community Coll., 1976—. Decorated Legion of Honor, Order of De Molay.; Named Omaha's Outstanding Young Man, 1945, Nebr. Outstanding Young Man, 1945. Mem. U. Omaha Alumni Assn., Pi Kappa Alpha. Republican. Episcopalian. Home: 6421 Glenwood Rd Omaha NE 68132

CUNNINGHAM, HARRY BLAIR, retired retail executive; b. Home Camp, Pa., July 23, 1907; s. Ezra James and Jane (Farley) C.; m. Margaret Diefendorf, Aug. 28, 1935; children: Jane (Mrs. William Herrington), Sally (Mrs. Gary Downey), Ann (Mrs. James A. Glime). Student, Miami U., Oxford, Ohio, 1925-27; D.B.A., Hillsdale (Mich.) College, 1963; LL.D., Tri-State Coll., 1967, Miami U., 1969. Reporter Harrisburg (Pa.) Patriot, 1927-28; with S.S. Kresge Co., Detroit, various exec. tng. and mgmt. positions including store mgr. and supt. stores, 1928-50, asst. sales dir., 1951-52, sales dir., 1953-57, gen. v.p., 1957-59, pres., chief exec. officer, 1959-67, chmn. bd., chief exec. officer, 1967-72, chmn. exec. com., 1972, hon. chmn. bd., 1973-77; hon. chmn. K-Mart Corp., 1977—, also dir.; dir. Nat. Steel Corp., NBD of Fla. Trustee Citizens' Research Council. Mem. Delta Upsilon. Presbyterian. Clubs: Orchard Lake Country (Birmingham, Mich.); Detroit; Lost Tree, Everglades (Palm Beach, Fla.); Bloomfield Hills (Mich.) Country. Home: 210 Lowell Ct Bloomfield Hills MI 48013 also 1887 Pine Ridge Ln Bloomfield Hills MI 48013

CUNNINGHAM, JACQUES, resource mgmt. exec.; b. Oklahoma City, June 22, 1920; s. Morrison B. and Lucy (Weaver) C.; m. Theda Mae Harrell, July 21, 1942; children—Jacqueline, Jacques H. B.S. in Bus. Adminstrn, Okla. State U., 1942. Personnel supr. Am. Airlines, Inc., Tulsa, 1946-48; indsl. mgr. Tulsa C. of C., 1948-54; v.p. Pub. Service Co. Okla., 1954-78; pres. Resource Mgmt. Co., Tulsa, 1978-80; port dir. Tulsa Port of Catoosa, 1980—. Author: Analysis of Industrial Foundations, 1949, Machine Tool Inventory—Tulsa Industry, 1950, (with Jack Story Jr.) Inland Waterways Port Analysis, 1962. Chmn. City of Tulsa-Rogers County Port Authority, 1963-65, Port of Catoosa Facilities Authority, 1969—; pres. Downtown Tulsa, Unltd., 1971; mem. City of Tulsa Econ. Devel. Commn., 1970-78, Okla. Gov.'s Com. on River Planning, 1970; pres. Ark. Basin Devel. Assn., 1972-73; mem. Okla. Water Resources Bd., 1972-78; pres. N.W. Passage Turnpike Assn., 1972-73; Okla. commr. Kans.-Okla. Arkansas River Commn., 1973—; mem. Gov.'s Econ. Devel. Mini-Cabinet, 1980—; bd. dirs. Water Resources Congress, 1971—. Served to capt. USAAF, 1942-45; Served to capt. USAF, 1951-52. Recipient Gold Knight award Nat. Mgmt. Assn., 1969. Mem. Sigma Alpha Epsilon. Democrat. Methodist (steward). Clubs: Mason (Shriner), Rotary, Propeller (nat. v.p. 1971). Home: 6725 S Gary St Tulsa OK 74136 Office: 5350 Cimarron Rd Catoosa OK 74015

CUNNINGHAM, JAMES GERALD, JR., transportation company executive; b. Morristown, N.J., Aug. 5, 1930; s. James Gerald and Kathryn Virginia (Cannon) C.; m. Marilyn Swanson, Sept. 22, 1956; children: Kathleen, Jean Marie, Barbara, James Gerald, III, Carl. B.S. in Civil Engring, Newark Coll. Engring., 1952. Civil engr. Pa. R.R., 1952-54; trainmaster Erie-Lackawanna R.R., 1956-62; div. mgr., dir. transp. Consol. Freightways, Menlo Park, Calif., 1962-69; sr. v.p., dir. REA Express, Inc., N.Y.C., 1969-75; also dir. REA Holding Corp.; pres., dir. Gateway Transp. Co., La Crosse, Wis., 1976-78; gen. mgr. intermodal ops. Consol. Rail Corp., Phila., 1978-79; pres., chief exec. officer Pa. Truck Lines Inc., Phila., 1980—. Served with Transp. Corps AUS, 1953-55. Mem. Assn. Am. Railroads (intermodal steering com.), Equipment Interchange Assn. (exec. com., past pres.), Intermodal Transp. Assn. (pres.). Clubs: N.Y. Athletic, Union League of Phila. Home: 3505 St Davids Rd Newtown Square PA 19073 Office: Six Penn Center Philadelphia PA 19104

CUNNINGHAM, JAMES VINCENT, poet; b. Cumberland, Md., Aug. 23, 1911; s. James Joseph and Anna Mattingly (Finan) C.; m. Barbara Francesca Gibbs, June 18, 1937 (div. 1942); 1 dau., Marjorie Ann (Mrs. George Lupien); m. Dolora Gallagher, Mar. 26, 1945 (div. 1949); m. Jessie MacGregor Campbell, June 3, 1950. Student, St. Mary's (Kans.) Coll., 1928; A.B., Stanford, 1934, Ph.D., 1945. Instr. Stanford, 1937-45; asst. prof. U. Hawaii, 1945-46, U. Chgo., 1946-52, U. Va., 1952-53; asso. prof. then prof. English Brandeis U., Waltham, Mass., 1953—, Univ. prof., 1976-80, emeritus, 1980—, chmn. dept., 1953-59, 61-62, 68-69, chmn., 1960-61, 70-71; Vis. prof. Harvard, 1952, U. Wash., 1956, Ind. U., 1961, U. Calif. at Santa Barbara, 1963, Washington U., St. Louis, 1976. Author: The Helmsman, 1942, The Judge is Fury, 1947, Doctor Drink, 1950, The Quest of the Opal, 1950, Woe or Wonder; The Emotional Effect of Shakespearean Tragedy, 1951, The Exclusions of a Rhyme: Poems and Epigrams, 1960, Tradition and Poetic Structure, 1960, The Journal of John Cardan, 1964, To What Strangers, What Welcome, 1964, The Renaissance in England, 1967, The Collected Poems and Epigrams, 1971, Collected Essays, 1977, Dickinson: Lyric and Legend, 1980. Guggenheim fellow, 1959-60, 67; Nat. Endowment for Arts grantee, 1966-67. Home: 17 Singletary Ln Sudbury MA 01776 Office: Dept English Brandeis Univ Waltham MA 02254

CUNNINGHAM, JOHN FRANCIS, computer company executive; b. Boston, Mar. 5, 1943; s. William J. and Rose L. (Mulhern) C.; m. Ellen M. Condon, June 25, 1966; children: Christopher, Erin, Trisha. B.A., Boston Coll., 1964; M.B.A., Amos Tuck Sch., Dartmouth Coll., 1966. V.p. mktg. Wang Labs., Inc., Lowell, Mass., 1972-76, sr. v.p., 1976-83, pres., chief operating officer, 1983—, dir.; trustee Wang Inst. Grad. Studies, Lowell; bd. dirs. Comml. Club, Boston. Bd. dirs. Boys & Girls Club Boston, Catholic Charitable Bur., Boston; bd. overseers Amos Tuck Sch., Dartmouth Coll., Hanover, N.Y.; trustee Boston Coll. Roman Catholic. Club: Weston Golf (Mass.). Office: Wang Labs Inc One Industrial Ave Lowell MA 01851

CUNNINGHAM, JULIA WOOLFOLK, author; b. Spokane, Oct. 4, 1916; d. John George and Sue (Larabie) C. Grad., St. Anne's Sch., Charlottesville, Va., 1933. Author: (juveniles): The Vision of Francois the Fox, 1960, Dear Rat, 1961, Macaroon, 1962, Candle Tales, 1964, Dorp Dead, 1965 (Children's Spring Book Festival award), Violet, 1966, Onion Journey, 1967, Burnish Me Bright, 1970, Wings of the Morning, 1971, Far in the Day, 1972, The Treasure Is the Rose, 1973, Maybe, A Mole, 1974, Come to the Edge, 1977, Tuppenny, 1978 (Christoper award 1978), A Mouse called Junction, 1980, Flight of the Sparrow, 1980 (Commonwealth Club Calif. award, Honor Book award Boston Globe), The Silent Voice, 1981, Wolf Roland, 1983. Mem. Authors Guild. Home: 33 W Valerio St Santa Barbara CA 93101

CUNNINGHAM, KEITH ALLEN, mining and manufacturing company executive; b. Weaver, W.Va., Aug. 21, 1922; s. James Arthur and Blanche (Proudfoot) C.; m. Jeanne Antoinette Viquesney, June 6, 1942; children: Keith Allen, Kathe Jan. B.S. in Bus. Adminstrn, W.Va. U., 1948, J.D., 1951. Bar: W.Va. 1951; C.P.A., Mich., Ohio, N.Y., Ind., La. Bldg. constrn. engr. Gibbs & Hills, Inc., N.Y.C., 1942-43; practiced law in, Belington, 1952; asso. Touche, Niven, Bailey & Smart (C.P.A.'s), Detroit, 1952-60; partner-in-charge Dayton (Ohio) office Touche, Ross, Bailey & Smart, 1960-65, dir. adminstrn. and office ops., 1965-67, exec. adminstrv. partner, vice chmn. bd. dirs., 1967-70; pres. Energy Conversion Devices, Inc., Troy, Mich., 1969-72, dir., 1969-74; exec. v.p. United Nuclear Corp., Falls Church, Va., 1973-75, pres., chief exec. officer, 1975—, chmn., 1982—, also dir.; lectr. W.Va. Tax Inst. Mem. Council for Reorgn. Ohio State Govt., 1963-64; treas. Mich. Employers Unemployment Compensation Bur., 1957-60; mem. advisory com. Mich. Security Commn., 1958-60. Served with USAAF, 1943-46. Mem. Am. Accounting Assn., Nat. Assn. Accountants, Am. Inst. C.P.A.'s, Mich. Soc. C.P.A.'s, Ohio Soc. C.P.A.'s (dir.), N.Y. Soc. C.P.A.'s, N.J. Soc. C.P.A.'s, Mich., W.Va. state bars, Detroit Bar Assn., Phi Beta Kappa, Phi Delta Phi. Methodist. Clubs: Mining (N.Y.C.); Detroit Athletic, Petroleum, Albuquerque Country, Congressional Country; Farmington Country (Charlottesville, Va.). Home: 12208 Meadow Creek Ct Potomac MD 20854 Office: UNC Crescent Plaza 7700 Leesburg Pike Falls Church VA 22043

CUNNINGHAM, KENNETH WAYNE, manufacturing company executive; b. Sandyville, Ohio, Jan. 12, 1919; s. Leroy Reed and Mary Ada (Johnston) C.; m. Miriam Katherine Schreiner, July 18, 1942; children: Sandra Kay, Carol Anne, Daniel David. Student, Canton Actual Bus. Coll., 1936-38. Cost acct. Monarch Rubber Co., Hartville, Ohio, 1936-41; with Ohio Ferro-Alloys Corp., Canton, 1945—, v.p. prodn., 1954-74, exec. v.p., 1974-76, pres., 1976—, dir.; dir. Citizens Savs. Assn., Canton. Served with AUS, 1941-46. Decorated Bronze star. Mem. Am. Soc. Metals, Ferro-Alloys Assn., Ala. Indsl. Group. Republican. Clubs: Congress Lake Country, Bob-o'Link Golf, Elks. Home: 2201 Applegrove Rd NW North Canton OH 44720 Office: 839 30th St Canton OH 44709

CUNNINGHAM, LEON WILLIAM, biochemist, educator; b. Columbus, Ga., June 9, 1927; s. Leon W. and Annie (Bussey) C.; m. Jean Swingle, Aug. 21, 1948; children—Hugh, Pamela, Sue Ellen. B.S., Auburn U., 1947; M.S., U. Ill., 1949, Ph.D., 1951. Research fellow protein chemistry U. Wash., Seattle, 1951-53; asst. prof. biochemistry Sch. Medicine, Vanderbilt U., Nashville, 1953-60, asso. prof., 1960-65, prof., 1965—, asso. dean, 1967-73, chmn. dept. biochemistry, 1973—; vis. staff Nat. Inst. for Med. Research, London, 1976; vis. prof. physiol. chemistry U. Utrecht, Netherlands, 1980. Served with USNR, 1945-46. USPHS spl. fellow Netherlands Nat. Def. Orgn., 1961-62. Mem. AAAS, N.Y. Acad. Sci., Chem. Soc., Soc. Biol. Chemistry. Home: 4619 Shys Hill Rd Nashville TN 37215

CUNNINGHAM, MARCUS EDDY, engineering executive; b. Lynn, Mass., Jan. 16, 1907; s. Daniel and Susie (Goad) C.; m. Mary Eloise Baird, Feb. 14, 1931 (dec. Nov. 1964); children: Charles Baird, Marcus Eddy; m. Marilyn A. Eneix, Oct. 1, 1966. B.S., Yale U., 1928; postgrad., Boston U., 1929. Gen. supt. Daniel Cunningham Constrn. Co., Boston, 1928-32, Austin Co., Cleve., 1932-40; pres., treas., dir. Brady Hill Co., Detroit, 1940—, Cunningham-Limp Co., 1948-70, chmn. bd., chief exec. officer, treas., dir., 1970-78, chmn. bd.; pres., treas., dir. Cunningham-Limp, Ltd., Toronto, Ont., Can., 1959—; chmn. bd., pres. Cunningham-Limp de las Americas, S.A., 1966—, Cunningham-Limp Internat., 1963—, Cunningham-Limp de Espana, 1966—, Cunningham-Limp (France) S.A.R.L., 1967-78, Cunningham-Limp Deutschland GmbH, 1970-78; chmn. bd., chief exec. officer, pres. Cunningham-Limp Holding Co., 1978—. Vice pres., dir. Gulfstream Park Racing Assn., Hallandale, Fla., 1963—; Bd. dirs. Detroit, Nat. councils Boy Scouts Am. Mem. Engring. Soc. Detroit, A.I.M. (pres.' council). Clubs: Yale (Detroit); Bloomfield Hills (Mich.) Country; Oakland Hills Country (Birmingham, Mich.); Indian Creek Country, Jockey (Miami Beach, Fla.); Kenilworth (Bal Harbour, Fla.); Le Mirador Country (Mont Pelerin, Lake Geneva, Switzerland). *

CUNNINGHAM, MARILYN ALICE ENEIX, advertising executive; b. Warren, Minn., Mar. 8, 1917; d. Frederick C. and Mary (Boman) Eneix; m. Marcus E. Cunningham, Oct. 1, 1966. B.A., U. Mich., 1937. Account supr. Grant Advt., Inc., Detroit, Chgo. and N.Y.C., 1945-60; dir. advt. Cunningham-Limp Co., Detroit, 1960-69, v.p., dir., Birmingham, Mich., 1969-72; vice chmn. bd., dir., 1972-78, Cunningham-Limp Holding Co., 1978—; v.p., dir. Brady Hill Co., Detroit, 1960—; vice chmn. bd., v.p., dir. Cunningham-Limp Internat., 1971—; vice-chmn. bd., dir. Cunningham-Limp de Las Americas, 1972—, Cunningham-Limp Ltd., 1972—. Author: The Right Plant on the Right Site for Maximum Profit, 1962, The Comprehensive Approach to Facility Expansion, 1967, Design and Engineering, 1970, The Facility Planning Services of Cunningham-Limp, 1973, Total Responsibility in Facility Expansion, 1975, Planning, Designing, Engineering and Building, 1976, Design-Engineering-Construction, 1977, Comprehensive Design, Engineering and Construction, 1978; Contbr. articles to profl. jours.; Author, pub.: SCOPE mag. Active civic, philanthropic activities. Mem. Fine Arts Soc. Detroit (Silver Anniversary mem.), Alpha Phi. Republican. Presbyn. Clubs: Kenilworth (Bal Harbour, Fla.); Jockey (Miami Beach, Fla.); Le Mirador Country (Switzerland). Home: Ocean Blvd Golden Beach FL 33160 Office: Kenilworth Condominium 10205 Collins Ave Bal Harbour FL 33154 Office: 1400 N Woodward Ave Birmingham MI 48011

CUNNINGHAM, MELVIN EUGENE, hospital administrator; b. Milw., Apr. 2, 1931; s. Melville E. and Nettie Ethel (Weston) C.; m. Ethel Christine Paulsen, July 18, 1959; children: Cynthia, Lisa, Lynda. Student, Trinity Bible Coll., 1954-55; B.S., No. Ariz. U., 1958; M.H.A., Washington U., St. Louis, 1964. Caseworker Cook County (Ill.) Welfare Dept., 1958; agt. IRS, Chgo., 1958-62; mem. hosp. adminstr. program Washington U., 1962-64; with Good Samaritan Hosp., Phoenix, 1963-73, asst. adminstrn., 1966-69, asso. adminstr., 1969-73; v.p., chief exec. officer Maryvale Samaritan Hosp., Phoenix, 1973—. Served with USAF, 1950-53. Recipient Service Citation award Samaritan Health Service, 1976, Distinguished Pub. Service medal Maricopa County (Ariz.) Med. Soc., 1976, Sammy award, 1983. Mem. Am. Coll. Hosp. Adminstrs., Ariz. Hosp. Assn. (pres. elect). Club: Optimists. Home: 2001 W Coolbrook St Phoenix AZ 85023 Office: 5102 W Campbell St Phoenix AZ 85031

CUNNINGHAM, MERCE, dancer; b. Centralia, Wash. Student, Cornish Inst. Allied Arts; hon. doctorate, U. Ill. Own dance co., 1953—; tchr. Sch. Am. Ballet, 1949-50; propr. own dance sch., N.Y.C., 1959—. Soloist, Martha Graham Co., 1939-45; 1st solo concert, 1944, several tours, U.S., Europe, 1949, 58, 60, 66, 69, 70, 72, 76, 77, 79-84, world tour, 1964, S.Am., 1968, 76, 82, Mideast, 1972, 76, Australia and Japan, 1976, Far East, 1984; prin. works choreographed include The Seasons, 1947, Sixteen Dances for Soloist and Company of Three, 1951, Septet, 1953, Minutiae, 1954, Suite for Five, 1956, Nocturnes, 1956, Antic Meet, 1958, Summerspace, 1958, Rune, 1959, Crises, 1960, Aeon, 1961, Story, 1963, Winterbranch, 1964, Variations V, 1965, How to Pass, Kick, Fall, and Run, 1965, Place, 1966, Scramble, 1967, RainForest, 1968, Walkaround Time, 1968, Canfield, 1969, Tread, 1970, Second Hand, 1970, Signals, 1970, Landrover, 1972, Changing Steps, 1973, Solo, 1973, Un Jour ou Deux, 1973, Sounddance, 1974, Rebus, 1975, Torse, Squaregame, 1976, Travelogue, 1977, Inlets, 1977, Fractions, 1977, Exchange, 1978, Locale, 1979, Duets, 1980, Fielding Sixes, 1980, Channels/Inserts, 1981, Trails, 1982, Quartet, 1982, Coast Zone, 1983, Roaratorio, 1983, Pictures, 1984. Decorated comdr. Order of Arts and Letters (France); recipient medal Soc. Advancement Dance in Sweden, 1964, Gold medal Internat. Festival Dance, 1966; Grand prix Belgrade Internat. Theatre Festival, 1972; Wash. State award, 1977; Creative Arts award Brandeis U., 1973; Capezio award, 1977; Samuel H. Scripps/Am. Dance Festival award, 1982; N.Y.C. Mayor's award of honor for arts and culture, 1983; Guggenheim fellow, 1954, 59. Mem. Am. Acad. and Inst. Arts and Letters (hon.). Office: 463 West St New York NY 10014

CUNNINGHAM, MORRIS, newspaperman; b. McMinnville, Tenn., July 27, 1917; s. Oscar Lafayette and Jessie Lee (Crawford) C.; m. Helen Henry Morris, Oct. 25, 1947; children: Diane, Morris Frank. Corr., state news editor, state capitol reporter Nashville Tennessean, 1935-43; reporter, news editor A.P., Nashville and N.Y.C., 1943-45; corr. Time, Life, Fortune mags., Nashville, 1945-53; Nashville corr. Memphis Comml. Appeal, 1945-53, Washington corr., 1953-78, bur. chief, 1978-84; Adv. com. tng. tchrs. deaf Office Edn., 1962-64. Mem. White House Corrs. Assn., State Dept. Corrs. Assn., Overseas Writers, Tenn. Squires, A.G. Bell Assn. for Deaf, Sigma Delta Chi. Methodist. Clubs: Kenwood Golf and Country; National Press (Washington). Home: 6002 Woodacres Dr Bethesda MD 20816

CUNNINGHAM, PATRICK JOSEPH, advt. agy. exec.; b. Kenosha, Wis., June 15, 1943; s. Patrick Joseph and Beatrice Mary (Ryan) C.; m. Ann Allen, June 29, 1968; children—Michael Patrick, Jennifer Ann. B.S., U. Wis., 1965. Copy supr. Lawler Ballard Little Advt., Norfolk, Va., 1969-70; Bonsib Advt., Ft. Wayne, Ind., 1970-72; with N.W. Ayer ABH Internat., N.Y.C., 1972—; exec. v.p., dir. creative services, 1980—, also dir. Served to lt. (j.g.) USNR, 1966-69. Recipient Clio award, 1973, 75, 76, 78, 79, Internat. Broadcasting award, 1973-75, 77, 78, Anny award, 1976, 78, 79. Mem. U. Wis. Alumni Assn., Evans Scholars Assn., Les Amis du Vin. Office: 1345 Ave Americas New York NY 10105

CUNNINGHAM, R. JOHN, consultant; b. Detroit, May 1, 1926; s. Richard John and Mary Gladys (Lahey) C.; m. Dorothy A. Clair, Nov. 29, 1947; children—Karen A., Richard J., William J., Patricia A., Cathy A., Kevin P., Maryann. Ph.B. in Commerce, U. Notre Dame, 1950; M.B.A., N.Y. U., 1954. Sr. v.p. Midwest Stock Exchange, Chgo., 1966-68; exec. v.p. New York Stock Exchange, 1968-71; dir. financial services Arthur Young & Co., N.Y.C., 1971-76; sr. v.p. Federated Dept. Stores, Inc., Cin., 1976-81; cons. Arthur D. Little, Inc., Cambridge, Mass., 1981—; chmn. adv. com. SEC Report Coordinating Group, 1974-76. Mem. Pres.'s Council, U. Notre Dame, 1968-75; mem. Parents Council, St. Marys Coll., South Bend, Ind., 1972-74. Served with AUS, 1944-47. Recipient certificate of appreciation U.S. SEC, 1975, SEC Report Coordinating Group, 1976; named Man of Year Chgo. Assn. Investment Bankers, 1967. Mem. Am. Mgmt. Assn. Club: City Midday (N.Y.C.). Home: 110 Hutchinson Rd Arlington MA 02174 Office: Acorn Park Cambridge MA 02140

CUNNINGHAM, R. WALTER, company executive; b. Creston, Iowa, Mar. 16, 1932; s. Walter Wilfred and Gladys (Backen) C.; m. Lo Ella Irby, July 8, 1956; children: Brian Keith, Kimberly Ann. B.S. in Physics, UCLA, 1960, M.A., 1961. Research asst. Planning Research Corp., Westwood, Calif., 1959-60; physicist RAND Corp., Santa Monica, Calif., 1960-64; astronaut NASA, 1964-71; crew member of first manned Apollo spacecraft Apollo 7; sr. v.p. Century Devel., 1971-74; pres. Hydrotech Devel. Co., Houston, 1974-76; sr. v.p. 3D/ Internat., Houston, 1976-79; founder The Capital Group, Houston, 1979—; dir. Nitron Inc. Author: The All American Boys, 1977. Served with USNR, 1951-52; as fighter pilot USMCR, 1952-56; col. Res. Recipient NASA Exceptional Service medal, also; Haley Astronautics award; Profl. Achievement award U. Calif. at Los Angeles Alumni, 1969; Spl. Trustee award Nat. Acad. Television Arts and Scis., 1969; medal of valor Am. Legion, 1975; Outstanding Am. award Am. Conservative Union, 1975. Fellow Am. Astronautical Soc.; mem. Soc. Exptl. Test Pilots, Am. Inst. Aeros. and Astronautics, Am. Geophys. Union, Sigma Pi Sigma. Office: The Capital Group 505 Stuart St Houston TX 77006

CUNNINGHAM, RALPH SANFORD, oil company executive; b. Albany, Ohio, Oct. 16, 1940; s. Harold Sanford and Julia Marie (Lasch) C.; m. Deborah Elaine Brookshire, Dec. 23, 1976; children: Ralph Sanford, Susan Ellen, Stephen Earl, Jennifer Marie. B.S. in Chem. Engring, Auburn (Ala.) U., 1962; M.S., Ohio State U., 1962, Ph.D., 1966. With Exxon Co. U.S.A., 1966-80, refinery mgr., Benicia, Calif., 1977-80; exec. v.p. processing and mktg. Tenneco Oil Co., Houston, 1980—; dir. IT Corp., Petro-Tex Chem. Corp. Chmn. United Way Solano-Napa Counties, Calif., 1979; exec. council, v.p. Silverado council Boy Scouts Am., 1978-79. Mem. Am. Inst. Chem. Engrs., Am. Petroleum Inst., Sigma Xi. Republican. Presbyterian. Office: PO Box 2511 Houston TX 77001 *

CUNNINGHAM, RICHARD GREENLAW, mechanical engineering educator, university official; b. Olney, Ill., Sept. 23, 1921; s. Rexford John and Florence (Greenlaw) C.; m. Suzanne Kimberly Barrett, Feb. 19, 1944; children: Stephen Barrett, Kimberly Ann, Elizabeth Ann. B.S. in Mech. Engring, Northwestern U., 1943, M.S., 1947, Ph.D., 1950. Research engr. research and devel. lab. Pure Oil Co., Crystal Lake, Ill., 1950-51; research engr. research lab. Shell Oil Co., Wood River, Ill., N.Y.C., 1954-55, research group leader, 1955-60, sr. research engr., 1960-61; project engr., asso. prof. engring. research Pa. State U. at University Park, 1951-54, prof. mech. engring., 1961—, head dept., 1962-71, v.p. research and grad. studies, 1971—, chmn. univ. senate, 1967-68. Contbr. articles to profl. jours. Trustee Centre Community Hosp., chmn. long-range planning com. Served with USNR, 1943-46. Mem. ASME (v.p. for edn. 1974-76, L.F. Moody award 1974, Outstanding Mech. Engr. award Central Pa. sect. 1974), Am. Soc. for Engring. Edn., Accreditation Bd. for Engring. and Tech. (dir. 1969-75, v.p. 1976-78, pres. 1978-80, chmn. accreditation coordination com. 1980-83), Am. Assn. Engring. Socs. (organizing com. 1978-79, exec. com. of ednl. affairs council 1980), Nat. Assn. Coll. and Univ. Bus. Officers (council govtl. relations, bd. mgmt. 1983—), Sigma Xi (pres. Pa. State U. chpt. 1966-67), Tau Beta Pi, Pi Tau Sigma, Phi Eta Sigma. Methodist. Patentee in field. Home: 900 Outer Dr State College PA 16801

CUNNINGHAM, ROBERT CYRIL, clergyman, editor; b. Peterborough, Ont., Can., Dec. 23, 1914; came to U.S., 1935, naturalized, 1942; s. John James and Cecelia (Simpson) C.; m. Helen Marian Platte, May 14, 1941; children—Robert Stephen, Philip Joseph, Andrew Platte, Bethel Marian. B.A., Central Bible Coll., 1962; M.A., Assemblies of God Grad. Sch., 1979. Ordained to ministry Assemblies of God, 1945; pastor Assembly of God, Ozark, Mo., 1943-47; mem. editorial staff Gospel Pub. House, Springfield, Mo., 1937—; editor Christ's Ambassadors Herald, 1940-45; asso. editor The Pentecostal Evangel, 1943-49, editor, 1949—. Author: Filled With The Spirit, 1972, Getting Together With Luke and Acts, 1973; contbr. articles to mags. Mem. Evang. Press Assn. (pres. 1961-63), Internat. Pentecostal Press Assn. (pres. 1973-76, pres. 80—), Central Bible Coll. Alumni Assn. (pres. 1946-48). Club: Univ. Home: 2338 E Bancroft St Springfield MO 65804 Office: 1445 Boonville Ave Springfield MO 65802

CUNNINGHAM, ROBERT LOUIS, educator; b. Birmingham, Mar. 22, 1926; s. Louis John and Marie Virginia (Schillinger) C.; m. Margery Ann Winters, Aug. 20, 1949; children—Christine, Michael, Sheila, Mark, Gregory, Virginia, Roberta, Lisa. B.A., St. Gregory Sem., 1947; Ph.D., Laval U., 1951. Asst. prof. philosophy Xavier U., Cin., 1951-53; asst. prof. philosophy San Francisco Coll. for Women, 1953-56, asso. prof., 1956-58; asso. prof. philosophy U. San Francisco, 1958-63, prof., 1963-81, asso. dean, 1981—; vis. prof. Rockford Coll., 1966, Queens Coll., summer 1967; research asso. in philosophy U. Calif. at Berkeley, 1967-68; distinguished vis. prof. philosophy USAF Acad., 1977-78. Author: Situationism and the New Morality, 1970, Liberty and the Rule of Law, 1979, also articles. Relm Found. grantee, 1965-66; Inst. for Interdisciplinary Research grantee, 1967-68; Carnegie fellow Inst. Legal and Polit. Philosophy, U. Calif. at Irvine, summer 1969; Nat. Endowment for Humanities fellow, summer 1975, 80; Earhart Found. grantee, 1981. Mem. Am. Philos. Assn., Am. Cath. Philos. Assn., Mont Pelerin Soc. Home: 2447 39th Ave San Francisco CA 94116

CUNNINGHAM, ROBERT MARIS, JR., editor; b. Chgo., May 28, 1909; s. Robert Maris and Beda (Dickson) C.; m. Deborah Libby, Nov. 24, 1934; children: Dennis, Damon, Margaret, Robert Maris. Ph.B., U. Chgo., 1931. Asst. to pres. Armour (now Ill.) Inst. Tech., Chgo., 1932-34; sales and sales promotion Shell Petroleum Corp., 1934-37; dir. pub. relations Chgo. Blue Cross hospitalization plan, 1938-41; asso. editor Hygeia (pub. by AMA), 1941-45; mng. editor The Modern Hosp. mag., 1945-51, editor, 1951-63, 67-73, pub., 1963-67; editorial dir. The Nations Schools, 1963-67, Coll. and Univ. Bus., 1967-73, pub., 1963-67, The Hosp. Purchasing File, 1963-67; editor Modern Nursing Home, 1964-73, pub., 1964-67; chmn. editorial bd. Modern Healthcare mag., 1974-75, contbg. editor, 1976, Hosps., Jour. Am. Hosp. Assn., 1977—; cons. ACS, 1955-59; v.p., dir. F.W. Dodge Corp., 1959-63; bd. dirs. Health Industries Assn., 1966-69, pres. (hon.). Author: Hospitals, Doctors and Dollars, 1961, The Third World of Medicine, 1968, Governing Hospitals, 1976, Asking and Giving, 1980, Wellness at Work, 1981, The Healing Mission and the Business Ethic, 1982; also articles on hosp. and med. subjects. Mem. Psi Upsilon. Home: 2126 N Dayton St Chicago IL 60614 Office: 676 St Clair St Chicago IL 60611

CUNNINGHAM, ROBERT MORTON, communications company executive; b. Ardmore, Pa., Nov. 27, 1907; s. Andrew and Mary (Neely) C.; m. Emily Thomas, June 23, 1934; children: Carol (Mrs. H.R. Reynolds), Robert A. B.S., Haverford Coll., 1929. With Bell Telephone Co., Pa., 1929-42, sr. staff engr., 1942; instr. elec. engring. Drexel Inst. Tech., evenings 1929-42; with Am. Tel. & Tel. Co., 1942-55, exec. asst., 1955; with Pacific Tel. & Tel. Co., 1955-72, asst. v.p., 1958-60, v.p. bus. research, 1960-66, v.p., sec., treas., 1966-72, also dir.; asso. dir. Security Pacific Nat. Bank; dir. Bell Telephone Co. Nev. Mem. borough council, Franklin Lakes, N.J., 1950-53; dir. Seascape Beach Assn., Aptos, Calif., 1973-75, pres., 1974-75; bd. dirs. Mid-Atlantic Center for Arts, 1976-79. Mem. Calif. Taxpayers Assn. (pres., dir. 1969-72), Taxpayers Assn of Cape May (dir. 1976—), IEEE, Newcomen Soc. N.Am., Cape May County Art League (dir. 1980—). Episcopalian (vestryman). Clubs: Wildwood Golf and Country (Cape May Court House, N.J.); Corinthian Yacht (Cape May, N.J.); Vesper (Phila). Home: 295 Windsor Ave Cape May NJ 08204

CUNNINGHAM, ROGER A., legal educator; b. 1921. J.D., Harvard U., 1948. Bar: Mass. 1948. Assoc. Nutter, McClennen and Fish, Boston, 1948-49; asst. prof. law George Washington U., 1950-54; assoc. prof. Rutgers U., New Brunswick, N.J., 1954-57, prof., 1957-59, U. Mich., Ann Arbor, 1959—. Author: (with Browder, Julin and Smith) Basic Property Law, 1966, 3d edit. 1979, (with Tischler) Law of Mortgages in New Jersey Practice, 2 vols., 1975. Office: U Mich Law Sch 304 Hutchins Hall 621 S State St Ann Arbor MI 48109

CUNNINGHAM, ROSS LEE, editor; b. St. Paul, Apr. 13, 1906; s. Ralph Lee and Agnes Mary (Tyrrell) C.; m. Charlotte Helen Logan, Mar. 7, 1931; children—Alan Tyrrell, Gayle Lee. Student, U. Wash., 1934-35; LL.D. (hon.), Seattle U., 1977. With Seattle Star, 1923-28; v.p. Alaska Washington Airways, 1928-31; staff Seattle Star-Seattle Post Intelligencer, 1931-38, Seattle Times, 1938-41, asso. editor, 1944-56, asso. editor, editorial page editor, 1956-68, editorial dir., 1968-77, columnist, 1977—; asst. to gov., Wash., 1941-44. Chmn. freedom of information com. Wash. Asso. Press Unit, 1953-56. Recipient Distinguished Service to Journalism award Wash. State Press Club, 1953. Mem. Seattle C. of C., Community Devel. Assn. Seattle, Am. Soc. Newspaper Editors, Philippine-Am. Soc. (bd. govs.). Clubs: Washington Athletic, Seattle Golf (Seattle); Port Ludlow Yacht. Home: 962 NW Elford Dr Seattle WA 98177 Office: Seattle Times Fairview Ave and John St Seattle WA 98111

CUNNINGHAM, THOMAS WILLIAM, clergyman, educator; b. Jersey City, June 7, 1911; s. Joseph A. and Mary A. (Snell) C. Student, St. Peter's Prep. Sch., 1923-27; A.B., Seton Hall U., 1931, Immaculate Conception Theol. Sem., 1931-35; M.A., Fordham U., 1943, Ph.D., 1950. Ordained priest Roman Cath. Ch., 1935; asst. pastor St. John's Ch., Orange, N.J., 1935-40; instr., later asst. prof. English lit. Seton Hall U., 1940-46, prof. English lit., head dept. English, 1946-53, dean coll. arts and scis., co-ordinating dean all schs., 1951-53, v.p. charge instrn., 1953-63; pastor Immaculate Conception Ch., Montclair, N.J., 1963-77; apptd. domestic prelate, 1964; Lectr. Cath. Forum Newark Critic's Circle N.Y.; Chmn. Newark Archdiocese Ecumenical Commn.; mem. Priest's Senate, Newark, 1971-77; synodal judge Archdiocesan Tribune, 1964-80. Author: Saints Off Pedestals, 1953; also articles, book revs. Appointed Papal Chamberlain, 1958. Recipient James Roosevelt Bayley award Seton Hall U., 1964; Coronat award St. Edward's U., 1964; For God and Country award Cath. War Vets., 1968. Mem. Modern Lang. Assn., Mediaeval Acad. Am., Am. Cath. Hist. Assn., Nat. Cath. Ednl. Assn., St. Paul's Guild N.Y. Clubs: K.C., Serra Vocation, Mercier. Home: 402 Central Ave Spring Lake NJ 07762 *The realization that God underlies our beginnings, our culture, our laws and our ideals gives me reason to participate in all phases of society's activities and bolsters my hopes in times of crisis. My love for my American roots urges me to greater efforts in creating a noble society around me so as to keep aglow the magnificent spirit of our founding fathers.*

CUNNINGHAM, WALTER JACK, electrical engineering educator; b. Comanche, Tex., Aug. 21, 1917; s. Walter Jack and Percy Adele (Moore) C.; m. Barbara Virginia Lynch, Feb. 26, 1944; children: Lawrence Bradford, John Hartwell. A.B., U. Tex., 1937, A.M., 1938; Ph.D., Harvard U., 1947. Instr. physics and communication engring. Harvard, 1939-46; part-time research OSRD, in acoustics and electric circuits, 1939-46; asst. prof. elec. engring. Yale U., 1946-50, assoc. prof., 1950-56, prof. engring. and applied sci., 1956-81, prof. elec. engring., 1981—, assoc. chmn. dept. engring. and applied sci., 1969-72. Author: Introduction to Nonlinear Analysis, 1958; tech. papers.; Bd. editors: Am. Scientist, 1955-81, Jour. Franklin Inst, 1962-75. Mem. Acoustical Soc. Am., IEEE, Am. Soc. Engring. Edn., Sigma Xi. (chmn. com. on publs. 1983—). Home: 200 Dessa Dr Hamden CT 06517 Office: Becton Center Yale U New Haven CT 06520

CUNNINGHAM, WILLIAM FRANCIS, JR., univ. adminstr.; b. Holyoke, Mass., Feb. 9, 1931; s. William Francis and Constance Emma (Cox) C.; m. Eleanor Mary Bissonette, Dec. 27, 1956; children—Margaret Ann, William John, Mary Elizabeth. A.B., Holy Cross Coll., 1954; M.A., Boston Coll., 1956; Ph.D., U. Pitts., 1961. Asst. prof. English Duquesne U., 1955-63; prof. Le Moyne Coll., 1963-78; dean (Coll. Arts and Scis.); prof. Creighton U., 1978—; Danforth asso., 1974—. Contbr. articles on 18th-century Brit. lit. to profl. jours. Mem. Coll. Bd. (council on coll.-level services, exec. com. Midwestern regional assembly 1980—), Am. Assn. Higher Edn., MLA, Am. Soc. 18th-century Studies, Assn. Jesuit Colls. and Univs. Office: Creighton U Omaha NE 68178

CUNNINGHAM, WILLIAM H., college dean. Dean Coll. Bus. Adminstrn., U. Tex., Austin. Office: Office of Dean Coll Bus Adminstrn U Tex Austin TX 78712§

CUNNINGHAM, WILLIAM PALMER, headmaster; b. Yonkers, N.Y., Oct. 5, 1922; s. George French and Elizabeth Austin (Purdy) C.; m. Mildred Jean Sutphen, June 11, 1949; children: Bruce Thayer, Scott Douglas. B.A., Wesleyan U., Middletown, Conn., 1947; M.A., Northwestern U., 1953. Chmn. history dept. Chgo. Latin Sch., 1947-54; chmn. history dept., asst. prin. Kinkaid Sch., Houston, 1954-61; headmaster Menlo Sch., Menlo Park, Calif., 1961-64, Newman Sch., New Orleans, 1964-77, Awty Sch., Houston, 1979-80, River Oaks Sch., Sherman Oaks, Calif., 1980—. Served with USAAF, 1942-45. Mem. Ind. Schs. Assn. S.W. (pres. 1974-75), Country Day Headmasters Assn. (life), Alpha Chi Rho. Home: 4500 Woodman Ave Apt A217 Sherman Oaks CA 91423

CUNNYNGHAM, JON, economics educator; b. Jefferson City, Mo., Mar. 3, 1935; s. Wilkie Burford and Modesta (Gutierrez) C.; m. Nancy Lou Bonte, June 21, 1958 (dec. 1981); children: Kathryn Lisa, Karen Elizabeth, Kristin Anne.; m. Mary Ellen Eschbach, Dec. 11, 1982. B.A., Oberlin Coll., 1957; Ph.D., U. Chgo., 1964. Instr. U. Chgo., 1961-62; asst. prof. econs. Columbia U., N.Y.C., 1963-65, asso. prof., 1965-66; assoc. prof. Ohio State U., Columbus, 1966-68, prof., 1969—, chmn. econs. dept., 1968-76, Mershon policy economist, 1976-80; econ. statistician U.S. Bur. Census, Washington, 1962-63; research asso. Nat. Bur. Econ. Research, 1963-68; dir. Fin. Research Center, Columbus, 1967-75. Ford Found. Faculty Research fellow, 1965-66. Mem. AAAS, Am. Econ. Assn., Am. Soc. for Cybernetics (treas. 1981-82, pres. 1983-85), Am. Statis. Assn., Econometric Soc., Soc. for Gen. Systems Research (treas. Central Ohio chpt. 1977-78, pres. 1978-79). Home: 66 W Jeffrey Pl Columbus OH 43214

CUNYUS, GEORGE MARVIN, oil company executive; b. Dallas, Jan. 13, 1930; s. Grady and Ruby (King) C.; m. Mary Ellen Faust, Apr. 24, 1952; children: Bruce, Stuart, John. B.A., Rice U., 1951; J.D., So. Meth. U., 1956. Bar: Tex. 1956. With Hunt Oil Co., Dallas, 1956—, sr. v.p., gen. counsel, 1962—, corp. sec., 1976—, dir., mem. exec. com.; chmn. bd, exec. com. E. Tex. Salt Water Disposal Co.; chmn. bd. Brooks Well Servicing, Inc. Trustees Disciples Found. of Dallas.; pres. Thai Christian Found. Served with U.S. Army, 1951-53. Mem. Mid-Continent Oil and Gas Assn. (dir. La. div.). Republican. Clubs: Dallas Petroleum, Lakewood Country. Home: 5634 Ledgestone Dr Dallas TX 75214 Office: Interfirst One Bldg Dallas TX 75202 *We start successful by being Americans. Everything beyond that is simply relative. Success is a frame of mind, the intention to do the best job possible under existing circumstances. Power, position and wealth do not denote success. The most successful person I have known was a teacher who had students come to his funeral 50 years after he had them in class.*

CUOMO, MARIO MATTHEW, governor of N.Y.; b. Queens County, N.Y., June 15, 1932; s. Andrea and Immaculata C.; m. Matilda Raffa; children: Margaret Cuomo Perpignano, Andrew, Maria, Amdeline, Christopher. B.A. summa cum laude, St. John's Coll., 1953; LL.B. cum laude, St. John's U., 1956. Bar: N.Y. 1956, U.S. Supreme Ct 1960. Confidential legal asst. to Hon. Adrian P. Burke, N.Y. State Ct. Appeals, 1956-58; assoc. Corner, Weisbrod, Froeb and Charles, Bklyn., 1958-63, partner, 1963-75; sec. of state State of N.Y., N.Y.C., 1975-79, lt. gov., 1979-82, gov., 1983—; mem. faculty St. John's U. Sch. Law, 1963-73; counsel to community groups, including Corona Homeowners, 1966-72; Charter mem. First Ecumenical Commn. of Christian and Jews for, Bklyn. and Queens, N.Y. Author: Forest Hills Diary: The Crisis of Low-Income Housing, 1974; Contbr. articles to legal publs. Recipient Rapallo award Columbia Lawyers Assn., 1976, Dante medal Italian Govt.-Am. Assn. Tchrs. Italian, 1976, Silver medallion Columbia Coalition, 1976, Pub. Adminstr. award C.W. Post Coll., 1977. Mem. Am., N.Y. State, Bklyn. Nassau and Queens County bar assns., Assn. Bar City N.Y., Am. Judicature Soc., St. John's U. Alumni Fedn. (chmn. bd. 1970-72), Cath. Lawyers Guild of Queens County (pres. 1966-67), Skull and Circle. Office: Office of Gov State Capitol Albany NY 12224 *

CUPP, DAVID FOSTER, photographer, journalist; b. Derry Twp., Pa., Feb. 4, 1938; s. Foster Wilson and Elizabeth (Erhard) C.; m. Catherine Lucille Lum, Nov. 20, 1965; children: Mary Catherine, Elizabeth, David Patterson, John. B.A. in Journalism, U. Miami (Fla.), 1960. Staff photographer Miami News, 1960-63, Charlotte (N.C.) Observer, 1963-66; photographer/writer Internat. Harvesters, Chgo., 1966-67; picture editor Nat. Geog. Mag., Washington, 1967, photographer, 1967-69; picture editor Detroit Free Press, 1969; writer/photographer Denver Post, 1969-77; freelance writer, photographer, 1977—; tchr. jr. and sr. high sch.-adult classes, including Journalist-in-the-schs., pilot program, Aurora, Colo., 1974-76, Nat. Endowment Arts poet-in-residence 5 Colo. schs. Contbg. author: Nat. Geog. books; co-author: Cindy, a Hearing Ear Dog, The Animal Shelter; contbr. article, photographs to popular mags. Bd. dirs. Friends of Children of Vietnam, adoption agy., 1973. Mem. Nat. Press Photographers Assn. (recipient numerous awards, citations, including, named Nat. runner-up Photographer of Year 1965, 72, named Regional Photographer of Year 1974, recipient 2nd Place News Picture Story award 1974, 3rd Place Sports Picture Story award 1974, McWilliams award for picture story 1974, McWilliams award for single picture 1974, 75, 2d Home, Family Picture Story award 1972, co-chmn. nat. conv.), Colo. Press Photographers Assn. (v.p.), Am. Soc. Mag. Photographers. Lutheran. Home: 2520 Albion St Denver CO 80207 Office: 2520 Albion St Denver CO 80207 *I don't think it's possible to sum life up in a few sentences, life is too complex, but if I were to try, I would have to say that I try to live my life in such a way that my children have pride in me, what I do, and how I do it. I don't feel I can tell my children to be honest, then I be dishonest, or tell them to have compassion, while I have none. I cannot punish a child for doing something at night, that I do during the day. In short, I try to be the person that I would want my children to be.*

CURATOLO, ALPHONSE FRANK, architect; b. Chgo., Sept. 20, 1936; s. Joseph and Pearl (Loizzo) C. B.A., U. Ill., 1961; grad., Barbizon Sch. Modeling, 1977; M.Arch., Calif. Western U., 1981, Ph.D. in Engring. and Architecture, 1983. Architect Masonite Corp., Chgo., 1963-66; exec. v.p., head architect Internat. Design Studios, Inc. Chief designer-architect, Playboy Clubs Internat., Chgo., 1966—; pres., Entertainment Enterprises. Served with AUS, 1961. Recipient award for Lake Geneva Playboy resort AIA, 1969, Earl prize for outstanding archtl. design, 1961, instns. award for outstanding design, Lake Geneva, 1969, trophy for outstanding entertainer of year, 1968-69, Universal Artists, Chgo., 1968; named Golden Gloves Fighter of Year, 1958, Barbizon Man of Month Fashion Contest Winner, 1977; recipient Archtl. award for Zorine's Lighting Inst., 1977; Service award March of Dimes, 1977; Disting. Leadership award, 1978. Mem. AIA, Assn. Registered Architects, Nat. Council Archtl. Registration Bds., Internat. Brotherhood Magicians, Internat. Detective Soc. Enterprises (pres.), Mensa. Republican. Roman Catholic. Winner U.S. Midwest Karate Championship, 1968, 69, 2d Place, World's 1st Karate Championships, 1968. Home: 5525 N Virginia Ave Chicago IL 60625 Office: 875 N Michigan Ave Chicago IL 60611

CURB, MICHAEL CHARLES, former lieutenant governor California; b. Savannah, Ga., Dec. 24, 1944; s. Charles M. and Stella L. (Stout) C.; m. Linda Dunphy; 1 dau., Megan Carole. Student pub. schs. With Sidewalk Prodns., 1965-68; pres. MGM Records, 1968-74; owner Mike Curb Prodns., Los Angeles, 1974-79; lt. gov. Calif., 1979-83; also chmn. Econ. Devel. Commn.; fin. chmn. Republican Nat. Com., 1982—; owner Curb Records, Burbank, Calif. Bd. dirs. Pepperdine U., Braille Inst. Am., Jr., Achievement of So. Calif.; Republican nat. committeeman from Calif., mem. nat. exec. com., chmn. program com. Nat. Conv.; chmn. Reagan campaign, Calif., 1975, Ford-Dole campaign, 1976. Named Record Producer of Yr. Billboard Mag., 1972; Calif. Mus. of Sci. and Industry Outstanding Bus. Achievement fellow. Mem. Nat. Conf. Lt. Govs. (chmn. 1982). Baptist. Office: Rep Nat Com 310 1st St SE Washington DC 20003

CURCIO, JOHN BAPTIST, truck manufacturing company executive; b. Hazleton, Pa., May 29, 1934; s. John B. and Bridget (Slattery) C.; m. Rosemary J. Kutash, Aug. 28, 1954; children: Mary Beth, John W., Kris Ann. LL.B., LaSalle Coll., 1963. Pres., chief exec. officer Montone Mfg. Co., Hazleton, 1954-67; v.p. Mack Trucks Inc., Allentown, Pa., 1967-73, exec. v.p., 1976-80, pres., chief operating officer, 1980-84, pres., chief exec. officer, 1984—; pres., chief exec. officer Crane Carrier Co., Tulsa, 1973-76. Served with USNR, 1951-54; Korea. Decorated Bronze Star, Purple Heart. Mem. Soc. Automotive Engrs. (nat. chmn. 1976). Club: Lehigh Valley Country. Office: Mack Trucks Inc 2100 Mack Blvd Allentown PA 18105

CURFMAN, LAWRENCE EVERETT, lawyer; b. Champaign, Ill., Apr. 13, 1909; s. Lawrence Everett and Winifred (Williams) C.; m. Margaret Sylvia Baldwin, May 1, 1937; children: Lawrence Everett III, Elizabeth Ann (Mrs. Peter Koch), John Edward. A.B., U. Mich., 1930, J.D., 1932. Bar: Kans. 1932. Since practiced in, Wichita; ptnr. Curfman, Harris, Stallings, Grace & Snow, 1982—. Contbr. articles to legal jours. Pres. Wichita Pub. Library Bd., 1954, 57, 58; Trustee E.A. Watkins Found. Mem. ABA (chmn. sect. local govt. law 1970- 71), Wichita Bar Assn. (pres. 1956), City Attys. Assn. Kan. (pres. 1953). Club: University (Wichita) (pres. 1965-66). Home: 122 N Pershing St Wichita KS 67208 Office: First Nat Bank Bldg Wichita KS 67202

CURIE, EVE, author, lectr.; b. Paris, Dec. 6, 1904; U.S., Jan. 1941; d. Pierre (Nobel prize winner for work in radium 1903) and Marie (Sklodowska) (Nobel prize winner in radio-active substances 1903, in chemistry 1911);; d. Pierre (Nobel prize winner for work in radium 1903) and Marie (Sklodowska) C.; m. Henry Richardson Labouisse, Nov. 19, 1954. B.S., Ph.B., Sevigne Coll.; L.H.D. (hon.), Mills Coll., 1939, Russell Sage Coll., 1941, Litt.D., U. Rochester, 1941. One of pubs. of Paris Presse (daily), resigned to return to ind. writing, 1949; and lectured on the war in, France and Eng.; Spl. adviser to Sec. Gen. NATO, 1952-54. Student music, first concert as pianist, Paris, 1925; later gave concerts in, France and, Belgium; musical critic for: weekly jour. Candide, for several years; also wrote articles on motion pictures and theater; Author: Madame Curie (selection Lit. Guild, Jr. Guild, Book-of-the-Month Club, Sci. Book of the month), 1937 (Nat. book award for non-fiction), Journey Among Warriors, 1943 (Literary Guild Selection). Served in Europe with Fighting French as officer in Women's div. of army, World War II. Decorated chevalier Legion of Honor, France, 1939; Order of Polonia Restituta, Poland, 1939; Croix de Guerre, France, 1944. Made first visit to U.S. with her mother, 1921; on 2d visit lectured in 10 U.S. cities (she speaks English, French and Polish), 1939; witnessed the fall of France, 1940, and went to London to work for the cause of Free France; because of pro-ally activities deprived of French citizenship by the Vichy Govt., Apr. 1941. Home: 1 Sutton Pl S New York NY 10022

CURL, RANE LOCKE, chemical engineering educator; b. N.Y.C., July 5, 1929; s. Herbert C. and Erna (Locke) C.; m. Katherine Ide, June 26, 1954 (div. 1961); children: Stefan Luther, Jocelyn Chandler; m. Shirley Anne Richardson, Sept. 26, 1963 (div. 1976); m. Alice Inez Rolfes, Feb. 27, 1982; 1 dau., Vittoria Sarah. B.S., MIT, 1951, Sc.D., 1955. Engr. Shell Devel. Co., Emeryville, Calif., 1955-61; hon. research asst. Univ. Coll., London, Eng., 1961-62; research asso. Technische Hogeschool Eindhoven, Netherlands, 1962-64; prof. chem. engring. U. Mich., 1964—; U.S. del. Internat. Congress Speleology, 1961, 65, 73, 77, 81; chmn. 8th Congress, 1981; adj. sec. Internat. Union Speleology, 1981—. Contbr. articles on chem. engring. and karst geomorphology to profl. jours. Fellow Nat. Speleol. Soc. (hon. mem., dir. 1958-61, 1967-70, 74—, pres. 1970-74, treas. sect. cave geology and geography 1974—), Explorers Club; mem. AAAS, Am. Chem. Soc., Internat. Assn. Hydrogeologists, Am. Inst. Chem. Engrs., Mich. Basin Geol. Soc., Nat. Assn. Watch and Clock Collectors, Mich. Karst Conservancy (pres. 1984—), Sigma Xi, Tau Beta Pi, Alpha Chi Sigma. Patentee acoustic process control, thermochem. prodn. of hydrogen and oxygen from water. Home: 2805 Gladstone Ave Ann Arbor MI 48104 Office: Dept Chem Engring U Mich Ann Arbor MI 48109

CURL, ROBERT FLOYD, JR., educator; b. Alice, Tex., Aug. 23, 1933; s. Robert Floyd and Lessie (Merritt) C.; m. Jonel Whipple, Dec. 21, 1955; children—Michael, David. B.A., Rice U., 1954; Ph.D. (NSF fellow), U. Cal. at Berkeley, 1957. Research fellow Harvard, 1957-58; asst. prof. chemistry Rice U., Houston, 1958-63, asso. prof., 1963-67, prof., 1967—; master Lovett Coll., 1968-72; Vis. research officer NRC Can., 1972-73; vis. prof. Inst. for Molecular Sc., Okazaki, Japan, 1977. Contbr. articles profl. jours. Alfred P. Sloan fellow, 1961-63; NATO postdoctoral fellow, 1964; recipient Clayton prize Instn. Mech. Engrs., London, 1958. Mem. Am. Chem. Soc., Phi Beta Kappa, Sigma Xi. Methodist. Home: 1824 Bolsover St Houston TX 77005

CURL, SAMUEL EVERETT, university dean, agriculturist; b. Ft. Worth, Dec. 26, 1937; s. Henry Clay and Mary Elva (Watson) C.; m. Betty Doris Savage, June 6, 1957; children: Jane Ellen, Julia Kathleen, Karen Elizabeth. Student, Tarleton State Coll., 1955-57; B.S., Sam Houston State U., 1959; M.S., U. Mo., 1961; Ph.D., Tex. A&M U., 1963. Mem. faculty Tex. Tech U., Lubbock, 1961, 63-76, 79—, tchr., researcher animal physiology and genetics, asst., asso. and interim dean Coll. Agrl. Sci., 1968-73, asso. v.p. acad. affairs, 1973-76, dean Coll. Agrl. Scis., prof., 1979—; pres. Phillips U., Enid, Okla., 1976-79; agrl. cons. Author: (with others) Progress and Change in the Agricultural Industry, 1974, Food and Fiber for a Changing World, 1976, 2d edit., 1982; contbr. 85 articles to profl. jours. Trustee, mem. exec. com. Consortium for Internat. Devel., High Plains Research Coordinating Bd., So. Regional Council, U.S. Joint Council Food and Agrl. Scis. Served as 2d lt. U.S. Army, 1959; capt. USAR. Recipient Faculty-Alumni Gold medal U. Mo., 1975; Am. Council Edn. fellow, 1972-73. Mem. Am. Soc. Animal Sci., Am. Assn. Univ. Agrl. Adminstrs., Assn. U.S. Univ. Dirs. Internat. Agrl. Programs, So. Assn. Agrl. Scientists, Sigma Xi, Phi Kappa Phi, Gamma Sigma Delta, Alpha Zeta. Club: Rotary. Home: 1810 Bangor Ave Lubbock TX 79416 Office: Office Dean Agrl Scis 108 Goddard Bldg Tex Tech U Lubbock TX 79409

CURLER, HOWARD J., business executive; b. 1925; (married). B.S. in Chem. Engring, U. Wis., 1948. With research dept. Marathon Corp., 1948-58; pres. Curwood Inc., 1958-68; corp. v.p. Bemis Co. Inc., 1965-76, exec. v.p., chief operating officer, 1976, pres., chief operating officer, 1977, pres., chief exec. officer, 1978—, also dir.; dir. Northwestern Nat. Bank Minn. Office: PO Box 1154 Appleton WI 54912

CURLEY, EDWIN MUNSON, philosophy educator; b. Albany, N.Y., May 1, 1937; s. Julius Edwin and Gertrude (Edwards) C.; m. Ruth Helen Snyder, Dec. 12, 1959; children: Julia Anne, Richard Edwin. B.A., Lafayette Coll., 1959; Ph.D., Duke U., 1963. Asst. prof. philosophy San Jose State Coll., 1963-66; research fellow Australian Nat. U., Canberra, 1966-68, fellow, 1968-72, sr. fellow, 1972-77; prof. philosophy Northwestern U., 1977-83, U. Ill.-Chgo., 1983—. Author: Hellenistic Philosophy, 1965, Spinoza's Metaphysics, 1969, Descartes Against the Skeptics, 1978; contbr. articles to profl. jours.; Am. co-editor: Archiv für Geschichte der Philosophie, 1979—. Mem. Am. Philos. Assn. Office: Dept Philosophy U Ill Chicago IL 60680

CURLEY, JOHN FRANCIS, JR., investment broker; b. Wollaston, Mass., July 24, 1939; s. John Francis and Ann (Omar) C.; m. Loretta Mae O'Keeffe, Oct. 20, 1962; children—William Laurance, Edward Reid, David Neil. Grad., Phillips Acad.; A.B., Princeton U., 1960; M.B.A., Harvard U., 1962. With Paine, Webber, Jackson & Curtis Inc., N.Y.C., 1964—, v.p., asst. to chmn. bd., 1970-72, exec. v.p., dir. adminstrv. div., 1972-77, pres., 1977-80, chmn. fin. com., 1980—, also dir.; pres., dir. Cashfund Inc.; dir. Paine Webber Inc., Paine Webber Mitchell Hutchins Inc., Constitution Reins. Corp. Treas. class of 1960, Princeton U., 1970-75. Served to 1st lt. AUS, 1962-64. Mem. Securities Industry Assn. (dir., exec. com. 1978-80), Investment Assn. N.Y. (past pres.), Bond Club N.Y.C. (gov.), Wall St. Planning Group. Clubs: Harvard Bus. Sch. of N.Y. (dir.), City Midday (N.Y.C.); Sleepy Hollow (Scarborough, N.Y.). Office: 140 Broadway New York City NY 10005

CURLEY, MICHAEL EDWARD, lawyer; b. Buffalo, Apr. 24, 1937. Student Inst. Lang. and Lingistics, Georgetown U., 1965-68; J.D., U. Buffalo, 1971. Bar: N.Y. 1974. Assoc. Nasca & Nasca, Buffalo, 1974-76; dep. commr., counsel N.Y. State Dept. Commerce, 1976-77; pres. N.Y. Job Devel. Authority, 1977-79; ptnr. Shea & Gould, N.Y.C., 1979—; chmn. bd. Niagara Frontier Tennis, Inc., 1973; parliamentarian N.Y. State Assembly, 1975-76; counsel N.Y. State Job Incentive Bd., 1976-77, N.Y. State Atomic Energy Council, 1975-76, N.Y. State Sci. and Tech. Found., 1979; chmn., pres. Econ. Devel. Publs., 1980, IDBI Mgrs., Inc., 1981. Bd. dirs. Buffalo Youth Bd., 1971-76. Mem. ABA, Am. Arbitration Assn., Am. Soc. Internat. Law. Home: 254 E 68th St New York NY 10021

CURLEY, WALTER JOSEPH PATRICK, JR., investment banker; b. Pitts., Sept. 17, 1922; s. Walter Joseph and Marguerite Inez (Cowan) C.; m. Mary Walton, Dec. 18, 1948; children: Margaret Cowan, Walter Joseph Patrick III, John Walton, James Mellon. Grad., Phillips Acad., Andover, Mass., 1940; B.A., Yale, 1944; certificate, U. Oslo, Norway, 1948; M.B.A., Harvard, 1948; LL.D., Trinity Coll., Dublin, 1976. Mgr. Caltex Oil Co., India, 1948-52, Italy, 1952-55, N.Y.C., 1955-57; v.p. San Jacinto Petroleum, 1957-60; ptnr. J.H. Whitney Co., 1961-75, dir. various subsidiaries; pres. Curley Land Co.; commr. pub. events, chief protocol, City N.Y., 1973-74, ambassador to Ireland, 1975-77; dir. Fiduciary Trust Co. of N.Y., N.Y. Life Ins. Co., Ind. Newspapers Ltd., Dublin, Crane Co., New Yorker mag., all N.Y.C., Inter-continental Energy Corp., Denver, Guinness Peat Aviation, Inc., Bank of Ireland, Am. Exploration Co., Houston, Visionaire Communications Inc. Author: Monarchs in Waiting, 1974. Bd. dirs. Barnard Coll., 1966-75, Buckley Sch., 1960-75, N.Y. Pub. Library, 1972-75, Am. Irish Found., Am. Irish Hist. Soc. Served as capt. USMC, 1943-46. Decorated Bronze Star; Cloud and Banner, Republic of China). Mem. Fgn. Policy Assn. (bd. govs.). Clubs: Yale, Union, Links, Racquet (N.Y.C.); Rolling Rock (Ligonier, Pa.); Kildare Street, St. Stephen's Green (Dublin, Ireland). Address: 630 Fifth Ave Suite 2920 New York NY 10111

CURLEY, WALTER WILLIAM, business executive, former librarian; b. Boston, Mar. 29, 1923; s. Walter Christopher and Lillian Elizabeth (Berg) C.; m. Marie Theresa Sullivan, Nov. 9, 1963; children: Celeste, Carolyn, Victoria, Alice. B.S., Northeastern U., 1947; M.S. in L.S, Simmons Coll., 1950. Asst. dir. Providence Public Library, 1950-62; dir. Suffolk Coop. Library System, N.Y.C., 1962-67; dir. info. services Arthur D. Little, Inc., Cambridge, Mass., 1967-70; dir. Cleve. Public Library, 1970-74; pres. Gaylord Bros. Inc., Syracuse, N.Y., 1974-80, Angle-Genessee, Inc., Sanford, N.C., 1974-80, Dolmar Inc., Milford, Conn., WFIF, Milford., until 1982, WBRL Radio, Berlin, N.H.; pres., owner Walter W. Curley, Inc., Rochester, N.Y.; chmn. bd. Forest Press, Albany, N.Y.; Nat. bd. dirs. Literacy Vols. of Am.; bd. dirs. Mid York Library System, South Yarmouth Library (Mass.); adv. com. White House Conf. on Libraries; bd. library trustees Found. N.Y. State. Served with AUS, 1943-46. Mem. ALA (council). Home: 8 Bass River Pkwy Bass River South Yarmouth MA 02664 Office: WFIF Kay St Milford CT

CURLOCK, WALTER, mining company executive; b. Coniston, Ont., Can., Mar. 14, 1929; s. William and Stephanie (Acker) C.; m. Jennifer Burak, May 28, 1955; children: Christine, William Paul, John Michael, Andrea. B.A.Sc., U. Toronto, 1950, M.A.Sc., 1951, Ph.D., 1953; D.Sc. hon., Laurentian U., 1983. Postdoctoral fellow Imperial Coll. Sci. and Tech., London, 1954; research metallurgist Inco, Sudbury, Ont., Can., 1954-59, supr. research sta., Port Colborne, Ont., 1959-60, supr.

research, Cooper Clif, Ont., 1960-64, asst. to gen. mgr., 1964-69, asst. gen. mgr. adminstrn., 1969-72, v.p. adminstrn., 1972-73, v.p. adminstrv. and engring. services, 1973-74, v.p., N.Y.C., 1974-77; tech. dir. Cofimpac, Paris, 1969-72; sr. v.p. prodn. Inco Metals Co., Toronto, 1977-80, pres., chief exec. officer, 1980-82; exec. v.p. Inco Ltd., Toronto, 1982—; dir. Great-West Life Assurance Co., Winnipeg., Man.; pres. Ont. Mining Assn., Toronto, 1981-82; 2d v.p. Mining Assn. Can., Ottawa, Ont., 1983—; dir. Centre for Resources Studies, Kingston, Ont., 1982—, Ont. Centre for Resource Machinery, Sudbury, 1983—; mem. Nat. Adv. Com. on Mining Industry, 1980—. Patentee in field. Bd. dirs. Foundation Cambrian Found., Sudbury, 1983; chmn. bd. Cambrian Coll. Applied Arts and Tech., Sudbury, Ont., 1980. Mem. Metall. Soc. of Can. Inst. Mining and Metallurgy (Airey 1979), AIME. Roman Catholic. Club: Board of Trade (Toronto). Home: 25 Cluny Dr Toronto ON Canada M4W 2P9 Office: Inco Ltd PO Box 44 1 First Canadian Pl Toronto ON Canada M5X 1C4

CURNIN, THOMAS FRANCIS, lawyer; b. Bklyn., Sept. 16, 1933; s. Thomas Francis and Marion (Wallace) C.; m. Miriam Johnson, Sept. 19, 1959; children: Thomas, Paul, Kevin, Mark. B.S., Mt. St. Mary's, 1955; LL.B., Fordham U., 1958. Bar: N.Y. 1959, U.S. Ct. Appeals (2d cir.) 1959, U.S. Dist. Ct. (so. dist.) N.Y. 1961, U.S. Dist. Ct. ea. dist.) N.Y. 1961, U.S. Ct. Appeals (5th cir.) 1978, U.S. Supreme Ct. 1979, U.S. Ct. Appeals (8th cir.) 1983. Ptnr. firm Cahill Gordon & Reindel, N.Y.C., 1968—; hearing panel chmn. dept. disciplinary com. First Jud. Dept., N.Y., 1980—. Mem. Bd. Arbitration Archdiocese n.Y., 1978—, Fordham Law Sch. Alumni Assn., N.Y.C., 1983. Served with USMC, 1958-59; served with USMCR, 1958-64. Mem. ABA (com. on corp. counsel litigation sect. 1980—). Democrat. Roman Catholic. Clubs: University (Larchmont, N.Y.); Down Town Assn. (N.Y.C.). Home: 4 Lyons Pl New York NY 10538 Office: Cahill Gordon & Reindel 80 Pine St New York NY 10005

CURRAN, DARRYL JOSEPH, photographer, educator; b. Santa Barbara, Calif., Oct. 19, 1935; s. Joseph Harold and Irma Marie (Schlagel) C.; m. Doris Jean Smith, July 12, 1968. A.A., Ventura Coll., 1958; B.A., UCLA, 1960, M.A., 1964. Designer, installer UCLA Art Galleries, 1963-65; mem. faculty Los Angeles Harbor Coll., 1968-69, UCLA Ext., 1972—, Sch. Art Inst. Chgo., 1975; prof. art Calif. State U., Fullerton, 1967—; curator various shows, 1971—; bd. dirs. Los Angeles Center Photog. Studies, 1973-77, pres., 1980-83; juror Los Angeles Olympics Photog. Commns. Project, 1983. One-man shows include, U. Chgo., 1975, U. R.I., Art Space, Los Angeles, 1978, Photoworks Gallery, Richmond, Va., 1979, Alan Hancock Coll., Santa Maria, Calif., G. Ray Howkins Gallery, Los Angeles, 1981, Portland Sch. Art (Maine), 1983, one-man shows include retrospectives, Chaffey Coll., Alta Loma, Calif., one-man shows include, Grassmont Coll., San Diego, represented in permanent collections, Mus. Modern Art, Royal Photog. Soc., London, Nat. Gallery Can., Ottawa, Mpls. Inst. Art, Oakland Mus., U. N.Mex., UCLA, Seagram's Collection, N.Y.C. Bd. dirs. Cheviot Hills Home Owners Assn., 1973. Served with U.S. Army, 1954-56. Mem. Soc. Photog. Edn. (dir. 1975-79). Home: 10537 Dunleer Dr Los Angeles CA 90064 Office: Dept Art Calif State Univ 800 N State College Blvd Fullerton CA 92634 *I am an artist with abstract expressionist sympathies who chooses to use the photographic medium in its broadest definition.*

CURRAN, DONALD CHARLES, government librarian; b. St. Louis, May 26, 1933; s. Thomas Francis and Dorothy Millie (Hackman) C.; m. Sandra Ann Connell, June 25, 1960; children: Maura Ann, Matthew Francis, Michael Connell. B.S. cum laude in Commerce, St. Louis U., 1959; postgrad. in public adminstrn., George Washington U., Washington, 1960-61. Mgmt. intern Bur. Old Age Survivors Ins., Balt., 1959-60; adminstrv. asst., adminstrv. officer, mgmt. analyst Library of Congress, Washington, 1961-69, budget officer, 1969-73, chief fin. mgmt. office, 1973-76, assoc. librarian of Congress, 1976—. Served with USAF, 1953-57. Office: 10 1st St SE Washington DC 20540

CURRAN, FRANK EARL, former mayor; b. Cleve., Dec. 19, 1912; s. William E. and Anna (Havert) C.; m. Florence McKenney, Apr. 15, 1936. Student, San Diego Jr. Coll., Balboa Law Sch., San Diego State Coll., U. Calif. extension. Dep. county assessor San Diego (Calif.) County, 1935-41; city storekeeper, Oceanside, Calif., 1937-38; supr. procurement critical materials Dept. Navy, 1940-49; sec.-mgr. Fraternal Order Eagles, San Diego, 1949-60; with Shoreline Ins. Co., San Diego, 1960-63; councilman, San Diego, 1955-63, vice mayor, 1957, 58, 61, 62, mayor, 1963-72; exec. v.p. Central City Assn. San Diego, Inc., 1972—; Gen. chmn. Inter-Am. Municipal Orgn. Congress, San Diego, 1960; presiding officer Punta del Este, Uruguay, 1962—, mem. nat. bd. dirs., 1962—; bd. dirs. League Calif. Cities, 1964-72, dir.-at-large exec. com., 1964-72, mem. resolutions coms., 1964-72; City rep. to league com. on internat. municipal coop., 1961—; mem. policy com. San Diego-Border Area Program, after 1963; bd. dirs. Palm City Sanitation Dist., after 1964; mem. Gov. Calif Adv. Com., after 1963; spl. rep. gov. Calif. to Commn. Californias, after 1964; mem. community relations com. U.S. Conf. Mayors, 1965-72; chmn. com. internat. municipal coop. Nat. League Cities, 1965-72, v.p., 1969, pres., 1970, bd. dirs., 1971; chmn. Coop. Area Manpower Planning System, 1970; mem. Govt. Task Force on Coastline Preservation, 1970. Contbr. articles to newspapers and mags. Bd. dirs. Nat. Center Voluntary Action, 1970. Recipient Mayor La Guardia Civic award, 1964, Elsie Wittmore award, 1966; decorated Order Queen Isabella The Catholic (Spain); Prince Henry The Navigator (Portugal); Cavaliere Order Stella della Solidarieta Italiana (Italy). Democrat. Home: 4901 Randall St San Diego CA 92109 Office: 625 Broadway Suite 901 San Diego CA 92101

CURRAN, JAMES ALBERT, constrn. co. exec.; b. Boston, Apr. 28, 1917; s. Sylvester Michael and Anne (Coyne) C.; m. Jane Eleanor Harvey, July 11, 1942; children—Jane Ann (Mrs. Marshall Chittenden Turner, Jr.), Michael Harvey. B.S., U.S. Naval Acad., 1941; M.B.A., U. So. Calif., 1956. Commd. ensign USN, 1941, advanced through grades to lt. comdr., 1945; damage control officer (U.S.S. North Carolina), 1945-46, tchr. tactics, Annapolis, 1943-44, ret., 1946; asst. gen. supt., project engr., project mgr., sr. v.p., sec., dir. C.F. Braun & Co., Alhambra, Calif., 1946—; Chmn. 42d Assembly Dist., United Republicans Calif., 1962-63. Decorated Bronze Star medal with combat V, Purple Heart, Letter of Commendation. Roman Catholic. Club: Annandale Golf (Pasadena). Home: 710 Pinehurst Dr Pasadena CA 91106 Office: CF Braun & Co Alhambra CA 91802 *I believe that a young man aspiring to reach the top should concentrate on doing the job assigned to him to the best of his ability. Success related to this method is the most satisfying. Success by political maneuvering is a shallow satisfaction.*

CURRAN, JOHN CHARLES, JR., financial company executive; b. N.Y.C., Aug. 21, 1932; s. John Charles and Mildred (Herrman) C.; m. Valerie E. O'Donovan, Sept. 13, 1958; children: Valerie Catherine, Cinnia DeClare, Mary Christina, Sheila Mairead. B.S., Georgetown U., 1954; postgrad., N.Y. U. Grad. Sch. Bus. Adminstrn., 1957-60. Ofcl. asst. First Nat. City Bank, N.Y.C., 1957-60; asst. to pres. Sears, Roebuck Acceptance Corp., 1960-62; financing mgr. Ford Motor Credit Corp., N.Y.C. and Dearborn, Mich., 1962-69; v.p., treas. Dayton Hudson Corp., Mpls., 1969-71; pres. White Motor Credit Corp., Cleve., 1972-75; v.p., treas. White Motor Corp., Cleve., 1972-75; exec. v.p., dir. Field Enterprises Ednl. Corp., Chgo., 1975-78; pres., chief exec. officer Deutsche Credit Corp., Deerfield, Ill., 1979—. Mem. bd. Woodlands Acad. Sacred Heart. Served to 1st lt., inf. AUS, 1954-56. Mem. Fin. Execs. Inst. Clubs: Econ., Mid-Am. (Chgo.); Knollwood (Lake Forest, Ill.). Home: 844 Timber Ln Lake Forest IL 60045 Office: 2333 Waukegan Rd Deerfield IL 60015

CURRAN, JOHN J., securities dealer; b. N.Y.C., Jan. 27, 1931. Student, Fordham U., 1949-53. Bar: N.Y. 1961. With Bache Halsey Stuart Shields, Inc., N.Y.C., 1955—, now chmn. exec. com., sec., gen. counsel, and dir. Served with USMCR, 1953-55. Mem. Nat. Assn. Securities Dealers, N.Y. Stock Exchange. Office: Bache Group Inc Bach Plaza 100 Gold St New York NY 10038

CURRAN, MARK CONNEY, lawyer; b. Chgo., Sept. 11, 1924; s. William Thomas and Josephine (Cooney) C.; m. Mary Gladys Wholey, May 12, 1962 (dec. June 1963); 1 son, Mark; m. Mary Jane McCarthy, Oct. 31, 1964; children: Mary Jane, Anthony, Nicholas. B.S., St. Ambrose Coll., 1947; J.D., Northwestern U., 1950. Bar: Ill., Iowa. Trial atty. NLRB, Washington, 1950-52, Chgo., 1952-55; asst. counsel P.P.G. Industries, Pitts., 1956-67; assoc. gen. counsel Montgomery Ward & Co., Chgo., 1967-76; ptnr. Sidley & Austin, Chgo., 1976—. Bd. dirs. United Way, 1973-79. Served to lt. (j.g.) USN, 1943-46; Atlantic. Mem. ABA, Chgo. Bar Assn. Democrat. Roman Catholic. Clubs: Mid-Day, Chicago. Office: Sidley & Austin One First National Plaza Chicago IL 60603 *

CURRAN, MARK COONEY, lawyer; b. Chgo., Sept. 11, 1924; s. William Thomas and Josephine Mercedes (Cooney) C.; m. Mary Gladys Wholey, May 12, 1962 (dec.); m. 2d Mary Jane McCarthy, Oct. 31, 1964; children: Mark, Mary Jane, Anthony, Nicholas. B.S., St. Ambrose Coll., Devenport, Iowa, 1947; J.D., Northwestern U., 1950. Bar: Ill. 1950, Iowa 1950. Trial atty. NLRB, Washington, 1950-52, Chgo., 1952-55; asst. counsel PPG Industries, Inc., Pitts., 1956-67; assoc. gen. counsel Montgomery Ward & Co., Chgo., 1967-76; ptnr. Sidley & Austin, 1976—. Mem. adv. com. Ill. State Toll Hwy. Com., 1975-80. Served to lt. (j.g.) USN, 1943-46. Mem. ABA, Chgo. Bar Assn. Roman Catholic. Club: MidDay (Chgo.). Home: 794 Cherokee S Lake Forest IL 60045 Office: One First Nat Plaza 4800 Chicago IL 60603

CURRAN, MICHAEL WALTER, management scientist; b. St. Louis, Dec. 6, 1935; s. Clarence Maurice and Helen Gertrude (Parsons) C.; m. Jeanette Lucille Rawizza, Sept. 24, 1955 (div. 1977); children: Kevin Michael, Karen Ann, Kathleen Marie (dec.), Kimberly Elizabeth; m. Mary Jane Lemanek, Aug. 18, 1981. B.S., Washington U., St. Louis, 1964. With Monsanto Co., St. Louis, 1953-65, supervisory positions dept. adminstrv. services, 1956-64, research technician inorganic chems. div., 1964-65; sr. ops. research analyst Pet Inc., St. Louis, 1965-68; pres. Decision Scis. Corp., St. Louis, 1968—, also dir.; dir. Am. Fin. Planning Inc., St. Louis; instr. physics Washington U., 1964-67; lectr. in field. Co-author: Handbook of Budgeting, 1981; contbr. articles to profl. jours. Adviser Jr. Achievement, St. Louis, 1958-59; active United Way, St. Louis, 1958-62. Mem. Inst. Mgmt. Scis. (chmn. St. Louis chpt. 1971-72), Ops. Research Soc. Am., Internat. Platform Assn., Mensa, Intertel, Sigma Xi, Alpha Sigma Lambda. Developer theories of bracket budgeting and range estimating. Office: Decision Scis Corp PO Box 28848 Saint Louis MO 63123

CURRAN, STUART ALAN, English language educator; b. Detroit, Aug. 3, 1940; s. Lawrence Charles and Margaret Rachel (Dalton) C. B.A., U. Mich., 1962, M.A., 1963; postgrad., Cornell U., 1963-64; Ph.D., Harvard U., 1967. Asst. prof. English U. Wis., 1967-70, asso. prof., 1970-74; prof. U. Pa., 1974—, chmn. dept. English, 1977-80; vis. asso. prof. Johns Hopkins U., 1974; adv. dir. Am. Blake Found. Author: Shelley's Cenci: Scorpions Ringed with Fire, 1970, Shelley's Annus Mirabilis: The Maturing of an Epic Vision, 1975; editor: Keats-Shelley Jour; contbr. essays, revs. to profl. jours.; editor: LeBossu and Voltaire on the Epic, 1970, (with Joseph Wittreich) Blake's Sublime Allegory: Essays on The Four Zoas, Milton, and Jerusalem, 1973. Woodrow Wilson Found. fellow, 1962-63; Am. Philos. Soc. fellow, 1969; Henry E. Huntington Library fellow, 1970, 72; NEH fellow, 1970-71, 83-84; John Simon Guggenheim Found. fellow, 1973-74. Mem. MLA, Keats-Shelley Assn., Byron Soc., Phi Beta Kappa. Home: 320 S 16th St Philadelphia PA 19102 Office: 121 Bennett Hall U Pa Philadelphia PA 19104

CURRENCE, RICHARD MORRISON, offshore marine transportation executive; b. Ashville, N.C., July 10, 1938; s. William Eugene and Lucille (Morrison) C.; m. Rebecca McDonald, July 8, 1962; children: John McDonald, Richard M. Student, U. S.-Columbia, 1956-59, Wake Forest U., 1959-61; LL.B., Tulane U., 1964. Contract atty. Texaco, Inc., New Orleans, 1964-67; asst. sec., adminstrv. mgr. Tidewater Marine Service, Inc., New Orleans, 1967-73; v.p. adminstrn., sr. v.p., mgr. North Sea and Europe Gulf Fleet Marine Corp., 1973-77, pres., chief exec. officer, New Orleans, 1978—. Mem. Offshore Marine Service Assn. (chmn. bd. dirs. 1980-82), Nat. Ocean Industries Assn., Tulane U. Sch. Law Energy Law Adv. Bd. Clubs: New Orleans Petroleum, Bienville, City, Plimsoll. Home: 541 Audubon St New Orleans LA 70118 Office: Gulf Fleet Marine Corp Suite 2400 Canal Pl One New Orleans LA 70130

CURRENT, RICHARD NELSON, educator, historian; b. Colorado City, Colo., Oct. 5, 1912; s. Park Curry and Anna (Christiansen) C.; m. Rose Metcalf Bonar, Dec. 20, 1937 (dec. Oct. 1983); children: Annabelle, Dana Bonar.; m. Maria E. Trelease, May 4, 1984. A.B., Oberlin Coll., 1934; M.A., Fletcher Sch. Law and Diplomacy, 1935; Ph.D., U. Wis., 1939. Instr. social sci. Salisbury State Coll., 1938-42; asst. prof. history and polit. sci. Rutgers U., 1942-43; asst. prof. history Hamilton Coll., 1943-44; prof. history No. Mich. Coll., 1944-45; assoc. prof. history Lawrence Coll., 1945-47; May Treat Morrison prof. Am. history Mills Coll., 1947-50; asso. prof. U. Ill., 1950-53, prof., 1953-55; prof., head dept. history and polit. sci. Woman's Coll., U. N.C., 1955-60; prof. history U. Wis., Madison, 1960-66, William F. Allen prof., 1964-66; Disting. prof. Am. history U. N.C., Greensboro, 1966-83; lectr. Doshisha U., Kyoto, Japan, summer 1958; Dept. State lectr., India, 1959; Fulbright lectr. U. Munich, Germany, May-July, 1959, U. Chile, 1968; Harmsworth prof. Oxford (Eng.) U., 1962-63. Author: Old Thad Stevens, 1942, Pine Logs and Politics, 1950, Secretary Stimson, 1954, The Typewriter and the Men Who Made It, 1954, Daniel Webster and the Rise of National Conservatism, 1955, (with J.G. Randall) Lincoln the President; Last Full Measure, 1955 (Bancroft prize 1956), The Lincoln Nobody Knows, 1958, (with T.H. Williams, F. Freidel) A History of the U.S, 1959, Lincoln and the First Shot, 1963, John C. Calhoun, 1963, Three Carpetbag Governors, 1967, The History of Wisconsin: The Civil War Era, 1848-1873, 1976, Wisconsin: A Bicentennial History, 1977, Northernizing the South, 1983, Speaking of Abraham Lincoln, 1983; bd. editors: Am. Hist. Rev., 1960-65. Mem. So. Hist. Assn. (pres. 1974-75), Am. Hist. Assn., Orgn. Am. Historians (mem. exec. com. 1966-69), Wis. Hist. Soc., Phi Beta Kappa. Home: 122 E 7th St Hinsdale IL 60521

CURRENT-GARCIA, EUGENE, emeritus English language educator; b. New Orleans, July 8, 1908; s. Joseph and Bertha (Ehrhardt) C.-G.; m. Alva Adele Garrett, June 18, 1935; children: William J., Alison Eugenia (Mrs. Raymond F. Heyd), Adele (Mrs. Charles MacLean). A.B., Tulane U., 1930, M.A., 1932; A.M., Harvard U., 1942, Ph.D., 1947. Teaching fellow Tulane U., 1930-33; instr. English U. Neb., 1936-39; tutor Harvard U., 1942-43; instr. La. State U., 1944-47; from asst. prof. to prof. Auburn U., 1947-64, Hargis prof. Am. lit., 1964-79, prof. emeritus, 1979—. Author: O. Henry, 1965, (with W.R. Patrick) American Short Stories, 3d rev. edit, 1976, 4th rev. edit., 1981, What Is the Short Story, 1961, rev. edit., 1973, Short Stories of the Western World, 1969, Realism and Romanticism in Fiction, 1962, (with Dorothy Hatfield) Shem, Ham, and Japheth: Papers of W.O. Tuggle, 1973; Editor: (with Norman A. Brittin) So. Humanities Rev, 1967-79. Ford Found. fellow, 1953; Fulbright lectr., Greece, 1956-58. Mem. Southeastern MLA (exec. com. 1967-70), So. Humanities Conf. (v.p., sec.-treas. 1960-64), Phi Beta Kappa, Phi Kappa Phi (scholar 1974), Omicron Delta Kappa, Delta Upsilon. Home: 510 E Samford Ave Auburn AL 36830

CURREY, BRADLEY NORTON, JR., manufacturing company executive; b. Chattanooga, June, 21, 1930; s. Bradley Norton and Louise Sevier (Giddings) C.; m. Sally McClellan, May 16, 1953; children: Bradley Norton III, Anne McClellan, Laura Louise, Russell McClellan. A.B., Princeton U., 1951. With Trust Co. Ga., Atlanta, 1953-76, exec. v.p., dir., 1974-76; pres. Rock-Tenn Co., Norcross, Ga., 1978—; dir. Standard Coosa Thatcher Co., Chattanooga. Pres. Atlanta Symphony Orch., 1980; trustee Lovett Sch., Randolph Macon Womans Coll., Emory U., Am. Assembly, Atlanta Arts Alliance; pres. Research, Atlanta, 1979-80. Served with AUS, 1951-53. Mem. Atlanta C. of C. (pres. 1974), Paperboard Packaging Council (dir.), Am. Paper Inst. (dir. recycled paperboard div.). Clubs: Piedmont Driving, Commerce, Princeton of N.Y. Home: 876 Crest Valley Dr NW Atlanta GA 30327 Office: PO Box 98 Norcross GA 30091

CURRIE, ALLAN BALDWIN, constrn. co. exec.; b. Atlanta, May 26, 1937; s. Clifford George and Lulu (Baldwin) C.; children—Kimberly Jean, Julie Anne, Lynn Robin. B.A., Mich. State U., 1961. C.P.A., Mich. Audit supr. Coopers & Lybrand, Detroit, 1961-68; sec.-treas. Utley-James, Inc., Pontiac, Mich., 1968-77, treas., 1977—; pres. U.J.A. Inc., Pontiac, 1977—. Past pres. Lake Angelus Shores Assn. Mem. Am. Inst. C.P.A.'s, Mich. Assn. C.P.A.'s. Home: 2080 Lake Angelus Shores Pontiac MI 48055 Office: 1100 Opdyke Rd Pontiac MI 48056

CURRIE, BRUCE, artist; b. Sac City, Iowa, Nov. 27, 1911; s. Malcolm and Clara Mabel (Austin) C.; m. Ethel Magafan, June 30, 1946; 1 dau., Jenne Magafan. Student, Northwestern U., 1930-32, U. Chgo., 1932-33. One man shows, Am. embassy, Athens, Greece, 1952, Ganso Gallery, N.Y.C., 1953, 54, Roko Gallery, 1958, 60, Albany Inst. History and Art, 1958, Ulster County Community Coll., Kingston, N.Y., 1967, Joseloff Gallery, U. Hartford, 1968, Schenectady Mus., 1970, Jacques Seligmann Galleries, N.Y.C., 1978, Midtown Galleries, N.Y.C., 1980, 83, represented in permanent collections, State U. N.Y. at Albany, Dwight Art Meml., Mt. Holyoke Coll., Butler Inst. Am. Art, Kalamazoo Inst. Arts, N.A.D., Ulster County Community Coll., Kingston, N.Y., Berkshire Community Coll. Served with USAAF, 1942-45; N. Am. Recipient Purchase award Henry Ward Ranger Fund, N.A.D., 1964, 75; Clarke prize, 1966; Benjamin Altman figure prize, 1979; Gold medal of honor Nat. Arts Club, 1964; Albany Inst. History and Art award, 1967; Berle award Berkshire Art Assn., 1967; purchase award, 1973; Charles Noel Flagg Meml. prize Conn. Acad. Fine Arts, 1968; Soletsky award Nat. Soc. Painters in Casein and Acrylic, 1973; Grumbacher award, 1974; John J. Newman Meml. award, 1976; Wallach Meml. award, 1980; Wright Meml. prize Cooperstown Art Assn., 1978; grand prize, 1981; also others. Mem. Audubon Artists (medal of honor 1963, other awards 1962, 68, 70, 71, 76, 79), Am. Watercolor Soc. (Whitney award 1975, Winsor-Newton award 1981), Conn. Acad. Fine Arts, Phila. Watercolor Club., Nat. Soc. Painters in Casein and Acrylic. Home: RFD Box 284 Woodstock NY 12498

CURRIE, CHARLES LEONARD, college president; b. Phila., July 9, 1930; s. Charles Leonard and Elizabeth Katherine (Harper) C. A.B., Boston Coll., 1955, M.A., 1956; Ph.L., Weston Coll., 1956; Ph.D., Cath. U. Am., 1961; S.T.B., Woodstock Coll., 1962, S.T.L., 1964; D.Sc. (hon.), Bethany Coll., 1975. Joined S.J., Roman Cath. Ch., 1950; vis. scientist Nat. Bur. Standards, Washington, 1961-62, Nat. Research Council, Ottawa, Can., 1963-65; postdoctoral research fellow Cambridge U., Eng., 1965-66; asst. prof. chemistry Georgetown U., Washington, 1966-72; pres. Wheeling (W.Va.) Coll., 1972-82, Xavier U., Cin., 1982—; Bd. dirs. Coll. of Holy Cross, Oak Knoll Sch., Summit, N.J., Linsly Inst., Wheeling, Council Ind. Colls., W.Va. Humanities Found., St. Joseph's U., Phila.; chmn. W.Va. Bd. Miner Tng. Contbr. articles to profl. jours. V.p., bd. dirs. United Way of Upper Ohio Valley. Mem. Am. Chem. Soc., Chem. Soc. (London), N.Y. Acad. Scis., Washington Acad. Scis., AAUP, Am. Assn. Univ. Adminstrs., Assn. Jesuit Colls. and Univs., W.Va. Assn. Pvt. Colls., W.Va. Assn. Coll. and Univ. Pres., W.Va. C. of C., Sigma Xi. Clubs: Rotary; University (Pitts.). Office: Xavier University 3800 Victory Parkway Cincinnati OH 45207 *

CURRIE, CLIFFORD WILLIAM HERBERT, librarian; b. Ramsgate, Kent, Eng., Nov. 24, 1918; s. William Albert and Gladys Irene (Slingsby) C.; m. Inga-Britta Olsson, Oct. 14, 1972. B.A., Fitzwilliam Coll., Cambridge (Eng.) U., 1949, LL.B., 1950, M.A., 1954; M.A., St. Edmund Hall, Oxford (Eng.) U., 1973, B.C.L., 1974. Asst. librarian Cambridge U., 1951-53; public library dir. London Borough of Bromley, Eng., 1953-59; librarian Imperial Coll. Sci. and Tech., London, 1959-68; exec. dir. Can. Library Assn., Ottawa, Ont., 1968-71; librarian Ashmolean Library, Oxford, Eng., 1972-78, Coll. William and Mary, Williamsburg, Va., 1978—. Author: Prospects in Librarianship, 58, 63; editor: Can. Library Jour, 1968-71; adv. editor: Eighteenth Century Life, 1980—. Served with Brit. Army, 1939-45. Fellow Library Assn. Eng. (bd. advanced studies 1966-68); mem. Internat. Assn. Tech. Univ. Libraries (v.p. 1968, sec. 1962-67, dir.), Working Party Librarians and the Book Trade (founding mem.), Soc. Bookmen (exec. com. 1976—). Clubs: Athenaeum, Arts, Authors, London, Frewen, Oxford; Grolier (N.Y.C.). Home: 200 Nelson Ave Williamsburg VA 23185 Office: Earl Gregg Swem Library Coll of William and Mary Williamsburg VA 23185

CURRIE, DAVID PARK, lawyer, educator; b. Macon, Ga., May 29, 1936; s. Gillette Brainerd and Elmyr (Park) C.; m. Barbara Suzanne Flynn, Dec. 29, 1959; children—Stephen Francis, Margaret Rose. B.A., U. Chgo., 1957; LL.B., Harvard U., 1960. Bar: Ill. bar 1963. Law clk. to Hon. Henry J. Friendly U.S. Ct. Appeals, Ltd. Circuit, N.Y.C., 1960-61; to Hon. Felix Frankfurter U.S. Supreme Ct., Washington, 1961-62; asst. prof. law U. Chgo., 1962-65, asso. prof., 1965-68, prof. law, 1968—; coordinator environ. quality State of Ill., Chgo., 1970; chmn. Ill. Pollution Control Bd., Chgo., 1970-72; vis. prof. Stanford U. Law Sch., 1965, U. Mich. Law Sch., 1964, 68, U. Hannover, W. Ger., 1981. Author: Cases and Materials on Federal Courts, 1968, 75, On Pollution, 1975, (with R. Cramton and H. Kay) On Conflict of Laws, 1968, 75, 81, Federal Jurdidiction in a Nutshell, 1976, 81, Air Pollution: Federal Law and Analysis, 1981. Office: 1111 E 60th St Chicago IL 60637

CURRIE, EARL JAMES, transportation company executive; b. Fergus Falls, Minn., May 14, 1939; s. Victor James and Calma (Hammer) C.; m. Kathleen E. Phalen, June 3, 1972; children: Jane, Joseph. B.A., St. Olaf Coll., 1961; cert. in transp., Yale U., 1963;

P.M.D., Harvard U., 1974. With Burlington No. Inc., 1964—, asst. v.p., St. Paul, 1977-78, Chgo., 1978-80, v.p., gen. mgr., Seattle, 1980-83, sr. v.p., St. Paul, 1983—; pres. Camas Prairie R.R., Lewiston, Idaho, 1982-83, Longview Switching Co., Wash., 1982-83. Bd. dirs. United Way, King County, Wash., 1980-83, Corp. Council for Arts, Seattle, 1980-83, Jr. Achievement, Seattle, 1980—; trustee St. Martins Coll., Lacey, Wash., 1982-83. Mem. Am. Assn. R.R. Supts. (bd. dirs. 1979-80), Seattle C. of C. (dir. 1980-83). Republican. Roman Catholic. Clubs: Harbor (Seattle); Overlake (Medina, Wash.); Blue Hills (Kansas City, Mo.). Office: Burlington Northern Inc. 176 E 5th St Saint Paul MN 55101

CURRIE, GLENN KENNETH, service company executive; b. Stoneham, Mass., Sept. 23, 1943; s. Kenneth Aubrey and Muriel Adeline (Berry) C.; m. Susanne Gosnell, Feb. 6, 1971; children: Diana, Lara. A.B., Dartmouth Coll., 1965. Security analyst Paul Revere Life Ins. Co., 1970-72; asst. pres. Paul Revere Life Ins. co., 1972-73; v.p. investments Paul Revere Life Ins. Co., 1973-78; v.p. fin. internat. srevices div. Avco Corp., Cin., 1978, v.p. internat. ops., 1979; pres. Avco Overseas Service Corp., Houston, 1979-82; group exec. Avco Corp., Greenwich, Conn., 1982—; dir. Village Nat. Bank, Houston. Bd. dirs. Fleetwood Homeowners Assn. Served with USN, 1965-69. Mem. Houston C. of C., N.Y. Soc. Security Analysts, Fin. Analysts Fedn., W. Houston C. of C. (dir.). Office: 1275 King St Greenwich CT 06830 also: 17200 Park Row Houston TX 77084

CURRIE, JAMES BRADFORD, aerospace consultant; b. Milw., Sept. 18, 1925; s. James Washburn and Lucille Bradford (Torrey) C.; m. Laura Betty Jensen; children by previous marriage: James S., Michael B. Student, U. Wis., 1946-48; B.B.A., U. Mich., 1958; grad., Indsl. Coll. Armed Forces, 1970. Joined U.S. Air Force, 1943, advanced through grades to maj. gen., 1977, 468 combat missions as pilot, Korea and Vietnam; assigned to Japan and Korea, 1948-51; assigned to Air Research Devel. Command U.S. Air Force, 1952-57; assigned to France (U.S. Air Force), France, 1958-62, served in, India, Iran, Norway, Turkey, Zaire, 1962-64, Vietnam, 1964-65, Germany, 1966-69; assigned Hdqrs. U.S. Air Force, Washington, 1970-78, dir. programs, 1977-78; ret., 1979, cons. to aerospace industries, 1979—. Decorated D.S.M., D.F.C., Air medal with 12 oak leaf clusters, Legion of Merit, Bronze Star, others. Mem. Air Force Assn., Order Daedalions. Presbyterian. Clubs: Army-Navy Country, Crystal City. Address: 307 S Yoakum Pkwy 1826 Alexandria VA 22304

CURRIE, JAMES SLOAN, state official; b. Clarkton, N.C., Mar. 17, 1919; s. George Hendon and Marie (Sloan) C.; m. Virginia Layton Spruill, Sept. 3, 1946; children: Marie Sloan Thursby, Mary Virginia Jones. Student, Davidson Coll., 1935-36; B.S., U. N.C., 1939, J.D., 1948, M.S., 1949. Bar: N.C. 1948. Securities analyst Jefferson Standard Life Ins. Co., 1940-41; underwriting aide FHA, 1941-42; practiced law Chapel Hill, 1948-50; dir. N.C. Dept. Tax Research; mem. State Bd. Assessments and Tax Rev. Bd., 1950-57; N.C. commr. revenue, chmn. State Bd. Assessments; mem. Tax Rev. Bd., 1957-61; asst. treas. Carolina Power & Light Co., Raleigh, N.C., 1961-67, treas., 1967-78; bd. mgrs. Wachovia Bank & Trust Co., Raleigh, 1967-78; commr. of banks State of N.C., 1978—. Exec. sec. N.C. Tax Study Commn., 1955-57, chmn., 1967-69; chmn. bd. Wake County chpt. ARC, 1960-61; pres. Wake County Opportunities, Inc., 1965-66; mem. Raleigh adv. bd. Salvation Army, 1967; bd. visitors Peace Coll., 1973-79; trustee Presbyn. Home, 1980-83. Served to maj. Transp. Corps, AUS, 1942-46; PTO. Decorated Bronze Star, Cross Mil. Service. Mem. Raleigh C. of C., N.C., Wake County bar assns., Conf. State Bank Suprs. (dir. 1980—), Adminstrv. Mgmt. Soc. (past chpt. pres.), Raleigh Execs. Club (past pres.), Pi Kappa Alpha, Phi Alpha Delta. Presbyterian. Club: Rotary. Home: PO Box 17171 Raleigh NC 27609 *My criterion for achieving personal and professional growth is to accept the maximum responsibility within my capabilities which opportunity affords so long as the requirements are ethical and constructive and do not jeopardize the honor, dignity or uniqueness of the individuals involved.*

CURRIE, LEONARD JAMES, architect, planner, educator; b. Stavely, Alta., Can., July 28, 1913; s. Andrew and Florence (McIntyre) C.; m. Virginia M. Herz, Feb. 8, 1937; children: Barbara E., Robert G., Elizabeth A. B.Arch., U. Minn., 1936; M. Arch., Harvard U., 1938, Wheelwright traveling fellow, 1940-41. Apprenticed with Walter Gropius, Marcel Breuer, Cambridge, Mass., 1938-40; archeologist div. hist. research Carnegie Instn. Expdn. to Copan, Honduras, 1941; airport constrn. Pan Am. Airways U.S. Govt., Guatemala and Nicaragua, 1941-42; asst. prof. architecture Harvard, 1946-51; architect Architects Collaborative, Cambridge, Mass., 1946-51; chief tech. aid mission on housing U.S. Govt., Costa Rica, 1951; organized, directed Inter-Am. Housing Center, Bogota, Colombia, 1951-56; prof., head dept. architecture Va. Poly. Inst., 1956-62; dean Coll. Architecture and Art, U. Ill., Chgo., 1962-72; prof. Coll. Architecture and Art, U. Ill., Chgo. Circle, 1972-81; Fulbright Sr. fellow, 1972-73; vis. prof. U. Sains Malaysia, 1972-73; hon. prof. Universidad Nacional de San Antonio Abad, 1977, Universidad Nacional Villarreal, 1977; former partner firm Atkins, Currie and Payne (architects, engrs. and planners); now prin. Leonard J. Currie, FAIA, Architect; AID campus planning cons. Central Am. univs., 1964; OECD cons. campus planning and chief adviser on tech. cooperation U. Patras, Greece, 1973—; Mem. City of Chgo. Cultural Com., 1963-66, Va. Com. on Sch. Bldg. Research, 1956-62; chmn. subcom. on comprehensive community planning, mem. exec. com. Community Improvement Adv. Com. of City of Chgo.; co-promulgator Charter of Machu Picchu, 1977; Bd. mem. Chgo. Sch. Architecture Found. Author: (with Rafaela Espino) Housing in Costa Rica, 1951, Planning of Central American Campuses, 1964, Designing Environments for the Aging, 1977; Contbr. articles to profl. publs.; prin. works include schs. and residences, New Eng., chs., Wesley Found. bldgs., residences in, Va., plan for resort in, W. Va., regional plan, Sogamoso Valley, Colombia, (with others), Six Moon Hill, coop. community, Lexington, Mass., Grad. Center, Harvard; cons., Rockefeller Found. phys. facilities planning, Colombia, 1967, campus planning cons., Nat. U. Nicaragua, 1969-70. Served as officer AUS, 1942-45; ret. lt. col. Res. Decorated Medalla de Merito, Colombia, 1956; recipient Disting. Service award U. Ill. Alumni Assn., 1982, Test of Time award for Va. residence, 1982. Fellow Internat. Inst. Arts and Letters, AIA (1st honor award 1963); mem. Sociedad Colombiana de Arquitectos (hon.), Soc. Archtl. Historians, American Inst. Cert. Planners, Inter-Am. Planning Soc. Home: 1506 Carlson Dr Blacksburg VA 24060

CURRIE, MALCOLM RODERICK, scientist, aerospace executive; b. Spokane, Wash., Mar. 13, 1927; s. Erwin Casper and Genevieve (Hauenstein) C.; m. Sunya Lofsky, June 24, 1951; children—Deborah, David, Diana; m. Barbara L. Dyer, Mar. 5, 1977. A.B., U. Calif. at Berkeley, 1949, M.S., 1951, Ph.D., 1954. Research engr. Microwave Lab., U. Calif. at Berkeley, 1949-52, elec. engring. faculty, 1953-54; lectr. U. Calif. at Los Angeles, 1955-57; research engr. Hughes Aircraft Co., 1954-57, v.p., 1965-66; head electron dynamics dept. Hughes Research Labs., Culver City, Calif., 1957-60, dir. physics lab., Malibu, Calif., 1960-61, asso. dir., 1961-63, v.p., dir. research labs., 1963-65, v.p., mgr. research and devel. div., 1965-69; v.p. research and devel. Beckman Instruments, Inc., 1969-73; dir. def. research and engring. Office Sec. Def., Washington, 1973-77; v.p. missile systems group Hughes Aircraft Co., Canoga Park, Calif., 1977-83, exec. v.p., 1983—; mem. Def. Sci. Bd. Author articles. Served with USNR, 1944-47. Decorated comdr. Legion of Honor, France; named nation's outstanding young elec. engr. Eta Kappa Nu, 1958, one of 5 outstanding young men of Calif. Calif. Jr. C. of C., 1960. Fellow IEEE, AIAA; mem. Nat. Acad. Engring., Am. Phys. Soc., Phi Beta Kappa, Sigma Xi, Lambda Chi Alpha. Patentee in field. Home: 28780 Wagon Rd Agoura CA 91301 Office: Hughes Aircraft Co 200 N Sepulveda Blvd Mail Sta C2/A103 El Segundo CA 90245 *

CURRIE, NORMAN THORNE, food corporate executive; b. Toronto, Ont., Can., Feb. 27, 1928; s. James Arthur C. and Ida Maude (Johnson) Brown; m. Mona Van Ark, May 7, 1949; children: Joan, Janet, James. Pres., chief exec. officer Corp. Foods Ltd., Toronto, 1964—. Gov. Internat. Devel. Research Ctr. Can., Ottawa, Ont., 1973—. Fellow Inst. Chartered Accts. Ont.; mem. Can. Inst. Chartered Accts. (gov. 1978-82). Home: 14 Pheasant Ln Islington On Canada M9A 1T2 Office: Corporate Foods Ltd 1243 Islington Ave Toronto On Canada M8X 2W1

CURRIE, OVERTON ANDERSON, lawyer; b. Hattiesburg, Miss., Nov. 28, 1926; s. Edward Alexander and Terry (Anderson) C.; m. Lavona Stringer, Dec. 31, 1949; children: Iva Terry, Overton Anderson, Martha Lavona, Lucy Flora, Judy Stringer. Asso. Sci., Marion Inst., 1944; B.B.A., U. Miss., 1948, LL.B., 1949; B.D., Emory U., 1958, M.Div., 1968; LL.M., Yale U., 1958. Bar: Miss. Bar 1949, Ga. bar 1959. Practice in, Hattiesburg, Miss., 1949-55, Atlanta, 1959—, county prosecuting atty., 1952-55, spl. asst. atty. gen. Miss., 1954-55; mem. faculty Yale U. Law Sch., 1958-59; partner Smith, Currie & Hancock, 1959—; adj. prof. Emory U. Law Sch., 1966-73, Fla. State U., 1973; lectr. chpt. seminars on constrn. law Asso. Gen. Contractors, Ga., 1967, 72-74, 76, 80, Fla., 1967-68, 71, 73-75, 78-83, Carolinas, 1968-83, Okla., 1968, 76, Ind., 1969, 71, 75, 77, Pa., 1969, 72, 73, 79, N.Y., 1969-70, Ky., 1972-74, Va., 1973-75, Tenn., 1974-79, Ala., 1974-83; lectr. constrn. law seminars Mech. Contractors Assn., various locations, 1971-77; lectr. numerous other constrn. industry trade assns. Author: Preparing Construction Claims for Settlement, 1968, Subcontracts and Labor Problems, 1969, Differing Site (Changed) Conditions, 1971. Bd. dirs. Ga. Assn. Pastoral Care; mem. profl. adv. com. Pastoral Counseling Service. Served with U.S. Mcht. Marine Corps USNR, 1944-46. Mem. Am. Bar Assn. (nat. chmn. sect. on public contract law 1971-72, mem. council ho. of dels. 1972-74, nat. chmn. constrn. cases com. 1978-80), Am. Trial lawyers. (past nat. v.p.), Am. Arbitration Assn. (bd. dirs.), State Bar Ga., Lawyers Club Atlanta, Phi Delta Theta, Phi Delta Phi, Omicron Delta Kappa, Phi Kappa Phi (nat. pres.), Beta Gamma Sigma, Phi Sigma Alpha. Clubs: Piedmont Driving, Capital City, Commerce (Atlanta). Home: 1055 Nawench Dr NW Atlanta GA 30327 Office: 2600 Peachtree Center Harris Tower Atlanta GA 30043

CURRIE, RICHARD JAMES, food store chain executive; b. St. John, N.B., Canada, Oct. 4, 1937; s. Hugh O'Donnell and Agnes Coltart (Johnstone) C.; m. Beverly Trites, Sept. 15, 1962; children: Jennifer Lee, Bryn Margaret, Elizabeth Gay. B.Engring. in Chemistry, Tech. Univ. N.S., 1960; M.B.A., Harvard U., 1970. Process engr. Atlantic Sugar Refineries, 1960-63, refining supt., 1963-68; sr. assoc. McKinsey & Co., 1970; v.p. Loblaws Cos. Ltd., 1972-74, exec. v.p., 1974-76, pres., 1976—; chmn. Nat. Tea Co., 1981—. Mem. bd. regents Mt. Allison U.; bd. govs. Bishop Strachan Sch. Clubs: York, Rosedale Golf, Granite. Office: Loblaw Cos Ltd 22 St Clair Ave E Suite 1901 Toronto ON Canada M4T 2S7 *

CURRIE, WILLIAM RICHARD, publicist; b. Chgo., June 25, 1941; s. Richard Boyd and Mary Jane (Leeds) C.; m. Susan Tourville; children: Heather Beatrice, Sean Emmett. B.S., U. Ill., 1965. Reporter City News Bur., Chgo., 1965-68; reporter Chgo. Tribune, 1968-73, asst. city editor, 1973-75, copy editor, 1973-75, reporter, 1975-82; press sec. City of Chgo., 1982-83; with Carl Byoir & Assocs., Chgo., 1983—. Pres. Pipe Fest USA Inc.; Chmn. Chgo. Highland Games. Served with U.S. Army, 1966-68. Recipient Ill. A.P. award, 1971, Pulitzer prize, 1972, certificate of merit Am. Bar Assn., 1972. Mem. Ill. St. Andrews Soc. Club: Chgo. Stockyard Kilty Bagpipe Band. Office: 401 N Michigan Ave Chicago IL 60611

CURRIER, ROBERT DAVID, neurologist; b. Grand Rapids, Mich., Feb. 19, 1925; s. Frederick Plummer and Margaret (Hoedemaker) C.; m. Marilyn Jane Johnson, Sept. 1, 1951; children—Mary Margaret, Angela Maria. A.B., U. Mich., Ann Arbor, 1948, M.D., 1952, M.S. in Neurology, 1956; postgrad., Nat. Hosp., U. London, 1955, Dublin, Ireland, 1972. Intern, then resident in neurology Univ. Hosp., Ann Arbor, 1952-56; from instr. to asso. prof. U. Mich. Med. Sch., 1956-61; mem. faculty U. Miss. Med. Center, Jackson, 1961—, prof. neurology, 1971—, chief div., 1961-77, chmn. dept., 1977—; med. adv. bd. Nat. Ataxia Found.; mem. clin. adv. council Amyotrophic Lateral Sclerosis Soc. Am., 1979—; mem. Ataxia com. World Fedn. Neurology, 1981—. Co-author: Neurology Notes, 1977; co-editor: Yearbook of Neurology and Neurosurgery, 1981—; asst. editor for history: Archives of Neurology, 1983—; contbr. articles to med. jours. Served with USAAF, 1943-45; ETO. Decorated Air medal with 2 oak leaf clusters; NIH grantee, 1961-74. Fellow Am. Acad. Neurology (chmn. history com. 1980—); mem. Am. Neurol. Assn., Central Soc. Neurol. Research (pres. 1971), Sigma Xi, Alpha Omega Alpha. Home: 5529 Marblehead Dr Jackson MS 39211 Office: 2500 N State St Jackson MS 39216

CURRIER, RUTH, dancer, choreographer; b. Ashland, Ohio, Jan. 4, 1926; d. Elmer MacDonald and Zada (Holliman) Miller. Student, Black Mountain Coll., 1942-44, N.Y. U., 1944-45. Asst. to Doris Humphrey, 1950-58; prin. Ruth Currier and Dance Co., 1957-68; asso. prof. dance, dir. Am. Dance in Repertory, Ohio State U., Columbus, 1968-73; artistic dir. José Limón Dance Co., N.Y.C., 1973-77; freelance choreographer, dir., tchr., 1977—; dir. Ruth Currier Dance Studio, N.Y.C., 1981—; adj. mem. faculty Bennington Coll., 1958-63. Soloist, José Limón Dance Co., N.Y.C., 1949-63. *I cherish the ballast of my history, but I continue to struggle to prevent past and present from tyrannizing my future.*

CURRIER, THOMAS SHOLARS, lawyer; b. Shreveport, La., Aug. 18, 1932; s. Charles Ford and Caroline (Sholars) C.; m. Barbara Ann Dawson, July 3, 1954; children: Charles Ford, II, Thomas Dawson, Henrietta Sholars. Student, Princeton U., 1950-52; LL.B., Tulane U., 1956. Bar: La. 1956, Va 1967, D.C 1970, N.Y 1970. Asso. firm Stone, Pigman & Benjamin, New Orleans, 1957-59; asst. prof. law Tulane U., 1959-62; asso. prof. La. State U., 1962-64, U. Va., 1964-67, prof., 1967-70; partner firm Mudge Rose Guthrie & Alexander, N.Y.C., 1971-77, Dewey, Ballantine, Bushby, Palmer & Wood, 1977—; lectr. Practicing Law Inst.; mem. labor arbitration panel Fed. Mediation and Conciliation Service, Am. Arbitration Assn.; Trustee South Kent (Conn.) Sch., 1969-74, Davis and Elkins Coll., 1971-83. Author: (with J.W. Moore) Moore's Federal Practice, vol. 1B, 1963, (with Forrester) Federal Jurisdiction and Procedure, 1962; contbr. articles in law revs. Mem. Am. Law Inst., Nat. Assn. Bond Lawyers (dir.), Order of Coif. Club: Downtown Assn. Home: 580 Park Ave New York NY 10021 Office: 101 Park Ave New York NY 10128

CURRIN, SAMUEL THOMAS, lawyer; b. Oxford, N.C., Dec. 13, 1948; s. Thomas Benjamin and Lois (Brady) C.; m. Margaret Person, June 24, 1973. B.A. cum laude, Wake Forest U., 1971; J.D., U. N.C., 1974. Bar: N.C. 1974. Asst. U.S. atty. Eastern Dist. N.C., Raleigh, 1976-78; legis. asst. to Sen. Jesse Helms, Washington, 1978-81; U.S. atty. Eastern Dist. N.C., Raleigh, 1981—. Chmn. pub. affairs com. So. Bapt. Conv., 1983—. Republican. Lodge: Lions (Raleigh). Home: 1700 Pineview St Raleigh NC 27608 Office: US Atty PO Box 26897 Raleigh NC 27611

CURRIS, CONSTANTINE WILLIAM, university president; b. Lexington, Ky., Nov. 13, 1940; s. William C. and Mary (Kalpakis) C.; m. Roberta Jo Hern, Aug. 9, 1974. B.A., U. Ky., 1962, Ed.D., 1967; M.A., U. Ill., 1965. Vice pres., dean of faculty Midway (Ky.) Coll., 1965-68; dir. ednl. programs W.Va. Bd. Edn., Charleston, 1968-69; dean student personnel programs Marshall U., Huntington, W.Va., 1969-71; v.p., dean of faculty W.Va. Inst. Tech., Montgomery, 1971-73; pres. Murray (Ky.) State U., 1973-83, U. No. Iowa, 1983—. Exec. council Four Rivers Boy Scouts Am.; trustee Midway Coll.; mem. adv. council Nat. Small Bus. Devel. Center. Recipient Algernon S. Sullivan medallion U. Ky., 1962; named outstanding young man in Ky., Jaycees, 1974. Mem. Phi Beta Kappa, Omicron Delta Kappa, Sigma Chi. Democrat. Greek Orthodox. Club: Rotary. Office: Office of the Pres U No Iowa Cedar Falls IA 50614 *I am very grateful for what America has given me. As the son of a Greek immigrant who possessed neither education nor a command of the English language, I am keenly aware of the opportunities a government of and for the people affords its citizens. If there is any quality to which I attribute what success I may have achieved it would be that of an abiding devotion to the "public interest" rather than allowing my decisions to be determined by vested or parochial interests.*

CURRY, ALAN CHESTER, insurance company executive; b. Columbus, Ohio, Oct. 15, 1933; s. Harold E. and Martha (Dew) C.; children: Diane, Thomas, Steven, Timothy, Jeffrey, Barry. Student, U. Ill., 1951-52; B.S. in Edn., Ill. State U., (Normal), 1957. Various actuarial positions State Farm Mut. Automobile Ins. Co., Bloomington, 1952-70, v.p., actuary, 1970—. Mem. bd. indsl. advisors Rose-Huilman Inst. Tech. Fellow Casualty Actuarial Soc. (dir. 1970-74); mem. Am. Acad. Actuaries (dir. 1977-80), Midwestern Actuarial Forum (pres. 1972-73), Am. Risk and Ins. Assn., Am. Statis. Assn., Pi Gamma Mu, Pi Omega Pi, Kappa Delta Pi. Lodge: Masons. Home: 7 Canterbury Ct Bloomington IL 61701 Office: State Farm Mut Automobile Ins Co One State Farm Plaza Bloomington IL 61701

CURRY, ALTON FRANK, lawyer; b. Dallas, Aug. 21, 1933; s. William Hadley and Myrtle Estelle (Posey) McKinney; m. Carole B. Piepgrass, Feb. 14, 1960 (div. Nov. 1979); children: Robyn, Mark, John; m. Ann O. Williams, Apr. 12, 1980. B.A., Baylor U., 1958, LL.B., 1960. Bar: Tex. 1960. Assoc. Fulbright & Jaworski, Houston, 1960-70, ptnr., 1970—; spl. asst. to Atty. Gen. of Tex., 1964-65, 71-72. Trustee Found. for Bus., Politics and Econs., 1979—; chmn. adminstrv. bd. Methodist Ch. Served to cpl. U.S. Army, 1953-55. Mem. ABA, Tex. Bar Assn., Houston Bar Assn., Baylor Law Alumni Assn. (pres. 1979-80, dir. 1977-79), Phi Alpha Delta. Clubs: Houstonian (trustee 1980-83); Houston Yacht (LaPorte, Tex.)). Lodge: Masons. Home: 2707 Weslayan St Houston TX 77027 Office: Fulbright & Jaworski 800 Bank of the Southwest Houston TX 77002

CURRY, BERNARD FRANCIS, banker; b. N.Y.C., Aug. 8, 1918; s. John F. and Mary F. (McKiernan) C.; m. Lorraine Vocco Kelly, Sept. 10, 1947; 1 dau., Catherine V. A.B., Coll. Holy Cross, 1939; J.D., Columbia U., 1942. Bar: N.Y. 1946. Sec. to Surrogate Delehanty, New York County, 1946-47; asso. Davis Polk Wardwell, Sunderl & Kiendl, N.Y.C., 1947-55; with Morgan Guaranty Trust Co. N.Y., N.Y.C., 1955—, sr. v.p., 1970-82; pres. Morgan Trust Co. of Fla., 1982—; mem. adv. council Labor Dept., 1976-79. Vice pres., bd. dirs. Dom Mocquereau Found., N.Y.C., 1967—; trustee W. Alton Jones Found., N.Y.C., Flower Hosp., 1979-82, W. Alton Jones Cell Soc. Center, 1980—. Served with AUS, 1942-46. Mem. Assn. Bar City N.Y., N.Y. State Bar Assn., Am. Bankers Assn. (pres. trust div. 1979-80). Club: Knight of Malta. Home: 350 S Ocean Blvd Palm Beach FL 33480 Office: 350 Royal Palm Way Palm Beach FL 33480

CURRY, BILL, journalist; b. Cin., July 27, 1943; s. Richard Nye and Virginia Dee C.; m. Rebecca Reed, Dec. 12, 1980. B.A., Ohio State U., 1967; M.S. in Journalism, Columbia U., 1968. Reporter Washington Post, 1968-72, asst. Va. editor, 1972-74, day city editor, 1974-75, Weekly editor, 1975-77, chief Houston bur., 1977-80; Denver bur. chief Los Angeles Times, 1980—. Recipient 1st Place award William Randolph Hearst Nat. Writing Competition, 1965.

CURRY, BRYCE QUENTION, banker; b. Hartselle, Ala., Nov. 9, 1923; s. James Gordon and Grace Flossy (Sparkman) C.; m. Caroly Jetty Evans, Sept. 2, 1970; children: James Bryce, Evan Andrew; 1 dau. by previous marriage, Janet Susan. B.A., George Washington U., 1951, J.D. with honors, 1955. Page, Ho. of Reps., Washington, 1941-43, legis. clk. to Ho. majority whip, 1946; legis. clk. to Senator John J. Sparkman, 1947-50; legis research asst. U.S. Senate, 1950-53; dir. research Nat. Savs. & Loan League, 1953-56, asst. gen. counsel, 1956-59, gen. counsel, 1959-63; pres. Fed. Home Loan Bank of N.Y., N.Y.C., 1963—; Mem. bd. regents Seton Hall U. Bd. editors: George Washington U. Law Rev. Served to lt. USNR, 1943-46. Mem. D.C. Bar Assn., N.Y. County Lawyers Assn. Democrat. Club: World Trade Center. Home: 21 North Star Dr Morristown NJ 07960 Office: Fed Home Loan Bank of NY One World Trade Center Floor 103 New York NY 10048

CURRY, DANIEL ARTHUR, lawyer, corporation executive; b. Phoenix, Mar. 28, 1937; s. John Joseph and Eva May (Wills) C.; m. Joy M. Shallenberger, Sept. 5, 1959; children: Elizabeth Marie, Catherine Jane, Peter Damien, Jennifer Louise, Julia Maureen, David Gordon. B.S., Loyola U., Los Angeles, 1957, LL.B., 1960; postgrad., U. So. Calif. Law Center, 1964-69; postgrad. exec. program, Grad. Sch. Bus., Stanford U., 1980. Bar: Calif. 1961, Hawaii 1972, U.S. Ct. of Appeals 9th Circuit 1972, U.S. Dist. Ct. Central Dist. Calif. 1972, Dist. of Hawaii 1972, U.S. Ct. Mil. Appeals 1972, U.S. Customs Ct 1972. Asso. Wolford, Johnson, Pike & Covell, El Monte, Calif., 1964-65, Demetriou & Del Guercio, Los Angeles, 1965-67; counsel, corporate staff divisional asst. Technicolor, Inc., Hollywood, Calif., 1967-70; v.p., sec., gen. counsel Amfac, Inc., Honolulu, 1970-78, sr. v.p., gen. counsel, 1978—; Bd. dirs. Amfac Found.; bd. regents Chaminade U. Served to capt. USAF, 1961-64. Mem. Sigma Rho, Phi Delta Phi. Clubs: Pacific (Honolulu); St. Francis Yacht (San Francisco). Office: 700 Bishop St PO Box 3230 Honolulu HI 96801 50 O'Farrell PO Box 7813 San Francisco CA 94120

CURRY, FRANCIS JOHN, physician; b. San Francisco, July 19, 1911; s. William Martin and Madonna (Burke) C.; m. Beryl Marguerite Swannel, Apr. 10, 1948; children: Francis John, Joan F., Elizabeth Anne, Patrick F., Thomas F., Robert, William, James. B.S., U. San Francisco, 1936; M.D., Stanford U., 1946; M.P.H., U. Calif., 1964. Diplomate: Am. Bd. Preventive Medicine. Teaching asst., research asst. Stanford U., 1942-43; intern San Francisco Gen. Hosp., 1945-46; resident Fresno (Calif.) Gen. Hosp., 1946-47; resident, asst. dir. Ahwahnee Tri-county Hosp., Madera, Calif., 1947-50; resident Santa Clara County (Calif.) Hosp., 1951-53; practice medicine specializing in pulmonary diseases and internal medicine, San Francisco, 1956—; chief Tb div. San Francisco Health Dept., 1960-74, dir. health, hosps. and mental health, 1970-76; prof., spl. lectr. U. Calif., Berkeley, 1966—; prof. health care adminstr. Golden Gate U., 1973—; mem. staff San Francisco Gen. Hosp., 1956—, dir. chest clinic, 1956-74; mem. staff U. Calif. Hosp.; asst. clin. prof. medicine Stanford

U., 1957-70, clin. prof., 1970—; asst. clin. prof. U. Calif., San Francisco, 1958-68, asso. clin. prof., 1968-70, clin. prof., 1970—; clin. prof. community dentistry U. Pacific, 1970—; project dir. Tb Control Project for San Francisco, USPHS, 1962-76; vice chmn. med. advisory com. San Francisco Hosp. Service Study Project, 1962—; mem. U. Calif. at San Francisco Gen. Hosp. Planning Com., 1963-78; mem. adv. council Tb Control Surgeon Gen. USPHS, 1965-78; cons., lectr. in field. Contbr. articles to profl. jours. Served as capt. AUS, 1953-55. Fellow ACP, Am. Coll. Preventive Medicine, Am. Coll. Chest Physicians (pres. Calif. chpt. 1962-63, regent 1971-78), Am. Pub. Health Assn.; mem. AMA, Calif. Med. Assn., Sci. Research Soc. Am., Am. Thoracic Soc., Royal Soc. Health, Acad. Preventive Medicine, Internat. Coll. Chest Physicians (dir. 1972-78), Am. Legion, Sigma Xi. Home: 217 Kensington Way San Francisco CA 94127 Office: Univ Calif Medical Center 1487 4th Ave San Francisco CA 94122

CURRY, JAMES TRUEMAN, JR., mining company executive; b. Nevada City, Calif., June 12, 1936; s. James Trueman and Nancy (Sherwin) C.; m. Barbara Hartman, June 21, 1958; children—James Trueman, Jennifer, Steven John. B.S. in Civil Engring, U. Calif. at Berkeley, 1959; M.B.A., Stanford, 1962. With Utah Internat. Inc., San Francisco, 1962—, adminstrv. asst. to pres., 1962-65; asst. to mgr. Navajo (N.Mex.) Mine, 1965-66, adminstrv. mgr., 1966-68; adminstrv. mgr. Australian operations Utah Devel. Co., subsidiary, 1969-70; treas. Utah Internat. Inc., 1970-72, v.p., treas., 1972-75, fin. v.p., 1975-82, also dir.; pres., mng. dir. Utah Devel. Co., 1982—; Bd. dirs. St. Luke's Hosp., San Francisco. Bd. dirs. St. Luke's Hosp. Served with AUS, 1959-60. Clubs: Burlingame Country, Pauma Valley Country, Pacific Union. Office: 167 Eagle St Brisbane Queensland Australia

CURRY, JANE LOUISE, writer; b. East Liverpool, Ohio, Sept. 24, 1932; d. William Jack and Helen Margaret (Willis) C. Student, Pa. State U., 1950-51; B.S., Indiana U. of Pa., 1954; postgrad., UCLA, 1957-59; A.M., Stanford U., 1962, Ph.D., 1969, U. London, 1961-62, 65-66. Tchr. art East Liverpool Schs., 1955, Los Angeles Schs., 1956-59; teaching asst. dept. English Stanford U., 1959-61, 64-65, acting instr., 1967-68. Author: Down from the Lonely Mountain, 1965, Beneath the Hill, 1967, The Sleepers, 1968, The Change-Child, 1969, The Daybreakers, 1970, Mindy's Mysterious Miniature, 1970, Over the Seas's Edge, 1971, The Ice Ghosts Mystery, 1972, The Lost Farm, 1974, Parsley Sage, Rosemary and Time, 1975, The Watchers, 1975, The Magical Cupboard, 1976, Poor Tom's Ghost, 1977, The Birdstones, 1977, The Bassumtyte Treasure, 1978, Ghost Lane, 1979, The Wolves of Aam, 1981, Shadow Dancers, 1983. Office: Atheneum Publishers 597 5th Ave New York NY 10017

CURRY, JERRY RALPH, army officer; b. McKeesport, Pa., Sept. 7, 1932; s. Jesse Aaron and Mercer Marion C.; m. Charlene Elaine Cooper, June 6, 1953; children: Jerry, Toni, Natasha. B.A., U. Nebr., 1960; M.S. in Internat. Relations, Boston U., 1970; D.Ministry, Luther Rice Sem., 1978; grad., U.S. Army War Coll., 1973, Command and Gen. Staff Coll., 1967. Commd. 2d lt. U.S. Army, 1952, advanced through grades to maj. gen., 1978, sr. advisor to 41st ARVN Regiment, Vietnam, 1970-71; ops. research analyst Office of Asst. Vice Chief of Staff, U.S. Army, Washington, 1971-72; brigade comdr. 3d Brigade, 8th Inf. Div., Germany, 1973; chief of staff V Corps, Frankfurt, Germany, 1975-76; dep. comdg. gen. Mil. Dist. of Washington, 1976-77; comdg. gen. Mil Dist. of Washington, 1977—; asst. div. comdr. 4th Inf. Div., Ft. Carson, Colo., 1977-78; comdg. gen. U.S. Army Test and Evaluation Command, Aberdeen Proving Ground, Md., 1978-79; dep. asst. sec. for pub. affairs Dept. Def., 1979—. Bd. dirs. Greenleaf Found., 1979—. Decorated Legion of Merit with oak leaf cluster, Bronze Star with V device, Silver Star, Cross of Gallantry with palm, Vietnam; recipient Disting. Alumni U. Nebr., 1979. Mem. Assn. U.S. Army, Am. Def. Preparedness Assn., Nat. Eagle Scout Assn., NAACP, Phi Alpha Theta. Office: US Army Military Dist Washington DC 20319

CURRY, NANCY ELLEN, educator; b. Brockway, Pa., Jan. 26, 1931; d. George R. and Mary F. (Covert) C. B.A., Grove City Coll., 1952; M.Ed., U. Pitts., 1956, Ph.D., 1972. Lic. psychologist, Pa. Tchr. public schs., East Brady and Oakmont, Pa., 1952-55; presch. demonstration tchr. Arsenal Family and Children's Center, U. Pitts., 1955-79, asso. dir., 1971-79; instr. Sch. of Health Related Professions, U. Pitts., 1956-61, asst. prof., 1961-72, asso. prof., 1972-75, prof., 1975—, acting chmn. dept. child devel./child care, 1972-73, chmn. dept., 1973—, also mem. faculty; asso. Pitts. Psychoanalytic Inst., 1974—; Fulbright exchange tchr. North Oxford Nursery Sch., Oxford, Eng., 1957-58; asso. dir. early childhood project Edn. Professions Devel. Act, U.S. Office of Edn., 1970-74; cons. in field. Co-producer 12 films on children's play; author numerous articles on child devel. Mem. AAUP, Assn. for Care of Children in Hosps., Nat. Assn. for Edn. of Young Children, Am. Psychol. Assn., Am. Psychoanalytic Assn. Office: 213 Pennsylvania Hall Univ Pittsburgh Pittsburgh PA 15261

CURRY, PETER DUNCAN, broadcasting and investment executive; b. Copenhagen, Denmark, July 12, 1912; s. Duncan Steele and Bertha (Laxdal) C.; m. Susan Lynne Guest; 1 dau., Tara Susan; children by previous marriage—Duncan Steele, Gerald Mark, Constance Kathleen, Patrick Murphy. Ed., Ridley Coll., St., Catharines, Ont., also Bishop's U., Lennoxville, Que.; LL.D. (hon.), U. Man., 1963. Dep. chmn. Power Corp. Can., Ltd.; chmn. bd., dir. Cablecasting Ltd.; dep. chmn., dir. Shawinigan Industries Ltd., Trans-Can. Corp. Fund; pres. Dromore Investment Co. Ltd., Greater Winnipeg Cablevision Ltd.; dir. Inco Ltd., CAE Industries Ltd. Trustee N. Am. Wildlife Found. Clubs: Manitoba, Toronto; Mount Royal (Montreal, Que.). Home: 7 Braeside Pl Westmount PQ H3Y 3E8 Canada Office: 759 Victoria Sq Montreal PQ H2Y 2K4 Canada

CURRY, PIERS LAND, telecommunications company executive; b. Armonk, N.Y., May 26, 1938; s. Robert Arthur and Sietske (Land) C.; m. Margaret Gossett, June 5, 1961; 1 dau., Sandra Byrd; m. Mona Faye Morrison, Mar. 11, 1973; 1 son, Piers Land. B.S., Columbia U., 1962. C.P.A. N.Y. Mgr. Arthur Young & Co., N.Y.C., 1962-70; asst. v.p. A.G. Becker, N.Y.C., 1970-77; dir. acquisitions SCM Corp., N.Y.C., 1977-80; v.p. corp. devel. Am. Express, N.Y.C., 1980-81; v.p. bus. devel. GTE Corp., Stamford, Conn., 1981—; mem. Conn. Venture Group, Stamford, 1981—. Pres. Byram Hills Bd. Edn., Armonk, N.Y., 1977-80; chmn. devel. com. North Castle Pub. Library, Armonk, 1981—; chmn. fin. com. St. Stephens Episcopal Ch., Armonk, 1982—; mem. Zoning Bd. Apls., Armonk, 1982—. Mem. Assn. Corp. Growth (sec. 1982—), Am. Inst. C.P.A.'s, N.Y. State Soc. C.P.A.'s. Clubs: Univ. (N.Y.C.); Whippoorwill (Armonk). Home: 441 Bedford Rd Armonk NY 10504 Office: GTE Corporation One Stamford Forum Stamford CT 06904

CURRY, RICHARD ORR, educator; b. White Sulphur Spring, W.Va., Jan. 26, 1931; s. Ernest Chalmers and Ida Mitt (Atkinson) C.; m. Patricia Leist, Apr. 6, 1954 (dec. 1967); children: Kimberly, Andrea, Jonathan; m. Patricia Montenegro, Feb. 11, 1968; 1 stepson, Michael Del Rosario. B.A., Marshall U., 1952, M.A., 1956; Ph.D., U. Pa., 1961; postdoctoral fellow, Harvard Div. Sch., 1965-66. Instr. European history Morris Harvey Coll., Charleston, W.Va., 1959-60; instr. Am. history Pa. State U., 1960-62; vis. asst. prof. Am. history U. Pitts., 1962-63; asst. prof. Am. history U. Conn., Storrs, 1963-66, assoc. prof., 1966-71, prof., 1971—; lectr., participant numerous seminars and symposia U.S., Philippines, Australia; assoc. dir. NDEA Inst. for High Sch. Tchrs. Am. History, (U. Conn.), summers 1965, 66; cons., critic Holt, Rinehard and Winston, Little, Brown & Co., Dodd, Mead & Cook, Allyn & Bacon, Dryden Press, Prentice-Hall, Iowa State U. Press, U. Mo. Press, La. State U. Press, Can. Research Council, NEH, others. Author: A House Divided: A Study of Statehood Politics and the Copperhead Movement in West Virginia, 1964, (with others) The Shaping of America, 1972, The Shaping of American Civilization, 2 vols., 1972; editor: The Abolitionists, 1965, (with others) Slavery in America: Theodore Weld's American Slavery As It Is, 1972; contbg. editor: Radicalism, Racism and Party Aligment: The Border States During Reconstruction, 1969, Conspiracy: The Fear of Subversion in American History, 1972; contbr. articles to profl. jours. Served with USN, 1952-54. Fellow Am. Assn. State and Local History, 1964, Soc. for Values in Higher Edn., 1965-66; named Ludwig von Mises fellow, 1982-83; fellow Social Sci. Research Council, 1966, NSF, 1966, NEH, 1967, Am. Philos. Soc., 1967, 70; named Fulbright lectr., 1981. Mem. New Eng. Hist. Assn., Soc. for Values in Higher Edn.

CURRY, ROBERT LEE, publishing company executive; b. Ossining, N.Y., Jan. 7, 1933; s. Vincent J. and Ruth (Brundage) C.; m. son, Michael R. Student, Fairleigh Dickinson U., 1955-58, Pace Coll., 1958-60; sr. mgmt. programs, U. Pa., UCLA, Harvard U., Dartmouth Coll., 1970-80. In sales Am. Cyanamid Co., N.Y.C., 1956-68; gen. mgr. Med. Econs. Co., Litton Industries, N.Y.C., 1968-75; pub. Mc-Graw-Hill Publs. Co., N.Y.C., 1975-81; pres. Hosp. Equities Inc., N.Y.C., 1981-82; chmn. Med. Pub. Enterprises, North Ft. Lee, N.J., 1982—. Mem. Ossining Zoning Bd. Appeals, 1966-68. Served with USN, 1950-55. Mem. Pharm. Mfrs. Assn., Pharm. Advt. Council, Midwest Pharm. Advt. Club, Nat. Wholesale Druggists Assn., Am. Public Health Assn., Am. Geriatric Soc. Clubs: Tuxedo Park Country, N.Y. Athletic. Home: 145 W 58th St New York NY 10019 44 Eileen Dr Mahwah NJ Office: 1 Bridge Plaza North Fort Lee NJ

CURRY, ROBERT LEE, lawyer; b. Lamont, Wis., May 10, 1923; s. Irving Gregg and Emma (Zimmerman) C.; m. Muriel Clapp, July 29, 1950; children—Robert Lee J., Laura Lynne, Melinda Ann. B.S., Lawrence U., 1948; LL.B., U. Wis., 1953. Bar: Wis. bar 1953. Asso. firm Boardman, Suhr, Curry & Field, Madison, Wis., 1953-56, sr. partner, 1956-73; v.p., gen. counsel CUNA Mut. Ins. Soc., Madison, 1964-73, pres., 1973—, dir., 1972—, CUNA Credit Union, 1965-70, pres., 1968-69; dir. Cumis Ins. Soc., 1972—, pres., 1973—. Served with USAAF, 1942-46. Mem. Am. Law Inst., U. Wis. Law Alumni Assn. (dir. 1967-70, pres. 1969-70), Order of Coif. Home: 4805 Fond du Lac Trail Madison WI 53705 Office: 5910 Mineral Point Rd Madison WI 53705

CURRY, STOWERS LEIGH, JR., govt. ofcl.; b. Bklyn., Sept. 19, 1924; s. Stowers Leigh and Frances (Upton) C.; m. Jacqueline F. Marois, Aug. 21, 1954. A.B., George Washington U., 1948, LL.B., 1950. Bar: D.C. bar 1950, also U.S. Supreme Ct. bar 1968. Atty.-adviser HHFA, 1950-54, asst. regional counsel San Francisco office, 1954-56; chief counsel Urban Renewal Adminstrn., 1956-66, Renewal Assistance Adminstrn., HUD, 1966-68; asso. gen. counsel for community devel. HUD, 1968-77, asso. dep. gen. counsel, 1977-79, dep. gen. counsel (ops.), 1979—. Served with AUS, 1943-46; PTO. Mem. Am., Fed. bar assns. Home: 6236 Lakeview Dr Falls Church VA 22041 Office: 451 7th St SW Washington DC 20410

CURSCHMANN, MICHAEL JOHANN HENDRIK, educator; b. Cologne, Germany, Jan. 11, 1936; came to U.S., 1963; s. Fritz Heinrich and Hanna Regine (Schinnerer) C.; m. Beryl G. Davis, Jan. 14, 1961; children—Jane, Paul. Student, Munich U., 1954-56, 58-60, Dr. phil., 1962, London U., 1956-57. Asst. prof. Munich U., 1961-63; asst. prof. dept. Germanic langs. and lit. Princeton U., 1963-65, asso. prof., 1966-68, prof., 1969—, chmn. dept., 1979—. Author works in field. Guggenheim fellow, 1970-71. Mem. Medieval Acad. Am., MLA, Internationale Vereinigung fur Germanische Sprachen und Literaturen. Home: 134 Sycamore Rd Princeton NJ 08540 Office: 230 East Pyne Princeton Univ Princeton NJ 08544

CURSON, THEODORE, musician; b. Phila., June 3, 1935; s. Leroy and Reava (Paige) C.; m. Marjorie N. Goltry, Apr. 1, 1967; children: Charlene, Theodore II. Student, Mastbaum Sch., Granoff Music Conservatory, Phila., 1952-53. Mem. Charles Mingus' Jazz Workshop, 1959-60; guest instr. U. Vt. Festival of Contemporary Music, 1968; instr. music Warsaw U.; pres. Nosruc Pub. Co., Jersey City, from 1961. Trumpeter with, Max Roach, Philly Joe Jones, Cecil Taylor, Eric Dolphy, 1960-63; appeared radio, TV, clubs, also, jazz festivals, including Nice, Jazz Yatra, India), Antibes, Aix en Provence, Lugano, Bologna, Macerata, Prague, Bled, Warsaw, Molde, Kongsberg, Ahus, Laren, Pori, 1964-81, U.S. festivals Birdland, Monterey, Newport/ N.Y., Newport Rebels Festival, Univ. concerts, including, Columbia, N.Y.U., Hobart Coll., Western Wash. Coll., Grinnell Coll., U. Calif. at Santa Monica, U. Calif. at Berkeley, U. Vt., toured India, Middle East and N. Africa for, State Dept., 1980; guest soloist, Norddoutscher Rundfunk TV; star, P.B.S. TV show Jazz Set, 1972; (Named New Star Monterey Jazz Festival 1962, winner Trumpet sect. Down Beat Internat. Critics Poll 1966, Ted Curson & Co. winner Down Beat Reader's Poll 1978, named New Jazz Artist Jazz Podium, Germany, recipient L.I. Musicians Soc. award 1970, Pori (Finland) City Standard 1978); Composer: Nosruc Waltz, 1960, Flatted Fifth, 1960, Straight Ice, 1965, Typical Ted, 1970, The Leopard, 1964, Reava's Waltz, Airi's Tune, Searchin for the Blues; rec. artist: Plenty of Horn, 1961, Fire Down Below, 1963, Tears for Dolphy, 1976, New Thing and Blue Thing, 1965, Urge, 1966, Ode to Booker Ervin, 1970, Pop Wine, 1972, Quicksand, 1975, Jubilant Power, 1976, Blue Piccolo, 1976, Flip Top, 1977, Typical Ted, 1977, The Trio, 1979, I Heard Mingus, 1980, Snake Johnson, 1981; music for films include Teorema, 1968, Notes for a Film on Jazz, 1968. Mem. Am. Fedn. Musicians. *

CURTHOYS, NORMAN P., biochemistry educator, consultant; b. Buffalo, Apr. 29, 1944; s. Albert J. and Emily M. (Ellman) C.; m. Linda H. Harriger, June 22, 1967; children: Paul, Michele. B.S. in Chemistry, Clarkson Coll., Potsdam, N.Y., 1966; Ph.D. in Biochemistry, U. Calif.-Berkeley, 1970. Postdoctoral fellow Washington U., St. Louis, 1970-72; asst. prof. biochemistry U. Pitts., 1972-77, assoc. prof., 1977-82, prof., chmn. dept., 1982—; vis. prof. U. Tubingen, W.Ger., 1977; mem. med. biochemistry study sect. NIH, 1982-85. Editorial bd.: Archives of Biochemsitry and Biophysics, 1977-82; contbr. articles to sci. jours., chpts. to books. Am. Cancer Soc. postdoctoral fellow, 1970-72; vis. fellow Alexander von Humboldt Found., 1977; research grantee NIH, 1973-87; recipient Research Career Devel. award NIH, 1976-81. Mem. Am. Chem. Soc., Am. Soc. Biol. Chemists. Office: Dept of Biochemistry U Pittsburgh Pittsburgh PA 15261

CURTI, MERLE EUGENE, historian; b. Papillion, Nebr., Sept. 15, 1897; s. John and Alice (Hunt) C.; m. Margaret Wooster, June 16, 1925 (dec. Sept. 1961); children—Nancy Alice Holub, Sister Felicitas Curti; m. Francis Bennett Becker, Mar. 9, 1968 (dec. Feb. 1978). A.B. summa cum laude, Harvard, 1920, A.M., 1921, Ph.D., 1927; student, Sorbonne, 1924-25; L.H.D., Northwestern U., 1950, U. Pa., 1962, Western Res. U., (now Case Western Res. U.), 1962, U. Mich., 1964, Adelphi U., 1965, U. Nebr., Drake U., 1967, U. Wis. at Milw., 1969; Litt.D., Rider Coll., 1970, Doane Coll., 1976; L.H.D., Beloit Coll., 1979. Vis. prof. Clark U., U. Chgo., UCLA, U. Vt.; instr. history Beloit Coll., 1921-22; asst. prof. Smith Coll., 1925-27, asso. prof., 1927-29, prof., 1929-35, Dwight Morrow prof., 1936-37; prof. history Tchrs. Coll., Columbia, 1937-42, U. Wis., 1942-68, Frederick Jackson Turner prof., 1947-68, now emeritus; Guggenheim fellow, 1929-30; vis. prof. Watumull Found. to univs. India, 1946-47; vis. prof. history U. Tokyo, 1959-60, U. Melbourne, 1964; vis. scholar Huntington Library, 1936-37, 69; Fulbright Conf. Am. Studies Cambridge, 1952, Hyderabad, 1964; mem. adv. com. to U.S. mem. commn. history Pan Am. Inst. History and Geography, 1949-54; emeritus advisor Friends Hist. Library Swarthmore Coll., 1975. Author: Austria and the U.S. 1948-1852, 1927, American Peace Crusade, 1929, Bryan and World Peace, 1931, Social Ideas of American Educators, 1935, The Learned Blacksmith: Letters and Jours. of Elihu Burritt, 1937, Growth of American Thought, 1943, 64 (Pulitzer award), Introduction to America, 1944, Roots of America Loyalty, 1946, (with Vernon Carstensen) University of Wisconsin, a history, 1949, (with L. P. Todd) America's History, 1950, (with W. Thorp and C. Baker) American Issues, 1950, (with R.H. Shryock, T.C. Cochran and F.H. Harrington) An American History, 1950, (with others) American Scholarship in the Twentieth Century, 1953, (with Kendall Birr) Prelude to Point Four, 1954, Probing Our Past, 1955, The American Paradox, 1956, The Making of an American Community, 1959, (with Paul Todd) Rise of the American Nation, 1960, 66, 74, 76, American Philanthropy Abroad: A History, 1963, (with Roderick Nash) Philanthropy in the Shaping of American Higher Education, 1965, Human Nature in American Historial Thought, 1969, Human Nature Nature in American Thought, A History, 1980; also articles. Bd. dirs. Harry S. Truman Library, 1958-61; Fellow Center Advanced Study in Behavioral Scis., 1956. Recipient award for distinguished scholarship Am. Council Learned Socs., 1960. Hon. fellow Wis. Acad. Sci., Arts and Letters, Wis. Hist. Soc. (bd. curators), Swedish Order of No. Star; mem. AAUP, Soc. Am. Historians, Social Sci. History Assn., Am. Hist. Assn. (pres. 1953-54), Orgn. Am. Historians (bd. editors 1936-40, pres. 1951-52), Soc. Sci. Research Council, Am. Council Learned Socs. (vice chmn. bd. dirs. 1958-59), Am. Philos. Soc., Am. Acad. Arts and Scis., Nat. Council for Social Studies, Am. Antiquarian Soc., Historic Madison (hon.), Phi Beta Kappa (senator 1947-52, pres. Wis. 1957-58), Phi Alpha Theta. Clubs: University, Madison. Lyme Center NH 03769

CURTIN, DAVID YARROW, educator, chemist; b. Phila., Aug. 22, 1920; s. Ellsworth Ferris and Margeretta (Cope) C.; m. Constance O'Hara, July 1, 1950; children—Susan McLean, Kathy Gardner, David Ferris, Jane Yarrow. A.B., Swarthmore Coll., 1943; Ph.D., U. Ill., 1945. Pvt. asst. Harvard, 1945-46; instr., then asst. prof. chemistry Columbia, 1946-51; mem. faculty U. Ill., Urbana, 1951—, prof. chemistry, 1954—, head div. organic chemistry, 1963-65; Vis. lectr. Inst. de Quimica, Mexico, summer 1955, U. Tex., 1959; Reilly lectr. U. Notre Dame, 1960. Mem. editorial bd.: Organic Reactions, 1954- 64; adv. bd., 1965—; mem. bd. editors: Jour. Organic Chemistry, 1962-66. Mem. Am., Brit., Swiss chem. socs., Nat. Acad. Sci., Am. Crystallographic Assn. Spl. research organic reaction mechanisms, stereochemistry, exploratory organic chemistry, reactions in solid state. Home: 3 Montclair Rd Urbana IL 61801

CURTIN, JANE THERESE, actress, writer; b. Cambridge, Mass., Sept. 6, 1947; d. John Joseph and Mary Constance (Farrell) C.; m. Patrick F. Lynch, Apr. 31, 1975. A.A., Elizabeth Seton Jr. Coll., 1967; student, Northeastern U., 1967-68. Appeared: in plays The Proposition, Cambridge and N.Y.C., 1968-72, Last of the Red Hot Lovers touring co., 1973; Broadway debut: Candida, 1981; author, actress: Off-Broadway mus. rev. Pretzels, 1974-75; star: TV series NBC Saturday Night Live, 1975-79, Kate & Allie, 1984—; appeared: in films Mr. Mike's Mondo Video, 1979, How to Beat the High Cost of Living, 1980; TV films include Divorce Wars-A Love Story. Recipient Emmy nomination, 1977. Mem. Screen Actors Guild, Actors Equity, AFTRA. Office: care Creative Artists Agy 1888 Century Park E Suite 1400 Los Angeles CA 90067 *

CURTIN, JOHN T., judge; b. 1921. B.S., Canisius Coll. Bar: N.Y. bar 1949. Formerly U.S. atty. for Western Dist. N.Y.; judge U.S. Dist. Ct. for Western N.Y., Buffalo, 1967—, now chief judge. Office: 624 US Court House Buffalo NY 14202 *

CURTIN, JOHN WILLIAM, plastic surgeon; b. Pitts., Mar. 1, 1922; s. Patrick John and Nelle (Joyce) C.; m. Jean Ellen Stewart, Dec. 29, 1951; childrenJohn William, Shawn Ellen. B.S., U. Pitts., 1943, M.D., 1947. Diplomate: Am. Bd. Plastic Surgery. Intern Mercy Hosp., Pitts., 1947-48; surg. resident Pitts. Hosp., 1948-50, U.S. Naval Hosp., 1950-51; resident plastic surgery U. Ill. Research and Ednl. Hosp., 1953-55; prof. surgery Rush Med. Sch., 1971—, chmn. dept. plastic and reconstructive surgery, 1971—; mem. faculty U. Ill. Coll. Medicine, 1953—, clin. prof. surgery, 1964—; attending plastic surgeon U. Ill. Hosp., 1953—, W. Side VA Hosp., 1954—, Cleft Palate Center, U. Ill. Coll. Medicine, 1955—, Presbyn.-St. Luke's Hosp., 1953—; cons. plastic surgery C., R. I. & P. R.R., Chgo.; Municipal Tb Sanitarium, Chgo. Tb Sanitarium, Great Lakes Naval Hosp. Contbr. med. jours. Chmn. med. adv. com. Chgo. Met. unit Nat. Found.-March Dimes, 1972—. Served with USNR, 1950-52; Korea. Mem. A.M.A. (chmn. sect. on plastic reconstructive and maxillofacial surgery 1972—), Ill., Chgo., Pa. med. socs., Chgo., Central surg. assns., A.C.S. (gov. 1974—, chmn. adv. council for plastic and maxillofacial surgery), Am. Soc. Plastic and Reconstructive Surgeons, Inst. Medicine Chgo., Midwest Surg. Assn., Am. Assn. Plastic Surgeons, Soc. Internat. de Chirurgie, Am. Cleft Palate Assn., Clin. Soc. U. Surgeons, Pan-Am., Pan-Pacific med. assns., Am. Assn. Surgery Trauma. Home: 1180 Hill Rd Winnetka IL 60093 Office: Prudential Bldg 130 E Randolph St Chicago IL 60601

CURTIN, MICHAEL EDWARD, international banking executive; b. Tulsa, Sept. 13, 1939; s. John D. and Agnes Marie (Meyercord) C.; m. Anne E. O'Grady, Aug. 17, 1963; children: Victoria Marie, Theodore Charles, Christianne Marie, Susan Marie. B.A., U. Notre Dame, 1961; M.A., U. Chgo., 1965. Asst. mgr. W.R. Grace & Co., N.Y.C., 1965-70, Chile, 1965-70; v.p. sec. Marine Insternat. Corp., Newark, N.J., 1970-72; chief fin. officer Satra Corp., N.Y.C., 1973-78; asst. treas. Revlon Inc., N.Y.C., 1978-81; exec. v.p. Inter-Am. Devel. Bank, Washington, 1981—; cons. Roburn Internat., N.Y.C., 1977-78. Pres. Princeton Skating Club, 1977; bd. trustees Princeton Pee-Wee Hockey Assn., 1975-80, Helen Kellogg Inst., U. Notre Dame, 1983—. Republican. Roman Catholic. Clubs: Springdale Golf (Princeton); Bretton Woods (Washington). Home: 3503 Springfield Ln NW Washinton DC 20008 Office: Inter-Am Devel Bank 808 17th St NW Washinton DC 20577

CURTIN, PHILIP DE ARMOND, history educator; b. Phila., May 22, 1922; s. Ellsworth F. and Margaretta (Cope) C.; children: Steven D., Charles G., Christopher C. B.A., Swarthmore Coll., 1948; M.A., Harvard U., 1949, Ph.D., 1953. Instr. then asst. prof. Swarthmore Coll., 1953-56; mem. faculty U. Wis., Madison, 1956-75, prof. history, 1961—, M.J. Herskovits prof. history and African studies, 1970-75, chmn. program comparative tropical history, 1959-75, chmn. African studies program, 1961-64, chmn. dept. African langs. and lit., 1963-66; prof. history Johns Hopkins U., Balt., 1975—, Herbert Baxter Adams prof., 1982—; Mem. joint com. Africa Social Sci. Research Council-Am. Council Learned Socs., 1963-73, chmn., 1971-73. Author: Two Jamaicas, 1955, The Image of Africa, 1964, (with Michael B. Petrovich) The Human Achievement, 1967, Africa Remembered, 1967, The Atlantic Slave Trade: A Census, 1969, (with Paul Bohannan) Africa and Africans, 1971, Imperialism, 1971, Africa and the West, 1972,

Economic Change in Pre-Colonial Africa, 1975, (with S. Feierman, J. Vansina and L. Thompson) African History, 1978; Mem. editorial bd.: Am. Hist. Rev, 1976-80. Served with U.S. Mcht. Marine, 1943-46. Ford fellow, 1958-59; Guggenheim fellow, 1966, 80; MacArthur fellow, 1983. Mem. African Studies Assn. (pres. 1971, past dir.), Am. Hist. Assn. (council 1967-70, pres. 1983), Social Sci. Research Council (dir. 1967-73), Internat. Congress Africanists (v.p. 1969-73), Phi Beta Kappa. Home: 3813 Fenchurch Rd Baltimore MD 21218

CURTIN, PHYLLIS, university dean, music educator; b. Clarksburg, W.Va.; d. E. Vernon and Betty R. (Robinson) Smith; m. Eugene Cook, May 6, 1956; 1 dau., Claudia Madeleine. Student, Monticello Coll., 1939-41; B.A., Wellesley Coll., 1943. Prof. Yale Sch. Music, New Haven, 1974-83; master Branford Coll. Yale U., New Haven, 1979-83; dean Sch. Arts, prof. music Boston U., 1983—; artist-in-residence Berkshire Music Center, Tanglewood, Lenox, Mass., 1965—. Made recital debut, Town Hall, N.Y.C., 1950, 53, 57, opera debut, N.Y.C. Opera in U.S. premiere of The Trial, 1953, recitals throughout, U.S. and fgn. countries; soprano soloist leading symphony orchestras; performer, tchr., Aspen Mus. Festival, 1953-57; appeared as Cressida in, Walton's Troilus and Cressida in, N.Y. premiere, 1955; title role in Floyd's: Susannah, world premiere, Tallahassee, 1955; title role in: Darius Milhaud's Medea, U.S. premiere, Brandeis U., 1955; world premiere Floyd's opera Wuthering Heights, 1958; leading soprano: Vienna Staatsoper, 1960, 61; debut as Fiordiligi in Cosi Fan Tutte, Met. Opera Co., 1961; debut, La Scala Opera, Milan, 1962; guest soloist, Stuttgart, Frankfurt opera cos., 1961-62, Passion of Jonathan Wade, N.Y.C. Opera, 1962; U.S. premiere Benjamin Britten's War Requiem, 1963; world premiere of Darius Milhaud's opera La Mère Coupable, Geneva, 1966; U.S. premiere Dimitri Shostakovitch's Symphony No. 14, with, Phila. Orch., 1971. Home: 24 Cottage Farm Rd Brookline MA 02146 Office: School for the Arts Boston Univ 855 Commonwealth Ave Boston MA 02215

CURTIN, RICHARD DANIEL, mgmt. cons., ret. air force officer; b. Taunton, Mass., Apr. 2, 1915; s. Patrick Henry and Della (Hart) C.; m. Mary Shirley Ray, May 10, 1969. Student, Brown U., 1933-35; B.Sc., U.S. Mil. Acad., 1939; M.Sc., U. Mich., 1950. Commd. 2d lt. U.S. Army, 1939; advanced through grades to maj. gen. USAF, 1963; various assignments, U.S., Panama, Eng., France, Germany, 1939-46; instr. Air U., Maxwell AFB, Ala., 1946-48; plans officer, war plans div. Hdqrs. USAF, Washington, 1950-54; dir. plans, later chief staff Hdqrs. 17th AF, N.Africa, 1954-56; exec. weapons systems Hdqrs. ARDC, Balt., 1956-58; asst. dep. comdr. tech. ops., dep. comdr. space programs AF Ballistic Missile Div., Inglewood, Calif., 1958-60; dir. systems devel., DCS/D, Hdqrs. USAF, Washington, 1960; dir. Office Space Programs, Office Sec. Air Force, Washington, 1960-62; dir. devel. plans DCS/R&D, Hdqrs. USAF, Washington, 1962-65; dep. U.S. def. advisor NATO, Paris, 1965-67, ret., 1967; dir. mgmt. enging. Bell Aerosystems Co., Buffalo, 1967-68; group v.p., dir. Southwestern Research Corp., Phoenix, 1968-70; pres. Dynamic System Electronics, Tempe, Ariz., 1968-70; v.p. Planning Research Corp., Chgo., 1970-73; gen. mgr. The Jacobs Co., Chgo., 1970-73; dir. tech. mgmt. Am. Def. Preparedness Assn., Washington, 1973-77; pres. Curtin Assos., Inc., Phoenix, 1977—, Petro Pure Corp., Palm Springs, 1981—. Mem. adv. bd. Heard Mus., Phoenix. Decorated Legion of Merit with clusters, Bronze Star with cluster; D.S.M.; Dept. Air Force; Croix de Guerre, etoile Vermeille. Asso. fellow AIAA; mem. Nat. Mcpl. League, Air Force Assn., Brown U. Alumni Assn., U. Mich. Alumni Assn., Assn. Grads. U.S. Mil. Acad. Club: Army-Navy. Home: 19 E San Miguel Phoenix AZ 85012

CURTIN, WILLIAM JOSEPH, lawyer; b. Auburn, N.Y., Mar. 9, 1931; s. William Joseph and Edith A. (Murray) C.; m. Helen Bragg White, Aug. 3, 1956; children: Helen Bragg, Caroline Goddard, William Joseph III, Christopher Newport. B.S., Georgetown U., 1953, J.D., 1956, LL.M., 1957. Bar: D.C. bar 1956, U.S. Supreme Ct. bar 1961. Asso. firm Morgan, Lewis & Bockius, Washington, 1960-64, partner, 1965—; public mem. Adminstrv. Conf. U.S., 1968-72; editor-in-chief Legal Legis. Reporter, 1968—; Chmn. trustees Norwood Sch., Bethesda, Md., 1976-79. Contbr. articles to legal jours. Recipient Labor Mgmt. Peace award Am. Arbitration Assn., 1966, John Carroll award Georgetown U., 1973. Fellow Am. Bar Found.; mem. Am. Bar Assn. (chmn. spl. com. nat. strikes in transp. industries 1968-70, chmn. labor relations law com., public utility sect. 1967-81, chmn. public utility law sect. 1982), D.C. Bar Assn. (chmn. labor law com. 1968-70). Office: Morgan Lewis & Bockius 1800 M St NW Suite 800 Washington DC 20036

CURTIS, BLAIR EDWARD, fin. exec.; b. Kansas City, Mo., Oct. 30, 1946; s. Edward A. and Eunice E. (Blair) C.; m. Martha Scott, Dec. 28, 1966; 1 son, Preston Nathaniel. B.A., Graceland, Coll., Lamoni, Iowa, 1968. Fin. sales rep. Allis Chalmers Credit Corp., 1971-73; asst. v.p. fin. Great Am. Mgmt. Co., Atlanta, 1973-76; treas., sec. Rhodes, Inc., Atlanta, 1976—. Mem. Fin. Execs. Inst., Nat. Cash Mgmt. Assn., Risk and Ins. Mgrs. Soc., Nat. Bus. Aircraft Assn., Assn. Cert. Fin. Analysts. Office: 1800 Century Blvd Atlanta GA 30345

CURTIS, CARL THOMAS, former U.S. senator; b. Minden, Nebr., Mar. 15, 1905; s. Frank O. and Alberta Mae (Smith) C.; m. Lois Wylie-Atwater, June 6, 1931 (dec. Sept. 1970); children: Clara Mae (Mrs. James A. Hopkins) (dec.), Carl Thomas; m. Mildred Genier Baker, Dec. 1, 1972. Ed., Nebr. Wesleyan U. Bar: Nebr. 1930. Tchr. Minden Schs.; practiced in, Minden, county atty., 1931-34; mem. 76th to 83d congresses from 1st Nebr. dist.; U.S. senator from, Nebr., 1955-79. Author: To Remind; Mem.: Forty Years Against the Tide. Mem. Am. Bar Assn., Nebr. Bar Assn., Theta Chi. Republican. Presbyn. Clubs: Mason, Odd Fellow, Elk. Home: 1300 G St Lincoln NE 68508 Office: 1200 N St Suite 500 Lincoln NE 68501

CURTIS, CHARLES EDWARD, Canadian government official; b. Winnipeg, Man., Can., July 28, 1931; s. Samuel and May (Goodison) C.; m. Hilda Marion Simpson, Oct. 30, 1954; 1 dau., Nancy Maude. C.A., U. Manitoba, 1949. Chartered acct. Dunwoody & Co., Winnipeg, 1949-54; chief assessor nat. revenue, income tax bd. Province of N.B., Can., 1954-67; dep. minister fin. Province of Man., Winnipeg, 1967—; vice chmn. Man. Hydro Electric Bd. Fellow Chartered Accts.; mem. Man. Inst. Chartered Accts. (pres. 1975-76). Club: Winter (Winnipeg) (bd. govs. 1974-79). Lodge: Rotary. Home: 596 South Dr Winnipeg MB Canada R3T 0B1 Office: Provincial Govt Province of Manitoba 109-450 Broadway Ave Winnipeg MB Canada R3C 0V8

CURTIS, CHARLES RAVAN, plant pathologist; b. Ault, Colo., Oct. 6, 1938; s. Charles Daniel and Lucile Eva (Seibel) C.; m. Louise Johnson Willett, Mar. 23, 1966; children—Robert Parks, Boyd Willett. B.S., Colo. State U., 1961, M.S., 1963, Ph.D., 1965. NSF grantee Colo. State U., 1961-63, NASA fellow, 1963-65; asst. prof. plant pathology U. Md., 1967-72, asso. prof., 1972-77, prof., 1977; prof., chairperson dept. plant sci. U. Del., Newark, 1978—, spl. asst. to pres., to provost for internat. devel., 1980—; Md. Dept. Natural Resources Power Plant Sitting Program contract, 1973-78; sci. textbook cons.; cons. EPA, NASA, pvt. industry. Contbr. sci. articles to profl. jours. Bd. dirs. Covered Bridge Farms Civic Assn., 1978; sec. Covered Bridge Farms Maintenance Corp., 1979; pres. Ptnrs. of the Ams. Del.-Panama, 1982-83. Served to capt. U.S. Army, 1965-67. Recipient Biomedical Research awards U. Md., 1968, 70, 71, 76; NSF grantee, 1969, 72; Delmarva Power and Light grantee, 1979. Mem. Am. Phytopathol. Soc. (pres. Potomac div. 1980-81, chmn. pollution effects on plants com. 1980-81), Bot. Soc. Am. (chmn. edn. com. 1978, chmn. teaching sect. 1978), Am. Soc. Plant Physiologists, Air Pollution Workshop Steering Com. Home: 3 The Horseshoe Covered Bridge Farms Newark DE 19711

CURTIS, CHARLOTTE MURRAY, columnist; b. Chgo.; d. George Morris and Lucile (Atcherson) C. B.A. in Am. History, Vassar Coll., 1950; L.H.D., St. Michael's Coll., 1974, Bates Coll., 1977; LL.D., Denison U., 1976; Litt.D. (hon.), Union Coll., 1979. Reporter, soc. editor Columbus (Ohio) Citizen, 1950-61; reporter N.Y. Times, 1961—, women's news editor, 1965-72, Family style editor, 1972-74, asso. editor paper, 1974—, editor Op-Ed page, 1974-82, columnist, 1982—; freelance writer, 1950—; tchr. narrative and short story writing Columbus YWCA, 1952-54; radio commentator Sta. WMNI, Columbus, 1959-60, Sta. WQXR, N.Y.C. Author: First Lady, 1963, The Rich and Other Atrocities, 1976; contbr. to: The Soviet Union: The Fifty Years, 1967, The Mafia: U.S.A, 1972, Assignment: U.S.A, 1974. Founder, pres. Young Assos. Columbus Symphony Orch.; chmn. edn. Columbus Jr. League, 1958-60; mem. N.Y. Jr. League, 1964—. Recipient various awards for reporting, writing and editing N.Y. Newspaper Women's Club, Ohio Newspaper Women's Assn., Am. Newspaper Women's Club, also awards N.Y. and Los Angeles chpts. Women in Communications; Ohio. Gov.'s award for journalism; U. So. Calif. Newspaper Journalism award. Mem. Am. Newspaper Guild (v.p. Columbus local 13 1956-60). Clubs: Washington Press, National Press; Cosmopolitan (N.Y.C.). Home: 40 E 10th St New York NY 10003 Office: 229 W 43d St New York NY 10036

CURTIS, CHRISTOPHER MICHAEL, editor; b. N.Y.C., May 7, 1934; m. Jean Getchell, Sept. 30, 1961; children: Christopher Michael, Hilary Ann, Hans Peter Kahn. B.A., Cornell U., 1957, postgrad., 1959-63. Sr. editor Atlantic Monthly, Boston, 1963—. Served with AUS, 1957. Clubs: St. Botolph, Union Boat (Boston). Home: 668 Bedford St Concord MA 01742 Office: 8 Arlington St Boston MA 02116

CURTIS, DENNIS EDWARD, lawyer, educator; b. New Orleans, Oct. 2, 1933; s. Arthur Mosby and Julia Marie (Flanahan) C.; m. Katherine Shea, Oct. 4, 1958; children: Lisa Brand, Stephanie Anne. B.S., U.S. Naval Acad., 1955; LL.B., Yale U., 1966. Bar: D.C. 1966, Conn. 1970, Calif. 1980. Assoc. Verner, Lipfert, Bernhard & McPherson, Washington, 1966-69; adj. prof. law Yale U. Law Sch., New Haven, 1969-80; prof. law U. So. Calif. Law Sch., Los Angeles, 1980—; of counsel O'Donnell & Gordon, Los Angeles, 1980. Bd. dirs. Legal Aid Found., Los Angeles. Lt. comdr. USN, 1955-63. Mem. ABA, D.C. Bar, Conn. Bar, Calif. Bar. Office: U So Calif Law Center Los Angeles CA 90089

CURTIS, DORIS S. MALKIN, geologist; b. Bklyn., Jan. 12, 1914; d. Meyer and Mary (Berkowitz) Malkin. B.A., Bklyn. Coll., 1933; M.A., Columbia, 1934, Ph.D., 1949. Paleontologist, stratigrapher, geologist Shell Oil, 1942-50, stratigrapher, 1959-61, sr. geologist, 1961-66, staff geologist, 1966-79; partner Curtis and Echols, 1979—; adj. prof. geology Rice U., 1979—; asst., then asso. prof. geology U. Houston, 1950-52; research geologist Scripps Instn. Oceanography, 1952-54; asst. prof. geology, then asso. prof. U. Okla., 1955-59; Mem. U.S. Nat. Com. on Geology, Nat. Acad. Scis., 1978—, chmn., 1981—; mem. com. global and internat. geology Bd. Earth Scis., Nat. Acad. Scis., 1982—; mem. sci. com. Internat. Geol. Correlation Program, 1979—; pres. Am. Geol. Inst., 1980-81. Fellow AAAS (chmn. sect. E 1980—), Geol. Soc. Am. (councillor 1982—); mem. LWV, Am. Assn. Petroleum Geologists (hon.), Internat. Assn. Sedimentologists, Soc. Econ. Paleontologists and Mineralogists (hon., pres. 1978-79), Sigma Xi. Home: 800 Anderson St Bellaire TX 77401 Office: Curtis & Echols 800 Anderson Bellaire TX 77401

CURTIS, DOUGLAS HOMER, electrical equipment manufacturing company executive; b. Jackson, Mich., July 19, 1934; s. Homer K. and Luella D. (Hall) C.; m. Jean A. Breaux; children: Rebecca, Linda, Colleen, Robert. B.A., Park Coll., Parkville, Mo., 1956. With Gen. Electric Co., 1958-69, mgr. Boston region, 1967-69; v.p. fin. and adminstrn. internat. Data Corp., Boston, 1969; v.p. fin. Franklin Electric Co. Inc., Bluffton, Ind., 1969-80; pres. Curtis Assocs., Inc., Bluffton, 1980-82; pres., chief operating officer Satelco, Inc., San Antonio, 1983-84; v.p. adminstrn. Lyall Electric Co., Kendallville, Ind., 1984—; Pres. Wells County (Ind.) Hosp. Authority, 1974-75. Served to 1st lt. USMCR, 1956-58. Mem. Nat. Assn. Securities Dealers (vicechmn. fin. 1980, chmn. fin. com. 1980), Fin. Execs. Inst. (chpt. dir. 1975). Home: 707 Oaktree Ct Fort Wayne IN Office: Hwy 6 and County Rd 400 E Kendallville IN 46755

CURTIS, JEROME NATHANIEL, lawyer; b. Cleve., July 13, 1902; s. Nathan and Leah (Goldsmith) C.; m. Iris Goldberg, June 12, 1938; 1 son, Robert M. A.B., Western Res. U., 1924, LL.B., 1926. Bar: Ohio bar 1926, also U.S. Supreme Ct 1926. Practiced in, Cleve., 1926—; mem. Ulmer, Berne, Laronge, Glickman & Curtis; asst. U.S. atty., 1936-41; chief asst. U.S. atty., 1942-43, spl. asst. to atty. gen. U.S. for hearing of conscientious objector cases, 1948-55; Mem. Ohio Bd. Bar Examiners, 1938-43, Ohio Ho. of Reps., 1933-34. Past pres. Cleve. Jewish Childrens Bur.; past v.p., bd. dirs. Cleve. Jewish Community Fedn.; past bd. dirs. Cleve. Community Fund, Cleve. Welfare Fedn., Cleve. Law Library Assn., Bellefaire, Nat. Council Jewish Welfare Fedns. and Welfare Funds, Jewish Family Service Assn., Mt. Sinai Hosp. Cleve. Mem. Am., Fed., Ohio, Cuyahoga County, Cleve. bar assns., Am. Judicature Soc., Order of Coif, Phi Beta Kappa, Delta Sigma Rho. Home: 17607 Fernway Rd Shaker Heights OH 44120 Office: Bond Court Bldg Cleveland OH 44114

CURTIS, JESSE WILLIAM, JR., U.S. district judge; b. San Bernardino, Calif., Dec. 26, 1905; s. Jesse William and Ida L. (Seymour) C.; m. Mildred F. Mort, Aug. 24, 1930; children: Suzanne, Jesse W., Clyde Hamliton, Christopher Cowles. A.B., U. Redlands, 1928, LL.D., 1973; J.D., Harvard U., 1931. Bar: Calif. 1931. Pvt. practice, 1931-35; mem. firms Guthrie & Curtis, San Bernardino, 1935-40, Curtis & Curtis, 1946-50, Curtis, Knauf, Henry & Farrell, 1950-53; judge Superior Ct. of Calif., 1953-62; U.S. judge Central Dist. of Calif., 1962—; Rep. dist. ct. on Jud. Council U.S., 1972-74. Chmn. San Bernardino Sch. Bd., 1942-46, mem., 1946-49; mem. Del Rosa Bd. Edn., 1950-53; Chmn. San Bernardino County Heart Fund; dir., past pres. YMCA; dir. Good Will Industries, Crippled Children's Soc., Arrowhead United Fund; adv. bd. Community Hosp. Mem. Am., Los Angeles County bar assns., Calif. State Bar, Am. Judicature Soc., Am. Law Inst., Los Angeles World Affairs Council, Town Hall, Phi Delta Phi. Democrat. Conglist. Club: Newport Harbor Yacht. Home: 305 Evening Star Ln Newport Beach CA 92660 Office: US Court House Los Angeles CA 90012

CURTIS, KEENE HOLBROOK, actor; b. Salt Lake City, Feb. 15, 1923; s. Ira Charles and Polley Francella (Holbrook) C. B.A., U. Utah, 1947, M.S., 1951. N.Y. debut in: The Shop at Sly Corner, 1949; stage dir. for tours, Martha Graham's Dance Co., 1949-54; stage mgr. various plays, 1950-60; actor, Assn. Producing Artists, 1962; toured, Australia and Far East as; stage mgr. for, Alvin Ailey-Carmen De Lavallade Am. Dance Co., 1962; returned to U.S. and, Assn. Producing Artists, 1962-69; latest plays include Patriot for Me, 1969; Indians, 1969, Blood Red Roses, 1970, Colette, 1970, The Rothschilds, 1970 (Tony award), A Ride Across Lake Constance, 1972, Night Watch, 1972, Via Galactica, 1972, St. Joan, 1974, Ring Round the Moon, 1975, Too Much Johnson, 1975, Life on a Limb, 1975, The Bakers Wife, 1976, The Comedians, 1977, Annie, 1978, Division Street, 1980, Chekhov in Yalta, Twelfth Night, Wild Oats, 1981, Flea in Her Ear, 1982, The Misanthrope, 1982; film debut in Orson Welle's: Macbeth, 1947; appeared in: films Blade, 1973, Rabbit Test, 1978, Heaven Can Wait, 1978; (Drama-Logue Critics award for outstanding achievement in theatre for Annie 1978). Served with USN, 1943-46. Recipient Disting. Alumni award U. Utah, 1973; named to Pioneer Meml. Theatre Hall of Fame, 1975. Mem. Actors Equity, AFTRA, Screen Actors Guild.

CURTIS, KENNETH STEWART, land surveyor; b. Lafayette, Ind., Oct. 10, 1925; s. Paul Byron and Mary Isabel (Stewart) C.; m. Mary Louise Dunbar, June 22, 1947; children: Teresa Ann, Charles Alan, Stephen Brian. B.S. in Civil Engring., Purdue U., 1946, M.S., 1949; Ford Found. fellow, Ohio State U., 1961-62. Registered land surveyor, Ind. Instr. surveying and mapping Purdue U. Sch. Civil Engring., West Lafayette, Ind., 1948-54, asst. prof., 1954-59, asso. prof., 1959-67, prof., 1967—; with U.S. Coast and Geodetic Survey, summers 1951-55, Jack Ammann Photogrammetric Engrs., summers 1953, RCA Missile Test Project, summer 1957; pvt. practice land surveying. Author various manuals on surveying practice.; editor: Purdue Land Surveying Proc., 1953-71, The Hoosier Surveyor, 1954-82. Recipient award for excellence Nat. Council Land Surveyors, 1972. Mem. Ind. Soc. Profl. Land Surveyors (Disting. Service award 1966, hon. pres. emeritus 1982), Am. Congress Surveying and Mapping (Earle J. Fennell award 1975), Nat. Soc. Profl. Surveyors, Am. Soc. Photogrammetry, Am. Assn. Geodetic Surveying, Am. Cartographic Assn., ASCE (Surveying and Mapping award 1976), Can. Inst. Surveying, Am. Soc. Enging. Edn., Soc. Am. Mil. Engrs., Internat. Soc. History of Cartography. Republican. Mem. Christian Ch. (Disciples of Christ). Club: Lafayette Lions (pres. 1964-65). Home: 2204 Happy Hollow Rd West Lafayette IN 47906 Office: Sch Civil Enging Purdue U West Lafayette IN 47907

CURTIS, LAWRENCE BUCK, oil company executive; b. Grand Junction, Colo., June 18, 1924; s. Chester E. and Leila C.; m. Rose A. Van, Sept. 16, 1949; children: Jennifer, Ann, David, Claudia. B.S., Colo. Sch. Mines, 1949. With Conoco, Inc., 1949—, chief engr. to mgr. ops. internat. prodn., 1963-71, from mgr. enging. to v.p. prodn. enging. services, 1971—, v.p. prodn. enging. services, Houston, 1981—; chmn. subcom. on enhanced oil recovery Nat. Petroleum Council, 1982-83. Served with USNR, 1942-46. Mem. Soc. Petroleum Engrs. (pres. 1971, vice-chmn. Wyo. Petroleum sect. 1957, chmn. 1958, vice-chmn. Denver sect. 1960), Am. Inst. Metall. Engrs. (v.p. 1972), Petroleum Club of Houston. Office: Conoco Inc 5 Greenway Plaza East Houston TX 77252

CURTIS, LAWRENCE LLOYD, zoo director, zoologist; b. Galveston, Tex., Apr. 20, 1930; s. Darwin Augustus and Frances (Gymer) C.; m. Kathryn Aaron, Dec. 27, 1952 (div. 1959); children: Chris, Cathy, Greg; m. Marilyn Hoffsommer, June 7, 1967; 1 dau., Pam. B.S., So. Meth. U., 1951, M.S., 1952. Asst. curator Dallas Aquarium, 1946-51; gen. curator Dallas Zool. Park, 1951-53; exec. dir. Ft. Worth Zool. Park, 1953-67; exec. sec. Portland Zool. Soc., Oreg., 1968-69; dir. Oklahoma City Zoo, 1970—; bd. dirs. Am. Assn. Zool. Parks and Aquariums, 1955-60, 66-69; pres. Tex. Acad. Sci., 1964; adj. prof. zoology Okla. State U., Stillwater, 1971—. Author: Zoological Park Fundamentals, 1967; contbg. author: Zoological Park and Aquarium Fundamentals, 1982; editor: Zoo Aviculturists Symposium, 1963, Aquarium-Herpetariums Symposium, 1963. Mem. Okla. Natural Heritage Council, Am. Soc. Ichthyologists and Herpetologists, Tex. Herpetological Soc., Nat. Species Council Soc., Am. Assn. Zoologists, Okla Herpetological Soc., Okla. Ornithol. Soc., Sigma Xi. Club: South Am. Explorers. Lodge: Rotary (Ft. Worth). Home: Oklahoma City Zoo Zoo Director's Residence Oklahoma City OK 73111 Office: Oklahoma City Zoo 2101 NW 50th St Oklahoma City OK 73111

CURTIS, MARCIA, university dean; b. Quincy, Mass., Aug. 8, 1931; d. Arthur Bicknell and Ethel Beatrice (Fraser) C. A.B. in Biology, Colby Coll., 1954; M. Nursing, Yale U., 1957; Ed.D., Boston U., 1969. Staff nurse Grace-New Haven Hosp., 1957; instr. Boston U. Sch. Nursing, 1959-65; staff nurse Carney Hosp., Dorchester, Mass., 1961-62, Univ. Hosp., Boston, 1965; instr., cons. Quincy City Hosp. Sch. Nursing, 1966; Human Relations Center teaching fellow in ednl. founds. Boston U. Sch. Edn., 1966-67; assoc. dean Med. U. S.C. Coll. Nursing, Charleston, 1968-69, dean, prof. Coll., 1969—; organizer nursing program Winthrop Coll., Rock Hill, S.C., 1977, Francis Manion Coll., Florence, S.C., 1982; cons. Jersey City Med. Center, 1967, S.C. Nurses Assn., 1969-71, S.C. Regional Med. Program, 1972; ednl. cons. Morris Coll., Sumter, S.C., 1973-74; cons. Handee Coll., Greenwood, S.C., 1981—; participant numerous workshops; mem. adv. council for comprehensive health planning S.C. Bd. Health; mem. Charleston Area Comprehensive Health Planning Com., Health Edn. Authority, Statewide Master Planning Com. on Nursing Edn., State Task Force on Health Resources; mem. adminstrv. adv. group sub com. for cancer S.C. Regional Med. Program; assoc. Boston U. Human Relations Center; mem. Def. Adv. Com. on Women in the Service, 1975-77. Patron Charleston Symphony Orch., Charleston Mus., Smithsonian Assos. Served to lt. Nurse Corps USNR, 1957-59. Mem. Am. Nurses Assn., S.C. Nurses Assn. (bd. dirs., joint commn. on practice, council on edn.), Nat. League Nursing, Am. Assn. Colls. Nursing, Am. Pub. Health Assn., Am. Assn. Higher Edn., Nat. Wildlife Assn., Audubon Soc., Pi Lambda Theta, Sigma Theta Tau. Home: 18 Charlestowne Ct Charleston SC 29401

CURTIS, MARK HUBERT, association executive, historian; b. Medford, Minn., July 7, 1920; s. James Hubert and Lydia Ethel (Krueger) C.; m. Maria Isabel bird y Zalduondo, Nov. 7, 1945; children: Mary Katherine, Thomas Mark. B.A., Yale U., 1942, M.A., 1947, Ph.D., 1953; L.H.D. (hon.), Washington and Jefferson U., 1978, Ill. Coll., 1979, Beaver Coll., 1979, Centre Coll., 1980, Southwestern at Memphis, 1981, Gettysburg Coll., 1982. Instr. history UCLA, 1953-59, assoc. prof. history, 1959-64, assoc. dean grad. div., 1962-64; pres. Scripps Coll., Claremont, Calif., 1964-76; cons. various colls. and orgns., 1976-78; pres. Assn. Am. Colls., Washington, 1978—; Danforth lectr. Pacific Sch. Religion, Berkeley, Calif., 1957; Folger Library research prof., 1964; dir. postdoctoral seminar William Andrews Clark Library, Los Angeles, 1969. Author: Oxford and Cambridge in Transition, 1558-1642, 1959 (Robert Livingston Schuyler prize 1961); contbr. articles to profl. jours. Social Sci. Research Council fellow, 1948-49; Guggenheim Found. fellow, 1959-60; Folger Shakespear Library fellow, 1962. Mem. Am. Hist. Assn. Presbyterian. Clubs: Yale (N.Y.C.); Cosmos (Washington). Home: 6112 River Rd Bethesda MD 20817 Office: Association of American Colleges 1818 R St NW Washington DC 20009

CURTIS, MORTON LANDERS, educator, mathematician; b. Port Lavaca, Tex., Nov. 11, 1921; s. David Morton and Rosena (Montier) C.; m. Eleanor Thomas, Aug. 12, 1944; children—Dana Allan, Jacquelyn Ann. B.S., Tex. Arts and Industries Coll., 1943; Ph.D., U. Mich., 1951. Instr. Northwestern U., 1950-51, asst. prof., 1953-56; mem. Inst. Advanced Study, Princeton, 1951-53; prof. math. U. Ga., 1956-59, Fla. State U., 1959-64, Rice U., Houston, 1964—, W.L. Moody, Jr. prof., 1966—, chmn. dept., 1964-69. Contbr. articles to profl. jours. Served to lt. USNR, 1943-46; capt. USCGR, 1968. Mem. Am. Math. Soc. (trustee 1966-69), Math. Assn. Am., Sigma Xi. Home: 4607 W Alabama Houston TX 77027

CURTIS, NEVIUS MINOT, utility executive; b. Holyoke, Mass., Aug. 16, 1929; s. Frederick A. and Janet H. (Nevius) C.; m. Muriel Acheson, Nov. 9, 1957; children: Jeffrey, Janet. B.A. in Econs. cum laude, Haverford (Pa.) Coll., 1951; M.B.A. in Fin., Stanford U., 1956. With acctg. dept. Calif.-Oreg. Power Co., Medford, Oreg., 1956-58; asst. to pres. Holyoke Water Power Co., 1958-65; asst. to comptroller Central Maine Power Co., Augusta, 1965-67; from asst. comptroller to sr. v.p. fin., dir. Central Maine Power Co., 1967-77; v.p. Detroit Edison Co., 1977-78; sr. v.p. fin. Delmarva Power & Light Co., Wilmington, Del., 1978-79, pres., chief operating officer, 1979-80, pres., chief exec. officer, 1980-83, chmn. bd., chief exec. officer, 1984—; dep. chmn. bd. Fed. Res. Bank Phila.; pres. Wilmington Econ. Devel. Corp. Served with USNR, 1952-55. Mem. Phi Beta Kappa. Home: 1912 Academy Pl Wilmington DE 19806 Office: 800 King St PO Box 231 Wilmington DE 19899

CURTIS, ORLIE LINDSEY, JR., lawyer; b. Hutchinson, Kans., Feb. 27, 1934; s. Orlie Lindsey and Lillian Esther (Barnes) C.; m. Idella Mae Krueger, June 5, 1955; children: Elizabeth, Victoria. B.A. with high distinction, Union Coll., Lincoln, Nebr., 1954; M.S., Purdue U., 1956; Ph.D., U. Tenn., 1961; J.D., U. So. Calif., 1977. Bar: Calif. 1977. Group chief Oak Ridge Nat. Lab., 1956-63; lab. dir., sci. fellow Northrop Corp., Hawthorne, Calif., 1963-77; since practiced in, Stockton; partner firm Kroloff, Belcher, Smart, Perry & Christopherson, 1980—; vis. lectr. physics U. Calif., Berkeley, 1970-71; adv. bd. physics dept. U. Ky., 1970-73; lectr. Nat. Symposia Products Liability. Author: Point Defects in Solids, 1975; contbr. articles to profl. jours. Bd. dirs. So. Calif. conf. Seventh-day Adventists, 1970-74, Newbury Acad. Park Acad., 1970-74, Lodi Acad., 1979—, No. Calif. conf. Seventh-day Adventists, 1980—. Fellow Am. Phys. Soc., IEEE (chmn. radiation effects com. 1970-73); mem. Am. Bar Assn., Def. Research Inst., State Bar Calif., San Joaquin County Bar Assn., Adventist Attys. Assn. (pres. 1983—), Order of Coif. Patentee in field. Home: 9794 N Fernwood Rd Stockton CA 95212 Office: 1044 N El Dorado St Stockton CA 95201

CURTIS, PHILIP C., artist; b. Jackson, Mich., May 26, 1907. B.A., Albion Coll., 1930; postgrad. law, U. Mich.; certificate, Yale Sch. Fine Arts, 1935; D.F.A. (hon.), Albion Coll., 1971, Ariz. State U., 1979, L.H.D., 1980. Supr. mural painting WPA Art Project, N.Y.C., 1935; Established Phoenix Art Center (now Phoenix Art Mus.), 1936. Subject of: movie The Time Freeze, 1974; One-man shows, San Francisco Mus. Art, 1949, Ariz. State U., Tempe, 1957, 70, Phoenix Art Mus., 1960, 63, Knoedler's, N.Y.C., 1964, Calif. Palace Legion of Honor, 1966, Feingarten Gallery, Los Angeles, Betty Thomen's Gallery, Basel, Switzerland, 1967, Galerie Krugier et Cie, Geneva, U. Ariz., Tucson, 1970, Amon Carter Mus. Western Art, Ft. Worth, Okla. Art Center, Oklahoma City, Coe Kerr Gallery, N.Y.C., Palm Springs (Calif.) Desert Mus., 1971, UCLA, 1972, U. Nev., Las Vegas, Utah Mus. Fine Arts, Galerie Ariadne, Vienna, 1974, Scottsdale (Ariz.) Center for Arts, 1978, C.M. Russell Mus., Gt. Falls, Mont., Phillips Collection, Washington, Ella Sharp Mus., Jackson, Mich., 1979, Gallery 609, Denver, 1980, Fine Arts Ctr., Tempe, 1984, retrospective exhbn., No. Ariz. U., 1967, group show, Weyhe Gallery, N.Y.C., 1950, Phoenix Art Mus., 1975, Santa Fe Festival of Arts, 1977, European tour, 1973-74. Served with OSS, World War II. Recipient gold medal Nat. Soc. Arts and Letters, 1976; Disting. Achievement award Ariz. State U., 1979; Ariz. Artist of Year, 1983; Benjamin Franklin fellow Royal Soc. Arts.; Curtis room established Phoenix Art Mus. Address: 109 Cattle Track Scottsdale AZ 85253

CURTIS, PHILIP CHADSEY, JR., mathematics educator; b. Providence, Mar. 6, 1928; s. Philip C. and Marion (Brown) C.; m. Dorothy K. Smith, July 15, 1950; children: Philip C. III, Anne, Peter, Marion, Alan. A.B., Brown U., 1950; M.A., Yale, 1952, Ph.D., 1955. Fulbright fellow, 1950-51; asst. prof. mathematics U. Calif. at Los Angeles, 1957-61, asso. prof., 1961-67, prof., 1967—, vice chmn. dept., 1967-71, chmn. dept., 1971-75; chmn. U. Calif. Bd. Admissions and Relations with Schs., 1983-85; vis. prof. U. Aarhus, Denmark, 1969-70, U. Copenhagen, 1975-76; cons. T.R.W., 1956-69. Served with AUS, 1946-47. Mem. Am. Math. Assn., Math. Assn. Am., Phi Beta Kappa, Sigma Xi. Home: 3441 Grandview Blvd Los Angeles CA 90066

CURTIS, PHILIP JAMES, lawyer; b. Denver, June 12, 1918; s. Philip C. and Anna J. (Jackson) C.; m. Betty D. Dodds, Mar. 17, 1943; children—Timothy, Anne, Nancy. A.B., Regis Coll., 1939; LL.B., Georgetown U., 1947. Bar: D.C. bar 1947, Ill. bar 1955. Atty. Gen. Counsel's Office, FTC, 1948-53, supr. antimonopoly sect. div. compliance, 1950-53; litigation atty. Zenith Radio Corp., Glenview, Ill., 1953-57, gen. counsel, 1959-70, v.p., gen. counsel, 1970—; asso. firm McConnell, Van Hook & Pashen, 1954-57, McConnell, Freeman, Curtis & McConnell, 1957-70. Served to maj. AUS and; Served to maj. USAAF, 1942-48; ETO. Mem. Am., Ill., Chgo. bar assns., Delta Eta Phi. Home: 1858 Habberton St Park Ridge IL 60068 Office: 1000 Milwaukee Ave Glenview IL 60025

CURTIS, RICHARD EARL, former naval officer, elevator company executive; b. Beckley, W.Va., Nov. 17, 1930; s. Herbert Earl and Lizzie Belle (Ramsey) C.; m. Martha Rhodes Lancaster, June 6, 1953; children: Steven Andrew, Richard Earl, Elizabeth Graham. B.S. in Elec. Engring, U.S. Naval Acad., 1953; M.B.A., Harvard U., 1961; grad., Indsl. Coll. Armed Forces, 1972. Commd. ensign U.S. Navy, 1953, advanced through grades to rear adm., 1980; logistics mgr. Strategic Systems Project Office, Washington, 1972-76; comdg. officer Naval Supply Center, Charleston, S.C., 1976-78; asst. for logistic project Naval Material Command, Washington, 1978-79; dep. dir. policy, programs, projects and systems Naval Supply System Command, Washington, 1979-81, vice comdr., 1981-82, ret., 1982; v.p. U.S. Elevator Co., Spring Valley, Calif., 1982—. Leader, dist. commr. Boy Scouts Am. Decorated Legion Merit, Bronze Star with combat V. Republican. Episcopalian. Home: 5130 Choc Cliff Dr Bonita CA 92002 Office: US Elevator Co 10728 US Elevator Rd Spring Valley CA 92010

CURTIS, RICHARD KENNETH, speech educator; b. Worcester, Mass., Jan. 22, 1924; s. Albert Wyman and Vena (Masters) C.; m. Elizabeth Fisher, July 7, 1945; children: Stephen Dana, David Alan, Laurel Elizabeth. Th.B., No. Bapt. Theol. Sem., 1950; M.S., Purdue U., 1951, Ph.D., 1954. Ordained to ministry Baptist Ch., 1951; pastor Russiaville (Ind.) Bapt. Ch., 1947-52; chmn. speech-English dept. Barrington (R.I.) Coll., 1952-56; chmn. speech dept. Bethel Coll., St. Paul, 1956-62; sr. minister Immanuel Bapt. Ch., Kansas City, Kans., 1962-67; chmn. speech dept. Muskingum Coll., New Concord, Ohio, 1967-69; prof., chmn. dept. communication Ind. U.-Purdue U. at Indpls., 1969-71, prof. speech, 1971—; gen. chmn. Community Coll. Expansion Council, Kansas City, Kans., 1966-67. Author: They Called Him Mister Moody, 1962, Evolution or Extinction: The Choice Before Us. A Systems Approach to the Study of the Future, 1982. Served to 1st lt. USAAF, 1943-46. Decorated D.F.C. Mem. Speech Communication Assn. (chmn. research com. religious interest group 1957-62, chmn. sr. coll.-univ. div. 1981-82), AAUP, World Future Soc. (coordinator Ind. mems.; pres. Central Ind. chpt. 1974—). Home: 636 Braeside N Dr Indianapolis IN 46260

CURTIS, ROBERT MCNOWN, lawyer; b. Tuscaloosa, Ala., Feb. 17, 1919; s. Nathan Stephenson and Harriet (Wilson) C.; m. Marie Collett, Mar. 21, 1944; children—Carol, Cay, Christopher Collett, Robert McNown. A.B., U. Ala., 1939; J.D., U. Fla., 1946. Bar: Fla. bar 1946, U.S. Supreme Ct. bar 1959. Law clk. firm Caldwell & Parker, Tallahassee, 1944-45, Gray, Waldo & Chandler, Gainesville, Fla., 1945-46; asso. firm Wallace E. Sturgis, Ocala, Fla., 1946-47; individual practice law, Ft. Lauderdale, Fla., 1947-53; with firm Saunders, Curtis, Ginestra & Gore (and predecessors), Fort Lauderdale, Fla., 1953—, sr. partner, 1959—; city atty., City of Fort Lauderdale, 1959, asso. town atty., Town of Lauderdale by the Sea, Fla., 1953-56; Chmn. Democratic Exec. Com., 1952-54, 67-72; chmn. N. Broward Hosp. Dist., 1961-65. Served with U.S. Army, 1941-44. Mem. Am., Broward County bar assns., Fla. Bar, Am. Coll. Mortgage Attys., Assn. Trial Lawyers Am., Acad. Fla. Trial Lawyers, Greater Fort Lauderdale C. of C. (dir. 1974-77, pres. 1976, chmn. bd. 1977), S.A.R., Sigma Chi. Clubs: Elks, Masons, Lauderdale Yacht, Tower. Home: 833 N Rio Vista Blvd Fort Lauderdale FL 33301 Office: PO Drawer 4078 Fort Lauderdale FL 33338

CURTIS, ROGER ERNEST, transportation and tire company executive; b. Greenwood, Ark., Mar. 26, 1928; s. Ernest Marshall and Nell (Rogers) C.; m. Charlene McCoy, May 4, 1947; children: Roger E., Terry Cutirs Cialone, Sally Caroline. Student pub. schs., Ft. Smith, Ark. Bookkeeper Tucker Duck & Rubber Co., Ft. Smith, 1949-54; office mgr. Ross Motor Co., Ft. Smith, 1954-56; mgr. People's Loan & Investment (Tucker Duck & Rubber Co.), 1956-59; v.p. customer service ABF Freight Systems, Inc., 1959-67; v.p., pres. ABC, ABF-Ark. Bandag ABF Systems, Inc., 1967-79, sr. v.p., pres. ABC, ABF-Tradco, 1979—; chmn. Traffic Safety Council, Ft. Smith, 1969-71. Adv. bd. dirs. Sparks Regional Med. Ctr., Ft. Smith, 1972-74; bd. dirs. Ft. Smith Girls' Club, 1979—; justice of peace Sebastian County Quorum Ct., Ft. Smith, 1967-76; mem. Com. of 21, United Fund of Ft. Smith, 1971-73. Mem. Ft. Smith C. of C. Methodist. Club: Hardscrabble (Ft. Smith). Home: 2415 Houston Fort Smith AR 72901 Office: Ark Best Corp 1000 S 21st St Fort Smith AR 72901

CURTIS, ROGER WILLIAM, artist, educator; b. Gloucester, Mass., Dec. 20, 1910; s. William Howard and Etta Elinda (Elwell) C.; m. Winifred Joan Fountain, Sept. 30, 1939; children: Hannah Joan, Alan Howard, William Arthur, David Philip. Grad., Burdett Coll., 1931; student, Boston U., 1938-39; also pvt. art studies. Treas. Cape Ann Festival of Arts, 1951-59; dir. Burlington Art Gallery, 1954-59, Boston Gallery, 1957-62; dir. For Mass. Nat. Art Week, 1958; founder New Eng. Artists Group, 1961—; art dir. Legendsea Gallery of A. T. Hibbard, 1960-77, Downtown Gallery, Boston, 1966-71; founder, owner Riverview Gallery, 1976—; Treas. Patterson Co. Inc., Boston, 1935-55, Com. for Fair Representation in Art Exhbns. Inc. Art instr. specializing marines painting demonstrations on technique of seascapes and landscapes; Exhibited in shows, Symphony Hall, Boston, Lever House, N.Y.C., Sheldon Swope Mus., Terre Haute, Ind., Chgo., Detroit, Fresno, Calif.; works in permanent exhbns. hosps., schs., art galleries, also pvt. collections; Author: Color in Outdoor Painting, How to Paint Successful Landscapes; cons. exhbns. for circulation. Recipient Waters of World award marine painting, 1968, 74; Painting awards Ogunquit Art Center (Maine), 1972, 77; Acad. Artists, Springfield, Mass., 1972, 77; Meriden (Conn.) Arts and Crafts, 1972, 77; Gordon Grant award; Meml. award North Shore Arts Assn., 1975; Seas of the World prize Rockport Art Assn., 1976; A.I. McCarthy award, 1979. Mem. Am. Artists Profl. League (v.p. Boston chpt. 1962, treas. Mass. chpt. 1972—), Copley Soc. (bd. govs. 1957-60), North Shore Arts Assn. (pres. 1955-59, dir. 1960—, treas. 1966—), Burlington Art Assn. (pres. 1958-62), New Eng. Guild Fine Arts (treas.), Concord Art Assn. (dir.), Guild Boston Artists (bd. mgrs. 1969, treas. 1970—), Mass. Art Assns. (co-founder), Italian Acad. Arts and Work. Club: Masons. Address: 30 Riverview Rd Gloucester MA 01930

CURTIS, SAMUEL RALSTON, JR., former iron ore company executive; b. Cleve., Dec. 3, 1919; s. Samuel Ralston and Mary Elizabeth (Steinen) C.; m. Betty Ethel Hillier, Feb. 12, 1944; children: Deborah (Mrs. David B. Puffer), Gary Ralston. B.A., Kenyon Coll., 1941; J.D., Cleve. Marshall Law Sch., 1953. With Cleve.-Cliffs Iron Co., Cleve., 1941—, asst. sec., 1961-70, sec., resident counsel, 1970-82; ret., 1982. Served as capt. USAAF, 1941-45. Mem. Am., Ohio, Cleve. bar assns., Am. Soc. Corporate Secs., Am. Iron and Steel Inst., Delta Kappa Epsilon. Club: Cleveland Athletic. Home: 3813-B Pinefield Ave New Port Richey FL 33552

CURTIS, STATON RUSSELL, univ. dean; b. Portland, Maine, Mar. 19, 1921; s. Clarence Leroy and Eva May (R) C.; m. Ruth Alden, Oct. 17, 1943; children—Sharon Leigh, Martha Gail. B.S., Gorham (Maine) State Coll., 1942; M. Ed., Springfield (Mass.) Coll., 1947. Tchr.-coach pub. schs., Barre, Vt., 1946; faculty chmn. student activities, instr. phys. edn., athletic coach, Brunswick campus U. Maine, 1947-49; dir. Hyde Meml. Rehab. Center and Pine Tree Camp, Bath, Maine, 1949-50; dir. municipal recreation, Brunswick, Maine, 1950-56; dir. Meml. Union, U. N.H., 1956-60; dean of men, dir. Univ. Union, Boston U., 1960-63, dean of students, 1963-69, dean student affairs, 1969-72, prof. edn., dean phys. devel. programs, 1972-77, prof. edn., internat. rep., 1977—. Served with USNR, 1943-45; lt. comdr. Res. Mem. Eastern Assn. Coll. Deans and Advisers to Students, Lambda Chi Alpha. Home: 19 Winsor Ln Topsfield MA 01983 Office: Boston Univ Boston MA 02215

CURTIS, TONY (BERNARD SCHWARTZ), actor; b. N.Y.C., June 3, 1925; s. Manuel and Helen (Klein) Schwartz; m. Janet Leigh, June 4, 1951 (div.); children: Ily, Jamie; m. Christine Kaufmann, Feb. 8, 1963; children: Alexandra, Allegra; m. Leslie Allen, Apr. 20, 1968. Student drama, New Sch. Social Research. Films include Houdini, 1953, Black Shield of Falworth, 1954, Six Bridges to Cross, 1955, So This is Paris, 1954, Trapeze, 1956, Mister Cory, 1957, Sweet Smell of Success, 1957, Midnight Story, 1957, The Vikings, 1958, Defiant Ones, 1958, Some Like It Hot, 1959, Perfect, Furlough, 1958, Spartacus, 1960, The Great Imposter, 1960, Pepe, 1960, The Outsider, 1961, Taras Bulba, 1962, Forty Pounds of Trouble, 1962, Paris When it Sizzles, 1964, The List of Adrian Messenger, 1963, Captain Newman, 1963, Wild and Wonderful, 1964, Sex and the Single Girl, 1964, Goodbye Charlie, 1964, The Great Race, 1965, Boeing, Boeing, 1965, Arriverderci, Baby, 1966, Not with My Wife, You Don't, 1966, Don't Make Waves, 1967, Boston Strangler, 1968, Lepke, 1975, The Bad News Bears Go to Japan, 1978, The Manitou, 1978, Sextette, 1978, Little Miss Marker, 1980, The Mirror Crack'd, 1980, Venom, 1982; star: TV series The Persuaders, 1971-72, McCoy, 1975-76, Vegas, 1978-81; TV films include The Users, 1978; Moviola: The Scarlet O'Hara War, 1980, The Million Dollar Face, 1981. Office: Kurt Frings Assocs 9440 Santa Monica Blvd Beverly Hills CA 90212 *

CURTIS, VERN O., restaurant chain executive; b. 1934; married. B.S. in Acctg., U. Utah, 1959. Acct. Arthur Young & Co, 1960-66; controller Data Dynamics, Inc., 1966-68; with Denny's Inc., La Mirada, Calif., 1968—, successively treas, treas. and asst. sec., v.p. fin. and treas., exec. v.p. and treas., now pres., chief exec. officer, dir. Served to capt. U.S. Army, 1959-60. Office: Dennys Inc 14256 E Firestone Blvd La Mirada CA 90638 *

CURTIS, WALTER W., bishop; b. Jersey City, May 3, 1913. Student, Fordham U., Seton Hall U., Immaculate Conception Sem., N.Am. and Gregorian U., Rome; S.T.D., Cath. U. Am. Ordained priest Roman Catholic Ch., 1937; appointed bishop of Bisica in Tunis and aux. bishop of Newark, 1957; bishop of Bridgeport, Conn., 1961—. Office: 238 Jewett Ave Bridgeport CT 06606 *

CURTIS, WILLIAM EDGAR, composer, conductor; b. Aberdeen, Scotland, Mar. 11, 1914; came to U.S., 1940, naturalized, 1944; s. William Alexander and Florence (Malseed) C.; m. Doris Gray Schauffler, June 20, 1942; children: Michael Gray, Julie Malseed (Mrs. Robert J. Reed), Anne Harvey (Mrs. Paul Chittenden). B.Mus. magna cum laude, Edinburgh U., 1935, M.A., 1936; M.A. Bucherand Frazer travel scholar in Europe, 1936-40; postgrad., Curtis Inst. and Berkshire Music Center, 1940-41, Cleve. Orch. Condrs. Workshop, 1956. Prof. music Union Coll., Schenectady, 1956-79, chmn. dept. arts, 1967-72; founder Northeastern N.Y. Student Orch., 1965; Adviser N.Y. State Council Arts, 1962—. Founder, Curtis String Orch., Boston, 1942; condr., 1942-44, Albany Symphony, 1948-66; founder, Northeastern N.Y. Philharmonia, 1966; conductor, 1966—; guest conductor, Boston Symphony, B.B.C. Radio Zürich, Oslo Philharmonic, Brabant Orkest, Rheinisches Kammerorchester; condr. (1965); (Recipient Am. Fedn. Musicians award 1952); Composer: Suite For Contralto, Viola and Orch, 1966, Concerto for Organ, 1967, Three Piano Pieces, 1968, Suite for Solo Flute, 1969, Double Exposure for String Quartet and Prerecorded Tape, 1969; music for film To Open Eyes, 1969; Music for Brass, 1973, Sonata for Two (flute and guitar), 1974, Brass Quintet, 1976, Music for Dance Perhaps (1 piano, 4 hands), 1976. Served with USNR, 1944-46. Mem. Am. Fedn. Musicians, AAUP. *Two lifelong convictions remain clear: that music, and each of the arts, is directly accessible to any person whose early exposure was a happy one; and that a piece of music, a painting...is revealed to be less an art work than a shared experience. For these reasons, teaching and learning is, in any field, a shared artistic experience, no less than the composing, conducting or performing of music. We need, in Josef Albers' phrase, "To teach the young more search, less research."*

CURTIS, WILLIAM HALL, lawyer; b. Arkansas City, Kans., Oct. 9, 1915; s. John Warner and Addie (Thompson) C.; m. Vivian Swearingen, Apr. 2, 1947; children—Gregory, Ann, John, Carolyn. A.B., U. Nebr., 1937; LL.B., Harvard U., 1940. Bar: Mo., Kans. bars 1941. Since practiced in, Kansas City; partner firm Morrison, Hecker, Curtis, Kuder & Parrish, 1950—; dir. Ednl. Credit Bus., Inc., Atlas Mut. Ins. Co., Kansas City, New Eng. Ranch & Oil Corp. Trustee Civic Health Found. Greater Kansas City; hon. trustee Kansas City (Mo.) Research Hosp. Served to maj. AUS, 1941-46. Fellow Am. Coll. Trial Lawyers; mem. Am., Kansas City bar assns., Lawyers Assn. Kansas City (pres. 1965-66), Assn. Life Ins. Counsel, Am. Council Life Ins. Cos., Assn. R.R. Trial Counsel, Am. Royal Assn. (bd. govs.). Clubs: Blue Hills Country (pres. 1960), River, Kansas City (dir.). Home: 6701 Rainbow St Shawnee Mission KS 66208 Office: Bryant Bldg Kansas City MO 64106

CURTISS, CHARLES FRANCIS, chemist, educator; b. Chgo., Apr. 4, 1921; s. Ralph Charles and Camille (Guthormsen) C.; m. Lois Pauline Hruska, Mar. 23, 1946; children: Larry A., Glenn D., Ned S. B.S., U. Wis., 1942, Ph.D., 1948. Faculty U. Wis., 1949—, prof. chemistry, 1960—. Author: (with others) Molecular Theory of Gases and Liquids, 1954, Dynamics of Polymeric Liquids, 1977; also research papers. Fellow Am. Phys. Soc., AAAS; mem. Am. Chem. Soc. Home: 6317 Keelson Dr Madison WI 53705

CURTISS, ELDEN F., bishop; b. Baker, Oreg., June 16, 1932; s. Elden F. and Mary (Neiger) C. B.A., St. Edward Sem., Seattle, M.Div., 1958; M.A. in Ednl. Adminstrn, U. Portland, 1965; postgrad., Fordham U., U. Notre Dame. Ordained priest Roman Catholic Ch., 1958; campus chaplain, 1959-64, 65-68; supt. schs. Diocese of Baker (Oreg.), 1962-70; pastor, 1968-70; pres./rector Mt. Angel Sem., Benedict, Oreg., 1972-76; bishop of Helena (Mont.), 1976—; mem. priests senate Archdiocese of Portland, 1974-76; mem. ecumenical ministries, State of Oreg., 1972; mem. pastoral services com. Oreg. State Hosp., Salem, 1975-76; Mem. adminstrv. bd. Nat. Conf. Cath. Bishops, 1976-80, mem. pro-life com., 1977—; bd. dirs. Cath. Mut. Relief Soc., 1977—, Mont. Cath. Conf., 1976—; mem. N.W. Assn. Bishops and Major Religious Superiors, 1976—, Mont. Assn. Chs., 1976—. Mem. Nat. Cath. Ednl. Assn. (Outstanding Educator 1973). Address: 515 N Ewing PO Box 1729 Helena MT 59601

CURTISS, HOWARD CROSBY, JR., mechanical engineer, educator; b. Chgo., Mar. 17, 1930; s. Howard Crosby and Susan (Stephenson) C.; m. Betty Ruth Cloke, Mar. 24, 1956; children: Lisa Crosby, Jonathan Cloke. B.Aero.Engring., Rensselaer Poly. Inst., 1952; Ph.D., Princeton U., 1965. Mem. research staff dept. aerospace and mech. scis. Princeton U., 1956-65, mem. faculty, 1965—, prof., 1970—; mem. Army. Sci. Bd., 1978-82, Army Sci. Adv. Panel, 1972-77; mem. Naval Research Adv. Com., 1978-80. Author: (with others) A Modern Course in Aeroelasticity, 1978; Editor: Jour. of Am. Helicopter Soc, 1972-74. Served with USN, 1952-54. Mem. Am. Helicopter Soc. (dir. 1978-79), AIAA, Sigma Xi, Tau Beta Pi. Clubs: Metedeconk, River Yacht. Home: 34 Southern Way Princeton NJ 08540 Office: Dept Mech and Aerospace Engring Princeton Univ Princeton NJ 08544

CURTISS, PAUL HERBERT, JR., physician, educator; b. Kokomo, Ind., June 2, 1920; s. Paul Herbert and Georgia Ella (Tanner) C.; m. Maria Elizabeth Moreton, June 29, 1945; children—Jonathan, Stacey. B.A., U. Wis., 1941, M.D., 1945. Diplomate: Am. Bd. Orthopaedic Surgery (treas. 1968). Intern Med. Sch. Hosp. and Clinic, U. Oreg., 1944-45; gen. surg. resident Beckman Downtown Hosp., N.Y.C., 1947-48; mem. staff N.J. Orthopaedic Hosp., Trenton, Hosp. for Spl. Surgery, N.Y.C., Kingsbridge VA Hosp., Bronx, N.Y., 1948-52; asso. prof. orthopaedic surgery Western Res. U. Med. Sch., 1952-65; prof., dir. orthopaedics Coll. Med., Ohio State U., 1965-78; editor Jour. Bone and Joint Surgery, 1979—; lectr. Harvard U.; vis. orthopedist Mass. Gen. Hosp.; chmn. dept. orthopaedics Children's Hosp., Columbus, 1965; cons. staff Riverside Methodist Hosp., Columbus. Trustee: Jour. Bone and Joint Surgery, 1972-78; Contbr. articles to research publs. Served to capt. AUS, 1945-47. Recipient Kappa Delta award for research, 1963; Traveling fellow to Great Britian Am. Orthopaedic Assn., 1957. Mem. Am. Orthopaedic Assn., A.C.S., Orthopaedic Research Soc., A.M.A., Franklin County, Columbus acads. medicine, Ohio Orthopaedic Soc., Russell E. Hibbs Soc., LeRoy G. Abbott Orthopaedic Soc., N. Am. Orthopaedic Travel Club, Am.-Brit. Canadian Club. Home: 17 Pleasant St South Natick MA 01760 Office: 10 Shattuck St Boston MA 02115

CURTISS, ROY, III, biology educator; b. May 27, 1934; m. Josephine Clark, Dec. 28, 1976; children: Brian, Wayne, Roy IV, Lynn, Gregory Clark, Eric Garth, Megan Kimberly. B.S. in Agr., Cornell U., 1956; Ph.D. in Microbiology, U. Chgo., 1962. Instr., research asst. Cornell U., 1955-56; jr. tech. specialist Brookhaven Nat. Lab., 1956-58; fellow microbiology U. Chgo., 1958-60, USPHS fellow, 1960-62; biologist Oak Ridge Nat. Lab., 1963-72; lectr. microbiology U. Tenn., 1965-72, lectr. Grad. Sch. Biomed. Scis., Oak Ridge, 1967-69, prof., 1969-72, assoc. dir., 1970-71, interim dir., 1971-72; Charles H. McCauley prof. microbiology U. Ala., Birmingham, 1972—83; sr. scientist Inst. Dental Research, 1972—83, Comprehensive Cancer Center, 1972—83; dir. molecular cell biology grad. program, 1973—82; acting chmn. dept.

microbiology Comprehensive Cancer Center, 1981—82; dir. Cystic Fibrosis Research Center, 1981—83; prof. cellular and molecular biology Sch. Dental Medicine Washington U., St. Louis, 1983, George William and Irene Koechig Freiburg prof. biology, 1984—; vis. prof. Instituto Venezolana de Investigaciones Científicas, 1969, U. P.R., 1972, U. Católica de Chile, 1973, U. Okla., 1983; Mem. NIH Recombinant DNA Molecule Program Adv. Com., 1974-77, NSF Genetic Biology Com., 1975-78; mem. NIH Genetic Basis of Disease Rev. Com., 1979—83, chmn., 1981—83. Contbr. articles to profl. jours.; Editor: Jour. Bacteriology, 1970-76. Mem. Oak Ridge City Council, 1969-72. Fellow Am. Acad. Microbiology; mem. Genetics Soc. Am., Soc. Gen. Microbiology, Am. Soc. Microbiology (parliamentarian 1970-75, dir. 1977-80), N.Y. Acad. Scis., AAAS, Council Advancement Sci. Writing (dir. 1976—82, v.p. 1978—82), Sigma Xi. Home: 6065 Lindell Blvd Saint Louis MO 63112 Office: Dept Biology Washington University Saint Louis MO 63130

CURTISS, URSULA REILLY (MRS. JOHN CURTISS, JR), author; b. Yonkers, N.Y., Apr. 8, 1923; d. Paul and Helen (Kieran) Reilly; m. John Curtiss, Jr., May 24, 1947; children: Katherine, John, Paul, Kieran, Mary. Student pub. schs. Fashion copywriter Gimbels, N.Y.C., 1944, Macy's, 1944-45, Bates Fabrics, Inc., 1945-47. Author: Voice Out of Darkness, 1948, The Second Sickle, 1950, The Noonday Devil, 1951, The Iron Cobweb, 1953, The Deadly Climate, 1954, The Stairway, 1955, Widow's Web, 1956, The Face of the Tiger, 1957, So Dies the Dreamer, 1960, Hours to Kill, 1961, The Forbidden Garden, 1962, The Wasp, 1963, Out of the Dark, 1964, Danger: Hospital Zone, 1966, Don't Open the Door!, 1968, Letter of Intent, 1971, The Birthday Gift, 1976, In Cold Pursuit, 1977, The Menace Within, 1979, The Poisoned Orchard, 1980, Dog in the Manger, 1982, Death of a Crow, 1983. Recipient Zia Award, 1963. Mem. Crime Writers' Assn. Home: 8408 Rio Grande Blvd Albuquerque NM 87114

CURTISS, WILLIS DAVID, lawyer, educator; b. Sodus, N.Y., May 31, 1916; s. Willis David and Louise Anna (Shoecraft) C.; m. Mary Melissa Fowler, June 29, 1951; children—David Fowler, Melissa Anne. A.B., Cornell U., 1938, LL.B., 1940. Bar: N.Y. bar 1940. Gen. practice, Sodus, 1940-42, dist. atty., Wayne County, N.Y., 1941; asst. prof. law U. Buffalo, 1946-47, Cornell U. Law Sch., Ithaca, N.Y., 1947-51, asso. prof., 1951-56, prof., 1956—, asso. dean, 1958-62; Vis. prof. U. Mich. Law Sch., summer 1950; spl. atty. Dept. Justice, 1954. Research cons. N.Y. State Law Revision Commn., 1952-56, exec. sec., 1956-60; mem. N.Y. Temporary Commn. on State Ct. System, 1970-73; Faculty trustee Cornell U., 1966-71. Served to lt. comdr. USNR, 1942-46. Mem. N.Y. State, Tompkins County bar assns., Am. Arbitration Assn., Am. Law Inst., Order of Coif, Phi Beta Kappa, Phi Kappa Phi, Delta Sigma Rho, Phi Delta Phi, Sigma Nu. Democrat. Presbyn. Home: 108 Hampton Rd Ithaca NY 14850 Office: Cornell Law Sch Ithaca NY 14853

CUSACK, ANNE MILLICENT, photojournalist; b. Chgo., July 21, 1951; d. Patrick F. and Ellen Torrey (Graham) Cusask; m. Richard Derk, Oct. 6, 1973. B.S. in Social Work, U. Ill., Champaign, 1973. Dir. photography Williams Press, Harvey, Ill., 1974-75; photojournalist Star Tribune Newspapers, Harvey, 1974-76; staff photographer Paddock Publs., Arlington Heights, Ill., 1976-78, Chgo. Tribune, 1978—. Recipient 1st pl. feature award Inland Press Assn.; named Chgo. Press Photographer of Yr., 1980; runner-up, 1981. Mem. Nat. Fedn. Press Women (Nat. Sweepstakes award 1974), Nat. Press Photographers Assn. (3d pl. award, home and family interest), Ill. Press Photographers Assn. (3d pl. Photographer of Yr., Photographer of Yr. 1976). Home: 122 S Scoville St Oak Park IL 60302 Office: Tribune Tower 435 N Michigan Ave Chicago IL

CUSHING, FREDERIC SANFORD, publishing co. exec.; b. Providence, June 13, 1920; s. Frederic Charles and Julia M. (Sanford) C.; m. Jean Marie Byers, Dec. 18, 1947; 1 son, James Byers. B.A., Colgate U., 1942; postgrad., Brown U., 1947, Carnegie Inst. Tech., 1949. With Rinehart & Co., Inc., 1947-59, asst. dir. coll. dept., nat. sales mgr., 1954-59; v.p., gen. mgr. coll. div. Holt, Rinehart & Winston, 1959-65, v.p. corporate mktg., 1965-66; dir. Holt, Rinehart & Winston, Ltd., London, Eng. and; Ont., Can., 1965-66; pres. Glencoe Press., 1966-72; v.p. Macmillan Co., 1966-74; mng. dir. Cassell and Collier and; Macmillan Pubs. Ltd., London, Eng., 1972-74; mng. dir. Collier Macmillan Schs. Ltd., Aldermaston, Eng., 1974-75; gen. mgr. ednl. pub. div. ITT Pub. Co., Indpls., 1975-76; dir. pub. Instrument Soc. Am., Research Triangle Park, N.C., 1976—; spl. cons. CIA, 1952-54; chmn. coll. sect. Am. Textbook Pubs. Inst., 1959-60, bd. dirs., 1965-66. Contbr. articles to profl. jours. Served to capt. USMCR, 1942-46; PTO. Mem. Beta Theta Pi. Democrat. Episcopalian. Office: PO Box 12277 Research Triangle Park NC 27709

CUSHING, HARRY COOKE, IV, retired investment banker; b. N.Y.C., Apr. 2; s. Harry Cooke and Cathleen (Vanderbilt) C.; m. Ruth Swift Dunbar, Jan. 14, 1961 (div.); 1 son, Harry Cooke V.; m. Laura Alvarez, Jan. 23, 1976. Student, Cornell U., 1945. Adviser for European ops. to chmn. bd. Ventures Ltd., 1955-59; pvt. adviser individuals and corps., 1966; ltd. partner Hallgarten & Co., N.Y.C., 1966-74. Chmn. polo com. People-to-People Sports Com., 1962—. Served with AUS, 1942-46. Decorated commendatore Order Crown of Italy. Mem. S.R. Clubs: Turf, White's (London); Travellers, Polo (Paris); Polo, Golf (Rome); Hurlingham (Buenos Aires, Argentina); Racquet and Tennis, Brook (N.Y.C.); Corviglia (St. Moritz, Switzerland); Palm Beach Polo and Country, Malta Polo. Address: 200 Park Ave Suite 2700 New York NY 10166 also Via Panama 48 Rome Italy

CUSHMAN, AARON D., public relations executive; b. Chgo., Aug. 29, 1924; s. Harry A. and Eva (Sternberg) C.; m. Doris Silverman, Mar. 8, 1948; children: Gary, Amy, Pamela. B.A., U. Ill., 1947. Publicity dir. Chgo. Lake Front Fair, 1950; pres. Aaron D. Cushman & Assos., Inc., Chgo., 1952—; dir. Chgo. White Sox, Mesa Electronics, Ltd. Mem. Adv. Council Kendall Coll.; mem. Mayor Daley's Adv. Com. Youth Welfare; mem. public relations com. Crusade of Mercy, Boy Scouts Am.; bd. dirs. Columbia Coll., Am. Sch. of Needlecraft. Served with USAF, 1943-45, 50-52. Mem. Public Relations Soc. Am. (past pres. counsellors sect. Chgo. chpt., Silver Anvil award 1983), Am. Coll. Radio Arts, Crafts and Scis. (regent), Welfare Public Relations Forum, Assn. Public Relations Round Table, Indsl. Editors Soc. (v.p.), Am. Acad. TV Arts, Crafts and Scis., Nat. Sci. Writers Assn., Nat. Assn. Real Estate Editors, Soc. Am. Travel Writers, Chgo. Dist. Tennis Assn. (dir.). Jewish. Clubs: Green Acres Country (dir.), Chgo. Publicity (past pres.). Home: 1093 Oak Ridge Dr Glencoe IL 60022 Office: 333 N Michigan Ave Chicago IL 60601

CUSHMAN, DAVID WAYNE, research biochemist; b. Indpls., Nov. 15, 1939; s. Wayne B. and Mildred M. (Coffin) C.; m. Linda L. Kranch, July 31, 1964; children: Michael, Laura. B.A., Wabash Coll., 1961; Ph.D., U. Ill., 1966. Research investigator Squibb Inst. for Med. Research, Princeton, N.J., 1966-69, sr. research investigator, 1969-73, research fellow, 1973-78, sr. research fellow, 1978-83, asst. dept. dir., 1983—. Recipient CIBA award, 1983; NSF fellow, 1961-63. Mem. Am. Soc. Pharmacology and Exptl. Therapeutics, Am. Chem. Soc. (Alfred Burger award in medicinal chemistry 1982), AAAS, N.Y. Acad. Sci., Am. Soc. Biol. Chemists, Phi Beta Kappa, Delta Phi Alpha, Sigma Xi. Home: RD 1 20 Lake Shore Dr Trenton NJ 08648 Office: Squibb Inst for Med Research PO Box 4000 Princeton NJ 08540

CUSHMAN, EDWARD L., univ. adminstr.; b. Boston, Apr. 6, 1914; s. Robert and Sarah C.; m. Katherine Jean Moore, Nov. 18, 1938; children—Robert Moore, Elizabeth Ann. A.B., U. Mich., 1937. Successively economist, civil service dir., asst. to employment service dir. Mich. Unemployment Compensation Commn., 1937-42; dep. dir. for Mich., War Manpower Commn., 1942-43, dir., 1943-46; spl. asst. to sec. of labor, 1946; prof. public adminstrn. Wayne U., 1946-54; v.p. indsl. relations Am. Motors Corp., 1954-59, v.p., 1959-66; now dir.; exec. v.p. Wayne State U., Detroit, 1966—, Clarence Hilberry U. prof., 1977—. Mem. Nat. Acad. Arbitrators, Indsl. Relations Research Assn. Office: 211 Walter P Reuther Library Labor and Urban Affairs Wayne State U Detroit MI 48202

CUSHMAN, HELEN MERLE BAKER, Consultant; b. Perth Amboy, N.J.; d. Ivan F. and Lucile (Atkinson) Baker; m. Robert Arnold Cushman, June 2, 1945; children—Lucinda Ann, Robert Rorem. A.B. in History, Barnard Coll., 1942; postgrad., NYU, 1944. Route analyst intelligence div. Air Transport Command, Washington, 1943-44; personnel asst. Gen. Cable Corp., N.Y.C., 1944-45; sr. staff asst. to chmn. bd. Trans World Airlines, N.Y.C., 1945-50; pres. H.M. Baker Assocs., Westfield, N.J., 1958—. Author articles, bus. histories, anniversary manual, manuals on archives and mgmt. Pres. Franklin PTA, 1963-64. Mem. Soc. Am. Archivists, Am. Records Mgmt. Assn. (past archivist-historian N.J. chpt., Lit. award 1972), P.E.O. Episcopalian. Club: Barnard Coll. of N. Central N.J. (past pres.). Address: Box 363 Westfield NJ 07090

CUSHMAN, JOHN HOLLOWAY, mgmt. cons.; b. Tientsin, China, Oct. 3, 1921; s. Horace Oscar and Kathleen (O'Neill) C. (parents Am. citizens); m. Nancy Townsend Troland, June 27, 1946; children—Constance, Cecelia, Kathleen, Mary, John, Theodore, Anne. B.S., U.S. Mil. Acad., 1944; M.S., Mass. Inst. Tech., 1950. Commd. 2d lt. U.S. Army, 1944, advanced through grades to lt. gen., 1976; various assignments, 1944-1960, mem. staff, Washington, 1961-62, mil. asst. to Sec. Army, 1962-63, sr. advisor, Vietnam, 1963-64, chief of staff, Fort Campbell, Ky., 1965-67, comdr. 2d brigade, Vietnam, 1967-68, commanding gen., Fort Devens, Mass., 1968-70, Vietnam, 1971-72, Fort Campbell, 1972-73; commandant U.S. Army Command and Gen. Staff Coll., Fort Leavenworth, Kans., 1973-75; comdg. gen. I Corps (ROK/US) Group, Korea, 1976-78, ret., 1978. Decorated D.S.M., Legion of Merit, Silver Star, D.F.C., Bronze Star, Air Medal. Roman Catholic. Address: 91 Warwick Rd Bronxville NY 10708

CUSHMAN, RICHARD DAVID, retail lumber company executive; b. Norwich, N.Y., Feb. 14, 1929; s. Edward V. and Dorothy D. (Schrader) C.; m. Pamela J. Decker, Mar. 27, 1954; children—Cynthia Louise, Melissa Dawn. B.A., Columbia U., 1950; M.B.A., CCNY, 1960. Credit investigator Nat. Credit Office, N.Y.C., 1954-57; with Diamond Internat. Corp., N.Y.C., 1957—; gen. mgr. Eastern and Western retail and wholesale ops., 1976-77, corp. v.p., 1977-79, group v.p. retail ops., N. Highlands, Calif., 1979—. Dir.-at-large Sacramento Safety Council, 1977—. Served with AUS, 1951-54. Mem. Sacramento Met. C. of C. (dir. 1977-82, v.p. small bus. council 1981, v.p. econ. devel. 1979-82). Home: 3663 Christian Valley Rd Auburn CA 95603 Office: PO Box 15377 Sacramento CA 95851

CUSHMAN, ROBERT, abrasives manufacturing company executive; b. Winchester, Mass., Apr. 29, 1916; s. Norman Locke and Madeline (Porter) C.; m. Mary Shorey, July 26, 1940; children: Mary Allerton (Mrs. Mary C. Higgins), Louise C. Paquette. Grad., Phillips Acad., Andover, Mass., 1935; B.A., Dartmouth, 1939. Salesman Gulf Oil Corp., 1939-44; with Norton Co., Worcester, Mass., 1944—, v.p., gen. mgr. abrasive div., 1961-67, exec. v.p., 1967-71, pres., chief exec. officer, 1971-79, chmn., chief exec. officer, 1979-80, chmn., 1980—, also dir.; dir. Houghton-Mifflin Co., State Mut. Life Assurance Co. Am., Hanover Ins. Co., Instron Corp., Paine Webber, Inc., Mass. Bay Ins. Co.; vice chmn. Polish-U.S. Econ. Council, 1974-80; mem. Czechoslovak-U.S. Econ. Council, 1976-79. Corporator Worcester Boys Club, Worcester Natural History Soc.; Mem. Community Services, Inc., Worcester County; chmn. United Negro Coll. Fund; dir. Mass. div. Am. Cancer Soc., 1970-75; hon. bd. dirs. Worcester Children's Theatre, Mohegan council Boy Scouts Am.; mem. Mass. Bd. Regents of Higher Edn.; trustee, past pres. bd. Shepherd Knapp Sch., Boylston, Mass.; past trustee Worcester Rehab. Center; trustee, chmn. bd. Worcester Found. Exptl. Biology; trustee New Eng. Aquarium, Boston, Worcester Polytech. Inst.; chmn. Greater Worcester Community Found.; bd. overseers Old Sturbridge Village, Amos Tuck Sch. Bus. Adminstrn., 1975-81, Boston Symphony Orch., 1973-79; bd. dirs. Asso. Industries Mass. Mem. Mass. Soc. Mayflower Descs., Research Inst. Am., Internat. Sales and Mktg. Execs., Bus. Roundtable, Theta Delta Chi. Unitarian. Clubs: Dartmouth (past pres. Worcester County), Tatnuck Country, Worcester, Laurel Brook, Black Brook Salmon, Worcester Fire Soc., Anglers of N.Y. Office: 1 New Bond St Worcester MA 01606

CUSHMAN, ROBERT EARL, clergyman, educator; b. Fall River, Mass., Dec. 26, 1913; s. Ralph Spaulding and Maud (Hammond) C.; m. Barbara Priscilla Edgecomb, Sept. 12, 1936; children—Robert Earl, Thomas Spaulding, Elizabeth Jane. Student, Denver U., 1932-34; A.B., Wesleyan U., Middletown, Conn., 1936; B.D., Yale, 1940, Ph.D., 1942; L.H.D., Belmont (N.C.) Abbey, 1966. Ordained elder Methodist Ch., 1940; asst. pastor, South Meriden, Conn., 1936-40, Hamilton, N.Y., 1941; instr. theology Yale Div. Sch., 1942-43; prof. religion U. Oreg., 1943-45; asso. prof. theology Duke Div. Sch., 1945-48, prof., 1948-58, dean, 1958-71, research prof., 1971—, Robert E. Cushman chair Christian theology, 1981; Ofcl. Meth. del. World Conf. Faith and Order, Lund, Sweden, 1952; founding mem. commn. ecumenical consultation Meth. Ch., 1958-64; mem. commn. ecumenical affairs United Meth. Ch., 1964-72, v.p., 1971-72; mem. N.A. commn. worship World Council Chs., 1954-63; ofcl. meth. del. 4th World Conf. Faith and Order, Montreal, 1963; Meth. ofcl. observer 2d Vatican Council, Rome, 1963-65; mem. N.C. conf. Wesley Soc., 1955-62; mem. commn. ecumenical affairs Nat. Council Chs., 1965-70; mem. World Meth. Council, 1970-72; chmn. bd. dirs. Oxford Edit. Wesley Works Project, 1959-71, gen. editor, 1971—, v.p., 1976—; fellow Ecumenical Inst. Advanced Theol. Studies, Jerusalem, 1971-72; del. Gen. Conf., Meth. Church, 1964, 66, 68, 70, 72; mem. univ. senate United Meth. Ch., 1966-71; Meth. del. N.C. Council Chs., 1970-74. Author: Therapeia; Plato's Conception of Philosophy, 1958, The Heritage of Christian Thought, 1966, Faith Seeking Understanding, 1981; Contbr.: Religion in Life. Recipient Tchr.-Scholar award Wesleyan U., 1967. Mem. Assn. United Meth. Theol. Schs. (pres. 1964-66, mem. exec. com.), Duodecim Theol. Group, Am. Theol. Soc., Phi Beta Kappa. Home: 2800 Croasdaile Dr J-6 Durham NC 27705 *Other things being more or less equal, I find achievement to be perseverance in worthy causes and, in the face of obstacles, a determination to give the job what it takes. In my observation, resiliency and attainment are closely paired. Yet resiliency without verve may become doggedness, so that loyalty that is sparked by vision is that quality in greater men that objectifies motivation. The latter sires the rarity of self-transcendence and perhaps is, in turn, the signature of something we call faith. It is this, I believe, that keeps endeavor from going stale, that outruns misgivings and weighty evidence to the contrary, and alone has survival value for imperfect fulfillments of which life is composed.*

CUSHMAN, ROBERT FAIRCHILD, emeritus political science educator, author, editor; b. Champaign, Ill, Nov. 28, 1918; s. Robert Eugene and Clarissa White (Fairchild) C.; m. Rhea Lillian Casterline, June 3, 1917; children: Leslee Fairchild, Linda Casterline. A.B., Cornell U., 1940, M.A., 1948, Ph.D., 1949. Grad. teaching asst. Cornell U., Ithaca, N.Y., 1946-49; instr. polit. sci. Ohio State U., Columbus, 1949-52, asst. prof., 1952-53; assoc. prof. NYU, N.Y.C., 1953-69, prof. govt., 1969-84, ret., 1984. Contbr. articles to law revs.; editor, contbg. author: Cases in Constitutional Law, 1958, Cases in Civil Liberties, 1968; series Leading Constitutional Decisions, 1969—. Served to sgt. AC U.S. Army, 1942-46; India. Mem. Am. Polit. Sci. Assn. Democrat. Quaker. Home: 27 Bennett Ave Huntington Station NY 11746

CUSHMORE, CAROLE LEE, publisher; b. Steubenville, Ohio; d. George E. and Adelma (Miller) Fithen; m. Taylor Cushmore, Oct. 28, 1967. B.F.A., Ohio U., 1962; postgrad., Pa. State U., 1964. Asso. producer CBS-TV, Phila., 1965-68; public relations officer Free Library of Phila., 1968-70; mgr. market devel. R.R. Bowker, N.Y.C., 1971-75, v.p., pub., book div., 1980—; v.p. mktg. Baker & Taylor, N.Y.C., 1975-80; mem. adv. bd. Center for the Book, 1981—; mem. pub. com. Info. Industry Assn., 1982-83; Trustee Ossining (N.Y.) Public Library, 1979—. Recipient Exec. Women Achievement award YMCA, 1979. Mem. ALA., Assn. Am. Pubs. (data base pub. com. 1983—), Internat Assn. Bus. Communicators. Home: PO Box 314 Scarborough NY 10510 Office: 205 E 42d St New York NY 10017

CUSICK, RALPH A., JR., investment banking company executive; b. Washington, July 25, 1934; m. Jaquelin Carter Ambler, June 15, 1957; children: Ralph A. III, James Ambler, Carter Marshall. With Alex Brown & Sons, Washington and Balt., from 1959, gen. ptnr., 1969—. Editor: Facts and Figures on Washington Securities, 1962-73. Pres. bd. dirs. Children's Hosp. Med. Research Ctr. Served with USNR, 1956-59. Mem. Washington Soc. Investment Analysts, Phi Delta Theta. Republican. Clubs: Metropolitan; Chevy Chase (Washington); Coral Beach (Paget, Bermuda). Office: 730 15th St NW Washington DC 20005

CUSSLER, CLIVE ERIC, author; b. Aurora, Ill., July 15, 1931; s. Eric E. and Amy (Hunnewell) C.; m. Barbara Knight, Aug. 28, 1955; children: Teri, Dirk, Dana. Student, Pasadena City Coll., 1949-51. Owner Bestgen & Cussler Advt., Newport Beach, Calif., 1961-65; creative dir. Darcy Advt., Hollywood, Calif., 1965-67; chmn. Nat. Underwater and Marine Agy. Author: novels The Mediterrranean Caper, 1973, Iceberg, 1975, Raise the Titanic!, 1976, Vixen 03, 1978, Night Probe, 1981, Pacific Vortex, 1982, Deep Six, 1984. Served in USAF, 1950-54. Recipient numerous advt. awards. Fellow Explorers Club, Royal Geog. Soc. Discoverer numerous historic shipwrecks.

CUSSON, RONALD YVON, theoretical physicist; b. Drummondville, Que., Can., July 3, 1938; came to U.S., 1960, naturalized, 1965; s. Roll and Jeannette (Thibeault) C. B.S. in Physics, Calif. Inst. Tech., 1960, Ph.D. in Physics and Math, 1965. Research fellow Calif. Inst. Tech., Pasadena, 1965-66; Alexander von Humbold fellow U. Heidelberg, 1966-67; research physicist Atomic Energy of Can., Chalk River, Ont., 1967-70; asso. prof. physics Duke U., Durham, N.C., 1970-77, prof. physics, 1977—; cons. O.R.N.L. Tenn., L.L.N.L. Calif., 1975—, G.S.I., Darmstadt, W. Ger., 1978—. Contbr. articles to various publs. Recipient Alexander von Humboldt Sr. Scientist award, 1978; NSF grantee, 1971-75; Amy Research Office grantee, 1971-74; Dept. of Energy grantee, 1983—. Mem. Am. Phys. Soc., AAAS, Sigma Chi. Office: Physics Dept Duke U Durham NC 27706 *The most exciting moments are those when one suddenly realizes that one is the first to possess the answer to some challenging problem. Then the work begins to communicate this new knowledge and carry forward the tide of human progress.*

CUSTIN, MILDRED, department store executive; b. Manchester, N.H., 1906. Grad., Simmons Coll., 1927; L.H.D., Temple U., 1966, Russell Sage Coll., 1968. With controller's office R.H. Macy Co., 1928; buyer gifts, china, glassware R.H. White & Co., Boston, 1933-35; buyer gifts John Wanamaker, Phila., 1935, then mdse. mgr. fashion div., v.p. and mdse. mgr. ready to wear and fashion accessories depts., 1951-58; pres. Bonwit Teller, Phila., 1958-65, Bonwit Teller N.Y. (subsidiary of Genesco) and 12 brs.), 1965-69, chmn. bd., chief exec. officer, 1969-70; pres. Mildred Custin Ltd., 1970—; also exec. cons. to Genesco, 1970—. Active civic, philanthropic endeavors; trustee Simmons Coll., Boston.; bd. overseers N.Y.U. Grad. Sch. Bus. Adminstrn. Decorated La Croix de la Chevalier del ' Ordre du Merite, France).; Recipient Distinguished Alumnae award Simmons Coll., 1964; Tobe award for distinguished contbn. to retailing, 1969. Home and office: 330 S Ocean Blvd Palm Beach FL 33480

CUSTIS, DONALD L., retired navy medical officer, VA medical administrator; b. Goshen, Ind., July 23, 1917; s. Lauren A. and Margaret (Shannon) C.; m. Phyllis Hodson, Apr. 6, 1942; children: Bruce L., Peter H. A.B., Wabash Coll., 1959, D.Sc. hon., 1977; M.D., Northwestern U., 1942. Diplomate: Am. Bd. Surgery. Intern. Presbyn.-St. Luke's Hosp., Chgo., 1942-43; resident in surgery Mason Clinic, Seattle, 1946-50; commd. lt. (j.g.) M.C. U.S. Navy Res., 1943, served, until 1946; recommd. comdr. M.C. U.S. Navy, 1946, advanced through grades to vice adm., 1973; surgeon naval hosps., Portsmouth, Va., 1956-58, Guantanamo Bay, Cuba, 1958-60, Gt. Lakes, Ill., Cuba, 1960-63, Beaufort, S.C., 1963-65, Phila., 1965-69, assigned, Danang, Vietnam, 1969; comdg. officer U.S. Naval Hosp., Bethesda, Md., 1970-73; surgeon gen. U.S. Navy, 1973-77; dep. for acad. affairs VA, Washington, 1977-78, dep. chief med. dir., 1978—; trustee Medic Alert, 1977—. Decorated D.S.M., Legion of Merit with combat V. Mem. ACS (bd. govs.), AMA (ho. of dels.), Uniformed Services U. of Health Scis. (past mem. bd. regents), Am. Hosp. Assn. (trustee), Assn. Mil. Surgeons U.S. (pres. 1974). Home: 10402 Windsor View Dr Potomac MD 20854 Office: Dept Medicine and Surgery VA 810 Vermont Ave NW Washington DC 20420

CUTCHINS, CLIFFORD ARMSTRONG, III, banker; b. Southampton County, Va., July 12, 1923; s. Clifford Armstrong Jr. and Sarah (Vaughan) C.; m. Ann Woods, June 21, 1947; children: Clifford Armstrong IV, William Witherspoon, Cecil Vaughan. B.S. in Bus. Adminstrn, Va. Poly. Inst. and State U., 1947; grad., Stonier Grad. Sch. Banking, 1953. From asst. cashier to pres., dir. Vaughan & Co., bankers, Franklin, Va., 1950-62; pres., cashier dir. Tidewater Bank & Trust Co., Franklin, 1962-63; (bank merged with Va. Nat. Bank), Norfolk, 1963, sr. v.p., dir., exec. v.p., 1965-69, pres., 1969-80, chmn. bd., chief exec. officer, dir., 1980—; pres., dir. Va. Nat. Bankshares, Inc., 1972-80, chmn. bd., chief exec. officer, dir., 1980—; dir. Franklin Equipment Co., Pulaski Furniture Corp. Bd. dirs. Camp Found., Franklin, 1962—; bd. dirs., trustee Alliance Health System; bd. dirs., pres. Va. Tech. Found.; trustee Va. Found. Ind. Colls., Sci. Mus. Va. Served to capt. AUS, World War II; PTO. Baptist. Clubs: Commonwealth (Richmond); Norfolk Yacht and Country, Virginia, Harbor (Norfolk); Princess Anne Country (Virginia Beach, Va.); Cypress Cove Country (Franklin, Va.). Home: 7320 Glenroie Ave Norfolk VA 23505 Office: One Commercial Pl Norfolk VA 23510

CUTHBERT, VIRGINIA (MRS. PHILIP C. ELLIOTT), artist; b. West Newton, Pa., Aug. 27, 1908; d. Richard Bruce and Frances Irene (Cartwright) C.; m. Philip Clarkson Elliott, June 8, 1935. B.F.A. (Augusta Hazard fellow), Syracuse U., 1930; postgrad., Academie de la Grande Chaumiere, Academie Colarossi, Paris, 1930, Chelsea Poly. Inst., London, 1931, George Luks, N.Y.C., 1932, U. Pitts., 1933-34,

Carnegie Inst. Tech., 1934-35. Instr. painting Albright Art Sch., Buffalo, 1943-54, U. Buffalo, 1954—, State U. N.Y. at Buffalo, 1962-65. Exhibited one-man shows, Carnegie Inst., 1938, Butler Art Inst., exhbns. include, Mus. Modern Art, N.Y.C., one-man shows, Syracuse Mus. Fine Arts, 1939, Syracuse U., 1945, Contemporary Arts, N.Y.C., 1945, 49, 53, Rehn Gallery, N.Y.C., 1958-66, N.Y. State Coll. Tchrs. Albany, 1959, Chautauqua (N.Y.) Art Assn., Albright-Knox Art Gallery, 1963, 74, 75, 76, Am. Acad. Arts and Letters, 1974, Rehn Gallery, N.Y.C., Gallery Without Walls, Buffalo, 1974, 75, 76, many others throughout U.S., exhbns. include, Met. Mus. Art, Whitney Mus. Am. Art, Westmoreland Mus. Art, Greensburg, Pa., Art Inst. Chgo., Pa. Acad. Fine Arts, Carnegie Internats., Ft. Worth Art Center, Butler Inst. Am. Art, Albright-Knox Art Gallery, Kenan Art Centre, Lockport, N.Y., 1975, others, retrospective exhbn., Charles Burchfield Center SUNY-Buffalo; represented in permanent collections, Albright-Knox Art Gallery, Hundred Friends of Pitts. Art, Syracuse U., Princeton Mus. Art, Rutgers U., Charles Burchfield Center SUNY, Everson Mus. Art, Syracuse, Canton (Ohio) Art Inst., Newark Mus. Art, also others, pvt. collections. Recipient prizes Asso. Artists Pitts. Ann., 1934, 36-40, Butler Art Inst., 1940, Western N.Y. Exhbn., 1944, 46, 50, 52, 55, 58, 65, 66, Pepsi-Cola Ann., 1946-47, Nat. Inst. Arts and Letters, 1954; Chataugua prize, 1955; prize Sisti Exhbn., Buffalo, 1956, 57; Albright Art Gallery, 1958, 80; Asso. Artists Orgn. Buffalo, 1976; Cover of Fortune, 1951. Mem. Patteran Artists, Kappa Alpha Theta. Methodist. Home: 147 Bryant St Buffalo NY 14222

CUTHBERTSON, RICHARD WILEY, advertising company executive; b. Warren, Pa., Oct. 21, 1935; s. James and Virginia C.; m. Margaret Ann Sampson, Aug. 1962; children: James, Jane, Craig. B.S., Rider Coll., 1961. C.P.A., N.Y., Ill. Mgr. audit and tax depts. Arthur Andersen & Co., N.Y.C., Tokyo, 1961-75; controller Foote, Cone & Belding, Chgo., 1975-80; exec. v.p. FCB Internat. Inc., Chgo., 1980—. Served to sgt. USMC, 1953-57; Korea, Japan. Mem. Am. Inst. C.P.A.'s, Fin. Execs. Inst., Tau Kappa Epsilon (pres. 1960-61). Roman Catholic. Club: Adventurers (Chgo.). Home: 2101 Grove St Glenview IL 60025 Office: FCB Internat Inc 401 N Michigan Ave Chicago IL 60611

CUTHRELL, CARL EDWARD, lawyer, educator, clergyman; b. Norfolk, Va., Aug. 13, 1934; s. Cecil Edward and Edna Catherine (Kirby) C.; m. Naomi Lorene Marshall, Dec. 23, 1960; children—Byron Eugene, Benjamin Dean. LL.B., LaSalle U. Law Sch., Chgo., 1959; B.A., Coll. William and Mary, 1962; B.D., Brantridge Forest Sch., Eng., 1970; M.A. in Med. History, Sussex (Eng.) Coll. Tech., 1972; B.A., Upper Iowa U., 1979. Bar: Va. bar 1960; Notary pub. at large, Va. Since practiced privately in, Hampton; tchr. history, geography Kecoughtan High Sch., 1964, Forest Glen High Sch., 1967-69, Central Christian Sch., Hampton, 1969—; ordained to ministry Evang. Friends Ch., 1972; pastor Rescue (Va.) Friends Ch., 1968—. Author: Ancient Mummies, 1967, Paul's Voyage, 1971; Contbr.: lit. criticisms to Times Herald Newspaper; also numerous short stories. Bd. dirs. Nat. Philatelic Inst.; trustee Quincy Coll., 1970, Nat. Coll. Surgeons Hall of Fame, 1972. Served with M.C. AUS, 1950-57; Korea. Decorated Silver Star; recipient Scouter's award medal Boy Scouts Am., 1956, Silver Beaver award, 1976, Nat. Tchrs. medal Freedoms Found., 1973, Peace medal UN, 1973, Good Citizenship medal SAR, 1976. Mem. U.S. Capital, Nat. hist. socs., SR, Sons Confederate Vets., Christian Educators Assn., Va. Herpetological Soc., Mil. Order Stars and Bars. Republican. Home: 307 Agusta Dr Newport News VA 23601 Office: PO Box 9033 Hampton VA 23670

CUTKOSKY, RICHARD EDWIN, physicist; b. Mpls., July 29, 1928; s. Oscar F. and Edna M. (Nelson) C.; m. Patricia A. Klepfer, Aug. 28, 1952; children: Mark, Carol, Martha. B.S., Carnegie Inst. Tech., 1950, M.S., 1950, Ph.D., 1953. Asst. prof. physics Carnegie-Mellon U., Pitts., 1954-61, prof. physics, 1961—, Buhl prof., 1963—. Fellow Am. Phys. Soc.; mem. AAAS. Home: 1309 Wightman St Pittsburgh PA 15217

CUTLER, ARNOLD R., lawyer; b. New Haven, Mar. 20, 1908; s. Max Nathan and Kate (Harder) C.; m. Hazel Lourie, Apr. 8, 1942; 1 son, David. B.A., Yale U., 1930, J.D., 1932. Bar: Conn. 1932, Mass. 1946. Mem. staff Office of Gen. Counsel, Pub. Works Adminstrn., Washington, 1933-36; chief counsel State of Wash., 1937-38; spl. asst. to chief counsel IRS, 1939-42, trial counsel New Eng. div., 1945-47; ptnr. Lourie & Cutler, Boston, 1947—; lectr. on taxation. Contbr. to books articles to legal jours. Trustee Beth Israel Hosp., Brandeis U.; trustee, past mem. exec. com. Combined Jewish Philanthropies Greater Boston; past. bd. dirs. Nat. Jewish Welfare Bd.; past pres. Brookline, Brighton and Newton Jewish Community Center; past. treas. Associated Jewish Community Centers of Greater Boston; past chmn. bd. Yale Law Sch. Fund; chmn. bequest com. Yale Law Sch. Lt. comdr. USCG, 1942-45. Fellow Am. Coll. Tax Counsel, Mass. Bar Found.; mem. ABA (past chmn. spl. adv. exempt orgns. com. tax sect.), Mass. Bar Assn., Boston Bar Assn. (past chmn. fed. tax com., past mem. council), Am. Law Inst. Clubs: New Century (past pres.), Greater Boston Brandeis (past pres.), Yale, Harvard, Wightman Tennis, Rotary (past bd. dirs.).

CUTLER, BERNARD JOSEPH, newspaperman; b. N.Y.C., May 26, 1924; s. Joseph Louis and Sophie (Appel) C.; m. Carol Ann Rataic, Mar. 6, 1948. B.S. in Mech. Engring, Pa. State Coll., 1945. Reporter Pitts. Press, 1945-51; reporter N.Y. Herald Tribune, 1951-56, Moscow corr., 1956-58, chief Paris bur., 1958-60, mng. editor European edition, Paris, 1960, editor European edition, 1961-66; European corr. Scripps-Howard Newspapers, Paris, 1966-69, fgn. editorial writer, Washington, 1969-72, chief editorial writer, 1972-80, editor-in-chief, 1980—. Author: Reactionary! Sgt. Lloyd W. Pate's Story, 1956. Recipient Disting. Alumni award Pa. State U., 1972. Clubs: Gridiron, National Press. Office: Scripps-Howard Newspapers 1110 Vermont Ave NW Washington DC 20005

CUTLER, CASSIUS CHAPIN, physicist, educator; b. Springfield, Mass., Dec. 16, 1914; s. Paul A. and Myra B. (Chapin) C.; m. Virginia Tyler, Sept. 27, 1941; children: (Cassius) Chapin, William (Urban) (dec.), Virginia Cutler Raymond. B.Sc., Worcester Poly. Inst., 1937, D.Eng. (hon.), 1975. With Bell Telephone Labs, 1937-78, asst. dir. electronics and radio research, Murray Hill, N.J., 1959-63, dir. electronic and computer systems research lab., Holmdel, N.J., 1963-78; prof. applied physics Stanford U., 1979—. Contbr. articles to profl. jours. Mem. 1st Ch. of Christ Scientist, Keyport, N.J., 1966-78 Mem. 1st Ch. of Christ Scientist, Menlo Park, Calif., 1979—, reader, chmn. bd., Plainfield, N.J., 1946-66. Fellow IEEE (Edison medal 1981), AAAS, mem.; Nat. Acad. Engring. Nat. Acad. Scis. Patentee numerous devices. Home: 1300 Oak Creek Dr Apt 318 Palo Alto CA 94304 Office: Ginzton Lab Stanford U Stanford CA 94305

CUTLER, EDWARD I., lawyer; b. Phila., Sept. 21, 1913; s. Samuel and Elizabeth (Esterman) C.; m. Roseline Adams, Aug. 12, 1938; children: Janet Kossman, Edward, Robin. A.B., U. Pa., 1934, J.D., 1937. Bar: Pa. 1938, Fla. 1948, U.S. Supreme Ct. bar 1966. Asst. law librarian U. Pa., 1937-39; law sec. to chief justice Pa., 1937-39, practiced in, Phila., 1938-44; exec. asst. Hooker's Point Shipyard, Tampa, Fla., 1944-46; engaged as real estate broker, Tampa, 1947, practice law, 1948—; mem. firm Carlton, Fields, Ward, Emmanuel, Smith & Cutler (P.A.), Tampa, Orlando, Tallahassee and Pensacola, Fla., 1961—, treas., 1969-76, pres., 1976-79; sec. C.W.A.G. Found., 1950-70, Indsl. Supply Corp., 1950-81; asst. procedural and equity rules coms. Supreme Ct. Pa., 1940-44; co-chmn. Nat. Conf. Lawyers and Collection Agys., 1970-72, Lawyers and C.P.A.s, 1973-76; commr. Uniform State Laws, 1974—; div. chmn. Nat. Conf. Commns. of Uniform State Laws, 1979-81; chmn. com. on Personal Property Leasing Act mem. news media com. Supreme Ct. Fla., 1975; bd. dirs. Nat. Lawyers' Com. for Civil Rights Under Law, 1976—. Note editor: U. Pa. Law Rev, 1936-37; Fla. contbr.: Compendium, Nat. Comml. Fin. Conf. Co-chmn. West Coast Fla. chpt. NCCJ, 1964-67; mem. exec. com. U.S. Fla. Found., 1962-66. Fellow Am. Bar Found., Fla. Bar Found.; mem. ABA (standing com. unauthorized practice law 1970-73, spl. com. coordination fed. jud. improvements 1976-80, chmn. 1980-83, bankruptcy task force 1982—), Phila. Bar Assn., Tampa Bar Assn., Hillsborough County Bar Assn., Fla. Bar (chmn. unauthorized practice law com. 1964-68, mem. com. on interest on trust funds 1975, lectr. continuing legal edn. on secured creditor's rights 1964—, on unauthorized practice of law 1968, 71, on uniform comml. code 1972), Am. Coll. Real Estate Lawyers (gov. 1981-83, pres.-elect 1983-84), Am. Judicature Soc., Comml. Law League Am., Am. Law Inst., U. Pa. Law Alumni (bd. mgrs. 1971-78), Order of Coif, Phi Beta Kappa. Clubs: Masons, Shriners, B'nai B'rith, Univ., Tower. Home: 192 Ceylon Ave Tampa FL 33606 Office: Exchange Nat Bank Bldg PO Box 3239 Tampa FL 33601

CUTLER, HOWARD ARMSTRONG, economics educator, emeritus chancellor; b. Webster City, Iowa, Apr. 27, 1918; s. Harry O. and Myrtle (Armstrong) C.; m. Enid Ellison, Jan. 2, 1943; children: Cheryl Varian, Kristen Ellison, Sherwood Thor. A.B., State U. Iowa, 1940, M.A., 1941; grad. certificate, Harvard U., 1943; Ph.D., Columbia U., 1952. Instr. econs. State U. Iowa, 1946; asst. to economist Irving Trust Co., N.Y.C., 1946-47; instr. econs. U. Ill., Urbana, 1948-50, asst. prof., 1950, asst. to dean, 1949-51; asst. prof. econs. Pa. State U., 1951-53, assoc. prof., 1953-56, prof., 1956-62, head dept., 1953-58, dir. gen. edn., 1957-62, asst. to v.p. academic affairs, 1958-61, asst. to pres., 1961-62; acad. v.p., prof. econs. U. Alaska, 1962-66, chancellor, 1976-81, chancellor emeritus, 1983—, Regent's prof. econs., 1981—; exec. v.p. Inst. Internat. Edn., N.Y.C., 1966-76; vis. prof. U. Chgo., 1955-56. Editor: Jour. Gen. Edn, 1960-62. Mem. Martin Luther King, Jr., Fellowship Selection Com., 1968-70; mem. pub.-at-large Ednl. Commn. for Fgn. Med. Grads., 1970—; mem. chancellor's panel on univ. purposes State U. N.Y., 1970-72; mem. Nat. Liaison Com. Fgn. Student Admissions, 1968-75; mem. adv. com. Carl Duisberg Soc., 1968-75; bd. dirs. Nat. Council for Community Services to Internat. Visitors, 1971-75, Internat. Schs. Services, 1971-75, Axe-Houghton Found., 1970—. Served to lt. USNR, 1942-46. Mem. Am. Econ. Assn., Am. Statis. Assn., AAAS, Am. Assn. Univ. Adminstrs. (dir. 1977-78), Internat. Assn. Univ. Presidents, Phi Beta Kappa, Beta Gamma Sigma, Pi Gamma Mu, Omicron Delta Epsilon. Office: Dept Econs U Alaska Fairbanks AK 99701 *At any given moment in time, one has everything he needs. One is impoverished only in his thoughts of the past and future. Remembering this, one can always act out of strength.*

CUTLER, JOHN CHARLES, physician, educator; b. Cleve., June 29, 1915; s. Glenn Allen and Grace Amanda (Allen) C.; m. Eliese Helene Strahl, Nov. 21, 1942. B.A., Western Res. U., 1937, M.D., 1941; M.P.H., Sch. Hygiene and Pub. Health, Johns Hopkins U., 1951. Diplomate: Am. Bd. Preventive Medicine and Pub. Health. Commd. asst. surgeon (lt. j.g.) USPHS, 1941, advanced through grades to asst. surgeon gen. (rear adm.), 1958; intern USPHS Hosp., S.I., N.Y., 1941; venereal disease investigations Pub. Health Service Venereal Disease Research Lab., Stapleton, N.Y., 1943-46; venereal disease research and demonstration, Guatemala, 1946-48; assigned WHO, 1949-50; with venereal disease div. USPHS, 1951-54; program office Bur. State Services, 1954-57; asst. dir. Nat. Inst. Allergy and Infectious Diseases, 1958; asst. surgeon gen. for program, 1958-59; health officer Central dist. Allegheny County Health Dept., 1959-61; dep. dir. Pan Am. San. Bur., regional office for Americas WHO, 1961-68; prof. internat. health, dir. population program Grad. Sch. Public Health, U. Pitts., 1968-79, chmn. dept. health services adminstrn., 1979-80, assoc. dept. chmn., prof. internat. health, 1980—; pres. Family Planning Council Southwestern Pa., 1971-72; sec. Am. Social Health Assn., 1972-76; pres. Internat. Health Soc., 1972-73, Am. Assn. World Health, 1973-75, Assn. Voluntary Sterilization, 1977-83; sec.-treas. World Fedn. Health Agys. for Advancement Vol. Surg. Contraception, 1975-81, pres.-elect., 1981—. Contbr. articles to med. publs. Fellow Am. Pub. Health Assn.; mem. Phi Beta Kappa. Home: 210 S Dallas Ave Pittsburgh PA 15208 Office: Grad Sch Pub Health U Pitts Pittsburgh PA 15261

CUTLER, KENNETH BURNETT, lawyer investment company executive; b. Muskegon Heights, Mich., June 19, 1932; s. Stanley and Lucile (Miles) C.; m. Cecelia Bilsly, Mar. 9, 1967; children: Kenneth Burnett, Randall Miles, Cynthia Bilsly, Robert Appleby, Jeffrey Lamont Derrick. B.B.A., U. Mich., 1954, J.D., 1957. Bar: Mich. 1957, N.Y. 1960. Assoc. firm Dewey Ballantine, Bushby, Palmer & Wood, N.Y.C., 1957-66; gen. counsel Lord, Abbett & Co., N.Y.C., 1966—, ptnr., 1972—; v.p., sec. Affiliated Fund; v.p. Lord Abbett Income Fund, Lord Abbett Bond-Debenture Fund, Lord Abbett Value Appreciation Fund, Lord Abbett Developing Growth Fund, Lord Abbett Cash Res. Fund. Served with AUS, 1957-63. Mem. Am., N.Y. State bar assns., Investment Co. Inst. (past bd. govs.), Nat. Assn. Security Dealers (arbitration panel), Phi Delta Phi. Clubs: City Midday, Winged Foot Golf, Bronxville Field. Home: 10 Westway Bronxville NY 10708 Office: 63 Wall St New York NY 10005

CUTLER, LEONARD SAMUEL, physicist; b. Los Angeles, Jan. 10, 1928; s. Morris and Ethel (Kalech) C.; m. Dorothy Alice Pett, Feb. 13, 1954; children—Jeffrey Alan, Gregory Michael, Steven Russell, Scott Darren. B.S., Stanford U., 1958, M.S., 1960, Ph.D., 1966. Vice pres. research and devel. Gertsch Products Co., 1949-57; with Hewlett Packard Co., 1957—, dir. phys. research lab., 1969-80, dir. phys. standards research lab., Palo Alto, Calif., 1980—; dir. Phys. sc lab., 1981—; mem. adv. panels Nat. Bur. Standards; cons. atomic frequency standards. Served with USNR, 1945-46. Fellow IEEE; mem. AAAS, Sigma Xi. Patentee in field. Home: 26944 Almaden Ct Los Altos Hills CA 94022 Office: 3500 Deer Creek Rd Palo Alto CA 94304

CUTLER, LLOYD NORTON, lawyer, company director; b. N.Y.C., Nov. 10, 1917; s. Aaron Smith and Dorothy (Glaser) C.; m. Louise W. Howe, Feb. 15, 1941; children: Deborah Norton (Mrs. James Notman, Jr.), Beverly Winslow (Mrs. Mark Weaver), Lloyd Norton, Louisiana Winslow. A.B. cum laude, Yale U., 1936, LL.B. magna cum laude, 1939, LL.D. (hon.), 1983. Bar: N.Y. 1940, D.C. 1946. Practiced in, N.Y.C., 1940-42, Washington, 1946—; partner Cox, Langford, Stoddard & Cutler, 1946-62, Wilmer, Cutler & Pickering, 1962-79, 81—; counsel to Pres. of U.S., 1979-81; dir. Am. Cyanamid Co., S.E. Bank Corp.; Lend-Lease mem. North African Econ. Bd., 1943; asst. fgn. liquidation commr. for Latin Am. Dept. State, 1945-46; sec. Lawyers Com. Civil Rights Under Law, 1963-65, co-chmn., 1971-73; chmn. D.C. Com. on Adminstrn. Justice under Emergency Conditions, 1968; exec. dir. Nat. Commn. on the Causes and Prevention of Violence, 1968-69; President's spl. rep. for maritime boundary and resource negotiations with Can., 1977-79, sr. cons. President's Commn. on Strategic Forces, 1983; Trustee Brookings Instn.; mem. Yale U. Council, 1966-71; chmn. Yale Devel. Bd., 1972—, Campaign for Yale, 1978-79; vis. lectr. Yale Law Sch., 1973-76, Yale Sch. Orgn. and Mgmt., 1977-79. Exec. dir. Met. Opera Assn., 1974-79. Mem. Am. Law Inst. (council), Am. Bar Assn. (chmn. sect. ind. rights and responsibilities 1968, mem. ho. dels. 1969), Council on Fgn. Relations (dir. 1977-79). Clubs: Federal City, Metropolitan, International, Chevy Chase (Washington); Yale, Century Assn. (N.Y.C.); Bath (London); Kittansett (Marion, Mass.). Home: 5215 Chamberlin Ave Chevy Chase MD 20015 Office: 1666 K St NW Washington DC 20006

CUTLER, MAX, lawyer; b. Athens, Ga., July 21, 1912; s. Louis and Gertrude (Narinsky) C.; m. Claire R. Mintz, Oct. 8, 1944; children: William L., John M. A.B., N.Y. U., 1934; J.D., Harvard U., 1937. Bar: N.Y. 1938. Practiced in, N.Y.C., 1938—; mem. firm John H. Levy, 1937-39, Davis & Gilbert, 1943-44; sr. partner Cutler & Cutler, 1944—; gen. counsel numerous bus. and profl. corps.; sec., gen. counsel Gabriel Industries, 1956-78; sec., gen. counsel Ophthalmic Research Found., Inc., 1975—, Ophthalmic Research Inst., Inc., 1975—, Inst. for Visual Scis., Inc., 1982—; pres., dir. Vanderbit Assocs., N.Y.C., 1944-55. Pres., founder Citizens Caucus for Stamford Bd. Edn.; bd. dirs. Citizens Sch. League, Stamford; founder, bd. dirs. N. Stamford Democratic Club; mem. legal com. Lexington Dem. Club, N.Y.C.; bd. visitors Washington Sq. Coll., 1957-60; pres., bd. dirs. Stamford Mid-Ridge Civic Assn., 1955-57; bd. dirs. Stamford Chamber Residences, 1956-60; bd. dirs., chmn. edn. com. Stamford Good Govt. Assn. Recipient N.Y. U. Alumni Gold medal, 1934; Meritorious Service award N.Y. U. Alumni Fedn., 1954; Crystal award N.Y. U. Alumni Fedn., 1982. Mem. Washington Sq. Coll. Alumni Assn. (dir., past pres.), N.Y. U. Alumni Fedn. (v.p., dir.), Am. Bar Assn., N.Y. County Lawyers Assn., Harvard Law Sch. Assn. (life), Alpha Gamma. Jewish. Clubs: Harvard, N.Y. U. (N.Y.C.). Home: 1175 York Ave New York NY 10021 Office: 150 E 58th St New York NY 10155

CUTLER, MAX, surgeon; b. Jitomir, Russia, May 9, 1899; came to U.S., 1907, naturalized, 1914; s. Sam and Esther (Tchudnowsky) C.; m. Bertie Burger, Apr. 12, 1946; children: Nina, Nancy, Susie. B.S., U. Ga., 1918; M.D., Johns Hopkins U., 1922; postgrad., Curie Inst., Paris and Radiumhemmet, Stockholm. Resident house surgeon Johns Hopkins Hosp., 1922-23; cons. in cancer, dir. cancer research Edward Hines VA Hosp. and; U.S. VA, 1931-46; asso. in surgery Northwestern Med. Sch., 1935-40; vis. prof. surgery Peking (China) Union Med. Coll., 1936-37; mem. surg. staff Cedars of Lebanon Hosp., Los Angeles, 1952-79, emeritus, 1979—; breast cons. dept. radiology UCLA, 1976-79, Century City Hosp., Brotman Meml. Hosp., 1967-79; founder, also dir. Chgo. Tumor Inst., 1938-52; dir. Beverly Hills Cancer Research Found., 1966-79; 1st pres. Am. Assn. Study Neoplastic Diseases, 1933-34; mem. Nat. Adv. Cancer Council, 1939-42. Author: (with Sir George Lenthal Cheatle) Tumors of the Breast, 1931, Cancer, Its Diagnosis and Treatment, 1938, Tumors of the Breast: Their Pathology, Symptoms, Diagnosis and Treatment, 1961; contbr. articles to profl. jours. Served in U.S. Army, World War I. Mem. N.Y. Acad. Medicine, Chgo. Inst. Medicine, Am. Radium Soc., Am. Assn. Cancer Research, AMA, Los Angeles County Med. Soc., Internat. Coll. Surgeons; hon. mem. Cuban Radiol. Soc., Radiol. Soc. Chile, Phi Epsilon Pi, Phi Delta Epsilon, Phi Beta Kappa, Alpha Omega Alpha. Jewish. Club: Masons. Home: 5950 Fremont Circle Camarillo CA 93010

CUTLER, PHYLLIS L., librarian; b. Boston, Mar. 31, 1928; d. Louis and Sadie (Ginsberg) Nanes; m. Maxwell Cutler, Dec. 23, 1948; children: Lewis Howard, Neal David, Jonathan Dana. A.B., Harvard U., 1962; M.L.S., Simmons Coll., 1966. Adminstrv. asst. Morrill Meml. Library, Norwood, Mass., 1968-71; asst. univ. librarian Brandeis U., Waltham, Mass., 1971-82; coll. librarian Williams Coll., Willimstown, Mass., 1982—; lectr. in field. Mem. ALA, Spl. Libraries Assn. (sec. 1973-74), New Eng. Library Assn. (chmn. coll. libraries sect. 1978), Simmons Coll. Alumni Assn. (pres. chpt. 1982-83, governing bd. 1976—). Home: 71 School St Williamstown MA 01267 Office: Williams College Sawyer Library Williamstown MA 01267

CUTLER, RICHARD WOOLSEY, lawyer; b. New Rochelle, N.Y., Mar. 9, 1917; s. Charles Evelyn and Amelia (MacDonald) Co.; m. Elizabeth Fitzgerald, Oct. 18, 1947; children: Marguerite Blackburn, Alexander MacDonald, Judith Elizabeth. B.A., Yale U., 1938, LL.B., 1941. Bar: Conn. 1941, N.Y. 1942, Wis. bar 1950, D.C. bar 1975. Practiced in, N.Y.C., 1941-49, Milw., 1949—; asso. firm Donovan, Leisure, Newton & Lumbard, 1941-42; atty. Legal Aid Soc., 1946-47, RCA Communications, Inc., 1947-49; partner firm Quarles & Brady (and predecessor firms), 1954—; dir. Steinman Lumber Co., Kelch Corp. Author: Zoning Law and Practice in Wisconsin, 1967. Chmn. Milw. br. Fgn. Policy Assn., 1951-53; Pres. Childrens Service Soc. Wis., 1961-63; pres. Neighborhood House, 1971-74; sec. Southeastern Wis. Regional Planning Commn., 1960—, Yale Devel. Bd., 1973-79; bd. dirs. Wis. Dept. Resource Devel., 1967-68; Met. Milw. Study Commn., 1957-61. Served to capt. USAAF, 1943-46. Mem. Am., Wis., Milw., D.C. bar assns., Phi Beta Kappa. Republican. Presbyterian. Clubs: Milwaukee Country, Milwaukee, University, Town (Milw.). Home: 7730 N Merrie Ln Milwaukee WI 53217 Office: 780 N Water St Milwaukee WI 53202

CUTLER, ROBERT H., motor freight company executive; b. Portland, Oreg., July 13, 1918; s. Frank W. and Hilma (West) C.; m. Ellouise Gunn, July 19, 1941; children: Virginia Forras, Cathryn Washburn. Student, U. Oreg., 1936-40. Asst. to pres. Consol. Freightways Co., Portland, 1938-48; pres. Bekins Van Line Co., Salt Lake City, 1948-51, Texas Arizona Motor Freight Co., El Paso, Tex., 1951-62; chmn. bd. Cutler Corp., Portland, Oreg.; pres. Cutler Industries, Rolison Industries; advisor, dir. Liberty Mut. Ins. Co.; dir. Marmon Group, Inc., Orchid Isle Auto Center, Inc., El Paso Electric Co., Am. Investors, El Paso Nat. Bank, Mid Am. Nat. Bank. Bd. dirs. El Paso Indsl. Corp.; pres. Rio Grande council Girl Scouts U.S.A. Served to capt. AUS, 1942-46. Mem. El Paso C. of C. (dir.), Am. Trucking Assns. (past chmn.), Western Hwy. Inst. (past pres.). Clubs: Pauma Valley Country (dir.); Calif., Arlington, Waverly Country., Rotary. Home: 6006 Balcones Ct El Paso TX 79912 Office: PO Box 9762 El Paso TX 79987

CUTLER, ROBERT WARD, architect; b. Ridgway, Pa., June 27, 1905; s. Robert Ward and Olga (Holmberg) C.; m. Doris Saxton, June 29, 1929 (dec.); children: Denise Cutler Kimball, Robert Ward; m. Morene Parten, Apr. 27, 1954. B.Arch., Syracuse U., 1928. Employed in various archtl. offices, N.Y.C., 1928-37; asso. Skidmore & Owings, N.Y.C., 1937-49; partner Skidmore, Owings & Merrill, N.Y.C., 1949-72; Mem. Art Commn. of City of N.Y., 1958-66; trustee Community Service Soc., N.Y.C., 1962-72, Syracuse U., 1964-72; cons. N.Y.C. Civic Center; mem. adv. council Architecture Found., U. Tex., Austin, 1979—. Recipient George Arents pioneer medal Syracuse U., 1968. Fellow AIA (pres. N.Y. chpt. 1956-58); mem. Archtl. League N.Y. (pres. 1961-63), Bldg. Research Inst. (pres. 1963-65), N.Y. Bldg. Congress (life; pres. 1965-69), Fifth Ave Assn. (pres. 1969-71), Sigma Chi, Tau Sigma Delta, Phi Kappa Phi. Episcopalian. Clubs: Century Assn., Met., N.Y. Athletic (N.Y.C.). Home: Salado TX 76571

CUTLER, STEPHEN JOEL, sociologist; b. Lawrence, Mass., Jan. 1, 1943; s. Lewis J. and Minnie C.; m. Karan Elizabeth Davis, Apr. 25, 1968; children: Ellen Min, Timothy Spence. B.A., Dartmouth Coll., 1964; M.A., U. Mich., 1965, Ph.D., 1969. Mem. faculty Oberlin (Ohio) Coll., 1969—, prof. sociology-anthropology, 1979—, chmn. dept., 1979-82; sr. fellow Center Study Aging and Human Devel., Duke U., 1975-76; adv. bd. nat. data program social scis. Nat. Opinion Research

Center, 1980—; mem. behavioral scis. study sect. NIH, 1979—. Co-author: Middle Start: An Experiment in the Educational Enrichment of Young Adolescents, 1978; co-editor: Major Social Problems: A Multidisciplinary View, 1979; asso. editor: Geront. Monographs, 1976-82; editorial bd.: Internat. Jour. Aging and Human Devel, 1980—, Jour. Gerontology, 1981—, Research on Aging, 1982—. Woodrow Wilson fellow, 1965; grantee NIMH, NSF. Fellow Gerontol. Soc. Am. (exec. com. behavioral and social scis. sect. 1979-81); mem. Am. Sociol. Assn. (council sect. on aging 1982-84). Home: 366 Reamer Pl Oberlin OH 44074 Office: Dept Sociology-Anthropology Oberlin Coll Oberlin OH 44074

CUTLER, THEODORE JOHN, appliances manufacturing company executive; b. Portland, Maine, July 11, 1941; s. Shepard Hugh and Dena C.; m. Julia C. Robb. A.B. in History with honors, Dartmouth Coll., 1963; M.B.A. with honors, U. Calif., Berkeley, 1965. With Procter & Gamble Co., Cin., 1965-72, brand mgr. and copy supr., to 1972; brand mgr. new product/acquisitions mgr. and co Clorox Co., Oakland, Calif., 1972-74; dir. mktg. audio div., then gen. mgr. div. Memorex Corp., Santa Clara, Calif., 1974-77, group v.p., 1977-80, pres. consumer products group, 1979-80; mng. partner Mktg. Corp. Am., Westport, Conn., 1980-82; v.p., gen. mgr. product mgmt. and mktg. div. major appliances Gen. Electric Co., Louisville, 1982—; dir. Patlex Corp., Ardmore, Pa., Pan Am. Banks, Inc., Miami. Active in charity work. Served with USAF, 1965. Home: 1220 Summit Ave Louisville KY 40204 Office: Appliance Park Louisville KY 40225

CUTLER, WALTER LEON, ambassador; b. Boston, Nov. 25, 1931; s. Walter Leon and Esther Dewey (Bradley) C.; m. Sarah G. Beeson, Mar. 16, 1957 (div. 1981); children: Allen Bradley, Thomas Gerard.; m. Isabel K. Brookfield, Nov. 28, 1981. B.A., Wesleyan U., Middletown, Conn., 1953; M.A., Fletcher Sch. Law and Diplomacy, 1954. Joined U.S. Fgn. Service, 1956; vice consul Am. consulate, Yaounde, Cameroon, 1957-59; fgn. affairs officer Dept. State, Washington, 1959-60, staff asst. to sec. of state, 1960-62; 2d sec. Am. Embassy, Algiers, Algeria, 1962-65, prin. officer Am. Consulate, Tabriz, Iran, 1965-67, polit. officer, 1st sec. Am. Embassy, Seoul, Korea, 1967-69, Saigon, Vietnam, 1969-71; fgn. affairs officer Dept. State, 1971-73; mem. Sr. Seminar in Fgn. Policy, 1973-74; dir. Office Central African Affairs, 1974-75; ambassador to Zaire, Kinshasa, 1975-79, ambassador-designate to Iran, 1979; dep. asst. sec. for congressional relations Dept. State, Washington, 1979-81; ambassador to Tunisia, Tunis, 1982-84, ambassador to Saudi Arabia, 1984—. Served with U.S. Army, 1954-56. Recipient Disting. Alumnus award Wesleyan U., 1983. Mem. Council Fgn. Relations, Am. Fgn. Service Assn. Office: NEA/ARP Dept State Washington DC 20520

CUTLER, WARREN GALE, manufacturing company executive; b. Avon, Ill., Jan. 31, 1922; s. Fred Lewis and Inez Faye (Beery) C.; m. Irene Baynok, Dec. 27, 1949; children: Alan, Brian, Larry, Melanie. B.S., Monmouth (Ill.) Coll., 1947; M.S., Pa. State U., 1953, Ph.D. (Am. Petroleum Inst. research fellow 1953-55), 1955; grad., Sloan Mgmt. Sch., M.I.T., 1966. Instr. physics and math. Monmouth Coll., 1947-51; grad. asst. Pa. State U., 1951-53; assoc. prof. physics Mankato (Minn.) State Coll., 1955-57, head dept., 1956-57; with Whirlpool Corp., Benton Harbor, Mich., 1957—, mgr. mech. engring. research, 1959-60, dir. research, 1960-67, dir. corporate research, 1967-84, v.p. univ. relations, 1984—; spl. extension lectr. Mich. State U., 1959-63, indsl. adv. com. dept. food sci., 1960-64; adv. com. Univ. Center, 1975—. Editor: Detergency: Theory and Test Methods, 1972-84. Served with AUS, 1942-46. Decorated Bronze Star, Commendation medal. Mem. Am. Phys. Soc., Am. Chem. Soc., Am. Oil Chemists Soc., Indsl. Research Inst. (chmn. research-on-research com. 1978-80, dir. 1980-84), Sigma Xi, Sigma Phi Epsilon. Roman Catholic. Club: Berrien Hills (Mich.) Country. Home: 218 Crofton Circle St Joseph MI 49085 Office: Research and Engring Center Whirlpool Corp Monte Rd Benton Harbor MI 49022

CUTLIP, RANDALL BROWER, former college president; b. Clarksburg, W.Va., Oct. 1, 1916; s. M.N. and Mildred (Brower) C.; m. Virginia White, Apr. 21, 1951; children: Raymond Bennett, Catherine Baumgarten. A.B., Bethany Coll., 1940; M.A., East Tex. U., 1949; Ed.D., U. Houston, 1953; LL.D., Bethany Coll., 1965, Columbia Coll., 1980; L.H.D., Drury Coll., 1975; Sc.D., S.W. Bapt. Coll., 1978; Litt.D., William Woods Coll., 1981. Tchr., adminstr. Tex. pub. schs., 1947-50; dir. tchr. placement U. Houston, 1950-51, supr. counselling, 1951-53; dean of students Atlantic Christian Coll., Wilson, N.C., 1953-56, dean coll., 1956-58; dean personnel, dir. grad. div. Chapman Coll., Orange, Calif., 1958-60; pres. William Woods Coll., Fulton, Mo., 1960-81, pres. emeritus, 1981—, trustee, 1981—; Chmn. bd. visitors Mo. Mil. Acad., 1968-73; chmn. bd. dirs. Mo. Colls. Fund, 1973-75; chmn. Mid-Mo. Asso. Colls., 1972-76; trustee Schreiner Coll., Kerville, Tex., 1983—; bd. dirs. Univ. of the Americas, Puebla, Mex., 1984—. Served with AUS, 1943-45. Recipient McCubbin award, 1968, Delta Beta Xi award, 1959. Mem. Am. Personnel and Guidance Assn., Alpha Sigma Phi, Phi Delta Kappa, Kappa Delta Pi, Alpha Chi.

CUTLIP, SCOTT MUNSON, university dean; b. Buckhannon, W.Va., July 15, 1915; s. Okey Scott and Janet (Munson) C.; m. Erna Katherine Flader, May 21, 1947; 1 son, George Carper. Student, W.Va. Wesleyan Coll., 1932-34; A.B., Syracuse U., 1939; Ph.M., U. Wis., 1941; Litt.D., W.Va. Wesleyan Coll., 1971. Reporter, editor various newspapers, W.Va., 1932-36; dir. pub. relations W.Va. Rd. Commn., 1941-42; asst. prof. U. Wis. at Madison, 1946-47, asst. to pres., 1947-49, assoc. prof., 1949-58, prof., 1958-75, U. Ga., Athens, 1975—, dean Henry W. Grady Sch. Journalism and Mass Communication, 1975—; Vis. prof. Cornell U., 1955-56, U. Idaho, 1954-58, Utah State U., 1967, U. Ga., 1975. Author: (with Allen Center) Effective Public Relations, 1952, rev. 5th edit., 1982, Fund Raising in the United States: Its Role in America's Philanthropy, 1965; Compiler: A Public Relations Bibliography, 2d edit, 1965. Served to maj. USAAF, 1942-46. Mem. Hist. Soc. Wis. (bd. curators 1958-75, pres. 1964-67), Assn. for Edn. in Journalism, Pub. Relations Soc. Am., Phi Kappa Phi. Clubs: Athens Country, Madison Literary. Home: 19 S Stratford Dr Athens GA 30605

CUTRELL, BENJAMIN ELWOOD, publisher; b. Scottdale, Pa., Mar. 28, 1923; s. George W. and Frances H. (Nissley) C.; m. Dorothy Lucille Stutzman, Dec. 2, 1944; children: Kathleen Cutrell Royer, David B. Student, Eastern Mennonite Coll., 1941-42; B.S., Carnegie-Mellon U., 1944. Gen. mgr., partner LeBlanc Printers, Denver, 1945-55; bus. mgr. Mennonite Pub. House, Scottdale, 1955-61, pub., 1961—; pres. Protestant Church-owned Pubs. Assn., 1974-76; mem. Scottsdale Community Civic and Indsl. Assn., 1983—. Mem. Mennonite Ch. (chmn. congregation 1962-66, elder 1966-70). Home: Route 1 Box 244-A Scottdale PA 15683 Office: 616 Walnut Ave Scottdale PA 15683

CUTRIGHT, PHILLIPS, educator, sociologist; b. Wooster, Ohio, Mar. 1, 1930; s. Clifford R. and Eva N. (Goddin) C.; m. Karen L. Bowles, Oct. 31, 1965; children: Anuschka, Jennifer. A.B., Coll. Wooster, 1955; Ph.D., U. Chgo., 1960. Mem. faculty Wash. State U., Pullman, 1960-61, Dartmouth, 1961-62; with Social Security Adminstrn., 1962-65; mem. faculty Vanderbilt U., Nashville, 1965-67, Washington U., St. Louis, 1967-68, Harvard-MIT, 1968-70; prof. sociology Ind. U., Bloomington, 1970—; cons. in field, 1971—. Contbr. articles to profl. jours. Bd. dirs. Planned Parenthood Monroe County, Ind. Served with USAF, 1951-53. Mem. Am. Sociol. Assn., Population Assn. Am. Home: 2106 Foxcliff N Martinsville IN 46151

CUTTER, CHARLES RICHARD, III, educator; b. Woodward, Okla., Feb. 8, 1924; s. Charles Richard and Mary (Lowry) C.; m. Phyllis Marie Fletcher, Nov. 15, 1942; children—Cynthia Marie (Mrs. Robert Wheeler Jr.), Marcia Ellen (Mrs. Douglas Walker). B.A., Baylor U.; B.D., Th.D., Ph.D., Southwestern Baptist Theol. Sem. Ordained to ministry Baptist Ch.; pastor Kopperl (Tex.) Bapt. Ch., 1957-72; prof. classics Baylor U., Waco, Tex., 1958—, Rev. Jacob Beverly Stiteler prof. Greek, 1962—; propr. Cutter Food Market, Gruver, Tex., 1946-51. Author: A Beginning Grammar of Classical and Hellenistic Greek, 1974, (with others) New Testament Studies. Served as navigator USAAF, 1942-45. Decorated Air medal with five clusters. Mem. Am. Philol. Assn., Soc. Bibl. Lit., Classical Assn. Midwest and South, AAUP (pres. Baylor chpt. 1980-81). Home: 2425 Charboneau St Waco TX 76710

CUTTER, DAVID LEE, pharmaceutical company executive; b. Oakland, Calif., Jan. 3, 1929; s. Robert Kennedy and Virginia (White) C.; m. Nancy Lee Baugh, Sept. 14, 1950; children: David Lee, Thomas White, William Baugh, Steven Kennedy, Michael Lee. Student, U. Calif. at Berkeley, 1947; A.B., Stanford U., 1950, M.B.A., 1952. C.P.A., Calif. Staff accountant Webb & Webb, C.P.A.'s, San Francisco, 1952-54; with Cutter Labs., Inc., 1954—, pres., 1967-74, chmn., 1974-80, vice-chmn., 1980-82, sr. cons., 1982—; dir. Bills Drugs, Inc., Lafayette, Calif., Chad Therapeutics, Inc., Woodland Hills, Calif. Active various community drives; mem. Citizens Com. to Study Discrimination in Housing, Berkeley, 1961-62; troop committeeman Boy Scouts Am., Berkeley, 1964-74; v.p. Mt. Diablo council, 1975-77, pres., 1978—; pres. Golden Gate Scouting, 1980—; Bd. dirs. Park Hills Homes Assn., 1961-63, HEALS, Emeryville, Calif., Alameda County (Calif.) Taxpayers Assn., 1967-69, Insts. Med. Scis., San Francisco, 1974-76; pres. Cutter Found., 1973—; trustee United Way of Bay Area, 1981—; mem. adv. bd. Herrick Hosp., 1968-76, trustee, 1976—, pres. bd. trustees, 1978—; mem. Accrediting Commn. on Edn. in Health Services Adminstrn., 1982—; bd. dirs. San Francisco Bay Area Council, 1968—; mem. adv. council Sch. Bus., San Francisco State Coll., 1966-70. Mem. Am. Inst. C.P.A.s, Calif. Soc. C.P.A.s, Med.-Surg. Mfrs. Assn. (dir. 1971-73), Pharm. Mfrs. Assn. (dir. 1972-78), Stanford Alumni Assn., Berkeley C. of C. (dir. 1977—, v.p. 1978-83), Delta Upsilon. Rotary. Home: 3749 St Francis Dr Lafayette CA 94549 Office: 2200 Powell St Emeryville CA 94608

CUTTER, EDWARD AHERN, III, pharmaceutical company executive; b. Berkeley, Calif., July 17, 1939; s. Edward Ahern and Helen (Westgate) C.; m. Susan Kren Cutter; children: Eric Alan, Spencer Edward. B.A., Stanford U., 1961, postgrad., 1964-65; J.D., Harvard U., 1964. Bar: Calif. 1965. Atty. Thelen, Marrin, Johnson & Bridges, San Francisco, 1965-67; mgr. legal services Cutter Labs. Inc., Berkeley, 1968-70, sec., corp. counsel, 1970-78, gen. counsel, sec., 1978-83, v.p. adminstrn., 1983-84. Mem. ABA, Calif., San Francisco bar assns. Home: Box 403 Belvedere CA 94920

CUTTER, JAMES ARTHUR, physician, educator; b. St. Louis, Sept. 22, 1924; s. Arthur L. and Ruth (Conway) C.; m. Norma Gloria Zynda, Sept. 1, 1949; children—Karen Anne Cutter Robison, Mark Alan, Brian David, Linda Marie Cutter Page, Nancy Jane Cutter Butson, Gary Lee, Keith Evan. M.D., Washington U., St. Louis, 1951. Diplomate: Am. Bd. Anesthesiology. Intern Percy Jones Gen. Hosp., Battle Creek, Mich., 1951-52; resident in anesthesiology Brooke Gen. Hosp., San Antonio, 1952-54; practice medicine, specializing in anesthesiology, Keesler AFB, Miss., 1954-57, Buffalo, 1957-61, Oklahoma City, 1961-70, Walnut Creek, Calif., 1970-76, Martinez, Calif., 1976—; asst. prof. anesthesiology U. Buffalo, 1957-60, asso. prof., 1960-61, U. Okla., 1961-62, clin. prof., 1962-65, prof., 1965-70, head dept. anesthesiology, 1965-70; chief anesthesiology Kaiser-Permanente Med. Center, Walnut Creek, 1970-76, Martinez, 1976—. Contbr. articles on anesthesiology to profl. jours. Served with AUS, 1944-46; to maj. USAF, 1951-57. Decorated Bronze Star, Purple Heart, U.S.; Croix de Guerre, France). Fellow Am. Coll. Anesthesiologists, Am. Coll. Chest Physicians, Assn. Univ. Anesthetists; mem. Am., Calif., No. Calif. socs. anesthesiologists, Internat. Anesthesia Research Soc. Home: Moraga CA 94556 Office: 200 Muir Rd Martinez CA 94553

CUTTER, RICHARD AMMI, retired judge; b. Salem, Mass., May 11, 1902; s. Louis Fayerweather and Mary Perkins (Osgood) C.; m. Ruth Dexter Grew, June 10, 1925; children: Louis Ammi, Henry Sturgis Grew and Helen (Mrs. Robert A.R. Maclennan). A.B., Harvard, 1922; LL.B., 1925; LL.D. (hon.), 1979, D.Sc.Jur, Suffolk U., 1960. Bar: Mass. 1926. Assoc. firm Goodwin, Procter, Field and Hoar, 1926-27; asst. atty. gen., Mass., 1927-30, adviser to gov. P.R., 1930-31; partner Storey, Thorndike, Palmer & Dodge (and successor firm Palmer, Dodge, Gardner & Bradford), Boston, 1931-42, 46-56; assoc. justice Supreme Jud. Ct., Boston, 1956-72; assigned on recall as ret. judge Appeals Ct., Boston, 1980—; Cons. to sec. air force, 1951, to dir. off-shore procurement, 1954; to dir. ICA, 1956; Mem. bd. overseers Harvard, 1966-72. Served from maj. to col. Gen. Staff Corps AUS, 1942-46. Decorated Legion of Merit with cluster. Mem. Am., Mass., Boston bar assns., Am. Law Inst. (pres. 1976-80, chmn. council 1980—), Harvard Law Sch. Assn. (pres. 1971-73), Colonial Soc. Mass., Am. Acad. Arts and Sci., Mass. Hist. Soc., Mass. Soc. of the Cincinnati (hon.). Episcopalian. Clubs: Harvard (N.Y.C.); Randolph (N.H.); Mountain; Country (Brookline, Mass.); Curtis, Tavern (Boston); Metropolitan (Washington); Appalachian Mountain. Home: 62 Sparks St Cambridge MA 02138

CUTTING, HEYWARD, designer, planner; b. N.Y.C., Dec. 3, 1921; s. Heyward and Constance (Roberson) C.; m. Jeremy Hohenstein, 1948 (div. 1978); children: Heyward, Francis Brockholst, William Bayard; m. Joan Faulkner Randell, Nov. 3, 1979; Stepson, Thomas William Randell. Grad., Eton, 1939; student, Harvard, 1939-41; B.Sc., Ill. Inst. Tech., 1953. Partner Chermayeff & Cutting (architects and indsl. designers), 1954-56; pvt. practice architecture, Cambridge, 1957; mem. Geometrics, Inc. (architects, engrs. and cons. specialized structures), Cambridge, 1958-68, 73—; asst. dir. adminstrn. Mus. Fine Arts, Boston, 1968-73, trustee, 1961-68, 73-78. Former trustee Mt. Auburn Hosp., Cambridge; past mem. vis. com. dept. archaeology, also dept. fine arts Harvard U. Served to maj. KRRC, 60th Rifles Brit. Army, 1941-45; Egypt, Italy. Mentioned in despatches. Club: Tavern (Boston). Home: 377 Main St Concord MA 01742 Office: Geometrics Inc 23 Arrow St Cambridge MA 02138

CUTTING, PHILIP FRANCIS, hotel exec.; b. Malden, Mass., Mar. 4, 1946; s. George Thompson and Mary Veronica C.; m. Paula Jean Lanchansky, July 20, 1968; children—Nikole Catherine, Megan Mary, Brendan Michael. B.S. in Hotel Adminstrn, U. Mass. Food and beverage mgr. Sheraton-Plaza Hotel, Boston, 1970-72; resident mgr. Sheraton-Carlton Hotel, Washington, 1972-73, Sheraton-Cleve. Hotel, 1973-74; mgr. Sheraton-Chgo. Hotel, 1974-76; gen. mgr. Sheraton-Ritz, Mpls., 1976—. Served with U.S. N.G., 1969-70. Recipient Hotel of Yr. award, N.Am. and Caribbean, 1978. Mem. Nat. Restaurant Assn., Minn. Hotel Assn. (dir., sec.-treas.), Mpls. Hotel Assn. (v.p.). Roman Catholic.

CUTTING, ROBERT THOMAS, army officer, physician; b. Winchendon, Mass., Oct. 28, 1929; s. Leon Louis and Albina Agnes (Duquette) C.; m. Ann Marie O'Brien, June 27, 1953; children: Mary Beth, Jeanne, Jonathan, Rosemary, Paul, Eileen, James. B.S., Holy Cross Coll., 1951; M.D., Boston U., 1955; M.P.H., Harvard U., 1959. Diplomate: Am. Bd. Preventive Medicine. Commd. officer U.S. Army; advanced through grades to brig. gen.; chief preventive medicine research div. U.S. Army Med. Research and Devel. Command, 1965-69; chief med. research team, Vietnam, 1969-70; dir. div. surgery Walter Reed Army Inst. Research, 1970-72; chief preventive medicine div. Office of the Surgeon Gen., Washington, 1972-75; command surgeon U.S. Army Materiel Devel. and Readiness Command, 1976-80; dir. health care ops. Office of the Surgeon Gen., Washington, 1980-82; comdg. gen. Dwight David Eisenhower Army Med. Ctr., Ft. Gordon, Ga., 1982—. Contbr. articles to profl. jours. Decorated Legion of Merit, Bronze Star (2), Air Medal (3). Fellow Am. Coll. Preventive Medicine; mem. AMA, Am. Public Health Assn., Assn. Military Surgeons, Am. Soc. Tropical Medicine and Hygiene, Aerospace Med. Assn. Republican. Roman Catholic. Home: 3803 Great Neck Ct Alexandria VA 22309 Office: Hdqrs Dwight David Eisenhower Army Med Center Fort Gordon GA 30905

CUTTINO, JOHN TINDAL, pathologist, educator; b. Sumter County, S.C., Aug. 15, 1912; s. Harry Wells and Lydia Beulah (Tindal) C.; m. Nell Parrott Seabrook, June 11, 1938; children—Harriette Wells, John Tindal.; m. Alma Chavers Patton, Apr. 23, 1983. B.S., Coll. of Charleston, 1934, LL.D. (hon.), 1961; M.D., Medical Coll. of S.C., 1936. Diplomate: pathologic anatomy Am. Bd. Pathology, 1947, clin. pathology, 1949. Rotating intern Roper Hosp., Charleston, S.C., 1936-37; asst. physician S.C. State Hosp., 1937-40; vol. fellow St. Elizabeth's Hosp., Washington, 1940; instr., sch. medicine Duke, 1946-47, asso. in pathology, 1947-50, asst. prof. pathology, 1950; acting dean med. coll. Med. Coll. S.C., 1950-51, dean, 1951-60, asso. prof. pathology, 1950-52, prof., 1952—, acting pres., 1960-62; dir. labs. Charlotte Meml. Hosp., 1965-70, dir., 1965-77. Contbr. articles to med. jours. Served to lt. col. M.C. AUS, 1941-45. Fellow Coll. of Am. Pathologists, Am. Soc. Clin. Pathologists; mem. Huguenot Soc., Am., So., N.C. med. assns., Am. Assn. Pathologists and Bacteriologists, Pi Kappa Phi, Phi Chi, Alpha Omega Alpha., Ind. Democrat. Presbyn. (elder). Club: Rotarian. Home: 101 Highland Forest Dr Matthews NC 28105 Office: Charlotte Meml Hosp Charlotte NC 28234

CUTTLE, TRACY DONALD, physician, former naval officer; b. Mont., Aug. 23, 1908; m. Hanna Lore Remmers, Dec. 22, 1960; children by previous marriage—Alexa (Mrs. Edward Cottingham), Lynn (Mrs. Henry Davis), Cynthia (Mrs. Roy Jackson). A.B., U. Calif. at Berkeley, 1931; M.D., U. Pa., 1935. Intern Pa. Hosp., 1935-37, research fellow, 1939-41; exchange fellow medicine St. Bartholomew's Hosp., London, Eng., 1937-39; asso. medicine Jefferson Med. Coll., Phila., 1939-41; research fellow, attending physician Pa. Hosp., 1939-41; commd. lt. (j.g.) M.C. USN, 1938, advanced through grades to capt., 1955; med. officer LST Flotilla 5, 1943-44, med. officer U.S.S. Bennington, 1944, med. officer 6th Marine Div., 1944-45, chief medicine U.S. Naval Hosp., Treasure Island, San Francisco, 1946, med. officer U.S. Naval Hosp., Oakland, Calif., 1946-51, chief medicine U.S. Naval Hosp., Chelsea, Mass., 1951-53, Yokosuka, Japan, 1953-55, asst. chief medicine Naval Hosp., Oakland, 1955-58, force med. officer CRU DES PAC, 1958-60, depot med. officer MCRD, San Diego, 1960-62, sr. med. officer U.S. Naval Shipyard, Portsmouth, N.H., 1962-64, comdg. officer Naval Hosp., Portsmouth, 1964-66, Chelsea, 1966-69, ret., 1969, practice medicine specializing in internal medicine, San Francisco, 1970—. Contbr. articles to profl. jours., sects. to books. Fellow ACP, Coll. Physicians Phila.; mem. Am. Fedn. Clin. Research. Clubs: Bohemian (San Francisco); Claremont Country (Oakland, Calif.). Home: 6006 Wood Dr Oakland CA 94611

CUTTS, CHARLES EUGENE, civil engineering educator; b. Sioux Falls, S.D., May 15, 1914; s. Charles Clifford and Ethel May (Gardner) C.; m. Jane Bebensee, Mar. 16, 1946; children: George Gardner, Elizabeth Ann. B.C.E., U. Minn., 1936, M.S. in Civil Engring, 1939, Ph.D., 1949. Registered profl. engr., Minn., Fla., Mich. Instrumentman Milw. R.R., 1936- 38; teaching asst. dept. civil engring. U. Minn., 1938-39, instr., asst. prof., 1946-50; engr. C.F. Haglin & Sons, summer 1939; asst. prof. dept. civil engring. Robert Coll., Istanbul, Turkey, 1939-42; engr. Braithwaite Co., Ltd., Iskenderun, Turkey, summer 1942, 43; asso. prof., asso. research engr. U. Fla., 1950-53; engr. Engring. Scis. Program NSF, Washington, 1953-56; profl. lectr. civil engring. George Washington U., 1955-56; prof., chmn. dept. civil engring. Mich. State U., 1956-69, prof., 1969—. Author: Structural Design in Reinforced Concrete, 1954, other tech. publs. Served to maj. C.E. AUS, 1943-46; lt. col. Res. ret. Mem. Nat. Acad. Scis. (fellowship com. 1961-63), ASCE (chmn. com. on mech. properties of materials 1965, pres. Mich. sect. 1967, chmn. com. on engring. edn. 1969-70), Am. Concrete Inst., Am. Soc. Engring. Edn. (chmn. civil engr. div. 1965-66, v.p. 1970—, chmn. constn. and bylaws com. 1981-83), Engrs. Council Profl. Devel. (chmn. region 5 1972-73), Nat. Soc. Profl. Engrs., Column Research Council, Tau Beta Pi, Chi Epsilon. Home: 4599 Ottawa Dr Okemos MI 48864 Office: Michigan State University East Lansing MI 48824

CUZZORT, RAY PAUL, sociology educator, writer; b. Cin., Dec., 1926; s. James Middleton and Clara Gertrude (Wolfhorst) C.; m. Phyllis Evelyn Taylor, Dec. 23, 1951 (dec. 1972); 1 dau., Barbara Rochelle. B.A., U. Cin., 1951, M.A., 1951; Ph.D., U. Minn.-Mpls., 1955. Research assoc. Population Research and Tng. Ctr., U. Chgo., 1956-57; asst. prof. sociology U. Kans., Lawrence, 1957-62; assoc. prof. U. Ill., Champaign, 1965-66; prof. U. Colo., Boulder, 1966—, chmn. dept. sociology, 1980—, research assoc. Inter-Univ. Com. on Superior Student, 1963-65. Author: (with Otis and Beverly Duncan) Statiscal Geography, 1961, Humanity and Modern Social Thought, 1969, (with E. King) 20th Century Social Thought 3rd edit., 1980. Served with USN, 1945-46. Fellow Ford Found., 1955. Mem. Western Social Sci. Assn. (editor 1983—), Am. Sociol. Assn., AAUP, Assn. Humanistic Sociology. Democrat. Unitarian. Home: 1300 Elder St Boulder CO 80302 Office: Dept Sociology Univ Colo Boulder CO 80309

CYERT, RICHARD MICHAEL, economist, university president; b. Winona, Minn., July 22, 1921; s. Walter Michael and Anne Fostine (Brown) C.; m. Margaret Shadick, Sept. 8, 1946; children: Lynn Cyert Westbrook, Lucinda Carol Steffes, Martha Sue. B.S. in Econs., U. Minn., 1943; Ph.D., Columbia U., 1951, U. Gothenburg, Sweden, 1972, U. Leuven, Belgium, 1973; LL.D. (hon.), Waynesburg Coll., 1979, Allegheny Coll., 1980, D.Sc., Westminster Coll., 1979. Instr. U. Minn., 1946, CUNY, 1948; instr. econs. Carnegie Inst. Tech. (now Carnegie-Mellon U.), Pitts., 1948-49, asst. prof. econs. and indsl. adminstrn., 1949-55, asso. prof. econs. and indsl. adminstr., head indsl. mgmt. dept., 1955-60, prof. econs. and indsl. adminstrn., 1960-62, dean, 1962-72, pres., 1972—; dir. Koppers Co., Inc., First Boston Corp., Inc., Am. Standard Inc., Allegheny Internat. Inc., White Consol. Industries, Inc., Copperweld Corp., H.J. Heinz Co., Regional Indsl. Devel. Corp. Author: (with R.M. Trueblood) Sampling Techniques in Accounting, 1957, (with H.J. Davidson) Sampling for Accounting Information, 1962, (with J.G. March) A Behavioral Theory of the Firm, 1963, (with K.J. Cohen) Theory of the Firm: Resource Allocation in a Market Economy, 1965; editor: (with L.A. Welsch) Management Decision Making, 1970; author: Management of

Non-Profit Organizations: With Emphasis on Universities, 1975, (with R.L. Ackoff and H.D. Wood) Decision Making Under Uncertainty and Managerial Leadership, 1977, (with C. Argyris) Leadership in the 80's: Essays on Higher Education, 1980, The American Economy 1960: 2000: A Retrospective and Prospective Look, 1983; bd. editors: Behavioral Sci; contbr. articles to profl. jours. Bd. dirs. Presbyn.-U. Hosp. Served USNR, 1943-46. Recipient Hofstra Disting. Scholar award, 1973, Outstanding Achievement award U. Minn., 1975; Ford fellow, 1959-60; Guggenheim fellow, 1967-68. Fellow Am. Statis. Assn., AAAS, Econometric Soc.; mem. Am. Econ. Assn., Am. Statis. Assn., Econometric Soc., Inst. Mgmt. Scis., Phi Beta Kappa, Beta Gamma Sigma. Home: 12 Edgewood Rd Pittsburgh PA 15215 Office: Carnegie-Mellon U 5000 Forbes Ave Pittsburgh PA 15213

CYKER, MARVIN MYER, dental equipment company executive; b. 1929; married. With Rower Dental Supply Co. (acquired by Healthco Inc. 1969), 1948-69; v.p. Healthco Inc., Boston, 1969-70, pres., 1970-76, chief exec. officer, 1972—, chmn. bd., 1976—, also dir. Office: Healthco Inc 11-25 Stuart St Boston MA 02116 *

CYKER, MICHAEL, dental equipment company executive; b. 1930; married. Pres. dental supply div. Healthco Inc., Boston, 1958—, corp. pres., 1976—, also dir. Office: Healthco Inc 11-25 Stuart St Boston MA 02116 *

CYLKE, FRANK KURT, librarian; b. New Haven, Feb. 13, 1932; s. Frank Anton and Helen Mary (Callahan) C.; m. Mary Elizabeth Zembroski, Dec. 28, 1962; children: Frank Kurt, Mary Amanda, Virginia Ann. B.A., U. Conn., 1954; M.L.S., Pratt Inst., 1957; postgrad., Fairfield U., Am. U., Georgetown U. Librarian Graham-Eckes Sch., Palm Beach, Fla., 1957-58; reference librarian Bridgeport (Conn.) Public Library, 1958-62; head public service New Haven Public Library, 1962-65; asst. librarian Providence Public Library, 1965-68; exec. dir. fed. library com. Library of Congress, 1970-73, dir. nat. library service blind and physically handicapped, 1973—; instr. U. R.I. Grad. Library Sch., 1967-68, Cath. U. Am. Grad. Library Sch., 1974—; exec. sec. panel edn. and tng. Com. Sci and Tech. Inst.; chmn. librarians tech. com. Met. Washington Council Govts., 1970-71; sec. U.S. Book Exchange, 1972-74; sec.-treas. Joint Venture Public Activity, 1970-74; mem. E. Greenwich (R.I.) Free Library Corp., 1967—; adv. bd. Ednl. Resources Info. Center/Clearinghouse Library and Info. Sci., 1970-72. Editor: Captains Shelf, 1964-66, FLC Newsletter, 1970-73. Grantee U.S. Office Edn., 1972. Mem. ALA, Spl. Libraries Assn. (pres. D.C. chpt. 1975-76), Am. Soc. Info. Sci. (sec. 1974-75), Pvt. Libraries Assn., Am. Assn. Workers Blind, Internat. Fedn. Library Assns. (founder/chmn. round table for blind), Shenandoah Natural History Assn. (exec. com. 1982—), Manuscript Soc., Lewes Hist. Soc. Roman Catholic. Club: Dinghy Cruising Assn. Home: 1032 Harriman St Great Falls VA 22066 Office: Library of Congress Washington DC 20542

CYPHERT, FREDERICK RALPH, educator; b. Brookville, Pa., Jan. 4, 1928; s. Ralph Leroy and Bessanna (Nail) C.; m. Lois Florence Grosz, June 1, 1957; children—Stacey Todd, Holly Susan. B.S., Clarion State Coll., 1949; M.A., Syracuse U., 1950; Ed.D., U. Pitts., 1957. Tchr., curriculum coordinator pub. schs., Penn Hills, Pa., 1950-56; asst. prof. Ball State U., Muncie, Ind., 1956-57; dir. instrn., pub. schs., Torrance, Cal., 1957-59; prof. Ohio State U., Columbus, 1959-65, asso. dean, 1965-68; dean Sch. Edn., U. Va., Charlottesville, 1968-74, Coll. Edn., Ohio State U., Columbus, 1974-79, dean emeritus, prof., 1979—. Author: Teaching in America, 1962, Teaching in the American Secondary School, 1964, An Analysis and Projection of Research in Teacher Education, 1965, A Taxonomy of Teacher Classroom Behavior, 1966; Contbr. articles to profl. jours. Served with USAAF, 1946-47. Recipient Distinguished Alumni award Clarion State Coll., 1967. Mem. Ohio Council on Tchr. Edn. (pres. 1966-68), Assn. Colls. and Schs. Edn. in State Univs. and Land Grant Colls. (pres. 1973-75), Assn. Supervision and Curriculum Devel., Am. Ednl. Research Assn., Am. Assn. Colls. Tchr. Edn. (pres. 1976-77), Am. Assn. Sch. Adminstrs., Phi Delta Kappa, Phi Sigma Pi, Pi Gamma Mu. Home: 267 Blandford Dr Worthington OH 43085

CYR, ARTHUR, association executive; b. Los Angeles, Mar. 1, 1945; s. Irving Arthur and Frances Mary C.; m. Betty Jean Totten, June 24, 1967; children: David Arthur, Thomas Harold. B.A., UCLA, 1966, M.A., 1967; A.M., Harvard U., 1969, Ph.D., 1971. Teaching fellow Harvard U., 1970-71; program officer internat. and edn.-research divs. Ford Found., 1971-74; asst. prof. polit. sci., adminstr. UCLA, 1974-76; program dir. Chgo. Council Fgn. Relations, 1976-81, v.p., program dir., 1981—; lectr. pub. policy and polit. sci. U. Ill., U. Chgo.; mem. vis. com. Ctr. for Far Eastern Studies, U. Chgo. Author: Liberal Party Politics in Britain, 1977, British Foreign Policy and the Atlantic Area, 1979; contbr. articles to profl. jours. Mem. Japan-Am. Soc. Chgo. (dir.), N.Y. Council Fgn. Relations, Internat. Inst. Strategic Studies, Am. Polit. Sci. Assn., Phi Beta Kappa. Clubs: Arts, Quadrangle; Univ. (Chgo.). Office: 116 S Michigan Ave Chicago IL 60603

CYR, CONRAD KEEFE, federal judge; b. Limestone, Maine, Dec. 9, 1931; s. Louis Emery and Kathleen Mary (Keefe) C.; m. Judith Ann Pirie, June 23, 1962; children: Keefe Clark, Jeffrey Louis Frederick. B.S. cum laude, Holy Cross Coll., 1953; J.D., Yale U., 1956. Bar: Maine 1956. Sole practice, Limestone, 1956-59; asst. U.S. Atty., Bangor, Maine, 1959-61; judge U.S. Bankruptcy Court, Bangor, 1961-81, U.S. Dist. Ct., 1981-83, chief judge, 1983—; standing spl. master U.S. Dist. Ct., Maine, 1974-76; chief judge Bankruptcy Appellate Panel Dist., Mass., 1980-81. Editor-in-chief, Am. Bankruptcy Law Jour., 1970-81; contbg. author, editor: Collier on Bankruptcy, Vol. 10. Treas. Limestone Republican Com., 1958; chmn. Town of Limestone Budget Com., 1959. Recipient Cert. of Appreciation Kans. State Bar Assn., 1979, U. Maine, 1983, Nat. Judge's Recognition award Nat. Conf. Bankruptcy Judges, 1979, Key to Town Limestone, 1983. Mem. ABA, Maine Bar Assn., Penobscot Bar Assn., Nat. Conf. Bankruptcy Judges (pres. 1976-77), Nat. Bankruptcy Conf. (exec. bd. 1974-77), Am. Judicature Soc., Limestone C. of C. (pres.). Roman Catholic.

CZAMANSKE, WILLIAM MARTEN, automotive diagnostic equipment company executive; b. Detroit, Feb. 10, 1932; s. Paul William and Lydia (Marten) C.; m. Carol Lee Durr, Aug. 15, 1954 (div. June 1976); children: Marten, John, Lynne, Thomas. B.S.B.A., U. Denver, 1957. Dir. mktg. Eastman Kodak Co., 1958-79; v.p. sales and mktg. Bell & Howell, 1979-82; sr. v.p. sales and mktg. Sun Electric Corp., Crystal Lake, Ill., 1982—. Served to 2d lt. U.S. Army, 1952-54. Home: 1158 Meadow Rd Northbrook IL 60062 Office: Sun Electric Corp One Sun Pkwy Crystal Lake IL 60014

CZARNECKI, GERALD MILTON, banker; b. Phila., Mar. 22, 1940; s. Casimir M. and Rose-Mary (Grajek) C.; m. Lois Rae DiJoseph, July 9, 1965; 1 dau., Robin Alexandra. B.S., Temple U., Phila., 1965; M.A., Mich. State U., 1967. C.P.A., Ill., Tex. With Continental Bank, Chgo., 1968-79, v.p., operating gen. mgr. trust ops. and gen. mgr. corp. services, 1971-78; pres. Fla. Computing Services, 1979; exec. v.p. Houston Nat. Bank, 1979-82; sr. v.p.-fin. Republic Bank Corp., 1982-83, exec. v.p., 1983-84; pres., chief exec. officer First So. Fed. Savs., 1984—; mem. faculty DePaul U., Chgo., 1975-78; mem. exec. com. Houston Clearing House Assn., 1980-82; adj. prof. econs. Houston Bapt. U., 1980-82; mem. faculty Bank Adminstrn. Inst., 1978—, Grad. Sch. Banking, U. Wis., 1979—; vis. prof. Jones Sch. Bus., Rice U., 1980; adj. prof. policy and strategy So. Methodist U., 1983-84; mem. adv. com. Banking Center, Tex. So. U., 1980-82; chmn. securities processing sub-com. Am. Nat. Standards Inst., 1974-79. Contbr. articles to profl. publs. Chmn. policy bd. Inroads Inc., Chgo., 1974-78; bd. dirs. Drug Abuse Council Ill., 1978, Jr. Achievement, Dallas; mem. exec. com., bd. dirs. Dallas Theatre Ctr. Mem. Am. Bankers Assn. (chmn. securities processing com. 1974-77, trust ops. com. 1978, mem. exec. com. ops. and automation div. 1980—, research com.), Corp. Fiduciaries Assn. Ill., Am. Inst. C.P.A.'s, Am. Econ. Assn., Tex. Soc. C.P.A.'s, Am. Inst. Banking (chmn. bd. govs. Houston chpt. 1980—, mem. Tex. state com. 1980—), Fin. Execs. Inst., N. Am. Soc. Corp. Planners (bd. dirs. Dallas Chpt. 1982-83), Assn. for Corp. Growth, Omicron Delta Epsilon, Alpha Delta Phi. Office: First So Fed Savs PO Box 16267 Mobile AL 36616

CZARNECKI, RICHARD EDWARD, business educator; b. Detroit, Jan. 6, 1931; s. Edward and Mary (Galazka) C.; m. Dolores C. Kadzielawski, Sept. 7, 1957; children: Christine, David, Carol, Paul. B.S., U. Detroit, 1953, M.B.A., 1956; Ph.D., Mich. State U., 1965. C.P.A., Mich. Sr. accountant Arthur Andersen & Co., Detroit, 1953-55; prof. accounting U. Detroit, 1956-68, chmn. dept. accounting and bus. law, 1960-67; asst. dir. edn. Am. Inst. C.P.A.s, N.Y.C., 1959; prof. bus. adminstrn. U. Mich., Dearborn, 1968—; cons. C.P.A. firms and industry. Mem. Am. Inst. C.P.A.s, Mich. Assn. C.P.A.s (dir. 1969—), Am. Accounting Assn., Nat. Assn. Accountants, Mich. Accountancy Found. (trustee), Am. Assn. U. Profs. (AAUP), Beta Gamma Sigma, Beta Alpha Psi, Delta Sigma Pi. Home: 6707 Plainfield St Dearborn Heights MI 48127 Office: 4901 Evergreen St U Mich at Dearborn Dearborn MI 48128

CZARNIECKI, MYRON JAMES, III, art museum director; b. San Francisco, May 28, 1948; s. Myron James, Jr. and Laura Maxine (Atwood) C.; m. Anne Frances Dixon, Nov. 20, 1976; children: Mark James, Laura Anne, Katherine Elizabeth. Student, Xaverius Coll., Antwerp, Belgium, 1966-67; B.A., Wabash Coll., 1971, Sch. Art Inst. Chgo., 1971-72. Instr. photography Wabash Coll., 1970-71; photographer Art Inst. Chgo., 1971-72, audio/visual supr., 1972-74; dir. edn. and state services The Ringling Museums, 1974-76; dir. Miss. Mus. Art, Jackson, 1976-83, Minn. Mus. Art, St. Paul, 1983—; curator-in-residence USIA, Sofia, Bulgaria, 1982; cons. Nat. Endowment for Arts and Humanities; lectr. Art Inst. Chgo; founding dir. Miss. Inst. Arts and Letters, 1978-83. Author or editor numerous exhbn. catalogs. Raymond Fund grantee, 1972-73; dir. more than 25 grants from Nat. Endowment Arts, Inst. Mus. Services. Mem. Internat. Council Mus., Am. Assn. Mus., Miss. Mus. Assn. (v.p.), Nat. Trust Hist. Preservation, Midwest Mus. Conf. Office: Minn Mus Art Landmark Ctr 5th at Market St Saint Paul MN 55102

CZARNIK, MARVIN RAY, aerospace engineer; b. St. Louis, Sept. 19, 1932; s. Stanley Bernard and Laura (Kramer) C.; m. Mary Ann Miller, Nov. 26, 1955; children—Kristy Kay, Carol Lee. Student, Valparaiso U., 1950-51; B.S. in Elec. Engring, Washington U., St. Louis, 1954; extension student, U. Mo., 1964. With McDonnell-Douglas Corp., St. Louis, 1955—, sr. group engr., guidance and control, 1964-68, Skylab program devel., 1968-72; mgr. software engring., 1972, 1973-78, 1978-79, 1978-81, 1982—, developed guidance system Gemini space rendevous. Fellow AIAA (asso.). Home: 8 Lakeside Circle Lake Saint Louis MO 63367 Office: PO Box 516 Saint Louis MO 63166

CZERWINSKI, CAROL LYNNE, endocrine physiologist; b. Milw., July 12, 1946; d. Harry T. and Florence Ann (Davis) C. B.S., Marquette U., 1968, M.S., 1970; Ph.D., Georgetown U., 1973. Research intern physiologist internal medicine dept. Nat. Naval Med. Ctr., Bethesda, Md., 1973-76, head Endocrinology lab, 1976—; clin. instr. pathology George Washington U., Washington, 1974-79, asst. professorial lectr. pathology, 1979—; instr. ob-gyn Uniformed Service U. of Health Scis., Bethesda, 1976-78, asst. prof., 1978—. Contbr. articles to profl. jours. Mem. Assn. Profs. Gynecology and Obstetrics, Am. Fedn. Clin. Research, N.Y. Acad. Scis., D.C. Endocrine Soc.

CZERWINSKI, EDWARD JOSEPH, language educator; b. Erie, Pa., June 6, 1929; s. Joseph and Anna (Branecka) C. B.A., Grove City Coll., 1951; M.A. in Drama and English, Pa. State U., 1955; postgrad., Emory U., 1955-57, Ind. U., 1960-61; M.A. in Russian, U. Wis., Madison, 1964; Ph.D. in Russian and Polish, U. Wis., Madison, 1965. Instr. English Ga. Tech. Inst., Atlanta, 1957-59; asst. prof. English and drama McNeese State Coll., La., 1959-60; assoc. prof. Russian and Polish lits. U. Pitts., 1965-66; assoc. prof. Russian and Polish U. Kans., Lawrence, 1967-70; prof. Russian and comparative lit. SUNY, Stony Brook, 1970—; ofcl. translator from Polish into English Interpress Pubs., Warsaw; founder, exec. and artistic dir. Slavic Cultural Center, Port Jefferson, N.Y., 1970—, pres. bd. trustees, 1970—. Editor: (with J. Piekalkiewicz) The Soviet Invasion of Czechoslovakia: The Effects on East Europe, 1972; editor, translator Pieces of Poland: Four Polish Dramatists, 1983; (with Mario Suško) Twenty Yugoslav Poets: the Meditative Generation, 1982; editor: Alternatives: An Anthology of Slavic and East European Drama, 1983; author also numerous articles and revs.; mem. editorial bd.: Books Abroad (now World Lit. Today), 1968—, Gradiva, 20th Century Lit, Comparative Drama; spl. editor, 1969-70; editor: Slavic and East European Arts Jour., 1982—, Polish lit. sect. Ency. Brit, 1975-78, East European sect. World Ency. Theater Ensembles. Served to 2d lt. USAF, 1951-53. Kosciuszko Found. grantee, 1962-64; Wanda Rohr Found. grantee, 1963; Internat. Dimensions grantee, 1966; Fulbright grantee, Yugoslavia, 1968-69; Inter-Univ. travel grantee, USSR, 1968-69, Czechoslovakia, 1969; Internat. Research and Exchange Bd. fellow, Yugoslavia, 1983-84; recipient Disting. Alumni award Grove City Coll., 1973; Chancellor's Excellence in Teaching award SUNY, 1973-74; Amicus Poloniae award, Poland, 1974; Disting. Prof. award N.Y. State Tchrs. of Fgn. Langs., 1975; Fulbright sr. scholar research award, Yugoslavia, 1983-84. Mem. MLA (exec. com. Slavic-Western lit. relations 1970-72), Polish Acad. Arts and Scis. Am., AAUP, Am. Assn. Tchrs. of Slavic and East European Langs., Am. Assn. Advancement of Slavic Studies. Home: Private Rd Box 127 Shoreham NY 11786 Office: SUNY Stony Brook NY 11794 *I was orphaned early in life. I had always felt that I had been cheated somehow until one day in high school a teacher befriended me. Within a year of our friendship, she died. Ever since I have tried to help others as she had helped me.*

CZERWINSKI, HENRY RICHARD, banker; b. Newark, Nov. 3, 1933; s. Henry Adam and Mary Josephine (Burkat) C. B.S. with honors, Kans. State U., 1959; postgrad., Stonier Grad. Sch. Banking, New Brunswick, N.J., 1966, Am. Inst. Banking, Kansas City, Mo., 1963. With Fed. Res. Bank, Kansas City, 1959—, auditor-acctg. mgr., 1959, acctg. officer, 1967, asst. v.p., 1969, v.p., 1972, sr. v.p., 1974, 1st v.p., 1977—; dir. Greater Kansas City Clearinghouse, 1977-83, Mid. Am. Automated Clearing House Assn., Kansas City, 1977—. Advisor Jr. Achievement, 1965-66; fund raiser United Way, 1967, Cancer Crusade, 1968, Heart Fund, 1970. Served with U.S. Army, 1954-56. Mem. Am. Inst. Banking (pres. Kansas City chpt. 1967), Alpha Kappa Psi, Phi Kappa Phi. Office: Red Res Bank Kansas City 925 Grand Ave Kansas City MO 64198

DAANE, ADRIAN HILL, chemist, university dean; b. Stillwater, Okla., June 18, 1919; s. Adrian and Bessie (Hill) D.; m. Jean Plunkett, June 22, 1944; children: Susan, Peter, Ann. B.S., U. Fla., 1941; Ph.D., Iowa State U., 1950. Research asso., group leader Manhattan Project Iowa State U., 1942-45, from grad. teaching asst. to prof. chemistry, 1946-63; grad. research asst., then sr. chemist Ames Lab., 1948-50, 58-63; prof. chemistry, head dept. Kans. State U., Manhattan, 1963-72; dean Coll. Arts and Scis. U. Mo., Rolla, 1972-79; dean Grad. Sch. Coll. Arts and Scis. U. Mo., 1979—; mem. adv. bd. Nat. Acad. Sci., 1958-72. Mem. bd. edn. Am. Baptist Conv., 1958-63; Trustee Bacone Coll., 1963-74. Mem. Am. Chem. Soc., Am. Inst. Mining, Metall. and Petroleum Engrs., AAAS. Home: Route 4 Box 187 Rolla MO 65401 *The real leaders in our civilization—in every part from small organizations up through our nation and the world—are those who have chosen carefully which organizations they will join and serve through, and then have served selflessly and with real committment.*

DAANE, JAMES DEWEY, banker; b. Grand Rapids, Mich., July 6, 1918; s. Gilbert L. and Mamie (Blocksma) D.; m. Blanche M. Tichenor, Apr. 28, 1941 (div. 1952); 1 dau., Elizabeth Marie Daane Mallek; m. Onnie B. Selby, Jan. 23, 1953 (dec. Dec. 1961); m. Barbara W. McMann, Feb. 16, 1963; children—Elizabeth Whitney, Olivia Quartel. A.B. magna cum laude, Duke U., 1939; M.P.A., Harvard U., 1946, D.P.A. (Littauer fellow), 1949. With Fed. Res. Bank, Richmond, Va., 1939-60, asst. v.p., 1953-57, v.p., 1957-60, also cons. to pres. bank; asso. economist Fed. Open Market Com., 1955-56, 58-59; chief IMF Fiscal Mission to Paraguay, 1950-51; adviser to pres. Fed. Res. Bank, Mpls., 1960; asst. to sec. treasury, 1960-61, dep. undersec. treasury for monetary affairs, 1961-63; bd. govs. Fed. Res. System, 1963-74; vice chmn. bd., dir. Commerce Union Bank, 1974-78; vice chmn. Tennessee Valley Bancorp, Inc., 1975-78; chmn. internat. policy com. Commerce Union Corp., 1978—; Frank K. Houston prof. banking and fin. Grad. Sch. Mgmt., Vanderbilt U., 1974—; dir. Whittaker Corp., Los Angeles, 1974—, Chgo. Bd. Trade, 1979-82, Nat. Futures Assn., 1983—. Bd. advisers Patterson Sch. Diplomacy and Internat. Commerce, U. Ky. Mem. J.F. Kennedy Sch. Govt. Assn. of Harvard U., Am. Econ. Assn., Am. Finance Assn. Home: 102 Westhampton Pl Nashville TN 37205 Office: Commerce Union Bank One Commerce Pl Nashville TN 37239

DABBS, HENRY ERVEN, TV art director producer, film producer, educator; b. Clover, Va., Oct. 15, 1932; s. Charles E. and Gertrude (Hudson) D.; m. Loretta D. Young, Jan. 9, 1957. B.F.A., Pratt Inst., 1955. Book designer Berton Wink, Inc., N.Y.C., 1958-62; pres., owner Henry Dabbs Prodns. (A Total Communication Complex), 1978—, partner, 1980—; instr. cinema Jersey City State Coll., 1977—. Art dir.-producer: Dancer, Fitzgerald Sample, N.Y.C., 1963—; editor, producer, dir.: motion picture Joshua, 1975-76; producer, dir.: documentary film The Movers, 1978; original paintings depicting famous Afro-Americans in Am. history in permanent collection, Frederick Douglass Mus., Washington.; Creator: Afro-American History Fact Pack, 1968; Author: Afro-American History Highlights, 1968, Black Brass, 1983; audio video series The ABC's of Black History, 1983. Served with AUS, 1955-58. Mem. N.A.A.C.P. Home: 24 Whittier Dr Englishtown NJ 07726

DABILL, PHILLIP ALVIN, wholesale foods executive; b. Pequot Lakes, Minn., Sept. 14, 1942; s. Gaylord D. and Faith A. (Brant) D.; m. Judith Salfisberg, Nov. 7, 1943; children: Julie, Barbara, Tom, Paul. A.B.A., Dakota Bus. Coll., 1962. Devel. mgr., store engr. Super Valu Stores, Inc., Fargo, N.D., 1962-72; dir. retail devel. Food Mktg. Corp., Ft. Wayne, Ind., 1972-74; retail ops. mgr. Super Valu Stores, Inc., Bismarck, N.D., 1974-77; gen. mgr. Plainfield Super Valu div., Ill., 1977-79; pres. Food Mktg. Corp., Ft. Wayne, 1979—; dir. Anthony Wayne Bank, Ft. Wayne. Bd. dirs. Jr. Achievement, 1979—; mem. planning com. ARC, 1980—; capt. United Way, 1981—. Mem. Plainfield C. of C. (dir. 1978). Republican. Lodge: Rotary. Home: 10809 Oaktrees Rd Fort Wayne IN 46825 Office: 4815 Executive Blvd Fort Wayne IN 46808

DABNEY, SETH MASON, III, lawyer; b. Bklyn., May 26, 1918; s. Seth Mason and Anna Sarsfield Tucker D.; m. Marian Jean Tomai, Dec. 28, 1946; children: Seth Mason IV, James Wilson. A.B., CCNY, 1939; LL.B., Columbia U., 1942. Bar: N.Y. 1942, Ill. 1964. Practiced in, N.Y.C., 1942-63, Peoria, Ill., 1963—; asso. firm Dorr, Hand, Whittaker & Watson, N.Y.C., 1942-55, partner, 1956-63; with Caterpillar Tractor Co., Peoria, 1963-83, asso. counsel, 1963-74, sec., gen. counsel, 1974-83; of counsel Westervelt Johnson Nicoll & Keller, 1983—. Contbr. articles to profl. jours. Peoria area chmn. Citizens Com. for Constl. Conv., 1968, Citizens for a New Constn., 1969; mem. Republican County Com., Ridgewood, N.J., 1956-63; bd. dirs. Peoria Symphony Orch., 1969-75, 76-79, pres., 1971-74; bd. dirs. Planned Parenthood Assn. Greater Peoria, 1977-83; bd. dirs., sec.-treas. Family Planning Found. Peoria, 1981—; v.p. Planned Parenthood Assn. Greater Peoria, 1978-80, 83—; mem. President's bus. adv. panel on antitrust export issues Nat. Commn. Rev. Antitrust Laws and Procedures, 1978-79; mem. Council Antitrust Policy, U.S. C. of C., 1981—. Served with AUS, 1943-45; ETO. Mem. Am., N.Y., Ill., Peoria County bar assns., Assn. Bar City N.Y., Phi Beta Kappa. Clubs: Country of Peoria, Creve Coeur. Home: 5903 Sherwood Dr Peoria IL 61614 Office: 1400 First Nat Bank Bldg Peoria IL 61602

DABNEY, VIRGINIUS, author; b. University, Va., Feb. 8, 1901; s. Richard Heath and Lily Heth (Davis) D.; m. Douglas Harrison Chelf, Oct. 10, 1923; children: Douglas Gibson (Mrs. James S. Watkinson), Lucy Davis (Mrs. Alexander P. Leverty), Richard Heath II. A.B., U. Va., 1920, A.M., 1921; D.Litt. (hon.), U. Richmond, 1940; LL.D., Lynchburg Coll., Coll. William and Mary, 1944; L.H.D., Va. Commonwealth U., 1976. Tchr. French Episcopal High Sch., 1921-22; reporter Richmond News Leader, 1922-28; editorial staff Richmond Times-Dispatch, 1928-34, chief editorial writer, 1934-36, editor, 1936-69; contbr. to N.Y. Times, Dictionary Am. Biography, Ency. Brit., London Economist.; Spent six months in Central Europe in 1934 under grant from Oberlaender Trust.; Lectr. on New South Princeton U. session, 1939-40; lectr. Fulbright Conf. Am. Studies, Cambridge U., 1954. Author: Liberalism in the South, 1932, Below the Potomac, 1942, Dry Messiah: The Life of Bishop Cannon, 1949, Virginia: The New Dominion, 1971, Richmond: The Story of a City, 1976, Across the Years: Memories of a Virginian, 1978, The Jefferson Scandals, 1981, Mr. Jefferson's University, 1981, Bicentennial History and Roster of the Society of the Cincinnati in the State of Virginia, 1783-1983, 1983, The Last Review, 1984; editor: The Patriots, 1975, Architectures in Downtown Richmond, 1982; Contbr. to nat. mags. Chmn. adv. bd. U.S. Hist. Soc.; bd. dirs. U. Press Va., 1966-70; chmn. Gov.'s Statewide Conf. on Edn., 1966; 1st rector Va. Commonwealth U., 1968-69, trustee, 1969-79. Recipient Lee Editorial award for disting. editorial writing Va. Press Assn., and Lee Sch. Journalism, Washington and Lee Univ., 1947; Pulitzer Prize for editorial writing, 1947; Nat. Editorial award Sigma Delta Chi, 1948, 52; Thomas Jefferson award for pub. Service, 1972, Raven award for service U. Va., 1973; Distinguished Service award Va. Social Sci. Assn., 1975; Jackson Davis medal for service to higher edn., 1975; spl. award Va. C. of C., 1975; Liberty Bell award Richmond Bar Assn., 1976; Guggenheim fellow. Mem. Am. Soc. Newspaper Editors (dir. 1946-59, pres. 1957-58), So. Acad. Letters, Arts and Scis., Authors League, Va. Hist. Soc. (pres. 1969-72), Raven, Omicron Delta Kappa, Delta Kappa Epsilon, Phi Beta Kappa, Sigma Delta Chi (fellow). Episcopalian. Club: Country of Virginia. Home: Tuckahoe Apts Apt 213 5621 Cary St Rd Richmond VA 23226

DABNEY, WATSON BARR, investment banker; b. Louisville, Dec. 24, 1923; s. William Cecil and Florence (Joyes) D.; m. Lucy Campbell

Mercer, July 23, 1953. Student, Phillips Exeter Acad., 1939-42, Princeton, 1942-43. With J.J.B. Hilliard, W.L. Lyons, Inc., Louisville, 1951—, partner, 1954-72, pres., chief exec. officer, 1972-82, chmn. bd., 1982—. Pres., trustee Am. Printing House for Blind, 1969-79. Served with AUS, 1942-45. Mem. Nat. Assn. Securities Dealers (bd. govs. 1968-70). Clubs: River Valley, Louisville Country (Louisville); Brook, City Midday (N.Y.); Mill Reef (Antiqua). Home: Mockingbird Valley KY 40207 Office: 545 S 3d St Louisville KY 40202

DABNEY, WILLIAM KROEHLE, manufacturing company executive; b. Cleve., June 22, 1933; s. John Carpenter and Mary Ellen (Kroehle) Dabney/C.; m. Valerie Daniels, Aug. 10 1962; children: Monica Kroehle, Joseph Daniels, Frona MacFarlane. A.B., Harvard U., 1955; M.B.A., Columbia U., 1960. Asst. treas. Internat. Paper Co., N.Y.C., 1975-78; pres. Diamond Sunsweet Inc., Stockton, Calif., 1978-80; exec. v.p. Sun*Diamond Growers Calif., Diamond Walnut Growers Inc., Stockton, Calif., Sun-Maid Growers Calif., Kingsbury, Sunsweet Growers Inc., Yuba City, Calif., 1980—. Mem. Fin. Execs. Inst., Nat. Council Farmer Coops., Walnut Mktg. Bd., Prune Mktg. Com., Sacramento Bank for Coops. (co-chmn. 1982—). Republican. Episcopalian. Home: 3423 Meade Dr Stockton CA 95209 Office: Sun Diamond Growers Calif 1050 S Diamond St Stockton CA 95201

DA CAL, ERNESTO GUERRA, educator; b. Ferrol, Spain, Dec. 19, 1911; s. Roman Perez and Laura (Guerra) Da C.; m. Elsie Allen, 1966. B.S., Inst. General y Tecnico de San Isidro, Madrid, 1928; M.A., U. Central, Madrid, 1936; Ph.D., Columbia, 1950; Dr. honoris causa, U. da Bahia, Salvador, Brazil, 1959. Instr. Bklyn. Coll., 1939-41; instr. to asso. prof. N.Y. U., 1941-56, prof., 1956-64, chmn. dept. Spanish and Portuguese, 1955-60; prof. Romance langs. Queens Coll., City U. N.Y., 1964—; Exec. officer doctoral program in Portuguese lang. and Luso-Brazilian lit. City U. N.Y., 1965-70; Vis. lectr. Princeton, 1942-43; lectr., asst. to dir. ASTP, Coll. City N.Y., 1943-44; lectr. Columbia, summer 1939-45; featured writer, broadcaster Western European div. Voice of Am. USIA, 1952-74. Author: Lengua y Estilo de Eca de Queiroz, 1954, Lua de Alen-Mar, 1959, Rio de Sonho e Tempo, 1963, Bibliografia Queirociana, 4 vols., 1975, 76, 80, 81; contbr. articles to profl. publs. Decorated Ordem Nacional do Cruzeiro do Sul, Brazil; Great Cross Order of St. James of Sword, Portugal; recipient Rosalia Castro prize for poetry, Portugal, 1960; named hon. citizen Rio de Janeiro, 1960; knight-comdr. Order Prince Henry The Navigator, Portugal, 1968; King Manual II prize for Portuguese bibliography, 1983; Guggenheim fellow, 1958; Fulbright grantee, 1970, 71. Mem. Internat. Acad. Portuguese Culture, Am. Assn. Tchrs. Spanish and Portuguese (pres. N.Y. chpt.), MLA (chmn. Portuguese bibliography), N.Y. Acad. Scis., Hispanic Inst. U.S., Hispanic Soc. Am. (trustee), Spanish Inst. N.Y., Acad. Scis. Lisbon (corr.), Phi Beta Kappa, Phi Lambda Beta (charter mem. exec. council 1966), Sigma Delta Pi, Trigonom. Home: Melrose Ave D Nuno Alvares Pereira 33-A Estoril 2765 Portugal Office: Queens Coll Flushing NY 11367 *My basic philosophy of life rests on the deep belief that while Man is forced to live by the harsh rule of facts, it is only by virtue of his dreams that he survives. So I have always been nurturing my capacities as a dreamer. On the other hand I have always guided my actions by the principle that one should never ask from life that which it cannot give you at that particular moment. If you deserve it, it will come to you later, unexpectedly, when you are not asking for it.*

D'ACCONE, FRANK A., music educator; b. Somerville, Mass., June 13, 1931; s. Salvatore and Maria (DiChiappari) D'A. Mus. B., Boston U., 1952, Mus.M., 1953; A.M., Harvard U., 1955, Ph.D., 1960. Asst. prof. music SUNY at Buffalo, 1960-63; assoc. prof. State U. N.Y. at Buffalo, 1964-68; prof. music UCLA, 1968—, chmn. dept., 1973-76, chmn. faculty, 1976-79; vis. prof. music Yale U., 1972-73. Editor: Music of the Florentine Renaissance, vols. 1-10, 1967-81; Contbr. articles to profl. jours. Am. Acad. Rome fellow, 1963-64; Fulbright fellow, 1963-64; Nat. Endowment for Humanities fellow, 1975; G.K. Delmas Venetian Studies award, 1977; J.S. Guggenheim Found. award, 1980. Mem. Am. (dir. 1973-74), Internat. musicological socs., Medieval Acad. Am. Compiler. Home: 725 Fontana Way Laguna Beach CA 92651 Office: Dept Music U Calif Los Angeles CA 90025

DACEY, GEORGE CLEMENT, laboratory administrator; b. Chgo., Jan. 23, 1921; s. Clement Anthony Dacey and Helyn MacLachan; m. Anne Zeamer, June 20, 1954; children: Donna Lynn, John Clement, Sarah Anne. B.S. in E.E, U. Ill., 1942; Ph.D. in Physics, Calif. Inst. Tech., 1951. Research engr. Westinghouse Research Labs, East Pittsburgh, 1942-45; mem. tech. staff transistor research Bell Telephone Labs, 1952-55, head transistor devel., 1955-58, dir. solid state electronics research, 1958-61, exec. dir. telephones div., 1963-68, v.p. customer equipment devel., 1968-70, v.p. transmission systems, 1970-79, v.p. ops. systems, 1979-81; pres. Sandia Nat. Labs., 1981—; v.p. research Sandia Corp., Albuquerque, 1961-63; dir. Perkin-Elmer Corp., Norwalk, Conn., 1st N.Mex. Bankshare Corp. Contbr. articles on transistor physics, lasers to tech. jours. Mem. exec. bd. Monmouth council Boy Scouts Am., 1970-75; bd. dirs. Monmouth Mus., 1972—. Recipient distinguished alumnus award U. Ill. Elec. Engring. Alumni Assn., 1970. Fellow IEEE, Am. Phys. Soc.; mem. Nat. Acad. Engring., Sigma Xi, Phi Kappa Phi, Tau Beta Pi, Eta Kappa Nu. Patentee transistors. Home: 1201 Cuatro Cerros TR SE Albuquerque NM 87123 Office: Sandia National Laboratories Albuquerque NM 87185

DACEY, MICHAEL FRANCIS, educator; b. Holyoke, Mass., Mar. 23, 1932; s. Francis L. and Florence (Hogkin) D.; m. Jeanette M. Mikula, May 30, 1960; 1 dau., Rachel Ann. Student, Bates Coll., 1950-51; B.A. in Geography, U. Kans., 1954, M.A., U. Wash., Seattle, 1955, Ph.D., 1960. Asst. prof. regional sci. U. Pa., 1960-64; asst. prof. geography Northwestern U., Evanston, Ill., 1964-65, asso. prof., 1965-68, prof., 1968—, prof. geol. scis., 1970—, chmn. geography dept., 1976—. Author: (with others) One Dimensional Central Place Theory, 1974, Christaller Central Place Structures: An Introductory Statement, 1977, An Introduction to the Mathematical Theory of Central Places: Central Place Geometry, 1979; contbr.: articles to profl. jours. An Introduction to the Mathematical Theory of Central Places: Central Place Geometry. Served with Army Map Service U.S. Army, 1956-58. Mem. Am. Statis. Assn., Assn. Am. Geographers (award for meritorious contbns. 1971), Inst. Math. Stats., Ops. Research Soc., Regional Sci. Assn. Home: 2023 Orrington St Evanston IL 60201 Office: 1936 Sheridan Rd Evanston IL 60201

DACEY, TIMOTHY JOHN, JR., banker, ret. air force officer; b. Marshfield, Mass., Aug. 12, 1917; s. Timothy John and Esther (Coleman) D.; m. Sara Rogers, Aug. 19; children—Timothy John III, Michael R., Mary P., Sara Ruth, Kathleen. B.A., Boston Coll., 1939. Commd. 2d lt. USAAF, 1940, advanced through grades to maj. gen., 1968; base comdr., wing comdr., personnel officer SAC, 1966-68, chief of staff, Offutt AFB, Nebr., 1968-72; ret.; pres. Bank Bellevue, Nebr., 1972—. Decorated Legion of Merit with oak leaf cluster, D.S.M. Home: 505 Edgewood Ct Bellevue NE 68005 Office: Bank Bellevue Bellevue NE 68005

DACHOWSKI, PETER RICHARD, financial executive; b. Hillington, Middlesex, Eng., June 2, 1948; came to U.S., 1969; s. Teodor and Mary (Stracey) D.; m. Victoria Kaplan Ortiz, May 1, 1977. M.A., Cambridge U., 1969; M.B.A., U. Chgo., 1971. Fin. analyst Exxon Corp., 1971-73; mgr. Boston Cons. Group, 1973-76; asst. treas. Certain-Teed Co., Valley Forge, Pa., 1976-78, asst. to chief exec. officer, 1979-80, v.p. planning and devel., 1980-81, v.p., treas., 1981-83, comptroller, 1983—; corp. devel staff Compagnie Saint Gobain, Paris, 1978-79; dir. Mexalit S.A. Recipient Wall St. Jour. award Dow Jones-Chgo., 1971. Mem. Fin. Mgmt. Assn., Fin. Execs. Inst., Beta Gamma Sigma. Home: 321 Woodmont Circle Berwyn PA 19312 Office: PO Box 860 Valley Forge PA 19482

DACIUK, MYRON MICHAEL, bishop; b. Mundare, Alta., Can., Nov. 16, 1919; s. Lucas and Ksenia (Bruchkowsky) D. D.D., Basilian Sem., Mundare, 1945. Ordained priest Ukrainian Catholic Ch., 1945, aux. bishop, 1982. Priest Ukrainian Cath. Ch., Can., 1945-82, bishop, Winnipeg, Man., Can., 19826; superior Basilian Fathers, Mundare, 1959-64, Edmonton, Alta., 1976-79, provincial superior, 1964-70. Home: 235 Scotia St Winnipeg MB Canada R2V 1V7 Office: Winnipeg Archeparchy 235 Scotia St Winnepeg MB Canada R2V 1V7

DACK, SIMON, physician; b. N.Y.C., Apr. 19, 1908; s. Isidore and Rebecca (Beitch) D.; m. Jacqueline Rosett, Jan. 23, 1949; children: Jerilyn Beth, Leonard. B.S., CCNY, 1928; M.D., N.Y. Med. Coll., 1932. Intern Mt. Sinai Hosp., N.Y.C., 1932-33, research fellow cardiology, 1934-38, clin. staff cardiology, 1938—, adj. physician cardiology, chief cardiac clinic, 1945-58, attending physician, 1966—; lectr. cardiology Columbia U.; asso. prof. medicine N.Y. Med. Coll., 1959—; asso. clin. prof. medicine Mt. Sinai Sch. Medicine, 1966-70, clin. prof. medicine, 1970-76, clin. prof. emeritus, 1976—; chief cardiac clinics Met. Hosp., N.Y.C., 1955-62, attending vis. physician, 1962—; asso. physician in cardiology Mt. Sinai Hosp., N.Y.C., 1958-70, attending physician cardiology, 1970-76, acting chief cardiology, 1972-74, cons. cardiologist, 1976—; attending physician Flower Fifth Ave. Hosp., 1966—; hon. prof. medicine U. Santo Tomas, Manila, 1961—. Contbr. articles to profl. jours.; editor-in-chief: Am. Jour. Cardiology, 1958-82, Jour. Am. Coll Cardiology, 1982—. Served as maj. M.C., AUS, 1942-45. Recipient Disting. Fellow award Am. Coll. Cardiology, 1969; presdl. citation Am. Coll. Cardiology, 1972; Jacoby medal Alumni Assn. Mt. Sinai Med. Center, 1979. Fellow ACP, Am. Med. Writers Assn. (editorial cons.), Am. Coll. Cardiology (trustee 1952—, pres. 1956-57, Spl. award 1961), N.Y. Cardiol. Soc. (hon.); mem. N.Y. Acad. Scis., A.M.A., Am. Heart Assn. (council on clin. cardiology 1962—), Am. Fedn. Clin. Research, Am. Coll. Chest Physicians, Philippine Heart Assn. (hon.), Alpha Omega Alpha. Home: 85 East End Ave New York NY 10028

DACKAWICH, S. JOHN, educator; b. Loch Gelley, W.Va., Jan 31, 1926; s. Samuel and Estelle (Jablonski) D.; m. Shirley Jean McVay, May 20, 1950; children—Robert John, Nancy Joan. B.A., U. Md., 1955; Ph.D., U. Colo., 1958. Instr. U. Colo., 1955-57; instr. Colo. State U., 1957-59; prof., chmn. sociology Calif. State U. at Long Beach, 1959-70; prof. sociology Calif. State U., Fresno, 1970-, chmn. dept., 1970-75; pvt. practice survey research, 1962—. Mem. Calif. Democratic Central Com., 1960-62; co-dir. Long Beach Central Area Study, 1962-64, Citizen Participation Study, Fresno. Served with USMCR, 1943-46; Served with AUS, 1950-53. Mem. Am., Pacific sociol. assns. Home: 1459 W Sample Ave Fresno CA 93705

DACOSTA, EDWARD HOBAN, plastics and electronics manufacturing company executive; b. Phila., Sept. 19, 1918; s. Robert C. and Edna (Hoban) DaC.; m. Joyce Jehl, Oct. 7, 1944 (dec. Nov. 1946); 1 son, Stephen Edward; m. Elizabeth Brendlinger, Feb. 26, 1949 (dec. 1968); 1 son, David Hoban; m. Sarah McDonnell Kratz, Dec. 28, 1968; stepchildren: Carolyn Ann Borlo, Beverly Randolph. Student, Villanova U., 1936-38, Wharton Sch. of U. Pa., 1946-47. With Synthane Taylor Corp., Valley Forge, Pa., 1938-76, gen. mgr., LaVerne, Calif., 1953-56, v.p. mktg., 1956-61, pres., dir., 1961-69, chmn., chief exec. officer, 1969-75; cons., 1975—; mng. dir. Alco Standard Corp., 1969-72; v.p., dir. C-W Industries, Inc., 1972—; pres. C-W Properties, Inc., 1977—; dir. Energy Sources Corp., Dallas, Gen. Devices, Inc., Norristown, Pa. Pres. Pa. United Fund, Harrisburg, 1964-67; past pres. Pathway Sch., Norristown, Phila. United Fund; pres. bd. trustees Norristown State Hosp., 1963-75; trustee Community Services of Pa., Harrisburg; mem. adv. bd. Bryn Mawr Coll. Grad. Sch., 1963—; bd. dirs. Community Services Planning Council, v.p., 1974-78, pres., 1978-80. Served to maj., pilot USAAF, 1942-46. Mem. Nat. Elec. Mfg. Assn. (dir., chmn. insulating materials div. 1963-70). Episcopalian. Clubs: Union League (Phila.); St. Davids Golf (Radnor, Pa.). Office: CW Industries Inc Southampton PA 18966

DACOSTA, JACQUELINE, advertising executive; b. N.Y.C., Jan. 21, 1927; d. Joachim and Tirsa (Olmeda) DaC. B.A. in Bus. Adminstrn., Hunter Coll., 1952. Asst. export mgr. Morse Internat., N.Y.C., 1946-52; supr. media research Biow, Beirn, Toigo, Inc., N.Y.C., 1952-55; media research analyst Ted Bates & Co., N.Y.C., 1955-63, asst. v.p. media research, 1963-65, coordinator internat. media, 1965—, v.p., dir. media info. and analysis, 1965-78, sr. v.p., 1977—, media dir., 1978—; cons. media, research, mktg., govt. and pvt. orgns.; internat. lectr. Contbr. articles to trade jours. Mem. adv. bd. Nat. Urban Coalition; bd. govs. Nat. Conf. Puerto Rican Women, 1975-77, Puerto Rican Family Inst., 1977—, Hamilton Madison Settlement House, 1977—; pres. Hamilton Madison Settlement House, 1981; bd. dirs. Bus. Council for UN Decade for Women, pres., 1979; bd. dirs. Broadcast Pioneers Found. Mem. Am. Advt. Fedn. (dir., named Advt. Woman of Yr. 1974), Advt. Research Found. (dir.), Advt. Women N.Y. (pres. 1973-74), Internat. Radio TV Soc., Internat. Radio TV Found., Hispanics in Communications (founder, pres. 1980-81). Home: 340 E 64th St New York NY 10021 Office: Ted Bates & Co 1515 Broadway New York NY 10036

DACOSTA, MORTON, producer-director theatre and films, actor; b. Phila., Mar. 7, 1914; s. Samuel and Rose (Hulnick) Tecosky. B.S. in Edu., Temple U., 1936, L.H.D., 1958. Broadway acting debut in: The Skin of Our Teeth, 1942; dir.: Broadway plays including The Gray Eyed People, 1952; Plain and Fancy, 1955, No Time for Sergeants, 1955, Auntie Mame, 1956, The Music Man, 1957, (libretto and co-producer) Saratoga, 1959, The Wall, 1960, (co-author) Maggie Flynn, 1966, Show Me Where the Good Times Are, 1970, The Women, 1973, A Musical Jubilee, 1975; plays at City Center, N.Y.C. including She Stoops to Conquer, 1949; Captain Brassbound's Conversion, 1950, Dream Girl and the Wild Duck, 1951; dir., producer: films Auntie Mame, 1958; The Music Man, 1961, Island of Love; conceived and directed: To Broadway with Love, Tex. Pavillion, N.Y. World's Fair, 1964. Recipient Golden Globe award Fgn. Press Assn., 1963. Mem. Soc. Stage Dirs. and Choreographers (treas. 1971-74), Dirs. Guild Am., Dramatists Guild Am., Actors Equity Assn. Democrat. Jewish.

DADDIEGO, VINCENT ANTHONY, advertising company executive; b. N.Y.C., Mar. 3, 1938; s. Nicholas Anthony and Concetta (Ferraro) D. Student, Hunter Coll., 1955-57, Arts Students League, 1955-57; A.A.S., CCNY, 1959. Art dir. McCann-Marshalk, N.Y.C., 1963-65; art supr., v.p. Young & Rubicam, N.Y.C., 1965—, sr. v.p. creative dir.; advisor, instr. Sch. Visual Arts, N.Y.C., 1975—; TV judge Art Dirs. Club, N.Y.C., 1970-81, Clio Com., 1970—. Contbr. articles to profl. jours. Recipient Clio award, 1966, Gold medals Art Dir. Club, 1970, 71, 72, Copy Club, 1973, 74, 75, awards Andy Com., 1975, 78. Office: Young & Rubicam Inc 285 Madison Ave New York NY 10017

DADISMAN, JOSEPH CARROL, newspaper executive; b. Statesboro, Ga., May 24, 1934; s. Howard Dean and Mary Lou (Moore) D.; m. Mildred Jean Sparks, Aug. 19, 1956; children: David Carrol, Ellen Clarice. A.B., U. Ga., 1956. Reporter, editorial writer, mng. editor Augusta (Ga.) Chronicle, 1956-66; editor Marietta (Ga.) Daily Jour., 1966-72; mng. editor Macon (Ga.) News, 1972-74; exec. editor, v.p. Columbus (Ga.) Ledger-Enquirer, 1974-80; gen. mgr. Tallahassee Democrat, 1980-81, pub., pres., 1981—. Pres. adv. bd. U. Ga. Sch. Journalism, 1979-81; pres. Jr. Achievement of Columbus-Phenix City, 1977-78. Served with AUS, 1957-59. Recipient Pub. Service award Cobb County C. of C., 1968, Fearless Editorial award Ga. Press Assn., 1963; named Young Man of Year Augusta Jaycees, 1962. Mem. Am. Newspaper Pubs. Assn., Am. Soc. Newspaper Editors, Ga. AP Assn. (pres. 1976-77), Sigma Delta Chi. Methodist. Clubs: Capital City, Governors, Fla. Econ., Forest Meadows Racquet, Capital Tiger Bay, Rotary. Home: 2424 Winthrop Rd Tallahassee FL 32312 Office: PO Box 990 Tallahassee FL 32302

D'ADOLF, STUART VICTOR, editor, publisher; b. Newark, July 6, 1925; s. Oscar and Cecil (Yudelowitz) d'A.; m. Edith Nelson, July 3, 1960; children: Miriam Beth, Joshua Meier. Student, CCNY, 1943; B.A., U. Calif.-Berkeley, 1949. Reporter-editor Ogdensburg (N.Y.) Jour., 1950-51, Parkersburg Sentinel, 1952-55, New Haven Jour.-Courier, 1955-60; asst. editor Rubber World, 1960-63, mng. editor, 1963-65; editor, pub. Ind. Agt., N.Y.C., 1965—. Bd. dirs. Friends of Cresskill (N.J.) Library, 1966-70, pres., 1971; mem. Bergen County (N.J.) Democratic Com., 1972-74; pres. Men's Brotherhood, Temple Sinai Bergen County, 1976-77. Served with USNR, 1943-46. Mem. Am. Soc. Bus. Press Editors, Ins. Advt. Conf., Am. Soc. Assn. Execs., Soc. C.P.C.U., Am. Risk and Ins. Assn., Soc. Ins. Risk, AAU, N.Y. Road Runners Club, Alliance Francais, Sigma Delta Chi. Home: 158 Lexington Ave Cresskill NJ 07626 Office: 100 Church St New York NY 10007

DADRIAN, VAHAKN NORAIR, sociology educator; b. Istanbul, Turkey, May 26, 1926; came to U.S., 1947, naturalized, 1961; s. Hagop and Mayreni (Der Garabedian) D. Ed. (Alexander von Humboldt fellow), U. Berlin, Germany, U. Vienna, Austria, U. Zurich, Switzerland; M.A., Wayne State U., 1950; Ph.D. (Reynolds fellow), U. Chgo., 1954. Asst. prof. sociology Washington Coll., Chestertown, Md., 1955-56, Boston U., 1957-59; research fellow Harvard Center for Middle Eastern Studies, 1961-62; sr. analyst dept. strategic studies div. missiles and space Raytheon, 1962-63; lectr. Boston Coll., 1963-65; asso. prof. Wis. State U., Superior, 1965-67, Fla. Atlantic U., 1967-68, prof., 1968-70, State U. N.Y. at Geneseo, 1970—; Vis. scholar Mass. Inst. Tech. Center Internat. Studies, 1960-61; guest researcher Inst. for Research on Soviet Union, Munich, Germany, summer 1962; participant, Am. Sociol. Assn. grantee 6th World Congress of Sociology, Evian, France, fall 1966; vis. prof. Duke, summer 1971; dir. genocide study project NSF, 1977—; lectr. at univs., confs. and on TV in, U.S., Europe, Soviet Union, S.Am. Contbg. author: World Book Ency., 1972—; Cons. editor: Internat. Jour. Contemporary Soc; translator, editor: United and Independent Turania (Zarevand), 1971; Contbr. articles to profl. jours., newspapers. Harvard Lab. Social Relations grantee, 1959; Am. Philos. Soc. grantee, 1961; Am. Com. Travel grantee-in-aid, 1962; Wenner-Gren Found. Anthropol. Research grantee, 1963, 65; Am. Council Learned Socs. grantee, summer 1966; recipient Wis. U. Bd. Regents award, 1966, St. Vardan medal for scholarship in field of Soviet nationalities Cardinal Aghadjanian, Rome, 1968; NSF grantee, 1968, 73, 76; State U. N.Y. grantee-in-aid, 1974. Mem. Delta Tau Kappa (hon.). Home: 1432 W Lake Rd Conesus NY 14435 Office: State U NY Geneseo NY 14454

DAEMMRICH, HORST SIGMUND, educator; b. Pausa, Germany, Jan. 5, 1930; s. Arthur M. and Gertrud A. (Orlamunde) D.; m. Ingrid H. Guenther, June 10, 1962; children: JoAnn, Arthur. A.B. C. Allen Harlan scholar, Wayne State U., 1958, M.A., 1959; Ph.D. (Petersen Kochs fellow, Goethe fellow), U. Chgo., 1964. Instr. U. Chgo., 1961-62; asst. prof. Germanic langs. and lits. Wayne State U., Detroit, 1962-66, asso. prof., 1967-70, prof., 1971—; resident dir. Jr. Year Inst. at U. Freiburg, Germany, 1972-73. Author: The Shattered Self, 1973, Literaturkritik in Theorie und Praxis, 1974, (with Ingrid Daemmrich) Themen und Motive in der Literatur, 1978, Karl Krolow, 1980, Wilhelm Raabe, 1981; editor: The Challenge of German Literature, 1971; contbr. articles to profl. jours. Mem. Am. Soc. Aesthetics, Acad. Lit. Studies, Am. Lessing Soc., Am. Assn. Tchrs. German (mem. commn. on higher edn. 1974—), Am. Comparative Lit. Assn., MLA (sec. and chmn. 19th century lit. 1972-73), Midwest MLA (sec., chmn. modern Germanic lit. 1966-67), Phi Beta Kappa. Home: 307 Suffolk Rd Flourtown PA 19031 Office: Dept Germanic Langs U Pa Philadelphia PA 19104

DAENZER, BERNARD JOHN, insurance executive; b. N.Y.C., Jan. 15, 1916; s. Bernard Cornelius and Amelia Catherine (Heinze) D.; m. Valerie Antoinette Lee, June 8, 1941; children—Peter, Jean Daenzer Aiken, John Richard. A.B., Fordham Coll., 1937; LL.D., 1942; LL.D., Coll. Ins. N.Y.C., 1981. Spl. agt. Loyalty Group, Westchester, N.Y., 1937-43; with Security-Conn. Group, 1943-57, exec. v.p., 1955-57; pres. Wohlrecich & Anderson Ltd., Cranford, N.J., 1957-81; chmn. bd. Limestone Agys. Ltd., Hamilton, Burmuda; dir. Alexander Howden Group Ltd., London, 1968-81; underwriter Lloyds of London, 1968—; dir. RLI Corp., Peoria, Ill. Columnist: Weekly Underwriter, 1964—; Author publs. in field. Trustee Ocean Reef Chapel Inc. Served with USNR, 1944-46. Mem. Coll. Ins. N.Y.C. (past chmn. bd.), Soc. Chartered Property and Casualty Underwriters (past pres. Conn. chpt., past pres. nat. assn.). Republican. Roman Catholic. Clubs: Ocean Reef, Toms River Country, Harbour Course, Card Sound Country, Racquet, Health and Tennis. Office: Ocean Reef Plaza Key Largo FL 33037

DAESCHNER, CHARLES WILLIAM, JR., physician, educator; b. Houston, Dec. 24, 1920; s. Charles William and Maxie Virginia (Hulsey) D.; m. Norma Sederholm, Nov. 14, 1948; children: Charles William III, Mary Lynn, Martha Ann. B.A., Rice Inst., 1942; M.D., U. Tex., 1945. Diplomate: Am. Bd. Pediatrics (dir., past pres., ofcl. examiner). Rotating intern Hermann Hosp., Houston, 1945-46; resident St. Louis Children's Hosp., 1948-50, Children's Med. Center, Boston, 1950-51; instr., then asso. prof. Baylor U. Med. Coll., 1951-60; prof. pediatrics, chmn. dept. U. Tex. Med. Br., Galveston, 1960—; mem.-at-large bd. Nat. Bd. Med. Examiners, 1978—, vice-chmn. exec. bd., 1981-83, chmn. exec. bd., 1983—, also mem. adv. com. undergrad. med. edn. Mem. sci. publs. com.: Tex. Medicine, 1973-81; mem. editorial bd., 1975-81; chmn., 1977—; editorial bd.: Am. Jour. Diseases of Children, 1973-81. Trustee Moody Retirement Home; bd. dirs. Galveston Hist. Dist., 1963-75; mem. Galveston Planning Commn., 1963-75. Served to capt., M.C. USAF, 1946-48. Mem. Am. Acad. Pediatrics (chmn. com. med. edn. 1965-70), Am. Pediatric Soc., So. Soc. Clin. Research, So. Soc. Pediatric Research, AMA, Tex. Pediatric Soc., Galveston County Med. Soc., Assn. Med. Sch. Pediatric Dept. Chmn. (pres. 1970—), Sigma Xi. Home: 1102 Harbor View Dr Galveston TX 77550

DAESCHNER, RICHARD WILBUR, food company executive; b. Preston, Nebr., July 5, 1917; s. Richard T. and Elma (Beckenhauer) D.; m. Prudence Armstrong, June 6, 1942; children: Richard, Rebecca, Martha. B.S. Edn., Kans. State Tchrs. Coll., 1937; J.D., Washburn U., 1941. Bar: Kans. 1941. Spl. agt. FBI, Washington, Boston, N.Y.C., Chgo., 1941-48; with employee relations dept. Beatrice Foods Co., Chgo., 1948—, dir. employee relations, 1963-68, dir. personnel and indsl. relations, asst. sec., 1968-73, asst. v.p., 1973-78, v.p., 1978—.

Mem. Chgo. Bar Assn., Grocery Mfrs. Assn., Ill. C. of C., Chgo. Assn. Commerce and Industry, Am. Mgmt. Assn., Chgo. Better Bus. Bur. (bd. dirs.), Phi Delta Theta. Republican. Presbyterian. Clubs: Exec. (Chgo.); Inverness Golf. Lodge: Elks.

DAEUBLE, LOUIS, architect; b. Leavenworth, Kans., June 7, 1912; s. Louis and Mary Frances (Flynn) D.; m. Margaret Elizabeth Barron, Feb. 25, 1941; children: Louis III, Jon Michael, Ann Barron. B.S. in Architecture, Tex. A&M U., 1932. Draftsman-designer with various architects, El Paso, 1933-41; ptnr. Carroll and Daeuble (later Carroll, Daeuble, DuSang and Rand), Architects), 1945-77; prin. Louis Daeuble (Architect), El Paso, Tex., 1977—; dir. Mut. Savs. Assn., Univ. Bank; mem. Tex. Bd. Archtl. Examiners, chmn., 1955. Mem. Plan Commn. City of El Paso, 1958-62; bd. dirs. El Paso Mus. Art, pres., 1966. Served to lt. col., C.E. and AC U.S. Army, 1941-46. Fellow AIA; mem. Tex. Soc. Architects (v.p. 1960), Tau Beta Pi. Roman Catholic. Club: Rotary (El Paso). Home: 2312 N Virginia St El Paso TX 79902

DAFERMOS, CONSTANTINE MICHAEL, educator; b. Athens, Greece, May 26, 1941; came to U.S., 1964; s. Michael Constantine and Sophia (Raptarchis) D.; m. Stella Theodoracopoulos, Sept. 6, 1964; children—Thalia, Michael. Diploma, Athens Nat. Tech. U., 1964; Ph.D., Johns Hopkins U., 1967. Fellow Johns Hopkins U., 1967-68; asst. prof. Cornell U., 1968-71; asso. prof. Brown U., 1971-76, prof. applied math., 1976—. Mem. editorial bd.: Archive for Rational Mechanics and Analysis, 1972—, Jour. of Thermal Stresses, 1978—; Contbr. articles in field to profl. jours. NSF grantee, 1970—; Office Naval Research grantee, 1972-80; USAF grantee, 1972-73; U.S. Army grantee, 1973—; NASA grantee, 1972-73. Mem. Soc. Natural Philosophy (treas. 1975-76, chmn. 1977-78), Am. Math. Soc., N.Y. Acad. Scis. Office: Division of Applied Mathematics Brown University Providence RI 02912

DAFFIN, IRL ALONZO, industrialist; b. Denton, Md., May 28, 1902; s. Alonzo S. and Arkansas Virginia (Dorsey) D.; m. Nancy Davis, Dec. 26, 1975; children—David K., Damaris Rebecca. Ed. Md. pub. schs. Sales mgr. Dellinger Mfg. Co., Lancaster, Pa., 1932-40; pres. New Holland Machine Co., 1940-47, New Holland Mfg. Co., Mountville, Pa., 1945-47; exec. v.p. New Holland Metals Co., 1947; sec. Lancaster Engring. Corp., Pa., 1946-47, pres., 1947—, Atlas Corp., 1948-49, Hertzler & Zook, Belleville, Pa., 1942-46, Daffin Mfg. Co., Lancaster, 1949-60, Narvon Mines, Ltd., 1962—, Irl Daffin Assos., Inc., 1962—, Warwick Corp., 1970—; chmn. Daffin Corp., Hopkins, Minn., 1960-62, Eastern Corp., Federalsburg, Md., 1970—, Hampden Color and Chem. Co.; dir. Daffin Mobile Products Co. div. Barber-Greene Co.; pres. Daffin Flying Service, 1976—; chmn. bd. Eastern Minerals & Chems. Co., 1982—. Bd. dirs. Lancaster Gen. Hosp.; trustee Lancaster Country Day Sch., Linden Hall Sch. for Girls, 1979-82. Mem. Newcomen Soc. Eng., C. of C. (dir.). Republican. Presbyterian. Clubs: Mason, Shriner, Elk, National Press, Lake Shore, Lancaster Country, Lancaster County Riding, Hamilton, Lancaster Country, University, Radnor Hunt, Beaufort Hunt, Great Oak Lodge and Yacht, Lyford Cay, Porcupine, Rose Tree Hunt, Caroline Country, Talbot Country. Home: Warwick Rd Lititz PA 17543 Office: Lancaster PA 17604

DAFT, JACK ROBERT, landscape architect, educator; b. St. Louis, Jan. 30, 1929; s. Robert and Mary Lillian (McCann) D.; m. Jimmie P. McClifford, Sept. 9, 1950; children: Steven R., Kate M. B.S.L.A., Tex. A & M U., 1957; M.A. in Urban Planning, Morgan State U., 1973. Registered landscape architect, Md., Pa. Asso. Lloyd Assos. (Landscape Architects), Balt., 1959-64; pres. Daft-McCune-Walker, Inc. (Landscape Architects and Engrs.), Balt., 1964-80; asso. prof. landscape architecture Morgan State U., 1979—, chmn. dept. built environ. studies, 1980—; chmn. Md. Bd. Examiners Landscape Architects, 1971—, Md. Interprofl. Com. on Environ. Policy, 1971; mem. Md. Task Force on Storm Water Mgmt., 1972-74. Designs include Eastpoint Mall, Balt., 1975 (Am. Soc. Landscape Architects Merit award), Heather Ridge Planned Community, Balt. (Nat. Assn. Home Builders and Better Homes and Gardens Mag. Grand award 1975, Md. chpt. Am. Soc. Landscape Architects Honor award 1977), Orchard Gardens, Balt., 1976 (Md. chpt. Am. Soc. Landscape Architects Honor award), Orchard Mews, Balt., 1976 (Md. chpt. Am. Soc. Landscape Architects Honor award), Hashawa Exptl. Area, Balt., 1977 (Md. chpt. Am. Soc. Landscape Architects Honor award), Quantico (Va.) Nat. Cemetery, 1979 (Md. chpt. Am. Soc. Landscape Architects Spl. award). Served with USMC, 1948-52. Recipient award of Merit C.E., Raystown Lake, Pa., 1974. Fellow Am. Soc. Landscape Architects (pres. Md. chpt. 1975-76, chmn. nat. films com. 1979-81, Mem., Service to Profession award 1979); mem. Council Landscape Archtl. Registration Bds. (cert.; pres. 1977-78, Mem., pres. Found. 1976-80, Service to Profession award 1980). Home: 302 E Joppa Rd Baltimore MD 21204 Office: Morgan State U Baltimore MD 21239

DAGENAIS, CAMILLE A., engr., corp. exec.; b. Montreal, Que., Can., Nov. 12, 1920. B.A.Sc., Ecole Polytechnique de Montreal, 1946; postgrad., Ecole des Hautes Etudes Commerciales, Montreal, 1969-70; LL.D., U. Toronto, 1973, Concordia U., 1979; D.Sc. (hon.), Royal Mil. Coll. Can., 1975, Laval U., 1977, D.A.Sc., U. Sherbrooke, 1975. Jr. engr. Can. Industries Ltd., Montreal, 1946-47; constrn. engr., Beloeil, Que., 1947-50; project engr. H.J. Doran, Morin Heights, Que., 1950-52, Montreal, 1952-53, Surveyer, Nenniger & Chenevert, 1953-59, partner, 1959—, chmn. bd., gen. mgr., 1965-66, pres., 1966-75, SNC Enterprises Ltd., 1967-75; chmn. bd., chief exec. officer The SNC Group, 1975—; dir. Can. Liquid Air Ltd., Royal Bank of Can., Spar Aerospace Ltd., Institut Armand Frappier, La Societe d'investissement Desjardins. Bd. govs. Conseil du Patronat du Quebec; mem. council Conf. Bd. Can., 1978—; mem. adv. com. Center for Internat. Bus. Studies, Ecole des Hautes Etudes Commerciales, NRC Can., 1972-74. Decorated officer Order of Can., 1973. Fellow Engring. Inst. Can.; mem. Order of Engrs. of Que., Assn. Cons. Engrs. Can. (pres. 1967-68, dir. 1966-70), Can. Soc. for Civil Engring. (pres. 1973), Can. Nuclear Assn. (pres. 1975-76), Internat. Commn. on Large Dams, Can. Export Assn. (dir. 1973-78). Office: The SNC Group 1 Complexe Desjardins PO Box 10 Desjardins Postal Station Montreal PQ H5B 1C8 Canada

DAGENHART, LARRY JONES, lawyer; b. Taylorsville, N.C., July 20, 1932; s. Luther Jones and Louise (Icenhour) D.; m. Sarah Katheryne Petty, June 23, 1956; children: Katie, Mary Louise, Larry Jones. B.S., Davidson (N.C.) Coll., 1953; LL.B., NYU, 1958. Bar: N.C. 1958. Since practiced in Charlotte; partner firm Helms, Mulliss & Johnston. Trustee Davidson Coll.; past pres. Charlotte Arts Council, Charlotte United Appeal. Served to 1st lt. AUS, 1954-56. Root-Tilden scholar. Mem. ABA, Am. Law Inst., Charlotte Bar Assn. (past pres.), Greater Charlotte C. of C. (chmn. 1983); fellow Am. Bar Found. Lutheran. Home: 1601 Biltmore Dr Charlotte NC 28207 Office: 227 N Tryon St Charlotte NC 28280

DAGER, WILLIAM ASHENFELTER, chemical company executive; b. Norristown, Pa., Aug. 4, 1920; s. William Wallas and Louise (Ashenfelter) D.; m. Edna Harriet Hipple, Sept. 27, 1947; children: Margaret Louise Dager Austin, Carol Anne Dager Teodoro. B.S., Chem. Engring., Pa. State U., 1941. Tech. supr. E.J. Levino, Plymouth Meeting, Pa., 1941-43; plant supr. Quaker Chem. Corp., Conshohocken, Pa., 1946-52, plant mgr., Wilmington and Conshohocken, 1952-63; plant and sales mgr. Wilmington and Conshohocken, Pomona, Calif., 1963-76; exec. v.p. Quaker Chem. Corp., Conshohocken, Pa., 1976—; pvt. practice cons. Simplex Precise Instruments, 1947-53. Mem. Lutheran Ch. Council, Blue Bell, Pa., 1956-60. Served with U.S. Army, 1943-46. Mem. Am. Chem. Soc., Am. Inst. Structural Engrs., Assn. Iron and Steel Engrs., Delta Sigma Phi. Office: Quaker Chem Corp Elm & Sanoy Conshohocken Pa 19428

DAGGATT, WALTER RUSSELL, soft drink mfg. co. exec.; b. Portland, Oreg., Mar. 16, 1919; s. Harold William and Eliza (Woodward) D.; m. Marjorie McKinlay, Sept. 2, 1942; children—Peter (dec.), Andrew, Scott, Russell. B.A. (sr. fellow 1942), Dartmouth Coll., 1943. Vice pres. Rubberset div. Bristol-Myers Co., Newark, 1943-57; v.p. Skinner Corp., Seattle, 1957-79, dir., cons., 1980—; pres., chmn. bd. Alpac Corp., Seattle, 1957-79, dir., cons., 1980—. Founder, mng. partner Seattle Sounders, profl. soccer team, 1973-79; Pres., chmn. bd. Seattle-King County Boys' Clubs, 1970-71. Served with USMCR, 1941-43. Mem. N.Am. Soccer League (exec. com.), Phi Beta Kappa, Phi Gamma Delta. Clubs: Seattle Golf (trustee 1980—), Wash. Athletic, University, Overlake Golf (past trustee), Harbor.). Home: 9000 NE 14th St Bellevue WA 98004 Office: 720 Skinner Bldg Seattle WA 98101

DAGGETT, ROBERT SHERMAN, lawyer; b. La Crosse, Wis., Sept. 16, 1930; s. Willard Manning and Vida Naomi (Sherman) D.; m. Lee Sullivan Burton, Sept. 16, 1960; children: Ann Sherman, John Sullivan; m. Helen Ackerman, July 20, 1976. A.B. with honors in Polit. Sci. and Journalism, U. Calif.-Berkeley, 1952, J.D., 1955. Bar: Calif. 1955, U.S. Supreme Ct. 1967. Assoc. firm Brobec, Phleger & Harrison, San Francisco, 1958-66, ptnr., 1966—; counsel Calif. Senate Reapportionment Com., 1972-73; adj. prof. evidence and advocacy Hastings Coll. Law, 1982—; demonstrator-instr. Nat. Inst. for Trial Advocacy, 1981—, Hastings Ctr. for Trial and Appellate Advocacy, 1981—, mem. adv. bd., 1983—; vol. pro tem small claims judge San Francisco Mcpl. Ct., 1981—. Bd. editors: Calif. Law Rev., 1953-55; contbr. articles to profl. jours. Rep. Pacific Assn. AAU, 1973; bd. dirs. San Francisco Legal Aid Soc.; bd. visitors Coll. V U. Calif.-Santa Cruz. Served to 1st lt. JAGC U.S. Army, 1958-62. Walter Perry Johnson scholar, 1953. Mem. ABA, State Bar Calif. (chmn. local adminstrv. com. 1964-65), San Francisco Bar Assn. (past dir.), Am. Judicature Soc., Order of Golden Bear, Phi Delta Phi, Theta Xi. Republican. Club: Bohemian (San Francisco). Office: Brobeck Phleger & Harrison Spear St Tower One Market Plaza San Francisco CA 94105

DAGIT, CHARLES EDWARD, JR., architecture educator, architect; b. Phila., July 1, 1943; s. Charles E. and Janet (Donnelly) D.; m. Alice M. Murdoch, June 3, 1967; children: Charles Edward, J. Murdoch. B.A., U. Pa., 1965, B.Arch., 1967, M.Arch., 1968. Registered architect, Pa.; registered architect, N.J. Designer Henry D. Dagit & Sons, Phila., 1965-68, Mitchell, Giurgola Assocs., 1968-69; project designer Henry D. Dagit & Sons, Phila., 1969-70; architect Dagit Saylor Architects, Phila., 1970—. Works include Serbin residence (Pa. award 1974), Phoenix City Ctr. for Arts (NEA grant), 1983. Pres. Gladwyne Civic Assn., 1981-82, Friends of St. Christopher's Hosp., Phila., 1977-78; trustee Bryn Mawr. (Pa.) Country Day Sch., 1975-79; bd. dirs. Phila. Zool. Soc., 1979—. Recipient Design award Progressive Architecture, 1974, 40 Under 40 award A&U Mag., Japan, 1977, View of World Contemporary Architecture award Japan Architect, 1977. Fellow AIA (Gold medal 1978). Republican. Roman Catholic. Clubs: Merion Golf (Ardmore, Pa.); Mask and Wig (Phila.). Home: 381 Williamson Rd Gladwyne PA 19035 Office: Dagit Saylor Architects 1133 Arch St Philadelphia PA 19107

DAGLEY, STANLEY, biochemist, educator; b. Burton-on-Trent, Eng., Apr. 1, 1916; came to U.S., 1963, naturalized, 1976; s. Arthur and Agnes Susannah (Walker) D.; m. Pasca Alice Stretton, June 24, 1939; children—Michael, Pauline Dagley White, Jane Dagley Bellion, Helen. B.A., U. Oxford, 1937, B.Sc., 1938, M.A., 1946; M.Sc., U. London, 1948, D.Sc., 1955. Sr. lectr. chemistry Sir John Cass Coll., London, 1945-47; lectr. biochemistry U. Leeds, Eng., 1947-52, reader, 1952-62, prof., 1962-66; vis. prof. U. Ill., 1963-64; prof. dept. biochemistry U. Minn., St. Paul, 1966-80, Regents' prof., 1980—. Author: (with Nicholson) An Introduction to Metabolic Pathways, 1970; Co-editor: Biochem. Edn, 1974—; Contbr. articles to profl. jours. Recipient Horace T. Morse award for outstanding contbns. to undergrad. edn. U. Minn., 1969; NSF Sr. Fgn. Scientist fellow, 1963. Mem. Biochem. Soc., Soc. for Gen. Microbiology, Am. Chem. Soc., Am. Soc. Microbiology, Am. Soc. Biol. Chemists (com. on ednl. affairs 1974—), Internat. Union Biochemistry (edn. com. 1976—). Episcopalian. Home: 2288 Carter Ave St Paul MN 55108

DAGNESE, JOSEPH MARTOCCI, librarian; b. Worcester, Mass., Oct. 10, 1927; s. Gennaro Francis and Carmella Veronica (Martocci) D.; (div.)children: Joseph Michael, Paul Andrew, Edward Peter. B.A., Boston Coll., 1949; M.A., Catholic U. Am., 1951, M.L.S., 1952; postgrad., Heidelberg (Germany) U., 1954-55. Cataloger Cath. U. Am., 1955-57; librarian Nuclear Metals, Inc., Concord, Mass., 1957-60; head acquisitions dept. Mass. Inst. Tech., 1960-62, sci. librarian, head circulation dept., 1962-66, asst. dir. tech. services, 1966-72; dir. libraries Purdue U., West Lafayette, Ind., 1972—; cons. Birla Inst. Tech., Pilani (Rajasthan), India, 1966-67, Delhi U., India, 1970; bd. dirs. Center for Research Libraries, 1981-84; v.p., pres.-elect Universal Serials and Book Exchange, 1984. Contbr. articles to profl. jours. Served with U.S. Army, 1952-54. Mem. Spl. Libraries Assn. (pres. Boston chpt. 1964-65, chpt. liaison officer 1970-72, John Cotton Dana lectr. 1972, chmn. com. on positive action 1972-74, dir. 1974-77, pres.-elect 1978-79, pres. 1979-80), Assn. Research Libraries. Home: 456 S 8th St Lafayette IN 47901

D'AGOSTINO, PETER PASQUALE, artist, educator; b. N.Y.C., July 29, 1945; s. Pasquale P. and Annunziata (Pitaniello) D'A.; m. Deirdre Dowdakin, Aug. 5, 1977. Student, Acad. Fine Arts, Naples, Italy, 1965-66; B.F.A. (Grad. Scholar), Sch. of Visual Arts, 1967; M.A., San Francisco State U., 1975. Instr. art and theatre arts Lone Mountain Coll., San Francisco, 1973-76; instr. San Francisco Art Inst., 1976-77, U. Calif., Berkeley Extension, 1977; asst. prof. art Wright State U., Dayton, Ohio, 1977-80; vis. artist UCLA, 1981; artist-in-residence TV Lab., WNET, N.Y.C., 1981. Producer various radio and TV shows, Calif., 1976, 77, Ohio, 1977-80, one-man shows include, Quay Gallery, San Francisco, 1973, Lone Mountain Coll., 1975, San Francisco Art Inst., 1976, Fine Arts Mus. of San Francisco, Floating Mus., San Francisco, San Francisco Mus. Modern Art, 1977, Ohio State U., Columbus, 1978, Lawson de Celle Gallery, San Francisco, Artists Space, N.Y.C., Mus. Modern Art, N.Y.C., 1979, Long Beach (Calif.) Mus. Art, Contemporary Art Center, Cin., Los Angeles Inst. Contemporary Art, 1980, Univ. Art Mus., Berkeley, Anthology Film Archives, N.Y.C., 1981, group shows include, Sch. of Visual Arts, N.Y.C., 1968, San Francisco Art Inst., 1975, Aarhus Mus. of Art, Denmark, 1976, Fine Arts Mus. of San Francisco, 1977, San Francisco Mus. Modern Art, 1976, 78, 79, Mus. of Modern Art, Bologna, Italy, 1977, Kemein Art Gallery, Tokyo, Japan, Ohio Wesleyan U., Delaware, 1978, Wright State U., 1979, Washington Project for the Arts, Washington, Everson Mus. Art, Syracuse, N.Y., Mus. of Contemporary Art, Chgo., Northwest Film Study Center, Portland, Oreg., 1979, Video 80, San Francisco, 1980, Whitney Mus. Am. Art, 1981; represented in permanent collections, Long Beach Mus. of Art, Oakland (Calif.) Mus., U. Calif., Berkeley, Sch. of Visual Arts, N.Y.C., San Francisco Public Library, San Francisco Mus. Modern Art. Nat. Endowment for the Arts fellow, 1974, 77, 79; Ohio Arts Council grantee, 1979, 80. Mem. Coll. Art Assn. Am., Internat. Art Network. Home: PO Box 566 Canal St Station NY 10013

D'AGOSTINO, RALPH BENEDICT, mathematician, statistician, educator; b. Somerville, Mass., Aug. 16, 1940; s. Bennedetto and Carmela (Piemonte) D'A.; m. Lei Lanie Carta, Aug. 28, 1965; children: Ralph Benedict, Lei Lanie Maria. A.B., Boston U., 1962, M.A., 1964; Ph.D., Harvard U., 1968. Lectr. math. Boston U., 1964-68, asst. prof., 1968-71, assoc. prof., 1971-76, prof., 1976—, lectr. law, 1975—, adj. prof. pub. health, 1982—, asso. dean, 1976-78; statis. cons. United Brands, 1968-76, Diabetes and Arthritis Control Unit, Boston, 1971-75, City of Somerville, Mass., 1972, ednl. div. Bolt, Beranek & Newman, 1971, Harvard Dental Sch., 1969; cons. biostats. Lahey Clinic Found., 1973—, Walden research, 1974-79, FDA, 1975—, Arnold & Porter, 1980, Bedford Research, 1976-81, GCA, 1979—, Lever Bros., 1982—, Conrail, 1981, also various research insts.; mem. Fertility and Maternal Health Drugs Adv. Com., FDA, 1978—; mem. life support subcom. FDA, 1979—, mem. task force on design and analysis in dental and oral research, 1979—; mem. task force Office of Tech. Assessment, 1980—; prin., co-prin. investigator, or sr. statistician Nat. Center Health Services Research, 1976—, U.S. Air Force, 1980—; prin., co-prin., investigator, or sr. statistician Nat. Inst. Criminal Justice, 1982—, Nat. Ctr. Child Abuse and Neglect, 1982—, Robert Wood Johnson Found., 1981—. Author: (with E.E. Cureton) Factor Analysis, An Applied Approach, 1981; assoc. editor: Am. Statistician, 1972-76, Stats. in Medicine, 1981—; editor: Health Service Research Quar, 1981—; book reviewer, Houghton Mifflin, Holden-Day, Duxbury Press, Prentice Hall, 1969—; contbr. articles to profl. jours. Recipient spl. citation FDA Commr., 1981. Mem. Am. Statis. Assn. (pres. Boston chpt. 1972, v.p. 1971, mem. nat. council 1973-75, vis. lectr. 1976-78, 80—), Inst. Math. Stats., Am. Soc. Quality Control, Phi Beta Kappa, Sigma Xi. Home: 5 Everett Ave Winchester MA 01890 Office: Dept Math Boston U 264 Bay State Rd Boston MA 02215

D'AGOSTINO, STEPHEN I., bottling company executive; b. N.Y.C., Oct. 23, 1933; s. Nicholas J. and Josephine D'A.; m. Mary Egan, July 2, 1955; children: Mary Jo, Joseph, Christopher, Gregory, Elizabeth, Sarah, Constance. B.A., Holy Cross Coll., 1955. With D'Agostino Supermarkets, New Rochelle, N.Y., 1955-82, controller, 1960-78, chmn., chief exec. officer, 1978-82; pres., chief operating officer JTL Corp., Chattanooga, 1982—; dir. Am. Nat. Bank, Chattanooga, Super Valu Stores, Mpls. Mem. Food Mktg. Inst. (chmn.), N.Y. State Food Mchts. (past chmn.), N.Y. Zool. Soc. Office: 700 Krystal Bldg Chattanooga TN 37402 *

DAHL, ADRIAN HILMAN, biophysicist; b. Modd, N.D., Dec. 6, 1919; s. Fredrick A. and Tonetta Martha (Fortney) D.; m. Norma Lee Hargadine, Nov. 9, 1979; children: David, Adrian, Sonje Ann. B.A., St. Olaf Coll., 1941; Ph.D., U. Rochester, 1953. Physicist Eastman Kodak Co., Rochester, N.Y., 1941-43, Oak Ridge, 1943-46; chief radiation instruments br. AEC, Washington, 1946-49; chief radiation physics sect. Atomic Energy Project U. Rochester Med. Sch., 1950-58; prin. scientist Oak Ridge Inst. Nuclear Studies, 1959-61; prof. physics and radiation biology Colo. State U., Ft. Collins, 1961-69; chief astrogeophysics sect. Martin Marietta Corp., Denver, 1969-71; chief environ. scis. br. ERDA, Idaho Falls, Idaho, 1971-76, tech. adv., 1976-77; tng. coordinator in health physics Los Alamos Sci. Lab., 1978—; Fulbright lectr. Argentina AEC, 1958; IAEA expert in radioisotopes, Indonesia, 1961; cons. Viking Search for Life on Mars Martin Marietta Corp. and TRW, 1971-74. Contbr. articles to profl. jours. Mem. Am. Inst. Physics, Am. Phys. Soc., Am. Assn. Physics Tchrs., Health Physics Soc., AAAS, IEEE, Sigma Xi, Sigma Pi Sigma. Lutheran. Lodge: Elks. Office: Los Alamos Nat Lab MS 401 PO Box 1663 Los Alamos NM 87545

DAHL, ARLENE, actress, beauty columnist, fashion designer, author, cosmetic exec.; b. Mpls., Aug. 11, 1928; d. Rudolph and Idelle (Swan) D.; m. Rounsevelle Schaum; children—Lorenzo Lamas, Carole Christine Holmes, Rounsevelle Andreas. Student (1st, 2d, 3d prizes for fashion designs), U. Minn., Minn. Inst. Art, Minn. Coll. Music, Minn. Bus. Coll. Pres. Woman's World div. Kenyon & Eckhart, 1967-72; also v.p. Kenyon & Eckhart, 1967-72; pres. Arlene Dahl Enterprises, 1967-77; nat. beauty adviser Sears Roebuck, 1970-75; internat. dir. Sales and Mktg. Execs. Internat., 1972-75; fashion dir. O.M.A., 1975-78; pres. Dahlia Parfums, Inc., 1975—, Dahlia Productions, Inc., 1978—. Author: Always Ask a Man, 1965, 12 Beautyscope books, 1968, rev. edit., 78, Arlene Dahl's Secrets of Hair Care, 1970, Beyond Beauty, 1980; played: Broadway appearances include One Touch of Venus; Applause, Questionable Ladies, Mr. Strauss Goes to Boston, Cyrano de Bergerac; played Chicago in: One Touch of Venus; played: Broadway appearances include The Camel Bell, Blithe Spirit; toured in, Liliom, The King and I, Roman Candle, I Married an Angel, Bell, Book and Candle, Applause, Marriage Go Round, Pal Joey, A Little Night Music, Forty Carats, Life With Father, Murder Among Friends, night 1967-77; act, Flamingo Hotel, Las Vegas, Latin Quarter, N.Y.C.; numerous motion pictures include debut in My Wild Irish Rose, 1947, Three Little Words, Desert Legion, Sangaree, Kisses for My President, Woman's World, Journey to the Center of the Earth, Les Poneyettes, The Landgrabbers, The Way to Kathmandu; internat. syndicated beauty columnist, 1950-70; designer sleepwear for, A.N. Saab & Co., 1952-57, In Vogue, (with Arlene Dahl Patterns), 1980—; TV appearances include Lux Video Theatre, 1952, 53; hostess: Pepsi-Cola Theatre, 1954, Opening Night series, 1958, Arlene Dahl's Beauty Spot series, 1966, Arlene Dahl's Starscope series, 1979-80; also guest starring appearances all networks, 1967—. Hon. life mem. Father Flannagan's Boys Town; bd. dirs. Hollywood Museum; internat. chmn. Pearl Buck Found., 1975—. Recipient Laurel award Box Office Mag., 8 times, 1948-63; named Best-Coiffed, 3 times, 1963-75; Woman of Yr. Advt. Club of N.Y.C., 1969. Mem. Author's Guild, Acad. Motion Picture Arts and Scis., Commanderie des Bontemps de Bordeaux.

DAHL, ARTHUR ERNEST, former manufacturing executive, consultant; b. Alexis, Ill., Sept. 16, 1916; s. Ernest Victor and Emma P. (Olson) D.; m. Dorothy Evelyn Peterson, Sept. 10, 1944; children: John Arthur, Robert Alan. Student, Augustana Coll., Rock Island, Ill., 1935-39. Head planning div. Home-O-Nize Co., Mascatine, Iowa, 1947-50; v.p., gen. mgr. The Prime Mover Co., Muscatine, 1950-70, chmn. bd., 1982, 83; sr. v.p. HON Industries Inc., Muscatine, 1970-81; dir. Bank of Alexis, 1979-83, pres., 1983; cons., 1981—; dir. J-Tel Assocs., Cedar Rapids, Iowa. Bd. dirs. Augustana Coll., 1976-82, mem. exec. com., 1979-82; mem. Iowa State Investment Adv. Bd., 1975-81; mem. council Grace Lutheran Ch., Muscatine. Served with U.S. Army, 1942-43. Republican. Home: 421 Parkington Dr Muscatine IA 52761

DAHL, CURTIS, educator; b. New Haven, July 6, 1920; s. George and Elizabeth Eudora (Curtis) D.; m. Mary Huntington Kellogg, Nov. 15, 1952; children: Julia Curtis, Winthrop Huntington Kellogg. B.A., Yale U., 1941, M.A., 1942, Ph.D., 1945. Dir. fellowships, asst. to editor Dodd, Mead & Co., 1944-46; instr. English, U. Tenn., 1946-48; mem. faculty Wheaton Coll., Norton, Mass., 1948—, prof., 1958—, Samuel Valentine Cole prof. English lit., 1966—; vis. prof. So. Ill. U., 1964, 66, 70, U. Wash., 1967, Brown U., 1970. Author: Robert Montgomery Bird, 1963; editor: "There She Blows": A Narrative of a Whaling Voyage, 1971; contbr. articles to profl. jours. Fence-viewer Town of

Norton, 1964-77, selectman, 1970-73; chmn. Norton Historic Dist. Commn., 1975—, Norton Hist. Commn., 1976-80. Carnegie fellow Harvard U., 1954-55; Guggenheim fellow, 1957-58; Fulbright prof. U. Oslo, 1965-66. Mem. MLA, Coll. English Assn., Melville Soc., Boston Browning Soc., Soc. Archtl. Historians, Presbyn. Hist. Soc., Victorian Soc. Republican. Home: 189 N Washington St Norton MA 02766 Office: Wheaton Coll Norton MA 02766 *Too few people today know the difference between "uninterested" and "disinterested."*

DAHL, ERNO JOYCE, coll. pres.; b. Waco, Tex., Nov. 11, 1928; s. Hans Bernhard and Sylvia (Nelson) D.; m. Suzanne Louise Preus, July 24, 1953; children—Jeremy Eliot Preus, Jeffrey Erno. B.A., Luther Coll., Decorah, Iowa, 1952; B.Th., Luther Theol. Sem., St. Paul, 1955; Ph.D., Durham (Eng.) U., 1957. Prof. theology Tex. Luth. Coll., Seguin, 1957-68, acad. dean, 1964-68; dean coll. Wittenberg U., Springfield, Ohio, 1968-70, v.p. academic affairs, 1970-77; pres. Carthage Coll., Kenosha, Wis., 1977—; ordained to ministry Luth. Ch., 1960; chmn. Luth. Faculty Conf. S.W., 1964-68; mem. commn. pub. relations Tex. Council Ch. Related Colls., 1964-68; mem. commn. standards and classification Assn. Tex. Colls. and Univs., 1967-68. Served with USMCR, 1946-48. Mem. Am. Assn. Higher Edn., Am. Assn. Colls. Tchrs. Edn., Am. Acad. Religion, Soc. Sci. Study Religion. Home: 623 17th Pl Kenosha WI 53140

DAHL, HARRY WALDEMAR, lawyer; b. Des Moines, Aug. 7, 1927; s. Harry Waldemar and Helen Gerda (Anderson) D.; m. Bonnie Sorensen, June 14, 1952; children: Harry Waldemar, Lisabeth (dec.), Christina. B.A., U. Iowa, 1950; J.D., Drake U., 1955. Bar: Iowa 1955, Fla. 1970. Practiced in Des Moines, 1955-59, 70—, Miami, Fla., 1972—; mem. firm Steward & Crouch, Des Moines, 1955-59; Iowa dep. indsl. commr., Des Moines, 1959-62, commr., 1962-71; mem. Dahl law firm, Des Moines, 1970—; mem. firm Underwood, Gillis and Karcher, Miami, 1972-77; adj. prof. law Drake U., 1972—; Exec. dir. Internat. Assn. Indsl. Accident Bds. and Commns., 1972-77; pres. Workers Compensation Studies, Inc., 1974—, Workers' Compensation Services, Inc., 1978—, Hewitt, Coleman & Assos. Iowa, Inc., 1975-79; mem. adv. com. Second Injury Fund, Fla. Indsl. Relations Commn. Author: Iowa Law on Workmen's Compensation, 1975; Editor: ABC Newsletter, 1964-77. Served with USNR, 1945-46. Adminstrs. award, 1967. Mem. Am. Trial Lawyers Assn., Am., Iowa, Fla. bar assns., Am. Soc. Law and Medicine (council 1975—), Iowa Assn. Workers' Compensation Lawyers (co-founder, pres.), Coll. of Workers Compensation Inc. (co-founder, regent), Swedish Pioneer Hist. Soc., Am. Swedish Inst., Des Moines Pioneer Club, East High Alumni Assn. (pres. 1975-76), Order of Coif. Lutheran. Clubs: Masons, Shriners, Sertoma (chmn. bd. 1974-75). Home: 3005 Sylvania Dr West Des Moines IA 50265 Office: 5835 Grand Ave Suite 201 Des Moines IA 50312

DAHL, JOHN ANTON, teacher educator; b. Ft. Dodge, Iowa, Feb. 14, 1922; s. Harry Arthur and Margaret (Schumacher) D.; m. May-Margaret Johnson, Sept. 8, 1964; children by previous marriage: John B., Kenneth M.; stepchildren: Douglas Wright, Kimberley Wright. B.A., San Jose (Calif.) State Coll., 1944; M.A., Stanford, 1950, Ed.D., 1952. Tchr., counselor, adminstr. Calif. pub. high schs., 1946-50; sec. coordinator and cons. guidance Tulare County (Calif.) schs., 1952-55; mem. faculty Calif. State U., Los Angeles, 1955—, prof. edn., 1960—, prof. counselor edn., 1972—; dean (Sch. Edn.), 1966-68, acting v.p. for bus. affairs, 1970-71, asst. v.p. acad. affairs, 1971-72, chmn. counselor edn. dept., 1978-81; vis. lectr. Claremont Grad. Sch., 1960-62, Occidental Coll., 1962-63, Fresno State Coll., 1953-54; cons. in field, 1956—. Author: (with others) Student, School and Society, 1964; also articles. Treas. H.B. McDaniel Found., 1977-83. Served with USAAF, 1943-45. Mem. San Joaquin Valley Guidance Assn. (pres. 1954-55), Calif. Assn. Secondary Secondary Sch. Curriculum Coordinator (pres. 1960-61), Calif. Assn. Secondary Sch. Adminstrs. (dist. officer, state rep.), Am. Assn. Colls. Tchrs. Edn. (state liaison rep.), AAUP, Nat. Soc. Study Edn., Am. Personnel and Guidance Assn., Calif. Assn. Humanistic Edn. and Devel. (exec. bd. 1977-79, pres. 1980-81), Phi Delta Kappa. Home: 930-D Ocean View Ave Monrovia CA 91016 Office: 5151 State University Dr Los Angeles CA 90032

DAHL, ROALD, writer; b. Llandaff, South Wales, Sept. 13, 1916; s. Harold and Sofie (Hesselberg) D.; m. Patricia Neal, July 2, 1953; children: Olivia (dec.), Tessa, Theo, Ophelia, Lucy. Student, Repton (Eng.) Sch., 1930-34. Author: juveniles The Gremlins, 1943, James and the Giant Peach, 1962, Charlie and the Chocolate Factory, 1964, The Magic Finger, 1965, Fantastic Mr. Fox, 1970, Charlie and the Great Glass Elevator, 1972, Danny, the Champion of the World, 1975, The Wonderful Story of Henry Sugar and Six More, 1977, The Enormous Crocodile, 1978, The Twits, 1981, George's Marvellous Medicine, 1981, Dirty Beasts, 1982, Revolting Rhymes, 1982, The BFG, 1983, The Witches, 1984; short story collections Over to You, 1945, Someone Like You, 1953, Kiss Kiss, 1960, Switch Bitch, 1974, Tales of the Unexpected, 1979, My Uncle Oswald, 1980, More Tales of the Unexpected, 1980; fable Sometime Never, 1948; plays The Honeys, 1953; screenplays You Only Live Twice, 1967, Chitty Chitty Bang Bang, 1968, Willy Wonka and the Chocolate Factory, 1971. Served to wing comdr. RAF, 1943. Recipient Edgar Allen Poe award Mystery Writers Am. Soc., 1954, 59. Address: Gipsy House Great Missenden Bucks England

DAHL, ROBERT KENNETH, electronics co. exec.; b. Oakland, Calif., Dec. 31, 1940; s. Peder Pederson and Ethel Lydia (Lilja) D.; m. Patricia Mitchell, Apr. 9, 1960; children—Kenneth Scott, Keith Allen. B.S. with honors, U. Calif., Berkeley, 1963. C.P.A., Calif. Auditor mgr. Price Waterhouse & Co., C.P.A., San Francisco, Sacramento, Oakland, Calif. and London, 1963-71; controller Fairchild Camera and Instrument Corp., Mountain View, Calif. and Wiesbaden, W.Ger., 1971-75; sr. v.p. fin. Measurex Corp., Cupertino, Calif., 1975-79; v.p. fin. Rolm Corp., Santa Clara, Calif., 1979—. Recipient Haskins & Sells Found. award, 1963; Alfred Sloan Meml. scholar, 1960-63. Mem. Fin. Execs. Inst., Am. Inst. C.P.A.'s, Calif. Bus. Sch. Alumni Assn., Calif. Soc. C.P.A.'s. Club: University. Home: 130 Willowbrook Dr Portola Valley CA 94025 Office: 4900 Old Ironsides Dr Santa Clara CA 95050

DAHL, THOMAS MOORE, engineering and construction company executive; b. Mpls., Aug. 8, 1918; s. Walter H. and Helen (Moore) D.; m. Gail Gilje, Feb. 20, 1943; children: Susan, Janet. Vice pres. United Engrs. & Constructors Inc., Phila., 1958-71, pres., chief operating officer, 1971-76, chmn. bd., chief exec. officer, 1976—; dir. Atomic Indsl. Forum, Jackson & Moreland Internat., UE&C Internat., United Mid-East, Inc., Piccon Inc. Bd. dirs. Med. Coll. Pa. Mem. Assn. Iron and Steel Engrs., IEEE. Clubs: Aronimink Golf; Union League (Phila.); Masons. Office: 30 S 17th St Philadelphia PA 19101

DAHLBERG, EDWIN LENNART, artist; b. Beloit, Wis., Sept. 20, 1901; s. Edwin Tore D. and Anna Sophia Eckholm; m. Gertrude Ernestine Seligman, Dec. 30, 1927; children: Eric Charles, Karen Dahlberg VanderVen, Clare Anna Dahlberg Horner. Grad., Art Inst., Chgo., 1924. Illustrator Graumen-Jennings Studio, Chgo., Il, 1925-32; free lance illustrator, N.Y.C, 1932-59, painter watercolors, Nyack, N.Y., 1959—. Recipient medal of honor Knickerboker Artists, 1970. Mem. Am. Watercolor Soc. (Gold medal 1972), Allied Artists Am., Nat. Acad. Design, Hudson Valley Art Assn. (Gold Medal of Honor and others 1974). Home: 6 South Blvd Nyack NY 10960

DAHLBERG, ERIC JOHN, JR., educator; b. Portland, Oreg., Oct. 13, 1934; s. Eric John and Evelyn Hazel (Ahnquist) D.; m. Carol Jean Edlund, Mar. 10, 1957; children—Nancy Lynn, Jane Ellen, Andrew William. B.A., Pacific Luth. U., 1957; M.A., Lewis and Clark Coll., 1962; Ed.D., U. Oreg., 1969. Tchr., adminstr. Beaverton (Oreg.) Public Schs., 1958-67; research asst. U. Oreg., 1967-69; field staff specialist Northwest Regional Ednl. Lab., Territory of Guam, 1969-70; prof. edn. Boise (Idaho) State U., 1970—; now also coordinator grad. studies Sch. Edn.; cons. to public schs. in, Oreg., Idaho.; Mem. rev. com. Am. Field Service, 1971—; adviser to Guam Dept. Edn., 1972. Contbr. articles to publs. in field. Mem. Comparative Edn. Soc., Comparative and Internat. Edn. Soc. (dir.), Western Region Comparative and Internat. Edn. Soc. (chmn., mem. exec. com.), Joint Council Econ. Edn., Oreg. Hist. Soc., Idaho Hist. Soc., Nat. Council Social Studies, Phi Delta Kappa (pres. local chpt.). Lutheran (pres. congregation). Clubs: Kiwanis (chmn. vocat. edn. com. 1972-73, chmn. external affairs com. Home: 4560 Cassia St Boise ID 83705

DAHLBERG, LEROY WALDO, lawyer; b. Boone, Iowa, Aug. 14, 1904; s. Oscar Frederick and Vendla Sophia (Johnson) D.; m. Julia France, Mar. 10, 1945; children: Christine, Lyle. Student, Wayne State U., 1920-22; A.B., U. Mich., 1925; J.D., U. Chgo., 1930. Bar: Ill. 1931, Mich. 1931. Partner firm Dahlberg, Mallender & Gawne, Detroit, 1931-; former dir. Mfrs. Nat. Bank Detroit. Trustee Wayne State U. Fund, Cranbrook Ednl. Community, Cranbrook Inst. Sci., Detroit Swedish Council; vestryman Christ Ch., Cranbrook. Fellow Am. Bar Found.; mem. Newcomen Soc., Econ. Club Detroit. Episcopalian. Clubs: Hidden Valley Ski (Gaylord, Mich.); Bloomfield Hills (Mich.) Country, Birmingham Tennis. Home: 3864 Peabody Dr Bloomfield Hills MI 48013 Office: 280 N Woodward Ave Birmingham MI 48011

DAHLEM, MAURICE JACOB, accountant; b. Rialto, Calif., Dec. 23, 1912; s. Rudolph Jacob and Lonie (Beckley) D.; m. Harriet Janet Ruth, Dec. 20, 1938; children: Susan Marie (Mrs. Craig K. Harris), John Stephen, Gregory Stewart. A.B. in Econs, UCLA, 1934. C.P.A., Calif., other states. With Price Waterhouse, C.P.A.s, Los Angeles, 1934-73, ptnr., 1952-73, ret., 1973. Past pres. Town Hall, Los Angeles; commr. Gt. Western council Boy Scouts Am., 1957-62; Past pres. Republican Assos., Los Angeles; hon. trustee, past treas. UCLA Found.; trustee Calif. Mus. Found. Mem. Am. Inst. C.P.A.s (mem. council 1962-68, exec. com. 1964-68), Calif. Soc. C.P.A.s (pres. 1962-63), Nat. Assn. Accts. (nat. dir. 1955-57), UCLA Alumni Assn. (bd. dirs. 1962-65, treas. 1963-65), Los Angeles Area C. of C. (past pres.). Episcopalian. Clubs: Rotarian., Los Angeles Country, California (Los Angeles). Home: 2141 La Mesa Dr Santa Monica CA 90402 Office: 606 S Olive St Los Angeles CA 90014

DAHLER, JOHN SPILLERS, chemist, educator; b. Wichita, Kans., May 7, 1930; s. Raymond Edward and Agnes (Spillers) D.; m. Lanaya Dorothy Williams, June 30, 1954 (dec. Feb. 1977); children: Kurt Williams (dec.), Gwendolyn Kay.; m. Dorothy Robinson, Feb. 27, 1982. B.S., U. Wichita, 1951, M.S., 1952; Ph.D., U. Wis., 1955. NSF postdoctoral fellow, Amsterdam, 1955-56; prof. chemistry and chem. engring. U. Minn., 1959—; NSF sr. postdoctoral fellow U. Calif., Berkeley, 1965; vis. prof. chemistry lab III U. Copenhagen, Denmark, 1973; vis. prof. theoretical chemistry inst. U. Wis., Madison, 1980. Asst. editor: Physics of Fluids, 1964-67; asso. editor: Chem. Engring. Sci, 1968, Jour. Statis. Physics, 1969-; mem. editorial bd. on chem. engring., Prentice-Hall, 1966; Contbr. articles to profl. jours. Del. Dem. State Conv., 1968; mem. Minn. Dem. Central Com., 1968-70. Served to 1st lt. USAF, 1956-58. Mem. Am. Phys. Soc., Soc. Natural Phil. Office: U Minn Dept Chemistry and Chem Engring Minneapolis MN 55455

DAHLGREN, CARL HERMAN PER, educator; b. N.Y.C., July 2, 1929; s. Harry W.A. and Ester Florence (Carlson) D.; m. Ella Kate Bowes, Oct. 8, 1960; children: Robert C., John L., Per M., Eva B. Mus.B., Westminster Choir Coll., Princeton, N.J., 1954. Project dir. Benson & Benson, Princeton, 1954-55; asst. head spl. research and analysis Gallup & Robinson, Princeton, N.J., 1956-57; v.p., artist mgr. Columbia Artists Mgmt., Inc., N.Y.C., 1958-68, dir., 1962-68; v.p. Hurok Concerts, Inc., N.Y.C., 1968-70, asso., 1970-74; pres. Dahlgren Arts Mgmt., Inc., Denver, 1970-78; sr. partner Dahlgren, Schiffmann & Assos., N.Y.C., 1978-80; asso. prof. U. Cin., 1978—, acting head broadcasting div., 1979-80; dir. masters program-arts adminstrn. Coll.-Conservatory Music, 1978—. Co-founder, exec. dir. Westminster Choir Coll. Alumni Fund Assn., 1954-59; mgr. Princeton Symphony Orch., 1957-59; dir. Central City (Colo.) Opera House, 1970-72; bd. dirs. Gilpin County Arts Assn., 1970-76; bd. dirs., sec. Colo. Celebration of Arts, 1974-76; pres. Classic Choral, 1975-78, Cin. Chamber Orch., 1982—; trustee Westminster Choir Coll., 1967-74. Served with AUS, 1947-49. Decorated knight 1st Class Order of Lion, Finland; recipient Merit award Westminster Choir Coll. Mem. Am. Symphony Orch. League, Nat. Assn. Concert and Festival Mgrs., Nat. Trust Historic Preservation. Republican. Episcopalian. Clubs: Faculty (U. Cin.); Nassau (Princeton). Home: 2216 Bedford Terr Cincinnati OH 45208

DAHLGREN, GEORGE, chemist, university dean; b. Chgo., Apr. 12, 1929; s. George Axel and Helen (Galloway) D.; m. Mary Basler, Sept. 1, 1951; children: Sarah Jane, Kirsten Anderson, Andrew Basler. B.S., Ill. Wesleyan U., 1951; M.S., U. Wyo., 1956, Ph.D., 1958. Postdoctoral fellow Cornell U., 1957-59; faculty U. Alaska, 1959-66, asso. prof. chemistry, 1962-66, head dept. chemistry, 1964-66; prof. chemistry U. Cin., 1966-75, head dept., 1971-75; dean Coll. Arts and Scis., U. Mo.-Kansas City, 1975-78; v.p. Franklin Inst., Phila., 1978-82; dean acad. affairs and faculties Ind. U. N.W., 1983—. Editor: Sci. in Alaska, Proc. Alaskan Sci. Confs., vols. 11-15, 1961-65; contbr. articles on periodate oxidations, hydrogen bonding, analysis, fast reaction kinetics to sci. jours. Fellow AAAS (exec. sec. Alaska div. 1960-65); mem. Am. Chem. Soc., AAUP, Sigma Xi. Home: 802 Brandonburr Dr Valparaiso IN 46383

DAHLGREN, JOHN ONSGARD, lawyer; b. Missoula, Mont., Sept 7, 1913; s. John and Geneva (Newhouse) D.; children: John Robert, Robin Reed. B.A., George Washington U., 1936; J.D., Georgetown U., 1939. Bar: D.C. 1939, Md. 1961. Chief counsel requisitioning div. Bd. Econ. Warfare, Washington, 1941-42; ptnr. firm Dahlgren & Close, Washington, 1946—. Pres. Internat. Humanities, Inc., 1960—; assoc. bd. dirs. Council of the Ams.; bd. dirs. Inter-Am. Bar Found. Served to comdr. USNR, 1942-45. Mem. Inter-Am. (sec.-gen. 1967—), Am., D.C. bar assns., Bar Assn. D.C. Clubs: Univ., Internat. (Washington). Home: 4952 Sentinel Dr Bethesda MD 20816 Office: 1000 Connecticut Ave NW Washington DC 20036

DAHLIN, DONALD C(LIFFORD), political science educator; b. Ironwood, Mich., June 18, 1941; (married); 2 children. B.A. magna cum laude in History, Carroll Coll., 1963; Ph.D. in Govt. (Univ. Departmental fellow), Claremont Grad. Sch., 1969; fellow in ct. mgmt., Inst. Ct. Mgmt., 1980. Asst. prof. govt. U. S.D., 1966-70, asso. prof., 1970-75, prof., 1975—, dir. criminal justice studies program, 1972-75, 78—, chmn. dept. polit. sci., 1978—; mgmt. analyst Law Enforcement Assistance Adminstrn., Dept. Justice, Washington, 1970-71; sec. S.D. Dept. Public Safety, Pierre, 1975-78; lectr., cons. in field; mem. S.D. Human Resource Cabinet Sub-Group, 1975-78, chmn., 1977-78; mem. S.D. Planning Commn., 1975-78; mem. adv. bd. Criminal Justice Statis. Analysis Center, 1975-78; chmn. S.D. Criminal Justice Commn., 1976-78; mem. U. So. Calif. Criminal Justice Tng. Center Planning Com., 1977-79, U. S.D. Research Inst. Adv. Panel, 1978-80; mem. acad. resource council S.D. Planning Agy., 1978-79. Contbr. articles to profl. publs. Recipient Sustained High Performance award Law Enforcement Assistance Adminstrn., 1971; Disting. Safety Service award S.D. Auto Club, 1978; Disting. Faculty award U. S.D., 1980; Haynes Found. research fellow, 1965-66; Am. Soc. Public Adminstrn. fellow, 1970-71; Bush Leadership fellow, summer 1975; Law Enforcement Edn. Program grantee, 1972-75; S.D. Criminal Justice Commn. grantee, 1972-74, 72-75; Criminal Justice Standards and Goals for S.D. grantee, 1974-75; Criminal Justice Data Collection grantee, 1974-75. Mem. Am. Soc. Public Adminstrn. (pres. Siouxland chpt. 1980-81), Am. Polit. Sci. Assn., Nat. Assn. Schs. Public Affairs and Adminstrn. (U. S.D. rep.), Am. Judicature Soc., Policy Studies Orgn. Home: 608 Poplar St Vermillion SD 57069 Office: U SD Dept Polit Sci Vermillion SD 57069

DAHLQUIST, ERIC EUGENE, publishing company executive; b. Niagara Falls, N.Y., Oct. 21, 1937; s. Charles Eugene and Cecile (LaPointe) D.; m. Linda Jeanne Molner, Nov. 17, 1961 (div. Sept. 1970); children: Eric Christopher, Karl Stanley; m. Carolyn Sue Carlton, Jan. 3, 1971; children: Scott Carlton, Jenniffer Leah. B.A., U. Buffalo, 1964. Tech. editor Hot Rod mag., 1964-66, feature editor, 1966-68; tech. editor Motor Trend mag., Los Angeles, 1968-69, editor, 1969-75; pres. Vista Pub., Inc., Sherman Oaks, Calif., 1975—. Vice pres. Sherman Oaks Homeowners Assn.; v.p. bd. dir. Our Lady of Corvallis Prep. Sch., Studio City, Calif. Mem. Internat. Motor Press Assn., Splty. Equipment Mfrs. Assn., Internat. Platform Assn. Republican. Roman Catholic. Address: 3761 Benedict Canyon Sherman Oaks CA 91423 *Goals, perserverance, and natural ability are the three obvious elements of a successful life. The secret is in realizing the first two attributes count far more in the equation than is popularly imagined. After that, time will judge if an individual achieves true greatness or merely celebrity status.*

DAHLSTROM, DONALD ALBERT, equipment manufacturing company executive; b. Mpls., Jan. 16, 1920; s. Raymond Estin and Dora Adina (Bloomgren) D.; m. Betty Cordelia Robertson, Dec. 4, 1942; children: Mary Elizabeth, Donald Raymond, Christine Dora, Stephanie Lou, Michael Jeffrey. Student, Macalester Coll., 1937-39; B.S. in Chem. Engring, U. Minn., 1942; Ph.D., Northwestern U., 1949. Petroleum engr. Internat. Petroleum Co., Ltd., Negritos, Peru, 1942-45; from instr. to asso. prof. chem. engring. Northwestern U., 1946-56; with Eimco Corp., Palatine, Ill., 1952—, v.p., dir. research and devel., 1960—, also dir.; v.p. research and devel. Envirotech Corp., Salt Lake City, 1969—; v.p., dir. Erco-Environtech, 1974—; sr. v.p. research and devel. Eimco Process Equipment Co., 1981—; dir. Process Engrs., Inc.; Am. mem. internat. sci. com. 6th Internat. Mineral Processing Congress, 1963; mem. adv. council on engring. NSF. Contbr. to handbooks. Mem. State Air Conservation Com. State Utah, 1971-78, vice chmn., 1977-78; Mem. sch. bd. dist. 110, Deerfield, Ill., 1959-61; pres. Riverwoods Residents Assn., 1962-63; chmn. bd. Northwestern YMCA, 1950-52; trustee Village of Riverwoods, 1966-69. Served with USNR, 1945-46. Recipient Merit award Northwestern U., 1965. Mem. Am. Inst. Chem. Engrs. (dir. 1960-62, v.p. 1963, pres. 1964-65, chmn. environ. div. 1971, Founders award 1972, Environ. award 1977), Am. Inst. Mining, Metall. and Petroleum Engrs. (chmn. minerals benefication div. 1963-64, bd. dirs. soc. mining engrs. 1965—, pres. soc. mining engrs. 1974-75, dir. 1973—, Rossiter W. Raymond award 1952, Richards award 1976, Krumb lectr. 1980, Taggart award 1983), Am. Chem. Soc., Nat. Acad. Engring., Water Pollution Control Fedn., Canadian Inst. Mining and Metallurgy, The Filtration Soc. (London), Air Pollution Control Assn., Mining and Metall. Soc. Am. (dir. Engrs. Council Profl. Devel.), Nat. Acad. Engrs., Sigma Xi (Holgate award Northwestern U. chpt. 1949), Phi Lambda Upsilon, Tau Beta Pi (nat. pres. 1958-62). Presbyterian. Home: 5340 Cottonwood Ln Salt Lake City UT 84117 Office: Eimco Process Equipment Co Box 300 Salt Lake City UT 84110

DAHLSTROM, WILLIAM GRANT, psychologist, educator; b. Mpls., Nov. 1, 1922; s. Arthur William and Elizabeth Pricilla (Baker) D.; m. Leona Erickson, Sept. 3, 1948; children: Amy Louise, Eric Lee. Student, UCLA, 1940-41; B.A. cum laude, U. Minn., 1944; Ph.D. in Psychology and Neuropsychiatry, U. Minn., 1949. Instr. psychology U. Minn., 1946-48, Ohio Wesleyan U., 1948-49; vis. asst. prof. State U. Iowa, 1949-53, research assoc., summer 1957; assoc. prof. psychiatry and psychology, dir. psychol. services Meml. Hosp., U. N.C., Chapel Hill, 1953-56, assoc. prof. psychology, 1956-60, research assoc. psychiatry, 1956-60, prof. psychology, 1960—, clin. prof. psychology in dept. psychiatry, 1960—; research prof. Inst. for Research in Social Sci., 1960—, chmn. dept., 1971-76; vis. scholar U. Calif., Berkeley, 1968, 76-77; field dir. Child Study Center U. N.C., 1962-63; chmn. mental health study sect. NIH, 1966-67. Author: (with G.S. Welsh) An MMPI Handbook, 1960, rev. edit. (with G.S. Welsh and L.E. Dahlstrom) Vol. I, 1972, Vol. II, 1975, (with E.E. Baughman) Negro and White Children, 1968; Co-editor: (with J.W. Thibaut) Jour. Personality, 1959-60; Cons. editor: Jour. Cons. Psychology, 1964—, Jour. Abnormal Psychology, 1964—; Contbr. articles to profl. jours. NIMH sr. postdoctoral fellow Menninger Found., Topeka, Kans., 1967-68; Co-recipient Anisfield-Wolf award for outstanding contbn. to race relations Sat. Rev. Lit., 1968. Fellow Soc. Personality Assessment, Am. Psychol. Assn.; fellow AAAS; mem. Am. Psychopath. Assn.; fellow N.Y. Acad. Scis.; mem. Sigma Xi. Democrat. Home: 322 Burlage Circle Chapel Hill NC 27514 Office: Dept Psychology University North Carolina Chapel Hill NC 27514

DAIGLE, JOHN MARTIN, banker; b. Houlton, Maine, Dec. 27, 1932; s. Philip S. and Christine (Lyons) D.; m. Dolores Dombek, Feb. 5, 1955; children—John Martin, Jeffrey, Judith, June. Student, Ricker Coll., 1950-51; B.S., Babson Coll., 1954. Sr. accountant Arthur Andersen & Co., Boston, 1954-58; controller Casco Bank & Trust Co., Portland, Maine, 1958-63, treas., 1963-69, dir., 1967—, pres., 1969—, chief exec. officer, 1971—; pres., dir. Casco No. Corp., 1972—; dir. Guy Gannett Pub. Co. Former chmn. Gov.'s Econ. Adv. Com.; bd. dirs. Portland Area Devel. Council, Greater Portland Bldg. Fund; past pres. United Way of Greater Portland; chmn. bd. trustees Babson Coll.; pres. Maine Econ. Soc. Named Man of Yr. Kiwanis Club, 1978. Republican (town com. Cumberland, Maine 1970—, budget com. 1971-72). Home: Box 80 RFD 4 Portland ME 04110 Office: 1 Monument Sq Portland ME 04104

DAIL, JOSEPH GARNER, JR., lawyer; b. Elloree, S.C., June 15, 1932; s. Joseph Garner and Esther Vernette (Harbort) D.; children: Edward Benjamin, Mary Holyoke. B.S., U. N.C., 1953, J.D. with honors, 1955. Bar: bar 1955. Practice in, Washington, 1959-76, McLean, Va., 1976—; partner firm Croft, Dail & Vance (and predecessor), 1966-76; counsel Gabeler, Ward & Griggs, 1983—. Assoc. editor: N.C. Law Rev, 1954-55. Served to lt. USNR, 1955-59; capt. Res. (ret.). Mem. Am., Fed., Va., N.C., D.C. bar assns., Motor Carrier Lawyers Assn. (Disting. Service award 1976), Assn. ICC Practitioners (treas. 1973-75), Order of Coif, Phi Beta Kappa. Republican. Club: Army and Navy (Washington). Office: 6623 A Old Dominion Dr McLean VA 22101

DAILEY, BENJAMIN PETER, chemistry educator; b. San Marcos, Tex., Sept. 1, 1919; s. Benjamin Peter and Anna Clementine (Waldo) D.; m. Beverly Elizabeth Holmes, June 30, 1945; children: Peter,

William Stephen. B.S., S.W. Tex. State U., 1938; M.A., U. Tex.-Austin, 1940, Ph.D., 1942. Group leader Nat. Def. Research Com., Pitts., 1942-45; postdoctoral fellow Harvard U., Cambridge, Mass., 1946-47; instr. to assoc. prof. chemistry Columbia U., N.Y.C., 1947-57, prof. chemistry, 1957—. Contbr. articles to profl. jours.; patentee in field. Recipient Presdl. Cert. of Appreciation, 1946; Sloan fellow, 1957-60; Adams fellow, 1962-63; NSF sr. postdoctoral fellow, 1962-63; Guggenheim fellow, 1970-71. Fellow Am. Acad. Arts and Scis., Am. Phys. Soc., Am. Chem. Soc. Home: 440 Riverside Dr New York NY 10027 Office: Dept Chemistry Columbia Univ New York NY 10027

DAILEY, DANIEL OWEN, artist, educator, designer; b. Phila., Feb. 4, 1947; s. David Bireley and Barbara Tarleton (Tricebock) D.; m. Linda MacNeil, Aug. 19, 1977; children: Allison MacNeil, Owen MacNeil. B.F.A., Phila. Coll. Art, 1969; M.F.A., R.I. Sch. Design, Providence, 1972. Tchr., fellow MIT Ctr. for Advanced Visual Studies, Cambridge, 1975-80; dir. glass program Mass. Coll. Art, Boston, 1973—; mem. faculty Pilchuck Glass Sch., Stanwood, Wash., 1974—; designer, artist Cristallerie Daum, Paris and Nancy, France, 1975—; designer Steuben Glass, Corning, N.Y., 1982—; owner Dailey Glass, Amesbury, Mass., 1977—; tchr. glass R.I. Sch. Design, 1970-72, Haystack Mountain Sch. Crafts, Deer Isle, Maine, 1976. Exhibited one-man shows, numerous U.S. and Europe, 1970—, numerous nat. and internat. group shows, 1970—; represented permanent collections, Met. Mus. Art, N.Y.C., Smithsonian Instn., Washington, Corning Mus. Glass, (N.Y.), Huntington Mus., (W.Va.), New Indian Mus., Flagstaff, Ariz., Les Archieves Daum, Nancy, France, U. Ill. Art Gallery, Normal, Brockton Art Mus., (Mass.), Nat. gallery Victoria, Melbourne, Australia, Nat. Mus. Modern Art, Kyoto, Japan, permanent collcetions, St. Louis Mus. Art, permanent collections, High Mus. Art, Atlanta. Trustee Haystack Mountain Sch., Deer Isle, Maine, 1983—. Fulbright Hayes fellow, Venice, Italy, 1972, 73; Nat. Endowment for Arts fellow, 1978; Mass. Council for Arts fellow, 1980. Mem. Glass Art Soc. (pres., chmn. bd. dirs. 1980-82), N.Y. Exptl. Glass Workshop (dir. 1979—). Home: 122 Market St Amesbury MA 01913 Office: Mass Coll Art 364 Brookline Ave Boston MA 02215

DAILEY, DONALD EARL, indsl. design cons.; b. Mpls., July 25, 1914; s. William Earl and Carrye Elizabeth (Fluhart) D.; m. Elizabeth Meall, Oct. 25, 1941; children—Deanne Carol, William Bruce. Student, U. Toledo, Toledo Museum Sch. Design, 1934-37. Design dir. Phila. office Harold Van Doran & Assos., 1940-46; propr. Donald Dailey Designers, Phila., 1946-50; v.p. Product Planning Servel, Inc., 1950-55; propr. Don Dailey & Assos., product design cons. to industry, Evansville, Ind., 1955—; lectr. U. Lehigh, Syracuse U., U. Mich., McGill U., others. Exhibited painting and sculpture museums, throughout Midwest. Chmn. city beautification Ohio Jr. C. of C., 1939; v.p., dir. Evansville Mus. Art and Sci., 1951-55, also chmn. bldg. com.; cons. city center devel. com. Evansville Future, Inc., 1964—. Recipient Bronze Medal award Indsl. Designers Inst., 1953, Master Design award Product Engring. mag., 1959, 64. Fellow Indsl. Design Soc. Am. (life mem.; founder jour.; v.p. 1965-66); mem. Mystic Marine Hist. Soc., Smithsonian Internat. Oceanographic Found., Am. Soc. Indsl. Designers (pres. 1964-65). Club: Oak Meadow Golf and Tennis. Patentee in field. Address: 9307 Petersburg Rd Evansville IN 47711

DAILEY, IRENE, actress, educator; b. N.Y.C., Sept. 12, 1920; d. Daniel James and Helen Therese (Ryan) D. Student of, Uta Hagen, N.Y.C., 1951-61, Herbert Berghof, N.Y.C., 1951-61. Cons. for Am. Nat. Theatre and Acad., 1965-68; cons. and coach for various theatre groups and individual artists, 1956—; guest artist and tchr. various univs. in, U.S., 1965—; founder Sch. of the Actors Co., N.Y.C., 1961, artistic dir., 1961-72, mem. faculty, 1961-72. Appeared in: films Daring Game, 1967, No Way to Treat A Lady, 1968, Five Easy Pieces, 1970, The Grissom Gang, 1970, The Last Two Weeks, 1977, The Amityville Horror, 1978; Broadway plays Andorra, 1962, The Subject Was Roses, 1964-65, Rooms, 1966-67, You Know I Can't Hear You When the Water's Running, 1968; appeared as Jasmin Adair in: Tomorrow With Pictures (London Mag. Critics award), Duke of York's, London, 1960; appeared as Beatrice in: The Effect of Gamma Rays on Man-In-the-Moon Marigolds, Chgo., 1970 (Sarah Siddons award); appeared as Banannas in: The House of Blue Leaves, Chgo., 1972 (Joseph Jefferson nomination); appears in: Another World, NBC-TV, 1973—; appeared in: Play Desire Under the Elms, Princeton, N.J., 1961; play The Sea Gull, 1973; Author: Waiting for Mickey and Ava, 1978. Mem. Actors Equity Assn., Screen Actors Guild, Nat. Acad. TV Arts and Scis. (Emmy award 1978-79), Am. Ednl. Theatre Assn., AFTRA. Unitarian.

DAILEY, JANET, romance novelist; b. Storm Lake, Iowa, May 21, 1944; m. William Dailey; 2 stepchildren. Student pub. schs., Independence, Iowa. Sec., Omaha, 1963-74. Author: No Quarter Asked, 1974, After the Storm, 1975, Sweet Promise, 1976, The Widow and the Wastrel, 1977, Giant of Medabi, 1978, The Bride of the Delta Queen, 1979, Lord of the High Lonesome, 1980, Night Way, 1981, This Calder Sky, 1981, This Clader Range, 1982, Stands a Calder Man, 1982, Lancaster Men, 1981, numerous other novels. Recipient Golden Heart award Romance Writers Am., 1981. Home: Star Route 4 Box 2197 Branson MO 95616 *

DAILEY, PETER HEATH, diplomat; b. New Orleans, May 1, 1930; s. John William and Abigail (Heath) D.; m. Jacqueline Ann Biggerstaff, 1953; children: Michael Ann, Sydney Jean, Peter Heath, Elizabeth Mary, Patricia Lynn. B.S., UCLA, 1954. Various positions to v.p. Erwin Wasey, Inc., Los Angeles, 1956-63; sr. v.p., dir. Western and Far Eastern regions Campbell-Ewald Co., Los Angeles, 1964-67; chmn. bd., chief exec. officer Dailey & Assocs., Los Angeles, 1968—; U.S. ambassador to Ireland, 1982—; partner Running Y Ranch, Klamath Falls, Oreg.; dir. Shamrock Broadcasting. Pres. November Group, spl. adv. agy. for Pres. Nixon; chmn. Campaign for Pres. Ford, 1976, dep. dir., 1980; Bd. dirs. St. Vincent's Found. and Hosp.; founding trustee UCLA Found.; trustee Villanova Prep. Sch. Served to lt. USNR, 1954-56. Mem. Los Angeles C. of C., San Francisco, Los Angeles advt. clubs, World Bus. Council, Chi Psi. Clubs: Family, Advertising, St. Francis Yacht (San Francisco); Sportsmen of the South, California, Advertising, Saddle and Sirloin, Bruin Football Alumni (Los Angeles); Rancheros Vistadores (Santa Barbara, Calif.); Lakeside Golf. Home: 1999 Oak Knoll Ave San Marino CA 91108 Office: 3055 Wilshire Blvd Los Angeles CA 90010

DAILEY, THOMAS EDWIN, construction company executive; b. Detroit, Mar. 25, 1932; s. Ralph Edwin and Margaret Eleanor (Longnecker) D.; m. Janice Ann Dempsey, Nov. 20, 1956; children: Jill Susan, Stephen Ralph. B.A., Denison U., Granville, Ohio, 1953. With R.E. Dailey & Co., Detroit, 1956—, exec. v.p., then pres., until 1976, chmn. bd., 1976—. Bd. dirs. Boys Clubs Met. Detroit, from 1975; Republican candidate for mayor of Detroit, 1977. Served with USNR, 1953-56; Korea. Named Man Who Made Marks Engring. New Record mag., 1968, 76, 78. Mem. Asso. Gen. Contractors Am. (pres. elect 1981, Man of Year award Detroit chpt.), Engring. Soc. Detroit, Detroit C. of C. (dir. 1979—). Clubs: Detroit Athletic, Orchard Lake Country, Plum Hollow Golf, Fairlane. Office: PO Box 19220 Detroit MI 48219 *

DAILY, JAMES L., JR., financial executive; b. Houston, Dec. 2, 1929; m. Virginia Teinert, Jan. 31, 1953; children: Kathy, Jimmy, Ricky. B.A. in Bus. Adminstrn, Rice U., 1951. C.P.A., Tex. Jr. accountant Tenneco, Inc., Houston, 1956-57, accountant, 1957-58, sr. accountant, 1958-59, acctg. supr., 1959-61, acctg. mgr., 1961-71, asst. controller, 1971-75, controller, 1975-78, v.p., controller, 1978—. Served to 1st lt. USAF, 1953-56. Mem. Am. Inst. C.P.A.'s, Fin. Execs. Inst., Tex. Soc. C.P.A.'s, Houston Soc. C.P.A.'s. Lutheran. Office: Tenneco Inc Tenneco Bldg llouston TX 77002

DAILY, JAMES WALLACE, engineering educator, consultant; b. Columbia, Mo., Mar. 19, 1913; s. Wallace Edgar and Marjory Isabel (McGrath) D.; m. Sarah Vanderlip Atwood, Sept. 10, 1938; children: John Wallace, Sarah Anne Vanderlip (Mrs. Charles Rosenberg). A.B., Stanford U., 1935; M.S., Calif. Inst. Tech., 1937, Ph.D., 1945. Registered profl. engr. Test engr. Byron Jackson Co., Berkeley, Calif., 1935; research asst. hydraulics Calif. Inst. Tech., 1936-37, research fellow, mgr. hydraulic machinery lab., 1937-40, instr. mech. engring., 1940-46; hydraulic engr. OSRD, Navy Research Projects, 1941-46; asst. prof. hydraulics M.I.T., 1946-49, asso. prof., 1949-55, prof., 1955-64; prof. engring. mechanics, chmn. dept. U. Mich., 1964-72, prof. fluid mechanics and hydraulic engring., 1972-81, prof. emeritus, 1981—; vis. prof. Tech. U. of Delft, Netherlands, 1971; vis. scientist Electricite de France Centre de Recherches et d'Essais, Paris, 1971; mem. U.S. del. water resources specialists to, People's Republic of China, 1974; vis. prof. East China Coll. Hydraulic Engring., Nanking, 1979; domestic and internat. cons. various firms. Author: (with D.R.F. Harleman) Fluid Dynamics, (with R.T. Knapp and F.G. Hammitt) Cavitation; Contbr. tech. articles Am., fgn. jours. Mem. sch. com. Town of Arlington, Mass., 1959-65. Recipient Naval Ordnance Devel. award, 1945. Mem. Nat. Acad. Engring., Internat. Assn. Hydraulic Research (hon. mem., pres. 1967-71, mem. Council 1963-65, 71-77), ASCE, ASME (hon.), Japan Soc. C.E. (hon.), Internat. House of Japan, Sigma Xi, Tau Beta Pi, Chi Epsilon. Congregationalist. Club: Cosmos (Washington). Home: 2968 San Pasqual St Pasadena CA 91107

DAILY, JAY ELWOOD, librarian, educator; b. Pikeview, Colo., June 17, 1923; s. Roy Raymond and Anna Olive (Baker) D.; m. Jennifer Mary Hole, Dec. 17, 1960. Student, So. Colo. State Coll., 1942-43, Grinnell Coll., 1943-44; B.A., N.Y. U., 1951; M.S., Columbia U., 1952, D.L.S., 1957. Adminstrv. officer Am. Edn. Mission Korea, 1952-53; head librarian Wagner Coll., N.Y.C., 1954-55; cons. librarian Office Prime Minister, Rangoon, Burma, 1957-59; adv. librarian U. Mandalay, Burma, 1959-62; library cons. Franklin Books Program, N.Y.C., 1962-65; asst. dir. U. Pitts. Libraries, 1965-66, asso. prof., 1967, prof. library sci., 1968—; cons. in field. Author: (with Mildred Myers) Cataloging for Library Technical Assistants, 1969, (with J. Phillip Immroth) Library Cataloging, 1971, (with James Williams and Martha Manheimer) Classified Library of Congress Subject Headings, 1972, 2d edit., 1982, Organizing Nonprint Materials, 1972, The Anatomy of Censorship, 1973—, Cataloging Phonorecordings, 1975, The Looking-Glass Decades, 1977; editor: (with Harold Lancour and Allen Kent) Ency. Library and Info. Sci., 1972-81, (with Allen Kent) Ency. Library and Info. Sci., 1982, Index to Ency. Library and Info. Sci., 1983, (with Harold Lancour and Allen Kent) Practical Books in Library and Info. Science. Served with AUS, 1943-46. Recipient Thomas Wolfe Poetry prize Washington Sq. Coll., N.Y. U., 1951; Paula K. Lazrus Meml. fellow NCCJ, 1955-57. Mem. Spl. Library Assn., Assn. Am. Library Schs., AAUP, ALA (exec. bd. cataloging and classification sect. 1967-71). Democrat. Anglican. Home: 709 S Negley St Pittsburgh PA 15232 *The technological changes in the transmission of knowledge should prove that understanding among all races and ages of people is possible and that the true enemy of everyone is ignorance. I consider it my good fortune to be on the leading edge of these changes.*

DAILY, LOWELL ROBERT, labor union official; b. Scandia, Minn., Sept. 5, 1927; s. Robert L. and Alice D. B.S., Mission House Coll., 1951. Pres. Bemis Workers Assn., Mpls., 1953-54; shop chmn. local 800 United Furniture Workers Am., Mpls., 1954-55, internat. rep., 1955-62, dir. dist. 7, 1962-74, internat. sec.-treas., Nashville, 1974—. Served with USN, 1945-46. Office: United Furniture Workers Am 1910 Airline Dr Nashville TN 37210 *

DAILY, THOMAS V., bishop; b. Belmont, Mass., Sept. 23, 1927. Student, Boston Coll., St. John's Sem., Mass. Ordained priest Roman Catholic Ch., 1952; missionary Peru as mem. Soc. St. James the Apostle; ordained titular bishop of Bladia and aux. bishop, Boston, 1975—. Office: 2121 Commonwealth Ave Brighton MA 02135 *

DAINES, WILLIAM PURDIE, hospital administrator, physician; b. Logan, Utah, Sept. 5, 1918; s. Lyman Luther and Agnes (Purdie) D.; m. Anne Marie Anstee, Sept. 19, 1941; children: William Fred, John Robert, Kathryn Lyn. B.A., U. Utah, 1938; M.D., Northwestern U., 1942, M.S., 1949. Diplomate: Am. Bd. Internal Medicine (bd. govs. 1975-81). Intern Passavant Hosp., Chgo., 1942-43; practice medicine specializing in internal medicine Odgen (Utah) Clinic, 1950-67; med. dir. McKay Dee Hosp., Ogden, 1967—; resident internal medicine Northwestern U. Med. Sptly. Tng. Program, 1976-79; asso. clin. prof. U. Utah. Med. Coll.; mem. Gov.'s Adv. Council on Comprehensive Health Planning, 1967-70. Served to lt. USNR, 1943-46; PTO. Fellow ACP; mem. Inst. Medicine of Nat. Acad. Sci., Am. Soc. Internal Medicine (trustee 1970-73, sec. treas. 1973-76, pres. 1977-78), AMA, Utah Med. Assn. Office: 3939 Harrison St Ogden UT 84409

DAISLEY, WILLIAM PRESCOTT, lawyer; b. Washington, Aug. 11, 1935; s. Gordon Walford and Augusta Greenleaf (Prescott) D.; m. Linda L. Thelin, Nov. 3, 1962; children: William Prescott Jr., Susan DeLeon. B.A., Randolph Macon Coll., 1959; LL.B., George Washington U., 1962. Bar: D.C. 1962, Md. 1968, U.S. Supreme Ct. 1978. Law clk. firm King & Nordlinger, Washington, 1960-62, assoc., 1963-69, ptnr., 1969—; dir. McLachlen Nat. Bank; Guest lectr. law George Washington U., 1972, 75, 78; mem. Montgomery County (Md.) Juvenile Ct. Com., 1970-73. Mem. Md., Am., Montgomery County, D.C. bar assns., Phi Delta Theta, Phi Delta Phi. Republican. Episcopalian. Club: Columbia Country. Home: 9817 Gartrell Pl Kensington MD 20895 Office: 1000 Connecticut Ave Washington DC 20036 also 7316 Wisconsin Ave Bethesda MD 20814 *Success, though rarely achieved with utter perfection, is a goal not to be eschewed, but rather one sought with diligent preparation. Those who achieve a fair modicum of success are often called "lucky". The lucky people I have known have one quality in common—they are invariably the best prepared.*

DAKAN, NORMAN EUGENE, librarian; b. Beaver City, Nebr., Sept. 16, 1926; s. Everett Sylvester and Avis Belle (Fowler) D.; m. Miyoko Muranaka, Jan. 24, 1957; 1 dau., Margot Toshiko. B.A., U. Calif.-Berkeley, 1953, B.L.S., 1954. Asst. reference and order librarian Calif. State Poly. Coll. Library, San Luis Obispo, 1954-56; base librarian, Ashiya AFB, Japan, 1956-57, chief librarian, Itazuke AFB, Japan, 1957-60, base librarian, Hickam AFB, Hawaii, 1960-62, chief librarian, Fuchu Air Sta., Japan, 1962-66, Kadena AFB, Okinawa, 1966-68, base librarian, Hickam AFB, Hawaii, 1968-70, chief librarian, Yokota AFB, Japan, 1970-71, 475th Air Base Wing supervisory librarian, 1971-75, base librarian, Hickam AFB, Hawaii, 1975, asst. Air Force librarian, Randolph AFB, Tex., 1976-77, dir. Air Force Library Program, 1977—. Compiler: Pacific Air Forces basic bibliographies Intelligence, Black Literature; editor: Air Force Monthly. Served with USN, 1944-46. Home: 9714 Meadow Dr Converse TX 78109 Office: AFMPC/MPCSOA Randolph AFB TX 78150

DAKIN, CHRISTINE WHITNEY, dancer, educator; b. New Haven, Aug. 25, 1949; d. James Irvin, Jr. and Jean Evelyn (Coulter) Crump; m. Robert Ford Dakin, June 21, 1969 (div. Sept. 1982). Student, U. Mich., 1967-71. Performer, teacher Ann Arbor Dance Theater, Mich., 1965-71; tchr. Ann Arbor Pub. Schs., 1967-70; tchr., choreographer Fairleigh Dickinson U., Rutherford, N.J., 1971-73; tchr. Lincoln Ctr. Inst., N.Y.C., 1978, Guanajuato Dance Festival, Mex., 1982; prin. dancer Martha Graham Dance Co., N.Y.C., 1976—; dancer, rehearsal dir. Pearl Lang Dance Co., 1971-79, Kazuko Hirahayashi Dance Co., 1974-76. Appeared: It's Hard to Be a Jew, 1972, The Dybuk, 1975; choreographer: My Fair Lady, 1969, Guys and Dolls, 1970, Amahl and the Night Visitors, 1968; guest dancer, Three's Co. Dance Co., San Diego, 1981, Three Raven Dance Festival, Lowman, Idaho, 1982; appeared (with Martha Graham Dance Co.), Covent Garden, London, 1976, Met. Opera, 1980, WNET Dance in Am. Series, 1979; performance at the White House, WNET, 1982. Scholar U. Mich., 1969, Conn. Coll., 1969. Mem. Am. Guild Mus. Artists (bd. govs.). Home: 207 E 202d St Bronx NY 10458 Office: Martha Graham Dance Co 316 E 63d St New York NY 10021

DALAND, ROBERT THEODORE, public administration educator, consultant; b. Janesville, Wis., Oct. 3, 1919; s. John Norton and Nellie Odessa (Furrow) D.; m. Dorothy Shaw, June 6, 1942; children: David Norton, William Christopher; m. Edwina Nary, Nov. 20, 1979. B.A., Milton Coll., Wis., 1942; M.A., U. Wis., 1947, Ph.D., 1979. Asst. prof. U. Ala., Tuscaloosa, 1949-56, U. Conn., 1956-59; assoc. prof. pub. adminstrn. U. N.C., Chapel Hill, 1959-61, prof., 1963—; assoc. prof. U. So. Calif., Rio de Janeiro, 1961-63. Author: Exploring Brazilian Bureaucracy, 1981, Brazilian Planning, 1967, Government and Health, 1955; editor: Comparative Urban Research, 1969; editorial bd.: Pub. Adminstrn. Abstracts, 1974—; editorial: Comparative Urban Research Trans., 1972—; book rev. editor: Pub. Adminstrn. Rev., 1966-74. V.p. N.C. Coastal Fedn., 1982—; coastal chair Sierra Club, Chapel Hill, 1982—. Served with AUS, 1942-45; PTO. Fellow Ford Found., 1954-55; postdoctoral fellow Columbia U. Met. Region Program, 1958-59; Fulbright fellow Rio de Janeiro, 1968-69. Mem. Am. Polit. Sci Assn., So. Polit. Sci. Assn., Policy Studies Orgn., Am. Soc. Pub. Adminstrn. Democrat. Home: 130 Justice St Chapel Hill NC 27514 Office: U NC 317 Hamilton Hall Chapel Hill NC 27514

DALBECK, RICHARD BRUCE, insurance executive; b. Cambridge, Mass., May 17, 1929; s. Harold Lewis and Elizabeth (Kessell) D.; m. Shirley Carolyn Wells, Apr. 7, 1956; children: Barbara Jane, Elizabeth Ann, Bruce Wells. A.B., Dartmouth Coll., 1952, M.B.A., 1953. Sales engr., market research specialist Gen. Electric Co., Lynn, Mass., 1956-57, Sales engr., mkt. research specialist, Lynchburg, Va., 1957-62; asso. mem. A.T. Kearney & Co., Inc. (Mgmt. Cons.), Chgo. and N.Y.C., 1962-66, prin., 1966-69; v.p. Union Mut. Life Ins. Co., Portland, Maine, 1969-74, sr. v.p., 1974—; dir. Unionmutual Stock Life Ins. Co. Am., Portland. Trustee Camp Bishopswood, 1975—, Park Danforth Home for Aged, Portland, Maine, 1982—; bd. dirs. United Way of Greater Portland, 1980—. Served with Supply Corps USNR, 1953-56. Mem. Life Office Mgmt. Assn., Am. Mgmt. Assn., Phi Beta Kappa. Episcopalian. Home: Spoondrift Ln Cape Elizabeth ME 04107 Office: 2211 Congress St Portland ME 04102

DALBY, ALAN JAMES, pharmaceutical executive; b. Glasgow, Scotland, Jan. 15, 1937; s. William J. P. and Elizabeth Jean (McKenzie) D.; May 21, 1960; children: A. Royce, Mark. B.S., Paisley Coll., 1958. Analytical chemist Smith Kline & French Labs., Can., 1958; mgmt. trainee SK&F, Phila., 1960-61; gen. mgr. consumer products div. Menley & James Labs., Can., 1963-65; dir. mktg. SK&F, Can., 1966-71; v.p. comml. devel. Worldwide Pharms., Phila., 1971-72, v.p., Europe, Africa, India, Brussels, 1972-75, v.p. internat., Phila., 1975-80, pres., 1980—; exec. v.p. Smith Kline Corp., Phila., 1980—. Trustee, Thomas Jefferson U. Mem. Pharm. Mfrs. Assn. (dir. Washington). Republican. Episcopalian. Clubs: Union League (Phila.); Aronimink Golf (Newton Square, Pa.); Seaview Country (Newtown Square, Pa.). Office: 1 Franklin Plaza Philadelphia PA 19101

DALE, AL, broadcast journalist. B.A., Mercer U.; attended, Columbia U. Reporter, anchorman Sta. WBTV, Charlotte, N.C.; reporter Sta. WGGA, Gainesville, Ga., Stas. WSB and WRNG, Atlanta; reporter, anchorman Sta. KPIX-TV, San Francisco; reporter Sta. WBBM-TV, Chgo.; now London corr. ABC-TV News. (Recipient Emmy award 1980). Office: ABC News 215 Great Portland St London W1 England

DALE, ERWIN RANDOLPH, lawyer, author; b. Herrin, Ill., July 30, 1915; s. Henry and Lena Bell (Campbell) D.; m. Charline Vincent, Aug. 27, 1955; children—Allyson Ann, Kristan Charline. B.A., U. Tex., El Paso, 1937, J.D., 1943. Bar: Tex. bar 1943, D.C. bar 1953, Mich. bar 1956, N.Y. bar 1960. Atty. Internal Revenue Service, 1943-56, chief reorgn. and dividend br., 1954-56; legal staff Gen. Motors Corp., 1956-57; partner firm Chapman, Walsh & O'Connell, N.Y.C. and Washington, 1957-59, Hawkins, Delafield & Wood, 1959—; lectr. tax matters. Dir. Md. Electronics Mfg. Corp., 1948-58; dir., treas. The Renaissance Corp., 1968-72; dir., asst. treas. Shancom Reconstrn. Corp., 1968-72, Newhaven Corp., 1968-72. Author numerous articles on fed. tax matters.; Bd. editors: Tex. Law Rev, 1941-42, 42-43. Mem. ABA (chmn. com. consol. returns sect. taxation 1959-60), Tex. Bar Assn., Mich. Bar Assn., N.Y. State Bar Assn. (chmn. corp. tax com. tax sect. 1967, 68, mem. exec. com. 1968-70), Tax Inst. of Am. (dir. 1967-69, treas. 1966), Assn. Bar City N.Y., Nat. Tax Assn., Ex-Students Assn. U. Tex. Clubs: Mason., Nat. Lawyers, Nat. Press (Washington); Bronxville (N.Y.) Field, Siwanoy Country. Home: 4 Crampton Rd Bronxville NY 10708 Office: 67 Wall St New York NY 10005

DALE, FRANCIS LYKINS, newspaper publisher, lawyer; b. Urbana, Ill., July 13, 1921; s. Charles Sherman and Sarah (Lykins) D.; m. Kathleen Hamlin Watkins, Mar. 20, 1947; children: Mitchell Watkins, Myron Lykins, Kathleen Hamlin, Holly Moore. A.B., Duke U., 1943; LL.B., U. Va., 1948; LL.D. (hon.), Eastern Ky. U., U. Cin., Ohio Wesleyan U., Salmon P. Chase Coll. of Law, Bloomfield Coll., Pepperdine Sch. of Bus. Bar: Ohio 1948. Assoc. Frost & Jacobs, Cin., 1948-53, partner, 1953-65; Asst. sec. Cin. Enquirer, Inc., 1952-65, pres., pub., 1965-73; pres. The Cin. Reds, Inc., 1967-73, vice-chmn., 1973-80; pub. Los Angeles Herald Examiner, 1977—; Chmn. Nat. Council Crime and Delinquency, 1973-74, vice chmn., 1975—; chmn. Commn. White House fellows, 1973-74; U.S. ambassador and rep. to European Office of UN and other internat. orgns., Geneva, Switzerland, 1974-76; spl. asst. to asst. sec. state, 1976; spl. adviser U.S. del. 31st Gen. Assembly. Active United Appeal, Cin.; bd. dirs. Goodwill Industries, Cin., v.p., 1968; bd. dirs., mem. exec. com. Cin. area chpt. ARC; bd. dirs. Boys Clubs' Am., Bethesda Hosp., Boys' Club Cin., Taft Inst., Natural History Museum, also symphony, opera, ballet cos.; trustee Occidental Coll., Claremont Sch. Theology; chmn. bd. councilors U. So. Calif. Coll. Continuing Edn.; bd. councilors Sch. Internat. Relations and Sch. Bus.; bd. dirs. Los Angeles chpt. ARC, Central City Assn., Meth. Hosp. So. Calif., Operating Co.-Music Center, Los Angeles World Affairs Council, Los Angeles chpt. NCCJ, Town Hall Calif., Greater Los Angeles Visitors and Conv. Bur.; bd. dirs., pres. Los Angeles County council Boy Scouts Am. Served with USNR, World War II. Named Outstanding Young Man of Year, Cin., 1951; recipient Gov.'s award for adding prestige Ohio, 1968; Superior Honor award State Dept., 1976; Freedoms Found. award, 1976; Silver Beaver award Boy Scouts Am., 1969. Fellow Am. Bar Assn.; mem.

Ohio Bar Assn. (pres. 1966-67), Cin. Bar Assn. (pres. 1961-62), Los Angeles C. of C. (v.p., dir.), Council Chs. Greater Cin. (pres. 1959-61), Frat. of Friends (v.p.), Order of Coif, Omicron Delta Kappa, Phi Kappa Psi, Sigma Nu Phi. Methodist (dist. lay leader 1958-64; mem. bd. publs.). Clubs: Lincoln, Rotary; Comml. (Cin.); Annandale Golf, Jonathan, Los Angeles Athletic, Calif. (Los Angeles); Bohemian (San Francisco). Home: 3634 San Pasqual Pasadena CA 91107 Office: Los Angeles Herald Examiner 1111 S Broadway Los Angeles CA 90015

DALE, HARVEY PHILIP, law educator; b. 1937. B.A., Cornell U., 1958; J.D., Harvard U., 1961. Bar: N.Y. 1962, D.C. 1966. Assoc. firm Curtis, Mallet-Prevost, Colt & Mosle, N.Y.C., 1962-66; ptnr. firm Schaeffer, Dale & Vogel, N.Y.C., 1966-76; ptnr.firm Conboy, Hewitt, O'Brien & Boardman, N.Y.C., 1976-77; councel Conboy, Hewittm O'Brien & Boradman, N.Y.C., 1977-80; asoc. prof. law N.Y.U., N.Y.C., 1977-79, prof., 1979—; counsel Cadwalader, Wickersham & Taft, N.Y.C., 1983—. Mem. Cornell U. Council, 1983—. Mem. N.Y. State Bar Assn. (mem. exec. com. tax sect. 1973-83), Assn. Bar City N.Y. (mem. tax com. 1982—). Home: 41 Stormowaye Chappaqua NY 10514 Office: NYY Law Sch 40 Washington Sq S New York NY 10012

DALE, JIM, actor; b. Rothwell, Northamptonshire, Eng., Aug. 15, 1935; s. William and Miriam Smith; m. Patricia Gardiner; children: Belinda, Murray, Adam, Toby. Actor, Nat. Theatre Co., Old Vic, England, plays touring Europe; plays Taming of the Shrew, N.Y.C.; actor, co-dir.: Scapino, N.Y.C.; actor: Barnum, N.Y.C.; film Raising the Wind, Carry on Spying, Carry on Cleo, The Big Job, Carry on Cowboy, Lock up Your Daughter, The National Health, Digby, Joseph Andrews, Pete's Dragon, Unidentified Flying Oddball; comedian (debut) solo, Savoy, London, 1951. Recipient Tony award for Barnum, 1980. Office: The Lantz Office 888 Seventh Ave New York NY 10106

DALE, LEON ANDREW, management sciences educator, arbitrator; b. Paris, May 9, 1921; (1 parent Am. citizen); m. Arlene R. Dale; children: Glenn Roy, Melinda Jennifer, Hilary Brooke, Amy Sue. B.A., Tulane U., 1946; M.A., U. Wis., 1947, Ph.D., 1949. Grad. asst. in econs. U. Wis., 1946-48; Asst. prof. labor econs. U. Fla., 1949-50; internat. economist AFL, Paris, 1950-53; AFL rep. at nat. labor convs., Greece, 1951, Naples, Italy, 1951, Switzerland, Sweden, Norway, Belgium, Austria, Luxembourg, Gt. Britain, France, 1950-53; cons. U.S. Govt., 1954-56; internat. economist U.S. Dept. Labor, Washington, 1956-59; chief econ. sect. Embassy of Morocco, Washington, 1959-60; prof., chmn. dept. mgmt. and indsl. relations, dir. internat. ctr., coordinator courses for fgn. students U. Bridgeport, Conn., 1960-69; prof. mgmt. Calif. State Poly. U., Pomona, 1969—, acting chmn. bus. mgmt. dept., summer 1973, coordinator internat. activities Sch. Bus. Adminstrn., 1969-77; lectr. Internat. Confedn. Tree Trade Unions Summer Sch., Wörgl, Austria, 1951; lectr. on Am. labor UN, Stockholm, 1952; lectr. U. Wis.-Milw., 1960; vis. prof. Columbia U., 1966, 67, Bernard Baruch Sch. Bus. and Pub. Adminstrn., 1966-69; cons., arbitrator; fact-finder State of Conn., 1964-69; Am. del., speaker 3d Internat. Symposium on Small Bus., Washington, 1976, 4th Internat. Symposium on Small Bus., Seoul, Korea, 1977, 5th Internat. Symposium on Small Bus., Anaheim, Calif., 1978, 6th Internat. Symposium on Small Bus., Berlin, 1979; also mem. U.S. steering com. Internat. Symposium on Small Bus.; sr. cons. Am. Grad. U., Covina, Calif., 1981-82; vis. prof. econs. Nat. U., San Diego, 1981-84; discussion leader Calif. Inst. Tech. Internat. Conf. on Combining Best of Japanese and U.S. Mgmt., Anaheim, 1981; speaker Pi Sigma Epsilon Ann. Conf., Anaheim, 1983; lectr. on indsl. relations to execs. Miller Brewing Co., Irwindale, Calif., 1983. Author: Marxism and French Labor, 1956, A Bibliography of French Labor, 1969; video tape Industrial Relations and Human Resources, 1982; Contbr. articles to profl. jours. Served with U.S. Army, 1942-45. Named Outstanding Educator for Conn., 1972, 73. Mem. Am. Arbitration Assn. (nat. panel arbitrators, nat. public employment disputes settlement panel), Indsl. Relations Research Assn., Am. Acad. Polit. and Social Sci., Soc. Profls. Dispute Resolution (charter). Club: Racing of France. (Paris). Home: 30 S La Senda South Laguna CA 92677 Office: Calif State Poly U Pomona CA 91768

DALE, MADELINE HOUSTON MCWHINNEY, banker; b. Denver, Mar. 11, 1922; d. Leroy and Alice Barse (Houston) McWhinney; m. John Denny Dale, June 23, 1961; 1 son, Thomas Denny. B.A., Smith Coll., 1943; M.B.A. in Fin, NYU, 1947. With Fed. Res. Bank N.Y., 1943-73; pres. First Women's Bank, N.Y.C., 1974-76; vis. lectr. N.Y. U. Grad. Sch. Bus., 1976-77; pres. Dale, Elliott & Co., Inc., N.Y.C., 1977—; dir. Carnegie Corp. N.Y., 1974-82, vice chmn. bd., 1980-82; asst. dir. Whitney Mus. Am. Art, 1983—; mem. adv. bd. N.Y. U. Grad. Sch. Bus. Adminstrn., U. Denver Grad. Sch. Bus. and Public Adminstrn.; dir. Atlantic City Electric Co. Mem. adv. bd.: Banking Law Jour. Trustee Retirement System, Fed. Res. Banks, 1955-58; trustee Inst. Internat. Edn., 1976—, treas., 1979—; bd. dirs. Investor Responsibility Research Center, 1975-80, Charles F. Kettering Found., 1975—; mem. President's Commn. on White House Fellows, 1975-77; bd. govs. Am. Stock Exchange, Inc., 1977—; commr. N.J. Casino Control Commn., 1980-82. Recipient medal Smith Coll., 1971, Alumni Achievement award N.Y. U., 1971. Mem. Am. Fin. Assn. (dir. 1955-57), Alumni Assn. N.Y. U.-Grads. Bus. Adminstrn. (pres. 1957-59), Money Marketeers (pres. 1960-61), Nat. Assn. Corp. Dirs., Am. Econ. Assn., Women's Bond Club, Nat. Assn. Bank Women, Fin. Women's Assn., Women's Econ. Round Table, Soc. Meml. Center, Phi Beta Kappa Assos. Home: PO Box 458 Red Bank NJ 07701 Office: 30 E 62d St New York NY 10021

DALE, ROBERT GORDON, business executive; b. Toronto, Ont., Can., Nov. 1, 1920; s. Gordon McIntyre and Helen Marjorie (Cartwright) D.; m. Mary Austin Babcock, Apr. 3, 1948; children: Robert Austin, John Gordon. Ed., U. Toronto Schs., 1930-39, Trinity Coll.; student, U. Toronto, 1939-40. Cert. in bus. adminstrn., 1946. With Maple Leaf Mills, Ltd., Toronto, 1947—, plant mgr., 1957-61, gen. product mgr., 1961-65, asst. to pres., 1965-67, exec. v.p., 1967-68, now chmn., pres., chief exec. officer, dir.; dir. Nat. Life Assurance Co. Can., CanPac Agri Products Ltd., McGavin Toastmaster Ltd., Baker Commodities Inc., Eastern Bakeries Ltd., Standard Chartered Bank Can., Manpower Services (Ont.) Ltd., Koppers Internat. Can. Ltd.; active Can. Exec. Service Overseas. Mem. adv. bd. Bloorview Children's Hosp.; past pres. Air Cadet League Can.; past chmn. Ont. Provincial Com.; trustee United Community Fund Greater Toronto; bd. govs. Can. Corps Commissionaires. Served with RCAF, 1940-45. Decorated D.F.C., Can. Forces Decoration, Disting. Service Order. Mem. Can. Nat. Millers Assn. (dir., past chmn.), Grocery Products Mfrs. Can. (dir.), Air Cadet League Can. (hon. pres.), Phi Kappa Pi. Conservative. Anglican. Clubs: Rosedale Golf, Nat., Badminton and Raquet, Bd. of Trade, Empire. Office: 2300 Yonge St Toronto ON Canada M4P 2X5 *

DALE, THOMAS MANFORD, JR., brokerage company executive; b. Dearborn, Mich., Nov. 22, 1931; s. Thomas Manford and Margaret Mary (Coffey) D.; m. Carole Jean Somond, Nov. 15, 1976; children: Corbin, Thomas, Terral Rae, Matthew, Peter, Patrick, Bret. B.B.A., LL.B., U. Mich. Assoc. Dorsey Windhorst Hannaford Whitney & Halladay, 1955-57; with Daine Kalman & Quail, Mpls., 1957—, now exec. v.p. Home: 111 Wayside Rd Hopkins MN 55343 Office: Dain Kalman & Quail 100 Dain Tower Minneapolis MN 55402

DALE, WESLEY JOHN, educator; b. Milw., Aug. 8, 1921; s. Colin B. and Irma P. (Pohl) D.; m. Pattie Surine, Aug. 20, 1949; 1 dau., Claudia. B.S. in Chemistry with highest honors, U. Ill., 1943; Ph.D., U. Minn., 1949. Teaching asst. U. Minn., 1943; research chemist Govt. Synthetic Rubber Research Program, 1943-46; mem. faculty U. Mo. at Columbia, 1949-66, prof. chemistry, 1958-66, chmn. dept., 1961-64, asst. to dean, 1954-55; staff asso. sci. facilities evaluation group, div. instl. programs NSF, 1964, sr. staff asso. sci. devel. evaluation group, div. instl. programs, 1964-66; dean Sch. Grad. Studies, U. Mo. at Kansas City, 1966-72, prof. chemistry, 1966—, univ. research adminstr., 1969-72, acting provost and dean faculties, 1971, provost, 1972-79, acting chancellor, 1976-77; cons. long range academic planning; chmn. Midwest Conf. Grad. Study and Research, 1970-71. Contbr. articles to profl. jours. Bd. dirs. Sci. Pioneers, Kansas City, Mo., 1967-78, Inst. Community Studies, Kansas City, Mo., 1970-73; trustee Mid-Continent Regional Ednl. Lab., Kansas City, 1972-73; mem. adv. com. U.S. Army Command and Gen. Staff Coll., Fort Leavenworth, Kans., 1973; bd. dirs. Harry S. Truman Library Inst., 1977, Kansas City Mus., 1976-77. Mem. AAAS, Am. Chem. Soc., Sigma Xi, Phi Kappa Phi, Phi Eta Sigma, Phi Lambda Upsilon, Pi Mu Epsilon, Gamma Alpha, Alpha Chi Sigma. Home: 310 W 49th St Kansas City MO 64112 Office: 5100 Rockhill Rd Kansas City MO 64110

DALE, WILLIAM ANDREW, surgeon; b. Nashville, Mar. 13, 1920; s. William Andrew and Lillias Wood (House) D.; m. Corinne Howell, Sept. 11, 1944; children—Mary Elizabeth, Corinne Howell, Virginia House, Catherine Craig. A.B., Davidson Coll., Davidson, N.C., 1941; M.D., Vanderbilt U., 1944. Intern, then resident in surgery U. Rochester (N.Y.) Med. Center, 1944-50, asst. prof., 1951-58; clin. prof. surgery Vanderbilt U. Med. Sch., 1958—; dir. Conf. Vascular Occlusin Disease, 1971; surg. cons. Office Surgeon Gen., USAF, 1971—. Author 3 books also articles. Served as officer M.C. USAF, 1946-48. Mem. Soc. Vascular Surgery (pres. 1975), Internat. Cardiovascular Soc. (pres. 1981), So. Vascular Assn., A.C.S. (gov.), Nashville Surg. Soc., Am. Surg. Assn., Am. Thoracic Surg. Assn., Internat. Surg. Soc., So. Surg. Assn., Sigma Xi. Home: 312 Lynwood Blvd Nashville TN 37205 Office: 2010 Church St Nashville TN 37203

DALE, WILLIAM BROWN, economist; b. Detroit, Mar. 24, 1924; s. William Holl and Grace May (Brown) D.; m. Deborah Jane Parry, July 27, 1946; children: William P., Susan D., Christopher A., Judith A., Katherine S. B.A. with honors, U. Mich., 1944; M.A., Fletcher Sch. Law and Diplomacy, 1947, Ph.D. candidate, 1948. Internat. economist U.S. Treasury, 1948-56; program mgr. internat. research Stanford Research Inst., 1956-61; U.S. exec. dir. Internat. Monetary Fund, Washington, 1962-74, dep. mng. dir., 1974-84. Served with USN, 1944-46. Mem. Council Fgn. Relations, Phi Beta Kappa. Democrat. Home: 6008 Landon Ln Bethesda MD 20817 Office: 700 19th St Washington DC 20431

DALE, WILLIAM SCOTT ABELL, visual arts educator; b. Toronto, Ont., Can., Sept. 18, 1921; s. Ernest Abell and Mary (Bulloch) D.; m. Jane Gordon Laidlaw, Apr. 19, 1952; children: Michael, John, Thomas. B.A., U. Toronto, 1944, M.A., 1946; Ph.D., Harvard, 1955. Research asst. Nat. Gallery Can., Ottawa, Ont., 1950-57; curator Art Gallery Toronto, 1957-59; dir. Vancouver (B.C.) Art Gallery, 1959-61; asst. dir. Nat. Gallery Canada, 1961-66, dept. dir., 1966-67; prof. dept. visual art U. Western Ont., London, 1967—, chmn. dept., 1967-75. Served with Royal Navy, 1944-45. Research fellow Dumbarton Oaks Research Library, Washington, 1956-57. Mem. Coll. Art Assn. Am., Mediaeval Acad. Am., Internat. Ctr. Medieval Art, Royal Soc. Arts. Club: Arts and Letters (Toronto). Home: 401 Huron St London ON N5Y 4J2 Canada Office: Dept Visual Arts U Western Ontario London ON N6A 5B7 Canada

DALEN, JAMES EUGENE, physician, educator; b. Seattle, Apr. 1, 1932; s. Charles A. and Muriel E. (Joanise) Robinson; m. Jan K. Daus, Sept. 17, 1955; children: James, Angela. B.S., Wash. State U., 1955; M.A., U. Mich., 1956; M.D., U. Wash., 1961; M.S., Harvard U., 1972. Intern and asst. med. resident Boston City Hosp., 1961-63; sr. resident New Eng. Med. Center, Boston, 1963-64; research fellow in cardiology Peter Bent Brigham Hosp., Boston, 1964-67, asso. dir. cardiovascular lab., 1967-75; instr., asst. prof., asso. prof. medicine Harvard Med. Sch., 1967-75; chmn. dept. cardiovascular medicine U. Mass. Med. Sch., 1975-77, prof., chmn. dept. medicine, 1977—; physician-in-chief U. Mass. Hosp., 1977—. Contbr. articles to med. jours. Served with USN, 1951-53. Mem. A.C.P., Am. Clin. and Climatol. Soc., Assn. Univ. Cardiologists, Am. Coll. Cardiology, Am. Coll. Chest Physicians, Am. Fedn. Clin. Research. Home: 15 High St Southboro MA 01772 Office: U Mass Med Sch Worcester MA 01605

DALENBERG, ROBERT VAN RAALTE, lawyer, utility company executive; b. Chgo., Nov. 1, 1929; s. John R. and Helene (Van Raalte) D.; m. Diane Curtis, June 19, 1954; children: Douglas, Donald, Betsy. Student, Morgan Park Jr. Coll., 1947-49; J.D., U. Chgo., 1953. Bar: Ill. bar 1956. Assoc. firm Essington, McKibben, Beebe & Pratt, Chgo., 1955-58, Schuyler, Stough & Morris, 1958-64, ptnr., 1965-67; gen. atty. Ill. Bell Telephone Co., Chgo., 1967-72; asso. gen. counsel Pacific Tel. & Tel. Co., San Francisco, 1972-76, v.p. and gen. counsel, 1976—. Served to lt. USCGR, 1953-55. Mem. Am., Ill., Chgo., Calif. bar assns., Am. Judicature Soc., Phi Kappa Psi, Legal Club Chgo., Law Club Chgo. Office: 140 New Montgomery St San Francisco CA 94104

DALES, RICHARD CLARK, history educator; b. Akron, Ohio, Apr. 17, 1926; s. Gerald Lee and Lucile (Miller) D.; m. Nancy Gene Vogeler, July 7, 1950; children—Susan Zoe, David Richard. A.B., U. Rochester, 1949; M.A., U. Colo., 1952, Ph.D., 1955. Instr. history N.D. State Coll., 1954-55; from instr. to asso. prof. Lewis and Clark Coll., Portland, Oreg., 1955-62; vis. asso. prof. U. Calif. at Santa Barbara, 1963-64; from asso. prof. to prof. U. So. Calif., 1964—, chmn. dept. history, 1969-72; mem. Inst. Advanced Study, 1966-67. Author: Robert Grosseteste's Scientific Works, 1961, Anonymi De Elementis, 1965, The Achievement of Medieval Science, 1973, A Medieval View of Human Dignity, 1977, A Twelfth-Century Concept of the Natural Order, 1978, The Intellectual Life of Western Europe in the Middle Ages, 1980, Malmonides and Boethius of Dacia on the Eternity of the World, 1982, Medieval Discussions of the Eternity of the World During the First Half of the Twelfth Century, 1982; editor: Roberti Grosseteste Commentarius in VIII Libros Physicorum Aristotelis, 1963, Marius On the Elements, 1974. Served with C.E. AUS, 1946-47. Am. Council Learned Socs. fellow, 1960-61. Home: 616 Chatham Pl Flintridge CA 91011

DALES, SAMUEL, microbiologist, virologist, educator; b. Warsaw, Poland, Aug. 31, 1927; emigrated to Can., 1948, naturalized, 1953; s. James and Helen (Ochs) D.; m. Laura L.R.J. Fischer, Dec. 28, 1952; children—Adam Charles, Pamela Ann. B.A. with honors, U. B.C., 1951, M.A., 1953; Ph.D., U. Toronto, 1956. Postdoctoral fellow Nat. Cancer Inst. Can., 1957-60; research asso., asst. prof. Rockefeller U., N.Y.C., 1960-66; asso. mem., mem., chief cytobiology Public Health Research Inst. City of N.Y., Inc., 1966-76; prof. U. Western Ont., Can., London, 1975—, chmn. microbiology and immunology, 1975-80; research prof. N.Y. U. Med. Sch., 1969-75; mem. adv. bd. spl. virus cancer program Nat. Cancer Inst., NIH, 1969-73; mem. virology study sect. NIH, 1971-75, ad hoc, 1977, 79; mem. sci. adv. bd. Banting Research Found., 1978-80; mem. rev. panels virology and cancer USPHS, Med. Research Council Can. Author: Biology of Poxviruses, 1981; asso. editor: Virology, 1963—, Intervirology, 1973—; editor: Jour. Cell Biology, 1973-76; contbr. sci. articles and revs. to profl. publs. Macy Found. scholar, 1981—; research grantee USPHS, Med. Research Council Can., Multiple Sclerosis Soc. Mem. Fedn. Am. Socs. for Exptl. Biology, Harvey Soc., Am. Soc. Cell Biology, N.Y. Soc. Electron Microscopy (council 1968-70), Amyotrophic Lateral Sclerosis Soc. An. (sci. adv. bd.). Home: 1588 Hillside Dr London ON N6E 2P8 Canada Office: Dept Microbiology Immunology Univ Western Ontario London ON N6A 5C1 Canada

DALES, WILLIAM, utility company executive; b. Anaheim, Calif., Aug. 19, 1924; s. William McKinley and Edith Irene (Flynn) D.; m. Marjorie Ann Rowcliffe, Nov. 15, 1952; children: Gary William, Ronald Jay, Robert Cecil. A.A., Santa Ana Jr. Coll., 1947; B.S., Oreg. State U., 1950. Dist. clk. Calif. Interstate Telephone Co., Bishop, 1950-54, traffic engr., Victorville, 1954-58, traffic mgr., 1958-61, plant mgr., 1961-64; v.p. ops. Continental Telephone Co. Calif., Victorville, 1964-68; pres. Continental Telephone Co. Ill., Sycamore, 1968-70; v.p. traffic Continental Telephone Service Corp., Bakersfield, Calif., 1970-73; pres. Continental Telephone Co. Va., Mechanicsville, 1973—. Served with USMC, 1943-46; PTO. Republican. Lodge: Elks. Home: 6402 Strawhorn Dr Mechanicsville VA 23111 Office: Continental Telephone Co Va PO Box 900 Mechanicsville VA 23111

D'ALESSANDRO, ROSEANNA MARIE, insurance company executive; b. Phila., Feb. 25, 1931; d. Peter Paul and Antoinette Mary (Dolente) D'A. Student, St. Joseph's U., 1950, Inst. Paralegal Training, 1973. With Ins. Co. N. Am., Phila., 1949-64; with Penn Mutual Life Ins. Co., Phila., 1964—, sr. office systems analyst, 1969-73, asst. sec., 1973-77, sec., 1977-79, asst. v.p., sec., 1980-81, sec. of 46 subsidiary cos., 1973—, asst. v.p., dir. public affairs, 1981—; dir. Hotel Brunswick, Inc., Indepno Corp., Penn Series Funds, Inc., WPI Investment Co., Penn Mut. Equity Services, Inc. Bd. dirs. Phila. Council for Community Advancement; chmn. Penn Mutual United Way campaign, 1976; active United Way of Southeastern Pa., 1977—; pres., dir. Washington Sq. Assn., 1977—; adv. council Women for Greater Phila., 1978-81, dir., 1981—; Republican committee-woman Lower Merion, Ward 8, Dist. 1, 1964—; sec. Lower Merion/Narberth Rep. Com., 1966-68, vice chmn., 1968-73, chmn., 1973-76; area leader Montgomery County Rep. com., Area 7, 1976-80; organizing bd. Women in Politics Polit. Action Com., 1979—; co-chmn. Internat. Friendship Fete, 1981; bd. dirs. Wynnewood Valley Civic Assn., 1978—, pres., 1984-85. Recipient Legion of Honor award Chapel of the Four Chaplains, 1967. Mem. Corporate Social Responsibility Assn. Roman Catholic. Home: 512 Twin Oaks Dr Wynnewood PA 19096 Office: Independence Sq Philadelphia PA 19172

D'ALESSIO, EDWARD RONALD, university president; b. West Orange, N.J., May 20, 1932; s. Gerardo K'Alessio and Angela (Picariello) D'A.; m. Rose M. Racanelli, Aug. 12, 1956; children: Judith A., Edward P., John G., Teresanne R. B.A. in social studies, Seton Hall U., 1954, L.H.D. (hon.), 1979; M.S. in edn., Fordham U., 1955; Ph.D. in hist. and philos. founds. of edn., Fordham U., 1967; postgrad., Advanced Adminstrv. Inst., Harvard U. Grad. Sch. Edn., 1967. Dir. div. elem. and secondary edn. U.S. Catholic Conf., 1970-76; with New Pres. Inst. Am. Council Edn., U. Wis., Madison, 1976; pres. Coll. of Our Lady of Elms, Chicopee, Mass., 1976-79; asst. U.S. sec. edn. Office Non-Pub. Edn. U.S. Dept. Edn., Washington, 1979-80, dep. U.S. commr. edn., 1980; exec. v.p. Seton Hall U., South Orange, N.J., 1980-81, pres., 1981—; cons. study Cath. edn. Archdiocese, N.Y., 1968; bd. dirs., charter mem. Council Am. Pvt. Edn., 1970-76; mem. Edn. Commn. of States; accreditor Conn. Dept. Higher Edn., 1979-83. Contbr. articles to porfl. and religious publs. Recipient 1st disting. alumnus of yr. Sch. Edn. Seton Hall U., 1976. Mem. Nat. Cath. Ednl. Assn., Am. Assn. Ch. Adminstrs., AAUP, Higher Edn. Group Washington D.C. Office: Office of Pres Seton Hall U South Orange NJ 07079

D'ALEXANDER, WILLIAM JOSEPH, pub. co. exec.; b. Cleve., Dec. 16, 1927; s. Silvio and Rose Margaret (DePhillips) D'A.; m. Mary Jo Comella, Apr. 15, 1961; children—William, Michael, James, Robert. B.S., B.A., Kent State U., 1951. Asst. advt. mgr. Gen. Electric Supply Co., Cleve., 1951-52; advt. mgr. No. Ohio Appliance Corp., Cleve., 1952-53; account exec. Fuller & Smith & Ross, Cleve., 1953-55; pub. Penton Pub. Co., Cleve., 1955-73; pres., chief exec. officer Delta Communications Inc., Chgo., 1973—. Served with AUS, 1946-47. Mem. Alpha Tau Omega. Roman Catholic. Home: 728 Glenayre Dr Glenview IL 60025 Office: 400 N Michigan Ave Chicago IL 60611

DALEY, ARTHUR JAMES, magazine pub.; b. St. Paul, Aug. 15, 1916; s. John and Mary (Mayer) D.; m. Lorayne Mary Mongan, June 7, 1941; children—Michael, Kay. Student pub. schs., Fond du Lac, Wis. Advt. salesman Fond du Lac Commonwealth Reporter, 1936, sports editor, 1937-40; sports writer Green Bay (Wis.) Press-Gazette, 1941-43, sports editor, 1946-68, telegraph, picture editor, 1968-78; pub. Green Bay Packer Yearbook, 1960—; columnist Green Bay Packer Report, 1974—. Mem. Wis. Hall of Fame Com.; mem. bd. of selectors Nat. Profl. Football Hall of Fame, Canton, Ohio. Served with AUS, 1943-46; ETO. Mem. Pro Football Writers Am., Nat. Football League Alumni Assn., Holy Name Soc. Roman Catholic. Club: Oneida Golf and Riding. Home: 1146 High View Ln Green Bay WI 54304 Office: PO Box 262 Green Bay WI 54305

DALEY, CHARLES LEON, banker; b. Phila., May 22, 1932; s. Patrick and Mary Veronica (Hagan) D.; m. Janet C. Toland, Sept. 29, 1962; children: Karen, Charles J., Carol Ann. B.S., LaSalle Coll., Phila., 1957. C.P.A., D.C., Pa. Mgr. Peat, Marwick, Mitchell & Co. (C.P.A.s), Phila., 1957-69; sr. v.p., controller First Pa. Corp., Phila., 1969-81; v.p. Burbidge Assocs., Phila., 1981-83; sr. v.p., chief fin. officer First Peoples Bank, Westmont, N.J., 1983—. Served with U.S. Army, 1953-55. Mem. Am. Inst. C.P.A.'s, Fin. Execs. Inst., Nat. Assn. Accountants, Pa. Inst. C.P.A.'s. Roman Catholic. Office: First Peoples Bank Cuthbert Blvd Westmont NJ

DALEY, DANIEL HAYES, air force officer; b. Elmira, N.Y., Mar. 9, 1920; s. Charles Augustine and Irene (Hayes) D.; m. Roberta Jean Buechele, Oct. 27, 1945; children: Martha Jean Daley Ferguson, Daniel Charles, David Keith, James Christopher. B.S. in Mech. Engring., Purdue U., 1942; S.M. in Aero. Engring., MIT, 1946. Registered profl. engr., Ohio. Commd. 2d lt. USAAF, 1942; advanced through grades to col. USAF, 1965; rated command pilot, 1958, assigned, U.S., 1942-44; asst. prof. aero. engring. Air Force Inst. Tech., 1946-49, asso. prof., acting head dept. mech. engring., 1949-55; pilot 4930th Test Support Group, Eniwetok Atoll, Pacific, 1955-56; wing flying safety officer 483d Troop Carrier Wing, Ashyia, Japan, 1956-58; chief aerodynamics sect. B-70 Weapon System Project Office, 1958-61; asso. prof. USAF Acad., 1961-64, prof., head dept. aero. engring., 1965, 67-72, 74—; prof., head dept. aerospace engring. Pakistan Air Force Coll. Aero. Engring., Karachi, 1965-67; chief scientist USAF European Office Aerospace Research, London, 1972-74; permanent prof., head dept. aeros. USAF Acad., 1967—; vis. prof. dept. mechanics U.S. Mil. Acad., 1980. Fellow Royal Aero. Soc. (asso.), AIAA (asso.), Pakistan Inst. Engrs. (life); mem. Sigma Xi, Tau Beta Pi, Sigma Gamma Tau, Pi Tau Sigma. Home: Quarters 4176 USAF Academy CO 80840 Office: Dept of Aeronautics USAF Academy CO 80840

DALEY, JOSEPH T., bishop; b. Connerton, Pa., Dec. 21, 1915. Ed., Charles Borromeo Sem., Phila.; D.D. Ordained priest Roman Cath. Ch., June 4, 1941; titular bishop Barca and aux. bishop, Harrisburg, 1963-67, coadjutor bishop with right of succession, 1967-71, bishop of, Harrisburg, Pa., 1971—. Address: 4800 Union Deposit Rd PO Box 2153 Harrisburg PA 17105 *

DALEY, PAUL HUBERT, steel co. exec.; b. Pawtucket, R. I., July 23, 1919; s. Joseph H. and Rosella (Coyle) D.; m. Mary D. Daley, Nov. 21, 1942; children—Mary Ellen Daley Etheridge, Paul Coyle, Steven Joseph. B.S., U. Paris, France, 1940; M.A., Fordham U., 1941. Mgmt. engr. Thompson & Lightner Co., Boston, 1944-46; with Heppenstall Co., Pitts., 1946—, v.p. sales, 1960-62, exec. v.p., 1962-76, pres., chief exec. officer, 1976—, also dir.; exec. v.p., dir. Midvale-Heppenstall Co., Phila., 1962-76, pres., chief exec. officer, 1976—; Heppenstall-Midvale A.G., Zug, Switzerland. Mem. adv. bd. Carnegie-Mellon Inst. Served to 2d lt. AUS, 1942-43. Mem. ASME, Forging Industry Assn., Open Die Forging Assn., Am. Mgmt. Assn. Home: 714 Cascade Rd Pittsburgh PA 15221 Office: 4620 Hatfield St Pittsburgh PA 15201

DALEY, ROBERT EMMETT, foundation executive; b. Cleve., Mar. 13, 1933; s. Emmett Wilfred and Anne Gertrude (O'Donnell) D.; m. Mary Berneta Fredericks, June 7, 1958; children: Marianne Fredericks, John Gerard. B.A. in English, U. Dayton, 1955; M.A. in Polit. Sci., Ohio State U., 1968, Ohio State U., 1976. Part-time copy boy, sports reporter Jour. Herald, Dayton, Ohio, 1953-55, local govt. reporter, Washington corr., fin. editor, 1957-65, pub. affairs reporter, 1967; staff writer Congressional Quar., Inc., Washington, 1966; traveling press sec. (for senatorial candidate John J. Gilligan), Ohio, 1968, 1970-71, asst. to Gov. Gilligan, 1971-75; pub. affairs reporter Dayton Daily News, 1969; media relations coordinator Nat. League Cities, Washington, 1976-77; dir. pub. affairs and communications Charles F. Kettering Found., Dayton, 1977—. Past pres. bd. trustees St. Joseph Home for Children. Served with U.S. Army, 1955-57. Mem. Nat. Press Club, Pub. Relations Soc. Am., Am. Polit. Sci. Assn., Am. Soc. Pub. Adminstrn., Communications Network in Philanthropy, Am. Acad. Polit. and Social Sci., Montgomery County Hist. Soc., Ind. Sector Pub. Info. and Edn. Com., Sigma Delta Chi. Roman Catholic. Lodges: K.C.; Ancient Order Hibernians. Home: 321 Whittington Dr Centerville OH 45429 Office: 5335 Far Hills Ave Dayton OH 45429

DALEY, WILLIAM PATRICK, art educator, artist; b. Hastings-on-Hudson, N.Y., Mar. 7, 1925; s. William Joseph and Alice Mary Ann (Doran) D.; m. Catherine S., Sept., 1950; children: Barbara, Charlotte, Thomas. B.S. In Edn., Mass. Coll.Art, 1950; M.A. in Art Edn., Columbia U., 1951. Instr. U. No. Iowa, Cedar Falls, 1951-54; asst. prof. art SUNY-New Paltz, 1954-57; assoc. prof. art SUNY-Fredonia, 1962-64; prof. art Phila. Coll. Art, 1957—; guest prof. U. N. Mex., Albuquerque, 1971-72, Calif. coll. arts and crafts, Oakland, 1973; guest instr. Tyler Sch. Art, Phila., 1970, Haystack Sch. Crafts, Deer Isle, Maine, 1969. Represented: permanent collections Phila. Mus. Art, St. Louis Mus. Art; permanent collection Everson Mus. Art, Syracuse, N.Y.; permanent collections Campbell Mus., Helen Drutt Gallery, Phila., Dienst Beeld ende Kunst, Kruithuis, Netherlands. Grantee NEA, 1977; recipient citation for Outstanding Achievement in Visual Arts Mass. Coll. Art, 1980. Mem. Am. Craftman's Council, Nat. Council on Edn. for Ceramic Arts (life mem.), Clay Studio (adv. bd.). Home: 307 Ashbourne Rd Elkins PA 19117 Office: Phila Coll Art Broad and Spruce Sts Philadelphia PA 19102

DALGARNO, ALEXANDER, astronomy educator; b. London, Eng., Jan. 5, 1928; s. William and Margaret (Murray) D.; m. Barbara W.F. Kane, Oct. 31, 1957 (div.); children: Penelope, Rebecca, Piers, Fergus; m. Emily K. Izsak, June 23, 1972. B.Sc., U. London, 1947, Ph.D., 1951; M.A. (hon.), Harvard U., 1967; D.Sc. (hon.), Queen's U. Belfast, 1980. Lectr., Queen's U., Belfast, No. Ireland, 1951-56, reader, 1956-61, prof. math. physics, 1961-67, dir. computation lab., 1961-66; prof. astronomy Harvard U., 1967—, Phillips prof., 1977—, chmn. dept., 1971-76; asso. dir. Center for Astrophysics Harvard U., 1973-80; acting dir. Harvard Coll. Obs., 1971-73; research scientist Smithsonian Astrophys. Obs., Cambridge, Mass., 1967—. Editor: Astrophys. Jour. Letters, 1973—; contbr. articles to profl. jours. Recipient Hodgkins medal Smithsonian Instn., 1977. Fellow Royal Soc., Phys. Soc. (London), Am. Phys. Soc. (Davisson-Germer award 1980); mem. Am. Geophys. Union, Am. Acad. Arts and Scis., Royal Astron. Soc., Internat. Acad. Astronautics (corr. mem.). Home: 244 Franklin St Newton MA 02158

DALINKA, MURRAY KENNETH, radiologist, educator; b. Bklyn., May 13, 1938; s. Joseph and Gertrude (Cohen) D.; m. Janice L. Kolber, Feb. 28, 1982; 1 son, Bradford Gordon; children by previous marriage: Ilene, Ian Scott. B.S., U. Mich., 1960, M.D., 1964. Am. Bd. Radiology. Intern Pa. Hosp., Phila., 1964-65; resident in radiology Montefiore Hosp., N.Y.C., 1965-68; instr. radiology Harvard Med. Sch., 1970-71; asst. prof. radiology Thomas Jefferson U. Hosp., Phila., 1971-73, assoc. prof., 1973-76, chief diagnostic radiology, 1974-76, prof., 1976—; chief orthopaedic radiology Hosp. U. Pa., 1976—; cons. Phila. Naval Hosp., 1974-79, Walson Hosp., Ft. Dix Army Base, 1972-77. Author: Arthrography, 1980, Symposium on Orthopedic Radiology, 1983; mem. editorial bd.: Bone Syllabus IV, 1982—, Skeletal Radiology, 1982—, Conversations in Radiology, 1977-79. Served to capt. USAF, 1968-70. James Picker research fellow, 1972-73. Mem. Internat. Skeletal Soc. (asst. sec.), Radiol. Soc. N. Am., Assn. Univ. Radiologists, Am. Coll. Radiology. Home: 318 S 21st St Philadelphia PA 19103 Office: Dept Radiology Hospital of Univ Pa 3400 Spruce St Philadelphia PA 19104

DALIS, IRENE, mezzo-soprano, opera director; b. San Jose, Calif.; d. Peter N. and Mamie (Boitano) D.; m. George Loinaz, July 16, 1957; 1 dau., Alida Mercedes. A.B., San Jose State Coll., 1946, M.S. (hon.), 1957; M.A., Columbia Tchrs. Coll., 1947; studied voice with, Edyth Walker, N.Y.C., 1947-50, Paul Althouse, 1950-51, Dr. Otto Mueller, Milano, Italy, 1952—. Prof. music San Jose (Calif.) State U., 1976—; gen. dir. Opera San Jose, 1979—. Operatic debut as dramatic mezzo-soprano, Berlin Staedtische Opera, 1955; debut, Met. Opera, N.Y.C., 1957; leading mezzo-soprano, to 1976; 1st Am.-born singer, Kundry Bayreuth Festival, 1961; opened, Bayreuth Festival in Parsifal, 1963; Commemorative: Wagner 150th Birth Anniversary; opened: 1963 Met. Opera Season in, Aida; premiered: Dello Joio's Blood Moon, 1961, Henderson's Medea, 1972; rec. artist, Philips Records. Recipient Fulbright award for study in, Italy, 1951; Tower award San Jose State U., 1974; Distinguished Service award Tchrs. Coll., Columbia U., 1961. Home: 1635 Mulberry Ln San Jose CA 95125 Office: 12 S 1st St Suite 900 San Jose CA 95113

DALLAS, SHERMAN FORBES, educator, labor arbitrator; b. Buffalo, May 22, 1919; s. Sherman L. and Mable (Forbes) D.; m. Betty Lou Sears, May 11, 1945; children: Barbara (Mrs. John L. Cox), George Sherman. B.A., Ohio No. U., 1949; M.A., Ind. U., 1951, Ph.D., 1955. Asst. prof. Ga. Inst. Tech., 1952-54; lectr. Ind. U., 1954-55; assoc. prof. Ind. State Coll., 1955-58; commr. Fed. Mediation and Conciliation Service, 1958-59; assoc. prof. Ga. Inst. Tech., 1959-61, prof., 1961—, Regents prof., 1982—, dir., dean Coll. Indsl. Mgmt., 1965-71; permanent arbitrator Process Piping Co., Plumbers and Pipefitters, Retail Clks. and Teamsters Union, Colonial Stores Inc., Alterman Bros., Inc., Teamsters and Assoc. Grocers, Inc., Ballet Fabrics Inc. and A.C.T.W.U., Bekaert Steel Wire Co., I.U.E., So. Assn. Colls. and Schs., Mr. V's and Bartenders Union.; cons. Center Disease Control, George C. Marshall Space Flight Center, Nuclear Assurance Corp., Lockheed Aircraft Co., Jacksonville Naval Air Sta.; Dir. internat. dept. Citizens & So. Nat. Bank, Ellijay Telephone Co. (Ga.), Goodwill Industries. Author: (with W. Propes and B. Schaffer) Labor Relations in the U.S. Nuclear Power Industry; Contbr. articles to profl. jours. Served to 2d lt. AUS, 1942-46. Mem. Am. Econ. Assn., Soc. Profls. in Dispute Resolution (v.p.), Nat. Acad. Arbitrators, Indsl. Relations Research Assn., Phi Kappa Phi, Beta Gamma Sigma, Omicron Delta Kappa, Pi Gamma Mu, Alpha Kappa Psi. Home: 3325 Valley Rd NW Atlanta GA 30305

DALLEY, GEORGE ALBERT, government official, consultant; b. Havana, Cuba, Aug. 25, 1941; s. Cleveland Ernest and Constance Joyce (Powell) D.; m. Pearl Elizabeth Love, Aug. 1, 1970; children: Jason Christopher, Benjamin Christian. A.B., Columbia U., 1963, J.D., 1966, M.B.A., 1966. Bar: N.Y. 1966, D.C. 1971, U.S. Supreme Ct. 1972. Asst. to pres. Met. Applied Research Center, N.Y.C., 1967-69; counsel The Children's Found., Washington, 1970-71; asso. counsel Stroock and Stroock and Lavan, Washington, 1970-71, Com. on Judiciary, U.S. Ho. of Reps., 1971-72; adminstrv. asst. to Rep. Charles B. Rangel, N.Y.C., Washington, 1973-77; dep. asst. sec. for human rights and social affairs Bur. Internat. Orgns. Affairs Dept. State, Washington, 1977-80; mem. CAB, 1980-82; dep. dir. Mondale for Pres. Com., 1983—; adj. prof. Am. U. Sch. Law. Mem. legal adv. com. Democratic Nat. Com., 1975-76. Mem. Am. Bar Assn., Nat. Bar Assn., Fed. Bar Assn., Nat. Conf. Black Lawyers. Presbyterian. Home: 1328 Vermont Ave NW Washington DC 20005 Office: Mondale for Pres 2201 Wisconsin Ave NW Washington DC 20007

DALLEY, JOSEPH WINTHROP, engineering educator, consultant; b. Aberdeen, Idaho, Aug. 12, 1918; s. Arthur Theophilis and Julia Frederickson (Amussen) D.; m. Alice Sawtelle, July 10, 1943; children: Joseph Winthrop, Amussen Ann, Nicholas Sawtelle, Theresa Jill, Sandra Kim. B.S.A.E., U. Tex., 1947, M.S.E.M., 1951, Ph.D., 1959. Diplomate: registered profl. engr., Tex. Asst. prof., research engr. U. Tex., Austin, 1948-59; prof., head aero. engrng. U. Wichita, 1959-60; prof., head engrng. mechanics U. Tex., Arlington, 1960-69, prof. aero. engrng. and engrng. mechanics, 1969-73, prof., assoc. dean Sch. Engrng., 1973-83; sr. ptnr. Dalley & Tucker, Arlington, 1965-73, Dalley, McWherter & Assocs., Arlington, El Paso, Tex., 1979—; assoc. Haneman Assocs. Inc., Richardson, Tex., 1961-68; vis. prof. U.S. Mil Acad., West Point, N.Y., 1983—. Author, editor: Review Notes for the EIT Exam, 1980. Served to lt. col. USAAF, 1940-46; PTO. Fellow Soc. Exptl. Stress Analysis (pres. 1975-76), Soc. Exptl. Stess Analysis (exec. com. 1971-73), AIAA (assoc. dir. North Tex. sect. 1966-70); mem. Am. Soc. Engrng. Edn., Tex. Soc. Profl. Engrs. (pres. Midcities chpt. 1979-80), Sigma Xi, Tau Beta Pi, Sigma Gamma Tau, Pi Tau Sigma. Lodge: Kiwanis. Home: 1911 Woods Dr Arlington TX 76010 Office: U Tex 1st and Yates Sts Arlington TX 76019

DALLIN, ALEXANDER, educator; b. Berlin, Germany, May 21, 1924; came to U.S., 1940, naturalized, 1943; s. David J. and Eugenia (Bein) D.; children—Linda, Natasha, Andrew. B.S., Coll. City N.Y., 1947; M.A., Columbia, 1948, Ph.D., 1953. Asso. dir. research program on USSR, N.Y.C., 1951-54; dir. research War Documentation Project, Washington, 1954-56; faculty Columbia, 1956-71, prof. internat. relations, 1961-65, Adlai Stevenson prof. internat. relations, 1965-71; former dir. Russian Inst.; prof. history and polit. sci. Stanford U., 1971—, chmn. dept. internat. relations, 1980—; cons. U.S. Govt., 1962-70; chmn. Nat. Council for Soviet and East European Research, 1978-80. Author: German Rule in Russia, 1941-1945, 1957, rev. edit., 1981, The Soviet Union at the United Nations, 1962, (with others) The Soviet Union and Disarmament, 1965, Political Terror in Communist Systems, 1970; editor: Soviet Conduct in World Affairs, 1960, Diversity in International Communism, 1963, Politics in the Soviet Union: Seven Cases, 1966, Soviet Politics Since Khrushchev, 1968, Women in Russia, 1977. Served with AUS, 1943-46. Fellow Social Sci. Research Council, 1950-51; Guggenheim fellow, 1961-62; Fulbright Hays fellow, 1965-66; Wilson Center fellow, 1978-79. Mem. Am. Assn. Advancement Slavic Studies, Western Slavic Assn. (pres. 1978-80), Council Fgn. Relations, Am. Hist. Assn. Home: 607 Cabrillo Ave Stanford CA 94305

DALLIS, NICHOLAS PETER, comic strip writer; b. N.Y.C., Dec. 15, 1911; s. Peter Nicholas and Sophia (Alexandre) D.; m. Sara Louise Luddy, May 29, 1939; children: Peter, Sally Dallis Anderson, Carolyn Dallis Uchman. A.B., Washington and Jefferson Coll., 1933; M.D., Temple U., 1938. Intern Washington (Pa.) Hosp., 1938-39; resident in psychiatry Henry Ford Hosp., Detroit, 1941-45; practice medicine specializing in psychiatry, Toledo, 1945-59. Creator: comic strip Rex Morgan, M.D, 1948—, Judge Parker, 1952—, Apt. 3-G, 1961—. Trustee Camelback Hosp., Phoenix. Recipient Decency award Kiwanis Internat., 1973, award on pub. health edn. AMA, 1954; Distinguished Service award Pres.'s Com. Employment of Handicapped, 1954. Charter fellow Am. Coll. Psychiatrists (life); life mem. Am. Psychiat. Assn. Address: 7315 E McLellan Blvd Scottsdale AZ 85253

DALLMAN, PAUL JERALD, engineer, writer; b. Washington, July 7, 1939; s. Paul Frederick and Helen Anna (Roloff) D. B.S. in Civil Engrng., U. Md., 1963, Mus.M., 1972. Registered profl. engr., Md., Va. Engr., Washington Surburban San. Commn., Hyattsville, Md., 1963-72; pvt. cons. engr., 1972—; music editor films and TV, USIA, Washington, 1967-68; critic Washington Star newspaper, 1970-73; now engr. and writer; dir. Nat. Assn. Ind. Record Distbrs. and Mfrs., Washington, 1975; also editor NAIRD News; lectr., demonstrator early music machines and phonographs Smithsonian Instn., 1977-81; jazz dir. Sta. WMUC-FM, 1980—; host, producer, engr. Sta. WDCU-FM, 1982, Sta. WAMU-FM, 1982—. Profl. singer, St. Paul's Ch., Alexandria, Va., 1967-71, Washington Camerata Chorus, 1968, St. John's Ch., Chevy Chase, Md., 1974—; Author: Guitar Teaching in the United States (The Life and Work of Sophocles Papas), 1978; contbr. articles to profl. jours.; writer, producer, narrator: Nat. Pub. Radio program Historical American Patriotic Recordings, 1976. Music Critics Assn. fellow Round Top, Tex., 1977; Nat. Endowment Arts grantee, 1976. Address: 3258 Queenstown Dr Mount Rainier MD 20712

DALLMAN, PETER RICHARD, pediatrician; b. Berlin, Nov. 19, 1929; U.S., 1938, naturalized, 1946; s. Max and Edith (Breslauer) D.; m. Mary Donaldson Fenner, May 29, 1959; children—Tom, Ann, Julia. B.A., Dartmouth Coll., 1951; postgrad., Med. Sch., 1950-52; M.D., Harvard U., 1954. Intern Hitchcock Hosp., Hanover, N.H., 1954; resident in pediatrics N.Y. Hosp.-Cornell Med. Center, 1957-59; fellow in pediatric hematology Boston Children's Hosp.-Harvard U., 1959-60, Stanford U., 1961-63, asst. prof. pediatrics, 1964-68; asst. prof. U. Calif., San Francisco, 1968-70, asso. prof., 1970-77, prof., 1977—; chmn. nutrition study sect. NIH; cons. Nat. Center Health Statistics; mem. com. on nutritional anemias Internat. Union Nutritional Scis. Contbr. numerous articles on iron metabolism and nutritional anemia to profl. jours. Served with M.C. USN, 1955-57. Recipient Research Career Devel. award NIH, 1966-73. Mem. Am. Acad. Pediatrics (vice chmn. com. nutrition), Am. Pediatric Soc., Soc. Pediatric Research, Am. Soc. Hematology, Am. Inst. Nutrition. Home: 2201 9th Ave San Francisco CA 94116 Office: U Calif Med Center M650 San Francisco CA 94143

DALLMANN, DANIEL F., artist, educator; b. St. Paul, Mar. 21, 1942; s. Otto and Marry D. B.S., Minn. State U., 1965; M.A., U. Iowa, 1968, M.F.A., 1969. Prof. Tyler Sch. Art, Phila., 1969—. One man shows, Schoelkopf Gallery, N.Y.C., 1980, Schoelkopf Gallery, 1984; group shows include, Allan Franklin Gallery, N.Y.C., 1982, Berkshire Mus., Pittsfield, Mass., 1983; represented in permanent collections, Chem. Bank N.Y., Am. Telephone and Telegraph, N.Y.C., J.B. Sneed Mus., Louisville. Office: Robert Schoelkopf Gallery 825 Madison Ave New York NY 10021

DALLMAYR, WINFRIED REINHARD (FRED), government educator; b. Ulm, Germany, Oct. 18, 1928; came to U.S., 1955, naturalized, 1962; s. Albert and Olga (Schnell) D.; m. Ilse Balzer, Aug. 24, 1957; children: Dominique Brigit, Philip Gregory. Dr. Law, U. Munich, Germany, 1955; M.A., So. Ill. U., 1956; Ph.D., Duke, 1960. Asst. prof. polit. sci. Milw.-Downer Coll., 1961-63; asst. prof. Purdue U., West Lafayette, Ind., 1963-65, asso. prof., 1965-68, prof., 1968-71, 73-78, head dept. polit. sci., 1974-78; prof. U. Ga., Athens, 1971-73; Dee prof. govt. U. Notre Dame, Ind., 1978—; research fellow Inst. European Studies, Turin, Italy, 1954-55, 56-57; vis. prof. Hamburg (Germany) U., 1968-69, 71, 76; vis. fellow Nuffield Coll., Oxford U., 1978. Author: (with R.S. Rankin) Freedom and Emergency Powers, 1964, Materials on Knowledge and Human Interests, 1974, (with T.A. McCarthy) Understanding and Social Inquiry, 1977, From Contract to Community, 1978, Beyond Dogma and Despair, 1981, Twilight of Subjectivity, 1981, Language and Politics, 1983; contbg. author: Law and Justice, 1970, Social Structure and Political Life, 1973, Phenomenological Sociology, 1973, Explorations in Phenomenology, 1974, Phenomenology and Social Science, 1978, Through the Looking-Glass, 1979; contbr. articles to social sci. and philosophy jours. Mem. Am. Polit. Sci. Assn., Am. Soc. Polit. and Legal Philosophy, Conf. for Study Polit. Thought, Soc. for Phenomenology and Existential Philosophy, Phi Beta Kappa. Home: 51888 Old Mill Rd South Bend IN 46637 Office: Dept Govt and Internat Studies U Notre Dame Notre Dame IN 46556

DALLOS, PETER JOHN, neurobiologist, educator; b. Budapest, Hungary, Nov. 26, 1934; came to U.S., 1956, naturalized, 1962; s. Ernest and Maria (Klein) D.; m. Cirla Joan Hammerman, Sept. 9, 1961 (div. 1974); 1 son, Christopher; m. Joan Badofsky, Aug. 18, 1977. Student, Tech. U. Budapest, 1953-56; B.S., Ill. Inst. Tech., 1958; M.S., Northwestern U., 1959, Ph.D., 1962. Research engr. Am. Machine and Foundry Co., 1959; cons. engr., 1959-60; mem. faculty Northwestern U., 1962—, prof. audiology and elec. engrng., 1969—, prof., chmn. dept. neurobiology and physiology, 1980—; vis. scientist Karolinska Inst., Stockholm, 1977-78; chmn. behavioral and neurosci. rev. panel Nat. Inst. Neurology, Communicative Disease and Stroke. Author: The Auditory Periphery: Biophysics and Physiology, 1973; also articles. Recipient 12th ann. award Beltone Inst. Hearing Research, 1977; Guggenheim fellow, 1977-78. Fellow Acoustical Soc. Am., IEEE; mem. AAAS, Internat. Soc. Audiology (exec. com.), Soc. for Neurosci., Assn. for Research in Otolaryngology, Soc. Contemporary Art (Chgo.), Sigma Xi, Tau Beta Pi, Eta Kappa Nu. Office: Frances Searle Bldg Northwestern Univ Evanston IL 60201

DALMAN, GISLI CONRAD, electrical engineering educator; b. Winnipeg, Man., Can., Apr. 7, 1917; s. Conrad Fred and Valgerdur (Thorsteinsdottir) D.; m. Catherine Stewart, Dec. 24, 1941; children: Diana Dalman Dotson, Kristine, Karen Dalman Nielsen, Conrad. B.E.E., Coll. City N.Y., 1940; M.E.E., Poly. Inst. Bklyn., 1947, D.E.E., 1949. Mfg. engr. RCA, 1940-45; mem. tech. staff Bell Telephone Labs., 1945-47; engrng. sect. head Sperry Gyroscope Co., Great Neck, N.Y., 1949-56; mem. faculty Cornell U., Ithaca, N.Y., 1956—, prof. elec. engrng., 1956—; acting dir. Sch. Elec. Engrng., 1972-73, dir., 1975-80; adj. prof. Poly. Inst. Bklyn., 1954-56; cons. to industry, 1956—; cons. on millimeter wave amplifiers to TRW, Redondo Beach, Calif., 1980-81. Contbr. articles on microwave solid stafe devices to profl. lit. Project mgr. UN Spl. Fund China Project, Chiao Tung U., Hsinchu, Taiwan, 1962-63. Fellow IEEE, AAAS; mem. Sigma Xi, Tau Beta Pi, Eta Kappa Nu. Home: 506 Hanshaw Rd Ithaca NY 14850

DALRYMPLE, GORDON BENNETT, engineering company executive; b. Williamsburg, Ky., Dec. 2, 1924; s. Ira Chase and Carrie Adelaide (Randolph) D.; m. Monalea V. Cooper, Dec. 23, 1950; children: Aaron Randolph, Gary Bryant, Mark Hamilton, Timothy Chase. B.S. in C.E, U. Ill., 1949, M.S., Ga. Inst. Tech., 1967; grad. advanced mgmt. program, Harvard U., 1969. Registered profl. engr., Ga. Jr. engr. Engrng. Works div. Dravo Corp., Pitts., 1951-52; with Law Engrng. Testing Co., Atlanta, 1952—, beginning as dir. engrng., successively v.p. and gen. mgr., exec. v.p., pres. and chief exec. officer, 1952-75, chmn. bd., 1975—; dir. Law Internat. Elder Sandy Springs Christian Ch.; bd. dirs. Nat. Benevolent Assn. Christian Ch. (Disciples of Christ); chmn. bd. Christian Coll. Ga., Interfaith Vol. Lawyers; chmn. bd., bd. dirs. Fla. Christian Center. Served with USNR, 1943-46. Named engr. of year Metro Atlanta, 1971; engr. of year State of Ga., 1977. Mem. Nat. Soc. Prof. Engrs., Ga. Soc. Profl. Engrs., Ga. Engrng. Found. (founding dir., past pres., life mem.), Southeastern Consortium for Minorities in Engrng. (past chmn., bd. dirs.), ASCE, ASTM. Club: Harvard Bus. Sch. of Atlanta. Home: 8125 Innsbruck Dr Dunwoody GA 30338 Office: 1140 Hammond Dr NE Suite 5150 Bldg E Atlanta GA 30356

DALRYMPLE, GUY HAROLD, hosp. pres.; b. Ft. Worth, July 1, 1920; s. O.C. and Bessie M. (Stout) D.; m. Betty Jane Williams, Aug. 1, 1942; children—Stephen, Chris, Bill. B.B.A., Baylor U., 1948. Office mgr. Bapt. Hosp., Alexandria, La., 1948-49; auditor-chief accountant Hendrick Meml. Hosp., Abilene, Tex., 1949; asst. adminstr. Bapt. Hosp., Beaumont, Tex., 1949, adminstr., 1953-76, pres., 1976—; Bd. dirs. Beaumont Blood Bank, 1954—, pres., 1967-68; chmn. bd. Hosp. Receivables Service Inc.; dir. Blue Cross-Blue Shield of Tex., 1975—; governing bd. Greater E. Tex. Health Systems Assn. Inc.; trustee Tex. Hosp. Ins. Exchange. Past pres. Beaumont Met. YMCA. Served with AUS, 1941-46. Mem. Am. Coll. Hosp. Adminstrs., Am. Hosp. Assn. (del.-at-large 1978-81), Bapt. Hosp. Assn. (pres. 1970-72), Tex. Hosp. Assn. (Earl M. Collier award 1975, pres. 1970-71, trustee pension plan 1978-81), Tex. Bapt. Hosp. Assn. (pres. 1978-80), Am. Protestant Hosp. Assn. (pres.-elect 1973, pres. 1974), Tex. Assn. Hosp. Governing Bds. (Founder's award 1981, pres. 1981), Beaumont C. of C. (past dir.). Baptist (trustee, deacon). Home: 6590 Windwood St Beaumont TX 77702 Office: PO Box 1591 Beaumont TX 77704

DALRYMPLE, JEAN, theatrical producer, publicist; b. Morristown, N.J., Sept. 2, 1910; d. George Hull and Elizabeth Van Kirk (Collins) D.; m. Ward Morehouse, Mar. 31, 1932 (div. 1937); m. Philip De Witt Ginder, Nov. 1, 1951. Ed. pvt. tutors; D.F.A. (hon.), Wheaton Coll., 1959. Bd. dirs. N.Y.C. Center Music and Drama, Soldiers, Sailors and Airmen's Club, N.Y.C., Friends of the Theatre and Music Collection of Mus. City N.Y., Profl. Children's Sch., N.Y.C., Am. Theatre Wing, ANTA., N.Y. World's Fair, 1964-65; cons. Performing Arts Program, N.Y. World's Fair; dir. U.S. Performing Arts Program, Fed. Pavilion, N.Y. World's Fair; Mem. adv. bd. N.C. Sch. Arts. Actress, writer, 1926-29; publicist for, John Golden, 1929-33; publicist, mgr. for artists including, Jose Iturbi, Grace Moore, Lily Pons, Bidu Sayoa, Glinka Milanov, Nathan Milstein, Leopold Stokowski, 1933-44; permanent dir., N.Y.C. Center Theatre Co.; theatre publicist, Tallulah Bankhead, Mary Martin, Margaret Sullivan; plays Ballet Russe de Monte Carlo, N.Y.C. Center; Lewisohn Stadium concerts; producer: Hope For The

Best, 1944, Brighten the Corner, 1945, Burlesque, 1946-48, Red Gloves, 1948-49; prod., dir.: summer circuit The Second Man, Harvey, Voice of the Turtle, Petrified Forest, 1950-53; permanent dir., Drama Co. N.Y. City Center; producer (with Jose Ferrer) 4 plays, 1953-54, Winter Play Festival of 1954-55, What Every Woman Knows, The Fourposter, Time of Your Life Wisteria Trees, 1955, King Lear, Marcel Marceau, Streetcar Named Desire, 1957; dir.: King Lear, Marcel Marceau, Streetcar Named Desire, Light Opera Co. N.Y. City Center; producer: Carousel (spl. Christmas Show); dir., producer numerous others; producer numerous TV programs and films; asso. producer: film Children of Theatre Street, 1976; producer: La Casa de Te de la Luna de Agosta, U.S. Dept. State, Mexico and S.Am., 1956-57, Variations on the Same Theme (Ionesco), Guggenheim Mus., N.Y.C., 1980; coordinator: U.S. Performing Arts Program, Brussels World's Fair, 1958; producer: Agnes de Mille Heritage Dance Theatre; coordinator: Internat. Festival Entertainment; Author: September Child, 1963, Careers and Opportunities in the Theatre, 1969, Jean Dalrymple's Pinafore Farm Cookbook, 1971, The Folklore and Facts of Natural Nutrition, 1973, From the Last Row, 1975, The Complete Handbook for Community Theatre, 1977, also articles, sketches, plays. Decorated knight Order Crown for Brussels World's Fair work, Belgium; recipient 4 citations for City Center Work from mayor N.Y.C. Mem. Nat. Council on Arts, Am. Nat. Theatre and Acad. (dir., treas.). Producer in prodn. operas, dramas for Pay-TV. Home: 150 W 55th St New York NY 10019

DALRYMPLE, RICHARD WILLIAM, banker; b. Somerville, N.J., May 27, 1943; s. Walter Andrew and Margaret Ann (Teston) D.; children: William Paul, Michael John, Kevin Scott, Craig Stephen, Debra Lyn, Bryan Tod. B.A., U. Norte Dame, 1965. With Chem. Bank, N.Y.C., 1965—, v.p., 1965-79; exec. v.p. European Am. Bank, N.Y.C., 1979—; chmn., dir. Eastern States Bankcard Inc., L.I., N.Y., 1982-83. Chmn. bd. dirs. Action Com. for L.I. Inc., 1982—; trustee Human Resources Ctr., Albertson, L.I., 1982—; chmn. SME campaign Boy Scouts of Greater N.Y., N.Y.C., 1982. Recipient Humanitarian award Am. Jewish Com. L.I., 1982. Roman Catholic. Club: Recess (N.Y.C.). Home: 104 Victoria Dr Basking Ridge NJ 07920 Office: European Am Bank 10 Hanover Sq New York NY 10015

DALRYMPLE, THOMAS LAWRENCE, lawyer; b. Wellsburg, W. Va., May 20, 1921; s. Lawrence Chester and Ethel May (Taylor) D.; m. Marjorie May Keeler; children: Bruce Lawrence, Dale Brian. A.B., U. Mich., 1943, J.D., 1947. Bar: Ohio 1947, U.S. Supreme Ct. Practiced in, Toledo, 1947—; assoc. Williams, Eversman & Morgan and successor firms, 1947-50, Welles, Kelsey, Fuller, Harrington & Seney and successor firms, 1950-52; ptnr. Fuller & Henry and predecessor firms, 1953—. Mem. Trout Unltd., Toledo Mus. Art. Served to capt. inf. AUS, 1943-46. Decorated Combat Inf. badge, Silver Star medal, Purple Heart. Fellow Am. Coll. Trial Lawyers, Ohio State Bar Found.; mem. Internat. Assn. Ins. Counsel, Am., Ohio, Toledo bar assns., Order of Coif, Phi Beta Kappa. Home: 4307 Stannard Dr Toledo OH 43613 Office: 300 Madison Ave Toledo OH 43604

DALSHAUG, ALLAN EMORY, banker; b. Buchanan, Sask., Can., May 19, 1931; s. Ellend Johann and Cornelia (Benson) D.; m. Elva Beatrice Smith, Mar. 24, 1955; children: Ellana Beatrice, Eric Justin Charles, Errin Jon. Grad. with honors, Lutheran Bible Inst., Outlook, Sask., Pacific Coast Banking Sch., 1967. With Security Pacific Bank, 1973-79, sr. v.p. strategic planning, Los Angeles, 1977-79; chmn. bd., chief exec. officer Sterling Bank, Los Angeles, 1980—; instr. S.W. Grad. Sch. Banking. Mem. Western Ind. Bankers Assn., Calif. Bankers Assn. Methodist. Club: Wilshire Country.

DALSTON, JEPTHA WILLIAM, hospital administrator, educator; b. Longview, Tex., Mar. 18, 1931; (married). B.A., Tex. A&M U., 1952; M.A., U. Okla., 1966, Ph.D. in Health Adminstrn. and Polit. Sci. 1970; postgrad., Columbia U., 1963-64; M.H.A., U. Minn., 1969. Controller Reynolds Army Hosp., Ft. Sill, Okla., 1959-60; adminstr. USPHS Indian Hosp., Lawton, Okla., 1960-65; chief planning and evaluation Indian Health Service USPHS, Oklahoma City, 1969-70; asst. adminstr. Univ. Hosp. and Clinics, Oklahoma City, 1970-73, adminstr., 1973-75; dir. Univ. Hosp., Ann Arbor, Mich., 1975—; asst. prof. U. Okla., 1970-73, asso. prof., 1973-76; prof. U. Mich., 1976—; preceptor Washington U., U. Minn. Served with U.S. Army, 1952-58; Served with Res., 1958—. Mem. Am. Hosp. Assn., Am. Public Health Assn., Am. Coll. Hosp. Adminstrn., Am. Acad. Polit. Sci. Office: U Mich Hosps 300 N Ingalls Bldg Ann Arbor MI 48109

DALTON, ALBERT JOSEPH, cancer researcher, educator; b. New London, Conn., Nov. 9, 1905; s. Joseph Aloysius and Serena (Olsen) D.; m. Leonie Ha, Dec. 8, 1977; children—Patricia Gade Dalton Tucker, Robert Paul, Celia Kay Dalton Clark. B.S., Wesleyan U., 1927; M.A., Harvard, 1929, Ph.D., 1934. Tutor Coll. City N.Y., 1929-32; instr. dept. anatomy Western Res. U. Sch. Medicine, 1934-38; lectr. dept. anatomy McGill U., 1938-41; research fellow Nat. Cancer Inst., 1941-42, biologist, 1942-61, chief biologist, 1961-75, scientist emeritus, 1975—; on leave as asso. sci. Sloan Kettering Inst. Cancer Research, 1958-59; prof. Cornell U. Grad. Sch., 1958—; Mem. molecular biology study sect. research grants rev. br. NIH, 1967-70. Co-editor: monograph series Ultrastructure in Biological Systems; asso. editor: Jour. Ultrastructure Research, Cancer Research, 1959-61. Recipient Superior Service award NIH, 1969. Fellow Royal Micros. Soc.; mem. Am. Assn. Anatomists, Soc. Exptl. Biology and Medicine, Soc. Exptl. Pathology, Am. Assn. Cancer Research, Electron Microscope Soc. Am., Am. Soc. Cell Biology, Am. Inst. Biol. Scis., Fedn. Am. Socs. Exptl. Biology, Sigma Xi. Home: 11916 Reynolds Ave Potomac MD 20854

DALTON, DENNIS GILMORE, political science educator; b. Morristown, N.J., Mar. 12, 1938; s. Andrew John and Emily Snow (Smith) D.; m. Sharron Louise Scheline, May 22, 1961; children: Kevin Andrew, Shaun Michael. B.A., Rutgers U., 1960; M.A., U. Chgo., 1962; Ph.D., U. London, 1965. Lectr. politics U. London, 1965-69; prof. polit. sci. Barnard Coll., Columbia U., N.Y.C., 1969—. Author: Indian Idea of Freedom, 1982; editor: States of South Asia, 1983. Mem. War Resisters League, N.Y.C., 1969—. Am. Council Learned Socs. grantee, 1975; Am. Philos. Soc. grantee, 1975; Am. Inst. Indian Studies fellow, 1974. Home: 105 Thompson St Apt 12 New York NY 10012 Office: Barnard Coll Columbia Univ 606 W 120th St New York NY 10027 *My research for the last two decades on the life and thought of Mahatma Gandhi has convinced me that his example carries universal implications for the study of conflict resolution. The theory and practice on non-violence offers us today a system of values and a hope for the future that should serve to inspire and energize humanity.*

DALTON, DONALD H., lawyer; b. Grant County, Wis.; s. Charles Christian and Alvina D.; m. Virginia Brady, Sept. 20, 1931; 1 dau., Sylvia Dalton Searight; m. Irene Martin, Sept. 16, 1939; children: Doris J. Dalton Harper, Donald H., Diane I. Student, U.S. Naval Acad., 1925-29, Columbia U., 1930; B.S., U. Chgo., 1931; postgrad., Yale U., 1934-35; J.D., Georgetown U., 1947. Bar: D.C. 1946, Ill. 1947, Md. 1952. Reporter, Washington Post, 1945; practice law, Washington, Ill., Md.; mem. firm Dalton & Brown, Washington; prof. pub. and bar relations Southeastern U., 1949-58. Mem. Republican Central Com. for Md., 1974-78, 82—, vice chmn., 1978—; trustee Legal Aid Soc. D.C. Served as war plans officer USN, World War II; lt. comdr. Res. ret. Recipient cert. of pub. relations achievement Am. Pub. Relations Assn., 1957; Disting. Alumni award Columbia U. Club, Washington, 1968. Mem. ABA (chmn. pub. relations com. gen. practice sect.), Fed. Bar Assn., D.C. Bar Assn. (1st v.p., dir., pres. found.), Md. Bar Assn. (mem. pub. relations com.), Chgo. Bar Assn., D.C. Bar Found. (pres. 1978), Am. Arbitration Assn., Assn. Plaintiffs Trial Attys. (dir.), English-Speaking Union, Am. Legion, Res. Officers Naval Service (pres.), Judge Advocates Gen. Assn. (dir.), 40 and 8, U.S. Capitol, Montgomery County hist. socs., Nat. Sojourners (chpt. pres.), U. Chgo. Alumni Assn., U.S. Naval Acad. Alumni Assn., Lincoln Group D.C. (pres. 1971—), SAR, Civil War Roundtable, Scribes (treas. 1975—), Delta Theta Phi. Clubs: Mason, Rotarian., Counsellors, Columbia U. (Washington) (pres. 1960-70); Army and Navy Country, Army and Navy, Capitol Hill, Lawyers, Nat. Press, Yale, Rotary of Washington (chmn. public relations com. 1974—), Saints and Sinners.). Home: 8603 Springdell Pl Chevy Chase MD 20015 Office: Fed Bar Bldg West 1819 H St NW Washington DC 20006

DALTON, DOUGLAS, lawyer; b. Astoria, Oreg., Sept. 1, 1929; s. Mervyn Edgar and Julia Margaret (Hitchcock) D.; m. Shirley Kirkpatrick, Aug. 29, 1953; children—Julia M., Douglas C., John D., Matthew J., Bartholomew P. B.A., UCLA, 1951; J.D., U. So. Calif., 1956. Bar: Calif. bar 1956. City prosecutor, Long Beach, Calif., 1956-60; partner Ball, Hunt, Hart, Brown & Baerwitz, Los Angeles, 1960-77; prin. Dalton & Buehler, Inc., Los Angeles, 1977—; adj. prof. law Pepperdine U. Sch. Law, Los Angeles, 1978-80. Counsel Pres. Nixon's Commn. on Campus Unrest, 1970. Served with USN, 1951-53. Fellow Am. Coll. Trial Lawyers; mem. State Bar Calif., County Bar Los Angeles, Am. Bar Assn. Republican. Office: 3660 Wilshire Blvd Suite 230 Los Angeles CA 90010

DALTON, HARRY, baseball exec.; b. Springfield, Mass., Aug. 23, 1928. Grad., Amherst Coll., 1950. With Balt. Orioles, 1953-71, v.p. and player personnel dir., 1965-71; exec. v.p., gen. mgr. Calif. Angels, 1971-77, Milw. Brewers, 1977—. Served as 1st lt. USAF. Decorated Bronze Star. Office: care Milw Brewers Milw County Stadium Milwaukee WI 53214 *

DALTON, JACK, librarian, educator; b. Holland, Va., Mar. 21, 1908; s. John Preston and Selma Hatcher (Butler) D.; m. Mary Armistead Gochnauer, Sept. 6, 1933; 1 son, John Preston, III. Student, Va. Poly. Inst., 1924-27; B.S., U. Va., 1930, M.S., 1935, U. Mich., 1935-36. Instr. in English, Va. Poly Inst., 1930-34; reference librarian U. Va., 1936-42, asso. librarian, 1942-50, librarian, 1950-56; dir. internat. relations office A.L.A., 1956-59; dean Sch. Library Service Columbia U., 1959-70, prof., dir. Library Devel. Center., 1970-79; cons., 1979—. Mem. ALA. Home: 445 Riverside Dr New York NY 10027

DALTON, JAMES EDWARD, air force officer; b. N.Y.C., Oct. 17, 1930; s. Edward A. and Marion (Conway) D.; m. Betty Jane Irwin, Nov. 29, 1958; children: Christopher, Stephanie, Todd. B.S., U.S. Mil. Acad., 1954; M.S.E. in Instrumentation Engring, U. Mich., 1960, U. Mich., 1960; grad. with distinction, Air Command and Staff Coll., 1965, Indsl. Coll. Armed Forces, 1970. Commd. 2d lt. U.S. Air Force, 1954, advanced through grades to lt. gen., 1981; served in numerous operational and research assignments, 1954-73; comdr. 39th Aerospace Rescue and Recovery Wing, Eglin AFB, Fla., 1973-75, Air Res. Personnel Center, Denver, 1975-76; dep. dir. concepts Hdqrs. USAF, Washington, 1976-77; dep. dir. Force Devel. and Strategic Plans, Plans and Policy Directorate, Office Joints Chiefs of Staff, Washington, 1977-78; vice dir. Joint Staff, 1978-80; commandant Indsl. Coll. of Armed Forces, Washington, 1980—; dir. Joint Staff, 1981—. Decorated Def. Disting. Service medal, Legion of Merit with oak leaf cluster, D.F.C., Bronze Star, Air medal with 5 oak leaf clusters, Meritorious Service medal with oak leaf cluster, Air Force Commendation medal. Mem. Air Force Assn., Assn. Grads. U.S. Mil. Acad. Roman Catholic. Home: 3723 Riverwood Rd Alexandria VA 22309 Office: Pentagon Washington DC 20301

DALTON, JOHN CHARLES, research adminstrator, physiologist; b. Clintwood, Pa., Apr. 11, 1931; s. Lewis Nathan and Thelma (Wallace) D.; m. Lillian Topalian, Feb. 15, 1964; children: Stephen Lewis, Irene Elizabeth. B.A., U. Va., 1951; A.M., Harvard U., 1952, Ph.D., 1955. From instr. to assoc. prof. biology U. Buffalo, 1952-62; scientist, adminstr. NIH, Bethesda, Md., 1962-70, 76-78, Health Resources Adminstrn., 1970-76; dir. extramural activities program Nat. Inst. Neurol. and Communicative Disorders and Stroke (NIH), 1978—. Contbr. articles to profl. jours. Served with USPHS, 1955-57. Recipient Sr. Exec. Performance award HHS, 1982. Democrat. Methodist. Home: 7005 Old Cabin Ln Rockville MD 20852 Office: Nat Inst Health 9000 Rockville Pike Bethesda MD 20205

DALTON, JOHN NICHOLS, lawyer, former governor Virginia; b. Emporia, Va., July 11, 1931; s. Ted R. and Mary (Turner) D.; m. Edwina Jeanette Panzer, Feb. 18, 1956; children: Katherine Scott, Ted Ernest, John Nichols, Mary Helen. A.B., Coll. William and Mary, 1953; J.D., U. Va., 1957. Bar: Va. 1957. Ptnr. Dalton & Jebo, Radford, Va., 1957-77; lt. gov. Va., 1974-78, gov., 1978-82; ptnr. McGuire Woods & Battle, Richmond, 1982—. Pres. Young Republican Fedn. Va., 1960; treas. Va. Rep. Com., 1960, gen. counsel, 1961-72; mem. Va. Ho. of Dels., 1966-72, Va. Senate, 1973. Served to 1st lt. AUS, 1954-56. Mem. Am. Legion, Sigma Alpha Epsilon. Clubs: Masons (33 deg.), Shriners (past potentate). Home: 8902 Ginger Way Ct Richmond VA 23229

DALTON, WILLIAM MATTHEWS, foundry executive; b. Chgo., June 27, 1922; s. Donald J. and Jessie (Shrimplim) D.; m. Gloria S. Schneider, Sept. 29, 1977; children: D.J., J.B., Katherine A. Ed., Pomona Coll., Claremont, Calif., Butler U., Indpls.; grad. Advanced Mgmt. Program, Harvard Bus. Sch., 1956. Pres. Dalton Foundries, Inc., Warsaw, Ind., 1959-68, chmn. bd., 1968—. Mem. Warsaw Community Sch. Bd., 1962-68, Kosciusko County Council, 1981—; trustee Ind. Vocat. Tech. Coll., 1964-68; chmn. Gov. of Ind. Com. on Youth Employment, 1979-82; pres. Lake Tippecanoe Property Owners Assn., 1979-82. Served with AUS, 1943-45. Mem. Ind. State C. of C. (chmn. 1983). Republican. Office: Dalton Foundries Inc PO Box 1388 Warsaw IN 46580

DALTREY, ROGER, musician; b. London, Mar. 1, 1944. Vocalist with: musical group The Who, 1965—; solo recs. include Daltrey, Ride A Rock Horse, Who Are You, 1980, Who's Next, 1980; appeared in: films Woodstock, 1970, Tommy, 1974, Lisztomania, 1975, The Kids are Alright, 1979, McVicar, 1983. Office: care Premier Talent Agy 3 E 54th St New York NY 10022 *

DALVIT, LEWIS DAVID, JR., symphony condr.; b. Denver, Dec. 11, 1925; s. Lewis David and Anita (Lyreman) D.; m. Patricia Dougan, Aug. 28, 1949; children—Jacqueline, Stephanie. B.A., Beloit Coll., 1950; M.S., Vandercook Coll., 1956. Joined music faculty, 1960; artist-in-residence Beloit (Wis.) Coll., 1964, acting chmn. music dept., 1965-66; condr. Beloit Symphony Orch., 1953-63, 64; asst. condr. Honolulu Symphony, 1963-64; mem. music faculty Milton Coll., 1952-63; now condr. Jackson (Miss.) Symphony.; Guest condr., U.S., 1964, 65, 70, 71, 72, Mexico, 1964, 65, Germany, 1965, Central Am., 1973, Japan, 1973. Served with USAAF, 1944-46. Recipient Orpheus award for excellence in music Phi Mu Alpha Sinfonia, 1973 *

DALY, CHARLES JOSEPH, professional basketball coach; b. St. Mary's, Pa., July 20, 1933. Student, St. Bonaventure U., 1948-49, Bloomsburg State Coll., 1949-52, Pa. State U. Asst. coach Duke U., Durham, N.C., 1963-69; coach Boston Coll., 1969-71, U. Pa., Phila., 1971-77; asst. coach Phila. 76ers, NBA, 1977-81; coach Cleve. Cavaliers, NBA, 1981-82, Detroit Pistons, NBA, 1983—. Office: Detroit Pistons Pontiac Silverdome 1200 Featherstone St Pontiac MI 48057 *

DALY, CHARLES ULICK, foundation executive, investor; b. Dublin, May 29, 1927; U.S., 1934, naturalized, 1940; s. Ulick deBurgh and Violet (Sealy-King) D.; m. Mary Larmonth, June 11, 1949; children: Michael, Douglas. B.A. Internat. Relations, Yale U., 1949; M.S. Journalism, Columbia U., 1959. Mgr. then v.p. Mexican subs. Pacific Molases Co., San Francisco, 1949-50, 52-58; congl. fellow Am. Polit. Sci. Assn., 1959-60; editor Stanford U., Calif., 1961; staff asst. Pres. Kennedy and Pres. Johnson, 1962-64; v.p. pub. affairs U. Chgo., 1964-67, v.p. devel. and pub. affairs, 1967-71; v.p. govt. and communtiy affairs Harvard U., Cambridge, Mass., 1971-76; editor Media and the Cities, The Quality of Inequality, Urban Violence; pres. Joyce Found., Chgo., 1978—; mem. Lloyd's of London, 1977—; free lance writer, 1958—. Mem. Commn. on Admistrv. Rev., U.S. Ho. of Reps.; chmn. Donor's Forum, Chgo., 1980; mem. Chgo. Council on Fgn. Relations. Served with USNR, 1945-46; served with USMCR, 1950-52. Decorated Silver Star, Purple Heart. Democrat. Clubs: Comml., Attic, Union League (Chgo.); University (Washington); Bantry Golf (Ireland). Home: 217 W Eugenie Chicago IL 60614 Office: Joyce Foundation 135 S LaSalle St Chicago IL 60603

DALY, GENE BENEDICT, justice; b. Great Falls, Mont., Dec. 13, 1917; s. Edward Jerome and Florence Avis (Jeffries) D.; m. Ruth Dorothy Richardson, May 2, 1942; children—Gene Jerome, Gregory Clark. Student, Carroll Coll., Helena, Mont., 1935, Gt. Falls Coll. Edn., 1949-50; J.D., U. Mont., 1953. Bar: Mont. bar 1953. Practiced in, Gt. Falls, 1953-70, city atty., 1955-59; atty. Cascade County, Gt. Falls, 1959—; justice Mont. Supreme Ct., Helena, 1970—. Served with USAAF, 1942-47. Mem. Am., Mont. bar assns., Am. Judicature Soc., Mont. Judges Assn., Mont. County Attys. Assn. (pres. 1969-70), Am. Legion, V.F.W., D.A.V. Elk, Moose, Eagle. Home: 805 Madison St Helena MT 59601 Office: State Capitol Bldg Helena MT 59601

DALY, GEORGE GARMAN, economist, educator; b. Painesville, Ohio, Oct. 5, 1940; s. George Fedinand and Helen May (Garman) D.; m. Barbara Leigh Anthony, Mar. 15, 1977. A.B., Miami U., Oxford, Ohio, 1962; M.A., Northwestern U., 1965, Ph.D., 1967. Asst. then assoc. prof. Miami U., Oxford, 1965-69; asst. prof. U. Tex., Austin, 1969-70; asst. prof., then prof. U. Houston, 1971-77, dean Coll. Social Sci., 1979-83; dean Coll. Bus. U. Iowa, Iowa City, 1983—; asst. dir. Inst. Defense Analysis, Arlington, Va., 1977-79; sr. economist Exec. Officer Pres., Washington, 1974; economist Fed. Energy Agy., Washington, 1975-76; adv. bd. Ctr. Pub. Policy, Houston. Mem. Am. Econs. Assn., Public Choice Soc., Phi Beta Kappa, Beta Gamma Sigma. Home: 14 Woods Ln Iowa City IA 52240 Office: U Iowa Coll Bus Iowa City IA 52242

DALY, JAMES JOSEPH, bishop; b. Bronx, N.Y., Aug. 14, 1921; s. Thomas and Catherine (Cass) D. Grad., Immaculate Conception Sem., Huntington, 1948; LL.D., Molloy Coll., Rockville Centre, N.Y., St. John's U., Jamaica, N.Y., 1979. Ordained priest Roman Catholic Ch., 1948; priest Our Lady of Snow, Blue Point, N.Y., 1948-51, Holy Child Jesus, Richmond Hill, 1951, St. William the Abbot, Seaford, 1951-58; procurator Immaculate Conception Sem., Huntington, 1958; dir. Priests' Personnel Bd., 1968-72; pastor St. Boniface, Elmont; aux. bishop of Rockville Centre, 1977—, Episcopal vicar Nassau County and vicar gen., 1977—, now aux. bishop, vicar of, Nassau County. Office: 50 N Park Ave Rockville Centre NY 11570

DALY, JAMES JOSEPH, newspaper exec.; b. Jersey City, June 11, 1916; s. Bernard B. and Anna (Leiner) D.; m. Catherine Mary Adams, June 26, 1937; children—Ann Daly Heller, Catherine Daly Kline. Student, St. Peters Coll. Classified advt. mgr. N.Y. Sun, 1946-49, World Telegram Sun, 1950-55; with Washington Post, 1955—, v.p., gen. mgr., 1965-72; exec. v.p. Washington Star, 1975-77, chmn. exec. com., dir., 1977-78; mem. exec. com. Newspaper I. Mem. exec. com. Washington Conv. and Visitors Bur., 1969-72; chmn. v.p. Tenafly (N.J.) Community Chest, 1955; budget com. Washington Health and Welfare Council, 1961-64; Bd. dirs. United Givers Fund, Washington Bd. Trade, Better Bus. Bur., ARC; trustee Am. Cancer Soc., Fed. City Council, 1977-78. Served with AUS, 1943-45. Mem. Washington Advt. Club, John Carroll Soc., Silurians. Clubs: Rotarian., Columbia Country, Pisces (Washington); Boca Raton (Fla.). Home: 700 S Ocean Blvd Boca Raton FL 33432 6905 Earlsgate Way Potomac MD 20852

DALY, JAMES WILLIAM, physician, educator; b. Chgo., Jan. 5, 1931; s. John F. and Helen L. (Hendricks) D.; m. Geraldine Callaghan, June 1953; children: Daniel, Timothy, Rebecca. Student, U. Santa Clara, (Calif.), 1948-51; M.D., Loyola U., Chgo., 1955. Diplomate: Am. Bd. Ob-Gyn (gynecologic oncology). Intern St. Mary's Mercy Hosp., Gary, Ind., 1955-56; resident in Ob-Gyn Wilford Hall USAF Hosp., San Antonio, 1959-62; M.D. Anderson Hosp. and Tumor Inst., Houston, 1962-63; mem. faculty U. Fla. Med. Sch., Gainesville, 1968-82, prof. ob-gyn, 1977-82; prof., chmn. dept. ob-gyn Creighton U. Sch. Medicine, Omaha, 1982—; dir. tumor registry Shands Teaching Hosp., 1980—, hosp. area clin. physician, 1969-80; project dir. North Central Fla. Maternity and Infant Care project, 1972-74; cons. Nat. Cancer Inst., VA Hosp., Gainesville. Author articles in field, chpts. in books. Served as officer M.C. USAF, 1956-68. Decorated Meritorious Service medal with oak leaf cluster. Fellow Am. Coll. Ob-Gyn; mem. Soc. Gynecologic Oncologists, AMA, Am. Radium Soc., S. Atlantic Assn. Obstetricians and Gynecologists, Felix Rutledge Soc., San Antonio Ob-Gyn Soc. (pres. 1967). Republican. Roman Catholic.

DALY, JOE ANN GODOWN, publishing company executive; b. Galveston, Tex., Aug. 7, 1924; d. Elmer and Jessie Fee (Beck) Godown; m. William Jerome Daly, Jr., Jan. 25, 1958 (dec.). B.A. in Journalism, U. Okla., 1945, 1952. Asst. editor house organ Southwestern Bell Telephone, St. Louis, 1945-47; sec. to city mgr. Okla. Daily News, Oklahoma City, 1947-49; pvt. piano tchr., Alva, Okla., 1952-54; sec. to editor Prentice-Hall, Inc., N.Y.C., 1954-55, asst. to children's book editor, 1955-58; asst. editor children's books Dodd, Mead & Co., N.Y.C., 1963, dir. children's books, 1965—; mem. Children's Book Council, N.Y.C., 1963, treas., 1969; mem. CBC/LA Com., N.Y.C., 1980, CBC/Prelude Com., 1983. Active Bklyn. Heights Assn., 1976—; friend Carnegie Hall, N.Y. Philharm.; mem. Met. Opera Guild, Mus. Modern Art, Mus. Natural History. Mem. Phi Beta Kappa, Sigma Delta Chi, Theta Sigma Phi, Mu Phi Epsilon. Democrat. Methodist. Home: 80 Cranberry St Brooklyn NY 11201 Office: Dodd Mead & Co Inc 79 Madison Ave New York NY 10016

DALY, JOHN CHARLES, JR., radio and TV consultant; b. Johannesburg, South Africa, Feb. 20, 1914; came to U.S., 1923; s. John Charles and Helene Grant (Tennant) D.; m. Margaret Criswell Neal, Jan. 7, 1937 (dec.); children: John Neal, John Charles, Helene Grant; m. Virginia Warren, Dec. 22, 1960; children: John Warren, John Earl Jameson, Nina. Student, Marist Bros. Coll., Johannesburg, 1920-23; grad., Tilton (N.H.) Sch., 1930; student, Boston Coll., 1930-33; D.Litt.,

St. Bonaventure U., 1959; D.H.L., Am. Internat. Coll., 1963; LL.D., Norwich U., 1964. Schedule engr. Capital Transit Co., Washington, 1935-37; corr. and news analyst CBS, 1937-49; spl. events reporter and White House corr., 1937-41; asst. producer-dir. and narrator Spirit of 41, Washington, 1941, N.Y.C., 1941-42, Middle East-Italy, 1943-44; service in U.S.A., Europe and South Am., for CBS, 1945-49; v.p. ABC in charge of news, spl. events and pub. affairs, 1953-60; dir. Voice of Am., 1967-68; cons. Citibank, N.Y.C., 1971—; forum moderator Am. Enterprise Inst., 1976—; lectr. Mem. Water Pollution Control Adv. Bd., 1960-62; moderator Nat. Town Meeting, 1974. Corr.-analyst, ABC; moderator programs on all networks (programs include) We Take Your Word, What's My Line, March of Time Thru the Years, News of the Week, etc., N.Y.C., 1949-53; Contbr. articles in nat. mags. Pres. bd. trustees Tilton (N.H.) Sch.; trustee Norwich U.; mem. adv. bd. Nat. Digestive Diseases Assn., 1982—. Mem. Artists and Writers Assn., Internat. Radio and TV Soc. (past pres.), Assn. Radio News Analysts, Radio Corr. Assn., Sigma Delta Chi. Episcopalian. Clubs: Burning Tree Country, Columbia Country, Country (Washington); Overseas Press of America (past pres.), Metropolitan (N.Y.C.); The Family, San Francisco Golf (San Francisco). Address: 1070 Park Ave New York NY 10028

DALY, JOHN DENNIS, utility company executive; b. Norwich, Conn., July 3, 1936; s. John J. and Frances J. (Donovan) D.; m. Jane M. McShera, Aug. 2, 1958; children: John Patrick, James T., Jeffrey M., Jill K. B.S.C.E., Worcester Poly. Inst., 1957; J.D., LL.D., Seton Hall U., 1967. Registered profl. engr., Ohio. Jr. engr. Columbia Gas System Service Corp., Columbus, Ohio, 1957-61, engr., supervising engr., N.Y.C., 1961-67, atty., Wilmington, Del., 1967-73, sr. atty., 1973-76; gen. counsel, sec. Columbia Gas Transmission, Charleston, W. Va., 1976-79; pres. Columbia Gas Distn. Cos., Columbus, 1979—. Bd. dirs. Ballet Met. of Columbus, 1979—; sponsor Hannah Neil Found., 1981. Served with U.S. Army, 1959-66. Mem. Am. Gas Assn., Pa. Gas Assn. (dir.). Republican. Roman Catholic. Clubs: Scioto Country, Athletic (Columbus); Edgewood Country (Charleston). Home: 1987 Chatfield Rd Columbus OH 43221 Office: Columbia Gas Distribution Cos 200 Civic Center Dr Columbus OH 43216

DALY, JOHN FRANCIS, indsl. mfg. co. exec.; b. N.Y.C., Dec. 13, 1922; s. John F. and Caroline (Pohl) D.; m. Casilda Boyd, July 16, 1953; children—Jo-Ann, Avis, Carol, Peter, Alexia. B.S., Rensselaer Poly. Inst., 1943. Vice pres. Internat. Steel Co., Evansville, Ind., 1956-59; exec. v.p. Universal Wire Spring Co., Bedford, Ohio, 1959-60; v.p. Hoover Ball & Bearing Co. (name Hoover Universal Inc. 1978), Ann Arbor, Mich., 1960-66, exec. v.p., 1966-68, pres., 1968—, chmn., chief exec. officer, 1972—, also dir.; dir. Detroitbank, Detroit, Comml. Savs. Bank, Adrian, Mich., Aluminum Extrusion Co., Cadiz R.R., Nat. Bank & Trust Co., Ann Arbor. Bd. dirs. Siena Heights Coll., Adrian, Mich. Served to capt. USAAF, 1943-46. Mem. Theta Xi. Home: 905 Berkshire Rd Ann Arbor MI 48104 Office: PO Box 1003 Ann Arbor MI 48106

DALY, JOHN NEAL, investment banker; b. Washington, Nov. 14, 1937; s. John Charles, Jr. and Margaret Criswell (Neal) D.; m. Barbara Claire Krueger, Apr. 2, 1966; children: John Gorman, Cristina Reed. B.A., Yale U., 1959, postgrad. Law Sch., 1959-60. With E.F. Hutton & Co., Inc., N.Y.C., 1960-83, exec. v.p., dir., to 1983; v.p. Salomon Bros. Inc., N.Y.C., 1983—; exchange ofcl. Am. Stock Exchange, 1979. Mem. Bond Club N.Y. (sec. 1973-74, gov. 1975-78), Securities Industry Assn. (chmn. nat. syndicate com. 1978-79), Comex Clearing Assn. (dir. 1981—). Clubs: Stanwich (Greenwich, Conn.); Burning Tree (Washington); Down Town Assn. (N.Y.C.); Mark's (London). Home: 390 Stanwich Rd Greenwich CT 06830 Office: One New York Plaza New York NY 10004

DALY, JOSEPH RAYMOND, advertising executive; b. N.Y.C., May 14, 1918; s. William C. and Mary (Hendrick) D.; m. Elizabeth R. Schulte, Apr. 19, 1947; children: Dorothy E., Suzanne J., Peter J., Timothy J., Mark, Andrew, Jennifer. A.B., Fordham U., 1940. With John A. Cairns (advt.), 1946-49; with Doyle Dane Bernbach Internat., Inc., N.Y.C., 1949—, sr. v.p., management supr., 1959-69, pres., 1968-74, chmn. bd., 1974—, chief exec. officer, 1976—. Served to lt. comdr., Air Corps USNR, 1940-46; PTO. Decorated Navy Cross, Purple Heart, Air medal. Clubs: Turf and Field (N.Y.C.); Huntington Country, Key Biscayne Yacht. Office: Doyle Dane Bernbach Internat Inc 437 Madison Ave New York NY 10022 *

DALY, LLOYD WILLIAM, classics educator emeritus; b. Plano, Ill., Oct. 6, 1910; s. William H. and Jessie H. (Fidlar) D.; m. Alice Bernadine Abell, Aug. 22, 1935; children: Caryl Abell Daly Johnson, Sara Sue Daly Rothenberger. A.B., Knox Coll., 1932, Litt.D., 1955; M.A., U. Ill., 1933, Ph.D., 1936. Research asst. in classics U. Ill., 1936; acting prof. Greek, Kenyon Coll., 1937; mem. Am. Sch. Classical Studies in Athens, 1937-38, mem. mng. com., 1953—; from instr. to asso. prof. classical langs. and lit. U. Okla., 1938-47; assoc. prof. classical studies U. Pa., 1947-54, prof., 1954—, Allen Meml. prof. Greek, 1958-77, prof. emeritus, 1977—; chmn. dept. classical studies U. Pa., 1960-67, vice dean Grad. Sch. Art and Scis., 1951-52, acting dean, 1966, dean of Coll., 1952-59. Author: (with W. Suchier) The Altercatio Hadriani Augusti et Epicteti Philosphi, 1939, Aesop Without Morals, 1961, History of Alphabetization, 1967, Brito Metricus, 1968, (with Bernadine A. Daly) Summa Britonis, 1975, Johannes Philoponus on the Accent of Homonyms; editor and author in part of Graeco-Roman articles in: Thesaurus of Book Digests, 1949; assoc. editor: Classical Philology, 1953-55; contbr. to: Am. Illustrated Med. Dictionary; contbr. articles to learned jours. Guggenheim fellow, 1959-60. Mem. Am. Philos. Soc., Mediaeval Acad. Am., Am. Philol. Assn., Archaeol. Inst. Am., Classical Assn. Atlantic States, Pa. State Assn. Classical Tchrs., Phi Beta Kappa, Phi Kappa Phi, Eta Sigma Phi. Home: 310 Morton Ave Ridley Park PA 19078 Office: Williams Hall U Pa Philadelphia PA 19104

DALY, MAGGIE (MRS. ARTHUR BAZLEN), columnist, lectr.; b. Castle Caufield, County Tyrone, Ireland, July 2; d. Joseph and Margaret D.; m. Arthur Bazlen, Aug. 31 (dec. Dec. 1954); 1 dau., Brigid. Now lectr. Nat. Lecture Tours; now daily columnist Chgo. Tribune.; Dir. Chgo. U.S.O. Profl. model, Chgo., 1946-52; fashion coordinator, hostess NBC radio show, 1952-54; columnist: Ladies Home Jour, 1954; appeared on: TV Home Show, 1954; Author: Guide to Charm, 1955, Kate Brennan, 1957. Hon. chmn. Chgo. Mental Health Assn. Mem. Adult Edn. Assn., Fashion Group of Chgo. Office: Chicago Tribune 435 N Michigan Ave Chicago IL 60611 *

DALY, NORMAN DAVID, artist; b. Pitts., Aug. 9, 1911; s. James Ambrose and Rose (Owens) D.; m. Helen Ogden Gebbie, Aug. 31, 1942; children—David, Nicholas (dec.). B.F.A., U. Colo., 1937; M.F.A., Ohio State U., 1940; postgrad., Inst. Fine Arts, N.Y. U., 1941. Prof. art Cornell U., 1942—. Creator: mythical culture Civilization of Llhuros, one-man shows, Durand-Ruel Galleries, N.Y.C., 1947, Betty Parsons Gallery, N.Y.C., 1945, Bertha Schaefer Gallery, N.Y.C., 1949, Arkron Art Mus., 1972, Rochester Meml. Art Gallery, 1973, State U. N.Y. at Albany, Indpls. Mus. Art, Roberson Art Center, 1974, Univ. Mus., U. Pa., Römisch-Germanisches Mus., Cologne, Germany, City Hist. Mus., Bochum, Germany, 1975, group shows, Met. Mus. Art, N.Y.C., 1946, Whitney Mus. Am. Art, N.Y.C., 1947, Art Inst. Chgo., 1945, Carnegie Internat., Pitts., 1948, Corcoran Gallery Art, Washington, 1951, Viromia Mus. Fine Arts, 1952, Calif. Palace of Legion of Honor, 1945, U. Ill. Ann., 1947, Inst. Contemporary Art, U. Pa., 1980; represented in numerous permanent collections, works in sound, writing, painting, sculpture and crafts. Nat. Endowment for Arts artist's fellow, 1974; Yaddo fellow, 1976, 71; N.Y. State Council Arts grantee, 1971; recipient awards Rochester Meml. Art Gallery, 1961, Chautauqua Nat., 1948, Denver Art Mus., 1943, Munson-Williams-Proctor Inst., Everson Mus., Syracuse, Syracuse Council Fine Arts, N.Y. State Fair; Cornell Disting. Teaching award, 1981; others. Home: 110 N Quarry St Ithaca NY 14850

DALY, ROBERT ANTHONY, motion picture company executive; b. Bklyn., Dec. 8, 1936; s. James and Eleanor D.; m. Nancy MacNeil, Oct. 7, 1961; children: Linda, Bobby, Brian. From dir. bus. affairs to v.p. bus. affairs, to exec. v.p. CBS TV Network, 1955-77; pres. CBS Entertainment Co., 1977—; chmn. Warner Bros., Inc., Burbank, Calif., 1981—; Bd. dirs. Am. Film Inst. Mem. Acad. Motion Picture Arts and Scis., Nat. Acad. TV Arts and Scis., Hollywood Radio and TV Soc., Motion Picture Pioneers. Roman Catholic. Club: Bel Air Country. Office: 4000 Warner Blvd Burbank CA 91522

DALY, T(HOMAS) F(RANCIS) GILROY, fed. judge; b. N.Y.C., Feb. 25, 1931; s. Paul Gerard and Madeleine (Mulqueen) D.; m. Stuart Stetson, Jan. 16, 1960; children—Timothy Francis Gilroy, Matthew M., Loan, Anna L. B.A., Georgetown U., 1952; LL.B., Yale U., 1957. Bar: Conn. bar 1957, N.Y. bar 1959. Mem. firm Simpson Thacher and Bartlett, N.Y.C., 1957-61; asst. U.S. atty. U.S. Dept. Justice, So. Dist. of N.Y., 1961-64; dept. atty. gen. State of Conn., 1967-71, spl. asst. to atty. gen., Conn., 1971-75, dep. state treas., 1976-77, ins. commr., 1976-77; U.S. Dist. Ct. judge, Conn., 1977—, individual practice law, Fairfield, Conn., 1964-77. Trustee Leukemia Soc. Am. (chmn. 1971). Served as 1st. lt. U.S. Army, 1952-54. Recipient Distinguished Service award Fairfield Jr. C. of C., 1967. Mem. Am., Conn., Fed. bar assns., Am. Judicature Soc., Fed. Bar Council, Assn. of Bar City of N.Y., Am. Legion, Phi Delta Phi. Democrat. Roman Catholic. Office: United States Courthouse 915 Lafayette Blvd Bridgeport CT 06604

DALY, WALTER JOSEPH, physician, educator; b. Michigan City, Ind., Jan. 12, 1930; s. Walter Hayes and Nellie Martha (Stipp) D.; m. Joan Brown, June 12, 1953; children—Lois Kay, Alice Louise. A.B., Ind. U., 1951, M.D., 1955. Intern Ind. U., 1955-56, resident, 1956-57, 59-62, instr. medicine, 1962-63, asst. prof., 1963-65, assoc. prof., 1965-68, prof., 1968-77, John B. Hickam prof., 1977-80, J.O. Ritchey prof., 1980—; chmn. dept. medicine, 1970-83, dean Sch. Medicine, 1983—; dir. Regenstrief Inst. Health Research, 1976—. Served to capt. M.C. U.S. Army, 1957-59. Fellow ACP (gov. 1980-84), Am. Coll. Cardiology; mem. Am. Physiol. Soc., Central Soc. Clin. Research (pres. 1980-81), Am. Soc. Clin. Investigation, Am. Clin. and Climatological Assn., Assn. Am. Physicians. Home: 4543 Manning Rd Indianapolis IN 46208 Office: 1100 W Michigan St Indianapolis IN 46223

DALY, WILLIAM GERALD, business executive; b. McKeesport, Pa., Sept. 13, 1924; s. William P. and Helen J. (McGowan) D.; m. Jean F. Wandrisco, June 24, 1950; 1 dau., Kathleen Jean. B.S. in Chem. Engring, Worcester Poly. Inst., 1946, Carnegie Mellon U., 1951; postgrad., Columbia U. Exec. Mgmt. Sch. Mfg. exec. Procter & Gamble, 1954-66; v.p. mfg. Heublein, Inc., Hartford, Conn., 1967-73; v.p. Riviana Foods, Inc., Houston, 1973-74; pres. Hills div. Riviana Foods, Topeka, 1974-80; pres. Gen. Plastics, Inc., Miami, Fla., 1980—; pres., owner BJ Restaurants, Inc., Key Largo, Fla., 1980—, WGD Assos., Key Largo, 1979—; sr. assoc. Baird Bus. Assocs., Inc., 1983—. Author: The Management Challenge, 1980. Served with USN, 1944-46, 52-54. Mem. Pet Food Inst. (dir.), Am. Pet Products Mfg. Assn. (dir.), C. of C. Republican. Roman Catholic. Clubs: Ocean Reef Health and Tennis (dir.), Ocean Reef, Ocean Reef Property Owners Assn. Home: FC-25A Barracuda Ln Ocean Reef Club Key Largo FL 33037

DALY, WILLIAM JAMES, health industry distributing company executive; b. Lawrence, Mass., Aug. 29, 1917; s. James W. and Alice Gertrude D.; m. Cornelia Mahony, July 18, 1942; children: Jane, Cornelius, James, William James, Christopher. B.S. in Elec. Engring, U.S. Naval Acad., 1941. With James W. Daly, Inc. (health care distbn.), Lynnfield, Mass., 1946—, pres., 1967—. Served to comdr. U.S. Navy, 1941-46. Mem. Nat. Wholesale Druggists Assn., Health Industry Distbrs. Assn. (pres.), Nat. Assn. Wholesalers, Am. Mgmt. Assn. Clubs: Salem Country, Lanam. Office: 66 Broadway Lynnfield MA 01940

DALY, WILLIAM JOSEPH, lawyer; b. Bklyn., Mar. 19, 1928; s. William Bernard and Charlotte Marie (Saunders) D.; m. Barbara A. Longenecker, Nov. 19, 1955; children: Sharon, Nancy, Carol. B.A., St. John's U., 1951, J.D., 1953. Bar: N.Y. 1954, U.S. Dist. Ct. (so. and ea. dists.) N.Y. 1958, U.S. Ct. Mil. Appeals 1969, U.S. Ct. Claims 1969, U.S. Tax Ct. 1969, U.S. Supreme Ct. 1973. Assoc. Garvey & Conway, Esquires, N.Y.C., 1954-55, Wing & Wing, Esquires, 1955-58; ptnr. Babchak, Daly & Lavery, Esquires and predecessor, Ossining, N.Y., 1958—. Bd. dirs. Legal Aid Soc., Westchester County N.Y., 1980—, v.p., 1983—; mem. 9th Jud. Dist. Grievance Com., 1981—. Served with U.S. Army, 1946-48; col. JAGC USAR, 1978. Fellow Am. Bar Found., N.Y. Bar Found.; mem. ABA, N.Y. State Bar Assn. (ho. dels. 1977—, exec. com. 1983—), Westchester County Bar Assn. (pres. 1979-81), Ossining Bar Assn. (pres. 1966-67), N.Y. State Trial Lawyers Am., Res. Officers Assn. U.S., Assn. U.S. Army, Phi Delta Phi. Roman Catholic. Home: 232 Hunter Ave North Tarrytown NY 10591 Office: Barclays Bank Bldg Ossining NY 10562

DALZELL, FRED BRIGGS, consultant; b. Bklyn., Sept. 23, 1922; s. Fred Briggs and Claire (Baxter) D.; m. Marie Conroy, Sept. 18, 1943; children: Victoria Ann Black, Fred Briggs Jr. Grad., Lawrenceville Sch., 1940, Amherst Coll., 1944. Cons. Sea Horse Marine, Inc.; trustee Dollar Savs. Bank N.Y., Dollar Dry Dock Savs. Bank; bd. mgrs. Seamen's House; sec., trustee South St. Seaport Mus.; trustee Am. Seamen's Friend Soc., Seamen's House YMCA; chmn. Internat. Seamen's Recreation Council; trustee N.Y. State Maritime Coll. Found.; bd. mgrs. Seamen's Ch. Inst. N.Y. and N.J. Served with USAAF, 1943-45. Mem. N.Y. Maritime Assn., Nat. Maritime Hist. Soc. (trustee, vice chmn.), St. Andrew's Soc., Pilgrims U.S. Clubs: India House, Yacht (N.Y.C.); Nat. Golf Links (Southampton, N.Y.). Home: Niamoque Ln Quogue NY 11959 Office: Sea Horse Marine Inc 515 Madison Ave New York NY 10022

DAM, KENNETH W., government official; b. Marysville, Kans., Aug. 10, 1932; s. Oliver W. and Ida L. (Hueppelsheuser) D.; m. Marcia Wachs, June 9, 1962; children: Eliot, Charlotte. B.S., U. Kans., 1954; J.D., U. Chgo., 1957; LL.D. (hon.), New Sch. Social Research, 1983. Bar: N.Y. State 1959. Law clk. to U.S. Supreme Ct. Justice Whittaker, 1957-58; asso. firm Cravath, Swaine & Moore, N.Y.C., 1958-60; mem. faculty U. Chgo. Law Sch., 1960—, prof. law, 1964-71, 74—, Harold J. and Marion F. Green prof., 1976—, provost univ., 1980-82; dep. sec. of state Dept. State, 1982—; asst. dir. nat. security and internat. affairs Office Mgmt. and Budget, 1971-73; exec. dir. Council Econ. Policy, 1973; vis. prof. U. Freiburg, Germany, 1964. Author: The GATT: Law and International Economic Organization, 1970, Oil Resources: Who Gets What How?, 1976, The Rules of the Game: Reform and Evolution in the International Monetary System, 1982; co-author: Federal Tax Treatment of Foreign Income, 1964, Economic Policy Beyond the Headlines, 1977, Energy: The Next Twenty Years, 1979. Mem. ABA, Am. Law Inst., Council Fgn. Relations, Chgo. Council on Fgn. Relations (dir. 1979—). Home: 3340 Reservoir Rd NW Washington DC 20007 Office: Dept State 2201 C St NW Washington DC 20520

DAMAN, ERNEST LUDWIG, mechanical engineer; b. Hannover, Germany, Mar. 14, 1923; came to U.S., 1940, naturalized, 1944; s. Fritz and Ruth Edith (Meyer) Dammann; m. Jan. 20, 1945 (div.); children: Diane Cathrine, Cynthia Ruth, Bruce Hershey; m. Dorothy Russo, June 21, 1980; stepchildren: Christopher Walsweer, Jonathan Walsweer. B.S. in Mech. Engring, Poly. Inst. Bklyn., 1943. With Foster Wheeler Corp., Livingston, N.J., 1947—, dir. research, 1960-73, v.p., 1973-81, sr. v.p., 1981—; chmn. Foster Wheeler Devel. Corp., Livingston, 1977—; dir. Foster Wheeler Solar Devel. Corp., Fluidized Combustion Co.; lectr. Chmn. Westfield (N.J.) Democratic Com., 1956-60, Westfield Area Com. for Human Rights, 1962-68; mem. Westfield Charter Study Commn., 1964. Served with U.S. Army, 1944-46. Decorated Bronze Star. Fellow ASME; mem. Inst. Fuel (U.K.), Am. Nuclear Soc., Pi Tau Sigma. Club: Westfield Tennis. Patentee. Home: 435 Wychwood Rd Westfield NJ 07090 Office: Foster Wheeler Corp 110 S Orange Ave Livingston NJ 07039 *As a naturalized citizen my life has been influenced by my strong admiration for American Democracy and all that it implies.*

DAMASKA, MIRJAN RADOVAN, legal educator; b. Brezice, Yugoslavia, Oct. 8, 1931; came to U.S., 1972; s. Radovan and Ljerka (Tkalcic) D.; m. Marija Brkoevic, Aug. 10, 1960. LL.M., U. Zagreb, Yugoslavia, 1956; D.Jurisprudence, Ljubljana Law Sch., 1960.. Prof. law U. Zagreb, 1960-72, acting dean Law Sch., 1970-71; prof. law U. Pa. Law Sch., Phila., 1972-76; Ford Found. prof. law Yale U. Law Sch., New Haven, Conn., 1976—; cons. Contbr. articles to legal jours.; author: Position of the Criminal Defendant, 1962. Nat. Found. for Study of Humanities fellow, 1978-79. Mem. Societe de Defense Sociale, Am. Assn. for Comparative Study of Law. Republican. Office: 117 Wall St New Haven CT 06520

D'AMATO, ALFONSE M., senator; b. Bklyn., Aug. 1, 1937; m. Penelope Ann Collenburg, 1960; children: Lisa, Lorraine, Daniel, Christopher. B.S., Syracuse U., 1959, J.D., 1961. Bar: N.Y. 1962. Adminstr., Nassau County, 1965-68; receiver of taxes Town of Hempstead, 1971-77, presiding supr., vice chmn. County bd. suprs., 1977-80; mem. U.S. Senate, 1981—. Mem. Island Park Vol. Fire Dept. Republican. Roman Catholic. Clubs: K.C., Lions, Sons of Italy. *

D'AMATO, ANTHONY ALFRED, legal educator; b. N.Y.C., Jan. 10, 1937; s. Anthony A. and Mary (DiNicholas) D'A.; m. Barbara S. Steketee, Sept. 4, 1958; children: Brian, Paul. B.A., Cornell U., 1948; J.D., Harvard U., 1961; Ph.D., Columbia U., 1968. Bar: N.Y. 1963, U.S. Supreme Ct. 1967. Instr. Wellesley Coll., 1963-65; of counsel S.W. Africa Cases, N.Y.C., 1965-66; Woodrow Wilson fellow U. Mich., Ann Arbor, 1966-67; prof. law Northwestern U. Law Sch., Chgo., 1968—, dir. Inst. Advancement of Prosthetics; dir. Globuscope Inc. Author: The Concept of Custom in International Law, 1971, (with O'Neil) The Judiciary and Vietnam, 1972, (with Hargrove) Environment and the Law of the Sea, 1976, (with Wasby and Metrailer) Desegregation from Brown to Alexander, 1977, (with Weston and Falk) International Law and World Order, 1980; bd. editors: Am. Jour. Internat. Law, 1981—. Recipient Annual Book award Am. Soc. Internat. Law., 1981. Mem. Internat. Law Assn., Am. Soc. Legal and Polit. Philosophy. Home: 716 Greenwood Ave Glencoe IL 60022 Office: Northwestern Law Sch Chicago IL 60601 *All goals in life pale in comparison to the one issue of transcendantplanetary importance: preventing nuclear war. We must establish mutually stable deterrence systems to prevent the temptation to initiate a nuclear attack. As a student of international and constitutional law, I will continue to use whatever I have learned in order to promote the recourse to law so as to establish conditions of international stability and trust.*

D'AMATO, ANTHONY ROGER, rec. co. exec.; b. N.Y.C., Jan. 21, 1931; s. Agostino and Luisa (Galiani) D'A.; m. Gabrielle Hilton, June 26, 1958; children—Luisa, Jennie, Tania, Joanna, Antonia. B.A. in Music and English Lit. cum laude (Founders Day award 1956), N.Y. U., 1956; M.A. (teaching fellow), Brandeis U., 1957. Artist and repertoire dir. stereophonic div. Decca Record Co., Ltd., Eng., 1958-78; pres. TDA Prodns. Ltd., N.Y.C., 1978—; exec. dir. Winnipeg (Man., Can.) Symphony Orch., 1979-80; v.p. artist and repertoire AudioFidelity Enterprises, N.Y.C., 1980—; mng. cons. Leopold Stokowski, 1964-72. Served with USMCR, 1951-53. Recipient Grand Prix du Disque, Charles Cros award rec., 1969. Mem. Assn. Cultural Execs. Can., Winnipeg C. of C., Phi Beta Kappa. Office: 221 W 57th St New York NY 10019

DAMAZ, PAUL F., architect; b. Portugal, Nov. 8, 1917; U.S., 1947, naturalized, 1953; s. Pierre L. and Maria A. (Leite) D.; m. Solange Guillon, Dec. 26, 1981. B.A. in Architecture, Ecole Speciale d'Architecture, 1941; M. Town Planning, U. Paris, Sorbonne, 1946. Archtl. designer UN Hdqrs., N.Y.C., 1948-51, Harrison & Abramowitz, 1951-53; chief designer Cajetan Baumann, N.Y.C., 1953-61; partner Damaz & Weigel, N.Y.C., 1962-76; pres. Adasco Tech Internat., N.Y.C., 1976-81; prin. Paul Damaz Assos., N.Y.C., 1981—; design critic Columbia, 1953; writer, critic, lectr. maj. univs. and TV. Dir. N.Y. Fine Arts Fedn.; Mem. nat. panel arbitrators Am. Arbitration Assn. Author: Art in European Architecture, 1956, Art in Latin American Architecture, 1962. Served as capt. French Army, 1941-45. Fellow A.I.A.; mem. French Ordre des Architectes, Archtl. League N.Y. (past v.p., Arnold W. Brunner award 1958), Municipal Arts Soc., French-Am. Soc., Am. Inst. Planners. Home: 302 E 88th St New York NY 10028 Office: 249 E 57th St New York NY 10022

D'AMBOISE, JACQUES JOSEPH, dancer, director, choreographer; b. Dedham, Mass., July 28, 1934; s. Andrew Ahearn and Georgette d'A.; m. Carolyn George, Jan. 1, 1956; children: George Jacques, Christopher R., Charlotte Lorraine and Catherine Liza (twins). Mem. N.Y.C. Ballet Co., 1949—; premier Danseur, 1953—; instr. Sch. Am. Ballet; prof., dean Sch. Dance, SUNY, Purchase, 1977-80; dir. Nat. Dance Inst. Motion pictures include The Best Things in Life are Free; Broadway prodn. Shinbone Alley; choreographer: TV spl. Sandlot Ballet. Office: NYC Ballet NY State Theatre Lincoln Center Plaza New York NY 10023 *

D'AMBROSIA, ROBERT DOMINICK, physician; b. Ellwood City, Pa., Dec. 25, 1938; s. Alphonse and Agnes Julia (D'Amore) D'A.; m. Barbara Ann Faycik, Oct. 17, 1964; children: Lisa Ann, Christopher John, Robert Matthew, Peter Alphonse. B.A., Washington and Jefferson Coll., 1964; M.D., U. Pitts., 1964. Diplomate: Am. Bd. Orthopaedic Surgery. Intern U. Colo., Denver, 1965; resident U. Pitts., 1970; fellow in rheumatology and rheumatoid surgery St. Margaret Meml. Hosp., U.Pitts., 1970; fellow in orthopaedic surgery Sacramento Med. Center, 1971; asst. prof. U. Calif., Davis, 1971-75, assoc. prof., 1975-76; prof., head dept. orthopaedics La. State U. Med. Center, New Orleans, 1976—; chief orthopaedic staff Hotel Dieu Hosp.; mem. staff Charity Hosp., Children's Hosp., Jo Ellen Smith Hosp., Mercy Hosp., So. Baptist Hosp., New Orleans; bd. examiner Am. Bd. Orthopaedic Surgery. Author: Musculoskeletal Disorders: Regional Examination and Differential Diagnosis, 1977, Prevention and Treatment of Running Injuries. Pres. Arthritis Found. Fellow. Served with USAF,

1965-67. Fellow Am. Acad. Orthopaedic Surgeons (bd. dirs.), A.C.S.; mem. AMA, Assn. Orthopaedic Chairmen (bd. dirs.), Orthopaedic Research Soc., Clin. Orthopaedic Soc., 20th Century Orthopaedic Soc., AAUP, Am. Assn. Med. Colls., Assn. Orthopaedic Chmn., Am. Orthopaedic Soc. Sports Medicine, La. State Med. Soc., La. Orthopaedic Assn., So. Med. Assn., Greater New Orleans Orthopaedic Soc., Orleans Parish Med. Soc., New Orleans Grad. Med. Assembly, Phi Beta Kappa, Alpha Omega Alpha. Office: 1542 Tulane Ave New Orleans LA 70112

DAMERON, THOMAS BARKER, JR., orthopaedic surgeon, educator; b. Rocky Mount, N.C., June 1, 1924; s. Thomas Barker and Rebecca (Sills) D.; m. Nancy Henry, Aug. 26, 1949; children: Thomas Barker III, David Henry, Christopher Buckston Williams, Nancy Vangleet Almquist, Rebecca Jane. M.D., Duke U., 1947. Diplomate: Am. Bd. Orthopaedic Surgery. Intern Baylor U. Hosp., Dallas, 1947-48; resident in gen. surgery Grady Meml. Hosp., Atlanta, 1948-49; resident in orthopaedic surgery Johns Hopkins Hosp., 1949-54; practice medicine specializing in orthopaedic surgery, Raleigh, N.C., 1954—; mem. staff Rex. Hosp., Wake Meml. Hosp., Raleigh Community Hosp.; instr. orthopaedic surgery Duke Sch. Medicine, Durham, N.C., 1954-62; adj. assoc. prof. poultry sci. N.C. State U., 1961-68; clin. prof. orthopaedic surgery U. N.C. Sch. Medicine, Chapel Hill, 1965—; physician cons. CARE, Tunis, Tunisia, African, 1969; cons. Sudan Interior Mission, Soddo, Ethiopia, 1973; dir. Carolina Fed. Savs. & Loan Assn. Contbr. numerous articles to med. jours., chpts. to books. Past chmn. Gov.'s Adv. Com. for Study of Crippled Childrens Facilities in N.C.; former bd. dirs. United Fund Raleigh and Wake County, Hayes Barton Methodist Ch., Wake County Muscular Dystrophy Assn., Hilltop Home, Wake County Cerebral Palsy and Rehab. Ctr.; founding pres. Parents of VA Episcopal Sch. Mem. Wake County Med. Soc. (pres. 1971), Raleigh Acad. Medicine, N.C. State Med. Soc. (chmn., mem. various coms., pres. elect 1983-84), N.C. Orthopaedic Assn. (past pres.), So. Med. Assn. (pres. 1978-79, past. chmn. exec. com., chmn. council), Am. Acad. Orthopaedic Surgeons (chmn. admissions com. 1978-79), Am. Orthopaedic Assn., Assn. Bone and Joint Surgeons, 20th Century Orthopaedic Assn., Internat. Soc. Orthopaedic Surgery and Traumatology, AMA (mem. ho. of dels. for orthopaedic surgery 1975-78, alt. del. from N.C. 1982-83), ACS, Orthopaedic Resident Assn. of Johns Hopkins Hosp. (founding pres.), Raleigh C. of C. Home: 414 Scotland St Raleigh NC 25609 Office: Raleigh Orthopaedic Clinic PA 3515 Glenwood Ave Raleigh NC 27612

DAMES, JOAN FOSTER (MRS. URBAN L. DAMES), editor; b. New Orleans, Sept. 29, 1934; d. Albert Steere and Lucia (Valdes) Foster; m. Urban Louis Dames, Feb. 10, 1959 (dec.); children: Alice Catherine, Lucia Ann, Cecilia Mary, Madeline Sophie. Student, St. Louis U., 1953-56. Seismograph rec. librarian St. Louis U., 1954-55; feature writer St. Louis Globe Democrat, 1955-60, St. Louis Post-Dispatch, 1966-68, women's editor, 1968—; editor Everyday mag., 1972-79, features editor, 1973-75, features dir., 1975-78, columnist, 1979—; Mem. pres.'s adv. council St. Louis U. High Sch., 1979-82; adv. Full Achievement, St. Louis U., 1982—; v.p. St. Louis Bridal Bur., 1959—; bd. dirs. Southside Day Nursery, 1983—. Radio personality: sta. KMOX-CBS, 1969-71; Author: Prelude, 1956. Mem. Soc. Am. Social Scribes (dir. 1969-72). Home: 7149 Lindell Ave University MO 63130 Office: 900 N Tucker Ave Saint Louis MO 63101

DAMGARD, JOHN MICHAEL, trade association executive; b. Ottawa, Ill., Dec. 7, 1939; s. Theodor Miller and Dorothy (Oughton) D.; m. Darcy Mead, Oct. 23, 1965 (div.); children: Michael, Theodor, Julie Mead. B.A., Knox Coll., Galesburg, Ill., 1964; student, U. Munich, Ger., 1962, U. Va., 1960. Vice-pres. Ill. Valley Investment Co., Dwight, Ill., 1966-70, dir., pres., 1976—; asst. to Vice Pres. U.S. White House, 1971-74; dep. asst. sec. U.S. Dept. Agr., Washington, 1974-77; v.p. ACLI Internat., Washington, 1977-82; pres., dir., exec. com. Futures Industry Assn., Washington, 1982—. Adv. Republican Heritage Group, 1976, Pres. Reagan Transition Team, 1980; mem. Rep. Nat. Com. Policy Group; bd. dirs. Washington Internat. Horse Show, 1975-81. Mem. Am. Soc. Assn. Execs., Aircraft Owners and Pilots Assn., Nat. Pilots Assn. Episcopalian. Clubs: Racquet (Chgo.); Meadow (Southampton, N.Y.). Home: 2439 Tracy Pl NW Washington DC 20008 Office: Futures Industry Assn 1825 I St NW Washington DC 20006

DAMIANOS, SYLVESTER, architect, sculptor; b. McKeesport, Pa., Dec. 31, 1933; s. Tsambikos and Melanie (Barboteau) D.; m. Lucille Spears, Dec. 28, 1957; children: Lynne Lucille, Laurie Elizabeth, Leigh Ann. B.Arch., Carnegie Inst. Tech., 1956; postgrad., Tech. Inst. Delft, Netherlands, 1957. Registered architect, Pa. Assoc. ptnr. Celli-Flynn, McKeesport, Pa., 1960-67; prin. Damianos & Pedone, Pitts., 1967-79; pres. Damianos & Assocs., Pitts., 1979—; pres. Pitts. Plan for Art, 1960-81. Architect bldg. renovation, PPA Gallery 407, 1978 (Design 1980); showroom design Franklin Interiors, 1969 (1st design 1969); exhibited works of sculpture, Mus. Art Carnegie Inst., 1975, Westmoreland County Mus. Art, 1966. Chmn. planning com. Borough of Edgewood, Pa., 1976-77, mem. council, 1977-81; bd. dirs. Met. Pitts. Pub. Broadcasting, 1980—, Am. Wind Symphony, Pitts., 1975-76; sec. Pitts. Art Commn., 1970-78. Fulbright grantee USIS, Netherlands, 1956. Fellow AIA; mem. Pa. Soc. Architects (v.p., Service 1978), Pitts. chpt. AIA (pres. 1980, Pres. 1981), Pitts Archtl. Club (pres. 1963-64), Soc. Sculptors (dir. 1977-79), Assoc. Artists Pitts. (pres., dir. 1963-65). Republican. Greek Orthodox. Club: Edgewood (pres., dir. 1969-75). Home: 328 Locust St Pittsburgh PA 15218 Office: Damianos & Assocs 322 Blvd of the Allies Pittsburgh PA 15222

DAMMAN, JAMES JOSEPH, real estate company executive; b. Grosse Pointe Park, Mich., Jan. 16, 1933; s. Adolph Louis and Rose Cecelia (Goddeeris) D.; m. Margaret A. Schulte, Oct. 6, 1956; children—James Joseph, Joan E., Stephen, Susan, Mark, Sandra. B.S. in Mktg, U. Detroit, 1954. With A.L. Damman Co. (retail hardware stores), Sterling Heights, Mich., 1956-74, sec., treas., controller, 1964-71, v.p., 1971-74; mem. Mich. Ho. of Reps., 1971-74; lt. gov. State of Mich., Lansing, 1975-78; sr. v.p. Real Estate One, Farmington Hills, Mich., 1978—. Mem. Troy (Mich.) City Commn., 1969-70. Mem. Nat. Assn. Realtors (bd. dirs. 1982—). Office: 29630 Orchard Lake Rd Farmington Hills MI 48018

DAMMANN, RICHARD WEIL, lawyer; b. N.Y.C., Oct. 23, 1911; s. Milton and Reta (Weil) D.; m. Marjorie Spiegel, Aug. 22, 1935; children: Deborah, Pamela, Penelope. A.B., Princeton U., 1932; LL.B., Harvard U., 1935. Bar: N.Y. 1935. Since practiced in, N.Y.C.; partner law firm Dammann, Edelman & Engel, 1935—; mem. adv. bd. Philip Morris Co., N.Y.C. Home: Kirby Ln Rye NY 10580 Office: 60 E 42d St New York NY 10165

DAMMERMAN, DENNIS DEAN, financial executive; b. Fairfield, Iowa, Nov. 4, 1945; s. Morris Melvin and Mary Louise (Watson) D.; m. Patricia Anne Bryk, July 9, 1967; children: Dwight David, Heather Lynne. B.S., U. Dubuque, 1967. Fin. mgmt. trainee Gen. Electric Co., 1967-69, corp. auditor, 1969-74, mgr. acquisitions analysis, lighting bus. group, 1974-76, mgr. ops. analysis, consumer products and services sector, 1976-78; v.p., comptroller Gen. Electric Credit Corp., Stamford, Conn., 1978—; dir. Trafalgar Developers, Inc., Miami, Fla., 1979—. Mem. Nat. Consumer Fin. Assn., Fin. Execs. Inst. Republican. Home: 21 Bellevale Dr Monroe CT 06468 Office: 570 Lexington Ave New York NY 10022

DAMMEYER, RODNEY F., business exec.; b. Cleve., Nov. 5, 1940; s. Frederick and Marion (Foster) D.; m. Diane Newins, Feb. 8, 1975; children: Paul, Scott, Tom, Kimberley, Alice. B.S. in Acctg., Kent State U., 1962. Ptnr. Arthur Anderson & Co., Seattle, 1962-79; exec. v.p. fin. Northwest Industries, Inc., Chgo., 1979-83; sr. v.p., chief fin. officer Household Internat., Prospect Heights, Ill., 1983—. Mem. Am. Inst. C.P.A.s, Fin. Execs. Inst., Nat. Assn. Accts. Presbyterian. Home: 11 Baneberry Ln Riverwoods IL 60015 Office: 2700 Sanders Rd Prospect Heights IL 60070

DAMMIN, GUSTAVE JOHN, medical educator; b. N.Y.C., Sept. 17, 1911; s. Gustave Frank and Anna Barbara (Anselm) D.; m. Anita Coffin, July 19, 1941; children: Susan, Tristram, Abigail. A.B., Cornell U., 1934, M.D., 1938; certificate in parasitology and tropical medicine, U. Havana, 1937; M.A. (hon.), Harvard, 1953. Diplomate: Am. Bd. Pathology, Nat. Bd. Med. Examiners. Intern medicine Johns Hopkins Hosp., 1939-40; asst. resident Peter Bent Brigham Hosp., Boston, 1940-41, pathologist in chief, 1952-74, cons., 1974—; mem. adv. med. bd. Leonard Wood Meml., 1969—; acting chief lab. service West Roxbury VA Hosp., 1976-77, asso. chief lab. service, 1978-81, cons., 1981—; instr. Columbia Coll. Phys. and Surg., 1941; asst. prof. pathology, then asso. prof. Washington U. Med. Sch., St. Louis, 1946-50, prof., chmn. bd., 1950-52; prof. pathology Harvard Med. Sch., 1952-62, Elsie T. Friedman prof. pathology, 1962-78, prof. emeritus, 1978—; lectr. tropical public health Harvard Sch. Public Health, 1978—; Niles lectr. Cornell Med. Coll., 1953; Phi Delta Epsilon lectr. Yale Sch. Medicine, 1956; I.W. Held lectr. Beth Israel Hosp., N.Y.C., 1963; Wadsworth lectr. N.Y. Lab Soc., Syracuse, 1970; cons. to surgeon gen. Dept. of Army, USPHS; nat. cons. global preventive medicine and epidemiology to surgeon gen. USAF; lab. cons. OCDM, 1950-60; pres. Armed Forces Epidemiological Bd., 1960-73; sci. adv. bd. Armed Forces Inst. Pathology, 1961-71; WHO expert adv. panel on enteric diseases, chmn. com., 1963; mem. subcom. geographic Pathology NRC, 1962-65; bd. dirs. Gorgas Meml. Inst., 1967—; nat. cons. to surgeon gen. USAF, 1968; mem. sci. adv. com. N.E. Regional Primate Research Center; mem. com. Yugoslavian Endemic Nephropathy, HEW, 1970-75; Kidney adv. com. Joint Commn. Accreditation Hosps., 1972-76; mem. Cholera adv. com. NIH, 1965—; mem. internat. Centers Com. NIH, 1972; del. U.S.-Japan Co-op. Med. Scis. Program, Dept. State, 1972—. Editorial com.: Ann. Rev. Medicine, 1957-60, Human Pathology, 1969—; Editorial bd.: Jour. Infectious Diseases. Served from 1st lt. to lt. col. M.C. AUS, 1941-46; dir. labs. div. Office Surgeon Gen., 1945-46; col. Res. ret. Decorated Legion of Merit with oak leaf cluster; recipient Walter Reed medallion, 1971, Distinguished Pub. Service medal Dept. Def., 1973, cert. of appreciation for cons. service Armed Forces Epidemiol. Bd., Dept. Def. and Surgeon Gen. Army, 1984; award of distinction Cornell U. Med. Coll. Alumni Assn., 1975; co-recipient Sci. achievement award Kidney Found. Mass., 1979. Mem. Nat. Acad. Sci. (mem. ad hoc coms. div. med. sci. 1970), N.Y. Acad. Scis., Am. Soc. Clin. Investigation, Am. Assn. Pathologists and Bacteriologists, Internat. Acad. Pathology (exec. council), AMA (vice chmn. sect. pathology and physiology), Transplantation Soc., Am. Soc. Tropical Medicine and Hygiene, Am. Soc. Exptl. Pathology, Assn. Am. Physicians, NIH (tropical medicine and parasitology study sect.), Soc. Med. Cons. to the Armed Forces (pres. 1963), Infectious Diseases Soc. Am., Assn. Mil. Surgeons, Assn. U.S. Army, Japanese-Am. Soc. Pathologists, Assn. Mexican Pathologists, Korean Med. Assn., 38th Parallel Med. Soc. Korea, AAUP, Sons and Daus. of Nantucket (pres. 1974-77), Sigma Xi, Alpha Omega Alpha. Home: 102 Sudbury Rd Weston MA 02193

DAMON, EDMUND HOLCOMBE, plastics company executive; b. St. Louis, Aug. 5, 1929; s. Ralph Shepard and Harriet (Dudley) Damon H.; m. Florence Elizabeth Drake, Apr. 14, 1956; children: Elizabeth, Leslie. B.A., Amherst Coll., 1951. Controller, treas. Strategic Materials Corp., N.Y.C., 1955-63; ops. analyst Norton Co., Troy, N.Y., 1964-65; v.p. corp. devel. Singer Co., Stamford, Conn., 1965-82; pres. Pantasote Inc., Greenwich, Conn., 1983—, dir.; dir. Milton Roy Co., St. Petersburg, Fla. Elder First Presbyterian Ch., Greenwich, 1970—; bd. dirs. Child Guidance Ctr., Stamford, 1983. Served to 1st lt. USAF, 1951-54. Mem. N.Am. Soc. Corp. Planning, Assn. Corp. Growth. Clubs: Stanwich (Greenwich); Webhannet Golf (Kennebunk, Maine). Office: Pantasote Inc 10 Valley Dr Greenwich Office Park 9 Greenwich CT 06830

DAMON, EDWARD KENT, office equipment co. exec.; b. Ft. Dodge, Iowa, Dec. 5, 1918; s. Edward Orne and Georgia (Mason) D.; m. Evelyn Wilcox Waddell, Oct. 4, 1940; children—Edward Kent, Bradley Mason, Kathleen Elizabeth Damon Shore, Sally Georgia Damon Turner. A.B., Amherst Coll., 1940; M.B.A., Harvard, 1942. Chief accountant Tobin Packing Co., Fort Dodge, 1946-49; asst. to controller Xerox Corp., Rochester, N.Y., 1949-52, asst. treas., 1952-53, treas., sec., 1953-60, v.p., 1960—, treas., 1960-76, sec., 1960—; dir. Bausch & Lomb, Inc., Rochester Gas & Electric Corp., Reckitt & Colman N. Am. Inc., Schlegel Mfg. Co.; trustee Community Savs. Bank. Bd. dirs. Sidney Hillman Health Center, Convalescent Hosp. For Children, pres., 1959-61; hon. bd. dirs. Rochester Philharmonic Orch.; trustee Monroe Community Coll., vice chmn., 1970-73; life trustee Center for Govtl. Research, Inc.; trustee, vice chmn. Rochester Inst. Tech.; mem. corp. Community Chest. Served to lt. USNR, 1942-46. Mem. Phi Beta Kappa. Republican. Episcopalian. Clubs: Rochester Country, Genesee Valley, Monroe Golf. Home: 65 Country Club Dr Rochester NY 14618 Office: Xerox Sq Rochester NY 14644

DAMON, RICHARD WINSLOW, physicist; b. Concord, Mass., May 14, 1923; s. Winslow Johnson and Florence Mabel (Smith) D.; m. Anna M. Trotter, Aug. 4, 1946; children: Laura, Louise, Paul Trotter. B.S., Harvard U., 1944, M.A., 1947, Ph.D., 1952. Teaching fellow Harvard U., Cambridge, Mass., 1946-48, 49-50; engr. Raytheon Co., Waltham, Mass., 1948-49; research assoc. Gen. Electric Research Lab., Schenectady, 1951-60; dept. mgr. Microwave Control Devices, Microwave Assocs., Burlington, Mass., 1960-62; dir. Applied Physics Lab. Sperry Research Center, Sudbury, Mass., 1962-82; dir. tech, 1982—; adv. group mem. on electronic materials NASA, 1967-71, adv. mem. subcom. on electrophysics, 1966-71, chmn., 1969-71, adv. com. on basic research, 1969-71; mem. panel to Nat. Bur. Standards, Nat. Acad. Sci./NRC, 1971-73; mem. evaluation panel to Nat. Bur. Standards, 1969-74, mem. electronics study group, 1972-74; adv. group on electron devices, working group A, under-sec. for research and engring. Dept. Def., 1973-80; mem. external adv. com. Lab. Surface Sci. and Tech., U. Maine, 1981—; dir. RSC Industries; lectr. Contbr. articles to profl. jours. Mem. Concord (Mass.) Spl. Sch. Salary Practices Com., 1964, Concord Comprehensive Town Plans Com., 1974-76. Served to lt. (j.g.) USNR, 1943-46; PTO. Fellow Am. Phys. Soc., IEEE (pres. 1981, bd. dirs. 1977-78, 81-83); mem. AAAS, IEEE Electron Devices Soc., IEEE Microwave Theory and Techniques Soc., IEEE Magnetics Soc., IEEE Sonics and Ultrasonics Group, Sigma Xi. Republican. Patentee in field. Home: 1623 Main St Concord MA 01742 Office: 100 North Rd Sudbury MA 01776

DAMON, STEWART WILBUR, export-import company executive; b. Maxwell, Nebr., Aug. 28, 1925; s. Harold Franklin and Ruth Margaret (Sargent) D.; m. Barbara Cottom, Jan. 15, 1946 (div. July 1956); 1 son, Stewart Wilbur; m. Paula Ilona Gerbasieh, July 30, 1956. B.A., U. N.C.-Chapel Hill, 1945. V.p. Schmetzer Inc., N.Y.C., 1956-59; pres. Transocean Trading, Geneva, 1959-60; sr. v.p. Premier Indsl. Corp., Cleve., 1960-82; pres. Damon & Assocs., Cleve., 1982—. Chmn. legis. com. U.S. Dept. Commerce Dist. Export Council, Cleve., 1981—. Served to lt. USN, 1945-56. Mem. Cleve. World Trade Assn. Republican. Methodist. Office: Damon & Assocs 21010 Ctr Ridge Rd Rocky River OH 44116 *International trade and commerce is the most certain way to international peace.*

DAMON, TERRY ALLEN, museum director, retired naval officer; b. Washington, Dec. 8, 1930; s. Norman Clare and Madeleine Bates (Hoag) D.; m. Janet Teeple, Apr. 12, 1980; children: Diane Clare, Denise Yvonne, Andrew Allen, Charles Ronald, Richard Teeple, David Shea. B.S., U. Mich., 1953. Commd. ensign U.S. Navy, 1955, advanced through grades to comdr., 1968; asst. naval attache, attache for air Am. Embassy, Tehran, Iran, 1961-63; pilot Heavy Attack Squadron Four Naval Air Sta., Whidbey Island, Washington, 1963-66; maintenance officer, flight instr. Attack Squadron 128, 1968-69, weapons officer Comdr. Carrier Div. 9, 1969-71; production mgmt. specialist Defense Intelligence Agy., 1971-76; asst. dir. Navy Meml. Mus., Washington, 1976-78, dir., 1978—; pres. Damon Galleries Ltd., 1974-81. Decorated Air medal (4). Mem. Council Am. Maritime Museums, Profl. Picture Framers Assn., Alpha Tau Omega. Republican. Episcopalian. Office: Navy Meml Mus Bldg 76 Washington Navy Yard Washington DC 20374

DAMON, WILLIAM VAN BUREN, child psychology, educator; b. Brockton, Mass., Nov. 10, 1944; Philip Arthur and Helen (Meyers) D.; (div.)children: Jesse Louis, Maria; m. 2d Anne Colby, Sept. 24, 1983. B.A., Harvard Coll., 1967; Ph.D., U. Calif.-Berkeley, 1973. Lic. psychologist, Mass. Social worker N.Y.C. Dept. Social Services, 1968-70; prof. psychology Clark U., Worcester, Mass., 1973—; dean Grad. Sch., Clark U., Worcester, Mass., 1983—; mem. study sect. NIMH, Bethesda, Md., 1981-84; cons. State Mass., 1976, State Coll., 1978, Allegheny County, Pa., 1979. Author: Social World of the Child, 1977, Social and Personality Development, 1983; editor: New Directions for Child Development, 1978—. Trustee Bancroft Sch., Worcester, Mass., 1982—. Grantee Carnegie Corp., N.Y., 1975-77, 77-79, Spencer Found., 1980-84. Mem. Jean Piaget Soc. (bd. dirs. 1983—), Am. Psychol. Assn., Soc. for Research in Child Devel. Democrat. Roman Catholic. Home: 20 Hillside Terr Belmont MA 02178 Office: Clark U Dept Psychology 950 Main St Worcester MA 02178 *Learn to thrive on the risks and challenges themselves rather than merely on the prospects of winning; expect that every right and privilege must be vigorously defended; and through it all never give up the principle of common decency.*

DAMONE, VIC (VITO FARINOLA), singer, actor; b. Bklyn., June 12, 1928; m. Pier Angeli, 1954 (div.); 1 son, Perry Rocco Luigi; m. Judy Rawlins, Nov. 1963 (div.); one dau. Appeared as singer: Godfrey Talent Scout show, 1945, night club debut, La Martinique, N.Y.C.; motion pictures include Rich, Young and Pretty, 1951, Athena, 1954, Hit the Deck, 1955, Kismet, 1955, Hell to Eternity, 1960; star: TV show Vic Damone Show, 1956, 57, Lively Ones, 1962, 63, Dean Martin Presents the Vic Damone Show, 1967; toured, Vietnam with, U.S.O., 1969; performed at White House dinner for former prisoners of war, 1973; recorded: album Best Feelings, 1980. Baha'i religion. Address: care Agy for Performing Arts Inc 120 W 57th St New York NY 10019 *

DAMORA, ROBERT MATTHEW, architect; b. N.Y.C., Mar. 2, 1912; s. Matthew Robert and Giacinta (Volonnino) d'Amora; m. Sirkka Heikkinen, Feb. 27, 1950; children: Jesa Sirkka, Matthew Robert. Student dept. architecture, NYU, evenings, 1932- 41; B.Arch., Yale U., 1953. Registered architect, N.Y., Conn., Mass., Vt., Fla. Archtl. journalist-photographer, designer, 1935—, practice architecture, 1955—; dir. Seeds for Architecture program Universal Atlas Cements div. U.S. Steel Corp., 1956- 58; asso. prof. architecture, design critic Columbia U., 1963-64. Prin. works include prefabricated interchangeable concrete components system for tract housing, Cape Cod, Mass., 1962, prefabricated custom house constructed 3 reduplicated concrete components, Ft. Lauderdale, Fla., 1967; Low-cost minimal housing Community Nassau, Bahamas, 1968; exhibited in Visionary Architecture show, Mus. Modern Art, 1960, Work featured on various TV programs, in numerous profl. jours. and newspapers. Served to lt. (j.g.), spl. devices div. Bur. Research and Invention USNR, 1943- 46. Recipient 1st prize Portland Cement Assn. Horizon Homes, 1962; Record House of Year Archtl. Record, 1962; Merit award AIA/House & Home, 1962; 1st prize AIA Conv. Products Exhibit, 1963, 64; Gold medal archtl. photography AIA, 1965; Honor award in architecture, 1965; Guggenheim fellow in archtl. research, 1966-67. Mem. AIA (nat. and local coms.), Archtl. Photographers Assn. (pres. 1947-49). Home: Pound Ridge Rd Bedford NY 10506

D'AMOURS, NORMAN EDWARD, congressman; b. Holyoke, Mass., Oct. 14, 1937; s. Albert L. and Edna (Laplant) D'A.; m. Helen E. Manning, Sept. 4, 1965; children: Danielle Ann, Susan Ellen, Norman Manning. A.B., Assumption Coll., 1960; LL.B., Boston U., 1963. Bar: N.H. 1964. Practiced in, Manchester, 1969—; asst. atty. gen. State N.H., 1966-69; city prosecutor, Manchester, 1970-72; mem. 94th-98th Congresses from 1st N.H. dist.; Instr. Anselm's Coll., 1971-73. Served with AUS, 1964-67. Democrat. Clubs: Optimists (treas. 1965-67), Elks, Richelieu (Manchester). Office: 922 Elm St Manchester NH 03101 also 2242 Rayburn House Office Bldg Washington DC 20515

DAMPEER, JOHN LYELL, lawyer; b. Cleve., June 3, 1916; s. James W. and Felicia (Gressitt) D.; m. Lucie Augustin Kennerdell, June 30, 1950; children: Lyell B., David K., G. Geoffrey. S.B., Harvard U., 1938, LL.B., 1942; student, New Coll., Oxford (Eng.) U., 1938-39. Bar: Ohio 1946. Since practiced in, Cleve.; ptnr. Thompson, Hine and Flory, 1955—; sec., dir. Fisher Foods, Inc., Van Dorn Co.; dir. Monarch Machine Tool Co., J.M. Smucker Co. Trustee Family Service Assn. Cleve., 1951-70. Henry fellow, 1938-39. Mem. ABA (Ohio Bar Assn., chmn. corp. law com. 1959-62), Greater Cleve. Bar Assn. (exec. com. 1958-61), Phi Beta Kappa. Republican. Baptist. Clubs: Union, Kirtland Country (Cleve.). Home: 2465 Marlboro Rd Cleveland Heights OH 44118 Office: Nat City Bank Bldg Cleveland OH 44114

DAMPIER, JOSEPH HENRY, clergyman, educator; b. Guelph, Ont., Can., Mar. 7, 1908; came to U.S., 1925, naturalized, 1940; s. Robert Alexander and Elizabeth (Hindely) D.; m. Ione Margaret Chandler, 1928 (dec. 1960); 1 dau., Phyllis (Mrs. Harry E. Fontaine); m. Mildred Feagans, 1963. A.B., Cin. Bible Sem, 1931; Ed.M., U. Pitts., 1941; D.D., Atlanta Christian Coll., 1952; LL. D., Johnson Bible Coll., 1957. Pastor Christian Church, Alfordsville, Ind. and Antioch, Ind., 1927-28, Lawrenceburg, Ind., 1929-34, First Christian Ch., McKeesport, Pa., 1934-41, First Ch., Johnson City, Tenn., 1941-58; provost Milligan Coll., Tenn., 1958-65; dean Emmanuel Sch. of Religion, 1965-69, prof. Christian ministries, 1969-82; pres. North Am. Christian Conv., 1950-51; mem. Commn. of Restudy, Disciples of Christ; external lectr. Maritime Christian Coll., Charlottetown, P.E.I., Can. Author: Workbook on Christian Doctrine, 1943; Mem. pub. com.: Standard Pub. Co, Cin.; Contbr. to religious mags. Recipient Fide et Amore award Milligan Coll., 1980. Mem. Am. Acad. Religion, Disciples of

Christ Hist. Soc. Clubs: Mason (32 deg.), K.T., Kiwanian (past pres.). Address: Grande Arms 4-W 216 University Pkwy Johnson City TN 37601

DAMRELL, CHARLES BRUCE, utility executive; b. Quincy, Mass., Dec. 8, 1932; s. Charles S. and Lillian May (Holden) D.; m. Janet Elizabeth Andersen, Apr. 6, 1956; children: Debra Jeanne, Jeffrey Bruce, David Charles. B.S.E.E., Northeastern U., 1955; P.M.D., Harvard U., 1970, A.M.P., 1983. With Boston Edison Co., 1955—, engring. sect. mgr., 1967-73, supt. engring. and constrn. dept., 1973-78, supt. engring., planning and research dept., 1978-79, v.p. engring. and distbn., 1979—; dir. Nuclear Electric Ins. Ltd., Hamilton, Bermuda. Deacon First Trinity Congl. Ch. of Scituate, 1974-78. Named Young Engr. of Year Mass. Soc. Profl. Engrs., 1976. Mem. IEEE (chmn. Boston sect. 1968-69), Eta Kappa Nu. Republican. Home: 40 Old Forge Rd Scituate MA 02066

DAMSBO, ANN MARIE, psychologist; b. Cortland, N.Y., July 7, 1931; d. Jorgen Einer and Agatha Irene (Schenck) D.; 6 foster children. B.S., San Diego State Coll., 1952; M.A., U.S. Internat. U., 1974, Ph.D., 1975. Commd. 2d lt. U.S. Army, 1952, advanced through grades to capt., 1957; staff therapist Letterman Army Hosp., San Francisco, 1953-54, 56-58, 61-62, Ft. Devers, Mass., 1955-56, Walter Reed Army Hosp., Washington, 1958-59, Tripler Army Hosp., Hawaii, 1959-61, Ft. Benning, Ga., 1962-64; chief therapist U.S. Army Hosp., Ft. McPherson, Ga., 1964-67; ret. U.S. Army, 1967; med. missionary So. Presbyterian Ch., Taiwan, 1968-70; psychology intern Naval Regional Med. Ctr., San Diego, 1975, pre-doctoral intern, 1975-76, postdoctoral intern, 1975-76, chief, founder pain clinic, 1976—; lectr., U.S., Can., Eng., France, Australia, cons. forensic hypnosis to law enforcement agys. Contbr. articles to profl. publs., chpt. to book. Tchr. Sunday sch. Methodist Ch., 1945—. Fellow Am. Soc. Clin. Hypnosis; mem. San Diego Soc. Clin. Hypnosis (pres. 1980), Am. Phys. Therapy Assn., Mem.; mem. Calif. Soc. Clin. and Hypnosis (bd. govs.), Internat. Soc. Clin. and Exptl. Hypnosis, Internat. Platform Assn. Republican. Club: Job's Daus. Home: 1062 W 5th Ave Escondido CA 92025 Office: Chief Pain Clinic Naval Regional Med Ctr San Diego CA 92134 *A purpose in life is essential to happiness. Success is a matter of making the most of the talents we are given, not receiving greater talents. Time is the most important gift. We can ill afford to waste it or wish it away. All accomplishment is meaningless unless one walks in harmony and fellowship with her maker and her fellow human beings. I am grateful to my parents and teachers for their examples and for providing me the opportunity for self-actualization.*

DAMSON, BARRIE MORTON, oil and gas exploration company executive; b. N.Y.C., Jan. 29, 1936; s. Harry and Ethel (Brody) D.; m. Joan Selig, Feb. 29, 1972; children: Blair, Laura, Bethany. A.B., Harvard U., 1956; LL.B., N.Y. U., 1959. Bar: N.Y. bar 1959. Pres. Damson Petroleum Corp., N.Y.C., 1963-69, Bronco Oil Corp., Midland, Tex., 1965-69, Delta Minerals Inc., Lake Charles, La., 1967-69; pres., chmn. bd. Damson Oil Corp., N.Y.C., 1969—; dir. Viking Resources Internat., N.V.; Bd. dirs., co-chmn. Children's Blood Found.-N.Y. Hosp.; bd. dirs. Independent Petroleum Assn. Am.; bd. dirs., past pres. Oil Investment Inst.; chmn. nominating com. Am. Stock Exchange, 1981. Mem. Bar Assn. N.Y., Am. Bus. Conf. (exec. com.). Clubs: Harvard, Board Room (N.Y.C.). Address: 366 Madison Ave New York NY 10017 *Perhaps it's the first creeping signs of age, conservatism, or merely the fact that I can't improve my backhand in tennis, but whatever it is I am sincerely concerned that so much of what is or was good in America now quietly erodes while we, the beneficiaries of this unique society do little but pay lip service to this. Are we really doing enough today? Should we not now give back a bit by directly involving ourselves in our government process? I believe this is the time for strong commitments and actions on our part to help perpetuate this truly grand society.*

DAMTOFT, WALTER ATKINSON, editor, publisher; b. Asheville, N.C., June 1, 1922; s. Walter Julius and Dorothy (Atkinson) D.; m. Janet Russell, Mar. 31, 1951; children—Russell Walter, Lisa. Student, Yale U., 1940-41; B.S. in Commerce, U. N.C., Chapel Hill, 1947. Salesman Sta. WKIX, Columbia, S.C., 1947; reporter Ark. Gazette, Little Rock, 1947-50; reporter, city editor Asheville (N.C.) Citizen, 1950-55; city editor Charlotte (N.C.) Observer, 1956-58, N.C. editor, 1958-60, Carolinas editor, 1960-62; writer Nat. Observer, Silver Spring, Md., 1962-69, news editor, 1969-72, sr. editor, 1972-77; editor, pub. Am. Way mag., Ft. Worth, 1977—. Editor: The Consumer's Handbook II, 1971, Here's Help, 1974. Pres. Garrett Park (Md.) Citizen's Assn., 1969-70; mem. Garrett Park Town Council, 1972-76. Served with USNR, 1943-46. Mem. Soc. Profl. Journalists, Phi Delta Theta. Democrat. Episcopalian. Home: 1307 Eastus Dr Dallas TX 75208 Office: Am Way Mag PO Box 61616 DFW Airport TX 75261

DANA, BILL, writer, performer, publisher; b. Quincy, Mass., Oct. 5, 1924; s. Joseph and Dena (Litchman) Szathmary; m. Evelyn Shular, Feb. 28, 1981. Grad., Emerson Coll., 1950, M.A. (hon.), 1959. Pres. Calif. Internat. Artists Mgmt., 1967-70, Bill Dana Productions, 1963-81; chmn. bd. Dana/Corwin Enterprises, Los Angeles, 1980—; gov. Grammy awards Nat. Assn. Rec. Artists. Head writer: Steve Allen Show, 1961; star: Bill Dana (Jose Jimenez) Show, 1963-64; producer: Spike Jones, 1962, Milton Berle Show, 1968; creative dir.: Adams Dana Silverstein, 1968-70; (nominated Grammy award 1961, 70, 6 time Emmy nominee.); Author: Jose the Astronaut, 1960, Ecolo-Jest, 1970, 80-81, (with Dr. Laurence J. Peter) The While Mirth Catalogue, 1981, Grate Expectations, The Name Book, The Unknown Comic Scrapbag, Would You Believe; TV script Sammy's Visit - All in the Family, 1973; film script Maxwell Smart, the Nude Bomb, 1979; appeared: film Hungry i Reunion, 1981; TV spl. No Soap, Radio, 1982. Served with Inf. U.S. Army, 1943-45. Decorated Bronze Star.; Recipient Peabody award (Steve Allen), 1957, Nat. Safety Council award, 1965, I.M.A.G.E. award, 1969, Aerospace award, 1964. Mem. Screen Actors Guild, AFTRA, Producers Guild Am., Equity, Writers Guild Am. West. Club. Office: care ICM 8899 Beverly Blvd Los Angeles CA 90048 *

DANA, EDWARD RUNKLE, physician; b. Columbus, Ohio, May 20, 1919; s. Lowell Brockway and Helen (Runkle) D.; m. Lorraine Kirschner, Aug. 2, 1945; children—Edward R., H. Richard. A.B., Wesleyan U., 1941; M.D., Johns Hopkins U., 1944. Diplomate: Am. Ed. Radiology. Intern Univ. Hosps., Cleve., 1944-45; resident radiology Johns Hopkins Hosp., 1947-50; dir. radiology Mercy Hosp., Balt., 1950-64; asst. prof. radiology Johns Hopkins Med. Sch., 1960-68, asso. prof., 1968-69; chief diagnostic radiology Orange County Med. Center, Orange, Calif., 1969—; asso. prof. radiology U. Calif. Med. Sch., Irvine, 1969-79, prof., 1979—, joint prof. gastroenterology, 1969—, chief gastrointestinal radiology, 1976-77, co-chief, 1977—; cons. gastroent. radiology Long Beach (Calif.) VA Hosp., 1974—. Contbr. articles to profl. jours. Served to capt. M.C. U.S. Army, 1945-47. Mem. Calif. Med. Soc., Orange County Med. Soc., Soc. Gastrointestinal Radiologists, Mensa, Sigma Chi, Phi Chi. Club: Md. Home: 2523 Altamar Dr Irvine Cove Laguna Beach CA 92651 Office: U Calif Irvine Med Center Orange CA 92668

DANA, FRANK MITCHELL, theatrical lighting designer; b. Washington, Nov. 14, 1942; s. John Daskum and Elizabeth Francis (Woods) D.; m. Wendy Karen Bensinger, Dec. 31, 1967; children: Scott Cameron, Ian Michael. B.F.A., Utah State U., 1964; M.F.A., Yale U., 1967. Tech. dir. Columbia Sch. Arts, N.Y.C., 1967-68; asst. to Jo Mielziner, N.Y.C., 1968-69; tech. dir. Yale Drama Sch., New Haven, Conn., 1970-71; prodn. mgr. Pitts. Civic Light Opera, Pitts., 1973-74; assoc. lighting dir. Fred Manning, N.Y.C., 1978—; lectr. U. Wash., So. Meth. U., San Francisco State U.; prodn. properties mgr. Sticks and Bones, Broadway; lectr. Rutgers U., New Brunswick, N.J., 1982—. Prodn. properties mgr.: Broadway Play Sticks and Bones; lighting designer: The Freedom of the City, 1974, Once in a Lifetime, 1978, Inspector General, 1978, Man and Superman, 1978, The Suicide, 1980, Mass Appeal, 1981, Monday After the Miracle, 1982; off-Broadway Play Three Acts of Recognition, A Coupla White Chicks, Mass Appeal, Oh Coward, Joseph and the Amazing Technicolor Dreamcoat; regional theatres, Am. Conservatory Theatre, Goodman Barn Theatre Co., Mark Taper Forum, McCarter Theatre, Cin. Playhouse, Seattle Repertory Theatre, Nat. Arts Ctr., Ottawa, Ont., Stratford Shakespeare Festival, Can., tours, opera, TV, spl. engagements. Mem. Internat. Alliance Theatrical Stage Employees, United Scenic Artists (trustee 1970-72). Republican. Office: 221 W 82nd St New York NY 10024

DANA, JERILYN DENISE, dancer; b. Portland, Maine, Aug. 16, 1949; d. Mark and Eleanore (Colvin) Doucette. Dancer Boston Ballet Co., 1967-74, Chgo. Lyric Opera, 1969-70, Les Grands Ballet Canadiens, Montreal, 1975—; prin. dancer Les Grands Ballets Canadiens, Montreal. Scholar Ford Found., 1963, 64. Office: Les Grands Ballets Canadiens 4869 Rue St Denis Montreal PQ Canada H2J 2L7

DANAHER, JOHN ANTHONY, ret. judge; b. Meriden, Conn., Jan. 9, 1899; s. Cornelius J. and Ellen (Ryan) D.; m. Dorothy King, Feb. 3, 1921; children—John A., Robert Cornelius, Jeanne. A.B., Yale, 1920; postgrad., Yale Law Sch., 1922; LL.D. (hon.), Georgetown U., 1979. Bar: Conn. bar 1922. Law clk. White & Case, N.Y.C., 1921-22; practiced, Hartford, Conn., and Washington, 1922-53, asst. U.S. atty., 1922-34; sec. State Conn., 1933-35; U.S. senator, 1939-45; counsel Rep. Senatorial Com., 1946-53; U.S. circuit judge U.S. Court of Appeals, Washington, 1953-69; sr. U.S. circuit judge, Hartford, Conn., 1969-80. Del. Rep. Nat. Conv., 1944; Congl. aide Rep. Nat. Com., 1945-46; exec. dir. U.S. Senatorial Campaign, 1948; Mem. Pres.'s Commn. Internal Security and Individual Rights, 1951; mem. Pres.'s Conf. Adminstrv. Procedure, 1953-54; dir. div. spl. activities Eisenhower campaign, 1952. Served as 2d lt. F.A. U.S. Army, 1918. Mem. D.C., Conn., Hartford County bar assns., Beta Theta Pi, Elihu. Republican. Roman Catholic. Club: Metropolitan (Washington). Home: 31 Wyndwood Rd West Hartford CT 06107

DANBY, KEN, artist, printmaker; b. Sault Ste. Marie, Ont., Can., Mar. 6, 1940; s. M.G. Edison and Gertrude L. (Buckley) D.; children—Sean, Ryan, Noah. Student, Ont. Coll. Art, Toronto, 1958-60. Profl. artist, 1962—. One-man shows, Gallery Moos Ltd., Toronto, 1964-83, Galerie Godard Lefort, Montreal, Que., Can., 1966, William Zierler Gallery, N.Y.C., 1972, 73, Images Gallery, Toledo, 1972, Fleet Gallery, Winnipeg, deVooght Gallery, Vancouver, 1977, 80, others; exhibited in numerous group shows including U.S. and European touring exhibit; represented in permanent collections, Mus. Modern Art, N.Y.C., Montreal Mus. Fine Art, Art Inst. Chgo., Nat. Gallery Can., Ottawa, also others; designer: Series III, Canadian Olympic Coins for, 1976 Olympics, Montreal. Decorated Queen's Can. Silver Jubilee medal; recipient R. Tait McKenzie chair for sport Nat. Sport and Recreation Centre, Ottawa, Ont., 1975. Mem. Royal Canadian Acad. Arts. Home: Rural Route 4 Guelph ON Canada Office: care Gallery Moos Ltd 136 Yorkville Ave Toronto ON Canada

DANCE, FRANCIS ESBURN XAVIER, communication educator; b. Bklyn., Nov. 9, 1929; s. Clifton Louis and Catherine (Tester) D.; m. Nora Alice Rush, May 1, 1954 (div. 1974); children: Clifton Louis III, Charles Daniel, Alison Catherine, Andrea Frances, Frances Sue, Brendan Rush; m. Carol Camille Zak, July 4, 1974; children: Zachary Esburn, Gabriel Joseph. B.S., Fordham U., 1951; M.A., Northwestern U., 1953, Ph.D., 1959. Instr. speech Bklyn. Adult Labor Schs., 1951; instr. humanities, coordinator radio and TV U. Ill. at Chgo., 1953-54; instr. Univ. Coll., U. Chgo., 1958; asst. prof. St. Joseph's (Ind.) Coll., 1958-60; asst. prof., then assoc. prof. U. Kans., 1960-63; mem. faculty U. Wis.-Milw., 1963-71, prof. communication, 1965-71; dir. Speech Communication Center U. Wis-Milw., 1963-70; mem. faculty U. Denver, 1971—; partner Helix Press, Shorewood, Wis., 1970-71; cons. in field. Author: The Citizen Speaks, 1962, (with Harold P. Zelko) Business and Professional Speech Communication, 1965, 2d edit., 1978, Human Communication Theory, 1967, (with Carl E. Larson) Perspectives on Communication, 1970, Speech Communication: Concepts and Behavior, 1972, The Functions of Speech Communication: A Theoretical Approach, 1976, Human Communication Theory, 1982; Editor: Jour. Communication, 1962-64, Speech Tchr, 1970-72; adv. bd.: Jour. Black Studies; editorial bd.: Jour. Psycholinguistic Research; Contbr. articles to profl. jours. Bd. dirs. Milw. Mental Health Assn., 1966-67. Served to 2d lt. AUS, 1954-56. Knapp Univ. scholar in communication, 1967-68; recipient Outstanding Prof. award Standard Oil Found., 1967. Fellow Internat. Communication Assn. (pres. 1967); mem. Speech Communication Assn. (pres. 1982), Psi Upsilon. Office: Dept Speech Communication Univ Denver Denver CO 80208 *Life should include a personal commitment to excellence with a corresponding humane tolerance for failure in self or in others. A belief in the progressive acquisition of autonomy can help guide both personal and professional decisions.*

DANCE, MAURICE EUGENE, college administrator; b. Bismarck, N.D., Jan. 14, 1923; s. Alvin Cecil and Jennie (Brown) D.; m. Margaret Thorstenson, Mar. 25, 1944 (dec. Apr. 1964); children—Michelle, Michael, Myles; m. Anita Ruth Bell, Apr. 10, 1965; children—Muriel, Jennifer, Kristina. B.A., U. Wash., 1947; M.S., U. Wis., 1949, Ph.D., 1953. Asst. prof. econs. Los Angeles State Coll., 1950-56; with San Fernando Valley State Coll., Northridge, Calif., 1956-69, prof. econs., 1956-69, chmn. dept., 1956-64, asst. to v.p. for acad. affairs, 1964-65; dean Sch. of Letters and Scis., 1965-69; v.p. acad. affairs Calif. State U., Hayward, 1969—; Econs. cons. Mem. Am. Econs. Assn., Indsl. Relations Research Assn., AAUP. Home: 5341 Greenridge Rd Castro Valley CA 94546

DANCEY, CHARLES LOHMAN, editor; b. Pekin, Ill., Nov. 28, 1916; s. Albert Duane and Bertha (Lohman) D.; m. Nina Evelyn Manker, Dec. 10, 1944; children: Richard, Burt Lee, Clinton Dancey. B.S., U. Ill., 1938. Reporter Peoria (Ill.) Star, 1938-40; reporter Peoria Jour., 1946-50; editor Peoria Jour. Star, 1958-80, asst. pub., 1980—; owner rep., mgmt. bd. WTVH-TV, Peoria, 1956-58. Ill. state comdt. Marine Corps League, 1947; City councilman, commr. fire and plice, Pekin, 1946-50. Served to col. USMCR, 1941-46, 50-51. Recipient Peoria chpt. B'nai B'rith Citizenship award, 1964. Mem. Inter-Am. Press Assn. (dir., exec. bd.), Am. Soc. Newspaper Editors. Club: Mason. Home: 419 Haines St Pekin IL 61554 Office: War Memorial Dr Peoria IL 61601

DANCO, LÉON ANTOINE, educator, mgmt. cons.; b. N.Y.C., May 30, 1923; s. Leon A. and Alvira T. (Gomez) D.; m. Katharine Elizabeth Leck, Aug. 25, 1951; children—Suzanne, Walter Ten Eyck. A.B., Harvard, 1943, M.B.A., 1947; Ph.D., Western Res. U., 1963. Asst. to div. pres. Interchem. Corp., N.Y.C., 1947-50; sales promotion mgr. Risdon Mfg. Co., Waterbury, Conn., 1950-55; mgmt. cons., Cheshire, Conn., 1955-57; prof., asso. dir. mgmt. program Case Inst. Tech., Cleve., 1957-58, lectr., 1959—; mgmt. cons. L.A. Danco & Co., 1957—; lectr. John Carroll U., Cleve., 1959-66, prof., dir. mgmt. confs., 1966—; vis. prof. econs. Cleve. Inst. Art, 1966-69, Kent State U., 1966-67; exec. dir. Univ. Services Inst., Cleve., 1967-69, pres., 1969—; pub. The Family in Business (newsletter), 1978—; pres. Center for Family Bus., 1978—. Author: Beyond Survival—A Business Owners Guide for Success, 1975, Inside the Successful Family Business, 1979, Outside Directors in the Family Owned Business, 1981; syndicated columnist: It's Your Business, 1973—. Served to lt. (j.g.) USCG, 1942-46; PTO. Mem. Am. Econ. Assn. Home: 28230 Cedar Rd Pepper Pike Cleveland OH 44122 Office: PO Box 24268 Cleveland OH 44124 *Whatever success we may achieve in this life will come from the purpose to which we put God's priceless gift of time.*

DANCY, JOHN ALBERT, news correspondent; b. Jackson, Tenn., Aug. 5, 1936; s. Albert Gallatin and Mabel Ann (Duck) D.; m. Ann Lewis, July 13, 1957; children: Christopher, Sara, John, Mary Katherine. Student, David Lipscomb Coll., Nashville, 1954-58; B.A. in English Lit, Union U., Jackson, 1959. News commentator Westinghouse Broadcasting Co., KYW-TV, Cleve., 1961-65; corr. NBC News, Los Angeles, Chgo., Berlin, London, Washington, 1965—. Recipient Columbia-Dupont award for documentaries, 1977, Overseas Press Club award for documentaries, 1977. Mem. Overseas Writers Washington, Radio-Television Corrs. Assn. Washington. Office: 4001 Nebraska Ave NW Washington DC 20016 *

DANDOY, MAXIMA ANTONIO, teacher educator emeritus; b. Santa Maria, Ilocos, Sur., Philippines; came to U.S., 1949, naturalized, 1951; d. Manuel and Isidra (Mendoza) Antonio; m. Apolinario M. Dandoy, Mar. 14, 1947. Teaching cert., Philippine Normal Coll., 1940; A.B., Nat. Tchrs. Coll., Manila, 1947; M.A., Arellano U., Manila, 1949; Ed.D. (John M. Switzer scholar, Newhouse Found. scholar), Stanford U., 1951; postgrad. (Calif. Fedn. Bus. and Profl. Women's Club scholar), Stanford U., 1952. Tchr. elem. sch., Philippines, 1927-37; lab. sch. tchr. Philippine Normal Coll., Manila, 1938-49; instr. Arellano U., Manila, 1947-49; lab. sch. prin. U. of East, Manila, 1953-54, asso. prof., 1952-55; prof. edn. Calif. State U., Fresno, 1956-82, prof. edn. emeritus, 1982—; curriculum writer, gen. office supr. Manila Dept. Edn., 1944-45; Mem. com. for the selection social studies textbooks for state adoption Calif., 1970-71; vis. prof. UCLA, 1956; Crisologo Meml. lectr. U. No. Philippines, 1977. Mem. Calif. Gov.'s Conf. on Traffic Safety, 1962, Calif. Gov.'s Conf. Delinquency Prevention, 1963. Named Disting. Woman of Year Fresno Bus. and Profl. Women's Club, 1957, Woman of Achievement, 1973, Outstanding Filipino, 1982. Mem. Nat. Council Social Studies (chmn. sec. internat. understanding, nat. conv. 1966), Calif. Fedn. Bus. and Profl. Women's Clubs (state chmn. scholarships 1961-63, treas. Fresno), Calif. Tchrs. Assn., AAUW (liaison Calif. State U. Fresno 1970-71), People to People of Fresno, Orgn. Filipino-Am. Educators Fresno (pres. 1977-84), Soc. Profs. Edn., Filipino-Am. Women's Club (adv. 1969-74), Internat. Platform Assn., Phi Delta Kappa, Pi Lambda Theta, Kappa Delta Pi (counselor 1972-79, nat. com. attendance and credentials 1975, nat. com. regional confs. 1966). Home: 1419 W Bullard Ave Fresno CA 93711 Office: Calif State U Fresno CA 93740

DANDOY, SUZANNE EGGLESTON, medical educator; b. Los Angeles, Jan. 2, 1935; d. Leonard Lester and Catherine (Wheelwright) Eggleston; m. Jeremiah Richard Dandoy, June 14, 1958; children: Kevin, Bret, Jolyn. B.A., U. Calif., Los Angeles, 1956; M.D., UCLA, 1960, M.P.H., 1963. Diplomate: Am. Bd. Preventive Medicine. Intern, Los Angeles Harbor Gen. Hosp., Torrance, Calif., 1960-61; resident Los Angeles Health Dept., 1961-62, 63-64; epidemiologist San Diego Dept. Pub. Health, 1967-68; chief Bur. Preventive Health Services, Ariz. Dept. Health, Phoenix, 1970-73, asst. commr., 1973-74, asst. dir., 1974-75, dir., 1975-80; prof. health adminstrn. Ariz. State U., Tempe, 1981—; adj. asso. prof. U. Ariz. Contbr. articles to profl. jours. Bd. dirs. Child Crisis Ctr., Tempe St. Lukes Hosp.; adv. com. on immunization practices HEW. Recipient award Ariz. Dietetic Assn., 1976, Maricopa County Med. Soc., 1980. Fellow Am. Pub. Health Assn., Am. Coll. Preventive Medicine; mem. Ariz. Pub. Health Assn., Ariz. Med. Assn., Phi Beta Kappa, Delta Omega. Democrat. Mormon. Home: 338 E Loma Vista Dr Tempe AZ 85282 Office: Ariz State U Tempe AZ 85287

D'ANDRADE, HUGH A(LFRED), pharmaceutical company executive, lawyer; b. Metuchen, N.J., Nov. 7, 1938; s. Herman and Lucille (Peticolas) D'A.; m. Nancy K. Koyen, June 1, 1963; 1 dau., Janine. B.A. in Econs., Rutgers U., 1961; LL.B. cum laude, Columbia U., 1964. Bar: N.J. 1964. Law sec. to assoc. justice N.J. Supreme Ct., 1964-65; assoc. Toner, Crowley, Woelper & Vanderbilt, Newark, 1965-68; gen. atty. CIBA Corp., Summit, N.J., 1968-70; counsel to pharms. div. CIBA-GEIGY Corp., Summit, 1970-75, v.p. and counsel pharms. div., 1975-77; sr. v.p. and counsel for planning and adminstrn. dept. CIBA-GEIGY, Summit, 1980-81; sr. v.p. adminstrn. Schering-Plough Corp., Kenilworth, N.J., 1981; dir. Biogen, N.V. Bd. overseers Found. at N.J. Inst. Tech., Newark. Mem. ABA, N.J. Bar Assn., Indsl. Biotech. Assn. (dir.). Home: 25 Clinton Pl Metuchen NJ 08840 Office: Galloping Hill Rd Kenilworth NJ 07033

D'ANDREA, ANTONIO, Italian educator; b. Messina, Italy, Nov. 22, 1916; s. Nunzio and Italia (Bassi) D'A. Doctor in Philosophy, U. Pisa, Italy, 1939. Faculty history of philosophy U. Pisa, 1944-45; dir. Central Bur. for Research in Social and Ednl. Affairs, Rome, 1945-49; vis. prof. McGill U., Montreal, Que., Can., 1949-56; asso. prof., 1956-63, prof. Italian, chmn. dept., 1964—; dir. Italian Inst., Montreal, 1962-64. Author: Le nome della storia, 1982; Co-editor: Yearbook of Italian Studies, 1971—, (with P.D. Stewart) Critical Edit., Introduction and Notes for Discours Contre Machiavel (I. Gentillet), 1974; Contbr. articles on history, lit. and philosophy to profl. jours. Decorated Stella Solidarieta Italiana grand ufficiale Order of Merit, Italy; UN grantee, 1948; UNESCO grantee, 1949; Can. Council grantee, 1958-59, 60, 73-74. Fellow Royal Soc. Can.; mem. Canadian Soc. for Italian Studies (pres.), Que. Assn. Profs. Italian, Soc. for History and Philosophy of Sci.

DANE, JOHN KENNETH, lawyer; b. Franklin, Maine, Mar. 29, 1920; s. John Churchill and Lettie Angie (Smith) D.; m. Shirley T. Van Wart, Apr. 6, 1941; children—John, Peter, Stephen, David, Richard, Jonathan. A.B., Harvard U., 1942; J.D., LL.M., Boston U., 1949. Bar: Mass. bar 1949, U.S. Supreme Ct. bar 1971. With Liberty Mutual Ins. Co., Boston, 1949—, v.p., 1971-78, gen. counsel, 1975—, sr. v.p., 1978—; vis. lectr. Harvard U., 1960-76. Contbr. articles to profl. jours. Mem. Lynnfield Town Fin. Com., 1960-61; mem. N.J. Workmen's Compensation Study Commn., 1973. Served with USN, 1944-46. Mem. Am., Mass., Boston bar assns., Am. Judicature Soc., Internat. Assn. Ins. Counsel (v.p. 1976-78). Republican. Clubs: Harvard, University, Algonquin. Home: 100 Moulton St Hamilton MA 01936 Office: 175 Berkeley St Boston MA 02117

DANE, MAXWELL, former advt. exec.; b. Cin., June 7, 1906; s. Abraham and Sophie (Sall) D.; m. Belle Sloan, Apr. 4, 1933; 1 son, Henry James. Advt. dept. Stern Bros., N.Y.C., 1928-32; retail promotion mgr. N.Y. Jour., 1933-36; account exec. Dorland Internat., 1937-39; advt. promotion mgr. Look mag., 1939-41; sales promotion mgr., radio sta. WMCA, 1941-44; pres. Maxwell Dane, Inc. (advt.), N.Y.C., 1944-49; founder, exec. v.p., sec.-treas., dir. Doyle Dane

Bernbach, Inc., N.Y.C., 1949-71, chmn. exec. com., 1969-71, dir., 1971—, mem. audit com., 1978—. Chmn. advt. and pub. div. United Jewish Appeal; chmn. exec. com. Jewish Week, N.Y.C., 1976—, pres., N.Y.C., 1982—; trustee emeritus Citizens' Budget Commn., N.Y.C.; trustee Haverford Coll., 1967—. Recipient Karl Menninger award Fortune Soc., 1983. Mem. N.Y. Civil Liberties Union (vice chmn. 1960-66, dir., treas. 1966—), Anti-Defamation League (chmn. nat. program com. 1969-76, hon. vice-chmn. 1976—), Fedn. Jewish Philanthropies (trustee, chmn. pub. relations com. 1971-76), Am. Arbitration Assn. (arbitrator 1972—), Internat. League Human Rights (treas. 1973—). Jewish. Clubs: City Athletic, City (N.Y.C.); Old Oaks Country (Purchase, N.Y.); Canyon Country (Palm Springs, Calif.). Home: 650 Park Ave New York NY 10021

DANELSKI, DAVID JOSEPH, political scientist, lawyer, educator; b. Green Bay, Wis., Oct. 29, 1930; s. Peter Anthony and Magdalen Agnes (Piontek) D.; m. Jeanne C. Parmer, June 12, 1954; children—Christine, Catherine, David, Ann, Rebecca. Student, St. Norbert Coll., 1948-50; LL.B., DePaul U., 1953; B.A., Seattle U., 1955; M.A., U. Chgo., 1957, Ph.D. (Louis E. Asher fellow 1957-58, Univ. fellow 1958-59), 1961. Bar: Ill. 1953, Wash. 1955. Partner firm Patrick & Danelski, Mt. Vernon, 1955-56; research atty. Am. Bar Found., Chgo., 1957-59; instr., asst. prof. polit. sci. U. Ill., Urbana, 1959-60; asst. prof. polit. sci. U. Wash., 1961-64; lectr., asso. prof. polit. sci. Yale U., 1964-70; prof. govt. Cornell U., Ithaca, N.Y., 1970-73, Goldwin Smith prof. govt., 1973-79, univ. ombudsman, 1973-75; partner firm Schroeter, Goldmark & Bender, Seattle, 1978-79, of counsel, 1979—; prof. polit. sci. Stanford U., 1979—. Author: A Supreme Court Justice Is Appointed, 1964, Rights, Liberties and Ideals, 1983; author, editor: (with Glendon Schubert) Comparative Judicial Behavior, 1969; editor: (with Joseph Tulchin) The Autobiographical Notes of Charles Evans Hughes, 1973; Contbr. articles to profl. jours. Served to lt. (j.g.) USNR, 1953-55. Recipient Sr. Fulbright-Hays award to Japan, 1968-69, E. Harris Harbison prize for gifted teaching Danforth Found., 1970, Humanities and Scis. Dean's award for disting. teaching Stanford U., 1981; Walter E. Meyer research fellow, 1962-63; John Simon Guggenheim fellow, 1968-69; Center for Advanced Study in Behavioral Scis. fellow, 1970-71; Japan Found. fellow, 1975; Sr. specialist East-West Center, 1965, 67. Mem. Am. Polit. Sci. Assn., Law and Soc. Assn., Wash. Bar Assn. Democrat. Home: 1474 Barton Dr Sunnyvale CA 94087 Office: Dept Polit Sci Stanford U Stanford CA 94305

DANENBARGER, WILLIAM FOWLER, radio station executive; b. Concordia, Kans., Apr. 7, 1910; s. William Henry and Lola (Fowler) D.; m. Winifred Wright, Mar. 30, 1934; children: William Wright, John K. A.B., U. Kans., 1933. Pres. radio sta. KNCK-KCKS, Concordia, 1954—; v.p., treas., dir. Gen. Fin. Inc., Concordia, 1975-; adv. bd. Creative Enterprises, Inc.; dir. Renewable Resources, Inc.; Chmn. Kans. Ednl. TV Authority, 1970-75. Commr. Edn. Commn. States, 1972-74, Kans. Econ. Devel. Commn., 1973-79; mem. Kans. Bd. Regents, 1960-65, 70-74, chmn., 1973-74; bd. regents Washburn U., 1961-65; mem. Concordia Library Bd., 1949-61, pres., 1960-61; chmn. adv. bd. St. Joseph's Hosp., 1976-81; trustee Kans. Council Econ. Edn., 1964-75; bd. dirs. Kans. State U. Research Found., 1972-74, Kans. Good Roads Assn., 1982—; v.p. Cook Found., Concordia, 1975—; mem. Kans. Indsl. Roundtable, 1976-79. Clubs: Elks, Concordia Country; Garden of Gods (Colorado Springs, Colo.). Address: 1250 Willow St Concordia KS 66901

DANENBERG, HAROLD, consumer products company executive; b. N.Y.C., Dec. 22, 1930; s. Isadore and Anna (Schiffrin) D.; m. Barbara Rosen, Aug. 22, 1954; children: Jill Audrey, Lori Sue. B.B.A., CCNY, 1953, M.B.A., 1959. With B. Manischewitz Food Co., 1955-57; product mgr. Best Foods div. CPC Internat. Co., 1957-64; group product mgr. Lehn & Fink Products Co. div. Sterling Drugs, 1964-71, v.p. consumer products, 1971-75, pres., also v.p. parent co., 1975-79; pres. Mennen USA, Morristown, N.J., 1979-81; pres., chief operating officer Mennen Co., Morristown, N.J., 1981—, The Mennen Co., 1981—; adj. prof. Pace U. Bd. dirs. Rockland County chpt. Am. Cancer Soc., 1971-77; chmn. Israel Bond drive, New City, N.Y., 1973-76; active March of Dimes. Served with AUS, 1953-55. Recipient Man of Year award Am. Cancer Soc., 1976, Fedn. Jewish Philanthropies-United Jewish Appeal, 1979. Mem. Nat. Wholesale Druggists Assn. (asso. mem. adv. com.). Club: Dellwood Country (New City). Office: Mennen USA Morristown NJ 07960

DANFORD, ARDATH ANNE, librarian; b. Lima, Ohio, Feb. 11, 1930; d. Howard Gorby and Grace Rose (Klug) D. B.A., Fla. State U., 1951, M.A., 1952. Head tech. services Lima Public Library, 1956-60; librarian Way Public Library, Perrysburg, Ohio, 1960-70; asst. dir. Toledo-Lucas County Public Library, 1971-77, dir., 1977—; bd. dirs. OHIONET. Author: The Perrysburg Story, 1966. Bd. dirs. Ohio Library Found.; Adv. bd. St. Charles Hosp. Recipient Toledo Headliner award Women in Communication, 1978, Boss of Yr. award PerRoMa chpt. Am. Bus. Women's Assn., 1978. Mem. ALA, Ohio Library Assn., League Women Voters., Maumee Valley Hist. Soc. Methodist. Clubs: Zonta (Toledo) (pres. club 1975-76); Toledo). Home: 2025 Sandringham St Toledo OH 43615 Office: 325 Michigan St Toledo OH 43624

DANFORTH, ARTHUR EDWARDS, financial executive; b. Cleve., Jan. 23, 1925; s. Arthur Edwards and Jane (Hillyard) D.; m. Elizabeth Wagley, Mar. 17, 1956; children: Hillyard Raible, Nicholas Edwards (dec.), Jonathan Ingersoll, Elizabeth Wagley, Michael Stowe. B.A., Yale, 1949. With Hayden Miller Co., Cleve., 1949-54, First Nat. City Bank (predecessor to Citibank N.A.), N.Y.C., 1954-63, asst. mgr. Buenos Aires office, 1959-61; treas. Bunge Corp., N.Y.C., 1963-65; sr. v.p., treas. Colonial Bank & Trust Co., Waterbury, Conn., 1965-70; chmn., chief exec. officer Farmers Bank of Del., Wilmington, 1970-76; prin. Danforth Group, New Canaan, Conn. Former bd. dirs. United Way of Del., Boys Club of Wilmington, Grand Opera House Inc. of Del., NCCJ, Audubon Soc. Conn., Greater Wilmington Devel. Council. Served as ensign USNR, 1945-46. Clubs: Nantucket (Mass.) Yacht; Yale (N.Y.C.). Home: 260 Whiting Pond Rd Fairfield CT 06430 Office: 82 Main St New Canaan CT 06840

DANFORTH, DAVID NEWTON, physician, educator; b. Evanston, Ill., Aug. 25, 1912; s. William Clark and Gertrude (MacLean) D.; m. Gladys Blaine, 1938; 1 son, David Newton. B.S., Northwestern U., 1934, M.S., 1936, Ph.D., 1938, M.D., 1939. Diplomate: Am. Bd. Obstetrics and Gynecology (dir. 1966-73, v.p. 1970-72). Intern N.Y. Postgrad. Hosp., N.Y.C., 1938-39; resident Sloane Hosp. for Women, Columbia, 1939-44; clin. asst. obstetrics and gynecology Northwestern U. Med. Sch., 1946-47, asst. prof. obstetrics and gynecology, 1947-52, asso. prof., 1952-59, prof., 1959-80, prof. emeritus, 1980—, chmn., 1965-72; asst. attending obstetrician and gynecologist Wesley Meml. Hosp., Chgo., 1946-47, chmn. dept. obstetrics and gynecology, 1965-71; chief dept. obstetrics and gynecology Evanston Hosp., 1947-65. Co-author: Pregnancy, 1975, The Complete Guide to Pregnancy, 1984; Editor, contbr.: Textbook of Obstetrics and Gynecology, 1966, 4th edit., 1982; assoc. editor: Obstet. and Gynecol. Survey; Contbr. articles to profl. jours. Served to lt. (s.g.), M.C. USNR, 1944-46. Recipient Capps prize for med. research, 1939; Gold Medal award Barren Found., 1965; Merit award Northwestern U., 1966; Silver Medal award Columbia, 1967. Mem. Am. Fertility Soc. (pres. 1963), A.C.S. (gov. 1959-61), Soc. Gynecol. Investigation, Am. Gynecol. Soc. (council 1962-64, pres. 1974), Chgo. Gynecol. Soc. (pres. 1961), Am. Coll. Obstetricians and Gynecologists (1st v. p. 1969), Am. Gynecol. Club (pres. 1974), Inst. Medicine Chgo., Soc. Exptl. Biology and Medicine, AAAS, AMA, Central Assn. Obstetricians and Gynecologists, Central Travel Club (sec. 1953-59, pres. 1960), Alpha Omega Alpha, Sigma Xi, Pi Kappa Epsilon. Home: 1630 Sheridan Rd Wilmette IL 60091

DANFORTH, DOUGLAS DEWITT, manufacturing company executive; b. Syracuse, N.Y., Sept. 25, 1922; s. Dewitt Ward and Ruth Cordellia (Ward) D.; m. Janet Mae Piron, May 15, 1943; children: Barbara Lee Danforth Osburn, Susan Jean Danforth Sutcliffe, Debra Lynn and Douglas Dewitt (twins). Student, Penn. Coll., Cleve., 1940-41; B.M.E., Syracuse U., 1947. Supt. planning Easy Washer Machine Co., Syracuse, N.Y., 1942-46; v.p., gen. mgr. in Mex. Internat. Gen. Electric Co., 1947-53; plant mgr. Gen. Electric Co., Balt., 1953-55; exec. v.p., gen. mgr. Industria Electrica De Mex., 1956-61, dir., 1958—; v.p. Westinghouse Electric Corp., Pitts., 1962-65, group v.p., 1965-69, exec. v.p., 1969-74; pres. Industry Products Co., Westinghouse, 1974-78, vice chmn., chief operating officer, 1978-83, chmn., chief exec. officer, 1983—; dir. Pitts. Nat. Corp., PPG Industries, Inc. Trustee Syracuse U., Carnegie Mellon U., Greater Pitts. Guild for Blind, Allegheny Health, Edn. and Research Corp., Com. for Econ. Devel.; bd. dirs. United Way Allegheny County. Clubs: Duquesne, Longue Vue (Pitts.); Laurel Valley, Rolling Rock (Ligonier, Pa.). Home: 272 Justabout Rd Venetia PA 15367 Office: Westinghouse Electric Corp Gateway Center Westinghouse Bldg Pittsburgh PA 15222

DANFORTH, JOHN CLAGGETT, U.S. senator, lawyer, clergyman; b. St. Louis, Sept. 5, 1936; s. Donald and Dorothy (Claggett) D.; m. Sally B. Dobson, Sept. 7, 1957; children: Eleanor, Mary, Dorothy, Johanna, Thomas. B.A. with honors, Princeton U., 1958; B.D., Yale U., 1963, LL.B., 1963, M.A. (hon.),; L.H.D., Lindenwood Coll., 1970; L.HD., Ind. Central U.; LL.D., Drury Coll., 1970, Maryville Coll., Rockhurst Coll., Westminster Coll., Culver-Stockton Coll.; D.D., Lewis and Clark Coll.; H.H.D., William Jewell Coll.; S.T.D., Southwest Bapt. Coll. Bar: N.Y. 1964, Mo. 1966. With firm Davis Polk Wardwell Sunderland & Kiendl, N.Y.C., 1964-66, Bryan, Cave, McPheeters and McRoberts, St. Louis, 1966-68; atty. gen. State of Mo., 1969-76; U.S. senator from Mo., 1976—; ordained deacon Episcopal Ch., 1963, priest, 1964; asst. rector, N.Y.C., 1963-66, assoc. rector, Clayton, Mo., 1966-68, Grace Ch., Jefferson City, 1969; hon. assoc. St. Albans Ch., Washington, 1977—; mem. governing bd. Nat. Cathedral.; chmn. Mo. Law Enforcement Assistance Council, 1973-74. Republican nominee U.S. Senate, 1970. Recipient Distinguished Service award St. Louis Jr. C. of C., 1969, Disting. Missourian and Brotherhood awards NCCJ; recipient Disting. Lectr. award Avila Coll.; named Outstanding Young Man Mo. Jr. C. of C., 1968; Alumni fellow Yale U., 1973-79. Mem. Mo. Acad. Squires, Alpha Sigma Nu (hon.). Republican. Office: 497 Russell Senate Office Bldg Washington DC 20510

DANFORTH, LOUIS FREMONT, banker; b. Los Angeles, Nov. 15, 1913; s. Louis F. and Louise (Bauerle) D.; m. Leota V. Schwulst, Sept. 9, 1944; children—David Louis, Victoria Leota. Grad., Columbia, 1934; postgrad., N.Y. U., 1952; D.B.A., Oklahoma City U., 1982. With Guaranty Trust Co., N.Y.C., 1946-55; chief fin. officer Liberty Nat. Bank & Trust Co., Oklahoma City, 1955-79; sr. v.p., treas. Liberty Nat. Corp., until 1979, cons., 1979—; adj. prof. econs. Oklahoma City U.; dir. Investors Trust Co., Duncan, Okla., 1st Nat. Bank, El Reno, Okla. Past pres., bd. dirs. Better Bus. Bur.; pres. Community Council Central Okla.; past pres. Central Okla. Council for Children with Learning Disabilities; bd. dirs., past pres. Sunbeam Home and Family Service; bd. dirs. Asso. Industries Okla., Okla. Council on Econ. Edn., Okla. State U., Okla. Lung Research Program, Am. Heart Assn.; bd. dirs., past pres. Community Council, United Appeal Greater Oklahoma City Area; mem. adv. council Oklahoma City U. Bus. Research Center; chmn. bd. commrs. Oklahoma City Pub. Housing Authority.; pres. Oklahoma County Mental Health Assn., 1983. Mem. Econ. Club Okla. (past pres.), Okla. Soc. Financial Analysts (past pres.), Okla. Financial Analysts Fedn. (past regional v.p.), Nat. Assn. Bus. Economists. Republican. Episcopalian. Clubs: Mens Dinner, Petroleum, Press (Oklahoma City). Home: 1135 NW 63d St Apt 8 Oklahoma City OK 73116 Office: PO Box 25848 Oklahoma City OK 73125 *The awareness of need for charity or compassion greater than the search for riches.*

DANFORTH, WILLIAM HENRY, physician, university chancellor; b. St. Louis, Apr. 10, 1926; s. Donald and Dorothy (Claggett) D.; m. Elizabeth Anne Gray, Sept. 1, 1950; children—Cynthia Danforth Noto, David, Ann, Elizabeth. A.B., Princeton U., 1947; M.D., Harvard U., 1951. Intern Barnes Hosp., St. Louis, 1951-52, resident, 1954-57; now mem. staff; asst. prof. medicine Washington U., St. Louis, 1960-65, asso. prof., 1965-67, prof., 1967—, vice chancellor for med. affairs, 1965-71, chancellor, 1971—; chmn. Med. Center Redevel. Corp., 1973—; pres. Washington U. Med. Sch. and Asso. Hosps., 1965-71; program coordinator Bi-State Regional Med. Program, 1967-69; dir. Ralston Purina Co., McDonnell Douglas Corp.; mem. nat. adv. heart and lung council Nat. Heart and Lung Inst., 1970-74. Trustee, chmn. bd. Danforth Found.; trustee Am. Youth Found., 1963—, Princeton U., 1970-74; pres. St. Louis Christmas Carols Assn., 1958-74, chmn., 1975—. Served with USN, 1952-54. Named Man of Yr. St. Louis Globe-Democrat, 1978. Fellow AAAS, Am. Acad. Arts and Scis.; Mem. Nat. Acad. Scis. Inst. Medicine. Home: 10 Glenview Rd Saint Louis MO 63124 Office: Washington U Saint Louis MO 63130

DANGEL, ROBERT FREDERICK, pipeline company executive; b. New Castle, Pa., June 29, 1926; s. Frederick M. and Sara (Artz) D.; m. Colleen H. Bottorf, Nov. 1, 1947; childern: Robert, Richard, Matthew. B.S. in Bus. Adminstrn., U. Pitts., 1950. Treas. Mich. Wis. Pile Line Co., Detroit, 1969-73, v.p. rates and certs., 1973-76, v.p. corp. planning, 1976-80, group v.p. fin. planning and regulatory affairs, 1980-83, sr. v.p., asst. to chmn., 1983—, dir., 1980—, ANR Storage Co., Detroit. Served with U.S. Army, 1944-46. Mem. Am. Gas Assn., Ind. Natural Gas Assn., Am. Econ. Club. Club: Detroit Athletic. Home: 12770 Veronica Southgate MI 48195 Office: Mich Wis Pipe Line Co 1 Woodward Ave Detroit MI 48226

D'ANGELO, JOSEPH FRANCIS, publishing executive; b. Astoria, N.Y., July 4, 1930; s. Frank and Matilda (Oliveri) D'A.; m. Marcia Elaine Mackie, Mar. 4, 1965; children: Elena, Joseph Francis. B.B.A., St. John's U., 1952. Mem. firm Haskins & Sells (C.P.A.'s), N.Y.C., 1952-61; treas., controller internat. operations Borden Co., Panama and P.R., 1961-65; v.p. King Features Syndicate div. Hearst Corp., N.Y.C., 1973-76, pres., 1976—; resident controller, 1965-73, bus. mgr., 1968-73, gen. mgr., 1973—; pres., dir. King Features Syndicate, Inc., 1973—, Features Music Corp., 1973—, KFS Music, Inc., 1973—, Telenews Film Corp., 1973—, King Features TV Prodns., Inc., N.Y.C., 1973—. Trustee Emerson Coll., Boston, North Shore Univ. Hosp.; bd. dirs. Saratoga Performing Arts Center, Saratoga Springs, N.Y., Mus. Cartoon Art and Hall of Fame, Greenwich, Conn., N.Y. Bd. of Trade. Mem. Artists and Writers Assn., Nat. Cartoonists Soc., Newspaper Comics Council, N.Y. State Soc. Newspaper Editors, So. Newspaper Pubs. Assn., Inst. Newspaper Controllers and Finance Officers, Met. Opera Guild, Sigma Delta Chi. Republican. Roman Catholic. Clubs: Union League, Dutch Treat, Friars, N.Y. Athletic, Overseas Press (N.Y.C.); Wheatley Hills Golf (East Williston, N.Y.); Strathmore-Vanderbilt Country (Manhasset, N.Y.); Knights of Malta. Home: 173 Chapel Rd Manhasset NY 11030 Office: 235 E 45th St New York NY 10017

D'ANGELO, ROBERT WILLIAM, lawyer; b. Buffalo, Nov. 10, 1932; s. Samuel and Margaret Theresa Guercio D'A.; m. Ellen Frances Neary, Sept. 17, 1959; children: Christopher Robert, Gregory Andrew. B.B.A., Loyola U. Los Angeles, 1954; J.D., UCLA, 1960. Bar: Calif. 1960. Since practiced in, Los Angeles; mem. firm. Myers & D'Angelo, Los Angeles, 1967—; adj. prof. law, taxation Whittier Coll. of Law., 1981. Served to capt. USAF, 1954-57. Mem. Am., Los Angeles County, Wilshire bar assns., State Bar Calif., Am. Inst. C.P.A.s, Calif. Soc. C.P.A.s, Am. Assn. Atty.-C.P.A.s, Calif. Assn. Atty.-C.P.A.s (pres. 1980), Phi Delta Phi, Alpha Sigma Nu. Home: 1706 Highland Ave Glendale CA 91202 Office: 3303 Wilshire Blvd Suite 500 Los Angeles CA 90010

DANGERFIELD, GEORGE, author; b. Newbury, Berkshire, Eng., Oct. 28, 1904; came to U.S., 1930, naturalized, 1943; s. George and Ethel Margaret (Tyrer) D.; m. Helen Mary Deey Spedding, June 28, 1928; m. Mary Lou Schott, June 29, 1941; children: Mary Jo, Hilary, Anthony. Student, Forest Sch., Walthamstow, Essex, Eng., 1916-22; B.A., Hertford Coll., Oxford U., 1927; M.A., Oxford U., 1968. Asst. editor Brewer, Warren & Putnam, N.Y.C., 1930-32; lit. editor Vanity Fair mag., 1933-35; writer, lectr., 1935—; lectr. history U. Calif. at Santa Barbara, 1968-72. Author: Bengal Mutiny, 1933, The Strange Death of Liberal England, 1935, Victoria's Heir, 1941, The Era of Good Feelings, 1952, Chancellor Robert R. Livingston of New York, 1960, The Awakening of American Nationalism, 1815-1828, 1965, Defiance to the Old World, 1970, The Damnable Question, 1976, (with Otey M. Scruggs) Henry Adams' History of the United States, 1963; contbg. author: (Allan Nevins) Times of Trial, 1958, (John A. Garraty) Shaping the Constitution, 1963, Interpreting American History, 1970. Served 102d inf. div. AUS, 1942-45. Recipient Bancroft prize in Am. history Columbia U., 1953, Pulitzer prize in Am. history, 1953; Benjamin D. Shreve fellow Princeton U., 1957-58; Guggenheim fellow, 1970. Fellow Soc. Am. Historians; mem. Ams. for Dem. Action, ACLU, Friends of Montecito Pub. Library, Am. Antiquarian Soc. Home: 883 Toro Canyon Rd Santa Barbara CA 93108

DANGERFIELD, RODNEY (JACK ROY), comedian, actor, author; b. Babylon, N.Y., 1922; m. Joyce Indig (dec.); children: Brian, Melanie. Performer in night clubs as Jack Roy, 1941-51, businessman, 1951-63, comedian, 1963—. Appeared in: numerous TV shows The Ed Sullivan Show, Tonight Show; host: TV show Saturday Night Live; appeared in: motion pictures The Projectionist, Caddyshack, 1980, Easy Money, 1983; founder Nightclub, Dangerfield's, 1969; rec.: albums The Loser, I Don't Get No Respect, No Respect, Rappin' Rodney; author: I Couldn't Stand My Wife's Cooking So I Opened a Restaurant, 1972, I Don't Get No Respect, 1973. Recipient Grammy award. Address: care Estelle Endler 3920 Sunny Oak Rd Sherman Oaks CA 91403 *

D'ANGIO, GIULIO JOHN, radiation therapist; b. N.Y.C., May 2, 1922; s. Carlo and Rosa (Calderazzo) D'A.; m. Jean Chittenden Terhune, Aug. 27, 1955; children: Carl, Peter. A.B., Columbia U., 1943; M.D., Harvard U., 1945; D. Medicine and Surgery (hon.), U. Bologna, 1983. Diplomate: Am. Bd. Radiology. Surg. intern Children's Hosp., Boston, 1945-46, tng. in pathology, 1948-49; resident in radiology Boston City Hosp., 1949-53; also mem. staff; radiation therapist Children's Hosp., 1956-62; researcher Donner Lab., also Lawrence Radiation Lab., U. Calif., Berkeley, 1962-63; dir. div. radiation therapy U. Minn. Med. Sch., 1964-68; chmn. dept. radiation therapy Meml. Hosp., N.Y.C., 1968-76; dir. children's cancer research center Children's Hosp., Phila., 1976—; prof. radiation therapy U. Pa. Med. Sch., 1976—, prof. pediatric oncology, 1976—; chmn. Nat. Wilms Tumor Study Com., 1968—; past chmn. cancer clin. investigation rev. com. Nat. Cancer Inst. Contbr. numerous articles med. jours. Served to capt. M.C. AUS, 1946-48. Decorated Commendation medal; recipient ann. award Am. Cancer Soc., 1978, Heath Meml. award M.D. Anderson Tumor and Cancer Inst., 1979. Fellow Royal Coll. Radiology; Mem. Am. Acad. Pediatrics (past chmn. sect. oncology-hematology), AAAS, Am. Assn. Cancer Research, Am. Coll. Radiology, Am. Soc. Therapeutic Radiologists, Royal Soc. Medicine, Internat. Soc. Pediatric Oncology, Radiol. Soc. N.Am., Am. Radium Soc., Soc. Pediatric Radiology, Phi Beta Kappa. Episcopalian. Home: 518 Cedar Ln Swarthmore PA 19081 Office: Children's Hosp 34th and Civic Center Blvd Philadelphia PA 19104

DANGREMOND, DAVID W., museum director; b. Norristown, Pa., June 8, 1952; s. James L. and Jean O. (Kross) D.; m. Mary Plant Spivy, Oct. 18, 1980. B.A. cum laude, Amherst Coll., 1974; M.A., U. Del., 1976. Dir. Webb-Deane-Stevens Mus., Wethersfield, Conn., 1976-80, Bennington Mus., Vt., 1980—; adj. prof. art history U. Hartford, Conn., 1977-80; tutor Historic Deerfield, Mass., 1975; trustee Williamstown Regional Art Conservation Lab., Mass., 1981; grant reviewer Inst. Mus. Services, Washington, 1982; dir. Attingham Summer Sch., Shropshire, England, 1980—. Foreward author: Heritage Houses: the American Tradition in Connecticut 1660-1900, 1979; contbr. articles to jours. Bd. dirs. Hartford Architecture Conservancy, Conn., 1978-80; mem. art and antiques council Conn. Pub. TV, Hartford, 1977-80; mem. long-range planning com. Bennington Free Library, 1981—; mem. concert com. Vermont Symphony Orch., Burlington, 1980—; div. head United Way of Bennington County, 1982—; del. Gov's Conf. on Future of Vt.'s Heritage, Montpelier, 1982. Fellow Historic Deerfield, 1973; Winterthur fellow H.F. duPont Winterthur Mus., 1974-76; Sir George Trevelyan scholar Attingham summer sch., Shropshire, Eng., 1976. Mem. Am. Assn. for State and Local History (state awards chmn.), New Eng. Mus. Assn. (planning com.), Vt. Council on Arts (membership com.), Vt. Mus. and Gallery Alliance (dir.), Greater Hartford Assn. of Historic Houses (bd. dirs.), Am. Assn. Museums (accreditation vis. com), Decorative Arts Soc., Greater Bennington C. of C. (bd. dirs.). Episcopalian. Clubs: Univ. (Hartford); Soc. Colonial Wars (New Haven). Lodge: Rotary Internat. (Bennington, Rotary Found. chmn.). Home: The Parsonage Monument Ave Old Bennington VT 05201 Office: Bennington Mus West Main St Bennington VT 05201

DANIAS, STARR, actress, dancer, singer; b. N.Y.C.; d. Spiro G. and Andrea Mae (Cocoros) D.; m. Douglas Wassell, Dec. 22, 1973. Leading dancer, London Festival Ballet, Joffrey Ballet; soloist, Am. Ballet Theater; prin. ballerina nat. touring co.: The Pavlova Celebration; appeared as Caroline in: film The Turning Point, 1978; appeared in musicals: El Bravo, 1981, On Your Toes, 1983; TV appearances include: daytime serial As the World Turns; Phil Donahue Show, Merv Griffin Show, 50th Acad. Awards Celebration. Mem. AFTRA, Screen Actors Guild, Actors Equity, Am. Guild Mus. Artists. Office: 130 W 56th St New York NY 10019

DANIEL, BETH, professional golfer; b. b. Charleston, S.C., Oct. 14; d. Robert and Lucia D. Grad., Furman U., 1978. Profl. golfer Ladies Profl. Golf Assn. tour, 1979—, Golden Lights Championship, 1980, World Series Women's Golf, 1980, World Championship Women's Golf, 1981, Lady Citrus Classic, 1981. Winner Patty Berg Classic, 1979, 80, U.S. Amateur Title, 1975, 77, Player of Year, Ladies Profl.

Golf Assn., 1980, Columbia Savings Classic, 1980, 82 Birmingham Classic, 1982

DANIEL, CHARLES DWELLE, JR., consultant, retired army officer; b. San Antonio, Oct. 30, 1925; s. Charles Dwelle and Jean Elizabeth (Stormont) D.; m. Ann Meredith Carter, June 7, 1946; children: Charles Dwelle III, Peter C. B.S., U.S. Mil. Acad., 1946; M.S., Tulane U., 1961, Ph.D., 1968. Joined U.S. Army, advanced through grades to maj. gen.; F.A. battery comdr., Korean War, 1950-52; adviser Ky. N.G., Louisville, 1953-55; F.A. missile officer 7th U.S. Army, Europe, 1956-59, physicist Def. Atomic Support Agy, Washington, 1963-66, F.A. bn. comdr. 1st inf. div., Viet Nam, 1966-67; div. chief, dir. Office of Chief of U.S. Army Research and Devel., 1968-71; comdg. gen. I Corps, Arty., Korea, 1971; dep. comdg. gen. Korean Support Command, 1971-72; dir. army research Dept. Army, Washington, 1972-74, dir. combat support systems, 1974; dep. comdt. Nat. War Coll., Ft. McNair, Washington, 1974-75; spl. asst. to comdg. gen. U.S. Army Materiel Command, Alexandria, Va., 1975-77; comdg. gen. U.S. Army Electronics Research and Devel. Command, Adelphi, Md., 1977-79; ret., 1979; dir. target acquisition BDM Corp., McLean, Va., 1979-80; cons. Burdeshaw Assos., 1981—. Decorated D.S.M., Silver Star, Legion of Merit with oak leaf cluster, D.F.C., Bronze Star with 4 oak leaf clusters, Air medal with 16 oak leaf clusters, Joint Service Commendation medal, Army Commendation medal, U.S.; Vietnamese Cross of Gallantry with Silver Star. Mem. Assn. U.S. Army, Assn. Grads. U.S. Mil. Acad., S.A.R. Home: 4904 Baltan Rd NW Washington DC 20016 Office: Burdeshaw Assocs Ltd 4701 Sangamore Rd Bethesda MD 20816

DANIEL, DAN, congressman; b. Chatham, Va., May 12, 1914; s. Reuben Earl and Georgia (Grant) D.; m. Ruby Gordon McGregor, Sept. 30, 1939; 1 son, Jimmie Foxx. Former asst. to chmn. bd. Dan River Mills, Inc., Danville, Va.; mem. 91st-98th congresses from 5th Dist. Va.; Dir. Bank of Va., Danville. Permanent mem. People-To-People Com.; Mem. Va. Ho. of Delegates, 1959-68. Served with USNR. Decorated Star of Solidarity, Italy, Croix de Merit; recipient Service to Mankind award; George Washington Honor medal. Mem. Am. Legion (past nat. comdr.), Va. C. of C. (past pres.). Office: 2368 Rayburn House Office Bldg Washington DC 20515 *

DANIEL, ELMER LEON, oil company executive; b. Ft. Worth, July 7, 1936; s. Elmer Clinton and Sallie Whittley (Thweatt) D.; m. Ann Lea Ball, Nov. 7, 1958; children: Michael Lee, Larissa Lyn, Suzanne Leigh. B.S. in Petroleum Engring, U. Tex., 1958. Petroleum engr. Plymouth Oil Co. and Marathon Oil Co., Midland, Tex., 1958-62, Sinclair Oil, 1962-64; field foreman Brit.-Am. Oil Co., Midland, 1964-66; sr. exploitation engr. Shell Oil Co., Midland, 1969; asst. v.p. ops Occidental of Libya, 1969-72; ops. mgr. Occidental of Nigeria, 1972-74; sr. v.p. Occidental of Britain, 1974-81; sr. v.p. North Sea ops. Occidental Calif., Bakersfield, 1981—. Chmn. Aberdeen Am. Sch. Ednl. Trust Ltd., 1979-81. Mem. Soc. Petroleum Engrs., Brit. Inst. Petroleum, Grampian-Houston Assn. Republican. Clubs: Aberdeen Petroleum, Ikoyi; Walden Yacht and Country (Houston); Lagos Yacht, Stockdale Country. Office: 5000 Stockdale Hwy Bakersfield CA 93309

DANIEL, EVELYN HOPE, university dean; b. Whitefield, Maine, Nov. 23, 1933; d. George Snowdeal and Evelyn Lura (Cole) Cunningham; m. Alfred Eugene Foulkes, Mar. 30, 1951 (div. 1956); children: Nancy Karen, George Warren; m. Harold Clifford Daniel, Jan. 1, 1957 (div. 1974); children: Jeffrey Martin, Dawn Hope. A.B. magna cum laude, U. N.C.-Wilmington, 1968; M.L.S., U. Md., 1969, Ph.D., 1974. Asst. prof. Coll. Library Sci. U. Ky., 1972-74; asst. prof. Grad. Sch. Library U. R.I., 1974-76; assoc. prof., asst. dean Sch. Info. Studies Syracuse U., N.Y., 1976-81, dean and prof., 1981—; cons. ednl. radio and TV, Tehran, Iran, 1976-77, Millersville State Coll., Pa., 1983, Fgn. Service Inst., U.S. Dept. State, Washington, 1983—. Co-author: Media and Microcomputers in the Library, 1983; contbr. articles to jours.; editorial bd. (Library Research), 1979—. NDEA fellow, 1968-69. Mem. ALA (chmn. standing com. on edn. 1980-83, coordinator Library Edn. Assembly 1980-83), N.Y. Statewide Continuing Library Edn. Adv. Com. (vice chmn. 1982-84), Assn. for Library and Edn. Sci. Educators (chmn. 1983-84). Home: 602 Jamesville Ave Syracuse NY 13210 Office: School Info Studies Syracuse Univ 200 Huntington Hall Syracuse NY 13210

DANIEL, GERARD, wire products company executive, religious organizational executive; b. Hamburg, Germany, June 6, 1916; s. Max and Wally (Kronheim) D.; m. Ruth Daniel, May 20, 1941; children: Ralph, Miriam. Pres. Fimex Middle East, Tel Aviv, Israel, 1944-48; export mgr. Berwick, Inc., N.Y.C., 1949-51, Toledano Pinto, Inc., 1951-53; pres. Gerard Daniel & Co., Inc., New Rochelle, N.Y., 1952—, City Wire Cloth, Paramount, Calif., 1975—. Pres. Larchmont Temple, N.Y., 1975; gov. Hebrew Union Coll., 1979; pres. World Union for Progressive Judaism, 1980—. Mem. Am. Importer's Assn., Filbration Soc. Home: Polly Park Rd Rye NY 10580 Office: 5 Plain Ave New Rochelle NY 10801 Office: World Union for Progressive Judaism 838 Fifth Ave New York NY 10021

DANIEL, HARBEN WINFIELD, broadcasting company executive; b. Nashville, Aug. 6, 1906; s. John and Grace Olive (Knight) D.; m. Catherine Murrey, Sept. 25, 1934; children—Catherine Daniel Long (dec.), Mary Daniel Cay; m. Caroline Noble Jones Wright, Dec. 30, 1970. Student, Vanderbilt U., 1924-26, Watkins Inst., 1927-28. From account exec. to comml. mgr. Sta. WSM, Nashville, 1930-39; pres. WSAV, Inc., Savannah, Ga., 1939—. Contbr. articles to profl. publs. Chmn. 3d Army Civilian Adv. Com., 1949-53; pres. Porter G. Pierpont Ednl. Fund, 1950-51; area chmn. Vanderbilt U. Alumni Endowment Devel., 1963—; mem. adv. council to edn. Chatham County Pub. Schs., 1969-70; mem. Savannah Airport Commn., 1968-76, Coastal Empire Council Boy Scouts Am.; bd. dirs. United Community Appeal; trustee Coastal Plains chpt. Ga. Conservancy. Recipient Silver medal Am. Advt. Fedn. Mem. Savannah C. of C. (dir.), Ga. Soc. Colonial Wars (governing council 1977—), Sigma Delta Chi, Sigma Chi. Clubs: Savannah Yacht and Country, Oglethorpe, Chatham (Savannah); Rotary (pres.). Home: 310 E 45th St Savannah GA 31405 Office: 901 E 70th St Savannah GA 31405

DANIEL, JAMES, writer, editor; b. Davidson County, N.C., June 6, 1916; s. James Manly and Bert (Fletcher) D.; m. Ramona Teijeiro, Apr. 15, 1939; children: Jane Clare (Mrs. John S. Nagy), Ramona Nina (Mrs. Mark Ritts). A.B., U. N.C., 1937; Nieman fellow, Harvard, 1942-43. Reporter Raleigh (N.C.) News & Observer, 1937-40; reporter Washington Daily News, 1941, city editor, 1946-47; with OWI in, CBI, 1943-45; Washington corr. Scripps-Howard Papers, 1948-56; contbg. editor Time mag., 1957-60; roving editor Reader's Digest, 1961-81; pres. Healing Springs Properties, Inc. Author: (with J. G. Hubbell) Strike in the West, The Complete Story of the Cuban Crisis, 1963; Editor: Private Investment, The Key to International Development, 1958. First selectman, Weston, Conn., 1967-69; sec. Natural Sci. for Youth Found. Club: Harvard (N.Y.C.). Home: 183 Good Hill Rd Weston CT 06883

DANIEL, JAQUELIN JAMES, lawyer, newspaper publisher; b. Jacksonville, Fla., Sept. 22, 1916; s. Richard Potts and Mary Goff (Palmer) D.; m. Anne Page Coachman, Oct. 18, 1947; children: Eleanor Page Daniel Porter, Jaquelin Palmer Daniel Haughton. A.B., Princeton U., 1939; LL.B., U. Fla., 1942; LL.D., Fla. State U., 1965. Bar: Fla. 1942. Mem. firm Daniel & Daniel, Jacksonville, 1942-60; pres., chmn. exec. com. Stockton, Whatley, Davin & Co., Jacksonville, 1960-76; chmn. exec. com. Ponte Vedra Co.; pub. Fla. Times Union and Jacksonville Jour., 1976-83; of counsel Pajcic Pajcic Dale & Bald, 1983—; dir. Atlantic Bancorp., Am. Gen. Corp., Freeport McMoran. Pres. United Way, 1955, 62; mem. bd. control Fla. Instns. Higher Learning, 1957-61, chmn., 1959-61; chmn. Duval County Local Govt. Study Commn., 1965-67; del. Democratic Nat. Conv., 1956; chmn. bd. visitors Davidson Coll., 1965; trustee Daniel Meml. Home for Children; chmn. bd. trustees George Peabody Coll., 1967-70; mem., chmn. bd. regents State Univ. System, 1971—; pres. Evergreen Cemetery Assn., 1956; trustee Princeton U., 1972-76, Episcopal Ch. Found. Served from ensign to lt. comdr. USNR, 1942-45. Decorated Bronze Star; recipient Disting. Service award U.S. Jaycees, 1950; Disting. Citizen award Nat. Mcpl. League, 1968; Brotherhood award NCCJ, 1970. Mem. Kappa Alpha. Democrat. Episcopalian. Clubs: Florida Yacht (commodore 1956), River (past pres.), Timuquana Country, Ponte Vedra (Jacksonville); Princeton (N.Y.C.). Home: 4985 Morven Rd Jacksonville FL 32210 Office: 2800 Independent Life Bldg Jacksonville FL 32202

DANIEL, KENNETH RULE, former iron and steel manufacturing company executive; b. Milford, Conn., Oct. 13, 1913; s. Cullen Coleman and Margaret Estelle (Elliott) D.; m. Virginia Moody Simpson, June 11, 1938; children: Kenneth Rule, Cullen Coleman, Robert Tennent Simpson, William Francis McKemie. B.S., U. Ala., 1936, Profl. Degree in Mech. Engring., 1957, D.Sc., 1980. Registered profl. engr. Ala. With Am. Cast Iron Pipe Co., Birmingham, Ala., 1936-78, chief engr., 1948-55, v.p. engring., 1955-59, v.p. engring and purchases, 1959-61, exec. v.p., 1961-63, pres., 1963-78, also dir., dir. various subsidiaries, 1963-78; vice chmn. bd. 1st Ala. Bank of Birmingham, 1977—; dir. 1st Ala. Bancshares, Inc.; emeritus dir. CSX Corp.; Sesquicentennial hon. prof. U. Ala., 1981. Mem. Ala. Bd. of Registration for Profl. Engrs. and Land Surveyors, 1967—; mem. regional adv. council Conf. Bd., 1967-78, Ala. Export Council, 1966-69; bd. dirs. Community Chest, 1965-78, Jr. Achievement, 1964-78, Birmingham Centennial Corp., 1968-73, Warrior Tombigbee Devel. Assn., 1963-78; gen. co-chmn. United Appeal, 1964, chmn. indsl. div., 1958; chmn. Radio Free Europe, Birmingham, 1966; mem. Jefferson County Judicial Commn., 1967-72; chmn. adv. bd. Salvation Army, 1968-69, mem. adv. council home and hosp., mem. nat. adv. council, 1976—; trustee Foundry Ednl. Found. (pres. 1964-65); trustee, mem. exec. com. So. Research Inst.; chmn. bd. trustees Jefferson County Cooper Green Hosp.; bd. visitors Berry Coll., Mt. Berry, Ga., 1968-78. Served to lt. col. AUS, 1941-46; ETO. Decorated Bronze Star, Legion of Merit; Croix de Guerre, France; recipient Gold Knight of Mgmt. award Nat. Mgmt. Assn., 1965, William Booth award Salvation Army, 1967, Henry Laurence Gantt medal Am. Mgmt. Assn. and ASME, 1977; Exec. of Yr. award Nat. Mgmt. Assn., 1978; named Engr. of Year Birmingham Engring. Council, 1967; elected to Ala. Acad. Honor, 1982. Fellow ASME (chmn. Birmingham sect. 1950-51); mem. NAM (dir. 1967-70), Asso. Industries Ala. (bd. dirs. 1963-78), Birmingham Area C. of C. (pres. 1969), Assn. Iron and Steel Engrs. (chmn. Birmingham Sect. 1954, nat. dir. 1955), Am. Ordnance Assn. (pres. Birmingham post 1964), Am. Foundrymen's Soc. (Thomas W. Pangborn Gold Medal award 1974), Am. Soc. for Engring. Edn., Engring. Soc. Birmingham, Newcomen Soc. N. Am., Sigma Alpha Epsilon, Theta Tau, Tau Beta Pi. Methodist (past chmn. bd. stewards). Clubs: Kiwanian., Birmingham Country, The Club, Mountain Brook, Shoal Creek, The Downtown (Birmingham); N.Y. Athletic (N.Y.C.). Home: 3212 Brookwood Rd Birmingham AL 35223 Office: PO Box 2727 Birmingham AL 35202

DANIEL, MICHAEL ROLAND, lieutenant governor South Carolina; b. Gaffney, S.C., Apr. 13, 1940; s. Dewey B. and Ruth (Chaney) D.; m. Margaret Ann Carr, May 25, 1965; children: Becky, Shelly, Barbara. Student, The Citadel, 1958-59; B.A., U. S.C., 1962, J.D., 1966. Formerly assoc. Hall, Daniel, Winter & Clary, Gaffney; mem. S.C. Ho. of Reps., 1973-83, speaker pro tem, 1980-83; lt. gov. State of S.C., Columbia, 1983—. Trustee Limestone Coll. Served with U.S. Army, 1967-68; capt. JAGC Res. Mem. Cherokee County Bar Assn., S.C. Bar Assn., ABA, Assn. Trial Lawyers Am. Democrat. Methodist. Lodges: Masons; Rotary. Office: State House Columbia SC 29201 *

DANIEL, RICHARD NICHOLAS, fabricated metals manufacturing company executive; b. Bklyn., Sept. 18, 1935; s. Louis V. and Jean (D'Andrea) D.; m. Elaine E. Sherman, Sept. 24, 1966; children: Matthew, Jeffrey. B.B.A., St. John's U., 1957; M.B.A., U. Pa., 1959. C.P.A., Tex. Planning assoc. Mobil Oil Corp., N.Y.C., 1962-70; v.p. fin. Laird Enterprises Inc., N.Y.C., 1970-71; v.p. ops. Wheelabrator-Frye, N.Y.C., 1971; v.p., controller Handy & Harman, N.Y.C., 1971-76, v.p.-fin., 1977-78, group v.p., 1978-79, pres., chief operating officer, 1979-83, pres., chief exec. officer, 1983—, also dir. Home: 91 Hawthorn Pl Briarcliff Manor NY 10510 Office: 850 3d Ave New York NY 10022

DANIEL, ROBERT EDWIN, church official; b. Joplin, Mo., Aug. 19, 1906; s. Robert Brown and Lilian (Boswell) D.; m. Margaret Moir, July 16, 1932; children: Robert William, Phillip Merrill, Linda Jane. A.B. magna cum laude, Ottawa U., 1927; LL.D., Whitworth Coll., 1971. With Blyth & Co., 1928-31, Pacific Northwest Co., Seattle, 1931-41, 46-66, pres., 1959-66; v.p. United Pacific Corp.; Chmn. regional bus. conduct com. Nat. Assn. Securities Dealers, 1959-60; gov. Midwest Stock Exchange, 1959-60. Trustee, treas. Wash.-Alaska Synod United Presbyn. Ch., dir. finance, 1966-72; trustee United Presbyn. Found., 1973-82. Served to maj. AUS, 1941-45. Republican. Presbyn. (elder). Home: 3214 8th St W Seattle WA 98119

DANIEL, ROBERT WILLIAMS, JR., former congressman; b. Richmond, Va., Mar. 17, 1936; s. Robert Williams and Charlotte (Bemiss) D.; m. Linda Hearne, Dec. 15, 1979; children by previous marriage—Robert, Charlotte, Nell. B.A., U. Va., 1954-58; M.B.A., Columbia U., 1961. Financial analyst J. C. Wheat Co., Richmond, 1961-62; instr. econs. U. Richmond Sch. Bus., 1963; officer CIA, Washington, 1964-68; owner, opr. Brandon Plantation, Prince George County, Va., 1968—; mem. 93d-97th Congresses from 4th Dist. Va.; cons. Dept. Def.; Mem. Commonwealth of Va. Bd. Conservation and Econ. Devel., 1972; mem., sec. Prince George County Planning Commn., 1972; mem. Va. Farm Bur. Mktg. Com., 1971-72. Trustee Atlantic Rural Exposition, Sheltering Arms Hosp., Richmond. Served with AUS, 1959. Recipient Disting. Service award Ams. for Constl. Action, 1973, 74, 75; Watchdog of Treasury award Nat. Associated Businessmen, 1973-74, 75-76; Freedom award Order of Lafayette, 1975. Mem. Phi Beta Kappa, Phi Kappa Psi. Republican. Episcopalian (vestryman 1968-72). Clubs: N.Y. Yacht (N.Y.C.); Metropolitan (D.C.); Commonwealth (Richmond); Moose. Home: Brandon Plantation Spring Grove VA 23881

DANIELEWSKI, WALTER EDWARD, delivery service co. exec.; b. Bklyn., May 10, 1933; s. Anthony and Mary (Buczkowska) D.; m. Claire Borny, Jan. 31, 1953; children—Walter Edward, Diana Lynn, Debra Mary, William G., Donna Ann. B.S. magna cum laude, Fordham U.; M.B.A. with distinction, Pace Coll. With United Parcel Service, 1956—, now sr. v.p., chief fin. officer; dir. United Parcel Service of Am., Inc. Served with USN, 1952-56. Office: United Parcel Service of Am Inc Greenwich Office Park 5 Greenwich CT 06830

DANIELIAN, ARTHUR CALVIN, architect; b. Pasadena, Calif., Jan. 18, 1935; s. Moses and Siranoush (Arsenian) D.; m. Martha Annette Landre, Feb. 19, 1966; 1 son, John. A.A., Pasadena City Co., 1954; B.Arch., U. So. Calif., 1963. Designer Edward Fickett, Architect, 1963-65, William Blurock & Ptnrs., Architect, 1965-68; pres. Danielian Assocs., Newport Beach, Calif., 1968—; mem. Inst. Residential Market; speaker in field. Served with U.S. Army, 1956-58. Recipient Gold Nugget, 1973-75, 77-79, award for wood sculpture, U. So. Calif., 1961. Mem. AIA (chmn. nat. housing com., pres. Orange County 1977-78, award Aquatic Village 1972). Office: Danielian Assocs 3848 Campus Dr Suite 210 Newport Beach CA 92660

DANIELIAN, LEON, ballet dancer, choregrapher; b. N.Y.C., Oct. 31, 1920; s. Frank and Varsik (Coolidganian) D. Student, Mikhail Mordkin Ballet Arts and Am. Ballet Sch., alternately for 5 yrs. With Ballet Russe de Monte Carlo, 1943—; dir. Am. Ballet Theatre Schs., 1967—; mng. dir. Enid Knapp Botsford Sch., Rochester, N.Y., 1978—. Repertoire includes Fokine's Spectre de la Rose; character roles in: Frankie and Johnny; guest artist, Ballet des Champs Elysées, Paris and North Africa, winter season 1951-52; star: dance film First Position, 1973; world tour as guest star with, San Francisco Ballet; ballet master, Ballet Russe Sch. Recipient Best Performing Male Dancer of Year award East Coast critics, 1949; Dance Masters of Am. Ann. award, 1971; Dance Educators of Am. award, 1979. Address: Univ of Texas Dept of Drama Austin TX 78712

DANIELL, HERMAN BURCH, pharmacologist; b. Cadwell, Ga., May 25, 1929; s. Walter and Ruby Florence (Burch) D.; m. Lorraine Smith, June 30, 1957; children—Kimberly Ann, Anthony Burch, Walter Herman. B.S. in Pharmacy, U. Ga., 1951, M.S. in Pharmacology, 1964, Ph.D.; USPHS trainee 1964-66, Med. Coll. S.C., Charleston, 1966. Owner-operator retail pharmacies, Savannah, Ga., 1953-62; instr. U. Ga., 1962-64; mem. faculty Med. U. S.C., 1966—, prof. pharmacology, 1978—. Author papers in field. Served to capt. Med. Service Corps AUS, 1951-53. Grantee USPHS, 1966-80, S.C. Heart Assn., 1966-73. Mem. Am. Soc. Pharmacology and Exptl. Therapeutics, Sigma Xi, Rho Chi, Kappa Sigma. Episcopalian. Home: 1549 Burning Tree Rd Charleston SC 29412 Office: 171 Ashley Ave Charleston SC 29403

DANIELL, JERE ROGERS, history educator, consultant; b. Millinocket, Maine, Nov. 28, 1932; s. Warren Fisher and Mary (Holway) D.; m. Sally Ann Wellborn, Dec. 1955 (div. 1969); children: Douglas, Alexander, Matthew; m. 2d Elena Lillie, July 19, 1969; stepchildren: Breena Brodsky, Clifford Brodsky. A.B., Dartmouth Coll., 1955; M.A., Harvard U., 1962, Ph.D., 1964. Asst. prof. history Dartmouth Coll., 1964-69, assoc. prof., 1969-74, prof., 1974—, chmn. dept., 1979-83; head tutor Heritage Found., Old Deerfield, Mass., 1960-64. Author: Experiment in Republicanism: N.H. Politics and the American Revolution, 1970, Colonial N.H.: A History, 1981; bd. editors: Univ. Press of New England, 1978—. Served to lt (j.g.) USN, 1955-58. Mem. Colonial Soc. Mass., Orgn. Am. Historians, N.H. Hist. Soc. Home: 11 Barrymore Rd Hanover NH 03755 Office: Dartmouth College Dept History Hanover NH 03755

DANIELLI, JAMES FREDERIC, scientist, educator, editor; b. Wembley, Eng., Nov. 13, 1911; s. James Frederic and Helena (Hollins) D.; m. Mary Guy, Jan. 4, 1937; children—Richard, Corinne. Ph.D., London (Eng.) U., 1933, Cambridge (Eng.) U., 1942; D.Sc., London U., 1938, Gent (Belgium) U., 1956, Med. Coll. Pa., 1970, Worcester Poly. Inst., 1972. Fellow Princeton, 1933-35, St. John's Coll., Cambridge (Eng.) U., 1942-45; physiologist Marine Biol. Assn., 1946; reader cell physiology Royal Cancer Hosp., 1946-49; prof. zoology, chmn. dept. King's Coll., London, Eng., 1949-61; prof. medicinal chemistry and biochem. pharmacology State U. N.Y. at, Buffalo, 1962-65, chmn. dept. biochem. pharmacology, 1962-65; prof. theoretical biology, dir. Center for Theoretical Biology, 1965-74, provost faculty natural sci. and math., 1967-69, asst. to pres., 1969-74; prof. Worcester (Mass.) Poly. Inst., 1974-80, emeritus prof., 1980—; vis. research prof. Salk Inst., 1973-75; cons. various indsl. firms, pubs., govt. orgns. Author: Permeability of Natural Membranes, 1942, Cell Physiology and Pharmacology, 1952, Cytochemistry, 1953; Editor: Symposia Soc. for Exptl. Biology, 1946-56, Symposia Internat. Soc. for Cell Biology, 1950-60, Internat. Rev. Cytology, 1951—, Jour. Theoretical Biology, 1960—, Gen. Cytochem. Methods, 1958-65, Progress in Surface and Membrane Sci, 1962-79, Jour. Social and Biol. Structures, 1978—; Contbr. articles to profl. jours. Fellow Royal Soc.; mem. Inst. Biology (past sec.), Biochem. Soc., Physiol. Soc., Soc. for Exptl. Biology (past sec.), Am. Soc. Cell Biology, Internat. Soc. for Cell Biology (past sec.), Am. Inst. Biol. Scis., Internat. Soc. for Study of Origin of Life. Office: Danielli Assos Inc 185 Highland St Worcester MA 01609

DANIELS, ALFRED HARVEY, merchandising executive; b. Pitts., Mar. 12, 1912; s. Harry and Irene D.; m. Ada M. Schoenberg, Oct. 1935; children—James, Molly; m. Stella Goldstein, 1959. B.A., Harvard, 1933, M.B.A., 1935. Divisional mdse. mgr. Abraham & Straus, 1940-48, mdse. v.p., 1948-55; v.p. Federated Dept. Stores, Inc., Cin., 1956—; also cons., group pres., dir. Federated Dept. Stores, 1969—; chief exec. officer I. Magnin, 1969-73; cons. Hudson's Bay Co. Can.; chmn. bd., chief exec. officer Burdine's, 1961-68; cons., dir. Gap Store's Inc., 1975—; dir. Asso. Merchandising Corp., 1st Nat. Bank Miami, 1963-68; sr. research asso. Columbia U. Sch. Bus. Contbr.: articles to trade revs. Columbia Hermes Exchange; Harvard Bus. Rev. Bd. dirs. Opera Guild; trustee United Fund, U. Miami; mem. Orange Bowl Com., 1963-68, 79—. Mem. Fla. Retail Fedn. (dir.), Nat. Retail Mchts. Assn. (exec. com.), Phi Beta Kappa. Clubs: Lotos, Harvard (N.Y.C.); Miami; Bankers, Concordia (San Francisco). Home: 1000 Mason St San Francisco CA 94108 *I have learned that success in life is in the quality of one's own sense of values, one's behavior, and one's loves.*

DANIELS, ARLENE KAPLAN, sociology educator; b. N.Y.C., Dec. 10, 1930; d. Jacob and Elizabeth (Rathstein) Kaplan; m. Richard Rene Daniels, June 9, 1956. B.A. with honors in English, U. Calif., Berkeley, 1952; M.A. in Sociology, 1954, Ph.D., 1960. Instr. dept. speech U. Calif., Berkeley, 1959-61; research asso. Mental Research Inst., Palo Alto, Calif., 1961-66; asso. prof. sociology San Francisco State Coll., 1966-70; chief Center for Study Women in Soc., Inst. Sci. Analysis, San Francisco, 1970—; mem. faculty Northwestern U., Evanston, Ill., 1975—, prof. dept. sociology, 1975—; cons. NIMH, 1971-73, Nat. Endowment for Humanities, 1975—, Nat. Inst. Edn., 1978—. Editor: (with Rachel Kahn-Hut) Academics on the Line, 1970; co-editor: Hearth and Home: Images of Women in the Mass Media, 1978, Education: Straightjacket or Opportunity?, 1979, Women and Work, 1982, Women and Trade Unions in Eleven Industrialized Countries; editor: Jour. Social Problems, 1974-78; asso. editor: Contemporary Sociology, 1980-82, Symbolic Interaction, 1979—. Trustee Bus. and Profl. Women's Research Found. Bd., 1980—, Women's Equity Action League Legal and Ednl. Def. Fund, 1979-81; mem. Chgo. Research Assos. Bd., 1981—. Recipient Social Sci. Research Council Faculty Research award, 1970-71; Ford Found. Faculty fellow, 1975-76; grantee Nat. Inst. Edn., 1978-79, 1979-80, NSF, 1974-75, NIMH, 1973-74. Mem. Sociologists Women in Soc. (pres. 1975-76), Am. Sociology Assn. (council 1979-81), Soc. Study Social Problems (v.p. 1981-82), Soc. Study Symbolic Inter-Action. Office: Dept of Sociology Northwestern University 1810 Chicago Ave Evanston IL 60201

DANIELS, CHARLIE, musician, songwriter; b. Wilmington, N.C., Oct. 28, 1936. Mem.: Jaguar band, 1958-67; sessionman in, Nashville, with Flatt and Scruggs, Marty Robbins, Claude King, Pete Seeger, Bob Dylan, others; founder, mem.: Charlie Daniels Band, 1971—; recorded for, Kama Sutra and Epic Records; records include Full Moon; songwriter; songs recorded by, Elvis Presley; songwriter, Gary Stewart, Tammy Wynette, others. Recipient 3 Country Music Assn. awards, 1979; named Instrumentalist of Yr., Instrumental Group of Yr.; Grammy award Single of the Yr. (Devil Went Down to Georgia); Grammy award Best Performance by a Country Group, 1980. Office: care Joseph E Sullivan Sound Seventy Mgmt Inc 210 25th Ave N Suite N-101 Nashville TN 37203

DANIELS, ELIZABETH ADAMS, educator; b. Westport, Conn., May 8, 1920; d. Thomas Davies and Minnie Mae (Sherwood) Adams; m. John L. Daniels, Mar. 21, 1942; children: John L., Eleanor B., Sherwood A., Ann S. A.B., Vassar Coll., 1941; A.M., U. Mich., 1942; Ph.D., N.Y. U., 1954. From instr. to prof. English Vassar Coll., Poughkeepsie, N.Y., 1948—, dean freshmen, 1955-58, dean studies, 1965-73, chmn. dept. English, 1974-76, 81—, acting dean faculty, 1976-78, chmn. self-study, 1978-80. Author: Jessie White Mario, Risorgimento Revolutionary, 1972; also articles. Bd. dirs. Poughkeepsie Day Sch. Recipient Grad. award Alumnae Assn. N.Y. U., 1954; Vassar fellow, 1941; Nat. Endowment Humanities summer stipend, 1981. Mem. Research Soc. Victorian Periodicals (exec. com.), MLA, AAUP, N.E. Victorian Soc., Phi Beta Kappa. Democrat. Club: Poughkeepsie Tennis. Home: 129 College Ave Poughkeepsie NY 12603 Office: Box 74 Vassar College Poughkeepsie NY 12601 *Growing up with intellectual ambitions, I was able to work out a very satisfactory career combining teaching, college administration, scholarship, family life, and a good marriage slightly forerunning the feminist movement of the late nineteen-sixties. I owe much of this to Vassar College, the first woman's college in the U.S.*

DANIELS, ELMER HARLAND, sculptor, architect; b. Owosso, Mich., Oct. 23, 1905; s. H. J. and Blanche (Tuthill) D.; m. Madge Kuhn, 1933; children: Stephen, Carol, Richard, Julia. Student, Grand Rapids (Mich.) Coll., 1924-25, John Herron Art Inst., Indpls., 1925-27, Beaux Arts Inst. Design, N.Y.C., 1927-29; study in, Europe, Eng., France and Italy (sculpture), 1931; student, Columbia, summer 1930. Tchr. Art Center Sch., Indpls., 1935-38; conducted pvt. studio classes, Indpls, 1938-40; organized Daniels Assos. (archtl. firm), 1943-50, Daniels and Zermack Assos., Ann Arbor, 1950-72.; Indsl. designer murals and, Oakland (Calif.), 1942—; designer, Domore Furniture Co.; designed bank buildings, Mich., Ohio, Ind., Ill; important works include Lincoln Meml, Lincoln City, Ind., (now owned by U.S. Dept. Interior and operated by Nat. Park Service) Lincoln Meml, commd. State of Ind., 1941, Heroic Head of Lincoln in Ala. marble, State Capitol Bldg, Indpls., 1939, Three Heroic Stone Figures, St. Joseph Ch., Jasper, Ind., 1941, six stone panels for Arts Bldg., Ball State Tchrs. Coll., Muncie, Ind., 1933, Brotherhood of Maintenance of Way meml, Detroit, Bay County War Meml, Bay City, Mich., Family Group, Detroit & No. Savs. & Loan, Flint, Mich., 5 terra figures, Loma Linda Restaurant, Ann Arbor, Mich., mural in oil, Union Bank, Steubenville, Ohio, also banks and instns. in, Indpls., Monroe, Mich., Grand Rapids, Mich., Petoskey, Mich., Pasadena, Calif. and Scottsdale, Ariz.; Portraits include Paul V. McNutt; bronze Ernest Hemmingway, Albert Switzer, Albert Einstein; Indsl. designer for, Kaiser Industries, Kaiser Aluminum, Kaiser Steel, Kaiser Community Homes, Kaiser Engrs., Standard Gysum, Heywood Wakefield Co., Plomb Tool Co., Steelcase, Inc., Stow-Davis Furniture Co., Bear Archery Co., etc., series bronze portraits of great fighting Indian chiefs of West; exhibited at, Deligny Galleries, Ft. Lauderdale, Fla., Deligny Galleries, Chgo. (Recipient Harry Johnson award 1931), Deligny Galleries, Chgo. (Ind. Artists Sculpture prize 1938), Deligny Galleries, Chgo. (C. V. Hickox prize 1942), Deligny Galleries, Chgo. (Grand prize Standard Oil Co. float Tournament of Roses.); Contbr.: articles on sculpture and art in gen., to Mich. Tradesman; Sculpture work; exhibited in: Sat. Eve. Post. Mem. Am. Soc. Indsl. Designers, Nat. Sculpture Soc., Archtl. League N.Y., Ind. Artists, Painters and Sculptors of N.J., Ind. Lincoln Union, Lincoln Fellowship of So. Calif. (hon. mem. 1944), Mich. Acad Sci., Arts and Letters, Pasadena, Palm Beach, Ann Arbor art assns., Washtenaw, Mich. hist. socs., Ann Arbor, Mich., Pompano Beach, Fla. chambers of commerce. Clubs: University of Pasadena, Pasadena Maestros; Miscowabik (Calumet, Mich.) (life); Ann Arbor (Mich.); Town, Barton Hills Country. Home: 9514 Burns Dr Sun City AZ 85351

DANIELS, FARRINGTON, JR., educator, physician; b. Worcester, Mass., Sept. 29, 1918; s. Farrington and Olive (Bell) D.; m. Alice Mae Monroe, June 9, 1951; children: Elizabeth, George, Christopher. A.B., U. Wis., 1940, M.A., 1942; M.D., Harvard U., 1943, M.P.H., 1952. Intern N.Y. Hosp., N.Y.C., 1944, resident and research fellow, 1947-49; head stress physiology br. U.S. Army Research and Devel. Command, Lawrence, Natick, Mass., 1950-55; asst. prof. dermatology U. Oreg., Portland, 1955-61; asso. prof. U. Ill., 1961-62; head dermatology div. N.Y. Hosp. Cornell Med. Center, N.Y.C., 1962-81, asso. prof. medicine, 1962-70, prof. medicine, 1970—, prof. public health, 1972—, prof. pathology, 1976—; mem. photobiology com. Nat. Acad. Scis., 1965-72; chmn. adv. com. on nonvisual effects of light, trustee Illuminating Engring. Research Inst., 1972-81; mem. climatic Impact assessment program (ozone) Dept. Transp., 1971-75. Contbr. articles to profl. jours. Served to capt., M.C. AUS, 1944-47. Fellow AAAS; mem. Soc. Investigative Dermatology, Am. Acad. Dermatology, Am. Dermatol. Assn., N.Y. Dermatol. Soc., N.Y. Acad. Medicine, N.Y. Acad. Sci., Internat. Soc. Biometerology. Home: 58 Harmon Ave Pelham NY 10803 Office: 1300 York Ave New York NY 10021

DANIELS, FRANK ARTHUR, newspaper exec.; b. Raleigh, N.C., June 8, 1904; s. Josephus and Addie Worth (Bagley) D.; m. Ruth Aunspaugh, Nov. 20, 1929; children—Frank Arthur, Patricia Woronoff. A.B., U. N.C., 1927. With mech. circulation, advt. depts. News and Observer, Raleigh, 1927-32, treas., 1932-56, gen. mgr., 1942—, pres., 1956—, pub., 1966—, chmn. bd., 1971—; mem. Raleigh bd. N.C. Nat Bank, 1969-73; dir. A.P., 1964-67, Atlantic & East Carolina Ry. Co., 1968-72. Past pres. Community Chest, Raleigh.; Chmn. N.C. Bd. Pub. Welfare, 1949-56; mem. N.C. Tax Study Commn., 1955-56; Bd. dirs. Research Triangle Inst., 1960-74; chmn. bd. trustees Rex Hosp., Raleigh, 1950-68; past trustee U. N.C., Chapel Hill. Mem. Am. Newspaper Pubs. Assn. (dir. 1956-64), So. Newspaper Pubs. Assn. (pres. 1951-52), Raleigh C. of C. (past pres.), Delta Kappa Epsilon. Presbyn. Clubs: Capital City, Carolina Country, Sphinx (Raleigh). Home: 1515 Glenwood Ave Raleigh NC 27608 Office: News and Observer-Raleigh Times 215 S McDowell St Raleigh NC 27601

DANIELS, FRANK ARTHUR, JR., newspaper publisher; b. Raleigh, N.C., Sept. 7, 1931; s. Frank Arthur and Ruth (Aunspaugh) D.; m. Julia Bryan Jones, June 4, 1954; children: Frank Arthur III, Julia Graham. A.B., U. N.C., 1953. With News and Observer Pub. Co., Raleigh, 1953—, bus. mgr., 1960-68, gen. mgr., 1968-71, pres., pub., 1971—; dir. A.P., Newspaper Advt. Bur., Mut. Ins. Co. Ltd., Hamilton, Bermuda, Bancshares of N.C., Inc., 1973-75. Bd. dirs., mem. exec. com., campaign chmn. United Way, 1964, pres., 1974-75; bd. dirs. Peace Coll., N.C. State U. Found., Rex Hosp., St. Mary's Coll.; chmn., pres. Am. Newspaper Pub. Assn. Found.; former mem. long-range planning com. Raleigh-Durham Airport.; past trustee Woodberry Forest Sch. Served with USAF, 1954-55. Named Outstanding Young Man of Yr. Raleigh Jaycees, 1963. Mem. So. Newspaper Pubs. Assn. (chmn. bd. 1973-74, pres. 1972-73, dir.), Am. Newspaper Pubs. Assn. (past bd. dirs., treas.), Eastern N.C. Press Assn. (pres. 1963-64), N.C. Press Assn. (past pres.), Delta Kappa Epsilon. Democrat. Presbyn. Clubs: Kiwanian., Capital City, Carolina Country, Sphinx (Raleigh). Home: 3514 Keats Pl Raleigh NC 27609 Office: 215 S McDowell St Raleigh NC 27601

DANIELS, GEORGE GOETZ, editor; b. Bklyn., Aug. 17, 1925; s. George Bryant and Katherine June (Goetz) D.; m. Doris Alden Billings, Dec. 19, 1965; 1 dau., Katherine Billings; children by previous marriage: Peter, Michael, Robert, Geoffrey. B.A. cum laude, Harvard U., 1949. Corr., Time mag., Detroit, 1949-50, contbg. editor, 1950-56, asso. editor, 1956-60, sr. editor, 1960-71; editor Time-Life Records, 1971-73; series editor Time-Life Books, 1973-82, exec. editor, 1982—; dir. Main-Pearl Corp., Buffalo. Served to 1st lt. USAAF, 1943-46. Mem. Am. Ornithologists Union, Am. Birding Assn. (dir.). Clubs: Harvard, Explorers, Bermuda Anglers. Home: Pleasant Hill Dr Potomac MD 20854 Office: Time-Life Books 777 Duke St Alexandria VA 22314

DANIELS, JAMES MAURICE, physicist; b. Leeds, Eng., Aug. 26, 1924; emigrated to Can., 1953, naturalized, 1971; s. Bernard and Mary Mahala (Proctor) D.; (married); children—Ian Nicolas James, Maurice Edward Bruce. B.A., Jesus Coll., Oxford (Eng.) U., 1945, M.A., 1949, D.Phil., 1952. Exptl. asst. Radar Research and Devel. Establishment, Malvern, Eng., 1944-46; tech. officer explosives div. Imperial Chem. Industries, Ardeer, Scotland, 1946-47; research fellow Clarendon Lab., Oxford U., 1951-53; asst. prof. physics U. B.C., Can., Vancouver, 1953-56, asso. prof., 1956-60; UNESCO expert U. Buenos Aires, Argentina, 1958-59; prof. U. Toronto, 1961—, chmn. dept. physics, 1969-73; vis. prof. Instituto de Fisica, S.C. de Bariloche Argentina, 1960-61, Helsinki U. Tech., 1974, Columbia U., 1978—. Author: Oriented Nuclei, Polarized Targets and Beams, 1965; contbr. numerous articles to profl. jours. Alfred P. Sloan fellow, 1962-65; Guggenheim fellow, 1978-79. Fellow Phys. Soc. (London), Inst. Physics (London), Royal Soc. Arts (London), Royal Soc. Can.; mem. Can. Assn. Physicists, Am. Phys. Soc., N.Y. Acad. Scis., Can. Inst. Particle Physics (sec-treas. 1971-73). Office: Dept Physics U Toronto Toronto ON M5S 1A7 Canada

DANIELS, JOHN HANCOCK, corp. exec.; b. St. Paul, Oct. 28, 1921; s. Thomas L. and Frances (Hancock) D.; m. Martha H. Williams, Dec. 23, 1942; children—Martha M. Daniels Jones, John Hancock, Jane P. Daniels Moffett, Christopher W. Student, St. Paul Acad., 1932-37; grad., Phillips Exeter Acad., 1939; B.A., Yale, 1943, Advanced Mgmt. Program, Harvard, 1957. With Archer-Daniels-Midland Co., Mpls., 1946—, successively mem. staff linseed oil div., prodn. mgr. alfalfa div., mgr. feed div., v.p., dir., 1946-53, pres., dir., 1958-67, chmn., 1967-72, dir., mem. exec. com.; pres. Mulberry Resources Inc.; dir. Soo Line R.R. Co. Bd. dirs. Bus. Council; trustee Com. Econ. Devel.; chmn. 1972 Decatur United Way Campaign. Served from 2d lt. to capt., F.A. AUS, 1943-46. Decorated Bronze Star medal. Mem. Masters of Foxhounds Assn. Am. Republican. Episcopalian. Clubs: Links (N.Y.C.); Minneapolis; Woodhill (Minn.); Sprindale Hall (Camden, S.C.). Home: 2472 Parkview Dr Hamel MN 55340 Office: PO Box 28 Long Lake MN 55356

DANIELS, MYRA JANCO (MRS. DRAPER DANIELS), advertising agency executive; b. Gary, Ind., June 25, 1925; d. Elias and Cecelia (Remstein) Janco; m. Draper Daniels, Aug. 19, 1967. B.S., Ind. State U., 1948, M.A., 1954; postgrad., Ind. U., 1955-57. Advt. dir. Meis Bros. Co., Terre Haute, Ind., 1944-50; v.p., account exec. Gregory & House Advt., Cleve., 1951-53; pres. Wabash Advt. Agy., Terre Haute, Ind., 1950-54; account supr. Kuttner & Kuttner, Chgo., 1954-62; v.p. Roche, Rickerd & Cleary (name later changed to Roche, Rickerd, Henri & Hurst, then to Roche, Rickerd, Henri, Hurst, Inc.), Chgo., 1962-63, exec. v.p., 1963-65; pres. Draper Daniels, Inc., Chgo., 1965-77, Daniels and Hawkins, Inc., Naples, Fla., 1984—; mem. faculty Ind. U., 1957—, asso. prof. advt., 1958-61; advt., sales cons. Bd. dirs. Nat. Advt. Review Bd., 1974—. Contbr. articles to profl. jours. Active Naples-Marco Philharmonic. Named Nat. Advt. Woman of Year, 1965; recipient Distinguished Alumni award Ind. State U., 1966. Mem. Am. Fedn. Advertisers (dir. 1973-75, pub. service com. 1974—), League Women Voters, Sales Execs. Club, Am. Mktg. Assn., AAUP, AAUW (pres. br. 1981), Gamma Alpha Chi, Kappa Delta Pi, Pi Omega Pi, Pi Lambda Theta, Delta Pi Epsilon, Tau Kappa Alpha, Theta Sigma Phi. Club: Altrusa. Home: 131 Stillwater Ct Marco Island FL 33937 *To have leadership you must want it and seek it. Whatever you build is a mirror of your values and interests. Take inventory of yourself. Surround yourself with people whose values you respect. Help others to succeed and it will insure your success.*

DANIELS, RALPH, chemistry educator, university dean; b. N.Y.C., May 2, 1921; s. Sidney M. and Helen (Finkel) D.; m. Shirley Wolhandler, July 1, 1944; children: Lesley Diane, Ethan Howard Michael, Brian Fredrick. A.B. magna cum laude, Bklyn. Coll., 1944; A.M., Harvard, 1949, Ph.D., 1950. Postdoctoral fellow U. Wis., 1950-51; instr. Purdue U., 1951-52; asst. prof. U. Ill. Med. Ctr., Chgo., 1952-58, assoc. prof., 1958-63, prof. medicinal chemistry, 1963-77, asst. dean, 1970-73; acting dean U. Ill. Med. Center at (Grad. Coll.), 1975-77; prof. medicinal chemistry, dir. (Office Research Adminstrn.); assoc. dean Grad. Coll., U. Okla. Health Scis. Center, Oklahoma City, 1977—; vis. scientist Chester Beatty Research Inst. of U. London, 1961-62. Author: Problems in Organic Chemistry; Contbr. to: also articles to profl. jours. Ency. Chemistry. Recipient award Am. Inst. Chemists, 1944; U.S. Rubber Co. fellow, 1949. Mem. Am. Chem. Soc., Am. Assn. Colls. Pharmacy, Nat. Council Univ. Research Adminstrs., Rho Chi. Research on medicinal agts., theoretical organic chemistry. Patentee in field. Home: 12800 Green Valley Dr Oklahoma City OK 73120 Office: 1000 Stanton L Young Blvd Oklahoma City OK 73104

DANIELS, ROBERT SANFORD, psychiatrist, university official and dean; b. Indpls., Aug. 12, 1927; s. Harry H. and Mary (Bassett) D.; m. Donna; children: Stephen, Allen, Lynn, Judith, James. B.S., U. Cin., 1948, M.D., 1951. Intern Cin. Gen. Hosp., 1951; resident U. Cin. Hosp., 1954-57; mem. faculty U. Chgo., 1957-71, dir. psychiat. cons. service, 1961-63, asso. prof. psychiatry, acting chmn. dept., 1963-66, clin. dir., 1966-68, asso. dean community and social medicine, 1968-71, prof. psychiatry and social medicine, 1970-71; dir. Center Health Adminstrn. Studies, Grad. Sch. Bus., 1970-71; dir. dept. psychiatry U. Cin., 1971-75, interim dean, 1972-75, dean Coll. Medicine,, 1975—, also sr. v.p., 1982—; chief staff Cin. Gen. Hosp., 1972—, Holmes Hosp., 1972—; vis. prof. social medicine and clin. epidemiology St. Thomas' Hosp. Med. Coll., London, Eng.; sci. exchange visitor Ministry Health, Moscow, USSR; vis. scholar King Edward VII Hosp. Fund, London, 1977; cons. Cook County Hosp., Ill. State Psychiat. Inst.; spl. research community and group psychiatry, health planning, community health, 1967-69; Chmn. Ill. Mental Health Planning Bd.; mem., chmn. rev. com., psychiatry edn. br. Health Services and Mental Health Adminstrn., 1971-75; mem. nat. mental health adv. bd. NIMH, 1975-79; bd. dirs. Hamilton County Bd. Mental Health and Retardation, 1974-78. Asso. editor: Social Psychiatry. Bd. dirs. Central Ohio River Valley Planning Authority, 1979—. Served with AUS, 1946-47; Served with USAF, 1952-54. Recipient Stella Feis Hoffheimer award U. Cin., 1951. Mem. A.M.A., Am. Psychiat. Assn., Am. Group Psychotherapy Assn., Assn. Am. Med. Colls., Ill. Group Psychotherapy Soc. (pres. 1965-66), Ill. Psychiat. Soc. (pres. 1967), Phi Beta Kappa, Alpha Omega Alpha. Office: Coll Medicine U Cin Cincinnati OH 45267

DANIELS, ROBERT VINCENT, history educator, former state senator; b. Boston, Jan. 4, 1926; s. Robert Whiting and Helen Underwood (Hoyt) D.; m. Alice May Wendell, July 2, 1945; children: Robert H., Helen L. Turcotte, Irene L. Nelson, Thomas L. A.B., Harvard U., 1945, M.A., 1947, Ph.D., 1951. Research assoc. M.I.T., 1951-52; mem. social sci. faculty Bennington Coll., 1952-53, 57-58; asst. prof. Slavic studies Ind. U., 1953-55; research assoc. Columbia U., 1955-56; asst. prof. history U. Vt., Burlington, 1956-57, 58-61, assoc. prof., 1961-64, prof., 1964—, chmn. dept., 1964-69, dir. exptl. program, 1969-71; mem. Vt. Senate, 1973-82, asst. minority leader, 1977-80, minority leader, 1981-82; chmn. Vt. Gov.'s Commn. Med. Care, 1974-75; mem. Vt. Health Policy Corp., 1977-80. Author: The Conscience of the Revolution, 1960, Documentary History of Communism, 1960, rev. edit., 1984, The Nature of Communism, 1962, Studying History, 1966, Red October, 1967, The Russian Revolution, 1972, Fodor's Europe Talking, 1975; co-editor: Dynamics of Soviet Politics, 1976; mem. bd. editors: Jour. Modern History, 1970-73. Mem. Chittenden County (Vt.) Democratic Com., 1959—; mem. Burlington City Dem. Com., 1965—; chmn. policy and planning platform com. Vt. Dem. Com., 1962-66, 69-73, 76-80, mem. exec. com., 1981—; alt. Dem. Nat. Conv., 1968; mem. Dem. Platform Com., 1980; bd. visitors USAF Acad., 1965-67. Served to ensign USNR, 1944-46. U.S.-Soviet Cultural Exchange scholar U. Moscow, 1966, USSR Acad. Scis., 1976, 84; NEH fellow, 1971-72; Guggenheim fellow, 1980-81. Mem. Am. Hist. Assn. (pres. conf. Slavic and East European History 1976-77), Am. Assn. Advancement Slavic Studies (dir. 1968-71), AAUP, ACLU, Vt. Hist. Soc. (trustee 1968-71), Vt. Council World Affairs. Club: Harvard of Vt. (pres. 1974-75). Home: 195 S Prospect St Burlington VT 05401

DANIELS, TERRENCE DAVID, business executive; b. St. Louis, Jan. 11, 1943; s. Edgar M. and Mary Jane (Phelan) D.; m. Courtnay Sylvan, July 24, 1966; children: Courtnay Phelan, Catherine McDuffie, Charles Page, Christopher Channing. B.A. in History, U. Va., 1966, M.B.A., 1970. With corp. fin. dept. W.R. Grace & Co., N.Y.C., 1970-72, asst. to chmn. of bd. and chief exec. officer, 1972-75, v.p. devel., consumer services group, 1975-77, now dir.; v.p. corp. devel. Mattel, Inc., 1977-79; chmn., pres., chief exec. officer Western Pub. Co., 1979-82; exec. v.p., group exec. Gen. Devel. Group W.R. Grace & Co.; dir. Allied Foods Inc., Faber-Castell Corp., Daniels Enterprises., Hal's Hardware and Lumber Stores Inc. Served to lt. U.S. Army, 1966-68. Roman Catholic. Club: Somerset Hills Country. Office: WR Grace & Co 1114 Ave of Americas New York NY 10036

DANIELS, WILBUR, union official; b. Detroit, Jan. 23, 1923; s. Max and Dora (Miller) D.; m. Patricia Heyman, Dec. 22, 1963; 1 dau., Ann G. B.S., CCNY, 1942; J.D., N.Y. U., 1950. Bar: N.Y. 1950, U.S. Supreme Ct. 1951. Research assoc., asst. dir. research Internat. Ladies' Garment Worker's Union, N.Y.C., 1943-50, assoc. gen. counsel, 1950-59, asst. to pres., 1959-61, dir. master agreements dept., 1965—, v.p., 1969-73, exec. v.p., 1973—; partner firm Vladeck & Elias, N.Y.C., 1961-63; exec. dir. Nat. Bd. Coat and Suit Industry, N.Y.C., 1963-65; asso. adj. prof. grad. div. N.Y. U. Law Sch., 1979—; mem. Fed. Adv. Council on Unemployment Ins., N.Y. State Adv. Council on Employment and Unemployment Ins.; vice chmn. N.Y. State Job Devel. Authority; mem. Nat. Commn. Unemployment Commn., 1977-80, U.S. Adv. Council on Employee Welfare and Pension Benefit Plans, 1962-69. Bd. mng. dirs., mem. exec. com. Met. Opera Assn.; bd. dirs. Lincoln Center for Performing Arts; bd. visitors Grad. Center, City U. N.Y.; bd. dirs. United Housing Found., N.Y. Urban Coalition, 1970-73. Served with U.S. Army, 1945-46. Mem. Am. Bar Assn., Indsl. Relations Research Assn., Assn. Bar of City N.Y., N.Y. County Lawyers Assn., N.Y. State Bar Assn., Am. Arbitration Assn. (bd. dirs., exec. com.), Phi Beta Kappa. Home: 242 E 19th St New York NY 10003 Office: 1710 Broadway New York NY 10019

DANIELS, WILLIAM BURTON, physicist, educator; b. Buffalo, Dec. 21, 1930; s. William C. and Sophia (Penner) D.; m. Adriana A. Braakman, Sept. 2, 1958; children—Charlotte, William Fredrik, Donald Christopher. B.S. in Physics, U. Buffalo, 1952; M.S., Case Inst. Tech., 1955, Ph.D., 1957. Instr. to asst. prof. Case Inst. Tech., 1957-59; research scientist Union Carbide Corp., 1959-61; mem. faculty Princeton, 1961-72, prof. solid state scis., 1967-72; Unidel prof. physics U. Del., Newark, 1972—; Research collaborator Brookhaven Nat. Lab.; cons. U.S. Army Research Lab.; guest scientist Research Establishment, Denmark, 1976; invitée Coll. France, 1977; exchange prof. U. Paris, 1977. John Simon Guggenheim Meml. fellow, 1976-77; recipient Alexander von Humboldt sr. scientist award, 1981. Fellow Am. Phys. Soc.; mem. AAAS. Research, publs. properties materials at high pressure, equation of state of solids, experimentation on solidified permanent gases, liquid crystals and plastic crystals, instrumentation high pressure research. Home: Physics Dept Univ of Delware Newark DE 19716

DANIELS, WILLIAM CARLTON, JR., construction executive; b. Birmingham, Ala., Mar. 18, 1920; s. William Carlton and Ethel Mae (Swift) D.; m. Harriet Virginia Millershan, Dec. 20, 1942; children: Harriet Diane Daniels Thomas, Margaret Duree Daniels Joseph. Student bus. adminstrn., Mars Hill (N.C.) Coll., 1938-40. With J.A. Jones Constrn. Co., Charlotte, N.C., 1940—, controller, 1966-76, treas., 1973—, v.p., 1976—. Served to 1st lt. AUS, 1942-46. Mem. Fin. Execs. Inst. (past pres. S.C. chpt.; chmn. profl. devel. nat. com. 1979-81), Asso. Gen. Contractors Am. (chmn. tax and fiscal affairs com. 1978-82), U. N.C. Exec. Program Grads. (past pres. Charlotte chpt.). Democrat. Presbyterian. Home: 4242 Kingswood Rd Charlotte NC 28211 Office: 6060 St Albans St Charlotte NC 28287

DANIELS, WILLIAM LEWIS, food company executive; b. Elmhurst, Ill., Apr. 14, 1944; s. Albert L. and Evelyn M. (Bousfield) D. B.S., Elmhurst Coll., 1970. With Keebler Co., Elmhurst, 1966—, sr. v.p., 1980—. Office: Keebler Co One Hollow Tree Ln Elmhurst IL 60126

DANIELSON, GORDON KENNETH, JR., cardiovascular surgeon, educator; b. Burlington, Iowa, Dec. 5, 1931; s. Gordon Kenneth and Helen H. (Hill) D.; m. Sondra Jean Bolich, Jan. 21, 1961; children: Gordon Kenneth III, Laura, Karen, Keith, Bruce, Susan, Jennifer. B.A. in Chemistry, U. Pa., 1953, M.D. (Pfizer, Senatorial, Clark scholar, Albert Einstein award 1956, Roche award 1956, Spencer Morris prize 1956), 1956; postgrad., Oak Ridge Inst. Nuclear Studies, 1960. Diplomate: Am. Bd. Surgery, Am. Bd. Thoracic Surgery. Intern U. Mich. Hosp., Ann Arbor, 1956-57; asst. resident in surgery Hosp. of U. Pa., 1957-61, chief resident in surgery, 1961-62, gen. and thoracic surgeon, 1962-65, asst. chief surg. div. I, 1962-65; vis. fellow in thoracic surgery Thorax Kliniken, Stockholm, 1963-64; practice medicine specializing in thoracic and cardiovascular surgery, Phila., 1963-65, Lexington, Ky., 1965-67, Rochester, Minn., 1967—; asst. attending physician dept. surgery Phila. Gen. Hosp., 1964-65; instr. surgery U. Pa Med. Sch., 1965; assoc. prof. surgery U. Ky. Med. Sch.; also chief cardiac surgery Univ. Hosp., 1965-67; cons. in surgery VA Hosp., Lexington, 1965-67; in cardiovascular surgery USPHS Hosp., 1965-67; mem. faculty Mayo Grad. Sch. Medicine, Rochester, Minn., 1967—, prof. surgery, 1975—; cons. cardiovascular and thoracic surgery Mayo

Clinic/Mayo Found., 1967—, St. Mary's Hosp., Meth. Hosp., Rochester, 1967—; Am. Heart Assn. vis. tchr., Amman, Jordan, 1981. Editor: Cardiovascular Surgery, 1972-78; editorial bd.: Modern Pediatric Cardiology, 1977—; contbr. numerous articles to med. jours. Markle scholar in acad. medicine, 1962-67. Fellow Am. Coll. Cardiology, A.C.S., Am. Coll. Chest Physicians; mem. Am. Assn. Thoracic Surgery, Am. Surg. Assn., Am. Heart Assn. (fellow council cardiovascular surgery), Internat. Cardiovascular Soc., Minn. Heart Assn., Ravdin-Rhoads Surg. Soc., Soc. Thoracic Surgeons (a founder), Soc. Univ. Surgeons, Soc. Vascular Surgery, Mexican Soc. Cardiology (hon.), Mayo Alumni Soc. Thoracic Surgery, Phi Beta Kappa, Alpha Omega Alpha. 1st fellow in congenital heart disease U.S.-USSR Health Exchange Program, 1973. Home: 6000 16th Ave NW Rochester MN 55901 Office: 200 1st St SW Rochester MN 55901

DANIELSON, MICHAEL NILS, political science educator; b. N.Y.C., Apr. 8, 1934; s. Virgil Andrew and Dorothy (DeLucas) D.; m. Ruth Patricia Schevon, Sept. 3, 1955 (dec. May 1979); children: Jessica Aidan, Jeffrey Andrew; m. Patricia R. Frank, Sept. 8, 1979. A.B., Rutgers U., 1955, M.A., 1956; Ph.D., Princeton, 1962. Instr. U. Omaha, 1957-59, Rutgers U., 1961; research asso. Inst. Pub. Adminstrn., N.Y.C., 1961-63; asst. prof. to prof. polit. sci. Princeton, 1963—; cons. to gov. N.J.; cons. N.J. Dept. Transp., N.J. Dept. Community Affairs, U.S. Dept. Housing and Urban Devel., Commn. on Populaton Growth and Am.'s Future, Ford Found., Kettering Found.; commr. Tri-state Transp. Commn., 1966-71. Author: Federal-Metropolitan Politics and the Commuter Crisis, 1965, Metropolitan Politics, 1966, Modern American Democracy, 1969, American Democracy, 1971, The Politics of Exclusion, 1976, One Nation, So Many Governments, 1977, New York: The Politics of Urban Regional Development, 1981. Trustee Glassboro State Coll., 1967-72. Served to lt. USAF, 1956-59. Mem. Am. Polit. Sci. Assn., Nat. Model R.R. Assn. Democrat. Home: 283 Hartley Ave Princeton NJ 08540

DANIELSON, WAYNE ALLEN, journalism and computer science educator; b. Burlington, Iowa, Dec. 6, 1929; s. Arthur Leroy and Bessie Ann (Bonar) D.; m. Beverly Grace Kinsell, Mar. 19, 1955; children: Matthew Henry, Benjamin Wayne, Grace Frances, Paul Arthur. B.A., State U. Iowa, 1952; M.A., Stanford U., 1953, Ph.D., 1957. Reporter, research mgr. San Jose (Calif.) Mercury-News, 1953-54; acting asst. prof. Stanford U., 1956-57; asst. prof. journalism U. Wis., 1957-59; mem. faculty U. N.C., 1959-69, prof. journalism, 1963-69; research prof. Inst. Research Social Sci., 1963-69, dean, 1964-69, Sch. Communication, U. Tex. at Austin, 1969-79, prof. journalism and computer sci., 1969—; mem. steering com. News Research Center, Am. Newspaper Pubs. Assn., 1964-73; mem. research com. AP Mng. Editors Assn., 1963—. Author: (with G. C. Wilhoit, Jr.) A Computerized Bibliography of Mass Communication Research, 1944-64, (with Blanche Prejean) Programed NewsStyle, 1977; contbr. articles to profl. jours.; editor: Journalism Abstracts, 1963-68, 71; editorial bd.: (with Blanche Prejean) Journalism Quar, 1964-72. Mem. pub. relations com. N.C. Heart Assn., 1963-67. Mem. Assn. Edn. Journalism (chmn. publs. com. 1968-72, research com. 1980-83, pres. 1970-71), Am. Assn. Schs. and Depts. Journalism (v.p. 1966-67, pres. 1967-68), Am., So. sociol. assns., Phi Beta Kappa, Sigma Delta Chi, Kappa Tau Alpha., Phi Kappa Phi. Office: Dept Journalism U Tex Austin TX 78712

DANILOV, VICTOR JOSEPH, museum official; b. Farrell, Pa., Dec. 30, 1924; s. Joseph M. and Ella (Tominovich) D.; m. Toni Dewey, Sept. 6, 1980; children: Thomas J., Duane P., Denise S. B.A. in Journalism, Pa. State U., 1945, M.S., Northwestern U., 1946; Ed.D. in Higher Edn, U. Colo., 1964. With Sharon (Pa.) Herald, 1942, Youngstown Vindicator, 1945, Pitts. Sun-Telegraph, 1946-47, Chgo. Daily News, 1947-50; instr. journalism U. Colo., 1950-51; asst. prof. journalism U. Kans., 1951-53; with Kansas City Star, 1953; mgr. pub. relations Ill. Inst. Tech. and IIT Research Inst., 1953-57; dir. univ. relations and pub. information U. Colo., 1957-60; pres. Profile Co., Boulder, Colo., 1960-62; exec. editor, exec. v.p. Indsl. Research Inc., Beverly Shores, Ind., 1962-69, pub., exec. v.p., 1969-71; dir., v.p. Mus. Sci. and Industry, Chgo., 1971-77, pres., dir., 1978—; Mem. rural industrialization adv. group Dept. Agr., 1967; panel internat. transfer tech. Dept. Commerce, 1968; sci. information council NSF, 1969-72; chmn. Conf. on Implications Metric Change, 1972; Nat. Conf. Indsl. Research; conf., 1966-70, Nat. Indsl. Research Week; chmn. observance, 1967-70; chmn. Midwest White House Conf. on Indsl. World Ahead, 1972, Internat. Conf. Sci. and Tech. Museums, 1976, 82; mem. task force on fin. acctg. and reporting by non bus. orgns. Fin. Acctg. Standards Bd., 1977-78. Author: Public Affairs Reporting, 1955, Starting a Science Center, 1977, Science and Technology Centers, 1982; also articles; editor: Crucial Issues in Public Relations, 1960, Corporate Research and Profitability, 1966, Innovation and Profitability, 1967, Research Decision-Making in New Product Development, 1968, New Products—and Profits, 1969, Applying Emerging Technologies, 1970, Nuclear Power in the South, 1970, The Future of Science and Technology, 1975, Museum Accounting Guidelines, 1976, Traveling Exhibitions, 1978, Towards the Year 2000, 1981; editor profl. procs. Trustee La Rabida Children's Hosp. and Research Center, 1973-83; mem. U. Chgo. Citizens' Bd., 1978—. Mem. Am. Assn. Museums (exec. com. 1976-77), AAAS, Am. Coll. Assn. Sci.-Tech. Centers (sec.-treas. 1973-74, pres. 1975-76), Internat. Council Museums (com. on sci. and tech. museums 1972-, vice chmn. 1977—, pres. 1982-83), Chgo. Council on Fine Arts (chmn. 1976-84), Sci. Mus. Collaborative (pres. 1983—), History of Sci. Soc., Soc. Indsl. Archeology, Soc. History of Tech., Chgo. Council Fgn. Relations (com. mem. 1980—), Sigma Delta Chi (chmn. Colo. 1959, chmn. nat. historic sites com. 1958). Clubs: Tavern, Univ. Home: 990 N Lake Shore Dr Chicago IL 60611 Office: Mus Sci and Industry 57th St and S Lake Shore Dr Chicago IL 60637

DANILOVA, ALEXANDRA, ballet dancer, choreographer; b. Peterhof, Russia; came to U.S., 1934; d. Dionis and Claudia (Gotovtzeva) D. Ed., Theatrical Sch. Petrograd. Now mem. faculty Sch. Am. Ballet; adjudicator Southeastern Ballet Conf., 1960. Mem., Russian State Ballet, Maryinsky Theater, 1922-24; soloist, Diaghileff Ballet, 1925; ballerina, 1929, Montecarlo Opera House, 1930-31; star: Oswald Stoll's prodn. Waltzes from Vienna, Alhambra Theatre, London, 1932; ballerina: Col. de Basil's Ballet Russe, 1933-38; prima ballerina: Ballet Russe de Monte Carlo, 1938-51; currently head own co. touring various countries, lecture tours, U.S., Europe; guest star: various ballets including Royal Ballet Covent Garden, 1946; star: Song of Norway, 1944; Broadway musical Oh Captain, 1958; choreographer, Met. Opera Co.; staged: (with George Balanchine for) Coppelia, N.Y.C. Ballet, 1974, Coppelia, and Los Angeles Ballet, 1980; works for, Nijinsky Festival Germany, 1975, for Md. Ballet. Recipient Capezio Dance award, 1958, Dance mag. award, 1984. Greek Orthodox. Address: 100 W 57th St New York NY 10019 *

DANILOWICZ, DELORES ANN, pediatric cardiologist, pediatrics educator; b. Bradford, N.Y., Feb. 3, 1935; s. Kajetan Joseph and Bronislawa Anna (Luta) D.; m. Hugh Paul Gabriel, June 3, 1960. A.B., NYU, 1956, M.D., 1960. Diplomate: diplomate am. bd. pediatrics. Inter, resident pediatrics Jacobi Hosp., Bronx, 1960-63, cardiac fellow, 1963-65; postdoctoral fellow Johns Hopkins, Balt., 1965-66, Nat. Heart Inst., Bethesda, Md., 1966-68; asst. prof. NYU Med. Ctr., N.Y.C., 1968-72; assoc. prof. NYU Med. Ctr., N.Y.C., 1972-80; prof. pediatrics NYU Med. Ctr., N.Y.C., 1980—; dir. pediatric cardiac catheterization lab. U. Hosp., 1968—; admitting physician Univ. Hosp., Bellevue Hosp., Lenox Hill Hosp.; chmn. N.Y. Heart Heart Assn. Com., N.Y.C., 1981—. Contbr. articles to profl. jours. NYU scholar, 1952-56; NYU Scholar, 1957-60; named Disting. Tchr. NYU Med. Sch., 1971, 1976; NYU Pediatric House Staff, 1975. Fellow Am. Acad. Pediatrics, Am. Coll. Cardiology; mem. Am. Heart Assn., N.Y. State-County Med. Soc.

DANIN, MARY ANN, artist, designer, educator; b. Los Angeles, Apr. 21, 1928; d. Dan and Edith (Shorr) D.; children: Sharon, David. A.B., UCLA, 1951, M.A., 1965; M.F.A., Claremont Grad. Sch., 1973. Pvt. practice textile design, 1947-52; high sch. tchr. Los Angeles Public Schs., 1951-55; instr. interior design and crafts Los Angeles Pierce Coll., 1954-55, 63-69; prof. art, weaving and design Calif. State U., Northridge, 1969—. Pvt. practice design cons., Venice, Calif., 1968—; colorist, designer: Colorways, 1980—, Am. Haiku Scrolls, Venice; (Recipient Pres.' Council Creativity award 1977); Author: Catalog Tapestry and Other Forms in Fiber, 1974; exhbns. Art Park-Los Angeles, 1976, Toys by Artists, Security Pacific Plaza, 1977-78, Fiber Artists, Ten from Calif, State U. Northridge, 1978, Los Angeles Mission Coll., 1977. Active program devel. interdisciplinary, univ. level fin. planning.; Mem. Venice Community Planning Council, 1975-77. Mem. World Craft Council, Am. Craft Council, Handweavers Guild Am., Craft and Folk Art Mus., Calif. Design, Los Angeles Inst. Contemporary Art, So. Calif. Handweavers Guild, Women in Design, Women's Caucus for Art, Los Angeles Costume Council, Town Hall Inter Soc. Color Council, Venice C. of C. Democrat. Jewish. Home: 1310 W Washington Blvd Venice CA 90291 Office: Art 3D Media California State U Northridge CA 91330

DANIS, PETER GODFREY, physician; b. Ottawa, Ont., Can., Apr. 12, 1909; s. Peter Godfrey and Helene (Burns) D.; m. Katherine Kramer, Apr. 6, 1931; children—Peter Godfrey, Richard, Joanne, Mary Katherine, James, Laura, David, Timothy and Thomas (twins), Deborah. Student, Gonzaga Coll., Spokane; B.S., St. Louis U., 1929, M.D., 1931, M.S., 1935. Diplomate: Am. Bd. Pediatrics. Intern St. Louis U. Group Hosps., 1931-32, fellow pediatrics, 1932-34; chmn. dept. pediatrics St. Louis U., 1947-57, asso. prof. pediatrics, 1948-51, prof. clin. pediatrics, 1951-79, emeritus prof. clin. pediatrics, 1979—, emeritus chmn. dept., 1979—; chief staff Cardinal Glennon Meml. Children's Hosp.; honor staff St. Mary's Hosp., 1969; chief pediatric cons., dir. health services Spl. Edn. St. Louis County. Bd. dirs. health and hosp. div. Social Planning Council, 1946-49; exec. bd. Cath. Charities, St. Louis, also med. dir. children's dept. Decorated Knight of Malta, Vatican; recipient Alumni Honor award St. Louis U., 1968, Staff award, 1974; Merit award St. Mary's Hosp., 1969; Health Care award Hosp. Assn. Met. St. Louis, 1974. Mem. Am. Acad. Pediatrics (state chmn. 1949-53, chmn. nat. com. hosps. and dispensaries 1950-52, gen. chmn. spring meeting 1971), St. Louis Med. Soc., St. Louis Pediatric Soc., A.M.A., Am. Acad. Cerebral Palsy, Am. Acad. Neurology (asso.). Home: 15022 Claymoor Ct Chesterfield MO 63017 Office: 2821 N Ballas Rd Town and Country Saint Louis MO 63131

DANIS, PETER GODFREY, JR., paper products executive; b. St. Louis, Jan. 20, 1932; s. Peter Godfrey and Katherine (Kramer) D.; m. Ann Wilmot, Apr. 14, 1934; children: Peter, Cathy, David, Mark, Laura. B.S., St. Louis U., 1953, M.B.A., 1958; postgrad., Columbia U., 1975. Sales mgr. Crown Zellerbach, San Francisco, 1955-68; gen. mgr. Boise Cascade, San Francisco, 1968-69, regional mgr., 1969-70, v.p., div. mgr., Chgo., 1976-80; dist. v.p. Boise, Idaho, 1980—; dir. Wholesale Stationers, 1980. Bd. dirs. Woodlands Acad. Served to 1st lt. U.S. Army, 1953-55. Republican. Roman Catholic. Clubs: Onwentsia (Lake Forest); Mid-Am.; Economic (Chgo.). Office: Boise Cascade Corp One Jefferson Sq Boise ID 83728

DANISH, ROY BERTRAM, broadcasting exec.; b. N.Y.C., Mar. 2, 1919; s. Max D. and Anne (Rich) D.; m. Jane Byington Millar, Apr. 12, 1953 (div. 1979); children—Elisabeth Jane, Caroline Anne. A.B., Columbia, 1940; M.B.A., Harvard, 1942. Asst. dir. research Mut. Broadcasting System, N.Y.C., 1946-47, sta. relations mgr., 1948-51, dir. sta. relations, 1952, dir. comml. operations, 1952-53, asst. to pres., 1953-54, v.p., 1954-55, McCann-Erickson, Inc., 1956-59; partner Smith/Greenland Advt., N.Y.C., 1959-60; asst. dir. TV Info. Office, Nat. Assn. Broadcasters, N.Y.C., 1960-62, dir., 1962—; Bd. dirs. Internat. Radio and TV Found., v.p., 1970-76. Served to lt. USNR, 1942-46. Mem. Nat. Acad. TV Arts and Scis. (nat. trustee, gov. N.Y. chpt. 1964-68), Internat. Radio and TV Soc. (v.p.), Broadcast Pioneers (pres. 1969-70), Columbia Coll. Alumni Assn., Beta Sigma Rho. Club: Harvard Business School. Home: 400 E 58th St New York NY 10022 Office: 745 Fifth Ave New York NY 10022

DANLY, DONALD ROBERT, manufacturing company executive; b. Chgo., Dec. 15, 1923; s. Philo Howard and Frances E. (Miller) D.; m. Mary Lyons, Dec. 21, 1945; children: Robert L., Christina, Beth, Amy, Thomas A., Catharine. B.M.E., Yale U., 1944. With Danly Machine Corp., Chgo., 1942—, v.p., 1955-78, pres., 1978—; pres. subs. Onsrud Machine Works, 1967-75. Served with USNR, 1943-46. Mem. Nat. Machine Tool Builders Assn., President's Forum. Roman Catholic. Clubs: Chgo. Yacht, Hinsdale Golf. Home: 1504 Burr Ridge Club Burr Ridge IL 60521 Office: 2100 S Laramie Ave Chicago IL 60650

DANNEMAN, FRED CHARLES, publisher, consultant; b. Des Moines, Aug. 30, 1919; s. Fred William and Vera (White) D.; m. Patricia Veatch, Feb. 14, 1948; children: Peggy, Elizabeth (Mrs. T. Kerry McCarter), Fred, David. B.J., U. Mo., 1941. Field advt. salesman Procter & Gamble, 1941-46; advt. mgr. asso. plants Swift & Co., 1946-48; space sales Boston Record Am., 1948-52; salesman Heart Advt. Service, 1952-60; advt. mgr. Am. Weekly, N.Y.C., 1960-63; with Ladies' Home Jour., N.Y.C., 1963—, salesman, advt. mgr., 1964-69, pub., v.p., 1969-74; exec. v.p. Downe Communications, Inc., 1974-77, pres., 1977-78, Downe Pub., Inc., Chartcom, Inc., 1977—, chmn. bd., 1980-83. Mem. Chappaqua (N.Y.) Dads Club, 1952-62, pres., 1956; Mem. Republican Com., Wellesley, Mass., 1949-52; mem. Rep. Town Com., Chappaqua, 1952-56. Served to 1st lt. AUS, 1942-46. Clubs: University (N.Y.C.); Sleepy Hollow Country (Scarborough, N.Y.); Saw Grass Country (Ponte Vedra Beach, Fla.). Home: 9742 Preston Trail W Ponte Vedra FL 32082 Office: 21 W Church St Jacksonville FL also

DANNEMEYER, WILLIAM EDWIN, congressman; b. South Gate, Calif., Sept. 22, 1929; s. Henry William and Charlotte Ernestine (Knapp) D.; m. Evelyn Hoemann, Aug. 27, 1955; children—Bruce, Kim, Susan. B.A., Valparaiso U., 1950; J.D., U. Calif., 1952. Bar: Calif. bar, U.S. Supreme Ct. bar. Individual practice law, Fullerton, Calif., 1957-79, asst. city atty., City of Fullerton, 1959-62; mem. Calif. Assembly, 1963-66, 77-78; judge pro tem Mcpl. Ct., 1966-76, Superior Ct., 1966-76; mem. 96th Congress from 39th Calif. Dist. Bd. dirs. Orange County Luth. High Sch., 1972-78; bd. dirs. Luth. Ch.-Mo. Synod, So. Calif. Dist.; spl. gifts chmn. Capital Fund drive Boy Scouts Am. Served with U.S. Army, 1950-52. Mem. Orange County Bar Assn. (dir.), Orange County Criminal Justice Council. Republican. Office: 1032 Longworth House Office Bldg Washington DC 20515

DANNENBERG, ARTHUR MILTON, JR., experimental pathologist, immunologist, educator; b. Phila., Oct. 17, 1923; s. Arthur Mansbach and Marion (Loeb) D.; m. Aileen Rose Hart, Mar. 30, 1948; children: Arlene Jane, Andrew Loeb, Audrey Ann. A.B., Swarthmore Coll., 1944; M.D., Harvard U., 1947; M.A., U. Pa., 1951, Ph.D., 1952. Diplomate: Nat. Bd. Med. Examiners. Intern Albert Einstein Med. Ctr., Phila., 1947-48; research resident Children's Hosp. (U. Pa.), 1948-49; fellow U. Pa., 1950-52, U. Utah, 1952-54; asst. prof. U. Pa., 1956-64; assoc. prof. environ. health scis. Johns Hopkins U. Sch. Hygiene, 1964-73, prof., 1973—, prof. joint faculty sch. medicine, 1976—. Contbr. articles to profl. jours., chpts. to books; assoc. editor: Am. Rev. Respiratory Diseases, 1979—; editorial bd., 1973-75, Infection and Immunity, 1976-78. Served as lt. Comdr. med. research unit 1 USN, 1954-56. Mem. Am. Soc. Exptl. Pathology, Histochem. Soc., Am. Soc. Microbiology, Reticuloendothelial Soc. (sec. 1975-76), Am. Assn. Immunologists. Home: 12 Lake Manor Ct Baltimore MD 21210 Office: Johns Hopkins U Sch Hygiene Baltimore MD 21205

DANNENBERG, MARTIN ERNEST, insurance company executive; b. Balt., Nov. 5, 1915; s. Martin Ernest and Wilhelmina (Wilfson) D.; m. Esther Salzman, May 29, 1941; children: Betsy, Richard. Student, Johns Hopkins U., U. Balt. Law Sch. With Sun Life Ins. Co. Am., Balt., 1932—, v.p. adminstrn., then sr. v.p., sec., 1966-76, dir., 1967—, vice chmn. bd., 1976-79, chmn. bd., 1979—; v.p., dir. Sun Life Group Am. (ins. holding co.), Atlanta; dir. Coastal States Life Ins. Co., Atlanta, Universal Guaranty Life Ins. Co., Columbus, Ohio. Bd. dirs. Associated Placement and Guidance Bur., Balt. Urban Coalition, Balt. Goodwill Industries, Balt. County Gen. Hosp., Balt. Choral Arts Soc., Sudden Infant Death Syndrome Inst.; mem. Mayor Balt. Adv. Com. Bus. Edn., Balt. County Phys. Fitness Commn., Md. Commn. Aging, Mayor Balt. Labor Market Adv. Commn.; asso. gen. campaign chmn. United Way of Central Md.; exec. bd., v.p. Balt. council Boy Scouts Am.; v.p. Balt. City Council P.T.A.'s. Served with CIC AUS, 1942-45; ETO. Decorated Bronze Star; named Distinguished Citizen Md. Mem. Life Office Mgmt. Assn. (past chmn. combination co. com., systems and procedures council), Adminstrv. Mgmt. Soc. (past pres. Balt.), Life Insurers Conf., Nat. Assn. Life Cos., Am. Council Life Ins. Home: 8107 Anita Rd Pikesville MD 21208 Office: Sun Life Ins Co Charles Center Baltimore MD 21201

DANNER, BLYTHE KATHARINE (MRS. BRUCE W. PALTROW), actress; b. Phila.; d. Harry Earl and Katharine D.; m. Bruce W. Paltrow, Dec. 14, 1969. B.A. in Drama, Bard Coll., D.F.A. (hon.), 1981, L.H.D., Hobart-Smith Coll., 1981. Appeared as Laura in: Glass Menagerie, 1965; repertory at, Theatre Co. Boston, The Knack, and 7 new Am. Plays, 1965-66; Appeared as Helena in: repertory Midsummer Night's Dream, Trinity Sq. Playhouse, R.I.; Appeared as Irena in: Three Sisters, Trinity Sq. Playhouse, R.I., 1967; with Lincoln Ctr. Repertory Co. in Summertree, 1968, Cyrano de Bergerac, 1968, Elise in the Miser, 1969 (Theatre World award); appeared on Broadway as Jill Tanner in: Butterflies Are Free (Tony award 1971); also appeared in: play Major Barbara, 1971; Twelfth Night, 1972, The Seagull, 1974, Ring Around The Moon, 1975, Betrayal, 1980 (Tony nomination); TV appearances include To Confuse the Angel (with Lee J. Cobb), George M. (with Joel Grey), 1970, Doctor Cook's Garden (with Bing Crosby), To Be Young, Gifted and Black, 1971, F. Scott Fitzgerald and 'The Last of the Belles', 1974, The Seagull, 1975, Eccentricities of a Nightingale, 1976, The Scarecrow, Adam's Rib; TV movies include A Love Affair: Eleanor and Lou Gehrig, 1978, Too Far to Go, 1979; movies include 1776, 1972, To Kill a Clown, 1972, Lovin' Molly, 1974, Hearts of the West, 1975, Futureworld, 1976, The Great Santini, 1980, Too Far to Go (with Michael Moriarty). Recipient Theatre World award, 1969; Best Actress award Vevey Film Festival, Switzerland, 1982. Care Agy for Performing Arts Inc 9000 Sunset Blvd Suite 315 Los Angeles CA 90069

DANNER, MARK STEVEN, retail holding company executive; b. Anderson, Ind., June 4, 1947; s. Max Smith and Joan Beigh (Yeager) D.; m. Margaret Ann Drockelman, Nov. 8, 1969; children: Alexandra Lynn, Ann Elizabeth, Noah Samuel. B.S., Ind. Central U., 1972. Asst. mgr. DDA Mchts. Bank, Indpls., 1968-71; various positions Danners, Indpls., 1971-74, exec. v.p., 1979-82, pres., 1982—; bd. dirs. Nat. Mass Retail Inst., N.Y.C., 1982. Mem. Boys Club Assn. of Indpls., 1983; bd. dirs. Hemophilia of Ind., Indpls., 1983. Club: Columbia (Indpls.). Home: 4154 Central Ave Indianapolis IN 46205 Office: Danners Inc PO Box 1146 Indianapolis IN 46206

DANNER, MAX SMITH, retail company executive; b. North Vernon, Ind, May 16, 1925; s. Harry Cleo and Genevieve Rose (Smith) D.; m. Joan b. Yeager, June 8, 1945 (div. 1961); children: Mark, Christopher, Jay, Lynn; m. Barbara E. Davis, Sept. 5, 1975; children: Derrik, Janalee, Bryan. Student, Wasbash Coll, 1943-44, Harvard U., 1945; B.S., Ind. U., 1947, postgrad., 1958. With Danners, Inc., Indpls., 1940-45, 1946-50, 1950-62; pres. chmn., Indpls., 1962-82, chmn., chief exec. officer, 1982—; dir. Ind. Retail Council, Indpls. Past bd. dirs. United Way, Better Bus. Bur., Boys Scouts Am, Indpls. Zoo; past. bd. dir. Jr. Achievement; past bd. dirs. Blue Cross; bd. dirs. Indpls. Indians Baseball Club, 1962—, Ind. Repertory Theatre, 1977—, 500 Festival Assocs., 1980—, Indpls. Kiwanis Found.; bd. dirs., past pres. Bosy Club of Indpls.; bd. dirs., trustee YMCA. Mem. Assn. Gen. Mdse. Chains (dir. 1963—, vice chmn. 1983, Navy League), Nat. Mass Retailers Inst., Ind. Presidents Orgn., Ind. State C. of C. (dir. 1963—), Beta Gamma Sigma. Republican. Methodist. Clubs: Downtown Indpls., Kiwanis; Skyline (Indpls.). Home: 4160 Washington Blvd Indianapolis IN 46205

DANNER, PATSY ANN (MRS. C.M. MEYER), businesswoman, state legislator; b. Louisville, Jan. 13, 1934; d. Henry J. and Catherine M. (Shaheen) Berrer; m. Lavon Danner, Feb. 12, 1951 (div.); children: Stephen, Stephanie, Shane, Shavonne.; m. C.M. Meyer, Dec. 30, 1982. Student, Hannibal-LaGrange Coll., 1952; B.A. in Polit. Sci. cum laude, N.E. Mo. State U., 1972. Dist. asst. to Congressman Jerry Litton, Kansas City, Mo., 1973-76; fed. co-chmn. Ozarks Regional Commn., Washington, 1977-81; owner, prin. Danner & Assocs., 1981—; mem. Mo. State Senate, 1983—. Sec. Macon County (Mo.) Tb Assn., 1963-66, Macon County Young Dems., 1966-70; pres. Macon Neighborhood council Girl Scouts U.S.A., 1968-70; chmn. Macon County Dem. Central Com., 1970-72; vice chmn. 9th Congl. Dist. Dem. Com., 1970-72. Mem. Bus. and Profl. Women, League Women Voters, Beta Sigma Phi. Roman Catholic. Home: 3910 N Central Kansas City MO 64119

DANOFF, I. MICHAEL, museum director, art critic, educator; b. Chgo., Oct. 22, 1940; s. Maurice and Matilda (Price) D.; m. Frances Evelyn Colker, May 31, 1964; children: Sharon, Brian. B.A., U. Mich., 1962; M.A., U. N.C., 1964; Ph.D., Syracuse U., 1970. Asst. prof. Dickinson Coll., Carlisle, Pa., 1970-73; curator U. Tex., Austin, 1973-74; chief curator Milw. Art Mus., 1974-80, assoc. dir., 1977-80; dir. Akron Art Mus., Ohio, 1980—; acquistions dir. HHK Found., Milw., 1977-82; panelist Nat. Endowment for Arts, Washington, 1976-82, Wis. Arts Bd., Madison, 1976-77, Ohio Mus. Assn., Columbus, 1980. Curator: art exhbns. Robert Mangold, 1984, Cindy Sherman, 1983, Emergence and Progression, 1979; co-organizer: art exhbn. Image in American Painting and Sculpture, 1981; art juror: Milw. Conv. Ctr., 1979, Akron State Office Bldg., 1983. Active Milw. Forum, 1976-80. Syracuse U. fellow, 1968-70; NEA Mus. Prof. fellow, 1973. Mem. Intermus. Conservation (trustee 1982—), Assn. Art Mus. Dirs., Coll. Art Assn. Club: Akron City. Office: Akron Art Mus 70 E Market St Akron OH 44308 *

DANOS, ROBERT MCCLURE, oil company executive; b. New Orleans, Dec. 9, 1929; s. Joseph A. and Muriel R. (McClure) D.; m. Barbara Umbach, Apr. 30, 1955; children: Robert M., Sally C., Susan M., Julie A., Richard F., Renee R. B.S. in Geology, Tulane U., 1950; M.S., La. State U., 1952. Geologist Texaco, Inc., New Orleans, 1955-67, staff geologist, Houston, 1967, div. geologist, Tulsa, 1968-70, exploration mgr., Denver, 1970-78; sr. v.p. K N Energy, Inc., Lakewood, Colo., 1980-83; pres., chief exec. officer Midlands Energy Co., Lakewood, 1983—. Served to 1st lt. U.S. Army, 1954. Mem. Am. Assn. Petroleum Geologists (del.), New Orleans Geologists Soc. (v.p. 1965-67), Rocky Mountain Assn. Geologists, Rocky Mountain Oil and Gas Assn., Rocky Mountain Natural Gasmen's Assn. Clubs: Cherry Hills Country; Denver Petroleum (Denver); Essex (New Orleans). Home: 4960 S Fulton St Englewood CO 80111 Office: Midlands Energy Co PO Box 15640 Lakewood CO 80215

DANSBY, JOHN WALTER, oil company executive; b. Logan, W.Va., Dec. 29, 1944; s. Charles Eugene and Lillian (Maggard) D.; m. Karen Navarin, June 20, 1970; children: Andrew, David. B.S. in Econs, U. Pa., 1966; M.B.A., Emory U., 1967; Ph.D. in Econs, U. Ky., 1976. Fin. analyst Ashland Oil, Inc., Ky., 1970-71, staff economist, 1975-77, mgr. fed. energy programs, 1977-81, exec. asst., 1981, v.p. strategic planning, 1981-84, v.p. planning, 1984—; vis. instr. Ohio U., 1980. Mem. U. Ky. Devel. Council, U. Ky. Fellows. Served to 1st lt. U.S. Army, 1968-69. Mem. Am. Econ. Assn., Nat. Assn. Bus. Economists, Internat. Assn. Energy Economists. Club: Bellefonte Country. Home: 280 Bellefonte Circle Ashland KY 41101 Office: PO Box 391 Ashland KY 41101

DANSEREAU, PIERRE, ecologist; b. Montréal, Can., Oct. 5, 1911; s. J. Lucien and Marie (Archambault) D.; m. Françoise Masson, Aug. 29, 1935. B.A., U. Montreal, 1932, B.S. Agr., 1936; D.Sc., U. Geneva, Switzerland, 1939, U. Sask., 1959, U. N.B., 1959, U. Strasbourg, France, 1970, U. Sherbrooke, 1971, Sir George Williams U., 1971, U. Waterloo, 1972, U. Guelph, 1973, U. Western Ont., 1973, Meml. U. Nfld., 1974, McGill U., 1976, U. Ottawa, 1978. Mem. faculty U. Montréal, 1940-42, 45, 55-61, 68-71; with Service de Biogéographie, 1943-50; prof. botany U. Mich., 1950-55; asst. dir., prof. ecology N.Y. Bot. Garden, 1961-68; adj. prof. Columbia U., 1962-68; mem. staff U. Qué. and Centre de Recherches Écologiques de Montréal, 1971-72; prof. ecology U. Qué, Montréal, 1972-76, prof. emeritus, 1976—; Vice chmn. Canadian Environ. Advisory Council, 1972-76, Can. Fed. Task Force Housing and Urban Devel., 1968, Natural Scis. and Engring. Research Council, 1978-80; mem. Sci. Council Can., 1968-72, Canadian Radio-TV Council, 1968; v.p. Canadian Commn. Internat. Biol. Programme, 1968; chmn. program urban devel. Sci. Council Can., 1970; pres. 1st Internat. Film Festival on Human Environment, 1973; sec. gen. Mich. Acad. Sci., Arts and Letters, 1953; 1st v.p. 9th Internat. Bot. Congress, 1959; chmn. bd. Gamma Inst., 1983—; hon. chmn. Fondation de l'ACFAS, 1984. Author: Biogeography: An Ecological Perspective, 1957, Phytogeographia laurentiana II, 1959, Contradictions & Biculture, 1964, (with co-author) Studies on the Vegetation of Puerto Rico I and II, 1966, (with others) A Universal System for Recording Vegetation II, 1966, Dimensions of Environmental Quality, 1971, Inscape and Landscape, 1973, La terre des hommes et le paysage intérieur, 1973, Harmony and Disorder in the Canadian Environment, 1975, Ezaim: Écologie de la Zone de l'Aéroport International de Montréal. Le cadre d'une recherche écologique interdisciplinaire, 1976; Co-author: Ecological Grading and Classification of Land-occupation and Land-use Mosaics, 1977; Author: An Ecological Grading of Human Settlements, 1978, Harmonie et désordre dans l'environnement canadien, 1980; Editor: Challenge for Survival, 1970. Guggenheim fellow, 1949; recipient Pierre Fermat medal, 1960; Commonwealth Prestige fellowship, 1961; Leo Pariseau medal, 1965; Pfizer prize, 1965; Prix David, Que., 1959; Distinguished Service award N.Y. Bot. Garden, 1969; companion Order Can., 1969; Massey medal, 1973; Molson prize, 1974; Esdras Minville meda, 1983; Marie-Victorin prize, 1983; named Great Montrealer in Sci., 1958-78. Fellow royal socs. Can., New Zealand (hon.); mem. Canadian Mental Health Assn. (pres. Que. 1972-74), Am. Teilhard de Chardin Assn. (pres. 1967), Ecol. Soc. Am. (v.p. 1968), Assn. Canadienne-Française pour l'Avancement des Scis. (sec. gen. 1945-46), Geog. Soc. Montreal (pres. 1957). Office: Univ du Québec à Montréal Case Postale 8888 Montreal PQ Canada H3C 3P8 *Teaching and research are parallel but complementary exercises. Contemplation and distillation in the ivory tower have to be fed by experience and exchange. My own experience has been mostly in the field: the sensorial witnessing of stones, plants, and animals, and men and cities, must be renewed all the time, in an endless addition to a personal treasury. But the translation into word-and-picture form needs interlocutors to test both the validity of perception and the communicability of rendering. This pulsation has varied in rhythm and content and has yielded both anxiety and happiness.*

DANSON, EDWARD BRIDGE, anthropologist; b. Glendale, Ohio, Mar. 22, 1916; s. Edward Bridge and Ann (Allen) D.; m. Jessica Harriet MacMaster, Nov. 7, 1942; children: Jessica Ann, Edward Bridge III. B.A., U. Ariz., 1940; M.A., Harvard, 1948, Ph.D., 1953. Asst. prof. anthropology U. Colo., 1948-50, U. Ariz., 1950-56; asst. dir. Mus. No. Ariz., 1956-58, dir., 1959-75; pres. Mus. of No. Ariz., 1975-79, bd. dirs., 1979-84; adj. prof. anthropology No. Ariz. U., 1973-75. Mem. adv. bd. Nat. Park Service, 1958-64, mem. adv. council, 1964—; mem. Ariz. Hist. Adv. Com., 1966—; chmn. Colo. Plateau Environmental Adv. Council, 1970-74; mem. Ariz. Council Humanities and Pub. Policy, 1973-75; Mem. adv. bd. Southwestern Parks and Monuments Assn., 1958—; trustee Folklife Center, Library of Congress, 1976—, chmn., 1979; bd. dirs. Flagstaff Symphony Assn., 1962-71, chmn., 1967-69; bd. dirs. Fred Harvey Fine Arts Found., 1970-77, Ariz. Hist. Soc., 1975—, Robert T. Wilson Found., 1971-74; v.p. Robert T. Wilson Found., 1972—. Served to lt. comdr. USNR, 1942-45. Fellow Am. Anthrop. Assn., A.A.A.S., Ariz. Acad. Sci. (pres. 1958-59); mem. Soc. Am. Archaeology, No. Ariz. Soc. Sci. and Art (dir. 1953-56), Am. Assn. Museums, Sigma Xi. Episcopalian. Home: PO Box 379 Sedona AZ 86336

DANSON, LAWRENCE NEIL, English educator; b. N.Y.C., Nov. 10, 1942; s. Harold and Henrietta (Steinberg) D.; m. Elizabeth A. Price, July 22, 1967; children: Benjamin, Joshua. B.A., Dartmouth Coll., 1964; M.A., Oxford U., 1966; Ph.D., Yale U., 1969. Instr. English Princeton U., 1968-69, asst. prof. English, 1969-75, assoc. prof. English, 1975-78, prof. English, 1978—; mem. faculty Bread Loaf Sch. English, Middelbury, Vt., 1977, 79, 81, 82; vis. assoc. prof. Dartmouth Coll., 1978. Author: Tragic Alphabet, 1974, The Harmonies of The Merchant of Venice, 1978, Max Beerbohm and The Mirror of the Past, 1982; editor: On King Lear, 1982. Fellow NEH, 1978. Mem. MLA, Shakespeare Assn. Am. Home: 158 Cedar Ln Princeton NJ 08540 Office: Dept English Princeton U Princeton NJ 08544

DANSON, STEPHEN MICHAEL, brokerage firm executive; b. N.Y.C., Mar. 31, 1943; s. Irving Samuel and Beatrice (Mach) D.; m. Emily Stark, Apr. 13, 1969 (div. Sept. 1980); children: Christopher Stark, Melissa Stark; m. Margaret Kessler, May 15, 1983. Student, Princeton U., 1962-66. Registered rep., asst. to sr. ptnr. Herzfeld & Stern, N.Y.C., 1968-70, head mcpl. bond dept., 1970-74, ltd. ptnr., 1974-78, gen. ptnr., 1978-84; pres. S.M.D. Assocs., Inc., N.Y.C., 1984—. Trustee Beth Isreal Hosp., N.Y.C., 1976—. Clubs: Tiger Inn (Princeton, N.J.); St. Andrews Country (Hastings-on-Hudson, N.Y.). Home: 1 Lincoln Plaza New York NY 10023

DANTAS, CARL E., photocomposition equipment company executive; b. Boston, 1934. Grad., Northeastern U. Pres., chief exec. officer Compugraphic Corp., Wilmington, Mass. Office: 200 Ballardvale St Wilmington MA 01887

DANTE, HARRIS LOY, emeritus history educator; b. Monticello, Ill., Feb. 17, 1912; s. Harris and Myrtle Thread (Loy) D.; m. Margaret June Miller, June 5, 1937; children: Susan Kay (Mrs. Robert L. Denniston), Nancy Jane (Mrs. Victor L. Bennison) John H. B.A. with honors, U. Ill., 1933, M.A., 1941; Ph.D., U. Chgo., 1950. Salesman Standard Oil Co., Chgo., 1933-36; tchr. Thornton (Ill.) Elementary Sch., 1936-38, Burlington (Ia.) Sr. High Sch., 1938-43, Burlington Jr. Coll., 1946-48; lectr. history U. Chgo., 1949-50; asst. prof. history and edn. Kent (Ohio) State U., 1950-52, assoc. prof., 1952-57, prof., 1957-82; cons. U.S. Office Edn., Ohio State Dept. Edn.; Co-dir. comparative edn. seminar to, Finland, USSR, Czechoslovakia and Spain, 1969, to USSR, 1972; mem. evaluation bd. Nat. Council Accreditation Tchr. Edn., 1976—. Co-author: U.S. History, 1967, Teachers Resources Book, 1967, United States History: Search for Freedom, 2 vols, 1974; Contbr.: articles Jr. Britannica Ency; also profl. jours. Served to lt. USNR, 1943-46. Recipient President's medal Kent State U., 1971. Mem. Nat. Council Social Studies (dir. 1959-63, 71-76, pres. 1973), Ohio Council Social Studies (pres. 1957, exec. com. 1979-82), Am. Hist. Assn., Orgn. Am. Historians, Ohio Acad. History (chmn. standards com. 1978—), NEA, AAUP (council State Univs. Ohio 1951—, pres. 1961), Phi Delta Kappa, Kappa Delta Pi, Phi Alpha Theta. Home: 502 Dansel Ave Kent OH 44240

DANTLEY, ADRIAN, professional basketball player; b. Washington, Feb. 28, 1956. Ed., U. Notre Dame. Profl. basketball player Buffalo Braves, 1976-77, Ind. Pacers, 1977, Los Angeles Lakers, 1977-79, Utah Jazz, 1979—; Mem. NBA All Star Team, 1980, 81, 82. Named NBA Rookie of the Yr., 1977. Leading scorer Nat. Basketball Assn., 1980-81. Office: care Utah Jazz the Salt Palace Suite 206 100 SW Temple Salt Lake City UT 84101

DANTO, ARTHUR COLEMAN, author, philosophy educator; b. Ann Arbor, Mich., Jan. 1, 1924; s. Samuel Budd and Sylvia (Gittleman) D.; m. Shirley Rovetch, Aug. 9, 1946 (dec. July 1978); children: Elizabeth, Jane; m. Barbara Westman, Feb. 15, 1980. B.A., Wayne State U., 1948; M.A., Columbia U., 1949, Ph.D., 1952; postgrad., U. Paris, 1949-50. Instr. U. Colo., 1950-51; mem. faculty Columbia U., 1952—, Johnsonian prof. philosophy, chmn. dept., 1979—, co-dir. Center for Study of Human Rights, 1978—. Author: Analytical Philosophy of Knowledge, 1968, What Philosophy Is, 1968, Analytical Philosophy of History, 1965, Nietzsche as Philosopher, 1965, Analytical Philosophy of Action, 1973, Mysticism and Morality, 1972, Jean-Paul Sartre, 1975, The Transfiguration of the Commonplace, 1981 (Lionel Trilling Book prize 1982); editor: Jour. Philosophy, 1965—. Bd. dirs. Amnesty Internat., 1970-75, gen. sec., 1973, nat. adv. council, 1975—. Served with AUS, 1942- 45. Fulbright fellow, 1949; Guggenheim fellow, 1969, 82; Am. Council Learned Socs. fellow, 1961, 70; Fulbright Disting. prof., Yugoslavia, 1976. Fellow Am. Acad. Arts and Sci.; mem. Am. Philos. Assn. (v.p. 1969, pres. 1983). Office: 710 Philosophy Hall Columbia U New York NY 10027

DANTON, JOSEPH PERIAM, librarian, educator; b. Palo Alto, Calif., July 5, 1908; s. George Henry and Annina (Periam) D.; m. Lois King, Dec. 25, 1948 (div.); children—Jennifer, Joseph Periam. Ed., U. Leipzig, Germany, 1925-26; A.B. magna cum laude, Oberlin Coll., 1928; B.S., Columbia, 1929; A.M., Williams Coll., 1930; Ph.D., U. Chgo., 1935,. With N.Y. Pub. Library, 1928-29; reference asst. Williams Coll. Library, 1929-30; with A.L.A., 1930-33; librarian, asso. prof. bibliography Colby Coll., Waterville, Maine, 1935-36, Temple U., Phila., 1936-46; dean Sch. Librarianship, U. Calif., 1946-61, asso. prof., 1946-47, prof., 1947-76, prof. emeritus, 1976—; Nat. library cons. U.S. Works Progress Adminstrn., 1937; vis. prof. Grad. Library Sch., U. Chgo., 1942, Columbia, 1946; vis. lectr. U. Toronto, 1963, Hebrew U., Jerusalem, Univs. of Belgrade, Ljubljana, Novi Sad, Zagreb, 1965, U. Brit. Columbia, 1968, 79, McGill U., 1969, U. P.R., 1970, U. N.C., 1977, U. Tex., 1979; Fulbright research scholar, Germany, 1960-61, Austria, 1964-65; surveyor and cons. numerous libraries, including Haile Selassie I Univ.; UNESCO Library Cons., Jamaica, 1968; Del. Internat. Fedn. Library Assns. meeting, The Hague, 1939, 66, Rome, 1964, Toronto, 1967, Frankfurt, 68, Copenhagen, 1969, Moscow, 1970, Liverpool, Eng., 1971, Budapest, 1972; dir. Dept. State-A.L.A. Multi-Area Group Librarian Program, 1963-64; Ford Found. cons. on libraries in S.E. Asia (with R. C. Swank), 1963; hon. research fellow U. London, 1974-75; Mem. exec. bd. Phila. Bibliog. Center, chmn. com. on microphotography, 1940-46. Compiler: (with others) Library Literature, 1921-32, 1934, (with M.F. Tauber) Theses and Dissertations, 1942, Union List of Microfilms, 1942-46; translator of: sects. on German libraries in Popular Libraries of the World, 1932; Author: Education for Librarianship, 1946, Education for Librarianship, Paris, 1950, United States Influence on Norwegian Librarianship, 1890-1940, 1957, Book Selection and Collections: A Comparison of German and American University Libraries, 1963, Index to Festschriften in Librarianship, 1970, (with Jane F. Pulis) vol. 2, 1967-1975, 1979, Between M.L.S. and Ph.D, 1970, The Dimensions of Comparative Librarianship, 1973; Editor: The Climate of Book Selection; Social Influences on Sch. and Pub. Libraries, 1959; Contbr. ednl. and book review jours.; Mem. editorial bd.: Coll. and Research Libraries Monograph Series, 1966-69, Library Quar., 1968—, Internat. Library Rev, 1968-77. Served as lt. USNR, 1942-45; PTO. Recipient Coll. and Research Libraries grant, 1960-61; Council on Library Resources grant, 1967-69; Berkeley citation, 1976; Beta Phi Mu award, 1983; Guggenheim fellow, 1971. Mem. A.L.A. (various coms. since 1934), Assn. Coll. and Ref. Libraries (treas. 1938-40), Calif. Library Assn., Assn. Am. Library Schs. (pres. 1949-50), Bibliog. Soc., Internat. Fedn. Library Assns. (chmn. com. library edn. 1967-72), Sigma Alpha Epsilon. Democrat. Club: Faculty (Berkeley, Calif.). Home: 500 Vernon St Apt 402 Oakland CA 94610 Office: Sch Library and Info Studies U Calif Berkeley CA 94720

DANTON, REBECCA *See* **ROBERTS, JANET LOUISE**

D'ANTONI, PHILIP, producer; b. Bronx, N.Y., Feb. 19, 1929; s. Peter and Josephine (Elici) D'A.; m. Ruth Ann Wiederecht, Sept. 12, 1953; children—Christopher, Jeanne, Carol, James, Robert. Student, Fordham U., 1948-50. Prodn. asst., asso. producer CBS-TV, 1949-53; v.p., dir. Mut. Broadcasting System, 1955-61; pres. D'Antoni/Weitz TV Prodns. Producers: weekly TV series Movin' On, NBC-TV, N.Y.C., 1961—; producer: films Bullitt, 1968, The French Connection, 1971 (Acad. award); producer, dir.: film The Seven Ups, 1973. Served with AUS, 1946-48. Mem. Dirs. Guild Am., Screenwriters Guild. Club: Dellwood Country. Home: 90 Cairnsmuir Ln New City NY 10956 Office: 8 E 63d St New York NY 10021

D'ANTONIO, NICHOLAS, bishop; b. Rochester, N.Y., July 10, 1916; s. Pasquale and Josephine (Salza) D'A. Student, St. Francis Seraphic Sem., Andover, Mass., 1931, St. Anthony Friary, Catskill, N.Y., 1939. Joined Order of Friars Minor; ordained priest Roman Catholic Ch., 1942; pastor, Trail, B.C., Can., 1943-45, provincial del. of U.S.A. Friars working in, Guatemala, Honduras and El Salvador, 1953-63, named prelate of, Olancho, Honduras, 1966; bishop Diocese Olancho, 1966-76; vicar gen. Archdiocese of New Orleans, 1977—; also vicar of Spanish-speaking Annunciation Ch., pastor, New Orleans, 1979—; Liaison Family Life and La. Cath. Conf. Home: 1221 Mandeville St New Orleans LA 70117

DANYLUK, STEVEN SIMEON, research executive; b. Winnipeg, Man., Can., Jan. 9, 1933; s. William W. and Olga (Senach) D.; m. Elizabeth E. Timlick, June 16, 1956; children: Lisa Gail, Steven David. B.Sc. with honors, U. Man., 1955, M.Sc., 1956; Ph.D., Rensselaer Poly Inst., 1958. Asst. prof. U. Toronto, Can., 1960-65; assoc. scientist Argonne Nat. Lab., Ill., 1965-70, sr. scientist, group leader, 1970-81, assoc. div. dir., 1975-81; v.p. research Domtar, Inc., Montreal, Que., Can., 1981—. Editor: Structural Molecular Biology, 1981. NRC postdoctoral fellow, Ottawa, Can., 1958-60; Japan Soc. Promotion Sci. sr. fellow, Toyko, 1980. Fellow Am. Inst. Chemists; mem. Am. Chem. Soc., Biophys. Soc., AAAS, Chem. Inst. Can., Can. Pulp and Paper Assn., TAPPI. Club: St. James (Montreal). Home: 84 Oakland Ave Hudson Heights PQ Canada J0P 1J0 Office: Domtar Inc 395 de Maisonneuve Blvd W Montreal PQ Canada H3C 3M1

DANZIG, FREDERICK PAUL, editor; b. Springfield, Mass., Sept. 17, 1925; s. Phillip and Sylvia (Levin) D.; m. Edith Goret, Mar. 16, 1952; children: Steven, Ellen Kay. B.A., Washington Sq. Coll., NYU, 1949. Copy boy AP, N.Y.C., 1943; reporter Herkimer (N.Y.) Evening Telegram, 1949, Port Chester (N.Y.) Daily Item, 1950-51; reporter, columnist UPI, N.Y.C., 1951-62; sr. editor Advt. Age, N.Y.C., 1962-68, exec. editor, 1969—; advt. newscaster Sta. WQXR, 1979-81, Sta. WMCA, 1982-83; adj. instr. New Sch. Social Research, N.Y.C. Author: (with Ted Klein) How to be Heard, 1974. Chmn., United Civic Orgn., Eastchester, N.Y., 1968-69. Served with inf. AUS, 1943-46. Decorated Bronze Star, Purple Heart, Presdl. Unit citation with oak leaf cluster; recipient NYU Alumni Achievement award, 1983. Mem. 29th Inf. Div. Assn., Sigma Delta Chi. Office: 220 E 42d St New York NY 10017

DANZIG, HAL, watch and jewelry mfg. co. exec.; b. Rochester, N.Y., Jan. 24, 1938; s. Clifford and Pauline D.; m. Carolyn King, Aug. 17, 1974; children—Tammra, Linda, Bryan, Carl. B.S.E.E., Bucknell U., 1959. Sales mgr. ITEK, Lexington, Mass., 1961-63; sales mgr. Midland Mfg. Co., Kansas City, Kans., 1963-65; pres. Electronic Research Co./ Textron, Overland, Kans., 1965-76, Waltham/Elgin Watch Co., Chgo., 1976—

DANZIG, JEROME ALAN, management consultant; b. N.Y.C., Feb. 7, 1913; s. Jerome J. and Helen Madeline (Wolf) D.; m. Sarah Palfrey, Apr. 27, 1951; 1 son, Jerome Palfrey; 1 stepdau., Diana Dupont. Grad., Horace Mann Sch. for Boys, 1930; B.A., Dartmouth, 1934. Staff reporter N.Y. Jour., 1934-35; spl. events dept., comml. program mgr., publicity dir. sta. WOR, N.Y.C., 1935-42; program dir. sta. WINS, N.Y.C., Crosley Broadcasting Co., 1946-48; asso. dir. network programs, supr. color broadcasting, producer CBS-TV, 1948-55; dir. program planning and devel. NBC owned stas. and spot sales, 1955-56; v.p. in charge radio network programs NBC, 1956-59; v.p. participating programs NBC-TV, 1959-61; TV-radio cons. N.Y. Republican City Com., 1961; spl. asst. to Gov. N.Y. (for radio-TV), 1962-69; spl. asst. to the dir. communications Gov.'s staff, 1969-72, spl. asst. to gov., 1972-74; cons. to v.p. U.S., 1975; partner Chester Burger & Co., Inc. (mgmt. cons.), 1976—; Mem. faculty telecommunications courses J. Walter Thompson Co., 1975-76; Mem. N.Y. State Commn. Cable TV, 1973—, vice chmn., 1973-78. Former chmn. public relations com. Alumni Council, Dartmouth; former trustee Jewish Bd. Guardians, N.Y.C., United Neighborhood Houses, N.Y.C.; trustee Jewish Home and Hosp. for Aged, N.Y.C. Served as officer USNR, 1942-46. Decorated Bronze Star. Mem. Public Relations Soc. Am. (accredited, pres. N.Y. chpt. 1981), Acad. TV Arts and Scis., Am. Arbitration Assn. (nat. panel arbitrators 1980—), Alpha Delta Phi. Clubs: Yale; Quaker Hill (Pawling, N.Y.). Home: 993 Park Ave New York NY 10028 Office: 171 Madison Ave New York NY 10016

DANZIG, RICHARD JEFFREY, lawyer; b. N.Y.C., Sept. 8, 1944; s. Aaron and Elinor (Moskowitz) D.; m. Andrea Auster, June 26, 1966; children: David, Lisa. B.A., Reed Coll., 1965; B.Phil., Magdalen Coll., Oxford U., 1967, D.Phil., 1968; J.D., Yale U., 1971. Bar: Calif. 1973. Asst. to pres. Rand Inst., N.Y.C., 1971; law clk. Justice White, U.S. Supreme Ct., Washington, 1971-72; fellow Harvard Soc. Fellows, 1975-77; asst. prof. Stanford Law Sch., 1972-75, assoc. prof., 1975-77; mem. faculty Harvard Program in the Law and Humanities, 1976; dep. asst. sec. of Def. for program devel. Dept. Def., Washington, 1977-79, acting prin. dep. asst. sec. of Def. for manpower, res. affairs and logistics, 1979, prin. dep. asst. sec., 1979-81; now mem. firm Latham, Watkins & Hills, Washington; vis. prof. Georgetown U. Sch. Law, 1979-80; cons. Police Found.; cons. Urban Affairs N.Y. Rand Inst., 1969-74. Author: The Capability Problem in Contract Law, 1978; Contbr. articles to profl. jours. Rockefeller Found. fellow, 1976-77; Rhodes scholar, 1965-68; Recipient Harlan Fiske Stone prize Yale Law Sch., 1970; Herbert prize Oxford U., 1967. Mem. Calif. Bar Assn., Phi Beta Kappa. Home: 3670 Upton St NW Washington DC 20008 Office: Latham, Watkins, & Hills 1333 New Hampshire Ave NW Suite 1200 Washington DC 20036

DANZIG, SARAH H. PALFREY, advt. exec., writer; b. Sharon, Mass., Sept. 18, 1912; d. John Gorham and Methyl (Oakes) Palfrey; m. Jerome A. Danzig, Apr. 27, 1951; children—Diana, Jerome Palfrey. Grad., Winsor Sch., 1930; spl. studies, Radcliffe Coll. Advt. cons. World Tennis mag., 1965—; sports editor NBC-TV Home program, 1956-57; sports commr., N.Y.C., 1966—; exec. com. Nat. Tennis Found. and Hall of Fame Inc. Author: Winning Tennis and How to Play It, 1946, Tennis for Anyone, 1966, rev. paperback, 1972, 80, also articles. Chmn. spl. events Child Study Assn. Am., 1963-67; chmn. ann. benefit Vis. Nurse Service, N.Y.C., 1961-63; mem. spl. events com. People to People Sports Com., 1962-64, Eastern Tennis Patrons, 1962-67; Trustee Community Service Soc. N.Y., 1966-76. Elected Mass. Greatest Woman Athlete Helms Hall of Fame, 1953; elected to Nat. Tennis Hall of Fame, 1963; recipient Service Bowl U.S. Tennis Assn., 1981. Mem. Lawn Tennis Writers Assn. Am., Internat. Lawn Tennis Club U.S. (hon.). Clubs: 7th Regiment Tennis (hon.), Jr. League, Town Tennis (hon.), English Speaking Union (N.Y.C.); Longwood Cricket (Chestnut Hill, Mass.) (hon.); Quaker Hill Country (Pawling, N.Y.); West Side Tennis (hon.). Winner 63 nat. and internat. tennis championships, 1927-45; mem. U.S. Wightman Cup team for ten consecutive years. Address: 993 Park Ave New York NY 10028

DANZIGER, FREDERICK MICHAEL, lawyer; b. N.Y.C., Mar. 12, 1940; s. Frederick Simon and Louise (Paskus) D.; m. Lucy Cullman, July 25, 1963; children: David M., Rebecca B. B.A., Harvard U., 1962; LL.B., Yale U., 1965. Law clk. Nixon Mudge Rose Guthrie & Alexander, N.Y.C., 1964, assoc., 1967-74, ptnr., 1974—; law clk. Kupfer, Silberfeld, Nathan & Danziger, N.Y.C., 1965-67; chmn. exec. com., dir. Culbro Corp., N.Y.C.; dir. B. Bros. Realty Corp., N.Y.C. Mem. ABA. Club: Century Country (Purchase, N.Y.). Home: 2 E 73d St New York NY 10021 Office: Mudge Rose Gutrie Alexander & Ferdon 20 Broad St 24th Floor New York NY 1005

DANZIGER, JERRY, broadcasting executive; b. N.Y.C., Jan. 23, 1924; s. Harry and Lillie (Lacher) D.; m. Zelda Bloom, Dec. 26, 1948;

children: Sydney, Alan, Lee. Grad. high sch. With WTTV, Bloomington, Ind., 1950-53; program mgr. WTSK-TV, Knoxville, Tenn., 1953; ops. mgr. WTTV, Indpls., 1953-57; gen. mgr. KOB-TV, Albuquerque, 1957—, v.p., 1983—; mem. Gov. N.Mex. Commn. for Film Entertainment, 1970-71. Bd. dirs. KIPC All Indian Pueblo Council, 1975—, Albuquerque Little Theatre, Albuquerque Pub. Broadcast, Albuquerque Jewish Welfare Fund, AP Broadcasting, 1980—, Goodwill Industries N.Mex., 1980. Served with USAAF, 1942-45. Recipient Compadre award Am. Women in Radio and TV, 1978, 80. Mem. N.Mex. Broadcasters Assn. (pres. 1972-73, Broadcaster of Year award 1976, 78), Press Club, Advt. Club. Club: Albuqerque Country. Office: Box 1351 Albuquerque NM 87103

DAPHNIS, NASSOS, artist; b. Krokeai, Greece, July 23, 1914; s. Panagiotes A. and Stamatico (Georgoulis) D.; m. Helen Avlonitis, Mar. 24, 1956; children: Artemis, Demetrios. Student, Art Students League, N.Y.C., 1946-49, Academie Frochot, Paris, 1950-51, Instituto Statale D'Arte, Florence, Italy, 1951-52. One-man shows, Contemporary Arts Gallery, N.Y.C., 1938-47, Mint Mus., Charlotte, N.C., 1949, Collette Allendy Gallery, Paris, 1950, Leo Castelli Gallery, N.Y.C., 1959-61, 63, 65, 68, 71, 73, 75, 80, 83, Toninelli Arte Moderna, Milan, Italy, 1961, Galerie Iris Clert, Paris, 1962, Franklin Siden Gallery, Detroit, 1967, Albright-Knox Mus., Buffalo, 1969, Everson Mus., Syracuse, N.Y., Brockton (Mass.) Art Center, 1970, Andre Zarre Gallery, N.Y.C., 1974, 76, 83, Printers Gallery, Ithaca, N.Y., 1975, Kingpitcher Gallery, Pitts., Phillips Gallery, Salt Lake City, 1980, Eaton/Shoen Gallery, San Francisco, one-man shows, Omega Gallery, Athens, 1983; exhibited in group shows, Pitts. Internat., 1958, 61, 70, Whitney Mus. Am. Art, N.Y.C., 1959, 61, 62, 64, 65, 67, Corcoran Gallery, Washington, 1959, 63, 69, Columbus (Ohio) Gallery Fine Art, 1960, Osaka (Japan) Mus. Fine Art, Guggenheim Mus., N.Y.C., 1961, Lever House, N.Y.C., Walker Art Center, Mpls., 1961, 62, Brandeis U., 1962, Washington Gallery Modern Art, 1963, Washington Sq. Galleries, N.Y.C., 1964, de Cordova Mus., Lincoln, Mass., 1965, Aldrich Mus., Ridgefield, Conn., 1969, Westbeth Ct. Gallery, N.Y.C., 1970, Tirca Karlis Gallery, Provincetown, Mass., 1972, Leo Castelli Gallery, N.Y.C., 1974, Birmingham (Ala.) Mus. Art, 1976, Albright Coll., Reading, Pa., numerous others; represented permanent collections at, Mus. Modern Art, N.Y.C., Whitney Mus. Am. Art, N.Y.C., Albright-Knox Gallery, Buffalo, Albany (N.Y.) Mall, Guggenheim Mus., N.Y.C., Balt. Mus., Providence Mus., Chrysler Mus., Norfolk, Va., Tel Aviv Mus., Israel, Munson-Williams-Proctor Mus., Utica, N.Y., Akron (Ohio) Art Inst., Reading (Pa.) Mus., Ann Arbor (Mich.) Art Mus., Balt. Mus., Pitts. Mus. Art, Hirshhorn Mus., Washington, Aldrich Mus., Ridgefield, Conn., Everson Mus., Syracuse, N.Y., Utah Mus. Fine Art, Salt Lake City., permanent collections, Vorres Mus., Athens, Goulandris Mus., Andros, Greece. Recipient Ford Found. award, 1962; Pitts. award, 1966; Nat. Found. Arts and Humanities award, 1966; Nat. Endowment on Arts award, 1971; A.P. Saunders medal, 1973; Guggenheim fellow, 1977. Office: 362 W Broadway New York NY 10013

DAPICE, RONALD R., government official; b. Utica, N.Y., Apr. 25, 1937; s. Rocco J. and Rose T. D.; m. Patricia Daedelow, May 18, 1963; children: Ronald, Traci, Diane. B.S. in Indsl. Mgmt, Syracuse U., 1960. With NASA, 1964—; dir. resource mgmt. Goddard Space Flight Center, 1974-80, Office Space Tracking and Data Systems, Washington, 1980—. Recipient Superior Performance award NASA, 1976, 78, Outstanding Achievement award, 1977. Office: 600 Independence Ave Washington DC 20546

DAPPLES, EDWARD CHARLES, geologist, educator; b. Chgo., Dec. 13, 1906; s. Edward C. and Victoria (Gazzolo) D.; m. Marion Virginia Sprague, Sept. 2, 1931; children—Marianne Helena, Charles Christian. B.S., Northwestern U., 1928, M.S., 1934; M.A., Harvard, 1935; Ph.D., U. Wis., 1938. Geologist Ziegler Coal Co., 1928; geologist Truax-Traer Coal Co., 1928-32, mine supt., 1932; instr. Northwestern U., 1936-41, asst. prof., 1941, asso. prof., 1942-50, prof. geol. scis., 1950-75, prof. emeritus, 1975—; geologist Ill. Geol. Survey, 1939, Sinclair Oil Co., 1945-50, Pure Oil Co., 1950; dir. Evanston Exploration Corp; sr. vis. scientist U. Lausanne, Switzerland, 1960-61; vis. prof. U. Geneva, Switzerland, 1970. Author: Basic Geology for Science and Engineering, 1959, Atlas of Lithofacies Maps, 1960. Fellow Geol. Soc. Am., Soc. Econ. Geologist, A.A.A.S.; mem. Am. Inst. Mining Engrs., Assn. Petroleum Geologists, Internat. Assn. Sedimentologists, Soc. Econ. Paleontologists and Mineralogists (pres. 1970, hon. mem. 1974), Am. Inst. Profl. Geologists (pres. Ill.-Ind. sect. 1979, pres. Ariz. 1982), Geochem. Soc., Assn. Engring. Geologists. Home: 13035 98th Dr Sun City AZ 85351

D'APPOLONIA, ELIO, civil engineer; b. Coleman, Alta., Can., Apr. 14, 1918; came to U.S., 1946, naturalized, 1959; s. Joseph S. and Constance (Piccinni) D'A.; m. Violet Mary D'Appollonia, May 2, 1942; children: David, Kenneth, Michael, Linda, Mark. B.S., U. Alta., 1942, M.S., 1946; Ph.D., U. Ill., 1948; D. Engring. (hon.), Carnegie-Mellon U., 1983. Cons. U.S. Army C.E., Alaska/No. Can., 1942-45; research asso. U. Ill., 1946-48; asst. prof. civil engring. Carnegie-Mellon U., 1948-56; pres., chmn. bd. D'Appolonia Cons. Engrs., Inc., Pitts., 1956—. Contbr. tech. articles to profl. jours. Recipient Keefer medal Engring. Inst. Can., 1948; William Metcalf award for outstanding engring. achievement Engrs. Soc. Western Pa., 1981; Disting. Alumnus award U. Ill., 1981; Disting. Service award Deep Founds. Inst., 1983. Mem. ASCE (Middlebrooks award 1969, Civil Engr. of Year, Pitts. sect. 1972), Nat. Acad. Engring., ASTM, Nat., Pa. socs. profl. engrs., Internat. Soc. Rock Mechanics, Internat. Assn. Bridge and Structural Engrs., Am. Underground Assn., Internat. Soc. Soil Mechanics and Found. Engrs., U.S. Nat. Com. Tunneling Tech., Deep Foundations Inst., Internat. Commn. Large Dams, Am. Inst. Cons. Engrs., Am. Water Resources Assn., Assn. Engring. Geologists. Republican. Roman Catholic. Club: Edgewood Country. Home: 1177 McCully Dr Pittsburgh PA 15235 Office: 10 Duff Rd Pittsburgh PA 15235

DARACK, ARTHUR J., editor; b. Royal Oak, Mich., Jan. 1, 1918; s. Edward Charles and Sonia (Resnikov) D.; m. Jean Claire Puttmyer, May 28, 1942; children—Glenn Arthur, Brenda Lee. Mus.M., Cin. Conservatory, 1949; Ph.D., Ind. U., 1951. Music editor Cin. Enquirer, 1951-61, feature writer, columnist, 1961-62, book and art editor, 1962-63; editor Dimension; Cin., monthly mag., 1963-65; asso. editor Ency. Brit., Chgo., 1967-70; sr. editor Actual Specifying Engr. (monthly mag.), 1971—; editor Consumers Digest mag., 1972-78; pres. Consumer Group Inc., 1978—; Program annotator Cin. Symphony Orch., 1952-61; adj. asso. prof. music Coll. Music, U. Cin. Author: Outdoor Power Equipment, 1977, Consumers Digest Automobile Repair Book; co-author: The Great Eating, Great Dieting Cookbook, 1978, Playboy's Book of Sports Car Repair, 1980; author: syndicated column Buy Right, 1977-81; contbg. editor, columnist: The Money Letter, 1979—. Served with AUS, 1941-45. Mem. Pi Kappa Lambda. Home and office: 9018 Sleeping Bear Rd Skokie IL 60076 *Two basic approaches to activity have motivated me—The theoretical and the practical. The practical involves self-help, which increasingly becomes a social engine for change and improvement, both for the individual and the society.*

DARBELNET, JEAN LOUIS, retired foreign language educator; b. Paris, Nov. 14, 1904; emigrated to Can., 1940; s. Louis and Augusta (Lailavoix) D.; m. Elizabeth Matheson, Aug. 20, 1938; children: Anne, Robert. Licence ès lettres, Sorbonne, U., Paris, 1925, Diplôme d'Etudes supérieures, 1926, Agrégé de l'Université, 1929. Mem. faculty dept. French U. Wales, 1925-26, U. Edinburgh, Scotland, 1926-27, U. Manchester, Eng., 1928-30; tchr. English, French lycées, 1932-37; instr. Harvard U., 1938-39; prof. French lang. and lit. McGill U., Montreal, Que., Can., 1940-46, chmn. French lang. and lit., 1940-46; prof. French Bowdoin Coll., 1946-62; prof. linguistics Laval U., Quebec, Que., 1962-75, prof. emeritus, 1975—. Author: books, most recent being Pensée et Structure, 1969, Le français en contact avec l'anglais en Amérique du Nord, 1976. Served with French Army, 1930-31, 39-40. Decorated chevalier de l'Ordre national du Mérite, France). Fellow Royal Soc. Can.; mem. MLA (life emeritus), Can. Linguistic Assn. (pres. 1966-68), Translators Soc. Que. (hon.), Assn. Translators and Interpreters of Ont. (hon.), Conseil international de la langue française. Roman Catholic. Home: 3034 Louvigny Quebec PQ G1W 1B1 Canada Office: Laval U Quebec PQ G1K 7P4 Canada

D'ARBELOFF, DIMITRI VLADIMIR, separations technology manufacturing executive; b. Paris, Oct. 8, 1929; naturalized, 1944; m. Vladimir A. and Catherine (Tiepolt) d'A.; m. Sybil Coe, Aug. 6, 1955; children: Melinda, John, Nicholas. A.B., Harvard U., 1951, M.B.A., 1955. Research asst. Harvard U. Grad. Sch. Bus. Adminstrn., 1955-57; pres. United Research Inc., Cambridge, Mass., 1957-62; v.p., then exec. v.p. Millipore Corp., Bedford, Mass., 1962-71, pres., chief exec. officer, 1971-80, chmn., chief exec. officer, 1980-84, chmn., 1984—; dir. Rexnord Inc., Mass. Fin. Services, Cambridge Trust Co., Black & Decker.; Bd. dirs., chmn. Mass. High Tech. Council; vice chmn. Am. Bus. Conf.; mem. Bus.-Higher Edn. Forum. Trustee Johns Hopkins U.; bd. dirs. Mass. Gen. Hosp.; chmn. trustees com. Applied Physics Lab., Johns Hopkins U., Balt. Served with USNR, 1951-53. Mem. Health Industry Mfrs. Assn. (dir.). Clubs: Harvard, Commercial (Boston); Cambridge Tennis, N.Y. Yacht; N.E. Harbor Fleet (Bar Harbor, Maine). Office: 80 Ashby Rd Bedford MA 01730

DARBY, EDWIN WHEELER, financial editor; b. Oakland, Md., Jan. 7, 1922; s. John Dade and Nell (Bosley) D.; children—Ann Wheeler, John Dade; m. Susan E. Kroening, Mar. 14, 1970; 1 son, George Kroening. B.S. in Journalism, Ohio U. White House corr. Time mag., 1948-55; midwest corr. Time and Fortune mags., 1956-58; financial editor, columnist Chgo. Sun-Times, 1958—. Recipient Marshall Field award, 1974, Loeb award, 1975. Clubs: Tavern, Attic (Chgo.). Home: 2703 W Logan Blvd Chicago IL 60647 Office: Chicago Sun-Times Chicago IL 60611

DARBY, HARRY, former U.S. senator, manufacturing company executive; b. Kansas City, Kans., Jan. 23, 1895; s. Harry and Florence Isabelle (Smith) D.; m. Edith Marie Cubbison, Dec. 17, 1917; children: Harriet Darby Gibson, Joan Darby Edwards, Edith Marie Darby Evans, Marjorie Darby Alford. B.M.E., U. Ill., 1917, M.E., 1929; LL.D., St. Benedict's Coll., Atchison, Kans., Westminster Coll., Fulton, Mo., Kans. State U., Manhattan and Washburn U., Topeka; D.C.S., Baker U., Baldwin City, Kans. With Mo. Boiler Works Co., Kansas City, 1911-19; with Darby Corp., 1920—; now chmn. bd., owner; founder, chmn. Leavenworth Steel, Inc., Darby Ry. Cars, Inc.; dir. numerous corps., U.S. senator from, Kans., 1949-50. Active 4-H Club, Boy Scouts Am.; mem. Republican Nat. Com. for Kans., 1940-64; trustee various cultural instns., assns.; trustee, chmn. Eisenhower Found., Abilene, Kans.; chmn. Eisenhower Presdl. Library Commn., Abilene; mem. Gov.'s Com. Kans. State Fair; chmn. emeritus Am. Royal Livestock and Horse Show; mem. exec. com. Kans. Livestock Assn., Agrl. Hall of Fame; dir., trustee Nat. Cowboy Hall of Fame. Served from 2d lt. to capt., F.A. U.S. Army, 1917-19; with AEF. Recipient numerous awards for civic activities. Fellow ASME; mem. Navy League U.S., Kansas City Crime Commn., Kans. Registration Bd. Profl. Engrs., U. Ill. Found., ASCE, Nat., Kans. soc. profl. engrs., Am. Hereford Assn., Am. Nat. Livestock Assn., Soc. Am. Mil. Engrs., Am. Soc. Agrl. Engrs., VFW, Am. Legion, 40 and 8, Mil. Order World Wars. Episcopalian. Clubs: Masons (32 deg.), Shriners, Jesters, Kansas City, Automobile of Mo., Saddle and Sirloin, Rotary, River, Terr., Man of the Month (Kansas City, Kans.); Chgo.; Chevy Chase, Capitol Hill (Washington); Cherry Hills (Denver); Burning Tree (Bethesda, Md.). Home: 1220 Hoel Pkwy Kansas City KS 66102 Office: 1st St and Walker Ave Kansas City KS 66110

DARBY, JOSEPH BRANCH, JR., metallurgist; b. Petersburg, Va., Dec. 12, 1925; s. Joseph Branch and Jessie Catherine (Frazier) D.; m. Eleanor Lee Daley, Mar. 25, 1951; children—Joseph III, John, Leslie, Peter. B.S., Coll. William and Mary, 1948, Va. Poly. Inst., 1951; M.S., U. Ill., 1955, Ph.D., 1958. Chemist Allied Chem. Corp., Hopewell, Va., 1948-49; devel. engr. Union Carbide Corp., Niagara Falls, N.Y., 1951-53; research scientist Argonne (Ill.) Nat. Lab., 1958—, asso. dir., 1974-78, 1978—; vis.sr. research fellow U. Birmingham, Eng., 1970-71. Co-editor: The Electronic Structure of the Actinides and Related Properties, 2 vols, 1974; mem. adv. bd.: Jour. of Less-Common Metals, 1971—; co-editor: Jour. Nuclear Materials, 1972—; contbr. articles to profl. jours. Mem. Nominating Com. for Sch. Bd., Wheaton, Ill., 1961-63, for Coll. of DuPage Bd. Trustees, 1963-65. Served with A.C. USMC, 1944-46. Sci. Research Council sr. fellow, 1970-71. Fellow Am. Soc. for Metals (mem. energy council div., mem. nuclear metallurgy com.); mem. Metall. Soc. Am. Inst. Mining, Metall. and Petroleum Engrs., ASTM, AAAS, Sigma Xi, Tau Beta Pi, Alpha Sigma Mu, Sigma Gamma Epsilon. Presbyterian (elder). Club: Wheaton Tennis Assn. Home: 1303 Marcey St Wheaton IL 60187 Office: 9700 S Cass Ave Argonne IL 60439

DARBY, MICHAEL RUCKER, economist; b. Dallas, Nov. 24, 1945; s. Joseph Jasper and Frances Adah (Rucker) D.; m. Joanne Tyndale Smith Gibbons, 1979; children—Margaret Loutrel, David Michael. A.B., Dartmouth Coll., 1967; M.A., U. Chgo., 1968, Ph.D., 1970. Asst. prof. econs. Ohio State U., 1970-73; vis. asst. prof. econs. UCLA, 1972-73, assoc. prof., 1973-78, prof., 1978—; research assoc. Nat. Bur. Econ. Research, 1976—; v.p., dir. Paragon Industries, Inc., Dallas, 1964-83. Author: Macroeconomics, 1976, Intermediate Macroeconomics, 1979, The Effects of Social Security on Income and the Capital Stock, 1979, International Transmission of Inflation, 1983; editor: Jour. Internat. Money and Fin, 1981—. Woodrow Wilson fellow, 1967-68; NSF grad. fellow, 1967-69; FDIC grad. fellow, 1969-70; Harry Scheman research fellow Nat. Bur. Econ. Research, 1974-75; vis. fellow Hoover Instn., Stanford U., 1977-78. Mem. Am. Econ. Assn., Am. Fin. Assn., Am. Statis. Assn., Econometric Soc., Mont Pelerin Soc., Royal Econ. Soc., Western Econ. Assn. Episcopalian. Home: 22414 De Kalb Dr Woodland Hills CA 91364 Office: Dept Economics UCLA Los Angeles CA 90024

DARBY, ROBERT FRED, architect; b. Statesboro, Ga., July 10, 1923; s. Fred Wigmore and Ollie Mae (Watson) D.; m. Sara Alice Bradley, June 29, 1943; children: Robert Bradley, Fred Leonard. B.S. in Arch, Ga. Inst. Tech., Atlanta, 1944, B.Arch., 1947. Registered architect, 25 states; cert. Nat. Council Archtl. Registration Bds. Archtl. designer, draftsman Reynolds, Smith & Hills, Jacksonville, Fla., 1947-50, designer, chief draftsman, 1950-53, project mgr., designer, chief architect, 1953-61, mgr. archtl. div., 1961-68, partner, 1968-70, sr. v.p., 1970-73, exec. v.p., 1973—; pres., dir. Reynolds, Smith & Hills of N.C.; v.p., dir. RSH of N.C., Greensboro; pres., dir. Reynolds, Smith & Hills of Conn.; v.p., dir. Trigon Constrn. Mgmt., Inc.; dir. Plantec Corp., Intraspace Designers, Inc., Lewis-Eaton, Inc., Jackson, Miss.; partner Reynolds, Smith & Hills, Lewis-Eaton, Jackson, Darby Lumber Co. Mem. Com. of 100; bd. dirs., past treas., past v.p. Jacksonville Symphony; sec.-treas. Jacksonville U. Council; chmn. City of Jacksonville Bldg. Codes Adjustment Bd.; former treas., v.p. and dir. Theatre Jacksonville; mem. Jacksonville adv. bd. Salvation Army; former mem. Jacksonville Housing and Urban Devel. Bd.; deacon Hendricks Ave. Bapt. Ch. Served to lt. (j.g.) USNR, 1944-46. Mem. AIA (past pres. Jacksonville chpt.), Constrn. Specifications Inst. (past dir. Jacksonville chpt.), Am. Hosp. Assn. (asso.), Am. Assn. Hosp. Planners, Alpha Tau Omega. Clubs: San Jose Country, Ponte Vedra, Univ., River, South Jacksonville Rotary (pres.). Home: 1125 Eutaw St Jacksonville FL 32207 Office: 6737 Southpoint Dr S Jacksonville FL 32207

DARBY, WILLIAM JEFFERSON, JR., physician; b. Galloway, Ark., Nov. 6, 1913; s. William J. and Ruth (Douglass) D.; m. Elva Louise Mayo, June 12, 1935; children—William J., James Richard, Thomas Douglass. B.S., U. Ark., 1936, M.D., 1937; M.S. (Univ. Sigma Xi fellow 1939-40, Horace H. Rackham fellow 1940-41), U. Mich., 1941, Ph.D., 1942, D.Sc. (hon.), 1966, Utah State U., 1973. Instr. phys. chemistry U. Ark. Sch. Medicine, 1937-39; asst. prof. biochemistry, also asst. prof. medicine Vanderbilt U. Sch. Medicine, 1944-46, asso. prof. biochemistry, 1946-48, prof. biochemistry, chmn. dept., dir. div. nutrition, 1949-71, prof. nutrition, 1964-79, prof. medicine in nutrition, 1965-79, prof. biochem. in nutrition, 1972-79, prof. emeritus, 1979—; pres. Nutrition Found., Inc., 1972—; mem. study sect. biochemistry and nutrition, div. research grants and fellowships USPHS, 1948-53, chmn. study sect. on metabolism and nutrition, 1948-53, chmn. study sect. on gen. medicine, 1956-59, mem. com. on selection sr. research fellowships, 1956-59, chmn. study sect. nutrition, 1959-61; mem. food and nutrition bd. NRC, 1949-71, mem. food protection com., 1950-71, chmn., 1954-71; mem. adv. bd. Inst. Nutrition Central Am. and Panama, 1950-64; mem. WHO Expert Adv. Panel on nutrition, 1950—, FAO and WHO Joint Expert Com. on Nutrition, 1954, 57, 61, 66; sci. adv. com. Samuel R. Noble Found., 1953-63, 78, chmn., 1955, 58, 61, 78, Joint FAO-WHO Expert Com. on Food Additives, 1956; cons. Interdeptl. Com. on Nutrition for Nat. Def., 1955-66; co-ordinator WHO Protein adv. group, 1956-60; mem. FAO/WHO/UNICEF Protein Adv. Group, 1960-62; mem. sci. adv. com. Nutrition Found., 1958-65, 67-71, Sci. Adv. Com. Nat. Vitamin Found., 1950-64; Kempner lectr. U. Tex. Med. Bd., Galveston, 1961; Negus lectr. Med. Coll. Va., 1972, Va. Acad. Sci., 1975; W.O. Atwater lectr. U.S. Dept. Agr., 1975, Underwood-Prescott Meml. lectr., 1979; chmn. adv. com. United Health Found., 1962-70; tech. adv. com. Inst. Nutrition Scis., Columbia U., 1966-70; vis. com. dept. nutrition and food sci. Mass. Inst. Tech., 1963-68, 74-76; nat. cons. USAF Surgeon Gen., 1967-72; mem. council on foods and nutrition AMA, 1948-62, 65-73, chmn., 1967-70; mem. commn. on pesticides sec. HEW, 1969-71; mem. long range planning com. FASEB, 1969-70; mem. Tenn. Gov.'s Adv. Commn. on Consumer Protection, 1969-70; mem. adv. com. on nutrition AID, 1968-72; vis. prof. U. Calif. at Davis, 1967; adv. com. on personnel for research Am. Cancer Soc., 1962-65; pub. trustee Food Law Inst., 1962—; mem. bd. basic sci. examiners State of Tenn., 1961-72, pres., 1962-72; mem. bd. commrs. Navajo Health Authority, 1972-77; adv. task force world hunger Presbyn. Ch. U.S., 1972-76; mem. Tenn. Gov.'s Commn. Aging, 1972-76; co-chmn. hazardous materials adv. com. EPA, 1971-74, environ. health adv. com., 1974-79. Co-author: Fermented Food Beverages in Nutrition; asso. editor: Nutrition Revs, 1944-50, Jour. Clin. Investigation, 1950-54. Decorated Order Rodolf Robles, Guatemala; Star of Jordan, 1963; Order Cedars of Lebanon, 1972; recipient Mead-Johnson B-Complex award, 1947; Joseph Goldberger Award AMA, 1964; Thomas Jefferson award Vanderbilt U., 1969; Charles Franklin Craig lectr. Am. Soc. Tropical Med., 1950; Roberts Meml. lectr. U. P.R., 1966; Phi Beta Kappa scholar, 1966-67; Forty-Niner award, 1975. Fellow A.C.P. (master 1973); mem. Nat. Acad. Scis., Am. Chem. Soc. (Spencer award 1972), Am. Inst. Nutrition (pres. 1958, Elvehjem award 1972, Osborne-Mendel award 1962), Am. Public Health Assn., AMA (chmn. council foods and nutrition 1960-62, 67-70), Am. Soc. Biol. Chemists, Soc. Exptl. Biology and Medicine, Nutrition Soc. (Gt. Britain), So. Soc. Clin. Research (v.p. 1948), Am. Fedn. Clin. Research, Am. Soc. Clin. Investigation, Assn. Am. Physicians, Austrian Pub. Health Assn. (hon.), Nat. Med. Assn. Panama, Am. Acad. Scis., Serbian Acad. Scis. (hon. mem.), Philippine Dietetic Assn. (hon.), L'Institute d'Egypte (asso.). Co-discoverer Vitamin M and of activity of pteroylglutamic acid in sprue.

DARBY, WILLIAM LEONARD, financial consultant; b. Eng., 1919; came to U.S., 1921, naturalized, 1928; s. Frederick and Mary (Simpson) D.; m. Dorothy Ruth Hyman, Mar. 14, 1941 (dec. Mar. 1977); 1 son, William Duane.; m. Judith H. Smith, May 16, 1981. B.A., Wayne U., 1942, M.A., 1955. Cost accountant Fisher Body div. Gen. Motors Corp., 1941-42, 46-47; with Allen Industries, 1948-72, v.p., controller, 1965—; v.p. Colonial Rubber Works, Inc., Star Textile & Research Co., Nat. Dyeing & Finishing Corp.; v.p., treas. Frisch Corp., Gordon Chapman Co., Allen Industries Can., Ltd., Dayco Corp., 1971-72; controller Taubman Co., 1972-73; v.p. fin., dir. F. Joseph Lamb Co., Warren, Mich., 1973-80; cons. Lamb Technicon, 1980—; dir. Q & Q Printing Co. Bd. dirs. Marygrove Coll., 1977-80. Served to capt. AUS, 1942-46, 51-52. Lutheran (v.p. congregation). Club: Gowanie Golf (treas. 1978). Home: 589 Anita St Grosse Pointe MI 48236 Office: 5563 E 9 Mile Rd Warren MI 48234

D'ARCAMBAL, THOMAS RADFORD, diversified industry executive; b. Hartford, Conn., Apr. 7, 1931; s. A.H. and Helen (Hathaway) d'A.; m. Joan Hooper, Aug. 9, 1958; children—Michelle, Melissa, Nicole. B.B.A., U. Mich., 1956, M.B.A., 1957. C.P.A., Calif. Auditor Price Waterhouse & Co. (C.P.A.'s), Los Angeles, 1957-59; controller Trousdale Constrn. Co., Los Angeles, 1959-60; treas. Trousdale Enterprises, Honolulu, 1960-65; financial v.p. Amfac Properties, Honolulu, 1965-68; controller Amfac Inc., Honolulu, 1968-83, v.p., 1969-73, sr. v.p., 1973-83, exec. v.p., 1983—; dir. Bay & River Nav. Trustee Le Jardin Acad. Sch., Honolulu Med. Group Research and Edn. Found.; dir. Oahu Devel. Conf.; mem. Hawaii Employers Council. Served with AUS, 1951-53. Mem. Am. Inst. C.P.A.'s, Hawaii Soc. C.P.A.'s, Financial Execs. Inst., Alpha Delta Phi. Clubs: Outrigger Canoe, Oahu Country, Pacific (Honolulu). Home: 919 Maunawili Rd Kailua HI 96734 Office: 700 Bishop St Honolulu HI 96801

D'ARCANGELO, ALLAN MATTHEW, artist; b. Buffalo, June 16, 1930; s. Bartholemew and Anna (Petrella) D'A.; m. Sylvia Rachel Resnick, Feb. 7, 1954; children—Christopher David (dec.), Gabrielle Anna, Gideon Bartholomew. B.S., U. Buffalo, 1952; postgrad., Coll. City N.Y., 1955-56, Mexico City Coll., 1957-59. Instr. Sch. Visual Arts, 1963-68; artist in residence Aspen (Colo.) Inst. Humanistic Studies, 1965, 67; prof. art Cornell U., 1968, Bklyn. Coll., City U. N.Y., 1973—. Vis. artist, Yale U., 1969, U. Syracuse, 1971, U. Ala., 1972, St. Cloud State U., U. Wis., Skowhegan Sch. Art, 1974, Memphis Acad. Art, 1975, one man shows at, Galerie Genova, Mexico City, 1958, L.I. U., 1961, Fischbach Gallery, 1963, 64, 65, 67, 69, Ileana Sonnabend Gallery, Paris, 1965, Rudolf Zwirner Gallery, Cologne, Germany, Hans Neuendorf Gallery, Hamburg, Germany, Gallery Muller, Stuttgart, Germany, Dwan Gallery, Los Angeles, 1966, Wurttembergischer Kunstverein, Stuttgart, Germany, 1967, Galerie Ricke, Kassel, Germany, Minami Gallery, Tokyo, Japan, Obelisk Gallery, Boston, 1967, 70, Franklin Siden Gallery, Detroit, 1968, 69, 72, Gergenverkehr, Aachen, West Germany, 1969, Skylite Gallery, U. Wis., Eau Claire, 1970, Inst. Contemporary Art, U. Pa., Phila., 1971,

Albright-Knox Gallery, Buffalo, Mus. Contemporary Art, Chgo., Marlborough Gallery, N.Y.C., 1971, 75, Elvehjem Art Center, U. Wis., Madison, 1972, Hokin Gallery, Chgo., 1974, Patricia Moore, Inc., Aspen, Schacht Fine Art Center, Russell Sage Coll., 1974, Gallery Kingpitcher, Pitts., 1975, Charles Burchfield Center, Buffalo, 1979-80, Mus. Art, Ft. Lauderdale, Fla., Univ. Gallery, Albany, N.Y., Wichita (Kans.) Art Mus.; exhibited numerous group shows including, Mexican Am. Inst., 1958, Inst. Contemporary Art, London, 1963, Albright-Knox Gallery, Buffalo, 1963, 69, Gemeente Mus., The Hague, 1964, Mus. Modern Art, 1964, 66, 68, Worcester (Mass.) Art Mus., 1965, 75, Milw. Art Center, 1965, Inst. Contemporary Art, Boston, Stedelijk Mus., Amsterdam, 1966, Am. Pavillion Expo 7, Montreal, 1967, IX Bienal de Sao Paulo, Brazil, Whitney Mus. Am. Art, N.Y.C., 1967, 69, 74, Biennal Americana de Artes Graficas, Calif., Columbia, 1973, 76, Weatherspoon Mus., Greensboro, N.C., 1975, Corcoran Gallery Art, Washington, Queens Mus., Flushing, N.Y., 1976, Hirshhorn Mus., Washington, Grey Art Gallery and Study Center, N.Y. U., numerous others; represented in pub. collections at, Mus. Modern Art, N.Y.C., Gemeente Mus., Aldrich Mus., Ridgefield, Conn., Whitney Mus. Am. Art, N.Y.C., Detroit Inst. Arts, Walker Art Center, Mpls., Albright-Knox Gallery, Buffalo, Mus. Contemporary Art, Nagaoka, Japan, Mus. Modern Art, Skopje, Yugoslavia, Mass. Inst. Tech., Whitney Mus. Am. Art, N.Y.C., Bklyn. Mus., N.Y. State Council Arts, Chase Manhattan Bank, N.Y.C., Joseph H. Hirshhorn Mus., Washington, Mus. Art, Cleve., Detroit Inst. Art, numerous others; executed mural for, Transp. and Travel Pavillion N.Y. World's Fair, 1963, mural, Bullfinch Bldg., Boston, N.Y.C. Parks Dept., 1970. Served with Signal Corps AUS, 1954-55. Recipient First Purchase award Nat. Small Painting Show U. Omaha, 1966, List Art Poster Program Commn. award, 1967, First prize Hofstra U., 1967; Annual award Nat. Inst. Arts and Letters, N.Y.C.

DARCY, DAVID KEENE, banker; b. Bklyn., July 21, 1922; s. David K. and Lillian (Webb) D.; m. Betty M. McDow, Sept. 5, 1947; children: Donna Marie, Linda Carol, Maureen Teresa. B.S., Lehigh U., 1946. Sr. v.p. Irving Trust Co., N.Y.C., 1946-79; pres. L.I. Trust Co., Garden City, N.Y., 1980-82, vice chmn., 1982—. Served to 2d lt. USAAF, 1942-45. Club: Garden City Country. Office: 1401 Franklin Ave Garden City NY 11530

DARCY, DONALD, banker; b. N.Y.C., Apr. 21, 1918; s. Michael Stephen and Marie J. (Ryan) D.; m. Geraldine K. Kindermann, Sept. 10, 1943; children: Dwight, Keith, Joan Sorgi. B.A., Fordham Coll., 1942. Exec. sec. Bronx Bd. Trade, N.Y.C., 1948-53; v.p. Bronx County Trust Co., N.Y.C., 1953-55; chmn., chief exec. officer North Side Savs. Bank, N.Y.C., 1956—; mem. Bronx adv. bd. Mfrs. Hanover Bank, N.Y.C., 1979—; trustee Savs. Banks Retirement System, 1982—. Bd. dirs. UN Devel. Corp., N.Y.C., 1982; chmn. bd. trustees Bronx Rotary Found., N.Y.C., 1975; sr. v.p., trustee St. Barnabas Hosp., N.Y.C., 1977; chmn. Bronx div. U.S. Savs. Bond Program, 1981. Recipient Good Scout award Greater N.Y. councils Boy Scouts Am., 1965, Bronze Pelican award Greater N.Y. councils Boy Scouts Am., 1966, Human Rights Citation N.Y. State Div. Human Rights, 1970, Humanitarian award Albert Einstein Med. Coll., 1976. Club: N.Y. Athletic. Home: 25 Parkview Ave Bronxville NY 10708 Office: 185 W 231 St New York NY 10463

DARCY, GEORGE ROBERT, public relations company executive; b. Rochester, N.Y., Aug. 23, 1920; s. George N. and Agnes (Hogan) D.; m. Martha Louise Harbrecht, Apr. 5, 1950; children: George H., Patricia A., Kevin B., Michael J., Elizabeth A. A.B., U. Rochester, 1942. Coll. rep. McGraw-Hill Book Co., N.Y.C., 1947-48, editor indsl. and bus. books, 1949-52; mgr. book div. F.W. Dodge Corp., N.Y.C., 1952- 54; sr. v.p. adminstrn. Rumrill Co., Inc., Rochester, 1954-59; pres. Darcy Communications, Inc., Rochester, 1959-76; also dir.; chmn. bd., chief exec. officer Hutchins/Darcy Inc., 1971-76; pres. Darcy Assoc. Counselors, Inc., 1976—; chmn., treas. DRC Internat. Inc., 1978—; chmn. bd. McGiffert, Mueller, Jones & Darcy Inc., Washington, 1983—; v.p. Internat. Public Relations Group Cos., Inc., 1977—; dir. Smith, Hazlett & Darcy, Inc., Marenco, Inc., Miami, Fla. Pub. information chmn. U.S. Golf Assn. Open Championship, 1968; mem. Monroe County Human Relations Commn., 1970-75, vice chmn., 1972-75; chmn. County Monroe Indsl. Devel. Agy., 1972-76, Independents for Rockefeller, Monroe County, 1970; mem. advisory bd. Am. Humane Assn., 1976-78; trustee Penfield (N.Y.) Bd. Edn., 1959-60, Meml. Art Gallery, U. Rochester, 1968-74; bd. dirs. Met. Rochester Devel. Council, 1972-77. Served to lt. (s.g.) USNR, 1942-46. Mem. Public Relations Soc. Am. (del. nat. assembly 1964-67), Rochester C. of C. (trustee), U. Rochester Assos. (chmn.). Home: 8 Oyster Rake Ln Hilton Head Island SC 29928 Office: 360 Lexington Ave New York NY 10017 also PO Box 1960 Hilton Head Island SC 29925 1701 K St Washington DC

DARCY, JOHN FRANCIS, electronic distribution company executive; b. Homestead, Pa., Aug. 10, 1932; s. Dominic Joseph and Florence Mary (Graham) D.; children: Mark, Christine, Stephanie, Jacqueline. B.S. in Bus. Adminstrn., U. Dayton, Ohio, 1955. With Tex. Instruments Inc., 1959-69; pres. Arrow Electronics Inc., Farmingdale, N.Y., 1969-76, Kierulff Electronics Inc., Los Angeles, 1976-83, Integrated Electronics Corp., Chatsworth, Calif., 1983—; sr. v.p. Ducommun Inc., 1981-83. Served with AUS, 1955-59. Decorated Commendation ribbon. Mem. Nat. Electronic Distbrs. Assn., Am. Electronics Assn. Roman Catholic. Club: North Ranch Country. Home: 23600 Strathern St Canoga Park CA 91304 Office: 20600 Plummer St Chatsworth CA 91311

D'ARCY, JOHN M., bishop; b. Brighton, Mass., Aug. 18, 1932. Student, St. John's Sem., Mass., Angelicum U., Rome. Ordained priest Roman Catholic Ch., 1957; spiritual dir. St. John's Sem.; ordained titular bishop of Medicana and aux. bishop of Boston, 1975—. Office: 127 Lake St Brighton MA 02135 *

DARDEN, EDWIN SPEIGHT, JR., architect; b. Stantonsburg, N.C., Oct. 14, 1920; s. Edwin Speight and Sally (Jordan) D.; m. s. Pauline K. Bartlett, Feb. 26, 1944; children: Edwin Speight, III, Judith Ann, Diane Russell. B.S. in Archtl. Engring., Kans. State U., 1947. Assoc., Fred L. Swartz and William G. Hyberg, Fresno, Calif., 1949-59; partner Nargis and Darden (Architects), Fresno, 1959-71; owner Edwin S. Darden Assos., Fresno, 1971—; mem. state adv. bd. Office of Agriculture and Constrn., 1970-78; cons. ednl. facilities, 1975—. Prin. works include Clovis (Calif.) High Sch., 1969, Clovis W. High Sch., 1976, Ahwahnee Jr. High Sch., Fresno, 1966, Tehipite Jr. High Sch., Fresno, 1973, Fresno County Dept. Health, 1978. Served to 1st lt. C.E., AUS, 1942-46. Fellow AIA; mem. Sigma Phi Epsilon, Alpha Kappa Psi. Presbyterian. Club: Fresno Rotary. Home: 7549 N Toletachi Rd Fresno CA 93711 Office: 5082 N Palm Suite G Fresno CA 93704

DARDEN, SEVERN TEACKLE, actor; b. New Orleans; s. Severn T. and Geraldine (Rubenstein) D.; m. Ann Barodel Grant, 1958 (div.); m. Cynthia Jane Williams, 1968. Ed., Mexico City Coll., U. Mexico, U. Chgo., Bard Coll. Appeared at, Barter Theatre, 1953—56, then, Compass Theatre, Chgo., St. Louis, N.Y.C., 1955-58, Second City, Chgo., Los Angeles, N.Y.C., London, Dublin, 1959-64; played in, Am. Shakespeare Festival, Stratford, 1957-59; in: A Murderer Among Us, 1964; asso. as actor, and/or producer, writer with: films Goldstein, 1963, Double Barreled Detective Story, 1964, Fearless Frank, 1965, The Virgin Pres, 1965, Dead Heat on A Merry-Go-Round, 1966, Luv, 1966, P.J, 1967, The President's Analyst, 1967, The Mad Room, 1968, The Model Shop, 1968; broadway Leda Had a Little Swan, 1968; films They Shoot Horses Don't They, 1969, Pussycat, Pussycat I Love You, 1969, Spanish Portrait, 1969, The Last Movie, 1970, The Hired Hand, 1970, Vanishing Point, 1970, Cisco Pike, 1972, Evry Little Crook And Nanny, 1972, Play it As it Lays, 1972, Conquest of the Planet of the Apes, 1972, The War Between Men and Women, 1972, The Battle For The Planet of the Apes, 1973, Day of the Dolphin, 1973, Skyway to Death, 1973, Hands of the Ripper, 1974, The American Revolution, 1974, Sandburg's Lincoln, 1974, The New Original Wonder Woman, 1975, The Prison Game, Jackson County Jail, The Disappearance of Aimeé, Victory at Entebbe, The Planet of the Apes, Skyway to Death, Stand Up and Blow, Wanda Nevada, 1979, In God We Trust, 1980, Why Would I Lie?, 1980; appeared in: Ovid's Metamorphoses, Festival of Two Worlds, Spoleto, Italy, 1973. Mem. Acad. Motion Picture Arts and Scis. Address: care Robert G Hussong Agy Inc 8271 Melrose Ave Suite 108 Los Angeles CA 90046 *

DARDEN, WILLIAM HOWARD, JR., biology educator; b. Tuscaloosa, Ala., Apr. 25, 1937; s. William Howard and Jannie Belle (Herring) D.; m. Caroline Jackson, July 15, 1959; children: Leanne Carol, Michael Howard. B.S., U. Ala., Tuscaloosa, 1959, M.S., 1961; Ph.D., Ind. U., 1965. Asst. prof. biology U. Ala., Tuscaloosa, 1965-68, assoc. prof., 1969-73, prof., assoc. chmn. dept. biology, 1973-74, prof., chmn. dept. biology, 1982—. Contbr. articles to sci. jours. Bd. dirs. Springhill lake Assn., 1980—, So. Grass Tennis Club, 1979-81, Ala. Credit Union, 1982—. Predoctoral fellow NIH, 1963-65; grantee NSF, 1972, U. Ala., Tuscaloosa, 1965-71. Mem. Am. Soc. Cell Biology, Assn. Southeastern Biologists, Southeastern Assn. Edn. Tchrs. of Sci., Sigma Xi, Beta Beta Beta, Omicron Delta Kappa. Am. Baptist. Home: 11B Springhill Lake Tuscaloosa AL 35405 Office: U Ala PO Box 1927 University AL 35486

DAREFF, HAL, author, editor, publisher; b. Bklyn., May 8, 1920; s. Barnett and Bessie (Littman) D.; m. Gladys Wilkowitz, Sept. 12, 1944; children: Scott, Brooks. Ed., New Sch. Social Research, N.Y.C., Washington and Lee U. Free-lance writer and editor, 1946-52; editor Children's Digest of Parents' Inst. and Better Reading Found., 1952-67; gen. editor Dell Seal Books of Dell Pub. Co., 1963-65; also editorial cons. pub. co.; contbg. editor Parents' mag., 1965-66; editor-in-chief juvenile and young adult books Grosset and Dunlap, Inc., N.Y.C., 1967-69; v.p., pub. Greenwood Press, Inc.; also affiliate Negro Univs. Press, Westport, Conn., 1969-70; pub. cons. New Am. Library, Inc., 1970—; pres., pub. Hyperion Press, Inc., 1972—; pub. cons., 1983—. Author: The First Microscope, 1962 (one of books of year Child Study Assn. 1962), Man in Orbit, 1962, Jacqueline Kennedy: A Portrait in Courage, 1965, Fun with ABC and 1-2-3, 1965, The Story of Vietnam (one of books of yr. Child Study Assn. Am.), 1966 (chosen 1 of 75 best books of yr. N.Y. Times 1966), From Vietnam to Cambodia, 1971 (Best Books of The Year list Library Jour. 1971). Served with AUS, 1941-45. Mem. Authors Guild, Artists and Writers Assn., Authors League Am. Home: RFD Box 4186 Beaucaire Ave Camden ME 04843

DARGEL, MERLE WILLIAM, tractor company executive; b. Peoria, Ill., June 12, 1920; s. Raymond D. and Mable E. (Arons) D.; m. Adeline M. Peterson, Dec. 11, 1943; children: Dennis K. (dec.), Kenneth B., Janet K. B.S. IN M.E., Ill. Inst. Tech, 1943; postgrad., MIT, 1963. Eastern div. service mgr. Caterpillar Tractor Co., Peoria, 1952-54, asst. gen. service mgr., 1954-60, gen. service mgr., 1960-64; mng. dir. Caterpillar of Australia, Melbourne, 1964-66, Caterpillar Tractor Co. Ltd., Glasgow, Scotland, 1966-76; v.p. Caterpillar Tractor Co., Peoria, 1976—; dir. Caterpillar Far East Ltd., Hong Kong, Caterpillar Mitsubishi Ltd., Tokyo, Caterpillar Australia Ltd., Caterpillar China Ltd., Tractor Engrs. Ltd., Bombay, others. Mem. exec. com. U.S.-ASEAN Bus. Council, Washington, 1982—. Served to lt. (j.g.) USN, 1944-46. Decorated comdr. Brit. Empire. Fellow Brit. Inst. Mgmt. Republican. Presbyterian. Clubs: Country of Peoria; St. George's Hill Lawn and Tennis (Wybridge Surrey, Eng.). Home: 7312 N Edgewild Dr Peoria IL 61614 Office: 100 NE Adams St Peoria IL 61629

DARGUSCH, CARLTON SPENCER, lawyer; b. Batavia, N.Y., Aug. 19, 1900; s. Julius Herman and Etta (Burnham) D.; m. Genevieve Johnston, Nov. 6, 1923; children—Carlton Spencer (dec.), Evelyn Byrd (Mrs. Charles A. Lanphere). Student, Ind. U., 1921-22, Ohio State U., 1922- 25. Legislative draftsman Ohio Gen. Assembly, 1925; atty. Tax Commn. of Ohio, 1925-33; tax commr. of, Ohio, 1933-37, resigned, Jan. 1937, engaged in pvt. practice of law, specializing in taxation, Columbus, Ohio, 1937—; dir. Clark Grave Vault Co.; cons. Engring. Manpower Commn.; Mem. com. specialized personnel, asst. dir. manpower ODM, 1955-57; mem. U.S. del. Conf. Applied Research in Europe, Vienna, Austria, 1956, India, 1958, USSR, 1960. Author: (with John R. Cassidy) Estate and Inheritance Taxation, 1930, rev. 1956, (with Jack H. Bertsch) The Operation of Selective Service in World War II, 1956. Trustee Ohio State U., 1938-59, 63-65, chmn. bd. trustees, 1944-45, 51-52, 58-59; dir. Ohio State U. Research Found., 1951-62. Active duty lt. col., Judge Adv. General's Dept. U.S. Army, 1940-47; dep. dir. nat. hdqrs. SSS; promoted colonel, 1942; brig. gen., 1946. Awarded D.S.M., 1946. Mem. Omicron Kappa Upsilon (hon.), Kappa Sigma, Phi Delta Phi, Mil. Order World Wars. Clubs: Mason., Chevy Chase (Md.); Army and Navy (Washington); Columbus Country, Columbus, Ohio State Faculty, Ohio State U. Sphinx (Columbus); Engineers, Chemists, The Players (N.Y.C.); Union (Cleve.); Queen City (Cin.). Helped draft plans for SSS, World War II and present; also plans for Universal Mil. Tng. Home: 271 N Columbia Ave Columbus OH 43209 Office: 218 E State St Columbus OH 43215

DARION, JOE, librettist, lyricist; b. N.Y.C., Jan. 30, 1917; s. Isak and Rose (Nadelle) D.; m. Hellen Solomon, June 8, 1940. Student journalism, CCNY. Lyricist of: popular songs, including Ricochet, Changing Partners, Midnight Train, 1954-58; librettist opera, cantatas, song cycles including: jazz opera Archy and Mehitabel; New Orleans Cantata, 1956-60; playwright, lyricist for: Broadway prodns. Shinbone Alley, 1957; lyricist: Man of La Mancha, 1965, Illya Darling, 1967; librettist for: oratorio Galileo, 1967; writer: English sect. bilingual musical The Megilla, 1968; screenplay, lyrics Archy and Mehitabel, 1969; librettist for: cantata And David Wept, 1970, The Questions of Abraham, 1972; for Christmas cantata A Handful of Souls, 1975, A Mass for Cain, 1978; opera Galileo Galilei, 1979; (Recipient Antoinette Perry award 1965, 66). Served with USNR, World War II; PTO. Recipient Antoinette Perry award, 1965, 66; Drama Critics Circle award, 1965-66; Outer-Critics Circle award, 1965, 66; Internat. Broadcasting award, 1964; Gold Records award; Gabriel award, 1974; Ohio State award Ohio State U. Telecommunications Center, 1975; Songwriters Hall of Fame Yr. Mem. A.S.C.A.P., Am. Guild Authors and Composers, Dramatists Guild, Nat. Acad. Rec. Arts and Scis. Jewish. Address: Pinnacle Rd Lyme NH 03768

D'ARISTA, ROBERT AUGUSTUS, artist; b. N.Y.C., July 2, 1929; s. Umberto and Caroline (Maruzzella) D'A.; m. Jane Webb, Oct. 30, 1954; children: Carla, Peter, Thomas, Antonia. Student, N.Y. U., 1948-50, Columbia U., 1950-52. Art instr. Wash. Bd. Edn., 1961; mem. teaching staff Am. U., 1961—; vis. prof. Boston U., summer 1970, 71, spring 1973, 78. Self employed as artist, 1954-61; one man shows, N.Y.C., 1955, 56, 59, 62, 64, 67, 68, Boston, 1971, Washington, 1957, 62, 77, 80, 81, group shows include, Carnegie Internats., Whitney Anns., Pa. Acad., Art Inst. Chgo., Guggenheim Mus., Ill. Biennial, Bogota Biennial, Detroit Mus., Bklyn. Mus., others; represented in permanent collections, Toledo Mus., Yale U., Hirshorn Mus., Neuberger., Nat. Collection. Recipient Richard and Hinda Rosenthal Found. award Nat. Inst. Arts and Letters, 1967. Home: 4805 Langdrum Ln Chevy Chase MD 20815

DARK, ALVIN RALPH, golf professional, former baseball executive; b. Comanche, Okla., Jan. 7, 1922; m. Jackie Dark; children: Allison, Gene, Eve, Margaret, Laura, Rusty. Student, La. State U., Southwestern La. Inst. Profl. baseball player, 1946-60; field mgr. San Francisco Giants, 1961-64, Kansas City Athletics, 1966-67, Cleve. Indians, 1968-71; mgr. Oakland (Calif.) Athletics, 1974, 75, San Diego Padres, 1977; coach Chgo. Cubs, 1965, spl. scout, 1981; now dir. golf, golf profl. Smithfield's, Easley, S.C. Served with USMCR. Named Rookie of Year Nat. League and Am. League, 1948. Mem. Nat. League All-Star Team, 1951, 52, 54, The Sporting News All-Star Major Team, 1954; All-Am. football player Southwestern La. Inst. Address: Smithfields 1311 Crestview Rd Easley SC 29640 *

DARK, PHILIP JOHN CROSSKEY, anthropologist, educator; b. London, Eng., May 15, 1918; s. John Noel and Annie (Crosskey) D.; m. Mavis Helena Boam, Mar. 7, 1942; children: Gail Susan, Victoria Eve. Student, Bradfield Coll., Berkshire, Eng., 1935; diploma in art, Slade Sch. Fine Art, London, 1948; M.A., Yale U., 1950, Ph.D. in Anthropology (spl. fellow social sci. 1950-51), 1954. Adminstrv. sec., asst. registrar W. African Inst. Social and Econ. Research, U. Ibadan, Nigeria, 1954-56; sr. research fellow U. Ibadan, 1957-60; prof. anthropology So. Ill. U., 1960-78, emeritus, 1978—, chmn. dept., 1963-66; research assoc. African ethnology Field Mus. Natural History, 1963—, Met. Mus. Art, 1977-80; Mem. Com. on Anthrop. Research in Museums, 1964-74; Bd. dirs. Human Relations Area Files, Inc., 1974-78; council for Museum Anthropology, 1974-78; mem. exec. com. Pacific Arts Assn., 1978—. Author: Bush Negro Art, 1954, 70, 71, Mixtec Ethnohistory: A Method of Analysis of the Codical Art, 1958, (with W. and B. Forman) Benin Art, 1960, The Art of Benin, A Catalogue of the A.W.F. Fuller and Chicago Natural History Museum Collections of Antiquities from Benin, Nigeria, 1962, An Introduction to Benin Art and Technology, 1973, Kilenge Art and Life: A Look at a New Guinea People, 1974, An Illustrated Catalogue of Benin Art, 1982; Editor: Pacific Arts Newsletter, 1975—. Served to lt. Royal Naval Vol. Res., 1940-46. Leverhulme Research fellow Univ. Coll., London, 1956-57; Sigma Xi-Kaplan Research award for anthropol. research in New Guinea, 1968. Fellow Am. Anthrop. Assn., Royal Anthrop. Inst.; mem. Soc. des Oceanistes, R.N.V.R. Officers Assn., Hakluyt Soc., Nigerian Hist. Soc., Soc. for Anthropology of Visual Communication (dir. 1974-78), Pacific Arts Assn. (exec. com. 1978—). Home: Saben Upper Castle Rd Saint Mawes Cornwall TR2 5BZ England

DARLING, BYRON THORWELL, physicist, educator; b. Napoleon, Ohio, Jan. 4, 1912; s. Frank Ellsworth and Evalyn Louise (Young) D.; m. Barbara Anne Borgogni, Aug. 24, 1946. B.Sc., U. Ill., 1933, M.Sc., 1936; postgrad., U. Mich., 1936-38, Ph.D., 1939, U. Wis., 1938-39. Instr. math. Mich. State Coll., 1939-41; instr. physics Pa. State Coll., 1941; research physicist U.S. Rubber Co., Detroit, 1941-46; research asso. U. Wis., 1946-47; research asso. with rank of instr. Yale U., 1947; asst. prof. physics Ohio State U., 1947-51, asso. prof., 1951-53; prof. theoretical physics Laval U., Quebec, Que., Can., 1955—; adj. vis. prof. U. Fla., Gainesville, 1980. Contbr. articles to sci. jours. Mem. Am. Phys. Soc., Can. Assn. Physicists, Assn. Canadienne Francaise pour l'Avancement des Sciences, N.Y. Acad. Scis., AAAS, Am. Assn. Physics Tchrs., Soc. Profl. Engrs. Que. Co-inventor synthetic rubber and various rubber machinery. Home: 2632 Chemin des Quatre Bourgeois Quebec PQ G1V 1W9 Canada Office: U Laval Faculte des Sciences Cite Universitaire Quebec PQ G1K 7P4 Canada

DARLING, CHARLES DOUGLAS, psychiatrist; b. Walkerton, Ind., July 7, 1905; s. Charles Davis and Gertrude (Peebles) D.; m. Ruth Walton, July 11, 1938; children—Charles (dec.), Barbara. B.S. summa cum laude, Lafayette Coll., 1929; M.D., U. Pa., 1933. Intern Presbyn. Hosp., Phila., 1933-35; physician George School, 1935-37; grad. tng. Pa. Hosp., Phila., 1937-38; mem. faculty Cornell U., 1938—, prof. clin. medicine (Ithaca) and head mental hygiene div. dept. univ. health services, 1944-69, prof. psychiatry emeritus, 1969—; practice medicine specializing in psychiatry, 1969—; attending physician Cornell U. and clinic, from 1940; cons. physician Tompkins County Meml. Hosp., from 1941; Mem. Med. Adv. Bd., World War II; Participated in insts. on mental and public health; lectr. Fellow Am. Psychiat. Assn. (life, chmn. com. on acad. edn. 1958-61); mem. N.Y. State Soc. Mental Health (pres.), AMA, N.Y. State Med. Soc. (life), Phi Beta Kappa. Home and Office: 111 Midway Rd Ithaca NY 14850 Office: 111 Midway Rd Ithaca NY 14850 *My essential philosophy is found in a poem I wrote: No matter what the age, the time is now. Since one is truly unprepared for joy or sorrow, choose now to drive, to work, to love; and not to fear, forever.*

DARLING, FRANK CLAYTON, political science educator; b. Chgo., May 8, 1925; s. Frank D. and Nora (Pomeroy) D.; m. Ann Bardwell, June 10, 1952; children: Diane Christine, Heather Ann, Elizabeth Carolyn. B.A., Principia Coll., Elsah, Ill., 1951; M.A., U. Chgo., 1957; Ph.D., Am. U., 1960. Lectr. Chulalongkorn U., Thailand, 1953-56; prof. U. Colo., 1960-67; prof. polit. sci., head dept. DePauw U., 1967-79; prof. polit. sci. Principia Coll., 1981—. Author: Thailand and The United States, 1965, Thailand: The Modern Kingdom, 1971, The Westernization of Asia: A Comparative Political Analysis, 1979. Served with USNR, 1943-46. Mem. Am. Polit. Sci. Assn., Assn. Asian Studies. Address: Principia Coll Elsah IL 62028

DARLING, GEORGE BAPST, JR., educator; b. Boston, Dec. 30, 1905; s. George Bapst and Alice Emma (Smith) D.; m. Ann F. Shaw, June 25, 1931. Ed., Phillips Acad., Andover Mass.; S.B., Mass. Inst. Tech., Cambridge, 1927; Dr.P.H., U. Mich., 1931, LL.D., 1975; M.A. (hon.), Yale, 1947. Research assoc., asst. epidemiologist Dept. Health, Detroit, 1927-32; with W. K. Kellogg Found., Battle Creek, Mich., 1932-43, beginning as asso. dir., mem. bd. trustees and asso. sec.-treas., 1934-37, comptroller, 1937, pres., 1940-43; dir. Atlas Properties, Inc., 1934-43, pres., 1940-43; dir. Kellogg Co., 1941-43; exec. sec. coms. on mil. medicine NRC, 1943-45, vice chmn. div. med. scis., 1944-45, 47-48; exec. sec. Nat. Acad. Sci. and NRC, 1946; dir. med. affairs Yale U., 1946-52, prof. human ecology, 1952-74, prof. emeritus, 1974—, life fellow emeritus Timothy Dwight Coll., 1974—; on leave as dir. Atomic Bomb Casualty Commn. NRC-Nat. Acad. Sci., Hiroshima and Nagasaki, Japan, 1957-72; on leave as Fogarty scholar Fogarty Internat. Center for Advanced Study in Health Scis., NIH, Bethesda, Md., 1973-74; vis. lectr. Hiroshima Sch. Medicine, Hiroshima Sch. Nursing.; Chmn. health div. New Haven Council Social Agys., 1954-57; bd. dirs. Grace New Haven Community Hosp., 1946-59, exec. com., 1946-53; bd. dirs. Conn. Health League. Civilian observer Joint Task Force 1, Bikini Atom Bomb test, 1946. Contbr. articles on public health and edn. to jours. Asso. Yale Med. Library, Art Gallery, Peabody Mus. Recipient Golden Orchid Supreme award Japan Med. Soc., 1967; Japan Red Cross medallion, 1967; Citation medal AEC, 1970; cert. of appreciation AEC, 1972; citations Japan Tb Assn., Combined Rotary Clubs, Hiroshima, gov. Hiroshima, mayor

Hiroshima, U. Hiroshima, Hiroshima Med. Assn., Japan Ministry Health and Welfare, 1972, U.S. sec. state, 1972; medallion Atomic Bomb Casulty Commn.-Japan Nat. Inst. Health; award for distinguished contbns. to research adminstrn. Soc. Research Adminstrs., 1974. Fellow Am. Pub. Health Assn. (mem. com. adminstrv. practice); mem. Washington Acad. Medicine, AAAS (life), Conn. Med. Soc. (Asso.), Radiation Research Soc. of Japan, Japan Pub. Health Assn., Hiroshima Med. Soc. (hon.), Am. C. of C. of Japan, Japan-Am. socs. Nagasaki, Hiroshima, Washington, Acad. Polit. Sci., N.Y. Acad. Scis., Delta Omega (past pres.), Pi Delta Epsilon, Theta Chi, Mortar and Ball, Ursa Major. Unitarian. Clubs: Mory's Assn., Rotary (Hiroshima and New Haven) (Paul Harris fellow); Beaumont Medical, Yale Faculty (New Haven); Yale (N.Y.C.); Cosmos (Washington). Address: Whitney Wood 1171 Whitney Ave Hamden CT 06517 Address: Cut in Two Island Stony Creek CT 06405

DARLING, JOHN ROTHBURN, JR., educator, univ. adminstr.; b. Holton, Kans., Mar. 30, 1937; s. John Rothburn and Beatrice Noel (Deaver) D.; m. Melva Jean Fears, Aug. 20, 1958; children: Stephen, Cynthia, Gregory. A.A., Graceland Coll., 1957; B.S., U. Ala., 1959, M.S., 1960; Ph.D., U. Ill., 1967. Divisional mgr. J.C. Penney Co., 1960-63; grad. teaching asst. U. Ill., Urbana, 1965-66; asst. prof. mktg. U. Ala., Tuscaloosa, 1966-68; assoc. prof. mktg. U. Mo., Columbia, 1968-71; prof. adminstrn., coordinator mktg. Wichita State U., 1971-76; dean, prof. mktg. Coll. Bus. and Adminstrn., So. Ill. U., Carbondale, 1976-81; v.p. acad. affairs Tex. Tech U., Lubbock, 1981—; mktg. research cons. Southwestern Bell, 1970; sr. v.p. Boothe Advt., Wichita, 1972; pres. Bus. Research Assos., 1972-76; cons. Bus. Research assocs., 1976—; spl. cons. FTC, Washington, 1972-75, U.S. Dept. Justice, 1973-74, Atty. Gen., State of Kans., 1972-76, Dist. Atty., 18th Jud. Dist., Wichita, 1972-76. Author: (with Harry A. Lipson) Marketing Fundamentals, Text and Cases, 1974; Contbr. articles to profl. jours. Bd. dirs. Outreach Found., 1973-79, v.p., 1975-77; bd. trustees Graceland Coll., Lamoni, Iowa, 1976—; mem. mgmt. com. Park Coll., Kansas City, 1976-79. Mem. Am. Assn. Higher Edn., Assn. Governing Bds. Univs. and Colls., Internat. Council Small Bus., Am. Mktg. Assn., Acad. Internat. Bus., Am. Econs. Assn., So. Bus. Adminstrn. Assn., So. Mktg. Assn., So. Econs. Assn., Midwest Bus. Adminstrn. Assn., Sales and Mktg. Execs. Internat., Beta Gamma Sigma, Alpha Kappa Psi, Chi Alpha Phi, Alpha Phi Omega. Mem. Reorganized Ch. of Jesus Christ of Latter Day Saints. Home: 3302 41st St Lubbock TX 79413 Office: Texas Tech Univ Lubbock TX 79409

DARLING, LOIS MACINTYRE (MRS. LOUIS DARLING), illustrator-author; b. N.Y.C., Aug. 15, 1917; d. Malcolm and Grace (Hamilton) McIntyre; m. Louis Darling, June 3, 1946. Student, Grand Central Sch. Art, and pvt. studies, 1935-40; student zoology, Columbia, 1947-51. Staff artist dept. paleontology, Am. Museum Natural History, N.Y.C., 1952-54; author, illustrator, 1948—; Author-illustrator: (with Louis Darling) Before and After Dinosaurs, 1959, Sixty Million Years of Horses, 1960, Turtles, 1962, The Science of Life, 1961, Bird, 1962, Coral Reefs, 1963, The Sea Serpents Around Us, 1965, A Place in the Sun, 1968, Worms, 1972, H.M.S. Beagle-Further Research or Twenty Years a-Beagling, 1977, A Study of H.M.S. Beagle, World Renowned Ship of the Royal Navy, 1982; illustrator: Sou'West and by West of Cape Cod, 1948, The Middle Road, 1961, Evolution of the Vertebrates, 1955, 69, 80, Where the Sea Breaks Its Back, 1966, Mystic Seaport Watercraft, 1980; others Silent Spring, 1962, The Birds, 1963, Animal Behavior, 1965, The Appalachians, 1965, others. Served with WAVES, 1943-45. Mem. Conn. Conservationists, Inc (dir., treas. 1955-56), Nat. Audubon Soc., Westport Audubon Soc. (conservation chmn 1955-61), Nature Conservancy, Am. Inst. Biol. Scis., Authors Guild, Soc. Illustrators, Catboat Assn., Thames Sci. Center. Nat. Women's Sailing Champion, 1941. Address: 4 Smith Neck Rd Route 5 Old Lyme CT 06371

DARLING, RALPH CLEMENT, peripheral vascular surgeon; b. Richmond, Calif., Aug. 28, 1927; s. Ralph Clement and Ruth (Alger) D.; m. Elaine Cicma, Mar. 25, 1948; children—Cynthia, Clement, Wendy, Beth. A.B., Boston U., 1949, M.D. cum laude, 1954. Diplomate: Am. Bd. Surgery, Am. Bd. Thoracic Surgery. Intern Mass. Gen. Hosp., 1953-54; asst. in pathology Children's Hosp., Boston, 1955; resident in surgery Children's Med. Center, Boston, 1955, cons. vascular surgery, 1969—; asst. resident, then clin. asst. surgery Mass. Gen. Hosp., 1956-59, chief vascular clinic, 1969—, sr. vascular surgeon, 1979—; chief resident in thoracic and cardiac surgery, asst. in surgery Baylor U. Hosp., Houston, 1959-60; mem. faculty Harvard U. Med. Sch., 1964—, asso. clin. prof. surgery, 1975—; cons. M.I.T., USPHS, USAF, Walter Reed Army Med. Center. Contbr. numerous articles to med. jours. Served with USMCR, 1944-46. Mem. AMA, Am. Thoracic Soc., A.C.P., Am. Fedn. Clin. Research, Mass. Med. Soc., New Eng. Cardiovascular Soc., Boston Surg. Soc., Soc. Vascular Surgery, Am. Coll. Chest Surgeons, Am. Geriatric Soc., Am. Assn. Surgery Traima, New Eng. Surg. Soc., Internat. Cardiovascular Soc., Pan-Pacific Surg. Assn., Am. Trauma Soc. (a founder), Am. Heart Assn. (exec. council cardiovascular surgery), Assn. Advanced Med. Instrumentation, New Eng. Soc. Vascular Surgery (pres. 1980), Royal Soc. Medicine, Am. Surg. Assn., Soc. Internat. Chirurgie, Alpha Omega Alpha. Home: 18 Emerson Pl Boston MA 02114 Office: 3 Hawthorne Pl Boston MA 02114

DARLING, RICHARD LEWIS, librarian, univ. dean; b. Great Falls, Mont., Jan. 19, 1925; s. Harry and Faye (Willey) D.; m. Persis Ann Williams, Dec. 11, 1947; children—Richard Lewis, Jere Andrew, Katherine Elizabeth; m. Pamela Ann Wood, May 5, 1973. B.A., U. Mont., 1948, M.A., 1950; M.L.S., U. Mich., 1954, Ph.D., 1960. Tchr. Choteau (Mont.) Pub. Schs., 1950-51; librarian U. Mich. High Sch., 1951-56; asst. prof. U. Mont., 1956-59; coordinator sch. libraries Livonia (Mich.) Pub. Schs., 1959-62; sch. library specialist U.S. Office Edn., 1962-64; supr. libraries Montgomery County Pub. Schs., Md., 1964-65, asst. dir. dept. edn. media and tech., 1965-66, dir., 1966-70; dean Sch. Library Service, Columbia, N.Y.C., 1970—. Author: Survey of School Library Standards, 1964, The Rise of Children's Book Reviewing in America, 1865-1881, 1968; editor: Extended Library Education Programs, 1980. Pres. Freedom to Read Found., 1974-77. Served with AUS, 1943-46. Recipient Dutton-MacRae award Am. Library Assn., 1959. Mem. Assn. Am. Library Schs., Am. Assn. Sch. Librarians (past pres.), A.L.A. (2d v.p. 1970-71, chmn. bldgs. and equipment sect. 1970-71)

DARLING, ROBERT EDWARD, opera company executive, stage director, designer; b. Oakland, Calif., Oct. 1, 1937; s. Irving Jackson and Helen Ellen (Hebel) D.; m. Ann Farris, Aug. 22, 1970. B.A., San Francisco State U., 1959; M.F.A., Yale U. Sch. Drama, 1963; student, Bayreuth Festspiel Meisterclasse, 1965. Mem. opera-musical theatre policy panel Nat. Endowment for Arts; panelist Nat. Opera Inst. Designer, dir. numerous opera, theatre and ballet prodns., throughout U.S. and Can., 1960—; N.Y.C. debut with Another Evening with Harry Stoones, 1962; San Francisco Opera debut with L'Elisir d'Amore, 1967; Chgo. Lyric Opera debut with Don Carlo, 1972; N.Y.C. Opera debut with Der Fliegende Hollander, 1976; dir. and designer for: world premiers of Medea, 1972, Colonel Johnathan the Saint, 1972, The Infanta, 1975, The Last of the Mohicans, 1976, The Face, 1978, Soyazhe, 1979; artistic coordinator, Spring Opera Theatre, San Francisco, 1972; artistic adv., Kansas City (Mo.) Lyric Theatre, 1973; co-founder/prin. dir., Hidden Valley Opera Ensemble, Carmel, Calif., 1974-77; artistic dir., Central City Opera House Assn., Denver, from 1977, designs represented in collection Am. design, Smithsonian Museum, N.Y.C.; Contbr. articles to profl. jours. Mem. United Scenic Artists, Am. Guild Musical Artists, Actors Equity-Can., Opera Am., Logan Circle Assn. Democrat. Lutheran. *

DARLINGTON, OSCAR GILPIN, historian, educator; b. Downingtown, Pa., Feb. 21, 1909; s. Oscar Gilpin and Emily Jane (Bareford) D.; m. Miriam Howe Wilson, Dec. 31, 1938; children: Helen Spear, Dawn, Mahlon Spear, Phoebe, Lynette, Gerbert, Eunice, Emily-Jane, Bernice. B.A., Pa. State Coll., 1932, M.A., 1933; Ph.D., U. Pa., 1938; student, Harvard U., summer 1931, Temple U., summer 1932. Asst. in ancient and mediaeval history U. Pa., 1934-38; instr. history Hofstra Coll., N.Y.U., 1938, asst. prof., 1939, assoc. prof., 1940, prof., 1941-50, chmn. dept. history, 1942-50, dir. summer session, 1949; prof. history, polit. sci., head dept., dir. area social scis. Champlain Coll., State U. N.Y., 1950-53; acad. dean InterAm. U. P.R., 1953-55; dean Coll. Liberal Arts, Ohio No. U., Ada, 1955-66, European-Am. Study Center, Basel, Switzerland, 1967-68, prof. European history, 1968—, dir. summer session, 1956-59; faculty adviser Student Christian Assn., Champlain Coll.; Bd. dirs. Regional Council for Internat. Edn., 1964-72. Author: The Travels of Odo Rigaud, Archbishop of Rouen (1248-1275), 1940, (with others) Contemporary Europe: A Symposium, 1941, Causes and Consequences of World War II, 1948, Glimpses of Nassau County History, 1949; newspaper column History Back of the News, 1942-45; articles (Gerbert [Pope Sylvester II] and 10th C. France), revs. hist. jours.; Editor, trustee: Nassau County Hist. Jour, 1944-50. Nat. trustee Children's Internat. Summer Villages; mem. Ada Sch. Bd., 1976-83. Mem. L.I. Hist. Soc., NEA, Mediaeval Acad. Am., Am. Hist. Assn., Am. Soc. Ch. History, Am. Acad. Social and Polit. Sci., Soc. Preservation and Encouragement Barbershop Quartet Singing in Am. (Lima Beane chpt.), U.S. Power Squadron, Phi Alpha Theta, Pi Gamma Mu, Phi Kappa Psi, Sigma Delta Pi. Republican. Methodist (lay preacher). Club: Torch (Lima) (pres. 1961). Lodge: Rotary. Home: 1731 Allentown Rd Apt 105 Lima OH 45205

DARLINGTON, RICHARD BENJAMIN, psychology educator, consultant; b. Woodbury, N.J., Nov. 16, 1937; s. Charles Joseph and Eleanor (Collins) D.; m. Elizabeth Day, June 13, 1959; children: Jean Susan, Lois Heather. B.A., Swarthmore Coll., 1959; Ph.D., U. Minn., 1963. Asst. prof. psychology Cornell U., Ithaca, N.Y., 1963-68, assoc. prof., 1968-80, prof., 1980—; v.p. Found. Human Service Studies, Ithaca, N.Y., 1979—. Author: Radicals and Squares, 1975, (with others) Lasting Effects of Early Education, 1982; contbr. articles to profl. jours., chpts. to books. Project dir. Am. Friends Service Com., 1960, 61. Fellow NSF, 1963-64, Woodrow Wilson Found., 1963-64; grantee HEW, 1977-81, Office of Edn., 1966-67, 70-71, Dept. of Labor, 1980-81. Mem. Phi Beta Kappa. Quaker. Home: 204 Fairmount Ave Ithaca NY 14850 Office: Dept of Psychology Uris Hall Cornell University Ithaca NY 14853

DARLINGTON, SIDNEY, educator, electrical engineer; b. Pitts., July 18, 1906; s. Philip Jackson and Rebecca Taylor (Mattson) D.; m. Joan Gilmer Raysor, Apr. 24, 1965; children: Ellen Sewall, Rebecca Mattson. B.S. magna cum laude, Harvard U., 1928, MIT, 1929; Ph.D. in Physics, Columbia U., 1940. Mem. tech. staff Bell Telephone Labs., Murray Hill, N.J., 1929-71, head dept., 1960-71; ret., 1971; adj. prof. elec. engring. U. N.H., Durham, 1971—; cons. in field, 1971—; Mem. U.S. commn. VI Internat. Sci. and Radio Union, 1959-75, del. gen. assemblies, 1960, 63, 66, 69. Author. Recipient Medal of Freedom U.S. Army. Fellow IEEE (Edison medal, Medal of Honor 1981), AIAA; mem. Nat. Acad. Engring., Nat. Acad. Scis., Phi Beta Kappa. Club: Appalachian Mountain. Patentee in field. Home: 8 Fogg Dr Durham NH 03824 *Life is a chancy business; my blessings have far outnumbered my adversities.*

DARLOW, JULIA DONOVAN, lawyer; b. Detroit, Sept. 18, 1941; d. Frank William Donovan and Helen Adele Turner; m. George Anthony Gratton Darlow (div.); 1 dau., Gillian; m. 2d John Corbett O'Meara. A.B., Vassar Coll., 1963; postgrad., Columbia U. Law Sch., 1964-65; J.D. cum laude, Wayne State U., 1971. Bar: Mich. 1971, U.S. Dist. Ct. (ea. dist.) Mich. 1971. Assoc. Dickinson, Wright, McKean, Cudlip and Moon, Detroit, 1971-78; ptnr. Dickinson, Wright, Moon, Van Dusen & Freeman, Detroit, 1978—; adj. prof. Wayne State U. Law Sch., 1974-75. Reporter: Mich. Nonprofit Corp. Act, 1977-82. Bd. dirs. Detroit Grand Opera Assn., 1978—; mem. Blue Cross-Blue Shield Prospective Reimbursement Com., Detroit, 1979-81; mem. allocation and rev. com. United Found., Detroit, 1982—. Fellow Am. Bar Found.; mem. State Bar Mich. (commr. 1977—, exec. com. 1979-83, sec. 1980-81, council Corp. Fin. and Bus. Law Sect. 1980—), Detroit Bar Assn. Found. (trustee 1982—), Women Lawyers Assn. (pres. 1977-78), Mich. Women's Campaign Fund (charter). Democrat. Club: Renaissance (Detroit). Office: 800 First Nat Bldg Detroit MI 48226

DARMAN, MORTON H., business exec.; b. Woonsocket, R.I., 1916. Grad., Brown U., 1937. Pres. dir. Top Co., Boston; pres., dir. Ivy Enterprises, Inc.; dir. Johnson Products, Inc., Washburn Energy Corp.; past pres. Am. Textile Mfrs. Inst.; mem. President's Adv. Com. on Trade Negotiations. Home: 231 Aspen Circle Lincoln MA 01773 Office: 51 Sleeper St Boston MA 02210

DARMAN, RICHARD GORDON, educator, business consultant, White House official; b. Charlotte, N.C., May 10, 1943; m. Kathleen Emmet, Sept. 1, 1967; children: William Temple Emmet, Jonathan Warren Emmet. B.A. cum laude, Harvard U., 1964, M.B.A., 1967. Dep. asst. sec. HEW, Washington, 1971-72; asst. to sec. Dept. Def., Washington, 1973; spl. asst. to atty. gen., Washington, 1973; fellow Woodrow Wilson Internat. Center for Scholars, Washington, 1974; prin., dir. ICF, Inc., Washington, 1975, 77-80; asst. sec. Dept. Commerce, 1976-77; vice chmn. U.S. del. UN Conf. on Law of Sea, 1977; lectr. public policy and mgmt. Harvard U., 1977-80; asst. to Pres. Reagan, White House, Washington, 1981—; Dir. Johnson Products, Inc., 1972-75; mem. U.S. del. Summit of Industrialized Countries, 1981, 82, 83, 84; mem. ocean policy com. Nat. Acad. Scis., 1978-80. Editor: Harvard Ednl. Rev, 1970; Author various articles on bus. and public policy. Trustee Bennington (Vt.) Coll., 1974-75. Mem. Council Fgn. Relations. Office: White House Washington DC 20500

DARMSTANDLER, HARRY MAX, business executive, retired air force officer; b. Indpls., Aug. 9, 1922; s. Max M. and Nonna (Holden) D.; m. Donna L. Bender, Mar. 10, 1957; children: Paul William, Thomas Alan. B.S., U. Omaha, 1964; M.S., George Washington U., 1965; grad., Nat. War Coll., 1965. Commd. 2d lt. USAAF, 1943; advanced through grades to maj. gen. USAF, 1973; served with (15th Air Force), Europe, 1943, Korea, 1952, comdr.-in-chief Pacific, 1960-63, served with joint chiefs of staff, 1965-68, supreme comdr., 1969-71; comdr. 12th Air Div. SAC, 1972, dep. chief of staff for plans, 1973; spl. asst. to chief of staff USAF, 1974-75; officer and/or dir. Ultra Systems Inc., Irvine, Calif., Rancho Bernardo Savs. & Loan, San Diego, DHA Group, Colorado Springs, Colo., Rakan Aviation and Leasing Corp., Oneida County Airport, N.Y. Author numerous articles on nat. def. requirements. Decorated D.S.M. with oak leaf cluster, Legion of Merit with oak leaf cluster, D.F.C., Air medal with 3 oak leaf clusters; research fellow U. Calif., Los Angeles, 1969-69. Mem. AIAA, Order Daedalians, Eagle Scout Alumni Assn., Phi Tau Alpha. Home: 12112 Fairhope Rd San Diego CA 92128

DARNALL, RAY O., diversified company executive; b. 1923; married. Dept. mgr. J.C. Penney Co., Inc., 1951-61; with Heck's Inc., Nitro, W.Va., 1961—, v.p. ops., 1969-72, asst. to pres., 1972-73, 1st v.p., 1973-79, pres., 1979—, also dir. Office: Heck's Inc Hub Indsl Park Box 158 Nitro WV 25143 *

DARNALL, ROBERT J., steel company excutive. Exec. v.p. Inland Steel Co., Chgo. Office: Inland Steel Co 30 W Monroe St Chicago IL 60603§

DARNTON, JOHN TOWNSEND, journalist; b. N.Y.C., Nov. 20, 1941; s. Byron and Eleanor (Choate) D.; m. Nina Lieberman, Aug. 21, 1966; children: Kyra, Liza, James. Student, Sorbonne U. and alliance Francais, Paris, 1960-61; B.A. in Psychology, U. Wis., 1966. With N.Y. Times, 1966—, Conn. corr., 1969-70, chief suburban corr., 1970-71, night rewrite, N.Y.C., 1971-72, reporter for N.Y.C. fiscal crisis in City Hall, 1972-75, corr., Lagos, Nigeria, 1976-77, Kenya, 1977-79, chief bur., Poland, 1979-82, Madrid, 1982—. Recipient George Polk award L.I.U., 1979, 82, Pulitzer prize, 1982. Office: NY Times Marques de Cubas 12-3oA Madrid Spain 14 *

DARNTON, ROBERT CHOATE, history educator; b. N.Y.C., May 10, 1939; s. Byron and Eleanor (Choate) D.; m. Susan Lee Glover, June 29, 1963; children: Nicholas Campbell, Catherine Choate, Margaret Townsend. B.A., Harvard U., 1960; B.Phil., Oxford U., Eng., 1962, D.Phil., 1964. Reporter N.Y. Times, N.Y.C., 1964; fr. fellow Harvard U., 1964-68; asst. prof. history Princeton U., N.J., 1968-71, assoc. prof., 1971-72, prof., 1972—. Author: Mesmerism and the End of the Enlightenment in France, 1968, The Business of Enlightenment: A Publishing History of the Encyclopedia, 1775-1800, 1979 (Am. Hist. Assn. Leo Gershoy prize 1979), The Literary Underground of the Old Regime, 1982, The Great Cat Massacre and Other Episodes in French Cultural History, 1984. Recipient Koren prize Soc. French Hist. Studies, 1973, MacArthur prize MacArthur Found., 1982. Fellow Am. Acad. Arts and Scis.; mem. Am. Hist. Assn., Am. Soc. Eighteenth-Century Studies (Clifford prize 1971, 73). Office: Dept History Princeton U Princeton NJ 08540

DAROFF, ROBERT BARRY, neurologist; b. N.Y.C., Aug. 3, 1936; s. Charles and May (Wolin) D.; m. Jane L. Abrahams, Dec. 4, 1959; children: Charles II, Robert Barry, William. B.A., U. Pa., 1957, M.D., 1961. Intern Phila. Gen. Hosp., 1961-62; resident in neurology Yale-New Haven Med. Center, 1962-65; fellow in neuro-ophthalmology U. Calif. Med. Center, San Francisco, 1967-68; prof. neurology, asso. prof. ophthalmology U. Miami (Fla.) Med. Sch.; also dir. ocular motor neurophysiology lab. Miami VA Med. Center, 1968-80; Gilbert W. Humphrey prof., chmn. dept. neurology Case Western Res. U. Med. Sch.; also dir. dept. neurology Univ. Hosps., Cleve., 1980—; staff neurologist Cleve. VA Med. Ctr.; mem. med. adv. bd. Myasthenia Gravis Found.; mem. nat. adv. eye council sensory and motor disorders vision panel NIH.; mem. motor disorders vision panel NIH, 1980-83. Editor neurol. progress: Annals of Neurology; book rev. editor: Neuro-ophthalmology, 1981—; assoc. editor: Jour. Biomed. Systems, 1970-72; mem. editorial bd.: Archives of Neurology, 1976; contbr. numerous articles med. jours.; mem. editorial bd.: Weekly Update: Neurology and Neurosurgery, 1978-80, Neurology and Neurosurgery Update Series, 1981—, Headache, 1980—. Chmn. Young Tae Kwon Do Acad., N. Miami, 1977-80; Bd. dirs. Benign Essential Blepharospasm Research Found., mem. sci. program com., 1980—. Served as officer M.C. USAR, 1965-67. Mem. Am. Neurol. Assn. (councillor 1980-82, chmn. membership adv. com. 1981-83, chmn. program adv. com. 1978), AMA, Am. Neurotology Soc., Am. Acad. Neurology (chmn. sci. program com. 1973-75), Soc. Neurosci., Rocky Mountain Neuro-ophthalmology Soc. (bd. dirs.), Assn. Research in Vision and Ophthalmology; mem. ACP (neurology subcom. med. knowledge self assessment program V 1977-80); Mem. Barany Soc., Am. Assn. Study Headache, Internat. Soc. Neuro-ophthalmology, Alpha Omega Alpha. Office: Dept Neurology Univ Hosps Cleveland OH 44106

DARR, JOHN WALKER, management educator; b. Terre Haute, Ind., Sept. 24, 1916; s. Barney and Hazle (Cooprider) D.; m. Marian Burnett, Dec. 28, 1968; 1 son, John Geoffrey. B.S., Ind. U., 1949, M.B.A., 1950; Ph.D., U. Ala., 1957. Grad. asst. Ind. U., 1950; asst. prof. U. Ga., 1950-53, Bowling Green (Ohio) State U., 1953-56, dir. mgmt. devel. programs and dir. internship program Sch. Bus., prof. bus. adminstrn., 1965-67; lectr. U. Ala., 1956-57; prof., chmn. dept. mgmt. Miss. State U., 1957-65; prof. mgmt., dir. mgmt. devel. program U. Mo., 1967-69; prof. mgmt. U. Dayton, Ohio, 1969—; Cons. numerous cos.; lectr., speaker in field. Author publs. in field. Mem. So. Econs. Assn., Am. Tng. Dirs. Assn., Personnel Dirs. Assn., Acad. Mgmt., Soc. Advancement Mgmt., So. Mgmt. Assn. (dir., chmn. membership com.), Beta Gamma Sigma, Chi Gamma Iota, Sigma Chi, Omicron Delta Kappa. Home: 922 Sunset Dr Bowling Green OH 43402 Office: Dept Mgmt Univ Dayton Dayton OH 45409

DARR, MILTON FREEMAN, JR., banker; b. Oak Park, Ill., Oct. 30, 1921; s. Milton Freeman and Frances Anna (Kaiser) D.; m. Margaret Claire Phipps, Jan. 27, 1945; children: Alan Phipps, Bruce Milton. B.S., U. Ill., 1942. With LaSalle Nat. Bank, Chgo., 1946-80, asst. cashier, 1950-53, asst. v.p., 1953, v.p., 1954-62, exec. v.p., dir., 1962-64, pres., 1964-68, chmn. bd., chief exec. officer, 1968-73, pres., 1974-77, vice chmn. bd., 1977-80. Mem. Bd. Edn. Dist. 88 Community High Sch., 1963-68; Chmn. commerce and industry com., treas. Chgo. Com. for Project Hope; state crusade chmn. Ill. div. Am. Cancer Soc., 1967, 68, chmn. bd., 1973-75, nat. bd. dirs., 1975-78; chmn. bd. mgrs. YMCA Met. Chgo., 1970-72; Bd. dirs. Chgo. Crime Commn., United Charities of Chgo., Mid-Am. chpt. A.R.C.; chmn. bd. trustees Elmhurst Coll.; trustee Ill. Cancer Council, Better Govt. Assn., YMCA Retirement Fund. Served to maj. USAAF, 1942-46. Recipient Distinguished Service award Am. Cancer Soc., 1976; Citizen fellow Inst. Medicine of Chgo. Mem. Am. Inst. Banking (pres. Chgo. chpt. 1955-56, mem. exec. council 1956-59, nat. v.p. 1959-60, nat. pres. 1960-61), Am. Bankers Assn. (mem. adminstrv. com., exec. council 1960-61), Assn. Res. City Bankers (treas. 1969-72), Robert Morris Assos. (pres. Chgo. chpt. 1965-66), Theta Chi. Presbyn. Clubs: Rotarian (Chgo.) (pres. 1973-74, Paul Harris fellow); Chicago, Bankers (pres. 1973), Economic, Executives, Union League (pres. 1968-69), Commerical (Chgo.) (treas.); Glen Oak Country.). Home: 316 Forest Trail Oakbrook IL 60521 Office: 135 S LaSalle St Chicago IL 60603

DARR, WILLIAM HUMISTON, educator, artist; b. Tuxedo, N.Y., June 20, 1920; s. John Whittier and Vera (Campbell) D.; m. Suanne Clark, Aug. 18, 1944 (div. 1970); children: Robin, Dorothy, Rebecca, Byrn. B.A., Wesleyan U., Middletown, Conn., 1951; M.F.A., Yale U., 1962; postgrad., Webb Sch., 1970. Instr. Amherst (Mass.) Coll., 1951-62; assoc. prof. Earlham Coll., Richmond, Ind., 1962-68; prof. art Drke U., Des Moines, 1968-79. Illustrator: the Goolibah Tree, 1944; author, artist: La Corida, 1949. Bd. dirs. Am. Friends Service Com., Torreon, Mexico, 1942; co-dir. Citizens Com. for Performing Arts Ctr., Des Moines, 1973, Studio Art Ctrs. Internat., Florence, Italy, 1976-79. Recipient Crye print award Richmond Art Assn., 1967; Carnegie grantee Great Lakes Colls., 1967; recipient Duncan Vaile award, 1941. Mem. Am. Watercolor Soc., New Eng. Mus. Assn., Phi Beta Kappa. Episcopalian. Address: PO Box 186 Woodstock CT 06281

DARRAGH, JAMES HILTON, physician; b. Montreal, Que., Can., Oct. 25, 1924; s. Herbert John and Eva Sarah (Dunlop) D.; m. Marna Gammell, 1950; children—Ian, Alexander, Jane. B.Sc., McGill U., Montreal, 1946, M.D., 1948, M.Sc., 1959. Intern Royal Victoria Hosp., Montreal, 1948-50; resident Boston City Hosp., 1950-51, Montreal Gen. Hosp., 1955-56; research fellow Yale Med. Sch., 1951-53; practice medicine specializing in internal medicine, Montreal, 1956-77; sr. physician Montreal Gen. Hosp., 1974-77; asso. prof. medicine, asso. dean Faculty Medicine McGill U., 1971-77; exec. dir. Royal Coll. Phys. and Surg. Can., Ottawa, 1980—; sr. lectr. Ottawa U. Faculty Medicine. Trustee Ottawa Gen. Hosp. Served as capt. M.C. AUS, 1953-55. Fellow Royal Coll. Phys. and Surg. Can., A.C.P.; mem. Can. Med. Assn. Club: Cercle Universitaire (Ottawa). Home: 64 Robert St Ottawa ON K2P 1G4 Canada Office: 74 Stanley Ave Ottawa ON K1M 1P4 Canada

DARRAGH, WILLIAM ROLAND, JR., insurance executive; b. Middletown, Ohio, Feb. 20, 1929; s. William Roland and Sarah Ruth (Freeze) D.; M. Martha Neely, Feb. 4, 1948 (div. 1966); children: William Roland III, Barbara, Timothy, Lee Patrick; m. 2d Myrna Haines, Aug. 13, 1966; 1 dau., Sarah Maude. Student, So. Meth. U., 1947-48, U. Ga., 1948-50; M.B.A., Loyola Coll.-Balt., 1975. Vice pres. data processing Md. Casualty Ins. Co., Balt., 1967-76, sr. v.p., chief fin., 1976-81; sr. v.p. data processing Am. Gen. Corp., Houston, 1981-82; exec. v.p. Am. Gen., Nashville, 1982—; dir. Nat. Life & Accident Ins. Co., 1983, Life & Casualty Ins. Co. Mem. Mayor's 2000 Today Com., 1983. Served with U.S. Army, 1947-48. Mem. Life Office Mgmt. Assn., Fin. Execs. Inst. Clubs: Hillwood Country, Maryland, Heritage. Office: Am General Center Nashville TN 37250

DARRELL, GEORGE ALBERT, architect; b. Wauconda, Ill., Nov. 9, 1931; s. William Erwin and Evelyn (Roether) D.; m. Betty J. Pracht, Feb. 2, 1953; children: David J., Steven sr. Douglas K. Student, U. Ill., 1949-52. With Holabird & Root (architects), Chgo., 1953-54; sr. v.p. Perkins and Will (architects), Chgo., 1954-73; exec. v.p. Urban Investment and Devel. Co., Chgo., 1973—; pres. Chgo. Bldg. Congress, 1978-80; mem. Western Springs (Ill.) Plan Commn., 1969-79. Prin. works include First Am. Tower, Nashville, 1973, 230 Monroe Bldg., Chgo., 1969, One America Place, Baton Rouge, 1974, First Fed. Bldg., Milw., 1974. Bd. dirs. N. Central Coll., Naperville, Ill., 1978—. Mem. AIA, Nat. Council Archtl. Registration Bds. Clubs: Econs. Club Chgo., Execs. Club Chgo., Tavern. Home: 5124 Ellington St Western Springs IL 60558 Office: 333 W Wacker Dr Suite 2100 Chicago IL 60606

DARRELL, NORRIS, lawyer; b. St. Kitts, W.I., Jan. 30, 1899; came to U.S., 1900, naturalized, 1910; s. Norris de Mouilpied and Maria Arabella MacDonald (Pandt) D.; m. Doris Clare Williams, June 24, 1925 (dec. 1943); children: Norris Jr., Richard Wheeler; m. Mary Hand Churchill, June 28, 1945; 1 stepson, Jonathan Churchill. LL.B., U. Minn., 1923. Bar: Minn. 1923, N.Y. 1927. Legal sec. Hon. Pierce Butler, asso. justice U.S. Supreme Ct., 1923-25; asso. firm Sullivan & Cromwell, N.Y.C., 1925—, Paris and Berlin rep., 1928-30, mem. firm, 1934-76, of counsel, 1976-79; Tech. adviser Fiscal Com. Econ. Devel., 1947-65; dir. Schroders Ltd., London, 1959-70, Schroders, Inc., 1968-73, J. Henry Schroder Banking Corp. and Schroder Trust Co., 1955-73, Oxford Paper Co., 1963-67, Harper & Row, Pubs., Inc., 1962-74, A. Johnson & Co., Inc., 1968-80, dir. emeritus, 1980—; Pres. Am. Law Inst., 1961-76, mem. council, 1947—, chmn. council, 1976-80, chmn. emeritus, 1980—; chmn. joint com. continuing legal edn. Am. Law Inst./Am. Bar Assn., 1966-74, alt. chmn./vice-chmn. com. continuing profl. edn., 1975-79, hon. mem., 1979—; mem. Lawyers' Com. for Civil Rights Under Law. Contbr. articles to legal jours. Bd. dirs. Goodwill Industries of Greater N.Y., Inc., 1943-74; bd. dirs. Pub. Health Research Inst. City N.Y., 1950-61, pres., 1953-61; trustee Practising Law Inst., 1941-75, trustee emeritus, 1975—, v.p., 1960-61; trustee Tax Found. Inc., 1963—, mem. exec. com., 1978—; Adv. bd. Internat. Bur. Fiscal Documentation, 1964-71; past. mem. various tax adv. coms. N.Y. State and U.S. govtl. bodies.; Trustee United Methodist Christ Ch., 1968—, mem. exec. com., 1971—, v.p., 1976—. Served in inf. U.S. Army, 1917-19. Recipient Merit award U. Minn. Law Alumni Assn., 1962; Outstanding Achievement award U. Minn., 1965; Marshall-Wythe medallion award Coll. William and Mary Marshall-Wythe Sch. Law, 1967; Harrison Tweed award Nat. Assn. Continuing Legal Edn. Adminstrs., 1977-78. Fellow Am. Bar Found., N.Y. Bar Found.; mem. Pilgrims U.S., Am. Bar Assn. (ho. of dels. 1965-77), N.Y. State Bar Assn. (Gold Medal award for disting. service in law 1978), Assn. Bar City N.Y. (v.p. 1956-58), Inst. Jud. Adminstrn., Inc., Am. Judicature Soc., Council Fgn. Relations, Scribes, Grey Friars, Order of Coif, Alpha Tau Omega, Phi Delta Phi. Clubs: Century, University (N.Y.C.). Home: 1107 Fifth Ave New York NY 10028 also Long Ridge Rd Bedford NY 10506 Office: 125 Broad St New York NY 10004

DARRELL, NORRIS, JR., lawyer; b. Berlin, Germany, May 10, 1929; s. Norris and Doris Clare (Williams) D. (parents Am. citizens); m. Henriette Maria Haid, July 31, 1962; 1 son, Andrew. A.B., Harvard U., 1951, LL.B. cum laude, 1954. Bar: N.Y. 1955, U.S. Supreme Ct. 1965. Asso. firm Sullivan & Cromwell, N.Y.C., 1956-65, partner, 1965—, in charge European office, Paris, 1968-71; dir. Schroders Inc., J. Henry Schroder Bank & Trust Co. Trustee Cold Spring Harbor Lab., Inc., 1974-81; Trustee United Student Aid Funds, Inc., N.Y.C., 1974—, E. Woods Sch., Oyster Bay, N.Y., 1974-79. Served with U.S. Army, 1954-56. Fellow Am. Bar Found.; mem. Am. Law Inst., Am. Bar Assn., N.Y. State Bar Assn., Assn. Bar City N.Y. Clubs: Down Town Assn., Harvard of N.Y., Pilgrims, River (bd. govs. 1978—). Home: 44 Walnut Tree Ln Cold Spring Harbor New York NY 11724 Office: 125 Broad St New York NY 10004

DARRELL, ROBERT DONALDSON, writer; b. Newton, Mass., Dec. 13, 1903; s. Ernest Willis and Elizabeth (Donaldson) D.; m. Emma Cartwright Bourne, Sept. 30, 1930 (div. 1936). Student, Harvard, 1922, New Eng. Conservatory Music, 1923-26. Staff writer, record reviewer Phonograph Monthly Rev., Boston and Cambridge, Mass., 1926-30, editor, pub., 1930-1931; free lance writer, 1932-34; asso. editor, reviewer Music Lovers' Guide, N.Y.C., 1932-34; record researcher Gramophone Shop, N.Y.C., 1934-39; editor Gramophone Shop Supplement, 1937-39, Steinway Rev. Permanent Music (later syndicated Rev. Recorded Music), N.Y.C., 1939-43; sr. writer, later supervising editor instrn. book dept. Hazeltine Electronics Corp., Little Neck, N.Y., 1943-46; editor Rev. Recorded Music, 1947-50; record revs. Down Beat, 1952; audio columnist Saturday Rev., 1953-55; columnist High Fidelity mag., 1955—, contributing editor, 1956—; also contributing editor Audiocraft magazine, 1955-58; Discographic cons. music div. N.Y.C. Pub. Library, 1952. Author: The Highroad to Musical Enjoyment, 1943, Good Listening, 1953; Compiler: Gramophone Shop Encyclopedia of Recorded Music, 1936, Schirmer's Guide to Books on Music and Musicians, 1951, Tapes in Review, 1963; Contbr. profl. publs. Guggenheim fellow, 1939. Fellow Radio Club Am.; mem. Audio Engring. Soc., Acoustical Soc. Am., Ulster County Hist. Soc., Assn. Recorded Sound Collections. Democrat. Home: Balmoral The Vly Stone Ridge NY 12484

DARRONE, DONALD WILLIAM, tool corp. exec.; b. Syracuse, N.Y., Feb. 20, 1916; s. Leon Oliver and Ethel (Halladay) D.; m. Doris Julia Allen, Sept. 10, 1938; children—Richard W., Allen E., Dorothy A., David A. B.S., N.Y. State Coll. Forestry, Syracuse U., 1937. With Allen Tool Corp., Syracuse, 1937—, pres., 1954—, also dir. Past v.p. Onondaga council Boy Scouts Am.; past dir Urban League; past pres. Syracuse U. Parents Assn., Alfred U. Parents Assn.; Past pres. bd. trustees Rescue Mission Alliance; past v.p., dir., trustee Syracuse YMCA. Mem. Nat. Tooling and Machining Assn. (past pres., trustee), Central N.Y. chpt. Tooling and Machining Assn., Met. Devel. Assn., Citizens' Found., Mfrs. Assn. Syracuse (dir.), Syracuse C. of C. (past dir.), Am. Welding Soc., Am. Soc. Metals, Soc. Mfg. Engrs. (past dir.), Syracuse U. Alumni Assn., Syracuse Tech. Club. Republican. Methodist (trustee). Clubs: Kiwanis; University (Syracuse). Home: 113 Bradford Ln Syracuse NY 13224 Office: 308 Maltbie St PO Box 1382 Syracuse NY 13201

DARROW, FRANK WILLIAM, educator; b. Syracuse, N.Y., Feb. 6, 1940; s. Frank Spengler and Elma (Herrick) D.; m. Catherine Twomey, Feb. 11, 1961; children—Carolyn, Gretchen. B.A., Williams Coll., 1961; Ph.D., U. Pa., 1965. Vis. asst. prof. Earlham Coll., 1965-66; asst. prof. chemistry Ithaca (N.Y.) Coll., 1966-70, asso. prof., 1971-72, 76—, asst. to provost, 1971-72, acting provost, 1972-73, provost, 1973-76. Recipient Kettering Found. grant, 1965-66. Home: 400 Gunderman Rd RD 1 Spencer NY 14883 Office: Ithaca Coll Ithaca NY 14850

DARROW, KATHARINE PRAGER, lawyer; b. Chgo., Dec. 26, 1943; d. Frank D. D. and Herta (Schild) Prager; m. Roger A. Boshes, June 16, 1963 (div. 1967); children: Alexander, Jessica, James. A.B., U. Chgo., 1965, student law, 1965-66; J.D., Columbia U., 1969. Bar: N.Y. 1970. Summer assoc. legal dept. N.Y. Times, 1968, staff atty., 1970-71, 1973-76, asst. gen. atty., 1977-80, gen. atty., 1980-81, gen. counsel, 1981—; assoc. Gottesman, Evans & van Merkenstein, London, 1971-73. Dir. Community Action for Legal Services, 1976-81; trustee U. Chgo., 1982—. Mem. Am. Newspaper Pubs. Assn., Assn. Bar City N.Y. Office: New York Times Co 229 W 43d St New York NY 10036

DARROW, ROBERT ARTHUR, plant physiologist, former government official; b. Saratoga Springs, N.Y., Dec. 15, 1911; s. Arthur Elliott and Edith (Foote) D.; m. Bertha Mathilda Schweitzer, Oct. 23, 1936; children: Gordon Roger, Janet Marjorie. B.S., N.Y. State Coll. Forestry, 1932; student, U. Idaho, 1932-33; M.S., U. Ariz., 1935, U. Chgo., 1934-36, Ph.D., 1937. Instr. dept. botany and range ecology U. Ariz., 1936-39, asst. prof., 1939-43, asso. prof., 1943-47, prof., 1947-48; asso. prof. dept. range and forestry Tex. A. & M. U., 1948-50, prof., 1950-62, acting head dept., 1959-60; chief chem. br. Crops div. U.S. Dept. Army, Ft. Detrick, Md., 1962-67; chief plant physiology div. Plant Scis. Lab., 1967-71, acting chief vegetation control div., 1972, chief, 1972-74; research leader, weed physiology lab. Agrl. Research Service, U.S. Dept. Agr., Frederick, Md., 1974-78; cons. prof. Tex. Tech. U., 1967-72. Author: (with L. Benson) The Trees and Shrubs of Southwestern Deserts, 3d edit, 1981; Contbr. numerous articles to sci. jours.; Editor plant ecology sect.: Biol. Abstracts, 1949-53; editor: Jour. Range Mgmt, 1954-56. Recipient Meritorious Civilian Service award Dept. Army, 1971. Fellow AAAS (mem. council 1972-75); mem. Soc. Range Mgmt. (life), Am. Bryological and Lichenological Soc., Ecol. Soc. Am., Internat. Assn. Plant Taxonomists, Assn. Tropical Biology, Weed Sci. Soc. Am., Sci. Research Soc. Am., Sigma Xi, Phi Kappa Phi, Alpha Xi Sigma. Home: 7613 Baltimore National Pike Frederick MD 21701

DART, CHARLES EDWARD, consultant; b. Port Huron, Mich., July 7, 1915; s. Charles Henry and Violet Marie (Rush) D.; m. Magdalene Gill Spencer, Oct. 31, 1942. A.S., Port Huron Jr. Coll., 1934; B.S. in Naval Architecture and Marine Engring, U. Mich., 1939; certificate, Grad. Sch. Bus. U. Pitts., 1961. With Newport News Shipbldg. & Dry Dock Co., 1939-81, exec. v.p., 1976-81; Mem. cost panel Navy and Marine acquisitions rev. com., 1974-75; mem. policy com. Council Def. and Space Industry Assns., 1970-76, vice-chmn., 1971-72, chmn., 1972-73; bd. visitors Def. Systems Mgmt. Coll., 1975, 79. Mem. Shipbuilders Council Am. (chmn. procurement adv. com. 1969-77), Soc. Naval Architects and Marine Engrs., Nat. Contract Mgmt. Assn. (bd. advisers 1977-80), Navy League U.S., Nat. Security Indsl. Assn. (hon. mem., trustee 1974-81), Propeller Club U.S. (gov. Newport News 1967-68, pres. 1966-67), Va. C. of C. (dir. 1976-79). Episcopalian. Club: Masons. Home: 135 Woodland Dr Newport News VA 23606

DARVIN, ROBERT W., furniture importing corporation executive; b. New Brunswick, N.J., Oct. 21, 1938; s. Julius and Goldie D.; m. Gretchen A. Gibbons, Oct. 28. Student, Rutgers U., 1956, 72, Columbia U., 1962-64. Midwest regional mgr. Walton Labs., Irvington, N.J., 1962-65; mgr. N.E. Fla. Jim Walter Corp., Tampa, 1963-66; founder, pres. Scandinavian Design Inc., Natick, Mass., 1965—; pres. Scandinavian Gallery Inc.; chmn. bd. Cambridge Dry Goods Co.; partner Am. Resource & Cons. Group; guest lectr. M.B.A. program Babson Coll. Editor, pub.: Darvin Theory econ. newsletter, 1977—. Mem. Mass. Fgn. Bus. Council. Served with USNAF, 1970-75. Recipient commendation Danish Minister Fgn. Affairs, 1978, Danish medal of honor and diploma Prince Henrik of Denmark; named One of Outstanding Retailers in Am. Home Furnishings Daily. Mem. Am. Mgmt. Assn., Nat. Home Furnishing Assn. (dir.), Furniture Assn. New Eng. (gov.), Young Presidents' Orgn., Am. Numismatic Assn., Nat. Speakers Assn. Named to speak as one of 3 leading internat. furniture retailers in world, Scandinavian Furniture Fair. Office: 575 Worcester Rd Natick MA 01760

DARY, DAVID ARCHIE, journalism educator, author; b. Manhattan, Kans., Aug. 21, 1934; s. Milton Russell and Ruth Engel (Long) D.; m. Carolyn Sue Russum, June 2, 1956; children: Catherine Lee, Carol Ann, Cynthia Kay, Cristina Sue. B.S. in Humanities, Kans. State U., 1956; M.S. in Journalism, Kans. U., 1970. Reporter, editor CBS News, Washington, 1960-63; mgr. local news NBC News, Washington, 1963-67; dir. pub. affairs Kans. Rep. State Com., Topeka, 1968; mem. faculty U. Kans., Lawrence, 1969—, prof. journalism, 1970—; cons. broadcast journalism, 1967—. Author: Radio News Handbook, 1967, Manual De Noticias Radiofonicas, 1970, Television News Handbook, 1970, How to Write News for Broadcast and Print, 1973, The Buffalo Book, 1974, Comanche, 1976, True Tales of the Old-Time Plains, 1979, Cowboy Culture, 1981, Lawrence, Douglas County Kansas: An Informal History, 1982, True Tales of Old-Time Kansas, 1984; Contbr. numerous articles to various mags. and newspapers. Mem. Kans. State Hist. Soc. (dir. 1972—), Western History Assn., Sigma Delta Chi, Kappa Tau Alpha. Lodge: Masons. Home: 1101 W 27th St Lawrence KS 66044

DASCHLE, THOMAS ANDREW, congressman; b. Aberdeen, S.D., Dec. 9, 1947; m. Linda Hall Daschle; children: Kelley, Nathan, Lindsay. B.A., S.D. State U., 1969. Fin. investment rep.; chief legis. aide, field coordinator Sen. James Abourzek, 1973-77; mem. 96th-97th Congresses from 1st S.D. Dist., 98th Congress at large. Served to 1st lt. USAF, 1969-72. Democrat. Office: 439 Cannon House Office Bldg Washington DC 20515

DAS GUPTA, SUBAL, physics educator, researcher; b. Calcutta, India, Aug. 11, 1939; emigrated to Can., 1968; s. Subodh Chandra and Pritilata (Sen) Das G.; m. Sanjukta Sen Gupta, Aug. 12, 1965; children: Monidipa, Nandini. M.Sc., Calcutta U., 1959; Ph.D., McMaster U., 1963. Asst. prof. physics McGill U., Montreal, 1967-71, assoc. prof., 1972-77, prof., 1978—. Contbr. articles to profl. jours. Office: Physics Dept McGill U 3600 University St Montreal PQ Canada H3A 2T8

DASH, LEON DECOSTA, JR., journalist; b. New Bedford, Mass., Mar. 16, 1944; s. Leon DeCosta and Ruth Elizabeth (Kydd) D. B.A., Howard U., 1968. Reporter Washington Post, 1966-68, 71-79, African bur. chief, 1979-83, with investigations desk, 1983—; vis. prof. U. Calif., San Diego, 1978. Author: (With Ben H. Bagdikian) The Shame of the Prisons, 1972. Peace Corps vol., Kenya, 1969-70. Recipient George Polk Meml. award Overseas Press Club, 1974; award for internat. news reporting Washington-Balt. Newspaper Guild, 1974; hon. mention Washington-Balt. Newspaper Guild, 1975. Office: Washington Post 1150 15th St NW Washington DC 20071

DASH, SAMUEL, lawyer, educator; b. Camden, N.J., Feb. 27, 1925; s. Joseph and Ida (Weinberg) D.; m. Sara Goldhirsh, July 14, 1946; children: Judy, Rachel. B.S., Temple U., 1947; J.D. cum laude, Harvard, 1950; LL.D. (hon.), Fairfield (Conn.) U., 1974, Georgetown U., 1983, PS.D., Temple U., 1978. Bar: Ill. 1950, Pa. 1952, U.S. Supreme Ct. 1955, D.C. 1978. Teaching fellow Northwestern, 1950-51; trial atty., criminal div. U.S. Dept. Justice, Washington, 1951-52; asst. dist. atty., chief appeals div., Phila., 1952-54, 1st asst. dist. atty., 1954-55, dist. atty., 1955-56; partner firm Blank and Rudenko, Phila., 1956-58, Dash & Levy, 1958-63; dir. Phila. Council Community Advancement, 1963-65; prof. law, dir. Inst. Criminal Law and Procedure and Appellate Litigation Clinic, Georgetown U. Law Sch., Washington, 1965—; chief counsel U.S. Senate select com. presdl. campaign activities (Senate Watergate com.), 1973-74; cons. Ford Found., 1958-63, Nat. Assn. Attys. Gen., 1971-73, Law Reform Com., Australia, 1977—; dir. Divi Hotels, Aruba; Mem. Human Relations Commn. Phila., 1957-65; exec. com. Community Relations Council, Phila., 1960-65, Met. Washington, 1973—; exec. dir. D.C. Jud. Conf. Mental Disorders and the Law, 1965-70. Author: The Eavesdroppers, 1959, Chief Counsel, 1976; Contbr. articles to profl. jours. Bd. dirs. Hebrew U., Jerusalem, 1975—, Fedn. Jewish Agys., Phila., 1960-65, Albert Einstein Med. Center, Phila., 1962-65, Internat. League Human Rights, 1972—; chmn. trustees Pub. Defenders Service D.C., 1967-76. Served to 2d lt. USAAF, 1943-46; ETO. Recipient civic awards various civic orgns.; Annual award Nat. Assn. Criminal Def. Lawyers, 1959; Commendation certificate Am. Bar Assn., 1971; others.; Sr. Fulbright scholar U. Melbourne, Australia, 1977. Mem. Am. Law Inst., Am. Bar Assn. (chmn. criminal law sect. 1971, del. 1972), Pa. Bar Endowment (dir. nationwide investigation wiretapping 1956-59), Nat. Assn. Criminal Lawyers (pres. 1958), B'nai B'rith (Phila. regional chmn. Anti-Defamation League 1960-63, nat. commr. 1960-63). Home: 110 Newlands St Chevy Chase MD 20815 Office: Georgetown U Law Center Washington DC 20001

DASHEFSKY, EDWARD LEO, cons., former electronics co. exec.; b. Malden, Mass., Nov. 4, 1914; s. Barnett and Rebecca (Bernstein) D.; m. Rose Zelermyer, Dec. 25, 1938; children—Gloria, Barry. B.S. in Aero. Engring, Mass. Inst. Tech., 1936. Aerodynamics and structural design engr. Sikorsky Aircraft Co., 1937, Curtiss-Wright Airplane Co., 1938-45; chief structures, project engr. Lark missile, guided missile div. Fairchild Engine and Airplane Co., 1946-51; with Raytheon Co., 1951-80, mgr. Sparrow III missile prodn., 1951-60, mgr. microwave and power tube div., 1961-80, v.p., 1962-69, sr. v.p., 1969-80; mgmt. cons., 1980—; dir. The Machlett Labs., Inc., Springdale, Conn., New Japan Radio Co., Ltd., Tokyo, Switchcraft, Inc., Chgo., Microsonics Inc. Mem. Am. Inst. Aeros. and Astronautics (past pres. Boston), Air Force Hist. Found., Am. Logistics Assn., Armed Forces Communications and Electronics Assn., Assn. U.S. Army. Club: Mason. Home: 69 Lincoln House Point Swampscott MA 01907

DA SILVA, HOWARD, actor; b. Cleve., May 4, 1909; s. Benjamin and Bertha (Sen) Silverblatt; m. Marjorie Nelson, 1950 (div. 1960); m. Nancy Nutter, June 30, 1961. Student, Carnegie Inst. Tech., 1928. Formerly with, Civic Repertory Theatre, Theatre Union Group, Mercury Theatre, also, Syracuse (N.Y.) Repertory Theatre; plays include Master Builder, Alice in Wonderland, Three Sisters, Alison's House, Lililom, A Doll's House, Sailors of Cattaro, Golden Boy, The Cradle Will Rock, 1776, Abe Lincoln in Illinois; films include Once in a Blue Moon, 1936, Abe Lincoln in Illinois, 1940, Sea Wolf, Sergeant York, Nine Lives Are Not Enough, Wild Bill Hickok Rides Again, Steel Against the Sky, 1941, Big Shot, Omaha Trail, Tonight We Raid Calais, Keeper of the Flame, 1942, The Lost Weekend, 1945 (nominated for Acad. award), Duffy's Tavern, Two Years Before the Mast, 1946 (nominated for Acad. award), Unconquered, 1947, They Live by Night, 1948, The Great Gatsby, 1949, Underworld Story, Three Husbands, 1950, Fourteen Hours, M, 1951, David and Lisa, 1962, The Outrage, 1964, Nevada Smith, 1966, "1776", 1972; dir.: N.Y. prodn. Cradle Will Rock, 1965, Purlie Victorious, My Sweet Charlie, The World of Sholom Aleichem, Tevya and His Daughters, Sandhog; radio) for Great Classics series, Fed. Theatre project, 1936; performed in plays of, Arch Oboler and, Norman Corwin, also radio, 1940; appeared in: TV spl. The Missiles of October, 1974, Stop Thief, 1976; episodes of TV series including The Fugitive; TV movies You're Dead, 1974, Hollywood On Trial, 1977, Verna: USO Girl, 1978; Author: (with Felix Leon) play The Most Dangerous Man in America *

DASMANN, RAYMOND FREDRIC, ecologist; b. San Francisco, May 27, 1919; s. William H. and Mary (McDonnell) D.; m. Elizabeth Sheldon, May 30, 1944; children—Sandra, Marlene, Lauren. A.B., U. Calif., Berkeley, 1948, M.A., 1951, Ph.D., 1954. Mem. faculty Humboldt State Coll., 1954-59, 62-66; research biologist Nat. Museums Rhodesia, 1959-61; lectr. zoology U. Calif., Berkeley, 1961-62; ecologist Conservation Found., Washington, 1966-70; sr. ecologist Internat. Union Conservation Nature, Morges, Switzerland, 1970-77; prof. U. Calif., Santa Cruz, 1977—. Author: Pacific Coastal Wildlife, 1957, Environmental Conservation, 1959, 76, African Game Ranching, 1963, Last Horizon, 1963, Wildlife Biology, 1964, 81, Destruction of California, 1965, A Different Kind of Country, 1968, No Further Retreat, 1971, Planet in Peril, 1972, Ecological Principles for Economic Development, 1973, The Conservation Alternative, 1975, California's Changing Environment, 1981; contbr. articles to profl. jours. Mem. Ecol. Soc. Am., Am. Soc. Mammalogists, Wildlife Soc. (pres.), Calif. Acad. Scis., Assn. Tropical Biology. Home: 116 Meadow Rd Santa Cruz CA 95060 Office: Environ Studies U Calif Santa Cruz CA 95064

DASSIN, JULES, motion picture dir.; b. Middletown, Conn., Dec. 18, 1911; s. Samuel and Berthe (Vogel) D.; m. Beatrice Launer, 1933 (div. 1962); children—Joseph, Richelle, Julie; m. Melina Mercouri, 1966. Dir.: motion pictures including Brute Force, 1946, Naked City, 1947, Thieves Highway, 1948, Night and The City, 1949, Du Rififi chez les Hommes, 1955, He Who Must Die, 1956, The Law, 1958, Never on Sunday, 1960, Phaedra, 1962, Topkapi, 1964, 10:30 P.M. Summer, 1966, Uptight, 1968, Promise At Dawn, 1969, The Rehearsal, 1974, A Dream of Passion, 1978, Circle of Two, 1980; Broadway play Ilya, Darling, 1967 (Recipient Dir.'s prize Cannes Film Festival 1955). Address: care Sue Mengers ICM Hollywood CA 90048 *

DASTYCK, GEORGE JOSEPH, newspaper publisher; b. Austin, Minn., Mar. 9, 1926; s. George Joseph and Helen Marie (Hogan) D.; m. Mary Elizabeth Melton, Dec. 17, 1945; 7 children. B.Psychology, U. Minn.-Mpls., 1949. Dir. employee relations Gannett Co., Inc., Rochester, N.Y., 1963-75; dir. adminstrn. and personnel Gannett

Rochester Newspapers, 1975-76; pub. Utica Observer-Dispatch & Daily Press, N.Y., 1976-80, Gannett Rochester Newspapers, 1980—; pres. Gannett N.E. Newspaper Group, Rochester, 1983—. Bd. dirs., 2d v.p. Rochester Downtown Devel. Corp., 1981; bd. dirs. Rochester C. of C., 1981—, Rochester Conv. and Visitors Bur., 1981—, Rochester YMCA, 1982—, Roberts Wesleyan Coll., 1983—; trustee St. John Fisher Coll., 1983—. Served with USAAF, 1944-46. Clubs: Oak Hill Country, Country of Rochester, Genesee Valley. Office: Gannett Rochester Newspapers 55 Exchange St Rochester NY 14614

DATARS, WILLIAM ROSS, physicist; b. Desboro., Ont., Can., June 14, 1932; s. Albert John and Leona Alberta (Fries) D.; m. Eleanor Wismer, Oct. 10, 1959; children—Timothy, Andrew, David. B.Sc., McMaster U., Hamilton. Ont., 1955; M.Sc., 1956; Ph.D., U. Wis., 1959. Physicist Def. Research Bd., 1959-62; mem. faculty McMaster U., 1962—, prof. physics, 1969—. E.W.R. Staecie fellow, 1968-70. Fellow Royal Soc. Can.; mem. Can. Assn. Physics, Am. Phys. Soc. Lutheran. Home: Rural Route 2 Lynden ON L0R 1T0 Canada Office: McMaster Univ Hamilton ON L8S 4K1 Canada

DATER, JUDY LICHTENFELD, photographer; b. Hollywood Calif., Calif., June 21, 1941; m. Dennis Dater, 1962 (div. 1964); m. Jack Welpott, 1970 (div. 1978). Student, UCLA, 1959-62; B.A., San Francisco State U., 1963, M.A., 1966. Free-lance photographer, Calif., 1967—; instr. photography U. Calif. Extension, San Francisco, 1966-74, San Francisco Art Inst., 1974-78. One-man shows, Aardvark Gallery, San Francisco, 1965, Sch. Art Inst. Chgo., 1972, Ctr. for Photog. Studies, U. Louisville, 1973, (with Jack Welpott), Internat. Mus. Photography, George Eastman House, Rochester, N.Y., Spectrum Gallery, Tucson, 1975, Witkin Gallery, N.Y.C., 1978, Kimball Art Ctr., Park City, Utah, 1979, Jeb Gallery, Providence, 1980, Catskill Ctr. Photography, Woodstock, N.Y., 1981, Camera Oscura Gallery, Denver, Yuen Lui Gallery, Seattle, 1982, Kathleen Ewing Gallery, Washington, exhibited in group shows including, MIT, Cambridge, 1967, Internat. Mus. Photography, George Eastman House, 1968, 74, Whitney Mus., N.Y.C., 1974, San Francisco Mus. Art, 1975, Mus. Modern Art, N.Y.C., 1978; represented in permanent collections, Mus. Modern Art, N.Y.C., Internat. Mus. Photography, George Eastman House, Fogg Art Mus., Harvard U., Cambridge, Ctr. for Creative Photography, U. Ariz., Tucson, San Francisco Mus. Modern Art, Bibliotheque Nationale, Paris. Recipient Dorthea Lange award Oakland Art Mus. (Calif.), 1974; Nat. Endowment for Arts Photography fellow, 1976; Guggenheim Photography fellow, 1978. Office: care Collected Vision Inc PO Box 5154 Berkeley CA 94705 *

DAUB, GUIDO HERMAN, chemist, educator; b. Milw., Dec. 16, 1920; s. Guido Ernst and Pauline Louise (Frentzel) D.; m. Katharine Powell, June 26, 1948; children—Guido William, Elisabeth, John Powell. B.S. in Chemistry, U. Wis., 1944, M.S., 1947, Ph.D. in Organic Chemistry, 1949. Chemist Rohm and Haas Co., Phila., 1944-45; faculty U. N.Mex., Albuquerque, 1949—, asst. prof. chemistry, 1949-54, asso. prof., 1954-61, prof. chemistry, 1961—, dept. chmn., 1970-81, dir., 1958-63. Co-author: Basic Chemistry, 1972, 77, 81; contbr. articles to publs. Recipient honor scroll N.Mex. Inst. of Chemists, 1975; recipient various research grants NIH, U.S. AEC, Dept. Energy. Mem. Am. Chem. Soc., Blue Key, Sigma Xi, Alpha Chi Sigma, Phi Lambda Upsilon, Phi Kappa Phi. Presbyterian. Club: University Golf Assn. Home: 1813 Miracorros Pl Albuquerque NM 87106 Office: Chemistry Dept U New Mexico Albuquerque NM 97131

DAUB, HAL, congressman; b. Fayetteville, N.C., Apr. 23, 1941; s. Harold John and Eleanor M. (Hickman) D.; m. Cindy S. Shin, Apr. 7, 1968; children: Natalie Ann, John Clifford, Tammy Renee. B.S. in Bus. Adminstrn, Washington U., St. Louis, 1963; J.D., U. Nebr., Lincoln, 1966. Bar: Nebr. Asso. firm Fitzgerald, Brown, Leahy, McGill & Strom, 1968-71; v.p., gen. counsel Standard Chem. Mfg. Co., 1971-80; mem. 97th-98th congresses from 2d Nebr. Dist.; mem. small bus. com., pub. works and transp. com., select com. on aging. 97th Congress from 2d Nebr. Dist.; Staff intern to U.S. Senator Roman Hruska from Nebr., 1966. Jr. pres. Nebr. Founders' Day, 1971; mem. exec. com., dir. Combined Health Agys. Drive, 1976; pres. Douglas-Sarpy unit Nebr. Heart Assn.; treas. Douglas County (Nebr.) Republican Party, 1970-73, chmn., 1974-77; mem. Nebr. Rep. Central Com., 1974-77, Congl. Rep. Def. Task Force, 1981—, Congl. Rep. Agrl. Task Force, 1981—; mem. exec. com. Rep. Nat. Congl. Com., 1981—. Served to capt. U.S. Army, 1963-68. Decorated Army Commendation medal with oak leaf cluster; named Outstanding Nebraskan, 1966; Most Outstanding Student Mem. in Nation Delta Theta Phi, 1966; 1 of 10 Most Outstanding Young Omahans Omaha Jaycees, 1976; recipient Service award SAC, 1976; Outstanding Vol. of Yr. award Douglas-Sarpy unit Nebr. Heart Assn., 1976; Recipient Leadership award Coalition for Peace Through Strength, Guardian of Small Bus. award Omaha C. of C., Watchdog of Treasury award. Mem. Nat. Assn. Credit Mgmt. (1st v.p. 1977), Omaha Bar Assn., Am. Legion, 40 and 8, VFW, NAACP, Urban League Nebr. Presbyterian. Clubs: Optimists, Masons. Office: 1019 Longworth Bldg Washington DC 20515

DAUBEN, WILLIAM GARFIELD, chemist, educator; b. Columbus, Ohio, Nov. 6, 1919; s. Hyp J. and Leilah (Stump) D.; m. Carol Hyatt, Aug. 8, 1947; children—Barbara, Ann. Edward. A.B., Ohio State U., 1941; A.M., Harvard, 1942; Ph.D., 1944; Ph.D. hon. degree, U. Bordeaux, France, 1980. Austin fellow Harvard, 1941-42, teaching fellow, 1942-43, research asst., 1943-45; instr. U. Calif. at Berkeley, 1945-47, asst. prof. chemistry, 1947-52, asso. prof., 1952-57, prof., 1957—; lectr. Am.-Swiss Found., 1962; pres. Organic Reactions, Inc., 1967; mem. med. chem. study sect. USPHS, 1959-64; mem. chemistry panel NSF, 1964-67; mem. Am.-Sino Sci. Cooperation Com., 1973-76; mem. assembly math. and phys. scis. NRC, 1977-80. Mem. bd. editors: Jour. of Organic Chemistry, 1957-62; bd. editors: Organic Syntheses, 1959-67; bd. dirs., 1971—; editor-in-chief: Organic Reactions, 1967—; Contbr. articles profl. jours. Recipient award Calif. sect. Am. Chem. Soc., 1959; Guggenheim fellow, 1951, 66; sr. fellow NSF, 1957-58; Alexander von Humboldt Found. Fellow, 1980. Fellow London, Swiss chem. socs.; mem. Am. Chem. Soc. (chmn. div. organic chemistry 1962-63, councilor organic div. 1964-70, mem. council publ. com. 1965-70, mem. adv. com. Petroleum Research Fund 1974-77, Ernest Guenther award 1973), Nat. Acad. Scis. (chmn. chemistry sect. 1977-80), Am. Acad. Arts and Scis., Phi Beta Kappa, Sigma Xi, Phi Lambda Upsilon, Phi Eta Sigma, Sigma Chi. Club: Bohemian. Home: 20 Eagle Hill Berkeley CA 94707

DAUBENSPECK, ROBERT DONLEY, advertising agency executive; b. Butler, Pa., Nov. 5, 1926; s. Frank Thorne and Virginia (Donley) D.; m. Susan May Alcorn, Oct. 28, 1967; children: Nancy, Joan, Jean, Thorne. A.B. in Econs. and Social Instns, Princeton U., 1949. Supr. Benson & Benson (mktg. research), Princeton, N.J., 1949-51; sales analyst Lever Bros., N.Y.C., 1951-52; mgr. sales devel. NBC, Chgo., 1952-61; with Foote, Cone & Belding Advt., Inc., 1961—, v.p., dir. media and programming, Chgo., 1974-79, sr. v.p., nat. broadcast dir., N.Y.C., 1979—. Author: Recall Technique As Measurement of Broadcast Audiences, 1949. Served with USAAF, 1945. Mem. Internat. Radio and TV Soc., Broadcast Advt. Club. Republican. Episcopalian. Clubs: Boyer, Whitehall, Barclay, St. Charles Country, Aspetuck Valley Country., Princeton. Home: 38 Old Orchard Dr Weston CT 06853 Office: 101 Park Ave New York NY 10166

DAUER, FRANCIS WATANABE, philosophy educator; b. Leipzig, Germany, Aug. 17, 1939; came to U.S., 1950, naturalized, 1954; s. Michael Satosi Watanabe and Dorothea W. D.; m. Margery Lilly Christensen, June 14, 1968 (div. Aug. 1982); children: Hilary Chisato Watahabe, Karen Aiko Watanabe. A.B., Dartmouth Coll., 1960; M.A., Harvard U., 1964, Ph.D., 1970; student, Oxford (Eng.) U., 1964-65. Lectr. philosophy U. Calif. at Santa Barbara, 1967-69, asst. prof., 1969-75, asso. prof., 1975-82, prof., 1982—, chmn., 1980—. Contbr. articles to profl. jours. Woodrow Wilson fellow, 1960; Harvard resident fellow, 1961, 62; Knox travelling fellow, 1964; U. Calif. summer faculty fellow, 1971. Mem. Am. Philos. Assn. Club: Harvard of Santa Barbara. Home: 3013 Lomita Rd Santa Barbara CA 93105

DAUER, MANNING JUILAN, JR., history educator; b. Wilmington, N.C., Aug. 12, 1909; s. Manning J. and Martha Eddins (Fitts) D. A.B., U. Fla., 1930, A.M., 1931, LL.D. (hon.), 1983; Ph.D., U. Ill., 1933; Litt.D. (hon.), U. West Fla., 1973. Instr. dept. history and polit. sci. U. Fla., 1933-34, asst. prof., 1934-41, asso. prof., 1941-46, prof., 1946-71, Distinguished Service prof., 1971—, head dept., 1950-75, dir. div. social scis., 1960-75; mng. editor Jour. Politics, 1939-41, 1946—; cons. govt. orgn. and adminstrn.; vis. prof. polit. sci. U. Ala., summer 1952; vis. prof. N.Y.U., 1957; Cons. Fla. Adv. Constl. Com., 1956, atty. gen. Fla.; cons. to legislature on reapportionment, 1972, 81; cons. So. Regional Edn. Bd. Author: The Basis of the Support of John Adams in the Federalist Party, 1933, The Adams Federalists, 1953, Florida Politics and Government, 1980, 2d edit., 1984; co-author: 200 Years of the Republic, 1976, Changing Politics in the South, 1976; author articles and pamphlets in field; contbr. to publs. Served as 2d lt. USAAF, 1942; 1st lt., 1943, 1944; maj., 1945-46; service with 5th Air Force, 1944-45; Australia; service with 5th Air Force; New Guinea; service with 5th Air Force; Netherlands; service with 5th Air Force; East Indies; service with 5th Air Force; Philippines; service with 5th Air Force; Okinawa, and; service with 5th Air Force; Japan (6 battle stars); lt. col. USAF Res., 1953—. Mem. Am. Hist. Assn., Am. Polit. Sci. Assn. (mem. council 1953-55, v.p. 1965-66), So. Polit. Sci. Assn. (pres. 1954-55), Fla. Polit. Sci. Assn. (pres. 1972), Fla. Hist. Soc., Am. Assn. U. Profs. (pres. Fla. chpt. 1939-41), Phi Beta Kappa (sec. Fla. chpt. 1938-41, pres. 1947-48), Phi Kappa Phi, Pi Gamma Mu, Kappa Delta Pi, Florida Blue Key. Designer reapportionment legislative dists. Fla., 1967. Home: 2255 NW 5th Pl Gainesville FL 32603

DAUGHADAY, WILLIAM HAMILTON, physician; b. Chgo., Feb. 12, 1918; s. C. Colton and Marion (Sharpe) D.; m. Hazel Judkins, Jan. 22, 1945; children: Elizabeth Colton (Mrs. Bruce Axelrod), John Freer. A.B., Harvard U., 1940, M.D., 1943. Diplomate: Am. Bd. Internal Medicine, mem., 1970-76. Intern Boston City Hosp., 1944; asst. resident Barnes Hosp., St. Louis, 1946-47, cons. clin. chemistry, mem. staff, 1950-69; mem. faculty Washington U. Sch. Medicine, St. Louis, 1949—, NIH fellow biol. chemistry, 1949-50, instr., then asst. prof. medicine, 1950-56, asso. prof., 1956-63, prof., 1963-, dir. metabolism dir., 1951—, dir. Diabetes and Endocrinology Research Center, 1975-77, dir. Diabetes Research and Tng. Center, 1977—; mem. endocrine study sect. NIH, 1967-71; mem. adv. bd. Nat. Pituitary Agy., 1964-70; mem. endocrinology and metabolism adv. com. FDA, 1976-81, chmn., 1980-81. Editor: Jour. Lab. and Clin. Medicine, 1960-66, Jour. Clin. Endocrinology and Metabolism, 1973-77; assoc. editor: Jour. Clin. Investigation, 1977-83; Author sci. papers on metabolism, endocrinology. Served as capt. M.C. AUS, 1944-46. Mem. Am. Diabetes Assn., Central Soc. Clin. Research, Am. Soc. Clin. Investigation, Endocrine Soc. (pres. 1971-72, Fred Conrad Koch medal 1975), Assn. Am. Physicians. Home: 1414 W Adams Kirkwood MO 63122 Office: Box 8127 Metabolism Div Washington U Sch Medicine 660 S Euclid Ave Saint Louis MO 63110

DAUGHDRILL, JAMES HAROLD, JR., college president; b. LaGrange, Ga., Apr. 25, 1934; s. James Harold and Louisa Coffee (Dozier) D.; m. Elizabeth Anne Gay, June 26, 1954; children: James Harold III, Louisa Rish, Elizabeth Gay. Student, Davidson Coll., 1952-54, D.D., 1974; A.B., Emory U., 1956; B.D., Columbia Theol. Sem., 1967, M.Div., 1969. Pres. Kingston Mills, Inc., Cartersville, Ga., 1956-64; ordained to ministry Presbyn. Ch., 1967; minister St. Andrews Presbyn. Ch., Little Rock, 1967-70; sec. of stewardship Presbyn. Ch. in U.S., Atlanta, 1970-73; pres. Coll. of Southwestern At Memphis, 1973—. Author: Man Talk, 1972; past assoc. editor: Presbyn. Outlook, 1972. Past chmn. Tenn. Council Pvt. Colls.; past pres. Coll. Athletic Conf.; past chmn. bd. So. Coll. Univ. Union; trustee Frank E. Seidman Award Found., Brooks Meml. Art Gallery; past trustee Brooks and Hutchison Sch.; past mem. adv. bd. Auburndale Sch. System; past bd. dirs. Tenn. Student Asst. Corp.; bd. dirs. Memphis chpt. NCCJ, Liberty Bowl; bd. dirs. Chickasaw council, exec. bd. Boy Scouts Am. Named Educator of Yr. Greater Memphis State, Pillar of Memphis Jewish Nat. Fund. Mem. Memphis C. of C. (bd. dir.), Assn. Am. Colls. (bd. dir.), Assn. Presbyn. Colls. (dir.), Phi Delta Theta, Omicron Delta Kappa. Clubs: University (N.Y.C.); Racquet, Memphis Country. Home: 671 West Dr Memphis TN 38112

DAUGHEN, JOSEPH ROBERT, journalist; b. Phila., June 12, 1935; s. John J. and Loretta (Sandone) D.; m. Joan Purdy, Dec. 30, 1961; 1 dau., Joan Patrice. B.S. in Bus. Adminstrn, Temple U., 1956. Reporter Phila. Daily News, 1956-63; Harrisburg corr. Phila. Bull., 1964-65, Washington corr., 1965-67, nat. corr., 1969-82; sr. writer Phila. Daily News, 1982—. Author: The Negro in Philadelphia, 1965, (with Peter Binzen) The Wreck of the Penn Central, 1971, The Cop Who Would Be King: The Honorable Frank Rizzo, 1977. Mem. Phila. Press Assn. Club: Nat. Press. Glenside PA 19038

DAUGHERTY, ALFRED CLARK, manufacturing company executive; b. Wilkinsburg, Pa., July 12, 1923; s. Horace William and Helen Claney (Bradley) D.; m. Janet Elliott, Dec. 14, 1946; 1 dau., Christine Daugherty Adams. B.A., Pa. State U., 1946. With Rockwell Mfg. Co., Pitts., 1946-57; v.p. Petroleum and Indsl. Meter Group, 1962, v.p. adminstrn., 1963; v.p., then pres. Republic Flow Meter Co., Chgo., 1957-61; pres. Rockwell Mfg. Co., Pitts., 1964-72, Dresser Industries Indsl. Spltys., Dallas, 1972-74, P.R. Mallory & Co., Indpls., 1975-78, chmn., chief exec. officer, 1978—; exec. v.p. Dart Industries Inc., Los Angeles, 1979—, also dir.; chmn. Duracell Internat., Bethel, Conn., 1979—; dir. Cin. Milacron Inc., Am. Precision Industries, Inc., Materials Research Inc., Grow Group Inc., Key Pharms., Inc. Served with U.S. Army, 1942-45. Mem. Machinery and Allied Products Inst. (exec. com.), Elec. Mfrs. Club. (gov.). Republican. Presbyterian. Clubs: Duquesne (Pitts.); Rolling Rock, Laurel Valley Golf (Ligonier, Pa.); John's Island Golf, Bent Pine Golf, Riomar Bay Yacht (Vero Beach, Fla.). Office: 622 Beachland Blvd Vero Beach FL 32963

DAUGHERTY, CARROLL ROOP, economist, labor arbitrator; b. Annville, Pa., Dec. 3, 1900; s. Benjamin Franklin and Della Frances (Roop) D.; m. Miriam Craiglow, 1928; children: James Carroll, David Henry; m. Marion Roberts, 1940; 1 dau., Frances Marion. A.B., Lebanon Valley Coll., 1921; A.M., U. Pa., 1924, Ph.D., 1927. Instr. Mercersburg (Pa.) Acad., 1921-23, Wharton Sch., U. Pa., 1925-28; prof. econs. U. Ala., 1928-31, U. Pitts., 1931-40; prof. econs., chmn. dept. Hunter Coll., 1940-46; prof. labor relations Northwestern U., 1946-68, chmn. dept., 1948-58; now labor arbitrator, cons.; prin. economist for labor productivity studies U.S. Bur. Labor Statistics, 1936; chief economist Wage and Hour div., U.S. Dept. Labor, 1938-40; mem. Com. on Postwar Price Problems, Nat. Bur. Econ. Research, 1944-46; nat. wage stblzn. dir. Nat. War Labor Bd., 1942-45; lend lease dir. in New Zealand for Dept. State, 1945-46; chmn. Pres.'s steel-labor fact-finding bd., 1949; Pres.'s R.R. labor emergency bds., 1951-52; referee Nat. R.R. Adjustment Bd., 1952—; tchr. mgmt. devel. U.S. and abroad. Author: Labor Problems in American Industry, 1933, 34, 38, 41, 48, Labor Under NRA, 1934; co-author: books including Economics of Iron and Steel Industry, 1937, Principles of Political Economy, 1950, Labor Problems of American Society, 1952, Conflict and Cooperation, 1968. Recipient Disting. Alumnus award Lebanon Valley Coll., 1965. Benjamin Franklin fellow Royal Soc. for Arts; mem. Indsl. Relations Research Assn. (exec. bd. 1954-56), Nat. Acad. Arbitrators, Lincoln Acad. Ill., Alpha Sigma Phi, Delta Sigma Pi, Beta Gamma Sigma. Home: 6621 Avenida de la Reina La Jolla CA 92037

DAUGHERTY, FRANKLIN W., geologist, educator; b. Alpine, Tex., June 20, 1927; s. William Adolph and Bertha (Carter) D.; m. Dorothy Cotten, July 18, 1945; children: Sheila B., Stephen F., Diana Claire. B.S., Sul Ross State Coll., 1950; M.A., U. Tex. at Austin, 1959, Ph.D., 1962. Rancher, Alpine, Tex., 1950-54, mineral exploration contractor, Alpine, 1955-58; geologist Dow Chem. Co., Douglas, Ariz., 1962-63; prof. geology, coordinator earth sci. research Killgore Research Center, West Tex. State U., 1963-76, chmn. dept. geology, 1976-77, adj. prof., 1977—; pres. Pinnacle Resources, Inc., Alpine, 1971—, D & F Minerals, 1980—; cons. in field. Contbr. articles to profl. jours. Chmn. Brewster County Hist. Commn., 1983. Served with AUS, 1946-47. Recipient excellence award West Tex. State U., 1967. Fellow Geol. Soc. Am.; mem. Geochem. Soc., West Tex. Geol. Soc., Tex. Mining Council, Sigma Xi. Home: Sunny Glen Rd PO Box 329 Alpine TX 79831

DAUGHERTY, FREDERICK ALVIN, U.S. judge; b. Oklahoma City, Aug. 18, 1914; s. Charles Lemuel and Felicia (Mitchell) D.; m. Marjorie E. Green, Mar. 15, 1947 (dec. 1964); m. Betsy F. Amis, Dec. 15, 1965. LL.B., Cumberland U., 1933; postgrad., Oklahoma City U., 1934-35, LL.B. (hon.), 1974, Okla. U., 1936-37. Bar: Okla. 1937. Practiced, Oklahoma City, 1937-40; mem. firm Ames, Ames & Daugherty, Oklahoma City, 1946-50; firm Ames, Daugherty, Bynum & Black, Oklahoma City, 1952-55; judge 7th Jud. Dist. Ct., Okla., 1955-61; U.S. dist. judge Western, Eastern and No. Dists. Okla., 1961—, chief judge., 1972-82; mem. Fgn. Intelligence Surveillance Ct., 1981—, Temporary Emergency Ct. Appeals, 1983—, Multi dist. Litigation panel, 1980—; mem. codes of conduct com. U.S. Jud. Conf., 1980—. Active local ARC, 1956—, chmn., 1958-60, nat. bd. govs., 1963-69, 3d vice chmn., 1968-69; active United Fund Greater Oklahoma City, 1957—, pres., 1961, trustee, 1963—; pres. Community Council Oklahoma City and County, 1967-69; mem. exec. com. Oklahoma City Council Alcoholism, 1964—; exec. com. Okla. Med. Research Found., 1966-69. Served as officer with AUS, 1940-45, 50-52. Decorated Legion of Merit with 2 oak leaf clusters, Bronze Star with oak leaf cluster; recipient award to mankind Oklahoma City Sertoma Club, 1962, Outstanding Citizen award Oklahoma City Jr. C. of C., 1965, Distinguished Alumni citation Samford U., 1974, Distinguished Service citation Okla. U., 1973; named to Okla. Hall of Fame, 1969. Mem. Am., Fed., Okla. bar assns., Am. Bar Found., Sigma Alpha Epsilon, Phi Delta Phi. Episcopalian (sr. warden 1957). Clubs: Kiwanian (pres. 1957, lt. gov. 1959), Mason (33 deg., Shriner, Jester), Men's Dinner Oklahoma City (pres. 1966-69). Office: US Courthouse Oklahoma City OK 73102

DAUGHERTY, FREDRICA, editor; b. Keller, Tex., Oct. 10, 1938; d. Fred Max and Bonnie Lou (Polley) D.; m. C.I. Cooper, Aug. 6, 1958; m. Steven Alan Bassion, May 30, 1976. Diploma, Famous Artists Comml. Art Sch., 1958; certificate, Rutherford Met. Sch. Bus., Fort Worth, 1958; postgrad., Tex. Christian U., 1958-60. Local operator Southwestern Bell Telephone Co., Ft. Worth, 1957-59; sec. Tandy Leather Co., Ft. Worth, 1959-60, advt. artist, 1960-62, chief copywriter, 1962-64; asst. advt. mgr. Tex Tan Western Leather Co., Yoakum, Tex., 1964-65; advt. prodn. mgr. Tandy Corp., Ft. Worth, 1965-70; editor-in-chief Decorating and Craft Ideas mag., Ft. Worth, 1970-78; editorial dir. Needlecraft for Today mag., Ft. Worth, 1978—, Needle and Thread mag., 1980—; v.p. Happy Hands Pub. Co., Ft. Worth, 1982—; founder Tall and II Internat. Sch. Equitation. Mem. Am. Crafts Council, Soc. Crafts Designers, Nat. Standards Council Am. Embroiders, Center History Am. Needlework., Dallas Dressage Club, U.S. Dressage Fedn., Legacy Arabian Horse Club. Mem. Unity Ch. Office: 4949 Byers St Fort Worth TX 76107

DAUGHERTY, ROBERT MELVIN, JR., physician, univ. dean; b. Kansas City, Mo., May 2, 1934; s. Robert Melvin and Mildred Josephine (Johnson) D.; m. Sandra Allison Keller, Aug. 10, 1957; children—Robert Melvin III, Allison, Christopher. B.A., U. Kans., 1956, M.D., 1960; M.S., U. Okla., 1963, Ph.D., 1964. Intern Jefferson Davis Hosp., Houston, 1960-61; resident U. Okla. Med. Center, Oklahoma City, 1961-64; asst. prof. physiology and medicine U. Okla. Med. Sch., Oklahoma City, 1964-66; asso. prof. physiology and medicine Mich. State U. Coll. Human Medicine, East Lansing, 1966-69; prof., dir. Office Curriculum Implementation, 1969-76; prof. physiology and medicine U. Wyo. Coll. Human Medicine, Laramie, 1976-78, dean, 1976-78; prof. physiology and medicine Ind. U. Sch. Medicine, Indpls., 1978-81, asso. dean, 1978-81, dir. continuing med. edn., 1978-81; dean Sch. Medicine, U. Nev., Reno, 1981—; teaching scholar Am. Heart Assn., 1970-75. Mem. Am. Physiol. Soc., Am. Heart Assn., AMA, Central Soc. for Clin. Investigation. Presbyterian. Home: 820 Marsh Ave Reno NV 89509 Office: Sch Medicine U Nevada Reno NV 89557

DAUGHTRY, DEWITT CORNELL, physician, surgeon; b. Clinton, N.C., Apr. 1, 1914; s. James Guilford and Lorena (Grantham) D.; m. Lucille Carr, June 3, 1939; children: Janet (Mrs. Lester E. Moody), James DeWitt. A.B., Atlantic Christian Coll., 1935; M.D., Med. Coll. Va., 1939, postgrad., 1945-46; postgrad., Wayne U. Coll. Medicine, 1939-42, George Washington U., 1948, Cook County Grad. Sch., 1951. Intern Detroit Receiving Hosp., 1939-40, sr. intern surgery, 1940-41; asst. resident surgery Alexander Blain Hosp., Detroit, 1941-42; resident surgery Med. Coll. Va. Hosp., 1945-46; resident thoracic surgery McGuire Gen. Hosp.; mem. dean's com. VA Hosp. Med. Coll. Va., 1946-48; pvt. practice medicine, specializing in thoracic and cardiovascular surgery, Miami, Fla., 1948—; instr. surgery Wayne U. Coll. Medicine, 1940-42, Med. Coll. Va., 1945-48; clin. prof. surgery U. Miami Sch. Medicine, 1969—, founder, endower sect. thoracic surgery, endower sect. gen. surgery chief dept., prof., 1978—; cons. thoracic surgery VA Hosp. and Regional Office, Southeast Fla. Tb Hosp.; Asst. sec.-treas. Papanicolaou Cancer Research Inst., Miami; chmn. asso. hosp. com. Jackson Meml. Hosp., U. Miami Sch. Medicine, 1967-68; mem. adv. bd. com. Internat. Congress on Smoking and Health, 1965-67; pres. med. staff Miami Heart Inst., 1970-72, chief of surgery, 1962-68, mem. med. exec. com., 1962-78, chmn. surg. audit com., 1965-70, 1972-74; chief thoracic surgery Mt. Sinai Med. Center of Greater Miami, 1949-63, also Baptist Hosp., and; Mercy Hosp.; chief surgery Nat. Children's Cardiac Hosp., 1950-60; chief thoracic surgery Dade County Hosp., 1950-65, McGuire Gen. Hosp., Richmond, Va., 1946-48; mem. staff Jackson Meml., Miami Heart Inst. (also mem. Endowment Fund and Benefactors Guild), Mt. Sinai, Cedars of Lebanon, Baptist, South Miami, Doctors, Variety Children's Mercy, St. Francis, North Shore, North Miami Gen., Palm Springs, Hialeah hosps.; ret. Pres. Anatomical Models, Inc.; Physician mem. Met. Pollution Control Bd., 1964-69; mem. exec. com. South Fla. Inter-Profl. Council, 1964, pres., 1976, 79; mem. med. adv. bd. Vocational

Rehab. Service, 1955-56; mem. Gov.'s Com. Employment Handicapped, 1962-64; Bd. govs. Com. of 100, 1970—, mem. exec. com., 1980—. Sr. author: Pulmonary Tumors for Tice's Practice of Medicine, 1967, Thoracic Trauma, 1980; contbr. numerous articles to med., sci. jours. Served with USPHS, 1942-45. Recipient Merit award Miami Med. Forum, 1968, 69; Silver medallion Miami Heart Inst., 1972; Benefactors Guild, 1978. Fellow A.C.S., Am. Coll. Chest Physicians (gov. 1964-70, bd. regents 1971-77), Am. Coll. Cardiology; mem. Am. Assn. Thoracic Surgery, Soc. Thoracic Surgeons, So. Thoracic Surg. Assn. (pres. 1964), Nat. Tb Assn. (dir. 1956-73), Am. Thoracic Soc. (council 1971-74), Am. Heart Assn., Am. Med. Assn., So. Med. Assn., Pan-Am. Med. Assn., Fla. Med. Assn., Dade County Med. Assn. (pres. 1964), Am. Med. Writers Assn., So. Tb Conf., So. Thoracic Soc., Fla. Thoracic Soc. (pres. 1956-57) thoracic socs), Fla. Tb and Health Assn. (pres. 1956-57), Dade County Tb Assn. (dir. 1950-81, v.p. 1960-61, exec. com. 1962-63), Heart Assn. Greater Miami (pres. 1967), Miami Med. Forum (pres. 1970), Hesperian Lit. Soc. (pres. 1934-35), So. Thoracic Surg. Assn. (v.p. 1957, pres. 1961, chmn. council 1962), So. Coll. Chest Physicians (sec. treas. 1959, v.p. 1960, pres. 1961), Fla. Tb and Respiratory Disease Assn. (v.p. 1955-56, dir. 1950—, mem. exec. com., pres. 1958, chmn. research com. 1956), Soc. Univ. Founders, Alpha Kappa Kappa. Clubs: Miami Shores Country; Ponte Vedra (Fla.); La Gorce Country (Miami). Home: 4201 Lake Rd Miami FL 33137

DAUGHTRY, JOHN CARY, photographer; b. Asheville, N.C., July 18, 1947; s. John Patrick and Eltas (Tucker) D.; m. Mary Ann Mee, May 25, 1974; 1 child, Alesha. B.A., Wake Forest U., 1968; M.F.A., Rochester Inst. Tech., 1971. Photography intern Greensboro (N.C.) Daily News, 1967, reporting intern, 1968; photography intern Sacramento (Calif.) Union, 1969-70; staff photographer Charlotte (N.C.) Observer, 1971-79; news photography services mgr. Charlotte Observer/Charlotte News, 1979—; grad. asst. instr. Rochester Inst. Tech., 1969-71; exhibited photography Wake Forest U., 1968, Rochester Inst. Tech., 1971, Mint Mus. Art, Charlotte, 1973. Named Photographer of Year Carolinas Press Photographers Assn., 1973, 74; recipient gold medal N.C. Arts Council, 1973. Mem. The Light Factory, Nat. Press Photographers Assn. (asso. dir. region 6 1976-80), Carolinas Press Photographers Assn. (pres. 1977). Baptist. Home: 2104 Charlotte Dr Charlotte NC 28203 Office: 600 South Tryon St Charlotte NC 28232

D'AULAIRE, EDGAR PARIN, artist, lithographer, author; b. Munich, Germany, Sept. 30, 1898; came to U.S., 1929, naturalized, 1939; s. Gino and Ella (d'Aulaire) Parin; m. Ingri Sandsmark Mortenson, July 24, 1925 (dec. 1980); children: Per Ola, Nils Maarten. Student, Inst. Tech., Munich, 1917-19, Sch. Applied Arts, Munich, 1919-22, Hans Hofman Sch., Munich, 1922-24, Ecole André Lhote, Paris, 1925-26, Ecole Pola Gauguin, Paris, 1926—. Lectr. with wife. Illustrator 17 books in, Germany, 1922-26; author-illustrator (with wife), 26 children's books, 1931—; painter, exhibited in, Norway and Paris; executed 2 frescoes, Norway, 1926-27; Author, illustrator: (with Ingri d'Aulaire) The Magic Rug, 1931, Ola, 1932, Ola and Blakken, 1933, Conquest of the Atlantic, 1933, The Lord's Prayer, 1934, Children of the Northlights, 1935, George Washington, 1936, East of the Sun and West of the Moon, 1938, Abraham Lincoln, 1939, Animals Everywhere, 1940, Leif the Lucky, 1941, The Star Spangled Banner, 1942, Don't Count Your Chicks, 1943, Wings for Per, 1944, Too Big, 1945, Pocahontas, 1946, Nils, 1948, Foxie, 1949, Benjamin Franklin, 1950, Buffalo Bill, 1952, The Two Cars, 1954, Columbus, 1955, The Magic Meadow, 1958, d'Aulaires' Book of Greek Myths, 1962, d'Aulaires' Norse Gods and Giants, 1967, d'Aulaires Trolls, 1972, The Terrible Troll Bird, 1976. Recipient Caldecott award A.L.A., 1940, Regina award Cath. Library Assn., 1970. Home: 74 Mather Rd Georgetown CT 06829

DAUM, GARY A., retail executive; b. Pitts., May 27, 1938; s. Alfred S. and Dorothy (Smith) D.; m. Linda Miller, Mar. 24, 1962; children: Brian, Lauren, Dana. B.S., Pa. State U. C.P.A. Auditor Touche Ross, Pitts., 1960-63; controller Gen. Nutrition, Pitts., 1963-70, v.p., 1970-79, pres., 1979—, dir. Served with U.S. Army, 1960-66. Mem. Pa. Soc. C.P.A.s, Am. Inst. C.P.A.s. Republican. Methodist. Home: 3000 Oakhurst Rd Bethel Park PA 15102 Office: 921 Penn Ave Pittsburgh PA 15222

DAUPHINAIS, GEORGE ARTHUR, importer; b. Waterbury, Conn., Apr. 11, 1918; s. Arthur J. and Nell (Phillips) D.; m. Sarah McConnell, Dec. 27, 1942; children: Carol Joe, George William, Sarah Marie. B.S. in Mech. Engring., La. State U., 1942. Advanced engring. program Gen. Electric Co., Schenectady, 1942, engr., 1942-47; with H.K. Porter Co., Inc., Phila., 1947-59, successively plant engr., works mgr., 1947-52, v.p., gen. mgr., 1952-59; v.p. Electric Autolite Co., Toledo, 1960—; pres. Prestolite Internat. Co. div. Eltra Corp., 1964—; group v.p. Sangamo Electric Co., Springfield, 1965-76; pres. Dauphin Company. Mem. ASME, Tau Beta Pi, Sigma Alpha Epsilon. Home: 2021 Willemoore St Springfield IL 62704 Office: PO Box 5137 Springfield IL 62705

DAUSCH, WILLIAM F., stainless steel manufacturing company executive; b. Hartford, Conn., Jan. 28, 1938; s. William F. and Mary P. D.; m. Elizabeth Claire Lock, Sept. 21, 1968; 1 son, Andrew Wood. B.S., U. Conn., 1960; J.D., U. Mich., 1968; M.B.A., Loyola Coll. Balt., 1982. Bar: N.Y. 1968. Asso. atty. firm LeBoeuf, Lamb, Leiby & MacRae, N.Y.C., 1968-73; v.p., gen. counsel CHC Corp., Towson, Md., 1973-77, Eastmet Corp., Cockeysville, Md., 1977—. Served with USNR, 1960-65. Mem. Am. Bar Assn., Bar Assn. State N.Y., Order of Coif. Club: Hillendale Country (Balt.) (gov.). Address: Eastmet Corp PO Box 507 Cockeysville MD 21030

DAUTEL, CHARLES SHREVE, mining company executive; b. Cleve., Apr. 5, 1923; s. Robert Poe and Frances (Shreve) D.; m. Isabell Francis Brown, June 11, 1947; Children: Charles Warren, Louis Craig. B.S.C., Ohio U., 1948; J.D., U. Cin., 1952. Bar: Ohio 1945. With firm Nichols, Wood, Marx & Ginter, Cin., 1952-55; with Eagle-Picher Industries, Inc., Cin., 1955—, asst. sec., asst. gen. counsel, 1958-70, sec., 1970—, v.p., 1980—; dir. Gateway Fed. Savs. & Loan Assn. Cin. Bd. dirs. Eagle-Picher Found. Served with AUS, 1942-46. Mem. Cin., Ohio, Am. bar assns., Phi Delta Theta, Phi Delta Phi. Clubs: Cincinnati, Hidden Valley Lake Country. Home: 5664 Candlelite Terr Cincinnati OH 45238 Office: 580 Bldg PO Box 779 Cincinnati OH 45201

DAVANT, JAMES WARING, investment banker; b. McComb, Miss., Dec. 1, 1917; s. Guy Hamilton and Em Reid (Waring) D.; m. Mary Ellis Westlake, Apr. 4, 1942; children—Mary Diane (Mrs. Harold F. Dietz, Jr.), John Hamilton, Patricia Jean (Mrs. Mark Honewell Reed). Student, U. Va., 1939. With Paine, Webber, Jackson & Curtis, 1945—, gen. partner, 1956—, mem. policy com., 1963—, mng. partner, 1964—, pres., chief exec. officer, 1970-71, chmn. bd., chief exec. officer, 1971-80, chmn. Paine Webber Inc., 1974-81, now dir.; ret., 1981; chmn. Assn. Stock Exchange Firms, 1966-68; bd. dirs. N.Y. Stock Exchange, 1972-77. Chmn. nat. adv. council Nat. Cystic Fibrosis Research Found.; Bd. dirs. Securities Industry Assn., 1973-78, Manhattan Eye, Ear and Throat Hosp., The Fresh Air Fund; chmn. central market com. Stock Exchange. Served to lt. comdr. USNR, 1940-45. Mem. Fgn. Policy Assn. Episcopalian. Clubs: Links, River, Brook, Downtown Assn., Economic (chmn. 1976-77), trustee, Pilgrims of U.S., Bond (gov. 1965—), Bond (N.Y.C.) (pres. 1972—); Minneapolis (Mpls.)). 200 E 66th St New York NY 10021 also Cherrywood Locust Valley NY 11560 Office: 1221 Ave of Americas 32d Floor New York NY 10020

DAVENPORT, CHESTER, lawyer; b. Athens, Ga.; m. Phyllis; children—Corey, Cece. Grad. cum laude, Morehouse Coll., 1963; law degree, U. Ga., 1966. Bar: Ga., D.C. bars. Atty. in appellate sect., tax div. U.S. Dept. Justice, Washington, 1966-69; legis. asst. to Senator Alan Cranston of Calif., 1969-71; v.p., gen. counsel R.H. Lapin & Co., mortgage bankers, San Francisco, 1971-73; coordinator Carter-Mondale policy planning group, 1976; team leader HUD/Dept. Transp. cluster for Pres. Carter's transition team, 1976; asst. sec. for policy, plans and internat. affairs U.S. Dept. Transp., 1977-79; ptnr. firm Hudson Leftwich & Davenport, Washington, 1979—. Democrat.

DAVENPORT, DONA LEE, television executive; b. Toledo, May 17, 1931; d. Juston Burns and Opal Thelma (Raines) D. B.A., tchrs.'s cert., U. Mich., 1953; summer postgrad., U. N.C., 1957, N.C. State U., 1958, Queens Coll., 1969. Tchr., Grosse Pointe, Mich., 1953-54, Jr. High Sch., Charlotte, 1955-58; radio-TV coordinator Charlotte Sch. System, 1958-60; co-founder, tchr. Am. Assn. U. Women Spl. Sch. for Academically Talented Children, Charlotte, 1960; radio-TV dir. Charlotte-Mecklenburg Schs., 1960-62; sta. mgr. WTVI, Charlotte, 1962-72, gen. mgr., 1972-77; exec. dir. WTVI, Inc., 1977-79; telecommunications mgmt. cons. Atlantic Research Corp., 1979—; Chmn. FCC Instructional TV Fixed Service Com. for N.C., 1968-71; Bd. dirs. Pub. Broadcasting Service, 1972-79. Named Charlotte's Outstanding Career Woman in Communications, Central Charlotte Assn., 1967; recipient Broadcast Preceptor award Broadcast Industry Conf, 1969; Regent's scholar U. Mich., 1949-53. Mem. So. Ednl. Communications Assn. (dir. 1968-78, treas. 1973-74, vice chmn. 1977-78), Nat. Assn. Ednl. Broadcasters, Am. Women in Radio and TV (named First Woman Public TV Sta. Mgr. 1980), N.C. Adminstrv. Women in Edn., Am. Assn. U. Women, Delta Kappa Gamma, Alpha Xi Delta. Baptist. Clubs: Business and Professional Women's (Charlotte); Charlotte-Mecklenburg Republican Women's. Home: 1510 Exeter Rd Charlotte NC 28211 Office: 1510 Exeter Rd Charlotte NC 28211

DAVENPORT, GUY MATTISON, JR., educator, author; b. Anderson, S.C., Nov. 23, 1927; s. Guy Mattison and Marie (Fant) D. B.A., Duke U., 1948; B.Litt., Oxford U., 1950; Ph.D., Harvard U., 1961. Instr. English Washington U., St. Louis, 1952-55; tutor Harvard U., 1957-60; ast. prof. English Haverford (Pa.) Coll., 1960-63; prof. English U. Ky., Lexington, 1963—. Author: The Intelligence of Louis Agassiz, 1963, Carmina Archilochi, 1964, Sappho:Songs and Fragments, 1965, Cydonia Flrentia, 1966, Pennant Key-Indexed Guide to Homer's Iliad, 1967, Pennant Key-Indexed Guide to Homer's Odyssey, 1967, Do You Have a Poem Book on e.e. cummings?, 1969, DaVinci's Bicycle, 1975, Geography and the Imagination, 1981, Ecolgues, 1981, Herakleitos, Diogenes and the Mimes of Herondas, 1981, Tatlin, 1982; contbr. articles to profl. jours. and mags. Served with AC U.S. Army, 1950-52. Rhodes scholar, 1948-50; recipient Zabel prize Am. Acad. Arts and Letters, 1981. Am. Baptist. Office: Dept English U Ky Lexington KY 40506

DAVENPORT, GWEN (MRS. JOHN DAVENPORT), author; b. Colon, C.Z., Oct. 3, 1910; d. James Farquharson and Gwen (Wigley) Leys; m. John Davenport, Feb. 5, 1937; children—Christopher, John Farquharson, Juliet Rathbone (Mrs. Bertrand Gilbert). A.B., Vassar Coll., 1931. Author: A Stranger and Afraid, 1943, Return Engagement, 1945, Belvedere; motion picture prodn. Sitting Pretty, 1947, Family Fortunes, 1949, Candy for Breakfast, 1950, The Bachelor's Baby, 1957, The Wax Foundation, 1961, Great Loves in Legend and Life, 1964; Contbr. short stories to nat. mags. Home: 308 Penruth Place Louisville KY 40207

DAVENPORT, HORACE ELSTUN, oil co. exec.; b. Buffalo, Jan. 26, 1907; s. William Ashley and Pauline (Tilley) D.; m. Elizabeth Rohrs, Dec. 14, 1932; children—Susan Davenport Peirce, Peter MacLaren, Michael Elstun. B.A., Columbia U., 1929. Pres. George W. Pickering Co., Salem, Mass., 1934-52, chmn., 1952-75; v.p. Pocahontas Fuel Co., Salem, 1952-57; pres. Pocahontas Steamship Co., 1952-69; pres. N.E. div. Consol. Coal Co., 1957-69; also corp. dir.; chmn. bd. Northeast Petroleum Industries, Inc., Boston, 1969-80, vice chmn., 1980—, also dir. Life trustee Salem Hosp. chmn. Nat. Rowing Found., 1966-78. Recipient Disting. Alumni award Columbia U., 1980; named to Rowing Hall of Fame, 1965. Clubs: Leander, Henley-on-Thames (Eng.); N.Y. Athletic, University (N.Y.C.); Algonquin (Boston); Essex Country (Manchester). Home: 505 Summer St Manchester MA 01944 Office: 100 Federal St Boston MA 02110

DAVENPORT, HORACE WILLARD, physiologist; b. Phila., Oct. 20, 1912; s. Horace Willard and Elizabeth (Langendorf) D.; m. Virginia Dickerson, Feb. 1, 1945 (dec. Mar. 1968); 2 sons; m. Ingeborg L. Epstein, Aug. 15, 1969. B.S., Calif. Inst. Tech., 1935, Ph.D., 1939; B.A., U. Oxford, Eng., 1937; B.Sc., 1938; D.Sc., 1961. Instr. physiology U. Pa. Med. Sch., Phila., 1941-1943; instr. physiology Harvard Med. Sch., 1943- 45; prof., head dept. physiology U. Utah Med. Sch., 1945-56; prof. dept. physiology U. Mich., Ann Arbor, 1956—, chmn. dept., 1956-78, William Beaumont prof., 1978-83, prof. emeritus, 1983—; vis. prof. Mayo Found., 1962-63. Contbr. to profl. jours. Recipient Friedenwald medal Am. Gastroent. Assn., 1980. Mem. Am. Physiol. Soc. (pres. 1961-62), Nat. Acad. Scis. Home: 1050 Wall St Apt 7D Ann Arbor MI 48105

DAVENPORT, MANUEL MANSON, philosophy educator; b. Colorado Springs, Colo., June 14, 1929; s. Ernest Alfred and Anna (Brauer) D.; m. Evi Gustafson; children: Marian, Mark, Mitchel, David, Brian, Linda. A.B., Bethany Nazarene Coll., 1950; M.A., Colo. Coll., 1954; Ph.D., U. Ill., 1957. Instr. Colo. Coll., 1956-57; asst., asso. prof. Colo. State U., 1957-67; prof. philosophy Tex. A& M U., College Station, 1967-, head dept., 1967-76; elem. sch. tchr., 1950-52, univ. lectr., 1978; disting. vis. prof. U.S. Air Force Acad., 1980-81. First v.p. Brazos Civil Liberties Union, 1968-71; campus liaison Peace Corps, 1968-72. Served with U.S. Army, 1952. Recipient Faculty Achievement awards, 1959, 60, 69, 78, 80; Rockefeller Found. grantee, 1962-63; Danforth Asso. Mem. AAUP (past chpt. pres.), Southwestern Philos. Soc. (past pres.), Am. Philos. Assn., Mountain Plains Philos. Assn. (past chmn.), Phi Kappa Phi, Omicron Delta Kappa. Home: 1206 Glade St College Station TX 77840 Office: Harrington Bldg College Station TX 77843 *Education must respect the right of the individual to be different as much as it demands respect for the wisdom of the past. The individual cannot achieve self-realization without learning from the past, but society cannot escape from the mistakes of the past unless individuals are free to deviate from tradition.*

DAVENPORT, WILBUR BAYLEY, JR., electrical engineering educator; b. Phila., July 27, 1920; s. Wilbur Bayley and Cora (Reifsnyder) D.; m. Joan Purington, Nov. 3, 1945; children: Mark Wilbur, Sally Davenport. B. Elec. Engring., Ala. Poly. Inst., 1941; M.S. in Elec. Engring, M.I.T., 1943, D.Sc., 1950. Mem. faculty M.I.T., 1949-82, prof. elec. engring., 1960-82, assoc. head dept. elec. engring., 1971-72, head dept. elec. engring. and computer sci., 1974-78; vis. prof. elec. engring. U. Hawaii, Manoa, 1982—; adj. research prof. elec. engring. Naval Postgrad. Sch., 1982-83; asst. dir. Lincoln Lab., 1963-65, assoc. dir. research lab. electronics, 1961-63; dir. Center for Advanced Engring. Study, 1972-74, Gen Rad, Inc., Concord, Mass., 1974-82; mem. sci. year editorial adv. bd. Field Enterprises Ednl. Corp., 1974-76; mem. Carnegie Commn. on Future Pub. Broadcasting, 1977—; cons. to govt. and industry, 1961—. Author: (with William L. Root) An Introduction to the Theory of Random Signals and Noise, 1958, Probability and Random Processes, An Introduction for Applied Scientists and Engineers, 1970. Served to lt. (j.g.) USNR, 1943-46. Recipient certification of commendation Navy Dept., 1960. Fellow IEEE, AAAS, Am. Acad. Arts and Scis.; mem. Nat. Acad. Engring., Sigma Xi, Tau Beta Pi, Phi Kappa Phi, Eta Kappa Nu, Spiked Shoe. Home: 1338 Aloha Oe Dr Kailua HI 96734 Office: Holmes 444 2540 Dole St Honolulu HI 96822

DAVENPORT, WILLIAM KIRK, automobile company executive; b. Ann Arbor, Mich., Dec. 22, 1928; s. Kenneth Mercereau and Florence Winifred (Pittelco) D.; m. Gertrude Baldwin Perkins, July 19, 1958; children: Kirk, Timothy, Nina. A.B., Harvard U., 1950; J.D., U. Mich., 1953. Bar: Mich. 1953, N.Y. 1958. Assoc. firm Cravath, Swaine & Moore, N.Y.C., 1957-63; sr. atty. Ford Motor Co., Dearborn, Mich., 1963-66, counsel, 1978-79, asst. gen. counsel, 1979—; sec. Ford Motor Credit Co., Dearborn, 1966—, counsel, 1975-77. Served to 1st lt. AUS, 1954-57. Mem. Am., Mich. bar assns., Order of Coif. Clubs: Chicago (Charlevoix, Mich.); Cranbrook (Mich.); Tennis. Home: 990 Burnham Rd Bloomfield Hills MI 48013 Office: Ford Motor Co WHQ Room 552 American Rd Dearborn MI 48121

DAVERN, CEDRIC INGLIS, university official, genetics educator; b. Hobart, Tasmania, Australia, Nov. 13, 1931; came to U.S., 1964; s. Aubrey Inglis and Sylvia Louise (Park) D.; m. Edith Charlotte Fickartz, Apr. 6, 1963 (div. 1980); children: James, Kathryn, Nicholas, Andrew; m. Gail Patty, Dec. 30, 1982; stepchildren: Jenny, Kyle, Luke. B.Sc. in Agr., U. Sydney, 1952, M.Sc., 1956; Ph.D., Calif. Inst. Tech., 1959. Research officer Commonwealth Sci. and Indsl. Research Orgn., Australia, 1953-64; asst. dir. Cold Spring Harbor (N.Y.) Lab. Quantitative Biology, 1965-67; asso. prof., then prof. genetics U. Calif., Santa Cruz, 1967-76, exec. officer dept., 1975-76; prof. genetics U. Utah, Salt Lake City, 1976—; dean Coll. Medicine, 1976-77, acad. v.p., 1977—; George and Dolores Eccles distinguished vis. prof., 1975-76; cons. NSF, NIH; cons. editor Freeman Pub. Co. Author papers in genetics, molecular biology. Sci. Books Internat. Sci. and Industry student fellow, 1956-59; NSF grantee. Office: Park Bldg U Utah Salt Lake City UT 84112

DAVEY, ANTHONY JOHN, ins. co. exec.; b. Bridgeport, Conn., May 31, 1925; s. Peter Martin and Janet (Otley) D.; m. Judith Crawford, Sept. 19, 1961. B. Social Studies cum laude, Holy Cross Coll., 1947; LL.B. (Root Tilden scholar), N.Y. U., 1955. Bar: N.Y. State bar 1956. Asso. firm Wilkie, Farr, Gallagher, Walton & FitzGibbon, N.Y.C., 1955-64; head legal dept., sec. Diamond Internat. Corp., N.Y.C., 1964-67, gen. counsel, 1967-69; v.p.-counsel USLIFE Corp., N.Y.C., 1969-76; v.p., asst. gen. counsel Prudential Ins. Co., Newark, 1977—. Served to lt. USNR, 1943-46, 50-52; MTO. Mem. Am., N.Y. State bar assns., Bar Assn. City N.Y., Phi Delta Phi, Delta Epsilon Sigma. Home: 420 E 23d St New York NY 10010 Office: Prudential Plaza Newark NJ 07101

DAVEY, BRUCE JAMES, insurance company executive; b. Montclair, N.J., Nov. 17, 1927; s. Reginald and Ellen Louis (Bragg) D.; m. Julia B. Twyford, June 21, 1958; children: Lynn Kathrine, Laurie Ellen, Bruce James. Suzanne Elizabeth. B.A., Colgate U., 1950. With Chem. Bank, N.Y.C., 1951-58, N.Y. Life Ins. Co., 1958—, asst. treas., 1960-76, treas., 1976—. Episcopalian. Home: 34 Battin Rd Fair Haven NJ 07701 Office: New York Life Ins Co 51 Madison Ave New York NY 10010

DAVEY, CHARLES BINGHAM, soil science educator; b. Bklyn., Apr. 7, 1928; s. Francis Joseph and Mary Elizabeth (Bingham) D.; m. Elizabeth Anne Thompson, July 11, 1952; children: Douglas Alan, Barbara Lynn, Andrew Martin. B.S., Syracuse U., 1950; M.S., U. Wis., 1952, Ph.D., 1955. Soil scientist Research Service, Dept. Agr., Beltsville, Md., 1957-62; asso. prof. N.C. State U., Raleigh, 1962-65, prof., 1965—, head dept., 1970-78, Carl Alwin Schenck disting. prof., 1978—. Editor: Tree Growth and Forest Soils, 1970; asso. editor: Soil Sci. Soc. Am. proc, 1967-72. Served with AUS, 1955-57. Fellow AAAS, Am. Soc. Agronomy, Soil Sci. Soc. Am. (pres. 1975-76); mem. Soc. Am. Foresters (Barrington Moore Research award), Internat. Soil Sci. Soc., Sigma Xi (Research award), Phi Kappa Phi, Gamma Sigma Delta, Xi Sigma Pi. Patentee, publs. in field. Home: 3704 Bryn Mawr Ct Raleigh NC 27606

DAVEY, CLARK WILLIAM, newspaper publisher; b. Chatham, Ont., Can., Mar. 3, 1928; s. William and Marguerite (Clark) D.; m. Joyce Gordon, Sept. 13, 1952; children: Richard Gordon, Kevin William, Clark Michael. B.A. in Journalism, U. Western Ont., 1948. With Chatham Daily News, 1948-51; mng. editor No. Daily News, Kirkland Lake, Can., 1951; hydro. seaway corr. Globe and Mail., 1951-55; mem. Parliamentary Press Gallery, Ottawa, 1956-60; fgn. editor Globe and Mail, 1960-63, mng. editor, 1963-78; pub. Vancouver (B.C., Can.) Sun, 1978-83, Montreal Gazette, 1983—; pres., chmn. The Canadian Press, 1981-83; v.p. Southam Inc., 1983—. Office: 250 Rue St Antoine Montreal PQ Canada H24 3R7

DAVEY, FRANK, poet, critic, educator; b. Vancouver, C., Can., Apr. 19, 1940; s. Wilmot Elmer and Doris (Brown) D.; m. Linda Jane McCartney, Nov. 20, 1969; children: Michael Gareth, Sara Geneve. B.A., U. B.C., 1961, M.A., 1963; Ph.D. (Can. Council fellow), U. So. Calif., 1968. Teaching asst. U. B.C., 1961-63; lectr. Royal Roads Mil. Coll., 1963-67, asst. prof., 1967-70, York U., Toronto, Ont., 1970-72, assoc. prof., 1972-80, prof., 1980—; Writer-in-residence Sir George Williams U., 1969-70; vis. prof. Shastri Indo-Canadian Inst., India, 1982. Author: poetry D-Day and After, 1962, City of the Gulls and Sea, 1964, Bridge Force, 1965, The Scarred Hull, 1966, Four Myths for Sam Perry, 1970, Weeds, 1970, Griffon, 1972, King of Swords, 1972, L'an trentiesme, 1972, Arcana, 1973, The Clallam, 1973, War Poems, 1979, The Arches: Selected Poems, 1981, Capitalistic Affection!, 1982, Edward and Patricia, 1983; criticism Earle Birney, 1971, From There to Here, 1974, 5 Readings of Olson's Maximus, 1970, Louis Dudek and Raymond Souster, 1981, Surveying the Paraphrase, 1983; Editor: Tish, 1961-63, Open Letter, 1965—, Tish No. 1-19, 1975, Mrs. Duke's Million, (Wyndham Lewis), 1977; mem. editorial bd.: Coach House Press. Nat. Dept. Def. arts research grantee, 1965, 66, 68; Can. Council travel grantee, 1971, 73; Can. Council leave fellow, 1974; Humanities Research Council Subvention, 1974, 80; Social Scis. and Humanities Research Council of Can. leave fellow, 1981. Home: 104 Lyndhurst Ave Toronto ON Canada

DAVEY, JACK, electric utility executive, electrical engineer; b. Alexandria, La., July 20, 1926; s. Marion Stephen and Margaret (Dunn) D.; m. Gloria Elizabeth Bitter, Oct. 14, 1940; children: Candace Jean, Kent Ritter. B.S., La. Tech. U., 1946; M.S., Iowa State U., 1947. Registered profl. engr., La. Assoc. engr. La. Power & Light, New Orleans, 1948, planning and budget mgr., then planning mgr., 1948-76; chief engr. La Power & Light, 1976-78; v.p., chief engr. La. Power & Light, 1978-81; v.p. planning and ops. Middle South Services, 1981—; tech. adv. com. FPC, Washington, 1970; chmn. Middle South Operating Com. for La., Ark. and Miss., 1978-79; chmn. reliability criteria com. S.W. Power Pool. Contbr. articles to tech. jours. Mem.

Baton Rouge Energy Adv. Com. Named Outstanding Engr. Region 3, 1982; recipient Edward Freitag award IEEE, 1979. Mem. IEEE(sr.), Edison Electric Inst. Democrat. Lutheran. Club: Amethyst (Algiers, La.). Office: Middle South Services 225 Baronne St New Orleans LA 70122

DAVEY, KENNETH GEORGE, biologist, university dean; b. Chatham, Ont., Can., Apr. 20, 1932; s. William and Marguerite (Clark) D.; m. Jeannette Isabel Evans, Nov. 28, 1959; children: Christopher Graham, Megan Jeannette, Katherine Alison. B.Sc., U. Western Ont., 1954, M.Sc., 1955; Ph.D., Cambridge (Eng.) U., 1958. NRC Can. fellow U. Toronto, Ont., 1958-59; Drosier fellow Gonville and Caius Coll., Cambridge U., 1959-63; asso. prof. parasitology McGill U., Montreal, Que., Can., 1963-67, prof. parasitology and biology, 1967-74, dir. Inst. Parasitology, 1964-74; prof., chmn. dept. biology York U., Downsview, Ont., 1974-81, dean of sci., 1982—; past pres. Huntsman Marine Lab.; pres. Biol. Council Can., 1979-81; mem. animal biology grant selection com. Natural Scis. and Engring. Research Council Can., 1980-83, group chmn. life scis., 1983—, mem. com. grants and scholarships, 1983—; mem. panel on tropical health NIH, 1978-82. Author: Reproduction in the Insects, 1965; contbr. numerous articles to profl. jours.; editor: Internat. Jour. Invertebrate Reprodn., 1978—; editorial bd.: Internat. Jour. Parasitology, 1973—, Exptl. Parasitology, 1970-75, Can. Jour. Zoology, 1966-76. Recipient Queen's Jubilee medal Govt. Can., 1977. Fellow Royal Soc. Can. (sec. Acad. Sci.), Entomol. Soc. Can.; mem. Soc. Exptl. Biology, Internat. Union Biol. Scis. (Can. nat. com. 1977—), Can. Soc. Zoologists (pres. 1981-82), Can. Com. Univ. Biology Chairmen (chmn. 1975-77). Office: Dept Biology York U Downsview ON M3J 1P3 Canada

DAVEY, LYCURGUS MICHAEL, neurosurgeon; b. N.Y.C., Feb. 20, 1918; s. Michael Marco and Elizabeth (Delaveris) D.; m. Artemis Diana Pappas, June 7, 1942; children—Michael Dean, Elaine Anne, Elizabeth. B.A., Yale U., 1939, M.D., 1943. Diplomate: Am. Bd. Neurol. Surgery. Surg. intern New Haven Hosp., 1943-44, asst. resident in surgery, 1946-50, William Harvey Cushing fellow, 1947-48, resident neurosurgeon, 1951-52; asst. resident in neurosurgery Hartford Hosp., 1950-51; clin. clk. Nat. Hosp., London, summer 1954; clin. instr. neurosurgery Yale U., 1952-60, asst. clin. prof., 1960-68, asso. clin. prof., 1968-77, clin. prof., 1977—; practice medicine, New Haven, 1952—; attending neurosurgeon Hosp. St. Raphael, VA Hosp., West Haven; asso. sect. chief Yale-New Haven Med. Center. Served to comdr. USNR, 1942-46, 52-54; capt. Res. ret. Fellow A.C.S., Internat. Coll. Surgeons; mem. AMA, Conn. Med. Soc., New Haven County Med. Soc., New Haven Med. Assn. (pres. 1972), Harvey Cushing Soc., New Eng. Neurosurg. Soc., Congress Neurol. Surgeons, Assn. Research in Nervous and Mental Diseases, Soc. Med. Consultants to Armed Forces. Home: 1010 Hartford Turnpike North Haven CT 06473 Office: 60 Temple St New Haven CT 06510 also 2 Church St S New Haven CT 06519 *My life has been enriched by treating tasks as a challenge to my resourcefulness, knowledge, originality, inventiveness and faith. The task becomes a game rather than a chore.*

DAVID, CLIVE, party architect; b. Manchester, Eng., June 6, 1934; came to US., 1957, naturalized, 1962; s. Marcus Wiener Kattenburg and Claire Rose (Levy) Wiener Kattenburg. Student, Blackpool Tech. Coll., 1951-52, Royal Coll. Art, 1955-57. Designer Chippendale's, London, Eng., 1955-57; asst. to pres., pub. relations Maybruck Assos., N.Y.C., 1959; Eastern regional dir. City of Hope, Phila., 1960-62; pres. Clive David Assos., N.Y.C., Party Enterprises, Ltd., Beverly Hills, 1962; Lectr. Party Planning par excellence, 1966—. Major parties arranged: Miss Universe Coronation Ball, Miami Beach, 1965, State visit of Queen Elizabeth & Prince Philip, Duke of Edinburgh, Bahamas, 1966, An Evening at the Ritz-Carlton, Boston, 1967, 69, Un Ballo in Maschera, Venice, 1967, An Evening over Boston, 1968, M.G.M. Cavalcade of Style, Los Angeles, 1970, Symposium on Fund Raising through Parties, Los Angeles, 1970, Great Midwest Limestone Cave Party, Kansas City, Une Soiree de Gala, Phila., Eleventh Anniv. of the Mike Douglas Show, Phila., The Mayor's Salute to Volunteers, Los Angeles, all 1972, Twenty Fifth Anniv. Salute to Israel, Jerusalem, 1973, The Bicentenary, 1976, The World Affairs Council Silver Ball, Boston, 1977, The Ohio Theatre Jubilee, Columbus, 1978, Mayors Salute to Vols, 1978, Dedication and Gala Performance, Northwestern U. Performing Arts Center, 1980, Metromedia Gala, Los Angeles Bicentennial, 1981; Contbr. articles to profl. publs. Served with Royal Arty. Brit. Army, 1953-55. Recipient Freedom Found. award, Valley Forge, Pa., 1961; City of Hope award, Phila., 1962; Mayor's medal for vol. services, Los Angeles, 1972; Shalom award State of Israel, 1974; named hon. citizen, also recipient mayor's medal City of Columbus. Mem. A.F.T.R.A. Jewish religion. Office: 282 S Reeves Dr Beverly Hills CA 90212 *I consider myself so fortunate to participate in events that bring joy, employment and funds to diversified causes, and maybe leave a miniscule contribution to history.*

DAVID, EDWARD EMIL, JR., electrical engineer, business executive; b. Wilmington, N.C., Jan. 25, 1925; s. Edward Emil and Beatrice (Liebman) D.; m. Ann Hirshberg, Dec. 23, 1950; 1 dau., Nancy. B.S., Ga. Inst. Tech., 1945; M.S., Mass. Inst. Tech., 1947, Sc.D., 1950; D.Engring. (hon.), Stevens Inst. Tech., 1971, Poly. Inst. Bklyn., 1971, U. Mich., 1971, Carnegie-Mellon, 1972, Lehigh U., 1973, U. Ill. at Chgo., 1973, Rose-Hulman Inst. Tech., 1978, U. Fla., 1982, Rensselaer Poly. Inst., 1982. Exec. dir. research Bell Telephone Labs., Murray Hill, N.J., 1950-70; sci. adviser to Pres. Nixon; dir. Office Sci. and Tech., Washington, 1970-72; exec. v.p. Gould, Inc., 1973-77; ind. cons., 1977; v.p. Exxon Corp., N.Y.C., 1978-80; pres. Exxon Research and Engring. Co., Florham Park, N.J., 1977—; dir. Materials Research Corp., Orangeburg, N.Y.; cons. Nat. Security Council, 1974-77; mem. def. sci. bd. Dept. of Def., 1974-75; chmn. Nat. Task Force on Tech. and Soc.; U.S. rep. to NATO Sci. Com. Author: (with Dr. J.R. Pierce) Man's World of Sound, 1958, (with Dr. J.R. Pierce and W.A. van Bergeikj) Waves and the Ear, 1960, (with Dr. J.G. Truxal) The Man-Made World, 1969 (Lanchester prize Operations Research Soc. Am. 1971); Contbr. articles to profl. jours. Mem. Bicentennial adv. com. Chgo. Mus. Sci. and Industry, 1974-75; mem. adv. bd. Office of Phys. Scis., NRC, 1976—; mem. Pres.'s Commn. on Nat. Medal of Sci., 1975-78; mem. vis. com. to div. phys. scis. U. Chgo., 1976—; mem. adv. council Humanities Inst., 1976—; trustee Aerospace Corp., 1974-81, chmn. bd. trustees, 1975-81; mem. corp. MIT, 1974—, also mem. exec. com., energy adv. bd.; bd. dirs. Summit (N.J.) Speech Sch., 1967-70; mem. Marshall Scholarships Adv. Council.; mem. adv. and resource council Princeton U.; mem. cons. sci. com. Chateaubriand Scholarships; trustee Carnegie Instn. of Washington. Served with USNR, 1943-46. Recipient George W. McCarty award Ga. Inst. Tech., 1958, award Summit Jr. C. of C., 1959; Am. Soc. M.E. award merit, 1971; Harold Pender award Moore Sch. U. Pa., 1972; N.C. award, 1972; award for disting. contbn. Soc. Research Adminstrs., 1980; N.J. Sci. and Tech. medal, 1982. Fellow IEEE, Acoustical Soc. Am., Am. Acad. Arts and Scis., AAAS (dir. 1974-75, 77-80, 80—, pres. 1977-78, chmn. bd. dirs. 1979-80), Audio Engring. Soc.; mem. Nat. Acad. Sci., Assn. Computing Machinery, Engring. Soc. Detroit, Nat. Acad. Engring. Patentee in field. Office: Exxon Research and Engring Co 180 Park Ave PO Box 101 Florham Park NJ 07932

DAVID, EDWARD M., lawyer; b. Phila., Dec. 26, 1916; s. William Morris and Frances Amelia (Cutler) D.; m. Mary Elizabeth Gass, Aug. 28, 1948; children—William, Peter, Elizabeth, Nancy. A.B., Princeton U., 1938; LL.B., U. Pa., 1941. Bar: Pa. bar 1942, U.S. Supreme Ct. bar 1972. Mem. firm Saul, Ewing, Remick & Saul, Phila., 1941—, partner, 1951—. Author, editor: Course Materials on Lifetime and Testamentary Estate Planning, 4th edit, 1982; editor: The Shingle, 1961; contbr. articles to profl. jours. Bd. dirs. Woodmere Art Gallery.; Trustee, former pres. bd First Presbyn. Ch. of Germantown. Served to lt. comdr. USNR, 1941-46. Mem. Am. Bar Assn., Pa. Bar Assn. (past chmn. real property, probate and trust law sect.), Phila. Bar Assn. (past chmn. orphans ct. com.), Am. Law Inst., Am. Coll. Probate Counsel. Club: Phila. Cricket. Office: 38th Floor Centre Sq W Philadelphia PA 19102

DAVID, HAL, lyricist; m. Anne; children: Jim, Craig. Ed., NYU Sch. Journalism. Books: What the World Needs Now and Other Love Lyrics, (with Burt Bacharach) Bacharach and David Songbook; Songs include: Raindrops Keep Fallin' On My Head (Acad. award), The Look of Love (Acad. award nomination), What's New Pussycat? (Acad. award nomination), Alfie (Acad. award nomination), Wives and Lovers, Casino Royale, It Was Almost Like a Song (all Grammy award nomination), What the World Needs Now is Love, To Love a Child (written for Foster Grandparents' Program), To All the Girls I've Loved Before (recorded by Julio Iglesias and Willie Nelson); chief collaborator: Burt Bacharach; other collaborators include, Henry Mancini, Joe Raposo; Broadway show Promises, Promises (Grammy award, Tony award nomination); films include: April Fools; record producer for, Dionne Warwick. Mem. ASCAP (pres. 1980—), Am. Guild Authors and Composers, Lyricists Guild Am., Dramatist Guild, Authors League. Address: 24 W 55th St New York NY 10019 *How do you create a hit? I don't know. When I sit down to work, I write what I feel. What happens afterwards is out of my hands. The only thing I'm sure of is you can't write a hit if you don't write a song. Of course, the act of creation, itself, is only one part of being a professional songwriter. To succeed and sustain, you have to have a knowledge of the other parts of the music business. You have to recognize that you are in business for yourself, and as president of your own company, you must be on top of all its aspects.*

DAVID, HERBERT ARON, statistics educator; b. Berlin, Dec. 19, 1925; U.S., 1957, naturalized, 1964; s. Max and Betty (Goldmann) D.; m. Vera Reiss, May 13, 1950; 1 son, Alexander John. B.Sc., Sydney U.(Australia), 1947; Ph.D., Univ. Coll. London U., 1953. Research officer Commonwealth Sci. and Indsl. Research Orgn., Sydney, 1953-55; sr. lectr. dept. stats. U. Melbourne (Australia), 1955-57; prof. stats. Va. Poly. Inst., 1957-64; prof. U. N.C., Chapel Hill, 1964-72; dir. stat. lab., head dept. stats. Iowa State U., Ames, 1972—, prof. stats., 1972—, Disting. prof. scis. and humanities, 1980—. Author: The Method of Paired Comparisons, 1963, 2d edit. 1981, Order Statistics, 1970. Recipient J. Shelton Horsley award Va. Acad. Scis., 1963. Fellow Am. Statis. Assn., Inst. Math. Stats.; mem. Biometric Soc. (editor biometrics 1967-72, pres. 1982-83), Internat. Statis. Inst. Jewish.

DAVID, MILES, association executive; b. Newark, Mar. 29, 1926; s. Samuel Harry and Estelle Rachel (Sklower) Ginsberg; m. Florence Cotton, Dec. 7, 1952; children: Steven, Amelia, Heidi. B.A., Univ. Heights Coll. Liberal Arts N.Y. U., 1946; postgrad. in English Lit, Columbia, 1946. Asso. editor Sci. Illustrated mag. McGraw-Hill Co., N.Y.C., 1946-48; editor Sponsor mag., N.Y.C., 1948-58; with Radio Advt. Bur., N.Y.C., 1958—, formerly v.p. and dir. promotion, exec. v.p., pres., now vice chmn., chief exec. officer, also dir.; Lectr. Tobe-Coburn Sch. for Fashion Careers; speaker in field to nat., internat. groups. Formerly bd. dirs. Brand Names Found.; bd. dirs. Advt. Council. Editor of: Sponsor mag. when it won George W. Polk award. Served with AUS, 1943-45; ETO. Recipient Morris Meister award; named Outstanding Alumnus Bronx High Sch. Sci. Man of Year Radio Trade Assn., 1975, 76. Mem. Internat. Radio, TV Soc., Broadcast Pioneers, Perstare et Praestare. Jewish. Clubs: Scarsdale (N.Y.); Town (com. pub. relations 1970-74). Adminstr. Higbee Study, use of radio for dept. stores, and All-Radio Methodology Study, how to measure radio. Home: 235 Fox Meadow Rd Scarsdale NY 10583 Office: 485 Lexington Ave New York NY 10017

DAVID, PAUL ALLAN, economics educator; b. N.Y.C., May 24, 1935; s. Henry and Evelyn (Levinson) D.; m. Sheila Ryan Johansson, Sept. 19, 1982; children: Rachel, Matthew. A.B. summa cum laude in Econs, Harvard U., 1956, Ph.D., 1973; postgrad., Pembroke Coll., Cambridge (Eng.) U., 1956-58. Asst. prof. econs. Stanford U., 1961-66, asso. prof., 1966-68, prof., 1969—, prof. history (by courtesy), 1976—, William Robertson Coe prof. Am. econ. history, 1978—, chmn. dept., 1979—; vis. prof. Harvard U., 1972-73; vis. professorial fellow Churchill Coll., Cambridge U., 1977-78; vis. fellow All Souls Coll., Oxford (Eng.) U., 1967-68; fellow Center for Advanced Study in Behavioral Scis., 1978-79; cons. in field. Author: Essays in Honor of Moses Abramovitz, 1974, Technical Choice, Innovation and Economic Growth: Essays on American and British Experience in the Nineteenth Century, 1975, Reckoning with Slavery: A Critical Study in the Quantitative History of American Negro Slavery, 1976; contbr. numerous articles to profl. jours.; editorial bd.: Explorations in Econ. History, 1974—, Jour. Econ. History, 1969-76, Hist. Methods, 1979—. Guggenheim fellow, 1975-76; Fulbright scholar, 1956-58. Fellow Am. Acad. Arts and Scis., Internat. Econometric Soc.; mem. Econ. History Assn. (v.p.), Inst. Polit. and Social Research (adv. com. on hist. archives), Am. Econ. Assn., Royal Econ. Soc. (U.K.), Econ. History Soc. (U.K.), Agrl. History Soc., Am. Hist. Assn. Office: Dept Econs Stanford U Stanford CA 94305

DAVID, PAUL THEODORE, polit. science educator; b. Brockton, Mass., Aug. 12, 1906; s. Ira E. and Bernice Grace (Harrison) D.; m. Opal Mary Davis, May 31, 1935. Student, Ga. Sch. Tech., 1924-26; A.B., Antioch Coll., 1928; A.M., Brown U., 1930, Ph.D., 1933. Instr. econs. Brown U., 1930-31; research fellow Brookings Inst., 1931-32; adminstrv. asst., economist TVA, 1933-36; staff mem. Pres. com. Adminstrv. Mgmt., 1936; sec., asst. dir. U.S. Adv. Com. on Edn., 1936-39; assoc. dir., chief economist Am. youth commn. Am. Council on Edn., 1939-42; mem. econ. staff, fiscal div. Bur. Budget, Washington, 1942-46; alt. U.S. rep. council Internat. Civil Aviation Orgn., Montreal, 1946-50; sr. staff mem. Brookings Instn., 1950-60; prof. govt. and fgn. affairs U. Va., 1960-77, prof. emeritus, 1977—; cons. Fed. Exec. Inst., Charlottesville, 1977-79; fellowship Center for Advanced Study in Behavioral Sciences, Stanford, Calif., 1959-60; vis. lectr. Salzburg Seminar in Am. Studies, summer 1963; vis. prof. U. Kent at Canterbury, 1974, U. Tasmania, 1978, Sangamon State U., Ill., 1980-81; cons. commn. rules Democratic Nat. Com, 1969-72. Author: Economics of Air Mail Transportation, 1934, The Politics of National Party Conventions, (with R. M. Goldman and R. C. Bain), 1960, (with Ralph Eisenberg) Devaluation of the Urban and Suburban Vote, Vols. I and II, 1962, Party Strength in the United States 1872-1970, 1972, (with James Ceaser) Proportional Representation in Presidential Nominating Politics, 1980, Sr. author Vol. I of Presidential Nominating Politics in, 1952; sr. editor other 4 vols. (with Moos and Goldman), 1954; editor: (with D. Everson) The Presidential Election and Transition 1980-81. Recipient Ford Found. faculty award, 1968-69. Mem. Am. Econ. Assn., Am. Polit. Sci. Assn., Phi Beta Kappa. Democrat. Clubs: Cosmos (Washington); Colonnade (Charlottesville Va.). Home: Route 5 Box 335-B Charlottesville VA 22901

DAVIDGE, ROBERT CUNNINGHAME, JR., hospital administrator; b. Schenectady, Jan. 1, 1942; s. Robert Cunninghame and Jean (Humphrey) D.; m. Margie Ann Green, May 20, 1961; children: Robert Cunninghame, III, Donna Marie, Christopher Hayne, Michael Rayburn. B.S., Fla. State U., 1965; M.B.A., U. Fla., 1967. Asst. adminstr. Tallahassee Meml. Hosp., 1967-69; adminstr. Cathedral Health and Rehab. Center, Jacksonville, Fla., 1969-73; exec. v.p. Tallahassee Meml. Regional Med. Center, 1973-79; exec. dir. Our Lady of Lake Regional Med. Center, Baton Rouge, 1979—; mem. Fla. Bd. Examiners Nursing Home Adminstrs., 1970-75; bd. dirs. Big Bend Med. Edn. Found., 1974-79, Neighborhood Health Center, Inc., Tallahassee, 1974-79, Big Bend Health Plan, 1974-79, Easter Seals N. Fla., 1971-73; mem. White House Health and Mental Health Task Force, 1971, Fla. Conf. Aging, 1971; mem. devel. bd. Fla. State Bank, 1973-79; Bd. dirs. Jacksonville Art Mus., 1972-73, Safety Council Greater Baton Rouge, 1981. Served with USAF, 1959-63. Grantee HEW, 1974. Fellow Am. Coll. Hosp. Adminstrs.; mem. Am. Hosp. Assn., La. Hosp. Assn. (sec.-treas. 1982-83, chmn. 1983-84), Res. Officers Assn., Beta Gamma Sigma. Republican. Roman Catholic. Clubs: Rotary (past dir. Tallahassee), K.C.). Home: 12115 Oakshire Ave Baton Rouge LA 70810 Office: Our Lady of Lake Regional Med Center 5000 Hennessy Blvd Baton Rouge LA 70809

DAVIDON, WILLIAM COOPER, physics and mathematics educator, scientist; b. Fla., Mar. 18, 1927; s. Jack and Ruth (Simon) D.; (div.)children: Alan, Ruth, Sarah, Martin. Student, Purdue U., 1943-44; B.S., M.S., Ph.D., U. Chgo. Engaged as research dir. Nuclear Chgo. Co., 1948-54; research asso. Fermi Inst., U. Chgo., 1954-56; asso. physicist Argonne Nat. Lab., 1956-61; asst. prof. physics Haverford Coll., 1961-69, prof. physics, 1969—, chmn. physics dept., 1969-70, 72-75, prof. math., 1982—; vis. asso. prof. U. Wash., 1958. Participant 3d, 10th, 17th and 22d Pugwash Confs. Scientists, 1958, 62, 67, 72; bd. dirs. for Phila. ACLU, 1971—. Named One of Ten Outstanding Young Men of Chgo. Chgo. Jaycees, 1960; Fulbright research scholar, 1966-67, 76-77. Mem. Soc. for Social Responsibility in Sci. (pres. 1965-67, edn. chmn.), Fedn. Am. Scientists (vice chmn. 1960-61), Am. Assn. Physics Tchrs., Soc. for Indsl. and Applied Math., Am. Math. Soc. Home: 410 W Lancaster Ave Haverford PA 19041

DAVIDOVICH, BELLA, pianist; b. USSR; m. Yulian Sitkovetsky (dec.); 1 son, Dimitri. Student, Moscow Conservatory. Formerly mem. faculty Moscow Conservatory. Concert pianist touring, Russia, Europe; performed with, Leningrad Philharmonic; U.S. debut, Newport Music Festival, 1979, Carnegie Hall, N.Y.C., numerous recs. Recipient 1st prize Chopin Competition, Warsaw, 1949. Office: care Jacques Leiser Artists Mgmt Dorchester Towers 155 W 68th St New York NY 10023 *

DAVIDOVSKY, MARIO, composer; b. Medanos, Buenos Aires, Argentina, Mar. 4, 1934; came to U.S., 1960; s. Natalio and Perla (Bulanska) D.; m. Elaine Blaustein, Nov. 19, 1961; children: Matias Gabriel, Adriana. Dir. Electronic Music Center, Princeton and Columbia univs., 1964—; vis. lectr. Sch. Music, U. Mich., 1964; guest prof. Inst. di Tella, Buenos Aires, 1965; prof. music CCNY, 1968-80, Columbia U., 1981—. Composer chamber music, orchestral works, also works for electronic music.; recs. on, Columbia, Sonnova, C.I.R. Nonesuch, Turnabout records. Guggenheim fellow, 1961-62, 62-63; Rockefeller fellow, 1964, 65; recipient award Koussevitzky Found., 1964, Library of Congress, 1964, Nat. Inst. Arts and Letters, 1965, Am. Acad. Arts and Letters, 1965; Creative Arts award Brandeis U., 1965; Aaron Copland award, Tanglewood, 1966; Naumburg award, 1971; Pulitzer prize in music, 1971. Mem. Am. Acad. and Inst. of Arts and Letters.

DAVIDOW, JEROME LEE, advertising agency executive; b. Boston, July 7, 1935; s. Morris Nathaniel and Estelle Anna (Cohen) D.; m. Barbara Carol Weiner, June 17, 1956 (div. July 1976); children: Amy Lynne, Judith Ann; m. Barbara Sue Mintzer, Oct. 11, 1981. A.B., Harvard Coll., 1956, M.B.A., 1958. Merchandising exec. R.H. Macy & Co., N.Y.C., 1958-65; product mgr. Sterling Drug Co., Montvale, N.J., 1965-67; exec. v.p. Leber Katz Ptnrs., N.Y.C., 1967—. Club: Harvard (N.Y.C.). Home: 80 Park Ave New York NY 10016 Office: Leber Katz Ptnrs 767 5th Ave New York NY 10153

DAVIDS, ANTHONY, psychology educator; b. Providence, Aug. 28, 1923; s. Anthony Notarangelo and Louise (Nahigan) D.; m. Martha J. St. Germain, Sept. 17, 1949. A.B. magna cum laude, Brown U., 1949; A.M., Harvard U., 1951, Ph.D., 1954. Research assoc., lectr. Harvard U., 1953-55; mem. faculty Brown U., Providence, 1955—, prof. psychology, 1964—; chief psychologist Emma Pendleton Bradley Hosp., Riverside, R.I., 1955-64, dir. psychology, 1965-80; USPHS spl. research fellow Inst. Personality Assessment and Research, U. Calif. at Berkeley, 1963-64. Author: Abnormal Children and Youth: Therapy and Research, 1972, Issues in Abnormal Child Psychology, 1973, Children in Conflict: A Casebook, 1974, Introductory Psychology, 1975, 2nd edit., 1982; Editor: Child Personality and Psychopathology: Current Topics, vols. 1-3, 1974-76. Fellow Am. Psychol. Assn., AAAS, Am. Orthopsychiat. Assn., Soc. for Personality Assessment; mem. Soc. for Research in Child Devel., Phi Beta Kappa, Sigma Xi. Research and publs. on personality assessment of normal and abnormal children and adults. Home: 218 Burgess Ave East Providence RI 02915 Office: Psychology Dept Brown U Providence RI 02912

DAVIDS, LEWIS EDMUND, educator, economist, author; b. N.Y.C., Apr. 21, 1917; s. William T. and Janet (Reid) D.; m. Anna Ruth Dornbush, May 29, 1941; children: Janet Ruth Davids Granthan, Judith Ann Davids Henson, Lewis Edmund. B.S., NYU, 1941, M.B.A., 1942, Ph.D., 1949; student, Wake Forest Coll., 1943, U. Paris, 1945; postdoctoral student, Southwestern Grad. Sch. Banking, So. Meth. U., 1958, Grad. Sch. Banking, U. Wis., 1966. Clk., Chase Nat. Bank, N.Y.C., 1935-39; acct. Williamsburgh Savs. Bank, N.Y.C., 1939-47; research asso. Inst. Internat. Finance, N.Y.C., 1947-48; economist Bankers Trust Co., N.Y.C., 1948; asst. prof. finance Drake U., 1949-51; prof. bus. adminstrn. Tex. A&M U., 1951-59; prof. econs. and finance U. Ga., 1959-61; Hill prof. bank mgmt. U. Mo.-Columbia, 1961-78, chmn. finance dept., 1977-78; Ill. Banker's prof. bank mgmt. So. Ill. U., Carbondale, 1978—; vis. prof. case method Harvard U., 1963; prof. fin. and control, Santiago, Chile, 1959; faculty fellow Sch. Mortgage Banking, Northwestern U., 1967; vis. prof. Southwestern Grad. Sch. Banking So. Meth. U., Sch. Banking South-La. State U., 1967-73; mem. faculty, counselor Assemblies for Bank Dirs. of So. Meth. U.; chmn. bd. Dir. Publs., Inc., 1968-75; chief econ. analyst Iowa dist. Econ. Stblzn. Agy. OPS, 1951; cons. Mo. Bankers Assn., 1961-78; economist Nat. Com. Monetary Policy, 1956-75; counselor Assemblies For Bank Dirs., 1968-75. Author: Problems of Small Business Financing, 1958, Dictionary of Insurance, 6th edit., 1983, Small Business Founders, 1963, Money and Banking Casebook, 1965, Money and Banking, 1969, 3d edit., 1970, Banking in Mid-America, 1969, Instant Business Dictionary, A Bank Director's Responsibilities, 1973, Conflicts of Interest, 1975, Board Policy and Risk Management, 1977, Audit Committee of the Board, 1977, Board Reports, 1978, Dictionary of Banking and Finance, 1978, Codes of Ethics, 1978, Contracts with Bank Executives, 1979, Effective Shareholder Meetings, 1980, Budgeting, Forecasting and Planning, 1982, Consumer Lending Policy, 1983; columnist: Mid-Continent Banker, Midwestern Banker, 1961—; editor: The Bank Board; cons. editor: Financial Handbook; contbg. editor: Banker's Mag., 1971-83; mem. editorial bd.: Jour. Bus. Research, 1972-76. Served with USAAF, 1943-45. Recipient cert. Council Internat. Progress Mgmt., 1960, Inst. Chileno de Adminstrn. Racional de Empresas, 1959. Mem. Am. Finance Assn. (chmn. So.

dist. 1960), So. Finance Assn. (pres. 1961), Mo. Bankers Assn. (chairholder banking 1961-78), Midwest Case Research Assn. (pres. 1964-66), Am., Midwest, So. econ. assns., Midwest Bus. Adminstrn. Assn. (dir.), Nat. Assn. Rev. Appraisers, Lakeshore Estates Assn. (pres. 1966-67), Alpha Kappa Psi, Beta Gamma Sigma. Club: Country of Missouri. Home: 27 Hillcrest St Carbondale IL 62901 Office: So Ill U Carbondale IL 62901

DAVIDS, NORMAN, engineering science and mechanics educator, researcher; b. N.Y.C., Mar. 17, 1918; s. Max and Sarah (Flint) Davidowitz; m. Frances White, Mar. 17, 1945; children: Gerald, Laura, Stuart. B.S., CCNY, 1937; M.S., NYU, 1938, Ph.D., 1940. Instr. CCNY, 1941; physicist C.E., Cin., 1942; mathematician Carnegie Inst. Tech., Washington, 1943-45; instr. Johns Hopkins U., Balt., 1945-47; assoc. prof. engring. sci. and mechanics Pa. State U., University Park, 1947-53, prof., 1958-78, prof. emeritus, 1978—; mem. Inst. Advanced Study, Princeton, N.Y., 1941-42; project dir. NIH, Bethesda, Md., 1968-78, Ballistics Research Labs., Aberdeen, Md., 1961-66; sr. sci. adviser Army Research Office, Durham, N.C., 1961. Editor: International Symposium on Stress Waves, 1960; contbr. articles to profl. jours. Recipient Naval Ordnance Devel. award Carnegie Inst., 1945; Fulbright scholar Israel Inst. Tech., 1959. Fellow Am. Acad. Mechanics (past treas., dir.); mem. ASME, Soc. Engring. Sci., Phi Beta Kappa, Sigma Xi. Democrat. Jewish. Home: 236 E Irvin Ave State College PA 16801 Office: Pennsylvania State University University Park PA 16802

DAVIDSEN, ARTHUR FALNES, astrophysicist, educator; b. Freeport, N.Y., May 26, 1944; s. Andrew and Anna (Falnes) D.; m. Anita Clare Salte, June 4, 1966; children: Andrew, Alexander, Austin. A.B., Princeton U., 1966; M.A., U. Calif.-Berkeley, 1972, Ph.D., 1975. Sci. liason officer Naval Research Lab., Washington, 1970-71; research asst. U. Calif., Berkeley, 1971-75; asst. prof. Johns Hopkins U., Balt., 1975-78, assoc. prof., 1978-80, prof. physics, 1980—; dir. Assn. Univs. for Research in Astronomy, Washington, 1979—; chmn. Johns Hopkins Space Telescope Inst. Com., 1979-81; mem. Space Telescope Inst. Council, 1982—; co-investigator Space Telescope Faint Object Spectograph, 1978—; prin. investigator Hopkins Ultraviolet Telescope Project, 1979—. Contbr. articles to profl. jours. Served to lt. (j.g.) USNR, 1968-71. Recipient Helen B. Warner prize Am. Astron. Soc., 1979; Alfred P. Sloan fellow, 1976-80. Mem. Am. Astron. Soc. (councilor), Internat. Astron. Union (U.S. nat. com.), Royal Astron. Soc., AAAS, Astron. Soc. Pacific, Explorers. Home: 4338 N Charles St Baltimore MD 21218 Office: Johns Hopkins U. 34th and Charles St Baltimore MD 21218

DAVIDSON, ABRAHAM A., art historian, photographer; b. Dorchester, Mass., June 27, 1935; s. Isaac and Ruth (Feinsilver) D. A.B. in Archtl. Scis. cum laude, Harvard U., 1957; postgrad., Hebrew U., Jerusalem, 1957-58; A.M. in Art History, Boston U., 1960; B. Jewish Edn., Hebrew Tchrs. Coll., Boston, 1960; Ph.D. in Art History, Columbia U., 1965. Vis. lectr. art history U. Iowa, 1963-64; instr. Wayne State U., Detroit, 1964-65; asst. prof. Oakland U., Rochester, Mich., 1965-68; vis. asst. prof. U. Colo., summer 1968; mem. faculty Tyler Sch. Art, Temple U., Phila., 1968—, prof. art history, 1975—; cons. Burlington County Community Coll., Pemberton, N.J., 1976-77. Author: The Story of American Painting, 1974, 79, The Eccentrics and Other American Visionary Painters, 1978, Early American Modernist Painting, 1910-1935, 1981; also articles.; one-man exhbns. of photographs, Temple U., 1972, 82, Painted Bride Gallery, Phila., 1974, Burlington County Community Coll., 1978, Gloucester County (N.J.) Coll., 1979, Villanova U., 1982; represented in permanent collections, Bank Leumi, Ins. Co. N.Am., Lehigh U., Sch. Pharmacy, Temple U., Villanova U., numerous TV appearances. Recipient Group 17 prize photography Detroit Inst. Arts, 1969. Office: Tyler Sch Art Beech and Penrose Aves Elkins Park PA 19126

DAVIDSON, ALFRED E., lawyer; b. N.Y.C., Nov. 11, 1911; s. Maurice Philip and Blanche (Reinheimer) D.; m. Claire Dreyfuss, June 28, 1934; children: Thomas, Kenneth. B.A., Harvard U., 1933; LL.B., Columbia U., 1936. Bar: N.Y. 1936, D.C. 1973. Asst. chief counsel codification div. N.Y.C. Charter Revision Com. and Bd. Statutory Consolidation, 1935-38; asst. to gen. counsel, wage and hour div. U.S. Dept. Labor, Washington, 1938-40, with rev. sect., office of solicitor, 1940-41; legislative counsel Office of Emergency Mgmt. in Exec. Office of Pres., 1941-43; asst. gen. counsel Lend-Lease Adminstrn., which later, with other agys., 1943-45, gen. counsel, 1945—, UNRRA, Nov., 1945; counsel Prep. Commn. for Internat. Refugee Orgn., 1947; dir. European hdqrs. UNICEF, 1947-51; econ. adviser Office of Sec. Gen. UN, 1951-52; gen. counsel UN Korean Reconstrn. Agy., 1952-54; exec. asst. to chmn. bd. Rio Tinto of Can., 1955-58; v.p., gen. counsel Tech. Studies, 1957-69, 73—; spl. rep. in Europe for Internat. Finance Corp., Paris, 1970-72, 76—; counsel Wilmer Cutler & Pickering, London, 1972-75; Dir. Channel Tunnel Study Group, 1959-69; lectr. internat. relations Am. Coll. in Paris, 1965-67; Chmn. Democratic Party Com. of France, 1964-70, 72, hon. chmn., 1973; co-chmn. Bi-Partisan Coms. on Absentee Voting and Medicare Overseas. Mem. Council Fgn. Relations, Assn. for Promotion of Humor in Internat. Affairs (co-founder), Assn. Ams. Resident Overseas (dir.), Common Cause Overseas (hon. chmn.). Clubs: Queens, Lansdowne (London); Standard Athletic, Paris. Home: 5 rue de la Manutention Paris 16 e France *Greed fuels the arms race, but I cling to the notion that even the greedy recognize that the use of nuclear arms will lead to self-destruction. That could come about only by mistake or lunacy. We should beef up our conventional arms so we have a better option than surrender or what amounts to suicide.*

DAVIDSON, ANDREA ALEXANDRA PATRICIA, ballet dancer; b. Montreal, Que, Canada, Sept. 17, 1953; d. John Richard and Joan Elizabeth (McBride) D. Grad., Nat. Ballet Sch., Toronto, Ont., Can.,; Profl. studies ballet, modern, jazz. Soloist Nat. Ballet Can., Toronto, 1971-74; prin. dancer Entre Sic Dance Co., Montreal, Que., Can., 1977-78; soloist Les Grands Ballet Canadiens, Montreal, 1981-82, sr. artist, 1982-83, prin. dancer, 1983—; dancer, tchr. Pavlychenko Studio, Toronto, 1980-81; tchr. L'Ecole Supierevre des Ballet Jazz, Que, Can., 1975-77, L'Acad. des Grands, 1976-77, La Compagnie de Danse, Danse Partout, Que, 1975-77, U. Toronto, 1980-81; choreographer ballets including Chopin Pas de Deux Danse Partout, 1977; choreographer Winterscapes Dance in Ca., 1981. Can. Council grantee, 1971, 73; Ont. Arts Council grantee for choreographer, 1981. Mem. Actor's Equity Assn., Dance in Can. Assn. Home: 5885 Jeanne Mance Apt 5 Montreal PQ Canada H2V 4K6 Office: Les Grands Ballets Canadiens 4869 rue St Denis Montreal PQ Canada H2J 2L7

DAVIDSON, BRUCE MERRILL, educator; b. Ironwood, Mich., Mar. 16, 1924; s. Harold Osborn and Alma (Knoepp) D.; m. Mary Catherine Wank, Jan. 29, 1949; children—Mark C., Diane M., Mary Ann. B.S. in Civil Engring, U. Mich., 1949; M.S., U. Wis., 1951, Ph.D., 1956. Adminstrv. asst. geog. sect. Allied Translation and Interpretation Sect., Tokyo, Japan, 1946-47; teaching asst. U. Mich., 1947-49; mem. faculty U. Wis., 1949-51, 53-55, 56-66; asso. dean Coll. Engring., 1962-66, prof. civil engring., 1964-66; traffic engr. Wis. Hwy. Commn., 1955-56; chmn. dept. civil engring. Wash. State U., Pullman, 1966-71; acad. dean U.S. Naval Acad., Annapolis, Md., 1971—; Mem. Gov.'s Sci. Adv. Council; NSF teaching cons. Roorkee (India) U., 1969; Mem. Madison Traffic Commn., 1960-64; U. Wis. chmn. Madison United Givers, 1964—. Alderman, Madison, 1956-64; del. Wis. Republican Conv., 1956; Bd. dirs. Madison Library, 1956-64, pres., 1960. Served with AUS, 1943-46, 51-53; maj. gen. Res. Mem. ASCE, Am. Soc. Engring. Edn. (dir. engring. coll. council), Am. Ry. Engring. Assn., Triangle, Scabbard and Blade (nat. dir.), Sigma Xi, Tau Beta Pi, Chi Epsilon, Phi Kappa Phi. Presbyn. Club: Rotarian. Research and publs. in field. Home: 15 Porter Rd US Naval Acad Annapolis MD 21402

DAVIDSON, CARL B., oil co. exec.; b. Trenton, N.J., Apr. 17, 1933; s. Jack O. and Pearl (Watkins) D.; m. Lois Greenwald, June 28, 1959; children—Andrew William, Jane Hope. A.B., Rutgers U., 1954, LL.B., 1957. Bar: D.C. bar 1957, N.Y. bar 1960. Asst. to gen. mgr. Koret Inc., N.Y.C., 1957-58; field atty. NLRB, N.Y.C., 1958-65; with Texaco Inc., N.Y.C. and Westchester, N.Y., 1965—, asst. to v.p., then asst. sec., 1971-74, corp. sec., 1974—. Address: 2000 Westchester Ave White Plains NY 10650

DAVIDSON, CHALMERS GASTON, historian, writer; b. Chester, S.C., June 6, 1907; s. Zeb V. and Kate (Gaston) D.; m. Alice G. Gage, Mar. 20, 1937; children: Robert Gage, Alice Graham (Mrs. Wm. H. Sims, III), Mary Gage. A.B., Davidson Coll., 1928; A.M., Harvard U., 1930, Ph.D., 1942; A.M., U. Chgo., 1936. Instr. Chamberlain Hunt Mil. Acad., Port Gibson, Miss., 1928-29, Blue Ridge Sch. for Boys, Hendersonville, N.C., 1933-34, The Citadel, Charleston, S.C., 1934-35; prof. history Davidson Coll., 1936-76, dir. library, 1936-75; Reynolda House lectr., N.C., 1967-68. Author: Rural Hill, 1943, Cloud over Catawba, 1949, Friend of the People, 1950, Mecklenburg Declaration of Independence Verse; editor: (1950) Piedmont Partisan, 1951, rev. edit., 1968, (1951) Mid-Point for '28, 1953, Gaston of Chester, 1956, Plantation World Around Davidson, 1969, rev. edit., 1973, 2d rev. edit., 1982, The Last Foray, 1971, The Generations of Davidson Coll, 1955, rev. edits., 1964, 72, 80, High-Point for '28, 1978; contbr.: hist. jours. Dictionary of N.C. Biography. Chmn. parents' adv. council Converse Coll., 1968-69; Mem. Carolina Charter Tercentenary Comm., 1963—; trustee Hezekiah Alexander Found., 1969-73; pres. Latta Place, Inc., 1972-73; mem. Charlotte-Mecklenburg Hist. Properties Commn., 1974-77, N.C. Exec. Mansion Fine Arts Com., 1976-79; bd. dirs. Edward Crosland Stuart Scholarship Program, 1976—. Served as armed guard comdr. Pacific area USNR, 1944-46. Recipient Charles A. Cannon award for contbn. to N.C. history, 1951; U.D.C. Mil. Cross, 1970; award of merit N.C. Soc. County and Local Historians, 1971; named Tchr. of Yr. S.C. Daus. Colonial Wars, 1972. Mem. N.C. Lit. and Hist. Assn. (pres. 1961-62), Hist. Soc. N.C. (pres. 1966-67), Mecklenburg Hist. Assn. (pres. 1956-57), N.C. Writers Conf. (chmn. 1960-61), Soc. Cincinnati, Huguenot Soc. Am., St. Andrews Soc. Carolina, Phi Beta Kappa, Omicron Delta Kappa, Beta Theta Pi (dist. chief 1952-57). Presbyn. Clubs: Charlotte Country, Blowing Rock Country. Home: Beaver Dam Davidson NC 28036

DAVIDSON, CHARLES HENRY, electrical engineering educator; b. Washington, Dec. 10, 1920; s. Charles Montgomery and Alice Maud (Rollins) D.; m. Hermine Elizabeth Sauthoff, Aug. 26, 1952; children: Elizabeth Lynn, Robert Montgomery. A.B. in Physics, Am. U., 1941, Ph.M., U. Wis., 1943, Ph.D., 1952. Instr. physics Mary Washington Coll. U. Va., 1946-47; engr. Continental Electric Co., Geneva, Ill., 1947-49; lab. asst. U. Wis., 1949-52, research asso. elec. engring., 1952-54, asst. prof., 1954-59, asso. prof., 1959-66, prof. elec. and computer engring. and computer sci., 1966—; dir. Engring. Computing Lab., 1961-82; asst. to dir. for instructional computing Madison Acad. Computing Ctr., 1982—; cons. in field; vis. prof. U. Edinburgh, Scotland, 1968-69; acad. dir. NSF Summer Inst. Introduction to Computing Machines, 1965-66. Author: (with Eldo C. Koenig) Computers: Introduction to Computers and Applied Computing Concepts, 1967. Mem. Assn. Computing Machinery (regional rep. to nat. council 1968-72, 78, chmn. spl. interest group on computers and soc. 1977—), Computer Soc., Sigma Xi, Omicron Delta Kappa, Tau Beta Pi. Unitarian-Universalist. Home: 2210 Waunona Way Madison WI 53713

DAVIDSON, CHARLES SPRECHER, physician; b. Berkeley, Calif., Dec. 7, 1910; s. Charles Sprecher and Mary (Blossom) D. A.B., U. Calif. at Berkeley, 1934; M.D., C.M., McGill U., 1939; M.A. (hon.), Harvard, 1953. Intern, house officer medicine San Francisco Hosp., 1939-41; research fellow medicine Harvard Med. Sch. and asst. resident physician Thorndike Meml. Lab., Boston City Hosp., 1941-42; various appointments, 1942-44, asso. dir. of II and IV Harvard Med. Services, Boston City Hosp. and asso. physician, 1948-63, asso. dir., 1964-70, acting dir., 1970-74, vis. physician, 1965, acting head dept. medicine, 1970-74; asso. prof. medicine Harvard Med. Sch., 1953-68, prof., 1969-73, William Bosworth Castle prof. medicine, 1974-77, prof. emeritus, 1977—; vis. prof. medicine Mass. Inst. Tech., 1974-77, sr. lectr. dept. nutrition and food sci., 1977—; asso. dir. Harvard med. unit Boston City Hosp., 1972—; program dir. Clin. Research Center, Mass. Inst. Tech., Cambridge, 1974-77; cons. Mt. Auburn Hosp., Cambridge, Cambridge Hosp.; hon. dir. Med. Found., Inc.; Scholar-in residence Fogarty Internat. Center NIH, 1972-73. Contbr. to profl. jours. Master A.C.P.; mem. Am. Gastroent. Soc., Am. Acad. Arts and Scis., Assn. Am. Physicians. Home: 100 Memorial Dr Cambridge MA 02142 Office: MIT Bldg 56 Room 216 Cambridge MA 02139

DAVIDSON, COLIN HENRY, university dean; b. Exeter, Eng., Mar. 4, 1928; emigrated to Can., 1968, naturalized, 1975; s. Douglas Nangle and Dulcie Rose (Winter) D.; m. Lucienne Fiant, Jan. 18, 1956; children: Dominique, Philip. Diploma architecture, Brussels Royal Acad., 1951; M.Arch., M.I.T., 1955. Archtl. asst. Lucccichenti/Monaco, Rome, 1951-54; asst. architect Architects' Collaborative, Cambridge, Mass., 1954-55, London County Council, 1956-60; pres. C.H. Davidson Cons., London, 1960-68; prof. architecture U. Montreal, 1968—; dean Faculty Environ. Design, 1976—; founder IF, 1969. Since editor: prin. works include Cosmos and SB2 industrialized bldg. systems; housing, Basildon, Essex, Eng., 1967; Co-author: Industrialized Building and the Architect, 1961, also thesauri in bldg. sci. and tech. Mem. Order Architects Que. Patentee bldg. components. Office: U Montreal PO Box 6128 Montreal PQ H3C 3J7 Canada *I have constantly been torn by the dilemma of the Architect: man-of-the-arts or man-of-science. Having opted for the second (perhaps out of fear of the former), I find I must work in a scientific near-vacuum. For this reason, I dedicate my life to problems of research and its application, to questions of information and organization in the building process, in practice and in education. This is my way of striving for a better built environment for mankind.*

DAVIDSON, CROW GIRARD, lawyer, former Democratic national committeman; b. Lafayette, La., July 28, 1910; s. James Joseph and Lilla May (Kennedy) D.; m. Mercedes Hester, Jan. 21, 1939 (div. Jan. 1952); children—Michael Cobb, Joan Hester; m. Joan F. Kaplan, Dec. 20, 1953 (div. Mar. 1967); children—John Matthew, Girard, Alice Elizabeth, Peter; m. Sylvia Nemer, Oct. 4, 1967. A.B., Southwestern La. Inst., 1930; LL.B., Tulane U., 1933, Yale, 1933-34, J.S.D., 1936. Bar: La. bar 1933. Atty. TVA, 1934-37; cons. atty. Bonneville Power Adminstrn., Portland, Oreg., 1940-42, gen. counsel, 1943-46; cons. OPM, Washington, 1941-42; asst. gen. counsel WPB, 1944-45; asst. sec. of the interior, 1946-50; now mem. law firm Davidson, Sharkey & Cummings.; Pres. Alaska Pacific Lumber Co.; cons. City N.Y., 1967-68; Mem. Oreg.'s Ednl. Coordinating Commn., chmn., 1974-77; Nat. Dem. elector, 1952; mem. Dem. Nat. Com. from Oreg., 1956-63; chmn. nat. Dem. Com. on Natural Resources; chmn. Western States Dem. Conf., 1960-63. Contbr. legal, other periodicals. Mem. Am., La., Oreg., Alaska bar assns., Order of Coif, Beta Theta Pi, Phi Alpha Delta, Omicron Delta Kappa. Democrat. Methodist. Club: Portland City. Home: 1054 SW Douglas Pl Portland OR 97205 Office: Park-Washington Bldg 519 SW Park St Portland OR 97205 also Commerce Bldg 1700 K St NW Washington DC 20006

DAVIDSON, DAVID SAMUEL, publishing company executive; b. N.Y.C., May 10, 1933; s. Samuel David and Anna (Negrin) D.; m. Edith Kahn, Dec. 6, 1953; children: Steven, Amy, Michael. B.B.A., CCNY, 1953; M.B.A., CUNY, 1961; B.A., Marymount Coll., 1979. C.P.A. Various fin. mgmt. positions Curtiss Wright Corp., 1953-62, Foster-Wheeler Corp., 1953-62; Hudson Pulp & Paper Corp., 1953-62; fin. mgmt. ITT, Los Angeles and N.Y.C., 1962-69; asst. group gen. mgr. ITT Consumer Services Group, N.Y.C., 1969-71; group gen. mgr. ITT N.Am. Ins. Group, 1972-77, ITT Ednl., Bldg. & Transport Services Group, 1977-79, ITT Pub. Group, N.Y.C., 1980—; chmn. bd. Howard W. Sams & Co., Indpls., 1982—, Bobbs-Merrill Co., N.Y.C. and Indpls., 1982—, Michie Co., Charlottesville, Va., 1982—, G.K. Hall & Co., Boston, 1982—, Marquis Who's Who, Chgo., 1982—, Intertec Pub. Corp., Overland, Kans., 1982—, Research & Rev. Service Am., Indpls., 1982—. Served with U.S. Army, 1954-56; Korea. Mem. Fin. Execs. Inst., Am. Inst. C.P.A.s, N.Y. State Soc. C.P.A.s. Home: Betmarlea Rd Norwalk CT 06850 Office: ITT Publishing 630 3d Ave New York NY 10017

DAVIDSON, DAVID SCOTT, architect; b. Great Falls, Mont., Dec. 17,, 1925; s. David Adams and Florence Mae (Scott) D.; m. Marjorie Luella Huffman, Sept. 10, 1949; children: Carol M., Marilyn S., Scott L., Bruce F., Craig S. Student, U. Utah, 1943, Pasadena City Coll., 1944; B.S. in Architecture, Mont. State U., 1950. Registered architect, Mont. Architect in tng. Shanley & Shanley Architects, Great Falls, 1950-52; architect van Teylingen, Knight, van Teylingen, Great Falls, 1952-54; prin. David S. Davidson, Architect, Great Falls, 1954-56; ptnr. Davidson & Kuhr Architects, Great Falls, 1956-75; pres. Davidson & Kuhr Architects, P.C., Great Falls, 1975—; dir., pres. Great Falls Arts Assn., 1980-83; dir., 2d v.p. Mont. Inst. Arts, 1981-84; mem. state constrn. adv. council State of Mont., 1983-84; dir. Paris Gibson Square, Great Falls, 1982-85. Mem. Great Falls Zoning Bd., 1972-75; mem. rehab. com. Great Falls Housing Task Force, 1975-78; chmn. architecture div. United Way, 1975-78. Served with U.S. Army, 1943-46. Recipient 1st honor Mont. chpt. AIA, 1973, 75, honor award in architecture Mont. chpt. AIA, 1973, 74, 78, 83, merit in architecture, 1965. Fellow AIA (chpt. pres. 1965-66, dir. 1962-66), Great Falls Soc. Architects (pres. 1958-59), Jr. C. of C. (dir. 1956-60). Lodge: Kiwanis. Home: 1212 Buena Ave Great Falls MT 59404 Office: Davidson and Kuhr Architects PC 309 Davidson Bldg Great Falls MT 59401

DAVIDSON, DONALD HERBERT, philosophy educator; b. Springfield, Mass., Mar. 6, 1917; s. Clarence Herbert and Grace (Anthony) D.; m. Nancy Hirschberg, Apr. 4, 1975 (dec. 1979); 1 dau. by previous marriage, Elizabeth Ann. B.A., Harvard U., 1939, M.A., 1941, Ph.D., 1949. Instr. philosophy Queen's Coll., 1947-50; from asst. prof. to prof. philosophy Stanford U., 1951-67; prof. philosophy Princeton U., 1967-70, chmn. dept. philosophy, 1968-70, lectr. with rank of prof., 1970-76; prof. philosophy Rockefeller U., 1970-76; Univ. prof. U. Chgo., 1976-81, U. Calif., Berkeley, 1981—; vis. prof. Tokyo (Japan) U., 1955; Gavin David Young lectr. U. Adelaide, 1968; John Locke lectr. Oxford (Eng.) U., 1970; vis. prof. U. Sydney, 1968, U. Pitts., 1972, U. Capetown, 1980; John Dewey lectr. U. Minn., 1975; Matchette Found. lectr. U. Wis., 1976; Carus lectr., 1980, Hägerstrom lectr., 1980; José Gaos vis. lectr. U. Mex., 1980. Co-Author: (with Patrick Suppes) Decision Making: An Experimental Approach, 1957; Author: Essays on Actions and Events, 1980, Inquiries into Truth and Interpretation, 1983; Co-editor: (with J. Hintikka) Words and Objections, 1969, (with Gilbert Harman) Semantics for Natural Language, 1970, The Logic of Grammar, 1975; mem. editorial bd.: Philosophia, 1970—, (with Patrick Suppes) Theoretical Linguistics, 1973—, Theory and Decision, 1974—, Erkenntnis, 1974—, Current Commentary in the Behavioral and Brain Sciences, 1976—. Served to lt. (s.g.) USNR, 1942-45; MTO. Teschemacher fellow in classics and philosophy, 1939-41; Rockefeller fellowship in humanities, 1945-46; Rockefeller fellowship for research, 1948; Ford Faculty fellowship, 1953-54; Am. Council Learned Socs. fellowship, 1958-59; NSF research grants, 1964-65, 68; fellow Center Advanced Study Behavioral Scis., 1969-70; Guggenheim fellow, 1973-74; fellow All Souls Coll. Oxford U., 1973-74; vis. fellow Research Sch. Social Scis., Australian Nat. U., 1977; hon. research fellow Univ. Coll., London, 1978. Fellow Am. Acad. Arts and Scis., Brit. Acad. Sci. (corr.); mem. Am. Philos Assn. (sec. Pacific Coast div. 1956-59, v.p. 1961, pres. Eastern div. 1973-74), Institute Internacional de Philosophie, Assn. Symbolic Logic, AAUP. Office: Philosophy Dept Univ Calif Berkeley CA 94720

DAVIDSON, ERIC HARRIS, devel. and molecular biologist; b. N.Y.C., Apr. 13, 1937; s. Morris and Anne D. B.A., U. Pa., 1958; Ph.D., Rockefeller U., 1963. Research asso. Rockefeller U., 1963-65, asst. prof., 1965-71; asso. prof. devel. molecular biology Calif. Inst. Tech., Pasadena, 1971-74, prof., 1974—. Author: Gene Activity in Early Development, 2d edit, 1976. NIH grantee, 1965—; NSF grantee, 1972—. Research, numerous publs. on DNA sequence orgn., gene expression during embryonic devel., gene regulation. Office: Div Biology Calif Inst Tech Pasadena CA 91125

DAVIDSON, ERNEST ROY, chemist, educator; b. Terre Haute, Ind., Oct. 12, 1936; s. Roy Emmette and Opal Ruth (Hugunin) D.; m. Reba Faye Minnich, Jan. 27, 1956; children: Michael Collins, John Philip, Mark Ernest, Martha Ruth. B.Sc. (Union Carbide fellow), Rose-Hulman Inst., 1958; Ph.D. (NSF fellow), Ind. U., 1961. NSF Postdoctoral fellow U. Wis.-Madison, 1961-62; asst. prof. chemistry U. Wash., 1962-65, asso. prof., 1965-68, prof., 1968—; Distinguished Vis. Prof. Ohio State U., 1974-75; cons. Lawrence Livermore Labs. Editor: Jour. Computational Physics, 1975—, Internat. Jour. Quantum Chemistry, 1975—, Jour. Chem. Physics, 1976-78, Chem. Physics Letters, 1977—, Jour. Am. Chem. Soc, 1978—; Contbr. numerous articles on density matrices and quantum theory of molecular structure to profl. jours. Battelle Meml. Inst. Sloan fellow, 1967-68; Guggenheim fellow, 1974-75; laureate l'Academie Internationale des Sciences Moleculaires Quantiques, 1971. Mem. Am. Chem. Soc., Am. Phys. Soc., Sigma Xi, Phi Lambda Upsilon, Tau Beta Pi. Home: 9809 220th SW Edmonds WA 98020 Office: Chemistry BG-10 U of Wash Seattle WA 98195

DAVIDSON, EUGENE ABRAHAM, biochemist, univ. adminstr.; b. N.Y.C., May 27, 1930; s. Jack and Sophie Miriam (Deutsch) D.; m. Alice Howell, Jan. 25, 1952; children—Mark, Robin, Steven, Ellen. B.S., UCLA, 1950; Ph.D., Columbia U., 1955. Postdoctoral fellow, instr. U. Mich., 1955-58; asst. prof. biochemistry Duke U., 1958-62, asso. prof., 1962-65, prof., 1965-67; prof., chmn. dept. biol. chemistry M.S. Hershey Med. Center, Pa. State U., 1967—, asso. dean for edn., 1975—; cons. in field. Author: Carbohydrate Chemistry, 1967; contbr. numerous articles to profl. publs.; Editorial reviewer for numerous jours. Guggenheim fellow, 1965-66; NIH grantee, 1958—. Mem. AAAS, Am. Soc. Biol. Chemists, Assn. Med. Sch. Depts. Biochemistry, Biochem. Soc., Am. Assn. Cancer Research, Soc. Complex Carbohydrates, Sigma Xi. Home: 131 E High St Hummelstown PA

17036 Office: Dept Biol Chemistry MS Hershey Med Center U Pa Hershey PA 17033

DAVIDSON, EUGENE ARTHUR, author; b. N.Y.C., Sept. 22, 1902; s. William and Bertha (Passarge) D.; m. Louise Keil, Apr. 6, 1928 (div.); children: Eugene Passarge, Lisa; m. Suzette Morton Zurcher, Nov. 1968. A.B., Yale, 1927, postgrad., 1927-28; Litt.D. (hon.), Park Coll., 1977. Mem. editorial dept. Yale Univ. Press, 1929-59, editor, 1931-59, dir., 1938-59, chmn. com. on publs.; editor Modern Age, 1960-70. Author: The Death and Life of Germany, 1959, The Trial of the Germans, 1967, The Nuremberg Fallacy, 1973, The Making of Adolf Hitler, 1977; Contbr.: book revs., articles and poetry to mags. including The Progressive. Pres. Found. Fgn. Affairs, Washington, 1957-70; Chmn. Conf. European Problems. Clubs: P.E.N. (N.Y.C.); Arts (Chgo.); Elizabethan (New Haven); Birnam Wood (Santa Barbara, Calif.). Address: 780 Riven Rock Rd Santa Barbara CA 93108

DAVIDSON, EZRA C., JR., physician, educator; b. Water Valley, Miss., Oct. 21, 1933; s. Ezra Cap and Theresa Hattie (Woods) D.; children: Pamela, Gwendolyn, Marc, Ezra K. B.S. cum laude, Morehouse Coll., 1954; M.D., Meharry Med. Coll., 1958. Diplomate: Am. Bd. Obstetrics and Gynecology (examiner 1973—). Intern San Diego County Gen. Hosp., 1958-59; resident in obstetrics and gynecology Harlem Hosp., N.Y.C., 1963-66, asst. attending obstetrics-gynecology, obstet. coordinator maternal and infant care clinics, 1967-68; dir. departmental research, asso. attending, acting chmn. obstetrics and gynecology, co-dir. coagulation research lab. Roosevelt Hosp., N.Y.C., 1968-70; fellow blood coagulation, asst. obstetrics and gynecology Columbia U. Coll. Physicians and Surgeons, N.Y.C., 1966-67, instr. dept. obstetrics-gynecology, 1967-69, asst. clin. prof., 1970; cons. obstetrics and gynecology Office Health Affairs, OEO, Washington, 1970-72; prof., chmn. dept. obstetrics and gynecology Charles R. Drew Postgrad. Med. Sch., Los Angeles, 1971—, acad. v.p., 1982—; prof. U. So. Calif., 1971-80, UCLA, 1980—; chief service dept. obstetrics and gynecology Martin Luther King, Jr. Gen. Hosp., Los Angeles, 1971—; attending physician dept. obstetrics and gynecology Los Angeles County-U. So. Calif. Med. Center, 1971—; mem. nat. med. advisory com. Nat. Found. March of Dimes, 1972—; bd. cons. Internat. Childbirth Edn. Assn., 1973—; mem. sec.'s adv. com. population affairs HEW, 1974-77, chmn. services task force, 1975-77; chmn. bd. dirs. Los Angeles Regional Family Planning Council, 1975-77; bd. dirs. Nat. Alliance Sch Age Parents, 1975-79; mem. Calif. Institutional Rev. Bd., 1977—. Served with USAF, 1959-63. Johnson Found. Health Policy fellow Inst. Medicine, Nat. Acad. Scis., 1979-80. Fellow Am. Coll. Obstetricians and Gynecologists (nat. sec. 1983—), A.C.S., Los Angeles Obstet. and Gynecol. Soc. (pres. 1982-83); mem. Los Angeles Regional Family Planning Council, Inc., Nat. Med. Assn. (mem. sci. council 1979—), Assn. Profs. Gynecology and Obstetrics (council 1978-81), Alpha Omega Alpha. Office: 12021 Wilmington Ave Los Angeles CA 90059

DAVIDSON, FRED, III, government official; b. Indpls., Oct. 3, 1941; s. Fred D. and Frances Louise (Lawler) Williams; m. Evelyn G. DeVane, July 30, 1966 (div. Sept. 1969); children: La Shavon, Freddia Gaynelle; m. Regenia Bridgeforth, Aug. 20, 1970. B.A., Central State U., Wilberforce, Ohio, 1965; L.H.D. (hon.), Nat. U., Vista, Calif., 1983. White House intern Dept. Treasury, Washington, 1959-63; zone mgr. Ford Motor Co., Indpls., 1969-77; govt. account rep. Xerox Corp., Indpls., 1977-80; v.p. Metro Fin. Group Ltd., Chgo., 1980-81; dep. asst. sec. Dept. Navy, Washington, 1981—. Bd. dirs. Greater Indpls. Housing Devel. Corp., 1978; pres. fin. bd. Washington Twp. (Ind.) Bd., 1979-81; trustee U.S. Naval Acad. Found., 1983—. Served to 1st lt. USMC, 1966-69; Vietnam. Decorated Cross of Gallantry, Vietnam. Mem. VFW, Aircraft Owners and Pilots' Assn., Am. Security Council, Marine Corps Res. Officers Assn., Nat. Pilots' Assn., Security and Intelligence Fund, Montford Point Marine Assn. (pres. Indpls. chpt. 1977-78), Montford Point Marines Assn. (pres. Chgo. chpt. 1980-82), Kappa Alpha Psi; life mem. NAACP (bd. dirs. 1975-77); mem. Res. Officers Assn. (nat. officer 1975-77), Naval Res. Assn. Republican. Methodist. Club: U.S. Senatorial. Lodges: Masons; Shriners. Office: Dep Asst Sec Navy Pentagon Room 4E775 Washington DC 20350

DAVIDSON, FREDERIC MCSHAN, educator; b. Glens Falls, N.Y., Feb. 11, 1941; s. Harry Stonewall and Jeanette D.; m. Linda M. Corcoran, Apr. 6, 1968; children—Susan, Julie. B. Engring. Physics, Cornell U., 1964; Ph.D. in Physics, U. Rochester, 1968. Asst. prof. elec. engring. U. Houston, 1968-70; asst., then assoc. prof., then prof. Johns Hopkins U., Balt. Mem. IEEE, Optical Soc. Am. Office: Dept Elec Engring Johns Hopkins U Baltimore MD 21218

DAVIDSON, GEORGE FORRESTER, former undersec. gen. UN; b. Bass River, N.S., Can., Apr. 18, 1909; s. Oliver Wendell and Emma (Sullivan) D.; m. Elizabeth Ruth Henderson, July 9, 1935; children—Roger Reynolds, Craig Sullivan, Barbara Louise; m. Anneke Irene Kuiper Henderson, June 15, 1975. A.B., U. B.C., 1928, LL.D., 1955; A.M., Harvard U., 1930, Ph.D., 1932; D.H.L., Brandeis U., 1961; LL.D., U. Victoria, 1968, Acadia U., 1973; D.H.L., Brandeis U., 1961; D.Litt., McMaster U., 1973; D.P.A., U. Ottawa, 1977. Supt. Welfare and Neglected Children, Provincial Govt. of B.C., 1934-35, dir. social welfare, 1939-42; exec. dir. welfare Fedn. and Council of Social Agys., Vancouver, B.C., 1935-39; exec. dir. Canadian Welfare Council at Ottawa, 1942-44; dep. minister Nat. Welfare, 1944-60, Citizenship and Immigration, 1960-63; dir. Bur. of Govt. Orgn., 1963-64; sec. Treasury Bd., 1964-68; pres. Canadian Broadcasting Corp., 1968-72; undersec. gen. UN, 1972-79; spl. adv. to exec. dir. UN Fund for Population Activities, 1980—; Canadian rep. Social Commn. of UN, 1947-52; mem. Canadian delegation to Econ. and Social Council, 1946-58, pres., 1958; chmn. social, humanitarian and cultural com. UN Gen. Assembly, 1953; 2d v.p. U.S. Nat. Conf. Social Work, 1951; pres. Canadian Inst. Pub. Adminstrn., 1950-51. Mem. Canadian Conf. Social Work (pres. 1952-54), Internat. Conf. Social Work (pres. 1956-60). Mem. United Ch. Can. Home: 400 E 54th St Apt 24C New York NY 10022

DAVIDSON, GORDON, theatrical producer, director; b. Bklyn., May 7, 1933; s. Joseph H. and Alice (Gordon) D.; m. Judith Swiller, Sept. 21, 1958; children: Adam, Rachel. B.A., Cornell U.; M.A., Case Western Res. U.; L.H.D. (hon.), Bklyn. Coll., D. Performing Arts, Calif. Inst. Arts, D.F.A., Claremont U. Ctr. Stage mgr. Phoenix Theatre Co., 1958-60, Am. Shakespeare Festival Theatre, 1958-60, Dallas Civic Opera, 1960-61, Martha Graham Dance Co., 1962; mng. dir. Theatre Group at UCLA, 1965-67; artistic dir. Center Theatre Group Mark Taper Forum, 1967—; co-founder New Theatre For Now, Mark Taper Forum, 1970; Past mem. theatre panel Nat. Endowment for Arts; past pres. Theatre Communications Group; mem. adv. council Internat. Theatre Inst.; mem. adv. com. Cornell Ctr. for Performing Arts; cons. Denver Center for the Performing Arts. Founder, Mark Taper Forum, 1970; prod., dir.: numerous theatrical prodns. including The Deputy, 1965, Candide, 1966, The Devils, 1967, Who's Happy Now, 1967, In the Matter of J. Robert Oppenheimer, 1968, Murderous Angels, 1970, Rosebloom, 1970, The Trial of the Catonsville Nine, 1971, Henry IV, Part I, 1972, Mass, 1973, Hamlet, 1974, Savages, 1974, Too Much Johnson, 1975, The Shadow Box, 1975, And Where She Stops Nobody Knows, 1976, Getting Out, 1977, Black Angel, 1978, Terra Nova, 1979, Children of a Lesser God, 1979, The Lady and the Clarinet, 1980, Chekhov in Yalta, 1981, Tales from Hollywood, 1982; prod.: numerous prodns. including Robert Frost: Promises To Keep, 1965, Yeats and Company, 1965, Oh What a Lovely War, 1965-66, Next Time I'll Sing to You, 1966, The Birthday Party, 1966, Poor Bitos, 1966, The Sorrows of Frederick, 1967, The Marriage of Mr. Mississippi, 1967, The Miser, 1968, Camino Real, 1968, The Golden Fleece, 1968, Muzeeka, 1968, The Adventures of the Black Girl in Her Search for God, 1969, Chemin de Fer, 1969, Uncle Vanya, 1969, Crystal and Fox, 1970, Story Theatre, 1970, Dream on Monkey Mountain, 1970, Rosebloom, 1970, Metamorphoses, 1971, Othello, 1971, Major Barbara, 1971, Godspell, 1971, Here Are the Ladies, Volpone, 1972, Old Times, 1972, Don't Bother Me I Can't Cope, 1972; numerous plays including Mass, 1973, The Mind with the Dirty Man, 1973, Forget-Me-Not Lane, 1973, The Hot'l Baltimore, 1973, The Mahoganny Songplay, 1973, The Measures Taken, 1973, Hamlet, 1974, The Charlatan, 1974, Juno and the Paycock, 1974, The Dybbuk, 1974, Me and Bessie, 1975, Sizwe Banzi Is Dead, 1975, Once in a Lifetime, 1975, Ashes, 1975, Cross Country, 1975, Three Sisters, 1975, Ice, 1976, Travesties, 1976, The Importance of Being Earnest, 1976, A History of the American Film, 1976, Angel City, 1976, Bugs/Guns, 1976, Leander Stillwell, 1976, For Colored Girls Who Have Considered Suicide/When the Rainbow Is Enuf, 1977, Comedians, 1977, Zoot Suit, 1978, Dusa, 1978, Fish, 1978; produced and directed: Stas & Vi, 1978, The Tempest, 1978; prod.: Talley's Folly, 1979, 5th of July, 1979, I Ought To Be in Pictures, 1979, Says I, Says He, 1979, Division Street, 1979, Billy Bishop Goes to War, 1980, Hoagy, Bix and Wolfgang Beethoven Bunkhaus, 1980, Tintypes, 1980, Twelfth Night, 1980, A Lesson from Aloes, 1981, A Tale Told, 1981, Number Our Days, 1981, A Flea in Her Ear, 1981, The Misanthrope, 1981, A Soldier's Play, 1982, Metamosphosis, 1982, Accidental Death of an Anarchist, 1982, Grownups, 1982, A Month in the Country, 1982, Richard III, 1982; dir.: operas including Cosi Fan Tutte, Otello, Beatrice and Benedick, Carmen, La Boheme, Il Trovatore; TV film The Trial of the Catonsville Nine, 1971; prod.: for TV Ifs the Willingness, PBS Visions Series, 1979, Who's Happy Now?, NET Theatre in Am. Series. Trustee Ctr. for Music, Drama and Art. Recipient N.Y. Drama Desk award for direction, 1969; recipient Los Angeles Drama Critics Circle awards for direction, 1971, 74, 75, Margo Jones award New Theatre for Now, 1970, 76, Obie award, 1971, 77, Outer Critics Circle award, 1977, Tony award for direction, 1977, award John Harvard, Nat. Acad. TV Arts and Scis., Nosotros Golden Eagle, N.Y. League for Hard of Hearing, N.Y. Speech and Hearing Assn., Am. Theatre Assn., Los Angeles Human Relations Commn.; Guggenheim fellow, 1983. Mem. League Resident Theatres (past pres.), ANTA (v.p. 1975). Office: Center Theatre Group 135 N Grand Ave Los Angeles CA 90012

DAVIDSON, GORDON BYRON, lawyer; b. Louisville, June 24, 1926; s. Paul Byron and Elizabeth (Franz) D.; m. Geraldine B. Geiger, Dec. 21, 1948; children: Sally Burgess, Stuart Gordon. A.B., Centre Coll., 1949; J.D., U. Louisville, 1951; LL.M., Yale U., 1952. Law clk. Supreme Ct. U.S., 1954; mng. partner firm Wyatt, Tarrant & Combs, Louisville, 1955—; lectr. U. Louisville Law Sch., 1958—; dir. Courier-Jour. & Louisville Times Co., WHAS Inc., Standard Gravure Co., Armor Elevator Co., Inc. Pres. Louisville Central Area, Inc., 1971-73; chmn. River City Mall Com., 1973-74, Louisville Devel. Com.; mem. Louisville Commn. Fgn. Relations; bd. dirs., chmn. Norton Childrens Hosps., Louisville Fund for Arts; bd. overseers U. Louisville; trustee Centre Coll., Project 2000; chmn. Ky. Center for Arts. Served with U.S. Mcht. Marine Acad., 1944-45; as 1st lt. JAGC U.S. Army, 1952-54. Recipient Louisville Citizens of Yr. award, 1973-74; Mayor's Fleur de Lis award, 1974; Louisville Man of Yr. award, 1981. Fellow Am. Bar Found.; mem. Am. Law Inst., Am. Ky., Louisville, Fed. bar assns., Louisville Area C. of C. (v.p., dir.), Phi Delta Theta, Omicron Delta Kappa, Phi Kappa Phi. Democrat. Presbyterian. Clubs: Harmony Landing Country, Jefferson, Louisville Country (bd. govs.); Tavern, Lawyers, Pendennis, Delray Beach. Home: 435 Lightfoot Rd Louisville KY 40207 Office: Wyatt Tarrant & Combs Citizens Plaza 28th Floor Louisville KY 40202

DAVIDSON, GORDON CHAMBERS, ins. co. exec.; b. Columbus, Ga., Oct. 27, 1927; s. Charles Jackson and Ethel Vivian (Spence) D.; m. Barbara VanAllen Scofield, Apr. 16, 1951; children—Gigi VanAllen, Michael Gordon, Gabrielle Scofield. B.A., Yale U., 1951; M.B.A., Harvard U., 1953. With Northwestern Mut. Life Ins. Co., Milw., 1953—, dir. real estate, then v.p. real estate, 1968-80, v.p., 1980—; chmn. bd. Marina Pacific Ltd.; pres., dir. NML Corp.; dir. numerous affiliated cos. Bd. dirs. Wis. Soc. Prevention Blindness, Goodwill Industries, Milw., Milw. Boys Club; adv. bd. YWCA Greater Milw.; corp. mem. Columbia Hosp., Milw. Served with USNR, 1945-46. Republican. Club: Milw. Country (dir.). Home: 7955 N Pheasant Ln Milwaukee WI 53217 Office: 720 E Wisconsin Ave Milwaukee WI 53202

DAVIDSON, HARVEY JUSTIN, university dean; b. Gentryville, Ind., Nov. 15, 1930; s. Harvey Harrison and Dorothy (Eberhardt) D.; m. Shirlee Jean Ploeger, Sept. 4, 1954; children: Charles Justin, John Clinton, James Christopher, Mary Jennifer. B.S. in Indsl. Mgmt, Carnegie-Mellon U., 1952, M.S. in Math. Econs, 1955; C.P.A. Staff asst. Operations Evaluation Group, U.S. Navy-Mass. Inst. Tech., 1955-56; economist Arabian-Am. Oil. Co., 1956-58; mgmt. cons. Touche Ross & Co., 1957-64; partner, 1964-69; dean Grad. Sch. Bus. and Pub. Adminstrn., Cornell U., 1969-79, Coll. Adminstrv. Sci., Ohio State U., Columbus, 1979—; Dir. Lukens, Inc., UNC Resources, Inc. Co-author: Statistical Sampling for Accounting Information, 1962, The Future of Accounting Education, 1961. Served to 1st lt., C.E. AUS, 1952-54. Decorated Bronze Star. Mem. Am., Pa. insts. C.P.A.s, Ill. Soc. C.P.A.s, Mich. Assn. C.P.A.s, Inst. Mgmt. Sci., Am. Statis. Assn. Unitarian. Home: 306 E Sycamore St Columbus OH 43206

DAVIDSON, HERBERT MARC, publisher, editor; b. N.Y.C., Nov. 8, 1895; s. Julius and Rose (Scharles) D.; m. Liliane Refregier, June 14, 1919; 1 son, Herbert Marc. B.Lit., Columbia U., 1918; LL.D. (hon.), Bethune-Cookman Coll., 1953. Reporter Kansas City (Mo.) Star, 1917, Portland (Oreg.) Jour., 1919, Fourth Estate, 1920, Los Angeles Examiner, 1920-21, Paris bur. Internat. News Service, 1922; rewrite man editorial writer, feature editor Chgo. Daily News, 1922-28; editor Daytona Beach (Fla.) News-Jour., 1928-62; v.p. News-Jour. Corp., Daytona Beach, 1928-62, pres., editor, pub., 1962—. Past bd. dirs. Daytona Beach chpt. A.R.C.; past pres. Daytona Beach Community Chest, 1953-54, Unitarian-Universalist Soc., Daytona Beach Area; trustee Bethune-Cookman Coll. Served with U.S. Army, 1918-19; Served with AEF in; France. Life fellow So. Regional Council; mem. Am. Soc. Newspaper Editors, Fla. Pubs. Assn. (past pres.), Am. Legion, Civic League Halifax Area, Sigma Delta Chi. Democrat. Club: Daytona Beach Rotary (past pres.). Home: 2 Braddock Ave Daytona Beach FL 32018 Office: 901 6th St Daytona Beach FL 32017 *At 33, I left metropolitan journalism in the North for family ownership of a paper in a small Southern city. We have endorsed liberal ideas and fought for clean government. It hasn't been easy, but we have enjoyed success. At 85, I can recommend a career in grassroots journalism and letting one's conscience be one's guide.*

DAVIDSON, HUGH MACCULLOUGH, educator; b. Lanett, Ala., Jan. 21, 1918; s. Robert Calvin and Anne Della (Stripling) D.; m. Loretta Miller, June 15, 1951; 1 dau., Anne Stripling. A.B., U. Chgo., 1938, Ph.D., 1946. Instr. French U. Chgo., 1946-48, asst. prof., 1948-53, asst. dean of Coll., 1949-52; chmn. Coll. French staff, 1951-53; asst. prof. romance langs., Dartmouth, 1953-56, prof. romance langs., 1956-62, chmn. dept., 1957-59; prof. French Ohio State U., Columbus, 1962-73; prof. French lit. U. Va., 1973; mem. Center Advanced Studies, 1973-75; vis. prof. French U. Mich., summer 1967; dir. Nat. Endowment for Humanities seminar, summer 1975, 77; Mem. vis. com. for humanities and arts Case-Western Res. U., 1971-77. Author: Words and Art: Studies in 17th Century French Rhetoric, 1965, also articles on French lit., fgn. lang. teaching, literary criticism, history of artistic and intellectual disciplines.; The Origins of Certainty: Means and Meanings in Pascal's Pensées, 1979; Editor: (with Pierre H. Dubé) A Concordance to the Pensées of Pascal, 1975, A Concordance to Pascal's Provinciales, 2 vols, 1980; Gen. editor: The Idea and Practice of General Education, 1950. Served as capt. USAAF, 1942-46. Fulbright research fellow, France, 1959-60; sr. fellow Nat. Found. Arts and Humanities, 1967-68; fellow Downing Coll., Cambridge (Eng.) U., 1979-80; Carnegie fellow in gen. edn., 1948-49. Mem. Modern Lang. Assn. (editorial bd. publs. 1967-72), Am. Assn. Tchrs. French, Am. Soc. 18th Century Studies, Assn. internationale des etudes françaises (mem. conseil 1976—), N. Am. Soc. for 17th Century Lit., Internat. Soc. History of Rhetoric (council mem. 1979—), Internat. Soc. Philosophy and Lit., Phi Beta Kappa. Episcopalian. Office: Dept French Lit U Va Charlottesville VA 22903

DAVIDSON, IAN BRUCE, investment company executive; b. Great Falls, Mont., Dec. 6, 1931; s. David Adam and Florence (Scott) D.; m. Nancy Ann Preston, June 18, 1961; children: Lauren Mae, Sydney Anne, Andrew Ian. B.B.A., U. Mont., 1953; M.B.A., U. Calif.-Berkeley, 1957. Finance instr. U. Mont., 1956-57; trainee J.A. Hogle & Co., Salt Lake City, 1957-58; with D.A. Davidson & Co., Great Falls, 1958—, pres., 1968—, chmn. bd. dirs., 1970—; mem. Mont. bd. advs. Mountain Bell Telephone Co.; dir. Mountain Bell, Denver, Sletten Constrn. Co., Pacific Hide & Fur Co., United Savs. Bank, Great Falls, Great Falls Gas Co.; owner, developer Davidson Bldg., Great Falls; mem. Midwest Stock Exchange, 1970, Pacific Stock Exchange. Pres. U. Mont. Found., 1972, now trustee; pres. United Fund Cascade County, Mont., 1973; mem. Mont. Commn. on Post Secondary Edn., 1973-75; mem. pres.'s council Coll. Great Falls; co-chmn. Citizens Involvement Com.; former trustee Mont. Physicians Service, Rocky Mountain Coll., Billings, Mont. Served with USAF, 1953-55. Named Disting. Alumnus U. Mont., 1980. Mem. Great Falls Area C. of C. (pres. 1975), Mont. C. of C. (dir.). Presbyterian (elder 1966—). Club: Rotary (pres. 1945—). Home: 3340 14th Ave S Great Falls MT 59405 Office: Davidson Bldg Great Falls MT 59401

DAVIDSON, IRA R., aluminum and chemical company executive; b. 1925; married. B.S. in Indsl. Engring., U. Pa. With Kaiser Aluminum & Chem. Corp., Oakland, Calif., yr. to present, mgr. maj. reduction and fabricating facilities U.S. and abroad; gen. mgr. products Kaiser Aluminum & Chem., 1972-75; corp. v.p. Kaiser Aluminum & Chem. Corp., 1975-80, exec. v.p., 1980—. Office: Kaiser Aluminum & Chem Corp 300 Lakeside Dr Oakland CA 94643 *

DAVIDSON, JACK LEROY, ednl. adminstr.; b. Indpls., July 14, 1927; s. Lawrence L. and Emma (Jones) D.; m. Ina Stanfill, June 20, 1948; children—William, Nancy, Evan. B.A., Franklin Coll., 1949; M.A., Ind. U., 1955, Ed. Adminstrn., 1961, Ph.D., 1967. Tchr., guidance counselor, coach Mitchell (Ind.) Pub. Schs., 1949-57; elem. prin., supervising prin. Vincennes (Ind.) Pub. Schs., 1957-59; supt. Worthington (Ind.) Pub. Schs., 1959-61, Salem (Ind.) Pub. Schs., 1961-65, Oak Ridge (Tenn.) Pub. Schs., 1965-68, Manatee County (Fla.) Pub. Schs., 1968-70, Austin (Tex.) Pub. Schs., 1970-80, Tyler (Tex.) Public Schs., 1980—; vis. prof. U. Tex.; chmn. Tex. Adv. Com. on Ednl. Improvement. Schs. Author: Effective School Board Meetings, 1970; Contbr. articles to ednl. jours. Chmn. United Fund, 1972-73; sch. chmn. local council Boy Scouts Am.; Bd. dirs., pres. Southwest Ednl. Devel. Lab.; charter mem. Tex. Commn. on Inter-Govtl. Relations; bd. dirs. Austin Jr. Achievement. Served with USNR, 1945-47. Mem. Am. Assn. Suprs. Curriculum Devel., Am., Tex. assns. sch. adminstrs. Meth. (deacon, dir.). Club: Rotarian. Home: 1807 Picadilly Pl Tyler TX 75703 Office: PO Box 2035 Tyler TX 75710

DAVIDSON, JAMES FREDERIC, political science educator; b. Newton, Kans., Oct. 4, 1924; s. Scoville E. and Margaret (Gates) D.; m. Mary Elizabeth Harnden, July 16, 1949; children: James Harnden, Margaret Foard, Mary Priscilla, John Ellsworth. B.A., Yale, 1945, postgrad., 1946-47; postgrad., Nat. Inst. Pub. Affairs, Washington, 1947-48; M.A., George Washington U., 1951; Ph.D., U. Chgo., 1954, Center for Study Higher Edn., U. Mich., 1962-63. Com. sec. Far Eastern Commn., Washington, 1948-50; adminstrv. asst. ECA, Washington, 1950-51; staff Pub. Adminstrn. Clearing House, Chgo., 1952-54; mem. faculty U. Tenn., 1954-64, prof. polit. sci., 1962-64; asst. dean Coll. Liberal Arts, 1959-61, asso. dean, 1963-64; dean faculty Concord Coll., Athens, W.Va., 1964-69; prof. polit. sci. Newcomb Coll., Tulane U., New Orleans, 1969-, dean, 1969-76. Contbr. articles to profl. jours. Served with USNR, 1943-46. Mem. Am. Polit. Sci. Assn. Unitarian. Home: 837 Short St New Orleans LA 70118

DAVIDSON, JAMES JOSEPH, JR., lawyer; b. Lafayette, La., June 24, 1904; s. James Joseph and Lilla May (Kennedy) D.; m. Virginia L. Dunham, Aug. 6, 1930; 1 son, James Joseph III. Student, Southwestern La. Inst., 1919-22; A.B., Tulane U., 1925, J.D., 1927. Bar: La. bar 1927. Practiced in, New Orleans, 1927-29, Lafayette, 1929—; mem. firm Davidson, Meaux, Sonnier, McElligott; Mem. La. Supreme Ct. Bar Examining Com., 1936-50. Vice pres. La. Civil Service League; mem. exec. com. Evangeline Area Council Boy Scouts Am., pres., 1967-68; mem. La. Commn. on Human Relations Rights and Responsibilities, 1965-70; bd. dirs. Council for a Better La., Public Affairs Research Corp.; La. com. Pres.' Cabinet Com. on Edn. Fellow Am. Bar Found., Southwestern Legal Found.; mem. La. Judiciary Commn. (1970-74), Nat. Municipal League (mem. council 1969-73), Internat. Assn. Ins. Counsel, ABA (mem. ho. of dels. 1964-68, 73-75), La. Bar Assn. (pres. 1958), Lafayette Bar Assn., 15th Jud. Dist. Bar Assn., Am. Law Inst., La. Law Inst. Council (pres. 1973-77), Am. Counsel Assn., Am. Judicature Soc., Am. Coll. Trial Lawyers, Am. Coll. Probate Counsel, Assn. of Bar City N.Y., Lafayette C. of C. (past pres.), Lafayette Library Assn. (past pres.), Lafayette Community Concert Assn. (past pres.), Order Coif, Phi Alpha Delta, Phi Kappa Phi. Methodist. Clubs: Masons, Rotary (past chpt. pres.), Internat. House, Boston (New Orleans). Home: 537 Girard Park Dr Lafayette LA 70503 Office: 810 Buchanan St Lafayette LA 70501

DAVIDSON, JOHN, entertainer. Grad., Denison U. Actor: film The Happiest Millionaire, 1967, The One and Only Genuine, Original Family Bank, 1968, Coffee, Tea, or Me?, 1973; numerous concerts; TV appearances, including John Davidson Show, 1976, 80—; host: That's Incredible, 1980—; guest host: Tonight Show; recording artist, Columbia Records, 1967-73, Mercury Records, 1973—; Record albums include Time of My Life, 1966, John Davidson, 1967, Kind of Hush, 1967, My Cherie Amour, 1969, Everything Is Beautiful, Well, Here I Am, 1973, Everytime I Sing. Address: care Artists Agy 190 N Canon Dr Beverly Hills CA 90210 *

DAVIDSON, JOHN, financial advisory executive; b. N.Y.C., Oct. 8, 1916; s. John and Elizabeth (Kelly) D.; m. Charlotte J. Duffy, Apr. 22, 1950 (dec.); m. Inge Riebeth, May 23, 1970; children—Jane K., Sara

G., Kirsten M. B.S., N.Y. U., 1944. With Consol. Natural Gas Company, Inc., N.Y.C., 1943-82, tax dept., 1943, asst. mgr. tax dept., 1953-58, mgr., 1958-61, asst. treas., 1961-63, asst. v.p. adminstrn., 1963-70, sec., 1967-70, v.p. adminstrn., 1970-82; pres. Capital Creation Co. of Pa., 1982—. Mem. Council on Employee Benefits. Mem. Beta Gamma Sigma. Club: Pitts. Field. Home: 114 Marvelwood Pl Pittsburgh PA 15215

DAVIDSON, JOHN KEAY, III, diabetologist; b. Lithonia, Ga., Mar. 30, 1922; s. John Keay, Jr. and Laura Elizabeth (Lovingood) D.; m. Mary Evelyn Coney, May 30, 1952; children—John Keay, IV, Dorothy Elizabeth, Anne Ralston, Georgia Dial. B.S., Emory U., 1943, M.D., 1945; Ph.D. in Physiology (Am. Diabetes Assn. research fellow), U. Toronto, Ont., Can., 1965. Surg. intern Grady Meml. Hosp., Atlanta, 1945-46, resident in medicine, 1948-49, Emory U. Hosp., Atlanta, 1949-50, New Eng. Center Hosp., Boston, 1950-51; asso. prof. physiology and medicine U. Toronto Faculty Medicine, 1966-68; mem. faculty Emory U. Med. Sch., 1968—, prof. medicine, dir. diabetes unit, 1970—. Author: (diet sect.): Diabetes Guide Book, 3d edit, 1979. Served with AUS, 1946-47. Fellow A.C.P.; mem. Am. Diabetes Assn. (dir. 1970-76, dir. postgrad. course 1980—, chmn. com. public affairs 1973-74, chmn. com. food and nutrition 1975-76, Outstanding Tchr. of Yr. award 1979), AMA, Am. Physiol. Soc., Endocrine Soc., Am. Soc. Internal Medicine, Can. Physiol. Soc. Methodist. Club: Druid Hills Golf. Home: 1075 Lullwater Rd NE Atlanta GA 30307 Office: 1365 Clifton Rd NE Atlanta GA 30322

DAVIDSON, JOHN KENNETH, SR., sociologist, educator; b. Augusta, Ga., Oct. 25, 1939; s. Larcie Charles and Betty (Corley) D.; m. Josephine Frazier, Apr. 11, 1964; children: John Kenneth, Stephen Wood. Student, Augusta Coll., 1956-58; B.S. in Edn, U. Ga., 1961, M.A., 1963; Ph.D., U. Fla., 1974. Asst. prof. dept. psychology and sociology Armstrong State Coll., Savannah, Ga., 1963-67; asst. prof. sociology Augusta Coll., 1967-74; acting chmn., asst. prof. dept. sociology Ind. U., South Bend, 1974-76; asso. prof. sociology U. Wis., Eau Claire, 1976-78, prof., 1978—, chmn. dept. sociology, 1976-80; cons. family life edn.; research cons. dept. ob-gyn Med. Coll. Ga., Augusta, 1969-74, pediatrics, 1972-73, also asso. dir. health care project, 1971-73, research instr., summer 1971, research asso., summer 1972-73, research cons. dept. community dentistry, 1974-79; program coordinator Community Devel. in Process Phase II and III, Title I Higher Edn. Act of, 1965, 1970; mem. sociology and anthropology com. Univ. System Ga., 1970-74, chmn. curriculum sub-com., 1970-72; dir. Sex Edn., The Public Schs. and You project Ind. Com. on Humanities, 1975. Asso. editor: Jour. Marriage and the Family, 1975—, Jour. Deviant Behavior, 1979—; contbr. articles to profl. jours. Past state chmn. public affairs Ind. Assn. Planned Parenthood Affiliates, 1975-76; past mem. Eau Claire Coordinating Council.; Former bd. dirs. Planned Parenthood North Central Ind., also past chmn. public affairs com., 1975-76; former bd. dirs., former 1st v.p. Wis. Family Planning Coordinating Council; bd. dirs., former mem. exec., info., internat. and edn. coms., chmn. social sci. research com. Assn. for Vol. Sterilization; former mem. resources allocation com. Planned Parenthood of Wis., Inc.; mem. Eau Claire County Adv. Health Forum, Eau Claire County Task Force on Family Planning. Mem. Am. Sociol. Assn., Wis. Sociol. Assn., So. Sociol. Soc., Mid-South Sociol. Assn., Midwest Sociol. Soc., Nat. Council Family Relations (chmn. com. standards and criteria for cert., mem. devel. com., chair cert. com.), Wis. Council Family Relations (exec. com., past pres.), Augusta Coll. Alumni Soc., U. Fla. Alumni Soc., U. Ga. Alumni Soc., Groves Conf., Pres.'s Club U. Wis.-Eau Claire, Kappa Delta Pi, Phi Kappa Phi, Phi Theta Kappa, Alpha Kappa Delta (nat. exec. com.; editor nat. newsletter 1979-83). Episcopalian. Home: 1305 Nixon Ave Eau Claire WI 54701 Office: Dept Sociology U Wis Eau Claire WI 54701

DAVIDSON, JOY ELAINE, mezzo-soprano; b. Ft. Collins, Colo., Aug. 18, 1940; d. Clarence Wayne and Jessie Ellen (Bogue) Ferguson; m. Robert Scott Davidson, Aug. 9, 1959; children: Lisa Beth, Scott, Jeremy Fergus, Bonnie Kathleen, Jordan Christian. B.A., Occidental Coll., Los Angeles, 1959; postgrad., Fla. State U., 1961-64. Co-founder Reward Inc. Debut, 1965; with, N.Y.C. Opera, Met. Opera, opera cos. throughout, U.S. and Can., also, opera cos. throughout, La Scala, Vienna State Opera, Bayerische State Opera, Lyons (France) Opera, Welsh Opera, Florence (Italy) Opera, Torino (Italy) Opera. (Recipient Gold medal Internat. Competition Young Opera Singers, Sofia, Bulgaria 1969), Rio de Janeiro. Mem. PEO; Mem. Sigma Alpha Iota, Zeta Tau Zeta. Democrat. Methodist. Home: 5751 SW 74th Ave Miami FL 33143 Office: Columbia Artists Mgmt 165 W 57th St New York NY 10019 *Success awaits those who dare to dream big enough. The success achiever is the possibility thinker.*

DAVIDSON, JOYCE, TV personality; b. Saskatoon, Sask., Can., Apr. 14, 1931; came to U.S., 1962; d. Eric Arthur and Myrtle Irene (Johnson) Brock; m. Douglas P. Davidson, 1948 (div. 1959); children—Shelley Irene, Constance Barbara; m. David Susskind, Apr. 22, 1966; 1 dau., Samantha Maria. Pres. Joyce Davidson Prodns., 1980—. Co-host: Tabloid, CBC, 1956-61; appeared on: Close-Up, CBC, 1958-61, Today Show, 1959-60, Jack Benny Show, 1959-60, PM East, 1962-63, Joyce Davidson Show, Authors, Con. Broadcasting Co., 1978-80, The World of Mother Teresa, 1981, the Entertainers with Joyce Davidson, 1981—. Mem. AFTRA, Assn. Can. TV and Radio Artists.

DAVIDSON, KEITH L., lawyer; b. Chgo., Il, Oct. 31, 1942; s. Louis G. and Anne Marie (Astley) D.; m. Wendy Sue Ruff, Nov. 22, 1980. A.B., U. Ill., 1965; J.D., Loyola U., 1969. Bar: Ill. 1968, U.S. Dist. Ct. (no. dist.) Ill. 1969, U.S Ct. Appeals (7th cir.) 1971, U.S. Ct. Appeals (4th cir.) 1973, U.S. Supreme Ct. 1978. Ptnr. Louis G. Davidson & Assocs., Ltd., Chgo., 1968—; participating adviser Nat. Ednl. TV Program, 1973; judge Moot Ct. Northwestern U., Chgo., Ill, 1973, 77, 78, Kent Law Sch., 1973, 77, 78, John Marshall Law Sch., 1973, 77, 78; lectr., trial demonstrator (various law sch., assns., seminars). Contbr. articles and book rev. to legal jours. other profl. mags. Fellow Am. Bar Found.; mem. ABA (council 1980-84), Ill. State Bar Assn. (gov. 1980—), Chgo. Bar Assn., Bar Assn. 7th Fed. Cir. Lawyers Am. (mem. com. on adminstrn. of justice 1975-76, 77-78), Assn. Trial Lawyers Am. (mem. internat. law and treaties com. 1980-81), Ill. Trial Lawyers Assn. (mem. bd. mgrs. 1976), Chgo Council Lawyers (v.p. 1974-76), World Assn Lawyers, Alliance Francaise (bd. dirs. 1975-79, 2d v.p. 1977-79). Club: Literary (Chgo.). Office: Louis G. Davidson & Assocs Ltd 111 W. Washington St Chgo. Il 60602

DAVIDSON, MARSHALL BOWMAN, editor, author; b. N.Y.C., Apr. 26, 1907; s. Henry F. and Frances Aubrey (Holt) D.; m. Ruth H. Bradbury, Aug. 20, 1935. B.S., Princeton, 1928. Asso. curator Am. wing Met. Mus. Art, N.Y.C., 1935-47, editor publs., 1947-61; mng. editor Horizon Books, 1961-63; editor Horizon mag., 1964-66, sr. editor, 1966—. Author: Life in America, 1951, The American Heritage History of Colonial Antiques, 1967, The American Heritage—History of American Antiques, 1784-1860, 1968, The American Heritage—History of Antiques, USA, 1865-1917, 1969, Bantam Book of Early American Furniture, 1980, The American Wing, A Guide, 1980, (with others) The History of the 20's and 30's, 1970, The American Heritage—History of Notable American Houses, 1971, A Concise History of France, 1971, The Artists' America, 1973, The Writers' America, 1973, Great Historic Places of Europe, 1974, The World in 1776, 1975, Fifty Early American Tools, 1975, The Drawing of America, 1983; contbg. author: The Romance of North America, 1958, America and Russia, 1962; contbr.: Dictionary American Biography; editor, commentator: A Pictorial History of Architecture in America, 2 vols., 1976, A Pictorial History of New York State, 1977; also articles in Am. decorative art jours., others.; adv. editor: Am. Heritage mag.; editor: The Original Water-color Paintings of John J. Audubon, 1966. Home: 140 E 83d St New York NY 10028

DAVIDSON, MICHAEL, lawyer; b. Bklyn., Feb. 20, 1940; s. Joseph H. and Alice (Gordon) D.; m. Karen Kreitler, May 10, 1969; children: Jesse, Kate. B.A., Cornell U., 1961; J.D., U. Chgo., 1964. Bar: N.Y. 1966. Vol. Peace Corps, Kenya, 1964-66; asst. counsel NAACP Legal Def. Fund., N.Y.C., 1966-73; dir. housing litigation bur. Housing and Devel. Adminstrn., N.Y.C., 1973-74; vis. assoc. prof. SUNY-Buffalo, 1974-77; chief staff counsel U.S. Ct. Appeals (D.C. Circuit), 1977-79; legal counsel U.S. Senate, Washington, 1979—. Home: 3753 McKinley St NW Washington DC 20015 Office: 642 Hart Senate Office Bldg Washington DC 20510

DAVIDSON, NORMAN RALPH, biochemistry educator; b. Chgo., Apr. 5, 1916; s. Bernard Ralph and Rose (Lefstein) D.; m. Annemarie Behrendt, Jull 11, 1942; children: Terence Mark, Laureen Davidson Reitman Agee, Jeffrey Norman, Brian Lee. B.S., U. Chgo., 1937, Ph.D. in Chemistry, 1941; B.Sc., Oxford (Eng.) U., 1939. Research scientist Manhattan Project U. Chgo., 1942-46; instr. chemistry Calif. Inst. Tech., Pasadena, 1946-49, asst. prof., 1949-52; assoc. prof. Calif Inst Tech, 1952-57; prof. Calif. Inst. Tech., 1957-82, Chandler prof. chem. biology, 1982—; mem. sci. adv. bd. Am Gen., Newbury Park, Calif., 1981—; mem. and chemn. biophysics and biophys. chemistry study sect. NIH, Bethesda, Md., 1964-68. Rhodes scholar, 1938-39. Recipient Calif. sect. award Am. Chem. Soc., 1954, Peter Debye award in phys. chemistry, 1971; named Calif. Scientist of Yr. Calif. Mus. Sci. and History, 1980. Mem. Nat. Acad. Scis.

DAVIDSON, RALPH KIRBY, economist, foundation executive; b. Webster, S.D., May 13, 1921; s. Alfred and Grace (Christensen) D.; m. Laura Agnes Devine, Dec. 28, 1940; children: Karen Ruth, Laura (Mrs. Dhiraj V. Tanna). Student, Mont. State U. at Missoula, 1946-48; B.A. (Rhodes scholar 1948-51), Keble Coll., Oxford (Eng.) U., 1950; M.A., Oxford (Eng.) U., 1954, Johns Hopkins U., 1953; Ph.D. with distinction, Johns Hopkins U., 1954. Printer Reporter and Farmer newspaper, Webster, 1936-41, printer, 1946; editor McPherson County Herald, Leola, S.D., 1942; part-time linotype operator Univ. Press, The Leader, also The Missoulian, Missoula, 1946-48; instr. McCoy Coll., Balt., 1952-53; linotype operator Balt. News Post, 1951-54; mem. faculty Purdue U., 1954-62, asst. prof., 1954-57, asso. prof., 1957-60, prof. econs., 1960-62, crew coach, 1955-61, asst. dean Grad. Sch., 1959-62; cons. Rockefeller Found., also vis. prof. econs., Makerere, Kampala, Uganda, 1962-63, asso. dir. for humanities and social scis., 1962-64, dep. dir., 1964-70, dep. dir. social scis., 1971-83, sr. scientist on research leave, 1983-84; Vice pres. West Lafayette (Ind.) Jr. High Sch. Bldg. Corp., 1961; Vice chmn. bd. trustees Internat. Food Policy Research Inst., 1975—; mem. sci. working group on social and econ. research WHO spl. program for research and tng. in tropical diseases, 1979—; chmn., 1982—. Author: Price Discrimination in Selling Gas and Electricity, 1955, reprinted 1976, (with V. L. Smith and J. W. Wiley) Economics: An Analytical Approach, rev. edit, 1962; editor: (with Coleman and Stifel) Social Sciences and Public Policy in the Developing World, 1982; contbr. also chpts. to books, articles, book revs. Trustee Grace Ch. Sch., 1982—. Served with AUS, 1943-46; PTO. Social Sci. Research Council fellow, 1953-54; Ford Found. fellow, 1958-59. Mem. Am., Royal econ. assns., Am. Assn. Rhodes Scholars, Asia Soc., AAAS, Econometrics Soc., Council Fgn. Relations, Keble Coll. Assn., Phi Beta Kappa. Episcopalian. Home: 2 Washington Sq Village Apt 8-O New York NY 10012

DAVIDSON, RALPH PARSONS, publishing company executive; b. Santa Fe, Aug. 17, 1927; s. William Clarence Davidson and Doris Parsons Stanton; m. Lou Hill; children: William A., R. Andrew. B.A. in Internat. Relations, Stanford U., 1950; postgrad., Alliance Francaise, Paris, 1951. With CIA, 1952-54; advt. salesman Life mag., 1954-56; European advt. dir. Time mag., London, 1956-62; mng. dir. Time-Life Internat., N.Y.C., 1967—; pub. Time mag., 1972-78; now chmn. bd. Time Inc.; publ. Time mag., 1972-78; dir. Signal Cos.; lectr. communications Stanford U., also mem. adv. bd. profl. journalism fellowships program. Trustee United Student Aid Funds, Nat. Urban League, Ocean Trust Found., Com. for Econ. Devel.; chmn. Bus. Com. for Arts; mem. Pres.'s Commn. Exec. Exchange; bd. dirs. World Wildlife Fund; vice chmn. Pres.'s Com. Internat. Youth Exchange; bd. dirs. N.Y. City Ballet.; mem. Statue of Liberty-Ellis Island Centennial Commn. Served with USNR, World War II. Mem. Stanford U. Alumni Assn. (pres. 1972-73). Clubs: Explorers, River (N.Y.C.); American (London). Office: Time Inc Time and Life Bldg Rockefeller Center New York NY 10020

DAVIDSON, RITA CHARMATZ, judge; b. Bklyn., Sept. 1, 1928; d. Michael and Eiga (Rokeach) Charmatz; m. David Sternheimer Davidson, Aug. 27, 1950; children: Minna Kohn, Leo Charmatz. B.A. with honors, Goucher Coll., 1948, LL.D., 1979; LL.B., Yale U., 1951. Bar: D.C. 1952, Md. 1963. Individual practice law, Washington and Montgomery County, Md., 1951-67; chairperson Montgomery County Bd. Appeals, 1960-64; commr. Md. Nat. Park and Planning Commn., 1967; zoning hearing examiner Montgomery County, 1967-70; sec. Md. Dept. Human Resources, 1970-72; asso. judge Ct. Spl. Appeals Md., 1972-79, Ct. Appeals Md., Annapolis, 1979—; chairperson Gov.'s Commn. on Jobs for Vets. and; Gov.'s Interagy. Com. on Childhood Devel., 1970-72. Recipient Woman of Year award Balt. Bus. and Profl. Women, 1971; Disting. Citizen's award State of Md., 1973; Leadership award Silver Spring C. of C., 1973; Focus Women's award Montgomery County, 1980; Humanitarian award Citizens Awards Com. Balt., 1980; others. Mem. Am. Bar Assn., Md. Bar Assn., Montgomery County Bar Assn., D.C. Bar Assn., Women's Bar Assn., Nat. Assn. Women Judges, Nat. Assn. Women Lawyers, Am. Judicature Soc., Md. Jud. Conf., Yale Law Sch. Assn., Am. Law Inst. Home: 8814 Altimont Ln Chevy Chase MD 20815 Office: 50 Courthouse Sq Room 305 Rockville MD 20850

DAVIDSON, RONALD CROSBY, physicist, educator; b. Norwich, Ont., Can., July 3, 1941; s. William Crosby and Annie Beatrice (Caley) D.; m. Jean Farncombe, May 18, 1963; children: Cynthia Christine, Ronald Crosby. B.Sc., McMaster U., 1963; Ph.D., Princeton U., 1966. Mem. faculty dept. physics U. Md., 1968-78; vis. scientist Los Alamos Sci. Lab., 1974-75; asst. dir. for applied plasma physics Office of Fusion Energy Dept. Energy, Washington, 1976-78; prof. physics, dir. Plasma Fusion Center MIT, Cambridge, Mass., 1978—; cons. Sci. Applications, Inc. Author: Methods in Nonlinear Plasma Theory, 1972, Physics of Nonneutral Plasmas, 1974. Ford Found. fellow, 1963-64; Imperial Oil fellow, 1963-66; Sloan Research Found. fellow, 1970-72. Fellow Am. Phys. Soc. (chmn. div. plasma physics); mem. Fusion Power Assn. (dir.), Sigma Xi. Home: 179 Morse Rd Sudbury MA 01776 Office: 167 Albany St Cambridge MA 02139

DAVIDSON, THOMAS MAXWELL, electronics company executive; b. N.Y.C., Dec. 14, 1937; s. Alfred Edward and Claire Helen (Dreyfus) D.; m. Ruth Elizabeth Bovenkerk, Dec. 8, 1962; children: Douglas Edward, Anne Elizabeth. B.A., Vanderbilt U., 1959; M.B.A., Columbia U., 1961. Mgr. Ford Motor Co., Dearborn, Mich., 1963-72; dir. credit ops. White Motor Corp., Eastlake, Ohio, 1972-73, v.p., treas., 1976-77; sr. v.p., chief ops. officer White Motor Credit Corp., Cleve., 1973-75, pres., chief exec. officer, 1975-77, also dir.; sr. v.p. fin., chief fin. officer, dir. Tex. Gas Transmission Corp., Owensboro, Ky., 1977-81; exec. v.p., chief fin. officer, dir. Arrow Electronics, Inc., Greenwich, Conn., 1981—. Bd. dirs. Wendell Foster Center. Served with U.S. Army, 1959. Mem. Am. Gas Assn. (fin. com.), Inst. Mgmt. Scis. Clubs: N.Y. Athletic, Wall Street. Home: 131 Doubling Rd Greenwich CT 06830 Office: 600 Steamboat Rd Greenwich CT 06830

DAVIDSON, VANDA ARTHUR, JR., obstetrician, gynecologist; b. Dubach, La., Oct. 9, 1918; s. Vanda Arthur and Flossie (Rainwater) D.; m. Earline Givens, Sept. 12, 1945; children: Vanda Lewis, Darrell Dale, Elizabeth Dianne. B.S., La. Poly. Inst., 1938; M.D., Tulane U., 1942. Diplomate: Am. Bd. Ob-Gyn. Intern Charity Hosp. of La., New Orleans, 1942-43; resident Tulane service Charity Hosp. La., 1946-49; practice medicine specializing in ob-gyn, Dallas, 1949—; mem. staff Baylor U. Med. Center, Dallas, Parkland Hosp., Presbyn. Hosp. of Dallas, Gaston Episcopal Hosp.; asst. clin. prof. U. Tex. Health Sci. Center, Dallas, 1951—; mem. original bd. dirs. Ling Electric, 1955; also on bds. Ling Electronics, 1958, Ling Temco and; Ling Temco Vaught, mem. exec. com., 1956-70, chmn. compensation com. and mem. exec. com. of bd., 1961-70; builder, chmn. bd. Med. Tower, 1962-69; founding mem., chmn. bd. Morgan Maxfield and Assos., 1964; chmn. bd. Sta.-KVIL, 1968-69; bd. govs. Tulane Med. Center, 1967—; dir. UTL, 1971—. Served to maj. U.S. Army, 1943-46. Decorated Bronze Star, Legion of Merit. Fellow A.C.S., Am. Coll. Ob-Gyn, Internat. Coll. Surgeons; mem. AMA, Central Assn. Ob-Gyn, Tex. Ob-Gyn. Soc., Dallas-Ft. Worth Ob-Gyn. Soc., N.Mex. Ob-Gyn. Soc. (hon.), Conrad G. Collins Ob-Gyn. Soc. (pres. 1958), Am. Fertility Soc., Explorers Club. Republican. Clubs: Chaparral, 2001, Dallas Gun, Hurricane Creek Country, Tex. Game Fishing, Safari, Game Coin Internat. Office: 8160 Walnut Hill Lane Suite 308 Dallas TX 75231

DAVIDSON, WILLIAM, clergyman; b. Miles City, Mont., July 20, 1919; s. Thomas and Catherine (Gold) D.; m. Mary Ernestine Shoemaker, June 3, 1942; children: Carol (Mrs. Ronald Carpenter), Thomas, George, Robert. B.S., Mont. State U., 1940; S.T.B., Berkeley Div. Sch., 1946; D.D. (hon.), Episcopal Theol. Sem., Lexington, Ky., 1966, LL.D. (hon.), 1978. Tchr. agr. Sidney (Mont.) High Sch., 1940-43; ordained to ministry Episcopalian Ch., 1947; minister, then rector various chs. in Mont., 1946-56; asso. sec. nat. council div. town and country, home dept. Episcopal Ch., 1956-62; rector Grace Ch., Jamestown, N.D., 1962-65; bishop of Western Kans., 1966-80, asst. bishop of Ohio, Cleve., 1980—. Chmn. trustees St. John's Mil. Sch., Salina, Kans., 1966-80, St. Francis' Boys' Homes, Salina, 1966-80. Named Young Man of Year Lewistown (Mont.) Jr. C. of C., 1954. Home: 1420 Westover Rd Cleveland Heights OH 44118 Office: 2230 Euclid Ave Cleveland OH 44115

DAVIDSON, WILLIAM M., managing partner professional sports team. Mng. ptnr. Detroit Pistons, NBA, Pontiac, Mich. Office: Detroit Pistons Pontiac Silverdome 1200 Featherstone Pontiac MI 48057

DAVIDSON, WILLIAM M., diversified company executive; b. 1921; (div.) LL.B., Wayne State U.; B.B.A., U. Mich. Pres. chief exec. officer Guardian Glass Co., Northville, Mich., 1957-68; pres., chief exec. officer, dir. Guardian Industries Corp., Northville, Mich., 1968—. Served with USN. Office: Guardian Industries Corp 43043W Nine Mile Rd Northville MI 48167 *

DAVID-WEILL, MICHEL ALEXANDRE, investment banker; b. France, Nov. 23, 1932; U.S., 1977; s. Pierre Sylvain and Berthe Marie (Haardt) David-W.; m. Helene Lehideux, July 20, 1956; children: Beatrice David-Weill Stern, Cecile David-Weill de la Baume, Natalie, Agathe. Ed., Inst. Scis. Politiques, 1953. Partner Lazard Freres & Co., 1961-65, Lazard Freres & Cie, 1965—; dir. Lazard Bros. & Co., Ltd., 1965—; sr. partner Lazard Freres & Co., N.Y.C., 1977—; chmn. bd., dir. Eurafrance, 1972—, BSN-Gervais-Danone, 1970—; dir. ITT. Mem. Security Industry Assn. (gov.), Academie des Beaux-Arts (mem. inst.). Clubs: Brook, Knickerbocker (N.Y.C.). Office: Lazard Freres & Co 1 Rockefeller Plaza New York NY 10020

DAVIE, JOSEPH MYRTEN, physician, pathology educator; b. La Porte, Ind., Oct. 14, 1939; s. John James and Dorothy Elizabeth (Hash) D.; m. Janet Sue Whorwell, Dec. 17, 1960; children: Shelley, Jennifer, Melissa. A.B., Ind. U., 1962, M.A., 1964, Ph.D., 1966; M.D., Washington U., St. Louis, 1968. Intern Washington U., 1968-69; staff asso. NIH, 1969-71; resident Nat. Cancer Inst., 1971-72; asso. prof. pathology Washington U. Sch. Medicine, 1972-75, asst. prof. microbiology, 1972-73, asso. prof. microbiology, 1973-75, prof., head microbiology and immunology, prof. pathology, 1975—. Asso. editor: Jour. of Immunology, 1975-78; sect. editor, 1978—. Served with USPHS, 1969-71. Mem. Am. Soc. Microbiology, Am. Assn. Immunologists, Am. Assn. Pathologists. Office: Dept Microbiology and Immunology Washington U Sch Medicine St Louis MO 63110

DAVIES, ALFRED ROBERT, physician, educator; b. Troy, Ohio, May 20, 1933; s. Alfred Willis and Lois Prugh (Shilling) D.; m. Shirley Gray Culp, June 23, 1956; children: Ann Borden, Robert Lane. A.B., Ohio Wesleyan U., 1955; M.D., U. Cin., 1959. Resident in internal medicine U. Cin., 1959-63; practice medicine specializing in internal medicine, Troy, Ohio, 1965-76; clin. prof. medicine Wright State U., 1977—, chmn. dept. medicine, 1977-81. Pres. Miami Valley (Ohio) Heart Assn., 1972-73; tchr. Sunday sch. First Methodist Ch., Troy, 1973—; trustee Stouder Meml. Hosp., Troy, 1977—; mem. Ohio Public Health Council, 1981—. Served with Med. Coprs USNR, 1963-65. Named One of Ohio's Outstanding Young Men, 1968; recipient Troy Community Service award, 1981. Fellow A.C.P.; mem. Miami County Med. Soc., Ohio State Med. Soc., AMA, Ohio Soc. Internal Medicine, Am. Soc. Internal Medicine, Am. Heart Assn., Wright State U. Acad. Medicine (exec. com. 1981), Omicron Delta Kappa, Pi Kappa Epsilon. Republican. Home: 1401 Peters Rd Troy OH 45373

DAVIES, ARCHIBALD DONALD, clergyman; b. Pitts., Apr. 15, 1920; s. Archibald Decimus and Velma Mercedes (Harris) D.; m. Mabel Myrtle Roberts, Dec. 25, 1939; 5 children. B.A., U. Tulsa, 1944; S.T.B., S.T.M., Seabury-Western Theol. Sem., 1947. Ordained deacon Episcopal Ch., 1950, priest, 1951; deacon-in-charge Trinity Ch., El Dorado, Kans., 1950-51, rector, 1951-52; chmn. dept. ch. edn. Kans. State U., 1951-54; rector St. Paul Ch. and Chapel, 1952-54; asso. sec. adult div. dept. ch. edn. Exec. Council Epis. Chs., 1954-56, exec. sec., 1956-58; rector Grace Ch., Monroe, La., 1958-61; asso. prof. ch. edn. Seabury-Western Theol. Sem., 1964-70; dean Trinity Cathedral, Omaha, 1968-70; bishop, Dallas, 1970—; Chaplain UAR, 1954—. Contbr. articles to mags. U.S. Army, 1962-64. Fellow Coll. Preachers. *

DAVIES, DANIEL R., educator; b. Plymouth, Pa., Feb. 21, 1911; s. John R. and Minnie (Kocher) D.; m. Winifred Evans, June 14, 1941 (div. July 1975); children: Cathie, Wendy; m. Nancy Church Edwards, Sept. 9, 1975. A.B., Harvard, 1933; A.M., Bucknell U., 1943; Ph.D., Columbia, 1946. Tchr. Forty Fort (Pa.) High Sch., 1934-44, head dept. English, 1940-44; asst. supt. schs., Briarcliff Manor, N.Y., 1944-45;

asst. dept. edn. adminstrn. Columbia, 1945-46, asst. prof. edn., exec. officer div. adminstrn. and guidance, 1946-49; asso. prof., exec. officer Tchrs. Coll., 1949-50, prof. edn., dir. coop. program in ednl. adminstrn., 1950-59; del. Coop. Center for Ednl. Adminstrn., 1955-59; asso. dir. Indsl. Mgmt. Work Conf., Columbia U. Sch. Engring., and Indsl. Research Conf., 1955-60; exec. dir. U. Council for Edn. Adminstrn., 1958-59; editorial cons. A.C. Croft Publs., New London, Conn., 1958-60; dir. research and devel. Croft Ednl. Services, 1960-66; v.p. research, devel. and dir. Croft Cons. Services, Tucson, 1966-71; pres. Davies-Brickell Assos., Ltd., 1972—; chmn. bd. Doris Lemke Realty, Inc., Bisbee, Ariz., 1981-83; Lectr. U. Ariz., 1962-64; vis. prof. San Diego State, summer 1957, U. N.Mex., summer 1960, Okla. A. and M., summer 1963, Tex. A. and M., U. Scranton, summer 1964, U. Nebr., summer 1971; mem. Nat. Com. Advancement Ednl. Adminstrn., 1955-57; cons. Lilly Endowment, Inc., 1976-77; head policy cons. Calif. Sch. Bds. Assn., 1976-81; dir. policy services Conn. Assn. Bds. Edn., 1978—; head policy cons. N.J. Sch. Bds. Assn., 1977-82; Spl. cons. on installing Davies-Brickell System in schs., U.S.A., Can., also Am. Schs., France, Holland, Greece, Italy.; organizing dir. First Nat. Bank Bisbee. Author: numerous books including Dynamics of Group Action, 8 vols, 1954; (with V. Anderson) Patterns of Educational Leadership, 1956, (with H.M. Brickell) Davies-Brickell System for School Board Policy Making, 1957, 13th edit., 1984, Calif. edits., 1977-80, Conn. edit., 1978-84, Nebr. edit., 1983-84, Board Policy Letter, 1958-71, (with R.T. Livingston) You and Management, 1958, (translated into Japanese, 1968), (with Margaret Handlong) Teaching of Art, 1962, The Administrative Internship, 1962, (with D.E. Griffiths) Executive Action, 1962-68, (with W.S. Elsbree, Louise H. Nelson) Educational Sec., 1962-67, Catholic Schools Adaptation of the Davies-Brickell System, 1968, (with Father James R. Dineen) New Patterns for Catholic Education, 1968, (with Catherine Davies Armistead) In-Service Education, 1975. Pres. bd. dirs. Ariz. Theatre Co., 1976-79. Named Citizen of Yr. Bisbee C. of C., 1983; Ford Found. grantee, Europe, 1961. Fellow AAAS; mem. NEA, AAUP, Nat. Soc. Study Edn. (contbr. Yearbook 1954), Am. Assn. Sch. Adminstrs., Nat. Conf. Profs. Ednl. Adminstrn. (exec. com., sec.-treas. 1948-58), Phi Delta Kappa. Clubs: Skyline Country (Tucson); Bisbee Country. Lodge: Bisbee Rotary (pres. 1984-85). Home: Casa del Jubilado PO Box 757 Naco AZ 85620 Office: Drawer 8 Bisbee AZ 85603 *People will say to me, in parting, "Have a good day!" My response is, "I always have a good day. They are too precious to waste." Their reaction is usually a thoughtful smile... My days are almost always happy ones. I start the day with thanks for another chance to see the sun, to be able to move about, to tackle challenges. A lame leg - result of an accident when I was 4 years old - put me on crutches until I went to college. Since then I have walked mostly without pain. What a joy it is to be able to join you with the good legs in viewing the beauty around us*

DAVIES, DAVID GEORGE, lawyer; b. Waukesha, Wis., July 19, 1928; s. David Evan and Ella Hilda (Degler) D.; m. Elaine Kowalchik, May 12, 1962; children: Thea Kay, Bryn Ann, Degler Evan. B.S., U. Wis., 1950, J.D., 1953. Bar: Wis. 1953, Ariz. 1959. Trust rep. First Nat. Bank of Ariz., Phoenix, 1957-58, asst. trust officer, 1958-62, trust officer, head bus. devel. in trust dept., 1962-66, v.p., trust officer, 1966; practice in Phoenix, 1967—; assoc. Wales & Collins, 1967-68; ptnr. Wales, Collins & Davies, 1968-75, Collins, Davies & Cronkhite, Ltd., 1975—; Instr. bus. law local chpt. C.L.U.s, 1965; instr. estate and gift taxation, 1973—; instr. estate planning Phoenix Coll., 1968—; past instr. Maricopa County Jr. Coll. Pres. Central Ariz. Estate Planning Council; pres., bd. dirs. Vis. Nurse Service, United Fund Agy.; chmn. bd. Beatitudes Campus of Care; bd. dirs. Phoenix chpt. Nat. Hemophilia Found.; bd. dirs., treas. trusteeship St. Luke's Hosp. Med. Ctr., Phoenix, 1982—. Served from 1st lt. to capt. JAGC, AUS, 1953-57. Mem. Central Assn. Life Underwriters (asso.), ABA, Wis. Bar Assn., State Bar Ariz., Am. Assn. Homes for Aged (legal affairs com., future com.). Congregationalist (chmn. bd. trustees, moderator). Home: 4730 E Exeter Blvd Phoenix AZ 85018 Office: Suite 220B 4350 E Camelback Rd Phoenix AZ 85018

DAVIES, DAVID GEORGE, economist, educator; b. Uniontown, Pa., May 27, 1924; s. Ernest John and Meta (Bailey) D.; m. Carol Kressen, Dec. 30, 1949; children—Richard, Lynn. A.B., Stanford, 1949; M.A., U. Cal. at Los Angeles, 1952, Ph.D., 1955. Research asst. Bur. Bus., Econ. Research, U. Cal., Los Angeles, 1951-52, teaching asst. econs. dept., 1952-54; asst. prof. U. Cin., 1955-58, asso. prof., prof., 1958-60; asso. prof. Duke, 1961-66, prof. econs., 1966—, chmn. dept. econs., 1970-73, dir. honors program, 1973—, dir. undergrad. studies, 1975-80; Dir. Econ. Inequities, Inc.; mem. univs. com. Nat. Bur. Econ. Research; mem. intergovtl. fiscal relations com. Nat. Tax Assn.-Tax Inst. Am., 1973—. Author: monograph International Comparisons of Tax Structures in Federal and Unitary Countries, 1976, The Economics and Politics of Financing Political Campaigns, 1976; mem. editorial bd.: Pub. Finance Quar; bd. editors: Jour. Law and Polit. Economy; contbr. articles to profl. jours. Haynes Found. Research fellow, 1954-55; Ford Found. Faculty Research fellow, 1960-61; Fulbright research scholar, Australia, 1968; sr. fellow Center for Commonwealth Studies; vis. research fellow Centre for Research on Fed. Financial Relations, Australian Nat. U., 1975, 80; Earhart research fellow, 1978-79. Mem. Am., So., Midwest econ. assns., Royal Econ. Soc., Nat. Tax Assn., Pub. Choice Soc., Assn. for Evolutionary Econs., AAAS, Pi Gamma Mu, Beta Gamma Sigma, Alpha Kappa Psi. Office: Econs Dept Duke U Durham NC 27706

DAVIES, DAVID KEITH, geologist; b. Barry, Eng., Oct. 10, 1940; came to U.S., 1966, naturalized, 1973; s. Buller T. and Muriel G. (Champ) D.; m. Ruth Margaret Mary Gilbertson, Dec. 12, 1964; children: Mark James, John Philip. B.S., U. Wales, 1962, Ph.D., 1966; M.S., La. State U., 1964. Asst. prof. Tex. A. and M. College Station, 1966-68, asso. prof., 1968-70, asst. dean, 1968-70; prof. U. Mo., Columbia, 1970-77; chmn. dept. geoscis., dir. Reservoir Studies Inst., Tex. Technol. U., Lubbock, 1977-80; pres. David K. Davies & Assos., Inc., Houston, 1980—. Contbr. articles to profl. jours. Mem. Planning and Zoning Commn. Columbia, Mo., 1979-80. Recipient A. I. Levorsen Meml. award Am. Assn. Petroleum Geologists, 1978. Fellow Geol. Soc. Am.; mem. Am. Assn. Petroleum Geologists, Soc. Econ. Paleontologists and Mineralogists, Soc. Petroleum Engrs. of AIME, Phi Kappa Phi. Home: 2210 Long Valley Kingwood TX 77339 Office: 1410 Stonehollow Dr Kingwood TX 77339

DAVIES, DAVID LLOYD, lawyer; b. Falls City, Nebr., Oct. 17, 1903; s. David Morris and Alice (Griffiths) D.; m. Barbara Coit Elliott, Sept. 10, 1930; children—Barbara Ann (Mrs. John H.V. Davies), David Coit. A.B., Stanford, 1925, J.D., 1927. Bar: Oreg. bar 1927. Since practiced in, Portland; mem. firm Stoel, Rives, Boley, Fraser & Wyse (and predecessors), 1937—; Dir. Leupold & Stevens, Inc. Trustee emeritus Med. Research Found. of Oreg.; past pres. Portland Art Assn.; dir., past pres. Oreg. Hist. Soc.; past pres. Portland Community Chest; bd. dirs., past pres. Library Assn. Portland; overseer emeritus Whitman Coll.; trustee Jackson Found. Mem. Am., Oreg., Multnomah County bar assns., Am. Law Inst., Automobile Club of Oreg. (dir., treas.). Republican. Presbyn. Clubs: Arlington, University (Portland); Century (N.Y.C.). Home: 01400 SW Military Rd Portland OR 97219 Office: 900 SW 5th Ave Portland OR 97204

DAVIES, DENNIS RUSSELL, pianist, music director, conductor; b. Toledo, Apr. 16, 1944; s. Harry and Lois (Schuller) D.; m. Molly Robison; children: Annabel, James, April. B.A., Julliard Sch. Music, 1966, M.A., 1968, D.Mus.Arts, 1972. Music dir., Norwalk (Conn.) Symphony Orch., 1968-72; condr., Juilliard Ensemble, 1968-74; music dir., St. Paul Chamber Orch., 1972-81, Cabrillo Music Festival, 1974—, White Mountains Festival of Arts, from 1975; regular guest condr., Netherlands Opera, from 1973; guest condr., Stuttgart Opera, 1976-80; music dir., 1980—; condr.: Flying Dutchman, Bayreuth Festival, from 1978. Address: Württembergisches Staatstheater Oberer Schlossgarten 6 D-7000 Stuttgart Germany *

DAVIES, FRANK EDWARD, advt. exec.; b. Nottingham, Eng., Mar. 18, 1923; s. Frank and Lily (Knight) D.; m. Annemarie Deutschmann, May 24, 1947; children—Bembo, Robin, Julia, Andrea. Student, Nottingham Coll. Art, U. London, Camberville Sch. Art, Guildford Sch. Art, Hillcroft Coll. Art dir. Maclean-Hunter, Toronto, Ont., Can., 1957-62; pres. Design Unit, Toronto, 1962-67, Davies/Collinson Ltd., 1968-70; partner Innovator Group, Toronto, 1971—; pres. Unimundus, 1980—; Lectr. U. Toronto, Ont. Coll. Art. Served with Royal Navy, 1942-46. Recipient Creative Printer of Year award, 1966; Chmn.'s award for design mgmt. Nat. Design Council, 1973; Benjamin Franklin award Printing Industries Assn., 1963; Gold medal Montreal Art Dirs. Show, 1962. Mem. Soc. Typog. Designers Can. (past pres.), Art Dirs. Club Toronto (past pres.). Home: 131 Bloor St W Toronto ON Canada Office: 45 Charles St E Toronto ON Canada

DAVIES, GARETH JOHN, trade association executive; b. Neath, Wales, Jan. 30, 1944; s. Gwyn and Molly D.; m. Maureen Martin, Sept. 1, 1973; children—Trudy, Allison. Solicitor and Notary, Coll. Law, London, 1969. Pros. solicitor South Wales Police Authority, 1969-70; asst. co. sec. Beecham Research Internat., London, 1970-71; partner Scott Jenkins and Davies, Swansea, Wales, 1972-76; chief adminstr. Ont. Travel Industry Conf., Toronto, 1977-78; exec. dir. Alliance Canadian Travel Assns., Ottawa, Ont., 1978—. Clubs: Rotary, Rideau (Ottawa, Ont., Can.); Royal Ocean Racing, Skal. Home: 906 Plante Dr Ottawa ON K1V 9E2 Canada Office: 1002 Albert St Suite 75 Ottawa ON Canada K1P 5E7

DAVIES, HORTON MARLAIS, clergyman, educator; b. Cwmavon, South Wales, Mar. 10, 1916; s. D. Marlais and Martha Reid (Davies) D.; m. Brenda Mary Deakin, Sept. 8, 1942; children—Christine Mary, Hugh Marlais, Philip Marlais; m. Marie-Hélène Baudy, Apr. 14, 1973. M.A. with high honors, U. Edinburgh, 1937, B.D. with highest honors, 1940; D.Phil., Oxford U., 1943, D. Litt., 1970; D.D., U. South Africa, 1950; D.Litt. (hon.), LaSalle Coll., 1966. Ordained to ministry Congl. Ch., 1942; minister Wallington Ch., South London, Eng., 1942-45; religious adviser, dir. edn. YMCA; operating with Brit. Army, 1945-46; prof., head dept. div. Rhodes U., Grahamstown, S. Africa, 1946-53, dean faculty, 1951-53; travelling fellow U.S., Carnegie Corp. of N.Y., also; Old St. Andrew's Meml.; lectr. Emmanuel Coll., U. Toronto, 1952; head joint dept. ch. history Mansfield and Regent's Park colls.; Oxford U., 1953-56; prof. religion Princeton U., 1956-59, Henry W. Putman prof., 1959—, chmn. dept., 1983-84; Guggenheim Found. fellow, 1959-60, 64-65; vis. prof. ch. history Union Theol. Seminary, N.Y.C., 1959, 1966; cons. on missionary research com. Joint Internat. Missionary Council and World Council Chs., 1954-60; Select preacher, vis. lectr. Cambridge U., Eng., 1960; Mullins lectr So. Bapt. Theol. Sem., Louisville, 1961; sr. F. Council Humanities Princeton U., 1961-62; vis. lectr. Princeton Theol. Sem., 1962, 65, 69, 71, 73, 75, 76, 77, 78, 79, 81, Pacific Sch. Religion, Berkeley, 1962, Eden Theol. Seminary, Webster Groves, Mo., 1965, Christian Theol. Sem., Indpls., 1977, Presbyn. Theol. Sem., Austin, Tex., 1977, St. John's U., Collegeville, Minn., 1967, 79; Zabriskie lectr. P.E. Sem., Alexandria, Va., 1963; vis. lectr. ecclesiastical art Union Theol. Sem., Richmond, Va.; vis. lectr. Mansfield Coll., Oxford, 1969; vis. prof. Drew U., 1969, adj. prof., 1978—; vis. prof. N.B. Theol. Sem., 1980; research grantee Huntington Library, San Marino, 1967-68, vis. fellow, 1981-82. Author: Christian Worship: Its Making and Meaning, 1946, The Worship of the English Puritans, 1948, The English Free Churches, 1952, Christian Deviations, 1954, A Mirror of the Ministry in Modern Novels, 1959, Worship and Theology in England, vols. 1-5, 1961-75, Varieties of English Preaching, 1900-1960, 1963, (with Hugh Davies) Sacred Art in a Secular Century, 1978, (with Marie-Helene Davies) Holy Days and Holidays, 1982; editor: (with R.H.W. Shepherd) An Anthology of South African Missions, 1953; Assoc. editor: Worship, 1967-72; Contbg. editor: Studia Liturgica (Rotterdam); Contbr. to periodicals. Founding trustee Inst. Ecumenical and Cultural Research, St. John's Abbey and U., Collegeville, Minn., 1967-72. Decorated Queen's Coronation medal, U.K.; recipient Berakah prize N.Am. Acad. Liturgy, 1979. Mem. Am. Soc. Ch. History, Am. Theol. Soc., Am. Acad. Religion. Home: 120 McCosh Circle Princeton NJ 08540 summer Milky Way Cream St Thetford Center VT 05075

DAVIES, JAMES ARTHUR, communications company executive; b. Honesdale, Pa., Sept. 13, 1930; s. William John and Marion Elizabeth (Edwards) D.; m. Carol Louise Fry, Aug. 14, 1954; children: Christina Marion, Stephen Scott. B.A., Pa. State U., 1958; postgrad., N.Y. U. Grad. Sch. Internat. Bus., 1965-67. With RCA Corp., N.Y.C., 1958—, staff v.p. major tech. projects, license ops., 1978—. Public relations officer N.J. CD Com.; commr. Pocantico Hills (N.Y.) Fire Dist. Served with USN, 1951-54. Mem. Am. Radio Relay League. Lutheran. Office: RCA Corp 2 Independence Way Princeton NJ 08540

DAVIES, JAMES CHOWNING, educator; b. Wauwatosa, Wis., May 6, 1918; s. Howell David and Julia (Merrell) D.; m. Eleanor Johnstone Getze, Jan. 10, 1943; 1 dau., Sarah Louise. A.B., Oberlin Coll., 1939; postgrad. in law, U. Chgo., 1939-40, U. Tex., 1945-46; Ph.D., U. Calif. at Berkeley, 1952. Supr. prodn. scheduling Consol. Vultee Aircraft Corp. (now Gen. Dynamics), San Diego, also Ft. Worth, 1942-45; research tng. fellow Social Sci. Research Council, 1950-51; Carnegie fellow polit. sci. U. Mich. Survey Research Center, 1951-53; asst. prof. to prof. polit. sci. Calif. Inst. Tech., Pasadena, 1953-63; faculty research fellow Social Sci. Research Council, 1961-62; prof. U. Oreg., Eugene, 1963—, head dept. polit. sci., 1964-67; vis. asst. prof. UCLA, summer 1956; vis. asso. prof. U. Calif., Berkeley, 1959-60; disting. vis. prof. U. Ariz., 1979. Author: Human Nature in Politics, 1963; Editor: When Men Revolt And Why, 1971. Served with AUS, 1946-47. Rockefeller Found. fellow, 1962-63; sr. research fellow U. Pa. Fgn. Policy Research Inst., 1969. Mem. Am. Polit. Sci. Assn. (council 1965-67), Western Polit. Sci. Assn. (pres. 1969-70), Internat. Polit. Sci. Assn., Internat. Soc. Polit. Psychology (councillor 1980—), AAAS, Phi Beta Kappa. Home: 1560 Prospect Dr Eugene OR 97403

DAVIES, JOHN ARTHUR, scientist; b. Prestatyn, North Wales, Mar. 28, 1927; emigrated to Can., 1940; s. Francis James and Doris Annie (Edkins) D.; m. Florence Smithson, July 29, 1950; children: Susan, Chris, Cathy, Paul, James, Anne. B.A. with honors in Chemistry, St. Michael's Coll., Toronto, 1947; M.A. in Phys. Chemistry, U. Toronto, 1948, Ph.D., 1950. With Atomic Energy of Canada, Chalk River, Ont., 1950—, prin. research officer solid state sci. br., 1972—; vis. prof. physics U. Aarhus, Denmark, 1964-65, 69-70; vis. scientist Nobel Inst. Physics, Stockholm, Sweden, 1962, Calif. Inst. Tech., 1969; prof. engring. and physics McMaster U., Hamilton. Author: (with J.W. Mayer, L. Eriksson) Ion Implantation, 1970; Contbr. over 150 articles in field to profl. jours. Ont. Ramsay Meml. fellow, 1954-56. Fellow Royal Soc. Canada, Kaiserlich Kongliche Bohmische Gesellachaften; mem. Danish Royal Soc. Roman Catholic. Home: Box 224 7 Wolfe Ave Deep River ON K0J 1P0 Canada Office: Atomic Energy of Canada Chalk River ON K0J 1J0 Canada

DAVIES, JOHN LOVATT, architect; b. Oswestry, Salop, Eng., Dec. 12, 1914; s. William and Florence (Goodyear) D.; m. Joan Haslam, Apr. 2, 1949; children—Kim Alan, John Anthony, Mary Megan. B.Arch., Liverpool U., 1937. Architect asst. Gordon Leith & Partners, South Africa, 1938-40; partner Grey Wornum & Partners, London, Eng., 1945-47; individual practice architecture, Vancouver, B.C., Can., 1949—. Served as pilot RAF, 1940-45. Fellow Royal Archtl. Inst. Can. (pres. 1962-64), AIA (hon.). Home: Gen Delivery Roberts Creek BC V0N 2W0 Canada Office: 923 Denman St Vancouver BC Canada

DAVIES, JOHN SHERRARD, former international trading company executive; b. Delphos, Ohio, Apr. 4, 1917; s. Homer M. and Elizabeth (Sherrard) D.; m. Marie Donat, July 8, 1940; children: John Morgan, Anne Donat Davies Hunter. B.A., Ohio Wesleyan U., 1939. Exec. Bell Telephone System, 1941-69; spl. asst. to Pres. Nixon and; dir. Office White House Visitors, 1969-71; dir. Hawaii-Pacific dist. office Industry and Trade Adminstrn., Dept. Commerce, 1971-79; pres. Davies & McMurtray, Ltd., Honolulu, 1979-83; mem. Nat. Visitor Facilities Adv. Commn., 1969-71; exec. sec. Hawaii Dist. Export Council; mem. policy com. Honolulu-Pacific Fed. Exec. Bd.; Mem. Gov.'s Adv. Com. for Hawaii World Trade Center. Served to capt. USAAF, 1942-46. Decorated Bronze Star; Order Brit. Empire. Mem. Hawaii World Trade Assn., Hawaiian Businessmen's Assn., Air Force Assn., Navy League U.S., Sigma Chi, Omicron Delta Kappa, Gamma Phi. Clubs: Rotary (Honolulu); (Atascadero).

DAVIES, MICHAEL JOHN, newspaper editor; b. Laindon, Eng., May 19, 1944; came to U.S., 1957, naturalized, 1972; s. George Charles and Hilda May (Epsley) D.; m. Carol Frances McCray, Dec. 18, 1965; children: Christopher, Adam. B.S. in Journalism, Ga. State U., 1966; M.S., Northwestern U., 1967. Reporter and/or copy editor Savannah (Ga.) Morning News, 1961-64, Atlanta Times, 1965, Atlanta Constn., 1966, Lloyd Hollister Newspapers, Chgo., 1967; successively copy editor, editor Scene mag.; mng. editor Louisville Times, 1968-76, Louisville Courier-Jour., 1976-78; editor Kansas City (Mo.) Star-Times, 1978—; juror Pulitzer prizes, 1977, 78. Lloyd Hollister fellow, 1966; recipient Northwestern Alumni Merit award, 1980. Mem. A.P. Mng. Editors Assn. (dir.), Am. Soc. Newspaper Editors, Com. Fgn. Relations, Soc. Profl. Journalists. Home: 1216 W 60th Terr Kansas City MO 64113 Office: 1729 Grand Ave Kansas City MO 64108

DAVIES, MICHAEL PETER, insurance broker; b. London, Eng., June 3, 1931; came to U.S., 1957, naturalized, 1967; s. John Bernard and Eleanor Dinsdale (Knight) D.; m. Dorothy Florence Warr, Dec. 10, 1955; children—Steven Richard, John Edward, Richard York. Grad. high sch. Ins. clk. Leroi, Flesch & Co., London, 1952-55; asst. buyer Goya Ltd., Eng., 1955-57; ins. clk. George Gordon & Son, N.Y.C., 1957-58; office mgr. Barr & Co., Inc., N.Y.C., 1958-66, pres., 1966—; Lectr. about Kent State U. for Program Corp. Am., 1973-76. Author: The Truth About Kent State: A Challenge to the American Conscience, 1973; Contbr. articles to newspapers., Kent State U. manuscript and, research papers donated to, Yale U. Library, 1977. Commr. S.I. Cath. Basketball Program, 1978-82. Served with RAF, 1950-52. Recipient S.I. Liberal Action Club award, 1974; nominee Nat. Book awards, 1974. Republican. Episcopalian. Home: 162 Fanning St Staten Island NY 10314

DAVIES, PAUL LEWIS, JR., lawyer; b. San Jose, Calif., July 21, 1930; s. Paul Lewis and Faith (Crummey) D.; m. Barbara Bechtel, Dec. 22, 1955; children: Laura Davies Mateo, Paul Lewis III. A.B., Stanford U., 1952; J.D., Harvard U., 1957. Bar: Calif. 1957. Assoc. Pillsbury, Madison & Sutro, San Francisco, 1957-63, partner, 1963—; dir. FMC Corp., Indsl. Indemnity Co., So. Pacific Co. Trustee Calif. Acad. Scis., 1971—, chmn., 1973-80; trustee Herbert Hoover Found., Inc.; bd. overseers Hoover Instn., chmn., 1976-82; bd. regents U. of Pacific; bd. dirs. Samuel Merritt Hosp., Merritt Peralta Med. Ctr. Served to 1st lt. U.S. Army, 1952-54. Mem. State Bar Calif., Am. Bar Assn. (com. on fed. regulation securities), San Francisco Bar Assn., Phi Beta Kappa, Pi Sigma Alpha. Republican. Clubs: World Trade, Pacific-Union, Bohemian, Stock Exchange, Villa Taverna, Bankers (San Francisco); Sainte Claire (San Jose); Claremont Country (Oakland, Calif.); Explorers, Links (N.Y.C.); Met. (Washington); Cypress Point (Pebble Beach, Calif.); Mid-Am., Chgo. (Chgo.); Farmington (Charlottesville, Va.). Office: 225 Bush St San Francisco CA 94104

DAVIES, RAYMOND DOUGLAS, musician, songwriter; b. North London, Eng., June 21, 1944. Student, Hornsey Art Coll., Croyden Coll. Singer, guitarist, composer, producer musical group, The Kinks, 1964—, numerous songs and recs. Office: care Internat Creative Mgmt 8899 Beverly Blvd Los Angeles CA 90048 *

DAVIES, RICHARD TOWNSEND, author, lectr., former fgn. service officer; b. Bklyn., May 28, 1920; s. John W.A. and Laura (Townsend) D.; m. Jean Stevens, Dec. 5, 1949; children—John Stevens, Michael Hardie, Glyn Townsend, Stephen Arthur. A.B., Columbia, 1942. Instr. German Poly. Inst. Bklyn., 1946-47; 3d sec. Am. embassy, Warsaw, Poland, 1947-49, 2d sec., Moscow, 1951-53, Kabul, Afghanistan, 1955-58; polit. officer internat. staff NATO, Paris, France, 1953-55; pub. affairs adviser Office Soviet Union Affairs, Dept. State, Washington, 1958-61, 1st sec., Moscow, USSR, 1961-62, counselor polit. affairs, 1962-63; dep. exec. sec. Dept. of State, Washington, 1964; asst. dir. (Soviet Union and Eastern Europe) USIA, Washington, 1965-68; U.S. consul gen., Calcutta, India, 1968-69; mem. planning and coordination staff Dept. State, 1969-70; dep. asst. sec. state for European affairs, 1970-72, U.S. ambassador to Poland, 1972-78; guest scholar Kennan Inst. Advanced Russian Studies, Washington, 1978-80; ret., 1980. Served with AUS, 1942-45. Recipient Honor award USIA, 1968. Address: 3511 Leland St Chevy Chase MD 20815

DAVIES, ROBERT ABEL, III, chemical and consumer products company executive; b. Englewood, N.J., Sept. 10, 1935; s. Robert Abel and Lillian Louise (Vila) D.; m. Marilyn Jean Doering, June 16, 1957; children: Bruce Gregory, Mark Richard, Eric Doering, Nancy Louise. A.B., Colgate U., 1957; M.B.A., Columbia U., 1963. Salesman Proctor & Gamble Co., Cin., 1960-61; product mgr. Colgate Palmolive Co., N.Y.C., 1963-66; group product mgr. Boyle-Midway div. Am. Home Products, N.Y.C., 1966-69; v.p. mktg. Church & Dwight Co. Inc., Piscataway, N.J., 1969-76, v.p., gen. mgr., 1976-81, pres., chief operating officer, 1981—, dir., 1981—; dir. Church & Dwight Ltd., Toronto, Can., 1969—. Served to lt. USNR, 1957-60. Mem. Columbia Bus. Sch. Alumni Assn. (dir. 1981—). Presbyterian. Home: 298 Nassau St Princeton NJ 08540 Office: Church & Dwight Co Inc 20 Kingsbridge Rd Piscataway NJ 08854

DAVIES, ROBERT ERNEST, educator, biochemist; b. Barton-upon-Irwell, Eng., Aug. 17, 1919; s. William Owen and C. Stella (Spencer) D.; m. Helen Jean Rogoff, Sept. 8, 1961; children—Daniel J., Richard D. B.Sc., U. Manchester, 1941, M.Sc., 1942, D.Sc., 1952; Ph.D., U. Sheffield, 1949; M.A., Oxford U., 1956, U. Pa., 1971. Mem. faculty U. Manchester, Eng., 1941-42, U. Sheffield, 1942-54, U. Heidelberg, Germany, 1954, Oxford (Eng.) U., 1954-59; mem. faculty U. Pa., 1955—, prof. biochemistry, 1955-70, Benjamin Franklin prof. molecular biology, 1970—, univ. prof. molecular biology, 1977—, chmn. Benjamin Franklin profs., 1978—; chmn. grad. group molecular biology, 1962-71, chmn. dept. animal biology, 1962-73. Mem. editorial bd.: Biochem. Jour, 1951-56; asso. editor: Jour. Mechanochemistry and Cell Motility, 1970—. Mem. Brit. Home Guard, 1940-45, Brit. Nat. Fire Service, 1940-45. Fellow Royal Soc.; mem. Am. Chem. Soc., Am. Soc. Biol. Chemists, Am. Physiol. Soc., N.Y. Acad. Scis. (hon. life), Sigma Xi, Phi Zeta. Spl. research biochemistry muscle contraction, function of kidney medulla, mechanism hydrochloric acid secretion in stomach. Home: 7053 McCallum St Philadelphia PA 19119

DAVIES, ROBERT MORTON, consultant; b. Carmi, Ill., Sept. 22, 1920; s. John Morton and Helen (Wallace) D.; m. Elizabeth Bell, July 2, 1955; children: Henry H., Robert W., J. Wallace. B.A., Wheaton (Ill.) Coll., 1941; M.A., U. Pa., 1945, Ph.D., 1954; postgrad., NYU, 1955-56. Asso. prof. The King's Coll., Briarcliff Manor, N.Y., 1943-50; dean men Perkiomen Sch., Pennsburg, Pa., 1951-52; asst. prof. English, adminstrv. asst. Valley Forge Jr. Coll., Wayne, 1952-55; instr. N.Y. Maritime Coll., 1955-58; prof., chmn. English dept. and div. humanities Thiel Coll., Greenville, Pa., 1958-64; dean Ithaca (N.Y.) Coll., 1964-66, provost, 1966-72, cons., 1972-73; v.p. adminstrn. State U. N.Y. at Purchase, 1973-78; dean acad. affairs Wilmington (Del.) Coll., 1979-80, v.p. acad. affairs, 1980—; chief exec. officer Belle-Day Enterprises, Inc.; Del. sr. cons.; Asst. instr. English U. Pa., Phila., part-time 1946; asst. prof. English Rutgers U., New Brunswick, N.J., parttime, 1955-58. Author: The Humanism of Paul Elmer More, 1958; Contbr. articles, book revs., essays to profl. jours. Mem. Am. Mgmt. Assn., Modern Lang. Assn., Phi Beta Kappa, Alpha Psi Omega, Pi Delta Epsilon, Delta Mu Delta. Home: 3 Pembrey Pl Wilmington DE 19803

DAVIES, ROBERT WYNTER, government official; b. Ft. Worth, Sept. 2, 1924; s. James Black and Belle Marie (Felland) D.; m. Valerie Edwards, Jan. 20, 1951; children: Kenneth, Margaret. B.S.M.E., Tex. A&M U., 1947; M.S. in Engring., Johns Hopkins U., 1950; cert, Oak Ridge Sch. of Reactor Tech., 1956. Registered profl. engr., Md. Text engr. Gen. Electric Co., Lynn, Mass., 1948; mgr. Balt. Gas & Electric Co., 1950-81; dep. asst. sec. U.S. Dept. Energy, Washington, 1981—; nuclear section chmn. Coordinating Agy. for Supplier Evaluation, Sacramento, 1975-77, pres., 1977-79. Served to capt. U.S. Army, 1943-46; PTO, ETO. Recipient Sr. Faculty Achievement award Tex. A&M U., 1947, Outstanding Leadership award Coordinating Agy. for Supplier Evaluation, 1979. Mem. Am. Nuclear Soc., ASME, Am. Soc. Quality Control. Home: 310 Felton Rd Lutherville MD 21093 Office: US Dept Energy 1000 Independence Ave SW Washington DC 20585

DAVIES, ROBERTSON, author; b. Thamesville, Ont., Can., Aug. 28, 1913; m. Brenda Mathews, 1940; three children. Student, Upper Can. Coll., Queen's U., Kingston, Ont., LL.D., 1962; B.Litt., Oxford (Eng.) U., 1938; LL.D., U. Alta., Edmonton, 1957, U. Man., 1972, U. Calgary, 1975, U. Toronto, 1981; D.Litt., McMaster U., Hamilton, Ont., 1959, U. Windsor, Ont., 1971, York U., 1973, Mt. Allison U., 1973, Meml. U., 1974, U. Western Ont., 1974, McGill U., 1974, Trent U., 1974, U. Lethbridge, 1981, U. Waterloo, 1981, U. B.C., 1983; D.C.L., Bishop's U., Lennoxville, Que., 1967; D. Hum. Litt., U. Rochester, 1983. Tchr., actor Old Vic Theatre Sch. and Repertory Co., London, Eng., 1938-40; lit. editor Saturday Night, Toronto, Ont., 1940-42; editor and pub. Examiner, Peterborough, Ont., 1942-68; prof. English U. Toronto, 1960-81; master Massey Coll., 1962-81; Past bd. govs. Stratford Ontario Shakespeare Festival. Author: Shakespeare's Boy Actors, 1939, Shakespeare for Young Players: A Junior Course, 1942, The Diary of Samuel Marchbanks, 1947, The Table Talk of Samuel Marchbanks, 1949; plays Hope Deferred, 1949, Fortune My Foe, 1949, Eros at Breakfast, 1949, Overlaid, 1949, At My Heart's Core, 1950, A Masque of Aesop, 1952, A Jig for the Gypsy, 1954, A Masque of Mr. Punch, 1963, Hunting Stuart and Other Plays, 1972, Question Time, 1975; novels Tempest Tost, 1951, Leaven of Malice, 1954, A Mixture of Frailties, 1958, Fifth Business, 1970, The Manticore, 1972; World of Wonders, 1975, (with Tyrone Guthrie) Renown at Stratford: A Record of the Shakespeare Festival in Canada, 1953, Twice Have the Trumpets Sounded: A Record of the Stratford Shakespearean Festival in Canada, 1954, Thrice the Brinded Cat Hath Mew'd: A Record of the Stratford Shakespearean Festival in Canada, 1955, A Voice from the Attic, 1960, The Personal Art: Reading to Good Purpose, 1961, Samuel Marchbanks' Almanack, 1967, Stephen Leacock: Feast of Stephen, 1970, The Enthusiasms of Robertson Davies, 1979, (with others) The Revels History of Drama in English, Vol. VI, 1975, One Half of Robertson Davies, 1977, The Rebel Angels, 1981, Enthusiasms of Robertson Davies (Judith S. Grant editor), 1979, Robertson Davies: The Well-Tempered Critic (Grant editor), 1981. Decorated companion Order of Can., 1972; recipient Louis Jouvet prize for directing Dominion Drama Festival, 1949; Leacock medal, 1955; Lorne Pierce medal, 1961; Gov. Gen.'s award for fiction, 1973. Fellow Royal Soc. Can.; mem. Am. Acad. and Inst. Arts and Letters (hon.). Address: Massey College 4 Devonshire Place Toronto M5S 2E1 ON Canada also care Curtis Brown Ltd 575 Madison Ave New York NY 10022

DAVIES, RONALD N., judge; b. Crookston, Minn., Dec. 11, 1904; s. Norwood S. and Minnie M. (Quigley) D.; m. Mildred M. Doran, Oct. 10, 1933; children: Timothy Q., Mary Jo, Thomas A., Catharine A., Jean M. A.B., U. N.D., 1927, LL.D. (hon.), 1961; LL.B., Georgetown U., 1930, LL.D. (hon.), 1982. Practiced in, Grand Forks, N.D., 1930-55; judge Municipal Ct., Grand Forks, 1932-40; lectr. U. N.D. Sch. Law, 1952-55; U.S. dist judge Dist. of N.D., Fargo, 1955—; Mem. N.D. Bd. Pardons, 1933, N.D. Athletic Commn., 1935. Served from 1st lt. to lt. col. AUS, 1942-46. Recipient Outstanding Alumnus award Georgetown U. Law Center, 1958, U. N.D., 1979; named to U. N.D. Athletic Hall of Fame, 1980. Fellow Am. Bar Found.; mem. N.D. Bar Assn. (Disting. Service award 1980, exec. dir. 1947-55), Grand Forks C. of C. (pres. 1953), Am. Legion, Am. Bar Assn., 40 and 8, Order of Coif, Sigma Nu, Phi Alpha Delta. Roman Catholic. Clubs: Elk, K.C. Home: 1449 S 10th St Fargo ND 58103 Office: US Courthouse Fargo ND 58107

DAVIES, THEODORE PETER, artist; b. Bklyn., 1928. Student, Art Students League, N.Y.C. Staff mem. Queens Council Arts; instr. Jamaica Arts Center. Exhbns. include, Print Club Phila., Queens Mus., Mus. Modern Art, N.Y.C., Boston Printmakers, 1959, SUNY, Albany, Art Students League, Brigham Young U., U. South, Columbia Coll., Guild Hall Mus.; represented in permanent collections, Mus. Modern Art, Phila. Mus. Art, Nat. Gallery Art, Washington, Brigham Young U., N.Y. Stock Exchange, U. South, Guild Hall Mus. Caps fellow in printmaking, 1973-74. Mem. Art Students League (past rec. sec.), Nat. Art Workers Community. Office: 30 E 14th St New York NY 10003 *I believe every new experience in life is judged, measured, and mirrored against our total life experience. We all have experiences in common which we can readily understand. It is the task of the artist to communicate these experiences through his work.*

DAVIES, THOMAS MOCKETT, JR., history educator; b. Lincoln, Nebr., May 25, 1940; s. Thomas Mockett and Faith Elizabeth (Arnold) D.; m. Eloisa Carmela Monzón Ábate, June 10, 1968; 1 dau., Jennifer Elena. B.A., U. Nebr., 1962, M.A., 1964; student, Universidad Nacional Autonóma de México, 1961; Ph.D., U. N.Mex., 1970; postdoctoral fellow, U. Tex., Austin, 1969-70. Lectr. U. N.Mex. Peace Corps Tng. Center, 1964-66; asst. prof. Latin Am. history San Diego State U., 1968-72, asso. prof., 1972-75, prof., 1975—; dir. Center Latin Am. Studies, Henry L. and Grace Doherty Charitable Found. fellow, 1966-68. Author: Indian Integration in Peru: A Half Century of Experience, 1900-1948, 1974 (co-winner Hubert Herring Meml. award Pacific Coast Council on Latin Am. Studies 1973), (with Victor Villaneuva) 300 Documentos Para la Historia del APRA; Conspiraciones Apristas de 1935 a 1939, 1979, Secretos Electorales del APRA: Correspondencia y Documentos de, 1939 1983, (with Brian Loveman) The Politics of Anti-Politics: The Military in Latin America, 1978; Contbr. articles to profl. jours. Summer research grants San Diego State U. Found., 1971-73, 75, 76, 79, 80; recipient Outstanding Faculty award San Diego State U. Alumni and Assos., 1981—. Mem. Latin Am. Studies Assn., Conf. Latin Am. History (exec. sec. 1979-84), Pacific Coast Council Latin Am., Rocky Mountain Council on Latin American Studies. Home: 4617 Edenvale Ave LaMesa CA 92041 Office: Dept History San Diego State U San Diego CA 92182

DAVIMOS, RICHARD H., stockbroker; b. Newark, N.J., May 18, 1922; s. Harry T. and Leonore L. D.; children: Richard, Robert, Steven, John. A.B., Lafayette Coll., 1944; M.B.A., Harvard U., 1947. Pres. Grand Award and Command Record Cos.; pres. V&R Advt., Mut. Broadcasting System; exec. v.p. Shearson Am. Express, Loeb Rhoades, Inc., N.Y.C. Home: 70 Winding Way West Orange NJ 07052 Home: 1401 S Ocean Blvd Boca Raton FL 33432 Office: Fed Hwy Boca Raton FL 33432

DAVIS, A. ARTHUR, lawyer; b. Sioux City, Iowa, Oct. 12, 1928; s. Edward R. and Isabel (Baron) D.; (div.)children: Pamela Benham, Mark Baron. B.S.S. with honors, Northwestern U., 1950, J.D., 1952. Bar: Iowa 1952, U.S. Circuit Ct. Appeals for 8th circuit, 1959, for 2d circuit 1975, D.C. 1968. Practice law, Des Moines, 1955—; asso. firm Brody, Parker, Roberts, Thoma & Harris, 1955-59; partner firm Davis, Hockenberg, Wine, Brown & Koehn, and predecessor firms, 1959—; lectr. pub. speaking Drake U., 1955-60; dir. Economy Forms Corp., Constrn. Products Inc., Triple F Inc., The Weitz Co., Inc., Midwest Limestone Co., Inc., Metal Products Mfg. Co., Robertson Cos., Inc.; chmn. joint com. Iowa Bar Assn.-Iowa Investment Bankers Assn., 1971-75; mem. U.S. 8th Circuit Judge Nominating Commn., 1978-80. Mem. Des Moines Commn. on Human Rights, 1960-63; mem. U.S. Holocaust Meml. Council, 1980—, Bd. Edn. Des Moines Ind. Community Sch. Dist., 1963-69; pres. Bd. Edn. Des Moines Ind. Community Sch. Dist., 1966-67; mem. vis. com. Northwestern U. Sch. Law, 1980—; mem. Gov.'s Commn. on State and Local Govt., 1964-68, Ins. Commr.'s Spl. Com. on State Regulation, 1967-68; bd. dirs. Planned Parenthood Assn. Iowa, pres., 1976; mem. adv. panel on making govt. work better Democratic Nat. Com., 1981—; bd. dirs. Iowa Product Devel. Corp., 1983—; mem. Lt. Gov.'s Iowa Tomorrow Com., 1983—. Served to 1st lt. AUS, 1953-55. Recipient Nat. award People to People Program, 1961, Brotherhood award Des Moines chpt. NCCJ, 1981. Mem. Des Moines C. of C. (dir. 1973-75, 80—, pres. 1979), Northwestern U. Law Alumni Assn. (pres. 1977-78), Order of Coif, Delta Sigma Rho, Phi Delta Phi, Phi Epsilon Pi. Democrat. Jewish. Clubs: Des Moines, Wakonda. Home: 3660 Grand Ave Des Moines IA 50312 Office: 2300 Financial Center Des Moines IA 50309 *I have made the basic assumption that what needs to be accomplished, I will have to accomplish by my own efforts, and then whatever help I have had - and it has been considerable - has been a gratuity.*

DAVIS, A. DAN, grocery store chain executive. Student, Stetson U. With Winn-Dixie Stores Inc., Jacksonville, Fla., 1968—, corp. v.p., mgr. Jacksonville div., 1978-80, sr. v.p. and regional dir. Jacksonville and Orlando (Fla.) and Atlanta divs., 1980-82, pres., 1982—, dir. Office: Winn Dixie Stores Inc 5050 Edgewood Ct PO Box B Jacksonville FL 32203 *

DAVIS, ALLEN, professional football coach and executive; b. Brockton, Mass., July 4, 1929; s. Louis and Rose (Kirschenbaum) D.; m. Carol Segall, July 11, 1954; 1 son, Mark. Student, Wittenberg Coll., 1947; A.B., Syracuse U., 1950. Asst. football coach Adelphi Coll., 1950-51; head football coach, Ft. Belvoir, Va., 1952-53; player-personnel scout Baltimore Colts, 1954; line coach The Citadel, 1955-56, U. So. Calif., 1957-59; asst. coach San Diego Chargers, 1960-62; gen. mgr., head coach Oakland Raiders (now Oakland Raiders), 1963-66, now owner, mng. gen. ptnr.; Football League, 1966; Former mem. mgmt. council and competition com. Nat. Football League. Served with AUS, 1952-53. Named Profl. Coach of Year A.P., U.P.I., Sporting News, Pro-Football Illustrated, 1963; Young Man of Yr., Oakland, 1963. Mem. Am. Football Coaches Assn. Only individual in history of profl. football to be an asst. coach, head coach, gen. mgr., league commr. and owner. Office: Los Angeles Raiders 332 Center St El Segundo CA 90245

DAVIS, ALLEN CLAYTON, ambassador; b. Glencliff, Tenn., Aug. 23, 1927; s. Floyd Spencer and Mildred Grace (Lee) D.; m. Marie-Therese Lamoitier, June 6, 1964; children: John Clayton, Ann Marie, Philip Lee. Student, Middle Tenn. State Coll., 1945, Duke U., 1945-47, George Washington U., 1953-54; B.S. Fgn. Service, Georgetown U., 1956; student, Fgn. Service Inst., 1965-66, U.S. Army War Coll., 1973-74. Asst. art gallery dir. Fantasy Gallery, Washington, 1954-56; personnel placement officer Dept. State, Washington, 1956-57; consular and polit. officer U.S. Embassy Monrovia, 1958-60; internat. relations officer Burs. of African and European Affairs, Dept. State, 1960-65; polit. officer U.S. Embassy Moscow, 1966-68; dep. chief mission U.S. Embassy Ouagadougou, 1968-70; polit. officer and dep. chief U.S. Interests Sect. Swiss Embassy, Algiers, 1971-73; dep. chief mission U.S. Embassy Dakar, 1974-77; dep. chief mission, minister-counselor U.S. Embassy Kinshasa, 1977-80; U.S. ambassador People's Revolutionary Republic of Guinea, 1980-83, Republic of Uganada, 1983—. Served to lt. comdr. USNR, 1945-46, 47-53. Mem. Am. Fgn. Service Assn., Flying Midshipmen Assn., Naval Aviation Mus. Found. Home: 211 College Heights Murfreesboro TN 37130 Office: Kampala Dept State Washington DC 20520

DAVIS, ALLEN FREEMAN, history educator, author; b. Hardwick, Vt., Jan. 9, 1931; s. Harold Freeman and Bernice Susan (Allen) D.; m. Roberta Hazel Green, June 16, 1956; children: Gregory Freeman, Paul Studley. A.B., Dartmouth Coll., 1953; M.A., U. Rochester, 1954; Ph.D., U. Wis., 1959. Instr. history Wayne State U., Detroit, 1959-60; asst. prof. history U. Mo., Columbia, 1960-63, assoc. prof., 1963-68; prof. Temple U., Phila., 1968—; vis. prof. U. Tex., Austin, 1983. Author: (with others) March of American Democracy, Vol. V, 1966, Spearheads for Reform, 1967, American Heroine, 1973, (with Jim Watts) Generations, 1974, 78, 83; co-author: (with Fredric Miller and Morris Vogel) Still Philadelphia, 1983; Author also numerous articles.; Editor: (with Harold D. Woodman) Conflict and Consensus in American History, 1966, 68, 72, 76, 80, 84, Eighty Years at Hull House, 1969, Jane Addams, The Spirit of Youth and the City Streets, 1972, (with Mark Haller), The Peoples of Philadelphia, 1973, Jane Addams on Peace, War and International Understanding, 1976, For Better or Worse, 1981; Editor series on Am. civilization. Served with AUS, 1954-56. Danforth Grad. fellow, 1953-59; Am. Philos. Soc. grantee, 1962, 65; Am. Council Learned Socs. sr. fellow, 1971-72. Mem. Am. Hist. Assn., Orgn. Am. Historians, Am. Studies Assn. (treas. 1971-72, exec. sec. 1972-77), Soc. Am. Historians. Home: 1934 Waverly St Philadelphia PA 19146 Office: History Dept Temple U Philadelphia PA 19122

DAVIS, ALVIA B., JR., hospital system executive; b. Hutchinson, Kans., Feb. 15, 1929; s. Alvia B. and Marie (Maresch) D.; m. Jacquelyn Aurell, June 17, 1950; children: Elizabeth, Stephanie, Grant. B.A., U. Kans., 1950. Wage and salary supr. Beech Aircraft Co., Wichita, Kans., 1951-55; with Wesley Med. Ctr., Wichita, 1955—, adminstr., 1970-76, exec. v.p., 1976-81, chief exec. officer, pres., 1982—; pres., chief exec. officer Health Frontiers, Inc., Wichita, 1982—; govt. appt. Statewide Health Coordinating Council, Topeka, 1976—; dir. Central Bank & Trust Co., Wichita, 1971—, Vol. Hosp. Am., Irving, Tex., 1982—. Fellow Am. Coll. Hosp. Adminstrs. (regent 1975-81); mem. Am. Hosp. Assn., Kans. Hosp. Assn. (chmn. 1977). Lodge: Rotary. Office: Health Frontiers Inc Wesley Med Ctr 550 N Hillside Ave Wichita KS 67214 *

DAVIS, ANDREW, conductor; b. Hertfordshire, Eng., Feb. 2, 1944; s. Robert James and Florence Joyce (Badminton) D. Mus.B. (Organ scholar), King's Coll., Cambridge (Eng.) U., M.A., 1967; student, Franco Ferrara, Rome, 1967-68. Pianist, harpsichordist, organist, Acad. of St. Martin-in-the-Fields, London, 1966-70; debut with, BBC Symphony Orch., 1970, BBC Scottish Symphony Orch., Glasgow, 1970-72; asso. conductor, New Philharmonia Orch., London, 1973-76; prin. guest conductor, Royal Liverpool (Eng.) Philharmonic Orch., 1974-77; music dir., Toronto (Ont., Can.) Symphony, 1975—; condr. tour in, China, 1978, Europe, 1983; conductor, Glyndebourne Opera Festival, summer 1973, 75-78; appeared with orchs. of, Detroit, N.Y.C., Chgo., Cleve., Los Angeles, Phila., Boston, London, La Scala, Rome, Berlin; appeared with festivals at, Berlin, Edinburgh; rec. artist for, CBS Records. Office: care The Toronto Symphony 60 Simcoe St Toronto ON Canada M5J 2H5

DAVIS, ANN BRADFORD, actress; b. Schenectady, May 5, 1926; d. Cassius Miles and Marguerite (Stott) D. B.A., U. Mich., 1948. Chmn., West Coast auditioning com. USO, 1969—, mem. Hollywood overseas com., 1969-70, nat. council, 1970, Calif. adv. com., 1971; mem. drama adv. panel Dept. State, 1972—. Actress plays, Erie, Pa., 1948-49, Porterville, Calif., 1949-51, Yosemite, Calif., 1950-51, Monterey, Calif., 1952-53, Hollywood, Calif., 1954-55, summer stock and dinner theatres, 1958—; nat. touring co. No No Nanette, 1972-73; actress: TV series Bob Cummings Show, 1955-59, Keefe Brasselle Show, 1963, John Forsythe Show, 1965-66, The Brady Bunch, 1969-74; Broadway play Once Upon a Mattress, 1960; toured with, USO, Asia, S. Pacific, Korea, 1967-70. Recipient Emmy award for Best Supporting Actress as Schultzy on Bob Cummings Show, 1957, 58, 59. Mem. Girls Friday of Showbiz, Spotlighters. Office: care Contemporary-Korman Artists Ltd 132 Lasky Dr Beverly Hills CA 90212

DAVIS, ARCHIBALD KIMBROUGH, banker; b. Winston-Salem, N.C., Jan. 22, 1911; s. Thomas W. and Frances (Conrad) D.; m. Mary L. Haywood, May 12, 1938; children: Archibald Hilliard, Louise Bahnson, John Haywood, Thomas Whitmell IV. A.B., U. N.C., 1932, M.A., 1975; student, Grad. Sch. Banking, Rutgers U., 1940. With Wachovia Bank and Trust Co. (N.A.), 1932—, asst. cashier, 1938-40, asst. v.p., 1940-42, v.p., 1942-46, sr. v.p. in charge, 1946-56, dir., 1956—; chmn. bd., 1956-74; dir. Norfolk So. Corp., Media Gen., Inc., Charlotte br. Fed. Res. Bank of Richmond, 1950-56. Founder, 1st pres., chmn. Northwest N.C. Devel. Assn.; chmn. dir. Research Triangle Found. of N.C.; Mem. N.C. Senate from Forsyth County, 1959, 61; trustee Duke Endowment.; Trustee Nat. Humanities Center, Salem Acad. and Coll. Fellow Am. Acad. Arts and Scis.; mem. U.S. C. of C. (dir. 1957-77, v.p. 1958-61, pres. 1971-72), Am. Bankers Assn. (pres. state bank div. 1957, pres. 1965-66), Robert Morris Assos. (former dir., mem. exec. com.), Old Salem, Inc. (pres. 1961-63), Salem Band, Phi Beta Kappa, Delta Kappa Epsilon. Democrat. Mem. Moravian Ch. Clubs: Grail, Golden Fleece, Forsyth Country, Rotary (pres. 1958-59). Home: 2828 Forest Dr Winston-Salem NC 27104 Office: 612 S Main St Winston-Salem NC 27108

DAVIS, ARTHUR HORACE, ambassador to Paraguay; b. Brockton, Mass., Oct. 6, 1917; s. Arthur Horace and Hazel E. (Cubbage) D.; m. Marian Esther James, Sept. 29, 1945; children: Cynthia, Karen, Susan, Arthur Horace. Student, U. Colo., 1956-62. Lic. real estate broker, Colo. Meteorologist Pan Am. Grace, Santiago, Chile, 1945-56, United Air Lines, Denver, 1956-62; v.p. Van Frellick Assocs., Denver, 1962-64; pres. New Englewood Colo., Denver, 1964-68, Villa Enterprises Inc., 1968-77, Arthur Davis Assocs., 1976-82; U.S. Ambassador to Paraguay, Asuncion, 1982—. Chmn. Jefferson County Republican Central Com., Denver, 1963-67. Served with USAAF, 1942-45. Mem. Am. Meteorol. Soc., Bd. Realtors, Inst. Real Estate Mgmt., Internat. Council Shopping Ctrs., Am. Fgn. Service Assn. Methodist. Club: International. Office: US Embassy Avenida Mariscal Lopez 1776 Asuncion Paraguay

DAVIS, ARTHUR QUENTIN, architect; b. New Orleans, Mar. 30, 1920; m. Mary H. Wineman, Aug. 30, 1942; children: Arthur Quentin, Pamela Henriette, James Matthew. B.S. in Architecture, Tulane U., 1940, B.Arch., 1941; M.Arch., Harvard, 1946. Partner Curtis & Davis Architects and Planners, New Orleans, 1946—; faculty Tulane U. Sch. Architecture, faculty mem. Pratt Inst. Bklyn., 1957, Harvard, 1960; mem. archtl. adv. com. U.S. Navy, 1968; chmn. Mayor's Adv. Com. Design, 1972, 73; hon. consul for Kingdom of Thailand, New Orleans. Prin. works include Thomy Lafon Sch, New Orleans, 1957, La. State Penitentiary, Angola, 1957, New Orleans Pub. Library, 1958, George Washington Carver Sch, 1958, Tulane U. Student Center, 1959, Berlin Med. Center, Berlin, West Germany, Am. Embassy, Saigon, Vietnam, 1964, Forestall Fed. Office Bldg, Washington, La. Superdome, 1965. Pres. Orleans Gallery Contemporary Art; trustee New Orleans Philharmonic Symphony, New Orleans Mus. Art, United Fund Greater, New Orleans; chmn. bd. New Orleans Jazz and Heritage Found., 1972-73; bd. dirs. Bur. Environ. Research, Am. Fedn. Arts. Served to lt. USNR, 1943-45. Recipient AIA 1st honor award for Thomy Lafton Sch., also La. State Penitentiary; 1st hon. award design competition House and Home, 1959; 1st award for Immaculate Conception Ch. Fellow AIA. Clubs: Harvard, So. Yacht; Cosmos (Washington); New Orleans Lawn Tennis., Century Assn. Home: 1440 Bourbon New Orleans LA 70116 Office: 512 S Peters St New Orleans LA 70115 257 Park Ave S New York NY 10010

DAVIS, B. DALE, newspaper editor educator; b. Bethesda, Ohio, Oct. 4, 1921; s. Harry A. and Mae Belle (Heskett) D.; m. Mary Patricia Talbot, Oct. 14, 1946; children: Claudia (Mrs. Douglas A. Witham), Hillary (Mrs. Frederic K. West), Melissa (Mrs. Peter Richmond). B.A., Ohio State U., 1944. Reporter Columbus (Ohio) Citizen, 1943; reporter-editor Lima (Ohio) News, 1945; with Detroit Free Press, 1946-63, asst. mng. editor, 1959-63; Sunday editor Phila. Bull., 1963-73, mng. editor, 1973-75, exec. editor, 1975-80, v.p., 1980-82; Atwood prof. U. Alaska, Anchorage, 1982-84; lectr. U. Pa., 1964-66, Am. Press Inst., Columbia U., N.Y.C., 1964-73. Contbg. author: Do You Belong in Journalism?, 1954. Mem. Am. Soc. Newspaper Editors, Phila. Com. on Fgn. Relations, Soc. Profl. Journalists. Clubs: Franklin Inn, Peale, Clover. 629 Seagrove Cape May NJ 08204 Office: 3221 Providence Dr Anchorage AK 99508

DAVIS, BENNIE LUKE, air force officer; b. McAlester, Okla., May 12, 1928; s. James Harry and Carrie (McBee) D.; m. Patricia Grafe, June 14, 1952; children—James Davis, Thomas. B.S., U.S. Mil. Acad., 1950; M.S., George Washington U., 1967; postgrad., Harvard Bus. Sch., 1969. Commd. 2d lt. USAF, 1950, advanced through grades to gen., 1979; staff officer (Hdqrs. Strategic Air Command), 1964-66, squadron comdr., Vietnam, 1968, with, Washington, 1969-71, dep.

asst. chief of staff for personnel, 1972-74, comdr., 1974-75, dir. personnel plans, Washington, 1975-77, dep. chief staff personnel, 1977-79, comdr., Randolph AFB, Tex., 1979-81, comdr.-in-chief, Offutt AFB, Nebr., 1981—. Decorated D.S.M., Silver Star, Legion of Merit, D.F.C., Bronze Star, Air medal, Joint Service Commendation medal, Air Force Commendation medal. Mem. Assn. Grads. U.S. Mil. Acad. Club: Harvard Business School (Washington). Home: Quarters 16 Offutt AFB NE 68113

DAVIS, BERNARD DAVID, med. scientist; b. Franklin, Mass., Jan. 7, 1916; s. Harry and Tillie (Shain) D.; m. Elizabeth Menzel, June 19, 1955; children—Franklin A., Jonathan H., Katherine J. A.B., Harvard, 1936, M.D., 1940. Intern, fellow Johns Hopkins Hosp., 1940-41; commd. officer USPHS, 1942-54; successively assigned NIH, Columbia, Pub. Health Research Inst. of N.Y., Rockefeller Inst., and charge; USPHS Tb Research Lab. at Cornell U. Med. Sch., 1947-54; prof. pharmacology, chmn. dept. N.Y. U. Med. Sch., 1954-57; prof. bacteriology, chmn. dept. Harvard, 1957-68, Adele Lehman prof. bacteriology and immunology, 1963-68, Adele Lehman prof. bacterial physiology, dir. bacterial physiol. unit, 1968—; div. com. for biology, medicine NSF, 1954-57; mem. med. adv. bd. Hebrew U., 1956-70; fellow Center for Advanced Study in Behavioral Scis., 1973-74. Trustee Worcester Found. for Exptl. Biology. Recipient Waksman medal Soc. Am. Bacteriologists, 1952. Mem A.A.A.S., Am. Soc. Biol. Chemists, Nat. Acad. Sci., Am. Acad. Arts and Scis. (v.p. 1977-79), Inst. of Medicine, Am. Soc. Microbiology, Soc. Gen. Physiology (pres. 1964-65), Harvey Soc., Phi Beta Kappa, Sigma Xi, Alpha Omega Alpha. Home: 23 Clairemont Rd Belmont MA 02178

DAVIS, BERTRAM GEORGE, lawyer, association executive; b. N.Y.C., Mar. 30, 1919; s. Maurice Bertram and Grace Elizabeth D.; m. Violet Timothy, Mar. 7, 1941; children: Grace Elizabeth Davis Hopper, Anne Whitfield Davis Wagman, Vivian Mary, Christine Anderson Davis Mobius, Gregory George. Student, St. Johns U., 1949-51, Am. U., 1951-52; LL.B., George Washington U., 1955. Bar: D.C. 1957, U.S. Supreme Ct. 1963. Passenger agt. Cunard White Star Ltd., N.Y.C., 1936-41; with The Am. Legion, Indpls., 1945—, nat. judge advocate, 1960—; pub. Am. Legion mag., 1978—, asst. nat. treas., 1963—; legal counsel Am. Legion Aux.; chmn. Am. Legion Retirement Com.; individual practice law, Washington, 1957-59. Served with U.S. Army, 1942-45. Mem. ABA, D.C. Bar Assn., Army, Navy and Air Force Vets. Can., Am. Legion, Delta Theta Phi. Democrat. Roman Catholic. Home: 106 1st St E Apt 302 Village at Tierra Verde Tierra Verde FL 33715 Office: 700 N Pennsylvania St Indianapolis IN 46206

DAVIS, BERTRAM HYLTON, educator; b. Ozone Park, N.Y., Nov. 30, 1918; s. Hubert Edwin and Gladys (Greenidge) D.; m. Ruth Austin Benedict, Jan. 11, 1946; children—Ralph Paul, Kathryn Austin (Mrs. Person), Richard Austin. Grad.—Phillips Acad., Andover, Mass., 1933-37; student, Hamilton Coll., Clinton, N.Y., 1937-39; A.B., Columbia, 1941, M.A., 1948, Ph.D., 1956; LL.D., Dickinson Coll., 1974. Lectr. English Hunter Coll., 1947-48; instr., then asst. prof. English Dickinson Coll., 1948-57; staff asso. Am. Assn U. Profs., 1957-63, dep. gen. sec., 1963-67, gen. sec., 1967-74; prof. English Fla. State U., Tallahassee, 1974—. Author: Johnson Before Boswell, 1960, A Proof of Eminence, 1973, Thomas Percy, 1981; editor (Sir John Hawkins): Life of Samuel Johnson LL.D, 1961; editor bull., AAUP, 1960-65; field editor: Twayne's English Authors Series, 1977—; mem. editorial com.: Yale Edition of Works of Samuel Johnson, 1979—. Served to capt. AUS, 1941-46. Guggenheim fellow, 1974. Mem. Modern Lang. Assn., Am. Soc. for 18th-Century Studies, Johnsonians, South Atlantic Modern Lang. Assn. Club: Cosmos. Home: 2309 Domingo Dr Tallahassee FL 32304 Office: Dept English Fla State U Tallahassee FL 32306

DAVIS, BETTE RUTH ELIZABETH, actress; b. Lowell, Mass., Apr. 5, 1908; d. Harlow Morrell and Ruth (Favor) D.; m. Harmon Oscar Nelson, Jr., Aug. 18, 1932 (div.); m. Arthur Farnsworth, Dec. 1940 (dec. Aug. 25, 1943); m. William Grant Sherry, Nov. 30, 1945; 1 dau., Barbara Davis; m. Gary Merrill, Aug. 1950 (div.); adopted children: Margot, Michael. Ed., Cushing Acad., Ashburnham, Mass. Began as motion picture actress, 1931; pictures include Dangerous (Acad. award Best Actress 1935), The Petrified Forest, Jezebel (Acad. award Best Actress 1938), Dark Victory, Juarez, The Old Maid, The Private Lives of Elizabeth and Essex, The Great Lie, The Bride Came C.O.D, All About Eve, 1950, Payment on Demand, 1951, Phone Call from a Stranger, 1952, The Star, 1953, The Virgin Queen, 1955, Storm Center, The Catered Affair, 1956, John Paul Jones, 1959, The Scapegoat, 1959, What Ever Happened to Baby Jane, Dead Ringer, Painted Canvas, 1963, Where Love Has Gone, Hush, Hush, Sweet Charlotte, 1964, The Nanny, The Anniversary, 1967, Connecting Rooms, 1969, Bunny O'Hare, 1970, Madam Sin, 1971, The Game, 1972, Burnt Offerings, 1977, Death on the Nile, 1979, Watcher in the Woods, 1979; TV movies Sister Aimee, 1977, The Dark Secret of Harvest Home, 1978, Strangers (Emmy award 1979), White Momma, 1980, Skyward, 1980, Family Reunion, 1981, A Piano for Mrs. Cimino, 1982, Little Gloria-Happy at Last, 1982, Right of Way, 1983; appeared in play The Night of the Iguana; Author: The Lonely Life, 1962; co-author: Mother Goddam, 1974. Recipient Am. Film Inst. Life Achievement award, Rudolph Valentino Life Achievement award, 1982, Am. Acad. Arts award, 1983, Disting. Pub. Service medal Dept. Def., 1983, Crystal award Women in Films, 1983. Office: care Gottlieb Schiff Ticktin Sternklar and Harris 555 Fifth Ave New York NY 10017

DAVIS, BRITT DUANE, banker; b. Lamesa, Tex., July 16, 1933; s. Dan Young and Dimple (Crain) D.; m. Mary Alice Horne, July 30, 1955; children: Britt Key, Collin Horne, Anne Caroline. B.A. in Econs, U. Tex., 1957. Various positions from personal trust adminstr., dept. head trust dept. Interfirst Bank Dallas, 1959-73, exec. v.p., sr. trust officer, Houston, 1973—; lectr. on arts fin./orgn. subjects. Bd. dirs. Houston Grand Opera Assn., Houston Ballet Fedn., Houston Symphony Soc., Greater Houston Conv. and Visitors Council; organizing dir. The Houston Festival Fedn., Inc., Cultural Arts Council Houston. Served with USN, 1950-54. Mem. Am., Tex. bankers assns., Houston Bus. Planning Council. Republican. Methodist. Clubs: Houston, Heritage, Lakeside Country. Office: First Internat Plaza 1100 Louisiana St Houston TX 77002

DAVIS, BRITTON ANTHONY, lawyer; b. Highland Park, Ill., Jan. 2, 1936; s. James Archie and Anita (Blanke) D.; m. Lynn Marriott Wegner, 1958 (dec. 1975); children: Hilary, Bradford, Shepard; m. Lynda L. Browning, 1976 (div. 1982). Student, Denison U., 1954-57; B.S. in Law, Northwestern U., 1959, LL.B., 1960. Bar: Ill. 1960. Asso. lawyer Haight, Simmons & Hofeldt, Chgo., 1959-67; partner Haight, Hofeldt, Davis & Jambor, Chgo., 1968—. Mem. Am. Bar Assn., Patent Law Assn. Chgo., Bar Assn. 7th Fed. Circuit. Clubs: Union League (Chgo.); Indian Hill (Winnetka, Ill.). Home: 285 Linden Ave Winnetka IL 60093 Office: 3614 Mid-Continental Plaza 55 E Monroe St Chicago IL 60603

DAVIS, BURL EDWARD, communications educator; b. Edenwold, Tenn., Sept. 8, 1930; s. John T. and Lydia Frances (Richards) D.; m. Frances Dawn Bartlett, Feb. 22, 1952; children: Kathy Aleta, Mary Kay, Phyllis Deanna, Michael Edward. B.A., David Lipscomb Coll., 1953; M.S., Clemson U., 1962; Ph.D., Mich. State U., 1968. Ordained to ministry, Ch. of Christ, 1946. Minister various locations, 1953-58; assoc. editor dept. agrl. communications Clemson (S.C.) U., 1958-65; research asst. dept. communications Mich. State U., East Lansing, 1964-68; prof. communications Abilene (Tex.) Christian U., 1969—, dir. mass communications program, 1975—; dir. Center for Communications Research, 1977—, World Christian Broadcasting Corp., Abilene, Tex., 1976-83, sec., 1976-77, mem. exec. bd., 1977-83, pres., 1977-80; cons. to numerous orgns. Contbr. articles to profl. jours. Advisor for campaigns various local, state polit. candidates, 1972-74; research dir. Citizens for Better Community, Abilene, 1976. Recipient Trustees award as outstanding tchr. Abilene Christian U., 1973, Spl. Recognition award Abilene Assn. Mental Health, 1972. Mem. Internat. Communications Assn., Assn. for Edn. in Journalism, Am. Speech Communication Assn., World Assn. Christian Communicators, So. Speech Assn. Mem. Ch. of Christ. Home: 2002 Cedar Crest Rd Abilene TX 79601 Office: Box 8034 Abilene Christian U Abilene TX 79601 *To achieve by serving other. . .to be ready when needed. . .to have something to offer. . .this is the secret of success.*

DAVIS, CABELL SEAL, JR., naval officer; b. Lakeland, Fla., July 20, 1926; s. Cabell Seal and Elizabeth (Massie) D.; m. Elizabeth Warner Holliday, Feb. 3, 1948; children: Carol, Cabell Seal III, Stephen. B.S., U.S. Naval Acad., 1947, U.S. Naval Postgrad. Sch., 1953, M.S., 1954. Commd. ensign U.S. Navy, 1947, advanced through grades to rear adm., 1975; service in aircraft carrier, destroyer, repair ship; project mgr. acquisition five gen. purpose amphibious ships, 1971-74, supr. shipbldg., Pascagoula, Miss., 1974-75; comdr. Charleston (S.C.) Naval Shipyard, 1975-78; dep. comdr. for indsl. and facility mgmt. Naval Sea Systems Command, Navy Dept., Washington, 1978-79; ret., 1979, cons., 1979—; extension tchr. Coll. William and Mary, Norfolk, Va., 1961-63. Asst. editor: Naval Engrs. Jour, 1964-68. Decorated Legion of Merit, Navy Commendation medal. Mem. Am. Soc. Naval Engrs. (asst. sec.-treas. 1964-68, President's award 1974), Naval Hist. Found., U.S. Naval Acad. Alumni Assn., Am. Philatelic Soc. Home and Office: 1673 Trap Rd Vienna VA 22180

DAVIS, CALVIN DE ARMOND, history educator; b. Westport, Ind., Dec. 3, 1927; s. Harry Russell and Abbie Jane (Moncrief) D. A.B., Franklin Coll., Ind., 1949; M.A., Ind. U., 1956, Ph.D., 1961. Tchr. Wilson Sch., Columbus, Ind., 1949-51, 53-54; asst. prof. history Ind. Central Coll., Indpls., 1956-57; teaching assoc. Ind. U., 1958-59; asst. prof. history U. Denver, 1959-62, Duke U., Durham, N.C., 1962-64, assoc. prof., 1964-76, prof., 1976—; cons. NEH, 1974. Author: The United States and the First Hague Peace Conference, 1962 (Albert J. Beveridge award 1961), The United States and the Second Hague Peace Conference, 1976. Served to cpl. U.S. Army, 1951-53. Mem. Am. Hist. Assn., Orgn. Am. Historians, Soc. Historians Am. Fgn. Relations, Conf. Peace Research in History (council 1979-81). Democrat. Mem. Christian Ch. Home: 907 Monmouth Ave Durham NC 27701 Office: Dept History Duke U. Durham NC 27706

DAVIS, CARL GEORGE, computer engineer; b. St. Louis, Nov. 30, 1937; s. Raymond Jefferson and Margaret (Peacock) D.; m. Joallen Guin, June 24, 1967; children: Jonathan, Allan, Steven. B.Aero. Engring., Ga. Inst. Tech., 1961; M.S. in Aero. Engring., U. Ala., 1966, U. Ala., 1972, Ph.D., 1972. Instr. U.S. Army Missile Command, Huntsville, 1964-69; research assoc. U. Ala., Tuscaloosa, 1969-72; sr. project engr. BMD Advanced Tech. Ctr., Huntsville, 1972-81, dir. data processing, 1981—; instr. Southeastern Inst. Tech., Huntsville, 1981-82; adj. assoc. prof. U. Ala., Huntsville, 1982—. Editor: Entity Relationship Approach to Software Engineering, 1983; contbr. articles to various publs. Mem. adv. com. U. Ala., 1982; mem. software com. Huntsville City Sch. System, 1983. Recipient Performance awards Dept. Army, 1977, 80, 82, R & D Achievement award Dept. Army, 1982. Fellow IEEE. Republican. Mem. Ch. of Christ. *

DAVIS, CAROLYNE KAHLE, government administrator; b. Penn Yan, N.Y., Jan. 31, 1932; d. Paul Frederick Kahle and Alice Edgerton (Kahle) Cargill; m. Ott Howard Davis, June 28, 1953; 1 son, Richard Ott. B.S., Johns Hopkins U., 1954; M.S., Syracuse U., 1965, Ph.D., 1972; D.Litt. (hon.), Georgetown U., 1982; D. Sc. (hon.), U. Evansville, 1982. Chmn. baccalaureate nursing program Syracuse U., 1969-73; dean Sch. Nursing, U. Mich., 1973-75, prof. nursing and edn., 1973-81, assoc. v.p. acad. affairs, 1975-81; adminstr. Health Care Financing Adminstrn., HHS, Washington, 1981—; bd. dirs. Johns Hopkins U., 1979-81, Am. Assn. Higher Edn., Washington, 1980-81. Contbr. articles to profl jours. Bd. dirs. Mich. Heart Assn., Detroit, 1973-81; mem. joint com. for health policy AAU, Nat. Assn. State Univs. and Land Grant Colls., Am. Council Edn.; mem. com. leadership devel. collegiate athletics Am. Council Edn., Washington, 1977-80. Recipient Disting. Alumnus award Johns Hopkins U., 1981; named Top Young Leaders in Am. Acad. Change Mag., 1978. Fellow Am. Acad. Nursing; mem. Nat. League for Nursing (dir. 1979-81), Sigma Theta Tau, Phi Delta Kappa. Repubican. Office: HHS Health Care Financing Adminstrn 200 Independence Ave SW Washington DC 20201

DAVIS, CHARLES ALEXANDER, public relations consultant; b. Mobile, Ala., Sept. 29, 1922; s. Robert A. and Clara Mae (Williams) D.; m. Rosalie M. Dorsey, Nov. 1, 1943; children—Charles Alexander, Daphne Kaye. Student, W.Va. State Coll., 1943-44, Roosevelt U., 1951-53; Dr. Human Services (hon.), Governor's State U., Park Forest South, Ill., 1975. Reporter, sportswriter Chgo. Defender newspaper, 1946-53, city editor, 1953-55, dir. pub. relations, 1955-57, dir. advt., 1957-59; info. officer Chgo. Commn. on Human Relations, 1959-61; pres. Charles A. Davis & Assos., Inc., Chgo., 1959—; exec. dir. Nat. Ins. Assn., 1962—; Pres. Inner City Industries, Inc.; gen. partner Adco Assos., real estate ltd. partnership; dir. Highland Community Bank.; Mem. Ill. Pub. Aid Adv. Commn., 1963-66, Health and Hosps. Governing Commn., Cook County, 1969-79. Author: (with R.E. Simon) On My Own. Bd. dirs. Chgo. State U. Found.; sec. Chgo. Southside br. NAACP; bd. govs. State Colls. and Univs., 1966-72; mem. Chgo. met. bd. NCCJ. Served with Q.M.C. AUS, 1943-46; PTO. Mem. Pub. Relations Soc. Am., Econ. Club Chgo., Press Club, Alpha Phi Alpha. Home: 2121 W Howland Ave Chicago IL 60620 Office: 2400 S Michigan Ave Chicago IL 60616

DAVIS, CHARLES CARROLL, aquatic biologist, educator; b. Azusa, Calif., Nov. 24, 1911; s. William Allen and Maude (Snyder) D.; m. Sally May Jacobsen, June 11, 1936; children: Peter Thomas, Betsy Ann. A.B., Oberlin Coll., 1933; M.S., U. Wash., 1935, Ph.D., 1940. Biologist II State of Md., 1942-43; instr. sci. Jacksonville Jr. Coll., 1944-46; asst. prof. zoology U. Miami, Coral Gables, Fla., 1946-48; asst. prof. biology Western Res. U., Cleve., 1948-52, asso. prof., 1953-63, prof., 1964-68; prof. biology Meml. U. of Nfld., 1968-78; ret., 1978; guest prof. aquatic biology U. Tromsø, Norway, 1975-76; cons. for zoology terms New World Dictionary, 1965-69, 82—. Author: The Pelagic Copepoda of the Northeastern Pacific Ocean, 1949, The Marine and Fresh-water Plankton, 1955; Co-editor: Internat. Revue der gesamten Hydrobiologie, 1974—; Contbr. numerous articles on plankton, eutrophication of Lake Erie, hatching mechanisms of invertebrate eggs, biol. prodn. to prof. jours. Fellow AAAS, Ohio Acad. Sci.; mem. Ecol. Soc. Am., Am. Soc. Limnology and Oceanography, Am. Micros. Soc., Plankton Soc. Japan, Internat. Soc. Limnology. Home: Site 3 Box 15 Rural Route 1 Paradise NF A0A 2E0 Canada Office: Dept of Biology Memorial Univ of Newfoundland St John's NF A1B 3X9 Canada *In all things, within the limits of my capabilities, to do what seems directly or indirectly of greatest value to humanity, regardless of its current popularity or unpopularity, and without aiming particularly at financial gain, honors or recognition, or especially at excelling over others. To trust all humans until they prove themselves untrustworthy, and to work towards a society in which no one will have occasion to be untrustworthy.*

DAVIS, CHARLES HARGIS, information scientist, university dean; b. Tell City, Ind., Sept. 23, 1938; s. Charles Alban and Ruth Elizabeth (Hargis) D. B.S. (State Merit scholar), Ind. U., 1960, A.M., 1966, Ph.D., 1969; postgrad. (German Govt. Fellow), U. Munich, W. Ger., 1960-61. Asst. editor Chem. Abstracts Service, Columbus, Ohio, 1962-65; chem. info. specialist Ind. U. Aerospace Research Applications Center, 1965-66; dir. systems Ind. U. ERIC Clearinghouse on Reading, 1967-69; asst. prof. library sci. Drexel U., 1969-71; asso. prof. U. Mich., 1971-76; prof., dean Faculty of Library Sci., U. Alta. (Can.), Edmonton, 1976-79, Grad. Sch. Library and Info. Sci., U. Ill., Urbana-Champaign, 1979—; speaker and condr. workshops and seminars in field; cons. in field; cons. editor Greenwood Press, Westport, Conn., 1974-79; pres. Can. Council Library Schs., 1978-79. Author: Illustrative Computer Programming for Libraries: Selected Examples for Information Specialists, 1974, 2d edit., 1981, (with James E. Rush) Information Retrieval and Documentation in Chemistry, 1974, Guide to Information Science, 1979; contbr. numerous articles, revs., bibliographies and columns to profl. publs. NSF research grantee, 1959-60. Mem. AAAS, Am. Chem. Soc., ALA (chmn. Library Research Round Table 1978-79), Am. Soc. Info. Sci. (chmn. Ind. U. student chpt. 1967-68, chmn. Ind. chpt. 1968-69, treas. Delaware Valley chpt. 1971, chmn. Mich. chpt. 1974-75, chmn. Western Can. chpt. 1978-79), Assn. Computing Machinery, Assn. Am. Library Schs. (chmn. research com. 1976-78), Phi Lambda Upsilon, Beta Phi Mu. Office: Grad Sch Library and Info Sci 410 DKH U Ill at Urbana-Champaign 1407 Gregory Dr Urbana IL 61801

DAVIS, CHESTER R., JR., lawyer; b. Chgo., Aug. 30, 1930; s. Chester R. and Mead (Scoville) D.; m. Anne Meserve, Mar. 3, 1962; children: John Chester, Julia Snow, Elizabeth Meserve. Grad., Phillips Exeter Acad., 1947; A.B., Princeton, 1951; LL.B., Harvard, 1958. Bar: Ill. 1958, U.S. Dist. Ct. (no. dist.) Ill. 1958. Mem. firm Bell & Boyd (and predecessor firm); partner Bell, Boyd & Lloyd and predecessor firm, 1968—. Asso. Rush-Presbyn.-St. Luke's Med. Center, Chgo., 1964—; Assoc. Adlai Stevenson Inst. Internat. Affairs, 1968—, Newberry Library, Chgo., 1974—; Mem. Winnetka (Ill.) Zoning Commn. and Bd. Appeals, 1974-79; mem. Winnetka Plan Commn., 1976-82; chmn. Spl. Joint. Com. of Winnetka Zoning Bd. and Plan Commn. to Revise Land Use Ordinances, 1978-83; village trustee Village of Winnetka, 1984—; Sec., bd. dirs. Vascular Disease Research Found.; mem. alumni council Phillips Exeter Acad.; chmn. Winnetka Interchurch Council., 1981—. Served to lt. (j.g.) USNR, 1952-56; now capt. USNR. Mem. ABA, Ill. Bar Assn., Chgo. Bar Assn. (chmn. com. civil practice 1969-70, chmn. land and zoning use com. 1980-82, chmn. real property law com. 1983—), Am. Soc. Internat. Law, Am. Judicature Soc., Am. Arbitration Assn. (nat. panel arbitrators), Am. Planning Assn., Urban Land Inst., Harvard Law Soc. Ill. (past pres.), Harvard Law Sch. Assn. (nat. v.p. 1970-71). Episcopalian. Clubs: University, Economic, Law, Legal (Chgo.); Princeton (N.Y.C.). Home: 670 Blackthorn Rd Winnetka IL 60093 Office: Three First Nat Plaza Chicago IL 60602

DAVIS, CLAUD MYRON, electrical engineer; b. Water Valley, Miss., Aug. 23, 1924; s. Claud Clifton and Anna Alta (Kelley) D.; m. Virginia Nenni, Nov. 10, 1956; children: Stephanie Anne, Claud Philip. B.S. in E.E., Okla. State U., 1950. Engr. IBM Computer Devel. Lab., Poughkeepsie, N.Y., 1950-58, mgr. 7074 Project, 1958-60, arch. for 360, 1961-63, mgr. FAA Project, 1963-68; with IBM Labs., Poughkeepsie and Fishkill, N.Y., 1968-83; program mgr. TPR White Plains, Poughkeepsie and Fishkill, 1983—. Fellow IEEE (sect. chmn. 1983-84); mem. Internat. Fedn. Info. Processing, Eta Kappa Nu (chpt. pres. 1948-49), Phi Kappa Phi, Sigma Tau, Pi Mu Epsilon. Baptist. Lodges: Masons (32 degree); Shriners. Office: IBM 44 S Broadway White Plains NY 10601

DAVIS, CLIVE JAY, lawyer, record co. exec.; b. Bklyn., Apr. 4, 1932; s. Herman and Florence (Brooks) D.; m. Janet Adelberg, Aug. 6, 1966; children—Fred, Lauren, Mitchell, Douglas. B.A. magna cum laude, N.Y. U., 1953; LL.B. cum laude, Harvard U., 1956. Bar: N.Y. bar 1957. Asso. firm Rosenman Colin Freund Lewis & Cohen, N.Y.C., 1958-60; gen. atty. Columbia Records, 1960-65, pres., 1966-73; pres., co-owner Arista Records, N.Y.C., 1974—. Author: Clive: Inside the Record Business, 1975. Recipient humanitarian award Anti-Defamation League, 1970, Martell Leukemia Found., 1980; named Man of Year Am. Parkinson Disease, 1972, Record Exec. of Year Nat. Assn. TV and Radio Announcers, 1973, Nat. Pop Music Survey, 1974, City of Hope, 1978. Mem. Record Industry Assn. Am. (pres., chmn. bd. 1972-73, now dir.). Home: 88 Central Park W New York NY 10023 Office: Arista Bldg 6 W 57th St New York NY 10019 *Experience has taught me to speak out again and again and, with right on one's side, the voice is eventually heard. Cheers for the reasoned vigilantes in society who prevent those in power from overwhelming the rights of the individual who otherwise cannot surface.*

DAVIS, COURTLAND HARWELL, JR., neurosurgeon; b. Alexandria, Va., Feb. 14, 1921; s. Courtland Harwell and Mary Helen (Fox) D.; m. Marilyn Bauer, Sept. 14, 1942; children: Courtland Harwell III, Randon, Richard, Jean Campbell, Cameron, Marilyn. A.B., George Washington U., 1941; M.D., U. Va., 1944. Diplomate: Am. Bd. Neurol. Surgery. Rotating intern U.S. Marine Hosp., New Orleans, 1944-45; asst. resident neurosurgery U. Va., 1945-46; postdoctoral research fellow neuropathology NIH, Duke Med. Center, 1948-49; asst. resident neurosurgery Duke Hosp., 1950-51, resident, 1951-52; practice medicine specializing in neurosurgery, Winston-Salem, N.C., 1952—; instr. medicine Duke Hosp., 1949-50; instr. neurosurgery Bowman Gray Sch. Medicine, 1952-55, asst. prof., 1955-59, asso. prof., 1959-67, prof., 1967—; mem. staff N.C. Bapt. Hosp., 1952—, asso. chief profl. services, 1975-82, chief profl. services, 1982—; mem. staff Kate Bitting Reynolds Meml. Hosp., 1953-58, City Meml. Hosp., 1953-58; cons. VA Hosp., Salisbury, N.C., 1954—, Regional Office VA, Winston-Salem, 1954; vis. prof. neurosurgery CARE-MEDICO, Malaysia, 1966, Christian Med. Coll., Vellore, India, 1966; vis. neurosurgeon HOPE, Cartagena, Colombia, S. Am., 1967, Kingston, Jamaica, 1971; chmn. med. care evaluation com. Piedmont Med. Found., 1978—; mem. N.C. Med. Peer Rev. Found., 1978—; dir. Land Title Corp. Alexandria, Inc. Vice chmn. Gov.'s Commn. on Mental Retardation, 1962-64, N.C. Legislative Council on Mental Retardation, 1964-71; Past pres. Bowman Gray Med. Found.; pres. Goodwill Industries, Assn. for Handicapped Childrens Center; bd. dirs. Forsyth County Rehab. House, Forsyth County Sheltered Workshop; trustee Found. for Internat. Edn. in Neurol. Surgery, 1969—; treas., bd. dirs. Piedmont Med. Found., Inc., 1980—. Served to capt. M.C. AUS, 1946-48. Fellow A.C.S. (com. on surg. edn. in med. schs. 1973—), Stroke Council Am. Heart Assn.; mem. AMA, So. Med. Assn., Med. Soc. N.C. (past del.), Forsyth County Med. Soc. (treas. 1980—), Congress Neurol. Surgeons, So. Neurosurg. Soc. (pres. 1976-77, mem. exec. council 1977—), Am. Assn. Neurol. Surgeons (mem. joint com. with Congress Neurol. Surgeons on continuing edn. 1972—, mem. subcom. structure of com. on edn. in neurol. surgery 1972—, mem. neurosurg. manpower monitoring com. 1975—), Neurosurg. Soc. Am. (pres. 1969, chmn. nominating com. 1979-80), N.C. Neurosurg.

Soc., Assn. for Research in Nervous and Mental Disease, Nat. Assn. Retarded Children (v.p. 1980-81, co-chmn. research com.), Am. Acad. Neurol. Surgeons (v.p. 1980-81), So. Neurol. Surgeons (mem. council 1977-79), Soc. Brit. Neurol. Surgeons (hon.), Alpha Omega Alpha, Theta Delta Chi, Nu Sigma Nu. Presbyterian (elder). Club: Rotarian (past pres.). Home: 921 Goodwood Rd Winston-Salem NC 27106 Office: Bowman Gray Sch Medicine 300 Hawthorne Rd Winston-Salem NC 27103

DAVIS, CRAIG ALPHIN, lawyer, manufacturing company executive; b. Oakland, Calif., July 28, 1940; s. Alphin Craig and Joyce Ida (Nevers) D.; m. Betty Rankin, July 13, 1963; children: Chelsea Alyson, Channing MacLaren. A.B. in Polit. Sci, U. Calif., Berkeley, 1964, J.D., 1967. Bar: Calif. 1968. Asso. firm Heller, Ehrman, White & McAuliffe, San Francisco, 1968-71; counsel Aluminum div. AMAX Inc., San Mateo, Calif., 1971-74; dir. law Alumax Inc., San Mateo, 1974, gen. counsel, sec., 1974—, v.p., 1978—, group v.p., gen. counsel, 1982—. Mem. editorial bd., research editor: Hastings Law Jour, 1966-67. Mem. Am. Bar Assn., State Bar Calif. Office: 400 S El Camino Real San Mateo CA 94402

DAVIS, CURTIS WHEELER, TV producer; b. New Haven, June 14, 1928; s. Malcolm Waters and Harriet Ide (Eager) D.; m. Julie Patricia Karras, Feb. 14, 1958; children: James Wheeler, Melissa Nina. B.A. with spl. distinction in music, Columbia, 1949. Prodn. mgr. W-N Recorder Corp., 1949-50; prodn. asst. and prodn. mgr. Louis de Rochemont Assos., 1953-58; prodn. mgr. Council Humanities, Boston, 1958-59; with Nat. Ednl. TV, N.Y.C., 1959-72, dir. cultural programs, 1965-72, ind. producer, 1972—; exec. producer ARTS, ABC Video Enterprises, 1981-82; dir. programs Arts, Hearst/ABC, 1982—; cons. Met. Opera, Cable Arts Found., Miss. Authority for Ednl. TV, Conn. Pub. TV, Fla. Pub. TV, TCR, Paris. Introduced: An American Family, NET Playhouse, NET Opera, Vibrations, USA: Arts; writer, producer: TV series The Music of Man for CBC, Toronto; producer, dir., writer: TV spl. Bartok: Concerto for CBC, Toronto and MTV, Budapest; Author: (with Yehudi Menuhin) The Music of Man, 1979 (Book of Month selection 1980), Leopold Stokowski, 1983; composer: Three Pictures for Piano, 1949, Concerto for Orchestra, 1949-53, Quintet for Harp and Strings, 1951, String Quintet, 1955, Recollections, 1969, Four Sonnets for Soprano and Orchestra, 1974-75. Served with AUS, 1951-53. Recipient Emmy award, 1969, 70, 71, Peabody award, 1967, 69, Am. Film Festival award, 1966, Anik award, 1979; recipient award Am. Council Better Broadcasting, 1981. Mem. Broadcast Music Inst., Nat. Assn. TV Arts and Scis. Episcopalian. Clubs: Century Assn. (N.Y.C.); American (London).

DAVIS, DANIEL EDWARD, museum director; b. Creston, Iowa, July 3, 1922; s. Fred M. and Myrtle A. D.; m. Mary Joan Kelly, July 15, 1947; children: Daniel B., Nancy, Terry, Barbara, Michelle. Student, U. Iowa, Nat. U. Mex., U. N.Mex., U. Mont. With Nat. Park Service, 1948-77, asso. regional dir., Omaha, 1973-77; dir. Ariz.-Sonora Desert Mus., Tucson, 1977—; adv. bd. Sch. Renewable Natural Resources, U. Ariz., 1980-81; adv. Arab Center Studies Arid Zones, Kouf Nat. Park, Libya.; cons. Egyptian Wildlife Service, Nat. Parks Netherlands West Indies. Author: Hikers Guide to Grand Canyon, 1956, Boatman's Guide to the Colorado River, 1957, The Little Colorado, 1958, Backcountry Travel, Sequoia National Park, 1961. Served with AUS, 1943-46. Recipient Meritorious Service award Dept. Interior, 1956, Environ. Leadership medal UN, 1982. Mem. Sierra Club, Nature Conservancy. Office: Route 9 Box 900 Tucson AZ 85743

DAVIS, DANIEL WALTER, commodity services co. exec.; b. Plainview, Tex., Oct. 5, 1930; s. Roy Bennett and Dennise (Cobb) D.; m. Mildred Drue Coffman, July 12, 1952; children—Dan Robert, Drue Ann, Paul Aubrey. B.B.A., Tex. A. and M. U., 1952; postgrad., U. Heidelberg, 1954-55. Pres. Commodity Exchange Services Co., Lubbock, Tex., 1978—; dir. Tex. Commerce Bank, Lubbock.; Councilor Tex. A. and M. Research Found., 1965—; mem. Tex. Natural Fibers & Textile Devel. Com., 1966—. Pres. Cotton Council Internat., 1975; Trustee Cotton Found. Served to lt. USAF, 1952-54. Named Cooperator of Year Tex., 1961. Mem. Nat. Cotton Council (dir. 1968-78), Tex. Fedn. Coops. (dir. 1956—, pres. 1960), Cotton Bd. (dir. 1975—). Methodist (bd. govs.). Home: 6610 Norwood St Lubbock TX 79413 Office: Suite 705 Metro Tower Lubbock TX 79401

DAVIS, DANNY (GEORGE JOSEPH NOWLAN), musician; b. Dorchester, Mass., May 29, 1925; s. Francis Parker and Elizabeth (Halpin) N.; m. Barbara Ann Bernier, Apr. 28, 1951; children: Kerry, Gavin, Kim, Tara. Attended pub. high sch. Owner, mng. dir. Daydan Music Inc., Nashville, Acoustic Music Inc., Lawday Music Inc., Nashville. Trumpist several orchs., including, Gene Krupa, 1944-45, Art Mooney, 1946, Sammy Kaye, 1950, Freddy Martin, 1951-52; producer, MGM Corp., N.Y.C., 1960-66, RCA, 1968-71; founder, leader, Nashville Brass, 1968—; composer. (Recipient Grammy awards for best instrumental group 1969-74). Mem. Nashville C. of C. (dir.), Country Music Assn. (best instrumental group year award 1969, 70, 71, 72, 73, 74), Am. Fedn. Musicians, Nat. Acad. Rec. Arts and Scis. (past pres.), AFTRA. Roman Catholic. Office: 1300 Division St Suite 104 Nashville TN 37203

DAVIS, DAVID, psychiatrist, educator; b. Liverpool, Eng., Oct. 5, 1927; came to U.S., naturalized, 1966; s. Solomon A. and Bertha (Finkelstein) D.; m. Phyllis Burman, 1952; children: Jonathan Paul, Jeremy Mark, Timothy Spenser. M.B., Ch.B., Glasgow (Scotland) U., 1949, M.D., 1974; Diploma in Psychol. Medicine, Conjoint Bd. of Royal Colls. Physicians and Surgeons, Eng., 1954. Lic. in medicine, U.K., Mo. House officer Stobhill Gen. Hosp., Glasgow, 1949-50; locum gen. practice, London, 1952; registrar in psychiatry St. Crispin Hosp., Northampton and South Ockendon Hosp., Essex, Eng., 1952-55; Fulbright traveling scholar, research fellow in psychiatry Washington U., St. Louis, vis. physician in psychiatry, 1955-57; registrar in psychiatry Bethlem Royal and Maudsley Hosps., U. London Postgrad. Inst. Psychiatry, 1957-59; sr. hosp. med. officer in psychiatry Borocourt Hosp., Henley, Eng.; with service at other hosps., 1959-60; asst. prof. psychiatry U. Mo., Columbia, 1960-61, assoc. prof., 1961-68, prof., 1968—, dir. inpatient psychiatry service, 1960-68, chief sect. gen. psychiatry, dir. edn. and tng., 1964-68, dir. community cons. program, 1966-72, chmn. dept. psychiatry, 1968-69, asso. chmn. dept. psychiatry, 1971-75, 77—; clin. dir. univ. service Mid-Mo. Mental Health Center, 1967-74, acad. head, 1968-69, asso. acad. head, dir. research and tng., chief sect. gen. psychiatry, 1970-75, chmn. dept. psychiatry, acad. head, 1975-76, chief psychiatry, 1977—, chmn. dept. psychiatry, acad. head, 1983-84; vis. scientist NIMH, 1969-70; vis. prof. U. Edinburgh, Scotland, 1976-77; vis. faculty fellow in community psychiatry Lab. Community Psychiatry, Harvard U. Med. Sch., 1965-67; disting. vis. prof. dept. psychology Bowling Green State U. (Ohio), Apr. 1983; examiner N.Y. State Dept. Mental Hygiene, 1970—; cons. in field. Contbr. articles to med. publs.; cons. editor: Jour. Operational Psychiatry. Pres. Congregation Beth Shalom of Mid-Mo., 1981-83. Served as flight lt. RAF, 1950-52. Recipient award for teaching excellence U. Mo. Residents, 1975; Royal Soc. Medicine Wellcome fellow, 1957-59; Am. Fund for Psychiatry teaching fellow, 1961-62; NIMH grantee, 1965-67. Fellow Am. Psychiat. Assn. (rep. and liaison Royal Coll. Psychiatrists 1979—), AAAS, Royal Soc. Health, Royal Coll. Psychiatrists, Am. Coll. Psychiatrists, Mo. Acad. Psychiatry (pres. 1970); mem. Can. Psychiat. Assn., Mid-Continent Psychiat. Assn., Boone County Assn. Mental Health, Mo. Assn. Mental Health (chmn. adv. com. 1968-74), AAUP, Internat. Assn. Social Psychiatry, N.Y. Acad. Scis., Central Mo. Psychiat. Soc. (pres. 1974, chmn. ethics com. 1977—), Mo. Psychiat. Assn. (pres. 1975), AMA, Brit. Med. Dir., Brit. Med. Register, Mo. Acad. Psychiatry (counselor 1975), N.Am. Soc., Royal Coll. Psychiatrists (founding chmn. 1978—), World Psychiat. Assn. (expert com. on clin. psychopathology), Sigma Xi, Phi Beta Pi. Clubs: B'nai B'rith (pres. 1965-66), University.). Office: Sch Medicine Dept Psychiatry U Mo 1 Hospital Dr Columbia MO 65201 *I have been helped by two principal notions - Awareness and Balance; awareness of my assets and liabilities; awareness of my tasks and obligations; awareness of the past implying a sense of history and language; awareness of the future by being open to new opportunities and interests. I have attempted to maintain a balance between work and leisure, science and humanism, reality and imagination, intellect and emotion, the serious and the humorous.*

DAVIS, DAVID BRION, historian, educator; b. Denver, Feb. 16, 1927; s. Clyde Brion and Martha (Wirt) D.; m. Frances Warner, Oct. 22, 1948 (div.); children: Jeremiah Jonathan, Martha Elizabeth, Sarah Brion; m. Toni Lisa Hahn, Sept. 9, 1971; children: Adam Jeffrey, Noah Benjamin. A.B. summa cum laude, Dartmouth Coll., 1950, Litt.D., 1977; A.M., Harvard, 1953, Ph.D., 1956; M.A., Oxford U., 1969. Scheduler Cessna Aircraft Co., Wichita, Kan., 1950-51; instr. history Dartmouth, 1953-54; mem. faculty Cornell U., 1955-69, prof. history, 1963-69, Ernest I. White prof. history, 1964-69; prof. history Yale, 1969—, Farnam prof. history, 1972-78, Sterling prof. history, 1978—, assoc. dir. Nat. Humanities Inst., 1975; Fulbright lectr., Hyderabad, India, 1967, univs. Guyana and W.I., 1974; Walter Lynwood Fleming lectr. So. history La. State U., 1969; Harmsworth prof. Oxford (Eng.) U., 1969-70; fellow Center Advanced Study Behavioral Scis., 1972-73, Henry E. Huntington Library, 1976; Benjamin Rush lectr. Am. Psychiat. Assn., 1976; French-Am. Found. chair in Am. civilization Ecole des Hautes Etudes en Sciences Sociales, Paris, 1980-81; Fulbright lectr., Israel, Holland, Italy, 1981; Patten lectr. Ind U., 1981; Hanes lectr. U. N.C., 1982; Thompson lectr. Vassar Coll., 1983; project dir. research grants Nat. Endowment for Humanities, 1980, 81. Author: Homicide in American Fiction, 1790-1860, A Study in Social Values, 1957, The Problem of Slavery in Western Culture, 1966, The Slave Power Conspiracy and the Paranoid Style, 1969, The Problem of Slavery in the Age of Revolution, 1770-1823, 1975, The Great Republic, 1977; editor: Ante-Bellum Reform, 1967, The Fear of Conspiracy, 1971, Ante-Bellum American Culture: An Interpretive Anthology, 1979. Mem. Subcom. internal security Democratic Nat. Policy Council. Served with AUS, 1945-46. Recipient Anisfield Wolf award in race relations, 1967, Pulitzer prize for nonfiction, 1967, Mass Media award NCCJ, 1967; Bancroft prize, 1976; Nat. Book award for history and biography, 1976; Guggenheim fellow, 1958-59; Fulbright grantee, 1980; NEH fellow, 1983-84. Fellow Am. Acad. Arts and Scis.; mem. Am. Philos. Soc., Am. Hist. Assn. (Albert J. Beveridge award 1975), Inst. Early Am. History and Culture (council 1976-79), Am. Antiquarian Soc., Soc. Am. Historians, Orgn. Am. Historians. Home: 733 Lambert Rd Orange CT 06477 Office: Dept History Yale University New Haven CT 06520

DAVIS, DAVID OLIVER, radiologist, educator; b. Danville, Ill., June 25, 1933; s. Oliver and Anna Marie (Collignon) D.; m. Agnes Layden, Dec. 26, 1955; children: Karen, Kathy, Diane, Janet, Nancy. B.S., U. Ill., 1954; M.D., St. Louis U., 1958. Diplomate: Am. Bd. Radiology. Intern Starkloff Meml. Hosp., St. Louis, 1958-59; resident USPHS Hosp., S.I., N.Y., 1959-61, Columbia Presbyn. Med. Center, N.Y.C., 1962-63; asst. prof. radiology Washington U., St. Louis, 1966-68, assoc. prof., 1968-70; prof. U. Utah, 1970-72, George Washington U., 1972—, chmn. dept. radiology, 1978-82; cons. USN; sec.-gen. 12th Internat. Symposium on Neuroradiology. Editor: Principles of Diagnostic Radiology, 1971, Reconstruction Tomography in Diagnostic Radiology and Nuclear Medicine, 1977; editorial bd.: Jour. Computer Assisted Tomography, 1977—, Am. Jour. Neuroradiology, 1979—, Neuroradiology, 1971-80; mem. editorial exec. com.: Jour. Investigative Radiology, 1971-80. Served with USPHS, 1959-64. NIH spl. fellow, 1964-66. Fellow Am. Coll. Radiology, Am. Heart Assn. (stroke council); mem. AMA, Am. Soc. Neuroradiology (sec. 1971-74, pres. 1979-80), D.C. Med. Soc., D.C. Radiol. Soc. (pres. 1983-84), Assn. Univ. Radiologists, Soc. Chmn. Acad. Radiology Depts. (sec.-treas. 1982-83), Internat. Microcirculation Soc., N. Pacific Soc. Neurology and Psychiatry (hon.), Am. Soc. Head and Neck Radiology, South Eastern Neuroradiology Soc., Phila. Roentgen Soc. (hon.), Western Neuroradiology Soc. Office: Dept Radiology George Washington U Med Center 901 23d St NW Washington DC 20037

DAVIS, DAVID WILLIAM, port authority executive; b. Belden, Nebr., June 2, 1932; s. Abner Paul Gries and Juanita (Jarvis) D.; m. Albie Muldavin, May 20, 1956 (div. 1972); children: Michelle, Matthew, Benjamin, Carol; m. Andronike E. Janus, Feb. 22, 1976. B.A., U. Calif.-Berkeley, 1954. With State of Calif., Sacramento, Calif., 1957-66; staff assoc. President's Task Force, Washington, 1966-67; research assoc. Brookings Instn., Washington, 1967-68; exec. dir.Econ. Devel. and Indsl. Connm., dir. Office Pub. Service, dept., adminstrv. services for fiscal affairs, City of Boston, 1968-71; dir. Office of Budgets Harvard U., Cambridge, Mass., 1971-75; exec. dir. Mass. Port Authority, Boston, 1975—; bd. dirs. Greater Boston Conv. and Tourist Bur., 1976—, Internat. Bus. Ctr. New Eng., Boston, 1977—, Fgn. Bus. Council, 1978—, Airport Operations Council Internat., Washington, 1979—. Author: (with others) Making Federalism Work, 1969 (Brownlow 1970). Chmn. Boston Indsl. and Fin. Authority, 1971-80; bd. dirs. Ford Hall Forum, 1981—, Boston Harbor Assocs., Inc., 1977—; mem. Marshall selection com. Brit. Consulate, Boston, 1982—. Mem. Am. Assn. Port Authorities, Nat. Acad. Pub. Adminstrn. Democrat. Home: 16 Acorn St Boston MA 02108 Office: Massachusettes Port Authority 99 High St Boston MA 02110

DAVIS, DEANE CHANDLER, former gov. Vt., lawyer; b. East Barre, Vt., Nov. 7, 1900; s. Earl Russell and Lois (Hillary) D.; m. Corinne Eastman, June 14, 1924 (dec. Mar. 9, 1951); children—Deane (dec.), Marian Davis Calcagni, Thomas C.; m. Marjorie Smith Conzelman, July 5, 1952. LL.B., Boston U., 1922, LL.D., 1969; LL.D., U. Vt., 1957, Middlebury Coll., 1964; Litt.D. (hon.), Norwich U., 1963, D.Pub.Service, 1976. Bar: Vt. bar 1922. Practiced law, Barre, Vt., 1922-31, 36-40, city atty., Barre, 1924-26, 28-30, states atty., Washington County, Vt., 1926-28, superior judge, State of Vt., 1931-36; mem. law firm Wilson, Carver, Davis & Keyser, Barre and Chelsea, Vt., 1936-40; gen. counsel Nat. Life Ins. Co., 1940-50, v.p., 1943-50, pres., chief exec. officer, 1950-66, chmn. bd., chief exec. officer, 1966-67, chmn. bd., 1967-68; now mem. exec. and fin. coms., dir.; dir. Union Mut. Fire Ins. Co.; gov., Vt., 1969-73; mem. Barre City Council, 1923-24. Author: Justice in Vermont, 1980. Pres. Vt. State C. of C., 1942-43; del. Republican Conv., 1948, 72, mem. resolutions com., 1948; pres. Calvin Coolidge Meml. Found.; bd. dirs. Life Ins. Med. Research Fund, 1955-57, Mary Fletcher Hosp., 1955-59; pres., mng. dir. Coop. Health Info. Center Vt., 1973-75, bd. dirs., 1973-77. Recipient Haugen award Vt. Soc. Public Adminstrs., 1980. Mem. ABA (gov. 1945-48, chmn. Vt. com. representing council on legal edn. and admissions to bar), Vt. Bar Assn. (pres. 1942), Life Ins. Assn. Am. (dir. 1953-63, pres. 1959-60), Am. Life Conv. (v.p.), Inst. Life Ins. (dir. 1961-64, chmn. bd. 1963), Am. Judicature Soc., Vt. Morgan Horse Assn. (chmn. bd.), Am. Morgan Horse Assn. (pres. 1963-64), Green Mountain Horse Assn. (v.p.), Delta Theta Phi. Methodist. Clubs: Masons, K.P. Home: 5 Dyer Ave RD 1 Montpelier VT 05602 Office: National Life Dr Montpelier VT 05602

DAVIS, DELMONT ALVIN, JR., manufacturing company executive; b. Hillside, Colo., June 11, 1935; s. Delmont A. and Zelma M. (Townsend) D.; m. L. June Clift, June 9, 1957; children: Terry, Curtis, Thayer. B.S.C.E., U. Colo., 1959. Registered profl. engr., Colo., Miss., La., Wis.; registered land surveyor, La. Project engr. Gen. Electric, Bay St. Louis, Miss., 1964-69, Ball Corp., Boulder, Colo., 1969, v.p. engrng., Lakewood, Colo., 1969-73, v.p. ops., 1973-76, group v.p., Westminster, Colo., 1976—; dir. PLM PAC AB, Malmo, Sweden, 1979—, PLM-BALL GmbH, Berlin, 1983—. Asst. chmn. United Way, Bay St. Louis, 1964-68; pres., civic chmn. Fountain Estates Homeowners' Assn., Slidell, La., 1967-69; asst. cub master, treas. Cub Scouts, 1970-72. Mem. ASCE, Nat. Soc. Profl. Engrs., Can. Mfrs.' Inst. (dir., mem. exec. com. 1976—), Tau Kappa Epsilon (pres. Boulder chpt. 1956-57, chmn. bd. dirs. chpt. 1957-58). Republican. Baptist. Home: 6608 Walker Ct Longmont CO 80501 Office: Ball Corp 9300 W 108th Circle Westminster CO 80020

DAVIS, DON R(AY), insurance consultant; b. Washingtonville, Ohio, Jan. 27, 1924; s. Ivan Wilbur and Sarah (Barton) D.; m. Louise Endress Hall, Nov. 15, 1952; children: Don Scott, Timothy John, Wendy Louise. B.A., Ohio Wesleyan U., 1948. Home office group rep. Aetna Life Ins. Co., Detroit, 1948-51; dist. group supr. N.Y. Life Ins. Co., Cleve., 1951-58; regional group mgr. Paul Reverse Life Ins. Co., Detroit, 1958-60; ins. agt. Dore Agy., Detroit, 1960-61; asst. v.p. sales Safeco Life Ins. Co., Seattle, 1961-68; pres. Am. Life Ins. Co. subs. Am. Internat. Group, Wilmington, Del., 1968-76; sr. v.p. Continental Corp., N.Y.C., 1976-82; cons. ins., Carmel, Ind., 1983—; mem.exec. com., mem. program com. Pacific Ins. Conf., 1981—. Fund dir. Continental Corp., United Way of Tri-State, N.Y.C., 1978, 79,80; trustee Ohio Wesleyan U., Delaware, 1982—. Served to sgt. USMC, 1943-46; PTO, China. Mem. Nat. Assn. Life Underwriters. Republican. Clubs: Wilmington Country; Essex Falls Country (N.J.). Home: 11330 E 550 S PO Box 262 Zionsville IN 46077

DAVIS, DONALD ALAN, news correspondent; b. Savannah, Ga., Oct. 5, 1939; s. Oden Harry and Irma Artice (Gay) D.; children: Russell Glenn, Randall Scott. B.A. in Journalism, U. Ga., 1962. Reporter Athens (Ga.) Banner-Herald, 1961-62, Savannah Morning News, 1962; with UPI, 1963-65; reporter, editor St. Petersburg (Fla.) Times, 1965-66; with UPI, 1967—, Vietnam corr., 1971-73, New Eng. editor, 1977-80, White House corr., 1981-83; polit. writer San Diego Union, 1983—; instr. journalism Boston U., 1979; lectr. U.S. Naval War Coll., 1983; bd. dirs. Fgn. Corr. Club, Hong Kong, 1974. Recipient award Fla. Bar Assn., 1966. Mem. Sigma Delta Chi. Presbyterian. Home: 541 Bonair St La Jolla CA 92037 Office: San Diego Union PO Box 191 San Diego CA 92112

DAVIS, DONALD JAMES, bishop; b. New Castle, Pa., Mar. 12, 1929; s. LeRoy Francis and Rya Anne (Stewart) D.; m. Gray Schofield, Sept. 6, 1952; children—Stewart, Kristin, Addison. B.A., Westminster Coll., 1949, D.D. (hon.), 1975; M.A., Bowling Green State U., 1971; M.Div., Princeton U., 1952; postgrad., Ind. U. Ordained priest Episc. Ch.; curate Ch. of the Epiphany and Christ Ch., Washington, 1955-57; rector St. Christopher's Ch., Indpls., 1957-63, Trinity Ch., Toledo, 1963-71, Bloomington, Ind., 1971-73; chaplain Ind. U., 1971-73; bishop co-adjutor Diocese of Erie, Pa., 1973, bishop, 1974—; press officer Ho. of Bishops, 1976—; chmn. Bd. of Hood Conf., 1976-77; mem. Standing Commn. on Ch. Music, Gen. Bd. of Examining Chaplains. Named Hon. Alumnus Bexley Hall Sem. Office: 145 W 6th St Erie PA 16501 *

DAVIS, DONALD RAY, entomologist; b. Oklahoma City, Mar. 28, 1934; s. Esker Arnold and Mildred Marie (Fortson) D.; m. Mignon Marie Bush, Sept. 29, 1972; 1 dau., Marisa Marie. B.A., U. Kans., 1956; Ph.D., Cornell U., 1962. Asso. curator, then curator entomology Smithsonian Instn., 1961-76, chmn. dept., 1976-81. Author papers in field. Recipient Smithsonian Instn. Fluid Research award, 1965, 73, 77-80, Smithsonian Instn. Research Found. award, 1966-67, 73-74; grantee Am. Philos. Soc., 1963. Mem. Lepidopterists Soc. (Jordan medal 1977), Assn. Tropical Biology, Entomol. Soc. Am., Nat. Speleological Soc., Soc. Systematic Zoology, Entomol. Soc. Washington (pres. 1979), Washington Biologists Field Club. Club: D.C. Grotto (Washington). Office: Smithsonian Instn NHB 430 Washington DC 20560 *I believe that life's major goal should be to contribute something of lasting value to earth's diverse heritage. Perhaps the most permanent heritage anyone can bequeath lies in the discovery of new knowledge. By thus enriching our common heritage, I feel that I can partially repay, in my own humble way, for the enormous privilege of having once lived on this interesting planet.*

DAVIS, DORLAND JONES, USPHS officer; b. Chgo., July 2, 1911; s. David John and Myra Helen (Jones) D.; m. Caroline Gertrude Baker, July 15, 1938; children: David Howard, Constance Elaine. Student, Internat. Sch., Geneva, Switzerland, 1927-28; B.S., U. Ill., 1933; M.D., Johns Hopkins, 1937, Dr.P.H., 1940. Commd. asst. surgeon USPHS, 1939, advanced through grades to asst. surg. gen.; assigned State Dept. for duty, North Africa, 1943-44; with NIH, 1939-43, 44—; chief lab. infectious diseases Nat. Mircrobiol. Inst., 1954-56; assoc. dir. Nat. Inst. Allergy and Infectious Dis., 1956-64, dir., 1964-75. Recipient Edward Rhodes Stitt award, 1955; Meritorious Service medal USPHS, 1967; Distinguished Service medal, 1971. Fellow Am. Acad. Microbiology, AAAS, Am. Pub. Health Assn., Am. Coll. Preventive Medicine, Coll. Physicians Phila.; mem. Soc. Am. Bacteriologists, Soc. Exptl. Biology and Medicine, A.M.A., Am. Assn. Mil. Surgeons, Am. Epidemiological Soc., Am. Assn. Immunologists, Johns Hopkins Univ. Soc. Scholars, Phi Beta Kappa, Beta Theta Pi, Delta Omega, Sigma Xi. Club: Cosmos (Washington). Investigations infectious diseases, including poliomyelitis, trypanosomiasis, psittacosis, hepatitis, conjunctivitis, influenza. Home: 7800 Carteret Rd Bethesda MD 20817 Office: Nat Insts Health Bethesda MD 20014

DAVIS, DOROTHY SALISBURY, author; b. Chgo., Apr. 26, 1916; d. Alfred Joseph and Margaret Jane (Greer) Salisbury; m. Harry Davis, Apr. 25, 1946. A.B., Barat Coll., Lake Forest, Ill., 1938. Mystery and hist. novelist; short story writer.; Author: A Gentle Murderer, 1951, A Town of Masks, 1952, Men of No Property, 1956, Death of an Old Sinner, 1957, A Gentleman Called, 1958, The Evening of the Good Samaritan, 1961, Black Sheep, White Lamb, 1963, The Pale Betrayer, 1965, Enemy and Brother, 1967, God Speed The Night, 1968, Where the Dark Streets Go, 1969, Shock Wave, 1972, The Little Brothers, 1973, A Death in the Life, 1976, Scarlet Night, 1980. Mem. Authors League, Mystery Writers of Am. (pres.), Writers Guild Am. Home: Palisades NY 10964

DAVIS, DOUGLAS MATTHEW, artist, educator, author; b. Washington, Apr. 11, 1933; s. Douglas Matthew and Pauline Elizabeth (Burton) D. B.A., Am. U., 1956; M.A., Rutgers U., 1958. Art critic Newsweek mag., 1969-77, gen. editor, 1977-80, sr. writer architecture, photography, contemporary ideas, 1980—; artist-in-residence TV Lab. Sta. WNET-TV, N.Y.C., 1972; lectr. Columbia U., UCLA, Osaka (Japan) U. of Arts; artistic dir. Internat. Network for the Arts, 1976—. Exhibited videotapes, films, drawings, prints, objects in one-man shows, including, San Francisco Mus. Modern Art, 1975, Everson Mus., Syracuse, N.Y., Whitney Museum Am. Art, N.Y.C., 1977, 81,

Neue Galerie, Aachen, W. Ger., 1978, Neuer Berliner Kunstverein, Berlin, Folkwang Mus., Essen, W. Ger., 1979, Galerie Stampa, Basel, Switzerland, P.S.I. Gallery, N.Y.C., 1980, Mus. Sztuki, Lodz, Poland, 1982; exhibited in group shows, including, Whitney Mus. Am. Art, 1971, 75, Mus. Contemporary Art, Chgo., 1975, Cracow (Poland) Bienale, 1976, Venice (Italy) Biennale, 1976, 78, Kassel (W. Ger.) Documenta 6, 1977, Ga. Mus. Art, 1978, Met. Mus., N.Y.C., 1982; represented in permanent collections, Hirschorn Mus., Washington, Ludwig Mus., Cologne, Victoria and Albert Mus., London, Met. Mus. Art, N.Y.C., Wadsworth Atheneum, Hartford, Conn., Dahlem Mus., W. Berlin; appeared in various telecasts and radio performances, U.S. and Europe, 1969—; Author: Art and the Future, 1973, Artculture: Essays on the Post-Modern, 1977. Nat. Endowment for Arts fellow, 1971, 75, 80; Deutscher Akademischer Austauschdient artists fellow, Berlin, 1977. Mem. Artist's Equity, Author's Guild. Office: 80 Wooster St New York NY 10012

DAVIS, DREXEL REED, treasurer State of Kentucky; b. Shelbyville, Ky., July 18, 1921; s. E. Forest and Myrtle Francis (Stacy) D.; m. Sarah Lillis, Oct. 15, 1947; children: Drexel R., Ann Lillis. Student, Georgetown Coll., 1940-42. Dep. clk. Ky.'s Ct. of Appeals, 1948-52, 56-63, clk., 1964-67; adminstrv. asst. Ky. Sec. of State, Frankfort, 1952-56; dist. mgr. Investors Heritage Life Ins. Co., Frankfort, 1969-72; treas. State of Ky., Frankfort, 1972-75, 79—, sec. of state, 1975-79. Served with Signal Corps U.S. Army, 1942-45. Mem. Southeastern Nat. Treas's. Assn. (chmn.). Democrat. Clubs: Lions (dist. govt.), Am. Legion, VFW, Masons, Shriners. Office: Treasury Dept New Capitol Annex Frankfort KY 40601 *

DAVIS, DWIGHT M., superintendent schools; b. Lynnville, Iowa, Mar. 12, 1920; s. Orland G. and Gertrude (McClung) D.; m. Alice Fredrickson, Aug. 20, 1941; children: Gilbert Kenneth, Trevor Dwight; m. Arleen M. Schultze, Nov. 2, 1980. B.A., Iowa State Tchrs. Coll., 1941; M.A., State U. Iowa, 1947, Ph.D., 1953. Tchr. math, Williamsburg, Iowa, 1941-42, Iowa Falls, Iowa, 1942-43, prin. high sch., dean jr. coll., Bloomfield, Iowa, 1947-48, prin. high sch., Hampton, Ia., 1948-50, U. High Sch. of State U. Iowa, Iowa City, 1950-53; dean Moline (Ill.) Community Coll., 1953-55; supt. schs., Moline, 1955-65, Des Moines, 1965-80, Colorado Springs, Colo., 1980—. Pres. Girls-Home Sch.; active Community Chest, Boy Scouts Am.; mem. Gov.'s Task Force on Edn.; life mem. P.T.A.; Trustee Joint Council Econ. Edn.; bd. dirs. Mid-Am. Arts Alliance. Served with C.E. AUS, 1943-46. Mem. NEA, Am. Assn. Sch. Adminstrs. (exec. com.), Phi Delta Kappa, Phi Mu Epsilon. Clubs: Kiwanian, Rotarian. Home: 2927 Highland Dr Colorado Springs CO 80909

DAVIS, E.M., manufacturing company executive. Pres., chief operating officer Hobart Corp., Troy, Ohio. Office: Hobart Corp World Hdqrs Ave Troy OH 45374

DAVIS, EARL JAMES, chemical engineering educator; b. St. Paul, July 22, 1934; s. Leo Ernest and Mary (Steiner) D.; m. Gretchen George Black, 1978; children: Molly Kathleen, David Leo. B.S. cum laude, Gonzaga U., 1956; Ph.D. (Leeds and Northrup fellow), U. Wash., 1960. Design engr. Union CarbideChems. Co., South Charleston, W.Va., 1956; research fellow chem. engring. U. Wash., 1957-60, asst. prof., 1960-64, asso. prof., 1965-68; research fellow Imperial Coll., London (Eng.) U., 1964-65; dir. computing center Gonzaga U., 1967-68; asso. prof. chem. engring. Clarkson Coll. Tech., 1968-73, head socio-environ. program, 1972-74, prof., 1973-78, chmn. chem. engring. dept., 1973-74, asso. dir., 1974-78; prof., chmn. chem. and nuclear engring. dept. U. N.Mex., 1978-80; dir. engring. div., prof. Inst. Paper Chemistry, Appleton, Wis., 1980-83; prof. chem. engring. U. Wash., Seattle, 1983—; adminstr. Am. Inst. Chem.Engrs.-Design Inst. Multiphase Processing, 1979—; sr. scientist, cons. Unilever Research Lab., Port Sunlight, Eng., 1974-75. NSF fellow, 1964-65; grantee, 1963-80. Mem. Am. Chem. Soc., Am. Inst. Chem. Engrs., Am. Soc. Engring. Edn., TAPPI, Sigma Xi, Phi Lambda Upsilon (pres. U. Wash. chpt. 1959-60). Democrat. Roman Catholic. Research and publs. on heat and mass transfer, math. modeling, aerosol, phys. chemistry. Office: Dept Chem Engring BF-10 U Wash Seattle WA 98195

DAVIS, EDDIE, jazz tenor saxophonist; b. N.Y.C., Mar. 2, 1921. Leader various jazz groups, N.Y.C., 1942-52; also played with, Cootie Williams, Andy Kirk, Louis Armstrong; played with, Count Basie Orch., 1952-53, 57, 66-73; co-leader groups with, Zoot Sims; also played in other groups with, Shirley Scott, Harry Edison, Johnny Griffin; albums include I Only Have Eyes For You, Heavy Hiller, Jaws Blues, Montreux '77, Stolen Moments, Straight Ahead, Sweet and Lovely. Office: care Pablo Records 1133 Ave of Americas New York NY 10036 *

DAVIS, EDGAR GLENN, pharmaceutical company executive; b. Indpls., May 12, 1931; s. Thomas Carroll and Florence Isabelle (Watson) D.; m. Margaret Louise Alandt, June 20, 1953; children: Anne-Elizabeth Davis Polestra, Amy Alandt, Edgar Glenn. A.B., Kenyon Coll., 1953; M.B.A., Harvard U., 1955. With Eli Lilly and Co., Indpls., 1958—, mgr. budgeting and profit planning, 1963-66, mgr. econ. studies, 1966-67, mgr. Atlanta sales dist., 1967-68, dir. market research and sales manpower planning, 1968-69, dir. mktg. plans, 1969-74, exec. dir. pharm. mktg. planning, 1974, exec. dir. corp. affairs, 1974-76, v.p. corp. affairs, 1976—; vis. fellow div. Health Policy Research and Edn., Kennedy Sch. Govt., Harvard U., 1981—; mem. adv. com. Bus. Roundtable Task Force on Health; U.S. rep. UN Indsl. Devel. Orgn. Conf., Lisbon, 1980; participant UNIDO meeting of experts on pharms., 1981; rep. to UN Commn. on Narcotic Drugs, Vienna, 1981, UN Econ. and Social Council, N.Y.C., 1981. Contbr. articles to profl. jours. Trustee Kenyon Coll., Gambier, Ohio, Christian Theol. Sem., Citizens' Research Found., U. So. Calif.; bd. dirs. Council on Religion and Internat. Affairs; v.p., bd. dirs. Washington Bus. Group on Health; dir. Public Affairs Council, Washington; chmn. bd. dirs. Ind. Repertory Theatre, 1980—; bd. visitors Bishops Sch., LaJolla, Calif.; v.p., bd. dirs. Indpls. Symphony Orch. and Ind. State Symphony Soc., 1977—; bd. dirs. Greater Indpls. Progress Com., 1977—, Met. Indpls. TV Assn., 1976—, Kenyon Festival Theatre, Nat. Health Council. Served to lt. USN, 1955-58. Mem. Inst. Medicine (resources devel. com.), Nat. Acad. Scis. Clubs: Met. (Washington); Harvard Overseas Press (N.Y.C.); Edgartown (Mass.); Yacht; Yacht (Chgo.); Woodstock, University, Contemporary, Lambs, Crooked Stick Golf (Indpls.). Home: 5635 Sunset Ln Indianapolis IN 46208 Office: 307 E McCarty St Indianapolis IN 46285

DAVIS, EDWARD BERTRAND, federal judge; b. W. Palm Beach, Fla., Feb. 10, 1933; s. Edward Bertrand and Mattie Mae (Walker) D.; m. Patricia Lee Klein, Apr. 5, 1958; children: Diana Lee Davis Gransden, Traci Russell, Edward Bertrand, III. J.D., U. Fla., 1960; LL.M. in Taxation, N.Y. U., 1961. Bar: Fla. bar 1961. Pvt. practice, Miami, 1961-79; counsel firm High, Stack, Lazenby & Bender, 1978-79; U.S. dist. judge So. Dist. Fla., 1979—. Served with AUS, 1953-55. Mem. Am. Bar Assn., Fla. Bar Assn., Dade County Bar Assn. Home: 6320 SW 50th St Miami FL 33155 Office: PO Box 013189 Miami FL 33101

DAVIS, EDWARD SHIPPEN, lawyer; b. N.Y.C., Jan. 23, 1932; s. Wendell and Lavinia (Riker) D.; m. Barbara Thompson, Sept. 13, 1980; children: Martha K., Edward Shippen. A.B., Harvard U., 1954, LL.B., 1959. Bar: Conn. 1959, N.Y. 1960, Wis. 1973, D.C. 1973. Assoc. Hughes Hubbard & Reed, N.Y.C., 1959-66, ptnr, 1967—; dir. Cognitronics Corp.; Hillenbrand Industries Inc. Author articles in field. Pres. bd. trustees Collegiate Sch., N.Y.C. Served with AUS, 1954-56. Mem. Am. Bar Assn., Conn. Bar Assn., Wis. Bar Assn., Assn. Bar City N.Y. Clubs: Harvard, Recess (N.Y.C.); University (Milw.). Home: 205 W 57th St New York NY 10019 Office: 1 Wall St New York NY 10005

DAVIS, EDWARD WILSON, educator; b. Thomaston, Ga., Aug. 4, 1935; s. James Royland, Jr. and Hazel (Bass) D.; m. Patricia Gail Forrest, Oct. 20, 1962; children—Matthew Wilson, Edward Royland. B.S. in Mech. Engring, Ga. Inst. Tech., 1957, M.S. in Indsl. Engring, 1959; postgrad., Swiss Fed. Inst. Tech., 1957-58; M.Phil., Yale U., 1967, Ph.D., 1968. Project leader Ops. Research, Inc., Washington, 1960-64; asst. prof. Harvard Bus. Sch., Cambridge, Mass., 1968-73; vis. asso. prof. Sloan Sch. Mgmt., M.I.T., Cambridge, 1973-74; asso. prof., prof. U. N.C., Chapel Hill, 1974-78; prof. Grad. Sch. Bus. Adminstrn., U. Va., Charlottesville, 1978—; cons. various pvt. and public cos., U.S. and Europe. Author: Case Studies in Material Requirements Planning, 1978; editor: Project Management, 1974, 2d edit., 1982. Council mem. Pilgrim Congregation Ch., 1972-74; cub scout and boy scout leader Occoneechee council Boy Scouts Am., 1974-77. IBM faculty fellow in internat. bus., 1976. Mem. Am. Mgmt. Assn., Inst. Mgmt. Scis., Am. Inst. Indsl. Engrs., Project Mgmt. Inst., Am. Inst. Decision Scis., Am. Prodn. and Inventory Control Soc. (dir. Ednl. and Research Found., presdl. award 1974). Presbyterian. Office: PO Box 6550 Charlottesville VA 22906

DAVIS, E. M., manufacturing company executive. Pres., chief operating officer Hobart Corp., Troy, Ohio. Office: Hobart Corp World Hdqrs Ave Troy OH 45374

DAVIS, EVELYN Y., editor, author, publisher; b. The Netherlands, Aug. 16; d. Herman H. and Marian (Witteboom) DeJong; m. William Henry Davis, 1957 (div. 1958); m. Marvin Knudsen, 1969 (div. 1970). Student, Western Md. Coll., George Washington U., N.Y. Inst. Fin. Lectr. on stockholder relations. Editor, pub., Highlights and Lowlights, 1964—; Contbr. articles on bus. and travel to various publs. Mem. Luther Rice Soc. (life). Republican. Home: Watergate East 2510 Virginia Ave NW Washington DC 20037 Office: 1127 Connecticut Ave NW Washington DC 20036 *I did not get where I am in life by standing in line. To me power is greater than love.*

DAVIS, FINIS E., business executive; b. Lead Hill, Ark., Aug. 29, 1911; s. John Preston and Mary Elizabeth (Cagle) D.; m. Ethlyn Watkins, July 15, 1933; children: Marybel (Mrs. Robert Black), Juliann (Mrs. Gary R. Edwards), Linda Sue (Mrs. Bruce Henry Broecker). Student, Ark. Polytech. Coll., 1932; B.S. in Edn, U. Ark., 1938. Tchr. Ark. Sch. for Blind, Little Rock, 1933-39, supt., 1939-47; v.p., gen. mgr. Am. Printing House for Blind, Louisville, 1947-76; pres. Label Specialties Inc., 1976—; Sponsoring com. Internat. Conf. Educators of Blind Youth, 1951-52, U.S. del. to conf., Bussum, Holland, 1952, mem. exec. council, 1952—, chmn. U.S. delegation to conf., Oslo, Norway, 1957. Mem. Lions Internat., 1941—, pres. Little Rock club, 1946-47, dist. gov. 7-B Ark., 1947, pres. Louisville club, 1950-51, dist. gov., 1953-54, internat. bd. dirs., 1954- 56, 1st v.p., 1959-60, pres., 1960-61; Mem. bd. Quapaw area council Boy Scouts Am., dist. commnr., also chmn. leadership tng., 1941-46; Bd. dirs. U. Louisville Internat. Center, Louisville Presbyn. Sem., Helen Keller Internat., N.Y., Nat. Soc. to Prevent Blindness, Ark. Enterprises for Blind, Kentuckiana Metroversity, Ky. Lions Eye Found.; chmn. United Appeal, 1968. Recipient Ambassador of Goodwill and Humanitarian awards Lions Internat., Disting. Service award Govt. of Peru, 1961, Disting. Merit award Govt. of Ecuador; named in his honor Library Bldg., Mich. Sch. for Blind, 1966. Mem. Am. Assn. Instrs. Blind (dir. 1950-55, pres. 1950-52), Am. Assn. Workers for Blind. Presbyn. (elder). Clubs: Masons (32 deg.), Executives, Pendennis (Louisville). Home: 6106 Rodes Dr Louisville KY 40222 Office: 8017 Catherine Ave Louisville KY 40222

DAVIS, FRANK ELWOOD, lawyer; b. Washington, Dec. 15, 1915; s. Leonard Henry and Anne Mae (MacCarthy) D.; m. Eleanor Louise Grunwell, Sept. 19, 1942; children: Robert Elwood, Anne Louise, Lynne Lockwood. LL.B., George Washington U., 1942; grad., Grad. Sch. Banking, Rutgers U., 1950. Bar: D.C. 1946. With Riggs Nat. Bank, 1934-50, now mem. adv. bd.; partner firm Reasoner Davis & Vinson (and predecessor firm), Washington, 1950—; gen. counsel Resources for Future, George Washington U.; counsel, dir. Acacia Mut. Life Ins. Co.; past pres. Washington Bd. Trade, 1965-66; gen. counsel, dir. Flakt Inc., Parsons Paper Co. Author: History of Trust Business for District of Columbia, 1950. Bd. dirs., pres. Met. Boys Club of Washington; Bd. dirs. Boys Club Am.; Chmn. Citizens Joint com. on Nat. Representation for D.C. Served to lt. USNR, 1942-46. Recipient Washingtonian award Jr. C. of C., 1954, Civic award Alpha Kappa Psi, 1960, Distinguished Service award Cosmopolitan Club, 1961. Mem. Soc. Friendly Sons of St. Patrick, Omicron Delta Kappa. Clubs: Metropolitan, Army and Navy, Chevy Chase Country, Columbia Country, Burning Tree, Kiwanis (Washington). Home: 2301 California St NW Washington DC 20008 Office: 888 17th St NW Washington DC 20006

DAVIS, FRANK TRADEWELL, JR., lawyer; b. Atlanta, Feb. 2, 1938; s. Frank T. and Sue (Burnett) D.; m. Winifred Storey, June 23, 1961; children: Frank, Frederick, Gordon. A.B., Princeton U., 1960; J.D., George Washington U., 1963; LL.M., Harvard U., 1964. Bar: Ga. 1963, U.S. Ct. Appeals (5th cir.) 1963, D.C. 1966, U.S. Supreme Ct. 1968, U.S. Ct. Appeals (11th cir.) 1982. Assoc. Hansell, Post Brandon & Dorsey, Atlanta, 1964-67; ptnr. Hansell & Post, Atlanta, 1968-77, 79—; mng. ptnr., gen. counsel Pres.'s Reorgn. Project office of Pres., 1977-79; vis. instr. U. Ga. Law Sch., 1964-66. Author: Business Acquisitions, 1977, (2d edit.) Business Acquisitions, 1982; contbr. articles to legal jours. Bd. dirs. Nat. Inst. Justice, 1980-81, Westminster Schs., 1969—; chmn. bd. dirs. Westminster Schs., 1984—; sr. warden All Saints' Episcopal Ch., 1982; bd. dirs. Va. Sem., 1980—; mem. Atlanta Charter Commn.; chmn. Atlanta Crime Commn., 1979. Served to lt. USNR, 1960-62. Mem. Am. Law Inst., Atlanta C. of C. (bd. dirs. 1975-77). Democrat. Clubs: Piedmont Driving (Atlanta); Chevy Chase (Md.). Home: 3229 Chateau Ct NW Atlanta GA 30305 Office: 3300 First Atlanta Tower Atlanta GA 30383

DAVIS, FREDERICK TOWNSEND, lawyer; b. Danbury, Conn., Dec. 28, 1945; s. Wendell and Lavinia (Riker) D.; m. Mary McGowan, June 8, 1968; children: Samuel, Benjamin, Eliza. B.A., Harvard U., 1967; J.D., Columbia U., 1972. Bar: N.Y. 1974, U.S. Dist. Ct. (so. dist.) N.Y. 1974, U.S. Ct. Appeals (2d cir.) 1974, U.S. Dist. Ct. (ea. dist.) Wis. 1979, Mass. 1980, U.S. Supreme Ct. 1981, U.S. Ct. Appeals (3d cir.) 1982, U.S. Dist. Ct. (ea. dist.) 1983. Law clk. to chief judge U.S. Ct. Appeals (2d cir.), 1972-73, U.S. Supreme Ct., 1973-74; asst. U.S. atty chief appellant atty. So. Dist. N.Y., 1974-78; assoc. Patterson, Belknap, Webb & Tyler, N.Y.C., 1978-80, ptnr., 1980—; bd. dirs. N.Y. Correctional Assn. Mem. Am. Law Inst., ABA (antitrust sect. 1980), N.Y.C. Bar Assn. (mem. criminal cts. com., fed. legislation com.). Club: Century Assn. (N.Y.C.). Office: Patterson Belknap Webb & Tyler 30 Rockefeller Plaza New York NY 10112

DAVIS, GALE ELWOOD, insurance company executive; b. Omaha, July 18, 1909; s. Stanley A. and Frances Mary (Evans) D.; m. Margaret Nell Lavelle, Nov. 30, 1933; children—Stanley L., Sally K., Molly F. LL.B., U. Nebr., 1931. Bar: Neb. 1931. With Mut. Omaha Ins. Co., 1932-65, v.p., 1950-59, exec. v.p., 1959-65; pres. United of Omaha Life Ins. Co., 1965-75, dir., 1959—; now mgr. Variable Fund B; dir. 1st Fed. Savs. & Loan Assn. Omaha.; Mem. pres.'s council Creighton U., Omaha. Trustee, dir. Clarkson Hosp.; trustee, past pres. Omaha Home for Boys; trustee, dir. U. Nebr. Found.; bd. dirs. Dr. C.C. and Mabel L. Criss Found. Mem. Omaha C. of C. (past dir.), Am., Nebr. bar assns., Delta Upsilon, Phi Delta Phi. Clubs: Mason (Shriner, Jester), Omaha, Omaha Country, Omaha Press; Nat. Lawyers (Washington); Garden of Gods (Colorado Springs, Colo.); Royal Poinciana Golf (Naples, Fla.); Plaza. Home: 939 S 106th Plaza Apt 201 Omaha NE 68114 Office: 3301 Dodge St Omaha NE 68131

DAVIS, GENE BERNARD, artist; b. Washington, Aug. 22, 1920; s. Arthur G. and Edna Mae (Stout) D.; m. Florence Elizabeth Coulson, Nov. 24, 1960. Student, U. Md., 1938-39, Wilson Tchrs. Coll., Washington, 1939-41. Asst. prof. Corcoran Gallery Art Sch. Painting, Washington; instr. painting and drawing Am. U., 1968-69; artist-in-residence Skidmore Coll., N.Y., summer 1969, U. Va., 1972. One man shows, Corcoran Gallery Art, 1964, 68, 70, 78, MIT, 1966, Hofstra U., San Francisco Mus. Art, 1968, Washington Gallery Modern Art, Jewish Mus., Walker Art Center, 1978, Bklyn. Mus., 1982, Carnegie-Mellon Mus., Pitts., 1983; group shows, Chgo. Art Inst., Los Angeles County Mus., Detroit Mus. Fine Arts, Brandeis U. Mus., Mus. Modern Art, Buenos Aires, Mus. Modern Art, Rio de Janeiro, Art Gallery of Toronto, Can., Munson-William-Proctor Inst., Utica, N.Y., Corcoran Gallery of Art, Washington, Walker Art Center, Mpls., Isaac Delgado Mus., New Orleans, Atlanta Art Assn., Mus. Modern Art, 1966, San Francisco Mus. Art, U.S. Embassies Art Program, White House Art Program, Los Angeles Country Mus., 1964, Whitney Mus., 1967, 69, 71. Recipient Bronze medal Corcoran Gallery Biennial Am. Painting, 1965; grant for contbn. to Am. art Nat. Council on Arts, 1967; Guggenheim fellow, 1974-75. Address: 4120 Harrison St NW Washington DC 20015

DAVIS, GENE CARLTON, lawyer; b. Chgo., June 15, 1917; s. Carl DeWitt and Alta (Hoff) D.; m. Roberta Wilson, Mar. 14, 1942; children: Bruce Carlton, Barbara Jean. A.B., U. Chgo., 1938; LL.B., Chgo. Kent Coll. Law, 1941. Bar: Ill. 1942. Practiced in, Chgo., 1942-79; with firm Isham, Lincoln & Beale, 1943-79, partner, 1953-79; individual practice law, Woodstock, Ill., 1979-82; mem. firm Davis & Holmes, Woodstock, Ill., 1982—; dir. So. Nev. Telephone Co., 1956-60, Parker Aleshire & Co., 1962-83. Author: Estate Planning A Client's Handbook, 1967. Trustee Orchestral Assn. Chgo., v.p., 1972-76. Served with AUS, 1942-43. Fellow Am. Coll. Probate Counsel; mem. ABA, Ill. Bar Assn., McHenry County Bar Assn., Chgo. Bar Assn. (chmn. admissions com. 1955, entertainment com. 1952, probate com. 1962). Presbyterian. Clubs: Law, Legal (pres. 1965), Saddle and Cycle, Union League (Chgo.); Racquet. Home: 3400 Raycraft Rd Woodstock IL 60098 Office: 666 Russel Ct Woodstock IL 60098

DAVIS, GEORGE ALFRED, financial executive; b. Montclair, N.J., Feb. 26, 1928; s. Robert Greener and Ruth (Conroy) D.; m. Maria Nekos, June 30, 1956; children—Stephen Greener, Carol Elizabeth, Leslie Ann. A.B. cum laude, Dartmouth Coll., 1952; M.B.A. with distinction, Amos Tuck Sch., 1953. C.P.A., N.J. Accountant Arthur Andersen & Co., N.Y.C., 1953-59; with Thomas J. Lipton, Inc., 1960-72, controller, 1965-72, Good Humor Corp., Continenal Foods, Inc., Good Humor Food Service, Inc., 1965-72; treas. C.R. Bard, Inc., Murray Hill, N.J., 1972-78, v.p., treas., from 1978, now v.p. fin., chief fin. officer. Mem. corps. com. Fairleigh Dickinson U.; Trustee, v.p. Tenafly Community Chest, 1969-71; trustee, treas. Mary Fischer Home, Tenafly, N.J. Served with AUS, 1946-48. Mem. Am. Inst. C.P.A.'s, Fin. Execs. Inst., Nat. Assn. Accts., N.J. Soc. C.P.A.s. Episcopalian (vestryman, treas. 1966-68). Clubs: Knickerbocker Country (Tenafly) (trustee 1978-80); Treasurers; Knickerbocker Country (Tenafly) (sec. 1979, v.p. 1980), Dartmouth of Bergen County (trustee, treas. 1965-68). Home: 144 Highwood Ave Tenafly NJ 07670 Office: 731 Central Ave Murray Hill NJ 07974

DAVIS, GEORGE DONALD, consultant, government official; b. Oneida, N.Y., Nov. 19, 1942; s. Pearl Floyd and Kathrine Virginia (Connolly) D.; m. Anita Face Riner, June 26, 1976; children: Maria Lisa, Brett Hollis, Sarah Bessie, Lara Emily; stepchildren: Andrea G. Riner, Joel S. Riner. B.S. in Forestry, SUNY, 1964; postgrad., Cornell U. Forester, pub. land adminstr. U.S. Forest Service, Dept. Agr., Colo., 1964-68; ecologist Gov. N.Y. State Temp. Study Commn. on Future of Adirondacks, 1969-71; pvt. land use and natural resources cons., Ithaca, N.Y., 1971; dir. planning Adirondack Park Agy., Ray Brook, N.Y., 1971-76; exec. dir. Wilderness Soc., Washington, 1976-77; spl. asst. U.S. Forest Service, Washington, 1977-79; dep. forest supr. Idaho Panhandle Nat. Forests, Coeur d'Alene, 1979-82; land use, natural resource cons. Wadhams, N.Y., 1982—; exec. dir. Adirondack Council, 1983—; spl. asst. U.S. Forest Service, 1982—; exec. dir. Adirondack Land Trust, 1984—; mem. environ. agenda task force Rockefeller Bros. Fund; mem. Hudson Basin project task force Rockefeller Found.; bd. dirs. N. Am. Loon Fund; bd. advisers Lake Champlain Com. Co-author: The Unfinished Agenda, 1977; Contbr. to profl. publs. Mem. Explorers Club. Roman Catholic. Home: Chevre Hill Farm Wadhams NY 12990 Office: Box D-2 Elizabethtown NY 12932 *The basic goal of my life has been to promote land and natural resource stewardship, through direct action and example, to help insure that our planet's resources are more equitably distributed among members of the present generation and are sufficient for future generations.*

DAVIS, GEORGE HOLMES, investment banker; b. Little Rock, Feb. 3, 1936; s. LaVonne Emerson D.; m. Irene Winnie Curtis, June 1960; children: George Holmes, Wallas Scott, Laura Emerson. B.A., Vanderbilt U., 1957. Exec. v.p. Dabbs, Sullivan, Trulock, Little Rock, 1959-70; sr. v.p. Stephens Inc., Little Rock, 1970—; dir. Dixie Current Mfg. Co., Little Rock, Stephens Fin. Ltd., Hong Kong. Bd. dirs. Easter Seal Rehab. Ctr., Little Rock. Served to lt. (j.g.) USN, 1957-59. Presbyterian. Office: Stephens Inc 114 E Capitol Ave Little Rock AR 72201 *

DAVIS, GEORGE KELSO, nutrition biochemist, educator; b. Pitts., July 2, 1910; s. Ross Irwin and Jennie (Kelso) D.; m. Ruthanna Wood, Jan. 25, 1936; children—Dorothy Jeanne (Mrs. Arthur C. Aikin, Jr.), Mary Ellen (Mrs. W. Edgar Benedict), Ruthanna Marie (Mrs. Donald W. Davidson), Virginia Kay (Mrs. John M. Fedison), Robert Wyatt, George William. B.S., Pa. State U., 1932; Ph.D., Cornell U., 1937. Research asst. Cornell U., 1932-37; research asst. prof. chemistry Mich. State U., 1937-42; prof. nutrition, animal nutritionist U. Fla., Gainesville, 1942-79, prof. emeritus, 1979—, dir. nuclear scis., 1960-65, dir. biol. scis., 1965-70, dir. research, 1970-75; Mem. Fla. Nuclear Commn.; chmn. Internat. Biol. Program Sect. Use and Mgmt. Biol. Resources, U. Fla. Council Oak Ridge Asso. Univs.; cons. minister agr., Costa Rica, univs. Costa Rica, Buenos Aires, San Marco, Peru, U. Agraria, Sao Paulo, Brazil, FAO, Dept. Agr., OEA-INTA, Argentina, Dept. Health, Edn. and Welfare, Nutrition Found., Fla. Dept. Agr.; mem. food and nutrition bd., com. animal nutrition, internat. biol. program com. Nat. Acad. Sci.-NRC, also chmn. bd. agr. and renewable resources, 1980-82; dir. human nutrition research grants program U.S. Dept. Agr., 1977-79; rev. bds. NSF, Nat. Acad. Scis.,

NIH; U. Fla. Faculty lectr., 1960; hon. prof. U. Chile, 1961—; Wellcome vis. prof. U. Ill., 1978; pres. Nat. Nutritional Consortium, 1977-78. Mem. editorial bd.: Jour. Animal Sci; Contbr. articles to profl. jours., chpts. books. Recipient Faculty award Fla. Blue Key, 1958, Disting. Faculty award U. Fla., 1960. Fellow Am. Inst. Nutrition (chmn. com. nutrition and trace elements 1961—, nat. exec. com. jour. 1961, Borden award 1964, mem. council 1971-74, pres. 1975-76); mem. Am. Inst. Biol. Scis. (chmn. S.E. regional council biol. satellite programs 1965—), Am. Chem. Soc. (sec.-treas. Fla. 1955, chmn. 1958, Fla. award 1956, Kenneth A. Spencer award 1980), Am. Soc. Animal Sci. (nat. v.p. 1961-62, sec. So. sect. 1960-61), A.A.A.S., Am. Soc. Biol. Chemists, Soc. Exptl. Biology and Medicine, Am. Dairy Assn., Am. Nuclear Soc., Soc. for Environ. Geochemistry and Health (pres. 1976-77), Fedn. Am. Socs. Exptl. Biology (chmn. pub. affairs com. 1975-77), Nat. Acad. Scis., Internat. Union Nutrition Scis. (chmn. U.S. nat. com., pres. XII Internat. Nutrition Congress), Sigma Xi (pres. Fla. 1956-57), Alpha Zeta, Phi Lambda Upsilon, Gamma Sigma Delta, Phi Eta Sigma, Phi Sigma, Gamma Sigma Epsilon, Blue Key; hon. mem. Sao Paulo Vet. Soc., Peruvian Vet. Assn. Home: 2903 SW 2d Ct Gainesville FL 32601

DAVIS, GEORGE LINN, banker; b. Des Moines, July 9, 1934; s. James Cox and Elizabeth (Linn) D.; m. Anne Roberts, May 1955 (div. Jan. 1967); children: James, Elliott, George Linn; m. Mary Elizabeth Graham, Apr. 27, 1968; children: Stephen, Thomas. B.A., Yale U., 1956; M.B.A., Harvard U., 1958. Sr. v.p. Citibank NA, N.Y.C., 1958-81; exec. v.p. First Chgo. Corp., Chgo., 1981. Mem. Res. City Bankers Assn., Robert Morris Assocs., Assn. Equipment Lessors (dir. 1974-76). Republican. Clubs: Chicago, Glenview. Office: 1st National Bank Chgo One 1st National Plaza Chicago IL 60670

DAVIS, GEORGE M., corporate executive. Pres., dir. Flint Industries, Inc. Office: PO Box 490 Tulsa OK 73101§

DAVIS, GEORGE WILMOT, naval officer; b. Columbia, S.C., May 29, 1933; s. George Wilmot and Susan (Hayne) D.; m. Jean Carroll, Aug. 16, 1957; children: Geroge W., Susan H., Robert D. B.S., U.S. Naval Acad., 1955; M.S. in E.E., U.S. Navy Postgrad. Sch., 1963. Commd. ensign U.S. Navy, 1955, advanced through grades to rear adm., 1981; comdg. officer nuclear cruiser, 1974-78, instr., Idaho Falls, Idaho, 1978-80; logistics NATO, Naples, Italy, 1980-81; dep. comdr. surface ships Naval Sea System Command, Washington, 1981—. Republican. Episcopalian. Home: 4912 Woodland Way Annandale VA 22003 Office: Naval Sea System Command Washington DC 20361

DAVIS, GINIA, singer, association executive; b. Phila., Mar. 10, 1923; d. Meyer and Hilda (Emery) D.; m. Morris M. Wexler, Oct. 1968. Student drama, Carnegie Inst. Tech., 1939-41; vocal pupil, Frances Lewando, Doris Monteux, 1939-50; coached with, Povla Frijsh, Pierre Monteux, Queena Mario, Pablo Casals, Madeleine Grey. Voice tchr. Mich. State U., East Lansing, 1962; dir. Hancock County Chamber Music Soc. (now Hancock County Friends of Arts), East Sullivan, Maine, 1962—. Performed as Polly Peachum in: The Beggar's Opera, 1941, Bar Harbor (Maine) Stock Co., Chautauqua, N.Y. Bucks County Playhouse; leading roles New Moon, Toledo Light Opera Co., 1945; appeared: on Broadway in Susan and God, 1942, Call Me Mister, 1946; made: operatic debut as Gretel in Hansel and Gretel with, Pitts. Opera Soc., 1943; ann. recital, N.Y.C., 1948-65; toured, U.S.A., 1947—, Europe, 1949, 50; appeared at, Holland Festival, 1950; in: 1st U.S. performances of Flaminio of Pergolesi, 1953; with, Royal Opera of Brussels, 1955, broadcasts, U.S., Europe; appeared with symphony orch., U.S., Europe, Middle-East, 1955—; made six months world tour, Africa, Asia, 1966, guitar concerts, 1965; dir. performing arts for children series, Hancock County Auditorium, 1976—, high sch. touring program, 1980—, recs. songs, Music Library Records, Inc., folk music div., Library of Congress; appearances Am. Folksong Festival; adviser folk music, Nat Arts Found.; authority on folksongs; collecter, transcriber, interpreter: (with Jean Thomas) folklore Ky. mountains (the Traipsin' Woman), 1950—; also other nations.; entertainer, Armed Forces, U.S., Europe. (Recipient grand prize Internat. contest interpretation French song 1958). Chmn. Sullivan (Me.) Conservation Commn., 1973—. Developer unique recital program Portraits in Song, 1947. Home: The Farmstead Gouldsboro ME 04607 also 3850 Galt Ocean Dr Fort Lauderdale FL 33308

DAVIS, GLENN ROBERT, lawyer, former congressman; b. Vernon, Wis., Oct. 28, 1914; s. Charles W. and Jennie (Wachendorf) D.; m. Kathryn J. McFarlane, Nov. 29, 1942; children—Kathleen, Margaret, James, Janet, Elizabeth. B. Edn., U. Wis.-Platteville, 1934; J.D., U. Wis.-Madison, 1940. Bar: Wis. bar 1940. Practiced in, Waukesha, 12 yrs; mem. firm Love, Davis & McGraw, 1957-64; mem. Wis. Assembly from Waukesha County, 1941-42, 80th-84th Congresses 2d Dist. Wis., 89th-93rd Congresses 9th Dist. Wis.; Pres., dir. New Berlin State Bank, 1959-65; cons. Potter Internat., Inc., Washington. Served with USNR, 1942-45. Named one of ten outstanding young men U.S. Jr. C. of C., 1947. Mem. Order of Coif. Clubs: Mason (Shriner), Kiwanian.). Home: 2729 S Grove St Arlington VA 22202

DAVIS, GORDON ALAN, museum administrator, educator; b. Wichita, Kans., Sept. 2, 1944; s. E.E. and Lucy (Graves) D.; m. Julanne McCarthy, Aug. 15, 1973. B.A., Wichita State U., 1966, M.A., 1969; M.S., Ind. U., 1971, M.A., 1971, Ed.D., 1973; cert. Mus. Mgmt. Inst., 1981; musems in edn. cert., Brit. Council, Commonwealth Inst., London, 1982. Research asst. Ind. U. Mus., Bloomington, 1970-73; dir. Salmon Ruins Archaeol. Research Ctr., Bloomfield, N. Mex., 1974, Mus. Man, Wichita State U., 1974-81; coordinator mus. Wichita Pub. Schs., 1975-82; dir. univ. musums Ill. State U., Normal, 1982—; pres. bd. Skinner-Lee Victorian House Mus., Wichita, 1982; chmn. Wichita Hist. Landmark Preservation Com., 1982. Recipient Courant award Nat. Mus. Art, Smithsonian Instrn., 1972-74, Award of merit Wichita Hist. Landmark Preservation Com., 1980, Wichita Preservation Alliance award, 1981; Nat. Trust Hist.Preservation scholar, 1979. Mem. Kans. Preservation Alliance (V.P. 1980-81, dir. 1979-82), Mountain Plains Mus. Assn. (v.p. 1980-81), Kans. Mus. Assn. (pres. 1981-82). Office: Univ Mueums Ill State U Normal IL 16716

DAVIS, GORDON RICHARD FUERST, research scientist; b. Prince Albert, Sask., Can., Apr. 5, 1925; s. Louis James D. and Nora Sylvia (Davis); m. Marie Berengere Pauline Berube, May 25, 1949; children: Joseph Richard Kevin, Marie Melanie Elise, Marie Raymonde Joceline, Marie-Therese Danielle. B.Sc. in Zoology with honors, McGill U., 1948, M.Sc., 1949, Ph.D., 1952. Agrl. scientist biol. control unit Can. Dept. Agr., Que., 1948-52, research officer research br., Saskatoon, Sask., 1952-65, research scientist research br., 1965—; mem. Div. III sci. curriculum com. Sask. Dept. Edn., 1974-80. Contbr. articles to profl. jours. Bd. trustees Sask. Catholic Bd. Edn., 1974-77. Served with Royal Can. Navy Vol. Res., 1944-45. Carpenter Teaching fellow, 1950-51. Mem. Nutrition Soc. Can. (sec. 1973-77, v.p. 1979-80, pres. 1980-81), Can. Fedn. Biol. Socs. (dir. 1973-77, 80-81, hon. sec.-treas. 1980—). Amglican. Home: 228 Campion Crescent Saskatoon SK Canada S7H 3T9 Office: Can Fedn Biol Scis 118 Veterinary Rd Saskatoon SK Canada S7N 2R4

DAVIS, HAMILTON SEYMOUR, anesthesiologist, educator; b. Pitts., Oct. 28, 1920; s. Karl Eugene and Vassie Sophia (Miller) D.; m. Marjorie Jean Wright, July 5, 1946; children: Eric Templeton, Scott Harold, Kim Elizabeth, Christopher Quay. A.B. cum laude, Colgate U., 1942; M.D., Western Res. U., 1945. Bar: Diplomate Am. Bd. Anesthesiology. Intern Grassland Hosp., Valhalla, N.Y., 1945-46, resident anesthesiology, 1948-50; asso. anesthesiologist VA Hosp.; also temporary chmn. dept. anesthesiology St. Mary's Hosp., Grand Junction, Colo., 1950-51; mem. faculty Western Res. U. Sch. Medicine, 1952-66, prof. anesthesiology, 1961-66; dir. dept. anesthesia Lakeside Hosp., 1953-66; attending anesthesiologist Met. Gen. Hosp., 1953-66; formerly cons. Cleve. VA Hosp., Lake County Meml. Hosp.; team physician Kenston Sch. Dist., 1957-66; mem. jet injection immunization programs, Cleve., 1955-66; prof. anesthesiology U. Calif. at Davis Sch. Medicine, 1966—, chmn. dept., 1966-79, 81-83; dir. dept. anesthesia U. Calif. at Davis-Sacramento Med. Center, 1966-79, chief of staff, 1976-77. Editor: Jour. Anesthesiology, 1965-71; Contbr. numerous articles in field to profl. jours. Camp physician Golden Empire council Boy Scouts Am., 1967-69; Pres. bd. dirs. Chagrin Falls Park Community Center, 1960-66; v.p. Geauga County Econ. Opportunities Council, 1966; founder, bd. dirs. Chagrin Falls Park Well-Baby Clinic, 1959-66. Served to capt. M.C. AUS, 1946-48. Mem. Am., Ohio, Cuyahoga County med. assns., Cleve. Acad. Medicine (pres. sect. anesthesiology 1957), Am. Standards Assn. (chmn. com z-79 1956-63, vice chmn. 1963-66), Am. Soc. Anesthesiologists (chmn. com. standardization and equipment 1956-63), Ohio Soc. Anesthesiologists, Cleve. Soc. Anesthesiologists (pres. 1956), Internat. Anesthesia Research Soc., Am. Coll. Anesthesiologists (bd. govs.), Assn. Univ. Anesthetists, Soc. Acad. Anesthesia Chairmen, Royal Soc. Medicine, Cal. Med. Soc. (sec. 1967, vice chmn. 1968, chmn. 1969, anesthesiology sect.), Yolo County Sacramento med. socs., Cal. Soc. Anesthesiologists. Home: 720 Peach Pl Davis CA 95616

DAVIS, HAROLD EUGENE, historian, educator; b. Girard, Ohio, Dec. 3, 1902; s. Henry E. and Katherine (Zeller) D.; m. Audrey Hennen, Aug. 31, 1929; 1 dau., Barbara Lee. A.B., Hiram (Ohio) Coll., 1924; A.M., U. Chgo., 1927; Ph.D., Case-Western Res. U., 1933. Prof. history, polit. sci. Hiram Coll., 1927-47, dean adminstrn., 1944-47; dir. div. edn. and tchr. aids (Office Inter-Am. Affairs), 1943-45; instr. Latin-Am. history Am.-Army U., Biarritz, France, 1945-46; organizer (Washington Semester program with cooperating colls. and univs.), 1947; prof. history and govt., chmn. div. social studies Am. U., Washington, 1947-59, prof. Latin Am. history, govt., 1959-63, Univ. prof. Latin Am. Studies, 1963-73, dean Coll. Arts and Scis., 1952-57, univ. prof. emeritus, 1973—; lectr., cons. Washington Internat Sch., 1975-76; lectr. U. Md., 1974-76; Lectr. (Washington Internat. Center); cons. Cin. Council on World Affairs Faculty Enrichment Program Latin Am. with cooperating colls., 1969-71, U.S. Armed Forces Inst.; Fulbright lectr. U. Chile, 1958-59; vis. prof. U. Mexico, 1962, India Sch. Internat. Studies, New Delhi, 1965-66; lectr. Inter-Am. Def. Coll., Nat. War Coll., Army War Coll., Fgn. Service Inst., Def. Intelligence Agy.; Mem. Internat. team observers Dominican Republic elections, 1962; mem. Gov.'s Commn. on History Ohio, World War II. Author: Makers of Democracy in Latin America, 1945, 68, Origins and Consequences of World War II, (with others), 1948, Latin American Leaders, 1949, 68, Social Science Trends in Latin America, 1950, The Americas in History, 1953, (with others) Contemporary Social Science, 1953, Development of Historiography, 1954, Development of Social Thought in Latin America, 1956, Government and Politics in Latin America, 1958, Material and Spiritual Factors in American History, 1958, Latin American Social Thought, 1961, 63, 66, The United States in History, 1968, (with Harold Durfee) The Study of Philosophy in the United States, 1964, Os Estados Unidos na História, 1966, Los Estados Unidos en la historia, 1967, History of Latin America, 1968, Points of Focus-Latin America, 1970, Hinsdale of Hiram, 1971, Latin American Thought—A Historical Introduction, 1972, 73, Report of Conference on Latin American Thought, 1972, Revolutionaries, Traditionalists and Dictators in Latin America, 1973, (with Larman Wilson and others) Latin American Foreign Policies, 1975, The Judaic-Christian View of History, 1976, (with J. Finan and F.T. Peck) Latin American Diplomatic History, 1977, Selected Poems, 1978, 150 Years of The American Peace Society, 1978, (with others) Homenaje a Luis Alberto Sánchez, 1981, Notes for a Dictionary of Ohio Indian Place Names, 1979, Homenaje a Luis Recasens Siches, 1982; editor: Inter-American Conferences, 1826-1954 (S.G. Inman), 1965, Autobiobliography, 1981, History and Power, 1983; contbr. to: Brit. encys. Americana; yearbooks Biog. Dictionary Internationalists; profl. jours.; Cons.: New Jefferson Ency; chmn. bd. editors: World Affairs. Decorated Order of Colón Dominican Republic; recipient Disting. Service award Ohio Acad. History, 1978, Inter-Am. Council, 1978. Fellow Garfield Soc. Hiram; mem. Instituto Indigenista Interamericano, Am. Hist. Assn., Latin Am. Studies Assn., Am. Polit. Sci. Assn., Instituto de Historia del Derecho Ricardo Levene (Argentina, corr.), Instituto Histórico y Geográfico del Uruguay (corr.), Omicron Delta Kappa, Phi Alpha Delta, Phi Kappa Phi, Phi Sigma Alpha, Phi Alpha Theta. Mem. Disciples Christ Ch. Club: Cosmos (Washington). Home: 4842 Langdrum Ln Chevy Chase MD 20815 Office: Dept History Am U Washington DC 20016

DAVIS, HAROLD FENIMORE, public relations executive; b. N.Y.C., May 17, 1916; s. Eddie and Anna (Tannenbaum) D.; m. Evelyn R. Leach, Apr. 6, 1941; children: Kenneth Edwin, Richard Paul, Marcy Ellen. Grad. high sch. News and publ. mgr. CBS, 1935-39; publ. and promotion mgr. Columbia Records, 1940-41; partner Davis-Lieber, 1941-42; v.p., promotion dir., dir. Kenyon & Eckhardt, Inc., 1945-56; v.p., asst. to pres., asst. to chmn., mgmt. supr. Grey Advt., Inc., 1956-68; pres. Grey & Davis, N.Y.C., 1968-79, Hal Davis & Assos., 1979—; lectr. N.Y. U. New Sch. Creator, producer: How to Form a Rock Group, 1968; producer: London Records. Trustee Brandeis U. Served with USNR, 1942-45. Mem. Pub. Relations Soc. Am. Clubs: Friars, Jazz of Sarasota (pres. 1980—). Home: 1529 Pelican Point Dr Pelican Cove Sarasota FL 33581

DAVIS, HAROLD L., psychoanalyst, editor; b. Phila.; m. Eleanor Morin; two children. B.S. in Physics, Carnegie-Mellon U., 1949; Ph.D. in Exptl. Physics, Cornell U., 1954. Formerly analytical physicist Pratt and Whitney Aircraft Co.; adj. asst. prof. Rensselaer Poly. Inst. Hartford (Conn.) Grad. Center; adj. prof. Union Grad. Sch.; faculty Center Modern Psychoanalytic Studies.; Chmn. Joint Council Mental Health Services.; Vice pres. Nat. Accreditation Assn. for Psychoanalysis. Asso. editor: Nucleonics mag, 1957-64; mag. editor, 1964-66; sr. editor: Scientific Research, 1966-69; editor: Physics Today, 1969—; Mem. editorial bd.: Modern Psychoanalysis, Psychoanalytic Rev. Served with AUS., World War II. Mem. Nat. Psychol. Assn. Psychoanalysis (dir., chmn. legislative com.), Am. Phys. Soc., N.Y. Acad. Scis., Am. Soc. Cybernetics, Sigma Xi, Gamma Alpha. Address: 3 Rutherford Pl New York NY 10003

DAVIS, HAROLD TRUSCOTT, lawyer; b. Worcester, Mass., June 15, 1895; s. Charles Francis and Eva Leolen (Truscott) D.; m. Ruth M. Lent, Oct. 26, 1956; 1 dau. (by previous marriage), Eleanor Davis Claff. A.B. magna cum laude, Harvard U., 1918, J.D., 1921. Bar: Mass. 1921. Since practiced in, Boston; partner firm Nutter, McClennen & Fish, 1930-76, of counsel, 1977—; counsel, Town of Hingham, Mass., 1955-74; dir. Carter Family Corp., EPP Corp.; dir. emeritus Hollingsworth & Vose Co.; past dir. other corps. Former corporator New Eng. Bapt. Hosp.; trustee, treas. Eliot A. Carter Found.; trustee Hingham Pub. Library, High St. Cemetery; clk. Olive Higgins Prouty Found.; hon. mem. Dean Found. Little Children. Fellow Am. Coll. Probate Counsel; mem. Am. Judicature Soc., Am.. Mass., Boston bar assns., Phi Beta Kappa, Alpha Sigma Phi. Republican. Congregationalist. Clubs: Union, Harvard (Boston); Hingham Yacht, Harvard (Hingham). Home: Bare Cove Ln Hingham MA 02043 Office: 600 Atlantic Ave Boston MA 02210

DAVIS, HARRY, cons. engr.; b. N.Y.C., Dec. 2, 1909; s. Joseph and Annie (Goldner) D.; m. Fay Oxhorn, 1931. B.S., Coll. City N.Y., 1931, E.E., 1933; M.E.E., Poly. Inst. Bklyn., 1948, Sc.D., 1973. Project engr. design and devel. meteorol. direction finders Signal Corps, sect. chief in charge devel. nav. systems, 1940-45; in charge devel. nav. equipment Air Force Watson Lab., 1945-50; chief (Nav. Lab.), 1949-51; tech. and sci. dir. Rome Air Devel. Center, 1951-60; dep. for research asst. sec. Air Force, Washington, 1960-66, dep. asst. sec. research and devel., 1966-68; dep. under sec. systems rev. Office Under Sec. Air Force, 1968-73; pres. Systems Rev. Assos., Inc., Arlington, Va., 1973—; Lectr. U. Cal. at Los Angeles, 1966-75; faculty elec. engring. staff Columbia, 1956—; mem. sci. adv. com. Harry Diamond Labs., US Army; mem., chmn. panels Def. Dept. Recipient George W. Goddard award Soc. Photog. Instrumentation Engrs., 1969; citation of honor Air Force Assn., 1969; named Man of Year award Hap Arnold chpt., 1970; Distinguished Alumni award Poly. Inst. Bklyn., 1973. Fellow IEEE (Harry Diamond Meml. award 1968, Man of Yr. award 1976), Am. Optical Soc., AAAS; mem. Am. Ordnance Assn., Am. Phys. Soc., Sigma Xi. Patentee communications and missile guidance, radar for def. against ballistic missiles. Home: 3536 Pinetree Terrace Falls Church VA 22041 Office: 1901 N Ft Myer Dr Arlington VA 22209

DAVIS, HARRY FLOYD, educator; b. Colby, Kans., Oct. 2, 1925; s. Leo Lloyd and Edna Mae (Miars) D.; m. Myrna Joan MacPhie, Sept. 9, 1961; children—Harry Floyd, Kenneth Hugh. B.S., Mass. Inst. Tech., 1948, M.S., 1953, Ph.D., 1954. Faculty U. B.C., 1955-58, Royal Mil. Coll. of Can., 1958-61; prof. U. Waterloo, Ont., Can., 1961—. Author: Introduction to Vector Analysis, 1960, Fourier Series and Orthogonal Functions, 1963. Served with USNR, 1944-46. Mem. Canadian Math. Congress, Am. Math. Assn., Soc. for Indsl. and Applied Math., Sigma Xi, Beta Theta Pi. Home: 355 Pommel Gate Cres Waterloo ON N2L 5X7 Canada

DAVIS, HARRY REX, educator; b. Ozona, Tex., Nov. 9, 1921; s. Rex Odice and Mima (Gowin) D.; m. Ruth Elizabeth Greenlee, Sept. 6, 1947; children—Peter Gowin, Scott Andrew, Martha Greenlee. B.A. summa cum laude, Tex. Christian U., 1942; A.M., U. Chgo., 1949, Ph.D., 1951; postdoctorate, Union Theol. Sem., 1952-53. Teaching fellow Tex. Christian U., 1945-46; mem. faculty dept. govt. Beloit (Wis.) Coll., 1948—, asso. prof., 1956-59, prof., chmn. dept., 1959—; Cons. ch. and soc. dept. World Council Chs., 1969. Author: (with others) Small City Government, 1962, Colleges and Commitments, 1971; Editor: Reinhold Niebuhr on Politics, 1960. Mem. Beloit City Council, 1959-60; chmn. Beloit Democratic Com., 1956, 61-63; mgr. campaigns Congl. candidates. Served with USAAF, 1942-45. Ford faculty fellow, 1952-53; Social Sci. Research Council grantee; Rockefeller Found. grantee. Mem. Midwest Polit. Sci. Assn. (sec.-treas. 1959-65, mem. exec. council 1966-68), Am. Polit. Sci. Assn. (chmn. Burdette award com. 1979), Am. Soc. Polit. and Legal Philosophy, Soc. Christian Ethics. Democrat. Presbyn. (elder, council on ch. and society 1965-72). Home: 735 Harrison Ave Beloit WI 53511 Office: Beloit Coll Beloit WI 53511

DAVIS, HARTWELL, lawyer; b. Auburn, Ala., Dec. 18, 1906; s. Christopher Hartwell and Elizabeth Myrick (Dowdell) D.; m. Elizabeth Mardre, Feb. 24, 1933; children—Hartwell, Letitia Dowdell Davis Hamill. Student, U. Fla., 1923-24; B.S., Auburn U., 1928; postgrad. (Woodrow Wilson Meml. scholar), U. Va. Law Sch., 1929-30; J.D., Emory U., 1931. Bar: Ga., Ala., Fla. bars 1931. Clk. Bradenton Bank & Trust Co., Fla., 1924-25; since practiced at, Opelika and Montgomery, Ala; asst. U.S. atty. Middle Dist. Ala., 1932-51, U.S. atty., 1953-62; city atty., Montgomery, 1951-53, spl. asst. atty. gen., Ala., 1964-71. Del. S.E. jurisdictional confs. Meth. Ch., 1948, 52, 56; mem. Meth. Gen. Bd. Evangelism, 1952-56; sec.-treas. Meth. Ala. Conf. Bd. Lay Activities, 1945-60; Pres. Montgomery YMCA, 1939-40, dir., 1935-57; chmn. Ct. of Honor, Tuckabatchee area Boy Scouts Am., 1951-52, chmn. merit badge com., 1953; Trustee George Wheeler Meml. Scholarship Fund, 1941-71; bd. dirs. Ala. Meth. Children's Home, 1953-76, 1st v.p., 1973-74. Mem. Am., Ala., Fed., Montgomery bar assns., Am. Judicature Soc., Ala. Hist. Assn., C. of C., Sigma Nu, Phi Alpha Delta, Theta Alpha Phi. Republican. Clubs: Kiwanian (pres. 1938), Capital City, Tuesday Evening Social, Fresh Air Domino. Home: 2216 Allendale Pl Montgomery AL 36111 Office: Suite 609 First Alabama Bank Bldg Montgomery AL 36104 *He only walks safely who walks uprightly.*

DAVIS, HENRY JEFFERSON, JR., former naval officer; b. Quincy, Fla., May 6, 1929; s. Henry and Sara Jewell (Davis) D.; m. Ernestine Hunt Tully, June 8, 1955; children: Frances Cornelia Davis Wallington, Jessica Leigh Davis Coughlin, H.J. Davis V, George Walton II. Student, U. Fla., 1947-48; B.S., Fla. State U., 1952; postgrad., U.S. Naval Acad., 1949-51; M.S., U.S. Naval Postgrad. Sch., 1962. Commd. ensign U.S. Navy, 1952, advanced through grades to rear adm., 1977; comdg. officer (Naval Security Group Activity), Winter Harbor, Maine, 1968-70, asst. chief of staff to comdr. in chief, 1973-76, chief, cryptologic adv. to comdr. in chief Pacific, 1976-77; asst. dir. plans and resources Nat. Security Agy.-Central Security Service, 1977-79, dep. dir. ops., 1979-82; ret., 1982. Decorated Def. Superior Service medal, Bronze star, Def. Meritorious Service medal, others. Mem. U.S. Naval Inst., IEEE, Sigma Xi. Baptist. Office: Dept Def Washington DC

DAVIS, HENRY LOUIS, bank holding company executive, accountant; b. St. Petersburg, Fla., Aug. 5, 1951; s. Norman Davenport and May (Gammelsetter) D.; m. Deborah Lynn Trimble, Aug. 2, 1964; children: Jared Blaine, Adria Leigh. B.B.A., Okla. U., Norman, 1973. Diplomate: C.P.A., Okla. Sr. auditor Peat, Marwick, Mitchell, Oklahoma City, 1973-78, Arthur Young & Co., 1978-79; sr. v.p., treas. First Okla. Bancorp. Inc., Oklahoma City, 1979—. Mem. Nat. Assn. Accts. (v.p. pub. relations Oklahoma City 1982-83), Am. Inst. C.P.A.'s, Okla. Soc. C.P.A.'s, Acctg. Research Assn. Democrat. Club: Young Men's Dinner (Oklahoma City). Office: First Okla Bancorp Inc PO Box 25189 Oklahoma City OK 73125

DAVIS, HERBERT LOWELL, utility co. exec.; b. Douds, Iowa, Feb. 18, 1933; s. John Herbert and Edna Belle (Frazier) D.; m. Roberta Willey Stearns, Sept. 10, 1955; children—Michael Stearns, Elizabeth Buchanan. Student, George Washington U., 1949-51; B.S. with distinction, U. Va., 1953; postgrad., U. Mich., 1953. C.P.A., Va. Sr. accountant Price Waterhouse & Co., Washington, 1957-61, mgr., 1961-66; asst. comptroller Potomac Electric Power Co., Washington, 1966-70, v.p., comptroller, 1970-72, sr. v.p., 1972-80, exec. v.p., 1980—, also dir.; dir. 1st Am. Bank (N.A.), Washington. Bd. dirs. Columbia Hosp. for Women, Washington, 1970—. Served to lt. (j.g.) USNR, 1954-57. Recipient Achievement award Va. Soc. Pub. Accountants, 1953. Mem. Met. Washington Bd. Trade, Financial Execs. Inst. (D.C. chpt. pres. 1974), Am., D.C. insts. C.P.A.'s. Episcopalian. Clubs: Rotarian, Metropolitan (Washington); Belle Haven Country. Home: 506 Richards Ln Alexandria VA 22302 Office: 1900 Pennsylvania Ave Washington DC 20068

DAVIS, HORACE CHANDLER, mathematics educator; b. Ithaca, N.Y., Aug. 12, 1926; emigrated to Can., 1962; s. Horace Bancroft and Marian (Rubins) D.; m. Natalie Ann Zemon, Aug. 16, 1948; children: Aaron, Hannah, Simone. B.S., Harvard U., 1945, M.A., 1947, Ph.D., 1950. Instr. math. U. Mich., Ann Arbor, 1950-54; assoc. editor Mathematical Revs., Providence, 1958-62; from assoc. prof. to prof. U. Toronto, Ont., Can., 1962—. Mem. Am. Math. Soc., Canadian Math. Congress, Soc. for Indsl. and Applied Math. Challenged constitutionality Com. on Un-American Activities of U.S. Ho. of Reps. in fed. courts, 1954-60. Office: Dept Math U Toronto Toronto ON M5S 1A1 Canada

DAVIS, HORANCE GIBBS, JR., educator, journalist; b. Manchester, Ga., July 14, 1924; s. Horance Gibbs and Florence Gray (Beavers) D.; m. Marjorie Lucile Davis, June 23, 1948; children: Gregory Rawson, Jennifer Diane. B.A. in Journalism with high honors, U. Fla., 1948, M.A., 1952. Reporter Fla. Times-Union, Jacksonville, 1949, state capitol corr., 1950-54; faculty U. Fla., Gainesville, 1954—, prof., 1965—, disting. service prof., 1977—; columnist Atlanta Jour.-Constn., 1977-78; editorial cons. Gainesville Daily Sun, 1962-83; columnist N.Y. Times Newspaper Group, 1983—. Served to 1st lt. USAAC, 1943-46; PTO. Decorated Air medal; recipient Pulitzer prize for editorial writing, 1971; Sidney Hillman award, 1963; Disting. Alumnus award U. Fla., 1971; merit cert. ABA, 1972, 76. Mem. Assn. Edn. in Journalism, Nat. Conf. Editorial Writers, Sigma Delta Chi (award for disting. service in journalism 1963, nat. v.p. 1969-72, Wells Meml. Key 1977), Omicron Delta Kappa, Phi Kappa Phi, Kappa Tau Alpha, Delta Tau Delta. Episcopalian (lay reader 1956-75). Home: 3290 NW 37th St Gainesville FL 32605

DAVIS, HOWARD ECKERT, polit. scientist, educator; b. Palmerton, Pa., Sept. 16, 1933; s. Howard Edward and Clara (Eckert) D.; m. Elizabeth Holbrook Forbes, June 29, 1957; children—Lisa Jeanne, Jill Rebecca, Thomas Howard. A.B., Dickinson Coll., 1955; M.A., Yale, 1956, Ph.D., 1962. Asso. prof. polit. sci. Randolph-Macon Coll., Ashland, Va., 1959-62, prof., chmn. dept. polit. sci., 1962-70, dean, 1970-77, prof. polit. sci., 1977—; lectr. Va. Commonwealth U., 1961-70, U. Richmond, 1961-64, Richmond Dept. Police Tng. Sch., 1961-72. Mem. Am. Polit. Sci. Assn., Phi Beta Kappa, Sigma Alpha Epsilon. Home: 111 Cub's Ln Ashland VA 23005

DAVIS, HOWARD HALSEY, supermarket company executive; b. Brockton, Mass., Mar. 21, 1902; s. Maynard Alton and Emma Smith (Walker) D.; m. Phyllis Caroline Smith, Oct. 19, 1926; 1 son, Howard Graham. B.S., Mass. Agrl. Coll., 1924; M.B.A., Harvard U., 1926. With Brockton Pub. Market, Mass., 1926-28, 29—, v.p., 1941—; with Ken Caryl Ranch Co., 1928-29; v.p. George C. Shaw Co., Portland, Maine, 1936-41, pres., 1941-74, chmn. bd., 1974-78; pres. Maine Savs. Bank, Portland, 1953-69, also trustee, 1953-69. Home: 178 Woodville Rd Falmouth ME 04105 Office: PO Box 3566 Portland ME 04104

DAVIS, HOWARD TED, chemical engineering educator; b. Hendersonville, N.C., Aug. 2, 1937; s. William Howard and Gladys Isabell (Rhodes) D.; m. Eugenia Asimakopoulos, Sept. 18, 1960; children: William Howard III, Maria Katherine. B.S., Furman U., 1959; Ph.D., U. Chgo., 1962. NSF postdoctoral fellow Free U. Brussels, 1962-63; asst. prof. U. Minn., Mpls., 1963-65, asso. prof., 1965-68, prof. chem. engring. and chemistry, 1968—, head dept. chem. engring. and materials sci., 1980—, chmn. exec. com. Microelectronic and Info. Scis. Ctr., 1982-84. Editor books.; Contbr. articles to tech. jours. Indsl. cons. NSF fellow, 1959-62; NSF postdoctoral fellow, 1962-63; Sloan Found. fellow, 1968-70; Guggenheim fellow, 1969-70. Mem. Am. Inst. Chem. Engring., Am. Chem. Soc., Am. Phys. Soc., Soc. Petroleum Engrs., Sigma Xi. Home: 1822 Mt Curve Ave Minneapolis MN 55403

DAVIS, HOWARD WALTER, advertising executive; b. Thomasville, Ga., Oct. 19, 1945; s. Howard Walter and Dorothy (Milton) Davis B.; m. Sharon Lou Getchell, Apr. 8,; children: Blake, Laurel. B.A., UCLA, 1967, M.B.A., 1970. With mktg. div. Am. Airlines, N.Y.C., 1970-73; with Tracy-Locke Batten Barton Durstine & Osborn, 1973—, pres., 1981—. Served with USAFR, 1967-73. Republican. Methodist. Office: Tracy-Locke Batten Barton Durstine & Osborn Plaza of Americas Dallas TX 75202 *

DAVIS, HUBERT EUGENE, college dean; b. Topeka, Feb. 2, 1926; s. Harold E. and Emma G. (Dickey) D.; m. Hermia Meeds, Aug. 19 (div. Dec. 1967). A.A., Ft. Scott Jr. Coll., 1946; B.A., Holy Cross Coll., 1948; M.A., St. Thomas Theol. Sem., 1953; M.L.S., Rosary Coll., 1955; postgrad., U. Chgo, 1955-57, 1962-63, 1968-69, Lutheran Sch. Theology, 1964, U. Marburg, (Germany), 1968. Librarian St. Thomas Coll., 1951-53; bus. mgr., editorial adviser Scepter Pub. Co., Chgo., 1953-55; prin. reference asst. Chgo. Pub. Library, 1955-57; librarian Tex. So. U., 1957-62; dir. Learning Resources Center, Southwest Coll., Chgo., 1962-72; dean student services Columbia Coll., Chgo., 1972-76, dean placement and institutional research services, 1976-81, dean instl. research, dir. grad. div., 1981—, also cons., media specialist; sr. staff cons. SYSCORP, Chgo., 1979—. Author: Learning Resources Centers—Concepts of Design, 1969. Mem. Am., Ill. library assns., Am. Philos. Assn., Am., Ill. assns. collegiate registrars and admission officers, Ill. Assn. Financial Aid Officers, Council on Library Technology, AAUP, Ill. Instl. Research Assn., Nat. Assn. Student Personnel Adminstr. Home: 7346 S Shore Dr Chicago IL 60649 Office: 59 E Van Buren St Chicago IL 60605

DAVIS, J., advertising agency executive; b. Alliance, Nebr., Feb. 26, 1945; s. John P. and Ruth M. (Annen) D.; m. Courtney Boyd Crowder, June 28, 1973; children: Cullen Boyd, Justin Scott, Robert Charles. B.A., U. Nebr., 1967. Asst. acct. exec. Benton & Bowles Inc., N.Y.C., 1972-73, acct. exec., 1973-76, v.p., acct. supr., 1976-79, sr. v.p., mgmt. supr., 1978-79, 81—, sr. v.p., account dir., Brussels, 1979-81. Served to capt. USAF, 1968-72. Office: Benton Bowles Inc 989 3rd Ave New York NY 10022

DAVIS, J. LUTHER, utility executive, lawyer; b. Memphis, May 8, 1924; s. Luther and Sarah (Carter) D.; m. Natalie Young, Jan. 26, 1947; children: James Luther, Fred C., Peggy E. B.S. in Bus. Adminstrn., U. Ariz., 1946, LL.B., 1949. Bar: Ariz. 1949. Pvt. practice, Tucson, 1949-52, asst. city atty., 1952-53, city mgr., 1953-55; with Tucson Gas & Electric Co. (name now Tucson Electric Power Co.), 1955—, exec. v.p., 1958-59, pres., 1959-76, chmn. bd., 1967—; dir. Fed. Res. Bd. Dallas (El Paso br.), 1974-77. Mem. City Tucson Charter Rev. Com., 1965-71; bd. dirs. Tucson Airport Authority, 1957-62, 1964-70, pres., 1965; bd. dirs. Tucson Med. Center, 1955-58, 59-65, pres., 1957-58; bd. dirs. Tucson Indsl. Devel. Bd., 1959-64, Ariz. Acad., 1962-74, 78-82, Health Planning Council Tucson, 1964-71, Green Fields Sch., 1964-69; chmn. bd. Green Fields Sch., 1964-66; bd. dirs. Tucson Regional Plan, 1966—; mem. U. Ariz. Found. Mem. Tex., Ariz. bar assns., NAM (dir. 1960-62), Pacific Coast Gas Assn. (dir. 1958-60), Tucson C. of C. (dir. 1958-60, 64-66, 80—), Pacific Coast Elec. Assn. (dir. 1972—, pres. 1978-79), Western Energy and Supply Assn. (dir. 1964-76), Blue Key, Phi Gamma Delta, Alpha Kappa Psi, Phi Delta Phi. Clubs: Tucson Country, Old Pueblo (dir. 1956-58), Old Pueblo (pres. 1957-58). Home: 6781 N Altos Primero Tucson AZ 85718 Office: 220 W 6th St Tucson AZ 85702

DAVIS, J. MORTON, investment company executive, economist; b. N.Y.C., Jan. 7, 1929; s. Morris and Sylvia (Mandel) Davidowitz; m. Rosalind Selengut, Sept. 24, 1949; children: Esther Davis Stahler, Ruki Davis Renov, Rivka, Lori. A.B. in Econs. magna cum laude, Bklyn Coll., 1957; M.B.A. with distinction, Harvard, 1959. Account exec. Shields & Co., N.Y.C., 1959-62; sr. pres. D.H. Blair & Co. Inc., N.Y.C., 1962—; pres. D.H. Blair Securities Corp., N.Y.C., 1967—; chmn. bd. Engex, Inc., XPLOR Energy Inc.; chmn., pres. Roundhill Capital, A Venture Capital SBIC Fund; dir. Satori Prodns. Inc.; lectr. econs. U. City, N.Y.; allied mem. N.Y. Stock Exchange, Am. Stock Exchange. Author: Making America Work Again, 1983. Treas. Independents, Republicans and Democrats for Good Govt., N.Y.C., 1969—; Trustee Yeshiva U., CUNY Grad. Sch. Mem. Phi Beta Kappa. Clubs: Harvard (N.Y.C.); Jockey, Racquet of Fla. (Miami); Lawrence (N.Y.) Tennis. Home: 7 Sutton Pl S Lawrence NY 11559 Office: 44 Wall St New York NY 10005 *I believe if you work very hard, it's easy to succeed! The corollary to that is that if you work easy, it's virtually impossible to succeed. If you contribute fully of your time, energy, knowledge, resources, etc., you ultimately get the rewards, at least commensurate with that contribution, and more, for you also have the joy of achieving and giving as much of what you are to this world. You not only are ultimately well paid but you make your mark. You achieve success with recognition and the gratifying feeling that you really earned it*

DAVIS, JACQUELINE MARIE VINCENT (MRS. LOUIS REID DAVIS), educator; b. Birmingham, Ala.; d. Jud Fred and Marie (Yates) Vincent; m. Louis Reid Davis, July 17, 1943. A.B. cum laude, Birmingham So. Coll., 1943; M.A., Columbia, U., 1950; M.S., U. Ala., 1958, Ed.D., 1961; postgrad., U. Va., George Washington U. Tchr. Fork Union (Va.) Mil. Acad., 1943-46, Ft. Belvoir, Va., 1946-48; tchr., adminstrv. asst., supr. Quantica (Va.) Post schs., 1950-52; instr., prof. dept. child devel and family life U. Ala. Sch. Home Econs., 1952-57, asso. prof., 1957-67, prof. child devel., dir., 1967—, mem. grad. council, adminstr. head start tng. program. Dir., 1964—; mem. NASA scholarship selection bd. U. Ala., 1966; mem. Gov.'s Advisory Com. on Day Care, 1963-66, State Adv. Com. on Children and Youth, 1960—; coordinator Head Start supplementary tng. programs State of Ala. Contbr. articles to profl. jours. Adviser, mem. selection com. Tombigbee council Girl Scouts U.S.A., 1961-66; cons. Tuscaloosa Community Action Program, 1965-66; chmn. Ala. Advisory Com. Children and Youth, 1978—. Mem. Nat. Assn. for Edn. of Young Children (mem. planning bd. 1963-64), U.S. Nat. Com. for Early Childhood Edn., World Orgn. for Early Childhood Edn., Southeastern Council Family Relations, So. Assn. Children Under Six (pres. 1961, mem. exec. bd. 1961—, chmn. 19th ann. conf.), Ala. Assn. Children Under Six (pres. 1963-64), Ala. Home Econs. Assn. (chmn. profl. sect. family life and child devel. 1963—, v.p. mem. governing bd. 1969-70), Comparative Edn. Soc., NEA, Am. Home Econs. Assn., Phi Beta Kappa, Kappa Delta Pi, Kappa Delta Epsilon. Methodist. Home: 47 Guilds Wood Tuscaloosa AL 35401 Office: PO Box 1211 University AL 35486

DAVIS, JAMES ALLAN, sociologist; b. Chgo., Nov. 2, 1929; s. Robert Gibson and Mary Adelaide (McMurray) D.; m. Martha Ann Hocking, Jan. 28, 1950; children: Mary, James, Andrew, Martha. B.S., Northwestern U., 1950; M.S., U. Wis., 1951; Ph.D., Harvard U., 1955. Research asso. Harvard U. Sch. Public Health, 1954-56; asst. prof. sociology Yale U., 1956-57; sr. study dir. Nat. Opinion Research Center, U. Chgo., 1957-67, asst. prof. sociology, 1957-64, asso. prof., 1964-67, dir. Nat. Opinion Research Center, prof. sociology, 1972-75; prof. Dartmouth Coll., 1967-72, 75-77; prof. sociology Harvard U., Cambridge, Mass., 1977—, chairperson dept. sociology, 1980-83, master, 1979—. Author: 7 books including Great Books and Small Groups, 1961, Undergraduate Career Decisions, 1965, Elementary Survey Analysis, 1971; contbr. articles to profl. jours. Mem. Am. Sociol. Assn. Home: Winthrop House Harvard Univ Cambridge MA 02138 Office: William James Hall Harvard Univ Cambridge MA 02138

DAVIS, JAMES ELSWORTH, food company executive; b. Henderson, Ark., July 31, 1907; s. William M. and Ethel (Chase) D.; m. Florence Novinger, Jan. 27, 1932; children: Dorothy Jean Davis Smith, Andrew Dano. Student, U. Idaho, 1926-27, U. Oreg., 1925; H.H.D., Stetson U., 1960; LL.D., Bethune-Cookman Coll., 1964; D.C.L., Jacksonville U., 1974. Pres. Economy Wholesale Grocery Co., 1939-42, v.p., dir., 1925-65; exec. v.p. Winn & Lovett Grocery Co., 1946-50; v.p., dir. Economy Wholesale Foods, Inc.; chmn. bd. Winn-Dixie Stores, Inc.; v.p. Economy Wholesale Distbrs., Inc.; chmn. bd., dir. Am. Heritage Life Ins. Co.; v.p. Crackin' Good Bakers Inc.; pres., dir. Danov Corp.; pres. Estuary Corp., D.D.I., Inc.; v.p., dir. Deep South Products; v.p. Astor Products, Inc.; hon. dir. Barnett Nat. Bank, Jacksonville, Monterey Canning Co., Bahamas Supermarkets, Nassau.; Trustee Bethune-Cookman Coll.; hon. bd. dirs. Bolles Sch.; bd. dirs. Am. Hist. and Cultural Soc.; v.p. Winn-Dixie Stores Found.; pres. James E. Davis Family-WD Charities, Inc.; trustee St. Luke's Hosp. Assn., Jacksonville, Fla.; mem. Citizens Council Budget Research, Tallahassee. Served from capt. to lt. col. AUS, 1943-45; ETOUSA, MTOUSA, NATOUSA; officer charge Q.M.C. Market Center, 1944-45; N.Y.C. Decorated Legion of Merit. Mem. Alpha Kappa Psi., Sigma Chi. Mem. Christian Ch. Clubs: Fla. Yacht, Ponte Vedra, River. Home: 3960 Ortega Blvd Jacksonville FL 32210 Office: Box B Jacksonville FL 32203

DAVIS, JAMES HORNOR, III, lawyer; b. Clarksburg, W.Va., Oct. 9, 1928; s. James Hornor II and Martha (Maxwell) D.; m. Ouida Caldwell, July 1, 1950; children—James Hornor IV, Lewis Caldwell. A.B., Princeton U., 1950; LL.B., U. Va., 1953. Bar: W.Va. bar 1953. Partner firm Preston & Davis, Charleston, 1953-65, Spilman, Thomas, Battle & Klostermeyer, 1965—; Mem. W.Va. Ho. of Dels., 1961-62, W.Va. Senate, 1963-66. Served with USAF, 1953-55. Fellow Am. Bar Assn.; mem. Am. Law Inst., Am. Judicature Soc. (dir. 1978-81), W.Va. Jud. Council (chmn. 1973-81), W.Va. Bar Assn., Kanawha County Bar Assn., Nat. Council Coal Lessors (pres.), W.Va. Mfrs. Assn. (chmn. 1973-75, dir.). Democrat. Episcopalian. Office: 1101 Kanawha Banking and Trust Bldg Charleston WV 25301

DAVIS, JAMES HORNOR, IV, museum director; b. Charlottesville, Va., May 16, 1953; s. James Hornor and Ouida (Caldwell) D.; m. Frederica Miller, Aug. 11, 1979. B.A. Archtl. History, U. Va., 1975; J.D., W.Va. U., 1978. Bar: W.Va. Assoc. Spilmen, Thomas, Battle & Klostermeyer, Charleston, W.Va., 1978-81; exec. dir. Sunrise Mus., Charleston, W.Va., 1981—. Home: 1568 Virginia St E Charleston WV 25311 Office: 746 Mytle Rd Charleston WV 25314

DAVIS, JAMES HOWARD, oil company executive; b. Marshalltown, Iowa, Aug. 6, 1935; s. Ralph Weldon and Ruth Loraine (Ware) D.; m. Karen Audely Swanson, June 9, 1956; children: Cynthia Ruth, Kimberly Diane. B.S., Iowa State U., 1956; M.B.A. with distinction, Harvard Grad. Sch. Bus., 1965. Vice pres. resins Ashland Chem. Co., Dublin, Ohio, 1972-75, group v.p., 1975-78, adminstrv. v.p., 1978-79; v.p. environ. affairs Ashland Oil Inc., Ky., 1979-80, adminstrv. v.p., 1980-81; pres. Ashland Services Co., 1981. Served to 1st lt. USMCR, 1956-58. Republican. Presbyterian. Home: 4839 Smoketalk Ln Westerville OH 43081 Office: Ashland Oil Inc 1000 Ashland Dr Ashland KY 41114

DAVIS, JAMES L., building products manufacturing company executive; b. Kansas City, Mo., 1927. Ed., Washington U., 1954. With H.H. Robertson Co., Pitts., 1954—; v.p., gen. mgr. Cuppiles Products div. H.H. Robertson Co., 1978-81; group exec. v.p., dir. H.H. Robertson Co., Pitts., 1981-83, pres., chief operating officer, dir., 1983—; dir. Overland Enterprises, Inc., Gleason Davis Co. Office: H H Robertson Co Two Gateway Ctr Pittsburgh PA 15222 *

DAVIS, JAMES MINOR, JR., utility company executive, mechanical engineer; b. Raeford, N.C., May 9, 1936; s. James Minor and Betsy S. (Sessoms) D.; m. Patsy Ann McLean, July 19, 1958; children: Martha Jeanette, James Owen, Julie Ann. B.S. in Mech. Engring., N.C. State U., 1958. Registered profl. engr., N.C. Test engr. Pratt & Whitney Aircraft Co., East Hartford, Conn., 1961-65; with Carolina Power & Light Co., Raleigh, N.C., 1965—, mgr. rates and regulation dept., 1976-79, sr. v.p. fuel and materials mgmt. group, 1979—. Pres. Episcopal Layman, Diocese of N.C., 1971-73; vestryman St. Michael's Episcopal Ch., Releigh, 1974-76. Served with USAF, 1958-61. Mem. N.C. Soc. Engrs., Profl. Engrs. N.C., Nat. Soc. Profl. Engrs., Am. Nuclear Soc., Health Physics Soc. Republican. Lodge: Kiwanis. Office: 411 Fayetteville St Raleigh NC 27602

DAVIS, JAMES (OTHELLO), physician, educator; b. Tahlequah, Okla., July 12, 1916; s. Zemry and Villa (Hunter) D.; m. Florrilla Louise Sides, Dec. 27, 1941; children: Janet Ruth, James Lawrence. M.A. in Zoology, U. Mo., 1939, Ph.D., 1942, B.S. in Medicine, 1943; M.D., Washington U., 1945. Intern Barnes Hosp., St. Louis, 1945-46; investigator Lab. Kidney and Electrolyte Metabolism, Nat. Heart Inst., Bethesda, Md., 1949-57, chief sect. on exptl. cardiovascular disease, 1957-66; asso. prof. physiology Temple U. Sch. Medicine, Phila., 1955-56; vis. asso. prof. physiology Johns Hopkins Sch. Medicine, 1961-64; vis. prof. physiology U. Va. Sch. Medicine, 1964; prof., chmn. dept. physiology U. Mo. Sch. Medicine, Columbia, 1966—. Mem. editorial bd.: Am. Jour. Physiology, 1961-63, 66-69, Endocrinology, 1962-65, Circulation Research, 1962-66, 71-76, 78-81, Hypertension, 1979-80. Served with AUS, 1943-45; Served with USPHS, 1946-66. Recipient AMA Golden Apple award for teaching U. Mo., 1968; Sigma Xi Research award U. Mo., 1971; Modern Medicine Distinguished Achievement award, 1973; Alumni gold medal U. Mo., 1973; Volhard award, 1974; CIBA award for hypertension research, 1975; Carl T. Wiggers award, 1976; citation of merit U. Mo. Sch. Medicine, 1981. Mem. Am. Heart Assn. (mem. med. adv. council, vice chmn. council for high blood pressure research 1970-72, chmn. council 1972-74), Am. Physiology Soc. (council 1974-78, steering com. circulation group 1978-81, pres. circulation sect. 1981), Endocrine Soc., Soc. Exptl. Biology and Medicine, Nat. Inst. Health Extramural Program, Assn. Physiology Dept. Chairmen (council 1971-74), Inter-Am. Soc. Hypertension (council 1978-80), Internat. Soc. Hypertension (pres. 1980-82), Nat. Acad. Scis., Sigma Xi, Alpha Omega Alpha. Home: 612 Maplewood Dr Columbia MO 65201

DAVIS, JAMES PAXTON, educator, novelist, journalist; b. Winston-Salem, N.C., May 7, 1925; s. James Paxton and Emily (McDowell) D.; m. Wylma Elizabeth Pooser, June 6, 1951 (div. 1971); children: Elizabeth Keith, Anne Beckley, James Paxton III; m. Peggy Painter Camper, July 21, 1973. Student, Va. Mil. Inst., 1942-43; A.B., Johns Hopkins, 1949. Reporter Winston-Salem Jour., 1949-51, Richmond (Va.) Times-Dispatch, 1951-52, Twin City Sentinel, Winston-Salem, 1952-53; faculty Washington and Lee U., 1953-76, prof. journalism, 1963-76, chmn. dept., 1968-74; vis. scholar Cambridge U., 1973. Book editor: Roanoke (Va.) Times & World News, 1961-81; contbg. editorial columnist, 1976—; Author: Two Soldiers, 1956, The Battle of New Market, 1963, One of The Dark Places, 1965, The Seasons of Heroes, 1967, A Flag at the Pole, 1976, Ned, 1978, Three Days, 1980. Served with AUS, 1943-46; CBI. Mem. Phi Beta Kappa, Omicron Delta Kappa. Home: PO Box 33 Fincastle VA 24090

DAVIS, JAMES ROBERT, cartoonist; b. Marion, Ind., July 28, 1945; s. James William and Anna Catherine D.; m. Carolyn L. Altekruse, July 26, 1969; 1 son, James Alexander. B.S., Ball State U., Muncie, Ind. Artist, Groves & Assocs., advt., Muncie, 1968-69; asst. to cartoonist: Tumbleweeds comic strip, 1969-78; cartoonist: Garfield comic strip, 1978—; TV script Here Comes Garfield, 1982; author: Garfield at Large, 1980, Garfield Gains Weight, 1981, Garfield Bigger Than Life, 1981, Garfield Weighs In, 1982, Garfield Takes the Cake, 1982, Garfield Treasury, 1982, Garfield Eats His Heart Out, 1983. Mktg. Hall of Fame award Am. Mktg. Assn., 1982. Mem. Nat. Cartoonists Soc. (Best Humor Strip of 1981), Newspaper Comics Council. Office: United Feature Syndicate Inc 200 Park Ave New York NY 10166

DAVIS, JAY MICHAEL, lawyer; b. Santa Barbara, Calif., Nov. 21, 1946; s. Jay, Jr. and June Coral (McDowell) D.; m. Christine Marie Durr, Sept. 11, 1971; 1 son, Byron Scott. B.S., Menlo Sch. Bus. Adminstrn., Menlo Park, Calif., 1968; J.D., U. San Diego, 1971. Bar: Calif. 1972. Dep. city atty., Los Angeles, 1971-64; atty. First Interstate Bank of Calif., Los Angeles, 1974-77; v.p., sec., gen. counsel Mitsui Mfrs. Bank, Los Angeles, 1977—. Mem. Am. Bar Assn., Am. Soc. Corp. Secs., Calif. Bar Assn., Calif. Bankers Assn., Los Angeles County Bar Assn., Delta Sigma Pi, Phi Delta Phi. Republican. Club: Los Angeles Athletic. Home: 2292 Kinneloa Canyon Rd Pasadena CA 91107 Office: 515 S Figueroa St Los Angeles CA 90071

DAVIS, JEFFERSON CLARK, JR., chemist; b. Jacksonville, Fla., Mar. 20, 1931; s. Jefferson Clark and Margaret Olivia (Pippin) D.; m. Sylvia Belle Conelly, June 4, 1954; children: Nancy, Susan, Gretchen. B.S., U. Ariz., 1953, M.S., 1954; Ph.D., U. Calif., Berkeley, 1959. DuPont teaching fellow U. Calif., Berkeley, 1956-59; instr., then asst. prof. chemistry U. Tex., Austin, 1959-65; mem. faculty U. S.Fla., Tampa, 1965—, prof. chemistry, 1971—, chmn. dept., 1978—; vis. prof. Calif. Inst. Tech., 1975; dir. Willard Grant Press; adv. council Coll. Chemistry, NSF, 1968; cons. in field. Author: Advanced Physical Chemistry, 1965, A Laboratory Manual for General Chemistry, 3d edit, 1980, Spectroscopy Film Series, 1970, Study Guide for General Chemistry, 3d edit, 1977, Chemistry Videotape Series, 2d edit, 1974; editorial bd.: Chemistry mag, 1969-72; editor: Am. Chem. Soc. Examinations, 1970—; contbr. to profl. jours. Served to 1st lt AUS, 1954-56. Fellow Am. Inst. Chemists, AAAS; mem. Am. Chem. Soc. (councilor), AAUP, Fla. Acad. Sci., Phi Beta Kappa, Sigma Xi, Phi Kappa Phi, Lambda Phi Alpha, Phi Lambda Upsilon, Sigma Pi Sigma. Unitarian. Address: 10615 Carrollwood Dr Tampa FL 33618

DAVIS, JEROME LEWIS, JR., writer, producer, director; b. N.Y.C., Sept. 26, 1917; s. Jerome L. and Maida May (Maibrunn) D.; m. Nancy Straus; m. Marilyn Maxwell; m. Beryl Reed Hammond; children: Jeffrey, Matthew, Joshua, Anthony. B.A., Franklin and Marshall Coll., 1939. Contbr. fiction to various mags., including, Esquire, New Yorker, Colliers, Cosmopolitan, 1942-45; author: screenplays, including Partners, Kind Lady, Apache Trail, Slight Case of Larceny, Duchess of Idaho; developer pilots and series, Universal City (Calif.) Studios, 1975-81; producer, writer, dir.: TV series Bewitched, 1963-66, Marlo Thomas Show, 1965-66, The Odd Couple, 1970-74, The Cop and the Kid; producer: CBS movie-of-the week The Golden Gate Murders, 1979; exec. producer: CBS TV series House Calls, 1979—. Served with Signal Corps U.S. Army, World War II. Mem. Writers Guild Am., East (tour lectr.), Dirs. Guild, Producers Guild. Office: Lorimar Prodns 3970 Overland Ave Culver City CA 90230

DAVIS, JERRY DONALD, lawyer, construction and engineering company executive; b. Minden, La., Sept. 6, 1938; s. Dean P. and Alice G. D.; m. Beryl Hutchings, Juns. 25, 1946; 1 dau., Elizabeth Ann. B.B.A., U. Tex., 1961, J.D., 1964. Bar: Tex. 1964. Adminstrv. asst., in house gen. legal work McCollough Tool Co., Houston, 1964-67; gen. legal work Gibson & Tatum, Houston, 1967-71; asst. gen. counsel Raymond Internat. Inc., Houston, 1971-78, v.p., sec., gen. counsel, 1979—; v.p., sec., gen. cousel Raymond Internat. Builders, Houston, 1978—. Mem. ABA, State Bar Tex., Am. Soc. Corp. Secs., Houston C. of C. Home: 11626 Cypresswood St Houston TX 77040 Office: Raymond International Inc 5065 Westheimer St Houston TX 77056

DAVIS, JOE WILLIAM, mayor; b. New Market, Ala., Oct. 22, 1918; s. Samuel Clifton and Sophie (Walker) D.; m. Dorothy Allen, Dec. 21, 1951; children—Joe William, Jeffrey Clifton, Julia Evelyn.; m. Hilda M. Crisco, Mar. 18, 1983. B.S. in Social Sci, E.Tenn. State Coll., 1941; M.A. in Edn. Adminstrn, Peabody Coll., 1953. Tchr., prin. Huntsville (Ala.) schs., 1946-55; personnel mgr. U.S. Indsl. Chem. Corp., Tuscola, Ill., 1955-59, asst. mgr. indsl. relations and safety, also security adminstr., 1959-63; adminstrv. asst. to mayor, Huntsville, 1964-68, mayor, 1968—. Served with USN, 1943-46. Mem. V.F.W., Am. Legion. Clubs: Elk, Mason (Shriner), Lion, Moose, Eagle. Home: 604 Greene St SE Huntsville AL 35801 Office: 308 Fountain Circle Huntsville AL 35804

DAVIS, JOEL, publisher; b. Chgo., Apr. 5, 1934; s. Bernard George and Sylvia (Friedman) D.; m. Carol Sue Barnett, Aug. 3, 1958; children: Charles Michael, Andrew Barnett, Jonathan William. B.A., Brown U., 1957; student, Columbia U., summer 1953. With Davis Publs., Inc., N.Y.C., 1957—, exec. v.p., 1959-68, pres., pub., 1969—; publishes 15 spl. interest publs. including Ellery Queen's Mystery Mag., Alfred Hitchcock's Mystery Mag., Isaac Asimov's Sci. Fiction Mag., Sylvia Porter's Personal Fin., 1969—; dir. Mut. N.Y. Mony Fund, Mony Variable Account-B-Fund. Mem. exec. com. gen. devel. council Brown U., 1962-77; vice chmn. Brown Devel. Council, 1968-69; nat. chmn. univ. fund Brown U., 1965-68; regional dir. Asso. Alumni Brown U., 1965-67, trustee, mem. corp., 1968-73; mem. adv. and exec. com. Brown U., 1971-73, chmn. budget, fin. com., 1971-73; bd. dirs. Brit. Am. Ednl. Found., 1977-80. Mem. Am. Arbitration Assn. (nat. panel), Mags. Pubs. Assn. (dir. 1969—, sec. 1979-81, vice chmn. mktg. com. 1969-73, exec. com. 1971-84, fin. com. 1974—), Young Pres.'s Orgn. Clubs: Union League, Brown (N.Y.C.) (gov. 1963-69); Weston Field). Home: 15 Crooked Mile Rd Westport CT 06880 Office: 380 Lexington Ave New York NY 10017

DAVIS, JOHN ANDERSON, economics educator; b. Springfield, Ill., June 8, 1924; s. Emerson and Mae (Denney) D.; m. Lois Colvin, Sept. 16, 1947; 1 son, Stephen Colvin. Student, Trinity U., San Antonio, 1942-43; B.A., So. Meth. U., 1949, M.A., 1950; Ph.D., U. Ala., 1957. Asst. state mgr. Inter-Ocean Ins. Co., Tex., 1945-50; asst. prof. econs. Lincoln Meml. U., Harrogate, Tenn., 1950-51; instr. social scis. Memphis State U., 1951-54; research asso. Ala. Bus. Research Council, U. Ala., 1955-56, univ. instr. econs., 1956-57; assoc. prof. econs. Miss. State U., 1957-59, prof. econs., 1959—, chmn. dept., 1959-83; Sec.-treas. Dallas Assn. Accident and Health Underwriters, 1945-50; mem. Ala. Bus. Research Council, 1955-56, Com. Miss. Economy, 1957-58; chmn. Miss. Council on Econ. Edn., 1968, now mem. exec. bd. Editor: Jour. So. Culture, 1965—, Midsouth Jour. Econs. Chmn. bd. advisers YMCA Miss. State U., 1963-64. Recipient Golden Triangle award YMCA, 1964, Outstanding Prof. award Grad. Coll. Bus. Students' Assn., Miss. State U., 1983. Mem. Miss. Econ. Assn. (sec. 1964-65), So. Econ. Assn., Miss. Mfrs. Assn., Am. Econ. Assn., AAUP, Southwestern Social Sci. Assn., Mid-South Acad. Economists (editor-in-chief jour., pres. 1966-67, exec. bd., Disting. Service award 1978, J. Anderson Davis lectureship established 1983), Beta Gamma Sigma, Alpha Kappa Psi, Delta Sigma Phi. Home: 103 Briarwood Dr Starkville MS 39759 Office: Dept Econs Miss State U State College MS 39762

DAVIS, JOHN BRADFORD, JR., college president; b. Haverhill, Mass., Sept. 14, 1921; s. John Bradford and Edna (Maxfield) D.; m. Barbara W. Burns, Feb. 20, 1943; children: Nancy (Mrs. Stephen Lasar), Martha (Mrs. Jeffrey Pattee), John Bradford III, Susan (Mrs. Anton Flygare), Lincoln, Deborah (Mrs. Daniel Glass), Rebecca, Sarah. B.A., U. N.H., 1944. Tchr. Laconia (N.H.) High Sch., 1944-45; asst. to pres. U. N.H., 1945-47, acting dean men, 1949-50; exec. sec. New Eng. Sch. Devel. Council, 1950-59; supt. schs., Lincoln, Mass., 1959-63, Worcester, Mass., 1963-66, Mpls., 1967-75; pres. Macalester Coll., St. Paul, 1975—; Lectr. Harvard Grad. Sch. Edn., 1955-56; dir. Cowles Media, Northwestern Nat. Life Ins. Co.; dep. chmn. Mpls. Fed. Res. Bank; Mem. spl. task force Pres.'s Sci. Adv. Com.; mem. Pres.'s Commn. on Sch. Fin., 1969—; pres. Minn. Pvt. Coll. Council, 1981—; mem. Rockefeller Panel Arts, Edn. and Americans, 1975—. Host: TV program Dimensions, Boston, 1955-57; Contbr. articles to profl. jours. Trustee Walker Art Center. Served with AUS, 1942-44. Mem. Harvard Grad. Sch. Edn. Alumni Assn. (pres. 1963-65), Phi Delta Kappa.

DAVIS, JOHN CHARLES, III, wholeslae drug company executive; b. Denver, Mar. 20, 1921; s. John C. and Dorothy (Mead) D.; m. Margaret Stenseth, Dec. 31, 1943; children: John C., Marne Davis Kellogg, Andrew. B.A., Princeton U., 1943. With Davis Cos., Denver, 1956—, chmn. bd., 1978—. Vice chmn. Colo. Blue Cross Blue Shield, Denver, 1976—; bd. dir. Mt. States Employment Council, 1966—; pres. Dist. Research and Edn. Found., Washington, 1973—. Served with USAAF, 1943-45. Republican. Episcopalian. Clubs: Denver Country, Pinehurst Country. Office: 501 W 44th Ave Denver CO 80216

DAVIS, JOHN DONALD, banker; b. Sheridan, Wyo., Apr. 27, 1927; s. Walter C. and Nell O. (Williams) D.; m. Janet B. Loeffler, Mar. 18, 1946; children—Jacqueline (Mrs. Sean Manering), Jerry Allen. Student, Colo. State Coll., Greeley, 1945-48. Sr. exec. v.p. United Bank of Ariz., 1979—, also dir.; dir. United Bancorp.; past pres. Phoenix Clearing House.; Pres. Tucson Econ. Devel. Corp. Bd. dirs., v.p. Tucson Met. YMCA; bd. dirs. Central Ariz. Project; trustee United for Ariz.; mem. Arizonans for Jobs and Energy. Mem. Am. Bankers Assn. (governing council, state v.p., mem. govt. relations council), Ariz. Bankers Assn. (past pres.), Tucson Met. C. of C. (past pres., named Man of Yr. 1979). Clubs: Rotary, Tucson Country, Old Pueblo. Home: 4930 Entrada Primera Tucson AZ 85718 Office: PO Box 3043 Tucson AZ 85702

DAVIS, JOHN DWELLE, psychology educator; b. Poughkeepsie, N.Y., Apr. 7, 1928; m. Jane Evans Peterson, June 9, 1954 (div. Sept. 1972); children: Philip Haldane, John Dwelle, Ward Peterson, Andrew Penistone. A.B., Brown U., 1954; M.A., U. Ill., 1956, Ph.D., 1962. Asst. prof. Am. U. Beirut, Lebanon, 1958-61, Yale U., 1961-65; faculty U. Ill., Chgo. Circle, 1965—, prof. psychology, 1968—; Vis. sr. research fellow U. Sussex, Brighton, Eng., 1970-71; ad hoc mem. psychobiology study sect. NIH, Brighton, Eng., 1970-71. Mem. Democratic Town Com., Branford, Conn., 1964-65. Mem. AAAS, Psychonomic Soc., N.Y. Acad. Scis., Soc. Neurosci., Midwestern Psychol. Assn. Home: 1875 N Orchard Chicago IL 60614

DAVIS, JOHN H, editor; b. Marion, Ill., Nov. 21, 1927; s. Chester Barnet and Sophia (Baker) D.; m. Anne Denise Neville, Mar. 3, 1956; children: Christopher, Alan; m. Melinda Wallace Williams, Jan. 24, 1981. B.S., U. Ill., 1951. Editor-in-chief Prentice-Hall Inc., Englewood Cliffs, N.J., 1970—, pres. coll. div., 1980—. Served with AUS, 1946-47. Home: Overlook Rd Alpine NJ 07620 Office: Prentice Hall Inc Englewood Cliffs NJ 07632

DAVIS, JOHN HERSCHEL, medical educator, surgeon; b. Coraopolis, Pa., May 11, 1924; s. John Herschel and Fern (:ew) D.; m. Peggy Lou Seyler, Sept. 7, 1946; children: Karen LaRue, Wendy Sue, Hale Rive'. Student, Allegheny Coll., 1942-43; M.D., Western Res. U., 1948. Diplomate: Am. Bd. Surgery. Intern Univ. Hosps., Celve., 1948-49, resident, 1955-56; asst. prof. surgery Western Res. U., Cleve., 1956-59, assoc. prof. surgery, 1959-64, prof., 1964-69; dir. surgery Cleve. Met. Hosp., 1966-69; prof., chmn. dept. surgery U. Vt., Burlington, 1969—; dir. Am. Bd. Surgery, Phila., Am. Bd. Emergency Medicine, East Lansing, Mich., Am. Trauma Soc., Chgo., 1978—; chmn. surgery sect. NIH, Washington, 1982—. Editor: Current Concepts of Surgery, 1965, Jour. of Trauma, 1974; Am. editor: Brit. Jour. Injury; editorial bd.: Medfact; corr. editor: Journal de Traumatologie, Jour. Injury. Mem. Bar. Rev. Com. Vt. Supreme Ct., 1982. Served to capt. U.S. Army, 1950-53. Recipient William Peck Research award Western Res. U., 1961, Surgeon of Year award Nat. Safety Council, N.Y.C., 1979. Mem. Am. Assn. for History of Medicine; fellow ACS (Scudder Oration award 1979); mem. AAAS, Am. Assn. for History of Medicine, Am. Asn. Surgery Trauma, Am. Burn Assn., Am. Fedn. Clin. Research, Am. Heart Assn., Am. Trauma Soc., Central Soc. Clin. Research, Central Surg. Soc., Chittenden County Med. Soc., Collegium Internationale Chirurgiae Digestivae, Digestive Disease Found., Eastern Surg. Soc., Halsted Soc., Internat. soc. for Burn Injuries, Italian Surg. Research Soc., Nat. Research Council of Nat. Acad. Scis., New Eng. Soc. for Vascular Surgery, New Eng. Surg. Soc., N.Y. Acad. Scis., Soc. Internationale de Chirurgie, Soc. Exptl. Biology and Medicine, Soc. Med. Cons. to Armed Forces, Soc. Surgery Alimentary Tract, Soc. Surg. Chairmen, Soc. for Vascular Surgery, Surg. Biology Club II, Thirty-eighth Parallel Med. Soc., Vt. State Med. Soc., Allen O. Whipple Med. Soc., Sigma Xi, Alpha Omega Alpha. Republican. Club: Ethan Allen (Burlington). Home: 21 Ridgewood Dr Burlington VT 05401 Office: Univ Vt Coll of Medicine Given Bldg Burlington VT 05405

DAVIS, JOHN KERRY, marine corps officer; b. Hagon, N.Mex., Mar. 14, 1927; s. Henry N. and Wilma (Meeks) D.; m. Jane Dickey, July 26, 1952; children: Keri, Gwendolyn Sue, Julie Leigh. B.A., U. N.Mex., 1951; M.P.A., George Washington U., 1962. Commd. 2d lt. U.S. Marine Corps, 1950, advanced through grades to gen., 1983; asst. wing comdr. Third Marine Aircraft Wing, 1975-76; comdr. Marine Corps Base Western Area, El Toro, Calif., 1976-77; comdr. gen. Third Marine Aircraft Wing, 1977-78; comdg. gen. First Marine Aircraft Wing, Okinawa, Japan, 1978-79, Fleet Marine Force, Camp Smith, Hawaii, 1981-83; asst. comdt. U.S. Marine Corps, 1983—. Decorated Legion of Merit with V, Air medal with numeral 12; recipient Disting. Citizen award Orange County Bd. Suprs., 1977. Mem. Marine Corps Assn., Marine Corps Aviation Assn., U.S. Naval Inst., Daedalians, Phi Delta Theta. Home: Quarters 1 Marine Barracks 8th and I Sts Washington DC 20390

DAVIS, JOHN MACDOUGALL, lawyer; b. Seattle, Feb. 20, 1914; s. David Lyle and Georgina (MacDougall) D.; m. Ruth Anne Van Arsdale, July 1, 1939; children: Jean, John, Bruce, Ann, Margaret, Elizabeth. B.A., U. Wash., 1936, LL.B., 1940. Bar: Wash. 1940. Partner Davis, Wright, Todd, Riese & Jones, Seattle; dir. Seattle-First Nat. Bank, ELDEC Corp., D.W. Close Co.; lectr. U. Wash. Law Sch., 1947-52. Bd. dirs. Virginia Mason Hosp., Seattle, 1952-79, pres., 1970-72; bd. dirs. Pacific Sci. Ctr., 1971—, past pres., past chmn.; trustee Whitman Coll., 1971—, chmn., 1983—; bd. dirs. Blue Cross Wash. and Alaska, 1982—, Diabetic Trust Fund, 1954—, Wash. Student Loan Guaranty Assn., 1978-83; mem. adv. bd. Chief Seattle council Boy Scouts Am. Served with USNG, 1931-34. Recipient Disting. Eagle Scout award, 1982. Mem. ABA, Wash. State Bar Assn., Seattle-King County Bar Assn. (pres. 1960-61), Order of Coif, Phi Delta Phi, Alpha Delta Phi. Presbyterian. Clubs: Rainier, Seattle Golf (Seattle); Mountaineers. Home: 7662 SE 22d St Mercer Island WA 98040 Office: 4200 Seattle-First Nat Bank Bldg Seattle WA 98154

DAVIS, JOHN MARCELL, psychiatrist; b. Kansas City, Mo., Oct. 11, 1933; s. Manvel H. and Genevieve (marcell) D.; m. Judith W. Malm, June 15, 1960; children: Richard Marcell, Katherine Judith. A.B., Princeton U., 1956; M.D., Yale U., 1960. Intern Mass. Gen. Hosp., Boston, 1960-61; resident in psychiatry Yale U. Med Center, 1961-64; clin. asso. NIMH, 1964-70; prof. psychiatry, asso. prof. pharmacology Vanderbilt U. Med. Sch., 1970-73; dir. research Ill. State Psychiat. Inst., Chgo., 1973—; Gilman prof. psychiatry U. Ill.-Chgo., 1981—; mem. sci. adv. com. McLean Hosp., Boston. Author: Diagnosis and Drug Treatment of Psychiatric Disorders, 1969, Practical Clinical Psychopharmacology, 1980, Tardive Dyskinesia, 1980, Psychopharmacology Update: New and Neglected Areas, 1980, Neurotransmitter Balance in Mental Illness, 1978. Fellow Am. Psychiat. Assn. (chmn. council research 1979-81), Am. Coll. Neuropsychopharmacology; mem. Am. Coll. Psychiatry. Address: 1601 W Taylor St Chicago IL 60612

DAVIS, JOHN MASON, economist, banker executive; b. Norwich, Conn., Aug. 2, 1935; s. John Mason and Alice L. (Burdick) D.; m. Joan Irene Bousquet, June 15, 1955; children: Joan Alice, Deborrah Anne, John Mason, Matthew Scott. B.S., 1957; M.S., U. Chgo., 1962. Research asst. dept. agr. U. Conn., Storrs, 1957-58; research assoc. Econ. Growth Ctr. Yale U., New Haven, 1962-63; economist First Nat. Bank, Chgo., 1965-73; spl. asst. chmn. Council Econ. Advs., Washington, 1973-77; sr. v.p. and economist Fed. Res. Bank, Cleve., 1977—. Nat. Assn. Bus. Economists. Office: Federal Reserve Bank 1455 E 6th St Cleveland OH 44114

DAVIS, JOHN MORGAN, judge; b. Shenandoah, Pa., Aug. 9, 1906; s. William J. and Sarah R. (Jones) D.; m. Eva B. Pierson, June 18, 1932; children: Patricia Anne, Carole Joan, John Morgan. B.S., U. Pa., 1929, LL.B., 1932; postgrad., Sch. Banking, Rutgers U., 1942. Bar: Pa. 1933, U.S. Supreme Ct. bar 1933. Practiced in, Phila., 1933-52; v.p. Seaboard Radio Broadcasting Corp., 1937-51; gen. counsel Nat. Assn. Broadcasters, 1944-46; chmn. Community Broadcasting Corp., 1951-64; judge Ct. Common Pleas, 1952-58; lt. gov. Pa., 1959-63; judge Fed. Dist Ct. for Eastern dist. Pa., 1964—, now. sr. judge.; Chmn. Gov.'s Com. on Edn.; former sec. Pa. Labor Relations Bd. Recipient numerous awards. Mem. Am. Judicature Soc., Lawyers Club Phila., Socialegal Club Phila., Welsh Soc., Phi Alpha Delta (hon.), Lambda Sigma Kappa. Baptist (trustee). Lodge: Masons. Office: Room 5614 US Courthouse Philadelphia PA 19106 *

DAVIS, JOHN PHILLIPS, JR., lawyer; b. Pitts., June 1, 1925; s. John Phillips and Jean Stout (Miller) D.; m. Mary McCreery Oates, Sept. 13, 1952; children: George B., John P. III, Elizabeth M., Mary O. Student, Williams Coll.; A.B., Harvard U., 1947, J.D., 1950. Bar: Pa. 1951. Since practiced in Pitts.; partner Reed Smith Shaw & McClay, 1961—; dir. Firth Stirling Inc., Pitts. Gage and Supply Co., Bloom Engrng. Co., Inc. Dir. Staunton Farm Found., 1964—, pres., 1968—; bd. dirs. Vis. Nurse Assn. Allegheny County, 1955-68, pres., 1962-64; trustee Shady Side Acad., Pitts., 1959—, chmn., 1971-74; trustee Ellis Sch., Pitts., 1969-74; bd. dirs. Pitts. Child Guidance Center, 1960-63; trustee Robert S. Waters Charitable Trust, 1971—; bd. dirs. Snyder Found., 1979—. Served with AUS, 1943-45; ETO. Decorated Bronze Star, Purple Heart. Mem. Am. Law Inst., ABA, Pa. Bar Assn. (chmn. jr. bar conf. 1957), Allegheny County Bar Assn. (pres. jr. bar sect. 1955). Republican. Episcopalian. Clubs: Duquesne, Fox Chapel Golf, Pitts. Golf, Harvard-Yale-Princeton (Pitts.). Home: 144 North Dr Pittsburgh PA 15238 Office: 747 Union Trust Bldg Pittsburgh PA 15230

DAVIS, JOHN ROWLAND, research adminstrator; b. Mpls., Dec. 19, 1927; s. Roland Owen and Dorothy (Norman) D.; m. Lois Marie Falk, Sept. 4, 1947; children—Joel C., Jacque L., Michele M., Robin E. B.S., U. Minn., 1949, M.S., 1951; postgrad., Purdue U., 1955-57; Ph.D., Mich. State U., 1959. Registered profl. engr., Calif., Oreg. Hydraulic engr. U.S. Geol. Survey, Lincoln, Nebr., 1950-51; instr. Mich. State U., 1951-55; asst. prof. Purdue U., 1955-57; lectr. U. Calif. at Davis, 1957-62; hydraulic engr. Stanford Research Inst., South Pasadena, Calif., 1962-64; prof. U. Nebr., Lincoln, 1964-65, dean, 1965-71; prof., head dept. agrl. engrng. Oreg. State U., Corvallis, 1971-75, dir. Agrl. Expt. Sta., asso. dean Sch. Agr.,, 1975—, instl. athletic rep., 1972—; mem. governing bd. Water Resources Research Inst., 1975—; dir. Western Rural Devel. Center, 1975—, Agrl. Research Found., Jackman Inst.; cons. Stanford Research Inst., Dept. Agr., Consortium for Internat. Devel.; dir. Engrs. Council Profl. Devel., 1966-72; pres. Pacific-10 Conf., 1978-79. Contbr. articles to profl. jours. Served with USNR, 1945-46. Fellow Am. Soc. Agrl. Engrs. (dir. 1971-73, agrl. engr. of year award Pacific Northwest region 1974); mem. AAAS, Nat. Coll. Athletic Assn. (v.p. 1979-83, sec.-treas. 1983—). Home: 2940 NW Aspen St Corvallis OR 97330

DAVIS, JOHN STAIGE, IV, physician; b. N.Y.C., Oct. 28, 1931; s. John Staige, III and Camilla Ruth (Cole) D.; m. Frederica Abbott, June 22, 1956; children—Susan, John, Stewart, Frederica, Rufus. B.A., Yale U., 1953; M.D., U. Pa., 1957. Diplomate: Am. Bd. Internal Medicine. Intern Hosp. U. Pa., Phila., 1957-58; resident in medicine U. Va. Hosp., Charlottesville, 1958-60; fellow in rheumatology, 1960-62; mem. faculty U. Va. Med. Sch., 1961—, prof. medicine, 1972—, chief div. rheumatology, 1967—; attending physician U. Va. Hosp., 1961—; vis. prof., chmn. dept. immunology U. Milan (Italy) Faculty Medicine, 1966-67; vis. prof. WHO Immunology Research and Tng. Center, Geneva, 1978-79; cons. WHO, 1979. Contbr. articles to med. jours., chpts. to books. Markle scholar acad. medicine, 1964-69; sr. investigator Arthritis Found., 1964-66, 67-70; Fogarty sr. internat. fellow, 1978-79. Fellow ACP; mem. AMA, Am. Fedn. Clin. Research, So. Soc. Clin. Investigation, Am. Clin. and Climatological Assn., Am. Rheumatism Assn., Am. Assn. Immunology, Albemarle County Med. Soc., Brit. Soc. Immunology, Med. Soc. Va., S.P.E.B.S.Q.S.A. Republican. Episcopalian. Club: Boar's Head Sports. Home: 325 Kent Rd Charlottesville VA 22903 Office: Sch Medicine Dir Rheumatology Dept Internal Medicine Charlottesville VA 22908

DAVIS, JOSEPH EDWARD, supermarket chain executive; b. Los Angeles, May 7, 1926; s. Joseph Edward and Myrtle Dorothy (Longstreet) D.; m. Marjorie Ann Mier, Mar. 27, 1953; children: Theresa, Sally, Victoria, Joseph. B.A., Occidental Coll., Los Angeles, 1949; M.B.A., U. Calif., Berkeley, 1951. C.P.A., Calif. Staff acct. Arthur Andersen & Co. (P.A.s), Los Angeles, 1951-59; with Alpha Beta Co., La Habra, Calif., 1959-83, controller, 1961-69, v.p., 1969-83, v.p. fin., 1973-83, Stater Bros. Markets, Colton, Calif., 1973-83. Treas. Museum Assn. North Orange County, 1975—, Fullerton-Morelia Sister City Assn., 1975—. Served with AUS, 1945-46. Mem. Am. Inst. C.P.A.s, Calif. Soc. C.P.A.s, Fin. Execs. Inst. Republican. Presbyterian. Club: Alta Vista Country. Office: 21700 Barton Road Coltonra CA 92324

DAVIS, JOSEPH LLOYD, educator, consultant; b. Crawfordsville, Iowa, May 4, 1927; s. Whitfield and Jane (Lloyd) D.; m. Margaret Florence Cooper, Dec. 28, 1949; children: Stephen Joseph, Thomas Whitfield, Jane Ellen. B.Sc., Ohio State U., 1949, M.A., 1955, Ph.D., 1967. Tchr. Morey Jr. High Sch., Denver, 1949-52; reporter Ohio State Jour., 1952-53; tchr. Central High Sch., Columbus, Ohio, 1953-54; asst. dir. adminstrv. research Columbus Public Schs., 1954-56, dir. publs. and public info., 1956-60, exec. asst. to supt., 1960-64, asst. supt. spl. services, 1964-77, supt. of schs., 1977-82; adj. prof. Ohio State U., 1983—; Trustee Columbus Convention and Visitors Bur., Center of Sci. and Industry, Ohio Council Econ. Edn. Mem. adv. bd. United Negro Coll. Fund.; bd. dirs. Franklin County Employment Commn. Served with USN, 1945-46, 50-51. Recipient award for civic leadership Columbus Area C. of C., 1980; Liberty Bell award Columbus Bar Assn., 1980. Mem. Am. Assn. Sch. Adminstrs., Nat. Sch. Public Relations Assn. (President's award 1980), Buckeye Assn. Sch. Adminstrs., Nat. Soc. Study of Edn., Phi Delta Kappa, Kappa Delta Pi. Presbyterian. Office: 270 E State St Columbus OH 43215

DAVIS, JOSEPH SAMUEL, department store executive; b. Chgo., Jan. 27, 1930; s. Joseph and Elizabeth (Cowen) D.; m. Martha Louise Gries, June 18, 1955; children: Elizabeth Louise, Katherine Ann, Mark Bennett, James Lincoln. B.A., Columbia U., 1951; M.B.A., Harvard U., 1953. From mgmt. trainee to buyer May D & F Co., Denver, 1956-61; from asst. div. mdse. mgr. to exec. v.p. Kaufmann's, Pitts., 1961-75; pres. G. Fox and Co., Hartford, Conn., 1975-79; pres., chief exec. officer M. O'Neil Co., Akron, Ohio, 1979-83, May D&F, Denver, 1983—; cons. dir. Banc-Ohio Nat. Bank, Akron, 1980-83; dir. Ohio Edison, 1982-83; adv. bd. Sch. Bus., Duquesne U., Pitts., 1974-79, Sch. Bus., U. Conn., 1977-79. Bd. dirs. Hartford Symphony Soc., 1977-79, Downtown Denver, Inc., 1983—, Nat. Jewish Hosp., 1984—; adv. bd. Akron Symphony, 1980-83, Jr. League Akron, 1979-83; trustee Akron Gen. Med. Center, 1980-83, Akron Art Mus., 1980-83, Akron Regional Devel. Bd., 1980-83, Denver Art Mus., 1984—. Served as officer USN, 1953-56. Mem. Harvard Bus. Sch. Club Colo. Clubs: Fox Chapel (Pa.) Racquet, Brown Palace. Office: May D&F 16th at Tremont Denver CO 80202

DAVIS, JOYCE STRIPLING, pathologist, educator; b. Big Spring, Tex., Feb. 18, 1924; d. Leslie Dayton and Alta Estelle (Hull) S.; m. Phil Davis, Mar. 27, 1946; children: Roger, Diane, Mark, Scott. B.S., Baylor U., 1945, M.D., 1947. Intern Washington U. Hosp., St. Louis, 1947-48; resident in pediatrics Methodist Hosp., Dallas, 1949; resident in pathology Baylor Hosp., 1952-53; asst. instr. Baylor Coll. Medicine, 1953-58, instr., 1954-60, asst. prof., 1960-65, asso. prof., 1965-79, adj. asso. prof., 1979—; gen. practice medicine, Mt. Vernon, Tex., 1950-51; prof., head dept. pathology and lab. medicine Tex. A&M U., College Station, 1975—. Mem. Assn. Pathology Chmn., Tex. Soc. Pathologists, Am. Soc. Clin. Pathologists, Houston Soc. Pathologists, Tex. Med. Assn., AMA. Democrat. Baptist. Home: 723 Shady Ln Bryan TX 77801 Office: College of Medicine Pathology and Laboratory Medicine College Station TX 77843

DAVIS, JULIA MCBROOM, speech and audiology educator; b. Alexandria, La., Sept. 29, 1930; d. Guy Clarence and Addie (McElroy) McBroom; m. Cecil Ponder Davis, Aug., Aug. 25, 1951 (div. 1981); children: Mark Holden, Paul Houston, Anne Hamilton. B.A., Northwestern State U., natchitoches, La., 1951; M.S., U. So. Miss., 1965, Ph.D., 1966. Cert. in clin. competence and audiology. Asst. prof. U. So. Miss., Hattiesburg, 1966-69; assoc. U. so. Miss., 1969-71; assoc. prof. Southwestern State U., Hammond, 1971; faculty U. Iowa, Iowa City, 1971—, prof., chmn. dept. speech pathology and audiology,

1980—, dir. Speech and Hearing Ctr., 1979-80. Author: (with Edward J. Hardick) Rehabilitative Audiology for Children and Adults, 1981; editor: Our Forgotten Children, 1977; assoc. editor Jour. Speech Hearing Research, 1975-77, Jour. Speech Hearing Disorders, 1982-83. Fellow Am. Speech-Hearing-Lang. Assn. (chmn. program com. 1980-81); mem. Acad. Rehabilitative Audiology (pres. 1979-80), Iowa Conf. for Hearing Impaired (pres. 1975-76), Iowa Speech and Hearing Assn. (v.p.-liaison 1972—), Sigma Xi. Democrat. Methodist. Office: Dept Speech Pathology and Audiology U Iowa Iowa City IA 52242

DAVIS, KEITH EUGENE, psychologist; b. Clifton, N.C., May 15, 1936; s. Ted Eugene and Mary Flossie (Rol) D.; m. Dorothy Ann Reeves, Feb. 23, 1968; 1 dau., Kristin Lee; children from previous marriage—Rachel, Rebecca, Jessica. B.A., Duke U., 1958, Ph.D., 1963. Instr. psychology Princeton U., 1961-62; asst. prof. U. Colo., Boulder, 1962-67, asso. prof., 1967-70; prof., chmn. dept. psychology Livingston Coll., Rutgers U., New Brunswick, N.J., 1970-73; prof. psychology U. S.C., Columbia, 1973—, provost of univ., 1974-78; found MAPS, mgmt. cons.; mem. population study sect. Nat. Inst. Child Health and Human Devel., 1973-76; mem. mental health research edn. rev. com. NIMH, 1979—, chmn., 1980—, State Plan Adv. Com., S.C. State Dept. Mental Health, 1976-78; bd. dirs. Columbia Area Mental Health Center, 1976-82, chmn. bd., 1981; pres. past participants (Greater Columbia Forum), 1975-76. Author: Advances in Experimental Social Psychology, 1963; author, editor: Advances in Descriptive Psychology, 1981; contbr. articles to profl. jours. Woodrow Wilson fellow, 1958-59; So. Fellowships Fund fellow, 1958-61. Mem. Am. Psychol. Assn., Am. Sociol. Assn., Mind Assn., Nat. Council Family Relations, Soc. Descriptive Psychology (1st pres. 1979-81), Phi Beta Kappa, Omicron Delta Kappa. Democrat. Home: 1808 Catawba St Columbia SC 29205 Office: Dept Psychology U of SC Columbia SC 29208

DAVIS, KENNETH A., retail executive; b. N.Y.C., May 13, 1949; s. Irving and Gloria (Schwartzbaum) D.; m. Marcie Brecker, June 15, 1975. B.S. in Econs., Cornell U., 1971. Vice pres. Weather All Fashions, N.Y.C., 1972-79; v.p. SE Nichols, Inc., N.Y.C., 1979-83, pres., 1983—. Club: Fresh Meadow (Great Neck, N.Y.). Office: SE Nichols Inc 275 7th Ave New York NY 10001

DAVIS, KENNETH CULP, lawyer, educator; b. Leeton, Mo., Dec. 19, 1908; s. Samuel Houston and Charlotte (Culp) D.; m. Carol Seeds, June 20, 1934; children—Malcolm Fletcher, Margaret Lynn; m. Inger Pedersen, June 14, 1962. A.B., Whitman Coll., 1931, LL.D., 1971; LL.B., Harvard, 1934. Bar: Ohio 1935. Practiced in, Cleve., 1934-35; asst. prof., then asso. prof. W.Va. U., 1935-39; with Dept. Justice, 1939-40; prof. law U. Tex., 1940-48, U. Minn., 1950-61; John P. Wilson prof. law U. Chgo., 1961-76; prof. law U. San Diego, 1976—; Vis. prof. law Harvard, 1948-50; staff mem. (Bd. Investigation and Research), 1942. Author: Administrative Law, 1951, Administrative Law Treatise, 4 vols, 1958, 2d edit., Vol. 1, 1978, Vol. 2, 1979, Vol. 3, 1980, Vol. 4, 1983, Administrative Law Cases-Text Problems, 6th edit, 1977, Administrative Law and Government, 1960; 2d edit., 1975, Discretionary Justice: A Preliminary Inquiry, 1969, Administrative Law Text, 3d edit, 1972, Police Discretion, 1975, Discretionary Justice in Europe and America, 1976. Mem. Phi Beta Kappa, Delta Sigma Rho, Phi Delta Theta. Home: 2480 Rue Denise La Jolla CA 92037

DAVIS, KENNETH EUGENE, chem. co. exec.; b. Portsmouth, Ohio, Nov. 19, 1935; s. Kenneth Wood and Freda Louise (Frese) D.; m. Reba Jeanne LeVally, Nov. 21, 1956; children—Jennifer Anne, Jeffrey Eugene, Gregory Brant. B.C.E., Ohio State U., 1958. With Ohio State U. Research Found., Columbus, 1955-58; supr. chem. research BSAF Wyandotte, Wyandotte, Mich., 1958-67; mgr. chem. engring. research Stauffer Chem. Co., Dobbs Ferry, N.Y., 1967-68, v.p., exec. asst. to pres., Westport, Conn., 1975-77, exec. v.p., 1977-80, pres., chief operating officer, 1980—, also mem. operating com., dir.; v.p., gen. mgr. SWS Silicone Corp., Adrian, Mich., 1968-75; dir. Conn. Nat. Bank. Mem. Am. Chem. Soc., Am. Inst. Chem. Engrs., Soc. Chem. Industry, Mfg. Chemists Assn. Clubs: Patterson, Aspetuck. Patentee in field.

DAVIS, KINGSLEY, sociologist, educator, researcher; b. Tuxedo, Tex., Aug. 20, 1908; s. Joseph Dyer and Winifred (Kingsley) D.; m. Jo Ann Daily, Aug. 20, 1936 (div.); children: Jo Ann Daily, Jefferson; m., Nov. 3, 1954 (div. 1977); 1 dau., Laura Isabelle. A.B. in English, U. Tex., 1930; M.A. in Philosophy, 1932, Harvard U., 1933, Ph.D., 1936. Instr. in sociology Smith Coll., 1934-36; asst. prof. sociology Clark U., 1936-37; assoc. prof., chmn. dept. Pa. State U., University Park, 1937-42, prof., chmn., 1942-44; vis. research assoc. Office Population Research, Princeton U., 1942-44; research assoc. Princeton U., 1944-48, assoc. prof. pub. affairs, 1944-45, assoc. prof. anthropology and sociology, 1945-48; prof. sociology U. Calif.-Berkeley, 1955-70, chmn. internat. population and urban research, 1956-77, chmn. dept. sociology, 1961-63, Ford prof. sociology and comparative studies, 1970-76, Ford prof. emeritus, recalled, 1976-77; disting. prof. sociology U. So. Calif., Los Angeles, 1977—; sr. research fellow Hoover Instn., Stanford U., Calif., 1981—; U.S. rep. Population Commn., UN, N.Y.C., 1954-61; mem. NASA Adv. Council, Washington, 1977-82, Adv. Council Sci. and Tech., Legis Assembly, Sacramento, 1970-71; disting. lectr. SUNY-Stony Brook, 1983. Author: Human Society, 1949, The Population of India and Pakistan, 1951, World Urbanization, 1972; editor: Cities, 1973. Recipient Irene Taeuber award for disting. research in demography, 1979, Commonwealth award for research in sociology, 1979; Oldright fellow, 1931-32; Henry Bromfield Rogers Meml. fellow, 1932-33; Social Sci. Research Council postdoctoral fellow, 1940-41; Carnegie Corp. traveling fellow, 1952; Ctr. Advanced Study Behavioral Scis. fellow, 1956-57, 80-81; NSF sr. postdoctoral fellow, 1964-65. Fellow AAAS (chmn. sect. 1963, 81, v.p. 1963), Am. Sociol. Assn. (pres. 1959, Disting. Career award 1982), Am. Statis. Assn. (liaison mem. council 1968-69); mem. Population Assn. Am. (pres. 1962-63), Sociol. Research Assn. (pres. 1960), AAUP (mem. council 1962—), Am. Eugenics Soc. (bd. dirs. 1953-55), Internat. Union Sci. Study Population (chmn. Am. com. 1967-68), Nat. Acad. Scis., Am. Acad. Arts and Scis., Am. Philos. Soc., World Acad. Art and Sci., Phi Beta Kappa (vis. scholar 1976-77). Home: 975 Wing Pl Stanford CA 94305 Office: Hoover Instn Stanford U Stanford CA 94305

DAVIS, LANCE EDWIN, economics educator; b. Seattle, Nov. 3, 1928; s. Maurice L. and Marjorie Dee (Seibert) D.; m. Susan Elizabeth Gray, Dec. 2, 1977; 1 dau., Maili. B.A., U. Wash., Seattle, 1950; Ph.D. (Ford Found. dissertation fellow summer 1956), Johns Hopkins U., 1956. Teaching asst. U. Wash., 1950-51, 52-53; teaching asst., then instr. Johns Hopkins U., 1953-55; from instr. to prof. econs. Purdue U., 1955-62; mem. faculty Calif. Inst. Tech., Pasadena, prof. econs., 1968—, Mary Stillman Harkness prof., 1980—; research asso. Nat. Bur. Econ. Research, 1979—. Author: The Growth of Industrial Enterprise, 1964; co-author: The Savings Bank of Baltimore, 1956, American Economic History: The Development of a National Economy, 2d rev. edit, 1968, Institutional Change and American Economic Growth, 1971; Co-editor: American Economic Growth: An Economist's History of the United States, 1971; bd. editors: Jour. Econ. History, 1965-73. Served with USNR, 1945-48, 51-52. Recipient Arthur Cole prize Econ. History Assn., 1966; Ford Found. Faculty fellow, 1959-60; Guggenheim fellow, 1964-65. Mem. Council Research Econ. History (chmn. 1973-74, 75-76), Econ. History Assn. (pres. 1978-79, trustee 1980-82), Anglo-Am. Hist. Assn. (gov. 1978-80). Home: 1746 Grevelia St South Pasadena CA 91030 Office: Humanities and Social Scis Div Calif Inst Tech Pasadena CA 91125

DAVIS, LAURENCE LAIRD, coal company executive; b. Cin., June 6, 1915; s. Thomas Jefferson and Jane (Brown) D.; m. Charlotte Rowe Nichols, Oct. 12, 1940 (dec. Sept. 1973); children: Sally Laird (Mrs. Arthur D. Pratt), Laurence Laird, Thomas Jefferson II; m. Onlee Partin, Nov. 7, 1973; 1 dau., Nancy Matilda Kathleen; stepchildren: Rickey Lee Foland, Stella Logan Turner, Samuel J. Logan, Gregory C. Logan. Grad., St. Mark's Sch., 1934; A.B., Harvard, 1938; postgrad., London (Eng.) Sch. Econs., 1939. With First Nat. Bank Cin., 1939-42, 46-70, v.p., 1949-64, vice chmn. bd., dir., 1964-70; also dir.; vice consul, econ. analyst State Dept., 1943-45; financial cons., 1970—; pres., dir. Roberta Coal Co., Elkhorn Collieries Co., Millers Creek Mineral Devel. Co., Burning Springs Land Co.; Chmn. English Speaking Union, 1965-72. Pres. Symphony Orch., 1965-68; Bd. dirs. Christ Hosp. Mem. Greater Cin. C. of C. (pres. 1965-68). Clubs: Commonwealth, Camargo, Queen City (Cin.). Home: 6910 Given Rd Cincinnati OH 45243 Office: 7710 Shawnee Run Rd Box 43096 Cincinnati OH 45243 Treasure Cay Abaco Bahamas

DAVIS, LEODIS, chemistry educator, researcher; b. Stamps, Ark., Sept. 25, 1933; s. Prentiss and Mary Ann (Anthony) D.; m. Norma June, Apr. 27, 1962; children: Melonie L., Leon E. B.S., U. Mo., Kansas City, 1956; M.S., Iowa State U., 1958, Ph.D., 1960. Asst. prof. chemistry Tenn. State U., Nashville, 1961-62; asst. prof. Howard U., Washington, 1962-67, assoc. prof., 1967-68, U. Iowa, Iowa City, 1969-76; prof., chmn. dept. chemistry Iowa City, 1976—; cons. in field. Recipient Lederle Med. Faculty award Lederle Pharm. Co., 1967-69; Victor Wilson scholar, 1952-56. Mem. Am. Chem. Soc., Am. Soc. Biol. Chemists, Sigma Xi, Phi Lambda Upsilon. Democrat. Office: U Iowa Dept Chemistry Iowa City IA 52242

DAVIS, LEONARD MCCUTCHAN, speech educator; b. Duffy, W.Va., July 14, 1919; s. Arch Goff and Ressie (McCutchan) D.; m. Mary Abrilla Bateman, Aug. 28, 1948; children: Leonard McCutchan, Anne Edmondson, James Mansfield. A.B., W.Va. U., 1948, M.A., 1950; Ph.D., Northwestern U., 1958. Dir. forensics Montevallo U., 1950-53; lectr. mgmt. communications U. Calif.—Berkeley; teaching fellow Northwestern U., 1953-54; instr. Nat. High Sch. Speech Inst., 1954; prof. W.Va. U., Morgantown, 1954—, chmn. dept. speech, 1966-72; Vis. prof. speech U. Calif.-, Santa Barbara, 1965-66, 67-68, U. Ariz, summer 1966; faculty Va. Banking Sch., 1961—; lectr. bus. and profl. communications UCLA; lectr. mgmt. communications U. Calif.-Berkeley; cons. in mgmt. communications for industry and hosps. Hist. preservation officer State of W.Va., 1973-78; chmn. (Gov.'s Bd. of Rev. for Hist. Preservation), 1975-78; mem. W.Va. Archives and History Commn., 1978-80; chmn. W.Va. Capitol Bldg. Commn.; mem. Hist. W.Va. Capitol Commn. Author: Mr. Lincoln Goes to Gettysburg, 1960, Night of Assassins (Death and Funeral of Abraham Lincoln), 1959, General Nathan Goff, Orator and Statesman, 1951, Communications in High-Risk Occupations, 1970, Perceived Power as a Mediator of Management Communication Style, 1980, Individual Differences Among Employees, 1982, Power in Organizations: Communications Techniques and Strategies, 1984; Editor: Official Statements and Papers of Governor Arch A. Moore, Jr., 3 vols; Contbr. monthly article: Banking News. Served with AUS, 1941-45. Mem. AAUP, Internat. Communication Assn., Eastern States Communication Assn., World Communication Assn., Beta Theta Pi, Delta Sigma Rho. Methodist. Clubs: Mason, Rotarian. Home: 401 Rotary St Morgantown WV 26505

DAVIS, LEVERETT, JR., educator; b. Elgin, Ill., Mar. 3, 1914; s. Leverett and Susan (Gulick) D.; m. Victoria Merrill Stocker, June 19, 1943; 1 son, Jeffrey Leverett. Student, U. Wash., 1930-32; B.S., Oreg. State Coll., 1936; M.S., Calif. Inst. Tech., 1938, Ph.D., 1941. Fellow faculty Calif. Inst. Tech., Pasadena, 1941—, prof. physics, 1956-81, prof. emeritus, 1981—. Recipient Exceptional Achievement award NASA, 1970. Mem. Am. Phys. Soc., Am. Astron. Soc., Internat. Astron. Union, Am. Geophys. Union. Home: 1772 N Grand Oaks Ave Altadena CA 91001 Office: Dept Physics California Inst Tech Pasadena CA 91125

DAVIS, LORRAINE JENSEN, magazine editor; b. Omaha, Apr. 2, 1924; d. Theron R. and L. Mildred (Henkel) Jensen; m. Richard Morris Davis, Apr. 4, 1959; 1 dau., Laura Jensen. B.A., U. Denver, 1946. Copywriter Glamour mag., N.Y.C., 1946-54, prodn. editor, 1954-61, Vogue Children mag., N.Y.C., 1963-66. Writer, asso. features editor, Vogue mag., N.Y.C., 1966-77; mng. editor, writer women's news column, 1977—; editor: Vogue Living and Food Guide, 1975; editorial cons.: Vogue Beauty and Health Guide, 1979-82; Editor: Cooking with Colette (by Colette Rossant), 1975, Fairchild Dictionary of Fashion (by Charlotte Calasibetta), 1975; English translation Paul Bocuse's French Cooking, 1977. Recipient Disting. Citizen award Alpha Gamma Delta, 1981. Mem. NOW, Am. Soc. Mag. Editors. Democrat. Episcopalian. Home: 425 E 63d St W3J New York NY 10021 Office: 350 Madison Ave New York NY 10017

DAVIS, LOUIS FREEMAN, ret. petroleum co. exec.; b. Longview, Tex., May 5, 1914; s. Edward William and Bertha Lee (Davis) D.; m. Elizabeth Murphy Mock, 1978; children by previous marriage—Fred Edward, Louis Freeman. B.S. in Mech. Engring, U. Tex., 1934; postgrad., Tex. A. and M. U., 1935. With Atlantic Richfield Co. (formerly Atlantic Refining Co.), 1935—, v.p., gen. mgr., 1965-66, sr. v.p., 1966-68, exec. v.p., dir., Dallas, 1968-72, Los Angeles, 1972-75, vice chmn., dir., 1975-79; pres., dir. Anaconda Co., 1978—; Mem. adv. council U. Tex. Coll. Engring. Mem. Soc. Petroleum Engrs., Am. Mining Congress, Am. Petroleum Inst. Clubs: Monterey Peninsula Country, Dallas Brook Hollow Golf, Dallas Petroleum. 17 Mile Dr and Spyglass Hill Rd Pebble Beach CA Office: 2929 LTV Tower Dallas TX 75201

DAVIS, LUTHER, writer-producer; b. N.Y.C., Aug. 29, 1921; s. Charles Thomas and Henriette (Roesler) D.; m. Dorothy deMilhau, Nov. 3, 1943 (div. 1961); children: Noelle, Laura Duval. B.A., Yale U., 1938. Author: play Kiss Them for Me, 1945; (with Charles Lederer) Libretto Kismet, 1953 (Tony award 1954), Timbuktu, 1978 (Tony award 1979); 15 screenplays including The Hucksters, 1946, A Lion Is In The Streets, 1950; producer-author: films Lady in a Cage, 1964, Across 110th Street, 1972. Served to maj. USAAF, 1942-45; CBI, ETO. Mem. Dramatists Guild Am., Writers Guild Am.-West, League N.Y. Theaters and Producers, Producers Guild Am. Club: New York Athletic (N.Y.C.).

DAVIS, LUTHER, JR., physicist; b. Mineola, N.Y., July 12, 1922; s. Luther and Anne Marie (Grod) D.; m. Joanne Wilder, Sept. 8, 1951; children—Hunt Collyer, Nancy Locke, Mark Wilder. B.S., Mass. Inst. Tech., 1942; Ph.D., 1949. Mem. staff Radiation Lab., Mass. Inst. Tech., 1942-45, research asso., 1945-49; with research div. Raytheon Co., Waltham, Mass., 1949—, asst. gen. mgr., 1958-69, gen. mgr., 1969—; cons. USAF Sci. Adv. Bd., 1958-60, NSF, 1975-78. Fellow IEEE; mem. Am. Phys. Soc. Episcopalian. Patentee microwave strip transmission line circulator. Office: 131 Spring St Lexington MA 02173

DAVIS, LYNN ETHERIDGE, polit. scientist, former government official; b. Miami, Fla., Sept. 6, 1943; d. Earl DeWitt and Louise (Featherston) Etheridge; m. John Roderick Davis, Aug. 6, 1966. B.A., Duke U., 1965; M.A., Columbia U., 1967, Ph.D., 1971. Asst. prof. polit. sci. Barnard Coll., Columbia U., N.Y.C., 1970-74; asst. prof. polit. sci. Columbia U., 1974-78; mem. staff Nat. Security Council, 1974, (Senate Select Com. on Intelligence), 1975-76; dep. asst. Sec. of Def. for Policy Plans and Nat. Security Affairs, Dept. Def., Washington, 1977-79; asst. dep. Under Sec. Def. for Policy Planning, 1979-81; sr. research Internat. Inst. Strategic Studies, London, 1981-82; prof. Nat. War Coll., Washington, 1982—. Author: The Cold War Begins, 1974. Woodrow Wilson fellow, 1965-66, 69-70; Columbia U. fellow, 1965-66, 68-69; Recipient David D. Lloyd prize Harry S Truman Library, 1976. Mem. Council Fgn. Relations, Phi Beta Kappa. Home: 205 Yoakum Pkwy Apt 1615 Alexandria VA 22304 Office: Nat War College Washington DC 20319

DAVIS, MAC, singer, songwriter; b. Lubbock, Tex., Jan. 21, 1942; s. T.J. and Edith Irene (Lankford) D.; 1 son, Joel Scott. Student, Emory U., Ga. State Coll. Employed as ditch digger, service sta. attendant, laborer, probation officer; dist. sales mgr. Liberty Records, 1965; profl. mgr. Metric Music, 1966-68. Entertainer, singer, 1969-77; TV spl. You Put Music in My Life, 1978; appeared in films: North Dallas Forty, 1979, Cheaper to Keep Her, 1980, The Sting II, 1983; rec. artist films; composer numerous popular songs. Office: Katz-Gallin-Morey Enterprises Inc 9255 Sunset Blvd Room 1115 Los Angeles CA 90069

DAVIS, MARTIN DAVID, mathematics educator; b. N.Y.C., N.Y., Mar. 8, 1928; s. Harry and Helen (Gotlieb) D.; m. Virginia Whiteford Palmer, Sept. 21, 1951; children—Harold, Nathan. B.S., CCNY, 1948; M.A., Princeton, 1949, Ph.D., 1950. Research instr. U. Ill., 1950-52; mem. (Inst. Advanced Study), 1952-54; asst. prof. U. Calif. at Davis, 1954-55, Ohio State U., 1955-56; asst. prof., then asso. prof. (Rensselaer Polytech. Inst.), 1956-59; mem. faculty N.Y.U., 1959-60, 65—, prof., 1969—; asso. prof. Belfer Grad. Sch. Sci., Yeshiva U., 1960-62, prof., 1962-65, 70-71; vis. prof. Westfield Coll., U. London, 1968-69, U. Calif., Berkeley, 1976-77, Santa Barbara, 1978-79; cons. Bell Telephone Labs., IBM. Author: Computability and Unsolvability, 1958, Applied Nonstandard Analysis, 1977, (with Elaine Weyuker) Computability, Complexity and Languages, 1983. Recipient Chauvent, Ford prizes Math. Assn. Am., Steele prize Am. Math. Soc. (all for articles on Hilbert's 10th problem).; Guggenheim Found. fellow, 1983. Mem. Am. Math. Soc., Assn. Symbolic Logic, Assn. Computing Machinery. Home: 326 W 85th St New York NY 10024

DAVIS, MARTIN S., diversified industry executive; b. N.Y.C. Student, N.Y. U., CCNY. Vice chmn., chief exec. officer mem. exec. com., dir. Gulf & Western Industries, Inc.; Bd. dirs. Nat. Multiple Sclerosis Soc., Found. for Children with Learning Disabilities; trustee John Jay Coll. Criminal Justice., Citizens Budget Commn. Office: 1 Gulf and Western Plaza New York NY 10023

DAVIS, MARVIN, petroleum company executive. Gen. ptnr. Davis Oil Co., Denver; co-owner 20th Century-Fox, 1981—. Office: care Sam Lusky Sam Lusky Assocs 633 17th St Suite 1616 Denver CO 80202§

DAVIS, MATTHEW DINSDALE, ophthalmologist; b. Madison, Wis., Oct. 25, 1926; s. Frederick A. and Edith Dinsdale (Swenson) D.; children—Matthew, Ann, Peter, Amelia, Lisa. B.A., U. Wis., 1947; M.D., U. Pa., 1950. Diplomate: Am. Bd. Ophthalmology. Intern, then resident U. Hosp., Madison; fellow Retina Service, Mass. Eye and Ear Infirmary, Boston; clin. instr. ophthalmology U. Wis., Madison, 1956-59, asst. clin. prof., 1959-65, asso. clin. prof., 1965-70, prof., chmn. dept. ophthalmology, 1970—. Mem. AMA, Wis. State Med. Soc., Dane County Med. Soc., Am. Acad. Ophthalmology, Wis.-Upper Mich. Soc. Ophthalmology, Assn. for Research in Vision and Ophthalmology, Soc. Heed Fellows, Retina Soc., Club Jules Gonin, Am. Ophthalmol. Soc. Home: 2106 Kendall St Madison WI 53705 Office: 600 Highland Ave Madison WI 53792

DAVIS, MATTIE BELLE EDWARDS, retired county judge; b. Ellabell, Ga., Feb. 28, 1910; d. Frank Pierce and Eddie (Morgan) Edwards; m. Troy Carson Davis, June 6, 1937 (dec. Aug. 1948); stepchildren: Jane (Mrs. Robert Gordon Potter), Betsy (Mrs. James W. Clark, Jr.). Student law in law office. Bar: Fla. 1936, U.S. Supreme Ct. 1950. Legal sec., 1927-36, practice with husband in, Miami, 1936-48, pvt. practice, 1948-59; judge Met. Ct. Dade County Fla., 1959-72, County Ct. Dade County, 1973-80; Mem. exec. com. Women's Conf. Nat. Safety Council, 1960-80, chmn., 1968-70; bd. dirs. Nat. Safety Council, 1965, v.p. women, 1973-80; mem. Fla. Gov.'s Hwy. Safety Com., 1970-81, Nat. Hwy. Safety Adv. Com., 1967-71; mem. registrants adv. bd. SSS, World War II. Pres. Dade County Tb Assn., 1960-62; exec. com. Fla. Tb and Respiratory Disease Assn., 1960-66; pres. Haven Sch. Mentally Retarded, 1958-60, sec., 1960-69; Trustee Andrew Coll., Cuthbert, Ga., 1960-81. Mem. Nat. Assn. Women Lawyers (treas. 1961-62, corr. sec. 1962-63, v.p. 1963-64, pres. 1965-66), Fla. Assn. Women Lawyers (pres. 1957-58), ABA (ho. of dels. 1967-75, 77-81, com. on constitution and by laws 1980—), Dade County Bar Assn., Fla. Bar, Internat. Fedn. Women Lawyers, Nat. Assn. Women Judges (a founder), Miami Bus. and Profl. Women's Club (pres. 1952-54), Nat. Fedn. Bus. and Profl. Women's Clubs (dir. dist. Fla. 1956-57), Kappa Beta Pi. Democrat. Methodist (supt. Sunday sch. 1948-54, chmn. ofcl. bd. 1957-60, trustee 1952-67, adminstrv. bd. 1968—). Club: Zonta Internat. Home: 402 Como Ave Coral Gables FL 33146

DAVIS, MELTON S., author; b. N.Y.C., Dec. 27, 1910; s. Charles Samillow and Jean (Zicklin) D.; m. Ferda Firat, Nov. 27, 1968 (div. May 1978). Student, U. Ala., 1928-30, U. Calif., 1936-37, Am. U., 1944, Centre Cultural Internat. de Royaumont, Asnieres, France, 1947-48. Pub. relations officer Office Fgn. Liquidation Commr., Dept. State, Paris, 1946-47; editor UNESCO, Paris, 1948-50; dir. radio Marshall Plan for Europe, Africa and Middle East, 1950-52; Mediterranean editor World mag.; also polit. columnist N.Y. Post, 1954-56; chief bur. Italy MBS, 1962—; editorial cons. Lancio Publs., Rome, Italy, 1972—. Author: All Rome Trembled, 1957, The Voluptuaries, 1964, Who Defends Rome, 1972; Contbr. to: Good Housekeeping, N.Y. Times Mag., Reader's Digest, Parade, Cosmopolitan, others. Served with AUS, World War II. Mem. Am. Soc. Journalists and Authors, Stampa Estera. Address: 11 Via Scipione Gaetano 00197 Rome Italy

DAVIS, MICHAEL DAVID, violinist; b. Hull, Eng., May 29, 1937; came to U.S., 1959; s. Jack W. and Hilda D.; 1 son, Steven Michael. Student, Guildhall Sch. Music, London, 1954-57, Staatliche Hochschule fur Musik, Koln, Germany, 1957-59; licentiate, Royal Acad. Music, London, 1955. Asso. Royal Coll. Music, London, 1955; Artist-in-residence Coll. Wooster, 1960-74; concertmaster Scottish Nat. Orch., 1974-76; artist prof. violin Ohio State U., 1976. Concertmaster, Columbus (Ohio) Symphony Orch., 1977—; rec. artist, Orion Records; recitalist, N.Y.C., Vienna, Austria, Athens, Greece, Amsterdam, Netherlands, Hague, Netherlands, Rotterdam, Netherlands, London, Brussels, Cologne, Germany, and others. (Winner Internat. Carl Flesch Competition 1957). Mem. N.Y. Musicians Club, Am. String Tchrs. Assn. (life), Pi Kappa Lambda. Office: Hughes Hall 1899 College Ave Columbus OH 43210

DAVIS, MILES DEWEY, trumpeter; b. Alton, Ill., May 25, 1926; m. Cicely Tyson, 1981. Student music, Juilliard Sch. Formerly played with, Eckstine Orch., Charlie Parker, Benny Carter, others; composer: film soundtracks Elevator to the Gallows, 1957, Jack Johnson, 1970 Recipient Grammy awards for recs. Sketches of Spain 1960, Bitches Brew 1970, numerous Down Beat mag. awards including Hall of Fame. Address: care Associated Booking Corp 445 Park Ave New York NY 10022 *

DAVIS, MILTON WICKERS, JR., chemical engineer; b. Frederick, Md., Apr. 5, 1923; s. Milton Wickers and Elizabeth Howard Griffith (Wood) D.; m. Roberta B. McIntyre, Dec. 18, 1948; 1 child, Gaither Griffith; m. Jane Crayton, May 21, 1955; 1 son, Richard Render; m. Harriett P. Ackerman, Dec. 24, 1977; 1 dau., Linda Marie Ackerman. B.E., Johns Hopkins U., 1943; M.S., U. Calif., Berkeley, 1949, Ph.D., 1951. Research asst. U. Calif. Radiation Lab., 1947-50; research engr. atomic energy div. duPont Co., Wilmington, Del., 1950-54, research supr., Aiken, S.C., 1954-62; Weisiger prof. chem. engring. U. S.C., Columbia, 1962—. Contbr.: Chemical Processing of Nuclear Fuels, 1970. Served to lt. USNR, 1943-46. Mem. Am. Inst. Chem. Engrs., Am. Chem. Soc., Md. Soc. War of 1812, Delta Phi. Episcopalian. Clubs: Sea Pines, Island (Hilton Head Island, S.C.). Address: PO Box 242 Columbia SC 29202 *Behave ethically in dealing with others. Be punctual in keeping appointments. Know that if you are doing the same things as all others in business, you are probably wrong. Be persistent. Your behavior in times of adversity is more important than your behavior in times of success.*

DAVIS, MONTE VINCENT, engineer, educator; b. Cove, Oreg., Apr. 29, 1923; s. Ruben Francis and Pomona Virginia (Stacklund) D.; m. Nancy Elaine Adler, May 5, 1973. B.A., Linfield Coll., 1949; M.A., Oreg. State U., 1951, Ph.D., 1956. Sr. scientist Gen. Electric Co., Richland, Wash., 1951-57; group leader, project dir. Atomics Internat. div. Rockwell Internat., Canoga Park, Calif., 1957-61; prof., dir. reactor lab. U. Ariz., 1961-73; dir. Neely Nuclear Research Center; prof. Ga. Inst. Tech., Atlanta, 1973-80, 1980—; pres. MND, Inc., Atlanta, 1975—; cons. U.S. Nuclear Regulatory Commn. Served with USAAF, 1943-46. Fellow Am. Nuclear Soc.; mem. Am. Phys. Soc., Soc. Nuclear Medicine, Internat. Solar Energy Soc., Sigma Xi. Clubs: Bent Tree Country (Jasper, Ga.); Druid Hills Country (Atlanta). Home: 1207 Reeder Circle NE Atlanta GA 30306 Office: 900 Atlantic Dr NW Atlanta GA 30318

DAVIS, MORRIS SCHUYLER, astronomer; b. Bklyn., Dec. 14, 1919; s. Nathan Samuel and Helen (Gross) D.; m. Dorothy Irene Hall, May 26, 1945; children—Glenn Craig, Elizabeth Davis Nyblade, Cynthia Louise, Deborah Susan Davis Toth, Nelli Katherine, Martha Davis Werlen. B.A., Bklyn. Coll., 1946; M.A., U. Mo., 1947; Ph.D., Yale U., 1950. Dir. Computer Center, Yale U., New Haven, 1956-66; also research asso. astronomy; pres. dir. Triangle Univs. Computation Center, Research Triangle Park, N.C., 1966-70; Morehead prof. astronomy U. N.C., Chapel Hill, 1970—. Fellow AAAS; mem. Univ. Research Assn. (trustee 1977—), Am. Astronom. Soc., Internat. Astron. Union. Unitarian. Home: 404 Estes Dr Chapel Hill NC 27514 Office: Dept Physics and Astronomy U NC Phillips Hall 039A Chapel Hill NC 27514

DAVIS, MOSHE, historian; b. Bklyn., June 12, 1916; s. William and Ida (Schenker) D.; m. Lottie Keiser, June 11, 1939; children: Zev, Tamar. B.S., Columbia U., 1937; Pd.B., Jewish Theol. Sem. Am., 1937, M.H.L., 1942; Ph.D., Hebrew U. Jerusalem, 1946; L.H.D. (hon.), Hebrew Union Coll.-Jewish Inst. Religion, 1974. Rabbi, 1942; registrar Jewish Theol. Sem. Am., N.Y.C., 1942-46, dean, 1946-51, provost, 1950-63, dir. Am. Jewish History Center, 1953-65, editor Regional History Series, 1963—, asso. prof. Am. Jewish history, 1956-63, research prof., 1963—; founding head Inst. Contempory Jewry, Hebrew U. Jerusalem, Israel, 1959—, vis. prof., 1959-63, assoc. prof. Am. Jewish history, 1963-70, Stephen S. Wise prof. Am. Jewish history and instns., 1970—; vis. scholar, cons. univs., Latin Am., U.S., Can., Europe.; mem. adv. com. Centre National des Hautes Etudes Juive, Brussels, 1962-75; chmn. Israel Pres.'s Study Circle on World Jewry, 1966—, Pres.'s Continuing Seminar on World Jewry and State of Israel, 1973—; Mem. adv. bd. Jewish Jour. Sociology, 1966—; committeeman Irving Neuman Hebrew Lit. award N.Y. U.; chmn. J. Machover Trust for Contemporary Jewish History, London. Program editor: Eternal Light, NBC-Radio, 1942-52, Frontiers of Faith, NBC-TV, 1951-53; Author: Shaping of American Judaism, 1951, Jewish Religious Life and Institutions, 1953, rev. edit., 1971, (with V. Ratner) Birthday of the World, 1959, Emergence of Conservative Judaism, 1963, From Dependence to Mutuality: The American Jewish Community and World Jewry, 1970; Editor: M.M. Kaplan Jubilee Volumes, 1951, Israel: Its Role in Civilization, 1956, Publications of Study Circle in Home of President of Israel, series I, 1967—, series XI, 1981, Contemporary Jewish Civilization Series, Vol. I, 1970, Vols. II and III, 1971—, (with A.J. Karp) Texts and Studies in American Jewish History, Vol. I, 1970, Vols. II, III, 1971, Vol. IV, 1976, Vol. V, 1979, The Yom Kippur War—Israel and the Jewish People, 1974, Hebrew vol., 1975, (with Y. Bauer and I. Kolatt) Studies in the History of Zionism, 1976, World Jewry and the State of Israel, 1977, With Eyes Toward Zion, 1977, Zionism in Transition, 1980; advisory editor: America and the Holy Land Collection, 1977; project dir.: Am. Holy Land Studies. Recipient Louis LaMed award for Hebrew Lit., 1951, citation B'nai B'rith, 1973, Lee M. Friedman Scholar's award, 1977; Lena Sokolow fellow, 1937-38; Guggenheim fellow, 1956, 59. Mem. Am. Jewish Hist. Soc. (hon. v.p. 1956—), Israel Hist. Soc. (exec. com. 1962—), Jewish Publ. Soc. (publ. com. 1963—), World Union of Jewish Studies (exec. council). Office: Inst Contemporary Jewry Hebrew U of Jerusalem Jerusalem Israel *"Success" is a complex word. How can it be gauged? Position? Public respect? Private welfare? Or is it creativity, dedication and search for truth. If the former, then others determine. If the latter, then I suggest success is continuing tension in the direction of one's goals. Above all, success is inviolate dedication. In my life—to the extent I know myself—my tension derives from my need to comprehend and interpret the meaning of the historic Jewish experience in our conflicted world, and to try to raise myself each day to live by Judaism's teachings.*

DAVIS, MULLER, lawyer; b. Chgo., Apr. 23, 1935; s. Benjamin B. and Janice (Muller) D.; m. Jane Lynn Strauss, Dec. 28, 1963; children: Melissa Jane, Muller, Joseph Jeffrey. B.A. magna cum laude, Yale U., 1957; J.D., Harvard U., 1960. Bar: Ill. 1960. Since practiced in Chgo.; asso. Jenner & Block, 1960-67; mem. Jones, Baer & Davis, 1967-; lectr. continuing legal edn., matrimonial law and litigation Legal adviser Michael Reese Med. Research Inst. Council, 1967-82. Contbr. articles to law jours.; author (with Sherman C. Feinstein) The Parental Couple in a Successful Divorce. Bd. dirs. Infant Welfare Soc., 1975—, pres., 1978-82. Served to capt. AUS, 1960-61; N.A., 1960-67. Fellow Am. Acad. Matrimonial Lawyers; mem. Fed. Bar Assn., ABA, Ill. Bar Assn., Chgo. Bar Assn. (matrimonial com., sec. civil practice com. 1979-80, vice chmn. 1980-81, chmn. 1981-82), Chgo. Estate Planning Council, Law Club Chgo. Republican. Jewish. Clubs: Tavern, Lake Shore Country. Home: 757 Bluff St Glencoe IL 60022 Office: 140 S Dearborn St Chicago IL 60603

DAVIS, NATALIE ZEMON, history educator; b. Detroit, Nov. 8, 1928; d. Julian Leon and Helen (Lamport) Zemon; m. H. Chandler Davis, Aug. 16, 1948; children: Aaron Bancroft, Hannah Penrose, Simone Weil. B.A., Smith Coll., 1949, D.H.L. hon., 1977; M.A., Radcliffe Coll., 1950; Ph.D., U. Mich., 1959; D. hon., Universite Lyon II (France), 1983, D.H.L., Northwestern U., 1983. Lectr. to asst. prof. Brown U., 1959-63; asst. prof. to assoc. prof. U. Toronto, 1963-71; prof. history U. Calif.-Berkeley, 1971-77; Henry Charles Lea prof. history Princeton U., 1978—. Author: Society and Culture in Early Modern France, 1975 (Berkeshire Conf. spl. award 1976), The Return of Martin Guerre, 1983. Recipient teaching citation U. Calif.-Berkeley, 1974, Outstanding Achievement award U. Mich., 1975; decorated Chevalier Ordre des Palmes Academiques, France, 1976. Fellow Am. Acad. Arts and Scis.; mem. Renaissance Soc. Am., Soc. French Hist. Studies (pres. 1976-77), Am. Hist. Assn. (council 1972-75, pres. modern history sect. 1980), Soc. Reformation Research. Democrat. Jewish. Home: 78 Alexander St Princeton NJ 08540 Office: Dept History Pirnceton U Princeton NJ 08544

DAVIS, NATHAN TATE, musician, educator; b. Kansas City, Kans., Feb. 15, 1937; s. Raymond and Rosemary (Green) D.; m. Ursula Broschke, Sept. 27, 1963; children—Joyce Nathalie, Pierre Marc. B.S. in Music Edn, U. Kans., 1960; postgrad., Sorbonne, Paris, France, 1967; Ph.D., Wesleyan U., 1974. Prof. music U. Pitts., 1969—; v.p. Seque Recording Co. Free lance profl. musician in, Europe, 1962-69; arranger, composer, Belgium Radio-TV, 1968; created: Grad. Program in Ethnomusicology, Undergrad. Program in Jazz Studies at, Paris Am. Acad.; Author: Jazz-Pop Improvisations for Flute, 1965; Composer: The United Spirit, 1972, A Tribute to Martin L. King, 1974, Writings in Jazz, 1977. Served with AUS, 1960-62. Nat. Found. for Arts grantee, 1972-73, 75—. Mem. Composers Soc. (Paris), Afro-Am. Music Hall of Fame, Inst. Black Am. Music, Nat. Gospel Adv. Bd. Home: 4125 Branding Pl Allison Park PA 15101

DAVIS, NATHANAEL VINING, aluminum company executive; b. Pitts., June 26, 1915; s. Edward Kirk and Rhea Ada (Reineman) D.; m. Lois Howard Thompson, 1941; children: James Howard Dow, Katharine Vining. Grad., Harvard, 1938. With Alcan Aluminium Ltd. (formerly Aluminium Ltd.), 1939—, pres., 1947-72, chmn. bd., chief exec. officer, 1972-79, chmn. bd., 1979—, also dir.; dir. Can. Life Assurance Co., Toronto, Bank of Montreal. Home: Osterville MA Office: Alcan Aluminium Ltd 1188 Sherbrooke St Montreal PQ H3A 3G2 Canada

DAVIS, NATHANIEL, humanities educator; b. Boston, Apr. 12, 1925; s. Harvey Nathaniel and Alice Marion (Rohde) D.; m. Elizabeth Kirkbride Creese, Nov. 24, 1956; children: Margaret Morton Davis Mainardi, Helen Miller, James Creese, Thomas Rohde. Grad., Phillips Exeter Acad., 1942; A.B., Brown U., 1944, LL.D., 1970; M.A., Fletcher Sch. Law and Diplomacy, 1947, Ph.D., 1960; postgrad. Russian lang. and area, Columbia, Cornell U., Middlebury Coll., 1953-54, U. Central de Venezuela, 1961-62. Asst. history Tufts Coll., 1947; joined U.S. Fgn. Service, 1947; 3d sec., Prague, Czechoslovakia, 1947-49, vice consul, Florence, Italy, 1949-52, 2d sec., Rome, Italy, 1952-53, Moscow, USSR, 1954-56; Soviet desk officer State Dept., 1956-60; 1st sec., Caracas, Venezuela, 1960-62, acting Peace Corps dir., Chile, 1962; spl. asst. to dir. Peace Corps, 1962-63, dept. asso. dir., 1963-65; U.S. minister to, Bulgaria, 1965-66; sr. staff Nat. Security Council (White House), 1966-68; U.S. ambassador to, Guatemala, 1968-71, to, Chile, 1971-73; dir. gen. Fgn. Service, 1973-75, asst. sec. of state for African affairs, 1975; U.S. ambassador to, Switzerland, 1975-77; State Dept advisor and Chester Nimitz prof. Naval War Coll., 1977-83; Alexander and Adelaide Hixon prof. humanities Harvey Mudd Coll., Claremont, Calif., 1983; lectr., U.S. history Centro Venezolano-Americano, 1961; lectr. Russian, Soviet history Howard U., 1962-65, 66-68. Bd. dirs., chmn. Inner City Childrens and Youth Program, Nat. Capital area Council Chs., 1958-59. Served to lt. (j.g.) USNR, 1944-46. Recipient Cinco Aguilas Blancas Alpinism award Venezuelan Andean Club, 1962. Mem. Am. Fgn. Service Assn. (bd. dirs., vice chmn 1964), Council on Fgn. Relations, Am. Hist. Assn., Phi Beta Kappa. Mem. United Ch. Christ. Club: Cosmos. Home: 1783 Longwood Ave Claremont Calif. 91711

DAVIS, OSCAR HIRSH, U.S. judge; b. N.Y.C., Feb. 27, 1914; s. Jacob and Minnie (Robison) D. A.B., Harvard U., 1934; LL.B., Columbia U., 1937. Bar: N.Y. 1938. Pvt. practice, N.Y.C., 1937-39; with Dept. Justice, 1939-42, 46-62, first asst. to solicitor gen., 1954-62; assoc. judge U.S. Ct. Claims, 1962-82, acting chief judge, 1977-78; judge U.S. Ct. Appeals (fed. cir.), 1981—. Served to capt. USAAF, 1942-46. Mem. Am., Fed. bar assns., Am. Law Inst., N.Y. County Lawyers Assn., N.Y. State Bar Assn. Home: 1101 3d St SW Washington DC 20024 Office: US Ct Appeals Fed Cir Washington DC 20439

DAVIS, OSSIE, actor, author; b. Cogdell, Ga., Dec. 18, 1917; s. Kince Charles and Laura (Cooper) D.; m. Ruby Ann Wallace (Ruby Dee), Dec. 9, 1948; children: Nora, Guy, LaVerne. Student, Howard U., 1935-38. Stage debut with, Rose McClendon Players, in Harlem, 1939; Broadway debut: Jeb, 1946; theatre appearances include A Raisin in the Sun, Purlie Victorious; writer, dir., actor: film Purlie Victorious, The Cardinal, The Hill; TV appearances include All God's Children; narrator: Freedom Road, With Ossie & Ruby, King; dir. films: Cotton Comes to Harlem, Gordon's War; author: Escape to Freedom: The Story of Young Frederick Douglass, 1978, Langston, 1982. Office: The Artists Agy 10000 Santa Monica Blvd Suite 305 Los Angeles CA 90067

DAVIS, OTTO ANDERSON, economics educator; b. Florence, S.C., Apr. 4, 1934; s. Otto and Pauline (Anderson) D.; m. Carolyn Quinn, Dec. 26, 1962; children—Craig, Wendy, Ross. A.B., Wofford Coll., 1956; M.A., U. Va., 1957, Ph.D., 1960. Asst. prof. econs. Grad Sch. Indsl. Adminstrn., Carnegie-Mellon U., Pitts., 1960-65; assoc. prof. Grad Sch. Indsl. Adminstrn. Carnegie-Mellon U., 1965-67, prof., 1967-68, prof. polit. economy Sch. Urban and Public Affairs, 1968-81, W.W. Cooper univ. prof. econs. and pub. policy, 1981—, assoc. dean, 1968-75, dean, 1975-81; research dir. Pa. Tax Commn., 1979—; Bd. visitors Air U., Maxwell AFB, 1980—. Contbr. book revs. and articles to profl. jours. Fellow Econometric Soc.; mem. Public Choice Soc. (pres. 1970-72), Assn. Public Policy Analysis and Mgmt. (policy council 1979, pres. 1982-83), Am. Econ. Assn., Am. Polit. Sci. Assn., Am. Soc. Public Adminstrn., Inst. Mgmt. Scis. Office: Dept Social Scis Carnegie-Mellon U Pittsburgh PA 15213

DAVIS, PAUL BROOKS, graphics designer, painter; b. Centrahoma, Okla., Feb. 10, 1938; s. Howard and Mary Susan (Brookhart) D.; m. Elise Hepburn, 1959; 1 son, John Philip; m. Myrna Rochelle Mushkin, Aug. 19, 1965; 1 son, Matthew Brookhart. Grad., Sch. Visual Arts, N.Y.C., 1955-59. Vis. lectr. U. Colo., 1967, Memphis State U., 1973, Memphis Acad. Art, 1973; adviser Tokyo Design Sch., 1974—. Graphic designer and illustrator, Push Pin Studios, N.Y.C., 1959-63; freelance artist, 1963—; one-man shows, Galerie Delpire, Paris, 1968, Benson Gallery, Bridgehampton, N.Y., 1973, Mus. Modern Art, Kamekura, Japan, 1975, Mus. Modern Art, Kyoto, Japan, 1976, Mus. Modern Art, Gumma, Japan, Centre Georges Pompidou, Paris, 1977, Galleria Gabbiano, Rome, Nishimura Gallery, Tokyo, Guild Hall, East Hampton, N.Y., 1978, Greengrass Gallery, N.Y.C., Sch. Visual Arts, Galleria Naviglio, Milan, Italy, Portland (Oreg.) Center for Visual Arts, Portland State U., Visual Arts Mus., N.Y.C., Art Center Coll. Design, Pasadena, Calif., 1979, Artcurial, Paris, Nishimura Gallery, Tokyo, 1979, 82, Artcurial, Paris, 1979, Art Ctr. Coll. of Design, Pasadena, Central Fall Gallery (N.Y.), 1981, Greengrass Gallery, N.Y.C., Central Falls Gallery, N.Y.C., Giraffics Gallery, Sag Harbor, N.Y., 1982, 83; group shows, Monocle Gallery of Polit. Art, N.Y.C., 1963, USIA Graphic Arts Exhbn., USSR, Van Bovenkamp Gallery, N.Y.C., 1964, Am. Fedn. Arts, 1964-65, Persona exhbn., Tokyo, 1965, Esquire Gallery, N.Y.C., 1966, D'Arcy Gallery, N.Y.C., The Bklyn. Mus., 1969, Musee des Arts Decoratifs, Louvre, Paris, 1970-71, Guild Hall East Hampton, L.I., 1971, Danenberg Gallery, N.Y.C., Galerie Delpire, Paris, 1974, The Corcoran Gallery, Washington, 1974-75, Lejeski Gallery, N.Y.C., 1975, Museo de Arte Contemporaneo de Caracas, Venezuela, 1976, The Greengrass Gallery, N.Y.C., 1977, others; represented in permanent collections, Playboy Club, Chgo., Olivetti Corp., Milan, Mus. Modern Art, N.Y.C., Museo Bogarin, Venezuela, Nat. Portrait Gallery, Washington, TochigL Prefectural Mus. Fine Art (Japan), Mus. of Racing, Saratoga, N.Y., Exxon Corp., Gen. Electric Co., Bolaffi Arte, Time, Inc., Paris Rev., prof. illustration, Syracuse U., 1972-74; Subject of books Paul Davis, 1976, Five Designers, 1976, Paul Davis Posters and Paintings, 1977, Artograph No. 2, 1980. Recipient Silver medal primera Bienal de Artes Graficas Museo de Tertulia, Colombia, S.Am., 1972; Gold medal N.Y. Art Dirs. Club, 1973, 74; Silver medal, 1977, Bronze medal 8th Internat. Poster Biennale, Warsaw, 1980; 2d prize Lahti Poster Biennale (Finland); named Outstanding Alumni Sch. Visual Arts, 1977. Mem. Alliance Graphique Internationale, Soc. Illustrators, Am. Inst. Graphic Arts. Home and office: PO Box 630 Sag Harbor NY 11963 *Perseverance.*

DAVIS, PAUL JOSEPH, endocrinologist; b. Chgo., Oct. 28, 1937; s. Paul Albert and Maxine Lydia (Mason) D.; m. Faith Ainsworth Baker, Dec. 8, 1962; children—Matthew, John, Sarah. B.A. magna cum laude, Westminster Coll., 1959; M.D. cum laude, Harvard U., 1963. Intern Bronx Municipal Hosp. Center, 1963-64, resident in medicine, 1964-67; clin. asso. NIH, Bethesda, Md., 1967-69, sr. staff asso., 1969-70; head endocrinology div. Balt. City Hosps., 1970-75; prof. medicine, head endocrinology div. SUNY, Buffalo Med. Sch., 1975—; also vice chmn. dept. medicine; chief med. service VA Med. Center, Buffalo, 1980—. Fellow A.C.P., Gerontol. Soc.; mem. Am. Fedn. Clin. Research, Am. Thyroid Assn., Am. Diabetes Assn., Endocrine Soc., Bd. Scientific Counselors, Nat. Inst. Aging, Nat. Inst. Health. Research and publs. on mechanisms of action of thyroid hormone, effects of aging on endocrine function. Home: 4012 Eckhardt Rd Hamburg NY 14075 Office: VA Med Center Buffalo NY 14215

DAVIS, PETER FRANK, film writer, producer; b. Los Angeles, Jan. 2, 1937; s. Frank and Tess (Slesinger) D.; m. Johanna Mankiewicz, Sept. 13, 1959 (dec. July 1974); children—Timothy, Nicholas; m. Karen Zehring, June 10, 1979; 1 son, Jesse. A.B. magna cum laude, Harvard, 1957. Editorial asst. N.Y. Times, 1958-59; asso. fellow Calhoun Coll., Yale, 1972—; univ. vis. lectr., 1974-75. Free-lance writer TV, mags., 1959-61; writer, Sextant Film Prodns., 1961-64; asso. producer television documentaries, NBC News, 1964; writer, producer, CBS News, N.Y.C., 1965-72; documentary cons.: Pumping Iron, 1978, Gilda Live, 1980; (Recipient awards for television documentary Saturday Rev. 1970, 71, award Nat. Acad. TV Arts and Scis. 1971, George Foster Peabody award 1971, award Nat. Acad. Motion Picture Arts and Scis. 1975); Television documentaries include The Heritage of Slavery, 1968, Hunger in America, 1968, The Battle of East St. Louis, 1969, The Selling of the Pentagon, 1971; film Hearts and Minds, 1975; co-writer: TV film Haywire, 1980. Served with AUS, 1959-60. Home: 320 Central Park W New York NY 10025

DAVIS, PHILIP J., mathematician; b. Lawrence, Mass., Jan. 2, 1923; s. Frank and Annie (Shrager) D.; m. Hadassah Finkelstein, Jan. 2, 1944; children: Abigail, Frank, Ernest, Joseph. B.S., Harvard U., 1943, Ph.D., 1950. Chief numerical analysis sect. Nat. Bur. Standards, Washington, 1958-63; prof. applied math. Brown U., Providence, 1963—. Author: Lore of Large Numbers, 1961, Interpolation and Approximation, 1963, Numerical Integration, 1967, The Schwarz Function, 1974, Circulant Matrices, 1979, The Mathematical Experience, 1981, The Thread, 1981 (Am. Book award 1983). Recipient Math. award Washington Acad. Scis., 1960, Chauvenet prize Math. Assn. Am., 1963. Mem. Math. Assn. Am., Am. Math. Soc. Home: 175 Freeman St Providence RI 02906 Office: Brown Univ Providence RI 02912

DAVIS, PHYLLIS BURKE, cosmetic company executive; b. Albany, N.Y., Dec. 24, 1931; d. J. Frank and Mary Catherine (Barnett) Burke; m. Edmund R. Davis, Nov. 22, 1968. B.A., U. Vt., 1953; LL.D., Babson Coll., 1974. Account exec. Norman Craig & Kummel, N.Y.C., 1965-68; product counselor Avon Products Inc., N.Y.C., 1968-69, group product counselor, 1969-71, mgr. sales promotions, 1971, dir. sales promotions, 1971-72, v.p. sales promotions advt., 1972-74, v.p. product mgmt., 1974-77, group v.p. product mgmt., 1977-80, group v.p. product quality and communications, 1980-83, group v.p. advt. and pub. relations, 1983—; dir. Nabisco Brands, Inc., N.Y.C., 1977—. Trustee U. Vt., Burlington, 1982—; bd. dirs. Multiple Sclerosis Soc., N.Y.C., 1983—. Named Cosmetic Women Achiever of Yr. Cosmetic Career Women, 1978, Econ. Equity Women's Equity Action League, 1979; named to Acad. Women Achievers YMCA, 1980. Mem. Cosmetic Toiletry and Fragrance Assn. (dir. 1974-80). Office: Avon Products Inc 9 W 57th St New York NY 10019

DAVIS, RALPH LANIER, educator; b. Kennedy, Ala., Sept. 10, 1921; s. Oran and Ethel (Richardson) D.; m. Betty Simpson, Aug. 20, 1943. B.S., Auburn U., 1943; M.S., Purdue U., 1948, Ph.D., 1950. Asst. prof. Prudue U., 1950-53, asso. prof., 1953-57, prof. dept. agronomy, 1957—, asst. dean, 1965-71, asso. dir. div. sponsored program, 1966—; vis. prof. Oreg. State U., 1959-60. Editor: Crop Sci, 1964-67. Chmn. Nat. Alfalfa Improvement Conf., 1963-64. Served to comdr. USNR, 1943-46. Fellow Am. Soc. Agronomy, A.A.A.S.; mem. Crop Sci. Soc. Am. (pres.-elect, gen. program chmn. 1962, pres. 1963), Sigma Xi (local v.p.), Alpha Zeta, Omicron Delta Kappa, Gamma Sigma Delta, Phi Kappa Phi. Home: 906 Essex St West Lafayette IN 47906

DAVIS, RAY C., manufacturing company executive; b. Canandaigua, N.Y., Dec. 18, 1941; m. Linda Beth Flash, May 30, 1961; children: Jeff, Jill, Kris. B.A., LeTourneau Coll., Longview, Tex. Sales engr. chem. div. Mobile Oil Co., Macedon, N.Y., 1966-71; gen. mgr. Marine div. Stemco Inc., Longview, Tex., 1971-72, v.p., gen. mgr., 1972-76; group v.p.Truck Prodn. div. Garlock Co., Longview, 1976-82; group pres. Colt Industries, Inc., Longview, 1982—; dir., mem. exec. com. First Nat. Bank, Longview. Bd. dirs. mem. exec. com. Good Shepherd Hosp., Longview; bd. dirs., mem. exec. com. LeTourneau Coll., Longview C. of C., Jr. Achievement, Longview. Mem. Soc. Automotive Engrs., Rubber Mfrs. Assn. Home: 1610 Pineland St Longview TX 75604 Office: Stemco Inc 300 E Industrial Blvd Longview TX 75606

DAVIS, RAYMOND, JR., chemist; b. Washington, Oct. 14, 1914; s. Raymond and Ida Rogers (Younger) D.; m. Anna Marsh Torrey, Dec. 4, 1948; children: Andrew Morgan, Martha Safford, Nancy Elizabeth, Roger Warren, Alan Paul. B.S., U. Md., 1937, M.S., 1939; Ph.D., Yale U., 1942. Chemist Dow Chem. Co., Midland, Mich., 1938-39, Monsanto Chem. Co., Dayton, Ohio, 1946-48; with Brookhaven Nat. Lab., Upton, N.Y., 1948—, now sr. chemist; adj. prof. dept. astronomy U. Pa. Contbr. articles to profl. jours. Served with USAAF, 1942-46. Recipient Boris Prejel prize N.Y. Acad. Scis., 1955; Comstock prize Nat. Acad. Scis., 1978; award for nuclear applications in chemistry Am. Chem. Soc., 1979. Mem. Am. Phys. Soc., Am. Geophys. Union, Am. Astron. Soc., AAAS, Meteoritical Soc., Nat. Acad. Scis. Office: Brookhaven Nat Lab Upton NY 11973

DAVIS, REX LLOYD, insurance company executive; b. Des Moines, Dec. 29, 1929; s. Leon Mack and Mercedes Johanna (Lamar) D.; m. Sally JoAnne Richard, Apr. 14, 1952; children: Kristine Lynn, Craig Thomas. J.D., Drake U., 1952. Bar: Iowa, U.S. Dist. Ct. Iowa, U.S. Supreme Ct.; C.P.C.U.; C.L.U. With Employers Mut. Casualty Co., Des Moines, 1954-66, regional v.p., Phila., 1966-72; exec. v.p. Ranger Ins. Co., Houston, 1972-75, pres., 1975—, chief operating officer; pres., chief operating officer Ranger Ins. Mgrs., Ranger Internat. Ins. Ltd., Ranger County Mut.; atty.-in-fact Ranger Lloyds, Houston; dir. Bank of Woodlake, Southwestern Ins. Info. Service., Anderson Clayton & Co. Bd. dirs. Salvation Army. Mem. Tex. Ins. Adv. Assn. Clubs: Lakeside Country, Houston City, Rotary (Houston). Home: 110 Sugarberry Circle Houston TX 77024 Office: Ranger Ins Co 5333 Westheimer Rd Houston TX 77056

DAVIS, RICHARD, musician; b. Chgo., Apr. 15, 1930; s. Robert and Elenora (King) Johnson; m. Patricia Jean Mulligan, Oct. 2, 1975; children—Robert, Richard, Joshua. B.M.E., Vandercook Coll. Music, Chgo., 1952. Asso. prof. bass and jazz studies U. Wis., Madison, 1976-77; clinician, adjudicator colls. in, U.S. and France; mem. Wis. Arts Bd. String bass player, 1945—; Author instrn. booklet.; appearances with major jazz groups, orchs., also, TV spls.; rec. artist, Muse, Galaxy, RCA Victor, Columbia, Milestone, others. Recipient Critics Poll award Down Beat mag., 1967-74, Reader's Poll award, 1967-72; Outstanding Musician's award Vandercook Coll., 1979; Outstanding prof. award U. Wis., Madison, 1978-79; grantee U. Wis., Wis. Arts Bd., Nat. Ednowment Arts. Mem. ASCAP (award 1976-79). Buddhist. Home: Route 1 Box 283 Barneveld WI 53507 Office: 4415 Humanities Bldg U Wis Madison WI 53706 *My high school teacher instilled in me the idea that it's not what you want to be in life, but what you do every day to attain that goal. That's the discipline I applied to achieve my success.*

DAVIS, RICHARD BRADLEY, physician; b. Iowa City, Iowa, Nov. 6, 1926; s. Bradley Nelson and Gladys Mae (Fairbanks) D.; m. Jean Nixeen Anderson, June 22, 1957; children—Janet, Stephen, Catharine. B.S., Yale U., 1949; M.D., State U. Iowa, 1953; Ph.D., U. Minn., 1964. Intern Mary Fletcher Hosp., Burlington, Vt., 1953-54, resident, 1954-56; instr. U. Minn., Mpls., 1959-64, asst. prof. medicine, 1964-69; vis. investigator Sir William Dunn Sch. Pathology, Oxford, Eng., 1964-65, MRC Blood Coagulation Research Unit, Churchill Hosp., Oxford, 1965; asso. prof. medicine U. Nebr., Omaha, 1969-73, prof. medicine, 1973—, acting dir. div. hematology, 1974-76, prof. pathology, 1976—, dir. hematology div., 1976-79; fellow grad. faculty, mem. exec. grad. council, exec. com. U. Nebr. Hosps., Med. Center. Contbr. articles to sci. publs. Served with U.S. Army, 1945-46. Borden Undergrad. Med. Research grantee, 1953; USPHS career devel. awardee, 1961-69. Fellow A.C.P., Central Soc. Clin. Research, Am. Fedn. Clin. Research, Am. Soc. Exptl. Pathology, N.Y. Acad. Scis., Am. Assn. History of Medicine Soc. Exptl. Biology and Medicine, Am. Soc. Hematology, Royal Micros. Soc., Internat. Soc. Haemostasis and Thrombosis, Omaha Mid-West Clin. Soc., Sigma Xi, Alpha Omega Alpha, Phi Beta Pi, Theta Kappa Psi. Home: 3514 S 94th St Omaha NE 68124 Office: 42d St and Dewey Ave Omaha NE 68105

DAVIS, RICHARD FRANCIS, city govt. ofcl.; b. Providence, Aug. 18, 1936; s. Walter Francis and Mary Elizabeth (Gearin) D.; m. Virginia Catherine Oates, Aug. 27, 1960; children—Walter Douglas, John Richard, Theresa Catherine. B.S., U. Ark., 1964; postgrad., M.I.T., 1964. Planner Met. Area Planning Commn., Little Rock, 1964-66; mem. Met. Planning Commn. Kansas City, Mo., 1966-67, dir. econs., 1967-69, dir. ops., 1969-71; exec. dir. Mid-Am. Regional Council, Kansas City, 1972-77; gen. mgr. Kansas City Area Transp. Authority, 1977—; instr. city planning U. Mo., Kansas City, 1973-74; Planning commr. City of Gladstone, Mo., 1967-69, 81, city councilman, 1969-71, mayor, 1971-72, chmn. park bd., 1972-76; mem. Clay County (Mo.) Indsl. Devel. Commn., 1972-77, Council on Edn., Kansas City, 1974—, treas., chmn. interdist. relations com. V.p. Brooktree Homeowners Assn., 1979-80. Served with USAF, 1955-59. Mem. Am. Soc. Public Adminstrn. (pres. Kansas City chpt. 1980, Public Adminstr. of Year 1973), Am. Planning Assn., Am. Public Transit Assn. (bd. dirs., mem. govtl. affairs and legis. steering com.). Home: 3612 N Brooktree Circle Gladstone MO 64119 Office: 1350 E 17th St Kansas City MO 64108

DAVIS, RICHARD FRANCIS, educator, university official; b. Keene, N.H., Aug. 30, 1924; s. Leston Francis and Bessie Viana (Barrett) D.; m. Carolyn Bernice Turner, June 18, 1950; children: Richard F., Rebecca L. B.S., U. N.H., 1950; M.S., Cornell U., 1952, Ph.D., 1953. Asst. prof. animal nutrition Cornell U., 1953-54; asst. prof. dairy sci. U. Md., College Park, 1954-56, asso. prof., 1956-58, prof., 1958—, head dept. dairy sci., 1956-81, acting chmn. div. agrl. and life scis., 1973-74, asso. provost agrl. and life scis., 1981—. Author: Modern Dairy Cattle Management, 1962; contbr. articles on animal nutrition to profl. jours. Served with U.S. Army, 1944-46. Mem. AAAS, Am. Inst. Nutrition, Am. Dairy Sci. Assn., Am. Soc. Animal Sci., N.Y. Acad. Sci., Washington Acad. Sci., Sigma Xi, Phi Kappa Phi, Alpha Zeta. Methodist. Club: Rotary (College Park) (pres. 1973-74). Office: Div Agrl and Life Scis U Md College Park MD 20742

DAVIS, RICHARD JOEL, lawyer, former govt. ofcl.; b. N.Y.C., Mar. 27, 1946; s. Herbert H. and Sylvia (Ginesin) D. B.A., U. Rochester, 1966; J.D., Columbia U., 1969. Bar: N.Y. State bar 1970. Law clk. to Judge Jack B. Weinstein, U.S. Dist. Ct. for Eastern Dist. N.Y., 1969-70; asst. U.S. atty. So. Dist. N.Y., 1970-73; task force leader Watergate Spl. Prosecution Force, Washington, 1973-75; asso. firm Weil, Gotshal and Manges, N.Y.C., 1976-77, partner, 1981—; asst. sec. of the treasury for enforcement and ops. Dept. Treasury, Washington, 1977-81; instr. in trial advocacy Harvard U.; instr. Nat. Inst. Trial Advocacy. Mem. Am. Bar Assn. Office: Weil Gotshal & Manges 767 Fifth Ave New York NY 10153

DAVIS, ROBERT ALDINE, college president; b. Broxton, Ga., June 15, 1928; s. Robert Aldine and Leda Estelle (Palmer) D.; m. Phyllis Clough, Aug. 5, 1955; children: Robert Aldine III, Phyllis Blaine, Palmer Clough. B.B.A., U. Ga., 1949; M.Div., Emory U., 1952; S.T.M., Yale U., 1959; D.D., Pfeiffer Coll., N.C., 1970; L.H.D., Westmar Coll., 1977. Ordained to ministry United Methodist Ch., 1952; dir. Wesley Found., Va. Poly. Inst., Blacksburg, 1952-59, Ga. Inst. Tech., Atlanta, 1959-62; assoc. dir. bd. higher edn. United Meth. Ch., Nashville, 1962-69; pres. Brevard (N.C.) Coll., 1969-76, Fla. So. Coll., Lakeland, 1976—; mem. univ. senate United Meth. Ch.; pres. Fla. Ind. Colls. Fund., 1978-80; mem. adv. com. bd. govs. U. N.C., 1972-76; sec. N.C. Assn. Ind. Coll., 1970-74; mem. 2d Dist. Ct. Appeal Jud. Nominating Com., 1982—. Pres. Brevard United Way, 1970, Brevard C. of C., 1975; bd. dirs. Lakeland YMCA, 1976-79; mem. Fla. Research and Devel. Com. Danforth scholar, 1958-59; named Young Man of Yr. Blacksburg C. of C., 1957, mem. Fla. Council of 100, 1979—; recipient Outstanding Service award Brevard C. of C., 1975. Mem. Nat. Assn. Ind. Colls. and Univs., Ind. Colls. and Univs. Fla. (pres. 1980—), Fla. Assn. Colls. and Univs. (v.p. 1984), Internat. Assn. Univ. Pres. (dir. N.Am. council), Lakeland C. of C. (dir. 1977—), Omicron Delta Kappa, Phi Kappa Phi, Beta Gamma Sigma. Club: Rotary (past pres. Brevard). Office: Fla Southern Coll Lakeland FL 33802

DAVIS, ROBERT EDWIN, chemical company executive; b. Madison, Ill., July 15, 1931; s. Harry Earl and Bernice (Prusak) D.; m. Shirley M. Krumbholz, Sept. 4, 1954; children: Tom, Barbara, Sue Ann. B.Ch.E., U. Mo., 1953. With Mobil Oil Co., St. Louis and Chgo., 1953-54, 56-57, petrochem. sales, 1953-54, dist. sales rep., 1956-57, Nalco Corp., Chgo. and Cleve., 1957-58; with Thiokol Corp., Newtown, Pa., 1958—, tech. dir., Dayton, 1958-60, Eastern dist. mgr., Washington, 1960-64, v.p. aerospace marketing, 1964-68, group v.p. gen. products, Newtown, 1968-70, pres., 1970—, chief exec. officer, 1973-83, chmn. bd., 1977-83; pres., chief exec. officer Sun Chem. Corp., 1983—; Mem. Pres.'s Commn. on Personnel Exchange, 1976-79. Bd. dirs. Pennsbury Scholarship Fund. Served with USAF, 1954-56. Mem. Am. Mgmt. Assn., Aerospace Industries Assn., Am. Inst. Aeros. and Astronautics. Clubs: Burning Tree, Brook of N.Y. Office: Sun Chem Corp 200 Park Ave New York NY 10166

DAVIS, ROBERT GORHAM, educator; b. Cambridge, Mass., June 8, 1908; s. Walter Burlingame and Mary Langdell (Millett) D.; m. Hope Hale, Sept. 3, 1939; children: Claudia Cockburn Flanders, Stephen Hale, Lydia Brooks. A.B., Harvard U., 1929, M.A., 1930. Instr. Rensselaer Poly. Inst., 1930-33; asst. Harvard U., 1933-34, instr., 1934-40, Briggs-Copeland Faculty instr., 1940-43; vis. lectr. Smith Coll., 1943-45, asso. prof. English, 1945-52, prof., 1952-57, chmn. dept. English, 1955-57; vis. prof. Columbia U., 1957-58, prof., 1958-76, spl. lectr., 1976-78, prof. emeritus, 1976—; Fulbright prof. U. Graz (Austria) and U. Innsbruck, Austria, 1954-55, U. La Plata, Argentina, 1965; vis. prof. U. Guanabara, Brazil, 1962; vis scholar Corpus Christi Coll., U. Cambridge, Eng., 1971; mem. Yaddo Corp., 1966-80. Author: John Dos Passos, 1962, C. P. Snow, 1965; Contbr.: articles and short stories to profl., popular publs., including O. Henry Memorial Award Prize Stories of 1942; editor: Ten Modern Masters, 1953, 3d rev. edit., 1972, Ten Masters of the Modern Essay, 1976. Chmn. Communist Party unit at Harvard U., 1938-39, Am. Com. for Cultural Freedom, 1953-54. Recipient Bowdoin prize Harvard U., 1929; Longview Found. award, 1958; Distinguished Tchr. award Sch. of Gen. Studies Columbia U., 1973; Guggenheim fellow, 1971-72. Mem. MLA (publs. editorial bd. 1955-65), PEN, Amnesty Internat., Corpus Christi Assn., Eng. Inst., Internat. Assn. Univ. Profs. English, Phi Beta Kappa. Democrat. Club: Harvard of Fairfield County (Conn.). Home: 4 Old Orchard Rd Westport CT 06880 *We are all too imperfect to take much satisfaction in success as the world measures it, except as we have loved and been loved by those around us, and in our work and social activity have, however slightly, made life better for humanity in general. But now, with organized killing going on everywhere, it is hard to consider any life successful that is not devoted to peace, world-sharing of goods and halting the drive toward nuclear war that may wipe out humanity completely.*

DAVIS, ROBERT LEACH, retired government official, consultant; b. Torrington, Conn., July 20, 1924; s. Clarence Adelbert and Ruth Mabel (Leach) D.; m. Lorraine Lillian Szabla, Sept. 16, 1950; children: Russell, Cynthia, Vicki, Scott, Gregg. B.A. in Psychology, U. Mich., 1949. Claims examiner Social Security Adminstrn., Chgo., 1950-52; investigator and personnel specialist U.S. CSC, Chgo., 1952-67; personnel dir. U.S. Post Office Region, Chgo., 1967-71; div. chief, asst. bur. dir. U.S. CSC, Washington, 1971-78; dep. asst. sec. for adminstrn. and mgmt. Dept. Labor, Washington, 1978-82. Served with AUS, 1943-46. Decorated Purple Heart. Mem. Internat. Personnel Mgmt. Assn. Democrat. Unitarian. Home: Route 1 Box 122 Montague MI 49437

DAVIS, ROBERT PAUL, physician, educator; b. Malden, Mass., July 3, 1926; s. Samuel and Sarah (Lemberg) D.; m. Ruby Black, Sept. 5, 1953; children—Edward L., John R., Elizabeth A. A.B. cum laude, Harvard, 1947, M.D. magna cum laude, 1951, A.M., 1955; A.M. (ad eundem), Brown U., 1967. Diplomate: Am. Bd. Internal Medicine, subsplty. bd. nephrology. Intern Peter Bent Brigham Hosp., Boston, 1951-52, asst. medicine, 1952-55, sr. asst. resident physician, 1955-56, chief resident physician, 1956-57; jr. fellow Soc. of Fellows Harvard, 1952-55; asst. medicine Harvard Med. Sch., 1956-57; asst. prof. medicine U. N.C., 1957-59, Albert Einstein Coll. Medicine, 1959-66, asso. prof., 1967; career scientist Health Research Council, N.Y.C., 1962-67; asst. vis. physician Bronx Mcpl. Hosp. Center, 1959-65, asso. vis. physician, 1966-67; physician in chief Miriam Hosp., Providence, 1967-74, dir. renal and metabolic diseases, 1974-79; prof. med. sci. Brown U., 1967—, chmn. sect. in medicine div. biol. and med. scis., 1971-74; Vis. scientist Ins. Biol. Chemistry of U. Copenhagen, 1965-66; mem. corp. Butler Hosp., Jewish Family and Children's Service; mem. sci. adv. council N.E. Regional Kidney Program; vice chmn. R.I. Advisory Commn. Med. Care and Edn. Found.; chmn. med. adv. bd. R.I. Kidney Found.; Bd. dirs. Asso. Alumni Brown U.; trustee Interhosp. Organ Bank, Boston, 1969—, treas., 1970—; pres. End-Stage Renal Disease Coordinating Council Network 28, New Eng., 1978-79. Asso. editor: R.I. Med. Jour, 1971—; Contbr. articles to profl. jours. Served as ensign USNR, 1944-46; as lt. (j.g.) M.C., 1951. Traveling fellow Commonwealth Fund, 1965-66; Willard O. Thompson Meml. traveling scholar A.C.P., 1965. Fellow AAAS, A.C.P.; mem. Am. Fedn. Clin. Research, Am. Soc. Transplant Physicians, Harvey Soc., Biophys. Soc., N.Y. Acad. Medicine, Am. Heart Assn., N.Y. Acad. Sci., Am. Soc. Cell Biology, Soc. Gen. Physiologists, Am. Physiol. Soc., Am. Soc. Artificial Internal Organs, Internat. Soc. Nephrology, Clin. Diabetes Assn. R.I. (pres. 1970-71), Providence, R.I. med. socs., Am. Soc. Nephrology, Am. Soc. Pediatric Nephrology, Soc. for Health and Human Values, Inst. of Society, Ethics and Life Scis., Am. Philos. Assn., Phi Beta Kappa, Sigma Xi. Home: 75 Prospect St Providence RI 02906 Office: Brown U 1 Randall Sq Providence RI 02904

DAVIS, ROBERT T., marketing educator. B.A., Harvard U., 1942, M.B.A., 1946, D.C.S., 1954. Mem. faculty St. Laurence U., 1946-48, Dartmouth Coll., 1948-52, Harvard U. Grad. Sch. Bus., 1952-57, IMEDE Mgmt. Devel. Inst., Harvard U., 1957-58, Stanford U. Grad. Sch. Bus., 1958—, Sebastian S. Kresge prof. mktg., 1974—, dir. Univ. Exec. Program, 1962-64, 67-68, dir. Stanford-Sloan Program, 1969-73; co-dir. Exec. Program for Smaller Cos., 1976—; v.p. mktg. Varia Assocs., Palo Alto, Calif., 1964-66. Author: Cases in Marketing Management and Performance, Development of Field Sales Managers; others books; contbr. articles to profl. jours. Trustee Mktg. Sci. Inst. Served with OSS, AUS, World War II. Recipient Salgo-Noren Disting. Teaching award, 1968. Office: Dept Mktg Stanford U Grad Sch Bus Stanford CA 94305 *

DAVIS, ROBERT THOMAS, JR., textile company executive; b. Columbus, Ga., May 3, 1927; s. Robert Thomas and Mary (Avant) D.; m. Barbara Ann Leeth, Feb. 10, 1951; children: Kelly, Rob, Louis. B.S. in Elec. Engring., Ga. Inst. Tech., 1947. Vice pres. Swift Spinning Mills Inc., Columbus, 1949-65, exec. v.p., 1965-66, pres., chief exec. officer, 1966-68; exec. v.p. Dixie Yarns Inc., Chattanooga, 1968-70, pres., 1970-81, chief exec. officer, 1973-81, chmn. bd., 1979-81; also dir., mem. exec. com.; pres. yarn div. Collins & Aikman, N.Y.C., 1981-82, exec. v.p., Charlotte, N.C., 1982-84; pres. Atree Industries, Inc., Shelby, N.C., 1984—; dir. Provident Life & Accident Ins. Co. City commr., Columbus, 1955-62, mayor, 1956; bd. dirs. Chattanooga Electric Power Bd. Named to Nat. Football Coll. Hall of Fame, 1978. Mem. Am. Textile Mfrs. Inst. (dir.), Ga. Textile Mfrs. Assn., Carpet and Rug Inst., Young Pres. Orgn., Carpet Yarn Assn. (pres. 1972-74), NAM (dir.). Clubs: Union League (N.Y.C.); Mountain City; Honors Golf (Chattanooga). Home: 3606 Furman Circle Gastonia NC 28054 Office: Artee Industries Inc PO Box 1485 Shelby NC 28150 *

DAVIS, ROBERT WILLIAM, congressman; b. Marquette, Mich., July 31, 1932; s. George Walter and Darlene Hazel (Hagen) D.; m. Martha Cole, Aug. 8, 1976; children: Robert, Lisa, George, Alexandra. Student, No. Mich. U., 1950, 52, Hillsdale Coll., 1951-52; B.S. in Mortuary Sci, Wayne State U., 1954. Funeral dir. Davis Funeral Home, St. Ignace, Mich., 1954-66; city councilman St. Ignace, 1964-66; mem. Mich. Ho. of Reps., 1966-70, Mich. Senate, 1970-78, Senate Republican leader, 1974-78; mem. 96th-98th Congresses from 11th Dist. Mich.; mem. armed services com., com. on mcht. marine and fisheries. Named Outstanding State legislator Nat. Council Sr. Citizens, 1973. Mem. Mich. Funeral Dirs. Assn., North-east Midwest Econ. Advancement Coalition, Mich. Cystic Fibrosis Assn., Young Ams. for Freedom. Republican. Episcopalian. Clubs: Lions, Elks, Eagles. Office: 1124 Longworth House Office Bldg Washington DC 20515

DAVIS, ROGER EDWIN, lawyer; b. Lakewood, Ohio, Dec. 29, 1928; s. Russell G. and Irma (Aboline) D.; m. Eva Grace Keeler, July 25, 1953 (div. Feb. 1980); children: Susan Lee, Lisa Ann, Steven Russell; m. Yvonne L. Berich, June 1, 1980. A.B., Harvard U., 1950; LL.B., U. Mich., 1953. Bar: Mich. 1953. Practice in Detroit, 1955—; asso. Langs, Molyneaux & Armstrong, 1955-60; counsel Avis Enterprises, 1961-62; with legal dept. S.S. Kresge Co. (now Kmart Corp.), 1963-70, v.p., gen. counsel, sec., 1970—. Trustee Arnold Home. Served with AUS, 1953-55. Mem. State Bar Mich., Fla. Bar, Am. Bar Assn., Am. Soc. Corp. Secs. Club: Pine Lake Country. Home: 3234 Pine Lake Rd Orchard Lake MI 48033 Office: 3100 W Big Beaver Rd Troy MI 48084

DAVIS, RON, artist; b. Santa Monica, Calif., June 29, 1937. Student, U. Wyo., 1955-56, San Francisco Art Inst., 1960-64. Announcer, Sta. KRWO, Cheyenne, Wyo., 1958-59; instr. U. Calif., Irvine, 1966. Works exhibited, Los Angeles County Mus., Mus. Modern Art, N.Y.C., Tate Gallery, London, Albright-Knox Art Gallery, Buffalo, San Francisco Mus. Art, San Antonio Mus. Art, Washington Gallery Modern Art, Whitney Mus., N.Y.C., Va. Mus., Richmond, Walker Art Center, Leo Castelli Galleries, Santa Barbara Mus. Art, Oakland Mus., also European galleries. Nat. Endowment Arts grantee, 1968. Office: Blum Helman Gallery 20 W 57th St New York NY 10019 *

DAVIS, ROSS DANE, lawyer; b. Bklyn., Mar. 21, 1919; s. Abraham N. and Gertrude (Ross) D.; m. Margaret Gould Roos, May 30, 1958. B.A., Brown U., 1941; LL.B., Columbia U., 1947. Bar: Admitted N.Y. 1948, D.C. 1968, U.S. Supreme Ct 1968. Assoc. firm Davis & Heffner, N.Y.C., 1947-51; with U.S. Govt., 1951-69; Exec. adminstr., acting adminstr. Small Bus. Adminstrn., 1965-66; adminstr. Econ. Devel. Adminstrn., 1966; asst. sec. econ. devel. U.S. Dept. Commerce, 1966-69; dir. Center for Program Implementation, Nat. League Cities-U.S. Conf. Mayors, Washington, 1969-74; partner firm Davis Simpich & Siena, Washington. Contbr. articles in field to profl. jours. Served to capt. AUS, 1942-46; PTO. Mem. Am., Fed. bar assns. Democrat. Clubs: Cosmos, Nat. Capital Democratic (Washington). Home: 3012 32d St NW Washington DC 20008 Office: 1301 Pennsylvania Ave NW Washington DC 20004

DAVIS, ROY TASCO, JR., retired foreign service officer, consultant; b. Columbia, Mo., Sept. 9, 1915; s. Roy T. and Loyce (Enloe) D.; m. Helen Elizabeth Winkler, Oct. 6, 1945; children: Roy Tasco III, John Albert, Susan Michael. A.B., U. Mo., 1937; student, George Washington U. Law Sch., 1947; grad., Nat. War Coll., 1958. Bar: D.C. 1947. Page U.S. Senate, 1927; asst. to pres. Nat. Park Coll., 1937-41; fgn. service officer, 1947-68, 2d sec., vice consul, Rio de Janeiro, Brazil, 1947-48, asst. cultural attache, Buenos Aires, Argentina, 1948-51, 2d sec., consul, 1952, 2d sec., consul, then 1st sec., Panama, 1952-55; staff asst., div. internat. orgns. Dept. of State, 1955-57; became consul, Naples, Italy, 1958, then consul gen., Rio de Janeiro; supr. consular services U.S. Consulate Gen., Hong Kong, 1967-68; fgn. affairs cons., 1968—. Served from ensign to lt. comdr. USNR, 1941-46. Mem. Am. Soc. Internat. Law, Fgn. Service Assn., Pima County Bar Assn., Tucson Com. on Fgn. Affairs, Phi Beta Kappa, Beta Theta Pi, Phi Alpha Delta, Sigma Delta Pi, Delta Sigma Pi. Club: Kiwanian. Home: 7222 Leonardo Da Vinci Tucson AZ 85704

DAVIS, RUSSELL LEONARD, librarian; b. Blackfoot, Ida., Oct. 25, 1924; s. John Leonard and Mary Verna (Robertson) D.; m. Emma Lou Barnes, June 10, 1949; childrenDan, Kathleen, Kirk, Susan, Eileen, Alan, Julie, Grant. Student, Weber Jr. Coll., 1948-50; B.S., Utah State U., 1952; A.M. in L.S, U. Mich., 1952-53. Teaching asst. U. Mich. Lib. Sch., 1952-53; engring. librarian Utah State U., 1953-54, circulation librarian, 1954-57, instr. library sci., 1953-57, extension librarian, 1955-57; dir. Utah State Library Commn., 1957—. Mem. A.L.A., Utah Library Assn. (pres. 1960-61), Mountain Plains Library Assn. (pres. 1964-65). Mem. Ch. of Jesus Christ of Latter-day Saints (bishop). Home: 575 E 1350 North Bountiful UT 84010 Office: 2150 S 3d W Salt Lake City UT 84115

DAVIS, RUSSELL STEWART, JR., plastics and steel manufacturing company executive; b. Cambridge, Md., Aug. 9, 1923; s. Russell S. and Mardelle V. D.; m. Gloria Gail Parker, June 7, 1945; children: Russell Stewart, Deborah P., Jeffrey P. B.S., U.S. Naval Acad., 1946. With NVF Co., 1948—, v.p., div. mgr., 1968-70, exec. v.p., chief operating officer, Yorklyn, Del., 1970—; also dir.; chmn. bd., chief operating officer, dir. Steel Corp. Tex., 1978—, NVF Can., 1970—; dir. NVF Europe, Chesapeake Ins. Co., Wilmington Savs. Fund Soc., Del., Mueller Brass Co., Air Cargo Equipment Co. Bd. dirs. United Fund Del. Served with USNR, 1942-48. Mem. Nat. Elec. Mfrs. Assn. (past dir.), Inst. Printed Circuits. Home: 7 Winding Way Greenville DE 19807 Office: PO Box 68 Yorklyn DE 19736

DAVIS, RUTH MARGARET (MRS. BENJAMIN FRANKLIN LOHR), former government official, business executive; b. Sharpsville, Pa., Oct. 19, 1928; d. W. George and Mary Anna (Ackermann) D.; m. Benjamin F. Lohr, Apr. 29, 1961. B.A., Am. U., 1950; M.A., U. Md., 1952, Ph.D., 1955. Statistician FAO, UN, Washington, 1946-49; mathematician Nat. Bur. Standards, 1950-51; head operations research div. David Taylor Model Basin, 1955-61; staff asst. Office Dir. Def. Research and Engring., Dept. Def., 1961-67; asso. dir. research and devel. Nat. Library Medicine, 1967-68; dir. Lister Hill Nat. Center for Biomed. Communications, 1968-70; dir. Inst. for Computer Scis. and Tech., Nat. Bur. Standards, 1970-77; dep. undersec. def. for research and engring., 1977-79; asst. sec. resource applications U.S. Dept. Energy, 1979-81; pres. Pymatuning Group Inc., 1981—; dir. United Telecom Inc., Comml. Credit Corp., Consol. Edison Inc., Varian Assocs., Aerospace Corp.; lectr. U. Md., 1955-57, Am. U., 1957-58; vis. prof. computer sci. U. Pa., 1969-72; adj. prof. U. Pitts.; cons. Office Naval Research, Washington, 1957-58; mem. Md. Gov.'s Sci. Adv. Council, 1971-77; chmn. nat. adv. council Electric Power Research Inst., 1975-76. Contbr. articles to profl. jours. Bd. dirs. Thayer Sch. Engring., Dartmouth Coll. Recipient Rockefeller Tech. Mgmt. award, 1973; Fed. Woman of Yr. award, 1973; Systems Profl. of Yr. award, 1973; Computer Sci. Man of Yr. award, 1979; Disting. Service medal Dept. Def., 1979, Dept. Energy, 1981; gold medal Dept. Energy, 1981. Fellow AIAA, Soc. for Info. Display; mem. AAAS, Am. Math Soc., Math Assn. Am., Nat. Acad. Engring., Nat. Acad. Pub. Adminstrn., Washington Philos. Soc., Operations Research Soc. Am., Phi Kappa Phi, Sigma Pi Sigma. Office: 1625 I St NW Washington DC 20006 *The rapid rate of change in our lives due principally to technology and changing personal values makes adaptability and flexibility key* *ingredients to success. The one essential invariant of success is integrity, accompanied by compassion.*

DAVIS, S. JOHN, educational administrator; b. Blacklick, Pa., Oct. 9, 1928; s. Spear J. and Elizabeth D. (Collins) D.; m. Janet Colson, June 14, 1952; children: Lisa Davis Kihm, Kara, John, Megan. B.S., Ind. U. of Pa., 1950, LL.D. (hon.), 1980; M.A., George Washington U., 1955; Ed.D., Am. U., 1972. Sci. tchr. Stratford Jr. High Sch., Arlington County (Va.) Public Schs., 1951-55; asst. prin. Kenmore Jr. High Sch., 1955-58; dir. Flint Hill Prep. Sch., Oakton, Va., 1958-63; asst. prin., acting prin. Ft. Hunt High Sch. (Fairfax County (Va.) Public Schs.), 1963-66; prin. W. Springfield High Sch., 1966-67, Area II supt., 1967-70, div. supt., 1970-79; supt. public instrn. Commonwealth of Va., Richmond, 1979—; cons. Fla. Gen. Assembly, 1973, U. Va., 1974, Japanese Govt., 1977, Ind. U. of Pa., 1977, Nat. Sch. Resource Network, 1980-81, So. Regional Edn. Bd., 1980-81. Bd. dirs. Fairfax Community Action Program, 1977—, Fairfax Symphony Orchestra, 1976—, Jr. Achievement, 1972-75; adv. com. Voluntary Action Center, 1977—; steering com. Virginians for Bonds, 1977; exec. bd. Ft. Belvoir Civilian-Mil. Adv. Council, 1972—; adv. bd. Memco Charitable and Scholarship Found.; adv. council No. Va. Hotline; dist. nominating com. Nat. Capital Area Council Boy Scouts Am.; final selection com. scholarship program Continental Telephone Service Corp. Recipient citation All Pa. Coll. Alumni Assn., 1981. Mem. Fairfax County C. of C. Methodist. Club: Masons. Office: Office Supt Pub Instruction 101 N 14th St Richmond VA 23216 *

DAVIS, S. ROBERT, bus. exec.; b. Columbus, Ohio, Oct. 31, 1938; s. Herman and Minnie (Newman) D.; (m), 1955; 4 children. Student, Ohio State U. Founder, pres. S. Robert Davis & Co., Inc., Columbus, Ohio, 1958-68; founder, now pres. and chmn. bd. Orange Co. Inc., Columbus, 1968—; dir. M.I.F. Funds; chmn. bd. Buckeye Fed. Savs. & Loan Assn., Strata Corp. Clubs: Columbus Athletic, Scioto Country.

DAVIS, SAMMY, JR., entertainer; b. N.Y.C., Dec. 8, 1925; s. Sammy and Elvira (Sanchez) D.; m. Loray White, 1958 (div. 1959); m. Mai Britt, Nov. 13, 1961 (div.); children: Tracey, Mark, Jeff; m. Altovise Gore, May 11, 1970. V.p. Tropicana Hotel, Las Vegas, Nev. Vaudeville appearances, Will Mastin Trio, 1930-48; singer, dancer, impressionist hotel, nightclub shows; rec. songs, Decca Records, 20th Century Records, Warner Records, (others); Broadway show Mr. Wonderful, 1956-57, Anna Lucasta, 1959; Broadway shows Porgy and Bess, 1959, Golden Boy; films Ocean's 11, Pepe, 1960, Sergeants Three, Convicts Four, Johnny Cool, Robin and the Seven Hoods, Sweet Charity, A Man Called Adam, Salt and Pepper, One More Time, The Pigeons, others; TV appearance Mod Squad, Name of the Game, Laugh-In, Lucy Show, All in the Family, Wednesday Night Mystery Movie Spl. Segment, 1973, Poor Devil, 1973, Sammy and Co., numerous spls.; producer: TV show The Trackers; author: autobiography Yes I Can, 1965. Served with AUS, 1943-45. Mem. Am. Soc. Mag. Photographers. Club: Friars (N.Y.C.). Address: care Mecca Artists 1650 Broadway Suite 1410 New York NY 10019

DAVIS, SAMUEL, hospital administrator, educator, consultant; b. N.Y.C., Sept. 30, 1931; s. Morris and Ethel (Levowitz) D.; m. Ellen Darce Kalker, June 16, 1957; children: Joseph Evan, Thomas Adam, Jonathan Edward, Jessica Ann. B.A., CCNY, 1952; M.S., Columbia U., 1957. Acct., Roosevelt Hosp., N.Y.C., 1954-55; relief adminstr. Meml. Center Cancer and Allied Diseases, N.Y.C., 1955-56; adminstrv. resident, then adminstrv. asst. to dir. and dir. ambulatory care services Roosevelt Hosp., 1956-59; mem. adminstrv. staff Hillside Hosp., Glen Oaks, N.Y.C., 1959-72, exec. v.p., 1970-72; exec. cons. L.I. Jewish-Hillside Med. Center, New Hyde Park, N.Y., 1972; exec. pres. Mt. Sinai Hosp., Mpls., 1972-75, dir., N.Y.C., 1975-81, pres., 1981—; sr. v.p. Mt. Sinai Med. Center, N.Y.C., 1975-77, exec. v.p., 1978—; assoc. prof. adminstrv. medicine Mt. Sinai Med. Sch., 1975-79, acting chmn., 1977-79, Edmond A. Guggenheim prof. health care mgmt., chmn. health care mgmt., 1979—; adj. prof. health care adminstrn. Baruch Coll., CUNY, 1978—; cons. corp. strategic planning, 1976—; vice chmn. bd. dirs. Hennepin County (Minn.) Health Coalition, 1973-75; mem. health adv. com. Minn. Met. Health Bd., 1974-75; mem. Hennepin County Health and Social Services Adv. Bd., 1974-75. Author: Decision Analysis in Hospital Administration, 1974; contbr. articles to profl. jours. Trustee Mpls. Fedn. Jewish Service, 1973-75; chmn. health and welfare div. N.Y.C. Fedn. Jewish Philanthropies, 1975-76. Served with AUS, 1952-54. Fellow social studies and humanities CCNY, 1952; WHO fellow, 1970. Fellow Am. Coll. Hosp. Adminstrs., Am. Pub. Health Assn.; mem. Am. Assn. Hosp. Planning, Am., N.Y. State hosp. assns., Am. Mgmt. Assn., Herman Biggs Soc. Office: Mt Sinai Hosp One Gustave L. Levy Pl New York NY 10029

DAVIS, SAMUEL BEVERLY, III, oil company executive; b. Louisville, Jan. 19, 1941; s. Samuel Beverly and Emmilee (Baker) D.; m. Judith Crawford, July 21, 1973; children: Connelly Stewart, Caren Davis, Merritt Stewart, Michael Davis, Samuel B. B.S., Fla. State U., 1963, M.B.A., 1964; grad. Advanced Mgmt. Program, Harvard U., 1979. Instr. Fla. State U. Sch. Mus., 1964-65; with Ashland Oil Inc., Ky., 1966-80, v.p. planning and analysis, 1972-74, adminstrv. v.p., 1974-80, chief fin. officer, 1978-79; sr. v.p. Belco Petroleum Co., N.Y.C., 1980-82; chmn., chief exec. officer Schroder Energy Assocs., Inc.,, N.Y.C., 1982—. Republican. Presbyterian. Office: One State St New York NY 10004

DAVIS, SAVILLE ROGERS, journalist; b. Watertown, Mass., Apr. 5, 1909; s. Francis Woodward and Esther (Saville) D.; m. Anita Pawolleck de Varon, Aug. 12, 1935; 1 dau., Julie Davis Jewett. A.B., Williams Coll., 1930; M.B.A., Harvard U., 1932. Reporter, Christian Sci. Monitor, Boston, N.Y.C., 1932-39, radio news writer, broadcaster, 1934-36, State Dept. corr., Washington, 1939, Mediterranean corr., Rome and Madrid, 1939-41, asst. to editor, 1941-45, chief London bur., roving corr. European internat. confs., 1945-47, Am. news editor, 1947-57, mng. editor, 1957-61, chief editorial writer, 1961-64, chief Washington news bur., White House corr., 1965-71, spl. corr., 1971—; BBC Washington corr., 1965-71, roving corr., South and East Asia, 1971-72, free lance journalist, 1971—; corr. in residence Fletcher Sch. Law and Diplomacy, 1974-76; seminar leader Brookings Instn., 1967-81; mem. adv. council NSF, 1976-80. Trustee, Wheelock Coll., chmn, 1963-65, hon. trustee, 1980—; pres. Christian Sci. Mother Ch., Boston, 1980-81; mem. U.S. Nat. Commn. for UNESCO, 1980—. Fellow Am. Acad. Arts and Scis. (sec., mem. council and exec. bd. 1976-80); mem. Harvard Bus. Sch. Alumni Assn. (pres. 1960-61), Internat. Inst. for Girls in Spain (pres. 1949-69), Phi Beta Kappa. Clubs: National Press, Federal City (Washington); Harvard (Boston). Address: Winter St Lincoln MA 01773

DAVIS, SHELBY CULLOM, investment banker, former ambassador; b. Peoria, Ill., Apr. 1, 1909; s. George Henry and Julia Mabel (Cullom) D.; m. Kathryn Edith Waterman, Jan. 4, 1932; children: Shelby Moore Cullom, Diana Cullom, Priscilla Alden (dec.). Student, Lawrenceville (N.J.) Sch., 1924-26; A.B., Princeton U., 1930; A.M., Columbia U., 1931; D. Polit. Sci., U. Geneva, 1934. Spl. corr., also asso. with Columbia Broadcasting Co., Geneva, 1932-34; economist Investment Corp. Phila., 1934-37; treas. Delaware Fund, Inc., 1937-39; econ. adviser Thomas E. Dewey, 1940; presdl. campaigns; mem. N.Y. Stock Exchange, 1941—; chief fgn. requirements sect. WPB, Washington, 1942, chief div. statistics and research, N.Y., No. N.J., 1943; 1st dep. supt. ins. N.Y. State, 1944-47; mng. partner Shelby Cullom Davis & Co. (investment bankers), N.Y.C., 1947-69, 75—; U.S. ambassador to, Switzerland, Bern, 1969-75; dir. Value Line Funds, Frankana Am. Re, Stella Re, Jackson Lab., Plimoth Plantation.; Chmn. history adv. council Princeton U.; bd. dirs. Nat. Right to Work Found., Accuracy in Media, Heritage Found. Author: Your Career in Defense, 1942, others; former bus. editor: Current History and Forum mags; contbr. articles to several jours. Mem. Fin. Analysts Assn. (pres. 1955-56), Gen. Soc. SR, Soc. Colonial Wars (gov.), Mayflower Soc. Republican. Clubs: Knickerbocker, Univ., Sleepy Hollow Country, Princeton, Players (N.Y.C.); Hartford; Harbor (Maine); Down Town Assn., Charter (Princeton); Everglades (Palm Beach, Fla.). Home: 193 Wilson Park Tarrytown NY Office: 70 Pine St New York NY 10270

DAVIS, SID, journalist; b. Youngstown, Ohio, Nov. 13, 1927; s. Morris and Hilda (Friedman) D.; m. Barbara J. Flint, July 21, 1960; children: Lawrence Jay, Morse Robert. B.S., Ohio U., 1952. News reporter Sta. WJEH, Gallipolis, Ohio, 1950-51; news dir. Sta. WKBN, Youngstown, 1952-59; White House corr. Westinghouse Broadcasting Co., Washington, 1959-68, chief Washington news bur., 1968-77; dir. news NBC News, Washington, 1977-79, bur. chief, 1979-80, v.p. and bur. chief, 1980-82, sr. Washington corr., 1982—. Producer: eyewitness account Kennedy assassination Dialogue on Dallas, 1963; dir. coverage all maj. news stories in U.S., presdl. trips abroad. Served with USN, 1946-48. Named Sigma Delta Chi Outstanding Journalism Grad. Ohio U., 1952. Mem. White House Corrs. Assn. Radio, TV News Dirs. Assn., Sigma Delta Chi, Omicron Delta Kappa, Tau Kappa Alpha. Clubs: National Press, Washington Press, Federal City (Washington). Covered Khrushchev's tour U.S., 1959, U.S. space launchings, 1960-63, Kennedy tours abroad as pres., Johnson's travels as pres., Nixon and Ford trips to China, USSR, Asia, and Europe; one of three reporters to witness swearing in of Pres. Johnson in Dallas, polit. reporting and analysis of major nominating convs., campaigns and elections beginning in 1960, including extensive travel with all Presdl. candidates. Home: 7103 Arran Pl Bethesda MD 20817 Office: NBC News 4001 Nebraska Ave Washington DC 20016

DAVIS, SIDNEY FANT, lawyer, textile manufacturing company executive; b. Louisville, May 14, 1934; s. Sidney Fant and Harriet Virginia (Price) D.; m. Sylvia Sue Hussey, Feb. 15, 1958; children: Susan, Kathleen, Sydney. B.S., U.S. Naval Acad., 1956; J.D., U. Fla., 1963. Bar: Fla. 1963, Ga. 1968, S.C. 1980. Asso., then partner firm Jennings, Watts, Clarke & Hamilton, Jacksonville, Fla., 1963-67; from atty. to v.p., asst. gen. counsel Delta Air Lines, Inc., Atlanta, 1967-79; v.p., gen. counsel Springs Industries, Inc., Ft. Mill, S.C., 1979—, sec., 1980—; guest lectr. Vandervilt U. Coll. Law. Exec. editor: U. Fla. Law Rev, 1962-63. Served as aviator USN, 1956-60. Mem. Am. Bar Assn. (1st prize article sect. corp., banking and bus. law 1969), Am. Soc. Corp. Secs. (pres. S.E. region 1974-75, nat. dir 1981—, chmn.-elect 1983-84, chmn. 1984-85). Republican. Clubs: Capital City (Atlanta); University (N.Y.C.). Home: 2318 Lathrop Ln Charlotte NC 28211 Office: Springs Industries Inc N White St Fort Mill SC 29715

DAVIS, STANLEY NELSON, hydrologist, educator; b. Rio de Janeiro, Brazil, Aug. 6, 1924; s. Nelson Caryl and Mary Faye (Caulkins) D.; m. Barbara Jean Wickham, Apr. 14, 1949 (div. Jan. 1982); children: Gerald Nelson, Ruth Ann, Darlene Grace, Randall Wayne, Betty Jean, Nancy Faye.; m. Augusta G. Felty, Feb. 12, 1982. B.S. in Geology, U. Nev., 1949; M.S., U. Kans., 1951; Ph.D., Yale, 1955. Geologist U.S. Bur. Reclamation, 1949, Mo. Geol. Survey, 1952, 53, 55; instr. U. Rochester, 1953-54; mem. faculty Stanford, 1954-67, prof. geology, 1965-67, U. Mo., 1967-73, chmn. dept., 1969-72; asso. dean Coll. Arts and Scis., 1972-73; prof. geology Ind. U., Bloomington, 1973-75; prof. hydrology U. Ariz., Tucson, 1975—, head dept. hydrology and water resources, 1975-79; Vis. prof. U. Chile, Santiago, 1960-61; tchr. Bowling Green U., summer 1963, Princeton, summer 1965, U. Hawaii, fall 1966; instr. U. Oriente in Venezuela, summer 1967-68, 72; lectr. Am. Geol. Inst.; mem. East Greenland Expdn., Arctic Inst. N. Am., summer 1959; cons. to govt. and industry, 1955—. Author: Hidrogeologia, 1961, (with R.M. DeWiest) Hydrogeology, 1966, (with P. Reitan and R. Pestrong) Geology, Our Physical Environment, 1976; also articles. Served with AUS, 1943-46; PTO. Fellow Geol. Soc. Am.; mem. Am. Geophys. Union, Assn. Engring. Geologists, AAAS, Soc. Econ. Paleontolgists and Mineralogists, Nat. Water Resources Assn., Sigma Xi. Home: 6540 W Box Canyon Dr Tucson AZ 85745 Office: Dept Hydrology and Water Resources U Ariz Tucson AZ 85721

DAVIS, STANTON WALKER, retail food company executive; b. Brockton, Mass., Dec. 12, 1908; s. Maynard W. and Emma S. (Walker) D.; m. Elisabeth Kaiser, Sept. 14, 1934; children: Anne Davis Peterson, Joan Davis Wheeler, Peter. B.S., Dartmouth Coll., 1930; M.B.A., Harvard U., 1932. With Brockton Public Markets, Inc. (merged with George C. Shaw Co. 1979, now Shaw's Supermarkets), East Bridgewater, Mass., 1932—, pres., 1950-75, chmn. bd., 1975—; dir. Kings Supermarkets Inc., West Caldwell, N.J. Past pres. Brockton Hosp. Clubs: Kittansett, Thorny Lea Golf. Home: 85 Crescent Dr Bridgewater MA 02324 Office: 140 Laurel St PO Box 600 East Bridgewater MA 02333

DAVIS, STEPHEN EDWARD, lawyer; b. Phila., Dec. 21, 1925; s. Edward and Josephine (Blitzstein) D.; m. Joyce Baldwin Kidder, July 30, 1955; children: Owen Kidder, Carolyn Woodbury, Charles Baldwin. B.S., U. Pa., 1946; M.S., Columbia, 1947, LL.B., 1952. Bar: N.Y. Assoc. Paul, Weiss, Rifkind, Wharton and Garrison, N.Y.C., 1952-54; sr. counsel Am. Electric Power Service Corp., N.Y.C., 1954-62; assoc. gen. counsel Universal Am. Corp., N.Y.C., 1962-68; asst. v.p and asst. res. counsel Gulf Western Industries Inc., N.Y.C., 1968-73; sr. v.p. and gen. counsel J. Henry Schroder Bank and Trust Co., N.Y.C., 1973—. Contbr. articles to profl. jours. Mem. ABA (com. on tax on banking and savs. instns., internat. bus. law com., sect. corp. banking and bus. law), Assn. Bar City N.Y. (banking law com.), Nat. Council for U.S.-China Trade (legal com.), Columbia Law Sch. Alumni Assn., Southwestern Legal Found. (adv. bd.), Phi Beta Kappa. Home: 130 Ridgewood Ave Glen Ridge NJ 07028 Office: J. Henry Schroder Bank and Trust Co One State St New York NY 10015

DAVIS, STEPHEN HOWARD, fluid dynamicist, educator; b. N.Y.C., Sept. 7, 1939; s. Harry Carl and Eva Leah (Axelrod) D.; m. Suellen Lewis, Jan. 15, 1966. B.E.E., Rensselaer Poly. Inst., 1960, M.S. in Math, 1962, Ph.D., 1964. Research mathematician Rand Corp., Santa Monica, Calif., 1964-66; lectr. in math. Imperial Coll., London U., 1966-68; asst. prof. mechanics and materials sci. Johns Hopkins U., 1968-70, asso. prof., 1970-75, prof., 1975-78; prof. engring. sci. and applied math. Northwestern U., 1979—; cons. in field; vis. prof. math. Monash U., Australia, 1973; vis. prof. chem. engring. U. Ariz., 1977; vis. scientist Institut fur Aerodynamik-ETH, Zurich, Switzerland, 1971; Mem. U.S. Nat. Com. for Theoretical and Applied Mechanics. Contbr. articles to profl. jours.; asst. editor: Jour. Fluid Mechanics, 1969-75; asso. editor, 1975—. Fellow Am. Phys. Soc. (chmn. div. fluid dynamics 1978-79, councillor div. fluid dynamics 1980-82); mem. Soc. Indsl. and Applied Maths., Sigma Xi, Pi Mu Epsilon. Home: 2735 Simpson St Evanston IL 60201 Office: Northwestern U Tech Inst Evanston IL 60201

DAVIS, STUART, Savings and loan association executive; b. Santa Monica, Calif.; s. William Arthur and Ida Mae (Hanson) D.; children—Lynn Fatti, Richard Edward. B.S., St. Mary's (Calif.) Coll., 1938. Vice chmn. Gt. Western Financial Corp., Los Angeles; Chmn. bd. Gt. Western Savs. & Loan Assn., Los Angeles, 1964-81, chmn. exec. com., 1981—. Trustee Pomona Coll. Recipient Alumnus of Yr. award St. Mary's Coll., 1964. Mem. U.S. League Savs. Assns. (chmn. legis. com. 1980-82, v.p. 1977, pres. 1978), Calif. Savs. and Loans League (pres. 1956), Savs. and Loan Found., Calif. C. of C. (past pres.). Clubs: St. Francis Yacht, Los Angeles Country, California., Thunderbird Country. Office: Gt Western Financial Corp 8484 Wilshire Blvd Beverly Hills CA 90211

DAVIS, THOMAS AUSTIN, university dean; b. Belgian Congo, May 31, 1934; s. William Ellsworth and Newell (Trimble) D. (parents Am. citizens); m. Patricia Denham, Mar. 31, 1959; children: Nancy, Timothy. B.A. in Math., Denison U., 1956; M.S., U. Mich., 1957; Ph.D., Cambridge U., 1963. Mem. faculty DePauw U., Greencastle, Ind., 1963-73, assoc. prof. math., 1967-73, dir. NSF Cosip program, Greencastle, 1971-72; asst. to provost for resource planning Princeton U., 1971-72; acad. adminstrn. intern Am. Council Edn., Princeton, 1971-72; acting pres. U. Puget Sound, Tacoma, 1979, prof. math, dean univ., 1973—. Author books; contbr. chpts. to books, articles to prof. jours. Mem. adminstrv. bd. United Meth. Ch., Greencastle, 1970; mem. steering com. Tacoma Area Council Giftedness, 1980-83; trustee Charles Wright Acad., Tacoma, 1980—. Danforth fellow, 1956; fellow Denison U. Research Found., 1956. Mem. Math. Assn. Am., Am. Soc. Values in Higher Edn., Assn. Acad. Deans, Phi Beta Kappa (past chpt. sec.), Phi Kappa Phi. Presbyterian. Lodge: Rotary. Office: Univ Puget Sound Tacoma WA 98416

DAVIS, THOMAS EDWARD, banker, economist; b. Detroit, Jan. 16, 1932; s. Edward Thomas and Margaret (Hughes) D.; m. Myra Sue Smith, Jan. 23, 1960; children: Bradley Edward, Gary Scott, Julie Elizabeth. B.A., Ohio Wesleyan U., 1954; M.A., U. Mich., 1960, Ph.D., 1965; attended, Brit. Council Sch. City of London, 1981. Asst. internat. economist Fed. Res. Bank N.Y., 1960-61; instr. U. Mich., 1964-65; with Fed. Res. Bank Kansas City, Mo., 1965—, v.p., 1971-77, sr. v.p., dir. research, 1977—; instr. Colo. Sch. Banking, 1968-73; assoc. economist Fed. Res. Open Market Com., 1977, 80, 83; trustee Livestock Mdsg. Inst., 1972—, Kans. Council Econ. Edn., 1980—, Mo. Council Econ. Edn., 1980—; chmn. conv. Allied Social Sci. Assn., 1980. Served with USAF, 1955-58. Mem. Am. Econ. Assn., Am. Inst. Banking, Kansas City C. of C. Home: 9217 Wedd Dr Overland Park KS 66213 Office: 925 Grand Ave Kansas City MO 64198

DAVIS, THOMAS HENRY, airline executive; b. Winston-Salem, N.C., Mar. 15, 1918; s. Egbert L. and Annie (Shore) D.; m. Nancy Carolyn Teague, Oct. 28, 1944; children: Thomas Henry, Winifred (Mrs. Blackwell Bennett Pierce), George Franklin, Nancy, Juliana Davis West. Student, U. Ariz., 1935-39. Aircraft salesman Piedmont Aviation, Inc., Winston-Salem, 1940, v.p., treas., 1941-43, pres., treas., 1943-81, chmn. bd., chief exec. officer, treas., 1981—; dir., mem. exec. com. Wachovia Corp.; dir. Midcontinent Telephone Corp., Duke Power Co.; Mem. Winston-Salem Redevel. Commn., Utilities Commn., 1955-75. Trustee Wake Forest U. Recipient Winston-Salem-Forsyth County. of C. Distinguished Service award, 1954, Frank Dawson trophy for outstanding service to aviation in N.C., 1949; U. Ariz. Alumni Achievement award, 1976; Tony Jannus award for service to air transp. industry, 1980; named to Va. Aviation Hall of Fame, 1980. Mem. Air Transport Assn. (dir.), Nat. Aviation Club, Soaring Soc. Am., Newcomen Soc., Winston-Salem C. of C. (past pres.), Pi Kappa Alpha. Democrat. Baptist. Clubs: Rotarian., Forsyth Country, Old Town (Winston-Salem); Wings (N.Y.C.). Home: 1190 Arbor Rd Winston-Salem NC 27104 Office: Smith Reynolds Airport Winston-Salem NC 27102 *Never depend on someone else to do for you what you can and should do for yourself.*

DAVIS, THURSTON N., clergyman; b. Phila., Oct. 12, 1913; s. Noble Thurston and Rose Mary (Carey) D. A.B., Georgetown Coll., 1937; S.T.L., Woodstock Coll., 1943; A.M., Harvard U., 1946, Ph.D., 1947; Litt.D., LaSalle Coll., 1959, Loyola Coll., Balt., 1964. Joined S.J., 1931; ordained priest Roman Catholic Ch., 1942; tchr. Regis High Sch., N.Y.C., 1938-39; instr. grad. sch. arts and scis. Fordham U., 1947-49; dean Fordham Coll., 1949-53; dir. John LaFarge Inst., John Courtney Murray Forum, 1967-70, 76—; with communications dept. U.S. Cath. Conf., N.Y.C., 1970-78. Contbg. editor: America, 1953-54; asso. editor, 1954-55; editor-in-chief, 1955-68; also: Cath. Mind, 1955-68; editor: A John LaFarge Reader, 1956, Between Two Cities, 1962. Club: Harvard (N.Y.C.). Address: 106 W 56th St New York NY 10019

DAVIS, TRUE, bus. exec.; b. St. Joseph, Mo., Dec. 23, 1919; s. William True and Helen (Marstella) D.; m. Virginia Bruce Motter, Jan. 24, 1948 (dec. Sept. 1969); children—William True, Bruce Motter, Lance Barrow. Student, Cornell, 1937-40; L.H.D., Tarkio U., 1963; J.D., Mo. Western Coll., 1979. Salesman Anchor Serum Co., St. Joseph, Mo., 1940-42, v.p., sales mgr., 1945-50, pres., 1950-60; pres., dir. Research Labs., Inc., 1952-60, Pet's Best Co., 1954-60, World Health Inst., Ltd., 1958-60, Peters Serum Co., Kansas City, 1956-60, Wilke Labs., Inc., West Plains, Mo., Wilke Labs. of Tenn., Memphis, 1956-60, Peerless Serum Co., St. Joseph, 1956-60, Med. Industries, Inc., 1957-60, Gothic Advt., Inc., 1956-60, Certified Labs., Inc., 1956-60, Davis Estate, Inc., 1958—, Carolina Vet. Supply, Inc., Charlotte, N.C., 1956-60, Anchor Serum Co. of Ind., Inc., Indpls., 1959-60, Anchor Serum Co. N.J., Camden, 1959-60, Anchor Serum Co. Minn., So. St. Paul, 1960; chmn., dir. Chemico Labs., Inc., Miami, Fla., 1960-63; chmn. Thompson Hayward Chem. Co., Kansas City, Mo., 1961-63; pres., dir. Philips Roxane, Inc., N.Y.C., 1959-63; v.p., dir. Philips Electronics and Pharm. Industries Corp., 1959-63; U.S. exec. dir. Inter-Am. Devel. Bank, 1966-68; ambassador to, Switzerland, 1963-65, asst. sec. treasury, 1965-68; pres., chmn. bd. dirs. Nat. Bank of Washington, 1969-73; dir. Laurel Race Course, Md., Tri Ltd., Bahamas; trustee Riviere Realty Trust, Washington.; Chmn. U.S. Port Security Com., 1965-68, N.Y. Pier Com., 1966-68, Pub. Adv. Com. Customs Adminstrn., 1966-68; mem. Fgn. Trade Zones Bd., 1965-68; U.S. del. Internat. Maritime Coordinating Orgn., London, 1966, GATT Conf. Anti-Dumping Laws, Geneva, 1966; adviser U.S. delegation to World Bank and IMF, 1966; chmn. Dept. Commerce Export Expansion Council, 1962-63, Washington Urban Coalition, 1971-72. Contbr. articles to trade, farm publs. Pres. Animal Health Inst., 1954-56, dir., 1946-59; mem. Nat. Serum Control Agy., 1947-58, chmn., 1954-55; exec. com. United Fund, 1960; bd. govs. Am. Royal, Kansas City, Mo., 1960—; mem. Cornell U. Council, 1962-68; bd. dirs. Washington Internat. Horse Show, 1975—, pres., 1978-80; Col., staff gov., Mo., 1949-54, 58-68 Col., staff gov., Ky., 1953-54. Served to lt. USNR, 1943-45. Recipient V.F.W. Outstanding Citizen award, St. Joseph, 1960; St. Joseph Jr. C. of C. Boy Year award, 1960. Mem. N.Y. Acad. Scis. (life), Thoroughbred Clubs Am., Newcomen Soc., Am. Legion, V.F.W. (mem. nat. Americanization com. 1961-63, chmn. state com. 1960-63, Nat. Gold Medal for Americanization 1967), Mo. Acad. Squires, Phi Gamma Delta. Democrat. Clubs: Minnesouri Angling (Alexandria, Minn.); F Street, Metropolitan (Washington). Home: 2860 Woodland Dr NW Washington DC 20008

DAVIS, VICTORIA (VICKY DAVIS), men's neckwear company executive; b. Detroit, Oct. 2, 1924; d. Isadore and Gussie (Garfunkel) Wolk; m. Lawrence Davis, Mar. 6, 1949; children—Robert M.,

Kenneth H. Student pub. schs., Detroit. Legal sec. firm Friedman, Meyers & Keys, Detroit, 1942-49; sec. Buick Motor Co., Flint, Mich., 1949-50; engring. sec. Fisher Body Co., Detroit, 1950-52; owner, designer Chest Knots, Oak Park, Mich., 1969-74; pres., designer Vicky Davis Ltd., N.Y.C., 1974—; lectr. fields of fashion, bus. opportunities for women. Pres. James N. Pepper Sch. PTA, Oak Park, 1965, 66; vol. worker Juvenile Ct., Detroit; active Detroit Assn. Retarded Children, Sinai Hosp. Women's Guild. Recipient Coty Am. Fashion Critics award, 1976; 1st Cutty Sark Fashion Designers award, 1980. Mem. Men's Fashion Assn., Men's Tie Assn., Council Fashion Designers Am. Home: 245 Fawn Hill Rd Tuxedo NY 10987 Office: 1123 Broadway New York NY 10010 *Having to succeed, rather than wanting to succeed, has not allowed me to accept anything less than success.*

DAVIS, VINCENT, educator; b. Chattanooga, May 3, 1930; (married); 3 children. B.A., Vanderbilt U., 1952; M.P.A., Woodrow Wilson Sch., Princeton U., 1959, M.A., 1960, Ph.D., 1961. Mem. faculty dept. politics, research asst. Center Internat. Studies, Princeton U., 1959-61, vis. research prof., 1969-70; mem. faculty Dartmouth Coll., 1961-62; mem. faculty Grad. Sch. Internat. Studies, research asso. Social Sci. Found. U. Denver, 1962-71; Patterson prof. internat. studies, dir. Patterson Sch. Diplomacy and Internat. Commerce, U. Ky., Lexington, 1971—; Nimitz prof. polit. sci. U.S. Naval War Coll., 1970-71; exec. council Inter-Univ. Seminar Armed Forces and Soc., U. Chgo., 1972-79; chmn. civilian adv. panel Sec. Def. Com. Excellence in Mil. Edn., 1974-76; cons., lectr. in field. Mem. internat. affairs fellowships com. Council on Fgn. Relations, N.Y.C., 1980—. Author: Postwar Defense Policy and the U.S. Navy, 1943-46, 1966, The Admirals Lobby, 1967, The Politics of Innovation, 1967, The Analysis of International Politics, 1971, Henry Kissinger and Bureaucratic Politics: A Personal Appraisal, 1979, The Post-Imperial Presidency, 1980; also monographs, spl. reports; editor: Sage Papers in Internat. Studies, 1971-77; contbr. profl. jours. Served with U.S. Navy, 1952-56; capt. Res. Mem. Internat. Studies Assn. (exec. dir. 1964-71, chmn. intensive panels 1972-74, pres. 1976-77), Am. Polit. Sci. Assn., AAUP, AAAS, Internat. Inst. Strategic Studies. Home: 3533 Gloucester Dr Westmorland Lexington KY 40510 Office: Patterson Sch Diplomacy and Internat Commerce Univ Ky Lexington KY 40506 *Young people coming of age in the 1980's and '90's are entering adulthood in a nation and world with rapidly shifting political-economic relationships dramatically different from anything we have known before. Trying to help students figure out the exact meaning of these shifts, and how to cope with them in their own professional and personal lives, is the central challenge to me for the remainder of my career.*

DAVIS, W. RICHARD, lawyer; b. Bryan, Texx, June 13, 1935; s. Halsell S. and Ara Lee (Simpson) D.; m. Sally Ann Kay Davis, Nov. 24, 1956; children—W. Richard, Jack Davies, Cynthia Kay. B.B.A., So. Meth. U., 1956, LL.B., 1958. Bar: Tex. bar 1958. Mem. firm Strasburger & Price, Dallas, 1958-63, partner firm, 1963—; bd. dirs. Def. Research Inst. Fellow Am. Coll. Trial Lawyers; mem. Dallas Bar Assn., Tex. Bar Assn., Am. Bar Assn., Tex. Assn. Def. Counsel, Dallas Assn. Def. Counsel, Internat. Assn. Ins. Counsel. Baptist. Club: Salesmanship (Dallas). Home: 4000 Shenandoah Dallas TX 75205 Office: 1200 1 Main Pl Dallas TX 75250

DAVIS, WALTER, professional basketball player; b. Pineville, N.C., Sept. 9, 1954. Student, U. N.C. Basketball player Phoenix Suns, NBA, 1977—. Mem. NBA All Star Team, 1978, 79, 80, 83. Office: care Phoenix Suns PO Box 1369 Phoenix AZ 85001 *

DAVIS, WAYNE ALTON, educator; b. Ft. Macleod, Alta., Nov. 16, 1931; s. Frederick and Anna Mary (Barr) D.; m. Audrey M. Zorolov, July 17, 1959; children: Frederick M., Peter W., Timothy M. B.S.E., George Washington U., 1960; M.Sc., U. Ottawa, 1963, Ph.D., 1967. Sci. officer Def. Research Bd., Ottawa, Ont., 1960-68; research scientist Dept. Communications, Ottawa, 1968-69; vis. scientist NRC, Ottawa, 1975-76; assoc. prof. U. Alta., Edmonton, 1969-77, prof. computing sci., 1977—, acting chmn. computing sci., 1982-83; lectr. U. Ottawa, 1965-69; sessional lectr. Carleton U., 1967; cons. Editor: The Barrs of Ardenville, 1978. Grantee NRC, 1970-78; research grantee Natural Scis. and Engring. Research Council, 1978—; syrategic grantee Natural Scis. and Engring. Research Council, 1981—; grantee Def. Research Bd., 1974-76. Mem. Can. Info. Processing Soc. (pres. 1978-79), Can. Man-Computer Communications Soc. (pres.), Can. Soc. Computational Study of Intelligence (treas. 1976—), IEEE, ACM. Anglican. Clubs: Faculty, Canadian Legion. Home: 11636 71 Ave Edmonton AB Canada T6G OA8 Office: U Alta Dept Computing Sci Edmonton AB Canada T6G 2HI

DAVIS, WENDELL, JR., lawyer; b. N.Y.C., June 22, 1933; m. Penelope Case, May 17, 1969; children: Jennifer C., Virginia W., Peter T. A.B. cum laude, Harvard U., 1954, LL.B., 1961. Bar: Conn. 1961, N.Y. 1963. Individual practice law, Brookfield, Conn., 1961; law sec. to Justice Charles D. Breitel, N.Y.C., 1964-65; mem. firm Scheuermann & Davis (and predecessor), N.Y.C., 1972-78, Emmet, Marvin & Martin, 1978—; Pres. Carnegie Hill-90th St. Inc., 1977-80. Mem. Am. Law Inst., Am., Conn., N.Y. State bar assns., Assn. Bar City N.Y. Home: 28 Huguenot Drive Larchmont NY 10538 Office: 48 Wall St New York NY 10005

DAVIS, W(ILLARD) KENNETH, management and engineering consultant; b. Seattle, July 26, 1918; s. Elbert Willard and Alice Marie (Kingman) D.; m. Margaret Ellen Bean, June 14, 1941; children—Kerry Suzanne, Warren Kenneth, Gail Marie Greene. Student, U. Calif. at Berkeley, 1936-38; B.S. in Chem. Engring, Mass. Inst. Tech., 1940, M.S., 1942. Asst. dir. Buffalo sta. Mass. Inst. Tech. Sch. Chem. Engring. Practice, 1941-42; sr. research engr. Calif. Research Corp., 1942-47; sr. engr. Ford, Bacon & Davis, Inc., 1947-49; asso. prof. engring. UCLA, 1949-53, prof. engring., 1953, Regents' lectr., 1961, 77-78, adj. prof. engring. and applied sci., 1980-81, 83; chief devel. engr. Calif. Research & Devel. Co., 1951-52, mgr. research, 1952-54; asst. dir. reactor devel. div. AEC, 1954, dep. dir., 1954, dir., 1955-58; v.p. Bechtel Corp., San Francisco, 1958-72, v.p. internat. power div., 1967-71, v.p. power and indsl. div., 1971-72; v.p. Bechtel Nuclear Corp., 1958-80, Bechtel Power Corp., 1973-81; dep. sec. energy Dept. Energy, Washington, 1981-83; dir. Mgmt. Analysis Co., 1983—; Mem. adv. bd. Naval Ordnance Test Sta., Inyokern, Calif., 1955-60; dir. Atomic Indsl. Forum, 1960-67, v.p., 1962-64, pres., chmn., 1964-67, hon. dir., 1967-81, 83; Mem. com. on radioactive waste mgmt. NRC, 1968-78, bd. energy studies, 1974-77, gov. bd., 1978-81, energy engring. bd., 1974-81; chmn. supply panel, com. on nuclear and alt. energy sources; mem. bd., exec. com. U.S. Nat. Com. World Energy Conf., vice chmn., 1972-74, 80-83, chmn., 1983; advisory com. on sci. and fgn. policy to sec. state, 1973-75; mem. tech. adv. bd. Panel on Project Independence, Dept. Commerce, 1974-75; advisory panel on nuclear engring. NSF, 1975; mem. corp. devel. com. M.I.T., 1973-81, energy advisory lab. bd., 1975-81, vis. com. dept. civil engring., 1976—, dept. chem. engring., 1980-81. Exec. v.p. Point Reyes Nat. Seashore Found. Recipient Flemming award, 1956; Profl. Progress award Am. Inst. Chem. Engrs., 1958; Robert E. Wilson award, 1969; Nat. Engring. award Am. Assn. Engring. Socs., 1982; Sec. of Energy's Gold medal for disting. service, 1983. Fellow Am. Nuclear Soc. (dir. 1957-60, Walter H. Zinn award 1983), Am. Inst. Chem. Engring. (chmn. nuclear engring. div. 1958, dir. 1972-74, chmn. energy com. 1973-75, pres. 1981, Founders award 1983), AAAS; mem. Am. Chem. Soc., ASME, Nat. Acad. Engring. (dir. 1972-81, v.p. 1978-81, exec. com. 1973-77, chmn. task force on energy 1973-74), Am. Soc. Engring. Edn., ASTM (dir. 1980-81, chmn. research and tech. planning com. 1976-79), Brit. Nuclear Energy Soc., Assn. Coop. in Engring. (chmn. energy coordinating com. 1974-75, vice chmn. 1978-79), Sigma Xi, Chi Phi. Presbyn. Clubs: World Trade; Commonwealth, Bankers, Villa Taverna (San Francisco); Sierra, Cosmos (Washington). PO Box 6269 3280 Edgewater Dr Dollar Point Tahoe City CA 95730

DAVIS, WILLIAM COLUMBUS, educator, author, lecturer; b. Birmingham, Ala., Aug. 28, 1910; s. William Columbus and Maude (Gray) D.; m. Mildred J. Dorman, July 24, 1948. A.B., U. Ala., 1931, M.A., 1932; M.A., Harvard U., 1943, Ph.D., 1948. Adminstrv. positions U.S. Senate, 1933-46; asst. prof. history U. Ga., 1948-51; faculty George Washington U., 1951-66, prof. Latin Am. history and govt., 1960-66, dir. Latin Am. studies, 1952-66; prof. internat. affairs, dir. Latin Am. studies, dir. lecture program, only permanent mem. faculty Nat. War Coll., Washington, 1963-74; dir., participant numerous radio, TV programs in field; lectr. various colls., univs., vis. prof. Samford U., 1983—. Author: The Last Conquistadores: The Spanish Intervention in Peru and Chile, 1863-1866, 1950, The Columns of Athens, 1951; co-author: Soviet Bloc Latin American Activities and Their Implications for United States Foreign Policy, 1960; editor: Index to the Writings on American History, 1902-1940, 1956, Am. Hist. Assn's Guide to Historical Literature, 1960; contbr. numerous articles on recent Latin Am. devels. to various publs. Mem. Phi Beta Kappa, Pi Kappa Phi. Baptist. Home: 1323 Darnall Dr McLean VA 22101

DAVIS, WILLIAM D(OYLE), banker; b. Yeagertown, Pa., May 13, 1931; m. Joyce E. Goss; children: William D., Susan E., Gregory L., Rebecca M. B.S. in Fin., Pa. State U., 1957; grad., Bank Adminstrn. Inst. Sch. U. Wis., 1968, Grad. Sch. Banking U. Wis., 1972. With Pa. Dept. of Banking, Harrisburg, 1957-67, No. Central Bank, Williamsport, Pa., 1967-79; pres., chief exec. officer Commonwealth Bank & Trust Co., N.A., Williamsport, 1979—, also dir.; dir., pres. Commonwealth Bancshares, Williamsport; dir. Pa. Enterprises, Inc., Pa. Gas & Water Co., Wilkes-Barre; treas. Indsl. Properties Corp., Williamsport. Bd. dirs. Greater Williamsport Partnership; adv. bd. Salvation Army; sec., bd. dirs. Mcpl. Authority, Williamsport. Served with U.S. Army, 1952-54. Mem. Pa. Bankers Assn. (chmn. fin. com. 1982-83), Pa. Econ. League, U.S. C. of C., Williamsport-Lycoming C. of C. (dir.), Appalachian Thruway Assn. Clubs: Williamsport Country, Eaglesmere Country, Ross. Home: 1207 Lafayette Pkwy Williamsport PA 17701 Office: Commonwealth Bank & Trust CoNA 101 W Third St Williamsport PA 17703

DAVIS, WILLIAM ERNEST, lawyer; b. Indpls., Jan. 26, 1921; s. William Ernest and Mary Ellen (Hoover) D.; m. Jane Ann Gentholts, Oct. 27, 1945 (div. 1967); children: William Arthur, Mark Howard, Lora Ann; m. Barbara B. Brown, Jan. 27,, 1968. Student, Miami U., Oxford, Ohio, 1940-42; A.B., Western Res. U., 1947, LL.B., 1978. Bar: Ohio. Ptnr. Falsgraf, Reidy, Shoup & Ault, Cleve., 1958-71, Baker & Hostetler, 1971—. Capt. U.S. Army, 1942-45. Fellow Am. Coll. Probate Counsel; mem. Phi Delta Phi, Phi Sigma. Republican. Episcopalian. Clubs: Mayfield Country, Hermit, Hunting Valley Gun, Rockwell Springs Trout. Home: 3835-3 Lander Rd Chagrin Falls OH 44022 Office: Baker & Hostetler 3200 National City Center Cleveland OH 44114

DAVIS, WILLIAM EUGENE, university administrator; b. Wamego, Kans., Feb. 15, 1929; s. Eugene Kenneth and Willa (Dickinson) D.; m. Pollyanne Peterson, Mar. 17, 1951; children: Deborah, Rebecca, Douglas, Brooke, Bonnie. B.S., U. Colo., 1951; M.A., U. No. Colo., 1958; Ed.D., U. Colo., 1963. Asst. to dean men U. Colo., 1951; tchr. English, coach Loveland Colo.) High Sch., 1954-55, Rapid City (S.D.) High Sch., 1955-59, Greeley (Colo.) High Sch., 1959-60; alumni dir., head football coach, dean men U. Colo., 1960-63; exec. asst. to pres. U. Wyo., 1963-65; pres. Idaho State U., Pocatello, 1965-75, U. N.Mex., Albuquerque, 1975-82; chancellor Oreg. System Higher Edn., Eugene, 1983—; Oreg. commr. Edn. Commn. of States, 1982—; Idaho commr. Western Interstate Commn. for Higher Edn., 1965-75, vice chmn., 1973-74, chmn., 1974-75; N.Mex. commr. Western Interstate Commn. Higher Edn., 1978-82; mem. N.Mex. Selection Com. for Rhodes scholars, 1976-82, Pres.'s Council Western Athletic Conf., 1975-82, chmn., 1978-79; mem. N.Mex. Gov.'s Com. on Tech. Excellence, 1975-82, Nat. Collegiate Athletic Assn. Theodore Roosevelt Award Jury, 1974-79; chmn. Idaho Rhodes Scholarship Selection Com., 1971-75; mem. Gov.'s Corp. Voluntarism Com., 1982—, Am. Council Edn., 1982—, AFL-CIO Labor/Higher Edn Council, 1982—. Author: Glory Colorado-A History of the University of Colorado, 1965, Nobody Calls Me Doctor, 1972. Served to capt. USMCR, 1951-54. Mem. Western Coll. Assn. (exec. com. 1981—), Oreg. Hist. Soc. (bd. dirs. 1982—), Am. Assn. State Colls. and Univs. (com. on acad. and student personnel 1982—, com. on student issues and affairs 1982—), Alpha Tau Omega, Phi Delta Kappa, Omicron Delta Kappa. Methodist. Clubs: Elk, Rotarian. Office: Oreg State System Higher Edn PO Box 3175 Eugene OR 97403

DAVIS, WILLIAM EUGENE, architect; b. Terre Haute, Ind., Sept. 4, 1921; s. William Eugene and Anne (Reese) D.; m. Carolyn Elaine Thompson, Oct. 23, 1964; children—Elizabeth Anne, John William. B.S., U. Ill., 1948, M.Arch., 1966. Structural designer Allen & Kelly, Architects, Indpls., 1948; field design engr. Girdler Corp., Louisville, 1950-52; constrn. engr. U.S. Army C.E. (Chgo. dist.), 1952-53; chief engr. design Liberty Powder Co., Newport, Ind., 1953-57; architect, prin., owner W.E. Davis, Architect, Rockville, Ind., 1957—; Lectr. archtl. tech. Ind. U.-Purdue U., Indpls., 1959-63, asst. prof., 1963-68, asso. prof., 1968-73, prof., 1973-77, chmn. dept. constrn. tech., 1966-77; prof., program dir. constrn. tech. Ind. State U., Terre Haute, 1977—. Prin. archtl. works include Holy Cross Luth. Ch, Crawfordsville, Ind., Southeastern Ch. Christ, Indpls., Billie Creek Village, Rockville, Ind. Served with USAAF, 1943-46. Mem. AIA, Soc. Archtl. Historians, Nat. Trust Hist. Preservation, AAUP, Ind. Soc. Architects. Club: Rotarian. Home: 411 Jackson St Rockville IN 47872 Office: Box 61 Rockville IN 47872

DAVIS, WILLIAM GRENVILLE, premier of Ont.; b. Brampton, Ont., Can., July 30, 1929; s. Albert Grenville D. and Vera M. (Hewetson); m. Helen MacPhee, 1953 (dec. 1962); children—Neil, Nancy, Catherine, Ian; m. Kathleen Mackay, 1963; 1 dau., Meg. B.A., U. Toronto, 1951; grad., Osgoode Hall Law Sch., 1954; LL.D. (hon.), Waterloo Luth. U., 1963, Western Ont. U., 1965, U. Toronto, 1967, McMaster U., 1968, Queen's U., 1968, Windsor U., 1969, D.U., Ottawa U., 1980. Bar: Called to Ont. bar 1955. Partner firm Davis, Webb and Hollinrake, Brampton, 1955-59; mem. Provincial Parliament Ont. from Peel Riding, 1959, 63, Peel North Riding, 1967, 71, Brampton Riding, 1975; 2d vice-chmn. Hydro-Electric Power Commn. of Ont., 1961-62; minister of edn., Ont., 1962-71, also minister of univ. affairs, 1964-71, premier of Ont., 1971—; leader Progressive Conservative Party of Ont., 1971—. Author: Education in Ontario, 1965, Building an Educated Society, 1816-1966, 1966, other publs. Mem. Ont., Can. bar assns. Mem. United Ch. Clubs: Kiwanis, Masons, Albany (Toronto). Address: Office of the Premier of Ont Parliament Bldgs Toronto ON Canada M7A 1A1

DAVIS, WILLIAM HOWARD, publishing company executive; b. Chgo., Mar. 6, 1922; s. Philip D. and Anne Helen (Tripp) D.; m. Chermaine Ryser, Oct. 11, 1952; 1 dau., Susie. B.S., Northwestern U., 1943. News editor Printer's Ink mag., Chgo., 1946-49; asst. to sales mgr. WGN-TV, Chgo., 1949-52; account exec. CBS-TV, Chgo. and N.Y.C., 1952-59; pres. Golf Digest, Inc., Norwalk, Conn., 1959-75; pres. mag. group N.Y. Times Co., 1975—. Author: Great Courses of the World, 1974, Greatest Golf Courses and Then Some, 1982. Bd. dirs. Big Brothers, Inc., N.Y.C. Served to lt. comdr. USNR, 1943-46. Mem. Mag. Pubs. Assn. (exec. com.), Phi Kappa Sigma. Christian Scientist. Clubs: Milbrook (Greenwich, Conn.); Winged Foot Golf (Mamaroneck, N.Y.). Office: 495 Westport Ave Norwalk CT 06856 *

DAVIS, WILLIAM POTTER, JR., university official; b. Cleve., Aug. 27, 1924; s. William Potter and Vesper (Wood) D.; m. Barbara Noel Day, Aug. 30, 1947; children: Glynis Wood, Jennifer Lanning, Christopher Lewis, Bethany Grinnel, Timothy Lord. A.B., Oberlin Coll., 1948; M.S., U. Mich., 1949, Ph.D., 1954; M.A. (hon.), Dartmouth Coll., 1967. Mem. faculty Dartmouth Coll., 1955—, instr. to prof. physics, asso. provost, 1967-70, acting dean Thayer Sch. Engring., 1969-70, budget officer, 1970-74, treas., 1974—; Asso. program dir., pre-coll. edn. sci. div. NSF, 1965-66; mem. corp. Dartmouth Savs. Bank; mem. adv. bd. N.H. div. Am. Automobile Assn. Contbr. articles to profl. jours. Mem. corp. Mary Hitchcock Meml. Hosp. Served with USNR, 1943-46. Mem. Nat. Council Univ. Research Adminstrs., AAAS, Sigma Xi, Phi Kappa Phi. Democrat. Conglist. Home: 7 Church St Norwich VT 05055 Office: Parkhurst Hall Dartmouth Coll Hanover NH 03755

DAVIS, WILLIAM ROBERT, physicist; b. Oklahoma City, Aug. 22, 1929; s. Cecil Samuel and Virgie Vinnolia (Fowler) D.; m. Robin Nell Reed, May 21, 1970; 1 son, Eric Reed. B.S., U. Okla., 1953, M.S., 1954; postgrad., U. Goettingen, W. Ger., 1955-56; Doktor der Naturwissenschaften, Tech. U. Hannover, W. Ger., 1956. Physicist Trisophia Enterprises, Oklahoma City, 1956-57; mem. faculty N.C. State U., Raleigh, 1957—, prof. physics, 1966—; cons. to govt. and industry, 1961—; pres. Regulus Corp. Okla., 1957-60; Bd. dirs. Am. Edn. and Advanced Studies Found., 1972—, Einstein Found. Internat., 1980—. Author: Classical Fields, Particles and the Theory of Relativity, 1970; also articles, chpts. in books. Guggenheim fellow, 1970. Fellow Am. Phys. Soc.; mem. Am. Assn. Physics Tchrs., Internat. Soc. for Gen. Relativity and Gravitation, AAAS, Sigma Xi, Sigma Pi Sigma, Pi Mu Epsilon, Tau Beta Pi, Sigma Tau. Address: PO Box 5383 Raleigh NC 27650

DAVIS, WYLIE HERMAN, lawyer, educator; b. Macon, Ga., May 26, 1919; s. Wylie Herman and Florine (Burdick) D.; m. June Marie Patterson, Nov. 9, 1957; children: Ann Marie, Neil, John, Alan; children by previous marriage: Louise, June Elizabeth. A.B., Mercer U., 1940, LL.B. magna cum laude, 1947, J.D., 1947; LL.M., Harvard U., 1948. Bar: Ark. 1953, Ill. 1958, Ga. 1968, U.S. Supreme Ct. 1958, U.S. Ct. Mil. Appeals 1958. Instr. English Mercer U., 1946; asst. prof. law U. Ark., Fayetteville, 1948-50, asso. prof., 1950-52, prof., 1952-55, 70-72, Disting. prof. law, 1972—, dean, 1973-78; prof. law U. Tex., 1955-56, U. Ill., 1956-67, U. Ga., 1967-70; Earl F. Nelson Disting. vis. prof. law U. Mo., Columbia, 1979-80; vis. summer prof. George Washington U., 1952, 64, U. Mich., 1958, U. Utah, 1960, U. N.C., 1968, U. S.C., 1974, U. Ala., 1982, Tex. Tech U., 1983; of counsel firm Davis, Cox and Wright, Fayetteville, 1976—; pvt. practice cons. ins., maritime law and labor arbitration, 1948—; chmn. drafting com. on contracts Nat. Conf. Bar Examiners, 1971—. Contbr. articles to legal jours. Bd. govs. Antaeus Inst., 1973—. Served with USNR, 1940-45; PTO. Recipient cert. of recognition Ark. Bar Assn., 1979. Mem. Ret. Officers Assn., Order of Coif, Phi Alpha Delta. Episcopalian. Clubs: Rotary (Fayetteville) (pres. 1978-79, Paul Harris fellow 1983—. Home: 1719 Carolyn Dr Fayetteville AR 72701 Office: Sch Law U Ark Fayetteville AR 72701

DAVISON, BEAUMONT, university administrator; b. Atlanta, May 30, 1929; s. Beaumont and Mellie (Zellars) D.; m. Ruth Wilson, June 12, 1952; children: Alan B., Lynne K. B.E., Vanderbilt U., 1950; M.E.E., Syracuse U., 1952, Ph.D., 1956. Instr., research asso. Syracuse (N.Y.) U., 1951-56; asst. prof. elec. engring. Case Inst. Tech., Cleve., 1956-59; exec. v.p., dir. Indsl. Electronic Rubber Co., Twinsburg, Ohio, 1959-67; chmn. dept. elec. engring. Ohio U., Athens, 1967-69, dean, 1969-71, v.p. regional higher edn., 1971-74; dean engring. Calif. State Poly. U., Pomona, 1974-83; pres. Tri-State U., Angola, Ind., 1983—; cons. microwave devices. Contbr. articles to profl. jours. Bd. dirs. chpt. ARC, 1976-83, chmn., 1978-79; trustee Meml. Hosp., Athens, 1971-74. Named Educator of Yr. Soc. Mfg. Engrs., 1977. Mem. Am. Soc. Engring. Edn., IEEE (sr.), Soc. Mfg. Engrs. (sr.), Sigma Xi, Tau Beta Pi, Phi Kappa Phi, Eta Kappa Nu, Phi Delta Theta. Office: Tri-State Univ Angola IN 46703

DAVISON, CHARLES HAMILTON, financial executive; b. Providence, Dec. 20, 1926; s. Ernest H. and Margery C. (Crowell) D.; m. Lessie Hall Lang Busbee, Aug. 16, 1958; children: Charles Hamilton, James Lang, Andrew Burwell. A.B., Dartmouth Coll., 1950; M.B.A., N.Y. U., 1953. C.P.A. Accountant Hurdman & Cranstoun, N.Y.C., 1950-55; partner firm Comery, Davison & Co., Providence, 1955-64; mng. partner Peat, Marwick, Mitchell & Co., Providence, 1964-65, mng. partner New Eng. Area, 1965-67, mng. partner Chgo. office, mem. exec. com. Midwest Area, 1967-77, dep. chmn., N.Y.C., 1977-80; vice chmn., chmn. fin. com., mem. exec. com. Smith Barney, Harris Upham & Co., N.Y.C., 1980-82; chmn., chief exec. officer Paramount Cards Inc., 1983—. Pres., bd. dirs. United Charities Chgo.; bd. dirs. Community Fund Chgo., Inc., R.I. Philharmonic; trustee Roosevelt U., Inst. on Man and Sci.; chmn. fin. com., mem. exec. com. Kenyon Coll.; mem. adv. council Northwestern U. Grad. Sch. Mgmt.; bd. overseers Amos Tuck Sch., Dartmouth Coll., NYU Grad. Sch. Bus.; mem. vis. com. Grad. Sch. Bus., U. Chgo. Serve with USAAF, 1944-46. Mem. Am. Inst. C.P.A.'s, Ill., N.Y. socs. C.P.A.'s, Chgo. Assn. Commerce and Industry (dir., v.p., policy com.). Republican. Congregationalist. Clubs: Commercial of Chgo.; Round Hill (Greenwich, Conn.); Indian Hill, Belle Haven; Agawam Hunt, Hope (Providence); Chicago (Chgo.); Johns Island (Vero Beach, Fla.). Home: 124 Glenwood Dr Greenwich CT 06830

DAVISON, DANIEL POMEROY, banker; b. N.Y.C., Jan. 30, 1925; s. Frederick Trubee and Dorothy (Peabody) D.; m. Catherine Cheremeteff, June 27, 1953; children: Daniel Pomeroy, George Peabody, Henry Pomeroy. Grad., Groton (Mass.) Sch., 1943; B.A., Yale, 1949; J.D., Harvard, 1952. Bar: N.Y. 1952. Assoc. firm White & Case, N.Y.C., 1952-55; asst. sec., then sec. J.P. Morgan & Co., Inc., N.Y.C., 1955-59; with Morgan Guaranty Trust Co., N.Y.C., 1959—, v.p., 1961-73, sr. v.p., 1973-76, exec. v.p., 1976-79; pres. U.S. Trust Co., N.Y.C., 1979-82, chmn. bd., pres., chief exec. officer, 1982—; dir. Atlantic Cos., Burlington No., Inc., Northwestern States Portland Cement Co. Trustee Met. Mus. Art, Markle Found. Served with USAAF, 1943-45. Home: Peacock Point Locust Valley NY 11560 Office: 45 Wall St New York NY 10005

DAVISON, EDWARD JOSEPH, educator; b. Toronto, Ont., Can., Sept. 12, 1938; s. Maurice and Agnes (Quinlan) D. Assoc., Royal Conservatory of Music, Toronto, 1957; B.A., U. Toronto, 1960, M.A., 1961; Ph.D., Cambridge U., 1964, Sc.D., 1977. Asst. prof. dept. elec. engring. U. Toronto, 1964-66, asso. prof., 1968-74, prof., 1974—; asst. prof. dept. elec. engring. and computer scis. U. Calif., Berkeley, 1966-67; dir. Elec. Engring. Consociates Ltd., Toronto, 1977—. Asso.

editor: Jour. Automatica, 1974—, Jour. Large Scale Systems: Theory and Applications, 1979—; Contbr. numerous articles infield to profl. jours. Athlone fellow, 1961-63; E.W.R. Steacie Meml. fellow, 1974-77; Killam Research fellow, 1979-80, 81-83. Fellow Royal Soc. Can., IEEE (v.p. Control Systems Soc. 1979-80, mem. adminstrv. com. 1977-83, dir. Soc. Mag. 1980—, assoc. editor jour. Trans. on Automatic Control 1974-76, editorial adv. bd. IEEE Procs. 1980-81); mem. IEEE Control Systems Soc. (pres.-elect 1982-83, pres. 1983—), Profl. Engrs. Ont. (cons. engr. 1979—), Internat. Fedn. Automatic Control (vice chmn. theory com. 1978—). Office: Department of Electrical Engineering University of Toronto Toronto ON M5S 1A1 Canada

DAVISON, ENDICOTT PEABODY, lawyer; b. N.Y.C., June 15, 1923; s. F. Trubee and Dorothy (Peabody) D.; m. Jane Ingalls, July 3, 1948; children—F. Trubee II (dec.), Endicott Peabody, Jane, David I., Malcolm. Grad., Groton Sch., 1941; B.A., Yale, 1948; LL.B., U. Va., 1951. Bar: N.Y. bar 1951, Conn. bar 1978. Partner Winthrop, Stimson, Putnam & Roberts, N.Y.C. and, Conn.; corp. officer for instnl. devel. and capital support Yale, 1971-76. Bd. dirs. Union Theol. Sem., Stamford Mus. and Nature Center, Seaport at Mystic, Que. Labrador Found.; trustee Groton (Mass.) Sch. Served with USAAF, World War II. Mem. Am. Bar Assn., Assn. Bar City N.Y., Nat. Recreation and Park Assn. (past chmn. bd.), Legal Aid Soc. N.Y. (dir., exec. com.). Home: Lord Hill Route 156 Lyme CT 06371 Office: 460 Summer St Stamford CT 06901

DAVISON, FREDERICK CORBET, univ. pres.; b. Atlanta, Sept. 3, 1929; s. Frederick Collins and Gladys (Carsley) D.; m. Dianne Castle, Sept. 3, 1952; children—Frederick Corbet, William Castle, Anne Harper. D.V.M., U. Ga., 1952; Ph.D., Iowa State U., 1963; H.H.D. (hon.), Presbyn. Coll., 1977, LL.D., Mercer U., 1979. Individual practice veterinary medicine, Marietta, Ga., 1952-58; research asst. Iowa State U., 1958-60, asst. prof., 1960-63; asso. Inst. Atomic Research, 1960-63; asst. dir. dept. sci. activities AVMA, 1963-64; dean U. Ga. Sch. Vet. Medicine, Athens, 1964-66, vice chancellor univ. system, 1966-67, pres. univ., 1967—; dir. Clarke Fed. Savs. & Loan Assn.; mem. Inst. Animal Resources, Nat. Acad. Sci.-NRC, 1965—. Contbr. articles to profl. jours. Mem. N.E. Ga. commn. Boy Scouts Am., past pres. Area 5; hon. mem. bd. counselors Oxford Coll. Recipient Disting. Achievement award Iowa State U., 1979. Mem. Am., Ga. vet. med. assns., Sigma Xi, Phi Kappa Phi, Sigma Alpha Epsilon, Omega Tau Sigma, Alpha Zeta, Phi Zeta, Gamma Sigma Delta. Club: Rotary. Home: 570 Prince Ave Athens GA 30601

DAVISON, JOHN HERBERT, educator; b. Istanbul, Turkey, May 31, 1930; came to U.S., naturalized, 1930; s. Walter Seaman and Eloise (Hollett) D.; m. Elizabeth Geary, Oct. 5, 1968; children—Alan, Sarah. B.A., Haverford Coll., 1951; M.A. (Woodrow Wilson fellow), Harvard, 1952; Ph.D., U. Rochester, 1959. Teaching asst. Eastman Sch. Music, Rochester, N.Y., 1958-59; faculty Haverford (Pa.) Coll., 1959—, now Ruth Marshall Magill prof. music, chmn. music dept., 1969-78; vis. lectr. Bryn Mawr (Pa.) Coll., 1968-70, 73. Composer: Symphonies No. 1, 1958, No. 2, 1959, No. 3 for Winds, 1964, No. 4 for Strings, 1966, Te Deum for Chorus and Orchestra, 1960, Sextet for English Horn, Piano and Strings, 1968, Communion Service, 1970, Cycle of Piano Music, 1972, Mass for Chorus and Orchestra, 1977, Symphony No. 5, 1980. Paine Traveling fellow Harvard, 1953-55; Ford Found.-Music Educators Nat. Conf. fellow for composer in residence Kansas City (Mo.) Pub. Schs., 1964-65. Mem. Nat. Assn. Am. Composers and Condrs. (Phila. chpt.), Phi Beta Kappa. Home: 3 College Circle Haverford PA 19041

DAVISON, JOSEPH WADE, petroleum company executive; b. Kansas City, Kans., Nov. 14, 1921; s. Elmer Joseph and Lucile (Ranney) D.; m. Leatha Belle Sanford, Feb. 3, 1951; children—Teresa Ann, Diane Leslie. B.S., U. Kans., 1943. Registered profl. engr., Okla. With Phillips Petroleum Co., Bartlesville, Okla., 1943—, chmn. operating com., 1973-75, mgr. research and devel., 1975-76, v.p. research and devel., 1976-80, sr. v.p. corp. planning and devel., 1980—; dir. McNally Pitts. Inc., Acurex Corp.; mem. bus. adv. com. Nat. Assn. Conservation Dists., 1975—. Chmn. Sch. Engring. adv. bd., exec. com. U. Kans., 1983—; exec. com. v.p. steering com. Frontiers of Sci. Fund Okla., 1974—, Cherokee council Boy Scouts Am., 1974—; mem. adv. bd. Coll. Engring. and Phys. Scis., U. Tulsa; bd. dirs. Jr. Achievement, Bartlesville, 1972-77. Served with USNR, 1944-46. Fellow Am. Inst. Chem. Engrs. (Founders award 1981); mem. World Petroleum Congress (U.S. nat. com. 1974-80, vice chmn. 1979—), Dirs. Indsl. Research, Coordinating Research Council (dir., pres. 1981-82), Bartlesville C. of C. (dir. 1975—, pres. 1982-83), Soc. Automotive Engring., Indsl. Research Inst., U. Kans. Alumni Assn. (past pres. county chpt.). Presbyterian (past pres. trustees). Patentee in field. Office: 17 Phillips Bldg Bartlesville OK 74004

DAVISON, KENNETH EDWIN, American studies educator; b. East Cleveland, Ohio, May 4, 1924; s. Gordon Edwin and Mildred K. (Smith) D.; m. Virginia Nell Rentz, June 14, 1959; children: Robert Edwin, Richard Allen. A.B., Heidelberg Coll., 1946; A.M., Western Res. U., 1951, Ph.D., 1953. Asst. prof. history, polit. sci. Heidelberg Coll., Tiffin, Ohio, 1952-56, assoc. prof. polit. sci., 1956-59, prof., 1959-64, prof. history, dir. Gen. Edn. Program, 1964-67, prof., chmn. Am. studies dept., 1967-83, prof., chmn. history and Am. studies dept., 1983—; vis. prof. Am. studies Bowling Green State U., 1972, 73, 74, 75; mem. bd. advisers Seneca County Mus., 1976—; cons. Tiffin Hist. Trust, 1976—. Author: Cleveland and the Civil War, 1962, The Presidency of Rutherford B. Hayes, 1972, The American Presidency: A Guide to Bibliographical Sources, 1983, (with others) Ohio Heritage, 1983; guest editor: Ohio History, 1968; editor: Hayes Hist. Jour., 1976-82; book rev. editor: Presdl. Studies Quar., 1978—; contbr. (to Collier's Ency.), 1964, 68, (to Am. Educator's Ency.), 1965, articles and revs. to profl. jours. Mem. lay bd. Mercy Hosp., 1983—; chmn. Heidelberg Community Lecture and Concert Series, 1956-63; mem. Ohio com. for pub. programs in humanities, 1973-80, mem. exec. com., 1977-80; chmn. Tiffin-Seneca Bicentennial Commn., 1974-77. Recipient Ohioana Library Bood award, 1973; grantee Am. Philos. Soc., 1963-64, Nat. Endowment Humanities summer seminar, 1978, 81, Can. Embassy Faculty Enrichment, 1979, 80, 81, Gerald R. Ford Found., 1983. Mem. Orgn. Am. Historians, Western History Assn., Ohio-Ind. Am. Studies Assn. (pres. 1965, 66), Am. Assn. State and Local History, Nat. Trust Historic Preservation, Soc. Ohio Archivists (exec. council 1970-73, v.p. 1972-73), So. Hist. Assn., Ohio Acad. History (editor newsletter 1971-74); Popular Culture Assn. adv. bd. (1972-75); Am. Studies Assn. nat. exec. council (1968-78); mem. Am. Studies Assn. (nat. treas. 1973-78), Ohio Hist. Soc. (research adviser 1968-75), Can. Am. Studies Assn., Assn. Can. Studies in U.S., Ctr. for Study of Presidency (bd. educators 1974—), Presidency Research Group, World Future Soc., Pi Kappa Delta, Phi Alpha Theta. Presbyterian. Home: 125 Hampden Park Tiffin OH 44883

DAVISON, PETER HUBERT, editor, poet; b. N.Y.C., June 27, 1928; s. Edward and Natalie (Weiner) D.; m. Jane Auchincloss Truslow, Mar. 7, 1959 (dec. July 1981); children: Edward Angus, Lesley Truslow. A.B. magna cum laude, Harvard, 1949, St. John's Coll., Cambridge (Eng.) U., 1949-50. Page U.S. Senate, 1944; asst. editor Harcourt, Brace & Co., 1950-51, 53-55; asst. to dir. Harvard U. Press, 1955-56; asso. editor Atlantic Monthly Press, 1956-59, exec. editor, 1959-64, dir., 1964-79, sr. editor, 1979—; poetry editor Atlantic Monthly, 1972—; mem. adv. bd. Nat. Transl. Center, 1965-68; policy panelist in lit. Nat. Endowment for Arts, 1980-83. Author: poems The Breaking of the Day, 1964, The City and the Island, 1966, Pretending to Be Asleep, 1970, Dark Houses, 1971, Walking the Boundaries, 1974, A Voice in the Mountain, 1977, Barn Fever and Other Poems, 1981; autobiography Half Remembered, 1973; editor: Hello, Darkness: The Collected Poems of L.E. Sissman, 1978, The World of Farley Mowat, 1980; contbr. poems, articles to numerous mags., anthologies. Trustee Fountain Valley Sch., 1967-75; mem. corp. Yaddo, 1978—. Served with AUS, 1951-53. Winner competition Yale Series Younger Poets, 1963; recipient poetry award Nat. Inst. Arts and Letters, 1972. Mem. Phi Beta Kappa. Clubs: Examiner, St Botolph (Boston); Harvard, Century (N.Y.C.). Office: 8 Arlington St Boston MA 02116

DAVISON, RODERIC HOLLETT, historian, educator; b. Buffalo, Apr. 27, 1916; s. Walter Seaman and Eloise (Hollett) D.; m. Louise Atherton Dickey, June 18, 1949; children—R. John, Richard H. A.B., Princeton, 1937; A.M., Harvard, 1938, Ph.D. (fellow Social Sci. Research Council, Kent fellow Nat. Council Religion in Higher Edn.), 1942. Instr. history Princeton, 1940-42, 46-47; faculty history George Washington U., 1947—, prof., 1954—, chmn. dept., 1960-64, 69-70; Lectr. diplomatic history Johns Hopkins Sch. Advanced Internat. Studies, 1951-52, 55-58; vis. lectr. Harvard, 1960. Author: The Near and Middle East: An Introduction to History and Bibliography, 1959, Reform in the Ottoman Empire, 1856-1876, 1963, Turkey, 1968; Contbg. author: The Diplomats 1919-1939, 1953, Guide to Hist. Lit, 1961; Adv. bd. editors: Middle East Jour, 1954—; Contbr. articles to profl. jours. Served with Am. Friends Service Com., 1942-44, Civilian Pub. Service Camp, 1944-46. Faculty fellow Fund for Advancement Edn., 1953-54; Guggenheim fellow, 1970-71. Mem. Am. Hist. Assn. (treas. 1974), Middle East Inst. (v.p. 1976-82), AAUP, Soc. for Values, Middle East Studies Assn. (pres. 1974-75), Turkish Studies Assn. (pres. 1980-81), Phi Beta Kappa. Home: 3506 Lowell St NW Washington DC 20016

DAVISON, STANLEY MARTIN, banker; b. Enderby, C., Can., Sept. 12, 1928; s. Ronald and Janet Grace (Livingstone) D.; m. Bette Irene Rusconi, June 12, 1957; children: Loreen Joyce, Diane Janine, Ronald James. Grad., Banff Sch. Advanced Mgmt., 1967, Sch. Advanced Mgmt., Harvard U., 1980. With Bank of Montreal, 1947—, sr. v.p. Man. and Sask. div., 1968-71, exec. v.p. domestic banking, 1971-73, exec. v.p., gen. mgr. domestic banking, 1973-74, exec. v.p., gen. mgr. credits and investments, 1974-76, exec. v.p., chief gen. mgr., 1976-80, vice chmn., dir., 1980—. Clubs: Toronto; Petroleum (Calgary, Alta., Can.). Home: 3125 Linden Dr SW Calgary AB Canada Office: 350 7th Ave Suite 2500 Calgary AB Canada

DAVISON, WALTER PHILLIPS, sociology educator; b. Bath, N.Y., July 15, 1918; s. Walter S. and Eloise (Hollett) D. A.B., Princeton U., 1939; M.A., Columbia U., 1941, Ph.D., 1954. Instr. Princeton U., 1948-49; editor Pub. Opinion Quar., 1948-51, 68-71; sr. research scientist Rand Corp., Washington, 1948-56, 57-61; vis. prof. MIT, Cambridge, 1956-57; sr. research fellow Council Fgn. Relations, N.Y.C., 1961-65; prof. journalism and sociology Columbia U., N.Y.C., 1965—. Author: The Berlin Blockade, 1958, International Political Communication, 1965, (with James Boylan and Frederick T.C. Yu) Resolving Nationality Conflicts, 1980, Mass Media:Systems and Effects, 1982. Trustee Bur. Social Sci. Research, Washington, 1956—, Inst. Internat. Social Research, Washington, 1969—. Served to 2nd lt. U.S. Army, 1943-45; ETO. Mem. Am. Sociol. Assn., Council Fgn. Relations, Internat. Inst. Communications, Am. Assn. Pub. Opinion Research (pres. 1971-72). Presbyterian. Home: RD 1 Princeton NJ 08540 Office: Grad Sch Journalism Columbia U. New York NY 10027

DAVISSON, LEE DAVID, electrical engineer educator; b. Evanston, Ill., June 16, 1936; s. Douglas David and Josephine May (Abbott) D.; m. Carol Jean Ishmael, Aug. 4, 1957 (div. 1975); children: Lee David, Lisa Jane, Linda Carol; m. Jan Bradbury Pfirrmann, July 17, 1975; stepchildren: Anne, Amy, Edward. B.S. in Engring, Princeton U., 1958; M.S., UCLA, 1961, Ph.D. (Ford Found. fellow 1963), 1964. Research engr. Aeronutronic Co., 1960-62; mem. tech. staff Hughes Aircraft Co., 1962-64; asso. prof. Princeton U., 1964-70; prof. elec. engring. U. So. Calif., 1969-76, U. Md., College Park, 1976—, chmn. dept., 1976—; cons. to govt. and industry. Co-author: Data Compression, 1976, Information and Ergodic Theory, 1978; contbr. articles to profl. jours. Served to 1st lt. AUS, 1958-60. Recipient award acad. promise Princeton Engring. Assn., 1965, award for ednl. innovation Md. Assn. Higher Edn. Fellow IEEE (gov. info. theory group 1972-82, pres. 1980, co-recipient Prize Paper award info. theory group 1976); mem. Sigma Xi, Eta Kappa Nu, Tau Beta Pi. Home: 1712 S Harbor Ln Annapolis MD 21401 Office: Elec Engring Dept U Md College Park MD 20742

DAW, HAROLD JOHN, lawyer; b. N.Y.C., July 6, 1926; s. Joseph and Dorothy (Dannenberg) D.; m. Meryl Kann, Sept. 25, 1960. A.B., Union Coll., 1950; LL.B., Columbia U., 1954. Bar: N.Y. 1955. Assoc. Shearman & Sterling, N.Y.C., 1954-62, ptnr., 1962—; dir. Nash Engring. Co., Norwalk, Conn., 1975—. Served with USN, 1944-46; ETO. Mem. ABA, N.Y. State Bar Assn., Bar Assn. City N.Y., Phi Beta Kappa. Clubs: University, Broad St. (gov. 1971—), Broad St. (pres. 1981, 82). Home: 10 Kempster Rd Scarsdale NY 10583 Office: 53 Wall St New York NY 10005

DAWBER, PAM, actress; b. Detroit, Oct. 18; d. Gene and Thelma D. Attended, Oakland Community Coll. Worked as model and; appeared in commls.; profl. acting debut in: Sweet Adeleine, East Haddam, Conn.; appeared on ABC-TV; appeared on: spl. Sister Terri; appears as Mindy on: TV series Mork and Mindy, 1978—; appeared in: TV movie The Girl the Gold Watch and Everything, Remembrance of Love, NBC, 1982, Last of the Great Survivors, CBS, 1983, Through Naked Eyes, ABC, 1983; film The Wedding; star: Joe Papp's Los Angeles prodn. of Pirates of Penzance, also Broadway prodn., 1982. Bd. dirs. Solar Lobby. Office: care ABC Press Dept 1330 Ave of Americas New York NY 10019

DAWES, ANDREW ALBERT, violinist, music educator; b. High River, Alta., Can., Feb. 7, 1940; s. Arthur Douglas and Lena Mae (Hill) D.; m. Karen Louise Whately, Oct. 14, 1967; children: Debra Louise, Adriana Tiamae. Student schs., Geneva, Switzerland, Clayton Hare, Murray Adaskin, Lorand Fenyves, Oscar Shumsky. Formerly instr. chamber music U. Toronto, Ont., now assoc. prof. music. Recitals in, Can., U.S., Europe; soloist with major orchs. of, Can.; a founder, 1st violinist, Orford String Quartet, 1965—; concertized throughout, Can., U.S., Western and Eastern Europe, USSR. Recipient Prix de Virtuosité Conservatoire de Geneve, Switzerland, 1964, Munich Internat. Competition, 1962, Montreal Internat. Competition, 1966, 69; 1st prize Jeunesses Musicales of Can. Nat. String Competition, 1967, Internat. String Quartet Competition, Stockholm, Sweden, 1974; Molson award Can. Council, 1976. Mem. Musicians Union. Mem. United Ch. of Can. Home: 17 Glen Stewart Crescent Toronto ON M4E 1P4 Canada Office: Faculty of Music Edward Johnson Bldg U Toronto Toronto ON Canada

DAWES, CAROL J., clinical psychologist; b. Villa Park, Ill., June 15, 1931; d. John I. and Anna J. (Eggum) Postula; children: Jennifer H., Molly M. B.A., Kalamazoo Coll., 1954; Ph.D., U. Mich., 1965. Psychology intern U. Mich. Psychology Clinic, 1959-65; staff psychologist U. Mich. Children's Psychiat. Hosp., 1965-67; pvt. practice psychology, Eugene, Oreg., 1969—; specialist in psychology Oreg. State System Higher Edn. Mem. Am. Psychol. Assn. Democrat. Address: 2328 Washington St Eugene OR 97405 also Address: 508 W Jefferson PO Box 1813 Corvallis OR 97339

DAWES, GEOFFREY SHARMAN, med. researcher; b. Derbyshire, Eng., Jan. 21, 1918; s. William and Olive (White) D.; m. Margaret Joan Monk, Apr. 15, 1941; children—Caroline Harriet, Alison Jennifer, Nicholas William, Martin Geoffrey. B.A., Oxford (Eng.) U., 1939, M.Sc., 1940, B.M., B.Ch., 1943, D.M., M.A., 1947; D.Med. (hon.), Gothenburg U., 1978. Fellow Worcester Coll., Oxford U., 1947; dir. Nuffield Inst. Med. Research, 1948-; mem. Med. Research Council, 1978—; vis. prof. U. Calif. at San Francisco, 1966. Author: Foetal and Neonatal Physiology, 1967. Gov. Sir John Port's Charity, Repton Sch., 1959—, chmn., 1971—. Recipient Max Weinstein award United Cerebral Palsy Assn., 1963; Gairdner Found. annual award, 1966; James Spence medal Brit. Pediatric Assn., 1969; Maternité award European Assn. Perinatal Medicine, 1976; decorated comdr. Order Brit. Empire; Rockefeller fellow Harvard, 1946. Fellow Royal Soc. (v.p. 1975-77, Blair Bell medal 1981), Royal Coll. Physicians, Royal Coll. Obstetricians and Gynecologists, Am. Coll. Obstetricians and Gynecologists (hon.), Am. Acad. Pediatrics (hon., Virginia Algor award 1980); mem. Neonatal Soc. (pres. 1965-69). Home: 8 Belbroughton Rd Oxford England Office: Nuffield Inst Med Research Headley Way Headington Oxford England

DAWES, RICHARD IRVING, metals company executive; b. Arlington, Mass., Nov. 24, 1919; s. Irving Desmond and Corinne Lee (Thies) D.; m. Elisabeth Hewitt Coffin, Apr. 2, 1949; children: Alan Stuart, Carol Winfield, Beverly Gail. A.B., Harvard U., 1940, M.B.A., 1942. Adminstrv. asst. inventory control dept. Reynolds Metals Co., Richmond, Va., 1946-48, scheduling mgr. printing div., 1948-53, staff asst. to gen. prodn. control mgr., 1953-57, asst. corporate sec., 1957-70, corporate sec., 1970—, sec., asst. sec. various subsidiaries and affiliates. Chmn. March of Dimes drive, 1953, chmn. Richmond-Henrico chpt., 1954; Bd. dirs. West End Community Center, Richmond, 1959—, treas., 1959-72. Served to lt. USNR, 1942-46. Mem. Am. Soc. Corporate Secs., Richmond C. of C., Va. Mfrs. Assn. (dir. 1979-80), Assn. Harvard Alumni (Middle Atlantic area v.p. 1961-64), Collegiate Schs. Patrons Assn. (v.p. 1971-72, pres. 1972-73, trustee 1974-76). Presbyterian (asst treas. 1963—, deacon, 1971-74, elder 1977-80). Clubs: Harvard of Va. (past pres.), Country of Va., Richmond Gentry (Richmond) (dir., sec.). Home: 8900 Watlington Rd Richmond VA 23229 Office: 6601 Broad St Rd PO Box 27003 Richmond VA 23261

DAWID, IGOR BERT, biologist; b. Czernowitz, Romania, Feb. 26, 1935; came to U.S., 1960, naturalized, 1977; s. Josef and Pepi (Druckmann) D.; m. Keiko Naito Ozato, Apr. 5, 1976. Ph.D., U. Vienna, 1960. Fellow dept. biology MIT, 1960-62; fellow dept. embryology Carnegie Instn. of Washington, Balt., 1962-66, mem. staff, 1966-78; chief devel. biochemistry sect. Lab. Biochemistry, Nat. Cancer Inst., Bethesda, Md., 1978-82; chief lab. molecular genetics Nat. Inst. Child Health and Human Devel. (NIH), Bethesda, 1982—; vis. scientist Max Planck Inst. for Biology, 1964-67; asst. prof. to prof. dept. biology Johns Hopkins U., 1967-78. Editor: Devel. Biology, 1971-75, Cell, 1977—; editor-in-chief: Devel. Biology, 1975-80; adv. editor, 1980—. Mem. Am. Soc. Biol. Chemists, Am. Soc. Cell Biology, Soc. Devel. Biology, Internat. Soc. Devel. Biologists, AAAS, Nat. Acad. Sci. Office: 9000 Rockville Pike Bethesda MD 20205

DAWIDOWICZ, LUCY S., historian, author; b. N.Y.C., June 16, 1915; d. Max and Dora (Ofnaem) Schildkret; m. Szymon M. Dawidowicz, Jan. 3, 1948. B.A., Hunter Coll., N.Y.C., 1936; postgrad. research fellow, Yivo Inst. Jewish Research, Vilna, Poland, 1938-39; M.A., Columbia U., 1961; L.H.D. (hon.), Kenyon Coll., 1978, Hebrew Union Coll.-Jewish Inst. Religion, 1978, Monmouth Coll., Yeshiva U., D.H.L., Spertus Coll. Asst. to research dir. Yivo Inst. Jewish Research, N.Y.C., 1940-46; edn. officer displaced persons camps Am. Jewish Joint Distbn. Com., Ger., 1946-47; research analyst, then research dir. Am. Jewish Com., N.Y.C., 1948-69; mem. faculty Yeshiva U., N.Y.C., 1969-78, prof. social history, 1974-78, Paul and Leah Lewis prof. holocaust studies, 1970-75, Eli and Diana Zborowski prof. interdisciplinary holocaust studies, 1976-78; vis. prof. Jewish civilization Stanford U., 1981; vis. prof. SUNY-Albany, 1982; bd. dirs. Leo Baeck Inst., N.Y.C., Library Corp., Jewish Theol. Sem., Conf. Jewish Social Studies; mem. President's Commn. on the Holocaust, 1978-79; adv. council Ctr. Modern Jewish Studies, Brandeis U. Author: (with L.J. Goldstein) Politics in a Pluralist Democracy, 1963, The Golden Tradition: Jewish Life and Thought in Eastern Europe, 1967, The War Against the Jews, 1933-1945, 1975, transl. into French, German, Japanese, Hebrew (Anisfeld-Wolf prize 1976), A Holocaust Reader, 1976, The Jewish Presence: Essays on Identity and History, 1977, The Holocaust and the Historians, 1981, On Equal Terms: Jews in America 1881-1981, 1982; editor: (with Joshua A. Fishman, others) For Max Weinreich: Studies in Jewish Languages, Literature and Society, 1964; Contbr. articles to jours. and newspapers. Recipient award Nat. Found. Jewish Culture, 1965, Meml. Found. Jewish Culture, 1968, 73, 74, 79, Atran Found., 1971, John Slawson Fund Research, Tng. and Edn., 1972, 79, Lucius N. Littauer Found., 1972, 80, Gustav Wurzweiler Found., 1974, 78; Outstanding Achievement award Hunter Coll., 1978; Guggenheim fellow, 1976. Mem. Am. Hist. Assn., Am. Jewish Hist. Soc., Conf. Jewish Social Studies, Assn. Jewish Studies. Home: 200 W 86th St Apt 20L New York NY 10024

DAWKINS, BEN C., JR., judge; b. Monroe, La., Aug. 6, 1911; s. Ben C. and Alice (McLeod) D.; m. Harriet White, Jan. 1, 1936; children—Cynthia, Ben C. III, Franklin White. A.B., Tulane U., 1932; J.D., La. State U., 1934. Bar: La. bar 1934. Practiced in, Monroe, 1934-35; sr. mem. firm Blanchard, Goldstein, Walker & O'Quin, Shreveport, La., 1935-53; chief U.S. dist. judge Western Dist. La., 1953-73, sr. judge, 1973—. Pres. Shreveport Recreation Council, 1941; dir. Children's Service Bur., 1947-51, Child Guidance Clinic, 1952; mem. sch. bd. Caddo Parish Sch., 1949-53, pres., 1950-52. Served as lt. comdr., air navigator USNR, 1942-45. Recipient Wisdom award of honor, 1969; Research fellow Southwestern Legal Found. Mem. ABA, La. Bar Assn. (bd. govs. 1950-52), Shreveport (v.p. 1941-42, sec.-treas. 1947-48, pres. 1949-50), Shreveport C. of C. (past dir.), Jr. C. of C. (past dir.), Am. Legion, V.F.W. (post comdr. 1946-47, judge adv. La. dept. 1947-48), Smithsonian Instn. Assos., Delta Kappa Epsilon, Phi Delta Phi, Omicron Delta Kappa. Episcopalian (past vestryman). Office: Fed Bldg Shreveport LA 71161 *

DAWN, CLARENCE ERNEST, history educator; b. Chattanooga, Dec. 6, 1918; s. Fred Hartman and Hettie Lou (Gibson) D.; m. Pansie Mozelle Dooley, July 8, 1944; children: Julia Anne, Carolyn Louise. B.A., U. Chattanooga, 1941; M.A., Princeton U., 1947, Ph.D., 1948. Instr. history U. Ill., Urbana, 1949-52, asst. prof., 1952-55, asso. prof., 1955-60, prof., 1960—; fellow Inst. Advanced Studies, Hebrew U., Jerusalem, 1981-82. Author: From Ottomanism to Arabism, 1973; Contbr. articles to profl. jours. Served with AUS, 1942-46; Served with U.S. Army, 1951-52. Social Sci. Research Council World Area fellow, 1948-49; fellow joint com. on Near and Middle East Social Sci. Research Council and Am. Council Learned Socs., 1966-67; Fulbright-Hays fellow, 1966-67. Mem. Am. Hist. Assn., Middle East Studies Assn., Middle East Inst. Home: 1504 S Grove St Urbana IL 61801

DAWSON, CLAYTON LEROY, Slavic language and literature educator, author; b. Seattle, Mar. 25, 1921; s. Charles Brady II and Lillie (Stenmoe) D.; m. Elizabeth Grace Abbott, Mar. 31, 1951; children: Robert Freeland, Margaret Ferne. B.A., U. Wash., 1949; M.A., Harvard U., 1951, Ph.D., 1954. Asst. prof., asst. dir. East European lang. program Syracuse U., 1953-57; lang. adviser Air Force Inst. Tech., 1957-59; prof., chmn. dept. Slavic langs. and lits. Syracuse U., 1959-66; prof. U. Ill., Urbana, 1966—, head dept. Slavic langs. and lits., 1966-74; cons. in field, 1961—; Mem. subcom. grants Russian and Soviet studies Am. Council Learned Socs., 1966-71; mem. inaugural selection com. Center for 20th Century Studies, U. Wis., Milw., 1969-71. Author: Intensive Russian, 5 vols, 1954-57, (with A. Humesky, C. Bidwell) Modern Russian I, 1964, (with A. Humesky) Modern Russian II, 1965, Modern Russian I Workbook, 1981. Served with AUS, 1942-45. Mem. Am. Assn. Tchrs. Slavic and East European Langs. (sec.-treas. Ill. 1968-69, pres. 1969-71), Dobro Slovo (pres. 1974-77), Phi Beta Kappa (pres. Gamma chpt. 1975-76), Phi Kappa Phi. Home: 1106 Silver St Urbana IL 61801 *One should not be ashamed of failed efforts; sometimes we learn more from failure than from success.*

DAWSON, DAVID CARLOUGH, management company executive; b. N.Y.C., Feb. 9, 1933; s. Frank J. and Margaret (Carlough) D.; m. Virginia F. Smith, Dec. 28, 1957; children: Kathryn, Gail, Steven, Mark. B.Metall. Engring., Cornell U., 1955; M.B.A., Duquesne U., Pitts., 1964. With duPont Co., 1955-56; with INCO Co., 1958-78, corp. v.p., 1976-78; pres., chief exec. officer battery subsidiary Electro Energy Corp., Phila., 1978—; dir. Pa. Mut. Ins. Co.; trustee Pa. Savs. Fund Soc. Served to lt. (j.g.) USNR, 1955-58. Mem. Am. Soc. Metals, Am. Mgmt. Assn., Conf. Bd., Am. Foundrymen, Phila. C. of C. (dir., exec. com.), Haverford (Pa.) Civic Assn. (dir.). Clubs: Broad Street, Union League, Phila. Country. Office: 1 Aldwyn Ctr Villanova PA 19085

DAWSON, GEORGE GLENN, educator; b. Shelter Island, N.Y., Aug. 16, 1925; s. Harry and Frances (Menafee) D.; m. Shirley Catherine Meader, Jan. 18, 1947. B.S. summa cum laude, NYU, 1956, M.A., 1957, Ph.D. (Danforth fellow), 1959. Instr. edn. NYU, 1957-59, asst. prof. social studies edn., 1959-62, asso. prof., 1962-65, prof., head social studies div., 1965-70, chmn. dept. social studies edn., 1965-70; dir. Peace Corps Somalia project, 1962-64, Center Econ. Edn., 1965-70; dir. research and publs. Joint Council Econ. Edn., 1970-75; dean Empire State Coll., 1975-78, prof. econs., 1978—, chmn. grad. program bus., 1982—; cons. econ. edn. to bus., labor unions, bds. edn. Mng. editor: Jour. Econ. Edn., 1970—, Econ. Topics Series, 1970-75; author: Guide to Economics, 1963; Author: Collegiate Guide to Economics, 2 vols., 1965, Our Nations Wealth, 1968, Foundations of Our Economy, 1969; co-author: The American Economy: Analysis and Policy, 1969, Teaching Economics in American History, 1973, Introductory Economics, 1980; editor: Communism-Menace to Freedom, 1962, Freedom-America's Choice, 1962, Economic Education Experiences Enterprising Teachers, Economics and Our Community, 1973; contbr. articles to profl. jours. Served with USNR, 1942-46, 50-51. Recipient Founders Day award NYU, 1956, 1st pl. in Kazanjian awards program, 1967. Mem. Am. Econ. Assn., Am. Ednl. Research Assn., Phi Delta Kappa, Kappa Delta Pi. Home: 2292 Arby Ct Bellmore NY 11710

DAWSON, GRAHAM RUSSELL, construction executive; b. Vancouver, C., Can., Nov. 18, 1925; s. Frederick James and Marion Patterson (Russell) D.; m. Dorothy Eva Drape Williams, May 19, 1949; children: Rebecca, Murray, Bruce, Marion, Ian. Student, Royal Can. Naval Coll., 1943-45; B.A.Sc. in Civil Engring, U. B.C., 1949. Project engr. Dawson Constrn., Ltd., 1949-52, v.p., 1952-56, pres., 1956-63, pres., chmn. bd., 1963—; chmn. bd. Daon Devel. Corp., Vancouver, 1964—. Mem. Vancouver Police Commn., 1970-75, chmn., 1977. Served to lt. Royal Can. Navy, 1943-46. Mem. Assn. Profl. Engrs. B.C., Roadbuilders and Heavy Constrn. Assn. B.C. (past pres.). Clubs: Shaughnessy Golf and Country, Vancouver (pres.). Office: Dawson Constrn Co Ltd 735 Clark Dr Vancouver V5L 3J4 Canada

DAWSON, HORACE GREELEY, JR., former diplomat, government official; b. Augusta, Ga., Jan. 30, 1926; s. Horace Greeley D.; m. Lula M. Cole, Aug. 30, 1953; children: Horace Greeley, III, Horace Gregory. A.B., Lincoln (Pa.) Coll., 1949; A.M., Columbia U., 1950; Ph.D., State U. Iowa, 1960. Instr. English So. U., Baton Rouge, 1950-53; asso. prof., dir. public relations N.C. Central U., Durham, 1953-62; joined U.S. Fgn. Service, 1962; service in, Uganda, Nigeria, Liberia and, Manila, ambassador to, Botswana, after 1979, now dep. examiner Fgn. Service, Dept. State; vis. prof. U. Nigeria, 1966-67, U. Md., 1971-79. Author: Handbook for High School Newspaper Advisors, 1961, also articles.; Co-editor: New Dimensions in Higher Education, 1961; mng. editor: Coll. Lang. Assn. Jour, 1957-60. Served with AUS, 1944-46. Recipient Superior Honor award USIA, 1965. Mem. Am. Fgn. Service Assn., Council Fgn. Relations, NAACP, Am. Legion, Alpha Phi Alpha. Mem. A.M.E. Ch. Address: Bd Examiners Fgn Service Dept State PO Box 9317 Arlington VA 22209

DAWSON, HOWARD ATHALONE, JR., U.S. judge; b. Okolona, Ark., Oct. 23, 1922; s. Howard Athalone and Mamie (Watson) D.; m. Marianne Atherholt, Feb. 2, 1946; children—Amy, Suzanne. B.S. in Commerce, U. N.C., 1946; J.D., George Washington U., 1949. Bar: D.C. bar 1949, Ga. bar 1958. Pvt. practice, Washington, 1949-50; atty. civil div. Office Chief Counsel, IRS, 1950-53, asst. regional counsel Atlanta region, 1953-56, regional counsel, 1957, asst. chief counsel adminstrn., Washington, 1958-62; judge U.S. Tax Ct., Washington, 1962—, chief judge, 1973-77. Served with AUS, 1943-45; ETO; capt. Res. Mem. Am., D.C., Fed. bar assns., Chi Psi, Delta Theta Phi. Club: National Lawyers (Washington). Home: 7408 Nevis Rd Bethesda MD 20817 Office: US Tax Ct 400 2d St NW Washington DC 20217

DAWSON, IRVING OWEN, polit. scientist; b. Lewistown, Mont., June 5, 1927; s. William and Ruby Aileen (Owens) D. B.A., N.Tex. State U., Denton, 1948; M.A., U. Tex., 1950, Ph.D., 1957. Instr. Lamar U., Beaumont, Tex., 1950, head govt. dept., 1960-70; mem. faculty U. Tex., Arlington, 1970—, prof. polit. sci., 1970—, chmn. dept., 1977—; cons. in field. Author: Governing Texas, 1966. Mem. Beaumont Civil Service Commn., 1968-70; chmn. Christian life com. Baptist Gen. Conv. Tex., 1966-71. Mem. Am. Polit. Sci. Assn., Am. Soc. Public Adminstrn., Internat. Personnel Mgmt. Assn., Southwestern Polit. Sci. Assn. (pres.). Democrat. Home: 1213 St Maria Ct Arlington TX 76013 Office: Dept Polit Sci Univ Tex Arlington TX 76019

DAWSON, JOHN FREDERICK, architect; b. Stambaugh, Mich., Sept. 4, 1930; s. Frederick John and Myrtle (Olson) D.; m. Ruth Jennette Opland, May 8, 1954; children—Craig Frederick, Cindy Paulette. B.Arch., U. Mich., 1953. Registered architect, Mich. Instr. U. Mich., 1956-60, asst. prof. architecture, 1960-63; dir. govtl. affairs A.I.A., Washington, 1963-65; v.p. Louis C. Kingscott & Assos. Inc., Washington and Kalamazoo, 1965-70; pres. Development Services, Inc., Kalamazoo, 1970-72; exec. v.p. Spanpark Corp., Kalamazoo, 1972-75; mgmt. cons. to architects, 1975-76; dir. adminstrn. Bus. and Instl. Furniture Mfrs. Assn., 1976-77; owner Solar Unltd., 1977—; pres. Solar Solutions, Inc., 1980—; Vice chmn. Kalamazoo Energy Policy Adv. Com., 1980—. Served with AUS, 1953-55. Home: 3604 Woodcliff Dr Kalamazoo MI 49008

DAWSON, JOHN HALLAM, banker; b. N.Y.C., Oct. 31, 1936; s. James Robertson and Margaret (Geny) D.; m. Mary Dee McVey, Apr. 19, 1975; 1 dau., Elizabeth McVey. B.A., Vanderbilt U., 1958; M.B.A., Harvard U., 1960. Various positions to sr. v.p. and dep. head internat. div. 1st Nat. Bank of Chgo., 1961-75; exec. v.p. internat. div. Crocker Nat. Bank, San Francisco, 1975-80, pres., 1981—. Served with AUS, 1960. Mem. Calif. Bankers Assn. (pres.), Bankers Assn. Fgn. Trade (past pres.), Phi Beta Kappa. Clubs: University, Bankers (San Francisco); Saddle and Cycle (Chgo.); (California). Office: 333 S Grand Ave Los Angeles CA 90071

DAWSON, JOHN MYRICK, plasma physics educator; b. Champaign, Ill., Sept. 30, 1930; s. Walker Myrick and Wilhelmina Emily (Stephan) D.; m. Nancy Louise Wildes, Dec. 28, 1957; children: Arthur Walker, Margaret Louise. B.S., U. Md., 1952, M.S., 1954, Ph.D., 1957. Research physicist Plasma Physics Lab. Princeton U., 1956-73, head theoretical group, 1965-73; prof. plasma physics UCLA, 1973—; dir. Center for Plasma Physics & Fusion Engring., 1976; cons. in field; John Danz lectr. U. Wash., 1974; guest Russian Acad. Scis., 1971; invited lectr. Inst. Plasma Physics, Nagoya, Japan, 1972. Contbr. articles in field to profl. jours. Recipient Exceptional Sci. Achievement award TRW Systems, 1977; James Clerk Maxwell prize in Plasma Physics, 1977; named Calif. Scientist of the Year, 1978. Fellow AAAS, Am. Phys. Soc. (chmn. plasma div. 1970-71); mem. Nat. Acad. Scis., N.Y. Acad. Scis., N.J. Acad. Scis., Sigma Pi Sigma, Phi Kappa Phi, Sigma Xi. Unitarian. Patentee in field. Home: 359 Arno Way Pacific Palisades CA 90272 Office: University of California 405 Hilgard Ave Los Angeles CA 90024

DAWSON, JOHN PHILIP, lawyer, educator; b. Detroit, July 24, 1902; s. John Philip and Cecile (Frumveller) D.; m. Emma Van Nostrand McDonald, Aug. 20, 1927; children: John Philip, David Michael, Peter McDonald. A.B., U. Mich., 1922, J.D., 1924, LL. D., 1968; D.Phil., Oxford U., Eng., 1930; LL.D., U. Edinburgh, U. Chgo., 1972, U. Frankfurt, 1977, Boston U., 1978. Bar: Mich. 1924. Asst. prof. law U. Mich., 1927-30, asso. prof., 1930-36, prof., 1936-57, Harvard Law Sch., 1956-73, Boston U. Law Sch., 1973-81; vis. prof. law U. Chgo., 1955, U. Colo., 1981; Storrs lectr. Yale U. Law Sch., 1978; chief counsel rent sect. OPA, 1942-43; chief Middle East div. Fgn. Econ. Adminstrn., 1943-45, spl. rep. Middle East area, 1945-46; dir. Fgn. Trade Adminstrn., Greek Govt., 1947-48; Democratic candidate for Congress, 2d Dist. Mich., 1950, 52; Sec.-treas. Assn. Am. Law Schs., 1947. Author: Unjust Enrichment, A Comparative Analysis, 1951, A History of Lay Judges, 1960, (with George E. Palmer) Cases on Restitution, 1958, 69, (with William B. Harvey) Cases on Contracts, 1958, 69, 77, The Oracles of the Law, 1968, Gifts and Promises, A Comparative Study, 1979; contbr. articles to law rev. Corr. fellow Brit. Acad.; mem. Am. Assn. Arts and Scis., Phi Delta Phi, Order of Coif (pres. 1956-58). Home: 17 Arlington St Cambridge MA 02140

DAWSON, LEONARD RAY, TV sportscaster, former profl. football player; b. Alliance, Ohio, June 20, 1935; 2 children. B.S., Purdue U., 1957. Profl. football player Pitts. Steelers, 1957-59, Cleve. Browns, 1960-61, Dallas Cowboys, 1962, Kansas City Chiefs, 1963-75; profl. football analyst NBC-TV, 1976—. Named Most Valuable Player, Super Bowl IV; participated in AFL All Star Fames, 1962, 64, 66, 67, 68, Pro Bowl, 1971. Address: NBC Sports Press Dept 30 Rockefeller Plaza New York NY 10020 *

DAWSON, MARY ANN WEFORTH (MIMI DAWSON), govt. ofcl.; b. St. Louis, Aug. 31, 1944; d. Francis Griffin and Jeanne (Gething) Weyforth; m. Rhett Brewer Dawson, Jan. 15, 1976. Grad., Washington U., St. Louis, 1966. Legis. asst., press sec. to Rep. Richard Ichord, Mo. Dist., 1969-72, 73; press sec., legis. asst. to Rep. James Symington, Mo. Dist.; press. sec. Sen. Bob Packwood, Oreg., 1973, adminstrv. asst., chief staff, legis. dir., 1975; commr. FCC, Washington, 1981—; Mem. steering com. Washington Women's Network. Mem. Am. Council Young Polit. Leaders, Women's Campaign Fund. Republican. Roman Catholic. Office: 1919 M St NW Washington DC *

DAWSON, MARY RUTH, curator; b. Highland Park, Mich., Feb. 27, 1931; d. John Elson and Olga Josephine (Down) D. B.S., Mich. State Coll., 1952; postgrad., U. Edinburgh, 1952-53; Ph.D., U. Kans., 1957. Instr. zoology Smith Coll., 1958-61; asst. program dir. NSF, Washington, 1961-62; mem. staff Carnegie Mus., Pitts., 1962—, curator, 1971—, chmn. earth sci. div., 1973—, acting dir., 1982-83; adj. assoc. prof. earth scis. U. Pitts., 1971—. Recipient Arnold Guyst award Nat. Geog. Soc., 1981, Woman in Sci. award Chatham Coll., 1983; Fulbright scholar, 1952-53; fellow AAUW, 1958-59; research grantee NSF, 1961-62, 65—. Fellow Geol. Soc. Am., Arctic Inst. N.Am., Explorers Club; mem. Soc. Vertebrate Paleontology (v.p. 1972-73, pres. 1973-74), Paleontol. Soc., Paläontologische Gesellschaft, Bernese Mountain Dog Club Am., Phi Beta Kappa. Research, publs. on Tertiary Lagomorpha, 1957—, early Tertiary rodents, 1960—, Arctic paleontology, 1975. Office: Carnegie Mus 4400 Forbes Ave Pittsburgh PA 15213

DAWSON, RAY FIELDS, research scientist, educator; b. Muncie, Ind., Feb. 13, 1911; s. Emmett Hamilton and Elsie (Fields) D.; m. Helen Dunham, Aug. 11, 1942. A.B. (Rector scholar), DePauw U., 1935; Ph.D. (Hooker fellow), Yale, 1938. NRC fellow Columbia U., 1938-39; instr. De Pauw U., 1939-40; asst. prof. U. Mo., 1940-42, Princeton U., 1942-45; asst. prof., assoc. prof., prof., Torrey prof. Columbia U., 1945-66; prof. dir. internat. programs Coll. Agr. and Environ. Sci., Rutgers U., New Brunswick, N.J., 1966-76, prof. emeritus, 1976—; dir. Lancaster Labs., Inc., 1961—; cons. Upjohn Co., 1958-79, Philip Morris, U.S.A., 1962—. Contbr. articles to sci. jours. Recipient Stephen Hales award Am. Soc. Plant Physiologists, 1945; 2d Ann. Research award Cigar Mfrs. Am. and Cigar Inst. Am., 1962; Disting. Alumnus award De Pauw U., 1953; Sigma Xi nat. lectr., 1959-60. Mem. Am. Chem. Soc. (emeritus), Am. Soc. Plant Physiologists (emeritus), Phi Beta Kappa, Sigma Xi. Clubs: Nassau (Princeton); Univ. (Winter Park, Fla.). Address: 40 Palmer Ave Winter Park FL 32789 *The business of education is disciplining mind and emotions while cultivating spirit.*

DAWSON, RAYMOND HOWARD, univ. adminstr.; b. Camden, Ark., Oct. 12, 1927; s. Hilary Herbert and Mildred Mae Pye; m. Alice Jo McKeehen, May 26, 1949; children—Alice Catherine, Carolyn Marie. A.B. summa cum laude, Coll. of Ozarks, 1949; M.A., Vanderbilt U., 1951; Ph.D., U. N.C., 1958. Asso. prof. Presbyn. Jr. Coll., Maxton, N.C., 1951-55; teaching fellow U. N.C., Chapel Hill, 1955-56, faculty, 1958—, prof., 1968, dean, 1968-72, sr. v.p. acad. affairs, 1972—; Mershon postdoctoral fellow Ohio State U., Columbus, 1959-60; Fulbright lectr. Kings Coll., U. London, Eng., 1964-65; vis. asso. prof. Inst. War and Peace Studies, Columbia, 1967-68; Bd. govs. Research Triangle Inst. Author: The Decision to Aid Russia, 1941, Foreign Policy and Domestic Politics, 1959, (with W. Lucas) The Organizational Policies of Defense, 1974. Served with AUS, 1945-47. Recipient Tanner award for excellence in undergrad. teaching U. N.C., 1962; E. Harris Harbison prize for distinguished teaching Danforth Found., 1968. Mem. Am., So. polit. sci. assns., Inst. Strategic Studies. Democrat. Presbyn. Home: 304 Glendale Dr Chapel Hill NC 27514

DAWSON, RICHARD, actor, comedian; b. Gosport, Hampshire, Eng., Nov. 20; married; children: Mark, Gary. Performed in repertory co. in, Eng., nightclubs in, Eng. and, U.S.; regular performer on: TV series Hogan's Heroes, 1965-71, Laugh-In, The New Dick Van Dyke Show, 1973-74; host: TV game show Family Feud, 1976—; other TV appearances on game shows, talk shows and series; appeared in: motion pictures King Rat, 1965, Munster Go Home, 1966, The Devil's Brigade, 1968, Promises, Promises; album The Children's Parade. Recipient Emmy award as outstanding game show host, 1978. Office: care ABC Press Relations 1330 Ave of Americas New York NY 10019 *

DAWSON, ROBERT KENT, government official; b. Scottsboro, Ala., Jan. 22, 1946; s. C. Paul and Lollie F. (Cook) D.; m. Susan Bernice Lee, Jan. 25, 1969; children: Amy Johanna, Stephen Paul. B.S., Tulane U., 1968; J.D., Cumberland Sch. Law, Samford U., 1971. Bar: Ala. 1971. Legis. asst. U.S. Rep. Jack Edwards, Washington, 1972-74; adminstr. com. pub. works and transp. U.S. Ho of Reps., Washington, 1974-81; prin. dep. asst. sec. for civil works U.S. Dept. Army, Washington, 1981—. Mem. adminstrv. bd. Trinity United Methodist Ch., Alexandria, Va., 1978—; mem. exec. bd. N. Ridge Citizens Assn., Alexandria, 1981—. Served to lt. U.S. Army, 1972-73. Recipient award Nat. Legal Aid and Defender Assn., 1971, Disting. Achievement in Art and Sci. Advocacy award Internat. Acad. Trial Lawyers, 1971. Mem. ABA (Silver Key award 1971), Ala. State Bar Assn. Office: Sec of Army Room 2E570 Pentagon Washington DC 20310

DAWSON, ROBERT OSCAR, lawyer, educator; b. St. Louis, Mar. 7, 1939; s. Lonnie McNeil and Thelma Kate (Hostetter) D.; m. Jana C. Zimmerman, Apr. 7, 1983; 1 dau., Katherine Irene. A.B., U. Mo., 1960; LL.B., Washington U., St. Louis, 1963; S.J.D., U. Wis., 1969. Bar: Tex. 1973. Asst. prof. law Washington U., 1964-67; vis. asso. prof. law U. Tex., Austin, 1967-68, prof. law, 1968-72; staff atty. Pub. Defender Service D.C., 1972-73; Wright C. Morrow prof. criminal law U. Tex., Austin, 1974—, William Benjamin Wynne prof., 1977-81, Judge Benjamin Harrison Powell prof., 1981—; mem. project staff Am. Bar Found. Survey of Criminal Justice in U.S., 1963-69; acad. adviser Tex. Family Code Project, 1968-73; reporter Juvenile Justice Standards Project, 1971—; bd. dirs. Travis County (Tex.) Legal Aid and Defender Soc. Author: Sentencing: The Decision as to Type, Length, and Conditions of Sentence, 1969, (with others) Criminal Justice Administration and Related Processes, 1971, Criminal Justice Administration, 1976, The Juvenile Justice Process, 2d ed, 1976. Mem. Order of Coif, Phi Beta Kappa. Home: 1900 Overland Hills Circle Austin TX 78746 Office: 727 E 26th St Austin TX 78705

DAWSON, SAMUEL COOPER, JR., motel company executive; b. Alexandria, Va., Sept. 21, 1909; s. Samuel Cooper and Edna French (Horner) D.; m. Frances Margaret Boatwright, Mar. 24, 1945; children: Samuel Cooper III, Marion Boatwright. Grad., Episcopal High Sch., Alexandria, 1928; B.A. in Commerce, U. Va., 1932. Tchr. sci. St. Christopher's Sch., Richmond, Va., 1932-36; underwriter Md. Casualty Co., Balt., 1936-39; mgr. Penn-Daw Motor Hotel, Alexandria, 1939-73; past pres. Penn-Daw Hotels Corp., Alexandria, Penn-Daw Shopping Center; past dir. Washington-Lee Savs. & Loan Assn. Past pres. Va. Travel Council.; Pres. Camp Alleghany for Girls, Lewisburg, W.Va.; bus. mgr. Episcopal High Sch., 1969-83. Served with USNR, 1942-46; capt. Res. ret. Recipient Hall of Fame award Hospitality magazine, 1961; Disting. Service award Am. Motor Hotel Assn., 1964. Mem. Am. Automobile Assn. (mem. No. Va. adv. bd.), Va. Hotel Assn. (past dir.), Va. Motel Assn. (past pres.), Alexandria Jr. C. of C. (past pres., Outstanding Young Man award 1942), Washington Restaurant Assn. (past pres.), Am. Motor Hotel Assn. (past pres.; chmn. legislative affairs com.), Washington Civil War Round Table, SAR (past pres. George Washington chpt.), Nat. Restaurant Assn. (dir.). Episcopalian. Club: Army Navy Country (Arlington). Home: 206 N Quaker Ln Alexandria VA 22304 Office: PO Box 56 Alexandria VA 22313

DAWSON, THOMAS CLELAND, government official; b. Washington, Mar. 9, 1948; s. Allan D. and Barbara Jane (Dodge) D.; m. Moira Jane Haley, June 1, 1974; children: Thomas, Andrew. B.A. with honors in econs., Stanford U., 1970, M.B.A., 1978; postgrad., Princeton U., 1970-71. Fgn. service officer U.S. Dept. State, Washington, 1971-76, economist, 1971-72, asst. to under sec. for econ. affairs, 1972-74; consul., econ. officer Am. Consulate Gen., Rio de Janeiro, Brazil, 1974-76; cons. McKinsey & Co., Washington, 1978-81; dep. asst. sec. U.S. Dept. Treasury, Washington, 1981—. Mem. Reagan-Bush Planning Task Force, Alexandria, Va., 1980; assoc. dir. Taft for Senate campaign, Cin., 1970. Woodrow Wilson fellow, 1970. Republican. Episcopalian. Home: 4210 Fordham Rd NW Washington DC 20016 Office: Dept Treasury 15th and Pennsylvania Ave NW Washington DC 20220

DAWSON, WALLACE DOUGLAS, JR., geneticist; b. Louisville, Mar. 15, 1931; s. Wallace Douglas and Ida Belle (Hieatt) D.; 3 children. B.S., Western Ky. U., 1954; M.S., U. Ky., 1959; Ph.D. (NSF Coop. fellow), Ohio State U., 1962. Asst. prof. biology U. S.C., 1962-66, asso. prof., 1966-71, prof., 1971—, chmn. dept. biology, 1974-77, George Bunch prof. biology, 1977—; vis. scientist div. mammals Smithsonian Instn., 1979. Served to 1st lt. USAF, 1955-57. Recipient Disting. Teaching award S.C. Honors Program, 1977; NIH grantee, 1964, 71. Mem. AAAS, Am. Genetic Assn., Am. Soc. Mammalogists, Assn. Southeastern Biologists, Genetics Soc. Am., Soc. Study Evolution, S.C. Acad. Sci., Sigma Xi. Republican. Research and publs. in field. Office: Dept Biology U SC Columbia SC 29208

DAWSON, WILFRED THOMAS, broadcast advertising executive; b. Galveston, Tex., Sept. 14, 1928; s. Wilfred Thomas and Margaret (Bishop) D.; m. Nita Logan, Feb. 1, 1949; children: June, Diane. B.F.A., U. Tex., 1949. Various broadcast positions, Los Angeles, Austin, Tex., Galveston, 1947-54; asst. sales promotion mgr. Sta. WBBM-TV, Chgo., 1954-56, sales promotion mgr., 1956-57, CBS-TV Spot Sales, N.Y.C., 1957-59, dir. sales promotion, research, 1959-60; v.p. advt., promotion CBS Radio, N.Y.C., 1960-61, v.p. info. services, 1961-69; dir. sales devel. CBS Radio Spot Sales, N.Y.C., 1970-73; v.p. div. services CBS Radio, N.Y.C., 1973—; v.p. market devel. CBS Radio Network and RadioRadio Network, N.Y.C., 1981—; advt., mktg. cons. Broadcasters Promotion Assn., N.Y.C., 1984—; Trustee Broadcasting Found. Am. Mem. Internat. Radio and TV Soc., Bus. and Profl. Advertisers Assn., Broadcast Pioneers. Broadcasters Promotion Assn. (pres. 1980), Mus. of Broadcasting, Galveston Hist. Soc., U. Tex. Ex's Assn., Theta Xi. Clubs: Sales Execs. N.Y., Montclair (N.J.) Beach. Home: 165 West End Ave New York NY 10023 Office: 51 W 52d St New York NY 10019

DAWSON, WILLIAM LEVI, composer, conductor; b. Anniston, Ala., Sept. 26, 1899; s. George W. and Eliza M. (Starkey) D.; m. Cornella D. Lampton, May 25, 1927 (dec. Aug. 1928); m. Cecile D. Nicholson, Sept. 21, 1935. Student composition, orchestration, Washburn Coll.; Mus. B., Horner Inst. Fine Arts, Kansas City, Mo., 1925; M. Composition, Am. Conservatory Music, Chgo., 1927; Mus. D., Tuskegee Inst., 1955, Ithaca Coll., 1982; postgrad., Eastman Sch. Music; LL.D., Lincoln U., 1978. Dir. music, Topeka, Kansas City, 1921-25; then 1st trombonist, Chgo. Civic Symphony Orch.; dir., Tuskegee Inst. Sch. Music, Tuskegee Choir; led: opening Tuskegee Choir at, Radio City Music Hall, 1932-33, on many tours, in concert series, NBC, CBS, ABC; guest condr. numerous state choral festivals, choral groups in, Spain, under auspices, Dept. State, 1956, Kansas City Philharmonic Orch., 1966, Nashville Symphony Orch., Talladega Choir and Mobile Symphony Orch., 1968, Wayne State U. Glee Club, 1970, 74, Balt. Symphony Orch., 1975; condr. symposium choral music, Huntingdon Coll., Montgomery, Ala., 1976 (Winner Rodman Wanamaker contest for composition 1930, 31), Huntingdon Coll., Montgomery, Ala. (Chgo. Daily News contest for band condrs. 1929); Composer: numerous arrangements Negro folk songs for voices Break, Break; with orch. Trio in A; violin, cello, piano Sonata in A; violin and piano Negro Folk Symphony. Recipient award and citation U. Pa. Glee Club, 1967, Alumni Achievement award U. Mo. at Kansas City, 1963, award and citation Am. Choral Dirs. Assn., 1975; named to Ala. Arts Hall of Fame, 1975; recipient Paul Heinecke citation of merit, 1983, Alumni Merit award Tuskegee Inst., 1983. Mem. Phi Mu Alpha Sinfonia (hon.). Address: PO Box 1052 Tuskegee Institute AL 36088 *I believe that an individual seldom does his best in any performance. Regardless of how well I perform an act, the feeling remains that it is possible to do it better; therefore, I always strive for improvement.*

DAWSON, WILLIAM RYAN, zoology educator; b. Los Angeles, Aug. 24, 1927; s. William Eldon and Mary (Ryan) D.; m. Virginia Louise Berwick, Sept. 9, 1950; children: Deborah, Denise, William. Student, Stanford, 1945-46; B.A., UCLA, 1949, M.A., 1950, Ph.D., 1953; D.Sc., U. Western Australia, 1971. Faculty zoology U. Mich., Ann Arbor, 1953—, prof., 1962—, D.E.S. Brown prof. biol. scis., 1981—, chmn. div. biol. scis., 1974-82, dir. mus. zoology, 1982—; Lectr. Summer Inst. Desert Biology, Ariz. State U., 1960-71; researcher Australian-Am. Edn. Found., U. Western Australia, 1969-70; mem. Speakers Bur., Am. Inst. Biol. Sci., 1960-62; Mem. adv. panel NSF environ. biology program, 1967-69; mem. adv. com. for research NSF, 1973-77; adv. panel NSF regulatory biology program, 1979-82; mem. R/V Alpha Helix New Guinea Expdn., 1969; chief scientist R/V Dolphin Gulf of Calif. Expdn., 1976; mem. R/V Alpha Helix Galapagos Expdn., 1978. Editorial bd.: Condor, 1960-63, Auk, 1964-68, Ecology, 1968-70, Ann. Rev. Physiology, 1973-79, Physiol. Zoology, 1976—; co-editor: Springer-Verlag Zoophysiology and Ecology series; asso. editor: Biology of the Reptilia, 1972. Served with USNR, 1945-46. USPHS Postdoctoral Research fellow, 1953; Guggenheim fellow, 1962-63; Recipient Russell award U. Mich., 1959, Distinguished Faculty Achievement award, 1976. Fellow AAAS, Am. Ornithol. Union (Brewster medal 1979); mem. Am. Soc. Zoologists, Am. Physiol. Soc., Ecol. Soc. Am., Cooper Ornithol. Soc. (hon., Painton award 1963), Internat. Soc. Biometeorologists, Phi Beta Kappa, Sigma Xi, Kappa Sigma. Home: 1376 Bird Rd Ann Arbor MI 48103

DAY, ANTHONY, newspaper editor; b. Miami, Fla., May 12, 1933; s. Price and Alice (Alexander) D.; m. Lynn Ward, June 25, 1960; children—John, Julia. A.B. cum laude, Harvard U., 1955, postgrad. (Nieman fellow), 1966-67; L.H.D. (hon.), Pepperdine U., 1974. Reporter Phila. Bull., 1957-60, Washington, 1960-69, chief Washington bur., 1969. Chief editorial writer: Los Angeles Times, 1969-71; editor editorial pages, 1971—. Bd. dirs. Caltech Y, 1980—. Served with AUS, 1955-57. Mem. Am. Soc. Newspaper Editors (chmn. freedom of info. com. 1977-79, com. on internat. communication 1981-83, dir. 1979—), Signet Soc. Harvard. Office: Los Angeles Times Times Mirror Sq Los Angeles CA 90053

DAY, ARTHUR GROVE, educator, author; b. Phila., Apr. 29, 1904; s. Arthur Sinclair and Clara T. (Hogeland) D.; m. Virginia Teresa Molina, July 2, 1928. A.B. in English, Stanford U., 1926, M.A., 1942, Ph.D., 1944. Tchrs. Coll., 1926-27, Stanford U., 1932-36, asst. dir. engring., sci. and mgmt. war tng., 1943-44; mem. faculty U. Hawaii, 1944-69, sr. prof. English, 1961-69, prof. emeritus, 1969—, chmn. dept., 1948-53; propr. White Knight Press, Honolulu, 1946—; chmn. pub. com. 10th Pacific Sci. Congress, 1961; Fulbright sr. research fellow, Australia, 1955; Smith-Mundt vis. prof. Am. studies U. Barcelona, Spain, 1957-58; Fulbright vis. prof. Am. studies U. Madrid, 1961-62. Author: (with F.J. Buenzle) Bluejacket, 1936, Coronado's Quest: The Discovery of the Southwestern States, 1940, The Sky Clears: Poetry of the American Indians, 1951, (with James A. Michener) Rascals in Paradise, 1957, Hawaii and Its People, 3d edit, 1968, Hawaii, Fiftieth Star, 1960, 69, The Story of Australia, 1960, (with R.S. Kuykendall) Hawaii, A History, 2d edit, 1961, They Peopled the Pacific, 1964, James A. Michener, 1964, 77, Louis Becke, 1966, Explorers of the Pacific, 1967, Coronado and the Discovery of the Southwest, 1967, Pirates of the Pacific, 1967, Adventurers of the Pacific, 1969, Jack London in the South Seas, 1971, Pacific Islands Literature, One Hundred Basic Books, 1972, (with Edgar C. Knowlton) V. Blasco Ibáñez, 1972, Robert D. FitzGerald, 1973, Eleanor Dark, 1976, Books About Hawaii, 1977, Captain Cook and Hawaii, 1977, (with Amos P. Leib) Hawaiian Legends in English, 1979, History Makers of Hawaii: A Biographical Dictionary; editor: (with Amos P. Leib) in Spanish Despatches from Mexico by Fernando Cortes, 1935; The Spell of the Pacific: An Anthology of Its Literature, 1949, (with W.F. Bauer) The Greatest American Short Stories, 1953, (with Carl Stroven) A Hawaiian Reader, 1959, Best South Sea Stories, 1964, Stories of Hawaii (Jack London), 1965, Mark Twain's Letters from Hawaii, 1966, 75, True Tales of the South Seas, 1966, (with Virginia M. Day) The Spanish in Sydney, 1793, 1967, South Sea Supercargo (Louis Becke), 1967, (with Carl Stroven) The Spell of Hawaii, 1968, Melville's South Seas, 1970, The Art of Narration: The Short Story, 1971, The Art of Narration; The Novella, 1971, Robert Louis Stevenson's Travels in Hawaii, 1973, Modern Australian Prose, 1901-1975, 1980; editor-in-chief: Pacific Science, 1947-49. Recipient Hawaii State award lit., 1979. Mem. Modern Lang. Assn., Honolulu Acad. Arts, Phi Beta Kappa. Clubs: Elks, Adventurers (Honolulu). Home: 1434 Punahou St Apt 1223 Honolulu HI 96822 Office: care The University Press of Hawaii 2840 Kolowalu St Honolulu HI 96822

DAY, BARRY LEONARD, advertising agency executive; b. Lincoln, Eng., Apr. 27, 1934; came to U.S., 1979; s. Samuel and Marguerite Bell. B.A., Balliol Coll., Oxford U., 1956, M.A., 1957. Creative dir. Lintas, Ltd., London, 1956-69; with McCann-Erickson (and affiliates), 1970—; vice chmn. McCann-Erickson Internat., N.Y.C., 1979-81, McCann-Erickson Worldwide, 1981—. Author: What We Have Here is a Failure to Communicate?, 1975, It Depends on How You Look at It, 1978, Political Communications, 1982, And You Call That Creative?, 1983; Editor: 100 Great Advertisements, 1978. Fellow Royal Soc. Arts, Inst. Practitioners Advt. Office: 485 Lexington Ave New York NY 10017

DAY, CASTLE NASON, foods company executive; b. Springfield, Mass., July 24, 1933; s. Chauncey Castle and Anne Frances (Nason) D.; m. Patricia Jarko, Feb. 1, 1956; children: Robert Castle, Anne Wilson. B.A., Williams Coll., 1955; M.S., MIT, 1957. Exec. v.p. McCall Pattern Co., N.Y.C., 1970-72; v.p. Norton Simon Inc., N.Y.C., 1973-74; exec. v.p. Max Factor Inc., Los Angeles, 1975-77; v.p. fin. Can. Dry Corp., N.Y.C., 1978-81; exec. v.p. Am. Bakeries Co., N.Y.C., 1982—. Home: 39 Driftway Ln New Canaan CT 06840 Office: Am Bakeries Co 100 Park Ave New York NY 10017

DAY, CECIL LEROY, agricultural engineering; b. Dexter, Mo., Oct. 4, 1922; s. Cecil Lawrence and Katherine (Kleffer) D.; m. Peggy Eunice Thrower, Aug. 29, 1948; children: Stanley K., Thomas L. B.S. in Agrl. Engring, U. Mo., 1945, M.S., 1948; Ph.D., Ia. State U., 1957. Mem. faculty U. Mo. at Columbia, 1945—, prof. agrl. engring., 1962—, chmn. dept., 1969-82; vis. prof. U. Thessaloniki, Greece, 1972; pres. Penreico, Inc., 1968-79. Author articles, bulls. Chmn. elec. appeals bd., Columbia, 1966-76. Fellow Am. Soc. Agrl. Engrs. (Outstanding Individual of Yr. Mo. sect. 1982); mem. Am. Soc. Engring. Edn. Mem. Ch. of Christ (elder). Home: 1103 Again St Columbia MO 65201 *"And we know that all things work together for good to them that love God."*

DAY, CHON, cartoonist; b. Chatham, N.J., Apr. 6, 1907; s. Lawrence and Nell Hunter (Van Orden) D.; m. Irene Townley, June 2, 1934; children—Clinton, Robert, Stephen. Student, Lehigh U., 1926, Art Students League, N.Y.C., 1929. Cartoons appearing in, New Yorker, Ladies Home Jour., Saturday Evening Post, numerous other mags.; author, illustrator: I Could Be Dreaming, 1945, What Price Dory, 1955, Brother Sebastian, 1957, Brother Sebastian Carries On, 1959, Brother Sebastian at Large, 1961 (Recipient Best gag cartoonist award Nat. Cartoonists Soc. 1956, 62, 70, Best Spl. Features award 1969, named to R.I. Heritage Hall of Fame 1972). Mem. Nat. Cartoonists Soc. Baptist. Clubs: Lions (past pres.), Westerly Yacht.). Address: 22 Cross St Westerly RI 02891

DAY, COLIN LESLIE, publisher; b. St. Albans, Eng., July 19, 1944; came to U.S., 1978; s. Archibald William Dagless and Jose (Greenfield) D.; m. Jennifer Ann Jones, July 30, 1966; children: Matthew, Gudrun. B.A., Oxford U., 1966, M.S., 1968; Ph.D., U. Stirling, 1973. Research officer N.I.E.S.R., London, 1966-68; research fellow Stirling U., Scotland, 1968-71, lectr. in econs., 1971-75; sr. econs. editor Cambridge Univ. Press, Cambridge, U.K., N.Y.C., 1976-81, editor-in-chief, 1981-82, editorial dir., 1982—. Co-author: Company Financing in United Kingdom, 1974; contbr. articles to prof. jours. Justice of peace County of Perthshire, Scotland, 1970-75; chmn. West Perthshire Labour Party, 1972-75. Home: 200 North St Rye NY 10580 Office: Cambridge Univ Press 32 E 57th St New York NY 10022

DAY, DANIEL EDGAR, government information officer; b. Montgomery, Ala., Dec. 10, 1913; s. Thomas and Gertrude (Ford) D.; m. Sanone Nickerson, Jan. 18, 1942; children: Sandra Ann (Mrs. James Johnson), Gregory Alan. Student, Crane Jr. Coll., Chgo., 1932-33, Am. U., 1946, 62, 64, U. Chgo., 1958. With Robert S. Abbott Pub. Co., Chgo., 1929-40, asst. city editor, 1936-40; enlisted USNG, 1938; enlisted as sgt. U.S. Army, 1941, advanced through ranks to lt. col., 1952; asst. chief, then chief Negro interest sect. Bur. Pub. Relations, War Dept., Washington, 1943-46; stationed (Hdqrs. 8th Army), Japan, 1946-49, Ft. Bragg, NC, 1950-51, Korea, 1952-53, Yokohama, 1953-55; prof. mil. sci. Fla. A & M U., Tallahassee, 1955-61; ret., 1961; Washington corr. Nat. Newspaper Pubs. Assn., 1961-66; adminstrv. officer USDA, Washington, 1966; info. specialist HUD, Washington, 1966-68, dep. dir. pub. information div., 1968-70, pub. information officer, 1970-73, dep. dir. news services div., 1973-74, info. officer, 1975—. Mem. Nat. Assn. Govt. Communicators (dir. 1974), Mil. Order World Wars. Clubs: Nat. Press (chmn. membership com. 1983), Pigskin (Washington)). Home: 8212 Eastern Ave NW Washington DC 20012 Office: Dept Housing and Urban Devel Washington DC 20410

DAY, DAVID ALLEN, civil engineer, educator; b. Ann Arbor, Mich., Nov. 22, 1924; s. Edmund Ezra and Emily Sophia (Emerson) D.; m. Mary Warrick Squires, Sept. 8, 1945; children: Marilyn, Barbara, Suzanne. Frederick, Caroline. Grad., Deerfield (Mass.) Acad., 1942; B.C.E., Cornell U., 1945; M.S., U. Ill., 1951. Registered profl. engr., Ill., Colo. Constrn. engr. Raymond Concrete Pile Co., 1946-47, Gen. Paving Co., 1947-48, Peter Kiewit Sons Co., 1950; cons. constrn. engring., 1952—; tchr. civil engring. U. Ill., 1948-58; prof. civil engring. U. Denver, 1958-74, dean engring., 1960-68; sr. staff engr. Stearns-Roger Inc., 1974—; Bd. dirs. Denver area Urban Drainage and Flood Control Dist., 1977—. Author: Survey of Construction Education, 1961, Associated General Contractors' Directory of Construction Education, 1968, Construction Equipment Guide, 1973, Maquinaria Para Construccion, 1978; Contbr. articles to profl. jours. Served to lt. USNR, 1943-46. Recipient Epstein award U. Ill., 1957. Mem. ASCE (Cornell sr. award Ithaca sect. 1945, exec. bd. constrn. div. 1967-72, mgmt. group 1972-78), Am. Soc. Engring. Edn. (chmn. RWI div. 1969), Nat. Soc. Profl. Engrs., Cornell Soc. Engrs., Profl. Engrs. Colo. (pres. 1971), Colo. Engring. Council (pres. 1975), Am. Arbitration Assn. (arbitrator 1979—), Theta Delta Chi, Chi Epsilon, Tau Beta Pi, Phi Kappa Phi. Episcopalian. Home: 2758 E Geddes Ave Littleton CO 80122

DAY, DONALD CLIFFORD, financial executive; b. Worcester, Mass., Mar. 2, 1928; s. Clifford Warren and Dorothy Seagrave (Southwick) D.; m. Suzanne Post, Dec. 31, 1953; children: Melissa, Jennifer, Geoffrey P., Peter K. (dec.). B.S., Bowdoin Coll., 1949. With State Mut. of Am., Worcester, Mass., 1949-72, v.p., 1970-72, New Eng. Mut. Life Ins. Co., Boston, 1972-81, sr. v.p., 1981—; pres., dir. NEL Equity Services Corp., Boston, 1972—; exec. v.p. NEL Cash Mgmt. Trust, 1978—, NEL Equity Fund, 1972—; v.p. NEL Growth Fund, 1972—, NEL Income Fund, 1973—, NEL Retirement Equity Fund, 1972—, NEL Tax Exempt Bond Fund, 1977—. Mem. Nat. Assn. Security Dealers (mem. dist. com. 1976-79, vice chmn. 1979), Beta Theta Pi. Office: 501 Boylston St Boston MA 02117

DAY, DONALD SHELDON, lawyer; b. Boston, Nov. 3, 1924; s. Israel and Frances (Goldberg) D.; m. Edythe Greenberg, July 8, 1945; children—Clifford L., Richard J., Halee Beth. B.A., Bates Coll., 1946; LL.B., Cornell U., 1948. Bar: N.Y. bar 1948. Since practiced in, Buffalo; now pres. firm Saperston, Day, Lustig, Gallick, Kirschner & Gaglione (P.C.); pres., Dir. various corps. Gen. chmn. United Jewish Fund campaign, Buffalo, 1971-73, 75; past co-chmn. Western N.Y. chpt. NCCJ; pres. United Jewish Fedn. Buffalo.; Trustee Children's Hosp. of Buffalo, Forest Lawn Cemetery and Crematory, Hebrew-Union Coll.; chmn. bd. Union Am. Hebrew Congregations; bd. dirs. Council Jewish Fedns. Served with AUS, 1942-45. Mem. Am., N.Y. State, Erie County bar assns., Order of Coif, Phi Kappa Phi.; mem. B'nai B'rith. Jewish religion (past pres. temple). Club: Mason. Home: 56 Devonshire Ct Kenmore NY 14223 Office: Goldome Ctr 1 Fountain Plaza Buffalo NY 14203

DAY, DORIS (DORIS VON KAPPELHOFF), singer; b. Cin., Apr. 3, 1924; d. Frederick Wilhelm and Alma Sophia von Kappelhoff; m. Al Jorden, Mar. 1941 (div. 1943); 1 son, Terry; m. George Weilder, 1946 (div. 1949); m. Marty Melcher, Apr. 3, 1951 (dec. 1968). Student pub. schs., Cin. Made profl. dancing appearances, Doherty & Kappelhoff, Glendale, Calif.; was singer: Karlin's Karnival, radio sta. WCPO; bands, Barney Rapp, Bob Crosby, Fred Waring, Les Brown; singer, leading lady, Bob Hope NBC radio show, 1948-50, Doris Day CBS show, 1952-53; singer, Columbia Records, 1950—; star, Warner Bros. Studio; motion pictures include Romance on the High Seas, 1948, My Dream is Yours, 1949, Young Man With a Horn, 1950, Tea For Two, 1950, West Point Story, 1950, Lullaby of Broadway, 1951, On Moonlight Bay, 1951, I'll See You in My Dreams, 1951, April in Paris, 1952, By the Light of the Silvery Moon, 1953, Lucky Me, Yankee Doodle Girl, 1954, Love Me or Leave Me, 1955 (selected as 1 of 10 best films by N.Y. Hearald Tribune), Pajama Game, 1957, Teacher's Pet, 1958, Tunnel of Love, 1958, It Happened to Jane, 1959, Pillow Talk, 1959, Midnight Lace, 1960, Jumbo, 1962, That Touch of Mink, 1962, The Thrill of It All, 1963, Please Don't Eat the Daisies, 1960, Lover Come Back, 1962, Send Me No Flowers, 1964, Do Not Disturb, 1965, The Glass Bottom Boat, 1966, Caprice, 1967, The Ballad of Josie, 1968, Where Were You When The Lights Went Out, 1968, With Six You Get Eggrolls, 1968; TV series The Doris Day Show, 1970-73; appeared on: TV spl. The Pet Set, 1972 (Winner 1st prize (with Jerry Doherty) as best dance team in Cin., Laurel award as leading new female personality in motion picture industry 1950, top audience attractor 1962). Christian Scientist. *

DAY, EDWARD W., judge; b. Cranston, R.I., May 24, 1901. Ph.B., Brown U., 1922; LL.B., Harvard, 1925. Bar: R.I. bar 1925. Practiced in, Providence; mem. Gardner, Day & Sawyer; clk. 8th Dist. Ct., 1929-30; 1st asst. atty. gen. of R.I., 1930-33, city solicitor, Cranston, 1935-43; chmn. R.I. Civil Service Commn., 1939-41; judge U.S. Dist Ct. R.I., Providence, 1953—, chief judge, 1966-71, sr. dist. judge, 1976—. Mem. Am., R.I. bar assns. Address: US Court House Providence RI 02903 *

DAY, EMERSON, physician; b. Hanover, N.H., May 2, 1913; s. Edmund Ezra and Emily Sophia (Emerson) D.; m. Ruth Fairfield, Aug. 7, 1937; children: Edmund Perry, Robert Fairfield, Nancy, Bonnie, Sheryl. B.A., Dartmouth Coll., 1934; M.D., Harvard U., 1938. Intern Presbyn. Hosp., N.Y.C., 1938- 40; fellow in cardiology Johns Hopkins U., 1940-42; asst. resident medicine N.Y. Hosp., 1942; med. dir. internat. div. Trans World Airline, N.Y.C., 1945-47; asst. prof. preventive medicine and pub. health Cornell U. Med. Coll., 1947-50, asso. prof. clin. preventive medicine and pub. health, 1950-54, prof. preventive medicine Sloan Kettering div., 1954-64; chmn. dept. preventive medicine Meml. Hosp., N.Y.C., 1954-63; dir. Strang Cancer Prevention Clinic, 1950-63; mem., chief div. preventive medicine Sloan-Kettering Inst., N.Y.C., 1954-64; cons. in geriatrics Cold Spring Inst., Cold Spring-on-Hudson, N.Y., 1952-57; dir. N.Y.C. Dept. Health Cancer Detection Center, 1947-50, Strang Clinic, Inc., 1963-66, PMI-Strang Clinic, 1966-69; pres. Preventive Medicine Inst., 1963-69, hon. pres., 1969—; v.p., med. dir. Medequip Corp., 1969-76, sr. med. cons., 1976—; nat. med. dir. Del. Profl. Services, Inc., 1980-82; med. v.p. Health Mgmt. Internat., Inc., 1982—; prof. medicine Northwestern U. Med. Sch., 1976-81, prof. emeritus, 1981—; assoc. dir. Northwestern U. Cancer Center, 1976-81; med. dir. Portes Cancer Prevention Center, 1978-79; attending physician Northwestern Meml. Hosp., 1976-81, sr. physician, 1981—; mem. Northwestern U. Med. Assocs., 1980-81; med. dir., chmn. dept. internal medicine Chgo. Specialty Hosp. and Med. Center, 1981—; affiliate staff physician Evanston, Glenbrook hosps., 1976—; attending physician, mem. med. bd. James Ewing Hosp., Meml. Hosp., N.Y.C., 1950-64; sr. mem. PMX Med. Group, N.Y.C., 1956—70; adj. prof. biology N.Y. U., 1965-70; mem. cancer detection com. Internat. Union Against Cancer, 1954-70; pres. N.Y.C. div. Am. Cancer Soc., 1963-64. Contbr. numerous articles to profl. jours. Served as flight surgeon ATC USAAF, 1942-45. Recipient Bronze medal Am. Cancer Soc., 1956, professorship in early detection Ill. div., 1976-79. Fellow ACP, N.Y. Acad. Medicine, N.Y. Acad. Scis. (pres. 1965), Am. Pub. Health Assn., Am. Occupational Med. Assn., Am. Geriatrics Soc., Internat. Acad. Cytology (hon.); mem. Am. Soc. Cytology (founding mem., pres. 1958, now hon. mem., Papanicolaou award 1978), Am. Soc. Preventive Oncology, Internat. Health Evaluation Assn., Soc. for Advanced Med. Systems (founding dir. 1969-81), Am. Assn. Med. Systems and Informatics (founding dir. 1981—), Harvey Soc., Ill., Chgo. med. socs., AMA, Phi Beta Kappa, Alpha Omega Alpha, Zeta Psi. Club: Century Assn. (N.Y.C.). Home: 320 Pebblebrook Dr Northbrook IL 60062 Office: 231 W Washington St Chicago IL 60606

DAY, EUGENE DAVIS, SR., immunology educator, researcher; b. Cobleskill, N.Y., June 24, 1925; s. Emmons Davis and Alice (McCartey) D.; m. Shirley M. Warner, Sept. 14, 1946; 1 son, Eugene Davis. B.S. in Chemistry, Union Coll., Schenectady, 1949; M.S., U. Del., 1950, Ph.D., 1952. Research assoc. Roscoe B. Jackson Meml. Lab., Bar Harbor, Maine, 1952-54; sr. cancer research scientist Roswell Park Meml. Inst., Buffalo, 1954-58, assoc. cancer research scientist, 1958-62; assoc. prof. immunology Duke U. Med. Ctr., Durham, N.C., 1962-65, prof., 1965-67, prof. immunology and exptl. surgery, 1967—. Author: The Immunochemistry of Cancer, 1966, Foundations of Immunochemistry, 1969, Advanced Immunochemistry, 1972; articles to profl. jours. Served with AUS, 1943-46. Grantee NIH, 1975—, Multiple Sclerosis Soc., 1973-82, AEC, 1964-72. Mem. Am. Assn. Immunologists, Am. Assn. Cancer Research, Am. Soc. Neurochemists, Sigma Xi. Home: 2727 McDowell St Durham NC 27705 Office: Duke U Med ctr PO Box 3045 Durham NC 27710

DAY, FRANK E., lawyer; b. Omaha, May 21, 1918; s. L.B. and Neva E. (Grimwood) D.; m. Geraldine Binning, Mar. 8, 1943; children: L.B., Chrisann, Linda. A.B., U. Nebr., 1940; student, U. Oreg. Law Sch. Individual practice law, 1945-47; partner firm Reiter, Day, Wall & Bricker, Portland, Oreg., 1951-72; partner Day, Prohaska, P.C., Portland, 1972—. Served to capt. AUS, 1942-45. Mem. Am. Bar Assn., Multnomah County Bar Assn., Am. Law Inst., Fedn. Ins. Counsel, Oreg. State Bar, Am. Legion. Clubs: Multnamah Athletic, Elks. Home: 8120 SW Parrway Dr Portland OR 97225 Office: 1240 Georgia Pacific Bldg Portland OR 97204

DAY, HORACE CORBIN, investment banker; b. Orange, N.J., July 7, 1937; s. Henry B. and Clementine (Corbin) D.; m. Dorothy Jemison, Dec. 9, 1961; children: Clementine Corbin, Horace Corbin Jr. B.A., Brown U., 1959; M.B.A., U. Pa., 1963. Gen ptnr. goldman, Sachs & Co., N.Y.C., 1963—; dir. Penn Corp., Princeton, N.J., Jemison Investment Co., Inc., Birmingham, Ala. Pres. bd. trustees Kent Place Sch., Summit, N.J.; v.p., bd. dirs. Frost Valley YMCA, Oliverea, N.Y.; trustee Kessler Inst. Rehab., West Orange, N.J., N.Y. Infirmary-Beekman Downtown Hosp. Clubs: Short Hills (N.J.); Hartwood (Monticello, N.Y.); Bay Head Yacht (N.J.); India House (N.Y.C.). Office: Goldman Sachs & Co 85 Broad St New York NY 10004

DAY, JACK GRANT, judge; b. Covington, Ky., Sept. 24, 1913; s. William Nicholas and Lilleon Ethel (Grant) D.; m. Ruth Angeline Schaefer, Feb. 29, 1936; children: John G., Thomas D., William S., Judith R., Kathleen L. B.S., Ohio State U., 1935, LL.B., 1938, A.M., 1940. Bar: Ohio 1939, U.S. Dist. Ct. 1946, U.S. Circuit Ct. 1950, Mich. 1957, U.S. Supreme Ct. 1959. Asst. prof. history and govt. Denison U., Granville, Ohio, 1942-43; individual practice law, Cleve., 1946-68; judge 8th appellate dist. Ct. of Appeals of Ohio, Cleve., 1968—, chief justice, 1970-72, 77, 82; chmn. VII region War Labor Bd., 1945; vice chmn. Nat. Wage Stabilization Bd., Washington, 1946; asso. prof. polit. sci. Western Res. U., 1946-49; lectr. law Case Western Res. U., 1967-68, 69-70, 79, 80, 80-81; mem. faculty Seminar for Intermediate Appellate Judges, N.Y. U., 1971—; mem. Am. delegation U. Bielefeld (Germany) Conf. on Research in Conflict with Law and Ethics, 1974. Co-editor: Labor Relations and the Law, 1953; Contbr. articles in field to profl. jours. Mem. NAACP (Distinguished Service award 1965), Nat. Assn. Def. Lawyers in Criminal Cases (sec. 1961-64, v.p. 1965, pres. 1966-68), Am. Bar Assn. (vice chmn. com. to implement standards for adminstrn. of criminal justice 1969-70, vice chmn. sect. criminal justice 1971-72, chmn. 1973-74, exec. com. appellate judges conf. 1976-83), Am. Law Inst. Home: 2854 Weybridge Rd Shaker Heights OH 44120 Office: Court House 1 Lakeside Ave Cleveland OH 44113

DAY, J(AMES) EDWARD, former postmaster general, lawyer; b. Jacksonville, Ill., Oct. 11, 1914; s. James Allmond and Frances (Wilmot) D.; m. Mary Louise, Burgess, July 2, 1941; children: Geraldine (Mrs. James A. Zurn), Molly (Mrs. John Himmelfarb), James Edward (dec.). A.B., U. Chgo., 1935; LL.B. cum laude, Harvard, 1938; LL.D., Ill. Coll., U. Nev. Bar: Ill. 1938, D.C. 1963, Md. 1972. With firm Sidley, Austin, Burgess & Harper, 1939-41, 45-49, 63-72; legal and legislative asst. to Ill. Gov. Adlai Stevenson, Springfield, 1949-50; mem., sec. Ill. Commn. Intergovtl. Coop., 1949-53; commr. ins., Ill., 1950-53; asso. gen. solicitor Prudential Ins. Co. Am., 1953-56, asso. gen. counsel, 1956, sr. v.p. charge Western operations, Los Angeles, 1957-61; postmaster gen. U. S., 1961-63; partner in charge Washington office Chgo. law firm Sidley and Austin, 1963-73; partner firm Cox, Langford & Brown, Washington, 1973—, Squire, Sanders & Dempsey, Cleve. and Washington, 1973—; dir., mem. exec. com. 4 cos. in Zurich Ins. Group; dir., mem. exec. com. Peoples Life Ins. Co., Washington; dir. Med. Mut. Liability Soc. Md.; voting trustee common stock Conrail; spl. counsel consumer electronics group Electronic Industries Assn.; Vice chmn. Gov.s' Commn. Met. Area Problems, Calif., 1959-61; mem. adv. bd. U.S. Customs Bur., 1966-68; mem. Calif. Gov.'s Bus. Adv. Council, 1959-61. Author: Humor in Public Speaking, 1965; Contbr. to legal and ins. publs. V.p. Nat. Capital council Boy Scouts Am.; gen campaign chmn. Los Angeles YMCA, 1959; chmn. adv. com. Md. Ins. Dept., 1966-69; chmn. Democratic Asso., Los Angeles County, 1958-61; del. Dem. Nat. Conv., 1960; Trustee Meridian House Found., Hood Coll., Frederick, Md., 1974—; trustee, sec. Project Hope, 1974—; mem. bd. fellows Claremont Coll., Calif., 1958-65; chmn. nat. devel. com. Georgetown U. Served to lt. USNR, 1940-45. Mem. Nat. Civil Service League (pres. 1964-66), Citizens Conf. State Legislatures (chmn. 1965-70), Nat. Assn. Ins. Commrs. (chmn. Midwestern zone 1950-53), Am., D.C., Md. Fed., Chgo. bar assns., Md. Farm Bur., Am., Eastern Devon cattle assns., Phi Kappa Psi. Democrat. Methodist. Clubs: Nat. Press, Internat., Nat. Lawyers, Touchdown (Washington); Union (Cleve.); Legal (Chgo.). Home: 5804 Brookside Dr Chevy Chase MD 20815 Office: 1201 Pennsylvania Ave Washington DC 20004 *Life isn't all that bad or all that serious, but it is all that short.*

DAY, JAMES MILTON, museum executive, English educator; b. Brownwood, Tex., June 7, 1931; s. William Joseph and Gladys Louise (Stuteville) D.; m. Doris Eugene Campbell, May 16, 1952 (div. Nov. 10, 1967); children: James Milton, Joseph Campbell. B.A., U. Tex., 1954, M.A., 1958; Ph.D., Baylor U., 1967. Asst. dir. legis reference Tex. State Library, Austin, 1958-59, dir. state archives, 1960-67; instr. in polit. sci. Howard County Jr. Coll., Big Spring, Tex., 1959-60; assoc. prof. English U. Tex.-El Paso, 1967-75, prof., 1975—, dir. El Paso Centennial Mus., 1980—, chmn. Tex. Western Press Editorial Bd., 1981—. Author: book Black Beans and Goose Quills: Literature of the Texan Mier Expedition, 1970, Captain Clint Peoples, Texas Ranger, 1980; compiler: The Texas Almanac 1857-1873, 1967 (Am. Assn. State and Local History cert. commendation 1967); editor: Maps of Texas/1527-1900, 1964 (ALA C.S. Hammond award 1965), Morris B. Parker's Mules, Mines and Me in Mexico, 1895-1932, 1979 (Border Regional Library Assn. award of Merit 1979). Served to 1st lt. U.S. Army, 1954-56. Fellow Tex. State Hist. Assn. (life mem.); mem. West Tex. Hist. Assn. (pres. 1977-78), El Paso Pub. Library Assn. (pres. 1980-81, 83—), Tex. Folklore Soc. (pres. 1978-79), Am. Folklore Soc., El Paso County Hist. Soc. (pres. 1982—), Southwestern Am. Lit. Assn. (pres. 1973-74), Western Lit. Assn. Clubs: Sons of Repubic of Tex. (sec.-gen. 1962-63); Knights of San Jacinto (Crosby, Tex.); El Paso Corral of Westerners Internat. (sheriff 1971-72). Lodge: Masons. Home: 3809 Pershing El Paso TX 79903 Office: El Paso Centennial Mus U Tex University at Wiggins El Paso TX 79968

DAY, JAMES VINCENT, government official; b. S. Brewer, Maine, Nov. 27, 1914; s. Thomas Patrick and Mary Ellen (Ryan) D.; m. Deima Irene McCormick, July 11, 1946; children: Teresa (Mrs. John P. Lynch), Daniel, James Vincent, Thomas, Timothy, Mary. Edn. certificate, Wash. State Tchrs. Coll., 1934, U. Me. at Machias, 1971. Sales Supr. H.J. Heinz Co., 1936-41; pres. Spillers, Inc., Kennebunk, Maine, 1951-55; nat. dir. pub. relations Am. Legion, 1956-61; vice chmn. Fed. Maritime Commn., from 1961, commr., 1980—; Mem. exec. com. Am. Legion PTA, 1961—; bd. advisers Blinded Vets. Assn., 1964—; bd. visitors Maine Maritime Acad., Castine.; Republican candidate for Congress from, Maine, 1956. Served to 1st lt. AUS, World War II. Named col., mil. staff Gov. Maine, 1955; recipient Pres.'s award Am. Legion Press Assn., 1961, ann. Golden Record award best services in nat. def., 1960, Big M award State of Maine Soc., 1965. Mem. Am. Legion (nat. vice comdr. 1956—), Maine Soc. Washington (pres. 1963), Pub. Relations Soc. Am., Kappa Delta Phi. Office: Fed Maritime Commn 1100 L St NW Washington DC 20537 *

DAY, JOHN FRANCIS, former savings and loan executive, mayor; b. Cleve., Mar. 14, 1920; s. Frank S. and Susan Josephine (O'Brien) D.; m. Gertrude Jane Schmitt, Dec. 29, 1941; children: Susan, Mary, Timothy, Gertrude, Kathryn, Patrick, Fanchon, Josephine. Ed., Western Res. U., Staunton (Va.) Mil. Acad. Formerly with Cosgrove & Co., Seaboard Fin.; former v.p. Calif. Fed. Savs. & Loan, Los Angeles; mayor, Glendale, Calif. Served with AUS, 1941-45. Decorated knight Equestrian Order of Holy Sepulchre of Jerusalem. Mem. League Calif. Cities, Am. Legion, Sierra Club. Democrat. Roman Catholic. Club: K.C. Home: 2327 Hollister Terr Glendale CA 91206 Office: 613 E Broadway Glendale CA 91206

DAY, JOHN FRANKLIN, charitable trust administrator; b. Cadillac, Mich., May 17, 1928; s. Karl S. and Margaret (Raine) D.; m. Gail Elizabeth Sunkenberg, Dec. 8, 1956; children: John Franklin, Thomas Raine, Richard Williams. Grad., Choate Sch., 1946; B.A. cum laude, Williams Coll., 1950; M.B.A., Harvard, 1955. Research asst. CIA, 1950-51; asst. to sr. partner Smith Barney & Co., N.Y.C., 1955-58; with Duke Endowment, N.Y.C., 1958—, asst. treas., 1961-66, treas., 1966-73, sec., 1973-79, sec.-treas., 1979-80, exec. dir., treas., 1980—; asst. sec. Duke Power Co., 1967-75; Treas. Angier B. Duke Meml., Inc., 1966-73, sec., 1973-79, sec.-treas., 1979-80, exec. dir., treas., 1980—; treas. Doris Duke Trust, 1966-73, sec., 1973-79, sec.-treas., 1979. Served as 1st lt. USMCR, 1951-53. Mem. Psi Upsilon. Clubs: City (Charlotte, N.C.); River Hills Country (Clover, S.C.). Home: 58 Honeysuckle Woods River Hills Plantation Clover SC 29710 Office: 200 S Tryon St Charlotte NC 28202

DAY, JOHN SIDNEY, management sciences educator; b. Newton, Mass., Oct. 13, 1917; s. Franklin Everett and Marion (Guild) D.; m. Barbara Jane Felch, Nov. 20, 1940; children: John Sidney, Stephen L. Student, Tufts U., 1935-37, Oxford Sch. Bus. Adminstrn., 1939; M.B.A. with distinction, Harvard U., 1950, D.C.S., 1956. Asst. to pres. C. Carlson Co., Boston, 1939-40, 45-46; instr. Oxford Sch. Bus. Adminstrn., Cambridge, Mass., 1946-48; research asst. Harvard Grad. Sch. Bus. Adminstrn., Cambridge, Mass., 1950-51, research asso., 1951-53, asst. prof., 1953-56; asso. prof. Purdue U., Lafayette, Ind., 1956-59, prof. indsl. mgmt., 1959-83, dean Krannert Grad. Sch. Mgmt., 1969-78, v.p. for devel., 1978-83, Krannert prof. mgmt., 1983—; dir. Mut. Trust Life, Purdue Nat. Bank, Gt. Lakes Chem. Co., Nat. Homes Corp. Author: (with L. Bollinger) Management of New Enterprises, 1952, Subcontracting Policy in the Airframe Industry, 1956, (with P. Donham) New Enterprise and Small Business Management, 1960. Bd. dirs. Purdue Research Found.; Mem. Tippecanoe County (Ind.) chpt. ARC, 1968-74, chmn., 1974; treas. Tippecanoe County Easter Seal Soc., 1972-78; mem. West Lafayette Economic Devel. Commn., chmn., 1975-83; mem. nat. adv. council SBA, 1976-78; trustee Joint Council on Econ. Edn., 1976-78; bd. dirs. Home Hosp., 1972-78, pres., 1977; bd. dirs. Am. Assemblies Collegiate Schs. Bus., 1974-78, pres., 1977-78. Served to col. USMC, 1940-45. Decorated Bronze Star (2); Ford Found. fellow, 1959-60. Mem. Am. Fin. Assn., Acad. Mgmt. Clubs: Lafayette Country, Masons, Rotary. Home: 6407 Division Rd West Lafayette IN 47906 Office: Hovde Hall Purdue U West Lafayette IN 47907

DAY, JOHN W., automotive company executive; b. 1933. B.S. in Bus., Northwestern U., 1955. With Chrysler Corp., Detroit, 1957—, quality control techician, 1957-58, budget investigator, 1958-59, cost analyst Missile div., 1959-61; supr. div. acctg. and travel audit, asst. fin. mgr. U.S. Assn. for Tech. Assistance, Italy and Turkey, 1961-62; asst. comptroller for Turkey, mgr. fin. and acctg. Chrysler Internat. Corp., 1962-63; acctg. and audit group exec. Chrysler Internat. S.A., 1963-64; treas., comptroller Chrysler Peru S.A., 1964-67; dir. fin. Chrysler do Brazil, 1967-69; mng. dir. Chrysler Colmotores, Colombia, 1969-71; v.p. Chrysler Internat. S.A., 1972-73; mng. dir. Chrysler Espana S.A., 1973-75; group dir. French and Spanish cos., then pres., mng. dir. Chrysler France, 1975-76; corp. v.p. Chrysler Corp., 1976-77; v.p. Europe, 1977-78; pres. Chrysler France, 1977-78; corp. group v.p. non auto, then group v.p diversified products Chrysler Corp., 1978-79, v.p., controller, 1979-81, group v.p. def. and internat., controller, now exec. v.p. def. and internat. ops., Detroit, 1981—. Office: Chrysler Corp 1200 Lynn Towsend Dr Box 1919 Detroit MI 48288 *

DAY, JOSEPH DENNIS, librarian; b. Dayton, Ohio, Sept. 23, 1942; s. John Albert and Ruth (Pearson) D.; m. Mary Louise Herbert, Oct. 10, 1964; children: Cindy, Jeff, Chris, Steve, Tom. B.A., U. Dayton, 1966; M.L.S., Western Mich. U., 1967. Community librarian Dayton-Montgomery Pub. Library, 1967-70; dir. Troy-Miami County Pub. Library, Troy, Ohio, 1970-76, Salt Lake City Pub. Library, 1976—; chmn. Miami Valley Library Orgn., 1971-73; pres. Ohio Library Assn., 1975-76; project dir. planning and constrn. first solar powered library in world, 1973-76. Pres., Troy Area Arts Council, 1973-74; mem. exec. bd. Freedom to Read Found., 1981—. Recipient Disting. Community Service award Troy C. of C., 1974; John Cotton Dana award, 1975, 77, 83; AIA-ALA architecture award, 1977. Mem. ALA (chmn. intellectual freedom com. 1981—), Utah Library Assn. (pres. 1979-80), Am. Soc. Pub. Adminstrn. Clubs: Kiwanis (pres. Troy 1975-76, Disting. Service award Troy 1973), Kiwanis (pres. Salt Lake-Foothill 1979-80). Address: 209 East 5th South Salt Lake City UT 84111

DAY, LEE MONROE, agricultural economics educator; b. Thayer, Iowa, Feb. 25, 1923; s. Samuel Gordon and Helen McCleary (Swindler) D.; m. Joan Meredith, Sept. 8, 1948; children: Michael Gordon, Meredith Lee. B.S., Iowa State U., 1947, M.S., 1948; Ph.D., U. Minn., 1953. Asst. prof. agrl. econs. U. Wis., 1950-55; agrl. economist USDA, 1955-67; prof. agrl. econs. Pa. State U., State College, 1967-74, head dept. agrl. econs. and rural sociology, 1969-74; prof. agrl. econs. Cornell U., Ithaca, N.Y., 1974—; Dir. designate NE Regional Center for Rural Devel., 1974-75, dir., 1975—. Served with USNR, 1943-46. Mem. Am. Agrl. Econs. Assn. (dir. 1971-74), N.E. Agrl. Econs. Assn. (Disting. Mem. award 1982, pres.-elect 1982-83, pres. 1983-84), Alpha Zeta, Phi Delta Kappa, Gamma Sigma Delta, Phi Kappa Phi. Democrat. Home: 6-D Sevanna Park Ithaca NY 14850

DAY, LEROY EDWARD, aerospace consultant; b. Doswell, Va., Jan. 2, 1925; s. Ira Eugene and Sallie (Lester) D.; m. Mary Elizabeth Hornbuckle, May 18, 1947; children: David, Jean, Michael. B. Aero. Engring., Ga. Inst. Tech., 1946; M.S. in Engring, UCLA, 1955, MIT, 1960. Dep. head missile program dept. U.S. Naval Missile Center, 1960-62; with NASA, 1962-81, dep. dir. space shuttle, 1969-79, dir. STS systems engring. and integration, 1980-81; lectr. U. Calif. at Los Angeles, 1958-59. Contbr. papers profl. lit. Local troop chmn. Boy Scouts Am., 1962; sr. warden Episcopal Ch. Served with USN, 1943-48. Sloan fellow, 1959; recipient Superior Achievement award NASA, 1967, Exceptional Service medal, 1969. Mem. Research Soc. Am., Tau Beta Pi, Phi Kappa Phi. Republican. Episcopalian. Home: 11709 Magruder Ln Rockville MD 20852 *I was fortunate to have lived and to have been involved in a great period of changes and advances in the aerospace field. . from jet aircraft to the flight to the moon and the space shuttle.*

DAY, MAURICE JEROME, automobile parts distributing company; b. Saginaw, Mich., Jan. 3, 1913; s. Thomas and Margaret (Cavanaugh) D.; m. Mary Fitzgerald, Aug. 12, 1944; children: Mary Joann, Jeanne Ellen, Paul Maurice, Barbara Claire. B.S., Mich. State Coll., 1934, M.S., 1935, Ph.D., 1937. Metallurgist Carnegie-Ill. Steel Corp., Gary, Ind., 1937-38, tech. trade rep., Chgo., 1941-45, mgr. alloy div., 1945-47; phys. chemist U.S. Steel Research Lab., Kearny, N.J., 1938-41; metall. engr. U.S. Steel Corp., Pitts., 1947-52; mgr. materials and processes div. Armour Research Found., Chgo., 1952-53, asst. dir., 1953-54; v.p. research and devel. Crucible Steel Co. Am., Pitts., 1955-57, v.p. tech., 1957-59, v.p. comml., 1959-63, sr. v.p., 1963-65; indsl. cons., 1965-68; pres., dir. Hawley Mfg. Co., San Francisco, 1966-76; chmn. bd. Argus, Inc, 1969—, pres., 1970-75; chmn. bd., chief exec. officer, dir. Seaport Corp., 1975—; pres., chief exec. officer, dir. Noma Worldwide, Inc., 1979—; dir. Brown Co. N.Y.C., Crucible Steel Co. Can., Oxford Electric Corp., Argus, Inc., Interphoto Corp., Crucible Steel Internat. (S.A.), Trent Tube Co.; Chmn. manganese panel, minerals and metals adv. bd., mem. panel guided missiles Nat. Acad. Scis.; Trustee Packaging Found., chmn. bd., 1963-65. Mem. Am. Ordnance Assn., Navy League U.S., Am. Soc. Metals, Def. Orientation Conf. Assn., A.I.S.I., Pa. Soc. Club: Duquesne (Pitts.). Office: 1155 7th St Oakland CA 94607

DAY, PATRICIA JEAN, publishing co. exec.; b. Villisca, Ia., Nov. 5, 1926; d. Russell Wayne and Brenice Leona (King) D.; m. Sol Stein, Mar. 31, 1962; children—Robert Bruce, David Day, Elizabeth Day. B.A., Barnard Coll., 1948; M.A., State U. Iowa, 1950; postgrad., U. Paris, 1951-52, Columbia, 1958-60. Vice pres. Mid-Century Book Soc., N.Y.C., 1959-62; v.p., sec.-treas. Stein & Day, Inc., N.Y.C., 1962—. Home: Linden Circle Scarborough NY 10510 Office: Scarborough House Briarcliff Manor NY 10510

DAY, PAUL RICHARD, adjutant general; b. Bangor, Maine, Dec. 12, 1922; s. Harry Wellington and Jennie Joyce (Ryan) D.; m. Mary Ellen Feeney, Mar. 24, 1945; children: Paul Richard, John Kevin, Brian Edward. Student, Colby Coll., 1942, Mich. State U., 1943, U. Maine, 1971. Customer services Northeast Airlines, Portland, Maine, 1947; sales rep. Met. Ins. Co., Portland, 1947-59; credit mgr. Mecaw Industries, Portland, 1960-66; adminstr. Dept. Commerce, 1966-68; asst. adj. gen. (air) Mil. Bur. Maine, Augusta, 1968-73; adj. gen. Maine Dept. Def., Augusta, 1973—; cabinet mem. Maine State Exec. Dept. Exec. officer Boy Scouts Am.; chmn. March of Dimes, 1970-71, U.S. Savs. Bonds, 1971-72, United Fund, 1971-72. Served with USAAF, 1942-45; to 1st lt. USAF, 1951-53; to maj. gen. Maine N.G., 1953—. Mem. N.G. Assn. U.S.; mem. Adjutants Gen. Assn. U.S.; Mem. Maine N.G. Assn., Credit Mgrs. Assn., Exec. Credit Mgrs. Assn., Soc. Profl. Emergency Planners, Am. Legion, VFW, Pi Phi. Clubs: Elks, Lions, Portland Toastmasters (treas.). Home: 29 Bedell St Portland ME 04103 Office: Camp Keyes Augusta ME 04330

DAY, POMEROY, banker; b. Hartford, Conn., June 21, 1906; s. Arthur Pomeroy and Lucy (Bunce) D.; m. Katherine Flateau Long, Feb. 11, 1938 (dec. Sept. 1966); children: Pamela (Mrs. Robert H. Pelletreau, Jr.), Elizabeth (Mrs. Thomas C. Bolton), Roger P., George C.; m. Ella M. Stover, May 1969. A.B., Yale U., 1928; LL.B., 1931; LL.D. (hon.), Trinity Coll., 1969. Bar: Conn. 1931. Practice, Hartford, 1931-58; mem. firm Robinson, Robinson & Cole, 1936-58; pres. Conn. Bank & Trust Co., 1961-66, chmn., 1966-70, chmn. exec. com., 1970-74; hon. dir. Conn. Bank & Trust Co.; past dir. various corps. Chmn. Hartford chpt. ARC, 1939-42; mem. Conn. Gov.'s Revenue Task Force, 1969-71; trustee Smith Coll., 1951-61; hon. bd. dirs. Hartford Hosp.; hon. trustee Wadsworth Atheneum, pres., 1970-72. Served to lt. col. M.I. AUS, 1942-45. Decorated Bronze Star. Mem. Soc. of Cin. Republican. Episcopalian. Clubs: Hartford (pres. 1955-56), Hartford Golf, Gulf Stream Golf, Gulf Stream Bath and Tennis, Everglades, Woods Hole Golf. Home: 2435 N Ocean Blvd Gulf Stream FL 33444

DAY, ROBERT EDGAR, artist, educator; b. Clinton Falls, Minn., Dec. 27, 1919; s. Judson LeRoy and Blanche Leone (Finch) D.; m. Helen Marie Hanson, Aug. 13, 1944 (dec.); children: Marion Eve, Cynthia, Brian Louis; m. Kathryn Jean Waitz, June 7, 1969. Student, U. Minn., 1937-39; B.A., St. Olaf Coll., 1943; M.A., U. Iowa, 1946, Ph.D., 1958. Instr. art and English, art supr. pub. schs., Winona, Minn., 1946-49; instr., asst. prof. art edn. and appreciation Kent State U., 1949-56; asso. prof. art history and sculpture No. Ill. U., 1958-60; prof., chmn. dept. art La. State U., 1960-65; prof. U. Colo., Boulder, 1965—, chmn. dept. fine arts, 1965-68; chmn. adv. com. Anglo-Am. Art Mus., 1961-63, dir. art history program in, Italy, 1971, 73, 74, 76, 77, 78, 81, 82. Exhibited the: Harvester, Regional Sculpture Invitational, Beaumont (Tex.) Art Mus., 1963. Danforth Found. tchr. grantee, 1957; Recipient Purchase award Ohio Printmakers Assn., Dayton (Ohio) Mus., 1951. Mem. Renaissance Soc. Am., Coll. Art Assn. Am. Home: 838 Spruce St Boulder CO 80302 *During my career in art and its history, I have come to realize in a deeper sense that people are more important than artifacts, and that underlying all values and meaningful human relationships is the working of an infinite and personal God. The great possibilities in any human creative effort can only be understood in this light.*

DAY, ROBERT J., mineral company executive; b. 1925. B.A., Pa. State U., 1947. With U.S. Gypsum Co., 1950—, dist. sales mgr., 1956, mktg. mgr. steel products, 1958, staff mktg. mgr. plastering materials, 1960, mdse. mgr., 1961, dir. product mgmt., 1966, div. gen. mgr. western div., Los Angeles, 1969, corporate v.p. mktg., 1974-77, sr. v.p., 1977-79, exec. v.p., 1979-81, pres., chief operating officer, 1981—, also dir. Served to capt. USAFR, 1943-45, 51-53. Address: U S Gypsum 101 S Wacker Dr Chicago IL 60606

DAY, ROBERT JAMES, magazine cartoonist; b. San Bernardino, Calif., Sept. 25, 1900; s. James Anderson and Estelle Strowbridge (Brooks) D.; m. Ethel H. Fabian, Aug. 29, 1904; children: Estelle E., James Anderson II. Student, Otis Art Inst., 1919-27. Mem. art dept. Los Angeles Times, 1919-27, Los Angeles Examiner, 1927-29, N.Y. Herald Tribune, 1930. Contbr.: other nat. mags. Punch, advt. campaigns nat. corps., cartoons exhibited throughout, U.S., Europe.; Author: All Out for the Sack Race, 1945; Illustrator: We Shook the Family Tree, 1946, Fun Fare, 1949, Lower Prices Are Coming, 1950, (Arthur Godfrey) Stories I Like to Tell, 1952, (Dorothy Rickard) Little Willie, 1953, (William Zunsser) Any Old Place With You, 1957, Seen Any Good Movies Lately, 1958, (Jack Olsen) The Mad World of Bridge, 1960, (Jonathan Rhodes) Over the Fence is Out, 1961, (Cory Ford) What Every Bachelor Knows, 1961, (Jane Goodsell) I've Only Got Two Hands and I'm Busy Wringing Them, 1966, (Leo Rosten) Rome Wasn't Burned in a Day, 1972. Address: Route 1 Gravette AR 72736

DAY, ROBERT WINSOR, medical center official; b. Framingham, Mass., Oct. 22, 1930; s. Raymond Albert and Mildred (Doty) D.; m. Jane Alice Boynton, Sept. 6, 1957 (div. Sept. 1977); children: Cristopher, Nathalia; m. Cynthia Taylor, Dec. 16, 1977. Student, Harvard U., 1949-51; M.D., U. Chgo., 1956; M.P.H., U. Calif. at Berkeley, 1958, Ph.D., 1962. Intern USPHS Hosp., Balt., 1956-57; resident U. Calif., Berkeley, 1958-60; research specialist Calif. Dept. Mental Hygiene, 1960-64; asst. prof. Sch. Medicine, U. Calif. at Los Angeles, 1962-64; dep. dir. Calif. Dept. Pub. Health, 1965-67; prof., chmn. dept. health services Sch. Pub. Health and Community Medicine, U. Wash., Seattle, 1968-72, dean, 1972-82, dean emeritus, 1982—; dir. Fred Hutchinson Cancer Research Center, Seattle, 1981—; cons. Govt. Affairs Inst., Washington, Battelle Meml. Inst., Northwest Labs., 1970—; Pres. Seattle Planned Parenthood Center, 1970-72. Served with USPHS, 1956-57. Fellow Am. Pub. Health Assn., Am. Coll. Preventive Medicine; mem. Soc. Pediatric Research. Office: Fred Hutchinson Cancer Research Ctr 1124 Columbia St Seattle WA 98104

DAY, ROLAND BERNARD, justice Wis. Supreme Ct.; b. Oshkosh, Wis., June 11, 1919; s. Peter Oliver and Joanna King (Wescott) D.; m. Mary Jane Purcell, Dec. 18, 1948; 1 dau., Sarah Jane. B.A., U. Wis., 1942, J.D., 1947. Bar: Wis. bar 1947. Trainee Office Wis. Atty. Gen., 1947; asso. mem. firm Maloney & Wheeler, Madison, Wis., 1947-49; 1st asst. dist. atty., Dane County, Wis., 1949-52; partner firm Day, Goodman, Madison, 1953-57; firm Wheeler, Van Sickle, Day & Anderson, Madison, 1959-74; legal counsel mem. staff Sen. William Proxmire, Washington, 1957-58; justice Wis. Supreme Ct., 1974—; Mem. Madison Housing Authority, 1960-64, chmn., 1961-63; regent U. Wis. System, 1972-74. Served with AUS, 1943-46. Mem. Am. Bar Assn., State Bar Wis., Am. Trial Lawyers Assn., Am. Judicature Soc., Ygdrasil Lit. Soc. (pres. 1968). Mem. United Ch. of Christ. Clubs: Madison, Madison Lit. Home: 4806 Sherwood Rd Madison WI 53711 Office: Supreme Ct Chambers State Capitol Madison WI 53702

DAY, STACEY BISWAS, physician, educator, author; b. London, Dec. 31, 1927; s. Satis B. and Emma L. (Camp) D.; m. Noor Kassam Kanji, May 6, 1952 (div. 1969); children: Kahlil A., Selim M.; m. Nasreen Y. Fazelbhoy, June 7, 1970 (div. 1973); m. Ivana Podvalova, Oct. 18, 1973. M.D., Royal Coll. Surgeons, Dublin, Ireland, 1955; Ph.D., McGill U., 1964; D.Sc., Cin. U., 1971. Intern King's County Hosp., State U. N.Y. Downstate Center, 1955-56; resident fellow in surgery U. Minn. Hosp., 1956-60; hon. registrar St. George's Hosp., London, Eng., 1960-61; lectr. exptl. surgery McGill U., Montreal, Que., Can., 1964; asst. prof. exptl. surg. U. Cin. Med. Sch., 1968-70; assoc. dir. basic med. research Shriner's Burn Inst., Cin., 1969-71; asso. prof. pathology, head Bell Museum Pathobiology U. Minn., Mpls., 1970-74; dir. biomed. communications and med. edn. Sloan-Kettering Inst., N.Y.C., 1974-80; mem. Sloan-Kettering Inst. for Cancer Research, 1974-80; mem. adminstrv. council, field coordinator, 1974-75; prof. biology Sloan Kettering div. Grad. Sch. Med. Sci. Cornell U., ret., 1980; clin. prof. medicine div. behavioral medicine N.Y. Med. Coll., from 1980; prof. biopsychosocial medicine, chmn. dept. comunity health U. Calabar Sch. Medicine, Calabar, Nigeria, 1982—; Arris and Gale lectr. Royal Coll. Surgeons, Eng., 1972, vis. lectr., Ireland, 1972; vis. prof. U. Bologna, 1977; vis. prof. health communications U. Santiago, Chile, 1979-80; vis. prof. Oncologic Research Inst., Tallinn, Estonia, 1976, All India Insts. Health, 1976, Univ. Maiduguri, 1982; moderator med. cartography and computer health Harvard U., 1978; cons. Pan Am. Health Assn., 1974—, U.S.-USSR Agreement for Health Cooperation, 1976; pres., chmn., pub.

Cultural and Ednl. Prodns., Montreal, U.S.A., 1966—; advisor to dean Med. Coll., Faculty Medicine and Health Scis., ABHA, Province of Asir, Saudi Arabia, 1981; bd. dirs., v.p. Am. sci. activities Mario Negri Research Found., 1975-80; pres., exec. dir. Internat. Found. for Biosocial Devel. and Human Health, 1978—; cons. Inst. Health, Lyfford Cay, Bahamas, 1981, Govt. Cross River State, Nigeria, Itreto State, Nat. Bd. Advs., Am. Biog. Inst., 1982—; founder, cons. Primary Self-Health Clinics, Oban, Ikot Oku Okono, and Ikot Imo, Nigeria, 1982—. Writer, 1965—; Author: verse Collected Lines, 1966; play By the Waters of Babylon, 1966; verse American Lines, 1967; play The Music Box, 1967; Three Folk Songs Set to Music, 1967, Poems and Etudes, 1968; novel Rosalita, 1968; The Idle Thoughts of a Surgical Fellow, 1968, Edward Stevens-Gastric Physiologist, Physician and American Statesman, 1969; novella Bellechasse, 1970; A Leaf of the Chaatim, 1970, Ten Poems and a Letter from America for Mr. Sinha, 1971, Curling's Ulcer: An Experiment of Nature, 1972, Tuluak and Amaulik: Dialogues on Death and Mourning with the Innuit Eskimo of Point Barrow and Wainwright, Alaska, 1974, East of the Navel and Afterbirth: Reflections from Rapa Nui, 1976, Health Communications, 1979, The Biopsychosocial Imperative, 1981, What Is Survival? The Physician's Way and the Biologos, 1981; editor: Death and Attitudes Toward Death, 1972, Membranes, Viruses and Immune Mechanisms in Experimental and Clinical Disease, 1972, Ethics in Medicine in a Changing Society, 1973, Communication of Scientific Information, 1975, Trauma: Clinical and Biological Aspects, 1975, Molecular Pathology, 1975; (with Robert A. Good) series Comprehensive Immunology, 9 vols., 1976-80; Cancer Invasion and Metastasis-Biologic Mechanisms and Therapy, 1977, Some Systems of Biological Communication, 1977, Image of Science and Society, 1977, What Is a Scientist, 1978, Sloan Kettering Inst. Cancer Series, 1974-80; editor-in-chief, mem. editorial bd.: Health Communications and Informatics, 1974-80; editor-in-chief: The American Biomedical Network: Health Care System in America Present and Past, 1978, A Companion to the Life Sciences, Vol. 1, 1979, A Companion to the Life Sciences, Vol. 2: Integrated Medicine, 1980, A Companion to the Life Sciences, Vol. 3: Life Stress, 1981, Advance to Biopsychosocial Health, 1984; editor-in-chief, mem. editorial bd.: Health Communications and Biopsycho. Social Health; editor: (with others) Cancer, Stress and Death, 1979, Computers for Medical Office and Patient Management, 1981, Readings in Oncology, 1980, Biopsychosocial Health, 1981; mem. editorial bd.: Psyche et Cancer, Switzerland, Psychoonocologia (Eupsycha); also co-editor various publs.; contbr. articles to profl. lit. Served with Brit. Army, 1946-49. Recipient Moynihan medal Assn. Surgeons Gt. Britain and Ireland, 1960, Reuben Harvey triennial prize Royal Coll. Physicians, Ireland, 1957, Disting. scholar award Internat. Communication Assn., 1980; recipient Sama Found. medal, 1982; named Ky. col., Chieftan Ntufam Ajan of Oban Oban People, Cross River State, Nigeria, 1983; recipient Chieftan Obong Nsong Idem Ibibio, Nigeria, 1983, Mgbe (Ekpe) honor, Nigeria, commendation WHO address Fed. Govt. Nigeria, Calabar, 1983, addresses presented by people of Ikot Imo, Nsit Anyang, Oban, 1982-84; Ciba fellow, Can., 1965. Fellow Zool. Soc. London, Royal Micros. Soc., Royal Soc. Health, World Acad. Arts and Scis., Japanese Found. for Biopsychosocial Health (internat. hon. fellow and most disting. mem.); mem. Am. Burn Assn., Internat. Burn Assn., Can. Authors Assn., N.Y. Acad. Scis., AAAS, AMA, Am. Assn. History Medicine, Am. Inst. Stress (dir.), Am. Anthrop. Assn., Am. Rural Health Assn. (v.p. internat. sci. affairs, dir.), Am. Cybernetics Assn., Soc. Med. Anthropology, Arctic Soc. N.Am., Harvey Soc., Council Biology Editors, Musk Ox Circle, Sigma Xi, numerous others. Club: U. Minn. Alumni (charter). Research in field. Home: 6 Lomond Ave Spring Valley NY 10977 Office: U Calabar Coll Med Scis Calabar Nigeria W Africa *I have tried to assimilate all that is good in many cultures and to bring about a synthesis of these expressions in my own life and writings. It is as if I must find a third eye that can see what is best in all men, to integrate them newly into a changing world, and to be as much a releasing force as to be an absorbing force.*

DAY, STANLEY R., construction company executive; b. 1925; married. B.A., Kenyon Coll., 1948. Exec. Aluminum Alloys Corp., 1948-66; bus. cons., Detroit, 1966—; chmn. bd. Champion Home Builders Co., 1977—, also dir. Office: Builders Co 5573 North St Dryden MI 48428

DAY, THOMAS BRENNOCK, educational administrator; b. N.Y.C., Mar. 7, 1932; s. Frederick and Alice (Brennock) D.; m. Anne Kohlbrenner, Sept. 5, 1953; children: Erica, Monica, Mark. B.S., U Notre Dame, 1953; Ph.D., Cornell U., 1957. Prof. U. Md., College Park, 1964-78, vice chancellor for acad. planning and policy, 1970-77, spl. asst. to pres., 1977-78, vice chancellor for acad. affairs Baltimore County, 1977-78; pres. San Diego State U., 1978—; cons. Bendix Corp., IBM Corp., Digital Equipment Corp.; vis. physicist Brookhaven Nat. Lab., 1963; cons. Argonne Nat. Lab., Ill., 1967. Contbr. articles to profl. jours. Mem. Am. Acad. Polit. and Social Sci., Am. Phys. Soc., Sigma Xi, Phi Kappa Phi. Republican. Roman Catholic. Lodge: Rotary. Office: Office of Pres San Diego U. San Diego CA 92182

DAY, TIMOTHY TOWNLEY, food company executive; b. Bklyn., May 9, 1937; s. David M. and Janice F. (Fowler) D.; children—Leslie, Timothy, Bryan. B.A., Wesleyan U., Middletown, Conn., 1959; M.B.A., Harvard, 1964. Fin. exec. Trans World Airlines, 1964-68; v.p., treas. Gen. Host Corp., N.Y.C., 1968-72, group v.p., 1972-79, exec. v.p., 1979-81; pres. Cudahy Foods Co. subs. Gen. Host Corp., 1975-81; pres., chief exec. officer Bar-S Foods Co., 1981—; Bd. dirs. Am. Meat Inst., 1976—. Co-author: Mangement of Racial Integration in Business, 1964. Served as officer USMC, 1959-61. Mem. Young Presidents Orgn., Chi Psi. Home: 5344 E Valle Vista Rd Phoenix AZ 85018 Office: 3443 N Central Ave Suite 1700 Phoenix AZ 85012

DAY, WILLIAM HUDSON, mechanical engr., turbomachinery company executive; b. Lynn, Mass., Feb. 4, 1937; s. Hudson Smith and Annie (Reynolds) D.; m. Susan Phelps, July 22, 1961; children: Andrew, Carolyn. B.M.E., Cornell U., 1960; M.S. in M.E., Poly. Inst. N.Y., 1966, Ph.D., 1970. Mgr. high temp. turbine project Gen. Electric Gas Turbine Div., Schenectady, 1967-71, mgr. systems engring., 1971-73, mgr. advanced product planning, 1973-77, mgr. advanced programs, 1977-79; v.p. advanced programs United Technologies, Hartford, conn., 1979-81; exec. v.p. Elliott Co., Jeanette, Pa., 1981—. Inventor in field; contbr. articles to profl. jours. Pres. Woodhaven Homeowners Assn., Scotia, N.Y., 1973-75; scoutmaster Boy Scouts Am., 1977-79; bd. dirs. Boy Scouts, Greensburg, Pa., 1983—. Served to 2d lt. U.S. Army, 1960-61. Mem. ASME. Republican. Home: 107 Rocky Dr Greensburg PA 15601 Office: Elliott Co N 4th St Jeannette PA 15644

DAY, WÖRDEN, sculptor, printmaker; b. Columbus, Ohio; d. Daniel E. and Amelia (Worden) D. M.A., NYU; student, Maurice Sterne, Vytlacil, Hoffmann, Hayter. Tchr. Va. Commonwealth U., U. Wyo., State U. Iowa, Pratt Inst., New Sch., Art Students League N.Y. Exhibited solo shows, Perls Gallery, Bertha Schaefer Gallery, Krasner Gallery, Grand Central Moderns, Smithsonian Instn., U. Minn., Cin., Norfolk and Balt. museums art, Va. Mus. Fine Arts, Phila. Art Alliance, Sculpture Center, N.Y., 1972, duo exhbn. sculpture, Montclair Art Mus., 1970; represented permanent collections, Mus. Modern Art, N.Y.C., Nat. Mus. Am. Art, Washington, Whitney Mus., Bklyn. Mus., Library of Congress, Phila. Mus. Art, Met. Mus. Art, many others. Guggenheim-Rosenwald fellow, 1951-53, 61-62. Mem. Fedn. Modern Painters and Sculptors, Sculptors Guild. Home: 427 Bloomfield Ave Montclair NJ 07042 *Art chose me when I was eight; I knew my life's journey from that date. Through weathers, wind and storm. When I shaped it, it shaped me, into larger and larger wholes, Eternally challenging, Forever encountering Today as now.*

DAYANANDA, MYSORE ANANTHAMURTHY, educator, engr.; b. Mysore City, India, July 1, 1934; came to U.S., 1958; s. Tekhalli Srinivasarao and Kapila Ananthamurthy; m. Prema Kumari Rao, July 5, 1972; 1 dau., Ila. B.Sc. with honors, Mysore U., 1955; D.I.I.Sc., Indian Inst. Sci., 1957; M.S., Purdue U., 1961, Ph.D., 1965. Sr. research asst. Indian Inst. Sci., Bangalore, 1957-58; postdoctoral research asso. Purdue U., 1965-66, asst. prof. materials engring., 1966-70, asso. prof., 1970-75, prof., 1975—; vis. prof. U. Munster, W. Ger., 1980. Contbr. articles to profl. jours. Fellow Am. Inst. Chemists; mem. Am. Inst. Mining, Metall. and Petroleum Engrs., Am. Soc. Metals, Microbeam Analysis Soc., AAAS, Am. Soc. Engring. Edn., Sigma Xi. Home: 461 Cumberland Ave West Lafayette IN 47906 Office: Sch Materials Engring Purdue U West Lafayette IN 47907 *Life in its limitless forms and manifestations offers man all opportunities for discovering its mysteries as well as his own. It is only through playing the game of Life and meeting its challenges that one embarks on the path of self-improvement, seeks self-fulfillment and travels towards the goal of universal knowledge and wisdom. My journey through life has so far taught me that disciplined effort and steady perseverance are the main requisites for success in any human endeavor.*

DAYNARD, JOHN A., retail executive; b. Amsterdam, N.Y., Feb. 9, 1929; s. Elwood L. and Isabel (Westall) D.; m. Dorothy Louise Shafer, May 14, 1948; children: Leslie, Andrew, April, Kelly, Kenneth, Courtney, Erin, Connie L., Lauren I. Grad. advanced mgmt. program., Harvard Bus. Sch., 1976. With Montgomery Ward & Co., Inc., 1945—, sr. vice-pres. Western region, 1980—; dir. Montgomery Ward Marcor, 1977—. Active Boy Scouts Am., United Way; mem. Pres. Reagan's Task Force. Mem. Calif. Retail Assn. (dir.). Republican. Methodist. Club: Diablo Country. Home: 265 Montair Dr Danville CA 94526 Office: 2825 E 14th St Oakland CA 94616

DAYTON, KENNETH NELSON, retail merchandise company executive; b. Mpls., July 20, 1922; s. G. Nelson and Grace (Bliss) D.; m. Julia Davis Winton, June 12, 1953; children: Judson McDonald, Duncan Nelson. B.A., Yale, 1944. With Dayton's, Mpls., 1946-65, gen. mdse. mgr., 1950-54, v.p., gen. mdse. mgr., 1954-65; exec. v.p., gen. mgr. Dayton Corp., Mpls., 1965-67, exec. v.p., 1967-69; pres. Dayton Hudson Corp., Mpls., 1969-74, chmn., 1974-77, chmn. exec. com., 1977—, also dir.; dir. N.W. Bancorp., Northwestern Nat. Bank, Gen. Mills, Inc., 1968-80; Bd. dirs. Rockefeller Found., 1977—, Mayo Found., 1977—, Mpls. Found., 1973—. Bd. dirs. Minn. Orchestral Assn., 1947-71, 73-75, 79—, pres., 1953-55; trustee Ordway Music Theatre, 1982, Carnegie Hall, 1983; mem. Bus. Com. for Arts, 1968-82, Nat. Council on Arts, 1970-76, Minn. State Arts Bd., 1971-77; vice-chairperson Ind. Sector, 1980—. Served with AUS, 1943-46. Office: 777 Nicollet Mall Minneapolis MN 55402

DAYTON, SAMUEL GREY, JR., investment banker; b. Media, Pa., Feb. 3, 1921; s. Samuel Grey and Mary S. (Wurts) D.; m. Frances Imbrie, June 17, 1943 (dec. Oct. 1974); children—Alice S., Samuel Grey 3d, Andrew I. A.B., Princeton U., 1943. Pres. Dayton Inc. (option specialists), Phila.; Partner Dayton, Fay, Heppe & Co. (investment broker, mems. Phila. Stock Exchange); mem. Phila. Stock Exchange; bd. govs., past pres. Phila.-Balt-Washington Stock Exchange. Served as lt. AUS, World War II. Mem. Fin. Analysts Phila., Nat. Assn. Securities Dealers (past dir. dist. 11), Phila. Securities Assn. Club: Bond (Phila.). Home: Cedar Hill Farm Box 317 Media PA 19063 Office: 1905 Architects Bldg 17th and Sansom Sts Philadelphia PA 19103

DAZEY, WILLIAM BOYD, lawyer; b. Chgo., Sept. 23, 1915; s. Alva William and Emma Mayo (Boyd) D.; m. Dolores Ann Melton, July 20, 1959; children: Barbara Ann Dazey Lantos, William Melton, Thomas Sumner, Daniel Putnam, Johnathan Mayo. Student, U. Ill., 1933; LL.B., Cumberland U., 1935. Bar: Tex. 1940. Ptnr. firm Godard & Dazey, Texas City, 1940-58; practiced in, Houston, 1960—; ptnr. firm Dazey & Newey, 1971-79. Bd. dirs. Galveston County chpt. ARC, 1947-58, Anti-Tb Assn. Galveston County, 1950-58. Served with U.S. Army, 1942-45. Decorated Bronze Star with oak leaf cluster, Purple Heart. Mem. Houston Bar Assn., ABA, State Bar Tex., Am. Judicature Soc., Legal Aid Soc. Harris County, UN Assn. Japan (cons.), UN Assn. Houston (pres.), Houston World Trade Assn. (dir.), Nat. Order Battlefield Commns., Tex. Internat. Trade Assn. (dir.), Tex. Assn. Steel Importers (hon.), Japan-Am. Soc. Houston (founder, past pres.), Phi Delta Theta. Democrat. Unitarian. Club: Houston Rotary. Home: 1029 Teresa Dr Houston TX 77055 Office: Buckley Bldg Suite 308 9225 Katy Freeway Houston TX 77024

D'AZZO, JOHN JOACHIM, electrical engineer, educator; b. N.Y.C., Nov. 30 1919; s. Domenick and Jacqueline (Capello) D'A.; m. Betty G. McBride, June 13, 1953; 1 son, Dennis. B.E.E., CCNY, 1941; M.S. E.E., Ohio State U., Columbus, 1950; Ph.D., Salford U., Eng., 1978. Registered profl. engr., Ohio. Quality control engr. Western Electric Co., Kearney, N.J., 1941-42; devel. engr. Air Material Command, Wright-Patterson AFB, Ohio, 1942-46; prof. elec. engring., dep. dept. head Air Force Inst. Tech., Wright-Patterson AFB, Ohio, 1947—. Author: Feedback Control System Analysis & Synthesis, 1960, (2d edit.) Feedback Control System Analysis & Synthesis, 1966, Linear Control System Analysis and Design, 1975, (2d edit.) Linear Control system Analysis and Design, 1981. Served to 2d lt. U.S. Army, 1945-46. Named Outstanding Engr. Affiliate Socs. Ohio, 1962. Fellow IEEE; mem. AIAA, Tau Beta Pi, Eta Kappa Nu. Roman Catholic. Home: 3923 Winthrop Dr Dayton OH 54531 Office: Air Force Inst Tech AFIT-ENG Wright-Patterson AFB OH 45433 *The spread of fundemental knowledge to new generations is a necessary task. Assisting individuals in developing approaches for applying theoretical results to practical applications is very rewarding. This must be done with understanding for the individual as a person.*

DEACON, PAUL SEPTIMUS, publisher; b. Toronto, Ont., Can., June 9, 1922; s. Frederick Herbert and Ethel Record (Emmerson) D.; m. Charlotte Adelle Smith, Feb. 25, 1950; children—Anne, Wendy, James, Andrew, Jennifer. B.A., U. Toronto, 1943, M.Com., 1947. With The Financial Post, Toronto, 1947-79, Eastern editor, Montreal, 1949-52, investment editor, Toronto, 1952-64, editor, 1964-77, pub., 1968-79; v.p. Maclean Hunter Bus. Pub. Co., Ottawa, Ont., 1979-82, Maclean Hunter Ltd., 1982—, also dir.; Pres. Nat. Ballet of Can., 1975-78; mem. adv. council Faculty Adminstrv. Studies, York U., Toronto; pres. Toronto Soc. Fin. Analysts, 1961-62. Served as pilot RCAF, 1942-45. Mem. United Ch. of Can. Clubs: Royal Ottawa Golf, Rideau, Canadian (Ottawa) (pres. 1982-83); University, Rosedale Golf (Toronto). Home: 112 Acacia Ave Rockcliffe Park Ottawa ON K1M 0P9 Canada Office: 151 Sparks St Room 309 Ottawa ON K1P 5E3 Canada

DEACY, THOMAS EDWARD, JR., lawyer; b. Kansas City, Mo., Oct. 14, 1918; s. Thomas Edward and Grace (Scales) D.; m. Jean Freeman, July 10, 1943; children: Bennette Kay Deacy Kramer, Carolyn G., Margaret Deacy Vickrey, Thomas, Ann. J.D., U. Mo., 1940; M.B.A., U. Chgo., 1949. Bar: Mo. 1940, Ill. 1946. Practice law, Kansas City, 1940-42; partner firm Taylor, Miller, Busch & Magner, Chgo., 1946-55, Deacy & Deacy, Kansas City, 1955—; lectr. Northwestern U., 1949-55, U. Chgo., 1950-55; dir., mem. exec. com. St. L.-S.F. Ry., 1962-80; dir. Burlington No. Inc., 1980—; mem. U.S. team Anglo-Am. Legal Exchange, 1973, 77; mem. com. on problems of discovery Fed. Jud. Center, 1976—. Mem. Juvenile Protective Assn. Chgo., 1947-55, pres., bd. dirs., 1950-53; mem. exec. bd. Chgo. council Boy Scouts Am., 1952-55; pres. Kansas City Philharmonic Orch., 1961-63, chmn. bd. trustees, 1963-65; trustee Sunset Hill Sch., 1963-73; trustee, mem. exec. com. U. Kansas City, 1963—; trustee Mo. Law Sch. Found., pres., 1973—. Served to capt. AUS, 1942-45. Fellow Am. Coll. Trial Lawyers (regent 1968—, treas. 1973-74, pres. 1975-76), Am. Bar Found; mem. Am. Law Inst., Jud. Conf. U.S. (implementation com. on admission of attys. to fed. practice 1979—), ABA (commn. standards jud. adminstrn. 1972-74, standing com. fed. judiciary 1974-80), Ill. Bar Assn., Chgo. Bar Assn., Mo. Bar Assn., Kansas City Bar Assn., Lawyers Assn. Kansas City, Beta Gamma Sigma, Sigma Chi. Clubs: Chgo. (Chgo.); Univ., Kansas City, Kansas City Country, River (Kansas City, Mo.). Home: 2722 Verona Circle Mission Hills KS 66208 Office: Bryant Bldg Kansas City MO 64106

DEAK, ISTVAN, historian; b. Szekesfehervar, Hungary, May 11, 1926; came to U.S., 1956, naturalized, 1962; s. Istvan and Anna (Timar) D.; m. Gloria Gilda Alfano, July 4, 1959; 1 dau., Eva. Student, U. Budapest, 1945-48, Sorbonne, 1950-51, U. Md., Munich, W. Ger., 1953-55; M.A., Columbia U., 1958, Ph.D., 1964. Journalist, librarian and bookseller, Budapest, Paris and Munich, 1945-56; instr. history Smith Coll., 1962-63; mem. faculty Columbia U., 1963—, prof. history, 1973—; dir. Inst. E. Central Europe, 1967-78; mem. Inst. Advanced Study, Princeton, N.J., fall 1981. Author: Weimar Germany's Left-Wing Intellectuals: A Political History of the Weltbühne and Its Circle, 1968, The Lawful Revolution; Louis Kossuth and the Hungarians, 1848-1849, 1979; Co-editor: Eastern Europe in the 1970's, 1972, Everyman in Europe: Essays in Social History, 2 vols., 2d edit, 1981. Recipient Lionel Trilling Book award Columbia U., 1979; German Acad. exchange fellow, 1960-61; Guggenheim fellow, 1970-71; Fulbright-Hays travel fellow, 1973. Mem. Mid-Atlantic Slavic Assn. (pres. 1977-78), Am. Assn. Study Hungarian History (chmn. 1980-81), Am. Hist. Assn., Am. Assn. Advancement Slavic Studies. Democrat. Home: 410 Riverside Dr New York NY 10025 Office: 1229 Internat Affairs Bldg Columbia U New York NY 10027

DEAK, NICHOLAS LOUIS, banker; b. Hateg, Hungary, Oct. 8, 1905; came to U.S., 1939, naturalized, 1943; s. Louis and Malvine (Billitz) D.; m. Liselotte Maria Potter, Dec. 21, 1939; 1 son, Robert Leslie. Grad., Acad. World Trade, Vienna, 1925; Ph.D. in Econs. and Finance, U. Neuchatel, Switzerland, 1929. With Royal Hungarian Trade Inst., 1930-35; mgr. Hungarian and Rumanian subsidiaries Brit. Overseas Bank, 1935-37; with econs. dept. League of Nations, Geneva, 1937-39; prof. econs. and internat. affairs Perkiomen Coll. Prep. Sch., Pennsburg, Pa., 1940-41, trustee, 1969—, chmn. bd. trustees, 1972; instr. econs. Coll. City N.Y., 1941-42; with Dept. State, 1945-46; chmn. Deak & Co., Inc., N.Y.C., 1946-80, chmn. bd., 1980—; pres. Deak Nat. Bank, Fleischmanns, N.Y., 1958—; chmn. bd. Perera Co., Inc., 1953—; prin. Bankhaus Deak & Co. Ltd., Vienna, 1968—; adj. prof. internat. finance Fairleigh Dickinson U., Teaneck, N.J., 1970-72; mem. faculty Am. Bankers Assn. Sch., U. Okla., 1972-79; adj. prof. N.Y. Law Sch., 1975; Vice pres. Internat. Comml. Exchange N.Y., 1970-74; bd. mgrs. N.Y. Produce Exchange, 1974; bd. dirs. N.Y. Futures Exchange of N.Y. Stock Exchange, 1980-83; mem. N.Y. Merc. Exchange, Chgo. Internat. Monetary Market of Merc. Exchange Chgo. Bd. dirs. Am.-Hungarian Found., Portuguese Am. Soc. Served to maj. AUS, 1942-46. Mem. Am. Bankers Assn. (chmn. internat. comml. lending div. 1974-76), AAUP, N.Y. C. of C. and Industry (chmn. export finance com.), Brit.-Am. (dir.), Danish chambers commerce, Am. Portuguese Cultural Soc., Newcomen Soc. N.Am., Econ. Research Round Table, Vets. of OSS (pres. 1974-75). Clubs: Downtown Athletic, N.Y. Athletic (N.Y.C.); Westchester Country, Touring de France (U.S. del.). Home: 24 Heathcote Rd Scarsdale NY 10583 Office: 29 Broadway New York NY 10006 also 111 Broad St Stamford CT

DEAKIN, DOUGLAS EDWARD, oil company executive; b. Edmonton, Alta., Can., June 21, 1938; s. Edward Thomas and Helen Irene (Stackhouse) D.; m. Helen E. Stakich, Sept. 11, 1959; children: Laurie Marie, Barbara Lee. B.Com., U. Alta., 1959. Chartered acct., 1962. Income tax assessor Dept. Nat. Revenue, 1959-66; income tax specialist Pan Am. Petroleum Corp., 1966-69; with Home Oil Co. Ltd., Calgary, Alta., 1969—, v.p., treas., 1978-80, v.p. fin., 1980—, treas., 1982—; treas. Scurry-Rainbow Oil Ltd. Mem. Tax Execs. Inst. (past pres. Calgary chpt.), Fin. Execs. Inst. Progressive Conservative. Anglican. Clubs: Pinebrook Golf and Country, Calgary Petroleum. Office: 324 8th Ave SW Calgary AB T2P 2Z5 Canada

DEAKIN, JAMES, writer, former newspaperman; b. St. Louis, Dec. 3, 1929; s. Rogers and Dorothy (Jeffrey) D.; m. Doris Marie Kanter, Apr. 14, 1956; 1 son, David Andrew. A.B., Washington U., St. Louis, 1951. Mem. staff St. Louis Post-Dispatch, 1951-81, Washington corr., 1953-80, White House corr., 1955-80; adj. asso. prof. journalism George Washington U., 1981—; fellow Woodrow Wilson Internat. Center for Scholars, 1980-81. Author: the Lobbyists, 1966, Lyndon Johnson's Credibility Gap, 1968, Straight Stuff, 1984; co-author: Smiling Through The Apocalypse, 1971, The Presidency and The Press, 1976, The American Presidency, Principles and Problems, Vol. II, 1983, The White House Press on the Presidency, 1983; also numerous articles. Recipient Distinguished Alumnus citation Washington U., 1973, Merriman Smith award for White House reporting, 1977; Markle Found. grantee, 1981. Mem. White House Corrs. Assn. (pres. 1974-75). Home: 6406 Whittier Ct Bethesda MD 20817 Office: Dept Journalism George Washington U Washington DC 20052

DEAKINS, JOHN DAVID, iron works executive; b. Kansas City, Mo., Sept. 12, 1942; s. John A. and M. Phyllis (Mast) D.; m. Beth L. Beamer, June 5, 1965; children: Derrick, David, Jennifer. B.S.M.E., U. Kans., 1965; M.S.M.E., U Kans., 1966; M.B.A., U. Pa., 1972. Diplomate: registered profl. engr., C.P.A. Mgr. treasury ops. Cameron Iron Works, Inc., Houston, 1975-80, v.p. fin., 1980-82, sr. v.p. fin., chief fin. officer, 1982—. Trustee Cypress-Fairbanks Ind. Sch. Dist., Houston, 1982—. Mem. Fin. Execs. Inst. (dir. Houston chpt. 1979-81), Am Inst. C.P.A.'s, Tex Soc. C.P.A.'s (membership com. 1983—), Tex. Soc. Profl. Engrs., Soc. Petroleum Engrs. Methodist. Office: Cameron Iron Works Inc PO Box 1212 Houston TX 77251

DEAKINS, WARREN WHITNEY, insurance company executive; b. Albuquerque, May 13, 1938; s. Warren Whitney and Nelleva (Booth) D.; m. Nancy J. Reynolds, June 21, 1959; children: Peter, Teri, Jay, Karen. B.S., Oreg. State U., Corvallis, 1959. Agt. Conn. Gen. Life Ins. Co., Oakland, Calif., 1962-65, asst. mgr., 1965-67, Fidelity Mut. Life Ins. Co., San Francisco, 1967-68, mgr., 1968-73, dir. agys., Santa Ana, Calif., 1973-75; v.p. agys. Fidelity Life Ins. Co., Phila., 1975-77, sr. v.p. agys., 1977-81, exec. v.p., 1981—. Bd. dirs. Am. Diabetes Assn., Phila. Served to lt. USAF, 1959-62. Mem. Life Ins. Mktg. and Research Assn. (chmn. 1983—), Agy. Officers Round Table (chmn. 1980-81), Am. Soc. C.L.U.s. Republican. Episcopalian. Office: Fidelity Mut Group 250 King of Prussia Rd Radnor PA 19087

DEAL, ERNEST LINWOOD, JR., banker; b. Florence, Ala., Jan. 5, 1929; s. Ernest Linwood and Nell W. (Willingham) D.; m. Mary Cooper, Dec. 27, 1952; children: Theresa Lynn, Sarah Street, Matthew Cooper, Jennifer Willingham. Student, Florence State Coll., 1947-49; B.S., U. Ala., 1952; postgrad., Southwestern Grad. Sch. Banking, So. Meth. U., 1961. Vice pres. Tex. Commerce Bank, Houston, 1956-65; sr. v.p. Capital Nat. Bank, Houston, 1965-71; pres., chief exec. officer Fannin Bank, Houston, 1971-82, chmn., chief exec. officer, 1982, InterFirst Bank, 1983, First City Nat. Bank, 1984—; governing council, state v.p., govt. relations council Am. Bankers Assn., 1977-82; v.p., 1978-79; dir. Adobe Oil & Gas Corp., Midland., Muse Air Corp. Chmn. Houston Parks Bd.; bd. dirs. Park Plaza Hosp.; trustee Kinkaid Sch., Southwestern Grad. Sch. Banking; bd. visitors M.D. Anderson Hosp. Served to lt. (j.g.) USNR, 1952-55. Mem. U. Ala. Alumni Assn., Houston C. of C. (dir., exec. com.), Tex. Bankers Assn. (dir.), Phi Gamma Delta, Delta Sigma Pi, Omicron Delta Kappa. Presbyn. Clubs: Houston Country, Ramada. Office: PO Box 2555 Houston TX 77252

DEAL, GEORGE EDGAR, management consultant; b. Marion, Ind., July 31, 1920; s. Harold Everett and Esther Victoria (Kendall) D.; m. Ruth Florence McFarland, Nov. 4, 1945; children: Joan Victoria, Georgia Lynn, Sharon Louise, Frank Kendall, Susan Melanie, Marylise Tobin. Student, Marion Coll., 1937-39; B.S. with high distinction, Ind. U., 1941, M.S., 1942; postgrad., Am. U., 1942, Harvard U., 1943, Columbia U., 1948; D.B.A., George Washington U., 1970. Indsl. specialist WPB, 1942; dept. mgr. Macy's, N.Y.C., 1947-49; supt. Bloomingdale's, N.Y.C., 1949-53; v.p. The Kroger Co., Washington, 1953-63; asst. to pres. Bionetics Research Labs., Falls Church, Va., 1964-67; dir. Grad. Mgmt. Sch., Am. Mgmt. Assn., Saranac Lake, N.Y., 1967-69; sr. research asso. Logistics Mgmt. Inst., Washington, 1969-70; pres. Mgmt. Factors Orgn., McLean, Va., 1970—; asso. prof. Central Mich. U.; faculty study dir. Nat. Grad. U.; chmn. sec. navy's adv. bd. edn. and tng., 1972-75; spl. asst. to dir. LIFE Internat.; cons. mgmt. orgn., mgmt. edn. Author; contbr. articles to profl. jours. Mem. Greater Washington Health and Welfare Council, 1966-67; mem.-at-large Nat. council Boy Scouts Am. Served to capt. USNR, 1942-47, 50-52. Fellow Washington Acad. Scis.; mem. Nat. Council Assns. in Policy Scis. (steering com.), Councils Retail Mchts. (dir. Tenn. and Ala. councils 1954-60), Inst. of Mgmt., AAAS, Ops. Research Soc. Am. (asso. editor 1969-73), Acad. Mgmt., Strategic Mgmt. Soc., Am. Mktg. Assn., World Future Soc., Soc. for Internat. Devel., Am. Inst. Mgmt., Internat. Inst. Strategic Studies, Navy League U.S., Beta Gamma Sigma. Republican. Roman Catholic. Club: Mason. Home and Office: 6245 Park Rd McLean VA 22101 *Rainbows are currently explained away scientifically, but the rainbows that I consider important are those of the mind—the dreams that create progress, hold out helping hands, bring smiles to the faces of the weary, and hope to the unbelieving.*

DEAL, JOE, photographer; b. Topeka, Kans., Aug. 12, 1947; s. Percy Harold and Laura Jean (Close) D.; m. Barbara Eckstrom, Aug. 16, 1969 (div. 1978); m. Christine Bertelson, Aug. 8, 1981; 1 dau., Meredith Ivy. B.F.A., Kansas City Art Inst., Mo., 1970; M.A., U. N.Mex., 1974, M.F.A., 1978. Dir. exhbns. Internat. Mus. of Photography, George Eastman House, Rochester, N.Y., 1975-76; prof. art U. Calif., Riverside, 1976—. Artist portfolio: The Fault Zone, 1981. Nat. Endowment for Arts photographers fellow, 1976, 1981; Guggenheim fellow, 1983. Democrat. Address: 3540 Watkins Dr Riverside CA 82507

DEAL, LANHAM, educational administrator; b. San Angelo, Tex., Apr. 8, 1921; s. James Culberson and Mary Elizabeth (Bates) D.; m. Anne L. Hunt, Aug. 23, 1943; children: Mary Christina, Carol Lanham, Louise Deal Pluymen, Lanham C. B.S., So. Meth. U., 1943. Mgr. Dallas Symphony Orch., 1946-50; sr. ptnr. Southwestern Concert Service, Dallas, 1950-67; gen. mgr. Seattle Symphony Orch., 1967-81; dir. Ctr. Arts Adminstrn. So. Meth. U., Dallas, 1981—; cons., panelist Nat. Endowment Arts; cons. Am. Symphony Orch. League. Served to lt. USNR, 1943-46. Mem. Am. Soc. Composers, Authors and Pubs., Am. Symphony Orch. League (Sudler award 1980). Home: 9510 Fair Oaks #108 Dallas TX 75231

DEAL, WILLIAM BROWN, physician, university dean; b. Durham, N.C., Oct. 4, 1936; s. Harold Albert and Louise Brown D.; m. Elizabeth French Grayson, Aug. 30, 1958; children: Kimberly Cawthorne, Kathleen Louise. A.A., Mars Hill Coll., 1956; A.B., U. N.C., 1958, M.D., 1963. Intern Shands Hosp., Gainesville, Fla., 1963-64; chief resident, instr. dept. medicine U. Fla., Gainesville, 1969-70, mem. faculty, 1970—, prof., 1975—, assoc. dean Coll. Medicine, 1973-77, v.p. health affairs, dean Coll. Medicine, 1978-80, dean, assoc. v.p. clin. affairs Coll. Medicine, 1980—; dir. Univ. Med. Ctr., Jacksonville, Fla., mem. liaison com. on med. edn., 1982—; dir. Atlantic 1st Nat. Bank, Gainesville; dir., sec.-treas. Shands Teaching Hosp., Inc. Contbr. articles to med. jours. Served with USNR, 1964-66. Recipient Disting. Service award U. N.C., 1979. Fellow ACP; mem. AMA, Assn. Am. Med. Colls. (adminstrv. bd. council of deans 1981—), So. Council Med. Deans (chmn. 1982-83), Alpha Omega Alpha, Beta Theta Pi. Republican. Presbyterian. Clubs: Lake Point Tower; Cosmos (Washington). Office: Box J-215 J Hillis Miller Health Center Gainesville FL 32610

DEALE, HENRY VAIL, JR., librarian; b. Balt., May 14, 1915; s. Henry V. and Sarah Lippincott (Sisson) D.; m. Jane Niehaus, June 7, 1944; 1 dau., Sarah Deale Gaskin. Student, Dickinson Coll., 1931-33; B.A., DePauw U., 1936; M. L.S., U. Ill., 1937; M.A. in English, Drake U., 1947-50. Circulation asst., stack supt. Northwestern U. Library, 1937-39; circulation asst., pub. relations dir. Bloomington (Ill.) Pub. Library, 1939-41; civilian pub. service, 1941-45; asst. librarian Ripon (Wis.) Coll., 1946; reference librarian Drake U. Library, 1946-48, humanities librarian, 1948-51; librarian Ill. Wesleyan U., 1951-53; dir. libraries Beloit Coll., 1953-80, dir. libraries emeritus, 1980—; also prof., chmn. dept. library sci.; cons. acad. libraries, 1980—; Fulbright scholar Pahlavi U., Shiraz, Iran, 1965-66; Fulbright lectr. faculty U. Tehran, Iran, 1970-71; mem. Gov.'s Council on Library Devel., 1974-77. Editor: Library Trends, July 1969; Contbr. articles to profl. jours. Recipient emeritus citation Beloit Coll., 1980. Life mem. ALA (mem. council 1972-74, chmn. grants com. 1967-70, internat. relations com. 1975-77); mem. Ill. Library Assn., Iowa Library Assn., Wis. Library Assn. (pres. 1959-60), AAUP, Midwest Acad. Librarians (chmn. 1957-59), Assn. Coll. and Research Libraries (pres. coll. sect. 1964-65). Home: 1427 Chapin St Beloit WI 53511

DEALESSANDRO, JOSEPH PAUL, insurance company executive; b. Bklyn., Apr. 9, 1930; s. Peter Charles and Lucy Rose (Doganiero) DeA.; m. Dorothy Joan Sivillo, Nov. 7, 1962 (dec. 1966). Student, Bklyn. Coll., 1947-51, N.Y. U. Coll. Ins., 1958. Mgr. Am. Ins. Co., N.Y.C., 1952-60, Century Ins. Co., 1960-62, St. Paul Ins. Co., 1962-67; pres. Nat. Union Ins. Co., N.Y.C., 1967—, also dir.; sr. v.p., dir. Am. Internat. Underwriters, 1970—; exec. v.p., dir. Am. Home Assurance Co., 1973—; pres., dir. Am. Internat. Global Assistance Corp.; chmn. bd. Am. Internat. Group Polit. Risk Inc.; tchr., condr. seminars Coll. of Ins.; dir. Commerce & Industry Ins. Co., United Guarantee Corp., Greensboro, N.C. Contbg. author: The Insurance Business Handbook; Contbr. articles to ins. jours. Mem. Am. Mgmt. Assn., Am. Risk Mgrs. Assn. Roman Catholic. Clubs: Grand Centurians, K.C. Home: 725 Dorian Rd Westfield NJ 07090 Office: 70 Pine St New York NY 10005

DEALEY, JOSEPH MACDONALD, former newspaper executive; b. Dallas, July 18, 1919; s. Edward Musgrove and Clara (MacDonald) D.; m. Doris Carolyn Russell, Jan. 18, 1947; children: Joseph MacDonald, Russell Edward, Pamela Carolyn, Frances Patricia. A.B., U. Tex., 1941. Reporter Dallas Morning News, 1942-50, asst. sec., 1950-55, dir., 1952—, sec., 1955-60, pres., 1960-80; chmn. bd., chief exec. officer A.H. Belo Corp., 1980-83, chmn. bd., 1983-84. Pres. Dallas County chpt. ARC, 1961-63; vice chmn., mem. bd. govs. Am. Nat. Red Cross, 1968-74; mem. exec. com. Community Council Greater Dallas, 1960—, pres., 1965-66; bd. dirs. Dallas Citizens Council, 1960—, pres., 1964-65; bd. dirs. Children's Med. Center, 1950—, pres., 1964-67; bd. dirs. Dallas Council Social Agys., 1958—; trustee Dallas Theater Center; bd. dirs. Dallas County United Fund, 1961—, mem. exec. com., 1962—, v.p., 1963-65, pres., 1967, campaign chmn., 1966-67; bd. dirs. United Community Funds and Councils Am., 1967-69, Dallas County Hist. Found., 1983—; bd. dirs., pres. State Fair Tex., 1983; mem. U. Tex. Devel. Bd. and Chancellor's Council, 1965-77, chmn., 1967-68; trustee Trinity U., San Antonio, 1972-76; bd. elders Highland Park Presbyn. Ch., 1969—. Served to lt. USAAF, 1942-46. Mem. Dallas C. of C. (dir.), Am. Newspaper Pubs. Assn. (dir.), So. Newspaper Pubs. Assn. (dir., pres. 1969), Tex. Daily Newspaper Assn. (exec. com., pres. 1969), Press Club Dallas, Sigma Delta Chi, Phi Delta Theta. Clubs: Dallas Country, Koon Kreek, Las Colinas Country, Masons (33 deg.). Office: 8333 Douglas St Suite 1575 Dallas TX 75225

DE ALVAREZ, RUSSELL RAMON, obstetrician, gynecologist, educator; b. N.Y.C.; s. John and Isidora (Torres y Sanchez) de A.; m. Betty Jane Casey, Sept. 11, 1943; children: Ann, Russell Ramon (dec.). B.S., U. Mich., 1931, M.D., 1935, M.S., 1940. Diplomate: Am. Bd. Obstetrics and Gynecology (asso. examiner). Intern U. Mich. Hosp., 1935-36, resident, 1937-38, lectr. maternal and child health, 1939-44, attending staff, 1938-44; assoc. attending gynecologist U. Oreg. Hosps., 1946-48; lst prof. and head dept. obstetrics and gynecology U. Wash. Med. Sch., 1948-64; prof., chmn. dept. obstetrics and gynecology Temple U.; also obstetrician, gynecologist-in-chief Temple Univ. Hosp., Phila., 1964—; obstetrician and gynecologist in chief U. Wash. Hosps., also King County Hosp., 1948-64; cons. Phila. Gen. Hosp., VA Hosp.; cons. in obstetrics-gynecology to surgeon gen. U.S. Army, HEW; cons. toxemia task force NIH (also high blood pressure edn. research program); cons. Commn. on Profl. and Hosp. Activities; cons. on gynecology Phila. Health Dept.; Bd. dirs. Planned Parenthood Assn. of Southeastern Pa., 1976—; bd. dirs. Family Planning Council of Southeastern Pa.; also treas. Phila. div.; mem. vis. com. U. Mich. Med. Center, 1978—. Editorial bd.: Am. Jour. Obstetrics and Gynecology; editor-in-chief: Quar. Rev. Obstetrics and Gynecology; editor: Clinical Obstetrics and Gynecology; editor-in-chief: Textbook of Gynecology, The Kidney in Pregnancy; co-editor: Textbook of Obstetric-Gynecologic Terminology; assoc. editor: Textbook of Obstetrics and Perinatology; contbr. numerous articles to med. publs. Served as lt. comdr. USNR, 1944-46. Fellow A.C.S., Am. Coll. Obstetricians and Gynecologists (asst. sec. 1958-59), Soc. Gynecologic Investigation (pres. 1959); mem. AMA (cons. Current Procedural Terminology, 3d and 4th edits.), Am. Assn. Obstetricians and Gynecologists, Soc. E-P-H Gestosis (U.S. chmn.), Am. Fedn. Clin. Research, Central Assn. Obstetrics and Gynecology, Wash. Soc. Obstetrics and Gynecology (hon. mem.), Ore. Soc. Obstetrics and Gynecology, Seattle Gynecol. Soc. (hon. life, pres. 1961-62), Pan Am. Med. Assn. (U.S. v.p. for Ob-Gyn), Western Soc. Clin. Research, Obstet. Soc. Phila. (council 1968-71, 1st v.p. 1970-71, pres. 1972-73), Pacific Northwest Soc. Obstetricians and Gynecologists (pres. 1962-63, hon. life mem.), Am. Gynecol. Soc. (v.p.), Am. Coll. Obstetricians and Gynecologists (asst. sec.), Nurses Assn. Am. Coll. Obstetricians and Gynecologists (exec. bd.), Research Soc. U. Wash., Norman F. Miller Gynecologic Soc. (pres. 1962-63), Pa., Phila. County med. socs., Am. Soc. Human Genetics, Soc. Obstetrics and Gynecology Can., Washington Obstet. Soc., Reno Surg. Soc., Assn. Profs. Gynecology and Obstetrics, Am. Nephrology Soc., Soc. Reprodn., AAUP, Venezuelan Obstet. and Gynecol. Soc. (hon. mem.), N.J. Obstet. and Gynecol. Soc. (hon. mem.), Pacific Coast Obstet. and Gynecol. Soc., S.W. Obstet. and Gynecol. Soc., Los Angeles Obstet. and Gynecol. Soc., Pacific Northwest Obstet. and Gynecol. Soc. (hon. life mem.), Honolulu Obstet. and Gynecol. Soc., AAAS, Hollywood (Calif.) Acad. Medicine, Pacific N.W. Obstet. and Gynecol. Assn. (pres. 1962), U. Mich. Med. Alumni Soc. (bd. govs.), Am. Legion, Sigma Xi, Alpha Omega Alpha, Nu Sigma Nu. Clubs: University, College, Seattle Golf (Seattle); Union League, Doctors Golf, Wayfair (pres. 1976-78), Phila. Country (Phila.)). Home: 1213 Pine Wood Rd Villanova PA 19085 Office: 3401 Broad St Philadelphia PA 19140

DEALY, JOHN MICHAEL, chemical engineer; b. Waterloo, Iowa, Mar. 23, 1937; s. Milton David and Ruth Marion (Dorton) D.; m. Jacqueline Dery, Aug. 22, 1964; 1 dau., Pamela. B.S., U. Kans., 1958; M.S., U. Mich., 1959; Ph.D., 1963; Ph.D. postdoctoral fellow, 1964. Asst. prof. chem. engring. McGill U., Montreal, Que., Can., 1964-67, asso. prof., 1967-72, prof., 1972—; cons. indsl. rheology and polymer processing. Author book on plastics testing; contbr. articles to profl. jours. Research grantee, 1965—. Mem. Am. Inst. Chem. Engrs., Canadian Soc. Chem. Engring., Soc. Rheology, Soc. Plastics Engrs., Am. Soc. Engring. Edn., Am. Chem. Soc., Sigma Xi, Tau Beta Pi, Phi Lambda Upsilon, Phi Kappa Phi, Omicron Delta Kappa, Theta Tau. Home: 305 Grosvenor Ave Montreal H3Z 2M1 Canada Office: Chem Engring Dept McGill U 3480 University St Montreal PQ H3A 2A7 Canada

DEAN, ALAN LOREN, government official; b. Portland, Oreg., July 27, 1918; s. Claude Lorenzo and Alfhild (Jacobson) D.; m. Vera Alta Sisson, Jan. 9, 1944; children—Claudia, Diana, Laura. B.A. in Polit. Sci. Reed Coll., 1941; M.A. in Pub. Adminstrn, Am. U., 1955. Dir. civilian personnel Umatilla Ordnance Depot, Dept. War, 1941-43; insp. civilian personnel programs Office Sec. War, 1943-45; dir. Dept. War Sch. Civilian Personnel Adminstrn., 1946-47; sr. analyst govt. orgn. Bur. Budget, 1947-59; asst. adminstr. mgmt. services FAA, 1959-61, asso. adminstr. for adminstrn., 1961-67; asst. sec. adminstrn. Dept. Transp., 1967-71; dep. asst. dir. Office Mgmt. and Budget, 1971-72; spl. adviser to undersec. Health, Edn. and Welfare, 1973-74; v.p. for adminstrn. U.S. Ry. Assn., 1974-79; Mem. bd. gen. adminstrn. Dept. Agr. Grad. Sch., 1961-70; mem. Interagy. Adv. Com. on Mgmt. Improvement, 1960-66; chmn. Am. Consortium for Internat. Publ. Adminstrn., 1973-75, mem. exec. com., 1976—; mem. Pres.'s Mgmt. Improvement Council, 1979-80; Mem. bd. suprs. Arlington County, 1952, planning commn., 1958-60; pres. Fairlington Civic Assn., 1950-51, Donaldson Run Civic Assn., 1955-56. Trustee Reed Coll., Portland, Oreg.; mem. governing bd. Center for Adminstrn., Nova U., Fla., 1979—. Recipient award for meritorious civilian service Dept. War, 1945, Career Service award Nat. Civil Service League, 1965; Exceptional Service award FAA, 1965; Outstanding Service award Dept. Transp., 1969; Exceptional Service award Office Mgmt. and Budget, 1972. Mem. Am. Polit. Sci. Assn., Am. Soc. Pub. Adminstrn. (pres. D.C. chpt. 1961-62, nat. council 1962-66), Fed. Exec. Officers Group (chmn. 1959-66), Internat. Inst. Adminstrv. Scis. (v.p. 1974-80), Nat. Acad. Pub. Adminstrn. (trustee 1972-76, chmn. 1978—), Nat. Civil Service League (dir. 1975—), Nat. Inst. for Public Mgmt. (dir. 1977-80). Conglist. Club: Cosmos. (Washington). Home: 3037 N Stafford St Arlington VA 22207 Office: 1120 G St NW Suite 540 Washington DC 20005

DEAN, BEALE, lawyer; b. Ft. Worth, Feb. 26, 1922; s. Ben J. and Helen (Beale) D.; m. Margaret Ann Webster, Sept. 3, 1948; children: Webster Beale, Giselle Liseanne. B.A., U. Tex., Austin, 1943, LL.B., 1947. Bar: Tex. 1946. Asst. dist. atty., Dallas, 1947-48; asso. Martin, Moore & Brewster, Ft. Worth, 1948-50; mem. Martin, Moore, Brewster & Dean, 1950-51, Pannell, Dean, Pannell & Kerry (and predecessor firms), 1951-65; partner Brown, Herman, Scott, Young & Dean, Ft. Worth, 1965-71, Brown, Herman, Scott, Dean & Miles, 1971—; dir. Security State Bank River Oaks. Served with AUS, 1942-45; ETO. Mem. ABA, Ft. Worth-Tarrant County Bar Assn. (past v.p., dir., pres. 1971-72), Am. Coll. Trial Lawyers, State Bar Tex. (dir. 1973-75), Am. Bar Found., Tex. Bar Found. (charter mem.). Presbyterian. Clubs: Ft. Worth Boat, Ridglea Country, Fort Worth. Home: 2008 Canterbury Dr Fort Worth TX 76107 Office: Ft Worth Club Bldg Fort Worth TX 76102

DEAN, BURTON VICTOR, educator; b. Chgo., June 3, 1924; s. Samuel and Dorothy (Eisner) D.; m. Barbara Louise Arnoff, Nov. 26, 1958; children: Howard David, Paul Evan, Heather Diana, Theodore Samuel. B.S., Northwestern U., 1947; M.S., Columbia U., 1948; Ph.D., U. Ill., 1952. Instr. math. Columbia U., 1947-49, Hunter Coll., 1949-50; research fellow math. U. Ill., 1950-52; mathematician Nat. Security Agy., 1952-55; research mathematician Ops. Research, Inc., 1955-57; assoc. prof. operations research Case Western Res. U., Cleve., 1957-65, prof. ops. research, chmn. dept., 1965-76, 79—, prof. ops. research, 1965—; on leave as vis. prof. indsl. and mgmt. engring. Technion-Israel Inst. Tech., 1962-63; assoc. Inst. Public Adminstrn., Washington, 1972-76, 79-82, Booz, Allen & Hamilton, 1980-82; cons. U.S. industry and govt., 1957—, TAHAL Water Planning for Israel, 1962-64; vis. prof. U. Louvain, Belgium, Ben Gurion U., U. Tel Aviv, 1978, Zero-Base Budgeting Seminars, Belgium, Egypt, Israel, Greece, Spain, 1978, Greece, Spain, Japan, 1979, 1980; lectr. U.S. CSC, 1977-80; dir. Intercapco, Inc., Advanced Drilling Corp. Author: Operations Research in Research and Development, 1963, reprinted, 1978, (with Sasieni and Gupta) Mathematics of Modern Management, 1963, reprinted 1978, Evaluation, Selection and Control of R & D Projects, 1968, (with Reisman, Salvador and Oral) Industrial Inventory Control, 1974, (with Goldhar) Management of Research and Innovation, 1980; also articles and chpts. in profl. jours, books Ency. Profl. Mgmt; editor: Mgmt. Sci, 1962—; assoc. editor: OPSEARCH, 1968-74; editor: IEEE Trans. on Engring Mgmt, 1968—, North Holland Studies in Management Science and Systems, 1974—. Bd. dirs. Friends of Cleve. Ballet; active Cleve. Inst. Music, Friends of Cleve. Orch., Cleve. Art Mus.; trustee Shaker Heights Library Bd. Fellow AAAS (chmn. indsl. sci. sect. 1976); mem. Ops. Research Soc. (council 1973-76, chmn. ORSA/AAAS com. 1976—), Inst. Mgmt. Scis. (chmn. coll. research and devel. 1969-73, council 1966-67, past chmn. No. Ohio chpt., council coll. engring. mgmt. 1978—), Am. Math. Soc., Omega Rho (founding mem. 1977, pres. 1980-82). Home: 2920 Broxton Rd Cleveland OH 44120

DEAN, CHARLES HENRY, federal agency administrator; b. Knoxville, Tenn., Oct. 22, 1925; s. Charles Henry and Helen (Ford) D.; m. Lottie Lavender, Dec. 30, 1947; children: Helen, James Miles, Camille. Student, U. Tenn., 1943-44; B.S., U.S. Naval Acad., 1947. Sales rep. Knoxville Fertilizer Co., Dean-Planters Warehouses, 1950-59; with Knoxville (Tenn.) Utilities Bd., 1959-81; chmn. bd. TVA, 1981—. Past pres. Knoxville Tourist Bur.; past chmn. Chancellors' Assos., U. Tenn.; trustee Knoxville Coll. Served with USMC, 1947-50. Recipient Profl. Mgrs. Citation Soc. Advancement Mgmt., 1972, Eminent Engr. award Tau Beta Pi, 1983. Mem. Am. Public Power Assn. (past dir.), Nat. Soc. Profl. Engrs., Tenn. Valley Public Power Assn. (past pres.), Knox County Indsl. Bond Bd. Republican. Presbyterian. Clubs: Civitan (past pres.), Racquet (Knoxville, Tenn.) (past pres.); LeConte (bd. govs.). Office: TVA Towers Knoxville TN 37902

DEAN, CHARLES THOMAS, industrial arts educator; b. Humboldt, Nebr., Feb. 11, 1918; s. Asa Franklin and Carrie Myrtle (Mort) D.; m. Marjorie Ellen Kennedy, Apr. 11, 1941; children: Carolyn Kay, Thomas Alan, Nancy Ann. B.A. (fellow chemistry 1941-42), Peru (Nebr.) State Tchrs. Coll., 1942; M.S., Iowa State U., 1948, Ph.D., 1951. Tchr. sci. and indsl. arts Indianola (Iowa) High Sch., 1946-47; asst. prof. indsl. edn. Iowa State U., 1947-51; prof. indsl. arts Calif. State Coll., Long Beach, 1952—, chmn. div. applied arts and scis., 1962—, dir., 1956—, 1963-68, dean, 1967-80, dean emeritus, 1980—; v.p. Overseas Constrn. Services Co., 1980—; Mem. tech. adv. coms. Compton (Calif.) Coll., Harbor Jr. Coll., Los Angeles, Orange Coast Coll., Costa Mesa, Calif., El Camino (Calif.) Coll.; mem. Calif. Curriculum Com. Indsl. Arts Edn.; membership com. Am. Council Indsl. Arts Tchr. Educators, 1957-63; cons. tech. edn., Cambodia, 1962-69; cons. AID, Swaziland, 1979; dir. research project NASA, 1962-64, 66; cons. tech. and vocat. edn. U.S. Office Edn.; mem. Calif. Bd. Vocat. Examiners, 1967. Co-author: Principles of Electricity, 1950; Editor: Wade Reynolds, The Man and His Art, 1968; Contbr. chpts. yearbooks. Mem. bd. mgmt. Armed Services YMCA, Long Beach, 1968—, Long Beach council United Way, 1969; bd. dirs. Long Beach Pacific Hosp., chmn., 1978-80; bd. dirs. 49er Athletic Found., Long Beach Pacific Hosp. Found., ARC; chmn. Greater Long Beach chpt., 1977-78; mem. Calif. Student Aid Commn., 1969-78; trustee Long Beach Community Coll., 1979—, pres. bd. trustees, 1981-83; cons. Samoa Community Coll., 1978. Served to lt. (j.g.) USNR, 1943-45, 51-52; capt. Res. Recipient Louise Mears geog. award Peru State Tchrs. Coll., 1941; Air Power award 1st Res. Squadron, Air Force Assn., 1960; named Outstanding Aviation Educator for Calif., 1961; recipient Aero. Space citation Calif. Aero. Commn., 1962, Merit award citation aviation edn. FAA, 1958, 64, 69, Aerospace Edn. Leadership award CAP, 1966, 69, 72, many others; named to Hall of Honor Nat. Aerospace Congress, 1976. Mem. Am. Indsl. Arts Assn. (co-chmn. nat. conv. 1959), Calif. Indsl. Edn. Assn. (pres. So. sect. 1958, co-chmn. conv. 1958, chmn. conv. 1982, pres. 1965-66), Calif. Aviation Edn. Assn. (v.p. 1960), Am. Vocat. Assn., Nat. Assn. Indsl. and Tech. Tchr. Educators (hon. mem.), Internat. Platform Assn., Calif. Coast U. Alumni Assn. (pres. 1981—), Blue Key, Epsilon Pi Tau (laureate mem., bd. dirs. 1979—, pres. bd. dirs. 1983—), Sigma Alpha Epsilon, Beta Beta Beta, Phi Delta Kappa, Psi Chi, Phi Kappa Phi (lectr. of year 1970), Kappa Delta Pi, Gamma Sigma Delta. Presbyn. (elder, trustee). Club: Mason. Home: 4602 Hazelbrook Ave Long Beach CA 90808 *Life is beautiful and should be lived to be shared with others. It is a mirror which reflects our inner feelings and allows those around us to enjoy our presence and company.*

DEAN, FRANCES CHILDERS, librarian; b. Parker County, Tex., Apr. 20, 1930; d. John and Audrey (Ribble) Childers; (div.)1 dau., Deborah Jane. B.S., Tex. Woman's U., Denton, 1959, M.L.S., 1962; postgrad., U. Md. Sch. librarian pub. schs. in Dallas and Fairfax, Va., 1959-63; sch. librarian, then coordinator evaluation and selection Montgomery County (Md.) pub. schs., 1963-76, dir. div. instructional materials, 1976-80, dir. dept. instructional resources, 1980—. Mem. Am. Assn. Sch. Librarians (pres. 1977-78, Intellectual Freedom award 1982), ALA (trustee Freedom to Read Found. 1974-76), Ednl. Film Library Assn. (dir. 1980—), Children's Book Guild Washington, Assn. Supervision and Curriculum, Beta Phi Mu. Democrat. Home: 528 Meadow Hall Rockville MD 20851 Office: 850 Hungerford Dr Rockville MD 20850

DEAN, FRANCIS HILL, landscape architect, educator; b. San Francisco, Oct. 1, 1922; s. John Samuel and Ethel (Hill) D.; m. Myrtle Oda Enoltt, Sept. 1, 1944 (div. 1969); children: Gary Dean, Tamara Dean; m. Carolyn Anderson Bower, Aug. 12, 1971; stepchildren: Deborah Friou, Linda Friou, Sally Friou, George Friou. B.S., U. Calif.-Berkeley, 1948; postgrad., U. So. Calif., 1984. Lic. landscape architect, Calif. Designer Eckbo, Royston & Williams, Los Angeles, 1948-58; prin. Eckbo, Dean & Williams, Los Angeles and San Francisco, 1958-64; prin., v.p. Eckbo, Dean, Austin & Williams, Pasadena and San Francisco, 1964-73, EDAW Inc., Newport Beach and San Fracisco, 1973-79; lectr. Calif. State Poly. U., Pomona, Calif., 1976—; vis. lectr. U. Guelph, Ont., 1981, La. State U., 1980, Osaka U., Japan, 1973; landscape cons. U. Calif.-Santa Barbara, 1972-76; mem. adv. council U. Calif. Ext. Landscape Arch. program, Irvine, 1979—; landscape archtl. works include Riverside Mall, Calif., Santa Ana-Santiago Creek Study. Mem. Fire Protection Task Force, Orange County, Calif., 1976-77; chmn. planning com. South Laguna Civic Assn., 1974—; mem. Save Elysian Park Com., Los Angeles, 1963-67. Served to capt. USAAF, 1942-45; ETO. Fellow Am. Soc. Landscape Architects; mem. AIA (jury mem.), Am. Soc. Landscape Architects (jury mem.), Sigma Lambda Alpha. Democrat. Office: Calif State Poly Univ 3801 W Temple Ave Pomona CA 91768

DEAN, FREDERICK BERNARD, holding co. exec.; b. N.Y.C., Sept. 21, 1927; s. Fred Carl and Loretta Regina (Dolloff) D. B.A., Columbia U., 1950, J.D., 1953. Bar: N.Y. State bar. Atty. Palmer, Serles, Delaney, Shaw & Pomeroy, 1953-59; v.p., dir. Atlas Gen. Industries, Inc., 1960-64, Coordinated Apparel, Inc., 1965-66, pres., chief exec. officer, 1966—; chmn. bd. dirs. Am. Argo Corp., N.Y.C., 1974—; chmn. exec. com. Group 800 N.V., 1980—. Served with USN, 1946-48. Club: Marco Polo (N.Y.C.). Home: Durham PA 18039 Office: 90 Park Ave New York NY 10016

DEAN, GEOFFREY, book publisher; b. Newcastle-upon-Tyne, Eng., Sept. 18, 1940; s. Thomas Craig and Mildred Catherine (Hoggard) D.; m. Philma Marina Patterson, Aug. 10, 1963; children: Andrea Samantha, Christopher Michael. B.A., U. Toronto, 1961. With McGraw-Hill Co. Can. Ltd., 1961-66, coll. editor, Scarborough, Ont., 1962-66; sales mgr. Methuen Publs., Toronto, 1966-70; mktg. mgr., then v.p. mktg. Van Nostrand Reinhold Ltd., Scarborough, 1970-76; pres., dir. John Wiley & Sons. Can. Ltd., Rexdale, Ont., 1976—; mem. adv. bd. on sci. pub. Nat. Research Council Can., 1982—. Mem. Book Pubs. Profl. Assn., Can. Book Pubs. Council (pres. 1983), Ont. Bus. Edn. Assn. (hon. pres. 1982-84). Club: Granite (Toronto). Office: 22 Worcester Rd Rexdale ON Canada M9W 1L1

DEAN, GEORGE ALDEN, advertising executive; b. Chgo., June 2, 1929; s. George Abiathar and Velma Clio (Shields) D.; m. Eleanor F. Tietig, June 18, 1955 (div. Feb. 1971); children: George Alden, Diane Flach; m. Jane Kentnor Pratt, Apr. 12, 1975. B.A., Princeton, 1952; M.B.A., Harvard, 1956. With Dancer Fitzgerald Sample, Inc., N.Y.C., 1956—, mgmt. supr., 1970—, exec. v.p., 1968—. Also dir. Fin. chmn. Mauwehu council Boy Scouts Am., 1968-73; bd. visitors Babcock Sch., Wake Forest U. Served to 1st lt., arty. AUS, 1952-54; Korea. Decorated Bronze Star. Republican. Episcopalian. Clubs: Colonial Princeton (bd. govs. 1964-70), Wilton (Conn.) Riding; Pequot Yacht (Southport, Conn.); Edgartown (Mass.) Yacht. Home: 944 Pequot Ave Southport CT 06490 Office: 405 Lexington Ave New York NY 10017

DEAN, H.R., utility company executive; b. 1926. B.S., Bowling Green Coll. Commerce, 1946. With Houston Light & Power Co., 1946—, v.p., 1970-73, group v.p., 1973-78, group v.p. acctg.-fin., 1978-81, exec. v.p., 1981—; dir. Houston Light & Power Co. Office: Houston Light & Power Co 611 Walker Houston TX 77001 *

DEAN, HOWARD BRUSH, stock broker; b. N.Y.C., Feb. 18, 1921; s. Howard B. and Maria (Cook) D.; m. Andree Maitland, Sept. 26, 1947; children: Howard Brush III, James Howell, William Gardiner. Grad., Pomfret Sch., 1938; student, Yale U., 1938-40. With Pan Am. Airways-Africa Ltd., 1941-43, China Nat. Aviation Corp., 1943-46; with Harris, Upham & Co., N.Y.C., 1946-69, partner, 1952-65; 1st v.p., dir. Harris Upham & Co., Inc., 1965-69; gen. partner Reynolds & Co, 1969-71; sr. v.p., dir. Reynolds Securities, Inc., N.Y.C., 1971-78, Dean Witter Reynolds Inc., 1978—; bd. govs. Assn. Stock Exchange Firms, 1959-65, exec. com., 1961-65, v.p., 1961-62; bd. govs. Am. Stock Exchange, 1961-64, Exchange ofcl., 1978-81. Trustee Browning Sch., N.Y.C., 1948-78, Pomfret (Conn.) Sch., 1951-60; trustee St. George's Sch., Newport, R.I., 1976—, pres. bd., 1980—; bd. dirs. N.Y. affiliate Nat. Council on Alcoholism, 1975-76, Freedom Inst., 1976—, Sears Roebuck Found. Mem. Investment Bankers Assn. Am. (gov. 1965-69). Episcopalian (vestry 1959-76, sr. warden 1966-71). Home: Hook Pond Rd Box 603 East Hampton NY 11937 Office: 83d Floor 1 World Trade Center New York NY 10048

DEAN, HOWARD M., JR., food company executive; b. 1937; married. B.B.A., So. Meth. U., 1960; M.B.A., Northwestern U., 1961. With Dean Foods Co., Inc., Franklin Park, Ill., 1955—, internal auditor, 1965-68, asst. to v.p. fin., 1968-70, pres., 1970—, also dir. Served to lt. (j.g.) USN, 1962-65. Office: Dean Foods Co Inc 3600 River Rd Franklin Park IL 60131 *

DEAN, JAMES FREDERICK, oil executive; b. Peoria, Ill., July 5, 1921; s. George A. and Myrtle Sarah (MacQuilkin) D.; m. Georgia E. Till, Dec. 25, 1942; children: Diana Rell, Sarah Gail, Hope Elizabeth. B.S. in Natural Sci., Centenary Coll., Shreveport, La.; M.S. in Chemistry, La. State U., Baton Rouge. With Exxon Corp. (and subs.), 1942—; pres. Esso Internat. div. Standard Oil Co., N.J., 1971-73; exec. v.p., dir. Esso Europe, Inc., London, 1973-74, pres., dir., 1974-78; sr. v.p., dir. Exxon Corp., N.Y.C., 1978-83. Mem. Soc. Petroleum Engrs. Republican. Clubs: Univ. (N.Y.C.); Blind Brook (Purchase, N.Y.); Royal Wimbledon Golf (London). Office: One Rockefeller Plaza Rm 1250 New York NY 10020

DEAN, JIMMY, meat-processing company executive, entertainer; b. Plainview, Tex., Aug. 10, 1928; s. G. O. and Ruth (Taylor) D.; m. Mary Sue Wittauer, July 11, 1950; children: Garry, Connie, Robert. Student public schs., Plainview. Pres. Jimmy Dean Meat Co., Plainview, Tex., 1969-72, chmn. bd., Dallas, 1972—. Entertainer, Washington area, 1948-57; host: Morning Show, CBS-TV, Washington, 1957, Jimmy Dean Show, N.Y.C., 1958-59, Jimmy Dean Show, ABC-TV, 1963-65; appeared on: radio and TV show Town & Country Jamboree, 1950's; entertained, U.S. Armed Forces, Caribbean, 1952, U.S. Armed Forces, Europe, 1953; rec. artist, 1953—; records include Big Bad John, 1961 (Gold Record); I.O.U, 1976 (Gold Record). Served with USAAF, 1946-48. Recipient Georgie award as outstanding performer in field of live entertainment for country music AGVA, 1972. Mem. Actors' Equity Assn., AFTRA, Screen Actors Guild, Tex. Spurs. Office: 1341 W Mockingbird Ln Suite 1100E Dallas TX 75247

DEAN, JOHN GUNTHER, ambassador; b. Germany, Feb. 24, 1926; came to U.S., 1939, naturalized, 1944; s. Joseph and Lucy (Askenaczy) D.; m. Martine Duphenieux, Dec. 26, 1952; children: Catherine, Curtis, Paul, Joseph. B.S. magna cum laude, Harvard U., 1947, M.A., 1950; Doctorate, U. Paris, 1949. With ECA, Am. embassy, Paris, 1950-51, Am. embassy, Brussels, 1951-53, asst. econ. commr., Saigon, 1953-56, polit. officer, Laos, 1956-58; consul Am. consulate, Togo, 1959-60; chargé d'affaires Am. embassy, Mali, 1960-61; with Dept. State, Washington, 1961-65; polit. officer Am. embassy, Paris, 1965-69; regional dir. CORDS in Central Vietnam, 1970-72; dep. chief mission Am. embassy, Laos, 1972-74; ambassador to Cambodia, 1974-75, to Denmark, 1975-78, to Lebanon, 1978-81, to Thailand, 1981—; adv. U.S. delegation to UN, 1963. Served to 2d lt. AUS, 1944-46. Fellow Center for Internat. Affairs Harvard, 1969-70. Clubs: Harvard (N.Y.C.); Kenwood Golf and Country (Washington). Home: Am Embassy-Bangkok Dept State Washington DC Office: Dept State Washington DC 20520

DEAN, JOHN WILSON, JR., ret. army officer, corp. exec.; b. Evanston, Wyo., Mar. 8, 1918; s. John Wilson and Reta (Murdock) D.; m. Lucille Lorraine Forster, July 3, 1942; children—Patricia Ann (Mrs. William J. Staffa), John Wilson III. Student, Brigham Young U., 1935-37, 39-41; grad., Armed Forces Staff Coll., 1954, Nat. War Coll., 1959. Commd. 2d lt. F.A. U.S. Army, 1941, advanced through grades to brig. gen., 1967; ret., 1971; pres. Tour Ice Nat. Sales Corp., Tour Ice Nat. Leasing Corp. Decorated D.S.M., Legion of Merit with 2 oak leaf clusters, Bronze Star with 2 oak leaf clusters, Army Commendation medal with 4 oak leaf clusters; also decorated by, France, Belgium, Italy, Netherlands. Mem. Assn. U.S. Army, Mil. Order World Wars. Home: 1921 Academy Blvd Colorado Springs CO 80909 Office: 1330 Ford St Colorado Springs CO 80915

DEAN, LAURA, choreographer/composer; b. S.I., N.Y., Dec. 3, 1945; d. Arthur Douglas and Esther Dorothy (Sweedler) D. Student public schs. Mem. N.Y. State Council on the Arts Dance Panel, 1974, 75. With 1st co. of dancers, Laura Dean and Dance Co., 1971; Stamping Dance, 1971, Circle Dance, 1972, Jumping Dance, Changing Pattern, Steady Pulse, Walking Dance, Sq. Dance, 1973, Spinning Dance, Response Dance, 1974, Drumming, 1975; choreographer/composer, Laura Dean Dancers and Musicians, 1976—, Song, 1976, Dance, 1976, Spiral, 1977, Music, 1979, (for Joffrey Ballet) Night, 1980, Tympani, 1980, Sky Light, 1982, (for Joffrey Ballet) Fire, 1982, Inner Circle, 1983, Enochian, 1983; appeared: PBS Dance in America series, 1980; contbr. articles to: Contemporary Dance. Creative Artist Public Service fellow, 1976; Guggenheim fellow, 1977, 82; Jerome Found. grantee, 1978-80; Mobil Found. grantee, 1979-82; Rockefeller Found. grantee, 1980; N.Y. State Council on Arts grantee, 1973-83; Nat. Endowment Arts grantee and fellow, 1977-83; Chem. Bank grantee, 1982-83; Con Edison grantee, 1983; Exxon Corp. grantee, 1983; IBM grantee, 1983; Philip Morris Co. grantee, 1983; challenge grant awarded to Dean Dance and Music Found., 1980. Office: Dean Dance and Music Found Inc 15 W 17th St New York NY 10011

DEAN, LELAND WILBUR, coll. dean; b. Mich., July 16; s. D.W. and Edna (Barton) D.; m. Frances Keller, Apr. 12, 1941; children—David, Janet, Deborah. A.B., Western Mich. U., 1939; M.A., Mich. State U., 1951, Ph.D., 1956. High sch. tchr., adminstr., 1939-42, 45-51; dir. confs. Mich. State U., 1951-54, asst. dean, 1954-70, dep. dean, 1970—. Served with USAAF, 1942-45. Mem. Phi Delta Kappa, Kappa Delta Phi. Club: Lions. Office: 517 Erickson Hall Mich State Univ East Lansing MI 48824

DEAN, LYDIA MARGARET CARTER (MRS. HALSEY ALBERT DEAN), author, food and nutrition consultant; b. Bedford, Va., July 11, 1919; d. Christopher C. and Hettie (Gross) Carter; m. Halsey Albert Dean, Dec. 24, 1941; children: Halsey Albert Jr., John Carter, Lydia Margerae. Grad., Averett Coll.; B.S., Madison Coll., 1941; M.S., Va. Poly. Inst. and State U., 1951; postgrad., U. Va., Mich. State U.; postgrad. in clin. nutrition, UCLA Med. Sch. Dietetic intern, therapeutic dietitian St. Vincent de Paul Hosp., Norfolk, Va., 1942; physicist U.S. Naval Operating Base, Norfolk, 1943-45; clin. dietitian Roanoke Meml. Hosps., 1946-51; asso. prof. Va. Poly. Inst. and State U., 1946-53; community nutritionist, Roanoke, Va., 1953-60; dir. dept. nutritions and dietetics Southwestern Va. Med. Center, Roanoke, 1960-67; food and nutrition cons. Nat. Hdqrs. A.R.C., Washington, 1967—, staff and vol., 1973—; nutrition scientist, cons. Dept. Army, Washington, 1973—, Dept. Agr., 1973—; pres. Dean Assos.; cons., asso. dir. Am. Dietetic Assn., 1975—; coordinator new degree program U. Hawaii, 1974-75; dir. nutrition programs HHS, Washington, 1975—; mem. task force White House Conf. Food and Nutrition, 1969—; chmn. fed. com. Interagy. Com. on Nutrition Edn., 1970-71; tech. rep. to AID and State Dept.; chmn. Crusade for Nutrition Edn., Washington, 1970—; participant, cons. Nat. Nutrition Policy Conf., 1974. Author: (with Virginia McMasters) Community Emergency Feeding, 1972, Help My Child How To Eat Right, 1973, rev., 1978, The Complete Gourmet Nutrition Cookbook: The Joy of Eating Well and Right, 1978, The Stress Foodbook, 1980; contbr. articles to profl. jours. Fellow Am. Pub. Health Assn., Internat. Inst. Community Service; mem. Am. Dietetic Assn., Bus. and Profl. Women's Clubs (cons. 1970—, pres. 1981-82), Am. Home Econs. Assn. (rep. and treas. joint congl. com.), AAUW, Inst. Food Technologists. Club: Zonta Internat. Home: 7816 Birnam Wood Dr McLean VA 22101 *In very early years of my life with the freedom to think and the background of family influence I realized that my life had a purpose and that I must work to fulfill that purpose. This belief has been my most motivating factor. Each day I have kept in mind the long-range goals for my life and on a daily basis I have set daily goals to be accomplished. In order to attain these goals I have used planning, self-discipline, willingness to sacrifice, hard work, a faith in and love for God, country, and individual people.*

DEAN, MORTON NISSAN, news correspondent; b. Fall River, Mass., Aug. 22, 1935; s. Joseph and Celia (Schwartz) Dubitsky; m. Valerie, July 25, 1965; children: Adam, Sarah, Jennie. B.A. in English, Emerson Coll., 1957, LL.D. (hon.), 1977. News dir. Herald Tribune Radio Network, N.Y. State, 1957-60; reporter, corr. Radio Sta. WBZ, Boston, 1960-64; legis. and polit. corr. WCBS-TV News, N.Y.C., 1964-67; corr., anchorman CBS News, N.Y.C., 1967—; also covered polit. campaigns, 1968—. Author: (with Sten Möllerström) Hello World, 1978; also news spls. Vietnam: A War That Is Finished, 1975, Energy: The Facts... The Fears... The Future, 1977, Iran: A Week of Tumult, 1979, Pope John Paul II: The American Journey, 1979. Recipient UPI Spl. award; Tom Phillips award, 1962; Overseas Press Club award for best interpretation fgn. affairs radio, 1975. Mem. AFTRA. Office: 524 W 57th St New York NY 10019 *

DEAN, PAUL JOHN, magazine editor; b. Pitts., May 11, 1941; s. John Aloysius and Perle Elizabeth (Thompson) D.; m. Jo-ann Tillman, Aug. 19, 1972; children: Jennifer Ann, Michael Paul. Student engring., Pa. State U., 1959-60. Gen. mgr. Civic Center Honda Co., Pitts., 1965-68, Washington-Pitts. Cycle Co., Canonsburg, Pa., 1968-70; nat. service mgr. Yankee Motor Co., Schenectady, 1970-73; competition congressman Am. Motorcyclist Assn., 1971, 72; adv. bd., guest speaker Los Angeles Trade Tech. Coll., 1974—. Engring. editor: Cycle Guide mag, Compton, Calif., 1973-74; editor-in-chief, 1974-80; editorial dir., 1980—; Author manuals. Served with AUS, 1964-65. Home: 5915 E Arabella St Lakewood CA 90713 Office: 20916 Higgins Ct Torrance CA 90501

DEAN, PAUL REGIS, legal educator; b. Leetonia, Ohio, July 12, 1918; s. Edward Joseph and Catherine (Sheets) D.; m. Delores M. Fitch, July 14, 1945; children—Mary E., Lawrence E. (dec.), Patricia, John, Paul, William, Delores, Teresa, Brian. Student, DeSales Coll., Toledo, 1936-38; B.A., Youngstown U., 1940; LL.B., Georgetown U., 1946, LL.M., 1952, LL.D., 1969. Bar: D.C. bar 1946, Va. bar 1954. Law clk. to Andrew M. Hood, D.C. Ct. of Appeals, 1946-47; prof. law Georgetown U., 1947-54, 69—, dean, 1954-69; Legal adviser to Pres.'s Com. Govt. Contract Compliance, 1952-53; Neutral trustee, United Mine Workers Am. Health and Retirement Funds, 1971—; mem. Pres.'s Commn. Pension Policy, 1979-81; trustee, v.p. Loyola Found. Inc., 1957—. Served to lt. USNR, 1942-46. Fellow Am. Coll. Probate Counsel; mem. Am., Va., D.C. bar assns., Am. Arbitration Assn., Delta Theta Phi. Home: 3313 Garland Dr Falls Church VA 22041 Office: 600 New Jersey Ave Washington DC 20001

DEAN, PETER, artist; b. Berlin, N.Y., July 9, 1941; s. William F. and Roza (Nathan) D.; m. Lorraine Otterson; 1 son, Gregory. Student, Cornell U., 1957-58; B.A., U. Wis., 1959. One man shows at, Darthea Speyer Gallery, Paris, 1981, Allan Stone Gallery, N.Y.C., 1970, 73, 78, 80, Bienville Gallery, 1975, 77, 79, 81; exhibited in group shows, Nat. Inst. Arts and Letters, N.Y.C., 1973, Corpus Christi Mus., 1981, Chrysler Mus., Norfolk, Va., Chgo. Art Inst., 1982; represented in permanent collection, Nat. Collection, Washington, Chgo. Art Inst., Madison (Wis.) Art Center, New Orleans Mus., Gray Gallery, N.Y. U.; vis. artist, Yale U., La. State U., N.D. U., U. Wis., Skidmore Coll. Founding mem. Rhino Horn Group, co-chmn., 1969-79. N.Y. Council Arts grantee, 1975-76. Mem. Spring St. Artists Marching and Drinking Club. Club: Zinnia Color Studio. Address: 2 Spring St New York NY 10012 *I'm a magician through whom the images of our time pass and become paintings. I'm an interpreter of reality into fantasy and back again. I'm a juggler of textures and color. I'm a seer of the past and a prophet of the future. I ride the hurricane, I walk the tightrope of sanity, I live on the edge of the world.*

DEAN, ROBERT CHARLES, architect; b. Memphis, Dec. 5, 1903; s. Charles and Martha (Little) D.; m. Ruth Andrew, Sept. 10, 1927; children: Robert C., Ruth Cameron, Nancy Elizabeth, Andrew John. B.S., Mass. Inst. Tech., 1926; M.Arch., 1927; M.Arch. traveling fellow, Fontainebleau Sch. of Fine Arts, 1925; LL.D. (hon.), Furman U., 1971. Asst. prof. Ga. Sch. Tech., 1927-28; instr. Mass. Inst. Tech., 1930-41; designer Perry, Shaw & Hepburn (now Perry, Dean, Stahl & Rogers, Inc.), Boston, 1930-40, ptnr., 1940—. Architect: Faulkner Hosp, Boston, Am. Mil. Cemetery, Cambridge, Eng., Furman U, Greenville, S.C., Bentley Coll, Waltham, Mass., Fine Arts and Sci. Center, Macalester Coll., St. Paul, Cox Bldg, Mass. Gen. Hosp., Greenville (S.C.) County Library, Liberty Mut. Ins. Co. Office Bldgs, Portsmouth, N.H. and Neshannock, Pa., Project 1B, New Eng. Med. Center Hosp. Mem. Mass. N.G., 1930-41. Served to col. AUS, 1941-45; brig. gen. ret. AUS. Decorated Bronze Star, Army Commendation medal, U.S.; Croix de Guerre; Etoile Vermeil, France; Croix de Guerre with palm, Belgium; officer Order of Orange Nassau, Netherlands. Fellow AIA; mem. Sigma Chi. Republican. Episcopalian. Clubs: City Club Corp. (Boston); Wellesley. Home: 29 Hundreds Rd Wellesley Hills MA 02181 Office: 177 Milk St Boston MA 02109

DEAN, ROBERT CHARLES, JR., mechanical engineer, business executive, educator; b. Atlanta, Apr. 13, 1928; s. Robert C. and Ruth (Andrew) D.; m. E. Nancy Hayes, Sept. 22, 1951; children: Margaret S., James C., Elizabeth S., Martha A., Charles E. B.S., M.S., MIT, 1949, Sc.D., 1954. Project engr. Ultrasonic Corp., 1949-51; head advanced engring. dept. Ingersoll-Rand Co., 1956-60; dir. research Thermal Dynamics Cor., 1960-61; dir. Ecol. Sci. Corp., 1968-70; co-founder, pres. Creare Inc., 1961-75; Ecol. Research Corp., 1968-70; co-founder, chmn. bd., prin. engr. Creare Innovations Co., 1976-79; founder 1979, since pres. Verax Corp., Hanover, N.H.; asst. prof. mech. engring. MIT, 1951-56; prof. engring. Thayer Sch. Engring., Dartmouth Coll., 1960—; mem. turbine and compressor subcom. NACA, 1954-55. Author numerous articles and patentee in field; editor: Jour. Fluid Engring., 1973-79. Recipient Gold medal Pi Tau Sigma, 1953, Master Designer award Product Engring. mag., 1967. Fellow ASME (chmn. hydraulics div. 1962-63, dir. Turbomachinery Inst. 1968—, Thurston lectr. 1977, Fluids Engring. award 1979); mem. Nat. Acad. Engring., Tau Beta Pi. Home: Hawk Pine Hill Norwich VT 05055 Office: PO Box B-1170 Hanover NH 03755

DEAN, SIDNEY WALTER, JR., business and marketing executive; b. Boston, May 20, 1905; s. Sidney W. and Marian (Perry) D.; m. Eugenia Serios, Nov. 2, 1963. A.B., Yale U., 1926. With J. Walter Thompson Co., 1927-42; mgr. Trade & Indsl. Dept., dir. media, v.p., 1937-42; exec. v.p., dir. Telecoin Corp., 1945-47; cons. marketing and mgmt., 1947-50; v.p. McCann-Erickson, Inc., 1950-61; pres. Ventures Devel. Co., 1961—; dir. Zip-A-Lope Corp., Marketmath, Inc., Fluted Paper Products Co., Inc.; Mem. FCC Adv. Com. Cable TV; chmn. N.Y.C. Adv. Com. Telecommunications.; Trustee Met. Ednl. TV Assn., 1954-59; dir. Audit Bur. Circulations, 1957-61. Author: Mass Communications in Modern Society, 1948, Planning for Integrated Marketing, 1949, Cable Television in New York, 1970. Vice chmn. Nat. Businessmen's Council. Served as capt. USAF; with OSS, Lend-Lease Adminstrn., 1943-45. Decorated Bronze Star medal. Mem. Am. Econ. Assn., Center for Policy Research (sr. asso.), Sigma Xi. Democrat. Clubs: Yale, City (N.Y.C.) (trustee). Home: 27 Washington Sq N New York NY 10011

DEAN, STANLEY ROCHELLE, psychiatrist; b. Stamford, Conn., Feb. 13, 1908; s. Jacob and Gerta (Rochelle) D.; m. Marion Jamieson, Nov. 8, 1967; children: Lori Dean Schonfeld, Michael Louis. B.S., U. Mich., 1930, M.D. cum laude, 1934. Diplomate: Am. Bd. Psychiatry and Neurology. Intern Hurley (Mich.) Hosp., 1934-35; resident in psychiatry Taunton (Mass.) State Hosp., Boston Psychopathic Hosp., 1935-37; sr. physician Fairfield State Hosp., Newtown, Conn., 1937-40; practice medicine specializing in psychiatry, Stamford, 1940-64, specializing in schizophrenia family and marriage counseling, Miami, Fla., 1964—; emeritus staff Stamford Hosp., St. Joseph's Hosp., Stamford; clin. prof. psychiatry U. Fla., U. Miami, Fla.; founder Research in Schizophrenia Endowment, 1958-62; chmn. internat. council coll. Human Sciences, Montreal, Que., Can. Author-editor: Schizophrenia: the First Ten Dean Award Lectures, 1973, Psychiatry and Mysticism, 1975; contbr. articles to profl. jours. Recipient prize for research New Eng. Psychiat. Assn., 1942; namesake Stanley R. Dean award Fund Behavioral Scis. and Am. Coll. Psychiatrists. Fellow Am. Psychiat. Assn. (joint commn. pub. affairs), Am. Coll. Psychiatrists, AAAS, Royal Soc. Medicine (Gt. Brit.), Royal Coll. Psychiatrists (Gt. Brit.); mem. Am. Assn. Social Psychiatry (pres. 1980-82), Alpha Omega Alpha, Phi Kappa Phi. Address: 1800 NE 114th St Miami FL 33181 *Thought is a form of energy. Psychogeny recapitulates cosmogeny; i.e., the mind has genesis in its genes.*

DEAN, THOMAS HAROLD, food products company executive; b. N.Y.C., Nov. 23, 1928; s. Joseph Richard and Helen Marie (Darby) D.; m. Geraldine Elizabeth Jackman, Aug. 7, 1954; children—Thomas R., Brian C., Leslie E., Cynthia A. B.S., Fordham U., 1952; postgrad. in Bus, N.Y. U., 1956-57. C.P.A., N.Y. Sr. accountant Price Waterhouse & Co., N.Y.C., 1954-63; asst. treas. Miles Labs., Inc., Ind., 1963-67; asst. to pres. Am. Home Products Corp., N.Y.C., 1967-68; controller Continental Grain Co., N.Y.C., 1968-73, v.p., treas., 1973-75, v.p. strategic planning and corp. devel., 1975-80, sr. v.p. corporate devel., 1981—; dir. Overseas Shipholding Group Inc., N.Y.C., Terminal Comml. Co. Inc., San Francisco, Calgene, Davis, Calif., Santek, Greensboro, N.C., Continental Grain Co., N.Y.C., Chia Tai Conti Ltd., Hong Kong; chmn. audit com. of bd. dirs. (Overseas Shipbldg. Group.). Served with USNR, 1952-54. Mem. Fin. Execs.

Inst., Am. Inst. C.P.A.'s, N.Y. State Soc. C.P.A.'s. Office: 277 Park Ave New York NY 10172

DEAN, WILLIAM GEORGE, geography educator; b. Toronto, Ont., Can., Nov. 29, 1921; s. William Ashton and Alice Mary (Firstbrook) D.; m. Elizabeth Efreda Johnston, Sept. 18, 1948; children: Peter Hugh, Robin Elizabeth. B.A. with honors, U. Toronto, 1949, M.A., 1950; Ph.D., McGill U., 1959. Research geographer Dept. Lands, B.C., 1953-55; asst. prof. United Coll. U., Winnipeg, Man., Can., 1953-56; lectr. geography U. Toronto, 1956-58, assoc. prof., 1958-69, prof., 1969—; research geographer Mines and Tech. Surveys, Ottawa, Ont., 1956-57; Arctice research cons. Rand Corp., Santa Monica, Calif., 1954-56; cons. Ont. Dept. Hwys., 1961-64; dir., editor Econ. Atlas of Ont., 1967-69; dir. Hist. Atlas of Can., 1975—. Editor: Canadian Geographer, 1960-67. Recipient Trinity Coll. prize, 1949; Arctic Research fellow Carnegie Found., 1950-52; NSF fellow, 1963; recipient W.W. Atwood Gold Medal Pan Am. Inst. Geography and History, 1973. Clubs: Nat. Yacht, Royal Canadian Curling. Office: Dept Geography U Toronto 100 Saint George St Toronto ON Canada M5S 1A1

DEAN, WILLIAM TUCKER, legal educator; b. Chgo., Aug. 31, 1915; s. William Tucker and Martha (Boldt) D.; m. Ann Coulson, May 15, 1943; children: Jonathan, Robert Coulson, Tobias, Sheila. A.B., Harvard, 1937, M.B.A., 1947; J.D., U. Chgo., 1940. Bar: D.C. bar 1940, N.Y. bar 1949, also U.S. Supreme Ct 1949. Atty. bituminous coal div. Dept. Interior, 1940-41; legal adviser fuel sect. OPA, 1941-42; atty. anti-trust div. Dept. Justice, 1943; asst. prof. law U. Kan. Law Sch., 1946-47; asst., then asso. prof. law N.Y. U. Law Sch., 1947-53; asso., then prof. law Cornell U., 1953—; gen. counsel, dir. Geotechnics and Resources, Inc., 1959-63; asso. dir. research N.Y. State Law Revision Commn., 1963-66. Author: (with C.O. Gregory and others) Illinois Annotations to Restatement of Torts, 1942; also numerous articles.; Editor: Annual Survey American Law, 1950-53, Survey of New York Law, 1950-53. Justice Village of Cayuga Heights, N.Y., 1962—; Co-chmn. N.Y. State Citizens Com. for Liquor Law Revision, 1964; Democratic candidate for Supreme Ct. from 6th Jud. Dist., 1982. Served to capt. AUS, 1942-46. Mem. Tompkins County Magistrates' Assn. (pres. 1969), Am., N.Y. State bar assns., Internat. Acad. Estate and Trust Law, Order of Coif, Phi Beta Kappa, Phi Kappa Phi. Mem. United Ch. Christ. Home: 206 Overlook Rd Ithaca NY 14850

DEANDA, JAMES, federal judge; b. Houston, Aug. 21, 1925; s. Javier and Mary Louise DeA.; m. Joyce Anita DeAnda; children: Louis, Christopher. B.A., Tex. A&M U.; LL.B., U. Tex., 1950. Bar: Tex. Pvt. practice, Houston, 1951-54, Corpus Christi, 1955-74, McAllen, 1974-79; U.S. dist. judge So. Dist. Tex., Houston, 1979—. Roman Catholic. Office: Federal Bldg Brownsville TX 78520

DEANE, FREDERICK, JR., banker; b. Boston, Aug. 5, 1926; s. Frederick and Julia (Coolidge) D.; m. Dorothy Legge, Dec. 21, 1948; children: Dorothy Porcher, Eleanor Dodds, Frederick III. Grad., Harvard, 1948, M.B.A. with distinction, 1951. With Bank of Va. and Bank of Va. Co., 1953—, now chmn. bd., chief exec. officer; dir. CSX Corp., Marriott Corp., Master Card Internat. Bd. dirs. Va. Mus. Found., Va. Found. Ind. Colls., Federated Arts Council Richmond, Va. Diocesan Center; trustee of the Funds of Protestant Episcopal Ch.; trustee Diocese of Va.; bd. dirs., vice chmn. Richmond Renaissance; trustee Westminster-Canterbury Found. Served to 1st lt. AUS, 1944-47; 1st lt., 1951-53. Mem. Assn. Res. City Bankers (dir.), Assn. Bank Holding Cos. (chmn. 1979-80), Richmond Soc. Fin. Analysts, Conf. Bd. (chmn. So. regional council). Republican. Episcopalian. Clubs: Harvard of Va., Harvard Bus. Sch. of Va.; Hasty Pudding-Inst. 1770, Delphic (Harvard); Commonwealth, Country of Virginia (Richmond); Harvard, Brook (N.Y.C.); Mid Ocean (Bermuda); Burning Tree (Bethesda, Md.); Metropolitan (Washington). Home: 110 W Hillcrest Ave Richmond VA 23226 Office: PO Box 25970 7 N 8th St Richmond VA 23260

DEANE, HERBERT ANDREW, educator; b. Bklyn., May 26, 1921; s. Andrew and Annette (Franzen) D. A.B., Columbia, 1942, Ph.D., 1953; postgrad., Harvard, 1946-47. Mem. faculty Columbia, 1948—, prof. govt., 1961—, vice provost acad. planning, 1968, Lieber prof. polit. philosophy, 1969—; Cons. legal and polit. philosophy Rockefeller Found., 1952-53. Author: The Political Ideas of Harold J. Laski, 1955, The Political and Social Ideas of St. Augustine, 1963; Editor: Jour. History Ideas, 1961—, Polit. Theory, 1972. Served with USNR, 1942-46. Rockefeller fellow, 1958-59; Guggenheim fellow, 1960-61; Nat. Endowment for Humanities sr. fellow, 1974-75. Mem. Am. Soc. Polit. and Legal Philosophy, Inst. Internat. de Philosophie Politique, Acad. Polit. Sci., Phi Beta Kappa. Democrat. Club: Century Assn. (N.Y.C.). Home: 423 W 120th St New York City NY 10027

DEANE, JAMES GARNER, editor, conservationist; b. Hartford, Conn., Apr. 5, 1923; s. Julian Lowrie and Miriam (Grover) D. B.A., Swarthmore Coll., 1943. Mem. editorial staff Washington Star, 1944-60, edn. editor, 1952-57, classical recs. critic, 1952-60; ind. researcher, vol. in conservation activity, 1961-68; asso. editor Nat. Parks Mag., 1968-69, editor, 1969; asst. editor The Living Wilderness, Washington, 1969-71, exec. editor, 1971-75, editor, 1975-81; now editor Defenders mag., Washington, 1981—; Washington corr. Mus. Courier, 1945-55; contbg. editor High Fidelity mag., 1953-55; mem. com. transp. environ. rev. process Transp. Research Bd. NRC, 1974-77; Am. co-chmn. Can. U.S. Environ. Council, 1975—. Bd. dirs. Arctic Internat. Wildlife Range Soc., 1979—; trustee Com. of 100 on Federal City, 1967—, 1st vice chmn., 1967-69; chmn. Potomac Valley Conservation and Recreation Council, 1967. Served with AUS, 1946-47. Recipient award Edn. Writers Assn., 1956, Public Service award Washington Newspaper Guild, 1956, Charles Carroll Glover award Nat. Park Service, 1967. Club: City Tavern. Home: 4200 Cathedral Ave NW Washington DC 20016 Office: 1244 19th St NW Washington DC 20036 *Protection of as many as possible of the remaining wild places and, with them, of the marvelous diversity of living species on our crowding planet is one of the imperatives of our time. This need can be met only by developing worldwide understanding of its crucial importance. That is the challenging task of the nature-conservation movement. I find it exhilarating to be making some contribution, however modest, to the accomplishment of that task through the techniques of journalism.*

DEANE, THOMAS ANDERSEN, banker; b. Los Angeles, Mar. 20, 1921; s. Thomas Clarke and Dorothy (Milbach) D.; m. Margaret Louise Noble, June 21, 1947; children: James C., William A. B.A., Pomona Coll., 1942; M.B.A., Stanford U., 1948. With Bank of Am. Nat. Trust & Savs. Assn., San Francisco, 1948—, exec. v.p., 1974—, vice chmn., 1982—. Trustee Pomona Coll., St. John's Hosp. and Health Center Found.; bd. dirs. Met. YMCA of, Los Angeles; mem. 100 Club of Los Angeles. Served with USMC, 1943-46. Mem. Calif. Bankers Assn. (dir. 1974—, pres. 1978), Central City Assn. Los Angeles (bd. dirs., mem. exec. com.), Assn. Res. City Bankers. Clubs: Los Angeles Country, California; Bankers (San Francisco). Office: Bank of Am 555 S Flower St Los Angeles CA 90071

DEANER, R. MILTON, steel co. exec.; b. Lynchburg, Va., June 26, 1924; s. Frank C. and Lucile (Woodall) D.; m. Jean D. Dow, Sept. 18, 1947; children—Pamela, Sandra, Robert. B.S., Tri-State Coll., 1948. Sales mgr. Arthur C. McKee (engring. contractor), Cleve., 1952-61, group v.p., 1964-71; chief engr. McLouth Steel Corp., Trenton, Mich., 1961-64, pres., chief operating officer, 1981—; v.p. engring. Nat. Steel Corp., Pitts., 1971-81. Served with USAAF, 1943-45

DEANTONI, EDWARD PAUL, state agency administrator; b. San Francisco, Mar. 7, 1941; s. Attilio Mario and Zita Elizabeth (Lolich) DeA.; m. Karen Dolores Thode, Jan. 22, 1966; children: Marc Edward, Christopher Earl. A.B., U. San Francisco, 1962; M.A., Cornell U., 1968, Ph.D., 1971. Vol. Peace Corps, Turkey, 1964-66; career counselor Cornell U., 1969-72; asst. prof. history Am. edn. Boston Coll., 1972-73; human resources planner, sr. analyst Planning Bur. State of S.D., Pierre, 1973-76; dir. health planning Dept. Health, 1976-77, sec. health, 1977-78, dir. state health planning and devel. agy., 1978-81; asst. dir. Associated Sch. Bds. S.D., 1981—. Woodrow Wilson fellow, 1962-63; ESEA fellow, 1966-69. Mem. Phi Kappa Phi. *The life of the mind, inspired by a classic liberal education and by a faith in truth, has been a major force in my life. I realize, however, that such learning enriches most when it is embedded in a life of practical affairs, when it enlivens my relationships with others, and when it is used to seek a good beyond myself.*

DEARDEN, DOUGLAS MOREY, educator; b. Echo, Utah, Aug. 25, 1923; s. Morey Thomas and Melba Viola (Richins) D.; m. Fay Rose Steuer, Oct. 9, 1948; children—Holly Kay, Mark Douglas, Laurie Ann. Student, Kansas City (Mo.) Jr. Coll., 1940-41, U. Colo., 1942-43; B.A., U. Utah, 1947, M.A., 1949; postgrad., U. Cal. at Berkeley, 1949-50; Ph.D., U. Minn., 1959. Grad. teaching asst. U. Utah, 1947-49; instr. U. Minn., 1950-51, prof., 1952—. Contbr. articles profl. jours. Served with USNR, 1943-46, 51-52. Recipient Tozer Found. grant field studies biology, 1958. Mem. AAAS, Nat. Assn. Reesearch Sci. Teaching, Phi Sigma, Phi Delta Kappa, Sigma Xi. Home: 2912 Orchard Ave North Minneapolis MN 55422

DEARDEN, JOHN, educator; b. Lancashire, Eng., Nov. 19, 1919; came to U.S., 1924, naturalized, 1933; s. Ernest and Florence (Curwen) D.; m. Helen-Marie Borden, June 25, 1945; children—John Curwen, Thomas Allen, Rachel Guerin, Ruth Anne. B.A., Am. Internat. Coll., Springfield, Mass., 1945; M.B.A., U. Pa., 1946; M.A., Harvard, 1964. C.P.A., 1948. Instr. accounting U. Pa., 1947-49; mem. central finance staff Ford Motor Co., 1949-59; mem. faculty Harvard, 1959—, Herman C. Krannert prof. bus. adminstrn., 1969—; vis. prof. IMEDE, Lausanne, Switzerland, 1970-71; Ford Found. cons. (Indian Inst. Mgmt.), Ahmedabad, 1966-67. Author: (with R. N. Anthony) Accounting Problems and Cases, 1961, Cost and Budget Analysis, 1962, (with R.N. Anthony) Management Control Systems, 1965, rev. edits., 1972, 76, 80, (with F.W. McFarlan) Management Information Systems, 1966, Computers in Business Management, 1966, Essentials of Cost Accounting, 1969, (with McFarland and Zani) Managing Computer Based Information Systems, 1970, (with Bursk, Hawkins, and Longstreet) Financial Control of Multi-national Operations, 1971, Cost Accounting and Financial Control Systems, 1973, (with Shank) Financial Accounting and Reporting: A Contemporary Emphasis, 1975, (with Bhattacharayya) Accounting for Management, 1976. Served with USNR, 1943-46. Recipient 50th Gold medal for contbn. to edn. Wharton Sch. Mem. Am. Inst. C.P.A.'s, Am. Accounting Assn., Financial Execs. Inst., Beta Gamma Sigma, Beta Alpha Psi. Home: 33 Summit Rd Lexington MA 02173 Office: Soldiers Field Boston MA 02163

DEARDEN, JOHN FRANCIS CARDINAL, former archbishop of Detroit; b. Valley Falls, R.I., Oct. 15, 1907; s. John S. and Agnes (Gregory) D. Grad., St. Mary's Sem., Cleve., 1929, N.Am. Coll., Rome, Italy, 1934; S.T.D., Gregorian U., Rome, 1934. Ordained priest Roman Catholic Ch., 1932; rector St. Mary's Sem., Cleve., 1944-48; apptd. papal chamberlain with title very rev. monsignor, 1945, consecrated coadjutor bishop Pitts., titular bishop Sarepta, 1948, bishop, Pitts., 1950-58; archbishop Archdiocese Detroit, 1959-80, apostolic adminstr., 1980-81. Elevated to cardinal, 1969. Mem. Nat. Conf. Cath. Bishops (pres. 1966-71).

DEARDEN, WILLIAM EDGAR CHAMBERS, chocolate company executive; b. Phila., Sept. 14, 1922; s. William Edgar Chambers and Nellie (Maloney) D.; m. Mary Kline, July 10, 1944; children: Bonnie Lynne, Pamela Kay. B.S. in Econs., Albright Coll., 1944, LL.D., 1974; postgrad., Harvard Bus. Sch., 1944-45, Temple U., 1953-54; D.Comml. Sci. (hon.), Am. Internat. Coll., 1984. Sales rep. Dun & Bradstreet, Inc., Reading, Pa., 1946-50, mgr., Trenton, N.J., 1950-51; asst. bus. mgr. Milton Hershey Sch., Hershey, Pa., 1953-57, bd. mgrs., 1964—; with Hershey Foods Corp., 1957—, dir. sales and marketing, 1965- 67, v.p. sales and marketing, 1967-71, group v.p., 1971-76, vice chmn., chief exec. officer, 1976-84, chmn. bd., 1984—, also dir.; chmn. bd. Hershey Trust Co.; dir. Dun & Bradstreet Corp., Carpenter Tech. Corp., Sterling Drug, Inc., AMP Inc. Bd. mgrs. M.S. Hershey Found.; chmn. bd. Milton Hershey Sch., 1981; trustee Albright Coll.; nat. chmn. Years of Challenge capital campaign, 1974-76; dir. Horatio Alger Awards Com., 1978; nat. food mfg. chmn. U.S. Indsl. Payroll Savs. Com., 1980. Served to lt. USNR, 1943-46, 51-53. Named Alumnus of Year Milton Hershey Sch., 1964; Dean of Confectionery Mfg. Industry, 1972; recipient Giant of the Industry award, 1971, Future Bus. Leaders Am./Phi Beta Lambda, 1979; Distinguished Alumnus award Albright Coll., 1975; Horatio Alger award, 1976; Hall of Fame award Tobacco Industry, 1978; Disting. Pennsylvanian award, 1980. Mem. Grocery Mfrs. Am. (dir. 1976—). Clubs: Econ. N.Y.; Masons (past pres. Hershey Shrine Club 1974—), Rotary (Hershey) (past pres.). Office: Hershey Foods Corp Hershey PA 17033

DEARIE, RAYMOND J., federal lawyer; b. 1944. A.B., Fairfield U.; J.D., St. John's U. Bar: N.Y. 1969. U.S. atty. (eastern dist. N.Y.), Bklyn., 1982—. Office: US Courthouse 225 Cadman Plaza E Brooklyn NY 11201 *

DEARING, AUDREY TRAUGOTT, electronics company executive; b. San Antonio, Sept. 27, 1929; d. Arthur Charles and Ella Christine (Bartels) Traugott; m. Harry Leonard Dearing, Aug. 18, 1950; children: Denise Elaine, Harry Leonard, Linda Claire. A.A., San Antonio Coll., 1949. With Tracor, Inc., Austin, Tex., 1961—, asst. corp. sec., adminstrv. asst. to pres., 1970-73, corp. sec., adminstrv. asst. to chmn. and pres., 1973—; sec. Westronics Inc., Ft. Worth, 1971—, dir., 1972—; sec. numerous subs. Tracor, 1972—. Sec. Dist. 10 Council 4-H Club, 1973-75, chmn. county council, 1972-74, sec.-treas., 1974-80; pres. Friends of Pflugerville Community Library. Recipient 4-H Club Leadership award, 1978., Silver Spur award, 1981. Mem. Am. Soc. Corp. Secs., Pflugerville C. of C., Phi Theta Kappa. Office: Tracor Inc 6500 Tracor Ln Austin TX 78721

DEARING, VINTON ADAMS, English educator; b. San Francisco, July 30, 1920; s. Henry H. and Estelle (Sosso) D.; m. Marion Elizabeth Miser, Dec. 3, 1946; children: Henry, Mary. A.B., Harvard, 1940, M.A., 1942, Ph.D., 1949. Mem. faculty UCLA, 1949—, prof. English, 1963-68, prof. English and computer applications in lit., 1969—. Author: A Manual of Textual Analysis, 1959, Principles and Practice of Textual Analysis, 1974; Editor: Poems and Prose of John Gay, 1974; textual editor: The Works of John Dryden, 1956—. Served with AUS, 1942-46. Guggenheim fellow, 1959-60; IBM Corp. research grantee, 1967; Fulbright research scholar, Eng., 1975-76. Mem. Bibliog. Soc., Inst. Antiquity and Christianity, Soc. Bib. Lit., Fulbright Alumni Assn., Assn. Lit. and Linguistic Computing, Assn. for Computers and the Humanities, Soc. Textual Scholarship. Home: 10542 Garwood Pl Los Angeles CA 90024

DE ARMAS, FREDERICK ALFRED, foreign language educator; b. Havana, Cuba, Feb. 9, 1945; came to U.S., 1959, naturalized, 1968; s. Alfredo and Ana Maria (Galdos) De A. B.A. magna cum laude, Stetson U., DeLand, Fla., 1965; Ph.D. (Carnegie fellow 1965-68), U. N.C., 1968. Mem. faculty La. State U., 1968—, prof. Spanish, 1978—, acting chmn. dept., 1979-80, dir. grad. studies, 1980—; vis. asso. prof. U. Mo., Columbia, summer 1977. Author: The Four Interpolated Stories in the Roman Comique, 1971, Paul Scarron, 1972, The Invisible Mistress, 1976; also articles.; Editor: (Luis de Belmonte Bermudez) El Sastre del Campillo, 1975; editorial adv. bd.: Bull. Comediantes, 1981—, Hispanófila, 1981; co-editor: Critical Perspectives on Calderón de la Barca, 1981. Grantee Nat. Endowment Humanities, summer 1979. Mem. MLA, Comparative Lit. Assn., Renaissance Soc. Am., Am. Assn. Tchrs. Spanish and Portuguese, Assn. Internat, Hispanistas, Assn. Filiologia y Linguistica America Latina., Hispanic Soc. Am. (Corr.). Home: 2376 Cherokee St Baton Rouge LA 70806 Office: Dept Spanish and Portuguese La State U Baton Rouge LA 70803

DEARMORE, THOMAS LEE, journalist; b. Mountain Home, Ark., Sept. 11, 1927; s. Benjamin and Ethel (Shiras) D.; m. Reba Byrd, Nov. 5, 1950; children—Diana, Jonathan. Student, N.Mex. A. and M. Coll., Las Cruces, 1944-45, Drury Coll., Springfield, Mo., 1958, Harvard, 1959-60. Editor Air Force newspaper, Spokane, Wash., 1945-46; reporter Daily Spokesman-Rev., Spokane, 1946; editor, co-owner Baxter Bull., Mountain Home, 1947-70; editorial writer Eve. Star Newspaper Co., Washington, 1970-76; asso. editor Ark. Gazette, Little Rock, 1976-78; editorial dir. San Francisco Examiner, 1978—. Contbr. articles mags. Served with USAAF, 1944-46. Mem. Am. Soc. Newspaper Editors, Soc. Nieman Fellows, Nat. Conf. Editorial Writers, Sigma Delta Chi. Home: 41 Valley Ct Pleasant Hill CA 94523

DEASY, CORNELIUS MICHAEL, architect; b. Mineral Wells, Tex., July 19, 1918; s. Cornelius and Monetta (Palmo) D.; m. Lucille Laney, Sept. 14, 1941; children—Diana, Carol, Ann. B. Arch., U. So. Calif., 1941. Practice architecture, Los Angeles, 1946—; partner, Robert D. Bolling, 1960-75; Prin. works include prin. offices student union, Calif. State U., Los Angeles.; Author: Design for Human Affairs, 1974. Vice pres. Los Angeles Beautiful; dir. Regional Plan Assn. Commr., Los Angeles Bd. Zoning Appeals, 1973—. Fellow A.I.A. (past pres., dir. So. Calif. chpt., chmn. com. research). Home: Davenport Creek Farm Route 3 Box 161-S San Luis Obispo CA 93401

DEASY, WILLIAM E., packaging co. exec.; b. Trenton, N.J., Jan. 10, 1920; s. Edward J. and Mary A. (Flanagan) D.; m. Bette M. Nedzbala, Sept. 13, 1947; children—Michael S., Mary Kay. B.Ch.E., Villanova U., 1941. Gen. mgr. Panelyte div. St. Regis Paper Co., N.Y.C., 1946-64; v.p. ops. Champion Packages Co., Chgo., 1965-69; pres., chief exec. officer RJR Archer, Inc., Winston-Salem, N.C., 1970—, dir. Served with USAAF, 1942-46. Mem. Flexible Packaging Assn. (vice chmn.), Aluminum Assn. (dir.), Winston-Salem C. of C. Republican. Roman Catholic. Office: RJ Reynolds Industries World Hdqrs Winston-Salem NC 27102

DEASY, WILLIAM JOHN, mining executive; b. N.Y.C., June 22, 1937; s. Jeremiah and Margaret (Quinn) D.; m. Carol Ellyn Lemmons, Feb. 1, 1963; children: Cameron, Kimberly. B.S. in Civil Engring, Cooper Union, 1958; LL.B., U. Wash., 1963. Asst. to pres. Morrison Knudsen Co., Boise, Idaho, 1970-72, v.p. N.W. region, 1972-75, v.p. mining, 1975-78, group v.p. mining, 1978-83, pres., chief operating officer, 1984—; exec. v.p. mining, mfg. and shipbuilding Nat. Steel & Shipbuilding Co.; dir. Morrison Knudsen Internat., Westmoreland Resources.; Mem. adv. bd. Coll. Mines, U. Idaho, 1979—. Mem. Soc. Mining Engrs., Soc. Mil. Engrs. Home: 3770 Coventry Dr Boise ID 83740 Office: PO Box 7808 Boise ID 83729

DEATHERAGE, FRED E., biochemistry educator; b. Waverly, Ill., Dec. 30, 1913; s. Fred E. and Marian Eve (Sevier) D.; m. Nellie Lou Carothers, Jan. 3, 1942; children: Fred Sevier, Catherine Margaret, Marilyn Nan. A.B., Ill. Coll., 1935, D. Sc., 1960; A.M., U. Ill., 1936; Ph. D., U. Iowa, 1938, Ohio State U., 1940-42. Instr. biochemistry U. Iowa, 1938-40; chemist Kroger Food Found., Cin., 1942-46; asst. prof. Ohio State U., 1946-48, asso. prof., 1949-51, prof., 1951-81, prof. emeritus biochemistry, 1981—, chmn. dept. agrl. biochemistry, 1951-64; asst. dept. animal sci. Ohio Agrl. Expt. Sta., 1949-51, asso., 1951-53, prof., 1953—; food scientist, technologist AID, Brazil, 1964-68; lectr. State U. of Campinas, 1974; cons. in field. Author: Food for Life, 1975. Mem. Am. Chem. Soc., Am. Inst. Nutrition, Inst. Food Technologists; AAAS Soc. for Nutrition Edn., Am. Meat Sci. Assn. Am. Soc. Biol. Chemists, Am. Soc. Animal Sci., Phi Beta Kappa, Sigma Xi, Sigma Pi, Phi Lambda Upsilon. Home: 4310 Colerain Ave Columbus OH 43214

DEATON, LOWELL S., appliance mfg. co. exec.; b. Springfield, Ohio, July 18, 1925; s. Walter C. and Mary Eloise (Webb) D.; m. Marcella E. Coleman, May 28, 1954. B.S. in Indsl. Engring, Ohio State U., 1952. Various positions Gen. Elec. Co., 1952-71; plant mgr. Carrier Corp., Carmel, Ind., 1971-74, v.p. mfg., 1974-76, exec. v.p., 1977—. Bd. dirs. Jr. Achievement, 1972-74; bd. govs. United Way, 1973-74. Served with USNR, 1943-45. Recipient Gen. Mgrs. award Gen. Elec. Co., 1960. Republican. Methodist. Clubs: Masons, Shriners. Office: Carrier Corp 1310 W Morris St Indianapolis IN 46331 *

DEATS, PAUL KINDRED, JR., educator, clergyman; b. Graham, Tex., Oct. 1, 1918; s. Paul Kindred and Agnes (Craig) D.; m. Ruth Miller Zumbrunnen, Sept. 10, 1941; children: Patricia Zee (Mrs. Alain Jehlen), Carolyn Kay, Frances Ann (Mrs. Donald Poe, Jr.), Randall Kin. A.A., Tarleton (Tex.) State Coll., 1937; B.A., So. Meth. U., 1939; B.D., Union Theol. Sem., N.Y.C., 1943; Ph.D. (Gen. Edn. Bd. (Rockefeller) fellow, Kent fellow), Boston U., 1954. Ordained to ministry Methodist Ch., 1944; asso. minister Highland Park Meth. Ch., Dallas and; Met. Duane Meth. Ch., N.Y.C., 1939-41, 41-42; dir. Wesley Found., U. Tex., 1942-51, United Ministry, Boston U., 1953-55, asst. prof. religion in higher edn., 1954-58, asso. prof. religion in higher edn. and social ethics, 1958-63, prof. social ethics, 1963—, Walter G. Muelder prof., 1979—, chmn. div. theol. and religious studies, 1969-81; Mem. Gen. Commn. on Ch.-Govt. Relations, 1965-68. Author: (with others) The Responsible Student, 1957, (with H.E. Stotts) Methodism and Society: Guidelines for Strategy, 1962; Editor: Toward a Discipline of Social Ethics, 1972. Trustee Car Eth Found. Am. Assn. Theol. Schs. fellow, 1961-62. Mem. Am. Anthrop. Assn., Soc. Christian Ethics, Soc. for Sci. Study Religion, Fellowship of Reconciliation. Democrat. Home: 106 Berkeley St West Newton MA 02165 Office: 745 Commonwealth Ave Boston MA 02215

DEAVER, DARWIN HOLLOWAY, former utility exec.; b. Topeka, Oct. 6, 1914; s. Glenn Harry and Mabel (Holloway) D.; m. Jane Harriet Miller, Apr. 26, 1941; children—James Miller, Robert Holloway Henry Crandon. Ph.B., Washburn Coll., 1935; M.B.A., Harvard, 1937. Investment analyst Delafield & Delafield, N.Y.C., 1937-39, Continental Casualty Co., Chgo., 1939-41, Harris Hall & Co., 1946-49; asst. to pres. Automatic Electric Sales Corp., Chgo., 1949-50, supply sales mgr., 1953-55, pres., 1955-62; exec. v.p., dir. Automatic Electric Co., 1962-64, pres., dir., 1964-67; exec. v.p. mfg. United

Telecommunications, Inc., Kansas City, Mo., 1967-75, exec. v.p. fin., 1975-79, also dir., 1968-79; chmn. bd., dir. Am. Bank & Trust Co.; dir. Conchemco, Labconco, Gladwin. Served to lt. USNR, 1941-45; as lt. comdr., 1950-52. Republican. Episcopalian. Clubs: Kansas City Racquet, Kansas City Country, River. Home: 5828 Pembroke Ct Shawnee Mission KS 66208 Office: PO Box 11315 Plaza Station Kansas City MO 64112

DEAVER, MICHAEL KEITH, govt. ofcl. business exec.; b. Bakersfield, Calif., Apr. 11, 1938; s. Paul Sperling and Marian Mack D.; m. Carolyn Judy, Jan. 17; children—Amanda Judy, Blair Clayton. B.A. in Public Adminstrn, San Jose State U., 1960. Adminstrv. trainee IBM, 1960-62; with Republican Central Com. of Santa Clara County (Calif.), 1962-66; cabinet sec. State of Calif., 1966-67, asst. to gov., dir. adminstrn., from 1967; partner, pres. Deaver & Hannaford Co., Los Angeles; asst. to pres. of U.S., also dep. chief of staff. Served with USAFR, 1961-66. Mem. Am. Council Young Polit. Leaders. Episcopalian.

DEAVERS, KARL ALAN, investment company executive; b. Hambleton, W.Va., Sept. 7, 1934; s. Okey B. and Kathleen (Bowley) D.; m. Ruth A. Hunt; 1 son, Kary A. B.S., W.Va. U., 1956, LL.B., 1959; LL.M., N.Y. U., 1960; grad. Advanced Mgmt. Program, Harvard, 1973. Bar: W.Va. bar 1959, N.Y. bar 1968. Tax atty. J. & W. Seligman & Co., N.Y.C., 1960-63; asst. to treas. Tri-Continental Corp., also Union Service Corp., N.Y.C., 1963-65, asst. treas., 1965-67, treas., 1967-80; also dir.; treas. Broad St. Investing Corp., also Union Income Fund, Inc.; treas. Nat. Investors Corp., 1967-80; treas., dir. Union Data Service Center, Inc., 1967-80; treas. Union Cash Mgmt. Fund, Inc., 1977-80; sr. v.p. Lehman Mgmt. Co., Inc., N.Y.C., 1980-82, exec. v.p., dir., 1982—; pres., dir. Lehman Cash Mgmt. Fund, Inc., N.Y.C., 1980—, Lehman Govt. Fund, Inc., 1981—, Lehman Tax-Free Reserves Inc., 1982-84, Mariner Instl. Funds Inc., 1982—, Mariner Tax-Free Instl. Funds Inc., 1983—, Lehman Internat. Dollar Fund Inc., 1984—. Trustee Northwestern Coll., Orange City, Iowa, 1980—. Mem. Am., W.Va., N.Y.C. bar assns., Phi Alpha Delta. Home: 47 E 63d St New York NY 10021 Office: Lehman Cash Mgmt Fund Inc 55 Water St New York NY 10041

DEBACCO, PAUL L., greeting card co. exec.; b. Newark, Sept. 13, 1929; s. Angelo and Teresa DeB.; m. Marilyn Metrione, May 31, 1952; children—Paul, John, Barbara, Thomas, Stephen, Mary Teresa. B.S., Seton Hall U., 1950; M.B.A., N.Y. U., 1955. Corp. dir. personnel adminstrn. Celanese Corp. Am., N.Y.C., 1958-62; asst. v.p. personnel and adminstrn. Inter-public Group of Cos., N.Y.C., 1962-65; corp. v.p. personnel and services Hallmark Cards, Inc., Kansas City, Mo., 1965—; dir. Old Am. Ins. Co., Kansas City; instr. principles of mgmt. Avila Coll., Kansas City, Mo. Bd. dirs. (hon.) Rockhurst Coll., 1969—; bd. counselors Avila Coll., 1972—; regent Conception Sem. Coll., 1973; trustee Notre Dame de Sion, 1973—; bd. dirs. Girl Scouts U.S.A., 1972—; ad. bd. Sch. Bus., Seton Hall U., 1975—; dir. Community Blood Bank, Kansas City, 1975—, St. Joseph Hosp., Kansas City, 1977—. Served with U.S. Army, 1951-53. Mem. Am. Soc. Personnel Adminstrn. (pres.'s council), Am. Mgmt. Assn., Citizens Assn. Kansas City, Kansas City C. of C., Mayor's Corps of Progress. Roman Catholic. Home: 11812 Pennsylvania St Kansas City MO 64114 Office: Hallmark Cards Inc PO Box 437 Kansas City MO 64141

DEBACHER, DONALD EDWARD, carbide, food processing equipment and steel company executive; b. Adams, Mass., Mar. 28, 1930; s. Nicholas J. and Jeanette M. (Debacher) D.; m. Eleanor L. Whitman, Jan. 27, 1951; children: Donald E., Boni A. Knight. B.Chem. Engring., Rensselaer Poly. Inst., 1951. Process engr. Ethyl Corp., Baton Rouge, 1951-55; with Gen. Electric Co., 1955-78, mgr. process devel., 1960-66, mgr. mfg., 1967-70, gen. mgr. Lexan products, 1970-73, gen. mgr. silicone products dept., 1973-74, gen. mgr. plastics div., v.p. co., 1974-78; pres., chief exec. officer Sandvik, Inc., Fairlawn, N.J., 1979—. Mem. Internat. Mgmt. and Devel. Inst., Am. Iron and Steel Inst. Republican. Roman Catholic. Clubs: Ridgewood Country, Ramsey Tennis. Office: Sandvik Inc 1702 Nevins Rd Fairlawn NJ 07410

DE BAKEY, LOIS, writer, lecturer, editor, educator; b. Lake Charles, La.; d. S.M. and Raheeja (Zorba) DeBakey. B.A. in Math., Tulane U., 1949, M.A. in Lit. and Linguistics, 1959, Ph.D. in Lit. and Linguistics, 1963. Asst. prof. English Tulane U.; asst. prof. sci. communication Tulane Med. Sch., 1963-65; asso. prof. sci. communication Tulane U. Med. Sch., 1965-67; prof. Tulane Med. Sch., 1967-68, lectr., 1968—, adj. prof., 1981—; prof. sci. communication Baylor Coll. Medicine, Houston, 1968—; mem. biomed. library rev. com. Nat. Library Medicine, Bethesda, Md., 1973-77, bd. regents, 1981—; dir. courses in med. communication A.C.S. and other orgns.; mem. nat. adv. council U. So. Calif. Center for Continuing Med. Edn., 1981—; mem. adv. com. Soc. Advancement Good English, 1984—; steering com. Plain English Forum, 1984—; former cons. in English Nat. Assn. Standard Med. Vocabulary. Sr. author: The Scientific Journal: Editorial Policies and Practices, 1976; Mem. editorial bd.: Tulane Studies in English, 1966-68, Cardiovascular Research Center Bull., 1971-83, Health Communications and Informatics, 1975-80, Forum on Medicine, 1977-80, Grants Mag, 1978-81, Internat. Jour. Cardiology, 1981—, Excerpta Medica's Core Jours. in Cardiology, 1981—, Health Communications and Biopsychosocial Health, 1981—; mem. usage panel: Am. Heritage Dictionary, 1980—; Contbr. articles on biomed. communication and sci. writing, audiovisual communication, also other subjects to profl. jours., books, encyclopedias. Recipient Distinguished Service award Am. Med. Writers Assn., 1970; Bausch & Lomb sci. award., John P. McGovern award Med. Library Assn., 1983. Mem. Internat. Soc. Gen. Semantics, Inst. Soc., Ethics and Life Scis., Council Biology Editors (dir. 1973-77, chmn. com. on editorial policy 1971-75), Council Basic Edn. (spl. commn. writing 1977-79), Soc. Tech. Communication, So. Assn. Colls. and Schs. (former exec. council Commn. on Colls.), AAAS, NIH Alumni Assn., Nat. Council Tchrs. English (com. on tech. sci. writing, conf. on coll. composition and communication), Assn. Tchrs. Tech. Writing, Dictionary Soc. N.Am., Nat. Assn. Sci. Writers, Soc. for Health and Human Values, Com. of Thousand for Better Health Regulations, Golden Key Nat. Honor Soc. (hon.), Phi Beta Kappa. Pioneered instruction in scientific communication in med. schs. Office: Baylor Coll Medicine One Baylor Plaza Houston TX 77030

DE BAKEY, MICHAEL ELLIS, surgeon; b. Lake Charles, La., Sept. 7, 1908; s. Shaker Morris and Raheeja (Zorba) DeB.; m. Diana Cooper, Oct. 15, 1936; children—Michael Maurice, Ernest Ochsner, Barry Edward, Denis Alton, Olga Katerina; m. Katrin Fehlhaber, July 1975. B.S., Tulane U., 1930, M.D., 1932, M.S., 1935, LL.D., 1965; Docteur Honoris Causa, U. Lyon, France, 1961, U. Brussels, 1962, U. Ghent, Belgium, 1964, U. Athens, 1964; D.H.C., U. Turin, Italy, 1965, U. Belgrade, Yugoslavia, 1967; LL.D., Lafayette Coll., 1965; M.D. (hon.), Aristotelean U. of Thessaloniki, Greece, 1972; D.Sc., Hahnemann Med. Coll., 1973, numerous others. Diplomate: Nat. Bd. Med. Examiners, Am. Bd. Surgery, Am. Bd. Thoracic Surgery. Intern Charity Hosp., New Orleans, 1932-33, asst. surgery, 1933-35, U. Strasbourg, France, 1935-36, U. Heidelberg, Germany, 1936; instr. surgery, Tulane U., 1937-40, asst. prof., 1940-46, assoc. prof., 1946-48; prof. surgery, chmn. dept. Baylor U., 1948—, v.p. med. affairs, 1968—; chief exec. officer Baylor Coll. Medicine, 1968-69, pres., 1969—, chancellor, 1979—; dir. Nat. Heart and Blood Vessel Research and Demonstration Center, Baylor Coll. Medicine, 1975—; surgeon-in-chief Ben Taub Gen. Hosp., 1963—; sr. attending surgeon Meth. Hosp.; cons. surgery VA, St. Elizabeth's, M.D. Anderson, St. Luke's, Tex. Children's Hosps.; clin. prof. surgery U. Tex. Dental Br., Houston; cons. Tex. Inst. Rehab. and Research, Brooke Gen. Hosp., Brooke Army Med. Center, Ft. Sam Houston, Tex.; cons. surgery Walter Reed Army Hosp., Washington.; mem. med. adv. com. sec. def., 1948-50; chmn. com. surgery NRC, 1953, mem. exec. com., 1953; mem. com. med. services Hoover Commn.; chmn. bd. regents Nat. Library Medicine, 1959; past mem. nat. adv. heart council NIH; mem. Nat. Adv. Health Council, 1961-65, Nat. Adv. Council Regional Med. Programs, 1965—, Nat. Adv. Gen. Med. Scis. Council, 1965, Program Planning Com., Com. Tng., Nat. Heart Inst., 1961—; mem. civilian health and med. adv. council Office Asst. Sec. Def.; chmn. Pres.'s Commn. Heart Disease, Cancer and Stroke, 1964. Author: (with Robert A. Kilduffe) Blood Transfusion, 1942, (with Gilbert W. Beebe) Battle Casualties, 1952, (with Alton Ochsner) Textbook of Minor Surgery, 1955, (with T. Whayne) Cold Injury, Ground Type, 1958, A Surgeon's Visit to China, 1974, (with A.M. Gotto) The Living Heart, 1977; editor: Yearbook of Surgery, 1958-70; chmn. adv. editorial bd.: Medical History of World War II. Mem. Tex. Constl. Revision Commn., 1973. Served as col. Office Surgeon Gen. AUS, 1942-46; now col. Res.; cons. to Surgeon Gen., 1946—. Decorated Legion of Merit, 1946; Rudolph Matas award, 1954; Independence of Jordan medal 1st class; Merit Order of Republic 1st class, Egypt; comdr. Cross of Merit Pro Utiliate Hominum Sovereign Order Knights of Hosp. of St. John of Jerusalem in Denmark; Hektoengold medal AMA; Internat. Soc. Surgery Distinguished Service award, 1957; recipient Modern Medicine award, 1957, Roswell Park medal, 1959; A.M.A. Distinguished Service award, 1959; Leriche award Internat. Soc. Surgery, 1959; Great medallion U. Ghent, 1961; Grand Cross of Order Leopold, Belgium, 1962; Albert Lasker award for clin. research, 1963; Order of Merit, Chile, 1964; St. Vincent prize med. scis. U. Turin, 1965; Orden del Libertador Gen. San Martin, Argentina, 1965; Centennial medal Albert Einstein Med. Center, 1966; Gold Scalpel award Internat. Cardiology Found., 1966; Distinguished Service prof. Baylor U., 1968; Distinguished Faculty award, 1973; Eleanor Roosevelt Humanities award, 1969; Civilian Service medal sec. def., 1970; USSR Acad. Sci. 50th Anniversary Jubilee medal, 1973; Phi Delta Epsilon Disting. Service award, 1974; La Madonnina award, 1974; 30 Yr. Service award Harris County Hosp. Dist., 1978; Knights Humanity award honoris causa Internat. Register Chivalry, Milan, 1978; Diploma de Merito Caja Costarricense de Seguro Social, San Jose, Costa Rica, 1979; Disting. Service plaque Tex. Bd. Edn., 1979; Britannica Achievement in Life award, 1979; Medal of Freedom with Distinction Presdl. award, 1969; Disting. Service award Internat. Soc. Atherosclerosis, 1979; Centennial award ASME, 1980; Marian Health Care award St. Mary's U., 1981; numerous others; named Dr. of Year Med. World News, 1965, Med. Man of Year, 1966, Humanitarian Father of Year award, 1974, Tulane U. Alumnus of Year, 1974, Tex. Scientist of Yr., Tex. Acad. Sci., 1979. Fellow A.C.S. (Ann. award Southwestern Pa. chpt. 1973), Inst. of Medicine Chgo. (hon.); mem. Am. Coll. Cardiology (hon. fellow), Royal Soc. Medicine, Halsted Soc., Am. Heart Assn., So. Soc. Clin. Research, AAAS, Southwestern Surg. Congress (pres. 1952), Soc. Vascular Surgery (pres. 1953), AMA, Am. Surg. Assn. (Disting. Service award 1981), So. Surg. Assn., Western Surg. Assn., Am. Assn. Thoracic Surgery (pres. 1959), Internat. Cardiovascular Soc. (pres. 1958, pres. N.Am chpt 1964), Mexican Acad. Surgery, hon.), Soc. Clin. Surg., Soc. Univ. Surgeons, Internat. Soc. Surgery, Soc. Exptl. Biology and Medicine, Hellenic Surg. Soc. (hon.), Bio-med. Engring. Soc. (dir. 1968), Houston Heart Assn. (mem. adv. council 1968-69), Sociedad Nacional de Cirugia (Cuba), C. of C., Sigma Xi, Alpha Omega Alpha. Democrat. Episcopalian. Club: University (Washington). Office: Baylor Coll Medicine 1200 Moursund Ave Houston TX 77030

DEBANE, PIERRE, Canadian government official, lawyer; b. Haifa, Palestine, Aug. 2, 1938; s. Gabriel and Marie (Gahel) DeB.; m. Elizabeth Nadeau, Dec. 22, 1980; children: Jean, Manuel. B.A. magna cum laude, Coll. St. Alexandre, Can.; postgrad., Seminaire in Trois-Rivieres, Can., Laval U.; postgrad. in law, U. Ottawa, Can. Bar: Que. 1964, Can. Supreme Ct. 1964. Prof. law Laval U.; spl. asst. to minister of justice Govt. of Can., 1967-68; mem. House of Commons, Govt. of Can., 1968—, Parliamentary com. on Transp.; Parliamentary sec. to Minister Urban Affairs, from 1974, Minister of External Affairs, 1972-74; also to Minister of Consumer and Corp. Affairs, 1974; minister of supply and services Govt. Can., 1978-80, minister of regional econ. expansion, 1980-82, minister of fisheries and oceans, 1982—; also dep. Matapedia-Metane, Govt. Can. Office: House of Commons Ottawa ON Canada K1A DA6 *

DE BARDELEBEN, ARTHUR, lawyer; b. Great Falls, Mont., July 12, 1918; s. John Arthur and Antoinette (Merselis) DeB.; children: Suzanne T. Fiedler, Joan T. Ph.B., U. Wis., 1940, LL.B., 1947. Bar: Wis. bar 1947. Since practiced in, Park Falls.; Bd. regents U. Wis., 1959-68, pres. bd. regents, 1964-67; bd. regents U. Wis. System, 1974-81; mem. U. Wis. System Task Force Faculty Compensation, 1983-84; mem. spl. adv. com. to Wis. Legis. Council on Wis. Guaranteed Higher Edn. Plan, 1974; mem. Wis. Coordinating Com. Higher Edn., 1959-67, Wis. Higher Ednl. Aids Bd., 1975-78, Fed. Judicial Nominating Commn. Western Dist. Wis., 1979-81; Presdl. elector, 1964. Author: (with Walter P. Metzger, Sanford H. Kadish, Edward J. Bloustein) Dimensions of Academic Freedom, 1969; Mem. bd.: Wis. Law Rev, 1940-41. Served with AUS, 1941-45. Mem. Am. Arbitration Assn. (nat. panel), ABA, 15th Jud. Circuit Bar Assn. (pres. 1959-60), State Bar Wis., Am. Acad. Polit. and Social Sci., Am. Civil Liberties Union, Am. Judicature Soc. Address: PO Box 280 Park Falls WI 54552

DEBARDELEBEN, JOHN THOMAS, JR., insurance company executive; b. Ft. Benning, Ga., Aug. 28, 1926; s. John Thomas and Erin Gautier (Howard) DeB.; m. Martha Evelyn Graves, Sept. 24, 1946; children: John T. III, Charles G., Eve Lamar. B.A., Vanderbilt U., 1947. C.L.U. Agent, asst. mgr. N.Y. Life Ins. Co., Nashville and Chattanooga, 1951-56, gen. mgr., Knoxville, Tenn., Savannah, Ga. and Montgomery, Ala.,, 1957-70, regional v.p., Chgo., 1971-76, v.p., N.Y.C., 1976-78, sr. v.p., 1978-82, exec. v.p., 1982—; dir. N.Y. Life & Health Ins. Co. Mem. Republican County Com., Montgomery, Ala., 1963-64; active Crusade of Mercy, Chgo., 1972-75, United Way of Tri-State, N.Y.C., 1979-81. Mem. Nat. Assn. Life Underwriters, Am. Soc. C.L.U.'s, Gen. Agts. and Mgrs. Conf., Montgomery, Chgo. chambers of commerce. Presbyterian (elder). Office: 51 Madison Ave New York NY 10010

DEBARE, CHARLES ALLEN, broadcasting executive; b. N.Y.C., May 15, 1924; s. Nathaniel J. and Lillian (Rubin) DeB.; m. Nancy Skutch, Apr. 28, 1956; children: Wendy, Deborah, Robert. A.B., Cornell U., 1944, J.D., 1949. Bar: N.Y. 1949. Pvt. practice law N.Y.C., 1950-55; staff atty. NBC, N.Y.C., 1955-59; v.p., dir. legal and bus. affairs ABC owned T.V. and radio stas. and radio network, N.Y.C., 1961-72; pres. ABC owner AM radio stas., 1972-82, ABC owned AM and FM stas., 1982—. Trustee Birch Wathen Sch., 1974—, chmn., 1978-80. Served with U.S. Army, 1943-46. Recipient citations Radio Advt. Bur. for mng. sales conf., 1981, Internat. Radio and T.V. Soc., 1981. Mem. Internat. Radio and T.V. Soc. (v.p. 1980—, bd. govs. 1972—), Bar Assn. City N.Y. Home: 25 E 86 St New York NY 10028 Office: 1330 Ave of the Americas New York NY 10019

DEBARTOLO, EDWARD J., real estate developer; b. Youngstown, Ohio, May 17, 1919; s Michael and Rose (Villani) DeB.; m. Maria Patricia Montani, Dec. 18, 1944; children: Edward J., Marie D. Grad., U. Notre Dame; D.Sc. hon., Fla. Inst. Tech., 1981. Registered profl. engr.; registered surveyor. Ptnr. Michael DeBartolo Constrn. Co., Youngstown, 1936-41, pres., 1946-48, Edward J. DeBartolo Corp., Youngstown, 1958-79, chmn. bd., chief exec. officer, 1979—; owner (3 race tracks), U.S. Football League franchise, (soccer team),. 2d lt. C.E. U.S. Army, 1941-46; Okinawa. Named Man of Yr. Mahoning Valley Econ. Devel. Corp., 1983, City of Pitts., 1983. Mem. Urban Land Inst., Nat. Realty Com., Internat. Council Shopping Ctrs. Roman Catholic. Office: DeBartolo Corp 7620 Market St Youngstown OH 44512

DE BARTOLO, EDWARD J., JR., owner pro football team; b. Youngstown, Ohio, Nov. 6, 1946; s. Edward J. and Marie Patricia (Montani) DeB.; m. Cynthia Ruth Papalia, Nov. 27, 1968; children: Lisa Marie, Tiffanie Lynne, Nicole Anne. Student, U. Notre Dame, 1964-68. With Edward J. DeBartolo Corp., Youngstown, Ohio, 1960—, v.p., 1972-75, exec. v.p., 1975—; pres. EJD Corp., 1979; owner, pres., mng. partner San Francisco 49ers, 1977—. Trustee Youngstown State U., 1974-77; mem. nat. adv. council St. Jude Children's Research Hosp., 1978—, local chmn., 1979-80; local chmn. fund drive Am. Cancer Soc., 1975—, City of Hope, 1977; mem. Nat. Cambodia Crisis Com., 1980—. Served with U.S. Army, 1969. Recipient Man of Yr. award St. Jude Children's Hosp., 1979. Mem. Internat. Council of Shopping Centers. Roman Catholic. Clubs: Tippecanoe Country, Fonderlac Country, Dapper Dan (dir. 1980—). Office: Edward J DeBartolo Corp 7620 Market St Youngstown OH 44512 *

DEBARTOLO, JACK, JR., architect; b. Youngstown, Ohio, May 6, 1938; s. Jack and Virginia (Sassinelli) DeB.; m. Pat. McLamore, Aug. 15, 1958; children: Ava, Gina, Jack III. B.Arch., U. Houston, 1962; M.Arch., Columbia U., 1964. Sr. v.p., dir. design Caudill Rowell Scott, 1964-73; sr. v.p. William Wilde & Assocs., Tucson, 1973; pres., gen. mgr., dir. design Anderson DeBartolo Pan Inc., Tucson, 1973—; mem. seminar faculties on hosp. design. Designer (award winning project), CRS Office Bldg., Houston, Joilet Jr. Coll., Ill., Pima Community Coll., Tucson, St. Mary's Convent, Tucson. Elder Grace Chapel, Tucson. Mem. AIA (pres. So. Ariz. chpt.), Internat. Hosp. Fedn., Am. Hosp. Assn., Assn. Western Hosps., Ariz. Soc. Architects, Tuscon Tomorrow. Republican. Club: Tucson Breakfast. Office: Anderson DeBartolo Pan Inc. 6339 E Speedway Blvd Tucson AZ 85710

DE BENKO, EUGENE, educator, librarian; b. Szaszregen, Hungary, June 2, 1917; came to U.S., 1950, naturalized, 1956; s. Jeno and Vilma (Simon) De B. B.A., Reg. Ferdinand U., Cluj, Rumania, 1939, M.A., 1940; Ph.D., Ferenc Jozsef U., Kolozsvar, Hungary, 1943; M.A., Ind. U., 1956. Jr. officer econ. affairs Hungarian Civil Service, 1940-47; bus. ops. analyst Assos. Investment Co., South Bend, Ind., 1952-55; mem. faculty Mich. State U., East Lansing, 1956—; head Internat. Library, 1964—, prof. social sci., 1970—; Lectr. cons. library U. Ryukyus, 1961-63; library cons. AID, India, 1963, Thailand, 1967, Africa, 1966, 70-71, 77, 78. Author: Research Sources for South Asian Studies in Economic Development, 1966, Research Sources for African Studies, 1969, Books and Publishing in Selected African Countries, 1973, Documentation for Development in the Sahel, 1977, Aspects of Rural Library and Information Service in Africa, 1978, Aid to the Sahel, 1978; contbr. articles to profl. jours. Recipient Disting. Faculty award Mich. State U., 1972. Mem. Nat. Council Cath. Men, ALA, African Studies Assn. (mem. com. archives 1967-70), Assn. Asian Studies (mem. com. Asian libraries 1964), Beta Phi Mu. Club: Michigan State Univ. Faculty (East Lansing). Home: 312 Lee Circle East Lansing MI 48823

DEBEVOISE, DICKINSON RICHARDS, judge; b. Orange, N.J., Apr. 23, 1924; s. Elliott and Josephine (Richards) D.; m. Katrina Stephenson Leeb, Feb. 24, 1951; children: Kate, Josephine Debevoise Davies, Mary Debevoise Rennie, Abigail H. B.A., Williams Coll., 1948; LL.B., Columbia U., 1951. Bar: N.J. 1953, U.S. Supreme Ct. 1956. Law clk. to Hon. Phillip Forman, chief judge U.S. Dist. Ct. for Dist. N.J., 1952-53; assoc. firm Riker, Emery & Danzig, Newark, 1953-56; partner firm Riker, Danzig, Scherer, Debevoise & Hyland, Newark, 1957-79; judge U.S. Dist. Ct. for N.J., 1979—; pres. Newark Legal Services Project, 1965-70; chmn. N.J. Gov.'s Workmen's Compensation Study Commn., 1972-73; mem. N.J. Supreme Ct. Adv. Com. on Jud. Conduct, 1974-78; chmn. N.J. Disciplinary Rev. Bd., 1978-79; mem. Lawyers Adv. Com. for 3d Circuit, 1975-79, chmn., 1979, N.J. Legal Services Adv. Council, 1976-78. Asso. editor: N.J. Law Jour, 1959-79. Trustee Ramapo Coll., N.J., 1969-73, chmn. bd., 1971-73; trustee Williams Coll., 1969-74, Hosp. Center at Orange, N.J.; v.p. Hosp. Center at Orange, 1975-79; pres. Democrats for Good Govt., 1956-60; active various presdl., senatorial, gubernatorial campaigns. Served from sgt. to 1st lt. U.S. Army, World War II, Korean War. Decorated Bronze Star. Fellow Am. Bar Found.; mem. Am. Bar Assn., N.J. Bar Assn., Fed. Bar Assn. (v.p. 1976), Assn. Fed. Bar State N.J. (v.p. 1977-79), Essex County Bar Assn. (treas. 1960-64, trustee 1968-71), Assn. Hosp. Attys., Am. Law Inst., Judicature Soc. Mem. United Ch. of Christ. Office: US Courthouse Newark NJ 07101

DEBEVOISE, THOMAS MCELRATH, lawyer, educator; b. N.Y.C., Aug. 10, 1929; s. Eli Whitney and Barbara (Clay) D.; m. Ann Taylor, Nov. 1951; children: Eli Whitney II, Albert Clay, Thomas McElrath III, Anne Elizabeth. B.A., Yale, 1950; LL.B., Columbia, 1954. Bar: N.Y. 1954, Vt. 1957, D.C. 1963. Asst. U.S. Atty. So. Dist. N.Y., 1954-56; pvt. practice law, Woodstock, Vt., 1957-59; dep. atty. gen. State of Vt., 1959-60, atty. gen., 1960-62; asst. gen. counsel Fed. Power Commn., 1962-64; pvt. practice law, D.C., 1964; partner Debevoise & Liberman, 1965-74, counsel, 1975-82, partner, 1982—; dean Vt. Law Sch., South Royalton, 1974-82, dean emeritus, 1982—, trustee, 1973—. Pres. Woodstock Found., 1982—; Bd. dirs. Lawyers Com. for Civil Rights Under Law, New Eng. Legal Found.; mem. Commn. on Instns. Higher Edn. of New Eng. Assn. Schs. and Colls. Fellow Am. Bar Found.; mem. Am. Law Inst., Fed. Energy (pres. 1973-74), Am., Vt. bar assns., Fed. Bar Council (trustee), Assn. Bar City N.Y., Phi Delta Phi. Republican. Episcopalian. Clubs: Masons, Lakota, National Lawyers, Century.; University, Yale (N.Y.C.). Home: Woodstock VT 05091 Office: 18 Elm St Woodstock VT 05091

DEBICKI, ANDREW PETER, educator; b. Warsaw, Poland, June 28, 1934; came to U.S., 1948, naturalized, 1955; s. Roman and Jadwiga (Dunin) D.; m. Mary Jo Tidmarsh, Dec. 29, 1959 (dec. 1975); children: Mary Beth, Margaret. B.A., Yale U., 1955, Ph.D., 1960. Instr. Trinity Coll., Hartford, Conn., 1957-60; asst. prof. Grinnell (Iowa) Coll., 1960-62, asso. prof., 1962-66, prof., 1966-68; prof. Spanish, U. Kans., Lawrence, 1968-76; Univ. Disting. prof. Univ. Kans., 1976—. Author: La poesia de Jose Gorostiza, 1962, Estudios sobre poesia espanola contemporanea, 1968, 81, Damaso Alonso, 1970, 74, La poesia de Jorge Guillen, 1973, Poetas hispanoamericanos contemporaneos: Punto de vista, perspectiva, experiencia, 1976, Poetry of Discovery, 1982; contbr. articles to various publs. Guggenheim fellow, 1970-71, 1980; Nat. Humanities Center fellow, 1980; Am. Council Learned Socs. fellow, 1966-67. Mem. MLA, Am. Assn. Tchrs. Spanish and Portuguese. Home: 2547 Alabama St Lawrence KS 66044 Office: Dept of Spanish and Portuguese Univ of Kansas Lawrence KS 66045

DE BLASI, ANTHONY ARMANDO, artist, educator; b. Alcamo, Italy, Jan. 1, 1933; came to U.S., 1938, naturalized, 1959; s. Frank and Josephine (Frisella) DeB.; m. Laurene Ann Hungle, July 28, 1972; children by previous marriage: Keith, Eric. Student, Art Students League, N.Y.C., 1957-59, Pan Am. Art Sch., 1957-58; B.A., U. R.I., 1961; M.F.A., Ind. U., 1963; student of, William Leete, Kingston, R.I., 1959-61, James McGarrell, Bloomington, Ind., 1961-63, William Bailey, Bloomington, 1961-63, Rudy Pozzatti, Bloomington, 1961-63, others. Artist-in-residence Washington and Jefferson Coll., Washington, Pa., 1963-66, also chmn. dept. art, 1963-66; prof. painting, drawing and design Mich. State U., East Lansing, 1966—. One-man shows of paintings, 1963—, latest being, Kresge Art Center, Mich. State U., E. Lansing, 1969, 72, 76, Spectrum Gallery, N.Y.C., 1968, 69, 71, 73, Detroit Art Inst., 1972, Razor Gallery, N.Y.C., 1975, 77, Western Mich. U., Kalamazoo, 1979, Wake Forest U., Winston-Salem, N.C., 1980, Urban Inst. Contemporary Art, Grand Rapids, Mich., 1981, numerous group shows, 1963—, latest being, Mus. of Modern Art, N.Y.C., 1968, Henri Gallery, Washington, 1968, 70, Riverside Mus., N.Y.C., 1970, Spectrum Gallery, 1970, 71, Calvin Coll., Grand Rapids, 1975, Eastern Mich. U., Ypsilanti, 1972, Corcoran Gallery, Washington, 1973, Razor Gallery, N.Y.C., 1975, 77, 78, 79, Gran Rapids Art Mus., 1980, Neill Gallery, N.Y.C., Detroit Inst. Arts, 1982, Birmingham (Mich.)-Bloomfield Art Assn.; represented in permanent collections, Detroit Art Inst., Ind. U. Mus. Fine Arts, Bloomington, Bethany (W.Va.) Coll., Ulrich Mus. Art, Wichita, Kans., Rose Art Mus., Brandeis U., Waltham, Mass., City Nat. Bank, Detroit and, numerous pvt. collections. Served with USN, 1951-55. Recipient Albert Kahn Associated Architects and Engrs. prize award, 1969, 1st Prize award Detroit Art Inst., 1970, Mich. Fine Arts Competition award of excellence Birmingham-Bloomfield Art Assn., 1982; Tiffany Found. grantee, 1966-67; Mich. Council for Arts Individual artist grantee, 1983. Office: Art Dept Mich State Univ East Lansing MI 48824

DE BLASIS, JAMES MICHAEL, opera association executive; b. N.Y.C., Apr. 12, 1931; s. James and Sarah (de Felice) de B.; m. Ruth Hofreuter, Aug. 25, 1957; 1 dau., Blythe. B.F.A., Carnegie Mellon U., 1959, M.F.A., 1960. Mem. drama faculty Carnegie Mellon U., 1960-62; head drama dept. Onondaga Community Coll., Syracuse, N.Y., 1963-72; head Opera Workshop, Syracuse, 1969-70; adv. of opera Corbett Found., Cin., 1971-76; gen. dir. Cin. Opera Assn., 1973—; internat. ind. stage dir. of opera, 1962—. Artistic advisor, Pitts. Opera, Inc., 1979-83. Served with U.S. Army, 1951-53. Recipient award Omicron Delta Kappa, 1959, Alumni award Bellaire High Sch., 1974. Mem. Actors Equity, Am. Guild Mus. Artists, Drama Alumni Carnegie Mellon U., Beta Theta Pi. Republican. Episcopalian. Office: 1241 Elm St Cincinnati OH 45210

DEBOCK, FLORENT ALPHONSE, corporation controller; b. LaLouviere, Belgium, Feb. 3, 1924; came to U.S., 1954, naturalized, 1959; s. Benoit and Elvire (Verbeke) DeB.; m. Mary C. Murray, July 2, 1960; 1 son, Mark Steven. Tchr. diploma, Inst. Ste. Marie, Arlon, Belgium, 1944; Accountant diploma, Inst. Professionel Superieur de Belgique, 1953; postgrad., La Salle Extension U., Chgo., 1956. C.P.A., D.C. Govt. auditor U.S. Army Audit Agy., Engr. Procurement Center, Europe, 1946-54; auditor Touche, Ross, Bailey & Smart, N.Y.C., 1954-61; controller Armor Elevator Co. (and affiliates), Queens, N.Y., 1962-64; controller subsidiary of Eaton, Yale & Towne, Dusseldorf, Germany, 1964-67; group controller bus. furnishings group Litton Industries, N.Y.C., 1967-68; controller Levitt & Sons, homebldg. div. ITT, Lake Success, N.Y., 1969-71, Intermodulex NDH Corp., White Plains, N.Y., 1971-74, Watch Case Corp. div. Zale Corp., Long Island City, N.Y., 1974-82, Baden & Foss, Inc. (div. Am. Gensmiths, Inc.), N.Y.C., N.Y., 1982—. Served with inf. Belgian Army, 1945-46. Decorated War of 1940-45 Commemorative medal, 1940-45 Vol. medal. Mem. Am. Inst. C.P.A.s, N.Y. State Soc. C.P.A.s, Nat. Assn. Accountants. Home: 123 99th St Brooklyn NY 11209 Office: 71 Fifth Ave. Long Island City New York 10003

DE BOER, PIETER CORNELIS TOBIAS, mechanical and aeronautical engineer, educator; b. Leiden, Netherlands, May 21, 1930; s. Pieter and Willemina (Zuydam) deB.; m. Joan Lieshout, June 7, 1956; children: Maarten P., Claire E., Yvette E. Mech. engr., U. Tech. Delft, 1955; Ph.D. in Physics, U. Md., 1962. Research asst., asso. U. Tech. Delft, 1954-55; research asso. U. Md., 1957-62, research asst. prof., 1962-64; asst. prof. Cornell U., 1964-68, asso. prof., 1968-74; prof. Sibley Sch. of Mech. and Aerospace Engring., Cornell U., 1974—, assoc. dir., 1982; mem. tech. staff Aerospace Corp., summer 1963, 65, 67; cons. in field to industry; vis. prof. von Karman Inst. for Fluid Dynamics, Belgium, 1968, Cornell Aero. Lab., Buffalo, 1969; cons. Ford Motor Co., 1971-73, gas turbine div. Gen. Electric Co., 1978-79. Contbr. articles to profl. jours. Served with Dutch Army, 1955-57. NATO fellow, 1968. Fellow AIAA (asso.); mem. ASME, Am. Phys. Soc., Internat. Assn., Hydrogen Energy, AAUP, Royal Inst. Ingenieurs (Netherlands), Sigma Xi, Sigma Pi Sigma. Clubs: Research (Cornell U.) (pres.); Finger Lakes Cycling (pres.), Finger Lakes Runners.). Office: 287 Grumman Hall Cornell Univ Ithaca NY 14853

DE BOOR, CARL, mathematician; b. Stolp, Germany, Dec. 3, 1937; m. Matilda C. Friedrich, Feb. 6, 1960; children—C. Thomas, Elisabeth, Peter, Adam. Student, Universitat Hamburg, 1956-59, Harvard U., 1959-60; Ph.D., U. Mich., 1966. Research mathematician Gen. Motors Research Labs., 1960-64; asst. prof. math., computer sci. Purdue U., 1966-68, asso. prof., 1968-72; prof. math., computer sci. Math. Research Center U. Wis.-Madison, 1972—; vis. staff mem. Los Alamos Sci. Labs., 1970—. Author: (with S. Conte) Elementary Numerical Analysis, 1972, 80, A Practical Guide to Splines, 1978, (with J.B. Rosser) Pocket Calculator Supplement for Calculus, 1979. Mem. Am. Math. Soc., Phi Beta Kappa. Office: 610 Walnut St Math Research Center Univ of Wis Madison WI 53706

DE BORCHGRAVE, ARNAUD, editor, author, lecturer; b. Brussels, Belgium, Oct. 26, 1926; s. Count Baudouin and Audrey (Townshend) de B.; m. Dorothy Solon, Apr. 1950; 1 son, Arnaud; m. Eileen Ritschel, Mar. 31, 1959; 1 dau., Trisha; m. Alexandra D. Villard, May 10, 1969. Student, Maredsous, Belgium, 1936-39, King's Sch., Canterbury, Eng., 1940-42. Freelance writer, Eastern Europe, 1946-47; staff United Press, Western Europe, 1947-51; mgr. Benelux Countries, 1949-51; European Corr. Newsweek, Paris, North Africa, Middle East, 1951-54, asso. editor fgn. reports, N.Y.C., 1954-55, gen. editor, fgn. editor, 1955, sr. editor, 1955-59, chief fgn. corr., 1959-62, mng. editor internat. edits., 1962-63, chief Newsweek Corr., 1964-80; columnist, TV host; sr. asso. Georgetown U. Center for Internat. and Strategic Studies. Served with Brit. Royal Navy, 1942-46. Decorated Medaille Maritime Belge; recipient Medal of Honor Def. Council, 1980, World Bus. Council, 1981, also numerous awards for fgn. reporting. Mem. Council on Fgn. Relations, U.S. Global Strategy Council. Clubs: Racquet and Tennis, Overseas Press; Traveller's (London, Eng.); Federal City (Washington). Home: 6 Chemin de la Tourelle Geneva Switzerland Office: CSIS 1800 K St NW Washington DC 20006

DEBOW, RUSSELL ROBINSON, judge; b. Lovejoy, Ill., Aug. 5, 1913; s. John W. and Bettie E. (Robinson) DeB.; m. Ruth Willa Duncan, Dec. 28, 1937; 1 dau., Dolores Diana. B.Ed., Ill. State Normal U., 1935; postgrad., Georgetown U. Law Sch., 1951-53; J.D., DePaul U., 1954. Bar: Ill. bar 1955. Dir. recreation, Lovejoy, 1935; asst. area dir. WPA, East St. Louis, Ill., 35-37, Nat. Youth Adminstrn., East St. Louis, 1937-41, state officer for Negro affairs, 1941-42, asst. to regional dir., Chgo., 1942-43; with Doehler-Jarvis Corp., Chgo., 1943-46; nat. field rep. Robert S. Abbot Pub. Co. (pubs. Chgo. Defender), 1946-49, sales mgr., 1949-51; asst. to dir. OPS, Washington, 1951-53; asst. to U.S. congressman, Chgo., 1954-61; practiced in Chgo., 1955-62, dep. commr. dept. investigation, City Chgo., 1962-65, adminstrv. asst. to mayor, 1965-67; magistrate Circuit Ct. Cook County, 1967-71, assoc. judge, 1971, judge, 1971—; Cons. spl. mission to Africa ICA, 1961; labor cons. USOM to Liberia, ICA, 1961. Mem. Cook County Bar Assn. (past v.p., gen. sec., dir.), Chgo. Bar Assn., ABA, Nat. Bar Assn. (past chmn. jud. council), World Assn. Judges, Am. Arbitration Assn. (nat. panel arbitrators). Home: 8055 S Paxton St Chicago IL 60617 Office: Richard J. Daley Center Chicago IL 60602

DEBRA, DANIEL B., mech. engr.; b. N.Y.C., June 1, 1930; s. Arthur H. and Gertrude Marie (Boyle) DeB.; m. Esther Slater Crosby, Apr. 3, 1954; children—Corinne, Elisabeth, Heidi, Jacques, David, Kathryn. B.E., Yale U., 1952; S.M., M.I.T., 1953; Ph.D., Stanford U., 1962. Project engr. Thermix Corp., Greenwich, Conn., 1953-54; supr. Lockheed, Sunnyvale, Calif., 1956-64; prof. aero. and astronautics Stanford U., 1964—. Served to 1st lt. USAF, 1954-56. Fellow AIAA; mem. Nat. Acad. Engring., IEEE, ASME, Soc. Automotive Engrs., Soc. Mfg. Engrs., Am. Geophys. Union, Am. Astronautical Soc., Instrument Soc. Am. Office: Dept Aeronautics and Astronautics Stanford Univ Stanford CA 94305

DE BREMAECKER, JEAN-CLAUDE, educator; b. Antwerp, Belgium, Sept. 2, 1923; came to U.S., 1948, naturalized, 1963; s. Paul J.C. and Berthe (Bouché) De B.; m. Arlene Ann Parker, Nov. 29, 1952; children—Christine, Suzanne. M.S. in Mining Engring, U. Louvain, Belgium, 1948, La. State U., 1950; Ph.D. in Geophysics, U. Cal. at Berkeley, 1952. Research scientist, sr. research scientist Inst. pour la Recherche Sci. en Afrique Centrale, Bukavu, Congo, 1952-58; Boese postdoctoral fellow, Columbia, 1955-56; postdoctoral fellow Harvard, 1958-59; faculty Rice U., Houston, 1959—, prof. geophysics, 1965—; research asso. U. Calif., Berkeley, 1966; vis. mem. Tex. Inst. for Computational Mechanics, U. Tex., Austin, 1977; vis. prof. U. Paris, 1980-81. Chmn. Citizens for McCarthy, Houston, 1968. Served with Belgian Army, 1944-45. Mem. Am. Geophys. Union, Fedn. Am. Scientists, Soc. Exploration Geophysicists, Internat. Assn. Seismology and Physics of Earth's Interior (asso. sec. gen. 1963-71), sec. gen. (1971-79), ACLU. Home: 2128 Addison St Houston TX 77030

DEBREU, GERARD, educator, economist; b. Calais, France, July 4, 1921; came to U.S., 1950, naturalized, 1975; s. Camille and Fernande (Decharne) D.; m. Francoise Bled, June 14, 1945; children—Chantal, Florence. Student, Ecole Normale Supérieure, Paris, France, 1941-44, Agrégé de l'Université, 1946; D. Sc., U. Paris, 1956; Dr. Rerum Politicarum honoris causa, U. Bonn, 1977; D. Scis. Economiques honoris causa, U. Lausanne, 1980; D. Sci.h.c., Northwestern U., 1981; D.h.c. U. des Sciences Sociales de Toulouse, 1983. Research asso. Centre Nat. De La Recherche Sci., Paris, 1946-48; Rockefeller fellow, U.S., Sweden and Norway, 1948-50; research asso. Cowles Commn., U. Chgo., 1950-55; asso. prof. econs. Cowles Found., Yale, 1955-60; fellow Center Advanced Study Behavioral Scis., 1960-61; vis. prof. econs. Yale U., fall 1961; prof. econs. U. Calif. at Berkeley, 1962—, prof. math., 1975—; Guggenheim fellow, vis. prof. Center Ops. Research and Econometrics, U. Louvain, 1968-69, vis. prof., fall 1971, winter, 1972; Erskine fellow U. Canterbury, Christchurch, New Zealand, summer 1969, vis. prof., summer 1973; Overseas fellow Churchill Coll., Cambridge, Eng., spring 1972; vis. prof. Cowles Found. for Research in Econs., Yale U., fall 1976; sr. U.S. scientist awardee Alexander von Humboldt Found.; vis. prof. U. Bonn, 1977; research asso. CEPREMAP, Paris, fall 1980. Author: Theory of Value, 1959; Asso. editor: Internat. Econ. Rev, 1959-69; mem. editorial bd.: Jour. Econ. theory, 1972—; mem. adv. bd.: Jour. Math. Econs, 1974—. Served with French Army, 1944-45. Decorated chevalier Légion d'Honneur. Fellow Am. Acad. Arts and Scis., Econometric Soc. (pres. 1971); Disting. fellow Am. Econ. Assn.; mem. Nat. Acad. Scis. Home: 267 Gravatt Dr Berkeley CA 94705

DE BRIER, DONALD PAUL, lawyer; b. Atlantic City, Mar. 20, 1940; s. Daniel and Ethel de B.; m. Nancy Lee McElroy, Aug. 1, 1964; children: Lesley Anne, Rachel Wynne, Danielle Verne. B.A. in History, Princeton U., 1962; LL.B. with honors, U. Pa., 1967. Bar: Tex. 1977, N.Y. 1967. Asso. firm Sullivan & Cromwell, N.Y.C., 1967-70, Patterson, Belknap, Webb & Tyler, 1970-76; v.p., gen. counsel, dir. Gulf Resources & Chem. Corp., Houston, 1976-82; v.p. law Kennecott Corp., Salt Lake City, 1983—. Served to lt. USNR, 1962-64. Club: Ft. Douglas. Home: 4242 Park Terr Dr Salt Lake City UT 84124 Office: Kennecott Bldg 10 E S Temple Salt Lake City UT 84133

DEBROUX, PIERRE ROBERT, diversified industry executive; b. Gembloux, Belgium, Mar. 23, 1925; came to U.S., 1955, naturalized, 1960; s. Robert and Genevieve (Leemans) D.; m. Anne Marie Balma, June 22, 1974; 1 dau., Dominique; children by previous marriage: Alain, Marc, Etienne, Patrick, Philippe, Jean Francois. B.S. in Elec. Engring, U. Louvain, 1946, M.B.A., 1948; postgrad., Syracuse U., 1955, Harvard, 1971. With Union Miniere du Haut Katanga (Africa) Uranium-Copper Mining, 1948-55; supr. market research Ford Motor Co., Detroit, 1955-57; mng. dir. Chrysler Corp., Antwerp, Belgium, 1957-63, Singer Co., Torino, Italy, 1964-67; group v.p. internat. Berol Corp., Danbury, Conn., 1967-72; group v.p. AMF Inc., White Plains, N.Y., 1972-78; pres., chief exec. officer Bandag, Inc., Muscatine, Iowa, 1978-80, Bastian Industries Inc., N.Y.C., 1980—. Office: Bastian Industries Inc 150 E 58th St New York NY 10015

DE BRUHL, ARTHUR MARSHALL, publishing company executive; b. Woodfin, N.C., Nov. 3, 1935; s. Arthur Marvin and Janie Myra (Wright) De B. A.B., Duke U., 1958. Editor U. Pa. Press, 1963-64; mem. editorial staff Crowell-Collier Macmillan, 1964-67; with Charles Scribner's Sons, N.Y.C., 1967—, mng. editor Dictionary Sci. Biography, Dictionary of Middle Ages, v.p., dir. Reference Book div., 1974—; sr. v.p. Scribner Book Cos., Inc., 1983—. Bd. dirs. Citizens Library Council of N.Y. State. Served to lt. (j.g.) USNR, 1959-62. Mem. History Sci. Soc.; mem. PEN. Club: Century Assn. Home: 347 E 52d St New York NY 10022 also Outlook Ave East Hampton NY 11937 Office: 597 Fifth Ave New York NY 10017

DE BRULER, ROGER O., justice Ind. Supreme Ct.; b. 1934. A.B., LL.B., Ind. U. Bar: bar 1960. Now justice Supreme Ct. of Ind., has also served as chief justice. Office: Supreme Court of Indiana 321 State House Indianapolis IN 46204 *

DEBRUNNER, PETER GEORGE, educator; b. Sitterdorf, Switzerland, Mar. 11, 1931; came to U.S., 1960; s. Rudolf Paul and Elisabeth (Keller) D.; m. Sigrid A. Muller, Sept. 2, 1955; children—Bettina A., Christian H., Susan E. Matura, Kantonsschule, Winterthur (Switzerland), 1949; diploma, Fed. Inst. Tech., Zurich, 1956, Ph.D., 1960. Research asst. Fed. Inst. Tech., 1956-60; research asso. U. Ill., 1960-62, research asst. prof., 1962-66, asst. prof., 1966-68, asso. prof., 1968-72, prof. physics, 1972—. Mem. Swiss Phys. Soc., European Phys. Soc., Am. Phys. Soc., Biophysical Soc., N.Y. Acad. Scis. Office: Physics Department University of Illinois Urbana IL 61801

DE BRUYN, PETER PAUL HENRY, anatomist, educator; b. Amsterdam, Holland, July 28, 1910; came to U.S., 1941, naturalized, 1947; s. Henry and Marianne (van den Nieuwenhuysen) DeB.; m. Jeannette Meershock, Sept. 6, 1931; children—Anneke, Yolande. M.D., U. Amsterdam, 1938, 1938. Asst. in histology Histological Lab., U. of Amsterdam, 1936-39; instr. anatomy U. Chgo., 1941, successively asst. and asso. prof., prof., 1952—, chmn. dept., 1946-61. Author articles in profl. jours.; Editor: Scientist's Library, U. Chgo. Press; asso. editor: Am. Jour. Anatomy; deptl. editor and advisor, adv. com.: Ency. Brit. Served as med. officer Dutch Army, 1939-40. Mem. Am. Assn. Anatomists, Am. Soc. Naturalists, Am. Soc. Cell Biology. Club: Quadrangle. Home: 2626 Lakeview Chicago IL 60614

DE BRUYN, ROBERT L., publishing company executive, educational consultant; b. Chgo., Aug. 3, 1934; s. Roy Charles and Anne Mae De B.; m. Eleanor Elizabeth Bartok, Mar. 9, 1957; children: Robert L., Gary Bruce, David Paul. B.S., Kans. State U., 1961, M.S., 1963. Account exec. Dun and Bradstreet, Chgo., 1955-57, Sta. WIBW-TV, Topeka, 1960-74; tchr., adminstr. Manhattan (Kans.) Pub. Schs., 1963-71; founder, pub., author The Master Teacher (staff devel. programs for tchrs.), Manhattan, 1970—, The Profl. Banker (staff devel. program for bankers), 1976—; pres. Master Tchr. Inst. Arts, Manhattan, 1977—; chmn. bd. Ednl. Pubs., Inc.; owner, mgr. R.L. De Bruyn and Assocs. (ednl. consultants), Manhattan, 1972—; dir. Kans. State Bank; v.p. Kans. Travel Agy., 1971—. Author: Causing Others To Want Your Leadership, 1976, Before You Can Discipline, 1983; co-author: Mastering Meetings, 1983. Mem. dean's exec. com. Coll. Edn. Kans. State U. Served with AUS, 1957-59. Mem. Jr. C. of C. (pres. 1961-62, state dir. 1963-64), Phi Delta Kappa. Republican. Methodist. Clubs: Mason (Shriner), Elk, Rotarian., Manhattan Country. Home: 220 Fordham Rd Manhattan KS 66502 Office: Leadership Ln Manhattan KS 66502

DE BRUYN KOPS, JULIAN, lawyer; b. Savannah, Ga., Nov. 8, 1908; s. Julian and May (Woodberry) de B.K.; m. Mary Virginia Thompson, July 1, 1939; children—Julianna, Virginia, Julian III. A.B., Harvard, 1929, LL.B., 1932. Bar: Md. bar 1932, Ohio bar 1946. Practice of law, Balt., 1932-41; also service with U.S. Govt., 1934-35; counsel Dayton Power & Light Co., O., 1946-69, gen. counsel, 1969-73; pvt. practice, Dayton, 1974—. Served with AUS, 1941-46. Mem. Am., Fed., Fed. Energy, Ohio, Dayton bar assns. Clubs: Lawyers, Engineers (Dayton). Home: 3 Forrer Blvd Dayton OH 45419 Office: 118 W 1st St Dayton OH 45402

DEBS, BARBARA KNOWLES, college president; b. Eastham, Mass., Dec. 24, 1931; d. Stanley F. and Arline (Eugley) Knowles; m. Richard A. Debs, July 19, 1958; children: Elizabeth, Nicholas. B.A., Vassar Coll., 1953, Scuola Normale, Pisa, Italy, 1953, U. Rome, 1954; postgrad., Radcliffe Coll., 1956-58; Ph.D., Harvard U., 1967; LL.D., N.Y. Law Sch., 1979. Instr. art dept. Vassar Coll., 1955-56; free lance translator editor Ency. of World Art, McGraw-Hill Pub., N.Y.C., 1959-62; asst. prof. art history dept. Manhattanville Coll., Purchase, N.Y., 1968-73, asso. prof., 1973-77, acting pres., 1975, pres., 1976—, prof. art history, 1977—; dir. AMF, Inc. Contbr. articles on Renaissance and contemporary art to profl. publs. Mem. N.Y. Council Humanities, 1978—; mem. Westchester Med. Center Hosp. Implementation Bd., 1978—, Westchester County Bd. Ethics, 1979—; trustee N.Y. Law Sch., 1979—, Commn. Ind. Colls. and Univs. of N.Y., 1975-79; exec. com. Commn. Ind. Colls. and Univs. of N.Y. 1977-79; mem. com. on higher edn., adv. council to Democrats in N.Y. State Senate, 1979—. AAUW Nat. fellow and Ann Radcliffe fellow, 1958-59; Radcliffe grant-in-aid, 1966-67; Am. Council Learned Socs. grantee, 1973. Mem. Am. Council on Edn. (chmn. commn. acad. affairs 1977-79), Young Audiences (nat. dir. 1977-80), Hundred Club of Westchester (dir.), Phi Beta Kappa. Home and Office: Manhattanville Coll Purchase NY 10577

DEBS, RICHARD A., investment banker, government official; b. Providence, Oct. 7, 1930; s. Abraham George and Madge (Fatool) D.; m. Barbara Knowles, July 19, 1958; children: Elizabeth Anderson, Nicholas. B.A. summa cum laude, Colgate U., 1952; postgrad. (Fulbright scholar), Cairo U., 1952-53; M.A., Princeton U., 1956, Ph.D., 1963; LL.B., Harvard U., 1958, grad. Advanced Mgmt. Program, Harvard Grad. Sch. Bus. Adminstrn., 1973. Bar: N.Y. 1960. Researcher joint project Harvard-Princeton, 1958-59; with Fed. Res. Bank of N.Y., N.Y.C., 1960-76, legal dept., 1960-64, asst. counsel, 1964-69, sec. of bank, 1965-69, v.p. govt. bonds and securities, 1969-72, v.p. loans and credits, 1969-72, v.p. open market ops., 1972, sr. v.p., 1973, 1st v.p., chief adminstrv. officer, 1973-76; alt. mem. Fed. Open Market Com., 1973-76; mng. dir. Morgan Stanley & Co., Inc., 1976—; pres. Morgan Stanley Internat. Inc., 1976—; chmn. com. fiscal agy. ops. Fed. Res. System, 1969-76; mem. Fed. Res. Steering Com. on Payments Mechanism, 1973-76, Fed. Res. Steering Com. on Internat. Banking, 1973-76; allied mem. N.Y. Stock Exchange; mem. adv. com. internat. capital markets; mem. com. multinat. enterprises U.S. council Internat. Bus.; Mem. Take Stock in Am. Com., 1973-76; mem. Egypt-U.S. Bus. Council.; Mem. adv. council Near Eastern program Princeton U.; mem. N.Y. State Savs. Bond Com., 1973-76; adv. council Am. Inst. Banking, 1973-76. Contbr. articles on internat. banking to profl. publs. Chmn. emeritus, trustee Carnegie Hall; bd. dirs. Fedn. Protestant Welfare Agys.; trustee Carnegie Endowment for Internat. Peace, Am. Univs. Field Staff, Am. U., Beirut; vice chmn. Am. U., 1981—; bd. dirs. Am. Council on Germany; mem. vis. com. Middle East Center Harvard U., 1976-82, mem. Ctr. Internat. Affairs. Mem. ABA (com. Middle Eastern law), Assn. Bar City N.Y., Council Fgn. Relations, C. of C. U.S. (internat. policy com., chmn. subcom. on internat. econ. devel.), Egyptian Am. C. of C. (chmn.), N.Y. C. of C. and Industry, Japan Soc., Asia Soc., Fgn. Policy Assn. Clubs: Econ. N.Y., Century Assn. (N.Y.C.); Larchmont Yacht (N.Y.). Address: Morgan Stanley Internat Inc 1251 Ave of Americas New York NY 10020

DE BURLO, COMEGYS RUSSELL, JR., banker, educator; b. Phila., Sept. 1, 1924; s. Comegys Russell and Margaret (Whitehurst) de B.; m. Edith Power Thatcher, May 4, 1948; children: Jane Thatcher, Charles Russell, John Todd. B.S., Swarthmore Coll., 1947; M.B.A., U. Pa., 1949; D.B.A., Harvard U., 1960. Lectr. Tufts U., Medford, Mass., 1954-56, asst. prof., 1956-61, asst. to preas., 1953-55, asst. comptroller, 1955-57, bus. officer, 1957-60, v.p., 1960-63, 65-82, sr. lectr., 1966-77, prof., 1977—, treas., 1968—; exec. v.p. U.S. Trust Co., 1983—; v.p. Ednl. Testing Service, Princeton, N.J., 1963-65; dir. U.S. Trust Co., Boston, UST Corp.; ednl. cons. Ednl. Research Assocs., Inc., 1950-56, NIH, Nat. Cancer Inst., Cancer Program Adv. Com., Cancer Research Centers Rev. Com., Am. Council on Edn., Com. on Taxation. Mem. advv. com. No. Calif. Cancer Program; mem. sci. adv. com. U. N.Mex. Cancer Treatment Ctr., Ohio State U. Comprehensive Cancer Ctr., 1983—; adv. bd. dirs. Middlesex Bank; trustee Cambridge Friends Sch., Belmont Hill Sch.; bd. mgrs. New Eng. Yearly Meeting; commr. public trust funds. Served with USNR, 1944-46. Fellow Royal Hort. Soc.; mem. Nat. Council Univ. Research Adminstrs., New Eng. Assn. Coll. and Secondary Schs., Assn. Computing Machinery, Eastern Assn. Coll. and Univ. Bus. Officers, Nat. Assn. Coll. and Univ. Bus. Officers, Am. Ednl. Research Assn., Am. Fin. Assn., Tau Beta Pi. Clubs: Belmont Hill, Harvard, Green Mountain, Appalachian Mountain. Home: 857 Concord Ave Belmont MA 02178 Office: Tufts U 50 Federal St. Boston MA 02110 40 Court St Boston MA 02108

DEBUS, ALLEN GEORGE, history educator; b. Chgo., Aug. 16, 1926; s. George Walter William and Edna Pauline (Schwenneke) D.;

m. Brunilda Lopez-Rodriguez, Aug. 25, 1951; children: Allen Anthony George, Richard William, Karl Edward. B.S., Northwestern U., 1947; A.M., Ind. U., 1949; Ph.D., Harvard U., 1961; postgrad., U. Coll. London, 1959-60. Research chemist Abbott Labs., North Chicago, Ill., 1951-56; asst. prof. U. Chgo., 1961-65, assoc. prof. history, 1965-68, prof., 1968-78, Morris Fishbein prof. history sci. and medicine, 1978—; dir. Morris Fishbein Center for Study History of Sci. and Medicine, 1971-77; mem. internat. adv. com. Inst. History of Sci. and Ideas Tel-Aviv U. and Ctr. for History and Philosophy of Sci. of Hebrew U. of Jerusalem. Author: The English Paracelsians, 1965, 66, (with Robert P. Multhauf) Alchemy and Chemistry in the 17th Century, 1966, The Chemical Dream of the Renaissance, 1968, 2d edit., 1972, Science and Education in the 17th Century, 1970, (with Brian Rust) The Complete Entertainment Discography, 1973, The Chemical Philosophy, 2 vols, 1977, Man and Nature in the Renaissance, 1978, 80, 81, 83, Italian transl., 1982, Robert Fludd and His Philosophical Key, 1979; editor: World Who's Who in Science from Antiquity to the Present, 1968, Science, Medicine and Society in the Renaissance, 2 vols, 1972, (1973) Medicine in Seventeenth-Century England, 1974; editor reprint: Theatrum Chemicum Britannicum (1652), 1967, (1973) John Dee's Mathematicall Praeface (1570), 1975; programmed: 3 records released by Smithsonian Instn. Music of Victor Herbert, 1979; contbr. (1973) articles to profl. jours. Social Sci. Research Council fellow, 1959-60; Fulbright fellow, 1959-60; Fels Found. fellow, 1960-61; Guggenheim fellow, 1966-67; overseas fellow Churchill Coll. Cambridge (Eng.) U., 1966-67, 69; mem. Inst. Advanced Study, Princeton, N.J., 1972-73; Nat. Endowment for Humanities fellow Newberry Library, Chgo., 1975-76; fellow Inst. for Research in Humanities U. Wis., Madison, 1981-82; research grantee Am. Philos. Soc., 1961-62, Wellcome Trust, 1962, NIH, 1962-70, 74-75, 77-78, NSF, 1961-63, 71-74, 77-78, 80-83, Am. Council Learned Socs., 1966, 70, 71. Fellow AAAS (mem. electorate nominating com., sect. L 1974-77, chmn. com. 1974); mem. History of Sci. Soc. (council 1962-65, program chmn. 1972, Pfizer award 1978), Soc. Study Alchemy and Early Chemistry (mem. council 1967—), Am. Assn. for History Medicine (program com. 1975), Brit. Soc. for History Sci., Internationale Paracelsus Gesellschaft, Am. Chem. Soc. (asso. mem. history of chemistry div., exec. com. 1969-72), Soc. Med. History of Chgo. (sec.-treas. 1971-72, v.p. 1972-74, pres. 1974-76, mem. council), Chgo. Lit. Club, Am. Hist. Assn., Académie Internat. d'Histoire de la Medecine, Société Internationale d'Histoire de la Medecine, Academie Internat. d'Histoire des Scis. (corr.), Am. Inst. History of Pharmacy (Edward Kremers award 1978, adv. panel hist. activity 1979-81, awards com. 1981—), Am. Soc. Reformation Research, Assn. Recorded Sound Collections., Midwest Junto for History of Sci. (pres. 1983-84). Patentee in field. Office: Dept of History U Chgo Chicago IL 60637

DEBUSK, EDITH M., lawyer; b. Waco, Tex., Apr. 12, 1912; d; Otto Clifton and Margaret (Hatcher) Mann; m. Manuel C. DeBusk, June 13, 1941. LL.B., Dallas Sch. Law, 1941; Certificate, So. Meth. U. Sch. Law, 1941. Atty. Regional Atty.'s Office (O.P.A.), Dallas, 1942; asso. atty. Office of Karl F. Steinmann, Balt., 1943-46; mem. firm DeBusk & DeBusk, 1946—; Vice pres. Killeen Savs. & Loan Assn., The Teeling Mortgage Co., Inc.; dir. DeBusk Corp.; officer East Town Osteo. Hosp. Corp. Former mem. Gov.'s Com. on Aging; dir. Dallas Citizens Commn. on Action for Aging, Inc.; del. to White House Conf. Children and Youth, 1960, Conf. on Aging, 1961; mem. Dallas Bd. Adjustment, 1963-65; former bd. dirs. Dallas United Cerebral Palsy Assn., Tex. Soc. Aging, Dallas County Community Action Com., Inc.; trustee Found. for Cranio-Facial Deformities, Nina Fay Calhoun Scholarship Fund Trust; former mem. adv. council Sr. Citizens Found., Inc.; former mem. div. aging Council of Social Agys., Citizens Traffic Commn.; former sec., legal adviser Tex. Fedn. Bus. and Profl. Women's Clubs. Named Woman of the Month Dallas Mag., 1948; Woman of Week, Balt., 1945; Bd. visitors Freedoms Found. at Valley Forge.; Recipient George Washington honor medal Freedoms Found. Fellow Tex. Bar Found. (life); mem. State Bar Tex., ABA (chmn. com. state and local taxation 1979-81), Dallas Bar Assn. (numerous coms.), Women's Council of Dallas County (legis. com.), Bus. and Profl. Women's Club Dallas (past pres.), Nat. Assn. Women in Constrn. (hon.), Delta Kappa Gamma (hon.), Kappa Beta Pi (past dean province IV). Presbyn. Club: Altrusa (Dallas) (pres. internat. 1963-65). Home: 7365 Elmridge Dr Dallas TX 75240 Office: 777 S Central Expressway Suite 7-F Richardson TX 75080

DEBUSK, MANUEL CONRAD, lawyer; b. Grosvenor, Tex., June 13, 1914; s. Elias C. and Ollie (Lewis) DeB.; m. Edith Mann, June 13, 1941. B.A., Tex. Technol. Coll., 1933; LL.B., So. Meth. U., 1941. Bar: Tex. 1942. Adminstrv. asst. FHA, Washington, Dallas, 1934-41; spl. agt. FBI, 1941-46; partner DeBusk & DeBusk, Dallas, 1946—; Chmn. bd. Debusk Corp.; pres. DeBusk Enterprises, Inc. Mem., chmn. coordinating bd. Tex. Colls. and Univs., 1969-70; Chmn. Dallas County Democratic Party, 1967-71; Bd. dirs., chmn. bd. regents Tex. Technol. Coll., 1959-65. Mem. Tex. Bar Assn., Tex., Nat. mortgage bankers assns., Nat. Lefthanded Golf Assn. (past pres.), Cosmopolitan Internat. (past internat. pres.). Home: 7365 Elmridge Dr Dallas TX 75240 Office: 777 S Central Expressway Richardson TX 75080 *One's yardstick, whether business or avocation, must be to leave the world a better place that it was before you touched it.*

DEBUSSHERE, DAVID ALBERT, professional basketball team executive; b. Detroit, Oct. 16, 1949; m. Gerri Warnock, 1968; children: Michelle, Peter, Dennis. Grad., Detroit U., 1962. Pitcher Chgo. White Soc, Am. League baseball, 1962-63; player, coach Detroit Pistons, NBA, 1962-68; player N.Y. Knickerbockers, NBA, 1968-74, exec. v.p., dir. basketball ops., 1982—; v.p., gen. mgr. N.Y. Nets, Am. Basketball Assn., 1974-75; commr. Am. Basketball Assn., 1975-76. Author: The Open Man, 1970. Mem. World Champion Team, 1970, 73, NBA All-Star Team, 1966-68, 70-73. Office: care New York Knickerbockers Madison Square Garden Four Penn Plaza New York NY 10001 *

DE BUTTS, JOHN DULANY, retired telephone company executive; b. Greensboro, N.C., Apr. 10, 1915; s. Sydnor and Mary Ellen (Cutchin) deB.; m. Gertrude Willoughby Walke, Nov. 4, 1939; children: Talbot (Mrs. Tyler Cain), Mary Linda (Mrs. R. Collins Couch). B.S. in Elec. Engring., Va. Mil. Inst., 1936; LL.D. (hon.), Knox Coll., 1966, Northwestern U., 1966, Lehigh U., 1975, Loyola U., Chgo., 1967, Hampden-Sydney Coll., 1978, Columbia U., 1978, Sc.D., Clarkson Coll. Tech., 1973, D.C.S., Pace Coll., 1977, Eng.D., Lafayette Coll., 1977, Worcester Poly. Inst., 1979, L.H.D., St. Augustine Coll., 1978. With Chesapeake & Potomac Telephone Co., 1936-49, 51-55, 59-62, v.p. ops. and engring., dir., 1959-62; with AT&T, N.Y.C., 1949-51, 55-57, 66—, asst. v.p. govt. relations, Washington, 1957-58, exec. v.p., N.Y.C., 1966-67, vice chmn. bd., 1967-72, chmn. bd., chief exec. officer, 1972-79, dir., 1967-81; gen. mgr. Westchester area N.Y. Telephone Co., 1958-59; pres., dir. Ill. Bell Telephone Co., 1962-66; dir. Hosp. Corp. Am., U.S. Steel Corp., Dart & Kraft, Inc., Gen. Motors Corp. Trustee Duke Endowment, 1973—, vice chmn., 1975-81; chmn. Va. Mil. Inst. Found., 1981—; vice chmn. Bus. Council, 1975-76, chmn., 1976-78, mem. exec. com., 1972—, chmn. membership com., 1979-80; bd. govs. United Way Am., 1972-79; bd. visitors Grad. Sch. Bus. Adminstrn., Duke U., 1974-81; hon. trustee Chicago Mus. Sci. and Industry; hon. life mem. bd. lay trustees Loyola U., Chgo.; trustee Tax Found., 1973-79; co-chmn. Bus. Roundtable, 1974-77, mem. exec. com., policy com., 1972-79; mem. sr. exec. council Conf. Bd., 1973-79, mem. policy com., 1974-79, vice chmn., 1974-79; mem. nat. com. Assn. Episc. Colls., 1966-79; Mem. O.R.C., 1936-39, U.S. N.G., 1939-40. Recipient Silver Beaver award Boy Scouts Am., 1964, Silver Antelope award, 1971; Silver Medal Brotherhood award NCCJ, 1966; Gold medal Brotherhood award, 1972; Charles Evans Hughes award, 1976; Washington award Engring. Socs., 1974; Ann. citation Midwest Research Inst., 1974; Gold medal USO, 1974; Founders Day award Loyola U., 1965; S. Byard Colgate award Jr. Achievement, 1970; Gold Achievement award, 1970; Highest Honor Leadership award, 1972; Corporate Man of Year award B'nai B'rith, 1973; Family of Man award Council of Chs., 1974; Distinguished Service award Va. Mil. Inst., 1975; Bus. Statesman award Harvard Bus. Sch., 1976; St. La Salla medal Manhattan Coll., 1977; medal of merit St. Nicholas Soc., 1977; Bus. Leadership award U. Mich., 1977; C. Walter Nichols award N.Y. U., 1978; Leaders in Mgmt. award Pace U., 1978; Disting. Citizens award Boy Scouts Am., 1978, Va. C. of C., 1979; Public Service award Advt. Council, 1978; N.C. award, 1978; Fairless Meml. medal, 1979; New Market medal Va. Mil. Inst., 1984. Mem. Western Soc. Engrs. (hon.), Navy League U.S., Northwestern U. Assos., Kappa Alpha, Beta Gamma Sigma (hon.). Republican. Episcopalian. Clubs: Metropolitan (Washington); Links (N.Y.C.); Commonwealth (Richmond, Va.). Office: 195 Broadway New York NY 10007

DECAIR, THOMAS PALMER, government official; b. Spartanburg, S.C., June 6, 1945; s. Theodore F. and Constance M. (Palmer) DeC.; 1 dau., Sara Diane. Student, Kalamazoo Coll., 1963-65; B.A. magna cum laude, Hope Coll., Holland, Mich., 1972. Dir. advt. and publicity Simicon Co., Holland, Mich., 1969-72; asst. press. sec. Pres. of U.S., Washington, 1972-75; exec. asst. Mich. gov. William G. Milliken, Lansing, 1975-77; pres., gen. mgr. Gilmroe Advt. Inc., Kalamazoo, 1977-78; v.p. McMaster Assocs. Pub. Relations, Troy, Mich., 1978-80; spl. asst. to atty. gen., dir. pub. affairs U.S. Dept. Justice, Washington, 1981—. Served with U.S. Army, 1967-69. Mem. Phi Beta Kappa. Republican. Episcopalian. Home: 1007 New Hampshire Ave NW DC 20037

DE CAMARA, RICHARD PAUL, franchising company executive; b. Ventnor City, N.J., Mar. 6, 1917; s. Alfonso Solis and Mary Helena (Conly) de C.; m. Marguerite Willey, Feb. 15, 1941; children: Joan, Richard Paul, Donna, Donald, Robert. B.A., George Washington U., 1949, M.B.A., 1950, D.B.A., 1966. With various brokerage businesses, Phila., 1935-41; commd. 2d lt. U.S. Army, 1941, advanced through grades to col., ret., 1962; mgr. market devel. Koppers Internat., 1962-63; v.p. staff St. Louis-San Francisco Ry. Co., 1963-66; v.p. info. and control systems ICRR, 1966-68, v.p. adminstrn., 1968-71; v.p. adminstrn., then exec. v.p. Midas Internat. Corp., Chgo., 1972-78, pres., chief exec. officer, 1978-82; owner Midas Muffler Shops, Chgo., 1982—, Mesa, Ariz, 1982—. Decorated Bronze Star with oak leaf cluster; recipient Morgan Richardson Goddard award George Washington U., 1949. Mem. Internat. Franchise Assn. (past pres., dir., mem. exec. com.), Motor and Equipment Mfrs. Assn. (gov., pres.'s council), Car Care Council (chmn. bd.), Phi Beta Kappa, Phi Eta Sigma. Roman Catholic.

DECAMP, GRAYDON, journalist; b. Cin., Feb. 6, 1934; s. James Milton and Anne Hetherington (Graydon) DeC.; m. Diane Johnson, Aug. 18, 1956; children: James Douglass. A.B., Williams Coll., 1956. Tchr. English Eaglebrook Sch., Deerfield, Mass., 1956-57; reporter, columnist Cin. Post, 1960-68, city editor, 1969-70; politics editor Cin. Enquirer, 1970-74, asst. city editor, 1975; editor Enquirer mag., Cin., 1976-81; freelance writer.; adj. faculty Coll. Mount St. Joseph, Cin., 1983—. Author: Blue and Gold: The Annapolis Story, 1975. Adv. bd. Hoxworth Blood Ctr., Cin., 1981—. Mem. Soc. Profl. Journalists (pres. chpt. 1974, dir. 1975).

DE CAMP, L(YON) SPRAGUE, author; b. N.Y.C., Nov. 27, 1907; s. Lyon and Emma Beatrice (Sprague) de C.; m. Catherine Adelaide Crook, Aug. 12, 1939; children: Lyman Sprague, Gerard Beekman. B.S., Calif. Inst. Tech., 1930; M.S., Stevens Inst. Tech., 1933. Instr. Inventors Found., 1933-36; prin. Sch. Inventing and Patenting, Internat. Corr. Schs., 1936-37; editor Fowler-Becker Pub. Co., 1937-38; asst. editor ASME, 1938; free lance writer, 1938-42, 46—. Author: (with Willy Ley) Lands Beyond, 1953 (Internat. Fantasy award), (with Fletcher Pratt) Tales From Gavagan's Bar, 1953 (Cleve. Sci. Fiction award), An Elephant for Aristotle, 1959 (Fiction award Athenaeum of Phila.), Lest Darkness Fall, Rogue Queen, the Ancient Engineers, Great Cities of the Ancient World, Lovecraft: A Biography, Literary Swordsmen and Sorcerers, The Hostage of Zir; numerous other books, articles and stories. Served from lt. to lt. comdr. USNR, 1942-46. Recipient J.R.R. Tolkien award for life work in fantasy, 1976, Grand Master Nebula award Sci. Fiction Writers Am., 1979. Mem. Univ. Mus. U. Pa., Phila. Acad. Natural Scis., History of Sci. Soc., Soc. History of Tech., Fellows in Am. Studies, Sci. Fiction Writers Am., Assn. Phonétique Internationale. Clubs: Trap Door Spiders, Hyborian Legion, First Fandom, Franklin Inn. Address: 278 Hothorpe Ln Villanova PA 19085 *As I contemplate my past, I am struck by the degree to which its course has been determined less by my own virtues and failings than by sheer luck—some good, some bad.*

DECAMP, ROSEMARY SHIRLEY, actress, enamelist; b. Prescott, Ariz., Nov. 14, 1910; d. William Val and Margaret Elizabeth (Hinman) DeC.; m. John Ashton Shidler, June 28, 1941; children—Margaret, Martha, Valerie, Nita. B.A., Mills Coll., 1932, M. A., 1933. Mem. faculty Mills Coll., 1932-33; State Dept. cultural grantee, tchr., Pakistan, 1963-64; participant State Dept. Tour, Pakistan, 1963-64. Appeared on radio, 1933-53, including, One Man's Family, 1933, Easy Aces, 1935, Dr. Christian, 1937-53, Hollywood Hotel, 1939, Lux Radio Theater; appeared in: feature films, including Yankee Doodle Dandy, 1942, Jungle Book, 1942, Hold Back the Dawn, 1941, Rhapsody in Blue, 1944, This is the Army, 1944, Shine on Harvest Moon, 1952; appeared on TV, 1947—, including, Life of Riley, 1949, Death Valley Days, 1952-77, Bob Cummings Show, 1954-58, That Girl, 1964-68, Love Boat, B.J. and the Bear; copper enamelist exhibited in one-woman shows, Los Angeles Museum Sci. and Industry, 1969, Jocelyn Center, Torrance, Calif., Highland-Hollywood Blvd. Savs. & Loan Gallery, 1970; exhibited in group show, Palos Verdes Community Art Gallery, 1981; represented in pvt. collections; Guest columnist: La Daily Jour, 1959-64; author children's novel: Here Duke, 1962. Fine arts commr. City of Torrance, 1971-73; bd. dirs. Torrance Meml. Hosp., 1970-75. Mem. Screen Actor's Guild (dir. 1953-65). Democrat. Episcopalian. Office: care Lew Sherrell Agy 7060 Hollywood Blvd Los Angeles CA 90028

DE CAMP, WILLIAM SCHUYLER, army officer; b. Ft. Monroe, Va., Sept. 24, 1934; s. John Taylor and Barbara Virginia (Meister) deC.; m. Anne Lindsey Draper, July 25, 1959; children: William Schuyler, Philip Draper, Timothy Laurent. A.A., U. Calif., Berkeley, 1954, A.B., 1956; M.A., Tulane U., 1965, Ph.D., 1970; student, Army War Coll., 1972-73, Armed Forces Staff Coll., 1969-70. Commd. 2d lt. U.S. Army, 1956, advanced through grades to maj. gen., 1980; bn. comdr., brigade exec. officer, Vietnam, 1968-69; spl. asst. to Army Chief of Staff, Washington, 1970-72; army asso. Sch. Advanced Internat. Studies Johns Hopkins, 1972-73; dep. to asst. dep. chief staff for ops. and planning U.S. Army, Washington, 1973-75; brigade comdr., W. Ger., 1975-76; spl. asst. to chief staff SHAPE, Belgium, 1976-77; asst. comdr. 3d Div., W. Ger., 1977-79; joint chiefs rep. NATO-Warsaw Pact MBFR Negotiations, Vienna, 1979-80; dir. Interam. region Office Sec. Def., 1981—. Pres. Mantua PTA, Fairfax, Va., 1973-74; instl. rep. Boy Scouts Am. Recipient awards Boy Scouts Am., PTA, Landkreis Kitzingen, W. Ger.; decorated Silver Star, Legion of Merit with oak leaf cluster, Meritorious Service medal with cluster, D.F.C., Bronze Star, Air medals with V, numerous others. Mem. Assn. U.S. Army, U.S. Armor Assn., Pi Sigma Alpha. Episcopalian. Home: 8912 Lynnhurst Dr Fairfax VA 22031 Office: Office Sec Def Washington DC 20301

DE CANI, JOHN STAPLEY, statistician, educator; b. Canton, Ohio, May 8, 1924; s. John Mustin and Ada Louise (Stapley) deC.; m. Jessie Montrose Farr, Dec. 17, 1955 (dec. Sept. 1969). B.S., U. Wis., 1948; M.B.A., U. Pa., 1951, Ph.D., 1958. Mem. faculty U. Pa., Phila., 1948—, assoc. prof. stats., 1963-72, prof., 1972—, chmn. dept. stats., 1972-78; cons. to cos., agys., including USN, 1957—, NAACP., 1967—, EEOC, 1976—. Author: (with R. C. Clelland) Basic Statistics, 1973; contbr. articles to profl. jours. Served with USAAF, 1943-45. Recipient Distinguished Teaching award Lindbach Found., 1964, Wharton disting. teaching award, 1978; Fulbright grantee, Norway, 1959-60. Fellow Am. Statis. Assn., Royal Statis. Soc.; mem. Inst. Math. Statistics, Biometric Soc. Clubs: Royal Norwegian Yacht (Oslo); Sailing of Chesapeake. Office: Dept of Statistics U of Pa E220 Dietrich Hall CC Philadelphia PA 19104

DECARAVA, ROY RUDOLPH, photographer, educator; b. N.Y.C., Dec. 9, 1919; s. Andrew DeC. and Alfreda (Ferguson) Anglero; m. Palma Burgess, 1941 (div.); children: Leslie, Vincent; m. Sherry Forsythe Turner, June 16; children: Susan, Wendy, Laura. Student, Cooper Union Inst. Assoc. Royer & Roger Art Studio, N.Y.C., 1943-48, Berman Studios, 1948-58; photographer Sports Illustrated mag., N.Y.C., 1965-75; prof. photography Hunter Coll., CUNY, 1975—. Author: (with others) The Sweet Flypaper of Life, 1955; catalog Roy DeCarava, Photographs, 1975; book Roy DeCarava, 1981; The Sound I Saw, 1983. Guggenheim fellow, 1952. Mem. Am. Soc. Mag. Photographers (spl. citation 1983). Office: Hunter coll 695 Park Ave New York NY 10021

DECARIE, THERESE GOUIN, psychology educator; b. Montreal, Que., Canada, Sept. 30, 1923; d. Leon Mercier and Yvette (Ollivier) Gouin; m. Vianney Decarie, Dec. 24, 1948; children: Pascale, Dominique, Jean-Claude, Emmanuel. B.A., U. Montreal, 1945, L.Ph., 1947, Ph.D., 1960; Ph.D. hon., U. Ottawa, Ont., 1981. Instr. psychology U. Montreal, 1949-51, assoc. prof., 1951-65, prof., 1965—. Decorated officer Order of Can., 1979. Mem. Royal Soc. Can., Nat. Research Council Can., Soc. canadienne de psychologie, Corporation des psychologues de la province de Quebec, Soc. Research in Child Devel., Societe canadienne de psychanlyse. Roman Catholic. Home: 77 ave McNider Outremont PQ Canada H2V 3X5 Office: U Montreal Dept Psychology CP 6128 Montreal PQ Canada H3C 3J7

DECARLO, CHARLES RAYMOND, college president emeritus; b. Pitts., May 7, 1921; s. Charles Raymond and Margaret (Lyons) DeC.; m. Dorothy Barrett, June 17, 1946; children—Tessa, Rachel, Elisa, Dean. B.S. in Engring, U. Pitts., 1943, Ph.D. in Math, 1951; D.Sc. (hon.), Newark Coll. Engring., 1969. With IBM Corp., 1951-69, dir. automation research, until 1969; pres. emeritus Sarah Lawrence Coll., Bronxville, N.Y.; Instr. U. Pitts., Am. Studies Inst., Salzburg, Austria; cons. U.S. Office Edn. Trustee Bank St. Coll. Edn., Inst. Man and Sci., Rennsselaerville, N.Y.; bd. dirs. Energy Fund. Author: (with Ormsbee Robinson) Education in Business and Industry, 1966. Served with USNR, 1943-46. Mem. Am. Acad. Arts and Scis. Office: Office of Pres Sarah Lawrence Coll Bronxville NY 10708

DE CASTRO, EDSON D., computer manufacturing corporation executive; b. 1938; married. Grad., Lowell Technol. Inst., 1960. Engring. positions Digital Equipment Corp., 1961-68; with Data Gen. Corp., Westboro, Mass., 1968—, pres., chief exec. officer, dir. Office: Data Gen Corp 4400 Computer Dr Westboro MA 01580 *

DE CASTRO, HUGO DANIEL, lawyer; b. Panama, Sept. 12, 1935; s. Mauricio Fidanque and Armida Rebecca (Salas) De C.; m. Isabel Shapiro, July 25, 1958; children: Susan M., Teresa A., Andrea L., Michele L. B.A. cum laude, UCLA, 1957, J.D., 1960. Bar: Calif. 1960; C.P.A., Calif. Since practiced in, Los Angeles; mem. firm De Castro, West & Chodorow, Inc., 1960—, pres., 1970—; lectr. UCLA, 1962-67, 68, counsel to dean Law Sch., 1963—; commr. tax adv. commn. State Bar Calif. Editor: UCLA Law Rev, 1959-60, Taxation for Lawyers, 1971—; Contbr. articles to profl. jours. Trustee, mem. exec. com. Westlake Sch.; trustee Stephen S. Wise Temple, UCLA Found.; bd. dirs., sec. Western Los Angeles Found. Mem. Am. (chmn. taxation subcom.), Los Angeles County Bar Assn., Beverly Hills Bar Assn. (dir. Law Found.), Western Los Angeles Regional C. of C. (chmn., dir.), ACLU, Los Angeles World Affairs Council, Am. Jewish Com., Pi Lambda Phi. Clubs: Del Rey Yacht (dir., officer); Founders of Music Center (Los Angeles); Las Hadas Country (Mex.); Mountain Gate Country, Lake Arrowhead Country, Monterrey Country. Office: Suite 1800 10960 Wilshire Blvd Los Angeles CA 90024

DE CHANTAL, RENÉ, diplomat; b. Moose Creek, Ont., Can., June 27, 1923; s. William Joseph and Antoinette (Ladouceur) deC.; m. Geneviève Penot, July 16, 1951; children: Marie-Laure, François. B.A., McGill U., 1948; licence ès lettres, U. Paris, 1951; diplôme de professeur de français, Ecole des professeurs de français à l'étranger, Sorbonne, 1951; doctorate, U. Paris, 1960, U. Ottawa, 1976. Mem. faculty U. Ottawa, Ont., 1951-62, asst. to dean, 1962; mem. faculty U. Montréal, 1962-65, 67-79, dean, 1967-71, 1971-75, v.p., 1975-79; head cultural affairs div. Dept. External Affairs, Ottawa, 1966-67; minister cultural affairs and info. Can. embassy, Paris, 1979—. Author: Chroniques de français, 1956, 61, Marcel Proust, critique littéraire, 2 vols, 1967. Served with Royal Canadian Air Force, 1942-45. Recipient Grand Prix Littéraire, Ville de Montréal, 1968, Médaille Broquette-Gonin Académie française, 1968. Fellow Royal Soc. Can.; mem. Acad. canadienne-française (sec.), La Société des Gens de lettres (France), Le Conseil international de la langue francaise (v.p.). Home: 55 rue de Babylone 75007 Paris France

DECHAR, PETER HENRY, artist; b. N.Y.C., Apr. 19, 1942; s. Edouard and Diane D. Prin. Peter Dechar Inc. Archtl. Furniture. Exhibited one-man shows, Cordier & Ekstrom Gallery, N.Y.C., 1967, 69, 75, Twentieth Century Art from the Rockefeller Collection, N.Y.C., 1969, Mus. Modern Art, N.Y.C., 1969, group shows, Larry Aldrich Mus., Ridgefield, Conn., 1967, Krannert Art Mus., Whitney Mus. Art, N.Y.C., 1967, 69; represented in permanent collections, Mus. Modern Art, N.Y.C., Whitney Mus. Art, N.Y.C., Larry Aldrich Mus., Ridgefield, Conn., Walker Art Ctr., Fiberglass Tower Art Collection. Office: 455 Carroll St Brooklyn NY 11215

DECHARIO, TONY HOUSTON, symphony orchestra executive; b. Girard, Kans., Sept. 25, 1940; s. Tony and Enid Eulalia (Frogue) D.; m. Mary Gill Ruby, Dec. 28, 1974; children: Samuel Paul, Rachel Christina, Toni Elizabeth, Mary Rebecca; stepchildren: Edmund Kidd II, Kenneth Kidd, Todd Kidd. Performer's cert., Eastman Sch. Music, U. Rochester, 1962, M.M., 1963; B. Music, Wichita U., 1962. Prin. Trombone, Dallas Symphony, 1964-65; 2d trombone, Rochester (N.Y.) Philharmonic Orch., 1972-75; gen. mgr. orch., 1975—. Lodge: Rochester Rotary. Home: 199 Oak Ln Rochester NY 14610 Office: 108 East Ave Rochester NY 14604

DE CHARMS, RICHARD, educator; b. Wilkes Barre, Pa., Dec. 13, 1927; s. Richard and Carita (Pendleton) deCharms; m. Marion Scranton Muir, Oct. 11, 1975. B.A., Swarthmore Coll., 1952; M.A., Wesleyan U., 1954; Ph.D., U. N.C., 1956. Asst. prof. dept. edn. Washington U., St. Louis, 1957-61, assoc. prof., 1961-65, prof., 1965—; vis. assoc. prof. U. Colo., Boulder, 1963-64; research assoc. Harvard U., Cambridge, Mass., 1965-66; vis. prof. U. Toronto, Ont., 1976; cons. Internat. Research Seminar, Munich, Ger., 1972, San Mateo Schs., Calif., 1967-68, Bellwood Sch., Chgo., 1978-81. Author: Personal Causation, 1968, (2d edit.) Personal Causation, 1983, Enhancing Motivation, 1976. Served to lt. (j.g.) USNR, 1946-52. Office Naval Research grantee, 1958-65; Carnegie Corp. grantee, 1966-70; NIMH grantee, 1973-76; Spencer Found. grantee, 1981-82. Fellow Am. Psychol. Assn.; mem. Internat. Soc. Polit. Psychology, Am. Ednl. Research Assn., AAAS, Sigma Xi. Home: 138 South Gore St. Saint Louis MO 63119 Office: Washington Univ Skinker and Lindell St Saint Louis MO 63130

DE CHASTELAIN, ALFRED JOHN GARDYNE DRUMMOND, army officer; b. Bucharest, Rumania, July 30, 1937; emigrated to Can., 1955, naturalized, 1962; s. Alfred George G. and Marion Elizabeth (Walsh) de C.; m. Mary Ann Laverty, Sept. 9, 1961; children: Duncan John, Amanda Jane. Student, Fettes Coll., Edinburgh, Scotland, 1950-55; B.A. with honors in History, Royal Mil. Coll., Can., 1960; grad., Brit. Army Staff Coll., 1966. Commd. 2d lt. Canadian Army, 1960, advanced through grades to maj. gen., 1983; comdg. officer 2d Bn. Princess Patricia's Canadian Light Inf., 1970-72; comdr. Canadian Forces Base, Montreal, Que., 1974-76; comdr. Canadian Contingent UN Force in Cyprus, 1976-77; comdt. Royal Mil. Coll. Can., Kingston, Ont., 1977-80; comdr. 4th Can. Mechanized Brigade Group, Lahr, Germany, 1980-82; dir. Gen. Land Doctrine Nat. Def. Hdqrs., Ottawa, 1982-83; dep. comdr. Mobile Command, St. Hubert, Que., 1983—. Recipient Canadian Forces Decoration. Mem. Royal United Services Inst., Royal Canadian Legion. Club: RMC of Can. Home: 366 Kitchener Westmount PQ Canada

DECHER, RUDOLF, physicist; b. Wuerzburg, W. Ger., Aug. 22, 1927; came to U.S., 1960, naturalized, 1967; s. Hermann Alexander and Karola (Krenig) D.; m. Christa Anna Hort, Jan. 7, 1956; children—Peter H., Marianne C. M. in Physics, U. Wuerzburg, W. Ger., 1950, Ph.D., 1954. Research scientist Dynamit AG, Troisdorf, W. Ger., 1955-60; with NASA Marshall Space Flight Center, Huntsville, Ala., 1960—, chief space physics div., space sci. lab., 1970—. Recipient Exceptional Service medal NASA, 1977. Mem. Am. Phys. Soc., AIAA. Roman Catholic. Home: 718 Owens Dr Huntsville AL 35801 Office: ES61 Marshall Space Flight Center Huntsville AL 35812

DECHERD, ROBERT WILLIAM, newspaper and broadcasting executive; b. Dallas, Apr. 9, 1951; s. Henry Benjamin, Jr. and Isabelle Lee (Thomason) D.; m. Maureen Healy, Jan. 25, 1975; 1 son, William Benjamin. A.B. cum laude (hon. freshman scholarship 1969, David McCord award 1973), Harvard U., 1973. Mgmt. trainee, then asst. to exec. editor Dallas Morning News, 1973-78, exec. v.p., 1980-83; v.p. corp. adminstrn. A.H. Belo Corp., Dallas, 1978-80, exec. v.p., 1981—, dir., 1976—, Belo Broadcasting Corp. Pres. Dallas Symphony Assn., 1979-80; treas. adv. bd. Dallas Salvation Army, 1978-80; trustee St. Mark's Sch. Tex., 1979—, chmn. exec. com., 1983—. Mem. Dallas Assembly (dir. 1978-80). Office: Communications Center Dallas TX 75265

DECI, EDWARD LEWIS, psychologist; b. Clifton Springs, N.Y., Oct. 14, 1942; s. Charles Henry and Janice Margaret (Upchurch) D. A.B., Hamilton Coll., Clinton, N.Y., 1964; postgrad., London Sch. Econs., 1965; M.B.A., U. Pa., 1967; Ph.D., Carnegie-Mellon U., 1970. Mem. faculty U. Rochester, N.Y., 1970—, prof. psychology, 1978—; pvt. practice psychotherapy, 1975—; orgnl. cons., 1970—. Author: The Psychology of Self-Determination, 1980, Intrinsic Motivation, 1975; co-author: Industrial and Organizational Psychology, 1977. Grantee NIMH, 1977-78, NSF, 1981-83. Fellow Am. Psychol. Assn. Home: 1410 East Ave Rochester NY 14610 Office: Psychology Dept U Rochester Rochester NY 14627

DECINCES, DOUGLAS VERNON (DOUG DECINCES), professional baseball player; b. Burbank, Calif., Aug. 29, 1950; m. Kristi Smith, Jan. 9, 1971; children: Timothy, Amy. Student, Pierce Jr. Coll., UCLA. Infielder Bluefield, Appalachian League, 1970, Dallas-Ft. Worth, Tex. League, 1970-71, Asheville, So. League, 1972, Rochester, Internat. League, 1973, Balt. Orioles, Am. League, 1973-81, Calif. Angels, Am. League, 1982—; mem. Am. League All-Star Team, 1983. Played in World Series. 1979. Office: c/o Calif Angels Anaheim Stadium 2000 State College Blvd Anaheim CA 92806 *

DECIO, ARTHUR JULIUS, manufacturing executive; b. Elkhart, Ind., Oct. 19, 1930; s. Julius A. and Lena (Alesia) D.; m. Patricia George, Jan. 6, 1951; children: Terrence, Jamee, Linda, Jay, Leigh Allison. Student, DePaul U., 1949-50; D.B.A. (hon.), Salem (W.Va.) Coll.; LL.D., U. Notre Dame, Ind. State U., Terre Haute. Pres., Skyline Corp., Elkhart, 1956-59, pres., chmn. bd., chief exec. officer, 1959—; pres., dir. Am. Fletcher Bank, Indpls.; dir. Schwarz Paper Co., Chgo.; past dir. Michiana Public Broadcasting Corp., South Bend, Ind., Centennial Corp., Grand Rapids, Mich., Fed. Res. Bank Chgo., Midwest Commerce Banking Co. Trustee U. Notre Dame; bd. dirs. Goshen (Ind.) Coll.; past mem. Commn. on Presidential Scholars; pres. Elkhart Gen. Hosp. Found.; dir. Nat. Italian-Am. Found., Washington; chmn. adv. council United Way, Elkhart, past dir., campaign chmn., 1966; dir. Cath. Diocese of Ft. Wayne-South Bend, Ind.; trustee Aux Chandelles Village Found., Elkhart; life mem. adv. bd. Salvation Army, Elkhart; life mem. bd. trustees Marmion Military Acad., Aurora, Ill.; past dir. Elkhart Urban League, Jr. Achievement Elkhart, Elkhart Gen. Hosp., N. Central Ind. Med. Edn. Found., South Bend, Nat. Jr. Achievement; past trustee Stanley Clark Sch., South Bend, LaLumiere Sch., Laporte, Ind.; mem. Council on Devel. Choices for the 80's, Urban Land Inst., Presidential Task Force on Low Income Housing, 1970. Recipient U. Portland (Oreg.) medal, Golden Plate award Acad. Achievement, Dallas, the Others award; Salvation Council of the Sagamores of the Wabash award State of Ind.; Community Service award Elkhart County br. NAACP, 1980; Marmion Centurion award Marmion Mil. Acad.; Others award Salvation Army; Achievement award Jr. Achievement; Humanitarian award, Community Service award Elkhart Urban League; Disting. Am. award Nat. Football Found. and Hall of Fame; Achievement award others. Mem. Manufactured Housing Inst. (dir.), Mobile Home Mfrs. Assn. (dir., past pres., past chmn. Washington affairs com.), Asso. Colls. Ind. (bd. govs.), Ind. Acad. Roman Catholic. Clubs: Elks, Knights of Malta. Home: 3215 Greenleaf Blvd Elkhart IN 46514 Office: 2520 By Pass Rd Elkhart IN 46514

DECK, JOSEPH FRANCIS, educator, chemist; b. St. Louis, Mar. 19, 1907; s. Michael and and Anna (Westerheide) D.; m. Lillian M. Schwalbe, June 30, 1937; children—Jerry Bothe, Mary Victory, Peter Mitchel. A.B., St. Louis U., 1928, M.S., 1930; Ph.D., U. Kan., 1932. With Stewart Inso Board Co., S. St. Joseph, Mo., 1932-36; quality supr. U.S. Gypsum Co., 1936; faculty U. Santa Clara, Calif., 1936—, dept. chemistry, 1945—, chmn. dept., 1936-72; Lectr. U. San Francisco, summers 1948, 49; research chemist Richmond Chase Co., 1940-49, Moyer Chem. Co., 1957-59, Food Machinery Corp., 1959-61. Named Chemist of Year St. Louis U. Chemists Club, 1965. Mem. Am. Chem. Soc., Albertus Magnus Guild, Cal. Assn. Chemistry Tchrs., Sigma Xi. Club: Rotarian (past pres. Santa Clara). Research on organic syntheses involving heterocyclic compounds, free radicals. Home: 937 Morse St San Jose CA 95126 Office: Dept Chemistry U Santa Clara CA 95053

DECK, RAYMOND HENRY, insurance company executive; b. St. Louis, June 26, 1922; s. Clemens Henry and Emma Frances (Grimm) D.; m. Veronica Ann Abbick, Feb. 7, 1946; children: Barbara, Raymond Henry, Michael, Mark, Kevin (dec.), Mary. B.S. in Commerce, St. Louis U., 1948; L.H.D. hon., St. Joseph Coll., West Hartford, Conn., 1982. Vice pres. Sentry Ins. Group, Stevens Point, Wis., 1941-62; sr. v.p. Am. Mut. Ins. Group, Wakefield, Mass., 1962-65; exec. v.p. Hartford Ins. Group, Conn., 1965—; dir. Hartford Fire Ins. Co., 1970—. Trustee St. Joseph Coll.; bd. dirs. United Way Capital Area, West Hartford, Combined Health Appeal, Hartford. Decorated Knight Order Saint Gregory the Great civil class Pope John Paul II, 1981. Roman Catholic. Club: Hartford Golf. Home: 47 West Hill Dr West Hartford CT 06119 Office: Hartford Ins Group Hartford Plaza Hartford CT 06115

DECKELBAUM, NELSON, lawyer; b. Washington, Apr. 1, 1928; s. Fred and Rose (Egber) D.; m. Louann Jacobs, Oct. 19, 1952; children: David Alan, Todd Stuart. B.S., Georgetown U., 1950, J.D., 1952. Bar: D.C. 1952, Md. 1957, U.S. Supreme Ct. 1966. Practice law, Washington, 1952—; sr. partner Deckelbaum, Wolpert & Ogens, 1974—; Staff mem. Commn. on Govt. Security, 1956. Chmn. Democratic precinct, Montgomery County, Md., 1958. Served with USAF, 1952-54. Mem. Am., Md., D.C. bar assns., Am. Judicature Soc., Georgetown University Alumni Assn. Democrat. Jewish. Clubs: Woodmont Country, Amity, Univ. Home: 4201 Cathedral Ave NW Washington DC 20016 Office: 1140 Connecticut Ave NW Washington DC 20036 also 7315 Wisconsin Ave Bethesda MD 20814

DECKER, BERNARD MARTIN, U.S. dist. judge; b. Highland Park, Ill., Apr. 2, 1904; s. Martin C. and Florence (Bryant) D.; m. Louise Armstrong, Aug. 15, 1928; children—Janine L. (Mrs. Jack G. Collins), Martin C. II. Student, Northwestern U., 1922-23; A.B., U. Ill., 1926; LL.B., Harvard, 1929. Bar: Ill. bar 1929. Law clk. Ralph J. Dady, 3d and 4th dists. Appellate Ct. Ill., 1938-43; gen. practice law firm Decker & Decker, Waukegan, Ill., 1929-51; judge Circuit Ct., 17th Circuit Ill., 1951-57; presiding judge (19th Circuit), 1957-62; U.S. judge No. Dist. Ill., Chgo., 1962—; Chmn. organizing com. Ill. Jud. Conf., 1957, mem. exec. com., 1958-62, chmn. conf., 1959; exec. com. Nat. Conf. State Trial Judges, 1961-63, del., 1961, 62; mem. com. ct. administrn. U.S. Cts., 1968-75, mem. rev. com., 1974-78, mem. jud. ethics com., 1978—. Pres. bd. edn. Waukegan Twp. High Sch., 1946-49. Mem. Harvard Law Soc. Chgo. (pres. 1964-65), ABA, Ill. Bar Assn., Lake County Bar Assn. (pres. 1955), Phi Beta Kappa, Delta Tau Delta. Office: US Ct House 219 S Dearborn St Chicago IL 60604

DECKER, CHARLES L., advertising agency executive; m. Carol A. Arne, Feb. 14, 1979; 1 dau., Katharine. B.A., Dartmouth Coll., 1959. With brand mgmt. Procter & Gamble, Cin., 1962-67; account mgr. Ogilvy & Mather, N.Y.C., 1967—, now sr. v.p., mgmt. supr. Lt. j.g. USCG, 1959-62. Home: 150 Corona Ave Pelham NY 10803 Office: Ogilvy & Mather 2 E 48th St New York NY 10017

DECKER, DAVID GARRISON, physician; b. Pittsford, N.Y., Sept. 14, 1917; s. Judson and Edith (Garrison) D.; m. Elizabeth Bavis, June 23, 1941; children: Margaret Louise, David Judson, Arthur Bavis, Ann Elizabeth. A.B., U. Rochester, 1939; M.D., Yale U., 1942; M.S., U. Minn., 1951. Diplomate: Am. Bd. Ob-Gyn. Intern Mary Imogene Bassett Hosp., Cooperstown, N.Y., 1942-43, asst. resident biochemistry and ob-gyn, 1946-47; resident ob-gyn Mayo Grad. Sch. Medicine, 1947-50, prof. ob-gyn, 1970—; mem. staff Mayo Clinic, Rochester, Minn., 1950—, chmn. dept. ob-gyn, 1969-76, sr. cons. dept. ob-gyn, 1976—. Contbr. articles profl. jours. Served to maj. M.C., AUS, 1942-46. Mem. Am. Assn. Obstetricians and Gynecologists, Am. Radium Soc., Am. Fertility Soc. (mem. exec. com. 1970—), Am. Coll. Ob-Gyn, Central Assn. Obstetricians and Gynecologists (sec.-treas. 1968-71, pres. 1973), Assn. Profs. Ob-Gyn, Soc. Gynecol. Oncologists, Minn. Obstet. and Gynecol. Soc., Obstet. and Gynecol. Travel Club, Central Travel Club (pres. 1970), Minn. Med. Assn., Sigma Xi. Presbyterian. Club: Masons. Home: 1106 Skyline Dr SW Rochester MN 55902

DECKER, FRANZ PAUL, symphony conductor, educator; b. Cologne, Germany; s. Caspar and Elisabeth (Scholz) D.; m. Christa Terka, May 26, 1969; children: Arabella, Ariadne. Grad. high sch.; student, State Inst. for Mus. Edn., Cologne; M.Conducting, U. Cologne; Dr.h.c., Concordia U., Montreal, Que., Can. Choir dir., asst. condr., Municipal Theater, Giessen, 1945; condr. opera, Cologne; municipal dir. music, Krefeld, from 1946; prin condr., State Opera house, Wiesbaden, 1950-53; permanent dir., Municipal Symphony Orch., Wiesbaden, 1953-56; general music director, Bochum, 1956-64; chief condr., artistical dir., Rotterdam Philharmonic Orch., 1962-68; permanent condr., mus. dir., Montreal Symphony Orch., 1967-76; guest condr. opera and concerts worldwide; Composer symphonies, opera, oratories, chamber music. Decorated Edgar Roquette Pinto medal, Brazil, 1963, Herscheppend Schep Ik medal, Netherlands, 1968; Order of Merit 1st class, Fed. Republic of Germany; Jubilee medal Queen Elizabeth II. Club: Rotarian. 2 Kronenburgerstrasse 5000 Cologne Federal Republic Germany

DECKER, FREDERIC CHARLES, magazine publisher, management consultant; b. South Bend, Ind., June 3, 1916; s. Charles Abram and Edith Gertrude (Heffer) D.; m. Lorayne Lutsch, Feb. 15, 1941 (dec. Nov. 1982); children: William F., Craig D., Keith P., Michael J. Pub. Printers Ink mag., N.Y.C., Consumer Advt., Bus. Advt. mags., 1960—; v.p. Physicians Info. Exchange, Inc.; pub. Mktg. Communications Mag., N.Y.C., The Chief Exec., New Products Report, coll. texts, bus. books; v.p. Vision, Inc., 1963-65; pres. Decker Communications, Inc., 1965—, Frederic C. Decker Co., Inc., 1972—, Frederic C. Decker Co., Inc., Mktg. Research Assocs., 1969, Decker Mgmt. Studies, 1974—, Counsel House Research, 1981—; dir. Hanley-Wood, Inc.; lectr. U. Bridgeport, George Washington U., Washingtonian Confs., Folio Mag. Week Seminars, Mag. Publishers Assn. Workshops, Face to Face, Mag. West Confs. Writer weekly column; contbr. articles to bus. and profl. jours. Trustee Inst. Advanced Mktg. Studies, Am. Health Found.; bd. dirs. Profl. Devel. Resources. Mem. Nat. Inst. Social Scis., Am. Advt. Fedn., Am. Bus. Press, Direct Mail Mktg. Assn., Mag. Pubs. Assn., Soc. Nat. Assn. Publs. Clubs: Princeton, Nat. Press. Home: High Ridge Rd Brookfield Center CT 06805 Office: Counsel House Brookfield Center CT 06805

DECKER, FREEMAN BERNARD, educator, city ofcl.; b. Arlington, Nebr., Feb. 26, 1908; s. Bernard and Keoka (Hagenbuck) D.; m. Constance Herndon, July 14, 1931; children—Karen, Judith. A.B., Wayne State Tchrs. Coll., 1930; M.A., U. Neb., 1945, Ed.D., 1956. Prin. Carroll (Nebr.) High Sch., then photographer, Wayne, Nebr., 1935-38; county supt. schs., Wayne, 1938-43; dep. Nebr. Dept. Pub. Instrn., 1943-51, state supt. schs., 1951-55, commr. edn., 1955-62; co-ordinator state colls., 1962; former dir. publs. Wayne State Coll., prof. edn., 1968-74; mayor of Wayne, 1974—. Home: 200 Blaine St Wayne NE 68787 *It takes so little effort to be nice to other people.*

DECKER, GILBERT FELTON, manufacturing company executive; b. Marietta, Ga., June 23, 1937; s. Felton Ambrose and Mary Irene (Pettyjohn) D.; children: Carlyle F., Donna L., Michael T. B.S.E.E., Johns Hopkins U., 1958; M.S., Stanford U., 1966. Systems engr. Sylvania Electronics Products, Mountain View, Calif., 1964-66; program mgr. ESL, Inc., Sunnyvale, Calif., 1966-69, v.p. engring., 1969-75, v.p. ops., 1975-77, pres., 1978-82; v.p. new ventures TRW Inc., 1982—. Chmn. fund-raising com. Jobs for Progress, Inc.; chmn. fund-raising div. United Way. Served with U.S. Army, 1958-64. Mem. Am. Electronics Assn., Santa Clara County Mfrs. Group (dir.), Res. Officers Assn., Assn. U.S. Army, Air Force Assn., Assn. Old Crows., Army Sci. Bd. Republican. Office: 1 Space Park Redondo Beach CA 90278

DECKER, JOHN CHARLES, utility company executive; b. Davenport, Iowa, July 19, 1941; s. Charles Edward and Louise Frances (Farmer) D.; m. Sue Ann Moeller, Aug. 12, 1966; children: John, Ed, Katy. B.A., Lawrence Coll., 1963; M.B.A., Wharton Grad. Sch. Finance and Commerce, U. Pa., 1965. With Iowa-Ill. Gas & Electric Co., Davenport, 1965—, asst. treas., 1973, treas., asst. sec., 1973-74, sec., treas., 1974—; dir. Bituminous Ins. Cos., Rock Island, Ill.; instr. St. Ambrose Coll., Davenport. Bd. dirs. Mercy Hosp., Jr. Achievement; vice-chmn. campaign United Way. Mem. Am. Gas Assn., Am. Soc. Corporate Secs. Clubs: Davenport, Rock Island Arsenal. Home: 2340 E 11th St Davenport IA 52803 Office: 206 E 2d St Davenport IA 52801

DECKER, JOHN LAWS, physician; b. Bklyn., June 27, 1921; s. John William and Margaret (Laws) D.; m. Lucille Macbeth, Nov. 13, 1954; children: Virginia Elliott, David Laws, Margaret Cauthorn, Susan Curtis. B.A., U. Richmond, 1942; M.D., Columbia U., 1951. Intern, asst. resident, chief resident medicine Presbyn. Hosp., N.Y.C., 1951-55; research fellow medicine Mass. Gen. Hosp., 1955-58; instr. medicine Columbia Coll. Physicians and Surgeons, 1954- 55; tutor med. scis. Harvard Med. Sch., 1957-58; from instr. to assoc. prof. medicine U. Wash. Med. Sch., 1958-65; chief arthritis and rheumatism br. Nat. Inst. Arthritis, Diabetes and Digestive and Kidney Diseases, NIH, Bethesda, Md., 1965-83; assoc. dir. clin. care, dir. Clin. Ctr. NIH, Bethesda, Md., 1983—; cons. U.S. Army, 1962—. Contbr. articles to profl. jours. Served to lt. USNR, 1942-46. Decorated Purple Heart. Fellow ACP (bd. govs. 1982—); mem. Am. Rheumatism Assn. (pres. 1972-73), Am. Fedn. Clin. Research, Phi Beta Kappa, Alpha Omega Alpha, Omicron Delta Kappa, Phi Gamma Delta, Nu Sigma Nu. Home: 4703 Broad Brook Dr Bethesda MD 20814 Office: Room 2C146 Bldg 10 Nat Institutes Health Bethesda MD 20205

DECKER, MARY TERESA, athlete; b. Bunnvale, N.J., Aug. 4, 1958; d. John and Jacquline D.; m. Ron Tabb, Sept. 12, 1981 (div. Dec. 1983). Student, U. Colo., 1977-78. Amateur runner, 1969—; cons. CBS Records, Times, Eastman Kodak; mem. U.S. Olympic Team, 1980. Holder 7 world track and field records, 1980-82; named Amateur Sportsman of Yr. Woman's Sports Found., 1982, 83; recipient Sullivan award AAU, 1982, Jesse Owens Internat. Amateur Athlete award, 1982, Gold medals at 1500 and 3000 meters World Track and Field Championship, Helsinki, Finland, 1983. Office: Athletics W 3968 W 13th St Eugene OR 97402 *

DECKER, OSCAR CONRAD, JR., retired army officer; b. Moorefield, Nebr., Oct. 10, 1924; s. Oscar Conrad and June L. (Brunner) D.; m. Ella Mae Tillson, Nov. 8, 1944; children: Kathleen, Linda, David. B.S. in Bus. Adminstrn., U. Nebr., 1951; M.S. in Internat. Affairs, George Washington U., 1969; student, Command and Gen. Staff Coll., 1959-60, Armed Forces Staff Coll., 1964, Navy War Coll., 1968-69. Served as enlisted man U.S. Army, 1943-46, commd. 2d lt., 1951, advanced through grades to maj. gen., 1976; mem. staff Dept. Army, Pentagon, Washington, 1964-67, comdr. bn., Vietnam, 1967; exec. to Asst. Sec. of Army for installations and logistics, Pentagon, 1972-73; project mgr. U.S. Army Tank Automotive Command, Warren, Mich., 1969-72, dir. procurement and prodn., 1973-75, dep. comdg. gen., 1975-76, comdg. gen., 1976-83; ret., 1983. Mem. exec. bd. United Found., Detroit. Decorated Legion of Merit with 3 oak leaf clusters, D.S.M., Army Commendation medal. Mem. Assn. U.S. Army, U.S. Armor Assn., Am. Def. Preparedness Assn. Lutheran.

DECKER, RAYMOND FRANK, scientist, university official, business executive; b. Afton, N.Y., July 20, 1930; s. Bernett Hurd and Mildred (Bisbee) D.; m. Mary Birdsall, Dec. 27, 1951; children: Susan, Elizabeth, Catherine, Laura. B.S., U. Mich., 1952, M.S., 1955, Ph.D., 1958. With Inco Ltd., 1958-82, v.p. corp. tech. and diversification ventures, 1978-82; v.p. research Mich. Technol. U., Houghton, 1982—; chief exec. officer, dir. Advanced Mineral Techs., Inc., Socorro, N.Mex., 1982—; dir. Inco U.S.; adj. prof. Poly. Inst. Bklyn., 1962-66, N.Y. U., 1968; Van Horn disting. lectr. Case-Western Res. U., 1975; mem. materials adv. bd. NRC-Nat. Acad. Scis., 1964, NASA, 1969, Mich. Technol. U., 1971, Nat. Bur. Standards, 1973, Poly. Inst. N.Y., 1977, NSF, 1978-80; mem. Nat. Materials Adv. Bd., 1982—; mem. feasibility panel Mich. State Research Fund, 1983—; mem. task force Molecular Biology Inst., 1983—; trustee Foundry Ednl. Found., 1975-77, Welding Research Council, 1975-80; keynote speaker on superalloys Seven Springs Conf., 1980, Nat. Acad. Engring., 1980—. Author: Strengthening Mechanisms in Nickel-base Superalloys; editor: Maraging Steels. Served to 1st lt. AUS, 1952-54. Recipient IR-100 award, 1964, Sesquicentennial award U. Mich., 1967. Fellow Am. Soc. metals (Achievement award N.Y. chpt. 1970, chmn. materials systems and design div. 1971-73, trustee 1976-79, Zay Jeffries lectr. 1978, Sauveur lectr. 1980, gold medal 1981, chmn. diamond decade com. 1980-81), Am. Inst. Chemists; mem. AIME (lectr. Inst. Metals div. 1973, R.F. Mehl medal 1973), ASTM, AAAS. Presbyterian. Club: Miscowaubik (N.Y.C.). Co-inventor maraging steels. Home: 701 E 7th Ave Houghton MI 49931 Office: Mich Technol U Houghton MI 49931 Advanced Mineral Techs Inc 1309 Lopezville Rd PO Box 1339 Socorro NM 87801

DECKER, RICHARD KNORE, lawyer; b. Lincoln, Nebr., Sept. 15, 1913; s. Fred William and Georgia (Kilmer) D.; m. Fern Iona Steinbaugh, June 12, 1938. A.B., U. Nebr., 1935, J.D., 1938. Bar: Nebr. 1938, U.S. Supreme Ct. 1941, D.C. 1948, Ill. 1952. Trial atty. antitrust div. Dept. Justice, 1938-52; partner firm Lord, Bissell & Brook, Chgo., 1953—. Trustee, Village of Clarendon Hills (Ill.), 1960-64; chmn. bd. elders Community Presbyn. Ch., Clarendon Hills, 1963-66; chmn. bd. Robert Crown Center Health Edn., Hinsdale, Ill., 1981-83. Served with USNR, 1942-45. Mem. ABA (chmn. antitrust sect. 1971-72), Ill. Bar Assn. (gov. 1969-73, chmn. antitrust sect. 1964-66), Chgo. Bar Assn. (chmn. antitrust law com. 1956-59), Law Club Chgo. Republican. Clubs: Mid-Day, Metropolitan, Hinsdale Golf (pres. 1968). Home: 20 Waverly Ave Clarendon Hills IL 60514 Office: 115 S LaSalle St Suite 3500 Chicago IL 60603

DECKER, ROBERT WAYNE, geophysicist, educator; b. Williamsport, Pa., Mar. 11, 1927; s. P. Harold and Catherine T. (Sullivan) D.; married; 4 children. B.S., MIT, 1949, M.S., 1951; D.Sc. (Sinclair fellow), Colo. Sch. Mines, 1953. Asst. geologist Bethlehem Steel Co., Venezuela, 1949; geophysicist New World Exploration Co., Reno, 1952-54; asst. prof. Dartmouth, 1954-61, asso. prof., 1961-67, chmn. dept. geology, 1963-65, 74-77, prof., 1967-79; geophysicist U.S. Geol. Survey, 1957—; scientist-in-charge Hawaiian Volcano Obs.,

1979—; asso. prof. Inst. Tech., Bandung, Indonesia, 1959-60; Mem. adv. panel for earth scis. NSF, 1971-74, chmn., 1972-73; chmn. geoscis. adv. panel Los Alamos Sci. Lab. Research affiliate Hawaii Inst. Geophysics, U. Hawaii, 1964—; participant Internat. Symposium on Volcanology, Japan, 1962, New Zealand, 1965; vis. scientist U.S. Geol. Survey Nat. Center for Earthquake Research, 1969-70; lectr. various colls., univs. Editor: Catalog of Active Volcanoes of the World, 1968-80; Am. editor: Bull. Volcanologique, 1967-75; author with Barbara Decker books on volcanoes; Contbr. articles to profl. jours. NSF grantee, 1968-71, 72-73. Fellow Geol. Soc. Am. (chmn. div.), Am. Geophys. Union (sect. v.p.); mem. Seismol. Soc. Am., Internat. Assn. Volcanology and Chemistry of Earth's Interior (pres. 1976-80), AAAS, Sigma Xi. Seismic and geodetic research on volcanism and tectonism of Hawaii, Iceland and Cascades; research on geothermal power. Home: PO Box 40 Hawaii National Park HI 96718

DECKER, THOMAS ANDREW, manufacturing company executive; b. Phila., Feb. 13, 1946; s. Arnold f. and Emma M. (Puhl) D.; m. M. Candace Jaeger; 1 dau., Samantha Elizabeth. B.A., U. Pa., 1968; J.D., U. Va., 1971. Bar: Pa. Assoc. law firm Pepper, Hamilton & Scheetz, Phila., 1971-73; counsel Lease Financing Corp., Bryn Mawr, Pa., 1973-74; gen. counsel Certain-Teed Corp., Valley Forge, Pa., 1974—. Served to capt. U.S. Army, 1972. Address: PO Box 860 Valley Forge PA 19482

DECKER, WAYNE LEROY, meteorologist, educator; b. Patterson, Iowa, Jan. 24, 1922; s. Albert Henry and Effie (Holmes) D.; m. Martha Jane Livingston, Dec. 29, 1943; 1 dau., Susan Jane. B.S., Central Coll., Pella, Iowa, 1943; postgrad., UCLA, 1943-44; M.S., Iowa State U., 1947, Ph.D., 1955. Meteorologist U.S. Weather Bur., Washington and Des Moines, 1947-49; mem. faculty U. Mo. at Columbia, 1949—, prof. meteorology, 1958-67, prof., chmn. dept. atmospheric sci., 1967—; chmn. com. climatic fluctuations and agrl. prodn. NRC, 1975-76; bd. dirs. Council for Agrl. Sci. and Tech., 1978—, mem. exec. com., 1981—. Mem. Am. Meteorol. Soc., Internat. Soc. Biometeorology, Am. Geophys. Union, Am. Agronomy Soc., Sigma Xi, Gamma Sigma Delta. Home: 1007 Hulen Dr Columbia MO 65201 Office: 701 Hitt St Columbia MO 65211

DECKERT, GORDON HARMON, psychiatrist, educator; b. Freeman, S.D., May 18, 1930; s. Herbert A. and Olivia Blanch (Graber) D.; m. Peggy Jane Chew, June 6, 1951; children: Chet, Carl. B.S., Northwestern U., 1952, M.D., 1955; D.Sc. (hon.), Albany Med. Coll., 1980, Georgetown U., 1982. Diplomate: Am. Bd. Psychiatry and Neurology. Intern Passavant Meml. Hosp., Chgo., 1955-56; fellow in medicine Mayo Clinic, Rochester, Minn., 1956-57; resident in psychiatry U. Okla. Hosp., 1959-62; clin. asst. to asst. prof. U. Okla. Coll. Medicine, 1959-69, prof. psychiatry, chmn. dept. psychiatry and behavioral scis., 1969—, David Ross Boyd Disting. prof., 1983; chief staff U. Okla. Hosps., 1970-72; chmn. psychiatry test com. Nat. Bd. Med. Examiners, 1973-78, chmn. interpersonal skills advisory com., 1974—, mem. at large, 1979—; Disting. Alumni prof. Northwestern U., 1978; nat. lectr. Author articles, book chpts., videotapes. Served to capt. M.C., USAF, 1957-59. Recipient Regents award superior teaching U. Okla., 1971, Aesculapian award Coll. Medicine, 1965, Disting. Service award Okla. Psychol. Assn., 1982. Fellow Am. Psychiat. Assn., Am. Coll. Psychiatrists; mem. AAUP, Assn. Am. Med. Colls., Am. Assn. Chmn. Depts. Psychiatry, Assn. Acad. Psychiatry (a founder), AMA, Sigma Xi, Alpha Omega Alpha. Home: 2237 NW 47th St Oklahoma City OK 73112 Office: Dept Psychiatry PO Box 26901 Oklahoma City OK 73190

DECKINGER, ELLIOTT LAWRENCE, advertising agency executive, marketing educator; b. N.Y.C., Apr. 17, 1917; s. Isaac and Mollie (Rose) D.; m. Adele Victoria Kay, June 7, 1941; children: Matthew, Nancy. B.S., N.Y. U., 1936, M.S., 1939, Ph.D., 1947. With Biow Co., N.Y.C., 1937-56, research and media dir., 1941-56; with Grey Advt., Inc., N.Y.C., 1956—, sr. v.p. charge internat. adminstrn., 1965-82, cons., 1982—; assoc. prof. mktg. St. John's U., 1982—. Author: Careers in Advertising, 1984; contbr. articles to profl. publs. Active Boy Scouts Am., 1955—, mem. nat. public relations com., 1972—, mem. nat. com. internat. scouting, 1973. Named Scouter of Year for communication arts in N.Y.C., 1976. Mem. Copy Research Council (past pres.), Market Research Council (past pres.), Radio and TV Research Council (past pres.), Advt. Research Found. (past chmn.), Internat. Advt. Assn., Am. Mktg. Assn. Home: Box 960 Jamaica NY 11431 Office: Grey Advt Inc 777 3rd Ave New York NY 10017 Office: St John's U Utopia and Grand Central Pkwys Jamaica NY 11439

DECKO, KENNETH OWEN, association executive; b. New Haven, Aug. 7, 1944; s. Charles C. and Frances D.; m. Marilyn Seaver, Oct. 21, 1972; children: Kurt, Amy. Student, Duke U.; J.D., U. Conn., 1969. With Conn. Bus. and Industry Assn., Hartford, 1970—, pres., 1981—. Served with USAR, 1969-70. Office: 370 Asylum St Hartford CT 06103

DECLARIS, NICHOLAS, educator, electrical engineer, medical scientist; b. Greece, Jan. 1, 1931; s. Elias and Helen (Georgiu) DeC.; m. Joan Giuffre, July 25, 1956 (dec. Jan. 1981); 1 son, John William. B.S., Tex. A. and M. Coll., 1952; M.S., Mass. Inst. Tech., 1954, Sc.D., 1959. Research engr. Cal. Research Corp., 1952; research asst., fellow Mass. Inst. Tech., 1952-56; asst. prof. to asso. prof. elec. engring. Cornell U., 1956-64, prof. elec. engring. and applied math., 1964-67; prof. elec. engring., research prof. Inst. for Fluid Dynamics and Applied Mathematics of U. Md., 1967—, head dept. elec. engring., 1967-74; prof. pathology Med. Sch. U. Md.; Cons. Gen. Elec. Co., IBM, NIH, AVCO, Md. Inst. for Emergency Med. Services, U. Chile, U. del Valle; research collaborator Tech. U. Gdansk, Poland. Author: (with R.E. Kalman) Aspects of Network and System Theory, 1971; Editor: Electrical Science Series, 1966—; Contbr. articles to profl. jours.; Reviewer: Math. Revs, 1962-65; adv. bd.: Clin. Engring. Trustee Glenelg (Md.) Sch.; trustee Guillemin Meml. Found.; chmn. Guillemin prize bd. Named Outstanding Educator of Am., 1972. Fellow IEEE (asso. editor Circuit Theory Trans. 1958-66); mem. Am. Math. Soc., Soc. Indsl. and Applied Math. Am. Soc. Engring. Edn., Assn. for Advancement Med. Instrumentation. Club: Cosmos. Home: Beaufort Dr Fulton MD 20759 Office: Elec Engring Dept U Md College Park MD 20742 Office: Dept Pathology U Md Sch Medicine 10 Pine St Baltimore MD 21201

DE CONCINI, DENNIS, U.S. Senator, lawyer; b. Tucson, May 8, 1937; s. Evo and Ora (Webster) DeC.; m. Susan Margaret Hurley, June 6, 1959; children: Denise, Christina, Patrick Evo. B.A., U. Ariz., 1959, LL.B., 1963. Bar: Ariz. bar 1963. Mem. firm Evo DeConcini, Tucson, 1963-65; partner firm DeConcini & McDonald, 1968-73; dep. Pima County atty. Sch. Dist. 1, 1971-72, county atty., 1973-76; mem. U.S. Senate from Ariz., 1977—; formerly pres., now dir. Shopping Centers, Inc. Chmn. legis. com. Tucson Community Council, 1966-67; mem. major gifts com., devel. fund drive St. Joseph's Hosp., 1970, mem. devel. council, 1971-73; mem. major gifts com. Tucson Mus. and Art Center Bldg. Fund, 1971; adminstr. Ariz. Drug Control Dist., 1975-76; precinct committeeman Ariz. Democratic Party, 1958—; mem. Pima County Dem. Central Com., 1958-67, Dem. State Exec. Com., 1958-68; state vice chmn. Ariz. Dem. Com., 1964-66, 70-72; vice chmn. Pima County Dem. Com., 1970-73. Served to 2d lt. JAG U.S. Army, 1959-60. Named Outstanding Ariz. County Atty., 1975. Mem. Am., Ariz., Pima County bar assns., Nat. Dist. Attys. Assn., Ariz. Sheriffs and County Attys. Assn., Am. Judicature Soc., Ariz. Pioneer Hist. Soc., NAACP, U. Ariz. Alumni Assn., Tucson Fraternal Order Police, Phi Delta Theta, Delta Sigma Rho, Phi Alpha Delta. Roman Catholic. Clubs: Nucleus, Old Pueblo, Pres.'s U. Ariz., Latin Am., Latin Am. Social (Tucson). Office: 328 Hart Senate Office Bldg Washington DC 20510

DECONCINI, JOHN CYRUS, labor organization executive; b. Phila., Sept. 14, 1918; s. Frank and Lillian Dec.; children: John, Thomas, Robert, Margaret Mary, Matthew. Student pub. schs., Kulpmont, Pa. With Bakery, Confectionery and Tobacco Workers Internat. Union, AFL-CIO, CLC, Washington, 1937—, successively mem. exec. bd., sec.-treas., exec. v.p., internat. rep., internat. v.p., 1951-57, internat. pres., 1957—. Chmn. bd. regents New Direction, Inc. Served to 1st lt. AUS, 1941-46. Democrat. Roman Catholic. Club: D.C. Friends of Ireland. Office: 10401 Connecticut Ave Kensington MD 20895 *

DE CONINGH, EDWARD HURLBUT, mfg. co. exec.; b. Chgo., July 2, 1902; s. Frederic Benjamin Edward and Lucy (Peck) de C.; m. Virginia Scott Mueller, Nov. 7, 1927 (dec. 1964); children—Mary (Mrs. Oliver F. Emerson), Edward Hurlbut, Virginia (Mrs. Harold C. Fleming); m. Martha Hooker Washburn, 1965. A.B., Princeton, 1922; student, U. Grenoble (France), 1922; B.S., Mass. Inst. Tech., 1925. Apprentice Am. Steel Foundries, 1925; sec. Laudryette Mfg. Co., Cleve., 1926-27; tech. editor Dust Recovering and Conveying Co., Cleve., 1928-33; partner, chief engr. Mueller Electric Co. (now Mueller Electric Co., Inc.), 1933-66, chmn. bd., 1966-; dir. Emerson Press, Inc., Midwest Screw Products, Inc. Pres. Cleve. Welfare Fedn., 1956-59; campaign chmn. Cleve. United Appeal, 1961, 62; pres. Cleve. Community Chest, 1964-65; Vice chmn. trustees Smith Coll., 1962-72; trustee Greater Cleve. Asso. Found., 1967-70, Cleve. Inst. Music; vice chmn. bd. trustees Case Western Res. Univ., 1973-75; trustee Laurel Sch., 1970-76. Recipient Outstanding Service award Cleve. Welfare Fedn., 1959, Distinguished Service award Cleve. United Appeal, 1963; 1967 Cleve. medal for pub. service. Mem. Phi Beta Kappa, Tau Beta Pi, Chi Phi. Clubs: Cleveland Skating, Kirtland Country, Union, University (Cleve.). Home: 23799 Stanford Rd Shaker Heights OH 44122 Office: 1583 E 31st St Cleveland OH 44114

DECOOK, RICHARD CYRIL, manufacturing company executive; b. Detroit, May 24, 1942; s. Cyril B. and Naomi C. DeC.; m. Mary Elizabeth Schwalm, Oct. 10, 1964; children: Elizabeth Anne, Susan Marie, Jennifer Lynne. B.B.A., U. Mich., 1965. C.P.A., Mich. Audit mgr. Ernst & Whinney C.P.A.s, Jackson, Mich., 1965-77; treas. Aeroquip Corp., Jackson, 1978-81, Libbey-Owens-Ford, Toledo, 1981-83, v.p., treas., 1983—; dir. Hubbard Apiaries, Onsted, Mich. Bd. dirs. Mich. Space Center, 1979-81, Jackson C. of C., 1979-81, Bishop's Edn. Council, Toledo, 1983. Mem. Mich. Assn. C.P.A.s, Am. Inst. C.P.A.s, Tax Execs. Inst., Fin. Execs. Inst., Am. Inst. Corp. Asset Mgrs. (bd. dirs.), Am. Inst. Corp. Treas. Republican. Roman Catholic. Club: Toledo. Home: 3851 Brookside Toledo OH 43606 Office: 811 Madison Ave Toledo OH 43695

DE CORDOVA, FREDERICK TIMMINS, TV producer-dir.; b. N.Y.C., Oct. 27, 1910; s. George and Margaret (Timmins) de C.; m. Janet Thomas, Nov. 27, 1963. B.S., Northwestern U., 1931. Producer-dir., Warner Pros. Pictures, 1943-48, Universal Internat. Pictures, 1948-53, CBS and NBC, 1953—; prodns. include: Tonight Show (Recipient Emmy award Acad. TV Arts and Scis. 1963, 68, 76, 77, 78, 79). Club: Bel Air Country (Los Angeles). Home: 1875 Carla Ridge Beverly Hills CA 90210 Office: NBC Burbank CA 91523

DE COSTA, EDWIN J., physician, surgeon; b. Chgo., Mar. 25, 1906; s. Lewis M. and Grace (Myers) DeC; m. Mari H. Bachrach, Jan. 5, 1935 (dec. 1970); children: Mari Jane De Costa Terman, Catherine De Costa Burstein, Louise De Costa Wides, John Lewis; m. Alyce H. Heller, Feb. 1, 1971. B.S., U. Chgo., 1926; M.D., Rush Med. Coll., 1929. Diplomate: Am. Bd. Obstetricians and Gynecologists (examiner 1955—). Intern Cook County Hosp., Chgo., 1929-30, resident obstetrics and pathology, 1930-32; resident gynecology Michael Reese Hosp., Chgo., 1932-33; attending Northwestern Meml. Hosp., Prentice Women's Hosp., Cook County Hosp.; prof. ob-gyn Northwestern U. Med. Sch., 1946—. Author: (with J.I. Brewer) Gynecology, 4th edit., 1967. Served as officer USNR, 1933-66; capt. ret. Mem. Chgo. Gynecol. Soc., Central Assn. Obstetricians and Gynecologists, Am. Coll. Obstetricians and Gynecologists, Am. Gynecol. and Obstetrical Soc., ACS, AMA, Ill., Chgo. med. socs., Central Travel Club, Chgo. Inst. Medicine, Pan-Pacific Surg. Assn., Pan-Am. Med. Assn., Phi Beta Kappa, Sigma Xi, Alpha Omega Alpha; hon. mem. Ark., Nebr. obstetrical and gynecol. socs., Am.-Brit. Cowdray Med. Soc., Tex. Assn. Obstetricians and Gynecologists. Home: 1540 N Lake Shore Dr Chicago IL 60610 Office: 670 N Michigan Ave Chicago IL 60611

DE COSTA, RENE, language educator, literary critic, writer; b. N.Y.C., Nov. 22, 1939; s. George and Anna J. de C.; m. Ayse Serpil Empe,, Aug. 9, 1964; 1 dau., Alev. A.B., Rutgers Coll., 1964; Ph.D., Washington U., 1970. Prof. Romance langs U. Chgo., 1970—, dir. Ctr. for Latin Am. Studies, 1979—. Author: The Poetry of Pablo Neruda, 1979, En pos de Huidobro, 1980, The Careers of a Poet, 1983; contbr. (writings to books in field); author articles to jours. and publes.; resident fellow: Ctr. for Studies in French Culture La Foundation Camargo, Cassis, France, 1974-75, 79; external examiner doctoral dissertations on Huidobro Neruda, U. Toronto, 1972, U. Toronto, 1981; vis. prof. (U. Ore. Summer), 1972, (Stanford U.), 1983. Research grantee Fulbright Commn., 1982; research fellow OAS, 1968; Ford Found. Fgn. Area Fellow, 1971-73; grantee Joint Com. Latin Am. Studies of Am. Council Learned Socs. and Social Sics; Research Council, 1971; travel grantee Am. Council Learned Socs., 1973; Social Sci. Research Council grantee, 1978-79; travel grantee Am. Philos. Soc., 1978.

DECOSTE, JOHN E. *See* **CARTER, TERRY**

DE COSTER, CYRUS COLE, educator; b. Leesburg, Va., Sept. 21, 1914; s. Cyrus C. and Jeanne (Brulay) DeC.; m. Barbara Krause, Dec. 28, 1948; children: Janine B., David C., Kenneth B., James K. A.B., Harvard, 1937; M.A., U. Chgo., 1940, Ph.D., 1951. Instr. romance langs. Carleton Coll., 1946-48, asst. prof., 1948-56, asso. prof., 1956-57; prof. romance langs. U. Kan., Lawrence, 1957-69, chmn. dept., 1962-65; prof. Spanish Northwestern U., Evanston, Ill., 1969—, chmn. dept., 1973-76, 79-83. Author: Correspondencia Inédita de Don Juan Valera, 1956, Obras Desconocidas de Juan Valera, 1965, Bibliografía crítica de Juan Valera, 1970, Juan Valera, 1974, Pedro Antonio de Alarcón, 1979; Editor: Juan Valera, Artículos de El Contemporáneo, 1966, Juan Valera, Las ilusiones del doctor Faustino, 1970, Juan Valera, Genio y figura, 1975. Served to lt. USNR, 1941-46. Home: 17 Martha Ln Evanston IL 60201

DE COUX, JANET, sculptor; b. Niles, Mich., Oct. 4, 1904; d. John Charles and Bertha (Wright) de C. Former student, Carnegie Inst. Tech., N.Y. Sch. Design, R.I. Sch. Design, Chgo. Art Inst. Apprentice C.P. Jennewein, N.Y.C., 1927-29, James Earl Fraser, Westport, Conn., 1932-35; apprentice to others; resident instr. Cranbrook Acad. Art, Birmingham, Mich., 1942-45; self-employed sculptor, Gibsonia, Pa., 1945—. Sculptures include Deborah Song, 1942 (Widener medal 1942), Heroic Portrait William Penn, State Capitol Pa., Harrisburgh, 1967. Fellow Tiffany Found., 1927, Guggenheim Found., 1939-42; grantee Am. Acad.-Nat. Inst. Art and Letters, 1945. Fellow Nat. Sculpture Soc. (Lindsay Meml. prize 1940); academician mem. Nat. Acad. Design. Democrat. Episcopalian. Home: 3930 Dickey Rd Gibsonia PA 15044

DECRANE, ALFRED CHARLES, JR., petroleum company executive; b. Cleve., June 11, 1931; s. Alfred Charles and Verona (Marquard) DeC.; m. Joan Elizabeth Hoffman, July 3, 1954; children: David, Lisa, Stacie, Stephanie, Sarah, Jennifer. B.A., U. Notre Dame, 1953; J.D., Georgetown U., 1959. Bar: Va. bar 1959, D.C. bar 1959, Tex. bar 1961, N.Y. bar 1966. Legal dept. Texaco, Inc., Houston, 1959-64, N.Y.C., 1964-66, asst. to vice chmn. bd., 1965-67, asst. to chmn. bd., 1967-68, gen. mgr. producing dept. Eastern hemisphere, 1968-70, v.p., 1970-76, sr. v.p., gen. counsel, 1976-77, sr. v.p., dir., 1977-78, exec. v.p., 1978-83, pres., 1983—; dir. CIGNA Corp., Arabian Am. Oil Co. Trustee Am. U., Beirut; mem. vis. com. Harvard U. Middle East Center. Served to lt. USMCR, 1954-55. Mem. ABA (sect. sec. 1964-67, co-founder Natural Resources Law Jour. mineral law sect., council mem. minerals sect.). Home: 55 Valley Rd Bronxville NY 10708 Office: 2000 Westchester Ave White Plains NY 10650

DE CRANE, RAYMOND EDWARD, editor; b. Cleve., Aug. 20, 1914; s. Bernard P. and Mary (Reeves) DeC.; m. Henriette Hasselo, Sept. 4, 1934 (dec.); children—Ruth (Mrs. George Mezera), Patricia (Mrs. Philip Cowan), Sandi (Mrs. Thomas Reddish), Raymond J., James E., Curtis A., Kenneth A., Terrence A., Kevin J. (dec.), Helen K., Kelly A.; m. Helen K. Abbott, Aug. 17, 1963. Ed., John Carroll U. With Cleve. Press, 1934-77, labor editor, 1942-45, asst. city editor, 1946-66, bus. editor, 1966-77; editor-in-chief No. Ohio Bus. Jour., 1977-78; pub. De Crane's Bus. Rev., 1978; v.p., fin. counselor Cuyahoga Savs. Assn., 1978—. Author: ann. Cut Your Own Taxes. Recipient Pub. Service award IRS, 1968. Mem. Cleve. C. of C., Sigma Delta Chi. Roman Catholic. Club: Mid-day (Cleve.). Home: 26123 Lake Rd Bay Village OH 44140 Office: One Erieview Plaza Cleveland OH 44114

DE CROW, KAREN, lawyer, author, lecturer; b. Chgo., Dec. 18, 1937; d. Samuel Meyer and Juliette (Abt) Lipschultz; m. Alexander Allen Kolben, 1960 (div. 1965); m. Roger Edward DeCrow, 1965 (div. 1972). B.S., Northwestern U., 1959; J.D., Syracuse U., 1972. Bar: N.Y., U.S. Dist. Ct. (no dist.) N.Y. Resorts editor Golf Digest mag., Evanston, Ill., 1959-60; editor Am. Soc. Planning Ofcls., Chgo., 1960-61; writer Center for Study Liberal Edn. for Adults, Chgo., 1961-64; editor Holt, Rinehart, Winston, Inc., N.Y.C., 1965, L.W. Singer, Syracuse, N.Y., 1965-66; writer Eastern Regional Inst. for Edn., Syracuse, 1967-69, Pub. Broadcasting System, 1977; tchr. women and law, 1972-74; nat. bd. mem. NOW, 1968-77, nat. pres., 1974-77, also nat. politics task force chmn.; cons. affirmative action, lectr. corps., polit. groups, colls. and univs., U.S., Canada, Finland, Peoples Republic of China, Greece, USSR; nat. coordinator Women's Strike for Equality, 1970; N.Y. State del. Internat. Women's Year, 1977; candidate for mayor, Syracuse, 1969; originated Schs. for Candidates; mem. chancellor's affirmative action com. Syracuse U.; mem. N.Y. State Ct. Arbitration Program, 1980; bd. advisors Working Women's Inst.; participant DeCrow-Schlafly ERA Debates, 1975—. Author: (with Roger DeCrow) University Adult Education: A Selected Bibliography, 1967, The Young Woman's Guide to Liberation, 1971, Sexist Justice, 1974, First Women's State of the Union Message, 1977; (with Robert Seidenberg) Women Who Marry Houses: Panic and Protest in Agoraphobia, 1983; Editor: The Pregnant Teenager (Howard Osofsky), 1968, Corporate Wives, Corporate Casualties (Robert Seidenberg), 1973; Contbr.: articles to Chgo. Sun-Times, N.Y. Times, Los Angeles Times, Boston Globe, Vogue, Mademoiselle, Miami Herald; other newspapers, mags.; columnist: Syracuse Post-Standard; Recording: Opening Up Marriage, 1980. Hon. trustee Elizabeth Cady Stanton Found. Mem. Am. Arbitration Assn., Dist. Attys. Adv. Council, ACLU, N.Y. State Women's Bar Assn. (chpt. dir.), N.Y. State, Onondaga County bar assns. Address: 7 Fir Tree Ln Jamesville NY 13078 *I feel especially lucky to be able to participate, as Holmes said, in the passion of our times. The movement to create equality between women and men is the most interesting and exciting place to be during this period in history. My goal is a world where the gender of a baby will have little or no relevance to future pursuits or pleasures - personal, political, economic, social, or professional. It is exhilarating to watch society change in that direction.*

DECTER, MIDGE, writer; b. St. Paul, July 25, 1927; d. Harry and Rose (Calmenson) Rosenthal; m. Norman Podhoretz, Oct. 21, 1956; children—Rachel, Naomi, Ruth, John. Student, U. Minn., 1945-46, Jewish Theol. Sem. Am., 1946-48. Asst. editor Midstream mag., 1956-58; mng. editor Commentary, 1961-62; editor Hudson Inst., 1965-66, CBS Legacy Books, 1966-68; exec. editor Harper's mag., 1969-71; book review editor Saturday Rev./World mag., 1972-74; sr. editor Basic Books, Inc., 1974—; exec. dir. Com. for Free World, 1980—. Author: The Liberated Woman and Other Americans, 1971, The New Chastity, 1972, Liberal Parents, Radical Children, 1975; Contbr. articles to popular publs. Bd. dirs. Heritage Found. Mem. Council Fgn. Relations. Home: 120 E 81st St New York NY 10028

DE CURTIS, DAVID SAMUEL, textile executive; b. Phila., June 26, 1930; s. Vincent and Iva R. (Elton) DeC.; m. Phyllis Macgeorge, Sept. 8, 1951 (dec.); children: David B., Sandra L.; m. Eloise Holt, Nov. 27, 1974. B.S., Drexel U., 1953. Accountant, plant controller Scott Paper Co., Chester, Pa., 1953-54, 57-61, Ft. Edward, N.Y., 1956-57, Mobile, Ala., 1962-64; plant controller, regional controller Ga.-Pacific Corp., Crossett, Ark., 1964-66, Stamford, Conn., 1966-71; controller Texfi Industries, Inc., Greensboro, N.C., 1971-72, v.p., controller, 1972-73, v.p. fin., 1974-78, pres., 1978-81, DeCurtis Trading Co., Greensboro, 1981—. Served to 1st lt. AUS, 1954-56. Mem. Fin. Execs. Inst. Home: 915 Sunset Dr Greensboro NC 27408 Office: 6202 Triport Ct Greensboro NC 27409

DECYK, ROXANNE JEAN, manufacturing company executive lawyer; b. Chgo., Nov. 5, 1952; d. Walter and Tillie (Kuzma) D.; m. William C. Young, Sept. 1, 1973; m. David Shute, Oct. 1, 1977. A.B., U. Ill.; J.D., Marquette U. Bar: Wis. 1977, Ill. 1981. Pres. Penta Advt., Champaign, Ill., 1972-73; staff journalist Coll. Medicine U. Ill., 1973-74; assoc. Foley & Lardner, Milw., 1977-79; pres. Corp. Legal Communications, Milw., 1980-81; v.p., sec., asst. to chmn. Internat. Harvester Co., Chgo., 1981-83, v.p. adminstrn., sec., 1983—; dir. Lincoln Nat. Pension, Ft. Wayne, Ind., First Trust, Chgo. Bd. dirs. YWCA, Greater Milw., 1980, Jr. Achievement, Chgo., 1982—. Recipient Nat. Merit Scholar award Outboard Marine Corp., 1970. Mem. Econ. Club Chgo., ABA, State Bar Wis., Ill. State Bar Assn., Am. Soc. Corp. Secs., Chgo. Network, Phi Beta Kappa. Club: Women's Athletic (Chgo.). Home: 1448 Lake Shore Dr Apt 10C Chicago IL 60610 Office: Internat Harvester Co 401 N Michigan Ave Chicago IL 60611

DEDELOW, DUANE WILLIAM, construction company executive; b. Hammond, Ind., July 31, 1937; s. William Edward and Helen Verna (Van Gorp) D.; m. Constance Brewster, May 21, 1978; children: Luke J. and Shannon A. (twins); children by previous marriage—Duane William, Doreen I., Dawn I. Dedelow Drutis, David E., Douglas C., Darryl and Darrin (twins), Dana M., Drew F. Student, Butler U., 1955-56, Purdue U., 1957-58. Vice pres. Dedelow, Inc., Gary, Ind., 1959-67, pres., chmn. bd., 1967—; pres. No. Ind. Heating and

Plumbing Contractors, 1967. Pres. Hammond Area YMCA, 1973; pres. Calumet council Boy Scouts Am., 1977. Home: 7505 W 118th Ave Crown Point IN 46307 Office: 6655 E Dunes Hwy PO Box 2440 Gary IN 46403

DEDERICH, SUSAN RUSSELL, harpist; b. Rockville Center, N.Y., Oct. 4, 1951; d. Robert Marwood and Martha Annette (Geffs) D.; m. Svetozar Pejovich. B. Performing Arts, Cleve. Inst. Music, 1973; student of, Alice Chalifoux. Prin. harpist Oklahoma City Symphony, 1973-74, New Orleans Symphony, 1974-77, Dallas Symphony, 1977—; adj. prof. harp So. Meth. U. Office: care Dallas Symphony Orch Music Hall PO Box 26207 Dallas TX 75226

DEDERICK, ROBERT GOGAN, government official; b. Keene, N.H., Nov. 18, 1929; s. Frederic Van Dyck and Margaret (Gogan) D.; m. Margarida N. Magalhaes, Aug. 24, 1957; children: Frederic, Laura, Peter. A.B., Harvard U., 1951, A.M., 1953, PhD., 1958; postgrad., Cornell U., 1953-54. Econ. research mgr. New Eng. Mut. Life Ins. Co., Boston, 1957-64; asso. economist No. Trust Co., Chgo., 1964, v.p., asso. economist, 1965-69, v.p., economist, 1969-70, sr. v.p., economist, 1970-81; mem. econ. adv. bd. U.S. Commerce Dept., 1968-70, 75-76, asst. to sec. commerce for econ. affairs, 1981-82, under sec. commerce for econ. affairs, 1982—. Fellow Nat. Assn. Bus. Economists (pres. 1973-74, governing council 1969-76); mem. Conf. Bus. Economists (sec.-treas. 1980-81), Discussion Group Indsl. Economists, Am. Statis. Assn., Am. Econs. Assn., Nat. Economists, Am. Finance Assn., Asso. Harvard Alumni (dir. 1980-82), Harvard Grad. Soc. Council. Clubs: Bankers, Economic, Executives, Harvard (Chgo.); Hinsdale Golf. Home: 113 S County Line Rd Hinsdale IL 60521 Office: northern trust company 50 s lasalle street chicago ill 60675

DEDEURWAERDER, JOSE JOSEPH, automotive executive; b. Brussells, Belgium, Dec. 31, 1932; s. Louis and Philippine (Paternote) D.; m. Nelly Antoinette Clemens, May 15, 1954; 1 dau., Joelle Cabassol. Grad. in tech. engring, Ecole Technique Moyenne Superieure, Belgium, 1953. Mfg. dir. Renault, Belgium, 1958-67, indsl. dir., Argentina, 1967-73; chief exec. officer Renault Mexicana, Mexico, 1973-76; plant dir. Renault, Douai, France, 1976-81; exec. v.p. Am. Motors Corp., Detroit, 1981-82, pres., chief operating officer, 1982—. Served as officer Belgium Navy, 1952-53. Mem. Automotive Hall of Fame (bd dirs.). Office: American Motors Corp 27777 Franklin Rd Southfield MI 48034

DEDINI, ELDON LAWRENCE, cartoonist; b. King City, Calif., June 29, 1921; s. Grutly Stefano and Oleta Regina (Loeber) D.; m. Virginia DeSales Conroy, July 15,1944; 1 son, Giulio. A.A., Hartnell Coll., Salinas, Calif., 1942; grad., Chouinard Art Inst., Los Angeles, 1942-44. Staff cartoonist: Salinas Morning Post, 1940-41; staff story dept., Walt Disney Studios, Burbank, Calif., 1944-46; staff cartoonist: Esquire mag, Chho., 1946-50, New Yorker mag, N.Y.C., 1950—, Playboy mag, Chgo., 1960—; Author: cartoon album The Dedini Gallery, 1961; anthologies of New Yorker, Playboy cartoons. Recipient Best Mag. Cartoonist award Nat. Cartoonists Soc., 1958, 61, 1964, ann. award for best color Cartoon Playboy, 1978. Mem. Nat. Cartoonists Soc., Cartoonists Guild Inc (2d v.p. N.Y.C. 1970). Address: Box 1630 Monterey CA 93940

DEDMAN, BERTRAM COTTINGHAM, retired insurance company executive; b. Columbia, Tenn., Dec. 24, 1914; s. Bertram Cottingham and Mary Ella (Fariss) D.; m. Rainsford Bayard MacDowell, June 16, 1938; children: Rainsford (Mrs. Theodore Harry Olson), Ella (Mrs. Channing Tai Yang). A.B., U. of South, Sewanee, Tenn., 1937; J.D., George Washington U., 1941. Bar: Tenn. 1941, D.C. 1977. Trial atty. Antitrust Div., Dept. Justice, Washington, 1941-54, Texaco, Inc., Los Angeles, 1954-57; asst. counsel, asso. gen. counsel, gen. counsel Ins. Co. of N.Am., Phila., 1957-70; v.p., gen. counsel INA Corp. (now CIGNA Corp.), Phila., 1968-77, v.p., sec., 1975-79. Editor, contbr.: Merger of Insurance Companies, 1966. Served with USNR, 1944-47. Mem. Am., Fed., Tenn., Phila. bar assns., Am. Judicature Soc., Internat. Assn. Ins. Law (past pres. U.S. chpt.). Home: 200 Winding Way Columbia TN 38401

DEDMON, DONALD NEWTON, university president; b. Mo., Aug. 13, 1931; s. Clarence R. and Ola Edith (Garner) D.; m. Geraldine Mary Sanders; children: Mary Elizabeth, Margaret Ann. B.S. in Edn, S.W. Mo. State U., Springfield, 1953; M.A., U. Iowa, 1956, Ph.D., 1961. Instr., dir. debate U. Iowa, 1955-59; asst., then asso. prof. speech, co-chmn. required communications courses St. Cloud (Minn.) State Coll., 1959-62; asso. prof., TV lectr. oral communications So. Ill. U., Carbondale, 1962-64; prof., chmn. dept. speech and arts Colo. State U., Boulder, 1964-66; communications cons., later head tng. and mgmt. devel. Smith, Kline & French Labs., 1966-68; dean Coll. Arts and Scis.; then exec. v.p., v.p. acad. affairs, acting pres. Marshall U., Huntington, W.Va., 1968-72; pres. Radford (Va.) U., 1972—, also mem. found. bd. dirs.; Dir. First and Merchants Nat. Bank, Radford.; dir. United Va. Bank, Radford; Mem. gen. profl. adv. com. Va. Council Higher Edn.; chmn. Council Pres. of Commonwealth Va.; state rep. Am. Assn. State Colls. and Univs. Contbr. numerous articles in field to profl. jours. Served with AUS, 1953-55. Mem. Va., Radford chambers commerce. Club: Rotarian. Home: Radford U Radford VA 24142

DE DUVE, CHRISTIAN RENE, educator, scientist; b. Thames-Ditton, Eng., Oct. 2, 1917; s. Alphonse and Madeleine (Pungs) de D.; m. Janine Herman, Sept. 30, 1943; children: Thierry, Anne, Francoise, Alain. M.D., U. Louvain, Belgium, 1941; M.Sc., 1946; M.Sc. Dr. honoris causa, univs. Turin, Leiden, Lille, Sherbrooke, Ghent, Liége, Catholic U. Chile, Université René Decartes, Paris, Gustavus Adolphus Coll., St. Peter, Minn., U. Rosario (Argentina), U. Aix-Marseille II. Prof. physiol. chemistry U. Louvain Med. Sch., 1947; prof. biochem. cytology Rockefeller U., N.Y.C., 1962-74, Andrew W. Mellon prof., 1974—. Recipient Prix des Alumni, 1949, Prix Pfizer, 1957, Prix Francqui, 1960, Prix Quinquennal Belge des Sciences Médicales, 1967; Belgium; Gairdner Found. Internat. award merit, Can., 1967; Dr. H.P. Heineken Prijs, Netherlands, 1973; Nobel prize, 1974. Mem. Royal Acad. Medicine, Royal Acad. Belgium, Am. Chem. Soc., Biochem. Soc., Am. Soc. Biol. Chemists, Pontf Acad. Sci., Am. Soc. Cell Biology, Deutsche Akademie der Naturforscher Leopoldina, Soc. Chim. Biol., Soc. Belge Biochim., Sigma Xi; fgn. mem. Am. Acad. Arts and Scis.; fgn. asso. Nat. Acad. Scis., Académie des Scis. de Paris, Academie des Sciences d'Athene. Home: 80 Central Park W New York NY 10023 Office: Rockefeller U York Ave and 66th St New York NY 10021

DEE, PETER ROGERS, playwright; b. Winchester, Mass., Apr. 11, 1939; s. Thomas Paul and Elizabeth (Rogers) D. A.B., Boston Coll., 1961; Assoc. Occupational Studies, Am. Acad. Dramatic Arts, 1973. Author: play A Sea of White Horses, 1976, Voices from the High School, 1982, Daughter of A Traveling Lady, 1967, Man Who Stayed by his Negative, 1971, No One Wants to Know, 1974. Served with USNR, 1961-65; PTO. Grantee Rinehart Found., 1981. Mem. New Dramatists, Circle Repertory Playwrights Workshop. Home: 341 W 88th St New York NY 10024

DEE, ROBERT F., pharmaceutical company executive; b. Cin., July 8, 1924; s. Raymond H. and Mary (Owen) D.; m. Virginia Winston Verner, Sept. 10, 1948; children: Jacqueline, Robert R., John, Catherine, Thomas. A.B., Harvard U., 1946; LL.D. (hon.), Phila. Coll. Pharmacy and Sci., 1978; L.H.D., Med. Coll. Pa., 1979. With Smithkline Corp., Phila., 1948—, successively market research analyst, asst. to adminstrv. v.p., dir. Animal Health div., dir. consumer, animal and instrument products, v.p., dir. consumer, animal and instrumental products,; exec. v.p. Smithkline Beckman Corp., 1971-72, pres., chief exec. officer, 1972-76, chmn. bd., chief exec. officer, 1976-82, chmn. bd., 1982—; dir. Fidelity Corp., Fidelcor Inc. Pres. PTA, Strafford, Pa., 1962-64; bd. dirs. Animal Health Assn., 1960-63, Pennsylvanians Effective Govt.; bd. mgrs. Pa. Hosp., 1972—; trustee United Way Southeastern Pa.; chmn. Found. Economic Freedom; mem. industry-labor council White House Conf. Handicapped Individuals; fin. com. Joint Council Economic Edn. Served with AUS. Mem. N.A.M. (dir.), Bus. Roundtable. Episcopalian. Office: Smithkline Beckman Corp 1 Franklin Sq Philadelphia PA 19101

DEE, RUBY, actress; b. Cleve., Oct. 27; d. Marshall Edward and Emma (Benson) Wallace; m. Ossie Davis, Dec. 9, 1948; children—Nora, La Verne, Guy. B.A., Hunter Coll., 1945, Fairfield U., Iona Coll., Va. State U.; apprentice, Am. Negro Theatre, 1941-44. Author: poetry Glowchild, 1972, Take It from the Top; columnist: N.Y. Amsterdam News; co-author: film Uptight; Stage appearances include Jeb, 1946, Raisin in the Sun, 1959, Purlie Victorious, 1961, The Imaginary Invalid, 1971, Wedding Band, 1972, Boesman and Lena, 1970, Anna Lucasta, Taming of the Shrew; others; motion pictures include Gone are the Days, The Jackie Robinson Story, Take a Giant Step, St. Louis Blues, A Raisin in the Sun, Purlie Victorious, To Be Young, Gifted and Black, Buck and the Preacher, Countdown at Kusini; numerous TV appearances including It's Good to be Alive, 1974, Today Is Ours, 1974, The Defenders, Police Woman, Peyton Place; TV films To Be Young, Gifted and Black, All God's Children, Roots: The Next Generation, I Know Why the Caged Bird Sings, Wedding Band, It's Good to Be Alive; co-producer: TV spl. Today is Ours; radio show Ossie Davis and Ruby Dee Story Hour, 1974-78; TV series With Ossie and Ruby, 1981; rec. artist poems and stories. (Recipient Obie award 1971, Ann. Martin Luther King, Jr. award Operation PUSH 1972), (with husband) (Frederick Douglass award N.Y. Urban League 1970, Drama Desk award 1974). Mem. NAACP, CORE, Student Non-Violent Coordinating Com., S.C.L.C. Address: care Blake Agy Ltd 409 N Camden Dr Suite 202 Beverly Hills CA 90210

DEECKEN, GEORGE CHRISTIAN, fin. exec.; b. Jersey City, Apr. 12, 1922; s. George R. and Florence C. (Foley) D.; m. Josephine J. Hennequin, Nov. 17, 1955; children—George W., John R., James R. B.S., N.Y. U., 1948. C.P.A., N.Y. Mgr. Price, Waterhouse & Co., N.Y.C., 1941-55; controller, treas. Christian Herald Assn., N.Y.C., 1955-59; v.p. finance and adminstrn. Remington Rand div. Sperry Rand Corp., N.Y.C., 1959-66; pres. lamp div. Internat. Tel. & Tel. Co., N.Y.C., 1966-68; sr. v.p., dir., chief financial officer Wickes Corp., Saginaw, Mich., 1968-71; sr. v.p., controller Chem. Bank, N.Y.C., 1971-81; exec. v.p., chief fin. officer, dir. Young & Rubicam, Inc., N.Y.C., 1981—. Served to capt. USAAF, World II. Mem. Am. Inst. C.P.A.'s, N.Y. State Soc. C.P.A.'s, Financial Execs. Inst. Club: Union League (N.Y.C.). Home: 19 Gault Park Dr Westport CT 06880 Office: 285 Madison Ave New York NY 10015

DEEDY, JOHN GERARD, JR., writer; b. Worcester, Mass., Aug. 17, 1923; s. John G. and Grace R. (McDonough) D.; m. Mary M. Noonan, Apr. 22, 1949; children: Mary Joan, John J., Justine A., Paul V. A.B., Holy Cross Coll., 1948; cert., Institut du Pantheon, Paris, 1949; A.B., Trinity Coll., Dublin, 1949, M.A., 1957. Reporter, corr. Boston Post, Boston Globe, Worcester Telegram, 1940-51; founding editor Cath. Free Press, Worcester, 1951-59; editor Pitts. Cath., 1959-67; mng. editor Commonweal, N.Y.C., 1967-78. Author: (with Jack Frost) The Church in Worcester New England, 1957, (with Martin Marty, David Silverman) The Religious Press in America, 1963, Eyes on the Modern World, 1965, The Vatican, 1970, What a Modern Catholic Believes About Conscience, Freedom and Authority, 1972, (with Philip Nobile) The Complete Ecology Fact Book, 1972, What a Modern Catholic Believes About the Commandments, 1975, Literary Places: A Guided Pilgrimage, New York and New England, 1978, Seven American Catholics, 1978, Apologies, Good Friends, An Interim Biography of Daniel Berrigan, S.J, 1981, The New Nuns: Serving Where the Spirit Leads, 1982. Served with USAAF, World War II. Recipient Pro Ecclesia et Pontifice, Pope Pius XII, 1954. Home: 28 Granite St Rockport MA 01966

DEEGAN, JOHN EDWARD, coll. pres.; b. Newburgh, N.Y., Mar. 31, 1935; s. John Francis and Kathleen Marguerite (McGrath) D. B.A., Villanova U., 1957, M.A., 1960, M.A. in Secondard Sch. Adminstrn, 1965; Ph.D. in Student Personnel Adminstrn. in Higher Edn, Am. U., 1971. Dir. studies Msgr. Bonner high Sch., Drexel Hill, Pa., 1961-69; asso. dean student activities Villanova U., 1972-73, asst. prof. edn., 1972-81, chmn. dept. edn., 1975-76, v.p. student life, 1976-81; pres. Merrimack Coll., North Andover, Mass., 1981—. Mem. Am. Personnel and Guidance Assn., Nat. Assn. Student Personnel Adminstrs., Phi Delta Kappa, Kappa Delta Pi. Roman Catholic. Club: K. of C.

DEEKEN, ALFONS THEODOR, philosopher; b. Emstek, Germany, Aug. 3, 1932; emigrated to U.S., 1966; s. Aloys and Paula (Nienaber) D. M.A., U. Munich, Germany, 1958; Ph.D., Fordham U., 1973. Asst. prof. philosophy Sophia U., Tokyo, Japan, 1973-75, asso. prof., 1975-81, prof., 1981—. Author: Growing Old and How to Cope With It, 1972, Process and Permanence in Ethics: Max Scheler's Moral Philosophy, 1974 (Best Ethics Book of 1974, Cath. Press Assn. Am). Mem. Am. Cath. Philos. Assn., Assn. for Philos. Anthropology, Japanese Soc. for Ethics. Address: Sophia U Kioicho 7 Chiyoda-ku Tokyo 102 Japan

DEEM, GEORGE, painter; b. Vincennes, Ind., Aug. 18, 1932; s. George C. and Laura (Bobe) D. Student, Vincennes U., 1951-52; B.F.A., Sch. Art Inst. Chgo., 1958. Tchr. painting Sch. Visual Arts N.Y.C., 1965-66, Leicester (Eng.) Coll. Art and Design, 1966-67, U. Pa., 1968; artist in residence Evansville Mus. Arts and Scis., 1979; vis. artist Ill. State U., Normal, 1982; sec. exec. com. MacDowell Colony Fellows, 1982-84. One man shows, Allan Stone Gallery, N.Y.C., 1963, 64, 65, 66, 68, 69, 75, 77, Sneed Gallery, Rockford, Ill., 1968, 69, 72, 76, 80, Merida Gallery, Louisville, 1966, 68, 69, 78, 83, Indpls. Mus. Art, 1974, Witte Meml. Mus., San Antonio, 1975, Evansville (Ind.) Mus. Arts and Scis., 1979, Greenberg Gallery, St. Louis, group shows include, Whitney Mus. Am. Art, N.Y.C., 1978, Pa. Acad. Fine Arts, 1981, Allentown (Pa.) Art Mus., 1983, Ft. Wayne (Ind.) Mus. Art, 1984; represented in permanent collections, Indpls. Mus. Art, Evansville Mus. Arts and Sci., Mus. Ludwig, Aachen, W. Ger., Vassar Coll. Art Gallery; contbr. articles to profl. jours. Served with U.S. Army, 1953-55. Home and Office: 10 W 18th St New York NY 10011

DEEMS, RICHARD EMMET, magazine publisher; b. N.Y.C., Jan. 19, 1913; s. Walter A. and Marie (Neufeld) D.; m. Jean S.; 1 dau., Cynthia. L.H.D. (hon.), Oglethorpe U., 1972. Propr. Interstate News Service, 1930-32; with circulation dept. New Yorker mag., 1932-33; circulation mgr. Esquire mag., 1933-39; with Harper's Bazaar, 1939-52, advt. mgr., 1947-52; v.p. charge advt. Hearst mags., 1952-55, exec. v.p., 1955-60, pres., 1960-76, chmn., 1976-78; dir., mem. fin. and exec. coms. Hearst Corp.; dir. Nat. Mag. Co., London, Prudential Bldg. Maintenance Corp., Drexel Burnham Fund, ISS Internat. Service System, Oriole Homes Corp., Lilli Ann Corp., DBL Cash Fund, Inc., DBL Tax-Free Cash Fund Inc., Meyers Parking Systems, Tesoro Petroleum Corp. Trustee William Randolph Hearst Found., The Hearst Found. Inc., Advt. Ednl. Found., Rochester Inst. Tech. Decorated Knight Order of St. Martin, 1972. Mem. Advt. Fedn. Am., Advt. Council (dir.), Mag. Pubs. Assn. (dir., Pub. of Yr. award 1979). Clubs: Bohemian (San Francisco); Madison Square Garden (N.Y.C.); Everglades (Palm Beach, Fla.). Home: Rural Route 1 South Salem NY 10590 also 325 S Lake Dr Palm Beach FL 33480 Office: 959 8th Ave New York NY 10019

DEEN, THOMAS BLACKBURN, transportation research executive; b. Lexington, Ky., Apr. 4, 1928; s. Encil and Utha Leola (Blackburn) D.; m. Bettie Marie Taylor, Nov. 28, 1954; children—Robin Elaine, Tomi Clair, Rebecca Lea, Samuel Encil. B.S.C.E., U. Ky., 1951; postgrad., U. Chgo., 1951-52; transp. cert., Yale U., 1956. Asst. city traffic engr., Nashville, 1956-57; dir. Nashville Met. Area Transp. Study, 1957-59; applied sci. rep. IBM, Nashville, 1959-60; dir. planning Nat. Capital Transp. Agy., Washington, 1960-64; sr. v.p. Alan M. Voorhees & Assos., McLean, Va., 1964-78; chmn., pres. PRC Voorhees, McLean, 1978-80; exec. dir. Transp. Research Bd., Nat. Acad. Scis., Washington, 1980—; vice chmn. bd. PADCO, Inc., Washington, 1973—; dir. Family Savs. and Loan, Springfield, Va., API Corp., Fairfax, Va.; lectr. various univs. Editorial bd.: Traffic Engring. and Control mag, London, 1981, Transp. Planning and Tech. Loughborough, U.K., 1978—. Bd. cons. ENO Found. for Hwy. Traffic, Saugatuck, Conn., 1981; research adv. bd. Joint Ctr. Urban Mobility, Houston, 1983—; Trustee Matson Meml. Fund, Washington, 1977-80; chmn. bd. Voorhees and Partners, Melbourne, Australia, 1975-78. Served to 1st lt. USAF, 1951-55. Recipient Outstanding ROTC Grad. medal U. Ky., 1951; Automotive Safety Found. fellow Yale U., 1956; Pike Johnson award for outstanding research Transp. Research Bd., Nat. Acad. Scis., 1976. Mem. Inst. Transp. Engrs., Tau Beta Pi, Sigma Pi Sigma. Baptist. Clubs: George Washington U. Faculty; Megalops (Nashville) (pres. 1959). Home: 611 Utterback Store Rd Great Falls VA 22066 Office: 2101 Constitution Ave NW Washington DC 20418

DEEP, IRA WASHINGTON, plant pathology educator; b. nr. Dover, Tenn., July 26, 1927; s. Ira W. and Fannie E. (Page) D.; m. Elsie Onifer, June 7, 1952; children—Michael W., Jeffrey W., Brian W., Craig W., Kathryn H. B.A., Miami U., Oxford, O., 1950; M.S., U. Tenn., 1952; Ph.D., Oreg. State U., 1956. Instr. Oreg. State U., 1953-57, asst. prof. botany and plant pathology, 1957-62, assoc. prof., 1962-68; asst. dean Grad. Sch., 1966-68; staff biologist Commn. Undergrad. Edn. Biol. Scis., 1966-67; prof. Ohio State U., 1968—, chmn. dept. plant pathology, 1968-83. Served with USMC, 1945-46. Mem. Am. Phytopath. Soc., AAAS, Am. Inst. Biol. Scis., Ohio Acad. Sci., Sigma Xi, Phi Kappa Phi. Home: 6859 Hayhurst Worthington OH 43085 Office: Dept Plant Pathology Ohio State Univ 2021 Coffey Rd Columbus OH 43210

DEER, JAMES WILLIS, lawyer; b. Reading, Pa., Mar. 14, 1917; s. Irvin E. and Rosemary (French) D.; m. Marion M. Hawkinson, July 31, 1943; 1 dau., Ann Marie. A.B, Oberlin Coll, 1938; J. D., U. Mich., 1941. Bar: Ohio 1941, N.Y. 1948. Legal staff SEC, 1942-45; practice in, N.Y.C., 1945—; mem. firm Holtzmann, Wise & Shepard, 1954—; chmn. bd. Western Auto Supply Corp., 1960; sec. Teleregister Corp., 1953-69, DuBois Chems., Inc., 1960-62; dir. Weigh-tronix Inc., Arts Way Mfg. Co., Inc., Selvac Corp., T-Bar, Inc., Am. Diversified Enterprises, Inc., Allegheny & Western Energy Corp., Techsci. Industries, Ampower Instrument Co., Inc. Mem. Am., N.Y. State bar assns., Phi Beta Kappa, Phi Alpha Delta. Home: 611 Shore Acres Dr Mamaroneck NY 10543 also Barr Terr 50 East Dr Delray Beach FL 33444 Office: 745 Fifth Ave: New York NY 10151

DEERE, CYRIL THOMAS, computer company executive; b. Rockville, Conn., Apr. 28, 1924; s. Albert Bertram and Belle Murdie (King) D.; m. Shirley Ann Scheiner, June 2, 1945; children: Sandra Deere Leinz, Kathryn Deere Bailey. B.S., Yale U., 1948. With Lee Paper Co., Vicksburg, Mich., 1949-50, Addressograph-Multigraph Corp., Hartford, Conn. and Cleve., 1950-69; founder Data Card Corp., Minnetonka, Minn., 1969-81, v.p. mktg., 1969-75, sr. v.p., 1975-77, exec. v.p., 1977-80, pres., 1980-82, dir. plastics div., 1974—; also dir.; pres., dir. Can. Data Card Ltd., Toronto, Ont., 1974—; founder, pres. Card Tech. Corp., Saddlebrook, N.J., 1983—; chmn. bd. Data Card Internat., 1977-78; dir. Data Card, Japan. Served with USMCR, 1943-44. Decorated Purple Heart. Mem. Am. Nat. Standards Inst. (1st chmn. credit card standards com. 1968-73), Input/Output Systems Assn. (pres. 1975). Clubs: Interlachen Country, Yale of Sarasota, Bent Tree Golf and Racquet. Home: 4915 Silver Fern Dr Sarasota FL 33583 Office: Card Tech Corp 280 Midland Ave Saddlebrook NJ 07662

DEERING, ANTHONY WAYNE MARION, real estate developer; b. Washington, Jan., 28, 1945; s. George Aloysius and Maude Emma (Matheys) D.; m. Kathryn Evelyn Regan, May 31, 1969; children—Heather, Spencer, Maron. B.S., Drexel U., Phila., 1968; M.B.A., Wharton Sch., U. Pa., 1970; postgrad., U. Exeter (Eng.). Bus. planner Exxon Co., N.Y.C., 1970-71; cons. Dunuck, Fulton Co., Phila., 1971—; sr. v.p., treas., chief fin. officer Rouse Co., Columbia, Md., 1971—; dir. T. Rowe Price Prime Res., T. Rowe Price New Income. Adv. bd. Fronkin Van Horn, Toronto, Ont., Can. Trustee Friends Sch., Balt. Home: 6011 Charlesmeade Baltimore MD 21212 Office: Rouse Co Columbia MD 21044

DEERING, FERDIE JACKSON, editor; b. Denison, Tex., Oct. 24, 1910; s. Norman Henry and Hattie (Br) D.; m. Flora Mildred Jennings, May 3, 1935; children: Cheryl Beth (Mrs. Richard Ralph Wilson), Robert E. Student, East Central State Coll., 1928-31. Reporter Ada (Okla.) Evening News, 1931-32; advt. salesman Denison (Tex.) Herald, 1932-33; night editor Ada News, 1934-37; asso. editor The Farmer-Stockman, Oklahoma City, 1937-42, editor, 1943-73; editor, mgr. RX Golf and Travel mag., 1967-68; editor Oklahoma's Orbit mag., 1961-69; mem. mgmt. com. Okla. Pub. Co., 1948-75, dir., asst. sec., 1958-75; editorial writer Daily Oklahoman-Oklahoma City Times, 1972-75; v.p., editorial dir. Farmer-Stockman Pub. Co., 1973—; editorial columnist Daily Oklahoman, 1975—; agri. bus. columnist Sunday Oklahoman, 1975—. Mem. gov. bd. Baptist Meml. Hosp., Oklahoma City, 1966-72; mem. weather modification adv. bd. Okla. Water Resources Bd., 1976-78; trustee Water Devel. Found. Okla., 1976-78, SW Am. Livestock Found.; bd. dirs. U. Okla. Research Inst., 1953-75, Bapt. Found. Okla., 1975-79, Okla. 4-H Found., 1979-82. Recipient Disting. Alumnus award East Central U., Ada, 1979, Henry G. Bennett Disting. Service award Okla State U., 1983. Mem. State Farm Mag. Bur. (dir. 1967-73), Agrl. Pub. Assn. (dir. 1967-73), Okla. City C. of C. (v.p. 1962-63), Am. Agrl. Editors Assn. (pres. 1951). Republican. Baptist. Clubs: Sirloin Okla. (pres. 1957-58, dir. Home: 11608 Susan Lane Oklahoma City OK 73120

DEERING, FRED ARTHUR, insurance company executive; b. Arkansas City, Kans., Jan. 12, 1928; s. Frederick A. and Lucile (Phillips) D.; m. Isabell Staufenberg, June 14, 1949; m. Elizabeth Kimball MacMillan, Apr. 12, 1979; children: Anne Deering Buchanan, Kate. B.S., U. Colo., 1951, LL.B., 1951. Bar: Colo. 1951. Asso. firm Gorsuch, Kirgis, Campbell, Walker & Grover, Denver, 1951-54, partner, 1954-62; v.p., gen. counsel Security Life & Accident Co., Denver, 1962-66, pres., chief exec. officer, dir., 1966—; pres.

Security Casualty Co., Denver, 1966-77; chmn. bd. Fin. Indsl. Fund, Denver, 1970—, Fin. Indsl. Income Fund, 1970—, Fin. Daily Income Shares, 1977—; Fin. Dynamics Fund, Denver, 1970—, Fin. Bond Fund, 1976—; chmn. chief exec. officer Midwestern United Life Ins. Co., 1983—; dir. Metal Fabricators, Inc., Denver, Kissinger Drilling Co., Inc., Columbia Savs. & Loan, 1st Columbia Fin.; instr. Am. Inst. Banking, 1953-57; lectr. Colo. Sch. Law, 1958-59. Trustee Loretto Heights Coll., 1968—, chmn. bd., 1968—; bd. dirs. Wallace Village for Children, 1968-78, Met. United Fund, 1969-71, Porter Hosp., 1970-79, U. Colo. Found., 1972-75; mem. adv. com. Met. Assn. for Retarded Children, Denver, 1970-71, Denver Research Inst., 1972-76. Served with U.S. Army, 1946-47. Mem. Am. Judicature Soc., Am., Colo., Denver bar assns., Assn. Life Ins. Counsel, Colo. Life Conv., Met. Denver Execs. Club (pres. 1970-71), Life Office Mgmt. Assn. (dir. 1977-81), Denver C. of C., Order of Coif, Sigma Alpha Epsilon. Clubs: Old Baldy (Saratoga, Wyo.); Cherry Hills (Englewood, Colo.) (dir. 1973-76, pres. 1975-76); Denver (dir. 1973-76), Univ., Castle Pines (Denver); Wigwam (Deckers, Colo.); Garden of Gods (Colorado Springs, Colo.). Home: 1551 Larimer St Apt 1701 Denver CO 80202 Office: 600 Security Life Bldg Denver CO 80202 also PO Box 2040 Denver CO 80201 *My life has been influenced more by a handful of people than by events or any other factors. Therefore, I am inclined to think that the lives of others may be more important than anything else in shaping our own careers and destinies.*

DEES, MORRIS SELIGMAN, JR., lawyer; b. Shorter, Ala., Dec. 16, 1936; s. Morris Seligman and Annie Ruth (Frazer) D.; m. Mary Farmer, Dec. 18, 1980; children by previous marriage: Morris Seligman III, John Fuller, Holly, Blakely, Ellie. B.S., U. Ala., 1958, LL.B., 1960. Bar: Ala. Chmn. bd. Fuller & Dees Pub., Inc., 1960-69; partner firm Levin & Dees, 1969-71; chief trial counsel So. Poverty Law Center, Montgomery, Ala., 1971—; pres. Funding Group, Inc., 1983—; Instr. criminal law Jones Law Sch., 1960-62; vis. fellow John F. Kennedy Sch. Govt. Harvard. Nat. fund raising dir. McGovern for Pres., 1972; nat. finance chmn. Carter for Pres., 1976; nat. fin. dir. Kennedy for Pres., 1980; trustee Miles Coll. Named One of 10 Outstanding Young Men of Am. U.S. Jaycees, 1967. Mem. Direct Mail Mktg. Assn. (dir., Showmanship award 1968), Am., Ala. bar assns., ACLU, Farm Bur., Beta Gamma Sigma, Sigma Delta Kappa. Democrat. Unitarian (pres. 1968). Home: Rolling Hills Ranch Mathews AL 36052 Office: 1001 S Hull St Montgomery AL 36104

DEESE, JAMES EARLE, psychologist, educator; b. Salt Lake City, Dec. 14, 1921; s. Thomas D. and Serena Jane (Johnson) D.; m. Ellin Ruth Krauss, Dec. 24, 1948; children: Elizabeth Ellin, James Lawrence. A.B., Chapman Coll., 1944; A.M., Ind. U., 1946, Ph.D., 1948; D.Litt., Chapman Coll., 1982. From asst. prof. to prof. psychology Johns Hopkins U., Balt., 1948-72; Commonwealth prof. U. Va., 1972-80, Hugh Scott Hamilton prof., 1980—; vis. prof. U. Calif.-Berkeley, 1958-59. Cons. editor: Psychol. Rev.; author: (with E.K. Deese) Psychology of Learning, 5th edit. (with S.H. Hulse and H. Egeth), 1980; Author: (with W. Lado and R. Goodale) Principles of Psychology, 2d edit., 1975, The Structure of Associations in Language and Thought, 1965, General Psychology, 1967, Psycholinguistics, 1969, Psychology as Science and Art, 1972, (with L.B. Szalay) Subjective Meaning and Culture, 1978, Thought into Speech, 1984; contbg. author: (with L.B. Szalay) Introduction to Psychology (C.T. Morgan), 1955; asso. editor: Jour. Exptl. Psychology, 1963-68; editor: Psychol. Bull., 1968-74. Fellow Soc. Exptl. Psychologists, Am. Psychol. Assn. (dir.); mem. Eastern Psychol. Assn. (pres. 1966-67), Linguistic Soc. Am., AAAS (v.p. 1971-72). Democrat. Clubs: 14 West Hamilton Street (Balt.); Greencroft, Colonnade (Charlottesville); Cosmos (Washington). Home: 1829 Westview Rd Charlottesville VA 22903

DEEVEY, EDWARD SMITH, JR., biologist; b. Albany, N.Y., Dec. 3, 1914; s. Edward Smith and Villa (Augur) D.; m. Georgiana Baxter, Dec. 24, 1938 (dec. Jan. 1982); children: Ruth (Mrs. Lehmann), Edward Brian, David Kevin.; m. Dian R. Hitchcock, Jan. 22, 1983. B.A., Yale, 1934, Ph.D., 1938. Instr. biology Rice Inst., Houston, 1939-43; research asso. biology Woods Hole Oceanographic Instn., 1943-46; asst. prof. biology Yale, 1946-51, asso. prof., 1951-57, prof., 1957-68; Dir. Geochronometric Lab., 1951-62; Killam research prof. biology Dalhousie U., Halifax, N.S., Can., 1968-71; grad. research prof. U. Fla., 1971—; curator paleoecology Fla. State Mus., 1971—; Sect. head environ. and systematic biology NSF, 1967-68; mem. Fisheries Research Bd., Canada, 1969-71, Nat. Acad. Scis. NSF sr. postdoctoral fellow; Fulbright travel grantee U. Canterbury, Christchurch, New Zealand, 1964-65; Recipient Fulbright research award, Denmark, 1953-54; Guggenheim fellow, Denmark, 1953-54. Fellow AAAS, Geol. Soc. Am.; mem. Am. Soc. Limnology and Oceanography (pres. 1974—), Ecol. Soc. Am. (pres. 1970), Am. Anthrop. Assn., Soc. Am. Archaeology, Am. Soc. Naturalists. Home: 1702 SW 35th Pl Gainesville FL 32608 also Sheldon Pl Pine Orchard Branford CT 06405

DE FABRY, DARRELL, financial executive; b. L.I., N.Y., Dec. 13, 1946; s. Arthur G. and Margot C. (Otto) de F.; m. Marjorie Breech, Apr. 17, 1976; children: Michele. Callie. Student, Calif. State U.-Long Beach, 1964-65; B.A., U. So. Calif., 1969, M.B.A., 1972. Internat. account officer Security Pacific Bank, Los Angeles, 1970-74; asst. v.p. European Am. Bank, Los Angeles, 1974-76; treas., corp. sec. Revell Inc., Venice, Calif., 1976-79; treas. Dillingham Corp., San Francisco, 1979—. Mem. Fin. Execs. Inst. Clubs: San Francisco Yacht; University (San Francisco). Office: Dillingham Corp 2 Embarcadero Center Suite 1600 San Francisco CA 94111

DEFALAISE, LOUIS, lawyer; b. Covington, Ky., Apr. 27, 1945; s. James Willard and Mildred Carolyn (Howard) DeF.; m. Susan Jane Court, June 12, 1968 (div.); children: David, Mary. B.A., Thomas More Coll., 1968; J.D., U. Ky., 1971. Bar: Ky. 1971, U.S. Dist. Ct. (eastern dist.) Ky. 1972, U.S. Ct. Appeals (6th cir.) 1972, U.S. Supreme Ct. 1975. Assoc. Adams, Brooking & Stepner, Covington, 1971, 74-81; asst. U.S. atty. Eastern Dist. Ky. Dept. Justice, Lexington, 1972-73, U.S. atty., 1981—; mem. Ky. Ho. of Reps., Frankfort, 1976-81, vice chmn. judiciary com., 1976-81; mem. Ky. gov.'s Select Com. on Implementation of New Jud. Article, 1976-78. Paliamentarian Republican Central Com., Frankfort, 1980-81. Mem. ABA, Fed. Bar Assn., Assn. Trial Lawyers Am., Ky. Bar Assn. Roman Catholic. Home: 129 Deauville Ct Fort Mitchell KY 41017

DEFEIS, ELIZABETH FRANCES, law educator, lawyer; b. N.Y.C.; d. Francis Paul and Lena (Amendola) D. B.A., St. John's U., 1956, J.D., 1958; LL.M., NYU, 1971; postgrad., U. Milan, Italy, 1963-64. Bar: N.Y. 1959, U.S. Dist. Ct.(so. dist.) N.Y. 1961, U.S. Dist. Ct. (ea. dist.) N.Y. 1978, U.S. Supreme Ct. 1963. With honors program Dept. Justice, Washington, 1958-61; asst. U. S. atty. So. Dist. N.Y., Dept. Justice, 1961-62; with RCA Corp., 1962-63; assoc. Carter, Ledyard & Milburn, N.Y.C., 1965-69; Reginal Heber Smith fellow Bedford Stuyvesant Legal Services Corp., 1969-70; prof. law Seton Hall U., N.Y.C., 1971—; dean Seton Hall U. sch. Law, N.Y.C., 1982—; project dir. Women and the Law TV sries, 1974-80; narrator Alts. to Violence TV Series, 1981—; bd. dirs. MFY Legal Services, Inc., 1971—; mem. N.J. Supreme Ct. task Force on Women and the Cts, 1982—. Bd. dirs. Nat. Orgn.Italian- Am. Women. Fulbright-Hays Scholar, Milan, Italy, 1963-64; Ford Found. fellow, 1970-71; Fulbright- Hays lectr., Iran, India, 1977-78. Mem. Fed. Bar Assn., ABA, Columbia Lawyers Assn., Assn. Bar City N.Y., Columbua Citizens found., Inc. Home: 111 Raymond Blvd Newark NJ 07102

DEFELICE, EUGENE ANTHONY, physician; b. Beacon, N.Y., Dec. 24, 1927; s. Domenick and Louise (Grippo) DeF.; m. Charlene C. Petsch, Dec. 21, 1957; children—Eugene Vincent, Charlene Deirdre. B.S., Columbia U., 1951; M.S., Boston U., 1954, M.D., 1956. Ciba fellow, lectr. pharmacology Boston U. Sch. Medicine, 1954-57; intern Newton (Mass.) Wellesley Hosp., 1957; practice medicine specializing in internal medicine, North Miami, Fla., 1958-61; asst. dir. clin. research Warner Lambert Research Inst., Morris Plains, N.J., 1961-64; dir. clin. pharmacology Bristol Labs., Syracuse, N.Y., 1965-66, Sandoz Inc. (formerly Sandoz-Wander, Inc.), East Hanover, N.J., 1967-68, exec. dir. clin. research, 1969-70, dir. sci. affairs and comml. devel., 1970-74, dir. corp. sci. devel., 1974, v.p. corp. sci. devel., 1974-77, v.p. internat. med. liaison, 1977-81, v.p., med. adviser, 1982-83; prof. biol. scis. New Eng. Coll. Pharmacy, 1956-58; cons. in medicine, Morristown, N.J., 1961—; clin. assoc. prof. medicine Coll. Medicine and Dentistry N.J.-Rutgers Med. Sch., 1977—; clin. prof. anesthesiology UCLA, 1978—. Contbr. numerous articles to profl. jours. cons. to editor; mem. internat. editorial com.: Triangle, Sandorama, 1979-81. Served with U.S. Army, World War II. Named hon. citizen of Alanno, Italy.; Named to Notable Italian-Am. Hall of Fame. Fellow Am. Geriatrics Soc., Acad. Psychosomatic Medicine; mem. AAAS, Am. Fedn. Clin. Research, Am. Heart Assn., AMA, Am. Soc. Artificial Internal Organs, Am. Soc. Clin. Pharmacology and Therapeutics, N.Y. Acad. Scis., Sigma Xi. Home: 11 Corn Hill Dr Morristown NJ 07960 Office: 11 Corn Hill Dr Morristown NJ 07960 *Success in life comes from constancy of purpose, diligent work, living according to sound moral and religious principles, and having faith and hope in the future. Helping to make the world a better place to live in, autographing one's work in excellence, and doing good by others are the rewards which bring happiness.*

DE FELITTA, FRANK PAUL, producer, writer, director; b. N.Y.C., Aug. 3, 1921; s. Pat and Genevieve (Sibilio) DeF.; m. Dorothy Gilbert, Aug. 4, 1945; children: Eileen, Raymond. Student, U. N.C., 1939, New Sch. Social Research, 1948. Dir.-writer, CBS, 1950-57; dir. programming, Nat. Telefilms Assos., 1959-61; producer, writer, dir., NBC, from 1962; producer, dir., writer, Universal Studios, 1968-69; film documentaries include Music of the South, 1955; sci. series Conquest, 1957; natural sci. series Adventure, 1953-55; hist. series Odyssey, 1958, The Chosen Child, 1962 (Writers Guild award), Emergency Ward, 1962 (Emmy award), Experiment in Excellence, 1963 (Sch. Bell award), Battle of the Bulge, 1964, The Stately Ghosts of England, 1964, The World of the Teenager, 1966 (Robert J. Flaherty award); dir., author: films Trapped, 1973, The Two Worlds of Jennie Logan, 1979 (Silver Halo award); dir.: film Dark Night of the Scarecrow, 1981; (Brotherhood award of Nat. Conf. Christians and Jews for film Mississippi- A Self Portrait, George Washington Honor medal of Freedoms Found. for film The American Image.); Author: films The First of January, 1970, The Savage Is Loose, 1971, Audrey Rose, 1977, The Entity, 1981; novels Oktoberfest, 1972, Audrey Rose, 1975, The Entity, 1978, Sea Trial, 1980, For Love of Audrey Rose 1982, Golgotha Falls, 1984. Served to capt. USAAF, 1941-45; ETO. Decorated D.F.C., Air medal (5), Presdl. citation; recipient Peabody award, 1954, 63, Ohio State U. award, 1957, Thomas Alva Edison award, 1958; CINE gold medal (2). Mem. Writers Guild Am., Dirs. Guild Am.

DE FEO, VINCENT JOSEPH, educator, biologist; b. N.Y.C., Oct. 1, 1925; s. Salvadore Francis and Teresa (Catalano) DeFeo; m. Elizabeth Ann Walling, Sept. 20, 1952 (div. 1973); children: Steven V., Ronald M. B.S., Juniata Coll., 1949; M.S., Rutgers U., 1951; Ph.D., Ohio State U., 1954; postdoctoral, Johns Hopkins U., 1955. Asst. prof. physiology Ohio State U., 1954-55; USPHS fellow Carnegie Inst. of Washington, Balt., 1955-57; asst. prof. anatomy U. Ill., 1957-63; vis. prof. anatomy U. Tenn. Med. Unit, 1961; USPHS postdoctoral tng. neuroendocrinology UCLA, 1959; electon microscopy Washington U., 1963; asso. prof. anatomy and obstetrics/gynecology Vanderbilt U. Sch. Medicine, 1963-66; asso. prof., asso. chmn. anatomy U. Hawaii, 1966-68, prof., 1968—, chmn. dept., 1969-73, 83—; dir. program on research and tng. in reproductive biology Ford Found., 1970-78. Mem. Soc. Study Reprodn., Soc. Study Fertility, Endocrine Soc., Am. Assn. Anatomists, Pan Am. Assn. Anatomy, Sex Info. and Edn. Council U.S., Soc. for Sci. Study Sex, Am. Assn. Sex Educators, Councilors and Therapists (cert. sex educator). Research and publs. on nervous and hormonal control reprodn., biology of implantation and embryo spacing, uterine decidualization, biol. clocks in reproductive phenomena, human sexuality. Office: U Hawaii Sch Medicine 1960 East West Rd Honolulu HI 96822

DEFFEYES, KENNETH STOVER, geologist; b. Oklahoma City, Dec. 26, 1931; s. Joseph Alfred and Hazel (Stover) D.; m. Nancy H. Swinski, Apr. 28, 1962; children—Stephen E., Sarah S. Geol. Engr., Colo. Sch. Mines, 1953; M.S. in Engring, Princeton U., 1956, Ph.D., 1958. Geologist Shell Devel. Co., Houston, 1959-63; asst. prof. U. Minn., Mpls., 1963-65; asso. prof. Oreg. State U., Corvallis, 1965-66; asso. prof. geology Princeton U., 1967-74, prof., 1974—, also master Stevenson Hall.; cons. in field. Co-author: Physical Geology, 1976. Served with C.E. AUS, 1953-55. NSF fellow, 1956-58; grantee NSF, Office Naval Research, Dept. Energy, NASA. Democrat. Patentee oil-well core orientation, precious metal recovery. Home: 115 Prospect Ave Princeton NJ 08540 Office: Geology Dept Princeton Univ Princeton NJ 08540

DEFIEBRE, CONRAD WILLIAM, microbiologist; b. Bklyn., Jan. 19, 1924; s. Conrad William and Barbara (Benisch) deF.; m. Harriet M. Hamm, Oct. 26, 1946; children—Conrad, Henry, Jeremy, Timothy, David, Christopher. B.S., Rensselaer Poly. Inst., 1949; M.S., U. Wis., 1950, Ph.D., 1952. Asst. bacteriologist U. Wis., 1949-52; research microbiologist duPont, Wilmington, Del., 1952-61; research dir. Wilson Labs. div. Wilson Pharm. & Chem. Corp., Chgo., 1961-67, v.p. research, 1967-69; with Ross Labs. div. Abbott Labs., Columbus, Ohio, 1969—, v.p. research and devel., 1971—; chmn. bd. infant formula council Abbott Labs., 1976-77, 81—; 2d vice chmn. Central Ohio Rehab. Ctr., Goodwill Industries, 1980. Served with AUS, 1943-46. Recipient award of merit Ohio State U., 1981. Fellow Am. Inst. Chemists; mem. Am. Chem. Soc., Am. Soc. Microbiology, Am. Inst. Biol. Scis., Sigma Xi. Roman Catholic. Clubs: Worthington Hills Country, Businessmen's Athletic. Home: 8000 Fairway Dr Worthington OH 43085 Office: 625 Cleveland Ave Columbus OH 43216

DEFLEUR, MELVIN LAWRENCE, sociologist, educator; b. Portland, Oreg., Apr. 27, 1923; s. Robert H. and Dorothy (Foster) DeF. B.S. cum laude, St. Louis U., 1949; M.S., U. Wash., 1952, Ph.D., 1954. Faculty Ind. U., 1954-63; prof. U. Ky., 1963-67, Wash. State U., Pullman, 1967—, chmn. dept. sociology, 1968-72, asso. dean for research Grad. Sch., 1974-76; prof. sociology U. N.Mex., 1976-80; prof., chmn. dept. sociology U. Miami, Coral Gables, Fla., 1981—. Author: (with Otto N. Larsen) The Flow of Information, 1958, Tecnicas y Metodos de Investigacion Social, 1965, (with Sandra Ball-Rokeach) Theories of Mass Communication, 4th edit, 1982, (with others) Sociology: Man in Society, 1971, Sociology: Human Society, 1973, 3d edit., 1981, (with Everette Dennis) Understanding Mass Communication, 1981, (with Shearon Lowery) Milestones in Mass Communication Research, 1983, Social Problems in American Society, 1983. Mem. Am. Sociol. Assn.; mem. Pacific Sociol. Assn., So. Sociol. Assn., Argentine Sociol. Soc., Internat. Institut de Sociologie. Home: 8225 SW 106th St Miami FL 33156

DEFLIESE, PHILIP LEROY, accountant, educator; b. Queens County, N.Y., Feb. 11, 1915; s. Philip and Frances (Ankenbr) D.; m. Pauline Harnisch, Apr. 28, 1946; children: Philip Leroy, Robert Wayne, Jeanne Marie. B.B.A., CCNY, 1938, M.S., 1940; D.C.S. (hon.), Villanova U., 1975. C.P.A., 1947. Tchr. accounting Grover Cleveland High Sch., N.Y.C., 1938-42; asst. prof. Adelphi U., 1947-48; adj. prof. Pace U., 1950-56; with Coopers & Lybrand, C.P.A.s, 1942-77, partner, 1956-77, mng. partner, chmn. exec. com., 1968-76, nat. dir. accounting, auditing and SEC services, 1962-68; prof. Columbia U., 1977—; dir. Veeco Instruments, Inc., ARA Services, Inc.; trustee Nat. Shoes Inc.; Mem. N.Y. State Bd. C.P.A. Examiners, 1964-69; chmn. N.Y.C. Audit Com., 1979—. Author: (with N.J. Lenhart) Montgomery's Auditing, 8th edit, 1957, (with others) 9th edit., 1975; Contbr. articles to prof. jours. Active local Boy Scouts Am., 1927-54. Served to lt. USNR, 1942-46. Recipient Silver Beaver award, 1947; Gold medal for distinguished service to acctg. profession Am. Inst. C.P.A.s, 1972. Mem. Am. Inst. C.P.A.s (chmn. bd. 1974-75, chmn. acctg. principles bd. 1971-73, past chmn. auditing procedure com.), N.Y. State Soc. C.P.A.s (past chmn. com. acctg. procedure), Am. Acctg. Assn., Nat. Assn. Accts. Clubs: Union League, Hemisphere (N.Y.C.); Garden City Country, Lake George. Home: 63 Princeton St Garden City NY 11530 also Bolton Landing NY 12814 Office: 1251 Ave of Americas New York NY 10020

DEFORD, SARA WHITCRAFT, educator; b. Youngstown, Ohio, Nov. 9, 1916; d. Union Corwin and Grace (Whitcraft) de Ford. A.B., Mt. Holyoke Coll., 1936, M.A., 1938; Ph.D., Yale, 1942. Instr. English Barnard Coll., 1942-46; asst. prof. Goucher Coll., Towson, Md., 1946-50, asso. prof., 1950-57, prof. English, 1957-81, prof. emeritus, 1981—; vis. prof. Tsuda College, Tokyo, 1969-70. Author 7 books, also poems.; contbr. articles to profl. jours. Nurse's aide A.R.C., 1950-71. Recipient Eugene F. Saxton Meml. fellowship, 1948; Alumnae Centennial award Mt. Holyoke Coll., 1972; Fulbright lectr., Japan, 1954-55, 61-62. Mem. Medieval Acad. Am., AAUP, AAUW. Mem. Soc. of Friends. Home: 1961 S Josephine St Apt 302 Denver CO 80210

DE FOREST, SHERWOOD SEARLE, agricultural engineer, agri-business services executive; b. Ames, Iowa, Sept. 20, 1921; s. Frank Ray and Clara Maud (Searle) De F.; m. Virginia Mary Flynn, June 20, 1947; children: David, Debra, Denise, Kimberly. Student, U. Cin., 1939-40; B.S., Iowa State U., 1943, M.S., 1947. Registered profl. engr., Iowa. Instr. agrl. engring. Iowa State U., 1946-47, extension agrl. engr., 1947-52; engring. editor Successful Farming mag., Des Moines, 1952-59; with U.S. Steel Co., Pitts., 1959-77, mgr. agrl. equipment mktg., 1964-70, indsl. rep., 1970-77; v.p. Montgomery Assos., Coraopolis, Pa., 1977—; owner De Forest Agri-Services, Coraopolis, 1977—; tech. transfer project leader No. Agrl. Energy Center, Sci. and Edn. Adminstrn., Dept. Agr., Peoria, Ill., 1980-81; mem. indsl. and profl. adv. com. Coll. Engring. Pa. State U., 1966-71; Mem. NE Regional Agrl. Research Planning Com., 1970-72. Contbg. author: Power to Produce, U.S. Dept. Agr. Yearbook, 1960, Steel in Agriculture, 1966; Contbr.: numerous articles to Successful Farming Mag. Served to 1st lt. USAAF, 1943-46. Recipient Am. Soc. Agrl. Engrs.-Metal Bldg. Mfrs. Assn. award for disting. work in advancing knowledge and sci. of farm bldgs., 1964. Fellow Am. Soc. Agrl. Engrs. (pres. 1975-76); mem. Sigma Delta Chi. Presbyterian (ruling elder). Patentee in field. Home and Office: 106 Fitzrandolph Rd Coraopolis PA 15108

DEFRANCEAUX, GEORGE WALDEMAR, mortgage banker, realtor, housing executive; b. Washington, Mar. 12, 1913; s. George and May Belle (LeDane) DeF.; m. Ada Moss, Oct. 13, 1934; children: George Jefferson, Donald Moss, Dianne Anna, Kaye Anne. Realtor, builder, Washington, 1932-40; v.p. Frederick W. Berens, Inc., Washington, 1940-53, pres., 1953-69, chmn. bd., 1957-69; asst. v.p. DeFranceaux Realty Group, Inc., and predecessor, 1940-53, exec. v.p., 1953-57, pres., chmn. bd., 1957-69; chmn., 1969—; pres., chmn. bd. F.W. Berens Ins. Service Inc., 1957-69; chmn. bd. Berens Mortgage Bankes Inc., 1940-69, Bankers Guaranty Corp., 1940-69; founder, pres. Assoc. Mortgage Cos., Inc., 1961-67; pres. Nat. Corp. Housing Partnerships, Washington, 1970—, chmn., 1972—. Mem. Washington Bd. Realtors (past pres.), Mortgage Bankers Assn. Met. Washington (past pres.), Nat. Assn. Realtors (past bd. dirs.). Clubs: Congl. Country (Potomac, Md.); Univ. (Washington); Poplar Island Yacht, Talbot Country (Easton, Md.). Home: 4200 Massachusetts Ave NW Washington DC 20016 Office: Nat Corp Housing Patnerships 1133 15th St NW Washington DC 20005

DE FRANCESCO, JOHN BLAZE, JR., public relations company executive; b. Stamford, Conn., May 22, 1936; s. John Blaze and Mae (Matyscyk) DeF.; m. Louise C. Terlizzo, Nov. 1, 1958 (div. 1983); children: Daryl, Jay, Dana, Dorian. B.S., U. Conn., 1958. Sr. v.p. Daniel J. Edelman, Inc., Chgo., 1967-77; v.p. Ruder Finn & Rotman, Inc., Chgo., 1977—, exec. v.p. Midwest region, 1980-81; dir. JLD Corp., Deerfield, Ill. Bd. dirs. Ill. Div. Vocat. Rehab., 1976-78. Served to lt. comdr. U.S. Navy, 1958-67; comdr. Res. ret. Recipient Silver Anvil award Public Relations Soc. Am., 1966, 75, 78, Golden Trumpet award Publicity Club, Chgo., 1976. Mem. Am. Mktg. Assn., Mktg. Communications Execs. Internat., Navy League U.S., Naval Res. Assn. Roman Catholic. Clubs: Tennaqua, Rotary. Home: 922 Osterman Ave Deerfield IL 60015 Office: 444 N Michigan Ave Chicago IL 60611 *

DE FRANCIS, JAMES UPTON, government official; b. Detroit, Dec. 23, 1943; s. Robert J. and Marjorie Upton (Sayre) De F.; m. Suzanne Chase Cox, Sept. 27, 1975; children: James Upton, Marcus Whitman. B.S., Albion Coll., 1965; postgrad., Detroit Coll. Law, 1965-67; M.P.A., Wayne State U., 1969. Spl. asst. to asst. minority leader U.S. Senate, Washington, 1968-79; dir. S.E. office Mich. Dept. Commerce, Detroit, 1979-80; prin. dep. asst. sec. for congl., intergovtl. and pub. affairs U.S. Dept. Energy, Washington, 1981—. Office: US. Dept Energy 1000 Independence Ave SW Washington DC 20585

DE FRANK, VINCENT, condr.; b. L.I. City, N.Y., June 18, 1915; s. Nicholas and Della (Proudford) DeF.; m. Jean Marie Martin, Aug. 26, 1960; children—Vincent Nicholas, Philip Martin. Student, Juilliard Sch. Music, 1934-36; grad., Ind. U., 1952; D.Mus. (hon.), Southwestern U., Memphis, 1974. Cellist, Detroit Symphony Orch., 1939-40, St. Louis Symphony, 1947-50; founder, condr., Memphis Symphony Orch., 1952—, also Memphis Little Symphony, Memphis Chamber Orch.; music supr., Memphis-Hebrew Acad., 1969—; mem. adv. panel, Tenn. Arts Commn., 1970—; guest condr., Memphis Civic Ballet, Memphis Opera Theatre, Tenn. All-State Orch., Sewanee Summer Music Center, Jackson (Miss.) Symphony, Nashville Symphony and Little Symphony, Quincy (Ill.) Symphony, Charlotte (N.C.) Symphony, Evansville (Ind.) Symphony; vis. prof., Southwestern at Memphis. Served with AUS, 1940-45. Mem. Memphis Music Inc., Am. Symphony Orch. League, Violoncello Soc., Condrs. Guild, Nat. Rifle Assn. Clubs: Masons, Petroleum (Memphis). Office: 3100 Walnut Grove Rd Memphis TN 38111

DEFTOS, LEONARD JOHN, endocrinologist, scientist, educator; b. Brockton, Mass., Dec. 3, 1937. B.A. cum honoribus, Brown U., 1959;

M.D. cum laude, U. Vt., 1964. Diplomate: Am. Bd. Internal Medicine. Intern in medicine Columbia-Presbyn. Med. Center, N.Y.C., 1964-65, resident in medicine, 1965-66; staff assoc. sect. polypeptide hormones and attending physician Clin. Center NIH, Bethesda, Md., 1966-68; instr. medicine Harvard U., 1968-70, asst. prof., 1970-71; clin. and research fellow Mass. Gen. Hosp., Boston, 1968-70, dir. immunoassey lab. endocrine unit, 1968-72; assoc. prof. medicine U. Calif., La Jolla, 1972-76, prof., 1976—; chief endocrine sect. VA Med. Center, San Diego, 1972—; Cons. U.S. Naval Hosp., San Diego, 1973—, Naval Regional Med. Center, Camp Pendleton, Cal., 1975—; clin. investigator VA, 1974-77; mem. study sect. gen. medicine B, NIH, 1975-79. Mem. editorial bd., reviewer, contbr. numerous articles to books and profl. jours. Served to lt. comdr. USPHS, 1966-68. Am. Cancer Soc. Research scholar, 1971. Mem. Am. Fedn. Clin. Research, Am. Soc. Clin. Investigation, Endocrine Soc. (chmn. postgrad. com. 1976-79), Western Assn. Physicians, Assn. Am. Physicians, Alpha Omega Alpha. Address: 3350 La Jolla Village Dr San Diego CA 92161

DE GAETANI, JAN, singer; b. Massillon, Ohio, July 10, 1933; m. Thomas De Gaetani (div.); m. Philip West, 1969; children: Mark, Francesca. B.S., Juillard Sch. Music, 1955. Mem. mus. group, Gramercy Chamber Ensemble; later sang with, Contemporary Chamber Ensemble; performed at, Am. Music Festival, Washington, 1962, concert series at, Met. Mus. Art, 1976-77, 79-82, Kaufman Auditorium, N.Y.C., 1981; mem. faculty, Eastman Sch. Music, U. Rochester, N.Y., 1972—; Kilbourn prof., 1976—; appeared with, N.Y. Philharmonic, Boston Symphony, Berlin Philharmonic, BBC Orch., Chgo. Symphony, others; recs. for, Nonesuch, Columbia, Decca, Vanguard, others; has recorded with, Gilbert Kalish, pianist, Abbey Singers, Riverside Chamber Singers, N.Y. Pro Musica, Waverly Consort.; Recs. include Songs of Stephen Foster (Stereo Rev. Record of Yr. 1972), Ancient Voices of Children, Schoenberg Book of the Hanging Gardens and Pierrot Lunaire, Songs from the Spanisches Liederbuch songs of Schubert, Chausson and Rachmaninoff, duets of Schumann, (Recipient Koussevitsky award for rec. Punch and Judy 1981). Office: Eastman Sch Music 26 Gibbs St Rochester NY 14604 *

DEGAVRE, ROBERT THOMPSON, consumer products company executive; b. Oxford, Eng., Oct. 31, 1940; came to U.S., 1949; s. Robert Thompson and Terena (Cameron) DeG.; m. Angela Jane Hulse, Feb. 28, 1966; children: Teresa, Timothy. B.A., Princeton U., 1962, M.P.A., 1968. With treasury dept. Exxon Corp., N.Y.C., 1968-72, Tokyo, 1968-72; fin. mgr., asst. treas. Inco Ltd., N.Y.C., 1972-77, treas., 1977-82; v.p., treas. Squibb Corp., Princeton, N.J., 1982—; dir. Toroonto-Dominion Trust Co., N.Y.C., 1981—. Mem. adv. council dept. econs. Princeton U., 1979—. Served to lt. USN, 1962-66. Mem. Phi Beta Kappa. Office: Squibb Corp PO Box 4000 Princeton NJ 08540

DEGEN, BERNARD JOHN, II, association executive; b. Washington, July 6, 1937; s. Bernard Everett D. and Pearl Vivian (Freeman) Degan; m. Evelyn Artemius Cocosis, Nov. 24, 1963; children: Stephanie Lisa, Bernard John. B.S., George Washington U., 1959; postgrad. in biochemistry and cellular physiology, Temple U., 1959-60, 61-62. Asst. bibliographer Biol. Abstracts, Phila., 1961-63; med. and surg. educator Lea Febiger, Phila., 1963-66; exec. dir. Am. Assn. Oral and Maxillofacial Surgeons, Chgo., 1966—; chief of staff Sec. of Energy, Washington, 1981; sec. Ednl. Found. Oral and Maxillofacial Surgery, Chgo., 1966—, Oral and Maxillofacial Surgery Polit. Action Com. Mem. Northbrook (Ill.) Planning Commn., 1982; mem. fin. com. 10th Congl. Disst. Rep. Orgn. Served to 1st lt. U.S. Army, 1960-61. Recipient Disting. Service medal U.S. Dept. Energy, 1981. Fellow (hon.) Internat. Coll. Dentists, Am. Assn. Oral and Maxillofacial Surgery (disting. service award 1979); mem. Am. Pub. Health Assn., Am. Hosp. Assn., Am. Soc. Assn. Execs.; mem. (affiliate) AMA. Republican. Greek Orthodox. Clubs: Sunset Ridge (Northbrook); Internat. (Chgo.). Home: 2780 Grace Ln Nothbrook Il 60062 Office: Am Assn Oral and Maxillofacial Surgeons 211 E Chicago Ave Chicago IL 60611

DEGENHARDT, RICHARD KENNEDY, china company executive; b. Clayton, Mo., Dec. 16, 1924; s. Louis Henry and Nelle (Kennedy) D.; m. Margaret Elizabeth Johnston, June 10, 1946; children: Katherine Ann Degenhardt Adair, Margaret Beth Degenhardt Alsup, Nancy Jean Degenhardt Roether, Richard K., William J. B.S., St. Louis U., 1949. Systems analyst Colo. Hosp. Service, Denver, 1949; mgr. C. of C., Estes Park, Colo., 1950-52, St. Augustine, Fla., 1952-54, exec. v.p., Asheville, N.C., 1954-71, C. of C. of Greater Kansas City, Mo., 1971-80, Belleek Ireland Inc., 1980—. Author: Belleek- The Complete Collectors Guild and Illustrated Reference, 1978. Served with AUS, 1943-45. Mem. So. Assn. C. of C. Execs. (past pres.), N.C. Assn. C. of C. Execs. (past pres.), Am. C. of C. Execs. (past v.p.), Travel Council N.C. (past pres.), Mo. C. of C. Execs. (past pres.). Roman Catholic. Office: 1001 US Hwy 1 Suite 202 Jupiter FL 33458

DEGENKOLB, HENRY JOHN, consulting structural engineer; b. Peoria, Ill., July 13, 1913; s. Gustav J. and Alice (Emmert) D.; m. Anna Alma Nygren, Sept. 9, 1939; children: Virginia A. Degenkolb Craik, Joan A. Degenkolb Boain, Marion S. Degenkolb Hune, Patricia H. Degenkolb Blanton, Paul H. B.S. in Civil Engring., U. Calif., Berkeley, 1936. With various engring firms, 1936-46; chief engr., then partner John J. Gould & H.J. Degenkolb, engrs., San Francisco, 1946-61; pres. H.J. Degenkolb & Assocs., San Francisco, 1961-79, chmn. bd., 1980—; lectr. U. Calif. extension, 1947-58; mem. Calif. Bldg. Standards Commn., 1971—, Calif. Seismic Safety Commn., 1975-77, Presdl. Task Force Earthquake Hazard Reduction, 1970-71; mem. engring. criteria rev. bd. Bay Conservation and Devel. Commn., 1970-76; Trustee Cogswell Coll., San Francisco. Contbr. profl. publns. Hon. mem. ASCE (Moiseiff award 1953, Ernest E. Howard award 1967); mem. Am. Concrete Inst., Am. Cons. Engrs. Council, Cons. Engrs. Assn. Calif., Structural Engrs. Assn. Calif. (pres. 1958), Earthquake Engring. Research Inst. (pres. 1974-78), Forest Hills Assn. (pres. 1957). Club: San Francisco Engineers. Home: 95 Linares Ave San Francisco CA 94116 Office: 350 Sansome St San Francisco CA 94104

DE GENNARO, RICHARD, university librarian; b. New Haven, Mar. 2, 1926; s. Ralph and Acquilina (Pedicini) De G.; m. Birgit M. Erikson, June 12, 1953; children—Ralph, George, Christina. B.A., Wesleyan U., Middletown, Conn., 1951, M.A., 1960; M.S. in L.S, Columbia U., 1956; postgrad., univs. Paris, Madrid and Perugia, 1951-55; grad. Advanced Mgmt. Program, Harvard U., 1971. Jr. accountant Atlas Constructors, Morocco, 1952-53; reference librarian N.Y. Pub. Library, 1956-58; successively reference librarian, asst. dir., asso. univ. librarian systems devel., sr. asso. univ. librarian Harvard U. Library, 1958-70; vis. prof. Grad. Library Sch., U. So. Calif., 1968-69; dir. libraries U. Pa., 1970—, adj. prof. English, 1979—; cons. library bldgs., tech. and mgmt.; mem. overseers com. to visit library Harvard U.; cons. MIT, Johns Hopkins U.; mem. adv. bd. Chem. Abstracts Service, 1967-70; mem. Palinet bd. Union Library Catalogue, 1970—; mem. com. internat. sci. and tech. info. programs Nat. Acad. Scis.-NRC, 1977—; governing bd. Research Libraries Group, 1979—, sr. vis. fellow, 1980-81; Bowker lectr., 1979. Author: Libraries, Technology, and the Information Marketplace, 1983; Contbr. articles to profl. jours. Bd. dirs. Center for Research Libraries, 1977-81; trustee U. Pa. Press, 1978-82. Served with USNR, 1942-45. Council Library Resources fellow, 1971; Rockefeller Found. Center, Bellagio, Italy, 1981. Mem. Assn. Research Libraries (pres. 1975, dir. 1973-76), ALA (pres. info. sci. and automation div. 1975), Am. Soc. Info. Soc. Club: Franklin Inn. Home: 201 Wakefield Rd Rosemont PA 19010 Office: Van Pelt Library 3420 Walnut St Philadelphia PA 19104

DE GEORGE, LAWRENCE JOSEPH, diversified company executive; b. N.Y.C., May 6, 1916; s. Frank Phillip and Frances (Cavallo) DeG.; m. Florence A. Efel, Dec. 18, 1943; children: Lawrence F., Peter R. B.S. in Elec. Engring, Princeton U., 1936; M.S., MIT, 1938. Asso. prof. elec. engring. Columbia U., 1938-39; field engr. Radio Engring. Lab., N.Y.C., 1939-41; pres. Times Wire and Cable Co., Inc., div. Internat. Silver Co., Wallingford, Conn., 1946; also v.p., dir. Times Wire and Cable div., 1958-64, pres., 1964-68; v.p., dir. Insilco Corp., Meridan, Conn., 1968-72, exec. v.p., 1972, vice chmn., 1976—; chmn., pres. Times Fiber Communications, Inc., Meriden, 1977—; pres. LPL Group Inc., N.Y.C., 1984—; dir. Travelers Equities Fund, Inc., Hartford, Conn.; Bd dirs. Gaylord Hosp., Wallingford, Conn. Past pres. Cheshire Community Theater. Served to lt. comdr. USNR, 1941-46. Mem. IRE, Electronic Industries Assn. (chmn. tech. com. high temperature cable). Republican. Clubs: Princeton, Engineers (N.Y.C.); Farms Country, Wallingford, Kiwanis. Home: 16904 Passage South Jupiter FL 33458 Office: 358 Hall Ave PO Box 384 Wallingford CT 06492

DE GEORGE, RICHARD THOMAS, educator; b. N.Y.C., Jan. 29, 1933; s. Nicholas and Carmelina (D'Ippolito) De G.; m. Fernande I. Melanson, June 15, 1957; children: Rebecca, Anne Marie, Catherine. B.A., Fordham U., 1954; Ph.B., U. Louvain, Belgium, 1955; M.A., Yale U., 1958, Ph.D., 1959. Faculty U. Kans., 1959—, prof. philosophy, 1964-72, Univ. prof., 1972—, chmn. dept., 1966-72; co-dir. Center for Humanistic Studies, 1977-82, dir., 1982-83; lectr., sr. research fellow Columbia U., 1965-66; asso. Inst. E. European Studies, Fribourg, Switzerland, 1962-63; Research fellow Yale U., 1969-70. Author: Patterns of Soviet Thought, 1966, The New Marxism, 1968, Soviet Ethics and Morality, 1969, A Guide to Philosophical Bibliography and Research, 1971, The Philosopher's Guide, 1980, Business Ethics, 1981, also articles.; Editor: Ethics and Society, 1966, Classical and Contemporary Metaphysics, 1962, Semiotic Themes, 1981; editor, contbr.: Reflections on Man, 1966; co-editor: The Structuralists, 1972, Marxism and Religion in Eastern Europe, 1976, Ethics, Free Enterprise and Public Policy, 1978. Served to 1st lt. AUS, 1955-57. Fulbright fellow, 1954-55; Ford fellow, 1962-63; recipient Hope Teaching award U. Kans., 1965; Nat. Endowment for Humanities fellow, 1969-70; project grantee, 1972-73; summer inst. dir., 1976, 77, 80, 81; Rockefeller Found. Humanities fellow, 1976-77. Mem. Am. Philos. Assn. (exec. com. 1976-79, nat. bd. officers 1982—), Internat. Fedn. Philos. Socs. (governing bd. 1979—), Internat. Assn. Philosophy Law and Social Philosophy (pres. Am. sect. 1977-79), Metaphys. Soc. Am. (v.p. 1981-82, pres. 1982-83), Internat. Fedn. Philos. Socs. (gov. bd. 1978—), Am. Assn. for Advancement Slavic Studies. Home: 945 Highland Dr Lawrence KS 66044

DE GERENDAY, LACI ANTHONY, sculptor; b. Budapest, Hungary, Aug. 17, 1911; came to U.S., 1912; s. Ladislaus and Helen (Jiraszek) de G.; m. Mary Ellen Lord, Dec. 19, 1969 (dec. 1976); 1 dau., Lynn; m. Elisabeth Gordon Chandler, May 12, 1979. Student, S.D. Sch. Mines, 1929-30, Ursinus Coll., 1930-31, NAD, Beaux-Arts Inst., 1934-35, U. Shrivenham, Eng. Sculpture, instr. Lyme Acad. Fine Arts. Exhbns., NAD, Pa. Acad., Boston Mus., Pa. Mus., Mus. San Francisco, Mus. Ariz., Cin. Mus., Mus. R.I., Mus. Modern Art, N.Y.C., Grand Central Galleries, Nat. Sculpture Soc., Archtl. League, Corning Glass Mus., N.J. Art Mus., N.Y. Coliseum, Salmagundi Club, Rockefeller Ctr., N.Y.C., Loeb Ctr. of NYU, Acad. Arts and Letters, Nat. Arts Club, Smithsonian Instn., Am. Bible Soc., Hudson Valley Art Assn., Mus. Fine Arts, Springfield, Mass., Nat. Collection Fine Arts, Washington, Art Ctr., Old Lyme, Conn., Foothills Art Ctr., Golden, Colo., Wall Focus Gallery, Chester, Conn.; prin. works include gold medal, Soc. Elec. Engrs., bronze equestrian relief of Lt. Junot, Mus. Algiers, Algeria, bronze medal, Soc. Medalists, bronze relief, NAD, numerous bronze relief protraits, silver coins. Recipient citation City of N.Y., 1st Sculpture prize N.J. Art Assn., Ellen Speyer award NAD, 1947, 63, Lindsey Morris Meml. award Nat. Sculpture Soc., 1955, 81, Bennet prize, 1963, Council of Am. Artists Soc. award, 1977, Roman Bronze Foundry award, 1980, Bedi-Makky Foundry prize, 1983, Lindsey Morris Meml. award Allied Artists Am., 1969, 76, 78, Silver medal of Honor, 1977, Wendel Clinedinst award, 1982, Mrs. John Newington award Hudson Valley Art Assn., 1979. Fellow Nat. Sculpture Soc.; mem. NAD, Allied Artists Am., Hudson Valley Art Assn., Nat. Soc. Lit. and the Arts, Nat. Arts Club. Address: Mill Pond Ln Old Lyme CT 06371

DEGHETTO, KENNETH ANSELM, engineering and construction company executive; b. Clifton, N.J., Apr. 1, 1924; s. Anselm and Linda (Zanetti) DeG.; m. Helen Zschack, Nov. 5, 1944; children: Donna, Glenn. B.S., U.S. Mcht. Marine Acad., 1943; B.Mech. Engring., Rensselaer Poly. Inst., Troy, N.Y., 1950. Registered profl. engr., N.Y., N.J., Wash., Fla., Alaska. With Foster Wheeler Corp., Livingston, N.J., 1951—, dir., 1973—, v.p., 1973-76, exec. v.p., 1976—; chmn. bd. Foster Wheeler Internat. Corp., 1975—. Served to lt. USNR, 1943-46. Mem. ASME, Nat. Assn. Corrosion Engrs., Sigma Xi (asso.), Tau Beta Pi, Tau Pi Sigma. Lutheran. Clubs: Royal and Ancient Golf (St. Andrews, Scotland); Montclair (N.J.) Country. Home: 42 Cornell Dr Livingston NJ 07039 Office: 110 S Orange Ave Livingston NJ 07039

DEGIUSTI, DOMINIC LAWRENCE, educator; b. Treviso, Italy, Mar. 30, 1911; came to U.S., 1916, naturalized, 1925; s. Angelo L. and Angela (DeNegri) DeG.; m. Dianna Dobrzechowski, June 28, 1974; children—Lenore (Mrs. Antoine Noujaim), Angelo, Peter. B.S., Coll. of St. Thomas, St. Paul, 1936; M.S., U. Mich., 1938; Ph.D. (DuPont fellow), U. Wis., 1943. Instr. Coll. of St. Thomas, 1936-38, asst. prof., 1942-43, 46-47; asst. in helminthology U. Mich. Biol. Sta., 1939-41, 46-51; instr., asst. prof. N.Y.U. Coll. Medicine, N.Y.C., 1943-46; research asso. U. Minn. Coll. Medicine, 1946-47; asst. prof. Catholic U. Am., Washington, 1947-49; asso. prof. dept. biology Wayne State U., Detroit, 1949-57, prof. dept. biology and Sch. Medicine dept. comparative medicine, 1957-81, prof. emeritus, 1981—, chmn. dept. biology, 1967-72, chmn. dept. comparative medicine, 1978-79; mem. staff dept. pathology Detroit Gen. Hosp. Hutzel Hosp. Markle Found. fellow to Central Am., 1945; Fulbright Research fellow to, Naples, Italy Zool. Sta., 1952; La. State U. fellow to, Caribbean, 1957. Fellow N.Y. Acad. Scis., AAAS, Am. Inst. Fishery Research Biologists; mem. Am. Soc. Parasitologist (mem. council 1964-67), Am. Soc. Tropical Medicine and Hygiene, Am. Soc. Zoology, Am. Soc. Protozoology, Am. Micros. Soc. (mem. council 1963-69, v.p. 1965, pres. 1966), Helminthology Soc. Washington, Mich. Acad. Sci., Arts and Letters, Mich. Entomol. Soc. (pres. 1954), Sigma Xi. Home: 18233 Pennington St Detroit MI 48221

DE GIVENCHY, HUBERT (GIVENCHY), fashion designer; b. Beauvais, France, Feb. 20, 1927; s. Lucien and Béatrice (Badin) Taffin de G. Ed., Ecole nationale supérieure des beauxarts. Faculty of Law U. Paris.; Apprenticeship fashion houses of Lelong, 1945-46, Piquet, 1946-48, Fath and Schiaparelli, 1948-51; opened his own fashion house, Paris, 1952; pres., dir. gen. Givenchy-Couture, after 1954. Address: Givenchy: 3 Ave George V 75008 Paris France *

DEGLER, CARL NEUMANN, educator, historian; b. Orange, N.J., Feb 6, 1921; s. Casper and Jewell (Neumann) D.; m. Catherine Grady, Nov. 19, 1948; children: Paul Grady, Suzanne Catherine. A.B., Upsala Coll., N.J., 1942, L.H.D., 1969; M.A., Columbia, 1947, Ph.D., 1952; M.A., Oxford (Eng.) U., 1973; LL.D., Ripon Coll., 1976, Colgate U., 1978. Instr. Hunter Coll., 1947-48, N.Y. U., 1947-49, Adelphi Coll., 1950-51, Coll. City N.Y., 1952; mem. faculty Vassar Coll., 1952-68, prof. history, 1962-68, chmn. dept., 1966-68; prof. Am. history Stanford, 1968—, Margaret Byrne prof. Am. history, 1972—; vis. prof. Columbia Grad. Sch., 1963-64, Stanford, summer 1964; Harmsworth prof. Oxford U., 1973-74; fellow Center Advanced Study in Behavioral Scis., 1979-80, Humanities Ctr., Stanford U., 1983-84; Mem. Calif. Council for Humanities, 1979—. Author: Age of Economic Revolution, 1967, rev. edit., 1976, Affluence and Anxiety, rev. edit, 1975, Out of our Past, 3d edit., 1983, Neither Black Nor White (co-winner Beveridge prize 1971, Pulitzer prize 1972), 1971 (Bancroft prize 1972), The Other South: Southern Dissenters in the Nineteenth Century, 1974, Place Over Time, 1977, At Odds: Women and the Family in America from the Revolution to the Present, 1980; Editor: Pivotal Interpretations of American History, 1966, Women and Economics (C.P. Gilman), 2d edit, 1970, The New Deal, 1970; Bd. editors: Am. Quar, 1967-70, Jour. So. History, 1967-71, Revs. in Am. History, 1972-75, Jour. Family History, 1977—; mem. editorial bd.: Plantation Society, 1979—; mem. editorial adv. bd.: Signs: Women in Culture and Society, 1974—. Served with AUS, 1942-45; CBI. Am. Council Learned Socs. fellow, 1964-65; Guggenheim fellow, 1972-73; NEH fellow, 1976-77, 83-84. Mem. Am. Acad. Arts and Scis., Antiquarian Soc., Am. Hist. Assn. (pres. Pacific Coast br. 1974-75), So. Hist. Assn., Econ. History Assn., Am. Studies Assn., Orgn. Am. Historians (exec. bd. 1970-73, 78-83, pres. 1979-80), AAUP. Home: 907 Mears Ct Stanford CA 94305

DEGNAN, HERBERT RAYMOND, financial exec; b. N.Y.C., Mar. 16, 1921; s. John T. and Florence R. (Schoonmaker) D.; m. Gertrude J. Fretterd, Oct. 3, 1943; children—Donald J., Regina (Mrs. Timothy Greiner), Raymond H., Robert W. Student, Columbia, 1938-40, postgrad., 1946-48; B.S., St. John's Coll., 1943; LL.B., Fordham U., 1955. Bar: N.Y. bar 1955. Accountant Scovell Wellington Co., N.Y.C., 1946-55; atty. Seghers & Reinhart, N.Y.C., 1955-57; sr. v.p., dir. Empire State Bldg. Corp., N.Y.C., 1957-62; v.p., dir. Nat. Car Rental System, N.Y.C., 1962-65; chief exec. officer, dir. 1st Fed. Savs. & Loan Assn., Tampa, Fla., 1965-67; pres., dir. Bermec Corp., N.Y.C., 1967-72; sr. v.p., chief fin. officer Tech. Tape, Inc., New Rochelle, N.Y., 1972-76; fin. cons., 1976-77; pres., dir. Cliffside Food Distbrs., Inc., Cliffside Park, N.J., 1977—. Served to lt. comdr. USNR, 1943-45. Decorated Bronze Star. Mem. Am., N.Y. State bar assns., N.Y. State Soc. C.P.A.'s, Am. Inst. C.P.A.'s, Skull and Circle, Delta Phi. Home: 161 S Maple Ave Ridgewood NJ 07450

DEGNAN, THOMAS LEONARD, lawyer; b. Waseca, Minn., Jan. 18, 1909; s. John James and Martha (Kurkowski) D.; m. Nan Glennon, Sept. 24, 1938; children—Nancy, Martha, Denise. Student, St. Mary's Coll., Winona, Minn., 1925-27; J.D., Georgetown U., 1930. Bar: Minn. bar 1930, N.D. bar 1933. With firm Sexton, Mordaunt, Kennedy & Carrol, St. Paul, 1930-38; founder, 1938; sr. partner firm Degnan, McElroy, Lamb, Camrud, Maddock & Olson, Ltd., Grand Forks, N.D.; mem. N.D. Jud. Council, 1961-63, N.D. Med. Center Adv. Bd., 1963-67, N.D. Jud. Survey Commn., 1965-67. Pres. Young Dems., N.D., 1940-44, nat. committeeman, 1944-48; Bd. dirs. St. James High Sch., 1954-56, Grand Forks Indsl. Found.; past pres., bd. dirs. Grand Forks Community Chest. Mem. ABA, N.D. Bar Assn. (pres. 1960-61), First Dist. Bar Assn. (pres. 1957-59), Grand Forks County Bar Assn. (pres. 1952-53), Edward Douglas White Law Club, Pierce Butler Law Club, Grand Forks C. of C. (past pres., dir.), Sigma Nu Phi., Elk (past exalted ruler). Home: 10318 Highwood Ln Sun City AZ 85373

DEGRAAF, DONALD EARL, educator; b. Grand Rapids, Mich., June 17, 1926; s. Benjamin and Mary (Stonehouse) DeG.; m. Malois Wieland, Aug. 20, 1948; children: Daniel M., Gwen L., David P. A.B., Calvin Coll., 1948; B.S. in Elec. Engring, U. Mich., 1947, M.S., 1950, Ph.D. in Physics, 1957. With dept. physics U. Mich., Flint, 1957—, asso. prof., 1961-67, prof., 1967—, chmn. dept., 1965-70, 71-75; dir. Flint Introductory Physics Sequence Curriculum Project, 1967—; visitor research center Mass. Inst. Tech., Cambridge, 1970-71; Fulbright fellow Murdoch U., Perth, Australia, 1976; pres. Crystal Press, 1977—; cons. on coll. physics curriculum devel. Corp. mem. Inter-Varsity Christian Fellowship, 1968-81, chmn. faculty com., 1970-74. Served to lt. USNR, 1944-46, 53-55. Fellow Am. Sci. Affiliation; mem. Am. Assn. Physics Tchrs., AAAS. Methodist. Home: 1909 Proctor St Flint MI 48504 *The institutional pressures toward conformity, routine, and paper-pushing must be resisted in order to maintain an emphasis on person-centered teaching, to respect the high value of every person.*

DEGRANDI, JOSEPH A., lawyer; b. Hartford, Conn., 1927; m. Yolanda Salica; children: Terese, Lisa, Donna. B.S., Trinity Coll., Hartford, 1949; M.S., George Washington U., 1950, LL.B., 1952. Bar: D.C. 1952, U.S. Supreme Ct. 1956. Now mem. firm Beveridge, DeGrandi & Kline, Washington.; Mem. adv. bd. Marymount Sch., Arlington, Va., pres., 1969-72; legal advisor U.S. delegation Diplomatic Conf. for Revision of Paris Conv., Nairobi, Kenya, 1981. Recipient Disting. Alumnus award George Washington U., 1982. Fellow Am. Bar Found.; Mem. ABA (chmn. sect. patent, trademark and copyright law 1981-82), Inter-Am. Bar Assn., Fed. Bar Assn., Internat. Bar Assn., Nat. Council Patent Law Assns. (sec. 1971-75, adv. panel 1975-79), Bar Assn. D.C. (dir. 1968-69, chmn. patent, trademark and copyright law sect. 1967-68), D.C. Bar Assn. (chmn. div. patent, trademark and copyright law 1978-79), Am. Patent Law Assn. (bd. mgrs. 1976-79), N.Y. Patent Law Assn., Patent Lawyers Club Washington (pres. 1959), Am. Judicature Soc., Am. Intellectual Property Law Assn. (dir., v.p. 1984—), Patent and Trademark Inst. Can., Chartered Inst. Patent Agts. (Gt. Britain), Internat. Patent and Trademark Assn. (exec. com. 1978-83, v.p. 1983—), Licensing Execs. Soc., Inter-Am. Assn. Indsl. Property, Assn. of Textile Industry, Inc., Federation Internationale des Conseils en Propriete Industrielle, Thomas More Soc. Am., Nu Beta Epsilon. Club: Rotary. Office: Beveridge DeGrandi & Kline Fed Bar Bldg W 1819 H St NW Washington DC 20006

DE GRANDPRÉ, ALBERT JEAN, telecommunications company executive; b. Montreal, Que., Can., Sept. 14, 1921; s. Rol and Aline (Magnan) de G.; m. Hélène Choquet, Sept. 27, 1947; children: François, Liliane, Suzanne, Louise. B.A., Coll. Jean de Brébeuf, 1940; B.C.L. (Gold medalist), McGill U., 1943. Bar: Montreal 1943. Partner firm Tansey, de Grandpré, Bergeron & Monet, Montreal, 1949-65; gen. counsel Bell Can. Co., Montreal, 1966, v.p. law, 1966-68, exec. v.p. adminstrn., 1968-70, exec. v.p. Eastern region, 1970-73, pres., 1973-76, dir., mem. exec. com., 1972—, chmn., chief exec. officer, 1976-83; chmn., chief exec. officer parent co. Bell Can. Enterprises, Inc., 1983—; dir. Dupont of Can. Ltd., Toronto-Dominion Bank, TransCan. PipeLines, No. Telecom. Ltd., Royal Ins. Group, Steel Co. Can., Ltd., Chrysler Corp. Chancellor McGill U., 1984—. Mem. Canadian Bar Assn. (life), Assn. Canadian Gen. Counsel (emeritus), Bar Province of Que. Roman Catholic. Clubs: St. James, St. Denis (Montreal); Toronto, Forest and Stream, Mt. Bruno Country. Office: 1050 Beaver Hall Hill Montreal PQ H3C 3G4 Canada *

DE GRAVELLES, WILLIAM DECATUR, JR., physician; b. Jennings, La., Feb. 20, 1928; s. William Decatur and Ara May (Zenor) deG. B.S., S.W. La. Inst., 1949; M.D., Tulane U., 1952. Diplomate: Am. Bd. Phys. Medicine and Rehab. Intern Charity Hosp. La., New Orleans, 1952-53; splty. tng. in phys. medicine, rehab. N.Y.U., Bellevue Med. Center, N.Y.C., 1953-56; practice medicine, specializing in phys. medicine and rehab.; dir. rehab. service Duke Med. Center, Durham, N.C., 1956-58; chief phys. medicine and rehab. Iowa Meth. Hosp., Des Moines, 1958—, Younker Meml. Rehab. Center, 1958—, med. dir., 1958—; Med. cons. Easter Seal's Camp Sunnyside, Des Moines. Chmn. med. adv. com. Polk County (Iowa) Nat. Found., 1958-65; mem. Gov's Com. on Employment Handicapped.; Bd. dirs. Iowa Easter Seal Soc., Goodwill Industries, Inc., Des Moines. Named Iowa Physician of Year Gov.'s Com. on Employment Handicapped, 1969; recipient citation for meritorious service Pres.'s Com. on Employment Handicapped; named Physician of Yr., 1978; recipient Cotton award Iowa chpt. Arthritis Found., 1969, Lay Individual award Iowa Park and Recreation Assn., 1974, Pub. Citizen of Year award Nat. Assn. Social Workers, 1977, Nat. Therapeutic Recreation Soc. citation, 1977, Distinguished Service award Gov.'s Com. Employment Handicapped, 1977, Gallantry award Easter Seal Soc. Crippled Children and Adults, Iowa, 1978. Mem. AMA, Iowa, Polk County med. socs., Muscular Dystrophy Assn., Am. (med. adviser Greater Iowa chpt.), Nat. Multiple Sclerosis Soc. (chmn. med. adv. com. central Iowa chpt. 1958-66), Iowa Rehab. Assn. (past dir., past pres.), Internat. Assn. Rehab. Facilities (dir.). Home: 6024 Ronwood Dr Des Moines IA 50312 Office: Iowa Meth Hosp 1200 Pleasant St Des Moines IA 50308

DEGRAZIA, ALFRED, educator, behavioral scientist; b. Chgo., Dec. 29, 1919; s. Alfred J. and Katherine (Lupo) deG.; m. Jill B.L. Oppenheim, May 11, 1942 (div.); m. Nina Mavridis, Dec. 21, 1972 (div.); children: Catherine deGrazia VanderPool, Victoria F., Jessica M. deGrazia Jeans, Paul R., John S., Carl M., Christopher; m. Anne-Marie Hueber, Apr. 23,1982. A.B., U. Chgo., 1939, Ph.D., 1948; student, Columbia Law Sch., 1940-41. Mem. faculty Northwestern U., 1948, U. Minn., 1948-50, Brown U., 1950-52, Stanford U., 1952-57; research prof. social theory NYU, 1959-83; vis. lectr. U. Istanbul, Turkey, U. Rome, U. Gothenburg, Sweden, U. Bombay, India; rector (pro tem) U. New World, Switzerland, 1971; cons. in field, 1948—; chmn. bd. Princeton Info. Tech., Inc., 1967-70; adv. bd. Simulmatics Corp., 1967. Author: Public and Republic, 1949, Elements of Political Science, 1952, World Politics, 1949, The Western Public, 1954, The American Way of Government, 1957, Grass Roots Private Welfare, 1958, American Welfare, 1960, Science and Values in Administration, 1961, Political Behavior and Organization, 2 vols, 1962, Apportionment and Representative Government, 1963, Republic in Crisis, Congress Against the Executive Force, 1965, The Velikovsky Affair, 1966, Congress and the Presidency, 1965; (poetry) Passage of the Year, 1967; Kalos: What Is to be Done with Our World, 1973, Politics for Better or Worse, 1973, 8 Bads-8 Goods: The American Contradictions, 1975, Art and Culture: 1001 Questions on Policy, 1979, Chaos and Creation: Quantavolution in Human and Natural History, 1981, Homo Schizo II: Human Nature and Behavior, 1983; editor: Congress: First Branch of Government, 1966; founder, editor jour.: Am. Behavioral Scientist, 1957-66. Mem. U.S. del. to UNESCO, 1960; first pres. Found. Vol. Welfare, 1957-59; chmn. research com. N.Y.C. Republican party, 1961; cons. Rep. Nat. Com., 1964; organizer Ind. Voters, Ill., 1946-48 organizer Ind. Voters, Calif., 1953-56. Served to capt. AUS, 1942-46; ETO; adv., Korea, 1951-52, Vietnam, 1967-68. Decorated Bronze Star, others. Mem. Am. Polit. Sci. Assn., Mediterranean Social Sci. Research Council, Internat. Polit. Sci. Assn., Fedn. Am. Scientists, Am. Assn. Pub. Opinion Research, AAAS. Designer computerized reference retrieval system in social scis., Universal Reference System, 1962-67. Office: care Metron Publs Box 1213 Princeton NJ 08540

DE GRAZIA, SEBASTIAN, political philosopher, author; b. Chgo., Aug. 11, 1917; s. Alfred Joseph and Catherine Cardinale (Lupo) de G.; m. Miriam Lund Carlson; children: Alfred Joseph III, Margherita, Sebastian; m. Anna Maria d'Annunzio di Montenevoso; children: Marco, Tancredi; m. Lucia Heffelfinger. A.B., Ph.D., U. Chgo. With FCC, 1941-43, OSS, 1943-45; mem. faculty U. Chgo., 1945-50; cons. bus. firms, state and U.S. Govt., 1947—; dir. research study time, work and leisure Twentieth Century Fund, 1957-61; prof. polit. philosophy Rutgers U., 1962—; vis. prof. U. Florence, Italy, 1950-52, Princeton U., 1957, U. Madrid, 1963, John Jay Coll. Criminal Justice, 1967-71, CUNY, 1967—, Inst. Advanced Study, Princeton, 1983. Author: The Political Community, 1948, Errors of Psychotherapy, 1953, Of Time, Work and Leisure, 1962, Masters of Chinese Political Thought, 1973. Grantee Am. Philos. Soc., Social Sci. Research Council, Am. Council Learned Socs.; Fulbright prof. Mem. Am. Polit. Sci. Assn., Am. Soc. Polit. and Legal Philosophy, Institut International de Philosophie Politique. Clubs: Cosmos (Washington); Nassau, Prettybrook (Princeton); Century (N.Y.C.). Home: Great Rd Princeton NJ 08540 Office: Eagleton Inst Rutgers U New Brunswick NJ 08903

DEGRIJS, LEO CHARLES, banker; b. Batavia, Java, 1926; married. Grad. Vrijzinning Christelijk Lyceum, The Hague, Netherlands, 1943. With Netherlands Post Tel & Tel Co., 1943-45, Netherlands-Indies Civil Adminstrn., 1945-49, Nederlandsche Handel-Maatschappij, bankers, Amsterdam, 1951-63, Continental Ill. Nat. Bank and Trust Co., Chgo., 1963—, internat. banking dept., 2d v.p. and head, Tokyo and Osaka, 1964, v.p., Chgo., 1967, head Far East group, 1968; head Asia Pacific and Africa-Middle East groups, 1973, sr. v.p., 1974, head internat. banking dept., 1976, head banking services dept., 1980, exec. v.p., 1981—; dir. Contiental Bank SA NV, Brussels, Continental Ill. Leasing Corp., Continental Ill. Bank Ltd., Hong Kong, Continental Bank Internat., Continental Internat. Fin. Corp., Continental Ill. Internat. Investment Corp.; cir. Continental Ill. Ltd., London; dir. Continental Ill. Bank (Can.). Address: Continental Illinois Corp 231 S LaSalle St Chicago IL 60697

DEGROAT, WILLIAM CHESNEY, pharmacology educator; b. Trenton, N.J., May 18, 1938; s. William Chesney and Margaret (Welch) deG.; m. Dorothy Marion Albertson, June 13, 1959; children: Allyson L., Cynthia L., Jennifer L. B.Sc., Phila. Coll. Pharmacology and Sci., 1960, M.Sc., 1962; Ph.D., U. Pa., 1965, postdoctoral, 1965-66; postdoctoral, Australian Nat. U., Canberra, 1966-67. Vis. research fellow John Curtin Sch. Med. Research, Canberra, 1967-68; asst. prof. U. Pitts., 1968-72, assoc. prof., 1972-77, adj. prof. pharmacy, 1978—, acting chmn. dept., 1978-80, prof. pharmacology, 1977—, prof. psychology, 1982—. Editorial bd.: Jour. Pharmacology and Exptl. Therapeutics, 1975-83, Jour. Autonomic Nervous System, 1979-83, Jour. Neurology and Urodynamics, 1982-83, Am. Jour. Physiology, 1983; editorial cons. profl. jours.; contbr. articles to profl. jours., chpts. in books. NSF predoctoral fellow, 1962-63; pharmacology fellow Riker Pharm. Co., 1966-67; NSF postdoctoral fellow, 1966-67; recipient research Career Devel. award NIH, 1972-77. Mem. AAAS, N.Y. Acad. Scis., Am. Soc. Pharmacology and Exptl. Therapeutics, Soc. for Neurosci., Internat. Brain Research Orgn., Urodynamics Soc., Sigma Xi, Rho Chi. Republican. Methodist. Home: 6357 Burchfield Ave Pittsburgh PA 15217 Office: Medical School University of Pittsburgh 572 Scaife Hall Terrace St Pittsburgh PA 15261

DEGROOT, JOHN DARRYL, broadcast executive; b. Detroit, Apr. 8, 1946; s. Donald F. and Iola (Shirley) DeG.; m. Carol Lynn Buxton, Sept. 1, 1973. B.A., Mich. State U., 1968. Announcer WHFI (WMJC), Birmingham, Mich., 1965-66, WTCM-AM & FM, Traverse City, Mich., 1968, WILS-AM & FM, Lansing, Mich., 1968, WPAG-AM & FM, Ann Arbor, Mich., 1971; sta. mgr. WATT, Cadillac, Mich., 1971-72; pres., gen. mgr. Alpine Broadcasting Co., WWRM-FM, Gaylord, Mich., WKZY-FM, Escanaba, Mich., WGRY-AM, Grayling, Mich., WMLQ-FM, Rogers City, Mich. Served to 1st lt. Signal Corps U.S. Army. Decorated Bronze Star; named Outstanding Grad. Mich. State U., 1968-69. Mem. Mich. Assn. Broadcasters (dir.-treas. 1974-75), Gaylord C. of C. (dir. 1974-76). Republican. Lutheran. Club: Rotary. Office: 308 1/2 W Main St Gaylord MI 49735

DE GROOT, MORRIS HERMAN, statistician, educator; b. Scranton, Pa., June, 8, 1931; s. Archibald L. and Florence (Dinner) DeGroot; m. Dolores Pine, Sept. 7, 1952 (dec. Sept. 1974); children: Jenny, Jeremy; m. Marilyn Dallolio Fischer, May 19, 1979. B.S., Roosevelt U., 1952; M.S., U. Chgo., 1954, Ph.D., 1958. Mem. faculty Carnegie-Mellon U. (and predecessor), 1957—, prof. math. statistics, 1966-77, prof. statistics and indsl. adminstrn., 1977—, head dept. statistics, 1966-72; adj. prof. psychiatry U. Pitts., 1978—; prof. European Inst. for Advanced Studies in Mgmt., Brussels, Belgium, 1971; mem. com. nat. statistics NRC, 1975-79, assoc. chmn., 1978-79, mem. Commn. on Behavioral and Social Scis. and Edn., 1980—. Author: Optimal Statistical Decisions, 1970, Probability and Statistics, 1975, also articles. Fellow Am. Statis. Assn. (asso. editor jour. 1970-74, book rev. editor 1971-75, editor 1976-78), Inst. Math. Stats. (asso. editor Annals of Statistics 1974-75, council 1975-78, 81—), Royal Statis. Soc., AAAS (mem.-at-large statistics sect. com. 1978—), Econometrics Soc.; mem. Internat. Statis. Inst. Home: 1236 Murdoch Rd Pittsburgh PA 15217

DEGRUSON, EUGENE HENRY, librarian; b. Girard, Kans., Oct. 10, 1932; s. Henry Dieudonne and Clemence (Merciez) DeG. B.S. in Edn., Pittsburg State U., (Kans.), 1954, M.S., 1958; postgrad., U. Iowa, 1958-60. Tchr. speech and theatre Highland Park High Sch., Topeka, 1954-58; grad. asst. in communications U. Iowa, 1958-60; instr. lang. and lit. Kans. State Coll., Pittsburg, 1960-63, asst. prof. English, 1962-68; assoc. prof. library sci. Pittsburg State U., 1968—, spl. collections librarian, 1968—. Author: Kansas Authors of Best Sellers, 1970, The Printer of Udell's: A Dramatization of Harold Bell Wright's Novel, 1975; contbg. author: First Printings of American Authors, 1978—; author: Bibliography of American Literature, 1973—; editor: Library Bull, 1968-74; poetry editor: Little Balkans Rev., 1980—. Mem. Kans. Library Assn., NEA, Bibliographical Soc. Am. Democrat. OFFICE: Pittsburg State University Pittsburg KS 66762

DEHAAN, NORMAN RICHARD, architect; b. Chgo., July 8, 1927; s. Peter Arend and Clara Anna (Nordstrom) DeH.; m. Christopher Welles, Dec. 1957 (div. Jan. 1963). Student, Ill. Inst. Tech., 1944-45. Project dir. AID, Dept. State, Korea, 1958-61; est. Norman DeHaan Asso., Chgo., 1964—; pres. Norman DeHaan Assos., Inc., 1967—; regional rep. Nat. Accessions Com., Dept. of State's Art in Embassies Program, 1965-75. Art dir., Country Life Ins. Co., Chgo., 1947-48; archtl. and interior designer, Sidney Morris & Assos., Chgo., 1948-53; designer, architect, UN Korean Reconstrn. Agy., 1953-54; archtl. adviser, Office of Pres. Korea, 1953-55; asst. dir. design, Container Corp. of Am., Chgo., 1955-57. Dir. Lake Michigan Regional Planning Council, 1963-76; trustee Columbia Coll., Chgo., 1976-84, Chgo. Sch. Architecture Found., 1966-71. Served with USNR, 1945-46; with C.E. U.S. Army, 1950-52. Fellow Am. Soc. Interior Designers (nat. pres. 1974-75, chmn. Ednl. Found.); mem. AIA (nat. chmn. com. interior architecture 1976-78, bd. dirs. Chgo. chpt. 1981—, pres. Chgo. chpt. 1984). Clubs: Cliff Dwellers (v.p., pres.-elect 1984—), Arts (Chgo.)). Home: 237 Menomonee St Chicago IL 60614 Office: 355 N Canal St Chicago IL 60606

DEHART, A. ROBERT, college president; b. Bonner Springs, Kans., Dec. 11, 1923; s. Arla Lando and Lona Maggie (Dodd) DeH.; m. Rena Frabony; children: David, Robert, Donald. B.S., U. Calif., Berkeley, M.S. in Mech. Engring, 1950; Ed.D., Stanford U., 1960. Lectr. engring. U. Calif., Berkeley, 1949-50; instr. engring. Monterey Peninsula Coll., 1950-55, dean students, 1955-57, Foothill Coll., Palo Alto, Calif., 1957-62, dir. research, 1962-67; pres. DeAnza Coll., Cupertino, Calif., 1967—; exec. dir. Mgmt. Devel. Inst., 1975—. Served with USNR, 1942-46. Mem. Assn. Calif. Community Coll. Adminstrs. (pres. 1975-77, dir), Am. Assn. Community and Jr. Colls. (bd. dirs.), Sigma Xi, Tau Beta Pi, Phi Delta Kappa. Democrat. Club: Rotary. Home: 18400-49 Overlook Rd Los Gatos CA 95030 Office: DeAnza Coll Cupertino CA 95014

DEHART, ROBERT CHARLES, research institute executive; b. Laramie, Wyo., Aug. 16, 1917; s. Charles Edward and Harriet Irene (Tapling) DeH.; m. Ethel Mitchell Thompson, Sept. 20, 1941 (dec.); children: Michael Robert, Dayle Ann; m. Marion Winifred McDonald, Aug. 21, 1970; 1 stepdau., Meghan Caughey. B.S. in Civil Engring, U. Wyo., 1938; M.S., Ill. Inst. Tech., 1940, Ph.D., 1955. Design engr. Standard Oil Co. Ind., Whiting, 1940-46; assoc. prof. civil engring. Mont. State U., Bozeman, 1946-53; structural analyst Armed Forces Spl. Weapons Project., Washington, 1953-58; with Southwest Reserach Inst., San Antonio, Tex., 1958—, now v.p. Contbr. articles to profl. jours. Mem. ASME, Sigma Xi, Tau Beta Pi, Sigma Tau, Phi Kappa Phi. Presbyterian. Home: 403 La Jara St San Antonio TX 78209 Office: Southwest Research Institute 6220 Culebra Rd San Antonio TX 78284 *I have always guarded against letting the fear of failure have an influence on my decision to undertake or not undertake a task.*

DE HARTOG, JAN, writer; b. Haarlem, Holland, Apr. 22, 1914; s. Arnold Hendrik and Lucretia (Meyjes) de H.; m. Marjorie E. Mein, Sept. 1961; children—Sylvia, Arnold, Nicholas, Catherine, Eva, Julia. Student, Amsterdam Naval Coll., 1930. Author: plays Skipper Next to God, 1946, This Time Tomorrow, 1947, The Fourposter, 1951, William and Mary, 1964; novels The Lost Sea, 1951, The Distant Shore, 1952, The Little Ark, 1954, A Sailor's Life, 1956, The Spiral Road, 1957, The Inspector, 1960, Waters of the New World, 1961, The Artist, 1963, The Hospital, 1964, The Call of the Sea, 1966, The Captain, 1966, The Children, 1968, The Peaceable Kingdom, 1971, The Lamb's War, 1979; musical I Do, I Do, 1966. Mem. Soc. of Friends.

DE HAVILLAND, OLIVIA MARY, actress; b. Tokyo, Japan, July 1, 1916; naturalized, 1941; d. Walter Augustus and Lilian Augusta (Ruse) de H. (parents British subjects); m. Marcus Goodrich, Aug. 26, 1946 (div.); 1 son, Benjamin Briggs Goodrich; m. Pierre Galante, Apr. 2, 1955; 1 dau., Gisele. Ed. in schools and convent in, Calif., Mills College. Pres., Jury Cannes Film Festival, 1965; Made stage debut as Hermia in: Midsummer Night's Dream (Max Reinhardt prodn.), Hollywood Bowl, 1934; 1st motion picture in same role, 1935; starred: in pictures, including Gone With the Wind (nominated for Acad. award 1939), Strawberry Blonde, Captain Blood, Anthony Adverse, Robin Hood, Hold Back the Dawn, (nominated for Acad. award 1941), Princess O'Rourke, To Each His Own, (Acad. award for best actress performance 1946), Dark Mirror, Snake Pit, (nominated for Acad. award 1948, N.Y. Critics award 1948), The Heiress, (Acad. award for best actress performance 1949, New York Critics award), The Snake Pit, (Laurel award, best performance 1948-53), My Cousin Rachel, 1952, Not As A Stranger, 1954, Ambassador's Daughter, 1955 (Belgian Critics Prix Femina), Proud Rebel, 1957, Light in the Piazza, 1961, Lady in a Cage, 1963 (British films and filming award), Hush, Hush Sweet Charlotte, 1964, The Adventurers, 1969, Pope Joan, 1971, Airport '77, 1976, The Swarm, 1978; appeared: in play A Gift of Time, 1962; summer stock What Every Woman Knows, Westport, Conn., Easthampton, L.I., 1946, Candida, 1951; 245 performances, Transcontinental Tour, 1951-52; 100 performances Juliet, 1951; TV performances Noon Wine, 1966, The Screaming Woman, 1972; TV appearances include The Next Generations, 1979; lecture tours, U.S., 1971-78; toured, Army and Navy hosps, in, U.S., Alaska, Aleutians, South Pacific, 1943-44, Army and Navy hosps, in, Europe, (1957-61); participant: narration of France's Bicentennial gift to U.S. Son et Lumiere, 1976, Bicentennial Service, Am. Cathedral in Paris, 1976; Author: Every Frenchman Has One, 1962. Trustee Am. Coll. in Paris, 1970, 71, Am. Library in Paris, 1974-78. Recipient Women's Nat. Press Club award for outstanding accomplishment in theater presented by Pres. Truman, 1950; Am. Legion Humanitarian award, 1967. Mem. Screen Actors Guild, Acad. of Motion Picture Arts and Scis. Democrat. Episcopalian (lay reader, mem. altar guild). Address: BP 156 75764 Paris Cedex 16 France *

DEHAY, JOHN CARLISLE, JR., lawyer; b. Jones Prairie, Tex., Mar. 30, 1922; s. John Carlisle and Valda (Drury) DeH.; m. Barbara Jean Smith, Nov. 30, 1956; 1 dau., Leslie. B.B.A., So. Meth. U., 1949, LL.B., 1949. Bar: Tex. bar 1948. Mem. legal dept. Employers Casualty Co., Dallas, 1949-51; pvt. practice law DeHay & Blanchard, Dallas, 1951—; Dir. Tex. Assn. Def. Counsel, 1968. Served with AUS, 1942-45. Decorated D.S.M. Mem. Am. Coll. Trial Lawyers, Internat. Acad. Trial Lawyers, Am., Dallas bar assns. Baptist. Clubs: Woodvale Fishing (Mineola, Tex.); Dallas, Dallas Idlewild (Dallas); Brookhollow Golf. Home: 3201 Villanova St Dallas TX 75225 Office: 2300 South Tower Plaza of Americas Dallas TX 75201

DEHLINGER, PETER, geophysics educator; b. Berlin, Germany, Oct. 3, 1917; U.S., 1925, naturalized, 1940; s. Walter H. and Isolde M. (Nebel) D.; m. Evelyn Jean Davis, Apr. 1, 1941; children: Margaret Ann (Mrs. C.K. Wildenthal), Peter Jean. B.S. with distinction, U. Mich., 1940; M.S., Calif. Inst. Tech., 1943, Ph.D., 1950. Seismologist Shell Oil Co., Los Angeles, 1943-48; research geophysicist Battelle Meml. Inst., Columbus, Ohio, 1950-53; asso. prof. to prof. Tex. A. and M. Coll., 1954-62; prof. Oreg. State U., 1962-68, U. Conn., Storrs, 1968—; dir. Marine Scis. Inst., 1968-76; univ. asso. U. Hawaii, 1964-69; on leave as dir. marine geology and geophysics programs, ocean sci. tech. group Office Naval Research, Washington, 1966-68; vis. prof. U. Alaska, summer 1966; prof. Am. U., Washington, part-time, 1966-67; geophys. cons; prin. investigator on research projects supported by different fed. agys., 1960-66, 68—; Mem. exec. com. Assn. Sea Grant Dirs., 1972-74; mem. Conn. Coastal Mgmt. Com., 1971-72, Conn. Environ. Policy Com., 1970-71. Asso. editor: Jour. Phys. Oceanography, 1970-76; Author monograph; contbr. articles to tech. jours. and books. Dehlinger Seamount named, 1973. Fellow Geol. Soc. Am.; mem. Am. Geophys. Union, Seismol. Soc. Am., AAAS, Conn. Acad. Sci. and Engring. (charter), Soc. Exploration Geophysicists, Sigma Xi, Phi Beta Kappa, Phi Kappa Phi, Tau Beta Pi. Home: 32 Woodmont Dr Rural Route 3 Willimantic CT 06226

DEHMELT, HANS GEORG, physics educator; b. Germany, Sept. 9, 1922; U.S., 1952, naturalized, 1962; s. Georg Karl and Asta Ella (Klemmt) D.; 1 son, Gerd. Grad., Graues Kloster, Abitur, 1940; Ph.D. summa cum laude, U. Goettingen, 1950. Postdoctoral fellow U. Goettingen, Germany, 1950-52, Duke U., Durham, N.C., 1952-55; vis. asst. prof. U. Wash., Seattle, 1955, asst. prof. physics, 1956, asso. prof., 1957-61, prof., 1961—; cons. Varian Assos., Palo Alto, Calif., 1956-76. Contbr. articles to profl. jours. Recipient Humboldt prize, 1974; award in basic research Internat. Soc. Magnetic Resonance, 1980; NSF grantee, 1958—. Fellow Am. Phys. Soc. (Davisson-Germer prize 1970); mem. Am. Acad. Arts and Scis., Nat. Acad. Scis. Home: 1600 43d Ave E Seattle WA 98112 Office: Physics Dept FM 15 U Wash Seattle WA 98195

DEHNER, DOROTHY, painter, sculptor; b. Cleve.; d. Edward P. and Louise (Uphof) D.; m. David Smith, 1927 (div. 1952); m. Ferdinand Mann, Sept. 9, 1955 (dec.); stepchildren: Irwin Mann, Abigail Mann Thernstrom. Student, UCLA, then Art Students League, 1927-31; study and research abroad; B.S. in Art, Skidmore Coll., 1952; Ph.D. (hon.), Skidmore Coll., 1982. Lectr. Skidmore Coll., 1947, 54; worked Atelier 17, 1952-55; tchr. Indian Hill Music Workshop, Stockbridge, Mass., 1953-54, Barnard Sch. for Girls, N.Y.C., 1954-56. Exhibited: with David Smith, Albany Inst., 1947; one-man shows, Albany Inst., 1953, Rose Fried Gallery, N.Y.C., 1952, U. Va. Mus. Fine Art, 1954, Chgo. Art Inst., 1955, Willard Gallery, N.Y.C., 1955, 57, 60, 63, 66, 70, 73, Wittenborn's Gallery, 1956, Gres Gallery, Washington, 1959, Parson's-Dreyfuss Gallery, N.Y.C., 1981, A.M. Sachs Gallery, N.Y.C., 1981, 82; exhibited retrospective, Jewish Mus., N.Y., 1965; retrospective, Marian Locks Gallery, Phila., 1975, Ft. Wayne (Ind.) Mus., Barbara Fiedler Gallery, Washington, 1980, A.M. Sachs Gallery, N.Y.C., 1981; one-man retrospective traveling show to 20 colls. and museums, 1953-54, 63-64; exhibited in group shows, Whitney Mus. Am. Art, watercolors, 1951, 52, 53, sculpture, 1960, 63, Bklyn. Mus. Internat. Watercolor show, 1953, 55, 59, Mus. Modern Art, 1952, 54, 59-71, Met. Mus., N.Y.C., 1953, also important museums, U.S.A., France, show, Am. Sculptors Gallery Bernard, Paris, Italy, Holland, Germany, New Sculpture group, Stable Gallery, N.Y.C.; works in permanent collections, Hirshhorn Mus., Washington, Met. Mus., N.Y.C., Dept. State, Columbia, Jewett Art Center, Wellesley Coll., Munson Williams Proctor Inst., Utica, N.Y., Mus. Modern Art, Columbus Gallery Fine Art, Hyde Collection, Glens Falls, N.Y., 1st Nat. Bank, Chgo., Biria Acad. Art, Calcutta, India, Cleve Mus., N.Y. Bank for Savs., Mus. Palm Beaches, Fla., Phoenix Mus. Art, Seattle Art Mus., Met. Mus. N.Y.C., Minn. Mus. Art, Newark Mus., Phila. Mus. Art, Phila. Mus., Storm King Art Center, Mountainville, N.Y.; exhibited in various colls., numerous others; executed bronze relief, Rockefeller Center, bronze sculpture, AT&T hdqrs., N.Y. Med. Coll., Phoenix Mus.; Appeared on radio, NBC; Author: art criticism Archtl. Forum, 1947; foreword John Graham's System and Dialectics of Art, 1971; also poetry. Fellow Tamarind Workshop, 1965; Recipient 1st prize for drawing Audubon Ann., 1947; Art U.S.A., 1959; 1st prize for sculpture Kane Meml. Exhbn., Yaddo Found.; Women's Art Caucus award, 1983. Mem. Sculptors Guild, New Sculpture group Fedn. Am. Painters and Sculptors. Home: 33 Fifth Ave New York NY 10003 Studio: 41 Union Sq New York NY 10003 *Dedication, rather than "work" better characterizes the attitude of the working artist.*

DE HOFFMANN, FREDERIC, nuclear physicist, research institute executive; b. Vienna, Austria, July 8, 1924; came to U.S., 1941, naturalized, 1946; s. Otto and Marianne (Halphen) de H.; m. Patricia Lynn Stewart, June 10, 1953. B.S., Harvard U., 1945, M.A., 1947, Ph.D. (fellow NRC, 1946-48), 1948. Staff mem. Los Alamos Sci. Lab., 1944-46, 48-55, alternate asst. dir., 1950-51; cons. AEC, 1947-48, com. sr. responsible reviewers, 1947-51; cons. Joint Congl. Com. Atomic Energy, 1954; asst. v.p. nuclear planning Convair (div. Gen. Dynamics Corp.), San Diego, 1955; v.p. Gen. Dynamics Corp., 1955-67; also gen. mgr. Gen. Atomic div., 1955-59, pres., 1959-67, Gen. Atomic Europe, Zurich, Switzerland, 1960-67; v.p. Gulf Oil Corp.; also pres. Gulf Gen. Atomic and Gulf Gen. Atomic Europe, 1967-69; chancellor Salk Inst. Biol. Studies, 1970-71, pres., 1972—; chmn., pres. Salk Inst. Biotech./Indsl. Assocs. (SIBIA), 1981—; hon. prof. theoretical physics U. Vienna, 1968—; sci. sec. UN Internat. Conf. Peaceful Uses Atomic Energy, 1955; pres. Conf. Future Sci. and Tech., Austria, 1972; Governing bd. Courant Inst. Math., N.Y. U., 1968—; dir. Atomic

Indsl. Forum, 1962-70; bd. dirs. Salzburg Sem. in Am. Studies, 1978-81; mem. Nat. Acad. Sci. subcom. mgmt. and tech. Internat. Inst. Applied Systems Analysis, 1978-82. Author: (with K. M. Case and G. Placzek), Vol. 1) Introduction to the Theory of Neutron Diffusion, 1954, (with H. A. Bethe and S. S. Schweber) Vols. 1 and 2) Mesons and Fields, 1955. Trustee Salk Inst., 1970—, Scripps Clinic and Research Found., 1956-66. Decorated Cross of Honour for Sci. and Arts, Decoration of Honour for Merit in Silver, Decoration of Honour in Gold, Republic Austria). Fellow Am. Phys. Soc., Am. Nuclear Soc. (bd. dirs. 1964-67); mem. Harvard Alumni Assn. (dir. 1961-64), Sigma Xi. Clubs: Bohemian (San Francisco); Duquesne (Pitts.); Cosmos (Washington); Univ. (N.Y.C.); Atheneum (London). Home: 9736 La Jolla Farms Rd LaJolla CA 92037 Office: PO Box 85800 San Diego CA 92138

DEIBLER, WILLIAM EDWIN, newspaper editor; b. Altoona, Pa., Apr. 18, 1932; s. Edwin Howard and Elizabeth Grace (Sheehan) D.; m. Phyllis Maxine Gates, Jan. 17, 1953; children—Gail Marie, William Eric. B.A. in Journalism, Pa. State U., 1959. Staff writer Centre Daily Times, State College, Pa., 1958-60; editor Daily Messenger, Homestead, Pa., 1960-63; writer AP, 1964-68; legis. corr., then city editor Pitts. Post-Gazette, 1968-74, mng. editor, 1979—. Served with USAF, 1952-56; Korea. Decorated Commendation medal; recipient award disting. reporting public affairs Am. Polit. Sci. Assn., 1971, award for cultural affairs writing Golden Quill, 1983, award for news feature writing Keystone Press, 1983. Mem. Internat. Press Inst., Am. Press Inst., AP Mng. Editors Assn., Pa. Soc. Newspaper Editors Assn., Sigma Delta Chi, Kappa Tau Alpha; mem. Sigma Delta Epsilon. Home: 1233 Satellite Circle Pittsburgh PA 15241 Office: 50 Blvd Allies Pittsburgh PA 15222

DEIKEL, THEODORE, business executive; b. Mpls., Oct. 5, 1935; m. Beverly Fern, Sept. 11, 1960; children: Eve Michelle, Laura D., Daniel Adam, Andrew Joseph. Ed., U. Minn. With Fingerhut Corp., Minnetonka, Minn., successively v.p., sr. v.p., then pres., 1974-79, chief exec. officer, 1975-79, chmn. bd., 1979—; also dir.; chmn. bd. Pickwick Internat., Inc., 1979—; sr. v.p. Am. Can Co., 1979-81, exec. v.p., 1981-83. Trustee Blake Sch., Hopkins, Minn.; bd. govs. Methodist Hosp., Mpls.; bd. dirs. Minn. Orch. Assn.; mem. Minn. Gov.'s Loaned Exec. Action Program. Served with USMC, 1953-57. Office: 4400 Baker Rd Minnetonka MN 55343

DEINERT, HERBERT, educator; b. Wiedenbrück, Germany, Dec. 13, 1930; came to U.S., 1954, naturalized, 1959; m. Waltraut von der Emde, 1957; children—Erika, Mark. Ph.D., Yale, 1960. Mem. faculty U. Ga., Athens, 1959-61, Duke, 1961-65; mem. faculty Cornell U., Ithaca, N.Y., 1965—, chmn. dept. German lit., 1968-74. Mem. MLA, Am. Assn. Tchrs. German (pres. central N.Y. chpt.). Home: 130 Honness Ln Ithaca NY 14850

DEINHARDT, FRIEDRICH WILHELM, microbiologist, educator; b. Guetersloh, Germany, May 26, 1926; emigrated to U.S., 1954, naturalized, 1961; s. Walter Ernst and Luise (Fischer) D.; m. Jean Bannister Brown, July 2, 1959; children—Tobias Friedrich, Nicholas George. Student, U. Gottingen, 1946-48, U. Zurich, 1948; M.D., U. Hamburg, 1951. Intern, resident internal medicine, pathology U. Hosp., Hamburg, 1951-54; research fellow, asst. prof. Childrens Hosp., U. Pa., Phila., 1954-61; asso. prof., chmn. dept. microbiology Rush-Presbyn. St. Lukes Med. Center, U. Ill., 1961-66, prof. microbiology, 1966-77; prof. hygiene and microbiology U. Munich, W.Ger., 1977—; cons. NIH, Surg. Gen. U.S. Army, Bd. Health, Chgo. Served with German Army, 1943-45. Fellow Am. Acad. Microbiology; mem. Am. Assn. Immunology, Am. Soc. Clin. Investigation, German Assn. Against Virus Diseases (pres. 1980—). Home: Schoenegger Weg 5 D8000 Munich 90 Federal Republic Germany Office: Max v Pettenkofer-Institut Pettenkoferstr 9a D8000 Munich 2 Federal Republic Germany

DEISLER, PAUL FREDERICK, JR., oil company executive; b. El Paso, Tex., Jan. 20, 1926; s. Paul Frederick and Jeanie Donnelly (Monroe) D.; m. Ellen Louise Bardwell, June 15, 1950; children: Jane Ellen, Paul Conrad, Julia Monroe. B.S. in Chem. Engring, Tex. A&M U., 1948; M.S., Princeton U., 1949, Ph.D., 1952. With Shell Oil Co., various locations, 1952—, v.p. transp. and supplies, 1969-71; dir. supply and refining compañía Shell de Venezuela, 1971-73; v.p. Chem. Co., Houston, 1973-74; v.p. research and engring. products Shell Oil Co., Houston, 1974-76, v.p. health, safety and environment, 1976—; dir. Chem. Industry Inst. Toxicology, 1975—; bd. dirs. Am. Indsl. Health Council, 1977-81, 84—; chmn. adv. council dept. chem. engring. Princeton U., 1978-81; alumni councilor Tex. A&M Research Found., 1977—. Bd. dirs. ARC, Houston, 1975-80; chmn. fin. com. Houston Sci. Fair, 1974-76. Served with USN, 1944-46; PTO. Mem. U.S. Naval Inst., Assn. Princeton Grad. Alumni (dir. 1976-79), Am. Petroleum Inst. (chmn. health, environ. and safety gen. com. 1983—), Soc. Chem. Industry, Am. Chem. Soc., AAAS, Am. Inst. Chem. Engrs., Soc. Risk Analysis, Sigma Xi, Tau Beta Pi, Phi Kappa Phi. Club: Petroleum. Home: 11215 Wilding Ln Houston TX 77024 Office: PO Box 2463 Houston TX 77001

DEISS, WILLIAM PAUL, JR., physician, educator; b. Shelbyville, Ky., Feb. 1, 1923; s. William Paul and Florence (Schilling) D.; m. Bettye Jane Baker, May 5, 1948 (div. 1979); children: Diana Elizabeth Deiss Mysliwiec, William David, Paula Jane Deiss Roberts.; m. Elizabeth Matson Benham, June 27, 1981. B.S., U. Notre Dame, 1943; M.D., U. Ill., 1945. Diplomate: Am. Bd. Internal Medicine (mem.). Intern U. Wis., 1945-46, resident, fellow in medicine, 1948-54; asst. prof., asso. prof. medicine Duke, 1954-58, asst. prof. biochemistry, 1954-58; assoc. prof., prof. medicine and biochemistry Ind. U., 1958-68; prof. U. Tex., Galveston, 1968—, chmn. dept. medicine, 1968-84; mem. adv. com. NIH. Contbr. articles to profl. jours. Served from 1st lt. to capt. M.C., U.S. Army, 1946-48. Fellow ACP; mem. Am. Fedn. Clin. Research (past sec.-treas.), Am. Soc. Clin. Investigation, Assn. Am. Physicians, Endocrine Soc., Central Soc. Clin. Research. Home: 7618 Beluche St Galveston TX 77550

DEITCHER, HERBERT, financial executive; b. Cohoes, N.Y., Oct. 27, 1933; s. John and Etta (Carr) D.; m. Barbara Judith Goldberg, Sept. 1, 1958; children: Janet Lee, Steven Robert.; B.B.A., Siena Coll., 1955; M.B.A., Boston U., 1960. With Raytheon Co., 1959—, asst. treas. fin. planning and controls, Lexington, Mass., 1967-69, asst. treas. ops., 1970-73, dir. internat. financing, 1973-78, v.p. internat. financing, 1979-83, v.p., treas., 1983—; instr. fin. Northeastern U., 1967-73; dir. Baybank Middlesex. Bd. dirs., treas. Lynnfield Inst. for Elderly (Mass.), 1982-83; bd. dirs., officer Temple Beth Shalom, Peabody, Mass., 1973-83. Served with U.S. Army, 1956-58; served to capt. USAAF, 1943-46. Fellow Planning Execs. Inst. (nat. v.p. 1964-72); mem. Fin. Execs. Inst. (internat. liason and Policy com. 1970—), Aerospace Industries Assn. Am. (interant. fin. group 1973—), Govt. Contract Mgmt. Assn., Beta Gamma Sigma, Delta Epsilon Sigma. Jewish. Home: 9 Longbow Circle Lynnfield MA 01940 Office: Raytheon Co 141 Spring St Lexington MA 02173

DEITRICK, JOHN ENGLISH, physician; b. Watsontown, Pa., Apr. 13, 1905; s. Edgar Dentler and Capitola H. (Heine) D.; m. Dorothy Geib, May 9, 1936; children—Sarah, John, William. B.S., Princeton, 1929; M.D., Johns Hopkins, 1933. Diplomate: Nat. Bd. Med. Examiners. Intern Johns Hopkins Hosp., 1933-34; resident medicine N.Y. Hosp., 1934-36; asst. Cornell Med. Coll., 1934-36, instr., 1936-42, asst. prof. clin. medicine, 1942-44, asso., 1944-52; dir. 2d Cornell Med. Div., Bellevue Hosp., N.Y.C., 1946-49; dir. survey med. edn. AMA and Assn. Am. Med. Colls., 1949-52; Magee prof. medicine Jefferson Med. Coll., Phila., 1952-57; dean prof. medicine Cornell U. Med. Coll., 1957-69; exec. dir. Assn. Med. Schs. Greater N.Y., 1969—; pres. N.Y. Acad. Medicine, 1970; attending physician N.Y. Hosp., N.Y.C.; Dir. Prudential Ins. Co., Prudential Life Ins. Co., Newark.; Bd. Dirs. N.Y.C. div. Am. Cancer Soc. Author: (with Robert C. Berson, M.D.) Medical Schools in the United States at the Mid-Century, 1953. Recipient Regional award Am. Cancer Soc., 1974. Fellow A.C.P.; mem. AMA, Harvey Soc., Pa., N.Y. County med. socs., N.Y. Acad. Medicine, Coll. Physicians Phila., Assn. Am. Physicians, Assn. Am. Med. Colls. (pres. 1963-64), Phi Beta Kappa, Sigma Xi. Club: Century Assn. University (N.Y.C.). Home: 69 Rocklege Bd Bronxville NY Office: 19 E 98th St New York City NY 10029

DEJARNETTE, EDWARD, ambassador; b. Richmond, Va, Jan. 15, 1938. B.A., U. Va., 1959, LL.B., 1963; M.S., George Washington U., 1978. Fgn. service officer U.S. Embassy, Niamey, 1965-67; state coordinator Pollard for Gov. campaign, 1968; fundraiser Capitol devel. Office, Randolph-Macon Coll., Richmond, VA, 1969-70; dep. dir. for Ecuador Peace Corps, Quito, 1970-72; dep. dir. for Lain Am. Peace Corps., 1972-73; dep. chief mission, Libreville, 1975-77; personnel offficer Bur. Personnel, Dept. State, Washington, 1978-80; dep. chief mission, Dakar, 1980-83, U.S. ambassador to Central African Republic, Bangui, 1983—. Served with USCG, 1960-64. Office: US Embassy Ave President Dacko BanguiCentral African Republic *

DE JART, JOHN EDWARD, association executive; b. Nacmine, Alta., Can., Apr. 20, 1920; s. Joseph Bertram and Marjory (Wright) de Hart. B.A., LL.B., U. Alta., 1942; grad., Can. Army Staff Coll., 1955. Commd. lt. Canadian Army, 1940, advanced through grades to lt. col., served various locations including Korea; ret., 1971; exec. Can. Corps of Commissionaires, Ottawa, Ont., 1974—; commr. Fed. Dist. St. John Ambulance Brigade; exec. dir. Conf. Def. Assns., Ottawa, 1980—. Decorated Mil. Cross Govt. of Can. Mem. Royal Can. Arty. Assn. (pres. 1978-79), Royal Can. Mil. Inst. Club: Laurentian. Home: 505 St Laurent Blvd #1602 Ottawa ON Canada K1K 3X4 Office: HQ Can Corps of Commissionaires 100 Gloucester St Ottawa ON Canada K2P 0A4

DE JESUS-TORE, ROBERTO, commercial banker; b. San Juan, P.R., Julu 27, 1918; s. Francisco R. de J. and Graciela Toro; m. Sylvia Pou, Aug. 17, 1946; children: Roberto, Sylvia, Nestor, Ani. B.S. in Econs., Wharton Sch.,, U. Pa., M.B.A. Vice-pres. Govt. Devel. Bank, San Juan, 1951-54; exec. v.p. Banco de Ponce, San Juan, 1954-59, pres. chief exec. officer, 1959-81, chmn. chief exec. officer, 1981-82, chmn. exec. com., 1983—; dir. Union Carbide Corp., Danbury, Conn., P.R. Cement Corp., San Juan. Bd. govs. ARS, Washington, 1981—. Served with U.S. Army, 1943-44. Office: Banco de Ponce GPO Box 3108 San Juan PR 00936

DE JOHNETTE, JACK, musician; b. Chgo., Aug. 9, 1942; s. Jack and Eva Jeanette (Wood) DeJ.; m. Lydia Ann Herman, Aug. 4, 1968; children: Farah, Minya Erica. Student, Wilson Jr. Coll., Chgo., 1959-60. Pianist with various jazz bands, Chgo., 1957-64; drummer, with John Coltrane, 1962, Miles Davis, 1967-70, Bill Evans, 1966, Charles Lloyd, 1963-65; band leader, with Directions and Spl. Edit., N.Y.C., 1975—; rec. artist, CBS, 1973-74, Fantasy Records, 1975-77, ECM records, 1978—; tchr., Creative Music Studio, Woodstock, N.Y.; Mem. in: Downbeat Mag, 1979; composer numerous rec. albums and compositions; author: The Art of Improvisation, 1981. Recipient numerous awards including Grand Prix Du Disque, Acad. Jazz, Paris, 1978; named Most Influential Musician on His Instrument for the 70's Musician Mag., 1980; NEA fellow, 1978; CAPS composers grantee, 1980. Office: care ECM Records/Warner Bros 75 Rockefeller Plaza New York NY 10019 *

DE JONG, ARTHUR JAY, college president; b. Paterson, N.J., Feb. 24, 1934; s. Peter A. and Anna (Vander Schaaf) De J.; m. Joyce Van Doorn, Dec. 21, 1957; children: Mark, Beth, Paul, Ruth and Richard (twins). B.A., Central Coll., Pella, Iowa, 1956; B.D., Western Theol. Sem., 1959; M.Th., Princeton Theol. Sem., 1962; S.T.D., San Francisco Theol. Sem., 1971. Chaplain Central Coll., 1960-66, dir. counseling, 1966-69, asso. acad. dean, 1969-71, acting acad. dean, 1971-72, asst. to pres., 1972-78, instr. in religion, 1960-62, asst. prof. religion, 1962-68, assoc. prof., 1968-72, prof., 1972-78; pres. Muskingum Coll., 1978—; cons. Council Advancement Small Colls., 1976-78. Author: Making It To Adulthood: The Emerging Self, 1972. Office: Muskingum Coll Office of Pres New Concord OH 43762

DEKKER, GEORGE GILBERT, language educator, writer; b. Long Beach, Calif., Sept. 8, 1934; s. Gilbert J. and Laura (Barnes) D.; m. Linda Jo Bartholomew, Aug. 31, 1973; children by previous marriage: Anna Allegra, Clare Joy, Ruth Siobhan, Laura Daye. B.A. in English, U. Calif.-Santa Barbara, 1955, M.A., 1958; M.Lit., Cambridge U. (Eng.), 1961; Ph.D. in English, U. Essex (Eng.), 1967. Lectr. U. Wales, Swansea, 1962-64; lectr. in lit. U. Essec, 1964-69; reader in lit. U. Essex, 1969-72, dean Sch. Comparative Studies, 1969-71; assoc. prof. English Stanford U. (Calif.), 1972-74, prof., 1974—, chmn. dept., 1978-81. Author: Sailing After Knowledge, 1963, James Fenimore Cooper the Novelist, 1967; auhtor: Coleridge and the Literature of Sensibility, 1978; editor: Donald Davie: The Responsibilities of Literature, 1983. Nat. Endowment Humanities fellos, 1977; Inst. Advanced Studies in Humanities fellow U. Edniburgh(Scotland), 1982. Mem. MLA, Internat. Assn. Univ. Profs. English. Democrat. Home: 1863 Park Blvd Palo Alto CA 94306 *Over the past twenty-five years I have divided my personal and professional life between the U.S. and Britian—not England alone, but Ireland, Scotland and Wales, too. This experience has given the distinctive stamp to my work as a teacher and writer, making me as much at home with Scott as with Hawthorne, with a British as well as an American university. I think I might write a good book on Henry James some day.*

DEKKER, MARCEL, pub. co. exec.; b. Amsterdam, The Netherlands, Feb. 12, 1931; came to U.S., 1939, naturalized, 1945; s. Maurits and Rozetta S. (Roos) D.; m. Harriett Gromb, July 21, 1967; children—Russell Maurits, David Robert, Jacqueline. B.S., N.Y. U., 1957. Advt. and import mgr. Intersci. Pub. Co., N.Y.C., 1958-62; pres., chief exec. officer Marcel Dekker, Inc., N.Y.C., 1963—; mng. dir. Marcel Dekker, AG, Basel, Switzerland, 1968—. Served with USAF, 1951-55. Club: Burning Tree Country (Greenwich, Conn.). Home: 41 Londonderry Dr Greenwich CT 06830 Office: 270 Madison Ave New York NY 10016

DEKKER, MAURITS, publisher, editor; b. Amsterdam, Holland, Mar. 18, 1899; s. Marcus and Elisabeth D.; m. Rozetta Sophia Roos, July 2, 1925; children: Elisabeth Emma, Andrew, Marcel. Degree in Chemistry, Physics and Microbiology, U. Amsterdam, 1923; D. honoris causa, N.Y. Poly. Inst., 1982. Pres., founder Dekker & Nordemann, Amsterdam; pres., founder Intersci. Pubs., N.Y.C., 1940-61, Elsevier Pub. Co., 1940-53; v.p. John Wiley, N.Y.C., 1961-64; chmn. Marcel Dekker, Inc., N.Y.C., 1966—; cons. Kodansha, Tokyo, 1966—. Mem. AAAS, N.Y. Acad. Sci. Office: 270 Madison Ave New York NY 10016

DEKMEJIAN, RICHARD HRAIR, political science educator; b. Aleppo, Syria, Aug. 3, 1933; came to U.S., 1950, naturalized, 1955; s. Hrant H. and Vahede V. (Matossian) D.; m. Anoush Hagopian, Sept. 19, 1954; children: Gregory, Armen, Haig. B.A., U. Conn., 1959; M.A., Boston U., 1960; Middle East Inst. cert. (pres's. fellow, Gulbenkian fellow), Columbia U., 1964, Ph.D., 1966. Mem. faculty SUNY, Binghamton, 1964—, prof. polit. sci., 1977—; also master Hinman Coll., 1971-72; vis. prof. Columbia U., U. Pa., 1977-78; v.p. Internat. Mktg. and Devel. Corp., 1978—; dir. Ctr. for Research and Devel. Inc. Author: Egypt Under Nasir, 1971, Patterns of Political Leadership: Israel, Lebanon, and Egypt, 1975; Contbr. articles to profl. jours. Pres. So. Tier Civic Ballet Co., 1973-76. Served with AUS, 1955-57. Mem. Am. Polit. Sci. Assn., Middle East Inst., Middle East Studies Assn., Internat. Polit. Sci. Assn., Pi Sigma Alpha, Phi Alpha Theta. Home: 917 Country Club Rd Binghampton NY 13903

DE KOONING, ELAINE, artist; b. N.Y.C., Mar. 12, 1920; d. Charles Frank and Mary Ellen (O'Brien) Fried; m. William de Kooning, Dec. 9, 1943. Hon. degree, Western Coll. Women, Oxford, Ohio, 1964. One-woman shows include, Stable Gallery, N.Y.C., 1954, 56, Tibor de Nagy Gallery, N.Y.C., 1957, Graham Gallery, N.Y.C., 1960, 61, 63, 65, U. N.M., 1957, Mus. N.M., Santa Fe, 1959, Gump's, San Francisco, Washington Gallery Modern Art, presdl. portraits, 1964, Lyman Allen Mus., New London, Conn., retrospective, 1959, Montclair (N.J.) Art Mus., 1973, Benson Gallery, Bridgehampton, N.Y., Ill. Wesleyan U., Bloomington, 1975, Coll. St. Catherine, St. Paul, rep. permanent collections, Mus. Modern Art. Loeb Center, N.Y.C., Kennedy Library, Cambridge, Mass., Truman Library, Independence, Mo., Elmira (N.Y.) Coll., Ark. Arts Center, Little Rock, Jewish Community Center, Bayonne, N.J., Montclair (N.J.) Art Mus., Ciba-Geigy Corp., Ardsley, N.Y., Neuberger Mus., Purchase, N.Y., also pvt. collections; tchr., U. N.Mex., 1959, Pa. State U., 1960, Contemporary Art Assn., Houston, 1952, U. Calif. at Davis, 1963-64, Yale, 1967, Carnegie-Mellon U., 1969-70, U. Pa., 1970-72, Wagner Coll., 1970, U. Pa., 1971—, N.Y. Studio Sch., Paris, France, 1974—, Parsons Sch. Fine Art, 1974-76; Lamar Dodd chair, U. Ga., Athens, 1976—. Home: 51 Raynor St Freeport NY 11520 Office: care Graham Gallery 1014 Madison Ave New York NY 10021

DE KOONING, WILLEM, artist; b. Rotterdam, Holland, Apr. 24, 1904; s. Leendert and Cornelia (Nobel) de K.; m. Elaine Marie Catherine Fried, Dec. 7, 1943. Student, Acad. Fine Arts, Rotterdam, 1916-24. Faculty Black Mountain Coll., N.C., 1948, Yale, 1950-51; Mem. Nat. Inst. Arts and Letters. Painter mural, Hall of Pharmacology, N.Y. World's Fair, 1939; Contbr. articles to popular and profl. publs.; one-man shows, Egan Gallery, 1948, 51, Sidney Janis Gallery, 1953, 56, 59, 62, Paul Kantor Gallery, 1961, M. Knoedler & Co. Inc., 1967, 69, Xavier Fourcade, Inc., N.Y.C., 1975, 76, 77, 78, Stedelijk Mus., Amsterdam, Netherlands, 1968, Mus. Modern Art, N.Y.C., 1969, Art Inst. Chgo., Los Angeles County Mus. Art, Balt. Mus., 1972, Seattle Art Mus., 1976, Stedelijk Mus., Amsterdam, Guggenheim Mus., N.Y.C., 1978, Carnegie Inst., Pitts., 1979-80, others, C. Grimaldis Gallery, Baltimore, 1982, Retrospective, Whitney Mus. Am. Art, N.Y.C., 1983; represented in permanent collections, Mus. Modern Art, St. Louis Art Mus., Chgo. Art Inst., Met. Mus. Art, Whitney Mus. Am. Art, N.Y.C., Guggenheim Mus., Carnegie Inst., Stedelijk Mus., Australian Nat. Gallery, also pvt. collections, Nelson Rockefeller, Mrs. John D. Rockefeller, III. Recipient Logan purchase prize Chgo. Art Inst., 1951 Gold medal for painting Am. Acad. Arts and Letters, 1975; Andrew W. Mellon prize, 1979; decorated officer Order of Orange-Nassau, Netherlands, 1979. Office: Woodbine Dr The Springs East Hampton Long Island NY 11937 *

DELACATO, CARL HENRY, educator; b. Pottstown, Pa., Sept. 10, 1923; s. Ercole S. and Julia (de Bartolomeo) D.; m. Janice E. Fernstrom, June 20, 1951; children—Elizabeth F., Carl Henry, David F. B.S. in Edn, West Chester State Coll., 1945, M.S., U. Pa., 1948, Ed.D., 1952. Asst. headmaster Chestnut Hill Acad., Phila., 1945-64; founder, dir. Chestnut Hill Reading Clinic, 1948; prof. Avery Postgrad. Inst., Phila., 1963-73; prof., chmn. dept. devel. edn. U. Plano, Tex., 1965-70; asso. dir. inst. Para Le Orgn. Neurologica, Buenos Aires, 1967-70, Insts. Achievement Human Potential, Phila., 1953-73; dir. Inst. Rehab. of Brain Injured, Morton, Pa., 1974—, Centrao de Rahabilitacao NS de Gloria, Sao Paulo, Brazil, 1976—; pres. Delacato & Delacato Consultants in Learning, Plymouth Meeting, Pa., 1970—; cons. Asociacion Para Ayuda Lesionados Cerebales, Barcelona, Spain, 1970—; hon. dir. of The Delacato Center, Holon, Israel, 1974—; dir. of Delacato project at Padagogische Hochschule Rheinland Abteilung fur Heilpadaggogik, Koln, W. Ger., 1975—, Delacato project TIKVA, Haifa, Israel, 1976—, others. Author: The Treatment and Prevention of Reading Problems, 1959, Diagnosis and Treatment of Speech and Reading Problems, 1963, Elementary School of the Future, 1964, Neurological Organization and Reading, 1966, A New Start for the Child with Reading Problems, 1970, The Ultimate Stranger, The Autistic Child, 1974, contbr. numerous articles on rehab. and edn. to profl. jours.; editor: Am. Lectures in Edn. and Learning, 1969—. Vice pres. U.S. World Orgn. Human Potential, 1968-73; mem. Pa. Commn. Human Potential, 1969-70, Gov. Sergipe (Brazil) Commn. Human Potential, 1968-70; bd. dirs. Centre for Neurol. Rehab., Morton, Pa., 1974—. Recipient Disting. Alumnus award West Chester Coll., 1978, award Greater Long Beach (Calif.) Soc. for Autistic Children, 1977, Diploma Socio-Benmento, Porto Allegra, Brazil, 1965, Diploma de Honra Ho Merito, Piracioba, Brazil, 1965, Diploma de Reconheciemen, to, Sao Paulo, 1965, Diploma e Medalha Comemorative de APAE, Rio de Janeiro, 1965, Gold Medal Honor, Brazil, 1960, Statuette with Pedestal award Internat. Rehab. Forum, 1966, 1st. Trailblazer award U. Plano, 1966. Mem. NSF. Address: Thomas Rd Philadelphia PA 19118

DE LA COLINA, RAFAEL, Mexican diplomat; b. Tulancingo, Hidalgo, Mexico, Sept. 20, 1898; s. Manuel and Maria (Riquelme) de la C.; m. Ruth Rosecrans, 1920 (dec. 1929); children: Ruth (Mrs. Francis W. Silk), Rafael; m. Amanda Steinmeyer, 1944. M.A., Nat. U. Mexico, 1918; postgrad., Fgn. Service Acad., Mexico, 1918. Held various posts in Consular Service, 1918-34; consul gen. of, Mexico, San Antonio, 1934-35, N.Y.C., 1936-43; minister counselor Mexican embassy, Washington, 1943-44; E.E. and M.P. of Mexico, Washington, 1944-48, A.E. and P., 1949-53; permanent rep. to UN, 1953-59; ambassador of Mexico, to Can., 1959-62, to Japan, 1962-64; ambassador, rep. of Mexico to OAS, Washington, 1965-84, ambassador emeritus, 1980—; Mexican del. Japanese Peace Conf., San Francisco, 1951; chmn. Mexican del. Conf. on Living Resources of Sea, Ciudad Trujillo, Dominican Republic, 1956; acting chmn. Mexican del. to Gen. Assembly of UN, 1953-57; chmn. Mexican dels. Inter-Am. Confs. and Gen. Assemblies Sessions, 1965—, Meeting of Consultation of OAS, 1965—, Intelsat, Washington, 1970-71. Author books on internat. law.; Contbr. articles to profl. jours. Founder, hon. pres. Mexican Welfare Com., Los Angeles. Decorated Order of Merit, Chile; Order Honneur et Merite, Haiti; Order of Merit Juan Pablo Duarte, Dominican Republic; Order Vasco Nunez de Balboa, Panama; Order Rising Sun, Japan; Order San Carlos, Colombia; Order Libertador, Venezuela; Order of Sun, Peru; Order Civic Merit Belisario Dominguez Mexican Senate, 1974. Mem. Am. Soc. Internat. Law, Mexican Acad. Internat. Law, Nat. Hist. and Lit. Soc. (Mexico City). Home: 6304 Evermay Dr McLean VA 22101 Office: 2440 Massachusetts Ave NW Washington DC 20008

DE LAET, WILLIAM THOMAS, restaurant executive; b. S.I., N.Y., June 28, 1942; s. William St. Claire de laet and Mildred (McClaughry) de L.; m. Ottilie de Laet-Wagenthaller, Dec. 27, 1971; children: Sonya, Sharon, Charles Hampton. A.A., S.I. Community Coll., 1965; B.A., Wagner Coll., 1968. Dir. tng. Wetson's Corp., Valley Stream, N.Y., 1966-68; regional mgr. Restaurant Assn., Miami, Fla., 1968-72; restaurant mgr. Burger King Corp., Miami, 1972-73, dist. mgr., 1973-75, v.p., regional mgr., 1975-81, sr. v.p., 1981—. Bd. govs. Barry U., Miami, 1980—, trustee, Miami, 1981—. Served with USAF, 1959-63. Mem. Nat. Restaurant Assn., Fla. Restaurant Assn. Republican. Roman Catholic. Home: 7300 SW 167 St Miami FL 33157

DE LA GARZA, E(KIKA), congressman; b. Mercedes, Tex., Sept. 22, 1927; s. Dario and Elisa (Villarreal) de la G.; m. Lucille Alamia, May 29, 1953; children: Jorge Luis, Michael Alberto, Angela Dolores. Student, Pan Am. Coll., Edinburg, Tex., 1947-48; LL.B., St. Mary's U., San Antonio, 1951. Bar: Tex. 1951. Mem. Tex. Ho. of Reps. from Hidalgo County, 1953-64, 89th-98th Congresses 15th Dist. Tex., chmn. Com. on Agr. Served with USNR, World War II; with AUS, Korea. Democrat. Office: 1401 Longworth House Office Bldg Washington DC 20515

DELAGI, EDWARD FRANCIS, physician; b. N.Y.C., Nov. 4, 1911; s. Michael Nicholas and Angela (Ciani) D.; m. Westa Vespa, Feb. 16, 1941; children—West Ann (Mrs. Richard Hanafin), Edwina (Mrs. Donald Askew). B.S., Fordham U., 1934; M.D., Hahnemann Med. Coll., 1938. Intern Fordham Hosp., Bronx, N.Y., 1938-40; resident Bronx VA Hosp., 1951-54, chief ward sect. phys. medicine and rehab., 1954-56; dir. phys. medicine and rehab. Misericordia Hosp., Bronx, 1958-65; attending physician Bronx Municipal Hosp. Center, 1956—; cons. phys. med. and rehabilitation No. Westchester Hosp., Misericordia Hosp., Bronx, St. Joseph's Hosp., Yonkers, N.Y.; asst. prof. dept. rehab. medicine Albert Einstein Coll. Med., Bronx, 1950-55, asso. prof., 1959, 64, prof., 1964—. Served with AUS, 1941-45. Decorated Bronze Star. Fellow A.C.P., Am. Acad. Phys. Medicine and Rehab., N.Y. Acad. Medicine; mem. AAAS, Am. Congress Phys. Medicine, N.Y. Acad. Sci. Home: 73 Heatherdell Rd Ardsley NY 10052 Office: Dept Rehabilitation Medicine Albert Einstein College of Medicine 1300 Morris Park Av Bronx NY 10461

DELAHANTY, DAVID, university president, educational administrator; b. N.Y.C., July 27, 1935; s. Patrick D. and Eileen (Keating) O'Connor. B.A., Catholic U., 1958; M.A., U. Detroit, 1961; M.S., Syracuse U., 1966, Ph.D., 1972. Tchr. St. Joseph High Sch., Detroit, 1958-62; tchr., prin. Christian Bros. Acad., Syracuse, N.Y., 1962-69; asst. prof. Manhattan Coll., Bronx, N.Y., 1970-75, assoc. prof., 1975-82, chmn. edn. dept., 1978-82, acting dean, 1979-80; pres. Lewis U., Romeoville, Ill., 1982—. Author: Helping Teachers Grow, 1975; editor: Manhattan College Self-Study, 1981. Trustee LaSalle Acad., N.Y.C., Christian Bros. Coll., Memphis. Syracuse U. fellow, 1969-70. Mem. Am. Assn. Higher Edn., Assn. Cath. Colls. and Univs., Fedn. Ind. Ill. Colls. and Univs., Phi Beta Kappa, Kappa Delta Pi. Roman Catholic. Lodge: Rotary/Joliet, Ill. Office: Lewis U Rt 53 Romeoville IL 60441

DELAHAY, PAUL, educator; b. Sas Van Gent, Netherlands, Apr. 6, 1921; came to the U. S., 1946, naturalized, 1955; s. Jules and Helene (Flahou) D.; m. Yvonne Courroye, 1962. B.S. in Gen. Engring, U. Brussels, 1941, M.S. in Chemistry, 1945, U. Liege, 1944; Ph.D. in Chemistry, U. Ore., 1948. Instr. chemistry U. Brussels, 1945-46; research asso. U. Ore., 1948-49; faculty La. State U., 1949-65, prof. chemistry, 1955-56, Boyd prof. chemistry, 1956-65; prof. chemistry N.Y. U., N.Y.C., 1965—, Frank J. Gould prof. sci., 1974—. Author: New Instrumental Methods in Electrochemistry, 1954, Instrumental Analysis, 1957, Double Layer and Electrode Kinetics, 1965; Editor: Advances in Electrochemistry, 1961-74. Guggenheim fellow Cambridge (Eng.) U., 1955-56, N.Y. U., 1971-72; Fulbright prof. Sorbonne, Paris, France, 1962-63; Recipient medal U. Brussels, 1963, Heyrovsky medal Czechoslovak Acad. Sci., 1965. Mem. Am. Chem. Soc. (award pure chem. 1955, Southwest award 1959), Electrochem. Soc. (Turner prize 1951, Palladium award 1967, chmn. theoretical div. 1957-59), AAAS, Am. Phys. Soc., Internat. Union Pure and Applied Chemistry (chmn. comm. electrochem. data 1959-63, titular mem. analytical sect. 1961-65), Sigma Xi. Home: 37 Washington Sq W New York City NY 10011

DELAKAS, DANIEL LIUDVIKO, retired foreign language educator; b. Springfield, Mass., Aug. 25, 1921; s. Alexander and Eva (Poska) D.; m. Mimi Cordich, July 22, 1945; 1 son, David Mark. Student, Smith Coll., summers 1936-40, U. Rochester, 1940-42; A.B., Bklyn. Coll., 1946; postgrad., Columbia, 1946, U. Paris (France), 1948; diploma, U. Firenze, Italy, 1957; postdoctoral, Sophia U., Tokyo, 1974, Ill. State U., 1974, Harvard Alumni Coll., 1977, 79, 81. From lectr. to asst. prof. Northwestern U., 1948-56; prof. Romance langs. Ripon (Wis.) Coll., 1956-83, chmn. dept., 1956-69, 74-83; fellow Harvard U., 1954, 73; vis. scholar Harvard Alumni Coll., 1975-79, vis. fellow, 1977, 78; fellow E. Asian Summer Inst. in Japanese, U. Ill., Urbana, 1972, Japanese Studies in Liberal Arts Coll., Monmouth Coll., 1974, Earlham Coll., 1975; vis. summer prof. U. Wash., 1960, U. Maine, 1961, U. Besançon, France, 1962, 63, Stillman Coll., Tuscaloosa, Ala., 1964, Tufts U. (also asso. dir. NDEA Inst.), 1965, U. Toulouse, France, 1966, 68, U. Alaska, 1967; fgn. lang. orientation officer NBBS-Holland-Am. Lines, summers 1950-56; reader French advanced placement Ednl. Testing Service, 1958-63; cons., fgn. lang. editor Sci. Research Assos., 1963-65; academic dir. Academic Year Abroad, Inc., Paris, 1969-70; cons., conf. participant UNESCO, Paris, 1970; Mem. charter com., constn. writer, regional pres. N.E. Wis. Fgn. Lang. Orgn. (New-Flo), 1968-69; exec. com. Insts. Coll. Teaching as a Career, Marquette U.-U. Wis. at Madison, 1960-63; mem. exec. steering com. Inst. Humanities for Mid-west Coll. Faculty Mems., U. Chgo., 1971-73; participant Mid-West faculty seminars U. Chgo. Center for Continuing Edn., 1974, 75, 77, 78, 80, 81, 82, 83; participant English as fgn. lang. seminar Harvard U., summer 1983; vis. cons. in English as fgn. lang. U. Oaxaca (Mex.), 1983. Contbr. to yearbooks, encys. Served with USAAF, 1942-43, 104th Inf. Div., 1944-45. Decorated Presdl. citation, Bronze Star; chevalier Palmes Académiques, 1967. Mem. AAUP, Modern Lang. Assn. (co-editor annual French 17th Century Studies 1952—), Wis. Assn. Presidents and Deans, Am. Assn. Tchrs. French, Am. Assn. Tchrs. Italian, Internat. Comparative Lit. Assn., Assn. Internat. des études françaises, Assn. Internat. des Docteurs de l'Univ. de Paris, Phi Sigma Iota (nat. exec. sec. 1964-74). Home: 74 Pigeon Hill St Rockport MA 01966 *There is great joy in the very process of learning, no matter what the age, no matter what the field.*

DE LA MADRID HURTADO, MIGUEL, president of Mexico; b. Colima, Colombia, Dec. 12, 1934. Law degree with hon. mention for thesis, Nat. Autonomous U. Mexico, 1957; M.P.A., Harvard U., 1965. With legal dept. Nat. Bank Fgn. Trade, 1953-57; adviser to mgmt. Bank of Mexico, 1960-65; asst. dir. gen. credit Mexican Ministry Treasury, 1965-70, gen. dir. credit, 1972-75, undersec. treasury and pub. credit, 1975-79; asst. dir. fin. PEMEX, 1970-72; minister nat. planning and budget Govt. of Mexico, 1979-82; pres. Mexico, Mexico City, 1982—; adviser Mexican Soc. Indsl. Credit, Mexican Ins. Co., Aeromexico, Nat. Bank Fgn. Commerce, Nat. Savs. Bank, Nat. Cinematographic Bank, Nat. Sugar Financing Commn., Nat. Pub. Works Bank; rep. Govt. of Mexico at internat. com. on econ. issues World Bank,, Interam. Devel. Bank, Interam. Econ. and Social Council. Office: Office of President Palacio Nacional Mexico Mexico DF

DELAMATER, JAMES NEWTON, physician; b. North Plainfield, N.J., Jan. 24, 1912; s. Van Ness and Jacqueline M. (Newton) DeL.; m. Harriet French, Sept. 1, 1934 (dec. Oct. 12, 1973); children—Steven French, Anne Terry, Sarah Van Ness; m. Elizabeth Clark, Oct. 25, 1974. Student, U. Va., 1930-31; A.B., Stanford U., 1934, M.D., 1938. Intern Los Angeles County Gen. Hosp., 1937-39, resident medicine, 1939-41; individual practice medicine, Los Angeles, 1946—; asst. prof. bacteriology U. So. Calif. Sch. Medicine, 1945, asso. prof., 1946, asso. prof. medicine, asso. dean, 1949-52, clin. prof. medicine, 1952—; affiliated Huntington Meml., Los Angeles County Gen. hosps.; epidemiologist Los Angeles County Med. Research Found., 1947—; med. cons. M.C. U.S. Army. Contbr. articles to med. jours. Served from lt. (j.g.) to comdr. M.C., 1941-45. Fellow A.C.P., Los Angeles Acad. Medicine; mem. AMA, AAAS, Am. Geriatrics Soc., Am. Soc. Tropical Medicine and Hygiene, Holland Soc. N.Y., Sigma Xi, Alpha Omega Alpha. Republican. Presbyn. Clubs: University (Pasadena); Hewlett, Toastmasters. Home: 2312 Pacific Dr Corona del Mar CA 92624

DELAMO, MARIO, dancer; b. Havana, Cuba, Jan. 30, 1946; s. Mariano and Mory V. (Alfonso) D. Grad. with honors in dance, High Sch. Performing Arts, 1966. Lectr. in field; tchr., choreographer Jacob's Pillow Dance Festival, 1971, Adelphi U., 1972, Steffi Nossen Sch. Dance, Scarsdale, N.Y., 1970-73; guest tchr. U. Calif. at Los Angeles, 1974. Prin. dancer on tours, Europe, with cos. of, Glen Tetley, Alvin Ailey and, Norman Walker, 1966-70; joined, Martha Graham Dance Co., N.Y.C., 1971—; now star dancer: TVS appearances Live from Wolftrap, 1976

DE LAND, EDWARD CHARLES, mathematician; b. Lusk, Wyo., May 16, 1922; s. Roy O. and Maude P. DeL.; m. Janet Murphy, Aug. 8, 1970; 1 dau., Katherine Eden. B.S., S.C. Sch. Mines and Tech., 1943; M.S., U. Calif., Berkeley, 1952; Ph.D., UCLA, 1956. Dir. quality control Corning Glass Works (N.Y.), 1946-48; instr. physics Calif. State U., 1948-50; sr. scientist Rand Corp., 1956-71; prof. surgery, anesthesiology and biomath. depts. UCLA, 1971—; dir. numerous corps.; cons. in field; vis. scientist NIH. Mem. editorial bd.: Jour. Assn. Advancement Med. Instrumentation, Biomaterials Devices and Artificial Organs; Contbr. articles to profl. jours.; Author 2 books. Mem. Soc. Computer Simulation, Assn. Computing Machinery, Biomed. Engring. Soc., AAAS, Assn. Internationale de Cybernetique, Phi Beta Kappa, Sigma Xi. Home: 23 Anchorage St Marina Del Rey CA 90291

DELANEY, ANDREW, insurance company executive; b. Vienna, Ohio, Aug. 2, 1920; s. John David and Elizabeth L. (Wurstner) D.; m. Wynelle Shellhouse, Apr. 5, 1947; 1 dau., Janet Lynn; m. Pauline Mills, July 31, 1982. B.A., Oberlin Coll., 1942; B.S., NYU, 1942. Actuarial trainee Equitable Life Assurance Co., N.Y.C., 1946-49; asst. actuary Union Central Life Ins. Co., Cin., 1949-54; v.p. actuary Am. Gen. Life Ins. Co., Houston, 1954-68, sr. v.p., 1968-76, sr. v.p., chief investment officer, 1976-82, vice chmn. bd., chief investment officer, 1982—; dir. Am. Gen. Life Ins. Co., Houston, Cullen Ctr. Bank & Trust, 1980—, Food Corp. Internat., 1978—. Life bd. dirs. Big Bros., Houston, 1969—; trustee Found. for Retarded, Houston, 1982—, Oberlin Coll., 1981—; past chmn. bd. trustees Emerson Unitarian Ch., Houston, 1966. Served to capt. USAF, 1942-46. Fellow Soc. Actuaries (bd. govs.). Republican. Clubs: Houston City, Houston Racquet; Forest Ramada (Houston). Home: 2831 Sackett Houston TX 77098 Office: Am Gen Corp 2727 Allen Pkwy Houston TX 77019

DELANEY, EDWARD NORMAN, lawyer; b. Chgo., Sept. 16, 1927; s. Frederick E. and Wynifred (Ward) D.; m. Carole P. Walter, May 31, 1950; children: Deborah Delaney Harris, Kathleen Delaney Cleveland, Edward Norman, Dorian A. LL.B., Loyola U., Chgo., 1951; LL.M., N.Y. U., 1959. Bar: Ill. 1952, Minn. 1961, U.S. Supreme Ct. 1963, Mo. 1974, D.C. 1975. Staff Office Chief Counsel, IRS, N.Y.C., 1955-60; atty. Investors Diversified Services Inc., Mpls., 1960-73, v.p., gen. counsel investment advisory group, 1968-73; sr. v.p., gen. counsel Waddell & Reed and United Investors Life Ins. Co., Kansas City, Mo., 1974; ptnr. firm Bogan & Freeland, Washington, 1975-81, Zuckert, Scoutt, Rasenberger & Delaney, 1982—; chmn. tax com. Investment Co. Inst., 1963-74; bus. advisory com. SEC Inter-Agy. Task Force Offshore Funds, 1970-71. Active fundraiser Center for Performing Arts, Kansas City, Mo., 1974; bd. dirs. Civic Orch., Mpls., 1963-68, pres., 1966-68. Served with USMCR, 1945-46. Mem. ABA (council tax sect. 1974-77, vice chmn. tax sect. 1978-81, chmn. tax sect. 1983-84), Fed., Minn., Hennepin County, Mo., D.C. bar assns. Clubs: Congressional Country, Univ., Georgetown (Washington). Home: 9405 Tobin Circle Potomac MD 20854 Office: 888 17th St NW Washington DC 20006

DELANEY, JOSEPH P., bishop; b. Fall River, Mass., Aug. 29, 1934. Student, Cardinal O'Connell Sem., Mass., Theol. Coll., Washington, N.Am. Coll., Rome, R.I. Coll. Ordained priest Roman Catholic Ch., 1960; ordained bishop of Fort Worth, 1981—. Office: 411 E Bolt Ave Fort Worth TX 76110 *

DELANEY, PATRICK JAMES, securities executive; b. N.Y.C., Dec. 15, 1940; s. James J. and Lola (Mathias) D.; m. Alexis Turpan, Mar. 31, 1975; children: Heather, James, Irene. B.S., Providence Coll., 1963; postgrad., Georgetown U. Law Sch., 1963-64, N.Y. Sch. Fin., 1965. Stockbroker, Harris Upham & Co., N.Y.C., 1965-73; spl. asst. to chmn. N.Y. State Racing and Wagering Bd., 1973-75; cons. to Vice-Pres. Nelson Rockefeller, 1975; asso. dir. intergovtl. relations Domestic Council, The White House, Washington, 1975-77; U.S. commr. Susquehanna River Basin Commn., Washington, 1977-81; v.p. Paine Webber, Hackensack, N.J., 1981—. Democrat. Roman Catholic. Club: University (Washington). Office: Paine Webber 433 Hackensack Ave Hackensack NJ 07601

DELANEY, THOMAS CALDWELL, JR., city ofcl.; b. Danville, Va., Jan. 1, 1918; s. Thomas Caldwell and Ethel Bernard (Loving) D.; m. Lois Jean Fitzsimmons, July 20, 1960. B.S., Spring Hill Coll., 1941; M.A., U. Ala., 1952. Dean, head dept. history Univ. Mil. Sch., Mobile, Ala., 1941-56; headmaster Wright Sch., Mobile, 1956-65; mus. dir., head dept. mus. City of Mobile, 1965—; mem. Nat. Hist. Records Adv. Bd., 1978-81; historian Mobile C.W. Centennial Commn., Mobile 250th Anniversary Celebration, 1961. Author: Deep South, 1942, 80, Remember Mobile, 1948, 69, 80, Story of Mobile, 1953, 61, 80, Phoenix Volunteer Fire Company of Mobile, 1838-1888, 1967, The First Hundred Years, 1968, Craigheed's Mobile, 1968, Confederate Mobile, 1971, Raphael Semmes, 1978, Mobile Sextet, 1981; author articles. Bd. dirs. Ala. First Capital Commn., 1961-65. Mem. Ala. Mus. Assn. (dir. 1978—), Southeastern Mus. Conf., Am. Assn. Museums, Ala. Hist. Assn. (pres. 1962), Hist. Mobile Preservation Soc. (dir. 1950-60), Smithsonian Assos., Nat. Archives, Fenollosa Soc. Japan (hon. charter). Presbyterian. Club: Rotary. Home: 8 S Ann St Mobile AL 36604 Office: 355 Government St Mobile AL 36602

DELANEY, WILLIAM FRANCIS, JR., insurance executive; s. William F. and Viola (Kelly) D.; m. Virginia Beers; children: Marcia, Gayle. Student, Ecole Albert de Mun Nogent sur Marne, France, Douai Sch., Eng.; certificate, Oxford and Cambridge; A.B., Princeton U.; LL.B., Harvard U.; student, N.Y. U., Practising Law Inst., Ins. Soc. N.Y.; Studied law, Paris. Bar: N.Y. bar, U.S. Supreme Ct. Atty. Irving Trust Co., N.Y.C.; gen. counsel Am. Internat. Underwriters Group; N.Y. reins. mgr. Fairfield & Ellis; pres. Delaney Offices, Inc., N.Y., 1954-; founding broker, mem. N.Y. Ins. Exchange; reins. intermediary and cons. for U.S. and world wide; reins. lectr. Ins. Soc. N.Y. Author: Reinsurance Laws of South America and Mexico; contbr. articles to ins. publs. Mem. Ins. Soc. N.Y. Roman Catholic. Clubs: Princeton, Drug and Chem., Deal Golf. Home: 215 Elberon Ave Allenhurst NJ 07711 Office: 99 John St New York NY 10038

DELANO, JACK, photographer, artist, composer; b. Kiev, Russia, Aug 1, 1914; came to U.S., 1923; s. William and Dries Ovcharov; m. Irene Esser Delano, July 5, 1940 (dec. 1982); children: Pablo Delano, Laura Delano. Diploma, Pa. Acad. Fine Arts, 1937. Photographer-artist Farm Security Adminstrn., Washington, 1940-43, 80-83; film maker Dept. Edn., San Juan, P.R., 1946-53; free lance film maker, San Juan, 1953-57; TV dir. WIPR-TV Channel 6, San Juan, 1957-63; gen. mgr. P.R. Radio and TV Service, San Juan, 1963-69; free lance photographer, illustrator, composer, film maker, San Juan, 1969—; tech. cons. P.R. Humanities Found., 1977—. Photographer photographs, Library of Congress, 1940-43; illustrator: books The Emperor's New Clothes, 1971; composer: ballet La Bruja de Loiza, 1950; film maker: Los Peloteros, 1952. Cresson Travelling scholar Pa. Acad. Fine Arts, 1936; Guggenheim fellow, 1945; UNESCO travelling fellow, 1960; NEH grantee, 1979. Mem. ASCAP. Address: RFD 2 Box 8 BB Rio Piedras PR 00928

DELANO, LESTER ALMY, JR., advertising executive; b. New Bedford, Mass., Nov. 28, 1928; s. Lester A. and Beatrice (Thomas) D.; m. Margaret Dent (div.); 1 dau., Leslie Ann; m. Helaine Shipper; children: Oliver Evan, Peter Franklin. Student, Amherst Coll., Brown U.; M.A., U. Chgo. Mktg. cons., Chgo., 1950-54; v.p. North Advt., Inc., Chgo., 1955-60; pres. Dodge & Delano, Inc., N.Y.C., 1961-71, Tinker, Dodge & Delano, Inc., 1971-76; chmn., chief exec. officer Tinker, Campbell-Ewald Inc., N.Y.C., 1976-77; pres. Campbell-Ewald Internat., London, Eng., 1977-80, Marshalk Campbell-Ewald Worldwide, N.Y.C., 1980—. Author: Creative Advertising Planning. Served with USN, 1945-48. Home: 115 Central Park W New York NY 10023 Office: 1290 Ave of Americas New York NY 10104 Williams House 30 Eastbourne Terr London W2 6LD England

DELANO, ROBERT BARNES, farmer, federation administrator; b. Richmond County, Va., July 8, 1924; s. Randolph O. and Bernice (Barnes) D.; m. Martha Webb, Aug. 21, 1948; children: Susan Webb, Robert Barnes. B.S. in Animal Husbandry, Va. Poly. Inst. and State U., 1944. Engaged in farming, 1946—; pres. Va. Farm Bur. Fedn., Inc., Richmond, 1962-80; v.p. Am. Farm Bur. Fedn., Park Ridge, Ill., 1976-80, pres., 1980—, bd. dirs., 1967-76; pres. So. Farm Bur. Life Ins. Co., 1975-80; dir. Dominion Nat. Bank, Richmond; pres. Richmond County Farm Bur., 1955-57; mem. Va. Air Pollution Control Bd., 1970-76, Gov.'s Commn. Industry of Agr., Pres.'s and Gov.'s trade missions to fgn. countries, 1968; U.S. pvt. sector rep. GATT, Geneva, 1982. V.p. Robert E. Lee council Boy Scouts Am., 1970-74; deacon Warsaw Bapt. Ch. Served with U.S. Army, 1944-46. Recipient Disting. 4-H Alumni award, 1981; named Man of Yr. in Va. Agr., 1978, among most influential nat. leaders U.S. News and World Report, 1981, 82, 83, Nat. Friend of Extension, Epsilon Sigma Phi, 1983; selected Outstanding Farm Family of Eastern Va., 1956. Mem. Alpha Zeta, Alpha Gamma Rho. Club: Block and Bridle. Home: Route 3 Warsaw VA 22572 Office: 225 Touhy Ave Park Ridge IL 60068

DELANO, VICTOR, retired naval officer; b. Washington, Dec. 20, 1919; s. Harvey and Marcia (Murdock) D.); m. Jacqueline Stinson, June 23, 1951; children: Katherine Stinson, Harvey II. B.S. in Elec. Engring, U.S. Naval Acad., 1941; M.S., Mass. Inst. Tech., 1949; grad., Indsl. Coll. Armed Forces, 1962. Commd. ensign U.S. Navy, 1941, advanced through grades to capt., 1959, ret., 1969; dir. Wichita Eagle & Beacon Pub. Co., Inc. (Kans.), 1957-72, treas., 1963-71, pres., 1970-71; gen. partner Forehand Assos., 1971—; Bd. advisers Victor Murdock Found. Bd. dirs. Friends of Nat. Zoo, Naval Hist. Found. (v.p., treas.), Avon Old Farms Sch. Decorated Bronze Star medal, Legion of Merit (2). Mem. Naval Inst., Naval Hist. Found., Sigma Xi. Clubs: Chevy Chase (Md.); Army and Navy, Metropolitan (Washington); University (San Francisco); Princess Anne Country, Wichita. Lodge: Mil. Order of Carabao. Home: 7111 Pyle Rd Bethesda MD 20817

DE LA OSSA, ERNEST GEORGE, food and drug company executive; b. Colon, Panama, Oct. 31, 1915; s. Ernesto and Estella Irene (Kerns) de la O.; m. Bonnie Eleanor Slattery, July 15, 1950; children: Donna Andrea de la Ossa Hultin, Richard William, William Haynie, Robin Lynn Estella de la Ossa DiCicco. B.A., Columbia U., 1937. With R.H. Macy & Co., 1937-42; with NBC, 1942-55, gen. mgr. radio and TV sta., 1953-55; chmn. Latin Am. planning and policy com. W.R. Grace & Co.; also v.p., dir. P.R., Mexican, Cuban, Colombian affiliates Latin Am. planning and policy com. W. R. Grace & Co.; v.p. paper div. W.R. Grace & Co., 1955-61; v.p. overseas ops. Internat. Paper Co., 1961-62; v.p. mgmt. planning Federated Dept. Stores, Inc., 1962-64; pres. internat. ops. Foremost Foods Co., 1964-70; pres. Foremost Internat., San Francisco, 1970-74, also dir.; v.p. govt. and internat. relations Foremost-McKesson, Inc., 1974-81; pres. Ossa Enterprises, Inc., 1981—, Enterprise Venture Capital Corp., 1982—; dir. Bank of the West, Joy Industries, Am. Microsystems, Inc., Polymetrics, Velo Bind, Inc., Tech. Equities Corp., Wind Baron Corp., Hygenics, Inc.; mem. adv. bd. Daleco; adj. prof. San Francisco State U.; Mem. salary stablzn. bd. U.S. Dept. Labor; bd. dirs. Latin Am. Inst.; vice chmn. S.E. Asia Trade and Investment, Calif. State Commn. Econ. Devel.; mem. Am.-Korean Found. Inc.; regional rep., bd. dirs. Agribus. Council Inc.; co-chmn. Inst. U.S.-Japan Relations; mem. San Francisco-Osaka Sister City Com., San Francisco-Sydney Sister City Com., Calif. Atty. Gen.'s Vol. Adv. Council; mem. adv. com. State of Calif.; co-chmn. for bus. orgn. UN U.; trustee, mem. exec. com. World Affairs Council; bd. dirs. Bus. Council for Internat. Understanding, Internat. Hospitality Center; chmn. dist. export council U.S. Dept. Commerce. Trustee emeritus Gonzaga U.; hon. trustee Meals for Millions—Freedom from Hunger Found.; bd. dirs. People for Peace Found., Nat. Council Asian Ams.; past pres. Peninsula Symphony Assn. Mem. N.Y. Personnel Mgmt. Assn. (past pres.), Am. Mgmt. Assn., Sales Execs. Club N.Y., Commerce and Industry Assn. N.Y. (chmn. personnel relations com.), Pan Am. Soc. (pres.), Korean-Am. (pres.), Brit. Am. (dir., hon. treas.), Argentine Am., U.S.-Mex. chambers commerce, Peninsula Symphony Assn. (dir., past pres.), Amigos de las Americas (trustee), Can.-Am. Soc. San Francisco (dir.), Assn. Corp. Growth, World Affairs Council No. Calif. (dir., exec. com.), San Francisco-Japan Bus. Forum (co-chmn.), Columbia Alumni Assn. (permanent pres. class 1937), Nat. Council U.S.-China Trade, Am. Arbitration Assn., UN Assn. San Francisco, Internat. Food and Wine Soc., Confrerie de la Chaine des Rotisseurs (dir., pres.). Clubs: Rotary; Hyde Park Golf and Country (Cin.); Westchester Country (Rye, N.Y.); Larchmont (N.Y.) Yacht; Pelham (N.Y.); Country; World Trade (San Francisco). Home: 1922 The Alameda San Jose CA 95126 Office: Crocker Plaza 1 Post St San Francisco CA 94104

DELAP, TONY, artist; b. Oakland, Calif., Nov. 4, 1927; s. Truman Henry and Catherine (Yontz) D.; m. Kathleen Rose Campbell, Dec. 27, 1964; children—Kelly Rose, Jack Henry. A.A., Menlo Jr. Coll.,

1947; student, Claremont Grad. Sch., 1947-49. Prof. U. Calif. at Irvine, 1965—. Exhibited group shows, San Francisco Mus., Oakland Mus., Whitney Mus., U. Ill., Mus. Modern Art N.Y., Los Angeles County Mus., Pasadena Mus., one man shows, Dilexi Gallery, San Francisco, Robert Elkon Gallery, N.Y.C., Felix Landau Gallery, Los Angeles, U. Calif. at Irvine, Nicholas Wilder Gallery, Los Angeles, Calif. Inst. Tech., Calif. State U., Long Beach, John Berggruen Gallery, San Francisco, Janus Gallery, Los Angeles, represented in permanent collections, Whitney Museum, Museum Modern Art N.Y.C., Walker Art Inst., Tate Gallery, London, Long Beach Mus. Art, Los Angeles County Mus. Art, Santa Barbara (Calif.) Mus. Art, Newport Harbor Art Mus., Newport Beach, Calif. Address: 225 Jasmine St Corona del Mar CA 92625

DE LA PARTE, LOUIS ANTHONY, JR., lawyer; b. Tampa, Fla., July 27, 1929; s. Louis and Dulce (Santa Cruz) de la P.; m. Helen C. White, Nov. 23, 1957; children: Louis David, Martha Ann. B.A., Emory U.; LL.B., U. Fla. Bar: Fla. 1953. Practice law, Tampa; spl. asst. atty. gen. State of Fla., 1953; asst. county solicitor and asst. state atty., Hillsborough County, Fla., 1957-61; mem. Fla. Senate, 1966-74, senate pres. pro tempore, 1972-74, pres., 1974; mem. Fla. Ho. of Reps., 1962-66; del. Dem. Nat. Conv., 1964; mem. Gov.'s Commn. on Capital Punishment, 1972, Gov.'s Task Force on Mental Health, Supreme Ct. Pub. Employees Rights Commn., 1973-74. Trustee U. Tampa. Served to capt. USAF, 1953-56. Recipient Allen Morris award, 1967, 71, 73; named Most Valuable Senator St. Petersburg (Fla.) Times, 1969, 70, 71, 74, Legislator of Year; Fla. Assn. Retarded Children, 1969-74; Legislator of Year Fla. Vol. Health Assns., 1970; Legislator of Year Pros. Attys. Assn., 1972. Mem. ABA, Fla. Bar (spl. com. on needs of children); Mem. Hillsborough County Bar Assn.; mem. D.C. Bar, Assn. Trial Lawyers Am., Am. Judicature Soc., Acad. Fla. Trial Lawyers; Mem. Greater Tampa C. of C. (past gov.), Fla. Blue Key, Phi Delta Phi, Eta Sigma Phi, Sigma Alpha Epsilon. Roman Catholic. Home: 8003 N Rome St Tampa FL 33604 Office: 705 E Kennedy Blvd Tampa FL 33602

DE LA PENA, GEORGE, ballet dancer; b. N.Y.C., 1956. Student, Ballet Theater Sch., Sch. Am. Ballet. Joined, Am. Ballet Theatre, 1974; promoted to soloist, 1975; many prin. roles throughout, U.S.; appeared in: film Nijinsky, 1980, Personal Best, 1982. Address: care William Morris Agy 1350 Ave of Americas New York NY 10019 *

DELAPENA, HARVEY V., JR., banker; b. Newark, Mar. 13, 1932; s. Harvey V. and Lucille (Slater) D.; m. Joanne Young, Aug. 15, 1959; children—Stephen, Brad, Susan. A.B., Colgate U., 1953; postgrad., N.Y. U. Bus. Sch. With Internat. div. Bank of N.Y., 1963—, assigned to London office, 1967-70, head Internat. div., N.Y.C., 1970—, also sr. v.p.; pres. Bank of N.Y. Internat. Bd. govs.; treas. India House. Mem. Am. Banking Assn., Netherlands C. of C. (dir.). Clubs: India House, Overseas Bankers (N.Y.C.). Home: 40 Dale Dr Summit NJ 07901 Office: 48 Wall St - 19th Floor New York NY 10015

DELAPLANE, STANTON HILL, newspaper columnist; b. Chgo., Oct. 12, 1907; s. Frank Hugh and Marion (Hill) D.; m. Miriam Moore, Dec. 6, 1940 (div. 1958); children: Kristin Moore, Thomas; m. Susan Aven, Feb. 2, 1961 (div. May 1973); children: Andrea Aven, John Berry Hill; m. Laddie Marshack, Oct. 19, 1979. Student, Hyde Park, Chgo., Santa Barbara, Cal., Monterey high schs., 1922-26. Editor Aperitif Mag. (pub. by Baroness Emily Von Romberg), 1933-36; reporter San Francisco Chronicle, 1936—, editor women's dept., 1937; now columnist; also columnist Chronicle Features, San Francisco; Organizer Calif. Young Democrats; and editor The Young Democrat, 1933-34; U.S. war corr. San Francisco Chronicle, 1944-45. Author: Pacific Pathways; Contbr. to: etc. Served to lt. comdr. USMC, Maritime Commn., 1942-44; Washington. Accredited corr. U.N. Conf., 1945; Recipient Pulitzer prize for regional reporting of movement of Calif.-Oreg. border counties to secede and form the 49th state, 1941, Nat. Headlines journalism award for feature series titles, Ding Dong Daddy of the D Car Line, 1946; Nat. Headlines award, 1959; 1st Ann. Writers award for best N. Am. article on sea travel Transpacific Passenger Conf. Club: San Francisco Press (pres. 1970-71, dir). Home: Mill Valley CA 94941 Office: San Francisco Chronicle San Francisco CA 94119

DELAPPE, IRVING PIERCE, scientist, government official; b. Boston, Oct. 28, 1915; s. Stephen Pierce and Sedley (Kirkpatrick) D.; m. Virginia R. Hebert, Sept. 19, 1942; children: Diane, Virginia, Stephen. S.B. (Stoughton scholar), Harvard U., 1942, A.M., 1946, Ph.D., 1953. Teaching fellow biology Harvard U., 1946-48, teaching asst. tropical medicine Med. Sch., 1947-48, asst. epidemiology exotic diseases Sch. Pub. Health, 1948; asst. prof. bacteriology and pub. health Mich. State U., 1948-54; dir. tech. info. Am. Cyanamid Co., N.Y.C., 1954-60; chief biochemistry and physiology, extramural programs Nat. Inst. Allergy and Infectious Diseases, NIH, 1960-76, chief parasitology and med. entomology, 1974-76, chief molecular microbiology and parasitology, 1977—. Author: (with Hawkins and Lindquist) Introduction to Parasitology, 1953; also articles. Mem. Explorers Club, Am. Soc. Tropical Medicine, Alliance for Prudent Use of Antibiotics, Sigma Xi. Clubs: East India (London); Harvard Mountaineering (Cambridge, Mass.); Harvard Varsity (Boston and Washington) (bd. dirs. Washington); Sierra (regional chmn. 1961-66); Potomac Appalachian Trail (Washington)). Home: 8907 Ridge Pl Bethesda MD 20817 also Office: Nat Inst Allergy and Infectious Disease NIH Bethesda MD 20205

DELAQUIS, NOEL, bishop; b. Notre-Dame de Lourdes, Man., Can., Dec. 25, 1934; s. Louis and Therese (Hebert) D. B.A., U. Man., 1954; B.Th., U. Laval, 1958; J.C.L., Latran, Rome, 1962. Ordained priest Roman Catholic Ch., 1958; asst. priest Christ the King Parish, St. Vital, Man., 1958-60; prof. canon law St. Boniface Sem., Man., 1962-68; chancellor Archdiocese of St. Boniface, Man., 1965-73; bishop of, Gravelbourg, Sask., Can., 1974—. Address: CP 690 Gravelbourg SK S0H 1X0 Canada *

DE LA RENTA, OSCAR, fashion designer; b. Santo Domingo, Dominican Republic, July 22, 1932; s. Oscar and Maria Antonia (deFiallo) de LaR.; m. Francoise deLanglade, Oct. 31, 1967. Student, Santo Domingo U., Academia de San Fernando, Madrid, Spain. Staff, Balenciaga's AISA, Madrid; asst. to: Castillo at, Lanvin, Paris; designer, Elizabeth Arden, N.Y.C.; now designer, Oscar de la Renta, Ltd., N.Y.C. Active Dominican Childhood Center, orphanage, Santo Domingo. Decorated Order Juan Pablo Duarte and; Order Cristobal Colon, Dominican Republic).; Recipient Coty awards, 1967, 68, Golden Tiberius award, 1968; named to Coty Hall of Fame, 1973. Mem. Council Fashion Designers Am. Office: 550 7th Ave New York NY 10018

DE LARROCHA, ALICIA, concert pianist; b. Barcelona, Spain, May 23, 1923; d. Eduardo and Teresa (De La Calle) de L.; m. Juan Torra, June 21, 1950; children: Juan, Alicia. Grad. (prize extraordinary, Gold medal), Acad. Marshall, Barcelona. Debut, Barcelona, 1927; solo recitalist, concert pianist maj. orchs. in, Europe, U.S., Can., Central and S. Am., S. Africa, N.Z., Australia, Japan; dir. Acad. Marshall, 1959—; rec. artist: Hispavox, CBS, Decca-London; records.; (Grammy award 1974, 75, 1st Gold medal Merito a la Vocación 1972). Recipient Harriet Cohen Internat. Music award, 1968; Paderewski Meml. medal, 1961; Grand prix du Disque Acad. Charles Cros, 1960, 74; Edison award, 1968; decorated Order Civil Merit Order Isabel la Catolica, Spain). Mem. Musica en Compostela (dir.), Hispanic Soc. Am. (corr.), Internat. Piano Archives (hon. pres.). Address: 119 W 57th St New York NY 10019

DELATTRE, EDWIN JULES, college president; b. Detroit, Sept. 4, 1941; s. Jules I. and Donna Marie (Abbott) D.; m. Alice Parker Boggs, Aug. 29, 1964; children: Donna (dec.), Lee. B.A., U. Va., 1963; Ph.D., U. Tex., 1970. Instr. Tex. Lutheran Coll., Seguin, 1967, U. Toledo, 1968-69, asst. prof., 1969-74; mem. Nat. Humanities Faculty, Concord, Mass., 1972-76, dir., 1974-80; pres. St. John's Coll., Annapolis, Md., 1980—, Santa Fe, 1980—; instr., cons. FBI Acad. Bd. dirs. NEH, Washington, Md. Commn. Humanities, Balt.; mem. adv. bd. Franklin J. Matchette Found., N.Y.C.; regional chmn. Pres.'s Commn. on White House Fellowships; vice chmn. Md. Hall of Records. Oldright fellow U. Tex., 1967; recipient Outstanding Tchr. award U. Toledo, 1973; named Young Leader Am. Acad. Change Mag., 1978. Mem. Am. Philosophy Group, Ohio Philosophic Assn., Philosophic Soc. Study of Sports, Metaphys. Soc. Am., Phi Beta Kappa. Clubs: Farmington Country (Charlottesville, Va.); Kiva (Santa Fe); University, Princeton (N.Y.C.). Home: 212 Norwood Rd Annapolis MD 21401 Office: St John's Coll 60 College Ave Annapolis MD 21404

DE LAUER, RICHARD D., govt. ofcl., former aerospace co. exec.; b. Oakland, Calif., Sept. 23, 1918; s. Michael and Matilda (Giambruno) DeL.; m. Ann Carmichael, Dec. 6, 1940; 1 son, Richard Daniel. A.B., Stanford, 1940; B.S., U.S. Naval Postgrad. Sch., 1949; Aero. Engr., Calif. Inst. Tech., 1950, Ph.D., 1953. Structrual designer Glenn L. Martin Co., Balt., 1940-42; design engr. Northrop Co., Hawthorne, Calif., 1942; commd. ensign USN, 1942, advanced through grades to comdr., 1958; assignments in, U.S., 1943-58, ret., 1966; lab. dir. Space Tech. Labs., El Segundo, Calif., 1958-60, Titan Program dir., 1960-62, v.p., dir. ballistic missile program mgmt., 1962-66; v.p., gen. mgr. systems engring. and integration div. TRW Systems Group, Redondo Beach, Calif., 1966-68, v.p., gen. mgr., 1968-70; exec. v.p. TRW, Inc., Redondo Beach, 1970-81; also dir.; undersec. for research and engring. Dept. Def., Washington, 1981—; dir. Ducommen, Inc., Los Angeles, Cordura, Inc., Chgo.; Vis. lectr. U. Calif., Los Angeles.; Chmn. Nat. Alliance Businessman, 1968-69; chmn. Region IX, 1970; mem. Def. Sci. Bd., Dept. Def. Author: (with R.W. Bussard) Nuclear Rocket Propulsion, 1958, Fundamentals of Nuclear Flight, 1965. Trustee U. Redlands. Fellow Am. Inst. Aeros. and Astronautics, Am. Astron. Soc.; mem. Nat. Acad. Engring., AAAS, Aerospace Industries Assn. (gov.), Sigma Xi. Home: 1101 S Arlington Ridge Rd Arlington VA 22202 Office: Dept Def Research and Engring Office of Undersec The Pentagon Washington DC 20301

DELAURA, DAVID JOSEPH, English language educator; b. Worcester, Mass., Nov. 19, 1930; s. Louis and Helen Adeline (Austin) DeL.; m. Ann Beloate, Aug. 19, 1961; children: Michael Louis, Catherine, William Beloate. A.B., Boston Coll., 1955, A.M., 1958; Ph.D., U. Wis., 1960. Mem. faculty U. Tex. at Austin, 1960-74, prof. English, 1968-74; Avalon Found. prof. humanities, prof. English U. Pa., Phila., 1974—. Author: Hebrew and Hellene in Victorian England: Newman, Arnold, and Pater, 1969; Editor: Victorian Prose: A Guide to Research, 1973; Contbr. chpts. to books, articles and revs. to profl. publs. Mem. Modern Lang. Assn. (ann. award for outstanding article 1964), AAUP. Home: 31 Orchard Ln Villanova PA 19085 Office: Dept English U Pa Philadelphia PA 19104

DE LAURENTIIS, DINO, motion picture producer; b. Torre Annunziata, Italy, Aug. 8, 1919; s. Rosario Aurelio and Giuseppina (Salvatore) De L.; m. Silvana Magnano, July 17, 1949; children: Veronica, Rafaella, Francesca. Ed. high sch. and comml. sch., Centro Sperimentale di Cinematografia, Rome. Mem. actor's sch., Expt. Film Center, Rome, 1937-39; organized first film prodn. co., 1941; productions include Bitter Rice, 1952, Ulysses, 1955, War and Peace, 1956, La Strada, 1956 (Acad. award), Nights of Cabiria, 1957 (Acad. award), This Angry Age, 1958, The Tempest, 1959, Under Ten Flags, 1960, The Best of Enemies, 1962, Barabbas, 1962, Three Faces of a Woman (Soraya), 1964, The Bible, 1966, Barbarella, 1967, Anzio, 1967, Waterloo, 1970, Valachi Papers, 1972, The Stone Killer, 1973, (moved to N.Y. 1973), Serpico, 1974, Death Wish, 1974, Mandingo, 1975, Three Days of the Condor, 1975, (moved to Los Angeles 1975), Lipstick, 1976, Face to Face, 1976, Buffalo Bill and the Indians, 1976, The Shootist, 1976, King Kong, 1976, Orca, 1977, The Serpent's Egg, 1977, King of the Gypsies, 1978, The Great Train Robbery, 1978, The Brink's Job, 1979, Hurricane, 1979, Flash Gordon, 1980, Ragtime, 1981, Striking Back, 1982, Conan The Barbarian, 1982, The Dead Zone, 1983, Firestarter, 1984, The Bounty, 1984, Conan The Destroyer, 1984, Dune, 1984. Office: Dino De Laurentiis Corp 1 Gulf and Western Plaza New York NY 10023

DELAWIE, HOMER TORRENCE, architect; b. Santa Barbara, Calif., Sept. 24, 1927; s. Fred Ely and Gertrude Elizabeth (Torrence) D.; m. Ethel Ann Sosna, Sept. 3, 1973; children: Gregory, Tracy, Scott, Claire, Shandell, Stephanie. B.S. in Archtl. Engring., Calif. Poly. U., 1951. Pvt. archtl. practice, San Diego, 1958—; pres. Homer Delawie Assos., 1970—; cons. architect Sea World, San Diego and Orlando, Fla.; guest lectr. environ. and community problems univ. extension. Mem. San Diego Planning Commn., 1969-82; mem. adv. com. Sta. KPBS-TV, pub. TV. Contbr. articles to profl. mags. Served with USNR, 1945-46. Fellow AIA (40 nat., regional or local design awards). Home: 2749 Azalea Dr San Diego CA 92106 Office: 2827 Presidio Dr San Diego CA 92110

DE LAY, DOROTHY (MRS. EDWARD NEWHOUSE), violinist, educator; b. Medicine Lodge, Kans., Mar. 31, 1917; d. Glenn Adney and Cecile (Osborn) DeLay; m. Edward Newhouse, Mar. 5, 1941; children: Jeffrey H., Alison Dinsmore. Student, Oberlin Coll., 1933-34, D.Music (hon.), 1981; B.A., Mich. State U., 1937; Artists diploma, Juilliard Grad. Sch. Music, 1941. Prof. violin The Juilliard Sch., N.Y.C., 1947—; mem. faculty Sarah Lawrence Coll., 1948—, Meadowmount Summer Sch. Music, Westport, N.Y., 1948-70, Aspen Summer Music Sch., 1971—; Starling prof. violin U. Cin., 1974—; vis. prof. violin Phila. Coll. Performing Arts, 1977-83, New Eng. Conservatory, 1978—; condr. Master classes univs. and conservatories in, U.S., Europe, Asia, Africa, Near East. Solo, chamber music performances in, U.S., Can., S.Am., 1937—; violinist, founder, Stuyvesant Trio, 1940-42; Contbr. articles on violins, violinists to various encys. Recipient Outstanding Artist-Tchr. award Am. String Tchrs. Assn., 1975, Highest honor citation Fedn. of Music Clubs, 1983. Mem. Mu Phi Epsilon. Home: 349 N Broadway Upper Nyack NY 10960 Office: Juilliard Sch Lincoln Center Plaza New York NY 10023

DE LAY, ROBERT FRANCIS, advt. exec.; b. Beresford, S.D., Jan. 4, 1919; s. John A. and Rosalie M. (Burns) DeL.; m. Bonnie C. Nelson, Jan. 24, 1942; 1 son, Stephen. Student, S.D. State U., 1941. With R.R. Donnelley, N.Y.C., 1946-49; advt. mgr. Victor Corp., Davenport, Iowa; advt. mgr., public relations dir. Am. Air Filter Co., Inc., Louisville, 1949-55; v.p. Burnett & Logan, Inc., Chgo., 1955-57; account exec. Waldie & Briggs, Chgo., 1957-59; pres. Direct Mail Mktg. Assn., Inc., N.Y.C., 1959—. Served from 2d lt. to lt. col. AUS, 1941-46. Decorated Bronze Star. Mem. Bus. Pubs. and Advt. Assn. (dir.), Am. Advt. Fedn. (dir.), Advt. Council, Inc. (dir.), Sigma Delta Chi. Home: 304 Bayberry Ln Westport CT 06880 Office: 6 E 43d St New York NY 10017

DE LAYO, LEONARD JOSEPH, ednl. adminstr.; b. N.Y.C., Feb. 14, 1921; s. Anthony and Mary (Antonucci) DeL.; m. Helen Griffith, Apr. 25, 1946; children—Leonard Joseph, Donna Marie, Dianne. B.S., U. N.Mex., 1949; M.A., Tchrs. Coll., Columbia, 1949. Tchr. pub. schs., Albuquerque, 1949-50; prin. Sandia Base Schs., Albuquerque, 1950-1958; exec. sec. Tchrs. Assn., Baltimore County, Md., 1959-63; supt. of pub. instrn. State of N.Mex., Santa Fe, 1963—; Chmn. Govs. Com. to Investigate State Hosp. for Mental Defectives, 1956; Govs. Commn. Mental Health, 1964; bd. mgrs. N.Mex. Congress Parents and Tchrs., 1952-58; mem. of Gov.'s coms. TV, 1963—, State Commn. Children and Youth, 1967—, Vocat. Rehab., 1964—, Adv. Council Spl. Edn., 1975-76; mem. Nat. Panel Cons. Pupil Personnel Services, 1969; chmn. Big Six Com. on Edn., 1973; mem. Nat. Adv. Com. on Guidance and Counseling, Rocky Mountain States Satellite Project. Mem. Commn. Edn. Nat. PTA, 1975; Bd. regents Am. Technol. U.; trustee St. Vincent Hosp., Santa Fe, 1975-78. Served with USMCR, 1943-46. Mem. Council Chief State Sch. Officers (dir. 1971—, pres. 1972-73), N.Mex., Nat., U.N.Mex. edn. assns., Albuquerque Pub. Schs. Edn. Assn. (past pres.), Phi Delta Kappa (past pres. U.N.Mex.), Kappa Delta Pi. Clubs: Rotary (pres. 1974-75), Optimist (Albuquerque) (past v.p.). Home: 114 La Paloma Santa Fe NM 87501 Office: State Dept Edn Sante Fe NM 87503 *My goal is to work unceasingly to promote standards of excellence in an educational program that involves all of our citizens of all ages.*

DEL BELLO, ALFRED BENEDICT, lieutenant governor N.Y.; b. N.Y.C., Nov. 3, 1934; s. Sylvester W. and Marie (Savio) Del B.; m. Dolores Virginia Rizzo, July 12, 1950; 1 son, Damon. B.A., Mahhattan Coll., 1956; LL.D. (hon.), Mercy Coll. Bar: N.Y. 1960. Practice, Yonkers, N.Y., 1961-73; ptnr. Del Bello and Belkin, 1962-66; councilman, Yonkers, 1966-69, mayor, 1970-73, county exec., Westchester County, N.Y., 1973-82; lt. gov. State N.Y., Albany, 1983—; pres. N.Y. State Assn. City Councilmen, 1968-69; dir. N.Y. State Conf. Mayors, 1970-73. Mem. adv. bd. Internat. Found. for Children's Hearing Edn. and Research; past v.p. Muscular Dystrophy Assn. Am.; bd. dirs. Renaissance Project, Westchester County; mem. adv. bd. Westchester County Hist. Soc. Mem. Am. Acad. Polit. and Social Sci. Roman Catholic. Club: K.P. Office: Lt Gov State Capitol Albany NY 12224

DEL CERRO, MANUEL, ophthalmology educator; b. Buenos Aires, Argentina, Aug. 20, 1931; came to U.S., 1964; s. Manuel and Julia (Caceres) del C.; m. Constancia Clotilde Nunez, May 17, 1958; children: Alicia, Marilu. B.A., B.S., Nat. Coll. Buenos Aires, 1951; M.D., U. Buenos Aires, 1958. Intern and resident in emergency medicine Buenos Aires Mcpl. Hosp., 1958-61, chief resident, 1961; postdoctoral Inst. Cell Biology U. Buenos Aires Med. Sch., 1958-59, 59-60; lectr. cytology NRC Argentina, 1962-63; assoc. prof. histology U. Buenos Aires, 1961-64; research assoc. U. Rochester, N.Y., 1965-69, 69-71, assoc. prof. Ctr. Brain Research and Neurology, 1971-79, assoc. prof. anatomy, 1976—, assoc. prof. ophthalmology, 1980—; prof. Ctr. Brian research and Ctr. Visual Sci., 1979—. Mem. N.Y. State Health Research Council, 1980-84. Served with Argentine Army, 1952. Grantee Nat. Eye Inst., 1978-81, Nat. Eye Inst., 1981-84. Fellow Royal Micros. Soc.; mem. Internat. Brain Research Orgn., Assn. Research in Vision and Ophthalmology, Soc. Neurosci., AAAS, Assn. Study of Mental and Nervous Diseases, Am. Assn. Neuropathologists, Am. Assn. Anatomists. Roman Catholic. Office: U Rochester Med Ctr Box 605 Rochester NY 14642

DELCHAMPS, ALFRED FREDERICK, JR., retail grocery chain executive; b. Mobile, Ala., June 30, 1931; s. Alfred Frederick and Sara Lucile (Crowell) D.; m. Carolyn Ann Weaver, Aug. 2, 1953; children: Alfred Frederick III, Thomas W., Carolyn M. Student, Duke U., 1948-50; B.S. in Commerce and Bus. Adminstrn, U. Ala., 1953. Supr. Delchamps, Inc., 1953-58, asst. sec., 1958-63, v.p. service ops., 1963-65, exec. v.p., 1965-76, pres., 1976—; dir. 1st Nat. Bank, Mobile.; Mem. bus. adv. council U. South Ala.; vice chmn. bd. trustees Huntingdon Coll., Montgomery, Ala. Past pres. Jr. Achievement of Mobile, Inc.; past 1st v.p. Community Chest and Council of Mobile County, past pres., Mobile Symphony and Civic Music Assn.; past disaster chmn. Mobile chpt. ARC; past gen. chmn. Group Aid for Retarded Children, Inc.; treas. Mobile Hist. Devel. Found., Mobile Track and Field Assn. Mem. Am. Mgmt. Assn. Republican. Methodist. Clubs: Country of Mobile, Isle Dauphine, Mystic Socs. Home: 163 S Georgia Ave Mobile AL 36604 Office: Delchamps Inc 305 Delchamps Ave Mobile AL 36633

DELCHER, EDWIN G., retired manufacturing executive; b. Balt. B.B.A., Loyola Coll., Balt. Controller, Martin-Marietta Corp., 1962-66; v.p. fin., sec. and treas. Black & Decker Mfg., 1966-78, sr. v.p., sec., 1978-83; dir. Union Trust Bancorp, Brown & Sharpe Mfg. Co. Trustee St. Joseph Hosp.; bd. dirs. MassMut Income Investors Inc. Mem. Fin. Execs. Inst., Md. Assn. C.P.A.s, Machinery and Allied Products, Inst. Home: 1612 Pot Spring Rd Timonium MD 21093

DEL CHIARO, MARIO ALDO, educator, art historian, archeologist, etruscologist; b. San Francisco, Apr. 22, 1925; s. Casimiro and Elisa (Bianchi) A.; m. Christina Falkman, Sept. 13, 1958; children: Kari Louise, Marco Claudio, Paola Christina. A.B., U. Calif. at Berkeley, 1950, M.A., 1951, Ph.D., 1956. Teaching asst. art history U. Calif. at Berkeley, 1950-51, 55, Univ. fellow in art, 1951-52; John Wesley Britton traveling fellow in classics, 1952-53, Met. Mus. Art fellow, N.Y.C., 1953-54, grantee Am. Numismatic Soc. Seminar, 1954; faculty U. Calif. at Santa Barbara, 1956—, prof. art history, 1966—, chmn. dept., 1969-72; Mem. archeol. staff for excavations in, Turkey, Yugoslavia, Egypt, Sicily and Italy; dir. U. Cal. Santa Barbara archeol. expdn. to, Tuscany, Italy. Author: The Genucilia Group: A Class of Etruscan Red-Figured Plates, 1957, Etruscan Red-Figured Vase-Painting at Caere, 1974, The Etruscan Funnel Group: A Tarquinian Red-Figured Fabric, 1974; exhbn. catalogues Greek Art in Private Collections of Southern California, 1963, Etruscan Art from West Coast Collections, 1967, Roman Art in West Collections, 1973, Etruscan Ghiaccio Forte, 1976, Re-exhumed Etruscan Bronzes, 1981; Contbr. book reviews, articles to profl. jours. Am. Philos. Soc. grantee, 1957, 75; Prix de Rome fellow Am. Acad. in Rome, 1958-60; Sr. Faculty fellow Humanities Inst. U. Calif. at Berkeley, 1967-68; Nat. Endowment for Humanities grantee, 1977. Mem. Archeol. Inst. Am., Explorers Club, Inst. Studi Etruschi ed Italici, Florence, Deutsches Archäologisches Inst., Instituto Archeologico Rome, Phi Beta Kappa. Home: 1376 Estrella Dr Hope Ranch Santa Barbara CA 93110

DELEHANTY, EDWARD JOHN, investment company executive; b. Wallingford, Conn., Oct. 14, 1929; s. Robert Thomas and Bertha (Slanec) D.; m. Margaret Marshall, July 18, 1969; children: Marke Cheryl, Dana Keith, Jeffrey Dean, Robin Lee. A.B., Clark U., Worcester, Mass., 1951. Agt., agy. supr., regional tng. supr., gen. agt. Paul Revere Life Ins. Co., Worcester, 1951-64; v.p., dir. agys. Boston Mut. Life Ins. Co., 1964-65; v.p., dir. Mut. Fund Assoc., Inc., San Francisco, 1965-68, exec. v.p., 1968-70; v.p., dir. Putnam Mgmt. Co., Boston, 1970-74; mem. exec. com. Putnam Cos., Inc.; dir. Putnam Fin. Services, Inc.; dir., mem. investment com. Putnam Capital Mgmt., Inc., exec. v.p., dir.; pres., dir. Putnam Capital Services, Inc.; sr. v.p., dir. Putnam Adv. Co. Inc.; pres. Acadian Fin. Services, Inc. Mem. alumni com. Clark U., 1962-65. Mem. Newcomen Soc., Sales and Mktg. Execs. Internat. Clubs: Mason., Commonwealth (San Francisco). Home: Seawall Rd Manset ME 04656 Office: 1 Post Office

Sq Boston MA 02109 *Be totally selfish—always treat others in a way that makes it possible for you to live with and like yourself.*

DELEONE, CARMON, conductor, musician, educator; b. Ravenna, Ohio, Mar. 23, 1942; s. Carmon and Julia Johanna (Klein) DeL.; m. Kathleen Virginia Hanna, Sept. 24, 1971; stepchildren: Tanya, Tina, Tara. B.M., Conservatory of Music, U. Cin., 1964, B.S. in Music Edn, 1965, M.M., 1967. Touring musician, State Theatre of N.Y., Henry Mancini and other orchs.; condr. univ. musicals, 1963-67; asst. condr., Cin. Symphony Orch., 1968-76; resident condr., 1976-80; music dir., Cin. Ballet Co., 1969—; prof., condr., Miami U., Oxford, Ohio, 1980—; music dir., Middletown Symphony, (Ohio), 1982—; guest condr. numerous orchs.; Mem. music panel, Ohio Arts Council; bd. dirs., Cin. Commn. Arts. (Recipient Corbett award Cin. Post-Times Star 1981), Cin. Commn. Arts. (Nutone prize Cin. Coll. Conservatory 1962), Cin. Commn. Arts. (T. Scott Huston prize 1963). Mem. Am. Symphony Orch. League, ASCAP, MacDowell Soc., Pi Kappa Lambda. Home: 4032 Rose Hill Ave Cincinnati OH 45229 Office: care Gordon Artists Mgmt Box 32105 Cincinnati OH 45232

DE LERMA, DOMINIQUE-RENE SEBASTIEN, musicologist, educator; b. Miami, Fla., Dec. 8, 1928; s. Daniel Robert Francois and Roberta De L. B.M., cum laude, U. Miami, 1953; postgrad., Berkshire Music Ctr., 1949, Curtis Inst. Music, 1949-50, U. Okla., 1962-63, Coll. Notre Dame, 1980-81; Ph.D. in Musicology, Ind. U., 1958; postgrad., Ind. U., 1963-65. Assoc. prof. music U. Miami, 1951-61, U. Okla., 1962-63, Ind. U., 1963-76; prof. Morgan State U., Balt., 1976—, Peabody Conservatory of Music, 1983—; lectr. tours U.S., Can., Caribbean, Europe; cons. in field; chief cons. black composers to CBS; v.p. Black Composers Project, 1977—; pres. Black Artists Collective, 1980—. Author: (books include) Bibliography of Black Music Series, 1981—; contbr. articles to profl. jours. Bd. dirs. Dance Theatre Harlem, Balt., Dance Theatre, Inst. for Research in Black Am. Music at, Fisk U., Creative Artists' Workshop, Bklyn. Philharm., Scott Joplin Found., Balt. Symphony Orch. Auditioning Com., Eubie Blake Cultural Ctr., Md. State Arts Council. Recipient Alice and Corin Strong award Scandinavian award, Scandinavian-Am. Found., 1969, Black Music Caucus award Music Educators Nat. Conf., 1982; grantee Found. Pro Helvetia, 1968-69, Scandianavian-Am. Found., 1969-70, Chapelbrook Found., 1968-70, Fondacaeo Calouste Gulbenkian, 1969-70. Mem. Music Library Assn., Soc. Ethnomusicology, Coll. Music Soc., NAACP. Roman Catholic. Home: 711 Stoney Springs Dr Baltimore MD 21210 Office: Music Dept Morgan State U. Baltimore MD 21239

DELEVIE, HAROLD JACOB, lawyer; b. Los Angeles, Apr. 24, 1931; s. Louis David and Rosa Reeva (Rubin) D.; m. Roberta Diane Bass, July 28, 1957; children: Mark Nathan, Elizabeth Susan. A.B., UCLA, 1953, J.D., 1956. Bar: Calif. 1957. Partner Epport & Delevie, Los Angeles, 1957-73; shareholder Epport & Delevie, a law corp., Beverly Hills, Calif., 1973-81; ptnr. Ervin, Cohen & Jessup, Beverly Hills, 1981—; Tchr. Los Angeles City Adult Schs., 1957-59. Bd. editors: UCLA Law Rev., 1955-56. Mem. ABA, Los Angeles County Bar Assn., Wilshire Bar Assn. (pres. 1970-71, bd. govs. 1967—), Beverly Hills Bar Assn., State Bar Calif. (mem. conf. state bar dels. 1969-71, chmn. local adminstrv. disciplinary com. 1969-70, hearing officer 1967-74), U. Calif. at Los Angeles Bus. Sch. Assn. (pres. 1960-61), UCLA (exec. council 1960-61), UCLA Law Alumni Assn. (dir. 1970-74, treas. 1972-73), Am. Arbitration Assn. (nat. panel arbitrators), Order Coif, Phi Beta Kappa. Democrat. Jewish. Home: 3638 Terrace View Dr Encino CA 91436 Office: 9401 Wilshire Blvd Beverly Hills CA 90212

DELEVORYAS, THEODORE, botanist, educator; b. Chicopee Falls, Mass., July 22, 1929; s. Basil John and Sophie (John) Dulchinos D.; m. Nancy Lou Foster, June 23, 1956 (div. Dec. 1978); children: Matthew Torrey, Christopher Theodore; m. Cecilia Ann Dean, Aug. 14, 1981. B.S., U. Mass., 1950; M.S., U. Ill., 1951, Ph.D., 1954; M.A. (hon.), Yale, 1968. Postdoctoral fellow NRC, U. Mich., Ann Arbor, 1954-55; asst. prof. botany Mich. State U., East Lansing, 1955-56; instr. botany Yale, New Haven, 1956-58, asst. prof., 1958-60, asso. prof. biology, 1962-68, prof. biology, 1968-72; asso. prof. botany U. Ill., Urbana, 1960-62; prof. botany U. Tex., Austin, 1972—, chmn. dept. botany, 1974—, chmn. dir. biol. scis., 1982—. Author: Morphology and Evolution of Fossil Plants, 1962, Plant Diversification, 1966, (with others) Morphology of Plants and Fungi, 1980; Contbr. numerous articles to profl. jours. Fellow Linnean Soc. London; mem. Bot. Soc. Am. (treas. 1967-72, v.p. 1973, pres. 1974), Paleontol. Soc., Palaeontol. Assn., Am. Inst. Biol. Scis., Internat. Assn. Plant Taxonomy, Internat. Soc. Plant Morphologists, Torrey Bot. Club, Am. Inst. Biol. Scis. (mem. bd. govs. 1975-77), Internat. Orgn. Paleobotany (pres. 1978-81), Phi Beta Kappa, Phi Kappa Phi. Club: Austin Yacht. Home: 4204 Zuni Dr Austin TX 78759

DEL GIUDICE, AMORE, hospital administrator; b. Waterbury, Vt., Oct. 31, 1913; s. Alfonso and Sebastiana (Imbruglia) Del G.; m. Helen E. Chubb, Oct. 1940; children: Richard, Joan; m. Marie Maschino Berning, Dec. 5, 1953. B.S., U. Vt., 1936, M.D., 1939. Diplomate: Am. Bd. Psychiatry and Neurology. Intern Vassar Bros. Hosp., Poughkeepsie, N.Y., 1939-40; resident psychiatrist Binghamton (N.Y.) State Hosp., 1946-51; asst. dir. St. Lawrence State Hosp., Ogdensburg, N.Y., 1961-66; dir. Middletown (N.Y.) Psychiat. Center, 1966-79. Served with M.C., AUS, 1940-46. Fellow Am. Psychiat. Assn. (life). Home: RD 1 Box 213A Hammond NY 13646

DEL GRECO, FRANCESCO, physician, educator; b. Italy, Aug. 23, 1923; came to U.S., 1951, naturalized, 1959; s. Gaetano and Gilda (Borga) del G.; m. Gerrie Flynn, June 23, 1956; 1 son, Paul. M.D., U. Rome, 1946; postgrad., Northwestern U., 1959-61. Intern Univ. Hosp., Rome, 1946-50, resident, 1950-51; research fellow Cleve. Clinc, 1951-54, asst. staff, 1955-57; vol. asst., research fellow Postgrad. Med. Sch. U. London, St. Thomas Hosp., 1954-55; intern Passavant Meml. Hosp., Chgo., 1957-58, resident, 1958-60, attending staff, 1960-72, dir. Dialysis Center, 1958—, dir. Clin. Research Center, 1961-81; attending staff VA Lakeside Med. Ctr., Chgo., 1960—, Northwestern Meml. Hosp., 1972—; prof. medicine Med. Sch. Northwestern U., Chgo., 1967—, chief sect. nephrology-hypertension, 1973; med. adv. bd. Ill. Kidney Found., chmn., 1975-79; mem. cardiovascular-renal study sect. Nat. Heart Inst.-NIH, 1975-79; mem. renal disease adv. com. State of Ill., 1974—. Danish Govt. scholar, 1951; Nat. Heart Inst. NIH fellow, 1952-53. Fellow ACP, AAAS; mem. Am. Physiol. Soc., Soc. Exptl. Biology and Medicine, Central Soc. Clin. Research, Am. Soc. Artificial Internal Organs, Council on Circulation, Council on High Blood Pressure Research, Council on Kidney in Cardiovascular Disease, Am. Heart Assn., Am. Soc. Nephrology, Am. Fedn. Clin. Research, Internat. Soc. Artificial Organs, AMA, Internat. Soc. Nephrology, Internat. Soc. Hypertension, Am. Soc. Clin. Pharmacology and Therapeutics, Assn. Clin. Scientists, N.Y. Acad. Scis. Office: Northwestern Meml Hosp Chicago IL 60611

DEL GUERCIO, LOUIS RICHARD MAURICE, surgeon, educator; b. N.Y.C., Jan. 15, 1929; s. Louis and Hortense (Ardengo) Del G.; m. Paula Marie Helene de Vautibault, May 18, 1957; children: Louis, Francsca, Paul, Catherine, Maria, Michelle, Christopher Anthony. B.S., Fordham U., 1949; M.D., Yale U., 1953. Diplomate: Am. Bd. Surgery, Am. Bd. Thoracic Surgery. Intern Columbia-Presbyn. Med. Center, N.Y.C., 1953-54; resident St Vincent's Hosp., N.Y.C., 1954-58, Cleve. City Hosp., 1958-60; practice medicine specializing in thoracic surgery, 1960—; mem. faculty Albert Einstein Coll. Medicine, N.Y.C., 1960-71, assoc. prof., 1966-70, prof. surgery, 1970-71, dir. Clin. Research Center-Acute, 1967-71; dir.; clin. prof. surgery N.J. Coll. Medicine, Newark, 1971-76; prof. surgery N.Y. Med. Coll., N.Y.C., 1976—, chmn. dept., 1976—; chief surgery Westchester County Med. Center, 1976—; cons. surgeon other hosps.; mem. surg. study sect. NIH, 1970-74; mem. com. on shock NRC-Nat. Acad. Scis., 1969-71; mem. merit rev. bd. VA, 1971-74; mem. health care tech. study sect. Dept. Health and Human Services, 1980—; cons. Nat. Center Health Services Research, 1980—; chmn. bd. dirs. Dalfex Med. Scis., Inc. Author: (with B.G. Clarke) Urology, 1956, The Multilingual Manual for Medical History Taking, 1972, (with S.G. Hershey, R. McConn) Septic Shock in Man, 1971; editor-in-chief: Critical Care Monitor, 1980—; contbr. articles to med. jours. Served with Mcht. Marine, 1946-47; served with AUS, 1949-50. Recipient award in medicine Fordham U. Alumni Assn., 1974, Gold award Am. Acad. Pediatrics, 1973, Alpha Omega Alpha Faculty award N.Y. Med. Coll., 1982; Am. Thoracic Soc fellow, 1959-60; grantee Health Research Council N.Y., 1965-71, NIH, 1962-71. Fellow A.C.S.; mem. Am. Trauma Soc. (founding mem.), Soc. Critical Care Medicine (founding mem., pres. 1976), Am. Surg. Assn., Am. Physiol. Soc., Soc. Univ. Surgeons, Equestrian Order of Holy Sepulchre of Jerusalem. Patentee in field. Home: 14 Pryer Ln Larchmont NY 10538 Office: NY Medical College Munger Pavilion Valhalla NY 10595 *Adaptability and the determination of what is possible are the keys to personal success and contentment.*

DELHEY, JOHN DONALD, mgmt. cons.; b. Chgo., Mar. 23, 1923; s. John Sullivan and Florence (Gorges) D.; m. Florence Elizabeth Britt, Sept. 8, 1951; children—Duncan C., Laura E., Christopher J. B.S., Northwestern U., 1949, M.B.A., 1953. Exec. trainee CECO Steel Products, Inc., Cicero, Ill., 1949-51; supr. A/C pay, aircraft engine div. Ford Motor Co., Chgo., 1951-54; sr. v.p. ops., dir. Sta-Rite Industries, Inc., Delavan, Wis., 1954-79; treas., dir. Keefe & Assos. Inc., Lake Geneva, Wis., 1979-80; dir. Barker Lumber Co., Inc., Delavan. Served to 1st lt. USAAF, 1942-47. Decorated Air medal. Home and Office: Route 5 Box 189 Delavan WI 53115

D'ELIA, FRANK ROLAND, lawyer, department store executive; b. Salerno, Italy, Mar. 5, 1931; s. Cony and Rose Mary (DiCandia) D'E.; m. Gloria J. Caruso, Oct. 19, 1963. B.A. in Polit. Sci, Bklyn. Coll., 1956; LL.B., N.Y. U., 1959. Bar: N.Y. 1960. With Allied Stores Corp., N.Y.C., 1959—, head corporate legal div., corporate atty., 1968—, asst. sec., 1968-76, sec., 1976—, v.p., 1977—. Mem. Consumer Affairs Citizens Adv. Com., Village of Lynbrook, N.Y., 1974-76. Mem. Am. Soc. Corporate Secs., Nat. Retail Mchts. Assn. (alt. mem. of govtl. and legal affairs com.). Clubs: Rockville Links (Rockville Centre, N.Y.); Princeton (N.Y.C.) (assoc.). Home: 30 Sunset Ave Lynbrook NY 11563 Office: Allied Stores Corp 1114 Ave of the Americas New York NY 10036

DE LISIO, STEPHEN SCOTT, lawyer; b. San Diego, Dec. 30, 1937; s. Anthony J. and Emma (Cheney) DeL.; m. Margaret I. Winter, June 26, 1964; children: Anthony W., Stephen Scott, Heather E. Student, Am. U., 1958-59; B.A., Emory U., 1959; LL.B., Albany Law Sch., 1962; LL.M., Georgetown U., 1963. Bar: D.C., N.Y. 1963, Alaska 1964. Practice law, Fairbanks, 1963-71, Anchorage, 1971—, asst. dist. atty., Fairbanks, 1963-65; asso. McNealy & Merdes, 1965-66; lectr. U. Alaska, 1965-67; partner Schaible, Staley, DeLisio & Cook, Inc., 1966—; dir. Woodstock Property Co., Inc., Pasit Inc.; city atty., Fairbanks, 1967-70, Barrow, 1969-72, Ft. Yukon and North Pole, 1970-72; past sec. U. Alaska Heating Corp., Inc.; past sec.-treas. Trans-Alaska Electronics, Inc., Baker Aviation, Inc.; arbitrator, mem. Alaska regional council Am. Arbitration Assn. Author: (with others) Law and Tactics in Federal Criminal Cases, 1964. Republican precinct committeeman, 1970-76; chmn. Alaska Republican Rules Com., Anchorage Rep. Com., 1973; v.p. We The People, 1977—; vice-chmn. Alaska Libertarian party, 1983—; mem. nat. com. Libertarian party, 1982—; past pres. Tanana Valley State Fair Assn.; past v.p. Fairbanks Mental Health Assn., Fairbanks United Good Neighbors Fund; past bd. dirs. Fairbanks Montessori Assn.; bd. dirs. Anchorage Community Chorus, 1975-77; former bd. dirs. Greater Fairbanks Community Hosp. Found. Recipient Jaycee Disting. Service award, 1968. Mem. ABA, Alaska Bar Assn., D.C. Bar Assn., Anchorage Bar Assn., Spenard Bar Assn. (pres. 1975-77), Am. Trial Lawyers Assn., Lawyer Pilots Bar Assn., Am. Judicature Soc., U.S. (past dir.), Alaska (past pres.), Fairbanks (past pres.), Jaycees (senator), Chi Phi, Pi Sigma Phi. Mem. Alaska Libertarian Party. Home: 5102 Shorecrest Dr Anchorage AK 99502 Office: 943 W 6th Ave Anchorage AK 99501 *A well-defined sense of values and the courage and determination to adhere to it is as essential to a life of purpose and fulfillment, as the rising of the sun is to life on this planet. The challenge is to develop values that are as relevant to the changes of tomorrow as to the reality of the now and the past. The "situation ethics" approach is as disastrous as a smashed rudder on a storm tossed vessel.*

DELL, ERNEST ROBERT, lawyer; b. Vandergrift, Pa., Feb. 6, 1928; m. Karen D. Reed, May 8, 1965; children: Robert W., John D., Jane C. B.S., U. Pitts., 1949, M.Litt., 1953; J.D., Harvard U., 1956. Bar: Pa. 1957, U.S. Supreme Ct. 1961; C.P.A., Pa. Ptnr. firm Reed Smith Shaw & McClay, Pitts., 1956—; adj. prof. law Duquesne U. Law Sch., Pitts., 1960. Mem. ABA, Pa. Bar Assn., Allegheny County Bar Assn., Pa. Inst. C.P.A.'s. Home: 119 Riding Trail Lane Pittsburgh PA 15215 Office: Reed Smith Shaw & McClay 747 Union Trust Bldg PO Box 2009 Pittsburgh PA 15230

DELLA FEMINA, JERRY, advt. agy. exec.; b. Bklyn., July 22, 1936; (married); three children. Former advt. copywriter; former pres., now chmn. bd. Della Femina, Travisano, & Partners Inc., 1967—. Author: (1970.) From Those Wonderful Folks Who Gave You Pearl Harbor. Named Advt. Exec. of Year, 1970. Office: 625 Madison Ave New York NY 10022

DELLAVECHIA, ANTHONY J., financial services company executive; b. Port Washington, N.Y., June 16, 1936; s. Pasquale and Margaret (Whyte) D.; m. Mary Ann Rybak, Oct. 30, 1960. Area v.p. Avco Fin. Services, Wellesley, Mass., 1957-76; sr. exec. v.p. Assos. Fin. Services, Irving, Tex., 1976-83, pres., 1983—. Served with AUS, 1955-57. Club: Bent Tree Country (Dallas). Home: 5940 Club Oaks Dr Dallas TX 75248 Office: 250 Carpenter Freeway Irving TX 75060 *Desire, hard work, sacrifice, and the ability to make a realistic self-evaluation of oneself daily are key ingredients to success.*

DELLENBACK, JOHN RICHARD, association executive; b. Chgo., Nov. 6, 1918; s. William H. and Margaret (Albright) D.; m. Mary Jane Benedict, Sept. 10, 1948; children: Richard Ludlow, David Albright, Barbara Clare. B.S. in Applied Econ. Sci, Yale U., 1940; J.D., U. Mich., 1949. Bar: Oreg. bar. Bus. tng. student Gen. Electric Co., 1940-42; instr. bus. law Oreg. State U., 1949-50, asst. prof., 1950-51; partner in law with Frank J. Van Dyke, Medford, Oreg., 1952-66; mem. Oreg. Ho. of Reps., 1960-66, (90th-93d Congresses, 4th Dist. Oreg.); dir. Peace Corps, Washington, 1975-77; pres. Christian Coll. Coalition, Washington, 1977—; dir. Nat. Bank Wash.; mem. Oreg. Bd. Bar Examiners. Pres. United Medford Crusade, Jackson County Cancer Soc.; active Boy Scouts Am.; moderator Oreg. Synod United Presbyn. Ch.; mem. Permanent Jud. Commn. Gen. Assembly United Presbyn. Ch., Commn. Ecumenical Mission and Relations; del. Republican Nat. Conv., 1964, 68, 72; bd. dirs. Medford YMCA, Kiwanis Found.; trustee Howard U., Lewis and Clark Coll. Served to lt. comdr. USNR, 1942-46. Named Jr. First Citizen Medford Jr. C. of C., 1953. Mem. Am., Oreg., Jackson County bar assns., Medford C. of C. (dir.), Oreg. Soc. of D.C. (pres.), Phi Beta Kappa, Phi Gamma Delta, Phi Alpha Delta. Clubs: Cosmos (Washington); Kiwanis (pres. Medford), Masons, Elks, Rogue Valley Univ., Rogue Valley Country. Home: 4100 Cathedral Ave NW Washington DC 20016 also 614 NW Westover Terr Portland OR 97210

DELLEUR, JACQUES WILLIAM, mechanical engineering educator; b. Paris, Dec. 30, 1924; U.S., 1952, naturalized, 1957; s. Georges Leon and Simone (Rossum) D.; m. DeLores Ann Horne, June 18, 1957; children: James Robert, Ann Marie. Civil and Mining Engr., Nat. U. Colombia, 1949; M.S. in Civil Engring., Rensselaer Poly. Inst., 1950; D.Engring. Sci., Columbia U., 1955. Civil engr. R.J. Tipton and Assos., 1950-52; from research asst. to instr. civil engring. and engring. mechanics Columbia, 1952-55; mem. faculty Purdue U., 1955—, prof. hydraulic engring. and hydrology, 1963—, head hydromechanics and water resources area, 1965-76, head hydraulic and systems engring. area, 1981—, asso. dir. Water Resources Research Center, 1971—, acting dir., 1983; research fluid mechanics U. Grenoble, France, 1961-62; research hydrology and environ. fluid mechanics French Nat. Hydraulics Labs., Chatou, France, 1968-69, 76-77. Co-author book on statis. hydrology, book on urban hydrology, also articles, reports in field. Fellow Ind. Acad. Sci.; Mem. ASCE (Freeman fellow 1961-62, chmn. fluid dynamics com. 1964-66, task com. mechanics of turbulence 1964-69, task com. hydraulics of bridges 1963-68), Am. Geophys. Union (chmn. urban hydrology com. 1978—), Am. Water Resources Assn., Am. Soc. Engring. Edn., Internat. Assn. Hydraulic Research, Internat. Assn. Sci. Hydrology. Home: 124 Mohican Pl West Lafayette IN 47906 Office: Sch Civil Engring Purdue Univ West Lafayette IN 47907

DELLINGER, DAVID, editor, printer; b. Wakefield, Mass., Aug. 22, 1915; s. Raymond Pennington and Marie E. (Fiske) D.; m. Elizabeth Peterson, Feb. 4, 1942; children: Patchen, Ray, Natasha Peterson, Daniel, Michele. B.A., Yale, 1936; student, Yale U. Div. Sch., 1937-39, New Coll., Oxford (Eng.) U., 1936-37; grad. sec., Dwight Hall, Yale U., 1937-39; student, Union Theol. Sem., N.Y.C., 1939-40. Assoc. minister Jube Meml. Ch., Newark, 1939-40; ptnr. Libertarian Press, workers coop., Glen Gardner, N.J., 1946-67; editor and pub. Liberation, 1956-75; editor Seven Days Mag., 1975-80. Author: Cuba: America's Lost Plantations, 1961, More Power than We Know, 1975; Editor: (with Michael Albert) Beyond Survival: New Directions for the Disarmament Movement, 1983; Contbr.: Seeds of Liberation, 1964, Nonviolence in America, 1966, Telling It Like It Was-The Chicago Riots, 1969, Against the Crime of Silence, 1969, Collected Essays—Revolutionary nonviolence, 1970, Nonviolent Action and Social Change, 1979. Mem. bd. dirs. Internat. Assn. Sociology Coop., 1955-65; chmn. Nat. Moblzn. Commn. to End War in Vietnam, 1967-71; coordinator Fifth Ave. Vietnam Peace Parade Com., 1965-73; mem. Bertrand Russell War Crimes Tribunal, 1966-67. Poynter fellow journalism Yale, 1969. Mem. Berzelius and The Colony Found. (Yale), Phi Beta Kappa. Office: care South End Press 302 Columbus Ave Boston MA 02116

DELLINGER, WALTER ESTES, III, lawyer; b. Charlotte, N.C., May 15, 1941; s. Walter Estes and Grace Phelan (Lawing) D.; m. Anne Elizabeth Maxwell, June 12, 1965; children—Hampton, Andrew. A.B. with honors, U. N.C., Chapel Hill, 1963; LL.B., Yale U., 1966. Bar: N.C. bar 1970. Asso. prof. law U. Miss., 1966-68; law clk. to Justice Hugo L. Black, U.S. Supreme Ct., 1968-69; asso. prof. law Duke U., 1969-72, prof., 1972—, asso. dean, 1974-76, acting dean, 1976-78; vis. prof. U. So. Calif. Law Center, 1973-74, U. Mich. Law Sch., 1977; prof. in residence U.S. Dept. Justice, Washington, 1980-81; cons., draftsman N.C. Criminal Code Commn., 1970-78. Mem. bd. editors: Yale Law Jour, 1965-66. Rockefeller Found. Humanities fellow, 1981-82. Mem. Am. Bar Assn., N.C. State Bar. Democrat. Home: 513 E Franklin St Chapel Hill NC 27514 Office: Duke U Law Sch Durham NC 27706

DELLIQUADRI, PARDO FREDERICK, former university dean; b. Pueblo, Colo., Jan. 20, 1915; s. Colombo Frederick and Rose Marie (Russo) D.; m. Velma Lee Ingram, Sept. 9, 1939; children—Toni Cheryl, Lyn Christine, Geri Martha. B.A. cum laude, U. Colo., 1938; M.S. in Social Work, U. Nebr., 1941. WPA investigator in, Wyo., 1938-39; research Brookings Instn., 1940; pub. welfare childrens worker, Yakima, Wash., 1941; state statistician Wyo. Pub. Welfare Dept., 1942, dir. childrens div., 1946-48; supt. child welfare Ill. Dept. Pub. Welfare, 1948-50; dir. div. children and youth Wis. Dept. Pub. Welfare, 1950-60; dean N.Y. Sch. Social Work, Columbia, 1960-67, Sch. Social Work, U. Hawaii, 1967-68; chief U.S. Children's Bur., Washington, 1968-69; dean Sch. Social Welfare, U. Wis., Milw., 1969-72, Sch. Social Work, U. Ala., 1972-81, Univ. prof., 1981; Exec. sec. Ill. Com. Children and Youth, 1948, Wis. Com. Children and Youth, 1950-60; tech. adv. com. White House Conf. Children and Youth, 1950; adv. council child welfare U.S. Congress, 1958-59; UN social welfare adviser to, El Salvador, 1959; U.S. rep. Inter-Am. Children's Inst., Montevideo, Uruguay, 1958-61, v.p., 1959-61; vice chmn. U.S. delegation Pan Am. Child Congress, Bogata, 1959; U.S. exec. bd. UNICEF, 1961-69; mem. of Mayor N.Y.C. Com. Pub. Welfare, 1961-67; mem. bd., exec. com. N.Y. Citizens Com. Children, 1961-67; ad hoc com. HEW, 1961; panel tng. grants Pres.'s Commn. Juvenile Delinquency, 1962-66, chmn., 1963-66; chmn. adv. group N.Y. State Legis. Com. on Child Care, 1965-67; chmn. N.Y. Adv. Welfare Study Com., 1965-66; del. White House Conf. on Children, 1970-71; exec. bd. Wis. Welfare Council, 1969; cons. Community Research Assos., N.Y.C., 1970-74; chmn. adv. com. Ala. Dept. Pensions and Security, 1975—; lectr. UCLA, 1981-82; cons. on volunteerism First Interstate Bank of Calif., 1983—. Mem. task force on leisure Nat. Council Chs. U.S.A., 1965-67; U.S. del. UN Conf. for Internat. Ministers Social Welfare, 1968; nat. bd. dirs. Am. Humane Assn., 1975—, v.p. children's div., 1974, pres., 1977—. Served to lt. USNR, 1942-46. Recipient FONEME Internat. award on youth, Milan, Italy, 1968; Norlin medal, 1969; Fulbright scholar fgn. exchange program to, Taiwan, 1980-81. Mem. Am. Pub. Welfare Assn. (chmn. membership com. 1950-52, dir. 1952, 54, 57, chmn. self-study com. 1965), Child Welfare League Am., Am. Assn. Social Workers (chmn. nominating com. 1954-55), Council Social Work Edn. (chmn. career com. 1961-67, chmn. com. on adminstrn. 1968-69, chmn. dean's steering com. 1971, nat. nominating com. 1975—), Nat. Assn. Social Workers (chmn. Wis. 1957-59, nat. dir. 1975—), Am. Council Nationality Services, Nat. Conf. Social Work (v.p. 1960-61, chmn. program com. 1970-71), confs. social welfare Wyo., Ill., Wis., N.Y., Wis. PTA (life), Ala. Conf. Social Work (pres. 1976-77), Alumni Assn. U. Colo. (pres. Northeastern chpt.), Phi Beta Kappa, Phi Kappa Phi. Office: 6527 W 6th St Los Angeles CA 90048

DELLO JOIO, NORMAN, composer; b. N.Y.C., Jan. 24, 1913; s. Casimir and Antoinette (Garramone) Dello J.; m. Barbara Bolton, 1974; children: Victoria, Justin, Norman Adrian. Student, All Hallows Inst., 1926-30, Coll. City N.Y., 1932-34, Inst. Mus. Art, 1936, Juilliard Grad. Sch., 1939-41, Yale Sch. Music, 1941; Mus.D. (hon.), Colby Coll., Lawrence Coll., U. Cin., 1967, St. Mary's Coll., 1969, Susequehanna U., 1980. Tchr. composition Sarah Lawrence Coll., 1945-50, Mannes Coll. Music, 1952—; commentator Met. Opera broadcasts; dean Sch. for the Arts, Boston U., 1972-78; Mem. research adv. council U.S. Office Edn.; adv. council State U. N.Y., Potsdam; chmn. policy com. contemporary music Ford Found. Composer: Ballet On Stage, 1944, Ricercari; for piano and orch., 1946, Variations-Chaccone-Finale, 1947, Diversion of Angeles; dance, 1948, Concerto for Clarinet and Orch, 1949, New York Profiles; for orch., 1949, The Triumph of St. Joan; opera, 1950, Psalm of David; chorus and orch., 1950, Song of Affirmation; soprano, chorus, narrator, orch., 1950, The Tall Kentuckian; score for musical play, 1952, Song of the Open Road; chorus, 1952, The Ruby; opera, 1953, The Lamentation of Saul, 1954, The Trial at Rouen, 1955, Mediations on Ecclesiastes, 1956, Air Power, symphonic suite, 1956, Ballad of the 7 Lively Arts, 1957, To St. Cecilia, 1958, Blood Moon; also: Variations and Fantasy for Piano and Orchestra, 1961; score Songs of Adieu, The Louvre, NBC TV, 1965 (Emmy award), Beyond Every Horizon; for Symphonic band Antiphonal Fantasy; organ, brass, strings, 1965, Songs of Walt Whitman for Orch. and Chorus, 1966, Capriccio; for piano, 1968, Fantasies on Theme of Haydn, 1968, Time of Snow; ballet, 1968, Proud Music of the Storm; chorus, brass, organ, 1967, Days of the Modern; chorus, brass, percussion, 1968, Evocations; chorus, orch., 1970, Psalm of Peace; chorus, organ, french horn, trumpet, 1971, Mass; chorus, organ, brass Concertante for Wind Instruments, 1972, Of Crows and Clusters; chorus and piano, 1972, Suite for Flute and Piano, 1973, Suite for Clarinet and Piano, 1973, Suite for Organ, 1973, Folio for Piano, 1973, Lyric Fantasies for Viola and Strings, 1973, The Poet's Song, 1973, Leisure, 1973, Mass to the Blessed Virgin; organ and chorus, 1974, Satiric Dances; band, 1974, Stage Parodies; piano 4 hands, 1974, Mass in honour of Pope John XXIII; organ, brass, strings and chorus, 1975, Notes from Tom Paine; chorus and piano, 1975, Colonial Variants; orch., 1976, Southern Echoes, 1976, Colonial Ballads; band, 1977, As of a Dream; orch., soloists, chorus, narrator and dancers, 1978, Sonata for Trumpet and Piano, 1978, Songs of Remembrance; voice solo and orch., 1978, Salute to Scarlatti; piano, 1978, The Psalmist's Meditation; chorus and piano, 1978, Variations; piano, 1980, Hymns Without Words; chorus and piano, 1979, Ballabili; dances for orch., 1981; chorus and piano Love Songs at Parting, 1982; string orch. East Hampton Sketches, 1983; piano and hands Song at Springtide, 1984; concert band Aria and Roulade, 1983; chorus and concert band Let Us Sing a New Song, 1984. Chmn. planning com. Ford Found.; Bd. dirs. Am. Music Center. Recipient Elizabeth Sprague Coolidge award, 1937, Town Hall Composition award, 1941, N.Y. Music Critics Circle award, 1949, 58, Pulitzer prize for music, 1957, Emmy award for TV Score; Guggenheim fellow, 1943-44; Am. Acad. Arts and Letters grantee, 1945. Mem. League Composers (dir.), Broadcast Music, Inc., Nat. Acad. and Inst. Arts and Letters (mem. council). Clubs: Century, Devon Yacht. Home: Box 154 East Hampton NY 11937 *Whatever recognition I have received for my creative work, I owe for the most part, to an understanding mother and disciplinarian father. In this, my 70th year, I give thanks for a loving wife and a composer son whose music I feel will be an extension of myself into the future.*

DELL'OLIO, LOUIS, fashion designer; b. N.Y.C., July 23, 1948; s. James and Edith Dell'O. Diploma, Parsons Sch. Design, N.Y.C., 1969. Tchr. spl. design Parsons Sch. Design, 1969. Design asst., Dominic Rompollo of Teal Traina, N.Y.C., 1969-71; chief designer, Giorgini div. of Originala, N.Y.C., 1971-74; designer, Anne Klein & Co., N.Y.C., 1974—. Recipient Coty award, 1977, 81, Coty Hall of Fame award, 1982, Coty Hall of Fame Citation, 1984; Norman Norell scholar, 1968. Mem. Fashion Designers Am. (council). Office: Anne Klein & Co 205 W 39th St New York NY 10016 *

DELLOMO, FRANK A., banker; b. Bklyn., Nov. 24, 1933; s. Anthony E. and Veronica K. (Jenson) D.; m. Pat Turvey, Oct. 24, 1962; children: Tracey, Alysen. Grad., Bklyn. Coll., 1957; postgrad., Brown U., 1963-66, Amherst Coll., 1968-69. Vice pres. Bklyn. Savs. Bank, 1968-72, sr. v.p., 1972-75, exec. v.p., 1975-81, pres., 1981—; sr. exec. v.p. Met. Savs. Bank, 1982—; mem. faculty Grad. Sch. Banking Brown U. Trustee Bklyn. Bur. Community Service; mem. exec. com. N.Y. div. Am. Cancer Soc., 1981. Mem. Savs. Instns. Mktg. Soc. Am. Clubs: Creek, N.Y. Athletic. Office: 211 Montague St Brooklyn NY 11201 *

DELL'OSSO, LOUIS FRANK, neuroscience educator; b. Bklyn., Mar. 16, 1941; s. Frank and Rose (Perrone) Dell'O.; m. Aquilina Marie Ferlo, May 22, 1965; single ptnr. Charlene Hale Morse, Sept. 29, 1977. B.E.E., Bklyn. Poly. Inst., 1961, postgrad., 1961-63; Ph.D., U. Wyo., 1968. Co-dir. Ocular Motor Neurophysiology Lab. VA. Med. Ctr., Miami, Fla., 1972-80; asst. prof. neurology U. Miami, 1972-75, assoc. prof. neurology, 1975-79, prof. neurology, 1979-80; dir. Ocular Motor Neurophysiology Lab. VA Med. Ctr., Cleve., 1980—; prof. neurology and biomed. engring. Case Western Res. U., Cleve., 1980—; cons. Westinghouse Research Lab, Pitts, 1966-67, 70-71, Mt. Sinai Hosp., Miami, FL, 1972-75. Bd. dirs. Vineland Galloway Civic Assn., Miami, 1973-76. Grantee NIH, 1971-77, VA Med. Ctr., 1972—, NSF, 1970. Mem. IEEE, Engring. in Medicine and Biology Soc. (chpt. chmn. 1977-78), Assn. Research in Vison and Ophthalmology, Rocky Mt. NeuroOphthalmology Soc., Soc. Neurosci., AAAS, Train Collectors Assn. Democrat. Home: 2356 Tudor Dr Cleveland Heights OH 44106 Office: VA Med Ctr Ocular Motility Lab 127A Cleveland OH 44106

DELLOW, REGINALD LEONARD, advertising executive; b. Detroit, Sept. 13, 1924; s. Reginald C. and Ethel (White) D.; m. Betsy Ann Paton, Feb. 26, 1949; children: John Paton, Elizabeth Diana, Tracy Susannah. Student, Wayne State U., 1941-43; B.S., Detroit Inst. Tech., 1946. Research dir., asst. to media dir. D.P. Brother & Co., Detroit, 1948-53; dir. media and research Allman Co., Detroit, 1953-56; exec. v.p. Grant Advt., Inc. (name changed to Harris-Grant, Inc.), Chgo., 1956-75; gen mgr. Meltzer, Aron & Lemen, Inc., Chgo., 1975-78; pres. Dellow & Assos., Chgo.; 1978—; Pres. Chgo. agy. Media Group, 1960. Named Media Man of Month, Apr. 1960; recipient Advt. award Am. Legion, 1958. Mem. Am. Marketing Assn. (pres. Mich. chpt. 1955, mem. nat. conv. com. 1963, 66, treas. Chi chpt. 1969-70), Council on Fgn. Relations, Presidents' Assn., Japan Am. Soc. (dir. 1976-83), Mid Am. Swedish Assn., Alpha Gamma Upsilon (pres. 1946), Omega Alpha Pi (pres. 1945). Republican. Mem. Christian Scientist Ch. Club: Union League (Chgo.). Home: 5445 N Sheridan Rd Chicago IL 60640 Office: 845 N Michigan Ave Suite 903 E Chicago IL 60611

DELLUMS, RONALD VERNIE, congressman; b. Oakland, Calif., Nov. 24, 1935; m. Leola Roscoe Higgs; 3 children. A.A., Oakland City Coll., 1958; B.A., San Francisco State Coll., 1960; M.S.W., U. Calif., 1962. Psychiat. social worker Calif. Dept. Mental Hygiene, 1962-64; program dir. Bayview Community Center, San Francisco, 1964-65; from assoc. dir. to dir. Hunters Point Youth Opportunity Center, 1965-66; planning cons. Bay Area Social Planning Council, 1966-67; dir. concentrated employment program San Francisco Econ. Opportunity Council, 1967-68; sr. cons. Social Dynamics, Inc., 1968-70; mem. 92d-98th Congresses from 8th Calif. dist.; Lectr. San Francisco State Coll., U. Calif. at Berkeley. Mem. Berkeley City Council, 1967-71. Served with USMCR, 1954-56. Democrat. Home: Washington DC Office: 2136 Rayburn House Office Bldg Washington DC 20515

DELMAR, EUGENE ANTHONY, architect; b. Gallitzin, Pa., June 8, 1928; s. Frank and Viola (Bocci) DiMaria; m. Bettie Hardin, Apr. 7, 1951; children: Diana, Daniel, David. B.Arch., Columbia U., 1954; M.Arch. in Urban Design, Catholic U. Am., 1971. Architect Ronald S. Senseman, Washington, 1954-59; prin. Eugene A. Delmar, Silver Spring, Md., 1959—; mem. vis. com. Sch. Architecture, U. Md. Important works include Electrophysics Lab, Columbia, Md., Montgomery County Jud. Ctr., Natatorium, Washington, Charlotte Hall Vets. Retirement Home, Denton Courthouse/Multi-Service Center. Active code enforcement bd. Dept. Econ. and Community Devel. Md.; mem. Montgomery County Beautification Com., 1965, Montgomery County Sign Rev. Bd., 1968-71. Served to 2d lt. C.E., U.S. Army, 1946-48. Recipient Disting. Service award U.S. Jaycees, 1964, E.B. Morris Disting. Service award, 1976. Fellow AIA (First award design 1966, award of merit for design Potomac Valley chpt. 1966); mem. Md. Soc. Architects (pres. 1972-73), Sigma Chi. Democrat. Episcopalian. Clubs: Silver Spring Lions (pres. 1978-79), Columbia University. Home: 2104 Hermitage Ave Silver Spring MD 20902 Office: 850 Sligo Ave Silver Spring MD 20910

DE LOACH, ANTHONY CORTELYOU, solar physicist; b. N.Y.C., July 9, 1934; s. Arthur Edwin and Helen Louise (Eagleton) de L. B.S. in Physics, U. S.C., 1961, Ph.D., 1966. Solar physicist NASA, 1966—; mission scientist for NASA/European Space Agy. Space Shuttle flight simulations, 1976-77, chief solar scis. br., Ala., 1974-80, staff scientist solar-terrestrial physics div., 1980—. Contbr. articles to sci. jours. Served with U.S. Army, 1954-56. Nat. Def. Grad. fellow, 1961-64; Oak Ridge Nat. fellow, 1964-66. Mem. AAAS. Home: 2612 Arrowwood Dr SE Huntsville AL 35803 Office: Solar-Terrestrial Physics Div ES51 Marshall Space Flight Center AL 35812

DELOACH, CARTHA DEKLE, corporate executive; b. Claxton, Ga., July 20, 1920; s. Cartha Calhoun and Eula Mary (Dekle) DeL.; m. Barbara Owens, Apr. 22, 1945; children: Barbara Elaine, Cartha Dekle, Thomas O., Theresa M., Gregory D., Sharon Marie, Mark Christopher. B.A., Stetson U., 1942; student, Law Sch., 1941-42, J.D. (hon.), 1966, Lincoln Coll., 1968. With FBI, 1942-70, asst. dir., 1959-65, asst. to dir., 1965-70; v.p. corporate affairs Pepsico, Inc., Purchase, N.Y., 1970—; dir. Piggly-Wiggly So., Inc. Chmn., pres. bd. dirs. J. Edgar Hoover Found., 1964—; bd. dirs. Banking Instns. Served with USN, 1944-46. Recipient Dist. Alumni award Stetson U., 1958; Pres.' Medal St. John's Coll., 1967; George Washington Honor medal Freedoms Found., 1967, 68, 69, 72; named Man of Year Nat. Assn. State Dirs. Vets. Affairs, 1964. Mem. Am. Legion (dept. comdr. 1958, nat. vice comdr. 1959, chmn. nat. pub. relations commn. 1959-78, Man of year award 1963), Stetson U. Alumni Assn. (dist. Alumnus award 1966), Knights of Malta, Pi Kappa Phi, Phi Alpha Delta. Home: 50 Gull Point Rd Hilton Head Island SC 29928 Office: PepsiCo Inc Purchase NY 10577

DELOGU, GAETANO, symphony music director, conductor; b. Messina, Sicily, 1934; s. Francesco Maria and Maria (Toraldo) D.; m. Teresa Deluca, Dec. 29, 1960; 1 son, Francesco. Grad., Universita di Catania, 1958. Permanent condr., Teatro Massimo di Palermo, Italy, 1975-78; music dir., Denver Symphony Orch., 1978—; guest condr. numerous orchs., including, N.Y. Philharmonic, London Philharmonic, others, recs. with, London Philharmonic and Czech Philharmonic. (Winner Young Condr.'s Competition, Florence, Dimitri Mitropoulos Internat. Competition, N.Y.C. 1968). Roman Catholic. Office: care Denver Symphony Orch 1245 Champa St Denver CO 80224

DE LONE, H. FRANCIS, lawyer; b. Phila., May 8, 1915; s. Louis S. and Helena L. (Lang) De L.; m. Madeline Heckscher, June 25, 1939; children: Richard Heckscher, H. Francis, Pamela S. Foster, Austin S. A.B. cum laude, Harvard U., 1937, LL.B., U. Pa., 1940. Bar: Pa. 1940. Since practiced, Phila.; partner firm Dechert Price & Rhoads (and predecessors), 1940—; mem. Fed. Jud. Nominating Commn. Pa., 1979—. Pres. United Way Southeastern Pa., 1978-80, Community Services Pa., 1970-73, Health and Welfare Council, Phila., 1967-69, 76-77, United Cerebral Palsy Assn., 1953-55. Served to 1st lt. USMC, 1944-46. Recipient Citizen Vol. award United Way Southeastern Pa., 1982. Mem. Am. Bar Assn., Am. Coll. Trial Lawyers, 3d Circuit Jud. Conf., Pa. Bar Assn., Phila. Bar Assn. Clubs: Merion Cricket, Phila. Racquet. Home: 10 Greenbriar Ln Paoli PA 19301 Office: 3400 Centre Sq W 1500 Market St Philadelphia PA 19102

DELONGA, LEONARD ANTHONY, artist, educator; b. Cannonsburg, Pa., Dec. 18, 1925; s. Raymond Peter and Emma (Bello) DeL.; m. Sandra Katz, Jan. 17, 1954; children: Roy, Beth Alison Senecal. B.A., U. Miami-Coral Gables, (Fla.), 1950; M.F.A., U. Ga., 1952. Asst. prof. Tex. Wesleyan Coll., Ft. Worth, 1954-56, U. Ga., Athens, 1956-64; prof. Mt. Holyoke Coll., South Hadley, Mass., 1964—, David B. Turman Disting. prof., 1981—; cons. Chatham Coll., Pitts., Wellesley Coll., 1978, Hamilton Coll., Clinton, N.Y., 1983. One-man shows, Kraushaar Galleries, N.Y.C., 1954, 67, 70, 74, 77, 78, Mt. Holyoke Coll., 1965-73, group shows include, NAD, 1974, group shows, Nat. Inst. Arts and Letters, 1961; represented in numerous public and pvt. collections. Chair Alumnae Found, Mt. Holyoke Coll., 1979. Served with USAAF, 1944-46. Grantee in field. Home: 23 Woodbridge St South Hadley MA 01075 Office: Mount Holyoke Coll South Hadley MA 01075

DE LOOPER, WILLEM JOHAN, artist, museum curator; b. The Hague, Netherlands, Oct. 30, 1932; came to U.S., 1950; s. Henri Bastiaan and Wilhelmina Johanna (Huizinga) De L.; m. Frauke Weber, Feb. 14, 1969. B.A., Am. U., 1957. Mem. staff Phillips Collection, Washington, 1959-72, asst. curator, 1972-74, assoc. curator, 1974—, curator, 1982—. Represented in permanent collections, Hirshhorn Collection and Sculpture Garden, Fed. Res. Bank, Richmond, Va., NSF, Phillips Collection, Corcoran Gallery Art.; One man shows include, Jefferson Place Gallery, 1966-74, Phillips Collection, Washington, 1975, Protech-McIntosh Gallery, 1975-80; group exhbns. include Group Seven, Washington Gallery Modern Art, 1968, Washington 20 Years, Balt. Mus. Art, 1970, Art Now, Kennedy Center, Washington, 1974, Golden Door—Artists Immigrants of Am. 1876-1976, Hirshhorn Mus. and Sculpture Garden, 1977, Nat. Acad. Sci., Galerie L., Hamburg, W. Ger., 1979, retrospective, No. Va. Community Coll., 1975, Fed. Res. Bd., Washington, 1978. Served with U.S. Army, 1957-59. Home: 2219 California St NW Washington DC 20008 Office: 1600 21st St NW Washington DC 20009

DE LORENZO, ANNETTE MARIE, farm equipment manufacturing company communications executive; b. Detroit, Nov. 10, 1941; d. Anthony George and Josephine (Paratore) De L. B.A., Manhattanville Coll, Purchase, N.Y., 1963; M.S., Columbia U., 1964. Research supr. Campbell-Ewald Co. Advt., Detroit, 1964-69; dir. housing and urban research Holmes-Harmon Corp., Birmingham, Mich, 1969-71; sr. info. analyst and research supr. Continental Ill. Nat. Bank, Chgo., 1971-74; v.p. Burson-Marsteller, Chgo., 1974-78, Hill and Knowlton, Inc., 1978-82; v.p. corp. communications Internat. Harvester Co., Chgo., 1982—. Jr. bd. dirs. Chgo. Symphony Orch.; bd. dirs. Mary Bartleme Homes, Chgo. Mem. Internat. Assn. Bus. Communicators, Chgo. Pub. Relations Clinic, Motor Vehicle Mfrs. Assn. U.S. (pub. info. policy com.). Club: Club Internat. (Chgo.). 1325 N State Pkwy Chicago Il 60610 Office: Internat Harvester Co 401 N Michigan Ave Chicago Il 60611

DE LORENZO, ANTHONY GEORGE, pub. relations exec.; b. Edgerton, Wis., Aug. 26, 1914; s. Joseph and Anna (Pipitoni) de L.; m. Josephine Paratore, Sept. 28, 1940; children—Annette M., Anthony J., Josephine M., Peter M. B.A., U. Wis., 1936; D.Sc. in Bus. Adminstrn. (hon.), Cleary Coll., 1958. Editorial staff Racine Jour.-Times, 1933-35; staff United Press Assn., Madison, Wis., also; Milw., Chgo., 1935-41, automotive editor, Mich. mgr., Detroit, 1941-44; pub. relations staff various accounts Kudner Agy., Inc., advt., 1944-49; staff dept. pub. relations Gen. Motors Corp., Detroit, 1949-56, v.p. charge public relations staff, 1957-79. Chmn. U. Wis. Found., 1979. Recipient Disting. Achievement in Journalism citation U. Wis., 1958. Mem. U. Wis. Alumni Assn. (nat. pres. 1965-66), Public Relations Soc. Am., Sigma Delta Chi. Roman Catholic. Clubs: Nat. Press, 1925 F St. (Washington); Detroit, Detroit Athletic, Recess (Detroit); Flint City, Bloomfield Hills Country; University (N.Y.C.). Home: Birmingham MI 48010 Office: 1700 N Woodward Bloomfield Hills MI 48013

DELORENZO, DAVID JOSEPH, public relations executive; b. Auburn, N.Y., Nov. 25, 1932; s. Joseph Robert and Marie (Hahn) DeL.; m. Margaret Mae Pinckney, July 21, 1956; children: David William, Mary Beth. Student public schs., Auburn. With lab. Gen. Electric Co., Auburn, 1951, 54-57; asst. bur. chief Elmira Star Gazette, 1957-58; bur. chief Syracuse (N.Y.) Post Standard, 1958-66, polit. writer, city hall reporter, 1966-71; asst. sports editor Auburn Citizen-Advertiser, 1971-77; editor Bowling mag. Am. Bowling Congress, Greendale, Wis., 1977-81, asst. mgr. pub. relations dept., 1981-82, mgr. pub. relations dept., 1982—. Sports chmn. Cayuga County (N.Y.) March of Dimes, 1965-77. Served with USCG, 1951-54. Recipient writing awards, including 5 1st pl. awards Cayuga County Fire-Police Assn., 1960-65; Journalism award Auburn Police Benevolent Assn., 1974; First place writing award Profl. Bowlers Assn., 1982; Bowling Mag. writing awards. Mem. Bowling Writers Assn. Am. (pres. 1974-75, meritorious service award 1976). Democrat. Roman Catholic. Club: K.C. Home: 3976 S 92d St Greenfield WI 53228 Office: 5301 S 76th St Greendale WI 53129 *Fortunate most aptly describes my life. With little background, I first was accepted as a newspaperman which led to being editor of a national publication and eventually to my present position of public relations manager of the world's largest sports membership organization. I sincerely appreciate the confidence so many others have had in me through the years.*

DELORIA, VINE VICTOR, JR., political science educator, author; b. Martin, S.D., Mar. 26, 1933; s. Vine Victor and Barbara (Eastburn) D.; m. Barbara Jeanne Nystrom, June 1958; children: Philip, Daniel, Jeanne Ann. B.S., Iowa State U., 1958; M.Th., Lutheran Sch. Theology, 1963; J.D., U. Colo., 1970; D.H. Litt., Augustana Coll., 1971. Staff asst. United Scholarship Service, Denver, 1963-64; exec. dir. Nat. Congress Am. Indians, 1964-67; lectr. West Wash. State Coll., 1970-72; chmn. Inst. for Devel. Indian Law, Washington, 1971-76; lectr. Pacific Sch. Religion, Berkeley, Calif., Summer 1975, New Sch. Religion, Pontiac, Mich., Summer 1976, Colo. Coll., Colorado Springs, 1977, 78; vis. prof. U. Ariz., Tucson, spring 1978, prof. polit. sci., 1978—. Author: Custer Died for Your Sins, 1969, We Talk, You Listen, 1970, Of Utmost Good Faith, 1972, God Is Red, 1973, Behind the Trail of Broken Treaties, 1974, The Indian Affair, 1974, Indians of the Pacific Northwest, 1977, The Metaphysics of Modern Existence, 1979, Red Man in New World Drama, 1972, American Indians, American Justice, 1983. Vice chmn. Am. Indian Resource Assocs., Oglala, S.D., 1973-75; Mem. Bd. Inquiry into Hunger and Malnutrition, 1967-68; mem. exec. council Episcopal Ch., 1969-70. Served with USMCR, 1954-56. Recipient Indian Achievement award Indian Council Fire, 1972. Mem. Authors Guild, Colo., Authors League, ABA, Am. Judicature Soc., Amnesty Internat., Advocates for the Arts. Office: Dept Polit Sci U Ariz Tucson AZ 85721

DELORME, JEAN-CLAUDE, telecommunications company executive; b. Montreal, Que., Can., May 22, 1934; s. Adrien and Marie-Anne (Rodrique) D.; m. Paule Tardif, Sept. 2, 1961; children: Catherine, Marie-Eve. B.A., Coll. Sainte-Marie, Montreal; Licentiate in law, U. Montreal, 1959. Bar: Que. bar 1960. Asso. firm Martineau Walker, Allison, Beaulieu, Tetley and Phelan, 1961-63; sec., gen. counsel Can. Corp. for 1967 World Exhbn., 1963-67; gen. counsel, asst. to chmn., chief exec. officer Standard Brands, Ltd., 1967-69; v.p. adminstrn., sec., gen. counsel Telesat Can., 1969-71; pres., chief exec. officer Teleglobe Can., Montreal, 1971—; Can. rep. Commonwealth Telecommunications Council, 1971—, chmn., 1973-80; dir. Interprovincial Pipe Line Ltd.; past mem. bd. dirs. Montreal Bd. Trade. Past pres. Régie de la Place des Arts; past pres. L'Opéra de Montréal; past mem. bd. dirs. Montreal Assn. Recreation and Culture, Nat. Ballet of Can., Internat. Inst. Music; bd. advisers McGill U. Decorated Officer Order Can., Centennial medal; recipient Gold medal Czechoslovakian Soc. Internat. Relations. Mem. Canadian Telecommunications Carriers Assn. (chmn. 1977-78), Can.-German Chamber Industry and Commerce, Que. Bar Assn. Clubs: Mt. Royal, St. James of Montreal, St. Denis, Le Cercle Universitaire d'Ottawa. Home: 3 Glendale Ave Beaconsfield PQ H9W 5P6 Canada Office: 680 Sherbrooke St West Montreal PQ H3A 2S4 Canada

DELP, WILBUR CHARLES, JR., lawyer; b. Cedar Rapids, Iowa, Oct.26, 1934; s. Wilbur Charles and Irene Frances (Flynn) D.; m. Patricia Lynn Vesley, June 22, 1963; children: Marci Lynn, Melissa Kathryn, Derek Charles. B.A., Coe Coll., 1956; LL.B., NYU, 1959. Bar: Ill. 1960, U.S. Supreme Ct. 1962. Assoc. Sidley & Austin, Chgo., 1959-68, ptnr., 1968; lectr. securities law seminars. Trustee Wayne Community Assn., 1975-78. Served with USAF, 1959-65. Mem. ABA (securities com.), Chgo. Bar Assn. (sub-com. chmn.), NYU Law Alumni Club (bd. dirs. 1976—), Phi Beta Kappa, Phi Kappa Phi. Republican. Episcopalian. Club: Mid-Day (Chgo.). Home: Box 97 Wayne IL 60184 Office: Sidley & Austin 1 First National Plaza Chicago IL 60603

DEL REAL, JUAN ANDRES, lawyer; b. Havana, Cuba, Nov. 4, 1939; came to U.S., 1960, naturalized, 1967; s. Gregorio and Marie Enriqueta Del R.; children: Marietta, Juan Carlos, Tad, Nimi; m. Clarie Luccaro Dorrell. Student, Tulane U., 1957-59, Havana U., 1960; J.D. cum laude, St. Louis U., 1966. Bar: Mo. 1967, D.C. 1967. Assoc. Surrey, Karasik, Gould & Green, Washington, 1966-67; asst. to pres. Central Aguirre Sugar Co., San Juan, P.R., 1967-68; ptnr. Surrey, Karasik, Green & Hill, 1968-71, Hill, Christopher & Phillips, 1971-80; asst. gen. counsel health care fin. div. HHS, 1980-81, gen. counsel, 1981—. Mem. ABA, D.C. Bar Assn. Republican. Office: Dept Health and Human Services Room 722A Hubert H Humphrey Bldg 200 Independence Ave SW Washington DC 20201

DEL REGATO, JUAN ANGEL, radio-therapeutist and oncologist, educator; b. Camaguey, Cuba, Mar. 1, 1909; came to U.S., 1937, naturalized, 1941; s. Juan and Damiana (Manzano) del R.; m. Inez Johnson, May 1, 1939; children: Ann Cynthia del Regato Jaeger, Juanita Inez del Regato Peters. John Carl. Student, U. Havana, Cuba, 1930; M.D., U. Paris, France, 1937, Laureat, 1937; Dr.S. (honoris causa), Colo. Coll., 1969; D.Sc. (honoris causa, ad gradum), Hahnemann Med. Coll., 1977, Med. Coll. Wis., 1981. Diplomate: Am. Bd. Radiology (trustee 1975—, historian 1976—). Asst. Radium Inst., U. Paris, 1934-37, Chgo. Tumor Inst., 1938; radiotherapeutist Warwick Cancer Clinic, Washington, 1939-40; research Nat. Cancer Inst., Balt., 1941-43; chief dept. radiotherapy Ellis Fischel State Cancer Hosp., Columbia, Mo., 1943-48; dir. Penrose Cancer Hosp., Colorado Springs, Colo., 1949-73; prof. clin. radiology U. Colo. Med. Sch., 1950-74; prof. radiology U. South Fla., 1974—; David Gould lectr. Johns Hopkins U., 1983. Author: (with L.V. Ackerman, M.D.)

Cancer; Diagnosis Treatment and Prognosis, 1947, 54, 62, 70, (with H.J. Spjut), 1977; Editor: Cancer Seminar, 1960—; Contbr. articles to profl. jours. Decorated Order of Carlos Finlay of Cuba; Order Francisco de Miranda Republic of Venezuela; Béclère medal à titre exceptionnel, 1980; recipient Gold medal Radiol. Soc. North Am., 1967, Inter-Am. Coll. Radiology, 1967, Am. Coll. Radiology, 1968; Gold plaque, 1975; Grubbe gold medal Ill. Radiol. Soc., 1973; Prix Bruninghaus French Acad. Medicine, 1979; Disting. Scientist award U. South Fla. Coll. Medicine, 1980; named Disting. Physician VA, 1974; Disting. physician VA, 1974—. Mem. Nat. Adv. Cancer Council, Bethesda, Md. (1967-71); mem. med. adv. com. Milheim Found., Denver.; Fellow Am. Coll. Radiology (bd. chancellors; chmn. commn. radiation therapy, com. awards and honors); mem. A.M.A., Nat. Acad. Medicine of France (Laureat 1948), Radiol. Soc. N.Am. (v.p. 1959-60, Arthur Erskine lectr. 1978), Am. Roentgen Ray Soc., Am. Radium Soc. (v.p. 1963-64, treas. 1966-68, pres. 1968-69, chmn. exec. com. 1971-72, historian 1969—, Janeway gold medal 1973), Assn. Am. Med. Colls., Internat. Club Radiotherapists (pres. 1962-65), Inter-Am. Coll. Radiology (pres. 1967-71, U.S. counselor 1971-79), Am. Soc. Therapeutic Radiologists (sec. 1958-68, historian 1968—, pres. 1974-75, chmn. bd. dirs. 1975-76, gold medal 1977), Fedn. Clin. Oncologic Socs. (pres. bd. dirs. 1976-77); hon. mem. Rocky Mountain, Pacific N.W., Tex., Oreg., Minn. radiol. socs., radiol. socs. Cuba, Mex., Panama, Ecuador, Peru, Paraguay, Can., Argentina, Buenos Aires (Argentina), Am. Inst. Radiology (historian 1978—). Home: 3101 Cocos Rd Carrollwood Tampa FL 33618 Office: Dept Radiology U South Florida Coll Medicine Tampa FL 33618 also VA Med Center 13000 N 30th St Tampa FL 33612

DEL REY, JUDY-LYNN, publishing executive; b. N.Y.C., Jan. 26, 1943; d. Zachary Harold and Norma Victoria (Breslau) Benjamin; m. Lester del Rey, Mar. 21, 1971. B.A., Hunter Coll., 1965. Mng. editor Galaxy mag. (UPD Pub. Corp.), N.Y.C., 1969-73; sr. editor Random House Inc. Ballantine Books, 1973-77, v.p., 1978—; editor-in-chief Del Rey Books, 1977-82, pub., 1982—. Editor: The Celtic Bull: Essays on James Joyce's Ulysses, 1966; book series Stellar Science Fiction Vols. 1-7, 1974-81; Stellar Short Novels, 1976; sci. fiction cons., contbr.: World Book Ency., 1972, 77. Recipient E.E. Smith Meml. New Eng. Sci. Fiction Assn., 1970; named to Hall of Fame Hunter Coll., 1972. Home: 310 E 46th St Apt 3M New York NY 10017 Office: Ballantine Books 201 E 50th St New York NY 10022

DEL REY, LESTER, author, editor; b. Saratoga, Minn., June 2, 1915; s. Franc and Jane (Sidway) del R.; m. Judy-Lynn Benjamin, Mar. 21, 1971. Student, George Washington U., 1931-33. Author, 1937—; sheet metal worker McDonnell Aircraft Corp., St. Louis, 1942-44; author's agt. Scott Meredith Lit. Agy., N.Y.C., 1947-50; tchr. fantasy fiction NYU, 1972-73; former editor sci. fiction mags.; editor Best Sci. Fiction Stories of Yr. E.P. Dutton & Co., 1971-75; fantasy editor Ballantine Books, 1975—. Author: sci. fiction and children's books including Marooned on Mars, 1952, Attack from Atlantis, 1953, Mission to the Moon, 1956, Step to the Stars, 1954, Cave of the Spears, 1957, Mysterious Earth, 1960, The Mysterious Sea, 1961, Moon of Mutiny, 1961, Mysterious Sky, 1964, Outpost of Jupiter, 1963, Runaway Robot, 1965, Infinite Worlds of Maybe, 1966, Rocket from Infinity, 1966, Tunnel Through Time, 1966, Prisoners of Space, 1968, The Eleventh Commandment, 1970, Nerves, 1970, Pstalmate, 1970, Gods and Golems, 1973, Early del Rey, 1975, Police Your Planet, 1975; others; Editor: Fantastic Science-Fiction Art, 1926-54, 1975, Garland Library of Science Fiction, 1975, The Best of John W. Campbell, 1976. Named guest of honor World Sci. Fiction Conv., N.Y.C., 1967. Mem. Soc. Illustrators. Club: Trap Door Spiders. Home: 310 E 46 St New York NY 10017

DEL RIO-ESTRADE, CARLOS, microbiologist; b. Mexico City, Feb. 28, 1923; s. Aurelio del Rio and Josefina (Estrada); m. Marta Elena Guerra, Sept. 23, 1964; children: Marta Sylvia, Carlos Renato, Alexandra Rosa, Eduardo Andres. Chemist-microbiologist, Inst. Politecnico Nacional, Mex., 1948; M.Sc. Buenos Aires Conv. fellow, Cornell U., 1950; Ph.D. NIH fellow, Cornell U., 1953. Dir. control. Syntex Labs., Mex., 1953-56; mem. faculty U. Nacional Autonoma de Mex., 1957—, prof. microbiology, 1965—, head dept., 1968-74; head spl. project Ctr. Econ. and Social Studies 3d World, Mexico City, 1978-79, adviser to dir. gen., 1979-80; dir. gen. Catmex, S.A., Mexico City, 1980—; vis. prof. Inst. Politecnico Nacional Grad. Sch., 1953, 56, U. Autonoma Metropolitana Xochimilco, 1977; invited lectr. U. Libre de Bruxelles, Belgium, 1979; organizer, participant (internat. confs.); pres. organizing com. Internat. Congress Clin Chemistry, Mex., 1978; pres. Leeuwenhoek Symposium, Mex., 1976; gen. coordinator XXIX Pugwash Conf., Mex., 1979. Mem. Am. Acad. Microbiology, Acad. de la Investigacion Cientifica, Assn. Mex. Microbiologia (founder 1949), Soc. Quimca de Mex. (founder 1956), Soc. Mex. de Bioquimica (founder 1957). Club: Cornell Mex. (pres. 1976-78). Home: 575 Las Flores Mexico Mexico 20 DF Office: 752 Ejercito Nacional Ave Mexico Mexico 5DF

DEL SANTO, L.A., retail merchandising company executive; b. 1934; m. B.S., U. San Francisco, 1955. With Household Merchandising Inc., Des Plaines, Ill., 1957—, with advt. dept. subs. Vons Grocery Co., 1957-58, asst. advt. mgr., 1958-61, advt. mgr., 1961-68, mgr. sales and mdse., 1968-71, sr. v.p., 1971-73, pres., chief exec. officer, 1973-75, corp. sr. v.p., 1975-79, exec. v.p., 1979—, dir. Served with U.S. Army, 1955-57. Office: Household Merchandising Inc 1700 Wolf Rd Des Plaines IL 60018 *

DELSON, ELIZABETH, artist; b. N.Y.C., Aug. 15, 1932; d. Julius and Emmy (Haas) Pfannmuller; m. Sidney L. Delson, Sept. 10, 1955; children—Karen Lee, Sara Jeanne, Matthew Robert. B.A., Smith Coll., 1954; M.A., Hunter Coll., 1972. Instr. graphic. arts Pratt Inst., 1962-66. Shows include USIA Travelling Exhibit, 1962-64, Bklyn. Museum Nat. Print Exhbn., 1966, L.I. U., 1969, others; one person exhbn., Hicks St. Gallery, 1964, L.I.U., 1969, 74, Peerdegat Library, 1971, 74, Park Gallery, 1972, Brownstone Gallery, 1974, others, represented in collections, N.Y. Pub. Library, L.I. U., U. So. Ill., Columbia, Boston Pub. Library, Bklyn. Mus. (Recipient medal of honor for graphics Audubon Artists 1961). Mem. Soc. Am. Graphic Artists, Contemporary Artists Guild, Audubon Artists. Address: 625 3d St Brooklyn NY 11215

DELSON, ROBERT, lawyer; b. N.Y.C., July 18, 1905; s. Louis and Ethel (Naum) D.; m. Majorie Delson, Dec. 25, 1941; children: Eric, James. B.A., Cornell U., 1926; LL.B., Columbia U., 1928. Bar: N.Y. 1929, D.C. 1971. Assoc. Wise & Seligsbert, 1929-31; assoc., gen. counsel Republic Pictures Corp., 1931-37; assoc. then ptnr. Delson & Gordon, N.Y.C., 1937-80, of counsel, 1981—; dir. Canon, U.S.A., Inc. Contbr. articles to legal jours. Mem. U.S. Com. Inter-Am. Assn. for Democracy and Freedom. AUS, 1942-45. Recipient Great Sign of Honor Pres. Republic of Australia, 1979. Mem. Am. Law Inst., ABA, Internat. Law Assn., Am. Soc. Internat. Law, Am.-Fgn. Law Assn., Consular Law Soc., Asia Soc., Maritime Law Assn., N.Y. State Bar Assn., N.Y. County Lawyers Assn., Phi Beta Kappa. Home: 11 E 86th St New York NY 10028 Office: 230 Park Ave New York NY 10169

DEL TORO, RUSSELL A., physician; b. Cabo Rojo, P.R., Nov. 1, 1924; s. Emiliano and Cornelia (Silva) Del T.; m. Ana L. Sosa, Sept. 3, 1948; children: Anna I., Russell A., Helga E. B.S., U. P.R., 1944; M.D., Temple U., 1949. Diplomate: Am. Bd. Internal Medicine. Intern, Ponce, P.R., 1949-50; resident in medicine Louisville VA Hosp., 1954-55; fellow in rheumatology Pa. Hosp., 1957-58; mem. faculty U. P.R. Med. Sch., 1958—, prof. medicine, 1977—, asso. dean clin. affairs, 1981—; mem. staff San Juan City Hosp., 1958—, chief medicine, 1976-80; practiced medicine specializing in internal medicine, San Juan, 1958—; mem. staff Ashford Med. Center, 1958—; pres. P.R. Bd. Med. Examiners, 1970-74. Contbr. articles to med. jours. Served with M.C. U.S. Army, 1955-57. Recipient cert. appreciation Fedn. States Med. Bds., 1972. Fellow A.C.P. (gov. 1980-84); mem. Am. Rheumatism Assn., AMA, P.R. Med. Assn., N.Y. Acad. Scis. Roman Catholic. Club: Dorado Beach Country. Home: 21 G Villa Caparra Guaynabo PR 00657 Office: Ashford Med Center Ashford Ave San Juan PR 00907

DEL TREDICI, DAVID, composer; b. Cloverdale, Calif., Mar. 16, 1937; s. Walter and Helen (Wagele) Del T. Piano student with, Bernhard Abramowitsch, Berkeley, Calif.; Robert Helps, N.Y.C.; B.A., U. Calif., Berkeley, 1959; M.F.A., Princeton U., 1964. Mem. faculty Harvard U., 1968-72, Buffalo U., 1973, Boston U., 1973—. Recital and symphony pianist; appeared with symphony orchs. including, San Francisco Symphony Orch.; composer-in-residence, Tanglewood Music Festival, 1964-65, Marlboro Music Festival, 1966-67, Aspen Music Festival, 1975; Received numerous commns. for compositions; works include I Hear an Army; Night Conjure-Verse; works include Syzygy, Pop-pourri, An Alice Symphony, Adventures Underground, Vintage Alice, Final Alice, Child (In Memory of a Summer Day), Quaint Events, Happy Voices; All in the Golden Afternoon. Bd. dirs. Yaddo, MacDowell Colony. Recipient Hertz award; Creative Arts award Brandeis U.; Naumberg Rec. award; award Nat. Council Arts and Letters; Pulitzer prize, 1980; Guggenheim fellow; Woodrow Wilson fellow. Mem. ASCAP, Phi Beta Kappa. Home: 463 West St Apt G121 New York NY 10014

DEL TUFO, ROBERT J., lawyer; b. Newark, Nov. 18, 1933; s. Raymond and Mary (Pellecchia) Del T.; m. Ann Hartley, Mar. 10, 1956; children: Barbara, Ann, Robert, David. B.A. cum laude in English, Princeton U., 1955; J.D., Yale U., 1958. Bar: N.J. 1959. Law sec. to chief justice N.J. Supreme Ct., 1958-60; assoc. firm Dillon & Bitar, Morristown, N.J., 1960-62, ptnr., 1962-74; asst. prosecutor, Morris County, N.J., 1963-65, 1st asst. prosecutor, 1965-67, 1st asst. atty. gen., State of N.J., 1974-77, dir. criminal justice, 1976-77; U.S. atty. Dist. of N.J., Newark, 1977-80; prof. Rutgers U. Sch. Criminal Justice, 1979-81; ptnr. firm Stryker, Tams & Dill, 1980—; mem. N.J. State Commn. of Investigation, 1981—; instr. bus. law Fairleigh-Dickinson U., 1964; mem. N.J. State Bd. Bar Examiners, 1968-74; mem. criminal law drafting com. Nat. Conf. Bar Examiners, 1972—; mem. com. on character N.J. Supreme Ct., 1982—. Editor: Yale U Law Jour; contbr. articles to profl. jours. Mem. law enforcement adv. com. County Coll. of Morris, 1970—; mem. Morris County Ethics Com., 1968-71, Morris County Jud. Selection Com., 1970-72, Essex County Jud. Selection Com., 1982—; v.p., mem. exec. com. United Fund of Morris County, 1966-70; chmn. Morris Twp. Juvenile Conf. Com., 1963-74; bd. dirs. Nat. Found. March of Dimes, 1966-68, Vis. Nurse Assn. Morris County, 1963-70, Morristown YMCA, 1970-74; trustee Newark Acad., 1976—; bd. regents St. Peter's Coll., 1979—. Fellow Am. Bar Found.; mem. Am., N.J., Morris County bar assns., Nat. Dist. Attys. Assn., Am. Judicature Soc., Yale Law Sch. Assn. (exec. com. 1978—), Order of Coif. Home: 7 Shelley Pl. Morristown NJ 07960 Office: 33 Washington St Newark NJ 07102

DELUCA, C. ROD, oil company executive; b. Temisdaming, Que., Can., Aug. 19, 1941; s. Eugene and Eda Anne (Merlongi) DeL.; m. Sue Ann Carlson, Dec. 22, 1962; 1 dau., Pamela Anne. PH.D. in Geophys. Engring., Colo. Sch. Mines, 1963; M.B.A., Harvard U., 1967. Cert. Assn. Profl. Engrs., Geologists and Geophysicists Alta. Seismologist Standard Oil Calif., 1963-65; with Occidental Petroleum Corp., 1967-69, Bow Valley Ind. Ltd., 1969—; pres. Bow Valley Exploration Inc., Denver, 1979—. Mem. adv. com. various post-secondary ednl. insts. Office: Bow Valley Exploration Inc 1700 Broadway (no.)900 Denver CO 80290

DELUCA, DONALD PAUL, metals co. fin. exec.; b. Newark, June 26, 1940; s. Daniel W. and Blanche H. (Chalupa) DeL.; m. Geraldine S. McNulty, Sept. 12, 1965; children—Susan E., Donald Paul. B.S. in Chemistry, Va. Mil. Inst., 1962; M.B.A. in Finance, Rutgers U., 1969; postgrad. sr. exec. program, Mass. Inst. Tech., 1977. Sr. chemist Hercules Inc., Parlin, N.J., 1965-67; asst. treas. Bank of N.Y., N.Y.C., 1969-72; mgr. bank relations PPG Industries, 1972-74; treas. Copperweld Corp., Pitts., 1974—, v.p., treas., 1976—. Contbr. articles to profl. jours. Served to 1st lt. U.S. Army, 1962-65. Mem. Fin. Execs. Inst., Am. Mgmt. Assn., Am. Iron and Steel Inst. Republican. Clubs: Pitts. Field, Duquesne. Home: 2635 Glenchester Rd Wexford PA 15090 Office: Two Oliver Plaza Pittsburgh PA 15222

DELUCA, JOSEPH R., business executive, retired air force officer; b. Greenville, Pa., Sept. 3, 1918; s. Pasquale and Concetta (Catullo) DeL.; m. Doris Colleen Hays, Jan. 22, 1944; children: Pat, Joel, Kathy, Barbara, Teresa, Michael, Tina, Marisa. M.A. in Internat. Relations, George Washington U., 1963. Commd. 2d lt. U.S. Air Force, 1942, advanced through grades to lt. gen., 1973; ret., 1975; v.p. Internat. Tech. Products Co., 1976-77; dep. under sec. Dept. Energy, Washington, 1978-79; exec. v.p. Inverness Resource Corp., Alexandria, Va., 1978-79; pres. Internat. Mktg. and Mgmt. Corp., Washington, 1980—. Decorated D.S.M. with oak leaf cluster, Legion of Merit with oak leaf cluster. Mem. Air Force Assn., Res. Officers Assn. Roman Catholic. Office: 655 15th St NW Suite 830 Washington DC 20005 *Persevere. Integrity and logic will prevail!*

DELUCA, PATRICK PHILLIP, pharm. scientist, ednl. adminstr.; b. Scranton, Pa., Sept. 7, 1935; m. Judy Beitzel, June 16, 1956; children—Paul, Thomas, Patrick, Donald, Michelle, Michael. B.S. in Pharmacy, Temple U., 1957, M.S., 1960, Ph.D. in Pharmacy (SKF W.G. Karr fellow), 1963. Analytical chemist SKF Co., 1957-59; instr., research asso. Temple U., 1959-62; sr. research pharmacist CIBA Co., Summit, N.J., 1963-66, plant mgr., 1966-69, Cormedics Corp., Somerville, N.J., 1969-70; mem. faculty U. Ky., 1970—, prof., asso. dean, 1972—; cons. to pharm. industry FDA. Recipient Leo G. Penn award Temple U., 1957; Lunsford-Richardson Pharmacy Research award Richardson Merrell Co., 1960, 62; Best Paper Toward Advancement Indsl. Pharmacy award N.J. Pharmacy Discussion Group, 1965; recipient numerous grants. Mem. Am. Pharm. Assn., Acad. Pharm. Sci. (pres. 1979-80), Parenteral Drug Assn. (Research Achievement award 1975), Am. Soc. Hosp. Pharmacists (Research award 1975), N.Y. Acad. Sci., Am. Soc. Enteral and Parenteral Nutrition, Sigma Xi, Rho Chi. Research, publs. in pharm. tech. Patentee in field. Home: 3292 Nantucket Dr Lexington KY 40502 Office: U Ky Coll Pharmacy Washington and Gladstone Sts Lexington KY 40506

DE LUCA, PETER J., lawyer, corporate executive; b. N.Y.C., Oct. 15, 1927; s. Thomas A. and Madeline (Insard) De L.; m. Marie Joan Macchia, Sept. 18, 1954; 1 son, David Laurence. LL.B. cum laude, N.Y. Law Sch., 1953. Bar: N.Y. Practice in, N.Y.C.; mem. firm Cravath, Swaine & Moore, 1953-59; with Pepsi Co., Inc., N.Y.C., 1959-71, v.p., 1963-65, v.p., gen. counsel, sec., 1965-71; sr. v.p. for corporate affairs, gen. counsel, dir. Revlon, Inc., 1971-73; sr. v.p., gen. counsel Gen. Foods Corp., N.Y.C., 1973. Author short stories under name Stephen Scott. Mem. Gov. Carey's Com. on Appointee Standards; bd. dirs. Heart Found., Burke Rehab. Hosp., NAACP Legal Def. and Ednl. Fund, N.Y. Foundling Com.; bd. dirs., vice chmn. Council of Better Bus. Bur.; trustee Food and Drug Law Inst. Served with U.S. Mcht. Marine USNR, 1945-47. Mem. Am., N.Y. State bar assns., Assn. Bar City N.Y., Delta Theta Phi, Sigma Pi Phi. Democrat. Clubs: Univ., Westchester Country, N.Y. Athletic, Lawyers. Home: 360 E 72d St New York NY 10021 Office: 250 North St White Plains NY 10625

DELUCA, RONALD, advertising agency executive; b. Reading, Pa., Oct. 28, 1924; s. Nicola and Grace (Carabello) DeL.; m. Lois Ann Hall, Nov. 27, 1952; children: Christine, Diane, Patricia, Maria, Lisa, Nicholas. Certificate comml. art, Pratt Inst., 1949; B.F.A., Syracuse U., 1951; B.A., New Sch. Social Research, 1966. Art dir. Roy S. Durstine (advt.), N.Y.C., 1954-56, Kenyon & Eckhardt (advt.), 1956-66; head creative group Grey Advt., N.Y.C., 1966-67; with Kenyon & Eckhardt Advt., N.Y.C., 1967—, exec. v.p., vice chmn., 1976—. Artist, J.C. Penney, N.Y.C., 1951-52; designer, Remington Rand, N.Y.C., 1952-53. Served with USAAF, 1942-46. Methodist (chmn. pastor parish relations com.). Home: Larchmont St Ardsley NY 10502 Office: 200 Park Ave New York NY 10017

DE LUCA, VINCENT ARTHUR, English literature educator; b. Bklyn., Jan. 9, 1940; s. A. Michael and Rose Catherine (Pully) De L. B.A., Hamilton Coll., 1961; M.A., Yale U., 1962, Ph.D., 1967. From instr. to prof. English Cornell U., Ithaca, N.Y., 1964-70; asst. prof. U. Toronto, Ont., Can., 1970-74, assoc. prof., 1974-81, prof. English, 1981—. Author: Thomas De Quincey: The Prose of Vision, 1980. Mem. MLA, Assn. Can. Univ. Tchrs. of English. Office: Erindale Coll U Toronto Mississauga ON Canada L5L 1C6

DE LUCCA, JOHN, educator; b. Bklyn., Oct. 8, 1920; s. Carlo and Adela (Ianniello) De L.; m. Margaret Louise Williams, June 10, 1956; children—Danielle S., David J. B.B.A., City Coll. N.Y., 1941; M.A., New Sch. for Social Research, 1950; postgrad., Harvard U., 1952-53; Ph.D. (Univ. fellow), Ohio State U., 1955. Lectr. philosophy Pace Coll., 1950-52; acting instr. English Ohio State U., 1955-56; instr. philosophy Wash. State U., 1956-58, asst. prof., 1958-62; asst. prof. philosophy U. Victoria, B.C., Can., 1962-64, asso. prof., 1964-68, first chmn. dept., 1963-68; prof. philosophy Queen's U., Kingston, Ont., 1968—; Pres., gen. mgr. Johart Internat. Corp., N.Y.C., 1946-51. Editor: Reason and Experience: Dialogues in Modern Philosophy, 1973; translator, editor: René Descartes' Meditations on First Philosophy, 1974, rev. edit., 1975; Contbr. articles to profl. jours., numerous book reviews. Served with AUS, 1942-45. Mem. Am. Philos. Assn. (mem. exec. com. Pacific div. 1965-67, program chmn. 1967), Can. Philos. Assn., Am. Assn. Advancement of Humanities (charter mem.), Philosophy of Sci. Assn., N.W. Conf. on Philosophy (pres. 1959-60), Humanities Assn. Can., Beta Gamma Sigma. Home: 10 Copperfield Dr Kingston ON K7M 1M4 Canada Office: Watson Hall Queen's U Kingston ON Canada

DELUCCA, JOHN JOSEPH, diversified company executive; b. Nutley, N.J., Apr. 25, 1943; s. Nicholas and Santa (Capalbo) D.; m. Patricia Ann Reid, Nov. 1, 1969; 1 son, Jonathan. B.A., Bloomfield (N.J.) Coll., 1966; M.B.A. cum laude, Fairleigh Dickinson U., Rutherford, N.J., 1969. Investment analyst Mut. Benefit Life Ins. Co., Newark, 1966-69; asst. v.p. US Life Corp., N.Y.C., 1969-72; v.p. investments Paul Revere Life Ins. Co., Greenwich, Conn., 1972-79; v.p., treas. parent co. Avco Corp., Greenwich, 1979—; asst. adj. prof. Seton Hall U., S. Orange, N.J., 1969-73; lectr. fin. Fordham U. Grad. Sch., 1973-79; dir. Enzo Biochem Inc., N.Y.C., RKO Century Warner. Served with USAR, 1965-66. Club: Apple Ridge Country. Home: 314 Ardmore Rd Ho-Ho-Kus NJ 07423 Office: 1275 King St Greenwich CT 06830

DELUCCIA, EMIL ROBERT, civil engineer; b. Brighton, Mass., Sept. 20, 1904; s. Emil James and Edna Laura (Hewes) de L.; m. Margaret McCutcheon, Jan. 16, 1932; children: Margaret Crichton, Jane Hewes. B.S. in Civil Engring, Mass. Inst. Tech., 1927. Registered profl. engr., D.C., Oreg. Surveyman and transitman Met. Water Supply Commn., Enfield, Mass., 1927-29; engr. designer Stone and Webster Engring. Corp., 1929-31; engr. insp. and designer U.S. Engr. Office, Charleston, W.Va., 1931-33, asso. engr. and chief of design sect., Huntington, W.Va., 1933-38, FPC, 1938-51; gen. engring. cons. and mgr. Yale hydroelectric project and others Pacific Power & Light Co., 1951, v.p., chief engr., 1952-66, sr. v.p., 1966-69; pres. Oreg. Grad. Center, 1969-72; cons. engr., 1969—; v.p. Overseas Adv. Assos., Inc., 1973—; sr. engr. cons. on dams and hydroelectric projects, 1938-40; chief, power supply br. Nat. Def. Power staff, 1940-41; asst. dir. Nat. Def. Power staff and asst. chief Bur. of Elec. Engring. (also cons. on power to OPM and WPB), chief Bur. of Power, 1944—; head group econ. and energy studies, South Vietnam, 1971-72, 74-75; U.S. del. Internat. Conf. on High Dams, Stockholm, 1948, Internat. Conf. on High Tension Elec. Systems, Paris, 1948; chief U.S. delegation Internat. Conf. High Tension Lines, Paris, 1950; U.S. del. World Power Conf., London, Eng., 1950; U.S. ofcl. Negotiation Treaty with Canada for division of water at Niagara Falls; cons. to UN, Japan, 1961, AEC, Nat. Security Resources Bd.; chmn. Internat. Passamaquoddy Bd. Engrs., U.S. Com. on Large Dams; mem. Tech. Indsl. Disarmament Com. for German and Japan Elec. Power Industry. Contbr. to: Ency. Brit. Served with R.O.T.C., Mass. Inst. Tech.; 2d lt. O.R.C., 1927; commd. capt. and advanced through grades to lt. col. AUS, 1942-45; with SHEAF, 1944; ETO; ret. as lt. col. O.R.C., 1956. Decorated medal of merit Legion of Merit; medal of Merit 1st class, South Vietnam; named Oreg. Engr. of Year, 1962. Fellow IEEE, ASCE; mem. Soc. Am. Mil. Engrs. (dir., recipient Goethals medal award 1963), A.I.M., V.F.W., Am. Geophys. Union, Am. Legion, Internat. Assn. High Tension Lines, Internat. Assn. Hydraulic Research, Internat. Assn. Large Dams. Clubs: Mason (Shriner), Army-Navy Country (Arlington, Va.); Cosmos (Washington); Arlington, University, Waverly Country (Portland). Home: 1275 S Skyland Dr Lake Oswego OR 97034

DELUE, DONALD HARCOURT, sculptor; b. Boston, Oct. 5, 1897; s. Harry Thornton and Ida Martha (DeLue) Quigley; m. Martha Naomi Cross, Oct. 5, 1931 (dec. 1981). Student, Boston Mus. Fine Arts Sch.; D. hon., Monmouth Coll., West Long Branch, N.J. Commns. The Rocket Thrower, World's Fair, N.Y.C., 1964-65, Boys Scout Meml. Tribute, Washington, Confederate Meml., Gettysburg, Pa., Fed. Court House, Phila., Fourteen Stations of Cross Loyola Jesuit Sem., Shrub Oak, N.Y., Edward Hull Crump Meml., Memphis, Lions of Judah Germantown Jewish Ctr., Phila., Chemistry Bldg., U. Pa., Meml. Urn., City Hall, Stockholm, Sweden, Bronze Door, Woodmont Shrine, Phila., also medals and replicas. Recipient Citation for Hist. Work DAR, J. Sanford Saltus medal, others, Guggenheim Found fellow; Nat. Inst. Arts and Letters fellow. Fellow Am. Numismatic Soc., Nat. Sculpture Soc. (pres. 1945-48, hon. pres. 1979—); mem. Am. Inst. Commemorative Art, Archtl. League (recipient Avery prize), Am. Artist Profl., Nat. Acad. Design (recipient Samuel B. Morse Gold medal), Allied Artists Am. Home: 82 Highland Ave Leonardo NJ 07737 Office: Sculpture Soc 15 E 26th St New York NY 10010

DELUGACH, ALBERT LAWRENCE, newspaper reporter; b. Memphis, Oct. 27, 1925; s. Gilbert and Edna (Short) D; m. Bernice Goldstein, June 11, 1950; children: Joy, David, Daniel, Sharon. B.J., U. Mo., 1951. Reporter Kansas City (Mo.) Star, 1951-60; St. Louis

Globe Democrat, 1960-69, St. Louis Post Dispatch, 1969-70; investigative reporter Los Angeles Times, 1970—. (Recipient Pulitzer prize for spl. local reporting 1969). Served with USNR, 1943-46. Recipient Gerald Loeb award for disting. bus. and fin. journalism, 1984. Mem. Sigma Delta Chi. Home: 4313 Price St Los Angeles CA 90027 Office: Los Angeles Times Times Mirror Square Los Angeles CA

DE LUGO, RON, congressman; b. St. Croix, V.I., Aug. 2, 1930; children: Maria Cristina, Angela Maria. Student, Colegio San Jose, P.R. Sta.-WIVI, St. Croix, 1950-55; mem. V.I. Territorial Senate, 1956-66; adminstr., St. Croix, 1961; rep. for V.I., Washington, 1968-72; mem. 93-98th Congress from V.I., Interior and Insular Affairs Com., Washington, Merchant Marine and Fisheries Co.; del. from V.I. U.S. Congress, 1972—. Founder V.I. Carnival, 1952; del. Democratic Nat. Convs., 1956, 60, 64, 68; mem. Dem. Nat. Com., 1959; del. V.I. Constl. Conv., 1971-72. Office: Room 2443 Rayburn House Office Bldg Washington DC 20515

DELUIGI, JANICE CECILIA WEIL LEFTON, painter, sculptor; b. Indpls., Nov. 27, 1915; d. Nathan Charles and Rosalind (Whitman) Weil; m. Ludovico DeLuigi, June 24, 1965; children by previous marriage: Larry, Margo. Student, Art Inst. Chgo., 1952, 62-64, U. Chgo., 1959; certificate, Accademia di Brera, Milan, Italy, 1965; also pvt. studies in, Austria; studied painting with, Constantine Pougialis and Oskar Kokoschka; studied sculpture with, Marini Marino; diploma, Instituto Nazionale Per L'Istruzione E L'Addestramento Nel Settore Artigiano, Venice, Italy, 1970. Tchr. painting, sculpture, history art George Williams Coll., Chgo., 1962, Contemporary Art Workshop, 1962-64; tchr. painting, sculpture history art Fondazione Cini, Venice, 1964-66, prof. art, 1966—; prof. edn. of culture Istituto Professionale Giorgio Cini, Venice; prof. English. lit. and visual arts Inst. Algarortti, Venice.; a founder of Poesia Veneta. Commn. from Italian Govt. for the: John F. Kennedy Meml. Monument in, Italy, Milan, 1967; Murano glass monument of Kennedy Bros, Benedictine Abbey, San Giorgio Maggiore, Venice. (Recipient 1st prize Internat. Painting and Sculpture, Fruili-Venezia Giulia 1971), San Giorgio Maggiore, Venice. (Silver medal for painting, Pope Paul VI 1973), San Giorgio Maggiore, Venice. (others.); One-woman shows, Chgo. Pub. Library, 1962, Juster Gallery, N.Y.C., 1961, Galerie Ror Volmar, Paris, France, 1964, Galleria d'Arte Il Camino, Rome, Galleria Santa Croce, Florence, Italy, Fondazione Cini, Venice, USIS, Milan, Studio Palazzi, Milan, 1983, Studio 3, Venice, glass sculpture of Murano, Galleria Bevilacqua La Masa, Venice, 1970, Galleria Santo Stephano, Venice, 1970, 72, Galleria d'arte TelEuropa, Rome, 1972, Encontro-Messina Gallery, 1976, Precious Peacock Gallery, Palm Desert, Calif., 1977, Beverly Wilshire Hotel, Los Angeles, others, group shows include, Art Inst. Chgo., Ill. State Fair, U. Ill., U. Chgo., Northwestern U., Roosevelt U., Evanston (Ill.) Art Center, Artists League Midwest, IV Biennale Internat. Sports, Culture, Fine Arts, U. Madrid, Spain, 1973; exhibited sculpture work murano glass, Biennale Venice, 1970, 72, Italy International Art exhibition, Ateneo San Basso, Venice, 1979; represented numerous pvt. collections, in permanent collections, Galleria del Naviglio, Milan, Galleria Naviglio Venzia, Venice, Santa Barbara (Calif.) Mus Art, Bradley Galleries, Santa Barbara, White House, Washington, Mus. Modern Art, Chgo., others, U.S. and, others, Italy. Mem. Arts Club Chgo., Renaissance Soc. of U. Chgo., Artists Equity Assn., Alumni Assn. Sch. Art Inst. Chgo. Address: Piscina San Moise 2053 San Marco 30124 Venice Italy

DE LUISE, DOM, actor; b. Bklyn., Aug. 1, 1933; s. John and Jennie (DeStefano) De L.; m. Carol Arata, Nov. 23, 1965; children—Peter John, Michael Robert, David Dominick. Student, Tufts Coll. Actor: off-Broadway plays Half Past Wednesday; actor: Broadway plays Luv; regular TV series The Dom De Luise Show; own TV series Lotsa Luck, 1973; appeared: TV shows Dinah; actor movies including History of the World Part I; actor, dir.: movie Hot Stuff, 1979. Office: care EBM 132 S Rodeo Dr Beverly Hills CA 90212

DEL VALLE, FRANCISCO RAFAEL, food science researcher, educator, consultant; b. Laredo, Tex., Oct. 19, 1933; s. Roberto and Margarita (Canesco) Del V.; m. Estela Alicia Urrutia, Aug. 6, 1961; children: Estela Margarita, Francisco Roberto. S.B. in Chemistry, MIT, 1954, M.S. in Biochem. Engring., 1956, S.M. in Chem. Engring., 1957, Ph.D. in Food Sci. and Tech., 1965. Prof. chem. engring. and food sci. Instituto Tecnologico y da Estudios Superiores de Monterrey, Mex.; Guaymas, 1961-77; dir. Instituto Chihuahuense de Investigacion y Desarollo de la Nutricion, Chihuahua, Mex., 1970-80; prof. Universidad Autonoma de Chihuahua, 1977—; pres. Fundacion de Estudios Alimentarios y Nutricianoles, 1980—; cons. to industry. Contbr. articles to tech. jours. Recipient Nat. Prize in Technology Pres. Mex., 1977, Nat. prize in Sci. and Tech. Banco Nacional de Mex., 1970, 81. Mem. Academia de la Investigacion Cientifica, Academia Nacional de Ingenieria, Asociacion de Tecnicos en Alimentos de Mex., Inst. Food Technologists, Sociedad Latinoamericana de Nutricion. Developed processes for prodn. of quick-salted fish cakes, soy-oats infant formula, other soy-oats high-nutrition, low-cost foods. Office: Apartado Postal Chihuahua ChihuahuaMexico

DEL VALLE, MANUEL LUIS, corporation executive; b. Santurce, P.R., Apr. 14, 1924; s. Manuel Luis and Matilda (Ganzalez) del V.; m. Isabelita Biascoechae, Nov. 8, 1947; children: Manuel Luis, Anibel. Chem. Engr., U. Mich., 1967. Engr. Davidson Chem. Co., Balt., 1947-48; exec. v.p. Caribe Nitrogen, Guanica, P.R., 1948-59; owner, operator Manuel del Valle, Inc., Carolian, P.R., 1959-79; pres. Bacardi Corp., Catano, P.R., 1979—; dir. Banco Popular de P.R., Mato Rey, Rexo, San Juan, P.R., Popular Bankshare, Miami, Fla. Pres. P.R. Cancer League Campaign, San Juan, P.R., 1970; bd. dirs. U. Sacred Heart, Santurce, 1981; chmn. Gt. Cities of Americas Conf., San Juan, 1983. Roman Catholic. Office: Bacardi Corp GPO Box 3549 San Juan PR 00936

DELWICHE, EUGENE ALBERT, microbiologist; b. Green Bay, Wis., Nov. 26, 1917; s. Edmond Joseph and Alice (Collin) D.; m. Constance Veronica Nott, July 9, 1949; children—Christine Jean, Michael Joseph, Anne Teresa, Stephen Richard. B.S. with honors, U. Wis., Madison, 1941; Ph.D., Cornell U., Ithaca, N.Y., 1948. Asst. prof. bacteriology Cornell U., 1948-51, asso. prof., 1951-55, prof., 1955-65, prof. microbiology, 1965—; prin. biologist Oak Ridge Nat. Lab., 1951, 52, 53, cons., 1951-59; bacteriologist Chem. Corps U.S. Army, Ft. Detrick, Md., 1957-58; cons., 1958; Guggenheim fellow Karolinska Inst., Stockholm, 1963-64; mem. sr.-postdoctoral fellowship program selection com. NSF, 1967-68. Contbg. author: Annual Review of Microbiology, 1955, Bergeys Manual Determinative Bacteriology, 8th edit, 1974; editorial bd.: Jour. Bacteriology, 1954-59; reviewer: Sci. 1966-70, Analytical Biochemistry, 1974-75; contbr. numerous articles to profl. jours. Served with inf. AUS, 1941-45. Mem. Can. Soc. Microbiologists, Soc. Indsl. Microbiology, Am. Soc. Biol. Chemists, Am. Acad. Microbiology (charter), Am. Soc. Microbiology (pres. div. 1952). Home: 117 Pine Tree Rd Ithaca NY 14850

DELYNN, HUBERT JAMES, broadcasting executive; b. Uniontown, Pa., May 28, 1921; s. Max and Irene (Goldstein) DeL.; m. Ruth H. Elow, Jan. 1, 1965; children: Irene, Nina, James, William. B.A., W.Va. U., 1941; J.D. (article editor law rev.), Harvard U., 1947. Bar: N.Y. 1947. Atty. firm Sullivan & Cromwell, N.Y.C., 1947-59; exec. Lazard Freres & Co., N.Y.C., 1959-67; with RKO Gen., Inc., N.Y.C., 1967—, exec. v.p., 1977-81, vice chmn., chief operating officer, 1981—, also dir.; dir., exec. com. Frontier Airlines, Inc.; dir. Sentinel Group Funds, Inc., Sentinel Cash Mgmt., Inc. Served to lt. USNR, 1942-46. Mem. ABA, Assn. Bar City N.Y. Clubs: Harvard (N.Y.C.); Longboat Key (Fla.); Golf and Tennis. Office: 1440 Broadway New York NY 10018 *

DE LYROT, ALAIN HERVE, editor; b. Paris, France, Aug. 19, 1926; s. Herve and Emilie (De Villahermose) De L.; m. Mary Elizabeth Allen, Dec. 21, 1961; children—Herve, Antoine. Student, Columbia, 1945-48, U. Paris, 1952-54. Researcher, reporter, corr. N.Y. Herald Tribune, Paris and N.Y.C., 1945-61; editor Continent, Paris, 1961-62; spokesman French Info. Ministry, Paris, 1962-64; European Bur. chief Copley News Service, Paris, 1964-66; editor-in-chief Selection du Readers Digest, Paris, 1966-70; exec. editor internat. edits. Readers Digest, Pleasantville, N.Y., 1971—. Decorated knight Legion of Honor, France, knight Order of Merit, France, comdr. Order of Merit, Luxembourg). Clubs: Travellers (Paris); Brook (N.Y.C.). Home: 23 Rue du Cherche-Midi Paris 75006 France Office: Readers Digest Pleasantville NY 10570 *Journalism has been my life's work—and love. Independence, objectivity, accuracy, imagination, and style are the essential ingredients of the trade. More than ever the press is needed to inform, to expose, to praise, to think. Let it observe the five above qualities and it will prevail. I've done my best to keep them in mind.*

DELZ, WILLIAM RONALD, petroleum company executive; b. N.Y.C., June 29, 1932; s. William W. and Mona M. (Hasler) D.; m. Joan C. Breitenbach, June 29, 1957; children: Pamela, Nicole. B.B.A., Iona Coll., New Rochelle, N.Y., 1957. C.P.A., N.Y. Public accountant, Hawaii and N.Y., 1957-65; treas. Troy Textiles Inc., N.Y.C., 1965-67, Royal Petroleum Corp., 1967-70; v.p., corp. controller New Eng. Petroleum Corp., N.Y.C., 1970-75, JOC Oil Inc., 1975-77; v.p., treas. Bantam Books Inc., N.Y.C., 1977-79; sr. v.p. Simon & Schuster Inc., N.Y.C., 1979-81; prin. Public Acctg., 1981—; pres. Prudential Funds Inc., 1981—. Pres. Sch. Holy Child Fathers Club, 1976-77. Served with U.S. Army, 1952-54. Mem. Am. Inst. C.P.A.s, N.Y. State Soc. C.P.A.s. Republican. Roman Catholic. Club: Westchester Country (Rye). Home and Office: Purchase St Rye NY 10580

DELZA-MUNSON, ELIZABETH, dancer, choreographer, educator; b. Russia; d. Solomon and Eva (Katcher) Hurwitz; m. Gorham B. Munson, Apr. 2, 1921. Dance tng., Neighborhood Playhouse, N.Y.C., 1917-24, Dalcroze Sch., Paris and N.Y.C., 1922-23, Gurdjieff Inst., Fontainbleau, France, N.Y.C., 1925-48; pupil of, Jessmin Howarth, Margot Duncan, Anna Duncan, Mary Porter Beegle, Alma Frank, Azuma; music pupil of, Sandra Levitski, Carol Robinson, Gertrude Wollner, Yella Pessl, Ralph Lawton, Thomas de Hartmann; auditor, Wanda Landowska seminar, 1944; scholarship, Seymour Sch. Mus. Re-edn., N.Y.C., 1924. Choreographer, tchr. movement drama dept. U. Calif. at Davis, 1967; tchr. spl. method in movement and coordination for singers in collaboration with Anna Hamlin. Festival dancer, Neighborhood Playhouse, 1922-28, 34; debut as soloist own concert group, Guild Theatre, N.Y.C., 1933; dir. dance, Walden Sch., N.Y.C., 1925-35, Elizabeth Delza Sch. Dance, 1936—; dir., dancer, Assn. Music and Art, Cape Cod, Mass., 1940; Contbr. to mags.; concerts various cities and colls., 1933—, concerts include modern dance forms, ancient sacred dances, dances with modern poetry, dances with contrapuntal music, dance dramas. Recipient citation drama dept. U. Cal. at Davis, 1967. Mem. Am. Dance Guild, Poetry Soc. Am., Nat. Soc. Lit. and Arts. Home: Hotel Wellington 7th Ave at 55th St New York NY 10019 Studio: care Carnegie Hall W 57th St Studio 607 New York NY 10019

DELZELL, CHARLES FLOYD, history educator; b. Klamath Falls, Oreg., Mar. 6, 1920; s. William Abner and Edith May (White) D.; m. Eugenia May Robertson, Mar. 21, 1948; children: William Robertson, Charles Neal, Pauline Ethel. B.S., U. Oreg., 1941; M.A., Stanford, 1943, Ph.D., 1951; postgrad., Istituto Italiano per gli Studi Storici, Naples, Italy, 1948-49. Curator, Mediterranean Area collections Hoover Instn., Stanford, 1946-49; asst. prof. history U. Hawaii, 1949-50; instr. history U. Oreg., 1950-51; asst. prof. history Vanderbilt U., 1952-55, assoc. prof., 1955-61, prof., 1961—, chmn. dept., 1970-73, 83, chmn. commn. on univ. governance, 1969-70, Harvie Branscomb distinguished prof. history, 1970-71, sr. research assoc. Inst. Pub. Policies, 1981—, mem. univ. senate, 1963-66, 68-71, 74-77, 82-85, chmn., 1976-77, Centennial fellow, 1974-75; Mem. Pres. Hoover's Spl. Food Mission to Europe, 1946; vis. prof. history U. Oreg., summer 1963, Stanford, summer 1966; dir. Nat. Endowment for Humanities Summer Seminars for Coll. Tchrs., 1976, 77. Author: Mussolini's Enemies: The Italian Anti-Fascist Resistance (George Louis Beer prize Am. Hist. Assn., Borden award Hoover Instn. and Library, Stanford 1961, 2d edit., 1974), Mediterranean Fascism, 1919-1945, 1970, Italy in Modern Times, 1963, The Unification of Italy, 1859-1861, 1965, (with John L. Snell) The Meaning of Yalta, 1956, 66, (with Hans A. Schmitt) Historians of Modern Europe, 1971, The Papacy and Totalitarianism between the two World Wars, 1973, The Future of History, 1977, Italy in the Twentieth Century, 1980; also articles. Served with AUS, 1943-45. Fulbright research scholar, Italy, 1964-65; Nat. Endowment for Humanities Sr. fellow, 1973-74; resident scholar Rockefeller Found. Bellagio Study and Conf. Center, Lake Como, Italy, 1978. Mem. Am. Hist. Assn. (chmn. nominating com. 1970, mem. council 1974-76, exec. com. 1975-76, mem. organizing com. XIV Internat. Congress Hist. Scis., bi-nat. conf. with Italian historians, Florence 1983), So. Hist. Assn. (exec. council 1969-71, chmn. European history sect. 1963-64), Soc. French Hist. Studies, AAUP (pres. Vanderbilt chpt. 1962-63), Soc. for Italian Hist. Studies (pres. 1968-69), Am. Com. on History 2d World War (chmn. 1972-75), Phi Beta Kappa (pres. Vanderbilt chpt. 1965-66), Phi Alpha Theta, Sigma Nu. Democrat. Methodist. Clubs: Mason., University (Nashville) (pres. 1982-83). Home: 2303 Bernard Ave Nashville TN 37212

DEMAIN, STANLEY, aerospace executive; b. N.Y.C., Nov. 8, 1923; s. Irving and May (Griffin) D.; m. Judith Schoenfeld, Feb. 12, 1946; children: Cathy Mann, Chris. M.S., MIT, 1960; B.E.E., Pratt Inst., 1950. Vice-pres. Fairchild Industries, Germantown, Md., 1950-63, Atlantic Aviation, Wilmington, Del., 1972-74; v.p., gen. mgr. Bendix Corp., Davenport, Iowa, 1974-76, v.p. group exec., Teterboro, N.J., 1976-79, corp. v.p., Arlington, Va., 1980—; v.p. Windsor Crest Assn., Davenport, 1975. Mem. adv. bd. Pratt Inst., Bklyn. USNR, 1941-45. Named Bendix Corp. Aerospace Man of Yr., 1983. Mem. Air Force Assn. Republican. Club: Kent Island Yacht. Home: 3939 Ft Worth Ave Alexandria VA 22304 Office: Bendix Corp Aerospace Electronics Group 1000 Wilson Blvd Arlington VA 22209

DEMARCO, MICHAEL JOSEPH, investment company executive; b. N.Y.C., Sept. 28, 1910; s. Pasquale and Adelaide DeM.; married, Nov. 10, 1946; children: Michael, Marianne, Jane. B.Social Sci., Bklyn. Coll., 1938. With Josephthal & Co., Inc., N.Y.C., 1929—, mng. partner, 1958-76, chmn., chief exec. officer, 1976—. Vice pres. Bklyn. Coll. Found., 1975-79. Served to 1st lt. U.S. Army, 1942-46. Mem. Data Mgmt. Assn. (pres. 1949-50), Nat. Assn. Securities Dealers (gov. dist. 12 com. 1969-72), Securities Industry Assn. (hon. mem. security op. div. and data mgmt. security), Am. Topical Assn. Clubs: South Fork Country, Rockville Links Corp., Am. Legion, Holy Cross Fathers. Lodge: K.C. Home: 84 Brompton Rd Garden City NY 11530 Office: 120 Broadway New York NY 10271

DE MARCO, THOMAS JOSEPH, periodontist, dean; b. Farmingdale, N.Y., Feb. 12, 1942; s. Joseph Louis and Mildred Nora (Cifarelli) De M.; children: Todd Gordon, Kristin Alice, Lisa Anne. B.S., U. Pitts., 1962; D.D.S., 1965; Ph.D., certificate in Periodontology, Boston U., 1968; cert. in fin. planning, Coll. Fin. Planning, Denver, 1976. Certificate in clin. hypnosis. Practice dentistry specializing in periodontics, Cleve., 1968—; mem. staff Met. Gen. Hosp., Cleve., Univ. Hosp., VA Hosp.; asst. prof. periodontics and pharmacology Case-Western Res. U., 1968-70, asso. prof., 1970-73, prof., 1973—, asso. dean, 1972-76, dean, 1976—. Author review books in dentistry, book on fin. planning, also articles on periodontology, pharmacology, fin. planning. Grantee Air Force Office Sci. Research, 1969, Upjohn Co., 1970, Columbus Dental Mfg. Co., 1971. Mem. Am. Acad. Periodontology, Internat. Assn. Dental Research, Am. Soc. for Preventive Dentistry (past pres. Ohio chpt.). Home: 12208 Fox Run Rd Chesterland OH 44026 Office: 2123 Abington Rd Cleveland OH 44106

DE MARGERIE, JEAN-M., ophthalmology educator; b. Prud'homme, Sask., Can., Dec. 11, 1927; s. Antonio (Agnes) and Lavergne de M.; m. Therese-E. Brochu, Aug. 31, 1955; children: Claudine, Michele, Andre, Monique, Jean-Pierre. B.A., U. Ottawa, 1947; M.D., U. Laval, Que., 1952; D.Phil., Oxford U., Eng., 1955. Intern Quebec City Univ. Hosps., 1951-52; resident in ophthalmology, Oxford, Eng., 1955-59, Edinburgh, Scotland, 1955-59; asst. prof. ophthalmology Queen's U., Kingston, Ont., 1960-66; prof. ophthalmology U. Sherbrooke, Que., 1966—, head dept., 1966-76, vice dean for research Faculty of Medicine, 1973-79, den Faculty of Medicine, 1979-83; exec. mem. Que. Health Research Council, 1974-78; v.p., then. pres. Med. Research Council Can., 1976-79. Assoc. editor: Can. Jour. Ophthalmology, 1965-79. Trustee Kingston Separate Sch. Bd., 1962-66; pres. Nat. Fedn. Can. Univ. Students, 1951-52. Fellow Royal Coll. Physicians and Surgeons Can., ACS; mem. Que. Assn. Opthalmologists (pres. 1976-77); kmem. Can. Ophthal. Soc. (pres. 1975-76). Office: Faculty of Medicine University of Sherbrooke CHUS Sherbrooke PQ Canada J1J 5N4

DE MARIA, ANTHONY J., electrical engineer; b. Santa Croce, Italy, Oct. 30, 1931; came to U.S., 1935; s. Joseph and Nicolina (Daddona) De M.; m. Katherine M. Waybright, Aug. 29, 1953; 1 dau., Karla Kay. B.S. in Elec. Engring, U. Conn., 1956, Ph.D., 1965; M.S., Rensselaer Poly. Inst., 1960. Acoustic research engr. Anderson Lab., West Hartford, Conn., 1956-57; magnetic research engr. Hamilton Standard Div. United Techs. Corp., Windsor Locks, Conn., 1957-58; scientist United Techs. Research Center, East Hartford, Conn., 1958—; instr. in electronics U. Hartford, 1957-60; adj. prof. physics Rensselaer Poly. Inst. Grad. Center, Hartford, 1970-77; lectr. in lasers UCLA, 1974—; mem. Dept. Def. Adv. Group on Electronic Devices, 1977-80, chmn., 1980—; mem. evaluation com. on electromagnetic tech. Nat. Bur. Standards, 1977-79; mem. Center Elec. and Electronic Engring., 1979—. Author: Lasers, Vol. III, 1972, Vol. IV, 1976; Contbr. articles to profl. jours. Mem. Air Force Sci. Adv. Bd., 1981—. Recipient Disting. Alumnus award U. Conn., 1978, Disting. Engring. award U. Conn., 1983, Davies medal and award Rensselaer Poly. Inst., 1980. Fellow IEEE (editor Jour. Quantum Electronics, Morris N. Liebman meml. award 1980), Optical Soc. Am. (v.p. 1979, pres. 1981); mem. Am. Phys. Soc., Nat. Acad. Engring., Conn. Acad. Scis. and Engring. Office: United Techs Research Center 400 Main St East Hartford CT 06108

DEMARIA, PETER JAMES, utility company executive; b. Blyln., Nov. 3, 1934; s. Anthony and Mary (Catalano) DeM.; m. Patricia K. Gilson, Sept. 1, 1962. B.A., Queens Coll., 1955; M.A., NYU, 1963. C.P.A., N.Y. With Apfel & Englander, C.P.A.s, N.Y.C., 1955-56, J. Henry Schroder Banking Corp., 1958-59, Niles & Niles, N.Y.C., 1962-64; treas., chief accounting officer, dir. AEP Service Corp., N.Y.C., 1978; treas. Am. Electric Power Co., Inc., Columbus, Ohio, 1978—. Served with USN; 1956-58. Mem. Am. Inst. C.P.A.s. Office: Amk Electric Power Co. Inc 1 Riverside Plaza Columbus OH 43215

DEMARIA, WALTER, sculptor; b. Albany, Calif., Oct. 1, 1935. B.A., U. Calif., Berkeley, 1957, M.A., 1959. Organized happenings U. Calif., Berkeley, Calif. Sch. Art, San Francisco, 1959-60. Exhbns. include Primary Structures, Jewish Mus., N.Y.C., 1966, Sculpture of the '60's, Los Angeles County Mus., 1967, Whitney Mus. Am. Art Sculpture Ann., 1968, When Activities Become Form, Bern, Switzerland, 1969, Information, Mus. Modern Art, N.Y.C., 1970, N.Y. Earth Room, 1977, Vertical Earth Kilometer, Kassel, Ger., 1977, Broken Kilometer, N.Y.C., 1979; represented in permanent collections, Mus. Modern Art, Dia Art Found., Whitney Mus. Am. Art, N.Y.C., Solomon R. Guggenheim Mus., Basel (Switzerland) Kunstmuseum. (Recipient Mather Sculpture prize Art Inst. Chgo. 1976). Guggenheim fellow, 1969-70. Office: PO Box 275 Canal Street Station New York NY 10013 *

DEMARIS, OVID (OVIDE E. DESMARAIS), author; b. Biddeford, Maine, Sept. 6, 1919; s. Ernest J. and Aurore (Casavant) D.; m. Inez E. Frakes, May 15, 1942; children: Linda Lee, Peggy Ann. A.B., Coll. Idaho, 1948; student, Syracuse U. Law Sch., 1948-49; M.S., Boston U., 1950. Reporter Quincy (Mass.) Patriot-Ledger, 1949-50, Boston Daily Record, 1950, Boston bur. U.P., 1950-52; advt. copy chief Los Angeles Times, 1953-59. Free-lance writer, 1959—; Author: Ride the Gold Mare, 1957, The Hoods Take Over, 1957, The Lusting Drive, 1958, The Slasher, 1959, The Long Night, 1959, The Extortioners, 1960, The Enforcer, 1960, The Gold-Plated Sewer, 1960, Lucky Luciano, 1960, The Dillinger Story, 1961, The Lindbergh Kidnaping Case, 1961, Candyleg, 1961, Chip's Girls, 1961, The Parasites, 1962, (with Ed Reid) The Green Felt Jungle, 1963, The Organization, 1964 (reissued as Fatal Mistake 1966, The Contract, 1970), (with Garry Wills) Jack Ruby, 1968, Captive City, 1969, America the Violent, 1970, Poso del Mundo, 1970, The Overlord, 1972, Dirty Business: The Corporate-Political Money-Power Game, 1974, The Director: An Oral Biography of J. Edgar Hoover, 1975, Judith Exner: My Story, 1976, Brothers in Blood: The International Terrorist Network, 1977, The Last Mafioso: The Treacherous World of Jimmy Fratianno, 1981, The Vegas Legacy, 1983. Served with USAAF, 1940-45. Address: PO Box 6071 Santa Barbara CA 93160

DEMARK, RICHARD REID, retired insurance company executive; b. Detroit, May 15, 1925; s. Charles and Hazel (Reid) DeM.; m. Dorothy Ann Goodin, Sept. 25, 1948; children: Deborah L., Richard R. B.A., U. Mich., 1947. Advt. mgr. Kemper Group, Chgo., 1960-65, resident v.p., Northeast mgr., Quincy, Mass., 1967-72, v.p., div. pres., 1972—. Bd. dirs. ARC of Massachusetts Bay, Boston, 1982; co-chmn. Republican Town Com., Boxford, Mass., 1970. Served to lt. USNR, 1943-52; PTO, Korea. Mem. South Shore C. of C. (bd. dirs. 1978). Republican. Episcopalian.

DE MARR, MARY JEAN, educator; b. Champaign, Ill., Sept. 20, 1932; d. William Fleming and Laura Alice (Shauman) Bailey. B.A., Lawrence Coll., 1954; M.A., U. Ill., 1957, Ph.D., 1963; postgrad., Universitaet Tuebingen, 1954-55, Moscow State U., 1961-62. Asst. prof. English Willamette U., 1964-65; asst. prof. English Ind. State U., 1965-70, asso. prof., 1970-75, prof., 1975—. Am. editor: Annual Bibliography of English Language and Literature, 1979—. Recipient Fulbright assistantship, 1954-55. Mem. MLA, Modern Humanities Research Assn., AAUP, Nat. Council Tchrs. English, Phi Beta Kappa,

Phi Kappa Phi. Home: 2841 Mariposa Dr Terre Haute IN 47803 Office: Dept English Ind State U Terre Haute IN 47809

DEMARS, DAN RICHARD, construction company executive; b. Indpls., Mar. 6, 1943; s. Richard Bruce and Joy Margurite (Geupel) DeM.; m. Sally Louise Shiel, Dec. 18, 1965; children: Christine Louise, Richard Geupel, Shiela Ann, Meghan Joy. B.A., Purdue U., 1965. Project mgr. Geupel Demars, Inc.,, Indpls., 1971-75; mktg.l mgr. Geupel DeMars, Inc.,, Indpls., 1975-77, v.p., 1977-79, exec. v.p. adminstrn., dir., 1979—; dir. Assoc. Gen. Constractors Ind., Indpls. Bd. dirs. Greater Indpls. Housing Devel. Corp., 1982—, Boys Coubs Am., 1983—, Central North Civic Assn., 1983—; bd. dir. Stanley K. Lacy Exec. Leadership Series, 1983—. Mem. Sigma Chi (alumni dir.). Clubs: Meridian Hills Country; Kiwanis (Indpls.). Home: 7630 Brookview Ln Indianapolis IN 46252 Office: Geupel DeMars Inc. PO Box 887, 1919 N. Meridian St. Indianapolis IN 46202

DEMARTINI, ROBERT JOHN, textile company executive; b. N.Y.C., Apr. 4, 1919; s. Andrew John and Regina Louise (Bosetti) D.; m. Carol Elaine Bauer, Feb. 5, 1945; children—Nancy Demartini Warner, David, Regina. B.S., MIT, 1941. Registered profl. engr., Mass. Textile engr. Russell Mfg. Co., Middletown, Conn., 1941-43; textile application engr. Gen. Electric Co., Schenectady, 1943-51; with Huyck Corp., 1951-79, exec. v.p. internat. ops., Wake Forest, N.C., 1973-79; pres. Demartini Devel. Industries, 1979—; gen. ptnr. REICO Ltd., 1980—; dir. King Fifth Wheel Co., 1975-81; adj. prof. N.C. State U., 1979—; Bd. dirs. N.C. World Trade Council, 1976-79, Center for New Bus. Devel., 1979-82. Contbr. articles to profl. jours. Mem. Am. Mgmt. Assn. Club: Raleigh Country. Patentee in field. Home and Office: 3500 Canter Ln Raleigh NC 27604

DEMARTINO, CARL, chemical company executive; b. Phila., Nov. 12, 1925; s. Vincent and Ophelia (LaMonaca) De M.; m. Betty Carr Wilson, June 22, 1946; children: Lee, Greg. B.S. in Chem. Engring, Villanova (Pa.) U., 1948. Chem. engr. Allied Chem. Corp., Phila., 1948-50; with E.I. du Pont de Nemours & Co., Wilmington, Del., 1950—, v.p. employee relations, 1979-83, v.p. internat. dept., 1983—; dir. Girard Bank, Wilmington. Bd. dirs. YMCA Wilmington and New Castle County, 1979—; co-founder, 1st pres. Opportunity Center, Wilmington, 1956, bd. dirs., 1956—; trustee Wilmington Med. Center, 1979—; mem. dean's adv. council U. Del., 1980—. Served with A.C. USNR, 1943-45. Republican. Presbyterian. Clubs: Wilmington, Vicmead Hunt, Wilmington Country, Sea Pines. Office: 1007 Market St Wilmington DE 19898

DEMASCIO, ROBERT EDWARD, judge; b. Coraopolis, Pa., Jan. 11, 1923; s. Peter and Rosa (Baretta) DeM.; m. Margaret Loftus, Aug. 6, 1955; children—Thomas, Robert, Mary. Student, Wayne State U., 1942-43, 47-51, LL.B., 1951, U. Ill., 1944. Bar: Mich. bar 1951. Practice law, Detroit, 1951-53, 61-66, asst. U.S. atty., chief criminal div., 1954-61; judge Recorders Ct., Detroit, 1967-71; U.S. dist. judge Eastern Dist. Mich., 1971—. Served with USNR, 1943-46. Mem. Am., Fed., Detroit bar assns., State Bar Mich. Office: US Courthouse Room 707 Detroit MI 48226 *

DEMATTEO, RONALD C(ASIMIR), hosp. adminstr.; b. Pitts., Mar. 11, 1940; s. Domenic and Edith (Liberatore) DeM.; m. Donna Whipple, July 8, 1961; children—Diane Elizabeth, Ronald Paul. B.S.B.A., U. Pitts., 1962; M.A. in Health Care Adminstrn, George Washington U., 1970. Controller St. Margaret Meml. Hosp., Pitts., 1958-69; adminstrv. resident Hosp. U. Pa., 1969-70; adminstr. gen. and spl. services John Hopkins Hosp., 1970-75; exec. v.p. Riverside Gen. Hosp., Secaucus, N.J., 1975-76, Englewood (N.J.) Hosp., 1976—. Mem. N.J. Hosp. Assn., Am. Coll. Hosp. Adminstrs. Club: Rotary. Home: 73 Heights Rd Clifton NJ 07012 Office: 350 Engle St Englewood NJ 07631 *I have always believed that no goal was too high or no problem too small for me to attempt. Striving to understand the other person's side has always guided my conduct.*

DEMATTIES, NICHOLAS FRANK, artist, art educator; b. Honolulu, Oct. 19, 1939; s. Ernest and Florence Adele (Sutherl) deM.; 1 son, Nicholas; 1 son by previous marriage, Seth. B.A., Long Beach State U., 1964; M.S., Ill. Inst. Tech., 1967. Instr. San Diego State Coll., 1967-69; asst. prof. Mt. St. Marys Coll., Los Angeles, 1969-70; guest lectr. U. Oreg., 1972; vis. artist Albion (Mich.) Coll., 1973-74; asst. prof. art Ariz. State U., Tempe, 1974-77, assoc. prof., 1977—; founder, dir. Pacific Northwest Graphics Workshop, Cheshire, Oreg., 1970-75. One-person shows, Scottsdale (Ariz.) Center for Arts, 1978, U. Houston, 1980, Suzanne Brown Gallery, Scottsdale, 1981, No. Ariz. U., Flagstaff, 1983; exhibited in group shows, Tulsa City Library, 1980, Sun Valley Center Gallery, 1981, Honey Sharp Gallery, Lenox, Mass., 1982, Phoenix Art Mus., 1983, Laguna Gloria Art Mus., Austin, Tex., 1984; represented in permanent collections, Los Angeles County Mus. Art, Bklyn. Mus. Art, Phoenix Art Mus., Biblietheque National de Paris, Library Congress, San Francisco Mus. Art, Portland Art Mus., Am. Republic Ins. Co. Des Moines. Served with USAF, 1956-60. Oreg. Arts Commn. fellow, 1972; Western States Arts Found. fellow, 1979; cash award Tex. Fine Art Assn., 1984. Mem. Coll. Art Assn., AAUP. Home: 4225 N 36th St Phoenix AZ 85018 Studio: 2337 N 10th St Phoenix AZ 85006

DEMAUSE, LLOYD, psychohistorian; b. Detroit, Sept. 19, 1931; s. Leon and Martha (Koren) DeMause; m. Susan Hein; children: Neil, Jennifer. Attended, Gen. Motors Inst., 1948-52; A.B., Columbia, 1957, postgrad., 1957-61; postgrad., Nat. Psychol. Assn. for Psychoanalysis, 1959-60. Founder Atcom Inc. (pub.), 1959; chmn. bd.; dir. Inst. for Psychohistory; pub. Psychohistory Press; mem. faculty N.Y. Center for Psychoanalytic Tng. Editor, author: Jimmy Carter and American Fantasy; editor, author: The History of Childhood, The New Psychohistory, A Bibliography of Psychohistory, Foundations of Psychohistory, Reagan's America. Served with AUS, 1952-54. Mem. Mediaeval Acad. Am., Am. Hist. Assn., Am. Anthropol. Assn., Internat. Psychohist. Assn. (pres.), Assn. Applied Psychoanalysis (exec. sec.). Home: 140 Riverside Dr New York NY 10024 Office: Inst for Psychohistory 2315 Broadway New York NY 10024

DE MAYO, PAUL, chemistry educator; b. London, Eng., Aug. 8, 1924; m. Mary Turnbull, May 28, 1949; children—Ann, Philip. B.Sc., U. London, 1944, Ph.D., 1954; D.es-Sc., U. Paris, 1970. Asst. lectr. Birkbeck Coll., London, 1954-55; lectr. U. Glasgow, Scotland, 1955-57, Imperial Coll., London, 1957-59; prof. chemistry U. Western Ont., Can., London, 1959—, dir. photochemistry unit, 1969-72. Author: Mono and Sesquiterpenoids, 1959, The Higher Terpenoids, 1959, numerous publs. in chem. lit.; editor: Molecular Rearrangements, vol. 1, 1963, vol. II, 1964, Rearrangements in Ground and Excited States, Vol. 1-3, 1980; editorial bd.: Nouveau Journal de Chimie. Recipient Merck, Sharp & Dohme Lecture award Chem. Inst. Can., 1966, Centennial medal Govt. Can., 1967, medal Chem. Inst. Can., 1982. Fellow Royal Soc. Can., Royal Soc. (London). Office: Chemistry Dept U Western Ont London ON Canada N6A 5B7

DEMAZIA, VIOLETTE, educator, foundation executive; b. Paris, U.S., 1927, 1934. Student, Ecole Superieure de la Rue Des Marais, Brussels, Priory House, St. John's Wood, Eng., Hampstead (Eng.) Conservatoire, Barnes Found., Merion, Pa., 1926-27; D.F.A. hon., St. Joseph's Coll., Phila., 1970, L.H.D., Lincoln U., 1969. Tchr. Barnes Found., Merion Station, Pa., 1927—, dir. edn., 1935—, v.p. bd. trustees, 1966—. Author: (with A.C. Barnes) Art and Education, 1929, Art and Education, rev. edit., 1947, 54, The Art of Henri Matisse, 1933, The French Primitives and Their Forms, 1931, The Art of Renoir, 1935, The Art of Cezanne, 1939; editor Barnes Found. Jour., 1970—; pub., editor: Vistas; contbr. articles to French and Am. mags. Decorated Knight Order of Arts and Letters French Ministry of Cultural Affairs; recipient Legion of Honor Chapel of Four Chaplains, Phila.; named Super Achiever Phila., Juvenile Diabetic Found., 1978. Home: PO Box 93 Merion Station PA 19066 Office: Barnes Found Merion Station PA 19066

DEMBER, WILLIAM NORTON, educator, psychologist; b. Waterbury, Conn., Aug. 8, 1928; s. David and Henrietta (Siegel) D.; m. Cynthia Fox, Dec. 21, 1958; children: Joanna, Laura, Gregory. A.B., Yale U., 1950; M.A., U. Mich., 1951, Ph.D., 1955. Instr. dept. psychology U. Mich., 1954-56; asst. prof. Yale U., 1956-59; mem. faculty U. Cin., 1959—, prof. psychology, 1965—, asst. dean, grad. sch., 1965-67, head dept. psychology, 1968-76, 79-81, dean Coll. Arts and Scis., 1981—. Author: Psychology of Perception, 1960, 2d edit., 1979, Visual Perception, 1964, General Psychology, 1970, 2d edit., 1984, Exploring Behavior and Experience, 1971; also articles. Fellow AAAS, Am. Psychol. Assn.; mem. Midwest Psychol. Assn. (pres. 1976), Eastern Psychol. Assn., Psychonomic Soc., N.Y. Acad. Scis. Developed and tested theory of motivation applying to behavior human beings and animals. Home: 920 Oregon Trail Cincinnati OH 45215

DEMBLING, PAUL GERALD, lawyer, former government official; b. Rahway, N.J., Jan. 11, 1920; s. Simon and Fannie (Ellenbogen) D.; m. Florence Brotman, Nov. 22, 1947; children: Ross Wayne, Douglas Evan, Donna Stacy. B.A., Rutgers U., 1940, M.A., 1942; J.D., George Washington U., 1951. Bar: D.C. 1952. Grad. asst., teaching fellow Rutgers U., 1940-42; economist, salary and wage analyst Office Chief Transp., Dept. Army, 1942-45; since practiced in, Washington; indsl. relations NACA, 1945-51, spl. counsel, legal adviser, gen. counsel, 1951-58; asst. gen. counsel NASA, 1958-61, dir. legis. affairs, 1961-63, dep. gen. counsel, 1963-67, gen. counsel, 1967-69, chmn. bd. contract appeals, 1958-61, vice chmn. inventions and contbns. bd., 1959-67; mem. and alt. rep. U.S. del. UN Legal Subcom. Com. on Outer Space, 1964-69; gen. counsel GAO, 1969-78; partner Schnader, Harrison, Segal & Lewis, Washington, 1978—; professorial lectr. George Washington U. Law Sch., 1965—. Editor-in-chief: Fed. Bar Jour., 1962-69; contbr. articles to profl. jours. Vice pres. Merrimack Civic Assn., 1956-57; bd. dirs. Merrimack Park Recreation Assn., 1956-59, 61-64. Recipient Meritorious Civilian Service award War Dept., 1945; Disting. Service award NASA, 1968; Nat. Civil Service League award, 1973. Fellow Nat. Contract Mgmt. Assn. (bd. advisers 1973—), AIAA (chmn. com. law and sociology 1969-71); mem. ABA (council public contract law), D.C. Bar Assn., Fed. Bar Assn. (nat. council 1963—, pres. Capitol Hill chpt. 1977-78, nat. sec. 1978-79, pres.-elect 1981-82, nat. pres. 1983-84), Internat. Inst. Space Law (pres. Am. assn. 1970-72), Nat. Acad. Pub. Adminstrn., Phi Delta Phi. Clubs: Cosmos, Nat. Lawyers (Washington). Home: 2131 N St NW Washington DC 20037 Office: 1111 19th St NW Washington DC 20036

DEMBNER, S. ARTHUR, magazine publisher; b. N.Y.C., Oct. 7, 1920; s. Jack D.;, Dec. 5, 1948; 3 children. A.B. (evenings), New Sch. Social Research, 1950; postgrad. Advanced Mgmt. Program, Harvard U., 1971. Account exec. Modern Mdse. Bur., 1945-47; circulation exec. Time, Inc., 1947-52; with Newsweek mag., 1952—, circulation dir., 1961—, v.p., 1962—, mem. exec. com., 1969—, dir., 1969—, also pub. book div.; sr. v.p. Newsweek, Inc., 1971-76; pres. Newsweek Books, 1973-76, Dembner Enterprises Corp., N.Y.C., 1976—; also pres. Dembner Books; dir. Alco Gravure Industries; Chmn. bd. govs. Direct Mail Advt. Assn., 1959-60; chmn. com. advisers on direct mail Dept. Agr., 1956-58; adv. com. sales and subscriptions Com. Econ. Devel., 1960. Editor: Modern Circulation Methods. Bd. dirs., v.p. Vis. Nurse Service N.Y.; Chmn. Vols. in Politics, N.Y.C., 1953; Bd. dirs. Encampment for Citizenship. Served to capt. USAAF, World War II. Mem. Advt. Fedn. Am., Assn. Am. Pub. (gov.), Hundred Million Club (past pres.), Sales Promotion Execs. Assn., Mag. Pubs. Assn. (chmn. circulation com.). Clubs: Players., Dutch Treat. Home: 140 Cabrini Blvd New York NY 10033 Office: 1841 Broadway New York NY 10023

DEMBO, LAWRENCE SANFORD, educator; b. Troy, N.Y., Dec. 3, 1929; s. Irving and Mildred (Spiwak) D.; m. Royce Benderson, Mar. 15, 1953. B.A., Syracuse U., 1951; M.A., Columbia, 1952; Ph.D., Cornell U., 1955. Instr. English Cornell U., 1959-60; asst. prof. U. Calif. at Los Angeles, 1960-65; Fulbright lectr., Montpellier, France, 1963-64; prof. English U. Wis., 1965—. Author: Hart Crane's Sanskrit Charge, a Study of the Bridge, 1960, The Confucian Odes of Ezra Pound, a Critical Appraisal, 1963, Conceptions of Reality in Modern American Poetry, 1966; Editor: Nabokov, The Man and His Work, 1967, Criticism, Speculative and Analytical Essays, 1968; Co-editor: The Contemporary Writer: Interviews with Sixteen Novelists and Poets, 1972, Doris Lessing, Critical Studies, 1974, Directions for Criticism, 1977; Editor: Contemporary Literature, 1966—; mem. editorial bd.: Am. Lit, 1973-76. Served to lt. (j.g.) USNR, 1956-59. Guggenheim fellow, 1968-69; Am. Council Learned Socs. fellow, 1977-78. Home: 5 Beach St Madison WI 53705

DEMBOFSKY, THOMAS JOSEPH, publisher; b. N.Y.C., July 5, 1927; s. Nathan and Alice (Meehan) D.; m. Constance Needle, Nov. 26, 1954; children—Karen, Charles, Bruce, Mathew. B.S., Columbia U., 1957. Sales rep. Coll. div. Alfred Knopf, N.Y.C., 1957, Ginn & Co., Boston, 1958-60; editor McGraw Hill Book Co., N.Y.C., 1961-63, sr. editor, 1963-65, editor-in-chief, 1965-67, editorial dir. coll. div., 1967-70, pub., 1970-72, gen. mgr., pub., 1974-81, gen. mgr., 1981—. Served with USNR, 1945-47, 1950-52. Clubs: Stamford Yacht, Stamford Power Squadron. Home: 85 Boxwood Dr Stamford CT 06906 Office: 1221 Ave of Americas New York NY 10020

DEMBOWSKI, PETER FLORIAN, language educator; b. Warsaw, Poland, Dec. 23, 1925; came to U.S., 1966, naturalized, 1974; s. Wlodzimierz and Henryka (Sokolowski) D.; m. Yolande Jessop, June 29, 1954; children—Anne, Eve, Paul. B.A. with honors, U. B.C., 1952; Doctorat d'Universite, U. Paris, France, 1954; Ph.D., U. Calif. at Berkeley, 1960. Instr. French U. B.C., 1954-56; asst. prof. French U. Toronto, 1960-63, asso. prof., 1963-66; mem. faculty U. Chgo., 1966—, prof. French, 1970—, dean students div. humanities, 1968-70, chmn. dept. Romance langs. and lits., 1976-83; resident master Snell-Hitchcock Halls, 1973-79; vis. mem. Sch. Hist. Studies, Inst. Advanced Study, Princeton, N.J., 1979-80. Author: La Chronique de Robert de Clari, 1963, Jourdain de Blaye, 1969, Ami et Amile, 1969, La Vie de sainte Maire l'Egyptienne, 1977, Jean Froissart and his Meliador, 1983. Served with Polish Army, 1944-46. Decorated Cross of Valor, Cross of Service with swords (Poland), Chevalier des Palmes Academiques (France); Guggenheim fellow, 1970-71; Danforth Found. asso., 1976—. Mem. MLA, Société de Linguistique Romane, Medieval Acad. Am. (councillor 1980—). Office: Dept Romance Langs and Lit 1050 E 59th St Chicago IL 60637

DEMBSKI, GREGORY ANTHONY, newspaper executive; b. Chgo., Mar. 12, 1917; s. Anthony J. and Frances (Mysliewiec) D.; m. Gladys Mary Hagenauer, Sept. 8, 1945; children: Gregory A. II, Timothy, Patrick, Jeffrey, Elizabeth. Sales exec. Chgo. Tribune, 1939-44, Cresmer & Woodward, Chgo., 1944-49, Scripps-Howard Newspaper, 1949-63; western mgr. Scripps-Howard Newspapers, Chgo., 1963-71; gen. mgr. Columbus (ohio) Citizen Jour., 1971-83, Jupiter (Fla.) Courier-Jour., 1983—. Chmn. bd. Salesian Boys Club, Columbus, Ohio, 1981-82, Better Bus. Bur., Columbus, 1981-82, Blue Cross of Central Ohio, Columbus, 1982-83. Named Outstanding Media Rep. Chgo. Media Assn., 1960. Mem. Am. Newpaper Pubs. Assn., Am. Newspaper Mktg. Execs. Assn., Am. Newpapers Rep. Assn. Roman Catholic. Lodges: Rotary; Elks. Office: Jupiter Courier Jour 800 Indiantown Rd Jupiter FL 33458

DEMELIO, JOSEPH JOHN, retail chain executive; b. N.Y.C., Nov. 30, 1930; s. John Joseph and Anna DeM.; m. Lorraine M. Quinones, May 31, 1952; children: Joanne, Carol, Lorraine, Anne, Katherine. B.A., Fordham Coll., 1952. Asst. actuary Nat. Bur. Casualty Underwriters, N.Y.C., 1952-60; sr. v.p., actuary Home Ins. Co., N.Y.C., 1960-76; pres., treas. J.C. Penney Casualty Ins. Co., Westerville, Ohio, 1976-82; v.p., dir. ins. J.C. Penney Co., N.Y.C., 1982—. Pres. Griffith Found., 1981; trustee St. Ann's Hosp. Fellow Casualty Acturarial Soc.; mem. Am. Acad. Actuaries, Ohio Ins. Inst., Westerville C. of C. (pres. 1979), Nat. Assn. Ind. Insurors (bd. govs.). Home: 51 Johnson Dr Chatham NJ 07928 Office: J C Penney Co Inc 1301 Ave of Americas New York NY 10019

DEMELLE, ARTHUR WILLIAM, service company executive; b. Natick, Mass., Sept. 16, 1940; s. Walter Earl and Lucille Elinor (Knott) DeM.; m. Deborah Jope, Aug. 3, 1963 (div. 1972); children: Jennifer, Todd; m. Madelaine Busch, Aug. 30, 1973; 1 dau., Sara. B.A. in Econs., Bowdoin Coll., 1962; M.B.A. in Acctg., Rutgers U., 1963. C.P.A., N.J. Audit staff Price Waterhouse, Morristown and Newark, 1963-75, audit ptnr., 1975-78; v.p. fin. Interpace Corp., Parsippany, N.J., 1978-80; sr. v.p. fin. Purolator, Inc., Piscataway, N.J., 1980—; dir. Marotta Sci. Controls, Boonton, N.J.; mem. acctg. adv. bd. Columbia U. Grad. Sch., N.Y.C. Mem. corp. United Way of Morris County, N.J. Mem. Am. Inst. C.P.A.s, Fin. Execs. Inst., N.J. Soc. C.P.A.s. Republican. Presbyterian. Home: 149 Mountain Ave Gillette NJ 07933 Office: Purolator Inc 255 Old New Brunswick Rd Piscataway NJ 08854

DE MENT, JACK (ANDREW), research chemist, author; b. Portland, Oreg., Feb. 6, 1920; s. Andrew Thomas and Bernadine (Michaels) De M. Student, Reed Coll., 1938-41; D.Sc. (hon.), Western States Coll., 1955. Diplomate: in Nuclear Physics, Am. Bd. Bio-Analysts. Chemist and metallurgist Mont. Assay Office, 1941; asst. spectroscopist Charlton Labs., Portland, 1941-42; research chemist, asso. editor Mineralogist Mag., Portland, 1940-51; research chemist and head De Ment Labs., Portland, 1941—; research asst. Sch. Dentistry, Oreg. Health Scis. U., 1948-50, research cons. biophysics and pharmacology, 1961-66; co-investigator USPHS, 1953-58; pres. Polyphoton Corp., 1955—; sci. editor Prevue Mag., 1958-65; research cons. Ultra-Violet Products, Inc., Los Angeles, 1942-50; Cons. Sec. of War (Project Crossroads (spent 2 mos. at Bikini atomic bomb tests), 1946; mem. Pres.' Conf. Tech. Distbn. Research, 1957; del. 1st Nat. Laser Safety Seminar, Orlando, Fla., 1966; Student of human strength, 1936-41; reviewer NSF, 1979-80. Author: (with H.C. Dake) Fluorescent Light and Its Applications, 1941, Uranium and Atomic Power, 1941 (rev. edn., 1945), Fluorescent Chemicals and Their Applications, 1942, Ultraviolet Light and Its Applications, 1942, Fluorochemistry, 1945, Rarer Metals, 1946 (English edition 1949), Handbook of Uranium Minerals, 1947, rev. edit., 1949, Handbook of Fluorescent Minerals, 1947, New Horizons in Cancer Control, 1954; prize essay Gravity Research Found., 1951; Contbr. to other books and encys. Recipient Wisdom Award of Honor, 1970, commendation Joint Com. Atomic Energy. Fellow Am. Coll. Med. Technologists; mem. Profl. Execs. Hall of Fame, Sigma Xi, Chi Beta Phi. Research: named and established fluorochemistry, 1942; Laser research, color radiography, quasitissue. Inventor radioactive and luminescent photographs, antifallout ship wash systems, fluidic optics; optoexplosive systems (explotron); first to separate blast-free light from explosions; discovered optoexplosion principle of physics; first to make lab. prototypes of radiological and weather warfare weapons, 1945-46; first to use for peaceful purposes radioactive isotopes made by atom bomb explosion; first delineated energy transduction disorders including cancer theory and biomed. piezoelectricity. Formally enunciated First Law of Fluorescence (Lommel-De Ment Absorption Law), new tests for uranium and ores; invented new weapons, radiological, weather warfare, directed energy, new methods for radioactive decontamination; several hundred discoveries and inventions described in over 300 papers in sci. jours.; U.S. and fgn. patents granted on new laser systems; holds or has filed 100 patents, assigned two dozen to AEC. Home: 4847 SE Division Portland OR 97206 *The bold idea carried by tenacity and hard work-albeit never perfect, magnifies as no other. To create energy and happiness lasting long into time is the way to spend a life. To make suns out of twinkles.*

DEMENT, WILLIAM CHARLES, sleep researcher, medical educator; b. Wenatchee, Wash., July 29, 1928; s. Charles Frederick and Kathryn (Severyns) D.; m. Eleanor Weber, Mar. 23, 1956; children: Catherine Lynn, Elizabeth Anne, John Nicholas. B.S., U. Wash., 1951; M.D., U. Chgo., 1955, Ph.D., 1957. Bd. cert. in clin. polysomography. Intern Mt. Sinai Hosp., N.Y.C., 1957-58, research fellow dept. psychiatry, 1958-63; assoc. prof. dept. psychiatry and behavioral scis. Stanford U., 1963-67, prof., 1967—; dir. Stanford Sleep Disorders Clinic and Lab., 1970—, Sleep Research Lab., Stanford, Calif., 1963—; chmn. U.S. Surgeon Gen.'s Joint Coordinating Council, Project Sleep, 1979—. Author: Some Must Watch While Some Must Sleep, 1972; editor-in-chief: Sleep, 1977—; mem. editorial bd.: Neurobiology of Aging, 1982—. Recipient medal Intra-Sci. Research Found., 1981, Disting. Service award U. Chgo. Med. Alumni Assn., 1978. Mem. Sleep Research Soc. (founder), Assn. Sleep Disorders Ctrs. (pres. 1982, Nathaniel Kleitman prize 1982), Inst. Medicine of Nat. Acad. Scis., Psychiat. Research Found., Soc. Neurosci., Western EEG Soc., Am. EEG Soc., Am. Physiol. Soc. Home: 440 Gerona Rd Stanford CA 94305 Office: Sleep Disorders Ctr TD 114 Stanford University Med Ctr Stanford CA 94305

DEMERATH, NICHOLAS JAY, III, sociology educator; b. Boston, Nov. 10, 1936; s. Nicholas J. and Helen Louise (Titus) D.; m. Judith Wood Richie, June 25, 1960; children: Loren Roberts, Peter Wells, Benjamin Burroughs. A.B. magna cum laude, Harvard U., 1958; M.A., U. Calif., Berkeley, 1962, Ph.D., 1964. Instr. to prof. sociology U. Wis., 1962-72; exec. officer Am. Sociol. Assn., Washington, 1970-72; prof., chmn. sociology U. Mass., Amherst, 1972—. Author: Social Class in American Protestantism, 1965, (with R.A. Peterson) System, Change and Conflict, 1967, (with P.E. Hammond) Religion in Social Context, 1968, (with M.T. Aiken and G. Marwell) Dynamics of Idealism, 1971, A Tottering Transcendence, 1973, (with K. F. Schuessler and O. N. Larsen) Social Policy and Sociology, 1974, (with G. Marwell) Sociology: Perspectives and Applications, 1976; Book rev. editor: Am. Sociol. Rev, 1965-68. Research fellow, grantee Danforth Found., 1965, NIMH, 1960-62, New World Found., 1966; grantee Lilly Endowment, 1983-84. Mem. Am. Sociol. Assn. (chmn. publs. com. 1975-77), Eastern Sociol. Soc. (v.p. 1975—), Soc. for Sci. Study Religion (council 1969-71), ACLU. Democrat. Home: 30 Harris Mountain Rd Amherst MA 01002

DEMERS, PHILIPPE, veterinary surgeon, zoological garden director; b. St.-Sebastian, Iberville, Que., Apr. 28, 1919; s. Charles-Emile and Amande (Desranleau) D.; m. A.J. Fortin, Oct. 14, 1948; children: Danielle, Josee, Jacques, Helene, Andrew; m. Danielle Demers, Sept. 1, 1975. B.A., St. Hyacinthe Sem., 1943; D.M.V., St. Hyacinthe Vet. Faculty, 1948. Practice vet. medicine, Shawinigan, Que., 1948-66, M.P., 1966-74; dir. Jardin Zool. de Que., Charlesbourg, 1981—; adminstr. Laurentide Chems., Shawinigan, 1983—. Mem. Shawinigan Sud Town Council, 1950-56, mayor, 1952-56; pres. Vet. Coll. St. Hyacinthe, 1975-81. Clubs: Richelieu; Kateri (Shawinigan). Lodge: KC (Shawinigan).

DEMETRION, JAMES THOMAS, art center administrator; b. Middletown, Ohio, July 10, 1930; s. Tom and Susie (Tsifiklis) D.; m. Barbara Parrish, 1954 (div. 1981); 1 dau., Elaine. Curator Pasadena (Calif.) Art Mus., 1964-66, dir., 1966-69, Des Moines Art Center, 1969—; Mem. museum advisory panel Nat. Endowment for Arts, 1973-76, co-chmn., 1974-76; mem. nat. exhbn. com. Am. Fedn. Arts, 1969-73; mem. nat. adv. com. Tamarind Inst., 1978—. Mem. internat. adv. com. Stuart Found., La Jolla, Calif. Mem. Assn. Art Mus. Dirs. (treas. 1976-77, pres. 1979-80). Office: Des Moines Art Center Greenwood Park Des Moines IA 50312

DEMETRIUS, JAMES KLEON, classics educator; b. Chicopee Falls, Mass., Aug. 23, 1924; s. James and Bess (Stephens) D. Student, NYU, 1945, U. N.D., 1946-47; B.A., U. Iowa and Bklyn. Coll., 1948; M.A., Columbia U., 1949, postgrad., 1950-58; Ph.D. (hon.), U. Ariz., 1982. Instr. Greek and Spanish Iona Coll., 1953-59; asst. prof. Spanish Widener Coll., 1959-62, Wash. Coll., 1962-63; asso. prof. Greek and Spanish Bloomfield Coll., 1963-68; vis. prof. fgn. langs. St. Francis Coll., 1971-72; prof. ancient and modern langs. Touro Coll., 1972; research in, Spain and Latin Am., 1973—; chmn. English and fgn. lang. dept. Interboro Jr. Coll., N.Y.C.; speaker U. Ky., 1958; honored speaker, Barry Chase Meml. lectr. The Grecian Concept of Education and Its Meaning to Us Today Bloomfield Coll., 1968; hon. speaker Unification Theol. Sem., 1978. Author: Greek Scholarship in Spain and Latin America, 1966; monographs An Essay on Greek Influences on Spanish Literature, 1961, Los Griegos en Espana, 1962, A Bibliography of Greek Studies in Spain, 1962, Nikos Kazantzakis in Spain, 1968, (with Dr. Luis Leon) Spanish Grammar Explained, 1972, Modern Greek Poetry, 1974, Homer: Europe's First Humanist, 1974; Columnist: Grecian World, 1961—; Numerous articles and studies and notes contbd. to Foliabiblia, Spain, St. Francis Bulletin, Greek Gazette London, Boletin de estudios helenicos, Spain, Greek Star, Slavic Rev, Filosofia Oggi, Balkan Studies; Book rev. editor, mem. editorial bd.: Hellenic Times, 1974—. Recipient awards for excellence in teaching, student bodies in Bloomfield Coll., 1968, St. Francis Coll., 1972; Fellow, Athens, Greece, 1977. Mem. Classical Assn. Spain, Hellenic Soc. London, Royal Inst. Philosophy (Eng.), Classical Assn. Spain, Internat. Hispanist Assn., Am. Assn. Teachers of Spanish and Portuguese, AAUP, Medieval Soc. Am., Am. Classical League, Soc. Ancient Greek Philosophy, Alpha Sigma Phi. *The guiding philosophy of my life has always been Homeric Humanism. When it is translated into every day terms, this philosophy embodies the thought that one must seek and strive after excellence, in everything one does. The individual must be highly individualistic and must constantly pursue knowledge. Good teachers in the past roamed bravely and defiantly afield, journeying through all of Western culture finding connections between one subject area and another. Their goal was not the training of specialists, but of humanists able to move gracefully within the spacious and orderly realm of learning.*

DE MICHELE, O. MARK, utility company executive; b. Syracuse, N.Y., Mar. 23, 1934; s. Aldo and Dora (Carno) De M.; m. Faye Ann Venturin, Nov. 8, 1957; children: Mark A., Christopher C., Michele M., Julianne; m. 2d Barbara Joan Stanley, May 22, 1982. B.S., Syracuse U., 1955. Mgr. Seal Right Co., Inc., Fulton, N.Y., 1955-58; v.p., gen. mgr. L.M. Harvey Co. Inc., Syracuse, 1958-62; v.p. Niagara Mohawk Power, Syracuse, 1962-78, Ariz. Pub. Service, Phoenix, 1978-81, exec. v.p., 1981-82, pres., 1982—, dir. Pres. Jr. Achievement, Syracuse, 1974-75 pres. Jr. Achievement, Phoenix, 1982-83, United Way of Central N.Y., Syracuse, 1978, Ariz. Opera Co., Phoenix, 1981-83. Named Outstanding Young Man of Yr. Syracuse Jaycees, 1968. Mem. Phoenix C. of C. (vice chmn. 1982-83). Republican. Clubs: Phoenix Country; Ariz. (Phoenix). Home: 7202 N 6th Way Phoenix AZ 85020 Office: Ariz Pub Service Co 411 N Central Ave Phoenix AZ 85036

DE MICOLI, SALVATORE, non-ferrous metals commodity executive; b. Pieta, Malta, May 21, 1939; came to U.S., 1954; s. Anthony and Jane (Camilleri) De M.; m. Irma L. Gil, Sept. 25, 1966; children: Mark, Marisa, Martin. Asst. sec. AMA Ametalco Inc., N.Y.C., 1956-72; v.p. N.C. Trading Co. Inc., N.Y.C., 1972-73; exec. v.p. Cerro Sales Corp., N.Y.C., 1973—; bd. govs. Commodity Exchange Inc., N.Y.C., 1982—. Mem. AIME(N.Y. sect.). Clubs: Copper, Mining (N.Y.C.). Home: 286 Bayview Ave S Massapequa NY 11758 Office: Cerro Sales Corp 250 Park Ave New York NY 10177

DEMIERI, JOSEPH L., diversified investment company executive; b. N.Y.C., Aug. 31, 1940; s. Leo A. and Frances (Garone) DeM.; m. Anne Patricia McCue, May 15, 1965. B.B.A., Tex. A. and M. U., 1962. C.P.A., N.Y. With Peat, Marwick, Mitchell & Co., N.Y.C., 1962-68; v.p., controller City Investing Co., N.Y.C. and Beverly Hills, Calif., 1968-82; exec. v.p. Motown Industries, Los Angeles, 1982—. Mem. Am. Inst. Corp. Controllers, Am. Inst. C.P.A.s, Fin. Execs. Inst., N.Y. State Soc. C.P.A.s. Home: 6259 Ebbtide Way Malibu CA 90265 Office: 6255 Sunset Blvd Los Angeles CA 90028

DE MILHAU, JOHN WADDINGTON, ret. banker; b. N.Y.C., Oct. 23, 1910; s. Louis J. deG. and Renee Noel (Gourd) de M.; m. Dorothea M. Harrison, Sept. 9, 1939; 1 son, David Livesey. Grad., Middlesex Sch., Concord, Mass., 1928; student, Harvard, 1932. With Chase Manhattan Bank, 1930-68, sr. v.p., 1962-68; with Altgelt & Co., Inc., 1968-80, pres., to 1980. Clubs: Riverside Yacht; Innis Arden Golf (Old Greenwich, Conn.). Home: Grosset Rd Riverside CT 06878

DE MILLE, AGNES, choreographer; d. William Churchill and Anna (George) de M.; m. Walter F. Prude, June 14, 1943; 1 son, Jonathan. A.B. cum laude, U. Calif.; Litt.D. (hon.), Mills Coll., 1952, Russell Sage Coll., 1953, Smith Coll., 1954, Western Coll., 1955, Hood Coll., 1957, Northwestern U., 1960, Goucher Coll., 1961, Clark U., 1962, U. Calif. at Los Angeles, 1964, Franklin and Marshall, 1965, Western Mich. U., 1967, Nasson Coll., 1971; L.H.D., Dartmouth Coll., 1974, Duke U., 1975, U. N.C., 1980, N.Y. U., 1981. Dance recitalist, U.S., Eng., France, Denmark, 1928-42; choreographer and dancer: The Black Crook, 1929; choreographer: film Romeo and Juliet, 1936; musicals Nymph Errant, 1933, Hooray for What, 1937, Oklahoma, 1943, One Touch of Venus, 1943, Bloomer Girl, 1944, Carousel, 1945, Brigadoon, 1947, Gentlemen Prefer Blondes, 1949, Paint Your Wagon, 1951, The Girl in Pink Tights, 1954, Goldilocks, 1958, Juno, 1959, Kwamina, 1961; ballets OBeah Black Ritual, 1940, Three Virgins and a Devil, 1942, Drums Sound in Hackensack, 1941, Rodeo, 1942, Tally-Ho, 1944, Fall River Legend, 1948, The Harvest According, 1952, Oklahoma; film, 1955, The Bitter Wierd, 1962, The Wind in the Mountains, 1965, The Four Mary's, 1965, The Golden Age, 1967, A Rose for Miss Emily, 1970, A Bridegroom Called Death, 1980, Texas 4th, 1977; choreographer, dir.: Allegro, 1947; dir.: Rape of Lucrecia, 1949, Out of this World, 1950, Come Summer, 1969; choreographer: musical 110 In the Shade, 1963; head, Agnes de Mille Dance Theatre, presented by S. Hurok, 6 mos. tour, 126 cities, 1953-54, Agnes de Mille Heritage Dance Theater, 1973, 74, Conversations About the Dance, 1974, 75, Omnibus lectrs. and ballets, 1956-57; choreographer for: Conversations About the Dance, Ballet Russe de Monte Carlo, 1942, Royal Winnipeg Ballet, 1972 (Recipient N.Y. Critics prize 1942-46), Royal Winnipeg Ballet (Donaldson award 1943-47), Royal Winnipeg Ballet (Madamoiselle merit award 1944), Royal Winnipeg Ballet (Antoinette Perry award 1947, 62), Royal Winnipeg Ballet (Lord and Taylor award 1947), Royal Winnipeg Ballet (Dancing Masters award of merit 1950), Royal Winnipeg Ballet (Dance Mag. award 1957), Royal Winnipeg Ballet (Capezio award 1966), Royal Winnipeg Ballet (Handel award Mayor N.Y.C. 1976), Royal Winnipeg Ballet (Kennedy award Pres. U.S. 1980), Royal Winnipeg Ballet (named Woman of Year by Am. Newspaper Woman's Guild 1946), Royal Winnipeg Ballet (named to Theatre Hall of Fame 1973), Royal Winnipeg Ballet (Agnes de Mille Theatre N.C. Sch. Arts, Winston-Salem named in her honor 1975); Author: Dance to the Piper, 1952, And Promenade Home, 1958, To A Young Dancer, 1962, The Book of the Dance, 1963, Lizzie Borden Dance of Death, 1968, Dance In America, 1970, Russian Journals, 1970, Speak to Me, Dance with Me, 1974, Where the Wings Grow, 1978, America Dances, 1980, Reprieve, 1981; contbr. to: McCalls mags. Recipient Commonwealth award in dramatic arts, 1980. Mem. Soc. Stage Dirs. and Choreographers (pres. 1965-66).

DEMING, FREDERICK LEWIS, banker; b. Des Moines, Sept. 12, 1912; s. Fred Kemp and Erva Pearl (Smyres) D.; m. Corinne Inez Wilson, Feb. 4, 1935; children: Frederick Wilson, Richard Louis. A.B., Washington U., St. Louis, 1934, M.A., 1935, Ph.D., 1941. Mgr. research dept to 1st v.p. Fed. Res. Bank, St. Louis, 1941-57, pres., Mpls., 1957-65; undersec. for monetary affairs U.S. Dept. Treasury, Washington, 1965-69; gen. ptnr. Lazard Freres & Co., N.Y.C., 1969-71; pres. Nat. City Bancorp., Mpls., 1971-82; dir. Nat. City Bancorp. Trustee Washington U., 1966—, Macalester Coll., 1959—, Endowment Fund, ARC, Washington, 1965—. Democrat. Clubs: Minneapolis, Minikahda, Met., Cosmos. Home: 4235 E Lake Harriet Blvd Minneapolis MN 55409

DEMING, FREDERICK WILSON, economist, banker; b. St. Louis, Dec. 29, 1935; s. Frederick Lewis and Corinne Inez (Wilson) D.; m. Lynne Eve Anken, Mar. 24, 1960; children—Susanne Lyn, Frederick Lawrence. B.A., Princeton U., 1957; M.A., Yale U., 1958. With Fed. Res. Bank of N.Y., 1961-71; sr. staff economist Council Econ. Advisers, 1968; exec. dir. Commn. Mortgage Interest Rates, 1969; spl. asst. to Sec. of HUD, 1970-71; sr. v.p., economist Chem. Bank, N.Y.C., 1971—. Home: 24 Colt Rd Summit NJ 07901 Office: 380 Madison Ave New York NY 10017

DEMING, ROBERT HERSCHEL, appliance manufacturing executive; b. Indpls., May 16, 1934; s. Herschel P. and Margaret T. D.; m. Beverly Ann Baker, May 16, 1953; children: Steve, Rob, Doug, Bruce. B.S. in Bus. Adminstrn., U. Colo., 1956, M.S., 1959; D.B.A., Harvard U., 1963. Ops. mgr., then dir. mktg. Black & Decker Mfg. Co., Towson, Md., 1964-68; chmn. bd., pres., chief exec. officer Desa Industries, Cockeysville, Md., 1968-76; group pres. portable appliance and tool group McGraw-Edison Co., Columbia, Mo., 1976-79, group pres. appliance group, corp. v.p., 1979—; chmn. bd., pres., chief exec. officer Toastmaster Inc., Columbia, 1980—; chmn. bd. Desa Industries; dir. Desa Industries Can., Insley Mfg. Co. Author: Characteristics of an Effective Management Control System in an Industrial Organization, 1968. Chmn. for Md., Harvard U. Bus. Sch. fund raising drive, 1969-72; bd. dirs. Md. YMCA, 1970-72, Friends Winston Churchill Meml., 1977. Rosenfeld scholar, 1952-56; grantee Ford Found., 1959-62. Mem. Young Pres. Orgn., Chief Execs. Orgn., Assn. Home Appliance Mfrs., Balt. C. of C. (life), U. Mo. Scholarship Assn., Beta Gamma Sigma (Key award 1955), Beta Alpha Psi (ann. award 1956). Clubs: Harvard Bus. Sch. (past pres. Md.), Columbia Coll. Medallion.). Home: 3008 Woodkirk Ln Columbia MO 65201 Office: 1801 N Stadium Blvd Columbia MO 65201

DEMING, WILLIS RILEY, business executive; b. Ada, Ohio, Nov. 28, 1914; s. Cliffe and Okla (Riley) D.; m. Dorothy Arline Hill, Aug. 19, 1950 (div. Aug. 1971); children: Susan Elizabeth, Deborah Anne, David Riley; m. Constance S. Mori, Nov. 6, 1971. B.A., Ohio State U., 1935, J.D., 1938. Bar: Ohio 1938, Calif. 1947, D.C. 1957. Pvt. practice, Columbus, Ohio, 1938-39; casualty claim examiner Am. Surety Co., N.Y.C., 1939-41; chief bds. and claims rev. br. San Francisco Port Embarkation, 1946-47; mem. firm Treadwell and Laughlin, San Francisco, 1947-54, Brobeck, Phleger & Harrison, 1954-56, Washington, 1956-60; pvt. practice, Washington, 1961-62; with Matson Nav. Co., San Francisco, 1962-71, 74—, now sr. v.p., gen. counsel; v.p., sec., gen. counsel Alexander & Baldwin, Inc., Honolulu, 1968-74. Served to lt. col. AUS, 1941-46; col., ret. Mem. Am., Fed., Hawaii, San Francisco, Maritime bar assns., D.C. Bar, State Bar Calif. Methodist. Clubs: Stock Exchange (San Francisco); Oahu Country (Honolulu); Metropolitan, Army and Navy (Washington). Home: 5649 Country Club Dr Oakland CA 94618 Office: PO Box 7452 San Francisco CA 94120

DEMMLER, RALPH HENRY, lawyer; b. Pitts., Aug. 22, 1904; s. Otto and Maud (Theobald) D.; m. Catherine Hollinger, Oct. 5, 1929; 1 son, John Henry. A.B., Allegheny Coll., Meadville, Pa., 1925, LL.D., 1965; LL.B., U. Pitts., 1928. Bar: Pa. 1928, Pa. and U.S. cts 1928. Faculty fellow Law Sch., U Pitts., 1928-30; practiced law in, Pitts., 1928—; partner firm Reed, Smith, Shaw & McClay, 1948-53, 55—; chmn. U.S. SEC, 1953-55, Fed. Home Loan Bank, Pitts., 1959-61; Mem. adv. com. on enforcement SEC, 1972; writer, lectr. securities regulation, 1953—. Author: The First Century of an Institution. Mem. Sch. Bd. of, Ross Twp., 1933-45 Mem. Sch. Bd. of, Allegheny County, Pa., 1938-45; treas. Pitts. Presbytery, 1941-45; trustee Allegheny Coll., 1957—, chmn. bd., 1968-72. Fellow Am. Bar Found.; mem. Am., Pa., Allegheny County bar assns., Am. Law Inst. (adv. com. on securities codification 1969—), Hist. Soc. Western Pa. (dir. 1977—), Order of Coif, Phi Beta Kappa, Delta Theta Phi, Delta Sigma Rho, Phi Gamma Delta. Presbyn. Clubs: Mason., Duquesne (dir. 1957-60), Rolling Rock, University (Pitts.). Home: Park Plaza 128 N Craig St Pittsburgh PA 15213 also Box 84 Ligonier PA 15658 Office: Union Trust Bldg Box 2009 Pittsburgh PA 15230

DEMOFF, SAMUEL LOUIS, retail chain exec.; b. Poland, Oct. 3, 1909; came to U.S., 1911; s. William and Fannie (Kout) D.; m. Clarice Cohen, Oct. 7, 1949; children—John M., Stephen E. Student, Am. Conservatory Music, 1923-28; B.A., Northwestern U., 1931. Mgr. Grossman Shoe Co., Chgo., 1931-35; with Edison Bros. Stores, Inc., St. Louis, 1935—, v.p., 1954-60, dir., exec. v.p., gen. mdse. mgr., 1960—. Mem. United Jewish Appeal Advisory com. Mem. Asso. Fashion Service (chmn. 1975-76, exec. com. 1970—), Volumne Footwear Retails Am, Nat. Soc. Retailers, Two/Ten Assos. Jewish. Club: Meadowbrook Country (gov. 1964-70). Home: 10358 Chimney Rock Dr St Louis MO 63141 Office: PO Box 14020 St Louis MO 63178 *What many people consider a great problem I look at as a challenge.*

DEMOLL, LOUIS, architect; b. Swarthmore, Pa., Aug. 19, 1924; s. Carl and Mary (Hitchner) DeM.; m. Carol Froebel, June 14, 1947; children: Lane, Cathy, Christopher, Meg., Lauri. B.A. with maj. honors, U. Pa., 1949. With Ballinger (Architects, Engrs., Planners), Phila., 1949—, partner in charge of design, 1955—, chmn. bd., 1974—; Lectr. in field. Pres. Delaware County Citizens Council, 1968-69; pres. The Sch. in Rose Valley Sch. Bd., 1968-69. Served with AUS, 1942-45. Recipient design awards Pa. Soc. Architects, Phila. chpt., and; Progressive Architecture. Fellow Royal Archtl. Inst. Can. (hon.), Hungarian Soc. Architects (hon.), AIA (pres. 1976); mem. Internat. Union Architects (pres. 1978—), Mexican Soc. Architects (hon.). Home: School Ln Rose Valley Moylan PA 19065 Office: Ballinger 211 S Broad St Philadelphia PA 19107

DE MONCHAUX, JEAN, educator. Dean Sch. Architecture & Planning MIT, Cambridge. Office: Office of the Dean Sch of Architecture and Planning MIT Cambridge MA 02139

DE MONEY, FRED WILLIAM, college president; b. Oak Park, Ill., Nov. 25, 1919; s. Fred Julius and Clara Louise (Linscheid) DeM.; m. Ione Christine Edstrom, June 3, 1944; children: Jennifer (Mrs. Murray Eagles McCord), Dale C. DeMoney Johnson, Charles F., Sarah (Mrs. Roger B. Gross), Elizabeth, Ellen. B.S., Ill. Inst. Tech., 1941; M.S., U. Minn., 1951, Ph.D., 1954. Research fellow U. Minn., 1951-54; research metallurgist Dow Chem. Co., Midland, Mich., 1954-55; research engr., br. head, tech. supr. Kaiser Aluminum & Chem. Corp., Spokane, Wash., 1955-69; tech. supr., project mgr. Center for Tech., Pleasanton, Calif., 1969-72; pres. Mont. Coll. Mineral Sci. and Tech., Butte, 1972—; Vice chmn. Cryogenic Engring. Conf., 1968. Bd. dirs. Mont. Tech. Found.; pres., chmn. bd. Mont. Energy and MHD Research and Devel. Inst.; adv. bd. Inst. Internat. Edn. Named Engr. of Yr. Inland Empire, 1962. Mem. AIME, ASME (cert. of merit 1969), Am. Soc. Metals (chpt. chmn. nat. long range planning com. 1961-62), Mining and Metall. Soc. Am., Am. Assn. State Colls. and Univs., Internat. Assn. Univ. Presidents, N.Y. Acad. Scis., Salamander, Sigma Xi, Tau Beta Pi. Club: Rotarian. Home: 1315 W Park St Butte MT 59701

DEMONTE, CLAUDIA ANN, artist, educator; b. Astoria, N.Y., Aug. 25, 1947; d. Joseph James and Ammeda Ellen (Heiss) DeM.; m. William Edward McGowin, May 28, 1977. B.A., Coll. Notre Dame, 1969; M.F.A., Cath. U., 1971. Instr. Bowie State Coll., Md., 1971-72, Prince Georges Community Coll., Largo, Md., 1972; assoc. prof. dept. art (U. Md.), College Park, 1972—; dir. Art Workshops, New Sch. Social Research, N.Y.C., 1980—; USIA artist in residence (Sofia), Bulgaria, 1982. Exhibited one-woman shows, Corcroan Gallery of art, Max Protetc Gallery, 1976, Contemporary Arts Center, New Orleans, Cranbrook Acad., 1978, Marianne-Deson Gallery, 1979, Miss. Mus., Fort Worth Mus., Washington Project for the Arts, 1980, Marion Locks Gallery, Miami Dade Gallery, Xochipilli, 1981, New Sch. Social Research, Swope Gallery, 1982; author: (with Judy Bachrach) The Height Report, 1983. Mem. adv. bd. Community Bd. 1, Astoria, N.Y., 1983; mem. Artists for Carter, 1980. Recipient award Am.-Italian Assn., 1971, Head Balt. Mus., 1972, Creative U. Md., 1974, 77, 83, artist-in-residence Nat. Endowment for Arts, 1979, 81. Democrat. Home: 96 Grand St New York NY 10013 Office: Art Dept U Md College Park MD 20742 Office: New Sch Social Research 66 W 12th St New York NY 10011

DE MONTE, ROBERT JACK, real estate investments company executive; b. Oakland, Calif., July 12, 1942; s. Mervin and Kathleen Irene (Murphy) De M.; m. Suzanne K. Whitney, Dec. 28, 1963; children: Michelle, Margaret. B.S., Calif. State U-Hayward, 1964; postgrad., Pepperdine U., 1977-78; LL.D., U. San Francisco, 1983. Jr. acct. supr. Moore Bus. Forms, Oakland, Calif., 1964-68; supr. pub. acctg. Coopers & Lybrand, San Francisco, 1968-71; dir. planning and resources Gov.'s Office, Sacramento, 1971-74; v.p. fin. and adminstrn. Johnstown Properties, Emeryville, Calif., 1974-76; sr. v.p. fin. and adminstrn. Consol. Capital Cos., Emeryville, 1976-83, exec. v.p. pub. programs, 1983—; pres., treas., trustee Consol. Capital Income Trust, Emeryville, Calif.; trustee Consol. Capital Realty Investors, Consol. Capital Spl. Trust; v.p. bd. govs. Nat. Assn. Real Estate Investment Trusts, Washington. Trustee Peralta Colls. Found., Oakland, Pitzer Coll., Claremont, Calif. Mem. Am. Inst. C.P.A.s, Calif. Soc. C.P.A.s. Republican. Home: 2045 Oakland Ave Piedmont CA 94611 Office: Consolidated Capital Cos 1900 Powell St Emeryville CA 94608

DE MONTEBELLO, PHILIPPE LANNES, museum administrator; b. Paris, May 16, 1936; U.S., 1951, naturalized, 1955; s. Roger L. and Germaine (de Croisset) de M.; m. Edith Bradford Myles, June 24, 1961; children: Marc, Laure, Charles. B.A. magna cum laude, Harvard U., 1961; M.A., NYU Inst. Fine Arts, 1963; LL.D., Lafayette Coll., 1979, Bard Coll., 1981. Asso. curator European paintings Met. Mus. Art, N.Y.C., 1963-69, vice dir. for curatorial and ednl. affairs, 1974-77, acting dir., 1977-78, dir., 1978—; dir. Mus. Fine Arts, Houston, 1969-74; mem. adv. bd. Skowhegan Sch. Painting and Sculpture, N.Y.C.; mem. Council Museums and Edn. in the Visual Arts, Columbia Adv. Council Depts. Art History and Archeology. Author: Peter Paul Rubens, 1969; contbr. to mus. bulls., various exhbn. catalogs. Trustee, mem. exec. com. NYU Inst. Fine Arts. Served to 2d lt. AUS, 1956-58. Recipient NYU Grad. Sch. Alumni Achievement award, 1978; Woodrow Wilson fellow, 1961-62; Gallatin fellow, 1981. Mem. Assn. Art Mus. Dirs. (ethics com.), Am. Fedn. Arts (trustee, exec. com.), Coll. Art Assn., Am. Assn. Mus. Home: 1150 Fifth Ave New York NY 10028 Office: Met Mus of Art 82d St at Fifth Ave New York NY 10028

DEMOPULOS, CHRIS, engineering company executive; b. Texarkana, Tex., Oct. 30, 1924; s. Frank and Helen G. (Murzicos) D.; m. Sophia S. Soteropulos, Nov. 12, 1950; children: Anastasia Elaine, Paul Chris. B.S. in Engring, Tex. A&M U., 1947. Registered profl. engr., La., Tex., Ark., Okal., Pa. Cons. engr. E.M. Freeman Assos., Shreveport, 1947-52; pres. Demopulos & Ferguson, Inc., Shreveport, 1953—; mem. Bd. Registration Profl. Engrs. and Land Surveyors La., 1977—. Bd. dirs. Met. YMCA Shreveport, 1966-79. Served with USAAF, 1943-45. Decorated Air medal with oak leaf cluster; recipient Engr. of Yr. award Engring. and Sci. Council of Shreveport, 1979; A.E. Wilder, Jr. award Cons. Engrs. Council of La., 1980. Fellow ASCE (pres. Shreveport chpt. 1960-61), Cons. Engrs. Council (dir. 1974-75); mem. Nat. Soc. Profl. Engrs., La. Engring. Soc. (dir. 1962-64), La. Cons. Engrs. Council (pres. 1973-74), Tex. Soc. Profl. Engrs., Soc. Am. Mil. Engrs. (pres. Shreveport post 1969-70), Am. Concrete Inst., Am. Legion, Shreveport Art Guild, Shreveport C. of C. Mem. Greek Orthodox Ch. Clubs: Tex. A&M Alumni, Houston Engrs., Shreveport Country. Lodge: Shreveport Rotary. Home: 331 Janie Ln Shreveport LA 71106 Office: 600 Petroleum Tower Shreveport LA 71101

DEMOREST, JEAN-JACQUES, educator; b. Lille, France, Oct. 31, 1920; s. Don Louis and Louise (Dury) D.; m. Karin E. Rosenthal, June 6, 1964. B.A., Ohio State U., 1940; M.A., 1940; Licence es lettres, Sorbonne, 1946; Ph.D., Princeton U., 1949. Instr. Duke U., 1948, asst. prof., 1950-53, assoc. prof., 1953-56, Cornell U., 1956, prof., chmn. dept. Romance lit., 1957-68; vis. prof. Harvard U., 1967-68, prof. Romance langs., 1968-75; vis. prof. U. Ariz., Tucson, 1975, prof. French and Italian, 1975—, head dept., 1981-83; Mem. cabinet French minister of nat. edn., 1964. Author: Dans Pascal, 1953, Les Passionnés ont vécu, 1956, Pascal Ecrivain, 1957; Translator: The French and The Republic (by Charles Moraze), 1958; Editor: Studies in XVIIth Century French Literature. Served as officer Free French Forces, 1941-47. Decorated officer Legion of Honor, Médaille de la Résistance, Croix de Guerre, France).; Fulbright research scholar, Paris, 1951-52; Guggenheim fellow, 1960; Am. Council Learned Socs. fellow, Paris,

1963-64. Mem. Association des Francais Libres, MLA, Internat. Assn. Philosophy and Lit. (co-founder 1974). Address: Dept French and Italian Univ Ariz Tucson AZ 85721

DEMOREST, ROBERT STEELE, editor; b. Toledo, Nov. 16, 1924; s. Herbert Steele and Gladys (Woodward) D. A.B., Boston U., 1950. Adminstrv. dir. outpatient services Children's Hosp., Columbus, Ohio, 1951-63; chief editor Ohio State Univ. Press, 1964—. Mem. German Village Soc. Columbus, Columbus Mus. Art. Served with AUS, 1943-46. Mem. Sierra Club, Audubon Soc., Nature Conservancy. Club: Ohio State U. Faculty (past pres.). Home: 559 City Park Ave Columbus OH 43215 Office: 1050 Carmack Rd Columbus OH 43210

DEMOS, GEORGE JAMES, manufacturing company executive; b. Phila., Mar. 9, 1928; s. Charles Anthony and Helen Veronica (Sucavage) D.; m. Jeannette Eden, June 7, 1952 (div.); children: Barbara, Brian, Christina. B.S.E.E., Drexel U., 1951; postgrad., Columbia U., 1953-54. Field sales engr. Leeds & Northrup Co., N.Y.C., 1951-57, resident field engr., Albany, N.Y., 1957-59, br. mgr., Balt., 1959-60, dist. mgr., Boston, 1960-65, central sales div. mgr., Phila., 1965-67, dir. sales dept., 1967, group v.p. mktg., North Wales, Pa., 1967-72, group v.p. systems, 1972-79, pres., chief exec. officer, 1980-83; group exec. Gen. Signal Corp., North Wales, 1980—, vice chmn., 1984—. Trustee Drexel U. Served with USN, 1945-46. Mem. Sci. Apparatus Makers Assn. (dir. 1980), Mfrs. Assn. Delaware Valley (dir. 1980), Instrument Soc. Am., Am. Soc. Metals, Indsl. Heating Equipment Assn. Office: 2 Highe Ridge Park Box 10010 Stamford CT 06904

DEMOS, JOHN PUTNAM, history educator, writer, consultant; b. Cambridge, Mass., May 2, 1937; s. Raphel D. and Jean Pauline (Demos) McMorran; m. Elaine Virginia Damis, July 27, 1963; children: Alison Virginia, Moira McMorran. B.A., Harvard U., 1959, postgrad., 1963-68; postgrad., Oxford U., Eng., 1959-60; M.A., U. Calif.-Berkeley, 1961. Teaching fellow Harvard U., Cambridge, Mass., 1966-68; from asst. prof. to prof. history Brandeis U., Waltham, Mass., 1968—, chmn. dept.; acad. cons. Author: A Little Commonwealth, 1970, Remarkable Providences, 1972, Entertaining Satan, 1982 (Bancroft prize 1983). Mem. council Carnegie Council on Children Carnegie Corp. N.Y., N.Y.C., 1972-77; mem. com. on child research and pub. policy Nat. Acad. Scis., Washington, 1978-81; vol. Peace Corps, Ghana, 1961-63. Recipient Horace Kidger award New Eng. History Tchrs. Assn., 1980. Mem. Am. Hist. Assn. Democrat. Office: Dept History Bradeis U South St Waltham MA 02254

DE MOSS, RALPH DEAN, microbiologist, educator; b. Danville, Ill., Dec. 29, 1922; s. Guy and Ruby (Walker) DeM; m. Patricia H. Day, June 2, 1946 (dec.); children: Susan L., G. Newton, Guy R., Kurt S.; m. Shirley R. Siedler, Nov. 22, 1975. A.B., Ind. U., 1948, Ph.D., 1951; student, Clemson Coll., 1943, St. Louis U., 1943-44. AEC postdoctoral fellow Brookhaven Nat. Lab., 1951-52; asst. prof. McCollum-Pratt Inst., Johns Hopkins U., 1952-56; asso. prof. microbiology U. Ill., Urbana, 1956-59, prof. microbiology, 1959—, head dept. microbiology, 1971—; mem. microbiology tng. com. NIH, 1967-69, chmn., 1969-71, mem. microbial chemistry study sect., 1976-80, chmn., 1978-80; mem. biomed. scis. panel NRC, 1976-80. Editor: Jour. Bacteriology, 1965-70. Served with AUS, 1942-46; ETO. Mem. Am. Soc. Microbiology, Am. Acad. Microbiology, Am. Soc. Biol. Chemists, Soc. Gen. Microbiology. Research and publs. in microbial biochemistry and physiology. Home: 801 Harmon Urbana IL 61801 Office: Dept Microbiology 131 Burrill Hall U Ill 407 S Goodwin Urbana IL 61801

DE MOTT, BENJAMIN HAILE, educator, author; b. Rockville Centre, N.Y., June 2, 1924; s. D. Gerard and Janet (Sanders) DeM.; m. Margaret Jane Craig, June 22, 1946; children—Joel, Thomas, Benjamin, Megan. B.A., George Washington U., 1949; Ph.D., Harvard, 1953; M.A., Amherst Coll., 1960; D.Litt., Franklin and Marshall Coll., 1970. Teaching fellow Harvard, 1950; from instr. to Mellon prof. humanities Amherst (Mass.) Coll., 1951—; columnist Harper's, 1962-64, 81—, Am. Scholar, 1962-64, Atlantic Monthly, 1973-80; prof. Mass. Inst. Tech., 1962; Fulbright prof. Birmingham (Eng.) U., 1965; vis. prof. Utah U., 1966, Yale, 1968-70; writer Nat. Ednl. TV, 1964; also cons.; mem. Columbia Seminar Am. Civilization; cons. Office Edn., Carnegie Commn. on Future Pub. Broadcasting, Soc. Mag. Writers, Nat. Inst. Edn., N.Y. State Arts Council, Nat. Endowment for Arts, Am. Council Learned Socs., Council Grad. Schs., Danforth, Rockefeller founds; Aspen Inst. Edn. dept. Amalgamated Clothing Workers Union, AFL-CIO; exec. com. Tchrs. and Writers Collaborative, N.Y.C.; seminar dir. Nat. Endowment for Humanities, 1973-74, 76-77, 78-79. Author: novels The Body's Cage, 1959, A Married Man, 1968; essays Hells & Benefits, 1962, You Don't Say, 1966, Supergrow, 1969, Surviving the Seventies, 1971, Scholarship for Society, 1974, America in Literature, 1977; Bd. editors: College English, 1964-70; contbg. editor: Sat. Review, 1972-73, Atlantic Monthly, 1977—; Contbr. articles to profl. jours. Bd. acad. advisers Marlboro Coll., 1963-65; mem. Presdl. Adv. Council Women's Ednl. Programs, 1975-76, Gov.'s Council Arts and Humanities, 1974-77; bd. dirs. Mass. Found. Humanities in Pub. Affairs, 1974—; mem. exec. bd. Fedn. Humanities Programs, 1979—; trustee Nat. Humanities Faculty; mem. selection com. Guggenheim Found., 1975—. Recipient Harbison award for distinguished teaching Danforth Found., 1969; Guggenheim fellow, 1964, 69. Mem. PEN, Nat. Book Critics Circle, Modern Lang. Assn., Phi Beta Kappa. Club: Century. Home: 22 Hitchcock Rd Amherst MA 01002

DEMOUTH, ROBIN MADISON, lawyer, corporate executive; b. Warwick, N.Y., Apr. 2, 1939; s. Claude Cornelius and Mary Louise (Shaw) D. B.A., U. Va., 1961; postgrad., U. Ill., 1962; J.D., John Marshall Law Sch., 1965; LL.M., Lawyers Inst., 1970; M.B.A., U. Chgo., 1976. Bar: Ill. 1966. With Stewart-Warner Corp., Chgo., 1965—, sr. atty., 1970-78, sec., counsel, 1978-81, sec., chief legal officer, 1981-82, v.p., sec., gen. counsel, 1982—. Mem. Gt. Lakes Commn., 1975-78; mem. adv. commn. Internat. Trade and Port Promotion, 1975-78; bd. dirs. Easter Seal Soc. Chgo., 1983. Mem. ABA (internat. law sect., bus. law sect.), Ill. Bar Assn., Chgo. Bar Assn., Am. Soc. Corp. Secs. Clubs: Chgo. Yacht, Columbia Yacht, Economics of Chgo. Home: 165 W Schiller St Chicago IL 60610 Office: 1826 Diversey Pkwy Chicago IL 60614

DEMPSEY, BRUCE HARVEY, museum director; b. Camden, N.J., July 4, 1947; s. Lawrence Aloysius and Esther Audrey (Harvey) D.; m. Gabriele Katharina Heerling, July 12, 1969; children: Gabriele Katharina, Lawrence Maximilian. B.A., Fla. State U., 1964, M.F.A., 1966, postgrad., 1966. Mem. faculty Fla. State U., Tallahassee, 1966-75, instr., 1969-75, dir. gallery, 1969-75; dir. Jacksonville (Fla.) Art Mus., 1975—; Mem. div. cultural affairs Fla. Visual Arts Panel, 1980-83; visual arts advisor Fla. Div. Cultural Affairs, 1973-76; art advisor Fla. Ho. of Reps., 1980; mem. fine arts adv. bd. Fla. Fine Arts Council, 1974-76, grants rev. panel, 1979; bd. dirs. Tallahassee Arts Council, 1973-77, Jacksonville Arts Assembly, 1979-80. Recipient travel aid grant U.S. Chinese Relations Council, 1975. Mem. Am. Assn. Mus., Fla. Art Mus. Dirs. Assn. (treas. 1977-79), Internat. Council Mus. Home: 2415 Mandarin River Ln Mandarin FL 32223 Office: 4160 Blvd Center Dr Jacksonville FL 32207

DEMPSEY, CHARLES GATES, art historian, educator; b. Providence., Mar. 11, 1937; s. Edward Wheeler and Betsey Mills (Beach) D.; m. Marjorie Elizabeth Cropper, Nov. 14. 1975; children: Martha Martin, Adam Sell, Catherine Wheeler. B.A., Swarthmore Coll., 1959; M.F.A., Princeton U., 1962, Ph.D., 1963. Asst. prof. dept. history of art Bryn Mawr Coll., 1965-70; asso. prof., 1970-76, prof., 1976-80, chmn. dept., 1975-80; prof. Renaissance and baroque art Johns Hopkins U., 1980—; sr. asso. deot. fine arts U. Melbourne, Australia, 1977; vis. prof. Folger Shakespeare Inst., 1977. Author: Annibale Carracci and the Beginnings of Baroque Style, 1977; contbr. articles to profl. jours. Fellow Am. Acad. in Rome, 1963-65; Am. Council Learned Socs. fellow, 1969-70; Harvard Center Renaissance Studies, Villa I Tatti fellow, 1973-74; Nat. Endowment Humanities fellow., 1978-79. Mem. Coll. Art Assn. Am., Renaissance Soc. Am. Home: 3918 Cloverhill Rd Baltimore MD 21218 Office: Dept History of Art Johns Hopkins U Baltimore MD 21218

DEMPSEY, CHARLES LADE, govt. ofcl.; b. Morristown, N.J., June 7, 1928; s. Louis F. and Clara V. (Lade) D.; m. Mary Mackenzie Dempsey, Oct. 17, 1954. B.S., Georgetown U., 1960; postgrad., Cath. U. Law Sch., 1962; grad., Fed. Exec. Inst., Charlottesville, Va., 1974. With HUD, 1957—, insp. gen., 1978—; Bd. dirs. Fed. Law Enforcement Tng. Center, Dept. Treasury. Served with U.S. Army, 1950-53. Decorated Bronze star; recipient John Marshall award Dept. Justice, 1981; Disting. Service award HUD. Mem. Assn. Fed. Investigators (nat. pres. 1977, exec. bd. 1979), Am. Soc. Public Adminstrn, Assn. Govt. Accts., Fed. Exec. Inst. Alumni Assn., Georgetown U. Alumni Assn. Roman Catholic. Office: HUD 451 7th St SW Washington DC 20410

DEMPSEY, FRANK JOSEPH, librarian; b. San Francisco, Nov. 8, 1925; s. Frank Joseph and Ruth M. (McPhedran) D. B.A., U. Calif.-Berkeley, 1950, B.L.S., 1953. Reference librarian Newark Pub. Library, 1953-54; tng. officer, head librarian Oakland (Calif.) Naval Supply Center, 1954-58; asst. city librarian Berkeley (Calif.) Pub. Library, 1958-62, city librarian, 1962-72; dir. Arlington Heights (Ill.) Meml. Library, 1973—; instr. reading improvement Oakland City Coll., 1957-58, U. Calif.-Berkeley Extension, 1966-67. Author: (with Craig McMicken) A Review of Library Administration, 1961; contbr.: numerous articles and book revs. profl. jours., also Ency. Americana. Mem. Berkeley Workreation Council.; bd. dirs. Friends of Calif. Libraries, Concert Theater, Inc., 1964-65; v.p. Berkeley chpt. ARC, 1971-72; chmn. Regional Library Adv. Council, Ill., 1974-75. Served with USNR, 1950-52. Recipient Superior Accomplishment award U.S. Naval Supply Center, 1956. Mem. ALA (chmn. friends of libraries com., chmn. pub. relations sect. 1978-79), Calif. Library Assn. (chmn. pub. relations com.), Ill. Library Assn. (pres. 1977-78), Pub. Library Execs. Central Calif. (pres. 1964-65), East Bay Library Council (chmn. 1965-66). Club: Chgo. Library (pres. 1981—). Home: 861 W Fletcher Chicago IL 60657 Office: 500 N Dunton Ave Arlington Heights IL 60004

DEMPSEY, HOWARD STANLEY, lawyer; b. LaPorte, Ind., Aug. 12, 1939; s. Howard Taft and Katheryn Alice (Prichard) D.; m. Judith Rose Enyart, Aug. 20, 1960; children: Howard Stanley, Whitney Owen, Bradford Evan, Matthew Charles. Student, Colo. Sch. Mines, 1956-57; B.A., U. Colo., 1960, J.D., 1964; cert., Harvard Sch. Bus., 1969. Ind. mine operator, Colo., Wyo., 1958-60; indsl. engr. Climax Molybdenum Co., Colo., 1960-61, asst. resident atty., 1964-65, resident atty., 1965-68, div. atty. western ops., Golden, Colo., 1968-72; gen. atty. law dept. western area also dir. environ. affairs AMAX, Inc., Denver, 1972-76, v.p., 1977-83; ptnr. Arnold & Porter, Denver, 1983—; chmn. AMAX Australia Ltd., 1980-83; chmn., exec. com. AMAX Iron Ore, 1980-83; dir., dep. chmn. Australian Consol. Mines Ltd., 1980-83. Contbr. articles to profl. jours. Trustee Rocky Mountain Mineral Law Found., pres., 1980-81. Mem. Am. Mining Congress (mem. public lands com. 1967-81), Am. Bar Assn. (chmn. hard minerals com. 1975-76), Colo. Bar Assn. (council mem. mineral law sect. 1971-73), Colo. Mining Assn. (pres. 1980-81), Continental Divide Bar Assn. (sec.-treas. 1969-73), Colo. Hist. Soc. (past dir.), Soc. Mining Law Antiquarians (pres. 1979-81). Methodist. Clubs: Rollings Hills Country (Golden); Am. Alpine, University, Colo. Mountain (Denver); Mining, Harvard (N.Y.C.); American National (Sydney, Australia); Capitol Hill. Lodge: Masons. Office: Arnold & Porter 1660 Lincoln St. Suite 2230 Denver CO 80264

DEMPSEY, JAMES HOWARD, JR., lawyer; b. Cleve., Oct. 18, 1916; s. James Howard and Ada (Hunt) D.; m. Julia C. Bolton, Aug. 2, 1942; children: Julia B. Dempsey Cox, Melissa Hunt Dempsey Gerrity. B.A., Yale U., 1938, LL.B., 1941. Bar: Ohio 1941. Practiced in Cleve., 1945—; gen. ptnr. Squire, Sanders & Dempsey, Cleve., 1958—; dir. Maynard H. Murch Co., Cleve., 1963—. Mayor, Hunting Valley Village, 1952-58; trustee Cleve. Mus. Art; Trustee U. Hosps., Home for Aged Women. Served to lt. comdr. USNR, 1941-45. Mem. ABA, Ohio, Cleve., D.C. bar assns. Clubs: Yale (N.Y.C.); Union, Tavern, Kirtland, Chagrin Valley Hunt. (Cleve.). Home: River Rd Chagrin Falls OH 44022 Office: 1800 Union Commerce Bldg Cleveland OH 44115

DEMPSEY, JAMES RAYMON, industrial executive; b. Red Bay, Ala., Oct. 4, 1921; s. Newman W. and Maude (Berry) D.; m. Dolores Barnes, Jan. 19, 1943; children—Susan, David Barnes, Anne. Student, U. Ala., 1937-39; B.S., U.S. Mil. Acad., 1943; M.S., U. Mich., 1947, D.Engring. (hon.), 1964. Commd. 2d lt. U.S. Army, 1943; advanced through grades to lt. col. USAF, 1951; with photo reconnaissance squadron, Eng., France, World War II, squadron comdr., 1945, guided missiles project officer, then chief guided missile projects, 1948- 49, exec. officer to, 1950-51, chief project sect., Patrick AFB, Fla., then operations officer missile test range, 1951-53, resigned, 1953; asst. to v.p. planning Convair div. Gen. Dynamics Corp., 1953-54, dir., 1954-57, mgr., 1957-58, v.p., 1958-61, sr. v.p.; pres. Gen. Dynamics Astronautics, 1961-65, Gen. Dynamics Convair, 1965-66; v.p. missiles, space and electronics group Avco Corp., 1966-68, v.p., group exec. govt. products group, 1968-75; pres. Digital Broadcasting Corp., 1978-79; mng. partner J.J. Finnigan Industries, Duluth, Ga., 1978—; trustee Phoenix-Chase Series Fund; dir. Precious Metals Holdings, Inc., Transatlantic Capital Corp.; dir Convest Energy Corp, Transatlantic Investment Corp.; dir. Superior Electric Co., P-C Capital Shares, Inc. Decorated Air Medal with clusters, D.F.C., U.S.; Croix de Guerre, France). Fellow Am. Inst. Aeros. and Astronautics, Am. Astronaut. Soc.; mem. Air Force Assn. (dir. 1958-59), NASA (spl. com. on space tech.). Clubs: Burning Tree, Congressional Country, Atlanta Athletic. Home: 4081 Ridgeview Circle North Arlington VA 22207 Office: JJ Finnigan Industries Old Peachtree Rd Duluth GA 30136

DEMPSEY, JERRY EDWARD, manufacturing company executive; b. Landrum, S.C., Oct. 1, 1932; s. Adolphus Gerald and Willie Ceyattie (Lee) D.; m. Harriet Coan Calvert; children: Jerrie E., Harriet R., Margaret. B.S., Clemson U., 1954; M.B.A., Ga. State Coll., 1968. With Borg-Warner Corp., 1962-84, gen. mgr. York div., 1972-77, exec. v.p. York div., Chgo., 1977-79, pres., chief operating officer York div., 1979-84, also dir. York div.; v.p., dir. Waste Mgmt. Inc., 1984—; dir. Nalco Chem. Corp. Mem. dean's adv. council Krannert Sch. Mgmt., Purdue U.; bd. dirs. Adler Planetarium; bd. visitors U. Pitts. Served to 1st. lt. U.S. Army, 1954-56. Mem. NAM (dir.), ASHRAE, Chgo. Assn. Commerce and Industry (dir.). Clubs: University (Chgo.); Butterfield Country, Economic, Chicago. Office: 200 S Michigan Ave Chicago IL 60604

DEMPSEY, JOHN CORNELIUS, manufacturing company executive; b. Cleve., July 14, 1914; s. John Henry and Anna Gertrude (Donavon) D.; children: Virginia Agnes (Mrs. Richard J. Ragan) Patricia Marie, Mary Theresa (Mrs. William J. McAlpin), Maureen Anne (Mrs. Daniel Phillip Kendall), Judith Marie (Mrs. Cecil J. Petitti), Michael Henry. Student, John Carroll U., 1932-35. With U.S. Steel Corp., Cleve., 1932-40; auditor Ernst & Ernst, Cleve., 1940-45; asst. comptroller Werner G. Smith, Cleve., 1945; sec. Greif Bros. Corp., Delaware, Ohio, 1946, chmn. bd., chief exec. officer, 1947—. Trustee Central Ohio council Boy Scouts Am.; trustee St. Ann Maternity Hosp., Cleve. City Hosp.; chmn. bd. trustees Cleve. City Hosp., 1949. Home: East Olentangy River Rd Route 4 Delaware OH 43015 Office: Greif Bros Corp 621 Pennsylvania Ave Delaware OH 43015

DEMPSEY, RAYMOND J., banker; b. Yonkers, N.Y., Mar. 4, 1935; s. John Raymond and Ruth D.; children—Christopher, Elizabeth. B.A., Colgate U., 1957. With Bankers Trust Co., N.Y.C., 1957-78, exec. v.p., 1975-78; chmn., pres. Fidelcor, Inc. and The Fidelity Bank, Rosemont, Pa., 1978-84; chmn., chief exec. officer European Am. Bancorp, N.Y.C., 1984—; also chmn., chief exec. officer European Am. Bank, European Am. Banking Corp. Trustee Phila. Found., 1978—. Served in USAR, 1958-64. Mem. Greater Pila. C. of C. (dir.). Office: European Am Bancorp 10 Hanover Sq New York NY 10015

DEMPSEY, WILLIAM HENRY, assn. exec.; b. New Ulm, Minn., Dec. 1, 1930; s. William Henry and Myra Louise (Seifert) D.; m. Mary Margaret Studer, Aug. 25, 1954; children—William Henry, III, Robert J., Timothy M., Elizabeth A., Thomas E., Mary C. Student, Coll. of St. Thomas, 1951; A.B., U. Notre Dame, 1952; LL.B., Yale U., 1955. Bar: D.C. bar 1955. Law clk. to Judge Charles Fahy, U.S. Ct. of Appeals for D.C. Circuit, 1955-56; chief law clk. to Chief Justice Earl Warren, U.S. Supreme Ct., 1959-60; partner firm Shea & Gardner, Washington, 1960-72; chmn. Nat. Ry. Labor Conf., Washington, 1972-77; pres., chief exec. officer Assn. Am. Railroads, Washington, 1977—. Served as 1st lt., Judge Adv. Gen. Corps U.S. Army, 1956-59. Mem. D.C. Bar Assn. Roman Catholic. Clubs: Met., Internat., Washington Golf and Country, F Street, Chevy Chase. Home: 3311 N Glebe Rd Arlington VA 22207 Office: 1920 L St NW Washington DC 20036

DEMSKE, JAMES MICHAEL, college president; b. Buffalo, Apr. 10, 1922; s. Albert J. and Augusta (Nagel) D. A.B., Canisius Coll., Buffalo, 1947, D.H.L. (hon.), 1981; Ph.L., Woodstock (Md.) Coll., 1951; S.T.L., U. Innsbruck, Austria, 1958; Ph.D., U. Freiburg, West Germany, 1962. Fingerprint technician FBI, 1942-43; joined Soc. of Jesus, 1947; ordained priest Roman Catholic Ch., 1957; instr. philosophy St. Peter's Coll., Jersey City, 1951-54; prof. theology, dir. students Bellarmine Coll., Plattsburgh, N.Y., 1963-66; pres. Canisius Coll., 1966—. Author: Introductory Metaphysics, 1955, Encounters with Silence, 1960, Sein, Mensch und Tod, 1963, Being, Man and Death, 1970, A Promise of Quality: the First 100 Years of Canisius College, 1970, The Irish and I, 1976, Alive and Well in Germany, 1977. Trustee Assn. Jesuit Colls. and Univs., Buffalo Gen. Hosp., Buffalo Studio Arena Theatre, Buffalo Philharmonic; trustee Empire of Am. F.S.A., Commn. Ind. Colls. and Univs., Ind. Coll. Fund N.Y., Western N.Y. Consortium Higher Edn., Friends of Hospice Buffalo, Friends of Copley Library-U. San Diego; adv. bd. Buffalo-Dortmund Sister City Com., Buffalo Urban League. Served to capt. AUS, 1943-46. Recipient Centennial Regents award Canisius Coll., 1970, 125th Anniversary Award for Distinguished Service State U. N.Y. at Buffalo, 1971, Brotherhood award Nat. Conf. Christians and Jews, 1971, Liberty Bell award Erie County Bar Assn., 1973, Silver Good Citizenship medal SAR, 1978; named Educator of Year Univ. Club Buffalo, 1970, Goodfellow of Year Buffalo Courier Express, 1971, Outstanding Citizen of Year Buffalo Evening News, 1971, Man of Year Bros. of Mercy, 1976. Mem. Buffalo and Erie County Hist. Soc., Buffalo Fine Arts Acad. Home: 2001 Main St Buffalo NY 14208

DEMSKI, JOEL S., business educator. Grad., U. Mich., 1962, M.B.A. with high distinction, 1963; Ph.D., U. Chgo., 1967. Mem. faculty Columbia U.; mem. Stanford U. Grad. Sch. Bus., 1968—, Paul E. Holden prof., 1979—; vis. prof. U. Chgo. Contbr. articles on acctg., econs. to profl. jours.; editorial bd.: Acctg. Rev., Jour. Acctg. Research. Mem. Am. Econ. Assn., Am. Acctg. Assn. Office: Stanford U Grad Sch Bus Stanford CA 94305 *

DEMUTH, CHRISTOPHER CLAY, lawyer, government official; b. Evanston, Ill., Aug. 5, 1946; s. Harry Clay and Ethel Marie (Schaiell) DeM.; m. Susan Ann Shultis, June 9, 1973; children: Christopher Clay, Elizabeth Ann, Catherine Leas. A.B., Harvard Coll., 1968; J.D., U. Chgo., 1973. Bar: Ill. 1973. Staff asst. to Pres. Richard Nixon, Washington, 1969-70; mem. Sidley & Austin, Chgo., 1973-76; assoc. gen. counsel Consol. Rail Corp., Phila., 1976-77; lectr., dir. regulatory studies Harvard Sch. Govt., Cambridge, Mass., 1977-81; adminstr. info. and regulatory affairs U.S. Office Mgmt. and Budget, Washington, 1981—, exec. dir. Presdl. Task Force on Regulatory Relief. Mem. ABA, Am. Econ. Assn. Republican. Episcopalian. Home: 3901 Fordham Rd NW Washington DC 20016 Office: Office Mgmt and Budget Old Executive Office Bldg Washington DC 20503

DEMUTH, RICHARD HOLZMAN, lawyer; b. N.Y.C., Sept. 11, 1910; s. Leopold and Dora (Holzman) D.; m. Eunice Burdick, June 14, 1947; 1 dau., Nancy Chase. A.B., Princeton, 1931; LL.B., Harvard, 1934. Bar: N.Y. State bar 1934, D.C. bar 1973. Law clk. to Circuit Judge Julian W. Mack, 1934-35; asso. Simpson Thacher & Bartlett, 1935-39; spl. asst. to U.S. atty. gen. Office Solicitor Gen., 1939-42; sr. officer IBRD, 1946-73, dir. devel. services dept., mem. pres.'s council, until 1973; partner law firm Surrey & Morse, Washington, 1973-80, of counsel, 1980—; Mem. adv. com. Woodrow Wilson Sch. Pub. and Internat. Affairs, Princeton, 1957-66; chmn. Consultative Group on Internat. Agrl. Research, 1971-73, Internat. Bd. for Plant Genetic Resources, 1974-80, chmn. emeritus, 1982—; Mem. governing bd. Internat. Inst. Ednl. Planning, 1964-73. Served from 2d lt. to lt. col. AUS, 1942-46. Decorated Legion of Merit; recipient Sears prize, 1933, Fay diploma Harvard Law Sch. Mem. D.C. Bar, Assn. Bar City N.Y., Soc. Internat. Devel. Clubs: Metropolitan (Washington); Princeton (N.Y.C.). Home: 5404 Bradley Blvd Bethesda MD 20814 Office: 1250 Eye St NW Washington DC 20005

DE NAGY, TIBOR JULIUS, art dealer; b. Debrecen, Hungary, Apr. 25, 1910; came to U.S., 1948, naturalized, 1953; s. Alexander and Anne (Kanitzde nagyecser) de N.; 1 dau., Marianne. Dr. Econs. and Philosophy, Basel U., 1931. Dir. Nat. Bank of Hungary, Budapest, 1931-47; pres. Tibor de Nagy Gallery Inc., N.Y.C., 1950—; chmn. bd. Watson-de Nagy Gallery Inc., Houston, 1973—; fgn. dep. Mfrs. Hanover Trust, N.Y.C., 1953-70. Author: Die Ungarische National Bank, 1932; contbr. articles to profl. jours. Recipient Arts award Syracuse U., 1980. Mem. Art Dealers Assn. Am., Mus. Modern Art, Whitney Mus. Home: 11 E 71st St New York NY 10021 Office: 29 W 57th St New York NY 10021

DENBEAUX, FRED, educator, writer; b. St. Louis, May 8, 1914; s. Ralph and Margaret (Langanke) D.; m. Jane van Voorst, June 9, 1937; children—Mark, Andrea. B.A., Elmhurst (Ill.) Coll., 1936; B.D.,

Union Theol. Sem., N.Y.C., 1939, S.T.M., 1940. Social worker Bklyn. Children's Aid Soc., 1937-39; ordained to ministry United Presbyn. Ch. USA., 1940; pastor in, Rebersburg, Pa., 1940-42; tchr. theology Dana Hall Schs., Wellesley, Mass., 1946-50; faculty Wellesley Coll., 1946—, prof. religion, 1958—, chmn. dept., 1955—, chmn. bd. preachers, 1964—; vis. prof. Brown U., 1960-61; vis. lectr. Trinity Coll., 1962-63. Author: Understanding the Bible, 1958, The Art of Christian Doubt, 1960, Guide to the Old Testament, 1964, Introduction to New Testament, 1965, Guide to the New Testament, 1965, The Premature Death of Protestantism, 1967, also articles. Served as chaplain AUS, 1942-46. Home: Box 211 Truro MA 02666

DENBESTEN, LAWRENCE, surgeon; b. Corsica, S.D., Oct. 4, 1926; s. Ed and Jennie DenB.; m. Shirley Langeland, June 12, 1952; children—Pamela K., David Lawrence. B.A., Calvin Coll. and Sem., Grand Rapids, Mich., 1949, B.S., 1952, Th.M., 1952; M.D., U. Iowa, 1956. Intern Hurley Hosp., Flint, Mich., 1956-57; chief surgeon, med. dir. Takum Hosp., Nigeria, 1957-60, Mkar Hosp., 1964-66; prof. surgery, vice chmn. dept. U. Iowa Hosps., 1966-67; prof. surgery, chief sect. gastrointestinal surgery UCLA Hosp. and Clinics, 1977—, vice chmn. dept., 1977-81; chief surg. services VA Center, Sepulveda, Calif., 1977-81; career investigator VA, 1972—. Author articles, abstracts in field, chpts. in books. Served with USNR, 1944-46. Advanced clin. fellow Am. Cancer Soc., 1964. Mem. A.C.S., Am. Surg. Assn., Am. Gastroenterol. Assn., Central Surg. Assn., Pacific Coast Surg. Assn., Western Surg. Assn., Alpha Omega Alpha. Home: 515 Ocean Ave 707N Santa Monica CA 90402 Office: Dept Surgery UCLA Sch Medicine Los Angeles CA 90024

DENBY, PETER, lawyer; b. Phila., Dec. 15, 1929; s. Charles and Rosamond (Reed) D.; m. Peggy Ann O'Hearn, May 19, 1956; children: Charles, Peter, Elizabeth Curtis. A.B., Princeton U., 1951; J.D., Harvard U., 1954. Bar: N.Y. 1957, Pa. 1960. Assoc. Davis Polk & Wardwell, N.Y.C., 1954-59, Reed Smith Shaw & McClay, Pitts., 1959-62, ptnr., 1962—; dir. Wheeling-Pitts. Steel Corp. Trustee Pressley Ridge Sch., Pitts., 1962-77, pres., Pitts., 1965-72; bd. dirs. Western Pa. Sch. for Blind Children, 1965—, pres., 1970-82; term trustee Carnegie Inst. Fine Arts Com., Pitts., 1965-72; trustee Sarah Scaife Found., Pitts, 1969—, Pitts. Plan for Art, 1970-73; mem. exec. com. Western Pa. Golf Assn., 1976—, sec., 1978—; bd. dirs. Pitts. Regional Planning Commn., 1971—; pres. Pitts Regional Planning Commn., 1974—. Mem. ABA, Allegheny County Bar Assn. Home: 518 Irwin Dr Sewickley PA 15143 Office: Reed Smith Shaw & McClay 747 Union Trust Bldg PO Box 2009 Pittsburgh PA 15230

DENCE, EDWARD WILLIAM, JR., banker; b. Newport, R.I., Feb. 25, 1938; s. Edward William and Dorothea Margaret (Conway) D.; m. Claire A. Guertin, Nov. 14, 1970; children: Suzanne Lynn, Christine Anne. A.B. summa cum laude, Providence Coll., 1959; LL.B., Harvard, 1963. Bar: Mass. 1963, R.I. 1965. Atty. New Eng. Electric System, 1963-68; sec., gen. counsel Fleet Fin. Group, Providence, 1968—; v.p., mem. mgmt. com. Indsl. Nat. Corp., 1980—; Mem. stockholders' adv. com. Fed. Res. Bank, Boston, 1976-77. Mem. R.I. Commn. Inter-Govtl. Relations, 1970-71; bd. dirs. R.I. Pub. Expenditure Council, 1969—; Mem. Providence Roman Cath. Diocesan Bd. Edn., 1970-73. Named One of Outstanding Young Men in Am., 1972. Mem. Am., R.I. bar assns. Home: 1485 High Hawk Rd East Greenwich RI 02818 Office: 55 Kennedy Plaza Providence RI 02903

DENCE, MICHAEL ROBERT, research director; b. Sydney, Australia, June 17, 1931; s. Robert Cecil and Barbara Sidney (Laurence) D.; m. Carole E. Paintin, Sept. 24, 1967; children: Alexandra C., Victoria C. B.Sc., Sydney U., 1953. Geologist Falconbridge Nickel Mines Ltd., 1953-54; research asst. U. Toronto, Ont., Can., 1955-58; tech. officer Geol. Survey Can., 1959-61; sci. officer Dominion Obs., Ottawa, 1962-65; research scientist earth physics br. Can. Dept. Energy, Mines and Resources, Ottawa, 1966-81, dir. gravity and geodynamics div., earth physics br., 1981-82, dir. gravity, geothermics and geodynamics div., earth physics br., 1982—; prin. investigator NASA Lunar Sample Program. Recipient Public Service award Can. Public Service, 1973. Fellow Royal Soc. Can., Meteoritical Soc., Geol. Soc. Can.; mem. AAAS, Am. Geophys. Union, Can. Geophys. Union. Home: 824 Nesbitt Pl Ottawa ON K2C 0K1 Canada Office: 3 Observatory Crescent Ottawa ON K1A 0Y3 Canada

DENECKE, ARNO HARRY, state justice; b. Rock Island, Ill., May 7, 1916; s. Harry and Gertrude (Etzel) D.; children—Virginia, David, William, John, Anne. A.B., U. Ill., 1937, LL.B., 1939. Bar: Ill. bar 1939, Oreg. bar 1946. Mem. law dept. Montgomery Ward & Co., Chgo. and Oakland, Calif., 1939-41; mem. firm Mautz, Souther, Spaulding, Denecke & Kinsey, Portland, Oreg., 1947-58; circuit judge State Oreg., Portland, 1959-62; asso. justice Supreme Ct. Oreg., 1963-76, chief justice, 1976—. Mem. sch. bd., Portland, 1957-58; Trustee Reed Coll., Portland, 1958—. Served from pvt. to maj. AUS, 1941-45. Mem. Am. Bar Assn. Episcopalian.

DENEGRE, GEORGE, lawyer; b. New Orleans, Oct. 10, 1923; s. Thomas Bayne and Alma (Baldwin) D.; m. Gayle Stocker, Oct. 4, 1950; children: Stanhope Bayne-Jones, Gayle Stocker Felchlin, George, John Gayle. B.A., Yale, 1943; LL.B., Tulane U., 1948. Bar: La. bar 1948. With firm Chaffe, McCall, Toler & Philips, 1948-49; assoc. firm Jones, Walker, Weachter, Poitevent, Carrère & Denègre, New Orleans, 1949-52; partner Jones, Walker, Waechter, Poitevent, Carrère & Denègre, 1952—; dir. Charter Security Life Ins. Co.; sec., dir. Canal Barge Co., Inc., Central Gulf Lines, Inc.; sec. Internat. Shipbldg. Corp.; dir. Dr. G.H. Tichenor Antiseptic Co. Bd. dirs. La. Assn. Mental Health, 1953-57, 58-77, pres., 1960-61; bd. dirs., sec. Greater New Orleans, Inc.; bd. dirs. Internat. House, 1964, 72—, Met. Crime Commn., 1965, Eugenie and Joseph Jones Family Found.; mem. adv. com. Tulane Med. Center; bd. administrs. Tulane U.; vice chmn. New Orleans and River Region Chamber. Served to lt. USNR, 1943-46. Hon. consul of India. Mem. Am., La., New Orleans, Maritime bar assns. Clubs: Metropolitan (Washington); Racquet and Tennis (N.Y.C.); Boston, Pickwick, Louisiana, New Orleans Country, Stratford (New Orleans). Home: 1525 Webster St New Orleans LA 70118 Office: 225 Baronne St New Orleans LA 70112

DENEMARK, GEORGE WILLIAM, education accreditation agency administrator; b. Chgo., Nov. 13, 1921; s. August Frederick and Harriet (Holly) D.; m. June Elaine Breidigam, Feb. 13, 1945; children: Eric, David, Gail. A.B., U. Chgo., 1943, M.A., 1948; Ed.D., U. Ill., 1956. Instr. U. Ill., Urbana, 1949-50; asst. prof. edn. Boston U., 1950-52; exec. sec. Assn. for Supervision and Curriculum Devel., Washington, 1952-56; asst. dean, prof. Coll. Edn. U. Md., 1956-58; dean, prof. Sch. Edn. U. Wis., Milw., 1958-67, Coll. Edn., U. Ky., Lexington, 1967-82, prof., 1982-83; dir. Nat. Council for Accreditation of Tchr. Edn., Washington, 1983—; cons. tchr. edn. and curriculum, Brazil, Colombia, P.R., V.I., Venezuela.; Chmn. adv. bd. ERIC Clearinghouse on Tchr. Edn. Editor: Ednl. Leadership, 1952-54; Chmn. editorial adv. bd.: Jour. Tchr. Edn, 1962-63. Trustee Joint Council on Econ. Edn.; bd. dirs. Escola Johnson, Fortaleza, Brazil; adv. bd. World Book, 1965-69. Served to lt. (j.g.) USNR, 1943-46. Mem. N.E.A. (life, chmn. nat. commn. on tchr. edn. and profl. standards 1967-68), Nat. Assn. State U. and Land Grant Colls. (chmn. com. on edn. for teaching profession 1968-69), Am. Assn. Colls. for Tchr. Edn. (pres. 1972-73), Assn. Supervision and Curriculum Devel., Nat. Soc. for Study Edn., Phi Delta Kappa. Home: 3510 39th St NW Washington DC 20016

DENENBERG, HERBERT SIDNEY, journalist, lawyer, former state official; b. Omaha, Nov. 20, 1929; s. David Aaron and Fannie (Rothenberg) D.; m. Naomi N. Glushakow, June 22, 1958. B.S., Johns Hopkins U., 1958; J.D., Creighton U., 1954; LL.M., Harvard U., 1959; Ph.D., U. Pa., 1962. Bar: Nebr. 1954, U.S. Supreme Ct. 1958, D.C. 1968, Pa. 1974; C.L.U.; C.P.C.U. Mem. firm Denenberg & Denenberg, Omaha, 1954-55; asst. prof. ins. U. Iowa, Iowa City, 1962, Wharton Sch. Finance and Commerce, U. Pa., 1962-65, assoc. prof., 1965-68, Harry J. Loman prof. ins., 1968-73; commr. ins., State of Pa., 1971-74; commr. Pa. Pub. Utility Commn., 1975; columnist Phila. Bull., 1975-79; consumer columnist Phila. Daily News, 1979-81, Phila. Jour., 1981—; consumer reporter Sta. WCAU-TV, CBS, Phila., WCAU-Radio, 1975-81, also talk-show host; columnist Sales and Mktg. Mag., 1976-80; regular on Real People, NBC-TV, 1979-80; consumer reporter Nat. Public Radio, 1979; Spl. counsel, research dir. Pres.'s Nat. Adv. Panel on Ins. in Riot-Affected Areas., 1967-68; spl. adviser to Gov. Pa. on consumer affairs, 1974-75; assc. dir. Wis. Ins. Laws Rev. Project, 1966-71; cons. Dept. Labor, 1965-68, Coop. Devel. Adminstrn. P.R., 1967-68, John F. Kennedy Center, Washington, 1966-71, Small Bus. Adminstrn., 1968-71, Dept. Justice, 1969, FTC, 1968, Dept. Transp., 1969-70, State of Nev., 1969-71, Alaska Legislature, 1976; spl. cons. to Mayor Washington, 1968-69; mem. Bd. of Health Promotion and Disease Prevention of Inst. Medicine, Nat. Acad. Scis., 1973—. Author: (with others) Risk and Insurance, 2d edit, 1973, (with Spencer L. Kimball) Insurance Government and Social Policy, 1969, (with J.R. Ferrari) Life Insurance and/or Mutual Funds, 1967, (with S.L. Kimball) Mass. Marketing of Property and Liability Insurance, 1970, The Insurance Trap, 1972, Shopper's Guide to Surgery, 1972, Shopper's Guide to Dentistry, 1973, Shopper's Guide to Insurance on Mobile Homes, 1973, A Citizens Bill of Hospital Rights, 1973, Shopper's Guide to Bankruptcy, 1974, Shopper's Guide Book, 1974, Herb Denenberg's Smart Shopper's Guide, 1980; also govt. reports and articles to jours.; columnist, mem. editorial bd.: Caveat Emptor, 1971—. Democratic candidate for U.S. Senator, 1974; Mem. adminstrv. bd. S.S. Huebner Found., 1968-71; bd. dirs. Consumers Union, 1973-76. Served to 1st lt. Judge Adv. Gen.'s Corps AUS, 1955-58. Recipient awards for articles Jour. Risk and Ins.; Lambert award, 1972; Nat. Press Club award, 1976, 77, 80; Journalism award Am. Osteo. Assn., 1976, Am. Chiropractors Assn., 1977-80. Mem. Am. Risk and Ins. Assn. (2d v.p. 1967-68, mem. bd. 1967-71, pres. 1969-70), Internat. Assn. Ins. Law (v.p. sci. sect. Am. chpt. 1967-71). Club: Old Clunker (founder, pres. 1982—). Home: PO Box 146 Wynnewood PA 19096 Office: WCAU-TV Philadelphia PA 19131 *Our governmental system is designed to make politicians fat and special interests groups rich. Government has become our number "one" consumer fraud. As a government official, educator, and author I have attempted to make government work for people instead of for special interests and politicians only. I have been willing to make waves and rock boats. I have tried to show that government can help people.*

DENENBERG, VICTOR HUGO, psychology educator; b. Chgo., Apr. 3, 1925; s. Jacob Herman and Gussie (Denenberg) D.; m. Ruth Adele Orner, Aug. 27, 1950 (div. Sept. 1975); children: Carol Faith, Susan Vicki, Nancy Gay, Julie Orner; m. Evelyn B. Thoman, Nov. 1975. B.A., Bucknell U., 1949; M.S., Purdue U., 1951, Ph.D., 1953. Research asso. Human Resources Research Office, Ft. Knox, Ky., 1952-54; from asst. prof. to prof. Purdue U., 1954-69; prof. biobehavioral scis. U. Conn., Storrs, 1969—; cons., writer in field.; Mem. study sect. NIH, 1967-71; mem. com. brain scis. NRC-Nat. Acad. Scis., 1967-73. Served with AUS, 1943-45. Decorated Purple Heart, Combat Inf. badge; NIH spl. fellow Cambridge (Eng.) U., 1963-64. Fellow Am. Psychol. Assn. (exec. com. div. exptl. psychology 1971-74, exec. com. div. comparative and physiol. psychology 1980-83), AAAS (council 1971-75), Animal Behavior Soc.; mem. Internat. Soc. Devel. Psychobiology (pres. 1970). Home: 796 Stafford Rd Storrs CT 06268

DENES, AGNES C., artist; b. Budapest, Hungary, 1938. Ed., CCNY, New Sch. Social Research; M.L. Robinson scholar, Columbia U., 1964-66. Instr. Sch. Visual Arts, N.Y.C., 1974-79, Skowhegan (Maine) Sch. Painting and Sculpture, 1979; guest lectr. N.Y. U., 1971, Guilford Coll., Greensboro, N.C., 1972, 75, 76, Syracuse U., 1973, Oberlin Coll., 1973, 74, N.Y. Inst. Tech., 1973, Corcoran Sch. Art, Washington, 1973, 74, Pratt Inst., 1974, 76, Moore Coll. Art, 1974, Ohio State U., 1974, Ohio Wesleyan U., 1974, San Francisco Art Inst., 1975, 76, Calif. Coll. Arts and Crafts, Oakland, 1975, Rutgers U., 1976, Douglass Coll., 1976, Palomar Coll., 1976, San Jose U., 1976, U. Calif., Berkeley, 1976, U. Akron, 1976, Otis Art Inst., Los Angeles, 1976, Tyler Sch. Art, Phila., 1977, Art Gallery of Ont., Toronto, 1977, UCLA, 1978, U. So. Calif., 1978, U. Calif., Northridge, 1978, Birmingham (Eng.) Poly. Inst., Rochester (N.Y.) Inst. Tech., 1979, M.I.T., 1980, Arkiv Museet, Lund, Sweden, 1980, Skidmore Coll., Saratoga Springs, N.Y., 1980, Hunter Coll., N.Y.C., 1980, 81, St. Lawrence U., N.Y., 1980. One-artist shows include, Columbia U., 1965, Ruth White Gallery, 1968, 69, A.I.R. Gallery, 1972, Corcoran Gallery Art, Washington, 1974, Ohio State U., Columbus, Stefanotty Gallery, N.Y.C., 1975, Rutgers U., 1976, U. Akron, Newport Harbor Art Mus., Newport Beach, Calif., Tyler Sch. Art, Phila., 1977, 112 Green St. Gallery, N.Y.C., Centre Culturel Americain, Paris, 1978, Amerika Haus, Berlin, Ikon Gallery, Birmingham, Eng., Inst. Contemporary Art, London, 1979, Studio d'arte Cannaviello, Milan, Italy, Galleriet, Lund, Sweden, 1980, Hayden Gallery, M.I.T., 1980, Galerie Aronowitsch, Stockholm, Elise Meyer Gallery, N.Y.C., 1980, retrospective, 1981, others; group shows include, Dwan Gallery, 1970, Nat. Acad. Galleries, Jewish Mus., Finch Coll. Mus., N.Y.C., 1971, Whitney Mus. Am. Art, 1971, 73, Mus. Modern Art, Buenos Aires, Argentina, 1971, Bklyn. Mus., 1972, 76, 77, Allen Meml. Art Mus., Oberlin (Ohio) Coll., 1972, Mus. Fine Arts, Santiago, Chile, Kent (Ohio) State U., N.Y. U., 1972, 75, Inst. Contemporary Art, Lima, Peru, 1972, N.Y. Inst. Tech., Museo Emilio A. Caraffa, Cordoba, Spain, 1973, Kunsthause, Hamburg, Germany, Asso. Am. Artists, 1973, 75, N.Y. Cultural Center, Neuer Berliner Kunstverein, Berlin, 1973, Mus. Modern Art, N.Y.C., 1973, 77, Calif. Inst. Arts, 1973, Indpls. Mus. Art, 1974, Kunsthalle, Cologne, Germany, Stadtisches Mus., Leverküsen, Germany, 1975, Basel Art Fair, Switzerland, Biennale of Sydney, Australia, 1976, Rockefeller Arts Center Gallery, State U. Coll. Fredonia, J.E. Lowe Gallery, Syracuse U., 1977, 80, Rush Rhees Gallery, U. Rochester, 1977, New Gallery Contemporary Art, Cleve. State U., Documenta VI, Kassel, Germany, Mus. Natural History, N.Y.C., Los Angeles Inst. Contemporary Art, Leo Castelli Gallery, N.Y.C., 1978, Rosa Esman Gallery, N.Y.C., 1978, 79, U. Mich. Mus. Art, 1978, Venice Biennale, Phila. Coll. Art, 1977, 78, Ackland Art Mus., U. N.C., Chapel Hill, 1979, Pace Gallery, N.Y.C., Galerie Aix, Stockholm, Seibu Art Mus., Tokyo, Kunstmuseum, Bern, Switzerland, U. Ariz., Tucson, 1980, Touchstone Gallery, N.Y.C., Venice Biennale, Musée National d'Art Moderne, Paris, New Mus., N.Y.C., U. Pa., Bklyn. Mus., Museu de Arte Contemporanea, U. Sao Paulo, Brazil, 1981, Douglass Coll., Rutgers U., Renaissance Soc., U. Chgo., Studio Arco d'Alibert, Rome, Mus. Contemporary Art, Chgo, Palais des Beaux-Arts, Brussels, NAD, N.Y.C., 1982; One-artist shows include numerous others; represented in permanent collections, Mus. Modern Art, N.Y.C., Whitney Mus. Am. Art, N.Y.C., Smithsonian Instn., Washington, Moderna Museet, Stockholm, Syracuse U., Allen Meml. Art Mus., Ohio State U., Oberlin Coll., Chase Manhattan Art Collection, U. Mass. Art Collection, Nat. Collection Fine Arts, Washington, Rutgers U., Roy R. Neuberger Mus., Corcoran Gallery, numerous others; (Recipient purchase prize Albion Coll. Nat. Print Competition 1973, purchase prize Rutgers U. Nat. Drawing Competition 1975); Author: Sculptures of the Mind, 1976, Paradox & Essence, 1976, Isometric Systems in Isotropic Space: Map Projections, 1979. Nat. Endowment fellow, 1974, 75, 81; Creative Artists Public Service grantee, 1972, 74, 80; C.A.S.T. fellow, 1977; DAAD fellow, 1978. Address: 595 Broadway New York NY 10012

DE NEUFVILLE, RICHARD LAWRENCE, educator; b. N.Y.C., May 6, 1939; s. Lawrence Eustace and Adeline de N.; 1 son, Robert. S.D., S.M., MIT, 1961, Ph.D., 1965. Asst. prof. to assoc. prof. dept. civil engring. MIT, Cambridge, Mass., 1965-75, prof., chmn. tech. and policy program, 1975—; vis. prof. Ecole Centrale de Paris, 1981-82, U. Calif.-Berkeley, 1974, 75, 76, London Grad Sch. Bus., 1973. Author: Airport Systems Planning, 1976, Systems Planning and Design, 1979, Systems Analysis for Engineers and Managers, 1971; editor: Jour. Transp. Research. Served to 1st lt. C.E. U.S. Army, 1961-62. White House fellow, 1964-65; Guggenheim fellow, 1973; recipient Systems Sci. prize NATO, 1974, Risk and Ins. prize Risk and Ins. Soc., 1976. Mem. ASCE, Ops. Research Soc. Am., AAAS. Clubs: Cambridge Boat, Cambridge Tennis. Office: MIT Room 1-138 Cambridge MA 02139

DENEUVE, CATHERINE (CATHERINE DORLEAC), actress; b. Paris, Oct. 22, 1943; d. Maurice Dorleac and Renee D.; m. David Bailey, 1965 (div. 1970); children: Christian Vadim, Chiara Mastroianni. Ed., Lycée La Fontaine, Paris. Motion picture appearances include Les Petits Chats, 1956, Les Collegiennes, 1956, Les portes claquent, 1960, Les Parisiennes, 1961, Et Satan conduit le bal, 1962, Vacances portugaises, 1963, Le Vice et la Vertu, 1963, Les Parapluies de Cherbourg, 1964 (Golden Palm of Cannes Festival), La Chasse à l'homme, 1964, Les Plus belles escroqueries du monde, 1964, Un Monsieur de compagnie, 1964, Repulsion, 1965, Coeur à la gorge, 1965, Le Chant de Ronde, 1965, La Vie de Chateau, 1965, Les créatures, 1966, Les Demoiselles de Rochefort, 1966, Benjamin, 1967, Manon 70, 1967, Belle de Jour, 1967 (Golden Lion of Venice Festival), Meyerling, 1967, La Chamade, 1968, The April Fools, 1968, La Sirène du Mississippi, 1968, Tristana, 1969, It Only Happens to Others, 1971, Dirty Money, Hustle, 1975, Lovers Like Us, 1975, Act of Aggression, 1976, March or Die, 1977, La Grande Bourgeoise, 1977, The Last Metro, 1980, A Second Chance, 1981, Reporters, 1982, The Hunger, 1983. Office: care Ufland-Roth Prodns 10201 W Pico Blvd Los Angeles CA 90035 *

DENEVAN, WILLIAM MAXFIELD, geographer; b. San Diego, Oct. 16, 1931; s. Lester W. and Wilda M. D.; m. Patricia Sue French, June 21, 1958; children: Curtis, Victoria. Ph.D., 1963. Mem. faculty dept. geography U. Wis., Madison, 1963—, prof., 1972—, chmn. dept., 1980-83. Author: The Upland Pine Forests of Nicaragua, 1961, The Aboriginal Cultural Geography of the Llanos de Mojos of Bolivia, 1966, The Native Population of the America in 1492, 1976; contbr. articles to profl. jours. Served with USN, 1953-55. Fulbright grantee, 1957; NRC grantee, 1961-62; Ford Found. grantee, 1965-66; NSF grantee, 1972-73; Guggenheim fellow, 1977-78. Mem. Assn. Am. Geographers, Am. Geog. Soc., AAAS, Am. Anthrop. Assn., Soc. for Am. Archaeology, Latin Am. Studies Assn. Office: Dept Geography Univ of Wis Madison WI 53706

DENHAM, FREDERICK RONALD, mgmt. cons.; b. Middlebrough, Eng., Oct. 21, 1929; s. Frederick and Gladys (Tattersall) D.; m. Lynn Hughes, Sept. 19, 1953; children—John, Gillian, Michael. B.Sc., U. Durham, Eng., 1950, Ph.D., 1953; M.B.A., U. Buffalo, 1960. Registered profl. engr., Ont.; cert. mgmt. cons. Sci. officer Def. Research Bd., Ottawa, Ont., Can., 1953-54; indsl. engr. Ford Motor Co. of Can., Ltd., Windsor, Ont., 1954-56; asst. supt. Union Carbide Can., Welland, Ont., 1956-61; cons. Thorne, Stevenson & Kellogg, Toronto, Ont., 1961-67, v.p., 1967—; prof. Faculty Adminstrv. Studies York U., 1967-71. Trustee North York Bd. Edn., 1974-78. Fellow Engring. Inst. Can. Anglican. Club: Masons. Home: 15 Danville Dr Willowdale ON M2P 1H7 Canada Office: 2300 Yonge St Toronto ON M4P 1G2 Canada

DENHAM, WILLIAM HAIG, mental health administrator; b. N.Y.C., Mar. 24, 1918; s. William E. and Nellie E. (Davis) D.; children—Lisa Ann, Stacey Lee. B.S., St. Johns U., 1942; M.S., Columbia U., 1950; Ph.D., Brandeis U., 1969. Profl. in mental health and social sci. areas at the practice, supervisory, edn. and managerial levels in, N.Y.C. and Washington, 1948-75; dir. div. manpower and tng. programs NIMH, U.S. Dept. Health and Human Services, Rockville, Md., 1975—; cons. Univ. Research Corp., Washington, U.S. Dept. Labor, Govt. of D.C.; mem. faculty Columbia U., 1952-54, Howard U., 1964-68, U. D.C., 1968-69, SUNY, Buffalo, 1969-71. Contbr. articles to profl. jours. Active Ams. for Dem. Action, Nat. Urban League, NAACP. Served with U.S. Army, 1942-45. NIMH fellow, 1962; NIMH trainee, 1963. Mem. AAUP, Nat. Assn. Social Workers, NEA, Am. Inst. Planning, Am. Polit. Sci. Assn., others. Home: 412 N Watergate East 2510 Virginia Ave NW Washington DC 20037 Office: 5600 Parklawn Dr Rockville MD 20857

DENHARDT, DAVID TILTON, educator; b. Sacramento, Feb. 25, 1939; s. David Burton and Edith (Tilton) D.; m. Georgetta Louise Harrar, July 1, 1961; children—Laura Jean, Kristin Ann, David Harrar. B.A. in Chemistry with high honors, Swarthmore Coll., 1960; Ph.D. in Biophysics, Calif. Inst. Tech., 1965. Instr. biol. labs Harvard, 1964-66, asst. prof., 1966-70; asso. prof. biochemistry McGill U., Montreal, Que., Can., 1970-77, prof., 1977-80; prof. biochemistry, microbiology and immunology, dir. Cancer Research Lab., U. Western Ont., London, 1980—. Editor: Jour. Virology, 1977—. Mem. Am. Chem. Soc., Am. Cancer Soc., Am. Soc. Biol. Chemists, Am. Microbiol. Soc., N.Y. Acad. Scis., Canadian Biochem. Soc., Phi Beta Kappa. Home: 96 Nathaniel Ct London ON N5X 2N6 Canada

DEN HARTOG, JACOB PIETER, cons. mech. engr.; b. Java, East Indies, July 23, 1901; came to U.S., 1924, naturalized, 1930; s. Marten and Elisabeth (Schol) Den H.; m. Elisabeth Stolker, July 29, 1926; children—Martin Dirk, Stephen Ludwig. E.E., U. Delft, Holland, 1924, Dr. Tech. Sci. (hon.), 1967; Ph.D., U. Pitts., 1929; A.M. (hon.), Harvard, 1942, D.Eng., Carnegie Inst. Tech., 1962; D.Sc., U. Ghent, Belgium, 1966, Salford U., 1970, U. Newcastle/Tyne, 1975. Engr. Westinghouse Research Labs., Pitts., 1924-32; asst. prof. mech. engring. Harvard, 1932-36, asso. prof., 1936-41; prof. Mass. Inst. Tech., 1945-67, emeritus, 1967—, head dept. mech. engring., 1954-58. Author: Mechanical Vibrations, 1934, 41, 46, 54, Mechanics, 1948, Strength of Materials, 1949, Advanced Strength of Materials, 1952. Served with USN, 1941-45; now capt. USNR; ret. Fellow Am. Inst. Aeros. and Astronautics, Am. Cons. Engrs. Council, Brit. Inst. M.E.; hon. mem. ASME, Japan Soc. M.E.; mem. Nat. Acad. Sci., Nat. Acad. Engring., Dutch Acad. Arts and Scis. Home: 150 Barnes Hill Rd Concord MA 01742 Office: Mass Inst Tech Cambridge MA 02139

DENHOF, MIKI, graphic designer; b. Triste, Italy; came to U.S., 1938, naturalized, 1944; d. Bernard and Olga (Krieger) Bardach; m. Hans Denhof. Ed., Reiman Sch. Art, Berlin, Germany. Asst. to art dir. Esquire mag., 1940-44; art dir. J. Walter Thompson (advt.), 1944-45;

promotion art dir. Conde Nast Publs., 1945-55; art editor Glamour mag., 1955-60, art dir., 1960-70; asso. editor House and Garden mag., 1970-78; creative dir. Conde Nast Books, 1978-81; graphic cons. Guild Hall, East Hampton, N.Y. Freelance designer of books, 1981—, work rep., Art Dirs. shows, also permanent graphic arts file, Mus. Modern Art.; also exhibited: one man show 35 Yrs. of Graphic Design (Recipient awards Am. Graphic Arts Soc.). Mem. Met. Mus. Art, Mus. Modern Art, Met. Opera Guild. Home: 118 E 60th St New York NY 10022 also 17 Barns Ln Easthampton NY 11937

DENIRO, ROBERT, actor; b. N.Y.C., 1945; m. Diahnne Abbott; 1 son, Raphael Eugene. Studied acting with, Stella Adler, Lee Strasberg. Motion pictures include The Wedding Party, 1969, Jennifer On My Mind, 1971, Bloody Mama, Born to Win, 1971, The Gang That Couldn't Shoot Straight, 1971, Bang the Drum Slowly, 1973, Mean Streets, 1973, The Godfather, Part II, 1974, The Last Tycoon, Taxi Driver, 1976, New York, New York, Bertolocci's 1900, 1977, The Deer Hunter, 1978, Raging Bull, 1980 (Recipient Acad. award as best supporting actor for The Godfather, Part II 1974, Hasty Pudding award Harvard U. 1979); motion pictures include True Confessions, 1981, The King of Comedy, 1982, Once Upon a Time in America, 1984. Office: 10125 Washington Blvd Culver City CA 90230

DENIS, PAUL, editor; b. N.Y.C., July 1, 1909; s. Nicholas and Amelia (Rozaky) Dejerenis; m. Helen Martin, May 17, 1942; children: Michael Stephan, Christopher Paul. Student, N.Y. U., 1931. Reporter Vaudeville News and Star, 1926-30; asso. editor N.Y. Star, 1930-31, The Billboard, 1931-43; drama reporter and vaudeville columnist N.Y. Post, 1943-45; radio TV editor N.Y. Post Home News, 1946-49; lectr. on radio, TV and show business; columnist N.Y. Daily Compass, 1949-51; columnist, book editor N.Y. Rev., 1951; asso. editor Why Magazine, 1951, Academy Mag., 1952-53; columnist TV World, TV People, Modern Screen mags., from 1953; TV editor Bklyn. Eagle; radio and TV commentator.; editorial dir. daytime TV mags. Sterling's Mags. Inc., 1969-78; founding editor Daytime Digest mag., 1982—. Author: Your Career in Show Business, 1948, Paul Denis' Celebrity Cook Book, 1952, Opportunities in Dancing, 1957, The Jackie Gleason Story, 1956, Super Sound, 1966, Daytime TV Star Directory, 1976, Opportunities in the Dance, 1980; Contbr. to nat. mags. Del. United Parents Assn., 1957-58; Bd. dirs. Parkinson's Disease Found. Recipient One More River award for promoting tolerance Sta. WNYC, 1947; Gagwriters Inst. award, 1948, citation Mag. Editors for Equal Rights Amendment, 1979, plaque for outstanding service to daytime TV community 1969 to 1978 Edge of Night, Internat. Club. Mem. Writers Guild Am., Radio Writers Guild, Newspaper Guild Club, Newspaper Guild N.Y., Radio-Television Critics Circle N.Y. (founder, chmn.), Assn. UN, Acad. Television Arts & Scis. Greek-Orthodox. Clubs: Silurians, Lambs. Home: 518 Tulfan Terr Bronx NY 10463 Office: 355 Lexington Ave New York NY 10017

DENISE, ROBERT PHILLIPS, financial executive; b. Montreal, Que., Can., Nov. 13, 1936; s. Warren Edward and Lorena Hyacinth (Patterson) D.; m. Margaret Ellen Maloney, June 30, 1937; children: Robert Phillips, William Joseph, Christopher Andrew. A.B., Duke U., 1959; postgrad., Northeastern U., Boston, 1970-71. With Gen. Electric Co., 1959-77, traveling auditor, 1965-66, fin. analyst, 1967-69, mgr. gen. acctg. and bus. analysis, 1970-72, mgr. fin. and adminstrn., 1972-74, chief fin. officer Irish affiliates, 1974-77; treas. Hoffman-LaRoche Inc., Nutley, N.J., 1978-82, controller, 1982—. Twp. committeeman, Millburn, N.J., 1981—, vice chmn., dep. mayor, Millburn, N.J., 1983-84, Mayor, chmn. twp. com., Millburn, N.J., 1984—; mem. Planning Bd., 1979-80; v.p., bd. dirs. Nat. Soc. to Prevent Blindness-N.J., 1980-82; chmn. Permanent Com. on Municipal Improvements, Ashland, Mass., 1971; active Boy Scouts Am. Served with U.S. Army, 1960-62. Republican. Office: 340 Kingsland St Nutley NJ 07110

DENISE, THEODORE CULLOM, educator; b. Whitewater, Wis., Mar. 9, 1919; s. Malcolm F. and Margaret E. (Lawrence) D.; m. Kathleen W. Cowles, Oct. 4, 1942; children—Patricia B. (Mrs. Nicholas White), Theodore Cullom. B.A., U. Mich., 1942, M.A., 1947, Ph.D., 1955. Teaching fellow U. Mich., 1946-48; mem. faculty Syracuse U., 1948—, assoc. prof. philosophy, 1959-64, prof. philosophy, 1964—, chmn. dept., 1959-72, chmn. humanities depts., 1973-76; dir. liberal studies Inst. Univ. Adminstrs., 1961-63, dir. of semester in, Italy, 1967-68, 76-77; dir. grad. studies in philosophy Inst. Univ. Adminstr., 1976—; mem. editorial com Univ. Press, 1972-78. Author: (with others) Great Traditions in Ethics, 1953, (with S.P. Peterfreund) Contemporary Philosophy and Its Origins, 1967; Editor: (with M.H. Williams) Retrospect and Prospect, 1956; Contbr. articles to philos. jours. Served with AUS, 1942-46. Mem. Assn. Symbolic Logic, Am. Philos. Assn., Alpha Kappa Lambda. Home: 301 Haddonfield Dr DeWitt NY 13214 Office: Dept Philosophy Syracuse U Syracuse NY 13210

DENISON, EDWARD FULTON, economist; b. Omaha, Dec. 18, 1915; s. Edward Fulton and Edith Barbara (Brown) D.; m. Elsie Lightbown, June 14, 1941; children: Janet Denison Howell, Edward. Student, Central YMCA Coll., Chgo., 1932-34, Loyola U., Chgo., 1935; A.B., Oberlin Coll., 1936; A.M., Brown U., 1938; Ph.D., 1941, Brookings Instn., 1939-40; grad., Nat. War Coll., 1951. Instr. Brown U., 1940-41; economist., nat. income div. Office of Bus. Econs., U.S. Dept. Commerce, 1941-47, acting chief, nat. income div., 1948; asst. dir. Office of Bus. Econs., 1949-56; assoc. dir. Bur. Econ. Analysis, 1979-82; economist Com. Econ. Devel., 1956-62; sr. fellow Brookings Instn., 1962-78, sr. fellow emeritus, 1978—; vis. research prof. U. Calif. - Berkeley, 1966-67; chief aggregates unit U.S. Strategic Bombing Survey, Germany, 1945; lectr. Am. U., Washington, 1946; Chmn. exec. com. Conf. Research Income and Wealth, 1957-59. Author: The Sources of Economic Growth in the United States and the Alternatives Before Us, 1962, Why Growth Rates Differ, 1967, Accounting for United States Economic Growth, 1929-1969, 1974, (with William K. Chung) How Japan's Economy Grew So Fast, 1976, Accounting for Slower Economic Growth, 1979. Recipient Woytinsky award, 1967. Fellow Am. Acad. Arts and Scis., Am. Econ. Assn. (Disting. fellow; v.p. 1978), Am. Statis. Assn.; mem. Internat. Assn. Research in Income and Wealth, Conf. Research in Income and Wealth. Club: Sherwood Forest (Md.). Home: Sherwood Forest Annapolis MD 21405 also 560 N St SW Washington DC 20024

DENISON, ROBERT HOWLAND, paleontologist; b. Somerville, Mass., Nov. 9, 1911; s. William Kendall and Florence Letchworth (Howland) D.; m. Marion Swift, June 29, 1940 (div. 1948); children: John Howland, David Oldmixen; m. Mary S. Maynard, Aug. 3, 1965; 1 son, Robert Wells. A.B., Harvard U., 1933; M.A., Columbia U., 1934, Ph.D., 1938. Asst. curator in mus. Dartmouth, 1937-47, instr. zoology, 1938-42, asst. prof., 1943-47; paleontologist African expdn. U. Calif., 1947-48; curator fossil fishes Field Mus. Nat. History, Chgo., 1948-70, research asso., 1971—; lectr. evolutionary biology U. Chgo., 1965-72; asso. Mus. Comparative Zoology, Harvard, 1973—; field trips in, U.S., Can., Europe, Africa, 1931—. Contbr. articles to profl. jours. Guggenheim fellow, 1953-54. Fellow AAAS; Mem. Soc. Vertebrate Paleontology (pres. 1962-63), Paleontol. Soc., Mass. Audubon Soc. Home: Todd Pond Rd Lincoln MA 01773

DENIUS, FRANKLIN WOFFORD, lawyer; b. Athens, Tex., Jan. 4, 1925; s. S.F. and Frances (Cain) D.; m. Charmaine Hooper, Nov. 19, 1949; children: Frank Wofford, Charmaine. B.B.A., LL.B., U. Tex. Bar: Tex. 1949. Practiced in, Austin, 1949—; sec.-treas., dir. Telcom Corp.; dir. So. Union Co., Tex. Commerce Bank-Austin; legal counsel Austin Better Bus. Bur. Chmn. spl. schs. div. United Fund, 1960, Pacesetters div., 1961, Schs. div., 1964; 1st v.p. United Fund; chmn. steering com. sch. bond campaign, past trustee Austin Ind. Sch. Dist., 1964; past pres. Young Men's Bus. League Austin; past pres., exec. council Austin Ex-Students Assn. U. Tex.; co-chmn. LBJ U Tex. Library Found.; mem. chancellor's council, pres.'s assos. U. Tex.; bd. dirs. Tex. Research League; trustee Schreiner Coll. Served with AUS, 1943-45. Decorated Silver Star medal with two oak leaf clusters, Purple Heart; recipient Outstanding Young Man of Austin award Jr. C. of C., 1959. Mem. Am., Tex., Travis County bar assns., Tex. Philos. Soc. Presbyterian (deacon, elder). Clubs: Mason., Longhorn (past pres.), West Austin Optimists (past dir.), Headliners (pres., sec. bd. trustees, mem. exec. com.). Home: 3703 Meadowbank Dr Austin TX 78703 Office: PO Box 2177 Austin TX 78768

DENIUS, HOMER RAINEY, electronics co. exec., rancher; b. Appomattox, Va., Jan. 31, 1914; s. Frank E. and Margaret (Watters) D.; m. Grace Evelyn Pence, June 26, 1936; children—Chris F., Sandra Jeanne (Mrs. Robert Keeley), Homer R. Student, U. Cin.; D.Sc. (hon.), Fla. Inst. Tech., 1964. Mgmt. exec., 1943—; chmn. bd. Electro-Sci. Mgmt. Corp., Orlando, Fla., 1968—. Methodist. Club: Mason (32 deg.). Home: Twin Creek Ranch Parkman WY 82838 Office: 600 Courtland St Suite 490 Orlando FL 32804

DENKER, ARNOLD, chess master; b. N.Y.C., Feb. 21, 1914; s. Max and Henrietta (Jorisch) D.; m. Nina Simmons, Dec. 27, 1936; children—Richard, Mitchell, Randy. B.A., N.Y. U., 1936. With Armour & Co., 1937-42; v.p., partner Jameco Trading Co., 1948-72; dir. Manhattan Chess Club, N.Y.C., 1972—; capt., trainer Ladies Olympic Chess Team, Medellin, Colombia, S.A., 1974; capt. U.S. Student Chess Team, Mexico City, 1980; co-chmn. internat. affairs com. U.S. Chess Fedn., 1980-81, v.p., 1981—; author columns on chess, also player and lectr., 1972—. Author: If You Must Play Chess, 1947, My Best Chess Games, 1981. Mem. Manhattan Chess Club, Fla. Chess Assn. (pres. 1980-81). U.S. champion, 1944-46; set world speed record for playing 100 chess players at one time, in 7 hours and 20 minutes, Cleve., 1946; granted internat. master status, 1950, internat. grandmaster title, 1981; Fla. state champion, 1976-78; 2d pl. Nat. Open Championship, 1977. Address: 2701 NE Ocean Blvd Fort Lauderdale FL 33308

DENKER, HENRY, playwright, author, director; b. N.Y.C., Nov. 25, 1912; s. Max and Jennie (Geller) D.; m. Edith Rose Heckman, Dec. 5, 1942. LL.B., N.Y. Law Sch., 1934. Bar: N.Y. 1935. Practiced law, N.Y.C., 1935-38; exec. Research Inst. Am., N.Y.C., 1936-37; tax cons. Standard Stats. subs. Standard and Poor, N.Y.C., 1937-39; lectr. dramatic writing Am. Theatre Wing, 1961-63, Coll. of the Desert. Writer, dir., producer: (radio series) The Greatest Story Ever Told, N.Y.C., 1947-57; author: (Broadway plays) Time Limit, 1956, A Far Country, 1961, Venus at Large, 1962, A Case of Libel, 1964, What Did We Do Wrong, 1968, Something Old, Something New, 1976, Horowitz and Mrs. Washington, 1979; (off-Broadway) The Name of The Game, 1967; A Sound of Distant Thunder, 1969, The Headhunters, 1974; (screenplays) The Heartfarm, 1970; The Hook, Twilight of Honor, Time Limit, A Time for Miracles, 1980, Outrage, 1984; writer, dir., producer numerous TV dramas, 1950-66; TV spls. include Give us Barrabas, 1964; Neither are we Enemies, 1971, The Choice, The Court Martial of Lieutenant Calley, Mother Seton, 1980; author: I'll Be Right Home, Ma, 1949, My Son, the Lawyer, 1950, Salome, Princess of Galilee, 1954, That First Easter, 1956, The Director, 1970, The Kingmaker, 1972, A Place for the Mighty, 1973, The Physicians, 1975, The Experiment, 1976, The Starmaker, 1977, The Scofield Diagnosis, 1977, The Actress, 1978, The Error of Judgement, 1979, Horowitz and Mrs. Washington, 1979, The Warfield Syndrome, 1981, Outrage!, 1982, The Healers, 1983, Kincaid, 1984. Mem. council Dramatists Guild, N.Y.C., 1967-69. Recipient Peabody award, 1949; Christopher award, 1953; Emmy award, 1948. Mem. Acad. TV Arts and Scis. (council). Jewish. Address: 241 Central Park West New York NY 10024

DENLINGER, JOHN KENNETH, journalist; b. Lancaster, Pa., Mar. 25, 1942; s. John Emory and Elizabeth (Smith) D.; m. Carol Ann Reilly, June 27, 1964; children: Lauri, Scott. B.S. in Econs, Pa. State U., 1964. Mem. staff Pitts. Press, 1964-66; mem. staff washington Post, 1966—; sports columnist, 1975—. Co-author: Athletes for Sale, 1975. Office: 1150 15th St NW Washington DC 20071

DENMAN, CHARLES FRANK, lawyer; b. Grapeland, Tex., May 8, 1934; s. James H. and Mary Jane D.; m. Carlene Smith, June 8, 1962; children: Kimberly, Yvonne. B.B.A., Sam Houston State U., 1955; J.D., South Tex. Coll. Law, 1967. Bar: Tex. 1965. Accountant Amoco Co., 1955-61; trust officer Houston Bank & Trust Co., 1967-69; gen. counsel Star Engraving Co., Houston, 1970-72, pres., 1973-77; sec., gen. counsel Sysco Corp., Houston, 1977-81; v.p. Oncor Corp., Houston, 1981—. Served with U.S. Army, 1957-59. Mem. ABA, Tex. Bar Assn., Houston Bar Assn., Corp. Secs. Assn., Nat. Realtors Assn. Republican. Presbyterian. Clubs: River Plantation Country (Conroe, Tex.); Rotary. Home: 93 Brandon Conroe TX 77302 Office: 17015 Aldine Westfield Houston TX 77073

DENMAN, EUGENE DALE, elec. engr.; b. Farmington, Mo., Mar. 15, 1928; s. Charles Mathias and Flora B. (Ward) D.; m. Lorene Norma J. Hodge, June 28, 1952; children—Stephen D., Laura K. B.S., Washington U., St. Louis, 1951; M.S., Vanderbilt U., 1955; D.Sc., U. Va., 1963. Engr. Magnavox Co., Ft. Wayne, Ind., 1951-52, Sperry Gyroscope Co., Gt. Neck, N.Y., 1954-56, Midwest Research Inst., Kansas City, Mo., 1956-60; research scientist U. Va., 1960-63; asso. prof. elec. engring., asst. prof. medicine Vanderbilt U., 1963-69; prof. elec. and systems engring. U. Houston, 1969—; cons. to govt. and industry, 1965—. Author: (with Roy N. Adams) Wave Propagation and Turbulent Media, 1966, Coupled Modes in Plasmas, Elastic Media and Parametric Amplifiers, 1970; editor: (with R.E. Bellman) Lecture Notes on Invariant Imbedding, 1971, (with B. Childs et al) Codes for Boundary-Value Problems in Ordinary Differential Equations, 1979. Com. chmn. Cub Scouts, Brentwood, Calif., 1967. Served with Signal Corps AUS, 1946-48. Mem. IEEE, Eta Kappa Nu, Tau Beta Pi. Methodist. Address: 13402 Taylorcrest St Houston TX 77079

DENMAN, JOE CARTER, JR., forest products company executive; b. Lufkin, Tex., Sept. 30, 1923; m. Ginia Beth Cox, Jan. 10, 1948; children: Joe Carter, III, Elizabeth Anne, Ginia Geanette. B.Arch., Tex. A&M U., 1950. Registered profl. engr., Tex. With Temple Industries, Diboll, Tex., 1950—, corporate v.p., 1964-66, exec. v.p., 1966-72, pres., 1972-77; exec. v.p. Temple-Eastex, Inc., 1974-77, pres., chief exec. officer, 1977—, chmn. bd., 1983—; exec. v.p. Temple-Inland, Inc., 1984—; v.p. Time, Inc., 1976-78, group v.p., 1978-84, dir., 1979-84; v.p. Angelina County Water Control and Improvement Dist. No. 2, 1963-68; v.p., dir. AFCO Industries, Inc., Diboll, Tex., 1973—; dir. Diboll State Bank, CRS Group, Inc., Houston, Pineland Bank (Tex.), Home Savs. & Loan Assn., Lufkin, Tex., Lumbermens Investment Corp., Austin, Tex., Sunbelt Ins. Co., Tex., Tex. South-Eastern R.R. Co., Diboll, Temple-White Co., Inc., Topaz Oil Co., Love Wood Products Co., Diboll., Angelina Free Press Inc., Inland Container Corp., Indpls.; v.p., dir. Sabine Investment Co., Diboll, Scotch Investment Co., Lufkin Steel Fabricators, RECO Inc. Pres. Diboll Booster Club, 1952, Quarterback Club, Diboll, 1952; mem. Diboll Sch. Bd., 1960-62; dir. Angelina County Community Fund, Inc., 1960-61, chmn. indsl. fund, 1965; pres., bd. dirs. Temple Industries Employees Fed. Credit Union, 1963-64; trustee Temple Pension Trust, 1964—, Meml. Hosp., Lufkin, 1978—, Angelina Coll., 1980—, Tex. Forestry Assn. Mus., Lufkin; past mem. adv. bd. Salvation Army, Lufkin.; mem. devel. council Coll. Agr., Coll. Architecture and Environ. Design Tex. A&M U. Served to lt. (j.g.), A.C. U.S. Navy, 1942-46. Named Disting. Alumnus Tex. A&M U., 1981. Mem. Nat. Forest Products Assn. (dir. 1968—), So. Forest Products Assn. (pres. 1969-70, dir. 1954—), Tex. Forest Products Mfrs. Assn. (pres. 1967-69, past dir.), Tex. Soc. Profl. Engrs., So. Pine Inspection Bur. (adv. bd.), So. Pines Plywood Standard (advisory com. 1961-64), Forest Products Research Soc. (dir. 1959-60), Am. Plywood Assn. (trustee 1973-74), Angelina County C. of C. (dir. 1966-68), Tau Beta Pi. Office: PO Drawer N Diboll TX 75941

DENMARK, BERNHARDT, business executive; b. Bklyn., June 6, 1917; s. William M. and Kate (Lazarus) D.; m. Muriel Schechter, Sept. 22, 1943; children: Richard J., Karen. A.B., NYU, 1941; postgrad., Am. U., 1941-42, Nat. Inst. Pub. Affairs, 1941-42. Vice pres. sales Telecoin Corp., N.Y.C., 1946-49; v.p. sales Internat. Latex Corp., N.Y.C., 1949-55; mgr. mktg. Playtex Co., N.Y.C., 1955-59, v.p., gen. mgr. family products div., 1959-63, v.p. mktg., 1963-65; pres. Playtex Co. Playtex div., 1965-67, Internat. Playtex Corp., N.Y.C., 1968-69, chmn. bd., 1969; exec. v.p., dir., mem. exec. com. Glen Alden Corp., N.Y.C., 1969-72; pres. Bevis Industries, Inc., White Plains, N.Y., 1972-76, Bus. Mktg. Corp. for N.Y.C., 1977-78; chmn. Denmark, Donovan & Oppel Inc., N.Y.C., 1978—; dir. Stanley Warner Corp., Schenley Industries, BVD Corp. Served to capt. AUS, 1942-46. Clubs: Fairview Country (Greenwich, Conn.); City Athletic (N.Y.C.). Home: 870 UN Plaza New York NY 10017 Office: 10 Rockefeller Plaza New York NY 10020

DENNARD, CLEVELAND LEON, univ. pres.; b. Sebring, Fla., Feb. 17, 1929; s. Nathaniel and Betsy Ann (Crocker) D.; m. Belle Brooks, Aug. 27, 1948; children—Judy, Sadie Jo, Beth Elaine, Ann. B.S., Fla. A&M U., 1948; M.S., Colo. State U., 1958; D.Ed., U. Tenn., 1964. Asso. prof. Ala. A&M U., 1957-60; prin. Carver Vocat. and Adult Sch., Atlanta, 1960-65; dep. commr. for manpower and program mgmt., City of N.Y., 1965-67; pres. Technol. Inst., Washington, 1967-77, Atlanta U., 1977—; dir. First Atlanta Corp., 1st Nat. Bank of Atlanta.; Chmn. So. Edn. Found., Atlanta; mem. Pres.'s Adv. Com. on Sci. and Tech. Policy, Sec. of Navy's Adv. Bd. on Edn. and Tng., Sec. of HEW adv. com. on accreditation and institutional eligibility, Nat. Acad. Sci.-Nat. Research Council Commn. on Human Resources. Trustee Robert F. Kennedy Meml. Found., Martin Luther King Jr. Center for Social Change, Metro Atlanta YMCA; bd. dirs., v.p. Island Teleradio Services, Inc.; bd. dirs., chmn. Dist. Communications, Inc.; bd. dirs., fin. chmn. Center for Community Change; dir. Central Atlanta Progress; bd. dirs. Nat. Manpower Inst.; bd. dirs., treas. African-Am. Scholars Council; bd. dirs. United Way, Atlanta. Named Washingtonian of Year, 1972. Mem. Phi Kappa Phi, Iota Lambda Sigma, Omega Psi Phi, Epsilon Boule. Democrat. Baptist. Clubs: Atlanta Guardsman, Masons. Office: 223 Chestnut St SW Atlanta GA 30314

DENNEAN, JOAN CLAIRE, oil company executive; b. Yonkers, N.Y., May 20, 1926; d. James Andrew and Marion Frances (Harrington) D. B.A., Coll. of New Rochelle, 1947. Exec. sec. Conoco Inc., Stamford, Conn., 1961-74, dep. corporate sec., 1974-75, corporate sec., 1975—. Mem. Pres.'s Adv. Council Coll. of New Rochelle, N.Y. Mem. Am. Soc. Corporate Secs. (sec.-treas. chpt.). Home: 26 Park Ln Westport CT 06880 Office: High Ridge Park Stamford CT 06904

DENNEN, DAVID WARREN, microbiologist; b. Clarks Summit, Pa., Mar. 20, 1932; s. William L. and Ruth L. (Lufkin) D.; m. Jane Dersheimer, Mar. 27, 1954; children: Laurie, Melinda, David H. B.S., MIT, 1954; M.S., Ind. U., 1964, Ph.D., 1966. With Eli Lilly & Co., 1954—, assoc. phys. chemist, 1954-56, phys. chemist, 1959-64, sr. microbiologist, 1966-69, mgr. antiobiotic devel., 1969-71, dir. antibiotic devel., 1971-74; mng. dir. Lilly Pharmachemie GmbH, 1974-75, dir. antibiotic prodn. and tech. services, Indpls., 1975-80; mng. dir. Lilly Research Centre, Ltd., Eng., 1980-82; exec. dir. Lilly Research Labs., 1982-83, v.p. biochem. devel. and biosynthetic ops., 1983—; dir. Lilly Industries, Ltd., Eli Lilly Group Pension Trustees, Ltd.; mem. research and tech. com. Confedn. Brit. Industry. Contbr. articles to profl. jours. Comdt. Ind. Mil. Acad.; dir. personnel Ind. Adj. Gen.'s Office; mem. dean's indsl. adv. com. Ind. U.-Purdue U., Indpls.; mem. Ind. Sci. Edn. Fund; edn. counselor MIT. Served with AUS, 1956-59; col. Ind. N.G. NIH fellow, 1965-66. Mem. Am. Chem. Soc., Am. Soc. Microbiology, Assn. Brit. Pharm. Industries (sci. com.), Theta Chi. Home: 6302 Woodwind Dr Indianapolis IN 46217

DENNER, MELVIN WALTER, educator; b. North Washington, Iowa, Aug. 27, 1933; s. Norbert William and Petronella Nettie (Eischeid) D.; m. N. Anne Greer, June 19, 1965; children: Mark Andrew, Michael Alan (twins). B.S., Upper Iowa U., 1961; M.S. (NSF fellow), U. Ky., 1963; Ph.D., Iowa State U., 1968. Asst. prof. life scis. Ind. State U., Evansville, 1968071, chmn. dept., 1969—, assoc. chmn. div. scis. and math., 1975—, assoC. prof., 1971-76, prof., 1976—, acting chmn. div. scis. and math., 1976-77, chmn., 1979—. Contbr. articles to profl. jours. Vice chmn. Iowa Young Democrats, 1958-60; Bd. dirs. Deaconess Hosp. Allied Health Programs., Evansville Mus. Arts and Scis. Served with USN, 1953-57. NIH fellow, 1966-67; Alumni Achievement fellow, 1967-68. Mem. Internat. Soc. Invertebrate Pathology (founding), Am. Soc. Parasitologists, Am. Micros. Soc. (nat. treas.), AAAS (film critic), Am. Inst. Biol. Sci., Sigma Xi, Sigma Zeta. Home: 100 S Peerless St Evansville IN 47712 Office: Div Sci and Math Indiana State University Evansville IN 47712 *The greatest gift we can have on earth is knowledge, for in knowledge we have truth.*

DENNERY, MOISE WALDHORN, lawyer; b. New Orleans, Apr. 29, 1915; s. Harry and Augusta (Waldhorn) D.; m. Phyllis Sugarman, June 7, 1941; children—Harry, Richard. B.A., Tulane U., 1935, LL.B., J.D., 1937. Bar: La. bar 1937, U.S. Dist. Ct. bar 1938, U.S. Circuit Ct. Appeals bar 1952, U.S. Supreme Ct. bar 1956, U.S. Tax Ct. bar 1953, U.S. Ct. Claims bar 1959, U.S. Ct. Customs and Patent Appeals bar 1952, U.S. Bd. Immigration Appeals 1952, ICC 1962. Asso. firm Schwarz, Guste, Barnett & Redmann, New Orleans, 1937-41; partner firm McCloskey, Dennery, Page & Hennesy (and predecessors), New Orleans, 1941—; lectr. in bus. law Tulane U., 1945-55. Bd. editors: Tulane U. Law Rev, 1935-36; statutory interpretation editor, 1936-37; editorial adv. bd.: Times Picayune. Sec. Charter Commn., City of New Orleans, 1950-52; trustee Isidore Newman Sch., New Orleans, 1946-69, chmn. bd., 1965-69; mem. La. State Civil Service Commn., 1952-62, chmn., 1956-62; trustee Touro Infirmary, New Orleans, 1955-65; bd. dirs. Met. Area Com., New Orleans, 1966-67; mem. steering com. Regional Planning Forum; pres. Bur. Govtl. Research New Orleans, 1967-69; mem. Goals for La. Com., Goals for New Orleans Com.; trustee New Orleans Jewish Ednl. and Charitable Fedn., New Orleans Jewish Welfare Fedn.; v.p., bd. dirs. Touro Synagogue, New Orleans; mem. La. Com. on Alcoholism, New Orleans Airport Commn.; chmn. United Negro Coll. Fund Campaign; mem. budget coms. Community Chest, United Fund; bd. dirs. Orleans Neighborhood Centers; chmn. legal com. Jewish Children's Home; mem. La. Commn. on Ednl. TV, 1970-71, La. Ednl. TV Authority, 1971-74; chmn. La. Ednl. TV

Authority, 1971-73; bd. dirs. Public Broadcasting Service, 1972-73; del., sec. La. Constl. Conv., 1973; mem. La. Commn. on Statutory Revision, 1974-75; chmn. Superdome Mgmt. Adv. Com., 1975-76, Mayor's Adv. Com. on Charter Revision, 1975-76, La. Constl. Conv. Records Commn., 1975-78. Recipient Weiss Brotherhood award NCCJ, 1976, Vol. Activist award, 1978. Mem. Am. Bar Assn., La. Bar Assn., New Orleans Bar Assn. (exec. com. 1964-67, 1st v.p. 1969-70, pres. 1972-73), Law Inst., Am. Judicature Soc., Notaries Assn. New Orleans, Am. Arbitration Assn. (nat. panel arbitrators), Tulane U. Alumni Assn., Am. Jewish Com. (nat. and New Orleans exec. bds.), La. Civil Service League (hon. life chmn., dir., Monte M. Lemann award 1964), La. State Personnel Council, Public Affairs Research Council, Order of Coif. Office: 505 Hibernia Bldg New Orleans LA 70112

DENNEY, ARTHUR HUGH, consultant; b. Rosendale, Mo., Sept. 25, 1916; s. Frank M. and Cora L. (Beatie) D.; m. A. Ilene Tucker, Aug. 5, 1939; children: Charles Hugh, Jo Ann (Mrs. Raymond Fisher). B.S., U. Mo., 1938, M.A. Econs., 1950; Diploma in Community Devel, U. London, 1969. Technician U.S. Forest Service, Mo., 1938; state coordinator Mo. Conservation Commn., Jefferson City, 1938-44; recreation dir. Mo. Dept. Resources and Devel., Jefferson City, 1944-45, dir., 1945-48; owner, operator Blue Springs (Mo.) Lodge Resort, 1948-50, 54-57; adminstrv. asst. McDonnell Aircraft, St. Louis, 1950-54; instr. regional and community affairs U. Mo., Columbia, 1958-67, asso. prof., 1967-70, prof., 1970-79, chmn. dept., 1968, 73-75; dir. rural planning and devel. Black and Veatch Internat., 1979-82; pvt. cons., 1982—; Cons. USDA, U.S. Dept. Labor, U.S. Dept. Commerce, Purdue U., U. Ark., Govt. of Indonesia. Author: Decongesting Metropolitan America, 1972; Contbr. articles to profl. jours. Chmn. civic improvement com. Columbia Indsl. Commn., 1966-68; chmn. Greater Columbia Planning Com., 1960-62. Danforth fellow, 1937. Mem. Community Devel. Soc. N. Am. (dir. 1973—, pres. 1976-77), AAAS, World Futures Soc., Nat. Univ. Ext. Assn. (adminstrv. bd. 1975-76), Alpha Gamma Rho, Alpha Zeta. Club: Mason. Home: 208 Westridge Columbia MO 65201

DENNEY, DONALD BEREND, educator; b. Seattle, Apr. 3, 1927; s. John Edwin and Catherine Boswell (Macgowan) D.; m. Dorothy Ziebell, Aug. 24, 1956. B.Sc., U. Wash., 1949; Ph.D., U. Cal., Berkeley, 1952. Research chemist E.I. duPont, 1952-53; with Hickrill Chem. Found., Katonah, N.Y., 1953-54; mem. faculty Rutgers U., 1955—, prof. chemistry, 1962—; cons. various chem. cos. Editor: Techniques and Methods in Organic and Organometallic Chemistry, 1970; editorial bd.: Phosphorus and Sulfur, 1971—. Mem. NIH Medicinal Panel B, 1965-69, 75-76, 79. Served with USCGR, 1944-45. A.P. Sloan fellow, 1955-59. Mem. Am. Chem. Soc., Phi Beta Kappa. Home: 20 Wakefield Ln Piscataway NJ 08854

DENNEY, GEORGE COVERT, JR., orgn. adminstr.; b. Pitts., July 18, 1921; s. George Covert and Ruth (Crowthers) D.; m. Alice McCauley, Apr. 13, 1946; children—Christopher Stock, Jill McCauley. B.S., Waynesburg Coll., 1942; LL.B., Harvard U., 1948; M.A., Columbia U., 1950. Bar: Mass. bar 1948, D.C. bar 1961. Fgn. affairs officer Dept. State, 1950-52; asst. gen. counsel Office Dir. Mut. Security, Exec. Office Pres., 1953-54; dep. asst. gen. counsel internat. matters Office Sec. Dept. Def., 1954-56; cons. com. fgn. relations U.S. Senate, 1956-62; dep. dir., bur. intelligence and research Dept. State, 1963-74; individual practice, Washington, 1974—; Fellow Inst. Current World Affairs, N.Y.C., 1962-63. Served to lt. USNR, 1942-46. Mem. Am. Bar Assn., Am. Soc. Internat. Law. Home and office: 2604 36th St NW Washington DC 20007

DENNEY, JAY RONALD, government official; b. Englewood, NJ, Nov. 2, 1936; s. Wells H. and Gertrude (Watson) D.; m. Fern Alexander, Dec. 15, 1963; children: Tracy A., Julie W., Allison Parke. B.S., U.S. Naval Acad., 1959. With U.S. Navy Dept., 1959-63; owner, pres. Arbonite Corp., Doylestown, Pa., 1963-81, The Denney Cos., 1981; prin. dep. asst. sec. manpower and res. affairs U.S. Navy Dept., Washington, 1981—; chmn. Liberty Bell Corrison Course, 1976-80. Elder Presbyterian Ch., Doylestown, 1974-77; bd. dirs. YMCA, 1977-81. Served to lt. USN, 1959-63. Mem. U.S. Naval Res., Bucks County C. of C. (v.p. 1978-81), Naval Res. Assn., Rubber Mfg. Assn. Republican. Presbyterian. Home: 6313 Beachway Dr Falls Church VA 22044 Office: Dept Navy Rm 4E780 Pentagon Washington DC 20350

DENNEY, K. DUANE, mfg. and service co. exec.; b. Plattsburg, O., May 27, 1923; s. Clark E. and Edith (Yeoman) D.; m. Patricia A. Nisley, Aug. 30, 1946; children—Susan A., Diane L. Student, Office Tng. Sch., Columbus, O., 1942-43, Franklin U., Columbus, 1946-49. Sr. v.p., chief fin. officer, dir., mem. exec. com. Automation Industries, Inc., Los Angeles, 1949—; dir. Frontier Savs. and Loan Assn., Cascade Steel Rollings Mills, Inc. Bd. govs. Shriners Hosps. for Crippled Children. Served with USNR, 1943-46. Decorated Bronze Star medal with 4 oak leaf clusters. Mem. Fin. Execs. Inst. (Los Angeles chpt.), Am. Mgmt. Assn., Los Angeles Treas. Club Assn., Los Angeles Pension Club. Clubs: Los Angeles Country, Masons, Shriner, Rotary, Elks. Home: 146 Via Monte D'Oro Redondo Beach CA 90277 Office: 1901 Bldg Century City Los Angeles CA 90067

DENNEY, ROGER PEARSON, JR., information systems company executive; b. Columbus, Ohio, Apr. 26, 1937; s. Roger Perle and Donna (Pearson) D.; m. Barbara Spicer, Aug. 6, 1956; children: Cynthia, Tobin. B.E.S. in Indsl. Engring., Johns Hopkins U., 1959, M.S.E., 1961. Registered profl. engr., Calif. Instr., mfg. planner Westinghouse Electric Corp., Pitts., 1961-65; editor-in-chief, dir. publs. Inst. Indsl. Engrs., N.Y.C., 1965-71; with Medicus Systems Corp., Evanston, Ill., 1971—, v.p. govt. services, 1975-77, sr. v.p. Eastern region, 1977-81, exec. v.p. ops., 1981—. Mem. adv. bd.: Handbook of Insustrial Engineering, 1982; editor-in-chief: Jour. Indsl. Engring., Indsl. Engring. mag., 1965-71. Mem. Inst. Indsl. Engr. (sr., v.p.-publs. 1981-83, chief fin. officer 1983-84, pres., chief exec. officer 1984-85), Alpha Pi Mu. Home: 551 Meadow Rd Winnetka IL 60093 *If I now enjoy some professional stature, then I am indebted to many people: the men and women who have worked for me over the years. Their skills, their industry, their attitudes, their creativity—these have been the building blocks of my career. I am convinced that hierarchies push from below, that leaders are made, not born. Leadership, after all, is simply a process of getting things done through people. You create an organizational culture, establish goals, prove guidance, and set a good example. Then watch it happen.*

DENNIN, JOSEPH FRANCIS, lawyer, government official; b. N.Y.C., June 9, 1943; s. William Wilfred and Kathryn L (Sever) D.; m. Sandra Earl Peek, Dec. 28, 1968; children: Theresa Michel, Allison Kathleen, James Joseph. B.A. magna cum laude, Stanford U., 1965, J.D., 1968; postgrad., U. Helsinki, Finland, 1968-69. Bar: Calif. 1969, N.Y. 1970. Assoc. Simpson, & Thacher & Bartlett, N.Y.C., 1969-75; counsel U.S. Senate Intelligence Com., Washington, 1975-76; staff asst. to Pres. White House, Washington, 1976-78; dir. ops. U.S. Internat. Trade Commn., Washington, 1978-79; dep. assoc. atty. gen. Dept. Justice, Washington, 1979-81; dep. asst. sec. Dept. Commerce, Washington, 1981—. Fulbright grantee Inst. Internat. Edn., 1968. Mem. ABA, Assn. Bar City N.Y. Club: Union League (N.Y.C.). Office: Dept Commerce 15th Between E and Constitution Ave NW Washington DC

DENNING, PETER JAMES, computer scientist; b. N.Y.C., Jan. 6, 1942; s. James Edwin and Catherine M. (Manton) D.; m. Dorothy Elizabeth Robling, Jan. 24, 1974; children—Anne, Diana. B.E.E., Manhattan Coll., 1964; M.S. in Elec. Engring. (NSF fellow 1964-67), MIT, 1965, Ph.D., 1968. Asst. prof. elec. engring. Princeton U., 1968-72; assoc. prof. computer scis. Purdue U., 1972-75, prof., 1975-84, head dept., 1979-83; dir. Research Inst. Advanced Computer Sci. NASA Ames Research Center, Mountain View, Calif., 1983; lectr. Author: Profl. Devel. Seminars, 1968—; Author textbooks, also numerous research papers. Recipient Outstanding Faculty award Princeton U. Engring. Assn., 1971, Best Paper award Am. Fedn. Info. Processing Socs., 1972. Fellow IEEE; mem. Assn. Computing Machinery (pres. 1980-82, editor-in-chief Computing Surveys 1977-79, Best Paper award 1968, editor communications of ACM 1983—, Recognition of Service award 1974), N.Y. Acad. Scis., Sigma Xi, Eta Kappa Nu, Tau Beta Pi. Home: 30 Bear Gulch Dr Portola Valley CA 94025 Office: Research Inst Advanced Computer Sci NASA Ames Research Center Moffett Field CA 94035

DENNIS, CARLETON CECIL, ecomomic consultant; b. Adrian, Mich., Oct. 21, 1923; s. Cecil Edward and Mabel Edna (Perkins) D.; m. Margaret Ann Harsh, Apr. 27, 1945; children: Michael C., Mark A., Thomas E. Student, Yale U., 1943-44; economist, Mich. State U., 1954, M.S., 1955; Ph.D., U. Calif.-Berkeley, 1959. Prof. econs. Mich. State U., East Lansing, 1959-62; economist Dept. of Agr., Washington, 1962-65; v.p. planning Agway, Inc., Syracuse, N.Y., 1965-82; cons. Dennis Cons., Bradenton, Fla., 1982—; adv. com. Bur. of Census, 1974-79, Dept. Agr., 1970-76; econ. devel. bd. State of N.Y., Albany, 1976-80. Dir. Central N.Y. Health Systems Agy., Syracuse, 1975-80; trustee Syracuse Rescue Mission, 1978-82. Served to lt. USN, 1943-46; served to lt. USN, 1950-53; PTO. Mem. Am. Agrl. Econs. Assn. (dir. 1979-82, Best Dissertation award 1959), Nat. Assn. Bus. Economists, N.E. Agrl. Econs. Assn. (dir. 1972-82), N.Am. Assn. Corp. Planners. Republican. Baptist. Home and Office: 6906 15th Ave Dr W Bradenton FL 33529

DENNIS, CLARENCE, surgeon, educator; b. St. Paul, June 16, 1909; s. Warren Arthur and Clara May (Van Orman) D.; m. Eleanor Mary Smith, June 17, 1939; children: Jane E. Dennis Wigertz, Richard, James, David; m. Mary Elise Mott, Mar. 12, 1977. B.S., Harvard U., 1931; M.D., Johns Hopkins U., 1935; M.S., U. Minn., 1938, Ph.D., 1940. Diplomate: Am. Bd. Surgery. Trained in surgery under Dr. O. H. Wangensteen, U. Minn., 1935-40; in physiology with Dr. M. B. Visscher, 1937-38, instr. in physiology, 1938-39, in surgery, 1940-41, asst. prof., 1941-44, asso. prof., 1944-47, prof. surgery, 1947-51, SUNY Downstate Med. Center, 1951-72, chmn. dept., 1952-72; dir. div. tech. applications Nat. Heart and Lung Inst., NIH, Bethesda, Md., 1972-73; spl. asst. for tech. Office of Dir., Nat. Heart, Lung and Blood Inst., 1973-74; prof. surgery State U. N.Y. at Stony Brook, 1974—; asso. chief staff for research and devel. VA Med. Center, Northport, N.Y., 1975—; former surgeon-in-chief Kings County Hosp., State U. Hosp. Contbr. articles to profl. publs. and textbooks. Recipient Modern Medicine award for disting. achievement, 1973; John H. Gibbon award Am. Soc. Extracorporeal Technicians, 1974. Fellow A.C.S. (past gov.); mem. Assn. Advancement Med. Instrumentation (pres. 1980-82, chmn. bd. 1982—), Am. Heart Assn., Am. Soc. for Artificial Internal Organs (past pres.), Internat. Surg. Soc. (past pres. U.S. chpt.), Soc. Vascular Surgery (past pres.), N.Y. Surg. Soc. (past pres.), Bklyn. Surg. Soc. (past pres.), Am. Assn. Surgery Trauma, Am. Assn. Thoracic Surgery, Soc. U. Surgeons, Am. Surg. Assn. (past v.p.), Soc. Clin. Surgery, Soc. Exptl. Biology and Medicine, N.Y. Cancer Soc. (past pres.), Internat. Cardiovascular Soc., Soc. Surgery Alimentary Tract, Nat. Soc. Med. Research (pres. 1977-79), N.Y. Soc. Thoracic Surgery, Soc. U. Surg. Chmn. (past pres.). Home: 28 View Rd Setauket NY 11733

DENNIS, DON W., artist; b. Reading, Pa., Jan. 21, 1923; s. Wilbur and Mary Pearl (Davies) D.; m. Gail Eileen Cullen, Feb. 17, 1952; children: Eileen, Lynne, Jay, Erin. B.S. in Art Edn., Kutztown U., 1950; postgrad., Pratt Inst., 1951-52. Designer, illustrator various companies, 1952-58; freelance artist, art tchr., 1958-62; art dir. Gibson Greetings, Cin., 1962-73; freelance artist, art tchr., Wyoming, Ohio, 1973—; commd. painter Phillips Petroleum, Norway. Represented: Phillips calendar, Phillips Petroleum, Norway, 1980; permanent and pvt. collections, Reading Mus. and Art Gallery, Pa., Miami U., Ohio, others. Served with USMC, 1942-45; PTO. Recipient Bronze Ga. Watercolor Soc., 1979. Mem. Nat. Acad. Design (assoc.), Am. Watercolor Soc. (Emily Lowes Meml. 1980, midwestern v.p. 1974-75, Walser Greathouse medal 1982), Ohio Watercolor Soc. (trustee, Silver 1978), Cin. Art Club (pres.), Artists Fellowship Inc. N.Y. Republican. Home: 731 Brooks Ave Wyoming OH 45215

DENNIS, DONALD DALY, librarian; b. Paris, France, Dec. 21, 1928; s. Alonzo Garcelon and Irene Eleanor (Daly) D.; m. Mary Lou Hartig, Oct. 17, 1964. B.A., Bowdoin Coll., 1951, U. Calif., Berkeley, 1956, M.L.S., 1957; postgrad., U. Mich., 1966-67. Reference librarian Free Library of Phila., 1957-60; dept. head Drexel Inst. Library, 1960-62, adj. prof. library sci., 1963-67; head librarian Cedar Crest Coll., Allentown, Pa., 1962-66, Dearborn Campus Library, U. Mich., 1966-67, health scis. librarian, 1967-68; chief reference services div. Nat. Library of Medicine, Bethesda, Md., 1969-71; univ. librarian Am. U., Washington, 1971—; lectr. Coll. Library and Info. Services, U. Md., College Park, 1980-83; library cons. Yarmouk U., Irbid, Jordan, 1983. Author: Simplifying Work in Small Public Libraries, 1965; Contbr. articles to profl. jours. Served to lt. USNR, 1951-55. Council on Library Resources grantee, 1963-65. Mem. ALA, D.C. Library Assn. (dir. 1973-75) library assns), Spl. Libraries Assn., Omicron Delta Kappa. Home: 9204 Seven Locks Rd Bethesda MD 20034 Office: Univ Library Am U Washington DC 20016

DENNIS, EDWARD S(PENCER) G(ALE), JR., lawyer; b. Salisbury, Md., Jan. 24, 1945; s. Edward Spencer and Virginia Monroe (Monroe) D.; m. Lois Juliette Young, Dec. 27, 1969; 1 son, Edward Brookfield. B.S., U.S. Merchant Marine Acad., 1967; LL.D., U. Pa., 1973. Bar: Pa. 1973. Law clk. Hon. A. Leon Higginbotham, Jr., U.S. Dist. Ct., Phila., 1973-75; asst. U.S. atty. U.S. Atty. Office, Phila., 1975-80, dep. chief.Criminal Div., 1978-80; chief Narcotic and Dangerous Drug sect. U.S. Dept. Justice, Washington, 1980-83; U.S. Atty. Eastern Dist. Pa., Phila., 1983—. Mem. ABA, Nat. Bar Assn., Fed. Bar Assn., Phila. Bar Assn., Delaware County Bar Assn., Nat. Orgn. Black Law Enforcement Execs. Office: U S Attys Office 3310 U S Courthouse 601 Market St Philadelphia PA 19106

DENNIS, JACK, political science educator; b. Tulsa, May 24, 1933; s. Joseph Stanley and Mary Jane (Wheeling) D.; m. Barbara Jeanne Lecture, June 18, 1960; children: Brent John, Mark William, Joseph Raymond. B.A., U. Okla., 1955, Oxford U., Eng., 1957, M.A., 1962, U. Chgo., 1960, Ph.D., 1962. Lectr. in polit. sci. Northwestern U., Evanston, Ill., 1962; asst. prof. polit. sci. U. Wis., Madison, 1963-68, assoc. prof., 1968-71, prof., 1971—, past dir. data and program library service, chmn. dept. polit. sci., 1978-81; vis. sr. lectr. in govt. Essex U., Colchester, Eng., 1968-69. Co-author: Children in Political System, 1969; editor: Socialization to Politics, 1973; contbr. articles to profl. jours., chpts. books. Served to 2d lt. U.S. Army, 1957-58. Rhodes scholar, 1955-57; Danforth fellow, 1958-62; Ford Found. faculty fellow, 1970-71; fellow Ctr. Advanced Study in Behavioral Sci., Stanford U., 1975-76, 82-83;. Mem. Am. Polit. Sci. Assn. (program chmn., mem. council 1979-80), Midwest Polit. Sic. Assn. (pres. 1982-83), So. Polit. Sic. Assn., Western Polit. Sci. Assn., Internat. Soc. Polit. Psychology. Democrat. Office: Dept Polit Sci North Hall U Wis Madison WI 53706

DENNIS, JAMES LEON, justice La. Supreme Court; b. Monroe, La., Jan. 9, 1936; s. Jenner Leon and Hope (Taylo) D.; m. Camille Smith; children: Stephen James, Gregory Leon, Mark Taylo, John Timothy. B.S. in Bus. Adminstrn, La. Tech. Inst., Ruston, 1959; J.D., La. State U., 1962; LL.M., U. Va., 1984. Bar: La. 1962. Asso. firm Hudson, Potts & Bernstein, Monroe, 1962-65, partner, 1965-72; judge 4th Dist. Ct. La. for Morehouse and Ouachita Parishes, 1972-74, La. 2d Circuit Ct. Appeals, 1974-75; asso. justice La. Supreme Ct., 1975—; coordinator La. Constnl. Revision Commn., 1970-72; del., chmn. judiciary com. La. Constnl. Conv., 1973; Mem. La. Ho. of Reps., 1968-72. Served with AUS, 1955-57. Mem. Am., La. 4th Jud. bar assns. Methodist. Club: Rotary. Office: Supreme Ct Bldg 301 Loyola Ave New Orleans LA 70112

DENNIS, JAMES LOUDON, medical educator; b. Oklahoma City, Aug. 8, 1913; s. William Bates and Artie (Abernathy) D.; m. Virginia Roueche, June 15, 1940; children: William H., James R., Constant Marie. B.S., U. Okla., 1936, M.D., 1940. Diplomate: Am. Bd. Pediatrics. Intern Highland-Alameda County Hosp., Oakland, Cal., 1941-42; resident medicine Merced County (Cal.) Hosp., 1941-43; resident pediatrics U. Tex. Med. Br., Galveston, 1950-52; asst. prof. pediatrics U. Tex. Med. Sch., 1952-54; dir. edn. Children's Hosp., Med. Center No. Cal., Oakland, 1955-62; prof. pediatrics U. Ark. Med. Sch., 1962-64; dean, dir. U. Okla. Med. Center, 1964-70, v.p., 1967-70; v.p. for health scis. U. Ark., Little Rock, 1970-75, chancellor, 1975-79; mem. Nat. Adv. Commn. Health Facilities, 1968-69; cons. Calif. Dept. Pub. Health, 1959-62, Am. Legion Child Welfare Com., 1962-69; mem. nat. com. Pediatric Research Edn. and Practice, 1961—; chmn. Okla. Commn. Med. Research, 1964-70, Okla. Commn. Handicapped, 1965-70; cons. Nat. Found., Com. Hosp. Care Children. Contbr. numerous articles in field. Bd. dirs. Okla. Med. Research Found., 1964-70, Okla. Health Sci. Fedn., 1965-70, Ark. Chamber Singers; pres. bd. dirs. Council on Aging, 1980-81. Served with M.C. USNR, 1943-46. Fellow Am. Acad. Pediatrics; mem. AMA (council sci. assembly 1965—, chmn. sect. pediatrics 1966), So. Soc. Pediatric Research, AAAS, Am. Pub. Health Assn., Assn. Acad. Health Ctrs. (nat. pres. 1971-72), Oklahoma City C. of C. (dir. 1969-70), Ret. Execs. Assn., Sigma Xi, Alpha Omega Alpha, Alpha Kappa Kappa. Democrat. Methodist. Home: 824 Ridgecrest Dr Little Rock AR 72205 Office: 4301 W Markham Little Rock AR 72201

DENNIS, JOE, educator; b. Sherman, Tex., Dec. 5, 1911; s. Elbert Leander and Maude Clay (Bernard) D.; m. Jeanette Wallis, Aug. 25, 1935; children—Nancy Clay, Linda Joan, Susan Moon. B.A., Austin Coll., 1933, D.Sc. (hon.), 1965; M.A., U. Tex., Med. Sch., 1937, Ph.D., 1942. Tutor biol. chemistry U. Tex. Med. Sch., 1934-36, instr., 1936-38; instr. chemistry Tex. Tech. U., 1938-41, asst. prof. chemistry, 1941-45, asso. prof., 1945-47, prof. chemistry, 1947-50, 69—, prof., head dept. chemistry and chem. engring., 1950-60, head dept. chemistry, 1960-69. Fellow AAAS (S.W. div. pres. 1955), Am. Inst. Chemists; mem. Am. Chem. Soc., Sigma Xi, Phi Kappa Phi. Presbyn. Home: 2718 29th St Lubbock TX 79410 *The only observation I have is: Life is "sorta" like a tube of toothpaste—a small portion of a limited supply is squeezed out for each day. You may as well use it as best you can for you certainly can not get it back in the tube.*

DENNIS, JOHN CARLTON, printing company executive; b. Wichita, Kans., Jan. 3, 1929; s. Carlton Edwin and Lottie (Blizzard) D.; m. Betty Ann Carmichael, Feb. 17, 1952; children: Diana, Robert, Cynthia. B.S. in Mech. Engring., Purdue U., 1951; M.S. in Engring. and Bus. Adminstrn., Ill. Inst. Tech., 1956; Advanced Mgmt. Program, Harvard U., 1981. Sr. engr. R.R. Donnelley & Sons Co., Chgo., 1957-59, various positions in mfg., 1959-65, v.p. mfg., 1965-75, group v.p., 1975-80, sr. group v.p., 1980-81, exec. v.p. ops., 1981—. Bd. dirs. Jr. Achievement Chgo., 1982; trustee Ill. Inst. Tech-, Chgo., 1983. Served to lt. comdr. USN; Korea. Mem. Gravure Tech. Assn. (pres. 1981-83, bd. dirs.). Republican. Episcopalian. Club: Chicago. Address: R R Donnelley & Sons Co 2223 King Dr Chicago IL 60616

DENNIS, JOHN MURRAY, physician, educator; b. Willards, Md., Jan. 31, 1923; s. John Murray and Betty (Hearne) D.; m. Mary Helen France, Oct. 8, 1947; children: Lori Ann, John Murray, Patrick France, Terry Elizabeth. B.S., U. Md., 1943, M.D., 1945. Intern U. Md. Hosp., 1945-46, resident radiology, 1948-50; fellow radiology U. Pa., 1950-51; mem. faculty U. Md. Sch. Medicine and Hosp., 1951—, prof., chmn. dept. radiology, 1953—, acting dean, 1973-74, dean, 1974—, vice chancellor health affairs, 1975—. Pres. Md. div. Am. Cancer Soc., 1962-65, bd. dirs. Md. div., 1955—, nat. bd. dirs., 1965-69. Served with AUS, 1946-48. Recipient Div. award outstanding service Am. Cancer Soc., 1966. Fellow Am. Coll. Radiology (vice chmn. council 1966-68, chmn. 1968-70, exec. com. bd. chancellors 1970—, chmn. bd. chancellors 1975-76, pres. coll. 1976-77, Disting. Service Gold medal 1980); mem. Med. and Chirurgical Faculty Md. (council 1968—, vice chmn. council 1970-71), Am. Roentgen-Ray Soc., Radiol. Soc. N.Am.; hon. mem. Rocky Mountain Radiol. Soc., Ind. Roentgen Soc. Home: 803 Huntsman Rd Towson MD 21204 Office: 655 W Baltimore St Baltimore MD 21201

DENNIS, KENNETH RALPH, hotel, construction, land development company executive; b. Martins Ferry, Ohio, Oct. 17, 1925; s. Ralph L. and Helen M. (McKim) D.; m. Judi Kay Espe, Apr. 30, 1955. B.S. in Math, Miami U., Oxford, O., 1946; postgrad., Ohio State U., 1948-50. Comml. audit mgr. Arthur Andersen & Co., Cin., 1950-65; exec. v.p., controller Del E. Webb Corp., Phoenix, 1966-82, fin. cons., 1983—. Served with USNR, 1944-47. Mem. Am. Inst. C.P.A.s, Ohio Soc. C.P.A.s, Nat. Assn. Accts., Beta Alpha Psi, Beta Gamma Sigma. Home: 3512 E Pasadena Ave Phoenix AZ 85018

DENNIS, PATRICIA DIAZ, government official, lawyer; b. Santa Rita, N.Mex., Oct. 2, 1946; d. Porfirio Madrid and Mary (Romero) Diaz; m. Michael John Dennis, Aug. 3, 1968; children: Ashley Elizabeth, Geoffrey Diaz. A.B. in English, UCLA, 1970; J.D., Loyola U., Los Angeles, 1973. Bar: Calif. 1973. Law clk. Calif. Rural Legal Asst., McFarland, Calif., 1971; assoc. Paul, Hastings, Janofsky & Walker, Los Angeles, 1973-76; atty. Pacific Lighting Corp., Los Angeles, 1976-78; atty., asst. gen. atty ABC, Hollywood, Calif., 1978-83; bd. dirs. NLRB, Washington, 1983-86. Exec. editor: Loyola Law Rev., 1972-73. Bd dirs. Nat. Network Hispanic Women, Stanford, Calif., 1983-84; com. mem. Coro Found. Hispanic Leadership Program, Los Angeles, 1981-82; bd. dirs. Resources for Infant Educarers, Los Angeles, 1981-83. Recipient cert. of Achievement YMCA, Los Angeles, 1979. Mem. Mex.-Am. Bar Assn. (sec. 1980-81, trustee 1979-80, 81-82), Los Angeles County Bar Assn. (child abuse subcom. chmn. barristers sect. 1980-81, exec. com. barristers sect. 1980-82), Hispanic Bar Assn. D.C., ABA (com. labor arbitration and the law in collective bargaining agreements, labor law sect. 1979-82). Democrat. Roman Catholic. Office: Nat Labor Relations Bd 1717 Pennsylvania Ave NW Washington DC 20570

DENNIS, RICHMOND BRAMWELL, corporation executive; b. Mobile, Dec. 14, 1920; s. James Albert and Belva (Morris) D.; m. Barbara Anne Deasy, July 26, 1958. Student, Spring Hill Coll., Mobile,

Loyola U., New Orleans; B.B.A., Tulane U., 1949. With Weis Fricker Mahogany Co., Pensacola, Fla., 1949-50, Otis J. Chamberlain (C.P.A.), New Orleans, 1950-51; successively audit, budget mgr., accounting mgr., regional controller, fin. analysis mgr. Montgomery Ward & Co., Chgo., 1951-66; controller Laclede Steel Co., St. Louis, 1966, treas., 1966, v.p., 1967-70; v.p. fin. and adminstrn. Automobile Club So. Cal., Los Angeles, 1970—; dir. ACSC Mgmt. Services, Inc.; Mem. nat. adv. bd. Am. Automobile Assn. Served with USNR, 1941-46; PTO. Mem. Fin. Execs. Inst. Clubs: Rotary, Annandale Golf, Birnam Wood, Valley Hunt. Home: 535 S Orange Grove Blvd Pasadena CA 91105 Office: 2601 S Figueroa St Los Angeles CA 90007

DENNIS, SANDY, actress; b. Hastings, Nebr., Apr. 27, 1937; d. Jack D.; m. Gerry Mulligan, June 1965. Student, Nebr., Wesleyan U., U. Nebr.; studied acting, Herber Berghof Studio, N.Y.C. Stage debut in: Bus Stop, Palm Beach, Fla.; N.Y. debut, 1957; appeared on: Broadway in Burning Bright, 1960, Face of a Hero, 1960, The Complaisant Lover, 1961, A Thousand Clowns, 1962, Any Wednesday, 1964; film debut in: Splendor in the Grass, 1961; later appeared in: Who's Afraid of Virginia Woolf?, 1965, Up the Down Staircase, 1967, The Fox, 1967, Sweet November, Daphne in Cottage D, The Millstone, Same Time Next Year; appeared in: films The Four Seasons, 1981; plays And Miss Reardon Drinks A Little; toured, 1971,72, Let Me Hear You Smile, 1973, Streetcar Named Desire, 1974, Born Yesterday, 1974, Absurd Person Singular, 1975, Cat on a Hot Tin Roof, 1975, Nasty Habits, 1977; Nasty Habits (Recipient Tony awards for A Thousand Clowns 1963, Any Wednesday 1964, Oscar award as best supporting actress for Who's Afraid of Virginia Woolf, N.Y. Critics Poll award, Moscow Film Festival best-actress award for Up the Down Staircase 1967). Address: care International Creative Mgmt 8899 Beverly Blvd Los Angeles CA 90048 *

DENNIS, WARD BRAINERD, aerospace co. exec.; b. Detroit Lakes, Minn., Aug. 28, 1922; s. Fred and Laura (Bergseng) D.; m. Bette Mae Evans, Mar. 16, 1948; children—Karen Christine, Patrick Ward. B. Aero. Scis., U. Minn., 1943; M.S., U. Mich., 1947; postgrad., Johns Hopkins, 1948-50. With Bell Aircraft Co., 1944-45, Cornell Aero. Lab., 1945-46; asst. prof. U.S. Naval Postgrad. Sch., 1947-50; with Rand Corp., 1950-53, Northrop Corp., 1953—, v.p. corp. devel. planning, 1963—. Pres. Great Western council Boy Scouts Am., 1980; bd. dirs. Los Angeles chpt. Soc. Prevention Cruelty to Animals, 1977-80. Home: 5224-5 Yarmouth Ave Encino CA 91316 Office: 1800 Century Park E Century City Los Angeles CA 90067

DENNIS, WARD HALDAN, university dean; b. Boston, Jan. 8, 1938; s. George Harold and Amarie (Whitters) D.; m. Janet Ruth Young, June 16, 1962; children—Ward Stuart, Heather Amarie, John Bradford. A.B., Middlebury (Vt.) Coll., 1960; M.A., Columbia U., 1961, Ph.D., 1965. Tng. officer Def. Lang. Inst., Monterey, Calif., 1965-67; asst. prof. Spanish Columbia U., 1967-69, asso. dean, then acting dean, 1969-76, dean, 1977, dir., 1974-77; co-founder, mem. Univ. Seminar Latin Am.; cons. in field. Author: Pérez Galdós: A Study in Characterization, 1968; also articles, revs. Served with AUS, 1965-67. Recipient Joint Service Commendation medal; Fulbright-Hays grantee, Quito, Ecuador, 1974. Mem. Latin Am. Studies Assn., Spanish Inst. (dir.), Sigma Delta Pi. Clubs: Niantic Bay Yacht, Nannahagan Swim. Home: 211 Broadway Pleasantville NY 10570 Office: 416 Lewisohn Hall Columbia Univ New York NY 10027

DENNIS, WILLIAM FRANCIS, merchandising company executive; b. Boston, Feb. 13, 1933; s. Edmund Gerard and Marie (Moretti) D.; m. Patricia Ann Terhune, July 18, 1959; children: Steven Craig, Sharon Marie. B.A., Harvard, U., 1954. Exec. trainee ABC, N.Y.C., 1957-59, asst. dir. merchandising, 1959-64, dir. merchandising, 1964-66, v.p. in charge merchandising, 1966-76; exec. v.p. Accent Merchandising Internat., Ltd., N.Y.C., 1976-77; dir. mdse. licensing United Artists Corp., N.Y.C., 1977-79, gen. mgr. merchandise and licensing, 1979-81, v.p., gen. mgr. licensing and merchandising, 1981-82; v.p. licensing and merchandising MGM/VA, 1982—. Served to lt. U.S. Army, 1954-57. Home: 872 Stockton Rd Valley Cottage NY 10989 Office: United Artists Corp 729 7th Ave New York NY 10019

DENNISON, ALFRED DUDLEY, physician, educator; b. Johnstown, N.Y., Jan. 6, 1914; s. Alfred Dudley and Marguerite (France) D.; m. Virginia Lee Beers, Oct. 24, 1940; children: Wayne, Norman, Melanie.; m. Gloria Dennison; children: Angelica, Gloria, Michelle. B.A., Hamilton Coll., 1939; M.D., Cornell U., 1939. Diplomate: Am. Bd. Internal Medicine. Intern, resident, destroyer in, World War II; fellow, instr. cardiology Postgrad. Med. Sch., NYU, N.Y.C., 1948-52; practice cons. cardiology, Indpls., 1953-68; dean Milligan (Tenn.) Coll., 1968-69; asso. in medicine Ind. U. Med. Sch., 1953—; chief of cardiology Meth. Hosp., Indpls., 1964-68, VA Hosp., Johnson City, Tenn., 1969-70, chief of cardiology, asst. chief medicine, Des Moines, 1970-72; asso. prof. medicine, chief cardiology Med. Sch., Tex. Tech. U., El Paso, 1975-77; med. dir. Project Bravo, Ysleta Clinic, El Paso, 1979—; ordained to ministry Christian Ch., 1977; cons. cardiology Univ. Heights and Community hosps., Indpls., Morgan County Hosp., Martinsville, Ind., Hendricks County Hosp., Danville, Ind., Clara Maas and Columbus hosps., Newark, Dallas County Hosp., Perry, Iowa, Greene County Hosp., Jefferson, Iowa; Cons. cardiology Guthrie County Hosp., Guthrie Center, Iowa; fellow in pediatric cardiology Victoria Heart Found., Morris Plains, N.J. Author: Shock It To Me Doctor, 1970, Give It To Me Straight Doctor, 1972, Prescription For Life, 1975, Windows, Ladders, Bridges, 1976; editorial adv. bd.: Emergency Medicine, 1969—; contbr. articles to profl. jours. Trustee Taylor U., Ind. Served to lt. comdr. M.C., USNR, World War II. Fellow ACP, Am. Coll. Chest Physicians (past pres., gov. Ind. chpt.), Am. Coll. Cardiology (past gov. Ind.), Am. Coll. Angiology, Am. Heart Assn. (council on clin. cardiology); mem. Polk County Heart Assn. (dir.), Am. Sci. Affiliation, Theta Delta Chi, Nu Sigma Nu, Alpha Phi Omega. Club: Masons (32 deg.). Office: PO Box 12900 Med Ctr Plaza 1600 Medical Center Dr El Paso TX 79902

DENNISON, BYRON LEE, electrical engineering educator; b. Clarksburg, W.Va., Dec. 8, 1930; s. Raymond Lewis and Edna (Sturm) D.; m. Betty Jean Davis, July 4, 1954; children: Diane Lee, Shirley Joanne. B.S. in Elec. Engring, W. Va. U., 1953, M.S., Va. Poly. Inst., 1962, Ph.D., Worcester Poly. Inst., 1967. Registered profl. engr., Mass., Va., W.Va. Sr. engr. govt. and indsl. div. Philco Corp., Phila., 1953-58; asst. asso. prof. Va. Poly. Inst., Blacksburg, 1958-66; prof. Lowell (Mass.) Tech. Inst., 1966-74, adj. prof., 1974-77, head dept. elec. engring., 1967-72; vis. prof. Va. Poly. Inst. and State U., 1977-79, Southeastern Mass. U., 1979-81, adj. prof., 1982, U. Lowell, 1982—, Merrimack Coll., 1983—; cons. Polysci. Corp., Blacksburg, 1961-63, Worcester Found. Exptl. Biology, Shrewsbury, Mass., 1966-68. Mem. I.E.E.E., Am. Soc. Engring. Edn., Sigma Xi, Eta Kappa Nu, Phi Kappa Phi. Research devel. math. model for motor activity of cat iris. Home: 70 Patten Rd RFD 4 Westford MA 01886

DENNISON, CHARLES STUART, institutional executive; b. N.Y.C., Mar. 21, 1918; s. Charles Stuart and Charlotte (Irwin) D.; m. Carol Frances Krueger, June 6, 1951; children: Laura Hardie, Deborah Irwin. Student, Columbia, N.Y.U. Exec. trainee Gen. Motors Corp., 1935-39; asst. mgr. advt. and sales promotion U.S. Steel Export Co., 1939-42; export sales mgr., acting gen. sales mgr. Willys Overland Motors, Inc., 1946-51; mng. dir. Olin Mathieson Ltd., also E.R. Squibb Ltd., London, Eng., 1951-57; v.p. Chrysler Export Corp., 1957-58; v.p. overseas Internat. Minerals & Chem. Corp., Skokie, Ill., 1958-70; dir. Internat. Minerals & Chem., Ltd., London, Eng., Internat. Minerals & Chem., Ltd. Pty., Australia, Internat. Minerals & Chem., Ltd. (Bahamas), Internat. Minerals & Chem., Ltd. (Can.), Panama, Coromandel Fertilisers, Ltd., Secunderabad, India, Compagnie Senegalaise des Phosphates de Taiba, Dakar, Azufrera Intercontinental S.A. de C.V., Mexico, until 1970; exec. Council Sci. and Tech., Washington; Mem. Pres.'s Sci. Advisory Com. Panel on World Food Supply, 1967; mem. exec. com. FAO Industry Coop. Program, Rome, until 1970; mem. industry adv. com. FAO, Rome; mem. council Soc. for Internat. Devel.; mem. com. on Internat. Devel. Inst., Nat. Acad. Scis.; mem. fgn. relations task force White House Conf. on Youth; mem. com. on tech. Council of Americas, 1973; bd. dirs. Assn. Internat. des Etudiants en Scis. Economiques et Commerciales; adv. mem. U.S. delegation OAS Conf. on Application Sci. and Tech. to Devel. Latin Am.; mem. bd. sci. and tech. for internat. devel. Nat. Acad. Scis., 1973-78; mem. Com. on Environ. Aspects U.S. Materials Policy; chmn. panel role U.S. firms R.D. & E. developing countries Nat. Acad. Scis.; mem. panel on internat. indsl. inst. Nat. Acad. Engring.; mem. com. pub. engring. policy NRC; sr. adviser UN Environment Program; exec. dir. Council Sci. and Tech. for Devel., 1977—; mem. Scowcroft panel on U.S. Security and Third World Policy Ctr. Strategic and Internat. Studies, 1980-82; dir. Bull. Atomic Scientists; lectr. univs. Trustee Agrl. Devel. Council, to 1974; bd. dirs. Overseas Devel. Council. Served to capt., parachute inf. AUS, World War II. Decorated Bronze Star, Combat Inf. badge; comdr. Order Merit, Senegal). Mem. English Speaking Union, Council Fgn. Relations. Clubs: Metropolitan (N.Y.C.); American (London). Box 369 Wainscott NY 11975

DENNISON, DAVID SHORT, JR., lawyer; b. Poland, Ohio, July 29, 1918; s. David Short and Cordelia (Whitman) D.; m. Dorothy Kelsey Houlette, May 11, 1973; children by previous marriage: Jennie, David Whitman. Student, Western Res. Acad., 1936; A.B., Williams Coll., 1940; LL.B., Western Res. U., 1945. Bar: Ohio 1946, D.C. 1959, Pa. 1975, Calif. 1977. Pvt. practice, Warren, Ohio, 1946-70, 74-75; v.p., gen. counsel, sec. Wheeling-Pitts. Steel Corp., 1975-78; of counsel firm Walker, McCure, Bonnen & Brehmer, Monterey, Calif., 1981—; mem. 85th Congress from Ohio, 1957-58; cons. (U.S. Civil Rights Commn.), 1959; mem. FTC, 1970-74. Chmn. Trumbull County (Ohio) Republican Central and Exec. Coms., 1964-66; mem. Ohio Republican Central Com., 1966-70, Trumbull County Bd. Elections, 1964-68; bd. dirs. Monterey Coll. Law. Served with Am. Field Service, World War II. Mem. ABA, Ohio, Calif., Monterey County bar assns. Home: 1004 San Carlos Rd Pebble Beach CA 93953 Office: PO Box LAW Monterey CA 93940

DENNISON, JOHN MANLEY, geologist, educator; b. Keyser, W.Va., Apr. 13, 1934; s. Raymond Lewis and Edna (Sturm) D.; m. Faye Lee, Mar. 7, 1981; 1 son by previous marriage, John Robert. B.S., W.Va. U., 1954, M.S., 1955; Ph.D., U. Wis., 1960. Asst. prof., then assoc. prof. U. Ill., Urbana, 1960-65; assoc. prof. U. Tenn., Knoxville, 1965-67; prof. geology U. N.C., Chapel Hill, 1967—, chmn. dept., 1967-74. Author: Concepts in Physical Science, 1965, Analysis of Geologic Structures, 1968, Geology, 1974, also articles. Served with U.S. Army, 1955-57. Fellow Geol. Soc. Am., AAAS; mem. Am. Assn. Petroleum Geologists, Paleontol. Soc. Address: 13 Bluff Trail Chapel Hill NC 27514

DENNISON, STANLEY SCOTT, lumber company executive; b. Mitchelville, Md., Sept. 1, 1920; s. Ralph Stanford and Cora Adeline (Scott) D.; m. Sharon Lee Johnson, June 1, 1968; children by previous marriage: Judith Dennison Tucci (dec.), Joan Dennison Daffron, Joyce D. Dennison Bischoff. Ed., Columbia Union Coll.; B.S., M.B.A., Calif. Western U., Ph.D., 1982. Operative builder Dennison Co., 1939-43; traffic rep. U.P. R.R., 1943-49; v.p. Arlington Millwork, Va., 1949-52, Internat. Filling Machine Co., Petersburg, Va., 1952-57, Atlanta Oak Flooring Co., 1957-62; regional mgr. Ga.-Pacific Corp., Portland, Oreg., 1962-70, v.p., 1970-78, sr. v.p., 1978-82, exec. v.p., 1982—. Bd. regents U. Portland; bd. advisors Calif. Western U.; bd. dirs. Atlanta Symphony, Central Atlanta Progress. Mem. Atlanta Commn. on Fgn. Relations, Western Forestry Assn. (charter), Alpha Kappa Psi. Democrat. Roman Catholic. Clubs: Capital City, Commerce (Atlanta). Home: 2575 Peachtree Rd NE Apt 14-c Atlanta GA 30305 Office: 133 Peachtree St NE Atlanta GA 30303

DENNISTON, F. EDWIN, industrial equipment company executive; b. Seattle, Jan. 25, 1922; s. Albert Glenn and Mary Malott (Day) D.; m. Anne Louise Edwardson, Jan. 22, 1949; children: Leslie Anne, Jeffrey Scott, Lory Louise. B.S., U. Oreg., 1947; J.D., U. San Francisco, 1952. Tax acct. U.S. Steel Corp., San Francisco, 1947-52; asst. controller Fibreboard Corp., San Francisco, 1952-67; corp. tax dir. Evans Products Co., Portland, Oreg., 1967-78, v.p. taxes, 1978—; lectr. taxes Portland State U. Author papers in field. Served with USAAF, 1943-45. Mem. Tax Execs. Inst. (past pres. San Francisco and Portland chpts., past nat. dir., v.p., mem. exec. com.), U.S. C. of C. Republican. Club: Masons. Office: PO Box 3295 Portland OR 97208

DENNLER, CARL, JR., accounting educator; b. Washington, Mo., Oct. 15, 1923; s. Carl L. and Lona (Rogers) D.; m. Mary Jeanne McDonald, June 3, 1951; children: McDonald K., Christine D. B.S. in Bus. Adminstrn, U. Mo., 1948, M.A. in Econs, 1950; Ph.D. in Accounting, U. Wis., 1962. Instr., then asst. prof. U. Maine, 1952-57; asso. prof. W.Va. U., 1957-63; mem. faculty U. Mass., 1963—, prof. accounting, 1968-80; prof. acctg. Fla. Atlantic U., 1980—. Editor: Acct.'s Digest. Served with USAAF, 1943-46. Mem. Am. Acctg. Assn., Beta Gamma Sigma, Beta Alpha Psi, Tau Kappa Epsilon. Club: Kiwanian. Home: 7765 Kenway Pl Boca Raton FL 33433

DENNLER, WILLIAM VAN AUKEN, zoo director; b. Schenectady, June 18, 1948; s. William Howard and Ruth (Van Auken) D.; m. Jeanne Strunk, Aug. 26, 1972; children: Kimberly Anne, Jeffrey Van Auken. B.S., Lake Forest Coll., Ill., 1970; M.B.A., Ind. U., 1973. Zoo keeper Cin. Zoo, 1972-75; curator of reptiles Toledo Zoo, 1975-80, exec. dir., 1981—. Fellow Am. Assn. Zool. Parks and Aquariums. Republican. Congregationalist. Lodge: Toledo Rotary. Office: Toledo Zoological Society 2700 Broadway Toledo OH 43609

DENNSTEDT, FREDERICK DEVERE, oil company executive; b. Harmony, Minn., Sept. 23, 1918; s. Frederick William and Ida Henrietta (Bruflodt) D.; m. Marjorie Ernst, July 7, 1948; children: Frederick Ernst, Sara Elizabeth. B.Chem. Engring., U. Minn., 1948; grad., Advanced Mgmt. Program, Harvard U., 1958. With Esso Standard Oil Co., 1948-61, asst. gen. mgr. Baton Rouge refinery, 1959-61; with Humble Oil & Refining Co. (now Exxon Co. U.S.A.), 1961-64, v.p. mfg. dept., 1962-63, v.p. supply and transp. dept., 1963-64, v.p. refining, Houston, 1969-79, sr. v.p., 1979—; refining coordinator Standard Oil Co, N.J., 1964-68; logistics ops. mgr., 1968-69. Mem. Am. Petroleum Inst. Home: 45 Briar Hollow 6 Houston TX 77027 Office: 800 Bell St Houston TX 77002

DENNY, BREWSTER CASTBERG, educator, university dean; b. Seattle, Sept. 5, 1924; s. Merle Wilson and Margaraith (Castberg) D.; m. Patricia Virginia Sollitt, June 14, 1950; 1 dau., Maria Janet. A.B., U. Wash., 1945; M.A., Fletcher Sch. Law and Diplomacy, 1948, Ph.D., 1959. Instr. Mass. Inst. Tech., 1948-52; with Office of Sec. of Def., 1952-60; profl. staff mem. Sub-Com. on Nat. Policy Machinery, U.S. Senate, 1960-61; asso. prof. pub. affairs U. Wash., 1961-64, prof. pub. affairs, 1964—, 1st dir., 1962-68, 1st dean, 1968-80, dean emeritus, 1980—, chmn. marine affairs bd., 1972-79; U.S. rep. to 23d gen. assembly UN, 1968; cons. to RAND Corp., 1961-68; mem. vis. com. dept. govt. Harvard, 1967-72; mem. Presdl. Adv. Council on Intergovtl. Personnel Policy, 1971-74; chmn. Gov.'s Task Force on Exec. Orgn., 1968-72; presdl. mem. U.S.-P.R. Commn. on Status of P.R., 1964-66; mem. bd. sci. and tech. in devel. Nat. Acad. Scis., 1976-81, co-chmn. Korean com. on sci. and tech., 1977—. Contbr. to: Am. Polit. Sci. Rev; author, co-author, editor articles, books, chpts., and reports. Trustee 20th Century Fund, 1975—, vice chmn., 1982—. Served to ensign USNR, 1943-46; to lt., 1952-54. Mem. UN Assn. U.S.A. (mem. nat. policy panel on UN capabilities in the 1970's 1970-71), Nat. Acad. Pub. Adminstrn., Am. Soc. for Pub. Adminstrn., Am. Polit. Sci. Assn., Council Fgn. Relations, AAAS (com. on new directions 1975-78, charter mem. com. on sci. and pub. policy 1968—, com. on arms control 1980—), Nat. Assn. Schs. Pub. Affairs and Adminstrn. (pres. 1968-69). Home: 5866 NE Parkpoint Dr Seattle WA 98115 Office: Grad Sch Pub Affairs U Wash Seattle WA 98195

DENNY, FLOYD WOLFE, JR., pediatrician; b. Hartsville, S.C., Oct. 22, 1923; s. Floyd Wolfe and Marion Elizabeth (Porter) D.; m. Barbara H. Denny, Apr. 27, 1946; children: Rebecca E., Mark W., Timothy P. B.S., Wofford Coll., 1944; M.D., Vanderbilt U., 1946. Diplomate: Am. Bd. Pediatrics. Intern Vanderbilt Hosp., Nashville, 1946-47, resident in pediatrics, 1947-48; instr. pediatrics U. Minn., 1951-52, asst. prof., 1952-53; asst. prof. pediatrics Vanderbilt U. Sch. Medicine, 1953-55; asst. prof. preventive medicine and pediatrics Western Res. U. Sch. Medicine, 1955-60, asso. prof. preventive medicine, 1960; prof. Sch. Medicine, U. N.C., Chapel Hill, 1960—, chmn. dept. pediatrics, 1960-81; vis. scholar dept. epidemiology Sch. Pub. Health and Child Devel. Inst., 1977-78; vis. worker Med. Research Council Clin. Research Centre, London, 1970-71; mem. Commn. on Streptococcal and Staphylococcal Diseases Armed Forces Epidemiol. Bd., 1954-72, dep. dir., 1959-63; mem. Commn. on Acute Respiratory Diseases Armed Forces Epidemiol. Bd., 1960-73, dep. dir., 1963-67, dir., 1967-73; mem. Inst. Medicine, Nat. Acad. Scis., 1981-86. Mem. editorial bd.: Am. Rev. Respiratory Diseases, 1971-74; mem. publs. com.: Jour. Infectious Diseases, 1973-78; Contbr. articles to med. jours. Served to maj. M.C. U.S. Army, 1948-51. Mem. Am. Acad. Pediatrics, Am. Assn. Immunologists, Am. Epidemiology Soc., Am. Fedn. Clin. Research, Am. Pediatric Soc. (pres. 1980-81), Am. Soc. Clin. Investigation, Am. Soc. Microbiology, Am. Thoracic Soc., Assn. Am. Physicians, Infectious Diseases Soc. Am. (pres. 1979-80), Soc. Exptl. Biology and Medicine, Soc. Pediatric Research (pres. 1968-69), So. Soc. Clin. Research, So. Soc. Pediatric Research, Phi Beta Kappa, Alpha Omega Alpha. Home: Route 10 Box 56 Chapel Hill NC 27514 Office: Dept Pediatrics 535 Burnett-Womack Bldg 229-H U NC Sch of Medicine Chapel Hill NC 27514

DENNY, JAMES MCCAHILL, pharmaceutical company executive; b. Mpls., Oct. 25, 1932; s. Charles M. and Mary (McCahill) D.; m. Catherine Mary Florence, Aug. 19, 1961; children: James, Philip F., Sarah, Matthew J., Catherine, William C. Student, Princeton U., 1950-54; B.A., U. Minn., 1957; LL.B., Georgetown U., 1960. Bar: N.Y. State 1963. Asso. firm Dewey, Ballantine, N.Y.C., 1960-65, Paris, 1965-68, N.Y.C., 1968; asst. counsel Firestone Tire and Rubber Co., Akron, Ohio, 1968-71, asst. treas., 1972-75, treas., 1975-78; sr. v.p. fin., chief fin. officer G.D. Searle & Co., Skokie, Ill., 1978—; dir. Gen. Binding Corp., Bankers Life Co. Treas. Children's Hosp., 1972-75, v.p., 1976. Served with U.S. Army, 1954-56. Mem. Assn. Bar of City of N.Y., Am. Bar Assn., Am. Soc. Internat. Law, Fin. Execs. Inst. Clubs: Princeton (N.Y.C.); Union Interallie (Paris). Office: GD Searle & Co Box 1045 Skokie IL 60076

DENNY, J(AMES) WILLIAM, utility executive; b. Nashville, Aug. 25, 1935; s. James R. and Margaret (Osment) D.; m. June Ralls, Aug. 31, 1957; children: Kevin, Steven, Jennifer. Student, Vanderbilt U., 1953-57. Road mgr. Philip Morris Country Music Show, 1957-58; pres. So. Star Investors Assos., 1960; account exec. McDonald & Alsup Advt. Agy., 1958-59; mgmt. trainee Third Nat. Bank, Nashville, 1959-61; mgr. Columbia Records Rec. Studio, also Columbia Records Custom Prodns., 1961-63; exec. v.p. Sta. WJAT, Swainsboro, Ga., Sta. WRBO, Waynesboro, Ga., Sta. WSNT, Sandersville, Ga., 1963-67; pres. Cedarwood Pub. Co., Inc., Nashville, 1963—; pres., dir. Nashville Gas Co., 1983—; partner Hatch Show Print, 1964—; pres., dir. Country Music Assn., 1966—, chmn. bd., 1974-75; asso. prof. Belmont Coll., Nashville, 1975—; dir. Tenn. Natural Gas Lines Inc., Nashville City Bank. Mem. Met. Nashville Auditorium Commn., 1977—; chmn. bd. Country Music Found., 1967, pres., 1968; Pres. Leadership Nashville Alumni Assn., 1977-78; bd. dirs. Nashville Cancer Soc., 1967-69, Brentwood Acad., 1971-80, Nashville Children's Hosp., 1978—; mem. Nashville Century III Com., 1978-79; trustee Wilkerson Speech and Hearing Center, 1975-79. Recipient Spl. Achievement award Record World mag., 1967; named Country Music Pub. of Year Music Bus. mag., 1964. Mem. Nat. Acad. Rec. Arts and Scis. (trustee 1965-82, pres. 1977-79), Nashville Jr. C. of C. (gov., Man of Year award 1967), Sigma Alpha Epsilon, Alpha Phi Omega. Methodist (dir. 1967—). Home: 800 Caldwell Ln Nashville TN 37204 Office: 815 16th Ave Nashville TN 37203

DENOON, DAVID BAUGH HOLDEN, ecoomist, educator, consultant; b. Toledo, Apr. 12, 1945; s. Clarence E. and Eleanor (Kratz) D. B.A., Harvard U., 1966; M.P.A., Princeton U., 1968; Ph.D., MIT, 1975. Asst. to chmn. Pa. State Bd. Edn., 1968; program economist U.S. AID, Dept. of State, Jakarta, Indonesia, 1969-71; asst. to pres. Nat. Bur. Econ. Research, N.Y.C., 1971-72; asst. prof. politics and econs. NYU, 1975-78, 79-80, assoc. prof. politics and econs., 1982—; v.p. U.S. Export-Import Bank, Washington, 1978-79; dep. asst. sec. U.S. Dept. Def., Washington, 1981-82; cons. Ford Found., N.Y.C., 1977-78-, 83—, U.S. Dept. Def., Washington, 1982—. Editor, contbr.: The New International Economic Order: A U.S. Response, 1979. Active Bucks County Land Use Task Force, 1975-78, Bucks Rep. Com., 1976-78. Mem. Asia Soc., Am. Econ. Assn., Am. Polit. Sci. Assn. Clubs: Harvard (N.Y.); Cosmos (Washington). Home: 3609 Creamery Rd Wycombe PA 18980 Office: NYU 25 Waverly Pl New York NY 10003

DENOV, SAM, musician; b. Chgo., Dec. 11, 1923; s. Jacob and Ida (Goldberg) D.; m. Charlotte June Jacobson, May 15, 1943; children—Donald Jack, Ernest Michael. Grad., U.S. Navy Sch. Music, 1943; B.G.S., Roosevelt U., 1973. Clinician Avedis Zildjian Co., Norwell, Mass. Cymbalist, San Antonio Symphony, 1947-50, Pitts. Symphony, 1950-52, Chgo. Symphony, 1954—; Author: The Art of Playing the Cymbals, 1963; featured in: ednl. film Cymbal Techniques, 1970 (honorable mention Am. Film Festival, N.Y. 1970). Chmn. Internat. Conf. Symphony and Opera Musicians, 1969-70. Served with USN, 1942-46. Recipient Chgo. Certificate of Merit, 1971; Commendation of both houses Ill. Gen. Assembly, 1971; named Chicagoan of Year Chgo. Press Club, 1971. Mem. Percussive Arts Soc. Inventor automatic electronic tuner for timpani. Home: 3200 N Lake Shore Dr Chicago IL 60657 Office: 220 S Michigan Ave Chicago IL 60604

DENOVO, JOHN AUGUST, history educator; b. Galva, Ill., Nov. 5, 1916; s. August and Paula (LaMantia) DeN.; m. E. Jeanne Humphreys, Dec. 22, 1948; children: Anne, John H. B.A., Knox Coll., Galesburg, Ill., 1938; M.A., U. Minn., 1940; Ph.D., Yale U., 1948;

postdoctoral student, Harvard U., 1956-57, Johns Hopkins U., 1957. Teaching asst. U. Minn., 1939-41; asst. in instrn. Yale U., 1947; from instr. to prof. Am. history Pa. State U., 1948-64; prof. history U. Wis., 1964-82, prof. emeritus, 1982—; vis. lectr. George Washington U., summer 1949; vis. asso. prof. U. Wis., summer 1961; vis. prof. Cornell U., 1963-64. Author: American Interests and Policies in the Middle East, 1900-1939, 1963; Editor: Selected Readings in American History, 2 vols, 1969, The Gilded Age and After, 1972; Contbr. articles, chpts. in books. Served to lt. USNR, 1941-45. Recipient Knox Coll. Alumni Achievement award, 1984; Grantee Social Sci. Research Council, summer 1956, 59; Ford Found. fellow, 1956-57; Faculty fellow Assn. Middle Eastern Studies, summer 1963; Rockefeller fellow, 1966-67; vis. scholar ERDA, 1976-77. Mem. Soc. Historians Am. Fgn. Relations (mem. council 1969-73), Am. Hist. Assn., Orgn. Am. Historians, Middle East Studies Assn., Phi Alpha Theta (Book prize 1964). Home: 4802 Regent St Apt 112B Madison WI 53705

DENOYER, JOHN MILFORD, geologist; b. Kalaw, Burma, May 19, 1926; s. Andrew J. and Mary (Gibbs) DeN.; m. Doris H. Hoffman, Nov. 3, 1951; children: Barbara J., Linda A., Perry H., Emily J. A.B., Chico State Coll., 1953; M.A., U. Cal.-Berkeley, 1955; Ph.D., U. Calif.-Berkeley, 1958. From instr. to assoc. prof. U. Mich., Ann Arbor, 1957-65, acting head acoustics and seismics lab., 1963-65; staff mem. Inst. for Def. Analyses, Washington, 1962-63; dep. dir. Nuclear Test Detection, Advanced Research Projects Agy., Washington, 1965-67; asst. dir. research U.S. Geol. Survey, Washington, 1967-69; dir. Earth Observations Programs Hdqrs. NASA, Washington, 1969-72, Earth Resources Observations Systems Program, U.S. Geol. Survey, 1972-79; research geophysicist U.S. Geol. Survey, 1978—. Served with AUS, 1944-46, 50-51. Recipient Henry Russel award U. Mich., 1964; Exceptional Service medal NASA, 1972; Meritorious Service award Dept. Interior, 1977; William T. Pecora award Dept. Interior and NASA, 1979. Fellow AAAS (council 1968-73); mem. Am. Geophys. Union (mem. council 1968-70), Seismol. Soc. Am., Geol. Soc. Am., Acoustical Soc. Am., Sigma Xi. Home: 4835 Drummond Ave Chevy Chase MD 20815 Office: Nat Center Stop 951 US Geological Survey Reston VA 22092

DENSEN, PAUL MAXIMILLIAN, health adminstr.; b. N.Y.C., Aug. 1, 1913; s. Charles Edwin and Carrie (Weinberg) D.; m. Elizabeth A. Reed, Dec. 19, 1939; children—Rebecca E. (Mrs. John Rothfuss), Peter. A.B., Bklyn.Coll., 1934; D.Sc., Johns Hopkins, 1939; M.A. (hon.), Harvard, 1968. From instr. to asso. prof. preventive medicine Vanderbilt U. Med. Sch., 1939-46; chief div. med. research statistics VA, Washington, 1946-49; asso. prof., then prof. biometry Grad. Sch. Pub. Health, U. Pitts., 1949-54; dir. div. research and statistics Health Ins. Plan Greater N.Y., 1954-59; dept. commr. N.Y.C. Dept. Health, 1959-66; dept. adminstr. N.Y.C. Health Services Adminstrn., 1966-68; dir. Harvard Center Community Health and Med. Care, 1968—; prof. community health Harvard Sch. Pub. Health, 1968—. Fellow Am. Statis. Assn., Am. Pub. Health Assn., AAAS; mem. Am. Epidemiol. Soc., Inst. Medicine. Home: PO Box 304 Sandown NH 03873 Office: 643 Huntington Ave Boston MA 02115

DENSEN-GERBER, JUDIANNE, psychiatrist, lawyer, educator; b. N.Y.C., Nov. 13, 1934; d. Gustave A. and Beatrice Densen; m. Michael M. Baden, June 14, 1958; children: Trissa Austin, Judson Michael, Lindsey Robert, Sarah Densen. A.B. cum laude, Bryn Mawr Coll., 1956; LL.B., Columbia U., 1959, J.D., 1969; M.D., NYU, 1963. Bar: N.Y. 1961. Rotating intern French Hosp., N.Y.C., 1963-64; resident psychiatry Bellevue Hosp., N.Y.C., 1964-65, Met. Hosp., 1965-67; mem. core staff Addiction Services Agy., N.Y.C., 1966-67; founder Odyssey House (psychiat. hosp. for rehab. narcotics addicts), N.Y.C., Mich., Maine, N.H., Utah, La., Australia, N.Z., 1967, clin. dir., 1967-69, exec. dir., 1969—, pres. bd., 1967—; pres. Odyssey Inst. Am., 1974—, Odyssey Inst. Australia, 1977—, Odyssey Inst. Internat., Inc., 1978—; asso. vis. prof. law U. Utah Law Sch., 1973-75; adj. prof. law N.Y. Law Sch., 1973-76; chairperson plenary session drug abuse Am. Acad. Forensic Scis., 1972, sec. psychiatry sect., 1973, chmn. sect., 1974—; founder, 1973, since pres. Inst. Women's Wrongs; founder, since pres. Odyssey Inst. (health care for socially disadvantaged), 1974—; bd. dirs. Simpson St. Devel. Assn., 1969, An Extraordinary Event (One to One for Mental Retardation), 1973—; mem. Nat. Adv. Commn. Criminal Justice Standards and Goals, 1971—, Pres.'s Commn. on White House Fellows, 1972-76; mem. drug experience adv. com. HEW, 1973-76; v.p. psychiat. sect. Internat. Forensic Medicine Conf., Budapest, 1967; pres. N.Y. Council Alcoholism, 1978—; guest lectr. narcotics addiction NYU Sch. Medicine, also Sch. Law; cons. in field; dir. Daitch Shopwell, Inc. Author: (with Trissa Austin Baden) Drugs, Sex, Parents and You, 1972, We Mainline Dreams, The Odyssey House Story, 1973, Walk in My Shoes, 1976; contbr. articles to profl. jours.; editor: Jour. Corrective and Social Psychiatry, 1975. Mem. N.Y.C. Crime Control Commn., 1975-79. Recipient Woman of Achievement award AAUW, 1970; Myrtle Wreath award Hadassah, 1970; B'nai B'rith Woman of Greatness award, 1971; Otty award for service to N.Y.C. Our Town Newspaper, 1977; named Dame of White Cross, Australia, Dame of Malta, Ky. Col., N.Y. State Hon. Fire Chief. Mem. AMA, N.Y. State, N.Y. County med. socs., Soc. Med. Jurisprudence, Therapeutic Communities of Am. (founding mem., 1st v.p. 1975—), Am. Acad. Psychiatry and Law, Am. Psychiat. Assn., N.Y. County Women's Bar Assn., N.Y. Assn. Vol. Agys. Narcotics Addiction and Substance Abuse (dir. 1968—). Republican. Unitarian. Club: Women's City (N.Y.C.). Office: 817 Fairfield Ave Bridgeport CT 06604

DENSMORE, WILLIAM PHILLIPS, management consultant; b. Brookline, Mass., June 16, 1924; s. Edward Dana and Annie Louise (Walley) D.; m. Martha Cox Lowell, Nov. 5, 1949; children: Elizabeth C., William P., Deborah L. B.S. M.E., Worcester Poly. Inst., 1945. With Norton Co., Worcester, Mass., 1946-82, v.p., gen. mgr., 1971-79, v.p. abrasive ops., U.S., Can., 1979-81, sr. v.p., 1981-82; v.p. L.F. McManus Inc., 1983—. Mem. Mass. State Bd. Edn., 1970-77; dir. Central Mass. Health Systems Agy., 1977-79; mem. mgmt. bd. U. Mass. Hosp., 1980—; bd. dirs. Worcester Heritage Preservation Soc., 1977-82; Trustee Worcester Poly. Inst.; chmn. Worcester Area Systems for Affordable Health Care, Worcester Area Sch./Bus. Partnership. Served with USNR, 1943-46. Mem. Worcester Area C. of C. Club: Worcester. Home: 10 Algonquin Rd Worcester MA 01609 Office: 446 Martin St Worcester MA 01606

DENT, BUCKY *See* **DENT, RUSSELL EARL**

DENT, FREDERICK BAILY, former ambassador, former secretary commerce, mill executive; b. Cape May., N.J., Aug. 17, 1922; s. Magruder and Edith (Baily) D.; m. Mildred C. Harrison, Mar. 11, 1944; children: Frederick Baily, Mildred Hutcheson, Pauline Harrison, Diana Gwynn, Magruder Harrison. B.A., Yale U., 1943. With Joshua L. Baily & Co., Inc., N.Y.C., 1946-47; with Mayfair Mills, Arcadia, S.C., 1947—, pres., 1958—, treas., 1977—, also dir.; sec. Dept. Commerce, Washington, 1973-75; ambassador, spl. rep. for trade negotiations, 1975-77; past dir. Gen. Electric Co., Crompton Co., Scott Paper Co., Mut. Life Ins. Co. N.Y.; dir. Armco Inc., Comsat, Internat. Paper Co., S.C. Johnson & Son, Inc., Joshua L. Baily & Co., S.C. Nat. Corp., S.C. Nat. Bank. Chmn. Spartanburg County Planning and Devel. Commn., 1960-72; Bus. Council. Trustee Inst. Textile Tech., Spartanburg Day Sch.; mem. corp. Yale U. Served with USNR, 1943-46. Episcopalian. Home: 19 Montgomery Dr Spartanburg SC 29302

DENT, HAROLD DUANE, manufacturing company executive; b. Kansas City, Mo., Aug. 9, 1938; s. Kenneth M. and Helen L. (Crumbaker) D.; m. Judith Marie Lassiter, May 30, 1959; children: Douglas D., Jeanne M. A.A., Kansas City Jr. Coll., 1950; B.S., Kans. State U., 1961; postgrad., Sloan Sch. Sr. Execs., M.I.T., 1980. With Internat. Harvester Co., Kansas City, Mo., 1961—, v.p. parts ops., Chgo., 1979-80, v.p., gen. mgr. medium truck div., 1980-81, v.p., gen. mgr. internat. ops., 1981-82; pres. Internat. Harvester Can. Ltd., Hamilton, Ont., Can., 1982—; v.p., dir. Internat. Harvester, Credit Corp. Can. Ltd., 1982—; dir. Internat. Harvester Can. Ltd., 1982—. Mem. Motor Vehicle Mfrs. Assn. (dir.), Canadian Farm and Indsl. Equipment Inst. (dir.), Hamilton Dist. C. of C., Ont. C. of C. Clubs: Hamilton, Royal Hamilton Yacht. Office: Internat Harvester Can Ltd 208 Hillyard St Hamilton ON Canada L8N 3S5

DENT, RUSSELL EARL (BUCKY DENT), professional baseball player; b. Savannah, Ga., Nov. 25, 1951; m. Stormy Dent. Student, Miami-Dade Community Coll. Baseball player Chgo. White Sox, 1973-76, N.Y. Yankees, 1977-82, Tex. Rangers, 1982—; player Am. League Championship Series, 1977, 78, 80, World Series, 1977, 78; mem. Am. League All-Star Team, 1975, 80. Named Most Valuable Player World Series, 1977. Office: care Texas Rangers Arlington Stadium PO Box 1111 Arlington TX 76010 *

DENT, V. EDWARD, former advertising and communications company executive; b. Green Bay, Wis., Oct. 17, 1918; s. Florian E. and Loretta M. (Castona) D. B.S., U. Wis., 1940. Mng. editor pharmacy publs. McGraw-Hill Co., N.Y.C., 1946-49; exec. v.p. L.W. Frohlich and Co. Intercon Inter Inc., N.Y.C., 1949-72; exec. dir. Nat. Sci. Network, N.Y.C., 1964-72; chmn. bd. Medicus Communications, Inc., 1972-78, Sci. and Medicine Pub. Co., Inc., 1977—, Cinemed Systems, Inc. (subs. Benton & Bowles, Inc.), N.Y.C., 1977-78. Exec. v.p. Aston Magna Found. Served to 1st lt. AUS, 1941-46; PTO. Home: Tater Hill Rd Old Lyme CT 06371

DENTLER, ROBERT ARNOLD, sociologist, educator; b. Chgo., Nov. 26, 1928; s. Arnold E. and Jennie (Munsen) D.; m. Helen Hosmer, Sept. 7, 1950; children: Deborah, Eric, Robin. B.S., Northwestern U., 1949, M.A., 1950; M.A., Am. U., 1954; Ph.D., U. Chgo., 1960. Reporter Chgo. City News Bur., 1949; tchr. Pomfret Sch., 1950-52; with U.S. Civil Service, 1952-54; instr. Dickinson Coll., 1954-57; fellow U. Chgo., 1957-59; researcher U. Kans., 1959-61; asst. prof. Dartmouth Coll., 1961-62; mem. faculty Tchrs. Coll., Columbia U., N.Y.C., 1962-72; prof. sociology, dep. dir. to dir. Tchrs. Coll., Columbia (Center for Urban Edn.), 1966-72; dean Sch. Edn., Boston U., 1972-79; sr. sociologist Abt Assocs., Cambridge, Mass., 1979-83; prof. sociology U. Mass., Boston, 1983—. Author: (with Peter Rossi) The Politics of Urban Renewal, 1961, (with Nelson W. Polsby and Paul A. Smith) Politics and Social Life, 1963, (with Phillips Cutright) Hostage America, 1963, (with B. Mackler and M.E. Warshauer) The Urban R's: Race Relations as the Problem in Urban Education, 1967, Major American Social Problems, 1967, (with M.E. Warshauer) Big City Dropouts and Illiterates, 1967, American Community Problems, 1967, Major Social Problems, 1973, Urban Problems, 1977, (with M.B. Scott) Schools on Trial: An Inside Account of the Boston School Desegregation Case, 1981, (with D.C. Baltzell and D.J. Sullivan) University on Trial, 1983. Home: 11 Childs Rd Lexington MA 02173 Office: Univ Mass Dept Sociology Boston MA 02125

DENTON, CHARLES MANDAVILLE, corp. exec.; b. Glendale, Calif., June 22, 1924; s. Horace Bruce and Marguerite (Mandaville) D.; m. Jean Margaret Brady, Dec. 10, 1955; children—Charles Mandaville II, Margot Elizabeth. Student, U. Calif., 1942, Okla. A. and M. Coll., 1943; B.A. in Journalism, U. So. Calif., 1949. Reporter San Fernando Valley Times, N. Hollywood, Calif., 1949-50, U.P., Los Angeles, 1950-52; reporter, sportswriter, columnist I.N.S., Los Angeles, 1952-59; reporter, feature writer, TV editor-columnist Los Angeles Examiner, 1959-62; free-lance TV and mag. writer, 1962-63; reporter Los Angeles Times, 1963; columnist San Francisco Examiner, 1963-68; communications dir. Leslie Salt Co., San Francisco, 1968-73; communications dir. Crown Zellerbach Corp., San Francisco, 1973—. Author: (with Dr. W. Coda Martin) A Matter of Life, 1964. Pres. Greater Los Angeles Press Club Welfare Found., 1961. Served with USNR, 1943-46. Mem. Phi Beta Kappa, Phi Kappa Phi, Sigma Delta Chi, Blue Key. Clubs: Greater Los Angeles Press (pres. 1955-57), Tiburon Peninsula, Bohemian. Home: 40 Seafirth Rd Tiburon CA 94920 Office: 1 Bush St San Francisco CA 94119

DENTON, DAVID EDWARD, psychology educator; b. Crossville, Tenn., Feb. 4, 1935; s. David Pyle and Orbie Loraine (McLarty) D.; m. Edith Ramona Lumpkin, Nov. 30, 1974; 1 dau., Mitzi Ann Wright. B.S. English, U. Tenn., 1958, M.S. Psychology, 1959, Ed.D., 1963. Asst., then assoc. prof. psychology and philosophy Austin Peay State U., Tenn., 1962-66; prof. dept. social and philos. studies in edn. U. Ky., Lexington, 1966—, chmn dept., 1979—; vis. prof. U. Tenn., 1964, 1965, W.Va. U., 1966; lectr. in field. Author: The Philosophy of Albert Camus, 1967, The Language of Ordinary Experience, 1970, Existential Reflections on Teaching, 1972, Existentialism and Phenomenology in Education, 1974, What Is Educational Research, 1979; contbr. articles to profl. jours. Fellow Philosophy of Edn. Soc. (sec.-treas.); mem. Ohio Valley Philosophy of Edn. Soc. (pres. 1970-71), Am. Edn. Studies Assn., Soc. Phenomenology and Existential Philosophy, World Future Soc. Episcopalian. Home: 125 Chenault Rd Lexington KY 40502 Office: Coll Edn U Ky Lexington KY 40506

DENTON, HAROLD RAY, government official; b. Rocky Mount, N.C., Feb. 24, 1937; s. Doc. S. and Sula Alga (Lamm) D.; m. Lucinda Vaden Oliver, July 11, 1959; children: Elizabeth Glass, Harold, Spencer Hilliard. B.S., N.C. State U., 1958; Ph.D. (hon.), Gettysburg Coll., 1979, Lebanon Valley Coll., 1979. With DuPont Savannah River Plant, Augusta, Ga., 1958-62, AEC-Nuclear Regulatory Commn., Washington, 1962-78; dir. Nuclear Regulatory Commn., Washington, 1978—. Named disting. exec. Pres. U.S., 1980. Mem. Am. Nuclear Soc. Home: 603 Smallwood Rd Rockville MD 20850 Office: Nuclear Regulatory Commn Nuclear Reactor Regulation 7920 Norfolk Ave Bethesda MD 20555

DENTON, JEREMIAH ANDREW, JR., U.S. senator, ret. naval officer; b. Mobile, Ala., July 15, 1924; s. Jeremiah Andrew and Irene Claudia (Steele) D.; m. Kathryn Jane Maury, June 6, 1946; children: Jeremiah Andrew III, Donald, James, William, Madeleine, Michael, Mary Elizabeth. Student, Spring Hill Coll., Mobile, 1942-43, L.H.D., 1974; B.S. in Engring, U.S. Naval Acad., 1946, Armed Forces Staff Coll., 1958-59, Naval War Coll., 1963; M.A. in Internat. Affairs, George Washington U., 1964; H.H.D. (hon.), St. Leo's Coll., LL.D., Troy State U. Commd. ensign U.S. Navy, 1946, advanced through grades to rear adm., 1973; aviator, flight instr., staff officer, 1946-65, combat pilot in, 1965, comdt., Norfolk, Va., 1974-77, ret., 1977; exec. asst. to pres. Spring Hill Coll., 1977-80; cons. to pres. Christian Broadcasting Network, 1978-80; Sol Feinstone lectr. U.S. Mil. Acad., 1975; U.S. senator from Ala., 1981—; mem. judiciary com., labor and human resources com., veterans affairs, chmn., mem. various subcoms. Author: When Hell Was In Session, 1976. Bd. regents Spring Hill Coll.; founder Coalition for Decency. Decorated Navy Cross, D.S.M. (Def. Dept. and Navy), Silver Star with two oak leaf clusters, Bronze Star with five oak leaf clusters, D.F.C., Purple Heart with oak leaf cluster, Air medal with oak leaf cluster, Navy Commendation medal; recipient John Paul Jones award Navy League, 1973, Ct. of Honor award Ala. Nat. Exchange Club, Ala. Legislature resolution, 1973, awards Valley Forge Freedoms Found., 1974, 76, For God and Country award Capitol Hill First Friday Club, 1974, Cross of Mil. Service UDC, 1975, Douglas MacArthur Meritorious Service award Norfolk chpt. Assn. U.S. Army, 1977. Mem. Ends of Earth Soc. (working com.), Am. Legion, VFW (Armed Forces award 1974), Catholic War Vets. (Celtic Cross award 1974), Res. Officers Assn. (hon. life). Roman Catholic. Clubs: K.C. (Patriot of Year award Princeton, N.J. 1975, Lantern award 1981), Knights of Malta. Research on prisoner of war behavior, attitudes and performance, 1973-74. Prisoner of war, North Vietnam, 1965-73. Home: Route 1 Box 305 Theodore AL 36582 Office: US Senate Washington DC 20510

DENTON, JOHN JOSEPH, ret. pharm. co. exec.; b. Newkirk, Okla., Nov. 24, 1915; s. Edwin Carlon and Anna Lee (Hart) D.; m. Anita R. Christoffersen, Nov. 30, 1949; children—Ann Hart, Margaret Canfield, Mary Elizabeth. B.S. in Chemistry, Okla. State U., 1937; Ph.D. in Organic Chemistry, U. Ill., 1941. Asst. chemistry U. Ill., 1937-40, spl. asst., 1940-41; with Am. Cyanamid Co., 1941-81, Pearl River, N.Y., 1956-81, dir. cardiovascular-renal research, 1971-73, dir. new product acquisitions, 1973-81. Fellow Chem. Soc. London, N.Y. Acad. Scis.; mem. Am. Chem. Soc., AAAS, Ridgewood (N.J.) Art Assn., Sigma Xi, Alpha Chi Sigma, Phi Kappa Phi, Phi Lambda Upsilon. Republican. Methodist. Home: 565 Upper Blvd Ridgewood NJ 07450

DENUNZIO, RALPH DWIGHT, investment banker; b. White Plains, N.Y., Nov. 17, 1931; s. Frank and M. Winifred (Sandbach) DeN.; m. Jean A. Ames, Sept. 25, 1954; children: David Ames, Peter Dwight, Thomas Richard. A.B., Princeton U., 1953. With Kidder, Peabody & Co., Inc. (and predecessor), N.Y.C., 1953—, exec. v.p., 1968-77, pres., chief exec. officer, 1977—, chmn. exec. com., 1970—, also dir.; dir. AMP Inc., Harrisburg, Pa., Fed. Express Corp., Securities Investor Protection Corp., Washington, Harris Corp., Melbourne, Fla.; bd. govs. N.Y. Stock Exchange, 1968—, vice chmn. bd., 1969-71, chmn. bd., 1971-72. Pres. bd. trustees Deerfield (Mass.) Acad.; past pres. bd. trustees Greenwich (Conn.) Country Day Sch.; trustee Princeton U. Mem. Securities Industry Assn. (chmn. 1980-81). Republican. Roman Catholic. Clubs: Bond (past officer, gov.), Links, Wall Street (gov.), Princeton (N.Y.C.); Stanwich (Greenwich); Riverside Yacht (Conn.). Home: Bridle Path Ln Riverside CT 06878 Office: 10 Hanover Sq New York NY 10005

DENVER, EILEEN ANN, editor; b. N.Y.C., Nov. 16, 1942; d. Daniel Joseph and Katherine Agnes (Boland) D. B.A., Coll. New Rochelle, 1964; certificate, Radcliffe Sch. Pub., 1964; M.A., Ind. U., 1967. Editorial asst. Mass. Inst. Tech. Tech. Review, Boston, 1965-66; instr. English St. Peter's Coll., Jersey City, 1967-70; asso. editor, writer Am. Home mag., N.Y.C., 1971-75; asst. editor Consumer Reports, Mt. Vernon, N.Y., 1975-77, asst. mng. editor, 1977-79, mng. editor, 1979—. Writer: pet column True Story mag, 1975-76; Author: Sacraments: Signs of Community, 1973. Home: 345 W 21st St New York NY 10011 Office: 256 Washington St Mount Vernon NY 10550

DENVER, JOHN (HENRY JOHN DEUTSCHENDORF JR), singer, songwriter; b. Roswell, N.Mex., Dec. 31, 1943; s. Henry John and Erma Deutschendorf; m. Ann Marie Martell, June 9, 1967. Student, Tex. Tech U. With, Chad Mitchell Trio, 1965-68; solo rec. and concert artist, 1968—; numerous recs.; has appeared on TV variety spls., 1973—; appeared in: film Oh, God!, 1977; Writer: numerous songs including Take Me Home, Country Roads, Leaving on a Jet Plane, Rocky Mountain High. Founder The Windstar Found., Snowmass, Colo., 1976; Mem. Presdl. Commn. on World Hunger, 1978. Recipient Golden Apple prize Hollywood Women's Press Club, 1977. Office: Aspen CO *

DENYSYK, BOHDAN, government official; b. Kornberg, Germany, Feb. 13, 1947; came to U.S., 1949; s. John and Maria (Zelenewich) D.; m. Halina Bubela, June 28, 1969; children: Maria H., Danya L., Adrienne Y., Alexis M. B.S., Manhattan Coll., 1968; M.S., Catholic U. Am., 1971; Ph.D., Union Exptl. Colls. and Univs., 1981. Project mgr. Naval Weapons Lab., Dahlgren, Va., 1968-72; scientist Naval Med. Research Inst., Bethesda, Md., 1972-75; program mgr. Naval Surface Weapons Ctr., Dahlgren, 1975-78; dept. head E.G. & G. Inc., Rockville, Md., 1978-81; dep. asst. sec. U.S. Dept. Commerce, Washington, 1981—; pres. DLR Assocs., Arlington, Va., 1972-80; cons. Dept. Def., 1979-80, mem. tech. working group, 1980. Author: Viscous Shock Layers, 1981; contbr. articles to profl. jours. Mem. Presdl. Transition Team, Washington, 1981; regional dir. Republican Nat. Com., 1980; dir. pub. relations Ukranian Nat. Info. Service, 1976-80; mem. Pres.'s Export Council, 1981—; pres. Phi Mu Alpha Sinfonia, 1967-68. Navy fellow, 1969-72; Regents scholar, 1964-68. Mem. AIAA, Am. Def. Preparedness Assn., Am. Phys. Soc. Republican. Roman Catholic. Home: 1301 19th Rd S Arlington VA 22202 Office: Dept Commerce 14th and Pennsylvania Ave Washington DC 20230

DEO, PATRICK A., business executive; b. 1930; married. B.S., Seton Hall U., 1952. With Grand Union Co., 1956—, v.p., gen. mgr. suburban div., 1965-70, exec. asst. to sr. v.p. ops., 1970-71, regional v.p., N.Y.C., 1971-73, corp. v.p., 1973-75, sr. v.p. supermarket ops., 1975-76, exec. v.p. supermarket div., 1976-78, exec. v.p., chief operating officer, 1978-79, pres., chief operating officer, 1979-81, chmn., chief exec. officer, 1981—, dir.; pres., chief exec. officer Cavenham (USA) Inc.; dir. Cavenham Holdings Inc.; bd. dirs. 1st State Bancorp of Newark. Served with U.S. Army. Mem. Food Mktg. Inst. Washington, N.J. Food Council, N.J. C. of C. Club: Braidburn Country. Office: G and Union Co 100 Broadway Elmwood Park NJ 07407 *

DEODATO, EUMIR, composer; b. Rio de Janeiro, Brazil, June 22, 1942; s. Belmiro and Eurydice Almeida; m. Ruth Santos, June 9, 1964; children—Cassius, Kennya, Karema. Owner Kenya Music, Inc., N.Y.C., 1972—. Keyboard player, Deodato Band, N.Y.C., 1973—; condr. studio orchs. in, N.Y., Calif., London, Brazil, Europe, Australia, 1960—; composer popular and symphonic works, 1958—; recs. for, Warner Bros. Records. (Recipient Best Arranger award for O Sabia, Rio Internat. Song Festival 1969), Warner Bros. Records. (golden record for arrangement Also Sprach Zarathustra from movie 2001, and Prelude, record album); composer: symphony The Legend of the Amazon Bird (Grammy award); producer, Kool and The Gang, Platinum Hook. Address: Suite 600 565 Fifth Ave New York NY 10017

DEONES, JACK E., corp. exec.; b. Mankato, Minn., Sept. 21, 1931; s. Nicholas H. and Beatrice R. (Viste) D.; m. Cleo Pat Peters, May 27, 1955; children—Gregg N., Alexa M. B.S.S., St. Mary's Coll., 1953; LL.B., Yale, 1956. Bar: Minn. bar 1956, N.J. bar 1974. Spl. agt. FBI, 1960-62; atty. Pfizer, Inc., 1962-65; div. counsel Honeywell, Inc., 1965-69; asst. gen. counsel Foster Wheeler Corp., Livingston, N.J., 1969-77, corp. sec., 1977—; dir. York Internat. Corp., Foster Wheeler Intercontinental Corp. Served with USN, 1956-60. Mem. Am., N.J., Minn. bar assns., Am. Soc. Corp. Secs. Home: 59 Briarcliff Mountain Lakes NJ 07046 Office: 110 S Orange Ave Livingston NJ 07039

DEPALMA, BRIAN RUSSELL, film director, writer; b. Newark, Sept. 11, 1940; s. Anthony Fredrick and Vivenne (Muti) DeP. B.A.,

Columbia Coll., 1962; M.A., Sarah Lawrence Coll., 1964. Dir. and writer: short film Woton's Wake, 1963 (Rosenthal Found. award 1963); documentary films Dionysus in '69, 1970, The Responsive Eye, 1966; feature films Murder a la Mod, 1968, Greetings, 1968 (Siher Bar Berlin Film Festival award 1969), The Wedding Party, 1969, Hi Mom, 1970, Get to Know Your Rabbit, 1972, Sisters, 1973, Phantom of the Paradise, 1974 (Grand prize 1975), Obsession, 1976, Carrie, 1976 (Avoriaz prize 1977), The Fury, 1978, Home Movies, 1979, Dressed to Kill, 1980, Blow Out, 1981, Scarface, 1983. Office: Fetch Prodns 25 Fifth Ave New York NY 10003 Office: 1600 Broadway New York NY

DEPALMA, RALPH GEORGE, surgeon; b. N.Y.C., Oct. 29, 1931; s. Frank and Maria (Sibilio) DeP.; m. Maleva Tankard, Sept. 23, 1955; children: Ralph L., Edward F., Maleva B., Malinda G. A.B., Columbia U, 1953; M.D., NYU, 1956. Diplomate: Am. Bd. Surgery. Resident in surgery Univ. Hosps., Cleve., 1962-64; instr. to assoc. prof. surgery Case Western Res. U., Cleve., 1964-80, prof. surgery, 1973-80; prof., chmn. surgery U. Nev., Reno, 1980-82, George Washington U. Sch. Medicine, Washington, 1982—; chief surgery George Washington U. Med. Ctr., Washington, 1982—. Contbr. articles to profl. jours. Served to capt. USAF, 1942-45; PTO. Grantee USPHS, 1974-82. Fellow ACS; mem. Cleve. Vascular Soc. (pres. 1977-78), Rocky Mt. Vascular Soc. (pres.), Am. Surg. Assn, Soc. Vascular Surgery. Clubs: Mentor Harbor Yacht (Mentor, Ohio); Cosmos (Washington).

DEPALMA, SAMUEL, internationalist analyst; b. Rochester, N.Y., June 22, 1918; s. Nicholas and Rose (Freda) DeP.; m. Grace E. Kilbourne, July 5, 1941; children: Cynthia M., Winifred R. A.B., U. Rochester, 1940; postgrad., Am. U., 1940-41. Econ. analyst, later air intelligence specialist USAAF, 1941-45; expert internat. orgn. affairs Dept. of State, 1945-58; polit. officer U.S. del. NATO, Paris, 1958-61; counselor polit. affairs, The Hague, Holland, 1961-63; chief office polit. affairs ACDA, 1963-66; asst. dir. U.S. ACDA, 1966-69; asst. sec. U.S. Dept. of State, 1969-73; dir. internat. relations ITT, 1973-83; ret., 1983; Adviser U.S. delegations numerous internat. confs. Mem. Am. Fgn. Service Assn., Council on fgn. Relations, Phi Beta Kappa. Club: Cosmos (Washington). Home: 6707 Rannoch Rd Bethesda MD 20817

DEPAOLO, RONALD FRANCIS, mag. editor; b. Jamaica, N.Y., July 12, 1938; s. Francis Edward and Evelyn Helen (Turck) deP.; m. Meredith Nell Mass, Aug. 12, 1967; children—Britton, Damon, Baird. B.A. cum laude, Moravian Coll., Bethlehem, Pa., 1964; M.S., Northwestern U., 1965. Reporter, corr., writer Life mag., 1965-70; news editor, corr. Business Week mag., 1970-72; freelance writer and editor, 1972-76; editor-in-chief, asso. pub. I-AM mag., N.Y.C., 1976-78; sr. editor Boardroom Reports, N.Y.C., 1978-80; editor-in-chief M.D. Mag., N.Y.C., 1980—; adj. prof. communications Ramapo Coll., Mahwah, N.J., 1974-75. Served with AUS, 1957-59, 60-61. Home: 49 Chilhowie Dr Kinnelon NJ 07405 Office: 30 E 60th St New York NY 10022

DE PASQUALE, JOSEPH, musician; b. Phila., Oct. 14, 1919; s. Horace and Rosa (Lanza) dep.; m. Maria M. von Leuchtenberg de Beauharnais, Aug. 7, 1949; children: Maria Alexandra, Elizabeth Ann, Joseph Serge, Charles Nicholas. Grad., Curtis Inst. Music, 1942. Tchr. Hart Sch. Music, Hartford, Conn., 1947-50, Boston Conservatory, 1947-48, New Eng. Conservatory, 1948-64, Tanglewood Summer Music Sch., 1947-64, Curtis Inst. Music, 1964—, Phila. Coll. Performing Arts, 1976—. Mem., All-Am. Youth Orch., 1941, ABC Symphony Orch., 1945-47; 1st violist, Boston Symphony Orch., 1947-64; prin. violist, Phila. Orch., 1964—; mem. various chamber music groups, Boston, 1948-60; formed (with brothers), dePasquale String Quartet, 1963; concertized in N. and S.Am., Europe, Japan; quartet in residence, Haverford Coll., 1977—, solo performances with orchs. in U.S., Europe and Can., U.S., recitals in U.S. and Bermuda; rec. artist, Columbia, RCA, Boston records. Served with USMCR, 1942-45. Decorated Star Italian Solidarity Pres. Italian Republic, 1969. Mem. Phila. Mus. Soc. Republican. Roman Catholic. Home: 532 General Lafayette Rd Merion PA 19066 Office: Acad of Music Locust and Broad Sts Philadelphia PA 19102

DEPATIE, DAVID HUDSON, motion picture company executive; b. Los Angeles, Dec. 24, 1930; s. Edmond LaVoie and Dorothy (Hudson) DeP.; m. Marcia Lee MacPherson, June 1972; children: David Hudson, Steven Linn, Michael Linn. Student, U. of South, 1947-48; A.B., U. Calif.-Berkeley, 1951. With Warner Bros. Pictures, Inc., 1951-63, v.p., gen. mgr. comml. and cartoon films div., 1963; pres. DePatie-Freleng Enterprises, Inc., Van Nuys, Calif., 1963—. Producer: Pink Panther and Inspector theatrical cartoon series; TV series The New Mr. Magoo; TV live-action and animation spl. The Hoober Bloob Highway; TV spl. Clerow Wilson Great Escape; TV series The Houndcats and the Barkleys; Christmas TV spls. The Tiny Tree; ABC aftersch. spl. My Mom's Having a Baby (recipient Emmy award); Dr. Seuss spl. Halloween Is Grinch Night (recipient Emmy award), Fantastic Four, Spider-Woman, The Pink Panther Christmas Special, The Bugs Bunny Christmas Special, Spider-Man & his Amazing Friends, The Pink Panther in Pink at First Sight; Dr. Seuss Spls. The Grinch Schplotzes the Cat-In-The-Hat; others.; (nominated for Emmy award 1974-75); exec. producer: The Incredible Hulk, Pandamonium, Meatballs and Spaghetti, Dungeons and Dragons. Recipient First award for the Lorax Zagreb Internat. Film Festival, 1972; recipient Emmy Award for Dr. Seus special The Grinch Grinches The Cat-in-the Hat, 1982. Mem. Acad. Motion Picture Arts and Scis. (Oscar award for Pink Panther 1964), Soc. Motion Picture Editors, Phi Gamma Delta. Republican. Episcopalian. Office: DePatie-Freleng Enterprises Inc 16400 Ventura Blvd Encino CA 91436

DEPAUW, GOMMAR ALBERT, educator, priest; b. Stekene, Belgium, Oct. 11, 1918; came to U.S., 1949, naturalized, 1955; s. Desiré and Anna (Van Overloop) De P. Diplomate Classical Humanities, Coll. St. Nicholas, Belgium, 1936; J.C.B., U. Louvain, 1943, J.C.L., 1945; Juris Canonici Dr., Catholic U. Am., 1953. Ordained priest Roman Cath. Ch., 1942; parish priest, chaplain Cath. Social Action, Ghent, Belgium, 1945-49, N.Y.C., 1949-52; with Mount St. Mary's, Emmitsburg, Md., 1952-65, successively prof. moral and fundamental dogmatic theology and canon law, sem. div., asso. prof. philosophy coll. div., 1952-65, dean studies, maj. sem. div., 1954-64, mem. council adminstrn., 1957-65; Theol. adviser II Vatican Ecumenical Council, 1962-65; founder-pres. Cath. Traditionalist Movement, Inc., 1964—. Author: The Educational Rights of the Church, 1953, The Rebel Priest, 1965, the Traditional Roman Catholic Mass, 1977; co-author: New Catholic Ency; contbr. to: Homiletic and Pastorial Review; editor: Sounds of Truth and Tradition; Producer Latin radio mass, various religious phonograph records. Served with Inf. M.C. Belgian Army, 1939-45. Decorated Honor cross Free Polish Forces. Mem. Cath. Theol. Soc. Am. Canon Law Soc. Am., Am. Cath. Philos. Assn., Nat. Cath. Ednl. Assn., Am. Assn. U. Profs. Address: 210 Maple Ave Westbury NY 11590 *Especially since my founding of the Catholic Traditionalist Movement in 1964 has made me somewhat "controversial," I draw great inspiration from two sayings adorning the walls of my office. One, attributed to Davy Crockett: "Be sure you're right. Then go ahead!" The other, quoting Saint Athanasius: "If the whole world goes against the truth, then Athanasius must go against the whole world!" And when living by those axioms becomes heavy at times, I just brace myself and coin another one of my own: "It's better to be right alone, than to be wrong with a thousand others!"*

DE PAUW, LINDA GRANT, history educator; b. N.Y.C., Jan. 19, 1940; d. Phillip and Ruth (Marks) Grant. B.A., Swarthmore Coll., 1961; Ph.D., Johns Hopkins U., 1964. Asst. prof. history George Mason Coll.-U. Va., Fairfax, 1964-65; spl. asst. to archivist U.S. Nat. Archives, Washington, 1965-66; asst. prof. history George Washington U., Washinton, 1966-69, assoc. prof., Washington, 1969-75, prof. Am. history, 1975—. Editor-in-chief, project dir. (Documentary History of the First Fed. Congress); author: The Eleventh Pillar: New York State and the Federal Constitution, 1966, Founding Mothers: Women of America in the Revolutionary Era, 1975, Remember the Ladies, 1976, Seafaring Women, 1982; editor, pub. (Minerva: Quarterly Report on Women and the Military). Woodrow Wilson fellow, 1961. Mem. Am. Hist. Assn. (Beveridge award 1964), Am. Mil. Inst., Assn. Documentary Editing, Authors Guild, Coordinating Com. on Women in Hist. Profession, Inter-Univ. Seminar on Armed Forces and Soc., Nat. Women's Studies Assn., Orgn. Am. Historians, So. Hist. Assn., U.S. Naval Inst. Home: 1101 S Arlington Ridge Rd Arlington VA 22202 Office: Dept History George Washington U Washington DC 20052

DEPEW, CHARLES GARDNER, manufacturing company executive; b. Palmerton, Pa., July 21, 1930; s. Harlan A. and Mary Louise (Gardner) D.; m. Heloise Gilmore, June 16, 1956; children—Mark G., Jane L., Anne G., Henry C. B.S. in Edn; A.B. in Natural Sci, Wittenberg U., Springfield, Ohio, 1952; M.B.A., U. Mich., 1956. With Owens-Ill., Inc., 1956—, v.p. adminstrv. div., 1969-72, v.p. glass container div., So. area mfg. mgr., 1972-73, v.p. glass container div., tech. dir., Toledo, 1973-79, v.p. corp. staff, energy and environ. tech., 1979-82; v.p., dir. govt. relations Owens-Ill. Inc. Trustee Nat. Sanitation Found.; bd. dirs., vice chmn. Am. Nat. Metric Council. Served to lt. (j.g.) USCGR, 1952-54. Presbyterian. Office: One Sea Gate Toledo OH 43666

DEPEYSTER, FREDERIC AUGUSTUS, surgeon; b. Chgo., Nov. 8, 1914; s. Frederic A. and Florence (Bryant) deP.; m. Marjorie Shay, June 18, 1948; children: Frances Lee, Deborah. B.A., Williams Coll., 1936; postgrad. med. sch., Harvard, 1938; M.D., U. Chgo., 1940. Diplomate: Am. Bd. Gen. Surgery. Intern Presbyn. Hosp., Chgo., 1940-41; surg. officer Peter Bent Brigham Hosp. & Children's Hosp., both Boston, 1941-43; resident surgeon Presbyn. Hosp., Chgo., 1946-48, Nicholas Senn fellow, 1948; Am. Cancer fellow U. Ill., 1949; practice medicine, specializing in surgery, Chgo., 1945—; sr. attending surgeon Presbyn.-St. Luke's Hosp., Chgo., 1948-62, chmn. gen. surgery sect., 1970—; mem. staff Cook County Hosp., Chgo.; mem. faculty surgery dept. U. Ill. Med. Sch., Chgo., 1946-71, prof., 1969-71; prof. surgery Rush Med. Coll., Chgo., 1971—. Contbr. profl. jours. Mem. Winnetka Community House Council, 1950-51; pres. 13th Gen. Hosp. Assn., 1949-50; sec. treas. Presbyn. Hosp. Staff, 1957-59; v.p. Presbyn.-St. Luke's Hosp. Staff, 1968-70, pres., 1970-72; chmn. bd. dirs. Med. and Nursing Services of Mid-America, ARC, 1964-66; Bd. dirs. Bishop Anderson Found., Chgo., 1950-69; trustee Rush Med. Coll., 1957-70, Rush-Presbyn.-St. Lukes Med. Center, 1971-74. Served to maj., M.C. AUS, 1943-46. Decorated Bronze Star, Sec. of War Commendation. Mem. AMA, A.C.S. (gov. 1978—), Ill., Chgo. surg. socs., Internat. Soc. Surgery, Soc. Surgery Alimentary Tract (founder mem.), Central Surg. Soc., Western Surg. Assn. (dir. 1978—), Nat. Soc. Med. Research, Rush Med. Coll. Alumni Assn. (pres. 1961-66), Am. Assn. Sr. Physicians (treas. 1980), Am. Soc. Cancer Research, Sigma Xi, Alpha Omega Alpha. Clubs: Williams (Chgo.); Holland Soc. N.Y. Home: 696 Prospect Ave Winnetka IL 60093 Office: 1725 W Harrison St Chicago IL 60612

DEPKOVICH, FRANCIS JOHN, retail chain executive; b. Anita, Pa., July 18, 1924; s. Michael John and Mary Elizabeth D.; m. Sophia S. Sokol, Jan. 28, 1950; children—Robert Francis (dec.), Diane Elizabeth. B.S. in Bus. Adminstrn, U. Pitts., 1949. With J.C. Penney Co. Inc., 1949—, corp. ops. mgr., N.Y.C., 1966-79, dir., v.p. store and Facilities planning and constrn., 1979—; seminar speaker. Mem. master plan project Citizens Com. Morris Twp., N.J., 1970; mem. Morris Twp. Planning Bd., 1972-78, chmn., 1979-83. Served with AUS, 1943-45. Decorated Bronze Star; recipient various certs. of appreciation. Republican. Roman Catholic. Office: 1301 Ave of the Americas New York NY 10019

DE-PODWIN, HORACE J., economist, educator; b. Bklyn., Oct. 28, 1922; s. Thaddeus and Lena (Kornat) DeP; m. Carolyn Prudence Ohlander, June 19, 1948; children: Andrew, Elizabeth, Margaret, David. A.B., Middlebury (Vt.) Coll.; A.M., Ph.D., Columbia U. Prof. econs., dean Grad. Sch. Mgmt., Rutgers State U., 1966-82; mgr. econ. research Gen. Electric Co.; pres. Econ. Studies, Inc.; dir. Mut. Benefit Funds, Seton Co.; vice chmn., dir Rutgers Minority Investment Co.; adviser Commonwealth P.R.; cons. GATT negotiations for U.S. Govt. Author: Discharging Business Tax Liabilities, 1954; also numerous econ. studies and articles. Trustee Sales Execs. Found.; bd. dirs. Interracial Council on Opportunity, New Brunswick Devel. Corp., N.J. Commn. on Criminal Justice Standards; vice chmn. N.J. Commn. on Efficiency in the Cts.; chmn. com. probation N.J. Supreme Ct. Served with inf. AUS, World War II. Decorated Bronze Star, Combat Infantryman's badge. Mem. Am. Econ. Assn., Am. Statis. Assn., AAUP, N.J. State C. of C. (dir.). Home: 145 Wyoming Ave Maplewood NJ 07040 Office: 92 New St Newark NJ 07102 also Economic Studies Inc 680 Fifth Ave New York NY 10019

DE POIX, VINCENT PAUL, diversified manufacturing company executive, retired naval officer; b. Los Angeles, Aug. 13, 1916; s. Elzear Paul and Grace (Howard) de P.; children: Suzanne, Carol, Christopher, Peter. B.S. in Elec. Engring, U.S. Naval Acad., 1939; student, U.S. Naval Postgrad. Sch., 1944-46; M.S. in Aero. Engring, M.I.T., 1946. Commd. ensign U.S. Navy, 1939, advanced through grades to vice adm., 1969, ret., 1974; served in U.S.S. Mpls. and U.S.S. Sicard, 1939-41; flight tng., 1941-42; fighter pilot Fighting Squadron Six on U.S.S. Enterprise, PTO, 1942-43; comdg. officer Fighting Squadron 172, 1948-50; first comdg. officer U.S.S. Enterprise, 1st nuclear aircraft carrier, 1960-63; comdr. Carrier Div. 7, 1966-67; asst. dep. chief naval operations (devel.), 1967-69; dep. dir. (adminstrn., evaluation and mgmt.) Office Dir. Def. Research and Engring., OSD, 1969-71; comdr. 2d fleet, Norfolk, Va., 1971-72; dir. Def. Intelligence Agy., Washington, 1972-74; asst. to pres. Teledyne, Inc., Los Angeles, 1974-75; pres. Teledyne Wah Chang Albany, Oreg., 1975—; group exec. N.W. group Teledyne, Inc., 1979—. Decorated D.S.M. with 3 gold stars, Legion of Merit, Air medal, Purple Heart. Office: Teledyne Wah Chang Albany PO Box 460 Albany OR 97321

DE POL, JOHN, artist; b. N.Y.C., Sept. 16, 1913; s. Joseph Zangrando and Theresa (Mariani) DeP.; m. Thelma June Roth, May 31, 1946; 1 dau., Patricia Gail. Student, Art Students League N.Y., Sch. Tech., Belfast, No. Ireland. Free lance wood engraver, printmaker, illustrator prints represented permanent collections, Cin. Mus., Library of Congress, N.Y. Pub. Library, Met. Mus. Art, Syracuse U. Library, others.; creator of, Woodcut Soc., presentation print, 1952, Miniature Print Soc., 1953, Albany Print Club, 1958-59; laureate, N.Y. Printers Wall of Fame, 1980. Served with USAAF, 1943-45. Recipient Richard Comyn Eames Mus. purchase prize, 1952, Kate W. Arms Meml. prize, 1955, 56, Albany Print Club Purchase prize, 1968, John Taylor Arms Meml. prize NAD, 1968, others; Named Academician Nat. Acad. Design. Mem. Art Students League (life), Soc. Am. Graphic Artists, Albany Print Club. Address: 280 Spring Valley Rd Park Ridge NJ 07656

DEPPERSCHMIDT, THOMAS ORLANDO, economist; b. St. Louis, Dec. 3, 1935; s. Robert O. and Marcella C. (Meier) D.; m. Bertha Marie Waldman, Nov. 28, 1957; children—M. Susan, Mark, Joel, Andrew, Amy, Joan. A.B., Ft. Hays (Kans.) State U., 1958; Ph.D., U. Tex., 1965. Asst. prof., then asso. prof. W. Tex. State U., Canyon, 1961-66; prof. econs., chmn. dept. Memphis State U., 1966—; treas., exec. com. Health First Memphis; research asso. study seasonality nat. constrn. industry TVA-Dept. Labor, 1978-79. Co-author: Encyclopedia of Economics, 1974; editor: Financial Policies in Transition, 1968. Trustee Immaculate Conception High Sch., Memphis, 1977—; mem. Gov. Tenn. Jobs Conf., 1978-79. Served with AUS, 1954-56. Mem. Am., So. econ. assns., Mid-South Acad. Economists. Home: 1246 Cherrydale Cove Memphis TN 38111 Office: Dept Econs Memphis State Univ Memphis TN 38152

DE PREIST, JAMES ANDERSON, conductor; b. Phila., Nov. 21, 1936; s. James Henry and Ethel (Anderson) DeP.; m. Betty Louise Childress, Aug. 10, 1963; children: Tracy Elisabeth, Jennifer Anne; m. Ginette Grenier, July 19, 1980. B.S., U. Pa., 1958, M.A., 1961, L.H.D. (hon.), 1976; student, Phila. Conservatory Music, 1959-61; D.Mus. (hon.), Laval U., 1980, D.F.A., U. Portland, 1983. Am. specialist music for State Dept., 1962-63; condr.-in-residence, Bangkok, Thailand, 1963-64. Am. debut with, N.Y. Philharmonic, 1964; asst. condr. to Leonard Bernstein, N.Y. Philharmonic Orch., 1965-66; prin. guest condr., Symphony of New World, 1968-70; European debut with, Rotterdam Philharmonic, 1969; asso. condr., Nat. Symphony Orch., Washington, 1971-75; prin. guest condr., Nat. Symphony Orch., 1975-76; music dir., L'Orchestre Symphonique de Que., 1976-83, Oreg. Symphony, 1980—; appeared with, Phila. Orch., 1972, Chgo. Symphony, 1973, Boston Symphony, Cleve. Orch., 1974; condr.: Am. premiere of Dvorak's First Symphony, N.Y. Philharmonic, 1972. Trustee Lewis and Clark Coll., 1983—. Recipient 1st prize gold medal Dimitri Mitropoulos Internat. Music Competition for Condrs., 1964; Merit citation City of Phila., 1969; medal of City of Que., 1983; Grantee Martha Baird Rockefeller Fund for Music, 1969. Address: Care Oreg Symphony 813 SW Alder St Portland OR 97201

DE PRIMA, CHARLES RAYMOND, educator; b. Paterson, N.J., July 10, 1918; s. Mario and Louise (Ruggiero) DeP.; m. Annemarie Boerschmann, June 15, 1951. A.B., Washington Sq. Coll., 1940; Ph.D., N.Y. U., 1943. Lectr. N.Y. U., 1942-46, vis. prof., 1962-63; mem. faculty Calif. Inst. Tech., Pasadena, 1946—, prof. math., 1956—; Mem. applied math. panel OSRD, 1942-46; head math. div. (Office Naval Research), 1951-52, mem., 1961—. Editor: Pacific Jour. Math, 1973—. Mem. Am. Math. Soc., Math. Assn. Am., Soc. Indsl. and Applied Math. (council 1961—), Phi Beta Kappa. Research and publs. on functional analysis, partial differential equations, gas dynamics, fluid mechanics. Home: Sea Ranch CA 95497 Office: Dept Math 253-37 Calif Inst Tech Pasadena CA 91125

DEPRIT, ANDRE ALBERT, mathematician, consultant; b. St. Servais, Belgium, Apr. 10, 1926; came to U.S., 1964, naturalized, 1974; s. Max Francois and Anne-Marie Caroline (Vasse) D.; m. Andree Jeanne Bartholome, Sept. 5, 1959; 1 son, Etienne. L.Ph., U. Louvain, Belgium, 1948, L.Sc., 1953, D.Sc., 1957. Sr. research asso. Nat. Bur. Standards, Gaithersburg, Md., 1977-79, mathematician, 1979-82, sr. mathematician, 1982—; assoc. prof. U. Kinshassa, Zaire, 1957-59, U. Louvain, 1957-61, prof., 1961-64; staff mem. Boeing Sci. Research Labs., Seattle, 1964-71; sr. research fellow NASA, Greenbelt, Md., 1971-72; prof. U. Cin., 1972-78, Charles Phelps Taft prof., 1979; cons. Charles Stark Draper Lab., Cambridge, Mass., 1977—, Naval Research Lab., Washington, 1976—, Nat. Bur. Standards, Boulder, Colo., 1974—; vis. prof. U. Wis., Madison, 1975, Yale U., New Haven, 1965-66, U. Liege, Belgium, 1970; vis. lectr. U. Wash., Seattle, 1965-66; resident visitor Bell Telephone Labs., 1968. Editor: Celestial Mechanics, 1969-73; Contbr. articles to profl. jours. Royal Acad. Scis. (Belgium) Agathon De Potter prize, 1957; Recipient Nat. Acad. Scis. Watson medal, 1972; Wettrems prize, 1971; Alan Berman award Naval Research Lab., 1982; Silver medal U.S. Dept. Commerce; NATO fellow, 1963; Nat. Acad. Sci.-NRC, 1971-72. Mem. Internat. Astron. Union, Am., Royal astronom. socs., AIAA, AAAS, Sigma Xi. Home: 19119 Roman Way Gaithersburg MD 20879

DEPUY, CHARLES HERBERT, educator, chemist; b. Detroit, Sept. 10, 1927; s. Carroll E. and Helen (Plehn) DeP.; m. Eleanor Burch, Dec. 21, 1949; children: David Gareth, Nancy Ellen, Stephen Baylie, Katherine Louise. B.S., U. Calif., Berkeley, 1948; A.M., Columbia U., 1952; Ph.D., Yale U., 1953. Asst. prof. chemistry Iowa State U., 1953-59, asso. prof., 1959-62, prof., 1962-63; prof. chemistry U. Colo., Boulder, 1963—, chmn. chemistry dept., 1966-68; vis. prof. U. Ill., summer 1954, U. Calif., Berkeley, summer 1960; NIH sr. postdoctoral fellow U. Basel, Switzerland, 1969-70; Cons. A.E. Staley Co., 1956-80, Marathon Oil Co., 1964—. Author: (with Kenneth L. Rinehart) Introduction to Organic Chemistry, 1967, rev. edit., 1975, (with Orville L. Chapman) Molecular Reactions and Photochemistry, 1970, (with Robert H. Shapiro) Exercises in Organic Spectroscopy; Mem. adv. bd.: Jour. Organic Chemistry, 1969-73; Contbr. articles profl. jours. Served wih AUS, 1946-47. John Simon Guggenheim fellow, 1977-78. Fellow AAAS, Chem. Soc. London; mem. Am. Chem. Soc. (mem. exec. com. organic div., chmn. Colo. sect., Gold medal), Sigma Xi. Home: 1509 Cascade Ave Boulder CO 80302

DERAMUS, WILLIAM NEAL, III, railroad executive; b. Pittsburg, Kans., Dec. 10, 1915; s. William Neal and Lucile Ione (Nicholas) D.; m. Patricia Howell Watson, Jan. 22, 1943; children: William Neal IV, Patricia Nicholas Fogel, Jean Deramus Wagner, Jill Watson Dean. A.A., Kansas City Jr. Coll., 1934; A.B., U. Mich., 1936; LL.B., Harvard U., 1939. Transp. apprentice Wabash R.R. Co., St. Louis, 1939-41, asst. trainmaster, 1941-43; asst. to gen. mgr. K.C.S. Ry. Co., Kansas City, Mo., 1946-48; asst. to pres. C.G.W. Ry. Co., Chgo., 1948, pres., dir., 1949-57, chmn. exec. com., 1954-57; pres., dir. M.-K.-T. R.R., 1957-61; chmn. bd. MAPCO, Inc., Tulsa, 1960-73, chmn. exec. com., 1973-81; pres., dir. Kansas City So. Lines, Mo., 1961-73, chmn. bd., 1966-80; pres. Kansas City So. Industries, Inc., Mo., 1962-71, chmn. bd., 1966—; dir. Employers Reins, Corp., Bus. Men's Assurance Co. Am., Kansas City Royals, all Kansas City, Mo. Served from capt. to maj. Transp. Corps, Mil. Ry. Service AUS, 1943-46; overseas, India; Served from capt. to maj. Transp. Corps, Mil. Ry. Service AUS, 1943-45; overseas, India. Mem. Beta Theta Pi. Clubs: Chicago; Kansas City, River, Mission Hills Country, Mercury, Rotary (Kansas City). Home: 37 LeMans Ct. Prairie Village KS 66208 Office: 114 W 11th St Kansas City MO 64105

DERBER, MILTON, labor and industrial relations educator; b. Providence, June 19, 1915; s. Harry and Sophie (Kalman) D.; m. Zelda Trenner, June 14, 1940; children: Clara Gail, Charles. Student, Springfield (Mass.) Jr. Coll., 1932-33; A.B., Clark U., 1936; A.M., U. Wis., 1937, Ph.D., 1940. Social Sci. Research Council fellow, 1936-39; research asso. 20th Century Fund, 1939-40; economist U.S. Bur. Labor Statistics, 1940-41, 46-47; field examiner NLRB, 1941-42; economist OPA, 1942-43; economist and research dir. Nat. War Labor Bd., 1943-45; coordinator of research Inst. Labor and Indsl. Relations, U. Ill., 1947-58, assoc. prof. labor and indsl. relations, 1947-49, prof., 1949—, acting dir., 1951-52; Chief economist Pres.'s Fact-Finding Bds. (Gen.

Motors and Pacific Coast Longshore Labor Disputes), 1945-46; vice chmn., project dir. Ill. Gov.'s Adv. Commn. on Labor-Mgmt. Policy for Pub. Employees, 1966; mem. Ill. Office Collective Bargaining, 1974-75, 76—. Contbg. author: How Collective Bargaining Works, 1942; Author: Labor-Management Relations under Industry-Wide Bargaining, 1955; co-author: The Local Union-Management Relationship, 1960, Plant Union-Management Relations, 1965, Research in Labor Problems in the United States, 1967, The American Idea of Industrial Democracy, 1865-1965, 1970, Strategic Factors in Industrial Relations Systems: The Metalworking Industry, 1976; Editor: Termination Report of Nat. War Labor Board, 1948; Co-editor: Problems and Policies of Dispute Settlement and Wage Stabilization during World War II, 1950, Labor and the New Deal, 1957; Project coordinator: Labor-Management Relations in Illini City, 1953. Fulbright sr. scholar, Australia, 1975-76. Mem. Indsl. Relations Research Assn. (editor 1948-50, mem. exec. bd. 1959-61, pres.-elect 1980-81, pres. 1982), AAUP (pres. U. Ill. chpt. 1959-60), B'nai B'rith. Home: 1103 Brighton Dr Urbana IL 61801

DERBES, DANIEL WILLIAM, manufacturing company executive; b. Cin., Mar. 30, 1930; s. Earl Milton and Ruth Irene (Grauten) D.; m. Patricia Maloney, June 4, 1952; children: Donna Ann, Nancy Lynn (dec.), Stephen Paul. B.S., U.S. Mil. Acad., 1952; M.B.A., Xavier U., Cin., 1963. Devel. engr. AiResearch Mfg. Co., Phoenix, 1956-58; with Garrett Corp., 1958-80, v.p., gen. mgr., then exec. v.p., Los Angeles, 1975-80, dir., 1976—; pres. Advanced Tech. Group, Signal Cos., Inc., La Jolla, Calif., 1980—, also dir.; dir. Kellogg Rust Inc., San Diego Gas & Electric Co., Ampex Corp. Pres. Palos Verdes (Calif.) Adv. Council, 1964; bd. dirs. Ind. Colls. So. Calif., 1980—, United Way, San Diego, 1981—; bd dirs. nat. exec. Boy Scouts Am., 1981—; trustee U. San Diego, 1981—. Served with AUS, 1952-56. Republican. Roman Catholic. Office: 11255 N Torrey Pines Rd La Jolla CA 92037

DERBY, PALMER PORTNER, industrial company executive; b. Washington, May 23, 1920; s. Calude Palmer and Hildagarde Rose (portner) D.; m. Marnie Holems Orborn, Dec. 29, 1941; children: Susan Palmer Derby Cox, Sally Margaret Derby Duffy. Student, Va. Poly. Inst., 1939-40, MIT, 1940-42. Registered profl. engr., Mass. With Raytheon Co., 1942—; jr. engr. Raytheon co., Waltham, Mass., 1942; various mgmt. positions in engring., research, mktg. Raytheon Co., 1942-62, asst. gen. mgr. microwave and power tube div., 1962-76, v.p., asst. gen. mgr., 1967-76, v.p. dir. new bus. analysis, Lexington, Mass., 1976—. Pioneer in devel. magnetron tubes for microwave ovens, microwave tubes for radar, electronic countermeasures missile and commnications application; patentee in field. Recipient Commendation medal, 1947. Mem. Assn. Home Appliance Mfrs. (asso. exec. bd. 1969—). Office: Raytheon Co. 141 Spring St Lexington MA 02173

DE REGNIERS, BEATRICE SCHENK, author, editor; b. Lafayette, Ind., Aug. 16, 1914; d. Harry and Sophia (Feinstein) Freedman; m. Francis de Regniers, May 2, 1953. Student, U. Ill., 1931-33; Ph.B., U. Chgo., 1935, Grad. Sch., 1936-37; postgrad., U. Toulouse, France, summer 1935, The Sorbonne, Paris, 1935-36; M.Ed., Winnetka (Ill.) Grad. Tchrs. Coll., 1941. Copywriter Scott Foresman & Co., Chgo., 1943-44; welfare officer UNRRA, Egypt, 1944-46; copywriter Am. Book Co., N.Y.C., 1948-49; dir. ednl. materials Am. Heart Assn., N.Y.C., 1949-61; editor Lucky Book Club of Scholastic Book Services, N.Y.C., 1961-81. Author: The Giant Story, 1953, What Can You Do With a Shoe?, 1955, A Little House of Your Own, 1955, Was It a Good Trade?, 1956, A Child's Book of Dreams, 1957, Something Special, 1958, Cats Cats Cats Cats Cats, 1958, What Happens Next?, 1959, The Snow Party, 1959, The Shadow Book, 1960 (also co-designer); author: Who Likes the Sun?, 1961, The Little Book, 1961 (also illustrator), The Little Girl and Her Mother, 1963, May I Bring a Friend?, 1964 (Caldecott award), The Abraham Lincoln Joke Book, 1965, David and Goliath, 1965, How Joe the Bear and Sam the Mouse Got Together, 1965; also illustrator: Penny, 1966, Circus, 1966, The Giant Book, 1966, The Day Everybody Cried, 1967, Willy O'Dwyer Jumped in the Fire, 1968, Catch a Little Fox, 1969, Poems Children Will Sit Still For, 1969, The Boy, the Rat, and the Butterfly, 1971, Red Riding Hood Retold in Verse for Boys and Girls to Read Themselves, 1972 (Bklyn. Art Books for Children citation 1973, 74), It Does Not Say Me-ow and Other Animal Riddle Rhymes, 1972, The Enchanted Forest, 1974, Little Sister and The Month Brothers, 1976, A Bunch of Poems and Verses, 1977, Laura's Story, 1979, Everyone is Good for Something, 1980, Picture Book Theater, 1982, Waiting for Mama, 1984; mem. Eloise Moore Dance Group, Chgo., 1942-43. Recipient Jr. Book award Boys Club Am., 1960, Most Disting. Work of Fiction for Younger Children award Ind. U. Writers Conf., 1964. Mem. Authors Guild Am., PEN, Loose-enders. Home: 180 W 58th St New York NY 10019

DERESIEWICZ, HERBERT, educator; b. Brno, Czechoslovakia, Nov. 5, 1925; s. William and Lotte (Rappaport) D.; m. Evelyn Altman, Mar. 12, 1955; children—Ellen, Robert, William. B.M.E., Coll. City N.Y., 1946; M.S., Columbia, 1948, Ph.D. (Univ. fellow 1949-50), 1952. Sr. staff engr. Applied Physics Lab., Johns Hopkins, 1950-51; mem. faculty Columbia, 1951—, prof. mech. engring., 1962—, chmn. dept., 1981—; cons. stress analysis, vibrations, elastic contact, wave propagation, mechanics granular and porous media., Fulbright sr. research scholar, Italy, 1960-61, Fulbright lectr., Israel, 1966-67, vis. prof., 1973-74. Contbr. profl. jours. Served with AUS, 1946-47. Mem. AAAS, ASME, Seismol. Soc. Am., N.Y. Acad. Scis., Sigma Xi. Home: 336 Broad Ave Englewood NJ 07631 Office: SW Mudd Bldg Columbia Univ New York NY 10027

DERGARABEDIAN, PAUL, energy and environ. co. exec.; b. Racine, Wis., Jan. 19, 1922; s. John and Mary (Hirmizian) D.; m. Mary A. Jansouzian, Dec. 27, 1947; children—Celeste, Claudia, Clarice, Paul. B.S., U. Wis., 1948, M.S., 1949; Ph.D. Shell Oil fellow), Caltech, 1952. Br. head U.S. Naval Weapons Center, Pasadena, Calif., 1952-55; lab. dir. TRW Systems, Redondo Beach, Calif., 1955-72, staff dir., 1974-80; dir. The Aerospace Corp., El Segundo, Calif., 1972-74, 80—; vis. prof. aeros. Caltech, 1971-72; founder, dir. Frontier Savs. & Loan; cons. in field. Served with USAAF, 1943-46. Fellow Inst. Advancement of Engring., Am. Astron. Soc. (dir. 1971—, nat. pres. 1969-71); mem. Phi Beta Kappa, Sigma Xi. Democrat. Armenian Apostolic. Club: Stereophonic of So. Calif. (pres. 1967-69). Home: 18 Poppy Trail Rolling Hills CA 90274 Office: 2350 E El Segundo Blvd El Segundo CA *As a scientist I have been moderately successful - and lucky - in doing what people in my field would consider creative work. The greatest contribution to this success, I feel, has been methodology which was gleaned from certain teachers and associates. If I have done the same for someone else, that would be the greater success.*

DERGE, DAVID RICHARD, educator; b. Kansas City, Mo., Oct. 10, 1928; s. David Richard and Blanche (Butterfield) D.; m. Elizabeth Anne Greene, Sept. 4, 1951 (dec. Mar. 1971); children—David Richard III, Dorothy Anne; m. Patricia Jean Williams, Sept. 2, 1972; children—William David, Mary Jennifer. A.B., U. Mo., 1950; A.M., Northwestern U., 1951, Ph.D., 1955; LL.D., Hanyang U., Korea, 1973. Instr. U. Mo., 1954-56, Northwestern U., summer 1955; mem. faculty Ind. U., 1956-72, prof. polit. sci., 1965-72, dean adminstrn., exec. v.p., 1968-72; pres. So. Ill. U., Carbondale, 1972-74, prof. polit. sci., 1974—, also dir. grad. studies, prof., 1976—; Pres. Behavioral Research Assos., 1968—; Mem. (U.S. Adv. Commn. Internat. Ednl. and Cultural Affairs), 1969-76; White House cons. Exec. Office of President, 1970-72; cons. higher and internat. edn. Dept. Health, Edn. and Welfare, 1971-72; sec., dir. Midwest Univs. Consortium for Internat. Activities, 1967-72; pres. Ill. Joint Council Higher Edn., 1972; bd. dirs. Ill. Ednl. Consortium for Computer Services, 1972; sec. Acad. Assn Midwest Univs. Author: Public Leadership in Indiana, 1969, Institution Building and Rural Development, 1968, The World of American Politics, 1968, also articles. Mem. City Council, Bloomington, Ind., 1963-67. Served with AUS, 1946-48; Served with USNR, 1952-73; comdr. Res. Grantee Social Sci. Research Council, 1957, Eagleton Inst. Practical Politics, 1959, Citizenship Clearing House, 1961; recipient Sigma Delta Chi Teaching award, 1963; Weatherly Distinguished Teaching award Ind. U., 1964; named Outstanding Young Man Ind. Ind. Jr. C. of C., 1963. Mem. Am. Polit. Sci. Assn., U.S. Naval Inst., Phi Beta Kappa, Pi Sigma Alpha, Alpha Pi Zeta, Alpha Kappa Psi, Phi Delta Kappa, Kappa Sigma. Presbyn. Clubs: Bloomington Squash Racquets, La Table Six. Home: Spring Arbor Lake Carbondale IL 62901

DER HAROOTIAN, KHOREN, sculptor; b. Ashodvan, Armenia, Apr. 2, 1909; came to U.S., 1921, naturalized, 1954; s. Haroutun and Nevart (Mouradian) Der Haroutunian; m. Hermine Ohanesyan, May 13, 1939 (dec. 1977); m. Yolanda Pirulis, 1979. Student, Worcester Art Mus. Sch. Sculptor, painter one-man shows, Caz-Delbos Galleries, N.Y.C., 1929, Jamaica (B.W.I.) Museum, Kingston, 1931, 38, 43, Worcester (Mass.) Art Museum, 1932, Kraushaar Galleries, N.Y.C., 1945, outdoor exhbn., N.Y.C., 1948, Art Alliance, Phila., 1950, Zwemmer Gallery, London, 1964, Armenian Gen. Benevolent Union Gallery, N.Y.C., 1965, Rockland Community Coll., Suffern, N.Y., 1967, Contemporaries Gallery, N.Y.C., Galerie Bernheim-Jeune, Paris, 1971, Artists' House and Gallery, Erevan, Armenia, USSR, Sculpture Center, N.Y.C., 1975; Mother of Ararat, Armenian Govt., 1977; exhbn., AGBU Gallery, N.Y.C., 1980, outdoor exhbn., Armenian Ch., N.Y.C., 1981, Armenian Ch., Worcester, Mass.; commd. 15 foot sculpture from native volcanic stone, Armenian Govt., 1982-84; Sculptor, painter retrospective exhbn., Mus. of Etchmiazin, Holy City of Armenia, 1983, two-man show, Gallery Ten, Inc., Mt. Vernon, N.Y., 1975, Gallery Ten, Inc., Mass., 1981, annual and group shows, Whitney Mus. Am. Art, Pa. Acad. Fine Arts, Chgo. Art Inst., U. Nebr., Worcester, Cranbrook, Springfield, Toledo, Cin. museums, Des Moines Art Center, Ohio U., Phila. Mus. Art, Audubon Artists exhbns., Sculptors Guild exhbns., John Herron Art Inst., Indpls., various London galleries, Royal Acad., London, 1964, 65, Royal Glasgow (Scotland) Inst., 1964; represented in permanent collections, Met. Mus. Art, N.Y.C., Worcester Art Mus., Jamaica (B.W.I.) Mus., Pa. Acad. Fine Arts, Whitney Mus. Am. Art, N.Y.C., Ariz. State Coll., Newark Art Mus., Bezelel Nat. Mus., Israel, Jerusalem Mus. Art, Our Lady Queen of Angels Sem., Albany, N.Y., Armenian State Art Mus., Erevan, pvt. collections in, U.S., Eng., Venezuela, Holland, France, Germany, Italy, W. Indies; exhibited work in marble, U.S. Pavilion, Brussels World's Fair, 1958, USIS, Florence, Italy, 1963; commd. to carve figure Christ and 4 Martyrs for, Diocese bldg. Armenian Ch. and Cultural Center, N.Y.C., 1959, Beaver for, Bernard Baruch City Coll., 1962, 2 8-foot bronze sculptures for facade, SS. Mesrob and Sahag Armenian Apostolic Ch., Wynnewood, Pa., 1973, 20-foot bronze sculpture Meher with 4 high relief panels by, Phila. Armenian Bicentennial Commemoration Com. for Fairmount Park, 1974. Recipient 1st prize Springfield Art Assn., 1944; Gold medal Audubon Artists 7th Ann. Exhbn., 1949; 1st prize sculpture 8th Ann. Exhbn., 1950; commn. Phila. Internat. Sculpture Exhbn., 1949; commn. for 29-foot granite Scientist Fairmount Park Art Assn., 1950; George D. Widener Meml. Gold Medal Pa. Acad. Fine Arts, 1954; exhbns. and monetary award with citation Nat. Inst. Arts and Letters, 1954; Medal of Honor Gruppo Donatello, Florence, 1962; Citation of Honor Gov. of Mass., 1981; Key to City, Worcester, Mass, 1981. Mem. Fedn. Modern Painters and Sculptors. Address: RFD 9 W Castle Rd Orangeburg NY 10962 *In my view, success has diverse aspects such as the financial, artistic, popular, personal and other forms. Success as such has not been my motivation in life. Each time I create a sculptural work or a public project, whenever I have brought my original conception, my ideas and thoughts to aesthetic fruition, I feel I have accomplished success. When my work is understood, appreciated and responded to by viewers, then that also to me is success.*

DERIAN, PATRICIA MURPHY, govt. ofcl.; b. N.Y.C., Aug. 12, 1929; d. Ronald T. and Ruby E. (Hardiman) Murphy; m. Paul S. Derian, 1952 (div. 1976); children—Michael T., Thomas Craig, Renee Brooke; m. W. Hodding Carter, III, Dec. 8, 1978. R.N. diploma, U. Va. Sch. Nursing, 1953. Dep. dir. Carter-Mondale Nat. Campaign, 1976; coordinator for human rights and humanitarian affairs Dept. State, Washington, 1977, asst. sec. for human rights and humanitarian affairs, 1977-81; Founder, organizer Loyalist Miss. Democratic Party, 1968; chmn. bd. Civic Communication Corp., Miss., 1968-76; mem. Dem. Nat. Com., 1968-80; pres. (So. Regional Council), Atlanta, 1976-77, mem. exec. com., 1966-77; mem. exec. com., bd. dirs. ACLU, 1971-77, mem. steering com. nat. prison project, 1975-77. Bd. dirs. Miss. Civil Liberties Union, 1969-77, Center for Community For Justice, Washington, 1974-77, Delta Ministry, Nat. Council Chs., 1974-77, Miss. Authority for Ednl. TV, 1975-77; mem. exec. com. Miss. Council Human Relations, 1964-77; bd. overseers Sch. Nursing, U. Pa., 1980—; bd. dirs. Fund for Free Expression, 1981—, Center for Democratic Policy, 1981—; convenor U.S. Friends of Mothers of Plaza de Mayo, 1981; mem. Americas Watch Com., 1981—

DERICCO, LAWRENCE ALBERT, college president; b. Stockton, Calif., Jan. 28, 1923; s. Giulio and Agnes (Giovacchini) DeR.; m. Alma Mezzetta, June 19, 1949; 1 son. Lawrence Paul. B.A., U. Pacific, 1949, M.A., 1971. Bank clk. Bank of Am., Stockton, 1942-43; prin. Castle Sch. Dist., San Joaquin County, Calif., 1950-53; dist. supt., prin. Waverly Sch. Dist., Stockton, 1953-63; bus. mgr. San Joaquin Delta Jr. Coll. Dist., Stockton, 1963-65, asst. supt., bus. mgr.; pres. San Joaquin Delta Coll., Stockton. Served with AUS, 1943-46; PTO. Mem. Calif. Assn. Pub. Sch. Bus. Ofcls., Assn. Sch. Bus. Ofcls. of U.S. and Can., Calif. Tchrs. Assn., NEA, Native Sons of Golden West, Phi Delta Kappa. Office: Office of the Pres San Joaquin Delta Coll 5151 Pacific Ave Stockton CA 95207 *

DE RIVAS, CARMELA FODERARO, psychiatrist, hospital administrator; b. Cortale, Italy, Nov. 25, 1920; came to U.S., 1935, naturalized, 1942; d. Salvatore and Mary (Vaiti) Foderaro; m. Aureliano Rivas, Oct. 30, 1948; children: Carmen, Norma, Sandra, David. Student, U. Pa., 1940-42; M.D., Women's Med. Coll. Pa., 1946. Diplomate: Am. Bd. Psychiatry and Neurology. Intern women's Med. Coll. Pa. Hosp., 1946; gen. practice, Phila. and, Tex., 1947-49; mem. staff Norristown (Pa.) State Hosp., 1949—, supt., 1963-70, dir. family planning, 1979—, clin. dir. spl. assignments, 1979—; assoc. psychiatry U. Pa., 1963—; psychiatrist Penn Found. for Mental Health, Sellersville, Pa., 1970-72; dir. intake coping services Central Montgomery Mental Health/Mental Retardation Center, Norristown, Pa., 1972-77, med. dir., 1977-79; dir. program evaluation Norristown State Hosp., 1979—. Bd. dirs., sec. Eastern Pa. Psychiat. Inst. Named to Hall of Fame S. Phila. High Sch., 1968; recipient citation Women's Med. Coll. Pa., 1968; Amite Achievement award, 1976; Achievement award Grad. Club Phila., 1976; named Woman of Yr. Pa. Fedn. Bus. and Profl. Women, 1979. Fellow Am. Psychiat. Assn., Pa. Psychiat. Soc. (dep. rep. assembly of dist. brs. 1979—); mem. Phila. Psychiat. Soc. (councilor), N.Y. Acad Scis., AMA, Montgomery County Med. Soc. (bd. dirs., past pres.), Pa. Med. Soc. (chmn. adv. com. to aux. 1981—, mem. ho. of dels.). Home: 700 Joseph Dr Wayne PA 19087 Office: Norristown State Hosp Norristown PA 19401

DE RIVERA, JOSE, sculptor; b. West Baton Rouge, La., Sept. 18, 1904; s. Joseph and Honorine (Montamat) Ruiz; m. Rose Covelli, 1926; 1 son, Joseph; m. Lita Jeronimo, 1955. Student drawing with, John W. Norton, Chgo., Spain, Italy, France, Greece, Egypt; D.F.A. (hon.), Washington U., St. Louis. Sculpture critic Yale, 1953-55; mem. faculty N.C. State Coll. Sch. Design, 1957-60. Exhibited numerous galleries, museums, univs., 1930—, including, De Cordova Mus., Whitney Mus. Am. Art, Ind. U., Smith, Mt. Holyoke colls., Galerie Claude Bernard, Paris, Zurich Art Mus., Stockholm Mus. Modern Art, Stedelijk Mus., Amsterdam, Seattle World Fair, Washington Gallery Modern Art, Battersea Park, London, Battersea Park, Pub. Edn. Assn. N.Y., Arts Club Chgo., White House, Washington, U. N.M., Los Angeles County Mus., Phila. Mus. Art, La Jolla (Calif.) Mus. Contemporary Art; represented in numerous permanent collections. Served with USAAF. Recipient Watson F. Blair prize Art Inst. Chgo., 1957; Creative Awards medal Brandeis U., 1969; others.; Nat. Inst. Arts and Letters grantee, 1959. Mem. Nat. Inst. Arts and Letters.; mem. Midwestern Psychol. Assn. Home: 435 E 57th St New York NY 10022 Office: Borgenicht Gallery 724 Fifth Ave New York NY 10019

DERK, RICHARD GEORGE, photojournalist; b. Chgo., Sept. 16, 1947; s. George R. and Maryjane (Lemmer) D.; m. Anne Cusack, Oct. 6, 1973. Student, MacMurray Coll., 1965-67, U. Ill., Champaign, 1967-71. Photographer Office Agrl. Communications U. Ill., 1970-73; staff photographer Rockford (Ill.) Newspapers Inc., 1973-74; photojournalist The Trib, Hinsdale, Ill., 1974-77, Chgo. Daily News, 1977-78; staff photojournalist Chgo. Sun-Times, 1978-84; freelance editorial photographer, Oak Park, Ill., 1984—; affiliate Picture Group, Inc., 1981—. Freelance promotional work with cities of, Louisville, 1973-77, Del Rio, Tex., 1973-75, Owensboro, Ky., 1973, Springfield, Ill., 1973-75. Mem. Nat. Press Photographers Assn. (Pictures of Year award 1974, 78, 80, 82, co-chmn. Ill. contest 1975-76, 77), Ill. Press Photographers Assn. (Pictures of Year award 1975, 76, 77, 78, 79, 80, 81, 82, 83). Office: 122 S Scoville Oak Park IL 60302

DERLACKI, EUGENE L(UBIN), physician; b. Chgo., Mar. 16, 1913; s. Walter and Jadwiga (Pamulowna) D. B.S., Northwestern U., 1936, M.D., 1939. Diplomate: Am. Bd. Otolaryngology. Intern Cook County Hosp., Chgo., 1939-40, jr. resident, 1941, sr. resident, 1942-43; postgrad. otolaryngology Rush Med. Coll., 1940, U. Ill., 1941-42; sr. attending staff Northwestern Meml. Hosp., 1946—; prof. otolaryngology Northwestern U. Med. Sch., 1957—. Served with M.C. AUS, 1943-46. Mem. AMA, Am. Acad. Otolaryngology, Coll. Allergists. Home: Surrey Rd Wayne IL 60184 Office: 55 E Washington St Chicago IL 60602

DERMAN, CYRUS, math. statistician; b. Phila., July 16, 1925; s. Samuel and Bessie (Segal) D.; m. Martha Winn, Feb. 24, 1961; childrenAdam Jason Winn, Hester Beth Rebecca. A.B., U. Pa., 1948, A.M., 1949; Ph.D., Columbia, 1954. Instr. Syracuse U., 1954-55; faculty Columbia, 1955—, prof. operations research, 1965—; vis. prof. Israel Inst. Tech., Haifa, 1961-62, Stanford, 1965-66, U. Calif., Davis, 1975-76, U. Calif., Berkeley, 1979. Author: (with Morton Klein) Probability and Statistical Inference for Engineers, 1959, Finite State Markovian Decision Processes, 1970, (with Leon Gleser and Ingram Olkin) A Guide to Probability Theory and Application, 1973, Probability Models and Applications, 1980. Fellow Inst. Math. Statistics, Am. Statis. Assn. Research and publs. on theory of Markov chains, Brownian motion, statis. inference, mgmt. sci. and ops. research. Home: 15 Pond Hill Rd Chappaqua NY 10514 Office: Mudd Bldg: Columbia New York NY 10027

DERMAN, DONALD ALLAN, govt. ofcl.; b. Bridgeport, Conn., May 27, 1933; s. Louis H. and Carrie R. (Reich) D.; m. Connie Lou Thumma, Apr. 1, 1977; 1 dau., Cheryl Lee. B.A., U. Conn., 1959, M.A., 1960. Program-budget analyst AEC, Chgo., Germantown, Md., 1960-65; sr. program analyst OEO, Washington, 1965-68; sr. budget examiner NASA Manned Space Flight Programs, Bur. of Budget, Washington, 1968-69, asst. div. chief space programs, 1969-70, dep. chief econs., sci. and tech. div., 1970-72; dep. chief human resources div. Office Mgmt. and Budget, Washington, 1972-73, dep. asso. dir. community devel. and veterans affairs div., 1973-76, dep. asso. dir. human resources div., 1976-81; asst. sec. Dept. Transp., Washington, 1981—. Served with USAF, 1952-56; to comdr. USNR, 1965—. Mem. U.S. Naval Inst., Naval Res. Officers Assn., Fed. Exec. Inst. Alumni Assn. Office: US Dept Transp 400 7th St SW Washington DC 20590

DERN, BRUCE MACLEISH, actor; b. Chgo., June 4, 1936; s. John and Jean (MacLeish) D.; m. Andrea Beckett, Oct. 20, 1969; 1 dau., Laura Elizabeth. Student, U. Pa., 1954-57. Appeared in numerous motion pictures, 1960—; including Wild River, 1960, Hush, Hush Sweet Charlotte, 1964, Marnie, 1964, Wild Angels, 1966, The Trip, 1967, War Wagon, 1967, Support Your Local Sheriff, 1968, Waterhole 3, 1967, Will Penny, 1968, Number One, 1969, Castle Keep, 1969, Bloody Mama, 1970, They Shoot Horses, Don't They?, 1970, Silent Running, 1972, Drive He Said, 1971 (Nat. Soc. Film Critics award), The Cowboys, 1972, King of Marvin Gardens, 1972, Laughing Policeman, 1973, The Great Gatsby (nominated Best Supporting Actor Hollywood Fgn. Press 1974), Smile, 1975, Posse, 1975, Family Plot, 1976, Won Ton Ton, 1976, Black Sunday, 1977, Coming Home (nominated Best Supporting Actor, Academy Motion Picture Arts and Scis), 1978 (named Best Supporting Actor, Your Choice for the Oscars-U.S. and Can.), Driver, 1978, Middle Age Crazy, 1980, Tattoo, 1981, That Championship Season, 1982; appeared in: Brodaway play Strangers, 1979 (Named Actor of Yr., Pacific Archives, Berkeley, Calif. 1972). Mem. Santa Monica Track Club. Office: care Creative Artists Agy Los Angeles 1888 Century Park E Los Angeles CA 90067 *

DE ROCCO, ANDREW GABRIEL, university president; b. Avondale, R.I., July 31, 1929; s. Joachim and Ida Lovat De R.; 1 son, J. Lovat. B.S. (Merit scholar), Purdue U., 1951; M.S., U. Mich., 1953, Ph.D. (Du Pont fellow), 1956; postdoctoral fellow, NRS, 1956-57. Mem. faculty U. Mich., Ann Arbor, 1957-62; vis. prof. U. Colo., Boulder, 1962-63; mem. faculty U. Md., College Park, 1963-79; prof. molecular physics, 1969-79; First Disting. vis. prof. USAF Acad., 1975-76; vis. prof. Tufts U., 1968, 69; dean of faculty and Coll. prof. natural scis. Trinity Coll., Hartford, Conn., 1979-84; pres. Denison U., Granville, Ohio, 1984—; mem. staff phys. scis. lab., div. computer research and tech. NIH, 1969—; cons. Bendix Corp., Office of Sec. Def., IBM, Medi-Sci. Corp., NIH, Teknekron Corp., Washington, VA Hosp., Washington Engring. Services Corp.; pres. Nat. Collegiate Honors Council, 1977-78; mem. bd. higher edn. State of Conn., vice chmn. standing. com. on accreditation. Contbr. numerous articles to profl. jours.; Editorial cons., Acad. Press, Cambridge Univ. Press, Harper & Row, Holt, Rinehart & Winston, others. Bd. dirs. Greater Washington Council for Clean Air, 1967-71; mem. village council Friendship Heights, Chevy Chase, Md., 1974-76; bd. dirs. World Affairs Ctr. NRC fellow, 1956-57; Am. Cancer Soc. fellow, 1956-57; NATO sr. fellow, 1964. Fellow AAAS; mem. Conn. Acad. Sci. and Tech., Am. Chem. Soc., Am. Phys. Soc., Biophys. Soc., Am. Assn. Physics Tchrs. (com. internat. edn.), Md. Acad. Scis. (sci. council 1970—), Sigma Xi, Phi Lambda Upsilon, Delta Rho Kappa, Sigma Pi Sigma. Office: Denison Univ Granville OH 43023

DE ROO, REMI JOSEPH, bishop; b. Swan Lake, Man., Can., Feb. 24, 1924; s. Raymond and Josephine (De Pape) De R. Student, St. Boniface (Man.) Coll.; S.T.D., Angelicum U., Rome, Italy. Ordained priest Roman Catholic Ch., 1950; curate Holy Cross Parish, St. Boniface, 1952-53; sec. to archbishop of St. Boniface, 1954-56; diocesan dir. Cath. action Archdiocese St. Boniface, 1953-54; exec. sec. Man. Cath. Con., 1958; pastor Holy Cross Parish, 1960-62; bishop of, Victoria, B.C., Can., 1962—; Canadian episcopal rep. Internat. Secretariat Apostleship See, 1964-78; chairperson Human Rights Commn. B.C., 1974-77; mem. social affairs commn. Can. Conf. Cath. Bishops, 1973-79, chmn., 1980—; pres. Western Cath. Conf. Bishops, 1980—. Address: 740 View St Victoria BC V8W 1J8 Canada

DE ROSIER, ARTHUR HENRY, JR., college president; b. Norwich, Conn., Feb. 18, 1931; s. Arthur Henry and Rose (Raymond) DeR.; m. Linda Preston Scott, Dec. 26, 1979; children: Deborah Ann, Marsha Carol, Brett Preston Scott, Melissa Estelle. B.S., U. So. Miss., 1953; M.A., U. S.C., 1955, Ph.D., 1959. Asst. prof. history The Citadel, 1956-57, Converse Coll., Spartanburg, S.C., 1957-59; asst. prof. U. So. Miss., 1959-60, assoc. prof., 1960-64, prof., 1964-65; assoc. prof. history U. Okla., 1965-67, asst. dean, 1966-67; dean Grad. Sch., prof. history E. Tenn. State U., Johnson City, 1967-72, v.p. for adminstrn., 1972-74; vice chancellor for acad. affairs, prof. history U. Miss., 1974-76, vice chancellor, 1976-77; pres. East Tenn. State U., 1977-80, Coll. Idaho, Caldwell, 1980—; vis. prof. history U. Mass., summer 1964; ednl. TV series on Am. history, 1966-72. Author: Through the South with a Union Soldier, 1969, The Removal of the Choctaw Indians, 1970, (with others) Four Centuries of Southern Indians, 1975, Forked Tongues and Broken Treaties, 1975, Appalachia: Family Traditions in Transition, 1975; Contbr. articles to hist. jours. Active numerous Indian philanthropies. Served with USAF, 1948-52. So. fellow, 1958; Am. Philos. Soc. grantee, 1964. Mem. Am. Hist. Assn., Orgn. Am. Historians, So., Western hist. assns., Am. Assn. State Colls. and Univs., Phi Beta Kappa. Club: Rotary. Home: 1923 Everett St Caldwell ID 83605 *A college is a place where educational opportunities are available for all who treasure learning. The testing, challenging, and expanding of the mind is our primary responsibility, and we should be graded on how successfully we complete that task. A college is also an integral part of society. It helps us develop and clarify ideals and goals; it challenges us to develop a civilized set of principles; and it affords us an opportunity to test those principles and goals in the greater society. And it must teach us to approach life with a sense of humor. We are human: we are capable of significant achievements and bumbling failures. An educated person learns to live with both, allowing success and failure to meet each other with good grace and a smile.*

DEROSIER, DAVID JOHN, biophysicist; b. Milw., Feb. 22, 1939; s. Herman Francis and Adell Marie (Hydar) D.; m. Anne Marie Schneider, Sept. 1, 1962; children: Elizabeth Anne, Charles David. B.S., U. Chgo., 1961, Ph.D., 1965. Postdoctoral fellow Lab. Molecular Biology, Cambridge, England, 1965-69; asst. prof. chemistry U. Tex., Austin, 1968-72, assoc. prof., 1972-73; assoc. prof. physics Brandeis U., Waltham, Mass., 1973-78, prof., 1978-79, prof. biology, 1979—, chmn. grad. program biophysics, 1978-79, 80-83. Coordinator Mason-Rice Community Sch., Newton, Mass., 1975-77. Air Force Office Sci. Research fellow, 1965; Am. Cancer Soc. fellow, 1966; NSF fellow, 1967; NIH grantee, 1970-83. Mem. Biophys. Soc., Am. Soc. Cell Biologists, AAAS. Home: 19 Manemet Rd Newton MA 02159 Office: Rosenstiel Ctr Brandeis U Waltham MA 02254

DEROUNIAN, STEVEN BOGHOS, state justice; b. Sofia, Bulgaria, Apr. 6, 1918; came to U.S., 1921; s. Boghos and Eliza (Aprahamian) D.; m. Emily Ann Kennard, Aug. 20, 1947; children: Ann Ashby, Eleanor Kennard. A.B., N.Y. U., 1938; LL.B., Fordham U., 1942. Bar: N.Y. 1942, D.C. 1959, Tex. 1981. Practiced in, Mineola, N.Y., Garden City, N.Y., also Washington; former mem. law firm Derounian, Candee, Guardino Murphy; mem. 83d-87th U.S. Congresses, 2d Dist. N.Y., 88th Congress 3d Dist. N.Y.; mem. com. on ways and means; now ret. justice Supreme Ct. State of N.Y.; Councilman, mem. bd., Town of North Hempstead, N.Y., 1948-52. Served to capt. inf., 103rd Div. AUS, 1942-46; maj. Res. Decorated Purple Heart, Bronze Star with cluster, Combat Infantryman's badge. Mem. Am., N.Y. State, Travis County bar assns., V.F.W., Am. Legion, Delta Theta Pi. Republican. Clubs: Capital; Chowder and Marching (Washington). Lodges: Masons; Elks. Home: 3103 Pleasant Run Pl Austin TX 78703

DEROW, PETER ALFRED, communications company executive; b. Boston, Apr. 18, 1940; s. Harry A. and Ruth (Dimond) D.; m. Ruth Joffe, June 13, 1965; children:Jonathan, Polly, James. B.A., Harvard U., 1962, M.B.A., 1965. Asst. to pres. Newsweek, Inc., N.Y.C., 1966, circulation dir., 1967, mktg. dir., 1968, mng. dir. internat. edits., 1969-74, v.p., 1969-73, sr. v.p., dep. to pub., 1973-75, exec. v.p., 1975-76, pres., 1976-77, 78-79, chmn. bd., pres., 1980-81; sr. v.p., dir. CBS, Inc., 1977-78, v.p., 1981—; pres. CBS Pub. Group, 1981—. Author: (with James C. Crimmins) Successful Publishing on Campus, 1967. Trustee Com. Econ. Devel. Club: Sky (N.Y.C). Office: 51 W 52d St New York NY 10019

DERR, K. T., petroleum co. exec. B.A., M.B.A., Cornell U. With Standard Oil Co. of Calif., 1960—, v.p., 1972—; Pres. Chevron U.S.A., Inc. subs. Standard Oil Co. of Calif., 1978-84; head merger program Standard Oil Co. of Calif. and Gulf Oil Corp., 1984—. Office: Standard Oil of Calif 225 Bush St San Francisco CA 94104 *

DERR, RICHARD EDWARD, aviation company executive; b. Warren, Ohio, Aug. 24, 1933; s. Harry Edward and Alfer (Robanke) D.; m. Doris Marie Congdon, June 29, 1956; children: Jacquelyn, Sandra, Dennis. B.S.E.E., U. Cin., 1956; M.S.E.E., U. So. Calif., 1959, M.P.I., 1959. Engr., dept. mgr. L-101 Lear-Siegler Astronics, Santa Monica, Calif., 1968-73; program mgr. IDAS Rockwell Internat., Cedar Rapids, Iowa, 1973-75, dir. program mgmt., 1975-77, dir. mfg., Cedar Rapids, 1977, dir. program mgmt., 1977-79, v.p., gen. mgr., 1979—. Mem. Iowa C. of C., Army Aviation Assn. (pres.), Nat. Contract Mgmt. Assn., Am. Helicopter Soc., Am. Def. Preparedness Assn., Armed Forces Communications and Electronics Assn. Republican. Home: 221 Forest Dr SE Cedar Rapids IA 52403 Office: Rockwell Internat 400 Collins Rd NE Cedar Rapids IA 52498

DERR, ROBERT JAMES, insurance company executive; b. Sterling, Nebr., Oct. 21, 1919; s. Herbert S. and Emma (Mahler) D.; m. Ana Paula Derr; children: Virginia Hall, Barbara, Thomas, Marcos, Regina. Student, U. Nebr., 1938-41, Los Angeles City Coll., U. So. Calif., U. Calif. at Los Angeles at Berkeley. Mfg. engr. Lockheed Aircraft Co., 1941-47; with Indsl. Indemnity Co., San Francisco, 1947—, exec. v.p., 1968-69, pres., 1970—, also dir., mem. exec. com.; dir. Crum & Forster Ins. Cos.; Guest lectr. Am. Mgmt. Assn., Stanford Grad. Sch. Bus., 1957-58. Bd. assos. Golden Gate Coll.; bd. dirs., past pres. Western Ins. Information Service; trustee Robert Louis Stevenson Sch., Pebble Beach, Calif.; v.p., bd. dirs. Inst. for Contemporary Studies. Methodist. Clubs: Commonwealth, World Trade, Merchants Exchange, Bankers (San Francisco); Round Hill Country (Alamo, Calif.). Home: 320 Lakeview Pl Alamo CA 94507 Office: 255 California St San Francisco CA 94111 *A philosophy I try to live by is: consistency of purpose; reverence for life; and respect for the dignity of others.*

DERRICK, A. M., petroleum engr.; b. Dublin, Tex., July 26, 1922; s. Alex M. and Velma W. (Thompson) D.; m. Margie Davidson, Jan. 10, 1946; children—Michael, Nancy, David, Patricia. B.S. in Petroleum Engring, U. Tex., 1947, M.S., U. Houston, 1956. Petroleum engr. Stanolind Oil and Gas Co., Pampa, Wink and Midland, Tex. and Tulsa, 1947-53; with El Paso (Tex.) Natural Gas Co., 1953—, sr. petroleum engr., 1953-59, mgr. reservoir engr., 1960-65, asst. v.p., 1966-71, v.p., 1972-76, sr. v.p., 1977—. Served with U.S. Navy, 1943-46. Mem. Soc. Petroleum Evaluation Engrs., Soc. Petroleum Engrs., Am. Assn. Petroleum Geologists, Am. Gas Assn., Pacific Coast Gas Assn. Republican. Baptist. Club: El Paso Country. Home: 4304 Santa Rita St El Paso TX 79902 Office: PO Box 1492 El Paso TX 79978

DERRICK, BUTLER CARSON, JR., congressman; b. Sept. 30, 1936; s. Butler Carson and Mary English (Scott) D.; m. Suzanne Mims, Dec. 29, 1960; children: Lydia Gile, Butler Carson, III. Student, U. S.C., 1954-58; LL.B., U. Ga., 1965; Hum.D. (hon.), Lander Coll., 1978. Bar: S.C. bar 1965. Partner firm Derrick & Byrd, Edgefield, S.C., 1970-75; mem. S.C. Ho. of Reps., 1969-74, 94th-98th Congresses from 3d S.C. Dist.; mem. house rules com., select com. on coms., exec. com. environ. study conf. 94th-97th Congresses from 3d S.C. Dist. Pub. study on Congl. Control of Expenditures. Pres. Edgefield County Fish and Game Assn. Named Outstanding Young Man of Year, 1971-72, S.C. Jaycees Assn.; Conservationist of Yr. S.C. Wildlife Fedn., 1977, Nat. Wildlife Fedn., 1977; one of Our Ten Best Friends in Congress Outdoor life mag.; Man of Yr. Anderson chpt. Ducks Unltd., 1980; recipient Disting. River Conservation award Am. Rivers Conservation Council, 1977. Mem. S.C. Bar Assn., ABA, Edgefield County Bar Assn. (past pres.). Democrat. Episcopalian. Home: Stonehenge Rd Edgefield SC 29824 Office: 201 Cannon House Office Bldg Washington DC 20515

DERRICK, MALCOLM, physicist; b. Hull, Eng., Feb. 15, 1933; came to U.S., 1963, naturalized, 1976; s. Arthur Henry and Gladys (Hopkinson) D.; m. Kathleen Allen, 1957; 1 son, Matthew; m. Christa Zars Baumgardner; 1966. B.Sc. with 1st class honours, U. Birmingham, 1954, Ph.D., 1959; M.A., Oxford U., 1961. Instr. Carnegie Inst. Tech., 1957-60; asst. prof. Oxford U., 1960-63; asst. physicist Argonne (Ill.) Nat. Lab., 1963-67, sr. physicist, 1967—, dir. high energy physics div., 1974-81; vis. prof. U. Minn., 1969-70, Univ. Coll., London, 1972-73; adv. com. Stanford U. Accelerator Center, Fermi Nat. Accelerator Lab.; mem. high energy physics adv. panel Dept. Energy. Author numerous research papers on high energy physics. Fellow Am. Phys. Soc. Home: 4717 Northcott Downers Grove IL 60515 Office: Argonne Nat Lab Bldg 362 Argonne IL 60439 *The opportunity to spend a lifetime's career investigating the Fundamental physical basis of matter is one that has been given to relatively few people. Such research requires large and expensive accelerators and particle detectors and so can only be funded by government agencies. It is to the credit of the United States that such support has been generously given, and the resulting revolution in our understanding of nature is the outstanding intellectual achievement of our times.*

DERRICK, WILLIAM SHELDON, physician; b. Millville, Pa., Mar. 5, 1916; s. Bruce Berger and Margaret (Mosteller) D.; m. Alice Marie Cowing, May 30, 1942; children: Lynn Sheldon, Bruce William. B.A., George Washington U., 1940, M.D., 1942. Diplomate: Am. Bd. Anesthesiology. Intern Allegheny Gen. Hosp., 1942-43; fellow in surgery Cleve. Clinic Found., 1943; resident in anesthesiology Walter Reed Gen., Mt. Alto VA, Gallinger Mcpl., also George Washington U. hosps., 1945-48; asso. anesthesiology Harvard U. Med. Sch., also head sect. anesthesiology Peter Bent Brigham Hosp., Boston, 1948-54; cons. anesthesia VA Hosp., Rutland Heights, Mass., Murphy Army Hosp., Waltham, Mass., also VA Hosp., W. Roxbury, Mass., 1950-54; head dept. U. Tex. System Cancer Center, M.D. Anderson Hosp., Houston, 1954-77; cons. St. Joseph's Hosp., Houston, 1955-77; prof. anesthesiology U. Tex. Med. Sch., 1954—; mem. staff (Center Pavilion Hosp.), 1967-77; vis. mem. grad. faculty Tex. A&M U., 1968-71; prof. U. Tex. Med. Sch., 1968—. Served to maj. M.C. AUS, 1943-46. Recipient Alumni Achievement award George Washington U., 1957; scholarship M.I.T., 1960; award for service as trustee Am. Registry Inhalation Therapists, 1972. Mem. Am. Coll. Anesthesiologists, Tex. Gulf Coast Anesthesia Soc. (pres. 1959-60), So. Soc. Anesthesiologists (pres. 1965-66, 83-84), New Eng. Soc. Anesthesiologists (pres. 1982-83), So. Med. Assn. (chmn. sect. anesthesiology 1967), Doctors Club Houston (pres., gov. 1969), Tex. Med. Found. (charter), AAUP (pres. Houston chpt. 1980-81). Presbyterian. Clubs: Aesculapian (Harvard U.); Bayou Rifles, Greater Houston Gun, Harvard, Racquet, Tennis Patrons, Knife and Fork, Les Amis du Vin (pres. 1971), University, U. Tex. Faculty (Houston) (pres. 1969-71); Congl. Country, George Washington U. (Washington). Devel. techniques of subarachnoid alcohol block for control of pain, 1956; co-devel. mech. respiratory assistor, 1949. Address: 2808 University Blvd Houston TX 77005

DERRY, R. MICHAEL, manufacturing company executive; b. Owosso, Mich., June 6, 1937; s. Arthur Leroy and Frances Lavonne (Medd) D.; m. Joma Jean Lauder, June 28, 1958; children: Verla Jo, David Dean, Kasandra Lee. B.B.A., Western Mich. U., Kalamazoo, 1960. C.P.A., Mich. Contrller, treas. J.P. Burroughs & Sons, Inc., Saginaw, Mich., 1968-74; pres. Ferrell-Ross Co., Saginaw, 1974-76; dir. long range planning, treas. Blount, Inc., Montgomery, Ala., 1976-79; sr. v.p. Hon Industries, Inc., Muscatine, Iowa, 1981—. Mem. Am. Inst. C.P.A.s, Mich. Assn. C.P.A.s. Club: Geneva Golf and Country (Muscatine) (treas. 1983). Lodge: Rotary. Home: 906 Sunrise Circle Muscatine IA 52761 Office: Hon Industries Inc 414 E 3d Ave Muscatine IA 52761

DERRYBERRY, WILLIAM EVERETT, former university president; b. Columbia, Tenn., Oct. 11, 1906; s. Felix Oscar and Bonnie Everett (McDonald) D.; m. Joan Pitt-Rew, Aug. 5, 1933; children: Walter Everett, June Elisabeth. B.A., U. Tenn., 1928, Oxford U., 1932, M.A., 1939; D.Litt., U. Chattanooga, 1965; LL.D., Pepperdine Coll., 1967. Prof. English Burritt Coll., Spencer, Tenn., 1932-33; head dept. English U. Tenn. Jr. Coll., 1933-38; head dept. langs. and lit. Murray (Ky.) State Coll., 1938-40; pres. Tenn. Technol. U., Cookeville, 1940-74, pres. emeritus, 1974—. Regional dir. U.S.O. and Nat. War Fund, 1943-46; Chmn. Tenn. Edn. Legislative Com., 1943, 44, 45; adv. bd. Tenn. Congress P.T.A.; sec. Conf. on Pub. Instns. in So. States, 1949; mem. Tenn. Jud. Council; pres. Tenn. Water Safety Congress, 1951; chmn. council univ. presidents Tenn. Bd. Edn. Recipient Outstanding Civilian Service medal U.S. Dept. Army, 1968, Distinguished Civilian Service decoration, 1974; Distinguished Am. award Nat. Football Found. and Hall of Fame, 1974; Merit award Gov. Tenn., 1974. Mem. AAUP, Nat. Council English Tchrs., U. Tenn. Alumni Assn. (pres. 1946), Tenn. Coll. Assn. (pres. 1945), So. Assn. Colls. (commn. on higher edn.), Phi Beta Kappa, Phi Delta Kappa, Sigma Chi, Phi Kappa Phi, Pi Kappa Delta, Omicron Delta Kappa, Kappa Delta Pi. Clubs: Rotarian, Lion. Address: Tenn Technol U Cookeville TN 38501

DERSHOWITZ, ALAN MORTON, lawyer, educator; b. Bklyn., Sept. 1, 1938; s. Harry and Claire (Ringel) D.; married; children: Elon Marc, Jamin Seth. B.A. magna cum laude, Bklyn. Coll., 1959, LL.B., Yale, 1962; M.A. (hon.), Harvard, 1967. Bar: D.C. 1963, Mass. 1968, U.S. Supreme Ct 1968. Law clk. to chief judge David L. Bazelon, U.S. Ct. Appeals, 1962-63; to justice Arthur J. Goldberg, U.S. Supreme Ct., 1963-64; mem. faculty Harvard, 1964—, prof. law, 1967—; Fellow (Center for Advanced Study of Behavioral Scis.), 1971-72; Cons. to dir. NIMH, 1967-69, 1967, 1968, 1967-68, 1972-73, 1972—, 1973-76; rapporteur Twentieth Century Fund Study on Sentencing, 1975-76. Author: (with others) Psychoanalysis, Psychiatry and the Law, 1967, Criminal Law: Theory and Process, 1974, The Best Defense, 1982; also articles.; Editor-in-chief: Yale Law Jours, 1961-62. Mem. commn. on law and social action Am. Jewish Congress, 1978—; bd. dirs. ACLU, 1968-71, 72-75, Assembly Behavioral and Social Scis. at Nat. Acad. Scis., 1973-76; chmn. civil rights com. New Eng. region Anti-Defamation League, B'nai B'rith, 1980. Guggenheim fellow, 1978-79. Mem. Order of Coif, Phi Beta Kappa. Jewish. Office: Harvard Law Sch Cambridge MA 02138

DERTOUZOS, MICHAEL LEONIDAS, computer scientist, electrical engineer; b. Athens, Greece, Nov. 5, 1936; came to U.S., 1954, naturalized, 1965; s. Leonidas Michael and Rosana G. (Maris) D.; m. Hadwig Gofferje, Nov. 21, 1961; children—Alexandra, Leonidas. B.S. in E.E, U. Ark., 1957, M.S., 1959; Ph.D., MIT, 1964. Head research and devel. Baldwin Electronics, Inc., 1958-60; research asst. MIT, Cambridge, 1960-64, asst. prof., 1964-68, assoc. prof., 1968-73, prof., 1973—, dir., 1974—; founder, chmn. bd. Computek, Inc., 1968-74; cons. in computers to industry. Author: Threshold Logic: a Synthesis Approach, 1966, (with Athans, Spann and Mason) Systems, Networks and Computation: Multivariable Methods, 1974, Systems, Networks and Computation: Basic Concepts, 1972, (with Clark, Halle, Pool and Wiesner) The Telephone's First Century—and Beyond, 1977, The Computer Age; A Twenty Year View, 1979; Contbr. articles profl. jours. Trustee Athens Coll., Greece, 1973—; chmn. bd. Boston Camerata, 1976—; dir. Cambridge Soc. Early Music, 1974-75. Recipient Terman Internat. Edn. award Am. Soc. Engring. Edn., 1975; Ford postdoctoral fellow, 1964-66; Fulbright scholar, 1954. Fellow IEEE (Thompson best paper prize 1968); mem. Sigma Xi, Tau Beta Pi, Pi Mu Epsilon. Greek Orthodox. Patentee in field. Home: 15 Bernard Ln Waban MA 02168 Office: 545 Technology Sq Cambridge MA 02139

DERWINSKI, EDWARD JOSEPH, government official; b. Chgo., Sept. 15, 1926; s. Casimir Ignatius and Sophia (Zmijewski) D.; m. Patricia Van Der Giessen; children: Maureen Sue, Michael Stephen. B.Sc. in History, Loyola U., 1951. Rep. 24th Dist., Ill. Gen Assembly, 1957-58; mem. 86th-97th Congresses from 4th Dist. Ill.; mem. fgn. affairs, post office, civil service coms.; counselor U.S. Dept. State, Washington, 1982—; Vice pres. exec. com., treas. Am. group Interparliamentary Union. Served with inf. AUS, 1945-46. Named one of ten Outstanding Young Men of Chgo., 1959, 61. Mem. VFW, Polish Highlanders (nat. dir.), Cath. War Vets., Polish Alma Mater, Am. Legion, Polish Legion Am. Vets (past state vice comdr.), Amvets, Polish Roman Cath. Union, Polish Nat. Alliance. Republican. Roman Catholic. Clubs: Moose, KC, Kiwanis. Office: Dept State Washington DC 20520 *

DERZON, GORDON M., hospital administrator; b. Milw., Dec. 28, 1934; married. B.A., Dartmouth Coll., 1957; M.H.A., U. Mich., 1961. Adminstrv. resident Bklyn. Hosp., 1960-61, adminstrv. asst., 1961-63, asst. exec. dir., 1963-65, exec. dir., 1966-67, State U. Hosp., Bklyn., 1967-68, Kings County Hosp. Center, 1968-74; supt. U. Wis. Hosps. and Clinics, Madison, 1974—; asso. prof. SUNY, 1967-74; clin. asso. prof. U. Wis. Contbr. articles to profl. jours. Mem. Am. Hosp. Assn., Am. Coll. Hosp. Adminstrs. Home: 3440 Topping Rd Madison WI 53705 Office: 600 Highland Ave Madison WI 53792

DERZON, ROBERT ALAN, health services administrator; b. Milw., Dec. 30, 1930; s. Matthew R. and Mildred L. (Gordon) D.; m. Margo Harris, Sept. 2, 1956; children: James, Andrea, Michael. A.B., Dartmouth Coll., 1953; M.B.A., Amos Tuck Sch. Bus. Adminstrn., 1954. Adminstrv. asst. R.I. Hosp., Providence, 1955-56; asst. dir. N.Y. U. Hosp., 1957-66; 1st dep. commr. of hosps. City of N.Y., 1966-70; dir. U. of Calif. Hosps. and Clinics, San Francisco, 1970-77; adminstr. health care financing adminstrn. HEW, Washington, 1977-78; sr. scholar Inst. of Medicine, Nat. Acad. Sci., Washington, 1978—; cons. U. Calif. Health Policy Program, 1978—; v.p. Lewin and Assos., 1979—; asst. prof. preventive medicine N.Y. U. Sch. Medicine, 1960-70; clin. asso. program in health care adminstrn. U. Chgo., 1972-77; lectr. dept. medicine U. Calif., San Francisco, 1970-77; lectr. program in health care adminstrn. U. Calif., Berkeley Sch. Public Health, 1972-77; cons. Cost of Living Council, Washington, Nat. Center for Health Services Research, U.S. Senate Budget Com., Office Tech. Assessment, Children's Med. Center, Krakow, Poland; del. 5th Pan Am. Conf. on Med. Edn., Caracas, Venezuela, 1974; vice chmn. Adv. Council to Calif. Health Facilities Commn., 1972-77; mem. bd. Bay Area Comprehensive Health Planning Council, 1974-77; mem. steering com. on social security studies Inst. Medicine, Nat. Acad. Sci., 1974-76; mem. Bd. of Standardization, N.Y.C., 1966-70; vice chmn. Dartmouth Hitcock Med. Ctr., 1983-84. Contbr. articles to profl. jours. Recipient award for exceptional integrity HEW, 1979. Mem. Am. Assn. Med. Colls. (chmn. council of teaching hosps. 1974, sec.-treas. 1974), Inst. Medicine (governing council 1983-86), Am. Hosp. Assn., Calif. Hosp. Assn. (trustee 1972-75). Jewish. Home: 6 Dawn Pl Mill Valley CA 94941 Office: Lewin & Assocs 5028 Geary Blvd San Francisco CA 94118

DESAI, CHANDRAKANT S., civil engineering and engineering mechanics educator; b. Nadisar, Gujarat, India, Nov. 24, 1936; came to U.S., 1964, naturalized, 1973; s. Sankalchand P. and Kamala M. (Kothari) D.; m. Patricia L. Porter, Apr. 28, 1969; children: Maya C., Sanjay C. B.Engring., U. Bombay, 1959; M.S. (Ideal Cement Co. fellow 1964), Rice U., Houston, 1966; Ph.D. (Am. Petroleum Inst. fellow 1966), U. Tex., Austin, 1968. Registered profl. engr., Miss. Civil engr. govt. and pvt. agencies, India, 1959-64; research civil engr. USAE Wayerways Expt. Sta., Vicksburg, Miss., 1968-74; prof. civil engring., dir. computational methods group Va. Poly. Inst. and State U., Blacksburg, 1974-81; prof., dir. engring. mechanics, geomech. and structural mechanics program dept. civil engring. and engring. mechanics U. Ariz., Tucson, 1981—; Erskine prof. U. Canterbury, Chistchurch, N.Z., 1980; chmn. Internat. Com. Numerical Methods in Geomechanics, 1976—. Author: Elementary Finite Element Method, 1979; co-author: Introduction to Finite Element Method, 1972, Constitutive Laws of Engineering Materials, 1983; co-editor, co-author: Numerical Methods in Geotechnical Engineering, 1977; gen. editor: Internat. Jour. Numerical and Analytical Methods in Geomechs; mem. editorial bds. profl. jours. Trustee Deep Founds. Inst., 1978-80; chmn./vice chmn. 1st, 2d, 4th Internat. Conf. Numerical Methods Geomechanics. Recipient Meritorious Civilian Service award C.E., U.S. Army, 1972, Alexander von Humboldt award W.German Govt., 1976, Theodore Cooke Meml. prize U. Bombay, 1958; grantee NSF, Dept. Transp., C.E. Mem. Inst. Structural Engrs. (Wallace Premium prize 1963), Internat. Soc. Rock Mechanics, Internat. Soc. Soil Mechanics and Found. Engring., ASCE (chmn. computer and numerical methods com. GT div. 1976-81), Earthquake Research Inst., Am. Underground-Space Assn., ASTM, Am. Acad. Mechanics, Am. Soc. Engring. Edn. Home: 6776 N Harran Dr Tucson AZ 85704 Office: Dept Civil Engring and Engring Mechanics U Arizona Tucson AZ 85721

DESAI, PADMA, economics educator, Sovetologist; b. Surat, Gujarat, India, Oct. 12, 1931; came to U.S., 1968; s. Kalidas L. and Shanta (Desai) D.; m. Jagdish N. Bhagwati; 1 dau., Anuradha Kristina. M.A.,

Bombay U., India 1953; Ph.D., Harvard U., 1960. Teaching fellow Harvard U., Cambridge, Mass., 1958-59, resarch assoc. Rusain Research Ctr., 1968-80, mem. vis com., 1982—; reader in econs. Delhi U., India, 1960-69; vis. prof. Boston U., 1977-79; prof. econs. Columbia U., N.Y.C., 1980—, mem. exec. com. W. Averell Harriman Inst. for Advance Study Soviet Union, 1980—. Author: books including India: Planning For Industrialization, 1970, Bokaro Steel Plant: Study of Soviet Assistance, 1971; editor: Marxism, Central Planning and The Soviet Economy, 1983. Mem. Am. Econ. Assn. Home: 25 Claremont Ave New York NY 10027 Office: Dept Econs Columbia U New York NY 10027

DE SAINT PHALLE, THIBAUT, educator, lawyer, investment banker; b. Tuxedo Park, N.Y., July 23, 1918; s. Fal and Marie (Duryee) de Saint P.; m. Rosamond Frame, Jan. 12, 1946 (dec. 1960); children: Fal, Pierre, Thérèse; m. Elene Canrobert Isles, June 21, 1965 (div. 1983); children: Marc, Diane; m. Mariana M. Smith, April 24, 1983. Student, Harvard U., 1935-37; A.B., Columbia U., 1939, J.D., 1941. Bar: N.Y. 1942. Asso. Chadbourne, Wallace, Parke & Whiteside, N.Y.C., 1941-50; partner, head corp. law dept. Lewis & McDonald, N.Y.C., 1950-58; v.p., treas. Becton, Dickinson and Co., Rutherford, N.J., 1958-62, dir., 1958-67; sr. partner Coudert Bros., N.Y.C., 1962-66, of counsel, 1966-77, Vorys, Sater, Seymour & Pease, Washington, 1983—; ltd. partner Dean Witter & Co., pres. Dean Witter Overseas Fin. Corp., N.Y.C., 1967-68; investment banker Stralem, Saint Phalle & Co., Inc., N.Y.C., 1968-70, vice chmn. bd. dirs., 1968-70; mem. faculty, prof. internat. fin. and law Centre d'Etudes Industrielles, Geneva, 1971-76; dir. Export-Import Bank U.S., Washington, 1977-81; Scholl prof. internat. bus. Georgetown U. Center Strategic and Internat. Studies, 1981—; chmn. exec. com. Crosby Internat. Group, 1981—. Author: (with others) The Dollar Crisis, 1963, Multinational Corporations, 1976, U.S. Productivity and Competitiveness in International Trade, 1980, Trade Inflation and the Dollar, 1981; contbr. numerous articles on internat. fin. and trade to profl. jours. Served with OSS USN, 1942-46. Decorated Navy Commendation medal, Bronze Star. Mem. ABA. Democrat. Roman Catholic. Clubs: Met. (Washington); River (N.Y.C.); Travellers (Paris). Home: 3227 Reservoir St NW Washington DC 20007 Office: 1800 K St NW Washington DC 20006 1828 L St NW Washington DC *By waking up every morning with the thought that this will be a day of adventure, good or bad, I have been prepared to take advantage of opportunities and to accept reverses, knowing that both good and bad events are transient phenomena in a long life.*

DESALVO, JOSEPH MICHAEL, geotechnical engineer; b. Rahway, N.J., July 4, 1931; s. Vincent and Josephine (Corrao) DeS.; m. Josephine C. Dragotta, Jan. 23, 1955; children: Steven, Thomas, Richard. B.S., Rutgers U., 1952; M.S., Columbia U., 1956. Registered profl. engr., 13 states. Instr. civil engring. Cooper Union for the Advancement of Art and Sci., N.Y.C., 1952-55, asst. prof., 1956-57; asso. engr. Joseph S.Ward & Assos. (Cons. Engrs.), Caldwell, N.J., 1952-57, chief engr., 1957-60; ptnr. Joseph S. Ward & Assos. (Cons. Engrs.), 1960-78; sr. v.p., ptnr., mng. officer N.J. office Converse Cons., 1978-79; dir. eastern ops. N.J. office Converse Ward Davis Dixon, 1980—; adj. instr. Rutgers U. Contbr. articles to profl. jours. Mem. ASCE, Am. Cons. Engrs. Council, Soc. Soil Mechanics and Found. Engring. (intern), Deep Founds. Inst., Assn. Soil and Found. Engrs., Chi Epsilon. Roman Catholic. Home: 264 Lynn Dr Franklin Lakes NJ 07417 Office: care of Converse Consultants PO Box 91 Caldwell NJ 07006

DESAN, WILFRID, philosophy educator. License en Philosophie, Lille (France) U.; Ph.D., Harvard U. Taught at Kenyon Coll., Harvard U.; now prof. philosophy emeritus Georgetown U. Author The Tragic Finale, The Marxism of Jean-Paul Sartre; The Planetary Man, Part I, A Noetic Prelude to a United World, Part II, An Ethical Prelude to a United World. Office: Dept Philosophy Georgetown Univ Washington DC 20057

DESANCTIS, ROMAN WILLIAM, cardiologist; b. Cambridge Springs, Pa., Oct. 30, 1930; s. Vincent and Margherita (Marini) DeS.; m. Ruth Ann Foley, May 7, 1955; children: Ellen Ruth, Lydia Marie, Andrea Jean, Marcia Louise. B.S. summa cum laude, U. Ariz., 1951; M.D. magna cum laude, Harvard U., 1955; D.Sc. (hon.), Wilkes Coll., 1984. Diplomate: Am. Bd. Internal Medicine, Sub Bd. Cardiovascular Diseases. Successively intern, asst. resident, sr. resident in medicine Mass. Gen. Hosp., Boston, 1955-56, 58-60, fellow in cardiology, 1960-62; dir. CCU, 1967-80, dir. clin. cardiology, 1980—, physician, 1970—; mem. faculty Harvard U. Med. Sch., 1964—, prof. medicine, 1973—. Co-author: Cardiac Clinico-Pathologica Conferences of the Mass. Gen. Hosp, 1972; contbr. articles to med. jours. Served as officer M.C. USNR, 1956-58. Recipient Excellence in Clin. Teaching award Harvard U. Med. Sch., 1980. Fellow A.C.P., Am. Coll. Cardiology; mem. Am. Heart Assn., Assn. Am. Physicians, Inst. of Medicine, New Eng. Cardiovascular Soc. (pres. 1979-80). Roman Catholic. Clubs: Winchester Country; Harvard (Boston); Aesculapian. Home: 5 Thoreau Circle Winchester MA 01890 Office: 15 Parkman Street Suite 367 Boston MA 02114

DE SANTIS, ANTHONY, theatre, restaurant executive; b. Gary, Ind., Jan. 5, 1914; s. Sam and Marie (DiVergilo) DeS.; m. Lucille Cuzeli, Feb. 12, 1945; children: Deborah, Diane. Student, Armour Inst., 1941. With research lab. staff Sherwin-Williams Paint Co., Chgo., 1934-39; owner, mgr. Embassy Club, Chgo., 1940-45, Martinique Restaurant, 1946—, Drury Lane Theatre, 1951—; dir. Heritage Pullman Bank & Trust Co., Chgo.; vice chmn. Heritage Standard Bank & Trust Co., Heritage Bank Corp.; pres. Martinique Co., Chgo., Evergreen Park Motel Corp., Drury Ln. Prodns., Inc., Water Tower Entertainment Inc.; treas. Martinique-Drury Ln. Corp; v.p. Indian Creek Investors, Inc. Mem. advisory bd. Sheriff of Cook County, Ill.; mem. citizens bd. U. Chgo.; bd. assos. De Paul U.; mem. advisory bd. Cath. Charities, Little Flower Soc. Recipient Humanitarian award, religious awards Little Flower Soc., 1966; decorated comdr. Order Holy Sepulchre, Knight of Malta; Knight comdr. Order St. John Jerusalem; Order St. Augustine Filius Ordinis; Knight comdr. Order St. Gregory; Order de Chasque; recipient Distinguished Service award Chgo. Police Capts. Assn., 8 Appreciation awards FBI, Chgo., 1969-78, Appreciation award Chgo. Fire Fighters, 1980; named Oaklawn Man of Year C. of C., 1965. Mem. Chgo. Patrolmen's Assn. (hon. life), Chgo. Conv. Bur. (1979). Clubs: Exec., Variety, Beverly Country (Chgo.); Quail Creek Country (Fla.); Mt. Kenya Safari.

DE SANTIS, VINCENT PAUL, educator, historian; b. Birdsboro, Pa., Dec. 25, 1916; s. Antonio and Martha Mae (Templin) DeS.; m. Helene O'Brien, June 24, 1946; children—Vincent, Edmund, Philip, John; m. Margaret Lois Lambert, May 13, 1978. B.S., West Chester (Pa.) State Coll., 1941; Ph.D., Johns Hopkins, 1952. Mem. faculty U. Notre Dame, 1949—, prof. history, 1962—, chmn. dept., 1963-71; summer vis. prof. Johns Hopkins, 1954, Bklyn. Coll., 1961, Georgetown U., 1962; vis. prof. U. Genoa, 1967-68, U. Queensland, Australia, 1976, 79. Author: Republicans Face the Southern Question, 1959, The Shaping of Modern America, 1877-1916, 1973, 77; co-author: Our Country, 1960, Roman Catholicism and the American Way of Life, 1960, America's Ten Greatest Presidents, 1961, The Democratic Experience, 1963, 68, 73, 76, 81, The Gilded Age, 1963, America Past and Present, 1968, American Foreign Policy in Europe, 1969, America's Eleven Greatest Presidents, 1971, Six Presidents from the Empire State, 1974, The Heritage of 1776, 1976, The Impact of the Cold War, Reconsiderations, 1977, A History of United States Foreign Policy, 4th edit, 1980, compiler The Gilded Age, 1973; editorial bd.: Hayes Jour. Mem. Cath. Commn. on Intellectual and Cultural Affairs. Served to capt. AUS, 1941-45. Recipient R.D.W. Connor award N.C. Lit. and Hist. Assn., 1959; award Am. Philos. Soc., 1955, 62, 63; Distinguished Alumni award West Chester State Coll., 1970; Guggenheim fellow, 1960-61; Fulbright lectr., 1967-68, 79; Henry E. Huntington grantee, 1973; Radcliffe Coll. grantee, 1982. Mem. Orgn. Am. Historians, Nat. Geog. Soc., Soc. Am. Historians, Am. Cath. Hist. Assn. (pres. 1963-64), Am. Hist. Assn., So. Hist. Assn., Am. Studies Assn., AAUP, Nat. Audubon Soc., No. Ind. Hist. Soc., Phi Alpha Theta. Home: Box 562 Notre Dame IN 46556

DESAUTELLE, WILLIAM PETER, financial executive; b. N.Y.C.; s. Alfred F. and Nora T. D.; m. Joan H. Hryharrow, Sept. 7, 1963; children: Christopher, W.P., Mark, Jill. B.A. in Math., Fairfield U., 1961; M.B.A., U. Conn., 1970. Mgr. fin. and adminstrn. Burndy Corp., Norwalk, Conn., 1967-71; group controller, treas. Smith & Wesson, Springfield, Mass., 1971-78; corp. treas. Kaman Corp., Bloomfield, Conn., 1979—. Office: Kaman Corp Blue Hills Ave Bloomfield CT 06002

DESBOIS, LOUIS CAMERON, airline executive; b. Montreal, Que., Can., July 20, 1931; s. Louis-Philippe and Helen Elizabeth (Cameron) DesB.; m. Louise Gareau, Apr., 1959; children: Valérie, Nicolas, Jean-François. Grad., Coll. Jean-de-Brébeuf, Montreal, 1952, McGill U., Montreal, 1955. Bar: Called to Que. bar 1956, created Queen's counsel 1974. Asso. firm Laidley, Howard, Lesage, McDougall, L'Ecuyer (and predecessor), Montreal, 1956-61; solicitor Air Can., Montreal, 1961-69, gen. atty., 1969-77, corp. sec., 1977-79, gen. counsel, 1979—; dir. Domaine d'Iberville Limitee; sec. Penair Investments Ltd., 1982. Mem. Internat. Law Assn. (past chmn. Montreal sect.), Air Transport Assn. Am., Assn. Am. Law Council, Can. Bar Assn. (past chmn. air and space law sec. Que. region, past nat. chmn. air and space law sect.), Internat. Air Transport Assn. (legal com.), Antiquarian and Numismatic Soc. Montreal (hon. pres., life gov.), Heraldry Soc. Can. Club: University (Montreal). Home: 102 de Touraine Preville St Lambert PQ J4S 1H2 Canada Office: Place Air Canada 500 Dorchester Blvd W Montreal PQ H3B 3P7 Canada

DESCH, CARL WILLIAM, banker, consultant; b. N.Y.C., Oct. 3, 1915; s. William and Marie (Mayerhofer) D.; m. Katharine Woerner, Aug. 31, 1940; children: Carol J. (Mrs. Russell R. Desoe), Carl William, Barbara K. (Mrs. Michael D. Lenihan). A.B., Columbia, 1937, M.A., 1939. With Citibank (N.A.), N.Y.C., from 1939, v.p., 1955-58, cashier, 1958-65, sr. v.p., cashier, from 1965; pres., dir. Exec. Air Fleet Inc.; chmn. Citibank (S.D.) N.A., Citibank (N.Y. State) N.A.; chmn., dir. SKF Industries, Inc., Pa., Skandia Am. Reins. Co., Hudson Ins. Co., Merc. Bank Can.; dir. Broadstone Group, Inc., Kimberly-Clark Corp., United Refrigerated Services Inc., Skandia Corp.; mem. trust adv. bd. USIF, real estate, Nassau, Bahamas. Treas. Greater N.Y. chpt. ARC; pres. Alumni Fedn. Columbia, 1969-71; trustee Columbia U. Served with USAAF, AUS, 1943-46. Clubs: University (N.Y.C) (council); Garden City Country.). Home: 121 Wilson St Garden City NY 11530

DESCH, THEODORE EDWARD, health insurance company executive, lawyer; b. Chgo., Oct. 1, 1931; s. Louis G. and Dorothy (Prieb) D.; m. Donna K. Thorsell, Feb. 3, 1951; children—Theodore M. (dec. 1968), Steven R., Katherine S., Gregory S. A.B., U. Ill., 1952, LL.B., 1954. Bar: Ill. bar 1954. Asst. gen. atty. C., R.I. & P. Ry., 1956-59, gen. atty., 1959-65, gen. counsel, 1965-68, v.p. and gen. counsel, 1968-70, vice chmn. bd., 1970-73, chmn. bd., 1973-74, chief exec. officer, 1970-74, dir., 1970-75; partner firm Kirkland & Ellis, Chgo., 1975-77; sr. v.p. law and pub. affairs Health Care Service Corp. (Blue Cross and Blue Shield Ill.), Chgo., 1977—. Trustee North Central Coll., Naperville; bd. dirs. Naperville Elderly Homes, Inc. Served to 1st lt., inf. U.S. Army, 1954-56. Mem. Am., Ill., Chgo. bar assns., Soc. Trial Lawyers, Delta Sigma Phi, Phi Alpha Delta. Lutheran. Clubs: Mason., Union League (Chgo.); Capitol Hill (Washington); Cress Creek Country (Naperville, Ill.). Home: 129 Springwood Dr Naperville IL 60540 Office: 233 N Michigan Ave Chicago IL 60601

DESCHENES, JULES OMER, judge; b. Montreal, Que., Can., June 7, 1923; s. Wilfrid and Berthe (Berard) D.; m. Jacqueline Lachapelle, June 26, 1948; children: Louise, Mireille, Pierre, Yves, Jean-Francois. B.A., Coll. de Montreal, 1943; M.Law, U. Montreal, 1946, LL.D. (hon.), 1981. Barrister, solicitor, Montreal, 1946-72; justice Ct. of Appeal, Quebec, 1972-73; chief justice Superior Ct. of Quebec, 1973-83; lectr. pvt. internat. law U. Montreal, 1962-69, bd. govs., exec. com., 1967-73, hon. mem. bd. govs., 1977. Author: The Sword and the Scales, 1979, Les Plateaux de la balance, 1979, Ainsi par lèrent les tribunaux, 1981, Masters in Their Own House, 1981. Pres. Montreal Port Council, 1969-70; pres. Quebec Adv. Council on Justice, 1972. Fellow Royal Soc. Can.; mem. Quebec Interprofl. Council (pres. 1965-67), Can. Jud. Council (exec. com. 1977-83), World Assn. Judges (com. on expanding Jurisdiction of Internat. Ct. of Justice, pres. 1977-82), Can. Bar Assn. (pres. Quebec br. 1966-67), Found. Law Research in Can. (trustee 1967-78). Roman Catholic. Club: Cercle de la Place d'Armes.

DESCHUTTER, RICHARD U., chemical company official; b. Detroit, May 25, 1940; s. Urbain and Margaret (Van de Veloe) DeS.; m. Carol Ann Desgranger, Apr. 2, 1966; children: Douglas and Debra (twins). B.S. in Chem. Engring., U. Ariz., 1964, M.S., 1965. Registered profl. engr., Ind. Regional sales mgr. detergents and phosphates Monsanto Co., N.Y.C., 1975-76, field sales dir. plasticizers div., St. Louis, 1976-77, dir. mktg., 1977-80, gen. mgr. detergents and phosphates div., 1980-82, gen. mgr. engring. products div., 1982—. Mem. devel. bd. St. Louis Children's Hosp., 1980. Office: Monsanto Co 803 N Lindbergh Blvd Saint Louis MO 63166 *

DE SCHWEINITZ, KARL, JR., economics educator; b. Phila., Mar. 16, 1920; s. Karl and Jessie (Dickson) de S.; m. Margery Anne Skinner, Aug. 8, 1945; children—Ellen, Deborah, Anne. B.A., Dartmouth Coll., 1941; Ph.D., Yale U., 1949. Prof. econs. Northwestern U., 1949-67, prof. econs. and law, 1967-79, prof. econs., 1979—. Author: Man and Modern Society, 1953, Industrialization and Democracy, 1964, The Rise and Fall of British India, 1983. Served with AUS, 1943-45. Mem. Am. Econ. Assn., AAUP, ACLU. Home: 2676 Orrington Ave Evanston IL 60201

DE SELDING, EDWARD BERTRAND, banker; b. Summit, N.J., June 15, 1926; s. Edward Fitzgerald and Alene (Rockwell) deS.; m. Joan Bulkley, Oct. 21, 1950; children—Peter, Ann, Edward Bertrand. B.A., Yale, 1950. With Spencer Trask & Co., Inc., N.Y.C., 1950-77, partner, 1962-68, v.p., dir., 1968-71, sr. v.p., dir., 1969-77, Hornblower, Weeks, Noyes & Trask, Inc., N.Y.C., 1977-79; 1st v.p. Loeb Rhoades, Hornblower & Co., 1978-79; v.p. Bruns, Nordeman, Rea & Co., N.Y.C., 1979-81, Bache Halsey Stuart, Inc., 1981-82, Conn. Nat. Bank, 1982—. Mem. com. on trust funds Domestic and Fgn. Missionary Soc., P.E. Ch. in, U.S.A. Served with USAAF, 1944-46. Mem. Nat. Assn. Securities Dealers Inc. (chmn. dist. 12 com. 1971, gov. 1972), Bond Club N.Y. (sec. 1967-68, gov. 1977-79). Republican. Episcopalian (vestryman 1961-63, 67-69, 77-79). Clubs: Yale (N.Y.C.); Landmark (Stamford, Conn.); Tokeneke (pres. 1974-75). Home: 18 Fox Hill Ln Darien CT 06820 Office: One Landmark Sq Stamford CT 06904

DESER, STANLEY, educator, physicist; b. Rovno, Poland, Mar. 19, 1931. B.S. summa cum laude, Bklyn. Coll., 1949; M.A., Harvard U., 1950, Ph.D., 1953; D.Phil. (hon.), Stockholm U., 1978. Mem. Inst. Advanced Study, Princeton, 1953-55, Parker fellow, 1953-54; Jewett fellow Inst. for Advanced Study, Princeton, 1954-55; NSF postdoctoral fellow, mem. Inst. Theoretical Physics, Copenhagen, 1955-57; lectr. Harvard U., 1957-58; mem. faculty Brandeis U., Waltham, Mass., 1958—, prof. physics, 1965—, chmn. dept., 1969-71, 76-77, Ancell prof. physics, 1979—; vis. scientist European Center Nuclear Research, Geneva, 1962-63, 76, 80-81; mem. physics adv. com. NSF, 1982—; Fulbright and Guggenheim fellow, vis. prof. Sorbonne, Paris, 1966-67, 71-72; Loeb lectr. Harvard U., 1975; vis. prof. College de France, Paris, 1976; vis. fellow All Souls' Coll., Oxford (Eng.) U., 1977; investigator titular ad honorem CIDA (Venezuela), 1983. Fellow Am. Phys. Soc., Am. Acad. Arts and Scis. Spl. research theoretical physics, field theory, relativity. Office: Physics Dept Brandeis Univ Waltham MA 02254

DE SERRES, FREDERICK JOSEPH, geneticist; b. Dobbs Ferry, N.Y., Sept. 24, 1929; s. Frederick J. and Helen Marie (Henshaw) de S.; m. Christine Marie Covone, Sept. 18, 1954; children—Mark, John, Paul, David, Jonathan, Lianne. B.S. in Biology, Tufts U., Medford, Mass., 1951; M.S. in Botany, Yale U., 1953; Ph.D. (Univ. fellow, Wadsworth fellow 1954-55), Yale U., 1955. Research asso. biology div. Oak Ridge Nat. Lab., 1955-57, sr. staff biologist, 1957-72; experimenters rep. NASA biosatellite program, 1964-68; coordinator environ. mutagenesis program Oak Ridge Nat. Lab., 1969-72; lectr. U. Tenn., 1971-73; adj. prof. dept. pathology U. N.C., Chapel Hill, 1973—; chief environ. mutagenesis br. Nat. Inst. Environ. Health Scis., Research Triangle Park, N.C., 1972-76; asso. dir. genetics, 1976—; U.S. coordinator biol. and genetic consequences project U.S.-USSR Environ. Protection Agreement, 1972—; chmn. panel mutagenesis and carcinogenesis U.S.-Japan Coop. Med. Sci. Program, 1972—; chmn. subcom. environ. mutagenesis, com. to coordinate toxicology and related programs Dept. Health and Human Services, 1972—; mem. com. on assessment nitrate accumulation in environ., div. biology and agr. NRC, 1970-72; cons. in govt., chmn. workshops on environ. pollutants and mutagenesis, 1961—. Editorial bd.: Radiation Botany, 1965-74, Mutation Research, 1969-72, Jour. Toxicology and Environ. Health, 1975-78, Carcinogenesis, 1979—; editor: Jour. Environ. and Exptl. Botany, 1975-77, Mutation Research, 1973—; sect. editor: Jour. Environ. Pathology and Toxicology, 1979; co-editor: Chemical Mutagens, Vol. 5, 1978, Vol. 6, 1980, Vol. 7, 1982, editor Vol. 8, 1983, 1978—; cons. editor: Environmental Research, 1981—; contbg. editor: Environmental Mutagenesis, 1979-81; author 207 publs. including research papers, abstracts, book chpts., editorials research interests: environ. mutagenesis, microbial genetics, mutagenicity of carcinogens, radiation and chem. mutagenesis, space biology. Nat. Cancer Inst. predoctoral fellow, 1952-54; Recipient Director's award NIH, 1976. Mem. Genetic Soc. Am. (rep. to NRC 1970-73), Internat. Assn. Environ. Mutagen Socs., Radiation Research Soc., Am. Soc. Cancer Research, Environ. Mutagen Soc. (council 1969-72, v.p., 1972-73, pres. 1973-76, editor newsletter 1969-72, ann. award 1979, contbg. editor jour. 1979), Internat. Commn. Protection Against Environ. Mutagens and Carcinogenesis (vice-chmn. 1976-83), AAAS., European Environ. Mutagen Soc. Home: 632 Rock Creek Rd Chapel Hill NC 27514 Office: Nat Inst Environ Health Scis Research Triangle Park NC 27709

DESFORGES, JANE FAY, physician; b. Melrose, Mass., Dec. 18, 1921; d. Joseph Henry and Alice (Maher) Fay; m. Gerard Desforges, Sept. 11, 1948; children—Gerard Joseph, Jane Alice. B.A. cum laude (Durant scholar), Wellesley Coll., 1942, M.D., Tufts U., 1945. Diplomate: Am. Bd. Internal Medicine, Am. Bd. Hematology. Intern in pathology Mt. Auburn Hosp., Cambridge, Mass., 1945-46; intern in medicine Boston City Hosp., 1946-47; USPHS research fellow in hematology Salt Lake Gen. Hosp., Salt Lake City, 1946-47; resident in medicine, then chief resident Boston City Hosp., 1948-50; research fellow in hematology hosp. Thorndike Lab., 1950-52; asst. dir. Tufts med. service, 1952-67; physician-in-charge RH lab., 1952-53; asso. dir. Tufts hematology lab., 1954-67, asst. dir. hosp. labs., 1958-67, asso. dir. Tufts med. service, physician in charge, 1967-73; acting dir. labs., 1967-68, dir. Tufts med. service, 1968-69, acting dir. I and II med. service, 1968-69; mem. faculty Tufts U. Med. Sch., 1952—, prof. medicine, 1972—; sr. physician, hematology, research asso. blood research lab. New Eng. Med. Center Hosp., Boston, 1973—; attending physician VA Hosp., Jamaica Plain; cons. hematology various area hosps., 1955—. Asso. editor: New Eng. Jour. Medicine, 1960—; editorial bd.: Blood, 1976-79; contbr. numerous articles med. jours. Bd. dirs. Med. Found., Inc., 1976-82; trustee Boston Med. Library, 1977-81; chmn. automation in med. lab. scis. rev. com. Nat. Inst. Gen. Med. Scis., 1974-76; mem. subcom. on hematology Am. Bd. Internal Medicine, 1976-82, bd. dirs., 1980—; chmn. blood diseases and resources adv. com. Nat. Heart, Lung and Blood Inst., 1978-81. Recipient Disting. Alumna award Wellesley Coll., 1981; Fellow, grantee NIH, 1955—. Mem. ACP, Am. Fedn. Clin. Research, Am. Soc. Clin. Pathology, Am. Soc. Hematology (exec. com. 1974-78, adv. bd. 1980-82, v.p. 1982-83), Internat. Soc. Hematology, Mass. Med. Assn., N.Y. Asad. Scis., Am. Assn. Physicians, Phi Beta Kappa, Alpha Omega Alpha. Home: 49 Lake Ave Melrose MA 02176 Office: 171 Harrison Ave Box 173 Boston MA 02111

DESHANE, WILLIAM WESLEY, business executive; b. London, Ont., Can., Sept. 23, 1938; s. Joel and Gertrude Alberta (Kelley) DeS.; m. Louise Arlene Sperry, June 26, 1965; 1 son, Peter. Student, Inst. Chartered Accts. Ont., 1957-62. Auditor and systems analyst Can. Gen. Electric, Toronto, Ont., 1962-65; comptroller Can. Gen. Electric, Toronto, Ont., 1973-78; sec.-treas. Emco Ltd., London, 1978—. Pres. United Way Greater London, 1981-83, bd. dirs., 1977-83; bd. dirs., treas. Jr. Achievement London, 1977-81. Mem. Fin. Exec. Inst. (v.p. 1983), Inst. Chartered Accts. Ont. Club: London (fin. com. 1982-83). Home: 462 Piccadilly St London ON Canada N5Y 3G3 Office: Emoc Ltd PO box 5300 London ON Canada N6A 4N7

DESHARNAIS, RICHARD PAUL, priest, philosopher, educator; b. Boston, May 30, 1931; s. Wilfrid and Juliette (Pedneault) D. M.A. in Theology, Holy Cross Coll., Washington, 1959, Cath. U. Am., 1961; Ph.D. in Philosophy, 1966; vis. scholar, Union Theol. Sem., N.Y.C., 1968. Ordained priest Roman Catholic Ch., 1958. Joined Congregation of Holy Cross, 1950; mem. faculty dept. philosophy King's Coll., Wilkes-Barre, Pa., 1962—, prof. philosophy, 1971—, dept. chmn., 1962-64, head various coms. Regular book reviewer: New Scholasticism Theological Studies, Sisters Today; contbr. articles to publs. in field. Active Roman Cath.-Luth. Ecumenical Dialogues; vol. Am. Assn. Nursing Homes; chmn. Learning and Resources Com., 1980-81; mem. Moreau Lecture Com., 1980—. Mem. Am. Cath. Philos. Assn., Internat. Soc. Thomas Aqinas. Home & Office: King's College Wilkes Barre PA 18711

DE SHAZOR, ASHLEY DUNN, retired retail company executive; b. Blackstone, Va., May 28, 1919; s. Francis Bertram and Carrie Lee (Joyner) DeS.; m. Margot Joy Best, Sept. 18, 1943 (dec. June 1966); children: Margot Joy DeShazor Brydon, Nancy Lee, Linda Louise; m. Shirley Dean Laffey, June 1, 1968; 1 son, Dean Laffey. B.S. in Bus.

Adminstrn, U. Richmond, Va., 1941. With Sears, Roebuck & Co., also pres. Sears, Roebuck de Colombia, 1941-63; with Montgomery Ward & Co., Chgo., 1963-80, procurement asst. to v.p. and gen. mdse. mgr., 1963-65, v.p., corp. credit mgr., 1966-80, also dir.; dir. Montgomery Ward Credit Corp. Trustee, exec. com. Nat. Found. Consumer Credit; bd. govs. Credit Research Center, Purdue U.; Bd. assos. U. Richmond, 1972-80; bd. dirs. Boys Clubs Chgo., 1981—. Served to lt. comdr. USNR, 1941-46. Mem. Nat. Retail Mchts. Assn. (past chmn. credit mgmt. div.), Acad. Polit. Sci. (life mem.), Sigma Alpha Epsilon. Episcopalian. Clubs: Economic, Mid-Am. (Chgo.); Westmoreland Country (Wilmette, Ill.); Camelback Country (Scottsdale, Ariz.). Home: 660 Winnetka Mews 313 Winnetka IL 60093 also 6712 E Maverick Rd Paradise Valley AZ 85253 Office: One Montgomery Ward Plaza Chicago IL 60671

DESHETLER, KENNETH EDWARD, insurance company executive; b. Toledo, Ohio, Aug. 17, 1928; s. Leo J. and Elsie M. (Caldwell) DeS.; children: Laura, J., Dana M. B.B.A., Toledo U., 1957; J.D., Ohio State U., 1958. Bar: Ohio 1958. Sole practice, Toledo, 1958-65; asst. dir. city law City of Toledo, 1961-62, prosecutor, 1963-64, chief pros. atty., 1964-65, judge mcpl. ct., 1965-71; commr. ins. State of Ohio, Columbus, 1971-75; of counsel Lane, Alton, Horst, Columbus, 1975-76; v.p. Nationwide Ins. Cos., Columbus, 1976—; dir. Ins. Info. Inst., N.Y.C., 1982—; pres. Ins. Fedn. Ohio, 1983; bd. electors Ins Hall of Fame, University, Ala., 1975—; pres. Nat. Assn. Ins. Commrs., 1974. Bd. dirs. Devel. Com. Greater Columbus, Greater Columbus Arts Council, Columbus Landmarks Found., Cystic Fibrosis Found., Columbus; mem. steering com. Kenyon Festival Theater, Gambier, Ohio, 1981; chmn. Citizens Com. for Community Mental Health, Columbus. Served with USAF, 1950-53. Mem. ABA, Ohio Bar Assn., Columbus Bar Assn. Democrat. Presbyterian. Office: Nationwide Ins Cos One Nationwide Plaza Columbus OH 43216

DESIDERIO, DOMINIC MORSE, JR., chemist; b. McKees Rocks, Pa., Jan. 11, 1941; s. Dominic Morse and Jewell Aline (Hull) D.; m. Julie Marie Thomas, Oct. 9, 1965; children—Annette Marie, Dominic Michael. B.A., U. Pitts., 1961; S.M., MIT, 1964, Ph.D., 1965. Organic control chemist Pitts. Coke & Chem. Co., 1958-60; research chemist U. Pitts., 1960-61; teaching asst. M.I.T., 1961-62, research asst., 1962-65; research chemist Am. Cyanamid Co., Stamford, Conn., 1966-67; asst. prof. chemistry Baylor Coll. Medicine, Houston, 1967-71, asso. prof. chemistry and biochemistry, 1971-78; prof. neurology (chemistry), dir. Stout Neurosci. Mass Spectrometry Lab., U. Tenn. Center for Health Scis., Memphis, 1978—; Internat. Assn. for Exchange of Students for Tech. Experience exchange student, polymer chemist, Badische Anilin and Sodafabrik, Germany, summer 1962. Author book, chpts. in books and articles. Recipient 1st Ann. Internat. award Mass Spectrometry in Biochemistry and Medicine, Alghero, Italy, 1975; Intra-Sci. Research Found. fellow, 1971-75. Mem. Am. Soc. Biol. Chemistry, Am. Chem. Soc., Am. Soc. Mass Spectrometry, AAUP, Japanese Soc. Biomed. Mass Spectrometry, AAAS. Home: 6602 Westminister Rd Memphis TN 38138 Office: 956 Court Ave Memphis TN 38163 *The principal standard of conduct in my life is belief, faith and trust in God, his son Jesus and his spirit. This belief has led to realization that I should develop both a persistence in whatever activity I undertake and a zest for life and for all the surprises it holds and to remember that whatever I may do is worth doing well.*

DE SILVA, COLIN, investment executive, author; b. Ceylon, Feb. 11, 1920; U.S., 1962, naturalized, 1972; s. John William and Rose Mary (Weerasinghe) de S.; children: Devayani, Cherine-Parakrama Chandrasoma. With Ceylon Civil Service, 1945-56, asst. sec. def., 1949-53, commr. nat. housing, 1953-56; mng. dir. Colombo Agencies, Ltd., also Colombo Indsl. Agencies, Ltd., 1957-62; exec. dir. Ceylon Mineral Waters, Ltd., 1957-62; dir. Vavasseur Trading Co., Ltd., 1957-62; pres., dir., owner Bus. Investment, Ltd., Honolulu, 1964—, West Coast Bus. Investment, Ltd., Portland, Oreg., 1970—, Econ. Devel. and Engring. Cons., Inc., Honolulu, 1965—; chmn. Gen. Mgmt. Corp., Honolulu, 1973—; pioneer in condominium devel., 1963—; chmn., dir. Condominium Mgmt., Inc.; lectr., cons. Peace Corps, 1962-66; econ. and fin. cons. nat. tourism studies. Del. Commonwealth Prime Ministers Conf., 1949, UN Housing Conf., 1955; chief liaison officer Commonwealth Fgn. Ministers Conf., 1949; pres. Ceylon Assn. Iron and Steel Mchts., 1956-62. Past chmn. bd. Opera Players of Hawaii; exec. com. Internat. C. of C., Ceylon, 1958-62; chmn. gen. importers com., mem. gen. council Ceylon Nat. C. of C., 1958-62; dir., past pres. McCully Bus. and Profl. Assn.; past dir. Waikiki Improvement Assn.; Trustee Kandyan Art Assn., 1946-49, Hawaii Pacific Coll., 1968-70. Mem. Screen Actors Guild, Honolulu, Portland chambers commerce, Smithsonian Instn. Home: 1040 Kealaolu Ave Honolulu HI 96816 Office: Suite 2320 Pacific Tower Honolulu HI 96813

DESIMINI, DONALD, manufacturing company executive; b. Medford, Oreg., 1939; married. B.S., Portland State U., 1962; postgrad. econs., U. Oreg., 1964. Credit analyst U.S. Nat. Bank of Oregon, 1964-67; with Evans Products Co. Inc., Portland, Oreg., 1967—, asst. treas., 1970-75, asst. v.p., then asst. to pres., 1981—; treas. Evans Transp. Co.; v.p., asst. treas., dir. Evans Fin. Corp. Office: Evans Products 1121 S W Salmon St Box 3295 Portland OR 97208 *

DE SIMONE, LOUIS A., bishop; b. Phila., Feb. 21, 1922. Student, Villanova U., Sr. Charles Borromeo Sem., Pa. Ordained priest Roman Catholic Ch., 1952; ordained titular bishop of Cillium and aux. bishop of Phila., 1981—. Office: St Monica Ch 2422 S 17th St Philadelphia PA 19145 *

DESIMONE, SALVATORE VINCENT, consulting engineer; b. N.Y.C., Jan. 25, 1924; s. Gabriel and Gemma (Amato) DeS.; m. Damaris Hamilton Smith, May 8, 1948; children: Ursula, Dorothy, Tiffany. B.C.E., Coll. City N.Y., 1948; postgrad., Columbia, 1948-49, 50-53. Registered profl. engr., N.Y., N.J., Conn., Mass., Fla., La., Ohio, Ky., D.C., Ga. Structural engr. Moran, Proctor, Freeman & Mueser, N.Y.C., 1948-51; chief structural dept. Brown Guenther, Booss, N.Y.C., 1952-53, structural engr., 1951-52; with Mueser, Rutledge, Johnston & DeSimone, N.Y.C., 1953—, asso., 1960-65, partner, 1966—; Vice pres. N.Y. Bldg. Congress, 1976—. Tech. adv. com. Village of N. Tarrytown, N.Y., 1976—, Ardsley, N.Y., 1956-59; mem. Ardsley Zoning Com., 1956-59; bd. dirs. Phelps Meml. Hosp., 1977-80. Served as 1st lt. inf. AUS, 1943-46. Decorated Purple Heart. Mem. N.Y. Assn. Cons. Engrs. (dir. 1976-80), ASCE, Am. Concrete Inst., Am. Cons. Engrs. Council, N.Y. Assn. Cons. Engrs., The Moles, Prestressed Concrete Inst., Concrete Industry Bd., Delta Kappa Epsilon. Club: Univ. Home: 457 Bellwood Ave North Tarrytown NY 10591 Office: 708 3d Ave New York NY 10017

DE SIPIO, GEORGE, lawyer; b. Phila., May 30, 1925; s. Jack and Amelia (Ricca) DeSipio; m. Carol Kahn, Sept. 4, 1954; children: George, Sally. B.A., U. Pa., 1949; LL.B., Harvard U., 1952. Bar: N.Y. 1953. Assoc. Clearly, Gottlieb, Steen & Hamilton, N.Y.C., 1952-63; ptnr. Cleary, Gottlieb, Steen & Hamilton, N.Y.C., 1963—; dir. Rosenbloom Securities, N.Y.C. Bd. dirs. Tebil Found., N.Y.C., 1972—, Henry Kaufman Found., N.Y.C., 1975—, Simon Found., N.Y.C., 1975—; chmn. Bd. Zoning Appeals, Saltaire, Fire Island, N.Y., 1976-81. Served with AUS, 1944-46; ETO. Fellow Am. Coll. Probate Council; mem. Estate Planning Council (dir.). Democrat. Club: Harvard (N.Y.C.). Home: 1035 Park Ave New York NY 10028 Office: Cleary Gottlieb Steen & Hamilton 1 State St Plaza New York NY 10004

DESJARDINS, PIERRE, consumer goods company executive; b. Montreal, Que., Canada, Oct. 28, 1941; s. Henri and Azilda (Tremblay) D.; children: Andre, Danielle, Patrick, Christian. B.Sc. in Bus. Adminstrn., U. Wyo., 1966; B.A., U. Montreal, 1962. Profl. football player Les Alouettes de Montreal, 1966-72; regional mgr. Atlantic Province Imperial Tobacco Co., Moncton, N.B., Can., 1973-75, Toronto, Ont., Can., 1975-78, v.p. sales, dir., Montreal, 1978-79; pres. La Brasseie Labatt Ltee. subs. Labatt Brewing Co., Ltd., Montreal, 1979—; v.p. parent co., London, Ont., 1979—. Pres. Grand Prix of Can., Montreal, 1979—. Mem. Que. Brewers Assn. (pres. 1981—). Clubs: St. Denis (Montreal); Business Schs. of Am. Office: La Brasserie Labatt Ltee 50 Labatt St LaSalle PQ Canada H8R 3E7

DESJARDINS, REGENT, constrn. co. exec.; b. Montreal, Que., Can., Sept. 30, 1926; s. Donat and Eliza (Paquin) D.; m. Jacqueline Dubuc, Apr. 1955; children—Regent-Yves, Johane, Line, Chantal, Benoit, Michel. Ed., Salaberry Sch., Tech. Sch., Montreal, Ecole des Beaux-Arts de Montreal. With firm Simard & Denis Inc., Montreal, 1965—, pres., 1971—; pres., gen. mgr. Montreal-Matin, newspaper, 1962-73, chmn. bd., 1973—; Pres. Regesco Inc.; dir. Mediacom Industries Inc. Mem. Montreal City Council, 1954—. Mem. Montreal C. of C., Jeune Chambre de Montréal (pres. 1953). Clubs: Laval-sur-le-lac, St. Denis, Canadien. Home: 90 Fernlea Crescent Ville Mont-Royal PQ Canada Office: 450 Sherbrooke E Suite 1001 Montreal PQ H2L 1J8 Canada

DESKINS, WILBUR EUGENE, educator, mathematician; b. Morgantown, W.Va., Feb. 20, 1927; s. Wilbur Lawrence and Avis (Creasy) D.; m. Barbara Brown, Apr. 18, 1953; children—Lucinda Eugenie, Samantha Eugenie. B.S., U. Ky., 1949; M.S., U. Wis., 1950, Ph.D., 1953. Teaching asst. U. Wis., 1949-51, fellow, 1951-52, teaching asst., 1952-53, instr., 1953, Ohio State U., 1953-55, asst. prof., 1955-56, Mich. State U., East Lansing, 1956-59, asso. prof., 1959-63, prof. math., 1963-71; prof. math., chmn. dept. U. Pitts., 1971—. Author: Abstract Algebra, 1964. Mem. Am., London math. socs., Math. Assn. Am., AAAS. Research and articles on algebra and group theory. Office: Univ Pittsburgh Pittsburgh PA 15260

DESLOGE, EDWARD AUGUSTINE, educator; b. St. Louis, Aug. 31, 1926; s. Louis Francis and Angela (Burdeau) D.; m. Moira Dunne, Dec. 15, 1958; children—Bryan, Matthew, Rosemary, Angela, Bruce. B.S. in Elec. Engring, U. Notre Dame, 1947; M.S. in Physics, St. Louis U., 1955, Ph.D., 1957. Instr. Yale, 1958-59; asst. prof. physics Fla. State U., 1959-65, asso. prof., 1965-69, prof., 1969—. Author: Statistical Physics, 1966, Thermal Physics, 1968, Classical Mechanics, 1982. Served with USNR, 1944-46. Mem. Am. Phys. Soc. Roman Catholic. Club: Elk. Home: 2213 Demeron Rd Tallahassee FL 32312

DESLOGE, TAYLOR STITH, steel company executive; b. St. Louis, June 16, 1921; s. George T. and Madeleine (Stith) D.; m. Marian Falk, July 7, 1950; children: M. Lindsay, Madeleine G., Stephen F., G. Taylor, M. Allan, Phillip G., Judeth C. A.B., St. Louis U., 1942; LL.B., Washington U., 1948. With Gen. Steel Industries, Inc., St. Louis, 1953—, asst. treas., 1955-61, sec., 1961-66, v.p., treas., 1966-73, v.p., treas., sec., 1973—, also dir.; dir. Brentwood Bancshares Corp., Christen, Inc.; chmn. Associated Industries of Mo. Vice pres. St. Louis Heart Assn., 1962-63, dir., 1960-63; trustee, fin. v.p. Mo. Hist. Soc., 1978—. Served to capt. AUS, 1942-46. Home: 1 Stoney Brook Ln Saint Louis MO 63124 Office: PO Box 16000 Saint Louis MO 63105

DESLONGCHAMPS, PIERRE, chemistry educator; b. St.-Lin, Que., Can., May 8, 1938; s. Rodolphe and Madeleine D.; children: Patrice, Ghyslain. B.Sc., U. Montreal, Que., 1959; Ph.D., U. N.B., 1964. Research fellow Harvard U., 1964, postdoctoral fellow, 1965; asst. prof. chemistry U. Montreal, 1966-67; asst. prof. U. Sherbrooke, Que., 1967-68, assoc. prof., 1968-72, prof., 1972—. Contbr. numerous articles to profl. jours. Recipient E.W.R. Steacie prize Nat. Research Council Can., 1974; Shell Can. Co. fellow, 1963; A. P. Sloan fellow, 1970-72; recipient Sci. prize, Province Que., 1971-72; E.W.R. Steacie fellow, 1971-74; Can. Council Izaak Walton Killam Meml. scholar, 1976-77; John Simon Guggenheim Meml. Found. fellow, 1979. Fellow Chem. Inst. Can. (Merck, Sharp and Dohme Lectures award 1976); fellow Royal Soc. Can.; mem. Corp. Profl. Chemists Que., Am. Chem. Soc., Swiss Chem. Soc., Assn. Harvard Chemists, AAAS, Association Canadienne-Francaise pour l'Avancement des Sciences (medaille Vincent 1975, medaille Pariseau 1979), Assn. Advancement Scis. Can. Inventor in field. Home: Rural Route 1 Ch McFarland North Hatley PQ J0B 2C0 Canada Office: Departement de Chimie U Sherbrooke PQ J1K 2R1 Canada

DESMARAIS, CHARLES JOSEPH, museum director, writer, editor; b. N.Y.C., Apr. 21, 1949; s. Charles Emil and Helen Barbara (Young) D.; m. Sharon McLeod, May 1, 1970; m. Patricia Jon Carroll, June 15, 1979. Student, Western Conn. State Coll., Danbury, 1967-71; B.S., SUNY-Rochester, 1975; M.F.A., SUNY-Buffalo, 1977. Curator Freinds of Photography, Carmel, Calif., 1973-74; asst. editor Afterimage, Rochester, 1975-77; dir. Chgo. Ctr. Contemporary Photography, Columbia Coll., Chgo., 1977-79, Calif. Mus. Photography, U. Calif.-Riverside, 1981—; guest curator Mus. Contemporary Art, Chgo., 1980, Los Angeles Ctr. Photog. Studies, 1981; arts adv. com. Riverside County Bd. Suprs., 1981—. Author, editor: Roger Mertin: Records 1976-78, 1978, Michael Bishop, 1979, The Portrait Extended, 1980. Art Critic's fellow Nat. Endowment Arts, 1979. Mem. Soc. Photog. Edn. (dir. 1979-83), Am. Assn. Museums, Coll. Art Assn., Nat. Stereoscopic Assn., Am. Photog. Hist. Soc. Office: Calif Mus of Photography U Calif Riverside CA 92521

DESMARAIS, OVIDE E. *See* **DEMARIS, OVID**

DESMARAIS, PAUL, business executive; b. Sudbury, Ont., Can., Jan. 4, 1927; s. Jean Noel and Lebea (Laforest) D.; m. Jacqueline Maranger, Sept. 8, 1953; children: Paul, Andre, Louise, Sophie. B.Comm., U. Ottawa, Ont., 1949; LL.D., U. Moncton, Wilfrid Laurier U., St. Francis Xavier U., Laurentian U., McMaster U., U. Montreal; D.Adm., U. Ottawa. Chmn. bd., chief exec. officer Power Corp. of Can., Montreal, Que., 1968—; chmn. exec. com., dir. Consol.-Bathurst Inc.; mem. exec. com., dir. Can. Pacific Ltd., Can. Pacific Enterprises Ltd.; dir. Domglas Inc., Gelco Enterprises Ltd., The Great-West Life Assurance Co., CB Pak Inc., Groupe Bruxelles Lambert S.A., Hilton Can. Ltd., Investors Group, Power Corp. Can., Power Fin. Corp., La Presse Ltée, The Seagram Co. Ltd., Lambert Brussels Corp., Pargesa Holdings S.A., others. Decorated officer Order of Can. Office: 759 Victoria Sq Montreal PQ H2Y 2K4 Canada

DESMARTEAU, DARRYL DWAYNE, chemistry and geology educator; b. Garden City, Kans., May 25, 1940; s. Arthur L. and Esther P. (Deines) DesM.; m. Genie L. Hardy, Sept. 16, 1962; children: Scott, Noel, Chad. B.S. in Chemistry, Wash. State U., Pullman, 1963; Ph.D., U. Wash, 1966. Acting asst. prof. U. Wash., 1966-67; asst. prof. Northeastern U., Boston, 1967-71, Kans. State U., Manhattan, 1971-73, assoc. prof., 1973-77, prof., 1977-82; prof., chmn. dept. chemistry and geology Clemson U., S.C., 1982—; cons. Monsanto Chem. Co., St. Louis, 1976-78, Hooker Chem. Co., Grand Island, N.Y., 1978-80. Bd. editors: Jour. Flourine Chemistry, 1981—; contbr. articles on fluorine chemistry to profl. jours. Served with USMCR, 1960-66. Sloan Found. fellow, 1975-77; Alexander von Humboldt Found. Research fellow, Bonn., W.Ger., 1979-80; numerous research grants. Mem. Am. Chem. Soc. (chmn. div. fluorine chemistry 1979, sec.-treas. 1976-78, exec. council 1973—, for creative work in fluorine chemistry 1983), Sigma Xi, Phi Lambda Upsilon, Alpha Chi Sigma. Republican. Roman Catholic. Home: 1007 Berkley Dr Clemson SC 29631 Office: Dept Chemistry Clemson Univ Clemson SC 29631

DESMOND, ALICE CURTIS (MRS. HAMILTON FISH), writer; b. Southport, Conn., Sept. 19, 1897; d. Lewis Beers and Alice (Beardsley) Curtis; m. Thomas C. Desmond, Aug. 16, 1923; m. Hamilton Fish, Oct. 16, 1976 (div. 1984). Grad., Miss Porter's Sch., Farmington, Conn., 1916; student, Parson's Art Sch., N.Y.C., 1920; Litt.D., Russell Sage Coll., 1946, Suffolk U., 1975. Has made three world tours. (Recipient Juvenile award Nat. League Am. Pen Women 1949); Author: Far Horizons, 1931, South American Adventures, 1934 (both books endorsed by Carnegie Endownment for Internat. Peace), The Lucky Llama, 1939, Soldier of the Sun, 1939, Feathers, 1940, For Cross and King, 1941, Jorge's Journey, 1942 (translated into Portuguese, Swedish, German), Martha Washington, 1942, The Sea Cats, 1944, Glamorous Dolly Madison, 1946, The Talking Tree, 1949 (translated into Swedish 1956), Alexander Hamilton's Wife, 1952, Barnum Presents: General Tom Thumb, 1954 (translated into French, Dutch 1956), Bewitching Betsy Bonaparte, 1958, Your Flag and Mine, 1960, George Washington's Mother, 1961, Teddy Koala: Mascot of the Marines, 1962, Sword and Pen for George Washington, 1964, Marie Antoinette's Daughter, 1967, Cleopatra's Children, 1971, Titus of Rome, 1976; Contbr. to anthologies: Roads to Travel, 1936, Boys of the Andes, 1941, Wonder and Laughter, 1947, Adventures in Reading Exploration, 1947, People and Progress, 1947, Told Under Spacious Skies, 1952, A Book of Gladness, 1953, American Backgrounds, 1959, This is Our Land, 1965, Cavalcades, 1965; Contbr. articles, fiction, verse to newspapers and mags. Rochester Mus. Arts and Scis. hon. fellow, 1946. Fellow Soc. Am. Historians; mem. Nat. League Pen Women, Am. Anthrop. Assn., Am. Folk Lore Soc., Nat. Assn. U. Women, Soc. Mayflower Descs., Colonial Dames Am., Daus. Founders and Patriots Am., N.Y. State Hist. Assn., Soc. Woman Geographers, Federated Garden Clubs N.Y. State (hon.), N.Y. Hist. Soc. (Pintard fellow), NAD, Am. Water Color Soc., Photog. Soc. Am., Royal Photog. Soc. Gt. Britain, Am. Numis. Assn., Am. Philatelic Soc., Nat. Assn. Women Artists, Print Club Albany, Authors League Am., Pen and Brush. Episcopalian. Clubs: Women's Nat. Republican, Colony, Junior League, Collectors (N.Y.C.); Garden of Am. Home: PO Box 670 Newburgh NY 12550

DESMOND, JOHN JACOB, architect; b. Denver, Apr. 5, 1922; s. Timothy and Rose (Dvorak) D.; m. Blanche Russell, Sept. 29, 1951 (div.); children—John Michael, Russell, Margaret. B.Arch., Tulane U., 1943; M.Arch., Mass. Inst. Tech., 1948. Archtl. draftsman Skidmore, Owings & Merrill, N.Y.C., 1947; archtl. designer, draftsman A. Hays Town, 1949-50, TVA, 1951-52; architect Desmond & Davis, 1954-58, Desmond-Miremont-Burks, Baton Rouge, Hammond, La., from 1958; now pres. John Desmond & Assos., Baton Rouge. Author: Louisiana's Antebellum Architecture, 1970; Contbr. articles to: AIA Jour.; Principal works include Southeastern La. Coll. Cafeteria, Hammond (1st honor award Gulf States region), Hammond, 1956 (Nat. Merit award AIA), St. Thomas More Ch. and Sch, Baton Rouge, 1960 (honor award Gulf States region AIA), Cath. Student Center, Southeastern La. Coll., 1960 (honor award Gulf States region AIA), La. State Library, Baton Rouge (nat. AIA-ALA award), Baton Rouge, 1954 (honor award Gulf States region AIA), Union Bldg, La. State U., Baton Rouge, 1963 (1st honor award Gulf States region AIA), Cath. Life Center, Baton Rouge, 1964 (honor award Gulf States region AIA); additions to Grace Meml. Episcopal Ch, Hammond, 1967 (honor award Gulf States region AIA), D.C. Reeves Elementary Sch, Ponchatoula, La., 1968 (honor award Gulf States regional Nat. Honor award AIA), Tangipahoa Parish Courthouse, Amite, La., 1969 (honor award AIA and Office Civil Def.); design architect: Pennington Biomed. Research Ctr., La. State Archives, U.S. Embassy, Monrovia, Liberia, La. Civil War Ctr. Served to lt. USNR, 1943-46. Recipient archtl. awards profl. orgns.; named Outstanding Alumnus Tulane U. Sch. Architecture. Fellow AIA (planning and urban design com., award for outstanding contbn. to design); mem. La. Architects Assn., La. Landmarks Assn., Soc. Archtl. Historians, Nat. Trust Historic Preservation. Club: Cosmos (Washington). Home: 1135 Carter Ave Baton Rouge LA 70806 Office: 703 Laurel St Baton Rouge LA 70802

DESNICK, ROBERT JOHN, human geneticist; b. Mpls., July 12, 1943; s. Theodore David and Celia Janice (Marcus) D. B.A., U. Minn., 1965, Ph.D., 1970, M.D., 1971. Diplomate: Nat. Bd. Med. Examiners. Research asso. U. Minn., Mpls., 1970-72, intern and resident dept. pediatrics, 1971-73, asst. prof. pediatrics, 1973-75, asst. prof. lab. medicine and pathology, 1973-75, asst. prof., 1973-75, asso. prof. pediatrics, 1976-77, asso. prof. genetics and cell biology, 1975-77, asso. prof., 1975-77, prof. pediatrics, 1977—; Arthur J. and Nellie Z. Cohen prof. pediatrics and genetics and chief div. med. genetics Mt. Sinai Sch. Medicine, N.Y.C., 1977—; attending physician pediatrics Mt. Sinai Hosp.; med. adv. bd. Nat. Tay-Sacks and Allied Diseases Assn., 1975—, Nat. Neurofibromatosis Found., 1978-81; Med. adv. bd. Nat. Found. Jewish Genetic Diseases, 1981—; bd. dirs. Soc. Inherited Metabolic Diseases, 1983—; mem. N.Y. Gov.'s Adv. Com. on Genetics, 1982—. Editor: Enzyme Therapy in Genetic Diseases, 1972, 79, Molecular Genetic Modification of Eucaryotes, 1978, Gaucher Disease: A Century of Delineation and Research, 1982, Animal Models of Inherited Metabolic Diseases, 1982; mem. editorial bd.: Enzyme, 1979—, Am. Jour. Human Genetics, 1980—; contbr. articles to sci. jours. USPHS fellow, 1968-70; recipient Ross award Soc. Pediatric Research, 1972; C.J. Watson award U. Minn. Med. Sch., 1973; NIH Research Career Devel. award, 1975-80; E. Mead Johnson award Am. Acad. Pediatrics, 1981. Mem. Am. Soc. Human Genetics, Genetics Soc. Am., Minn. Human Genetics League (dir. 1970-77), Soc. Complex Carbohydrates, Behavior Genetics Assn., Am. Fedn. Clin. Research, Am. Soc. Biol. Chemists, AAAS, Midwest Soc. Pediatric Research, Soc. Pediatric Research, Soc. Exptl. Biology and Medicine, Am. Soc. Exptl. Pathology, Central Soc. Clin. Research, Soc. Study Social Biology, N.Y. Acad. Sci., European Soc. Human Genetics, Am. Soc. Clin. Investigation, Sigma Xi. Office: Mt Sinai Sch Medicine of City U NY Fifth Ave and 100th St New York NY 10029

DESOER, CHARLES AUGUSTE, electrical engineer; b. Ixelles, Belgium, Jan. 11, 1926; came to U.S., 1949, naturalized, 1958; s. Jean Charles and Yvonne Louise (Peltzer) D.; m. Jacqueline K. Johnson, July 21, 1966; children—Marc J., Michele M., Craig M. Ingenieur Radio-Electricien, U. Liege, Belgium, 1949, D.Sc. (hon.), 1976; Sc.D. in Elec. Engring, M.I.T., 1953. Research asst. M.I.T., 1951-53; mem. tech. staff Bell Telephone Labs., Murray Hill, N.J., 1953-58; asso. prof. elec. engring. and computer scis. U. Calif., Berkeley, 1958-62, prof., 1962—, Miller research prof., 1970-71. Author: (with L. A. Zadeh) Linear System Theory, 1963, (with E. S. Kuh) Basic Circuit Theory, 1969, (with M. Vidyasagar) Feedback Systems: Input Output Properties, 1975, Notes for a Second Course on Linear Systems, 1970, (with F. M. Collier) Multivariable Feedback Systems; contbr. numerous articles on systems and circuits to profl. jours. Served with Belgian Arty., 1944-45. Decorated Vol.'s medal; recipient Best Paper prize 2Joint Automatic Control Conf., 1962, Univ. medal U. Liege, 1970, Disting. Teaching award U. Calif., Berkeley, 1971, Prix

Montefiore Inst. Montefiore, 1975; award for outstanding paper Control Systems Soc., 1981, IEEE, 1979; Guggenheim fellow, 1970-71. Fellow IEEE (Edn. medal 1975), AAAS; mem. Nat. Acad. Engring., Am. Math. Soc., Math. Assn. Am., Soc. Indsl. and Applied Math. Office: Dept Elec Engring and Computer Sci U Calif Berkeley CA 94720

DESOTO, CLINTON BURGEL, psychologist, educator; b. Hartford, Conn., Jan. 13, 1931; s. Clinton Burgel and Ruth Esther (Higbie) D.; m. Jane Louise Everhardt, Feb. 4, 1956; children: Brian, William, Stewart; m. Janet Louise Tolbert, Feb. 7, 1975. Student Eau Claire State Coll., Wis., 1948-50; B.A., U. Wis., 1952, M.A., 1953, Ph.D., 1956. Instr. Johns Hopkins U., 1956-57, asst. prof., 1957-61, assoc. prof., 1961-69, prof. psychology, 1969—. Contbr. chpts. to books, articles to profl. jours. Mem. Am. Psychol. Assn., Psychonomic Soc., Soc. Exptl. Social Psychology, Eastern Psychol. Assn., AAAS, Sigma Xi. Home: 923 Beaverbank Circle Towson MD 21204 Office: Dept Psychology Johns Hopkins U. Baltimore MD 21218

DE SOTO, SIMON, mech. engr.; b. N.Y.C., Jan. 8, 1925; s. Albert and Esther (Eskenazi) Soto; 1 dau., Linda Jane. B.M.E., CCNY, 1945; M.M.E., Syracuse U., 1950; Ph.D., UCLA, 1965. Lic. profl. engr., Calif., N.Y. Engr. Johns-Manville Corp., N.Y.C., 1946-48; instr. in engring. Syracuse U., 1948-50; research engr. Stratos-Fairchild Corp., Farmingdale, N.Y., 1950-54; research specialist Lockheed Missile Systems div. Lockheed Corp., Van Nuys, Calif., 1954-56; sr. tech. specialist Rocketdyne Rockwell Internat., Canoga Park, Calif., 1956-69; asso. prof. mech. engring. Calif. State U., Long Beach, 1969-72, prof., 1972—; lectr. UCLA, 1954-70; cons. engr.; dir., sec.-treas. Am. Engring. Devel. Co.; mem. tech. planning com. Public Policy Conf.: The Energy Crisis, Its Effect on Local Govts., 1973; founding mem. Calif. State U. and Colls.; Statewide Energy Consortium and cons. tech. assistance program. Author: Thermostatics and Thermodynamics: An Instructor's Manual, 1963. Served with U.S. Mcht. Marine, 1945-46. Recipient Outstanding Faculty award UCLA Engring. Student Body, 1962, Calif. State U., Long Beach, 1971, 73, 76. Mem. AAAS, Am. Soc. Engring. Edn., Tau Beta Pi, Pi Tau Sigma. Research publs. in field. Office: Calif State U Long Beach CA 90840

DESPATIE, ROGER, bishop; b. Sunbury, Ont., Can., Apr. 12, 1927. Ordained priest Roman Catholic Ch., 1952; Titular bishop, Usinaza, 1968-73; aux. bishop Sault Ste. Marie, Can., 1968-73; bishop Hearst, Ont., 1973—. Office: PO Box 1330 Hearst ON Canada POL INO

DESPRES, LEO ARTHUR, educator; b. Lebanon, N.H., Mar. 29, 1932; s. Leo Arthur and Madeline (Bedford) D.; m. Loretta A. LaBarre, Aug. 22, 1953; children—Christine, Michelle, Denise, Mary Louise, Renee. B.A., U. Notre Dame, 1954, M.A., 1956; Ph.D., Ohio State U., 1960. Research asso. Columbia Psychiat. Inst. and Hosp., 1957-60; postdoctoral fellow Social Sci. Research Council, Guyana, 1960-61; asst. prof. Ohio Wesleyan U., 1961-63; faculty Case Western Res. U., Cleve., 1963-74, prof. anthropology, 1967-74, chmn. dept., 1968-74; prof. sociology, anthropology U. Notre Dame, Ind., 1974—, chmn. dept., 1974; Cons. in field. Author: Cultural Pluralism and Nationalist Politics in British Guyana, 1968; Editor: Ethnicity and Resource Compeition in Plural Societies, 1975. Fulbright scholar U. Guyana, 1970-71. Mem. Am. Anthrop. Assn., Am. Ethnol. Soc., African Studies Assn., Central States Anthrop. Soc. (exec. com., pres. elect), AAUP. Home: 16587 Bennington Ct Granger IN 46530 Office: Dept Sociology and Anthropology U Notre Dame Notre Dame IN 46556

DESPRES, LEON MATHIS, lawyer, former city ofcl.; b. Chgo., Feb. 2, 1908; s. Samuel and Henrietta (Rubovits) D.; m. Marian Alschuler, Sept. 10, 1931; children—Linda Baskin, Robert Leon. Ph.B., U. Chgo., 1927, J.D., 1929. Bar: Ill. bar 1929. Pvt. practice law, Chgo., 1929-; trial examiner NLRB, Chgo., 1935-37; instr. U. Chgo., 1936, U. Wis., summers 1946-49; alderman 5th Ward Chgo. City Council, 1955-75, parliamentarian, 1979—. Mem. Chgo. Plan Commn., 1979—. Mem. Am., Ill., Chgo. bar. assns., Chgo. Council Lawyers, Order Coif, Phi Beta Kappa. Home: 1220 E 56th St Chicago IL 60637 Office: 77 W Washington St: Chicago IL 60602

DESPRES, ROBERT, atomic energy company executive; b. Quebec City, Que., Can., Sept. 27, 1924; s. Adrien and Augustine (Marmen) D.; m. Marguerite Cantin, Sept. 10, 1949; children: Laurent, Marie, Esther, Louis. Student, Coll. Levis, 1936-41; B.A., Acad. Que., 1944; M. Com., Laval U., 1946-47; postgrad., Western U., 1960. Comptroller Que. Power Co., Quebec, 1947-63; regional mgr. Adminstrn. & Trust Co., Quebec, 1963-65; dep. minister Que. Dept. Revenue, Quebec, 1965-69; pres., gen. mgr. Que. Health Ins. Bd., Quebec, 1969-73; pres. U. Que., Quebec, 1973-78; pres., chief exec. officer Nat. Cablevision, Ltd., 1978-80, also dir., 1978-80; pres. Netcom Inc., 1978—; chmn.bd. Atomic Energy of Can. Ltd., 1980—; dir. Campeau Corp., Can. Malting Co. Ltd., Can. Union Ins. Co. Ltd., Domtar Inc., Drummond McCall Inc., Corp. Falconbridge Copper, Gaz Inter-Cite' Québec Inc., Flakt Can. Ltd., McNeil, Mantha, Ltée, Mfrs. Life Ins. Co., Nat. Trust Co. Ltd., Norcen Energy Resources Ltd., Sidbec, Sidbec-Dosco Ltd.; mem. Montreal Bd. Trade; formerly mem. Royal Commn. on Fin. Mgmt. and Accountability, Govt. Can. Contbr. articles to mgmt. publs. Bd. dirs., pres. Que. Heart Inst.; Bd. dirs. Société du Musée du Séminaire de Que. Served with Armed Forces, 1942-45. Decorated officer Order of Can. Fellow Soc. Mgmt. Accts. Can.; mem. Pres.'s Assn. Am., Can. Nuclear Assn., C. of C. Française du Can. Clubs: Le Cercle de la Garnison de Québec, Golf Lorette, La Gorce Country, Rideau, Mt. Royal. Home: 890 Dessane St Quebec PQ Canada G1S 3J8 Office: 275 Slater St Ottawa ON Canada K1A 0S4

DES ROCHES, ANTOINE, newspaper executive; b. Quebec, P.Q., Can., Jan. 9, 1924; s. Francis and Antoinette DesR.; m. Monique Nuytemans, Jan. 24, 1969. Reporter Le Soleil, 1942-47; news editor Le Soleil, also L'Evenement-Jour., Quebec, P.Q., 1947-52, Sta. CHLN, also Le Nouveau Jour., Montreal, P.Q., 1958-62; info. expert UNESCO, 1962-63; news editor La Presse, Montreal, 1964-67, 70-72, dir. pub. relations, 1972—, asst to pres., 1982—; pres. Les Editions La Presse. Mem. Assn. des Editeurs Canadiens (pres. 1983), Canadian Daily Newspaper Pubs. Assn. Roman Catholic. Home: 24 Buttonwood St Dollard-des Ormeaux PQ H9A 2N2 Canada Office: La Presse 7 St Jacques St Montreal PQ H2Y 1K9 Canada

DES ROCHES, RALPH A., management consultant; b. Rumford, Maine, Sept. 10, 1916; s. Alex and Angelina (Doiron) Des R.; m. Yvonne C. Stone, Oct. 8, 1946; children: Laurel, Alexis, Aimee, Alec. Student, U. N.H., Durham. Dir., owner Doc Des Roches Ski Sch., 1946-63; buyer, supr. ski shop Laurel Mountain, Ligonier, Pa., 1945-63; asst. to mgr. Laurel Mt. Slopes Co., 1945-57, pres., 1957-63; exec. v.p. Ski Industries Am., Washington, 1963-81; prin. Doc Des Roches & Assocs. (mgmt. cons.), Farmington, Maine, 1981—; coordinator Nat. Ski Week, 1965-73; mem. N.Y. Com. U.S. Ski Team, 1967-68; participant numerous intercollegiate, Eastern, nat. and regional ski meets. Served with AUS, 1942-43. Recipient John M. Clair Meml. award U.S. Ski Team, 1974, Service to Sport award Nat. Ski Hall of Fame, 1977. Mem. Eastern Profl. Ski Instrs. Assn., Profl. Ski Instrs., Assn., Applachian Mt. Ski Area Operators (chmn.), Fedn. Internat. de Ski, U.S. Ski Writers Assn. (charter Golden Quill award 1968), Eastern Ski Writers Assn. (charter), Am. Ski Fedn. (asst. sec.-treas. 1972-79), U.S. Ski Assn. (dir. 1962-67, chmn. coms., Julius P. Blegen Meml. award 1963), U.S. Eastern Amateur Ski Assn. (2d v.p. 1964-65); hon. mem. numerous ski assns. and teams. Home: Clearwater Pond PO Box 470 Farmington ME 04938 Office: Doc Des Roches & Assocs PO Box 470 Farmington ME 04938

DESSART, DONALD JOSEPH, mathematics educator; b. Green Bay, Wis., Apr. 2, 1928; s. Eli Joseph and Mary Octavia (Warrichaiet) D.; m. Gloria Jean Clemons, June 17, 1950; children: Mary, Thomas, Jean, Brian, Ruth Anne. B.S., U. Wis., 1950, M.S., 1955; Ph.D., U. Md., 1961. Tchr. math., Escanaba, Mich., 1953-54, Madison, Wis., 1954-56; prof. State U. N.Y. at Oneonta, 1956-62; prof. math., math. edn. U. Tenn., Knoxville, 1962—; profl. asso. Office Program Integration, NSF, Washington, 1978-79. Editorial bd.: Jour. for Research in Math. Edn, 1973-76; chmn., 1975-76; Contbr. articles to profl. math., ednl. jours. Served as line officer USNR, 1950-53; PTO. Named Danforth Tchr., 1959-60; Outstanding Educator Am. Am. Ednl. Research Assn., 1972. Fellow AAAS; mem. Math. Assn. Am., Nat. Council Tchrs. Math. (chmn. research adv. com. 1975-76), Tenn. Math. Tchrs. Assn. (pres. 1967-69, lectr. of yr. 1983-84), Phi Beta Kappa, Sigma Xi, Phi Delta Kappa, Phi Eta Sigma, Phi Kappa Phi, Pi Mu Epsilon. Episcopalian. Home: 8012 Bennington Dr Knoxville TN 37919

DESSAUER, HERBERT CLAY, biochemist; b. New Orleans, Dec. 30, 1921; s. Herbert Andrew and Shirley Ross (Patin) D.; m. Frances Jane Moffatt, Dec. 10, 1949; children: Dan Winston, Rebecca Lynn, Bryan Clay. Profl. cert. in meteorology, Calif. Inst. Tech., 1945; B.A., La. State U., 1949, Ph.D., 1952. Mem. faculty La. State U. Med. Center, New Orleans, 1951—, prof. biochemistry, 1963—, acting dept. head, 1977-78; research asso. dept. herpetology Am. Mus. Natural History, 1978—; mem. Alpha Helix Expdn. to New Guinea, 1969; cons. VA Hosp., New Orleans, 1962—; mem. panel advanced sci. edn. NSF, 1965-67, panel in systematic biology, 1972-75, panel workshop on frozen tissue collection mgmt., 1983; mem. task force on fluoridation New Orleans Health Planning Council, 1971-72. Editorial bd.: Herpetologica, 1967-79; contbr. articles to profl. jours. Served to 1st lt. USAAF, 1943-46. Grantee NSF, 1961—, Am. Philos. Soc., 1964. Fellow AAAS, Herpetologists League; mem. Am. Physiol. Soc., Soc. Exptl. Biology and Medicine (sect. sec. 1959-61), Soc. Study Amphibians Reptiles (bd. dirs. 1981), Am. Soc. Icthyology and Herpetology, Soc. Systematic Zoology, Sigma Xi, Phi Kappa Phi. Address: 7100 Dorian St New Orleans LA 70126

DESSAUER, JOHN HANS, chemist; b. Aschaffenburg, Germany, May 13, 1905; came to U.S., 1929, naturalized, 1936; s. Hans and Bertha (Thywissen) D.; m. Margaret B. Lee, June 29, 1935; children: John Philip, Margot, Thomas David. B.S., Inst. Tech., Munich, Germany, 1924-26, M.S., D.Eng., 1929; L.H.D., Le Moyne Coll., 1963; D.Sc. (hon.), Clarkson Coll., 1975, LL.D., Fordham U., 1979. Chemist Ansco, Binghamton, N.Y., 1929-35; chemist Haloid Co., Rochester, N.Y., 1935-38, research dir., 1938-46, v.p. charge research and product devel., dir., 1946-59; (name changed to Haloid Xerox, Inc., 1958); exec. v.p. research and engring. div. Xerox Corp., 1959-68, vice chmn. bd., until 1970, dir., until 1973. Co-author: Xerography and Related Processes; author: My Years with Xerox, or the Billions Nobody Wanted. Trustee emeritus Fordham U. Fellow Photog. Soc. Am., N.Y. Acad. Scis., Am. Inst. Chemists; mem. Am. Chem. Soc., Nat. Acad. Engring. Roman Catholic. Home: PO Box 373 Pittsford NY 14534 also Hillsboro Beach FL Office: 57 Monroe Ave Pittsford NY 14534

DESSER, MAXWELL MILTON, art director, producer; b. N.Y.C., Aug. 7 1909; s. Solomon and Saide Franklin and Desser; m. Mary Alice Natkin, Mar. 7, 1953. Student, Queens Coll., Pratt Inst., Cooper Union, N.Y. U, Am. U. Free lance art dir., film-strip producer, N.Y.C., 1935—; owner Desser Prodns., N.Y.C.; producer filmstrips Crawl (Internat. TV and Film Festival N.Y. Silver medal 1967), Dun's Market Identifiees (Internat. TV and Film Festival N.Y. gold medal 1968). Author: Using the Library, 1957. Served to lt. USNR, 1942-45. Recipient Nat. Art League Gold medal, 1962, 1968; Knickerbocker Artists gold medal, 1973. Dolphin fellow Am. Watercolor Soc. (Silver medal 1975, Dolphin fellow, sec., dir. 1973-83); asoc. mem. Nat. Acad. Design; mem. Allied Artists Am. (Silver medal 1978), Audubon Artists (Silver medal 1981, bd. dirs. 1979-82). Club: Salagundi. Office: Desser productions 22 E 49 St New York NY 10017

DESSLER, ALEXANDER JACK, space scientist; b. San Francisco, Oct. 21, 1928; s. David Alexander and Julia (Shapiro) D.; m. Lorraine Hudek, Apr. 18, 1952; children: Pauline Karen, David Alexander, Valerie Jan, Andrew Emory. B.S., Calif. Inst. Tech., 1952; Ph.D., Duke, 1956. Sect. head Lockheed Missiles & Space Co., 1956-62; prof. Grad. Research Center, Dallas, 1962-63; prof., chmn. space sci. dept. Rice U., Houston, 1963-69, prof. space physics and astronomy, 1970-82, chmn. dept., 1979-82, campus bus. mgr., 1974-76; sci. adviser Nat Aeros. and Space Council, 1969-70; pres. Univs. Space Research Assn., 1975-81. Editor: Jour. Geophys. Research, 1965-69, Revs. of Geophysics and Space Physics, 1969-74, The John Wiley Space Science Text Series, 1968-76; adv. bd.: Planetary and Space Sci. Served with USN, 1946-48. Recipient Outstanding Young Scientist award Tex. wing Air Force Assn., 1963. Fellow Am. Geophys. Union (Macelwane award 1963), AAAS; mem. Am. Astron. Soc., Internat. Assn. Geomagnetism and Aeronomy (exec. com., v.p. 1979—). Home: 6907 Steeplechase Dr Huntsville AL 35806

DESTEVENS, GEORGE, chemist, educator; b. Tarrytown, N.Y., Aug. 21, 1924; s. Samuel and Celeste (Leggin) deS.; m. Ruby deVico, Nov. 30, 1950. B.S., Fordham U., 1950, M.S., 1951, Ph.D., 1953. Research chemist Remington Rand, Middletown, Conn., 1953-55; research chemist CIBA Pharm. Co., Summit, N.J., 1955-60, dir. medicinal chemistry, 1960-65, dir. chem. research, 1965-67, v.p., dir. research, 1967-70; exec. v.p., dir. research CIBA-Geigy Corp., Summit, 1970-79; prof. chemistry Drew U., Madison, N.J., 1979—, dir., 1980—; frontiers in chemistry lectr. Wayne State U., 1961; vis. professorial lectr. medicinal chemistry U. Vienna, 1961, U. Kans., 1964, Weizmann Inst., Israel, 1965, U. Kyoto, Japan, 1965; chmn. award com. CIBA-Geigy-Drew Award in Frontiers in Biomed. Research, 1976—; mem. research adv. bd. Frito-Lay, 1979—; chmn. bd. Med. Mark Corp., 1983—; cons. chem. cos., 1979—. Author: Diuretics, Chemistry and Pharmacology, 1963, Analgetics, 1965; editor: Medicinal Chemistry Monographs, 1963—, Medicinal Research Revs, 1981—; mem. editorial bd.: Organic Preparations and Procedures, 1969—, Synthetic Reactions, 1971—, Chemistry in the Economy, 1973; contbr. articles to various publs. Trustee St. Barnabas Med. Center, 1970—; bd. dirs. N.J. chpt. Huntington's Disease, 1980—. Served with U.S. Army, 1942-46. Recipient Outstanding Achievement award in Sci. Fordham Coll. Alumni Assn., 1966; Walter J. Hartung Meml. award in medicinal research U. N.C., 1979. Fellow N.Y. Acad. Scis. (research award in chemistry 1961); mem. Am. Chem. Soc., Am. Inst. Chemistry, AAAS, Assn. Research Dirs. (exec. council), Am.-Swiss Found. Sci. Exchange (trustee), Soc. Chem. Industry, Indsl. Research Inst., Sigma Xi, Phi Lambda Upsilon. Clubs: Morris County Golf (Convent Station, N.J.); Summit Tennis. Home: 2 Warwick Rd Woodland Park Summit NJ 07901 Office: Dept of Chemistry Drew U Madison NJ 07940 *Those who surrender principle for security risk losing both security and principle.*

DESTINE, JEAN-LEON, choreographer, dancer, teacher; b. St. Marc, Haiti, Mar. 26, 1928; came to U.S., 1944; s. Leon and Lucienne (Joseph) D. Student, Lycee Petion, Port-au-Prince, Haiti, 1940-43, Ethnol. Inst., Haiti, 1941-42. Pres., dir. Destine Dance Found., Ltd.; Hon. cultural attache in U.S. for, Republic of Haiti; adv. bd. UNESCO Dance, 1978. Choreographer, dancer; founder, dir., Troupe Nationale Folklorique, Haiti's Internat. Expn., 1950; choreographer, dancer: Troubled Island, N.Y.C. Opera, 1949-50, Witch Doctor; motion pictures, 1950-51, Cantiones Unidas, 1957; guest artist, Internat. Dance Workshop, Bonn, W.Ger., 1980, 81, 82, 83; artistic dir., choreographer, lead dancer, Jean-Leon Destine Afro-Haitian Dance Co. appearing, U.S., Can., Europe, Asia, Latin Am. Decorated chevalier Order Honneur et Merite Haitian Govt., 1951, officer, 1958; recipient Caribbean Arts and Cultural award, 1979, Thelma Hill Dance award, 1981; Rockefeller Found. scholar, 1944-46; Nat. Endowment Arts Choreographer's fellow, 1980-81. Address: 676 Riverside Dr New York NY 10031

DESTINO, RALPH, JR., retail executive; b. Providence, Apr. 7, 1936; s. Ralph R. and Josephine D.; (div.)1 son, Ralph, III. B.A., Dartmouth Coll., 1954. Vice pres. Ralph Destino Ltd., 1955-70; pres. Kenton Wholesale Corp., 1971-73, Cartier (Far East) Ltd., 1974-75, Cartier Inc., N.Y.C., 1976—; dir. Fashion Inst. Tech.; chmn. jewelry div. Channel 13 Public TV Auction, 1978-79. Bd. dirs. N.Y.C. div. Am. Cancer Soc., 1980, crusade chmn., 1981-84; mem. president's council Museum City N.Y., 1979—. Recipient Humanitarian award Am. Jewish Com., 1979. Mem. Jewelry Inst., Jewelry Industry Council (dir.), DeBeers Carat Club. Clubs: Doubles, Le Club (N.Y.C.). Office: 653 Fifth Ave New York NY 10022

DESTLER, I. M(AC), political scientist, foreign policy writer; b. Statesboro, Ga., Aug. 21, 1939; s. Chester McArthur and Katharine (Hardesty) D.; m. Harriett Kirkham Parsons, July 27, 1968; children: Mark Dodson, Katharine Elizabeth. B.A. magna cum laude, Harvard U., 1961; M.P.A., Princeton U., 1965, Ph.D., 1971. Peace Corps vol. U. Nigeria, Nsukka, 1961-63; asst. Senator Walter Mondale, Washington, 1965-67; staff assoc. Pres.'s Task Force on Govt. Orgn., Washington, 1967; analyst, acting coordinator for Asia, Internat. Agrl. Devel. Service, U.S. Dept. Agr., Washington, 1967-69; Internat. Affairs fellow Council on Fgn. Relations, Washington, 1969-70; vis. lectr. Woodrow Wilson Sch., Princeton U., (N.J.), 1971-72; research assoc. Brookings Inst., Washington, 1972-76, sr. fellow, 1976-77; sr. assoc. Carnegie Endowment for Internat. Peace, Washington, 1977-83; sr. fellow Inst. Internat. Econs., Washington, 1983—; cons. Am. Fgn. Service Assn., 1970-71, U.S. State Dept., 1976; cons. on reorgn. U.S. Office Mgmt. and Budget, 1977, 79; dir. study on politics of econ. disputes U.S.-Japan Econ. Relations Group, Washington, Tokyo, 1980. Author: Presidents, Bureaucrats and Foreign Policy - The Politics of Organizational Reform, 1972, 74, (with others) Managing an Alliance - The Politics of U.S.-Japanese Relations, 1976, (with Fukui and Sato) The Textile Wrangle - Conflict in Japanese-American Relations, 1969-71, 1979, Making Foreign Economic Policy, 1980, (with Leslie H. Gelb) Our Own Worst Enemy: The Unmaking of American Foreign Policy, 1984; co-editor: Coping with U.S.-Japanese Economic Conflicts, 1982. Mem. Council Fgn. Relations, Am. Polit. Sci. Assn. (publs. com. 1982-83). Democrat. Presbyterian. Home: 1478 Waggaman Circle McLean VA 22101 Office: Inst Internat Econs 11 Dupont Circle NW Washington DC 20036

DE STWOLINSKI, GAIL ROUNCE BOYD, educator; b. Sidney, Mont., Nov. 8, 1921; d. Harold Lowell and Alice (Hardenburgh) R.; m. David Robinson Boyd, Sept. 4, 1943 (dec. 1944); 1 son, David Robinson Boyd; m. Louis Charl de Stwolinski, June 15, 1951. Mus.B., U. Mont., 1943; M.Music Theory, Eastman Sch. Music U. Rochester, 1946, Ph.D. in Music Theory, 1966. Instr. U. Okla., 1946, asst. prof. music theory, 1949-55, asso. prof., 1955-66, prof., 1966—, Distinguished prof., 1970—, chmn. dept. music theory and composition, 1953-60; Adviser, cons. in field. Author: also articles in mus. jours. Form and Content in Instrumental Music. Recipient Regents award superior teaching, 1966; named David Ross Boyd prof., 1970; recipient Distinguished Service citation U. Mont., 1974. Mem. Okla. Music Tchrs. Assn., Okla. Theory Roundtable, Music Tchrs. Nat. Assn., Music Educators Nat. Conf., AAUP, Coll. Music Soc., Soc. Music Theory, Mortar Bd., Phi Beta Kappa (hon.), Pi Kappa Lambda, Mu Phi Epsilon, Kappa Kappa Gamma. Democrat. Home: 1037 Cruce St Norman OK 73069

DE TAKACSY, NICHOLAS BENEDICT, physicist, educator; b. Budapest, Hungary, Feb. 24, 1939; s. Constantin and Katalin (Jellenz) de T.; m. Mickey Mary Dawson, June 16, 1962; children: Victoria, Christine, Frederica. B.Sc., Loyola Coll., Montreal, Que., Can., 1959; M.Sc., U. Montreal, 1963; Ph.D., McGill U., 1966. Research asso. Calif. Inst. Tech., Pasadena, 1966-67; asst. prof. Loyola Coll., Montreal, 1967-68; mem. faculty McGill U., Montreal, 1968—, prof. physics, 1978—, chmn. dept., 1979-82. Mem. Can. Assn. Physicists, Am. Phys. Soc. Roman Catholic. Office: 3600 University St Montreal PQ H3A 2T8 Canada

DETELS, ROGER, epidemiologist, physician, university dean; b. Bklyn., Oct. 14, 1936; s. Martin P. and Mary J. (Crookr) D.; m. Mary M. Doud, Sept. 14, 1963; children: Martin, Edward. B.A., Harvard U., 1958; M.D., NYU, 1962; M.S. in Prevention Medicine, U. Wash., 1966. Am. Bd. Preventive Medicine. Intern U. Calif. Gen. Hosp., San Francisco, 1962-63; resident U. Wash., Seattle, 1963-66, practice medicine specializing in preventive medicine, 1966—; med. officer, epidemiologist Nat. Neurol. Diseases, Bethesda, Md., 1969-71; assoc. prof. epidemiology Sch. Pub. Health, UCLA, 1971-73, prof., 1973—; dean, 1980—; head div. epidemiology Sch. Pub. Health, UCLA, 1972-80; guest lectr. various univs., profl. confs. and med. orgns., 1969—; research physician Wadsworth Hosp. Center, Los Angeles, 1972. Contbr. articles to profl. jours. Served as lt. comdr. M.C. USN, 1966-69. Grantee in field. Fellow Am. Coll. Preventive Medicine; mem. Am. Epidemiological Soc., Soc. Epidemiologic Research (pres. 1977-78), Assn. Tchrs. Preventive Medicine, Calif. Acad. Preventive Medicine (chmn. essay com. 1971), Am. Public Health Assn., Am. Assn. Cancer Edn. (membership com. 1979-80), Am. Thoracic Soc., Internat. Epidemiologic Assn., AAAS, Sigma Xi, Delta Omega. Office: UCLA Sch Public Health Los Angeles CA 90024

DETERLING, RALPH ALDEN, JR., surgeon, educator; b. Williamsport, Pa., Apr. 29, 1917; s. Ralph Alden and Edith Pauline (Ritter) D.; m. Mary Ann Gilson, June 21, 1947; children: Ralph III, William R., John S., Paul A. A.B., Stanford U., 1938, M.D., 1942; M.S. in Surgery, U. Minn., 1946, Ph.D., 1947. Diplomate: Nat. Bd. Med. Examiners, Am. Bd. Surgery, Am. Bd. Thoracic Surgery. Intern Hosp. U. Pa., 1941-42, resident, 1942-43; fellow surgery Mayo Found., 1943-47; staff physician Nopeming Sanatorium, 1947; asst. attending surgeon Presbyn. Hosp., N.Y.C., 1948-50, asso. attending surgeon, 1950-59; surg. cons. U.S. Naval Hosp., St. Albans, Manhattan VA Hosp., N.Y.C., Paterson (N.J.) Gen. Hosp.; asso. surgeon attending Francis Delafield Hosp., N.Y.C.; asst. prof. surgery Columbia Coll. Phys. and Surg., 1948-50, asso. prof., 1950-54, asso. clin. prof. surgery, 1954-59; dir. surg. research labs.; chmn. dept. surgery Tufts U. Sch. Medicine, Boston, 1959-75, prof. surgery, 1959—; lectr. Boston U., 1963—, Northwestern U., 1973-75; surgeon-in-chief New Eng. Med. Center Hosp., 1959-75; dir. first surg. service Boston City Hosp., 1959-70, cons., 1970—; cons. Newton-Wellesley, Boston VA, Mt. Auburn, St. Elizabeth's, Lemuel Shattuck, Waltham, Nashoba Community, Emerson, Choate, Framingham Union hosps., Huggins Hosp.,

Wolfeboro, N.H., Bayshore Med. Ctr., Springfield, Mass. Contbr. articles to med., sci. jours. Fellow A.C.S., Am. Coll. Chest Physicians; mem. Am., N.Y. thoracic socs., Harvey Soc., Whipple Soc., Colombian Coll. Surgeons (hon. mem.), Brazilian Coll. Surgeons (hon. mem.), N.Y. Soc. Cardiovascular Surgery (sec.-treas. 1957, v.p.), Med. Strollers (pres. 1957), Soc. Vascular Surgery, Internat. Cardiovascular Soc. (treas.-gen. 1953-57, sec.-gen. 1961-67, v.p. 1969, pres. 1969-71, N.Am. chpt. pres. 1965, co-chief editor Jour. Cardiovascular Surgery 1973—), AAAS, Am. Soc. Artificial Internal Organs, Argentina Angiology Soc. (hon. mem.), Uruguay Angiology Soc. (hon. mem.), Chile Angiology Soc. (hon. mem.), Colombia Angiology Soc. (hon. mem.), Brazil (corr.), Assn. Surgeons Gt. Britain and Ireland (corr.), Soc. Surgery Alimentary Tract, N.Y. acads. medicine, Soc. Univ. Surgeons, N.Y. Acad. Scis., Internat. Soc. Surgery, Soc. for Surg. Alimentary Tract, Am. Trauma Soc., Am. Assn. Surgery Trauma, Am. Assn. Thoracic Surgery, Am., Mass. heart assns., Am. Philatelic Soc., Stanford, Mayo Found. alumni assns., Am. Acad. Arts and Scis., Am. Surg. Assn., Mass. Med. Soc., New Eng. Surg. Soc., Boston Surg. Soc. (pres. 1970), St. Paul Surg. Soc. (hon. mem.), North Pacific Surg. Soc. (hon. mem.), N.Y. Surg. Soc., Lombard Surg. Soc. Italy (hon.), Nat. Surg. Soc. Cuba (hon.), Phi Beta Kappa, Sigma Xi (chpt. sec.), Alpha Omega Alpha, Alpha Kappa Kappa. Home: 62 Conant Rd Lincoln MA 01773 Office: 171 Harrison Ave Boston MA 02111

DETERMAN, JOHN DAVID, lawyer; b. Mitchell, S.D., Feb. 18, 1933; s. Alred John and Olive Gertrude (Lovinger) D.; m. Gloria Esther Rivas, Nov. 15, 1980; children by previous marriage: James Taylor, Mark Sterling. B.Engring. in Elec. Engring. cum laude, U. So. Calif., 1955; LL.D. magna cum laude, UCLA, 1961. Electronics engr. Hughes Aircraft Co., Los Angeles, 1955-60; sr. partner Tuttle & Taylor, Inc., Los Angeles, 1961—; dir. Sav-On Food Co., Inc., Thiem Industries, Inc., Early Calif. Industries, Inc., 1973-79, 82—; founder Stanford U. Law Sch. Carl D. Spaeth Scholarship Fund, 1972; arbitrator Am. Arbitration Assn., mem. nat. panel arbitrators, 1962—, mem. adv. council, Los Angeles, 1982—. Mem. State Bar Calif., Los Angeles County Bar Assn., Am. Coll. Constrn. Arbitrators (charter 1982—), Order of Coif, Eta Kappa Nu, Tau Beta Pi. Office: 609 S Grand Ave Los Angeles CA 90017 *Tolerate even intolerance but never cruelty*

DETERS, JAMES RAYMOND, manufacturing company executive; b. Cin., June 18, 1937; s. Joseph Gerald and Elsie Marie (Murphy) D.; m. Jacklyne Florence Eaton, Feb. 20, 1960; children—James, Deborah. B.S.C., Ohio U., 1959; M.B.A., Ohio State U., 1963. Acctg. mgr. Procter & Gamble Co., Cin., 1963-66; asst. controller Boise Cascade Corp., Mpls., 1967; controller Lindsay div. TransUnion Corp., Mpls., 1968-69; group controller Borg-Warner Corp., Chgo., 1970-72, asst. corp. controller, 1973-75, corp. controller, 1975—, v.p., 1978-82, v.p. human resources, 1982—; exec. in residence Purdue U., 1976. Pres. Kidney Found. Ill., 1974-77; bd. dirs. Chgo. Youth Centers, 1974-76; trustee Grant Hosp., Chgo., 1978-82, Barat Coll., Lake Forest, Ill., 1978-82, Lake Forest Sch. Mgmt., 1980-83; adv. bd. U. Ill., 1983—; mem. Leadership Council for Chgo. Open Communities, 1983—. Served to capt. AUS, 1960-63. Mem. Fin. Execs. Inst., Am. Mgmt. Assn. (lectr.), Machinery and Allied Products Inst. (fin. council), Ill. C. of C. (trustee 1980—), Delta Tau Delta. Republican. Roman Catholic. Clubs: Economic, Chgo. Athletic Assn., Onwentsia Country. Home: 1300 Loch Ln Lake Forest IL 60045 Office: 200 S Michigan Ave Chicago IL 60604

DETHERO, J. HAMBRIGHT, banker; b. Chattanooga, Jan. 2, 1932; s. Jacob Hambright and Rosalie Frances (Gasser) D.; m. Charlotte Nixon Lee, Sept. 19, 1959; children: Dinah Lee, Charles Drew. B.S. in Bus. Adminstrn., U. Fla., 1953; B.F.T., Am. Grad. Sch. Internat. Mgmt., Phoenix, 1958. With Citibank, N.Y.C., P.R., Caracas, Venezuela, San Francisco, 1958-69; mgr. First Nat. City Bank (Internat.), San Francisco, until 1969; v.p. internat. div. Crocker Nat. Bank, San Francisco, 1969-75, sr. v.p., 1976—, London, 1977-80, San Francisco, 1980-84, Bank America World Trade Corp., 1984—. Bd. dirs. Calif. Council Internat. Trade, 1972-77, pres., 1974-76; trustee World Affairs Council No. Calif.; vice chmn. Dist. Export Council No. Calif.; mem. world bus. adv. council Am. Grad. Sch. Internat. Mgmt. Served with USN, 1953-57. Mem. Bankers Assn. Fgn. Trade, World Trade Club San Francisco, Brit.-Am. C. of C. (v.p., dir.). Club: Orinda (Calif.) Country. Home: 694 Old Jonas Hill Rd Lafayette CA 94549 Office: 915 Front St San Francisco CA 94111

DETHLOFF, HENRY CLAY, history educator; b. New Orleans, Aug. 10, 1934; s. Carl Curt and Camelia (Jordan) D.; m. Myrtle Anne Elliott, Aug. 27, 1961; children: Clay, Carl. B.A., U. Tex., Austin, 1956; M.A., Northwestern State U., Natchitoches, La., 1960; Ph.D., U. Mo., Columbia, 1964. Instr., then asst. prof. history U. Southwestern La., 1962-68; asso. prof. U. So. La., 1966-69; mem. faculty Tex. A&M U., 1969—, prof. history, 1975—, chmn. dept., 1981—. Author: Thomas Jefferson and American Democracy, 1971, The Pictorial History of Texas A&M University, 1876-1976, 1975, The Centennial History of Texas A&M University, 1876-1976, 1975, Americans and Free Enterprise, 1979, A History of American Business, 1983. Served to lt. (j.g.) USNR, 1956-58. Mem. Agrl. History Assn., Econ. History Assn., So. Hist. Assn., Tex. Hist. Assn., La. Hist. Assn., Phi Kappa Phi, Phi Alpha Theta, Sigma Chi. Democrat. Methodist. Home: 8709 Bent Tree St College Station TX 77840 Office: Dept History Tex A&M U College Station TX 77843

DETHY, RAY CHARLES, university dean; b. Louisville, Nov. 3, 1928; s. Raymond A. and Ellen (Beach) D.; m. Gloria A. Hegenberger, June 6, 1953 (div.); children: David Lee, Stephen Ray, Christine Elise; m. Carol A. Weiss, May 28, 1972 (div.); m. Virginia Willis, July 4, 1982. B.Sc., Ohio State U., 1951, M.A., 1959, Ph.D., 1963; M.B.A., Rensselaer Poly. Inst., 1981. Elementary tchr., Whitehall, Ohio, 1954, football and track coach, tchr. Latin, 1955-56, supt. schs., Knox County, Ohio, 1956-57, asst. supt. schs., Newark, O., 1957-60; asst. to dean Ohio State U., 1960-63; assoc. prof., chmn. depts. instrn. and adminstrn. Northeastern U., 1963-65; prof. edn., dir. grad. sch. edn., dir. Urban Edn. Center, 1965-69; dean Sch. of Edn. St. John's U., Jamaica, N.Y., 1969-72, dean spl. programs, 1972-73; dean Sch. Edn. and Profl. Studies Central Conn. State Coll., New Britain, 1973—; dean acad. affairs Lyndon State Coll. (Vt.), 1973—; co-chmn. Conn. Human Resources Commn., 1980; chmn. Conn. Tchr. Edn. Program Rev. Com., 1978; v.p. Conn. Assn. Colls. and Univs. for Tchr. Edn.; project dir. Conn. Competency Based Tchr. Edn. Consortium, 1974—, Capitol Regional Edn. Council, 1978; cons., evaluator New Eng. Competency Based Tchr. Edn. and Adminstrv. Programs.; Incorporating mem. Edn. Devel. Center, Boston; partner GDH Assos., Boston. Author: (with R. Ostrander) A Values) Approach to Educational Adminstration, 1969. Vice pres. Plymouth County Hosp. Served with AUS, 1951-53. Mem. Am. Ednl. Research Assn., Hartford Area Supts. Assn., Am. Assn. Sch. Adminstrs., Phi Delta Kappa. Home: 144 Holabird Ave Winsted CT 06098 Office: Central Conn State Coll New Britain CT 06050

DETLEFSEN, GUY-ROBERT, management consultant; b. Chgo., May 3, 1919; s. Gustav C. and Elsa L. (Larrieu) D.; m. Merry Campbell, May 30, 1941; children: Guy-Robert, Keith Campbell, Joan Andre. B.A. cum laude, Harvard U., 1941. Cert. chem. dependency counselor. With shipbldg. div. Bethlehem Steel Co., Quincy, Mass., San Francisco, 1941-44; research tech. Pillsbury Co., 1945-52, dir. comml. research and devel., 1952-58, v.p. growth and tech., 1959-66, v.p. comml. devel. div., 1966-69; exec. v.p., gen. mgr., dir. Maple Island, Inc., Mpls., 1970-73; pres., chmn. Barberio Cheese Houses, Inc., Mpls., 1973-77; pres. Detlefsen and Assos., Mpls., 1977—; ptnr. Chem. Dependency Recovery Assocs.: Program Devel. Cons., Mpls., 1983—; Dir. research adv. council Nat. Indsl. Conf. Bd.; mem. social policy task force Minn. Chem. Health Assn. Mem. Am. Mktg. Assn. (award for product testing 1949, past v.p. mktg. mgmt. div.), Am. Econ. Assn. Home: 231 Glenmoor Ln Long Lake MN 55356 Office: Box 5 Long Lake MN 55356

DET LIMA, RICHARD FORD, photographic company executive, lawyer; b. N.Y.C., Oct. 19, 1930; s. Edwin A. and Ora M. (Ford) detLima; m. Sarah Elizabeth Boulton, Dec. 14, 1969; children: Harriet Jane, Jonathan Ford, Catherine Elizabeth, Caroline Frances. B.A. magna cum laude, Amherst Coll., 1951; M.A., Harvard U., 1952, J.D., 1955. Bar: N.Y. 1959, Ohio 1971. Atty., Cravath, Swaine & Moore, N.Y.C., 1959-65; asst. counsel Firestone Tire & Rubber Co., Akron, Ohio, 1965-68; asst. area mgr. for Europe Firestone Internat. Co., Rome, 1968-69, area mgr. Asia and S. Pacific, Akron, 1969, pres., 1970-72; v.p., sec. Polaroid Corp., Cambridge, Mass., 1972—. Served to lt. USNR, 1955-58. Home: 55 Summer St Cohasset MA 02025 Office: 549 Technology Sq Cambridge MA 02139

DE TONNANCOUR, PAUL ROGER GODEFROY, library adminstr.; b. Fall River, Mass., May 22, 1926; s. R. Godefroy and Emilie (St. Germain) de T.; m. Mary E. Fenno, Apr. 9, 1955; children—Paul Godefroy, Camille Marie. A.B., Providence Coll., 1952; M.S., Simmons Coll., 1953; postgrad., Western Res. U., U. So. Cal. Asst. librarian Enoch Pratt Library, Balt., 1953-54; chief librarian, tech. analyst Armco Steel Corp., Balt., 1954-56; dir. research library Gen. Dynamics (Ft. Worth div.), 1956—, dir. tech. information programs, 1964—; Cons. Modern Lang Assn. Am., U.S. Office Edn. on sci. information personnel; John Cotton Dana lectr., 1966. Singer, Ft. Worth Opera Assn. Chorus; Author: The Exploitation of Technical Information, 1966; co-author: Science Information Personnel, 1963; Contbr. articles to profl. jours. Active United Fund and Community Council; mem. exec. com. Big Bros. Tarrant County.; Trustee Cosmopolitan Internat., 1961-63. Served with USNR, 1943-46. Named Boss of Year Am. Bus. Women's Assn., 1965. Mem. ALA, AAAS, Am., Nat. mgmt. assns., Ft. Worth Art Assn., Spl. Libraries Assn., Am. Soc. Information Sci., Delta Epsilon Sigma. Episcopalian. Clubs: Mason., Fort Worth Boat. Home: 6332 Genoa Rd Fort Worth TX 76116 Office: PO Box 748 Fort Worth TX 76101 *Above all, don't take yourself too seriously; Seek wisdom for itself and nurture a sense of humor. Most of the world's troubles are caused by grim egocentrics; so earnest, so persuasive, so single-minded; Wisdom and a balanced sense of humor will protect one from their unrelenting pressures.*

DE TORNYAY, RHEBA, nurse, university dean; b. Petaluma, Calif., Apr. 17, 1926; d. Bernard and Ella Fradkin; m. Rudy de Tornyay, June 4, 1954. Student, U. Calif., Berkeley, 1944-46; diploma, Mt. Zion Hosp. Sch. Nursing, 1949; A.B., San Francisco State U., 1951, M.A., 1954; Ed.D., Stanford U., 1967; Sc.D. (hon.), Ill. Wesleyan U., 1974, L.H.D., U. Portland, 1974. Faculty San Francisco State U., 1957-67, prof. nursing, 1966-67, chmn. dept., 1959-67; asso. prof. U. Calif. Sch. Nursing, San Francisco, 1968-71, prof., 1971; dean, prof. Sch. Nursing, UCLA, 1971-75, U. Wash., Seattle, 1975—. Author: Strategies for Teaching Nursing, 1971, 2d edit., 1982, Japanese transl., 1974. Mem. Am. Nurses Assn., Am. Acad. Nursing (charter fellow, pres. 1973-75), Inst. Medicine (governing council 1979-81), Am. Edn. Research Assn., Western Soc. Research in Nursing, Soc. Health and Human Values, Western Coucil Higher Edn. in Nursing (dir. 1976-79). Office: Sch Nursing SC-72 U Wash Seattle WA 98195

DETORO, FREDRIC EDWARD, chemical executive; b. Providence, Nov. 29, 1932; s. Ferdin and Teresa (Corsi) D.; m. Dorothy Silvestri, Aug. 28, 1954; children: Donna Louise, Kathleen Joyce, Steven Edward, Michael Kenneth. Sc.B., Brown U., 1954; Ph.D., Duke U., 1957. With Am. Cyanamid Co., Wayne, N.J., 1957—, v.p. div. organic chems., 1975-77, v.p. fibers div., 1977-78, pres. div. indsl. chems., 1978—, group v.p. chems., 1980—. Office: Am Cyanamid Co One Cyanamid Plaza Wayne NJ 07470

DETRA, RALPH WILLIAM, research laboratory administrator; b. Thompsontown, Pa., Mar. 23, 1925; s. Ralph Emerson and Sara Jane (Portzline) D.; m. Charlesanna Francis Eberly, June 21, 1947; children—Stephen William, David Eberly. B.S. in Mech. Engring, Cornell U., 1946, M. Aero.Engring, 1951; Dr. sc. techn. (NRC fellow 1951-52), Fidgenossische Technische Hochschule, Zurich, Switzerland, 1953. Supr. aerodynamic research, aviation gas turbine div. Westinghouse Corp., Kansas City, Mo., 1953-55; prin. research scientist Avco Everett Research Labs. Inc. (Mass.), 1955-59, v.p. fossil energy tech., 1972-81, exec. v.p., gen. mgr., 1981—, v.p., gen. mgr. systems div., Wilmington, Mass., 1966-71; pres. Tyco Labs. Inc., Waltham, Mass., 1971-72. Author papers in field. Served with USN, 1943-47. Asso. fellow AIAA; mem. Sigma Xi, Tau Beta Pi. Republican. Episcopalian. Club: Winchester Country. Home: 15 Frost St Arlington MA 02174 Office: 2385 Revere Beach Pkwy Everett MA 02149

DETRE, THOMAS, psychiatrist, educator; b. Budapest, Hungary, May 17, 1924; came to U.S., 1953, naturalized, 1958; m. Katherine Maria Drechsler, Sept. 15, 1956; children: John Alan, Antony. B.A., Gymnasium of Piarist Fathers, Kecskemet, Hungary, 1942; postgrad., Horthy Miklos U. and Pazmany Peter U., 1945-47; M.D., Rome U., 1952. Diplomate: Am. Bd. Psychiatry and Neurology (assoc. examiner). Intern Morrisania City Hosp., N.Y.C., 1953-54; resident inpsychiatry Mt. Sinai Hosp., N.Y.C., 1954-55; resident in psychiatry Yale U., 1955-57, chief resident, instr., 1957-58, instr., 1958-59, asst. prof., 1959-62; dir. psychiat. inpatient service Yale-New Haven Hosp., 1960-68, assoc. prof., 1962-70, asst. chief psychiatry div., 1965-68, psychiatrist in chief, 1968-73, prof., 1970-73; prof., chmn. dept. psychiatry U. Pitts., 1973-82, assoc. sr. vice chancellor, disting. service prof. health scis., 1982—; dir. Western Psychiat. Inst. and Clinic, Pitts., 1973—. Author: (with H.G. Jarecki) Modern Psychiatric Treatment, 1971; contbr. chpts. to books. Fellow Am. Coll. Psychiatrists, Am. Psychiat. Assn.; mem. Am. Coll. Neuropsychopharmacology, Collegium Internat. Neuropsychopharmacologicum, Pan Am. Med. Assn., AAAS, Assn. Psychophysiol. Study Sleep, Am. Soc. Clin. Pharmacology and Therapeutics, Phi Beta Kappa. Office: 3811 O'Hara St Pittsburgh PA 15213

DETREVILLE, ROBERT TREAT PAINE, physician; b. Beaufort, S.C., Feb. 19, 1925; s. Benjamin Ellis and Ruth Claghorn (Saffold) DeT.; m. Janice Suzanne Mundy, Nov. 26, 1953; children: Suzanne, Anne Hamilton, Janice Mundy, Nancy Beaumont, George Mundy. B.S., The Citadel, 1948; M.D., Med. Coll. S.C., 1948; Sc.D. in Indsl. Medicine, U. Cin., 1956; grad., Sch. Aviation Medicine. Diplomate: occupational medicine Am. Bd. Preventive Medicine. Rotating intern St. Francis X. Infirmary, Charleston, S.C., 1947-48, Roper Hosp., Charleston, 1948-49; practice gen. medicine, Charleston County, 1949-51; commd. 1st lt. USAF, 1951, advanced through grades to col. M.C.; chief phys. standards, Wright-Patterson AFB, Ohio, 1952-53, dep. chief profl. services div., 1956-59; chief Aerospace Med. Br., Norton AFB, Calif., 1959-60; chief health and safety, ballistic systems div. Air Force Systems Command, Inglewood, Calif., 1960-61; comdr. Tactical Airlift Clinic (AFRES) Greater Pitts. Internat. Airport, 1974-75; maj. command asst. occupational med. services Air Force Logistics Center, Wright-Patterson AFB, 1975-77; dir. aerospace medicine USAF Med. Center, Wright-Patterson AFB, 1977-79, spl. asst. to comdr. for occupational and hyperbaric medicine, dir. base med. services, 1979-80; cons. occupational medicine to comdr. USAF Occupational Environ. Health Lab., Brooks AFB, Tex., 1980—; asst. clin. prof. indsl. health U. Cin., 1958-59; asst. prof. indsl. health, dept. preventive medicine and indsl. health Coll. Medicine, 1961-63; vis. lectr. occupational medicine U. Calif. Med. Center, Los Angeles, 1960-61, USAF Sch. Aerospace Medicine, 1965—, U. Tex. Grad. Sch. Pub. Health, San Antonio, 1981—; co. physician Ethyl Corp., 1961-62, asst. med. dir., 1962-63; mng. dir. Indsl. Hygiene Found. Am., Mellon Inst., Pitts., 1963-68; adv. fellow Mellon Inst. of Carnegie-Mellon U., 1968-72; pres. Indsl. Health Found. Am., Inc., 1968-72; cons. Triangle Health Ctr., 1972-75; adj. prof. occupational medicine U. Pitts. Grad. Sch. Pub. Health, 1963-75; asso. clin. prof. community medicine dept. Wright State U., 1977-80; cons. staff div. medicine dept. occupational health West Pa. Hosp., 1963-75; sr. research cons. Inst. for Devel. Human Resources, Am. Insts. for Research, 1972-73; mil. cons. USAF surgeon gen., 1977—; USAF liaison mem. NRC Com. on Toxicology, 1956-60, occupational health med. surveillance com., Dept. Def., 1982—. Editorial bd.: Jour. Occupational Medicine, 1961-67. Mem. bd. Oakmont Carnegie Library, 1966-75. Fellow Am. Acad. Occupational Medicine (chmn. publs. com. 1962-65), Indsl. Medicine Assn. (chmn. com. indsl. hygiene and clin. toxicology 1960-62), A.C.P., Am. Coll. Preventive Medicine, Aerospace Med. Assn.; mem. Air Force Assn., Am. Conf. Govtl. Indsl. Hygienists, Am. Indsl. Hygiene Assn. (biol. monitoring com.), AMA, Assn. Mil. Surgeons, Tex. Med. Assn., Bexar County Med. Soc. Episcopalian. Home: 6310 Mallard Point San Antonio TX 78239

DETTBAN, WOLF-DIETRICH, pharmacologist; b. Berlin, Jan. 30, 1928; U.S., 1958, naturalized, 1968; s. Erwin Bruno and MariaMagdalena (Courady) D.; m. Christine Anneliese Keune, Sept. 15, 1960; children: Donata-Andrea, Henning-Christian. M.D.l, D. Gottingen, 1953. Intern Univ. Clinic, Gottingen, 1953-54; research assoc. biol. dept. Ciba Co., Basel, 1954-55; research assoc. Physiol. Inst., U. Saarland, Homburg, Saar, 1955-58; research assoc. neurology Columbia U., N.Y.C., 1958-61, asst. prof., 1961-67, assoc. prof., 1967-68; prof. pharmacology Vanderbilt U., Nashville, 968—; mem. corp. Marine Biol. Lab., Woods Hole, Mass.; mem. com. on toxicology of anticholinesterase chems. NRC; cons. U.S. Army Med. Research and Devel. Command. Contbr. articles in field to profl. jours. Grantee NIH, 1958. Mem. Am. Physiol. Soc., Am. Soc. Pharmacology and Exptl. Therapeutics, Am. Soc. Neurchem., Soc. Gen. Physiologists, Soc. for Neurosci., Soc. Toxicology, Harvey Soc., AAAS. Home: 4422 Wayland Dr Nashville TN 37215 Office: Vanderbilt U Med Center S 2100 Pierce Ave Nashville TN 37232

DETTINGER, GARTH BRYANT, physician, ret. air force officer, county health officer; b. Syracuse, N.Y., Dec. 23, 1921; s. Maurice and Maxine Bryant (Giddings) D.; m. Gladys Ruth Hickingbotham, Aug. 5, 1939; children—Holly Maxine Dettinger Dixon, Ronald Mark, Michael James. A.B., Harvard U., 1948; M.D., Columbia U., 1952; M.S. in Surgery, Baylor U., 1956. Diplomate: Am. Bd. Surgery. Commd. officer U.S. Air Force, 1952, advanced through grades to maj. gen., 1977; intern Valley Forge Army Hosp., Phoenixville, Pa., 1952-53; resident in surgery Brooke Army Hosp., San Antonio, 1953-57; chief surgery MacDill Hosp., Tampa, Fla., 1957-59, Elmendorf Hosp., Alaska, 1959-62, Davis-Monthan Hosp., Tuscon, 1962-64; hosp comdr., Roswell, N.Mex., 1964-67; chief profl. services Air Forces Europe, 1967-70; hosp. comdr., Vandenberg, Calif., 1970-72; surgeon Air Force Mil. Personnel Center, San Antonio, 1972-74; command surgeon Air Tng. Command, 1974-75; dir. plans and resources U.S. Air Force, Washington, 1975-77, dep. surgeon gen., 1977-80; asst. health dir., Fairfax County, Va., 1980—; surg. cons. Surgeon Gen. U.S. Editor-in-chief: Surgeons Comments, 1967-70. Fellow A.C.S. (bd. govs.); mem. AMA, Va. Assn. Health Dirs., Royal Soc. Medicine, Alpha Omega Alpha. Republican. Episcopalian. Home: 9337 Tovito Dr Fairfax VA 22031 Office: Fairfax County Health Dept 4080 Chainbridge Rd Fairfax VA 22030

DETUNO, JOSEPH EDWARD, lawyer; b. Chgo., Jan. 2, 1931; s. Robert and Sarah (Laurenzana) D. Student, De Paul U., 1949-51, LL.B., 1954. Bar: Ill. 1954. Atty. Security Mut. Casualty Co., Chgo., 1956-63; partner Gifford, Detuno & Gifford, Chgo., 1963—. Served with AUS, 1954-56. Mem. ABA, Ill. Bar Assn., Chgo. Bar Assn. (chmn. com. indsl. commn. 1967-68), Am. Judicature Soc., Chgo. Trial Lawyers. Home: 201 E Chestnut St Chicago IL 60611 Office: 221 N LaSalle St Chicago IL 60601

DE TURK, FREDERICK WALTER, copper company executive; b. W. Reading, Pa., May 29, 1928; s. Elmer F. and Sara M. (Snyder) DeT.; m. Carolyn Nubel, Oct. 14, 1950; children—Deborah DeTurk Amato, Eric, Nancy. B.A., U. Mich., 1950; grad., Advanced Mgmt. Program Harvard U., 1978. Mgmt. trainee Jos. G. Pollard Co., Garden City Park, N.Y., 1950; acct. exec. O.E. McIntyre Inc., Gt. Neck, N.Y., 1951; mktg. and sales positions Phelps Dodge Copper Products Corp. and Phelps Dodge Electronic Products Corp., N.Y.C., 1953-68; asst. v.p. Phelps Dodge Industries, Inc., N.Y.C., 1968-69; now pres.; pres. Phelps Dodge Communications Co., White Plains, N.Y., 1969-78; v.p. personnel Phelps Dodge Corp., N.Y.C., 1978-79; dir. Phelps Dodge Overseas, Shared Med. Systems Corp., Phelps Dodge Industries Inc. Contbg. author: How I Made the Sale That Did the Most for Me, 1981. Served with U.S. Army, 1951-53. Mem. Soc. Mining Engrs. Congregationalist. Clubs: Univ., Mining, Wilton Riding., Woodway Country. Home: 104 Olmstead Hill Rd Wilton CT 06897 Office: 300 Park Ave New York NY 10022

DETVOSS, JAMES THOMAS, philatelist; b. Ocheyedan, Iowa, Mar. 22, 1916; s. Jesse Franklin and Ada Calista (Johnson) DetV.; m. Dorothy Alberta Durr, Oct. 10, 1938; children: Richard Allan, Robert Neal, Rosalie Jean DetVoss Starr. Student, U. Iowa, 1933-37; B.S., U. Md., 1958. Circulation supr. Des Moines Register and Tribune, 1938-40; commd. 2d lt., inf. ORC, 1937; called to active duty, 1941, advanced through grades to col., 1961; grad. Command and Gen. Staff Coll., 1953; mem. mil. staff Big Three Conf., Bermuda, 1953; spl. security officer U.S. Army, Pacific, 1949-52, U.S. Forces, Austria, 1954-55, SHAPE, 1955-58; Joint Chief Staff and Sec. Def., 1958-61; ret., 1961; asst. exec. sec. Am. Philatelic Soc., 1961-63, exec. dir., 1963-81. Contbr. profl. handbooks.; Editor: Am. Philatelic Congress Book, 1953. Pres. Phila. Internat. Philatelic Exhbn., 1974—, Am. Philatelic Research Library, 1980—; trustee Philatelic Found., Centre County Community Found. Decorated Legion of Merit; recipient McCoy award Am. Philatelic Congress, 1953, 59, John N. Luff award Am. Philatelic Soc., 1955, 58, Tilleard medal Royal Philatelic Soc., 1957; Jere Hess Barr award Am. Philatelic Congress, 1959; Hanford cup Garfield-Perry Stamp Club, Cleve., 1964; Outstanding Achievement in Philately award, 1967; Alfred F. Lichtenstein Meml. award for disting. service to philately, 1977; named to Roll of Disting. Philatelists, Gt. Brit., 1981. Fellow Royal Philatelic Soc. (London), Royal Philatelic Soc. Can.; mem. Am. Philatelic Soc., Am. Philatelic Congress, Collectors Club N.Y., Fédération Internationale de Philatélie (v.p. 1976—), Postal History Soc. (hon.), Am. Soc. Assn. Execs. (life).

Presbyterian (elder). Club: Rotary. Home: 9 Nittany View Circle State College PA 16801

DETWEILER, DAVID KENNETH, veterinary physiologist, educator; b. Phila., Oct. 23, 1919; s. David Rieser and Pearl Irene (Overholt) D.; m. Inge E. A. Kludt, Feb. 2, 1965; children: Ellen, Diane, Judith, David, Inge, Kenneth. V.M.D., U. Pa., 1942, M.S., 1949; Sc.D. (hon.), Ohio State U., 1966, M.V.D., U. Vienna (Austria), 1968, D.M.V., U. Turin (Italy), 1969. Asst. instr. physiology and pharmacology Sch. Vet. Medicine, U. Pa., Phila., 1942-43, instr., 1943-45, assoc. in physiology, pharmacology, 1945-47, asst. prof., 1947-51, assoc. prof., 1951-62,, chmn. dept. vet. med. scis., 1956-68, dir. comparative cardiovascular studies unit, 1960—, prof., head lab. physiology and pharmacology, 1962-68, prof., head lab. physiology, 1968—, prof. faculty arts and scis., 1968—, chmn. grad. group comparative med. scis., 1971—; mem. Inst. Medicine, Nat. Acad. Scis., 1974—; cons. cardiovascular toxicology, 1950—. Contbr. numerous articles to various publs. Guggenheim fellow, 1955-56; Recipient Gaines award and medal Am. Vet. Med. Assn., 1960; D.K. Detweiler prize in cardiology established in his honor German Group of World Vet. Med. Assn., 1982. Fellow AAAS; mem. Am. Physiol. Soc., Am. Assn. Vet. Physiology and Pharmacology (pres.), N.Y. Acad. Scis., Am. Vet. Med. Assn., Council Basic Scis., Am. Heart Assn., Acad. Vet. Cardiology (pres.), Am. Coll. Vet. Internal Medicine (cardiology group), Phi Zeta. Office: Sch Vet Medicine 3800 Spruce St Philadelphia PA 19104

DETWEILER, JOSEPH HALL, retired manufacturing executive; b. Aurora, Ill., Aug. 12, 1920; s. Harry Rutt and Verne (Hall) D.; m. Catherine Ann Lawrence, Apr. 19, 1945; children: Peter Hall, Steven Lawrence, Nancy Ross, Carol Norton. B.S., Princeton U., 1941; I.A., Harvard U., 1943, M.B.A. with distinction, 1946. C.P.A., Mich. Engr., Lockeed Aircraft, 1941-42; acct. Arthur Andersen & Co., 1946-48; cons. Sanderson & Porter, 1948-49; treas. Argus Cameras, Inc., Ann Arbor, Mich., 1949-55, v.p., 1955-57; v.p., gen. mgr. Argus Cameras div. Sylvania Electric Products, Inc., 1957-59; dir. corp. planning Louis Allis Co., Milw., 1959-61; fin. v.p. Hamilton Mfg. Co., Two Rivers, Wis., 1961-63, exec. v.p., 1963-65; treas., dir., v.p. fin. Kroehler Mfg. Co., Naperville, Ill., 1965-80. Past chmn. Ann Arbor Republican Com. Served as lt. USNR, 1943-46. Mem. Fin. Execs. Inst., Phi Beta Kappa. Home: 57th St nr County Line Rd Hinsdale IL 60521

DETWEILER, ROBERT CHESTER, university dean, historian; b. French Camp, Calif., Dec. 8, 1938; s. Chester and Alice Mae (Gallagher) D.; m. Susan Jan Krudwig, Nov. 22, 1978; 1 dau., Lara Anne. B.A., Humboldt State U., 1960; M.A., San Francisco State U., 1965; Ph.D., U. Wash., 1968. Asst. prof. history San Diego State U, 1968-71, assoc. prof., 1971-74, prof., 1974-78, chmn. dept. history, 1977-78, assoc. dean Coll. Arts and Letters, 1978-80, dean coll., 1980—. Author: Richard Bland and the Origins of the Virginia Revolt, 1982; editor: Environmental Decay in Its Historial Context, 1973, Race, Prejudice and the Origins of Salvery in America, 1975, Liberation in the Americas,, 1978. Served to col. USMCR, 1960—. Mem. Orgn. Am. Historians, Am. Hist. Assn., USMCR Officers Assn. (pres. chpt. 1977-79). Lodge: Kiwanis. Home: 4333 Caminito de la Escena San Diego CA 92108

DETWILER, PETER MEAD, investment banker; b. Detroit, June 7, 1928; children: Mary, Elizabeth, Susan. B.A., Trinity Coll., 1950; M.B.A., Harvard, 1953. With Holly Carburetor Co., Detroit, 1953; research analyst, asst. to dir. Schroder Wagg & Co. Ltd., London, Eng., 1954-55; exec. asst. to mng. dir. and chmn. Ever-Ready Razor Products, London, 1955-57; asst. to pres. A.S.R. Products Co., N.Y.C., 1957-61; with Philip Morris, Inc., N.Y.C., 1961; v.p. E.F. Hutton & Co., Inc., N.Y.C., 1961-64, v.p., voting stockholder, 1964-70, dir., 1968—, sr. v.p., 1970-72, mem. exec. and fin. coms., 1970—, vice chmn. bd., dir., mem. exec. and fin. coms., 1972—; dir., mem. exec. and finance coms. E.F. Hutton Group Inc., 1974—; dir., chmn. exec. com. Verex Corp., Madison, Wis., 1966-79; dir., mem. exec. com. Albion Malleable/Hayes Albion Corp., Jackson, Mich., 1965-72, Puritan Fashions Corp., N.Y.C., 1974-76; dir., chmn. fin. com. Handleman Co., Detroit, 1963-78, Tesoro Petroleum Corp., San Antonio, 1967—; dir., chmn. exec. com. S-A-L Inc., Summit Airlines, Inc.; chmn. fin. com., mem. exec. com. Commonwealth Oil Refining Co., Inc., P.R., 1975-77; dir., mem. fin. com. Trinidad-Tesoro Petroleum Co. Ltd., 1969—; dir. Ferro Mfg. Co., Detroit, 1979—, Gulfstream Aerospace Corp., Savannah, Ga., 1980-82; dir., chmn. exec. com. S-A-L, Inc., Summit Airlines, Inc., Phila., 1983—. Trustee Upper Raritan Water-Shed Assn., Far Hills, N.J., Purnell Sch., Pottersville, N.J.; bd. dirs. Am.-Swiss Assn.; bd. govs., mem. exec. com. Flight Safety Found., 1981—. Mem. N.Y. Soc. Security Analysts, Fin. Analysts Fedn., Am. Petroleum Inst. Clubs: Essex Hunt (Peapack, N.J.); Somerset Lake and Game (Far Hills, N.J.); City Midday, Knickerbocker (N.Y.C.). Home: 969 Fifth Ave Apt 4 New York NY 10021 also High Stoy Farm Larger Cross Rd Gladstone NJ 07934 Office: 1 Battery Park Plaza New York NY 10004

DETZER, KARL, writer; b. Fort Wayne, Ind., Sept. 4, 1891; s. August J. and Laura (Goshorn) D.; m. Clarice Nissley, Nov. 26, 1921; children—Karl (dec.), Mary-Jane (Mrs. J.C. Moench). L.H.D. (hon.), Ind. U., 1979. Reporter, photographer Ft. Wayne newspapers, 1909-16, advt. writer, Chgo., 1920-23, screen play writer and tech. dir., Hollywood, 1934-36; roving editor Reader's Digest, 1939-42, 46-77; pub. Enterprise-Tribune, Leland, Mich., 1947-51. Author: books and screen plays; latest book Myself When Young, 1968; Contbr. articles to leading mags. Mem. Mich. State Corrections Council, 1948-49; chmn. Mich. Citizens Com. on Reorgn. State Govt., 1950-51; spl. adviser to Mil. Govt., Berlin, Germany, 1948. Served from pvt. to capt., inf. U.S. Army, 1916-1919; from maj. to col. Gen. Staff Corps. AUS, 1942-46. Decorated D.S.M. Mem. Authors League Am., Internat. Assn. City Mgrs., Mich. State Police (hon.), V.F.W. (hon. life Floyd Gibbons Post, N.Y.C.). Democrat. Unitarian. Clubs: Deadline (N.Y.C.); National Press, Overseas Press. Home: Leland MI 49654 Office: The Reader's Digest Pleasantville NY 10570

DEUCHLER, PHILIP GEORGE, precious metals co. exec.; b. Neward, N.Y., Oct. 8, 1927; s. Philip George and Helen Katherine (Keane) D.; m. Shirley L. Rand, Sept. 20, 1952; children: William P., Barbara Deuchler Maher, Carol L. B.S. in Metall. Engring, Purdue U., 1949. Registered profl. engr., Calif. Sales engr. Handy & Harman, Chgo., 1949-56, dist. sales mgr., 1956-65, mgr. plant and sales, Los Angeles, 1965-69, plant mgr., Attleboro, Mass., 1969-71, v.p. mktg., 1969-71, 71-79, group v.p., 1979—; dir. Lucas-Milhaupt Inc., Am. Chem. and Refining Co., Inc., Handy & Harman, Handy & Harman of Can. Ltd. Served with USN, 1945-46. Mem. Profl. Engrs. Soc. Republican. Clubs: University (N.Y.C.); Noroton Yacgt, Wee Burn Country (Darien, Conn.). Home: 14 Kerry Ln Darien CT 06820 Office: 850 3d Ave New York NY 10022

DEUKMEJIAN, GEORGE, governor California; b. Albany, N.Y., June 6, 1928; s. C. George and Alice (Gairdan) D.; m. Gloria M. Saatjian, 1957; children—Leslie Ann, George Krikor, Andrea Diane. B.A., Siena Coll., 1949; J.D., St. John's U., 1952. Bar: N.Y. 1952, Calif. 1956, U.S. Supreme Ct. 1970. Partner firm Riedman, Dalessi, Deukmejian & Woods, Long Beach, Calif., to 1979; mem. Calif. Assembly, 1963-67, Calif. Senate, 1967-79, minority leader; atty. gen. State of Calif., 1979-82, gov., 1983—; former dep. county counsel Los Angeles County. Mem. exec. bd. Long Beach council Boy Scouts Am. Served with U.S. Army, 1953-55. Mem. Long Beach Bar Assn., Am. Bar Assn., State Bar Calif., Long Beach C. of C. (past dir.), Navy League, YMCA. Republican. Episcopalian. Clubs: Lions, Elks. Office: Office of Gov State Capitol Sacramento CA 95814

DEUPREE, MARVIN MATTOX, business consultant, accountant; b. Woodbine, Iowa, Oct. 8, 1917; s. Archie Orin and Pearl (Mattox) D.; m. Katherine Anita Beard, Aug. 18, 1951; children: Marvin Mattox, Meredith Ann. B.A. with high distinction, State U. Iowa, 1941; M.B.A. with distinction, U. Pa., 1948. C.P.A., N.Y., Ill., Mich., La., Iowa, Va., N.C. Instr. acctg. U. Pa., 1947-48; with Arthur Andersen & Co. (C.P.A.s), 1948-75, partner, 1960-75, mem. policy com. on acctg. and auditing, 1962-72; bus. cons., 1975—; pres. Emporium Specialties Co., Inc., 1977—; adj. asso. prof. NYU Grad. Sch. Bus. Adminstrn., 1973-76. Contbr. articles to profl. jours. Served as officer USNR, 1943-46. Mem. Am. Inst. C.P.A.s, N.Y. State, Ill. socs. C.P.A.s, Nat. Assn. Accts., Am. Acctg. Assn., Phi Beta Kappa. Episcopalian. Clubs: Wall Street (N.Y.C.); Executives, Wharton Graduate Business School, University (Chgo.). Home: 5 Academy Rd Ho-Ho-Kus NJ 07423 Office: 1345 Ave of Americas New York NY 10019

DEUSCHLE, KURT WALTER, physician, educator; b. Kongen, Germany, Mar. 14, 1923; came to U.S., 1924, naturalized, 1949; s. John and Marie (Schaefer) D.; m. Jeanne Magagna, 1975; children by previous marriage—Kurt J., Sally, James. B.S. cum laude, Kent State U., 1944; M.D., U. Mich., 1948. Intern Colo. Gen. Hosp., Denver, 1948-49; resident medicine, fellow oncology Upstate Med. Center of State U. N.Y. at Syracuse, 1950-52, instr. medicine, 1954-55; asst. prof. pub. health and preventive medicine Cornell Med. Coll., 1955-60; prof., chmn. dept. community medicine U. Ky., 1960-68; Ethel H. Wise prof., chmn. and dir. dept. community medicine Mt. Sinai Sch. of Medicine of City U. N.Y., 1968—; Merrimon lectr. U. N.C., Chapel Hill, 1975; vis. prof. U. Lagos, Nigeria, 1977; mem. tech. bd. Milbank Meml. Fund; mem. Tb control adv. com. Center Disease Control Dept. HEW; cons. manpower intelligence NIH; mem. Inst. Medicine of Nat. Acad. Scis., Washington; mem. rural health systems del. to China, 1978. Author: (with J. Adair) The People's Health: Anthropology and Medicine in a Navajo Community, 1970; Contbr. to: (ed. John Norman) Medicine in the Ghetto, 1969, Community Medicine: Teaching, Research and Health Care, (ed. Lathem and Newberry), 1970. Served with AUS, 1943-46. Commonwealth Fund sr. health fellow, 1966-67. Fellow Am. Coll. Preventive Medicine (past pres., Distinguished Service award 1975); mem. Am. Pub. Health Assn. (award for excellence in domestic health 1975), Am. Thoracic Soc., Assn. Tchrs. Preventive Medicine, Internat. Epidemiol. Assn., Alpha Omega Alpha. Home: 1212 Fifth Ave New York NY 10029 Office: Fifth Ave and 100th St New York NY 10029

DEUSING, MURL, producer; b. Milw., Sept. 5, 1908; s. Henry and Olga (Henning) D.; m. Mildred Nickels, May 25, 1928. B.E., U. Wis., 1933. Asst. curator edn. Milw. Pub. Mus., 1932-45, curator edn., 1945-59; during this period adminstr. audiovisual library serving Milw. schs., also pioneered mus. TV Programs; photographer wild life Walt Disney's True Life Adventures, Zoo Parade, Warner Bros., also lectr. wild life and travel, 1939—; owner Murl Deusing Film Prodns., classroom teaching films, 1946- -; dir. Mus. Sci. and Natural History, St. Louis, 1959-61; producer TV programs Nat. Ednl. TV and Radio Center, N.Y.C., 1961-77; producer Murl Dausing Safari TV series, 1964-77. Author: Soil, Water and Man, 1936. Recipient Distinguished Alumnus award U. Wis.-Milw. Alumni Assn., 1971. Mem. AAAS, Wis. Soc. Ornithology (past pres.), Am. Assn. Museums (counselor 1959), Izaak Walton League (past nat. dir., past sec. Wis.), Midwest Mus. Conf. (past pres.), Acad. Sci. St. Louis, Wis Acad. Sci., Nat. Conservancy, Wilderness Soc., Nat. Parks Assn. Address: 1401 W Hwy 50 Box 163 Clermont FL 32711

DEUTCH, JOHN MARK, chemist, college dean; b. Brussels, Belgium, July 27, 1938; came to U.S., 1940, naturalized, 1946; s. Michael Joseph and Rachel Felicia (Fisher) D.; m. Samayla Dodek; children—Philip, Paul, Zachary. B.A., Amherst Coll., 1961, D.Sc. and Humane Letters (hon.), 1978; B. Chem. Engring, M.I.T., 1961; Ph.D. in Phys. Chemistry, M.I.T., 1965. System analyst Office Sec. Def., 1961-65; fellow Nat. Acad. Scis./NRC, Nat. Bur. Standards, 1966-67; asst. prof. Princeton U., 1967-70; mem. faculty MIT, 1970—, prof. chemistry, 1971—, chmn. dept., 1976, dean sci., 1982—; chmn. adv. panel chemistry NSF, 1974; mem. Nat. Def. Sci. Bd., 1977—, Pres.'s Nuclear Safety Oversight Com.; dir. Office Energy Research U.S. Dept. Energy, Washington, 1977-79, acting asst. sec. for energy tech., 1979, under sec., 1979-80; mem. Army Sci. Adv. Panel, 1975-78, Pres. Commn. on Strategic Forces, 1983. Author research articles. Sloan fellow, 1969-71; Guggenheim fellow, 1974. Mem. Am. Phys. Soc., Am. Chem. Soc., Council Fgn. Relations, Am. Acad. Arts and Scis. Home: 6 Belfry Terr Lexington MA 02173 Office: Dept Chemistry MIT Room 6123 Cambridge MA 02139

DEUTSCH, ARNOLD REID, business executive, consultant; b. Budapest, Hungary, Oct. 9, 1919; U.S., 1925; s. Louis G. and Sadie (Kaufman) D. B.A., Columbia U. Editorial writer N.Y. Sun, N.Y.C., 1935-40, N.Y. Jour., 1940-42; creative dir. Brown Advt. Agy., N.Y.C., 1945-50; chmn. Deutsch, Shea & Evans, Inc., N.Y.C., 1950—. Author: Human Resources Revolution, 1978, How to Find a Job, 1980, How to Hold a Job, 1983. Lt. j.g. USN, 1942-45; ETO. Mem. Friends of Mozart (bd. dirs.), Concert Artists Guild (bd. dirs.), Morality in Media (bd. dirs.), Am. Assn. Advt. Agys. Home: 35 Park Ave New York NY 10016 Office: Deutsch Shea & Evans Inc 49 E 53d St New York NY 10022

DEUTSCH, GEORGE CARL, metallurgical engineer; b. Budapest, Hungary, Apr. 19, 1920; s. Frank and Jennie (Greenbaum) D.; m. Ruth Amster, Oct. 4, 1942; children—Fred, Harvey, Marilyn. B.S. in Phys. Metallurgy, Case Western Res. U., 1942. With Copperweld Steel Co., Warren, Ohio, 1942-44; with Nat. Adv. Com. for Aero., to 1969, chief high temperature materials br., to 1969; with NASA, 1960-81, dir. research and tech. div., to 1981, cons., 1981—; cons. aerospace research and tech.; mem. adv. group for aerospace devel. NATO; mem. nat. materials adv. bd. Nat. Acad. Sci. Contbr. articles to profl. jours. Served with U.S. Navy, 1944-46. Recipient Disting. medal NASA, 1980. Fellow Am. Soc. Metals; mem. AIME. Jewish. Office: 8303 Whitman Dr Bethesda MD 20817

DEUTSCH, JAN C., legal educator; b. 1935. B.A., Yale U., 1955, Ph.D., 1962; M.A., Cambridge U., Eng., 1963. Bar: D.C. 1963, Ohio 1965. Law clk. to Justice Stewart U.S. Supreme Ct., 1962-66; assoc. Jones Day Cockley & Reavis, Cleve., 1964-66; asst. prof. Yale U. Law Sch., New Haven, Conn., 1966-67, assoc. prof., 1967-68, prof., 1968—; lectr. Case Western Res. U., 1965-66; cons. Pres' Commn. on Law Enforcement And Adminstrn. of Justice, 1966, Pres' Task Force on Telecommunications, 1968, Aetna Life and Casualty Co., 1979—. Author: (with Bianco) International Transactions: The Law of Corporations, 1976, Selling the People's Cadillac, 1976. Mem. Order of Coif. Office: Yale Law Sch Drawer 401A Yale Sta New Haven CT 06520

DEUTSCH, KARL W(OLFGANG), political scientist, emeritus educator; b. Prague, Czechoslovakia, July 21, 1912; came to U.S., 1938, naturalized, 1948; s. Martin M. and Maria (Scharf) D.; m. Ruth Slonitz, Apr. 2, 1936; children: Mary Elizabeth Deutsch Edsall, Margaret Deutsch Carroll. Candidatus Juris, German U., Prague, 1934; D. Law and Polit. Sci., Charles U., Prague, 1938; Ph.D. in Govt., Harvard U., 1951; D. Econs. and Social Scis. (hon.), U. Geneva, 1973; LL.D. (hon.), U. Mich., 1975, U. Ill., 1976, Northwestern U., 1980, Ph.D., U. Mannheim (Germany), 1977, Tech. U. Berlin, 1983, D.Litt., U. Pitts., 1980. From instr. to prof. M.I.T., Cambridge, Mass., 1942-52, prof. history and polit. sci., 1952-58; prof. polit. sci. Yale U., New Haven, 1958-67; prof. govt. Harvard U., Cambridge, Mass., 1967-71, Stanfield prof. internat. peace, 1971-83; emeritus (Harvard U.), 1983—; also dir. Internat. Inst. Comparative Social Research, West Berlin, 1976—; vis. prof. Princeton (N.J.) U., 1953-54, U. Chgo., 1954, Heidelberg (Germany) U., 1960, Frankfurt (Germany) U., 1968, U. Geneva, 1971, 72, 74, 75, U. Paris, 1973, 74, U. Zurich, 1975; U. Mich., 1977, U. Hamburg, 1983; chmn. faculty Am. seminar, Salzburg, 1981; vis. fellow Nuffield Coll., Oxford U., Eng., 1962; specialist U.S. Dept. State, India, 1963, 73, Poland, 1967, Afghanistan and Nepal, 1973. Author: Nationalism and Social Communication, 1953, rev. edit., 1966, The Nerves of Government, 1963, rev. edit., 1966, Arms Control and the Atlantic Alliance, 1967, The Analysis of International Relations, 1968, rev. edit., 1978, Nationalism and Its Alternatives, 1969, Politics and Government: How People Decide Their Fate, 1970, rev. edits., 1974, 80, Tides Among Nations, 1979; co-author or contbg. author: Political Community and the North Atlantic Area, 1957, Germany Rejoins the Powers, 1959, World Handbook of Political and Social Indicators, 1964, France, Germany and the Western Alliance, 1967, Mathematical Approaches to Politics, 1973, Mathematical Political Analysis, 1976, Eco-Social Systems and Eco-Politics, 1977, Problems of World Modelling, 1977, Decentralization, 1980, Fear of Science-Trust in Science, 1980, Comparative Government, 1981, Advances in the Social Sciences, 1984; editorial bd.: Behavioral Sci., 1965—, Comparative Studies in Society and History, 1966-80, Polit. Theory, 1975—, Zeitschrift für Politik, 1976—, Jerusalem Jour. Internat. Relations, 1976—, Jour. Policy Modeling, 1978—. Decorated Grand Cross of Merit (W. Ger.), 1977, with star, 1983; recipient Sumner prize Harvard U., 1951; Sudeten German prize of culture, 1977; in Medias Res research prize, 1979; Prix de Talloires, 1982; Guggenheim fellow, 1954, 71. Fellow Nat. Acad. Scis., Am. Acad. Arts and Scis.; mem. Am. Polit. Sci. Assn. (pres. 1969-70), Internat. Polit. Sci. Assn. (pres. 1976-79), Soc. for Gen. Systems Research (pres. 1983-84), Peace Sci. Soc. (pres. 1973-74), Internat. Inst. Polit. Philosophy (pres. 1983-84), Am. Unitarian Assn. Office: 226 Littauer Bldg Harvard U Cambridge MA 02148 *My life's aim has been to study politics in order to help people to overcome the four chief dangers of our time: large wars, hunger, poverty and vast population growth. For this end, I have sought more knowledge for greater competence and more compassion.*

DEUTSCH, MARTIN BERNARD JOSEPH, editor, publisher; b. Karlsruhe, Germany, Apr. 7, 1931; came to U.S., 1939, naturalized, 1948; s. Benedickt and Margarethe (Zivi) D.; m. son, Kenneth. Student in Journalism, CCNY, 1953, Columbia U., summer 1955. CCNY coll. corr. N.Y. Times, 1953-55; mng. editor The Beachcomber, Long Beach I., N.J., summers 1952, 53; reporter Southwest American, Ft. Smith, Ark., 1954-55; mng. editor Travel Courier and Travel Weekly, 1955-67; sr. v.p., editor, pub. OAG Travel Mags. (div. Ofcl. Airline Guides, Inc.); (Dun & Bradstreet Co.), N.Y.C., 1967—; guest instr. U. Mass., 1975; speaker travel and transp. industry. Mem. Upper Manhattan Community Planning Bd., 1965; mem. travel adv. bd. U.S. Dept. Commerce, U.S. Travel Service, 1977-81. Served with U.S. Army, 1953-55. Recipient various awards for travel journalism. Mem. Travel Industry Assn. Am. Club: Sky (N.Y.). Home: 106 Pinehurst Ave New York NY 10033 Office: 888 Seventh Ave New York NY 10019

DEUTSCH, MORTON, psychologist, educator; b. N.Y.C., Feb. 4, 1920; s. Charles and Ida (Prager) D.; m. Lydia S. Shapiro, June 1, 1947; children—Anthony Charles, Nicholas Andrew. B.S., Coll. City N.Y., 1939; M.A., U. Pa., 1940; Ph.D., Mass. Inst. Tech., 1948. From asst. to asso. prof. psychology N.Y. U., 1948-56; dir. research interpersonnel processes Bell Telephone Labs., Murray Hill, N.J., 1956-63; prof. psychology, edn. Tchrs. Coll. Columbia, N.Y.C., 1963—, Edward Lee Thorndike prof., 1981—; vis. scholar Russell Sage Found., 1976-77; Cons. Nat. Inst. Mental Health, VA. Author: Interracial Housing, 1951, Research Methods in Social Relations, 1951, Preventing World War III; Some Proposals, 1962, Theories in Social Psychology, 1965, The Resolution of Conflict: Constructive and Destructive Processes, 1973, Applying Social Psychology, 1975. Trustee Marshall Fund. Served to 1st lt. USAAF, 1942-45. Decorated D.F.C. with cluster, Air medal with three clusters.; Recipient AAAS Socio-Psychology prize, 1961; Samuel Flowerman Meml. award, 1963; Hovland Meml. award, 1967; Kurt Lewin Meml. award, 1968; Gordon Allport prize, 1973. Mem. Soc. Psychol. Study Social Issues (pres. 1960-61), Am. Psychol. Assn., N.Y. State Psychol. Assn. (pres. 1965-66), Eastern Psychol. Assn. (pres. 1968-69), Am. Sociol. Assn., AAAS, Internat. Soc. Polit. Psychology (pres. 1981-82). Home: 161 W 86th St New York NY 10024

DEUTSCH, ROBERT WILLIAM, physicist; b. Far Rockaway, N.Y., Mar. 21, 1924; s. Nathan and Lena (Berger) D.; m. Florence Kadish, Sept. 11, 1949; children—Jane Lisa, David Jeffrey. B.S., Mass. Inst. Tech., 1948; Ph.D., U. Calif., 1953. Physics cons. Martin-Marietta Corp., Balt., 1962-64; pres. Gen. Physics Corp., Columbia, Md., 1966; Prof., chmn. dept. nuclear sci. and engring. Cath. U. Am., 1964-72. Contbr. articles to profl. jours.; author newspaper articles and pub. info. booklets on nuclear power. Served with AUS, 1943-46. Fellow Am. Nuclear Soc.; mem. Am. Phys. Soc., Am. Soc. Engring. Edn., AAAS. Research on tng. programs and facilities for nuclear power plant personnel. Home: 8502 Arbor Wood Rd Baltimore MD 21208 Office: 1000 Century Plaza Columbia MD 21044

DEUTSCH, STANLEY, anesthesiologist, educator; b. N.Y.C., Apr. 4, 1930; s. Elias and Estelle (Press) D.; m. Margaret R. Zuanic, July 11, 1971; children: Susan, Ellen, Nina, Eva. B.A., NYU, 1950; M.A., Boston U., 1951, Ph.D., 1954, M.D., 1957. Diplomate: Am. Bd. Anesthesiology. Research and teaching fellow in physiology Boston U. Sch. Medicine, 1951-55; intern Grad. Hosp., U. Pa., 1957-58, resident in anesthesiology, 1958-61; asst. prof. anesthesiology U. Pa., 1963-65; asst. prof. Harvard U., 1965-69; prof. U. Chgo., 1969-71; prof., head. dept. anesthesiology U. Okla. Health Scis. Center, 1971-82; prof. anesthesiology U. Tex. Med. Sch., Houston, 1982—; cons. VA Med. Center, Oklahoma City. Contbr. articles to profl. publs. Served as capt., M.C. USAR, 1961-63. Mem. Am. Soc. Anesthesiologists (dir.), Okla. Med. Assn., AMA, Sigma Xi, Alpha Omega Alpha. Home: 3711 Crystall Falls Dr Missouri City TX 77459 Office: 6431 Fannin MSMB 5020 Houston TX 77030

DEUTSCH, STUART JAY, industrial and systems engineer; b. N.Y.C., Mar. 11, 1943; s. Meyer and Pauline D.; m. Carol A. Powers, Jan. 20, 1968; children: Geoffrey, Jason. B.S., Mich. State U., 1965; Ph.D., U. Wis., 1970. Project engr. Shulton Inc., Clifton, N.J., 1965-66; spl. process engr. Avco Co., Lycoming, Stratford, Comm., 1966-68; asst. prof. ops. research Poly. Inst. Bklyn., 1970-72; mem. faculty Ga. Inst. Tech., Atlanta, 1972—, prof. indsl. and systems engring., 1978—; cons, in field. Author books in field; Mem. editorial bd.: Evaluation Quar, 1976—, Transactions Inst. Indsl. Engring., Urban Geography; contbr. articles to profl. jours. Ford Found. grantee, 1969-70; Nat. Inst. Law Enforcement and Criminal Justice grantee, 1974—; Nat.

Inst. Justice grantee. Mem. Ops. Research Soc. Am., Am. Statis. Assn., Inst. Indsl. Engrs., Sigma Xi. Club: Atlanta Lawn Tennis Assn. Address: 1604 Withmere Way Dunwoody GA 30338

DEV, VASU, chemistry educator; b. Lahore, India, Mar. 18, 1933; s. Bhim Dev and Satyavat (Pandey) Shastri; m. Barbara C. Zimmerman, Dec. 19, 1963; children—Rajan, Nisha. B.S., Punjab (India) U., 1951, 1953, M.S., 1954; Ph.D., U. Calif., Davis, 1962. Chemist Regional Drug Research Lab., Jammu, India, 1955-56; chemist Med. Coll., Patiala, India, 1956-59; research asso. U. Chgo., 1963-64; asst. prof. dept. pharm. medicinal chemistry U. Tenn., Memphis, 1964-65; prof. chemistry Calif. State Poly. U., Pomona, 1965—, chmn. dept., 1971-78; U.S. India exchange scientist, 1982. Contbr. articles to profl. jours. NSF research grantee, 1966-67; Calif. Poly. U. Creative Activity League grantee, 1970. Mem. Am. Chem. Soc., Chem. Soc. London, Am. Soc. Pharmacognosy, Calif. Assn. Chemistry Tchrs., Sigma Xi. Home: 1210 Cambridge Ave Claremont CA 91711 Office: Dept Chemistry Calif Poly U Pomona CA 91768

DEVAN, CHRISTOPHER BARTRAM, former librarian, restauranteur; b. Plainfield, N.J., Nov. 15, 1926; s. Samuel Arthur and Winifrede (Richards) D.; m. Margaret Brice, Feb. 23, 1963; children: Cathryn A. Devan Conroy, Elizabeth Devan Marrs, Caroline G. Devan Morris, William Arthur, Margaret Richards. B.A., George Washington U., 1950; M.S. in L.S, U. Ill., 1954. Asst. field dir. ARC, 1952-53; br. librarian Milw. Pub. Library, 1954-57; county librarian Greene County Library, Springfield, Mo., 1957-60; county and extension librarian pub. libraries, Springfield and Greene County, 1960-61, Pa., 1961-63; asst. dir. Wilmington (Del.) Inst. Free Library, 1963-64; dir. libraries Wilmington Inst. Free Library and New Castle County Free Library, 1964-70; dir. Cuyahoga County Pub. Library, Cleve., 1970-75, Jefferson-Madison Regional Library, Charlottesville, Va., 1975—. Chmn. Central Va. chpt. ARC, 1979—. Served with AUS, 1945-46, 50-51. Mem. ALA (council 1966-70), Del. Library Assn. (pres. 1968-69), Va. Library Assn., Southeastern Library Assn., Middle Atlantic Regional Library Fedn., SAR, Religious Soc. Free Quakers. Episcopalian. Club: Rotarian. Home: 2817 Northfield Rd Charlottesville VA 22901 Office: Pan & Pantry 1715 C Seminole Trail Charlottesville VA 22901

DEVANE, DENIS JAMES, health care company executive; b. N.Y.C., Feb. 11, 1938; s. Eugene and Deborah (Courtney) D.; m. Margaret Mary Walsh, Oct. 14, 1961; children: Denise, Daniel, Deborah, Tara. B.S., Fordham U., 1959. Asst. v.p. nat. sales mgr. C.I.T. Bldgs. Corp., N.Y.C., 1971-74, v.p., gen. mgr., 1973-74, pres., 1974-75; v.p. Lifemark Corp., Houston, 1975-80, sr. v.p., 1980—. Mem. Am. Hosp. Assn., Fedn. Adm. Hosps., Am. Mgmt. Assn., Tex. Hosp. Assn. Clubs: Univ. (chmn. athletic com. 1983-84); Westlake (Houston)). Home: 15214 Turkey Creek Houston TX 77079

DEVANE, WILLIAM, actor; b. Albany, N.Y., Sept. 5, 1937; m. Eugenie; children—Josh, Jake. Attended, Am. Acad. Dramatic Arts, N.Y.C. Movie appearances include: The Bad News Bears in Breaking Training, 1977, Marathon Man, Family Plot, Rolling Thunder, Butch and Sundance: The Early Years, Yanks, Honky Tonk Freeway, 1980; appeared in: TV films Shirts/Skins, Crime Club, The Bait; TV miniseries From Here to Eternity, Black Beauty; numerous other TV appearances, including: Judgement: The Court Martial of the Tiger of Malaya—General Yamashita, on Stage, Medical Center, Ironside, Hawaii Five-O, The Missiles of October, Fear on Trial, The Snoop Sisters; series Knots Landing; stage appearances include: One Flew Over the Cuckoo's Nest; dir. play: G.R. Point at, Playhouse Theater, N.Y.C. Office: care Agy for Performing Arts Inc 120 W 57th St New York NY 10019 *

DEVANEY, JOHN FRANCIS, aluminum company executive; b. Toronto, Ont., Can., Sept. 19, 1924; s. Leo Murray and Mary Margaret (Campbell) DeV.; m. Gertrude Iona Stuart, June 18, 1949; 1 dau., Lynn Elizabeth. B.S.A.E.M.E., Cornell U., 1949. With U.S. Steel Corp., Reynolds Metals, Harvey Aluminum, Hunter Engring, Amax, Nat. Steel; pres. Nat. Aluminum Corp., Pitts. Mem. Aluminum Assn. (dir., exec. com.). Clubs: Duquesne, Met., Field. Office: Nat Aluminum Corp 20 Stanwix St Pittsburgh PA 15222

DE VARON, LORNA COOKE, choral conductor; b. Western Springs, Ill., Jan. 17, 1921; d. Vernon Walter and Hazel Mildred (Watts) Cooke; m. Jose de Varon, May 14, 1944; children: David, Joanna, Cristina, Alexander. A.B., Wellesley Coll., 1942; A.M., Radcliffe Coll., 1945. Asst. condr. Radcliffe Choral Soc., Radcliffe-Harvard Choir, 1942-44; condr. Bryn Mawr Coll. Choir, 1944-47; condr. chorus, chmn. choral dept. New Eng. Conservatory Music, Boston, 1947—; concert tours, U.S., Europe, Russia, Israel; condr. Israel Summer Festival, 1977-79; tchr. choral conducting, conductor Tanglewood Festival Chorus, 1952-66. Editor, arranger choral works, E.L. Schirmer, Boston. Mem. Cambridge Arts Council. Recipient medal for Disting. Achievement City of Boston, 1967, Radcliffe Grad. Soc., 1972, Wellesley Coll., 1978, medal of Israel, 1977, Ludi award New Eng. Conservatory, 1983. Mem. Pi Kappa Lambda. Home: 94 Lake View Ave Cambridge MA 02138 Office: 290 Huntington Ave Boston MA 02115 *I have always tried to be a musician who lives the compleat (sic) life: to study and to perform music of many different eras, doing justice to its spirit and genius, and to live a life enriched by family, a large number of students and as much knowledge as possible of other art forms.*

DE VAUCOULEURS, GERARD HENRI, astronomer, educator; b. Paris, Apr. 25, 1918; U.S., 1957, naturalized, 1962; m. Antoinette Pietra, Oct. 31, 1944. Ph.D., U. Paris, 1949; D.Sc., Australian Nat. U., Canberra, 1957. Research attache Nat. Center Sci. Research, Sorbonne and Astrophysics Inst., Paris, 1943-49; research fellow Australian Nat. U. Mt. Stromlo Obs., 1951-54; observer-in-charge Yale-Columbia So. Sta., 1954-57; astronomer Lowell Obs., Flagstaff, Ariz., 1957-58; research asso. Harvard U. Obs., 1958-60; asso. prof. astronomy U. Tex., Austin, 1960-63, prof., 1964-80, Ashbel Smith prof., 1981-82, Blumberg prof., 1983—; vis. prof. Coll. de France, Paris, 1976, Royal Obs., Edinburgh, Scotland, 1976; cons. in field. Author 20 books, 350 research papers in field. Grantee NSF, NASA, others. Mem. Internat. Astron. Union, Am. Astron. Soc., Royal Astron. Soc. (Herschel medal 1980), Astron. Soc. Pacific, French Phys. Soc. Address: Astronomy Dept RLM 16 316 U Tex Austin TX 78712

DE VAULT, VIRGIL THOMAS, physician; b. White County, Ind., July 16, 1901; s. Thomas and Bertha (Summers) De V.; m. Arilla Spence, June 23, 1930. B.S., Ind. U., 1927, M.D., 1929, Sc.D. (hon.), 1977; M.D., San Marcos U., Lima, Peru, 1934; postgrad. in surgery, London, Heidelberg, Munich, Edinburgh, Vienna, 1935. Intern Gorgas Hosp., Panama C.Z., 1929-30; chief med. officer Anglo-Ecuadorian Oil Field, ltd., Salinas, Ecuador, 1930; asst. resident surgeon St. Agnes Hosp., Balt., 1930-31; chief surgeon Williston (N.D.) Clinic, 1931-32; chief surgeon, med. officer Compania Petrolera Lobitos, Ltd., Peru, 1932-34, 36-37; chief surgeon, dir. Anglo-Am. Hosp. and Clinc, Lima, 1937-50; med. dir. Fgn. Service and Dept. State, Washington, 1950-63; med. dir. all personnel State Dept. and agys., 1952-63; capt. USPHS Res., 1950-59; internat. rep. A.M.A., Chgo., 1965-67, dir. dept. internat. health, 1967-70; internat. exec. sec. Internat. Coll. Surgeons, Washington, 1971—; Mem. adv. bd. CARE-Medico, 1961—. Contbr. med articles to profl. publs. Bd. dirs. Music Research Found., Inc., Internat. Mus. of Surg. Sci. and Hall of Fame, Chgo.; trustee German Med. Soc. Chgo. Ednl. Found. Recipient diploma of honor Municipality San Isidro, Peru, 1946; decorated knight comdr. Orden del Sol, Orden Daniel Carrion (both Peru). Fellow A.C.S. (mem. internat. relations com. 1964-70), Internat. Coll. Surgeons (hon. fellow; dir. Gen. North Am. Fedn. 1961-64, asso. internat. sec. gen. 1964-65, mem. qualifications council 1965—, v.p. U.S. sect. 1969—, life hon. internat. sec. gen. 1978—), Sociedad de Cirugia de Madrid (hon.); mem. Pan Am. Med. Soc. (v.p. 1958, trustee 1959-64, pres. 1963-64), Am. Hosp. Assn., A.M.A., Washington Med. Soc., Am. Med. Soc. Vienna (life, chmn. surg. group Vienna 1935), Accion Medico del Peru, Assn. Mil Surgeons, Internat. Med. Assn., Am. Soc. Peru (gov. 1938, pres. 1940), Pan Am. Assn., Inc. (trustee 1952—), Indiana Soc., Theta Kappa Psi. Baptist. Clubs: Mason (33), Lima Country, Lima Golf (Peru); Cosmos (Washington); Explorers (N.Y.); Pan Am. Clipper. Home and office: Westchester Apts 3900 Cathedral Ave NW Washington DC 20016

DEVAUX, PETER FORDNEY, advertising agency executive; b. Detroit, Aug. 21, 1944; s. Arthur Flavian and Irene Claire (Fordney) deV.; m. Paula Turner, Aug. 4, 1967. B.A., U. Mich., 1966, M.B.A. with high distinction, 1970. With Indsl. Capital Corp., Providence, 1970-71; dir. comml. credit Trans World Airlines, N.Y.C., 1971-75; asst. treas., then v.p., treas. Young & Rubicam Inc., N.Y.C., 1975-78, sr. v.p., 1978—, controller, 1979, dir. corp. info. services, 1980—, dir. fin. and adminstrn., 1983—. Served with U.S. Army, 1966-68. Mem. Soc. Mgmt. Info. Systems, Advt. Data Processing Assn., U. Mich. Bus. Sch. Alumni Assn. (chmn. bd. govs.), Phi Kappa Phi, Beta Gamma Sigma. Democrat. Clubs: Iroquois Hunting and Fishing, Union League, U. Mich. N.Y. Office: 285 Madison Ave New York NY 10017

DEVEAU, THOMAS C., hotel exec.; b. Schenectady, June 19, 1906; s. Thomas R. and Anne (Hughes) D.; m. Elizabeth Reardon, July 27, 1929; children—Thomas C., John R. A.B., Cornell U., 1927. Gen. mgr. Sheraton-Biltmore Hotel, Providence, 1948-52; gen mgr. Sheraton-Mt. Royal Hotel, Montreal, Can., 1952-56; v.p., gen. mgr. Park Sherton Hotel, N.Y.C., 1956-62; Midwest div. mgr., v.p. Sheraton Corp. Am., St. Louis, 1962—. Mem. Canadian Hotel Assn. (past v.p.), R.I. Hotel Assn. (past pres.), Montreal Hotel Assn. (past pres.), Am. Hotel Assn., Greater St. Louis Hotel Assn., Sigma Nu. Home: 5028 Clayridge Dr St Louis MO 63129

DEVELLANO, JAMES CHARLES, professional hockey manager; b. Toronto, Ont., Can., Jan. 18, 1943; came to U.S., 1979; s. James Joseph and Jean (Piter) D. Ont. scout St. Louis Blues NHL, Toronto, 1967-72; eastern Can. scout N.Y. Islanders, Toronto, 1972-74, dir. scouting, 1974-82; asst. gen. mgr. Islanders, L.I., N.Y., 1981-82; gen. mgr. Detroit Red Wings, 1982—. Home: 1300 E Lafayette St Apt 1203 Detroit MI 48226 Office: Detroit Red Wings Hockey Club Joe Louis Arena 600 Civic Center Dr Detroit MI 48226

DEVENDORF, DAVID STUART, rubber company executive; b. Baldwinsville, N.Y., May 29, 1935; s. Carl Marvin and Belle (Richie) D.; m. Joan Arlene Olson, May 19, 1961; children: Jill A., Lynn F. B.S. in Chem. Engring., 1957; M.B.A., Stanford U., 1961. Engr. Proctor & Gamble, Cin., 1957-59; mem. treasury dept. Exxon Corp., N.Y., 1961-73, London, 1961-73, Caracus, Venezuela, 1961-73; v.p., treas. B.F. Goodrich Co., Akron, Ohio, 1973—. Mem. Cleve. Treas. Club, fin. Execs. Inst. Home: 2958 Bonnebrook Dr Akron OH 44313 Office: BF Goodrich Co 500 S Main St Akron OK 44318

DEVENING, ROBERT RANDOLPH, food company executive; b. San Francisco, Mar. 8, 1942; s. John I. and Jean (Devening) Bolen; m. Susan Church Willis, Feb. 8, 1964; children: Jennifer McQueen, Brian Willis, Jason Bolen. A.B. in Internat. Relations, Stanford U., 1963; M.B.A., Harvard U., 1966. With Price Waterhouse & Co. (C.P.A.s), 1963-64, Applied Power Industries, Inc., Milw., 1966-67; with Jos. Schlitz Brewing Co., 1967-70, dir. distbn. planning and research, 1969-70; controller Fairmont Foods Co., Omaha, 1970-72; exec. v.p., treas. Ponderosa System, Inc., Dayton, Ohio, 1972-75; v.p. fin. Wilson Foods Co. (subs. LTV Corp.), Oklahoma City, 1975-79; exec. v.p. fin. and adminstrn., dir. Fleming Cos., Inc., Oklahoma City, 1979—; adv. dir. Arkwright Boston Ins. Co. Pres. Stanford Alumni Club Wis., 1968; bd. dirs. Ballet Okla.; sec.-treas. Harvard Bus. Sch. Club Milw., 1968-69; trustee Casady Sch., Oklahoma City. Mem. Fin. Execs. Inst., Delta Tau Delta. Home: 6921 Avondale Ct Oklahoma City OK 73116 Office: 6601 N Broadway Box 26647 Oklahoma City OK 73126

DEVEREAUX, ALFRED BOYCE, JR., army officer; b. Ithaca, N.Y., Sept. 21, 1937; s. Alfred Boyce and Margaret Webb (Boddie) D.; m. Melissa Elsie Potter, Sept. 8, 1962; children: Melissa Inez, Stephen Boyce. B.S., U.S. Mil. Acad., 1959; M.S., Ohio State U., 1963, Ph.D., 1973; diploma, U.S. Command and Gen. Staff Coll., 1970, Army War Coll., 1978. Registered profl. engr., N.H. Commd. 2d lt. U.S. Army, 1959, advanced through grades to col., 1979; service in, Korea, W. Ger. and Vietnam; comdr. 649th Engr. Battalion, W. Ger., 1975-77; comdr., dir. U.S. Army Cold Regions Research and Engring. Labs., Hanover, N.H., 1978-81; comdr., dist. engr. C.E. U.S. Army, Jacksonville, Fla., 1981—. Active local Episcopal Ch., Boy Scouts Am. Decorated Legion of Merit, Meritorious Service medal (2), Bronze Star, Commendation medal. Mem. Soc. Am. Mil. Engrs., Am. Soc. Photogrammetry. Home: 4121 Old Mill Cove Trail W Jacksonville FL 32211 Office: Jacksonville Dist US Army Corps Engrs Jacksonville FL 32201

DEVEREUX, LAWRENCE HACKETT, indsl. exec.; b. N.Y.C., Aug. 14, 1929; s. Philip L. and Agnes (Hackett) D.; m. Alice Fraser, Nov. 17, 1956; children—Lawrence, Elizabeth, Alison. A.B., Holy Cross Coll., 1951; M.B.A., N.Y. U. Grad. Sch. Bus., 1958. Asst. treas., asst. controller Hewitt Robins, 1956-65; asst. comptroller Ingersoll Rand Corp., 1965-68; v.p., controller Amerace Corp. (name formerly Amerace Esna Corp.), N.Y.C., 1968-72, v.p. adminstrn., treas., 1972-77; v.p. fin. Bell & Howell Co., Chgo., 1977-80; sr. v.p., chief fin. officer CF Industries, Inc., Long Grove, Ill., 1980—. Served to 1st lt. USMC, 1951-53. Mem. Fin. Execs. Inst. Club: Chgo. Economic. Home: 69 Indian Hill Rd Winnetka IL 60093 Office: CF Industries Inc Salem Lake Dr Long Grove IL 60047

DEVEREUX, TIMOTHY EDWARD, advertising company executive; b. Chgo., Jan. 13, 1932; s. James Matthew and Nellie (Fitzmaurice) D.; m. Ann Sullivan, Apr. 2, 1956; children: Timothy Jr., Colette Marie, Jennifer Ann, Peter Gerard, Nora Marie, Matthew. B.A., U. Notre Dame, 1955. Copywriter Montgomery Ward & Co., Chgo., 1957-58; pub. relations dir. Victor Comptometer Corp., Chgo., 1958-60; sales promotion mgr. Bankers Life & Casualty Co., Chgo., 1960-61; dir. advt. and pub. relations Mid-America Foods, Inc., River Forest, Ill., 1961-62; mdse. mgr. Marshall John & Assos., Chgo. also Northbrook, 1962-65; acct. supr. Marshall John/Action Advt., Northbrook, Ill., 1965-70, exec. v.p., chief exec. officer, 1970—; also dir.; pres. Devereux Direct, Ltd., 1977-79; v.p. direct response group Frankel & Co., Chgo., 1979—. Served with USMCR, 1955-57. Home: 735 S Wesley St Oak Park IL 60304 Office: 111 E Wacker Dr Chicago IL 60601

DEVINATZ, ALLEN, mathematician; b. Chgo., July 22, 1922; s. Victor and Kate (Bass) D.; m. Pearl Moskowitz, Sep. 16, 1956; children: Victor Gary, Ethan Sander. B.S., Ill. Inst. Tech., 1944; A.M., Harvard U., 1947, Ph.D., 1950. Instr. Ill. Inst. Tech., 1950-52; NSF Postdoctoral fellow, 1952-53, fellow, 1953-54; asst. prof. U. Conn., 1954-55; faculty Washington U., St. Louis, 1955-67, prof., 1961-67; prof. math. Northwestern U., Evanston, Ill., 1967—; vis. mem. Weizmann Inst., Israel, 1980, Inst. Hautes Etudes Sci., Paris, 1982. Contbr. articles profl. jours. Sr. NSF Postdoctoral fellow, 1960-61. Mem. Am. Math. Soc., Sigma Xi, Tau Beta Pi. Home: 626 Lavergne Ave Wilmette IL 60091 Office: Dept Math Northwestern U Lunt Bldg Evanston IL 60201

DEVINE, B. MACK, petroleum company executive; b. Gadsden, Ala., Feb. 23, 1945; s. Charles Durwood and Ida Nell (Blanton) DeV; m. Shirley Jean Fitzpatrick, Mar. 16, 1966; children: Charles, Cynthia. B.S. in Acctg., Jacksonville (Ala.) State U., 1968; postgrad., U. South Fla., Harvard U. Bus. Sch. Vice pres., dir. Bay-Con Industries, Tampa, Fla., 1971-74; v.p., treas. Automatic Mdsg. Co., Tampa, 1974-75; chief fin. officer So. Equipment Co., Tampa, 1975-76; v.p. Am. Agronomics Corp., Tampa, 1976-77, pres., dir., 1977-82; chmn., pres., dir. Key Energy Enterprises Inc., Tampa, 1982—. Served with USAR, 1968-70. Decorated Army Commendation medal. Mem. Am. Mgmt. Assn. (president's assn.), Young Presidents Orgn. Republican. Clubs: Palma Ceia Country, University. Lodge: Rotary. Home: PO Box 1665 119 Hickory Creek Blvd Brandon FL 33511 Office: 9250 Bay Plaza Blvd Tampa FL 33619

DEVINE, BING *See* **DEVINE, VAUGHAN P.**

DEVINE, C. ROBERT, publishing company executive; b. Clarksburg, W.Va., June 13, 1917; s. James J. and Frances M. (Ryan) D.; m. Louise C. Williams, Mar. 27, 1943 (div.); children: Mallory C., Rodney W., Ian C.; m. Gisele Edenbourgh Lichine, Dec. 23, 1966. Grad., Princeton U., 1938; L.H.D., Fairleigh Dickinson U., 1976. Promotion, research dir. U.S. News Pub. Co., 1946-48, asst. advt. dir., 1948-55; exec. bus. dept. Reader's Digest, N.Y.C., 1955-58, advt. dir. internat. edits., 1958-60, pres. Latin Am. div., 1960, asst. gen. mgr., 1960-66, dep. gen. mgr. internat. edits., 1966; v.p., dir. dir. corp. and public affairs Reader's Digest Assn., Inc., 1970-82. Bd. dirs. Met. Opera Assn.; bd. dirs. Am. Hosp. Istanbul; trustee Am. U. Cairo, chmn. nominating com.; trustee MacArthur Meml. Found., Vail-Deane Sch.; mem. West Point Constn. Island Com. Served from pvt. to maj. AUS, World War II. Decorated Bronze Star medal. Mem. Council on Fgn. Relations, Sales Exec. Club, Internat. Advt. Assn. (chmn., chief exec. officer 1976-80, pres. 1962-64, mem. exec. com., dir. at large), Internat. Execs. Assn. (dir.), Assn. Ex-Mems. Squadron A, Mag. Pubs. Assn. (chmn. internat. com. 1964-70, past chmn. conf. arrangements com.), XIIIth Corps Assn., Mil. Order Fgn. Wars, Assn. U.S. Army (v.p. N.Y. chpt.), Fgn. Policy Assn., Fedn. Internat. Periodical Press (v.p. 1978-79, pres. 1979-81, chmn. 1981—), English-Speaking Union, World Press Inst., Soc. for Rehab. Facially Disfigured (trustee), Pub. Relations Soc. Am. Clubs: Union, Squadron A, Dutch Treat, River (N.Y.C.); Pilgrims U.S.; Travellers (Paris). Home: 101 E 69th St New York NY 10021

DEVINE, CHARLES JOSEPH, JR., urologist, educator; b. Norfolk, Va., Feb. 23, 1923; s. Charles Joseph and Julia Vera (Campbell) D.; m. Rae Lou Ellis, Sept. 30, 1950; children—Charles Joseph III, Paul E., Jane C., David C., Rachael A. B.A., Washington and Lee U., 1943; M.D., George Washington U., 1947. Diplomate: Am. Bd. Urology, Nat. Bd. Med. Examiners. Intern Brady Inst., Johns Hopkins Hosp., 1947-48; fellow in urology Cleve. Clinic, 1948-50; resident in urology U.S. Naval Hosp., Phila., 1951; with Devine-Poutasse-Fiveash Assos., Ltd., Norfolk, Va., 1952—, pres., 1975—; chief urology Med. Center Hosps., 1979-80; pres. med. staff Norfolk Gen. Hosp., 1970; chmn. dept. surgery DePaul Hosp., 1965-66; chief of urology Children's Hosp. of King's Daus., 1977—; cons. staff Bayside Hosp., Virginia Beach, Va.; cons. in urology Lake Taylor City, U.S. Naval hosps., VA Center, Hampton, Va.; clin. coordinator for urology Eastern Va. Med. Sch., 1973-75, prof., chmn. dept. urology, 1975—; clin. dir. pediatric urology program Bur. Crippled Children of Va., Norfolk; mem. Project Hope, Alexandria, Egypt, 1977; Royal Australasian Coll. Surgeons Found. lectr., 1982, condr. symposia; producer med. motion pictures, TV surg. presentations; vis. prof. univs.; presenter profl. meetings. Author: Urology in Practice, 1978; mem. editorial bd.: Jour. Urology, 1978—, Weekly Updates in Urology, 1978—; contbr. numerous articles to profl. jours., chpts. in books. Served to lt. M.C. USNR, 1950-52. Fellow A.C.S. (pres. Va. chpt. 1967), Am. Acad. Pediatrics, Am. Soc. Plastic and Reconstructive Surgeons (asso.); mem. AMA, Med. Soc. Va., Norfolk Acad. Medicine, Am. Urol. Assn. (awards), Va. Urol. Soc. (pres. 1968), Tidewater Urol. Assn., Societe Internationale d'Urologie, Am. Assn. Genitourinary Surgeons, Soc. Pediatric Urology, Soc. Univ. Urologists, So. Med. Assn., Southeastern Surg. Congress, Seaboard Med. Soc., AAAS, N.Y. Acad. Scis., Alpha Tau Omega, Nu Sigma Nu. Roman Catholic. Clubs: Norfolk Yacht and Country, Harbor (Norfolk); U.S. Yacht Racing Union, Cruising of Va. Home: 2034 Hunters Trail Norfolk VA 23518 Office: 400 W Brambleton Ave Suite 100 Norfolk VA 23510

DEVINE, DONALD J., government official; b. Bronxville, N.Y., Apr. 14, 1937; s. John and Frances M. D.; m. Ann Delia Smith, Aug. 29, 1959; children: William, J. Michael, Patricia, Joseph. B.B.A., St. John's U., Jamaica, N.Y., 1959; M.A., City U. N.Y., 1965; Ph.D., Syracuse (N.Y.) U., 1967. Asst. prof. govt. and politics U. Md., 1967-81; dir. U.S. Office Personnel Mgmt., 1981—. Author: The Attentive Public, 1970, The Political Culture of the United States, 1972, Does Freedom Work? Liberty and Justice in America, 1978, Reagan Electionomics, 1983. Parliamentarian, mem. exec. com. Md. Republican Com., 1974-79; Md. chmn. Reagan for Pres., 1976, 80; mem. rules com. Rep. Nat. Com., 1973-75, floor officer conv., 1972, 76, del., 1976-80. Served with USAR, 1960-66. Mem. Am. Polit. Sci. Assn., Am. Assn. Public Opinion Research, Mt. Pelerin Soc., Phila. Soc. Roman Catholic. Office: 1900 E St NW Washington DC 20415 *

DEVINE, GRANT, Canadian premier; b. Regina, Sask., Can., 1944; m. Chantal Guillaume, July 1966; children: Michelle, Monique, David, John William. B.S.A., U. Sask., 1967; M.Sc. in Agr. Econs., U. Alta., 1969, M.B.A., 1970; Ph.D., Ohio State U., 1976. Assoc. prof. agr. U. Sask., 1975-79; mktg. specialist Fed. Govt. Ottawa Agr. Commodity Legislature, 1970-72; leader Progressive Conservative Party of Sask., 1979; premier of Province of Sask., 1982—; adv. to Food Prices Rev. Bd. and Province Govts. Contbr. articles to profl. jours. Mem. Am. Econ. Assn., Am. Mktg. Assn., Am. Assn. Consumer Research, Canadian Agr. Econ. Soc. (recipient Cert. of Merit), Consumers Assn. Can. Office: Legislative Bldg 2405 Legislative Dr Regina SK Canada S4S 0B3 *

DEVINE, JAMES BRENDAN, government agency official; b. N.Y.C., Nov. 14, 1936; s. John Joseph and Anna (Mangan) D.; m. Lynda Bernice Purvis, Mar. 17, 1967. A.B., Merrimack Coll., 1959; M. Pub. Adminstrn, U. Mich., 1962; student, Nat. War Coll., 1969-70. Instr. Lowell (Mass.) Sch. System, 1959; reporter Lowell Sun, 1960; exec. trainee Office Sec. Def., 1961-62, asst. tng. officer, 1962-64, asst. Vietnam affairs, 1964-66; polit.-mil. officer Am. embassy, Bangkok, Thailand, 1966-67; asst. Thailand and SEATO affairs Office Asst. Sec. Def., 1967-69; joined U.S. Fgn. Service, 1970; counselor polit.-mil. affairs Am. embassy, Rome, 1970-74; counselor polit.-mil. affairs Am. Embassy Saigon, 1974-75; dir., dep. dir. Office Nuclear Energy and Energy Tech. Affairs, Bur. Oceans, Internat. Environ. and Sci. Affairs, Dept. State, Washington, 1975-77; sr. internat. policy analyst Nuclear Regulatory Commn., Washington, 1977-80; asst. dir. for exports-imports and internat. safeguards Office of Internat. Programs, NRC, 1980-82; dep. asst. sec. for nuclear energy and energy tech. affairs Bur. Oceans, Internat Environ. and Sci. Affairs, Dept. State, Washington, 1982—; Mem. U.S. Sr. Exec. Service, 1980—. Served with AUS, 1959-60. Office Sec. Def. fellow, 1966. Address: 3524 King Arthur Rd Annandale VA 22003

DEVINE, (JOSEPH) LAWRENCE, drama critic; b. N.Y.C., Sept. 21, 1935; s. John Justin and Hazel (Tippit) DeV.; m. Genevieve Christian, Aug. 29, 1959 (div. 1968); children: John Justin II, Ellen Morse; m. Lucy Memory Williamson, July 26, 1968. Student, Georgetown U., 1953-54, U. Mich., 1954; B.S. in Journalism, Northwestern U., 1957. Drama critic Miami (Fla.) Herald, 1962-67; entertainment editor, drama and film critic Los Angeles Herald-Examiner, 1967-68; entertainment editor, drama critic Detroit Free Press, 1968—; mem. faculty drama critics U. Detroit, 1974—; asso. dir. Critics Inst., Eugene O'Neill Meml. Theater Center, Waterford, Conn., 1973—; Nat. Endowment for Humanities profl. fellow U. Mich., 1975-76, fellow seminar for critics of arts, Washington, 1977; mem. nat. new playwrights jury Am. Coll. Theatre Festival, critic-in-residence festivals, 1978-79; mem. Pulitzer prize nominating jury in drama, 1981-82. Contbr. articles to profl. jours., revs. to newspapers, mags. Served with AUS, 1958-62. Mem. Am. Theater Critics Assn. (chmn. exec. com. 1979-81), Internat. Assn. Theater Critics (U.S. del. biennial congresses Tel Aviv, Mexico City 1981, 83), Beta Theta Pi, Sigma Delta Chi. Home: 17315 E Jefferson Grosse Pointe MI 48230 Office: 321 W Lafayette Blvd Detroit MI 48231

DEVINE, SHANE, fed. judge; b. 1926. B.A., U. N.H.; J.D., Boston Coll. Bar: bar 1952. Now judge U.S. Dist. Ct. N.H. Mem. Am. Bar Assn. Office: US Dist Ct PO Box 892 Concord NH 03301 *

DEVINE, VAUGHAN P. (BING DEVINE), professional football team executive; b. Mar. 1, 1917; m. Mary Anderson; children: Joanne (Mrs. Schaumburg), Janice, Jane. Grad., Washington U. Mem. staff stats. dept. St. Louis Cardinals Nat. League baseball team, until 1939, asst. pub. relations dept., 1939-41, mgr. bus., Johnson City, Tenn., 1941-42, Fresno, Calif., 1942, Decatur, Ill., 1942, mgr. farm system team, Columbus, Ga., 1946-49, gen. mgr. farm system team, Rochester, 1949-55, exec. asst. to gen. mgr. parent orgn., St. Louis, 1955-57, gen. mgr., 1957-64, 67—; exec. v.p., 1973-78; former v.p. adminstrn., now pres., chief operating officer St. Louis Cardinals, NFL; pres., gen. mgr. N.Y. Mets, 1965-67. Served with USNR, 1943-46; PTO. Recipient Major League Exec. of Year, 1963, 64. Office: St Louis Cardinals 200 Stadium Plaza Saint Louis MO 63102 *

DEVINE, WILLIAM J., consumer finance company executive; b. Clintonville, Wis., 1930; married. B.S., U. Wis., 1953, J.D., 1960. Supr. Assoc. Investment Co., 1953-58; sole practice finance, 1960-62; staff atty. Gen. Fin. Corp., Evanston, Ill., 1962-64, asst. gen. counsel, 1964-66, asst. v.p., 1966-69, v.p., gen. counsel, Evanston, Ill., 1969-72, v.p., sec., gen. counsel, Evanston, Ill., 1972-73, sr. v.p., sec., gen. counsel, 1973-80, exec. v.p., gen. counsel, 1980-81, chmn. bd., chief exec. officer, gen counsel, 1981—, dir. Office: General Finance Corp 1301 Central St Evanston IL 60201 *

DEVINO, GARY THOMAS, agricultural economic educator, consultant; b. Middlebury, Vt., Nov. 9, 1937; s. Rollie E. and Hazel S. D.; m. Carol E. Wiley, June 28, 1959; children: Daine, Nancy, Mark, Glenn. B.S., Cornell U., 1959, M.S., 1960; Ph.D., Pa. State U., 1965. Asst. prof. agrl. econs. U. Vt., Burlington, 1965-66; asst. prof. Rutgers U., New Brunswick, N.J., 1966-69, assoc. prof., 1969-70, U. Mo., Columbia, 1970-78, prof., 1978—; cons. agri-bus. firms, 1965—. Author: Agribusiness Finance, 1981. Mem. Am. Agrl. Econs. Assn., Gamma Sigma Delta, Omicron Delta Epsilon. Home: Route 4 Box 232A Columbia MA 65201 Office: U Mo 322 Mumford Hall Columbia MO 65211

DEVINO, WILLIAM STANLEY, educator, economist; b. Burlington, Vt., Nov. 17, 1926; s. William Arthur and Elaine Anna (Blaise) D.; m. Raphaella Frances Gillespie, Aug. 27, 1948; children: Bonnie Ann, Denise Marie. B.A., U. Vt., 1951; M.A., U. Conn., 1953; Ph.D., Mich. State U., 1959. Instr. econs. Mich. State U., 1955-57, Ford Found. dissertation fellow econs., 1957-58, research asso., 1958-59, lectr. econs., 1959-60; faculty U. Maine, Orono, 1960—, prof. bus. and econs., 1963—, dir., 1963-65, dean, 1965—; Cons. Mich. Senate Labor Com., 1955; mem. Gov. Mich. Task Force on Labor, 1959; mem. arbitration roster Fed. Mediation and Concilation Service; mem. Gov. Maine Adv. Com. on Bus. Taxation, 1971-72; mem. pub. disputes settlement panel Nat. Center for Dispute Settlement; mem. fact-finding and mediation panels N.H. Pub. Employees Labor Relations Bd.; mem. fact finding panel Maine Labor Relations Bd. Author: Exhaustion of Unemployment Benefits During a Recession, 1960; co-author: A Study of Textile Mill Closings in Selected New England Communities, 1966; Contbr. articles to profl. jours. Served with AUS, World War II. Mem. Am. Arbitration Assn. (nat. labor panel, Maine adv. council), Am. Econ. Assn., Indsl. Relations Research Assn., Nat. Acad. Arbitrators. Home: 358 Howard St Bangor ME 04401

DEVISÉ, PIERRE ROMAIN, city planner, educator; b. Brussels, Belgium, July 27, 1924; came to U.S., 1935, naturalized, 1958; s. Victor Pierre and Madeleine (Cupers) deV.; m. Margaret Ahern, Nov. 17, 1978; children: Peter Charles, Daniel Romain. B.A., U. Chgo., 1945, M.A., 1958. Chancellor Belgian Consul, Chgo., 1945-47, comml. attache, 1947-56, Belgian Consulate Gen., Chgo.; planning dir. Hyde Park-Kenwood Conf., 1956-57; research planner Northeastern Ill. Planning Commn., 1958-60; sr. planner Chgo. City Planning Dept., 1961-63; asst. dir. Hosp. Planning Council for Met. Chgo., 1964-70, Ill. Regional Med. Program, 1971-73; prof. urban scis. U. Ill., 1973-81; prof. pub. adminstrn. Roosevelt U., Chgo., 1982—; Lectr. De Paul U., 1962—; vis. lectr. U. Mich., 1966, U. Hawaii, 1968, U. Ill., 1969, 70, U. Iowa, 1971, U. Chgo., 1972; prin. investigator Chgo. Regional Hosp. Study, 1966—; exec. dir. Chgo. Commn. to Study Conv. Week Disorders, 1968-70; cons. Chgo. Commn. on Human Relations, 1966—, Chgo. Model Cities Program, 1968—, Cook County Council Govts., 1968—, Comprehensive Health Planning, Inc., 1971—; Census Bur., 1973—, U.S. Senate Health Subcom., 1974, HEW, 1975—, Ho. Ways and Means Com., 1975—, Senate Banking Com., 1976—. Author: monographs including Suburban Factbook, 1960, Social Geography of Metropolitan Chicago, 1960, Chicago's People, Jobs and Homes, 1963, Chicago's Widening Color Gap, 1967, Chicago's Apartheid Hospital System, 1968, Chicago, 1971, Ready for Another Fire, 1971, Misused and Misplaced Hospitals and Doctors, 1973, Chicago's Future, 1976, Chicago: Transformations of an Urban System, 1976, Chicago in the Year 2000, 1978. Mem. Am. Statist. Assn., Chgo. Assn. Commerce and Industry, Am. Pub. Health Assn., Assn. Am. Geographers, Planned Parenthood Assn. Chgo., Old Town Boys Club. Club: City (Chgo.). Home: 1712 W Henderson Chicago IL 60657 Office: Roosevelt U 430 S Michigan Ave Chicago IL 60605

DEVITA, VINCENT THEODORE, JR., oncologist; b. Bronx, N.Y., Mar. 7, 1935; s. Vincent Theodore and Isabel DeV.; m. Mary Kay Bush, Aug. 3, 1957; children: Teddy (dec.), Elizabeth. B.S., Coll. William and Mary, 1957; M.D., George Washington U., 1961. Diplomate: Nat. Bd. Med. Examiners, Am. Bd. Internal Medicine. Intern U. Mich. Med. Center, Ann Arbor, 1961-62; resident in medicine George Washington U. Med. Service D.C. Gen. Hosp., 1962-73; sr. resident in medicine Yale New Haven Med. Center, 1965-66; clin. asso. lab. chem. pharmacology Nat. Cancer Inst. NIH, Bethesda, Md., 1963-65, mem. staff, 1966—, chief med. br., 1971-74, dir. div. cancer treatment, 1974-81, clin. dir. inst., 1975-81, dir., 1981—; mem. faculty George Washington U. Med. Sch., 1971—, prof. medicine, 1975—; mem. expert advisory panel WHO, 1976; mem. Lasker Award Jury, 1976; chmn. Com. French-Am. Agreement on Cancer Treatment Research, 1976—; vis. prof. Stanford U. Med. Sch., 1972; 1st ann. Clowes lectr. Roswell Park Meml. Inst. Buffalo, 1973. Contbr. numerous articles to med. jours. Served with USMCR, 1955-61. Tobacco Research Industry fellow, 1959; recipient Albert and Mary Lasker Med. Research award, 1972; Superior Service award HEW, 1975; Esther Langer Found. award, 1976; Alumni medallion Coll. William and Mary, 1976; Jeffrey Gottliev award, 1976; decorated Oren del Sol en el Grando Oficial, Peru, 1970. Fellow A.C.P.; mem. Am. Soc. Clin. Oncology (chmn. program com. 1972, dir. 1973-76, pres. 1977-78), Am. Cancer Soc., Am. Soc. Hematology, Am. Assn. Cancer Research (dir. 1976-79), AMA, Am. Fedn. Clin. Research, Am. Soc. Clin. Investigation, Soc. Surg. Oncology, Smith-Reed-Russel Med. Soc., Alpha Omega Alpha. Office: Bldg 31 Room 11A52 9000 Rockville Pike Bethesda MD 20014 *

DEVITO, FRANCIS JOSEPH, advertising agency executive; b. N.Y.C., July 13, 1938; s. Basil and Mary (Mincielli) DeV.; m. Lynn R. Brauneiss; children: Christopher F., Anthony P. B.F.A., Pratt Inst., 1961. Asst. art dir. Batton, Barton, Dursteen & Osborne, N.Y., 1965-67; art dir. Young & Rubicam, N.Y.C., 1967-73, creative supr., 1973-76, v.p. assoc. creative dir., 1976-80, sr. v.p. group creative dir., 1980—. Served to capt. U.S. Army, 1961-65. Home: 20 Harbor Hill Rd Huntington NY 11743 Office: Young & Rubicam 285 Madison Ave New York NY 10017 *The ability to be creative in a business world is what makes advertising one of the most exciting and rewarding of jobs. Consumers are bored and unmotivated by the trite, ordinary, hum-drum advertising they are bombarded with. To push yourself and others to do it fresher, bolder, different than it's ever been done is the everday challange. When you succeed, the personal rewards are outstanding.*

DEVITO, MATHIAS JOSEPH, real estate executive; b. Trenton, N.J., Aug. 23, 1930; s. Charles P. and Margaret L. DeV.; m. Rosetta Kormuth, July 26, 1956; children: Ann Margaret, Charles Michael. B.A., U. Md., 1954, LL.B. with highest honors, 1956. Bar: Md. bar. Asst. atty. gen. State of Md., 1963-64; partner firm Piper & Marbury, Balt., 1965-70; sr. v.p., gen. counsel, then exec. v.p. Rouse Co., Columbia, Md., 1968-73, pres., chief exec. officer, dir., 1973—; dir. First Nat. Bank Md., Balt., U.S. Air and Trizec Corp. Ltd. Editor: Md. Law Rev, 1955-56. Mem. Mayor Balt. Bus. Adv. Council, 1977—; Chmn. bd. trustees Md. State Colls., 1970-73; trustee Johns Hopkins U., 1983—. Mem. Order of Coif. Roman Catholic. Clubs: Elkridge, Union League, Adirondack League. Office: Rouse Hdqrs Bldg Columbia MD 21044

DEVITO, RICHARD A(NTHONY), publisher; b. Boston, Nov. 30, 1940; s. Louis and Marie C. DeV.; m. Eileen F. Dunn, Aug. 16, 1973; children: Richard A., Laura Ann. B.S. in Public Relations, Boston U., 1961. Public relations trainee Gen. Electric Co., Schenectady, Columbia, S.C. and Pittsfield, Mass., 1961-66; public relations rep. Charles Brunelle Co., Hartford, Conn., 1967; public relations mgr. chems. div. Cabot Corp., Boston, 1967-68; pres. DeVito Labs., Inc., Boston, 1968-71; fin. cons. DeVito & Assos., Weston, Mass., 1971-73; pub. New Eng. Sr. Citizen and Nursing World Jour. mags., Weston, 1973—; v.p. Prime Nat. Pub. Corp., Weston; initiated Sr. American of Yr. awards, 1977. Contbr. articles to profl. publs. Roman Catholic. Club: Mercedes Benz Am. Home: 706 Boston Post Rd Weston MA 02193 Office: 470 Boston Post Rd Weston MA 02193 *Vision, perserverance, determination, humor, and luck, in that order, are the backbone of my success.*

DEVITT, EDWARD JAMES, judge; b. St. Paul, May 5, 1911; s. Thomas Phillip and Catherine Ethel (McGuire) D.; m. Marcelle M. LaRose, Apr. 22, 1939; children: Marcelle Terese, Timothy Patrick. LL.B., U. N.D., 1935, B.S., 1936, also LL.D. Bar: D.C., Minn., Ill., N.D. Practiced law, East Grand Forks, Minn., 1935-39, St. Paul, 1946—, mcpl. judge, 1935-39, asst. atty. gen. Minn., 1939-42; instr. law U. N.D., 1935-39, St. Paul Coll. Law, 1945—; mem. 80th Congress from 4th Minn. Dist.; probate judge Ramsey County, St. Paul, 1950-54; judge U.S. Dist. Ct., 1954—. Author: (with Blackmar) Federal Jury Practice and Instructions. Bd. dirs. Fed. Jud. Center. Served as intelligence officer USNR, 1942-46. Decorated Purple Heart. Fellow Am. Bar Found.; mem. Am., Minn., Ramsey County bar assns., Am. Judicature Soc., Am. Legion, VFW, DAV, Order of Coif, Blue Key, Phi Delta Phi, Beta Gamma Sigma, Delta Sigma Rho. Republican. Roman Catholic. Clubs: K.C., Athletic (St. Paul). Office: Federal Courts Bldg Saint Paul MN 55101 *

DE VIVO, DARRYL CLAUDE, pediatric neurologist; b. Everett, Mass., Aug. 28, 1937; s. Ottavio Joseph and Alyce Irene (Thurston);; s. Ottavio Joseph and Alyce Irene (De Vivo); m. Ruth Marie Crock, Feb. 6, 1965; children: Cynthia, Jessica, Kristin. B.A., Amherst Coll., 1959; M.D., U. Va., 1964. Intern Univ. Hosp., Boston, 1964-65; resident in pediatrics and neurology Mass. Gen. Hosp., Boston, 1965-67; clin. asso. NIH, 1967-69; fellow in pediatric neurology St. Louis Children's Hosp., 1969-70; mem. faculty Washington U. Sch. Medicine, St. Louis, 1970-78, prof. pediatrics and neurology, 1977-78; Sidney Carter prof. neurology and prof. pediatrics Coll. Physicians and Surgeons Columbia U., N.Y.C., 1979—; dir. pediatric neurology Columbia-Presbyn. Med. Center, N.Y., 1979—. Asso. editor: Annals of Neurology, 1979-83; asso. editor: Textbook of Pediatrics, 17th edit, 1982; contbr. articles to med. jours. Served with USPHS, 1967-69. NIH grantee. Mem. Am. Neurol. Assn., Am. Acad. Neurology, Child Neurology Soc., Am. Pediatric Soc., Soc. Pediatric Research, Am. Soc. Neurochemistry, Internat. Child Neurology Assn., Soc. Neurosci., Alpha Omega Alpha. Club: Ardsley (N.Y.) Country. Office: 710 W 168th St New York NY 10032

DEVIVO, SAL J., newspaper exec.; b. Saratoga Springs, N.Y., Feb. 3, 1937; s. Salvatore and Sabine (Lobombardo) DeV.; m. Carolyn Ann Turney, Dec. 17, 1961; children—Sally, Karen, Michael, Darin. B.A. in Journalism, St. Bonaventure U., 1962. Reporter The Saratogian, Saratoga Springs, 1956-58, Schenectady Gazette, 1959, Niagara Falls (N.Y.) Gazette, 1962, Sunday editor Niagara Gazette, 1964, city editor, 1966-68; mng. editor The Saratogian, 1968-72, editor, pub., 1972-74, Niagara Gazette, 1974-75; editor Camden (N.J.) Courier-Post, 1975, pub., 1976-79; exec. editor, asso. pub. Binghamton (N.Y.) Press and Sun-Bull., 1979-80; pres., pub. Utica (N.Y.) Observer-Dispatch and Daily Press, 1980—. Pres. Saratoga County United Way, 1973; gen. campaign chmn. Niagara Falls United Givers Fund, 1975; pres. adv. council St. Bonaventure U., 1978-79; bd. dirs. Cooper Med. Center, Camden, 1978-79. Mem. N.Y. State Soc. Newspaper Editors (past pres.), N.J. Press Assn. (dir.), Am. Newspaper Pubs. Assn., Am. Soc. Newspaper Editors. Roman Catholic. Home: Indian Field Rd Clinton NY 13323 Office: 221 Oriskany Plaza Utica NY 13503

DEVLIN, JEFFREY ANTHONY, advertising executive, television producer; b. Orange, N.J., Mar. 30, 1947; s. Harry Arthur and Dorothy (Wende) D.; m. Nancy Wilson, Sept. 2, 1972; children: Matthew Carry, Elizabeth Wande. B.S., Bethel Coll., 1969; postgrad., Dartmouth Coll., 1970-71. Assoc. producer Cannon Films, N.Y.C., 1971-72; with SSC & B Lintas Worldwide, N.Y.C., 1972—, v.p., 1979-80, dir. broadcast prodn., 1980-81, sr. v.p., 1981—. Bd. dirs. YMCA, WestfieldN.J., 1980—. Recipient Clio award, 1980, Gold medal Soc. Illustrators, 1980, Gold and Silver medals Art Dirs. Club, 1979, Silver medal Internat. TV and Film awards, 1980. Mem. Dirs. Guild Am. Clubs: Dutch Treat; Squadron A (N.Y.C.); St. James (London). Home: 521 Park Ave New York NY 10013 Office: SSC & B Advt Inc 1 Dag Hammarskjold Plaza New York NY 10017

DEVLIN, JOHN H., metals manufacturing company executive; b. 1921. B.B.A., U. Ill., 1943. C.P.A., Ill. With Libby, McNeill & Libby, Inc., 1946-47, Laramore & Douglas, C.P.A.s, 1947-51, Fansteel, Inc., North Chicago, Ill., 1951—, v.p. adminstrn., 1963-77, exec. v.p. fin. and adminstrn., 1977—, also dir. Served with AUS, 1943-46. Office: Fansteel Inc 1 Tantalum Pl North Chicago IL 60064 *

DEVLIN, JOHN H, corporate executive; b. Toronto, Ont., Can., Mar. 23, 1920; s. Charles D. and Florence D. Student, Upper Can. Coll. Advt. mgr. Duplate Can., Ltd. and asso. cos., Toronto, 1946-53; gen. sales mgr. Smith & Stone Ltd., 1953-59; pres. Rothmans of Pall Mall Can., Ltd., 1959-69; chmn. Carling O'Keefe Ltd., 1968, Rothmans of Pall Mall Can., Ltd., Don Mills, Ont., 1969—, chmn. bd.; chmn. bd. Alfred Dunhill of London Ltd.; dir. Rothmans Internat. Ltd., Bank of Montreal, Crown Life Ins. Co. Mem. Bus. Com. for Arts, Toronto; bd. dirs. Council for Bus. and Arts in Can.; mem. World Wildlife Fund. RCAF. Clubs: Badminton and Racquet, Toronto, Turf, York. Address: 1500 Don Mills Rd Don Mills Rd Ont. Can. M3B 3L1 Also: 75 Dufflaw Rd Toronto Ont. Can. M6A 2W4

DEVLIN, JOSEPH PAUL, chemist, educator; b. Hale, Colo., Jan. 11, 1935; s. Bernard Leo and Mary Agnes (O'Rourke) D.; m. Margaret Mary Bowe, June 1, 1957; children: Jeanne Marie, Bonnie JoAnn, Rebecca, Matthew Shawn. B.S. in Chemistry, Regis Coll., Denver, 1956; Ph.D. (NSF fellow 1959-60), Kans. State U., 1960. Research asso. U. Minn., 1960-61; mem. faculty Okla. State U., Stillwater, 1961—, prof. chemistry, 1970—, chmn. dept., 1976-81; Primary sch. soccer coach, 1979-81. Author papers in field, chpts. in books. NSF grantee, 1962—; AEC, 1966-71. Mem. Am. Chem. Soc. (chmn. Okla. sect. 1980-81), AAAS, Sigma Xi, Phi Lambda Upsilon. Democrat. Roman Catholic. Home: Route 3 Box 337 Stillwater OK 74074 Office: Dept Chemistry Okla State Univ Stillwater OK 74078

DEVLIN, MICHAEL COLES, bass-baritone; b. Chgo., Nov. 27, 1942; s. John Stott and Jane (Coles) D.; m. Theresa A. Padvorac. Mus.B., La. State U., 1965. Debut, N.Y.C. Opera, 1966; appeared with, Santa Fe Opera, Houston Opera and Symphony, San Francisco Symphony, symphonies in, Los Angeles, Phila., Boston, Chgo., New Orleans, Washington, N.Y. Philharm., opera cos. in, Boston, New Orleans, Washington, Ft. Worth, English debut, Glyndebourne Festival, 1974; appeared at, Covent Garden, 1975, 77, European debut, Holland Festival, 1977; appeared with, Frankfurt and Munich operas, 1977, Can. opera and symphony work in, Winnipeg, Toronto and Ottawa; debut, Met. Opera, 1978, San Francisco Opera, 1979, Hamburg and Paris operas, 1980, Miami and Monte Carlo operas, 1981, Dallas opera, 1983, Chgo. Opera, 1984.

DEVLIN, ROBERT MANNING, insurance company executive; b. Bklyn., Feb. 28, 1941; s. John Manning and Norma (Hall) D.; m. KatharineBareis, Sept. 13, 1961; children: Michael Hall, Matthew Bareis. B.A. in Econs., Tulane U., 1964. C.L.U. Various positions Mut. Life Ins. Co. N.Y., 1964-77; v.p., asst. to pres. Calif. Western States Life Ins. Co., Sacramento, 1977-80, sr. v.p., 1980; exec. v.p., dir. Life and Casualty Ins. Co. Tenn., Nashville, 1980—, Nat. Life and Accident Ins. Co., 1983—; dir. Am. Gen. Life Ins. Co. Okla., Am. Gen. Life Ins. Co. Del. Bd. dirs., mem. exec. com., v.p. Jr. Achievement, Nashville, 1981—; trustee, mem. exec. com. Father Ryan High Sch., Nashville, 1981—. Mem. Am. Soc. C.L.U.s, Nat. Assn. Life Underwriters. Roman Catholic. Clubs: Belle Meade Country, Nashville City. Home: 4417 Howell Pl Nashville TN 37205 Office: Life and Casualty Ins Co Tenn American General Center Nashville TN 37250 *Success in life is in direct relation to the commitments you make and keep.*

DEVLIN, ROBERT MARTIN, plant physiology educator; b. Albany, N.Y., Oct. 13, 1931; s. Patrick C. and Katherine (Martin) D.; m. Wanda T. Karandy, July 10, 1960; children: Kristin M., Theresa A., Michael P. B.S., SUNY, Albany, 1959; M.S. (grad. fellow), Dartmouth Coll., 1961; Ph.D., U. Md., 1963. Grad. teaching asst. botany dept. U. Md., 1961-63; asso. prof. plant physiology U. Mass., 1965-72, prof., 1972—; instr. grad. courses Northeastern U., 1968-75. Author: Plant Physiology, 1966, 4th edit., 1983, Experiments in Plant Physiology, 1970, Photosynthesis, 1971, Biology of Human Concern, 1972; contbr. articles to profl. jours. Town mem., Barnstable, Mass., 1970-73. Served with U.S. Amry, 1952-54. EPA research grantee, 1969-74. Mem. Am. Soc. Plant Physiologists, Am. Council on Sci. and Health (bd. sci. advisors), Am. Soc. Hort. Sci., Internat. Platform Assn., Nat. Council Environ. Balance, Council Agrl. Sci. and Tech. (dir.), Sigma Xi, Phi Siga. Club: Explorers. Home: 157 Bristol St Hyannis MA 02601 Office: U Mass East Wareham MA 02538 *Contemporary man is now more numerous and lives longer than in any previous epoch and his greatest present concern is the maintenance of his environment and his health. It is my sincere hope that the "ecology movement" so widely current today is not merely a fad but a trend for the future, a trend that will secure man's own existence as well as that of all the ancient and various life forms that preceded him on this planet, and remain with him today.*

DEVLIN, THOMAS MCKEOWN, biochemist; b. Phila., June 29, 1929; s. Frank and Ella Mae (McKeown) D.; m. Marjorie Adele Paynter, Aug. 15, 1953; children—Steven James, Mark Thomas. B.A., U. Pa., 1953; Ph.D., Johns Hopkins U., 1957. Research asso. Merck Inst., Rahway, N.J., 1957-61, sect. head, 1961-66, dir. enzymology, 1966-67; prof., chmn. dept. biol. chemistry Hahnemann U. Sch. Medicine, 1967—; acting dean Hahnemann Med. Coll. (Sch. Allied Health Professions), 1972-74, 80-81; vis. scientist U. Brussels, 1964-65; Inst. Genetics, Naples, Italy, 1965; mem. NSF rev. panels, 1976, 77; mem. council acad. soc. Assn. Am. Med. Colls., 1975-79; mem. com. on sci. and arts Franklin Inst., 1977—; mem. test com. Nat. Bd. Med. Examiners, 1983—. Editor: (J. Wiley) Textbook of Biochemistry, 1982; Contbr. numerous articles to profl. jours. Mem. Commn. on Evaluation, Retention and Selection of Judges, Phila. Bar Assn., 1976-79, vice chmn., 1979; vis. com. Lehigh U., 1982—. Mem. Am. Soc. Biol. Chemists, Am. Assn. Cancer Research, Am. Soc. Cell Biology, Soc. Exptl. Biology and Medicine, Biophys. Soc., N.Y. Acad. Scis., Biochem. Soc., Phi Beta Kappa, Sigma Xi. Episcopalian. Club: Ocean City (N.J.) Yacht. Home: 1100 Norsam Rd Gladywyne PA 19035 Office: Dept Biol Chemistry Hahnemann U Sch Medicine Philadelphia PA 19102

DE VOE, IRVING WOODROW, microbiologist, educator; b. Brewer, Maine, Oct. 4, 1936; s. Woodrow Donnison and Maydelle Muir (Fielding) De V.; m. Lynne Rae Parker, June 21, 1960; children—Scott Irving, David Brookfield, Steven Patrick, Christopher James, Samantha Rae. B.S., Aurora Coll., 1964; Ph.D. in Microbiology, U. Oreg., 1968. Asst. prof. microbiology Aurora (Ill.) Coll., 1969-70; research asso. Argonne (Ill.) Nat. Labs., 1969-70; asst. prof. microbiology McGill U., 1970-75, asso. prof., 1975-78, prof., chmn. dept. microbiology and immunology, 1978—. Contbr. articles to profl. jours. Served with U.S. Army, 1954-57; Served with USN, 1957-61. NIH fellow, 1964-68; Nat. Research Council Can. fellow, 1968-69. Mem. Am. Soc. Microbiology, Can. Soc. Microbiologists, Que. Soc. Microbiologists, Sigma Xi. Home: 115 Chestnut Dr Baie-D'Urfe PQ H9X 2M2 Canada Office: 3775 University St Montreal PQ H3A 2B4 Canada

DEVOL, KENNETH STOWE, journalism educator; b. Los Angeles, Apr. 3, 1929; s. Howard Putnam and Gladys (Harris) D.; m. Shirley May Dixon, Dec. 30, 1951; children: Sharon Marie, Randall Putnam. A.B., U. So. Calif., 1951, M.S., 1954, Ph.D., 1965; postgrad. (Nat. Endowment Humanities grantee), Stanford U., 1969. Publicity work Hollywood Bowl, 1946-50; chmn. journalism Los Angeles Valley Coll., 1955-61; asst. prof. Calif. State U. Northridge, 1961-65, assoc. prof., 1965-69, prof., 1969—, chmn. journalism, 1969-81, acting asso. dean, 1975-76; sr. lectr. U. So. Calif., 1978-82; Reporter-editor Valley Times, 1957-60; researcher, writer Andrews-Yagemann TV Prodns., 1965. Author: (with Esther Davis) Writing Style For Journalists, 1962, Mass Media and the Supreme Court: The Legacy of the Warren Years, 3d edit, 1982; Contbr.: Readings in Mass Communications, 5th edit, 1983; contbr. to: Justice Hugo Black and the First Amendment, 1978. Mem. Assn. for Edn. in Journalism and Mass Communication (nat. pres. 1975-76), mem. exec. com. (1970-71, 75-78), Assn. Schs. Journalism and Mass Communication (nat. pres. 1979-80), Am. Assn. Schs. and Depts. Journalism (mem. exec. com. 1973-74, 75-81), Am. Soc. Journalism Sch. Adminstrs., Western Assn. Univ. Publs. Mgrs. (pres. 1980-81), Am. Newspaper Pubs. Assn. (coop. com. on edn. 1975-77), Accrediting Council in Journalism and Mass Communication (accrediting com. 1975-78), Soc. Prof. Journalists, AAUP, Kappa Tau Alpha (recipient recognition for research in journalism 1972). Office: 18111 Nordhoff St Northridge CA 91330

DEVONS, SAMUEL, educator, physicist; b. Bangor, N.Wales, U.K., Sept. 30, 1914; came to U.S., 1959; s. David Isaac and Edith (Edlestein) D.; m. Celia Ruth Toubkin, Sept. 7, 1938; children—Susan Danielle, Judith Rosalind, Amanda Jane, Cathryn Ann Julie. B.A., Trinity Coll., Cambridge (Eng.) U., 1935, M.A., Ph.D. (Exhbn. 1851 scholar), 1939; M.Sc., Manchester (Eng.) U., 1959. Sr. sci. officer Air Ministry, Ministry Supply, U.K., 1939-45; fellow, dir. studies, lectr. physics Trinity Coll., 1946-49; prof. physics Imperial Coll., London, Eng., 1950-55; Langworthy prof. physics, dir. phys. labs. U. Manchester, 1955-60; prof. physics Columbia, 1960—, chmn. dept., 1963-67; Royal Soc.-Leverhulme vis. prof., Andhra, India, 1967-68; Racah vis. prof. physics Hebrew U., Jerusalem, 1973; Balfour vis. prof. history of sci. Weizman Inst., Israel, 1974, bd. govs., 1971—; Mem. Tech. Assistance-UNESCO Team of UN to S. Am., 1957. Author: Excited States of Nuclei, 1949; Editor: Biology and the Physical Sciences, 1969, High Energy Physics and Nuclear Structure, 1970. Served with RAF, 1944-45. Recipient Rutherford medal and prize Inst. Physics, U.K., 1970. Fellow Phys. Soc. London (past v.p.), Royal Soc. London, Am. Phys. Soc. Home: Lewis Rd Irvington-on-Hudson NY 10533 Office: Dept Physics Columbia U New York NY 10027

DEVORE, MARGARET BOWEN, anesthesiologist; b. Troy, S.C., Dec. 29, 1930; d. William Reese and Ruth (McAlister) Bowen; m. Robert N. DeVore, Aug. 31, 1952; children—Robert Douglas, John Anthony and Thomas Lee (twins), William George, and Margaret Ann (twins). B.A., Winthrop Coll., Rock Hill, S.C., 1951; M.D. magna cum laude, Med. Coll. S.C., 1955. Diplomate: Am. Bd. Anesthesiology. Intern Med. Coll. S.C., 1955-56; gen. practice medicine, Oceana, W.Va. and, Jackson, S.C., 1956-62; resident in anesthesiology Med. Coll. Ga. Hosp., Augusta, 1962-64, mem. faculty, 1964—, 1964—, prof. anesthesiology, 1973—, asso. dean students, 1979—; clin. dir. anesthesia Eugene Talmadge Meml. Hosp., 1976-79. Author articles, revs. in field. Recipient Disting. Faculty award Med. Coll. Ga., 1978. Mem. Am. Soc. Anesthesiologists, AMA, Internat. Anesthesia Research Soc., Assn. Am. Med. Colls., Ga. Soc. Anesthesiologists, Med. Assn. Ga., Richmond County Med. Soc., Am. Med. Women's Assn., Alpha Omega Alpha. Home: 1949 Bolin Rd North Augusta SC 29841 Office: Med Coll Ga Augusta GA 30912 *Life is a marvelous gift! This thought is responsible for my ambition to pursue excellence and is basic to my caring for others. How fortunate I am that parents, teachers and friends convinced me that being a woman would only be an asset, never a stumbling block. Thus I have enjoyed the best of all worlds—wife, mother, physician, teacher and myself—with just the proper doses of failure to assure humility.*

DEVORE, PAUL CAMERON, lawyer; b. Great Falls, Mont., Apr. 25, 1932; s. Paul Theodore and Maxine (Cameron) DeV.; m. Roberta Humphrey, Feb. 3, 1962; children: Jennifer Ross, Andrew Cameron, Christopher Humphrey. B.A., Yale U., 1954; M.A., Cambridge U., 1956; J.D., Harvard U., 1961. Bar: Wash. 1961. Assoc. Wright, Innis, Simon & Todd, Seattle, 1961-66; ptnr. Davis, Wright, Todd, Riese & Jones, Seattle, 1967—, chmn. exec. com., 1983—; sec. Seattle Times Co., 1976—, Walla Walla Union-Bull., Inc., Wash., 1976—; mem. adv. bd. Media Law Reporter, Washington, 1978—. Chmn. Seattle Community Coll., 1967-68; pres. A Contemporary Theatre, Seattle, 1972-74; sec. Seattle Art Mus., 1973—; pres. The Bush Sch., Seattle, 1976-79; chmn. Va. Mason Research Ctr., Seattle, 1983—. Mem. ABA (chmn. forum com. on communications law 1981), Wash. State Bar Assn. (chmn. sect. of corp. bus. and banking law 1981-82), Seattle-King County Bar Assn. (trustee 1975-76), Phi Beta Kappa, Beta Theta Phi. Clubs: Seattle Tennis, University, Rainier, Monday (Seattle). Home: 1516 E Howe St Seattle WA 98112 Office: Davis Wright Todd Riese & Jones 4200 SeaFirst Bank Bldg Seattle WA 98154

DE VORE, PAUL WARREN, technology educator; b. Parkersburg, W.Va., July 18, 1926; s. Harry and Eleanor Sarah (Dunn) DeVore; m. Eleanor Condron, Apr. 7, 1952; children: Michelle Ann, Phillip Charles. B.S., Ohio U., 1950; M.S., Kent State U., 1954; Ed.D., Pa. State U., 1961. Postdoctoral fellow U. Md., 1965-66; instr. pub. schs. Chagrin Falls, Ohio, 1950-53; asst. prof. engring. Grove City Coll., 1953-56; asst. prof. SUNY-Oswego, 1956-60, dir. div. indsl. arts and tech., 1960-67; prof. tech. edn. W. Va. U., Morgantown, 1967-75, prof., chmn. tech. edn., 1975—; cons. NSF, Dept. Edn. Author: Technology: An Intellectual Discipline, 1964, Education in a Technological Society, 1971, Technology and the New Liberal Arts, 1976, Technology: An Introduction, 1980, Introduction to Transportation, 1983; cons. editor: Tech. Edn. Series, 1974—. Chmn. campaign United Fund, Oswego, 1962-63. Served with USN, 1944-46. Named Outstanding Tchr. W. Va. U., 1970-71; recipient Outstanding Research award Phi Delta Kappa, 1978. Mem. Am. Council Indsl. Arts Edn., Soc. History of Tech., AAAS, World Future Soc., Epsilon Pi Tau (Disting. Service award 1976). Home: 668 Colonial Dr Morgantown WV 26505 Office: Allen Hall Dept Tech W Va U Morgantown WV 26506

DE VOS, PETER JON, ambassador; b. San Diego, Dec. 24, 1938. B.A., Princeton U., 1960; M.A., Johns Hopkins U., 1962. Fgn. service officer for Brazil Dept. State, Washington, 1962-66, polit. officer, Naples, 1966-68; dep. prin. officer, Luanda, 1968-70, polit. officer, Sao Paulo, 1970-71, Brasilia, 1971-73; spl. asst. Bur. Inter-Am. Affairs, Washington, 1973-75; polit. officer, Athens, 1975-78, Nat. War. Coll., 1978-79; dep. dir. So. African Affairs, Dept. State, Washington, 1979-80; U.S. ambassador to Republic of Guinea-Bissau and to Republic of Cape Verde, 1980-83, Mozambique, Maputo, 1983—. Office: US Embassy 35 Rua Da Mesquita 3d Floor Maputo Mozambique *

DEVOS, RICHARD MARVIN, chemical company executive; b. Grand Rapids, Mich., Mar. 4, 1926; s. Simon C. and Ethel R. (Dekker) DeV.; m. Helen J. Van Wesep, Feb. 7, 1953. Student, Calvin Coll., 1946; LL.D. (hon.), Oral Roberts U., Grove City (Pa.) Coll., Northwood Inst., Midland, Mich., Dickinson Sch. Law, Carlisle, Pa., 1980, Pepperdine U., 1980, Lubbock Christian Coll., 1981, D.Litt., Hope Coll., 1982. Partner Wolverine Air Service, 1945-48; co-founder, pres. Ja-Ri Corp., 1949, Amway Corp., 1959—; pres. Amway of Can. Ltd., Amway Pty. Ltd. Australia, Amway Hotel Corp., Amway Global, Inc., Ada, Mich., Amway Internat., Inc., Amway (U.K.) Ltd., Amway Mgmt. Co., Amway Stock Co., Amway Ja-Ri Corp., Amway (OHK) Hong Kong Ltd., Amway GmbH (W.Ger.), Amway Intercontinental, Inc., Amway (Ireland) Ltd., Amway (Nederland) Ltd., Statitrol, Inc., Nutrilite Products Inc., Buena Park, Calif.; dir. Amway (Malaysia), Sdn. Bhd., Amway Communications, Old Kent Bank & Trust, Grand Rapids, Amway (Malaysia) Sdn. Bhd., Amway (Japan) Ltd.; dir., sec. Amway Distbrs. Assn. U.S., Amway Distbrs. Assn. Can.; co-chmn. Mut. Broadcasting System, Inc., Amway Communications Corp.; pres. Amway Stock Transfer Co., Mut. Sports, Inc., Ada Report, Inc.; chmn. bd. Reference Map Internat. Author: Believe!. Chmn. Gospel Films, Muskegon, Mich.; dir. BIPAC.; bd. dirs. past pres. Grand Rapids Jr. Achievement, 1966-67; bd. control Grand Valley State Colls.; bd. dirs. United Way Kent County, Robert Schuller Ministries, Nat. Legal Center for Public Interest; trustee Butterworth Hosp., Grand Rapids; past chmn. New Grand Rapids Com.; chmn. Nat. Office Disability; mem. corp. Northwood Inst. bd. advisers St. Mary's Hosp.; mem. council trustees Freedoms Found. Served with USAAF, 1944-46. Recipient Alexander Hamilton award Econ. Edn. from Freedoms Found.; Disting. Salesman of Year award Grand Rapids Sales and Mktg. Execs.; Bus. Leader of Yr. award Religious Heritage Am.; Industry Week Excellence in Mgmt. award; Thomas Jefferson Freedom of Speech award Kiwanis Internat.; Mich. Week Vol. Leadership award; Mktg. Man of Yr. award West Mich. chpt. Am. Mktg. Assn.; Am. Enterprise Exec. award Nat. Mgmt. Assn.; Golden Plat award Acad. of Achievement; George Washington Honor medal Freedoms Found.; Free Enterprise award Americanism Ednl. League. Mem. NAM (past dir.), Direct Selling Assn. (past chmn., dir., Champion of Free Enterprise and Knights of Royal Way awards, Hall of Fame award), Newcomen Soc., Round Table. Mem. Christian Reformed Ch. (elder, chmn. fin. com.; past pres. missionary soc.; mem. bd. missions). Clubs: Economic (dir.), Rotary (Disting. Service award) (Grand Rapids); Pillars bd. dirs. Home: Grand Rapids MI Office: 7575 E Fulton Rd Ada MI 49355

DEVRIES, BERNARD JERIN, architect; b. Chgo., June 21, 1909; s. Christian W.B. and Johana (Zicterman) DeV.; m. Jean Ann Frissel, June 27, 1936; 1 dau., Jo-Ann C. Student, Mich. State U., 1929-30; B.S. in Architecture, U. Mich., 1934. Registered architect, Mich., Ill., Ind., Ohio, Mass., Conn., Tex., N.J. Asst. engr. City of Ann Arbor (Mich.), 1934-37; designer Lewis J. Sarvis (architect), Battle Creek, Mich., 1937-38; pvt. practice architecture Bernard J. DeVries (now DeVries Assos., Inc.), architects and planners), Muskegon, Mich., 1938-83; profl. community planner; architect Gen. Telephone Co. Mich., Master City Plan Muskegon, CBD Redevel. Plan Muskegon, Muskegon Marquette Urban Renewal Project; also schs., churches, indsl. and apt. bldg. complexes. Chmn. Mich. Bd. Registration for Architects; mem. Mich. Bd. Registration for Land Surveyors.; Commr. Muskegon City Planning Commn., 1944-65, chmn., 1947-65; commr. Muskegon Bd. Appeals, 1954-65; charter mem. Muskegon Community Services Planning Council, 1963-70, dir., 1963; founder, charter mem. Lake Michigan Region Planning Council, Inc., 1960—, vice chmn., 1964, chmn. Mich. delegation, 1961-70; Mem. Nat. Council Archtl. Registration Bds. Co-author: Dunes Area Regional Planning, 1962, Regional Highways and Population Growth Report, 1963. Trustee C.W. Smith Kiwanis Found., 1980—; bd. dirs. Hackley Heritage Assn., 1960—. Recipient Disting. Service award Jr. C. of C., 1943, hon. mention Am. Gas Assn. Residence Competition, 1939, Mich. Sch. Bds. Sch. Design Competition, 1963; 1st place Design award for Branch Bank, Muskegon AIA, 1964; named Muskegon's Mr. Planner Muskegon Chronicle, 1963. Fellow A.I.A. (sec., dir. Western Mich. chpt. 1945-47, v.p. Grand Valley chpt. 1963, pres. 1964); mem. Mich. Soc. Architects (bd. mem. 1967—, gold medal 1966), Am. Soc. Planning Ofcls., Mich. Soc. Planning Ofcls. (founder, charter dir. 1956, bd. mem. 1967-73, pres. 1970), Mich. Assn. of Professions (charter), Muskegon C. of C. (Builders award 1956). Clubs: Kiwanian (pres. 1952, mem. Legion Honor), Muskegon Century, Muskegon Yacht. Home: 1387-D Creek Dr Muskegon MI 49441

DEVRIES, DONALD LAWSON, retired business executive; b. Sykesville, Mo., Mar. 29, 1917; s. John Oliver and Emma (Koller) DeV.; m. Jeanne Louise Coleman, Jan. 1, 1946; children: Donald Lawson, Mary Deborah. B.S., Lehigh U., 1939; cert., Harvard Bus. Sch., 1962. With Koppers Metal Products, Balt., 1940-77, v.p., 1963-77, gen. mgr., 1972-77; sr. v.p. Koppers Co. Inc., Balt., 1978-82; dir. 1st Nat. Bancorp, Balt., Eastmet Corp., Cockeysville, Md., Slaysman Co., Balt. Chmn. The Balt. Opera Co., 1979—; chmn. bd. trustees Goucher Coll., Towson, Md., 1979-82; trustee Md. Hist. Soc., Balt., 1980—; chmn. The Community Found. of Greater Balt. Area, Inc., 1982—. Recipient John Goucher award Goucher Trustees, 1982. Republican. Episcopalian. Clubs: Elkridge, Chesapeake Bay Yacht, Talbot Country, L'Hirondelle, Maryland. Home: Hunting Point Farm Route 1 Box 233 Easton MD 21601

DEVRIES, JOHN ADRIAN, electronic systems company executive; b. Clifton, N.J., Sept. 7, 1923; s. Daniel A. and Margaret (Redling) DeV.; m. Irene Balogh, Aug. 9, 1945; children: John Adrian, Karen A. Smith, Janet E. Rooney, Brian R., William F., Michael V. B.M.S., U. Note Dame, 1945; B.S., U. Notre Dame, 1946, M.S., 1947. Pres., chmn. bd. Computer Applications, Inc., N.Y.C., 1961-70; sr. v.p. Gen. Instrument Co., N.Y.C., 1970—; chmn. bd. subs. Am. Totalisator Co.; dir. Sytek, Inc., Mountain View, Calif., 1981—. Served to lt. USN, 1943-46; PTO. Mem. AIAA, Assn. Computing Machinery. Office: Gen Instrucment Corp 1775 Broadway New York NY 10019

DE VRIES, KENNETH LAWRENCE, mechanical engineer, educator; b. Ogden, Utah, Oct. 27, 1933; s. Sam and Fern (Slater) DeV.; m. Kay M. DeVries, Mar. 1, 1959; children—Kenneth, Susan. A.B., Weber State Coll., 1953; B.S., U. Utah, 1959, Ph.D., 1962. With Convair, Fort Worth, 1957; mem. faculty U. Utah, Salt Lake City, 1961—, prof. mech. engring., 1969-76, prof. dept. mech. and indsl. engring., 1976—, chmn. dept., 1970-81; head polymer program NSF, 1975-76; mem. Utah Council Sci. and Tech., 1973-77. Author: Analysis and Testing of Adhesive Bonds, 1977; contbr. articles on polymers, dental materials, rock mechanics, adhesive design to profl. jours. Mem. ASME, Am. Phys. Soc., Internat. Soc. Dental Research, Am. Chem. Soc., ASTM, Material Soc. Mormon. Home: 1466 Penrose St Salt Lake City UT 84103 Office: 3008 Mech Engring Bldg U Utah Salt Lake City UT 84112

DE VRIES, MARGARET GARRITSEN, economist; b. Detroit, Feb. 11, 1922; d. John Edward and Margaret Florence (Ruggles) Garritsen; m. Barend A. de Vries, Apr. 5, 1952; children: Christine, Barton. B.A. in Econs. with honors, U. Mich., 1943, Ph.D., MIT, 1946. With IMF, Washington, 1946—, sr. economist, 1949-52, asst. chief multiple currency pratices div., 1953-57, chief Far Eastern Div., 1957-59, econ. cons., 1963-73, historian, 1973—; professorial lectr. econs. George Washington U., 1946-49, 58-63. Author: (with Irving S. Friedman) Foreign Economic Policy of the United States in the Postwar, 1947, (with J. Keith Horsefield and others) The International Monetary Fund, 1945-1965, Twenty Years of International Monetary Cooperation, 3 vols., 1969, The International Monetary Fund, 1966-71, The System Under Stress, 2 vols., 1977; contbr. articles to profl. jours. Recipient Disting. Alumni award U. Mich., 1980; AAUW scholar, 1939-42; U. Mich. Univ. scholar, 1942; MIT fellow, 1943-46; Ford Found. grantee, 1959-62. Mem. Am. Econ. Assn., Internat. Studies Assn., Washington Women Economists Assn., U. Mich. Alumni Assn., MIT Alumnae Assn., Phi Beta Kappa, Phi Kappa Phi. Mem. United Church of Christ. Office: IMF 700 19th St NW Washington DC 20431 *Probably the greatest factor in my life has been a sense of direction. Growing up in Detroit in the Great Depression of the 1930's, as a child I became aware of the problem of extensive unemployment. Then, as now, Detroit was the the hardest hit cities. I knew I wanted to be an economist and to work in the public sector. Motivation, determination, a coutinuing interest in economics, and a feeling of the need for public service have carried me the rest of the way.*

DE VRIES, PETER, writer, editor; b. Chgo., Feb. 27, 1910; s. Joost and Henrietta (Eldersveld) De V.; m. Katinka Loeser, Oct. 16, 1943; children: Jan, Peter Jon, Emily, Derek. A.B., Calvin Coll., 1931; student, Northwestern U., summer 1931. Editor community newspaper, Chgo., 1931, free lance writer, 1931; asso. editor Poetry Mag., 1938, co-editor, 1942; mem. editorial staff New Yorker Mag., 1944—. Author: No But I Saw the Movie, 1952, The Tunnel of Love, 1954, Comfort Me with Apples, 1956, The Mackerel Plaza, 1958, The Tents of Wickedness, 1959, Through the Fields of Clover, 1961, The Blood of the Lamb, 1962, Reuben, Reuben, 1964, Let Me Count the Ways, 1965, The Vale of Laughter, 1967, The Cat's Pajamas and Witch's Milk, 1968, Mrs. Wallop, 1970, Into Your Tent I'll Creep, 1971, Without a Stitch in Time, 1972, Forever Panting, 1973, The Glory of the Hummingbird, 1974, I Hear America Swinging, 1976, Madder Music, 1977, Consenting Adults, or The Duchess Will Be Furious, 1980, Sauce for the Goose, 1981, Slouching Towards Kalamazoo, 1983. Mem. Am. Acad. and Inst. Arts and Letters. Home: 170 Cross Hwy Westport CT 06880 Office: care New Yorker Mag 25 W 43d St New York NY 10036

DE VRIES, RIMMER, economist; b. Utrecht, Netherlands, Jan. 20, 1929; came to U.S., 1951, naturalized, 1957; s. Jacob and Mettje (Verburg) de V.; m. Ruth Berg, May 24, 1958; children—Rimmer D., Jacqueline R., Joyce C. B.A., Netherlands Sch. Econs., 1951; M.A., Ohio State U., 1952, Ph.D., 1955. Economist Fed. Res. Bank N.Y., 1956-61; economist, then v.p. Morgan Guaranty Trust Co., N.Y.C., 1961-78, sr. v.p., 1978—; Mem. econ. adv. bd. U.S. Dept. Commerce. Editor: World Fin. Markets, 1968—. Trustee, treas. N.J. Conservation Found., 1979; bd. dirs. Inst. Internat. Devel., 1973. Mem. Conf. Bd. Econ. Forum, Council Fgn. Relations, Inst. Internat Econs. adv. com. Republican. Mem. Christian Reformed Ch. Home: Hill and Dale Rd RFD 3 Lebanon NJ 08833 Office: 23 Wall St New York City NY 10015

DEVRIES, WILLIAM CASTLE, surgeon, educator; b. Bklyn., Dec. 19, 1943; s. Hendrik and Cathryn Lucille (Castle) DeV.; m. Ane Karen Olsen, June 12, 1965; children: Jon, Adrie, Kathryn, Andrew, Janna, William, Diana. B.S., U. Utah, 1966, M.D., 1970. Intern Duke U. Med. Center, 1970-71, resident in cardiovascular and thoracic surgery, 1971-79; asst. prof. surgery U. Utah; chmn. div. cardiovascular and thoracic surgery; chief thoracic surgery Salt Lake VA Hosp. Recipient Wintrobe award, 1970. Mem. A.C.S., Utah Med. Assn., AMA, Intermountain Thoracic Soc., Salt Lake Surg. Soc., Utah Heart Assn., Assn. VA Surgeons, Utah Lung Assn., Alpha Omega Alpha. Mormon. Office: 50 N Medical Dr Salt Lake City UT 84132

DEW, CHARLES BURGESS, historian, educator; b. St. Petersburg, Fla., Jan. 5, 1937; s. Jack Carlos and Amy (Meek) D.; m. Robb Reavill Forman, Jan. 26, 1968. A.B., Williams Coll., 1958; Ph.D., Johns Hopkins, 1964. Instr. Wayne State U., 1963-64, asst. prof., 1964-65, La. State U., 1965-68; asso. prof. U. Mo., Columbia, 1968-72, prof., 1972-78; vis. asso. prof. U. Va., 1970-71; vis. prof. history Williams Coll., Williamstown, Mass., 1977-78, prof. history, 1978—. Author: Ironmaker to the Confederacy: Joseph R. Anderson and the Tredegar Iron Works, 1966, The Meanings of American History, 1972; contbr.: chpt. to Origins of the New South, 1877-1913 (C. Vann Woodward), rev. edit., 1972. Recipient Fletcher Pratt award N.Y. Civil War Round Table, 1966, award of merit Am. Assn. for State and Local History, 1967. Mem. Am. Hist. Assn., Orgn. Am. Historians, Phi Beta Kappa, Delta Psi. Home: 218 Bulkley St Williamstown MA 01267

DE WAART, EDO, conductor; b. Amsterdam, Netherlands, June 1, 1941; came to U.S., 1959. Grad. with honors for oboe, Amsterdam Conservatoire, 1962. Oboist, Concertgebouw Orch., Amsterdam, 1963-64, asst. condr., 1966-67; asst. to Leonard Bernstein, N.Y. Philharm., 1964-65; condr. Rotterdam (Netherlands) Philharm., 1967—, also prin. condr., music dir.; founding condr. Netherlands Wind Ensemble, 1967-71; condr., music dir., San Francisco Symphony Orch., 1977—; guest condr., Amsterdam Concertgebouw, Berlin Philharm., Boston Symphony, Chgo. Symphony, London Symphony, Cleve. Orch., N.Y. Philharm., Phila. Orch.; condr.: new prodn. Lohengrin, Beyreuth Festival, summer 1979; rec. artist, Philips Records; rec. with major European orchs. including, New Philharmonia, English Chamber Orch., Royal Philharmonic Orch., Dresden State Orch. Recipient 1st prize Metropoulos Competition, N.Y.C., 1964. Office: San Francisco Symphony Orch Davies Symphony Hall San Francisco CA 94102

DE WAHL, DAVID ALLEN, manufacturing company executive; b. Mpls., June 3, 1924; s. Arvid Rutherford and Gertrude Sophia De W.; m. Lois Martha Dann, July 24, 1953; children: David Allen, Elizabeth Ann, Duncan Comrie. B.A. summa cum laude, U. Minn., 1946; J.D. cum laude, Harvard U., 1949. Bar: N.Y. 1949, Mich. 1973. Asso. firm Sullivan & Cromwell, N.Y.C., 1949-52; from atty. to v.p., gen. counsel, sec. Am. Standard, Inc., N.Y.C., 1952-73; v.p., gen. counsel Fruehauf Corp., Detroit, 1973-75, Airco Inc., Montvale, N.J., 1975—; pres., dir. MDF Tech., Inc., Deposit, N.Y.; dir. Mountain Med. Equipment, Inc., Denver. Mem. ABA, Assn. Bar City N.Y., Phi Beta Kappa. Clubs: University (N.Y.C.); Ridgewood Country. Home: 205 Wearimus Rd HoHoKus NJ 07423 Office: 85 Chestnut Ridge Rd Montvale NJ 07645

DEWALD, ERNEST LEROY, landscape architect; b. Cleve., Oct. 15, 1907; s. Frank Ernest and Bessie Mary (Stutzman) D.; m. Edna E. Kummer, Oct. 9, 1935. B.F.A. in Landscape Architecture, Ohio State U., 1931; postgrad. (Found. scholar), Lake Forest Found. for Architects and Landscape Architects, 1931. Registered landscape architect, Calif., N.Y., Ohio, Pa. Landscape architect U.S. Forest Service and Nat. Park Service, McGregor, Iowa, Lynn, Minn., and Hinckly, Minn., 1933-38; Works Progress adminstr. Cleve. City Parks and City of East Cleveland, 1938-41, Albert D. Taylor, Cleve., 1941-43, City of Cleve., 1945-56, Outcalt, Guenther (Architects), Cleve., 1956-59; pvt. practice landscape architecture, Shaker Heights, Ohio, 1959—. Co-author: Cleve. Region Airport Plan, 1946. Active Nat. Council Landscape Archtl. Registration Bds., 1967-74, pres., 1968-69, 72-73; mem. Nat. Interprofl. Council Registration, 1972-73; exec. sec. Ohio Roadside Council, 1959-67, vice chmn., 1968—; mem. Forest Hill Park Adv. Commn., 1977—, People to People Internat., 1981—, del. to China, 1981. Fellow Am. Soc. Landscape Architects (nat. 2d v.p. 1969-71, sec.-treas. Council Fellows, Ky-Ohio chpt. medal 1974);

mem. Cleve. Mus. Art (life), Internat. Fedn. Landscape Architects, Ohio State Alumni Assn. (life). Home: 12910 Fairhill Rd Shaker Heights OH 44120 Office: 3570 Warrensville Center Rd Shaker Heights OH 44122 *To create a better environment and a better way of life for mankind one must harmoniously integrate his work with that of nature. To be successful one must have enthusiasm for the work at hand.*

DEWALD, PAUL ADOLPH, psychiatrist; b. N.Y.C., Mar. 12, 1920; s. Jacob Frederick and Elsie (Wurzburger) D.; m. Eleanor Whitman, Sept. 1, 1961; children—Jonathan S., Ellen F. B.A., Swarthmore Coll., 1942; M.D., U. Rochester, 1945; cert. psychoanalysis, SUNY, 1960. Intern, Strong Meml. Hosp., Rochester, N.Y., 1945-46, resident, 1948-52; instr. U. Rochester, 1952-57, asst. prof. psychiatry, 1957-61; pvt. practice psychoanalysis, St. Louis, 1961—; asst. clin. prof. psychiatry Washington U., St. Louis, 1961-65; asso. clin. prof. St. Louis U., 1965-69, clin. prof. psychiatry, 1969—; dir. treatment service Psychoanalytic Found. St. Louis, 1961-72, med. dir., 1972-73, St. Louis Psychoanalytic Inst., 1973-83, supervising and tng. analyst, 1973—; mem. faculty Chgo. Inst. Psychoanalysis, 1961—, supervising and tng. analyst, 1965—; vis. prof. U. Cin., 1968—; mem. Mo. State Mental Health Commn., 1978-83. Author: Psychotherapy: A Dynamic Approach, 1964, 2d edit., 1969, The Psychoanalytic Process, 1972; also articles. Served to capt. M.C., AUS, 1946-48. Fellow Am. Psychiat. Assn.; mem. Mo. Psychiat. Assn. (pres. 1970-71), Eastern Mo. Psychiat. Assn. (pres. 1969-70), Am. Psychoanalytic Soc., St. Louis Psychoanalytic Soc. (pres. 1970-71). Home: 60 Conway Ln Saint Louis MO 63124 Office: 4524 Forest Park Saint Louis MO 63108 *I was encouraged by my parents to see my career as a potential source of creative enjoyment, fulfillment and self-esteem. I was fortunate to choose a field that encouraged those attitudes, and a wife who supported me in them. I have other interests and sources of fulfillment, but when there is nothing better or more enjoyable to do, I work.*

DEWALL, RICHARD ALLISON, surgeon; b. Appleton, Minn., Dec. 16, 1926; s. Herman H. and Grace G. (Gardner) DeW.; m. Diane B. Prettyman, Oct. 24, 1952; children—Beth B., Amy, Melissa. B.A., U. Minn., 1949, B.S., 1950, B.M., 1952, M.D., 1953, M.S. in Surgery, 1960. Diplomate: Am. Bd. Surgery, Am. Bd. Thoracic Surgery. Research asst. dept. surgery U. Minn., 1954-56, instr. surgery, 1960, asst. prof., 1962; research fellow Am. Heart Assn., 1956-58; advanced research fellow, 1958-60, established investigator, 1960-62; prof. surgery, chmn. dept. Chgo. Med. Sch., 1962-66; chief surgery Cox Heart Inst., Kettering, Ohio, 1966—; staff Kettering Hosp.; coordinator surgery residency tng. program Kettering Meml. Hosp., 1968-75; Co-chmn. med. sch. planning com. Wright State U., Dayton, Ohio, 1968-73. clin. prof. surgery, 1975—. Recipient award U.S. Jr. C. of C., 1957. Fellow A.C.S., Am. Coll. Cardiology; mem. Soc. for Thoracic Surgery, AMA, AAAS (co-recipient Ida B. Gould Meml. award 1956), Soc. Univ. Surgeons, Am. Assn. Thoracic Surgery, Dayton Surg. Soc., Nu Sigma Nu, Sigma Chi. Research on perfusion techniques as an aid to open cardiac surgery. Home: 421 Thornhill Rd Dayton OH 45419 Office: 111 W 1st St Dayton OH 45402

DEWAR, JOHN STUART, retired chemical company executive; b. Guelph, Ont., Can., June 24, 1918; s. John George and Effie (Marshall) D.; children: Helen, John, Peter, Kenneth; m. Marian E. Prowse; 3 stepchildren. Student, Upper Can. Coll., 1936; B.S. in Chem. Engring. Queen's U., 1941. Staff Def. Industries Ltd., 1941, supt. nitroglycerine dept. Winnipeg Works, 1942; Chem. sales engr. Nat. Carbon Co. div. of Union Carbide Can. Ltd., Toronto, 1943-46; v.p. Union Carbide Can. Ltd., 1956-63, exec. v.p., 1963-65, pres., 1965-81, chmn., chief exec. officer, 1981-83, now dir.; dir. Toronto-Dominion Bank, Mfrs. Life Assurance Co., Thomson Newspapers Ltd., Ralston Purina Can.; bd. govs. Ont. Research Found.; mem. NRC Can., 1968-69. Mem. Toronto chpt. Ludwig Inst. Cancer Research; past chmn. Canadian Council; chmn. Conf. Bd., 1970-72. Mem. Can. Chem. Producers Assn. (chmn. 1968-69). Office: 123 Eglinton Ave E Toronto ON M4P 1J3 Canada

DEWAR, MARION, mayor; b. Montreal, Que., Can., Feb. 17, 1928; d. Wilson and Agnes (Cunningham) Bell; m. Kenneth J. Dewar, Sept. 15, 1951; children: Robert, Elizabeth, Catherine, Paul. Grad., St. Joseph's Sch. Nursing, 1949; B.N.Sc., U. Ottawa, 1969. Public health nurse Ottawa-Carleton Health Unit, 1968-72; alderman City of Ottawa, Ont., Can., 1972-74, dep. mayor, controller, 1974-78, mayor, 1978—; mem. exec. com. Ottawa-Carleton Regional Council. Bd. dirs. Riverside Hosp., Ottawa Civic Hosp., Ottawa-Carleton Bd. Health. Mem. Can. Colls. Nurses. Mem. New Democratic Party of Can. Office: City Hall 111 Sussex Ottawa ON Canada KIN 5A1

DEWAR, MICHAEL JAMES STEUART, chemistry educator; b. Ahmednagar, India, Sept. 24, 1918; came to U.S., 1959, naturalized, 1980; s. Francis and Nan (Keith) D.; m. Mary Williamson, June 3, 1944; children: Robert Berriedale Keith, Charles Edward Steuart. B.A., Oxford (Eng.) U., 1940, D.Phil., 1942, M.A., 1943. Imperial Chem. Industries fellow Oxford U., 1945; phys. chemist Courtaulds Ltd., 1945-51; prof. chemistry, head dept. Queen Mary Coll., U. London, Eng., 1941-59; prof. chemistry U. Chgo., 1959-63; Robert A. Welch prof. chemistry U. Tex., 1963—; Reilly lectr. U. Notre Dame, 1951; Tilden lectr. Chem. Soc. London, 1954; vis. prof. Yale U., 1957; Falk-Plaut lectr. Columbia U., 1963; William Pyle Phillips visitor Haverford Coll., 1964, 70; Arthur D. Little vis. prof. MIT, 1966; Marchon vis. lectr. U. Newcastle (Eng.), 1966; Glidden Co. lectr. Kent State U., 1967; Gnehm lectr. Eldg. Technische Hochschule, Zurich, Switzerland, 1968; Barton lectr. U. Okla., 1969; Disting. vis. lectr. Yeshiva U., 1970; Kahlbaum lectr. U. Basel, Switzerland, 1970; Benjamin Rush lectr. U. Pa., 1971; Kharasch vis. prof. U. Chgo., 1971; Phi Lambda Upsilon lectr. Johns Hopkins U., 1972; Firth vis. prof. U. Sheffield, 1972; Foster lectr. SUNY-Buffalo, 1973; Five Colls. lectr., Mass., 1973; Sprague lectr. U. Wis., 1974; Disting. Bicentennial prof. U. Utah, 1976; Bircher lectr. Vanderbilt U., 1976; Pahlavi lectr., Iran, 1977; Michael Faraday lectr. U. No. Ill., 1977; Priestley lectr. Pa. State U., 1980; cons. to industry. Author: Electronic Theory of Organic Chemistry, 1949, Hyperconjugation, 1962, Introduction to Modern Organic Chemistry, 1965, Computer Compilation of Molecular Weights and Percentage Compositions of Organic Compounds, 1969, The Molecular Orbital Theory of Organic Chemistry, 1969, The PMO Theory of Organic Chemistry, 1975; also articles. Recipient Harrison Howe award Am. Chem. Soc., 1961, S.W. regional award, 1978; Robert Robinson Lecture, Chem. Soc., 1974; G.W. Wheland Meml. medal U. Chgo., 1976; Evans award Ohio State U., 1977; hon. fellow Balliol Coll., 1974. Fellow Royal Soc. (Davy medal 1982), Am. Acad. Arts and Scis., Chem. Soc. London; mem. Am. Chem. Soc., Nat. Acad. Sci., Sigma Xi. Home: 6808 Mesa Dr Austin TX 78731

DEWAR, ROBERT EARL, chain store corporation executive; b. Traverse City, Mich., Nov. 20, 1922; s. Floyd C. and Irlene (Nash) D.; m. Nancy Jane Miller, Sept. 26, 1944; children: Robert Earl, Jane Elizabeth, John. Student, Alma Coll., 1940-42; LL.B., Wayne State U., 1948; postgrad., U. Mich. Sch. Bus. Adminstrn., 1963. Bar: Mich. 1948. Gen. practice law, Detroit, 1948-49; with S.S. Kresge Co., 1949—, asst. v.p. fin., 1963-65, v.p. fin., 1965-66, adminstrv. v.p., 1966—, exec. v.p. adminstrn., fin., 1968-70, pres., Troy, Mich., 1970-72, chmn. bd., 1972—, now chmn. exec., fin. cons. dir. Served as pilot USNR, 1942-45. Decorated Air medal with oak leaf cluster. Office: K Mart Corp 3100 W Big Braver Rd Troy MI 48084

DEWART, LESLIE SUTHERLAND, educator, philosopher, lawyer; b. Madrid, Spain, Dec. 12, 1922; s. Gerardo and Adamina (Duarte) Gonzalez; m. Joanne McWilliam, Aug. 26, 1954 (div. Aug. 1972); children: Leslie, Elizabeth, Sean, Colin; m. Doreen Brennan, Aug. 20, 1976. B.A., U. Toronto, 1951, M.A., 1952, Ph.D., 1954; LL.B., 1979. Teaching fellow dept. philosophy St. Michaels Coll., U. Toronto, 1952-54, asst. prof., 1956-61, asso. prof., 1961-68, prof. faculty theology, 1968-69, prof. dept. religious studies, 1968—, prof., 1969-78, prof. faculty of theology, 1979—; chmn. combined depts. religious studies, 1970-71; instr. dept. philosophy U. Detroit, 1954-56; prof. Toronto Grad. Sch. Theol. Studies (now Toronto Sch. Theology), 1968—. Author: Christianity and Revolution, 1963, The Future of Belief, 1966, The Foundations of Belief, 1969, Religion, Language and Truth, 1970; Asso. editor: Continuum, 1964-71, Internationale Dialog Zeitschrift, 1967-78, Concurrence, 1968-70; Contbg. editor: The Ecumenist, 1968—; Editorial bd.: Studies in Religion-Sciences Religeuses, 1970-80; Contbr. articles profl. jours. Served to flying officer RCAF, 1942-47. Recipient Can. Council Research grant, 1970. Mem. Société Europeenne de Culture, Europeénne de Culture, Canadian Soc. for Study Religion. Address: 14 Prospect St Toronto ON M4X 1C6 Canada

DEWBERRY, LAWRENCE GLENN, JR., steel executive; b. Atlanta, Sept. 7, 1919; s. Lawrence Glenn and Florence (Bowen) D.; m. Sylvia Snow, Aug. 14, 1942; children: Lawrence Glenn III, Lewis S. Student, Ga. State U., Atlanta, 1939-40; Asso. Sci. in Indsl. Tech., So. Tech. Inst., 1949. With Atlantic Steel Co., Atlanta, 1949—, v.p. operations, 1961-63, exec. v.p., 1963-65, pres., 1965-78, chmn., chief exec. officer, 1978—, also dir.; chmn. exec. com. Atlantic Bldgs. Systems, Inc. Mem. NAM (past dir.), Am. Iron and Steel Engrs., Am. Iron and Steel Inst. (dir.), Ga. Bus.-Industry Assn. (past pres., dir.). Methodist. Club: Rotary. Office: Atlantic Steel Co PO Box 1714 Atlanta GA 30301 *

DEWBRE, J. W., lawyer, business executive; b. May, Tex., Dec. 31, 1933; s. John Henry and Zula Faye (Williams) D.; m. Anna Victoria Cranmer, Nov. 22, 1973; 1 son, Jonathan Owen. B.S., Tex. A&M U., 1955; LL.B., So. Meth. U., 1963. Bar: Tex. With Republic Nat. Life Ins. Co., 1960-81, computer programmer, systems analyst, 1960-63, atty., 1963-66, asst. counsel, 1966-72, asso. counsel, 1972-75, v.p., asso. counsel, 1975-77, head legal div., 1977, sr. v.p., gen. counsel, 1978-80, exec. v.p., gen. counsel, 1980-81; v.p., regional counsel USLife Corp., 1981—; sr. v.p., gen. counsel Gt. Nat. Life Ins. Co., Dallas, 1981—; mem. adv. com. Tex. State Bd. Ins. Contbr. profl. jours. Served to 1st lt. U.S. Army. Mem. Dallas Assn. Life Ins. Counsel, Assn. Life Ins. Counsel, Am. Judicature Soc., Internat. Assn. Ins. Counsel, ABA, Tex. (chmn. corp. counsel sect.), Dallas, Tex. Aggie bar assns., Phi Delta Phi. Republican. Club: Austin (Tex.). Home: 13335 Rolling Hills Ln Dallas TX 75240 Office: 6500 Harry Hines Dallas TX 75235

DEWEESE, DAVID DOWNS, physician, surgeon, emeritus educator; b. Columbus, Ohio, Mar. 16, 1913; s. Bernard D. and Vilette Downs (Gilfillan) DeW.; m. Mary Dorothy Jones, June 24, 1938 (dec. Aug. 1974); adopted children: Diane Downs, Dana Evelyn; m. Edna Elaine Kuckenberg, July 19, 1975; stepchildren: Peter William, Karen Anna. A.B., U. Mich., 1934, M.D., 1938. Diplomate: Am. Bd. Otolaryngology (pres. 1972-76). Intern U. Hosp., Ann Arbor, Mich., 1938-39, resident otolaryngology, 1939-40; instr. otolaryngology U. Mich. Med. Sch., 1941-44, U. Oreg. Med. Sch., 1944-45, clin. prof., 1951-61, chmn. dept. otolaryngology, 1958-79, prof., 1961-80, prof. emeritus, 1980—; trustee Health Scis. Center Found., 1975-78; otolaryngologist Portland (Oreg.) Clin., 1944-61; Bd. dirs. Portland Center for Hearing and Speech, 1947—, pres., 1949-59, med. dir., 1958—; chmn. communicative disorders research tng. com. NIH, 1965-66, mem. dirs. adv. com., 1982—; mem. adv. council Nat. Inst. Neurol. Diseases and Stroke, 1968-70; Bd. dirs. U. Oreg. Med. Sch. Advancement Fund, v.p., 1971-75. Sr. author: Textbook of Otolaryngology, 1960, 6th edit., 1982; Editorial bd.: AMA Archives of Otolaryngology, 1961-64, Laryngoscope, 1972—. Trustee Marylhurst Coll., 1965-74. Jr. fellow ACS; mem. AMA, Ore., Multnomah County med. socs., Oreg. Acad. Ophthalmology and Otolaryngology (pres. 1958), Pacific Coast Oto-Ophthal. Soc. (pres. 1964), Am. Laryngol., Rhinol., Otol. Soc. (pres. 1974-75), Am. Acad. Ophthalmology and Otolaryngology (2d v.p. 1957-58), Portland Acad. Medicine, Am. Otol. Soc., Am. Broncho-Esophageal Assn., Am. Laryngol. Assn., Soc. Univ. Otolaryngologists (pres. 1968), Am. Council Otolaryngology (dir. 1968-74), Soc. Acad. Chairmen Otolaryngology, Sigma Chi (Significant Sig 1979), Nu Sigma Nu (nat. pres. 1959- 60), Alpha Omega Alpha. Clubs: Waverly Country, Golf, Multnomah Athletic, Rotary, Arlington. Home: 1200 SW 61st Dr Portland OR 97221

DEWEESE, MARION SPENCER, educator, surgeon; b. Corydon, Ind., Aug. 17, 1915; s. Arville Otis and Vergie (Jenkins) DeW.; m. Helen Sosnoski, June 25, 1941; children—Diane Hope, Dawn Cheryl, Pamela Lea. B.A., Kent State U., 1935; M.D., U. Mich., 1939, M.S. in Surgery, 1948. Intern, then resident gen. surgery U. Mich. Hosp., 1939-41, 45-48; instr., then asst. prof. surgery U. Mich. Med. Sch., 1948-51; pvt. practice gen. surgery, San Diego, 1951-53; asso. prof., then prof. surgery U. Mich. Med. Sch., 1953-64; prof. surgery, chmn. dept. U. Mo. Med. Sch., 1964-74; also W. Alton Jones distinguished prof.; clin. prof. surgery U. Mich., 1974—; practice gen. and vascular surgery, Ann Arbor; chief surgery Ann Arbor VA Hosp., 1953-56; chief staff St. Joseph Mercy Hosp., Ann Arbor, 1979-81. Contbr. profl. jours. Served to lt. col. M.C. AUS, 1941-45. Mem. A.C.S., Am., Central, Western, So. surg. assns., Soc. Vascular Surgery, Internat. Cardio-Vascular Surgery Soc., AMA, Am. Acad. for Surgery Trauma, Am. Burn Assn., Soc. for Surgery Gastrointestinal Tract, others. Home: 2229 Glendaloch Ann Arbor MI 48104 Office: 3505 E Huron River Dr Ypsilanti MI 48197

DEWELL, MICHAEL, theatre executive, writer, producer; b. West Haven, Conn., Mar. 21, 1931; s. Mansfield Humphrey and Minnie (Dwy) D.; m. Nina Foch, Oct. 31, 1967. B.A., Yale U., 1952; M.A., U. London, 1953; R.A.D.A., Royal Acad. Dramatic Arts, London, 1954. Stage mgr. Cherry Lane Theatre, N.Y.C., 1954-56; writer-producer Sta. WRAMC-TV, Dept. Def., Washington, 1956-58; producer Nat. Phoenix Theatre, N.Y.C., 1958-60; founder, producer Nat. Repertory Theatre Found., N.Y.C., 1961-67, pres., Los Angeles, 1969—; producer Nat. Repertory Theatre at Ford's Theatre, Washington, 1967-68; bd. dirs., mem. exec. com. Am. Nat. Theatre and Acad., N.Y.C., 1960-68; adviser N.Y. State Arts Council, Albany, 1962-64; trustee Co. Theatre Found., Los Angeles, 1968-71; founder, trustee, mem. exec. com. Free Shakespeare Festival, Los Angeles, 1973; founder, pres. Los Angeles Free Pub. Theatre Found., 1974. Producer: Broadway plays, musicals The Crucible, 1964, The Seagull, 1964, Tonight at 8:30, 1967, A Touch of the Poet, 1967, The Imaginary Invalid, 1967; opera The Turn of the Screw, Am. premier at Am. Festival, Boston, 1961; touring plays Once Upon a Mattress, 1959-60, Mary Stuart, 1958-59, 61-62, Ring Around the Moon, 1963-64, Elizabeth the Queen, 1961-62, The Trojan Women, 1965-66, The Madwoman of Chaillot; As You Like It, 1973, Macbeth, 1974, Comedy of Errors, 1974; nat. TV prodns. CBS All-Star Gala, Inaugural Night at Ford's, 1968; translator: (with Carmen Zapata) plays Blood Wedding, 1979; Yerma, 1981 (Drama Logue award 1981), House of Bernarda Alba, 1982; contbr. articles on theatre to newspapers and mags., N.Y. Herald Tribune, Dallas News, Boston Globe; editor: short-story anthology Hell and High Water, 1956; asst. editor, Yale Rev., 1950-52; editorial asst.: Time and Tide, London, 1953-54; mng. editor: Man's Mag., Challenge Mag., N.Y.C., 1954-56; author: narration for compiliation film Ole Hollywood, 1981. Trustee, mem. exec. com. El Peublo Park Assn., Los Angeles, 1983—; trustee Bilingual Found. of Arts, Los Angeles, 1977—, sec., Los Angeles, 1982-83, v.p., Los Angeles, 1982—. Recipient Antoinette Perry award Am. Theatre Wing, N.Y.C., 1965, Outer Circle award Nat. Critics N.Y.C., 1959, 65. Club: University (Los Angeles). Office: Nat Repertory Theatre Found PO Box 71011 Los Angeles CA 90071

DEWERTH, GORDON HENRY, media company executive; b. Milw., Sept. 3, 1939; s. Henry Andrew and Elizabeth Barbara (Schlitt) DeW.; m. Karen Lillian Overson, July 7, 1962; children: Julie, Christine, Amy. B.B.A., U. Wis., 1961; M.B.A., Bradley U., 1964. Asst. to treas. Jos. Schlitz Brewing Co., Milw., 1968-71; asst. treas. ITT Grinnell, Providence, also mgr. pension fund trust ITT, N.Y.C., 1971-76; treas. Macmillan, Inc., N.Y.C., 1976-82; sr. v.p. fin., treas. Cowles Media Co., Mpls., 1982—. Served with U.S. Army, 1961-63. Mem. N.Y. Treasurers Group, Mensa. Lutheran. Home: 17105 5th Ave N Plymouth MN 55447 Office: 329 Portland Ave Minneapolis MN 55415

DEWEY, ARTHUR EUGENE, diplomat; b. Mainesburg, Pa., Feb. 18, 1933; s. Glenn Cecil and Florence (Tice) D.; m. Priscilla ann Parce, June 24, 1956; 1 dau., Elisabeth Parce. B.S.E., U.S. Mil. Acad., 1956; M.S.E., Princeton U., 1961; postgrad., Grad. Inst. Internat. Studies, Geneva, Switzerland, 1972-73. Enlisted U.S. Army, 1956, advanced through ranks to col., 1973, ret., 1981; White House fellow Dept. State, Washington, 1968-69, dir. Pres's Commn. on White House Fellowships, 1971-72, dep. asst. sec. Bur. Refugee Program, 1981—; v.p. Bus. Consortium for Gifted and Talented, Washington, 1981—. Decorated Legion of Merit, D.F.C., Def. Superior Service medal, Army Commendation medal. Mem. Internat. Inst. Strategic Studies. Republican. Presbyterian. Club: Army and Navy (Washington). Home: 5219 Westbard Ave Bethesda MD 20816 Office: Dept State 2201 C St NW Washington DC 20520

DEWEY, DONALD ODELL, univ. dean; b. Portland, Oreg., July 9, 1930; s. Leslie Hamilton and Helen (Odell) D.; m. Charlotte Marion Neuber, Sept. 21, 1952; children—Leslie Helen, Catherine Dawn, Scott Hamilton. Student, Lewis and Clark Coll., 1948-49; B.A., U. Oreg., 1952; M.S., U. Utah, 1956; Ph.D., U. Chgo., 1960. Mng. editor Condon (Oreg.) Globe-Times, 1952-53; city editor Ashland (Oreg.) Daily Tidings, 1953-54; asst. editor, asso. editor The Papers of James Madison, Chgo., 1957-62; instr. U. Chgo., 1960-62; asst. prof., asso. prof., prof. Calif. State U., Los Angeles, 1962—, dean, 1970—. Author: The Continuing Dialogue, 2 Vols, 1964, Union and Liberty: Documents in American Constitutionalism, 1969, Marshall versus Jefferson: The Political Background of Marbury v. Madison, 1970. Recipient Outstanding Prof. award Calif. State U., 1976. Mem. Am. Hist. Assn. (mem. exec. council Pacific Coast br. 1971-74), Orgn. Am. Historians, Am. Soc. Legal History (adv. bd. Pacific Coast br.), Phi Alpha Theta, Pi Sigma Alpha, Sigma Delta Chi, Phi Kappa Phi. Home: 3891 Hampstead Rd Flintridge CA 91011 Office: Dept History Calif State U Los Angeles CA 90032

DEWEY, DONALD WILLIAM, magazine editor and publisher, author; b. Honolulu, Sept. 30, 1933; s. Donald William and Theckla Jean (Engeborg) D.; m. Sally Rae Ryan, Aug. 7, 1961; children: Michael Kevin, Wendy Ann. Student, Pomona Coll., 1953-55. With Pascoe Steel Corp., Pomona, Calif., 1955-56, div. Reynolds Aluminum Co., Los Angeles, 1956-58, Switzer Panel Corp., Pasadena, Calif., 1958-60; sales and gen. mgr. Western Pre-Cast Concrete Corp., Ontario, Calif., 1960-62; editor, pub. R/C Modeler Mag., Sierra Madre, Calif., 1963—, Freshwater and Marine Aquarium Mag., Sierra Madre, 1978—; pres., chmn. bd. R/C Modeler Corp., Sierra Madre, 1963—. Author: Radio Control From the Ground Up, 1970, Flight Training Course, 1973, For What It's Worth, Vol. 1, 1973, Vol. 2, 1975; contbr. articles to profl. jours. Sustaining mem. Rep. Nat. Com., 1981—; charter mem. Nat. Congl. Club, 1981—; mem. Rep. Presdl. Task Force, 1981—, 1984 Presdl. Trust, Conservative Caucus, Nat. Tax Limitation Com., Nat. Conservative Polit. Action Com. Served with Hosp. Corps, USN, 1951-53. Mem. Oceanic Soc., AAAS, Internat. Oceanograpnic Found., Internat. Assn. Aquatic Animal Medicine, Fedn. Am. Aquarium Socs., Am. Philatelic Soc., Nat. Rifle Assn., Am. Topical Assn., Marine Aquarium Soc., APS Writers Unit 30, Nat. Trust for Historic Preservation, Am. First Day Cover Soc., United Postal Stationery Soc., Confederate Stamp Alliance, Am. Air Mail Soc., Bur. Issues Assn., Am. Revenue Assn., C.Z. Study Group, Pitcairn Islands Study Group, Pet Industry Joint Adv. Council, Sierra Madre Hist. Soc., Friends of Sierra Madre Library, U.S. Naval Inst., Internat. Betta Congress, Nat. Fisheries Assn., Am. Killifish Assn., Am. Catfish and Loach Assn., Am. Wildlife Fedn. Republican. Episcopalian. Home: 410 W Montecito Ave Sierra Madre CA 91024 Office: 120 W Sierra Madre Blvd Sierra Madre CA 91024

DEWEY, LEWIS WILLIAM, JR., corporate executive; b. Milw., June 16, 1934; s. Lewis William and Marion Louise (Coke) D.; m. Ann Heizer McMaster, Feb. 28, 1976. B.A., U. Wis., Madison, 1956. Export sales rep. Outboard Marine Corp., Waukegan, Ill. and Nassau, Behamas, 1956-60; asst. export mgr. Briggs & Stratton Corp., Milw., 1960-66, mgr. internat. sales, 1966-72, v.p. internat. sales, 1972-76, v.p. sales and service, 1976-77, exec. v.p., 1977—, also dir.; dir. 1st Wis. Trust Co., 1st Wis. Nat. Bank, DEC Internat., Inc., Mgmt. Resources Assocs. Bd. dirs. Elmbrook Meml. Hosp., Milw. Symphony Orch.; trustee Alverno Coll. Mem. Outdoor Power Equipment Inst., Engine Service Assn., World Trade Assn. Milw., Inc., YMCA. (dir.). Clubs: Univ., Western Racquet, Chenequa Country. Home: 1205 Lakeside Dr Elm Grove WI 53122 Office: PO Box 702 Milwaukee WI 53201

DEWEY, PHELPS, newspaper executive; b. Mpls., Mar. 23, 1928; s. Maurice Adams and Alice (Wheelwright) D.; children: Richard, (dec.) Susan, Kimberley, Peter. Student, Dartmouth, 1947-48. Promotion dir. San Francisco Chronicle, 1953-60; press relations mgr. Los Alamos Sci. Lab., 1960-62; promotion mgr. Chgo. Daily News/ Chgo. Sun Times, 1962-63; promotion dir. San Francisco Chronicle, also gen. mgr. Chronicle Features Syndicate, 1963-65, San Francisco Newspaper Printing Co., 1965-70; gen. mgr. Chronicle Books div. Chronicle Pub. Co., 1965-77; asst. pub. San Francisco Chronicle, 1978—; v.p. dir. Chronicle Videotex, Inc.; dir. San Francisco Newspaper Agy., Planetree, Inc. Mem. Golden Gate Nat. Parks Assn. (dir.), Calif. Newspaper Pubs. Assn. (dir.), Round Valley Conservation League (pres.). Office: 901 Mission St San Francisco CA 94103

DEWEY, ROBERT MANSON, JR., investment company executive; b. Bronxville, N.Y., July 1, 1931; s. Robert Manson and Helen (Sjoblom) D.; m. Rowena Bauer, Sept. 20, 1958 (div. 1970); children: Robert Manson III, Grant G., Bradley M.; m. Harriet Blees, Dec. 19, 1981. B.A. in History, Yale U., 1953. Adminstrv. asst. Citicorp, N.Y.C., 1954-59; v.p. State Nat.Bank Conn., Stamford, 1959-64; sr. v.p., dir. Laird Inc., N.Y.C., 1964-72, F.S. Smithers & Co., 1972-74; mng. dir. Donaldson Lufkin & Jenrette, Inc., N.Y.C., 1974—; dir. Donaldson Lufkin & Jenrette Securities Corp.; dir. Telecredit Inc., Los Angeles. Served with USNR, 1953-54. Mem. New Canaan C. of C. (pres. 1962-63). Republican. Club: New Canaan Country (Conn.). Office: Donaldson Lufkin & Jenrette 140 Broadway New York NY 10005

DEWHURST, CHARLES KURT, museum director, curator, folklorist; b. Passaic, N.J., Dec. 21, 1948; s. Charles Allaire and Minn Jule (Hanzl) D.;; m. Marsha MacDowell, Dec. 15, 1972; 1 dau., Marit Charlene. B.A., Mich. State U., 1970, M.A., 1973, Ph.D., 1983. Editorial asst. Carlton Press, N.Y.C., 1967; computer operator IBM, N.Y.C., 1968; head advisor Mich. State U., East Lansing, 1970-74; project dir. Mich. State U. Mus., 1975, curator, 1976-83, dir., 1982—; guest curator Mus. Am. Folk Art, N.Y.C., 1978-83, Artrain, Detroit, 1980-83; visual arts panelist Mich. Council Arts, Detroit, 1981-83; cons. City of Cleve., 1983. Auhtor: Reflections of Faith, 1983; author: Artists in Aprons, 1979, Rainbows in the Sky, 1978, Michigan Folk Art, 1976 (Am. Assn. State and Local History award 1977). Mus. profl. grantee Smithsonian Instn., Scandinavia, 1978; project grantee Mich. Council Humanities, 1979-80, Nat. Endowment Humanities, 1979-83, Nat. Endowment Arts, 1982. Mem. Am. Folklore Soc., Mich. Folklore Soc., Midwest Soc. Lit., Popular Culture Assn., Mich. Hist. Soc. Democrat. Roman Catholic. Home: 212 N Harrison St East Lansing MI 48823 Office: The Museum Michigan State U Circle Dr East Lansing MI 48824

DEWHURST, COLLEEN, actress; b. Montreal, Que., Can., June 3; m. James Vickery, 1947 (div. marriage dissolved); m. George C. Scott; 2 sons. Student, Downer Coll., Milw., Am. Acad. Dramatic Art; pupil of Harold Clurman and Joseph Anthony. First profl. appearance in The Royal Family, 1946; Broadway appearances include Desire Under the Elms, 1952, Tamberlain the Great, 1956, Camille, 1956, The Eagle Has Two Heads, 1957, The Country Wife, 1957, All the Way Home, 1960, Great Day in the Morning, 1962, Ballad of the Sad Cafe, 1963, Taming of the Shrew, The Eagle Has Two Heads, Macbeth, Hello and Goodbye, Good Woman of Setzuan, Children of Darkness, Moon for the Misbegotten, The Big Coca-Cola Swamp in the Sky, Mourning Becomes Electra, An Almost Perfect Person, The Queen and the Rebels, The Dance of Death, You Can't Take It With You; appearances with, N.Y. Shakespeare Festival; motion picture appearance in The Nun's Story, 1959, The Cowboys, 1972, McQ, 1974, Annie Hall, 1977, Ice Castles, 1979, When a Stranger Calls, 1977, Final Assignment, 1980, Tribute, 1980; dir.: Broadway play Ned and Jack, 1981; numerous TV appearances, 1957— (Recipient Obie award 1957, 63, Lola D'Annunzion award 1961, Tony award 1961, 74, Sylvania award 1960, Theatre World award, Sarah Siddons award for A Moon for the Misbegotten 1974). Address: care STE Representation Ltd 1776 Broadway New York NY 10019 *

DEWHURST, STEPHEN, government official, lawyer; b. N.Y.C., Aug. 1, 1942; s. Henry S. and Jeanne A. (Dunne) D.; m. Miriam E. Petty, May 18, 1974. B.A., George Washington U., 1964, J.D., 1967. Bar: D.C. 1967. With Office Budget and Program Analysis, U.S. Dept. Agr., Washington, 1966-68, 70—, asst. dir. ops. revs., 1974-76, dep. dir. program revs., 1976-78, dir., 1978—. Served with U.S. Army, 1968-70. Decorated Army Commendation medal; recipient cert. of merit Dept. Agr., 1973, 77, Presdl. award as meritorious exec. Dept. Agr., 1980. Mem. ABA, Am. Assn. for Budget and Program Analysis (pres.-elect). Home: 3237 Dye Dr Falls Church VA 22042 Office: US Dept Agr 14th and Independence Ave Washington DC 10150

DEWILDE, DAVID MICHAEL, lawyer, financial services executive; b. Bridgeton, N.J., Aug. 11, 1940; s. Louis and Dorothea (Donnelly) deW.; m. Sally Stockdale (div.); children: Holland Stockdale, Christian Ducroix. A.B., Dartmouth Coll., 1962; LL.B., U. Va., 1967. Bar: N.Y. 1968, D.C. 1972. Assoc. Curtis, Mallet-Prevost, Colt & Mosle, N.Y.C., 1967-69; assoc. gen. counsel Dept. HUD, Washington, 1969-72; investment banker Lehman Bros., Washington, 1972-74; dep. commr. FHA, Washington, 1974-76; pres. Govt. Nat. Mortgage Assn., Washington, 1976-77; mng. dir. Leperc and DeNeuflize & Co., N.Y.C., 1977-81; exec. v.p. policy and planning Fed. Nat. Mortgage Assn., Washington, 1981-82; pres. deWilde & Assocs., Washington, 1982—. Served to lt. USN, 1962-64. Office: deWilde & Assocs Suite 370 2501 M St NW Washington DC 20037 *Loving and living have made my life fulfilling.*

DE WIND, ADRIAN WILLIAM ANDREWS, lawyer; b. Chgo., Dec. 1, 1913; s. Norman and Ethel (Andrews) De W.; m. Joan Elizabeth Mosenthal, June 21, 1941; children—Barbara (Mrs. Edward Fiske Mooney), Adrian William Andrews, Susan (Mrs. Robert R. Kesner), John Stone. A.B., Grinnell (Iowa) Coll., 1934; student, U. Paris, Sorbonne, 1932-33; LL.B., Harvard U., 1937; LL.D., CCNY, 1976. With Sage, Gray, Todd & Sims, N.Y.C., 1937-43; with U.S. Treasury Dept., 1943-48, asst. tax legis. counsel, 1945-47, tax legis. counsel, 1947-48; mem. firm Paul, Weiss, Rifkind, Wharton & Garrison, 1948—; lectr. taxation N.Y. U. Sch. Law, 1948-54; chief counsel, subcom. on adminstrn. of internal revenue laws Com. on Ways and Means, Ho. of Reps., Washington, 1951-52; mem. Pres.'s Task Force on Tax Policy, 1961; mem. adv. group to Commr. Internal Revenue, 1966-67; mem. Mayor's Task Force on N.Y. Constnl. Conv., 1967; del. Democratic Nat. Conv., 1968; chmn. spl. task force on taxation Council on Economy of N.Y., 1976; Bd. dirs. Revson Found., Inc. Contbr. articles to legal periodicals. Bd. dirs., mem. exec. com. NAACP Legal Def. and Ednl. Fund, Inc.; bd. dirs. New World Found., Nat. Com. Against Discrimination in Housing, Com. for Modern Cts., Lawyer's Com. for Civil Rights Under Law, Lawyers' Com. for Internat. Human Rights; chmn. bd. dirs. Natural Resources Def. Council; trustee New Sch. Social Research; bd. visitors CCNY. Fellow Am. Bar Found., N.Y. Bar Found.; mem. Am. Law Inst., Am. Bar Assn., N.Y. County Lawyers Assn., Assn. Bar City N.Y. (v.p. 1975-76, pres. 1976-78), N.Y. State Bar Assn., Fed. Bar Council. Sherman CT 06784 also RFD 2 Stowe VT 05672 Office: 345 Park Ave New York NY 10022

DE WINDT, EDWARD MANDELL, manufacturing executive; b. Great Barrington, Mass., Mar. 31, 1921; s. Delano and Ruth (Church) de W.; m. Betsy Bope, June 21, 1941; children: Pamela, Delano II, Dana, Elizabeth, Edward Mandell. Student, Williams Coll., 1939-41. With Eaton Corp., Cleve., 1941—, gen. mgr. stamping div., 1954-59, v.p. sales, 1959-61, group v.p. internat., 1961-66, pres., 1967-69, chmn. bd., 1969—, also dir., chief exec. officer; mem. exec. com., dir. Ohio Bell Telephone Co.; dir. Dart & Kraft, Inc., Fed. Res. Bank Cleve., Sears, Roebuck and Co., Allstate Ins. Co., UAL, Inc., United Airlines, Inc. Trustee Cleve. Ednl. TV Assn., Cleve. Clinic; bd. dirs. United Way Am., Berkshire Sch., Univ. Sch., NCCJ. Decorated comdr. Order Brit. Empire; commendatore Italian Republic. Mem. Soc. Automotive Engrs., Soc. Cin., Am. Soc. Corp. Execs., Bus. Council. Clubs: Union, Tavern, Pepper Pike Country, Kirtland (Cleve.); Bloomfield Hills (Mich.) Country, Augusta (Ga.) Nat.; Blind Brook (N.Y.); Laurel Valley (Ligonier, Pa.); Links (N.Y.C.); Seminole, Jupiter Island (Fla.). Office: 100 Erieview Plaza Cleveland OH 44114 *

DE WITT, EUGENE A., advertising agency executive; b. Norwalk, Conn., Feb. 3, 1943; s. Albert W. and Anna (Astrab) DeW.; m. Juliana Fera, July 31, 1965. A.B. magna cum laude, Tufts U., 1965. Media planner, buyer Dancer-Fitzgerald-Sample, Inc., N.Y.C., 1965-66; broadcast buyer BBDO, Inc., N.Y.C., 1966; asst. media dir. Ogilvy & Mather, Inc., N.Y.C., 1966-71; exec. v.p., dir. media and bus. affairs Rosenfeld, Sirowitz & Lawson, Inc., N.Y.C., 1971-77; sr. v.p., dir. media and network programming BBDO, Inc., N.Y.C., 1978-79; exec. v.p., dir. U.S.A. media services McCann Erickson, Inc., 1979—. Mem. Am. Assn. Advt. Agencies (mem. media policy com., media tng. subcom.), Advt. Research Found. (mem. media communications council). Home: 106 W 74th St New York NY 10023 Office: 485 Lexington Ave New York NY 10017

DE WITT, JESSE R., clergyman; b. Detroit, Dec. 5, 1918; s. Jesse A. and Bessie G. (Mainzinger) DeW.; m. Annamary Horner, Apr. 19, 1941; children—Donna Lee (Mrs. William Wegryn), Darla Jean (Mrs. William Inman). B.A., Wayne State U., 1948; B.D., Garrett Theol. Sem., 1948; D.D., Adrian Coll., 1965, Northland Coll., 1976, Wiley Coll., 1981; H.H.D. (hon.), North Central Coll., 1977. Ordained deacon, received in full membership Methodist Ch. (Detroit conf.), 1945, ordained elder, 1948; student pastor, 1944-46; minister Aldersgate Ch., Detroit, 1946, Faith Ch., Oak Park, Mich., 1952-58; exec. sec. Detroit Conf. Bd. Missions, 1958-67, dist. supt., 1967-70; asst. gen. sec. sect. ch. extension Nat. Bd. Missions, 1970-72; bishop United Meth. Ch., resident bishop, 1972-80, bishop, 1980—; del. gen. conf. Meth. Ch., 1964, 66, 68, 70, 72, 76; past epis. rep. Commn. on Status and Role Women; epis. rep. Consultation on Ch. Union, Bd. Ch. and Society (other coms. and task forces); pres. nat. div. Bd. Global Ministries, 1976-80, pres., 1980—; past pres. North Central jurisdiction Coll. Bishops; chmn. pastoral concerns com. Council Bishops, United Meth. Ch. Trustee North Central Coll., Naperville, Ill., Garrett Evang. Sem.; bd. dirs. No. Ill. Conf., Meth. Youth Services, Marcy-Newberry Assn., United Meth. Homes and Services, Lake Bluff-Chgo. Homes for Children. Address: No Ill Conf United Meth Ch 77 W Washington St Suite 1806 Chicago IL 60602

DE WITT, JOYCE, actress; b. Wheeling, W.Va., Apr. 23, 1949. B.A., Ball State U.; M.F.A., UCLA. Directed, staged and starred in dinner theatre musicals; performed in summer theatre, Rockford, Ill.; co-star: TV series Three's Company, 1977—; other TV appearances include With This Ring, Baretta, Tony Randall Show; TV spls. include John Ritter, Being of Sound Mind and Body, others. Office: care ABC Public Relations 1330 Ave of Americas New York NY 10019 *

DE WITT, LEW CALVIN, song writer; b. Roanoke, Va., Mar. 12, 1938; s. L.C. and Rose E. (Hogan) De W.; m. Judy Wells, Feb. 16, 1980; children: Denver Dale, Donna Kay, Brain Zachary, Shannon Lee. With Statler Bros., Nashville, 1955—, v.p. prodn., 1973—; v.p. Am. Cowboy, Nashville, 1973—. Songs include Just in Time, 1965, Samson, 1971, Is That What You'd Have Me Do, 1969, Flowers on the Wall, 1963, So This Is Love, 1970, Pictures, 1970, Ten Commandments, 1967, The Strand, 1973, The Boy Inside of Me, 1972, The Kingdom of Heaven is at Hand, 1974, The Dreamer, 1974, The Teacher, 1975, The Song of Solomon, 1975, Things, 1972, Thank You World, The Movies, Quite a Long Long Time, others. Recipient Grammy and Country Music Assn. awards. Office: care Dick Blake Internat 38 Music Sq E Nashville TN 37203 *

DEWITT, PAUL BURTON, lawyer; b. Sheldon, Iowa, Apr. 15, 1910; s. Jesse Arthur and Pearl (Monk) DeW.; m. Else Hvistendahl, May 31, 1943; 1 son, Jon Lance. A.B., A.M., U. Iowa, 1931; A.M., Harvard, 1934; LL.B., U. Mich., 1937. Bar: Iowa bar 1937, N.Y. bar 1969. Practiced with Shull and Marshall, Sioux City, 1937-38; chief legislative drafting bur. and state law librarian State of Iowa, 1939-40; asst. sec. Am. Judicature Soc., Ann Arbor, Mich., 1941; reporter, rules com. Supreme Ct. Iowa, Des Moines, 1941-42; exec. sec. Assn. of Bar City of N.Y., 1945-81; sec. Nat. Conf. of Judicial Councils, 1941. Editor: Annual Handbook Nat. Conf. of Jud. Councils. Served as lt. USNR, 1942-46; now lt. comdr. Recipient medal Assn. Bar City N.Y., 1970. Mem. Am. Bar Assn. (alternate del. to UN 1946, sec. spl. com. on improving jud. adminstrn., chmn. sect. bar activities 1947-49, dir. state coms., sect. jud. adminstrn. 1948-51, mem. ho. of dels.), Iowa Bar Assn. (sec. 1941-42), Phi Beta Kappa, Phi Delta Theta. Episcopalian. Club: Century (N.Y.). Home: 601 E 20th St New York NY 10010

DEWITT, THOMAS DAVID, filmmaker; b. N.Y.C., Aug. 11, 1944; s. David and Madlyn (Weiner) DeW. Student, Columbia Coll., 1962-65; B.A., San Francisco State Coll., 1968. Partner TaV Media Prodns. (WTV Video Group.); adj. research assoc. SUNY, Albany, 1974—; artist in residence WNET-TV Lab, 1974-78; artist Electronic Body Arts, Inc., 1978—; adj. research assoc. Image Processing Lab. Rensselaer Poly. Inst., 1982—. Films include Fall, 1971, Cathode Ray Theater, 1974, CRT, 1975, Zierot in Outta Space, 1978, This is TV-America, 1979, TeleVisions, 1981, The Video Artist, 1982. Bd. dirs. Albany Community Video Project, 1976-79. Guggenheim Found. fellow, 1978-79; Nat. Endowment Arts grantee, 1975-79. Address: Box 83 Ancramdale NY 12503

DE WITT-MORETTE, CÉCILE, physicist; b. Paris, Dec. 21, 1922; U.S., 1948; d. André and Marie Louise (Ravaudet) Morette; m. Bryce S. DeWitt, Apr. 26, 1951; children—Nicolette, Jan, Chris, Abigail. B.S., U. Caen, 1943; Ph.D., U. Paris, 1947. With Centre Nat. de la Recherche Sci., 1944-65; prof. Maitre de Confs., 1965—; mem. Inst. Advanced Studies in Dublin, 1946-47, Copenhagen, 1947-48, Princeton, 1948-50; lectr. U. Calif. at Berkeley, 1952-55, U. N.C., Chapel Hill, 1956-71; prof. astronomy U. Tex., 1972—; founder, dir. Ecole d'ete de Physique Theorique, Les Houches, France, 1951-72. Author: Particules Elementaires, 1951, (with Y. Choquet-Bruhat and M. Dillard-Bleick) Analysis, Manifolds and Physics, 1977, rev. edit., 1981, (with A. Maheshwari, B. Nelson) Path Integration in Non Relativistic Quantum Mechanics, 1979; also articles. Rask-Oersted fellow, 1947-48. Fellow Am. Phys. Soc.; mem. Internat. Astron. Union, European Phys. Soc. Home: 3300 Jamesborough Austin TX 78703 Office: Dept Astronomy U Tex Austin TX 78712

DEWOLFE, JOHN CHAUNCEY, JR., lawyer; b. Chgo., June 9, 1913; s. John Chauncey and Mabel (Spafford) DeW.; m. Dorothy Fulton, May 9, 1942; children: John Chauncey, III, George F. B.S., U. Ill.; J.D., U. Wis., 1939. Bar: Wis. 1939, Ill. 1940. Ptnr. firm DeWolfe, Poynton & Stevens and predecessor firms, 1946—. Contbr. articles to profl. jours. Trustee Village of Riverside, Ill., 1963-70; Chmn. West Suburban Mass Transit Dist., 1974-76; trustee Knock Research Found. Served from lt. to maj. AUS, 1942-45, 51-52; lt. col. USAR ret. Mem. Am., Ill., Wis. bar assns., Chgo. Bar Assn. (chmn. corp. law com. 1973-74), Bar Assn. 7th Fed. Circuit, Assn. Trial Lawyers Am., SAR, Sigma Phi Epsilon. Republican. Episcopalian. Clubs: Chgo. Yacht, Univ. (Chgo.). Home: 1448 N Lake Shore Dr Chicago IL 60610 Office: 135 S La Salle St Chicago IL 60603

DEWS, PETER BOOTH, medical researcher, educator; b. Eng., Sept. 11, 1922; came to U.S., 1948, naturalized, 1957; s. George Ashley and Ella (Booth) D.; m. Grace Miller, Dec. 6, 1949; children: Pamela, Kenneth, Alan, Michael. M.B., Ch.B., U. Leeds, Eng., 1944; Ph.D., U. Minn., 1952; M.A. (hon.), Harvard, 1959. House physician Grimsby (Eng.) Dist. Hosp., 1944-45; lectr. pharmacology U. Leeds, 1945-47; Wellcome research fellow, Tuckahoe, N.Y., 1948-49; fellow, then research asso. physiology and biometrics Mayo Clinic, Rochester, Minn., 1950-52; instr. to asso. prof. pharmacology Harvard Med. Sch., Boston, 1953-62, Stanley Cobb prof. psychiatry and psychobiology, 1962—; Mem. adv. coms. NIH, USPHS, NASA. Editorial bd. jours. in field.; Contbr. articles profl. jours. Fellow Am. Acad. Arts and Scis.; mem. Physiol. Soc., Am. Soc. Pharmacology and Exptl. Therapeutics., Inst. of Medicine. Home: 181 Upland Rd Newtonville MA 02160 Office: 25 Shattuck St Boston MA 02115

DEWSBURY, DONALD ALLEN, comparative psychologist; b. Bklyn., Aug. 11, 1939; s. Edwin Leroy and Carol Wieler (Neil) D.; m. Joyce Ruth Kraekel, June 8, 1963; children: Bryan Bradley, Laura Alison. A.B., Bucknell U., 1961; Ph.D., U. Mich., 1965. NSF postdoctoral fellow U. Calif., Berkeley, 1965-66; mem. faculty dept. psychology U. Fla., Gainesville, 1966—, prof., 1973—, mem. Center for Neurobiol. Scis., 1967—. Author: Comparative Animal Behavior, 1978; Editor: (with D. Rethlinghshafer) Comparative Psychology: A Modern Survey, 1973, (with T. McGill, B. Sachs) Sex and Behavior: Status and Prospectus, 1978. Mem. Animal Behavior Soc. (pres. 1978-79), Am. Psychol. Assn., Psychonomic Soc., Am. Soc. Mammalogists, Am. Soc. Zoologists, Behavior Genetics Assn., AAAS, Fla. Acad. Scis., Phi Beta Kappa, Psi Chi. Home: 840 NW 20th St Gainesville FL 32603 Office: Dept Psychology Univ of Fla Gainesville FL 32611

DEXTER, DONALD HARVEY, surgeon; b. Maywood, Ill., Apr. 8, 1928; s. Harry Malcolm and Theodora Jane (Trelawny) D.; m. Esther Ruth Reeve, May 16, 1953; children: Donald Harvey, Scott Reeve, Bryce Malcolm, Margaret Helen. B.S., Tulane U., 1948; M.D., Northwestern U., 1950. Diplomate: Am. Bd. Surgery. Intern Cook County Hosp., Chgo., 1950-51; resident in surgery Ill. Central Hosp., Chgo., 1951-52, Cook County Hosp., 1955-58; practice medicine specializing in surgery, Macomb, Ill., 1958—; sr. mem. Macomb Clinic; prof. dept. health scis. Western Ill. U., 1975—; team physician; coroner McDonough County, Ill., 1964-76. Mem. Western Ill. U. Found. Served with USNR, 1953-54. Named Outstanding Citizen of Macomb Jaycees, 1972, Macomb Area C. of C., 1973; recipient award of recognition Devel. Center of Western Ill. U. and Macomb Area C. of C., 1977. Fellow A.C.S. (pres. Ill. chpt. 1972, gov.-at-large Ill. chpt. 1983—, state chmn. field liaison program commn. on cancer, 1983—); mem. AMA, Ill. Med. Soc., Ill. Surg. Soc., M.W. Surg. Assn., Internat. Assn. Coroners and Med. Examiners, Phi Beta Kappa. Republican. Episcopalian. Club: Rotary. Home: Tower Rd Rural Route 1 Macomb IL 61455 Office: Macomb Clinic 505 E Grant St Macomb IL 61455

DEXTER, JOHN, opera, stage and film director, 0; b. Derby, Eng., Aug. 2, 1925; s. Harry James and Rose D. Dir., English Stage Co.; dir.: plays Yes - and After, 1957, Each in His Wilderness, 1958, Chicken Soup with Barley, 1958, Roots, 1959, The Kitchen, 1959, This Year, Next Year, 1960, I'm Talking About Jerusalem, 1960, South, 1961, The Keep, 1961, England, Our England, 1962, The Blood of the Bambergs, 1962, Jackie the Jumper, 1963; assoc. dir., Nat. Theatre, 1963-66, 71-75; dir.: Saint Joan, 1963, Hobson's Choice, Othello, Royal Hunt of the Sun, 1964, Armstrong's Last Goodnight, 1965, Black Comedy, 1965, The Storm, 1966, A Woman Killed with Kindness, 1971, Tyger, 1971, The Misanthrope, 1973, Equus, N.Y.C., 1973, 74, The Party, 1973, Phaedra Britannica, 1975, Do I hear a Waltz?, N.Y.C., 1965, Benevenuto Cellini, 1966, Black Comedy and White Lies, N.Y.C., 1967, Wise Child, 1967, The Old Ones, 1972, In Praise of Love, 1973, Equus, N.Y.C., 1974, Pygmalion, 1974; prodns. of Un Ballo in Maschera, Hamburg State Opera, I Vespri Siciliani, Hamburg State Opera, From the House of the Dead, Hamburg State Opera, Boris Godurov, Hamburg State Opera, Billy Budd, Hamburg State Opera; Sadler's Wells Opera prodn. The Devils of Loudon; Nat. Theatre prodn. Gallileo, 1980, Shoemaker's Holiday, 1981; Paris Opera prodn. I Vespri Siciliani; prodn., Met. Opera, N.Y.C., 1974—; prodns. include Le Prophete, Dialogues of the Carmelites, Lulu, 1976-77, Rigoletto, 1977-78, Billy Budd, The Bartered Bride, Don Pasquale, Don Carlo, 1978-79, Die Entfuhrung aus dem Serail, 1979, The Rise and Fall of the City of Mahagonny, Don Carlo, 1979, Parade, 1981, Stravinsky, 1981, The Portage to San Cristobal, 1982; films The Virgin Soldiers, 1969, The Sidelong Glances of a Pigeon Kicker, 1970, I Want What I Want, 1972. Recipient Tony award for Best Dir. of a Drama, 1975. Office: Metropolitan Opera Lincoln Center New York NY 10023

DEXTER, LEWIS, physician; b. Concord, Mass., Mar. 1, 1910; s. Smith Owen and Helen (Denison) D.; m. E. Cassandra Kinsman, Dec. 12, 1941; children—Lewis, Smith Owen, Cassandra Kinsman Short. B.A., Harvard, 1932, M.D., 1936. Diplomate: Am. Bd. Internal Medicine. Intern Presbyn. Hosp., N.Y.C., 1936-38; staff mem. Peter Bent Brigham Hosp., 1941—, physician, 1952—; faculty mem. Med. Sch., Harvard, 1941—; tutor medicine, 1948—; prof. medicine Peter Bent Brigham Hosp., 1969-76, prof. emeritus hosp. and med. sch., 1976—; prof. emeritus U. Mass. Sch. Medicine, 1980—. Fellow A.C.P. under Doctor Bernardo A. Houssay Inst. Physiology, Buenos Aires, Argentina, 1940-41. Fellow ACP, Am. Coll. Cardiology; mem. Am. Soc. Clin. Investigation, Assn. Am. Physicians, Am. Heart Assn., Am. Physiol. Soc., Am. Acad. Arts and Scis., Am. Clin. and Climatological Assn., N.Y. Acad. Scis., Assn. Univ. Cardiologists, Brit. Cardiac Soc. (corr.); hon. mem. Argentine, Peruvian socs. cardiology, Argentine Med. Assn. Club: Interurban Clin. Home: 108 Upland Rd Brookline MA 02146 Office: 75 Francis St Boston MA 02115

DEYOUNG, LILLIAN JEANETTE, nurse, edn. adminstr.; b. Ogden, Utah, July 26, 1926; d. Peter and Gertrude (Dallinga) DeY. R.N., Dee Meml. Sch. Nursing, Utah, 1947; B.S. in Nursing Edn, U. Utah, 1950; M.S. in Ednl. Adminstrn, U. Utah, 1955, Ph.D., 1975. Asso. dir. nursing edn. Latter Day Saints Hosp., Salt Lake City, 1954-55; dir. Sch. of Nursing, instr. St. Luke's Hosp. Sch. of Nursing, Denver, 1955-72; asso. prof., curriculum coordinator Intercollegiate Center for Nursing Edn., Spokane, Wash., 1972-73; asst. dir. nursing service U. Utah Med. Center, Salt Lake City, 1973-75; prof., dean Coll. of Nursing, U. Akron, Ohio, 1975—; cons. Duquesne U. Sch. Nursing, 1980, Youngstown State U. Dept. of Nursing, 1979; mem. State of Ohio Bd. of Nursing Edn. and Nurse Registration, 1979—, v.p., 1980—. Author: Dynamics of Nursing, 4th edit, 1981. Active ARC. Isobel Robb scholar, 1974-75; recipient pearl pin Am. Nurses Assn., 1972; named Colo. Nurse of Yr., 1965. Mem. Ohio League for Nursing, Ohio Nurses Assn. (dir. 1977-81), Am. Assn. Collegiate Nursing (by—laws com. 1980—). Mormon. Office: College of Nursing Univ Akron Akron OH 44325 *Throughout my life, I have prepared myself academically, experientially, and spiritually to accept any challenge required of me as I focused my entire life to the cause of Nursing as a profession.*

DEYOUNG, MELVIN HOWARD, insurance executive; b. Salt Lake City, Nov. 2, 1928; s. Henry and Marion C. (Smith) DeY.; m. Kathryn Jean Beckstead, Dec. 11, 1953; children: Howard Lynn, Sandra Kay, Bryan Garth. B.S. in Math. and Acctg, U. Utah, 1961. Insp. Pacific Fire Rating Bur. (Utah Office), 1954-63; mgr. schedule rating, 1963-68; adminstrv. asst. Nat. Ins. Actuarial and Statis. Assn., N.Y.C., 1968-70; asst. mgr. actuarial (Ins. Services Office), N.Y.C., 1970-72, asst. gen. mgr., 1974-75; pres., gen. mgr. Am. Assn. Ins. Services, Chgo., 1975—. Contbr. articles on ins. to profl. publs. Served with USAAF, 1947-50. Mem. Nat. Assn. Mut. Ins. Cos. (dir. 1977-83), Profl. Ins. Agents Am., Ind. Ins. Agts., Soc. of Ins. Research (research com. 1978-82), Soc. Planning Execs., Alliance Am. Insurers. Mormon. Office: 1035 S York Rd Bensenville IL 60106 *I have always been guided by my convictions for better or worse. Education, discipline and work habits have been difficult to master. I have worked extra hard to achieve "success." I believe it has been this extra effort, mixed with confidence in myself, integrity, respect for others, and faith, that has guided my life to my present position.*

DEYOUNG, RUSSELL, rubber company executive; b. Rutherford, N.J., Apr. 3, 1909; s. Abram and May (Thompson) DeY.; m. Lois E. Bishop, May 1, 1937; children: Bruce Russell, Ralph Earl, Janet Lois (Mrs. James Mungo). B.S., Akron U., 1932, D.Sc., 1960; M.S., M.I.T., 1940. With Goodyear Tire & Rubber Co., Akron, Ohio, 1928—, v.p.,

1956-58, pres., 1958-64, chmn. bd., 1964-74, chief exec. officer, 1964-74, chmn. exec. and finance com., 1974-79; dir. First Fla. Banks, LTV Corp.; Mem. corp. M.I.T. Clubs: Portage Country (Akron); Naples Yacht, Royal Poinciana Golf (Naples, Fla.). Home: 2777 Gulf Shore Blvd N Naples FL 33940

DEZEMBER, RAYBURN STUART, banker; b. Evansville, Ind., Jan. 24, 1931; s. Larry O. and Dalpha Fay (Haley) D.; m. Joan Erreca, Sept. 11. 1954; children: Rebecca, Brent, Cherilee, Kathleen. B.A. in Sociology, Whittier Coll., 1953. Chmn., pres. Am. Nat. Bank, Bakersfield, Calif., 1967-83, chmn., 1983—, Bakersfield Ready Mix Inc., 1967—; owner Service Transport Inc., Bakersfield, 1966—; chmn., pres., chief exec. officer Central Pacific Corp., Bakersfield, 1981—; dir. Bakersfield Californian Newspaper, Fed. Res. Bank San Francisco Los Angeles br., 1972-77, Fed. Res. Bank San Francisco, 1984—; mem. Stanford Ado Group, Palo Alto, Calif., 1975-77. Bd. dirs. Pacific Coast Banking Sch. U. Wash.-Seattle, 1972-78; bd. trustees Whittier Coll., (Calif.), 1970—, Kern High Sch. Dist., Bakersfield, 1968-80. Mem. Bank Adminstrn. Inst. (bd. dirs., exec. com., chmn. 1983—), Am. Bankers Assn. (leadership council 1982-83), Calif. Bankers Assn. (pres. 1980-81, bd. dirs 1983—). Republican. Congregationalist. Clubs: Jonathan (Los Angeles); Stockdale County (Bakersfield). Lodge: Elks. Office: Central Pacific Corp PO Box 5500 5016 California Ave Bakersfield CA 93309

DHALIWAL, RANJIT SINGH, mathematician, educator; b. Bilaspur, India, June 21, 1930; s. Bharpur Singh and Bachan Kaur (Grewal) D.; m. Gurdev Kaur, July 1, 1958; 1 son, Gurminder Singh. M.A., Punjab U., 1955; Ph.D., Indian Inst. Tech., Kharagpur, 1960. Lectr. Indian Inst. Tech., New Delhi, 1961-63, asst. prof., 1963-66; asso.prof. U. Calgary, Alta., Can., 1966-71, prof. math., 1971—; visitor Imperial Coll. Sci. and Tech., London, 1964-65; vis. prof. City U. London, 1971-72. Author book; contbr. articles to profl. jours. Mem. Am. Math. Soc., Soc. Indsl. and Applied Math., Can. Math. Congress, London Math. Soc. Home: 44 Patterson Dr Calgary AB Canada Office: Dept Math U Calgary Calgary AB Canada

DHANAK, AMRITLAL MAGANLAL, engineering educator; b. Bhavnagar, India, July 13, 1925; came to U.S., 1947, naturalized, 1953; s. Maganlal Sojabhai and Nathiben (Valera) D.; m. Harriet Cook, Aug. 28, 1954; children: Eric, Lynn, Michelle. B.Sc., Royal Inst. Sci., Bombay, 1947; B.S., U. Calif. at Berkeley, 1950, M.Engring., 1951, Ph.D., 1956. Asso. mech. engring., research engr. U. Calif. at Berkeley, 1950-56; project engr. Gen. Electric Co., Schenectady, 1956-58; asso. prof. Rensselaer Poly. Inst., Troy, N.Y., 1958-61; prof. mech. engring. Mich. State U., East Lansing, 1961—; cons. to industry. Sir. Jaswantsinghji scholar U. Bombay, India, 1943-46. Mem. ASME (exec. com. tech. and soc. div. 1974—), Internat. Solar Energy Soc., Sigma Xi. Home: 333 University Dr East Lansing MI 48823

DHARMAPURI, VIDYASAGAR, pediatrician, medical educator; b. India, Aug. 16, 1939; came to U.S., 1963, naturalized, 1979; s. Chakradhara Swamy and Venkatamma D.; m. Nagamani R. Beligere, June 6, 1968; children: Sahana, Sadhana, Sanjay. M.B.B.S., Osmania Med. Coll., Hyderabed, 1961; M.S.C. in Physiology, U. Man., Can., 1971. Diplomate: Am. Bd. Pediatrics. Intern Vassar Hosp., Poughkeepsie, N.Y., 1963-64; resident in pediatrics Grassland Hosp., Valhalla, N.Y., and Albany Med. Center, 1964-65, Pitts. Children's Hosp., 1965-66; fellow in neonatology Pa. Hosp. and Phila. Children's Hosp., 1965-68; teaching fellow U. Man., 1971; asso. dir. nurseries Cook County Hosp., Chgo., 1971-74; dir. newborn nurseries U. Ill. Med. Center, Chgo., 1974—, prof. pediatrics and ob-gyn, 1977—, dir. neonatology, 1974—. Editorial bd.: Perinatology/Neonatology Jour. Pres. Hindu Temple Greater Chgo., 1977-79; mem. adv. bd. India Abroad Found. Fellow Royal Coll. Physicians and Surgeons Can.; mem. Am. Thoracic Soc., Royal Soc. Medicine, Soc. Critical Care Medicine (council, pres.-elect), Soc. Pediatric Research, Chgo. Lung Assn., Am. Pediatric Soc., Midwest Soc. Pediatric Research, Chgo. Pediatric Soc., Perinatal Research Soc. Home: 804 Wild Wood Ct Oak Brook IL 60521 Office: 840 S Wood St Chicago IL 60612

D'HARNONCOURT, ANNE, museum curator; b. d., Rene, D'Harnoncourt; Sarah, Carr, naturalized, D'Harnoncourt; m. Joseph J. Fishel, June 19, 1971. B.A., Radcliffe Coll., 1965; M.A. with distinction, Courtauld Inst. Art, U. London, 1967. Curatorial asst. Phila. Mus. Art, 1967-69, curator 20th Century painting, 1971—; asst. curator 20th Century art Art Inst. Chgo., 1969-71. Organizer: (with McShine) exhbn. Marcel Duchamp, 1973-74, (with others) Philadelphia: Three Centuries of American Art, 1976, Eight Artists, 1978, (with Percy) Violet Oakley, 1979, Futurism and the International Avant-Garde, 1980, (with Sims) John Cage: Scores and Prints, 1982; author: (with Walter Hopps) Etant Donnes...Reflections on a New Work by Marcel Duchamp, 1969, The Cubist Cockatoo: Preliminary Exploration of Joseph Cornell's Hommages to Juan Gris, 1978. Office: Phila Mus Art 26th St and Benjamin Franklin Pkwy PO Box 7646 Philadelphia PA 19101

DHRYMES, PHOEBUS JAMES, economist, educator; b. Cyprus, Oct. 1, 1932; s. Demetrios and Kyriaki (Neophytou) Dhrymiotis; m. Beatrice Bell Fitch, Dec. 10, 1972; children: Phoebus James, Philip Andrew, Alexander Robert. B.A. with highest honors, U. Tex., 1957; Ph.D., M.I.T., 1961. Asst. prof. econs. Harvard U., 1962-64; assoc. prof. econs. U. Pa., 1964-67, prof., 1967-73; prof. econs. Columbia U., N.Y.C., 1973—. Author: Econometrics: Statistical Foundations and Applications, 1971, 74, Distributed Lags: Problems of Estimation and Formulation, 1971, 81, Russian edit., 1982, Introductory Econometrics, 1978, Mathematics for Econometrics, 1978, 2d edit., 1984; Mng. editor, editor: Internat. Econ. Review, 1965-72; co-editor: Jour. Econometrics, 1972-77. Served with U.S. Army, 1952-54. Fellow Econometric Soc., Am. Statis. Assn.; mem. Am. Econ. Assn. Office: Dept Econs Columbia Univ New York NY 10027

DIAB, GEORGE, television executive; b. Moundsville, W.Va., Mar. 4, 1924; s. George S. and M.J. (Azaar) D.; m. Catherine A. Scherrer, Jan. 24, 1953; children: Barbara, Robert, Stephen. B.S.J., Ohio U., 1949. Vice pres. Sta. WTRF-TV, Wheeling, W.Va., 1953-69; v.p., gen. mgr. Sta. WCHS-TV, Charleston, W.Va., 1969-70; v.p. Rollins Inc. Broadcasting, Atlanta, 1970-71; pres. Clay Broadcastings, Sta. WWAY-TV, Wilmington, N.C., 1971—, Sta. KFDX-TV, Wichita Falls, Tx, 1971—, Sta. KJAC-TV, Port Arthur, Tex., 1971—, Sta. WAPT-TV, Jackson, Miss., 1971—; v.p., dir. Clay Communications, Inc. Bd. dirs. Salvation Army, Wilmington, 1975-78, U. N.C.-Wilmington Student Aid Assn., 1979—. Served to sgt. U.S. Army, 1942-45; ETO. Named Outstanding Broadcaster Phoenician Club, Wheeling, 1954, Disting. West Virginian Gov. of W.Va., 1970. Mem. N.C. Assn. Broadcasters (v.p.), Wilmington C. of C. (dir. 1980). Republican. Roman Catholic. Club: Cape Fear Country (Wilmington). Office: WWAY-TV PO Box 2068 Wilmington NC 28402

DIAL, MORSE GRANT, JR., chemical company executive; b. Watertown, N.Y., June 21, 1925; s. Morse Grant and Ethelwyn D.; m. Mary Taylor Johnston, Aug. 5, 1965. A.B., Princeton U., 1949; J.D., Columbia U., 1952. Bar: N.Y. 1953. With firm Kelley, Drye, Warren, Clark, Carr & Ellis, N.Y.C., 1953-54; with Union Carbide Corp., N.Y.C., 1954—, v.p., 1973—, sec., 1976—; Mem. econs. adv. bd. Columbia U. Grad. Sch. Bus. Served with USNR, 1943-45. Mem. Bus.-Govt. Relations Council, Inst. Jud. Adminstrn. (fin. com.), Mgmt. Policy Council, Phi Delta Phi. Address: Old Ridgebury Rd E4 Danbury CT 06817

DIAL, OLIVER EUGENE, political scientist, educator; b. Woodriver, Ill., Nov. 10, 1922; s. Oliver Lee and Julia Lavina (Botkin) D.; m. Bette Jeanne Wynkoop, Dec. 28, 1944; 1 son, Oliver Eugene. LL.B., Blackstone Coll. Law, 1954; B.A., San Diego State Coll., 1959, M.S. in Pub. Adminstrn, 1962; Ph.D. in Polit. Sci. (Sch. fellow), Claremont Grad. Sch., 1965. Time motion study engr. Owens Ill. Glass Co., Alton, 1940-42; commd. 2d lt. U.S. Marine Corps., 1942, advanced through grades to maj., 1953; ret., 1963; lectr. govt. San Diego State Coll., 1963-64; asst. prof. govt. Calif. Poly. U., San Luis Obispo, 1964-65; chmn. dept. govt. Idaho State U., 1965-68; vis. prof. polit. sci., mem. staff Urban Systems Lab., Mass. Inst. Tech., 1968-69; mem. faculty Joint Center Urban Studies, Harvard U., 1968-69; chmn. dept. polit. sci., supr. grad. program pub. adminstrn. Baruch Coll. City U. N.Y., 1969-70; prof. urban affairs U. Colo. Grad. Sch. Pub. Affairs, 1973-81; prof. elec. engring. U. Colo., 1981—; cons. fed. intergovtl. agys. com. urban regional info. systems, Washington, 1968-80. Author: Programming and Statistics for Basic Research, 1969, Bibliography on Urban Affairs, 1970, (with Kraemer, Mitchell, Weiner) Municipal Information Systems: The State of the Art in 1970, 1971, Integrated Municipal Information Systems: The USAC Approach, 1972, Integrated Municipal Information Systems: The Use of the Computer in Local Government, 1973, (with Goldberg) Privacy, Security, Computers and the City: Guidelines for Municipal Information Systems, 1974; Editor: policy forum info. systems dedication Bureaucrat, 1972; editor: Urban Geocoding, 1975; Contbr. numerous articles to profl. publs. and popular computer mags. Mem. Am. Bar Found. (adv. com. land records improvement 1973—), Urban Regional Info. Systems Assn. (pres. 1979-80), Am. Polit. Sci. Assn., AAUP, Am. Soc. Pub. Adminstrn., AAAS. Home: 7086 Indian Peaks Boulder CO 80301 *Much of my life has been, and continues to be, as a student. When I consider the diversity of subjects I have studied, I am deeply impressed with the surprising contribution each has made at one time or another to the solution of a problem, or to the introduction of a valued opportunity. What one has done in the past is much like seeds planted and forgotten; yet, time and time again to be harvested in unexpected times and places.*

DIAL, WILLIAM HENRY, banker; b. Lake City, Fla., Dec. 12, 1907; s. John Clarke and Katie Belle (Woltz) D.; m. Grace Franklin, Feb. 9, 1935; children: Joan (Mrs. E. Daniel Ruffier), Patricia (Mrs. Peter Vig). LL.B., U. Fla., 1932. Bar: Fla. bar 1932. Practiced in, Orlando, 1932-58; mem. firm Akerman, Dial & Akerman; atty. Fla. Bankers Assn., 1946-58; of counsel Akerman, Senterfitt & Eidson (and predecessor), 1974—; exec. v.p. First Nat. Bank, Orlando, 1958-61, pres., 1961-68, chmn. bd., 1968—, also dir.; chmn. Sun Banks of Fla., Inc., 1967-74, chmn. exec. com., 1974-77. Author: Florida Banking Code, 1953, History of the Banking Laws of Florida, 1953. Chmn. bd. United Appeal, Orange County, 1961; mem. Fla. Council 100, 1962-75, Fla. Road Bd., 1955-58, Fla. Bd. Control, 1953-54; former mem. regional adv. com. 6th Nat. Bank Region, Comptroller of Currency, treas. Central Fla. Devel. Com., 1963; mem. adv. bd. Fla. Inst. Tech., 1967—. Served to lt. col. AUS, World War II. Mem. Orange County Bar Assn. (past pres.), Orlando Area C. of C. (past pres.), Am. Bankers Assn., Fla. Bankers Assn. (pres. 1966-67). Presbyn. (deacon). Clubs: Rotarian., Orlando Country, Executives, University, Citrus. Home: 1059 Edgewater Dr Orlando FL 32804 Office: PO Box 231 Orlando FL 32802

DIAMANDOPOULOS, PETER, educator; b. Irakleion, Crete, Greece, Sept. 1, 1928; came to U.S., 1948, naturalized, 1964; s. Theodore George and Rita (Mouzenides) D.; m. Maria Blackstock, 1980; children: Theodore, Cybele, Ariadne. Diploma with honors, Athens Coll., 1947; B.A. cum laude, Harvard, 1951, M.A., 1956, Ph.D., 1957. Instr. philosophy Bates Coll., 1958; instr., then asst. prof. philosophy U. Md., 1958-62; mem. faculty Brandeis U., 1962-77, prof. philosophy, 1964-77, dean faculty, 1965-71, chmn. dept. philosophy and history of ideas, 1972-76, faculty mem. bd. trustees, 1974-77; pres. Sonoma State U., Rohnert Park, Calif., 1977-83; Univ. Trustees' prof. Calif. State U., San Francisco, 1983—; dir. studies, fellow Adlai Stevenson Inst., Chgo., 1969-74; cons. history of sci. Smithsonian Instn., 1959-61. Mem. Am. Philol. Assn., Am. Philos. Assn., Mind Assn., Aristotelian Soc., Hellenic Soc., AAAS. Office: Trustees Prof Calif State U care San Francisco State U San Francisco CA 94132

DIAMANT, ALFRED, educator; b. Vienna, Austria, Sept. 25, 1917; came to U.S., 1940, naturalized, 1942; s. Ignatz and Julia (Herzog) D.; m. Mary Ann Redmon, Mar. 18, 1943; children—Steven R., Alice L. Student, Textilschule Vienna, 1935-36; A.B. with highest honors, Ind. U., 1947; M.A., Yale, 1950, Ph.D., 1957. Textile engr., Austria, Yugoslavia, U.S., 1936-38, 40-42; from instr. to assoc. prof. polit. sci. U. Fla., 1950-60; assoc. prof. to prof. polit. sci. Haverford Coll., 1960-67, chmn. dept., 1963-67; prof. polit. sci. and west European studies Ind. U., Bloomington, 1967—, chmn. dept., 1977-80, dir. grad. studies, 1969-71, dir. West European studies program, 1971-77; Vis. assoc. prof. polit. sci. Yale U., 1958-59, Columbia, summer 1961; vis. prof. Ruhr U. Bochum, 1966-67, U. Alta., 1983; co-chmn. (Council for European Studies), 1976-79; cons. U.S. Office Edn., 1965-66, sr. research asso. European adminstrn. research project, 1966-70. Author: Austrian Catholics and the First Republic: Democracy, Capitalism and the Social Order, 1918-34, 1960 (trans. into German, Italian 1964), Modellbetrachtung der Entwicklungsverwaltung, 1967; co-author: Temporal Dimensions of Development Administration, 1970, Frontiers of Developmental Administration, 1971, Sozialstruktur and Politik in Frankreich, 1976, Worker's Self-Management: The West European Experience, 1977, The Cost of Federalism, 1984; Asso. mng. editor: Jour. Politics, 1950-55; editorial bd., 1968-74, Adminstrn. and Society, 1968—; Contbr. chpts. to 7 books, numerous articles to profl. jours. Served to 1st lt. AUS, 1942-45. Decorated Purple Heart, Bronze Star.; Tchr. study grantee Danforth Found., 1955; Fulbright travel grantee, 1966; Guggenheim fellow, 1973-74; Fulbright sr. research grantee, 1973-74; AMOCO Teaching award, 1975; guest scholar Brookings Instn., 1980-81. Mem. Am. Polit. Sci. Assn., Midwest Polit. Sci. Assn. (v.p. 1971-72), AAUP (chmn. Haverford Coll. chpt. 1962-64), Phi Beta Kappa. Democrat. Episcopalian. Home: 2033 Montclair Ave Bloomington IN 47401

DIAMENT, PAUL, electrical engineering educator, consultant; b. Paris, Nov. 14, 1938; U.S., 1948; s. Zajwel Matys and Rywka (Szmerlowska) D.; m. Carol Goldstein, July 7, 1963; children: Edith Zoe, Theodore Mathis, Benjamin Jay. B.S., Columbia U., 1960, M.S., 1961, Ph.D., 1963. Asst. prof. elec. engring. Columbia U., N.Y.C., 1963-69, assoc. prof., 1969-76, prof., 1976—; research assoc. Stanford U. (Calif.), 1966-67; vis. assoc. prof. Tel Aviv U., 1970-71; mem. research staff IBM, Yorktown Hieghts, N.Y., 1974, Yorktown Heights, N.Y., 1982; cons. in field. Contbr articles to profl. jours. Mem. Am. Phys. Soc., Optical Soc. Am., IEEE(sr.), Sigma Xi, Tau Beta Pi, Eta Kappa Nu. Home: 148 Wellington Ave New Rochelle NY 10804

DIAMOND, ABEL JOSEPH, architect; b. S.Africa, Nov. 8, 1932; naturalized, 1969; s. Jacob and Rachel (Werner) D.; m. Gillian Mary Huggins, Aug. 11, 1959; children: Andrew Michael, Alison Suzanne Katherine. B.Arch. with distinction, U. Capetown, 1956; M.A., U. Oxford, 1958; M.Arch., U. Pa., 1962. Certificate Nat. Registration Bds. U.S.A. Partner Diamond & Hallen, S.Africa, 1959-61; architect office of Louis Kahn, Phila., 1962-64; pvt. practice architecture, Toronto, Ont., Can., 1965—; prin. A.J. Diamond and Ptnrs. (Architects and Planners), Toronto, 1975—; asst. prof. U. Pa., 1962-64; asso. prof. U. Toronto, 1964-69; adj. prof. York U., 1969-72. Editorial bd.: Canadian Forum, 1976-79; archtl. works include York Sq, Toronto, Ont. Med. Assn. Hdqrs, Student Union Housing, U. Alta., Citadel Theatre, Edmonton, Innis Coll. U. Toronto, Hydro Block Housing, Toronto, 322 King St W, Arvida Med. Clinic for Alcan, Village Terraces Housing, Toronto, Alcan Exec. Offices, Toronto, Montreal, Cleve, Central YMCA, Toronto, Berkeley Castle, Toronto, Burns Bldg, Calgary. Adv. bd. Taragon Theatre, 1978-79; registration bd. Ont. Assn. Architects, 1976-79; chmn. vis. com. Schs. of Architecture, Ont. Recipient Oxford Rugby Blue. Fellow Royal Archtl. Inst. Can.; asso. Royal Inst. Brit. Architects; mem. Can. Inst. Planners, Am. Inst. of Planners, Royal Can. Acad. Arts. Clubs: Vincents (Oxford); University (Toronto). Office: 2 Berkeley St Toronto ON M5A 2W3 Canada

DIAMOND, BERNARD LEE, educator, psychiatrist; b. San Francisco, Dec. 8, 1912; s. Leon Isaac and Rose (Cohen) D.; m. Ann Landy, Feb. 10, 1946; children: Joan, Lynn (Mrs. Alan Feiger), Larry, Lisa, Judy, Jan. A.B., U. Calif. at Berkeley, 1935; M.D., U. Calif. at Berkeley and San Francisco, 1939. Intern, resident psychiatry U. Mich. Neuropsychiat. Inst., 1938-40, 41-42; grad. San Francisco Psychoanalytic Inst., 1952; pvt. practice psychiatry and psychoanalysis, San Francisco, 1945-64; faculty U. Calif. at Berkeley, 1963—, prof. law, 1964-80, emeritus, 1980—, clin. prof. psychiatry, 1968—, acting dean Sch. Criminology, 1969-70, 74-76; dir. Dr. of Mental Health program U. Calif.-San Francisco, 1981—; Mem. Calif. Commn. Insanity and Criminal Offenders, 1960-63. Contbr. articles to profl. jours. Bd. advisers Atascadero State Hosp., 1974-76. Served to lt. col. M.C. AUS, 1940-41, 42-45. Recipient J. Elliot Royer award U. Calif., 1964; Gold medal award Mt. Airy Found., 1972. Fellow AAAS, Am. Psychiat. Assn. (Isaac Ray award 1968), Am. Orthopsychiat. Assn. (bd. dirs. 1968-71); mem. Am. Bd. Forensic Psychiatry (dir. 1978-82), Am. Sociol. Assn., Am., Internat. psychoanalytic assns., Am. Acad. Psychiatry and Law (Golden Apple award 1975), No. Calif. Psychiat. Soc. (past pres.). Home and Office: PO Box 999 Ross CA 94957

DIAMOND, CORA ANN, philospher, educator; b. N.Y.C., Oct. 30, 1937; d. Abraham and Sylvia (Goldhaar) D. B.A., Swarthmore Coll., 1957; B.Phil., Oxford U., 1961. Asst. lectr. Univ. Coll. Swansea, 1961-62, U. Sussex, 1962-63; lectr. moral philosophy U. Aberdeen (Scotland), 1963-71; assoc. prof. philosophy U. Va., 1971-82, prof. philosophy, 1982—. Editor: Wittgenstein's Lectures on the Foundations of Mathematics, 1976; co-editor: (with Jenny Teichman) Intention and Intentionality, Essays in Honour of G.E.M. Anscombe, 1979. Fellow Am. Council Learned Socs., 1976-77, Woodrow Wilson Found., 1957-58. Mem. Am. Philos. Assn., Aristotelian Soc. Home: 655 Kearsarge Circle Charlottesville VA 22901 Office: Dept Philosophy U Va Charlottesville VA 22901

DIAMOND, DAVID LEO, composer; b. Rochester, N.Y., July 9, 1915; s. Osias and Anna (Schildhaus) D. Student, Cleve. Inst. Music, 1927-29, Eastman Sch. Music (U. Rochester), 1930-34, Am. Conservatory, Fountainebleau, France, summers 1937, 38, New Music and Dalcroze Inst., N.Y. C., 1934-36. Tchr. composition Met. Music Sch., N.Y.C., 1950; lectr. on Am. music Seminar in Am. Studies Schloss Leopoldskron, Salzburg, Austria, 1949; Fulbright prof. U. Rome, 1951-52; Slee prof. music U. Buffalo, 1961, 63; prof., chmn. dept. composition Manhattan Sch. Music, N.Y.C., 1965-67; vis. prof. U. Colo., Boulder, 1970; composer-in-residence Am. Acad. in Rome, 1971-72, Juilliard Sch. Music, 1973; vis. prof. U. Denver, 1983. Contbr. to: Music Jour; compositions include 8 symphonies, concertos, 11 string quartets, chamber music, 52 preludes and fugues for the piano, sonatas, choral music and songs, scores for motion pictures, and other forms of instrumental music; composer music for: Columbia albums Fourth String Quartet; Romeo and Juliet, 4th Symphony; composer, condr.: original score for Margaret Webster prodn. of The Tempest, 1944-45; also incidental music for Cheryl Crawford prodn. of Tennessee Williams' The Rose Tatoo, 1962; music for This Sacred Ground (setting of Lincoln's Gettysburg Address), 1962; commd. works include: The Noblest Game, Nat. Opera Inst., Secular Cantata (James Agee poems), N.Y. State Arts Council, Second Sonata for Violin and Piano, Library of Congress McKim Fund; works performed by major orchs. and other well known music orgns., throughout U.S. and abroad. Recipient numerous major awards and prizes, 1935—, including; Prix de Rome; Paderewski award; Guggenheim fellow, 1938, 42, 58; Juilliard Pub. award; Stravinsky award ASCAP; Naumberg Rec. award for Nonet and String Quartet No. 9; Nat. Endowment for Arts grantee.; Rockefeller Found. grantee, 1983. Mem. Nat. Inst. of Arts and Letters. Home: 249 Edgerton St Rochester NY 14607 *To have felt out of step in one's first years confirms one's invalidism in these last years: a sad story at best, with just a glimmer of hope before the next catastrophe.*

DIAMOND, DONALD, professional basketball team executive. V.p. Phoenix Suns, NBA. Office: care Phoenix Suns 2910 N Central Phoenix AZ 85012

DIAMOND, FRED I., electronic engineer; b. Bklyn., Dec. 13, 1925; s. Joseph and Celia (Just) D.; m. Edna R. Hutt, Sept. 2, 1956; children: Celia, Joel, Shari. S.B.E.E., MIT, 1950; M.E.E., Syracuse U., 1953, Ph.D., 1966. Electronic engr. Rome Air Devel. Center, Griffiss AFB, N.Y., 1950-51, sr. scientist, 1961-70, chief plans, 1970-73, tech. dir. communications and control div., 1973-81, chief scientist, 1981—; chmn. avionics panel NATO Adv. Group for Aerospace Research and Devel.; U.S. leader communications subgroup Australian, Canadian, N.Z., U.K., U.S. Tech. Coordination Program; instr. dept. math. Utica Coll., 1957-59; lectr. dept. elec. engring. Syracuse U., 1959-61; Mem. ednl. council MIT, 1968—. Contbr. articles to profl. jours. Bd. dirs. Rome Community Concert Assn., 1968-80; trustee Jervis Public Library, 1977—, pres., 1980-83; mem. indsl. adv. com. U. Mass. Sch. Engring., dept. engring. Rensselaer Poly. Inst. Served with U.S. Army, 1944-46. Recipient Meritorious Civilian Service medal U.S. Air Force, 1968, decoration for exceptional civilian service, 1978. Fellow IEEE, AAAS, AIAA (asso.). Club: Lake Delta Yacht. Office: Rome Air Devel Center Griffiss AFB NY 13441

DIAMOND, FREDA, designer, home furnishings consultant, lecturer; b. N.Y.C.; d. Jack and Ida (Levine) D.; m. Alfred Baruch. Grad., Woman's Art Sch., Cooper Union; hon. degree, Cooper Union, 1975; study archtl., decorative design in, France, Eng., Italy, Belgium, Sweden, Denmark. Designer, home furnishings products cons., stylist, coordinator dept. stores and mfrs. in, U.S., Mexico, Europe, India and South Africa; Sent to Italy as tech. adviser rehab. of Italian craftsmen, after World War II, went to Japan as adviser to Japanese Govt., 1957, 68, adviser for Am. trade and indsl. devel. with Israel, 1969, 73, adviser retailers, mfrs. govts., India, USSR, Czeckoslovakia, South Africa, Dominican Republic; lectr., adviser World Trade Inst. Export Industry and Trade Devel. Program for developing countries, 1973-81; lectr. seminars. Author: The Story of Glass, 1953; Contbg. author: Your Future in the Fashion World; designs displayed, Mus. Modern Art, N.Y.C., Toledo Mus., Akron (Ohio) Art Inst., Avery Mus., Hartford, Conn., also Paris Expn. Mem. Am. Soc. Interior Designers,

Indsl. Designer Soc. Am., Nat. Home Fashions League, The Fashion Group. Address: 440 E 56th St New York NY 10022

DIAMOND, GUSTAVE, fed. judge; b. Burgettstown, Pa., Jan. 29, 1928; s. George and Margaret (Solinsky) D.; m. Emma L. Scarton, Dec. 28, 1974; 1 dau., Margaret Ann; 1 stepdau., Joanne Yoney. A.B., Duke U., 1951; J.D., Duquesne U., 1956. Bar: Pa. bar 1958, U.S. Ct. Appeals bar 1962. Law clk. to judge U.S. Dist. Ct., Pitts., 1955-61; 1st asst. U.S. atty. Western Dist. Pa., 1961-62, U.S. atty., 1963-69; partner firm Cooper, Schwartz, Diamond & Reich, Pitts., 1969-75; formerly individual practice law, Washington, Pa.; former solicitor washington County, Pa.; now judge U.S. Dist. Ct. Western Dist. Pa. Mem. Am. Bar Assn., Pa. Bar Assn., Allegheny County Bar Assn., Washington County Bar Assn., Fed. Bar Assn. Office: US Dist Ct 7th and Grant St Pittsburgh PA 15230

DIAMOND, IRVING T., physiology educator. James B. Duke Prof. physiology Duke U., Durham, N.C. Office: Duke U Dept Physiology Durham NC 27710

DIAMOND, ISIDORE, screenwriter; b. Ungheni, Rumania, June 27, 1920; came to U.S., 1929; s. David and Elca (Waldman) D.; m. Barbara Bentley, July 21, 1945; children—Ann Cynthia, Paul Bentley. B.A., Columbia, 1941. Screenwriter, Hollywood, Calif., 1941—; collaborator with Billy Wilder, 1955— (Recipient Acad. award 1960, N.Y. Film Critics award 1960, Writers Guild award 1957, 59, 60, Laurel award 1980); Screenwriter: Love in the Afternoon, 1957, Some Like It Hot, 1959, The Apartment, 1960, One, Two, Three, 1961, Irma La Douce, 1963, Kiss Me, Stupid, 1964, The Fortune Cookie, 1966, Cactus Flower, 1969, The Private Life of Sherlock Holmes, 1970, Avanti, 1972, The Front Page, 1974, Fedora, 1978, Buddy Buddy, 1981. Mem. ASCAP, John Jay Assos. Columbia. Beverly Hills CA 90212

DIAMOND, ISRAEL, pathologist, educator; b. Flint, Mich., Aug. 1, 1914; s. Leo and Nessie (Jenchelska) D.; m. Thelma Greenberg, May 6, 1942; 1 son, Jonathan R. B.Sc., Coll. City N.Y., 1934; M.D., U. Edinburg, Scotland, 1939. Intern Met. Hosp., N.Y.C., 1940, Lincoln Hosp., 1941; practice medicine specializing in pathology, 1942—; resident Univ. Hosp., 1946-47; asso. pathologist Children's Hosp., Boston, 1948-52; dir. labs. Childrens Hosp., Louisville, 1952-60, Luth. Med. Center, N.Y.C., 1960-68; now cons.; chmn. dept. lab. medicine Roger Williams Gen. Hosp., Providence, also prof. pathology Brown U., 1968—; cons. VA Hosp., Miriam Hosp., Providence. Served with AUS, 1942-46. Fellow Coll. Am. Pathologists, Am. Soc. Clin. Pathology. Club: University (Providence). Home: 54 Brimmer St Boston MA 02108 Office: Brown Univ Program in Medicine Dept Pathology Providence RI 02912

DIAMOND, JARED MASON, biologist; b. Boston, Sept. 10, 1937; s. Louis K. and Flora K. D. B.A., Harvard U., 1958; Ph.D., Cambridge (Eng.) U., 1961. Jr. fellow Soc. Fellows, Harvard U., 1962-65; asso. in biophysics (Med. Sch.), 1965-66; asso. prof. physiology U. Calif. Med. Center, Los Angeles, 1966-68, prof., 1968—; cons. in conservation and nat. park planning govts., Papua New Guinea, Solomon Islands, Indonesia. Author: Avifauna of the Eastern Highlands of New Guinea, 1972, Ecology and Evolution of Communities, 1975. Recipient Burr medal Nat. Geog. Soc., 1979, Bowditch prize Am. Physiol. Soc., 1976, Disting. Achievement award Am. Gastroent. Assn., 1975. Fellow Am. Acad. Arts and Scis.; mem. Nat. Acad. Scis. Research in membrane physiology, ecology. Office: Physiology Dept UCLA Med Center Los Angeles CA 90024

DIAMOND, JOSEPH, lawyer; b. Washington, Dec. 22, 1935; s. Leo Aaron and Dora S. D.; m. Susan Kaplan, Dec. 25, 1965; children: Sara, David. A.B., Columbia U., 1957; LL.B., Cornell U., 1960. Bar: N.Y. 1961, D.C. 1964, U.S. Supreme Ct. 1964. Mem. LeBoeuf, Lamb & Leiby, N.Y.C., 1961-63, Melrod, Redman & Cartlan, Washington, 1963-65; comptroller of currency Office of Chief Counsel U.S. Dept. Treasury, Washington, 1966-67; assoc. Rogers & Wells, N.Y.C., 1967-69, ptnr., 1969—. U.S. Army. Mem. ABA. Office: Rogers & Wells 200 Park Ave New York NY 10017

DIAMOND, M. JEROME, former attorney general Vermont; b. Chgo., Mar. 16, 1942; s. Leo and Sonya (Peusner) D.; m. Carol English Robinson; 8 children. A.B., George Washington U., 1963; M.A., U. Tenn., 1965, J.D., 1968. Bar: Vt. 1968, U.S. Supreme Ct. 1975. Law clk. U.S. Dist. Judge Ernest Gibson, 1968-69; asso. firm Kristensen, Cummings & Price, Brattleboro, Vt., 1969-70; state's atty. Windham County, Vt., 1970-74; atty. gen. State of Vt., 1975-81. Bd. trustees Brooks Meml. Library, 1970-73; chmn. Putney Zoning Bd. Adjustment, 1971-74; mem. Vt. Criminal Justice Tng. Council, 1974-81, Vt. Commn. Adminstrn. of Justice, 1975-81. Mem. Vt. State's Attys. Assn. (past pres.), Vt. Bar Assn., Washington County Bar Assn., Nat. Assn. Atty. Gens. (v.p. 1978-79, pres. 1980), Eastern Regional Conf. Attys. Gen. (chmn. 1975-76). Democrat. Jewish. Clubs: Shriners, Masons, B'nai B'rith. Office: PO Drawer J Montpelier VT 05602

DIAMOND, MALCOLM LURIA, religion educator; b. Bklyn., Nov. 6, 1924; s. Walter Joseph and Jeannette Civia (Luria) D.; m. Barbara Reingold, June 1953 (div. 1974); children: Michael, Jonathan; m. Denise J. Landry, July 1976. B.Engring., Yale U., 1945; postgrad., Trinity Coll., Cambridge (Eng.) U., 1947-48; Ph.D., Columbia U., 1956. Mem. faculty Sarah Lawrence Coll., Bronxville, N.Y., 1950-51, N.Y. U., 1951-53; mem. faculty Princeton U., 1953—, prof. religion, 1968—, William J. Danforth prof., 1978—. Author: Martin Buber: Jewish Existentialist, 1960, Contemporary Philosophy and Religious Thought, 1974; co-editor: The Logic of God, 1975. Served with USNR, 1942-45. Recipient Harbison Teaching award Danforth Found., 1970; Kent fellow, 1951; Guggenheim fellow, 1976. Mem. Am. Acad. Religion (exec. com. 1975-77), Soc. Values in Higher Edn., Princeton Assn. Human Rights. Jewish. Home: 24 Wheatsheaf Ln Princeton NJ 08540 Office: Dept Religion 613 Seventy Nine Hall Princeton NJ 08544

DIAMOND, MATTHEW PHILIP, choreographer, dancer; b. N.Y.C., Nov. 26, 1951; s. Irwin and Pearl (Ziffer) D. B.A., CCNY, 1972. Co-founder, 1979; artistic dir., choreographer Diamond., 1979-83. Prin. dancer, Louis Falco Dance Co., 1970-74, Jennifer Muller and the Works, 1975-76; choreographer: 3 of Diamond's, 1977, Handful of Diamond's, 1978, 3 By Matthew Diamond, 1978, (feature film) Phi Beta Rockers, 1982; guest choreographer, Batsheva Dance Co., Tel Aviv, 1978, Bet-Dor Dance Co.; dir. 3 operas, Children's Free Opera, 1983. Nat. Endowment Arts fellow, 1977, 79. Office: 29 W 21st St 4th Floor New York NY 10010

DIAMOND, MURRAY ALLEN, hosp. exec.; b. Phila., Mar. 2, 1910; s. Edward L. and Rose (Roth) D.; m. Irene Roth, June 14, 1936; children—Stephen P., Richard D. B.S., Tulane U., 1933, M.D., 1936; M.P.H., Johns Hopkins, 1947. Diplomate: Am. Bd. Psychiatry and Neurology. Intern Trinity Hosp., Bklyn., 1936-37; sr. intern USPHS Hosp., Lexington, Ky., 1937-39, staff physician internal medicine, 1938-39; psychiat. fellow U. Colo., 1939-40; psychiat. resident USPHS Hosp., Ft. Worth, 1940-42, clin. dir., 1942-44; practice medicine specializing in psychiatry, New Orleans, 1947-49, N.Y.C., 1949-53, Lexington, 1953-57, Washington, 1962—; exec. officer, chief psychiat. service USPHS Hosp., New Orleans, 1944-46; regional mental health cons. Dept. Health. Edn. and Welfare (Region I and II), N.Y.C., 1946-47; dir. edn. USPHS Hosp., Lexington, 1949-51, clin. dir., 1951-54, med. officer-in-charge, 1958-62; asst. chief div. hosps. USPHS, Washington, 1954-55, spl. asst. to surgeon gen. for health preparedness, 1955; dep. chief div. personnel Office Surgeon Gen., 1955-58, asst. surgeon gen. for personnel, 1962-66; exec. dir. Touro Infirmary, 1966-73; instr. psychiatry Tulane U. Sch. Medicine, 1944-46, clin. prof. psychiatry, 1967—, adj. prof., 1967—; asso. prof. psychiatry U. Ky. Sch. Medicine, 1960-62. Recipient USPHS Commendation medal, 1962, USPHS Meritorious medal, 1966. Fellow Am. Psychiat. Assn., Am. Pub. Health assns., A.C.P., A.A.A.S.; mem. A.M.A., Am. Hosp. Assn., Am. Soc. Pub. Adminstrn., Soc. for Personnel Adminstrn., Nat. Health Council (dir.), Armed Forces Relief and Benefit Assn. (v.p.), Alpha Omega Alpha. Clubs: Mason (32 deg., Shriner), Lion.). Home: 2423 Oriole St New Orleans LA 70122 Office: 4226 Chef Menteur Hwy New Orleans LA 70126

DIAMOND, NEIL, singer, composer; b. Bklyn., Jan. 24, 1941; m. Marcia Diamond; children: Jesse, Marjorie, Elyn. Student, N.Y.U. Formerly with, Bang Records, Uni, MCA Records, Los Angeles; now rec. artist, singer, composer, Columbia Records; songs include September Morn, Kentucky Woman, Cherry, Song Sung Blue, numerous others; also numerous albums; also composer: film score Jonathan Livingston Seagull (Grammy award 1973), Every Which Way but Loose; composer film score, actor: The Jazz Singer; guest artist network TV shows. Recipient Gold records. Address: care Columbia Records 1801 Century Park W Los Angeles CA 90067 *

DIAMOND, NORMA JOYCE, anthropologist; b. N.Y.C., Feb. 12, 1933; d. Simon Bernard and Mary (Carush) D. A.B., U. Wis., 1954; Ph.D., Cornell U., 1966. Asst. prof. anthropology U. Mich., Ann Arbor, 1963-70, asso. prof., 1970-75, prof., 1975—; vis. prof. Shandong U., China, 1979-80. Author: K'un Shen: A Taiwan Village, 1969; contbr. articles on women and on rural orgn. and devel. in China and Taiwan to publs.; mem. editorial bd.: Modern China. Ford fgn. areas fellow, 1960-61; Social Sci. Research Council fellow, 1969, 79; Am. Philos. Soc. grantee, 1969, 75. Fellow Am. Anthrop. Assn.; mem. Assn. Asian Studies, Soc. Applied Anthropology, Com. Concerned Asian Scholars. Office: Dept Anthropology U Mich Ann Arbor MI 48109

DIAMOND, PATRICK HENRY, financial executive; b. N.Y.C., June 10, 1943; s. Joseph Bertram and Marie (Lynch) D. B.C.E., Manhattan Coll., 1963; J.D., Columbia U., 1966, M.B.A., 1967; LL.M. in Taxation, NYU, 1971. Bar: N.Y. 1967, U.S. Supreme Ct. 1972; C.P.A., N.Y.; registered profl. engr., N.Y. Fin. planner Exxon, Inc., 1967-69; asst. to chmn. and chief exec. officer Amax, Inc., 1969-72; mem. firm Hynes, Diamond & Reidy, 1972-75; v.p. fin. Maule Industries, 1975-78; v.p. fin., chmn. fin. com., dir. Robertshaw Controls Co., Richmond, Va., 1978—. Mem. Fin. Execs. Inst. (internat. liaison and policy com., Corp. fin. com.), Council Fgn. Relations, Machinery and Allied Products Fin. Council, Econ. Club N.Y.C., Newcomen Soc. N.Am., English Speaking Union. Clubs: Deep Run Hunt, Westwood Racquet, N.Y. Yacht. Address: 1701 Byrd Ave Richmond VA 23230

DIAMOND, PETER ARTHUR, economics educator; b. N.Y.C., Apr. 29, 1940; s. Daniel and Dora (Kolsky) D.; m. Priscilla Gibbs Myrick, Oct. 16, 1966; children: Matthew, Andrew. B.A., Yale U., 1960; Ph.D., MIT, 1963. Asst. prof., acting assoc. prof. U. Calif.-Berkeley, 1963-66; from assoc. prof. to prof. econs. MIT, Cambridge, 1966—. Social Sci. Research Council fellow, 1965; Guggenheim Found. fellow, 1966, 82; recipient Mahalanobis Meml. award Indian Econometric Soc., 1980. Fellow Econometric Soc. (council 1981-84), Am. Acad. Arts and Scis.; mem. Am. Econs. Assn. Democrat. Office: MIT Dept Econs Cambridge MA 02139

DIAMOND, RICHARD EDWARD, publisher; b. S.I., N.Y., May 24, 1932; s. Joseph H. and Gertrude (Newhouse) D.; m. Alice W. Blach., July 27, 1963; children: Caroline. Alison. Richard Edward. Student, Cornell U., 1953. With S.I. Advance, 1953—; publisher, 1979—; bd. dirs. Newspaper Advt. Bur. Trustee. S.I. Acad., 1967—, pres. bd., 1977—; bd. dirs. S.I. Hosp., 1978—. Recipient Disting. Citizens award Wagner Coll., S.I., 1976. Mem. Am. Newspaper Pubs. Assn. Jewish. Office: 950 Fingerboard Rd Staten Island NY 10305

DIAMOND, RICHARD JOHN, investment company executive; b. Phila., Aug. 6, 1941; s. Joseph John and Helen Rose D.; m. Doris Gruber, June 8, 1963; children: Laura Ann, Richard John. B.S., LaSalle Coll.; M.B.A., Temple U. Acctg. mgr. Campbell Soup Co., Camden, N.J.; controller Fed. Sweet & Biscuit Co., Clifton, N.J.; exec. v.p., chief operating officer Mickelberry Corp., N.Y.C.; pres., dir. Newcourt Industries, Inc. Served with U.S. Army, 1963-65. Decorated Army Commendation medal. Mem. Fin. Execs. Inst., Nat. Assn. Accts. Clubs: Montclair Golf, Univ. (N.Y.C.). Office: Mickelberry Corp 405 Park Ave New York NY 10022

DIAMOND, ROBERT STEPHEN, publishing co. exec.; b. Phoenix, Jan. 9, 1939; s. Bert A. and Rose (Garfinkle) D.; m. Susan E. Arnsberg, May 30, 1964. B.A., Claremont (Calif.) Men's Coll., 1961; M.S. in Journalism, Columbia U., 1967. Staff writer Ariz. Republic, Phoenix, 1962-64, Los Angeles Times, 1964-66; asso. editor Fortune mag., N.Y.C., 1967-70; v.p. Reliance Group, Inc., N.Y.C., 1970-75; v.p., dir. public relations Chase Manhattan Corp., N.Y.C., 1975-77; sr. v.p. corp. communications Dun & Bradstreet Corp., N.Y.C., 1977—, sec. polit. action com., 1980—. Bd. dirs. Old Scarsdale Assn., 1977—; mem. president's adv. council Claremont Men's Coll., 1975—. Mem. Sigma Delta Chi. Club: Quaker Ridge. Home: 5 Carstensen Rd Scarsdale NY 10583 Office: 299 Park Ave New York NY 10171

DIAMOND, SEYMOUR, physician; b. Chgo., Apr. 15, 1925; s. Nathan Avruum and Rose (Roth) D.; m. Elaine June Flamm, June 20, 1948; children: Judi, Merle, Amy. Student, Loyola U., 1943-45; M.B., Chgo. Med. Sch., 1948, M.D., 1949. Intern White Cross Hosp., Columbus, Ohio, 1949-50; gen. practice medicine, Chgo., 1950—; dir. Diamond Headache Clinic, Ltd., Chgo., 1970—; mem. staff St. Joseph Hosp., Chgo., Weiss Meml. Hosp.; prof. neurology Chgo. Med. Sch., 1970-82, adj. assoc. prof. pharmacology, 1982—; lectr. dept. community and family medicine Loyola U. Stritch Sch. Medicine, 1972-78; cons. mem. FDA Orphan Products Devel. Initial Rev. Group. Co-author: The Practicing Physician's Approach to Headache, 3d edit, 1982, More Than Two Aspirin: Help for Your Headache Problem, 1976, Advice from the Diamond Headache Clinic, 1982, Coping with Your Headache, 1982, Headache in Contemporary Patient Mgmt. series, 1983; contbr. numerous articles on headache and related fields to books and profl. jours. Pres. Skokie (Ill.) Bd. Health, 1965-68. Recipient Disting. Alumni award Chgo. Med. Sch., 1977. Mem. AMA (Physicians Recognition awards 1970-73, 74, 77, 79, 82, alt. del. sect. on clin. pharmacology and therapeutics, mem. health policy agenda for Am. People, mem. Cost Effectiveness Conf.), Am. Assn. Study of Headache (exec. dir. 1971—, pres. 1972-74), Nat. Migraine Found. (pres. 1971-77, exec. dir. 1977—), World Fedn. Neurology (exec. officer 1980—, research group on migraine and headache), Ill. Acad. Gen. Practice (chmn. mental health com. 1966-70), Ill., Chgo. med. socs., Biofeedback Soc. Am., Internat. Assn. Study of Pain, Am. Soc. Clin. Pharmacology and Therapeutics (chmn. headache sect. 1982—, mem. com. coordination sci. sects. 1983—), Postgrad. Med. Assn. (pres. 1981), Am. Med. Electroencephalographic Assn. Home: 9543 N Springfield St Evanston IL 60203 Office: 5252 N Western Ave Chicago IL 60625 *I derive great satisfaction from helping a person who is totally disabled from pain to again lead a normal, functional life.*

DIAMOND, SIDNEY, chemist, educator; b. N.Y.C., Nov. 10, 1929; s. Julius and Ethel D.; m. Harriet Urish, May 2, 1953; children: Florence, Julia. B.S., Syracuse U., 1950; M.F., Duke U., 1951; Ph.D., Purdue U., 1963. Research engr. U.S. Bur. Public Rds. (now Fed. Hwy. Adminstrn.), Washington, 1953-61, research chemist, 1961-65; asso. prof. engring. materials Purdue U., 1965-69, prof., 1969—; pres. Sidney Diamond and Assos., Inc. (engring. materials cons.); mem. Nat. Materials Adv. Bd. Com. on Status of Research in U.S. Cement and Concrete Industries. Contbr. numerous articles on cement and concrete to profl. jours.; editor: Cement and Concrete Research. Served with U.S. Army, 1951-53. Fellow Am. Ceramic Soc. (trustee, Copeland award); mem. Clay Minerals Soc., Internat. Congress on Chemistry of Cement (pres. sect. 6 of 8th congress), Am. Concrete Inst., Concrete Soc. (Gt. Britain), ASTM, Materials Research Soc. Home: 819 Essex St West Lafayette IN 47906 Office: Sch Civil Engring Purdue U West Lafayette IN 47907

DIAMOND, SIGMUND, educator, editor; b. Balt., June 14, 1920; s. Isidor and Yetta (Mirtenbaum) D.; m. Shirley Welson, Jan. 4, 1945; children—Stephen Mark, Betty. A.B., Johns Hopkins, 1940; Ph.D. in History, Harvard, 1953. With U.S. Govt., 1942-43; internat. rep. UAW-CIO, 1943-47; lectr. Am. history Sarah Lawrence Coll., 1955-56; mem. faculty Columbia, 1955—, prof. hist. sociology, 1964—, Giddings prof. sociology, 1978—; editor Polit. Sci. Quar., 1963-75; Fulbright prof. Am. history Tel-Aviv U., 1975-76. Author: The Reputation of the American Businessman, 1955, In Quest: Journal of an Unquiet Pilgrimage, 1980; Editor: The Nation Transformed, 1963. Fellow Center Advanced Study Behavioral Scis., 1959-60; sr. research fellow Newberry Library, 1967. Mem. Am. Hist. Assn., Am. Sociol. Assn., Econ. History Assn. Home: 15 Claremont Ave New York NY 10027

DIAMOND, STANLEY JAY, lawyer; b. Los Angeles, Nov. 27, 1927; s. Philip Alfred and Florence (Fadem) D.; m. Lois Jane Broida, June 22, 1969; children: Caryn Elaine, Diana Beth. B.A., UCLA, 1949; J.D., U. So. Calif., 1952. Bar: Calif. 1953. Practiced law, Los Angeles, 1953—; dep. Office of Calif. Atty. Gen., Los Angeles, 1953; ptnr. Diamond & Tilem, Los Angeles, 1957-60, Diamond, Tilem & Colden, 1960-79, Diamond & Wilson, 1979—; lectr. music and entertainment law UCLA; Mem. nat. panel arbitrators Am. Arbitration Assn. Bd. dirs. Los Angeles Suicide Prevention Center, 1971-76. Served with 349th Engr. Constrn. Bn. AUS, 1945-47. Mem. Am., Calif., Los Angeles County, Beverly Hills bar assns., Assn. Trial Lawyers Am., Calif., Los Angeles trial lawyers assns., Am. Judicature Soc., Lawyers Club Los Angeles, Calif. Copyright Conf., Nat. Acad. Rec. Arts and Scis., Zeta Beta Tau, Nu Beta Epsilon. Home: 608 N Linden Dr Beverly Hills CA 90210 Office: 12304 Santa Monica Blvd 3d Floor Los Angeles CA 90025

DIAMOND, STUART, journalist; b. Camden., N.J., June 20, 1948; s. Irving H. and Ruth (Safran) D. B.A. in English, Rutgers U., 1970. Mcpl. and investigative reporter New Brunswick (N.J.) Daily Home News, 1969-73; mcpl. reporter. energy and environ. writer Newsday, Long Island City., N.Y., 1973—; contbg. editor Omni mag., 1978-81; lectr., TV commentator., 1978—. Author: It's In Your Power, 1978, No-Cost, Low-Cost Energy Tips, 1980; documentary films The Energy War, 1980, The Future is Now, 1981; also nat. mag. cover stories. Recipient N.J. Publishers Assn. award, 1972; N.Y. State Press Assn. award, 1976, 78, 80, 82; Amos Tuck award nat. econ. reporting., 1978, 80, 82; Deadline Club Sci. Writing prize, 1979, 80; U. Mo. award nat. bus. writing, 1979, 82; Polk award nat. reporting, 1980; award for public service reporting Scripps Howard Found., 1980; award for conservation reporting Scripps Howard Found., 1982; Front Page award for nat. reporting., 1980. Mem. AFTRA, Sigma Delta Chi. Home: 340 Woodbine Ave Northport NY 11768 Office: Newsday Long Island NY 11747

DIAMONSTEIN, BARBARALEE DWORKIN, writer, television interviewer, producer; b. N.Y.C.; d. Rubin Robert and Sally H. Simmons; m. Alan A. Diamonstein, July 22, 1956; m. Carl Spielvogel, Oct. 27, 1981. B.A., B.C., M.A., N.Y. U., 1954, doctorate, 1963. Staff asst. White House, 1963-66; dir. cultural affairs City of New York, 1966-67; dir. of forums McCall Corp., 1967-69; editor spl. supplements, columnist Harper's Bazaar, 1969-71; spl. project dir., guest editor Art News, 1973—; columnist Ladies Home Jour., 1979—; contbr. to Saturday Rev., Vogue, Partisan Rev., N.Y. Times, others; mem. faculty Hunter Coll., City U. N.Y., 1974-76, New Sch., 1976—, Duke U. (Inst. Policy Scis.), 1978; arts cons. CBS-TV, 1978-82; curator Buildings Reborn, Collaborations, Visions and Images (nat. travelling museum exhbns.), 1978—. TV interviewer, producer: About the Arts, WNYC-TV, 1975-79, ABC-TV Arts, 1980—; Author: Open Secrets: 94 Women in Touch With Our Time, 1972, The World of Art, 1902-77, 75 Years of Art News, 1977, Buildings Reborn: New Uses, Old Places, 1978, Inside New York's Art World, 1979, American Architecture Now, 1980, Collaboration: Artists and Architects, 1981, Visions and Images: American Photographers on Photography, 1981; Interior Design: The New Freedom, 1982, Handmade in America, 1983; editor: Our 200 Years: Tradition and Renewal, 1975, MoMA at 50, 1980. Commr. N.Y.C. Landmarks Preservation Commn., 1972—; dir. Mcpl. Art Soc., 1973—; commr. N.Y.C. Cultural Commn., 1975—; Bd. dirs. N.Y.C. Bicentennial Commn., 1973-77; bd. dirs. Bklyn. Acad. Music, 1969-74, N.Y. Landmarks Conservancy, 1973—; vice chmn. N.Y. Landmarks Conservancy, 1983—; bd. advisers Film Anthology Archives, 1969—; mem. vis. com. Met. Mus. Art., 1982—; bd. dirs. Am. Council Arts, 1982—, Fresh Air Fund, 1983—. Home: 720 Park Ave New York NY 10021

DIANA, JOHN NICHOLAS, physiologist; b. Lake Placid, N.Y., Dec. 19, 1930; s. Alphonse Walton and Dolores (Mirto) D.; m. Anita Louise Harris, May 8, 1966; children: Gina Sue, Lisa Ann, John Nicholas. B.A., Norwich U., 1952; Ph.D., U. Louisville, 1965. Asst. prof. physiology Mich. State U. Med. Sch., 1966-68; asso. prof., then prof. U. Iowa Med. Sch., 1969-78; prof. physiology, chmn. dept. La. State U. Med. Center, Shreveport, 1978—; cons. Nat. Inst. Neurol. Diseases and Stroke, 1973-75, Nat. Heart, Lung and Blood Inst., 1974—, mem. cardiovascular and renal study sect., 1980—; research com. Iowa Heart Assn., 1974-77, bd. dirs., 1977-79; mem. cardiovascular study sect. Am. Heart Assn., 1981-84. Author papers, abstracts in field. Served with AUS, 1952-54; Served with USAR, 1961-62. NIH postdoctoral fellow, 1965-67. Mem. Am. Fedn. Clin. Research, Am. Physiol. Soc. (editorial bd. jour. 1974-78), Microcirculation Soc. (pres. 1977-78, editorial bd. jour. 1979—), Am. Heart Assn. (fellow council circulation), N.Y. Acad. Scis., La. Heart Assn. (dir. 1979-81, research com. 1978-82), Sigma Xi. Democrat. Patentee coronary vasodilator. Home: 3081 Dartmoor Ct Shreveport LA 71115 Office: 1501 Kings Hwy Shreveport LA 71103 *Progress related to the health and welfare of any nation can only be accomplished by programs directed at the development of human thought and human thought processes. The ultimate fate of man will rest upon the success of all societies to stimulate human vital curiosity, talents. energies. basic scholarship and research to address those factors which will preserve man's natural cultural heritage and his ability to lead a free and independent existence.*

DIANA, JOSEPH A., foundation executive; b. New Castle, Pa., June 26, 1924; s. Joseph Anthony and Emma (Eardly) D.; m. Kathryn June Matthews, June 26, 1946; children: Mark Steven, Chris Joseph, Todd Francis, Paul Jeffrey. Student, Notre Dame U., 1942; B.A., U. Mich., 1950, postgrad., 1950-51. Mem. adminstrv. staff U. Mich., 1950-70, sec. to faculty Med. Sch., 1956-69, asst. controller, 1969-70; v.p. fin. and mgmt. SUNY, Stony Brook, 1970-75; assoc. v.p. bus. affairs, vice chancellor adminstrv. affairs U. Ill., Champaign-Urnana, 1975-79; v.p. adminstrn., treas. John C. and Catherine T. MacArthur Found., Chgo., 1979—. Republican. Roman Catholic. Home: 2011 Silver Ct W Urbana IL 61801 Office: 140 S Dearborn St Chicago IL 60603

DIANIS, JOHN EDWARD, association executive; b. McHenry, Ill., May 1, 1925; s. John and Anna (Danovsky) D.; m. Mary Alice Johnston, May 27, 1950; children: Nancy Dianis Hanna, John W. Diploma acctg., Lake Coll. Commerce, Waukegan, Ill., 1948; B.B.A., Northwestern U., 1965. Staff assoc. Nat. Selected Morticians Assn., Evanston, Ill., 1948-68; exec. v.p. Monument Builders N. Am., Evanston, 1968—; mgmt. and tax cons., real estate broker. Mem. bd. Wauconda (Ill.) Unit Sch. Dist. 118, 1947-54, Wauconda Zoning Bd., 1965-71; mayor Village of Wauconda, 1973-77; bd. dirs. Lake County Mcpl. League, 1976-77. Served with USAAF, 1943-45. Mem. Am. Soc. Assn. Execs. (cert.), Meeting Planners Internat., Nat. Assn. Exposition Mgrs., Ill. Soc. Assn. Execs., Chgo. Soc. Assn. Execs., Nat. Tax Practitioners Assn., Assn. Econ. Council, Am. Legion, Antique Automobile Club Am. Republican. Mem. Evang. Free Ch. Clubs: Shriners, Lions (past dist. govt.). Home: 211 Lewis Ave Wauconda IL 60084 Office: 1612 Central St Evanston IL 60201

DIANIS, WALTER JOSEPH, banker; b. Greenwich, Conn., Aug. 12, 1918; s. Joseph and Susie (Sumka) D.; m. Pauline Frano, Oct. 11, 1942; children: Charles, Thomas. B.B.A., Iona Coll., 1950; M.B.A., NYU, 1952; cert., Rutgers U., 1959. Auditor Port Chester Savs. Bank, N.Y., 1936-48; sr. accountant Dusenbury & Hogenauer, Port Chester, 1948-53; 1st sr. v.p. Home Savs. Bank, White Plains, N.Y., from 1953, now pres., also trustee. Active Community Chests, Port Chester and White Plains, 1948-57; trustee White Plains YWCA. Served with USCG, 1942-45. Mem. White Plains C. of C. (treas. 1968-72). Lutheran (chief financial officer). Clubs: University, Westchester County Assn. (White Plains). Home: 12 Hartford Ave Greenwich CT 06830 Office: 170 Hamilton Ave White Plains NY 10601

DIASSI, PATRICK ANDREW, pharm. co. exec.; b. Morristown, N.J., July 1, 1926; s. Frank P. and Angelina (Larezza) D.; m. Louise R. Pallotta, Sept. 28, 1952; children—Patricia L., Michael A. B.S., St. Peter's Coll., 1946; M.S., Rutgers U., 1950, Ph.D., 1951. Mem. staff organic chemistry dept. E.R. Squibb & Sons, Inc., Princeton, N.J., 1951-68, asst. dep. dir. organic chemistry dept., 1968-71, dir. chem. process devel. dept., 1971-72, dir. chem. and microbiol. research and devel. dir., asso. dir., Princeton, 1972-76, v.p. chem. research and devel., 1977—. Contbr. articles to profl. jours. Served with U.S. Army, 1944-46. Roman Catholic. Holder numerous U.S. patents. Home: 744 Norgate St Westfield NJ 07090 Office: Squibb Inst for Med Research PO Box 4000 Princeton NJ 08540

DIAZ, JUSTINO, bass; b. San Juan, P.R., Jan 29, 1940; s. Justino and Gladys Villarini; children: Natascia, Katya. Student, U. P.R., 1958-59, New Eng. Conservatory Music, 1959-62. Appearances with, New Eng. Opera Theatre, 1961, Opera Co. Boston, 1966, Am. Opera Soc., 1963-64, 69, Dallas Civic Opera, opera cos. of, New Orleans, Ft. Worth, San Juan, N.Y.C., Balt., Memphis, San Francisco, Boston, Miami, Fla., symphony orchs. of, N.Y.C., Cleve., Boston, philharm. orchs. of, Phila., Chgo., Dallas, Indpls., Detroit, N.Y.C., Los Angeles, also Spoleto, Casals and Salzburg festivals and La Scala, Milan, Italy, Gran Teatro del Liceo, Barcelona, Spain, Teatro Colon, Buenos Aires, Argentina, Hamburg State Opera, Germany, Vienna (Austria) State Opera, Munich State Opera; leading bass, Met. Opera Co., 1963—; rec. artist for, Columbia, London, Vanguard, ABC, RCA, Angel records. Recipient Handel medalion N.Y.C., 1966; recipient Family of Man citation Soc. Family of Man, 1966. Home: 140 West End Ave New York NY 10023

DIAZ, RAMON V., judge. Judge Superior Ct. of Guam, Agana. Office: Superior Ct of Guam Judiaciary Bldg Agana Guam 96910

DIAZ-COLLER, CARLOS, physician; b. Villahermosa, Tabasco, Mexico, Sept. 2, 1916; s. Jose and Maria Gonzalez; m. Anna Maria de la Garza, Dec. 17, 1945; children—Carlos, Jose Alberto, Mario, Juan Antonio and Anna Maria Elisa (twins). M.D., Army Med. Sch., Mexico, 1945; M.P.H., Harvard, 1948. Del. from Mexico WHO, 1956, 57, 58, exec. bd. alternate, 1956-57, v.p. exec. bd., 1958-59; del. from Mexico to directing council Pan-Am. San. Orgn., 1956, 57, exec. com., 1957-58, pres. exec. com., 1958-59; del. from Mexico XV Pan Am. San. Conf., 1958; dir. div. exptl. studies in pub. health Ministry Pub. Health and Welfare, Mexico, 1957, 58; chief dept. of profl. edn. and editorial and reference services Pan Am. Health Orgn. of WHO, 1960-73; dir. gen. research and reference services Ministry Health and Welfare, Mexico, 1973—; Pub. health supr. Mexican Army, 1948-56; dir. (Sch. Pub. Health), Mexico, 1953. Editor: Jour. of Mexican Pub. Health Soc, 1955-58. Mem. Mexican Pub. Health Soc. (pres. 1957-58), Am. Pub. Health Assn., Nat. Geog. Soc. Home: California 180 Churubusco Mexico City 21 DF Mexico Office: Secretaría de Salubridad y Asistencia Mexico 6 DF Mexico *Man is reaching for the stars because he worries not only for himself but also for his descendants-his society.*

DIAZ-LLANEZA, JOSE ANTONIO, flower export company executive; b. Mexico City, Mexico, Jan. 15, 1938; s. Jose Ramon and Concepcion Elena (Llaneza) Diaz y Diaz; m. Candace Ann Loren, July 15, 1972; children: Ana Tarina, José Antonio. B. Humanities, Centro U. Mexico, 1955; grad. pub. accounting, Nat. U. Mexico, 1960; M.B.A. (Ford Internat. fellow), Columbia, 1963; C.P.A., Mexico. Partner Roberto Casas Alatriste, Coopers & Lybrand, C.P.A.s, Mexico City and N.Y.C., 1957-69; with div. ITT companies, 1970-74; gen. mgr. Sistemas de Bombeo ITT, pump mfrs., Mexico City, 1973-75; gen. mgr. USM Mexicana, S.A. de C.V., also area dir. USM Corp. and United Machinery Group for Mexico, Caribbean, C. Am., Andean region, 1975-80, 1980—; dir. food div. Grupo Visa, 1981—. Co-author: Modern Management Techniques, 1969. Mem. Mexican Inst. and Coll. C.P.A.s, Mexican Coll. Bus. Adminstrn., Nat. Assn. Accts., Alpha Kappa Psi. Clubs: Lo Peña Sailing, Raqueta Bosques. Home: Galileo 16-2 Mexico City 5 Mexico Office: Reforma 116-17 Mexico DF Mexico

DIAZ-VERSON, SALVADOR, JR., insurance company executive; b. Havana, Cuba, Dec. 31, 1951; s. Salvador and Metodia Diaz-V.; m. Patricia Dianne Floyd, Apr. 24, 1976; 1 son, Salvador III. B.A. in Fin., Fla. State U., Tallahassee, 1973. Chief investment officer Am. Family Life Assurance, Columbus, Ga., 1977-79; exec. v.p. Am. Family Corp., Columbus, 1980-83, pres., 1983—, also dir.; dir. Phenix Girard, Phenix City, Ala., 1978—. Sec. Am. Family Polit. Action Com., 1983; bd. dirs. United Way, Columbus, 1983—; mem. vocat. tng. adv. com. Muscogee County Sch. Dist., Columbus, 1983—. Mem. Columbus C. of C. (dir. 1983—). Democrat. Roman Catholic. Clubs: Green Island Country, Country of Columbus. Office: American Family Corp 1932 Wynnton Rd Columbus GA 31999

DI BACCO, THOMAS VICTOR, historian; b. Bellaire, Ohio, June 8, 1937; s. Achille and Jennie (Varanese) Di B.; m. Mallie Zidenah Rowe, Aug. 8, 1959; children: Deborah, Thomas. B.A. with highest distinction, Rollins Coll., 1959; M.A., Am. U., 1962, Ph.D., 1965. Instr. history U. South Fla., 1964-65; asst. prof. history Am. U., Washington, 1965-69, assoc. prof., 1969-77, prof. bus. adminstrn., 1977—, dean faculty affairs, 1974-81; cons. to assns., govt. agys., lectr. on Am. history for religious groups, radio, TV appearances. Author: Jeremiah Moore and Moorefield, 1971, Presidential Power in Latin American Politics, 1977; contbr. articles to profl. jours. Named Best Prof. Am. U., 1971. Mem. Am. Hist. Assn., Orgn. Am. Historians, Omicron Delta Kappa, Pi Gamma Mu, Phi Alpha Theta, Theta Alpha Phi, Phi Kappa Phi. Office: American U. Washington DC 20016

DI BARI, NICHOLAS MICHAEL, marketing executive; b. Bklyn., Jan. 28, 1945; s. Nicholas and Carmela E. (DeRosa) Di B.; m. Donna Marie Bergeron, Oct. 30, 1970; children: Nicholas Michael, Danielle Marie. B.S., U. Dayton, 1966; postgrad., U. Nev. Underwriter Allstate Ins. Co., Huntington, N.Y., 1968-69; comml. dist. mgr. Comml. Computers Inc., Huntington, 1970-71; br. mgr. Storage Tech. Corp., Louisville, Colo., 1972-76; sr. v.p. mktg. Comadisco Inc., Rosemont, Ill., 1977—. Served with U.S. Army, 1966-68. Recipient Hi Paid Mktg. Exec. in U.S. award Wall St. Jour. Proxy Revs. of SEC, 1979, 80, 81, 82, 83. Republican. Roman Catholic. Office: 6400 Shafer Ct Rosemont IL 60018 *In order to accurately assess your success, one must first have his-her ego satisfied. This can only come as a result of acceptance by his-her peer group as "the best in the business."*

DIBBLE, CHARLES ELLIOTT, anthropologist, educator; b. Layton, Utah, Aug. 18, 1909; s. George Elliott and Ella Annice (Tolman) D.; m. Audrey Nelson, Dec. 16, 1936; children: Nelson, Ella, Charlene, Carlos. B.A., U. Utah, 1936; M.A., Nat. U. Mexico, 1938, Ph.D., 1942. Faculty U. Utah, Salt Lake City, 1939—, prof. anthropology, 1952—, head dept., 1960-64, now disting. prof. emeritus anthropology; vis. prof. U. Minn., 1957, 59; spl. research Nahautl lang. Author: El Codice en Cruz, 1942, El Codice Xolotl, 1951, Codice de 1576, 1963; Co-translator: Florentine Codex Volumes, 1950-82. Recipient Disting. Research Prof. award U. Utah, 1970; decorated Mexican Order Aztec Eagle. Fellow Hist. Soc. N.Mex.; mem. Academia Mexicana de la Historia, Sociedad Mexicana de Antropologia, Inst. Andean Research, Asociacion Internacional de Nahuatlatos, Phi Beta Kappa, Phi Kappa Phi. Home: 335 East Center North Salt Lake UT 84054

DIBENEDETTO, ANTHONY THOMAS, university official; b. N.Y.C., Oct. 27, 1933; s. Thomas and Mathilda DiB.; m. Rose Marie Lima, Feb. 12, 1955; children: Diane, Laura, Thomas, David, Stephen. B.Ch.E., CCNY, 1955; M.S., U. Wis., 1956, Ph.D., 1960. Chem. engr. Union Carbide Corp., 1954-55; prof. chem. engring. U. Wis., 1960-67; prof., dir. materials research lab. Washington U., 1967-71; head dept. chem. engring. U. Conn., 1971-77, v.p. grad. edn. and research, 1979-81, v.p. acad. affairs, 1981—; cons. in field. Author: The Structure and Properties of Materials, 1967. Recipient Ednl. Service award Plastics Inst. Am., 1973; NSF profl. devel. award, 1977-79; Disting. Service award U. Wis., 1981. Mem. Soc. Plastics Engrs., Am. Inst. Chem. Engring., Sigma Xi, Tau Beta Pi. Home: 1 Brookside Ln Mansfield Center CT 06250 Office: Gulley Hall U-86 U Conn Storrs CT 06268

DIBERARDINO, MARIE ANTOINETTE, biologist, educator; b. Phila., May 2, 1926; d. Henry and Adelina (Belfi) DiB. B.S. in Biology, Chestnut Hill Coll., 1948; Ph.D. in Zoology, U. Pa., 1962. Research asst. Inst. for Cancer Research, 1951-58, research asso., 1960-64, asst. mem., 1964-67; asso. prof. anatomy Med. Coll. Pa., Phila., 1967-71, prof. anatomy, 1971—, prof. physiology, 1981—. Adv. bd.: Internat. Rev. of Cytology, 1976, Differentiation, 1981—; Contbr. articles on devel., genetics and cell biology to sci. jours.; contbr. book revs. in field. NSF grantee; NIH grantee. Fellow AAAS; mem. Am. Soc. Cell Biology, Soc. for Devel. Biologists (treas., trustee 1975-78), Am. Soc. Zoologists, Am. Assn. Anatomists, Internat. Soc. of Differentiation (exec. com. 1978—), Sigma Delta Epsilon. Office: Med College of Pennsylvania 3300 Henry Ave Philadelphia PA 19129

DIBIAGGIO, JOHN A., university president; b. San Antonio, Sept. 11, 1932; s. Ciro and Acidalia DiB.; m. Carolyn Mary Enright, June 29, 1957; children: David John, Dana Elizabeth, Deirdre Joan. A.B., Eastern Mich. U., 1954; D.D.S., U. Detroit, 1958; M.A., U. Mich., 1967; D.Sc. (hon.), Fairleigh Dickinson U., 1981. Practice dentistry, New Baltimore, Mich., 1958-65; asst. prof., asst. to dean U. Detroit Sch. Dentistry, 1965-67; asso. prof., asst. dean U. Ky. Sch. Dentistry, 1967-70; prof., dean Sch. Dentistry, Va. Commonwealth U., 1970-76; v.p. for health affairs, exec. dir. U. Conn. Health Center, Farmington, 1976-79; pres. U. Conn., 1979—; dir. Colonial Bancorp; cons. Nat. Cancer Inst., Jour. ADA. Contbr. articles to profl. jours. Pres. Anchor Bay (Mich.) Sch. Bd., 1960-64; corporator, bd. dirs. Hartford Hosp., Mt. Sinai Hosp., St. Francis Hosp., Hartford, Conn.; bd. dirs. Am. Cancer Soc., Nat. Alliance Businessmen, Hartford Hosp., March of Dimes; trustee U. Detroit; bd. overseers Sch. Dentistry, U. Pa. Decorated Order of Merit, Italy; recipient award for leadership in ethnic heritage Sacred Heart U. Fellow Am. Coll. Dentists, Internat. Coll. Dentists; mem. ADA, Am. Assn. Dental Schs., Internat. Assn. Dental Research, Am. Public Health Assn., Am. Assn. Higher Edn., Assn. Acad. Health Centers, Phi Kappa Phi, Omicron Kappa Upsilon, Beta Gamma Sigma, Alpha Omega, Alpha Sigma Chi, Alpha Lambda Delta. Home: Oak Hill Rd Storrs CT 06268 Office: Gulley Hall Univ of Conn Storrs CT 06268

DIBIASE, JOSEPH L., business executive. Pres. John A. Eberly, Inc., Reading, Pa. Office: John A Eberly Inc PO Box 201 Reading PA 19603§

DIBLE, WILLIAM TROTTER, chemical company executive; b. Oakmont, Pa., Sept. 7, 1925; s. William T. and Lois Sarah (Croll) D.; m. Sara S. Stierstorfer, Sept. 19, 1948; children: William S., John Rend, Jeffrey Croll, Charles Kendig. B.S., Pa. State U., 1947; M.S., U. Wis., 1949, Ph.D. in Soil Chemistry and Plant Physiology, 1951. With Internat. Minerals and Chems. Corp., Chgo., 1951-64; an organizer, 1964, since pres., chief exec. officer Terra Chems. Internat. Inc., Sioux City, Iowa. Bd. dirs. Morningside Coll., Iowa Coll. Found. Served with USNR, 1943-46. Mem. Am. Chem. Soc., Am. Soc. Agronomy, Soil Sci. Soc., Sigma Xi. Home: 4327 Country Club Blvd Sioux City IA 51104 Office: Plaza Bldg 600 4th St Sioux City IA 51101

DIBNER, DAVID, elec. machinery mfg. co. exec.; b. N.Y.C., Apr. 18, 1927; s. Bern and Barbara (Druss) D.; m. Frances Kessler, Aug. 13, 1950; children—Brent, Daniel, Mark. B.S., Columbia, 1950; certificate bus. adminstrn., London (Eng.) Sch. Econs., 1951; post-grad., Harvard, 1968. Dir. advt. and sales promotion Burndy Corp., Norwalk, Conn., 1963-66, dir. corp. and marketing communications, 1966-67, dir. planning, 1967-69, v.p. planning and bus. devel., 1969-70, group v.p. power products, 1970-71, vice-chmn. bd. dirs., 1971-72, chmn. bd., 1972—; dir. Holson Co., Work Bench. Vice-pres. Burndy Library, 1957—; nat. asso. Boys' Clubs Am., 1971—; trustee Poly. Inst. N.Y., Norwalk Hosp. Served with USNR, 1945-46. Mem. Am. Technion Soc. (dir. 1972—). Patentee in field. Office: Burndy Corp Norwalk CT 06856

DI BONA, CHARLES JOSEPH, association executive; b. Quincy, Mass., Feb. 26, 1932; s. Guido Ralph and Helen Elizabeth (Pangraze) DiB.; m. Evelyn Rauch, July 2, 1959; children—Caroline Anne, Charles J. B.S., U.S. Naval Acad., 1956; M.A. (Rhodes scholar), Oxford U., Eng., 1962. Pres., chief exec. officer Center for Naval Analyses, 1967-73; spl. cons. to Pres. U.S., dep. dir.; White House Energy Policy Office, 1973-74; exec. v.p., chief operating officer Am. Petroleum Inst., Washington, 1974-78, pres., chief exec. officer, 1979—; Bd. dirs. U.S. Nat. Com. World Energy Conf., Nat. Energy Found., World Affairs Council of Washington; trustee Meridian House Internat.; vice chmn. U.S. nat. com. World Petroleum Congress; bd. dirs. U.S. Navy Meml. Found.; mem. Fed. City Council. Served to lt. comdr. U.S. Navy, 1956-67. Roman Catholic. Clubs: Cosmos, F Street, City Tavern, Met. Home: 9306 Georgetown Pike Great Falls VA 22066 Office: 1220 L St NW Washington DC 20005

DI CAPUS, MICHAEL, editor; b. N.Y.C., Aug. 2, 1938; s. Giuseppe and Angelina (Coppa) di Capua. Student, Brown U., 1955-58. Editor Farrar, Straus and Giroux, N.Y.C., 1966-81, v.p., 1975—, editor-in-chief, 1981—, dir., 1974—. Recipient Roger Klein award for editing, 1975. Office: Farrar Straus and Giroux 19 Union Sq W New York NY 10003

DICARLO, DOMINICK L., lawyer, government official; b. Bklyn., Mar. 11, 1928; m. Esther Hansen; children: Vincent, Carl, Robert, Barbara. B.A., St. John's Coll., 1950, LL.B., 1953; LL.M., NYU. Asst. U.S. atty. Eastern Dist. N.Y., 1959-62, chief organized crime and racketeering sect., 1959-62; spl. asst. to U.S. atty., 1962; counsel to minority leader N.Y. Council, 1962-64; sole practice, 1954—; mem. N.Y. State assembly, 1964-81, dep. minority leader, 1975-78; asst. sec. state for internat. narcotics matters Dept. State, Washington, 1981—; vice chmn. N.Y. State Legis. Commn. on Crime, 1969-70, Select Commn. on Correctional Insts. and Programs, 1972-73. Office: Dept State Internat Narcotics Matters 2201 C St NW Washington DC 20520 *

DICARLO, LOUIS MICHAEL, educator; b. N.Y.C., Jan., 17, 1903; s. Amedeo and Theresa (Glacomo) DiC.; m. Marian E. Warcup, Sept. 17, 1947. B.A., Union Coll., 1932; certificate of proficiency, Clarke Sch. for Deaf, 1936; M.S., Mass. State U., 1937; Ed.D., Columbia, 1948. With N.Y. State Police, 1923-26; social worker, 1932-35, tchr. pub. schs., New Rochelle, N.Y., 1938-47; faculty Ind. U., 1942; faculty dept. audiology and speech pathology Syracuse U., 1947—, prof., 1952—, chmn. dept., 1952-62; clin. prof. otolaryngology Upstate Med. Sch., Syracuse, 1979—; vis. prof. audio and speech pathology U. Hawaii, 1964-65; vis. prof. Ithaca Coll., 1968-69, acting dean, 1971-73; chief audiology and speech pathology VA Hosp. Syracuse, N.Y. State Crippled Children's Assn., Sunnyview Orthopaedic and Rehab. Hosp., Schenectady; with Gordon D. Hoople Hearing and Speech Center; dir. speech pathology Syracuse Rehab. Center; cons. Pineland Hosp. and Tng. Center, Pownal, Maine. Author: Speech after Laryngectomy, 1958, Our Educational Dilemma; The Deaf, 1964; Contbr. articles profl. jours., fiction to mags. Bd. dirs. United Cerebral Palsy Assn. of Syracuse; aux. bd. Graham Alexander Assn. Served with U.S. Army, 1919-23; with AUS, 1942-45. Recipient Archibold high scholarship prize, Warner prize, meritorious award VA, 1981. Fellow Am. Speech, Lang. Hearing Assn. (award 1980); mem. Am., N.Y. State, Syracuse psychol. assns., Alexander Graham Bell Assn. for Deaf, Speech Assn. Eastern States, Acoustical Soc. Am., Nat. Council Psychol. Aspects of Disability, Am. Assn. Mental Deficiency, Council Exceptional Children (Hammond prof. 1960), N.Y. State Speech and Hearing Assn. (pres.). Home: 1030 E Genesee St Syracuse NY 13210

DI CENZO, COLIN DOMENIC, university dean; b. Hamilton, Ont., Can., July 26, 1923; s. Ferdernado and Kathleen (Quickenden) diC.; m. Patricia Evelyn Wright, Sept. 12, 1950; children: Colin, Eileen, Brian, Mark, Peter, Pamela. B.Sc. in Elec. Engring, U. N.B., 1952; D.I.C., Imperial Coll. Sci. and Tech., London, 1954; M.Sc. in Elec. Engring, U. N.B., 1957. Comd. artificer apprentice Can. Navy, 1941, advanced through grades to comdr., 1965; trans. Naval Res., 1966; Control engr. Met. Vickers, Eng., 1953-54; lectr. Royal Mil. Coll. Can., 1954-57; dep. head sonar engring. Naval Hdqrs., Ottawa, Ont., 1957-60, head underwater fire control system design group, 1960-62; squadron staff officer 2d Destroyer Squadron, Pacific, 1962-64; project engr. hydrofoil ship HMCS Bras d'Or, Naval Hdqrs., 1964-65; Comdg. officer HMCS Star, 1969-71; assoc. prof. McMaster U., Hamilton, 1965-72, prof. elec. engring., 1972-79, prof. elec. and computer engring., 1979-80, dir. studies faculty engring., 1968-75, asso. dean engring., 1975-79; dean engring. and applied sci. Meml. U. Nfld., St. John's, 1980—. Bd. govs. Labrador Inst. No. Studies, 1980—, Centre for Cold Oceans Resource Engring., 1980—. Decorated Order Can.; recipient Can. Decoration, 1953, Centennial medal, 1967; Queen's Silver Jubilee medal, 1977; award Public Servants Invention Act; Gov.-Gen.'s Commemorative medal, 1978; Athlone fellow, 1952-54; Brydone-Jack scholar, 1952. Fellow IEEE (asso. editor transactions 1975-78), Engring. Inst. Can. (Julian C. Smith medal 1977, pres. 1979-80); mem. Can. Soc. Elec. Engring. (pres. 1976-78), Assn. Profl. Engrs. Ont. (Engring. medal 1977), Commonwealth Engrs. Council, Pan Am. Union Engring. Socs. (dir. 1981—), Instn. Engrs. (Australia). Patentee, also numerous publs. in field. Home: 28 Millen Ave Hamilton ON L9A 2T4 Canada Office: Meml U Nfld St John's NF A1B 3X5 Canada

DI CHIERA, DAVID, performing arts impresario; b. McKeesport, Pa., Apr. 8, 1937; s. Cosimo and Maria (Pezzaniti) DiC.; m. Karen VanderKloot, July 20, 1965; children: Lisa Maria, Cristina Maria. B.A. summa cum laude in Music, UCLA, 1956, M.A. in Composition (scholar), 1958, Ph.D. in Musicology, 1962; certificate in composition and piano (Fulbright Research grantee), Naples Conservatory of Music, 1959. Instr. music U. Calif., Los Angeles, 1960-61; asst. prof. music Oakland U., Rochester, Mich., 1962-65, chmn. music dept., 1966-73; founder, gen. dir. Mich. Opera Theatre, Detroit, 1971—; founding dir. Music Hall Center for the Performing Arts, Detroit, 1973—; artistic advisor to pres. Oakland U.; artistic dir. Dayton Opera Assn., 1981—; trustee Nat. Opera Inst. Producer, dir.: Overture to Opera series for, Detroit Grand Opera series, 1963-71; Composer various works for piano, violin, orch., voice; author articles on Italian opera for various encyclopedias; contbr. revs. and articles to music jours. Mem. Arts Com. New Detroit, Inc.; trustee, mem. exec. com. Music Center for Performing Arts; mem. Arts Task Force City of Detroit. Recipient Atwater Kent award U. Calif., Los Angeles, 1961; Certificate of Appreciation City of Detroit, 1970; citation Mich. Legislature, 1976; Michaelangelo award Boys' Town of Italy, 1980; award Mich. Found. for Arts, 1981; President's Cabinet award U. Detroit, 1982; George Gershwin fellow, 1958; named A Michiganian of Yr., 1980; cavaliere della Repubblica Italiana. Mem. Am. Arts Alliance (exec. com.), Central Opera Service, Nat. Opera Assn., Am. Symphony League, Am. Musicol. Soc., OPERA Am. (pres.), AAUP, Phi Beta Kappa, Phi Mu Alpha Sinfonia. Club: Detroit Athletic. Office: Mich Opera Theatre 350 Madison Ave Detroit MI 48226

DICHTER, ERNEST, consulting psychologist; b. Vienna, Austria, Aug. 14, 1907; s. William and Mathilde (Schneider) D.; m. Hedy Langfelder, 1935; children—Thomas William, Susan Jane. Ph.D., U. Vienna; licenciés es lettres, Sorbonne. Research psychologist J. Stirling Getchell, Inc. (advt. agy.), N.Y.C.; now pres. Ernest Dichter, Assocs. Internat. Ltd.; cons. psychologist on programs CBS; ind. cons. psychologist; prof. Nova U., Ft. Lauderdale, Fla. Author: chapter in Radio Research The Psychology of Radio Commercials, 1943-44; Television Research; series of 9 articles in Tide mag., 1945; The

Psychology of Everyday Living, 1946, Motivational and Market Behavior; chpt. on testing techniques, 1958; The Strategy of Desire, 1960, Handbook of Consumer Motivations, 1964, Motivating Human Behavior, 1971, The Naked Managers, 1974, The New World of Packaging, 1975, Why Not, Management Problems of the '70's, 1973, Sascha and the Onion, 1974, Sascha and the Suppose Store, 1974, Sascha is Not Afraid, 1974, Comment Vivrons Nous en L'An 2000, 1979, Getting Motivated, 1979, The National Manager Test, 1984; frequent speaker acad., bus. and advt. groups; contbr. articles on market research. Mem. Am. Psychol. Assn. Introduced depth interviewing into marketing research, adapted numerous clin. techniques to gen. consumer testing. Home and Office: 24 Furnace Brook Drive Peekskill NY 10566 *I believe that the definition of happiness is constructive discontent. Getting there is all the fun; the goal itself is much less important than growth, striving, and self-fulfillment.*

DICHTER, MISHA, concert pianist; b. Shanghai, China, Sept. 27, 1945; came to U.S., 1947, naturalized, 1953; s. Leon and Lucy (Lhevine) D.; m. Cipa Glazman, Jan. 21, 1968; 2 sons. Student, UCLA, 1963-64; B.S., Juilliard Sch., 1968. Performed world concert tours, 1966—; appeared with maj. world orchs. including, Phila., Boston Symphony, Chgo. Symphony, N.Y. Philharmonic, Cleve. orchs.; Rec. artist, RCA, now, Phillips. Recipient Silver medal Moscow Tschaikovsky competition, 1966. Office: ICM Artists Ltd 40 W 57th St New York NY 10019

DICK, ALBERT BLAKE, III, former manufacturing company executive, corporate director; b. Chgo., Mar. 10, 1918; s. Albert Blake and Helen (Aldrich) D.; m. Elisabeth York, Sept. 14, 1940; children: Albert Blake IV, John Howard, Frederick Aldrich; m. Susan Drake Bent, Aug. 20, 1960. Student, Yale U., 1938-39. With A.B. Dick Co., 1939-82, holding various positions in purchasing, mfg., sales, and controllers divs., dir., 1946-82, treas., 1947-60, pres., 1947-61, chmn., 1961-82; dir. No. Trust Co., No. Trust Corp., Commonwealth Edison Co., First Nat. Bank of Lake Forest, Ill., First Nat. Bank of Lake Bluff; Life trustee Ill. Inst. Tech. Trustee, mem. exec. bd. Rush-Presbyn.-St. Luke's Med. Center; chmn., dir. Lake Forest Hosp. Served in USN, 1942-45. Clubs: Economic, Executives, Chicago, Attic, Commercial, Metropolitan (Chgo.); Onwentsia (Lake Forest); Cotton Bay (Eleuthera, Bahamas); Old Elm (Ft. Sheridan, Ill.); Birnam Wood Golf (Santa Barbara, Calif.). Home: 1550 N Green Bay Rd Lake Forest IL 60045 Office: 135 S LaSalle St Room 2514 Chicago IL 60603

DICK, BERTRAM GALE, JR., educator; b. Portland, Oreg., June 12, 1926; s. Bertram Gale and Helen (Meengs) D.; m. Ann Bradford Volkmann, June 23, 1956; children—Timothy Howe, Robin Louise, Stephen Gale. B.A., Reed Coll., 1950, Wadham Coll., Oxford (Eng.) U., 1953, M.A., 1958; Ph.D., Cornell U., 1958. Research asso. U. Ill., 1957-59; mem. faculty U. Utah, 1959—, prof. physics, 1965—, Univ. prof., 1979-80, chmn. dept., 1964-67; cons. Minn. Mining and Mfg. Co., 1960-67; vis. prof. Technische Hochschule, Munich, 1967-68; vis. scientist Max Planck Institut Für Festkörperforschung, Stuttgart, W. Ger., 1976-77. Mem. Alta Planning and Zoning Commn., 1972-76; pres. Chamber Music S56392alt Lake City, 1974-76. Served with USNR, 1944-46. Fellow Am. Phys. Soc.; mem. AAAS, Am. Alpine Club, Sierra Club, Phi Beta Kappa, Sigma Xi. Research in theory solid state. Home: 1377 Butler Ave Salt Lake City UT 84102

DICK, CHARLES HOWARD, college president; b. Hutchinson, Kans., June 11, 1930; s. Charles Otto and Mary Elizabeth (Combs) D.; m. BarbarAnn Deren, June 14, 1969. B.A., U. Kans., 1953; Ph.D., Northwestern U., 1957; M.S., Calif. State U., Fresno, 1971; D.Sc., Hamilton State U., Tucson, 1973. Dir. public edn. Am. Cancer Soc., N.Y.C., 1957-61, Roswell Park Meml. Inst., Buffalo, 1961-67; asst. v.p. SUNY, Buffalo, 1967-69; asst. to pres. Calif. State U., Fresno, 1969-71, prof. health sci., 1970-71; asst. commr. HEW, Washington, 1971-73; v.p. Cornell U. Med. Center, N.Y.C., 1973-76; pres. Centenary Coll., Hackettstown, N.J., 1976—, prof. allied health, 1978-80; trustee Assn. Ind. Colls. and Univs. N.J., 1978-80, N.J. Coll. Fund Assn., 1978-80; chmn. nat. freedom info. task force HEW, 1972-73. Author articles, reports, monograph, films. Chmn. exec. com. Am. Cancer Soc., 1968-69; bd. dirs. Muscular Dystrophy Assn. Am., Buffalo, 1968-69; mem. Nat. Conf. High Blood Pressure, 1972-73. Recipient award Public Relations Soc. Am., 1972, Nat. Safety Council, 1972. Mem. Assn. Am. Colls., Am. Council Edn., Council Advancement and Support Edn., Nat. Assn. Sci. Writers. Episcopalian. Office: 400 Jefferson St Hackettstown NJ 07840 *

DICK, DOUGLAS PATRICK, construction company executive; b. Pitts., Jan. 5, 1953; s. Dorsey W. and Loretta L. D.; m. Deborah Genge, Dec. 11, 1976; children: Alexander Genge, Cameron. Student, Hawthorne Coll., 1971-72, Robert Morris Coll., 1972-73. Asst. sales mgr. Dick Corp., Pitts., 1971-75, constrn. mgr., 1975-79, treas., 1979—. Trustee Teamster Welfare and Pension Fund. Office: PO Box 10896 Pittsburgh PA 15236

DICK, HENRY HENRY, clergyman; b. Russia, June 1, 1922; s. Henry Henry and Mary (Unger) D.; m. Erica Penner, May 25, 1946; children—Janet (Mrs. Arthur Enns), Judith (Mrs. Ron Brown), James, Henry. Th.B., Mennonite Brethren Bible Coll., 1950. Ordained to ministry Mennonite Brethren Ch., 1950; pastor in, Orillia, Ont., Can., 1950-54, Lodi, Calif., 1954-57, Shafter, Calif., 1958-69; faculty Tabor Coll., 1954-55; gen. sec. Mennonite Brethren Conf. of U.S.A., 1969-72; pres. Mennonite Brethren Bibl. Sem., Fresno, Calif., 1972-76; vice moderator Gen Conf. Mennonite Brethren Ch., 1975-78, moderator, 1979—; pastor Reedley Mennonite Brethren Ch., 1976—; moderator Pacific Dist. Conf., 1959-60, 61-63, 75-77; mem. exec. com. Mennonite Central Com. Internat., 1967-75, mem. bd. reference and counsel, 1966-69, 72-75, mem. bd. missions and services, 1969-72; exec. sec. Bd. Edn. (Mennonite Brethren), 1969-72, chmn, 1979—; dir. Mennonite Disaster Service (Yuba City (Calif.) Flood), 1955, Eureka, Calif., 1966; pres. Mennonite Brethren Chs. N.Am., 1979—. Columnist: bi-weekly publ. Christian Leader, 1969-75. Bd. dirs. Bob Wilson Meml. Hosp., Ulysses, Kans., 1969-72. Recipient Humanitarian award Shafter C. of C., 1969, Citation bd. dirs. Bibl. Sem. Clubs: Kiwanis, Reedley Rotary. Home: 783 W Carpenter St Reedley CA 93654 Office: 1632 L St Reedley CA 93654

DICK, NANCY E., state lieutenant governor; b. Detroit, July 22, 1930; m. Stephen Barnett; children: Margot, Timber, Justin. B.A. in Resort Mgmt., Mich. State U. Worked in resort mgmt., conv. dir., interior design, bookkeeping;; mem. Colo. Gen. Assembly, 1974-79, vice chmn. transp. and energy com.; lt. gov. State of Colo., 1979—; fin. chmn. Fedn. Rocky Mountain States; mem. adv. panel U.S. Oil Shale Environ. Com., 1974-78; del. Nat. Democratic Party Convention, 1980; mem. Fordham Planning Commn., U.S. Health Care Cost Containment, 1981; Rocky Mt. bd. dirs. Inst. Internat. Edn., 1980-87; exec. bd. Gov's. Interstate Indian Council, 1981-83; chmn. regional selection White House Fellows, 1981, panelist, 1979-80; chmn. Colorado-Human Indsl. Conf. Planning Com.; del. Women's Leadership Conf. on Nat. Security. Trustee Denver Symphony Assn.; hon. chmn. Friends of the Urban League; mem. rural health com. Colo. Med. Soc., 1975-76; exec. bd. U.S. Army War Coll., 1981. Recipient Disting. Alumni award Mich. State U., 1980, Florence Sabin award Colo. Pub. Health Care Assn., 1980, Outstanding Alumnus award Coll. Bus., Mich. State U., 1981, Outstanding Citizen Nat. Rural Primary Care Assn., 1981, Found. scholarship Nat. Ctr. Creative Leadership, 1981. Democrat. Office: Office of Lt Gov State Capitol Bldg Room 144 Denver CO 80203 *

DICK, RAYMOND DALE, psychology educator; b. Toledo, Ohio, July 16, 1930; s. Floyd Edward and Clara Belle (Spilker) D.; m. Beverly Ann Sparks, June 18, 1955; children: Gregory Dale, Jeffrey Clayton. B.S., Northwestern U., 1952; M.A., U. Mo., 1955, Ph.D., 1958. Asst. prof. psychology Fort Hayes (Kans.) State Coll., 1958-62, assoc. prof., 1962-64, prof., 1964-66, acad. chmn. psychology dept., 1959-66; prof. psychology U. Wis., Eau Claire, 1966—, dean Sch. Grad Studies, 1966—82; Assoc. Danforth Found., 1962—, also chmn. Upper Midwest selection com., 1969-72; mem. com. liberal arts edn. North Central Assn. Colls. and Secondary Schs., 1963-66, coordinator liberal arts com., 1965-68, cons-examiner, 1971—. Contbr. profl. jours. Mem. Am., Midwestern, Wis. psychol. assns., AAUP, AAAS, Am. Assn. Higher Edn. Home: 2823 Irene Dr Eau Claire WI 54701

DICK, RICHARD IRWIN, environmental engineer, educator; b. Sanborn, Iowa, July 18, 1935; s. Laurence Irwin and Lillian Marie (Riesser) D.; m. Delores Kay Den Beste, Aug. 31, 1958; children: Natalie Ann, Kevin Irwin, Laura Lynn, Craig David. B.S., Iowa State U., 1957; M.S., State U. Iowa, 1958; Ph.D., U. Ill., 1965. Sanitary engr. USPHS, Kansas City, Mo., 1958-60; sanitary engr. Clark, Daily and Dietz (Cons. Engrs.), Urbana, Ill., 1960-62; prof. civil engrng. U. Ill., 1962-72, U. Del., Newark, 1972-77; Joseph P. Ripley prof. engrng. Cornell U., Ithaca, N.Y., 1977—; Thomas R. Camp lectr. Boston Soc. Civil Engrs., 1981. Contbr. 125 articles to profl. jours. Served with USPHS, 1958-60. Recipient Harrison Prescott Eddy medal Water Pollution Control Fedn., 1968. Mem. Assn. Environ. Engrng. Profs. (past pres., Disting. lectr. 1980), Internat. Assn. Water Pollution Research (past mem. exec. com., bd. govs.), ASCE, Water Pollution Control Fedn., Am. Water Works Assn., Brit. Instn. Water Pollution Control, Sigma Xi, Tau Beta Pi, Chi Epsilon, Phi Kappa Phi. Home: 115 W Upland Rd Ithaca NY 14850 Office: 118 Hollister Hall Cornell U Ithaca NY 14853

DICKASON, JAMES FRANK, land and farming company executive; b. San Francisco, July 5, 1922; s. James Frank and Jean Dempster (Humbird) D.; m. Linda Celeste Stewart, Dec. 9, 1961; children: James B., Thomas H., Margaret J., Bradford S. B.A., Harvard U., 1944; M.B.A., Stanford U., 1951. Successively asst. sec., sec., v.p., dir. White Investment Co., San Francisco, 1951-63; exec. v.p. Newhall Land & Farming Co., Valencia, Calif., 1963-71, pres., 1971—, chief exec. officer, 1971-79, chmn. bd., 1979—, dir., 1963—; dir. Wells Fargo & Co., Pacific Lighting Corp. Vice pres., dirs. United Way Los Angeles; v.p., bd. dirs. Southwest Museum; bd. dirs. Automobile Club of So. Calif.; trustee Calif. Inst. Arts. Served with U.S. Army, 1943-46. Mem. Urban Land Inst., Calif. Roundtable, Calif. C. of C. (bd. dirs., treas.), Lambda Alpha. Republican. Presbyterian. Clubs: California (Los Angeles); Pacific Union, Bohemian (San Francisco); Knickerbocker (N.Y.C.). Home: 930 Rosalind Rd San Marino CA 91108 Office: PO Box 55000 Valencia CA 91355

DICKASON, JOHN HAMILTON, association executive; b. Wooster, Ohio, June 3, 1931; s. Donald Eugene and Martha Himes (Hamilton) D.; m. Barbara Helen Fee, June 20, 1953; children: John Harold, Kathryn Helen. A.B., Dartmouth Coll., 1953, M.B.A., 1954; grad., Inst. Orgn. Mgmt., Mich. State U., 1965, Advanced Mgmt. Program, Harvard U., 1980. With Scott Paper Co., 1954-58; personnel technician Ill. Civil Service Commn., Springfield, 1958-60; bus. mgr., then asso. dir. Ill. Bar Assn., 1960-70, exec. dir., 1970—. Pres. Springfield Mental Health Assn., 1965-66; sr. warden Christ Episcopal Ch., Springfield, 1973-75, lic. lay reader, 1970—, treas., 1966-69, 76—; mem. fin. com. Diocese Springfield, 1975-77; troop leader local Boy Scouts Am., 1966—, mem. council exec. com., 1978-80. Served with AUS, 1954-56. Mem. Am. Bar Assn. (asso.), Am. Soc. Assn. Execs., Ill. Soc. Assn. Execs. (pres. 1972), Nat. Assn. Bar Execs. (pres. 1976-77, Man of Yr. 1983), Am. Judicature Soc. Republican. Clubs: Sangamo, Racquet, Surf (Springfield). Home: 11 Boulder Point Springfield IL 62702 Office: Ill Bar Center Springfield IL 62701

DICKE, RICHARD MAC LANE, lawyer; b. Boise, Idaho, Dec. 26, 1915; s. Henry F. and Louise (Traub) D.; m. Elizabeth Cantlin, Aug. 15, 1942; children: Richard, Cynthia, Mary, David, Deborah. B.A., Princeton U., 1937; LL.B., U. Pa., 1940. Bar: N.Y., Pa. Assoc. Simpson Thacher & Bartlett, N.Y.C., 1940-41, 1946-52, partner, 1952—; dir. Am. Electric Power Co., Inc., Atlantic City Electric Co. Editor: U. Pa. Law Rev. Mem. bd. overseers U. Pa. Law Sch.; chmn. bd. trustees Human Resource Sch. Served with USN. Republican. Episcopalian. Clubs: Princeton, Downtown Assn., Garden City Golf, Lawrence Beach., Cherry Valley Country, Cap and Gown. Home: 26 Cathedral Ave Garden City NY 11530 Office: One Battery Park Plaza New York NY 10004

DICKE, ROBERT HENRY, educator, physicist; b. St. Louis, May 6, 1916; s. Oscar H. and Flora (Peterson) D.; m. Annie Henderson Currie, June 6, 1942; children: Nancy Jean Dicke Rapoport, John Robert, James Howard. A.B., Princeton U., 1939; Ph.D., U. Rochester, 1941, D.Sc. (hon.), 1981; D.Sc. (hon.), U. Edinburgh, 1972, Ohio No. U., 1981. Microwave radar devel. Radiation Lab., MIT, 1941-46; physics faculty Princeton U., 1946—, Cyrus Fogg Brackett prof. physics, 1957-75, Albert Einstein Univ. prof. sci., 1975—, chmn. physics dept., 1967-70; mem. adv. panel for physics NSF, 1959-61; chmn. adv. com. atomic physics Nat. Bur. Standards, 1961-63; mem. com. on physics NASA, 1963-70, chmn., 1963-66; chmn. physics adv. panel Com. on Internat. Exchange of Persons (Fulbright-Hays Act), 1964-66; chmn. adv. com. on radio astronomy telescopes NSF, 1967, 69; mem. Nat. Sci. Bd., 1970-76; vis. com. Nat. Bur. Standards, 1975-79, chmn., 1979; vis. prof. Harvard U., 1954-55; Sherman Fairchild Disting. scholar Calif. Inst. Tech., 1975; Walker Ames prof. U. Wash., Seattle, 1979; Jaynes lectr. Am. Philos. Soc., 1969; Scott lectr. Cambridge U. (Eng.), 1977. Author: (with Montgomery, Purcell) Principles of Micro-wave Circuits, 1948, (with J.P. Wittke) An Introduction to Quantum Mechanics, 1960, The Theoretical Significance of Experimental Relativity, 1964, Gravitation and the Universe, 1970. Trustee Asso. Univs. Inc., 1980—. Recipient Nat. Medal Sci., 1970, NASA medal for exceptional sci. achievement, 1973, Cresson medal Franklin Inst., 1974. Mem. Nat. Acad. Scis. (Comstock prize 1973), Am. Philos. Soc., Am. Geophys. Union, Am. Phys. Soc., Am. Astron. Soc., Am. Acad. Arts and Scis. (Rumford medal 1967), Royal Astron. Soc. (assoc.). Home: 321 Prospect Ave Princeton NJ 08540

DICKELMAN, HOWARD CLARENCE, food chain executive; b. Exland, Wis., Sept. 27, 1918; s. Lawrence Henry and Elsie (Skode) D.; m. Dorothy Jane Finkler, Dec. 16, 1939; children: Judith Ann, James Howard, Vicky Lynn. Student, Marquette U., Milw., 1936-39. With sales div. Gen. Foods Corp., 1938-46; mgr. produce div. Schultz Sav-O Stores Inc., Sheboygan, Wis., 1946-60, pres., 1964—, chmn. bd., 1974—, also dir.; dir. Security First Bank, Sheboygan. Bd. dirs. Topco Assn., Skokie, Ill., St. Nicholas Hosp., Sheboygan; chmn. Topco Credit Com., 1977; adv. com. Kohler (Wis.) Village, 1979—. Served with USNR, 943-46. Mem. Nat. Assn. Food Chains, Wis. Food Dealers Assn., Food Mktg. Inst., Sheboygan Area C. of C., Econ. Club Sheboygan. Roman Catholic. Club: Pine Hill Country. Office: Schultz Sav-O Stores Ave 2215 Union Ave Sheboygan WI 53081

DICKENS, BERNARD MORRIS, legal educator; b. London, Nov. 4, 1937; emigrated to Can., 1974; s. David and Rose (Jacobs) D. LL.B., King's Coll., U. London, 1961, LL.M., 1965, Ph.D., 1971; LL.D., U. London, 1978. Barrister, Inner Temple, 1963; barrister and solicitor, Law Soc. Upper Can. (Ont. bar), 1977. Tutorial student King's Coll., U. London, 1962-63; lectr. Coll. Law, London, 1964-68, sr. lectr., 1968-72, prin. lectr., 1972-74; research prof. law U. Toronto, Ont., Can., 1974-80, prof. law, 1980—; cons. panel human research WHO/CIOMS, Geneva, 1979-83; legal cons. abortion law Commonwealth Secretariat, London, 1976-83; project cons. Ont. Law Reform, Toronto, 1982—; cons. mem. com. on ethics Can. Med. Assn., Ottawa, 1982—. Author: Abortion and the Law, 1966, Medico-Legal Aspects of Family Law, 1979, (with R.J. Cook) Abortion Laws in Commonwealth Countries, 1979, Emerging Issues in Commonwealth Abortion Law, 1982. Mem. Atty. Gen.'s Com. on Children's Representation, Toronto, 1977-78; mem. editorial adv. bd. Bibliography of Bioethics, Kennedy Inst., 1978—; bd. dirs. Can. Found. for Children and Law, 1979-83, Advocacy Resource Centre for Handicapped, 1981—. Connaught grantee U. Toronto, 1974, 78; John T. Law lectr. Hosp. for Sick Children Found., 1982. Mem. Can. Bar Assn., Can. Assn. Law Tchrs., Am. Soc. Law and Medicine, N.Y. Acad. Sci., Medico-Legal Soc. Toronto. Jewish. Home: 55 Charles St W # 1504 Toronto ON Canada M5S 2W9 Office: Faculty of Law Univ Toronto 84 Queen's Park Toronto ON Canada M5S 1A1

DICKENSON, R. KEITH, energy company executive; b. Grand Rapids, Mich., June 19, 1930. B.S., U.S. Mil. Acad. With Tex. Eastern Corp., Houston, 1969—, now sr. v.p. Office: Tex Eastern Corp PO Box 2521 One Houston Ctr Houston TX 77001

DICKENSON, RUSSELL ERRETT, government official; b. Melissa, Tex., Apr. 12, 1923; s. John Errett and Lexie (Davis) D.; m. Ollie Maxine Moran, Dec. 23, 1947; children: Vickie Lee, Russell Steven. Student, N. Tex. State Coll., 1940-42; B.A., Ariz. State Coll., 1947; D.Sc. (hon.), No. Ariz. U., 1982. Assoc. regional dir. Nat. Capital Parks-Nat. Park Service, Washington, 1968-70, gen. supt., 1970-71, regional dir., 1971-73; dep. dir. Nat. Park Service, 1973-75, regional dir. Pacific N.W. Region, Seattle, 1975-80, dir., Washington, 1980—; exec. sec. Nat. Park Found., Washington, 1980—. Bd. dirs. J.F. Kennedy Ctr., Washington, 1980—, Wolf Trap Found., Vienna, Va., 1980—, Pennsylvania Ave. Devel. Corp., Washington, 1981—, Statue of Liberty-Ellis Island Centennial Com., N.Y.C., 1982—. Served to capt. USMC, 1942-46; PTO. Recipient Meritorious Service award Dept. Interior, 1971, Disting. Service award Dept. Interior, 1972, Cornelius Amory Pugsley award Am. Scenic and Hist. Preservation Soc., 1975, Disting. Alumni award No. Ariz. U., 1978, award for Excellence Nat. Soc. Park Resources, 1981, George Washington medal U.S. Capitol Hist. Soc., 1982, Golden Flower of Rheydt award, W. Germany, 1983. Club: Cosmos (Washington). Office: Nat Park Service Dept Interior 18th and C Sts NW Washington DC 20240

DICKER, MARVIN, lawyer; b. Bklyn., July 14, 1933. B.A., Bklyn. Coll., 1954; LL.B., Columbia U., 1957. Bar: N.Y. 1958, U.S. Supreme Ct. 1965. Law clk. U.S. Dist. Ct. (so. dist.) N.Y., 1957-58; assoc. Proskauer, Rose, Goetz & Mendelsohn, N.Y.C., 1958-68, ptnr., 1968—; adj. prof. Adelphi U., Long Island, N.Y., 1972—; faculty mem. New Sch. for Social Research, N.Y.C., 1978—. Mem. Am. Arbitration Assn., N.Y. State Bar Assn., Westchester Bar Assn., Assn. Bar City of N.Y. Office: Proskauer Rose Goetz & Mendelsohn 300 Park Ave New York NY 10022

DICKERSON, EARL BURRUS, retired insurance company executive; b. Canton, Miss., June 22, 1891; s. Edward and Emma (Garrett) D.; m. Kathryn Kennedy, June 15, 1930; 1 dau., Diane. A.B., U. Ill., 1914; J.D., U. Chgo., 1920; H.H.D., Wilberforce U., 1961; LL.D., Northwestern U., 1977, U. Ill.-Chgo., 1984. Bar: Ill. 1920. Exec. v.p. Supreme Life Ins. Co. of Am., 1954-55, gen. counsel, 1921-55, gen. mgr., 1955-62, pres., also chief exec. officer, 1955-71, chmn. bd., 1971-73, hon. chmn. bd., financial cons., 1973—; asst. corp. counsel, City of Chgo., 1923-27, asst. atty. gen., Ill., 1933-39. Mem. City Council Chgo., 1939-43; dir. emeritus Hyde Park Fed. Savs. & Loan Assn.; Bd. dirs. S.E. Chgo. Commn., 1953—; mem. Pres.'s Com. Fair Employment Practice, 1941-43; Trustee emeritus La Rabida Jackson Park Sanitarium. Served as lt. inf. AEF, World War I. Recipient citation for pub. service Alumni Assn. U. Chgo., 1961; Legal Def. award NAACP, 1975; Olive H. Crosthwait award Chgo. Ins. Assn., 1976; Humanitarian award Abraham Lincoln Center, 1977, Henry A. Booth House, affiliate Hull House Assn., 1981; Disting. Legislator award Black Ill. Legis. Lobby, 1979; award for community service Negro Joint Appeal, 1970; Black Businessman of Yr. Black Book, 1971; James H. Tilghman award Washington Park and Wabash Ave YMCAs, 1979; Illini Achievement award U. Ill., 1981; Heritage award DuSable Mus. African Am. History, 1982. Mem. Chgo. Urban League (past pres.), NAACP (dir. emeritus), ABA, Ill. Bar Assn., Cook County Bar Assn. (Presdl. award 1979, spl. honoree 25th ann. lawday 1983), Chgo. Bar Assn., Nat. Lawyers Guild (past pres.), U. Ill. Alumni Assn. (Earl B. Dickerson achievement award 1982), Northwestern U. Alumni Assn., U. Chgo. Law Sch. Assn., Am. Legion (founder), Kappa Alpha Psi (past grand polemarch). Episcopalian. Club: Original Forty (Man of Year award 1976) (Chgo.). Home: 4800 Chicago Beach Dr Chicago IL 60615 Office: 3501 Martin Luther King Jr Dr Chicago IL 60653

DICKERSON, FREDERICK REED, lawyer, educator; b. Chgo., Nov. 11, 1909; s. Fred George and Rena (Reed) D.; m. Jane Morrison, June 14, 1939; children: Elizabeth Ann (Mrs. David D. Brown), John Scott, Martha Reed. Grad., Lake Forest Acad., 1927; A.B., Williams Coll., 1931; LL.B., Harvard U., 1934; LL.M. (Univ. fellow 1938-39), Columbia U., 1939, J.S.D., 1950. Bar: Mass. 1934, Ill. 1936, U.S. Supreme Ct. 1943. Assoc. firm Goodwin, Procter & Hoar, Boston, 1934-35, McNab, Holmes & Long, Chgo., 1936-38; asst. prof. law Washington U., St. Louis, 1939-40, U. Pitts., 1940-42; atty. OPA, 1942-47; asst. legis. counsel U.S. Ho. of Reps., 1947-49, Joint Army-Air Force Statutory Revision Group; chmn. com. on codification, dep. asst. gen. counsel U.S. Dept. Def., 1949-58; prof. law Ind. U., 1958-83, prof. emeritus, 1983—, asso. dean, 1971-75; distinguished vis. prof. law So. Ill. U., 1976, 80; Pres. F.G. Dickerson Co., Chgo., 1948-82; chmn. commn. on uniform laws State of Ind., 1969-81; mem. Ind. Statute Revision Commn., 1969-70; cons. Dept. Def., 1958-59, 66, FAA, 1960-65, Dept. Transp., 1967-69, Pres.'s Com. on Consumer Interests, 1967-68, Commn. on Govt. Procurement, 1971-72, Gen. Accounting Office, 1973-76; lectr. Northwestern U., 1938, Am. U., 1956, 58, Practising Law Inst., 1961, 79, U.K. Govt. Legal Officers' Course, 1972, U.S. CSC, 1971-76, lectr. Center for Adminstrv. Justice, 1975-79. Author: Products Liability and the Food Consumer, 1951, Legislative Drafting, 1954, Fundamentals of Legal Drafting, 1965, Interpretation and Application of Statutes, 1975; Editor: Legal Problems Affecting Private Swimming Pools, 1961, Product Safety in Household Goods, 1968, Professionalizing Legislative Drafting—The Federal Experience, 1973, Proc. International Seminar and Workshop on the Teaching of Legal Drafting, 1977, Cases and Materials on Legislation, 1978, Materials on Legal Drafting, 1981; mem. editorial bd.: Jurimetrics Jour, 1962—; bd. advisors: Jour. of Legislation, 1977—; contbr.: articles to Harper's mag., Esquire, Ency. Americana. Pres. Chevy Chase Citizens Assn., 1955-56, Friends of Music, Ind. U., 1972-73. Recipient Distinguished Civilian Service award Dept. Def., 1957, award Assn. Am. Law Schs., 1983; Ford Found. law faculty fellow Harvard U., 1961-62; Am. Assembly fellow, 1968. Mem. Am. Law

Inst., Nat. Conf. Commrs. on Uniform State Laws, ABA (chmn. standing com. law and tech. 1968-69, chmn. standing com. legis. drafting 1969-73, chmn. com. on lang. sci. and formal systems 1982—), Ind. Bar Assn., Pierian Sodality of 1808, Order of Coif, Phi Alpha Delta, Phi Gamma Delta. Methodist. Home: 870 Woodscrest Dr Bloomington IN 47401

DICKERSON, GEORGE WILLIAM, city ofcl., ret. army officer; b. Warrenton, Va., Aug. 29, 1918; s. Broadus Charles and Ada Montz (Davis) D.; m. Lois Ann Wood, Apr. 22, 1946. B.S., Va. Poly. Inst., 1941; M.S., Ohio U., 1956; M.B.A., George Washington U., 1963. Commd. 2d lt. U.S. Army, 1941, advanced through grades to brig. gen., 1967; served with (24th Div.), PTO, 1942-45, inf. officer, 1946-50, comdr., Austria, 1950-53; mil. prof. Ohio U., 1953-56; regtl. comdr., Korea, 1957-59; mem. staff Dept. Army and Joint Chiefs Staff, 1959-63, 1963-66; prof. (Army War Coll.), 1967, comptroller, 1967-68, comdg. gen., Vietnam, 1967-69; comptroller U.S. Army, Europe, 1970-72; city mgr., Poquoson, Va., 1972-80; instr. U. Md. Overseas Div., 1957-59. Contbr. articles service jours. Active Girl Scouts, Boy Scouts Am.; bd. dirs. chpt. ARC. Decorated D.S.M. with oak leaf cluster, Silver Star, D.F.C., Soldier's Medal, Bronze Star with 2 oak leaf clusters, Air medal with 18 oak leaf clusters, Joint Service Commendaion medal, Army Commendation medal with 2 oak leaf clusters. Mem. Assn. U.S. Army, S.A.R., Phi Kappa Phi, Alpha Kappa Psi, Omicron Delta Kappa. Baptist. Clubs: Kiwanis, Army-Navy Country. Home: Dickerwood Poquoson VA 23662

DICKERSON, NANCY HANSCHMAN, television producer, news correspondent; b. Milw.; d. Frederick R. and Florence (Conners) Hanschman; m. Claude Wyatt Dickerson, Feb. 24, 1962 (div. 1983); children: Elizabeth, Ann, Jane, Michael, John. Student, Clarke Coll., Dubuque, Iowa; grad., U. Wis., 1948; postgrad., Harvard U.; H.H.D., Am. Internat. Coll., Springfield, Mass. Sch. tchr., Milw.; staff asst. Senate Fgn. Relations Com., Washington; producer CBS News, 1956-60, 1st woman news corr., 1960-63; news corr. NBC, 1963-70; news analyst Inside Washington (syndicated nationally for TV stas.), 1971—; producer spl. syndicated TV programs, pres. Dickerson Co., 1971—; polit. commentator Newsweek Broadcasting Service; founder, exec. producer Television Corp. Am., 1980—; reporter Pres. Kennedy's funeral, Republican and Democratic convs., Civil Rights March on Washington, Kennedy, Johnson and Nixon inaugurations; represented Pub. Broadcasting Corp. (on all-network Conversation with Pres. Nixon), 1970; lectr. Author: Among Those Present, 1976. Trustee Am. U. Recipient Collegian award LaSalle Coll., Phila; Spirit of Achievement award Albert Einstein Coll., Yeshiva U.; Sigma Delta Chi award Boston U.; Pioneer award New Eng. Women's Press Assn.; Assoc. fellow Pierson Coll., Yale, 1972—; Peabody award for 1982 TV program on Watergate; Silver Gavel award for 1982 TV program on Watergate ABA. Mem. Radio-Television News Analysts. Clubs: Washington Press (past v.p.), Federal City).

DICKERSON, NORVIN KENNEDY, contractor, investor; b. Louisville, Mar. 3, 1917; s. Norvin Kennedy and Clara (Mertinkate) D.; m. Sara McCarten Craig, June 7, 1939; children: Norvin Kennedy III, Ann Gillam. Ed. pub. schs., Louisville. From gen. supt. to Southeastern mgr. R.B. Tyler Co., Louisville, 1935-45; founder Dickerson Inc., Monroe, N.C., 1945, pres., 1945-58, chmn. bd., 1958—; chmn. bd. 5 other corps.; dir. N.C. Nat. Bank, Monroe; dir., chmn. bd. Dickerson Group, Inc.; dir. Comml. Products Inc., Monroe; ptnr. Wilson Woods Real Estate Co.; owner Sally Mae Farms, Sally Mae Greenhouses; co-owner Ridgewood Devel. Co., Monroe, Monroe Devel. Assn., Inc. Mem. council Boy Scouts Am., past pres. Central N.C. council; mem. N.C. State Engring. Found.; past jr. and sr. warden St. Paul's Episcopal Ch., Monroe, N.C., now sr. warden emeritus; trustee St. Marys Coll., Raleigh, N.C. Symphony; bd. visitors Johnson C. Smith U. Mem. Assoc. Gen. Contractors Am. (hon. life dir.; dir past chmn. hwy. div.; past pres. Carolinas br.), N.C. Arts Assn., N.C. Soc. Engrs. Clubs: Charlotte City; City, Capitol City (Raleigh); Country of N.C. (Pinehurst); Rolling Hills Country (Monroe, N.C.); Hounds Ears. Home: 2001 Griffith Rd Monroe NC 28110 Office: Box 400 Monroe NC 28110

DICKES, ROBERT, psychiatrist; b. N.Y.C., Apr. 15, 1912; s. Benjamin and Anna (Adler) D.; m. Bernice Livingston, June 12, 1938; children: Richard A., Susan R. Dickes Hubbard. B.S., CCNY, 1933; M.S., Emory U., 1934, M.D., 1938. Diplomate: Am. Bd. Internal Medicine, Am. Bd. Psychiatry and Neurology. Intern L.I. Coll. Hosp., Bklyn., 1938-39, asst. resident in internal medicine, 1938-39, resident in medicine, 1939-41, dir. med. clinics, 1946-50; asso. in medicine L.I. Coll. Medicine, 1946, asst. prof. psychiatry, 1949; fellow in medicine Western Res. U.-Lakeside Hosp., 1941-42; fellow in psychiatry Kings County Hosp. Center-SUNY Bklyn., 1950-52, mem. staff, 1952—, pres. med. br., 1977-78; clin. asso. prof. psychiatry Downstate Med. Center SUNY, Bklyn., 1950-54, asso. prof., 1954-56, clin. asso. prof., 1956-61, asso. prof., 1961-63, prof., 1963, 78-82, prof. emeritus, 1982—, tng. and supervising analyst, 1965—, acting chmn. dept. psychiatry, 1965-66, 71-72, dir. infant behavior study lab., 1973, dir. center human sexuality, 1973—, chmn. dept. psychiatry, 1975-78; clin. prof. psychiatry NYU Coll. Medicine, 1982—; cons. VA hosps., Bklyn., Northport, N.Y. Contbr. articles to profl. publs. Bd. govs., mem. acquisitions com. Bklyn. Museum. Served to maj. M.C. U.S. Army, 1942-46. Commonwealth fellow, 1941-42, 48-49. Fellow A.C.P., Am. Psychiat. Assn., Am. Coll. Psychiatry; mem. Am. Psychoanalytic Assn., Psychoanalytic Assn. N.Y. (treas. 1962-64), Bklyn. Psychiat. Soc. (pres. 1967), Kings County Med. Soc., Kings County Psychiat. Soc. (pres. 1967-68), Soc. Sex Therapy and Research (pres. 1979-81), Soc. Consultants to Armed Forces of U.S.

DICKESON, ROBERT CELMER, political science educator., university president; b. Independence, Mo., June 28, 1940; s. James Houston and Sophie Stephanie (Celmer) D.; m. Ludmila Ann Weir, June 22, 1963; children: Elizabeth Ann, Cynthia Marie. A.B., U. Mo., 1962, M.A., 1963, Ph.D., 1968; postgrad., U. No. Colo., 1971, 72; postgrad. inst. ednl. mgmt., Harvard U., 1973. Adminstrv. asst. U. Mo., Columbia, 1962-64, dir. student activities, 1964-68, asst. dean students, 1968-69; dean student affairs No. Ariz. U., Flagstaff, 1969-70, asso. prof. polit. sci., 1970-76, prof., 1976-81, on leave, 1979-81, v.p. student affairs, 1970-79, v.p., univ. relations, 1973-79; dir. Ariz. Dept. Adminstrn., Phoenix, 1979-81; pres. U. No. Colo., Greeley, 1981—, prof. polit. sci., 1981—; adj. prof. Ariz. State U., Tempe, 1979-81; nat. vice-chmn. Cert. Public Mgr. Policy Bd., 1980-81; planning and mgmt. cons.; mem. univ. adv. council Am. Council on Life Ins.; dir. United Bank of Greeley. Contbr. articles to profl. jours. Active Boy Scouts Am.; v.p. Grand Canyon council, Flagstaff, 1974-76, pres., 1976-79, mem. nat. council, 1976-81, T. Roosevelt council, 1979-81, Long's Peak Council, 1981—; mem. state com. Ariz. Democratic Com., 1970-72; chmn. Gov.'s Commn. on Merit System Reform, 1979-80, Gov.'s Regulatory Rev. Council, 1980-81, Gov.'s Commn. Higher Edn., 1983—; mem. Gov.'s Commn. Excellence in Edn., 1983—. Recipient Dist. award of Merit., 1973, Silver Beaver award, 1975; Recipient Disting. Service award Sigma Alpha Epsilon, 1969. Mem. Am. Polit. Sci. Assn., Am. Soc. Public Adminstrn. (Ariz. exec. bd., Superior Service award 1981), Am. Acad. Polit. and Social Sci., Coll. Student Personnel Inst. (acad. council 1969-73), Nat. Assn. Student Personnel Adminstrs. (regional council 1974-79), Newcomen Soc., Phi Kappa Phi. United Methodist (pres. bd. trustees 1974). Lodges: Kiwanis (pres. 1975-76); Rotary. Office: Office of President U No Colo Greeley CO 80639

DICKEY, DUVAL FREDERICK, bus. cons., former energy company executive; b. New Orleans, June 16, 1916; s. Charles E. and Alma G. D.; m. Margaret V. Stewart, Sept. 26, 1942; children: DuVal Frederick, Virginia Dickey Nelson. B.B.A., Tulane U., 1939; grad. advanced mgmt. program, Columbia U., 1958. With Exxon Co. U.S. A. (and predecessor cos.), 1939—, v.p. mktg., Houston, 1972—, sec., 1978-81; bus. cons., 1981—. Mem. pres.'s council, chmn. bus. sch. council Tulane U. Served with USN, 1942-46. Mem. Am. Soc. Corp. Secs., Am. Petroleum Inst., Phi Kappa Sigma, Beta Gamma Sigma. Republican. Lutheran. Club: River Oaks Country (Houston). Home and Office: 354 Westminster Houston TX 77024

DICKEY, ERVIN JOHN, JR., insurance company executive; b. Atlanta, 1919; m. Dorothy Ann Davis, 1943; 1 son, Trent Stevenson. Ed., U. Va., 1942. Chmn., chief exec. officer Carlton Holdings Co., N.Y. Casualty Ins. Co.; dir. Marine Midland Co. N.Y., Phoenix Mut. Life Ins. Co. Trustee House of Good Samaritan Hosp.; bd. dirs., pres. Samaritan Keep Home, Watertown, N.Y.; past trustee Clarkson Coll., Potsdam, N.Y. Clubs: Metropolitan (N.Y.C.); Capital City (Atlanta); Black River Valley (Watertown, N.Y.). Home: 221 Clinton St Watertown NY 13601 Office: 120 Washington St Watertown NY 13601

DICKEY, GLENN ERNEST, JR., sports columnist; b. Virginia, Minn., Feb. 16, 1936; s. Glenn Ernest and Madlyn Marie (Emmert) D.; m. Nancy Jo McDaniel, Feb. 25, 1967; 1 son, Kevin Scott. B.A., U. Calif., Berkeley, 1958. Sports editor Watsonville (Calif.) Register-Pajoronian, 1958-63; sports writer San Francisco Chronicle, 1963-71, sports columnist, 1971—. Author: The Jock Empire, 1974, The Great No-Hitters, 1976, Champs and Chumps, 1976, The History of National League Baseball, 1979, The History of American League Baseball, 1980, (with Dick Berg) Eavesdropping America, 1980, America Has a Better Team, 1982, The History of a Professional Basketball, 1982; contbr.: stories to Best Sports Stories, 1962, 68, 71, 75, 76. Home: 120 Florence Ave Oakland CA 94618 Office: Chronicle Publ Co 901 Mission St San Francisco CA 94119

DICKEY, JAMES, poet, novelist, film-maker, critic; b. Atlanta, Feb. 2, 1923; s. Eugene and Maibelle (Swift) D.; m. Maxine Syerson, Nov. 4, 1948 (dec. 1976); children—Christopher Swift, Kevin Webster; m. Deborah Dodson, Dec. 30, 1976; 1 dau., Bronwen Elaine. Student, Clemson Coll., 1942; B.A., Vanderbilt U., 1949, M.A., 1950. Poet in residence Reed Coll., Portland, Oreg., 1963-64, San Fernando (Calif.) Valley State Coll., 1964-64, U. Wis., 1966; cons. in poetry Library of Congress, 1966-68; now poet in residence, prof. English U. S.C., Columbia. Author: poems Into The Stone, 1960, Drowning with Others, 1962, Helmets, 1964, Two Poems of the Air, 1964, Buckdancer's Choice, 1965, reissued 1982 (Nat. Book Award of poetry 1966); criticism The Suspect in Poetry, 1964; Poems, 1957-67; poems The Eye-Beaters, 1970; criticism Babel to Byzantium, 1968, reissued 1981; novel Deliverance, 1970; belles-lettres Self-Interviews, 1970; criticism Sorties, 1971; prose poem Jericho, 1974; poems The Zodiac, 1976; prose poem God's Images, 1977; children's poems Tucky the Hunter, 1978; poems The Strength of Fields, 1979, Scion, 1980; Deliverance: A Screenplay, 1981; poems Puella, 1982, Falling, May Day Sermon and Other Poems, 1982; author: False Youth: Four Seasons, 1983; belles-lettres Night Hurdling, 1983; poems The Central Motion, 1983. Served with USAAF and USAF, World War II; Korea. Decorated Air medal.; Recipient Union League prize, 1958, Vachel Lindsay award, 1959, Longview award, 1959; Melville Cane award, 1965-66; Sewanee Rev. fellow, 1954-55; Guggenheim fellow, 1962-63; Nat. Inst. grantee, 1966. Mem. Nat. Inst. Arts and Letters. Address: 4620 Lelias Ct Lake Katherine Columbia SC 29206 Office: Dept of English Univ of SC Columbia SC 29208

DICKEY, JOHN HORACE, lawyer; b. Edmonton, Alta., Can., Sept. 4, 1914; s. Horace Arthur and Catherine (Macdonald) D.; m. Eleanor Joyce Carney, Apr. 18, 1959; children—Thomas, Michael, John Robert, Stephen, Gregory, Mary. B.A., St. Mary's U., 1936, LL.D., 1980; LL.B., Dalhousie U., 1940; L.H.D., Mt. St. Vincent U., 1981. Bar: N.S. 1940, Apptd. Queen's Counsel 1957. Practiced in, Halifax, 1940—; partner McInnes, Cooper & Robertson, 1947—; pres. N.S. Pulp, Ltd.; chmn., dir. Atlantic Trust Co. of Can.; dir. Dover Mills, Ltd., Atlantic Trust Co., Can. Comml. Corp.; Mem. Canadian-Am. com. C.D. Howe Research Inst.; Canadian rep. Econ. and Social Council of UN, 1950; mem. Canadian Delegation to UN, 1950. Mem. Canadian Ho. of Commons rep. Constituency Halifax, 1947-57; parliamentary asst. to minister Def. Prodn. and minister Trade and Commerce, 1952-57; Chmn. bd. Mt. St. Vincent U., 1969-73. Served to maj. Canadian Army, 1942-47. Mem. Canadian Bar Assn. (past v.p.), N.S. Barristers Soc. (past pres.), Liberal Fedn. Can. (past v.p.). Home: 1532 Larch St Halifax NS B3H 5W8 Canada Office: PO Box 730 1673 Bedford Row Halifax NS B3J 2V1 Canada

DICKEY, JOHN MILLER, architect; b. Chgo., Jan. 9, 1911; s. Samuel and Louise (Atherton) D.; m. Harriet Marcy Hunt, Oct. 11, 1941; children—Samuel, Alice John. A.B., Princeton U., 1933, M.F.A., 1935. Partner firm Price & Dickey, Media, Pa., 1947-62; propr. John M. Dickey (specializing in historic research and restoration), Media, Pa., 1962—; mem. properties com. Nat. Trust Historic Preservation, 1973-80; mem. Pa. Rev. Bd., 1970-80, 1972-77, 1980—. Author articles in field.; prin. restorations include Walnut St. Theatre, Phila., City Tavern, Phila., Cliveden, Phila., Stenton, Phila., Andalusia, Phila., George Read, II House, New Castle, Del. Recipient Nat. award Historic House Assn. Am., 1980. Fellow AIA (preservation coordinator Pa. 1972-76), Soc. Archtl. Historians (treas. 1962-66, dir. 1968-71), Assn. Preservation Tech. (v.p. 1973-75), Phila. Art Alliance. Democrat. Club: Princeton. Address: 207 W Baker St Media PA 19063

DICKEY, JOHN SLOAN, university president emeritus; b. Lock Haven, Pa., Nov. 4, 1907; s. John W. and Gretchen (Sloan) D.; m. Christina M. Gillespie, Nov. 26, 1932; children—Sylvia Alexander, Christina Louise (Mrs. Stewart P. Stearns, Jr.), John Sloan. A.B., Dartmouth Coll., 1929; J.D., Harvard U., 1932. Bar: Mass. bar 1932. Practiced in, Boston, 1932; asst. to commr. Mass. Dept. Correction, 1933; asst. to asst. sec. of state and asst. to legal adviser U.S. Dept. State, 1934-36; law practice with Gaston, Snow, Hunt, Rice & Boyd, Boston, 1936-40; spl. asst. to sec. of state, 1940, spl. asst. to, 1940-44; and detailed to U.S. Dept. State as chief (World Trade Intelligence div.); Dir. Office Pub. Affairs, Dept. State, 1944-45; pub. liaison officer U.S. delegation to UN Conf. on Internat. Orgn., San Francisco, 1945; lectr. in Am. fgn. policies Sch. Advanced Internat. Studies, Washington, 1944-45; pres. Dartmouth Coll., 1945-70, pres. emeritus, Bicentennial prof. pub. affairs, 1970—; Sr. vis. fellow (Council on Fgn. Relations), 1971. Author: The Dartmouth Experience, Canada and the American Presence; Contbg. author: The Secretary of State; Editor: The United States and Canada; Contbr. law and fgn. affairs jours. Mem. Phi Beta Kappa. Address: Dartmouth Coll Hanover NH 03755

DICKEY, ROBERT PRESTON, author, educator, poet; b. Flat River, Mo., Sept. 24, 1936; s. Delno Miren D. and Naomi Valentine (Jackson) Dikey; m. Victoria Anne McCabe, Jan. 9, 1969; children: Georgia Rae, Shannon Ezra, Rain Dancer. B.A., U. Mo., 1968, M.A., 1969; Ph.D., Walden U., 1975. Instr. U. Mo., 1967-69; asst. prof. English and creative writing U. So. Colo., 1969-73; assoc. mem. faculty Pima Coll., Tucson, 1975—. Author: (with Donald Justice, Thomas McAfee, Donald Drummond) poetry Four Poets, 1967, Running Lucky, 1969, Acting Immortal, 1970; Concise Dictionary of Lead River, Mo., 1972, The Basic Stuff of Poetry, 1972, Life Cycle of Seven Songs, 1972, McCabe Wants Chimes, 1973, Admitting Complicity, 1973; opera librettos Minnequa, 1976, The Witch of Tucson, 1976; Jimmie Cotton!, 1979, (with Mary K. O'Brien) Exercise Anytime, 1980, Way Out West, 1979, (The Poetica Erotica of R.P. Dickey), 1979; contbr. Poetry to popular mags, poetry, Saturday Rev., Commonweal, Prairie Schooner; founder, editor: The Poetry Bag quar., 1966-71; poetry editor: So. Colo. Standard, 1973-74. Served with USAF, 1955-57. Recipient Mahan award for poetry U. Mo., 1965-66. Home: 339 E 94th St Apt 2F New York NY 10128

DICKEY, WILLIAM (HOBART DICKEY), humanities educator, poet; b. Bellingham, Wash., Dec. 15, 1928; s. Paul Condit and Anne Marie (Hobart) D. B.A., Reed Coll., 1951; M.A. (Woodrow Wilson fellow), Harvard, 1955; M.F.A., U. Iowa, 1956; postgrad., Jesus Coll. U. Oxford, Eng., 1959-60. Instr. Cornell U., Ithaca, N.Y., 1956-59; asst. prof. English Denison U., 1960-62; asst. prof. San Francisco State U., 1962-65, asso. prof., 1966-69, prof. English and creative writing, 1970—, chmn. creative writing, 1974-77; vis. prof. English U. Hawaii, 1972. Author: Of the Festivity, 1959, Interpreter's House, 1964, Rivers of the Pacific Northwest, 1969, More Under Saturn, 1971, The Rainbow Grocery, 1978 (Juniper prize), The Sacrifice Consenting, 1981, Six Philosophical Songs, 1983; Contbr. poems, revs. to lit. jours. Fulbright fellow, 1959-60; Nat. Endowment Arts creative writing fellow, 1978-79; recipient Union League prize Poetry mag., 1961; Commonwealth Club of Calif. medal, 1972; Juniper prize U. Mass. Press, 1978; Creative Writing award Am. Inst. Arts and Letters, 1980. Mem. United Profs. Calif., Philol. Assn. Pacific Coast, Modern Lang. Assn. (del. assembly 1974-76), Phi Beta Kappa. Home: 486 Chenery St San Francisco CA 94131

DICKHONER, WILLIAM HAROLD, utility company executive; b. Cin., Sept. 2, 1921; s. Harry Frank and Matilda (Klicke) D.; m. Helen Emma Ludwig, Feb. 20, 1944; children: William H., Thomas Lee. B.S. in Mech. Engring, U. Cin., 1950. With Cin. Gas & Electric Co., 1941—, supt. power plant, 1961-64, dept. electric prodn., 1964-68, mgr. electric ops., 1968-70, v.p. electric engring. and prodn., 1970-72, sr. v.p. electric engring. and ops., 1972-74, exec. v.p., 1974-75, pres., chief exec. officer, 1975—; dir. Central Bancrop., Inc., Ohio Nat. Life Ins. Co., Central Trust Co., Ohio Valley Electric Corp.; Pres. Union Light, Heat & Power Co., Covington, Ky.,. Mem. adv. bd. Greater Cin. Salvation Army; Bd. dirs. Dan Beard council Boy Scouts Am., Ohio Electric Utility Inst., Helium Breeder Assos.; trustee Clovernook Home and Sch. for Blind, Zool. Soc. Cin., U. Cin. Found., Herman Schneider Found., Cin. Served to capt., inf. AUS, World War II; Korea. Mem. Am. Nuclear Soc., Engring. Soc. Cin., Helium Breeder Assos., ASME, Ohio C. of C. (dir.), Cin. C. of C. (dir.). Clubs: Queen City, Cincinnati, Western Hills Country (Cin.). Home: 6018 Countryhills Dr Cincinnati OH 45238 Office: 139 E 4th St Cincinnati OH 45202

DICKIE, GEORGE THOMAS, educator, philosopher; b. Palmetto, Fla., Aug. 12, 1926; s. George Harrison and Emily (Brown) D.; m. Ruth Joyce Petty, Aug. 5, 1950 (dec. Apr. 26, 1975); children: Garrick George, Blake Allen; m. Suzanne Cunningham, June 25, 1977. A.B., Fla. State U., 1949; Ph.D., U. Calif. at Los Angeles, 1959. From instr. to asso. prof. Wash. State U., 1956-64; asso. prof. U. Houston, 1964-65; mem. faculty U. Ill.-Chgo., 1965—, prof. philosophy, 1967—. Author: Aesthetics: An Introduction, 1971, Art and the Aesthetic: An Institutional Analysis, 1974; Editor: (with others) Aesthetics: A Critical Anthology, 1977; Contbr. to profl. jours. Served with USMC, 1944-46. Nat. Endowment for Humanities fellow, 1971-72; Guggenheim fellow, 1978-79. Mem. Am. Philos. Assn., Am. Soc. Aesthetics (trustee 1966-69). Democrat. Home: 1050 W North Shore Ave Chicago IL 60626 Office: Dept Philosophy U Ill Chgo Chicago IL 60680

DICKIE, HELEN AIRD, physician, educator; b. North Freedom, Wis., Feb. 19, 1913; s. Robert Bruce and Anna (Adams) D. B.A., U. Wis., 1935; M.D., 1937. Intern, chest resident Los Angeles County Hosp., 1937-40; resident medicine U. Wis. Med. Sch., 1940-42, staff instr. medicine, 1942-43, asst. prof., 1943-45, asso. prof., 1945-55, prof. medicine, 1955—; cons. VA Hosp. Master A.C.P.; mem. Central Soc. Clin. Research, Am. Thoracic Soc., Am. Fedn. Clin. Research, Wis. Tb and Respiratory Diseases Assn. (pres. 1968, dir.), Alpha Omega Alpha. Research on farmer's lung, Tb, acute histoplasmosis, spontaneous mediastinal emphysema. Home: 501 Clifden Dr Madison WI 53711

DICKIE, MARGARET MCKENZIE, English educator; b. Bennington, Vt., Sept. 13, 1935; d. Henry Hodgeson and Dorothy (Sweet) D.; children: Elizabeth Uroff, Catherine Uroff. A.B., Middlebury Coll., 1956; Ph.D., Brown U., 1965. Mem. faculty U. Ill., Urbana, 1967—, prof. English, 1979—, head dept., 1983—, fellow Ctr. for Advanced Studies, 1978; vis. prof. U. Reading (Eng.), 1979-80, U. Fla., Gainesville, 1983. Author: Becoming a City, 1980, Hart Crane-The Patterns of His Poetry, 1975, Sylvia Plath and Ted Hughes, 1979. Mem. MLA. Home: 305 W Michigan St Urbana IL 61801 Office: Dept English U Ill 608 S Wright St Urbana IL 61801

DICKINSON, ALFRED JAMES, realtor; b. Eufaula, Ala., Dec. 19, 1916; s. Alfred J. and Bertha (Trotter) D.; m. Elsie Vick Mattingly, Mar. 21, 1942; children—Alfred James IV, Paul Mattingly, Elsie Stringfellow, Mary Bridgers. B.A., U. Richmond (Va.), 1937; M.B.A., Harvard, 1939. Asst. to comptroller Virginia-Carolina Chem. Corp., Richmond, Va., 1939-41, v.p., 1952-56, v.p., asst. to pres., 1956-57; v.p. Freeport Sulphur Co., 1957-60; exec. v.p. W.M. Brown & Son, Inc., Richmond, 1960-63; pres. Alfred J. Dickinson, Inc., Richmond, 1963—; Spl. agt. FBI, 1941-44. Served as capt. USMCR, 1944-46. Mem. Harvard Bus. Sch. Alumni Assn., Phi Beta Kappa, Omicron Delta Kappa, Phi Gamma Delta. Baptist. Clubs: Country of Virginia, Commonwealth. Home: 6101 Three Chopt Rd Richmond VA 23226 Office: 4900 Augusta Ave Richmond VA 23230

DICKINSON, ALICE BRAUNLICH, mathematics educator; b. N.Y.C., Apr. 11, 1921; d. Hans and Dorothy (Harding) B.; m. David J. Dickinson, Dec. 10, 1944; children: Sara, Dan. B.A., U. Mich., 1941, Ph.D., 1952; M.A., Columbia U., 1947. Asst. project engr. Sperry Gyroscope Co., Garden City, N.Y., 1942-44; mem. staff MIT Radiation Lab., Cambridge, 1944-45; lectr. Pa. State U., 1950-56; vis. prof. U. Baroda, India, 1962, 68, 77, U. Aligarh, 1961-62; mem. faculty Smith Coll., 1959—, prof., 1970-81, prof. emeritus, 1981—, chmn. math. dept., 1970-73, dean of coll., 1973-77; cons. Hampshire Coll., 1965-68. Author: Differential Equations: A Study in Time and Motion, 1972. Recipient Hampshire Coll. Founders award, 1970. Mem. Ely Ringing Guild, N.Am. Guild Change Ringers, AAUW. Home: Graves Rd Ashfield MA 01330

DICKINSON, ANGIE (ANGELINE BROWN), actress; b. Kulm, N.D., Sept. 30; m. Burt Bacharach, 1 dau., Lea Nikki. Ed., Immaculate Heart Coll., Glendale Coll. Motion pictures include Rio Bravo, 1959, Bramble Bush, 1960, The Sins of Rachel Cade, 1961, Jessica, 1962, Captain Newman, M.D, 1963, The Art of Love, 1965, The Chase, 1966, Cast a Giant Shadow, 1966, Point Blank, 1968, Sam Whiskey, 1968, Some Kind of a Nut, 1969, The Killers, 1964, The Last

Challenge, 1967, Young Billy Young, 1969, Pretty Maids All in a Row, 1971, Big Bad Mama, 1974, Dressed to Kill, 1980, Death Hunt, 1982, Charlie Chan and the Curse of the Dragon Queen, 1982; others; star: TV series Policewoman, 1974-78. Address: care The Black-Glenn Agy Ltd 409 N Camden Dr Beverly Hills CA 90212 *

DICKINSON, CHARLES ARTHUR, computer company executive; b. Warroad, Minn., Oct. 30, 1923; s. Arthur Job and Josephine D.; m. Jean Louise Senstad, Aug. 2, 1947; children—Peter Arthur, Joseph Charles, Richard Paul, Thomas George, Anne Louise. B.E.E., U. Minn., 1949, M.B.A., 1951. Vice pres., gen. mgr. Oklahoma City ops. MPI Co. (subsidiary Control Data Corp.), 1975-77; v.p. mfg. Memorex Co., Santa Clara, Calif., 1977-78; sr. v.p. ops. Data Products Corp., Woodland Hills, Calif., 1978-79, pres., 1980—, chief exec. officer, 1982—. Served to 1st lt. USAAF, 1943-46. Office: 6200 Canoga Ave Woodland Hills CA 91365

DICKINSON, CHARLES CAMERON, III, theologian, educator; b. Charleston, W.Va., May 13, 1936; s. Charles Cameron and Frances Ann (Saunders) D., Jr. B.A. cum laude, Dartmouth Coll., 1958; B.D., Pitts. Theol. Sem., 1965; Ph.D., U. Pitts., 1973. Prof. English, Greek and N.T. Ecole de Theologie Kimbanguiste, Zaire, 1972; asst. prof. systematic theology and philosophy Union Theol. Sem., Richmond, Va., 1974-75; asst. prof. religion and philosophy Morris Harvey Coll., Charleston, 1975-79; prof. Am. Coll. of Rome, 1979; research prof. U. Charleston, 1980-81; curatorial assoc. manuscript collections Andover-Harvard Theol. Library, 1981—; vis. scholar Christ Ch., Oxford (Eng.) U., 1979, Harvard U. Div. Sch., 1980; prof. linguistics and lit. Hebei Tchrs U., Shijiazhuang, Hebei Province, China, 1983-84; dir. Univ. Press Edits./Mountain State Press, Charleston, 1980-83. Author articles, revs. in field. Bd. dirs., mem. ednl. council River Sch., Charleston, 1978-81; bd. dirs. Charleston Chamber Music Soc., Kanawha Valley Youth Orch., Charleston Ballet, W.Va. Opera Theater, Kanawha Pastoral Counseling Center. Served as enlisted man USMC, 1958-61. Entrance fellow Chgo. Theol. Sem., 1962; Chgo. U. Div. Sch. scholar, 1962. Fellow Royal Soc. Arts; mem. Karl Barth Soc. N.Am. (dir.), Am. Acad. Religion, Soc. Bibl. Lit., Am. Theol. Soc., Am. Philos. Assn., Am. Assn. Advancement Humanities, AAAS, W.Va. Philos. Soc., W.Va. Assn. Humanities, Internat. Bonhoeffer Soc. Democrat. Clubs: Charleston Rotary (chmn. student exchange com. 1978-79); Edgewood Country (Charleston); Wichita (Wichita Falls, Tex.); University (Pitts.). 1111 City National Bldg Wichita Falls TX 76301 45 Francis Ave Cambridge MA 02138

DICKINSON, ELEANOR CREEKMORE, artist, educator; b. Knoxville, Tenn., Feb. 7, 1931; d. Robert Elmond and Evelyn Louise (Van Gilder) C.; m. Ben Wade Oakes, June 12, 1952; children: Mark Wade, Katherine Van Gilder, Peter Somers. B.A., U. Tenn., 1952; postgrad., San Francisco Art Inst., 1961-63; M.F.A., Calif. Coll. Arts and Crafts, 1982. Escrow officer Security Nat. Bank, Santa Monica, Calif., 1953-54; mem. faculty Calif. Coll. Arts and Crafts, Oakland, Calif., 1971—, assoc. prof. art, 1974-84, prof., 1984—, dir. galleries, 1976—. Author: Revival, 1974, That Old Time Religion, 1975, The Complete Fruit Cookbook, 1972; also museum catalogs; one person exhbns. include, Corcoran Gallery Art, Washington, 1970, 74, San Francisco Mus. Modern Art, 1965, 68, Fine Arts Mus. San Francisco, 1969, 75, touring exhbn., Smithsonian Inst., 1974-80, Oakland Mus., 1979, Tenn. State Mus., 1981-82; represented in permanent collections, Nat. Collection Fine Arts, Corcoran Gallery Art, Library of Congress, Smithsonian Instn., San Francisco Mus. Modern Art, Butler Inst. Art, Oakland Mus., Santa Barbara Mus. Bd. dirs. Center for Visual Arts, San Francisco, 1976-78; mem. council bd. and alumni bd. San Francisco Art Inst., trustee, 1964-67; sec., bd. dirs. YWCA, 1955-62; treas., bd. Westminster Center, 1955-59; bd. dirs. Children's Theater Assn., 1958-60, Internat. Child Art Center, 1958-68, Calif. Confedn. for the Arts, 1983—. Mem. Coalition of Women's Art Orgns. (dir., v.p. 1978-80), Coll. Art Assn., AAUP, San Francisco Art Assn. (sec., dir. 1964-67), NOW, Artists Equity Assn. (nat. v.p., dir. 1978-84), Arts Advocates, Women's Caucus for Art (nat. Affirmative Action officer 1978-80). Democrat. Episcopalian. Home: 2125 Broderick St San Francisco CA 94115 Office: 5212 Broadway Oakland CA 94618

DICKINSON, ELMER NEWTON, JR., ins. exec.; b. Hartford, Conn., Jan. 5, 1924; s. Elmer N. and Florence Alberta (Martin) D.; m. Josephine Pawsey, May 16, 1945; children—Robert, John, Sherry-Lee. Student, U. Conn., 1942; B.S., Trinity Coll., Hartford, 1948. With Commerce and Industry Ins. Co., N.Y.C., 1948—, pres., 1968—; pres., dir. Am. Home Assurance Co., 1971-78, chmn., chief exec. officer, 1978—; also dir.; chmn., chief exec. officer, dir. Commerce & Industry Ins. Co., 1978—; exec. v.p. Am. Internat. Group, Inc., 1976—; chmn., chief exec. officer AIU Ins. Co., Ins. Co. State Pa., Birmingham Fire Ins. Co. Pa., Nat. Union Fire Ins. Co., Pitts., 1978—; dir. Am. Internat. Life Assurance Co. N.Y. Served with USAAF, 1943-45. Club: Union League (N.Y.C.). Home: Tulip Tree Ln Norwalk CT 06851 Office: 70 Pine St New York NY 10270

DICKINSON, ERNEST MILTON, veterinary educator; b. Boston, Ohio, May 12, 1905; s. Ernest Samuel and Mary Lily (English) D.; m. Celeste Snyder, Sept. 30, 1927; children: Milton Zan, Bess Celeste. D.V.M., Ohio State U., 1927; M.S., Oreg. State U., 1935. Asst. prof. Oreg. State U., Corvallis, 1927-36; asso. prof., 1938-41, prof., 1941—, head dept. vet. medicine, 1955-70; veterinarian U. Calif. at Berkeley, 1936-38; cons. U.S. Dept. Agr., Agrl. Research Service, Dept. Interior, Wildlife Service, Dept. Health, Edn. and Welfare, NIH, USPHS. Contbr. articles to sci. jours. Recipient Meritorius Service award Oreg. Turkey Industry, 1947; Dedicated Service award Oreg. Poultry and Hatchery Assn., 1970. Fellow AAAS; mem. AVMA (chmn. poultry disease sect. 1942-45), Oreg. Vet. Med. Assn., Am. Assn. Avian Pathologists, Poultry Sci. Assn., U.S. Animal Health Assn., Wildlife Disease Assn., Sigma Xi, Gamma Sigma Delta. Lodges: Masons; Rotary. Research avian diseases, coccidiosis, pullorum diseases, salmonellosis, erysipelas, ornithosis, fowl pox. Home: 231 NW 30th St Corvallis OR 97330

DICKINSON, FAIRLEIGH STANTON, JR., former manufacturing company executive; b. Rutherford, N.J., Dec. 9, 1919; s. Fairleigh Stanton and Grace Bancroft (Smith) D.; m. Mary Elizabeth Harrington, June 25, 1946; children—Ann Bancroft (Mrs. Stephen C. Turner), Tracy Harrington. B.A. cum laude, Williams Coll., 1941, LL.D., 1973; L.H.D., Bard Coll., St. Peter's Coll. With Becton, Dickinson & Co., Rutherford, 1941-77, pres., 1948-73, chmn. bd., 1973-77, chief exec. officer, 1973-74, also dir.; chmn. bd., dir. Nat. Community Bank, Rutherford; dir. Prudential Ins. Co. Am. Mem. N.J. Senate, 1968-71; Bd. dirs. N.J. Symphony Orch.; hon. bd. govs. Hackensack (N.J.) Hosp.; bd. dirs. Coast Guard Acad. Found., Nat. Center Health Edn.; trustee Vineyard Open Land Found., Bennington Coll., Edward Williams Coll., N.Y. Mil. Acad., Kent Sch., Fairleigh Dickinson U. Served to lt. comdr. USCGR, 1941-46. Decorated Order Vasco Nunez de Balboa, Panama; recipient Distinguished Pub. Service award USCG; Pres.'s medal Hunter Coll. of CUNY; Hon. fellow Wolfson Coll. Cambridge, Eng.). Fellow Royal Soc. Arts; mem. N.Y. Acad. Scis., N.J. Hist. Soc. (trustee), Phi Beta Kappa, Delta Upsilon. Clubs: University, N.Y. Yacht, Williams (N.Y.C.); Edgartown (Mass.) Yacht, St. Croix (V.I.) Yacht. Home: 160 Fairmount Rd Ridgewood NJ 07450 Office: Rutherford NJ

DICKINSON, JOHN HAROLD, airport manager; b. Los Angeles, Mar. 24, 1920; s. John Fred and Alivia Mary (Swinnerton) D. Student, Los Angeles City Coll., 1941-42. Asst. supt. ops. City of Los Angeles Dept. of Airports, 1947-55, supt. ops., 1955-63; airport mgr. Van Nuys Airport, Calif., 1963-75, Ontario Internat. Airport, 1975-79, Los Angeles Internat. Airport, 1979—. Mem. Los Angeles Mayor's Adv. Com., 1968; v.p. Indsl. Assn. San Fernando Valley, 1971-72; pres. West Van Nuys C. of C. Served to capt. U.S. Army, 1942-46, 51-53. Mem. Calif. Assn. Airport Execs. (cert., pres. 1963-83, Airport Mgr. of Yr. 1971-72, Pres.'s award 1974), Am. Assn. Airport Execs. Republican. Episcopalian. Club: Kiwanis (charter pres. 1969-75). Home: 508 W 64th Pl Inglewood CA 90302 Office: City of Los Angeles Airports One World Way Los Angeles CA 90009

DICKINSON, JOSHUA CLIFTON, JR., museum director, educator; b. Tampa, Fla., Apr. 28, 1916; s. Joshua Clifton and Mary (Martin) D.; m. Lucy Jackson, Apr. 13, 1936; children: Joshua Clifton III, Martin Freeman, Susan Ellissa. Student, U. Va., 1936-39, Cornell U., summer 1938; B.S., U. Fla., 1940, M.S., 1946, Ph.D., 1950. Faculty U. Fla., 1946—, asst. prof. biology, 1950-55, asso. prof. biology, 1955, prof. zoology, 1973-79; curator Fla. State Mus., 1952-79, chmn. natural scis., 1953-60, acting dir., 1959-61, dir., 1961-79, dir. emeritus, 1979—, adj. curator, 1980—; Research fellow Harvard, 1951-52; vis. investigator Woods Hole Oceanographic Inst., 1952; expdns. to, Honduras, 1946, Bahamas, 1958-62, 66-67, Jamaica, 1946, Baffin Island, 1955, Sombrero Island, 1964, Navassa Island, 1967, Turks and Caicos Islands, 1974. Contbr. monographs, sci. papers to profl. lit. Chmn. Fla. Bd. Archives and History, 1967-69; mem. mus. adv. panel Nat. Endowment for Arts, 1970-72, co-chmn., 1972-74; panelist fellowship program NSF, 1966-68; mem. Nat. Council on Arts, 1976-82, also chmn. com. planning and policy. Served to comdr. USCGR, 1942-45; ret. Grantee Nat. Park Service, 1954, NSF, 1955-57. Fellow AAAS; mem. Am. Ornithologists Union, Am. Soc. Naturalists, Am. Assn. Museums (chmn. sci. mus. sect. 1961, mem. council 1964-70, sec. 1970), Am. Soc. Zoologists, Wilson Ornithol. Soc., Am. Assn. Sci. Mus. Dirs. (v.p. 1967-69), Assn. Systematic Collections (pres. 1972-75, dir. 1974-76, chmn. membership com. 1976-79), Bahamas Nat. Trust, Assn. S.E. Biologists (sec. 1955-58), Fla. Acad. Scis. (chmn. biology sect. 1952, editor quar. jour. 1955-63), N.E. Birdbanding Assn., Eastern Birdbanding Assn., Conf. Biol. Editors, Conf. Dirs. Systematics Collections, Fla. Audubon Soc. (dir. 1958-64, 79—), S.E. Museums Conf. (v.p. 1971-72, pres. 1972), Internat. Council Museums (exec. com. 1974-77), Am. Assn. Museums (vis. accreditation team 1973-75), Sigma Xi, Phi Sigma, Alpha Tau Omega. Democrat. Presbyn. Club: Rotarian (pres. Gainesville 1967-68). Home: 6320 SW 30th Ave Gainesville FL 32608 Office: Fla State Mus U Fla Dickinson Hall Museum Rd Gainesville FL 32611

DICKINSON, RICHARD DONALD NYE, clergyman, educator, theological seminary dean and official; b. Monson, Mass., Aug. 1, 1929; s. Richard Donald Nye and Phoebe Abigail (Naylor) D.; m. Nancy Leland Stone, Nov. 26, 1955; children: Elizabeth Stone, Richard Donald Nye III, Edward David McCrea. B.A., Am. Internat. Coll., 1950, M.A., 1951; S.T.B., Boston U., 1954, Ph.D., 1959; Certificate, Institut Oecumenique, Geneva, 1955. Ordained to ministry United Ch. of Christ; chaplain, instr. Wheaton Coll., Norton, Mass., 1957-62; asso. dir. Quaker Confs. in So. Asia, 1962-64; sr. research officer Inst. for Social Studies, The Hague, Netherlands, 1964-67; sec. for specialized assistance World Council Chs., 1967-68; now cons.; prof. Christian social ethics Christian Theol. Sem., Indpls., 1968-74, v.p., dean, 1974—; commr. devel. com. World Council Chs.; Mem. edn. commn. Nat. Council Chs., 1972-74; now mem. ch. world service com.; incorporating mem. Center for Exploration Values and Meaning.; Bd. dirs. internat. affairs div. Am. Friends Service Com., div. overseas ministries of Christian Ch. Author: The Christian College and National Development, 1967, Line and Plummet, 1968, The Christian College in Developing India, 1969, To Set at Liberty the Oppressed, 1975, Poor, Yet Making Many Rich, 1983. Mem. Am. Soc. for Christian Ethics, Soc. for Sci. Study Religion. Home: 5173 N Kenwood Ave Indianapolis IN 46208 Office: 1000 W 42d St Indianapolis IN 46208

DICKINSON, RICHARD RAYMOND, oil company executive; b. Orange, Calif., Jan. 28, 1931; s. Raymond Russel and Florence Marie (Jacobson) D.; m. Barbara Jean Morrison, June 16, 1957; children: Roderick, Christine. B.S., Calif. Inst. Tech., 1952; M.S., U. So. Calif., 1960. Chem. engr. Los Angeles Refinery Texaco, 1952-68, gen. mgr. supply and distbn., London, 1968-76, plant mgr. Eagle Point plant, Westville, N.J., 1976-79, gen. mgr. alternate energy group, White Plains, N.Y., 1979, v.p. strategic planning, 1979-82, sr. v.p. U.S. refining, mktg., supply and transp., Houston, 1982—. Served with USNR, 1955-58. Home: 13126 Paradise Valley Dr Houston TX 77069

DICKINSON, ROGER ALLYN, educator; b. Bklyn., Sept. 8, 1929; s. Robert Albert and Esther (Odl) D.; m. Ruth Nordis, June 1, 1957; children: Robert Allyn, Roger Perry, Todd Charles, Bruce Gregory. A.B., Williams Coll., 1951; M.B.A., UCLA, 1955; Ph.D., Columbia U., 1967. Lectr., asst. prof. bus. adminstrn. U. Calif., Berkeley, 1964-69; asso. prof. Rutgers Grad. Sch. Bus., Newark, N.J., 1969-70, prof., 1970-75, Coll. Bus., U. Tex., Arlington, 1975—, dean, 1975-79; dir. Tandycrafts, Inc. Author: Retail Management: A Channels Approach, 1974, (with others) A Basic Approach to Executive Decision Making, 1978, Retail Management, 1981; Contbr. articles to profl. jours. Mem. Am. Collegiate Retailing Assn. (pres. 1980-82). Home: 2104 Tretorn Ct Arlington TX 76017 Office: Coll of Bus U Tex Arlington TX 76019

DICKINSON, WILLIAM BOYD, editor; b. Kansas City, Mo., Feb. 21, 1931; s. William Boyd and Aileen (Robinson) D.; m. Betty Ann Landree, Feb. 1, 1953; children: William Boyd IV, David Alan. A.B., U. Kans., 1953; student, George Washington U. Law Sch., 1957-58. With U.P.I., 1955-59, mem. staff overnight desk, Washington, 1957-59; staff writer Editorial Research Reports, Washington, 1959-66, editor, 1966-73; editor, v.p. Congl. Quar., Inc., 1972-73; gen. mgr., editorial dir. Washington Post Writers Group, 1973—; Winston Churchill Traveling fellow, summer 1968. Supervisory editor: Congl. Quar.'s Complete Guide to Congress. Served with AUS, 1953-55. Mem. Internat. Press Inst., English-Speaking Union (dir. Washington chpt.), Alpha Tau Omega, Omicron Delta Kappa. (Washington). Home: 3719 T St NW Washington DC 20007 Office: 1150 15th St NW Washington DC 20071

DICKINSON, WILLIAM LOUIS, congressman; b. Opelika, Ala., June 5, 1925; s. Henry K. and Bernice (Lowe) D.; m. Barbara Edwards; children—Christopher, Michael, Tara, William Louis. LL.B., U. Ala., 1950. Bar: Ala. bar 1950. Practiced in, Opelika, 1950-63; judge, Opelika City Ct., 1951-53; judge Ct. Common Pleas, 1953-59, Juvenile Ct. Lee County, 1953-59, Fifth Judicial Ct. Ala., 1959-63; asst. v.p. So. Ry. System, Montgomery, 1963-64; mem. 89th-97th congresses, 2d Dist. Ala., asst. minority whip, 1973—, ranking Rep. mem. armed services com., armed services research and devel. subcom.; mem. ho. administrn. com., armed services readiness subcom., exec. com. of com. on committees of Rep. conf. in House, armed services mil. installations and facilities subcom. Served with USN, World War II. Named One of Four Outstanding Young Men in Ala., 1961; recipient Disting. Service award Ams. for Constl. Action; Watchdog of Treasury award Nat. Associated Businessmen; Statesman award Am. Conservative Union; Congressional Appreciation award Army Aviation Assn. Am.; Peace through Strength medal Am. Security Council. Mem. Ala. Bar Assn., Sigma Alpha Epsilon. Clubs: Shriner, Kiwanian. Office: 2406 Rayburn House Office Bldg Washington DC 20515

DICKINSON, WILLIAM TREVOR, hydrologist; b. Toronto, Ont., Canada, Aug. 30, 1939; s. Clarence Heber and Katie Isobel (Kneen) D.; m. Sharon Lucille Tutt, Aug. 24, 1963; children: Michael Trevor, Cathryn Ruth. B.S.A., U. Toronto, 1961, B.A.Sci., 1962, M.S.A., 1964; Ph.D., Colo. State U., 1967. Research assoc. Colo. State U., 1964-67; asst. prof. engring. U. Guelph, Ont., 1967-70, assoc. prof., 1970-78, prof., 1978—, coordinator instructional devel., 1979-82; pvt. cons. water resources engring. Contbr. articles to profl. jours. Mem. Assn. Profl. Engrs. Ont., Can. Assn. Univ. Tchrs., Soil Conservation Soc. Am. (pres. Ont. chpt.), Ont. Water Mgmt. Research Com., Soc. Preservation and Encouragement Barbershop Quartet Singing Am. Mem. United Ch. of Can. Home: 44 Hickory St Guelph ON Canada N1G 2X3 Office: Univ Guelph Guelph ON Canada N1G 2W1

DICKLER, ROBERT M., hospital administrator; b. Chgo., Sept. 5, 1945; s. Jerome A. and Josephine R. (Sweet) D.; m. Susan Baskin, Sept. 3, 1967; 1 dau., Miriam. B.A., Case-Western Res. U., 1967; M.H.A., U. Minn., 1972. Social worker, sch. counselor Longview State Hosp.-Children's Unit Sch., Cin., 1967-70; with U. Minn. Hosp. and Clinics, Mpls., 1971-81, assoc. dir. ops., 1977-78, sr. assoc. dir., 1978-81; dir. U. Colo. Hosp., Denver, 1981—; editorial bd. Jour. Ambulatory Care Mgmt., 1978. Bd. dirs. Rocky Mountain Multiple Sclerosis Found., 1981—. Recipient Am. Surg. Trade Assn. Acad. Honors award U. Minn., 1971-72, Faculty Excellence in Teaching award U. Minn., 1979-80, Disting. Service award Mpls. C. of C., 1981, commendation U. Minn. Bd. Regents, 1981. Mem. Assn. Am. Med. Colls. (assembly council teaching hosps. rep. 1983—), Colo. Hosp. Assn. (legis council 1982). Office: U Colo Hosp Room A-020 4200 E 9th Ave Denver CO 80262

DICKMAN, FRANCOIS MOUSSIEGT, ambassador; b. Iowa City, Iowa, Dec. 23, 1924; s. Adolphe Jacques and Henriette Louise (Moussiegt) D.; m. Margaret Hoy, June 3, 1947; children: Christine, Paul. B.A., U. Wyo., 1947; M.A., Fletcher Sch. Law and Diplomacy, Medford, Mass., 1948. Research asst. Brookings Instn., Washington, 1950; with U.S. Fgn. Service, 1951—; consular/comml. officer, Barranquilla, Colombia, 1952-54, Arabic lang. trainee, Beirut, Lebanon, 1955-57, econ./comml./consular officer, Khartoum, Sudan, 1957-60; Egyptian-Syrian affairs desk officer Dept. State, 1961-65; econ. officer, Tunis, Tunisia, 1965-68; student U.S. Army War Coll., Carlisle, Pa., 1968-69; econ. counselor, Jidda, Saudi Arabia, 1969-72; dir. Arabian Peninsula affairs Dept. State, 1972-76; ambassador to, United Arab Emirates, 1976-79, to Kuwait, 1979—. Served with AUS, 1943-46, 50-51. Recipient Dept. State Meritorious Honor award, 1965, Disting. Alumni award U. Wyo., 1980. Mem. U.S. Army War Coll. Alumni Assn., U. Wyo. Alumni Assn., Phi Beta Kappa, Phi Kappa Phi. Office: Am Embassy Box 77 (Safat) Kuwait Kuwait

DICKMAN, JAMES BRUCE, photojournalist; b. St. Louis, Mar. 25, 1949; s. Joseph Edward and Isabel Catherine (Brown) D.; m. Mary Kay Thomas, Sept. 23, 1968 (div.); children: Kristi Michele, Gavin Thomas; m. 2d Rebecca Lauren Skelton, Sept. 16, 1983. Student, U. Tex., 1967-69. Photographer McKinney Job Corps., Tex., 1969-70, Dallas Times Herald, 1970—. Recipient Pulitzer prize for photography Columbia U., 1983, World Press Photo of Yr. award World Press Photo Orgn., Holland, Amsterdam, 1983, awards Dallas Press Club, AP and UPI, Tex. Headliners, others. Mem. Nat. Press Photographers Assn. Home: 6522 Walnut Hill Ln Dallas TX 75230 Office: Dallas Times Herald 1101 Pacific Dallas TX 75202 *I've always felt that I've had a guardian angel pointing me in the correct directions. But it's always been up to me to do something with the opportunities once they're presented.*

DICKS, JOHN BARBER, educator, physicist; b. Natchez, Miss., Mar. 10, 1926; s. John Barber and Pauline (Merrill) D.; m. Eleanor Ann Burdeshaw, Jan. 5, 1973; children: Pauline, Dunbar.; children (by previous marriage): Ian, Ayers Merrill, Agnes, Josephine. B.S., U. South, 1948; Ph.D., Vanderbilt U., 1955. Asso. prof. Tenn. Technol. U., Cookeville, 1953-54; asst. prof., asso. prof. U. of South, Sewanee, Tenn., 1954-64; prof. physics U. Tenn. Space Inst., Tullahoma, 1964—, Alumni distinguished prof., 1972—, chief scientist, 1982—, dir. energy conversion div., 1967-82; Pres. J.B. Dicks & Assos., 1967—, Applied Energetics, Inc., 1967—; Chmn. steering com. Symposium on Engring. Aspects of Magnetohydrodynamics, 1971; pres. Tenn. Energy Inst., 1980—. Contbr. articles profl. jours. Asso. fellow AIAA (asso. editor jour.); mem. Am. Phys. Soc., AAUP (Tenn. state chmn. 1962-64), ASME (chmn. energetics div. 1972-73, chmn. synthetic fuels com. 1981-82, chmn. synthetic fuels symposium Energy Sources Tech. Conf. and Exhbn.), Sigma Xi, Sigma Pi Sigma. Home: 710 N College St Tullahoma TN 37388

DICKS, NORMAN DE VALOIS, Congressman; b. Bremerton, Wash., Dec. 16, 1940; s. Horace D. and Eileen Cora D.; m. Suzanne Callison, Aug. 25, 1967; children: David, Ryan. B.A., U. Wash., 1963, J.D., 1968. Bar: Wash. 1968. Salesman, Boise Cascade Corp., Seattle, 1963; labor negotiator Kaiser Aluminum Co., Seattle, 1964; legis. asst. to Senator Warren Magnuson of Wash., 1968-73, adminstrv. asst., 1973-76; mem. 95th-98th Congresses from 6th Wash. Dist.; mem. appropriations com., interior, mil. constrn., def. subcoms. 95th-97th Congresses from 6th Wash. Dist. Mem. U. Wash. Alumni Assn., Sigma Nu. Democrat. Lutheran. Office: 2429 Rayburn House Office Bldg Washington DC 20515

DICKSON, CARROLL J., lawyer; b. Mpls., Aug. 6, 1905. LL.B., U. Minn., 1927; LL.M., Columbia, 1930. Bar: Minn. bar 1927, N.Y. bar 1933. Now Counsel to firm Whitman & Ransom, N.Y.C. Mem. Phi Delta Phi. Office: 522 Fifth Ave New York NY 10036

DICKSON, DAVID N., food company executive; b. 1943. B.A., Stanford U., 1965, M.B.A., 1967. With Carnation Co., Los Angeles, 1967—, trainee, Los Angeles, 1967-68, asst. product mgr., Los Angeles, 1968-70, product mgr., 1970-72, group product mgr., 1972-74, asst. gen. mgr., 1974-75, v.p., gen. mgr. instant div., 1975-77, group v.p., 1977-79, exec. v.p., dir., 1979—. Office: Carnation Co Inc 5045 Wilshire Blvd Carnation Bldg Los Angeles CA 90036 *

DICKSON, DAVID WATSON DALY, college president; b. Portland, Maine, Feb. 16, 1919; s. David Augustus and Mary Marguerite (Daly) D.; m. Vera Mae Allen, Aug. 5, 1951 (dec. July 5, 1979); children: David Augustus II, Deborah Anne, Deirdre Elizabeth; m. Barbara Childs Mickey, Feb. 14, 1981. A.B., Bowdoin Coll., 1941, L.H.D., 1974; M.A., Harvard U., 1942, Ph.D., 1949; L.H.D., Bloomfield Coll., 1983. Instr. to assoc. prof. English Mich. State U., 1948-63; prof., head English dept. No. Mich. U., Marquette, 1963-66, dean, 1966-67, v.p. acad. affairs, 1967-68; provost, v.p. acad. affairs, prof. English Fed. City Coll., Washington, 1968-69; prof. English, asst. to pres. State U. N.Y. at Stony Brook, 1969-72, dean continuing and developing edn., prof. English, 1972-73; pres. Montclair State Coll., Upper Montclair, N.J., 1973-84, Disting. Service prof., 1984—; Cons. Nat. Found. for Humanities, 1969-71, Mott Found., 1973-74. Bd. dirs. Nat. Com. on Future of State Colls. and Univs.; trustee Montclair Art Mus., North Essex Devel. and Action Council; bd. overseers Bowdoin Coll., 1966-

75, trustee, 1975-82; mem. policy bd. Project Change. Served to 1st lt. AUS, 1944-46. Recipient Distinguished Teaching award Mich. State U., 1952; Distinguished Educator award Bowdoin Coll., 1971; Rosenwald fellow, 1942-43; Smith Mundt fellow, 1958-59. Mem. MLA, Milton Soc., Am. Assn. State Colls. and Univs. (chmn. com. on undergrad. studies), Am. Assn. Colls. (commn. on liberal learning), Phi Beta Kappa, Omega Psi Phi, Sigma Psi Phi., Phi Kappa Phi. Roman Catholic. Lodge: Rotary. Home: 18 Prospect St South Orange NJ 07679

DICKSON, HORATIO LOVAT, author; b. Victoria, Australia, Jan. 30, 1902; s. Gordon Fraser and Mary Josephine (Cunningham) D.; m. Marguerite Brodie, Dec. 26, 1934; 1 son, Jonathan. M.A., U. Alt., Can., 1929; LL.D. hon., U. Alta., U. Western Ont., Can., D. Litt., York U., Toronto, Ont. Editor Fortnightly Rev., London, 1929-32, Rev. of Revs., 1931-32, Lovat Dickson's Mag., 1934-37; mng. dir. Lovat Dickson Ltd., Pubs., London, 1932-38; dir. Macmillan & Co., London, 1938-64. Author: biography H.G. Wells, Wilderness Man, Radcliffe Hall; autobiography The Ante Room, The House of Words. Decorated Order of Can. Fellow Royal Soc. Can.

DICKSON, JAMES LOTHAR, playwright, stage director, impresario; b. Chgo., Mar. 25, 1949; s. Vincent Brackley and Carol Lois (Schaffner) D. B.A., Harvard U., 1970. Stage dir. Manhasset Bay Opera, 1975-77, N.J. State Opera, 1975-78, N.Y. Lyric Opera, 1977-78, Pa. Opera Theatre, 1977, N.Y. City Opera, 1982; artistic adminstr. Santa Fe Opera, 1978-80; mng. dir. Chamber Opera Theatre N.Y., 1982; gen. mgr. June Opera Festival N.J., 1982—. Playwright: Monmouth, 1968, Fear of Success, 1971, Summer in the Midwest, 1975, Chiliasm, 1972, The Princess of the Suburbs, 1973, Banjo, 1981; (musical) Pippin, 1969. Recipient Phyllis Anderson award, 1969. Mem. Am. Guild Musical Artists, Dramatists Guild. Home: PO Box 22 Tesuque NM 87574 Office: 165 Perry St New York NY 10014

DICKSON, JENNIFER JOAN, photographer, graphic artist; b. Piet Retief, S. Africa, Sept. 17, 1936; d. John Liston and Margaret Joan (Turner) D.; m. Ronald Andrew Sweetman, Apr. 13, 1962; 1 son, William David. Student, Goldsmith's Coll. Sch. Art, London, Atelier 17, Paris. Tchr. art, Eng., U.S., W. Indies and Can., 1961—. One-woman exhbns. include, New Vision Centre, London, 1962, Editions Alecto, London, 1964, Adler Fielding Gallery, Johannesburg, S. Africa, 1965, Zwemmer's Gallery, London, 1966, Cultural Centre, St. Peter's Abbey Mus., Ghent, Belgium, 1967, Ball State U., Muncie, Ind., U. Sussex, Eng., U. W. Indies, Jamaica, 1969, Saidye Bronfman Centre, Montreal, 1970, Galerie Dresdnere, Toronto, 1973, 75, 78, 81, Madison (Wis.) Art Centre, 1972, Galerie Martal, Montreal, 1972, 80, Gallery 1640, Montreal, 1974, 76, Oxford (Eng.) Gallery, 1973, 79, Nat. Film Bd. Photo Gallery, Ottawa, 1975, 78, 80, Denison U. Art Gallery, Granville, Ohio, 1976, Wallack Galleries, Ottawa, 1977, 79, 80, 83, Heal's Art Gallery, London, 1977, Agnes Etherington Art Centre, Queen's U., Kingston, Ont., Iconography of Desire, U. B.C. Fine Arts Gallery, Vancouver, 1978, numerous group exhbns., 1959—, including biennales of, Bradford, Eng., Crakow, Poland, Llubljana, Yugoslavia, Tokyo. Recipient Jeunes Artistes pour Gravures prize Paris Biennale, 1963, George A. Reid award Can. Painters, Etchers and Engravers, 1973, spl. edit. purchase award world print competition San Francisco Mus. Art, 1973, 1st Can. Biennale Prints and Drawings award, Calgary, 1978, Walter Moos award, Biennale prize Norwegian Internat. Print Biennale, 1980. Mem. Royal Can. Acad., Royal Acad. Arts (London), Royal Soc. Painters-Etchers and Engravers. Address: 508 Gilmour St Ottawa ON K1R 5L4 Canada

DICKSON, PAUL, clergyman; b. Lakeland, Fla., Sept. 9, 1905; s. David B. and Coral (Patrick) D.; m. Anna Elizabeth Clarke, May 24, 1930; 1 son, David Franklin. Student, Stetson U., 1922-26; Ph.D. cum laude, Ludwigs-Maxmillians U., Munich, Germany, 1951; M.A., Columbia, 1954, Ed.D., 1960. Commd. 1st lt. U.S. Army, 1934-38; exec. asst. mgr. Southwest Hotels Co., Memphis and Kansas City, Mo., 1938-39; gen. mgr. Commonwealth Hotel, Kansas City, Mo., 1939-40; returned to active duty as capt. U.S. Army, 1940, advanced through grades to col., 1953; various assignments U.S. mil. schs. and inf. divs., 1940-45; prof. mil. sci. and tactics Denver pub. schs., 1945-47; assigned U.S. Army Europe, 1947-49; mem. faculty (U.S. Mil. Acad.), 1949-55, ret., 1956; dean Munich Campus U. Md., 1957-61; asso. prof. fgn. lang. edn. Fla. State U., 1961-63, prof., 1963-69; dir. staff devel. Pinellas County schs., Fla, 1969-72; ordained to ministry Episcopal Ch., 1970; asst. rector Ch. of Ascension, Clearwater, Fla., 1972-77, asso. rector, 1978—; lang. cons. south Fla. Edn. Center, 1962-64; adv. council N.E. Conf. Teaching Fgn. Langs, 1963-67. Author: Das Amerikabild in der deutschen Emigrantenliteratur seit 1933, 1951, Visible Vocabulary to Accompany German Military Readings, 1954, Foreign Language Instruction, 1960, Ins Deutsche Hinein, 1963, Articulated Language Learning, 1964, Foreign Language Education, 1966; Editor: Deutsche Sprachlehre, 1954, German Military Readings, 1954. Pres., chmn. bd. Fla. Gulf Coast Art Center, 1974-77. Decorated Bronze Star medal; Medaille de Reconnaissance, France; named officer d'Academie Francaise. Mem. Modern Lang. Assn. Am. (regional fgn. lang. cons. 1963—), Am. Assn. Tchrs. French, German, Spanish and Portuguese, NEA, Fla. Edn. Assn. (pres. modern lang. sect. 1965-68), Assn. Higher Edn., South Atlantic Modern Lang. Assn., Assn. Supervision and Curriculum Devel., So. Humanities Conf., Pi Kappa Phi. Episcopalian (lay reader, vestryman, clk. deacon, priest). Home: 50 Harbor View Ln Belleair Bluffs FL 33540

DICKSON, ROBERT CLARK, retired physician, educator; b. St. Marys, Ont., Canada, Sept. 24, 1908; s. William M. and Mabel Earl (Clark) D.; m. Constance Fraser Grant, Sept. 16, 1939 (div. 1983); children: William Fraser, Shelagh Margaret, Jane Alice Constance. M.D., U. Toronto, 1934, LL.D., 1983; LL.D. hon., Dalhousie U., 1978. Jr. asst. physician dept. medicine U. Toronto, Ont., 1939-56; from assoc. prof. to prof. and head dept. medicine Dalhousie U., Halifax, N.S., Can., 1956-78, prof. emeritus, 1979—; chmn. Can. Armed Forces Med. Council, 1971-83. Lt. col. M.C. Can. Army, 1939-45; ETO, Natousa. Decorated comdr. Order of Can., Order of Brit. Empire. Fellow Royal Coll. Physicians and Surgeons Can. (council 1960-68, pres. 1968-70); mem. Can. Med. Assn., Med. Soc. N.S. Conservative. Mem. United Ch. Can. Home: 2803 W 41 Ave Vancouver BC Canada V6N 4B4

DICKSON, ROBERT GEORGE BRIAN, chief justice of Canada; b. Yorkton, Sask., Can., May 25, 1916; s. Thomas and Sarah Elizabeth (Gibson) D.; m. Barbara Melville Sellers, June 18, 1943; children: Brian H., Deborah I. Dickson Shields, Peter G., Barry R. LL.B., U. Man., 1938, LL.D., 1973; D.Cn.L., St. John's Coll., 1965; LL.D., U. Sask., 1978, U. Ottawa, 1979, Queen's U., 1980, Dalhousie U., 1983. Bar: Man. 1940, created Queen's counsel 1953. Mem. firm Aikins, MacAulay & Co., Winnipeg, Man., 1945-63; judge Ct. of Queen's Bench of Man, 1963-67, Ct. of Appeal för Man., 1967-73; justice Supreme Ct. of Can., Ottawa, Ont., 1973-84, chief justice, 1984—. Trustee Sellers Found., Winnipeg; chancellor Diocese of Rupert's Land, Ch. of Eng., 1960-71; chmn. bd. govs. U. Man., 1971-73. Served with Royal Canadian Arty., 1940-45; hon. lt. cvl. 30th Field Regiment Royal Can. Arty. Mem. Law Soc. Man. (life bencher). Home: Marchmont Dunrobin ON Canada K0A 1T0 Office: Supreme Ct of Can Ottawa ON Canada K1A 0J1

DICKSON, RUSH STUART, holding company executive; b. Charlotte, N.C., Aug. 18, 1929; s. Rush Smith and Lake (Simpson) D.; m. Joanne Shoemaker, Oct. 12, 1951; children: Rush Stuart, Thomas Walter, John Alexander, Laura Lake. Grad., Davidson Coll., 1951. With Am. & Efird Mills, Mt. Holly, N.C., 1951, Goldman, Sachs & Co., N.Y.C., 1951-52; pres. R. S. Dickson & Co., Charlotte, 1952-68; chmn. bd. Ruddick Corp., Charlotte, 1968—; dir. Am. & Efird Mills, Harris-Teeter Supermarkets, Hemby Investments. Chmn. Charlotte-Mecklenburg Hosp. Authority; bd. dirs., officer Rush S. Dickson Family Found., The Dickson Found.; bd. dirs. Found. U. N.C., Charlotte; trustee Arts and Sci. Council, Heineman Found., U.N.C.-Charlotte, Wake Forest U.; bd. visitors Johnson C. Smith U.; chmn. bd. visitors Davidson Coll., Charlotte Country Day Sch. Served with USAR. Mem. Charlotte C. of C. (dir.), Newcomen Soc. N.C. Democrat. Clubs: Boston (New Orleans); Charlotte City, Charlotte Country, Quail Hollow Country (Charlotte); Capital City (Raleigh, N.C.); Country of N.C. (Pinehurst); Grandfather Golf and Country, Linville (N.C.) Country. Home: 2235 Pinewood Circle Charlotte NC 28211 Office: 2000 First Union Plaza Charlotte NC 28282

DICKSON, SALLY ISABELLE, retired public relations executive; b. Westport, Conn.; d. William D. and Lula B. (Taylor) D. Student pub. schs., Katherine Gibbs Sch., N.Y.C. Pres. Nat. Needlecraft Bur., 1940-43; Sally Dickson Assocs., N.Y.C., 1943-71, Creamer, Dickson, Basford Inc., 1971-79, co-chmn. agy. policy and planning com., 1979-81. Author: (with Joyce Clarke) Woman's Guide to Financial Security, 1953; Contbr. articles to profl. jours. Active Literacy Vols. Am. Recipient Silver Anvil Am. Pub. Relations Assn., 1945. Mem. Advt. Women N.Y. Club: Cedar Point Yacht (Westport, Conn.). Home: 20 Cross Way Westport CT 06880

DICKSON, WILLIAM MURRAY, lawyer; b. Pitts., Dec. 2, 1926; s. Edward Joseph and Nora (McDonough) D.; m. Jane Rowles, Feb. 20, 1965. A.B., U. Notre Dame, 1950, LL.B., 1951. Bar: Ill., D.C. Mem. Mayer, Brown & Platt, Chgo. Home: 1449 Lake Shore Dr Chicago IL 60610 Office: Mayer Brown & Platt 231 S LaSalle St Chicago IL 60610

DICKSTEIN, SIDNEY, lawyer; b. Bklyn., May 13, 1925; s. Charles and Pearl (Stahl) D.; m. Barbara H. Duke, Sept. 20, 1953; children: Ellen Simeon, Matthew Howard, Nancy Joy. A.B., Franklin and Marshall Coll., Lancaster, Pa., 1947; J.D., Columbia U., 1949. Bar: N.Y. State 1949. Law clk. to Joseph Richter, N.Y.C., 1949-50; asso. law office Herman E. Cooper, 1950-53; founder firm Dickstein & Shapiro, N.Y.C., 1953; now sr. partner successor firm Dickstein, Shapiro & Morin, Washington and N.Y.C. Trustee Franklin and Marshall Coll. Served with AUS, 1943-44; Served with USNR, 1944-46. Mem. ABA, Bar Assn. D.C. Home: 9050 Bradgrove Dr Bethesda MD 20817 Office: 2101 L St NW Washington DC 20037

DICTEROW, GLENN EUGENE, violinist; b. Los Angeles, Dec. 23, 1948; s. Harold Joseph and Irina (Lourier) D.; m. George-Ann Tobin, June 27, 1980; children—Laura Michele, Julie Erin. B.Mus., Juilliard Sch., 1970. Judge Young Musician Found. competition, Los Angeles, 1979, 80; tchr. orch. repertoire U. So. Calif., 1979; pvt. tchr. of violin, 1972—. Soloist, N.Y. Philharmonic, Los Angeles Philharmonic, San Francisco Symphony, Indpls. Symphony, Seattle Symphony, N.J. Symphony; premiered: Holdridge Violin Concerto, 1978; asso. concertmaster, then concertmaster, Los Angeles Philharmonic, 1972-79; concertmaster, N.Y. Philharmonic, 1980—; (Recipient 1st prize Young Musicians Found. 1962, Coleman Chamber Music 1st prize, Los Angeles 1961, 63, 3d prize Merriweath Post Competition, Washington 1963, Kimber 1st prize, San Francisco 1964, Julia Klumpkey 1st prize, San Francisco 1965, Bronze medal Tchaikovsky competition, Moscow, USSR 1970). Mem. Musicians Union. Office: Avery Fisher Hall Lincoln Center Broadway at 65th St New York City NY 10023

DICUS, CLARENCE HOWARD, JR., lawyer; b. Poplar Bluff, Mo., Apr. 26, 1921; s. Clarence H. and Lena (Hardey) D.; m. Edith Helen George, June 20, 1942; children: Linda Ornes, Laurie Rasmussen, Stephen, Paul, Todd, Kent, Brian. A.B., U. Mo., 1941; J.D., Harvard, 1947. Bar: Mo. bar 1947. Since practiced in, Kansas City; partner firm Dietrich, Davis, Dicus, Rowlands & Schmitt, 1957—. Pres. Unity Soc. Practical Christianity, 1957; Bd. dirs. Citizens Assn. Kansas City, 1964—, Met. YMCA, 1981—. Served to comdr. USNR, 1942-45. Fellow Am. Coll. Probate Counsel; mem. Am., Kansas City bar assns., Lawyers Assn. Kansas City (pres. 1972-73), Am. Judicature Soc., Estate Planning Council Kansas City (pres. 1963), Pi Kappa Alpha. Clubs: University (Kansas City); Leawood Country. Home: 601 W 114th Terr Kansas City MO 64114 Office: City Center Sq Kansas City MO 64105

DICUS, JOHN CARMACK, savings and loan association; b. Hutchinson, Kans., May 16, 1933; s. George Byron and Desda (Carmack) D.; m. Barbara Elizabeth Bubb, Feb. 4, 1956; children: Debra Elizabeth, John Bubb. B.S., U. Kans., 1955. With Capitol Fed. Savs. & Loan Assn., Topeka, 1959—, exec. v.p., 1963-69, pres., 1969—; dir. First Nat. Bank, Manhattan Mut. Life Ins. Co., Columbian Nat. Title Co., Security Benefit Life Ins. Co., all Topeka; Mem. Fed. Savs. and Loan Adv. Council, 1973. Chmn. Shawnee Country chpt. ARC, 1965; treas. Jayhawk area council, Boy Scouts Am., 1967-68; pres. Topeka United Way, 1972-73; trustee Stormont-Vail Regional Med. Center, Menninger Found.; past pres. Native Sons of Kansas. Served to lt. (j.g.) USN, 1956-59. Mem. U.S. League Savs. Assns. (exec. com. past dir.), Kans. Savs. and Loan League (pres. 1974-75), Topeka C. of C. (dir. 1962, v.p. 1965-66, 71, pres. 1978, pres. Indsl. Devel. Corp.), U. Kans. Alumni Assn. (pres. Shawnee County chpt. 1966, dir.), Kans. Assn. Commerce and Industry (past dir.), Phi Delta Theta. Episcopalian (sr. warden, vestryman). Clubs: Masons (32 deg.), Shriners (potentate Arab Temple 1975), Jesters, Rotary (past dir.), Topeka Country (dir., pres. 1968), Topeka Town (dir., pres. 1972). Home: 1524 Lakeside Dr Topeka KS 66604 Office: 700 Kansas Ave Topeka KS 66603

DIDIO, LIBERATO JOHN ALPHONSE, anatomist, educator; b. Sao Paulo, Brazil, May 7, 1920; s. Pascoal and Lydia (Cacace) DiD.; m. Lydia S. Silva, Mar. 12, 1960; children: Vera, Rubens, Lydia N.S., Arthur S. B.S., Dante Alighieri Coll., 1939; M.D. summa cum laude, U. São Paulo, 1945, M.S., 1949, Ph.D., 1951; postgrad., Nat. Coll. War, Rio de Janeiro, 1957. Instr. physiology Faculty Medicine, U. Sao Paulo, Brazil, 1942-43; instr. anatomy Faculty Medicine U. Sao Paulo, 1943-45, asst. prof. anatomy, 1945-51, asso. prof., 1952-53; tchr. chemistry Roosevelt State Coll., Sao Paulo, 1943-44; prof., chmn. dept. topog. anatomy Faculty Ciencias Medicas, Cath. U. Minas Gerais, 1954-55; chmn. dept. anatomy med. sch. Belo Horizonte, U. Minas Gerais, 1954-63, dir. Inst. Morphology, 1962-63; prof. anatomy Med. Sch., Dental Sch., Grad. Sch., Northwestern U., Chgo., 1963-67; prof. anatomy, chmn. dept. Med. Coll. Ohio, Toledo, 1967—, dean grad. sch., 1972—; vis. prof. U. Messina, Italy, 1955; Vis. prof. U. Brazil, 1957, U. Parma, Italy, 1958; vis. prof. anatomy, Rockefeller Found. fellow Sch. Medicine, U. Wash., 1960-61; guest investigator Rockefeller Inst. Med. Research, N.Y.C., 1961, Med. Sch., Harvard U., 1961; Co-chmn. 41st session 7th Internat. Congress Anatomy, N.Y.C., 1960; chmn. session on heart and arteries Internat. Congress Anatomy, Leningrad, 1970; del. Internat. Congress for Electron Microscopy, Phila., 1962, 8th Internat. Congress Anatomy, Wiesbaden, Ger., 1965; del., co-chmn. Session on Embryology I, Panam. Congress Anatomy, Mexico City, 1966; pres. III Congress, New Orleans, 1972; hon. pres. IV Pan Am. Congress Anatomy, Montreal, Can., 1975, V Congress, São Paulo, 1978, VI Congress, Buenos Aires, 1981; pres. 4th Symposium on Morphol. Scis., Toledo, Ohio, 1979; chmn. sect. meeting Chgo. Heart Assn. U. Chgo., 1967; adj. prof. biology U. Toledo, 1967—, adj. prof. forensic medicine Coll. Law, 1973—; adj. prof. biology Bowling Green U., 1967; seminars at numerous univs., U.S., Germany, Italy, Latin Am.; cons. Dep. Assuntos U.-Ministry Edn. Cult. Brazil, Pan Am. Health Orgn., WHO; mem. adv. com. on grad. edn. Ohio Bd. Regents. Contbr. articles to profl. jours. Trustee Siena Heights Coll., Adrian, Mich. Decorated gt. of cl. Ipiranga Order Govt. State of Sao Paulo; recipient William H. Rorer award Am. Coll. Gastroenterology, 1970; Andreas Vesalius award Mexican Assn. Anatomy, 1971; Honor Magistro award Brazilian Soc. Anatomy, 1976; Gold medal Alumni Assn. Faculty Medicine, U. Sao Paulo, 1977; Anatomist of Yr. award 4th Internat. Symposium on Morphological Scis., 1979, 5th edit., 1981; medal Arnaldo V. Carvalho Faculty Medicine, U. São Paulo, 1979; named hon. citizen Belo Horizonte, Brazil, 1963, New Orleans, 1972, hon. prof. Cath. U. Chile, 1980. Fellow AAAS; mem. Am. Assn. Cell Biology, Am. Assn. Anatomists, AAUP, Anat. Soc. Gt. Britain and Ireland, Assn. Am. Med. Colls., Electron Microscopy Soc. Am., Pan Am. Med. Assn., Internat. Coll. Surgeons, N.Y. Acad. Scis., Pan Am. Assn. Anatomy (hon. pres.), Midwest Soc. Anatomists (former pres.), Sigma Xi (former sec.). Home: 3563 Edgevale Rd Toledo OH 43606

DIDION, JOAN, author; b. Sacramento, Calif., Dec. 5, 1934; d. Frank Reese and Eduene (Jerrett) D.; m. John Gregory Dunne, Jan. 1964. B.A., U. Calif., Berkeley, 1956. Asso. feature editor Vogue mag., 1956-63; former columnist Saturday Evening Post; former contbg. editor National Review. Now freelance writer: novels Run River, 1963, Play It As It Lays, 1971, A Book of Common Prayer, 1977, The White Album, 1979; author: book of essays Slouching Towards Bethlehem, 1969; co-author: screenplays for films The Panic in Needle Park, 1971, A Star Is Born, 1976. Recipient 1st prize Vogue's Prix de Paris, 1956, Morton Dauwen Zabel prize AAAL, 1978; Breadloaf Writers Conf. fellow, 1963. Office: care Wallace & Sheil 118 E 61st St New York NY *

DI DOMENICA, ROBERT ANTHONY, musician, composer; b. N.Y.C., Mar. 4, 1927; s. Angelo and Philomena (Mosca) DiD.; m. Leona Knopf, Feb. 6, 1951; children—David, Peter Josef, Claude Robert. B.S., N.Y. U., 1951. Mem. theory faculty New Eng. Conservatory, 1969-73, asso. dean performing orgns., 1973-76, dean, 1976-78. Flutist, N.Y.C. Center Opera, N.Y. Philharmonic, Symphony of Air; soloist, Composers Forum, 20th Century Innovations; rec. artist, RCA, Columbia, Colpix, MGM, Atlantic, Deutsche Grammophon records; albums include Leona DiDomenica In Live First Performance of the Solo Piano Music of Robert DiDomenica; composer: Symphony, 1961, Concerto for Violin and Chamber Orch, 1962, Quintet for Clarinet and String Quartet, 1965, Sonata for Violin and Piano, 1966; opera The Balcony, 1972, Black Poems (baritone, piano and tape), 1976. Served with USNR, 1944-46. Guggenheim fellow, 1972-73; grantee Rockefeller Found., 1965; commd. by Goethe Inst., Boston, 1975. Mem. Broadcast Music Inc. Home: 17 Paul Revere Rd Needham MA 02194 Office: 290 Huntington Ave Boston MA 02115

DIDOMENICO, MAURO, JR., communication executive; b. Bronx, N.Y., Jan. 12, 1937; s. Mauro and Elizabeth DiD.; m. Angela M. Carracino, Aug. 29, 1964; children—Catherine Lee, David M. B.S., Stanford U., 1958, M.S., 1959, Ph.D., 1963. Mem. tech. staff Bell Labs., Murray Hill, N.J., 1962-66, supr., 1966-70, head optical device dept., 1970-80; dept. head integrated customer service dept. AT&T, Basking Ridge, N.J., 1980-82, div. mgr. strategic planning, 1982—. Contbr. numerous articles to profl. lit. Fellow IEEE, Am. Phys. Soc.; mem. N.Y. Acad. Scis., Sigma Xi, Tau Beta Pi. Roman Catholic. Office: AT&T 295 N Maple Ave Basking Ridge NJ 07920

DIEBENKORN, RICHARD CLIFFORD, JR., painter; b. Portland, Oreg., Apr. 22, 1922; s. Richard Clifford and Dorothy (Stephens) D.; m. Phyllis Gilman, June 16, 1943; children—Gretchen Gilman, Christopher Calif. B.A., Stanford, 1949; student, U. Calif. at Berkeley, 1943, Calif. Sch. Fine Arts, 1946; M.A., U. N.Mex., 1952. Tchr. San Francisco Art Inst., 1959-67; prof. art U. Calif. at Los Angeles, 1966-73; artist-in-residence Stanford, 1963-64. Author: Drawing, 1965; one man shows, Calif. Palace of Legion of Honor, San Francisco, 1948-60, San Francisco Mus. Art, 1954, 72, Oakland Mus., 1956, Pasadena Mus. Art, 1959, Phillips Meml. Gallery, Washington, 1961, Nat. Acad. Arts and Letters, N.Y.C., 1962, Carnegie Inst., Pitts., Washington Gallery Modern Art, 1964, Jewish Mus., N.Y.C., 1965, Tate Gallery, London, Eng., 1964, De Young Mus., San Francisco, 1963, Nelson Gallery, Kansas City, Mo., 1968, Pa. Acad. Fine Arts, Phila. (Carol H. Beck Gold Medal award), Los Angeles County Mus. Art, 1969, U. Calif. at Los Angeles, 1976, Albright-Knox Art Gallery, Buffalo, retrospective, 1976-77, others; exhibited, Venice Biennale, 1968, 78; works represented in permanent collections, Bklyn. Mus., Chgo. Art Inst., Met. Mus. Art, Mus. Modern Art, Whitney Mus. k5ll N.Y.C., Toronto Mus., Nelson Gallery, Kansas City, Phoenix Mus., Albright-Knox Gallery, Buffalo, Santa Barbara (Calif.) Mus., Cleve. Art Mus., Milw. Mus., Stanford U., Houston Mus., Oberlin Coll. Gallery, San Francisco Mus. Art, Pasadena Art Mus., Phillips Meml. Gallery, Hirschorn Mus., Washington, Carnegie Inst., U. Iowa, U. Mich., Los Angeles County Mus. Art. (Recipient Skowhegan medal for painting 1979). Mem. Nat. Found. on Arts and the Humanities, Nat. Inst. Arts and Letters. Office: care Knoedler Gallery 19 E 70th St New York NY 10021

DIEBOLD, ALBERT RICHARD, rancher; b. Cleve., Jan. 13, 1906; s. Albert Henry and Treva (Couch) D.; m. Dorothy Roosen, June 5, 1930; children: Albert Richard, Diane Treva Diebold Terni, Dudley George. Grad., Hotchkiss Sch., Lakeville, Conn., 1924; student, Princeton U., 1929. Mem. N.Y. Stock Exchange; also firm Bell & Beckwith, Toledo, 1929-38; engaged in drug and cosmetic bus., 1939-42, 45-61; pres. Double-D Ranch, Inc., N.Y.C., 1958—; owner Toplands Farm (Holstein cattle), Roxbury, Conn., 1945—; dir. Am. Home Products Corp. Bd. dirs. Christian Herald Assn., Penney Retirement Community, Penney Farms, Fla. Served to maj. AUS, 1942-45. Clubs: N.Y. Yacht, Racquet and Tennis, Church (N.Y.C.); Bath and Tennis, Everglades, Poinciana (Palm Beach, Fla.). Home: Toplands Farm Roxbury CT 06783 also 35 Sutton Pl New York NY 10022 also 400 S Ocean Blvd Palm Beach FL 33480 Shore Ln Boca Grande FL 33921 Office: 375 Park Ave New York NY 10152

DIEBOLD, FOSTER FRANK, university president; b. Orange, N.J., Oct. 24, 1932; s. Barnard A. and Gladys Lillian (Neer) D.; m. Patricia Elizabeth Gorski, Apr. 27, 1974; children: Jessica, Stacey. B.S. in Edn, Monmouth Coll., West Long Branch, N.J., 1959; M.A. in Ednl. Adminstrn, Seton Hall U., East Orange, N.J., 1964; postgrad. (Wall St. Jour. fellow 1963), Rutgers U. Tchr. English and psychology, asst. to supt. schs. Neptune Twp. (N.J.) Public Schs., 1965-69; supr. Arthur Brisbane Child Treatment Center for Emotionally Disturbed, Farmingdale, N.J., 1957-58; dir. div. coll. devel. and planning Kean Coll. of N.J., 1969-76; exec. sec. to bd. regents, spl. asst. to pres. U. Alaska Statewide System, 1976-77, pres., 1977-79, also Regent's prof.; pres. Edinboro U. (Pa.), 1979—; mem. adminstrn. and fin. com. Pa. State Colls. and Univs. Commn.; participant profl. confs.; mem. adv.

bd. Marine Bank. Mem. corp. bd. Hamot Med. Ctr., Erie, Pa.; bd. govs. State System Higher Edn. Com. Long-Range Planning; mem. Pa. State Bd. Edn. Task Force and Articulation; mem. adv. bd. William J. McMannis and A. Haskell McMannis Ednl. Trust Fund. Recipient Exceptional Service award Pa. Sociol. Soc., 1983. Mem. Commn. Univ. Presidents of State System of Higher Edn. (coms. adminstrn. and fin., ednl. policies and human resources mgmt.), World Future Soc. (edn. policy com. 1983-84, charter), Pa. Assn. Colls. and Univs. (mem. govt. relations com.), Sr. Colleague Adv. Network. Office: President's Office Edinboro Univ Edinboro PA 16444

DIEBOLD, JOHN, business executive; b. Weehawken, N.J., June 8, 1926; s. William and Rose (Theurer) D.; m. Doris Hackett, Nov. 22, 1951 (div. 1975); 1 dau., Joan. B.S. (Regtl. Acad. award), U.S. Mcht. Marine Acad., 1946; B.A. with high honors in Econs, Swarthmore Coll., 1949; M.B.A. with distinction, Harvard, 1951; LL.D. (hon.), Rollins Coll., 1965, Sc.D., Clarkson Coll., 1965, D. Engring., Newark Coll. Engring., 1970, L.H.D., Canaan Coll., 1972, D.C.S., Manhattan Coll., 1973. With Griffenhagen & Assos. (mgmt. cons.), N.Y.C., also Chgo., 1951-57; owner Griffenhagen & Assocs. (mgmt. cons.), 1957-60, 1960; chmn. bd. Griffenhagen-Kroeger, Inc., 1960—; founder Diebold Group, Inc. (mgmt. cons.), N.Y.C., 1954, pres., chmn. bd., 1954—; founder Diebold Europe S.A., 1958, chmn. bd., 1958—; founder, chmn. bd. Mgmt. Sci. Tng. Inst., 1958—; founder John Diebold Inc. (mgmt. and investment), 1967, chmn., 1967—, DCL Inc. (holding co. of Diebold Computer Leasing, Inc.), 1967—, Gemini Computer Systems, Inc., 1968-75; dir. Genesco, Prentice Hall, Inc. Author: Automation, The Advent of the Automatic Factory, 1952, republished, 1983, Beyond Automation, 1964, Man and the Computer—Technology as an Agent of Social Change, 1969, Business Decisions and Technological Change, 1970, The Role of Business in Society, 1983; also articles.; Editor: World of the Computer, 1973. Mem. Sec. Labor Adv. Com. Manpower and Automation, 1962-66, Pres. Kennedy's Com., Dept. Labor's 50th Anniversary, 1963; mem. U.S. delegation UN Sci. Conf., Geneva, Switzerland, 1963; mem. adv. council Soc. for Technol. Advancement of Modern Man, Switzerland, 1963-76; men. com. human values Soc. Advancing Tech., Nat. Council Chs., 1965-68; presdl. appointee nat. adv. council Peace Corps, 1965-70; mem. Com. on 2d Regional Plan for N.Y.C., 1966-70; trustee, treas., mem. exec. com. Nat. Com. on U.S.-China Relations, 1969—; trustee, sec. Bus. Council for Internat. Understanding, 1970-83; mem. Internat. Inst. Strategic Studies, London, 1971—; bd. consultants, mem. adv. com. UN We Believe, 1972—; mem. Adv. Council on Japan-U.S. Econ. Relations, 1972-74; mem. steering com. Atlantic Conf., 1972-82; mem. Council on Fgn. Relations, 1967—; mem. adv. group developing fgn. affairs program, planning and budgeting system sec. state, 1966-67; Chmn. vis. com. Sch. Bus. Adminstrn., Clarkson Coll. Tech., 1961-66; vice chmn. vis. com. econs. Harvard U., 1963-69, 70-76, mem. vis. com. engring. and applied physics, 1974-80; adv. council Inst. for Crippled and Disabled N.Y.C., 1957—; mem. U.S. adv. com. European Inst. Bus. Adminstrn., 1965—; mem. bus. adv. com. Grad. Sch. Indsl. Adminstrn., Carnegie-Mellon U., 1969—; trustee Freedom House, 1969—, Com. for Econ Devel., 1970—; vice chmn. Am. Council on Germany, 1970-80, trustee, 1980-83; founder, pres. Diebold Inst. Pub. Policy Studies, 1967—; trustee Carnegie Instn., Washington, 1975—; trustee, vice chmn. legislation com. N.Y. Met. Reference and Research Library Agy., 1974-80; mem. com. for African industrialization Club de Dakar, Paris, 1973—; pub. mem. Hudson Inst., 1967—; mem. vis. com. Center for Research in Computing Tech. and Office for Info. Tech., Harvard U., 1971-74; mem. organizing com. on Harvard and East Asia, 1974—; mem. adv. council Grad. Sch. Bus. Adminstrn., Columbia U., 1968-75; mem. vis. com. Grad. Sch. Mgmt., Vanderbilt U., 1969-74; bd. dirs. Acad. for Ednl. Devel., 1972—, Young Audiences, 1980-82, Parent Participation Workshop, 1982—; trustee, mem. exec. com. Council of Ams., 1971-74; trustee Nat. Planning Assn., 1973—; founding mem., mem. exec. com. council Rockefeller U., 1973—; mem. adv. com. ethical and human values of sci. and tech. NSF, 1973—, indsl. panel on sci. and tech., 1974—; trustee Overseas Devel. Council, 1974—, Found. for Teaching Econs., 1980—; mem. Nat. Acad. Sci. Evaluation Panel for Oversight over Inst. Computer Scis. and Tech., Nat. Bur. Standards, 1975-79, N.Y. Gov.'s Planning Commn. for Conf. on Libraries, 1976-79, N.Y. Sheriff's Jury, 1976-80; chmn. East Asian History of Sci., Inc., 1980—; mem. exec. com. Public Agenda Found., 1981—; mem. Friends of History of Sci. Harvard U., 1982—; trustee adv. bd. Found. Student & Communication, Inc., 1983—; bd. dirs. U.S. organizing com. Air and Space Bicentennial, 1983-84; mem. ALA Commn. on Freedom and Equality of Access to Info., 1983—. Served with USNR, World War II. Decorated grand officer Order of Istiqlal, Jordan; grand cross Eloy Alfaro Found., Panama, Order St. Martin, Vienna; commendatore Order Merit, Italy; Order Merit, Germany; Chevalier Legion of Honor, France; Named one of ten outstanding young men U.S. Jr. C. of C., 1962; recipient Disting. Info. Scis. award Data Processing Mgmt. Assn., 1980; Fellow J. Pierpont Morgan Library, 1973—. Fellow Internat. Acad. Mgmt.; Mem. Internat. Cybernetics Assn. (dir. 1957—), AAAS (chmn. sect. com. on indsl. sci. 1981—), Am. Printing History Assn., U.S.C. of C. (council on trends and perspectives 1969-81), Internat. C. of C. (trustee U.S. council 1971-74), Center for Inter-Am. Relations, Mid-Atlantic Club N.Y., Author's Guild (com. on the 70's 1970-73). Clubs: Harvard Business School, Economic, Union League, Harvard (N.Y.C.); Metropolitan (Washington); Chicago; Bohemian (San Francisco); Reform, Burkes (London). Home: 1 East End Ave New York NY 10021 Office: The Diebold Group Inc 475 Park Ave S New York NY 10016

DIEBOLD, ROBERT ERNEST, physicist; b. Rhinelander, Wis., Aug. 31, 1937; s. Charles Harbou and Elizabeth (Strong) D.; m. Bobbie Fortun Lively, Mar. 28, 1981; children by previous marriage: Daniel, Michael, Steven, Bruce. B.S., U. N.Mex., 1958; M.S., Calif. Inst. Tech., 1960, Ph.D., 1963. NSF postdoctoral fellow European Orgn. for Nuclear Research, Geneva, 1962-64; research asso. Stanford (Calif.) Linear Accelerator Center, 1964-69; physicist Argonne (Ill.) Nat. Lab., 1969-75, sr. physicist, 1975—, asso. lab. dir., 1979-80, div. dir., 1981—; program adv. com. Brookhaven Nat. Lab., 1972-74, Fermi Nat. Accelerator Lab., 1973-76, Stanford Linear Accelerator Center, 1973-75; mem. high energy physics adv. panel Dept. of Energy, 1975-80. Fellow Am. Phys. Soc. (sec.-treas. div. particles and fields 1980-83). Home: 8116 Fairmount Ave Downers Grove IL 60516 Office: Argonne Nat Lab 9700 S Cass Ave Argonne IL 60439

DIECKE, FRIEDRICH PAUL JULIUS, physiologist; b. Holzen, Germany, June 27, 1927; s. Walter Wilhelm and Emma S. D.; m. Elizabeth Bennett, Nov. 26, 1955; children—Dietrich W., Friedrich K. Doctor rer. nat. magna cum laude in Comparative Physiology, Universitat Wurzburg, 1953. Asst. Universitat Wurzburg, 1955-56; instr. U. Tenn. Coll. Medicine, 1956-57, asst. prof., 1957-59; vis. investigator Rockefeller Inst., 1959; asso. prof. physiology George Washington U. Coll. Medicine, 1959-63; prof. U. Iowa Coll. Medicine, 1963-75, acting head dept., 1973-75; prof., chmn. dept. physiology Coll. Medicine and Dentistry of N.J., N.J. Med. Sch., Newark, 1975—. Mem. AAAS, Am. Physiol. Soc., Soc. Gen. Physiologists, Biophys. Soc., Soc. Neurosci., Assn. Chairmen Depts. Physiology, Sigma Xi. Office: Dept Physiology Coll Medicine and Dentistry NJ Med Sch 100 Bergen St Newark NJ 07103

DIEDERICH, J(OHN) WILLIAM, newspaper executive; b. Ladysmith, Wis., Aug. 30, 1929; s. Joseph Charles and Alice Florence (Yost) D.; m. Mary Theresa Klein, Nov. 25, 1950; children: Mary Theresa Diederich Evans, Robert Douglas, Charles Stuart, Michael Mark, Patricia Anne, Donna Maureen (dec.), Denise Branden, Carol Lynn Diederich Weaver, Barbara Gail, Brian Donald, Tracy Maureen, Theodora Bernadette, Tamara Alice, Lorraine Angela. Ph.B., Marquette U., Milw., 1951; M.B.A. with high distinction (Baker scholar), Harvard U., 1955. With Landmark Communications, Inc., Norfolk, Va., 1955—, v.p., treas., 1965-73, exec. v.p. fin., 1973-78, exec. v.p. community newspapers, 1978-82, exec. v.p., chief fin. officer, 1982—, also dir.; chmn. bd. dirs. Landmark Community Newspapers, Inc., 1977—; pres. Exec. Productivity Systems, Inc., 1982—; instr. Boston U., 1954, Old Dominion U., 1955-59. Bd. dirs. Landmark Charitable Found. Served as officer USMCR, 1951-53; lt. col. Res. (ret.). Mem. Inst. Newspaper Controllers and Fin. Officers, Nat. Assn. Accts., Am. Numismatic Assn., S.A.R., Nat. Geneal. Soc., Wis. Geneal. Soc., Pa. Geneal. Soc., Sigma Delta Chi. Roman Catholic. Club: Harbor (Norfolk). Home: 3751 Little Neck Point Virginia Beach VA 23452 Office: 150 W Brambleton Ave Norfolk VA 23501

DIEDRICH, WILLIAM LAWLER, lawyer; b. De Kalb, Ill., Nov. 17, 1923; s. William Leo and Marie Antoinette (Lawler) D.; m. Margaret Lucille Benson, Aug. 6, 1949; children: Peter, Louise, Anne. B.A., St. Benedict's Coll., 1949; LL.B., Georgetown U., 1951. Bar: D.C. 1952, Calif. 1954, U.S. Supreme Ct. 1956. Assoc. Pillsbury, Madison & Sutro, San Francisco, 1952-36, ptnr., 1963—; dir. San Francisco Com. Urban Affairs, 1972-74. Co-author: How to Defend an Employment Discranimation Case, 1982. Pres. bd. dirs. Catholic Social Service, San Francisco, 1980, 81; bd. dirs. Cath. Charities, 1982—, Benedictine Coll., 1972-80. Served to sgt. U.S. Army, 1943-46; Burma, India. Recipient Kans. Monk award Benedictine Coll., Atchison, 1977. Mem. State Bar Calif., Bar Assn. San Francisco (joint chmn. com. equal employment 1969-72, chmn. com. labor laws 1979-81), Bar Assn. D.C. Democrat. Roman Catholic. Club: Commonwealth (San Francisco). Home: 355 Santa Clara Ave San Francisco CA 94127 Office: Pillsbury Madison & Sutro 225 Bush St San Francisco CA 94104

DIEFENBACH, ALLAN BERLEMAN, lawyer; b. Bluffton, Ind., May 18, 1909; s. Howard Berleman and Josephine C. (Zartman) D. A.B. cum laude, Heidelberg Coll., 1931; J.D., U. Mich., 1934; postgrad., U. Akron. Bar: Ohio bar 1934. Since practiced in, Akron; mem. firm Chapman, Thomson, Diefenbach & Hardesty; dir. Fair Finance Co. Co-author: Ohio Probate Practice. Exec. com. Gov. Ohio Traffic Safety Conf., 1959-61; organizing pres. Greater Akron Council Chs., 1947-50; mem. com. Akron Pub. Sinking Fund, 1937-44; chief tng. officer Summit County Civil Def., 1943-45; Trustee Ohio Presbyn. Homes, 1960—, Heidelberg Coll., Goodwill Industries, Akron, 1971-77; bd. visitors law sch. U. Mich., 1963-66. Fellow Am. Bar Found., Ohio Bar Found. (dir. 1963-69); mem. ABA (mem. award of merit com. 1975-79), Ohio Bar Assn. (pres. 1959-60), Akron Bar Assn. (Charles Travers Grant Meml. prize 1942, 56, pres. 1952-53), Am. Judicature Soc. (dir. 1966-69), Nat. Huguenot Soc. (past counselor gen.), Summit County Hist. Soc. (trustee 1973—, pres. 1974-78), Pi Kappa Delta, Tau Kappa Alpha. Republican. Presbyn. Clubs: Kiwanian., Franklin, City (Akron). Home: 356 S Rose Blvd Akron OH 44313 Office: Centran Bldg Akron OH 44308

DIEFENBACH, VIRON LEROY, university dean emeritus, dental educator; b. Balt., Feb. 9, 1922; s. William Lewis and Ardie Gertrude (Von Wachter) D.; m. Adele Larson, Apr. 18, 1956; children: Kathryn Louise, Arthur Karl, William Henderson, Sue Henderson. Student, Western Md. Coll., 1940-42, Pratt Inst. Engring., 1943, Harvard U., 1944; D.D.S., U. Md., 1949; M.P.H., U. Pitts., 1954. Diplomate: Am. Bd. Dental Pub. Health. Dental intern USPHS Hosp., Norfolk, Va., 1949-50, various clin. assignments, 1950-52, dental pub. health field tng., 1952-53; asst. regional dental cons. USPHS, Chgo., Office Personnel, Office Surgeon Gen., USPHS, Washington, 1955-56, information dir. div., 1957-59; regional dental cons. USPHS, Denver, 1959-61, dep. chief div., Bethesda, Md., 1962-65, acting chief and dir., 1966, asst. surgeon gen., 1966-70; asst. exec. dir. Am. Dental Assn., 1970-72; prof. health resources mgmt. Grad. Sch. Public Health, U. Ill., 1973—, assoc. dean, 1977, dean, 1978-83. Served with AUS, 1942-44; with USPHS, 1949-70. Recipient Scholarship Gold medal U. Md., 1949, Meritorious Service medal USPHS, 1966. Fellow Am. Pub. Health Assn. (past sect. chmn., sec.), AAAS, Am. Coll. Dentists; mem. Commd. Officers Assn. USPHS (mem. exec. bd., past chmn. bd.), ADA, Am. Assn. Pub. Health Dentists, Fedn. Dentaire Internationale. Home: 1405 N Sandburg Terr Chicago IL 60610 Office: Sch Public Health U Ill Health Sci Center Chicago IL 60680

DIEFENDERFER, WILLIAM MARTIN, III, lawyer; b. Sharon, Pa., May 3, 1945; s. William M. and Bernadine M. (Freeborn) D.; m. Sandra J. Hoover, Aug. 7, 1976; children: William Martin IV, Barret. B.A., Dickinson Coll., 1967; J.D., Duquesne U., 1973; LL.M., U. London, Eng., 1974. Bar: Pa. 1975. Regional dir. Pa. Higher Edn. Agy., Harrisburg, 1972-73; staff atty. com. on edn. and labor U.S. Ho. of Reps., 1975-76; asst. dir. domestic council The White House, Washington, 1976-77; adminstrv. asst. and legal counsel to Congressman from 23d Dist. of N.Y., 1977-79; chief counsel com. on commerce, sci. and transp. U.S. Senate, Washington, 1979-83; mem. McNair, Glenn, Konduros, Corley, Singletary, Porter & Dibble, P.A., Washington, 1983—. Served with U.S. Army, 1970-72. Mem. Am. Bar Assn., Fed. Bar Assn. Republican. Office: 1155 15th St NW Washington DC 20005

DIEHL, DIGBY ROBERT, journalist; b. Boonton, N.J., Nov. 14, 1940; s. Edwin Samuel and Mary Jane Shirley (Ellsworth) D.; m. Kay Beyer, June 6, 1981; 1 dau., Dylan Elizabeth. A.B. in Am. Studies (Henry Rutgers scholar), Rutgers U., 1962; M.A. in Theatre Arts, UCLA, 1966, postgrad., 1969—. Editor Learning Center, Inc., Princeton, N.J., 1962-64; dir. research Creative Playthings, Los Angeles, 1964-66; editor Coast mag., Los Angeles, 1966-68, Show mag., 1968-69; book editor Los Angeles Times, 1969-78; v.p., editor-in-chief Harry N. Abrams, Inc., N.Y.C., 1978-79; book editor Los Angeles Herald Examiner, 1980—; instr. journalism UCLA, 1969-78; jurist Nat. Book Awards, 1972; mem. nominating com. Nat. Medal for Lit., 1972-75; v.p. Nat. Book Critics Circle, 1975-78, bd. dirs., 1981—; jurist Am. Book Awards, 1981. Author: Supertalk: Extraordinary Conversations, 1974, Front Page, 1981. Trustee KPFK-Pacifica Found. Recipient; Irita Van Doren award, 1977. Mem. Am. Soc. Journalists and Authors, AAUP, Phi Beta Kappa, Phi Sigma Delta. Office: Los Angeles Herald Examiner 1111 S Broadway Los Angeles CA 90015

DIEHL, RICHARD KURTH, savs. and loan assn. exec.; b. Chgo., July 6, 1935; s. George Henry and Agnes Martha (Kurth) D.; m. Barbara Louise Clark, June 9, 1957; children—Clark Kurth, Scott Richard, Stacy Louise. B.A., Beloit Coll., 1957; postgrad., Harvard U., 1957-58; M.B.A., U. Chgo., 1959. Dir. mktg. Kimberly-Clark Corp., Neenah, Wis., 1968-70; pres., chief exec. officer Purnell, Inc., Santa Monica, Calif., 1970-72; v.p., chief operating officer Theta Cable TV, Santa Monica, 1972-74; exec. v.p., chief savs. officer Western Fed. Savs. and Loan Assn., Los Angeles, 1974-80; exec. v.p., a founding officer Centurion Savs. and Loan Assn., Century City, Calif., 1980—. Mem. Citizens Adv. Council Los Angeles Schs., 1970-72. Woodrow Wilson fellow, 1957-58; Harvard Austin fellow, 1957-58; Sears Roebuck Found. fellow, 1958-59. Mem. Calif. Savs. and Loan League, Phi Beta Kappa, Sigma Alpha Epsilon. Clubs: Rotary Internat., Riviera Tennis, Santa Monica Tennis Patrons. Home: 17155 Palisades Circle Pacific Palisades CA 90272 Office: 2049 Century Park E Los Angeles CA 90067

DIEHL, VAL BURL, biscuit co. exec.; b. Mitchell, S.D., Sept. 4, 1916; s. Maurice Blake and Alene (Wallace) D.; m. Mary Ellen Condon, Sept. 7, 1940; children—Barbara Mae (Mrs. W. Wilson), James Maurice, Julie Ann (Mrs. G.D. Holloway). B.S., Dakota Wesleyan U., 1938; student, Navy Supply Corps Sch., 1943, advanced mgmt. program Harvard, 1962. Distbr. Royal Typewriter Co., Mankato, Minn., 1940-42; with Nabisco, Inc. (formerly Nat. Biscuit Co.), 1942-43, 54—, asst. dir. internat. operations, 1955-61; chmn. Nabisco Foods Eng., 1962; asst. to pres. Nat. Biscuit Co., N.Y.C., 1962-68, v.p. internat. div., 1968, exec. v.p., now pres., chief operating officer, 1973—, also dir., Eng., France, Italy, Can., Nicaragua, Panama; dir. Gen. Pub. Utilities Corp. Trustee Council of Americas. Served to lt. USNR, 1943-45. Mem. Biscuit and Cracker Mfrs. Assn. (dir.). Republican. Roman Catholic. Clubs: Baltusrol Golf, John's Island. *

DIEHL, WALTER FRANCIS, labor union ofcl.; b. Revere, Mass., Apr. 13, 1907; s. John H. and Mary J. (Levinus) D.; 3 children. Student, Northeastern U., 1925-27. Moving picture machine operator, 1927-46; with Internat. Alliance Theatrical Stage Employees and Moving Picture Machine Operators U.S. and Can., 1944—; mem. exec. bd. local 182, Boston, 1944-46, bus. agt., 1946-53, internat. rep., 1953-57, asst. internat. pres., 1957-74, internat. pres., 1974—. Mem. Catholic Actors Guild (v.p. 1964). Office: 1515 Broadway Suite 601 New York NY 10036

DIEKEMA, ANTHONY J., college president; b. Borculo, Mich., Dec. 3, 1933; m. Jeane Waanders, Dec. 20, 1957; children: Douglas, David, Daniel, Paul, Mark, Maria, Tanya. B.A., Calvin Coll., Grand Rapids, Mich., 1956; M.A. in Sociology and Anthropology, Mich. State U., 1958, Ph.D., 1965. Field interviewer Bur. Bus. Research, Mich. State U., East Lansing, 1955-56, asst. dir. housing, 1957-59, instr. and lectr. sociology and anthropology, 1959-64, admissions counselor, 1959-61, asst. dir. admissions and scholarships, 1961-62, asst. registrar, 1962-64; asst. dean admissions and records, research asso. in med. edn. and asst. prof. sociology U. Ill. Med. Center, Chgo., 1964-66, dir. admissions and records, asst. prof. sociology and edn., 1966-70, asso. chancellor, asso. prof. med. edn., 1970-76; pres. Calvin Coll., 1976—; dir. Union Bancorp. Contbr. articles to profl. jours. Trustee Blodgett Meml. Med. Center, Grand Rapids, 1979—; bd. dirs. Met. YMCA, Grand Rapids, 1979—, Project Rehab, 1978—; treas. Back-to-God Hour Radio Com., 1970-76; chmn. Synodical Com. on Race Relations, 1973-75; pres. Strategic Christian Ministry Found., 1969-73; mem. bd. curators Trinity Christian Coll., 1969-73, chmn., 1972-73, mem. presdl. search com., 1972-73. Mem. Am. Assn. Pres.'s Ind. Colls. and Univs. (dir. 1978—), Assn. Ind. Colls. and Univs. Mich. (exec. com. 1979—), Am. Assn. Higher Edn., Am. Sociol. Assn., Soc. Health and Human Values, Soc. Values in Higher Edn., Nat. League Nursing (accreditation com. 1974-79), Alpha Kappa Delta. Club: Rotary. Office: 390 College Center Calvin Coll Grand Rapids MI 49506

DIEMAR, ROBERT EMERY, JR., investment banker; b. Covington, Ky., July 7, 1942; s. Robert E. and Eloise (Wehry) D.; m. Eleanor S. Griggs, Sept. 12, 1970; children: Robert III, John, Thomas, Caroline. A.B., Princeton U., 1965; M.B.A., Dartmouth Coll., 1967. Assoc. Dillon, Read & Co., N.Y.C., 1967-73, Donaldson, Lufkin & Jenrette, 1973-74, v.p., 1974-76, sr.v.p., 1976—. Trustee Lawrence Country Day Sch., Hewlett, N.Y., 1982-83; bd. dirs. Henry St. Settlement, N.Y.C., 1976—; vestry Trinity-St. John's Episcopal Ch., Hewlett, N.Y., 1978-83. Served with USCGR, 1967-73. Office: Donaldson Lufkin & Jenrette 140 Broadway New York NY 10005

DIEMER, EMMA LOU, composer, organist; b. Kansas City, Mo., Nov. 24, 1927; d. George Willis and Myrtle (Casebolt) D. B.Mus., Yale U., 1949, M.Mus., 1950; Ph.D., Eastman Sch. Music, 1960. Composer-in-residence (Ford Found. Young Composers grantee) Arlington, Va. Schs., 1959-61; asst. prof. theory and composition U. Md., 1965-70; prof. theory and composition U. Calif., Santa Barbara, 1971—; organist 1st Ch. of Christ, Scientist, Santa Barbara, 1973—. Over 100 choral and instrumental compositions including Music for Woodwind Quartet, 1976, Four Poems of AliceMeynell for Soprano and Chamber Ensemble, 1977, Concerto for Flute, 1978, Symphony No. 2, 1980, Suite for Orchestra, 1981. Fulbright scholar, 1952-53; Kindler Found. Commn. grantee, 1963; Nat. Endowment Arts grantee, 1981. Mem. Am. Guild Organists, League Women Composers, Am. Women Composers, ASCAP (ann. awards 1962-83), Mu Phi Epsilon. Democrat. Home: 2249 Vista del Campo Santa Barbara CA 93101 Office: Dept Music U Calif Santa Barbara CA 93106 *A composer who succeeds in some measure must have talent, encourage- ment, strong self-motivation, an almost obsessive need for self-expression through music, a belief in the importance of one's own contribution, the ability to appraise one's own work, the desire, at least part of the time, to communicate.*

DIENER, BERT, food broker, artist; b. N.Y.C., Mar. 21, 1915; s. Frederick and Lena (Rublin) D.; m. Hermine Van Baarn, Nov. 14, 1940; children: Francine Carol, Fredric Jay. B.S., U. Va., 1937. Partner Gold-Rose Diener, N.Y.C., 1939-45, Rich-Diener, 1945-63; pres. Pratico-Diener Corp., Fort Lee, N.J., 1963-68; exec. v.p. Pratico, Diener & Stein, Inc., 1968-69, Diener & Stein, Inc., 1969-74; chief operating officer Diener-Stein Sales, 1974—; pres. Quad Media Concepts, 1978-79, Bert Diener, Inc., 1980—; pres. Telestar Products Corp., Grocery Industry Services, Inc., Living Arts Force; mem. marketing adv. com. U.S. Banknote Corp. Exhibited in one-man shows, Southhold Gallery, L.I., 1967, Frankel Gallery, Roslyn, N.Y., 1968, Center Art Gallery, N.Y.C., 1970, three man show, Sears-Vincent Price Gallery, Chgo., 1969, group show, Grand Prix International D'Art Contemparin De la Principaute de Monaco, 1970; Pub., editor: Grocery Industry Directory Met. N.Y, 1961-65. Trustee Sculpture Ctr. Mem. Grocery Mfrs. Reps. N.Y.C. (past pres.), Nat. Food Brokers Assn. (past dir.), Assn. Food Distbrs. (past chmn. brokers div.), Artists Welfare Fund (pres.), N.Y. Artists Equity (pres.), Internat. Assn. Art (coordinator), Fine Arts Fedn. of N.Y. (v.p.), Met. Painters and Sculptors, Youth Art Program (founder, chmn.), Sales Execs. Club N.Y. Republican. Club: New York Athletic. Home: 177 E 75th St New York NY 10021 Office: 111 Mineola Ave Roslyn Heights NY 11577 *The good that has come into my experience has only been meaningful when I in turn did some good. I am merely a medium through whom the good passes and the goods pass.*

DIENER, ROYCE, health services company executive. Chmn., chief exec. officer Am. Med. Internat. Inc., Beverly Hills, Calif. Office: Am Med Internat Inc 414 N Camden Dr Beverly Hills CA 90212

DIENER, STEPHEN I., video company executive; b. Jersey City, Dec. 17, 1938; s. Maurice and Ruth (Tarchis) D.; m. Yannick Diener; children: Hollis, James. B.A. in English, Tulane U., 1960. Dir. mktg. Revlon Internat., N.Y.C., 1968-71; dir. mktg. Europe CBS Internat., Paris, 1972-75; pres. Internat. div. ABC Records, Inc., Los Angeles, 1975-77, pres., 1977-79; exec. v.p. Latin Am. ops. CBS Records Internat., Coral Gables, Fla., 1979—; exec. v.p. CBS/Fox Video Internat. Mem. Rec. Industry Assn. Am. (adv. bd.), Internat. Music Industry Conf. (adv. com.), Los Angeles C. of C. Jewish. Home: 754 Kitchawan Rd Ossining NY 10562 Office: 1211 Ave of Americas New York NY 10036

DIENER, THEODOR OTTO, plant pathologist; b. Zurich, Switzerland, Feb. 28, 1921; came to U.S., 1949, naturalized, 1955; s. Theodor Emanuel and Hedwig Rosa (Baumann) D.; m. Sybil Mary Fox, May 11, 1968; children by previous marriage: Theodor W., Robert A., Michael S. Dipl. Sc. Nat. E.T.H., Swiss Fed. Inst. Tech., 1946, D. Sc. Nat., 1948. Asst. Swiss Fed. Inst. Tech., Zurich, 1946-48; plant pathologist Swiss Fed. Exptl. Sta., Waedenswil, 1949-50; asst. prof. plant pathology R.I. State U., Kingston, 1950; asst. plant pathologist Wash. State U., Prosser, 1950-55, asso. plant pathologist, 1955-59; research plant pathologist Agrl. Research Service, USDA, Beltsville, Md., 1959—; lectr. univs. and research insts.; Regents' lectr. U. Calif., Riverside, 1970; Andrew D. White prof.-at-large Cornell U., 1979-81. Author: Viroids and Viroid Diseases, 1979; asso. editor: jour. Virology, 1964-66, 74-76; editor, 1967-71; mem. editorial com.: Ann. Rev. Phytopathology, 1970-74, Annales de Virologie, 1980—; contbr. articles to sci. publs. Recipient Campbell award Am. Inst. Biol. Scis., 1968; Alexander von Humboldt award, 1975; Superior Service award USDA, 1969; Distinguished Service award, 1977. Fellow Am. Phytopath. Soc. (Ruth Allen award 1976), N.Y. Acad. Scis., Am. Acad. Arts and Scis.; mem. AAAS, Nat. Acad. Scis., Leopoldina, German Acad. Natural Scientists. Discoverer novel class of pathogens (viroids), 1971. Home: 4530 Powder Mill Rd PO Box 272 Beltsville MD 20705 Office: Plant Virology Lab Agrl Research Center USDA Beltsville MD 20705

DIENSTFREY, HARRIS DAVID, editor; b. N.Y.C., May 14, 1934; s. Joseph Leon and Elizabeth (Hertz) D.; m. Jane Winborne Olds, May 29, 1970; stepchildren: Elizabeth Tobier, Natalie Tobier, Lincoln Tobier. B.A., U. Chgo., 1954, M.A., 1956. Asst. editor Commentary mag., 1959-61; editor Center for Urban Edn., 1965-68; co-founder, editor-in-chief Outerbridge & Dienstfrey, N.Y.C., 1969-71; editor Charles Scribner's Sons, N.Y.C., 1973-74; fiction and book editor Cosmopolitan mag., 1975-80; sr. editor Psychology Today mag., 1980-83; editor, dir. publs. Inst. for Advancement Health, N.Y.C., 1983—. Co-author: What Do You Want To Be When You Grow Old?, 1979. Served with AUS, 1956-58. Home: 75 Prospect Park W Brooklyn NY 11215 Office: 16 E 33d St New York NY 10022

DIERCKS, CHESTER WILLIAM, JR., capital goods manufacturing company executive; b. Urbana, Ill., Oct. 15, 1926; s. Chester William and Anna (Gude) D.; m. Marie Johnson, Aug. 5, 1950; children: Chester William, III, Lisa Beth. B.S. in Gen. Engring, Iowa State U., Ames, 1950; M.S. in Indsl. Mgmt. (Sloan fellow), Mass. Inst. Tech., 1962. Gen. mgr. med. services, x-ray and splty. transformer div. Westinghouse Electric Co., Pitts., 1950-71; with Allis-Chalmers Corp. (and subs.), 1971-77; exec. v.p. elec. group, pres. Allis-Chalmers Power Systems, Inc., Milw., 1976—, sr. exec. v.p., chief fin. officer, 1976-77; pres., chief exec. officer Siemens-Allis, Inc., 1977—, Utility Power Corp., Atlanta, 1978—; dir. Clow Corp., 1st Atlanta Corp., 1st Nat. Bank Atlanta, Siemens Electric Ltd.; Mem. Industry Sector Adviory Com. to 1974 Trade Reform Act, 1976-77; mem. mgmt. adv. com. Coll. Indsl. Mgmt., Ga. Inst. Tech.; dir. Siemens Electric Ltd. Bd. visitors Emory U., Berry Coll., Mt. Berry, Ga. Served to 1st lt. U.S. Army, 1945-47. Mem. Nat. Elec. Mfrs. Assn. (bd. govs.), Machinery and Allied Products Inc., Atlanta C. of C. (dir.), Fin. Execs. Inst. Clubs: Capital City (Atlanta); University (Milw.). Home: 4545 Powers Rd Marietta GA 30067 Office: PO Box 89000 Atlanta GA 30338

DIERCKS, FREDERICK OTTO, government official; b. Rainy River, Ont., Can., Sept. 8, 1912; s. Otto Herman and Lucy (Plunkett) D.; m. Kathryn Frances Transue, Sept. 1, 1937; children: Frederick William, Lucy Helena. B.S., U.S. Mil. Acad., 1937; M.S. in Civil Engring., MIT, 1939, Syracuse U., 1950. Registered profl. engr., D.C. Commd. 2d lt. U.S. Army, 1937, advanced through grades to col., 1952; comdg. officer U.S. Army Map Service, Washington, 1957-61, dir. U.S. Army Coastal Engring. Research Center, 1964-67, ret., 1967; assoc. dir. U.S. Coast and Geodetic Survey (now Nat. Ocean Survey), Rockville, Md., 1967-74; U.S. mem. commn. cartography Pan Am. Inst. Geography and History, OAS, 1961-67, alternate U.S. mem. directing council, 1970-74, exec. sec. U.S. sect., 1975—. Decorated Legion of Merit, (U.S.); grand cross Order of King George II, (Greece); most Exalted Order of White Elephant, (Thailand). Fellow ASCE; mem. Am. Soc. Photogrammetry (pres. 1970-71, dir.), Sigma Xi. Republican. Presbyterian. Clubs: Army-Navy, Cosmos (Washington). Lodge: Masons (Ft. Leavenworth, Kans.). Home: 9313 Christopher St Fairfax VA 22031 *One is better off starting life with little or nothing and having to earn one's way. There is then little time for pondering what is wrong with life, and resenting it, and fighting or withdrawing from it; but only for working, first to stay alive and then from the sense of achievement and possible service to others.*

DIERCKS, WALTER ELMER, lawyer; b. Irvington, N.J., July 6, 1945; s. Elmer Jules and Evelyn Sophie (Lauster) D.; m. Mary-Jane Atwater, Apr. 16, 1977; children: Emily Jane, Gillian Ruth. B.Chem. Engring., Rensselaer Poly. Inst., 1967; J.D., U. Va., 1972. Bar: Va. 1972, D.C. 1973. Devel. engr. Diamond Shamrock Corp., Balt., 1969-70; pub. Charlottesville (Va.) Consumer, 1970-72; atty. FTC, Washington, 1972-76; dep. asst. dir. compliance Bur. Consumer Protection, 1976-77; gen. counsel, sec. Washington Star Co., 1977-81; ptnr. Rubin, Winston & Diercks, Washington, 1981—. Chmn. Alexandria (Va.) Landlord-Tenant Relations Bd., 1976; mem. Alexandria Charter Rev. Commn., 1980-81, Alexandria Democratic Com., 1979-81, 83—. Recipient award excellence FTC, 1977. Mem. ABA. Democrat. Unitarian. Home: 304 Lamond Pl Alexandria VA 22314 Office: 1730 M St NW Suite 708 Washington DC 20036

DIERDORFF, JOHN AINSWORTH, editor; b. Chgo., Feb. 1, 1928; s. John and Phoebe (Frary) D. B.A., Yale, 1949. Staff writer Yakima (Wash.) Morning Herald, 1950-52; staff writer Portland Oregonian, 1952-56; copy editor Bus. Week, N.Y.C., 1956-60, asst. editor, 1960-61, asst. mng. editor, 1961-66, 76-77, mng. editor, 1966-69, 77—, sr. editor, 1969-76. Mem. Am. Soc. Mag. Editors, Soc. Profl. Journalists. Club: Coffee House (N.Y.C.). Home: 335 W 11th St New York NY 10014 also Rhinecliff NY 12574 Office: 1221 Ave of Americas New York NY 10020

DIERKER, CHARLES TORRANCE, holding co. exec.; b. Pitts., July 24, 1920; s. Carl Theodore and Jessie Torrance (Wilbraham) D.; m. Marilynn Keller, June 20, 1943; children—Lawrence E., Richard T., Laura Lynn. B.S. in Metall. Engring, Carnegie Inst. Tech., 1942. Indsl. gas engr. So. Calif. Gas Co., Los Angeles, 1946-49, mgr. sales promotion, until 1964; mgr. operations Central Plants Inc., Los Angeles, 1964-70; pres. Central Plants, Pacific Lighting Leasing, Los Angeles, 1970—, Dual Fuel Systems, Inc., 1979—. Served with C.E. U.S. Army, 1942-46. Mem. Am. Gas Assn., Tau Beta Pi. Home: 5906 Oakdale Ave Woodland Hills CA 91367 Office: 6140 Bristol Pkwy Culver City CA 90230

DIERKS, RICHARD ERNEST, veterinarian, ednl. adminstr.; b. Flandreau, S.D., Mar. 11, 1934; s. Martin and Lillian Ester (Benedict) D.; m. Eveline Carol Amundson, July 20, 1956; children—Jeffrey Scott, Steven Eric, Joel Richard. Student, S.D. State U., 1952-55; B.S., U. Minn., 1957, D.V.M., 1959, M.P.H., 1964, Ph.D., 1964. Supervisory microbiologist Communicable Disease Center, Atlanta, 1964-68; prof. coll. veterinary medicine Iowa State U., Ames, 1968-74; head dept. veterinary sci. Mont. State U., Bozeman, 1974-76; dean Coll. Veterinary Medicine, U. Ill., Urbana, 1976—; mem. tng. grant rev. com. Nat. Inst. Allergy and Infectious Diseases, 1973-74. Contbr. articles to profl. jours. Served with USPHS, 1964-67. Career Devel. awardee Nat. Inst. Allergy and Infectious Diseases, 1969-74. Mem. Am., Ill. veterinary medicine assns., Am. Soc. Microbiologists, Am. Coll. Veterinary Microbiologists, Am. Coll. Vet. Preventive Medicine, Am. Assn. Immunologists, Soc. Exptl. Biology and Medicine, Gamma Sigma Delta, Phi Kappa Phi, Phi Zeta. Republican. Lutheran. Club: Rotary. Home: 2801 E Holcolm Dr Urbana IL 61801 Office: College of Veterinary Medicine University of Illinois Urbana IL 61801

DIERS, DONNA KAYE, nurse educator; b. Sheridan, Wyo., May 11, 1938; d. Don Carlos and Ilene Helen (Poffenberger) D. B.S.N., U. Denver, 1960; M.S.N., Yale U., 1964. Staff nurse Yale Psychiat. Inst., New Haven, 1960-62; mem. faculty Yale U. Sch. Nursing, New Haven, 1964—, prof., 1979—, dean, 1972—; dir. Yale Health Services, Community Health Care Plan, New Haven, 1972—. Author: Research in Nursing Practice, 1979. Mem. adv. com. Robert Wood Johnson Found., Princeton, N.J., 1980—; mem. research rev. com. Nat. Ctr. Health Services Research, Washington, 1981—. Recipient Henderson award Conn. Nurses Assn., 1980, Disting. Alumna award Yale U. Sch. Nursing, 1983. Fellow Am. Acad. Nursing, Inst. Nursing; mem. Am. Nurses Assn. Home: 220 Osborn Ave New Haven CT 06510 Office: Yale U Sch Nursing 855 Howard Ave New Haven CT 06510

DIERS, HANK, drama educator; b. Dubuque, Iowa, Sept. 23, 1931; s. Hermann Henry and Elfriede Johanna (Langholz) D.; m. Doris Elaine Blumreich, Sept. 5, 1953; children: Daniel, Deborah, John, Alicia, David. B.A., Wartburg Coll., 1953; postgrad., U. Dubuque, 1949, 53-54; M.A., U. Ill., 1957, Ph.D., 1965. Faculty drama dept. U. Miami, Coral Gables, Fla., 1960—, chmn. dept. drama, 1967—, prof., 1968—, dir. univ. theatres, 1973—; acting dir. theatre, guest cons. SUNY-Old Westbury; exec. dir. So. Shakespeare Repertory Theatre, Coconut Grove Playhouse, 1961-68; exec. producer Ring Theatre Arts Festival Theatre, 1969—; founder Fumpets Puppet Theatre, ASTA Fair, Amsterdam, Netherlands, 1970. Dir.: plays including Hamlet, 1968, The Royal Hunt of the Sun, 1968, The Boy Friend, 1971 (winner Am. Coll. Theatre Festival 1972), The Apple Tree, 1970, Jacques Brel (winner Am. Coll. Theatre Festival 1973); original producer: Miami; Author: play Doctor, Doctor, 1971, 307 Defense of Hermann Goering, 1972, Mine Eyes Have Seen the Glory, 1976. Mem. alumni bd. Wartburg Coll., 1968—, Omni Theatre.; Trustee 3rd Century Bicentennial. Served with AUS, 1954-56. Recipient Silver medal for Photography N.Y. World's Fair, 1964; Angel award for Theatre The Miami Herald, 1966, 67; Iron Arrow U. Miami, 1970. Mem. Am. Theatre Assn., SCA, Southeastern Theatre Conf. (sec. 1962-64), Fla. Theatre Conf. (v.p.), Fla. Arts Congress (dir.), Alpha Psi Omega, Alpha Phi Gamma. Lutheran (Dade County council 1969-72). Home: 6830 SW 104th St Miami FL 33156

DIES, DOUGLAS HILTON, association executive; b. St. Paul, Sept. 9, 1913; s. Edward Jerome and Mareeta (Cole) D.; m. Mary Frances Doreen Harding, Nov. 25, 1939; children—Harding Mogridge, Andrea Frances. A.B., Harvard, 1934; postgrad., Oxford U., 1934-35. Editorial staff Grand Forks (N.D.) Herald, summer 1933, Mpls. Star, summer 1934, London Sunday Chronicle, summer 1935; staff London bur. U.P., 1935-38, Knoxville (Tenn.) Jour., 1938-40; pub. relations dept. Westinghouse Electric Co., 1940-41; staff A.P., Cleve., 1941-42; pub. info. staff U.S. Bd. Econ. Warfare, Washington, 1942-43; pub. relationist, Washington, 1946—, asso. world trading corps., 1947—; asst. to pres. Nat. Inst. Oilseed Products, 1947—; Washington rep. Pillsbury Co., 1956-64, East Asiatic Co., 1956-78, Woodward & Dickerson, Inc., 1958—; asst. sec., bur. raw materials Am. Vegetable Oils and Fats Industries, 1961-62, sec., 1962—; exec. sec. Am. Council Ind. Labs., 1963-81; cons., 1981—; Guest lectr. Georgetown U. Sch. Fgn. Trade; mem. Agrl. Tech. Adv. Com. on Oilseeds and Products for Multilateral Trade Negotiations, 1975—; mem. adv. State Tech. Services Act D.C. Editor: Chemurgie Digest, 1950-58, Washington Correspondence, 1947—. Mem. Republican City Com., Alexandria, 1958-61. Served from ensign to lt. comdr. USNR, 1943-46. Mem. S.R. (gov. D.C. 1956-65), Mil. Order World Wars, Sigma Alpha Epsilon. Episcopalian (vestryman). Clubs: Harvard (N.Y.C., Washington); Metropolitan, Univ., Oxford-Cambridge (Washington). Home: 505 Robinson Ct Alexandria VA 22302 Office: 1725 K St N W Washington DC 20006

DIESEL, JOHN PHILLIP, multinat. corp. exec.; b. St. Louis, June 10, 1926; s. John Henry and Elsa A. (Poetting) D.; m. Rita Jan Meyer, June 12, 1949; children—Holly, Gretchen, John, Dana. B.S., Washington U., St. Louis, 1951. Exec. asst. div. mgr. McQuay-Norris Mfg. Co., St. Louis, 1951-57; partner Booz, Allen & Hamilton, Inc., Chgo., 1957-61; v.p. ops. Ops. Research, Inc., Santa Monica, Calif., 1961-62; v.p., treas., dir. Mgmt. Tech., Inc., Los Angeles, 1962-63; dir. mktg. and planning A.O. Smith Corp., Milw., 1963-65, dir. mfg. and engring., 1965-67, v.p. mfg. and planning, 1967-70, group v.p., 1970-72; chmn. bd. Armor Elevator Can., Ltd., 1970-72; chmn. bd., pres. Armor Elevator Co., Inc., 1970-72; pres., chief exec. officer Newport News (Va.) Shipbldg. & Dry Dock Co., 1972-78, chmn. bd., 1976-78; exec. v.p. Tenneco Inc., 1976-79, pres., 1979—, also dir.; dir. Cooper Industries, Inc., First City Nat. Bancorp. Tex., Inc. Served with USNR, 1944-47. Methodist. Clubs: Pine Valley Golf, Seminole Golf, Metropolitan. Home: 327 Longwoods Ln Houston TX 77024 Office: Tenneco Inc PO Box 2511 Houston TX 77001

DIESEM, JOHN LAWRENCE, publishing executive; b. Albuquerque, July 16, 1941; s. Walter Franklin and Glen Ethel (Helpbringer) D.; m. Barbara Jane Willmarth, Feb. 25, 1967 (div. Oct. 10, 1976); m. Kathleen Terese Walsh, Feb. 2, 1979. B.A., George Washington U., 1964, M.A., 1965. Group mgr. Electronic Data Systems, N.Y.C., 1970-74; N.Y. State dep. commr., 1974-75; sr. mgr. Arthur Andersen, N.Y.C., 1975-80; v.p., dir. bus. systems devel. McGraw-Hill, N.Y.C., 1980, v.p., dir. tech. services, 1983—. Dir. George Washington U. dean's alumni adv. bd., 1981. Served to capt. USAF, 1965-69; Vietnam; to major USAF Res. Intelligence. Decorated Bronze Star. Mem Omicron Delta Kappa; mem. Sigma Chi. Republican. Episcopalian. Club: N.Y. Athletic (N.Y.C.). Home: 20 W 90th St New York NY 10024 Miller Rd Claverack NY 12513 Office: McGraw-Hill Book Co. 1221 Ave of Americas New York NY 10020

DIETCH, HENRY XERXES, judge; b. Bklyn., Nov. 13, 1913; s. Isadore J. and Mary (Krieg) D.; m. Shirley Friedman, Jan. 11, 1941; children: William A., Nancie I., James T. A.A., Crane Coll., 1933; J.D., John Marshall Law Sch., 1937; grad., Nat. Jud. Coll. Bar: Ill. 1937. Ptnr. firm Davis, Dietch & Ryan, Chgo., 1954-77; assoc. judge Circuit Ct. Cook County, 1977—; hearing officer Dept. of Labor, Chgo., 1937-46; v.p., dir. Unity Savs. of Park Forest, Ill., to 1977. Columnist: Judiciously Speaking, 1979—; Contbr. articles to profl. jours. Mayor City of Park Forest, 1949-55, corp. counsel, 1958-77, vice chmn. Chgo. adv. bd., Salvation Army, 1969—. Served to lt. USAAC, 1942-45; ETO. Recipient Citation of Merit John Marshall Law Sch., 1972. Mem. Am., Ill., Chgo. bar assns., Am. Judicature Soc., Nat. Inst. Mcpl. Law Officers. Clubs: Rotary, B'nai B'rith. Home: 332 Oakwood St Park Forest IL 60466 Office: Civic Center Chicago IL 60602

DIETEL, WILLIAM MOORE, charitable foundation executive; b. Islip, N.Y., Aug. 14, 1927; s. Frederick William and Zillah Yolanda (Vannuccini) D.; m. Linda Remington, June 16, 1951; children: Elizabeth Lynn, Cynthia Lyon, Lisa Remington, John Frederick, Victoria Moore. A.B., Princeton U., 1950; M.A., Yale U., 1952, Ph.D., 1959; postgrad., London U. Inst. Hist. Research, 1953-54. Instr. history U. Conn. Extension Sch., Stamford, 1952-53; instr. history U. Mass., Amherst, 1954-59; asst. dean of coll., asst. prof. humanities Amherst Coll., 1959-61; prin. Emma Willard Sch., Troy, N.Y., 1961-70; pres. Rockefeller Bros. Fund, N.Y.C., 1975—; dir. Spears, Benzak, Salomon & Farrell, Inc. Trustee Colonial Williamsburg Found., N.Y. Public Library, N.Y.C.; chmn. Winrock Internat. Livestock Research and Tng. Center, Morrilton, Ark.; mem. nat. adv. council Hampshire Coll.; governing council Rockefeller Archive Center.; bd. dirs. Am. Pub. Radio, St. Paul. Fellow World Acad. Art and Sci.; Mem. Council on Fgn. Relations., Soc. for Values in Higher Edn. (Kent fellow 1952). Clubs: University, Century Assn. (N.Y.C.); Cosmos. Office: 1290 Ave of Americas New York NY 10104

DIETER, GEORGE E., JR., university dean; b. Phila., Dec. 5, 1928; s. G. Ellwood and Emily (Muench) D.; m. Nancy Joan Russell, June 21, 1952; children: Carol Joan, Barbara June. B.S. in Metall. Engring, Drexel Inst. Tech., 1950; Sc.D., Carnegie Inst. Tech., 1953. Research engr. E.I. duPont Engring Research Lab., Wilmington, Del., 1955-59, research supr., 1959-62; prof., head dept. metall. engring. Drexel Inst. Tech., 1962-69; dean Coll. Engring. Drexel U., 1969-73; dir. Processing Research Inst., Carnegie-Mellon U., 1973-77; dean Coll. Engring., U. Md., 1977—; cons. in field. Author: Mechanical Metallurgy, 1961, 2d edit., 1976, Engineering Design, 1983. Mem., 1953-55; AUS. Fellow Am. Soc. for Metals; mem. Am. Inst. Mech. Engring., Am. Soc. for Metals, Am. Soc. Engring. Edn., AAAS, Sigma Xi, Tau Beta Pi. Home: 1 Locksley Ct Silver Spring MD 20904 Office: U Md College Park MD 20742

DIETERLE, DONALD LYLE, accountant, educator; b. Sterling, Ill., Nov. 27, 1908; s. John George and Edith Marie (Carolus) D.; m. Mary Elizabeth Paul, Dec. 20, 1935; 1 son, Donald Paul. B.S., U. Ill., 1930, M.S., 1931, postgrad., 1931-32. C.P.A., Ill., Ind. Instr. accounting U. Ill., 1930-32; auditor RFC, 1932-35; prof. accounting Southeastern U., Washington, 1932-35; asst. fin. examiner SEC, 1935; prin. Lyle Dieterle & Co. (C.P.A.'s), Bloomington, Ind., 1935—; prof. acctg. Ind. U., 1935—, now prof. emeritus, asso. dir. engring., sci. sci. mgmt. war tng. program, 1941-45, dir. small bus. programs, 1945—, chmn. dept. accounting, 1955-67; Sec.-treas. Bus. & Real Estate Trends, Inc., Bloomington, 1949—; sec.-treas., dir. Universal Life & Accident Ins. Co., Bloomington, 1955—; treas. Univ. Underwriting Co., Inc.; partner Cardinal Oil Co.; dir., mem. exec. and finance coms. Gt. No. Life Ins. Co., Indpls.; v.p., treas., dir. Mohawk Oil Co., Inc.; Mem. bd. certified accountants, Ind., 1948—. Author: (with J.K. Lasser, others) Tax Accounting Methods, 1952, C.P.A. Coaching Problems, revised edit, 1954, (with Seawell) CPA Problems, 1959. Served as lt. (j.g.), Supply Corps USN, 1935-41. Mem. Am. Inst. Accountants (bd. examiners 1954-55), Ind. Soc. of Chgo., Am. Accounting Assn., Nat. Accounting Assn., C.P.A. Examiners, Financial Execs. Inst., C. of C., Beta Alpha Psi, Acacia, Beta Gamma Sigma, Alpha Kappa Psi. Presbyn. Clubs: Mason (Shriner), Rotarian., Columbia (Indpls.). Office: 621 N Walnut St Bloomington IN 47401

DIETHELM, ARNOLD GILLESPIE, surgeon; b. Balt., Jan. 13, 1932; s. Oskar Arnold and Grace Elizabeth D.; m. Nancy Lee Lane, June 21, 1951; children: Nancy Elizabeth, Linda Lane, Eugene Arnold, Ellen Jeanette, Richard Gillespie. A.B., Wash. State U., 1953; M.D., Cornell U., 1958. Intern, then resident in surgery N.Y. Hosp., 1958-65; asst. in surgery, research fellow Peter Bent Brigham Hosp., Boston, 1965-66; research fellow surgery Harvard U. Med. Sch., 1966-67; instr. Cornell U. Med. Sch., 1964-65; mem. faculty U. Ala. Med. Center, Birmingham, 1967—, prof. surgery, 1973—, vice chmn. dept., 1973-82, chmn. dept. surgery, 1982—, dir. div. gen. surgery, 1977—, chmn. dept. surgery, 1982—. Contbr. articles med. jours. Mem. AAAS, A.C.S., AMA, Am. Soc. Nephrology, Am. Soc. Transplant Surgeons, Am. Surg. Assn., Assn. Acad. Surgery, Transplanatation Soc., So. Surg. Assn. Home: 3248 Sterling Rd Birmingham AL 35213 Office: Dept Surgery Univ Ala Med Sch Birmingham AL 35294

DIETHRICH, EDWARD BRONSON, heart institute executive, cardiovascular surgeon; b. Toledo, Aug. 6, 1935; m. Gloria Baldwin, June 17, 1956; children: Lynn, Edward Bronson II. A.B., U. Mich., 1956, M.D., 1960. Diplomate: Am. Bd. Surgery, Am. Bd. Thoracic Surgery. Intern. St. Joseph Mercy Hosp., Ann Arbor, Mich., 1960-61; resident in surgery St. Joseph Mercy Hosp. and U. Mich. Med. Ctr., Ann Arbor, 1961-62, 64-65, Henry Ford Hosp., Detroit, 1963-64; resident in thoracic and cardiovascular surgery Baylor Coll. of Medicine Hosp., Houston, 1965-66, instr., 1966-67, asst. prof. surgery, 1967-71; med. dir. Ariz. Heart Inst., Phoenix, 1971—; pres. Internat. Heart Found., Phoenix, 1971—. Author: Heart Test, 1981; editor: Noninvasive Cardiovascular Diagnosis, 1978, 80, Noninvasive Assessment of the Cardiovascular System, 1982. Mem. Pres.'s Council for Phys. Fitness and Sports. Recipient U. Mich. Regents Alumni Honor award, 1953-54, Med. Research award St. Joseph Mercy Hosp., 1963, 64, San Francisco Film Festival 1st prize, 1967, Cardiovascular Surgery Adv. Panel citation Ethicon, Inc., 1976. Fellow Am. Coll. Cardiology, Am. Coll. Chest Physicians (merit cert 1970, Outstanding Film award 1973, 77); mem. AMA (Hektoen Gold Medal award 1970), Am. Coll. Angiology, ACS, Am. Fedn. for Clin. Research, Am. Heart Assn. (council on cardiovascular diseases), Am. Trauma Soc., Assn. for Acad. Surgery, Denton A. Cooley Cardiovascular Surg. Soc. (exec. com. 1977-78), Frederick A. Coller Surg. Soc. (award 1963), Internat. Cardiovascular Soc., Michael E. DeBakey Internat. Cardiovascular Soc., Samson Thoracic Surg. Soc., Surg. Soc. Chile, Soc. for Vascular Surgery, Soc. Thoracic Surgeons, Soc. Acad. Surgeons, Southwestern Surg. Congress, Jordanian Surg. Soc., Nu Sigma Nu. Office: Ariz Heart Inst PO Box 10000 Phoenix AZ 85064

DIETMEYER, DONALD LEO, electrical engineer; b. Wausau, Wis., Nov. 20, 1932; s. Henry Joseph and Erna M. (Zastrow) D.; m. Carol White, Jan. 26, 1957; children—Karl Peter, Elizabeth Mary, Anne Katherine, Diana Lee. B.S. in Elec. Engring, U. Wis., Madison, 1954, M.S., 1955, Ph.D., 1959. Mem. faculty U. Wis., Madison, 1958-63, 64—, prof. elec. and computer engring., 1967—, assoc. dean Coll. Engring., 1983—; sr. engr. IBM Corp., Poughkeepsie, N.Y., 1964. Author: Logic Design of Digital Systems, 1978, Conlan Report, 1983. Served with AUS, 1957. Recipient Western Electric Fund award, 1972. Sr. mem. IEEE; mem. Computer Soc., Assn. Computing Machinery, Sigma Xi. Home: 2211 Waunona Way Madison WI 53713 Office: 1425 Johnson Dr Madison WI 53706

DIETRICH, JOSEPH JACOB, research executive; b. Bismarck, N.D., Oct. 31, 1932; s. Jacob Peter and Elizabeth (Janzer) D.; m. Florence Kolodziejczak, June 27, 1959; children: Ann Marie, Michael, John, James. B.A. in Chemistry, St. John's U., Collegeville, Minn., 1953; Ph.D. in Organic Chemistry, Iowa State U., Ames, 1957. Research chemist PPG, Inc., Barberton, Ohio, 1957-59, Spencer Chem. Co., Kansas City, Kans., 1960-64; with Diamond-Shamrock Corp., Cleve., 1964—, dir. research, 1973-78, dir. tech. devel., 1978-82; dir. tech. Eltech Systems Corp., 1982—. Contbr. articles to profl. jours. Mem. Am. Chem. Soc., Soc. Plastic Engrs., Indsl. Research Inst., Cleve. Assn. Research Dirs. Republican. Roman Catholic. Clubs: Elks, Serra. Patentee in field. Home: 6958 Pennywhistle Circle Painesville OH 44077 Office: Box 348 Painesville OH 44077

DIETRICH, MARION CLARENCE, manufacturing company executive; b. Billing, Mont., July 12, 1922; s. Marion Clarence and Edna (Tharp) D.; m. Katharine Lowry, Feb. 2, 1944; children: Katharine Dietrich Werber, Stephen L., John M., Jane E. B.A., Yale U., 1944; M.B.A. with high distinction, Harvard U., 1947. Dir. comml. research Nat. Tube div. U.S. Steel Co., 1947-49; dist. sales positions Ford Motor Co., 1950-58, nat. dealer advt. coordinator, 1959; gen. sales mgr. Kiekhaefer Corp., 1959-61; v.p. spl. sales Cummins Engine Co., Inc., Columbus, Ind., 1962-65, v.p., corp. devel. and planning, 1965-66, v.p., dir. mktg. Europe, Africa, Middle East, India, 1966-67, v.p. mktg., 1968-71, exec. v.p., 1971—, gen. mgr. indsl. group; pres. Cummins Corp.; pres., dir. Cummins Ams., Inc., Cummins Diesel Sales Corp.; chmn., dir. Cummins Diesel Internat., Ltd.; v.p., dir. Cummins Diesel of Can., Ltd. Dist. chmn. Boy Scouts Am., 1974-75; chmn. Bicentennial Com. Bartholomew County, Ind., 1975—; chmn. Bd. Indsl. Devel., Columbus, 1977. Served to 1st lt. F.A. AUS, World War II; ETO. Decorated Bronze Star medal with 2 oak leaf clusters, Purple Heart with oak leaf cluster. Mem. Soc. Automotive Engrs., Am. Mktg. Assn., Constrn. and Machinery Mfrs. Assn. (v.p., dir., mem. exec. com.), Mgmt. Policy Council, Columbus C. of C. (chmn. bd.). Republican. Home: 2730 Washington St Columbus IN 47201 Office: Cummins Engine Co Inc PO Box 3008 Columbus IN 47201

DIETRICH, MARLENE (MARIA MAGDALENA VON LOSCH), actress; b. Berlin, Germany; came to U.S., 1930; d. Edward and Josephine (Felsing) von Losch; m. Rudolf Sieber, May 13, 1924; 1 dau., Maria. Ed., Augusta Victoria Sch., Berlin. Began as violinist; debut as: actress in Broadway, Berlin, 4 years; with, Max Reinhardt's Sch. Dance; later in: film The Blue Angel (German); and since starred in: motion pictures, including Martin Roumagnec (French), 1946, Golden Earrings, 1947, Foreign Affair, 1948, Stage Fright, 1950, No Highway in the Sky, 1951, Rancho Notorious, 1952; numerous others the latest including the Monte Carlo Story, 1957, Around the World in 80 Days, 1956, Witness for the Prosecution, 1958, Judgement at Nuremberg, 1961, Just a Gigolo, 1981; also appears in night clubs and, theatres. (Recipient Spl. Tony award 1967-68); Author: Marlene Dietrich's ABC, 1962, My Life Story, 1979; Toured, Army Service Camps, Europe, 1945, concert tour, U.S., 1973. Address: care Regency Artists Ltd 9200 Sunset Blvd Suite 823 Los Angeles CA 90069

DIETRICH, PAUL EMIL, architect; b. Hammond, Ind., Apr. 23, 1926; s. Emil and Bertha (Fritzen) D.; m. Eleanor Stahl, 1950; children: Andrea, Kristen, Eric, Lars, Britt. B.S., U. Nebr., 1949; B.Arch., Harvard U., 1956, M.Arch., 1970. Cert., Nat. Council Archtl. Registration Bds. Engaged in architecture, 1956—; founding partner Cambridge Seven Assos., Inc., Mass., 1962—; founding mem. Cambridge Arts Council, 1976; mem. Cambridge Planning Bd., 1972; mem. faculty Harvard U., 1966, Northeastern U., Boston, 1981. Prin. works include New Eng. Aquarium (Design award Progressive Architecture mag. 1967); U.S. Pavilion at Expo '67, Montreal, Que., Can., 1967 (AIA Design award 1967), Children's Museum Visitors' Center, Boston, 1968, MBTA Sta. modernization, Boston, 1965-70, New Bedford (Mass.) Whaling Mus., 1974, N.C. Marine Sci. Center, Wilmington, 1971, office and distbn. Center, Knapp Shoes, Inc., Brockton, Mass., 1966; prin. works include Garvan exhibit, Yale U., 1973; Porter Sq. Sta., Boston, 1976, office and distbn. center, Talbots Inc., Hingham, Mass., 1978, Solar Energy Exhibit, Washington, 1976, Digital Equipment Corp. bldg., Spit Brook, N.H., 1980, Markem office bldg., Keene, N.H., 1981, Charles Sq., Cambridge, Mass., Basketball Hall of Fame, Springfield, Mass.; Gen. Cinema Theatres renovations. Served with A.C., USNR, 1944-46. Fellow AIA; mem. Boston Soc. Architects. Address: Cambridge Seven Assocs Inc 1050 Massachusetts Ave Cambridge MA 02138

DIETRICH, RICHARD VINCENT, geologist; b. LaFargeville, N.Y., Feb. 7, 1924; s. Roy Eugene and Mida Amy (Vincent) D.; m. Frances Elizabeth Smith, Dec. 28, 1946; children: Richard Smith, Kurt Robert, Krista Gayle Brown. A.B., Colgate U., 1947; M.S., Yale U., 1950, Ph.D., 1951. Geologist Iowa Geol. Survey, 1947, N.Y. State Sci. Service, summers 1949-50; asst. prof. geology Va. Poly. Inst., Blacksburg, 1951, asso. prof., 1952-56, prof., 1956-69, asso. dean arts and scis., 1966-69, dean, 1969; prof. geology Central Mich. U., Mt. Pleasant, 1969—, dean arts and scis., 1969-75; dir. Econ. Geol. Pub. Co., 1966-72. Author books; contbr. articles to profl. jours.; Editor: Mineral Industries Jour, 1953-61; mng. editor: Bull. Econ. Geology, 1966-73; exec. editor: Rocks and Minerals, 1980—; mem. editorial bd.: Mineral. Record; author poems, haiku, essays, cartoons. Organizer N. Am. for Mineral. Abstracts, 1976-80. Served with USAAF, 1943-46. Recipient Acad. citation Mich. Acad. Sci., Arts and Letters, 1978; Fulbright research prof. U. Oslo, 1958-59. Fellow Geol. Soc. Am., Am. Mineral. Soc.; mem. Soc. Econ. Geology, Norsk Geologisk Forening, Geol. Soc. Finland, Am. Geol. Inst. (gov. 1972-74), Assn. Earth Sci. Editors (pres. 1972-73), Sigma Xi, Phi Beta Kappa, Phi Kappa Phi., Sigma Gamma Epsilon. Presbyterian. Home: 2499 E Broomfield Rd Mount Pleasant MI 48858 Office: 311 Brooks Hall Central Mich U Mount Pleasant MI 48859 *My parents were supportive although they had hoped for a different direction. Education, the work ethic, and retention of individualism and imagination were promoted.*

DIETRICH, WILLIAM ALLEN, retired air force officer, association executive; b. Oklahoma City, Nov. 12, 1923; s. William Montgomery and Edna Lillian (Williamson) D.; m. Mary Ethel Rupert, Dec. 25, 1945; children: Linda Ann Dietrich Morris, Jackie Lynn Dietrich Daniel, Jeanne Sue Dietrich King, Donald Allen. Student, Southeastern Coll., Durant, Okla., 1941-42, Sophia U., Tokyo, 1952-54; B.A., George Washington U., 1956. Commd. 2d lt. USAAF, 1942; advanced through grades to maj. gen. USAF, 1973; air ops. officer joint staff comdr.-in-chief U.S. Naval Forces Eastern Atlantic and Mediterranean, 1960-63; dep. comdr. 516th Tactical Airlift Wing, Dyess AFB, Tex., 1965-66; comdr. 313th Tactical Airlift Wing, Forbes AFB, Kan., 1968-70, USAF Tactical Airlift Center and 839th Air Div., Pope AFB, N.C., 1970-71; vice comdr. 22d Air Force, Travis AFB, Cal., 1971-73; chief of staff Mil. Airlift Command, Scott AFB, Ill., 1973-75; ret., 1975; exec. dir. Uniformed Services Benefit Assn., Kansas City, Mo., 1975—; pres. USBA Services, Inc., USBA Realty Inc., INSERV, Inc., Kansas City Emergency Preparedness Group, Inc. Dir. Kansas City Bank & Trust Co.; Bd. dirs. Trinity Luth. Hosp., Kansas City, Mo. Decorated D.S.M., Legion of Merit with 2 oak leaf cluster, D.F.C. with oak leaf cluster, Air medal with 2 oak leaf clusters, Joint Service Commendation medal, Air Force Commendation medal, Chinese Breast Order Yun Hui; recipient Disting. Service medal State of Okla. Mem. Order Daedalians, Kansas City C. of C., Navy League, Assn. U.S. Army, Mil. Order World Wars, Airlift Assn., Ret. Officers Assn., Combat Pilots Assn., Army Aviation Assn. Am., Air Force Assn., Hump Pilots Assn. Clubs: Kansas City, Leawood Country, Kansas City Navy Aero, Rotary. Home: 835 W 55th St Kansas City MO 64113 Office: USBA Bldg 3822 Summit St Kansas City MO 64111

DIETRICH, WILLIAM GALE, lawyer, shopping center consultant; b. Kansas City, Mo., Mar. 6, 1925; s. Roy Kaiser and Gale (Gossett) D.; m. Marjorie Nell Reich, July 14, 1945; children: Meredith Gale Dietrich Steinhaus, Ann E. Dietrich Cooling, Walter Reich. A.B., Yale U., 1948, LL.B., 1951. Bar: Mo. 1951. Practiced law, Kansas City; partner Dietrich, Davis, Dicus, Rowlands & Schmitt (and predecessors), 1953-73; project dir., gen. counsel Blue Ridge Shopping Center, Inc., Kansas City, Mo., 1955-73, pres., gen. mgr., 1964-73, Blue Ridge Tower, Inc., Kansas City, 1967-73; sec.-treas. Sun-Ra Frozen Foods, Inc., 1973-80, pres., 1980; sec.-treas. A. Reich & Sons, Inc., 1973—, A. Reich & Sons Gardens, Inc., 1973—. Trustee, asst. sec. Research Med. Center, Kansas City, 1977-80, vice chmn., 1980-83, chmn., 1983—; trustee Research Med. Found., 1980—; bd. dirs. Research Health Services, 1980—, vice-chmn., 1983—; bd. dirs., sec. Mahana Condominium Assn., Maui, Hawaii, 1977—. Served to 1st lt. AUS, 1943-46; PTO. Mem. Am., Kansas City bar assns., Mo. Bar, Blue Ridge Mall Mchts. Assn. (dir. 1958-73), Internat. Council Shopping Centers (past dir. for Mo., Kans., Iowa), Lawyers Assn. Kansas City, Phi Beta Kappa, Phi Delta Phi. Episcopalian (vestry). Clubs: Kansas City Rotary (dir., sec. found. 1978—), University, Mission Hills Country, Yale, Kansas City (Kansas City, Mo.). Home: 1000 Huntington Rd Kansas City MO 64113 Office: 900 Blue Ridge Tower Kansas City MO 64133

DIETSCH, ROBERT WILLIAM, govt. ofcl., journalist; b. Cleve., Oct. 23, 1919; s. William and Emma (Schurig) D.; m. Paulene F. Gatz, Dec. 24, 1942; children—John, Deborah, Douglas, Craig. B.A. magna cum laude, Western Res. U., 1941. Asst. city editor, then asst. bus. editor Buffalo Evening News, 1948-51; World news editor, then bus. editor Cleve. Press, 1951-61; bus. editor Scripps-Howard Newspapers, Washington, 1961-77; asst. to dir. for pub. affairs Office Mgmt. and Budget, Washington, 1977-79; dep. asst. adminstr. Office Public Communications SBA, Washington, 1979—. Mem. South Euclid-Lyndhurst (Ohio) Sch. Bd., 1958-61; bd. dirs. Cleve. World Affairs Council, 1955-59, Cleve. chpt. ACLU, 1959-61. Served with, USAAF; Served with, 1942-45. Woodrow Wilson sr. fellow, 1973—; fellow Internat. Press Inst., 1959; recipient award Cleve. Newspaper Guild, 1955, 57, 59. Mem. Nat. Soc. Bus. Editors, Phi Beta Kappa, Sigma Delta Chi. Club: Nat. Press (Washington). Home: 5303 Elliott Rd Bethesda MD 20816 Office: SBA 1441 L St NW Washington DC 20416

DIETZ, ALBERT GEORGE HENRY, engineering educator; b. Lorain, Ohio, Mar. 7, 1908; s. Peter and Adele (Grevsmuhl) D.; m. Ruth Avery, Sept. 9, 1936; children: Margaret, Henry Avery. A.B., Miami U., 1930; Sc.D., MIT, 1941. With dept. bldg. engring. and constrn. MIT, Cambridge, 1934-62, asst., instr., 1936-41, asst. prof., 1941-46, assoc. prof., 1946-50, prof., 1950-62, prof. bldg. engring. depts. civil engring. and architecture, 1962-73, emeritus, 1973—, dir. plastic research lab., 1946-62; on leave of absence to Forest Products Labs. as sr. cons. engr., 1942; field service cons. office Field Service OSRD, 1944-45; cons. constrn. and materials, 1940—. Author: Dwelling House Construction, 1946, 4th edit., 1975, Materials of Construction: Wood, Plastics, Fabrics, 1949, (with Marcia Koth, Julio Silva) Housing in Latin America, 1965, Plastics for Architects and Builders, 1970; Editor: Engineering Laminates, 1949, Composite Engineering Laminates, 1970, (with Laurence Cutler) Industrialized Systems for Housing, 1971; Contbr. articles to profl. jours. Mem. Engring. Edn. Mission to Japan, 1952; Chmn. bldg. research adv. bd. Nat. Acad. Sci.-NRC. Sr. fellow East-West Center, 1973-74; Recipient John Derham Internat. award Plastics Inst. Australia, 1962; New Eng. award Engring. Socs. New Eng., 1968; named Constrn. Man of Quarter Century Bldg. Research Adv. Bd., Nat. Acad. Scis.-Nat. Acad. Engrs., 1977. Fellow AAAS, Am. Acad. Arts and Scis., ASCE (hon.), Royal Soc. Arts; mem. ASTM (hon., Richard L. Templin award 1948, Walter Voss award 1974, award merit 1957), Soc. Plastics Industry, ASME, Soc. Engring. Edn., Forest Products Research Soc., Soc. Plastics Engrs. (past nat. dir., Internat. Gold medal 1971), Boston Soc. Civil Engrs. (Desmond Fitzgerald award 1945, 56), Bldg. Research Inst. (past dir.), Phi Beta Kappa Assos., Sigma Xi, Tau Beta Pi. Home: 19 Cambridge St Winchester MA 01890 Office: Mass Inst Tech Cambridge MA 02139

DIETZ, CECIL EUGENE, media consultant, TV administrator; b. Cookeville, Tenn., Apr. 7, 1925; s. Harry Denney and Emma Jane (Bilbrey) D.; m. Imogene Rockwell, June 29, 1946; children: Charles Harold, Cecil Burton, Brenda Carol Dietz Valiquette, Wallace Wordsworth, Franz Gerald. B.S., Tenn. Tech. U., 1950. With Nashville Tennessean, 1950-70, edn. editor, city editor, 1962-70; publs. dir., journalist-in-residence Peabody Coll. Tchrs., 1970-74; pres. Dietz Enterprises, 1974-75; exec. dir. Tenn. Pub. TV, 1975-80; media cons. U.S. SBA, Washington, 1980-81, Nat. Seminar Resources and Retrieval Race Relations Info., 1974; communications dir. Met. Nashville Schs., 1983—; exec. adminstr. Sta. WDCN-TV, 1983—; cons. Assn. Colls. Univs. for Internat.-Intercultural Studies Inc., 1974—; regional rep. USIA, also Newsweek, 1950's-60's. Exec. producer, writer films, 1969—; regional editor, Nat. Ednl. TV, 1965-68; writer, host: NET spl. Of Monkeys and Men, 1967. Served with USNR, 1943-46. Recipient Tenn. Sch. Bell award, 1962. Mem. Nashville Pub. TV Council. Methodist (adminstrv. bd. 1968-72). Home: 3614 Woodmont Blvd Nashville TN 37215 *If man learns to respect others, including their views even though he may disagree with them, he has begun to acquire knowledge and wisdom.*

DIETZ, CHARLTON HENRY, lawyer; b. LeMars, Iowa, Jan. 8, 1931; s. Clifford Henry and Mildred Verna (Eggensperger) D.; m. Viola Ann Lange, Aug. 17, 1952; children: Susan (Mrs. Jay Kakuk), Robin (Mrs. Jack Mayfield), Craig. B.A., Macalester Coll., 1953; J.D., William Mitchell Coll. Law, 1957. Bar: Minn. 1957. Mem. public relations staff Minn. Mining and Mfg. Co., St. Paul, 1952-58, atty., 1958-70, asso. counsel, asst. sec., 1970-72, asst. gen. counsel, sec., 1972-75, gen. counsel, sec., 1975-76, gen. counsel, v.p. legal affairs, 1976—, also dir.; dir. Eastern Heights State Bank, chmn., 1981—; dir. State Bond and Mortgage Co.; instr. William Mitchell Coll. Law, 1960-74, trustee, 1974—, pres., 1980—. Bd. dirs. St. Paul Area YMCA, 1973-80, chmn., 1978-80; bd. dirs. Minn. Citizens Council on Crime and Justice, 1976—, pres., 1982—; trustee United Theol. Sem., 1976-82; bd. dirs. St. Paul United Way, 1980—, Ramsey County Hist. Soc., 1979—; mem. Conferees of Minn. Citizens Conf. on the Cts., 1981-82. Fellow Am. Bar Found.; Mem. ABA, Fed. Bar Assn., Ramsey County Bar Assn., Am. Soc. Corporate Secs., Assn. Gen. Counsel. Republican. Mem. United Ch. of Christ. Clubs: Mason (Shriner, Jester), St. Paul Athletic, North Oaks, Minn. Home: 1 Birch Ln North Oaks MN 55110 Office: Minn Mining and Mfg Co 3M Center St Paul MN 55144

DIETZ, EARL DANIEL, manufacturing company executive; b. Avon, Ohio, Jan. 22, 1928; s. Herman Joseph and Viola Katherine (Blaser) D.; m. Joan Batteiger, June 10, 1950; 1 dau., Kerry Leigh. B.S., Ohio State U., Columbus, 1959, M.S., 1959, Ph.D., 1965. Lab. technician Battelle Meml. Inst., Columbus, 1954-58; with Owens-Ill., Inc., Toledo, 1959—, project engr., research scientist, dir. glass and ceramic research, dir. corporate research labs., v.p., tech. dir. consumer and tech. products group, 1959-73, v.p. corporate staff, 1973—, dir. engring., Commack, N.Y., 1973-77, mgr. engring. services for paper, Toledo, 1977-79, mgr. mfg. services, 1979-81, dir. corporate energy, environ. and tech. services, 1981—. Served with CIC AUS, 1952-54. Recipient Texnikoi Outstanding Alumnus award Ohio State U. Coll. Engring., 1970. Fellow Am. Ceramic Soc.; mem. Soc. Glass Tech. Pantee tooth filling compositions, laser glass melting. Home: 4700 Turnbridge Rd Toledo OH 43623 Office: Owens Illinois 1 Seagate Toledo OH 43666

DIETZ, FRANK TOBIAS, educator; b. Bridgeport, Conn., Aug. 13, 1920; s. Frank Charles and Otillia (Wasserman) D.; m. Thera Louise Bushnell, Feb. 24, 1945; children: Martha Dietz Beyersdorf, Thomas Frank. B.S., Bates Coll., 1942; M.A., Wesleyan U., Middletown, Conn., 1946; Ph.D., Pa. State U., 1951. Instr. physics Pa. State U., 1947-49, research asst., 1949-51; asso. underwater acoustics Woods Hole (Mass.) Oceanographic Inst., 1951-54; asst. prof. physics, research asso. phys. oceanographer U. R.I., 1954-56, asst. prof. physics, 1956-58, asso. prof., 1958-64, prof., 1964—, prof. physics and oceanography, 1968-76, prof. physics, 1976-83, prof. emeritus, 1983—, acting chmn. dept. physics, 1971-73, asst. dean, 1973, asso. dean, 1974-76; vis. asso. prof. marine sci. U. Miami, 1963-64. Served with USNR, 1944. Fellow Acoustical Soc. Am.; mem. Am. Assn. Physics Tchrs., Am. Geophys. Union, Delta Phi Alpha, Sigma Xi, Pi Mu Epsilon, Phi Kappa Phi, Sigma Pi Sigma. Home: 28 Spring Hill Rd Kingston RI 02881

DIETZ, JOHN RAPHAEL, consulting engineer; b. Carbondale, Pa., Jan. 31, 1912; s. John A. and Bridget (Barrett) D.; m. Elizabeth Harding Bezilla, Mar. 15, 1983; children by previous marriage: Robert J., Elizabeth Dietz Brown. B.S. in Civil Engring, Drexel U., Phila., 1934. Registered profl. engr., Pa. Contract estimator J.A. Dietz Co., 1934-35; designer Pa. Dept. Hwys., 1935-38; designer, resident engr. Pa. Turnpike Commn., 1938-40; san. engr. for J.E. Greiner Co., Camp Meade, Md., 1940; designer Caribbean Architect-Engrs., 1941-42; chief designer for Gannett Eastman & Fleming, Inc., Andrews Air Field, Washington, 1942-43; civilian with U.S. Engr. Corps on study Potomac River Basin flood control, 1943-44; with Gannett Fleming Corddry and Carpenter, Inc., cons. engrs., 1942—, dir. hwy. div., then pres., Harrisburg, Pa., 1950-76, chmn. bd., 1970—; dir. CCNB Bank (N.A.). Trustee Drexel U. Bd.; dirs. Holy Spirit Hosp., Camp Hill, Pa., 1965—, pres., 1983; bd. dirs. Villa Teresa Nursing Home, Harrisburg, Pa., 1973—, pres., 1973-75. Recipient A.J. Drexel Paul award Drexel U., 1973. Life fellow ASCE (past pres. Central Pa. chpt.); mem. Am. Council Cons. Engrs., Nat. Soc. Profl. Engrs., Am. Road and Transp. Builders Assn. (past dir.), Pa. Hwy. Info. Assn. (past pres.), Pa. Soc. Profl. Engrs. (Profl. Engrs. Disting. Service award Harrisburg chpt. 1965). Roman Catholic. Home: 511 Arlington Rd Camp Hill PA 17011 Office: PO Box 1963 Harrisburg PA 17105

DIETZ, WILLIAM RONALD, banker; b. Seattle, Nov. 25, 1942; s. William Phillip and Helen Mae (Wilson) D. B.A., U. Wash., 1964; M.B.A., Stanford U., 1968. Fin. cons. 1st Nat. City Bank, N.Y.C., 1968-70; v.p., mgr. Citicorp Subs. Mgmt. Office, Citicorp, N.Y.C., 1971-74; chmn. Citicorp Factors, Inc., N.Y.C., 1974-75; v.p., mgr. N.Y., N.J. and Conn. comml. banking Citibank N.A., N.Y.C., 1976-78, sr. v.p., gen. mgr. Eastern region corp. banking, 1978-81; sr. v.p., head Caribbean Basin div., 1982—; also dir. Citibank Internat.; dir. Chase Bag Co., United Bank Trinidad and Tobago., Banco Internacional de Colombia, Caribbean Fin. Services Corp. Mem. policy com. advanced credit mgmt. program SUNY-Buffalo; assoc. U. Miami Grad. Sch. Internat. Studies; mem. policy com. Internat. Ctr. Miami. Served to lt. USNR, 1964-66. Mem. Delta Tau Delta. Clubs: University (N.Y.C.); Bankers (Miami); Old Lyme Country. Home: One Grove Isle Dr Apt 603 Coconut Grove FL 33133 also Lieutenant River Ln Old Lyme CT 06371 Office: One SE 3d Ave Miami FL 33131

DIETZE, GOTTFRIED, political science educator; b. Kemberg, Germany, Nov. 11, 1922; came to U.S., 1949; s. Paul and Susanne (Pechstein) D. Dr.Jur., U. Heidelberg, Germany, 1949; Ph.D., Princeton U., 1952; S.J.D., U. Va., 1961. Instr. polit. sci. Dickinson Coll., 1952-54; mem. faculty Johns Hopkins, 1954—, prof. polit. sci., 1962—; vis. prof. U. Heidelberg, 1956, 58-60, Brookings Instn., 1960-61, 67. Author: Ueber Formulierung der Menschenrechte, 1956, Kandidaten, 1982, The Federalist, 1960, In Defense of Property, 1963 (Monks award), Magna Carta and Property, 1965, America's Political Dilemma, 1968, Youth, University and Democracy, 1970, Bedeutungswandel der Menschenrechte, 1971, Academic Truths and Frauds, 1972, Two Concepts of the Rule of Law, 1973, Deutschland—Wo bist Du?, 1980, Kant und der Rechtsstaat, 1981; Editor: Essays on the American Constitution, 1964. Mem. Am. Polit. Sci. Assn., Am. Soc. Polit. and Legal Philosophy, Deutsche Gesellschaft fur Amerikastudien, Acad. Human Rights, Mont Pelerin Society. Lutheran. Office: Johns Hopkins Univ Baltimore MD 21218

DIEVLER, DAVID HAROLD, investment mgmt. exec.; b. Willow Grove, Pa., Oct. 23, 1929; s. Harold Gilbert and Lillian (Pierce) D.; m. Hilda Marie Maron, May 31, 1954; children—Maria, Anne, James, Elise, Marguerite. B.S., U. Pa., 1950. C.P.A., N.Y., D.C. Mgr. Price Waterhouse & Co. (C.P.A.'s), N.Y.C., 1950-65; asst. controller W.R. Grace & co., N.Y.C., 1965-68; with F. Eberstadt Co., Inc., N.Y.C., 1968-79; vice chmn. Eberstadt Asset Mgmt., 1979—. Mem. Financial Execs. Inst., N.Y. State Soc. C.P.A.'s, Am. Inst. C.P.S.'s. Club: Downtown Athletic (N.Y.C.). Home: 100 Crest Rd Ridgewood NJ 07450 Office: 61 Broadway New York NY 10006

DIFFORD, WINTHROP CECIL, educator; b. East Liverpool, Ohio, Nov. 12, 1921; s. Lionel Cecil and Pamela (Grice) D.; m. Nedra Arline Erisman, Nov. 28, 1944; children—Pamela Arline (Mrs. Clyde Hinkle), Phyllis Ann (Mrs. Larry Studinski), Kenneth Edel. B.S., Mt. Union Coll., 1942; postgrad., Ohio State U., 1942-43; M.S., W.Va. U., 1947; Ph.D., Syracuse U., 1954. Asst. area engring. geologist Nebr., area engring. geologist Colo. U.S. Bur. Reclamation, 1948-51; asst. state geologist, Harrisburg, Pa., 1955-56; prof., chmn. dept. geology Dickinson Coll., 1954-65; E.L. Phillips Found.; intern acad. adminstrn. U. R.I., 1965-66; asst. dean grad. studies U. Bridgeport, Conn., 1966-68; dean (Grad. Coll.); dir. summer session U. Wis.-Stevens Point, 1968-78, now prof., adminstr. semester-in-Britain, 1972; vis. scientist Am. Geol. Inst.; cons. in S. Vietnam under U.S. AID Higher Edn. contract; cons. U.S. Naval Oceanographic Office. Author: (with R. Jankowski) Introduction to Oceanography-Science of the Seventies, (1967.); Editor: Proceedings of Nat. Conf. on the Concept of a Sea-Grant College, 1965. Served with USNR, World War II; Korean Conflict. Fellow Geol. Soc. Am., Royal Soc. Arts (London), Explorers Club; mem. Marine Tech. Soc., Sigma Xi, Sigma Gamma Epsilon, Phi Delta Kappa, Phi Kappa Tau, Gamma Alpha. Episcopalian. Clubs: Mason, Rotarian. Home: 7252 6th St Custer WI 54423

DIFFRIENT, NIELS, industrial designer; b. Star, Miss., Sept. 6, 1928; s. Robert Ethan and Dovie Lee (Peacock) D.; m. Helena Hernmarck, May 29, 1976; children—(by previous marriage) Scott, Julie, Emily. Student, Wayne State U., 1951-52; B.F.A., Cranbrook Acad., 1954; hon. doctorate, Art Center Coll. of Design, 1975. Architect Eero Saarinen, Bloomfield Hills, Mich., 1948-53; with Walter B. Ford, Detroit, 1953-54, Marco Zanuso, Milan, Italy, 1954-55; gen. partner Henry Dreyfuss Assocs., N.Y.C., 1955-80; head ind. indsl. design studio, Ridgefield, Conn., 1981—; mem. faculty indsl. design UCLA, 1961-69. Mem. editorial bd.: Indsl. Design mag, 1976—; contbr. articles to profl. jours. Fulbright fellow, 1954-55; Nat. Endowment for Arts grantee, 1975-80; recipient nat. award design for transp. U.S. Dept. Transp., 1981; Resource Council awards, 1979, 81; gold medal Inst. Bus. Designers, 1980; ann. award Design and Environ. mag., 1975; (with Marco Zanuso) Compasso d'Oro, 1957. Fellow Indsl. Design Soc. Am. (Design Excellence award 1980); mem. Internat. Design Conf. Aspen (dir. 1974—), Internat. Design Edn. Found. (exec. bd. 1976—). Inventor, designer human engineered comml. chairs for Knoll Internat., 1979, 80, for Sunar Co., 1981. *The conscious intellect is but the policeman ordering the facts around. All real insight comes from* *the sub-conscious which resists regimentation. One must have patience and trust to ease the passage of true innovation from within.*

DIFORIO, ROBERT G., publisher; b. Mamaroneck, N.Y., Mar. 19, 1940; s. Richard John and Mildred (Kuntz) D.; m. Birgit Rasmussen; 1 son, Stephen Christopher. B.A., Williams Coll., 1964. From book sales rep. to v.p. book sales Kable News Co., 1964-72; with New Am. Library, Inc., N.Y.C., 1972—, exec. v.p., 1980-81, pres., publisher, 1981—, chmn. bd., chief exec. officer, 1983—. Served with USCGR. Club: N.Y. Athletic. Home: Arrowhead Ln Larchmont NY 10538 Office: 1633 Broadway New York NY 10019

DI FRANCO, LORETTA ELIZABETH, lyric coloratura; b. Bklyn., Oct. 28, 1942; d. Philip Carl and Lavinia (Russo) Di F.; m. Anthony Martin Pinto, June 15, 1968; 1 dau. Student, Hunter Coll., Julliard Sch. Music. Mem. chorus, Met. Opera Assn., N.Y.C.; now soloist N.Y. Met. Opera debut in, Pique Dame, 1965, performances in, Paris, also summer concerts, Lewisohn Stadium, 1966; mem. various choruses, festivals and concert series, including, Empire State Music Festival, Mozart Opera Festival, Chautauqua, N.Y., 1964; also performed on radio and TV. (Recipient 1st prize Met. Opera Nat. Auditions 1965). Stuart and Irene Chambers award, 1965; Kathryn Turney Long scholar, 1965-66; Martha Baird-Rockefeller Fund for Music grantee, 1964. Mem. Am. Guild Musical Artists. Office: care Met Opera Guild Inc 1865 Broadway New York NY 10023 *

DI FURIA, GIULIO, psychiatrist; b. Ariano, Irpino, Italy, Oct. 24, 1925; came to U.S., 1953, naturalized, 1959; s. Oto Maria and Vincenza (Scauzillo) di F.; m. Marion Ann Rampuli, Mar. 27, 1955; children: Renzo, Diane, Robert, Richard, Julieann, Paul. M.D., Bologna (Italy) U., 1951. Chief hosp. services Medfield State Hosp., Harding, Mass., 1957-58; mem. staff Western State Hosp., Fort Stellacoom, Wash., 1958—, supt., 1963-80; asst. clin. prof. psychiatry and pharmacology U. Wash. Sch. Medicine, 1965—. Contbr. profl. jours. Recipient citation for outstanding service to Wash. in mental health, 1964. Fellow Am. Psychiat. Assn., Am. Geriatric Soc., N. Pacific Soc. Neurology and Psychiatry; mem. Am. Assn. Med. Supts. Mental Hosps. (mem. council 1971—). Address: 34 Country Club Dr SW Tacoma WA 98498

DIGANGI, FRANK EDWARD, ednl. adminstr.; b. West Rutland, Vt., Sept. 29, 1917; s. Leonard and Mary Grace (Zafonti) DiG.; m. Genevieve Frances Colignon, June 27, 1946; children—Ellen (Mrs. Philo David Hall), Janet (Mrs. W. Dale Greenwood). B.S. in Pharmacy, Rutgers U., 1940; M.S., Western Res. U., 1942; Ph.D., U. Minn., 1948. Asst. prof. U. Minn. Coll. Pharmacy, 1948-52, asso. prof., 1952-57, prof. medicinal chemistry, 1957—, also asso. dean adminstrv. affairs. Author: Quantitative Pharmaceutical Analysis, 7th edit, 1977; Contbr. articles to pharm. jours. Served with USNR, 1943-46; PTO. Recipient Alumni Assn. Disting. Pharmacist award, 1977; Faculty Recognition award Coll. of Pharmacy Alumni Soc., 1981. Mem. Am. Pharm. Assn., Minn. Pharm. Assn. (pres. 1971, chmn. bd. 1972-73, Pharmacist of Year award 1972, Harold R. Popp Meml. award 1979), AAUP, Am. Chem. Soc., Am. Assn. Colls. Pharmacy, Sigma Xi, Phi Beta Phi, Phi Lambda Upsilon, Rho Chi. Clubs: University Campus, University Faculty Golf, Gown-in-Town (Mpls.). Home: 1684 Pinehurst Ave Saint Paul MN 55116 Office: College of Pharmacy University of Minnesota Minneapolis MN 55455

DI GENOVA, MARIO HENRY, hotel company executive; b. Marseilles, France, Nov. 9, 1927; came to U.S., 1949; s. Alfredo and Alphonsine (Tulimiero) Di G.; 1 dau. by previous marriage, Alexandra. Sacre Coeur, 1947; Dr. (hon.), Mexican Acad. Internat. Law. Sr. v.p. ops. Inter-Continental Hotels Inc., N.Y.C., 1964-70; pres., chief exec. div. Europe-Africa, Paris, 1970-73; mng. dir., chief exec. officer Ciga Hotels, Rome, 1973-74; pres., chief exec. officer Americana Hotels Inc., N.Y.C., 1974-77; vice chmn., chief exec. officer Grand Met. Hotels, Paris, 1978-80, gen. dir., 1981; mng. dir. Intercontinental Hotels, Miami, 1983—. Mem. Pres. Ford's Ethnic Affairs Com.; bd. dirs Am.-Korean Cultural Soc.; bd. dirs. I Love A Clean N.Y. Com., N.Y.C. Visitors and Conv. Bur. Served with AUS, 1951-53. Decorated knight comdr. Order of Merit, Ivory Coast, Knight comdr. Order of Merit, Gabon, knight comdr. Order Holy Sepulchre, Jerusalem, Knight Order of Merit, Italy; recipient Arts Sci. and Letters medal, France. Mem. Am. Hotel and Motel Assn. (dir. industry adv. council), Nat. Acad. Geography and History Mexico. Clubs: Knickerbocker, Doubles (N.Y.C.); Grove Isle (Miami); Maxim's Bus. (Paris); Roma Polo (Rome). Home: 720 Coral Way Coral Gables Fl 33134 Office: 2655 LeJeune Rd Suite 601 Coral Gables Fl 33134

DIGGES, DUDLEY PERKINS, editor; b. Bklyn., July 11, 1918; s. Dudley McDaniel and Caroline Semple (Fleet) Diggs; m. Betty Lee Belt, Nov. 27, 1947; children: Deborah H., Sally S., Diana L., Mallory F. B.A., Va. Mil. Inst., 1939; postgrad., Harvard U., 1940-41. Tchr. Staunton (Va.) Mil. Acad., 1939-40; asst. U.S. sec. Allied Control Authority, Berlin, 1946-48; editorial writer Balt. Eve. Sun, 1948-52, 54-78, European corr., 1953, editor editorial page, 1979-81; dir. C.B. Fleet Co. Served with AUS, 1941-46. Mem. Nat. Conf. Editorial Writers. Club: Hamilton St. (Balt.). Home: 217 Club Rd Baltimore MD 21210 Office: Evening Sun Baltimore MD 21203

DIGGES, SAM COOK, broadcasting executive; b. Columbia, Mo., Jan. 8, 1916; s. Charles William and Frances (Cook) D.; m. Carol Jean Ellis, Dec. 16, 1961; 1 son by previous marriage, Sam Cook. B.A. in Journalism, U. Mo., 1937. Advt. salesman, columnist Washington Daily News, 1937-42; time salesman sta. WMAL/WMAL- TV, Washington, 1942-49; with CBS, Inc., 1949-81; gen. mgr. sta. WCBS-TV, N.Y.C., 1954-58; adminstrv. v.p. CBS Films Inc., N.Y.C., 1958-67; exec. v.p. CBS-owned AM stas. CBS Radio div., 1967-70, pres., 1970-81, Radio Sta WSBR, Boca Raton, Fla., 1982—; commentator Sta WPTV, Palm Beach, Fla., 1982—; Bd. curators Stephens Coll., 1970-82; bd. dirs. Advt. Council, 1976-81, Radio Advt. Bur., 1969-81. Served with U.S. Mcht. Marine, 1944-45. Recipient medal of honor U. Mo. Sch. Journalism, 1973, Faculty-Alumni gold medal U. Mo.-Columbia Alumni Assn., 1974; Communicator of Year award Sales and Mktg. Execs. Internat., 1977; Maj. League Baseball Commr.'s award, 1980. Mem. Internat. Radio and TV Soc. (pres. 1963-65, bd. govs. 1959-67, gold medal 1981), Nat. Acad. TV Arts and Scis. (bd. trustees 1966-67, gov. N.Y.C. chpt. 1965-67), Phi Delta Theta. Republican. Lutheran. Clubs: Woodway Country (Darien, Conn.); Everglades, Beach (Palm Beach, Fla.). Home: 241 Tradewind Dr Palm Beach FL 33480

DIGGINS, PETER SHEEHAN, ballet co. adminstr.; b. Rochester, N.Y., June 23, 1938; s. Bartholomew A. and Mona (Sheehan) D. B.A. in English, Georgetown U., 1959. Staff reporter Washington Post, 1960-65; asst. artistic adminstr. Met. Opera, N.Y.C., 1965-72; dir. dance programs N.Y. State Council on the Arts, 1972-75; gen. adminstr. The Joffrey Ballet, N.Y.C., 1975-79; pres. Peter S. Diggins Assos., 1979—; cons. in arts mgmt. dance and opera cos. Contbr.: articles to Opera Mag. Recipient grant for European work-study tour Met. Opera, 1968. Home: 133 W 71st St New York NY 10023 Office: 133 W 71 St New York NY 10023

DIGGS, J(ESSE) FRANK, retired magazine editor; b. Hagerstown, Md., Nov. 21, 1917; s. Jesse Franklin, Jr. and Oleita (Mearns) D.; m. Tracy Evalyn Briscoe, Oct. 6, 1942; children—Margaret, Deborah. B.A. in Econs., Am. U., 1938; postgrad., George Washington U. Reporter Washington Post, 1938-41; mem. staff U.S. News & World Report, 1945-82, nat. editor, then asso. editor, 1965-78, sr. editor, Washington, 1978-82. Served with AUS, 1941-45. Decorated Silver Star, Bronze Star, Purple Heart. Mem. Sigma Delta Chi. Clubs: Washington Golf and Country, Washington Post E-Streeters.

DIGGS, MATTHEW O'BRIEN, JR., air conditioning and refrigeration company executive; b. Louisville, Jan. 11, 1933; s. Matthew O'Brien and Dorothy Leroy (Leary) D.; m. Nancy C. Brown, Nov. 5, 1955; children: Elizabeth, Joan, Judith, Matthew O'Brien III. Student, Hanover Coll., 1950-52; B.S. in Mech. Engring, Purdue U., 1955; M.B.A., Harvard U., 1961. Engr. Lincoln Electric Co., Cleve., 1955-59, Toledo Scale Corp., 1961-63; v.p., mng. officer east central region Booz, Allen & Hamilton Inc., Cleve., 1963-72; v.p. mktg. Copeland Corp., Sidney, Ohio, after 1972, then exec. v.p., now pres. Dir. Bank One of Dayton, (Ohio). Served to 1st lt., C.E. AUS, 1955-57. Mem. Air-Conditioning and Refrigeration Inst. (chmn. bd. dirs.). Home: 1160 Lytle Ln Dayton OH 45409 Office: Campbell Rd Sidney OH 45365

DIGGS, WALTER EDWARD, JR., lawyer, aerospace company executive; b. St. Louis, Apr. 17, 1936; s. Walter Edward and Louree (Peoples) D.; m. Carol Ann Kent (June 30, 1962); children: Sally Ann, Thomas Kent. B.A., Amherst Coll., 1958; J.D., Washington Coll., St. Louis, 1961. Bar: Mo. Law clk. chief judge Fed. Dist. Ct., St. Louis, 1961-62; assoc. Bryan, Cave, McPheeters & McRoberts, St. Louis, 1962-65, Peper, Martin, Jensen, Maichel & Hettlage, 1965-66; asst. gen. counsel Anheuser-Busch Inc., St. Louis, 1966-70; dir., pres. Busch Properties Inc., St. Louis, 1971-76; sec., counsel McDonnell Douglas Corp., St. Louis, 1976—. Mem. bd. commrs. St. Louis Mus. Sci. and Natural History. Mem. St. Louis Bar Assn., Mo. Bar Assn., ABA, Am. Soc. Corp. Secs. (pres.), Order of Coif, Phi Delta Phi. Republican. Presbyterian. Home: 9966 Old Chatham Rd Saint Louis MO 63124 Office: McDonnell Dougals Corp PO Box 516 Saint Louis MO 63166

DI GIOIA, ANTHONY MICHAEL, JR., civil engineer; b. Pitts., Aug. 24, 1934; s. Anthony Michael and Elvira (Luongo) DiG.; m. Carole V. Kerr, Sept. 1, 1956; children: Anthony Michael, III, Christina, Stephen, Robert, Paula, David, Deanna, Matthew. B.S.C.E., Carnegie-Mellon U., 1956, M.S., 1957, Ph.D., 1960. Vice pres. Gen. Analytics, Inc., Pitts., 1958-65, pres., 1965-74; asst. prof. civil engring. Carnegie-Mellon U., 1960-62, lectr., 1962-65; pres. GAI Cons., Inc., Monroeville, Pa., 1974—. Contbr. articles to profl. jours. Mem. council St. Bartholomew's Ch., Pitts., 1977-81. Served with C.E. U.S. Army, 1961-62. Mem. ASCE (Young Civil Engr. of Yr. award Pitts. sect. 1970, pres. Pitts. sect. 1973, dist. 4 dir. 1974-77, Civil Engr. of Yr. award Pitts. sect. 1981), Soc. Am. Mil. Engrs. (pres. Pitts. post 1973-74, regional v.p. Ohio Valley region 1974-76). Republican. Roman Catholic. Home: 11 Wisteria Dr Pittsburgh PA 15235 Office: 570 Beatty Rd Monroeville PA 15146

DIGIORGIO, CHRISTINE, diversified consumer products company executive; b. San Francisco, June 29, 1946; d. Robert J. and Eleanor (Vollman) DiG.; m. Ray J. Timmerman, Jan. 14, 1983. A.A., Pine Manor Coll., 1967; B.A., San Francisco State U., 1968; M.B.A., Golden Gate U., 1980. Asst. v.p. Bank of America, San Francisco, 1975-80; treas. DiGiorgio Corp., San Francisco, 1980—. Home: 71 DeBell Dr Atherton CA 94025 Office: DiGiorgio Corp One Maritime Plaza San Francisco CA 94111

DIGIORGIO, ROBERT, diversified consumer products company executive; b. N.Y.C., Dec. 2, 1911; s. Salvatore and Marie (Meyer) Di G.; m. Eleanor Vollmann, Jan. 20, 1940 (div.); children: Ann, Barbara, Christine, Dorothy; m. Patricia Kuhrts Sharman, Aug. 7, 1964. A.B., Yale, 1933; B.L., Fordham U., 1936. Bar: N.Y. 1937. With Di Giorgio Corp., San Francisco, 1937—, pres., 1962-71, chmn. bd., chief exec. officer, 1971-82, chmn. bd., 1982—; dir. Carter Hawley Hale Stores, Inc., Pacific Telephone & Telegraph Co., all San Francisco. Clubs: Metropolitan (N.Y.C.); California (Los Angeles); Pacific-Union, Commonwealth, Bohemian, Golf (San Francisco). Office: One Maritime Plaza San Francisco CA 94111

DI GIOVANNI, ANTHONY, coal mining company executive; b. Phila., May 10, 1919; s. Charles and Josephine (Giacobbe) Di G.; m. Rose Persichetti, July 28, 1946; children: Joanne, Diane, Rosemary, Charles. B.S. in Bus. Adminstrn, St. Joseph's U., 1940. C.P.A., Pa. Accountant Service Supply Corp., Phila., 1940-42; account supr. Ernst & Ernst, 1942-51, mgr., 1952-65; former v.p., dir. United Eastern Coal Sales Corp.; exec. v.p. finance and adminstrn., dir. Barnes & Tucker Co., Valley Forge, Pa., 1965-72, pres., dir., 1972—; group pres. resources div. Alco Standard Corp., 1973—, v.p., 1976—; pres. Alco Standard Canadian Coal Corp., 1976—; dir. Upshur Coals Corp. Bd. dirs. St. Joseph's U. Recipient ACE award, 1974, Spl. Dirs. award, 1976; both from Alco Standard Corp. Mem. Nat. Coal Assn. (dir. 1973—, fin. com. 1978—), Am. Inst. C.P.A.s, Pa. Inst. C.P.A.s (past dir., com. chmn.). Roman Catholic. Clubs: Southwark, Overbrook Golf (Phila.). Home: 2745 Overbrook Terr Merion Golf Manor Ardmore PA 19003 Office: PO Box 883 Valley Forge PA 19482

DIGIOVANNI, JACK LEONARD, newspaper financial executive; b. N.Y.C., Nov. 18, 1935; s. Sebastian and Maria Concetta (CAruso) DiG.; m. Patrina Barone, Jan. 19, 1957; children: Diane Marie, Patricia. B.B.A., CCNY, 1956; M.B.A. with distinction, Pace U., 1975. Fine. exec. Dow Jones & Co., Inc., N.Y.C., 1956-64; fin. exec. N.Y. News Inc., N.Y.C., 1965; treas. Daily News Charities, N.Y.C., Gaynor News Co., Daily News Found., N.Y. News Inx.; mem. pension coms. N.Y. News Retirement Plans, N.Y.C., 1982; trustee Guild-News Pension Plan, N.Y.C., 1982. Treas., trustee Oradell Swim Club, (N.J.), 1978; pres., trustee Oradell Pub. Library, 1982. Mem. Inst. Newspaper Controllers and Fin. Officers. Roman Catholic. Club: UNICO (dir. 1982-83). Lodge: Lions. Home: 250 Morris St Oradell NJ 07649 Office: New York News Inc 220 E 42d St New York NY 10017

DI GIROLAMO, JOSEPH, electronic components co. exec.; b. Boston, Nov. 15, 1923; s. Frank and Rose (Blanda) DiG.; m. Dorothea Leona Jahnke, Nov. 28, 1948; children—Janet Sue, Joel Alan. B.S. in Elec. Engring, Purdue U., 1948. Relay and controls engr. Ind. & Mich. Electric Co., South Bend, Ind., 1948-53; project engr. CTS Corp., Elkhart, Ind., 1953-61, asst. gen. mgr., Berne, Ind., 1961-65, gen. mgr., 1965-67; pres., gen. mgr. CTS of Berne Inc., 1967-70; v.p. CTS Corp., Elkhart, 1969-71, group v.p., 1971-76, exec. v.p., 1976-79, exec. v.p., chief operating officer, 1979-80, chmn. bd., 1980—, also dir.; dir. Keene Products, Inc., CTS Keene, Inc., CTS Tool, Die & Machine, Inc., CTS of Asheville, Inc., CTS of Brownsville, Inc., Keene Monon, Inc., CTS Halex, Inc., CTS Microelectronics, Inc., others. Trustee CTS Found.; mem. pres.'s council Purdue U. Served with USN, 1943-46. Mem. Purdue Alumni Assn., Purdue Research Found., Berne C. of C., Elkhart C. of C. Republican. Lutheran. Clubs: Rotary, Oak Hills Golf, Elcona Country. Patentee in field. Home: 3125 Greenleaf Blvd Elkhart IN 46514 Office: 905 N West Blvd Elkhart IN 46514

DIGNAC, GENY (EUGENIA M. BERMUDEZ), sculptor; b. Buenos Aires, Argentina, June 8, 1932; came to U.S., 1954; d. Jose Victor Marenco and Margarita Eugenia D.; m. Jose Y. Bermudez, Apr. 7, 1958; children—Alexander, Melanie. Ed., U. Buenos Aires, 1952-54. Lectr. in field. Exhibited in one-woman shows, Galeria 22, Caracas, Venezuela, 1967, Michael Berger Gallery, Pitts., 1969, Cinema 2, Caracas, 1971, Pyramid Gallery, Washington; exhibited in numerous group shows, including, Corcoran Gallery of Art, Washington, 1958, 59, Inst. Contemporary Arts, Washington, 1967, Bklyn. Mus., 1968, Mus. Modern Art, Buenos Aires, 1971, Mus. Fine Arts, Boston, Palais des Beaux Arts, Brussels, 1974, Inst. Contemporary Arts, London; represented in permanent collections, Fundacio Joan Miro, Barcelona, Spain, Palazzo Dei Diamanti, Ferrara, Italy, Museo La Tertulia, Cali, Colombia, Galeria del Banco Central, Quito, Ecuador., The Latinoamerican Art Found., San Jaun, P.R., and others in, Argentina, Chile, Germany, Italy, Ireland, Spain, U.S. and, Venezuela; works include: 19 Fire Gestures-, 1970-80, 1971; radio and TV interviews, U.S. and abroad; Works with lights, fire and temperatures; subject of profl. articles, films. Recipient prize for light sculpture IX Festival of Art, Cali, 1969. Home: 4109 E Via Estrella Phoenix AZ 85028

DIGNAM, ROBERT JOSEPH, physician; b. Manchester, N.H., July 8, 1925; s. Walter Joseph and Margaret Veronica (Lowe) D.; m. Evelyn Pettitt, Aug. 4, 1961; children—Stephen Mark, Lyn Shore, Margaret Gale. B.S., Bates Coll., 1945; M.D., Tufts U., 1949. Intern Boston City Hosp., 1949-50, resident in orthopedic surgery, 1954-57, Lahey Clinic, Boston, 1953-54; practice medicine specializing in orthopedic surgery, Santa Monica, Calif., 1960—; mem. staff St. Johns Hosp. UCLA Med. Center; clin. prof. orthopedic surgery UCLA. Served to lt., M.C. USN, 1951-54. Fellow A.C.S.; mem. AMA, Mass. Med. Soc., Calif. Med. Assn., Am. Acad. Orthopedic Surgeons. Club: Jonathan. Home: 821 Alma Real Pacific Palisades CA 92072 Office: 2021 Santa Monica Blvd Santa Monica CA 90404

DIGNAN, THOMAS GREGORY, JR., lawyer; b. Worcester, Mass., May 23, 1940; s. Thomas Gregory and Hester Clare (Sharkey) D.; m. Mary Anne Connor, Sept. 16, 1978; 1 dau., Kellyanne E. B.A., Yale U., 1961; J.D., U. Mich., 1964. Bar: Mass. 1964, U.S. Supreme Ct. 1968. Assoc. firm Ropes & Gray, Boston, 1964-74, ptnr. firm, 1974—; spl. asst. atty. gen. State of Mass., 1974-76; dir. Boston Edison Co. Editor: Mich. Law Review, 1963-64; Contbr. articles to profl. jours. Bd. dirs. Family Counseling and Guidance Centers, Inc., 1967-76, 78—, v.p., 1983—; Bd. dirs. Gov.'s Mgmt. Task Force, 1979-81; mem. fin. com. Town of Sudbury, 1982—; bd. advisers Environ. Law Ctr., Vt. Law Sch., 1981—; mem. lawyers com. Atomic Indsl. Forum. Mem. Am. Bar Assn., Mass. Bar Assn., Boston Bar Assn., Assn. Internationale du Droit Nucleaire, Am. Nuclear Soc., Am. Law Inst., Order of the Coif.; mem. Phi Delta Phi. Republican. Roman Catholic. Clubs: Downtown, Union. Asst. Home: 17 Robert Best Rd Sudbury MA 01776 Office: 225 Franklin St Boston MA 02110

DI JAMES, PASCAL, labor union official; b. Buffalo, Aug. 1, 1926; s. Daniel and Agnes DiJ.; m. Lenora, 1967; children: Daniel, Leonard. Student, Chown Sch. Bus., 1948-50. Mem. Local 8, Internat. Assn. Marble, Slate and Stone Polishers, Rubbers & Sawyers, Tile & Marble Setters Helpers & Terrazzo Helpers, 1952—; fin. sec. Local 8, Marble, Slate & Stone Polishers, 1952-54, bus. agt., 1954-71, internat. union rep., 1971-75, gen. pres.-sec.-treas., Alexandria, Va., after 1975; pres. reorganized union Tile, Marble, Terrazzo, Finishers, Shopworkers and Granite Cutters Internat. Union, 1980—. Served with U.S. Army, 1945-47. Office: 801 N Pitt St Alexandria VA 22314

DIKE, PHIL, artist, educator; b. Redlands, Calif., Apr. 6, 1906; s. Andrew Noble and Jennie E. (Twigg) D.; m. Betty Love Woodward, June 17, 1933; 1 son, Philip Woodward. Student, Chouinard Art Inst., 1924-28, Art Students League, 1928, Am. Acad., Fontainbleau, France, 1930. Color cons. Walt Disney, 1935-45; instr. figure painting Chouinard Art Inst., 1945- 50; instr. painting Scripps Coll., 1950; now prof. emeritus art Scripps Coll. and; Claremont Grad. Sch. (Dana Mention, Pa. Acad. Fine Arts 1947, Nat. Acad. Water Color prize 1950, 58, 1st prize Calif. Water Color Soc. 1931, 1st prize Watercolor Butler Inst. Am. Art 1959, Albert Dorne purchase prize Am. Water Color Soc. 1960, Grumbacher prize Calif. Water Color Soc. 1960, Paul B. Remmy Meml. award Am. Water Color Exhbn. 1962, purchase prize Springfield Nat. Watercolor Exhbn., 1967, Calif. Nat. Watercolor Exhbn. 1969, Water Color U.S.A. 1972, Watchung award Calif. Nat. Watercolor Exhbn. 1974, Richard S. Grant Meml. award Nat. Watercolor Exhbn. 1976), Exhbns., Carnegie, 1936, 37, 50, Chgo. Art Inst., Pa. Acad. Fine Arts, Salon, Paris, France, Met. Mus. Art, 1951, Nat. Acad., Works in permanent collection, Met. Mus. Art, Wood Mus., Santa Barbara Mus. (Awarded 1st prize oil painting, Golden Gate Expn. 1940). Medal Achievement Pepsi Cola, 1946; Hatfield prize, 1946; Cole prize, 1952; Pottinger award, 1953; Brugger award, 1957, 66; John L. Ernst award, 1965; Nat. Academician. Mem. Am. Watercolor Soc. (hon. v.p. 1954), Calif. Watercolor Soc., Nat., West Coast Watercolor Soc. (v.p. 1964-65). Home: 2272 N Forbes Ave Claremont CA 91711 *There is a deep satisfaction in the rhythm of the waves; the changing light; the smells; the sand and rock that change from day to day; the sun, moon and the tides; and the innate dependability of the universal reality, and the belief that this can bring to me a better understanding.*

DIKE, SHELDON HOLLAND, computer programmer/analyst; b. Atlantic City, Oct. 23, 1916; s. Clarence Sheldon and Ethelyn Flora (Holland) D.; m. Joan Arlene Rebyor, Nov. 28, 1971; children: by previous marriage—Lawrence Sheldon, Walter Hopcraft, Robert Lindsay, Martin Spencer, Martha Mary. Student, Colgate U., 1934-36; B.S. in E.E, U. N.Mex., 1941; Ph.D., Johns Hopkins U., 1951. With dept. terrestrial magnetism Carnegie Inst., Washington, 1941-42; faculty U. N.Mex., Albuquerque, 1942-43, U. Mich., Ann Arbor, 1943-44, Los Alamos Sci. Lab., 1944-45, Glenn L. Martin Co., Balt., 1946-47; radiation lab. Johns Hopkins U., Balt., 1947-51; with Sandia Corp., Albuquerque, 1951-56; pres. The Dikewood Corp., Albuquerque, 1956-69, cons., 1970—; pres. S.H. Dike & Co., Inc., Albuquerque, 1967—; programmer/analyst Hancock Dikewood Services, Inc., Albuquerque, 1980—; pres. Edde Fund, Inc., Albuquerque, 1967—. Author: The Territorial Post Offices of New Mexico, 1958, The Territorial Post Offices of Arizona, 1958, New Mexico Territorial Postmark Catalog, 8th edit, 1981; Contbr. articles to profl. jours. Mem. State Small Bus. Council N.Mex., 1967; mem. Gov.'s Commn. on Humanities, 1967, Com. Econ. Devel., 1967, N.Mex Amigos, 1966—. Recipient Naval Ordnance Devel. award, 1945. Fellow Am. Phys. Soc., IEEE; mem. Sigma Xi. Patentee in field. Home: 3700 Aspen St NE Albuquerque NM 87110 Office: 1420 Carlisle Blvd NE Albuquerque NM 87110

DIKOV, JOSEPH, bishop; b. Pelovo, Pleven, Bulgaria, July 11, 1907; s. Diko Ivanov and Valka Baleva (Marinova) D. Grad., Spiritual Sem., Sofia, Bulgaria, 1930. Ordained priest Bulgarian Orthodox Ch., 1938; sec. Rila Monastery, 1935-36; protosingel of Metropolitan of Vratza, 1936-41, Plovdiv, 1941-42; chief cultural dept. Holy Synod, 1943-45, 51-57; rector Spiritual Sem., Plovdiv, Bulgaria, 1947-51; vicor bishop to Bulgarian Patriarch Kiril, 1957-70; adminstr. Bulgarian Akron, Ohio diocese, 1970-72; metropolitan of N.Y. Dioceses N.Y.C., 1972—; del. to Prague Peace Conf. Home: 550 A W 50th St New York NY 10019

DILDAY, WILLIAM HORACE, JR., broadcasting executive; b. Boston, Sept. 14, 1937; s. William Horace and Alease Virginia (Scott) D.; m. Maxine Carol Wiggins, Nov. 5, 1966; children: Erika Lynn, Kenya Alease. B.S., Boston U., 1960. Ops. supr. IBM, Boston, 1963;

pub. relations and personnel dir. E.G. & G. Roxbury, minority bus., Roxbury, Mass.; personnel dir. WHDH Radio, TV, Boston, 1969-72; gen. mgr. WLBT-TV, Jackson, Miss., 1972—; dir. NBC-TV Affiliates, 1979-83, vice-chmn., 1982-83, chmn. affiliates sports com., 1981-83. Mem. Jackson Urban League, pres., 1978-79; bd. dirs. Jackson-Hinds Comprehensive Health Center; mem. Hinds County Democratic Exec. Com. Served with AUS, 1960-62. Mem. Nat. Assn. Black Journalists, Nat. Assn. Broadcasters (TV bd. dirs.). Home: 855 Rutherford Dr Jackson MS 39206 Office: PO Box 1712 Jackson MS 39205

DI LELLA, ALEXANDER ANTHONY, educator; b. Paterson, N.J., Aug. 14, 1929; s. Alexander and Adelaide (Grimaldi) Di L. B.A., St. Bonaventure U., 1952; S.T.L., Cath. U.Am., 1959, Ph.D., 1962; S.S.L., Pontifical Bibl. Inst., Rome, 1964. Entered Franciscan Order, Roman Catholic Ch., 1949; ordained priest, 1955. Lectr. O.T. and bibl. Greek Holy Name Coll., Washington, 1964-67; asst. prof. Semitic lang. Cath. U. Am., 1966-68, assoc. prof., 1968-76, assoc. prof. O.T., 1976-77, prof., 1977—; adj. prof. O.T. Washington Theol. Union, 1969-72; mem. Rev. Standard Version Bible Com., 1982—. Author: The Hebrew Text of Sirach: A Text, Critical and Historial Study, 1966, The Book of Daniel, 1978, Proverbs in the Old Testament in Sriac According to the Peshitta Version, 1979. Am. Sch. Oriental Research fellow, 1962-63; Guggenheim fellow, 1972-73; Assn. Theol. Schs. in U.S. and Can. fellow, 1979-80. Mem. Soc. Bibl. Lit. (pres. Chesapeake Bay region 1972-73), Cath. Bibl. Assn. (pres. 1975-76, del. to Council on Study of Religion 1971-72), Izaak Walton League. Home: Curley Hall Cath U Am Washington DC 20064 Office: Room 420 Caldwell Cath U Am Washington DC 20064 *Most of my adult life I have been a student of biblical languages and literatures, interpretation and theology. Teaching, research and publications enable me to convey to others the value of the Bible as a primary document of Judaism and Christianity and as a significant factor in Western culture and civilization.*

DILIDDO, BART A., chemical engineer, chemical company executive; b. Cleve., Mar. 5, 1931; s. Donato and Lucia (Simone) DiL.; m. Roseann L. Canalaz, Aug. 13, 1955; children: Kara Marie, David Anthony. B.S. in Chem. Engring., Cleve. State U., 1954; M.S., Ill. Inst. Tech., 1956; Ph.D., Case-Western Res. U., 1960. With Brecksville Research and Devel. Ctr. B.F. Goodrich Co., 1956-67, With Avon Lake Tech. Ctr., 1967-70, process mgr., Orange, Tex., 1970-72, dir. latex chems., 1972-73, dir. R&D, Cleve., 1973-75, div. v.p. tire tech., Akron, 1975-78, div. v.p. spl. projects, Cleve., 1978, div. v.p. plastics, 1978-79, sr. v.p. and gen. mgr. plastics, 1979-80, exec. v.p., 1980—; pres. Chem. Group, 1980—; dir., vice-chmn. Chlorine Inst. Mem. Am. Inst. Chem. Engrs., Vinyl Inst. (chmn.), Chem. Mfrs. Assn., Soc. Plastics Industry (dir.). Republican. Roman Catholic. Patentee in field. Office: 6100 Oak Tree Blvd Cleveland OH 44131

DILKS, PARK BANKERT, JR., lawyer; b. Phila., Mar. 25, 1928; s. Park Bankert and Gertrude Scott (Hilton) D. A.B., U. Pa., 1948, J.D., 1951. Bar: Pa. 1952, D.C. 1951, U.S. Supreme Ct. 1962. Asst. dist. atty., Phila., 1952; assoc. firm Souser & Schumacker, Phila., 1953-60, Morgan, Lewis & Bockius, 1961-63, ptnr., 1964—; chmn. bd. U.S. Investment Fund, 1973—; dir. Broadstone Group, Inc., N.Y.C. Served as 1st lt. USAR, 1952-58. Mem. ABA, Pa. Bar Assn., Phila. Bar Assn., D.C. Bar Assn., Fed. Bar Assn., Assn. Bar City N.Y., Phi Beta Kappa. Club: Union League. Home: William Penn House 1919 Chestnut St Apt 2604 Philadelphia PA 19103 Office: 2000 One Logan Sq Philadelphia PA 19103

DILL, CHARLES ANTHONY, manufacturing company executive; b. Cleve., Nov. 29, 1939; s. Melville Reese and Gladys (Frode) D.; m. Louise T. Hall, Aug. 24, 1963; children: Charles Anthony, Dudley Barnes. B.S. in Mech. Engring, Yale U., 1961; M.B.A., Harvard U., 1963. With Emerson Electric Co., 1963—, corp. v.p. internat., 1973-77; pres. subsidiary A.B. Chance Co., 1977-80, corp. group v.p., St. Louis, 1980—; sr. v.p. Emerson Electric, 1982—; dir. First Nat. Bank, Centralia, Mo. Adv. bd. Coll. Engring. U. Mo. Republican. Congregationalist. Clubs: St. Louis Country, Fox Chapel (Pa.) Racquet. Home: 1298 Mason Rd St Louis MO 63131 Office: 8000 W Florissant Ave St Louis MO 63136

DILL, ELLIS HAROLD, univ. dean; b. Pittsburg County, Okla., Dec. 31, 1932; s. Harold and Mayme Doris (Ellis) D.; m. Cleone June Granrud, Sept. 12, 1953; children—Michael Harold, Susan Marie. A.A., Grant Tech. Jr. Coll., 1951; B.S. in Civil Engring, U. Calif. at Berkeley, 1954, M.S., 1955, Ph.D., 1957. Asst. prof. to prof. aeros. and astronautics U. Wash., 1956-77, chmn. dept. aeros. and astronautics, 1976-77; dean engring. Rutgers U., New Brunswick, N.J., 1977—. Mem. Soc. Natural Philosophy. Research, numerous publs. on mechanics of solids. Home: 436 Brentwood Dr Piscataway NJ 08854 Office: Rutgers U Coll Engring New Brunswick NJ 08903

DILL, GUY, artist; b. Duval County, Fla., May 30, 1946; s. James Melvin and Virginia Crane D.; m. Mary Ann Hinkey, Sept. 14, 1975. B.F.A. with honors, Chouinard Sch. Art, Los Angeles, 1970. Mem. faculty dept. sculpture UCLA, 1977-82. Represented in permanent collections, Mus. Modern Art, N.Y.C., Guggenheim Mus., N.Y.C., Whitney Mus., N.Y.C., Newport Harbor Art Mus., Newport Beach, Calif., Stedelijk Mus., Amsterdam, Netherlands., Mus. Contemporary Art, Los Angeles; One man exhbns. include, Felicity Samuel, London, 1972, Ace Gallery, Los Angeles, 1971, 73, 77, Pace Gallery, N.Y.C., 1974, 76, Thomas Gallery, Los Angeles, 1975, Tortue Gallery, Los Angeles, 1976, Dobrick Gallery, Chgo., 1977, Felsen Gallery, Los Angeles, 1978, 79, Janus Gallery, Los Angeles, 1980, 81; One man exhbns. include, Flow Ace Gallery, Los Angeles, 1982. Served with USCG, 1963-67. Home: 819 Milwood Ave Venice CA 90291

DILL, LADDIE JOHN, artist; b. Long Beach, Calif., Sept. 14, 1943; s. James Melvin and Virginia (Crane) D.; m. Ann Cathrine Thornycroft, Jan. 13, 1976; 1 dau., Ariel Dill. B.F.A., Chouinard Art Inst., 1968. Lectr. painting and drawing UCLA, 1976—. Exhns. include, San Francisco Mus. Modern Art, 1977-78, Albright Knox Mus., Buffalo, 1978-79, The First Show, Los Angeles, represented in permanent collections, Los Angeles County Mus., Santa Barbara Mus., San Francisco Mus. Modern Art, Seattle Mus., Newport Harbor Art Mus., Oakland Mus., Smithsonian Instn., IBM. Nat. Endowment Arts grantee, 1975, 82; Guggenheim Found. fellow, 1979-80; Calif. Arts Council Commn. grantee, 1983-84. Address: 1625 Electric Ave Venice CA 90291

DILL, WILLIAM JOSEPH, editor; b. Carmi, Ill., May 8, 1935; s. Hurshell Lloyd and Alma Lucille (Newby) D.; m. Marie Emilie Hubert, Aug. 14, 1965; children—Kevin Joseph, Kathleen Marie, Lisa Marie, Christopher Hubert. B.S., So. Ill. U., Carbondale, 1961. Reporter, editor Chgo. AP, 1961-65, asst. bur. chief, 1965-69, chief bur., Balt., 1969-71, Nashville, 1971-73, Charlotte, N.C., 1973-76, Mpls., 1976-81; editor The Forum of Fargo-Moorhead, N.D., 1981—. Served with USN, 1953-57. Named Journalism Alumnus of Yr. So. Ill. U., 1970. Mem. Sigma Delta Chi. Roman Catholic. Home: 105 19th Ave N Fargo ND 58102 Office: PO Box 2020 Fargo ND 58102

DILL, WILLIAM RANKIN, college president; b. Sewickley, Pa., Aug. 18, 1930; s. Frederick Hayes and Caroline (Rankin) D.; m. Jean McLeod, June 13, 1953; children: Jens McLeod, Holly Ruth, Harrison Rankin, Cynthia Wightman. A.B., Bates Coll., 1951; M.S., Carnegie Inst. Tech., 1953, Ph.D., 1956; postgrad., U. Oslo, 1953-54. Sr. research fellow Grad. Sch. Indsl. Adminstrn., Carnegie Inst. Tech., Pitts., 1955-56, asst. prof., 1956-60, asso. prof., 1960-65, asst. dean, 1959-62, asso. dean, 1962-65; program dir. edn. research and devel. IBM, White Plains, N.Y., 1965-70; dean Grad. Sch. Bus. Adminstrn., NYU, N.Y.C., 1970-80, U.S.-Chinese Nat. Center for Devel., Dalian, China, 1980; pres. Babson Coll., Wellesley, Mass., 1981—; dir. One William St. Fund, Technicorp Internat., Union Mut. Life Ins. Author: The New Managers, 1962, The Carnegie Tech. Management Game, 1964, The Organizational World, 1973, Running the American Corporation, 1978, Planning in the US and USSR, 1978. Trustee Carnegie Found. for Advancement Teaching. Fulbright scholar, 1953-54; Ford Found. Faculty Research fellow, 1964-65. Mem. Phi Beta Kappa, Sigma Xi, Delta Sigma Rho, Beta Gamma Sigma. Unitarian. Office: Babson Coll Babson Park MA 02157

DILLARD, ANNIE, author; b. Pitts., Apr. 30, 1945; d. Frank and Pam (Lambert) Doak. B.A., Hollins Coll., 1967, M.A., 1968. Columnist The Living Wilderness, Wilderness Soc., 1973-75; contbg. editor Harper's mag., N.Y.C., 1973-81; scholar-in-residence Western Wash. U., Bellingham, 1975-78; disting. vis. prof. Wesleyan U., 1979-83, adj. prof., 1983—; Phi Beta Kappa orator Harvard/Radcliffe, 1983; mem. U.S. Writers' del. UCLA U.S.-Chinese Writers' Conf., 1982; mem. U.S. Cultural Del. to China, 1982. Author: poetry Tickets For A Prayer Wheel, 1974; Pilgrim at Tinker Creek, 1974 (Pulitzer prize for gen. non-fiction 1974), Holy the Firm, 1977, Living by Fiction, 1982, Teaching a Stone to Talk, 1982, Encounters with Chinese Writers, 1984. Mem. Nat. Com. on U.S.-China Relations, 1982—. Recipient N.Y. Presswomen's award for excellence, 1975, Wash. Gov.'s award for contbn. to lit., 1978. Mem. Poetry Soc. Am., Authors Guild, Nat. Citizens for Public Libraries, Phi Beta Kappa. Address: care Blanche Gregory 2 Tudor City Pl New York NY 10017

DILLARD, DAVID HUGH, physician, educator; b. Spokane, Wash., May 14, 1923; s. James Pitt and Mabel (Carlson) D.; m. Virginia Foster, July 7, 1948; children: Kristine, David, James, Julia, Robert, Jennifer, Geoffrey. Student, Gonzaga U., 1942-43; A.B., Whitman Coll., 1946, D.-Sc. (hon.), 1979; M.D., John Hopkins U., 1950. Diplomate: Nat. Bd. Med. Examiners, Am. Bd. Surgery, Am. Bd. Thoracic Surgery. Intern Johns Hopkins Hosp., 1950-51; resident U. Wash., Seattle, 1951-59; research fellow Nat. Cancer Inst., 1953-54, trainee, 1954-55, 57-58; instr. dept. surgery U. Wash., 1954-59, asst. prof., 1959-63, assoc. prof., 1963-69, prof., 1969—, chief div. cardiac surgery, 1972-78. Served with USNR, 1955-57. Fellow A.C.S.; mem. Sociètè Internationale de Chirurge, Am., North Pacific, Pacific Coast, Seattle surg. assns., Am. Heart Assn. (fellow council on cardiovascular surgery), Am. Assn. Thoracic Surgery, Western Thoracic Surg. Assn., Wash. State Heart Assn., Wash. State, King County (Wash.) med. assns., Sigma Xi. Home: 12712 39th NE Seattle WA 98125

DILLARD, DUDLEY, economist, educator; b. Ontario, Oreg., Oct. 18, 1913; s. John James and Frances (Cunning) D.; m. Louisa Gardner, August 22, 1939; children: Lorraine Gardner (Mrs. William C. Gray), Amber Frances (Mrs. Douglas G. Kelly). B.S., U. Calif., 1935, Ph.D., 1940; vis. scholar, Harvard, 1939, Columbia, 1940. Teaching asst. U. Calif., 1935-36, Flood fellow in econs., 1936-37, research asst., 1937-38, teaching asst., 1938-39; Newton Booth Travelling fellow, 1939-40; instr. econs. U. Colo., 1940-41, U. Del., 1941-42; faculty U. Md., 1942—, chmn. dept. econs., 1951-75, acting provost div. behavioral and social scis., 1976-77; vis. asso. prof. econs. Columbia, 1948-50, vis. prof., summer, 1951, 55, 58; cons. U.S. Army, 1945-46. Author: The Economics of John Maynard Keynes, 1948, (with others) Post-Keynesian Economics, 1954, Economic Development of North Atlantic Community, 1967; Editorial bd.: Jour. Econ. History, 1948-54; Contbr. profl. jours. Chmn. Gov.'s Com. on Employment in Md., 1962-64; mem. Gov.'s Adv. Com. on Manpower Devel. and Tng., 1962-67; Mem. U.S. exec. bd. Am. Coll. in Paris, 1966—, chmn., 1979-81. Mem. Am. Econ. Assn., So. Econ. Assn. (pres. 1976-77), Assn. Evolutionary Econs. (pres. 1979), History Econs. Soc. (v.p. 1982-83), Econ. History Soc., AAUP, Phi Beta Kappa, Pi Gamma Mu, Beta Gamma Sigma, Beta Alpha Psi. Club: Cosmos (Washington, District of Columbia). Home: 7007 Forest Hill Dr College Heights Estates Hyattsville MD 20782 Office: Dept Econs U Md College Park MD 20742

DILLARD, JOSEPH KING, electrical engineer; b. Westminster, S.C., May 10, 1917; s. Joe King and Daysie (Holcombe) D.; m. Elizabeth Wash, Dec. 8, 1939; children: William King, John Holcombe. B.S. in Elec. Engring, Ga. Inst. Tech., 1947, M.S., MIT, 1950; grad. Advanced Mgmt. Program, Harvard U., 1960. Instr. elec. engring. MIT, 1947-50; electric utility engr. Westinghouse Electric Corp., East Pittsburgh, 1950-56, mgr. electric utility engring., 1956-69, gen. mgr. advanced systems tech., 1969-80, sr. cons., 1980-82, ret., 1982. Contbr. articles to profl. jours. Past chmn. nat. adv. bd. Ga. Tech. U. Served with USNR, 1939-46. Fellow IEEE (pres. 1976, dir. 1970-76), Nat. Soc. Profl. Engrs., Engring. Soc. Western Pa., Nat. Acad. Engring. Republican. Presbyterian. Clubs: Edgewood Country, Univ. (Pitts.). Home: 3323 Scathelocke Rd Pittsburgh PA 15235 Office: 777 Penn Center Blvd Pittsburgh PA 15235

DILLARD, RICHARD HENRY WILDE, author, educator; b. Roanoke, Va., Oct. 11, 1937; s. Benton Oscar and Mattie Lee (Mullins) D.; m. Cathy Anne Hankla, Mar. 24, 1979. B.A., Roanoke Coll., 1958; M.A. (Woodrow Wilson fellow), U. Va., 1959, Ph.D., 1965. Instr. in English, Roanoke Coll., summer 1961; Instr. in English U. Va., 1961-64; asst. prof. English, Hollins Coll., 1964-68, asso. prof., 1968-74, prof., 1974—. Author: The Day I Stopped Dreaming About Barbara Steele, 1966, News of the Nile, 1971, After Borges, 1972, The Book of Changes, 1974, Horror Films, 1976, The Greeting: New and Selected Poems, 1981, The First Man on the Sun, 1983; (with others) screenplay Frankenstein Meets the Space Monster, 1965; editorial bd.: Hollins Critic, 1966-77. Mem. Roanoke County (Va.) Democratic Com., 1976—. Ford Found. grantee, 1972; recipient Acad. Am. Poets award, 1961. Mem. Authors Guild, Bibliog. Soc. U. Va., Count Dracula Soc., Internat. PEN, Melville Soc., Truman Library Inst., Phi Beta Kappa. Democrat. Baptist. Office: PO Box 9671 Hollins College VA 24020

DILLARD, ROBERT CARL, retail company executive; b. Prattville, Ala., Apr. 9, 1931; s. Joseph Samuel and Verna Marie (Meek) D.; m. Wanda Charlene Chapman, Aug. 5, 1951 (dec. 1976); 1 son, William Douglas; m. Linda Sue Snow, May 13, 1977. B.A., Marshall U., 1955. Controller Hudson-Thompson Inc., Montgomery, Ala., 1961-64; controller, treas. M. Loeb Corp., Chgo., 1964-66; dir. fin. and adminstrn. New Eng. Grocery Supply Co., Worcester, Mass., 1966-68; sr. v.p. Loblaw, Inc., Buffalo, 1976-77; v.p., fin., dir. McLain Grocery Co., Masillon, Ohio, 1977-79; v.p., sec.-treas. A. J. Bayless Markets, Inc., Phoenix, 1968-76, 79—; dir. Brewster Savs. and Loan Co., Ohio, 1978-79; prin., dir. DC Sign & Graphics Co., Glendale, Ariz., 1982—. Served to sgt. USMC, 1949-52. Republican. Unitarian. Clubs: Lions (Phoenix) (v.p. 1973-74); Rotary (Massillon)). Home: 13202 N 13th Ln Phoenix AZ 85029 Office: A J Bayless Markets Inc 111 E Buckeye Rd Phoenix AZ 85004

DILLARD, ROBERT LIONEL, JR., lawyer, former life insurance executive; b. Corsicana, Tex., Sept. 30, 1913; s. Robert Lionel and Mattie Sam (Jack) D.; m. Dundee Sheeks, Jan 3O, 1937; children: Robert Lionel III, Diane Dillard More, Deborah (Mrs. John B. Cullen III). B.S. in Commerce, So. Meth. U., 1934, J.D., 1935; LL.M., Harvard U., 1936. Bar: Tex. 1935. With firm Saner, Saner & Jack, Dallas, 1936-41; asst. city atty. Dallas, 1941-45; with Southland Life Ins. Co., Dallas, 1945—, v.p., gen. counsel, sr. v.p., gen. counsel, 1968-70, exec. v.p., gen. counsel, 1970-77, also dir.; with firm Saner, Jack, Sallinger & Nichols, Dallas, 1978—; city atty. Carrollton, Tex., 1947-75. Author articles in field. Mem. bd. edn. Dallas Ind. Sch. Dist., 1953-62, pres., 1961-62; trustee pub. TV, Dallas, 1957-74; pres. Dallas Council Social Agys., 1963-65, Dallas Council Camp Fire Girls, 1960-61; chmn. nat. bd. Camp Fire Girls, 1965-68; officer, dir. Dallas Symphony Orch., 1961-74. Recipient Disting. Law Alumnus award So. Meth. U., 1958, Disting. Alumnus award, 1963. Fellow Am. Bar Found.; mem. ABA (ho. of dels. 1956-58), Inter-Am. Bar Assn., Tex. Bar, Dallas Bar Assn. (pres. 1948), Am. Judicature Soc., Nat. Legal Aid Soc., Assn. Life Ins. Counsel (pres. 1973—), Alpha Tau Omega, Delta Theta Phi (past dist. chancellor), Order Woolsack. Methodist (chmn. ofcl. bd., tchr. adult Sunday sch.). Club: Mason (33 deg.; grand master Tex. 1961-62). Home: 6624 Lakewood Blvd Dallas TX 75214 Office: 1200 Republic Nat Bank Bldg Dallas TX 75201

DILLARD, WILLIAM T., department stores company executive; b. Mineral Springs, Ark., 1914. B.B.A., U. Ark., 1935; M.S., Columbia U., 1937. Pres. Dillard Dept. Stores Inc., Little Rock, until 1977, chmn. bd., chief exec. officer, 1977—; dir. First Nat. Bank, Little Rock. Office: Dillard Dept Stores Inc 900 W Capitol St Little Rock AR 72203 *

DILLE, EARL KAYE, elec. utility exec.; b. Chillicothe, Mo., Apr. 25, 1927; s. George Earl and Josephine Christina (Kaye) D.; m. Martha Virginia Merrill, Sept. 8, 1951; children—Thomas Merrill, James Warren. B.S., U.S. Naval Acad., 1950; M.S., St. Louis U., 1961. With Union Elec. Co., St. Louis, 1957—, exec. v.p., 1971—, also dir.; dir. Elec. Energy, Inc., Mo. Power & Light Co., Mo. Edison Co., Mo. Utilities Co., Union Colliery Co., Merc. Trust Co., Merc. Bancorp. Inc., Civic Employment Corp.; pres. Asso. Industries Mo., 1974-76. Mem. adv. council Coll. Engring., U. Mo.; mem. exec. bd. St. Louis Area council Boy Scouts Am.; bd. dirs. St. Louis Symphony Soc., Ranken Tech. Inst., St. Louis Regional Commerce and Growth Assn., 1976-79. Served with USN, 1950-57; comdr. Res. Recipient U. Mo. award for distinguished service in engring., 1973, Alumni Merit award St. Louis U., 1974; Outstanding Engr. in Industry award Mo. Soc. Profl. Engrs., 1976. Mem. Engrs. Club St. Louis (pres. 1977-78), IEEE, Sigma Xi. Episcopalian. Clubs: Mason. (Grand master Mo. 1982-83), Bellerive Country, Noonday, St. Louis. Home: 27 Dunleith Dr Saint Louis MO 63131 Office: 1901 Gratiot St Saint Louis MO 63166

DILLE, JOHN ROBERT, physician; b. Waynesburg, Pa., Sept. 2, 1931; s. Charles Emanuel and Ruth Emma (South) D.; m. Joan Marie Sirtosky, Dec. 17, 1955; children: Paul Andrew, John Alan. B.S., Waynesburg Coll., 1952; M.D., U. Pitts., 1956; M.Indsl. Health, Harvard U., 1960. Diplomate: Am. Bd. Preventive Medicine. Intern Akron City Hosp., 1956-57; resident in aerospace medicine USAF Sch. Aerospace Medicine, San Antonio, 1960-62; program adv. officer FAA Civil Aeromed. Research Inst., Oklahoma City, 1961-64, regional flight surgeon, Los Angeles, 1965; chief FAA Civil Aeromed. Inst., U.S. Dept. Transp., Oklahoma City, 1966—; asso. prof. U. Okla., 1961—, dir. tng. residency aerospace medicine, 1967-72. Asso. editor: Ag Pilot Internat. mag, 1980—; contbr. articles to profl. jours. Served with USAF, 1957-59; col. M.C. Army N.G. Recipient Meritorious award William A. Jump Found., 1968. Fellow Aerospace Med. Assn. (exec. council 1978-81, chmn. history and archives com. 1982—, Theodore C. Lyster award 1978, chmn. history and archives com. 1982-84), Am. Coll. Preventive Medicine (regent 1974-77); mem. Flying Physicians Assn., Civil Aviation Med. Assn., Assn. Mil. Surgeons U.S., Internat. Acad. Aviation and Space Medicine, Sigma Xi, Nu Sigma Nu. Presbyterian. Home: 335 Merkle Dr Norman OK 73069 Office: 6600 S MacArthur Blvd Oklahoma City OK 73125

DILLE, ROLAND PAUL, coll. pres.; b. Dassel, Minn., Sept. 16, 1924; s. Oliver Valentine and Eleanor (Johnson) D.; m. Beth Hopeman, Sept. 4, 1948; children—Deborah, Martha, Sarah, Benjamin. B.A. summa cum laude, U. Minn., 1949, Ph.D., 1962. Instr. English U. Minn., 1953-56; asst. prof. St. Olaf Coll., Northfield, Minn., 1956-61; asst. prof. English Calif. Lutheran Coll., Thousand Oaks, Calif., 1961-63; mem. faculty Moorhead (Minn.) State U., 1963—, pres., 1968—. Author: Four Romantic Poets, 1969. Treas. Am. Assn. State Colls. and Univs., 1977-78, bd. dirs., 1978-80, chmn., 1980-81; mem. Nat. Council for Humanities, 1980—. Served with inf. AUS, 1944-46. Mem. Phi Beta Kappa. Home: 516 9th St S Moorhead MN 56560

DILLENBERGER, JOHN, educator, clergyman; b. St. Louis, July 11, 1918; s. Charles and Bertha (Hoffmann) D.; m. Jane Daggett Karlin, July 19, 1962; children by previous marriage: Eric John, Paul Gregor. B.A., Elmhurst Coll., 1940, D.D., 1959; B.D., Union Theol. Sem., 1943; Ph.D., Columbia, 1948; D.D., U. Vt., 1957; S.T.D., Ch. Divinity Sch. Pacific, 1965, Ripon Coll., 1966; L.H.D., U. San Francisco, 1966. Ordained to ministry United Ch. of Christ, 1943; tutor asst. theology Union Theol. Sem., N.Y.C., 1947-48; instr. religion Princeton, 1948-49; asst. prof. religion Columbia, 1949-52, asso. prof., 1952-54; asso. prof. theology Harvard Div. Sch., 1954-57, Parkman prof. theology, 1957-58; Ellen S. James prof. systematic and hist. theology, grad. sch. and seminary Drew U., Madison, N.J., 1958-62; prof. hist. theology, dean grad. studies San Francisco Theol. Sem., San Anselmo, Calif., 1962-64; dean, pres., prof. hist. theology Grad. Theol. Union, Berkeley, Calif., 1962-72, prof. hist. theology, 1962-78; pres. Hartford Sem., 1978—; Research scholar Nat. Collection Fine Arts Smithsonian Instn., 1973-74. Author: God Hidden and Revealed, 1953, (with Claude Welch) Protestant Christianity: Interpreted Through Its Development, 1954, Protestant Thought and Natural Science, 1960, Contours of Faith, 1969; Editor: Martin Luther: Selections from his Writings, 1961, John Calvin: Selections from His Writings, 1971; Chmn. editorial bd.: Library of Protestant Thought, 1958-72; author: Benjamin West; The Context of His Life's Work, 1977, (with Jane Dillenberger) Perceptions of the Spirit in 20th Century American Art, 1977. Mem. exec. com. Assn. Theol. Schs. U.S. and Can., 1970-74. Served with Chaplain's Corps USNR, 1943-46. Fellow Soc. for Values in Higher Edn. Home: 1536 LeRoy Berkeley CA 94708

DILLER, BARRY, motion picture company executive; b. San Francisco, Feb. 2, 1942; s. Michael and Reva (Addison) D. Vice pres. feature films and movies of week ABC, 1971-73, 1973-74; chmn. bd. Paramount Pictures Corp., 1974—; pres. Gulf & Western Leisure Time Group, 1983—. Mem. Am. Film Inst., Variety Clubs Internat., Hollywood Radio and TV Soc., Acad. Motion Picture Arts and Scis., ACLU, NCCJ. Home: 5555 Melrose Ave Los Angeles CA 90038

DILLER, PHYLLIS, actress, authoress; b. Lima, Ohio, July 17, 1917; d. Perry Marcus and Frances Ada (Romshe) Driver; m. Sherwood Anderson Diller, Nov. 4, 1939 (div. Sept. 1965); children: Peter III, Sally, Suzanne Diller Mills, Stephanie Diller Waldron, Perry; m. Warde Donovan, Oct. 7, 1965 (div. July 1975). Student, Sherwood Music Conservatory, Chgo., 1935-37, Bluffton (Ohio) Coll., 1938-39; D.H.L., Nat. Christian U., 1973. (Best TV Comedienne award TV Radio Mirror 1965); Author: Phyllis Diller Tells All About Fang, 1963, Phyllis Diller's Housekeeping Hints, 1966, Phyllis Diller's Marriage Manual, The Complete Mother, The Joys of Aging and How to Avoid Them, 1981; Accompanied Bob Hope entertainment group to, South Vietnam, Christmas, 1966, symphony appearances soloing on piano.; Theatrical prodns. include Dark at the Top of the Stairs, 1961, Wonderful Town, 1962, Happy Birthday, 1963, Hello, Dolly!, i970, Everybody Loves Opal, 1972, What Are We Going to Do With Jenny, 1977; numerous appearances TV and radio, concerts, supper clubs and hotels, 1955—; producer, writer: Phyllis Diller Shows, 1963, 64; rec. artist, Verve Records, Columbia Records; pres., BAM Prodns., Ltd., 1965—, PhilDil Prodns., Ltd., 1966—; motion pictures include Eight on the Lam, 1967, The Private Navy of Sergeant O'Farrell; star: TV series The Pruitts of Southampton, 1966-67, Beautiful Phyllis Diller Show, 1968-69 (Recipient honors including Star of Year award Nat. Assn. Theatre Owners). Minuteman award U.S.; Treasury Dept.; Distinguished Service citation Ladies Aux. VFW; Woman of Year award Variety Club Women Balt.; Golden Apple; Hollywood Women's Press Club, 1967; Woman of Year award St. Louis chpt. Nat. Bus. and Profl. Women's Club, 1971; named hon. mayor, Brentwood, Calif., 1971; Hon. life mem. San Francisco Press and Union League Club. Office: care PhilDil Prodns Ltd 230 Park Ave New York NY 10169

DILLER, THEODORE CRAIG, lawyer; b. Pitts., Aug. 3, 1904; s. Theodore and Rebecca (Craig) D.; m. Barbara Cox, May 16, 1936; children: Anne Cox Diller Sterling, Rebecca Crossette Diller Howe, Deborah Howard Diller Trianta. Ph.B., Kenyon Coll., 1925; LL.B., Harvard U., 1928. Bar: Pa. 1928, Ill. 1929. Practice law, Chgo., 1929—; partner Lord, Bissell & Brook, 1946—; sec. Magnaflux Corp., 1940-59. Mem. Am., Ill., Chgo. bar assns., Law Club Chgo., Legal Club Chgo. Republican. Episcopalian. Clubs: University., Mid-Am. (Chgo.). Home: 416 Cumnor Rd Kenilworth IL 60043 Office: 115 S LaSalle St Chicago IL 60603

DILLEY, FRANK B., educator; b. Athens, Ohio, Nov. 17, 1931; s. Frank Brown and Geneva (Steiner) D.; m. Jane Long, Sept. 10, 1953; children—F. Brian, Carol Jane, Kathryn Elizabeth. A.B., Ohio U., 1952, M.A., 1953; M.Div., Union Theol. Sem., 1955; Ph.D., Columbia, 1961. Instr. Smith Coll., 1957-60, asst. prof., 1960-62; asso. prof. Millikin U., Decatur, Ill., 1962-67; prof., chmn. dept. philosophy U. Del., 1967-70, 74—, asso. provost, 1970-74; Bd. advisers Walden U., Naples, Fla. ACE Acad. Adminstrn. intern, 1965-66. Author: Metaphysics and Religious Language, 1965, also articles. Mem. Am. Philos. Assn., Metaphys. Soc. Am., Am. Acad. Religion, Phi Beta Kappa. Home: 106 Tanglewood Ln Newark DE 19711

DILLHOFF, J. THOMAS, life insurance company executive; b. Cin., Sept. 1, 1925; s. Edward Bernard and Gertrude Matilda (Kennedy) D.; m. Mary M. Martin, June 12, 1948; children: Richard, Nancy, Mary Susan, Thomas Allen, Paul, James. Student, U. Cin. C.L.U. With Western & So. Life Ins. Co., 1946-55; with Farmers New World Life Ins. Co., Mercer Island, Wash., 1955-75, 78—, exec. v.p., 1958-75, pres., 1978—, Investors Guaranty Life Ins. Co., 1975-76, Ohio State Life Ins. Co., 1976-78. Served with USNR, 1943-45. Fellow pLife Mgmt. Inst.; mem. Am. Soc. C.L.U.'s, Submarine Vets. World War II Assn. Office: 3003 77th Ave Mercer Island WA 98040

DILLIN, JOHN WOODWARD, JR., newspaper correspondent; b. Miami, Fla., July 6, 1936; s. John Woodward and Alberta (Thompson) D.; m. Gay Andrews, Oct. 1, 1966; 1 dau., Katherine. B.S.J. with honors, U. Fla., 1958, postgrad. in U.S. history, 1961-63. Reporter St. Augustine (Fla.) Record, 1958, Tampa (Fla.) Tribune, 1960-61; reporter Christian Sci. Monitor, Boston, 1964-66, corr., Vietnam, 1966-67, city editor, Boston, 1967-71, corr., Atlanta and Washington, 1971-79, mng. editor for news, Boston, 1979-83, nat. polit. corr., Washington, 1983—. Served with AUS, 1958-59. Christian Scientist. Home: 5525 N 15th St Arlington VA 22205 Office: 910 16th St NW Washington DC 20006

DILLIN, SAMUEL HUGH, U.S. judge; b. Petersburg, Ind., June 9, 1914; s. Samuel E. and Maude (Harrell) D.; m. Mary Eloise Humphreys, Nov. 24, 1940; 1 dau., Patricia Jane. A.B. in Govt, Ind. U., 1936, LL.B., 1938. Bar: Ind. bar 1938. Partner firm Dillin & Dillin, Petersburg, 1938-61; U.S. dist. judge So. Dist. Ind., 1961—; Sec. Pub. Service Commn. Ind., 1942; mem. Interstate Oil Compact Commn., 1949-52, 61. Mem. Ind. Ho. of Reps. from Pike and Knox County, 1937, 39, 41, 51, floor leader, 1951; mem. Ind. Senate from Pike and Gibson County, 1951, 61, floor leader, pres. pro tem, 1961; candidate for gov. Ind., 1956. Served to capt. AUS, 1943-46. Mem. Am. Bar Assn., Am. Judicature Soc., Delta Tau Delta, Phi Delta Phi. Democrat. Presbyn. Club: Indianapolis Athletic. Home: 4710 Laurel Circle North Dr Indianapolis IN 46226 Office: Federal Bldg Indianapolis IN 46204

DILLINGHAM, CHARLES, III, theatre manager; b. Washington, Nov. 25, 1942; s. Charles and Barbara (Kibler) D.; m. Susan D. Clines, June 7, 1975; 1 son, Jonathan Charles. B.A., Yale U., 1965, M.F.A., 1969. Gen. mgr. Am. Conservatory Theatre, San Francisco, 1969-78; free lance producer, mgr., San Francisco, 1978-79; gen. mgr. Bklyn. Acad. Theatre Co., N.Y.C., 1979-81, Am. Ballet Theatre, 1981—. Founding mem., treas. Calif. Theatre Council, San Francisco, 1974-77. Democrat. Unitarian. Home: 50 Morningside Dr Apt 53 New York NY 10025 Office: Am Ballet Theatre 890 Broadway New York NY 10025

DILLMAN, BRADFORD, actor; b. San Francisco, Apr. 14, 1930; s. Dean and Josephine Moore D.; m. Frieda Harding, 1956 (div.); m. Suzy Parker, 1963; 5 children. B.A., Yale U., 1951; student, Actors' Studio, N.Y.C., 1955. Profl. stage debut The Scarecrow, N.Y.C., 1953; appeared in: Profl. stage debut in Third Person, N.Y.C., 1955, Long Day's Journey Into Night, N.Y.C., 1956 (Theatre World award 1957), The Fun Couple, N.Y.C., 1962; film debut in A Certain Smile, 1958; other films include Compulsion, 1959 (Cannes Film Festival Best Actor award 1959), Sancutary, 1961, Francis of Assisi, 1961, Jigsaw, 1968, Suppose They Gave a War and Nobody Came, 1970, Mephisto Waltz, 1971, Escape From the Planet of the Apes, 1971, The Iceman Cometh, 1973, The Way We Were, 1973, Gold, 1974, The Swarm, 1978, Piranha, 1978, The Amsterdam Kill, 1978, Guyana: Cult of the Damned, 1980, Sudden Impact, 1983; appeared on numerous TV dramas, 1953-62; since 1962 has guested on many: TV series, including Wide World of Mystery; TV movies Black Water Gold, 1970, Revenge, 1972, Deliver Us From Evil, 1973, Murder or Mercy, 1974, Disappearance of Flight 412, 1974, Force Five, 1975, Widow, 1976. Served to 1st lt. USMC, 1951-53. Office: care Contemporary-Korman Artists Ltd 132 Lasky Dr Beverly Hills CA 90212 *

DILLMAN, GRANT, news executive; b. Columbus, Ohio, May 4, 1918; s. Herschel G. and Daisy L. (Fothergill) D.; m. Audrey Maslow, June 30, 1945; children: Darryl, Craig; 1 dau. by previous marriage, Jo Kunkle. Student, Franklin U., Columbus, 1940-41. With Columbus Dispatch, 1939-42; with pub. relations div. Curtiss-Wright Co., 1942; with UPI (and predecessor), 1942-83, night editor, then news editor Washington bur., 1950-73, v.p. and Washington mgr., 1973-83; exec. dir. Nat. Press Found., 1983—; mem. com. on nat. disaters and the media NRC, 1981-82; chmn. com. on nat. reporting The Pulitzer Prize 1983. Named to Sigma Delta Chi Washington Hall of Fame, 1978. Mem. Sigma Delta Chi (chmn. nat. freedom of info. com. 1973-76). Clubs: Gridiron (pres. 1980), Washington Press, Nat. Press. Home: 6604 Rosecroft Pl Falls Church VA 22043 Office: 315 Nat Press Bldg Washington DC 20045

DILLMAN, L. THOMAS, physicist; b. Huntington, Ind., Au. 26, 1931; s. Lloyd Everett and Nancy (Walther) D.; m. Mary Alice Bagwell, Apr. 18, 1954; children: John Mark, Anne Elizabeth, Mary Susan, Bradford Louis. B.A., Manchester Coll., 1953; M.S., U. Ill., 1955, Ph.D., 1958. Research asst. Los Alamos (N.Mex.) Sci. Lab, summer, 1958; prof. physics Ohio Wesleyan U., 1958—; lectr. physics U. Ill., summers 1960-61; health physics research Oak Ridge Nat. Lab., summers 1967—; cons. Health and Safety Research Div., Oak Ridge (Tenn.) Nat. Lab., 1967—. Contbr. articles health physics, nuclear medicine, nuclear gamma-ray spectroscopy. Mem. Am. Assn. Physicists in Medicine, Am. Phys. Soc., Am. Assn. Physics Tchrs., Health Physics Soc., Nat. Council on Radiation Protection (mem. com. 33 1969—), Sigma Xi. Home: 184 W Lincoln Ave Delaware OH 43015

DILLON, CLARENCE DOUGLAS, investment company executive; b. Geneva, Switzerland, Aug. 21, 1909; s. Clarence and Anne McE. (Douglass) D.; m. Phyllis C. Ellsworth, Mar. 10, 1931 (dec.); children: Phyllis Ellsworth (Mrs. Phyllis Collins), Joan Douglas (Duchesse de Mouchy); m. Susan S. Sage, Jan. 1, 1983. Grad., Groton Sch., 1927; A.B., Harvard, 1931; LL.D., N.Y. U., 1956, Lafayette Coll., 1957, U. Hartford, 1958, Columbia U., 1959, Harvard, 1959, Williams Coll., 1960, Rutgers U., 1961, Princeton, 1961, U. Pa., 1962, Middleburg Coll., 1963, Tufts U., 1982. Mem. New York Stock Exchange, 1931-36; dir. U.S. & Foreign Securities Corp. and U.S. & Internat. Securities Corp., 1937-53; pres. U.S. & Fgn. Securities Corp. and U.S. & Internat. Securities Corp., 1937-53, pres., dir., 1967-71, chmn. bd., 1971—; dir. Dillon, Read & Co., Inc., 1938-53, chmn. bd., 1946-53, chmn. exec. com., dir., 1971—. A.E. & P. to, France, 1953-57; under sec. of state for econ. affairs Dept. State, 1958-59, under sec. of state, 1959-61; sec. of treasury, 1961-65; Pres. Met. Mus. Art, N.Y.C., 1970-78, chmn., N.Y.C., 1978—; hon. gov. N.Y. Hosp.; chmn. Rockefeller Found., 1972-75, Brookings Instn., 1970-76; former pres. bd. overseers, Harvard Coll. Served from ensign to lt. comdr. USNR, 1941-45. Decorated Air medal, Legion of Merit. Mem. Soc. Colonial Wars N.Y., Soc. of Cincinnati. Clubs: Racquet and Tennis, Knickerbocker, Links, River, Recess, Century, Pilgrims (N.Y.C.); Metropolitan (Washington). Office: 767 Fifth Ave New York NY 10153

DILLON, CLIFFORD BRIEN, lawyer; b. Amarillo, Tex., Oct. 25, 1921; s. Clifford Newton and Leone (Brien) D.; m. Audrey Catherine Johnson, Jan. 16, 1945; children: Audrey Catherine Dillon Peters, Robert Brien, Douglas Johnson. B.B.A., U. Tex., 1943, LL.B. with honors, 1947. Bar: Tex. 1947. Practiced in, Houston, 1947—; ptnr. Baker & Botts, 1957—; mem. faculty Southwestern Legal Found., 1968—. Author articles in field. Bd. dirs. Antitrust Inst., U. Tex. Health Sci. Ctr., Houston; mem. antitrust adv. bd. Bur. Nat. Affairs; Past bd. dirs., Houston Vis. Nurses Assn. Served to lt. (j.g.) A.C. USNR and USCGR, 1943-45. Fellow ABA (chmn. sect. antitrust law 1975-76), State Bar Tex., Am. Judicature Soc.; mem. Houston Bar Assn., U.S. C. of C. (adv. council antitrust policy), Houston C. of C., Phi Kappa Psi, Phi Delta Phi. Presbyterian. Clubs: Houston Country, Petroleum (Houston); Riverhill Country, Old Baldy, Headliners. Office: Baker & Botts 3000 One Shell Plaza Houston TX 77002

DILLON, DIANE CLAIRE SORBER, illustrator; b. Glendale, Calif., Mar. 13, 1933; d. Adelbert Paul and Phyllis Mabel (Worsley) Sorber; m. Lionel John Dillon, Mar. 17, 1957; 1 son, Lionel J. Student, Los Angeles City Coll., 1950-51, Skidmore Coll., 1952-53, Parsons Sch. Design, 1954-56, Am. Inst. Graphic Arts, 1955, Sch. Visual Arts, 1957. Staff artist Dave Fris Advt. Agy., Albany, N.Y., 1956-57; free lance illustrator for pub. cos., advt. agys., publs., and others, 1957—; instr. Sch. Visual Arts, 1971-74. Illustrator: (with Leo Dillon) numerous children's books including Whirlwind is a Ghost Dancing (Belting), 1974; Stories and Songs From Uganda (Serwadda), 1974, The Third Gift (Jan Carew), 1974, Song of the Boat (Graham), 1975 (Boston Globe-Horn Book Award Honor book 1976), The Hundred Penny Box (S. Bell Mathis), 1975, Why Mosquitoes Buzz in People's Ears (Aardema), 1975 (Caldicott medal 1976, N.Y. Times Best Book 1975, ALA Notable Book 1975), Ashante to Zulu (Muskgrove), 1976 (Caldicott medal 1977), numerous children's books, the most recent being, 1976 (N.Y. Times Best Book for 1976, Caldecott medal 1977, ALA Notable Book 1976); Children of the Sun, 1980, Two Pairs of Shoes, 1980; artist (with Leo Dillon) stained glass ceiling in, Master Eagle Gallery, N.Y.C.; nat. poster for movie The Fox, 1967; Subject of: book The Art of Leo and Diane Dillon, 1981. Active Neighborhood Assn., Bklyn. Co-recipient Norescon-Hugo Sci. Fiction Achievements award, 1971. Mem. Soc. Illustrators (Certs. of Merit 1968-77), Nat. Graphic Artists Guild. (pres. 1981-83). Office: care Dial Press 1 Dag Hammarskjold Plaza 245 E 47th St New York NY 10017

DILLON, DONALD WARD, management consultant; b. Wichita, Kans., Jan. 31, 1936; s. Maurice B. and Helen M. (Ward) D.; m. Jacquelyn A. Hicks, Dec. 28, 1958; m. Brenda Marie Rager, July 9, 1983. B.Music Edn., Wichita State U., 1959, M.Music Edn., 1961; D.Music. Edn., U. Okla., 1970. Tchr. music Derby (Kans.) public schs., 1959-66; mem. faculty Southeastern La. U., Hammond, 1968-69; exec. dir. Okla. Arts and Humanities Council, 1969-73; asst. dir. fed.-state partnership Nat. Endowment Arts, Washington, 1973-79, dir. grants office, 1979; exec. dir. Music Educators Nat. Conf., Reston, Va., 1979-83; pres. Don Dillon Assocs., Dallas, 1983—; exec. mgmt. cons., bd.dirs. Fund Advancement Music Edn., 1979—. Exec. editor: Music Educators Jour, 1979—, Design for Arts Edn, 1980—; Contbr. articles profl. jours. Bd. dirs. Nat. Com. Arts for Handicapped, 1980—. Mem. Am. Soc. Assn. Execs. Methodist. Home and Office: 4023 High Summit Dr Dallas TX 75234

DILLON, EDWARD, government official, retired air force officer; b. Santa Monica, Calif., Mar. 29, 1932; s. Frank A. and May Florence (Banks) D.; m. Helga Louise Bess, May 26, 1956; 1 dau., Bettina Louise. B.S., Troy (Ala.) State U., 1971; grad., Air War Coll., 1970. Joined U.S. Air Force, 1951, commd. 2d lt., 1953, advanced through grades to maj. gen., 1978; comdr. C-141 assoc. units, Dover AFB, Del., Norton AFB, Calif., 1970-73, comdr. 459 TAW, Andrews AFB, Md., 1973-75, dep. to chief Air Force Res., U.S. Air Force Hdqrs., Washington, 1975-76, comdr. 14th Air Force, Dobbins AFB, Ga., 1976-79, vice comdr., chief operating officer, Robins AFB, Ga., 1979-82, ret., 1982, dep. dir. operational plans, Colorado Springs, Colo., 1982—. Decorated Legion of Merit with 1 oak leaf cluster. Mem. Air Force Assn., Res. Officers Assn., Order of Daedalians. Club: Rotary. Home: 120 Miramar Dr Colorado Springs CO Office: Space Com/ DOX Peterson AFB CO 80914

DILLON, GARY G., manufacturing company executive; b. Eaton, Ohio, May 21, 1934; s. M.H. and E.L. (Clensy) D.; m. Beverly Mulholland, Jan. 2, 1954. B.S. in Bus. Adminstrn, Miami U., Oxford, Ohio, 1955. With Philip Carey Corp., Cin., 1955-57; with Pillsbury Co., Mpls., 1957-78; exec. v.p., chief operating officer King-Seeley Thermos Co./Household Internat., Chgo., 1978-81, pres., chief exec. officer, Prospect Heights, Ill., 1981—; Pres., chief exec. officer Household Mfg. Inc./Household Internat., Prospect Heights, 1982—. Office: Household Mfg Co 2700 Sanders Rd Prospect Heights IL 60070 *

DILLON, GEORGE CHAFFEE, manufacturing company executive; b. Kansas City, Mo., Oct. 29, 1922; s. Edward J. and Mary (Coon) D.; m. Joan Alamo Kent, Sept. 11, 1948; children: Kent, Courtney, Emily. B.S., Harvard U., 1944, M.B.A., 1948. Adminstrv. asst. J. A. Bruening Co., Kansas City, Mo., 1948-51; with Butler Mfg. Co., Kansas City, Mo., 1951—, treas., 1960—, v.p., 1961-63, exec. v.p., 1963-67, pres., 1967-78, chmn. bd., chief exec. officer, 1978—; dir. Johns Manville Corp., Phelps Dodge Corp., Newhall Land and Farming Co. Past. chmn. bd. trustees Midwest Research Inst., Kansas City, Mo.; trustee Mayo Found., Rochester, Minn., Children's Mercy Hosp., Kansas City, Mo. Served to lt. USNR, 1943-46. Home: 600 Westover Rd Kansas City MO 64113 Office: Butler Mfg Co BMA Tower Penn Valley Park Kansas City MO 64141

DILLON, JOHN B., medical educator; b. San Benito, Tex., Oct. 11, 1911; s. John Harper and Lillian (Mitchell) D. M.D., St. Louis U., 1943. Intern Wis. Gen. Hosp., Madison, 1943; cons. anesthesiology Huntington Meml. Hosp., Pasadena, Calif., 1943-46; chief anesthesia service Los Angeles County Hosp., 1946-51, cons., 1951—; asso. clin. prof. surg. anesthesiology U. So. Calif. Med. Sch., 1946-51; mem. faculty U. Calif. at Los Angeles Med. Sch., 1950—, prof., chief anesthesiology, 1953-71, prof., chmn. dept., 1971-73, asst. dean, 1966—; field rep. Joint Commn. on Accreditation Hosps., 1979—, cons., 1980—; cons. anesthesiology Harbor Gen. Hosp., Torrance, Calif., Olive View Sanitarium, San Fernando, Calif., VA Hosp., San Fernando, Cedars of Lebanon Hosp., Los Angeles, St. John's Hosp., Santa Monica, Calif.; cons. Am. Arbitration Assn., 1979—. Served to capt. M.C. AUS, 1944-46. Fellow A.C.P.; mem. A.M.A. (mem. council on assemblies 1970—, chmn, com. emerging health manpower 1971-72, past ho. of dels.), Am. Soc. Anesthesiology. Home: PO Box 759 Koloa Kauai HI 96756

DILLON, MERTON LYNN, historian; b. nr. Addison, Mich., Apr. 4, 1924; s. Henry J. and Cecil Edith (Sanford) D. B.A., Mich. State Normal Coll., 1945; M.A., U. Mich., 1948, Ph.D., 1951. Asst. prof. history N.Mex. Mil. Inst., Roswell, 1951-56; asst. prof. Tex. Tech. Coll., Lubbock, 1956-59, asso. prof., 1959-63, prof., 1963-65; asso. prof. Northern Ill. U., DeKalb, 1965-67; prof. Ohio State U., Columbus, 1967—. Author: Elijah P. Lovejoy, Abolitionist Editor, 1961, Benjamin Lundy and the Struggle for Negro Freedom, 1966, The Abolitionists, the Growth of a Dissenting Minority, 1974; Contbr. articles to profl. jours. Nat. Endowment for the Humanities fellow, 1973-74. Mem. Am. Hist. Assn., Orgn. Am. Historians, So. Hist. Assn. (bd. editors 1959-63), A.A.U.P., A.C.L.U., Phi Beta Kappa. Home: 10460 Addison Rd Jerome MI 49249 Office: Dept History Ohio State U Columbus OH 43210

DILLON, OSCAR WENDELL, JR., mech. engr.; b. Franklin, Pa., May 27, 1928; s. Oscar Wendell and Maude Lena (Gilmore) D.; m. Jane Fruechtemeyer, June 4, 1960; children—Diane, Jane, Donald, David. M.S., Columbia, 1955, D. Engrng. Sci., 1959; Aero. Engr., U. Cin., 1951. Asst. prof. Johns Hopkins, Balt., 1958-63; lectr. Princeton, 1963-65; mem. faculty U. Ky., Lexington, 1965—, prof. engring. mechanics, 1969—, chmn. dept., 1969-72. Contbr. articles to profl. jours. Served to 1st lt. USAF, 1951-53. Recipient Weston award U. Cin., 1951; Outstanding Research award Am. Soc. Engring. Edn., 1966; U. Ky. Research award, 1967; named Outstanding Engring. Alumnus U. Cin., 1970. Mem. ASME. Home: 203 Kirk Dr Nicholasville KY 40356

DILLON, PAUL SANFORD, artist; b. Newport, Vt., Aug. 5, 1943; s. Peter Leo and Ruth Marjorie (Searles) D.; m. Stephanie Jackson, 1975; 1 son, Jesse Sanford. Student, St. Michael's Coll., 1962-65. Constrn. worker, surveyor, musician, sign painter, 1963-65. Performing and rec. musician, 1965-69; painter one-man shows include, Iolas Gallery, N.Y.C., 1978, 80, Asher/Favre Gallery, Los Angeles, 1980; participant various group exhbns. Bd. dirs., mem. artists cons. com. Cedars Hosp., Los Angeles. Recipient New Talent award Los Angeles County Mus. Art, 1975, purchase prize Wash. State Mus., 1977. Mem. Los Angeles Inst. Contemporary Art. Home: 3660 W Pico Blvd Los Angeles CA 90019

DILLON, PAUL WILSON, supermarket chain executive; b. Hutchinson, Kans., Aug. 4, 1926; s. Clyde Wilson and Flora L. (Jones) D.; m. Ruth Muirhead, Aug. 19, 1949; children—David B., Elizabeth Ann Dillon Ramseyer, Mary M. Dillon Esau. B.S. in Bus, U. Kans., 1950. With Dillon Cos., Inc., Hutchinson, 1950—, sec.-treas., 1965-80, sr. v.p., 1980—, also dir. Dir. First Fed. Savs. & Loan Assn., Hutchinson.; Active local Boy Scouts Am., 1955—; trustee, treas. Wesley Towers Methodist Retirement Home, 1970. Served with USNR, 1944-45. Mem. Am. Soc. Corp. Secs., Am. Legion, VFW, Phi Kappa Psi. Republican. Presbyterian. Club: Elks. Home: 207 Kisiwa Pkwy Hutchinson KS 67501 Office: 700 E 30th St Hutchinson KS 67501

DILLON, RAY E., retail and supermarket stores executive; b. 1924. Student, Kans. U. With Dillon Cos., Hutchinson, Kans., 1946—, pres., 1962-79; former chmn. bd., now hon. chmn. Dillon Cos.; also dir. Dillon Cos. Office: Dillon Cos Inc 700 E 30th Ave PO Box 1266 Hutchinson KS 67501 *

DILLON, RICHARD HUGH, author, librarian; b. Sausalito, Calif., Jan. 16, 1924; s. William T. and Alice M. (Burke) D.; m. Barbara A. Sutherland, June 9, 1950; children: Brian, David, Ross. A.A. with hon. mention, U. Calif.-Berkeley, 1943, A.B. with honors in History, 1948, M.A., 1949, B.S. in L.S, 1950. Head Sutro Library, San Francisco, 1953—; tchr. summer sessions UCLA, 1964, U. San Francisco, 1959—, U. Hawaii, 1962. Author: Embarcadero, 1959 (2d place nonfiction Phelan awards 1959), The Gila Trail, 1960, Shanghaiing Days, 1961, California Trail Herd, 1961, The Hatchet Men, 1962, Meriwether Lewis, 1965 (Gold medal Commonwealth Club Calif. 1966), J. Ross Browne, 1965, The Legend of Grizzly Adams, 1966, Fool's Gold, 1967 (Silver medal Commonwealth Club Calif. 1967), Humbugs and Heroes, 1970, Burnt-Out Fires, 1973; K3Exploring the Mother Lode Country, 1974 (Spur award Western Writers Am. 1974), Siskiyou Trail, 1975, We Have Met the Enemy, 1978, High Steel, 1979, Great Expectations, 1980, Delta Country, 1982. Served with inf. AUS, World War II; ETO. Decorated Purple Heart; recipient awards of merit Calif. Hist. Soc., Am. Assn. State and Local History for all-around research and pub.; Laura Bride Powers award for disting. service to city of San Francisco, 1970. Fellow Calif. Hist. Soc.; mem. Western History Assn.; Mem. Book Club Calif. (pres. 1977-79), Phi Beta Kappa. Home: 98 Alta Vista Ave Mill Valley CA 94941

DILLON, RICHARD WAYNE, supermarket executive; b. Hutchinson, Kans., Sept. 8, 1927; s. Ray E. and Stella A. (Schmitt) D.; m. Carolyn A. Critser, May 3, 1952; children: Bradley D., William R., Steven R. Student, Kans. U., 1949-51. Meat supr. Dillon Food Stores, 1953-57, v.p., 1957-65; exec. v.p. Dillon Co., Inc., Hutchinson, 1965-79, pres., 1979-82, vice chmn., 1982—. Dir. Salt City Fed. Savs. & Loan Assn.; Trustee Kans. 4-H Found.; former pres., mem. Hutchinson Sch. Bd. Served with USAAF, 1945-46. Home: 4600 E 28th St Hutchinson KS 67501 Office: 700 E 30th St Hutchinson KS 67501

DILLON, ROBERT MORTON, architect, research executive; b. Seattle, Oct. 27, 1923; s. James Richard and Lucille (Morton) D.; m. Mary Charlotte Beeson, Jan. 6, 1943; children: Robert Thomas, Colleen Marie Dillon Brown, Patrick Morton. Student, U. Ill., 1946-47; B. Arch., U. Wash., 1949; M.A. in Architecture, U. Fla., 1954.

Registered architect, Fla. Designer-draftsman Williams and Longstreet (Architects), Greenville, S.C., 1949-50, William G. Lyles, Bissett, Carlisle & Wolff (Architects), Columbia, S.C., 1949-1950, Robert M. Dillon and Wm. B. Eaton (Architects), Gainesville, Fla., 1952-55; staff architect Bldg. Research Adv. Bd., Nat. Acad. Scis.-NRC, Washington, 1955-56, project dir., 1956-58, exec. dir., 1958-77; exec. sec. U.S. nat. com. for Conseil Internat. du Batiment, 1962-74; Sec. U.S. Planning Com. 2d Internat. Conf. on Permafrost, Yakutsk, USSR, 1972-74; exec. asst. to pres. Nat. Inst. Bldg. Scis., Washington, 1978-81, v.p., 1982-84; exec. v.p. Am. Council Constrn. Edn., Washington, 1984—; Asst. prof. architecture Clemson Coll., 1949-50; instr., asst. prof. architecture U. Fla., 1950-55; lectr. structural theory and design Catholic U. Am., 1956-62; guest lectr. Air Force Inst. Tech., Wright-Patterson AFB, 1964-65; distinguished faculty Acad. Code Adminstrn. and Enforcement, U. Ill., 1972; Professorial lectr. engring. George Washington U., 1973-77, 81-82; vis. prof. architecture U. Utah, 1978; vis. prof. Coll. Environ. Design, U. Okla., 1984. Author: (with S.W. Crawley) Steel Buildings: Analysis and Design, 1970, 3d edit., 1983; contbg. author: Funk and Wagnall's New Ency, 1972. Cons. Ednl. Facilities Labs., N.Y.C., 1958-71; Mem. adv. com., low-income housing demonstration program HUD, Washington, 1964-67; mem. working groups U.S.-USSR Agreement on Housing and Other Construction, 1975—; mem. sub-panel on housing White House Panel on Civilian Tech., Washington, 1961-62; mem. advs. to the F. Stuart Fitzpatrick Meml. Award Trustee, 1969—, chmn., 1974-78; mem. adv. panel Basic Homes Program OEO and HUD, 1972-77; mem. Nat. Adv. Council on Research in Energy Conservation, 1975-78; mem. adv. com. Council Am. Bldg. Ofcls., 1976—; mem. tech. council on bldg. codes and standards Nat. Conf. of States, 1977-78. Served with USNR, 1942-45. Mem. AIA (mem. com. on research for architecture 1962-67, chmn. 1969, chmn. com. archtl. barriers 1967-68, mem. nat. housing com. 1970-72, 84—), Nat. Acad. Code Adminstrn. (trustee 1976-80, mem. exec. com. 1978-82, mem. new bd. dirs. 1980-82, 83—, sec.-treas. 1981-82), Am. Real Estate and Urban Econs. Assn., Md. Soc. Architects, ASCE (task com. on cold regions 1977-79, tech. council on codes and standards, exec. com. 1976-81, sec, tech. council on codes and standards, exec. com. 1977-78, mem. tech. council on cold regions engring., exec. com. 1979—, vice chmn. 1980-81, chmn. 1981), Am. Inst. Steel Constrn., Sigma Lambda Chi. Home: 811 Arrington Dr Silver Spring MD 20901 Office: 1015 15th St NW Suite 700 Washington DC 20005

DILLON, ROBERT SHERWOOD, ambassador; b. Chgo., Jan. 7, 1929; s. Dale Crowell and Viola May (Sherwood) D.; m. Caroline Sue Burch, June 16, 1951; children: Dale Kathleen Dillon Lips, Robert S., John Irving, Elizabeth Sue, Thomas Carter. B.A., Duke U., 1951; postgrad., Princeton U., 1959. Commd. fgn. service officer Dept. State, 1956, vice consul, Puerto La Cruz, Venezuela, 1956-58, Izmir, Turkey, 1960-62, polit. officer, Ankara, Turkey, 1962-66, personnel officer, Washington, 1966-68; spl. asst. Sec. State for Polit. Affairs, 1968-70; dep. prin. officer Am. Consulate Gen., Istanbul Dept. State, Washington, 1971-74, dep. chief of mission, Kuala Lumpur, Malaysia, 1974-77, Ankara, Turkey, 1977-80, Cairo, Egypt, 1980-81, ambassador to Lebanon, Beirut, 1981—. Served with U.S. Army, 1947-49. Mem. Am. Fgn. Service Assn., Sigma Alpha Epsilon. Unitarian. Home: American Embassy-Beirut Dept State Washington DC 20520 Office: American Embassy Ave de Paris Beirut Lebanon

DILLON, THOMAS ANDREW, government official; b. White Plains, N.Y., June 30, 1944; s. Daniel Aloysius and Dorthy (James) D.; m. Carol Nell Armstrong, Dec. 28, 1968; children: Daniel Parker, Katherine Grace. A.B., Harvard Coll., 1966; Ph.D., U. Colo., 1969. Sect. chief Nat. Bur. Standards, Boulder, Colo., 1969-73, sr. program analyst, Gaithersburg, Md., 1973-76, dep. dir., Gaithersburg, 1978-80; div. dir. ERDA Dept. Energy, Germantown, Md., 1976-78, dep. asst. sec., Washington, 1980—. Home: 11901 Clover Knoll Gaithersburg MD 20878 Office: Dept Energy 1000 Independence Ave SW Washington DC 20585

DILLON, THOMAS CHURCH, advertising executive; b. Seattle, Mar. 27, 1915; s. Thomas J. and Clarissa (Church) D.; m. Georgiana Adams, Nov. 8, 1939 (dec. May 1964); children: Thomas Adams, Victoria Caroline, George Anthony; m. Patricia Doran, 1965. Student, Harvard U., 1933-36. With Batten, Barton, Durstine & Osborn, Inc., 1938-80, successively copy writer, Mpls., creative head, San Francisco, Los Angeles, 1938-48, v.p., 1948-59, mgr., 1957-58, treas., 1958-62, exec. v.p., 1959-64, gen. mgr., 1962-64, pres., 1964-75, chief exec. officer, 1967-77, chmn. bd., 1975—; pres. (BBDO Internat., Inc.), 1971-75, chief exec. officer, 1971-77, chmn. bd., 1975-80, now dir.; pres. Mintaka, Inc., 1980-83, Am. Bloodpressure Ctrs., Inc., 1983—; dir. MTC Properties, Inc., Midwest Communications, Inc. Elected to Advt. Hall of Fame, 1980. Clubs: Economic, Harvard (N.Y.C.). Home: 870 UN Plaza New York NY 10017 Office: 866 UN Plaza New York NY 10017

DILLON, W. MARTIN, steel and wire manufacturing executive; b. Sterling, Ill., Mar. 19, 1910; s. Paul Washington and Crete (Blackman) D.; m. Helene Reynolds, June 20, 1931; children—Peter W., Margo, Gale (Mrs. Philip Inglee). Grad., Culver Mil. Acad., 1929; student, Babson Inst., 1929-30; H.H.D., DePaul U., U. Chgo., U. Dubuque, Iowa. Asst. to pres. Northwestern Steel & Wire Co. (name formerly Northwestern Barb Wire Co.), 1939-48, pres., 1951-80, chmn. bd., 1980—; pres. Northwestern Products Co., 1950—. Bd. dirs. Sterling-Rock Falls Community Trust. Mem. Assn. Iron and Steel Engrs., C. of C., Am. Iron and Steel Inst. (dir.), NAM, Cum Laude Soc. (Culver Mil. Acad.). Clubs: Metropolitan, Union League (Chgo.). Home: PO Box 537 Sterling IL 61081 Office: Northwestern Steel & Wire Co Sterling IL 61081

DILLON, WILTON STERLING, anthropologist, ofcl. Smithsonian Instn.; b. Yale, Okla., July 13, 1923; s. Earl Henry and Edith Holland (Canfield) D.; m. Virginia Leigh Harris, Jan. 20, 1956; 1 son, Wilton Harris. B.A., U. Calif., Berkeley, 1951; postgrad., Inst. Ethnology, U. Paris, U. Leyden, 1951-52; Ph.D., Columbia U., 1961. News reporter Holdenville (Okla.) Daily News, 1936-41; publicity dir. Okla. Bapt. U., 1941-42; news reporter U. Ala. News Bur., 1942-43; info. specialist, civilian mem. Civil Info. and Edn. Sect. SCAP, Tokyo, 1946-49; vis. lectr. sociology and anthropology Hobart and William Smith colls., Geneva, N.Y., 1953-54; staff anthropologist Japan Soc. N.Y.; also lectr. Japanese studies Fordham U., 1954; dir. Clearinghouse for Research in Human Orgn., Soc. Applied Anthropology, N.Y.C., 1954-56; cons. Overseas Tng. and Research, Inc., Washington, 1956; exec. sec., dir. research Phelps-Stokes Fund N.Y.; including dir. research project on higher edn. and African nationhood U. Ghana, 1961-62; vis. lectr. Columbia U., New Sch. Social Research, 1957-63; mem. staff Office Fgn. Sec. Nat. Acad. Scis., 1963-69; dir. seminars Smithsonian Inst., Washington, 1969-75, dir. symposia and seminars, 1975—; adj. prof. U. Ala., 1971—; chmn. Battle of Yorktown Bicentennial observance Smithsonian Instn., 1981. Author: Gifts and Nations, 1968, also articles.; Editor: (with John F. Eisenberg) Man and Beast: Comparative Social Behavior, 1971, The Cultural Drama, 1974; editorial bd.: Human Orgn, 1956-66. Del. numerous internat. confs. including UNESCO, Pugwash; mem. adv. council on Africa Dept. State, 1964-68; mem. Hazen Found., Danforth Found., 1962—; mem. adv. com. internat. div. Am. Friends Service Com., 1962-83; hon. commr. Internat. Year of Child, 1979-80; pres. bd. dirs. Inst. Intercultural Studies, N.Y.C.; sec. bd. trustees Phelps-Stokes Fund; sec.-treas., bd. dirs. Inst. Psychiatry and Fgn. Affairs; mem. bd. visitors Wake Forest U., 1978-81. Served with USAAF, 1943-46. Decorated Chevalier de l'ordre les arts et lettres, 1983; Woodrow Wilson Internat. Center for Scholars guest scholar, 1970. Fellow Am. Anthrop. Assn., African Studies Assn., Soc. Applied Anthropology, AAAS; mem. Lit. Soc. Washington Anthrop. Soc. Washington. Episcopalian (lay reader N.Y. diocese 1958-60). Home: 1446 Woodacre Dr McLean VA 22101 Office: Smithsonian Instn Washington DC 20560

DILLOW, NANCY ELIZABETH, museum curator; b. Toronto, Ont., Can., 1928. B.A. in Art and Archaeology with honours, U. Toronto, 1952. With Crown Trust Co., 52-53; mem. staff Art Gallery Toronto, 1956-67, curator extension and edn., 1965-67; dir. Norman Mackenzie Art Gallery, U. Regina, Sask., 1967-79; chief curator Winnipeg (Man.) Art Gahlery, 1980—; mem. fine arts adv. com. Dept. Public Works, 1968-72; pres. Sask. Museums Assn., 1976-78; adv. com. mus. policy Sask. Heritage Bds., 1977-79; mem. Prairie regional adv. com. Can. Conservation Inst., 1978—. Author mus. catalogues. Chmn. bd. Regina Modern Dance Works, 1979. Grantee Can. Council, 1957. Mem. Can. Museums Assn. (council 1967-69), Western Can. Art Assn. (dir. 1971-73), Can. Art Mus. Dirs. Orgn. (sec. 1971-75, pres. 1977-79), Nat. Museums Can. (cons. com. 1972-74). Address: Winnipeg Art Gallery 300 Memorial Blvd Winnipeg MB R3C 1V1 Canada

DILLS, JAMES ARLOF, publishing company executive; b. Guelph, Ont., Can., Aug. 11, 1930; s. George Arlof and Isma Marie (MacPherson) D.; m. Shirley Jean Elliott, Aug. 16, 1952; children—Steven George, James Mark, Paul David, Catherine Jane, Carolyn Shirley. Grad. in journalism, Ryerson Poly. Inst., 1951. Pub. The Can. Champion, Milton, Ont., 1966-78, The Georgetown (Ont.) Ind., 1973-78; sec.-treas. Dills Printing and Pub. Co. Ltd., Acton, Ont., 1954—; exec. dir. Can. Community Newspapers Assn., Toronto, Ont., 1979—; mem. adv. com. journalism program Sheridan Coll., 1965-78; pres. Ont. Weekly Newspapers Assn., 1975—. Pres. Milton Hist. Soc., 1977-80. Named Citizen of Yr., Milton, 1978. Mem. Inst. Assn. Execs., Newspaper Mgrs. Assn. Club: Milton Rotary (pres. 1957). Office: 705 University Ave Toronto ON M5J 1T6 Canada

DILUGLIO, THOMAS ROSS, state lieutenant governor; b. Providence, Nov. 25, 1931; s. Thomas and Elvira (Rossi) DiL.; m. Loretta Agnes Migliaccio; children: Thomas A., Mark W., Anthony R., Vera H., Beth E. A.B., Brown U.; LL.D., Boston U. Pres. Highland Orchards, Inc., 1972—, Queen Restaurant, 1972—; town solicitor, 1970—; lt. gov. State of R.I., Providence, 1976—. Treas. Johnston Democratic Town Com., 1958-64, chmn., 1964-78; mem. R.I. State Senate, 1960-64; chmn. legis. com. R.I. Constl. Conv., 1964-67; del. Dem. Nat. Conv., 1976, 80. Mem. Phi Delta Theta. Roman Catholic. Lodge: United Comml. Travelers. Office: State House 317 Providence RI 02903 *

DILUZIO, NICHOLAS ROBERT, educator, physiologist; b. Hazleton, Pa., May 4, 1926; s. Nicholas and Carmela (Searfella) DiL.; m. Gertrude Alma Dezagottis, June 10, 1948; children—Nicholas Mark, Tamara Ann, Daniel Val. B.S., U. Scranton, 1950; Ph.D. (USPHS fellow), U. Tenn., 1954. Investigator Dorn Lab. for Med. Research, Bradford, Pa., 1954, Oak Ridge Nat. Lab., 1956, U.S. Naval Radiol. Def. Lab., 1958; mem. faculty U. Tenn. Med. Units, Memphis, 1955-68, prof., 1962-64, chmn. physiology and biophysics dept., 1965-68; prof., chmn. dept. physiology Tulane U. Med. Sch., 1968—. Editor: Advances in Experimental Medicine and Biology; Contbr. articles profl. jours. Mem. Tenn. Adv. Com. on Atomic Energy, 1958-68; mem. sci. adv. bd. Nat. Council on Alcoholism, 1963-68. Recipient Lederle Med. Faculty award, 1958-61. Mem. AAAS, Am. Physiol. Soc., Am. Heart Assn., Soc. for Exptl. Biology and Medicine, Reticuloendotheliel Soc. (pres. 1966-68). Patentee in field. Home: 732 Fairfield Ave Gretna LA 70053 Office: Tulane U Sch Medicine New Orleans LA 70112

DILWORTH, EDWIN EARLE, obstetrician, gynecologist; b. Jasper, Ala., June 28, 1914; s. Tranny and Bertie (Caldwell) D.; m. Neida May Humphrey, June 17, 1939; children: John Edwin, Robert Earle, Nancy. A.B., U. Ala., 1936; M.D., Tulane U., 1940. Diplomate: Am. Bd. Ob-Gyn. Intern, then resident in ob-gyn Shreveport (La.) Charity Hosp., 1940-44; practice medicine specializing in ob-gyn, Shreveport, 1959-60; chief ob-gyn Schumpert Meml. Med. Center, 1951, pres. staff, 1954; chief ob-gyn Confederate Meml. Med. Center, Shreveport, 1954-76, pres. staff, 1959; clin. prof. La. State U. Med. Sch., Shreveport, 1967—. Contbr. articles to profl. jours. Head med. div. Shreveport United Way, 1972. Served to capt. M.C. AUS, 1944-46. Recipient Disting. Service award Shreveport Med. Soc., 1980. Fellow Am. Coll. Ob-Gyn (a founder), ACS; mem. Central Assn. Ob-Gyn, Southeastern Assn. Ob-Gyn, So. Gynec. and Obstet. Soc. Club: Shreveport Skeet. Home: 660 Thora Blvd Shreveport LA 71106 Office: 865 Margaret Pl Shreveport LA 71101

DILWORTH, JOSEPH RICHARDSON, investment banker; b. Hewlett, N.Y., June 9, 1916; s. Dewees Wood and Edith (Logan) D.; m. Elizabeth Cushing, June 15, 1940; children—Joseph Richardson, Melissa McKay (Mrs. Herbert Gold), Alexandra Cushing, Charles Dewees. A.B., Yale, 1938, LL.B., 1942. Bar: Conn. bar 1942. Buying dept. Kuhn, Loeb & Co., 1946-51, partner, 1951-58; with Rockefeller Family & Assocs., 1958-81; chmn. bd., now dir. Rockefeller Center, Inc.; dir. R.H. Macy & Co., Inc., Pan Holding, Squibb Corp., Chrysler Corp., Selected Risk Investments. Mem. Council Fgn. Relations.; Successor trustee Yale Corp.; trustee Colonial Williamsburg Found.; chmn., trustee Inst. for Advanced Study; trustee, vice chmn. Met. Mus. Art; trustee Rockefeller U. Served as lt. comdr. USNR, 1942-45. Mem. Am. Legion, Pilgrims of U.S., Phi Beta Kappa. Republican. Clubs: Links, Century Assn., Knickerbocker (N.Y.C.). Home: 141 Hodge Rd Princeton NJ 08540 Office: care metropolitan museum of art 5th ave at 82nd street New York NY 10028

DIMAGGIO, FRANK LOUIS, civil engineering educator; b. N.Y.C., Sept. 2, 1929; s. Serafino and Maria (Barbuto) DiM.; m. Irene C. Koehn, Dec. 15, 1963; children: Samuel, Peter. B.S., Columbia U., 1950, M.S., 1951, Ph.D., 1954. Registered profl. engr., N.Y. Prof. civil engring. Columbia U., 1956—, chmn. dept., 1975-78, Carleton prof., 1978—; cons. in field, 1956—. Served with AUS, 1954-56. NSF sr. postdoctoral fellow, 1962-63. Fellow ASCE (exec. com. engring. mech. div. 1982-83); mem. Sigma Xi. Home: 138 Van Orden Ave Leonia NJ 07605 Office: Dept Civil Engring and Engring Mechanics Columbia Univ New York NY 10027

DIMAN, WILLIAM ALEXANDER, life insurance company executive; b. Greenwood, Miss., Mar. 31, 1917; s. Harry and Wheat (Burkhalter) D.; m. Phyllis H. Heath, Feb. 23, 1976; children: Charles N., Alice B. Diman Pratt, Margaret C. Diploma, Bentley Sch. Acctg., 1936-38; student, Life Office Mgmt. Inst., 1948-53; degree, MIT, 1958, Aspen Inst., 1968. C.P.A., Mass. Auditor Charles F. Rittenhouse & Co., Boston, 1938-42; with John Hancock Mut. Life Ins. Co., Boston, 1942—, controller, 1964—, sr. v.p., 1975—; dir. John Hancock Advisers, Inc., John Hancock Distbrs., Inc., John Hancock Realty Devel. Corp.; trustee Newton Savs. Bank. Alderman City of Newton, Mass., 1952-55, 62-63; treas. Rebecca Pomeroy Found.; trustee Newton Cemetary Corp. Served to lt. USNR, 1944-46. Fellow Life Office Mgmt. Inst.; mem. Am. Inst. C.P.A.s, Fin. Execs. Inst. (v.p. N.E. area 1973—). Home: 157 Lowell Rd Wellesley MA 02181 Office: John Hancock Mutual Life Ins Co John Hancock Pl PO Box 111 Boston MA 02117

DIMARTINO, JOSEPH SALVATORE, investment company executive; b. Bklyn., Oct. 2, 1943; s. Raymond and Celia (Mecurio) DiM.; m. Linda Jeanne Rappa, Oct. 21, 1967; children: Joseph James, Jennifer Lynne. B.S. in Econs., Manhattan Coll., 1965; postgrad., NYU, 1966-68. Credit analyst Dun and Bradstreet, N.Y.C., 1965-66; investment officer Chase Manhattan Bank, N.Y.C., 1966-70, 2d v.p., 1971; investment officer, dir. various mut. funds Dreyfus Corp., N.Y.C., 1973—, pres., chief operating officer, 1982—. Office: Dreyfus Corp 767 Fifth Ave 35th Floor New York NY 10153

DI MARTINO (DENDARIARENA), RITA, utility company executive, government representative; b. Bklyn., Mar. 7, 1937; d. Juan and Paquita (Cruz) Dendariarena; m., Oct. 5, 1957 (div. Aug. 1979); children: Vickie Ann, Anthony Robert, Celeste Frances. A.A., S.I. Community Coll., 1974; B.A., Richmond Coll., 1976; M.P.A., C.W. Post Coll., L.I. U., 1977. Sr. bus. cons. N.Y. State Dept. Commerce, N.Y.C., 1974-78; alt. U.S. rep. UNICEF, 1982, U.S. rep., 1983—; dist. mgr.-corp. relations AT&T Co., N.Y.C., 1979—; pres. AVC Cons. Corp., N.Y.C.; mem. bd. vistors Nat. Ctr. Bilingual Research, 1980—. Mem. adv. bd. Doctors Hosp., S.I., 1977—; mem. pres.'s adv. council Coll. S.I.; bd. dirs., sec. bd. United Way S.I., 1975-78; loanee exec. United Way, 1983; chairperson Republican Nat. Hispanic Assembly N.Y. State, 1977—; vice chairperson, mem. exec. com. Rep. Com. N.Y. State. Recipient award or Merit Office of Pres. Borough S.I., N.Y. State Dept. Commerce award, cert. recognition U.S. Immigration and Naturalization Service, 1977, cert. appreciation Pace U. Ctr. Minority Bus. Edn., 1978, Roberto Clemente Humanitarian award Boricua Coll., 1983; honoree Richmond County Spanish Am. Club, 1975, S.I. Community Corp., 1976, Kings County Puerto Rican Leadership Conf., Rep. Nat. Hispanic Assembly N.Y. State, 1982; contbns. to Small Bus. Community honoree Spanish Merchants and Grocers Assn., 1983. Mem. Nat. Council La Raza (exec. com. 1978—, bd. dirs. 1978—, chairperson nominations com.), Nat. Assn. Lationo Elected and Appted. Ofcls. (bd. dirs. 1978—), N.Y. State Hispanic C. of C. (v.p. 1983—). Club: Women's Nat. Rep. Home: 1337 Arden Ave Staten Island NY 10022 Office: AT&T 550 Madison Ave Room 2435 New York NY 10022

DI MATTEO, JOHN R., newspaper executive; b. Portland, Maine, Sept. 13, 1931; s. Rosario and Josephine (Prioetti) Di M.; m. Patricia H. Huddleston, Sept. 9, 1956; children: Susan, Martha, Andrew. B.S., Babson Coll., 1953. C.P.A., Maine. With Arthur Andersen & Co. (C.P.A.s), Boston, 1955-59; with Jordan & Jordan, Portland, 1959-72, partner, 1963-72; exec. v.p., gen. mgr. Guy Gannett Pub. Co., Portland, 1972-78, pres., dir., 1978—; dir. Guy Gannet Broadcasting Services. Trustee Maine Savs. Bank, Portland.; Trustee, treas. Westbrook Coll.; trustee Maine Med. Center, Portland. Served with AUS, 1953-55. Mem. Am. Inst. C.P.A.s. Office: 390 Congress St Portland ME 04104

DI MEO, DOMINICK, artist, sculptor; b. Niagara Falls, N.Y., Feb. 1, 1927; s. Antonio and Michelina (Sandonato) Di M.; m. Judith S. Cousins, Dec. 26, 1963. B.F.A., Sch. Art Inst., Chgo., 1952; M.F.A., State U. Iowa, 1953. Vis. artist Sch. of Art Inst. Chgo., 1977; instr. Chgo. Acad. Fine Arts, 1967-69. One man shows include, Lake Forest (Ill.) Coll., 1955, Bemidji (Minn.) Coll., 1963, Fairweather-Hardin Gallery, Chgo., 1964, 68, 71, Barat Coll., Lake Forest, 1966, Chgo. Public Library, Kendall Coll., Evanston, Ill., 1967, Westbroadway Gallery, N.Y.C., 1973, 75, 76, Project Studios One, Long Island City, N.Y., 1982, group exhbns. include, Albright-Knox Art Gallery, Buffalo, 1953, 54, Art Inst. Chgo, 1959, 60, 61, 63, 65, 66, 67, 68, 71, 76, 79, Mus. Contemporary Art, Chgo., 1969, Joan Miro Internat. Drawing Prize Competition, Barcelona, Spain, 1977, 78, 79, 80; represented in: permanent collections Art Inst. Chgo, Art Inst. Chgo., Whitney Mus. Am. Art, N.Y.C., U. Mass., Amherst, Nat. Collection Fine Arts, Smithsonian Instn., Elmhurst Coll. Guggenheim Found. fellow, 1972; NEA fellow in sculpture, 1982. Mem. Momentum (founding mem.), Participating Artists Chgo.), Artists Collaborative. Address: 429 Broome New York NY 10013

DIMICHAEL, SALVATORE GEORGE, psychologist; b. N.Y.C., Apr. 21, 1914; s. George and Carmela (Pellettiere) DiM.; m. Eleanor Marie Gasparovich, June 1, 1946; children—Nicholas James, Carmelita, Stephen M. B.S. cum laude, Fordham Coll., 1935; M.A., Fordham U., 1939, Ph.D., 1943. Diplomate: Am. Bd. Examiners in Profl. Psychology. Asst. dir., supr. teaching methods AAF Instrs. Sch., St. Louis, 1942-43; asst. prof., dir. tchr. tng. St. Louis U., 1943-44; cons., psychol. services Vocational Rehab. Adminstrn., HEW, Washington, 1944-53, regional rep., 1957-66, regional asst. commr., 1966-67; dir. ICD Rehab. and Research Center, 1968-76; cons., 1977—; lectr. psychology, supr. counsel-trainees Cath. U. Am., 1946-53. Author: Vocational Rehabilitation: A Major Social Force, 1964; Mem. editorial adv. bd.: Personnel and Guidance Jour, 1959-62, Jour. of Rehab, 1963-69. Exec. dir. Nat. Assn. for Retarded Children, N.Y.C., 1954-57; Exec. sec. Nat. Psychol. Research Council for the Blind, 1949-53; Exec. com. Pres.' Com. Employment Handicapped. Recipient Family Action award Nat. Catholic Welfare Conf., 1955; Merit award Phi Mu Sigma, 1956; Encaenia award Fordham Coll., 1960; Outstanding Contbr. award Am. Rehab. Counseling Assn., 1972; Distinguished Service award Pres.'s Com. on Employment Handicapped, 1977. Fellow Am. Psychol. Assn. (pres. div. psychologists in rehab. 1961-62), Am. Assn. on Mental Deficiency; mem. Am Personnel and Guidance Assn. (pres. div. rehab. counseling 1957-58), D.C. Personnel and Guidance Assn. (pres.), Am. Cath. Psychol. Assn. (pres. 1958-59, Nat. Vocat. Guidance Assn.). Home and Office: 13-38 Parsons Blvd Whitestone NY 11357

DI MITRI, PIERO, fashion designer; b. Palermo, Italy, July 1, 1933; came to U.S., 1963, naturalized, 1970; s. Raffaele and Michelangela (Mirabella) Dimitri; m. Maria Parisi, Nov. 9, 1955; children: Rafael, Michele, Robert, Peter. Diploma, Milan (Italy) Fashion Inst., 1956. Designer, tailor Caraceni, Rome, 1950-52, Litrico, 1953-56; owner, mgr. Custom and Design Studios, Milan, 1957-63, Palermo, Sicily, 1957-63, DiMitri of Italy, N.Y.C., 1964—, DiMitri Couture, Ltd., 1980—; designer, cons. Michael Stern Menswear Co., Rochester, N.Y., 1972—, Melbo Clothing Inc., Osaka, Japan, 1976—, Malcolm Kenneth Coats, Phila., 1974—, Bert Paley Leathers, 1974—. Creator: Pia by DiMitri (women's cologne and perfume), 1978, DiMitri (men's cologne), 1978. Recipient Coty Fashion Critics award for menswear, 1973, Coty Return award, 1974, Coty Hall of Fame award, 1975. Mem. Am. Fashion Designers, Mens' Fashion Assn. Roman Catholic. Clubs: Jockey (Miami); Atrium, Le Club (N.Y.C.); Club A. Office: 110 Greene St New York NY 10012

DIMITRIADIS, ANDRE C., airline executive; b. Istanbul, Turkey, Sept. 29, 1940; s. Constantine N. and Terry D. B.S., Robert Coll., Istanbul, 1964; M.S., Princeton U., 1965, NYU, 1967, Ph.D., 1970. Analyst Mobil Oil Internat., N.Y.C., 1965-67; mgr. TWA, N.Y.C., 1967-73; dir. Pan Am. Airways, N.Y.C., 1973-76, asst. treas., 1976-79; v.p., chief fin. officer Air Calif., Newport Beach, 1979-82; sr. v.p., chief fin. officer Western Airlines, Los Angeles, 1982—, dir. Democrat. Greek Orthodox. Home: Marquesas Way Apt 309D Marina del Rey CA 90292 Office: Western Airlines 6060 Avion Dr Los Angeles CA 90045

DIMITRIOS I (DIMITRIOS PAPADOPOULOS), archbishop, ecumenical patriarch; b. Istanbul, Turkey, Sept. 8, 1914. Student, Theol. Sch. Halki, Heybeliada-Istanbul. Ordained dean Greek Orthodox Ch., 1937, ordained priest, 1942; preacher, Edessa, Greece, 1937-38, Parish of Ferikoy-Istanbul, 1939-45; priest Orthodox community, Teheran, Iran, 1945-50, head priest, Ferikoy-Istanbul, 1950-64, bishop of, Elaia; aux. bishop of Patriarch Athenagoras, Istanbul, 1964-72; metropolitan of Imvos and Tenedos, 1972; Archbishop of Constantinople and Ecumenical Patriarch, 1972—. Office: Rum Ortoks Patrikhanesi H Fener Istanbul Turkey *

DIMITRY, JOHN RANDOLPH, college president; b. Detroit, Feb. 15, i929; s. Dracos Alexander and Elizabeth Stanton (Bisl) D.; m. Audrey Oktavec, Aug. 20, 1952; children: Mark, Jane, Kate. Student, Spring Hill Coll., 1948-49; B.A., Wayne State U., 1952, M.S., 1954, Ed.D., 1966. Tchr., Highland Park (Mich.) Jr. Coll., 1954-61; also instr. Wayne State U., part-time 1957-61; research asso. Macomb County Community Coll., Warren, Mich., 1962-63, adminstrv. asst., 1963, asst. to pres., 1963-65, dir. div. research and devel., 1965-66, dean center campus, 1966-67, pres., 1967-75, No. Essex Community Coll., Haverhill, Mass., 1975—; mem. Gov.'s Commn. on Higher Edn., 1973—; pres. Mich. Community Coll. Assn., 1972-73. Mem. state adv. council on vocat. edn. Mich. Dept. Edn., 1969-72, council on higher edn., 1972—; mem. pres.'s adv. com. ACCT. Served with AUS, 1947-48, 52-53. Kellogg Found. fellow Community Coll. Adminstrn., 1961-63. Home: Old Wharf Rd West Newbury MA 01985

DIMITRY, THEODORE GEORGE, lawyer; b. New Orleans, Jan. 15, 1937; s. Theodore Jospeh and Ouida Marion (Seiler) D.; m. Sara Elizabeth; 1 son, Theodore Warren. B.S., Tulane U., 1958, J.D., 1960. Bar: La. 1960, Tex. 1964. Assoc. firm Phelps, Dunbar, Marks, Claverie & Sims, New Orleans, 1965-69, ptnr., 1969-75; ptnr. firm Vinson & Elkins, Houston, 1975—; research fellow Southwestern Legal Found., Dallas, 1973—; speaker on maritime law, offshore contracting, resource devel. at profl. seminars, 1975—. Contbr. articles to profl. jours. Mem. Maritime Law Assn. U.S., Southeastern Admiralty Law Inst., Am. Soc. Internat. Law, ABA. Office: Vinson & Elkins First City Tower Houston TX 77002

DIMMA, WILLIAM ANDREW, real estate executive; b. Montreal, Que., Can., Aug. 13, 1928; s. William Roy and Lillian Noreen (Miller) D.; m. Katherine Louise Vacy Ash, May 13, 1961; children: Suzanne Elizabeth Irene, Katherine Lillian Louise. B.A. in Sci, U. Toronto, 1948; M.M.P., Harvard U., 1956, D.B.A., 1973; M.B.A., York U., Toronto, 1969. Registered profl. engr., Ont. With Union Carbide Can. Ltd., 1948-69, exec. v.p., dir., 1967-69; dean Faculty Adminstrv. Studies; prof. bus. adminstrn. York U., 1973-75; pres., dir. Torstar Corp., Toronto, 1976-78, Toronto Star Newspapers Ltd., 1976-78, A.E. LePage Ltd., Toronto, 1979—; chmn. bd. Polysar Ltd.; chmn. Fed. Govt Com. Fin. Services; dir. Continental Bank, Simpsons-Sears Ltd., Gen. Accident and Assurance Co., Canron Inc., Capstone Investment Trust, Silverwood Industries Ltd., Interprovincial Pipelines Ltd., Niagara Fin. Co., Delta Hotels. Chmn. bd. dirs. Niagara Inst.; Bd. dirs. Toronto Symphony Orch.; bd. govs. York U.; trustee Toronto Hosp. for Sick Children. Sir Bertram Whindle scholar; Elmslie Meml. scholar, 1944; Can. Council fellow, 1970-73. Clubs: Toronto, Toronto Golf, York (Toronto); Mark's (London). Home: 17 Dunloe Rd Toronto ON M4V 2W4 Canada Office: Suite 1000 33 Yonge St Toronto ON M5E 1S9 Canada

DIMMERLING, HAROLD J., bishop; b. Braddock, Pa., Sept. 23, 1914. Ed., St. Fidelis Prep. Sem., Herman, Pa., St. Charles Sem., Columbus, Ohio, St. Francis Sem., Loretto, Pa. Ordained priest Roman Catholic Ch., 1940; consecrated bishop, 1969; bishop Diocese of Rapid City, S.D., 1969— *

DIMMICK, CAROLYN REABER, justice Washington Supreme Court; b. Seattle, Oct. 24, 1929; d. Maurice C. and Margaret T. (Taylor) Reaber; m. Cyrus Allen Dimmick, Sept. 10, 1955; children: Taylor, Dana. B.A., U. Wash., 1951, J.D., 1963; LL.D., Gonzaga U., 1982. Bar: Wash. Asst. atty. gen., Wash., 1953-55; judge Dist. Ct., 1965-75, Superior Ct., 1976-80; justice Wash., Supreme Ct., 1981—; pros. atty. King County, Wash., 1959-60, 62-65; individual practice law, 1959-60. Recipient Matrix Table award, 1981, World Plan Execs. Council award, 1981, others. Mem. Am. Judges Assn. (gov.), Nat. Assn. Women Judges, World Assn. Judges, Am., Wash. bar assns., Am. Judicature Soc. Clubs: Wash. Athletic, Wingpoint Golf and Country, Harbor. Office: Temple Justice Olympia WA 98504

DIMMICK, WILLIAM ARTHUR, bishop, seminary president; b. Paducah, Ky., Oct. 7, 1919; s. James Oscar and Annis Amanda (Crouch) D. B.A., Berea Coll., 1946; M.Div., Yale U., 1949; M.A., George Peabody Coll., 1955; D.D., Berkeley Divinity Sch., 1975; D.C.S., Christian Bros. Coll., Memphis, 1982. Ordained priest Episcopal Ch., 1955; rector St. Philips Ch., Nashville, 1955-60; dean St. Marys Cathedral, Memphis, 1960-73; rector Trinity Ch., Southport, Conn., 1973-75; bishop Episcopal Diocese No. Mich., Marquette, 1975-82; asst. bishop Episcopal Ch., Mpls., 1981—; interim dean, pres. Seabury Western Theol. Sem., Evanston, Ill., 1983—; mem. standing liturgical commn. Episcopal Ch. Assoc. Parishes. Pres. Memphis and Shelby County Health and Welfare Planning Council, 1970-73. Office: 2112 Sheridan Rd Evanston IL

DIMOCK, EDWARD JORDAN, judge; b. Elizabeth, N.J., Jan. 4, 1890; s. George Edward and Elizabeth (Jordan) D.; m. Constance Bullard, June 20, 1912; children: Constance D. (Mrs. Frank H. Ellis), Mary D. Robbins, Elizabeth D. (Mrs. William B. Ryan), Lucy D. Lieberfeld, Emily D. (Mrs. Ignatius G. Mattingly). Student, Pingry Sch., Elizabeth, N.J., 1901-06; A.B., Yale U., 1911; LL.B., Harvard U., 1914. Bar: N.Y. 1914. Mem. law firm Hawkins, Delafield & Longfellow, N.Y.C., 1918-41; state reporter editing ofcl. law reports State N.Y., Albany, 1942-45; chmn. appeal bd. Office Contract Settlement, Washington, 1945-48, mem. appeal bd., 1948-51; U.S. dist. judge So. N.Y., 1951-61, sr. dist. judge, 1961—; Lectr. law municipal corps. Yale Law Sch., 1941-46; Asso. fellow Berkeley Coll., Yale. Chmn. joint com. N.Y.C. Bar Assns., 1937-39, Yale Alumni U. Fund, 1938-40; rep. U.S. Dist. Cts. 2d Circuit on Jud. Conf., 1957-59. Mem. Assn. Bar City N.Y. (exec. com. 1938-42), N.Y. State Bar Assn., Fed. Bar Assn., Sullivan County Bar Assn., ABA (ho. of dels. 1943, bd. editors Jour. 1944-68, bd. govs. 1948-51), Am. Law Inst. (past mem. council), N.Y. County Lawyers Assn., Psi Upsilon. Democrat. Episcopalian. Clubs: Century (N.Y.C.); Elihu, Elizabethan (Yale). Home: Route 1 Forestburgh NY 12777

DIMOCK, MARSHALL EDWARD, political science educator; b. San Bernardino, Calif., Oct. 24, 1903; s. Milton Edward and Anne (Behrens) D.; m. Lucy Butler Stotesbury, Sept. 14, 1926 (dec.); children: Milton Marshall, Mark, Marianne; m. Gladys Gouverneur Ogden, June 29, 1940; 1 son, Davis Ludlow. B.A., Pomona Coll., Claremont, Calif., 1925; Ph.D., Johns Hopkins, 1928. Instr. polit. sci. UCLA, 1928-30, asst. prof., 1930-32; assoc. prof. pub. adminstrn. U. Chgo., 1932-41; lectr. Sch. Pub. Law and Adminstrn., NYU, 1941-44, prof., head govt. dept., 1955-62; 2d asst. sec. of labor, 1938-40; asso. commr. Immigration and Naturalization Service Dept. of Justice, 1940-42; dir. Recruitment and Manning Orgn. and asst. dept. war shipping adminstr., 1942-44; prof. polit. sci. Northwestern U., 1944-1948; rep. tech. assistance bd. UN, Turkey, 1953-54; co.-dir. Pub. Adminstrn. Inst. for Turkey and Middle East, 1953-54; cons. Adminstrv. Staff Coll., Eng., 1954; Ford vis. prof. pub. adminstrn. Internat. Christian U., Tokyo, 1966-67; vis. prof. U. Va., Mich., P.R., Carleton Coll., U. Ankara, Fla. State U., Adminstrv. Staff Coll., Eng., U. Colo., Indian Inst. Pub. Adminstrn., U. Tex.; Fellow Social Sci. Research Council, 1932-33; Made studies for Sec. of War on Panama Canal enterprises and inland waterway transp., 1933-35; cons. Nat. Resources Com., 1935-39; chmn. Sec. of Labor's Commn. on Immigration Adminstrn., 1938-39; cons. War Dept., 1944, GAO, 1946-48; office of Sec. of Def., 1948-49; cons. Pres.'s Adv. Council Exec. Orgn., 1969-71. Author: several books; later ones American Government in Action, 1951, Business and Government, 1957, Free Enterprise and the Administrative State, 1951, Public Administration, 5th edit, 1983, A Philosophy of Administration, 1958, Administrative Vitality, 1959, The New American Political Economy, 1962, Creative Religion, 1963, The Japanese Technocracy, 1968; autobiography The Center of My World, 1980; Law and Dynamic Administration, 1980, (with Edgar N. Jackson) Doubting is not Enough, 1983; editor: Goals for Political Science, 1951. Dir., mem. exec. com. United Seamen's Service, chmn. 1946-56; Pres. Shinner Found., 1947-50. Mem. Vt. State Legislature (1949-50), Fellow (council mem. 1955- 59), A.A.A.S.; mem. Internat. Inst. Adminstrv. Scis., Royal Inst. Pub. Adminstrn. (London), Internat., Am. polit. sci. assns., Nat. Acad. Pub. Adminstrn., Unitarian Universalist Assn. (moderator 1961-64), Am. Soc. Pub. Adminstrn., Soc. for Advancement of Mgmt. (pres. Washington Chapt. 1941-42, nat. dir. 1942-43, nat. v.p. 1945-46), Am. Econ. Assn., Pi Sigma Alpha (nat. pres. 1962-64). Unitarian. Club: Rotarian. Home: Scrivelsby Bethel VT 05032

DIMON, GARTH FREMONT, pharmaceutical company executive; b. Minot, N.D., July 23, 1926; s. Leslie F. and Lora E. (Johnson) D.; m. Sarah Eysenbach, Aug. 28, 1948; children: Gary, Lee, Carl, Leslie. A.B., Oberlin Coll., 1950; M.B.A., Syracuse U., 1951. Personnel mgr. Proctor & Gamble Co., 1951-66; v.p. employee relations Clairol, Stamford, Conn., 1966-78, N.Y.C., 1966-78, Bristol-Myers Co., 1978-79, v.p. human resources, 1979-82, sr. v.p. human resources, 1982—. Office: 345 Parke Ave New York NY 10154

DIMOND, EDMUNDS GREY, medical educator; b. St. Louis, Dec. 8, 1918; s. Edmunds Grey and Gertrude Ruth (Schmidt) D.; m. Mary Dwight Clark, Nov. 28, 1968; children: Sherri Grey (Mrs. Charles Allenbaugh), Lark Grey, Leagrey. Student, Purdue U., 1938-39; B.S., Ind. U., 1942, M.D., 1944; D.Sc. (hon.), Hahnemann Grad. Sch., 1976. Mem. faculty U. Kans. Med. Center, Kansas City, 1950-60, prof., chmn. dept. medicine, 1953-60, dir. cardiovascular lab., 1950-60; mem., dir. Inst. for Cardiopulmonary Diseases, Scripps Clinic and Research Found., 1960-67; prof.-in-residence U. Calif. at San Diego Sch. Medicine, 1967-68; research asso. physiology Scripps Inst. Oceanography, La Jolla, Calif., 1960-68; scholar-in-residence Nat. Library Medicine, 1967; spl. asst. to asst. sec. HEW, Washington, 1968; disting. prof. medicine U. Mo., Kansas City, 1968—, provost for health scis., 1968-79, chmn. dept. medicine, 1981—; Fulbright prof., Netherlands, 1956; vis. prof. Nat. Heart Inst., London, Eng., 1959; Ministry of Health vis. prof., Israel, 1978; scholar-in-residence Rockefeller Found. Study Center, Bellagio, Italy, 1978; chmn. overseas edn. team Dept. State, 1962, 64, 65, 66, 73; guest lectr. Chinese Med. Assn., China, 1971, 72, 73, 76, 77, 78, 79, 80, 82. Author: Electrocardiography, 1952, Rev. edit., 1955, 60, 64, Digitalis, 1957, Exercise Electrocardiograms, 1961, More Than Herbs and Acupuncture, 1975; Editor-in-chief: Accel, 1968-77; editor: Diastole on Hospital Hill Audiotape, 1980; Contbr. articles to profl. jours. Bd. dirs. Truman Med. Center, Kansas City, Mo.; trustee LaJolla Museum Art; bd. dirs. Grenville Clark Fund at Dartmouth Coll. Served with M.C. AUS, 1945-47. Recipient Distinguished Service award Am. Coll. Cardiology, 1969; Paul Dudley White Traveling scholar, 1956-57. Fellow A.C.P., Coll. Physicians Phila., Am. Coll. Cardiology (pres. 1962). Home: 2501 Holmes St Kansas City MO 64108 Office: 2411 Holmes St Kansas City MO 64108

DIMOND, ROBERT EDWARD, publisher; b. Washington, Dec. 12, 1936; s. James Robert and Helen Marie (Murphy) D.; m. Patricia Ann Berger, Jan. 22, 1966; children: Mark Edward, Michele Lynn, Melinda Ann. B.A. in Journalism, George Washington U., 1961. Mng. editor Nat. Automobile Dealers Assn. mag., Washington, 1955-63; editor, pub. Bus. Products mag., Washington, 1963-69; v.p. Hitchcock Pub. Co.; pub. Infosystems mag., Office Products mag., Wheaton, Ill., 1969-81; pres. R.E. Dimond & Assocs., Hinsdale, Ill., 1981-83; pub. Telecommunication Products and Tech., Penn Well Pub. Co., Littleton, Mass., 1983—. Served with USAF, 1961-62. Democrat. Roman Catholic. Home: 23 Lynn Rd Needham Ma 02194 Office: 119 Russell St Littleton MA 01462 *Never, ever lose your sense of humor, there is no situation in which it cannot be used; be nice to all on the way up because you're likely to meet them on the way down.*

DI MONTEZEMOLO, ALESSANDRO C., insurance brokerage executive; b. Rome, Nov. 25, 1918; U.S., 1954; s. Alberto C. and Maria Alessandra di M.; m. Catherine B. Murray, May 27, 1960. Grad., Royal Cav. Acad., 1938, Royal Cav. Sch., 1940. Officer Italian mil. forces, 1938; advanced through grades to maj.; served with SHAPE, Paris, 1949-52; ret., 1952; with internat. div. (N.Am. area) Piaggio Corp., 1953-59; rep. for U.S. and Can. Assicurazioni Generali Group, 1959-72; pres., dir. prin. U.S. ins. and fin. affiliates including Genamerica Mgmt. Corp., Transocean Holding Corp., Rogen Mgmt. Corp.; central mgr. fgn. ops. Riunione Adriatica di Sicurta, 1973-74; with Marsh & McLennan Internat., Inc., 1974—, mng. dir., Europe, 1974-76, pres., N.Y.C., 1976—; dir., sr. v.p. Marsh & McLennan Cos., Inc.; chmn. Marsh & McLennan World Services, 1981—, Marsh & McLennan, Inc., 1982—; officer or dir. dir. all subs. of Marsh & McLennan Inc., including Marsh & McLennan Ltd., Can.; Marsh & McLennan Italia & Co. SpA, Société Faugere & Jutheau (S.A.), France, Henrijean & Cie (S.A.), Belgium, Marsh & McLennan Espana (S.A.), Spain, Baillieu Bowring Marsh & McLennan Pty. Ltd., Australia, Marsh & McLennan South East Asia, Ltd., Hong Kong, Marsh & McLennan Japan, Ltd., Bowring Burgess Marsh & McLennan Ltd., N.Z., Marsh & McLennan (Singapore) Pte. Ltd., Marsh & McLennan U.K. Ltd., Bowring Barclays & Assos. Holdings (South Africa) Ltd.; mem. coordinating com. Hudig-Langeveldt Groep BV, Netherlands; adv. council Tudor-Marsh & McLennan, Brazil; mem. adv. com. Bourchier, Marquard, Zepeda & Asociados, S.C. (Mex.). Clubs: River (N.Y.C.); Meadow (Southampton, N.Y.); Circolo della Caccia (Rome). Home: 870 UN Plaza New York NY 10017 Office: 1221 Ave of Americas New York NY 10020

DI MUCCIO, MARY JO, librarian; b. Hanford, Calif., June 16, 1930; d. Vincent and Theresa (Yovino) DiMuccio. B.A., Immaculate Heart Coll., 1953, M.A., 1960; Ph.D., U.S. Internat. U., 1970. Tchr. parochial schs., Los Angeles, 1949-54, San Francisco, 1954-58; tchr. Govt. of Can., Victoria, B.C., 1959-60; asst. librarian Immaculate Heart Coll. Library, Los Angeles, 1960-62, head librarian, 1962-72; adminstrv. librarian, City of Sunnyvale, Calif., 1972—. Pres. exec. bd., past pres. Sunnyvale Community Services. Mem. ALA, Spl. Library Assn., Cath. Library Assn. (past pres.), Calif. Library Assn., Sunnyvale Bus. and Profl. Women, Peninsula Dist. Bus. and Profl. Women (pres.). Club: Soroptimist (past pres.). Home: 720 C Blair Ct Sunnyvale CA 94087 Office: 665 W Olive Ave Sunnyvale CA 94086 *My goal has been to become a universal person, and that is my responsibility as a professional person-to see that the society we are building for tomorrow is appropriate to the needs of the people we serve.*

DI NARDO, BRUNO, internaional lawyer; b. Gamberale, Chieti, Italy, Nov. 1, 1939; came to U.S., 1954; s. Francesco and Ida (Gizzi) Di N.; (div.)1 son, Thomas. B.A., Duquesne U., 1961; J.D., Fordham U., 1964. Bar: Ill. 1969, N.Y. 1973. Jr. atty. Burroughs Corp., Detroit, 1969-71; corp. devel. mgr. Lever Bros., N.Y.C., 1971-73; gen. counsel French Am. Banking Corp., N.Y.C., 1973—; pres., owner Law Offices Di Nardo and Co, P.C., N.Y.C., 1978—. Mem. N.Y. County Lawyers Assn. Republican. Office: Di Nardo and Co One World Trade Ctr New York NY 10048

DINCULEANU, NICOLAE, mathematician; b. Padea, Romania, Feb. 26, 1925; U.S., 1976, naturalized, 1981; s. Nicolae and Frusina (Lusca) Dobrescu; m. Elena Constantinescu, Feb. 9, 1959. Engr., Poly. Inst., Bucarest, 1950; licencie math., U. Bucarest, 1951, Ph.D. in Math, 1957. Prof. math. U. Bucarest, 1950-77; vis. prof. Queen's U., Kingston, Ont., Can., 1966-67, U. Rennes, France, U. Erlangen, w. Ger., 1970; Disting. vis. prof. U. Pitts., 1970-71; vis. research prof. U. Fla., Gainesville, 1972-77, prof. math., 1977—. Author: Vector Measures, 1967, Integration on Locally Compact Spaces, 1974, Textbook of Mathematical Analysis, 2 vols, 1962; also articles. Recipient Stoilov prize Romanian Acad., 1964. Mem. Am. Math. Soc. Mem. Romanian Orthodox Ch. Club: Torch. Office: Math Dept Walker Hall 312 U Fla Gainesville FL 32611

DINE, JIM, painter; b. Cin., June 16, 1935. B.F.A., U. Cin., Boston Mus. Sch. Tchr. Yale, 1965. Artist in residence Oberlin Coll., 1965, Cornell U., 1966-67; instr. Royal Coll. Art, London, 1967-68. Author, illustrator: Welcome Home Lovebirds, 1969; co-author: Work from the Same House, 1969; co-author, illustrator: The Adventures of Mr. and Mrs. Jim & Ron, 1970; illustrator: The Poet Assassinated, 1968; prod. happenings, including Car Crash, 1960; one-man shows, 1959—, including, N.Y.C., Milan, Brussels, Paris, Chgo., Washington; exhibited in groups shows, Venice, London, Dallas, Buenos Aires, Phila., Pasadena, Tokyo, The Hague, Brussells, Vienna, Buffalo, Munich, W.Ger., Stockholm, Atlanta, Los Angeles, others, The Hague, Chgo., The Hague, London, The Hague, N.Y.C.; represented in permanent collections, Brandeis U., Mus. Modern Art, Guggenheim Mus., Albright Mus., N.Y. U., Tate Gallery, London, Stedelijk Mus., Amsterdam, Whitney Mus., N.Y.C., others. Mem. Am. Acad. and Inst. Arts and Scis. Address: care The Pace Gallery 32 East 57th Street New York NY 10022 *

DINEEN, CAROLE JAMES, government official; b. Trquisate, Guatemala, Sept. 12, 1941; d. Edwin Yowell and Florence (Murtagh) Jones; m. Robert Emmet Dineen, Jan. 25, 1974. B.A., Brown U., 1963. Mgr. airport ops. TWA J.F. Kennedy Airport, 1977-78; v.p. Bankers Trust Co., 1978-83; with Dept. Treasury, Washington, 1983—, fiscal asst. sec., 1983—.

DINEEN, ROBERT JOSEPH, diversified manufacturing company executive; b. Cin., Dec. 3, 1929; s. Thomas Leo and Stella Patricia (Finnegan) D.; m. Marilyn Kamp, May 4, 1957; children: Brian, Lynn, Erin, Kerrie, Kevin, Mary Shannon, Patricia. B.E.E., U. Cin., 1952. With Allis-Chalmers Corp., Milw., 1951—, group exec., v.p. power generation and transmission group, 1971-76; pres. Allis-Chalmers Power Systems, Inc., Fiat-Allis Constrn. Machinery Inc., Deerfield, Ill., 1976—; pres., chief exec. officer White Farm Equipment Co., 1981—; exec. v.p., chief operating officer Marley Co., 1983—. Bd. dirs. Cin. Indsl. Inst. Served with AUS, 1952-54. Recipient distinguished alumnus award U. Cin., 1971. Mem. Nat. Elec. Mfrs. Assn. (gov.), Constrn. Industry Mfrs Assn. (2d v.p.), Am. Mgmt. Assn. Home: 2122 Middlefork Rd Northfield IL 60093 Office: 1900 Johnson Dr Mission Woods KS 66205

DING, GAR DAY, architect; b. Canton, China, Nov. 14, 1929; came to U.S., 1966; s. Chew Cheung and Ngan She (Ho) D.; m. Maisie Young, Aug. 24, 1954; children—David, Judy, Derek, Walter. B.Arch., U. Auckland, N.Z., 1953; B.Engring., U. Canterbury, N.Z., 1959; M.Engring.Sci., U. New S. Wales, Australia, 1961. Lectr., then sr. lectr. archtl. scis. U. Sydney, Australia, 1959-66; prof. architecture, chmn. environmental systems studies Va. Poly. Inst. and State U., Blacksburg, 1966-72; prof., dir. grad. studies architecture Miami U., Oxford, Ohio, also U. Cin., 1972-73; prof. architecture, head dept. U. Ill., Urbana, 1973-80, research prof., 1980—; mem. bldg. research adv. bd. Nat. Acad. Scis., 1976-80; mem. housing com. New River Valley Dist. Planning Commn., 1970-72; mem. public adv. panel region 5 GSA, 1978; cons. in field. Co-author: Models in Architecture, 1968; contbg. author: Metropolitan Transportation Planning, 1975; Contbr. to profl. jours. Humes Industries scholar, 1956; C.S. McCully scholar, 1957; recipient research award Royal Inst. Brit. Architects, 1966; grantee Dept. Army, 1966, NSF, 1976, 81. Fellow N.Z., Royal Australian insts. architects; mem. ASCE, Instn. Engrs. Australia. Home: 10 Forest View Mahomet IL 61853 Office: Univ Ill Urbana IL 61801

DINGELL, JOHN DAVID, JR., congressman; b. Colorado Springs, Colo., July 8, 1926; s. John D. and Grace (Bigler) D. B.S. in Chemistry, Georgetown U., 1949, J.D., 1952. Bar: D.C. bar 1952, Mich. bar 1953. Park ranger U.S. Dept. Interior, 1948-52; asst. pros. atty., Wayne County, Mich., 1953-55; mem. 84th-88th congresses from 15th Dist. Mich., 89th-97th congresses from 16th Dist. Mich.; mem. migratory bird conservation commn., chmn. Com. on energy and commerce, sub. com. chmn. oversight and investigation; mem. Office Tech. Assessment. Served as 2d lt. inf. AUS, 1945-46. Home: Trenton MI 48121 Office: Room 2221 Rayburn House Office Bldg Washington DC 20515

DINGEMAN, JAMES HERBERT, industrial executive, consultant; b. Detroit, July 31, 1917; s. Harry J. and Bessie (Schafer) D.; m. Ann R. McGillivray, Apr. 26, 1941; children: Patricia D. (Mrs. Thomas J. Moran), James Herbert, Peter J., Mary Ann. LL.B., U. Detroit, 1939. Bar: Mich. 1939. Practice in, Detroit, 1939-43; mem. firm Dingeman & DeGalan, 1939-43; legal adviser Fed.-Mogul Corp., Detroit, 1943-46, asst. dir. indsl. relations, 1946-60, dir. orgn. planning exec. devel., 1960-68, sec., 1965-68; v.p. legal and corp. planning affairs, sec. Parke, Davis & Co., 1968-70, group v.p. legal and corp. planning affairs, sec., 1970-71, v.p. adminstrn., sec., 1971-77, dir., 1970—; v.p. Warner-Lambert Co., 1970-77, cons., 1977—; dir. Bank of Commerce, Mich. Consol. Gas Co., Detroit Ball Bearing Co., Bush Mfg. Co., Genova Corp., Primark Corp., Commerce Bancorp; instr. Detroit Coll. Law, 1940, Walsh Inst. Accountancy, 1945. Founder Little League Baseball, Grosse Pointe Farms, 1952, pres., 1954-55; area chmn. United Fund, 1965; Mem. Republican Fin. Com., 1950—; councilman, Grosse Pointe Farms, 1966—, mayor pro-tem, 1969-75, mayor, 1975—; Mem. exec. bd. Detroit Area council Boy Scouts Am. Trustee, St. John Hosp., Citizens Research Council, Oxford Inst., Detroit Sci. Center, U. Detroit, Grosse Pointe Farms Found., St. Clair Health Services Corp.; pres. Bus./Edn. Alliance, 1975-77. Mem. Am., Mich. bar assns., Assn. Gen Counsel, Am. Soc. Corp. Secs., Nat. Health Lawyers Assn., Am. Mgmt. Assn., Greater Detroit C. of C. (dir.), Lambda Sigma (past nat. pres.), Delta Theta Phi. Clubs: Detroit Athletic (dir.), Detroit Country, Cardinal (Detroit); Otsego Ski (Gaylord, Mich.); The Little (Gulfstream, Fla.); Delray Beach (Fla.); Port Huron (Mich.) Golf.

Home: 4 Radnor Circle Grosse Pointe Farms MI 48236 Office: 22151 Moross Rd Detroit MI 48236

DINGES, EDWARD ARTHUR, army officer; b. Newburgh, N.Y., Apr. 5, 1931; s. John Edward and Helen Emma (Post) D.; m. Marjorie Sue Dunnington, June 7, 1959; children: Kristan, Jennifer, Pamela. B.S., U.S. Mil. Acad., 1953; grad., Command and Gen. Staff Coll., Ft. Leavenworth, Kans., 1968, Army War Coll., 1971; M.A. in Internat. Studies, Am. U., 1972. Commd. 2d lt. U.S. Army, 1953, advanced through grades to maj. gen., 1977; div. arty. comdr. 3d Armored Div., Hanau, Germany, 1975-76, chief of staff, Frankfurt, Ger., 1976-77, asst. div. comdr., Giessen, Ger., 1977-78; asst. comdt. U.S. Army F.A. Sch., Ft. Sill, Okla., 1978-80, comdr., 1980-82; dep. chief of staff ops. and intelligence Hdqrs Allied Forces Central Europe, Brunssum, Netherlands, 1982—. Decorated Legion of Merit with 2 oak leaf clusters, D.F.C., Bronze Star medal with oak leaf cluster, Air medal with 3 oak leaf clusters. Mem. Assn. U.S. Army, West Point Alumni Assn. Episcopalian. Lodge: Masons. Home: Hommerterallee 16 Amstenrade Limburg Netherlands 6436 AR Office: NATO AFCENT Akerstraat 7 Brunssum Limburg Netherlands 6445 CL

DINGLE, RAYMOND, research scientist; b. Perth, Western, Australia, Sept. 5, 1935; U.S., 1966; s. Harry and Nora (Weedon) D.; m. Regina Vida Jonikis, Mar. 6, 1959; children: Joanna Bronwyn, Nicholas Andrew, Andrew Christian. B.S., U. Western Australia, 1957, Ph.D. in Chemistry, 1962. Fellow Univ. Coll., London, 1963; lectr. Orsted Inst., U. Copenhagen, 1963-66; mem. research staff Bell Labs., 1966-72; sr. fellow dept. solid state physics Australian Nat. U., 1972; mem. research staff Bell Tel. Labs., Murray Hill, N.J., 1973-79, group supr. exploratory III-V high speed device dept., 1979—; sci. cons. to govt. agys.; dir. NATO ARI on microelectronics, 1982. Contbr. research and devel. articles to profl. jours. Served with Royal Australian Navy, 1953-54. Mem. Am. Phys. Soc., AAAS. Club: Canoe Brook Country (Summit, N.J.). Patentee in solid state electronics, device physics and materials sci. Home: 50 Wildwood Ln Summit NJ 07901 Office: 600 Mountain Ave Murray Hill NJ 07974

DINGMAN, MAURICE J., bishop; b. St. Paul, Iowa, Jan. 20, 1914; s. Theodore and Angela (Witte) D. Ed., St. Ambrose Coll., Davenport, Iowa, 1936, N.Am. Coll. and Gregorian U., Rome, Catholic U. Am. Ordained priest Roman Cath. Ch., 1939; instr. St. Ambrose Acad., 1940-43; vice chancellor Diocese of Davenport, Iowa, 1942-45; prin. Hayes High Sch., Muscatine, Iowa, 1950-53; domestic prelate, 1956; appointed bishop Diocese of Des Moines, 1968—. Office: PO Box 1816 2910 Grand Ave Des Moines IA 50306 *

DINGMAN, MICHAEL DAVID, engineering and high technology company executive; b. New Haven, Sept. 29, 1931; s. James Everett and Amelia (Williamson) D.; m. Jean Hazlewood, May 16, 1953 (div.); children: Michael David, Linda Channing (Mrs. Michael S. Cady), James Clifford.; m. Elizabeth G. Tharp, Apr. 13, 1984. Student, U. Md. Gen. partner Burnham & Co. (investment bankers), N.Y.C., 1964-70; pres., dir., chief exec. officer Wheelabrator-Frye Inc., Hampton, N.H., 1970-83, chmn. bd., 1977—; pres., dir. The Signal Cos., Inc., La Jolla, Calif., 1983—; dir. Mellon Nat. Corp., Time Inc., AMCA Internat., Ltd., McFaddin Ventures, Inc., Pogo Producing Co., Ford Motor Co. Trustee John A. Hartford Found. Mem. IEEE, Mus. Fine Arts (Boston), Mus. Sci. (Boston). Clubs: Links, Board Room, N.Y. Yacht (N.Y.C.); Union (Boston); Cruising of Am. (Conn.); Bohemian, Fairbanks Ranch Country; Lyford Cay (Nassau); La Jolla Country. Office: 11255 N Torrey Pines Rd La Jolla CA 92037

DINGMAN, REED OTHELBERT, surgeon, educator; b. Rockwood, Mich., Nov. 4, 1906; s. Wilbert Alva and Gertrude (Scherer) D.; m. Thelma Agnes Muir, Nov. 24, 1932; children—David Lyons, Sue Muir, Sally Fae. A.B., U. Mich., 1928, D.D.S., 1931, M.S., 1932, M.D., 1936; D.Sc., U. Miami, 1974. Diplomate: Am. Bd. Oral Surgery, Am. Bd. Plastic Surgery (chmn. 1964-65). Oral and plastic surgeon Gelsinger Meml. Hosp., Danville, Pa., 1937-39; pvt. practice oral and plastic surgery, Washington, 1939-40; asst. prof. oral surgery U. Mich., 1940-45, assoc. prof. oral surgery, 1945—; prof. surgery, head sect. plastic surgery Med. Sch., 1965-76, prof. surgery emeritus, 1976—, acting head sect. plastic surgery, 1982—; chief dept. plastic surgery St. Joseph Mercy Hosp., Ann Arbor, 1960-75. Author: (with Paul Natvig) Surgery of Facial Fractures; Editor: Jour. Oral Surgery, 1948-52; asso. editor: Year Book of Plastic Surgery; Contbr. articles to med., dental publs. Fellow A.C.S., Am. Coll. Dentists; mem. Am. Dental Assn., AMA, Am. Soc. Oral and Maxillofacial Surgeons, Am. Soc. Plastic and Reconstructive Surgeons (pres., dir. found., pres. 1963-64), Western surg. socs., Am. Assn. Plastic Surgeons, Am. Cleft Palate Soc., Am. Soc. Maxillo-facial Surgeons (pres. 1952), Am. Soc. Trauma, S. African Soc. Plastic Surgeons (hon.), Am., Internat. socs. aesthetic plastic surgeons. Home: 2125 Nature Cove Ct Ann Arbor MI 48104 Office: Univ Mich Hosp Ann St Ann Arbor MI 48109

DINIELLI, NICHOLAS ANTHONY, canteen co. exec.; b. Jersey City, Apr. 4, 1930; s. Felix and Josephine (Rella) D.; m. Jeanne Frances Elphinstone, Oct. 14, 1951; children—Jacqueline Dinielli King, Constance Dinielli Miller, Philip. B.B.A., Pace U., 1952; M.B.A., Rutgers U., 1962. With budget and fin. analysis dept. Getty Oil Co., N.Y.C., 1952-61; mgr. acctg., taxes, consolidations, ins. Fed. Electric Corp., Paramus, N.J., 1962-67; mgr. fin. controls ITT World Hdqrs., N.Y.C., 1967-70; controller Canteen Corp. (subsidiary TWC, Chgo.), 1970—, v.p., 1973—; lectr. corp. acctg. Upsala Coll., East Orange, N.J., 1965-67. Served with USNR, 1947-53. Mem. Fin. Execs. Inst., Am. Inst. Corp. Controllers. Home: 1406 N Salem Blvd Arlington Heights IL 60004 Office: Canteen Corp Merchandise Mart Chicago IL 60654

DINITZ, SIMON, sociology educator; b. N.Y.C., Oct. 29, 1926; s. Morris and Dinah (Schulman) D.; m. Mildred H. Stern, Aug. 20, 1949; children: Jeffrey, Thea, Risa. Student, CCNY, 1943-44; B.A., Vanderbilt U., 1947; M.A., U. Wis., 1949, Ph.D., 1951. Successively scholar, teaching asst., research asst., fellow U. Wis., 1947-50; mem. faculty Ohio State U., 1951—, prof. sociology, 1958—, research asso. psychiatry, 1956-74; vis. lectr. U. Wis., summers 1951, 52; George J. Beto prof. criminal justice Sam Houston State U., 1983; vis. prof. U. So. Calif., summer 1968, U. Wis., summer 1969, Tel Aviv U., autumn 1970-73, U. Haifa (Israel), 1982; cons. UN Social Def. Research Inst., Rome, 1970-73; sr. fellow Acad. Contemporary Problems, 1974—; vis. prof. U. South Fla., 1980, 81; Sir John Barry Meml. lectr. U. Melbourne (Australia), 1981. Co-author: Social Problems, 1964, Schizophrenics in the Community, 1967, Women After Treatment, 1968, Critical Issues in the Study of Crime, 1968, Deviance, 1969, 2d edit., 1975, The Prevention of Juvenile Delinquency: An Experiment, 1972, Schizophrenics in the New Custodial Community, 1974, Delinquents and Nondelinquents in the Puerto Rican Slum, 1975, Juvenile Victimization: The Institutional Paradox, 1976, In Fear of Each Other, 1977, The Violent Few, 1978, Restraining the Wicked, 1979, Careers of the Violent, 1982; also articles.; co-editor: Criminal Justice Planning, 1977. Mem. Ohio Task Force Community Mental Health, 1965-66; mem. Gov.'s Adv. Panel for Rehab. and Correction, 1974-75, Gov.'s Youth Services Adv. Panel, 1976—. Served with USNR, 1945-46. Recipient Hofheimer prize Am. Psychiat. Assn., 1968, Outstanding Teaching award Ohio State U., 1968, 70, Outstanding Research award, 1979; Louis Nemzer award Ohio State U. chpt. AAUP, 1980. Fellow Am. Sociol. Assn., Am. Psychopath. Assn.; mem. N. Central Sociol. Assn. (v.p. 1968, pres. 1982-83), Am. Soc. Criminology (pres. 1970-71, Sutherland award 1974), Phi Beta Kappa (hon.). Home: 298 N Cassady St Columbus OH 43209

DINKEL, JOHN GEORGE, magazine editor; b. Bklyn., Aug. 1, 1944; s. Charles Ernest and Loretta Gertrude D.; m. Leslie Hawkins, Oct. 25, 1969; children: Meredith Anne, Kevin Carter. B.S. in Mech. Engring, U. Mich., 1967, M.S., 1969. Staff engr. Chrysler Corp., Highland Park, Mich., 1967-69; engring. editor Car Life Mag., Newport Beach, Calif., 1969-70, Road & Track Mag., Newport Beach, 1972-79, editor, 1979—. Mem. Soc. Automotive Engrs., Am. Racing Press Assn., Internat. Motor Press Assn., Sports Car Club Am., Internat. Motor Sports Assn., Pi Tau Sigma. Office: 1499 Monrovia Newport Beach CA 92663

DINKELSPIEL, RICHARD COLEMAN, lawyer; b. Oakland, Calif., Feb. 13, 1913; s. Edward and Ellen (Gaines) D.; m. Miriam Cutter, Dec. 9, 1939; children: Susan (Mrs. Joseph Cerny), Robin (Mrs. Anthony Miller), Joan, Anne, Richard Coleman. A.B., U. Calif., 1934, J.D., 1937. Bar: Calif. 1937. City judge, Suisun, Calif., 1937-42, practice law, Suisun, 1937-42, San Francisco, 1946—; partner Dinkelspiel, Donovan & Reder; justice of peace Suisun Twp., 1939-42; Chmn. citizens adv. com. to review lien laws Calif. Legislature, 1963-64. Chmn. Adv. Com. to State Senate on Lien Law Revision, 1965-69; mem. Gov.'s Adv. Com. Children and Youth, 1967—; co-chmn. Gov.'s Commn. on Family, 1966; bd. dirs. San Francisco Lawyers Com. for Urban Affairs, 1970—, co-chmn., 1969; mem. exec. com., bd. trustees Lawyers Com. for Civil Rights Under Law, 1970—, co-chmn., 1981-83; Bd. regents Holy Name Coll., 1973-76; pres.'s council Jesuit Sch. Theology at Berkeley, 1971-74; trustee San Domenico Sch. Found., 1971—, chmn., 1973-75. Served from lt. to lt. col. AUS, 1942-46. Recipient award of pub. recognition St. Thomas More Soc., 1970. Fellow Am. Bar Found.; mem. Bar Assn. San Francisco (pres. 1968, dir.), San Francisco Bar Found. (pres. 1972-73), State Bar of Calif. (gov. 1974-77, commn. on jud. nominees 1978-79), Am. Bar Assn., Nat. Conf. Bar Presidents, St. Thomas More Soc. San Francisco (pres. 1960), Sigma Alpha Epsilon, Phi Delta Phi. Clubs: Commonwealth (Quar. chmn. 1969, bd. govs. 1972—), Commonwealth (pres. 1982), Meadow, The Family. Home: Box 511 Kentfield CA 94914 Office: One Embarcadero Center 27th Floor San Francisco CA 94111

DINKINS, CAROL EGGERT, lawyer, former government official; b. Corpus Christi, Tex., Nov. 9, 1945; d. Edgar H., Jr. and Evelyn S. (Scheel) Eggert; m. O. Theodore Dinkins, Jr., July 2, 1966; children: Anne, Amy. B.S., U. Tex., 1968; J.D., U. Houston, 1971. Bar: Tex. 1971. Adj. asst. prof. law U. Houston Coll. Law, also prin. asso. Tex. Law Inst. Coastal and Marine Resources, U. Houston, 1971-73; assoc., then partner firm Vinson & Elkins, Houston, 1973-81, 83—; asst. atty. gen. land and natural resources Dept. Justice, 1981-83; chmn. Pres.'s Task Force on Legal Equity for Women, 1981-83; mem. Hawaiian Native Study Commn., 1981-83; dir. Nat. Consumer Coop. Banks Bd., 1981. Author articles in field. Chmn. Tex. Gov.'s Task Force Coast Mgmt., 1979, Tex. Gov.'s Flood Control Action Group, 1980-81. Mem. ABA, State Bar Tex., Houston Bar Assn., Tex. Water Conservation Assn., Houston Law Rev. Assn. (dir. 1978—). Republican. Lutheran. Office: 2828 First City Tower Houston TX 77002 *

DINMAN, BERTRAM DAVID, aluminum company executive; b. Phila., Aug. 9, 1925; s. Meyer and Minnie (Kaufman) D.; m. Gabrielle Stamm, June 11, 1950; children: Stefanie, Jonathan David, Emily, Joshua. Student, Temple U., 1944-46, 67, M.D., 1951; Sc.D., U. Cin., 1957. Asst. prof. to prof. Ohio State U. Coll. Medicine, 1957-65; prof., dir. Inst. Indsl. Health, U. Mich. Sch. Pub. Health, 1965-73; corp. med. dir. Aluminum Co. Am., Pitts., 1973-78, v.p. health and safety, 1978—; trustee Am. Bd. Preventive Medicine; cons. U.S. Army, USN, WHO; mem. U.S. del. ILO, 1980-81, 84; adj. prof. pub. health U. Pitts., 1975—. Served with C.E. U.S. Army, 1944-46. Mem. Permanent Commn. and Internat. Assn. Occupational Health (dir.), Am. Acad. Occupational Medicine (pres. 1973-74, award of merit). Club: Duquesne (Pitts.). Office: Aluminum Company of America 1501 Alcoa Bldg Pittsburgh PA 15219

DINNEEN, JAMES FRANCIS, lawyer, business executive; b. Malden, Mass., July 24, 1915; s. James C. and Frances K. (Callahan) D.; m. Margaret Mary Quinn, Dec. 7, 1943; children: James F.X., Patricia M., Margaret R. A.B., Boston Coll., 1937; LL.B., 1942. Bar: Mass. 1943. Atty. Dept. Justice, Washington, 1946-47; trial atty., spl. counsel Liberty Mut. Ins. Co., Boston, 1947-62; spl. counsel Raytheon Co., Lexington, Mass., 1962-70, dir. govt. relations, 1970—, v.p., 1977—. Chmn. Boston Sch. Bldg. Commn., 1960-63, Milton (Mass.) Sch. Needs Com., 1972-73; mem. town meeting, Milton, 1973—. Served with USNR, 1942-46. Mem. Mass. Bar Assn. (chmn. legis. com. 1963-71, v.p. 1967-70, chmn. com. legal clinics 1976, bd. dels. 1965-70, exec. com. 1967-70). Clubs: University (Washington); Wollaston Golf (Milton). Home: 21 Hilltop St Milton MA 02186 Office: Raytheon Co Lexington MA 02173

DINNERSTEIN, HARVEY, artist; b. N.Y.C., Apr. 3, 1928; s. Louis and Sarah (Kobilansky) D.; m. Lois Behrke, May 24, 1951; children: Rachel, Michael. Student of, Moses Soyer, 1944-46, Art Students League, 1946-47, Tyler Art Sch., Temple U., 1950. Instr. drawing and painting Sch. Visual Arts, N.Y.C., 1963-80, N.A.D., 1974—, Art Students League, 1980—. Exhibited works in one-man shows at, Davis Galleries, N.Y.C., 1955, 60, 61, 63, Kenmore Galleries, Phila., 1964, 66, 69, 70, F.A.R. Galleries, N.Y.C., 1972, 79, Sindin Galleries, 1983; exhibited in group shows at, Whitney Mus. Am. Art, N.Y.C., 1955, New Britain (Conn.) Mus. Am. Art, 1964, Am. Acad. and Inst. Arts and Letters, N.Y.C., 1974, Pa. State U. Mus. Art, others, works represented in collections at, Met. Mus. Art, Whitney Mus. Am. Art, Martin Luther King Labor Center, N.Y.C., New Britain Mus. Art, Fleming Mus. at U. Vt., Burlington; Author: A Portfolio of Drawings, 1968, Harvey Dinnerstein—Artist at Work, 1978. Served with U.S. Army, 1951-53. Recipient Temple Gold medal Pa. Acad. Fine Art, 1950; Allied Artist Gold medal, 1977; President's award Audubon Artists, 1978; Arthur Ross award Classical Am.; others; Tiffany Found. grantee, 1948, 61. Mem. N.A.D. Home and Office: 933 President St Brooklyn NY 11215

DINNERSTEIN, LEONARD, historian, educator; b. N.Y.C., May 5, 1934; s. Abraham and Lillian (Kubrik) D.; m. Myra Anne Rosenberg, Aug. 20, 1961; children: Andrew, Julie. B.A., CCNY, 1955; M.A., Columbia U., 1960, Ph.D., 1966. Instr. N.Y. Inst. Tech., N.Y.C., 1960-65; asst. prof. Fairleigh Dickinson U., Teaneck, N.J., 1967-70; adj. prof. Columbia U., summers 1969-72, 74; adj. asst. prof. N.Y. U., 1969-70; prof. Am. history U. Ariz., Tucson, 1970—. Author: The Leo Frank Case, 1968 (Anisfield-Wolf award 1969), (with David M. Reimers) Ethnic Americans: A History of Immigration and Assimilation, 1975, (with Roger L. Nichols, David M. Reimers) Natives and Strangers, 1979, America and the Survivors of the Holocaust, 1982; contbr. articles and book revs. to hist. jours.; editor: (with Roger L. Nichols, David M. Reimers) American Vistas, 1971, Jews in the South, 1973, Decisions and Revisions: Interpretations of 20th Century American History, 1975, America Since World War II, 1976. Mem. Orgn. Am. Historians, Am. Hist. Assn., Am. Jewish Hist. Assn. Democrat. Jewish. Home: 5871 E 7th St Tucson AZ 85711 Office: Dept History U Ariz Tucson AZ 85721 *

DINNING, JAMES SMITH, biochemist; b. Franklin, Ky., Sept. 28, 1922; s. James Starks and Fanny Blanche (Smith) D.; m. Sally Sue Hensley, Oct. 28, 1944; children: Katherine Sue, James Michael, Robin Joann, Randall Starks. B.S., U. Ky., 1946; M.S., Okla. State U., 1946, Ph.D., 1948; D.Sc. (hon.), Mahidol U., Bangkok, Thailand, 1974. Mem. faculty U. Ark. Med. Sch., Little Rock, 1948-63, prof. and chmn. dept. biochemistry, 1957-59, asst. dean Grad. Sch., 1959-63; dir. Rockefeller Found., Bangkok, 1963-75; research scientist U. Fla., Gainesville, 1975—. Author research papers in field. Served with AUS, 1942-46. Recipient Lederle Med. Faculty award, 1954, Jordan Medal of Independence, 1963. Mem. Am. Inst. Nutrition (Meade-Johnson award 1964, editor jour. 1979—), Soc. Exptl. Biology and Medicine, Am. Soc. Biol. Chemists, Sigma Xi. Home: 2554 SW 14th Dr Gainesville FL 32608

DINOSO, VICENTE PESCADOR, JR., physician, educator; b. San Marcelino, Philippines, Oct. 17, 1936; came to U.S., 1961, naturalized, 1973; s. Vicente Dinoso and Eugenia Corpus (Pescador) D.; m. Alice M. Dinoso, June 19, 1965; children—Vincent, David. B.S., U. Philippines, 1955, M.D., 1960. Intern Mt. Sinai Hosp., Hartford, Conn., 1961-62; resident St. Mary's Hosp., Waterbury, Conn., 1962-64, Lahey Clinic Found., Boston, 1964-65; research fellow Temple U. Sch. Medicine, Phila., 1965-66, 68-69, instr. medicine, 1969-72, asst. prof., 1972-74; asso. prof. medicine Hahnemann Med. Coll. and Hosp., Phila., 1974-78, prof. medicine, asso. prof. physiology, 1978—; practice medicine specializing in gastroenterology, 1969—. Co-editor: Gastrointestinal Emergencies, 1976; contbr. articles to med. jours. Mem. Am. Gastroenterol. Assn., Am. Physiol. Soc., Am. Fedn. for Clin. Research, AAAS, Sigma Xi. Republican. Office: Hahnemann U Hosp 230 Broad St Philadelphia PA 19102

DINSDALE, HENRY BEGG, neurologist, educator; b. Kingston, Ont., Can., Sept. 22, 1931; s. Harry Hamlin and Doris Eileen (Donnelly) D.; m. Lyla June Yates, June 11, 1955; children: Janice, Scott, Henry, Martha. M.D., C.M., Queen's U., Ont., Can., 1955. Resident in medicine Queen's U., 1955-57; registrar Maudsley Hosp., London, 1957-59; Nuffield fellow Queen's Sq., London, 1959-60; resident, research fellow Harvard neurol. unit Boston City Hosp., 1960-73; lectr.-prof. medicine div. neurology Queen's U., Kingston, Ont., chmn. div. neurology, 1971—, head dept. medicine, 1983—; mem. Med. Research Council; chmn. various provincial and fed. research coms. Author: The Nervous System, Structure and Function Disease, 1972; contbr. articles in cerebral circulation and stroke to med., sci. jours. Recipient Brown prize, 1950; Morris prize, 1950; Weil award, 1976; Nuffield fellow, 1959-60; MacLachlan fellow, 1961-62; Bullard fellow, 1962-63. Mem. Royal Coll. Physicians and Surgeons Can., Can. Neurol. Assn., Am. Neurol. Assn., Am. Acad. Neurology, Can. Med. Assn., Coll. Physicians and Surgeons Ont. and Que., Royal Soc. Medicine. Home: 95 Hill St Kingston ON K7L 2M8 Canada Office: Etherington Hall Queen's U Kingston ON K7L 3N6 Canada

DINSE, JOHN MERRELL, lawyer; b. Rochester, N.Y., June 26, 1925; s. Frank John and Lois Vanlora (Merrell) D.; m. Ann Thompson (Goodenough), Dec. 27, 1948; children—Jeffrey P., Pamela R. A.B., U. Rochester, 1947; LL.B., Cornell U., 1950. Bar: N.Y. State bar 1950, Vt. bar 1951, U.S. Dist. Ct. bar 1952, U.S. Ct. Appeals 1957. Asso. firm Austin & Edmunds, Burlington, Vt., 1950-57; partner firm Dinse, Allen & Erdmann (and predecessor firms), Burlington, 1957—. Dir. Vt. Municipal Bond Bank.; Mem. Vt. Waterways Commn., 1962-63; chmn. Vt. Jud. Nominating Bd., 1967-77; fin. chmn. Vt. Republican Party, 1967; campaign chmn. Gov. Deane C. Davis, 1968, 70. Served with U.S. Army, 1943-46. Decorated Bronze star. Fellow O2Am. Coll. Trial Lawyers Am. Bar Found., Am. Law Inst.; mem. Chittenden County Bar Assn., Vt. Bar Assn. (bd. mgrs. 1974—, pres. 1978-79), Am. Bar Assn., Am. Judicature Soc. (dir. 1975-79), No. New Eng. Def. Counsel Assn. (past pres.), Assn. Ins. Attys., Internat. Assn. Ins. Counsel, Def. Research Inst. (dir., pres. 1980, chmn. bd. 1981), New Eng. Bar Assn. (dir.). Club: Lake Champlain Yacht. Home: Harbor Rd Shelburne VT 05482 Office: 209 Battery St Burlington VT 05402

DINSMOOR, JAMES ARTHUR, psychology educator; b. Woburn, Mass., Oct. 4, 1921; s. Daniel Stark and Jean Erskine (Masson) D.; m. Anne Darrow Berninger, July 17, 1943 (div. Mar. 1953); 1 son, Daniel Stark; m. Marise Kay Sawyer, Jan. 1, 1956; children: Mara Jean, Robert Scott. B.A., Dartmouth Coll., 1943; M.A., Columbia U., 1945, Ph.D., 1949. Instr. Newark Colls., Rutgers U., 1945-46; lectr. Columbia U., N.Y.C., 1946-51; asst. prof. Ind. U., Bloomington, 1951-58, assoc. prof., 1958-63, prof. psychology, 1963—. Author: Operant Conditioning: An Experimental Analysis of Behavior, 1970. Mem. nat. bd. Nat. Com. for a Sane Nuclear Policy, Washington, 1966-68. Fellow Am. Psychol. Assn. (dir. v.p. 1977-80); mem. Soc. Exptl. Analysis of Behavior (pres. 1979-81), Midwestern Psychol. Assn. (council 1973-82, pres. 1980-81). Home: 1511 Maxwell Ln Bloomington IN 47405 Office: Dept Psychology Ind U Bloomington IN 47405

DINSMORE, GORDON GRIFFITH, management consultant; b. Passaic, N.J., Jan. 25, 1917; s. Edward Griffith and Elizabeth (Gordon) D.; m. Anne McGuire, June 22, 1946; children: Lois Marie, Gordon Griffith, Diane Elizabeth. B.A., Washington Sq. Coll., NYU, 1944; postgrad., Grad. Sch. Arts and Scis., NYU, 1944-46. With Met. Life Ins. Co., N.Y.C., 1937-82, v.p. personal ins. ops., 1971-72, v.p. corp. planning, 1972-76, sr. v.p. adminstrn., 1976-82; disting. visitor in residence Grinnell Coll. (Iowa), 1981; mgmt. cons., 1982—; cons. sec. HEW, 1957-58. Mem. council Borough of Oradell, N.J., 1956-62, pres., 1959-62; mem. Bergen County (N.J.) Republican Com., 1954-55. Mem. Pi Mu Epsilon. Club: Hackensack Golf. Home and Office: 671 Briarwood Ct Oradell NJ 07649

DION, GERARD, social science educator; b. Ste. Cecile de Frontenac, Que., Can., Dec. 5, 1912; s. Albert and Georgianna (LeBlanc) D. B.A., Levis Coll., 1935; L.Th., Laval U., Quebec, Que., 1939, L.Ph., 1942, M.S.S., 1943; LL.D. (hon.), McGill U., Montreal, Que., 1975, U. B.C., Can.), Vancouver, 1976, U. Toronto, Ont., 1978, Concordia U., Montreal, 1980, D.Litt., St. Francis Xavier U., Antigonish, N.S., 1977. Ordained priest Roman Catholic Ch., 1939; asst. prof. social sci. Laval U., 1944-49, prof. social sci., 1949-80, prof. emeritus, 1980—, prof. indsl. relations, 1944-80, asst. dir. dept. indsl. relations, 1946-56, dir. dept. indsl. relations, 1956-63; mem. Can. Prime Minister's Task Force on Labor Relations, 1966-68; chmn. Can. Textile Labour-Mgmt. Com., 1967—. Author: Vocabulaire francais-anglais des relations professionnelles/Glossary of Terms Used in Industrial Relations, 1972, Dictionnaire canadien des relations du travail, 1976; editor: Relations industrielles/Indsl. Relations, 1945—; assoc. hon. editor: Royal Soc. Can., 1975—. Mem. Econ. Council Can., 1976-80, Acad. Panel Can. Council, 1976-78, Can. Social Scis. and Humanities Research Council, 1978-81. Decorated officer Order Can.; Killam scholar, 1975-77. Mem. Can. Indsl. Relations Assn., Assn. Internationale des relations professionnelles, Indsl. Relations Research Assn., Association internationale des sociologues de langue francaise, Association canadienne de sociologie et d'anthropologie, Association canadienne de theologie, Academie des lettres et des sciences humaines. Home: 909 Mgr Grandin Quebec PQ Canada G1V 3X8 Office: Universite Laval Quebec PQ Canada G1K 7P4

DIONNE, JOSEPH GERARD, bishop; b. St. Basile, N.B., Can., June 19, 1919; s. Aurele and Octavie (Pelletier) D. B.A., Laval U., 1944; Ph.D. in Canon Law, Angelicum U., 1963. Ordained priest Roman

Cath. Ch., 1948. Asst. pastor Parish Our Lady of Sorrows, Edmundston, N.B., Can., 1948-56, pastor, 1971-75; chaplain orphanage, Edmundston, 1956-60, Hotel-Dieu, St. Basile, 1963-67; dir. Nat. Missions Office Cath. Bishops, Ottawa, Ont., 1967-71; aux. bishop Diocese Sault Ste.-Marie, Ont., 1975-83; bishop Roman Catholic Diocese, Edmundston, 1984—. Lodge: K.C. (4 degree). Home and Office: Centre Diocesain Edmundston NB Canada E3V 3K1

DIONNE, JOSEPH LEWIS, publishing company executive; b. Montgomery, Ala., June 29, 1933; s. Antonio Ernest Joseph and Myrtle Mae (Armstrong) D.; m. Joan F. Durand, June 12, 1954; children: Marsha Joan Dionne Guerin, Gary Joseph, Darren Durand. B.A., Hofstra U., 1955, M.S., 1957; Ed.D., Columbia U., 1965. Guidance counselor L.I. Public Schs., 1956-61; asst. prof. Hofstra U., Hempstead, N.Y., 1962-63; dir. instrn., project dir. Ford Found. Sch. Improvement grant Brentwood (N.Y.) Pub. Schs., 1963-66; v.p. research and devel. Ednl. Developmental Labs., Huntington, N.Y., 1966-68; v.p., gen. mgr. CTB/McGraw-Hill, Monterey, Calif., 1968-73; sr. v.p. corp. planning, McGraw-Hill, Inc., N.Y.C., 1973-77; pres. McGraw-Hill Info. Systems Co., N.Y.C., 1977-79; exec. v.p. ops. McGraw Hill, Inc., 1979-81, pres., 1981—, chief exec. officer, 1983—; dir. Equitable Life Ins. Co. Am. Past moderator, alumni council Tchrs. Coll., Columbia U., now trustee; elder Presbyn. Ch. of New Canaan; past pres. Soc. To Advance Retarded. Served as 2d lt. AUS, 1955-56. Mem. Phi Alpha Theta, Kappa Delta Pi, Phi Delta Kappa. Club: Woodway Country (Darien, Conn.). Home: 198 N Wilton Rd New Canaan CT 06840 Office: 1221 Ave of Americas New York NY 10020

DIONNE, MAURICE ADRIAN, member Canadian Parliament, educator; b. Bath, N.B., Aug. 26, 1936; s. George P. and Mary E. (McLaughlin) D.; m. Precille Babin, Aug. 12, 1961; 5 children. Student, N.B. Tchrs. Coll., St. Thomas U. Prin./high sch.; elected in gen. election House of Commons, Ottawa, 1974—, apptd. Parliamentary sec. to minister of nat. def., 1975, chmn. standing com. on transport. Liberal. Roman Catholic. Office: House of Commons Ottawa ON Canada K1A 0A6 *

D'IORIO, ANTOINE, university adminstr., chemist; b. Montreal, Que., Con., Apr. 22, 1925; s. Joseph and Assunta (Torino) D'I.; m. Ghislaine Chatel, Sept. 9, 1950 (dec. Mar. 1977); children: Michele, Luc, Marie, Johanne, Helene, Marc, Andre. B.Sc., U. Montreal, 1946, M.Sc., 1947, Ph.D., 1950. Lectr. U. Montreal, 1949-50; postdoctoral fellow U. Wis., 1950-51; asst. prof. U. Montreal, 1951-56, asso. prof., 1956-61; vis. scientist U. Oxford, Eng., 1955-56; chmn. dept. biochemistry U. Ottawa, 1961-69, dean sci. and engring., 1969-76, v.p., 1976—; editor Can. Jour. Biochemistry, 1973—. Contbr. numerous articles biogenic amines to sci. jours. Fellow Royal Soc. Can.; mem. Am. Soc. Biol. Chemists, Am. Chem. Soc., Am., Internat. socs. neurochemistry, Can. Biochem. Soc., Biochem. Soc. (London). Home: 509 Wilbrod St Ottawa ON Canada

DIOTTE, ALFRED PETER, pen company executive; b. Newport, N.H., Apr. 16, 1925; s. J. Alfred and Mary Ellen (Perry) D.; m. Helen M. Foote, June 12, 1948; children: Cathy, Cere, Peter. B.S., Marquette U., 1950; J.D., U. Wis., 1953, M.B.A., 1979; postgrad., Harvard, 1961. Bar: Wis. bar 1953. Partner Fett, Murphy & Diotte, Janesville, 1953-54; with Parker Pen Co., Janesville, 1954—, asst. sec., asst. to exec. v.p., 1957-59, asst. sec., gen. counsel, 1959-62, corporate sec., gen. counsel, 1962-68, v.p. adminstrn., sec., 1968-77, exec. v.p. adminstrn., 1977-83, sr. v.p. adminstrn., 1983—, also dir. Dir. Bancwis Corp., Bank of Wis., Janesville. Served with A.C. USNR, 1943-45. Mem. Am., Wis., Rock County bar assns. Home: Janesville WI 53545 Office: One Parker Pl Janesville WI 53545

DIPALMA, JOSEPH RUPERT, pharmacology educator; b. N.Y.C., Mar. 21, 1916; s. Frank and Anna (Attanasio) DiP.; m. Mary Solowey, June 26, 1948; children: Maria, Dorothea, Joan, Yvonne, Mary-Jo. B.S., Columbia U., 1936; M.D., SUNY, Downstate Med. Center, 1941; D.Sc. (hon.), Hahnemann Med. Coll., 1981. Intern, resident in internal medicine Kings County Hosp., Bklyn., 1942-44; asst. prof. medicine and pharmacology State U. N.Y. Downstate Med. Sch., 1946; prof. pharmacology, chmn. dept. Hahnemann Med. Coll. and Hosp., Phila., 1951-67, dean, 1967-82, v.p., 1971-72, sr. v.p., 1972-82, prof. pharmacology and medicine, 1982—; mem. bd. Regional Med. Program Southeastern Pa., 1967-75, Health Systems Agy., 1977—. Editor: Pharmacology in Medicine, 1971, Basic Pharmacology in Medicine, 1976, 2d edit., 1982; Contbr. med. jours. Recipient Alumni medallion State U. N.Y. Downstate Med. Sch., 1966. Mem. Coll. Physicians Phila. (council 1969-78), AMA, Pa., Phila. County med. socs., Am. Physiol. Soc., Am. Soc. Pharmacology and Exptl. Therapeutics, Am. Soc. Clin. Pharmacology, Alpha Omega Alpha. Home: 100 Pembroke Ave Wayne PA 19087 Office: 235 N 15th St Philadelphia PA 19102 *The creation of new ideas and approaches is always the ultimate goal.*

DIPALO, ERNEST G., government official; b. Jersey City, Nov. 30, 1932; s. Ernest Michael and Minnie (Resigno) DiP.; m. Donna Miriam Derow, Oct. 23, 1966; children: Robert Victoria, Dina. B.S., Fairleigh Dickinson U., 1962. Advt. mgr. Ridgewood Newspaper, Inc., N.J., 1957-61; social ins. specialist Social Security Adminstrn., Balt., 1961-70, chief program tng., 1973-76, dep. dir. office human resources, Balt., 1976-79, dep. assoc. commr. for pub. affairs, 1979—; exec. asst. Pres.'s Welfare Reform Program, Balt., 1970-73. Pres. Strawbridge Community Assn., Carroll County, Md., 1972, Freedom Swim Club Inc., Carroll County, Md., 1973; chmn. constrn. com. Liberty High Sch., Carroll County, Md., 1974, Am. Cancer Soc., Carroll County, Md., 1976. Served with USN, 1951-55. Recipient Superior Performance award Social Security Adminstrn., 1982, 83. Mem. Am. Soc. Tng. and Devel. Club: K.C. (Carroll County, Md.). Office: Social Security Adminstrn 6401 Security Blvd Baltimore MD 21235

DI PAOLO, JOSEPH AMEDO, geneticist; b. Bridgeport, Conn., June 13, 1924; s. John Anthony and Nancy (Montagano) Di P.; m. Arleta Mae Schrieb, June 14, 1952; children: Nancy, John. B.A., Wesleyan U., 1948; M.S., Western Res. U., 1949; Ph.D., Northwestern U., 1951. Instr. genetics bacteriology dept. biology Loyola U., Chgo., Il., 1951-53; instr. clin. and exptl. pathology Northwestern U. Med. Sch., Chgo., 1953-55; sr. cancer research scientist Roswell Park Meml. Inst., Buffalo, 1955-63; research pharmacologists, cell biologist biology br., div. cancer cause and prevention Nat. Cancer Inst., Bethesda, Md., 1963-76, chief lab. biology, div. cancer cause and prevention, 1976—; assoc. prof. lectr. anatomy George Washington U., Washington, 1973—; chmn. U.S.-Germany Cancer Program Area for Environ. Carcinogenesis, 1979—. Editor, co-author: Chemical Carcinogenesis, 1974; assoc. editor: Jour. of Nat. Cancer Inst., 1968-71, Cancer Research, 1970-78, Teratogenesis, Carcinogenesis, Mutagenesis, 1982—. Served with USN, 1943-46. Fellow N.Y. Acad. Sci., AAAS; mem. Am. Assn. Cancer Research (bd. dirs. 1983—), Am. Soc. Human Genetics, Am. Soc. Exptl. Pathology, Genetics Soc. Am., Teratology Soc., Hamster Soc., Tissue Culture Assn., Sigma Xi. Roman Catholic. Home: 6605 Melody Ln Bethesda MD 20817 Office: Bldg 37-2A-19 Rockville Pike Bethesda MD 20205

DI PASQUALE, PASQUALE, JR., coll. pres.; b. Boston, Oct. 6, 1928; s. Pasquale and Lucrezia (Caruso) Di P.; m. Charlotte Rose Fasnacht, Aug. 12, 1961; children—Theresa M., Catherine S., Maria E. B.A., U. Notre Dame, 1955; M.A., Oxford U., 1961; Ph.D., U. Pitts., 1965. Head English dept. St. Mary's Sem., Mwanza, Tanganyika, 1957-61; asst. prof. English Seton Hill Coll., 1961-65; asso. prof. Middle English lang. and lit. U. Oreg., 1965-69; prof. Ill. State U. at Normal, 1969-72; pres. Assumption Coll., Worcester, Mass., 1972-77, Loras Coll., Dubuque, Iowa, 1977—. Served with USMCR, 1950-52. Fulbright scholar, 1955-56; Fulbright grantee, 1956-57; Office of Sci. and Scholarly Research grantee U. Oreg., 1968. Mem. Modern Lang. Assn., Nat. Council Tchrs. English, AAUP, Am. Assn. U. Adminstrs., Benedictine Acad. Am., Conf. Christianity and Lit., Medieval Acad. Am., Coll. English Assn., N.Y. C.S. Lewis Soc. Address: Office of Pres Loras Coll 1450 Alta Vista Dubuque IA 52001

DI PIETRO, ROBERT JOSEPH, linguist; b. Edicott, N.Y., July 18, 1932; s. Americo Dominick and Mary Agnes Di P.; m. Vincenzina Angela Giallo, Sept. 5, 1953; children: Angela Maria, Mark Andrew. B.A. cum laude, SUNY, Binghamton, 1954; M.A., Harvard U., 1955; Ph.D., Cornell U., 1960. Project linguist Center Applied Linguistics, Rome, 1960-61; mem. faculty Georgetown U., 1961-78, prof. linguistics, 1969-78, chmn. Italian dept., 1966-68; dir. Inter-Univ. English Program, Madrid, 1963-64; prof. linguistics and Italian, chmn. dept. lang., dir. inter-deptl. program in linguistics U. Del., Newark, 1978—; Fulbright lectr., Italy, 1960-61, Spain, 1963-64, W. Ger., 1978; Andrew Mellon disting. lectr. Georgetown U., 1975-78; lectr. Internat. Communications Agy., Yugoslavia, 1978-80, Finland, 1981; Spanish lang. proficiency tester Dept. State, Venezuela, 1965; bd. dirs. Nat. Italian Am. Found., 1979—; developer Strategic Interaction (methodology for fgn. lang. instrn.). Author: Language Structures in Contrast, 2d edit, 1978, Japanese edit., 1974, Italian edit., 1978, Language as Human Creation, 1978; editor: Linguistics and the Professions, 1982, New Perspectives in American Literature, 1983; founder, editor: Interfaces, 1974—. Decorated Cavaliere Ufficiale, Italy, 1977. Mem. MLA, Linguistic Soc. Am., Linguistic Assn. Can. and U.S. (a founder), Soc. Italiana di Linguistica, Am. Assn. Tchrs. Italian, Am. Anthrop. Assn., AAAS. Club: Chesterbrook Swim (McLean). Home: 1706 Woodman Dr McLean VA 22101 Office: Dept Langs U Del Newark DE 19711 *Personal ambition must always be tempered by concern for the welfare of others.*

DIPRIMA, DIANE, poet, playwright; b. N.Y.C., Aug. 6, 1934; d. Francis and Emma (Mallozzi) diP.; m. Alan S. Marlowe, 1962; children: Jeanne, Dominique, Alexander. Student, Swarthmore Coll., 1950-52. Co-editor: The Floating Bear, 1961-63; editor: Kulchur, 1960-61, Signal mag., 1963; editor, pub.: (with Alan S. Marlowe) Poets Press, N.Y.C., 1964-69; books include Dinners and Nightmares, 1961, New Handbook of Heaven, 1963, Earthsong: Poems, 1957-59, 1968, Hotel Albert, 1968, Revolutionary Letters, 1969, The Book of Hours, Loba, 1973; pub.: Eidolon Edits., San Francisco, 1972-76; dir.: N.Y. Poets Theatre, 1961-65; author: This Kind of Bird Flies Backward, 1958; (play) Murder Cake, 1960, Paideuma, 1960, The Discontent of a Russian Prince, 1961, Like, 1964; (poetry) The Monster, 1961, Poets Vaudeville, 1964, Haiku, 1967, The Star, The Child, The Light, 1968; (novel) Memoirs of a Beatnik, 1969, L.A. Odyssey, 1969, New As . . ., 1969, Notes on a Summer Solstice, 1969, Prayer to the Mothers, 1971, So Fine, 1971; (novel) The Calculus of Variation, 1972; Poems for Freddie, 3 vols., 1972-78, Selected Poems, 1956-75, 1975; editor: (with LeRoi Jones) The Floating Bear: A Newsletter, Nos. 1-37, 1974, War Poems, 1968, Various Fables from Various Places, 1960. Nat. Inst. Arts and Letters grantee, 1965; Nat. Endowment Arts grantee, 1966. *

DI PRIMA, RICHARD CLYDE, educator, mathematician; b. Terre Haute, Ind., Aug. 9, 1927; s. Clyde and Ethel (Phillips) DiPrima; m. Maureen P. Clune, Nov. 27, 1954; children: Shivaun, Richard Clyde. B.S., Carnegie Inst. Tech., 1950, M.S., 1951, Ph.D., 1953. Research asso. MIT, 1953-54; research fellow Harvard U., 1954-56; research physicist Hughes Aircraft Co., 1956-57; mem. faculty Rensselaer Poly. Inst., 1957—, prof. math., 1962—, asso. dean Grad. Sch., 1968-72, chmn. Faculty Council, 1969-70, chmn. dept. math. scis., 1972-81, Eliza Ricketts Found. prof. math., 1979—; cons. to industry, 1961—; Fulbright lectr. Weizmann Inst. Sci., Rehovoth, Israel, 1964-65; mem. com. recommendations U.S. Army basic sci. research Nat. Acad. Sci.-NRC, 1976—, chmn., 1981—; mem. sci. council Inst. Computer Application, Sci. and Engring., NASA-Langley Research Center, 1977—, chmn., 1981-82; mem. adv. bd. Office Math. Scis. NRC, 1979—; mem. vis. com. Center for Application of Math.; also dept. math. Lehigh U. Author: Elementary Differential Equations and Boundary Value Problems, 1965, 3d edit., 1977, Elementary Differential Equations, 1965, 3d edit. 1977, Introduction to Differential Equations, 1970; editor: Physics of Fluids, 1973-76; mem. editorial bd.: Mechanics Research Communications, 1973—. Mem. budget com. Troy United Fund, 1960-64; mem. adv. bd. Albany Diocesan Office Health and Social Services, 1966-70, v.p., 1969-70. Served with AUS, 1946-48. Guggenheim fellow, 1982-83; Fulbright research fellow Weizmann Inst., 1983. Fellow Am. Acad. Mechanics (pres. 1976-77), Am. Phys. Soc., ASME (exec. com. 1977-82, chmn. 1981-82, William H. Wiley Disting. Faculty award 1980); mem. Am. Math. Soc., Am. Math. Assn., Soc. Indsl. and Applied Math. (mem. council 1970—, v.p. for programs 1975-77, trustee 1977-80, pres. 1978-80), Soc. Natural Philosophy, Conf. Bd. Math. Scis. (exec. com. 1975-78), Sigma Xi. Home: 3 Meadowbrook Ln Troy NY 12180

DIQUINZIO, PASQUALE JOSEPH, lawyer, lecturer; b. Phila., Dec. 31, 1925; s. Domenic and DiSantis DiQ.; m. Bernice Amelia Canzanese, Sept. 8, 1953; children: Patrice, Mark, Mary, David. B.A., Temple U., 1951; J.D., U. Pa., 1954. Bar: Pa. 1955. Law clk. J. Goodrich 3d Circuit Ct. Appeals, Phila., 1954-55, Justice H. H. Burton U.S. Supreme Ct., Washington, 1955-56; assoc. Dechert Price & Rhoads, 1956-63, ptnr., Phila., 1963—; lectr. law Temple U., Phila., 1971-80, Willanova U., Pa., 1980—; vice chmn. plannig commn. Pa. State U. Tax Conf., 1981, chmn., 1982. Mng. editor: U. Pa. Law Rev., 1953-54; contr. articles on taxes to legal jours. Served with USN, 1944-46. Mem. ABA (tax sect. 1957-83), Phila. Bar Assn. (tax sect. 1956-83). Roman Catholic. Clubs: Rolling Green Gold (Springfield, Pa.); Racquet (Phila.). Home: 521 Williamson Ln Springfield PA 19064 Office: Dechert Price & Roads 3400 Centre Square W 1500 Market St Philadelphia PA 19102

DIRAC, PAUL ADRIEN MAURICE, physicist, educator; b. Bristol, Eng., Aug. 8, 1902; s. Charles Adrien Ladislas and Florence Hannah (Holten) D. D.Sc., Bristol U., 1921; Ph.D., U. Cambridge, 1926. Vis. lectr. U. Wis., 1929, U. Mich., 1929, Princeton U., 1931; Lucasian prof. math. U. Cambridge, 1932-69; mem. Inst. Advanced Studies, Princeton, NJ, 1947-48, 58-59; prof. physics Fla. State U., Tallahassee, 1971—. Author: Principles of Quantum Mechanics, 1930, 4th edit., 1958, Lectures on Quantum Mechanics, 1966, The Development of Quantum Theory, 1971, Spinors in Hilbert Space, 1974, General Theory of Relativity, 1975. Recipient Nobel prize in physics (with Erwin Schrodinger), 1933, Royal Medal, 1939, Copley medal Royal Soc. London, 1952, Order of Merit, 1973. Fellow Royal Soc.; mem. Nat. Acad. Scis. (fgn. assoc.). Office: Dept Physics Fla State U Tallahassee FL 32306 *

DIRCKS, WILLIAM JOSEPH, govt. ofcl.; b. N.Y.C., Sept. 20, 1929; s. Bruno and Irene (McCartney) D.; m. Rosemarie Van Eycken Barrett, June 11, 1966; 1 dau., Elizabeth Barrett; stepchildren—Clare Killeen, Barrett Killeen. B.A., Fordham U., 1951; M.A., Clark U., 1958; postgrad., U. Calif., Berkeley, 1959-60. Asst. instr. U. Calif., Berkeley, 1959-60; with AEC, Washington, 1960-66, OEO, 1966-67; dir. research and analysis U.S. Travel Service, Commerce Dept., 1967-71; sr. staff mem. Pres.'s Council on Environ. Quality, 1971-74; exec. asst. to adminstr. EPA, 1974-75; dep. exec. dir. Nuclear Regulatory Commn., Washington, 1975-78, dir. nuclear material safety and safeguards, Silver Spring, Md., 1978-80, exec. dir., Washington, 1980—. Author: Urban and America: Policies for Future Growth. Served with USAF, 1951-59. Clubs: Fordham, Cosmos (Washington). Home: 5104 Baltan Rd Washington DC 20016 Office: Nuclear Regulatory Commn 1717 H St NW Washington DC 20555

DIRECTOR, STEPHEN WILLIAM, electrical engineering educator, researcher; b. Bklyn., June 28, 1943; s. Murray and Lillian (Brody) D.; m. Lorraine Schwartz, June 20, 1965; children: Joshua, Kimberly, Cynthia, Deborah. B.S., SUNY-Stony Brook, 1965; M.S., U. Calif.-Berkeley, 1967, Ph.D., 1968. Prof. elec. engring. U. Fla., Gainesville, 1968-77; vis. scientist IBM Research Labs., Yorktown Heights, N.Y., 1974-75; prof. elec. and computer engring. Carnegie-Mellon U., Pitts., 1977—, U.A. and Helen Whitaker prof. electronics and elec. engring., 1980—, prof. computer sci., 1981—; head dept. elec. and computer engring. U.A. and Helen Whitaker prof. electronics and elec. engring., Pitts., 1982—; cons. Intel Corp., Santa Clara, Calif., 1977—, Digital Equipment Corp., Hudson, Mass., 1982—; cons. editor McGraw-Hill Book Co., N.Y.C., 1976—; dir. Research Ctr. Computer-Aided Design, Pitts., 1982—. Author: Introduction to System Theory, 1972, Circuit Theory, 1975; editor: Computer-Aided Design, 1974. Recipient Frederick Emmons Terman Am. Soc. Engring. Edn., 1976. Fellow IEEE (W.R.G. Prize 1979, Centennial medal 1984); mem. IEEE Circuits and Systems Soc. (pres. 1981, Best Paper 1970, assoc. editor jour 1973-75), IEEE Computer Soc. Office: Dept Elec and Computer Engring Carnegie-Mellon U Schenley Park Pittsburgh PA 15213

DIRENZO, GORDON JAMES, sociology educator, social psychologist; b. North Attleboro, Mass., July 19, 1934; s. Santo and Giulia (Petti) DiR.; m. Mary Kathleen Ryan, July 6, 1968; children: Maria Giulia, Chiara Veronica, Marco Santo. B.A., U. Notre Dame, 1956, M.A., 1957, Ph.D., 1963; postgrad., Harvard U., 1959, Columbia U., 1963-65, U. Colo., 1964. Diplomate: Cert. social psychologist. Instr. Coll. of St. Rose, Albany, N.Y., 1957-59, U. Portland, Oreg., 1961-62; asst. prof. Fairfield (Conn.) U., 1962-66; asso. prof. Ind. U., South Bend, 1966-70; prof. sociology U. Del., Newark, 1970—; mem. faculty Siena Coll., Albany (N.Y.) Med. Center, 1958-59, U. Notre Dame, 1960-61, Coll. White Plains, 1963-65, Bklyn. Coll., 1965, Western Conn. State Coll., 1964, SUNY, Stony Brook, 1964; affiliate mem. med. and dental staff Wilmington (Del.) Med. Center, 1976—, St. Francis Hosp., Wilmington, 1980—, Northeastern Hosp., Phila., 1982—; dir. Sociol. Cons. Group, North Attleboro, 1963—; Fulbright-Hays prof. U. Rome, 1968-69, U. Bologna, Italy, 1980-81. Contbr. articles to profl. jours.; author: Personality, Power and Politics, 1967, Concepts, Theory and Explanation in the Behavioral Sciences, 1966, Personality and Politics, 1974, We, the People: American Character and Social Change, 1977, Sociological Perspectives, 1984. U. Notre Dame fellow, 1959-60; Ford Found. grantee, 1960; Italian Ministry of Edn. fellow, 1960; NSF fellow, 1964; Nat. Endowment for Humanities grantee, 1975; Del. Inst. Med. Edn. and Research grantee, 1975; recipient Disting. Service award Am. Assn. Family Practice, 1980, 82, 84. Fellow Am. Sociol. Assn.; mem. Am. Psychol. Assn., AAUP, AAAS, Assn. Behavioral Scis. in Med. Edn., Soc. Personality and Social Psychology, Am.-Italian Hist. Assn. (nat. exec. council 1977-80), Fulbright Alumni Assn., Internat. Sociol. Assn., Clin. Sociology Assn., Internat. Soc. Polit. Psychology (charter), Soc. Psychologists in Medicine, Internat. Polit. Sci. Assn., Soc. for Study Social Problems, Soc. Psychol. Study Social Issues, Eastern Sociol. Soc., Alpha Kappa Delta. Home: 28 Deer Run Little Baltimore Farms Newark DE 19711 Office: Dept Sociology U Del Newark DE 19711

DIRIDON, RODNEY JOHN (ROD), county official; b. Dunsmuir, Calif., Feb. 8, 1939; s. Claude and Rhoda Middleton (Covert) D.; m. Mary Ann Fudge, July 4, 1964; children: Rodney John, Mary Margaret. Student, Chico State U., 1958-59; M.S., San Jose State U., 1963. Service sta. attendant Lamberts Texaco, 1953-56; carpenter's apprentice De Borre Constrn. Co., 1956-58; fireman/brakeman S.P. R.R., 1958-63; skiing instr. Mt. Shasta Ski Bowl, 1960-63; fraternity comptroller Sigma Phi Epsilon, 1960-62; research asst. San Jose State U. Inst. Bus. Econ. Research, 1963, mem. dean's council, 1971-73, pres.'s council, 1969-72; mgmt. systems analyst Lockheed Missiles Co., 1967-69; pres., chief exec. officer Diridon Research Corp., San Jose, Calif., 1969-75, chmn., 1978, 81; bd. suprs. Santa Clara County, 1975-83; adj. prof. San Jose State U.; dir. League Calif. Cities Environ. Com., 1973—; mem. exec. com. Assn. Bay Area Govts., 1972—, pres., 1976-78; cons. Saratoga City Council, 1972-74, Save San Francisco Bay Assn., 1971-77; county chmn. State Bd., 1970-72; chmn. Santa Clara County Employment Tng. Bd., 1977; mem. Transit Bd. Santa Clara County, 1975-83, chmn., 1979, 82; mem. Met. Transp. Commn., 1979—; chmn. bd. Calif. Library Authority for Systems and Services, 1976; mem. transp. steering com. Nat. Assn. Counties; chmn. Citizens for Transit Action Com., 1976-79, Santa Clara County Energy Task Team, 1976-77. Publisher: The County Report, 1969-74. Bd. dirs. Mental Health Assn. Calif.; promotion chmn. Spl. Olympics for Mentally Retarded Children, 1971-72, 75-77; chmn. citizens adv. bd. County Methadone Program, 1970-71; mem. adv. com. San Jose-Santa Clara Water Pollution Control Treatment Plant; mem. joint conf. com. Valley Med. Center, 1978; chmn. and vice-chmn. San Jose Citizens Community Improvement Com., 1969-73; founding chmn. County Research Soc., 1971-72; pres. San Jose Symphony Assn., 1973-75; founder Nat. Council on Alcoholism; bd. dirs. Multiple Sclerosis Soc., Am. Heart Assn., 1971-72, Dental Health Council Calif., Retirement Jobs, Inc., Santa Clara Central div. United Way, 1975-77; chmn. Scout-O-Rama, 1976-83; chmn. bd. govs. Central Santa Clara County YMCA, 1973; chmn. Solar Energy Tech. Adv. Com., 1978-79; chmn. bd. control Guadalupe Corridor Study, 1979-82; chmn. Guadalupe Corridor Joint Powers Bd., 1983; mem. Intergovtl. Council mem. Intergovtl. Council; chmn. Peninsula Transp. Alternatives Program, 1978-83; mem. State Solar Calif. Local Govt. Commn.; vice chmn. Bay Area Air Quality Mgmt. Dist., 1983. Served with USNR, 1963-67. Named Disting. Citizen San Francisco area San Jose City Council, 1973, One of Five Outstanding Young Men Calif., 1973, One of Ten Outstanding Young Men Am., 1973. Mem. County Suprs. Assn. Calif. (chmn. transp. and public works com.), Calif. Assn. Regional Councils San Jose State U. Alumni Assn. (dir. 1969-72), Calif. Jr. C. of C. (pres.), Jaycees (senator), San Jose Jr. C. of C. (pres., chmn. bd. 1969-70). Episcopalian. Clubs: Rotarian., Commonwealth (San Francisco). Home: 870 Camino Dr Santa Clara CA 95050 Office: 70 W Hedding St 10th Floor San Jose CA 95110

DIRKS, KENNETH RAY, pathologist, army officer, medical educator; b. Newton, Kans., Feb. 11, 1925; s. Jacob Kenneth and Ruth Viola (Penner) D.; m. Betty Jean Worsham, June 9, 1946; children: Susan Jan, Jeffrey Mark, Deborah Anne, Timothy David, Melissa Jane. M.D., Washington U., St. Louis, 1947. Diplomate: Am. Bd. Pathology. Rotating intern St. Louis City Hosp., 1948, asst. resident in gen. surgery, 1948-49; resident in pathology VA Hosp., Jefferson Barracks, Mo., 1951-53, resident in pathology, asst. chief lab. service, Indpls., 1953-54; resident in pathology Letterman Army Hosp., San Francisco, 1956-57; fellow in tropical medicine and parasitology La. State U., Central Am., 1958; asst. in pathology Washington U. Sch. Medicine, 1952-53; asst. chief lab. service VA Hosp., Jefferson Barracks, 1953; instr. pathology U. Ind. Med. Center,

Indpls., 1953-54; commd. capt. M.C. U.S. Army, 1954, advanced through grades to maj. gen., 1976; dir. research Med. Research and Devel. Command, Washington, 1968-69, comdr., 1969-71, comdr, dep. comdr., 1973-76, Med. Research Inst. Infectious Diseases, Ft. Detrick, Frederick, Md., 1972-73, comdr., 1973, Fitzsimons Army Med. Center, Denver, 1976-77; supt. Acad. Health Scis., Ft. Sam Houston, Tex., 1977-80; asso. prof. pathology and lab. medicine Coll. Medicine, Tex. A&M U., College Station, 1980—. Contbr. articles to med. jours. Decorated D.S.M., Legion of Merit with oak leaf cluster, Meritorious Service medal, Army Commendation medal with oak leaf cluster. Fellow Coll. Am. Pathologists, Internat. Acad. Pathology. Address: 2513 Oak Circle Bryan TX 77801 *1) Know your job and work hard. 2) Respect all persons. 3) Be candid and honest always. 4)Persevere in the face of adversity. 5) Love God, country, and other people. 6) Help others.*

DIRKS, LEE EDWARD, newspaper executive; b. Indpls., Aug. 4, 1935; s. Raymond Louis and Virginia Belle (Wagner) D.; m. Barbara Dee Nutt, June 16, 1956; children: Stephen Merle, Deborah Virginia, David Louis. B.A., DePauw U., 1956; M.A., Fletcher Sch. Law and Diplomacy, 1957. Reporter Boston Globe, 1957, Nat. Observer, Washington, 1962-65, news editor, 1966-68; securities analyst specializing in newspaper stocks Dirks Bros., Ltd., Washington, 1969-71, Delafield, Childs, Inc., 1971-75, C.S. McKee & Co., 1975-76; asst. to pres. Detroit Free Press, 1976-77, v.p., gen. mgr., 1977-80; pres. Lee Dirks & Assos., Detroit, 1980—; lectr. Am. Press Inst., 1971—; cons. newspaper econs., 1971-76. Author: Religion in Action, 1965; pub.: Newspaper Newsletter, 1970-76. Bd. dirs. Nat. Ghost Ranch Found., Santa Fe, 1973—. Served to capt. USAF, 1957-61. Named Religion Writer of Yr. Religious Newswriters Assn., 1964. Fellow Religious Pub. Relations Council; mem. Phi Beta Kappa, Lambda Chi Alpha. Methodist. Clubs: Nat. Press (Washington); Renaissance, Oakland Hills (Detroit). Home: 3150 Kenway Dr Bloomfield Hills MI 48013 Office: Suite 3870 400 Renaissance Center Detroit MI 48243

DIRKS, LESLIE CHANT, government official; b. New Ulm, Minn., Mar. 7, 1936; s. Emereld Francis and Eva (Gay) D.; m. Eleanor G. McPeake, Feb. 10, 1959; children: Anthony, Jason, Elizabeth. B.S. in Physics, MIT, 1958, Oxford (Eng.) U., 1960. Instr. physics Phillips Acad., Andover, Mass., 1960-61; with CIA, 1961—, dep. dir. sci. and tech., 1976—. Recipient Disting. Intelligence medal CIA, 1977, Nat. Security medal, 1978; ann. award IEEE, 1980. Mem. Nat. Acad. Engring. Home: 45 Hancock St Lexington MA 02173 Office: Raytheon Co Lexington MA 02173

DIRKSEN, RICHARD WAYNE, canon precentor, organist, choirmaster; b. Freeport, Ill., Feb. 8, 1921; s. Richard Watson and Maude (Logeman) D.; m. Joan Milton Shaw, Jan. 9, 1942; children: Richard Shaw, Geoffrey Paul, Laura Gail, Mark Christopher. C.O.C., Peabody Conservatory, 1942; D.F.A. (hon.), George Washington U., 1981. Asst. organist-choirmaster Washington Cathedral, 1942-47, assoc. organist-choirmaster, 1947-69, dir. program, 1964-69, precentor, 1969—, organist-choirmaster, 1977—. Composer sacred music and secular operettas. Served to sgt. U.S. Army, 1942-45. Named Disting. Alumnus Peabody Conservatory, 1980. Mem. AM. Guild Organists, Assn. Anglican Musicians, ASCAP. Episcopalian. Office: Washington Cathedral Mount Saint Alban Washington DC 20016

DIRVIN, GERALD VINCENT, consumer products company executive; b. Phila., Mar. 28, 1937; s. Vincent A. and Mary (Fitch) D.; m. Polly Burnett, June 27, 1959; children: John, David, Barbara. B.A., Hamilton Coll., Clinton, N.Y., 1959. With Procter & Gamble Co., 1959—, sales mgr., then v.p. coffee div., 1975-80, group v.p., Cin., 1980—, dir., 1981—; bd. dirs., Nat. Coffee Assn. Am. Mem. exec. bd. Dan Beard council Boy Scouts Am.; trustee Creater Cin. Cancer Control Program, Hamilton Coll., Cin. Zoo; mem. president's council Xavier U., Cin. Republican. Roman Catholic. Clubs: Commonwealth, Camargo, Queen City. Office: Procter & Gamble Co PO Box 599 Cincinnati OH 45201

DI SABATO, LOUIS ROMAN, zoo dir.; b. Columbus, Ohio, Oct. 7, 1931; s. Roman John and Lucille Katherine (Bernard) DiS.; m. Phyllis Ann Thompson, July 8, 1953; children—Christopher R., Julie Ann, Maura L., Carol N., Kathleen. Student, Ohio State U., 1949-52. With Columbus Municipal Zoo, 1955-63, dir., 1961-63, Seneca Park Zoo, Rochester, N.Y., 1963-68, San Antonio Zool. Gardens and Aquarium, 1968—. Served to 2d lt. U.S. Army, 1952-55. Fellow Am. Assn. Zool. Parks and Aquariums; mem. Internat. Wild Waterfowl Assn. Roman Catholic. Club: Rotary (sec.). *

DI SANT'ANGELO, GIORGIO, designer; b. Florence, Italy, May 5, 1939; came to U.S., 1962; s. Domingo Imperatrice and Leila (Ratti) di Sant'A. Grad., U. Architecture, Buenos Aires, 1960. With indsl. design studio in, Argentina, 1960-61; tchr. indsl. design Rodari Sch. Design, Rosario, Argentina, 1959; textile designer Gloria Buse Studio, N.Y.C., 1962; stylist Ameritex, N.Y.C., 1962, Marcus Bros., 1963; propr. Sant'Angelo Ready-to-Wear, N.Y.C., 1966-67, di Sant'Angelo, Inc., 1968—. Free-lance architect and indsl. designer, Rome, Italy; indsl. designer, decorator: Caribean Hotel, Nassau, 1963; free-lance accessories designer, 1966. Served as lt. Argentine Army, 1954. Recipient 1st prize ceramics, Argentina, 1959, 1st prize sculpture, 1968, 1st prize animation, Buenos Aires, 1961; Spl. Coty award, 1968, 70; Winnie award, 1970; Tommy award Am. Printed Fabric Council, 1975; Inspiration Home Furnishings award, 1978. Mem. Fashion Designers Am. (council 1969). Office: 20 W 57th St New York NY 10019 *For a creator, it is more important to meet one's own standards than it is to please others. It is only then that one becomes an individual.* *

DISBROW, RICHARD EDWIN, utility executive; b. Newark, Sept. 20, 1930; s. Milton A. and Madeline Catherine (Segal) D.; m. Patricia Fair Warner, June 27, 1953 (div. Sept. 1972); children: John Scott, Lisa Karen; m. Teresa Marie Moser, May 12, 1973. B.S., Lehigh U., 1952; M.S. in elec. engring., Newark Coll. Engring., 1959, MIT, 1965. With Am. Electric Power Service Corp., N.Y.C., 1954—, Columbus, Ohio, 1954—, transmission and distbn. mgr., 1967-70, controller, 1970-71, v.p., controller, 1971-74, exec. v.p., 1974-75, vice chmn. bd.,, 1975-79, pres., chief adminstrv. officer, 1979—, dir.; pres., dir. Am. Electric Power Co.; instr. Newark Coll. Engring., 1959-64; mem. N.J. Engrs. Com. For Student Guidance, 1960-64; mem. vis. com. dept. mech. engring. and mechanics Lehigh U. Indsl. com., 1960-64; trustee Franklin U. Served to 1st lt. USAF, 1952-54. Sloan fellow MIT. Mem. Edison Electric Inst. (dir.), Psi Upsilon, Eta Kappa Nu. Clubs: Columbus Athletic, Worthington Hills Country. Office: Am Electric Power Service Corp 1 Riverside Plaza Columbus OH 43216

DISCH, THOMAS MICHAEL, author; b. Des Moines, Iowa, Feb. 2, 1940; s. Felix H. and Helen M. (Gilbertson) D. Student, Washington Sq. Coll., 1959-62. Mem. faculty U. Minn., Mpls., Wesleyan U., Conn. Free lance writer novels, short stories, poetry and criticism, 1964—; author: over 20 books including The Genocides, 1965, Camp Concentration, 1968; 334, 1972, Getting Into Death and Other Stories, 1976, Clara Reeve, 1975, On Wings of Song, 1979 (John W. Campbell Meml. award), (with Charles Naylor) Neighboring Lives, 1981; The Businessman: A Tale of Terror, 1984; poetry ABCDEFG HIJKLM NPOQRST UVWXYZ, 1981, Here I Am, There You Are, Where Were We, 1984; books editor: Twilight Zone; contbr.: numerous poems and articles, lit. criticism to publs. including Poetry; libretto opera Frankenstein. Recipient Brit. Sci. Fiction award, 1981. Mem. PEN., NBCC. Office: care John Schaffner Assoc New York NY *

DISCHER, CHARLES DALE, manufacturing and marketing company executive; b. Kalamazoo, July 22, 1924; s. Charles V. and Ethel (Bailor) D.; m. Patricia E. Krause, June 12, 1948; children: Brett, Christine. A.B., Kalamazoo Coll., 1949; M.A., Mich. State U., 1951. C.P.A., Mich.; registered prin. Nat. Assn. Securities Dealers. Staff mem. firm Seidman & Seidman, Grand Rapids, Mich., 1951-54; servicing mgr. Albert Mortgages, Inc., Grand Rapids, 1954-56; sec. treas. Baxter Laundries Corp., Grand Rapids, 1956-63; v.p., investment officer Amway Corp., Ada, Mich., 1963—; pres., dir. Amway Mgmt. Co., Amway Mut. Fund, Amway Stock Transfer Co.; chmn. bd. Halcyon Petroleum, Inc.; dir. Preferred Properties Inc. Mem. exec. bd. Grand Valley Council Boy Scouts Am., 1968—; Bd. assos. Carthage Coll., Kenosha, Wis., 1971—; bd. advisers Ferris State Coll., Big Rapids, Mich., YWCA, Grand Rapids. Served with AUS, 1943-46. Decorated Purple Heart. Mem. Am. Inst. C.P.A.s, Mich. Assn. C.P.A.s Lutheran (treas.). Clubs: D.A.V., Peninsular. Home: 2705 Hall St SE Grand Rapids MI 49506 Office: 7575 E Fulton Rd Ada MI 49355

DISHAROON, LESLIE BENJAMIN, insurance company executive; b. Phila., Aug. 6, 1932; s. Theodore Lee and Sally (Oglesby) D.; m. Ann Merriwether, June 26, 1954; children: Lee Ann Disharoon Tolzmann, Beth Disharoon Morris, Martha Disharoon French, Carrie Disharoon Souter. B.A., Brown U., 1954; M.B.A., Columbia U., 1956. C.L.U. With Conn. Gen. Life Ins. Co., 1956-60, Conn. Mut. Life Ins. Co., Hartford, Conn., 1960-77; chmn. bd. Monumental Life Ins. Co., Balt., 1977-83; pres., dir. Monumental Corp., 1978—, chmn. bd., 1979—; dir. 1st Md. Bancorp., Balt. Gas & Electric, Preston Trucking Co., Vol. State Life Ins. Co., Chattanooga. Trustee Johns Hopkins Hosp., Balt., Goucher Coll., Towson, Md., 1977—; mem. Greater Balt. Com., 1977—. Mem. Beta Gamma Sigma. Clubs: Farmington Country (Charlottesville, Va.); Md., Center (Balt); Green Spring Valley Hunt (Garrison, Md.); Swan Island (Currituck, N.C.); Princess Anne Country (Virginia Beach, Va.). Office: 2 E Chase St Baltimore MD 21202

DISHER, JOHN HOWARD, aerospace consultant; b. Olmstead, N.D., Dec. 23, 1921; s. Howard Merlin and Mary Christine (Johnston) D.; m. Lillian Helen Rusnak, Apr. 19, 1948; children—James Howard, John Thomas. B.M.E., U. N.D., 1943; grad., Advanced Mgmt. Program, Harvard U., 1969. With NASA, 1943-81; aero. research scientist Lewis Propulsion Lab., Cleve., 1943-51, head flight research sect., 1951-58; project engr. Mercury, Langley Field, Va., 1959-60, head advanced manned systems, Washington, 1960-61; asst. dir. Apollo spacecraft devel., 1961-63; dir. Apollo Test, 1963-65; dep. dir. Skylab program, 1965-74, dir. advanced programs manned spaceflight, 1974-80; aerospace cons., 1981—; Mem. tech. com. Indpls. 500 Automobile Race. Author articles on hypersonic heat transfer, propulsion and aerodynamics. Mem. alumni adv. council U. N.D. Coll. Engring. Recipient Sustained Superior Performance award NASA, 1965, Exceptional Service medal, 1969, 80, Disting. Service medal, 1974. Asso. fellow Am. Inst. Aeros. and Astronautics; mem. Harvard Alumni Assn., U.S. Auto Club (tech. com.), Sigma Nu. Presbyterian. Home and office: 8407 Whitman Dr Bethesda MD 20817 *When I started with NASA/NACA in 1943 we were struggling to get our fighter planes to 400 miles an hour. Four years later we'd broken the sound barrier and in the next 15 we'd send John Glenn around the earth at 17,000 miles an hour and were getting ready to land men on the moon before the decade was through. Now we have the space shuttle that takes men and cargo into space in a rocket ship and returns like a plane. Truly its been an incredible 40 years and more downright pleasure, fun and excitement than I can describe! I believe that NASA's record demonstrates that we can excel as a nation when the goal is clear and the motivation strong.*

DISHMAN, LEONARD I., accountant; b. Chgo., May 4, 1920; s. Morris and Jennie (Siegel) D.; m. Frances J. Bernstein, Sept. 26, 1942; children: Ethelynn Dishman Kleiman, Michael. B.S.C., Central YMCA Coll., Chgo., 1942; postgrad., Northwestern U., 1948. Office mgr. Witco Chem. Co., Chgo., 1947-48; nat. credit mgr. Philip Blum & Co., Chgo., 1948-51; asst. comptroller, office mgr., personnel mgr. Triangle Distbrs. Inc., Chgo., 1951-53; comptroller Lee Shell Co., Chgo., 1953-55; pub. acct., Chgo., 1947—; gen. partner Torrence Assns., Chgo., 1963—; pres. The Ozark Co., Len Ber Ltd.; partner 5700 Co.; dir. Welstead & Welstead, Inc. Bd. dirs. Ill. Wildlife Endowment, 1971-82, pres., 1971-73. Mem. Ind. Accts. Assn. Ill. (pres. chpt. 1972-73). Home: 5104 W Fitch Ave Skokie IL 60077 Office: 5799 N Lincoln Ave Chicago IL 60659

DISHY, BOB, actor; b. Bklyn.; s. Nathan and Amy (Barazani) D. Ed. in drama, Syracuse U. Appeared: in Broadway plays Damn Yankees, 1955, From A to Z, Flora The Red Menace, The Unknown Soldier and His Wife, Something Different, The Goodbye People, A Way of Life, The Creation of the World and Other Business, An American Millionaire, Sly Fox, Murder at the Howard Johnsons, Grown Ups; off-Broadway plays Chic, There Is A Play Tonight, Can-Can, By Jupiter; also appeared in various regional theaters; appeared in: films, including The Tiger Makes Out, Lovers and Others Strangers, The Big Bus, Last Married Couple in America, First Family, Author, Author; numerous network and Pub. Broadcasting System show; mem. co.: TV series That Was The Week That Was; actor, dir.: Story Theatre. Served with U.S. Army, 1957-59. Winner All-Army Entertainment Contest.

DISNEY, POLEY H., consumer products company executive; b. Harrisburg, Ill., Sept. 3, 1939; s. Poley H. and Mary Elizabeth (Parrot) D. Cert. in acctg., Southeastern Ill. Coll., 1964; B.S., U. Evansville, 1966. With Mead Johnson, Evansville, Ind., 1966-80, controller, 1975-80; sr. v.p. Drackett Co., Cin., 1980-82; v.p., controller Bristol Myers Co., N.Y.C., 1982-83, pres. products div., 1983—. Mem. Pres. Collegium Eckerd Coll. Mem. Proprietary Assn. Office: Bristol-Myers Products 345 Park Ave New York NY 10154 *

DISNEY, ROY EDWARD, broadcasting company executive; b. Los Angeles, Jan. 10, 1930; s. Roy Oliver and Edna (Francis) D.; m. Patricia Ann Dailey, Sept. 17, 1955; children: Roy Patrick, Susan Margaret, Abigail Edna, Timothy John. B.A., Pomona Coll., 1951. Guest relations exec. NBC, Hollywood, Calif., 1952; apprentice film editor Mark VII Prodns. Hollywood, Calif., 1942; asst. film eidtor, cameraman prodn. asst., writer, producer, dir. Walt Disney Prodns., Burbank, Calif., 1954-77; pres. Roy E. Disney Prodns. Inc., Burbank, Calif., 1978—; chmn. bd. dir. Shamrock Broadcasting Co., Hollywood, Calif., 1979—, Shamrock Holdings Inc., Burbank, CALIF., 1980—; dir. Walt Disney Prodns., 1967—; trustee Calif. Inst. Arts, Valencia, 1967—. Author: novelized adaptation of Perri; producer movie: Pacific High; writer, dir., producer numerous TV prodns. Bd. dirs. Big Bros. of Greater Los Angeles; mem. adv. bd. dirs. St. Joseph Med. Ctr., Burbank; mem. U.S. Naval Acad. Sailing Squadron, Annapolis, Md.; fellow U. Ky. Recipient Acad. award nomination for Mysteries of the Deep. Mem. Dirs. Guild Am. West, Writers Guild Am. Republican. Clubs: 100, Confrerie des Chevaliers du Tastevin, St.Francis Yacht, St. Francis Yacht, Calif. Yacht, San Diego Yacht, Transpacific Yacht. Office: Shamrock Holdings Inc 4421 Riverside Dr Suite 207 Burbank CA 91505

DISPEKER, THEA, artists' rep.; b. Munich, Germany; d. Moritz and Emma Schlesinger; m. Lawrence Greig. Ph.D. in Musicology, U. Munich. Dir. music edn. Central Inst. Edn., Berlin, children's div. N.Y. World's Fair; founder, mgr. Little Orch. Soc., N.Y.C.; personal rep. for singers, instrumentalists and conductors, N.Y.C. Recipient Bundesverdienstkreuz govt. W. Ger.; Handel medallion City of N.Y. Mem. Concert Artists Guild, Am. Symphony Orch. League, Internat. Soc. Performing Arts Adminstrs. Inc., Assn. Coll., Univ. and Community Arts Adminstrs. Inc. Home: 175 E 79th St New York NY 10021 Office: 59 E 54th St New York NY 10022

DISTEFANO, JOSEPH JOHN, III, computer science, bioengineering and medicine/biocybernetics educator, consultant; b. Bklyn., Apr. 30, 1938; s. Joseph and Angelina (Vannata) DiS.; children: Joseph, Allegra. B.E.E., CCNY, 1961; M.S., UCLA, 1964, Ph.D., 1966. Registered profl. engr., Calif. Research engr. Autonetics, Anaheim, Calif., 1961-63; asst. prof. UCLA, 1966-72, assoc. prof., 1972-76, prof. dept. computer sci., dept. medicine, 1976—. Mem. editorial bd.: Optimal Control Applications and Methods, 1983—; mem. editorail bd.: Am. Jour. Physiology-Intergrative, Regulatory and Comparative Physiology, 1980—; mem. editorial bd.: Annals of Biomed. Engring., 1971—; author: Feedback and Control Systems, 1967. Recipient NASA traineeship grad. edn. award, 1963-66, Dist. Teaching award Engring. Systems, UCLA, 1971; N.Am. Rockwell sci. engring. fellow, 1962-63; Fulbright Hays sr. scholar, 1979. Mem. Endocrine Soc., Am. Thyroid Assn., Control Systems Soc., Am. Fedn. Clin. Research. Office: UCLA 4731 Boelter Hall Los Angeles CA 90024

DI STEFANO, VICTOR, pharmacology educator; b. Rochester, N.Y., Mar. 17, 1924; s. Anthony N. and Rose M. (Ricci) Di S.; m. Shirley Jean End, Aug. 16, 1946; children: Mark, Lynne, Paul, Peter John. A.B., U. Rochester, 1949, Ph.D., 1953. Asst. prof. pharmacology U. Rochester, 1957-63, assoc. prof., 1963-72, prof., 1972—, prof. radiation, biochemistry and biophysics, 1970—; adj. prof. biomed. edn. CCNY, 1980—. Contbr. articles to profl. jours. Chmn. Zoning Bd. Appeals, Wheatland, N.Y., 1959—; mem. Wheatland-Chili Sch. Bd., Scottsville, N.Y., 1963-69. Served with inf. U.S. Army, 1943-46; ETO. Mem. Am. Soc. Pharmacology, Sigma Xi. Home: 1055 Quaker Rd Scottsville NY 14546 Office: U Rochester 601 Elmwood Ave Rochester NY 14642

DISTELHORST, GARIS FRED, association executive; b. Columbus, Ohio, Jan. 21, 1942; s. Harold Theodore and Ruth (Haywood) D.; m. Helen Cecilla Gillen, Oct. 28, 1972; children: Garen, Kristen. B.Sc., Ohio State U., 1965. Cert. assn. exec. Vice pres. Smith, Bucklin & Assocs., Washington, 1969-80; exec. dir. Nat. Assn. Coll. Stores, Oberlin, Ohio, 1980—; mem. exec. council Internat. Booksellers Fedn., Vienna, Austria. Bd. dirs. Washington Choral Arts Soc., 1975-76; treas. Old Mill Community Council, Alexandria, Va., 1977-79; commr. Citizens Cable TV commn., Oberlin, Ohio, 1982-83; chmn. Sesquicentennial com., Oberlin, 1983; bd. dirs. Library of Congress, Washington. Served to lt. USN, 1965-69. Deocrated USN Achievement medal, 1969. Mem. Inst. Assn. Mgmt. Cos. (treas. 1979-80, award merit 1979), Am. Soc. Assn. Execs. (dir.), Greater Cleve. Soc. Assn. Execs., Nat. Assn. Expn. Mgrs., Trade Show Bur. Republican. Presbyterian. Lodges: Kiwanis; Rotary. Office: National Association of College Stores 528 E Lorain Oberlin OH 44074

DISTLER, WILLIAM FRANCIS, mining engineer; b. Denver, Aug. 17, 1917; s. Robert E. and Carolyn D.; m. Della Price Cole, June 14, 1942; children: Bruce R., Marilyn J. Distler Bugg, Emily Anne Distler Kraus. E.M., Colo. Sch. Mines, 1939; grad., Advanced Mgmt. Program, Harvard U., 1966. With Miami Copper Co., 1939-54, mine supt., until 1954; with Climax Molybdenum Co. div. AMAX, Inc., 1954-83, pres., Greenwich, Conn. Bd. dirs. Luth. Med. Center Found., Denver, 1976—, Community Electrogardiogram Interpretive Service, Denver, 1976—. Recipient Distinguished Achievement medal Colo. Sch. Mines, 1977. Mem. Colo. Mining Assn. (dir. 1971—), Colo. Assn. Commerce and Industry (dir. 1973), AIME, Mining and Metall. Soc. Am. Home: PO Box 327 Frisco CO 80443 12405 E Gold Dust Dr Tucson AZ 85749

DI SUVERO, MARK, sculptor; b. Shanghai, China, Sept. 18, 1933; s. Vittorio and Matilde (Millo) DiS. B.A., U. Calif., Berkeley, 1957. Co-founder Park Place Gallery, N.Y.C., 1963. One-person shows, Green Gallery, N.Y., 1960, Parl Place Gallery, N.Y., 1966, Van Abbemuseum, Eindhoven, Netherlands, Gardin des Tuileries, Paris, 1975, Whitney Mus., N.Y.C., group exhbns., Palais des Beaux-Arts, 1981, Construct Gallery, Chgo., 1982, San Francisco Mus. Modern Art; represented in permanent collections, Art Inst. Chgo., Whitney Mus., N.Y.C., Wadsworth Atheneum, Hartford, N.Y. U., City Art Mus., St. Louis, others. Recipient grant Longview Found., Walter K. Gutman Found., award Art Inst. Chgo., 1963, Creative Arts award Brandeis U., Skohegan Sch. award. Office: care Oil and Steel Gallery 157 Chambers St New York NY 10007 *

DITKA, MICHAEL KELLER, professional football coach; b. Carnegie, Pa., Oct. 18, 1939; s. Mike and Charlotte (Keller) D.; m. Margery Ditka, Jan. 21, 1961 (div. 1973); children: Michael, Mark, Megan, Matthew; m. Diane Ditka, July 8, 1977. Student, U. Pitts. Profl. football player Chgo. Bears, Phila. Eagles, Dallas Cowboys, asst. coach, 1973-81; head coach Chgo. Bears, 1982—. Roman Catholic. Home: 18581 Brooke St Grayslake IL 60030 Office: Chicago Bears Football Club 55 E Jackson St Chicago IL 60604

DITOMASSI, GEORGE ROBERT, toy manufacturing company executive; b. Holyoke, Mass., Oct. 27, 1934; s. George and Nancy (Morini) D.; (div.)children: G. Robert, Mark, Dawn, Beth. B.B.A., U. Mass., 1957; A.M.P., Harvard U., 1980. Prodn. mgr. edn. div. Milton Bradley Co., Springfield, Mass., 1962-64, sales mgr., Springfield, 1964-68, v.p. Whiting div., 1970-76, sr. v.p. mktg., Springfield, 1979-83, exec. v.p., 1983—, dir., Porfl. Data Services, East Longmeadow, Mass. Trustee Baystate Med. Ctr., Springfield, 1981, Springfield Coll, 1983. Served to 2d lt. U.S. Army, 1958. Roman Catholic. Clubs: Colony (Springfield); Field (Longmeadow, Mass.). Home: 15 Park St Springfield MA 01105 Office: Milton Bradley Corp 111 Maple St Springfield MA 01115

DITTENHAFER, BRIAN DOUGLAS, banker, economist; b. York, Pa., Aug. 15, 1942; s. Nathaniel Webster and Evelyn Romaine (Myers) D.; m. Miriam Marcy, Aug. 22, 1964; 1 son, Daniel Webster. B.A., Ursinus Coll., 1964; M.A., Temple U., 1966, postgrad. (Univ. fellow) (G.E. Found fellow), 1967-71. Personnel asst. Philco Corp., Phila., 1965-66; teaching asst. Temple U., Phila., 1966-67, research asso., 1968-69; bus. economist Fed. Res. Bank of Atlanta, 1971-76; v.p., chief economist Fed. Home Loan Bank of N.Y., N.Y.C., 1976-79, sr. v.p., chief fin. officer, 1979-80, exec. v.p., 1980—. Deacon Central Presbyn. Ch., 1981-84; bd. dirs. N.Y. Council Econ. Edn., 1983—. Mem. Nat. Assn. Bus. Economists, Am. Econ. Assn., Am. Fin. Assn., Am. Real Estate and Urgan Econ. Assn., N.Y. Assn. Bus. Econs., Omicron Delta Epsilon. Club: Forecaster's of N.Y. (sec.-treas. 1982-84). Office: Federal Home Loan Bank of New York One World Trade Center 103rd Floor New York NY 10048

DITTER, JOHN WILLIAM, JR., judge; b. Phila., Oct. 19, 1921. B.A., Ursinus Coll., 1943, LL.D., 1970; LL.B., U. Pa., 1948. Bar: Pa. 1949. Clk. Ct. Common Pleas, Montgomery County, Pa., 1948-51, judge,

1964-70; asst. dist. atty., Montgomery County, 1951, 53-55, 1st asst. dist. atty., 1956-60; mem. firm Ditter and Jenkins and predecessor firm, Ambler, Pa., 1953-63; judge U.S. Dist. Ct. Eastern Dist. Pa., Phila., 1970—; lectr. Villanova U. Past pres. bd. trustees Calvary Methodist Ch.; charter pres. Ambler Jaycees, 1954-55; bd. dirs. Riverview Osteo. Hosp., Norristown, Pa., 1964-71; bd. consulters Villanova U. Sch. Law. Served to capt. USNR, 1943-68. Mem. Am., Fed., Pa., Montgomery County bar assns., Ambler C. of C. (pres. 1959-61). Office: 6614 US Court House Philadelphia PA 19106

DITTERT, J. LEE, JR., lawyer; b. Houston, Sept. 22, 1931; s. J. Lee and Hazel Lenore (Young) D.; m. Dinah Lee VanSandt, July 10, 1955; children: Theresa Ann, Diana Lynn, Christopher Lee, Johanna Marie. B.A., U. Tex., 1952, LL.B., 1957. Bar: Tex. 1957. Since practiced in, Bellville; co-owner mng. ptnr. radio sta. KACO, Bellville, Tex.; Land title examiner Bellville (Tex.) Abstract Co., Stewart Title Co., 1959—, Chgo. Title Co., 1974—; county judge, Austin County, Bellville, 1967-74; county atty. Austin County, 1979-81. Pres. Silver Spurs Service Orgn., U. Tex., 1955-56, Bellville Indsl. Found., 1961-71, 78—; pres. Bellville Little League, 1970, mgr., 1971-77; Mem. exec. com. Houston-Galveston Area Council, projects rev. chmn., 1972, sec., treas., 1973; state del. to Dem. Conv., 1968; trustee Bellville Hosp. Authority, 1975-81, chmn., 1980. Served to lt. comdr. USNR, 1954-66; Korea. Mem. ABA, Austin County Bar Assn. (pres. 1970-71, sec. 1977), State Bar of Tex. (mem. dist. commn. on admissions), Bellville C. of C., VFW, Phi Delta Phi. Episcopalian (mem. diocesan constn., canons com. 1965-70, layreader 1964—, vestryman). Clubs: Lions., Booster, Golf. Home: 18 N Cummings Bellville TX 77418 Office: PO Box 99 Bellville TX 77418

DITTERT, LEWIS WILLIAM, coll. dean; b. Phila., Jan. 22, 1934; s. Charles Frick and Carolyne (Obermiller) D.; m. Starr Nancy Winkler, Aug. 31, 1957; children—Anne Marie, Steven Daniel. B.S., Temple U., 1956; M.S., U. Wis., 1960, Ph.D., 1961. Research phamacist, group leader Smith Kline & French Labs., Phila., 1961-67; mem. faculty U. Ky., Lexington, 1967-78, prof. pharmacy, 1973-78; dean Sch. Pharmacy U. Pitts., 1978—; cons. pharm. mfg. firms. Contbr. articles to profl. jours. Fellow Acad. Pharm. Scis.; mem. Am. Pharm. Assn., Am. Assn. Colls. Pharmacy, Pa. Pharm. Assn., Sigma Xi, Rho Chi. Home: 222 Carriage Ln Upper St Clair PA 15241 Office: 3501 Terrace St Pittsburgh PA 15261

DITTES, JAMES EDWARD, psychology of religion educator; b. Cleve., Dec. 26, 1926; s. Mercein Edward and Mary (Freeman) D.; children: Lawrence William (dec.), Nancy Eleanor, Carolyn Ann, Joanne Frances. A.B., Oberlin Coll., 1949; B.D., Yale U., 1954, M.S., 1955, Ph.D., 1958. Instr. Am. Sch., Talas, Turkey, 1950-52; ordained to ministry United Ch. Christ, 1954; mem. faculty Yale U., 1955—, prof. psychology of religion, 1967—, chmn. dept. religious studies, 1975-82; chmn. Council on Grad. Studies in Religion in U.S. and Can., 1970-71. Author: The Church in the Way, 1967, Minister on the Spot, 1970, Bias and the Pious, 1973, When the People Say No, 1979, (with Robert Menges) Psychological Studies of Clergyman, 1965. Served with USNR, 1945-46. Guggenheim fellow, 1965-66; Fulbright Research fellow, Rome, 1965-66; sr. fellow NEH, 1972-73. Fellow Am. Psychol. Assn.; mem. Soc. Sci. Study of Religion (exec. sec. 1959-63, editor jour. 1966-71, pres. 1971-73). Home: 140 Captain Thomas Blvd West Haven CT 06516 Office: 409 Prospect St New Haven CT 06510

DITTMAN, DUANE ARTHUR, university official; b. Yonkers, N.Y., Nov. 19, 1924; s. Willis Arthur and Marion (Wilson) D.; m. Virginia Scott, May 31, 1952; children: D. Scott, Sharon J., Douglas A., Donna L. B.A., Colgate U., 1950. Coll. rep. Am. Book Co., N.Y.C., 1950-52; asst. sales mgr. Krementz & Co., Newark, 1952-55; asst. dir. devel. Colgate U., Hamilton, N.Y., 1955-58; dir. devel. St. Lawrence U., Canton, N.Y., 1958-63, v.p., 1963-76, Davidson (N.C.) Coll., 1976-80, Coll. William and Mary, Williamsburg, Va., 1980—. Served with USNR, 1943-47. Recipient Maroon citation Colgate U., 1970. Mem. Am. Coll. Pub. Relations Assn. (trustee 1966-68, sec. 1969, pres. 1970-71), Beta Theta Pi. Presbyterian (elder). Club: Rotary (pres. Canton 1968-69). Home: 103 Overlook Dr Williamsburg VA 23185 Office: Coll William and Mary Williamsburg VA 23185

DITTMANN, REIDAR, art educator; b. Tonsberg, Norway, Jan. 15, 1922; came to U.S., 1945, naturalized, 1950; s. Gustav Adolf and Solveig (Tovsen) D.; m. Chrisma J. Skoien, Dec. 18, 1947; children: Reidar, Solveig, Rolf, Kristin, Lisa. Student, Oslo Conservatory, Oslo U., 1941-43; B.Mus., St. Olaf Coll., 1947, B.A., 1949; M.A., U. Wash., 1954, Ph.D., 1975. Mem. faculty St Olaf Coll., Northfield, Minn., 1946—; dir. internat. studies St. Olaf Coll., Northfield, Minn., 1964-75, prof. art and Norwegian, dir. galleries, 1975—; cons. Mpls. Inst. Arts. Author: The Educational System of Norway, 1969, Edvard Munch and Henrik Ibsen, 1977; translator, editor: Edvard Munch: Close-up of a Genius, 1968; Ibsen and Munich, 1978; picture editor: Franklin Library Ibsen edit., 1981, Eros and Psyche: Strindberg and Munch in the 1890s, 1982; composer. Chmn. Rice County Democratic-Farmer Labor Party, 1961-62. Served with Norwegian Resistance, 1941-43; interned in Buchenwald Camp Norwegian Resistance, 1943-45; served with Norwegian Army Intelligence, 1945. Recipient award for inter-religious service Jewish Community Council, 1968; decorated St. Olav medal, Norway. Mem. Norwegian-Am. Hist. Assn. (exec. bd.), Soc. Advancement Scandinavian Studies, Coll. Art Assn. Home: 908 W 1st St Northfield MN 55057 Office: Saint Olaf Coll Northfield MN 55057

DITTMEIER, THOMAS EDWIN, lawyer; b. St. Louis, Apr. 10, 1944; s. Edwin A. and Mildred P. (Braun) D.; m. Janet A. West, June 18, 1966; children: Thomas, Ann, Stephen. B.S. in Bus. Adminstrn., U. Mo., 1966; J.D., St. Louis U., 1969. Bar: Mo. 1969. Asst. prosecuting atty. St. Louis County (Mo.), 1969-77; asst. circuit atty. Circuit Attys. Office, St. Louis, 1977-81; U.S. atty. U.S. Dist. Ct. (ea. dist.) Mo., St. Louis, 1981—; mem. atty. gen.'s adv. com. Dept. Justice, 1982—; lectr. Nat. Coll. Dist. Attys., Houston, 1980. Recipient Achievement award St. Louis U. Law Sch., 1969. Mem. Nat. Dist. Attys. Assn., Mo. Prosecutors Assn. Republican. Roman Catholic. Office: US Attorney Eastern Dist Mo 1114 Market St Room 414 Saint Louis MO 63101

DITTRICH, RAYMOND JOSEPH, medical device company executive; b. Wichita, Kans., Feb. 17, 1932; s. Raymond Joseph and Helen Sue (Sheehan) D.; m. Paula Ann Makielski, Feb. 20, 1954; children: Lisa Ann, Claire Louise, David Thomas, Mark Alan. A.B. magna cum laude, U. Notre Dame, 1953; LL.B., U. Mich., 1958. Bar: Minn. bar 1958, Fla. bar 1973. Atty. Cargill, Inc., Mpls., 1958-71; v.p., gen. counsel, sec. Burger King Corp., Miami, Fla., 1971-74; v.p., gen. counsel Pillsbury Co., Mpls., 1974-80, sec., 1977-80; v.p., gen. counsel Ga. Pacific Corp., 1980; v.p., sec., gen. counsel Medtronic, Inc., Mpls., 1980—. Mem. Charter Commn., Minnetonka, Minn., 1968-70; bd. dirs., pres. Mpls. Aquatenniel Assn., 1984. Served with USMCR, 1953-55; lt. col. Res. Mem. ABA, Fla. Bar Assn., Minn. Bar Assn. (v.p., dir. corporate counsel sect.), Food and Drug Law Inst. (trustee), Phi Alpha Delta. Republican. Roman Catholic. Clubs: Royal Palm Tennis (Miami); Wayzata Country, Mpls., Mpls. Home: 685 Old Long Lake Rd Wayzata MN 55391 Office: 3055 Old Hwy 8 PO Box 1453 Minneapolis MN 55440

DITUNNO, JOHN F., JR., physiatrist, educator; b. Phila., June 8, 1932; s. John F. and Catherine D.; m. Patricia Lyons, Oct. 23, 1965; children—Christine, Anna Marie, Lauri, Theresa. B.S., St. Joseph Coll., Phila., 1954; M.D., Hahnemann Med. Coll., 1958. Diplomate: Am. Bd. Phys. Medicine and Rehab. (vice chmn. 1972-81, chmn. 1981-82). Intern Hahnemann Med. Coll., Phila., 1958-59, resident in medicine, 1962-64, instr. medicine, 1964, head sect. phys. medicine and rehab. dept. medicine, 1966, dir. sect. phys. medicine and rehab., 1966-67; resident in phys. medicine and rehab. Jacobi Hosp., Albert Einstein Med. Sch., N.Y.C., 1963-64, U. Pa. Hosp., Phila., 1964-65; asso. prof. phys. medicine and rehab. Temple U. Health Scis. Center, Phila., 1967-69; prof. rehab. medicine dept. rehab. medicine Jefferson Med. Coll., Phila., 1969—, chmn. dept., 1969—; chief phys. medicine Lankenau Hosp., Phila., 1971—; med. dir. dept. phys. medicine and rehab. Daroff div. Albert Einstein Med. Center, Phila., 1975—; dir., chief phys. medicine and rehab. Crozer-Chester Med. Center, Pa., 1976—; cons. Wilmington Med. Center, 1971—, Magee Meml. Rehab. Center, Phila., 1975—, Wills Eye Hosp., Phila., 1980—. Contbr. articles to med. jours. Mem. Phila. Soc. Phys. Medicine and Rehab. (v.p. 1970-71, pres. 1971-72), Philadelphia County Med. Soc., Pa. Acad. Phys. Medicine and Rehab. (pres.-elect 1971-72), Am. Heart Assn. (gov. S.E. Pa. 1971-73), Am. Congress Rehab. Medicine (pres. Eastern sect. 1971-72), Am. Rheumatism Assn., Am. Acad. Phys. Medicine and Rehab. (v.p. 1979, pres.-elect 1980-81, pres. 1981-82, gov. 1976—), Phila. Rheumatology Soc., Assn. Acad. Physiatrists (pres. 1973-74, v.p. 1975), AMA, Assn. Am.Med. Colls., Hosp. Assn. Pa., Am. Spinal Injury Assn. (chmn. task force in physician manpower 1980—). Office: Dept Rehab Medicine Thomas Jefferson U Hosp 111 S 11th St Philadelphia PA 19107

DITZ, JOHN ADAMS, construction company executive; b. Stockton, Calif., Mar. 4, 1921; s. George Armand and Janet (Adams) D.; m. Elizabeth Ann Goodwin, June 14, 1947; children: Susan, Elizabeth, Nancy, Janet. A.B., Stanford U., 1942. Vice-pres., Ditz Bros., San Jose, Calif., 1948-60, Ditz-Crane, Santa Clara, Calif., 1954-82, pres., 1982—; v.p. McKesson Corp., San Francisco, 1975—; pres. Foremost Homes Hawaii, Honolulu, 1975-80, McKesson Property Co., San Francisco, 1975—; chmn. bd. Aqua Media Inc., Sunnyvale, Calif., 1970-75; dir. Ditz-Crane, Santa Clara, Calif., Pacific Pure Water Co., Sunnyvale. Chmn. Santa Clara Heart Assn., San Jose, 1951; trustee Stanford U., Palo Alto, Calif., 1982—, Palo Alto Med. Found., 1982—. Served to lt. USN, 1942-46; PTO. Republican. Episcopalian. Clubs: Bohemian, Pacific Union (San Francisco). Office: McKesson Corp 1 Post St 27th Floor San Francisco CA 94104

DIVALERIO, RICHARD MICHAEL, utility executive; b. Erie, Pa., Sept. 30, 1930; s. Constantino and Elvita Marie (BelPorto) DiV.; m. Carmela Ursula Caracciolo, Dec. 29, 1956; children: Lisa Ann, Diane Marie, Richard Michael, Mark John, Robert Alan, David James. B.S.C., U. Notre Dame, 1953, J.D., 1954. Bar: Pa. 1955, N.Y. 1978. From asst. to sec. and gen. counsel United Natural Gas Co., Oil City, Pa., 1957-74; sec., gen. counsel, dir. Nat. Fuel Gas Supply Corp., Buffalo, 1974—; sec., dir. Penn-York Energy Corp.; sec. Seneca Resources Corp.; Vice chmn. Oil City Redevel. Authority, 1973-76. Editorial bd.: Notre Dame Lawyer, 1953-54. Served with AUS, 1955-56. Mem. Am. Gas Assn., Am. Bar Assn., Fed. Energy Bar Assn., Am. Mgmt. Assn., N.Y. State Bar Assn., Pa. Bar Assn., Buffalo C. of C. Roman Catholic. Home: 11 Pawtucket Row Orchard Park NY 14127 Office: 10 Lafayette Sq Buffalo NY 14203

DIVELY, GEORGE SAMUEL, communications and information processing equipment manufacturing company executive; b. Claysburg, Pa., Dec. 17, 1902; s. Michael A. and Martha A. (Dodson) D.; m. Harriett G. Seeds, June 30, 1933 (dec. Aug. 1968); 1 son, Michael A.; m. Juliette Gaudin, Feb. 1969. B.S. in E.E, U. Pitts., 1925, D.Sc. in Engring. (hon.), 1962; M.B.A., Harvard U., 1929; D.Eng. (hon.), Case-Western Res. U., 1961; D.Sc. (hon.), Fla. Inst. Tech., 1972. With Harris Corp., 1937—, successively asst. to sec.-treas., asst. treas., sec.-treas., dir., v.p. and gen. mgr., 1937-47, pres., 1947-61, chief exec. officer, 1952-68, chmn. bd., 1954-72, chmn. exec. and fin. com., 1972-78, hon. chmn. bd., 1972—. Author: The Power of Professional Management. Hon. trustee Case Western Res. U.; trustee Ednl. TV Met. Cleve.; dir. assocs. Harvard Grad. Sch. Bus. Adminstrn. Fellow Am. Mgmt. Assn. (life mem.). Clubs: Masons, Pepper Pike Country, The Country, Union, Harvard (Cleve.); Harvard (N.Y.C); Royal Palm Yacht and Country (Fla.). Home: 13515 Shaker Blvd Apt 3A Cleveland OH 44120 Office: 1450 Illuminating Bldg 55 Public Sq Cleveland OH 44113

DIVER, WILLIAM, linguistics educator; b. Chgo., July 20, 1921. B.A., Lawrence Coll., 1942; M.A., Harvard U., 1947; Ph.D., Columbia U., 1953. Instr. English Ripon (Wis.) Coll., 1947-49; tchr. Latin Blake Sch., Minn., 1954-55; from asst. prof. to prof. linguistics Columbia U., 1955—. Served from ensign to lt. (j.g.) USNR, 1942-45. Decorated Legion of Merit. Mem. Societe de Linguistique de Paris. Office: 401 Philosophy Hall Columbia Univ New York City NY 10027

DI VESTA, FRANCIS JOHN, psychologist; b. Bridgeport, Conn., Mar. 8, 1920; s. Patrick and Marion (Lepore) Di V.; children: Carol Lynn, Laurence Aldrich. B.S., U. Conn., 1942; M.S., Cornell U., 1945, Ph.D., 1948. Asst. prof. edn. Bucknell U., 1948-49; assoc. program dir. Human Resources Research Ctr. (USAF), 1949-54; assoc. prof. to prof. Syracuse U., 1954-64; prof. edn. and psychology Pa. State U., University Park, 1964—; cons. to govt. and industry, lectr., Europe and S.Am. Author: (with G.G. Thompson) Educational Psychology, 1970, Language, Learning and Cognitive Processes, 1974; editorial: (with G.G. Thompson and J. Horrocks) Social Development and Personality, 1971; bd. cons. editors: Jour. Ednl. Psychology, 1966—, Ednl. and Communication Tech. Jour., 1975—, Research and Devel. in Edn., 1978—, Interam. Jour. Psychology, 1982—; contbr. articles to profl. and tech. jours. Fellow Am. Psychol. Assn. (exec. com. 1975-78), AAAS; mem. Am. Ednl. Research Assn., Soc. Research in Child Devel., Psychonomic Soc., Sigma Xi. Office: Pa State U 314 Cedar Bldg University Park PA 16802

DIVINE, ROBERT ALEXANDER, history educator; b. Bklyn., May 10, 1929; s. Walter E. and Emily (Mable) D.; m. Barbara C. Renick, Aug. 6, 1955; children—J. Douglas, Elisabeth T., Richard L., Kirk M. B.A., Yale, 1951, M.A., 1952, Ph.D., 1954. Instr. U. Tex., Austin, 1954-57, asst. prof., 1957-61, asso. prof., 1961-63, prof. history, 1963—, chmn. dept. history, 1963-68, Piper prof., 1972, George W. Littlefield prof. Am. history, 1981—; fellow Center for Advanced Study in Behavioral Scis. Stanford, Calif., 1962-63; Albert Shaw lectr. in diplomatic history, Johns Hopkins, 1968. Author: American Immigration Policy, 1924-52, 1957, The Illusion of Neutrality, 1962, The Reluctant Belligerent, 1965, Second Chance, 1967, Roosevelt and World War II, 1969, Foreign Policy and U.S. Presidential Elections, 1940-1960, 2 vols, 1974, Since 1945: Politics and Diplomacy in Recent American History, 1975, Blowing on the Wind, 1978, Eisenhower and the Cold War, 1981. Mem. Orgn. Am. Historians, Am. Hist. Assn., Soc. for Historians of Am. Fgn. Relations, Am. Com. on History 2d World War. Democrat. Methodist. Home: 2402 Rockingham Circle Austin TX 78704

DIVINE, WILLIAM ROBINSON, mgmt. cons.; b. Los Angeles, Sept. 13, 1915; s. Thomas J. and Lucy A. (Robinson) D.; m. Leir O. Clifford, Feb. 23, 1941; children—William Robinson, Suzanne (dec.), Phillippe Alvin. B.A., Pomona Coll., 1937; M.A., U. Cin., 1939; J.D., George Washington U., 1947. Bar: D.C. bar 1947. With Bur. Budget, 1941-51, chief mgmt. improvement staff, 1948-51; dir. budget and mgmt. U.S. Regional Office, Paris, France, 1951-54; v.p. Lester B. Knight and Assos. (cons. engrs.), Chgo., 1954-56; asst. comptroller So. Ry. System, 1956-61, comptroller, 1961-70, v.p., 1967-70; v.p. finance Penn Central Transp. Co., 1971-74, fin. adviser, 1974-76; mgmt. cons., 1976—; prof. bus. and econs. Wingate Coll., N.C., 1980-81; bus. asso. Greenwich Research Assos., 1981—; adj. prof. bus. finance and data processing Am. U. Sch. Bus. Adminstrn., 1951-65; mem. orgn. planning council Nat. Indsl. Conf. Bd., 1963-71. Editor: George Washington U. Law Rev, 1946-47. Mem. Fin. Execs. Inst. (pres. Washington chpt. 1965-66), Soc. Advancement Mgmt. (pres. Washington chpt. 1961-62, internat. pres. 1964-65, chmn. bd. 1965-66), Am. Mgmt. Assn., U.S. C. of C., Phi Beta Kappa, Order of Coif. Clubs: University (Washington); Congressional Country (Bethesda, Md.). Home and office: 647 N Ithan Ave Rosemont PA 19010

DIWAN, ROMESH KUMAR, economics educator; b. Sabathu, India, Dec. 20, 1933; came to U.S., 1967; s. Fatehchand and Lila D.; m. Joyce Johnson, Oct. 25, 1970. M.S., Delhi Sch. Econs., 1955; Ph.D. in Ecns., U. Birmington (Eng.), 1965. Lectr. dept. econs. Panjab U., Chandigarh, India, 1958-61; lectr. econometrics U. Glasgow (Scotland), 1964-65; cons. to UN, N.Y.C., 1965-66, 67-68; vis. assoc. prof. dept. econs. U. Hawaii, Honolulu, 1966-67; assoc. prof. dept. econs. Rensselaer Poly. Inst., Troy, N.Y., 1968-73, prof., 1973—; vis. profl. Washington U., St. Louis, 1971; acad. visitor London Sch. Econs. and Polit Sci., 1976-77; mem. exec. bd. N.Y. State Conf. for Asian Studies, 1974-77. Author: (with Dennis Livingston) Alternative Development Strategies and Appropriate Technology, 1979; contbr. numerous articles on prodn. function and econ. devel. to profl. jours. NSF grantee, 1978, 81. Fellow Inst. Mgmt. Sci.; mem. Econometric Soc., Assn. for Social Econs., Am. Econs. Assn., Assn. for Asian Studies, Internat. Inst. Social Econs., Assn. for Indian Studies (chmn. 1978-81), Fedn. Am. Scientists, Friends of Earth Internat. (editorial bd.), N.Y. State Assn. for Asian Studies, Internat. Soc. for Tech. Assessment, Internat. Inst. Social Econs. Office: Econs Dept Rensselaer Poly Inst Troy NY 12181

DIWOKY, ROY JOHN, petroleum exec.; b. Council Bluffs, Iowa, Dec. 4, 1910; s. Adolph and Ann and Koncal (Diwoky); m. Doris M. Hendricks, Apr. 17, 1933; children—Roy James (dec.), Linda. B.S., State U. Iowa, 1933, M.S., 1934; student, Harvard Bus. Sch., 1948. With Standard Oil Co., Ind.), Whiting (Ind.) Refinery, 1935-49, asst. gen. supt., 1948-49; exec. asst. to pres., dir., v.p. Pan-Am. So. Corp., New Orleans, 1949, exec. v.p. and dir., 1950-56; gen. mgr. mfg., dir. Am. Oil Co., 1956-57; pres., chief exec. officer, dir. Commonwealth Oil Refining Co., Inc., 1957-61, Crown Central Petroleum Corp., 1961-67, cons. and dir.; treas., sec., dir. Liquilux Gas Service, Inc., also Bottle Service, Inc., 1968-74; cons., dir. Liquilux Gas Service, Ponce, P.R., 1974—. Mem. Am. Petroleum Inst. (mem. gen. refining com.), Am. Chem. Soc., Am. Inst. Chem. Engrs., New Orleans C. of C., Nat. Petroleum Refiners Assn. (dir.), 25 Yr. Club Petroleum Industry, Phi Gamma Delta. Clubs: Internat. House, Petroleum (New Orleans); Chicago (Ill.); Dorado Beach (San Juan, P.R.); Deportivo, Yacht (Ponce, P.R.); Maryland, Baltimore Country; Ridglea Country (Ft. Worth). Home: 4005 Winding Way Fort Worth TX 76126

DIX, FRED ANDREW, JR., professional society executive; b. Connellsville, Pa., Aug. 27, 1931; s. Fred Andrew and Freda Pearl (Horton) D.; m. Jean Carol Bacon, July 18, 1953; children: Cynthia Carol, Jennifer Jean, Stephen Bacon. B.S., Rutgers U., 1953, M.S., 1957. Petroleum geologist Standard Oil Co. of Calif., Salt Lake City, 1957-62, Denver, 1962-64, Mobil Oil Corp., Jackson, Miss., 1965-66, Corpus Christi, Tex., 1966-72, Houston, 1972, div. exploration data processing coordinator, 1967-72; exec. dir. Am. Assn. Petroleum Geologists, Tulsa, 1973—. Contbr. articles to profl. jours. Served with USAF, 1954-55. Mem. Rutgers Geology Club (pres.), Geol. Soc. Am., Tulsa, Houston, Oklahoma City geol. socs., Council Engring. and Sci. Soc. Execs., Am. Assn. Petroleum Geologists (chmn. com. on statistics of drilling 1969-70, treas. 1972, Disting. Service award 1983), Petroleum Club Tulsa, Tulsa C. of C., Kappa Sigma. Republican. Presbyn. Home: 6815 E 52d St Tulsa OK 74145 Office: PO Box 979 1444 S Boulder St Tulsa OK 74101

DIX, ROLLIN C(UMMING), mechanical engineering educator, consultant; b. N.Y.C., Feb. 8, 1936; s. Omer Houston and One Mae (Cumming) D.; m. Elaine B. VanNest, June 18, 1960; children: Gregory, Elisabeth, Karen. B.S.M.E., Purdue U., 1957, M.S.M.E., 1958, Ph.D., 1963. Registered profl. engr., Ind., Ill. Asst. prof. mech. engring. Ill. Inst. Tech., Chgo., 1964-69, assoc. prof., 1969-80, prof., 1980—, assoc. dean for computing, 1980—; cons. mech. design Bronson & Bratton, Inc., Chgo., 1965—; chmn. bd. Nat. Conf. Fluid Power, Chgo., 1978—; dir. Bimet Corp., Morris, Ill. Patentee road repair vehicle, method for vestibular test. Served to 1st lt. U.S. Army, 1960-61. Mem. ASME, Am. Soc. Engring. Edn. Republican. Home: 10154 S Seeley Ave Chicago IL 30343 Office: Ill Inst Tech 10 W 31st St Chicago IL 60616

DIXIT, BALWANT NARAYAN, pharmacology and toxicology educator, adminstrator; b. Kerawade, India, Jan. 7, 1933; came to U.S., 1962; s. Narayan V. and Janakibai N. (Gokhale) D.; m. Vidya B. Ghanekar, Dec. 26, 1969; children: Sunil, Sanjay. B.S. in Chemistry and Biology, Fergusson Coll., Poona, India, 1954, U. Poona, 1955; M.S. in Biology with honors, U.Poona, 1956, U. Baroda, India, 1962; Ph.D., U. Pitts., 1965. Sr. research fellow Baroda U., 1960-61; asst. prof. pharmacology U. Pitts., 1965-68; assoc. prof., U. Pitts., 1968-75; asst. chmn. U. Pitts., 1969-74; acting dean U. Pitts. 1976-78; chmn., assoc. dean U. Pitts., 1978—. Recipient Disting. Alumnus award U. Pitts. Sch. Pharmacy, 1982; fellow Internat. Union Physiological Scis., 1962. Mem. Am. Soc. Pharmacology and Explt. Therapeutics, Soc. Neurosci., N.Y. Acad. Sci., Am. Assn. Colls. Pharmacy, Internat. Soc. Xenobiotic Metabolsim. Home: 608 Ravencrest Rd Pittsburgh PA 15215 Office: U Pitts 1100 Salk Hall Pittsburgh PA 15261

DIXON, ALAN JOHN, U.S. Senator; b. Belleville, Ill., July 7, 1927; s. William G. and Elsa (Tebbenhoff) D.; m. Joan Louise Fox, Jan. 17, 1954; children: Stephanie Jo, Jeffrey Alan, Elizabeth Jane. B.S., U. Ill., 1949; LL.B., Washington U., St. Louis, 1949. Bar: Ill. 1950. Practiced in, Belleville, 1950-76; police magistrate City of Belleville, 1949; asst. atty., St. Clair County, Ill., 1950; mem. Ill. Ho. of Reps., 1951-63, Ill. Senate, 1963-71; minority whip; treas. State of Ill., 1971-77, sec. of state, 1977-81; U.S. Senator from, Ill., 1981—. Mem. Am. Legion, Belleville C. of C. Democrat. Office: US Senate Washington DC 20510

DIXON, ARTHUR GEORGE JOHN, engring. exec.; b. East St. Louis, Ill., June 13, 1897; s. Robert John and Wilhelmina (Schlosser) D.; m. Dorothy Jane McConnell, June 16, 1928; children—David Arthur, Diana Jane. B.S. in Engring, U. Ill., 1924; LL.D., Carthage Coll., 1974. With Modine Mfg. Co., Racine, Wis., 1926—, successively engr., sales mgr., sec. corp., 1926-54, v.p. engring. and research, 1954-57, exec. v.p., 1957-60, pres., 1960-63, vice chmn. bd., 1963-72, chmn. bd., 1972-73, dir. emeritus, 1973—; Mem. fed. industry adv. coms. Pres. Village of North Bay, Wis. Served with USMC, World War I. Mem. Am. Legion. Mason. Clubs: Rotarian., Racine Country. Home: 401 Cross Creek Rd Racine WI 53402 Office: 1500 DeKoven Ave Racine WI 53403

DIXON, FITZ EUGENE, JR., professional sports executive; b. Winter Harbor, Maine, Aug. 14, 1923; s. Fitz Eugene and Eleanor

Elkins (Widener) D.; m. Edith B. Robb, June 5, 1952; children: George Widener, Edith Eleanor. Student, Harvard U., 1942-43; L.H.D. (hon.), Pa. Mil. Coll., Lafayette Coll., Hahnemann Med. Coll., Cabrini Coll., Pa. Coll. Podiatric Medicine, LL.D., Widener Coll., Chestnut Hill Coll., D.Pub. Service, Temple U., Sc.D., Spring Garden Coll. Ltd. ptnr. Phila. Phillies Baseball Team; dir. Provident Nat. Bank, Phila., 1971—, Provident Nat. Corp., 1975—, PNC Fin. Corp.; pres. Phila. Art Commn., 1977—, Phila. Internat. City Coordinating Com., 1979—, Phila. Council for Progress, 1979. Dir. Phila. Facilities Mgmt., Inc., 1971—; life trustee Phila. Free Library, 1974—; commr. Fairmount Park, Phila., 1977—; chmn. Del. River Port Authority, 1979-81, vice chmn., 1981-83, chmn., 1983—; trustee Abington (Pa.) Meml. Hosp., 1944—, sec. bd., 1947-53, v.p., 1953-68, chmn. bd., 1968-74; chmn. bd. govs. State System Higher Edn.; dir. Devon Horse Show, 1975—; trustee Ellis Fund Adv. Com., Newtown, Pa., 1972—, Nat. Mus. Racing, 1971, Pop Warner League, 1976, Episcopal Acad., Merion, Pa., 1961—; chmn. bd. Episcopal Acad., 1972-75; bd. dirs. Maxwell Meml. Football Club, 1977-80, Police Athletic League, 1976—, Mann Music Center, 1979—, U.S. Equestrian Team, Inc.; trustee Juvenile Law Ctr. of Phila.; mem. Nat. Maritime Adv. Com.; trustee Maine Coast Meml. Hosp., Ellsworth, 1951—, chmn. bd., 1971-75, hon. chmn. bd., 1975—; trustee Phila. Mus. Art, 1979—; trustee emeritus Germantown Dispensary and Hosp.; pres. Widener Meml. Found. in Aid of Handicapped Children; chmn. trustees Temple U., 1977-83, chmn. exec. com., 1975-77, hon. life trustee; chmn. bd. govs. Temple U. Hosp., 1975-77; chmn. bd. Widener U., 1972—; co-chmn. American Gold Cup, 1973—; bd. mgrs. Franklin Inst. Mem. Marquis Soc. Lafayette Coll., Nat. Steeplechase and Hunt Assn. (life, past pres.), Am. Sail Tng. Assn., Am. Horse Show Assn. (life), Am. Grand Prix Assn. (dir.), Phila. Soc. Promotion Agr., Soc. War of 1812, Soc. Colonial Wars, Swedish Colonial Soc. Episcopalian. Clubs: Athenaeum, Phila. Corinthian Yacht, Phila., Phila. Cricket, Phila. Racquet, Union League (Phila.); Palm Beach (Fla.) Everglades, Bath and Tennis, Jockey, Vesper Boat, Key Largo (Fla.) Anglers, Locust, Orpheus, Radnor Hunt, Sunnybrook Golf, Whitemarsh Valley Country, Winter Harbor Yacht (treas. 1948—); Bal Harbour, Delray Beach Yacht (Fla.); Yacht; Univ. & Whist (Wilmington, Del.); Farmers of Pa. Office: PO Box 178 Lafayette Hill PA 19444

DIXON, FRANK JAMES, medical scientist, educator; b. St. Paul, Mar. 9, 1920; s. Frank James and Rose Augusta (Kuhfeld) D.; m. Marion Edwards, Mar. 14, 1946; children: Janet Wynne, Frank, Michael. B.S., U. Minn., 1941, M.B., 1943, M.D., 1944. Diplomate: Am. Bd. Pathology. Intern U.S. Naval Hosp., Great Lakes, Ill., 1943-44; research asst. dept. pathology Harvard, 1946-48; instr. dept. pathology Washington U., 1948-50, asst. prof., 1950-51; prof., chmn. dept. pathology U. Pitts. Med. Sch., 1951-60; chmn. dept. exptl. pathology Scripps Clinic and Research Found., La Jolla, Calif., 1961-74, chmn. biomed. research depts., 1970-74, dir. research inst., 1974—; research assoc. dept. biology U. Calif. at San Diego, 1961-64, prof. in residence in dept. biology, 1965-68, adj. prof. dept. pathology, 1968—; sci. adviser NIH, Nat. Found., Helen Hay Whitney Found., St. Jude's Med. Center, Christ Hosp. Inst., Cin.; mem. expert adv. panel on immunology WHO; sci. adv. bd. Nat. Kidney Found.; Pahlavi lectr. Ministry of Sci. and Higher Tech., Iran, 1976. Co-editor: Advances in Immunology; Editorial bd.: Excerpta Medica, Jour. Exptl. Medicine, Am. Jour. Pathology, Cellular Immunology, Kidney Hosp. Practice, Perspectives in Biology and Medicine; Contbr. articles to profl. jours. Served with M.C. USNR, 1943-46. Recipient Theobald Smith award, 1952; Parke-Davis award in exptl. pathology, 1957; Disting. Achievement award Modern Medicine, 1961; Martin E. Rehfuss award in internal medicine, 1966; Von Pirquet medal Ann. Forum on Allergy, 1967; Bunim medal Am. Rheumatism Assn., 1968; Internat. award Gairdner Found., 1969; Mayo Soley award Western Soc. Clin. Research, 1969; Albert Lasker Basic Med. Research award, 1975; Dickson prize U. Pitts., 1975; Homer Smith award N.Y. Heart Assn., 1976; Rous-Whipple award Am. Assn. Pathologists, 1979. Mem. Nat. Acad. Scis., N.Y. Acad. Scis. Western Assn. Physicians, Western Soc. Clin. Research, Soc. Exptl. Biology and Medicine, Transplantation Soc., AAAS, Am. Soc. Clin. Investigation, Am. Acad. Allergists, Interurban Path. Soc., Harvey Soc. (lectr. 1962), Am. Soc. Exptl. Pathology (pres. 1966), Am. Assn. Immunologists (pres. 1972), Am. Assn. for Cancer Research, Assn. Am. Physicians, Am. Acad. Arts and Scis., Sigma Xi, Nu Sigma Nu, Alpha Omega Alpha. Home: 2355 Avenida de La Playa La Jolla CA 92037 Office: 10666 N Torrey Pines Rd La Jolla CA 92037

DIXON, GEORGE FRANCIS, JR., manufacturing company executive; b. Jersey City, Feb. 24, 1918; s. George F. and Frances (Martin) D.; m. Lottie Ivy Carter, Dec. 1, 1950; children: George Francis III, Richard Elliott, Marshall Lawrence, Charlotte Ivy. B.S., U.S. Mil. Acad., 1940; M.S., Cornell U., 1947; D.Eng., Grenoble U., France, 1949. Dist. engr. Vicksburg Dist. Corps Engrs., 1949-53; pres. Dart Truck Co., Kansas City, Mo., 1955-57; also dir.; with Carlisle Corp., Pa., 1954—, pres., 1957-70, chmn., 1970—, also dir.; dir. Dauphin Deposit Trust Co., Harrisburg, Pa., CDI Corp., Phila.; Chmn. Pa. Div. Trauma. Trustee Dickinson Sch. Law, Gettysburg Coll. Served at lt. col. AUS, World War II; div. engr., comdg. officer 65th Engrs., 25th Inf. Div. Mem. ASCE, Assn. Grads. U.S. Mil. Acad. (trustee, pres.), Soc. Automotive Engrs., Soc. Am. Mil. Engrs. Home: RD I Box 6 Boiling Springs PA 17007 Office: Carlisle Corp Carlisle PA 17013

DIXON, GEORGE HALL, banker; b. Rochester, N.Y., Oct. 7, 1920; s. George H. and Frances (Wheeler) D.; m. Marjorie Freeman, Apr. 3, 1948; children: George E., Andrew T., Candis H. B.S., Wharton Sch., U. Pa., 1942; M.B.A., Harvard, 1947. With Brown Bros. Harriman & Co., N.Y.C., 1947-50; gen. partner Davis & Davis, Providence, 1950-56; v.p. finance, treas. Sperry & Hutchinson Co., N.Y.C., 1956-68; chmn., pres., dir. First Nat. Bank Mpls., 1968-76; dep. sec. of treasury, 1976-77; now chmn., chief exec. officer First Bank System, Inc., Mpls., also dir.; dir. Northwestern Nat. Life Ins. Co., Mpls., Internat. Multifoods Corp., Soo Line R.R. Co., Donaldson Co.; banking adv. council Am. Gas Assn. Mem. Viking council Boy Scouts Am.; bd. dirs. Minn. Orch. Assn.; bd. dirs., past pres. United Way Mpls. Area; trustee Sci. Mus. Minn.; chmn., trustee Carleton Coll.; mem. Minn. Bus. Partnership. Served to capt. AUS, 1943-46. Mem. Atlanta Inst. Internat. Affairs., Assn. Res. City Bankers, Assn. Bank Holding Cos. (dir., exec. com.). Presbyn. Clubs: Links (N.Y.C.); Minneapolis; Minn. (St. Paul). Office: 1200 First Bank Pl E Minneapolis MN 55402

DIXON, GORDON HENRY, biochemist; b. Durban, South Africa, Mar. 25, 1930; s. Walter James and Ruth (Nightingale) D.; m. Sylvia W. Gillen, Nov. 20, 1954; children: Frances Anne, Walter Timothy, Christopher James, Robin Jonathan. M.A. with honors, U. Cambridge, Eng., 1951; Ph.D., U. Toronto, 1956. Research asso. U. Wash., 1956-58; research asso. U. Oxford, Eng., 1958-59; asst. prof. biochemistry U. Toronto, 1959-61, asso. prof., 1961-63; prof. U. B.C., 1963-72; prof., chmn. dept. biochemistry U. Sussex, Eng., 1972-74; prof. med. biochemistry U. Calgary, Alta., Can., 1974—, chmn., 1983—. Contbr. articles to profl. jours. Recipient Steacie prize, 1966. Fellow Royal Soc. London, Royal Soc. Can. (Flavelle medal 1980); mem. Am. Soc. Biol. Chemists, Can. Biochemistry Soc. (pres. 1982-83, Ayerst award 1966). Home: 3424 Underwood Pl NW Calgary AB Canada T2N 4G7 Office: Dept Med Biochemistry Health Scis Centre 3330 Hospital Dr NW Univ of Calgary Calgary AB Canada T2N 4N1

DIXON, HARRY FAULKNER, apparel company executive; b. Westmont, N.J., July 22, 1923; s. Henry and Elizabeth Donaldson (Faulkner) D.; m. Mary Lou O. Irwin, Mar. 22, 1946; children—Elizabeth Marie, Christina Carol, Cynthia Louise, Robert Dean. B.S. with honors, Temple U., 1949; postgrad., Calif. State U., Fullerton, 1965, U. Cin., 1977-78. Div. controller, plant mgr. Playtex, Newman, Ga., 1949-63; mfg. controller Wesson Co., Fullerton, Calif., 1963-66; controller Rexene div. Dart Industries, Paramus, N.J., 1966-71; v.p. fin. and adminstrn. B.V.D. Corp., N.Y.C., 1971-75; treas., controller Palm Beach, Inc., Cin., 1976-79; v.p., asst. to chmn. Eagle Shirtmakers div. Palm Beach, Inc., Quakertown, Pa., 1980-82; controller Pines Shirt and Pajama Co., Inc. Served with USMC, 1942-45. Decorated D.F.C., Air medal with four clusters. Mem. Nat. Assn. Accts. Republican. Presbyterian. Home: 40 Estates Dr Center Valley PA 18034

DIXON, HARVEY LEWIS, electronics manufacturing executive; b. Lawrence County, Tenn., Oct. 15, 1927; s. Henry M. and Ruth (McMackin) D.; m. Beverly Dorothy Bigger, Sept. 10, 1950; children: Ronald, Debra, Sharon, Sandra. B.S. in Indsl. Engring. with distinction, Stanford U., 1952, M.S., 1953. Mgr. quality control def. lab. Sylvania Electric Co., Mountain View, Calif., 1953-54; with SRI Internat. (formerly Stanford Research Inst.), Menlo Park, Calif., 1954-82, mgr. logistic systems research, 1963-68, exec. dir. urban and social systems div., 1968-75, v.p. fin. and adminstrn., 1954-82; v.p. adminstrn. semiconductor equipment ops. Eaton Corp., 1982—; speaker in field. Contbr. articles to profl. publs. Mem. White House Nat. Goals Working Group, 1970; mem. adv. council Sch. Edn., U. San Francisco, 1975-78; mem. Govtl. Research Council of San Mateo County, Calif., 1975—. Served with USN, 1945-48. NSF fellow, 1952-53. Mem. Am. Inst. Indsl. Engrs. (Peninsula chpt. Indsl. Engr. of Yr. 1975), Phi Beta Kappa, Sigma Xi. Methodist. Home: 1448 Kyle Ct Sunnyvale CA 94087 Office: 655 River Oaks Parkway San Jose CA 95135

DIXON, JAMES PAYSON, JR., college president; b. Portsmouth, N.H., Mar. 15, 1917; s. James Payson and Mary (Russell) D.; m. Edla Denton Mills, Aug. 31, 1941; children—Linn, Russell M., Pamela, Deborah, Donna, Peter C. B.S., Antioch Coll., 1939; M.D., Harvard, 1943; M.S., Columbia, 1947. Diplomate: Am. Bd. Preventive Medicine and Public Health. Intern Boston City Hosp., 1944; fellow W.K. Kellogg Found., 1945-46, Rockefeller Found., 1946-47; med. dir. Denver Gen. Hosp., 1947-48; asso. prof. preventive medicine and public health U. Colo.; mgr. health and hosps., Denver, 1948-52; prof. public health and preventive medicine U. Pa., 1952-59; commr. health, Phila., 1952-59; pres. Antioch Coll., 1959-75; vis. prof. Sch. Pub. Health, U. N.C., 1976-77, clin. prof., 1977—; interim pres. Eastern Va. Med. Authority, 1978-79. Author public health, social welfare and ednl. articles. Overseer Coll. of V.I.; trustee Goddard Coll., Inst. for Policy Studies. Served from surgeon to med. dir. USPHS, 1952-54; asst. dir. clin. center NIH. Home: 3406 Dover Rd Durham NC 27707

DIXON, JEANE, author, lecturer, real estate broker, columnist; b. Medford, Wis.; d. Gerhart and Emma (von Graffee) Pinckert; m. James L. Dixon. Founder, chmn. bd. Children to Children Inc.; sec.-treas. James L. Dixon & Co., Realtors, Washington. Author articles, books; Author: My Life and Prophecies, 1969, Reincarnation and Prayers to Live By, 1970, The Call to Glory, 1972, Yesterday, Today and Forever, 1976, Horoscopes for Dogs (Pets and Their Planets), 1979; Syndicated columnist: Horoscope and Predictions, Los Angeles Times Syndicate.; featured in Rupert Murdoch's Star. Chmn. Easter Seal campaign, Washington, 1968. Recipient Loreto Internat. award Loreto Shrine in, Italy; Internat. L'Enfant award Holy Family Adoption League; named Woman of Year Internat. Orphans; knight Internat. Order of St. Martin, Vienna; award Md. chpt. Cystic Fibrosis Found.; St. John of Jerusalem Internat. Humanitarian Christian Chivalry award; knighted Dame of Humanity; Imperial Byzantine Order of St. Constantine the Great of St. George; Fall Gal award Nat. Saints and Sinners Conv.; Unsung Heroine award Ladies aux. VFW; Golden Lady Humanitarian award AMITA Internat.; Internat. Nostradamus award Internat. Platform Assn.; Leif Erikson Humanitarian award Sons of Norway; First Anglo hon. Navajo princess. Mem. Nat. League Am. Pen. Women, A.S.C.A.P., Internat. Platform Assn. Club: Internat. (Washington). Exponent of extrasensory perception (subject of book A Gift of Prophecy). Address: care James L Dixon & Co 1225 Connecticut Ave NW Washington DC 20036

DIXON, JOHN ALDOUS, surgeon; b. Provo, Utah, July 16, 1923; s. Henry Aldous and Lucille (Knowlden) D.; m. Karma Jeppsen, Sept. 28, 1944; children—Stephen, Kay, Lisa. Student, Weber Coll., Ogden, Utah, 1940-42, Idaho State U., 1942; B.S., U. Wash., 1943; M.D., U. Utah, 1947. Diplomate: Am. Bd. Surgery. Surg. resident U. Rochester Med. Center, 1947-50; pvt. practice surgery, Odgen, Utah, 1953-68; part-time tchr. U. Utah Med. Sch., 1953-68, asso. clinical prof. surgery, 1965-68, asso. prof. surgery, 1968-70, prof. surgery, 1970—, dir. endoscopic and laser surgery, 1978—, exec. v.p. of univ., 1970-72, dean, 1972-76, v.p. for health scis., 1973-78; chief surgery McKay-Dee Hosp., 1965-67; mem. nat. adv. council on health professions edn., 1976-80. Contbr. to: Am. Med. Jour. Chmn. Utah Bd. Health, 1960-63; Bd. regents U. Utah, 1963-66; trustee Intermountain Health Care, 1974-78; Mem. Ogden City Council, 1956. Served with USNR, 1943-46; served to capt. USAF, 1951-53. Fellow A.C.S.; mem. Am. Gastroent. Assn., Soc. for Surgery Alimentary Tract, Western Surg. Assn., Utah Soc. Bio-med. Research, Internat. Collegium Cirurgicum, Am. Soc. Gastrointestinal Endoscopy, Soc. Am. Gastrointestinal Endoscopic Surgeons, Utah Med. Assn. (pres. 1980-81), Alpha Omega Alpha, Phi Kappa Phi. Home: 875 Donner Way Salt Lake City UT 84108 Office: 50 N Medical Dr Salt Lake City UT 84132

DIXON, JOHN ALLEN, JR., chief justice La. Supreme Ct.; b. Orange, Tex., Apr. 8, 1920; s. John A. and Louella (Stark) D.; m. Imogene K. Shipley, Oct. 20, 1945; children: Stella (Mrs. Paul Shepard), Diana (Mrs. L.C. Morehead, Jr.), Jeannette (Mrs. Michael Downing). B.A., Centenary Coll., 1940; LL.B., Tulane U., 1947. Bar: La. 1947. Tchr., coach Tallulah High Sch., 1940-42; pvt. practice law, Shrveport, La., 1947-57, asst. dist. atty., Shreveport, 1954-57; judge 1st Dist. Ct., 1957-68, La. Ct. Appeal, Shreveport, 1968-70; asso. justice La. Supreme Ct., 1971, now chief justice. Served with AUS, 1942-45. Democrat. Methodist. Club: Mason. Office: Supreme Ct La 301 Loyola Ave New Orleans LA 70112 *

DIXON, JOHN CURTIS, JR., naval officer; b. N.Y.C., Jan. 24, 1926; s. John Curtis and Blanche Pearce (Williams) D.; m. Elizabeth Earnest Matthews, June 7, 1949; children: Laura Kellie, Robert Aubrey. Student, Mercer U., 1943; B.S., U.S. Naval Acad., 1949. Served as enlisted man U.S. Army, 1944, U.S. Navy, 1944-45, commd. ensign, 1949, advanced through grades to rear adm., 1974; naval aviator, fighter pilot, 1950-66; comdr. VF-191 Flying Crusaders, Vietnam, 1965-66, Air Wing Eight, 1967-68, U.S.S. Canisteo (A0-99), 1971-72, U.S.S. John F. Kennedy (CV-67), 1972-74, Tactical Wings Atlantic, 1974-75, Carrier Group Six; also Carrier Striking Force Atlantic Fleet, 1975-77; dep. chief of staff Pacific Fleet, 1977-80; dir. strike and amphibious warfare div. Dept. Navy, 1980-81. Decorated Legion of Merit (3), D.F.C. (2), Air medal (10), Navy Commendation medal. Episcopalian.

DIXON, JOHN MORRIS, magazine editor; b. Long Branch, N.J., June 22, 1933; s. Abram C. and Emily (Minton) D.; m. Carol Ruth Nipomnich, Dec. 27, 1959; children: Peter, Susannah. B.Arch., MIT, 1955. From asst. editor to sr. editor Progressive Architecture, 1960-65, editor, 1971—; sr. editor Archtl. Forum, 1965-71. Author: Architectural Design Preview, U.S.A, 1962, (with N. White and E. Willensky) A.I.A. Guide to New York City, 1967. Served to 1st lt. AUS, 1955-57. Fellow A.I.A. (chmn. exhibits com. N.Y. chpt. 1964-65, co-chmn. visitors com. N.Y. chpt. 1965-66, chmn. pub. relations com. N.Y. chpt. 1970-71, mem. design com. 1978—, chmn. 1983). Home: 382 Sound Beach Ave Old Greenwich CT 06870 Office: 600 Summer St Stamford CT 06904

DIXON, JOHN WAINWRIGHT, corporate executive; b. Lexington, Ky., Mar. 12, 1920; s. Thomas H. and Mary (Edmonds) D.; m. Doris I. Sowell, May 13, 1961; children: Jacqueline P., Frederick D.R., Clinton M. Student, George Washington U., 1948-49; A.B., U. Houston, 1948; M.A., U. Miami, Fla., 1951. Asst. prof. So. Miss. Coll., 1952-53; asst. to v.p. planning Convair Gen. Dynamics, San Diego, 1956-61; asst. comptroller, dir. systems planning Office Asst. Sec. Def., Washington, 1961-62; dir. planning Ling Temco Vought, Inc., Dallas, 1962-67, v.p. planning, 1967-69; chmn., pres. E-Systems, Inc., Dallas, 1969-82, chmn., chief exec. officer, 1982—; dir. MKT R.R., Katy R.R. Mem. Dallas Citizens Council; mem. nat. adv. council Inf. Museum Assn.; Bd. dirs. Christmas Pageant of Peace, 1973—, Center for Internat. Bus. S.W., Dallas Civic Opera, Dallas Community Coll. Dist. Found., Dallas Symphony Assn., Nat. Park Found., United Way, USO, Wolf Trap Found., So. Meth. U. Found. for Sci. and Engring.; mem. adv. com. Honor Am.; chmn. Dallas County U.S. Savings Bonds, 1975-81. Served with AUS, 1941-46. Named to Honor Role Inf. Officer Candidate Hall Fame, Ft. Benning, Ga. Mem. Air Force Assn., Aerospace Industries Assn. (bd. govs.), Am. Def. Preparedness Assn. (dir.), U.S. Army Assn. (chmn. 1979-80), Armed Forces Communications and Electronics Assn. (dir.), U.S. C. of C., Dallas Council World Affairs, Nat. Security Indsl. Assn. (trustee, exec. com.), Assn. Unmanned Vehicle Systems (hon. trustee), Phi Beta Kappa. Club: Dallas Economists (pres. 1968). Office: PO Box 226030 Dallas TX 75266 *Believe that hard work, integrity and fair dealings with all people above, below, and on equal level has always been, and will always be, the keys to success.* *

DIXON, JOHN WESLEY, JR., religion and art educator; b. Richmond, Va., Aug. 18., 1919; s. John Wesley and Margaret (Denny) D.; m. Vivian Ardelia Slagle, Jan. 9, 1943; children: Susan Raglan, Judith Ann, Miriam Elizabth. B.A., Emory & Henry Coll., 1941; Ph.D., U. Chgo., 1953. Instr. Mich. State U., East Lansing, 1950-52; asst. prof. Emory U., Atlanta, 1952-57; exec. dir. Faculty Christian Fellowship, N.Y.C., 1955-57; assoc. prof. Dickinson Coll., Carlisle, Pa., 1957-60; prof. Fla. Presbyn. Coll., St. Petersburg, 1960-63; prof. religion and art U. N. C., Chapel Hill, 1963—. Author: Nature and Grace in Art, 1964, Art and the Theological Imagination, 1978; auhtor: The Physiology of Faith, 1979. Served to 1st lt. U.S. Army, 1941-45. Democrat. Episcopalian. Home: 216 Glenhill Ln Chapel Hill NC 27514 Office: U NC Dept Religion Chapel Hill NC 27514

DIXON, JULIAN CAREY, congressman; b. Washington, Aug. 8, 1934; m. Betty Lee; 1 son, Cary Gordon. B.S., Calif. State U., Los Angeles, 1962; LL.B., Southwestern U., Los Angeles, 1967. Mem. Calif. State Assembly, 1972-78; mem. 94th-98th Congresses from Calif. 28th Dist., mem. House Appropriations Com., Com. on Standards Ofcl. Conduct, chmn. Black Caucus. Chmn. Calif. State Democratic Caucus. Served with U.S. Army, 1957-60. Mem. NAACP, Urban League, Calif. Arts Commn. Democrat. Office: Room 423 Cannon House Office Bldg Washington DC 20515 *

DIXON, LOUIS M., hotel and casino company executive. Chmn. Harrah's Hotels and Casinos, Reno, NV. Office: Harrah's 300 E Second St Reno NV 89504

DIXON, RICHARD CRESSIE, natural gas co. exec.; b. Guymon, Okla., Mar. 24, 1929; s. Homer E. and Esta (Hayes) D.; m. Georgianna Sweet, Aug. 27, 1950; children—Richard Phillip, James Douglas, Daniel Kent. B.S. in Petroleum Engring, Okla. U., 1952. With Panhandle Eastern Pipe Line Co. (and subs. cos.), 1952—, mgr. gas purchase, Liberal, Kans., 1952-66; v.p. Anadarko Prodn. Co. subs., Liberal, 1961-65; pres. Anadarko, Ft. Worth, 1968-71; v.p., prodn. and gas supply divs. Panhandle Eastern Pipe Line Co., Kansas City, Mo., 1966-68, sr. v.p., Houston, 1971—. Mem. Am. Petroleum Inst., Ind. Petroleum Assn. Am., Mid-Continent Oil and Gas Assn., Soc. Petroleum Engrs., Ind. Natural Gas Assn. Republican. Presbyn. Clubs: Houston, Petroleum, Univ., Lakeside Country (Houston). Home: 334 Fawnlake Dr Houston TX 77079 Office: PO Box 1642 Houston TX 77001

DIXON, RICHARD WAYNE, communications co. exec.; b. Hubbard, Oreg., Sept. 25, 1936; s. Harlow C. and Mabel (Nielson) D.; m. Rosina O. Berry, July 4, 1970; children—Erica, Douglas, Andrew. B.A. (Nat. scholar 1955-58), Harvard U., 1958, M.A., 1960, Ph.D., 1964. Tech. staff mem. Bell Labs., Murray Hill, N.J., 1965, supr. lightwave lasers group, 1968-79, head optoelectronics devices dept., 1979—. Editor: IEEE Electronic Device Letters, 1980—; Contbr. articles to various publs. NSF fellow, 1959-63. Fellow IEEE; mem. Am. Phys. Soc., AAAS. Asso. Home: 43 Old Wood Rd Bernardsville NJ 07924 Office: Bell Labs 600 Mountain Ave Murray Hill NJ 07974

DIXON, ROBERT JAMES, aerospace consultant, former air force officer, former aerospace company executive; b. N.Y.C., Apr. 9, 1920; s. William H. and Mary A. (Smith) D.; m. Elizabeth Harriman (dec.); m. Lamana M. Kelly, July 19, 1958; children: Kelly Lee, Thomas Fries, Roland Cahill, Mary Lucinda. Grad., Collegiate Sch., N.Y.C., 1937; A.B., Dartmouth, 1941, Air War Coll., 1959. Enlisted RCAF, 1941; trans. USAAF, 1943; advanced through grades to gen. USAF, 1973; served as pilot, ETO, World War II, Korea; vice comdr. 7th Air Force, Vietnam, 1969-70; dep. chief staff personnel Hdqrs. USAF, Washington, 1970-73; comdr. TAC Air Command, Langley, Va., 1973-78; ret., 1978; pres. Fairchild Republic Co., Farmingdale, N.Y., 1978-81, chmn., 1982, ret., 1982; aerospace Fairchld Republic Co., Farmingdale, N.Y., 1982—. Decorated D.S.C., D.S.M. (4), Legion of Merit (2), U.S.; D.F.C. (2), U.S. and U.K.; Legion of Honor, France; recipient Collier trophy, 1978. Home and Office: 29342 Ridgeview Trail Boerne TX 78006

DIXON, ROBERT W., diversified manufacturing corporation executive; b. 1918; married. With H.K. Porter Co., 1962; v.p., gen. mgr. Kellems Co., subs., 1962—; with Hubbell, Harvey Inc., Orange, Conn., 1962—, corp. v.p. domestic ops., 1966-68, group v.p., 1968-70, exec. v.p. ops., 1970-73, pres., 1973-80, chmn. bd., chief exec. officer, dir., 1980—. Office: Hubbell Harvey Inc 584 Derby Milford Rd Orange CT 06477 *

DIXON, THOMAS FRANCIS, aviation company executive; b. Nashville, Mar. 15, 1916; s. Sam Jones and Mary (Francis) D.; m. Margaret Ann Donovan, July 6, 1943; children: Thomas A., Neil E., Nancy A., Jane E. B.E. in Engring, Vanderbilt U., 1938; B.S. in Chem. Engring; M.S., U. Mich., 1940, Calif. Inst. Tech., 1945. Vice pres. research and engring. Rocketdyne div. (N.Am. Aviation Co.), 1946-61; dep. asso. adminstr. NASA, 1961-63; v.p. N.Am. Aviation, Inc., 1963-

68; chmn. bd. Airtronics, Inc., 1968-69, pres., 1969-73, chmn. bd., 1973—; exec. v.p. program devel. Teledyne McCormick Selph, 1975-76, pres., 1976—, Application Planning Inc., 1982—. Served to lt. comdr. USNR, World War II. Recipient Robert H. Goddard Meml. award Am. Rocket Soc., 1957; Louis W. Hill Space Transp. award Inst. Aero. Scis., 1960. Fellow Am. Inst. Aeros. and Astronautics, Am. Rocket Soc. (pres. So. Calif. sect.); mem. Soc. Automotive Engrs. Home: 7 Via Las Encinas Carmel Valley CA 93924

DIXON, WENDELL L., financial company executive; b. Harrisburg, Ill., Aug. 2, 1923; m. Martha Anne Dixon; 4 children. Grad., U. Evansville. Mgmt. trainee Credithrift Fin., Inc., Houston and Evansville, Ind., 1946, br. mgr., 1947-53, dist. mgr., 1953-54, personnel dir., Houston and Evansville, 1954-55, dir. ops., Houston and Evansville, Ind., 1955-68; v.p., chief ops. Credithrift Fin. Corp., Houston and Evansville, Ind., 1968-71, exec. v.p., chief ops., 1971, pres., chief ops., 1971-73, chmn., chief exec. officer, 1973—; pres., dir. Credithrift Fin. Mgmt. Corp., Houston and Evansville, Ind., 1968—; dir. Citizens Nat. Bank; mem. Ind. Dept. Fin. Instns. Trustee U. Evansville; bd. dirs. Evansville's Future, Welborn Bapt. Hosp.; past pres. Welborn Bapt. Hosp. Found. Mem. Nat. Consumer Fin. Assn. (exec. com.), Evansville C. of C. (dir.). Baptist. Lodge: Shriners. Office: Credit Thrift Fin Inc 601 NW 2d St Evansville IN 47701

DIXON, WESLEY MOON, JR., pharmaceutical executive; b. Evanston, Ill., Oct. 18, 1927; s. Wesley Moon and Katherine (Strawn) D.; m. Suzanne Searle, May 23, 1953; children: Katherine Dixon Thomson, Carolynn Frances, John Wesley. B.A., Yale U., 1950. Salesman, Owens-Ill. Co., 1950-54; with G.D. Searle & Co., Chgo., 1954—, pres., 1972, now vice chmn., dir. Dir. No. Trust Co.; Trustee Lake Forest (Ill.) Coll., Art Inst. Chgo.; bd. dirs. Lake Forest Hosp., Up With People, Rehab. Inst. Chgo., John Crerar Library, Center for Am. Archeology. Mem. Chgo. Council Fgn. Relations (dir.). Republican. Episcopalian. Clubs: Onwentsia, Shoreacres (Lake Forest); Chgo., Casino, Mid-Am., Comml., Econ., Commonwealth (Chgo.). Office: GD Searle and Co PO Box 1045 Chicago IL 60076 *

DIXON, WILFRID JOSEPH, statistics educator; b. Portland, Oreg.; m. Glorya Duffy, June 25, 1983; children—Janet Dixon Elashoff, Kathleen Dixon Nebent. B.A., Oreg. State Coll., 1938; M.A., U. Wis., 1939; Ph.D., Princeton, 1944. Asst. prof. math. U. Okla., 1942-44, 45-46; mem. joint Army-Navy Target Group, Washington and, Guam, 1944-45; asso. prof., then prof. math. U. Oreg., 1946-55; prof. preventive medicine UCLA, 1955-67, prof., 1967—, chmn. dept. biomath., 1967-74; pres. BMDP Statis. Software, Inc., 1981—; math. stat. VA Brentwood. Author: (with F.J. Massey) Introduction to Statistical Analysis, 4th edit., 1982; also articles.; Asso. editor: Biometrics, 1955-65, Annals of Math. Statistics, 1955-58. Cons. NIH, 1960—, NRC, 1948—, NSF, 1968—, Calif. Dept. Mental Hygiene and Public Health, 1963—. Fellow AAAS, Royal Statis. Soc.; mem. Inst. Math. Statistics, Internat. Statis. Inst., Am. Statis. Assn. (v.p. 1969-70, 78-81). Home: 1909 Pelham Ave Apt 308 Los Angeles CA 90025 Office: Univ Calif Los Angeles CA 90024

DIXON, WILLIAM CORNELIUS, lawyer; b. Dexter, N.Y., July 1, 1904; s. Frank and Celia (Potter) D.; m. Arvilla Pratt, Nov. 20, 1934; children—Anne Arvilla, Nancy Cornelia. A.B., U. Mich., 1926, J.D., 1928. Bar: Ohio bar 1928, Calif. bar 1948, bar Supreme Ct. U.S 1948. Asso. with firm Holliday-Grossman-McAfee, Cleve., 1928-32; asst. dir. law, Cleve., 1932-33, practiced law, 1933-38; judge Supreme Ct. Ohio, 1938; spl. asst. to atty. gen. U.S., anti-trust div., 1944-54; chief asst. trial sect. anti-trust div., 1945; Legal adviser and mem. Joint War and State Depts. Zaibatsu Mission to Japan, 1946; apptd. chief West Coast offices Anti-trust Div., 1946; chief trial counsel for Govt. U.S. versus Standard Oil Co. Calif. et al, 1948, chief, 1948-54; pvt. law practice, Los Angeles, 1954-59, asst. atty. gen., Calif., in charge state anti-trust enforcement, 1959-63. Dir. relief for Ohio under Emergency Relief Act, 1938-39; Moderator Los Angeles Assn. Congl. Chs., 1957; moderator Congl. Conf. So. Calif. and S.W., 1960; mem. constn. commn. United Ch. of Christ; mem. United Ch. Bd. for Homeland Ministries, 1962-65. Mem. Calif., Los Angeles bar assns., Delta Sigma Rho, Pi Kappa Alpha. Democrat. Home: 1188 Romney Dr Pasadena CA 91105 Office: Subway Terminal Bldg 417 S Hill St Los Angeles CA 90013 *The past and unachieved goals in life soon pass into history. The goals of today become the achievements and successes of tomorrow.*

DIXON, WILLIAM ROBERT, musician, composer, educator; b. Nantucket, Mass., Oct. 5, 1925; s. William Robert and Louise Ann (Wade) D.; children: William, Claudia Gayle, William. Diploma, Hartnette Conservatory Music, 1951. Clk., internat. civil servant UN Secretariat, N.Y.C., 1956-62; free lance musician, composer, N.Y.C., 1962-67; mem. faculty Columbia U. Tchrs. Coll., 1967-70; composer-in-residence George Washington U., Washington, 1967; dir. Conservatory of Univ. of the Streets, N.Y.C., 1967-68; guest artist in residence Ohio State U., 1967; mem. faculty dept. dance Bennington (Vt.) Coll., 1968—, chmn. dept. black music, 1973—; vis. prof. U. Wis., Madison, 1971-72; lectr. painting and music Mus. Modern Art, Verona, Italy, 1982. Recs. include Archie Shepp-Bill Dixon Quartet, 1962, Bill Dixon 7-Tette, 1963, Intents and Purposes: The Bill Dixon Orchestra, 1967, For Franz, 1976, New Music, Second Wave, 1979, Bill Dixon in Italy, 1980, considerations 1 and 2 Bill Dixon, 1980, 82, Bill Dixon in the Labyrinth, 1983; paintings exhibited, Ferrari Gallery, Verona, Italy, 1982; exhibited paintings Multimedia Contemporary Art Gallery, Brescia, Italy, 1982. Served with U.S. Army, 1944-46. Mem. Am. Fedn. Musicians, Duke Ellington Jazz Soc. (hon.). Office: Bennington Coll Bennington VT 05201

DIXON, W(ILLIAM) ROBERT, educator; b. Hudson, Pa., Sept. 16, 1917; s. William Robert and Mary (George) D.; m. Carol Everson Lewis, Dec. 20, 1940; children: William R., Barbara Ann. A.B., Syracuse U., 1938, M.A., 1939; Ph.D. (Horace H. Rackham fellow 1947-48, Burke Aaron Hinsdale scholar 1948), U. Mich., 1948. Tchr., prin. W. Canada Valley Central Schs., Middleville, N.Y., 1940-42; asst. prof. U. Ill., 1948-49, U. Mich., 1949-52, asso. prof., 1952-56, prof. ednl. psychology, 1956—; vis. prof. edn. U. Bombay, India, 1964-65. Contbr. articles to profl. jours. Dir. Mich. Interdisciplinary Research Tng. Program, 1967-72. Served with USAAF, 1942-45. Decorated Air Medal with 10 oak leaf clusters, D.F.C. Fellow Am. Psychol. Assn.; mem. Am. Ednl. Research Assn., N.Y. Acad. Scis., AAAS, Nat. Council Measurement in Edn. Nationally ranked tennis player Men's Singles, 1945, Vets. Singles, 1962. Home: 671 Skynob Dr Ann Arbor MI 48105 Office: Sch Edn U Mich Ann Arbor MI 48109

DIXON, WILLIE JAMES, musician; b. Vicksburg, Miss., July 1, 1915; s. Charlie and Daisey D. Founder Blue Heaven Found. Inc. Composer: for groups The Four Jumps of Jive, 1939, The Big Three Trio, 1940; producer, composer, rec. artist, Chess; rec. artist, Columbia, 1969; Ovation Records, 1973, 76; compositions include I'm Your Hoochie Cooche Man, I'm Ready, I Ain't Superstitious, I Can't Quit You Baby, You Can't Judge a Book by its Cover, You Shook Me, Built for Comfort. Mem. Am. Fedn. Musicians, Nat. Acad. Rec. Arts and Scis. Winner Chgo. Golden Glove Boxing Championship, 1939 *

DIZARD, WILSON PAUL, JR., international affairs consultant, educator; b. N.Y.C., Mar. 6, 1922; s. Wilson Paul and Helen Marie (Oliver) D.; m. Lynn Margaret Wood, Mar. 11, 1944; children: John William, Stephen Wood, Wilson Paul III, Mark Christopher. B.S., Fordham Coll., 1947; postgrad., Columbia, 1947-49. Writer, editor Time Inc., N.Y.C., 1947-51; with Dept. State and USIA, 1951-80; vice consul, Istanbul, Turkey, 1951-53; chief Greece-Turkey-Iran br., 1953-55; info. officer Am. embassy, Athens, Greece, 1955-60; public affairs officer consulate-gen., Dacca, 1960-62, spl. asst. dep. dir., 1964-65, asst. dep. dir., 1966-67; 1st sec. Am. embassy, Warsaw, Poland, 1968-70; asst. dir. Public Affairs Office, Saigon, Vietnam, 1970; spl. adviser polit. sect. U.S. embassy, Saigon, 1971; communications adviser to dir. USIA, Washington, 1971-73, chief plans and program policy, 1973-77; vice-chmn. U.S. del. to 1979 World Adminstrv. Radio Conf. Dept. State, Washington, 1978-79; v.p. Kalba-Bowen Assocs., Cambridge, Mass., 1980—; adj. prof. internat. affairs Georgetown U., 1975—, sr. assoc. Ctr. Strategic and Internat. Studies, 1983—; mem. U.S. del. and exec. asst. to conf. dir. Internat. Telecommunications Satellite Conf., Washington, 1968-69; research assoc. Center Internat. Studies, M.I.T., 1962-63; sr. adviser Dept. State, Washington, 1984—. Author: The Strategy of Truth, 1961, Television—A World View, 1966, The Coming Information Age, 1981; Contbr. articles profl. jours. Cons. Carnegie Found. Commn. on Ednl. TV. Served with AUS, 1943-46. Recipient distinguished alumni award Fordham Coll., 1962. Clubs: International, Cosmos (Washington). Home: 2811 28th St NW Washington DC 20008 Office: Ctr Strategic and Internat Studies Georgetown U 1800 K St NW Washington DC 20006

DI ZEREGA, THOMAS WILLIAM, gas company executive, lawyer; b. Round Hill, Va., Sept. 27, 1927; s. Augustus and Susan Martha (Nichols) diZ.; m. Mary Howe Glascock, Sept. 15, 1956; 1 dau., Mary Bryan. B.A., U. Wichita, 1953; J.D., George Washington U., 1956. Bar: Va. 1958, D.C. 1964, U.S. Supreme Ct. 1965, Pa. 1968, N.Y. 1971, Utah 1980. V.p. Atlantic Richfield Co., Los Angeles, 1967-74; exec. v.p. Northwestern Energy Co., Salt Lake City, 1974-80, also dir.; pres. N.W. Energy Co., Salt Lake City, 1980—; pres. Apco Oil Corp., Houston, 1975-78, also dir.; pres. Apco Argentina, Inc., also dir. Trustee Apco Liquidating Trust; v.p., dir. Energy Ventures, Inc.; Mem. exec. com. Can.-Am. Com.; bd. dirs. Nat. Planning Council. Served in U.S. Army, 1946-47. Mem. ABA. Democrat. Episcopalian. Clubs: Calif. (Los Angeles); Country, Alta (Salt Lake City); Met., Chevy Chase (Washington). Home: Oakdale Farm Upperville VA 22176 Office: PO Box 247 Upperville VA 22176

DIZON, REYNALDO CRUZ, ballet dancer; b. Navatas, Manial, Feb. 13, 1955; emigrated to U.S., 1979; s. Wenceslao and Juliana (Dela Cruz) D. Soloist Ballet Philippines, Manila, 1973-79, Les Grands Ballet Canadiens, Montreal, 1979-81, prin. dancer, 1981—. Home: 1090 Laurier West Apt 9 Montreal PQ Canada H2V 2K8

DJERASSI, CARL, educator, chemist; b. Vienna, Austria, Oct. 29, 1923; s. Samuel and Alice (Friedmann) D.; m. Norma Lundholm (div. 1976); children: Dale, Pamela (dec.). A.B. summa cum laude, Kenyon Coll., 1942, D.Sc. (hon.), 1958; Ph.D., U. Wis., 1945; D.Sc. (hon.), Nat. U. Mex., 1953, Fed. U., Rio de Janeiro, 1969, Worcester Poly. Inst., 1972, Wayne State U., 1974, Columbia, 1975, Uppsala U., 1977, Coe Coll., 1978, U. Geneva, 1978. Research chemist Ciba Pharm. Products, Inc., Summit, N.J., 1942-43, 45-49; asso. dir. research Syntex, Mexico City, 1949-52, research v.p., 1957-60; v.p. Syntex Labs., Palo Alto, Calif., 1960-62, Syntex Research, 1962-68, pres., 1968-72, Zoecon Corp., 1968—; Prof. chemistry Wayne State U., 1952-59, Stanford, 1959—; dir. Cetus Corp., Ridge Vineyards, Teknowledge, Inc.; Andrews lectr. U. New South Wales, Australia; Debye lectr. Cornell U.; Reynaud lectr. Mich. State U.; Venable lectr. U. N.C.; Edgar Fahs Smith Meml. lectr. U. Pa.; O.H. Smith lectr. Okla. State U.; Stieglitz lectr. U. Chgo.; Bachman lectr. U. Mich.; Mack lectr. Ohio State U.; Dreyfus lectr. Dartmouth; Fuson lectr U. Nev.; Dreyfus Disting. scholar Duke U.; Gregory Pincus Meml. lectr. Worcester Found.; Baker lectr. U. Calif. (Santa Barbara); Osborne lectr. Rockefeller U.; Purves lectr. McGill U.; Redman lectr. McMaster U.; ann. chemistry lectr. Royal Swedish Acad. Engring.; Scheele lectr. Swedish Pharm. Soc. Mem. editorial bd.: Jour. Organic Chemistry, 1955-59; Editorial bd.: Tetrahedron, 1958—, Steroids, 1963—, Proc. of Nat. Acad. Scis, 1964-70, Jour. Am. Chem. Soc, 1966-75, Organic Mass Spectrometry, 1968—; Author 7 books.; Contbr. numerous articles to profl. jours. Recipient Intrasci. Research Found. award, 1969; Freedman Patent award Am. Inst. Chemists, 1970; Chem. Pioneer award, 1973; Nat. Medal Sci., 1973; Perkin medal, 1975; Wolf prize in chemistry, 1978; John and Samuel Bard award in Sci. and Medicine, 1983; named to Nat. Inventors Hall of Fame, 1978. Mem. Nat. Acad. Scis., Am. Chem. Soc. (award pure chemistry 1958, Baekeland medal 1959, Fritzsche award 1960, award for creative invention 1973), Swiss Chem. Soc., Royal Soc. Chemistry (hon. fellow, Centenary lectr. 1964), Am. Acad. Arts and Scis., German Acad. (Leopoldina), Royal Swedish Acad. Scis. (fgn.), Royal Swedish Acad. Engring. Scis. (fgn.), Am. Acad. Pharm. Scis. (hon.), Brazilian Acad. Scis. (fgn.), Mexican Acad. Sci. Investigation, Bulgarian Acad. Scis. (fgn.), Phi Beta Kappa, Sigma Xi, Phi Lambda Upsilon (hon.). Office: Dept Chemistry Stanford U Stanford CA 94305

DJERASSI, ISAAC, physician; b. Sofia, Bulgaria, July 27, 1925; came to U.S., 1954, naturalized, 1962; s. Rahamim and Adela (Tadjer) D.; m. Nira Eskenazy, Jan. 31, 1954; children—Ram Isaac, Ady Lynn. Student, Sofia U. Med. Sch., 1944-49; M.D., Hebrew U., Jerusalem, 1952; D.H. (hon.), Villanova U., 1977. Intern Hadassah Hosp., Tel Aviv, 1951-52, resident, 1953-54; research asso. Harvard U. Med. Sch., Boston, 1955-60; asst. prof. pediatrics U. Pa., Phila., 1960-69; dir. research Mercy Cath. Med. Center, Phila., 1969—, also dir. hematology. Contbr. articles to profl. jours. Mem. med. advisory bd. Nat. Hemophilia Found., Phila., 1964—, Leukemia Soc., Phila., 1970—. Recipient Albert Lasker award Albert and Mary Lasker Found, 1972. Mem. Am. Soc. Cancer Research, Soc. Pediatric Research, Am. Soc. Exptl. Pathology, Am. Assn. Blood Banks. Inventor filtration leukophersis system and machine for white blood cell transfusions, 1970; discoverer high methotrexate-citrovorum rescue chemotherapy of cancer, 1964-77; developer platelet transfusions, 1955-62. Home: 2034 Delancey Pl Philadelphia PA 19103 Office: Mercy Catholic Med Center PO Box 19709 Philadelphia PA 19143

DJORDJEVIC, DIMITRIJE, historian; b. Beograd, Yugoslavia, Feb. 27, 1922; came to U.S., 1970, naturalized, 1977; s. Vladimir and Jelena (Rasic) D.; m. Nan Fletcher, June 1981; 1 dau. Student, U. Beograd, 1950-54, Ph.D., 1962. Jelena. Sr. staff mem. Inst. History, Serbian Acad. Scis. and Arts, 1958-69, Inst. Balkan Studies, 1969-70; prof. U. Calif., Santa Barbara, 1970—, chmn. Russian area studies, 1976—; mem. Nat. Com. to Promote History of Habsburg Monarchy, 1973-79. Author: Austro-Serbian Customs War 1906-1911, in Serbian, 1962, Revolutions nationales des peuples balkaniques, 1904-1914, 1965; co-author: The Balkan Revolutionary Tradition, 1981, also papers, essays, revs.; editor: The Creation of Yugoslavia, 1914-1918, 1980; editorial bd. profl. jours. Mem. Am. Hist. Assn., Am. Assn. Advancement Slavic Studies, Modern Greek Studies Assn., N.Am. Soc. Serbian Studies, Conf. Slavic and East European History (pres. 1984), Santa Barbara Com. Fgn. Relations. Serbian Orthodox. Office: Dept History U Calif Santa Barbara CA 93106

DJORDJEVICH, MICHAEL, ins. co. exec.; b. Belgrade, Yugoslavia, Aug. 24, 1936; U.S., 1956, naturalized, 1961; s. Dragoslav R. and Ruzica J. Georgevich; m. Marie Louise Hohman, Jan. 20, 1963; children—Marie, Alexander, Michelle. B.S., U. Calif., Berkeley, 1968; M.B.A., San Francisco State U., 1962. With Fireman's Fund Ins. Co., San Francisco, 1962—, supr. cost and standards, 1965-70, asst. treas., 1970-74, v.p. investments, 1974-78, v.p., treas., 1978—; dir. Spanek, Inc. State pres. Calif. Young Republicans, 1965-66; vice chmn. United Republicans of Calif., 1968-69; dir. First Serbian Benevolent Soc., 1976-80. Served with U.S. Army, 1962-63. Mem. Treasurers Club of San Francisco. Republican. Serbian Orthodox. Club: University. Home: 74 Arguello Circle San Rafael CA 94901 Office: 3333 California St San Francisco CA 94119 *In the dark shadows of Nazi and Communist tyranny and then in the steady glow of freedom in America, I have grown to understand: that human dignity and integrity can be maintained even under most adverse conditions; that one can remain true to oneself regardless of outside forces; that we have a choice to do or not to do what is right, just and noble.*

DLESK, GEORGE, industry consultant; b. Chgo., Dec. 13, 1914; s. John J. and Anna (Dedic) D.; m. Jacquelyn McCredie, Mar. 16, 1940; children: Lynn, Devi, Andrea. B.S. in Indsl. Mgmt, U. Ill., 1939; postgrad., U. Calif., Berkeley, 1942, Inst. Paper Chemistry, Appleton, Wis., 1955, U. Sarasota, 1979; grad., Advanced Mgmt. Program, Harvard, 1967. With Booz, Allen & Hamilton (mgmt. cons.), Chgo., 1943-46; with Packaging Corp. Am., 1946-74, v.p. paperbd. div., 1956-67, sr. v.p., Evanston, Ill., 1967-74; sr. v.p. mills, dir. Consol. Packaging Corp., Chgo., 1975-76; pres. Mgmt. Services for the Paper Industry, Chgo., 1976-78; with Am. Inst. Fin. and Mgmt., 1979-81; pres. Computer Program Builders, Inc., 1981—. Mem. Sarasota Power Squadron. Episcopalian. Clubs: University (Grand Rapids, Mich.); Sarasota Yacht. Home: Islander Club 2301 Gulf of Mexico Dr Longboat Key FL 33548 Office: PO Box 32009 Sarasota FL 33578

DMTRYSHYN, BASIL, historian; b. Poland, Jan. 14, 1925; U.S., 1947, naturalized, 1951; s. Frank and Euphrosinia (Senchak) Dmytryshyn; m. Virginia Roehl, July 16, 1949; children: Sonia, Tania. B.A., U. Ark., 1950, M.A., 1951; Ph.D., U. Calif.-Berkeley, 1955. Asst. prof. history Portland State U., Oreg., 1956-59, assoc. prof., 1959-64, prof., 1964—; vis. prof. U. Ill., 1964-65, Harvard U., 1971, Hawaii U., 1976, Hokkaido U., Sapporo, Japan, 1978-79. Author: (most recent) Colonial Russian America 1817-1832, 1976, A History of Russia, 1977, U.S.S.R.: A Concise History, 4th edit., 1984, The End of Russian America, 1979, Civil and Savage Encounters, 1983, Russian Statecraft, 1984, The Subjugation of Siberia, 1984; contbr. articles to profl. jours. State bd. dirs. PTA, Oreg., 1963-64; mem. World Affairs Council, Oreg., 1965—. Fulbright-Hays fellow W. Germany, 1967-68; fellow Kennan Inst. Advanced Russian Studies, Washington, 1978; recipient John Mosser award Oreg. State Bd. Higher Edn., 1966, 67. Mem. Am. Assn. Advancement Slavic Studies (dir. 1972-75), Am. Hist. Assn., Western Slavic Assn., Can. Assn. Slavists, Oreg. Hist. Soc., Nat. Geog. Soc., Conf. Slavic and East European History (nat. sec. 1972-75). Office: Dept History Portland State U Portland OR 97207

DOAN, CORTLAND CHARLES, educator; b. Glendale, Calif., Aug. 9, 1926; s. Cortland Palmer and Laura (Ott) D.; m. Virginia Evalyn Malmgreen, Oct. 10, 1947; children—Laurie Evalyn, Charles Cortland, Robyn Lillian. A.A., Pasadena City Coll., 1951; B.A., U. Calif., Santa Barbara, 1953; M.A., Calif. State Coll., 1965. Tchr. indsl. arts San Diego city schs., 1953-56, Citrus Coll., 1959-61, Glendora, Calif., 1959-65; engring. supr. Consol. Electrodynamics Corp., 1956-59; mem. faculty dept. indsl. studies Calif. State U.-, Los Angeles, 1965—; now prof. Calif. State U.; engring. cons. Electro-Mech. Design, 1960—; vocat. edn. adviser to, Brit. Honduras, 1970. Contbr. articles to profl. jours. Planning commr. City Duarte, Calif., 1961-63. Served with USNR, 1943-46. Recipient Laureate citation Epsilon Pi Tau, 1972; Indsl. Educator of Year Coll. Level Los Angeles County Indsl. Edn. Assn., 1978. Mem. Robotics Internat. of Soc. Mfg. Engrs. (sr.), Calif. Tchrs. Assn., Calif. Coll. and Univ. Faculty Assn., Am. Vocat. Assn., Am. Indsl. Arts Assn., Calif. Indsl. Edn. Assn., Calif. Council of Indsl. Art Tchr. Educators. Office: 5151 State University Dr Los Angeles CA 90032

DOANE, JOHN PHILIP, bus. exec.; b. Lincoln, Nebr., Mar. 3, 1935; s. Gilbert Harry and Susan Howland (Sherman) D.; m. Stephanie Jay Etnier, Jan. 26, 1957; children—Charles Jay, Peter Etnier, Harry Sherman (dec.). Student, Mass. Inst. Tech., 1953-57; B.B.A., U. Wis., 1962, M.B.A., 1963. With Standard Oil Co., N.J., 1963-73; asst. treas. The Budd Co., Troy, Mich., 1973-74, treas., 1974—. Mem. Phi Beta Kappa, Delta Psi, Beta Gamma Sigma. Episcopalian. Home: 3666 Burning Bush Birmingham MI 48010 Office: Budd Co 3155 W Big Beaver Troy MI 48084

DOBAN, ROBERT CHARLES, glass co. exec.; b. Kenosha, Wis., Feb. 25, 1924; s. Charles and Mary D.; m. Eleanore Szatko, July 25, 1947; 1 son, Geoffrey Robert. B.S., Yale U., 1949; Ph.D., U. Wis., 1952. Research chemist E.I. DuPont de Nemours & Co., Inc., Wilmington, Del., 1952-57, various research mgmt. positions, 1957-68, lab. dir., 1968-70, venture mgr., 1970-72, research dir., 1972-74; v.p. tech. services Owens-Corning Fiberglas Corp., Toledo, 1974-77, sr. v.p. sci. and tech., 1978—; dir. Sherwin-Williams Co., Cleve. Bd.dirs. WGTE-TV-FM, pub. broadcasting, 1978—. Served to lt. USN, 1944-46. Mem. Am. Chem. Soc., AAAS, Indsl. Research Inst., Chem. Soc. (London). Clubs: Toledo, Belmont Country, Caranor Hunt and Polo; Internat. (Washington). Home: 30761 E River Rd Perrysburg OH 43551 Office: Owens-Corning Fiberglas Fiberglas Tower 1 Levis Sq Toledo OH 43659

DOBBIE, GEORGE HERBERT, textile mfg. co. exec.; b. Galt, Ont., Can., Nov. 15, 1918; s. George Alexander and Edith (Scott) D.; m. Marie L. Reiser, Mar. 15, 1941; children—George C., Murray S., Brian H., Alexander M. Student, Bishop Ridley Coll., 1934-35, McGill U., 1936-39. With Newlands & Co., Galt, 1939—, sales mgr. hand knit div., 1947-51, pres., 1951-63; chmn. bd. Glenelg Textiles Ltd., Agatex Devel. Ltd., both Galt; dir. Can. Trust Co., London, Ont., Dominion Life Assurance Co., Waterloo, Ont.; hon. dir. Domtar, Inc., Montreal, Que. Past chmn. Can. Textile Inst., Galt Bd. Trade, Galt Bd. Edn.; past bd. govs. U. Waterloo, Lakefield Coll. Sch., Ont. Served from pvt. to capt. Royal Canadian Army, 1941-45. Mem. Canadian Woolen and Knit Goods Mfrs. Assn. (pres. 1956-58), Primary Textiles Inst. Can. (chmn.), Can. Mfrs. Assn. (past v.p.), Pacific Basin Econ. Council (past v.p.). Home: 45 Blair Rd Galt ON Canada Office: 1201 Franklin Blvd S Galt ON Canada

DOBBIN, ROBERT FRANCIS, lawyer; b. N.Y.C., Sept. 6, 1931; s. James Joseph and Mary Teresa (Cusker) D.; m. Jean Marie Harrington, Apr. 30, 1955; children: Kathleen M., Robert F., Sarah J., Courtney A. B.S., Fordham U., 1953, LL.B., 1959. Bar: N.Y. 1959, U.S. Supreme Ct. 1968, U.S. Dist. Ct. (so. and ea. dists.)N.Y. 1962. Assoc. Davis Polk & Wardwell, N.Y.C., 1959-69; ptnr. Shearman & Sterling, N.Y.C., 1971—. Served to 1st lt. U.S. Army, 1953-55. Mem. ABA, Fed. Bar Council, N.Y. State Bar Assn., Assn. Bar City N.Y. Roman Catholic. Office: Shearman & Sterling 53 Wall St New York NY 10005

DOBBINS, CHARLES GORDON, educator, editor; b. Greensboro, Ala., Aug. 15, 1908; s. John Gordon and Mantie Edgar (Wolf) D.; 1 son, Peter Young; m. Sylvie Buffet, Dec. 21, 1963. A.B., Samford U., 1929; M.A., Columbia, 1931; postgrad., U. Wis., 1931-33; L.H.D., Judson Coll., 1967; Litt.D., Jamestown Coll., 1971; LL.D., Coll. St. Francis, 1973. Reporter Birmingham Age-Herald, 1929; instr. English

U. Wis., 1931-34; dir. Fed. Emergency Relief Adminstrn. Transient Camp, Ft. McClellan, Ala., 1935; dist. dir. Nat. Youth Adminstrn., Gadsden, Ala., 1936; asst. prof. English, asst. to pres. Ala. Coll., 1936-39; editor, pub. Anniston (Ala.) Times, 1939-42; editor Montgomery (Ala.) Advertiser, 1946-47; editor, pub. Montgomery Examiner, 1947-55; staff asso. Am. Council on Edn., 1956-62, dir. commn. on fed. relations, 1962-63, exec. sec., 1963-73, dir. acad. adminstrn. internship program, 1967-73; cons. Acad. Edn. Devel., 1974-75, Am. Council on Edn., 1975-77, Office Sec. HEW, 1976-77. Author: American Council on Education: Leadership and Chronology, 1918-1968, 1968, American Council on Education, Programs and Services, 1958-75, 1976; Editor: Educational Record, 1968-73; The Strength to Meet our National Need, 1956, Expanding Resources for College Teaching, 1956, Higher Education and the Federal Government: Programs and Problems, 1963, The University, The City, and Urban Renewal, 1964; co-editor: Whose Goals for American Higher Education?, 1968; Contbr.: articles to Ency. Americana; others. Pres. Ala. Press Assn., 1942; v.p., exec. dir. Nat. Home Library Found., 1978—; Dir. OPS, Ala., 1951-53; mem. Nat. Planning Assn. (Com. of South), 1946-55, Ala. Bd. Edn., 1951-59; bd. visitors Eckerd Coll., 1968-72; trustee Judson Coll., 1942-58, Alderson Broaddus Coll., 1975—. Served with USNR, 1942-46. Mem. Omicron Delta Kappa, Sigma Delta Chi, Sigma Nu. Democrat. Baptist. Club: Cosmos (Washington). Home: Lovettsville VA 22080 Home: 1545 18th St NW Washington DC 20036

DOBBINS, HARRY MICHAEL, electronics engineer; b. Lincoln, Nebr., Dec. 27, 1945; s. Harry Lee and Irene Mildred D.; m. Kathleen Ann Gorman, May 4, 1974; 1 dau., Elizabeth Ann. B.S. in Physics, U. Notre Dame, 1967, Ph.D., 1972. Chief scientist tech. group USAF, Wright Patterson AFB, Ohio, 1972-80; Alaska area engr. USPHS, Anchorage, 1980—; cons. in field. Author. Recipient Outstanding Performance Recognition award USAF, 1974, 79, 80. Patentee in field. Office: PO Box 7-741 Anchorage AK 99510

DOBBINS, JAMES FRANCIS, JR., foreign service officer; b. N.Y.C., May 31, 1969; s. James Francis and Agnes Ann (Bent) D.; m. Toril Kleivdal, Dec. 31, 1969; childrenL Colin, Christian. B.S.F.S., Georgetown U., 1963. Commd. fgn. service officer Dept. State, 1967; mem. staff U.S. del. Vietnam Peace Talks, Paris, 1968; mem. policy planning staff Dept. State, Washington, 1969-71; cousul., Strasbourg, France; spl. asst. to U.S. rep. UN, N.Y.C., 1973-75; polit.-mil. officer Am. Embassy, London, 1978-81; dep. asst. sec. U.S. Dept. State, Washington, 1982—. Served to lt. (j.g.) USN, 1963-66. Recipient Supervisor Honor award Dept. State, 1982. Mem. Internat. Inst. Strategic Studies-London. Office: Dept State (EUR) 2210 C St NW Washington DC 20520

DOBBINS, JAMES JOSEPH, artist; b. Woburn, Mass., Aug. 12, 1924; s. William John and Delia (Feeney) D.; m. Dorothy Esther Fitzpatrick, Jan. 20, 1951; children: Patricia Dobbins Osborn, William, Mary Dobbins Hintlian, James Joseph, Rita Dobbins McGoldrick, Mark, Dorothy Dobbins Claplin, Christopher, John, Maura. Student, Cornell Coll., Mt. Vernon, Iowa, 1945; B.S., Mass. Coll. Art, 1951, Boston U. Grad. Sch. Edn., 1951-52. Tchr. Boston pub. schs., 1952; editorial cartoonist Woburn (Mass.) Times, 1947-51, Lowell (Mass.) Sun, 1952-53, N.Y. Daily News, 1953, Boston Post, 1953-56, Boston Herald Traveler, 1956-72, Boston Herald Am., 1972-76, Manchester Union Leader, N.H. Sunday News, 1977—. Author: Dobbins Diary of the New Frontier, 1964; Original drawings donated to, Syracuse U. Library. Mem. Diocese of Boston Ecumenical Commn., 1975-77; trustee Cath. Charities for Diocese of Boston.; bd. dirs. Marr Boys and Girls Club, Dorchester, Mass. Served with USNR, 1943-45. Decorated D.F.C., Air medal; recipient two Freedoms Found. 1st prizes, 14 honors medals; Christopher Lit. award, 1958; grand prize Internat. Competition Wayne State U., 1960; certificate of merit Syracuse U., 1969; named Outstanding Young Man Boston Jaycees, 1957. Mem. Nat. Cartoonist Soc., Assn. Am. Editorial Cartoonists. Democrat. Catholic. Clubs: Boston Press (pres. 1967-68), Winchester Country.). Home: 1 Swan Rd Winchester MA 01890 Office: 35 Amherst St Manchester NH 03105 *Life is but a moment on the clock of eternity—don't waste any of it. Keep busy and keep happy.*

DOBBINS, RICHARD ANDREW, engineering educator; b. Burlington, Mass., July 15, 1925; s. William John and Catherine (Porter) D.; m. Iona Mae Blake, Nov. 28, 1953; children: Deborah Anne, Catherine Blake. Sc.B., Harvard U., 1948; M.S., Northeastern U., 1956; Ph.D., Princeton U., 1961. With Eastern Inspection Bur., Boston, 1948-50, Arthur D. Little, Inc., Cambridge, Mass., 1950-53, Sylvania Electric Products Inc., Waltham, Mass., 1953-55; mem. faculty Brown U., 1960—, prof. engring., 1968—, chmn. exec. com. div. engring., 1983—; vis. research asso. Calif. Inst. Tech., 1967-68, U. Essex, Eng., 1971; vis. prof. Abadan (Iran) Inst. Tech., 1975; vis. scientist Nat. Bur. Standards, 1981-82; cons. to govt. and industry. Author: Atmospheric Motion and Air Pollution: An Introduction for Students of Engineering and Science, 1979; Editorial adv. bd.: Combustion Sci. and Tech, 1969-73; Contbr. articles to profl. jours. Served with USNR, 1943-46. Mem. ASME, Combustion Inst., Am. Phys. Soc., Am. Meteorol. Soc., Sigma Xi, Tau Beta Pi. Home: 11 President Ave Providence RI 02906 Office: Div Engring Brown Univ Providence RI 02912

DOBBINS, WILLIAM OCTAVIUS, III, physician; b. Phoenix, Oct., 15, 1932; s. William Octavius and Mary (Kimbell) D.; m. Ellen Scott-Smith, June 29, 1958; children: Laura Diane, Sharon Elene. Student, Davidson Coll., 1950-53; M.D., Med. Coll. Ala., 1957. Diplomate: Am. Bd. Internal Medicine, Am. Bd. Gastroenterology. Resident and fellow U. Wash., Seattle, 1960-65; asst. prof. medicine Duke U., 1965-67, asso. prof., 1967-68; asso. prof. medicine George Washington U., 1969-73, prof., 1973—; pvt. practice medicine, Washington, 1970-79; prof. internal medicine U. Mich. Med. Sch., 1979—; asso. chief staff research VA Med. Center. Author: (with Shingleton) Malabsorption Syndromes, 1968; contbr. articles to med. jours. Served to capt. U.S. Army, 1958-60. USPHS grantee, 1965, 78. Mem. Am. Fedn. Clin. Research (pres. Eastern sect. 1973-74), Am. Digestive Disease Soc. (trustee), AAAS, So. Soc. Clin. Investigation, Am. Gastroenterol. Assn., Alpha Omega Alpha. Democrat. Home: 1719 Hermitage Ann Arbor MI 48104 Office: VA Med Center 2215 Fuller Rd Ann Arbor MI 48105

DOBBS, DAN BYRON, lawyer; b. Ft. Smith, Ark., Nov. 8, 1932; s. George Byron and Gladys Pauline (Stone) D.; m. Betty Jo Teeter, May 31, 1953 (div. 1978); children: Katherine, George, Rebecca, Jean. B.A., U. Ark., 1956, LL.B., 1956; LL.M., U. Ill., 1961, J.S.D., 1966. Bar: Ark. 1956. Partner firm Dobbs, Pryor & Dobbs, Ft. Smith, 1956-60; asst. prof. law U. N.C., Chapel Hill, 1961-63, asso. prof., 1963-66, prof., 1967, Aubrey L. Brooks prof. law, 1975-77; Rosenstiel prof. law U. Ariz., 1978—; vis. asst. prof. U. Tex., summer 1961; vis. prof. U. Minn., 1966-67, Cornell Law Sch., 1968-69, U. Va. Law Sch., 1974, U. Ariz. Law Sch., 1977-78. Author: Handbook on the Law of Remedies, Damages, Equity, Restitution, 1973, Problems in Remedies, 1974; Contbr. articles to legal jours. Office: Law Coll U Ariz Tucson AZ 85721

DOBBS, FRANK WILBUR, chemistry educator; b. Chgo., Sept. 8, 1932; s. Frank W. and Mabelle (Schueler) D.; m. Caroline Starr, Aug. 23, 1958; children: Catherine, Frank, Seth. B.A., U. Chgo., 1953, M.S., 1955; Ph.D., MIT, 1961. Instr. Kennedy King Coll., Chgo., 1959-63; asst. prof. Northeastern Ill. U., Chgo., 1963-64, assoc. prof., 1964-68, prof., 1968—; chmn. natural scis. Northeastenr Ill. U., Chgo., 1967-68; chmn. phys. scis. Northeastern Ill. U., Chgo., 1968-71, chmn. dept. chemistry, 1971-77; dean Coll. Arts and Scis. Northeastern Ill., Chgo., 1977—. Auhtor: The Age of the Molecule, 1976; author: (with Forsler and Gilbert) The Physical Sciences, 1972. Recipient award for excellence in chemistry teaching Ill. Drug and Chem. Industries Activity Com., 1964; fellow Ethyl Corp., 1957. Mem. AAAS, Am. Chem. Soc., Ill. Acad. Sci. Office: Northeastern Ill U 5500 N Saint Louis Ave Chicago IL 60625

DOBBS, GREGORY ALLAN, journalist; b. San Francisco, Oct. 9, 1946; s. Harold Stanley and Annette Rae (Lehrer) D.; m. Carol Lynn Walker, Nov. 25, 1973; children: Jason Walker, Alexander Adair. B.A., U. Calif., Berkeley, 1968; M.S.J., Northwestern U., 1969. Assignment editor, reporter Sta. KGO-TV, San Francisco, 1966-68; news dir. San Francisco Tourist Info. Program Service, 1968; editor ABC Radio, Chgo., 1969-71; producer ABC News, Chgo., 1971-73, corr., 1973-77, London, 1977-82, Paris, 1982—; lectr. Northwestern U. Sch. Journalism, 1975, 76. Walter Lippmann fellow Ford Found., 1975; recipient Sigma Delta Chi Disting. Service award for TV reporting Soc. Profl. Journalists, 1980, Emmy award for outstanding program achievement, 1981. Mem. Assn. Am. Corrs. in London., Anglo-Am. Press Assn. in Paris. Office: ABC News 22 Avenue D'Eylau Paris 16 France *"Truth" often is cited as journalism's guiding principle. However, many journalists pay little attention to the "truth" of what they cover. Moreover, none can claim always to know the "truth" about what he or she has seen, for where there is more than one side to a story, there is, at least in the perception of those involved, more than one "truth." Therefore it is our responsibility as journalists not always to seek the "truth" but rather to try to be thorough, to tell all we've learned, and to let the public draw its own conclusions.*

DOBBS, JOHN BARNES, artist, educator; b. Nutley, N.J., Aug. 2, 1931; s. John Montgomery and Catherine (Barnes) D.; m. Anne Baudement, 1959; children: Nicolas, Michel. Student, 1949, Bklyn. Mus. Art Sch., 1950-52, Skowhegan Sch., 1952. Assoc. prof. studio art John Jay Coll., CUNY, N.Y.C., 1978—. 20 one man shows in, U.S. and France, group exhibitions include, Nat. Inst. Arts and Letters (Childe Hassam purchase prize 1972), Whitney Mus., Nat. Acad. Design (Ranger Fund purchase prize 1966, 80), Nat. Acad. Design (Benjamin Altman prize 1980), Mus. Modern Art, Butler Inst. Am. Art, Salon des Independents; represented by, A.C.A. Galleries, N.Y.C. Served to cpl. U.S. Army, 1952-54; ETO. Louis Comfort Tiffany grantee, 1967. Mem. Nat. Acad. Design (acadamician). Home: 436 West St New York NY 10014 Office: City University of New York John Jay College 444 W 56th St New York NY 10019

DOBBS, MATTIWILDA, opera and concert singer, coloratura soprano; b. Atlanta, Georgia; d. John Wesley and Irene Ophelia (Thompson) D.; m. Luis Rodriguez Garcia, Apr. 4, 1953 (dec. June 26, 1954); m. Bengt Janzon, Dec. 23, 1957. B.A. with honors, Spelman Coll., Atlanta, 1946; M.A., Tchrs. Coll. Columbia, 1948; studied voice with, Mme. Lotte Leonard, N.Y.C., 1946-50; student, Mannes Music Coll., 1948-49, Berkshire Music Festival, 1949; studied French music with, Pierre Bernac, Paris, 1950-52. Performing prof. voice U. Tex., Austin, 1973-74. Appeared: Dutch Opera, Holland Festival, 1952, also recitals, Holland, Paris, Stockholm; appeared: LaScala Opera, Milan, Italy, 1953, also concerts, Eng., France, Italy, Scandinavia, Austria, Belgium, command performance, Covent Garden, London, 1954, concert tours, U.S., 1954—. Australia, 1955, 59, 72, Israel, 1957, 59, USSR, opera and concerts, 1959, Hamburg State Opera, 1961-62, Am. opera debut, San Francisco Opera, 1955, debut, Met. Opera, N.Y.C., 1956, recitals, orchestral concerts in, N.Y.C., Phila., Va., Tex., Kan., N.C., Fla., Ala., Ga., La., midwest, 1972, 73, 74, 75; artist-in-residence, Spelman Coll., 1974-75 (Recipient 2d prize Marian Anderson awards 1947); (1st prize Internat. Competition Mus. Performers, Geneva Conservatory Music 1951). John Hay Whitney fellow, Paris, 1950. Conglist. Office: care Joanne Rile Mgmt Box 27539 Philadelphia PA 19118

DOBELL, BYRON MAXWELL, editor; b. Bronx, N.Y., May 30, 1927; s. Jacob and Marie (Schaeffer) D.; m. Edith Spielberg, 1952 (div. 1957); m. Ande Rubin, 1958 (dec. 1967); 1 dau., Elizabeth; m. Elizabeth Rodgers Dempster, 1969. A.B., Columbia U., 1947. Picture editor U.S. Camera, 1952-55; asso. editor Popular Photography, 1956-57; feature editor Pageant, 1957-58, This Week, 1958-60; sr. editor Time-Life Books, 1960-62, asso. dir. editorial planning, 1971-72; mng. editor Esquire mag., N.Y.C., 1962-67, 79—, editor-in-chief, 1977, Book World (weekly lit. supplement Chgo. Tribune and Washington Post), 1967-69; editor-in-chief book div. McCall Pub. Co., 1969-71; editorial dir. New York mag., 1972-77; sr. editor Life mag., N.Y.C., 1978-79; editor Am. Heritage mag., 1982—; Bd. dirs. Am. Inst. Graphic Arts, 1971-74. Editor: Life Guide to Paris. Served with AUS, 1946-47. Clubs: P.E.N., Coffee House (N.Y.C.). Home: 150 E 69th St New York NY 10021 Office: Am. Heritage Mag 10 Rockefeller Plaza New York NY 10020

DOBELLE, EVAN SAMUEL, polit. ofcl.; b. Washington, Apr. 22, 1945; s. Martin and Lillian (Mendelsohn) D.; m. Kit Huntington Jones, June 7, 1970. Student, The Citadel, 1962-65, Am. U. Sch. Govt., 1965; B.S., M.Ed., U. Mass., 1970. Research asso. Pres.'s Commn. Campus Unrest, 1970; exec. asst. to U.S. Sen. Edward Brooke, 1971-73; mayor, Pittsfield, Mass., 1973-76; commr. environ. mgmt. Commonwealth of Mass., 1976-77; chief of protocol U.S. with rank of ambassador, 1977-78; coordinator Carter Presdl. Campaign, 1979-81; dep. chmn. Democratic Nat. Com., 1980—; treas. Nat. Dem. Party, 1978-79; faculty Calif. State U., Los Angeles, 1970, John F. Kennedy Inst. Politics, Harvard U., 1971-73. Chmn. bd. advisers Berkshire (Mass.) Community Coll., 1972-76. Served as maj. USAF; Aux. Sr. CAP. Recipient Berkshire Nat. Resources award, 1976; Pittsfield Dem. City Com. award, 1976; award for distinction in service Mass. League Cities and Towns, 1977; Nat. Youth Service award B'nai B'rith, 1977; U.S. Office Edn. fellow, 1969. Mem. AAUP, Phi Delta Kappa. Jewish. Clubs: Masons, Shriners, Eagles, Lions (dir. Pittsfield 1974-75); Internat. (Washington)). Office: 816 Connecticut Ave NW Washington DC 20520

DOBERENZ, ALEXANDER R., chemist, nutrition educator; b. Newark, Aug. 17, 1936; s. Alexander J. and Marie (Zink) D.; m. Angela Rajoppi, June 7, 1958; children: Annamarie, Judith Lynn. B.S. in Chemistry, Tusculum Coll., 1958; M.S., U. Ariz., 1960, Ph.D. in Biochemistry and Nutrition, 1963. Research assoc. dept. physics U. Ariz., Tucson, 1963-69; vis. assoc. prof. nutrition U. Hawaii, 1969; assoc. prof. nutritional scis. U. Wis., Green Bay, 1969-71, prof., 1971-76, assoc. dean Coll. and Sch. Profl. Studies, 1969-76, prof. growth and devel., 1975-76; prof. food sci. and human nutrition U. Del., Newark, 1976—, dean Coll. Human Resources, 1976—, coordinator home econs. research Coll. Agrl. Scis., 1978—; cons. food industry, 1976—; mem. nat. steering com. new initiatives for home econs. U.S. Dept. Agr., 1979—. Contbr. numerous articles on food chemistry and nutrition to profl. publs. Head underwater recovery unit Pima County Sheriff's Dept., 1966-68; warrant officer CAP, 1965-69; mem. Brown County Comprehensive Health Planning Council, 1973-76; bd. dirs. Pima County Sheriff's Search and Rescue, 1968. Recipient Research Career Devel. award NIH, 1966-69. Fellow Am. Inst. Chemists; mem. Am. Chem. Soc., Am. Home Econs. Soc., Am. Inst. Nutrition (Mead Johnson award nominating com. 1973-76), Nutrition Soc. Today, Soc. for Nutrition Edn., Nutrition Soc. London Soc. Exptl. Biology and Medicine, Am. Soc. Clin. Nutrition, AAAS, Assn. Adminstrs. of Home Econs., Del. Gerontol. Soc. (exec. com. 1978), Nat. Council Adminstrs. Home Econs. (exec. bd. 1982-83), Assn. for Devel. Computer Based Instruction, Del. Acad. Sci., Sigma Xi, Phi Lambda Upsilon., Phi Kappa Phi. Roman Catholic. Clubs: University and Whist, Whist. Office: 101 Alison Hall Univ of Delaware Newark DE 19711

DOBERSTEIN, AUDREY K., college president; b. June 12, 1932; m. Stephen C. Doberstein; children: Carole, Stephen, Anne, Curt. B.S. in Elem. Edn, East Stroudsburg State Coll., 1953; M.Ed., U. Del., 1957; Ed.D., U. Pa., 1982. Exec. dir. Title I ESEA, Del. Dept. Public Instrn., 1965-69; pres. Ednl. Research and Services, Inc., 1969-79; asso. prof. Cheyney State Coll., 1969-79; pres. Wilmington Coll., New Castle, Del., 1979—. Mem. NEA, Am. Assn. Higher Edn., AAUW, Del. Assn. Bus. and Profl. Women, Phi Delta Kappa. Office: Wilmington College 320 DuPont Hwy New Castle DE 19720

DOBEY, JAMES KENNETH, banker; b. Vallejo, Calif., June 20, 1919; s. Austin E. and Margaret (Hansen) D.; m. Jean Smith, Apr. 18, 1942; children: James A., Peter M. A.B., U. Calif., Berkeley, 1940; postgrad., Rutgers U., 1956. With Shell Oil Co., Comml. Credit Corp., 1940-42, Wells Fargo Bank, San Francisco, 1946—, exec. v.p., 1965—, vice chmn. bd., 1973, chmn. bd., 1977-80; dir. Wells Fargo & Co., Nat. Gypsum Co., Tex. Utilities Co., Ampex Corp. Trustee Wells Fargo Mortgage & Equity Trust. Served to capt. airborne inf. AUS, 1942-46. Mem. Delta Chi. Club: Pacific Union. Office: PO Box 1419 Aptos CA 95001

DOBKIN, IRVING BERN, entomologist, sculptor; b. Chgo., Aug. 9, 1918; m. Frances Berlin, July 1, 1941; children: Jane, Joan, David, Jill. B.S. cum laude, U. Ill., 1940; postgrad., Ill. Inst. Tech., 1941-42. With War Dept., 1942; chmn., pres. Dobkin Pest Control Co., Chgo., 1946—; Pres., dir. Sculptors Guild Ill., 1964-65; lectr. schs. and assn.; life mem. Art Inst. Chgo., Chgo. Natural History Museum, N. Shore Art League, Evanston Art Center, Mus. Contemporary Art, Chgo. Exhibits include, Art Inst. Chgo., McCormick Pl., Chgo., Old Orchard. Asso. mem. Smithsonian Instn., Peabody Mus. Natural History, Yale U.; pres. Fine Art Ctr., 1983—; asso. mem. Adler Planetarium Assn. Served to lt. USNR, 1943-46. Mem. Entomol. Soc. Am., Fedn. Am. Scientists, AAAS, Am. Inst. Biol. Scis., UN Assn., Oceanographic Soc., Malacology Soc. Am.; asso. mem. Sierra Club, Chgo. Acad. Sci., Archeological Inst. Am., Calif. Acad. Sci., AIA, Am. Schs. Oriental Research, Geog. Soc. Am., Nat. Audubon Soc., Ill. Audubon Soc., Am. Indian Affairs Fedn., S.W. Indian Fedn., Nat. Wildlife Soc., Save the Redwoods Soc., Wilderness Soc., Nat. Parks and Conservation Assn., Am. Harp Soc., Am. Forestry Assn., Am. Fedn. Mineral Socs., Explorers Club, Primitive Arts Soc. Chgo., Chgo. Zool. Soc., Midwest Paleontol. Soc. Home: 306 Maple Ave Highland Park IL 60035 Office: 505 N Lake Shore Dr Chicago IL 60611

DOBKIN, JAMES ALLEN, lawyer, artist; b. N.Y.C., Sept. 9, 1940; s. Louis Robert and Eve (Gartner) D.; m. Irma Laufer, Aug. 4, 1964; children: Jill, David. B.S. in Chem. Engring., Poly. Inst. N.Y., 1961; J.D., NYU, 1964; LL.M., Georgetown U., 1968. Bar: N.Y. 1965, U.S. Supreme Ct. 1968, D.C. 1969. Assoc. Arnold & Porter, Washington, 1968-72, ptnr., 1973—; atty. advisor Pres.'s Commn. on Govt. Procurement, Washington, 1972-73. Contbr. numerous articles to legal jours., numerous group and one-man art exhbns., throughout U.S. Served to capt. U.S. Army, 1964-68. Mem. ABA, Fed. Bar Assn., D.C. Bar Assn. Democrat. Jewish. Home and Studio: 8810 Fernwood Rd Bethesda MD 20817 Office: Arnold & Porter 1200 New Hampshire Ave NW Washington DC 20036 *As an engineer, abstract artist and attorney, I have found a single approach increasingly governing my diverse endeavors. It is closely related to the techniques of trial and error in that it entails the meticulous pursuit of alternatives. The approach thus fores the exercise of imagination in a linear fashion until a problem is satisfactorily resolved.*

DOBKIN, JOHN HOWARD, art administrator; b. Hartford, Conn., Feb. 19, 1942; s. Louis P. and Ruth D.; m. Immaculada de Habsburgo-Lorena, Dec. 18, 1969; children: Carlos, Leopoldo, Anthony. B.A., Yale U., 1964; cert., Institut d'etudes Politiques, 1965; J.D., NYU, 1968. Exec. asst. to sec. Smithsonian Inst., Washington, 1963-71; adminstr. Cooper-Hewitt Mus., N.Y.C., 1971-78; dir. NAD, N.Y.C., 1978—; chmn. Art Com. for Gracie Mansion; mem. adv. bd. Archive Am. Arts; mem. corp. McDowell Colony. Author catalogue, organizer exhb.: Edwin Dickinson-Draftsman, Painter, 1982; organizer catalogue and exhbn.: Samuel F.B. Morse, 1982; organizer, curator catalogue and exhbn.: From All Walks of Life, 1979, Next to Nature, 1980. Mem. Arthur Ross Found. Recipient Smithsonian Instn. Exceptional Service award, 1969. Mem. Conn. Bar Assn. Club: Century Assn. (N.Y.C.). Home: 137 E 95th St New York NY 10028 Office: National Acad Design 1083 Fifth Ave New York NY 10028

DOBLER, DONALD WILLIAM, college dean; b. Rocky Ford, Colo., Apr. 18, 1927; s. William L. and Anna (Nelson) D.; m. Elaine Carlson, Dec. 27, 1951; children: Kathleen, David, Daniel. B.S. in Engring., Colo State U., 1946-50; M.B.A., Stanford U., 1958, Ph.D., 1960. Application and sales engr. Westinghouse Elec. Corp., Pitts. and Phila., 1950-53; mgr. purchasing and materials FMC Corp., Green River, Wyo., 1953-57; guest lectr. Stanford Sch. Bus., 1960; asst. prof. mgmt. State U. Utah, Logan, 1960-63, asso. prof., 1964-66, head dept. bus. adminstrn., 1964-66; vis. prof. mgmt. Dartmouth Coll., 1963-64; dean Coll. Bus., Colo. State U., Ft. Collins, 1966—; dir. U. Nat. Bank, 1967-73, Home Fed. Savs. & Loan Assn., 1973—; pres. Parklane Arms, Inc., 1967-77; part-time mgmt. cons., 1960—; cons. European Logistics Mgmt. Program, 1970, 72, 77, European Fedn. Purchasing, 1970; faculty Mgmt. Center Netherlands, 1972. Author: Purchasing and Materials Management: Text and Cases, 1965, 71, 77, 84; contbg. author mgmt. books.; Contbr. to profl. jours. Mem. Colo. Gov.'s Adv. Com., 1968-77, Ft. Collins Mayor's Budget Com., 1968-71; dist. chmn. Boy Scouts Am., 1974-77; mem. adv. council Colo. Region, SBA, 1973-79, No. Region, Colo. Div. Employment, 1975-77; bd. dirs., div. chmn. Ft. Collins United Way, 1973-80, pres., 1977; bd. dirs. Ft. Collins Jr. Achievement, 1973—. Served with USNR, 1945-46. Mem. Acad. Mgmt., Nat. Assn. Purchasing Mgmt. (chmn. nat. acad. plan com. 1976-81, mem. profl. cert. bd. 1982—, assoc. editor Jour. Purchasing and Materials Mgmt. 1975-80, editor 1980—), Denver Purchasing Mgmt. Assn. (dir. 1975-83, v.p. 1977, pres. 1979, asso. editor Jour. Purchasing and Material Mgmt. 1975-80, editor 1980—), Am. Prodn. and Inventory Control Soc., Green River C. of C. (pres. 1955), Am. Assn. Collegiate Schs. Bus. (nat. com. accreditation 1972-76, nat. standards commn. 1978-81, dir. 1980-83, chmn. fin. and audit com. 1983), Sigma Tau, Phi Kappa Phi, Beta Gamma Sigma (nat. gov. 1975-78). Congregationalist. Club: Rotary.

DOBLER, WILLIAM O., newspaper editor; b. St. Joseph, Mo., Mar. 18, 1926; s. William O. and Rose (Beardsley) D.; m. Mary Nancy McMullen, Aug. 21, 1948; children—James, Lisa, Gregory, Christine. B.A., U. Nebr., 1950. Reporter Lincoln (Nebr.) Star, 1950-57, editorial page editor, 1957-59, also currently, editor, 1959—. Pres. Lincoln Park and Recreation Bd., 1970-73, Lincoln Hosp. and Health Council, 1970-72, Lincoln Children's Zoo Assn., 1970-71, Nebr. Commn. for Higher Ednl. Aid, 1972; vice chmn. Pius X Found., 1970; bd. dirs.

Lincoln Found., 1980—. Served with USNR, 1944-46. Mem. Am. Soc. Newspaper Editors, Sigma Delta Chi (pres. Nebr. 1958). Roman Catholic (mem. Nebr. Cath. Conf., v.p. parish council 1970). Clubs: Elk., Lincoln Serra (pres. 1967-68). Home: 2600 S 75 St Lincoln NE 68506 Office: The Lincoln Star 926 P St Lincoln NE 68501 *The ultimate measure of satisfaction in life comes from the contribution you make to the well-being of your fellow man.*

DOBLIN, JAY, designer, educator; b. N.Y.C, Dec. 10, 1920; s. Frank C. and Evelyn (McElroy) D.; m. Annette Woodward, Mar. 27, 1949. Grad., Pratt Inst., 1942. Indsl. designer, devel. work govt. projects, camouflage Raymond Loewy Assos., N.Y.C., 1942-49, exec. designer, 1952-55; indsl. designer Singer, Frigidaire, Schick, Coca Cola, Shell Oil Co., Nat Biscuit Co.; dir. Inst. Design, Ill. Inst. Tech., 1955-69, prof., 1955-69; sr. v.p., dir. Unimark Internat. Chgo., until 1972; affiliated with Delta Planning Group, Chgo., to 1983; prin. Jay Doblin Assocs., Chgo., 1983—; cons. J.C. Penney Co., Inc., Standard Oil Co., Ind., Am. Hosp. Assn.; chmn. indsl. design dept. night sch. Pratt Inst.; prof. Sch. Art Inst., Chgo., 1975—; vis. prof. London Bus. Sch., 1979-80; lectr. Author: Perspective—A New System for Designers, 1955, 100 Great Product Designs, 1970. Recipient honor student award Pratt Inst., 1942, Disting. Alumna award, 1973; Kaufmann Internat. Design award Internat. Inst. Edn. Fellow Royal Soc. Arts (London), Indsl. Designers Soc. Am. (pres. 1956, dir., Outstanding Design Programs award 1974, Personal Recognition award 1982), Internat. Council Socs. Indsl. Design (v.p.), Internat. Design Conf. (dir.); mem. Indsl. Design Educators Assn. (past pres.). Home: 2235 N Cleveland Ave Chicago IL 60614

DOBRIANSKY, LEV EUGENE, educator, economist, diplomat; b. N.Y.C., Nov. 9, 1918; s. John and Eugenia (Greshchuk) D.; m. Julia Kusy, June 29, 1946; children: Larisa Eugenia, Paula Jon. B.S. (Charles Hayden Meml. scholar), NYU, 1941, M.A., 1943, Hirshland polit. sci. fellow, 1943-44, Ph.D., 1951; LL.D., Free Ukrainian U. at U. Munich, Germany, 1952. Faculty, NYU, 1942-48; asst. prof. econs. Georgetown U., 1948-52, asso. prof., 1952-60, prof., 1960—, chmn. dept., 1953-54; exec. mem. Inst. Ethnic Studies, 1957—; dir. Inst. Comparative Econ. and Polit. Systems, 1970—; faculty Nat. War Coll., 1957-58; U.S. ambassador to Bahamas, 1983—; cons. Dept. State, 1971—, USIA, 1971—; lectr. on Soviet Union, Communism, U.S. fgn. policy; chmn. Nat. Captive Nations Com., Inc., 1959—; pres. Ukrainian Congress Com. Am., 1949—, Am. Council for World Freedom, 1976-79; mem. Economists Nat. Com. on Monetary Policy; strategy staff mem. Am. Security Council, 1962—; econs. editor Washington Report; mem. Pres.'s Commn. on Population, 1974-75; cons. Corpus Instrumentorum, Kreber Found.; mem. Am. Com. to Aid Katanga Freedom Fighters, Emergency Com. Chinese Refugees. Author: A Philosophico-Economic Critique of Thorstein Veblen, 1943, The Social Philosophical System of Thorstein Veblen, 1950, Free Trade Ideal, 1954, Communist Takeover of Non-Russian Nations in USSR, 1954; co-author: The Great Pretense, 1956, Veblenism: A New Critique, 1957, Captive Nations Week Resolution, 1959, The Crimes of Khrushchev, 1959, Decisions for a Better America, 1960, Vulnerabilities of USSR, 1963, Nations, Peoples, and Countries in the USSR, 1964, The Vulnerable Russians, 1967, U.S.A. and the Soviet Myth, 1971; pub.: Revista Americana, 1977; editor: Europe's Freedom Fighter: Taras Shevchenko, 1960, Tenth Anniversary of the Captive Nations Week Resolution, 1969, The Bicentennial Salute to the Captive Nations, 1977, Twentieth Observance and Anniversary of Captive Nations Week, 1980; asso. editor: (1946-62) Ukrainian Quar., chmn. editorial bd., 1962; contbr.: Peace and Freedom Through Cold War Victory, 1964, Nationalism in the USSR and Eastern Europe, 1977, Ukraine in a Changing World, 1978; articles to profl. jours. Planning mem. Freedom Studies Center, Boston; asst. sec. Republican Nat. Conv., 1952; adviser Rep. Nat. Com., 1956; mem. Com. on Program and Progress of Rep. Party, 1959; asst. to chmn. Rep. Nat. Conv., 1964; vice chmn. nationalities div. Rep. Nat. Com., 1964; sr. adviser United Citizens for Nixon-Agnew, 1968; exec. mem. ethnic div. Com. to Reelect the Pres., 1972; advisor to Gov. Reagan, 1980; issues dir. Republican Nat. Com., 1980; chmn. Ukrainian Catholic Studies Found., 1970-73; bd. govs. Charles Edison Youth Fund, 1976—; mem. expert adv. bd. NBC, Washington, 1977—. Lt. col. (res.) 352d Mil. Govt. Civil Affairs, 1958; col. U.S. Army Res., 1966. Recipient Freedoms Found. award, 1961, 73; Shevchenko Freedom award Shevchenko Meml. Com., 1964; Shevchenko Sci. Soc. medal, 1965; Hungarian Freedom Fighters' Freedom award, 1965; Latvian Pro Merito medal, 1968; Freedom Acad. award, Korea, 1969; Wisdom award of honor, Calif., 1970; named Outstanding Am. Educator, 1973; decorated D.S.M., 1973. Mem. Free World Forum (exec. com.), Acad. Polit. Sci., Nat. Acad. Econs. and Polit. Sci., AAUP, Am. Acad. Polit. and Social Sci., Am., Cath. econ. assns., Am. Finance Assn., Nat. Soc. Study Edn., Shevchenko Sci. Soc., NYU Alumni Assn., Internat. Cultural Soc. Korea (hon.), Gold Key Soc., Beta Gamma Sigma, Delta Sigma Pi. Clubs: Capitol Hill, International, University (Washington). Home: 4520 Kling Dr Alexandria VA 22312 Office: US Embassy Mosmar Bldg Queens St Nassau Bahamas

DOBROVOLNY, JERRY STANLEY, engring. educator; b. Chgo., Nov. 2, 1922; s. Stanley and Marie (Barone) D.; m. Joan Gretchen Baker, June 14, 1947; children—James Lawrence, Janet Lee. B.S. in Mech. Engring, U. Ill., 1943, M.S., 1947. Registered profl. engr. Faculty U. Ill., Urbana, 1945—, asso. prof., 1957—, prof., head dept. gen. engring., 1959; Geophys. research engr. Ill. Geol. Survey, summers 1949-52; design and traffic survey engr. Ill. Div. Hwys., summers 1948, 53, 54; cons. soil mechanics, 1955—; Mem. Ill. Adv. Council on Vocational Edn., 1969-72, Nat. Adv. Council on Vocational Edn., 1970-73. Author: (with others) Basic Drawing for Engineering Technology, (with R.P. Hoelscher and C.H. Springer) Graphics for Engineers, 1968. Past pres. Champaign County Young Republican Club; mem. Champaign County Rep. Central Com. Served with C.E. AUS, 1942-44. Fellow A.A.A.S.; mem. Am. Legion, 40 and 8, Soc. for History and Tech., Ill. Acad. Sci., Am. Soc. Engring. Edn. (Arthur Williston award 1971), Am. Soc. C.E., Am. Tech. Edn. Assn. (trustee 1964-67, 69-74, pres. 1967-68), Nat. Soc. Profl. Engrs., Ill. Soc. Profl. Engrs. (pres. Champaign County chpt. 1964-65, state v.p. 1971-73, pres. 1974-75), Champaign County Soc. Profl. Engrs., Newcomen Soc. N.Am., Sigma Xi, Scabbard and Blade, Sigma Iota Epsilon, Tau Nu Tau. Home: 1104 S Prospect Ave Champaign IL 61820 Office: Coll Engring U Ill Urbana IL 61801

DOBSON, HERBERT GORDON, mgmt. cons.; b. Can., Dec. 19, 1900; came to U.S., 1919, naturalized, 1938; s. Joseph Bent and Minnie (Steeves) D.; m. Frances Garland Roberts, June 21, 1930; children—Ann Garland, Jane Frances. Student pub. schs. of, N.B. Auditor Can. Nat. Rys., 1918-19; insp. Bank Am. Nat. Trust Savs. Assn., Los Angeles, 1920-43; v.p., controller Occidental Life Ins. Co., Los Angeles, 1943-62, sr. v.p., 1962-65; pres. Angeles/Cardillo Travel Agy., 1965-67; mgmt. cons., 1969—. Pres. Episcopal Ch. Home for Children, 1965-69, 70-72; coordinator Episcopal Ch. Cathedral Project, 1970-71, Vis. Nurse Assn., 1972—. Home: 410 Church Rd Apt 24 Ojai CA 93023

DOBSON, JOHN MCCULLOUGH, historian; b. Las Cruces, N.Mex., July 20, 1940; s. Donald Duane and Carolyn Margaret (Van Anda) D.; m. Cynthia Davis, Aug. 29, 1963; children: David, Daniel. B.S., MIT, 1962; M.S., U. Wis., 1964, Ph.D., 1966. Asst. prof. history Calif. State U., Chico, 1966-67; fgn. service officer U.S. Dept. State, Washington, 1967-68; asst. prof. history Iowa State U., Ames, 1968-72, assoc. prof., 1972-78, prof., 1978—; vis. assoc. prof. history U. Md., 1972, 76; Fulbright lectr. Univ. Coll., Dublin, 1979-80. Author: Politics in the Gilded Age: A New Perspective on Reform, 1972, Two Centuries of Tariffs: The Background and Origins of the U.S. International Trade Commission, 1977, America's Ascent, 1978. Grantee U.S. Internat. Trade Commn., 1976. Mem. Am. Hist. Assn., Orgn. Am. Historians, Soc. Historians of Am. Fgn. Relations, AAUP. Home: 2019 Kildee St Ames IA 50010 Office: Dept History Iowa State U Ames IA 50011

DOBSON, RICHARD LAWRENCE, dermatologist, educator; b. Boston, Apr. 12, 1928; s. Joseph William and Celia Beatrice (Siegler) D.; m. Marie C. Mollomo, Aug. 19, 1950; children: Richard Lawrence, Pamela Blair, Lisa Marie. M.D., U. Chgo., 1953; B.S., U. N.H., 1981. Diplomate: Am. Bd. Dermatology. Intern Cin. Gen. Hosp., 1953-54; resident Hitchcock Clinic, Hanover, N.H., 1954-57; asst. prof. dermatology U. N.C., Chapel Hill, 1957-61; prof. U. Oreg., Portland, 1961-72, SUNY-Buffalo, 1972-79, Med. U. S.C., Charleston, 1980—; vis. prof. U. Nijmegan (Netherlands), 1969-70; v.p. Med-Ed Inc. (Rosslyn), Va., 1978—; pres. Can-Do Inc. (Mt. Pleasant), S.C., 1982—. Editor: Year Book of Dermatology, 1979-82, Clinical of Dermatology, 1972-82, Contemporary Review, 1973—, Clinical Dermatology, 1972-82; asst. editor: Jour. Am. Acad. Dermatology, 1979—. Served with USN, 1946-47. Fellow ACP, Am. Acad. Dermatology (pres. 1983-84); mem. Am. Dermatologic Assn. (pres. 1977-82), Soc. Investigative Dermatology (pres. 1975-76), Oreg. Dermatol. Soc. (pres. 1971-72); hon. mem. Polish Dermatology Soc.; mem. Brit. Dermatology Soc., Dutch Dermatology Soc., N.Am. Clin. Dermatol. Soc., Ga. Dermatology Soc. Republican. Roman Catholic. Clubs: Snee Farm (Mt. Pleasant); Beach and Racquet (Isle of Palms, S.C.). Home: 1105 Deleisseline Blvd Mount Pleasant SC 29464 Office: Med U SC 171 Ashley Ave Charleston SC 29425

DOBSON, WILLIAM DAVID, agricultural economist; b. Black River Falls, Wis., Sept. 12, 1937; s. Luther and Agnes Ragna (Olson) D.; m. Ruby Lucille Enloe, Dec. 27, 1958; children—Jeffrey, Diane. B.S., Wis. State Coll., River Falls, 1959; M.S., Iowa State U., 1961; Ph.D., Purdue U., 1969. Mktg. specialist Dept. Agr., Washington, 1962-66; grad. instr. Purdue U., 1966-69; mem. faculty U. Wis., Madison, 1969-82, prof. agrl. econs., chmn. dept., 1976-81; sr. staff economist Pres' Council Econs. Advisers, 1981-82; prof. agrl. econs. Purdue U., Lafayette, Ind., 1982—, chmn. dept. agrl. econs., 1982—; cons. in field. Corr. editor: Malaysian Econ. Jour. Chmn. Madison Bus. and Devel. Commn., 1977-79. Recipient Fulbright Hays award, 1974, Excellence in Teaching award Coll. Agrl. and Life Scis., U. Wis.-Gamma Sigma Delta, 1975. Mem. Am. Agrl. Econs. Assn. (Published Research award 1972, Distinguished Undergrad. Teaching award 1976), Am. Econs. Assn., Ind. Farm Mgmt. Assn. Home: 337 Laurel Dr West Lafayette IN 47906 Office: Dept Agrl Econs Purdue U West Lafayette IN 47907

DOBYNS, BROWN MCILVAINE, educator, surgeon; b. Jacksonville, Ill., May 14, 1913; s. Henry D. and Leah (McIlvaine) D.; m. Mary Meredith Davis, Sept. 21, 1940; children—Mary Meredith, Courtney Sara, Brown McIlvaine. B.A., Ill. Coll., 1935; M.D., Johns Hopkins, 1939; M.S., U. Minn., 1944, Ph.D., 1946. Diplomate: Am. Bd. Surgery. Intern surgery Johns Hopkins Hosp., 1939-40; fellow surgery Mayo Found., 1940-43; resident surgery Kahler Hosp., Mayo Clinic, 1943-45, 1st asst. surgery, 1945-46, asst. surg. staff, 1946; research fellow surgery, med. sch. Harvard, 1946-48, asst. prof. surgery, 1948-51; grad. asst. surgery Mass. Gen. Hosp., 1946-48, asst. surgery, 1946-51; asso. prof. surgery Western Res. U. Med. Sch., 1951-58, prof. surgery, 1958—; asst. chief surg. service Cleve. Met. Gen. Hosp., 1951-66, assoc. chief surg. service, 1967—; asst. surgeon Univ. Hosp., Cleve., 1951—; Fulbright lectr., Australia, 1966. Mem. fellowship subcom. Com. on Growth NRC, 1950-54; mem. fellowship com. NSF, 1954-61, chmn., 1955-61; adv. screening com. med. scis. Fulbright, 1955-58; adv. com. research on etiology cancer Am. Cancer Soc., 1956-59, chmn. adv. com. on instnl. grants, 1963-65; mem. Dernham Scholarship com. Calif. Cancer Soc., 1964-74. Recipient Van Meter prize, 1946, award of merit, 1954, Disting. Service award, 1978; all Am. Thyroid Assn.; citation for disting. public service Ill. Coll. Fellow A.C.S.; mem. Soc. Univ. Surgeons, Am. Soc. Clin. Investigation, Am., Central surg. assns., Am. Fedn. Clin. Research, Am. Thyroid Assn. (pres. 1956-57), Cleve. Surg. Soc. (pres. 1966-67), Halstead Soc., Societé Internationale de Chirurgie, AAAS, Endocrine Soc., Sigma Xi. Home: 9930 Kirtland Rd Chardon OH 44024 Office: 3395 Scranton Rd Cleveland OH 44109 *Try to have a new experience every day.*

DOBYNS, LLOYD ALLEN, JR., broadcast journalist; b. Newport News, Va., Mar. 12, 1936; s. Lloyd A. and L. Helen (Stokes) D.; m. Patricia Louise Parker, Mar. 16, 1956; children: Denise Dobyns Honig, Brian, Alison, Kenneth. B.A., Washington and Lee U., 1957. Reporter WDBJ-AM/TV, Roanoke, Va., 1957-58; news dir. WCUM-AM, Cumberland, Md., 1960; reporter WAVY-AM/TV, Norfolk, Va., 1960-63, news dir., 1963-68; mng. editor WNEW-TV, N.Y.C., 1968-69; asst. news dir. WNBC-TV, N.Y.C., 1969-70; news dir. WMAQ-TV, Chgo., 1970-72; corr. NBC, Paris, 1972-74; prin. writer-reporter Weekend, NBC, N.Y.C., 1974-79; corr. NBC, N.Y.C., 1979-82, prin. writer, co-anchor NBC News Overnight, 1982, prin. writer, anchor, editor Monitor/First Camera, 1982. Served with U.S. Army, 1958-60. Recipient Christopher award for writing-reporting NBC News TV documentary If Thats a Gnome, This Must Be Zurich, 1974, for NBC White Paper: Gambling, 1980; George Foster Peabody Broadcasting award for Weekend, 1976; TV award Am. Inst. Indsl. Engrs.; Martin R. Gainsburgh award; Dupont-Columbia award; Nat. Headliners award for writing-reporting NBC White Paper: If Japan Can, Why Can't We, 1980; Aviation and Space Writers award; Nat. Soc. Profl. Engrs. award for NBC Reports; Janus award; San Francisco Film Festival award, Gabriel award, Golden Eagle award for NBC Reports: Bataan, The Forgotten Hell, 1982. Home: 300 Central Park W New York NY 10024 Office: 30 Rockefeller Plaza New York NY 10020

DOCKERAY, JAMES CARLTON, economist; b. Grand Rapids, Mich., Aug. 16, 1907; s. Floyd Carlton and Katherine Caroline (Eddy) D.; m. Isabel Ruth McRoberts, Sept. 2, 1935; children: George Carlton, William Floyd, Susan Ruth. B.A., Ohio Wesleyan U., 1929; M.A., Ohio State U., 1931, Ph.D., 1936. Student acct. Chesapeake & Potomac Telephone Co., 1929-30; asst. econs. Ohio State U., 1931-35; instr. Iowa State Tchrs. Coll., 1935-36; asso. prof. econs. and bus. adminstrn. James Millikin U., 1936-42; prof. fin. U. Md., 1942-46; fiscal and fin. economist Dept. Commerce, 1946-61; professorial lectr. George Washington U., 1946-55, prof. fin., chmn. dept. govt. and bus., 1955-64, asst. dean Sch. Govt. Bus. and Internat. Affairs, 1964-66, dean, 1966-73, emeritus, 1973—; now cons.; lectr. Grad. Sch. Banking, Rutgers U., 1952-55; dep. mem. FHLB, 1938; cons. statis. control div. USAAF, 1943-45. Author: Public Utility Taxation in Ohio, 1938, (with W.H. Husband) Modern Corporation Finance, 7th edit, 1972. Mem. Am. Econ. Assn., Nat. Acad. Pub. Adminstrn. (study panel), Am. Finance Assn., Washington Soc. Investment Analysts. Club: Econs. (Orlando, Fla.). Home and Office: 100 Minnehaha Circle Maitland FL 32751

DOCKHORN, ROBERT JOHN, physician; b. Goodland, Kans., Oct. 9, 1934; s. Charles George and Dorotha Mae (Horton) D.; m. Beverly Ann Wilke, June 15, 1957; children: David, Douglas, Deborah. A.B., U. Kans., 1956, M.D., 1960. Diplomate: Am. Bd. Pediatrics. Intern Naval Hosp., San Diego, 1960-61, resident in pediatrics, Oakland, Calif., 1963-65; resident in pediatric allergy and immunology U. Kans. Med. Center, 1967-69, asst. adj. prof. pediatrics, 1969—; resident in pediatric allergy and immunology Children's Mercy Hosp., Kansas City, Mo., 1967-69, chief div., 1969—; practice medicine specializing in allergy and immunology, Prairie, Kans., 1969—; clin. prof. pediatrics and medicine U. Mo. Med. Sch., Kansas City, 1972—. Contbr. articles to med. jours.; co-editor: Allergy and Immunology in Children, 1973. Fellow Am. Acad. Pediatrics, Am. Coll. Allergists (bd. regents 1976—, v.p. 1978-79, pres.-elect 1980-81, pres. 1981-82), Am. Acad. Allergy; mem. AMA, Kans. Med. Soc., Johnson County Med. Soc., Kans. Allergy Soc. (pres. 1976-77), Mo. Allergy Soc. (sec. 1975-76), Joint Council Socio-Econs. of Allergy (dir. 1976—, pres. 1978-79). Home: 8510 Delmar Ln Prairie Village KS 66208 Office: 5300 W 94th Terr Prairie Village KS 66207

DOCKING, THOMAS ROBERT, state lieutenant governor, lawyer; b. Lawrence, Kans., Aug. 10, 1954; s. Robert Blackwell and Meredith (Gear) D.; m. Jill Sadowsky, June 18, 1977; 1 son, Brian Thomas. B.S., U. Kans., 1976, M.B.A., J.D., 1980. Bar: Kans. Assoc. Regan & McGannon, Wichita, Kans., 1980-82, ptnr., 1982—; lt. gov. State of Kans., Topeka, 1983—; mem. Gov.'s Task Force on High Tech. Devel.; mem. adv. commn. Dans. Dept. Econ. Devel. Mem. Big Bro.-Big. Sister Program. Mem. Kans. Bar Assn., ABA, Kans. Cav. (bd. dirs., v.p. adminstrn.), U. Kans. Alumni Assn. (treas.), Pi Sigma Alpha, Beta Gamma Sigma, Beta Theta Pi. Democrat. Presbyterian. Home: 8525 Limerick Ln Wichita KS 67206 Office: Regan & McGannon Suite 1400 KSB Bldg 125 N Market Wichita KS 67202

DOCKRAY, GEORGE HENRY, editor, publisher; b. Phila., May 4, 1920; s. George L. and Mary (Finan) D.; m. Louise Stedman, Nov. 9, 1942 (dec. May 1970); children: Karen E., George Henry, Andrea; m. Audrey Laney Cochran, June 2, 1973. B.S., Phila. Coll. Textiles and Sci., 1948. Textile research asso. Research Inst. Temple U., 1948-49; textile engr. Nat. Cotton Council Am., Washington, 1949-53; asso. editor Textile Industries, Atlanta, 1953-56, exec. editor, 1956-57, editor, 1957-68, editor-in-chief, 1968-79; pub. Textiles Panamericanos, Atlanta, 1978-83; group pub. Textile Group W.R.C. Pub. Co., Atlanta, 1983. Served with AUS, 1941-45. Mem. Fiber Soc., Textile Inst. (Eng.), Am. Assn. Textile Chemists and Colorists, Sigma Delta Chi, Delta Kappa Phi. Home: 4064 Navajo Trail NE Atlanta GA 30319 Office: 1760 Peachtree Rd NW Atlanta GA 30357

DOCKSON, ROBERT RAY, savings and loan executive; b. Quincy, Ill., Oct. 6, 1917; s. Marshall Ray and Letah (Edmondson) D.; m. Katheryn Virginia Allison, Mar. 4, 1944; 1 dau., Kathy Kimberlee. A.B., Springfield Jr. Coll., 1937; B.S., U. Ill., 1939; M.S. in Fgn. Service, U. So. Calif., 1940, Ph.D., 1946. Lectr. U. So. Calif., 1940-41, 45-46, prof., head dept. mktg., 1953-59, dean; and prof. bus. econs., 1959-69; vice chmn. bd. Calif. Fed. Savs. & Loan Assn., Los Angeles, 1969-70, pres., 1970-77, chmn., 1977—, chief exec. officer, 1973-83; chmn. chief exec. officer CalFed Inc., 1984—, also dir.; instr. Rutgers U., 1946-47, asst. prof., 1947-48; dir. Bur. Bus. and Econ. Research, 1947-48; economist Western home office Prudential Ins. Co., 1948-52, Bank of Am., San Francisco, 1952-53; econ. cons., 1953-57; dir. McKesson Corp., IT Corp., Pacific Lighting Corp., Transam. Capital Fund, Inc., Transam. Income Shares, Inc., Olga Co., Internat. Lease Fin. Corp., Computer Scis. Corp., Fed. Res. Bank of San Francisco. Am. specialist for U.S. Dept. State; mem. Town Hall, 1954—, bd. govs., 1963-65, hon. bd. govs., 1965—, pres., 1961-62; Trustee John Randolph Haynes and Dora Haynes Found., Rose Hills Meml. Park Assn., Com. for Econ. Devel., Calif. Council for Econ. Edn.; trustee, pres. Orthopedic Hosp.; bd. councilors Grad. Sch. Bus. Adminstrn., U. So. Calif.; bd. regents, chmn. univ. bd. Pepperdine U.; chmn. housing task force Calif. Roundtable. Served from ensign to lt. USNR, 1942-44. Decorated Star of Solidarity Govt. of Italy.; Recipient Asa V. Call Achievement award; Disting. Community Service award Brandeis U.; Whitney M. Young Jr. award Urban League, 1981; Man of Yr. award Nat. Housing Conf., 1981; Industrialist of Yr. award Calif. Mus. Sci. and Industry, 1984. Mem. Calif. C. of C. (pres. 1980, dir. 1981—), Los Angeles C. of C. (dir.), Am. Arbitration Assn., Newcomen Soc. North Am., Phi Kappa Phi (Diploma of Honor award 1984), Beta Gamma Sigma. Clubs: Rotarian., Bohemian, California, Los Angeles Country, One Hundred, Silver Dollar, Birnam Wood Golf, Thunderbird Country. Office: 5670 Wilshire Blvd Los Angeles CA 90036

DOCKSTADER, FREDERICK J., museum director; b. Los Angeles, Feb. 3, 1919; s. Fred and Dorothy D.; m. Alice Elizabeth Warren, Dec. 25, 1951. A.B., Ariz. State Coll., A.M.; Ph.D., Western Res. U., 1951. Tchr. Flagstaff (Ariz.) City Schs., 1936-41, Cranbrook (Mich.) Schs., 1942-50; staff ethnologist Cranbrook Inst. Sci., 1950-52; faculty, also curator anthropology Dartmouth Coll., 1952-55; asst. dir. Mus. Am. Indian, Heye Found., N.Y.C., 1955-60, dir., 1960-75; adv. editor Ency. Americana, 1957—; commr. U.S. Indian Arts and Crafts Bd., 1955-67; vis. prof. art and archeology Columbia U., 1961-64; adj. prof. art history Ariz. State U., Tempe, 1983—; mem. N.Y. State Mus. Adv. Council, 1960-65. Author: The Kachina and the White Man, 1954, Indian Art in America, 1960, Indian Art in Middle America, 1964, Kunst in Amerika: I, 1965, Indian Art in South America, 1967, Kunst in Amerika: II, 1968, Kunst in Amerika: III, 1969, (with Ferdinand Anton) Pre-Columbian Art, 1968, Indian Art of the Americas, 1973, Great North American Indians, 1977, Weaving Arts of the North American Indian, 1978, Compiler: The American Indian in Graduate Studies, 1957, supplement, 1973. Trustee Huntington Free Library, Futures for Children Found., Fred Harvey Found., Thomas Jefferson Forum, 1983—. Fellow Rochester Mus. Arts and Scis.; Recipient 1st prize silversmithing Cleve. Mus. Art, 1950; award Lotos Club, 1972. Fellow AAAS, Cranbrook Inst. Sci., Am. Anthrop. Assn.; mem. Soc. Am. Archeology. Clubs: Cosmos, Century. Home: 165 W 66th St New York NY 10023

DOCQUIER, EDGAR GERARD, labor union executive; b. Liege, Belgium, Nov. 7, 1929; emigrated to Can., 1950, naturalized, 1956; s. Jules Chislain D. and Rosalie Collinge; m. Gabrielle St. Pierre, Sept. 5, 1953; children: Daniel, Stephane, Isabelle, Fabienne. B.A., Coll. St. Berthuin, Pce Namur, Belgium, 1949. Pres. Local Union 3953 United Steelworkers Am., St. Jean, Que., Can., 1953-59, staff rep., 1959-65, asst. to dir. Dist. 5, Montreal, 1965-77, nat. dir. for Can., Toronto, 1977—; mem. gen. council Que. Fedn. Labour, Montreal, 1969—; v.p. Can. Labour Congress, Ottawa, Ont., 1977—; mem. central com. Internat. Metalworkers Fedn., Geneva, 1977—; Can. Labour Congress rep. Internat. Confedn. Free Trade Unions, Brussels, 1977—. Mem. Que. Legal Aid Commn., Montreal, 1969—, Royal Commn. on Econ. Union and Devel. Prospects for Can., Ottawa, 1982—. Mem. New Democratic Party (federal) and Parti Quebecois (provincial). Roman Catholic. Home: 33 Orchardview Blvd 1412 Toronto ON Canada M4R 2E9 Office: United Steelworkers Am 234 Englinton Ave E Toronto ON Canada M4P 1K7

DOCTER, CHARLES ALFRED, lawyer, former state legislator; b. Hamburg, Germany, Aug. 5, 1931; s. Alfred Joseph and Annie Beatrice D.; m. Marcia Kaplan, Nov. 27, 1958; children: Will Henry, Michael Warren, Adina Jo. B.A. magna cum laude, Kenyon Coll., 1953; J.D., U. Chgo., 1956. Bar: Md., D.C., U.S. Supreme Ct. Former aide to late Sen. Paul H. Douglas; practice law, specializing in bankruptcy and reorgn., Washington, 1959—; sr. partner firm Docter,

Docter & Salus, Washington, 1967—; Pres. Montgomery County (Md.) Com. for Fair Representation, 1962-65. Pres. Western Suburban Democratic Club, 1965-66; mem. Md. Ho. of Dels., 1967-78; serving variously as chmn. Montgomery and Prince George's counties Bi-County Dels.; dirs. Met. Washington Council Govts., 1970. Served to lt. USNR, 1956-59. Sponsor Md. tenants' rights laws, Md. Pub. campaign financing law, Md. revolving credit law and other consumer measures. Home: 9810 Hillridge Dr Kensington MD 20795 Office: 1612 K St NW Washington DC 20006

DOCTOR, HENRY, army officer; b. Oakley, S.C., Aug. 23, 1932; s. Henry and Annie Bell (Aiken) D.; m. Janie Mae Manigault, Dec. 31, 1956; children: Constanza, Kenneth, Lori Ann, Cheryl Lynn. B.S., S.C. State Coll., 1954; M.A., Ga. State U., 1973; postgrad., U.S. Army War Coll., 1974. Commd. U.S. Army, advanced through grades to maj. gen.; comdg. officer, Ft. Benning, Ga., 1970-71, dep. comdr., 1971; chief modern army vol. army control group (Inf. Center), 1971-72, dir. psychometrics, 1974-75, comdg. officer, Hawaii, 1974-77, dir. enlisted personnel mgmt., Alexandria, Va., 1977-79, asst. div. commander, Ft. Stewart, Ga., 1979-80, dir. personnel, tng. and force devel., Alexandria, Va., 1980-83; comdg. gen. Second Inf. Div., Korea, 1983—. Decorated Legion of Merit, Bonze Star. Mem. Assn. U.S. Army, Omega Psi Phi. Baptist. Club: Mason. Home: Camp Casey Korea Office: 5001 Eisenhower Ave Alexandria VA 22333 *

DOCTOROFF, MARTIN MYLES, lawyer; b. Cambridge, Mass., Jan. 27, 1933; s. Abraham M. and Rose (Blackstone) D.; m. Allene Ruth Miller, Aug. 26, 1956; children: Daniel Louis, Mark Howard, Andrew Seth and Thomas David (twins). A.B., Harvard Coll., 1954; J.D., U. Mich., 1957. Bar: Mich. 1957, Mass. 1957. With FBI, 1957-60; practiced in, Detroit, 1960-64, Oak Park, Mich., 1964-74, Southfield, Mich., 1975—; partner firm Bellinson & Doctoroff, 1960-64, Bellinson, Doctoroff & Wartell, 1964-74, Zussman, Doctoroff & Wartell, Southfield, 1975-79, Bushnell, Gage, Doctoroff & Reizen, 1980—; spl. asst. atty. gen., Mich., 1969—, pub. adminstr., Oakland County, Mich., 1975—; Mem. planning commn. City of Birmingham, Mich., 1970-75, chmn., 1973-75; chmn. hearing panel Grievance Commn., State Bar of Mich., 1971—, chmn. standing com. on grievance, 1979—, mem. jud. qualifications com., 1981—. Chmn. Mich. regional adv. bd. Anti-Defamation League of B'nai B'rith, 1972-74, mem. nat. law com., civil rights com., 1972—; mem. Nat. Commn. Anti-Defamation League, B'nai B'rith, 1975—. Mem. Am., Mass., Mich., Detroit, Oakland County, South Oakland bar assns., Am. Trial Lawyers Assn., Soc. Former Agts. FBI (chmn. 1973-74), B'nai B'rith. Home: 1270 Lake Park Birmingham MI 48009 Office: 3000 Town Center 15th Floor Southfield MI 48075

DOCTOROW, EDGAR LAWRENCE, novelist, English educator; b. N.Y.C., Jan. 6, 1931; s. David Richard and Rose (Levine) D.; m. Helen Esther Setzer, Aug. 20, 1954; children: Jenny, Caroline, Richard. A.B. in Philosophy with honors, Kenyon Coll., Gambier, Ohio, 1952; L.H.D. (hon.), 1976, Hobart Coll., 1979. Editor New Am. Library, N.Y.C., 1960-64; editor-in-chief Dial Press, N.Y.C., 1964-69, pub., 1969; mem. faculty Sarah Lawrence Coll., Bronxville, N.Y., 1971-78; creative writing fellow Yale Sch. Drama, 1974-75; writer-in-residence U. Calif, Irvine, 1969-70; vis. sr. fellow Council on Humanities Princeton U., 1980; vis. prof. English, NYU, N.Y.C., 1982—. Author: Welcome to Hard Times, 1960, Big as Life, 1966, The Book of Daniel, 1971, Ragtime, 1975 (Nat. Book Critics Circle award); play Drinks Before Dinner, 1979; Loon Lake, 1980, Lives of the Poets, 1984. Served with AUS, 1953-55. Recipient Arts and Letters award Am. Acad. and Nat. Inst. Art, 1976; Guggenheim fellow, 1973; Creative Artists Program Service fellow, 1973-74. Mem. Authors Guild (dir.), Am. Acad. and Inst. Arts and Letters, Am. P.E.N. (dir.), Writers Guild Am. East, Century Assn. Address: care Random House Publishers 201 E 50th St New York NY 10022

DODD, CHARLES GARDNER, phys. chemist; b. St. Louis, Jan. 26, 1915; s. Harry Gardner and Ruth Esther (Hauskins) D.; m. Edel Marie Bovbjerg, June 10, 1943; children—Sally Little, Karen Elise, Mary Bartlett, Frederick Porter. B.S., Rice U., 1940; M.S., U. Mich., 1945, Ph.D., 1948. Chief advanced materials research sect. Owens-Ill. Tech. Center, Toledo, 1962-68; asso. prin. scientist Philip Morris Research Center, 1968-74; sr. research asso. Warner Lambert Co., 1974-80; pres. Conn. Technology Cons.'s, Inc., Stratford, 1980—; cons. ion implantation for materials modification, surface chemistry. chmn. Gordon Research Conf. on Chemistry at Interfaces, 1957. Contbr. articles to sci. and tech. publs. Fellow A.A.A.S., Am. Inst. Chemists; mem. Microbeam Soc. Am., Mineral. Soc. Am., N.Y. Acad. Scis., Clay Minerals Soc., Am. Vacuum Soc., Am. Chem. Soc., Am. Soc. Metals, Am. Crystallographic Assn. Club: Chemists. Home: 581-B North Trail Stratford CT 06497 Office: PO Box 524 Stratford CT 06497

DODD, CHRISTOPHER J., senator; b. Willimantic, Conn., May 27, 1944; s. Thomas J. and Grace (Murphy) D. B.A. in English Lit, Providence Coll., 1966; J.D., U. Louisville, 1972. Bar: Conn. bar 1973. Vol. Peace Corps, Dominican Republic, 1966-68; mem. 94th-97th Congresses from 2d Conn. Dist. Served with AUS, 1969-75. Democrat. Office: Hart Senate Office Bldg Washington DC 20510

DODD, ED(WARD BENTON), cartoonist; b. La Fayette, Ga., Nov. 7, 1902; s. Jesse Mercer and Effie (Cooke) D.; m. Miriam Croft, Feb. 26, 1938 (dec. 1943); m. Elsa Norris, July 25, 1958 (div. 1968); m. Rosemary Wood Johnston, Nov. 7, 1981. Student, Ga. Inst. Tech., 1921-22, N.Y. Art Students League, 1923-24; under, Daniel Beard. Instr., dir. Dan Beard Camp for Boys, 1920-38; instr. outdoor activities N.Y. Mil. Acad., Cornwall, N.Y., 1926-27; comml. artist, N.Y.C., 1929-30. Drew: humor panel Back Home Again, United Feature Syndicate, 1930-45; cartoonist: Mark Trail, Field Syndicate, 1946—; Author: Mark Trail's Camping Tips; Contbr. articles to popular publs. Recipient award for service to conservation Nat. Forestry Assn.; outstanding cartoon strip Sigma Delta Chi, 1948; for conservation wildlife Wis. Humane Soc.; for conservation edn. Detroit Sportsman's Congress; hon. chmn. Nat. Wildlife Week, 1952-53; Conservation award Nat. Wildlife Fedn., 1967. Mem. Outdoor Writers Am., Delta Tau Delta (Nat. Achievement award 1972). Presbyn. Clubs: Homosassa, Piedmont Driving (Atlanta). Office: Field Syndicate 1703 Kaiser Ave Irvine CA 92714

DODD, EDWARD HOWARD, JR., retired publishing executive, author; b. N.Y.C., June 25, 1905; s. Edward Howard and Mary Elizabeth (Leggett) D.; m. Roxana Foote Scoville, Aug. 6, 1932 (div. May 1950); children: Louise Armstrong, Roxana Foote, Edward H. III; m. Camille O. Gilpatric, Oct. 1952. A.B., Yale U., 1928. With Dodd, Mead & Co. (pubs.), 1929-82, head editorial dept., 1937—, dir., 1938—, v.p., 1941, pres., 1953-57, chmn., 1966-76, chmn. editorial bd., 1976-82; with OSS, Washington, 1942-45. Author: Great Dipper to Southern Cross: The Cruise of the Schooner Chance through the South Seas, 1930, The First Hundred Years: A History of Dodd, Mead & Co, 1939, Of Nature, Time and Teale, 1960, Tales of Maui, 1964, Polynesian Art, 1967, Polynesian Seafaring, 1972, Polynesia's Sacred Isle, 1976, The Rape of Tahiti, 1983. Trustee Marlboro Sch. Music. Served with Squadron A, 101st Cav. N.Y. N.G., 3 yrs. Mem. Elihu Soc., Alpha Delta Phi. Clubs: Century, Yale (N.Y.). Cruised through South Seas on small schooner, 1928-29. Address: Windmill Hill Putney VT 05346 *Retire early enough to develop and pursue an alternate career that has no ending. Mine at age 55 is anthropology—Polynesian culture.*

DODD, EDWIN DILLON, container manufacturing company executive; b. Point Pleasant, W.Va., Jan. 26, 1919; s. David Rollin and Mary Grace (Dillon) D.; m. Marie Marshall, Apr. 18, 1942; 1 dau., Marjorie Lee (Mrs. Jay Wannamaker). B.S., B.A., Ohio State U., 1941; Indsl. Adminstr., Harvard, 1943; LL.D., U. Toledo, 1970, Washington and Jefferson Coll., 1972, Coll. of William and Mary, 1982. Engr. airplane div. Curtiss-Wright Corp., 1941-42; pub. relations rep. Owens-Ill. Glass Co., 1946-49, pub. relations dir., 1949-54, prodn. mgr. Libbey Glass div., 1954-56, factories mgr. libbey glass div., 1956-58, v.p., asst. gen. mgr. libbey glass div., 1958, gen. mgr. paper products div., 1959-61, gen. mgr. forest products div., 1961-68; exec. v.p. Owens-Ill., Inc., Toledo, 1964-68, pres., chief exec. officer, 1968-76, chmn. bd., 1976—, dir., 1966—; chmn. bd. Bahamas Agrl. Industries Ltd., 1966-68, pres., 1962-66, dir., 1962—; pres. Forest Products Corp., 1959-68; also dir.; pres. Sabine River & No. R.R., 1966-68, dir., 1966—; pres. Valdosta So. R.R. Co., 1961-68, dir., 1966; pres. Marinette, Tomahawk & Western R.R. Co., 1961-68, dir., 1966—; pres., chmn. bd. Owens-Ill. Timber Corp., 1962-68, dir., 1962—, Ohio Bell Telephone Co., Toledo Trust Co., Goodyear Tire & Rubber Co., Nat. Petro Chems. Corp., Toledo Trustcorp., Inc.; Mem. industries adv. com. Advt. Council; mem. U.S. sect. European Community-U.S. Businessmen's Council; mem. Nat. Commn. on Air Quality, Nat. Indsl. Energy Conservation Council. Past chmn. and trustee Fourdinier Kraft Bd. Inst.; past pres. Toledo Bd. Edn.; dir., mem. Toledo-Lucas County Port Authority, Toledo Labor-Mgmt. Citizens Com.; 1st chmn. Greater Toledo Corp.; mem. Pres.'s Indsl. Pollution Control Council, 1970—; Bd. dirs. Florence Crittenton Home, Toledo Council of Social Agencies; trustee Toledo Art Mus., Inst. Paper Chemistry; mem. adv. council Nat. 4H Club; mem. Nat. Corporations Com. United Negro Coll. Funce; asso. trustee Toledo Boys' Club; mem. bd. devel. council Med. Coll. Ohio, Toledo; bd. visitors Berry Coll.; trustee U. Toledo Corp., Com. Econ. Devel., Council of Ams.; former trustee The Toledo Hosp.; mem. centennial commn. Riverside Hosp. Served as maj. AUS, 1943-46. Decorated Legion of Merit; Mil. Merit Medal, P.I.).; Recipient Distinguished Citizen award Toledo Jr. C. of C., 1955, Ohio Jr. C. of C., 1955; Distinguished Citizens award Nat. Municipal League; Phoenix award; Pacemaker award U. Toledo; named Packaging Man of Yr., 1977. Mem. Toledo C. of C. (post. chmn.), Fibre Box Assn. (dir. 1960-68, pres. 1965), Internat. Corrugated Case Assn. (pres. 1967, dir. 1967—), Nat. Paper Board Assn. (dir. 1964-68), Am. Paper Inst. (dir. 1966-68), Am. Soc. Corp. Execs., Ohio Soc. N.Y., Nat. Municipal League (regional v.p. 1967, council), Bus. Roundtable, U.S. C. of C. (chmn. 1983), Nat. Indsl. Conf. Bd., Harvard Bus. Sch. Assn. (former pres. exec. council), Phi Gamma Delta. Presbyn. Clubs: Toledo, Toledo Country, Belmont Country, Inverness (Toledo); Mid-America (Chgo.); Economic (N.Y.C.); Cloud (N.Y.C.); Links (N.Y.C.); Augusta (Ga.) Nat. Golf; Lyford Cay (Bahamas); Blind Brook (Purchase, N.Y.); Muirfield Village Golf (Dublin, Ohio); Burning Tree (Bethesda, Md.). Office: Owens-Ill Inc One Sea Gate Toledo OH 43666

DODD, GERALD DEWEY, JR., radiologist, educator; b. Oaklyn, N.J., Nov. 18, 1922; s. Gerald Dewey and Anne Aloysius (Keveney) D.; m. Helen Carolyn Glenzing, Apr. 5, 1946; children: Patricia, Michael, Barbara, Gerald Dewey III, Anne, Susan, Thomas. A.B., Lafayette Coll., 1945; M.D., Jefferson Med. Coll., 1947. Diplomate: Am. Bd. Radiology. Intern Fitzgerald Mercy Hosp., Darby, Pa., 1947; resident Jefferson Med. Coll., Phila., 1948-50; asst. radiologist, instr. radiology Jefferson Med. Coll. and Hosp., Phila., 1952-55, asst. radiologist, clin. prof. radiology, 1961-66; assoc. prof. radiology, assoc. radiologist U. Tex. M.D. Anderson Hosp. and Tumor Inst., Houston, 1955-61, prof., chmn. dept. diagnostic radiology, 1966—; prof. radiology U. Tex. Med. Sch., Houston, 1971—; chmn. dept. radiology, 1971-74, prof. radiology, 1971—; cons. radiologist St. Luke's Hosp., Tex. Children's Hosp., Houston, 1966—, St. Joseph's Hosp., 1969—; vis. mem. grad. faculty Tex. A&M U., College Station, 1969—; adj. prof. radiology Baylor Coll. Medicine, 1983—. Assoc. editor: Radiology, 1977—; mem. editorial bd.: Acta Thermographica, 1976—, Gastrointestinal Radiology, 1976—; cons. editor: The Cancer Bull, 1979—; mem. editorial adv. bd.: Cancer, 1979—; referee: CRC Critical Revs. in Radiol. Scis, 1969—; contbr. articles in field to profl. jours. Bd. dirs. Am. Cancer Soc., 1977—, mem. med. and sci. exec. com., 1979—; mem. public edn. com. Nat. Council Radiation Protection and Measurement, 1980—, bd. dirs., 1981—. Fellow Am. Coll. Radiology (vice chmn. bd. chancellors 1980-82, chmn. bd. chancellors 1982—); mem. Radiol. Soc. N.Am. (magna cum laude award 1972, 74), AMA, Am. Roentgen Ray Soc. Gastrointestinal Radiologists, Assn. Univ. Radiologists, Am. Gynecol. Soc. (hon.), Argentine Soc. Gastroenterology (corr.), Pacific N.W. Radiol. Soc. (hon.), Blue Grass Radiol. Soc., Tex. Med. Assn., Tex. Radiol. Soc., Harris County Med. Soc., Houston Radiol. Soc. (mem. exec. com. 1975—), Phila. Roentgen Ray Soc. (hon.), Alpha Omega Alpha, Phi Delta Theta, Phi Chi. Republican. Roman Catholic. Home: 1749 South Blvd Houston TX 77091 Office: 6723 Bertner Dr Houston TX 77030

DODD, JACK GORDON, JR., physicist, educator; b. Spokane, Wash., June 19, 1926; s. Jack Gordon and Mary Ida (Stuart) D.; m. Mary Ann Howell, June 11, 1951; children—Jeffrey John, Laura Jean. Student, State Coll. Wash., 1946-48; B.S. in Physics, Ill. Inst. Tech., 1951, M.S., U. Ark., 1957, Ph.D., 1965. With Argonne (Ill.) Nat. Lab., 1951-53; tchr. Fourche Valley High Sch., 1953-55, 56-57; asst. prof. Drury Coll., 1957-60; asso. prof. Ark. Poly. Coll., 1960-65, U. Tenn., Knoxville, 1965-69; Charles A. Dana prof. physics and astronomy Colgate U., Hamilton, N.Y., 1969—; cons. on phys. optics, microscopy, detonation theory. Served with USN, 1944-46. Mem. Am. Assn. Physics Tchrs., Am. Phys. Soc., Am. Astron. Soc., Optical Soc. Am., Soc. Photographic and Instrumentation Engrs., Inst. Optical Engrs., Sigma Xi. Office: Dept Physics Colgate U Hamilton NY 13346

DODD, JAMES CHARLES, architect; b. Texarkana, Tex., Jan. 17, 1923; s. Richard and Pearl (Smith) D.; m. Constance M. Curry, Sept. 17, 1947; children: Florenda Dodd Mitchell, James Charles. B.A., U. Calif.-Berkeley, 1952. Designer Calif. Div. Architecture, Sacramento, 1953-56; project architect Barovetto & Thomas Architects, Sacramento, 1956-61; prin. Dodd & Assocs., Architects Y Planners, Sacramento, 1960—; owner Urban Constrn. Co., Sacramento, 1972—; guest lectr. architecture Calif. Poly State U. Mem. Citizens Adv. Com. Sacramento Unified Sch. Dist., 1965-66; v.p. Sacramento NAACP, 1968-70; mem. Community Welfare Council, 1967-69, Calif. Coordinating Council Higher Edn., 1968-70; bd. dirs. Goodwill Industries; chmn. bd. govs. Calif. Community Colls., 1972-73; chmn. planning com., bd. dirs. Meth. Hosp. AUS, 1943-46. Recipient Masonry Honor award for Archtl. Design, 1971, Achievement award NAACP, 1972, Concrete Design award, 1974. Fellow AIA (dir. Calif. council 1969-70, 74—, Merit Design award 1974, nat. dir. 1978—); mem. Nat. Orgn. Minority Architects (v.p. 1973). Office: 2710 X St Sacramento CA 95818

DODD, JAMES ROBERT, geologist, educator; b. Bloomington, Ind., Mar. 11, 1934; s. James Edgar and Margaret Elizabeth (Hatcher) D.; m. Margaret Joann Emerson, Aug. 19, 1956; children: Mark Alan, Paul Emerson. A.B., Ind. U., 1956, A.M., 1957; Ph.D. (NSF fellow), Calif. Inst. Tech., 1961. Ford Found. Postdoctoral fellow Calif. Inst. Tech., 1961; geologist Texaco Inc. Research Labs., Bellaire, Tex., 1961-63; asst. prof. geology Case Western Res. U., 1963-66; asso. prof. Ind. U., 1966-73, prof., 1973—. Contbr. articles on chemistry of invertebrate skeletons and carbonate sedimentology. Petroleum Research Fund grantee, 1964-69; NSF grantee, 1971-76, 78-82. Fellow Geol. Soc. Am.; mem. Paleontol. Soc., AAAS, Soc. Econ. Paleontologists and Mineralogists, Phi Beta Kappa, Sigma Xi. Presbyn. (elder). Home: 6875 E Trailway Dr Bloomington IN 47401

DODD, LAMAR, artist, art educator; b. Fairburn, Ga., Sept. 22, 1909; s. Francis Jefferson and Etta Irene (Cleveland) D.; m. Mary Lehmann, Sept. 25, 1930; 1 dau., Mary Irene. Student, Ga. Sch. Tech., 1926-27, Art Students League of N.Y., 1929-33; L.H.D., LaGrange Coll., 1949; A.F.D., U. Cahttanooga, 1959; D.F.A., Fla. State U. Art tchr., Five Point, Ala., 1927-28; asst. mgr. Spivy-Johnson Co., Birmingham, Ala., 1933-37; assoc. prof. art U. Ga., 1937-40, prof., 1940—, head dept. fine arts, 1960—; ant. academician. Exhibited, Whitney Mus. Ann Exhbn., 1937-57, nebr. Ann. Exhbn., 1940, Carnegie Internat., Pitts., 1936, N.Y. World's Fair, 1939-40, San Francisco Fair, 1939; represented permanent collections, Met. Mus., N.Y.C., Telfair Acad., Savannah, High Mus., Atlanta, Pa. Acad. Fine Arts, Whitney Mus. Am. Art, pvt. collections; exhibited one-man show, Corcoran Mus., Washington, 1942, Grnd Central Art Gallery, N.Y., Rochester Meml. Art Gallery, 1949, Witte Meml. Mus., San Antonio, 1951, others; contbr. articles to art jours. Recipient numerous awards and prizes, 1936-57, 2d award, Painting of the Yr. Pepsi-Cola Art Exhbn., 1947, Va. Bienniel Purchase award, 1948, 1st Purchase prize southeastern Art Exhbn., 1949, Nat. Inst. Arts and Letters grantee, 1950, Grumbacher Oil award Fla. Internat. Exhibit, 1952, Edwin Palmer Meml. prize N.A.D., 1953, 1st Transparent Watercolor prize Southeastern Art Assn. Exhbn., 1953, Exhbn. am. Art (N.Y. World's Fair), 1940. Address: 590 Springdale Athens GA 30601

DODD, PAUL A(LBERT), economics educator; b. at Greenwood, Mo., July 26, 1902; s. William R. and Eva (Powless) D.; m. Bonnie N. Jennings, June 18, 1928; 1 son, Paul David. A.B., Park Coll., 1924, LL.D., 1950; Ph.D., U. Pa., 1932. Instr., U. Pa., 1926-28, Harrison grad. fellow, 1930-31; asso. in econs. UCLA, 1928-30, asst. prof., 1932-38, asso. prof., 1939-45, prof., 1945-61, prof. emeritus, 1961—; dean Coll. Letters and Sci. (UCLA), 1946-61, emeritus Coll. Letters and Sci., 1961—, mem. adminstrv. com. of deans, 1950-52, acting vice chancellor, 1959-60; spl. cons. Middle East Tech. U., 1960-61; pres. San Francisco State U., 1962-66; dir. Calif. Med.-Econ. Survey, 1934-39; fed. maritime arbitrator for So. Calif., 1935-39; dir. Study of Problem of Extra Player in Motion Picture Industry, 1939-40; mem. Gov.'s Com. on Health Ins., 1939-40; Rockefeller Found. fellow, Australasia, 1940-41; asso. mem. Nat. W.L.B., 1942-45; vice chmn. 10th regional W.L.B., 1942-43; co-chmn. Nat. Shipbuilding Com., 1943-44; chmn. N.W.L.B. Wartime Incentive Com., 1943; arbitrator in various indsl. disputes including agrl., aircraft, furniture, hosiery, jewelry, lumber, motion picture, newspaper, petroleum, shipbuilding and textile industries; spl. econ. adviser to Gov. Sask., Can., 1945-46. Author: Financial Policies in the Aviation Industry, 1933, California Medico-Economic Survey, 1937, (with G. S. Watkins) Management of Labor Relations, 1938, (with E. F. Penrose) Economic Aspects of Medical Services, 1939, (with G. S. Watkins) Labor Problems, 1940; co-author: The Management of Personnel and Labor Relations, 1950; also various articles on labor and social ins. Bd. dirs. Inst. Indsl. Relations, 1945-47; mem. Presdl. Emergency Ry. Labor Bd., 1947, Ford Found. Fund for Advancement Edn. Nat. Com., 1950-55; adviser Middle East Tech. U., 1961-62; trustee Park Coll., 1964-70. Haines Found. research fellow, 1937-38; Russell Sage research fellow, 1938; Dodd Hall dedicated UCLA, 1974; Disting. Univ. Service award UCLA, 1984. Fellow AAAS; mem. Am. Arbitration Assn., Am. Acad. Arbitrators (charter mem.), Am. Assn. Emeriti (dir. 1965—), Pi Gamma Mu. Presbyterian. Home: 1380 Running Springs Rd 2 Walnut Creek CA 94595

DODD, ROBERT BRUCE, physician, educator; b. Fairbury, Nebr., Apr. 12, 1921; s. Cyrus Milo and Blanche (Kohl) D.; m. Mary Elinor Karll, Dec. 30, 1949; children: Hollyce Ann (Mrs. Thomas Gregory Rose), Robert Bruce, David Karll. Student, U. Chgo., 1939-41; M.D., U. Nebr., 1945. Intern Research and Edn. Hosps. U. Ill., 1945-46; dir. anesthesia Columbia Hosp., Milw., 1948-49; trainee in anesthesia Mass. Gen. Hosp., 1950-51, asst. anesthetist, 1951; practice medicine specializing in anesthesiology, Milw., 1948-49, Dallas, 1951-53, Balt., 1953-56, St. Louis, 1956-69, Springfield, Ill., 1969—; instr., asso. prof. anesthesiology Southwestern Med. Sch. U. Tex., Dallas, 1951-53; prof., head dept. anesthesia Sch. Medicine U. Md., 1953-56; Henry E. Mallinckrodt prof. anesthesiology, head div. anesthesiology Sch. Medicine, Washington U., 1956-69; anesthesiologist-in-chief Barnes Hosp., 1956-68; cons. VA Hosps., Dallas, McKinney, Tex., 1951-53, USPHS Hosp., Balt., 1955-56, VA Hosp., St. Louis City Hosps., 1956-69; clin. prof. anesthesiology So. Ill. U. Sch. Medicine, Carbondale, 1969-83, prof., head dept. anesthesiology, 1983—; anesthesiologist Meml. Hosp., Springfield, 1969—, head dept. anesthesia, 1975—. Author: Diethyl Ether, 1962; Contbr. articles to profl. jours. Served with M.C. AUS, 1946-48. Mem. AMA, Am. Soc. Anesthesiologists (2d v.p. 1967-68), Ill. Soc. Anesthesiologists (1st speaker ho. dels., pres.), St. Louis Soc. Anesthesiologists (past pres.), Internat. Anesthesia Research Soc., Assn. U. Anesthetists (past treas.), Sangamon County Med. Soc., So. Med. Assn. (past sect. chmn.), Alpha Omega Alpha. Home: 2178 Huntleigh Rd Springfield IL 62704 Office: Meml Med Center Springfield IL 62702

DODDS, ROBERT JAMES, JR., lawyer; b. Pitts., Mar. 5, 1916; s. Robert James and Agnes Julia (Raw) D.; m. Kathryn Moore Bechman, June 6, 1942 (dec. Sept. 1943); 1 son, Robert James III; m. Virginia T. Enright, Feb. 13, 1961; children: Dana, Anthony. Grad., Shady Side Acad., Pitts., 1933; A.B., Yale, 1937; LL.B., U. Pa., 1940. Bar: Pa. 1940. Since practiced, Pitts.; mem. firm Reed, Smith, Shaw & McClay; gen. counsel U.S. Dept. Commerce, 1959-61. Trustee Shady Side Acad. (emeritus), YMCA, Pitts.; trustee, past pres. bd. Children's Hosp. of Pitts.; former dir. Blue Cross Western Pa.; bd. dirs., sec. Pitts. Symphony Soc. Served from pvt. to maj., inf. AUS, 1941-45; ETO. Decorated Bronze Star medal. Mem. Am., Pa., Allegheny County bar assns. Presbyn. (trustee). Clubs: Duquesne (Pitts.); Pitts. Athletic Assn.; Longue Vue Country, Rolling Rock, Yale (N.Y.C.); Metropolitan (Washington); Wilderness Country (Naples, Fla.). Home: 1740 Beechwood Blvd Pittsburgh PA 15217 Office: Reed Smith Shaw & McClay Union Trust Bldg Pittsburgh PA 15230

DODENHOFF, WILLIAM, forest products company executive; b. Bklyn., July 16, 1920; s. William D. and Christine (Dehne) Weggeland; m. Shirley Blair, Sept. 16, 1948; children: William, Deborah, Susan, Robert. B.A., Rochester, 1950; M.B.A., Harvard U., 1950. Asst. to pres., mktg. mgr., N.Y. div. sales mgr. Lever Bros., N.Y.C., 1950-54; v.p., gen. mgr. Mobil Chem., Macedon, N.Y., 1954-71; v.p., sr. v.p. pulp and paper Internat. Paper Co., N.Y.C., 1971—; dir. S.A.Y. Industries, Leominster, Mass., Sealed Air Corp., Saddle Brook, N.J.; advisor Sprout Venture Capital Group D.L.J., N.Y.C., 1976-83. Served with USMC, 1943-46. Republican. Clubs: Harvard, Sky (N.Y.C.); Siwanoy Country; Annabels (London). Home: 24 Gramatan Ct Bronxville NY 10708 Office: Internat Paper Co 77 W 45th St New York NY 10036

DODER, DUSKO, foreign correspondent; b. Yugoslavia, July 22, 1937; emigrated to U.S.; s. Vaso and Maria (Gjurchu) D.; m. Karin Rasmussen, Mar. 6, 1963; 1 son, Peter. B.A., Washington U., St. Louis, 1962; M.S., Columbia, 1964, M.A. in History, 1965. Reporter A.P., N.Y.C., Concord, N.H., Albany, N.Y., 1965-68; reporter U.P.I., N.Y.C., fgn. corr., Moscow, Russia, 1968-70, 78; asst. fgn. editor Washington Post, 1970-73, East European, Mediterranean corr., 1973-76, Moscow corr., 1978, 81—, asst. fgn. editor, Can. corr., 1978-81. Author: The Yugoslavs, 1978. Recipient Citation for excellence for articles on Soviet Union Overseas Press Club, 1982; fellow Woodrow Wilson Internat. Center for Scholars, 1977—. Office: American Embassy (m) Helsinki Finland 00140

DODGE, CHARLES MALCOLM, composer, music educator; b. Ames, Iowa, June 5, 1942; s. Albert Francis and Constance (Ruth) D.; (div. 1971); 2 children; m. Katharine King Schlefer, July 1, 1978. B.A. with honors and high distinction in music, U. Iowa, 1964; M.A., Columbia U., 1966, D.M.A., 1970. Pres. Am. Music Center, 1979-82; instr. music Columbia U., 1967-69, asst. prof., 1970-77; asso. prof. music Bklyn. Coll., 1977-79, prof., 1980—; instr. Princeton U., 1969. Composer: Composition in Five Parts for Cello and Piano, 1964, Solos and Combinations, 1964, Folia, 1965, Rota for Orch., 1966, Changes, 1970, Earth's Magnetic Field, 1970, Speech Songs, 1972, Extensions, 1973, The Story of Our Lives, 1974, In Celebration, 1975, Palinode, 1976, Cascando, 1978, Any Resemblance is Purely Coincidental, 1980, Han Mötte Henne I Parken, 1981, Distribution, Redistribution, 1982, He Met Her In the Park, 1983, The Waves, 1984; Compositions have been performed by, Univ. Symphony Orch., Iowa City, 1963, Nat. Gallery Art, 1964, Group Contemporary Music, Columbia, Tanglewood, Lenox, Mass., Composer's Forum, N.Y.C., 1965, Columbia Group, Tanglewood Festival Am. Music, 1965, 73, Library of Congress, Coolidge Festival, 1970, Bourges Festival, 1974, 76, 83, Am. Composers Orch., 1977, New Music, N.Y. Festival, 1979, Internat. Festival of Electronic Music, Stockholm, 1980, 82, Venice Biennale, 1982, Calarts Festival, 1983, Hudderfield Festival, Eng., 1983, MIT Exptl. Music Studio, 1983, N.Y. Philharm., 1984, Olympic Arts Festival, Los Angeles, 1984; Co-author: Computer Music-Synthesis, Composition and Performance, 1984. Woodrow Wilson fellow, 1964-65; Lydia C. Roberts fellow, 1965-66; Guggenheim fellow, 1972-73, 75-76; Recipient Broadcast Music awards, 1963, 64, 66, 67; 1st pl. Joseph H. Bearnes prize, 1964, 67; Raphael Sagalyn award, 1964; citation AAAL, 1975; commd. Fromm Music Found., 1965, Contemporary Music Soc., Koussevitzky Found., 1969, Nat. Endowment for Arts, 1974, 75, 79, Am. Composers Orchs., 1976, Stephen Montague, 1980, Swedish Radio Co., 1980, MIT Exptl. Music Studio, 1983. Mem. Am. Soc. Univ. Composers, Am. Composers Alliance (pres. 1971-75), Phi Beta Kappa, Pi Kappa Lambda, Phi Eta Sigma. Home: 56 Garden Pl Brooklyn NY 11201 Office: Bklyn Coll Conservatory of Music Bedford Ave and Ave H Brooklyn NY 11210

DODGE, CLEVELAND EARL, JR., manufacturing executive; b. N.Y.C., Mar. 7, 1922; s. Cleveland Earl and Pauline (Morgan) D.; m. Phyllis Boushall, Dec. 19, 1942; children: Alice Berkeley, Sally Mole, Cleveland III. B.S. in Mech. Engring., Princeton U., 1943. With DeLaval Steam Turbine Co., 1942, Gen. Electric Co., 1946-51; v.p., dir. Warren Wire Co., Pownal, Vt., 1951-55; pres., dir. Dodge Industries, Inc., Hoosick Falls, N.Y., 1955-67; v.p., dir. Engineered Yarns, Inc., 1962-68; pres. Internat. Dodge, Inc., 1968—, also treas., dir.; pres., dir. Dodge Machine Co., 1968—, Alta Energy Corp., 1968—; v.p., dir. Amex Plastics Inc., 1972-74; dir. Phelps Dodge Corp., Centenial Ins. Co., Key Bank, N.A., Albany, N.Y.; trustee Atlantic Mut. Ins. Co. Pres., bd. dirs. Cleveland H. Dodge Found.; trustee Thousand Island Shipyard Mus., YMCA Retirement Fund, Springfield Coll., Bennington Mus. Served to lt. USNR, World War II. Mem. Princeton Engring. Assn., Princeton Rowing Assn. Congregationalist. Clubs: Laurentian Lodge (Shawbridge, Que., Can.); Princeton (N.Y.C.); Berkshire Tennis, San San Bay Golf; Taconic Golf (Williamstown, Mass.); Kiwanis. Home: Quarry Hill Farm Pownal VT 05261 Office: Dodge Machine Co Inc PO Box 178 Hoosick Falls NY 12090

DODGE, EARL FARWELL, political party executive; b. Malden, Mass., Dec. 24, 1932; s. Earl Farwell and Dorothy Mae (Harris) D.; m. Barbara Viola Regan, July 20, 1951; children: Earl, Barbara, Allen, Calvin, Faith, Karen, Michael. Student public schs., Malden. Exec. sec. Prohibition Nat. Com., 1957-63, 67-79, chmn., 1979—, Colo. Prohibition party, Denver, 1971—, candidate for many offices including v.p., U.S., 1976, 80; sec. Colo. Alcohol Drug Edn., 1972-81, exec. dir., 1981—; sec. Nat. Temperance and Prohibition Council, 1974—; pres. Nat. Civic League, Colo. Right to Life Com., 1976—. Author numerous pamphlets, booklets on alcohol problems; editor: Nat. Statesman, 1960—. Mem. Kalamazoo Community Relations Bd., 1968-71; pres. Kalamazoo Good Govt. Assn., 1968-71; deacon Beth Eden Baptist Ch., Denver, chmn. sch. bd., 1973—. Recipient Ann. Good Govt. awards, 1971, 78. Mem. Am. Polit. Collector Items Assn., Colo. Polit. Collector Items Assn., SAR. Home: 10105 W 17th Pl Lakewood CO 80215 Office: Prohibition Nat Com 128 W 11th Ave Denver CO 80204

DODGE, JOHN VILAS, editor; b. Chgo., Sept. 25, 1909; s. George Dannel and Mary Helen (Porter) D.; m. Jean Elizabeth Plate, Aug. 17, 1935; children—Ann, John M., Gerald C., Kathleen. B.S., Northwestern U., 1930; postgrad., U. Bordeaux, France, 1930-31. Editor Northwestern U. Alumni News and ofcl. publs. of Northwestern, 1932-37; exec. sec. Northwestern U. Alumni Assn., 1937-38; asst. editor Ency. Brit.; asso. editor Brit. Book of Year, 1938-43, Ten Eventful Years (4 vol. history 1937-46), 1947; asst. editor Ency. Brit., 1946-50, mng. editor, 1950-60, exec. editor, 1960-64, sr. v.p.-editorial, 1964-65, sr. editorial cons., 1965-70, 72—, v.p. internat. editorial, 1970-72; editor Brit. World Lang. Dictionary, 1954; Editorial counselor Ency. Universalis, Paris, Japanese Internat. Ency., Tokyo, Enciclopedia Barsa, Mexico City, Enciclopédia Mirador Internacional, Rio de Janeiro. Free-lance writer, 1931-32; Chmn. bd. editors, Ency. Brit. Publs., Inc., 1976—. Served from pvt. to 1st lt. A.A.A., M.I. AUS, 1944-46. Recipient staff citation War Dept. Mem. Sigma Delta Chi. Home: 3851 Mission Hills Rd Northbrook IL 60062

DODGE, PETER HAMPTON, architect; b. Pasadena, Calif., July 1, 1929; s. Irving C. and Edna D. (Allison) D.; m. Janice Coor-Pender, Aug. 30, 1952; children: Susan Julia, Sarah Caroline. Student, Art Center Sch., Calif., 1947-49; A.B. with honors in Architecture, U. Calif., Berkeley, 1956. Cert. architect, Calif., Hawaii, Nev., Idaho, Colo. Apprentice Alvin Lustig (designer), Los Angeles, 1949-50; draftsman Joseph Esherick (AIA), 1956, architect, 1959-63; asso. architect Joseph Esherick and Assos. (architects), San Francisco, 1963-72; prin. Esherick, Homsey, Dodge and Davis (architects and planners, P.C.), San Francisco, 1972—, pres., 1979—; lectr. dept. architecture U. Calif., Berkeley, 1961-64, 71; vis. lectr. dept. design San Francisco Art Inst., 1965. Prin. archtl. works include Shortstop Inc; markets office and warehouse, Benicia, Calif., 1976, Great American Hamburger Place Bldg, Davis, Calif., 1977; interim expansion of Transworld Airlines, 1975, Western Airlines, 1977, at, San Francisco Internat. Airport, Grad. Residence Facility, U. Calif., Davis, 1970, Ekahi Village; 297 condominium units) in resort community of, Wailea, Hawaii, 1976. Mem. Rockridge Community Planning Council, Oakland, Calif., 1971. Served with C.E. U.S. Army, 1957-58. Fellow AIA (dir. Calif. council 1979-81, dir. San Francisco chpt. 1977-78, sec. 1979, v.p. 1980, pres. San Francisco chpt. 1981, Honor award 1970, Bartlett award 1970). Clubs: Sierra, Commonwealth. Office: 2789 25th St San Francisco CA 94110 *

DODGE, PHILIP ROGERS, physician, educator; b. Beverly, Mass., Mar. 16, 1923; s. Israel R. and Anna (McCarthy) D.; children: Susan, Judith. Student, U. N.H., 1941-43, Yale, 1943; M.D., U. Rochester, 1948. Diplomate: Am. Bd. Psychiatry and Neurology. Intern Strong Meml. Hosp., 1948-49; asst. resident neurology Boston City Hosp., 1949-50, resident, 1950, sr. resident, 1951-52; practice medicine, specializing in child neurology, Boston, 1956-67, St. Louis, 1967—; teaching fellow neurology Harvard Med. Sch., 1950, 51-53, instr. neurology, 1956-58, asso. in neurology, 1958-61, asst. prof., 1962-67; asst. neurologist Mass. Gen. Hosp., 1956-59, dir. pediatric neurology program, 1958-67, asso. neurologist, 1959-63, neurologist, 1963-67, asso. pediatrician, 1961-62, pediatrician, 1962-67; investigator Joseph P. Kennedy, Jr. Meml. Labs. for Study Mental Retardation, 1962-67; pediatric neurologist Boston Lying-In Hosp., 1961-67; cons. in neurology Walter E. Fernald State Sch. for Retarded Children, 1963-67; med. dir. St. Louis Children's Hosp., 1967—; asso. neurologist Barnes Hosp., 1967—; prof., head Mallinckrodt Dept. Pediatrics, Washington U. Sch. Medicine, 1967—, prof. neurology, 1967—; Vis. scientist Clin. Research Center, U. P.R., 1965-66, hon. vis. prof. physiology, 1967; cons. collaborative project on cerebral palsy Nat. Inst. Neurol. Diseases and Blindness, 1958; bd. dirs., chmn. research adv. com. Mass. Soc. for Prevention Cruelty to Children, 1961-67; mem. sci. research adv. bd. Nat. Assn. for Retarded Children, 1963-67; bd. dirs. Central Midwestern Regional Lab., Inc., 1968-70; mem. gen. clin. research centers adv. com. USPHS, 1971-74; mem. Mo. Gov.'s Council on Developmental Disabilities, 1971-74; chmn. Mo. Mental Health Commn., 1974-78; mem. nat. adv. child health and human devel. council NIH, 1974-77; chmn. panel on neurol. disorders, developmental, long-range program strategies NINCDS, 1977-79; panel chmn., consensus devel. conf. on diagnosis and treatment of Reye's Syndrome, 1981. Author: (with others) Nutrition and the Developing Nervous System, 1975; Editorial bd.: Jour. Developmental Medicine and Child Neurology, 1965—, Jour. Pediatrics, 1970-80, Pediatric Research, 1970-78, Current Problems in Pediatrics, 1969—, Neurology, 1973-76; Contbr. articles to profl. jours. Served from 1st lt. to maj. M.C. U.S. Army, 1950-56. Mem. Am. Pediatric Soc. (council 1972-78, chmn. council 1978-1979), Am. Acad. Neurology (past com. chmn.), Am. Neurol. Assn., Assn. for Research in Nervous and Mental Disease, Soc. Pediatric Research, Soc. Biol. Psychiatry, St. Louis Soc. Neurol. Scis., Assn. Med. Sch. Pediatric Dept. Chmn. (pres. 1975-77), Alpha Omega Alpha. Home: 410 N Newstead Saint Louis MO 63108 Office: 500 S Kingshighway Saint Louis MO 63110

DODGEN, HAROLD WARREN, educator; b. Blue Eye, Mo., Aug. 31, 1921; s. James Monroe and Lora (Myers) D.; m. Harriet Keddie Ralston, Jan. 20, 1945; children—Cynthia Jeanne, Gilbert Keddie, Stephen LaRele. Student, Long Beach Jr. Coll., 1939-41; B.S., U. Calif. at Berkeley, 1943, Ph.D., 1946. Research asst. Manhattan Dist. Project, U. Calif. at Berkeley, 1943-46; post-doctorate fellow Inst. Nuclear Studies, U. Chgo., 1946-48; asst. prof. chemistry Wash. State U., 1948-52, asso. prof., 1952-59, prof. chemistry, 1959-63, dir. chemistry and physics, 1963—, dir., 1954-68, chmn. chem. physics program, 1968-77. Fellow Am. Inst. Chemists; mem. Am. Chem. Soc., Am. Phys. Soc., Am. Nuclear Soc., AAUP, AAAS, Phi Beta Kappa, Sigma Xi, Alpha Chi Sigma. Home: NW 905 Fisk St Pullman WA 99163

DODSON, DARYL THEODORE, ballet administrator, arts consultant; b. Warrensburg, Mo., Oct. 9, 1934; s. Theodore and Ada Marie (Ayres) D. B.S., Central Mo. State U., 1956. Mem. Gov. S.C.'s Council of the Arts, 1974; mem. adv. panel Vt. Council on Arts, 1978; mgr. Am. tour 1st cultural exchange, People's Republic of China and U.S., 1978, Nat. Ballet Cuba, 1979, Royal Ballet Eng., 1981; pres. Pine Cone Enterprises, Ltd., 1977-81; propr. Pine Cone Inn, Haverhill, N.H., 1978-81; mgr. Opera House, John F. Kennedy Ctr., Washington, 1981; mgr. U.S. and Can. tour Sweeney Todd, 1982; mgr. U.S. tour Amadeus, 1982-83. Asst. dir.: The Mikado, N.Y. City Opera, 1959; regisseur, Chgo. Opera Ballet, 1960; asst. stage mgr., Am. Ballet Theatre, N.Y.C.; stage mgr., Am. Ballet Theatre, 1961; prodn. stage mgr., Am. Ballet Theatre; prodn. mgr., Am. Ballet Theatre, 1963; gen. mgr., Am. Ballet Theatre, 1968—. Served with U.S. Army, 1957-59. Mem. Theta Chi, Theta Alpha Phi. Episcopalian. Home: 328 W 86th Street New York NY 10024 Home: On the Common Haverhill NH 03765 Office: Met Opera House Lincoln Center New York NY 10023

DODSON, EDWARD GRIFFITH, JR., lawyer; b. Norfolk, Va., Feb. 11, 1914; s. Edward Griffith and Harriotte Jones (Winchester) D.; m. Mary Archer Talcott, Oct. 26, 1940; children: Elizabeth Archer (Mrs. James R. Heinzen), Harriotte Winchester (Mrs. E.R. McDannald), Edward Griffith III. B.A., U. Va., 1937, LL.B., 1937. Bar: Va. bar 1937. Since practiced in, Roanoke; asso. firm Cocke, Hazlegrove & Shackelford, 1937-42, 46-47; sr. partner firm Dodson, Pence, Viar, Young & Woodrum (and predecessor), Roanoke, 1948—; substitute justice Juvenile and Domestic Relations Ct., 1947-48; dir., past chmn. Roanoke bd. Bank Va.; dir. Richardson-Wayland Elec. Corp. Mem. Roanoke Youth Commn., 1946-49, Charter Study Commn., 1961; pres. Roanoke City-County Pub. Forum, 1948-49, Roanoke Guidance Center, 1963-64; mem. Roanoke Charter Commn., 1965, Roanoke Citizens Blue Ribbon Long-Range Planning and Goal Setting Com., 1977-78, Va. Ho. of Dels., 1948-54; trustee, past vestryman, sr. warden St. John's Episcopal Ch.; past bd. dirs.; past v.p. Family Service Assn.; past bd. dirs. ARC, Children's Home Soc., Travelers Aid Soc.; past mem. social planning council Roanoke Community Fund; past mem. adv. com. Sch. Social Work; past vice chmn. adv. com. Va. Commonwealth U.; trustee Episcopal High Sch., 1965-71, Jamestown Corp., 1974-76; pres. bd. trustees Diocese S.W. Va., 1971-74; chmn. bd. Mental Health Services of Roanoke Valley, 1972-73. Served to lt. USNR, 1942-46. Fellow Am. Coll. Probate Counsel, Am. Bar Found.; mem. ABA, Va. Bar Assn. (v.p. 1948), Roanoke Bar Assn. (pres. 1953), Va. State Bar (pres. 1961-62), Roanoke Jaycees (pres. 1941-42), Va. Inland Sailing Assn., Newcomen Soc., Delta Kappa Epsilon, Phi Delta Phi. Democrat. Clubs: Roanoke German, Shenandoah. Home: PO Box 1371 Roanoke VA 24007 Office: Bank of Virginia Bldg Roanoke VA

DODSON, GLENN ARTHUR, musician, music educator; b. Berwick, Pa., Feb. 17, 1931; s. Clayton Irvin and Louise (Moore) D.; 1 dau., Tonda Darice. Grad., Curtis Inst. Music, Phila., 1953. Prin. trombonist New Orleans Symphony Orch., 1965-68, Phila. Symphony Orch., 1968—; instr. trombone Loyola U., New Orleans, 1960-65, Am. Conservatory Music, Chgo., 1965-68, U. Wis., Madison, 1967-68, Curtis Inst. Music, 1969—, Phila. Mus. Acad., 1968—. Served with USMCR, 1953-56. Home: 1831 Brandywine St Philadelphia PA 19130 Office: Phila Orch 1420 Locust St Philadelphia PA 19102

DODSON, OSCAR HENRY, numismatist, museum consultant; b. Houston, Jan. 3, 1905; s. Dennis S. and Maggie (Sisk) D.; m. Pauline Wellbrock, Dec. 17, 1932; 1 son, John Dennis. B.S., U.S. Naval Acad., 1927; grad., U.S. Naval Postgrad. Sch., 1936; M.A. in History, U. Ill., 1953. Commd. ensign USN, 1927, advanced through grades to rear adm., 1957; moblzn. planning officer Bur. Naval Personnel, 1945-48; comdg. officer U.S.S. Thomas Jefferson, 1949-50; prof. naval sci. U. Ill., 1950-53; comdr. Landing Ship Flotilla, Atlantic Fleet, 1954-55; chief staff U.S. Naval mission to Greece, 1955-56, 1st Naval Dist., Boston, 1956-57; ret., 1957; asst. prof. history U. Ill., 1957-59; dir. Money Mus., Nat. Bank Detroit, 1959-65, World Heritage Mus., U. Ill., Urbana, 1966-73, now dir. emeritus; acting dir. Champaign County Hist. Mus., 1980—; mem. numis. adv. com. Smithsonian Instn., 1946; mem. Ann. Assay Commn., 1948, U. Ill. Found. Pres.'s Council, U.S. Naval Acad. Found.; visited numis. socs. under auspices State Dept., USSR, Finland, Poland, Austria, Denmark, 1959. Author: Money Tells the Story, 1962; contbg. editor: Coinage Mag., 1973—; contbr. articles to profl. and numis. jours. Decorated Silver Star. Fellow Am., Royal (London) numis. socs., Explorers Club; mem. Am. Numis. Assn. (life, Farran Zerbe award 1968, bd. govs. 1950-55, pres. 1957-61), Am. Mil. Inst., Archeaeol. Inst. Am., U. Ill. Alumni Assn. (Loyalty award 1966), U.S. Naval Acad. Alumni Assn. Clubs: Rotary (pres. Champaign 1972-73), Yacht (N.Y.C.); Army-Navy (Washington); Champaign Country, Circumnavigators, Torch. Office: 486 Lincoln Hall U Ill 702 S Wright St Urbana IL 61801 *We must know the past, for we are becoming one huge family. We either understand and appreciate each other, or we eliminate each other.*

DODSON, RAYMOND M., educator, chemist; b. West Hazleton, Pa., July 8, 1920; s. Curvin E. and Lena (Correll) D.; m. Margaret Ann Ward, Feb. 6, 1943 (div. 1982); children: Karen L. (Mrs. Terry Bloom), Steven R., Debra L., Rebecca D. (Mrs. Stanley Johnson); m. Elizabeth Ann Brenner, Aug. 7, 1982. B.S. summa cum laude, Franklin and Marshall Coll., 1942; postgrad., U. Wis., 1944; Ph.D., Northwestern U., 1947. Asst. prof. U. Minn., 1947-51; chemist G.D. Searle and Co., Chgo., 1951-55, asst. dir. chem. research, 1956-60; prof. chemistry U. Minn., 1960—; Mem. endocrinology study sect. NIH, 1962-66. NRC fellow, 1946-47. Mem. Am. Chem. Soc., A.A.A.S., N.Y. Acad. Sci., Chem. Soc. (London, Eng.), Phi Beta Kappa, Sigma Xi. Dir. research aldactone (spironolactone), 1956-59, microbiol. aromatization steroids, 1960, reactions sulfur monoxide, 1967, reactions of disulfur monoxide, 1970, rearrangements of thietanes, 1972. Co-inventor syncromate, cronolone, 1959. Home: 1920 S 1st St 1404 Minneapolis MN 55454

DOE, BRUCE ROGER, geologist; b. St. Paul, Apr. 24, 1931; s. Richard Harding and Ruth (Schoen) D.; m. Nellija Valida Oleks, Mar. 21, 1958. B.S., B.Geol. Engring., U. Minn., 1954; M.S., Mo. Sch. Mines, 1956; Ph.D., Calif. Inst. Tech., 1960. Postdoctoral fellow Geophys. Lab., Washington, 1960-61; geologist U.S. Geol. Survey, Washington, 1961-63, Denver, 1963-68, 71—, chief br. isotope geology, 1976-81; staff scientist Lunar Sample Program, NASA, Washington, 1969-71; mem. Lunar Sample Analysis Planning Team, 1970-72, vice chmn., 1973-74; mem. Comet and Asteroid Missions Adv. Panel, 1971-72, Comet and Asteroid Sci. Working Group, 1972-73; vis. investigator Geophys. Lab., 1961-62; lectr. Am. Geophys. Union, 1963-65, 70; acad. guest Swiss Fed. Inst., Zurich, 1968-69; lectr. Vernadsky Meml. Lecture, Moscow, 1976; dir. Economic Geology Pub. Co. Author: Lead Isotopes, 1970; editorial bd.: Econ. Geology, 1970-74; mem., Econ. Geology Pub. Co., 1974—; contbr. articles to sci. jours. Ruling elder First Presbyn. Ch., Lakewood, Colo., 1974-76. Fellow Geol. Soc. Am. (subcom. on hon. fellows 1974-76, chmn. 1976); mem. Soc. Econ. Geologists (chmn. research com. 1979, chmn. disting. lectr. com. 1979, trustee Found. 1981—), AAAS, Geochem. Soc. (standards com. 1969—, council 1974-77, 80, v.p. 1980-81, pres. 1981-82), Am. Geophys. Union (editor EOS 1982—). Home: 11721 Dry River Ct Reston VA 22091 Office: Stop 981 US Geol Survey Reston VA 22092 *Although there are short-term unpleasantnesses in giving one's honest opinions and advice, I have found that people and organizations keep coming back for more. In addition, people of action are needed in this life even at the sacrifice of perfection and without assurance of progress.*

DOE, RICHARD PHILIP, educator, physician; b. Mpls., July 21, 1926; s. Richard Harding and Ruth Elizabeth (Schoen) D.; m. Shirley Joan Cedarleaf, Sept. 15, 1950; children—Nancy Jean, Charles Jeffrey, Robert Bruce. B.S., U. Minn., 1949, M.B., 1951, M.D., 1952, Ph.D., 1966. Intern Oakland (Cal.) Hosp., 1951-52; resident internal medicine Mpls. VA Hosp., 1952-55, chief chemistry sect., 1956-60, chief metabolic endocrine sect., 1960-69, endocrine staff, 1976—; head metabolic endocrine sect. U. Minn. Hosp., 1969-76; faculty U. Minn. Med. Sch., Mpls., 1955—, prof. medicine, 1969—. Served with USNR, 1944-46. USPHS grantee, 1958—. Mem. Am. Soc. Clin. Investigation, Mpls. Soc. Internal Medicine, Minn. Soc. Internal Medicine, Central Soc. Clin. Research, Endocrine Soc., Am. Fedn. Clin. Research, Internat. Soc. Chronology. Home: 5613 Hawkes Dr Edina MN 55436 Office: Metabolic-Endocrine Sect VA Hosp 54th St and 48th Ave Minneapolis MN 55417

DOELITZSCH, DENNIS FRANK, broadcasting executive; b. Red Bud, Ill., Feb. 13, 1947; s. Elmer Frank and Aleda Ann (Mueller) D.; m. Joann Francis Boyd, June 14, 1969; children: Dinah Jo, Deanna Beth. B.S., So. Ill. U., 1969. Radio announcer, engr., salesman various stas., 1965-69; sales specialist Gates Radio Co., Quincy, Ill., 1969-70; owner, mgr. sta. WDDD-TV-FM, WDDW, Marion, Ill., 1970—; dir. Peoples Bank, Marion, So. Ill. Inc., Crab Orchard and Egyptian R.R., Marion. Mem. Nat. Radio Broadcasters Assn. (dir.), Nat. Assn. TV Program Execs., AP Broadcasters Assn., Ill. Broadcasters Assn. (dir.), Marion C. of C. (pres. 1978). Club: Rotary (Marion) (pres. 1979). Office: Route 37 N Marion IL 62959

DOENGES, BYRON FREDERICK, economist, educator, govt. ofcl.; b. Ft. Wayne, Ind., June 18, 1922; s. Arthur Philip and Elsie (Mesing) D.; m. Elaine Aiken, June 15, 1947. Diploma, Internat. Bus. Coll., 1941; A.B., Franklin (Ind.) Coll., 1946; M.B.A., Ind. U., 1948, Ph.D., 1962. Instr., headmaster boarding dept. Punahou Sr. Acad., Honolulu, 1948-50; dir. scholarships and loans Ind. U. at Bloomington, 1951-56, asst. dean, 1955-65; prof. econs., dean Coll. Liberal Arts, Willamette U., 1965-71; econ. cons. Gov. Oreg., 1971-72; dep. asst. dir. U.S. Arms Control and Disarmament Agy., Washington, 1972-73, chief econs. and spl. studies div., 1973-76, sr. econs. adviser, 1976—; Program devel. head Title II Nat. Def. Edn. Act, U.S. Office Edn., Washington, 1958-59; asso. dir. Salzburg (Austria) Seminar Am. Studies, 1962-64; mem. Higher Commn. N.W. Assn. Secondary and Higher Schs., 1968-71; mem. exec. bd. N.W. Assn. Pvt. Colls. and Univs., 1969-70. Editor: Accountability, 1973; Contbr. articles to profl. jours. Served to lt. comdr. USNR, 1943-46; PTO. Recipient alumni citation Franklin Coll., 1977. Mem. Am. Econ. Assn., Soc. Internat. Devel., Western Econ. Assn., Lambda Chi Alpha (mem. nat. fellowship bd. 1965—), Pi Gamma Mu, Omicron Delta Kappa. Club: Cosmos (Washington). Spl. research internat. capital movements, econs. higher edn., econs. arms control. Home: 700 New Hampshire Ave NW Washington DC 20037 Office: Dept State Washington DC 20451

DOENGES, NORMAN ARTHUR, educator; b. Ft. Wayne, Ind., Aug. 23, 1926; s. Arthur Philip and Elsie (Mesing) D.; m. Pamela Lee Wiegand, Aug. 23, 1952; children—Cynthia Lee, Stephanie Lynn, Jonathan Philip. B.A., Yale, 1947, Balliol Coll., Oxford (Eng.) U., 1949; M.A., Princeton, 1951, Ph.D., 1954; Fulbright scholar, Am. Sch. Classical Studies, Athens, Greece, 1951-52. Instr. Princeton, 1949-50, 52-53; mem. faculty Dartmouth, 1955—, prof. classics, 1965—, chmn. dept., 1959-63, 67-71, 78-79, chmn. humanities div., 1963-67, asso. dean faculty, 1964-66. Author: The Letters of Themistokles, 1981. Served with AUS, 1953-55. Mem. Am. Philol. Assn., Soc. Promotion Hellenic Studies, Classical Assn. Can., Classical Assn. New Eng. (sec.-treas. 1963-68), Assn. Ancient Historians, Phi Beta Kappa. Home: 34 Rip Rd Hanover NH 03755

DOENGES, RUDOLPH CONRAD, finance educator; b. Tonkawa, Okla., Dec. 7, 1930; s. Rudolph Soland and Helen Elizabeth (Lower) D.; m. Ellen Ione Gummere, Oct. 5, 1963; children: Rudolph Conrad, John Soland, William Gummere. A.B. magna cum laude (scholar 1948-52), Harvard U., 1952, M.B.A., 1954; D.B.A. (Ford Found. fellow 1963-64), U. Colo., Boulder, 1965. Mktg. analyst Ford Motor Co., Dearborn, Mich., 1954; gen. mgr. Doenges-Long Motors and Western Auto Rentals, Colorado Springs, 1958-61; mem. faculty U. Tex., Austin, 1964—; prof. fin., 1974—, assoc. dean, 1972-76, chmn. dept. fin., 1976-80; dir. Doenges-Glass Motors, Aurora, Colo. Author: (with E. W. Walker) Case Problems in Financial Management, 1968, Consumer Credit in Texas, 1970; editor: Readings in Money and Banking, 1968, (with H. A. Wolf) Corporate Planning Models, 1971; contbr. articles in field to profl. jours. Served with USN, 1955-58. Mem. Austin C. of C., Fin. Mgmt. Assn. (dir. 1980—), Southwestern Fin. Assn. (pres. 1973-74), Southwestern Fedn. Adminstrv. Disciplines (pres. 1975-76), Austin-San Antonio Soc. Fin. Analysts, Phi Beta Kappa, Beta Gamma Sigma. Republican. Methodist. Club: El Paso (Colorado Springs). Home: 3500 Hillbrook Circle Austin TX 78731 Office: Dept of Finance U Tex Austin TX 78712

DOERFLER, LEO G., educator; b. N.Y.C., June 25, 1919; s. Gustav S. and Anna (Steiner) D.; m. Alice Laura Turecheck, Dec. 19, 1943; children—Dennis Lee, Donald Lee, David Lee, Ann Laura. A.B., N.Y.U., 1939; M.S., Washington U., St. Louis, 1941; Ph.D., Northwestern U., 1948. Tchr.- psychologist Iowa Sch. Deaf, Council Bluffs, 1941-43; instr. audiology Northwestern U., 1946-48; chief dept. audiology-speech pathology Latrobe Area Hosp., 1976—; prof. audiology emeritus (Sch. Medicine); dir. doctoral program bioacoustics U. Pitts., 1948-76; dir. dept. audiology Eye and Ear Hosp., Pitts., 1948-76; Cons. in field, 1946—, Nat. Inst. Neurol. and Communicative Diseases and Stroke. Contbr. articles to profl. jours. Bd. dirs. Cerebral Palsy Assn. Pitts., 1958—. Served with AUS, World War II. C.C. Bunch fellow Northwestern U., 1946-47. Fellow AAAS, Am. Speech and Hearing Assn. (pres. 1967); mem. Am. Indsl. Hygiene Assn. (com. on noise), Indsl. Med. Assn. (com. on noise), Am. Acad. Ophthalmology and Otolaryngology (com. on hearing and equilibrium), Am. Bd. Examiners in Speech Pathology and Audiology (pres. 1960), Acad. Dispensing Audiologists (pres. 1978-79), Sigma Xi. Inventor D-S test for psychogenic deafness. Home: 4533 Barlind Dr Pittsburgh PA 15227 Office: Central Med Arts RD 7 Greensburg PA 15601

DOERING, WILLIAM VON EGGERS, educator, organic chemist; b. Ft. Worth, June 22, 1917; s. Carl Rupp and Antoinette (von Eggers) D.; m. Ruth Haines, 1947 (div. 1954); children: Christian, Peter, Margaretta; m. Sarah Cowles Bullitt, 1969 (div. 1981). B.S., Harvard U., 1938, Ph.D., 1943; D.Sc. (hon.), Tex. Christian U., 1974. Faculty, Columbia U., 1943-52; prof. Yale U., 1952-67, dir. div. sci., 1962-65; prof. Harvard U., 1967—; hon. prof. Fudan U., Shanghai, China, 1980; research chemist Nat. Def. Research Council, Harvard U., 1941-42, Polaroid Corp., 1943, Office Prodn. Research and Devel., 1944-45; dir. Hickrill Chem. Research Found., Katonah, N.Y., 1947-59; cons. Upjohn Co., 1956—. Contbr. articles to profl. jours.; hon. regional editor: Tetrahedron, 1958-60. Chmn. Council for Livable World, Washington, 1962-72, pres., 1973-78. Recipient John Scott award City of Phila., 1945; Pure Chemistry award Am. Chem. Soc., 1953; Synthetic Organic Chem. Mfrs. Assn.; medal for creative work in synthetic organic chemistry, 1966; Hofmann medal German Chem. Soc., 1962; William C. DeVane medal Yale Phi Beta Kappa, 1967; Theodore William Richards medal, 1970. Mem. Nat. Acad. Sci., Am. Acad. Arts and Scis. Office: Dept Chemistry Harvard 12 Oxford St Cambridge MA 02138

DOERMANN, HUMPHREY, foundation administrator;; b. Toledo, Nov. 13, 1930; s. Henry John and Alice (Robbins Humphrey) D.; m. Elisabeth Adams Wakefield, Jan. 7, 1956; children: Elisabeth M., Eleanor H., Julia L. A.B., Harvard, 1952, M.B.A., 1958, Ph.D., 1967. Asst. to com. on admissions and scholarships Harvard, 1955-56; reporter Mpls. Star, 1958-60; asst. to bus. mgr. Mpls. Star & Tribune Co., 1960-61; dir. admissions Harvard, 1961-66, asst. to dean, 1966-69, asst. dean, 1970-71, lectr. on edn., 1967-71; exec. dir. Bush Found., St. Paul, 1971-78, pres., 1978—; Mem. selection com. Nat. Merit Scholarships, 1965-67; cons. Council Higher Edn. Va., 1969, W.Va. Bd. Regents, 1970. Author: Crosscurrents in College Admissions, rev. edit, 1970, Toward Equal Access, 1978; Contbr. articles to Found. News; others. Mem. Belmont (Mass.) Town Meeting, 1969-70; Trustee Found. Center, N.Y.C., 1975-83, chmn. bd., N.Y.C., 1982-83; bd. overseers Harvard Coll., 1973-79; chmn. Minn. Council on Founds., 1981—. Served to lt. (j.g.) USN, 1952-55. Home: 736 Goodrich Ave Saint Paul MN 55105 Office: Bush Found E-900 First Nat Bank Bldg Saint Paul MN 55101

DOERMER, RICHARD T., banker; b. Ft. Wayne, Ind., Dec. 12, 1922; s. John S. and Kathryn (Morris) D.; m. Mary Louise McNabb, June 18, 1949; children—Richard D., Kathryn A. B.S., U. Notre Dame, 1943; LL.B., Cornell U., 1949. Bar: Ind. bar 1949. Practiced in, Ft. Wayne, until 1956; chmn., pres., dir. Ind. Bank & Trust Co., Ft. Wayne, 1957—; dir. Kendallville Bank & Trust Co., Decatur Bank & Trust Co., Frances Slocum Bank, Wabash, Ind., Internat. Gen. Industries Inc., Washington, Burro Crane Co., Inc., Chgo., Old Fort Industries, Inc., Ft. Wayne, Kingsford Industries, Inc., Avis Indsl. Corp., Heckman Bindery, Inc., Citizens No. Bank of Elkhart, Western-Cullen-Hayes, Inc., Chgo., Pacific Forge, Inc., Fontana, Calif.; chmn. bd. First Equity Security Life Ins. Co., Anderson, Ind. Pres., past campaign chmn. Allen County United Way.; Trustee St. Francis Coll., Ft. Wayne. Served as lt. (j.g.) USNR, 1943-46. Named Ft. Wayne area Outstanding Young Man of Year, 1956; Man of Year Met. Notre Dame Club Ft. Wayne, 1960. Mem. Ft. Wayne Press Club (bd. dirs.), Ind. Bankers Assn., Ind., Am. bar assns., Ft. Wayne Met. C. of C. (pres.). Roman Catholic. Club: K.C. (4 deg.). Office: 915 S Clinton St Fort Wayne IN 46801 *

DOERR, ARTHUR HARRY, univ. adminstr.; b. Johnston City, Ill., Aug. 28, 1924; s. Arthur H. and Nettie Esther (Felts) D.; m. Dale A. Lantrip, Aug. 15, 1947; 1 son, Marc M. Student, U. Cal. at Berkeley, 1943-44; B.A. with high honors, So. Ill. U., 1947; M.A., Ind. U., 1948; Ph.D., Northwestern U., 1951. Grad. asst. Ind. U., 1947-48; grad. asst., then half-time instr. Northwestern U., 1948-51; field team chief rural land classification program of P.R. and P.R. Dept. Agr. and Commerce and Social Sci. Research Center at U. P.R., 1950; mem. faculty U. Okla., 1951-70, Regents prof. geography, 1969, dean, 1961-65; prof. geography U. Pa., 1966-67; chief party AID devel. project to Pahlavi U., Shiraz, Iran, 1966-67; v.p. acad. affairs U. W. Fla., Pensacola, 1970—; vis. summer prof. Eastern Ill. State Coll., 1951, Central Wash. Coll., 1952, George Peabody Coll., 1953, Wis. State U., Stevens Point, 1955, Western Wash. U., 1957, Northwestern U., 1960; Fulbright prof. U. Philippines, 1958-59; intelligence expert Dept. Army, summer 1956; geologist Okla. Geol. Survey, summer 1959; geologist, phys. geographer Dorudzhan Excavation, Iran, 1967. Author: (with Lee Guernsey) Principles of Geography, Physical and Cultural, 1959, 2d edit., 1975, Principles of Physical Geography, 1964, 2d edit., 1976, An Introduction to Economic Geography, 1969, Coal Mining in Oklahoma and Its Landscape Modifications, 1960, also articles, chpts. in books. Served to 2d lt. AUS, 1943-46. Recipient Teaching award U. Okla., 1955; Alumni award distinguished profl. achievement So. Ill. U., 1965. Fellow Okla. Acad. Sci.; mem. Sigma Xi (past sec., v.p. U. Okla. chpt.), Phi Delta Kappa, Gamma Theta Upsilon, Pi Kappa Sigma, Phi Kappa Phi. Home: 66 Blithewood Dr Pensacola FL 32514

DOERR, HOWARD P., telephone co. exec.; b. Lincoln, Nebr., June 3, 1929; s. Julius Henry and Kathryn (Kister) D.; m. ArVella Florence Stroh, Sept. 10, 1950; children—Cathleen K., Steven B., David S. B.S. in Bus. Adminstrn, U. Nebr., 1950. With Northwestern Bell Telephone Co., 1950—, asst. v.p. ops., Omaha, 1966-69, v.p., gen. mgr. Nebr. area, 1969-72, v.p. revenues, 1972-78, sr. v.p. fin., Omaha, 1978-81, sr. v.p. fin. and external affairs, 1981—; dir. Northwestern Nat. Bank, Omaha. Trustee Omaha Indsl. Found., Nebr. Ind. Coll. Found., Luth. Med. Center, Omaha; bd. dirs. Urban Housing Found., Omaha, Park East, Inc., Gt. Plains council Girl Scouts U.S.A. Served to lt. USAF, 1951-52. Mem. Nebr. Assn. Commerce and Industry (dir.). Lutheran. Home: 3605 S 94th Ave Omaha NE 68124 Office: 1314 Douglas On-The-Mall Omaha NE 68102

DOERRE, KARL HAROLD, insurance company executive; b. Alton, Ill., Oct. 13, 1921; s. Benjamin Orville and Frances (Karel) D.; m. B. Irene Buck, Oct. 9, 1948; children Dorene Doerre Ross, Karl E., Marietta E. B.S. in Bus. Adminstrn., Washington U., St. Louis, 1947. With U.S. Fidelity & Guaranty Co., Balt., 1947—, v.p., 1966-72, exec. v.p., 1972—; dir. Del Mar Co., Thomas Jefferson Life Ins. Co.; dir. Fidelity Ins. Co.; dir. Fidelity & Guaranty Ins. Underwriters Inc. Served with AUS; World War II. Mem Surety Assn. Am. Home: 11 E Aylesbury Rd Timonium MD 21093 Office: US Fidelity & Guaranty Co. 100 Light St PO Box 1138 Baltimore MD 21203

DOGANÇAY, BURHAN CAHIT, painter, photographer; b. Istanbul, Turkey, Sept. 11, 1929; s. Adil and Hediye D.; m. Angela Hausmann, Dec. 11, 1978. Ed., Academie de la Grande Chaumiere, 1955; Ph.D. in Econs., U. Paris, 1956. Exhibited works at, Centre Georges Pompidou, Paris, 1982, Palais des Beaux-Arts, Brussels, Musée St.-Georges, Liege, Belgium, Musée d'Art Contemporain, Montreal, 1983. Recipient cert. of appreciation City of N.Y., 1964; fellow Tamarind Lithography Workshop, 1969. Design selected for UNICEF card, 1974. *Mostly unshattered self-confidence, hard work and the willingness to meet new challenges are the basis of my success and happiness.*

DOGGETT, AUBREY CLAYTON, JR., mortgage banker; b. Greensboro, N.C., Nov. 8, 1928; s. Aubrey Clayton and Ann (Blevins) D.; m. Judy Perier, July 26, 1952; children: Aubrey Clayton III, Kathryn Ann, Russell Lee, Robert Keith, Karen Michelle. B.S., U. N.C., 1950. Salesman Richardson Realty, Inc., Greensboro, 1950, 52-53; reviewing appraiser Prudential Ins. Co. Am., Greensboro, 1953-58; exec. v.p., dir., mem. exec. com. Key Co., Greensboro, 1958-63; v.p. mortgage loan dept. Wachovia Bank & Trust Co., Winston-Salem, N.C., 1963-66, sr. v.p., 1966-70; pres. Wachovia Mortgage Co., 1970-71; also dir.; pres., trustee Wachovia Realty Investments, 1970-71; pres., dir. Wingreen Corp., Winston-Salem, 1971—; sr. v.p., dir. AMIC Corp. (and subs.), 1981-83; dir. Amreal Corp., H. G. Smithy Co., U.S. Shelter; Mem. Gov. N.C. Com. Low Income Housing, 1964-68; chmn. ad hoc com. Winston-Salem Model Cities Commn., 1969; mem., past chmn. N.C. Housing Adv. Council; bd. dirs. Winston-Salem Housing Found. Exec. Bd.; pres. Granville Place, Inc., Kenner Homes & East Salem Homes, Inc. (housing for elderly). Chmn. Greater Greensboro Open Golf Tournament, 1960. Served to 1st lt. USMCR, 1950-52; lt. col. Res. ret. Decorated Purple Heart. Mem. Mortgage Bankers Assn. Carolinas (pres. 1970, dir. 1966-71), Mortgage Bankers Assn. Am. (gov. at large 1971-82, legis. and income property coms.), Winston-Salem Real Estate Bd., Nat. Assn. Real Estate Investment Trusts (gov. 1971-74), SAR, Sigma Chi. Episcopalian. Club: Old Town. Home: 2813 Galsworthy Dr Winston-Salem NC 27106 Office: 915 W 4th St Winston-Salem NC 27101

DOGGETTE, HERBERT RICHARD, JR., government official; b. Bklyn., Dec. 7, 1933; s. Herbert Richard and Sally Blanche (Robertson) D.; m. Elizabeth Burton Branch, May 24, 1959; children: Michelle, Carol, David. B.A.B.A., U. Md., 1974; M.P.A., George Washington U., 1978. Various positions Social Security Adminstrn., Los Angeles, 1958-65; staff asst. San Francisco Regional Office, Los Angeles, 1965, dist. mgr., Watts, Calif., asst. dist. mgr., Hollywood, Calif., 1965-67, asst. regional rep. Bur. Dist. Office Ops, San Francisco, 1967-68; with Bur Retirement and Survivors Ins, San Francisco, 1968, 69-78; asst dir. mgmt. Chgo Payment Ctr. Bur. of Retirement and Survivors Ins., 1968; chief orgn. and staff devel. br. Bur. Retirement and Survivors Ins., Balt., 1968, dir. labor relations-equal opportunity, 1969-73; asst. bur. dir. for adminstrn. Bur Retirement and Survivors Ins, 1973-75; dep. bur. dir Bur. Retirement and Survivors Ins, 1975-78; assoc. commr. for mgmt., budget and personnel Social Security Adminstrn., Balt., 1979, dep. commr. for ops, 1979—; Am. Polit. Sci. Assn. congl. fellow, Washington, 1968-69; acting dep. asst. sec. for equal opportunity programs HEW, Washington, 1978. Vice chmn. Balt. Fed. Exec. Bd., 1979-80, chmn., 1980-81, chmn. combined fed. campaign com., 1981-82. Served in U.S. Army, 1952-54. Recipient Commr.'s citation Social Security Adminstrn., 1966, 73, cert. of merity Oakwood Coll., Huntsville, Ala., 1977, Sec.'s Spl citation HEW, 1979, Nat. Civil Service League, 1970; named Disting. Exec. Sr. Exec. Service, 1980; recognition outstanding leadership Fed. Exec. Bd., 1981; Mgmt. Nat. Council Social Security, 1982. Mem. Am. Soc. Pub. Adminstrn. (Md. chpt., Clifford R. Gross 1981). Democrat. Seventh-Day Adventist. Office: Social Security Adminstrn 6401 Security Blvd Baltimore MD 21235

DOGOLE, SAUL HARRISON, security co. exec.; b. Phila., Jan. 16, 1922; s. Irving M. and Ethel (Kreager) D.; m. Marilyne Zucker, July 27, 1967; children—James E., Ian M. B.A., U. Pa., 1943. Partner Globe Internat. Detective System, 1950-60; pres. Globe Security Systems, Inc., 1960-72, chmn., chief exec. officer, 1972—; sr. v.p. Walter Kidde & Co., Inc., Clifton, N.J., 1976—. Mem. Phila. Gas Commn., 1977—; fin. dir. Humphrey for Pres. Campaign, 1972; del. Nat. Democratic Conv., 1972, 76; bd. dirs. Coalition for a Democratic Majority. Recipient Humanitarian award Kain Moses group Am. Cancer Soc.; Cyrus Adler Community Service award, 1969. Mem. World Bus. Council, Pa. Chiefs of Police Assn., Phila. C. of C. Jewish. Clubs: Variety, Locust, Masons, Shriners. Home: Apt 709 41 Conshohocken State Rd Bala Cynwyd PA 19004 Office: 2503 Lombard St Philadelphia PA 19146

DOHANIAN, DIRAN KAVORK, art historian, educator; b. Somerville, Mass., Mar. 26, 1931; s. Hagop Mardiros and Esther (Babigian) D. B.F.A., Mass. Sch. Art, 1952; A.M. in Teaching, Harvard, 1953, M.A., 1955, Ph.D., 1964. Instr. art Eastern Nazarene Coll., Wollaston, Mass., 1952-55; reader in fine arts Harvard, 1954-55, 56-57, teaching fellow fine arts, 1955-57; vis. asst. prof. history art U. Ala., 1957-58; vis. asst. prof. history Oriental art U. Hawaii, 1959-60; asst. prof. fine arts, dir. course in Oriental humanities U. Rochester, N.Y., 1960-65, asso. prof. fine arts, 1965-71, prof., 1971—, chmn. dept. fine arts, 1980-83; cons. curator Oriental art The Meml. Art Gallery, Rochester, 1976—, bd. mgrs., 1977-78, 80-83; Cooke-Daniels Meml. lectr. art Cooke-Daniels Found. and Denver Art Mus., 1965; Louise Weiser lectr. Mt. Holyoke Coll., 1983; cons. Choice, Jour. Assn. Coll. Research Libraries. Author: The Mahayana Buddhist Sculpture of Ceylon, 1977, also articles in profl. jours. C.R.B. fellow Belgian Art Seminar, Brussels and Antwerp, 1956; Fulbright fellow, India, 1958-59; sr. research fellow Am. Inst. Ceylonese Studies, Colombo, 1968; Am. Council Learned Socs. fellow, India, 1973. Mem. Am. Inst. Indian Studies (trustee 1964-65), Am. Com. for History South Asian Art (dir. 1969-71). Home: 269 Payson Rd Belmont MA 02178 Office: Dept Fine Arts U Rochester Rochester NY 14627

DOHENY, DAVID ARMOUR, lawyer; b. Cobourg, Ont., Can., July 2, 1931; came to U.S., 1931, naturalized, 1955; s. Clarence William and Kate (Armour) D.; m. Olga Kean, June 13, 1959 (div.); children: John Douglas Armour, Jennifer; m. Carmen Teresa Fajardo, Dec. 20, 1975; 1 stepson, Brett Bibeau. A.B. cum laude, Williams Coll., 1953; LL.B., Harvard U., 1958. Bar: Ill. 1959, Fla. 1966. Asso. Taylor, Miller, Busch & Magner, Chgo., 1958-63; asst. gen. counsel Am. Photocopy Equipment Co., Evanston, Ill., 1963-65; sec., gen. counsel legal dept. Gen. Devel. Corp., Miami, Fla., 1966-68, v.p., sec., gen. counsel, 1968-77, exec. v.p., gen. counsel, 1977-81; asst. state's atty. 11th Jud. Circuit, Dade County, Fla., 1981-82; asst. U.S. atty. So. Dist. Fla., 1982—; hon. consul Netherlands, Miami, 1978-80. Republican precinct capt., Chgo., 1962-65; bd. dirs. Fla. Philharmonic Soc., 1970-82, Spectrum Programs, Inc. (drug rehab.); mem. Met. Dade County Council Arts and Scis., 1976-80; adv. council Center Law and Econs., U. Miami. Served with C.E., U.S. Army, 1953-55. Mem. Am., Fla., Chgo., Dade County bar assns., Lincolns Inn Soc., N.Y. Geneal. and Biog. Soc., Am. Soc. Corp. Secs. (past pres. Southeastern regional group), Fla. C. of C. (dir. 1978-81), Zeta Psi. Episcopalian. Home: 1778 S Bayshore Ln Miami FL 33133 Office: 151 S Miami Ave Miami FL 33131

DOHERTY, EDWARD DENVIR, II, petroleum company executive; b. Chgo., Oct. 3, 1935; s. Edward Den vir and Charlotte D.; m. Alison Ramsey Ferguson, Dec. 4, 1971; children: Christina, Seana, Neal. B.A., LaFayette Coll., 1957; LL.B., Columbia U., 1960. Sr. internat. atty. Richardson-Merreell, Inc., N.Y.C., 1965-70; asst. gen. counsel E. R. Squibb & Sons, Inc., N.Y.C., 1970-72; sr. atty. Commonwealth Oil Refining Co., San Antonio, 1972-75, exec. v.p., gen. counsel, 1975—, also dir. Mem. ABA, N.Y. State Bar Assn., Assn. Bar City N.Y., State Bar Tex., Inter-Am. Bar Assn. Home: 700 Elizabeth Rd San Antonio TX 78209 Office: 8626 Tesoro Dr San Antonio TX 78217

DOHERTY, HERBERT JOSEPH, JR., historian, educator; b. Jacksonville, Fla., Feb. 4, 1926; s. Herbert Joseph and Marie (Bishop) D. B.A., U. Fla., 1948, M.A., 1949; Ph.D., U. N.C., 1953. Mem. faculty U. Fla., 1949-50, 53—, chmn. social scis., 1963-79, prof. history and social sci., 1964—, dir. gen. edn. programs in behavioral studies, humanities and social scis., 1979—, dir. Honors Program, 1980—; lectr. Far East div. U. Md., 1959-60, 1960-61; Chmn. Alachua County Hist. Commn., 1974-77; Mem. adv. commn. Fla. Bd. Archives and History, 1968-70; Fla. rev. bd. Nat. Register Historic Places, 1969—; adv. bd. Fed. Records Center, Atlanta, 1967-71; adv. council Fed. Regional Archives, 1971-77; Fla. adv. bd. Nat. Hist. Pubis. and Records Commn., 1976—. Author: Richard Keith Call: Southern Unionist, 1961, The Whigs of Florida, 1845-1854, 1959; also articles. Served with USAAF, 1944-46. Mem. Nat. Trust Historic Preservation, Orgn. Am. Historians, Am. Hist. Assn., So. Hist. Assn., Fla. Hist. Assn. (bd. dirs. 1962-68, 70-72, 77-80, pres. 1968-70, editor quar. 1962-64), Phi Beta Kappa, Phi Kappa Phi, Phi Alpha Theta, Delta Tau Delta, Fla. Blue Key. Democrat. Home: 415 NE 5th Ave Gainesville FL 32601

DOHERTY, JAMES EDWARD, III, physician, educator; b. Newport, Ark., Nov. 22, 1923; s. James Edward and Ida Josephine (Parish) D.; married; children: Richard Edward, Margaret Elise. B.S. Medicine, U. Ark., 1944, M.D., 1946. Diplomate: Am. Bd. Internal Medicine (cardiovascular disease). Intern Columbus (Ga.) City Hosp., 1946-47; resident internal medicine U. Ark. Sch. Medicine, 1949-52, instr. medicine, 1952-53, asst. prof., 1953-61, assoc. prof., 1962-68, prof., 1968—, dir. cardiology div., 1969-77, dir. cardiovascular research, 1977—, dir. continuing med. edn., 1977—; chief cardiology sect. VA Hosp., Little Rock, 1956-68; Del. U.S. Pharmacopeial Conv., 1970; mem. so. regional research and adv. com. Am. Heart Assn., 1969-70. Contbr. articles to profl. publs. Bd. dirs. Ark. Heart Assn., 1960—, sec., 1955-56, pres., 1959-60. Served with AUS, 1943-46; Served with USAF, 1947-49. Recipient Casimir Funk award, 1975. Mem. A.C.P. (gov. Ark. 1979—), Am. Coll. Cardiology (gov. Ark. 1962-65, 68-71), Soc. Nuclear Medicine, N.Y. Acad. Scis., A.M.A., So. Soc. Clin. Investigation, Assn. Univ. Cardiologists, Sigma Xi, Alpha Omega Alpha, Alpha Epsilon Delta, Sigma Chi. Clubs: Mason., Medical Center Camera, Raquet., Med. Ctr. Scuba (v.p. 1983-84). Pioneer research tritium labelled digoxin. Office: 300 E Roosevelt Rd Little Rock AR 72206

DOHERTY, JAMES MARTIN, advertising consultant; b. Sharon, N.D., June 23, 1916; s. David James and Anne (Westlund) D.; m. Virginia Mae Deitch, June 20, 1956 (div. 1961); m. Rosella Marie Rauh, Feb. 2, 1963; children: Shawn, Dennis, Randall. Student, Buena Vista Coll., Storm Lake, Iowa, 1938-40. Underwriter Nationwide Ins. Co., Columbus, Ohio, 1948-51, dir. advt. and promotion, 1952-72, v.p. advt. and promotion, 1973-81; advt. cons., Columbus, 1982—. Served with U.S. Mcht. Marine, 1943-45. Recipient best of show awards Life Ins. Advertisers Am., 1976, 77, 78. Mem. Sales Promotion Execs., Advt. Fedn. Am., Columbus Advt. Fedn. Democrat. Roman Catholic. Club: Brookside Country (Columbus) (dir. 1960-63). Home: 2761 Helston Rd Columbus OH 43220

DOHERTY, JOSEPHINE KRISTAN, research administrator; b. Glen Cove, N.Y., Sept. 2, 1924; d. John Jacob and Joan (Blazic) Kristan; m. Joseph C. Doherty, Nov. 21, 1952. A.B., Hunter Coll., 1945; postgrad., N.Y. U., 1950-52. Research asst. Hodgkins Disease Research Lab., 1948-52, Columbia U. Coll. Physicians and Surgeons, 1950-52, NIH, 1952-54; research analyst Sci. Info. Exchange, 1954-57; research mgr. NSF, Washington, 1957-76, with Div. Applied Research, 1976-81, with Div. Environ. Biology, 1981-82; detailed to Dept. State-UNESCO Commn., 1976-77; exec. dir. Inst. Ecology, Arlington, VA., 1982—; mem. U.S. nat. com. UNESCO Man and Biosphere Program, 1973-76. Fellow AAAS; mem. Ecol. Soc. Am. (council), Am. Inst. Biol. Scis., Am. Soc. Limnology and Oceanography. Home: 810 S Royal St Alexandria VA 23314 Office: Inst Ecology 1401 Wilson Blvd PO Box 9197 Arlington VA 22209

DOHERTY, THOMAS, publisher; b. Hartford, Conn., Apr. 23, 1935; s. Thomas and Elizabeth (Story) D.; m. Barbara Slocum, Feb. 15, 1958; children: Linda, Kathleen, Thomas W. Student, Trinity Coll., Hartford, 1957. From salesman to div. sales mgr. Pocket Books, 1958-69; nat. sales mgr. Simon & Schuster, 1969-76; pub. Tempo Books, 1971-75; pub., gen. mgr. Ace and Tempo divs. Grossett & Dunlap Inc., 1976-80; founder, pres. Tom Doherty Assos., Inc. (pub. Tor Books), N.Y.C., 1980—; cons. Richard Gallen Inc. Mem. World Sci. Fiction Assn. (charter). Republican. Roman Catholic. Home: 56 Jefferson Ave Rockville Centre NY 11570 Office: 8 W 36th St New York NY 10018

DOHERTY, THOMAS JOSEPH, brokerage company executive; b. Cambridge, Mass., Oct. 20, 1933; s. Thomas Joseph and Margaret Cecelia (O'Connell) D.; m. Carol Anne Conroy, Jan. 5, 1957; children: William, John, Robert, Susan. A.B. cum laude, Suffolk U., Boston, 1961. With Merrill Lynch, Pierce, Fenner & Smith Inc., N.Y.C., 1958—, v.p., 1978—; mng. dir. Merrill Lynch White Weld Capital Markets Group, 1979—; trustee Cin. Stock Exchange, 1979-83; mem. Am. Stock Exchange, N.Y. Stock Exchange; bd. govs. Pacific Stock Exchange. Served with AUS, 1953-55. Mem. Security Traders Assn.

N.Y., Gen. Alumni Assn. Suffolk U. (dir. 1976-77). Republican. Roman Catholic. 06820

DOHERTY, WILLIAM THOMAS, JR., history educator; b. Cape Girardeau, Mo., Mar. 30, 1923; s. William Thomas and Kittie (Baird) D.; m. Dorothy Ashley Huff, Aug. 13, 1947; children: Victor Sargent, Dorothy Ashley, Catherine Baird, Julia Holbrook, William Thomas III. A.B., B.S., S.E., Mo. State Coll., 1943; M.A., Am. U., 1950; Ph.D., U. Mo., 1951. Instr. history Westminster Coll., Fulton, Mo., 1947-48, Christian Coll., 1949-50, U. Mo., 1948-49, 50-51; asst. prof. history U. Miss., 1951-53; asst. prof., then assoc. prof. history U. Ark., 1953-56; assoc. prof. history U. Miss., 1956-58, prof., chmn. dept. history, 1958-61; prof. history, dir. Ford Found. 3 yr. Master's program Kan. State U., Manhattan, 1961-63; prof. history, chmn. dept. W.Va. U., Morgantown, 1963-79, univ. historian, 1979. Author: Louis Houck: Missouri Historian and Entrepreneur, 1960, Berkeley, U.S.A.: A Bicentennial History of a Virginia and West Virginia County 1772-1972, 1972, West Virginia History, 1974, West Virginia University: Symbol of Unity in a Sectionalized State, 1982, West Virginia Social Studies, 1984; Editor: Minerals, Vol. IV in Conservation History of the United States, 1971; editor-in-chief: West Virginia History Jour., 1979. Mem. Am. Hist. Assn., So. Hist. Assn., Orgn. Am. Historians, AAUP. Home: 140 Waitman St Morgantown WV 26505

DOHLMAN, CLAES HENRIK, physician; b. Uppsala, Sweden, Sept. 11, 1922; came to U.S., 1958, naturalized, 1965; s. Gösta Fritz and Ebba Gustava (Ribbing) D.; m. Carin Björklund, Apr. 24, 1948; children—Lena, Jan, Ebba, Henrik, Peter, Erik. M.D., U. Lund, Sweden, 1950, Ph.D., 1957. Resident in ophthalmology U. Lund, 1950-52; asst. surgeon Univ. Eye Clinic, Lund, Sweden, 1954-58; research asso. Retina Found., Boston, 1958-62; fellow in ophthalmology Mass. Eye & Ear Infirmary, Boston, 1958-63, asst. in ophthalmology, 1963-66, dir. cornea service, 1964-75, surgeon, 1972—, chief of eye services, 1974—; dir. dept. cornea research Retina Found., 1962—; asso. prof. ophthalmology Harvard Med. Sch., 1969-73, prof., chmn. dept., 1974—, dir., 1974—. Contbr. articles to profl. jours. Served as lt. comdr. Swedish Navy, 1948. Decorated Order of Vasa; recipient New Eng. Ophthal. Soc. award, 1966; Friedenwald award for research in ophthalmology, 1971. Home: 49 Newton St Weston MA 02193 Office: 243 Charles St Boston MA 02114

DOHSE, FRITZ-EGBERT, university dean, mechanical engineering educator; b. Goettingen, Germany, Feb. 6, 1925; came to U.S., 1950; s. Johannes A. and Annemarie L. (Hesemann) D.; m. Helga E. Encke, July 30, 1953; children: Lothar A., Hans J., Dirk M. B.S., Tech. W. Berlin, 1945; M.S., La. State U.-Baton Rouge, 1954; Ph.D., U. Ill., 1962. Registered profl. engr., La. Chmn. dept. mech. engring. U. New Orleans, 1964-72, dean coll. engring., 1973—; dir. La. Maritime Devel. Corp., New Orleans, 1982. Pres. Univ. Terr. Nieghborhood Assn., New Orleans, 1980—; bd. dirs. German Seamen's Home, New Orleans, 1972—. NSF fellow, 1961-62. Mem. Gauss Soc., Am. Soc. Engring. Edn. Home: 6242 Curie St New Orleans La 70122 Office: U New Orleans Lakefront New Orleans LA 70148

DOI, JAMES ISAO, educator, univ. dean; b. Stockton, Calif., Feb. 28, 1923; s. Goichi and Asako (Asahi) D.; m. Mary Yamashita, July 11, 1945; 1 dau., Mary Margaret. Student, Muskingum Coll., 1943-44; M.A., U. Chgo., 1950, Ph.D., 1952. Asst. to textbooks and curriculum officer CIE-GHQ-SCAP, Occupation of Japan, 1946-48; research asst. dept. edn. U. Chgo., 1951; budget analyst, asst. to chancellor N.Mex. Bd. Ednl. Finance, Santa Fe, 1952-56, asst. chancellor, 1956-57; dir. instl. research, asso. prof. edn. U. Colo., 1957-60, asso. provost, 1960-63, prof. edn. and sociology, 1962-63; dir. instnl. research, prof. edn. N.Y. U., 1963-64; prof. higher edn. U. Mich., Ann Arbor, 1964-71, dir., 1970-71; dean Grad. Sch. Edn. and Human Devel., U. Rochester, N.Y., 1971-79, Coll. Edn., U. Wash., Seattle, 1979—; cons. Nat. Endowment for Humanities, 1968-72; Dir. studies Colo. Assn. State-Supported Instns. Higher Edn., 1957-60; cons. U.S. Office Edn., 1965-71. Contbr. articles to profl. jours. Trustee Alice Lloyd Coll. Served with AUS, 1944-46. Mem. Am. Ednl. Research Assn., Assn. Higher Edn., Assn. Instnl. Research (exec. com. 1965-67), Am. Sociol. Assn., Phi Beta Kappa. Address: College of Education Univ of Wash Seattle WA 98195

DOIG, JAMESON WALLACE, politics educator; b. Oakland, Calif., June 12, 1933; s. James Rufus and Mary (Jameson) D.; m. Joan Nishimoto, Oct. 8, 1955; children: Rachel, Stephen, Sarah. A.B., Dartmouth Coll., 1954; M.P.A., Princeton U., 1958, M.A., 1959, Ph.D., 1961. Research asst. N.J. Republican Com., 1957; staff mem. Brookings Instn., 1959-61; from asst. prof. to prof. politics Princeton, 1961—, asso. dean, 1972-73, dir. univ. research program in criminal justice, 1973—; Cons. Fels Fund, 1966-68, Daniel and Florence Guggenheim Found., 1970—, Nat. Prison Overcrowding Project, 1983—, Lavanburg Found., 1983—; vis. prof. John Jay Coll. Criminal Justice, 1967-68, 70-72; Mem. adv. com. Gov. N.J., 1965-70; mem. adv. coms. Am. Bar Assn., 1974-78; mem. adv. bd. Police Found., 1977-78; mem. adv. council N.J. Dept. Corrections, 1974-82, vice-chmn., 1980-82; cons. on parole to gov. of N.J., 1975-78; Bd. dirs. N.J. Assn. on Correction, 1971-74, 80-82, N.J. Bar Inst. & Law Center, 1974-78, Nat. Center for Adminstrv. Justice, 1979-82, S. Forty Corp., 1980-82. Author: Metropolitan Transportation Politics and the New York Region, 1966, (with D.E. Mann) The Assistant Secretaries, 1965, (with D.T. Stanley and D.E. Mann) Men Who Govern, 1967, (with M. Danielson) New York: The Politics of Urban Regional Development, 1982; Co-author, editor: Criminal Corrections: Ideals and Realities; contbr.: Governing the States and Localities, 1969, Agenda for a City, 1970, Metropolitan Politics, 1971, Urban Politics and Policy-Making, 1973, Crime and Criminal Justice, 1975, Public Administration and Public Policy, 1977, Determinants of Law Enforcement Policies, 1979; Adv. editor, Clark Boardman Pubs., 1980-83. Served to lt. (j.g.) USNR, 1954-56. Mem. Am. Correctional Assn., Am. Polit. Sci. Assn., Am. Soc. Pub. Adminstrn., Policy Studies Orgn. Home: 122 Moore St Princeton NJ 08540 Office: Woodrow Wilson School Princeton NJ 08544

DOIRON, JOSEPH AUBIN, Can. provincial ofcl., dentist; b. North Rustico, P.E.I., Can., June 10, 1922; s. Adolphe O. and Mary E. (Pineau) D.; m. Rose Bernice Gallant, June 17, 1950; children—Paul, Robert, Pierre, Simonne, Colette, Omer, Marc. B.A., St. Anne's Coll., Can., 1946, H.H.D. (hon.), 1980; D.D.S., U. Montreal, Can., 1951; LL.D. (hon.), Dalhousie U., 1981. Practice dentistry, Summerside, P.E.I., 1951-79, lt. gov. of, P.E.I., 1980—. Founding pres. Acadian Mardi Gras Assn., 1964; pres. Summerside (P.E.I.) Kinsmen, 1956-57, St. Paul's Parish Council, St. Paul's Roman Cath. Ch., 1969; P.E.I. rep Can. Folk Arts Council, 1968; bd. dirs. P.E.I. Heritage Found., 1970, Summerside Co-op Assn.; trustee Summerside Sch. Bd., 1956-68. Decorated knight of grace Order of St. John. Mem. Dental Assn. P.E.I. (pres.), Can. Dental Assn. (gov. 1971-76), La Societe Saint Thomas d'Aquin, Acadian Mus. Assn., Greater Summerside C. of C. Club: K.C. (grand knight 1956-57). Office: Province House Charlottetown PE C1A 7L9 Canada

DOISY, EDWARD ADELBERT, biochemist; b. Hume, Ill., Nov. 13, 1893; s. Edward Perez and Ada (Alley) D.; m. Alice Ackert, July 20, 1918 (dec. 1964); children—Edward Adelbert (dec.), Robert Ackert, Philip Perez, Richard Joseph (dec.); m. Margaret McCormick, Apr. 19, 1965. A.B., U. Ill., 1914, M.S., 1916; Ph.D., Harvard U., 1920; D.Sc., Washington U., 1940, Yale U., 1940, U. Chgo., 1941, Central Coll., 1942, U. Ill., 1960, Gustavus Adolphus Coll., 1963; LL.D., St. Louis U., 1955; Docteur Honoris Causa, U. Paris, 1945. Asst. in biochemistry Harvard Med. Sch., 1915-17; instr., asso. and asso. prof. biochemistry Washington U. Sch. Medicine, St. Louis, 1919-23; prof. biochemistry, dir. dept. St. Louis U. Sch. Medicine, 1923-65, Distinguished Service prof. biochemistry, emeritus, also dir. emeritus Edward A. Doisy dept. biochemistry, 1965—; adminsrv. bd.; dir. dept. biochemistry, biochemist St. Mary's Hosp., St. Louis, 1924—; Several named lectures at various univs. and soc. meetings.; Mem. League of Nations com. for standardization sex hormones, London, 1932, 35. Author: (with Edgar Allen and Charles H. Danforth) Sex and Internal Secretions, 1939; Contbr. articles on blood buffers, sex hormones, vitamin K, and antibiotic compounds to profl. jours. Served to 2d lt. U.S. Army, 1917-19. Recipient Gold medal St. Louis Med. Soc., 1935; Philip A. Conne medal Chemists Club N.Y., 1935; St. Louis award, 1939; Willard Gibbs medal, 1941; Am. Pharm. Mfg. Assn. award, 1942; Squibb award, 1944; Barren Found. medal, 1972. Mem. Am. Soc. Biol. Chemists (council 1926-27, 34-37, 40-45, pres. 1943-45), Am. Chem. Soc., Nat. Acad. Scis., Am. Philos. Soc., Pontifical Acad. Scis., Am. Acad. Arts and Scis., Phi Beta Kappa, Sigma Xi, Phi Kappa Phi, Alpha Omega Alpha. Shared Nobel prize in physiology and medicine with Dr. Henrik Dam, 1943. Home: 4B Colonial Village Ct Webster Groves MO 63119 Office: 1402 S Grand Blvd Saint Louis MO 63104

DOJNY, RICHARD FRANCIS, publishing company executive; b. Norwalk, Conn., Apr. 24, 1940; s. Francis Joseph and Mary (Ross) D.; m. Brooke Maury, July 16, 1966; children: Matthew, Maury. B.A., Dartmouth Coll., 1962. Sales rep. McGraw-Hill Book Co., N.Y.C., 1964-69, editor, 1969-73, field mgr., 1973-76, regional mgr., 1976-77, dir. mktg., 1977-79, v.p., gen. mgr., 1979—. 1st lt. U.S. Army, 1962-64. Mem. Assn. Am. Publishers (head com. 1981—), Nat. Assn. Coll. Stores, Am. Mgmt. Assn. Roman Catholic. Home: 39 Burr Farms Rd Westport CT 06880 Office: McGraw Hill Book Co 1221 Ave of the Americas New York NY 10020

DOKE, MARSHALL J., JR., lawyer; b. Wichita Falls, Tex., June 9, 1934; s. Marshall J. and Mary Jane (Johnson) D.; m. Betty Marie Orsini, June 2, 1956; children: Gregory J., Michael J., Laetitia Marie. B.A. magna cum laude, Hardin-Simmons U., 1956, LL.B., So. Meth. U., 1959. Bar: Tex. 1959. Asso. firm Thompson, Knight, Wright & Simmons, Dallas, 1959, 62-65; founding partner firm Rain Harrell Emery Young & Doke, Dallas, 1965—; lectr. govt. contract law So. Meth. U., 1965—; gen. counsel Tex. Republican Com., 1976-77; mem. adv. council U.S. Claims Ct., 1982—. Editor-in-chief: Southwestern Law Jour, 1958-59; editor: ABA Ann. Devels. in Govt. Contract Law, 1975—. Pres. Hope Cottage-Children's Bur. Inc., 1969-70; visitor Law Sch., So. Meth. U., 1966-69; mem. law com. So. Meth. U. Bd. Trustees, 1977—; bd. dirs. Dallas Theater Center, 1976—, chmn. exec. com., 1981—, pres., 1983—; chmn. bd. dirs., pres. World Trade Assn. Dallas-Ft. Worth, 1979-80; bd. dis., sec. Theater Trustees Am., 1983—. Served to 1st lt., JAGC U.S. Army, 1959-62. Fellow Am. Bar Found., Tex. Bar Found.; mem. ABA (chmn. sect. pub. contract law 1969-70, ho. of dels. 1970-72, 74—, bd. govs. 1980-82), Tex. Bar Assn. (chmn. com. responsible citizenship 1971-73), Am. Bar Retirement Assn. (dir., trustee 1980—, pres. 1982—), Nat. Conf. Lawyers and C.P.A.s (co-chmn. 1983—), Nat. Contract Mgmt. Assn. (nat. bd. advisors 1983—), Dallas C. of C. (chmn. com. consular corps 1972—, chmn. internat. com. 1979—), U.S. C. of C. (council on procurement policy 1983—), So. Meth. U. Law Alumni Assn. (pres. 1976-77). Home: 6910 Dartbrook St Dallas TX 75240 Office: 4200 Republic Bank Tower Dallas TX 75201

DOKTOR, PAUL, musician; b. Vienna, Austria, Mar. 28, 1919; came to U.S., 1947, naturalized, 1952; s. Karl and Georgine Stefanie (Engelmann) D.; m. Caryn G. Friedman, June 17, 1979; 1 dau., Alexis-Karla. Diploma, Vienna State Acad. Music, 1938. Mem. viola and chamber music faculty U. Mich., mem. Stanley Quartet, 1948-51; mem. viola and chamber music faculty Mannes Coll. Music, 1952—, N.Y. U., 1965—, Juilliard Sch., 1971—; guest faculty mem. Mozarteum Salzburg, Institut de Hautes Etudes Musicales Montreux, Saratoga String Quartet Program, Bowdoin Coll. Summer Music Festival, 1977—. Second viola in Quintet series with, Busch Quartet, Europe, 1936-38; mem., Lucerne String Quartet; viola prin., Lucerne Symphony and Paul Sacher's Collegium Musicum, Zurich, Switzerland, 1939-47; founder, mem., Rococo Ensemble, The Duo Doktor-Menuhin, N.Y. String Sextet, New String Trio of N.Y.; solo concert tours in, Europe, Can., South Am., U.S., Mexico and Orient; contbr. articles to music jours. Recipient 1st prize Internat. Music Competition Geneva, 1942; Artist Tchr. of Year award Am. String Tchrs. Assn., 1977. Mem. Am. Viola Soc. (dir.), Am. String Tchrs. Assn. (hon. life mem.), The Bohemians (dir.). Home: 215 W 88th St New York NY 10024

DOKU, HRISTO CHRIS, dental educator; b. Istanbul, Turkey, Apr. 17, 1928; s. Anastas C. and Despina M. (Zumbuli) D.; 1 dau., Deadra. Certificate of physics, chemistry and biology, U. Istanbul, 1947, D.D.S., 1951; D.M.D., Tufts U., 1958, M.S.D., 1960. Diplomate: Am. Bd. Oral and Maxillofacial Surgery. Instr. oral surgery Sch. Dental Medicine, Tufts U., Boston, 1957-59, asst. prof., 1959-63, asso. prof., 1963-67, prof., 1967—, chmn. dept. oral and maxillofacial surgery, 1965, assoc. dean for hosp. and clin. affairs, 1966-76, asso. dean, 1976—; vis. surgeon Boston City Hosp.; chief dental service New Eng. Med. Center Hosps.; cons. VA Hosp., Boston, USPHS Hosp.; USPHS tchr. trainee, 1958-60. Contbr. articles to profl. jours. Recipient Hatton award Internat. Assn. Dental Research, 1960. Mem. N.E. Soc. Oral Surgeons, Am. Assn. Oral and Maxillo-facial Surgery., Omega Kappa Upsilon. Home: 37 Maugus Hill Rd Wellesley Hills MA 02181

DOLAN, ANTHONY ROSSI, journalist, speechwriter; b. Norwalk, Conn., July 7, 1948; s. Joseph William and Margaret (Kelley) D. Student, Yale U., 1970. Dep. press sec. Buckley for Senate, N.Y.C., 1970; assoc. creative dir. Agora Group, N.Y.C., 1972; press sec. Sandman for Gov., 1973; research dir. OEO, Washington, 1972-73; reporter Stamford (Conn.) Advocate, 1974-80; spl. research dir. and speechwriter Reagan-Bush Com., 1980; chief speechwriter, spl. asst. to Pres. White House, 1981—. Folk singer, N.Y.C., 1971-72; Recorded: album Tony Dolan, 1969. Served with U.S. Army Res., 1970-76. Recipient Nat. Headliners award for investigative reporting, 1977, Pulitzer prize for investigative reporting, 1978, Thomas Brindley award for pub. service New Eng. News Execs., 1978, Roy Howard citation for pub. service, 1978, Salurians medal for investigative reporting, 1978; Edwin Blair scholar Yale U., 1966-70. Mem. ASCAP, Investigative Reporters and Editors. Republican. Roman Catholic. Office: White House 1600 Pennsylvania Ave Washington DC 20500

DOLAN, JAMES FRANCIS, lawyer; b. Orange, N.J., Jan. 5, 1930; s. Thomas and Edna (Monahan) D.; m. Rita Hughes, June 27, 1953; children: James E., Stephen T., Michael, Richard F. B.S., Seton Hall U., 1950; LL.B., Columbia U., 1953. Bar: D.C. 1953, N.Y. 1957. Assoc. atty. Davis Polk & Wardwell, N.Y.C., 1957-66, ptnr., 1966—; dir. Triangle Pubs., Inc., Radnor, Pa. Served to lt. USN, 1953-57. Mem. ABA, N.Y. State Bar Assn., Assn. Bar City N.Y. Clubs: Knickerbocker (N.Y.C.); Seminole Golf (North Palm Beach, Fla.). Home: N Beach Rd Town of Jupiter Island Hobe Sound FL 33455 Office: 1 Chase Manhattan Plaza New York NY 10005

DOLAN, JAMES VINCENT, lawyer; b. Washington, Nov. 11, 1938; s. John Vincent and Philomena Theresa (Vance) D.; m. Anne Reilly, June 18, 1960; children: Caroline, James. A.B., Georgetown U., 1960, LL.B., 1963. Bar: U.S. Dist. Ct. 1963, U.S. Ct. Appeals (D.C.) cir. 1964, U.S. Ct. Appeals (4th cir.) 1976. Law clk. U.S. Ct. Appeals D.C., 1963-64; assoc. Steptoe & Johnson, Washington, 1964-71, ptnr., 1971-82; mem. Steptoe & Johnson Chartered, Washington, 1982-83; v.p. law Union Pacific Systems, Omaha, 1983—. Co-author: Construction Contract Law, 1981; contbr. articles to legal jours.; editor-in-chief: Georgetown Law Jour., 1962-63. Mem. ABA, D.C. Bar Assn., Barristers. Democrat. Roman Catholic. Clubs: Congressional Country (v.p. 1982, pres. 1983), Metropolitan). Office: Union Pacific Systems 1416 Dodge St Omaha NE 68179

DOLAN, JOHN E., utilities co. exec.; b. N.Y.C., May 9, 1923; s. John A. and Marie C. (Comiskey) D.; m. Anne Dolan, Feb. 16, 1952; children—John E., Bryan, Vincent, Robert, Raymond, Philip, Lawrence, Paul. Student, Rensselaer Poly. Inst., 1946-47; B.S.M.E., Columbia U., 1950. With Am. Electric Power Service Corp., N.Y.C., 1950—, chief mech. engr., 1966-67, sr. exec. v.p. engring., 1975-79, vice chmn. engring. and constrn., 1979—, dir., v.p. subs. cos. Served to 1st lt. USAAF, 1942-46. Decorated Air medal. Fellow ASME; mem. Nat. Acad. Engring., Tau Beta Pi. Roman Catholic. Home: 1487 Oakview Dr Worthington OH 43085 Office: 180 E Broad St Columbus OH 43215

DOLAN, JOHN RALPH, corp. exec.; b. Peabody, Mass., Apr. 20, 1926; s. John L. and Ethel M. (Tierney) D.; m. Lois M. Burkhart, Jan. 24, 1948; children—Mary Ellen, Geraldine (Mrs. Paul Bonardi), Dorothy, John, Peter. Student, Boston Coll., 1943, Bryant and Stratton Coll., 1945-46, Bentley Coll., 1948-50. Passenger accountant Cunard Steamship Co., 1947-50; office mgr. Dolan Tanning Co., 1950-56; gen. mgr. Flash Sportswear, 1957-59; budget mgr. CBS Electronics Co., 1959-62; controller/treas. Am. Polymer & Chem. Co., 1962-63; dir. financial planning E.G. & G., Inc., Bedford, Mass., 1963-71, controller, 1971—; dir. Eagle Industry Co. Ltd., Japan. Mem. Town Meeting, Danvers, Mass., 1964-70, Sch. Bldg. Com., Danvers, 1966-69. Served with USNR, 1943-45. Mem. Financial Execs. Inst. Club: Corinthian Yacht (Marblehead, Mass.). Home: 7 Ft Beach Way Marblehead MA 01945 Office: Wellesley Office Park Wellesley MA 02181

DOLAN, JOSEPH FRANCIS, lawyer, state official; b. Woodhaven, N.Y., Nov. 21, 1921; s. Joseph and Helen (Carlin) D.; m. Martha McMillen, July 3, 1959; children—Thomas, Peter (dec.). A.B., LL.B., St. John's U., 1947. Bar: Colo. 1949. Atty. U.S. Dept. Justice, Denver and Washington, 1947-51; practice law, Denver, 1953-60, asst. dep. atty. gen. U.S., 1961-65; adminstrv. asst. to U.S. Senator Robert Kennedy, 1965-68; pres. Shakey's Inc., Englewood, Colo., 1969-73; exec. dir. Colo. Dept. Revenue, 1975-77; U.S. atty., Colo., 1977-81; exec. dir. Colo. Dept. Hwys., Denver, 1982—; Mem. Colo. Legislature, 1959-61; asst. counsel spl. U.S. Senate Com. Investigating Lobbying and Campaign Finance; also asst. to Sen. John F. Kennedy, 1956-57; chief counsel House Select Com. on Lobbying Activities, 1950; mem. Colo. Commn. for Promotion Uniform State Laws, 1955-67. Author legal articles. Served with AUS, World War II. Home: 4101 S Colorado Blvd Englewood CO 80110 Office: 4201 E Arkansas Ave Denver CO 80222

DOLAN, MICHAEL WILLIAM, lawyer, government official; b. Kansas City, Mo., Dec. 13, 1942; s. William Michael and Vivian (Bush) D.; m. Laurel C. Cummings, June 13, 1964; children: Matthew, Abigail. B.A., U. Kans., 1964; J.D. with honors, George Washington U., 1969; M.L.T., Georgetown U., 1981. Bar: Va. 1969, D.C. 1970, U.S. Ct. Claims 1981, U.S. Tax Ct. 1981, U.S. Supreme Ct. 1973. Atty. Dept. Justice, Washington, 1971-73, dep. legis. counsel, 1973-79, dep. asst. atty. gen., 1979—; with Fed Exec. Devel. Program, 1978-79. Contbr. numerous articles to profl. jours. Served to 1st lt. U.S. Army, 1964-66. Recipient John Marshall award Dept. Justice, 1978. Mem. ABA. Office: Dept Justice 10th and Constitution Ave Washington DC 20530

DOLAN, RAYMOND BERNARD, ins. co. exec.; b. Chgo., Feb. 13, 1923; s. Christopher P. and Florence M. (Taylor) D.; m. Theresa, May 25, 1946; children—Paul, Ronald, Donald, Sharon. Student, No. Mich. U., 1942; D.Arts and Scis. (hon.), Mt. Marty Coll., Yankton, S.D., 1980. With Equitable Life Assurance Soc. U.S., 1946—, v.p., chief line ops., N.Y.C., 1971-74, sr. v.p. corp. communications, 1974-79, exec. v.p., chief agy. officer, 1979—; Inst. Life Ins. prof. in residence, econs. dept. St. Olaf Coll., 1975; dir. Equitable Variable Life Ins. Co. Vice chmn. Holy Spirit Ch. Parish Council, Stamford, Conn., 1968-71; chmn. Stamford dist. Boy Scouts Am., 1970-73; chmn. bd. dirs. Nat. Council Better Bus. Burs. Served to lt. col. USAF, 1942-45, 51-52, 61-62. Decorated D.F.C., Air medal with 4 oak leaf clusters. Mem. Nat. Assn. Life Underwriters, C.L.U.'s N.Y., Nat. Guard Assn. (life), Consumer Council, Am. Council Life Ins., Res. Officers Assn., Conf. Bd., Pub. Affairs Research Council. Republican. Roman Catholic. Club: K.C. (4th deg.). Home: 5 Kings Grant 377 S Main St New Canaan CT 06840 Office: 1285 Ave of the Americas New York NY 10019

DOLAN, THOMAS IRONSIDE, manufacturing company executive; b. Hastings, Mich., Mar. 31, 1927; s. Clifford and Katherine (Ironside) D.; m. Barbara Jane Sisson, June 11, 1948; children—Nancy, Sarah. B.S. in Indsl.-Mech. Engring, U. Mich., 1949. Pres. Kelvinator, Inc., Grand Rapids, Mich., 1969-75; sr. group v.p. White Consol. Industries, Inc., Cleve., 1975-80; sr. v.p. A.O. Smith Corp., Milw., 1980-82, pres., dir., 1982—, also dir. subs. Mem. Greater Milw. Com.; corp. mem. Milw. Sch. Engring. Mem. Met. Milw. Assn. Commerce (bd. dirs.), Machinery and Allied Products Inst. (exec. com.), Soc. Automotive Engrs. Clubs: Milw. Country, Milw. University. Lodge: Rotary.

DOLAND, JACK VAN KIRK, university president; b. Lake Arthur, La., Mar. 3, 1928; s. Earl A. and Irma (Williams) D.; m. Nell Richardson, Oct. 17, 1952; children: Diane, Connie. B.Ed., Tulane U., 1950; M.Ed., La. State U., 1954, Ed.D., 1977. Tchr., coach Sulphur (La.) High Sch., 1950-66, Dequincy (La.) High Sch., 1953-57; asst. football coach La. State U., Baton Rouge, 1966-70; athletic dir. McNeese State U., Lake Charles, La., 1970-79, pres., 1980—. Contbr. articles to profl. jours. Bd. dirs. So. Regional Edn. Bd., 1980—; mem. council Nat. Collegiate Athletic Assn. Bd., Kansas City; v.p. ARC, Lake Charles, 1982—; dir. First Methodist Ch., Lake Charles, 1970—. Served with La. N.G., 1948-54. Mem. Am. Football Coaches Assn. Methodist. Home: 4130 Ryan St Lake Charles LA 70609 Office: McNeese State U Ryan St Lake Charles LA 70609

DOLBEAR, F. TRENERY, JR., economics educator; b. Scranton, Pa., 1935. B.A., William Coll., 1957; M.A., Yale U., 1958, Ph.D., 1963. Asst. prof. econs. Carnegie-Mellon U., 1963-68; mem. faculty Brandeis U., Waltham, Mass., 1968—, Clinton S. Darling prof. econs.; vis. asst. prof. bus. econs. Stanford U., 1966-67; vis. assoc. prof. econs. U. Essex, 1975-76. Contbr. articles to profl. jours. Office: Dept Econs Brandeis U Waltham MA 02254 *

DOLBY, RAY MILTON, engring. co. exec., elec. engr.; b. Portland, Oreg., Jan. 18, 1933; s. Earl Milton and Esther Eufemia (Str) D.; m. Dagmar Baumert, Aug. 19, 1966; children—Thomas Eric, David Earl.

Student, San Jose State Coll., 1951-52, 55, Washington U., St. Louis, 1953-54; B.S. in Elec. Engring, Stanford U., 1957; Ph.D. in Physics (Marshall scholar 1957-60, Draper's studentship 1959-61, NSF fellow 1960-61), Pembroke Coll. Cambridge (Eng.) U., 1961. Electronic technician/jr. engr. Ampex Corp., Redwood City, Calif., 1949-53, engr., 1955-57, sr. engr., 1957; Ph.D. research student in physics Cavendish Lab., Cambridge U., 1957-61, research fellow in long wavelength x-rays, 1961-63; UNESCO adviser Central Sci. Instruments Orgn., Chandigarh, Punjab, India, 1963-65; owner, pres. Dolby Labs. Inc., San Francisco and London, 1965—; cons. U.K. Atomic Energy Authority, 1962-63. Trustee Univ. High Sch., San Francisco; bd. dirs. San Francisco Opera; bd. govs. San Francisco Symphony. Served with U.S. Army, 1953-54. Recipient Beech-Thompson award Stanford U., 1956; Emmy award for contbn. to 1st video recorder, 1957; Trendsetter award Billboard, 1971; Top 200 Execs. Bi-Centennial award, 1976; Lyre award Inst. High Fidelity, 1972; Emile Berliner Maker of the Microphone award Emile Berliner Assn., 1972; Sci. and Engring. award Acad. Motion Picture Arts and Scis., 1979. Fellow Audio Engring. Soc. (bd. govs. 1972-74, Silver Medal award 1971, pres. 1980-81), Brit. Kinematograph, Sound, TV Soc., Soc. Motion Picture and TV Engrs. (Samuel L. Warner award 1978); mem. IEEE, Tau Beta Pi. Club: St. Francis Yacht. Inventions, research, publs. in video tape rec., x-ray microanalysis, noise reduction and quality improvements in audio and video systems; patentee. Office: 731 Sansome St San Francisco CA 94111

DOLCH, WILLIAM LEE, educator; b. Kansas City, Mo., July 11, 1925; s. Bruce Eugene and Mary (Mullinnix) D.; m. Elaine Thome Byers, June 27, 1948; children—Kathryn Marie, Eric Alan. B.Ch.E., Purdue U., 1947, M.S., 1949, Ph.D., 1956. Research asst. Civil Engring. Sch. and Joint Hwy. Research Project, Purdue U., 1949-56, asst. prof., 1956-60, asso. prof., 1960-64, prof. engring. materials, 1964—; cons. problems of cement and concrete. Served with USN, 1944-46. Recipient Dudley medal ASTM, 1966; Wason medal Am. Concrete Inst., 1968. Fellow ASTM (award of merit 1977); mem. Transp. Research Bd., Am. Concrete Inst., Sigma Xi. Research engring. materials, especially portland cement, concrete, aggregates. Home: 1407 N Grant St West Lafayette IN 47906 Office: Civil Engring Sch Purdue U Lafayette IN 47907

DOLE, ARTHUR ALEXANDER, psychology educator; b. San Francisco, Oct. 25, 1917; s. Arthur Alexander and Ella Elizabeth (Duncan) D.; m. Marjorie Elizabeth Welsh, Mar. 19, 1949; children: Peter, Steven, Barbara. B.A., Antioch Coll., Yellow Springs, Ohio, 1946; M.A., Ohio State U., 1949, Ph.D., 1951; M.A. (hon.), U. Pa., 1973. Diplomate: Am. Bd. Examiners in Profl. Psychology. Asst. psychology and edn. Antioch Coll., 1946-48; counselor Ohio State U., 1948-51; dir. Bur. Testing and Guidance, U. Hawaii, 1951-60, from asst. prof. to prof. psychology, 1951-67; prof. psychology in edn. U. Pa., 1967—, chmn. dept., 1967—; cons. Phila. Dept. Edn. Author articles in field.; Cons. editor profl. jours. Fellow Am. Psychol. Assn.; mem. AAAS, AAUP, Am. Ednl. Research Assn., Am. Personnel and Guidance Assn., Internat. Council Psychologists, Internat. Rehab. Assn., Nat. Rehab. Assn., Sigma Xi. Home: 543 Manor Rd Wynnewood PA 19096 Office: 3700 Walnut St Philadelphia PA 19104

DOLE, ELIZABETH HANFORD, secretary U.S. Dept. Transportation; b. Salisbury, N.C., July 29, 1936; d. John Van and Mary Ella (Cathey) Hanford; m. Robert Joseph Dole (U.S. Senator from Kans.), Dec. 6, 1975. B.A. with honors in Polit. Sci., Duke, 1958; postgrad., Oxford (Eng.) U., summer 1959; M.A. in Edn., Harvard U., 1960, J.D., 1965. Bar: D.C. 1966. Staff asst. to asst. sec. for edn. HEW, Washington, 1966-67; practiced law, Washington, 1967-68; asso. dir. legis. affairs, then exec. dir. Pres.'s Com. for Consumer Interests, Washington, 1968-71; dep. dir. Office Consumer Affairs, The White House, Washington, 1971-73; commr. FTC, Washington, 1973-79; chmn. Voters for Reagan-Bush, 1980; dir. Human Services Group, Office of Exec. Br. Mgmt., Office of Pres.-Elect, 1980; asst. to Pres. for public liaison, 1981-83; sec. U.S. Dept. Transp., 1983—; mem. nominating com. Am. Stock Exchange, 1972; mem. N.C. Consumer Council, 1972. Trustee Duke U., 1974—; mem. council Harvard Law Sch. Assos. Recipient Arthur S. Flemming award U.S. Govt., 1972; named one of Am.'s 200 Young Leaders, Time mag., 1974. Mem. Am. Newspaper Women's Club (asso.), Phi Beta Kappa, Pi Lambda Theta, Pi Sigma Alpha. Office: 400 7th St SW Washington DC 20590

DOLE, HOLLIS MATHEWS, cons. geologist; b. Paonia, Colo., Sept. 4, 1914; s. Edwin Enyart and Mary Velma (Mathews) D.; m. Ruth Josephine Mitchell, Sept. 29, 1942; children—Michael Hollis, Stephen Eric. B.S., Oreg. State Coll., 1940, M.S., 1942; student, U. Calif., 1941, U. Utah, 1951-52; D.Engring., Mont. Tech., 1972. With U.S. Bur. Mines, 1942, U.S. Geol. Survey, 1946; staff Oreg. Dept. Geology and Mining Industry, 1946-69, successively field geologist, geologist, asst. dir., 1946-55, acting dir., 1955-56, state geologist, 1956-69; asst. sec. mineral resources Dept. Interior, Washington, 1969-73; gen. mgr. Colony devel. operation Atlantic Richfield Co., Denver, 1973-76, Washington rep., 1976-79; mineral resource cons., 1980—; instr. geology Vanport Coll., Oreg. Extension, 1949-52; adj. prof. Portland State U., 1969-73, Oreg. State U., 1980—; mem. Nat. Petroleum Council, 1973-79, Law of Sea Adv. Commn., U.S. State Dept., 1974, 79, Antarctic sect. Ocean Affairs Adv. Commn., 1978-80; mem. fed. energy adv. com. U.S. Dept. Energy, 1974-78; govt. rep. SEA USE Council, 1979—; mem. adv. com. OSU Sea Grant, 1980—; mem. bd. mineral and energy resources NRC, 1981—. Councilor AGI Minority Commn., 1974—. Served from ensign to lt. USNR, 1942-46. Recipient Gold medal hon. award U.S. Dept. Interior, 1972; Disting. Service award Oreg. State U., 1973. Mem. Soc. Mining Engrs. of AIME, Am. Assn. Petroleum Geologists, Geol. Soc. Am., Soc. Econ. Geologists, Can. Inst. Mining, Assn. Am. State Geologists, Oreg. Acad. Sci., Sigma Xi, Sigma Gamma Epsilon, Kappa Kappa Psi, Delta Sigma Phi. Republican. Presbyn. Home and Office: 75 Condolea Way Lake Oswego OR 97034

DOLE, MALCOLM, physical chemist; b. Melrose, Mass., Mar. 4, 1903; s. William Andrews and Grace Weld (Soper) D.; m. Frances Hibbard Page, Oct. 27, 1928; children: Priscilla Page, Malcolm. A.B., A.M., Harvard U., Ph.D., 1928. Research phys. chemist Rockefeller Inst. Med. Research, 1928-30; instr. Northwestern U., 1930-35, asst. prof., 1935-38, asso. prof., 1938-43, on leave, 1943-45, prof., 1945-69, prof. emeritus, 1969—, chmn. Materials Research Center, 1964-68; Robert A. Welch prof. chemistry Baylor U., Waco, Tex., 1969-82, prof. emeritus, 1982—; dir. Nat. Def. Research Com. Lab., Dugway Proving Ground, 1943-44; research physicist radiation lab. U. Calif. and Oak Ridge, 1944-45; cons. Oak Ridge Nat. Lab., 1953-63, NSF, 1962-65; hon. mem. faculty U. San Marcos, Lima, Peru, U. Chile; mem. phys.-chemistry adv. panel Office Naval Research, 1948-50; trustee Gordon Research Conf., 1958-61. Author: Experimental and Theoretical Electrochemistry, 1935, The Glass Electrode, 1941, Introduction to Statistical Thermodynamics, 1954; editor: The Radiation Chemistry Macromolecules, vols. I, II; asso. editor: Chem. Revs., 1956-59; contbr. sci. articles to profl. jours. Awarded Army-Navy cert. of appreciation, 1948; named Most Outstanding Scholar, Baylor U., 1977; recipient Alumnus Honoris Causa award Baylor U., 1982, S.W. regional award Am. Chem. Soc., 1979. Fellow Am. Phys. Soc., Electrochem. Soc. (v.p. 1940); mem. Assn. Harvard Chemists (pres. 1942-43), Acad. Scis. Argentina (fgn. mem.). Episcopalian. Clubs: Ridgewood Country, Sheridan Shore Yacht. Home: 5813 Mt Terminal Dr Waco TX 76710

DOLE, RICHARD FAIRFAX, JR., lawyer, educator; b. Lowell, Mass., July 12, 1936; s. Richard Fairfax and Grace Priscilla (Haynes) D.; m. Linda Ann Ingols, Nov. 12, 1961; children: Richard Fairfax III, Robert Paul, Mary Grace. A.B. magna cum laude, Bates Coll., Lewiston, Maine, 1958; LL.B. with distinction, Cornell U., 1961, LL.M., 1963; S.J.D., U. Mich., 1966. Bar: Iowa 1966, Tex. 1979. Mem. faculty U. Iowa Coll. Law, 1964-78, prof., 1969-78; commr. uniform state laws, Iowa, 1969-79, Tex., 1981—; B.W. Young prof. U. Houston Ctr. Law, 1978—; Adv. mem. Iowa Uniform Comml. Code Legis. Study Com., 1973; cons. commn. Bankruptcy Laws U.S., 1972-73, Nat. Commn. Product Safety, 1969-70; cons. on bankruptcy revision U.S. Senate Jud. Com., 1974-76. Draftsman laws; author monograph. Legis. research fellow U. Mich. Law Sch., 1962-64. Mem. Am. Law Inst., Am. Arbitration Assn. Home: 9144 Kenilworth Dr Houston TX 77024

DOLE, ROBERT J., U.S. Senator; b. Russell, Kans., July 22, 1923; s. Doran R. and Bina D.; m. Elizabeth Hanford, Dec. 1975. Student, U. Kans., U. Ariz.; A.B., Washburn Mcpl. U., Topeka, 1952, LL.B., 1952; LL.D. (hon.), Washburn U., Topeka, 1969. Bar: Kans. Mem. Kans. Ho. of Reps., 1951; practice law, Russell, Kans., 1953-61, Russell County atty., 1953-61; mem. 87th Congress from 6th Dist., Kans., 88th-90th congresses from 1st Dist., U.S. Senate from Kans., 1968—; chmn. Republican Nat. Com., 1970-73; Rep. vice-presdl. candidate, 1976. Served with AUS, World War II. Decorated Purple Heart (2), Bronze Star with cluster. Mem. Am. Legion, VFW, 4-H Fair Assn., Kappa Sigma. Methodist. Clubs: Masons, Shriners, Elk, Kiwanis. Home: Russell KS 67665 Office: 141 Hart Senate Office Bldg Washington DC 20510 *

DOLE, ROBERT PAUL, appliance manufacturing company executive; b. Freeport, Ill., Nov. 12, 1923; s. Herman Walter and Louise Marie (Bornemeier) D.; m. Joyce Lindsay, Mar. 14, 1947; 1 dau., Luanne Dole Cloyd. B.A., Cornell Coll., Mt. Vernon, Iowa, 1948. Personnel mgr. Green Giant Co., Lanark, Ill., 1948-50, controller, 1951-52; asst. treas. Henney Motor Co., Inc., Freeport, 1952-53, Eureka Williams Corp., Bloomington, Ill., 1954-62; v.p. and asst. gen. mgr. The Eureka Co., Bloomington, 1962-79, sr. v.p., 1980, pres., 1980—; exec. v.p., dir. parent co. Nat. Union Electric Corp., 1980—; pres. affiliate Kent Co., Elkhart, Ind., 1980—; trustee Internat. Assn. Machinists Nat. Pension Fund, 1972-80; dir. Dometic, Inc., Bloomington, Ill., Appliance Components S.A. de C.V., Juarez, Mex., Tappan Co., Mansfield, Ohio, First Fed. Savs. & Loan Assn., Bloomington. Served in U.S. Army, 1943-46. Republican. Clubs: Masons, Elks. Office: 1201 E Bell St Bloomington IL 61701

DOLEY, HAROLD EMANUEL, JR., government official; b. New Orleans, Mar. 8, 1947; s. Harold E. and Kathryn (Wall) D.; children: Harold E. III, Aaron M. B.S., Xavier U., New Orleans, 1968. Account exec. Bache & Co., N.Y.C. and New Orleans, 1968-73; mem. N.Y. Stock Exchange, 1973-74; v.p. Howard, Weil, Labouisse & Fredericks, New Orleans, 1974-76; pres. Doley Securities Inc., New Orleans, 1976-82; dir. minerals mgmt. service Dept. Interior, Washington, 1982—; instr. So. U., 1970-81; fin. advisor Greater New Orleans Ednl. TV, 1970-81; mem. La. Minerals Bd., Baton Rouge, chmn. royalty acctg. com., 1980-81. Mem. fin. com. for Gov. David C. Treene of La., 1980. Named Outstanding Stockbroker of Yr. Shareholders Mgmt. Co., 1972. Mem. N.Y. Stock Exchange, N.Y. Futures Exchange, Nat. Assn. Security Dealers. Republican. Home: 616 Baronne St New Orleans LA 70113 Office: US Dept Interior 18th and C Sts NW Washington DC 20240

DOLEZELOVA-VELINGEROVA, MILENA, Chinese literature educator; b. Prague, Czechoslovakia, Feb. 8, 1932; emigrated to Can., 1968; d. Josef and Marie (Vichrova) Velinger; m. Lubomir Dolezel, Nov. 27, 1961; children: Marketa, Milena. M.A., Charles U., Prague, 1955; Ph.D., Oriental Inst., Prague, 1964. Research asst. Oriental Inst., Prague, 1955-58, research assoc., 1958-68, U. Mich., Ann Arbor, 1967-68; assoc. prof. Chinese lit. (U. Toronto), 1969-75, prof., 1975—; editorial bd. Project Chinese Lit. 1900-1949, European Sci. Found., 1979-83. Author: Ballad of the Hidden Dragon, 1971; editor, author: The Chinese Novel at the Turn of the Century, 1980. Fellow Social Scis. and Humanities Research Council of Can., France, 1977-78, Social Scis. and Humanities Research Council of Can., Stockholm, 1980-83, 1982. Mem. Assn. Asian Studies, Chinese Tchrs. Assn., Can. Asian Studies Assn. Office: Dept of East Asian Studies University of Toronto Toronto ON Canada M5A 1A5

DOLGER, JONATHAN, editor, literary agent; b. N.Y.C., Sept. 3, 1938; s. Henry and Laura (Zeck) D. A.B., Brown U., 1960. Asst. publicity dir. Simon and Schuster, 1962-65; asso. editor Fawcett Crest Books, 1965-66; mng. editor Dell Books, 1966-68; sr. editor New Am. Library, 1968; v.p., mng. editor Simon and Schuster, 1968-78; editor-in-chief Fireside Paperbacks, 1968-78; sr. editor Trade div. Harper & Row, 1978-79; pres. The Jonathan Dolger Agy., N.Y.C., 1979—; lectr. pub. procedures course Radcliffe Coll., New Sch. Social Research; pub. course NYU. Author: The Expense Account Diet, 1969; also articles. Office: 49 E 96 St New York NY 10128

DOLGIN, MARTIN, cardiologist; b. N.Y.C., Apr. 12, 1919; s. Samuel and Betha (Brodsky) D.; m. Jeanne Rydell, Feb. 12, 1950; children: Barbara, Deborah, Stuart. A.B., NYU, 1939, M.D., 1943. Diplomate: Am. Bd. Internal Medicine. Intern, resident in medicine Lincoln Hosp., N.Y.C., 1943, 44; fellow in intenal medicine Lahey Clinic, Boston, 1945, 46; fellow in cardiovascular disease research Michael reese Hosp., Chgo., 1947; instr. to assoc. prof. medicine NYU, N.Y.C., 1948-73, prof. clin. medicine, 1973—; attending physician Bellevue Hosp. and Univ. Hosp., N.Y.C., 1973—; adj. attending physician Montefiore Hosp., N.Y.C., 1948-68; cons. in cardiology Will Rogers Hosp., Saranac Lake, N.Y., Columbus Hosp., N.Y.C., 1960-70; chief cardiology sect. N.Y. VA Hosp., 1955—. Editorial bd.: Jour. Electrocardiology; contbr. articles in electrocardiography to publs. Served with M.D. U.S. Army, 1952-54. Fellow ACP, Am. Coll. Cardiology, N.Y. Acad. Sci.; mem. Am. Fedn. Clin. Research, Am. Heart Assn., AAAS, Alpha Omega Alpha. Home: 32 Mountain View Ave Ardsley NY 10502 Office: NY VA Hospital 24th St and First Ave New York NY 10010

DOLIBOIS, JOHN ERNEST, diplomat; b. Luxembourg, Dec. 4, 1918; U.S., 1931, naturalized, 1941; s. Charles Nicholas and Maria M. (Winter) D.; (m); m. Winifred Helen Englehart, Jan. 17, 1942; children: John Michael, Robert Joseph, Brian Charles. A.B., Miami U., Oxford, Ohio, 1942. Indsl. engr. Procter & Gamble, Cin., 1942, 46-47; alumni dir. Miami U., 1947-66, v.p. for devel. and alumni affairs, 1966-81; ambassador to, Luxembourg, 1981—; hon. consul of Luxembourg for, Ohio, 1977-81, also mem. bd. econ. devel., 1977-81. Contbr. articles on alumni programming and fund raising to profl. jours. Mem. Talawanda Sch. Dist. Citizens Com., 1960—; mem. Community Improvement Corp., Oxford, 1966-69; v.p. Dan Beard Council Boy Scouts Am.; bd. dirs. Oxford Community Chest; trustee Miami U. Found.; bd. dirs. Am. Alumni Council, 1970-74; chmn. internat. alumni com. Council Advancement and Support of Edn., 1972-76. Served to capt. U.S. Army, 1942-46. Decorated officer Grand Ducal Order Crown of Oak, comdr. Grand Ducal Order of Merit, Luxembourg; recipient A.K. Morris award, 1966; Benjamin Harrison medal, 1977; Frank L. Ashmore award Council Advancement and Support of Edn., 1982. Mem. Phi Beta Kappa, Beta Theta Pi, Phi Kappa Phi, Phi Eta Sigma, Omicron Delta Kappa, Psi Chi. Presbyterian. Clubs: Hamilton City, Oxford Country. Office: US Embassy 22 Blvd Emmanuel Servais 2535 Luxembourg

DOLICH, ANDREW BRUCE, professional baseball team administrator; b. Bklyn., Feb. 18, 1947; s. Mac and Yetta (Weiselter) D.; m. Ellen Andrea Fass, June 11, 1972; children: Lindsey, Caryn, Cory Daniel. B.A., Am. U., 1969; M.Ed., Ohio U., 1971. Adminstrv. asst. to gen. mgr. Phila. 76ers, NBA, 1971-74; v.p. Md. Arrows Lacrosse, Landover, 1974-76; mkg. dir. Washington Capitals, NHL, Landover, 1976-78; exec. v.p., gen. mgr. Washington Diplomats Soccer, 1978-80; v.p. bus. ops. Oakland A's Baseball, Calif., 1980—; dir. Sports Adminstrs. Program Ohio U., Athens, 1978-82, U. Mass., 1979—. Bd. dirs. Oakland YMCA, Calif., 1982—. Recipient Alumni of Yr. award Ohio U. Sports Adminstrs. Program, Athens, 1982, Clio award Am. Advt. Fedn., 1982. Democrat. Jewish. Office: Oakland A's Baseball Oakland Coliseum Oakland CA 94621

DOLIN, ALBERT HARRY, lawyer; b. Chgo., Nov. 28, 1913; s. Harry and Esther (Klitzky) D.; m. Ada Wohl, July 20, 1982; 1 son, Barry M. B.S., Northwestern U., 1936; LL.B., Loyola U., Chgo., 1943. Bar: Ill. 1943. Gen. counsel Goldblatt Bros., Inc., Chgo., 1951-63, financial v.p., sec., 1963-68, exec. v.p., 1968-79, also dir.; dir. Prospect Plaza State Bank, Mt. Prospect, Ill., 1961-63; Chmn. taxation com. State St. Council, Chgo., 1960-79; gen. counsel Chgo. Heart Research Found., 1962—; chmn. appeal bd. SSS, No. Jud. Dist. Number 4, 1970-76; mem. Ill. Internat. Trade and Port Promotion Adv. Com., 1974-78. Trustee Goldblatt Bros. Found., 1968-79, Spertus Coll. Judaica, 1970-73, Cancer Research Found., U. Chgo., 1963—; bd. dirs. Jewish Vocational Service, 1968-69, Highland Park (Ill.) Hosp., 1956-61, Civic Fedn. Chgo., 1971-79, Jewish Home for Aged, Chgo., 1961-67; bd. govs. State of Israel Bonds, 1961-67. Mem. Am., Ill., Chgo. bar assns., Ill. Retail Mchts. Assn. (sec., dir. 1971-79), Am. Technion Soc. (bd. dirs. 1962-68). Jewish (chmn. trustees synagogue 1960-63, pres. temple 1957-60). Clubs: Covenant (Chgo.); Green Acres Country (Northbrook, Ill.); Westview Country, Neptune Flamingo Yacht (Miami, Fla.). Home: 68 Lakeview Terr Highland Park IL 60035 Office: 55 E Monroe St Suite 4444 Chicago IL 60603

DOLIN, SAMUEL JOSEPH, educator, composer; b. Montreal, Can., Aug. 22, 1917; s. Joseph and Freda (Levin) D.; m. Inthia Leslie Pidgeon, Mar. 7, 1953; children: Leslie Elizabeth, John Joseph. Mus.B., U. Toronto, 1942, Mus.D., 1956. Tchr., Royal Conservatory of Music, Toronto, 1945—, also lectr.; dir. Can. Music Center, 1970-75. Compositions include: (for orch.) Symphony No. 2; chamber music Sonatina; 3 sonatas for flute, violin and violoncello with tape, 1973; opera Casino; cantata Ricercar for Guitar Solo, 1974, Concerto for Piano and Orchestra, 1974, Adikia for 1-5 accordions and tape, Fantasy for guitar solo, Symphony No. 3, Prelude, Interlude and Fantasy for violoncello, Sonata for Violoncello and Piano, 1978, Deuteronomy XXXII for flute and voice, Concerto for 4 (2 pianos and percussion, Sonata Fantasia for Baroque Flute and Forte Piano, Trio for Piano, Violin and Cello, Golden Section (various instruments, dancer, slides, lighting), 1981, Kinesis I and II (trombone, cello), 1981, Quintet for Brass, 1981; films The Meeting Point; rec. artist. Can. Council grantee (5); recipient numerous commns. Mem. Can. League Composers (pres. 1969-73, dir. 1963—), Internat. Soc. Contemporary Music (v.p. 1972-75). Office: 273 Bloor St W Toronto 5 ON Canada *

DOLINAY, THOMAS V., bishop; b. Uniontown, Pa., July 24, 1923. Student, St. Procopius Coll., Ill. Ordained priest Roman Catholic Ch., 1948. Ordained titular bishop Tiatira and aux. bishop Byzantine rite Diocese of Van Nuys, Calif., 1981, installed, 1982—. Editor: Eastern Cath. Life, 1966-82. Office: Chancery Office 5335 Sepulveda Blvd Van Nuys CA 91411 *

DOLIVE, EARL, business; b. 1917; married. Mgr. charlotte ops. Genuine Parts Co., 1937-59, mgr. Mpls. ops., 1959-62, various positions, Atlanta, 1962-65, exec. v.p., 1965-73, vice chmn. bd., 1973—; dir. Office: Genuine Parts Co 2999 Circle 75 Pkwy Atlanta GA 30339

DOLKART, RALPH ELSON, physician; b. Moline, Ill., Feb. 1, 1913; s. Leo and Clara (Elson) D.; m. Marjorie Holbrook Ballou, Oct. 11, 1940; children: Pamela Dolkart Gorin, Jennifer (dec.), Lucy, John E., Catherine Dolkart Davidson, David R., Kimberley. B.S., Northwestern U., 1934, M.S. in Physiol. Chemistry, 1935, M.D., 1938. Diplomate: Am. Bd. Internal Medicine. Intern St. Luke's Hosp., Chgo., 1938; med. house officer Peter Bent Brigham Hosp., Boston, 1939-40; practice medicine, specializing in internal medicine, Chgo., 1940—; attending physician St. Luke's Hosp., 1941-51, Passavant Meml. Hosp., 1951—, pres. staff, 1969—; attending physician VA Research Hosp., Chgo., 1952-60; mem. faculty Med. Sch., Northwestern U., Chgo., 1942—, asso. prof. medicine, 1956-66, prof., 1966-78, prof. emeritus, 1978—; med. dir. USPHS (R), 1966—, now med. dir. Europe; sr. cons. med. affairs Europe, Travenol Internat. Services, Inc.; cons. Chgo. Bd. Health, 1946—, HEW, 1971—, Simon Stevin Inst. Med. Research, Brugge, Belgium, 1971—; mem. health care adv. com. Health Edn. Commn., Ill. Bd. Higher Edn., 1969-71; mem. adv. council div. health planning, resource devel. Ill. Dept. Pub. Health, 1968-70; mem. exec. com. blood donor program Mid-Am. chpt. ARC, 1965-68. Contbr. profl. jours. Chmn. bd. dirs. coordinating council Comprehensive Health Care Agys. North Eastern Ill., 1973-74; bd. dirs. Comprehensive Health Care Planning Inc., Chgo. (pres. 1968-71), Chgo. Health Research Found. Elizabeth Ward fellow, 1941-45. Fellow Royal Soc. Medicine; mem. Chgo. Med. Soc. (pres. 1968-69), Ill. Med. Assn. (mem. task force on physician shortage, service to medically deprived areas), Diabetes Assn. Greater Chgo. (dir. 1954-69, pres. 1969-71), Am. Diabetes Assn. (mem. nat. program com. 1966-67), ACP (life; com. internat. med. activities 1965-68), Central Soc. Clin. Research (emeritus mem.). Home: 18C Kastanjeboomstraat Brugge 8000 Belgium Office: 20 Kastirnseboomstraat 8000 Brugge Belgium *The achievement of "success" in my own concept of thinking is a term for the beholder. If, indeed, there is such a thing as success, it means to me only that one has attained a status of respect in the pursuit of life by one's peers in a chosen profession and/or the people one has served, and by the family one has reared.*

DOLLARD, ELIZABETH K., lawyer; b. Bklyn., Mar. 16, 1913; d. Hans C. and Lydia (Warner) Klintrup; m. Charles Dollard, Oct. 8, 1949. Student, Conn. Coll., 1932-34; A.B., U. Wis., 1936; LL.B., Yale U., 1939. Bar: N.Y. 1941, Vt. 1956. Practiced in, N.Y.C., 1941-56, Bennington, Vt., 1956-71; mem. exec. com. Bennington County Indsl. Corp. Founder Bennington Mental Health Clinic, 1956, Red Brick Sch., Bennington, Bennington Mus.; mem. exec. com., fellow Inst. Soc. Ethics and Life Scis., Hastings Center; mem. exec. com., v.p. St. Joseph's Coll., Paran Recreations, Yale Law Sch. Fund. Mem. Am. Bar Assn., Vt. Bar Assn. (treas.), N.Y. State Bar Assn., Internat. Bar Assn., Assn. Bar City N.Y., World Assn. Lawyers for World Peace Through Law, ACLU, Common Cause, Children's Def. Fund, Phi Beta Kappa. Address: 30 Sutton Pl New York NY 10022

DOLLEY, STEPHEN HAYDEN, real estate investment company executive; b. San Francisco, Apr. 21, 1920; s. Frank Stephen and Sarah Helena (McCormick) D.; m. Martha Jean, Apr. 6, 1961. B.A.,

Brown U., 1942. Vice-pres., dir. Winter Mortgage Co., 1946-62; v.p. Colwell Co., 1962-65; mng. dir. John Hayden Co., Los Angeles, 1965—; pres., chief exec. officer Colwell Mortgage Trust, 1969-80; chmn., pres., chief exec. officer CMT Investment Co., Los Angeles, 1981—. Served with USNR, 1942-46. Mem. Calif. Mortgage Assn. (dir. 1960-63), So. Calif. Mortgage Bankers Assn. (pres. 1961), Nat. Assn. Real Estate Investment Trusts (gov. 1980—), Lambda Alpha Land. Republican. Presbyn. Clubs: Colony Hunt, Los Angeles Country., Los Angeles Gruela. Home: Circle Four Ranch San Miguel CA 93451

DOLLIVER, JAMES MORGAN, state supreme court justice; b. Ft. Dodge, Iowa, Oct. 13, 1924; s. James Isaac and Margaret Elizabeth (Morgan) D.; m. Barbara Babcock, Dec. 18, 1948; children: Elizabeth, James, Peter, Keith, Jennifer, Nancy. B.A. in Polit. Sci, Swarthmore Coll., 1949; LL.B., U. Wash., 1952. Bar: Wash. State bar 1952. Law clk. to Judge Fred Hamley, Wash. Supreme Ct., 1952-53; individual practice law, Port Angeles, Wash., 1953-54, Everett, Wash., 1961-64; adminstrv. asst. to Congressman Jack Westland, 1955-61, Gov. Daniel J. Evans, 1965-76. Chmn. United Way Campaign Thurston County, 1975, pres., 1976, mem. exec. bd., 1977—; chmn. Wash. chpt. Nature Conservancy, 1981—; mem. exec. bd. Tumwater Area council Boy Scouts Am., 1972—; trustee Deaconess Children's Home, Everett, 1963-65, U. Puget Sound, 1970—, Swarthmore Coll., 1980—, Wash. 4-H Found., 1977—; bd. dirs. Thurston Mason Community Health Center, 1977—; mem. exec. com. Thurston Youth Service Soc., 1970—. Served as ensign USCG, 1945-46. Recipient award Nat. Council Japanese Am. Citizens League, 1976; Silver Beaver award, 1971; Silver Antelope award, 1976. Mem. Am., Wash. bar assns., Am. Judges Assn., Am. Judicature Soc., State Capitol Hist. Soc. (pres. 1976-81). Clubs: Masons, Rotary. Office: Wash Supreme Ct Temple of Justice Olympia WA 98504

DOLMAN, JOHN PHILLIPS, JR., magazine publishing company executive; b. Phila., May 22, 1944; s. John Phillips and Dodie Lewis (Porter) D.; m. Rebecca Critchlow, Oct. 29, 1977; 1 son, John P. III. A.B. in History, Wagner Coll., 1966; M.B.A. in Internat. Bus, Wharton Grad. Div., U. Pa., 1971. Asst. account exec. Benton & Bowles Inc., N.Y.C., 1971-72, account exec., 1972-73, account supr., Amsterdam and London, 1973-75, v.p., account supr., 1975-78; pub. Motor Boating & Sailing mag., 1978-80; gen. mgr. mag. devel. Hearst Mags., N.Y.C., 1980-82; v.p., asst. pub. Pub. div. Playboy Enterprises, Inc., Chgo., 1983-84, sr. v.p., 1984—. Contbr.: Marine Bus. mag, 1977-78. Served to 1st lt. U.S. Army, 1966-68; Vietnam. Decorated Bronze Star. Mem. Mag. Pubs. Assn., U.S. Power Squadron, U.S. Yacht Racing Union. Republican. Episcopalian. Clubs: N.Y. Yacht, Norwalk (Conn.) Yacht, Corinthians. Home: 657 Glenwood Rd Lake Forest IL 60045 Office: Playboy Enterprises, Inc 919 N Michigan Ave Chicago IL 60611

DOLMATCH, THEODORE BIELEY, consultant; b. N.Y.C., Apr. 22, 1924; s. Aaron and Diana (Bieley) D.; m. Blanche Ormont, Dec. 28, 1948; children: Karen Ann, Stephen Joseph. B.A., N.Y. U., 1947, M.A., 1948; student, Columbia, 1948-50. Tchr. Queens Coll., 1948-50; asst. supr. Sch. Gen. Studies, Bklyn. Coll., 1950-55; publs. bus. mgr. Am. Mgmt. Assn., 1955-62; pres. Pitman Pub. Corp., N.Y.C., 1962-71, Intext Publishers Group, N.Y.C., also Intext Ednl. Devel. Group, 1971-75, Info. Please Pub., Inc., 1976-80, Dolmatch Publs., Inc., 1979-81; cons. to govt. agys. and corps., 1981—. Author (sometimes under pseudonym Stephen Josephs) books and articles. Home: 298 Law Rd Briarcliff Manor NY 10510

DOLMETSCH, CARL (RICHARD), (JR.), English language educator; b. Kingston, Pa., July 5, 1924; s. Carl Richard and Margaret (Hollister) D.; m. Joan Downing, Feb. 7, 1948; children—Carl Richard III, Christoph. B.A., Drake U., 1948, M.A., 1949; Ph.D., U. Chgo., 1957. Faculty Drury Coll., 1949-51; tchr. Oak Park-River Forest High Sch., Oak Park, Ill., 1951-56; faculty Drake U., 1956-59, Coll. William and Mary, Williamsburg, Va., 1959—, chmn. dept. English, 1970-76; John Hay fellow Columbia, 1954-55; Fulbright lectr. Free U. Berlin, 1964-66, U. Erlangen-Nuernberg, 1977; vis. prof. U. Ga., summer 1968, Free U. Berlin, 1981-1982; lectr. Falkenstein Seminar in Am. Studies, W. Germany, 1966, 69, 71. Author: The Smart Set: A History and Anthology, 1966, (Co-editor) The Poems of Charles Hansford, 1961; Contbr. to: Literatur und Sprache der Vereinigten Staaten, 1969, American Literature in the 20th Century, 1971, Ency. Am. Biography, 1974, Southern Literary Study: Problems and Possibilities, 1975, Essays in Early Virginia Literature Honoring Richard Beale Davis, 1977, Southern Writers: A Biographical Dictionary, 1979; Music critic: Va. Gazette; staff contbr.: Orpheus, W. Berlin, Opera Can., Toronto, Opera Mag., London. Served with USAAF, 1943-45. Mem. MLA, AAUP, Music Critics Assn. Address: Dept English Coll William and Mary Williamsburg VA 23185

DOLPH, CHARLES LAURIE, educator; b. Ann Arbor, Mich., Aug. 27, 1918; s. Ray Aaron and Olive (Epker) D.; m. Marjorie L. Tibert, Apr. 15, 1944 (div. Nov. 1964); children—Lawrence Ray, Milton Charles (dec.), Noel Thomas (dec.); m. Brita Wilhelmina Thelin, May 12, 1965. B.A., U. Mich., 1939; M.A., Princeton, 1941, Ph.D., 1944; student, Brown U., 1941. Instr. Princeton, 1941-42; theoretical physicist Naval Research Lab., Washington, 1943-45; mem. tech. staff Bell Tel. Labs., Murray Hill, N.J., 1945-46; lectr. U. Mich., 1946-47, asst. prof., 1947-52, head theoretical div., 1952-54, asso. prof., 1954-59, prof., 1960—; guest prof. Tech. Universities of Munich and Aachen, Germany, 1957-58, Rockefeller U., 1971, U. Stuttgart, Germany, 1972; cons. Thompson Ramo Wooldridge, 1954-57, Hughes Research Lab., 1960, Rand Corp., 1960-66, Gen. Elec. Tempo., 1965—. Asso. editor: Jour. Math. Analysis, 1960—; Author numerous research articles areas of non-linear integral equations; gas dynamics; antenna theory; stochastic processes; non-self-adjoint operator theory; scattering theory; electro-magnetic theory; meteorology. Served with USNR, 1944-45. Jr. fellow Princeton, 1939-40; sr. fellow, 1941-42; Guggenheim fellow, 1957-58. Mem. Am. Math. Soc., I.E.E.E., A.A.A.S., Phi Beta Kappa, Sigma Xi, Phi Eta Sigma, Phi Kappa Phi. Patentee in field. Home: 3 Haverhill Ct Ann Arbor MI 48105

DOLPH, ROBERT NORMAN, oil company executive; b. Phila., Oct. 18, 1925; s. Norman L. and Eleanor A. (Morrison) D.; m. Eileen Wanamaker, May 17, 1946; children: Charles D., Russell G., Barbara L., David N., Douglas R. B.S. in Chem. Enging, U. Mich., 1946. Chem. engr. Exxon Research and Enging. Co., 1946-51; with Creole Petroleum Corp., Venezuela, 1951-75, pres., 1971-75, bd. dirs., 1970-75; exec. v.p. Esso Inter-Am., 1976, Exxon Internat. Co., N.Y.C., 1976, pres., 1976-79, Esso Middle East, 1979-81, Exxon Internat. Co., N.Y.C., 1981—. Served with USNR, 1944-46. Mem. Am. C. of C. in Argentina (past dir.), Venezuelan-Am. C. of C. (past dir.). Office: 200 Park Ave Florham Park NJ 07932

DOLPH, WILBERT EMERY, lawyer; b. Palatka, Fla., Dec. 29, 1923; s. Wilbert Emery and Ophelia (Reynolds) D.; m. Roberta Hundley; children: Wilbert Emery III, Kenneth Alan, Scott Marshall, Cheryl. Student, U. Ariz., 1941-42, LL.B., 1949. Bar: Ariz. 1949. Asst. city atty., Tucson, 1949-50, asst. atty. gen., Ariz., 1950-51, practice in, Tucson, 1951—; shareholder firm Bilby, Shoenhair, Warnock & Dolph, P.C., 1953—; counsel jud. com. Ariz. Senate, 1952. Pres. Pima County Young Democrats, 1952-53; v.p. Ariz. Young Dems., 1952-53; Trustee Tucson Med. Center, pres., 1973-75; mem. U. Ariz. Found., U. Ariz. Pres.'s Club; bd. visitors U. Ariz. Law Coll.; past bd. dirs. Ariz. Sonora Desert Mus., Ariz. Heart Assn., So. Ariz. Heart Assn., Tucson Festival Soc., Ariz. Children's Home Assn., Tucson YMCA; bd. dirs. Friends of the Library, U. Ariz. Served with USNR, 1942-43; to capt. USMCR, 1943-46. Decorated Air medal. Mem. ABA, Ariz. Bar Assn., Pima County Bar Assn. (exec. com., pres. 1974-75), Am. Bd. Trial Advocates, Navy League, Tucson Fgn. Relations Com., Phi Delta Phi, Sigma Chi. Episcopalian (vestryman, parish warden 1974-76). Clubs: Marching & Chowder Soc., Old Pueblo, Graduate, Skyline Country (Tucson); Quail Valley Tennis. Home: 6145 N Mina Vista Tucson AZ 85718 Office: Valley Nat Bldg Tucson AZ 85701

DOLPHIN, DAVID HENRY, chemistry educator; b. London, Jan. 15, 1940; s. Henry William and Isabella (Christmas) D. B.Sc., U. Nottingham, Eng., 1962, Ph.D., 1965, D.Sc., 1982. Research fellow Harvard U., 1956-66, instr. chemistry, 1966-69, asst. prof., 1969-71, asso. prof., 1971-74, vis. prof., 1980; asso. prof. U. B.C., 1979—; mem. study sect. NIH Bioanalytical and Metallobiochemistry. Author: Tabulation of Infrared Spectroscopy, 1977; editor: Biological Aspects of Inorganic Chemistry, 1977, The Porphyrins, 1979; bd. editors: Inorganic Biochemistry. Guggenheim fellow, 1980. Fellow Chem. Soc. London; mem. Am. Chem. Soc., N.Y. Acad. Scis., Can. Chem. Soc. Home: 3091 W 38th Ave Vancouver BC V6N 2X4 Canada Office: Dept Chemistry U B C 2036 Main Hall Vancouver BC V6T 1Y6 Canada

DOLSON, CHARLES HERBERT, air line exec.; b. St. Louis, May 13, 1906; s. Frank Edward and Hattie Mae (Harbison) D.; m. Bonnie Gooch, May 27, 1935 (dec.); m. Clara Allison, Aug. 30, 1962. B.S. in C.E, Washington U., St. Louis, 1928. Test pilot Curtiss Wright Airplane Co., St. Louis, 1930-31; pilot Am. Airlines, Inc., 1931-34, Delta Air Lines, Inc., Atlanta, 1934-40, chief pilot, 1940-42, 1945-47, operations mgr., 1947-48, v.p. operations, 1948-59, exec. v.p., 1959-65, pres., 1965-70, chief exec. officer, 1966—, chmn. bd., 1970-71, chmn. exec. com., 1971—, also dir.; mem. adv. council Trust Co. Ga. Served as lt. comdr. USNRF, 1928-30, 42-45. Recipient Sec. Navy Commendation with ribbon, 1945; Alumni award Washington U., St. Louis, 1967; Gold medal for extraordinary service FAA, 1972. Mem. Alpha Tau Omega. Club: Elk. Home: 660 W Conway Dr NW Atlanta GA 30327 Office: Delta Air Lines Inc Atlanta Airport Atlanta GA 30320

DOLUISIO, JAMES THOMAS, educator; b. Bethlehem, Pa., Sept. 28, 1935; s. Dominic and Sue (Powell) D.; m. Phyllis M. Sabolski, June 20, 1959; children—Thomas, James, Rebecca. B.S. in Pharmacy, Temple U., 1957, M.S., 1959; Ph.D., Purdue U., 1962. From asst. prof. to asso. prof. pharmacy Phila. Coll. Pharmacy and Sci., 1961-67, also asso. dir. dept., 1965-67; prof., chmn. dept. pharmacy U. Ky., Lexington, 1967-73; prof., dean U. Tex., Austin, 1973—; Cons. Smith Kline & French Labs., Phila., 1962-67, McNeil Labs., Ft. Washington, Pa., 1967-72, Hoechst Labs., Somerville, N.J., 1973—, Nat. Inst. Drug Abuse, 1976-78, HEW, U.S. Surgeon Gen., 1975-83. Contbr. to profl. and sci. jours. NSF fellow, 1959-61; Am. Found. Pharm. Edn. fellow, 1957-59. Mem. Am. Pharm. Assn., Am. Assn. Colls. Pharmacy, Am. Soc. Hosp. Pharmacy, Rho Chi. Office: Office of Dean Coll Pharmacy U Texas Austin TX 78712

DOMAN, NICHOLAS R., lawyer; b. Budapest, Hungary, Apr. 10, 1913; s. Odon and Irene (Parkany) D.; m. Katharine Huntington Bigelow, Aug. 25, 1951; children: Daniel Bigelow, Alexander Macdonald. Student, London Sch. Econs., 1932; M.A. in Law, U. Colo., 1935; J.D., U. Budapest, 1936; postgrad., Geneva Sch. Internat. Studies, 1937. Bar: D.C. 1947, N.Y. 1948, U.S. Supreme Ct 1948. Mem. research faculty U. Chgo., 1939-40; lectr. Rotary Internat. Inst., Chgo., 1940-41, 46-47; asst. prof. govt. and econs. Coll. William and Mary, 1941-42; asst. to U.S. Chief Prosecutor Nuremberg Trial, 1945-46; practice law, N.Y.C. and Washington, 1948—; adj. prof. taxation Sch. Law N.Y.U., 1967-77; founder Nicholas R. Doman Soc. Internat. Law U. Colo., 1967; symposium leader on internat. transactions Am. Law Inst.-ABA, Am. Soc. Internat. Law, World Peace Through Law; v.p., dir., gen. counsel Fed. Union, Washington; panelist, commentator on internat. politics for TV and radio. Author: The Coming Age of World Control, 1942; Contbr. articles to profl. jours., popular publs. Trustee Pitzer Coll., 1975—. Served to 1st lt. AUS, 1942-45; Italy. Recipient George Washington award, 1979; Norlin award U. Colo., 1980. Mem. Internat. Law Assn. (exec. com. 1965—), Am. Law Inst., Internat. Bar Assn., Union Internationale des Avocats. Clubs: Regency, Williams (N.Y.C.); Shelter Island Yacht. Home: 1185 Park Ave New York NY 10028 Office: 420 Lexington Ave New York NY 10017 *The one who strives merely to preserve the status quo may be respected by his community but will accomplish little for the betterment of society.*

DOMAR, EVSEY DAVID, economics educator; b. Lodz, Poland, Apr. 16, 1914; came to U.S., 1936, naturalized, 1942; s. David O. and Sarah (Slonimsky) Domashevitsky; m. Carola Rosenthal, Apr. 16, 1946; children—Erica, Alice. Student, State Faculty of Law, Harbin, Manchuria, 1930-31; B.A., U. Calif. at Los Angeles, 1939; M.A., U. Mich., 1941; postgrad., U. Chgo.; M.A., Harvard, 1943, Ph.D., 1947. Teaching fellow U. Mich., 1940-41, lectr., summer 1946; teaching fellow Harvard, 1941-43; economist Bd. Govs. Fed. Res. System, 1943-46; lectr. George Washington U., summer 1944; asst. prof. econs. Carnegie Inst. Tech., 1946-47; asst. prof. econs., research asso. Cowles Commn., U. Chgo., 1947-48; asso. prof. polit. economy Johns Hopkins, 1948-55, prof., 1955-58, dir. Russian studies, 1949-51; vis. prof. Mass. Inst. Tech., 1957, prof. econs., 1958-72, Ford prof. econs., 1972—; Vis. lectr. U. Buffalo, 1949; vis. asso. prof. Russian Inst., Columbia, 1951-55; vis. Fulbright prof. Oxford U., 1952-53; vis. prof. Stanford, summer 1957, Harvard, 1962, summer 1958, 76, Universidad de Los Andes, Bogota, Colombia, summer 1965, UCLA, summer 1968, Stockholm Sch. Econs., 1972, La Trobe U., Melbourne, Australia, summer 1974, Hebrew U., Jerusalem, 1979; disting. exchange scholar People's Republic of China, summer 1981; research asso. Harvard Russian Research Center, 1958—; exec. com. Conf. Research in Income and Wealth, 1966-68; cons. Rand Corp., 1951-81; lectr. Centro de Estudios Monetarios Latino- americanos, Mexico City, 1954; cons. fgn. study, research fellowship program Ford Found., 1954-58; chmn. com Slavic grants Am. Council Learned Socs., 1960-62; cons. Brookings Instn., 1956-59, NSF, 1958, 67-69. Author: Essays in the Theory of Economic Growth, 1957; Contbr. articles profl. jours.; Mem. bd. editors: Am. Econ. Review, 1957-59, The American Economist, 1963—, Jour. Comparative Econs, 1976-82. Center for Advanced Study in Behavioral Scis. Stanford fellow, 1962-63; John R. Common award Omicron Delta Epsilon, 1965. Trustee Omicron Delta Epsilon.; Fellow Am. Acad. Arts and Scis., Econometric Soc.; mem. Am. Econ. Assn. (exec. com. 1963-65, v.p. 1970), Royal Econ. Soc., Assn. for Comparative Econs. (pres. 1970), A.A.U.P., Phi Beta Kappa, Pi Gamma Mu. Home: 264 Heath's Bridge Rd Concord MA 01742 Office: Dept Econs E52-303F Mass Inst Tech Cambridge MA 02139 *If you do something, do it well.*

DOMARADZKI, THEODORE FELIX, educator, editor; b. Warsaw, Poland, Oct. 27, 1910; s. Joseph and Maria (Tomaszewska) D.; m. Maria Teresa Dobija, Apr. 22, 1954. Bac., Polish Coll., Zakopane, 1930; M.A., U. Warsaw, 1939; Litt.D., U. Rome (Italy), 1941; diploma, Acad. Polit. Sci., Warsaw, 1936. Asst. in diplomatic history Acad. Polit. Sci., 1936-39; assoc. prof. Pontificio Inst. Orientale, Gregorian U., Rome, 1943-47; prof. Polish lit. and dir. Polish Program and Paderewski Collection U. Montreal, Que., Can., 1948-76; prof., pres. Inst. Comparative Civilizations Montreal, 1976—; dir. dept. Slavic studies Inst. Comparative Civilizations, 1948-63; dir. Polish Research Center Inst. comparative Civilizations, 1963—; vis. prof. Fordham U., 1948-50; prof., dir. dept. Slavic studies U. Ottawa, 1949-53; lectr. Polish lang. State U. Rome, 1941-47. Author: Les Consideration de C.K. Norwid sur la liberte de la parole, 1971, Le Symbolism et L'Universalisme de C.K. Norwid, 1974; editor: Slavic and East European Studies, 1956-76. Head demographical div. Warsaw City Hall, 1932-35; chief edn. div. for Poles Brit. Embassy, Rome, 1945-46; v.p. Can. Inter-Amk. Research Inst., Montreal, 1964—; pres. Can. Com. for Orgn. World U., 1971—; dir. gen. Inst. Comparative Civilizations. Served to maj. Polish red Cross, 1944-46; Italy. Mem. Eastern Can. Assn. Slavic and Eastern Europe Specialists (hon. pres. 1976), Assn. Can. Writers, Can. Soc. Comparative Study Civilizations (hon. life mem.. pres. 1972-76), Can. Internat. Acad. Humanities and Social Scis. (v.p. 1975—), Can. Assn. Slavists (hon. life), Com for Can.-Polish Univ. and Sci. Cooperation (pres. Que. sect. 1969—), Que. Ethnic Press Assn. (v.p. 1979-81). Home: 5601 Ave des Cedres Montreal PQ Canada HIT 2V4 Office: Inst Comparative Civilization Montreal 5155 Ave de Gaspe Montreal PQ Canada H2T 2A1

DOMENICI, PETE (VICHI DOMENICI), U.S. senator; b. Albuquerque, May 7, 1932; s. Cherubino and Alda (Vichi) D.; m. Nancy Burk, Jan. 15, 1958; children: Lisa, Peter, Nella, Clare, David, Nanette, Helen, Paula. Student, U. Albuquerque, 1950-52; B.S., U. N.Mex., 1954, LL.D. (hon.); LL.B., Denver U., 1958; LL.D. (hon.), Georgetown U. Sch. Medicine; H.H.D. (hon.), N.Mex. State U. Bar: N.Mex. 1958. Tchr. math. pub. schs., Albuquerque, 1954-55; ptnr. firm Domenici & Bonham, Albuquerque, 1958-72; mem. U.S. Senate from N.Mex., 1972—; mem. energy and natural resources com., chmn. subcom. on energy research and devel.; mem. com. on environ. and public works; chmn. budget com.; mem. spl. com. on aging; mem. Presdl. Adv. Com. on Federalism. Mem. Gov.'s Policy Bd. for Law Enforcement, 1967-68; chmn. Model Cities Joint Adv. Com., 1967-68; mem. Albuquerque City Commn., 1966-68, chmn. and ex-offico mayor, 1967. Mem. Nat. League Cities, Middle Rio Grande Council Govts. Home: 11110 Stephalee Ln Rockville MD 20852 Office: Suite 434 Dirksen Senate Office Bldg Washington DC 20510

DOMINGO, PLACIDO, tenor; b. Madrid, Spain, Jan. 21, 1941; s. Placido and Pepita (Embil) D.; m. Marta Domingo; children: Jose, Placido, Alvaro Maurizio. Student, Conservatory in Mexico City. Made operatic debut, 1961; debut, Met. Opera, 1968; star tenor with opera cos. including, La Scala, Covent Garden, Hamburg State Opera, Vienna State Opera, N.Y.C. Opera, San Francisco Opera, Nat. Hebrew Opera in, Tel-Aviv; leading roles: 50 operas including Don Rodrigo, Tosca, Andrea Chenier, Don Carlo, Carmen, La Boheme, Errani; appeared in film: La Traviata, 1983; recs. for, RCA. Office: care Eric Semon Assos Inc 111 W 57th St New York NY 10019 *

DOMINGUE, EMERY, cons. engring. co. exec.; b. Scott, La., Jan. 9, 1926; s. Lucien and Mathilde (Hebert) D.; m. Beatrice Broussard, Dec. 30, 1950; children—Dave, Cal James, Kevin Drew. B.S., U. Southwestern La., 1949; M.S., U. Ill., 1955. Engr. La. Dept. Hwys., 1949-50, E. Tex. Constrn. Co., 1950-51; tchr. civil engring. U. Southwestern La., 1951-61; prin. Domingue, Szabo & Assos., Inc., Lafayette and Baton Rouge, La., 1957—, pres., 1964—. Mem. Lafayette Parish Planning Commn.; pres. La. Intracoastal Seaway Assn. Served with U.S. Army, 1944-46; ETO. Fellow ASCE (pres., cert. of appreciation Baton Rouge br.), Am. Cons. Engrs. Council.; mem. Am. Soc. Profl. Engrs., Profl. Engrs. Pvt. Practice, Am. Concrete Inst., Am. Congress Surveying and Mapping, Am. Public Works Assn., Am. Ry. Enging. Assn., Cons. Engrs. Council La. (A. E. Wilder award), C. of C. (exec. com., dir.). Democrat. Roman Catholic. Clubs: Kiwanis (Lafayette) (pres.); Century.). Home: 203 Beverly Dr Lafayette LA 70503 Office: 117 Pinhook Rd Lafayette LA 70501

DOMINGUEZ, JOHN HENRY, mental health administrator; b. Westfield, Mass., Dec. 23, 1945; s. Henry S. and Theresa Pauline (Calamitini) D.; m. Kathryn Lee Cameron, Oct. 21, 1967; children: Lisa, Stacy. B.A., St. Michael's Coll., 1967; M.S.W., SUNY-Albany, 1970. Cert. social worker, N.Y.; cert. mental health adminstr. Tng. team leader Hudson River Psychiat. Ctr., Poughkeepsie, N.Y., 1972-74, exec. dir., 1980—; treatment team leader Harlem Valley Psychiat. Ctr., Wingdale, N.Y., 1974-75, chief mental hygiene treatment services, 1975-78; dep. dir. Hudson River Regional Office, Poughkeepsie, 1978-80. Bd. dirs. Am. Heart Assn., Dutchess County, 1981-82. Named Most Disting. Grad. Rockefeller Coll. SUNY-Albany, 1983. Mem. Assn. Mental Health Adminstrs., N.Y. State Cert. Social Workers, Acad. Cert. Social Workers. Roman Catholic. Home: 33 Gilbert Dr Hyde Park NY 12538 Office: Hudson River Psychiat Center Branch B Poughkeepsie NY 12601

DOMINGUEZ, JORGE IGNACIO, government educator; b. Havana, Cuba, June 2, 1945; came to U.S., 1960; s. Jorge Jose and Lilia Rosa (de la Carrera) D.; m. Mary Alice Kmietek, Dec. 16, 1967; children: Lara Lisa, Leslie Karen. A.B., Yale U., 1967; A.M., Harvard U., 1968, Ph.D., 1972. Asst. prof. govt. Harvard U., Cambridge, Mass., 1972-77, assoc. prof., 1977-79, prof., 1979—. Author: Cuba: Order and Revolution, 1978, Insurrection or Loyolty, 1980; editor, author: Economic Issues and Political Conflict, 1982, Mexico's Political Economy, 1982; editorial bd.: Am. Polit. Sci. Rev., 1979-81, Internat. Orgn., 1982—, Social Sci. Quar., 1972-82, Mexican Studies, 1983—; editor: (with others) Pub. Policy, 1973-74. Mem. Inter-Am. Dialogue, 1982-83, UNA-USA Panel on U.S.-Soviet Relations, 1981; steering com. Aspen Inst. Governors Western Hemisphere, 1980-82; chmn. bd. trustees Latin Am. Scholarship Program of Am. Univs., Cambridge, Mass., 1981-82. Fulbridge-Hays fellow, 1983; mem. Antilles Research Program Yale U., New Haven, 1974-75; jr. fellow Harvard U., 1969-72. Mem. Latin Am. Studies Assn. (pres. 1982-83), New Eng. Council Latin Am. Studies (pres. 1980), Social Sci. Research Council, Pan Am. Soc. New Eng. (gov. 1979-82). Club: Elihu (New Haven). Office: Dept Govt Harvard U. Littauer M 37 Cambridge MA 02138

DOMINGUEZ, STEVEN, health care company financial executive; b. Tucumcari, N.Mex., July 10, 1942; s. Isamel and Fidelia (Benavidez) D.; m. Roberta Ann Jean, June 20, 1970; children: Steven Robert, Kristina Danielle, Jon Marie. B.A., Eastern N.Mex. U., 1968, M.B.A., 1969. Auditor Price, Waterhouse & Co., Los Angeles, 1969-72; sr. auditor Blue Cross So. Calif., Woodland Hills, Calif., 1972-73; asst. dir. cost reimbursement Nat. Med. Enterprises Inc., 1973-77, v.p. cost reimbursement, 1977—. Office: National Medical Enterprises Inc 11620 Wilshire Blvd Los Angeles CA 90025

DOMINIAK, GERALDINE FLORENCE, accountant; b. Detroit, Sept. 28, 1934; d. Benjamin Vincent and Geraldine Esther (Davey) D. B.S., U. Detroit, 1954, M.B.A., 1956; Ph.D., Mich. State U., 1966. C.P.A., Mich. Audit supr. Coopers & Lybrand, 1958-63; asst. prof. U. Detroit, 1965-68; assoc. prof. Mich. State U., 1968-69; prof. acctg. Tex. Christian U., Ft. Worth, 1969—, chmn. dept. acctg., 1974—; Arthur Young prof. acctg. Fla. A&M U., 1977. Author: (with J. Edwards and T. Hedges) Interim Financial Reporting, 1972, (with J. Louderback) Managerial Accounting, 1975, Managerial Accounting, 2d edit., 1978, Managerial Accounting, 3d edit., 1982. Ford Found. fellow, 1964-65. Mem. Am. Inst. C.P.A.'s, Am. Acctg. Assn., Assn.

Govt. Accts., Nat. Assn. Accts., Am. Woman's Soc. C.P.A.'s, Tex. Soc. C.P.A.'s, AAUP, ACLU, Beta Alpha Psi, Beta Gamma Sigma. Roman Catholic. Home: 4401 Cardiff St Fort Worth TX 76133 Office: Sch Bus Tex Christian U Fort Worth TX 76129 *To teach is to learn.*

DOMINICK, DAVID DEWITT, lawyer; b. Phila., Jan. 24, 1937; s. DeWitt and Elizabeth (Pullman) D.; m. Mary Helen Stein, Sept. 8, 1966; children: Buck, Andrew, DeWitt. B.A., Yale U., 1960; J.D., U. Colo., 1966. Bar: Colo. 1966, Wyo. 1966, D.C. 1974. Legis. asst. U.S. Senator Clifford P. Hansen, Wyo., 1966-69; commr. Fed. Water Quality Adminstrn., Dept. Interior, 1969-71; asst. adminstr. for hazardous materials control EPA, Washington, 1971-73; practice law, Washington, 1974-75, Denver, 1975—. Contbr. articles profl. jours. Vice-pres., Rocky Mountain Planned Parenthood; mem. Colo. Land Use Commn. Served to capt. USMCR, 1960-63. Mem. Am., Colo., Wyo., D.C. bar assns., Wyo. Hist. Soc., Nature Conservancy, Audubon Soc. Clubs: Met. (Washington); Denver Country, Univ. (Denver). Home: 300 Humboldt St Denver CO 80218 Office: 837 Sherman St Denver CO 80203

DOMINIK, JACK EDWARD, lawyer; b. Chgo., July 9, 1924; s. Ewald Arthur and Gertrude Alene (Crotzer) D.; children—Paul, David, Georgia Lee, Elizabeth, Sarah, Clare. B.S. in Mech. Engring. with distinction, Purdue U., 1947; J.D., Northwestern U., 1950. Bar: Ill. bar 1950, U.S. Patent Office 1953, Wis. bar 1959, Fla. bar 1964. Founder, sr. partner firm Dominik, Knechtel, Godula & Demeur (patent, trademark, and copyright attys.), Chgo., 1962-78, Jack E. Dominik (P.A., patent, trademark and copyright attys.), Miami, Fla., 1974—. Served to 1st lt., C.E. AUS, 1943-46; ETO. Mem. Am., Wis., Fla., Chgo. bar assns., Am., Chgo., Milw. patent law assns., Tau Beta Pi, Pi Tau Sigma, Tau Kappa Alpha. Clubs: Chgo. Yacht, Union League. Office: Suite 2110 One SE 3d Ave Miami FL 33131

DOMINO, EDWARD FELIX, educator, pharmacologist; b. Chgo., Nov. 20, 1924; s. James I. and Mary (Dolerzek) D.; m. Antoinette Kaczorowski, Nov. 20, 1948; children: Karen Barbara, Laurence Edward, Debra Ann, Kenneth Edward, Steven Edward. B.S., U. Ill., 1948, 1949, M.S. in Pharmacology, M.D. with honors, 1951. Rotating intern Presbyn. Hosp., Chgo., 1951-52; mem. faculty U. Ill., 1951-53, U. Mich. Med. Sch., 1953—, prof. pharmacology, 1962—; dir. pharmacology div. Lafayette Clinic, Detroit, 1967-81; vis. prof. neuropsychopharmacology Wayne State U., from 1959, clin. prof. psychiatry, 1973-80; Mem. study sect. pharmacology and chemistry Nat. Inst. Mental Health, 1965-69; vis. pharmacologist U.S.-USSR Cultural Exchange Program, 1971; mem. com. on nicotine and smoking antagonist drugs Nat. Cancer Inst., 1972-76; rep. U.S. Pharmacopeia, 1976—; spl. fellow Nat. Inst. Gen. Med. Scis., 1972-73; mem. ad hoc com. Sci. Adv. Bd., USAF, 1977-78; mem. med. research and devel. adv. panel to surgeon gen. U.S. Army, 1979—; mem. nat. sci. adv. bd. Brain Info. Service, UCLA, 1975-81; mem. ad hoc com. on marijuana and health Nat. Acad. Scis., 1981. Author and editor books in field.; Mem. editorial bd.: Jour. Pharmacology and Exptl. Therapeutics, 1958-65, Jour. Neuropharmacology, 1962—; cons. editor: Psychophysiology, 1968-75, Jour. Clin. Pharmacology and Therapeutics, 1973—, Pharmacology, Biochemistry and Behavior, 1973—, Research Communication on Substance Abuse, 1980—, Neurobiol. Aging, 1980—; supporting editor: Psychopharmacology, 1966-78, Archives Inter. de Pharmacodynam. et Ther, 1976—; asso. editor: Exptl. Neurology, 1975-80; contbr. articles to med. jours. Served with USNR, 1943-46. Recipient Sigma Xi prize medicine, 1951; Research award Mich. Soc. Neurology and Psychiatry, 1955; Sci. Exhibit 1st prize Am. Soc. Anesthesiologists, 1963; Sci. Exhibit cert. of merit AMA, 1964; Kravkov Meml. medal acad. bd. Inst. Pharmacology and Chemotherapy of Acad. Med. Sci., USSR, 1968; Cert. of Merit in Teaching and Research Mich. Psychiat. Assn., 1981; Alumnus award in research and edn. U. Ill., 1981. Fellow AAAS; mem. Am., Central electroencephalographic socs., Am. Soc. Pharmacology and Exptl. Therapeutics, N.Y. Acad. Sci., Internat. Soc. Cerebral Blood Flow and Metabolism, Washtenaw County Med. Soc., Soc. Exptl. Biology and Medicine, Internat. Brain Research Orgn., Soc. Psychophysiol. Research, Am. Coll. Neuropsychopharmacology (councilor 1969-71, 83-85, v.p. 1975-76), Soc. Biol. Psychiatry, Am. Coll. Clin. Pharmacology and Therapeutics, Nat. Assn. Standard Med. Vocabulary, Soc. for Neuroscis., Japanese Pharmacology Soc., Mich. Med. Soc. (del. to U.S. Pharmacopeia conv. 1979—, chmn. sect. clin. pharmacology and therapeutics 1973-77), Soc. Med. Cons. to U.S. Armed Forces, Internat. Soc. Neurochemistry, Mich. Psychiat. Assn. (asso.), Am. Psychiat. Assn., Sigma Xi (councilor 1961-63), Alpha Omega Alpha. Home: 3071 Exmoor Ann Arbor MI 48104 *My goal in life is to meet all of its challenges, pursuing a career in science and teaching, but above all living a wholesome and happy life as a husband and father.*

DOMJAN, JOSEPH (SPIRI DOMJAN), artist; b. Budapest, Hungary, Mar. 15, 1907; s. Paul and Maria (Lika) D.; m. Evelyn A. Domjan, Mar. 13, 1944; children—Alma Domjan Melbourne, Michael P., Daniel G. B.A., Hungarian Royal Acad. Fine Arts, 1940, M.A., 1942. Founder Domjan Mus., Sarospatek, Hungary, 1977. Exhibited in over 400 one-man shows including, Ernst Mus., Budapest, 1955, Mus. Art and History, Geneva, 1957, Cin. Art Mus., 1958, 74, N.J. State Mus., Trenton, 1966, 73, Dallas Public Library, 1964, 77, Museo della Bellas Artes, Mexico City, 1966, Cuyuga Mus., Auburn, N.Y., 1975; represented in numerous permanent collections including, Met. Mus., Victoria and Albert Mus., Tate Gallery, London, Mus. Modern Art, Paris, Albertina Graphische Sammlung, Vienna, Nat. Gallery Fine Arts, Library of Congress, Washington, Nat. Mus., Stockholm, Mus. Modern Art, Tokyo; author, illustrator 24 books; Author: The Proud Peacock, 1966, The Little Cock, 1966, The Artist and the Legend, 1975, Bellringer, 1975, Wing Beat, 1976, Edge of Paradise, 1979. Rockefeller Found. grantee, 1958; Recipient numerous prizes Soc. Illustrators, Am. Inst. Graphic Arts, Print Club of Albany, Am. Color Print Soc. Mem. Nat. Acad. Design, Soc. Am. Graphic Artists, Soc. Illustrators, Print Council Am., Silvermine Guild, Internat. Platform Assn. Address: West Lake Rd Tuxedo Park NY 10987

DOMKE, HERBERT REUBEN, state ofcl.; b. Hillsboro, Kans., Apr. 6, 1919; s. Henry and Lydia (Steltzer) D.; m. Joan Marie Sullivan, June 14, 1946; children—Catherine (Mrs. James Teague), Jane Alice, Elizabeth Marie, Henry Francis. Student, Wright Jr. Coll., Chgo., 1935-37; S.B., U. Chgo., 1939, M.D., 1942; M.P.H., Harvard, 1948, Dr.P.H., 1959; D.Sc. (hon.), Central Methodist Coll., Fayette, Mo., 1975. Intern Billings Meml. Hosp., Chgo., 1942-43, Chgo. Meml. Hosp., 1943-44; chief med. officer Chgo. Health Dept., 1944-47; health commr. St. Louis County Health Dept., 1949-58; dir. Pitts.-Allegheny County (Pa.) Health Dept., 1959-66, Health and Hosps., St. Louis, 1966-70, Mo. Div. Health, Jefferson City, 1971-80, dir. sect. med. care, 1980—; instr. U. Chgo., 1944-46; asst. prof. Washington U., St. Louis, 1949-58, prof. pub. health, prof. medicine, 1966; adj. asso. prof. U. Pitts., 1959-66; clin. prof. preventive medicine St. Louis U., 1966; prof. dept. community health and med. practice U. Mo., Columbia.; Mem. Pa. Gov.'s Commn. Health Services for Appalachia, Mo. Gov.'s Council Comprehensive Health Planning; med. adv. com. Mo. Div. Welfare, Bi-State (Mo.-Ill.) Regional Med. Program; mem. commn. to USSR urban health planning, 1966; co-founder Conf. Urban Health Providers; pres. U.S. Conf. City Health Officers, 1968-70. Editorial bd.: Pub. Health Reports, 1960-68; Contbr. articles to pub. health jours. Bd. dirs. Blue Cross Western Pa., St. Louis Tb Health Soc., Pitts. Tb League, Pitts. United Mental Health Services, St. Louis Hosp. Planning Commn.; trustee Cancer Research Center, Columbia, Mo.; Med. dir. USPHS, 1966—. Recipient Nat. Med. Assn. award, 1967; Mayor's Civic award City of St. Louis, 1970; Mo. Nursing Home Assn. award, 1971; Milton research fellow Harvard Sch. Pub. Health, 1948-49. Mem. Mo. State Med. Assn., Mo. Public Health Assn., Assn. State and Territorial Health Officers, A.A.A.S. (mem. commn. air conservation). Club: University (St. Louis). Home: Route 2 New Bloomfield MO 65063 Office: Missouri Div Health 221 W High St Jefferson City MO 65101

DOMMEN, ARTHUR JOHN, agricultural economist; b. Mexico City, Mexico, June 24, 1934; came to U.S., 1940, naturalized, 1958; s. John Henry and Sarah (Hall) D.; m. Phan Thi Hong Loan. B.Sc., Cornell U., 1955; Ph.D., U. Md., 1975. Mem. staff U. P.I., 1957- 63, bur. chief, Hong Kong, 1961-63; mem. staff Los Angeles Times, 1965-71, bur. chief, New Delhi, India, 1966-68, Saigon, Vietnam, 1968-71; agrl. economist Intech, Inc., Silver Spring, Md., 1975-77; mem. AID Mission to, Tunisia, 1977-79; with U.S. Dept. Agr., Washington, 1980—. Author: Conflict in Laos, The Politics of Neutralization, 1964. Served with AUS, 1955-57. Press fellow N.Y. Council Fgn. Relations, 1963-64. Home: 7716 Radnor Rd Bethesda MD 20817 Office: 500 12th St SW Room 342 Washington DC 20250

DOMMERMUTH, WILLIAM P., marketing educator; b. Chgo., June 29, 1925; s. Peter R. and Gertrude (Schnell) D.; m. H. Joan Hasty, June 6, 1959; children: Karin Jo, Margaret, Jean. B.A., U. Iowa, 1948; Ph.D., Northwestern U., 1964. Advt. copywriter Sears, Roebuck & Co., Chgo., 1949-51, sales promotion mgr., 1951-58; asst., then asso. prof. mktg. U. Tex., Austin, 1961-67; asso. prof. U. Iowa, Iowa City, 1967-68; prof. So. Ill. U., Carbondale, 1968—; Cons. bus. firms. Author: (with Kernan and Sommers) Promotion: An Introductory Analysis, 1970, (with Andersen) Distribution Systems, 1972, (with Marcus and others) Modern Marketing, 1975, Modern Marketing Management, 1980, Promotion: Analysis, Creativity and Strategy, 1984; contbr. articles to profl. jours. Mem. Am. Mktg. Assn., Am. Inst. Decision Scis., Phi Beta Kappa, Beta Gamma Sigma, Theta Xi, Delta Sigma Pi. Club: Court. Home: Six Rolling Acres Murphysboro IL 62966 Office: Dept Marketing So Ill Univ Carbondale IL 62901

DOMNICK, DONAL FREDERICK, tractor company executive; b. Danville, Kan., Aug. 12, 1921; s. Mahlon and Josephine A. (Clements) D.; m. Norma Jean Shoemaker, Nov. 7, 1943; children: Donna J., Dennis F., Terrence M., Stanley R., David D., Dee Anne, Elizabeth S. Grad., Wabash Inst. Personnel Devel., 1974. Dir. mfg. G.O. Caterpillar Tractor Co., Peoria, Ill., 1966-69; plant mgr. Caterpillar Tractor Ltd., Glasgow, Scotland, 1969-72, mng. dir., Gosselies, Belgium, 1972-74; plant mgr. Caterpillar Tractor Co., Joliet, Ill., 1974-77; v.p. mfg. and facility planning Caterpillar Tractor, Peoria, Ill., 1977-83; v.p. European mfg. facilities Caterpillar Tractor Co., Peoria, Ill., 1983—. Bd. advisors, exec. com. St. Francis Med. Ctr., Peoria, 1979—; bd. dirs. Med. Ctr. Facilities Corp., 1982—; trustee Peoria Civic Ctr. Authority, 1983—. Served with U.S. Army, 1944-46; ETO. Mem. Soc. Mfg. Engrs. (Internat. Engring. Citation award 1983), Robot Inst. Am. (dir.), Machinery and Allied Products Inst. (v.p. mfg. council). Republican. Roman Catholic. Home: 4716 Knoxville Ave Peoria IL 61614 Office: Caterpillar Tractor Co. 100 NE Adams St Peoria IL 61629

DOMOKOS, GABOR, physicist; b. Budapest, Hungary, Mar. 5, 1933; s. Laszlo and Aranka (Szekely) D. Dipl.Phys. with Highest Honors, Eötvös Lorand U., Budapest, 1956; postgrad., Central Inst. for Physics, Budapest, 1956-60, Dr. Phys. Math Scis., 1963. Research physicist Joint Inst. Nuclear Research, Dubna, 1960-63; sr. research physicist Central Research Inst., Budapest, 1964-65, 67—; lectr. Johns Hopkins, 1965-66; now prof. physics; research physicist U. Calif. at Berkeley, 1966-67. Fellow Am. Phys. Soc.; mem. Am. Math. Soc., European Phys. Soc., Italian Phys. Soc. Research and publs. on theory of interactions of elementary particles at high energies. Office: Johns Hopkins Dept Physics Baltimore MD 21218

DOMS, KEITH, librarian; b. Endeavor, Wis., Apr. 24, 1920; s. Reinhard Edward and Lillian (Gohlke) D.; m. Margaret Ann Taylor, Apr. 1, 1944; children: Peter Edward, David Laurance. B.A., U. Wis., 1942, B.L.S., 1947. City librarian Concord (N.H.) Pub. Library, 1947-51; dir. Grace A. Dow Meml. Library, Midland, Mich., 1951-56; asso. dir. Carnegie Library of Pitts., 1956-64, dir., 1964-69, Free Library of Phila., 1969—; cons. pub. library devel. programs and pub. library bldgs.; specialist, dir. library seminar for State Dept., Pakistan, 1964; pres. Pitts. Regional Library Center, 1967-69; Pa. del. to White House Conf. on Libraries and Info. Services, 1978—. Contbr. articles to tech. lit. Pres. United Mental Health Services of Allegheny County, 1963-65, Pa. Home Teaching Soc., 1969-76, Union Library Catalogue Pa., 1974-75, Palinet/Union Library Catalogue, 1975-77; vice chmn. Gov.'s Council on Library Devel., 1968-76; mem. Pa. State Bd. Edn. and Council of Higher Edn., 1975—; trustee On Line Computer Library Center, 1982—; Bd. visitors Grad. Sch. Library and Information Scis., U. Pitts., 1968—; mem. Museum Council; bd. dirs. Greater Phila. Cultural Alliance, 1972-75, Reading is Fundamental Found., 1971-72, Freedom to Read Found., 1970-73. Served with AUS, 1942-46. Mem. ALA (mem. council 1960-63, exec. bd. 1963-67, v.p. 1970-71, pres. 1971-72, chmn. com. on freedom access to libraries 1966-68, coordinating com. on library services to disadvantaged 1968-70, pres. library adminstrn. div. 1963-64, Lippincott award 1982), Pa. Library Assn. (pres. 1961, Disting. Service award 1976), World Affairs Council Phila. (bd. 1969-73), Internat. Fedn. Library Assns. (dir. pub. library sect. 1978—), Internat. Assn. 1972, City Libraries (pres. 1974-77), Spl. Library Assn., Community Leadership Seminar Assos. U. Pa., Beta Phi Mu (pres. 1962-64). Clubs: Pittsburgh Bibliophiles, Philobiblon, Franklin Inn (pres. 1978—), Art Alliance, Sunday Breakfast; Science and Arts (Germantown). Home: 3101 W Coulter St Philadelphia PA 19129 Office: Logan Sq Philadelphia PA 19103

DON, CONWAY JOSEPH, physician, educator; b. Newcastle, Eng., Dec. 1, 1922; s. Frank Austin and Rozanne (McHatton) D.; m. Jean Mary Wylie, Feb. 26, 1949; children: Felicity, Rosemary Don Light, Caroline, Paul, Penelope. M.B., B.S., Univ. Coll. Hosp., London, 1946, L.M.C.C., 1957. House physician Univ. Coll. Hosp., London, 1946, resident med. officer radiology, 1948-56; house physician Addenbrooke's Hosp., Cambridge, Eng., 1947; teaching fellow Harvard U., 1956-57; clin. fellow Mass. Gen. Hosp., 1956-57, vis. fellow, 1970; now prof., chmn. dept. radiology U. Ottawa, Ont., Can.; vis. prof. Vanderbilt U., 1977, U. Jeddah, Saudi Arabia, 1980, U. Calif.-San Francisco, 1984; dir. dept. radiology Ottawa Gen Hosp.; cons. radiologist Ont. Cancer Found., Ottawa Civic Hosp., St. Vincent Hosp., Ottawa, Riverside Hosp., Ottawa. Fellow Royal Coll. Physicians (London and Can.); mem. Can. Assn. Radiologists, Radiol. Soc. N.Am., Assn. Univ. Radiologists, Soc. Chmn. Radiol. Depts., Can. Med. Assn. Clubs: Rideau Squash and Racquet, Ottawa Athletic, Cercle Universitaire (Ottawa). Home: 20 Rideau Terr Ottawa ON Canada Office: X ray Dept Ottawa Gen Hosp Ottawa ON Canada

DONABEDIAN, AVEDIS, physician; b. Beirut, Lebanon, Jan. 7, 1919; came to U.S., 1955, naturalized, 1960; s. Samuel and Maritza (Der Hagopian) D.; m. Dorothy Salibian, Sept. 15, 1945; children: Haig, Bairj, Armen. B.A., Am. U., Beirut, 1940, M.D., 1944; M.P.H., Harvard U., 1955. Physician, acting supt. English Mission Hosp., Jerusalem, 1945-47; instr. physiology, clin. asst. dermatology and venereology Am. U. Med. Sch., 1948-51, univ. physician, dir. univ. health service, 1949-54; med. asso. United Community Services Met. Boston, 1955-57; asst. prof., then asso. prof. preventive medicine N.Y. Med. Coll., 1957-61; mem. faculty U. Mich. Sch. Pub. Health, Ann Arbor, 1961—, prof. med. care orgn., 1964—, Nathan Sinai disting. prof. public health, 1979—. Author: A Guide to Medical Care Adminstration: Medical Care Appraisal—Quality and Utilization, 1969, Aspects of Medical Care Administration, 1973, Benefits in Medical Care Programs, 1976, The Definition of Quality and Approaches to Its Assessment, 1980, Medical Care Chartbook, 1980, The Criteria and Standards of Quality, 1982. Recipient Dean Conley award Am. Coll. Hosp. Adminstrs., 1969; Norman A. Welch award Nat. Assn. Blue Shield Plans, 1976; Elizur Wright award Am. Risk and Ins. Assn., 1978; Nat. Merit award Delta Omega, 1978. Mem. Inst. Medicine, Assn. Tchrs. Preventive Medicine; fellow Am. Pub. Health Assn., Am. Coll. Hosp. Adminstrs. (hon.). Home: 1739 Ivywood Dr Ann Arbor MI 48103 Office: MCO-SPH II 109 Observatory St Ann Arbor MI 48109

DONACHIE, JAMES ROSS, hospital administrator; b. Dundee, Scotland, May 13, 1923; came to U.S., 1925, naturalized, 1946; s. John and Janet (Blair) D.; m. Evelyn Lacaeyse, June 30, 1954; children: Michael, David, John. B.S., U Iowa, 1949, M.A., 1954; M.S., U. So. Calif., 1950; postgrad., Columbia U. Resident in hosp. adminstrn. Memphis VA Hosp. and Bapt. Meml. Hosp., 1953-54; adminstrv. asst. to dir. Bklyn. VA Hosp., 1954-56; spl. asst. to dir. Salt Lake City VA Hosp., 1956-58; asst. dir. Roseburg (Oreg.) VA Hosp., 1958-61, Denver VA Hosp., 1961-68, Durham (N.C.) VA Hosp., 1968-70, North Chicago (Ill.) VA Hosp., 1970-74; dir. Grand Island (Nebr.) VA Hosp., 1974-75, Battle Creek (Mich.) VA Med. Center, 1975—; dir. Med. Dist. 14, 1981; lectr. U. Colo., 1962-68, also mem. pharmacy adv. council; asst. preceptor hosp. adminstrn. program Duke U., 1968-70; preceptor health care and hosp. adminstrn. Northwestern U. Grad. Sch., 1972-74; v.p. Nebr. div. Am. Cancer Soc., 1974-75; chmn. health facilities regional adv. com. Central Nebr. Comprehensive Health Planning Council, 1974-75; mem. Mich. Statewide Health Coördinating Council, 1981; trustee S.W. Mich. Health Systems Agy., 1975-79; mem. dean's com. Coll. Human Medicine, Coll. Osteo. Medicine, Mich. State U., 1976-79; bd. dirs. Central Nebr. Health Edn. Corp., 1974-75; mem. Denver Met. Hosp. Council, 1962-68. Bd. dirs., v.p. Grand Island Goodwill Industries, 1974-75; charter mem. Sr. Exec. Service U.S., 1979. Served with AUS, 1943-46. Recipient President's key Colo. Hosp. Assn., 1968; Appreciation award Nebr. post Am. Legion, 1975; President's gavel Grand Island chpt. Fed. Exec. Assn., 1975; Nat. Comdr.'s award Mil. Order Purple Heart, 1979; Dedicated Service award Marine Corps League, Dept. Mich., 1978; citation for meritorious service Mich. dept. Am. Legion; Nat. Comdr. award DAV; Outstanding Service plaque Mich. dept. Am. Vets. World War II, Korea and Viet Nam; Nat. Disting. Service award Marine Corps League; Silver Citizenship medal Marine Corps League; Disting. Service award Mich. dept. VFW, 1981; Cert. of appreciation Mich. Assn. County Vets. Counselors; Resolution of tribute for outstanding service to vets. Mich. Ho. of Reps. Fellow Am. Coll. Hosp. Adminstrs.; mem. Royal Soc. Health, Assn. Mental Health Adminstrs., Assn. Mil. Surgeons U.S., Fed. Hosp. Inst., U. Iowa (life, nat. council) alumni assns., Colo. Hosp. Assn. (dir. 1962-68, v.p. 1968), Profl. Golfers Assn. Am. (hon. com. Mich. sect.), Am. Legion, Alpha Delta Tau. Roman Catholic. Home: 56 Rock Creek Ln Battle Creek MI 49016 Office: VA Med Center Battle Creek MI 49016

DONADIO, JAMES VINCENT, JR., physician; b. Indpls., Mar. 12, 1935; s. James Vincent and Bonita Margaret (Frede) D.; m. Mary Jane Fitzaimmons, Aug. 16, 1958; children: Katherine Anne, Elizabeth Mary, James Vincent, Joseph William. B.S., Georgetown U., 1957; M.D., Ind. U., 1961. Diplomate: Am. Bd. Internal Medicine. Intern Marion County Gen. Hosp., Indpls., 1961-62; resident in internal medicine Mayo Grad. Sch. Medicine, Rochester, Minn., 1962-64, fellow in nephrology, 1964-66, instr. medicine, 1968-73; asst. prof. medicine Mayo Med. Sch., Rochester, 1973-76, assoc. prof., 1976-80, prof. medicine, 1980—; cons. in internal medicine and nephrology Mayo Clinic, 1966—, chmn. div. nephrology, 1978—; exec. com. Nat. Kidney Found., 1980—; cons., grant site reviewer NIH, Bethesda, 1980—. Contbr. articles to profl. jours. Served to capt. U.S. Army, 1966-68. Decorated Bronze Star. Fellow ACP, Internat. Soc. Nephrology; mem. Am. Soc. Nephrology, Am. Fedn. Clin. Research, Central Soc. Clin. Research, Sigma Xi. Roman Catholic. Club: YMCA. Home: 1205 E Silver Lake Dr Rochester MN 55904 Office: Mayo Clinic 200 1st St SW Rochester MN 55905

DONAGAN, ALAN, educator, philosopher; b. Melbourne, Australia, Feb. 10, 1925; came to U.S., 1956, naturalized, 1983; s. Harry Cyril and Ruby Evaline (Evans) D.; m. Barbara Lynn Galley, Aug. 18, 1951. B.A., Queen's Coll., U. Melbourne, 1946, M.A., 1951; B.Phil., Oxford (Eng.) U., 1953; Litt. D. (hon.), Ripon Coll., 1983. Lectr. philosophy U. Western Australia, 1946-48, Univ. Coll., Canberra, Australia, 1949-51, sr. lectr., 1954-55; vis. asst. prof. U. Minn., 1953-54, asst. prof., 1956-57, asso. prof., chmn. dept. philosophy, 1957-61; prof. philosophy, chmn. dept. Ind. U., 1961-65; prof. philosophy U. Ill., 1965-70, U. Chgo., 1970—, Phyllis Fay Horton prof. humanities, 1977—. Author: The Later Philosophy of R.G. Collingwood, 1962, (with Barbara L. Donagan) Philosophy of History, 1965, The Theory of Morality, 1977; Contbr. articles to profl. jours. Am. Council Learned Socs. fellow, 1972-73; Guggenheim fellow, 1976-77; fellow Center for Advanced Study in the Behavioral Scis., Stanford, 1976-77. Mem. Am. Philos. Assn. (pres. Western div. 1980-81), Institut International de Philosophie, Aristotelian Soc. Home: 5844 Stony Island Ave Chicago IL 60637

DONAGHY, PATRICK CHRISTOPHER, publisher; b. N.Y.C., June 9, 1933; s. John and Catherine (Hartigan) D.; m. Mary Ann Bachtel; 1 son, Patrick. B.A. cum laude, Marist Coll., Poughkeepsie, N.Y., 1956; postgrad., CUNY, NYU, Ohio State U. Elem. and High sch. tchr., 1954-57, engaged in pub., 1957—; editor-in-chief sch. div. Charles E. Merrill Pub. Co., Columbus, Ohio, 1972, v.p., gen. mgr., 1973-81; pres. Silver Burdett Co. (subs. SFN Coms.), Morristown, N.J., 1981—. Home: 11 Harter Rd Morristown NJ 07960 Office: 250 James St Morristown NJ 07960

DONAHOE, DAVID LAWRENCE, county government official; b. Pitts., June 5, 1949; s. Thomas Kernan and Anna Mae (Lawrence) D.; m. Judith DiNardo, June 5, 1971; children: Jennifer, Jeffrey. B.A. in Secondary Edn., U. Pitts., 1971, M.A. in Pub. Adminstrn., 1978. Asst. dir., adminstr. Allegheny County, Pitts., 1974-76, dep. controller, 1976-77, county clk., 1977-78, dir. aviation, 1980-83; sch. treas. City of Pitts., 1978-80; exec. dir. Pa. Econ. League, Pitts., 1983—; sec. bd. Port Authority Allegheny County, 1975-80; teaching asst. U. Pitts, 1976; dir., sec. Pittsburgh Countywide Corp., 1979-83. Adv. com. Salvation Army Pitts., pres., 1981; treas. Irish Room Com., U. Pitts., pres., 1981. Recipient cert. achievement Allegheny County, 1977, Disting. Service award Port Authority of Allegheny County, 1982. Mem. Mcpl. Fin. Officers Am. (debt. com. 1979), Am. Soc. Pu. Adminstrn., Airport Operators Council Internat., league Municipalites (bd. dirs. Pitts. 1975-76). Democrat. Roman Catholic. Office: Pa Econ League 3 Gateway Ctr Pittsburgh PA 15222

DONAHOE, FRANCIS MARION, retired savings and loan executive; b. Salem, Oreg., June 16, 1907; s. Thomas Malcolm and Florence (Coffman) D.; m. Nan Saunders, Oct. 17, 1931; children: Nancy (Mrs. John J. Wall), Thomas S., Francis C., Kathleen (Mrs. Randy Cofer). A.B., U. Wash., Seattle, 1930. Asst. mgr. Olympia Fed. Savs. and Loan, Wash., 1935-44; exec. sec. Capitol Savs. & Loan Assn., Olympia, 1944-51, dir., 1949-51, 65-70; sr. v.p. Fed. Home Loan Bank of San Francisco, 1951-53; pres., chmn., dir. Citizens Savs. & Loan Assn., San Francisco, 1953-74, chmn. exec. com., 1974-83, United Fin. Corp. Calif., 1974-83, ret., 1983. Bd. dirs. Calif. Tax Payers Assn., 1965-73, v.p., 1970—; bd. dirs. Downtown Assn. San Francisco, 1962-74; trustee Savs. and Loan Found., 1969-71; bd. dirs., treas. Mission Hospice Inc. of San Mateo County, 1979—. Mem. San Francisco C. of C. (v.p. 1964-67), Calif. Savs. and Loan League (pres. 1962), Phi Delta Theta. Roman Catholic. Clubs: Stock Exchange of San Francisco (bd. dirs.), Peninsula Golf and Country, K.M., Kiwanis. Home: 110 Park Rd Burlingame CA 94010

DONAHUE, CHARLES, JR., legal educator, author; b. N.Y.C., Oct. 4, 1941; s. Charles James and Rosemary (Spang) D.; m. Sheila Finn, Aug. 8, 1964; 1 dau., Sarah. A.B., Harvard Coll., 1962; LL.B., Yale U., 1965. Bar: N.Y. 1966, Mich. 1969, U.S. Supreme Ct. 1971. Atty.-adv. Office Gen. Counsel of Air Force, Washington, 1965-67; asst. gen. counsel Pres.'s Commn. on Postal Orgn., Washington, 1967-68; asst. prof. law U. Mich., 1968-70, asso. prof., 1970-73, prof., 1973-79; prof. law Harvard U., 1980—; acad. visitor law dept. London Sch. Econs. and Polit. Sci., 1972-73; vis. prof. law Vrije Universiteit Brussel, 1975, Columbia U., 1976, U. Calif. Boalt Hall, 1976, Harvard U., 1978-79. Author: (with others) Cases and Materials on Property: An Introduction to the Concept and the Institution, 1974, 2d edit, 1983, (with P. Martin) A Course in Basic Property, 1975, (with N. Adams) Select Cases from the Ecclesiastical Courts of the Province of Canterbury, c. 1200-1301, 1981; articles editor: Yale Law Jour, 1963-65; bd. editors: Am. Jour. Legal History, 1977—. Served with USAF, 1965-68. Mem. Am. Law Inst., Am. Soc. Legal History (dir. 1977-79, v.p. 1981—), Selden Soc., Société d'histoire du droit, Société pour l'histoire des droits de l'antiquité, Medieval Acad. Am. Roman Catholic. Home: 584 Centre St Newton MA 02158 Office: Harvard Law Sch Cambridge MA 02138

DONAHUE, DONALD JORDAN, packaging co. exec.; b. Bklyn., July 5, 1924; s. John F. and Florence (Jordan) D.; m. Mary Meyer, Jan. 20, 1951; children: Mary G., Judith A., Donald Jordan, Thomas, Nicholas P. B.A., Georgetown U., 1947; M.B.A., NYU, 1951. With Chem. Corn Exchange Bank, N.Y.C., 1947-49; with Am. Metal Climax Inc. (name changed to AMAX, Inc.), N.Y.C., 1949-75, treas., 1957-67, v.p., 1963-65, exec. v.p., 1965-69, pres., 1969-75, also dir., 1964-75; vice chmn. Continental Can Co., Inc. (name changed to Continental Group, Inc.), N.Y.C., 1975—; dir. Nat. Starch & Chem. Co., Northwest Utilities, Inc. Chmn. bd. trustees Georgetown U.; v.p., trustee ICD Research Center; trustee Joint Council Econ. Edn. Served with AUS, 1943-46. Clubs: Greenwich Country (Greenwich); Blindbrook Country, University; River (N.Y.C.). Home: Meads Point Greenwich CT 06830 Office: 1 Harbor Plaza Stamford CT 06902

DONAHUE, ELINOR, actress; b. Tacoma, Wash., Apr. 19, 1937; d. Thomas William and Doris Genevieve (Gelbaugh) D.; m. Harry Stephen Ackerman, Apr. 21, 1961; children—Brian Patrick, Peter Kyran, James Jay, Christopher Asher. A.A., UCLA. Began show bus. career singing on Radio KMO, Tacoma, 1939; song and dance act Bert Levy Vaudeville Circuit, 1944-46; appeared in: films Tenth Ave. Angel; others; appeared on: TV series Father Knows Best, 1954-60, Andy Griffith Show, 1960, Odd Couple, 1972-74, Mulligan's Stew, 1977-78, Please Stand By, 1978-79, Drs. Private Lives; numerous guest roles on: Tv including No Margin for Error on Police Story, 1978. Bd. dirs. Y.E.S., Share Inc. Democrat. Episcopalian. Office: 3575 Cahuenga-West Los Angeles CA 90068 *

DONAHUE, KENNETH, museum director; b. Louisville, Jan. 31, 1915; s. Samuel J. and Ida (Walton) D.; m. Daisy Cain, Aug. 13, 1940; children: L. Nicaea, Craig R. A.B., U. Louisville, 1936; A.M., N.Y. U., 1942, postgrad., 1946-47. Lectr. Mus. Modern Art, 1938-43; research fellow Am. Council Learned Socs., Italy, 1947-49; lectr., curatorial asst. Frick Collection, 1949-53; curator John and Mable Ringling Mus. Art, Sarasota, Fla., 1953-57, dir. mus., 1957-64; dep. dir. Los Angeles County Mus. Art, 1964-66, dir., 1966-79, dir. emeritus, 1979—; founding cons. Nev. Mus. Fine Art, 1982—; Mem. art adv. panel to commr. internal revenue, 1970-74; mem. conseil de direction Gazette des Beaux-Arts, 1975—. Contbr. articles to profl. jours. Served with AUS, 1943-45. Decorated comdr. Order of Merit, (Italy). Mem. Assn. Am. Museums (v.p. 1970-72, council 1968-77), Coll. Art Assn. (dir. 1967-71), Assn. Art Mus. Dirs. (v.p. 1971-72). Home: 245 S Westgate Los Angeles CA 90049 Office: 5905 Wilshire Blvd Los Angeles CA 90036

DONAHUE, PHIL, TV personality; b. Dec. 1935; m. Marge Cooney, 1958 (div. 1975); children: Michael, Kevin, Daniel, Jim, Maryrose; m. Marlo Thomas, 1980. Grad., U. Notre Dame. Host: Donahue (formerly The Phil Donahue Show), Dayton, Ohio, 1967-74, Chgo., 1974—; regular appearances Today show, from 1979 (Recipient Emmy award for Best Daytime Talk Show 1977, 79, 82). Roman Catholic. Office: WBBM-TV 630 McClurg Ct Chicago IL 60611 *

DONAHUE, ROBERT JAMES, army officer; b. Boston, Mar. 15, 1932; s. Patrick James and Anna Loretta (Moynihan) D.; m. Elyse Jean Cavalli, Feb. 26, 1957; children; Patrick, Brian, Robert James, Elyse. B.S., Ohio State U., 1968; M.P.A., Pa. State U., 1975; D.B.A., Far East Mgmt. Soc., Tokyo, 1979. Commd. 2d lt. U.S. Army, 1953, advanced through grades to maj. gen., 1980; comdr. U.S. Army Strategic Communications Commands, Camp Darby, Italy, 1970-73, U.S. Army Strategic communications Commands, Heidelberg, Germany, 1970-73; dep. dir. telecommunications Hdqrs. Dept. Army, Washington, 1973-77; comdr. U.S. Army Communications Command Japan, Camp Zama, 1977-79; dep. comdg. gen. U.S. Army Signal Ctr., Ft. Gordon, Ga., 1979-81; dir. joint tactical communications office Office Sec. Def., Ft. Monmouth, N.J., 1981—. Contbr.: articles on mil. communications electronics, Signal mag. Served with U.S. Army, 1952-53. Decorated Legion of Merit with 2 oak lead clusters, Bronze Star, Meritorious Service medal, Air medal, Joint Service Commendation medal. Mem. Armed Forces Communications Electronics Assn. (bd. dirs. 1981—), Armed Forces Comunications Electronics Assn. (internat. v.p. 1981-83), Armed Forces Communications Electronics Assn. (chmn. awards com. 1981-83), Assn. U.S. Army. Club: Exchange (Augusta, Ga.) (chmn. awards com. 1979-80). Home: 36 Russel Ave Fort Monmouth NJ 07703 Office: Joint Tactical Communications Office of Def Fort Monmouth NJ 07703

DONAHUE, ROBERT WILLIAM, ret. petroleum co. exec.; b. Chgo., Apr. 25, 1916; s. Frank H. and Hattie (Rogers) D.; m. Carolyn Maloy, Nov. 7, 1942; children—Ann (Mrs. Leonard Giunta), Mary (Mrs. Stephen O'Neill), Katherine (Mrs. John Mink), Patricia (Mrs. Thomas Pleatman), Margaret, Richard. B.S., Purdue U., 1941. With Sun Oil Co. (name now Sun Co. Inc.), 1941-80, dir. comml. devel., 1964-67, dir. purchasing, 1967-70, exec. v.p. products group, 1970-71; also dir.; pres., dir. Sun Oil Co. Pa., 1971-73, exec. v.p., 1973-75, vice chmn., 1975-79, sr. v.p., dep. chief exec. officer, 1979-80. Mem. Am. Petroleum Inst., Soc. Automotive Engrs. Republican. Roman Catholic. Home: 1777 Hamilton Dr Valley Forge PA 19481

DONAHUE, THOMAS MICHAEL, educator; b. Healdton, Okla., May 23, 1921; s. Robert Emmett and Mary (Lyndon) D.; m. Esther Marie McPherson, Jan. 1, 1950; children: Brian M., Kevin E., Neil M. A.B., Rockhurst Coll., 1942, D.Sc., 1981; Ph.D., Johns Hopkins U., 1947. Research asso., asst. prof. Johns Hopkins U., 1947-51; asst. prof. U. Pitts., 1951-53, assoc. prof., 1953-57, prof., 1957-74, dir. Lab. Atmospheric and Space Sci., 1966-74, dir. Space Research Coordination Center, 1966-74; chmn. dept. atmospheric and oceanic sci. and Space Physics Research Lab., U. Mich., Ann Arbor, 1974—; mem. phys. scis. com. NASA, 1972-77, adv. council, 1982—, Mars sci. working group, 1976—, solar system exploration com., 1981—, chmn. Space Sci. Bd., 1982—; mem. Arecibo adv. bd. Cornell U., 1971-76; chmn. solar terrestrial relations com., mem. atmospheric scis. com., geophysics research bd., climate bd. Nat. Acad. Scis.; chmn. sci. steering groups Pioneer Venus multi-probe and orbital missions to Venus; trustee-at-large Upper Atmosphere Research Corp., 1975—; vice-chmn. exec. com., trustee Univ. Corp. for Atmospheric Research, 1978—; chmn. bd. trustees Univs. Space Research Assn., 1978—. Editor: Space Research X, 1969; assoc. editor numerous publs., particularly specializing in atomic physics and properties of planetary atmospheres.; editor: Venus, 1983; assoc. editor: Planetary and Space Sci. Served with AUS, 1944-46. Recipient Public Service award NASA, 1977, 7 achievement awards, Disting. Public Service medal, 1980; Arctowski medal Nat. Acad. Sci., 1981; Fleming medal Am. Geophys. Union, 1981; Guggenheim fellow U. Paris, 1960. Fellow Am. Phys. Soc., Am. Geophys. Union (pres. solar-planetary relations 1972-75, v.p. 1969-72, pres., 1972-75), AAAS.; Mem. Nat. Acad. Scis. Club: Cosmos. Participant Voyager mission to outer planets, Galileo mission to Jupiter, Spacelab 1. Home: 1781 Arlington Blvd Ann Arbor MI 48104

DONAHUE, THOMAS REILLY, trade union official; b. N.Y.C., Sept. 4, 1928; s. Thomas Reilly and Mary E. (Purcell) D.; children: Nancy Angela, Thomas Reilly III. B.A., Manhattan Coll., 1949; J.D., Fordham U., 1956; LL.D., U. Notre Dame, 1980, Loyola U.-Chgo., 1984. Dir. edn., bus. agt. local 32B, Bldg. Service Employees Internat. Union, AFL-CIO, 1949-52; dir. contract dept., 1952-57, European labor program coordinator, Paris, 1957-60; asst. to pres. Bldg. Service Employees' Internat. Union, 1960-67; asst. sect. for labor-mgmt. relations Dept. Labor, 1967-69; exec. sec. Service Employees Internat. Union, 1969-71, v.p., 1971-73; exec. asst. to pres. AFL-CIO, 1973-79, sec.-treas., 1979—. Mem. U.S. Catholic Conf. Com. on Social Devel.; Bd. dirs. Muscular Dystrophy Assn., Carnegie Corp., Nat. Urban League, Brookings Instn. Served with USNR, 1945-46. Democrat. Home: 613 G St SW Washington DC 20024 Office: 815 16th St NW Washington DC 20006

DONAHUGH, ROBERT HAYDEN, library adminstr.; b. St. Paul, May 20, 1930; s. Robert Emmett and Elmyra Elanore (Hayden) D. B.A., Coll. St. Thomas, 1952; M.A., U. Minn., 1953. Instr. English and speech Robert Coll., Istanbul, Turkey, 1956-57; head tech. services Canton (Ohio) Public Library, 1957-62; asst. dir. Public Library of Youngstown and Mahoning County, Ohio, 1962-79, dir., 1979—. Author: Evaluation of Reference Resources in 8 Public Libraries in 4 Ohio Counties, 1970; contbr.: book revs. to Library Jour, 1958—. Served with M.P. U.S. Army, 1954-56. Mem. ALA, Ohio Library Assn. (pres. 1975), Midwest Fedn. Library Assns. (pres. 1979-83). Clubs: Elks, Rotary. Home: 509 Ferndale Ave Youngstown OH 44511 Office: 305 Wick Ave Youngstown OH 44503

DONALD, ALEXANDER GRANT, psychiatrist; b. Darlington, S.C., Jan. 24, 1928; s. Raymond George and Chesnut Evans (McIntosh) D.; m. Emma Louise Coggeshall, Oct. 25, 1958; children—Sandy, Mary Chesnut, Marion Lide. B.S., Davidson Coll., 1948; M.D., Med. U. S.C., 1952. Diplomate: Am. Bd. Psychiatry and Neurology. Intern Jefferson Med. Coll., 1952-53; resident in psychiatry Walter Reed Hosp., 1956-59; dir. Mental Health Clinic, Florence, S.C., 1962-66; dept. commr. S.C. Dept. Mental Health, 1966-67; dir. William S Hall Psychiat. Inst., Columbia, 1967—; prof., chmn. dept. neuropsychiatry and behavioral scis. Sch. Medicine, U. S.C., Columbia, 1975—, assoc. dean student affairs, dir. admissions, 1982—. Served to maj. U.S. Army, 1953-62. Fellow Am. Coll. Psychiatrists, So. Psychiat. Assn.; mem. Am. Psychiat. Assn. (pres. S.C. dist. br. 1967), AMA, Columbia Med. Soc. (v.p. 1981, del. 1981). Presbyterian. Office: PO Box 202 Columbia SC 29202 *Probably the highest function of man's God-given mind is that of introspection—the understanding of oneself and others through thinking.*

DONALD, DAVID HERBERT, author, history educator; b. Goodman, Miss., Oct. 1, 1920; s. Ira Unger and Sue Ella (Belford) D.; m. Aida DiPace, 1955; 1 son, Bruce Randall. Student, Holmes Jr. Coll., 1937-39; A.B., Millsaps Coll., 1941, L.H.D., 1976; A.M., U. Ill., 1942, Ph.D., 1946; teaching fellow, U. N.C., 1942; M.A. (hon.), U. Oxford, 1959, Harvard U., 1973. Research asst. history U. Ill., 1943-45, research asso., 1946-47; fellow Social Sci. Research Council, 1945-46; instr. history Columbia, 1947-49; asso. prof. history Smith Coll., 1949-51; asst. prof. history Columbia U. Grad. Faculty, 1951-52, asso. prof., 1952-57, prof. history, 1957-59, Princeton U., 1959-62; prof. Am. history Johns Hopkins U., Balt., 1962-73, Harry C. Black prof., 1963-73, dir. Inst. So. History,, 1966-72; Charles Warren prof. Am. history and prof. Am. civilization Harvard U., 1973, chmn. grad. program in Am. civilization, 1979—; vis. asso. prof. Amherst Coll., 1950; Fulbright lectr. Am. history U. Coll. North Wales, 1953-54; mem. Inst. Advanced Study, 1957-58; Harmsworth prof. Am. history Oxford U., 1959-60; John P. Young lectr. Memphis State U., 1963; Walter Lynwood Fleming lectr. La. State U., 1965; Benjamin Rush lectr. Am. Psychiat. Assn., 1972; Commonwealth lectr. Univ. Coll., London, 1975. Author: Lincoln's Herndon, 1948, Divided We Fought, A Pictorial History of the War, 1861-1865, 1952, Inside Lincoln's Cabinet: The Civil War Diaries of Salmon P. Chase, 1954, Lincoln Reconsidered: Essays on the Civil War Era, 1956, rev., 1961, A Rebel's Recollections, (G.C. Eggleston), 1959, Charles Sumner and the Coming of the Civil War, 1960 (Pulitzer prize in biography), Why the North Won the Civil War, 1960, (with J.G. Randall) The Civil War and Reconstruction, 2d edit, 1961, rev., enlarged edit., 1969, The Divided Union, 1961, The Politics of Reconstruction, 1863-67, 1965, The Nation in Crisis, 1861-1877, 1969, Charles Sumner and the Rights of Man, 1970, (with Sidney Andrews) The South Since the War, 1970, Gone for a Soldier, 1975, (with others) The Great Republic, 1977, rev. edit., 1981, Liberty and Union, 1978; editor: War Diary and Letters of Stephen Minot Weld, 1979; Gen. editor: Documentary History of American Life, The Making of America Series, 6 vols.; co-editor: (with wife) Diary of Charles Francis Adams, 2 vols, 1964; Contbr. articles to periodicals. Guggenheim fellow, 1964-65; fellow Am. Council Learned Socs., 1969-70, Center for Advanced Study Behavioral Scis., 1969-70, George A. and Eliza G. Howard fellow, 1957-58; Nat. Endowment for Humanities sr. fellow, 1971-72. Fellow Am. Acad. Arts and Scis.; mem. Orgn. Am. Historians, Am. Hist. Assn., So. Hist. Assn. (v.p. 1968, pres. 1969), Soc. Am. Historians, Mass. Hist. Soc., Am. Antiquarian Soc., Phi Beta Kappa, Phi Kappa Phi, Pi Kappa Delta, Pi Kappa Alpha, Omicron Delta Kappa. Episcopalian. Clubs: Harvard (N.Y.C.); Cosmos, Signet, Fox. Home: PO Box 158 Lincoln Rd Lincoln Center MA 01773

DONALD, DAVID RICHARD, banker; b. Needham, Mass., July 3, 1930; s. Thomas Husson and Harriet May (Pike) D.; m. Jo-Ann Marks, Sept. 18, 1954; children: Joy Ann, Thomas Philip. Certificate, Am. Inst. Banking, 1958; postgrad., Grad Sch. Nat. Assn. Mut. Savs. Banks, 1963, 1965. Asst. mgr. grocery div. Crossman's Market, Needham, Mass., 1948-51; with Mut. Savs. Bank for Savs., Boston, 1954—, treas., 1968—, v.p., 1971-76, sr. v.p., 1976-82, exec. v.p., 1982—. Treas. Am. Cancer Fund, Newton, 1958-59, Needham Cub Scouts, 1968—, Needham YMCA, 1971; vice chmn., treas. Needham Housing Authority, 1974-77; mem. Needham Personnel Bd., 1979-81, chmn., 1980-81; trustee Glover Meml. Hosp. Served with USCG, 1951-54. Mem. Newton-Needham C. of C., Savs. Banks Assn. Mass. Conglist. Club: Mason. Home: 323 Dedham Ave Needham MA 02192 Office: 1188 Centre St Newton Center MA 02159

DONALD, ERIC PAUL, aeronautical engineer, inventor; b. Sunderland, Eng., Feb. 23, 1930; came to U.S., 1964, naturalized, 1970; s. Norman and Dorothy (Dobson) D.; m. Christine Juliet Allen, Dec. 26, 1966; children: April Elise America, Paul Allen Hertford. Student, Sunderland Tech. Coll., 1949; H.N.C., Acton Tech. Coll., 1957; M.Sc., Cranfield Inst. Tech., 1974. Engr. Fairey Aviation Co., London, 1953-59; research engr. English Electric Co., 1959-64; indsl. engring. cons., N.Y.C., 1965-66; cons. engr. Lockheed Corp., 1966-67, Boeing, 1967-69, Grumman, 1969-70, Hawker Siddeley, 1970-71; chief stress analyst Guided Weapons div. Brit. Aircraft Corp., 1973-79; sr. engring. scientist Douglas Aircraft Co., Long Beach, Calif., 1979—; founder Donald Research, 1978, E.P. Donald Ltd., 1979; mng. dir. Blee-Bolt Indicators Ltd., 1979—. Contbr. articles to profl. jours.; patentee in field. Served with RAF, 1950-52. Assoc. fellow AIAA; mem. Royal Aero. Soc., Inst. Patentees and Inventors (Richardson gold medal 1977); Assoc. fellow Soc. Geneologists, AIAA. Anglican. If I had done no more than solve the world metal fatigue detection problem, I should have considered my life worthwhile. Home: 1855 Petaluma Ave Long Beach CA 90815 Office: 3855 Lakewood Blvd Long Beach CA 90846

DONALD, LARRY WATSON, sports journalist; b. Dayton, Ohio, Mar. 10, 1945; s. Carl V. and Ruth L. (Sanders) D.; m. Nancy Lynn Higgins, Jan. 27, 1968; 1 son, David Alan. B.S. in Journalism, Bowling Green (Ohio) State U., 1967. Sports editor Fostoria (Ohio) Review Times, 1967-71; mng. editor Football News, also editor Basketball Weekly, Detroit, 1971-79; pub. Baseball Bull., 1979—, Basketball Times, 1980—; editor Medalist Industries Sports News, 1979—, Inside Coaching, 1982; pub. mag. Mich. Publinx Golf Assn., 1980. Recipient award for best sports story Nat. Newspaper Assn., 1969. Mem. U.S. Basketball Writers Assn. (awards 1976, 77), Sigma Delta Chi, Delta Tau Delta. Democrat. Presbyterian. Clubs: Foxfire Golf and Country (Pinehurst, N.C.); Elks. Home: 6578 Emerald Lake Dr Troy MI 48098

DONALD, PAUL AUBREY, insurance company executive; b. Prince Frederick, Md., July 6, 1929; m. Anne Harris, Nov. 5, 1966; children: Cynthia Binz, Jan Donald, Glenn White, Mike Donald, Ken Donald, Steve Donald. B.Com., U. Balt., 1956. Vice pres., regional mgr. Nationwide Ins., Lynchburg, Va., 1975-79, v.p. property casualty mktg., Columbus, Ohio, 1979-80, v.p. western devel., 1980-81, v.p., adminstrv. asst. to pres., 1981, pres., gen. mgr., 1981—; chmn. bd. Neckura Life Ins. Co., Auto Direkt Ins. Co., Pioneer Auto Ins. Co.; vice chmn. Farmland Ins. Co., Farmland Life Ins. Co., Neckura Casualty Ins. Co.; pres. Nationwide Found., Nationwide Transport, Inc., Colonial Ins. Co., Scottsdale Ins. Co., Nat. Annuity Advisors, Inc., Multi-Flex Advisors, Inc., Nationwide Cash Mgmt. Co., Farmland Ins. Co., others. Pres.-elect United Way of Franklin County, Inc., Columbus, 1983—; trustee Columbus Symphony Orch., 1982—, Meth. Theol. Sch., Delaware, Ohio, 1983—; v.p. Council for Study of Ethics and Econs., Columbus, 1983—. Mem. Nat. Assn. Health Underwriters, Am. Soc. C.I.U.s, Soc. C.P.C.U.s. Methodist. Home: 8016 Park Ridge Ct Worthington OH 43085 Office: Nationwide Ins One Nationwide Plaza Columbus OH 43216

DONALD, ROBERT GRAHAM, retail food chain personnel executive; b. Vancouver, B.C., Can., May 22, 1943; came to U.S., 1946; s. H. Graham and Marion O. (Benoit) D.; m. Patricia K. Shea, Oct. 17, 1970; children: Linda M., Lisa A. Student Delaware Valley Coll., Doyleston, Pa., 1961-63; B.S., Iowa State U., 1965; grad. exec. program food industry mgmt., Cornell U., 1972. With Grand Union Co., Elmwood Park, N.J., 1968—, labor relations asst., 1974-75, dist. sales mgr., 1976-78, dir. personnel, 1978-81, v.p.-personnel, adminstrv. services, 1981—. Served in U.S. Army, 1966-68. Mem. Am. Soc. Personnel Adminstrn. Office: The Grand Union Co 100 Broadway Elmwood Park NJ 07407

DONALDSON, CHARLES RUSSELL, chief justice Idaho Supreme Court; b. Helena, Mont., Feb. 2, 1919; s. Charles Mortimer and Mabel (King) D.; children: Karen, Holly, Jean, Laurel, Sarah, Charles. Student, Willamette U., 1937-38; B.A., U. Idaho, 1941, LL.B., 1948; postgrad., George Washington Law Sch., 1943-44. Bar: Idaho 1948. Practice law, Boise, 1948-64, dist. judge, 1964-68; justice Idaho Supreme Ct., Boise, 1969—, chief justice, 1973, 79-80, 83—; mem. Idaho Ho. of Reps., 1955-57; justice of peace, 1960-64. Served with Signal Corps, AUS, World War II. Office: Supreme Ct Bldg Boise ID 83707 *

DONALDSON, COLEMAN DUPONT, consulting engineer; b. Phila., Sept. 22, 1922; s. John W. and Renee (duPont) D.; m. Barbara Goldsmith, Jan. 17, 1945; children: B. Beirne, Coleman duPont, Evan F., Alexander M., William M. B.S. in Aero. Engring., Rensselaer Poly. Inst., 1943; M.A., Princeton U., 1954, Ph.D., 1957. Staff, NACA, Langley Field, Va., 1943-44, head aerophysics sect., 1946-52; gen. aerodynamics USAC, Wright Field, Ohio, 1945-46; aerodynamic evaluation Bell Aircraft, Niagara Falls, N.Y., 1946; sr. cons., pres. Aero Research Assos. of Princeton, N.J., 1954-79, chmn. bd., 1979—; cons. missile guidance and control Gen. Precision Equipment Corp., 1957-68; cons. magnetohydro-dynamics Thompson Ramo Wooldridge, Inc., 1958-61; cons. aerodynamic heating, gen. aerodynamics Martin Marietta Corp., 1955-72; gen. editor Princeton series on high speed aerodynamics and jet propulsion, 1955-64; cons. boundary layer stability, aerodynamic heating, missile and ordnance systems dept. Gen. Electric Co., 1956-72; cons. Grumman Aerospace Corp., 1959-72; Robert H. Goddard vis. lectr. with rank of prof. Princeton U., 1970-71; mem. research and tech. adv. council panel on research NASA, 1969-76; mem. indsl. profl. adv. com. Pa. State U., 1970-77; mem. Pres.'s Air Quality Adv. Bd., 1973-74; chmn. lab. adv. bd. for air warfare Naval Research Adv. Com., 1972-77; mem. Marine Corps panel Naval Res. Adv. Com., 1972-77; chmn. adv. council dept. aerospace and mech. scis. Princeton U., 1973-78. Author articles on aerodynamics. Fellow AIAA (Dryden Research lecture award 1971, gen. chmn. 13th aerospace scis. meeting 1975), Nat. Acad. Engring., Am. Phys. Soc., Sigma Xi, Delta Phi. Home: PO Box 279 Gloucester VA 23061 Office: 1800 Old Meadow Rd Suite 114 McLean VA 22102

DONALDSON, DAVID MARBURY, lawyer; b. Lincoln, Mass., Apr. 27, 1938; s. Donald P. and Astrid (Lorentzon) D.; m. Lynn Burrows, Aug. 18, 1962; children: Sarah, Robert, Rachel. A.B., Harvard U., 1960, LL.B., 1963. Bar: Mass. 1965, U.S. Tax Ct. 1974. Lectr. law U. Singapore, 1963-65; ptnr. Ropes & Gray, Boston, 1965—; lectr. Harvard U. Extension; dir. Charrette Corp., Lemire & Co., Inc. Author: Harvard Manual on Tax Aspects of Charitable Giving, 1980,

5th edition, 1983. Trustee Carroll Sch.; mem. Planning Bd. Town of Lincoln, Mass., 1967-68, moderator Planning Bd., 1978—; corporator Emerson Hosp., Concord, Mass.; deacon First Parish Ch., Lincoln. Mem. ABA, Mass. Bar, Boston Bar, Nat. Health Lawyers Assn., Nat. Assn. Coll. and Univ. Attys. Club: Harvard (Boston). Office: Ropes & Gray 225 Franklin St Boston MA 02110

DONALDSON, ETHELBERT TALBOT, educator; b. Bethlehem, Pa., Mar. 18, 1910; s. Francis and Anne H. (Talbot) D.; m. Christine H. Hunter, June 24, 1941 (div. 1967); 1 dau., Deirdre H.; m. Jacqueline Sissa Filson, Mar. 23, 1967 (div. 1969); m. Judith H. Anderson, May 18, 1971. B.A., Harvard U., 1932; Ph.D., Yale U., 1943; Litt.D. (hon.), Lehigh U., 1980. Tchr. French, English, Latin and Greek Kent Sch., Conn., 1932-38, 39-40; faculty Yale U., 1946-67, 70-74, research instr. to assoc. prof., 1946-56, prof., 1956-66, Bodman prof. English, 1966-67, 70-74; acting master of Saybrook Coll., Yale U., 1963; prof. English Columbia U., 1967-70, Ind. U., Bloomington, 1974-76, Disting. prof. English, 1976-80, emeritus, 1980—; vis. prof. U. Coll., London, 1951-52, King's Coll., 1971-72, U. Mich., 1973-74. Author: Piers Plowman: The C-Text and Its Poet, 1949, Speaking of Chaucer, 1970; also articles in profl. jours.; Editor: Chaucer's Poetry, 1958, (with George Kane) B Version of Piers Plowman, 1975. Served to capt. USAAF, 1943-46. Guggenheim fellow, 1951-52, 77-78. Fellow Mediaeval Acad. (pres. 1980-81, Haskins medal 1978), Am. Acad. Arts and Scis., Brit. Acad. (corr.); mem. MLA, Conn. Acad. Arts and Scis. (pres. 1966-67), Acad. Lit. Studies, New Chaucer Soc. (pres. 1978-79), Phi Beta Kappa. Clubs: Savage, Athenaeum (London). Home: 2525 E 8th St Bloomington IN 47401

DONALDSON, FRANK ARTHUR, JR., manufacturing executive; b. Mpls., Aug. 19, 1919; s. Frank Arthur and Ruth (Chase) D.; m. Irene Elizabeth Sweeney, Mar. 1, 1954; children: Frank Arthur III, John Andrew. Engring. degree cum laude, Harvard U., 1942. Engr. Donaldson Co., Inc., Mpls., 1941-44, v.p., 1947-51, pres., gen. mgr., 1951-73, chmn. bd., chief exec. officer, 1973-82, chmn. bd., 1982—; dir. 1st Bank System, Inc., 1st Nat. Bank Mpls., Graco Inc., North Central Cos., St. Paul, Magnetic Controls Co. Served with USN, 1944-45. Mem. Soc. Automotive Engrs., Minn. Bus. Partnership. Clubs: Desert Forest (Carefree, Ariz.); Minneapolis, Woodhill Country (Mpls.). Office: 1400 W 94th St Minneapolis MN 55431

DONALDSON, JEFF RICHARDSON, artist, educator; b. Pine Bluff, Ark., Dec. 15, 1932; s. Sidney Frank and Clementine Frances (Richardson) D.; 1 dau., Jameela Kaneeka. B.A., Ark. State Coll., 1954; M.S., Inst. of Design, Ill. Inst. Tech., 1963; Ph.D., Northwestern U., 1974. Chmn. art dept. Marshall High Sch., Chgo., 1958-65; asst. prof. art Northeastern U., Chgo., 1965-69; lectr. Northwestern U., Evanston, Ill., 1969-70; prof., chmn. dept. art, art gallery dir. Howard U., Washington, 1970—; art cons. Student Non-Violent Coordinating Com., 1963-66, CORE, Chgo., 1962-63; organizer, contbg. artist Wall of Respect, Chgo., 1967; chmn. N. Am. zone, 2d World Black and African Festival of Arts and Culture, Lagos, Nigeria, 1975; advisor art assessment div. IRS, Washington, 1976; cons. Nat. Endowment for Humanities, 1975—; v.p. internat. festival com., U.S. and Can.; FESTAC 77, 1975—. (Recipient first prize for painting, Art and Soul Competition, Chgo. 1968, first prize award, Black Expressions Competition, Chgo. 1969); Editor: Ill. Art Edn. Yearbook, 1969; Contbr. articles to mags. Bd. dirs. Nat. Center for Afro-Am. Artists, Boston, 1970—; mem. adv. bd. Studio Mus. in Harlem, 1970-74; mem. corp. bd. Children's Hosp., Washington, 1974—; mem. D.C. Art Commn., 1977—. Served with AUS, 1955-57. Ford Found. fellow, 1967-68; Northwestern U. fellow, 1968-69. Home: 504 T St NW Washington DC 20001

DONALDSON, LAUREN R., emeritus radiobiology educator; b. Tracy, Minn., May 13, 1903; s. Russell C. and Jessie M. (Moses) D.; m. Lenora E. Carney, June 25, 1927; children: John Russell, Joann Lauren. A.B., Intermountain Union Coll., 1926; M.S., U. Wash., 1931, Ph.D., 1939; D.Sc. (hon.), Rocky Mountain Coll., 1958, Hamline U., 1965. Prin., tchr. sci. and athletics Shelby (Mont.) High Sch., 1926-30; summer mem. staff Mont. Dept. Fish and Game, 1926-31; asst. to asso. prof. fisheries U. Wash., Seattle, 1932-48, prof., 1948-73, prof. emeritus, 1973—, dir., 1943-57, 1958-66; asst. prof. U. Oreg., summer 1941; biologist Wash. Dept. Fish, summers 1942-43; chief div. radiobiology Operation Crossroads, 1946, Bikini Sci. Resurvey, 1948; radiobiol. observer Operation Sandstone, Eniwetok, 1948; biologist Operation Ivy, 1952; dir. U. Wash. radiobiol. studies Pacific weapons testing program, 1954-64; rep. AEC, Japan, 1954; lectr. U. Oslo, Norway, 1952, U. Helsinki, Finland, 1959; cons. fisheries U.S. Fish and Wildlife Service, 1935-40, Internat. Pacific Salmon Fisheries Commn., 1941-43; cons. biol. effects radiation Gen. Electric Co., Richland, Wash., 1947-56; cons. mineral metabolism Gen. Mills, Inc., 1963-72; cons. planning Nat. Fisheries Center and Aquarium, U.S. Fish and Wildlife Service, 1965-66; vis. prof. Tokyo Fisheries U., Japan, 1973; mem. Nat. Sea Grant coll. rev. panel U.S. Dept. Commerce, 1980—; guest lectr. Shangdong Coll. Oceanography, Qingdao, China, 1983—. Contbr. numerous articles to profl. jours. and reports on fisheries mgmt. and radiobiology. Mem. Seattle CD Bd., 1946-50; chmn. Wash. Gov.'s Adv. Com. on Fisheries, 1957-64; chmn. Aquarium com. Oceanographic Commn. Wash., 1967-70; mem. Bonneville regional adv. council U.S. Dept. Interior, 1968-73; sci. adv. group Internat. Atlantic Salmon Found., 1970—. Recipient Nat. Sea Grant Coll. award, 1971; Lockheed award for Ocean Sci. and Engring., 1971; award for contbns. to improvement and propagation salmon in Japan Gov. Hokkaido, 1972; Shinkishi Hatai medal for contbns. to marine biology in Pacific area Japan Soc. for Promotion Sci., 1975; Tokai U. teaching award, 1980. Mem. Am. Fisheries Soc., AAAS, Phi Sigma, Sigma Xi. Home: 6201 51st NE Seattle WA 98115 Office: Fisheries Center U Wash Seattle WA 98195

DONALDSON, RICHARD MIESSE, oil company executive, lawyer; b. Columbus, Ohio, Apr. 8, 1929; s. Maynard McClure and Mary Ann (Miesse) D.; m. Carolyn Jean Cray, Aug. 30, 1952; children: Nancy Ann, Susan Beth Donaldson Hill, Richard Cray. B.S., Northwestern U., 1950; J.D., U. Mich., 1953; LL.M., Harvard U., 1957. Bar: Ohio bar 1953. Spl. partner McAfee, Hanning, Newcomer, Hazlett & Wheeler, Cleve., 1957-67; gen. partner Squire, Sanders & Dempsey, Cleve., 1967-70; v.p., gen. counsel Standard Oil Co., Ohio, Cleve., 1970-74, v.p. govt. and pub. affairs, 1974—; dir. Broadview Fin. Corp., 1978—. Trustee Children's Aid Soc. of Cleve., 1965—, pres., 1967-69; trustee Planned Parenthood of Cleve., 1966-72; bd. dirs. Cleve. Council World Affairs, 1970-75; bd. dirs., exec. com. Cleve. Internat. Program, 1972-75; com. mem. Young Life in Cleve., 1970-75, chmn., 1971-72; trustee Great Lakes Shakespeare Festival, 1979—, v.p., 1981—; mem. Rocky River (Ohio) Bd. Edn., 1962-69, 81, pres. bd., 1965-68; bd. mgrs., treas. The Brush Found., 1977—; trustee Ohio Pub. Expenditure Council, 1976—; bd. dirs. Govt. Research Inst., 1976—; mem. Lutheran Hosp. Found., 1978—, chmn., 1979-80. Served to capt., JAGC USAF, 1953-56. Mem. Am., Ohio, Cleve. bar assns., Am. Petroleum Inst., Ohio C. of C. (bd. dirs.). Republican. Mem. United Ch. of Christ (mem. session 1970, chmn. ch. and ministry dept. 1973, moderator 1974-75, chmn. council 1979-80). Clubs: Cleve. Yachting, Clevelander, Midday (Cleve.); River Oaks Racquet. Home: 21418 Kenwood Ave Rocky River OH 44116 Office: Guildhall Bldg Cleveland OH 44115 *Trust in the Lord with all your heart, and do not lean on your own understanding. In all your ways acknowledge Him and He will make your paths straight. Proverbs 3:546.*

DONALDSON, ROBERT CHARLES, educator; b. San Francisco, Jan. 28, 1924; s. Donald and Cora Priscilla (Donaldson) Wood; m. Persis Chapple, Jan. 4, 1975; children by previous marriage—Diane Margery, Robert Charles. Student, U. Ariz., 1942; B.A., U. So. Calif., 1950, M.A., 1951; Ph.D., U. Mich., 1954; Fulbright scholar, U. Brussels, 1953-54. Asst. prof. Eastern Ky. State Coll., 1954-57; asst. prof. history Calif. State U., Sacramento, 1957-62, asso. prof., 1962-67, prof., 1967—, chmn. dept., 1969-75, chmn. acad. senate, 1968-69, coll. ombudsman, 1969-70, presiding officer faculty, 1972-75; Senator Acad. Senate of Calif. State Univs. and Colls., 1970-76. Served with AUS, 1943-46. Mem. Am. Hist. Assn., Phi Kappa Phi, Phi Alpha Theta, Blue Key. Democrat. Home: 1516 Little Ct Carmichael CA 95608

DONALDSON, ROBERT HERSCHEL, college provost; b. Houston, June 14, 1943; s. Herschel Arthur and Vera Edith (True) D.; m. Judy Carol Johnston, June 27, 1964 (div. Apr. 30, 1984); children: Jennifer Gwynne, John Andrew. A.B., Harvard U., 1964, A.M., 1966, Ph.D., 1969. Prof. polit. sci. Vanderbilt U., 1968-81, asso. dean, 1975-81; provost, v.p. acad. affairs, prof. polit. sci. Herbert H. Lehman Coll. CUNY, 1981—; vis. research prof. U.S. Army War Coll., 1978-79. Author: Stasis and Change in Revolutionary Elites, 1971, Soviet Policy toward India, 1974, The Soviet-Indian Alliance: Quest for Influence, 1979, The Soviet Union in the Third World: Successes and Failures, 1981, Soviet Foreign Policy since World War II, 1981. Council Fgn. Relations fellow, 1973-74. Mem. Am. Assn. Advancement Slavic Studies, Internat. Studies Assn., Phi Beta Kappa. Republican. Methodist. Home: 2400 Johnson Ave Apt 14A Bronx NY 10463 Office: Bedford Park Blvd W Bronx NY 10468

DONALDSON, ROBERT MACARTNEY, JR., physician; b. Hubbardston, Mass., Aug. 1, 1927; s. Robert Macartney and Helen Mildred (Morrow) D.; m. Priscilla Hurd, Sept. 1, 1950; children: Robert M., John H.; m. Phyllis Bodel, Jan. 14, 1974. B.S., Yale U., 1949; M.D., Boston U., 1952. Intern Mass. Gen. Hosp., 1952-53; resident Boston VA Hosp., 1955-57; fellow in gastroenterology Peter Bent Brigham Hosp., Boston, 1957-59; instr. Harvard U. Med. Sch., 1957-59; asst. prof. medicine Boston U., Med. Sch., 1959-64, prof., chief gastroenterology, 1967-73; assoc. prof. U. Wis. Med. Sch., 1964-67; prof. medicine, dir. med. studies, dept. internal medicine Yale U. Med. Sch., 1973—; chmn. adv. bd. Nat. Center Ulcer Research and Edn., 1975—; chmn. adv. tng. grant com. NIH, 1967-73; chmn. adv. research com. VA, 1968-71. Editor: Jour. Gastroenterology, 1970-77; contbr. chpts. med. textbooks. Served with USNR, 1953-55. Recipient Clin. Investigator award VA, 1959-64; spl. fellow NIH, 1957-59. Fellow A.C.P.; mem. Am. Gastroenterol. Assn. (pres. 1979-80), Am. Fedn. Clin. Research, Am. Soc. Clin. Investigation, Assn. Am. Physicians. Office: Yale U Sch Medicine 333 Cedar St New Haven CT 06510

DONALDSON, SAMUEL ANDREW, journalist; b. El Paso, Tex., Mar. 11, 1934; s. Samuel Andrew and Chloe (Hampson) D.; m. Billie Kay Butler, Nov. 30, 1963; children: Samuel, Jennifer, Thomas, Robert.; m. Janice Claire Smith, Apr. 16, 1983. B.A., U. Tex., El Paso, 1955; postgrad., U. So. Calif., 1955-56. Radio/TV news reporter/anchorman WTOP, Washington, 1961-67; Capitol Hill corr. ABC News, Washington, 1967-77, White House corr., 1977—. Served to capt. AUS, 1956-59. Mem. Congl. Radio-TV Corrs. Assn. (exec. com.), AFTRA (past pres. Washington-Balt. chpt.). Home: 1125 Crest Ln McLean VA 22101 Office: 1717 deSales St NW Washington DC 20036

DONALDSON, STEPHEN REEDER, author; b. Cleve., May 13, 1947; s. James R. and Mary Ruth (Reeder) D.; m. Stephanie Rae Boutz, Sept. 20, 1980. B.A., Coll. of Wooster, 1968; M.A., Kent State U., 1971. Asst. dispatcher Akron City Hosp., 1968-70; teaching fellow Kent State U., 1971; acquisitions editor Tapp-Gentz Assos., West Chester, Pa., 1973-74; instr. Ghost Ranch Writers Workshops, N.Mex., 1973-77. Author: Lord Foul's Bane, 1977, The Illearth War, 1977, The Power That Preserves, 1977, The Wounded Land, 1980, (as Reed Stephens) The Man Who Killed His Brother, 1980, The One Tree, 1982, White Gold Wielder, 1983, Daughter of Regals, 1984. Recipient John W. Campbell award for best new writer World Sci. Fiction Conv., 1979, Best Novel award Brit. Fantasy Soc., 1979, Balrog award for best novel, 1981, 1983, Saturn award for best fantasy novel, 1983. Mem. Am. Contract Bridge League. Clubs: Duke City Bridge, Showdown Tennis. Office: care Del Rey Ballantine 201 E 50th St New York NY 10022

DONALDSON, WILLIS LYLE, research institute administrator; b. Cleburne, Tex., May 1, 1915; s. Charles Lyle and Anna (Bell) D.; m. Frances Virginia Donnell, Aug. 20, 1938; children: Sarah Donaldson Seaberg, Susan Donaldson Pollock, Sylvia Donaldson Nelson, Anthony Lyle. B.S., Tex. Tech. U., 1938. Distbn. engr. Tex. Electric Service Co., 1938-42, supervisory engr., 1945-46; asst. prof. elec. engring. Lehigh U., 1946-51, assoc. prof., 1953-54; with S.W. Research Inst., San Antonio, 1954—, v.p., 1964-72, v.p. planning and program devel., 1972-74, sr. v.p. planning and program devel., 1974—. Bd. dirs. San Antonio Chamber Music Soc., pres., 1962-72. Served to capt. USNR, 1942-45, 51-53. Named Disting. Engr. Tex. Tech. U., 1969. Fellow IEEE, Am. Soc. Nondestructive Testing; mem. Nat. Soc. Profl. Engrs., Tex. Soc. Profl. Engrs., Am. Optical Soc., Armed Forces Communications and Electronics Assn., Am. Mgmt. Assn., Sigma Xi, Tau Beta Pi, Eta Kappa Nu, Alpha Chi. Mem. Christian Ch. (Disciples of Christ). Home: 104 Pontiac Ln San Antonio TX 78232 Office: 6220 Culebra Rd San Antonio TX 78284

DONAT, GEORGE, management consultant, business executive; b. Vienna, Austria, June 19, 1920; came to U.S., 1940, naturalized, 1943; s. Lewis and Margaret (Csillagh) D.; m. Glenna Gienty, Oct. 9, 1948; children: Stephanie, Jeffrey M. Grad., Royal Acad. Econs., Budapest, Hungary, 1938; student, George Washington U. Sch. Law, 1950-53. Mem. Allied Control Commn.; sr. investigator Dept. Justice, 1948-50; with Dept. Commerce, 1950-53, Parke-Davis & Co., 1953-68, dir. comml. devel., 1967-68, dir. European and Can. ops., 1965-67; dep. dir. Bur. Internat. Commerce, Washington, 1962-64; adminstr. bus. and def. services Dept. Commerce, Washington, 1964-65; v.p. E.R. Squibb & Sons, N.Y.C. and Princeton, N.J., 1968-79; pres. ICN Pharms., Inc., Covina, Calif., 1979-80; also dir.; pres. Geo. Donat Assocs., Inc., Princeton, 1980—; chmn. bd. Schwarzhaupt Corp., Las Vegas, 1980—, Rom-Am. Pharm., 1983—; leader various profl. seminars. Bd. dirs. Detroit Bd. Commerce, 1965-68, U.S. C. of C., 1965-71, N.J. Trade Expansion Adv. Council, 1975-79; pres. Wrightstown Twp. (Pa.) Civic Assn., 1975-79; bd. dirs. Warsaw Children's Hosp. Found., Wilmington, Del., 1977-83. Served with inf. U.S. Army, 1941-45; PTO. Decorated Bronze Star. Clubs: Univ. (Detroit); Nat. Capital Democratic. Office: The Office Center Suite 2D Princeton Meadows Plainsboro NJ

DONATH, FRED ARTHUR, geologist, geophysicist; b. St. Cloud, Minn., July 11, 1931; s. Arnold C. and Elizabeth (Crary) D.; m. Mavis Eleanor Hagen, July 19, 1952; children: Robert William, Deborah Ann. B.A., U. Minn., 1954; M.S., Stanford U., 1956, Ph.D., 1958. Mem. faculty San Jose (Calif.) State Coll., 1957-58; mem. faculty Columbia U., N.Y.C., 1958-67, prof. geology, 1966-67, U. Ill., Urbana, 1967-80, head dept. geology, 1967-77; cons. U.S. Nuclear Regulatory Commn., 1977-80; pres. CGS, Inc., Urbana, 1980-83; dir., prin. geoscientist Ertec Western Inc., Long Beach, Calif., 1983—; adv. Office Sci. and Tech. Policy, 1978-79; mem. U.S. Nat. Com. Rock Mechanics, 1978-81. Editor: Ann. Rev. Earth and Planetary Scis, 1970-80; asso. editor: Geol. Soc. Am, 1963-73; acting editor, 1964; mem. editorial bd.: Engring. Geology, 1964-83, Tectonophysics, 1964-77; contbr. numerous articles on geophysics to sci. jours. Recipient Semicentennial Medallion Rice U., 1962. Fellow Geol. Soc. Am., Geol. Soc. London, AAAS; mem. Am. Geophys. Union (sec. tectonophysics sect. 1964-68, vis. lectr. 1967-72), Am. Assn. Petroleum Geologists (lectr. continuing edn. program 1965-78), Phi Beta Kappa, Sigma Xi. Research in exptl. high pressure geophysics, deep geol. disposal of nuclear waste. Designer high pressure equipment. Office: Earth Technology Corp 3777 Long Beach Blvd Long Beach CA 90807

DONATI, ENRICO, painter, corporate executive; b. Milan, Italy, Feb. 19, 1909; came to U.S., 1934, naturalized, 1945; s. Federico and Marianna (Vita) D.; m. Claire Javal, 1934; children: Marina (Mrs. Serge Lier), Sylviane (Mrs. Claude Mahias); m. Adele Schmidt, 1965; 1 dau., Alexandra. D. Econs. and Social Scis., U. Pavia, Italy, 1929. Chmn. bd. Houbigant, Inc., 1965—; vis. lectr., critic Yale U., 1960-62; Mem. jury Fulbright Scholarship Program, 1954-56, 61-64; mem. Yale Council Arts and Architecture, 1962-69; mem. adv. bd. Parsons Sch. Design, N.Y.C., 1959; chmn. nat. com. Univ. Art Mus., Berkeley, Calif., 1970-72; adv. bd. regents Brandeis U., 1956-65. Mem. Surrealist group, until 1950; one-man shows include, Staempfli Gallery, N.Y.C., 1962, 63, 66, 68, 70, 72, 74, 76, 80, 82, J. L. Hudson Gallery, Detroit, 1964, 66, 69, Mass. Inst. Tech., 1964, Obelisk Gallery, Washington, 1965, Minn. Mus. Art, 1977, Ankrum Gallery, Los Angeles, 1977, 79, 82, Chrysler Mus., Norfolk, Va., 1977; one-made shows include, Tenn. Fine Arts Center, Nashville; one-man shows include, Gairweather Hardin Gallery, Chgo., Hunter Mus. Art, Chattanooga, 1978, Davenport (Iowa) Mcpl. Art Gallery, Wildenstein Art Center, Houston, Norton Gallery, Palm Beach, Fla., 1979, Osuna Gallery, Washington, Palm Springs (Calif.) Desert Mus., 1980, Grand Palais, Paris; represented in permanent collections, Am. Republic Ins. Co., Des Moines, Mus. Modern Art, Whitney Mus., Washington U., St. Louis, Houston Mus. Fine Arts, Muses Royaux des Beaux-Arts de Belgique, Mus. Internat. Center Aesthetic Research, Turin, Italy, Albright-Knox Art Gallery, Detroit Inst. Art, U. Mich., Balt. Mus. Art, Newark Mus. Art, Galleria Nazionale d'Arte Moderna, Rome and Milan, Michener Found., Allentown, Pa., IBM Corp., Mass. Inst. Tech., Chase Manhattan Bank, Rockefeller collection, Johns Hopkins U., Yale Art Gallery, Washington Gallery Modern Art, Tougaloo (Miss.) Coll., Univ. Art Mus., Israel Mus., Jerusalem, U. Miami, St. Paul Art Center, U. Tex. at Austin, Hudson Mall, N.Y.C., Mus. Fine Arts, St. Petersburg, Fla., Prudential Life Ins. Co., Newark, Tacoma Art Mus., Lowe Mus. U. Miami, High Mus. Art, Atlanta, Pitts. Nat. Bank, Avon Products, Inc., N.Y.C., Doane Coll., Crete, Nebr., also collections numerous bus. corps., pvt. collections. Served as lt. Italian Mountain Troops. Decorated cavaliere Della Corona D'Italia. Clubs: New Canaan (Conn.) Country; Bohemian (San Francisco). Studio: 222 Central Park S New York NY 10021 Office: 1135 Pleasantview Terr Ridgefield NJ 07657 also Gimpel and Weitzenhoffer 1040 Madison Ave New York NY 10021

DONATI, ROBERT MARIO, physician, educator; b. Richmond Heights, Mo., Feb. 28, 1934; s. Leo S. and Rose Marie D. B.S. in Biology, St. Louis U., 1955, M.D., 1959. Diplomate: Am. Bd. Nuclear Medicine, bd. dirs., 1980—. Intern St. Louis City Hosp., 1959-60; asst. resident John Cochran Hosp., St. Louis, 1960-62; fellow in nuclear medicine St. Louis U., 1962-63; practice medicine specializing in nuclear medicine, St. Louis, 1963—; mem. staff John Cochran Hosp., 1963-83, St. Louis U. Hosp., 1963—; mem. faculty (St. Louis U. Sch. Medicine), 1963—, asst. prof. internal medicine, 1965-68, assoc. prof., 1968-74, prof., 1974—, prof. radiology, 1979—, dir. div. nuclear medicine, 1968—, sr. assoc. dean, 1983—; chief nuclear medicine services St. Louis VA Med. Center, 1968-79, chief of staff, 1979-83; adj. prof. medicine Washington U. Sch. Medicine, 1979-83; Del. Am. Bd. Med. Spltys., 1982—; councilor Federated Council Member Medicine Orgns., 1981—. Editor: (with W. T. Newton) Radioassay in Clinical Medicine, 1974; Contbr. articles to profl. jours. Mem. Presdl. Adv. Commn. on VA, 1972; Bd. dirs. Inst. for Health Mgmt., Inc., 1976-78; mem. HEW Task Force on Health Effects of Ionizing Radiation, 1978-79; mem. desegregation monitoring and adv. com. U.S. Dist. Ct., 1980-82; mem. Multi-Hosp. Systems Nat. Adv. Com., 1982—. Served to capt. AUS, 1966-68. Decorated Army Commendation medal. Mem. AMA (residency rev. com. for nuclear medicine 1978-80), St. Louis Med. Soc., Am. Fedn. for Clin. Research (councilor 1967-70), Central Soc. Clin. Research, AAUP, N.Y. Acad. Scis., Soc. Exptl. Biology and Medicine, Soc. Nuclear Medicine (acad. council 1970—, bd. trustee 1977-81, assoc. chmn. sci. program 1978, mem. publs. com. 1979—, chmn. 1982-83), Am. Coll. Nuclear Physicians, Am., Internat. socs. hematology, Soc. Med. Consultants to Armed Forces, Sigma Xi. Roman Catholic. Clubs: Cosmos (Washington); Racquet (St. Louis). Research in clin. investigative nuclear medicine and humoral control of cellular proliferation. Home: 5335 Botanical Ave Saint Louis MO 63110 Office: St. Louis U. Sch Medicine 1325 S Grand Blvd Saint Louis MO 63104

DONAVAN, GEORGE EDGAR, banker; b. Jackson, Miss., Feb. 23, 1916; s. George Edgar and Annie Mivian (Nelson) D.; m. Katie Bell Holmes, Dec. 3, 1938; children—George Edgar III, Carl Howard. Student, Miss. State U., 1933-34; B.S.C., U. Miss., 1937. With Lamar Life Ins. Co., Jackson, 1937-42, Scharff & Jones, Inc. (investments), 1946-60; with 1st Nat. Bank, Jackson, 1960-74; v.p. Unifirst Fed Savs. & Loan Assn., Jackson, 1974—. Served with USNR, 1943-46. Mem. Omicron Delta Kappa, Pi Kappa Alpha. Clubs: Rotarian (pres. Jackson 1972-73), Capital City, Petroleum, Jackson Country, University. Home: 3949 Eastwood Dr Jackson MS 39211 Office: Capitol at State St Jackson MS 39205

DONAVAN, GEORGE FRANCIS, real estate development company executive; b. Worcester, Mass., Jan. 6, 1939; s. Ethel May (Dowell) Donovan; m. Diane Marie Vuona, Aug. 20, 1960; children: Lisa, David. B.S. in Elec. Engring., Norwich U., 1961. Mktg. rep. IBM Corp., Hartford, Conn., 1964-68; v.p. Computer Property Corp., N.Y.C., 1968-71; pres. Gemcor, Ramsey, N.J., 1971-72; v.p. Fairfield Communities Inc., Little Rock, 1972-77, sr. v.p., 1977-81, pres., Knoxville, 1981—, dir. Trustee Dulin Gallery Art, Knoxville, 1983. Served to lst lt. U.S. Army, 1961-63. Mem. Am. Land Devel. Assn. (dir., chmn. 1982-84), Knoxville C. of C. (dir. 1983). Republican. Roman Catholic. Clubs: Cherokee Country, Fox Den Country (Knoxville); Little Rock Country. Office: Fairfield Communities Inc 408 Cedar Bluff Knoxville TN 37923

DONCHI, DON JOSEPH, foreign service officer; b. Newark, Aug. 30, 1938; s. Sol M. and Celia B. D.; m. Margaret Dunn, Dec. 29, 1963; children: Michael, Julia, Sarah. A.B., NYU, 1961, M.A., 1962, postgrad., 1962-64. Commd. U.S. Fgn. Service; 3d sec. Am. Embassy, Yaonde, Camproun, 1964-66, 2d sec., Sofia, Burgaria, 1967-69; 1st sec. Am Embassy, Oslo, Norway, 1973-76; congl. fellow U.S. Congress, Washington, 1978-79; dir. tng. State Dept., U.S. Congress, 1980-82; Am. consul gen. U.S. Consulate Gen., Zagreb, Yugoslavia, 1982—. Sch. bd. chmn. Am. Sch. of Zagreb, 1982—. Recipient Meritorious Honor award U.S. State Dept., 1972. Office: Brace Kavurica 2 Zagreb Yugoslavia 41000

DONCHIAN, RICHARD DAVOUD, investment firm executive; b. Hartford, Conn., Sept. 21, 1905; s. Samuel B. and Armenouhi A.

(Davoud) D.; m. Alma C. Gibbs, Feb. 9, 1957. A.B., Yale U., 1928. Chartered fin. analyst U. Va. and Inst. Chartered Fin. Analysts, 1964. Market technician Hemphill Noyes & Co., N.Y.C., 1933-35; v.p. Samuel Donchian Rug Co., Hartford, Conn., 1933-38; pres. Fin. Supervision, Inc., N.Y.C., 1938-42; econ. analyst, market letter writer Shearson Hammill & Co., N.Y.C., 1946-48; pvt. investment adviser, N.Y.C., 1948-60; pres. Futures, Inc., N.Y.C., 1948-60; account exec., dir. commodity research, v.p. Hayden Stone, Inc. (name changed to Shearson, Am. Express), 1960—, sr. v.p. investments, Greenwich, Conn., 1971—; pres. Donchian Commodities, Inc., Greenwich, 1973—, Donchian Mgmt., Inc., Ft. Lauderdale, Fla., 1976—; sr. adviser Commodity Trend Timing Fund, N.Y.C., 1980—, 1982—. Author articles and monographs. Served as statis. control officer with USAAF, 1942-45. Mem. Commodity Exchange, Inc., N.Y. Cotton Exchange, N.Y. Futures Exchange, N.Y. Soc. Securities Analysts, Am. Statis. Assn., Nat. Assn. Futures Trading Advs., Fin. Forum, N.Y. Rug Soc. Republican. Presbyterian (elder). Clubs: Yale, Down Town Assn. (N.Y.C.); Scarsdale Golf; Deerfield Country (Deerfield Beach, Fla.); Yale (Ft. Lauderdale); Univ. (Hartford); Appalachian Mountain. Home: 133 N Pompano Beach Blvd Pompano Beach FL 33062 also Bomoseen VT 05732 Office: 2 Greenwich Plaza Greenwich CT 06830 also 3099 E Commercial Blvd Fort Lauderdale FL 33308

DONCHIN, EMANUEL, psychologist, educator; b. Tel Aviv, Apr. 3, 1935; U.S., 1961; s. Michael and Guta D.; m. Rina Greenfarb, June 3, 1955; children: Gill, Opher, Ayala. B.A., Hebrew U., 1961, M.A., 1963; Ph.D., UCLA, 1965. Teaching and research asst. dept. psychology Hebrew U., 1958-61; research asst. dept. psychology UCLA, 1961-63, research psychologist, 1964-65; research asso. div. neurology Stanford U. Med. Sch., 1965-66, asst. prof. in residence, 1966-68; research asso. neurobiology br. NASA, Ames Research Center, Moffett Field, Calif., 1966-68; asso. prof. dept. psychology U. Ill., Urbana-Champaign, 1968-72, prof. psychology and physiology, 1972—, head dept. psychology, 1980—. Author: (with Donald B. Lindsley) Averaged Evoked Potentials, 1969; contbr. articles to profl. jours. Served with Israeli Army, 1952-55. Fellow AAAS, Am. Psychol. Assn.; mem. Soc. Psychophysiol. Research (pres. 1980), Fedn. Behavioral, Cognitive and Psychol. Socs. (v.p. 1981—), Am. EEG Soc., Psychonomic Soc., Soc. Neuroscis., AAAS. Office: Dept Psychology U Ill 603 E Daniel St Champaign IL 61820

DONEGAN, CHARLES EDWARD, lawyer, educator; b. Chgo., Apr. 10, 1933; s. Arthur C. and Odessa (Arnold) D.; m. Patty Lou Harris, June 15, 1963; 1 son, Carter Edward. B.S.C., Roosevelt U., 1954; M.S., Loyola U., 1959; J.D., Howard U., 1967; LL.M., Columbia, 1970. Bar: N.Y. 1968, D.C. 1968, Ill. 1979. Pub. sch. tchr., Chgo., 1956-59; with Office Internal Revenue, Chgo., 1959-62; labor economist U.S. Dept. Labor, Washington, 1962-65; legal intern U.S. Commn. Civil Rights, Washington, summer 1966; asst. counsel NAACP Legal Def. Fund, N.Y.C., 1967-69; lectr. law Baruch Coll., N.Y.C., 1969-70; asst. prof. law State U. N.Y. at Buffalo, 1970-73; assoc. prof. law Howard U., 1973-77; vis. assoc. prof. Ohio State U., Columbus, 1977-78; asst. regional counsel U.S. EPA, 1978-80; prof. law So. U., Baton Rouge, 1980—; arbitrator steel industry, 1972—, U.S. Postal Service, New Orleans; vis. prof. law La. State U., summer 1981; real estate broker. Author: Discrimination in Public Employment, 1975; Contbr. articles to profl. jours., to Dictionary Am. Negro Biography. Active Americans for Democratic Action. Named Most Outstanding Prof. So. U. Law Sch., 1982; Ford Found. scholar, 1965-67; Ford Found. fellow Columbia U., 1972-73; Nat. Endowment for Humanities postdoctoral fellow in Afro-Am. studies Yale, 1972-73. Mem. ABA (vice chmn. com. edn. and curriculum local govt. law sect. 1972—, mem. pub. edn. com. sect. local govt. 1974—, chmn. liaison com. AALS), Nat. Bar Assn., D.C. Bar Assn., Chgo. Bar Assn., Fed. Bar Assn., Cook County Bar Assn., Am. Arbitration Assn. (arbitrator), Nat. Conf. Black Lawyers (bd. organizers), Assn. Henri Capitant, Roosevelt, Loyola, Howard and Columbia alumni assns., Alpha Phi Alpha, Phi Alpha Kappa, Phi Alpha Delta. Home: 10837 Flintwood Ave Baton Rouge LA 70811 Office: So U Sch Law Baton Rouge LA 70813

DONEGAN, THOMAS JAMES, lawyer; b. Bklyn., Feb. 27, 1907; s. Thomas James and Mary F. (Carey) D.; m. Dorothy N. Reynolds, May 2, 1936; 1 son, Thomas James. A.B., Columbia U., 1929; LL.B., Fordham U., 1931. Bar: N.Y. 1932, U.S. Supreme Ct., U.S. Dist. Ct. (so. and ea. dists.) N.Y. Practice N.Y.C., 1932-33, 46-57; agt. FBI, 1933-46; spl. asst. atty. gen. U.S., 1947-57; chmn. interdeptl. com. internal security Nat. Security Council, 1953-54; chmn. personnel security adv. com. Exec. Office Pres., 1954-57; mem. U.S. Subversive Activities Control Bd., 1957-67; exec. dir. Indian Claims Commn., Washington, 1968-70; hearing examiner U.S. Dept. Health, Edn. and Welfare, San Diego, 1970-72; fed. adminstrv. law judge, 1972-77. Lt. USNR, 1937-40. Mem. ABA. Office: PO Box 10149 Bainbridge Island WA 98110

DONELAN, FRANCIS PATRICK, construction company executive; b. N.Y.C., Apr. 13, 1939; s. Joseph and Eileen (Meehan) D.; m. Katherine Munafo, July 20, 1963; children: Francis, Douglas. B.S. in Acctg., Fordham U., 1960, LL.B., 1963. Ptnr. firm Hynes & Diamond, N.Y.C., 1963-80; v.p., sec., gen. counsel George A. Fuller Co., N.Y.C., 1980—. Mem. ABA, Am. Arbitration Assn. Panel of Arbitrators, N.Y. State Bar Assn. Club: Marco Polo (N.Y.C.). Home: 78 Russell Rd Garden City NY 11530 Office: George A Fuller Co 919 3d Ave New York NY 10022

DONELAN, WILLIAM JOSEPH, hospital adminstrator; b. Washington, Oct. 2, 1946; s. William Joseph and Anna Grayson (Curtice) D.; m. Mary Anne McGuinness, Aug. 17, 1968. B.A., Wheeling Coll., 1968; M.S., Duke U., 1974. Asst. bus. mgr. Duke U. Med. Ctr., Durham, N.C., 1969-70, adminstrv. asst., 1970-74, bus. mgr., 1974-81; chief operating officer Duke U. Hosp., Durham, N.C., 1981—; adj. asst. prof. Duke U., 1982—. Trustee Kidney Found. N.C., Chapel Hill, 1971-78, Nat. Kidney Found., N.Y.C., 1973-76; bd. dirs. Lincoln Community Health Ctr., Durham, 1977-82. Recipient pres.'s award Kidney Found. N.C., 1976. Democrat. Roman Catholic. Club: Duke Mgmt. (Durham) (pres. 1981-82). Home: 150 Dixie Dr Chapel Hill NC 27514 Office: Duke U Hosp Durham NC 27710

DONELANI, JACK EDWARD, institute executive; b. Montreal, Que., Can., Dec. 6, 1946; s. Eric Edward Donegani and Daisy Harriet (Welch) D.; m. Denise Elizabeth Ballagh; 1 son, Neal. B.Sc., 1969; M.Sc., U. Toronto, 1975; M.B.A., York U., 1980. Head mktg. unit Computer Centre, AES, 1976-78; head climate archive unit Data Adminstrn. br., 1978-80; pres. Profl. Inst. Public Service of Can., Ottawa, Ont., 1980—. McGill scholar; NRC Scholar. Mem. Canadian Meteorol. and Oceanographic Assn., Public Adminstrn. Assn. Home: 23 2d Ave Ottawa ON K1S 2H2 Canada Office: 786 Bronson Ave Ottawa ON K1S 4G4 Canada

DONEN, STANLEY, film producer, director; b. Columbia, S.C., Apr. 13; s. Mortie and Helen D. Ed., U. S.C. Dir.: films including Saturn 3, 1980; co-dir.: On the Town; producer-dir.: The Little Prince, 1974, Lucky Lady, 1975, Movie Movie, 1978. Mem. Dir. Guild Am. Office: care Dirs Guild Am 7950 W Sunset Blvd Hollywood CA 90046 *

DONER, DEAN BENTON, educator; b. Brookings, S.D., May 1, 1923; s. David Benton and Edna (Beals) D.; m. Lois Jacobsen, Dec. 23, 1944; children—Kalia Louise, Margaret, Lauren Elizabeth. B.S., S.D. State U., 1947; M.F.A., U. Ia., 1948, Ph.D., 1953. Instr. English U. Ida., 1950-53; instr., prof. English, asso. dean Sch. Humanities, Purdue U., 1953-67; dean (Coll. Liberal Arts and Scis.); prof. English U. Ill., Chgo. Circle, 1967-73; v.p., prof. English Boston U., 1973—; vis. prof. U. Hamburg, 1967; faculty Salzburg Seminar in Am. Studies, 1967. Contbr. short stories, poems, article to mags. Served with USAAF, 1943-46. Democrat. Unitarian. Home: Wolfsbrunnensteige 2B 6900 Heidelberg Federal Republic Germany Office: Boston U Tompkins Barracks APO New York NY 09081

DONEY, WILLIS FREDERICK, educator; b. Pitts., Aug. 19, 1925; s. Willis Frederick and Ora (Powell) D. B.A., Princeton, 1946, M.A., Ph.D., 1949; M.A., Dartmouth, 1966. Instr. Cornell U., 1949-52; vis. lectr. U. Mich., 1952; asst. prof. Ohio State U., 1953-56, 57-58; George Santayana fellow, 1956-57; mem. faculty Dartmouth, 1958—, prof. philosophy, 1966—; mem. Inst. for Advanced Study, Princeton, N.J., 1972-73; vis. lectr. Harvard, 1963; vis. prof. Edinburgh U., 1980. Author articles on 17th Century philosophy.; Editor: Descartes: A Collection of Critical Studies, 1967, Malebranche: Entretiens sur la Métaphysique, 1980. Ford-Dartmouth fellow, 1970; Camargo Found. fellow, 1978-79. Home: N Main St Norwich VT 05055 Office: Philosophy Dept Dartmouth Coll Hanover NH 03755

DONFRIED, KARL PAUL, minister, theology educator; b. N.Y.C., Apr. 6, 1940; s. Paul and Else (Schmuck) D.; m. Katharine E. Krayer, Sept. 10, 1960; children: Paul Andrew, Karen Erika, Mark Christopher. A.B., Columbia U., 1960; B.D., Harvard U., 1963; S.T.M., Union Theol. Sem., 1965; Th.D., U. Heidelberg, (Ger.), 1968. Ordained to ministry, 1963; named ecumenical canon Christ Ch. Cathedral, Springfield, Mass., 1977. Assoc. pastor ch., N.Y.C., 1963-64, acting Luth. chaplain, 1963-64; mem. faculty Smith Coll., Northampton, Mass., 1968—, prof. N.T. and early Christianity, 1968—, chmn. dept. religion and mem. N.T. panel Nat. Luth.-Roman Cath. Dialogue, 1971-73, 75-78; chmn. Columbia Seminar for Study of N.T., 1976-77; vis. prof. Assumption Coll., Worcester, Mass., 1975, Amherst Coll., 1976, 78, St. Hyacinth Coll. and Sem., Granby, Mass., 1976, Brown U., 1979, Mt. Holyoke Coll., 1983. Author: (with R.E. Brown, J. Reumann) Peter in the New Testament, 1973, The Setting of Second Clement in Early Christianity, 1974, (with others) Mary in the New Testament, 1978, The Dynamic Word, 1981; editor: The Romans Debate, 1977; editorial bd.: Jour. Bibl. Lit., 1975-81. Mem. Am. Acad. Religion (dir. 1972-73, pres. New Eng. region 1971-72), Studiorum Novi Testamenti Societas (chmn. Paul seminar 1975-78, exec. com. 1979-83), Soc. Bibl. Lit. (pres. New Eng. region 1975-76), Cath. Bibl. Assn. Address: Dept Religion Smith Coll Northampton MA 01063 *As the son of immigrant parents, I learned early the value of hard and honest work, the necessity for intergrity in all human relations and the blessings of generosity to those less fortunate. These values, together with my commitment to Christianity, have shaped, and continue to shape, my life.*

DONINO, FRANK DONALD, advertising agency executive; b. Greenwich, Conn., Oct. 8, 1938; s. Frank Andrew and Jennie Lena (Bruno) D.; children—Thomas, Gary, Frank, Jennifer, Maria. B.A., Fairfield U., 1960. Vice-pres. Grey Advt., N.Y.C., 1961-72; exec. v.p. McCann-Erickson, Inc., N.Y.C., 1972-79; pres. John H. Murray Advt. Agy., 1979—; bd. dirs. career adv. com. Fairfield U. Mem. Byram Hills Bd. Edn., 1976-81, pres., 1978-81; Councilman Town of North Castle, 1981-85. Club: Whipporwill Country. Address: 373 Taconie Rd Greenwich CT 06830

DONIS, PETER P., agricultural machinery manufacturing company executive; b. Madison, Wis., May 30, 1924; s. Peter A. and Katherine A. (Gray) D.; m. Mildred Eva Niesen, June 23, 1948; children: David Lee, Diana Louise, Paul Andrew. B.B.A., U. Wis., 1948. With Caterpillar Tractor Co., 1956—, plant mgr., Joliet, Ill., 1963-74, v.p., Peoria, Ill., 1975-77, exec. v.p., 1977—; dir. Home Fed. Savs. and Loan Assn., Peoria. Trustee Joint Council on Econ. Edn., Western U. Regional Adv. Council, Adv. Council of Ill. 2000 Found. Mem. Ill. State C. of C. (bd. dirs.). Club: Country (Peoria). Home: 7610 N Edgewild Dr Peoria IL 61614 Office: 100 NE Adams St Peoria IL 61629

DONLEAVY, JAMES PATRICK, writer; b. Bklyn., Apr. 23, 1926; m. Valerie Heron (div.); children: Philip, Karen; m. Mary Wilson Price; children: Rebecca, Rory. Student, Trinity Coll., Dublin, Ireland. Author: novel, later adapted as play The Ginger Man, 1955, Fairy Tales of New York, 1960; A Singular Man novel, later adapted as play, 1963, Meet My Maker the Mad Molecule, short stories, sketches, 1964, The Saddest Summer of Samuel S, novella, later adapted as play, 1966, The Beastly Beatitudes of Balthazar B, novel, later adapted as play, 1968, The Onion Eaters, 1971, The Plays of J.P. Donleavy, 1972; novel A Fairy Tale of New York, 1973; The Unexpurgated Code, A Complete Manual of Survival and Manners, 1975, The Destinies of Darcy Dancer, Gentleman, 1977; novel Schultz, 1979, Leila, 1983; J.P. Donleavy's de Alfonce Tennis, The Superlative Game of Eccentric Champions. Its History, Accoutrements, Rules, Conduct and Regimen, 1984. Served with USNR, World War II. Recipient Creative Arts award Brandeis U., 1961-62; AAAL grantee, 1975. Home: Levington Park Mullingar County Westmeath Ireland

DONLEVY, JOHN DEARDEN, lawyer; b. Chgo., May 29, 1933; s. Frank and Alice Genevieve (O'Connor) D.; m. Kristin Bach Donlevy-Minnick, Apr. 20, 1963; 1 son, John Dearden. Student, Stanford U., 1950-52; B.S., Northwestern U., 1954; J.D., U. Chgo., 1957; postgrad., Northwestern U., 1958. Bar: Ill. 1957, U.S. Dist. Ct. (no. dist.) 1957, U.S. Ct. Appeals (7th cir.) 1969, U.S. Supreme Ct. 1972. Asst. state's atty. Cook County Criminal Div., Chgo., 1958-61; city prosecutor City of Evanston, Ill., 1961; assoc. Mayer, Brown & Platt, Chgo., 1962-73, ptnr., 1974—; participant Hinton Moot Ct. Competition U. Chgo., 1955-56, judge Hinton Moot Ct. Competition, 1972. Bd. dirs. English-Speaking Union, Chgo., 1964-65; active Republican Orgn., 1958-60. Recipient Disting. Legal award Am. Legion, Chgo., 1960; named spl. prosecutor-labor racketeering Cook County State's Atty., Chgo., 1959-61. Mem. ABA, Ill. State Bar Assn. (workers' compensation, criminal law sections), Chgo. Bar Assn., Workers' Compensation Lawyers Assn. (Ill.). Republican. Roman Catholic. Home: 945 Ravine Rd Winnetka IL 60093 Office: Mayer Brown & Platt 231 S LaSalle St Chicago IL 60604 *I have always sought to examine problems carefully in order to obtain the fullest possible understanding of them, as I believe that with proper understanding, there is nothing in life which need be feared.*

DONLEY, EDWARD, manufacturing company executive; b. Highland Park, Mich., Nov. 26, 1921; s. Hugh and Frances (Gavin) D.; m. Inez Cantrell, Oct. 24, 1946; children: Martha Donley Robb, Thomas, John. B.M.E., Lawrence Inst. Tech., 1943; grad., Advanced Mgmt. Program, Harvard, 1959. Vice pres. Air Products and Chems. Inc., Allentown, Pa., 1950-66, exec. v.p., 1966, pres., 1966—, chief exec. officer, 1973—, chmn. bd., 1978—, also dir.; dir. Am. Standard, Inc., Mellon Bank N.A., Pa. Power & Light; bd. overseers Coll. Engring. and Applied Sci. U. Pa.; corp. mem. Lawrence Inst. Tech.; trustee, mem. bus. adv. council Carnegie-Mellon U.; mem. bus.-higher edn. forum Am. Council on Edn.; chmn. exec. com. Bus. Council Pa.; mem. Dun's Pres.'s Panel. Mem. adv. bd.: Chem. and Engring. News. Mem. Conf. Bd., Am. Inst. Chem. Engrs., Soc. Chem. Industry, Chem. Mfrs. Assn. (chmn. 1978-79). Home: 326 N 27th St Allentown PA 18104 Office: PO Box 538 Allentown PA 18105

DONLEY, RUSSELL LEE, III, engineer, state representative; b. Salt Lake City, Feb. 3, 1939; s. R. Lee and Leona (Sherwood) D.; m. Karen Kocherhans, June 4, 1960; children: Tammera Sue, Tonya Kay, Christina Lynn. B.S. in Civil Engring. with honors, U. Wyo., 1961; M.S. in Engring., U. Fla., 1962. Registered profl. engr., Wyo., Mont., Colo., N.Y.; land surveyor, Wyo. Mem. Wyo. Ho. of Reps., 1969—, chmn. appropriations com., 1975-78, mem. rules com., 1973-84; chmn. rules com. Wyo. Ho. Reps., 1983-84; majority floor leader Wyo. Ho. of Reps., 1979-80, speaker pro tem, 1981-82, chmn. legis. mgmt. council, 1983-84, speaker of house, 1983-84; with Russel L. Donley and Assocs. Inc., Casper, Wyo., 1983—. Chmn. Western Region Council State Govts., 1982-83; precinct committeeman Republican Party, 1967; chmn. Wyo. Young. Reps., 1968; fin. chmn. Natrona County Rep. Party, 1970; pres. bd. dirs. YMCA, Casper, 1976—. Recipient award for engring. excellence Am. Cons. Engrs. Council, Legislator of Yr. award Nat. Republican Legislators Assn., 1981; named Wyo. Outstanding Young Engr. Sigma Tau, 1974, Disting. Wyo. Engr. Tau Beta Pi., 1976. Mem. Am. Water Works Assn., Nat. Soc. Profl. Engrs., Wyo. Soc. Profl. Engrs., Wyo. Engring. Soc., Wyo. Assn. Cons. Engrs. and Surveyors. Mormon. Home: 1140 Ivy Ln Casper WY 82609 Office: Wyo Ho of Reps Office of Speaker State Capitol Cheyenne WY 82002 Office: 240 S Wolcott St Casper WY 82601

DONNA, JAMES MICHAEL, news service executive; b. Wilkes-Barre, Pa., July 15, 1946; s. Michael and Dolores (Slattery) D.; m. Patricia Lukaszewska, Aug. 18, 1979. B.A., Mt. St. Mary's Coll., Emmitsburg, Md., 1971; M.A., Pa. State U., 1972. Editorial researcher Look mag., N.Y.C., 1966-68; reporter Reading (Pa.) Eagle, 1972-73; with AP, 1973—, enterprise editor, N.Y.C., 1977-79, bur. chief, 1979-83, dir. wide world photos, 1983—. Dept. State fellow Yugoslavia, 1972. Office: 50 Rockefeller Plaza New York NY 10020

DONNAHOE, ALAN STANLEY, newspaper executive; b. Asheville, N.C., Aug. 27, 1916; s. Paul Albert and Kate (Stanley) D.; m. Elsie Pitts, 1938; children—Kate Stanley Donnahoe Vaughan. Student pub. schs. Bar: Va., N.C. Dir. research Richmond (Va.) C. of C., 1936-46, asst. exec. mgr., 1946-50; exec. sec. Richmond Inter-Club Council, 1938-41, Va. Soc. Pub. Accountants, Richmond, 1946-50; dir. research Richmond Newspapers, Inc., 1950-55, v.p., 1956-59, exec. v.p., asst. pub., 1959-65, pres., dir., 1966—; pres., chief exec. officer, dir. Media Gen., Inc., 1969-81, vice chmn., chief exec. officer, dir., 1982—; pres., dir. Southeast Media, Inc., Richmond Newspapers, Inc., all Richmond, Va., Cablevision of Fredericksburg, Inc., Va., Tribune Co., Tampa, Fla., Piedmont Pub. Co., Winston-Salem, N.C., Golden Triangle Printing Co., Greensboro, N.C.; dir. Security Fed. Savs. & Loan Assn. (and subs.'s), Golden West Pub. Co., Inc., William B. Tanner Co., United Va. Bankshares, Inc., Beacon Press, Media Gen. Fin. Services, Inc., Garden State Paper Co., all Richmond, Tampa TV Inc., Purolator, Inc., Piscataway, N.J., Cliggott Pub. Co., Greenwich, Conn., Pronapade, Mexico City, Highlander Publs. Inc., Hacienda Heights, Calif.; mem. bus. adv. com. U.S. Bur. Labor Statistics, 1948-49, U.S. Bur. Census, 1948-49; lectr. statistics U. Richmond, 1948-49; mem. Tax Study Commn., 1963-64, Va. Met. Area Study Commn., 1966-67; mem. fiscal study com. Va. Adv. Legis. Council, 1956-58; mem. adv. com. to sec. edn. State of Va., 1973; mem. listed co. adv. com. Am. Stock Exchange, 1975—. Former mem. bd. dirs. Richmond Meml. Hosp.; bd. dirs. Nat. Center for Resource Recovery, Inc., Washington, Richmond Area Community Council, 1972, Citizens Study Council, 1973; bd. govs. United Givers Fund, 1960-63, 66-69; pres. Collegiate Schs., 1967-68; bd. dirs., past pres. Richmond Eye Hosp., RPI Found., Va. Commonwealth U., Richmond; mem. Nat. Commn. on Taxes and IRS, 1979—; chmn. Bus. Adv. Commn. on White Collar Crime, 1980—. Served from pvt. to 1st lt., C.E. AUS, 1943-46; ETO; as 1st lt. Gen. Staff U.S. Army, 1950-52. Recipient Good Govt. award Richmond First Club, 1967; Distinguished Service award Richmond Urban League, 1969. Mem. Am. Statis. Assn., Am. Newspaper Pubs. Assn. (newsprint com. 1976—), Am. Mktg. Assn. (pres. Va. chpt. 1954-55), C. of C. U.S. (communications com. 1970-75, chmn. postal service panel 1976-80), Richmond C. of C. (pres. 1968), Beta Gamma Sigma. Presbyterian. Clubs: Commonwealth (dir. 1972), Country of Va., Downtown (Richmond). Home: 8912 Alendale Rd Richmond VA 23229 Office: 333 E Grace St Richmond VA 23219

DONNELL, HAROLD EUGENE, JR., assn. exec.; b. Balt., Mar. 12, 1935; s. Harold Eugene and Ruth Elizabeth (Meeth) D.; m. Rosemary Gatch, Apr. 25, 1959; children—David Crawford, Laurette Butler. B.A., Amherst Coll., 1957. Field asst., agent Equitable Life Assurance Soc., Balt., 1958-61; salesman Eastern Products Corp., Balt., 1961-64, asst. nat. sales mgr., 1964-66; exec. dir. Md. Dental Assn., Towson, 1966-74, Acad. Gen. Dentistry, Chgo., 1974—. Trustee Am. Fund for Dental Health, 1976—. Served with U.S. Army, 1957-58. Recipient Disting. Service award N.C. Acad. Gen. Dentistry, 1980; ann. Walter E. Levine Meritorious Service award Alpha Omega, 1970. Mem. Am. Soc. Assn. Execs., Chgo. Soc. Assn. Execs., ADA. Republican. Lutheran. Office: 211 E Chicago Ave Chicago IL 60611 *Any degree of success I have achieved in this life is a result of dedicatedly applying the talents I have been given or acquired with single minded drive to accomplish specific goals.*

DONNELL, JAMES C., II, retired oil company executive; b. Findlay, Ohio, June 30, 1910; s. Otto Dewey and Glenn (McClell) D.; m. Dolly Louise DeVine, July 2, 1932; 1 dau., Susan (Mrs. Harry W. Konkel). A.B., Princeton, 1932. Mgr. crude oil sales Marathon Oil Co., Findlay, 1932-36, dir., 1936-75, v.p., 1937-48, pres., 1948-72, chmn., 1972-75. Mem. world council, nat. council YMCA. Mem. Am. Petroleum Inst., Am. Assn. Petroleum Geologists, Sigma Xi, Phi Beta Kappa. Republican. Presbyn. Clubs: Elk., Country (Findlay); Princeton. Links, University (N.Y.C.); Union (Cleve.); Inverness (Toledo); Bohemian (San Francisco). Home: 839 S Main St Findlay OH 45840 Office: 539 S Main St Findlay OH 45840

DONNELL, JOHN RANDOLPH, petroleum executive; b. Findlay, Ohio, June 22, 1912; s. Otto Dewey and Glenn (McClelland) D.; m. Margaret Louise Watt, Feb. 1, 1939 (dec.); children: John Randolph, Ann (Mrs. R. Kennedy Davis), William Watt, Thomas Blakeman, Richard Holmes; m. Maureen Nahas, July 31, 1981. B.S., Case Inst. Tech., 1934. Spl. rep. Marathon Oil Co., Findlay, 1938, asst. to mgr. prodn., 1944-50, treas., 1950-54, v.p. supply and transp., 1954-61, dir., 1954-73, v.p. charge internat. activities, 1961-65, sr. v.p. internat., 1965-67, sr. v.p. corporate planning, 1967-69, sr. v.p. finance and planning, 1969-73; pres. Marathon Internat. Oil Co., 1961-67; dir. First Nat. Bank Findlay, 1939-83, chmn. bd., 1947-83; dir. Toledo Trust Co., 1958-80, Toledo Trustcorp., Inc., 1970-80. Pres. Bd. Edn. Findlay, 1944-54; Trustee Case Western Res. U., Cleve.; Regional chmn. Boy Scouts Am., 1953-56, mem. nat. exec. bd., 1953-83; bd. dirs. World Scout Found. Mem. Sigma Xi, Tau Beta Pi. Presbyn. Clubs: Country (Findlay); Toledo; Belmont Country (Toledo); Union, The Country (Cleve.); Sky (N.Y.C.); Beach, Everglades (Palm Beach, Fla.). Home: 77 Locust St Perrysburg OH 43551 Office: 539 S Main St Findlay OH 45840

DONNELL, JOSEPH STOVER, III, naval officer, consultant; b. Annapolis, MN, Jan. 21, 1932; s. Joseph Stover and Alice (Crane) D.; m. Diane Parker, June 21, 1958 (div. Aug. 1966); 1 dau., Sandra; m. 2d Judith Swan, Dec. 30, 1972; 1 son, Brian Joseph. B.S.C.E., Tufts U., 1954; M.S. in Fgn. Affairs, George Washington U., 1965, George Washington U., 1974. Commd. ensign U.S. Navy, 1954, advanced through grades to rear adm., 1981; comdg. officer U.S.S. Richard E. Byrd, 1971-73; ops. analyst Office of Chief Naval Ops., 1973-74; detailed to Indsl. Coll. Armed Forces, Washington, 1974-75; plans officer Seventh Fleet, Yukosuka, Japan, 1975-77; comdg. officer U.S.S. Sterett, San Diego, 1977-79; chief of staff Comdr. Carrier Group Five, Subic Bay, Philippines, 1979-80; dep. dir. for ops. (J-33) U.S. Navy, Washington, 1980-83; comdr. Cruiser Destroyer group Twelve, Mayport, Fla., 1983—. Decorated Legion of Merit, Meritorious Service medal, others. Republican. Home: 212 Moale Ave Mayport FL 32227 Office: Comdr Cruiser Destoryer Group Twelve FPO Miami FL 34099

DONNELLAN, SHAUN KEVIN, manufacturing company executive; b. Durban, South Africa, Oct. 5, 1944; came to U.S., 1980; s. Bernard Joseph and Martha (Ridl) D.; m. Sheila Frances Hanks, July 9, 1969; children: Patrick, Brendon, Charles, Katherine. B.S. with honors, U. Natal, South Africa, 1964; M.A., Cambridge U., England, 1968; A.M.P., Harvard U., 1980. Corp. planning mgr. Messina Devel. Co., Johannesburg, South Africa, 1970-72; mng. dir. Premier Metal Co., Johannesburg, 1972-76; v.p. internat. Grove Mfg. Co., Oxford, Eng., 1976-79, sr. v.p., Shady Grove, Pa., 1980—. Home: 201 Clayton Ave Waynesboro PA 17268 Office: Grove Mfg Co PO Box 21 Shady Grove PA 17256

DONNELLAN, THOMAS A., archbishop; b. N.Y.C., Jan. 24, 1914; s. Andrew and Margaret (Egan) b. A.B., Cathedral Coll., 1933; student, St. Joseph's Sem., 1933-39; J.C.D., Catholic U. Am., 1942. Ordained priest Roman Catholic Ch., 1939; synodal judge Marriage Tribunal, 1950-58; vice chancellor Archdiocese N.Y., 1947-50, chancellor, 1958-62, vocation dir., 1957-62; rector St. Joseph's Sem., 1962-64; bishop of, Ogdensburg, N.Y., 1964-68, archbishop of, Atlanta, 1968—, also chaplain del., vicar gen., mil. ordinariate for, Ga., Fla., N.C., S.C., 1972—; Treas., chmn. region, com. hispanic affairs Nat. Conf. Catholic Bishops; Treas., com. capitalism and Christianity, com. pro-life activities U.S. Catholic Conf.; mem. exec. bd. Catholic Near East Relief.; bd. govs. Cath. Ch. Extension Soc. Decorated knight comdr. Knights Holy Sepulchre. Address: Chancery Office 680 W Peachtree St NW Atlanta GA 30308 *

DONNELLY, BRIAN J., congressman; b. Dorcnester, Mass., Mar. 2, 1946; m. Virginia Norton. Grad., Boston U., 1970. Tchr. Boston Trade Sch., 1970-72; mem. Mass. Ho. of Reps. from 20th Dist., 1973-78, 96th-98th Congresses from 11th Dist. Mass., budget com., pub. works and transp. com. Named Legislator of Year Mass. Ho. of Reps., 1978, Outstanding Young Leader of Boston, 1981. Democrat. Roman Catholic. Address: 438 Cannon House Office Bldg Washington DC 20515

DONNELLY, CHARLES FRANCIS, management consultant; b. Toronto, Ont., Can., Jan. 19, 1924; s. Edward A. and Margaret Jane (Doyle) D.; m. JoAnn McCarthy, June 28, 1952; children: Charles Francis, Mary, Kathleen, Mark, David, Joanna. B.Commerce, U. Toronto, 1949; LL.D., Fordham U., 1953. Bar: N.Y. 1953, Mich. 1964. Assoc. Hughes Hubbard & Reed, N.Y.C., 1953-58; v.p., gen. counsel S.H. Kress & Co., N.Y.C., 1958-64; assoc. counsel Ford Motor Co., Dearborn, Mich., 1964-67; exec. v.p. Bendix Corp., Detroit, 1967-77, vice chmn., chief adminstrv. officer, 1977-80, dir., 1968-80; counsel firm Clark, Klein & Beaumont, Detroit, 1980-82; management consultant, 1982—. Mem. adv. bd. Providence Hosp., Southfield, Mich.; trustee No. Mich. Hosps., Inc., Petoskey. Served with RCAF, 1942-45. Mem. Am., N.Y., Mich. bar assns. Clubs: Union League (N.Y.C.); Little Harbor (Harbor Springs, Mich.). Office: 4 Meadowgate Harbor Springs MI 49740

DONNELLY, CHARLES LAWTHERS, JR., air force officer; b. Barberton, Ohio, Aug. 24, 1929; s. Charles Lucius and Flora (Riley) D.; m. Carolyn Marie Vandersall, Mar. 30, 1952; 1 dau., Linda Marie. B.A., Otterbein Coll., 1950; grad., Air Command and Staff Coll., 1964, Royal Coll. Def. Studies, London, 1971; M.P.A., George Washington U., 1964. Served as aviation cadet U.S. Air Force, 1951-52, commd. 2d lt., 1952, advanced through grades to maj. gen., 1977; fighter interceptor pilot, Selfridge AFB, Mich. and Wheelus Air Base, Libya, 1952-56, jet instr., asst. ops. officer for, 1956-60, a.d.c. to comdr., 1960-63, instr., Maxwell AFB, Ala., 1963-66, F-4 tng., George AFB, Calif., 1966, combat pilot, S.E. Asia, 1966-67; served in various staff positions Hdqrs. USAF, Washington, 1967-70; vice comdr., comdr. (401st Tactical Fighter Wing, Torrejon Air Base), Spain, 1972-75; dep. dir. plans Hdqrs. USAF, Washington, 1975-77; comdr. (Sheppard Tech. Tng. Center), Sheppard AFB, Tex., 1978-79, chief, Saudi Arabia, 1979—. Bd. dirs. United Way of Greater Wichita Falls, Tex., Wichita County chpt. ARC, Wichita Falls Bd. Commerce and Industry. Decorated D.S.M., Legion of Merit with 2 oak leaf clusters, D.F.C., Air medal with 12 oak leaf clusters, Air Force Commendation medal. Mem. Air Force Assn., Order Daedalians, Eta Phi Mu. Episcopalian. Club: Wichita Falls Country (Wichita Falls)

DONNELLY, CHARLES ROBERT, community coll. pres.; b. Allen, Mich., Apr. 3, 1921; s. Peter Joseph and Florence Veronica (Stitt) D.; m. Marilynn Elaine Jones, Sept. 15, 1945; children—Maureen, Michael, Mark, Bridget, Patrick, Kathleen. B.A., Hillsdale (Mich.) Coll., 1941; M.A., U. Mich., 1947, Ph.D., 1961. Tchr. English Rockwood (Mich.) High Sch., 1941-42; tchr. English, baseball coach Flint (Mich.) Community Jr. Coll., 1947-60, dean, then pres., 1960-70; pres. Community Colls. of U. Nev. System, 1970-77, Alpena (Mich.) Community Coll., 1977—; mem. Western States Regional Manpower Adv. Com., 1970-74; pres. Mich. Assn. Jr. Colls., 1964-65. Served with AUS, 1942-46. Recipient Alumni Achievement award Hillsdale Coll., 1968; Athletic award Nat. Assn. Jr. Colls., 1970. Mem. Am. Vocat. Assn., Mich. Community Coll. Assn. Democrat. Roman Catholic. Clubs: Kiwanis, K.C. Home: 2130 S 2d Ave Alpena MI 49707 Office: 666 Johnson St Alpena MI 49707

DONNELLY, JOHN, psychiatrist, educator; b. Liverpool, Eng., 1914; m. Mabel W. Collins, Aug. 27, 1949. M.B., Ch.B., U. Liverpool, 1938; D.P.M., Royal Coll. Physicians and Surgeons, U.K., 1948; Sc.D., Trinity Coll., Hartford, Conn., 1979. Diplomate: Am. Bd. Psychiatry and Neurology., Certified psychiat. hosp. adminstr. Intern David Lewis No. Hosp., Liverpool, 1938-39; resident, postgrad. tng. program Psychiat. Inst., U. London-Maudsley Hosp.; clin. asst. Sutton Emergency Hosp., 1947, Manor Hosp., Epsom, Eng., 1948; sr. registrar Cane Hill Hosp., Surrey, Eng., 1948-49; clin. dir. Inst. of Living, Hartford, Conn., 1952-54, exec. officer, 1954-57, med. dir., 1957-65, psychiatrist-in-chief, chief exec. officer, 1965-79, sr. cons., 1979—; prof. psychiatry U. Conn., 1977—; cons. Hartford Hosp., St. Francis Hosp. and Med. Center, 1965—; mem. nat. mental health adv. council NIMH, 1971-75; mem. Conn. Bd. Mental Health, 1957-72, chmn., 1963-67. Editor: Digest Neurology and Psychiatry, 1965-79; editorial bd.: Psychiat. Jour. of U. Ottawa Faculty Medicine, 1976—. Mem. Conn. Jud. Rev. Council, 1977—. Fellow Am. Coll. Psychiatrists, A.C.P., Am. Psychiat. Assn. (life), Royal Coll. Psychiatrists (U.K.), Royal Soc. Medicine, AAAS; mem. Group for Advancement of Psychiatry (pres. 1969-71), AMA (chmn. council on mental health 1973), Nat. Assn. Pvt. Psychiat. Hosps. (pres. 1977-78). Office: Inst of Living 200 Retreat Ave Hartford CT 06106

DONNELLY, JOSEPH LENNON, utility company executive; b. Scranton, Pa., Mar. 17, 1929; s. Joseph L. and Irene (Dougher) D.; m. Lynn Haakonsen, Aug. 4, 1974; children: David Charles, Joseph Lennon III, Haakon Thomas. B.S., U. Scranton, 1950; J.D., U. Pa., 1953. Bar: Pa. 1954. Dep. atty. gen. Commonwealth Pa., 1955-58; with Pa. Power & Light Co., Allentown, 1958-79, v.p. fin., 1975-79; exec. v.p., chief fin. officer Gulf States Utilities Co., Beaumont, Tex., 1979—. Pres. bd. trustee Allentown State Hosp., 1968-69; chmn. Lehigh County Mental Health, Pa. Mental Retardation Bd., 1968-71. Mem. ABA, Fin. Execs. Inst., Edison Electric Inst., Pa. Bar Assn. Democrat. Roman Catholic. Clubs: Tower, Beaumont Country. Office: Gulf States Utilities Co. 350 Pine Beaumont TX 77701

DONNELLY, MARIAN CARD, educator, art historian; b. Evanston, Ill., Sept. 12, 1923; d. Harold S. and Ethel (Gates) Card; m. Russell J. Donnelly, Jan. 21, 1956; 1 son, James Armstrong. A.B. summa cum laude, Oberlin Coll., 1946, M.A., 1948; Ph.D., Yale U., 1956. Instr. fine arts Upsala Coll., 1948-50; art librarian U. Rochester, 1951-53; research asso. decorative arts Art Inst., Chgo., 1956-57; vis. lectr. U. Chgo., 1965; asst. prof. dept. art history U. Oreg., Eugene, 1966-68, asso. prof., 1969-73, prof., 1973-81, prof. emeritus, 1981—; participant Attingham (Eng.) Summer Sch., 1972, 75; vis. research scholar in art history U. Copenhagen, 1972; lectr. U. Oreg. Center for Internat. Music, Stuttgart, Germany, 1972. Author: The New England Meeting Houses of the Seventeenth Century, 1968, A Short History of Observatories, 1973; Contbr. articles to profl. jours. Am. Council Learned Socs. grantee, 1959-60. Fellow Royal Soc. Arts (London); mem. AAUP, Archeol. Inst. Am., Nat. Trust for Hist. Preservation, Nat. Trust for Scotland, Soc. for Preservation New Eng. Antiquities, Soc. Archtl. Historians (dir. 1964-67, 78-81, asso. editor newsletter 1966-72, 2d v.p. 1972-74, 1st v.p. 1974-76, pres. 1976-78, gen. chmn. Bicentennial programs 1975-76), Phi Beta Kappa. Home: 2175 Olive St Eugene OR 97405

DONNELLY, ROBERT LEO, rubber co. exec.; b. Springfield, Mass., May 9, 1925; s. Leo Joseph and Ruth Gertrude (Meramble) D.; m. Elizabeth Anne Lyons, Nov. 29, 1947; 1 son, Robert Leo. B.A. with honors, U. Conn., 1951, LL.B., 1955. Bar: Conn. bar 1955; C.P.A., Conn. With Ernst & Ernst, Hartford, Conn., 1951-59; with Armstrong Rubber Co., West Haven, Conn., 1959—, sec., corp. atty., 1966—. Served with AUS, 1943-46. Mem. Am. Bar Assn., Am. Inst. C.P.A.'s. Home: 680 S Greenbrier Dr Orange CT 06477 Office: 500 Sargent Dr New Haven CT 06507

DONNELLY, ROBERT TRUE, state supreme court justice; b. Lebanon, Mo., Aug. 31, 1924; s. Thomas John and Sybil Justine (True) D.; m. Wanda Sue Oates, Nov. 16, 1946; children: Thomas Page, Brian True. Student, Tulsa U., 1942-43, Ohio State U., 1943; J.D., U. Mo., 1949. Bar: Mo. 1949. Mem. firm Donnelly & Donnelly, Lebanon; city atty., Lebanon, 1954-55, asst. atty. gen., Mo., 1957-61; justice Supreme Ct. Mo., Jefferson City, 1965—, chief justice, 1973-75, 81-83; bd. govs. Mo. Bar, 1957-63. Mem. Lebanon Bd. Edn., 1959-65; trustee Sch. Religion, Drury Coll., Springfield, Mo., 1958-66, Mo. Sch. Religion, Columbia, 1971-72. Served with inf. AUS, World War II. Decorated Purple Heart. Mem. Am., Mo. bar assns., Phi Delta Phi. Presbyterian. Club: Mason. Home: 3459 Hobbs Ln Jefferson City MO 65101 Office: Supreme Ct Bldg Jefferson City MO 65101

DONNELLY, RUSSELL JAMES, physicist, educator; b. Hamilton, Ont., Can., Apr. 16, 1930; s. Clifford Ernest and Bessie (Harrison) D.; m. Marian Card, Jan. 21, 1956; 1 son, James. B.Sc., McMaster U., 1951, M.Sc., 1952; M.S., Yale, 1953, Ph.D., 1956. Faculty U. Chgo., 1956-66, prof. physics, 1965-66, U. Oreg., Eugene, 1966—, chmn. dept., 1966-72, 82-83; vis. prof. Niels Bohr Inst., Copenhagen, Denmark, 1972; co-founder Pine Mountain Obs., 1967—; cons. Gen. Motors Co. Research Labs., 1958-68, NSF, 1968-73, 79—, mem. adv. panel for physics, 1970-73, chmn., 1971-72, mem. adv. coms. on materials research, 1979—; cons. Jet Propulsion Lab., Calif. Inst. Tech., Pasadena, 1973-82. Contbr. papers to profl. lit.; editor: (with Herman, Prigogine) Non-Equilibrium Thermodynamics Variational Techniques and Stability, 1966, (with Parks, Glaberson) Experimental Superfluidity, 1967; assoc. editor: Physics of Fluids, 1966-68; mem. editorial bd.: Phys. Rev. A, 1978—. Bd. dirs. U. Oreg. Devel. Fund, 1970-72, Lane County Coop. Mus. Commn., 1975—; chmn. Lane County Coop. Mus. Commn., 1975-82. Alfred P. Sloan fellow, 1959-63; sr. vis. fellow Sci. Research Council, U.K., 1978. Fellow Am. Phys. Soc. (exec. com. div. fluid dynamics 1966-72, 80—, sec-treas. 1967-70, chmn. 1971-72, 82-83, Otto Laporte Meml. lectr. 1974), AAAS; mem. AAUP, Am. Assn. Physics Tchrs. Episcopalian. Club: Cosmos (Washington). Research on physics fluids, especially hydrodynamic stability and superfluidity. Home: 2175 Olive St Eugene OR 97405 Office: Dept Physics Univ Oreg Eugene OR 97403

DONNELLY, THOMAS JOSEPH, lawyer; b. Pitts., Mar. 4, 1925; s. Thomas E. and Ruth L. (Beitzer) D.; m. Marilyn A. Pfohl, Apr. 16, 1955; children: Thomas C., Elizabeth A., Daria, Heather, Michael, Marilyn, Peter. Student, M.I.T., 1943-44; B.S. in Engring, U. Mich., 1946, J.D., 1950. Bar: Pa. bar 1951. Student engr. Westinghouse Electric Corp., 1946-47; since practiced in, Pitts.; partner firm Houston, Houston & Donnelly; dir. Pabst Brewing Co., Federated Research Corp., Federated Investors, Inc. Bd. dirs. Young Republicans Allegheny County, 1954-55; Chmn. bd. trustees Carlow Coll., Pitts.; bd. dirs. Human Life Found. Am. Served as apprentice seaman USNR, 1943-46. Mem. Barristers Soc., Am., Pa., Allegheny County bar assns., Tau Beta Pi. Roman Catholic. Clubs: Knight of Malta., Toastmasters, U. of Mich. Lawyers (Ann Arbor); University, Duquesne, Chatham (Mass.) Yacht. Home: 1085 Shady Ave Pittsburgh PA 15232 Office: 2510 Centre City Tower Pittsburgh PA 15222

DONNELLY, THOMAS RENN, JR., government official; b. Steubenville, Ohio, May 25, 1939; s. Thomas R. and Flora D. (Conti) D.; m. Christine McCafferty, Feb. 23, 1963; children: Thomas R. II, Derek S., Terence R. Student, U. Pitts., 1960-61; B.S.E., Princeton U., 1962. Salesman John Manville Corp., 1962-63; supr. Air Products & Chems., 1963-67; exec. v.p. U.S. Jr. C. of C., 1967-70, Nat. Center for Vol. Action, 1970-72; cons. Cost of Living Council, 1972-74; mng. partner Louis C. Kramp & Assos., 1974-81; dep. asst. sec. for legislation HHS, Washington, 1981-83, asst. sec. for legislation, 1983—. Active Nat. council Boy Scouts Am., 1969—. Mem. U.S. Jr. C. of C. (life). Clubs: Princeton (N.Y.); Dial Lodge (Princeton U.). Office: Dept Health Human Services 200 Independence Ave S W Washington DC 20201 *

DONNEM, ROLAND WILLIAM, lawyer, business executive; b. Seattle, Nov. 8, 1929; s. William Roland and Mary Louise (Hughes) D.; m. Sarah Brandon Lund, Feb. 18, 1961; children: Elizabeth Prince, Sarah Madison. B.A., Yale U., 1952; J.D. magna cum laude, Harvard U., 1957. Bar: N.Y. 1958, Supreme Ct. 1963, D.C. 1969, Ohio 1976. With Davis Polk & Wardwell, N.Y.C., 1957-63, 64-69; law sec. appellate div. N.Y. Supreme Ct., N.Y.C., 1963-64; dir. policy planning antitrust div. Justice Dept., Washington, 1969-71; v.p., sec., gen. counsel Standard Brands Inc., N.Y.C., 1971-76; v.p. law Chessie System, Cleve., 1976-78, sr. v.p. law, 1978—. Bd. dirs., fin. v.p. Presbyn. Home for Aged Women, N.Y.C., 1972-76; bd. dirs., treas. James Lenox House, Inc., 1972-76; trustee Food and Drug Law Inst., 1974-76; trustee, sec. Brick Presbyterian Ch., 1974-76. Served from ensign to lt. (j.g.) USNR, 1952-54. Mem. ABA; Mem. Fed. Bar Assn., N.Y. State Bar Assn., N.Y.C. Bar Assn., D.C. Bar Assn., Ohio Bar Assn., Greater Cleve. Bar Assn., Am. Corp. Counsel Assn., Am. Law Inst., Nat. Panel Arbitrators, Am. Arbitration Assn., Def. Orientation Conf. Asn., Grocery Mfrs. Assn. (legal com. 1971-76), Corn Refiners Assn. (lawyers adv. com. 1971-76), Assn. Am. Railroads (legal affairs com. 1976—), Yale Alumni Assn. Cleve. (treas. 1982-84, del. 1984—), Phi Beta Kappa. Republican. Presbyn. Clubs: Tuxedo, Union (N.Y.C.); Nat. Lawyers, Capitol Hill, University, Metropolitan, Chevy Chase (Washington); Center (Balt.); Cleve. Racquet, Kirtland, Cleve. Wine and Food, Fork and Fiddle, Mid Day (Cleve.). Home: 2945 Fontenay Rd Shaker Heights OH 44120 Office: Terminal Tower PO Box 6419 Cleveland OH 44101

DONNER, FRANK JORIS, lawyer; b. Bklyn., Feb. 25, 1911; s. Samuel and Sophie (Kaufman) D.;, 1938; children—Eleanor, Daniel. B.A., U. Wis., M.A., 1934; LL.B., Columbia U., 1937. Counsel United Elec. Workers, N.Y.C.; asso. gen. counsel CIO, N.Y.C.; individual practice law, N.Y.C. Author: The Age Surveillance; contbr. articles to jours., mags. Mem. Phi Beta Kappa. Home: South Norwalk CT 06854 Office: 36W 44M St New York NY 10036

DONNER, MARTIN WALTER, physician; b. Leipzig, Germany, Sept. 5, 1920; s. Walter T. and Else (Ruehl) D.; m. Adelheid I. Wimmer, Apr. 28, 1951; children—Cornelia, Stephanie, Thomas. M.D., U. Leipzig Med. Sch., 1945. Resident in internal medicine U. Hosp., Leipzig, 1945-50; resident fellow Radiology Center, Cologne, 1950-54; resident Mound Park Hosp., St. Petersburg, Fla., 1954-57; radiologist Johns Hopkins Hosp., Balt., 1957—, asso. prof. radiol. scis., 1964-68, prof. radiology, 1966—, dir. div. diagnostic radiology, 1967-73, prof. radiol. sci., 1968—, chmn. dept. radiology, 1972—, radiologist-in-chief, 1972—; vis. investigator Carnegie Inst., Washington; vis. prof. Free U. of Berlin, State U., Ohio U., Heidelberg, U. Calif. at San Francisco, Guys Hosp., London, Eng. Editorial staff: Am. Jour. Med. Sci, 1961-68, Johns Hopkins Med. Jour, 1973-76, Investigative Radiology, 1974-79, Radiologica clinica, 1976-79, Gastrointestinal Radiology, 1976—, Diagnostic Imaging, 1979—. Fellow Am. Coll. Radiology; mem. A.M.A., Radiol. Soc. N.Am., Am. Roentgen Ray Soc., Md. Radiol. Soc., Md. Med. and Chirurgical Faculty, Johns Hopkins Med. Soc., Assn. U. Radiologists, Soc. Gastrointestinal Radiologists, German Soc. Internal Medicine, German Soc. Radiology (corr.). Home: 317 Southwind Rd Baltimore MD 21204 Office: Johns Hopkins Hosp 606 N Broadway Baltimore MD 21205

DONNER, RICHARD, movie director. Director: Salt and Pepper, 1968, Twinky, 1969, The Omen, 1976, Superman, 1978, Inside Moves, 1981, The Toy, 1982. Office: Gelfand Breslauer 1880 Century Park E Los Angeles CA 90067 *

DONNESON, SEENA SAND, artist; b. N.Y.C., May 2; d. Max and Ann (Silber) S; m. Sam Gershwin; children: Erika, Lisa. Student, Pratt Inst., 1941-43, Art Students League, 1943-45, 58. Mem. art staff N.Y. U., 1962-63, Nassau County Office Cultural Devel., 1972-79, New Sch. for Social Research, 1974; guest artist Tamarind Lithography Workshop, 1968; vis. artist Clayworks, N.Y.C., 1981. Exhibited one-woman shows at, Pietrantonio Gallery, Brooks Meml. Art Gallery, Sheldon Swope Art Gallery, Portland (Maine) Mus. Art, Tenn. Fine Arts Center, Terrain Gallery, N.Y.C., univs. of Ariz., Oreg. Ala., Okla. and Calif., L.I. U., George Washington U., Princeton U., numerous others; exhibited in: group shows Sculpture in Color, N.Y.C., Ft. Lauderdale (Fla.) Mus., Norfolk Mus. Arts and Scis., Bklyn. Mus., San Francisco Mus. Art, DeCordova Mus., Pratt Graphic Art Center, N.Y.U., Lehigh U., New Sch. for Social Research, others, fgn. traveling exhbns., T.S.S. Olympia, Am. Gallery of U.S. Embassy, Athens and Salonika, Greece, Brussels (Belgium) Worlds Fair, USIS, 1957-58, Mcpl. Art Mus., Tokyo, Japan, also on tour throughout Japan, 1960-61, Argentine Artists-NAWA Exchange Exhbn., Museo de Belles Artes, Buenos Aires, Argentina, 1962-63, Argentine Artists-NAWA Exchange Exhbn., Museo de Belles Artes, Scotland, Eng., 1963-64, Contemporary Minature Prints, 1966—; represented in permanent collections, White Mus. Art, Washington Mus. Fine Arts, Jacksonville Art Mus., Va. Mus. Fine Art, Bklyn. Mus., Norfolk Mus., USIA Art in Embassies, Los Angeles County Mus. Art, Museum Modern Art, N.Y.C., Smithsonian Mus., N.J. State Mus., N.Y. Public Library, Ft. Lauderdale Mus. Fine Art, Snug Harbor Cultural Center N.Y.C., also numerous colls., univs., and bus. corps. Recipient art awards Suffolk (L.I., N.Y.) Mus., 1956, Ball State 13th Annual, 1967; Abbott Treadwell meml. prize Nat. Assn. Women Artists, 1966; purchase award Washington State U., 1970; others.; Edward Mac Dowell Found. fellow, 1963, 64; Tamarind guest and artist fellow, 1968; grantee Mcpl. Art Soc., N.Y. Art in Park, 1974; CAPS fellow. Mem. Artists Equity, Nat. Assn. Women Artists, Women in the Arts. Studio: 319 Greenwich St New York NY 10013

DONOFRIO, FRANCIS JOSEPH, retired judge; b. Phoenix, Aug. 8, 1913; s. Salvatore and Angela Marie (Fisher-Pesqueira) D.; m. Cora Bradley, July 9, 1936; children: Carole Donofrio Wilks, Richard. Student, Phoenix Coll., 1931-33; J.D., U. Ariz., 1936. Bar: Ariz. 1936. Assoc. firm Marks & Marks, 1936, Townsend & Jenckes, 1937; dep. clk. Superior Ct. of, Maricopa County, 1937-42; dep. county atty., Maricopa County, 1942-47, chief dep. county atty., 1947, county atty., 1947-49; judge Ariz. Superior Ct., Phoenix, 1949-65, Juvenile Ct., Maricopa County, 1957-65, Ariz. Ct. Appeals, Phoenix, 1965-81, ref., 1981. Bd. dirs. T.R. council Boy Scouts Am., Boys Club of Phoenix, Maricopa County Community Coll. Dist. Found., Phoenix, New Chance Industries, Phoenix, Mercy Care Found. of St. Joseph's Hosp., Phoenix, Alexander Sch., Phoenix, Patterdell Sch., Phoenix, Good Shepherd Sch. for Girls, Phoenix; mem. steering com. Christian Conf. on Adult and Youth, Phoenix; mem. adv. bd. St. Joseph's Hosp. and Med. Center, Phoenix. Recipient Outstanding Service award Maricopa County Bar Assn., 1946, Outstanding Service to Youth award Ariz. Delinquency Control Inst., 1960, awards Valley of Sun Sch. for Handicapped Children, 1951, Nat. Council on Crime and Delinquency Local Bd., 1950, Ariz. Children's Home, 1948, Gov.'s Adv. Council on Mental Retardation, 1965, N.Y. U. Appellate Judges Seminar, 1966. Mem. Ariz. Judges Assn., Nat. Council Juvenile Ct. Judges, State Bar Ariz., Am. Bar Assn. (Airz. chmn. Jr. Bar Conf. 1946-48), Am. Judicature Soc., Ariz. Acad., NCCJ, Justinian Soc., Phi Alpha Delta. Democrat. Roman Catholic. Clubs: Kiwanis, Moose, Elks, Eagles (Reverence of Law award 1975), Woodmen of World (pres. Ariz.-N.Mex. Jurisdiction 1961-63), Woodmen of World (Outstanding Service award 1963), Woodmen of World (Mr. Woodman 1958, 79). Home: 116 W Marlette St Phoenix AZ 85013

DONOGHUE, JOHN DANIEL, judge; b. Springfield, Mass., May 12, 1909; s. John F. and Margaret Ellen (Curran) D.; m. Rosemary Lynch, Sept. 15, 1936 (dec. 1979); children: John W., Mary Frances (Mrs. John M. Collins), James D., Michael.; m. Faith Williams, Apr. 4, 1982. A.B., St. Michael's Coll., 1932, M.A., 1961, J.D. (hon.), 1981. Announcer WMAS, Springfield, 1932-34; reporter, editor, critic Springfield Daily News, 1934-44; dir. pub. relations, faculty St. Michael's Coll., Winooski Park, Vt., 1947-66, acting chmn. journalism dept., 1974-75, adj. prof. journalism, 1983—; asst. to provost Vt. State Colls., 1966-69; editor Vt. Catholic Tribune, 1969-74; asst. judge Superior Ct., Chittenden County, 1975-83; Music critic Burlington Free Press, 1952—. Editor: Assistant Judges, handbook. Sch. dir., South Burlington, 1952-67; chmn. Task Force on Vt. Parochial Schs., 1967-68; charter mem. Vt. Ednl. TV Broadcast Council, 1968-75;

Justice of Peace, South Burlington, 1968-75; Asso. trustee St. Michael's Coll. Served with AUS, 1944-46. Decorated Army Commendation medal; named Alumnus of Yr. St. Michael's Coll., 1972, presdl. citation, 1978; Layman of Yr. Vt. Edn. Assn., 1960. Mem. New Eng. Press Assn. (dir.), Am. Coll. Pub. Relations Assn. (past New Eng. dir.), Vt. Sch. Dirs. Assn. (past pres.). Roman Catholic. Club: K.C. Home: 40 Hayden Pkwy South Burlington VT 05401 Office: St Michael's Coll Winooski VT 05404

DONOGHUE, MILDRED RANSDORF, educator; b. Cleve.; d. James and Caroline (Sychra) Ransdorf; m. Charles K. Donoghue (dec. 1982); children: Kathleen, James. Ed.D., UCLA, 1962; J.D., Western State U., 1979. Asst. prof. edn. Calif. State U., Fullerton, 1962-66, assoc. prof., 1966-71, prof., 1971—. Author: Foreign Languages and the Schools, 1967, Foreign Languages and the Elementary School Child, 1968, The Child and the English Language Arts, 1971, 75, 79, 85; co-author: Second Languages in Primary Education, 1979; Contbr. articles to profl. jours., Ency. of Edn. Mem. Nat. Council Tchrs. English, Am. Dialect Soc., Am. Ednl. Research Assn., AAUP, Nat. Soc. for Study of Edn., Am. Assn. Tchrs. Spanish and Portuguese, Internat. Reading Assn., Nat. Assn. Edn. Young Children, Orange County Med. Assn. Women's Aux., Authors Guild, Phi Beta Kappa, Phi Kappa Phi, Pi Lambda Theta. Office: Div Tchr Edn Calif State U Fullerton CA 92634

DONOHUE, ALBERT F., investment banker; b. Scott, N.Y., Sept. 1, 1909; s. Jeremiah G. and Mary J. (Sweeney) D.; m. Barbara A. Braun, Oct. 17, 1935; children—James, Thomas, Mary, John. A.B., U. Mich., 1932, J.D., 1936. Bar: N.Y. bar. Investment banker, 1936—; asso. Kidder, Peabody & Co., N.Y.C., 1944—, partner, 1950—, v.p., dir., 1957—; dir. Giant Food Properties, Inc., Washington, Handy Andy, Inc., San Antonio, Alterman Foods, Inc., Atlanta, others. Mem. Am., N.Y. bar assns., Bar Assn. City N.Y. Roman Catholic. Clubs: St. Andrews Golf (Hastings, N.Y.); Bronxville (N.Y.) Field; Shenorock Shore (Rye, N.Y.); Bond, Recess (N.Y.C.). Home: 9 Essex Pl Bronxville NY 10708 Office: 10 Hanover Sq New York City NY 10005

DONOHUE, CARROLL JOHN, lawyer; b. St. Louis, June 24, 1917; s. Thomas M. and Florence (Klefisch) D.; m. Juanita Maire, Jan. 4, 1943 (div. July 1973); children: Patricia Carol Donohue Stevens, Christine Ann Donohue Smith, Deborah Lee Donohue Wilucki; m. Barbara Lounsbury, Dec. 1978. A.B., Washington U., 1939, LL.B. magna cum laude, 1939. Bar: Mo. 1939. Asso. Hay & Flanagan, St. Louis, 1939-42, Salkey & Jones, 1946-49; partner Husch, Eppenberger, Donohue, Elson & Jones, St. Louis, 1949—. Author articles in field. Campaign chmn. ARC, St. Louis County, 1950; mem. adv. com. Child Welfare, St. Louis, 1952-55; exec. com. Slum Clearance, 1949, bond issue com., 1955; bond issue com. St. Louis County Bond Issue; screening and supervisory coms., 1955-61, county citizen's com. for better law enforcement, 1953-56, chmn. com. on immigration policy, 1954-56, Mayor, Olivette, Mo., 1953-56; chmn. County Bd. Election Commrs., St. Louis County, 1960-65; chmn. speakers com. Non-Partisan Ct. Plan; vice-chmn. bd. Regional Commerce and Growth Assn. Served to lt. USNR, 1942-45. Decorated Bronze Star medal, Navy and M.C. medal. Mem. Mo. Bar Assn. (past mem. bd. govs., chmn. annual meeting, editor jour. 1940-41), ABA, St. Louis Bar Assn. (past pres., v.p., treas.), Order of Coif, Omicron Delta Kappa, Sigma Phi Epsilon, Delta Theta Phi. Club: Mo. Athletic. Address: 100 N Broadway Saint Louis MO 63102

DONOHUE, JERRY, chemist, educator; b. Sheboygan, Wis., June 12, 1920; s. Jerry and Leila Marian (Bishop) D.; m. Patricia Ann Schreier, Feb. 10, 1945; children—Terence, Nora. A.B., Dartmouth, 1941, M.A., 1943; Ph.D., Calif. Inst. Tech., 1947. Instr. chemistry Dartmouth, 1941-43; sr. research fellow Calif. Inst. Tech., 1947-52; prof. chemistry U. So. Calif., 1953-66, U. Pa., 1966—. Mem. Am. Crystallographic Assn., Phi Beta Kappa, Sigma Xi. Office: Dept Chemistry Univ Pa Philadelphia PA 19104

DONOUGH, ROBERT JOHN, banker; b. Lebanon, Pa., July 20, 1924; s. Leroy B. and Kathryn M. (Karch) D.; m. Joyce Foote, Jan. 24, 1945; children: Robert, Michael, James, Kathleen. B.S. in Bus. Adminstrn., Lebanon Valley Coll., 1946; M.B.A., Harvard U., 1947. With State Bank Albany, N.Y., 1947-72, sr. v.p., 1969-72; exec. v.p., sec. United Bank Corp., N.Y., Albany, 1972-75, pres., chief adminstrv. officer, 1975-76, also dir.; pres., chief exec. officer, dir. Liberty Nat. Bank & Trust Co., Buffalo, 1976-83; vice-chmn. Norstar Bancorp., Buffalo, 1983—; pres., dir. U.B.C. Leasing N.Y., Inc.; dir. Blue Cross Western N.Y. Mem. Greater Buffalo Devel. Found., 1975; bd. dirs. Deaconess Hosp., Buffalo, United Way Buffalo and Erie County. Served to lt. USNR. Mem. N.Y. State Bankers Assn., Assn. Res. City Bankers, Fin. Execs. Inst., Buffalo Found. (dir.). Presbyterian. Clubs: Buffalo, Buffalo Country. Office: Norstar Bancorp 10 Fountain Plaza Buffalo NY 14202 *

DONOVAN, ALLEN FRANCIS, aerospace company executive; b. Onondaga, N.Y., Apr. 22, 1914; s. Paul Andrew and May (Hudson) D.; m. Beverly Fay, Aug. 14, 1940 (div.); 1 son, Allen Michael; m. Doris Mildred Efram, Apr. 17, 1953 (div.); children: Kathryn Ellen, Marshall Stephen; m. June Wallace Healy, Aug. 30, 1974. B.S. in Aero. Engring., U. Mich., 1936, M.S., 1936, D. Engring. (hon.), 1964. With Curtiss-Wright Corp., Glenn L. Martin, Stinson Aircraft, Vultee Aircraft, 1936-46; head aero. mechanics dept. Cornell U. Aero. Lab., 1946-55; dir. aero. research and devel. staff Ramo-Woolridge Corp. (name changed to Space Tech. Labs., Inc.), 1955-58, v.p., 1958-60; sr. v.p. tech. Aerospace Corp., 1960-78; exec. cons., 1978—; cons. Pres.'s Sci. Adv. Com., 1957-72; mem. Air Force Sci. Adv. Bd., 1948-57, 59-68; U.S. del. Geneva Conf., 1959; mem. space systems com. NASA, 1972-77; cons. Sci. and Tech. Policy Office, NSF, 1973-76. Editor vols. on high speed aerodynamics, jet propulsion.; Author tech. papers on space vehicles, aeronautics. Recipient Medal for exceptional civilian services U.S. Air Force, 1968; recipient Sci. award Air Force Assn. Fellow AIAA; mem. Nat. Acad. Engring., Sigma Xi. Club: Calif. Yacht. Home: 35 Beachcomber Dr Corona del Mar CA 92625

DONOVAN, ARTHUR JOSEPH, surgeon, educator; b. Concord, N.H., Jan. 10, 1925; s. Joseph Casey and Mary Elizabeth (Callahan) D.; m. Jane Wooddell, Jan. 8, 1955; children: John Arthur, Rachel Jane. Three-yr. cert., Harvard U., 1944; M.D., Tufts U., 1948. Diplomate: Am. Bd. Surgery. Intern Grace-New Haven Community Hosp., 1948-49, resident, 1949-52, 54-55; instr. surgery Tufts U., 1955-57, assoc. prof., 1959-61; asst. clin. prof. U. So. Calif., 1961-64, asst. prof., 1964-67, assoc. prof., 1967-69, prof., 1969—, chmn. dept. surgery, 1979—; prof., chmn. dept. surgery U. South Ala., 1973-79, acting dean, 1974-76, v.p. health affairs, 1976-77. Served to lt. USNR, 1952-54; Korea. Mem. Alpha Omega Alpha. Club: University (Los Angeles). Office: U So Calif 1200 N State St Los Angeles CA 90033

DONOVAN, BRUCE ELLIOT, classics educator, University dean; b. Lawrence, Mass., Mar. 8, 1937; s. Harry Albert and Ruth Hannah (Kent) D.; m. Doris Louise Stearn, Sept. 7, 1959; children: Gregory Stearn, Erika Ruth. A.B., Brown U., 1959; postgrad., U. Bristol, Eng., 1959-60; M.A., Yale U., 1961, Ph.D., 1965, Rutgers Center for Alcohol Studies, 1976. Cert. alcoholism counselor, R.I. Instr. Yale U., 1962-65; from instr. to prof. classics Brown U., Providence, 1965—, asso. dean for chem. dependency, 1977—, dean freshmen and sophomores, asso. dean coll., 1981—; pvt. cons. on alcoholism. Author: Euripides Papyri from Oxyrhynchus, 1969; author articles and revs. on ancient Greek lit. and alcohol issues. Bd. dirs., mem. Lippitt Hill Sch. Vol. Program; Bd. dirs., Vols. in Action; mem. R.I. Council for Community Services.; founding mem. New Eng. Coll. Alcohol Network. Fulbright fellow, 1959-60; Woodrow Wilson fellow, 1960-61; fellow Center for Hellenic Studies, Washington, 1971-72. Mem. Am. Philol. Assn., Classical Assn. New Eng., Am. Soc. Papyrologists, Assn. Labor-Mgmt. Adminstrs. and Consultants on Alcoholism, Alcohol and Drug Problems Assn. N. Am., R.I. Assn. Alcoholism Counselors. Club: Review. Home: 261 President Ave Providence RI 02906 Office: Box 1935 Brown U Providence RI 02912:

DONOVAN, CHARLES FRANCIS, ednl. adminstr.; b. Boston, Mar. 28, 1912; s. John J. and Mary E. (Doyle) D. A.B., Boston Coll., 1933; A.M., Fordham U., 1938; S.T.L., Weston (Mass.) Coll., 1944; Ph.D., Yale, 1948. Joined S.J., 1933; ordained priest Roman Catholic Ch., 1943; faculty Boston Coll., 1938-39, 48—, prof. edn., 1948—, chmn. dept., 1948-63, dean, 1952-66, acad. v.p. univ., 1961-68, sr. v.p., dean faculties, 1968-79, univ. historian, 1979—. Address: Boston Coll Chestnut Hill MA 02167

DONOVAN, DAVID GERARD, librarian; b. Boston, May 27, 1921; s. David Joseph and Margaret Elizabeth (Sullivan) D.; m. Katharine E. Hickey, Mar. 16, 1951; 1 dau., Jane Elizabeth. A.B., Boston U., 1949; M.A., Simmons Coll., Boston, 1951. Librarian U.S. Govt., 1951-61, Gen. Electric Co., Croton-on-Hudson, N.Y., 1961-62; cultural affairs officer USIA, New Delhi, India, 1962-65; field dir. Library of Congress, Karachi, Pakistan, 1965-67; dir. internat. relations ALA, Washington, 1967-72; assoc. dir. libraries U. Notre Dame, 1972-76; tech. info. officer AID, Washington, 1976-82, cons., 1982—; adviser UNESCO and UNDP, 1978-79; adminstr. Ford and Rockefeller found. grants to ALA for library devel. abroad, 1967-72; mem. Govt. Adv. Com. Internat. Book and Library Programs; cons. in field. Contbr. to profl. publs. Bd. dirs. Karachi Am. Sch., 1965-67, Music Soc. Pakistan, 1965-67. Mem. ALA, Indian Libary Assn. (life mem.), Phi Beta Kappa, Delta Phi Alpha. Home: 211 Halyard Ln Mashpee MA 02649

DONOVAN, EGBERT HERBERT, clergyman, consultant; b. Buffalo, Jan. 15, 1913; s. James D. and Laura-Mary (Thompson) D. A.B., St. Vincent Coll., Latrobe, Pa., 1936; M.A., 1940; M.Ed., Cath. U. Am., 1945; Ed.D. (hon.), St. Francis Coll., 1968, LL.D., Seton Hill Coll., 1969. Headmaster St. Vincent Prep. Sch., Latrobe, Pa., 1945-54; dean of men St. Vincent Coll., 1957-62; chaplain Pa. State U., 1962-67; archabbot, chancellor St. Vincent Archabbey and Coll., Latrobe, 1967-79; now cons. Bd. dirs. St. Vincent Coll., 1947-62, 67-79. Mem. Nat. Newman Chaplains Assn., Am. Benedictine Acad., Conf. Major Superiora of Men. Club: K.C. Address: St Vincent Archabbey Latrobe PA 15650

DONOVAN, FRANK WILLIAM, lawyer; b. Washington, Sept. 12, 1905; s. Frank Dennis and Catherine (Connor) D.; m. Helen Turner, June 25, 1938 (div. May 1947); children: Frank William, Julia Donovan O'Meara, Russell Hodges; m. Elizabeth Chetwoode Hodges, June 19, 1947 (dec. Nov., 1968); m. Ana Maria Fuentes-Munizaga, Dec. 8, 1969. A.B., Notre Dame U., 1926; LL.B., Harvard U., 1929. Bar: Mich. 1930. Partner Yerkes, Goddard & McClintock, Detroit, 1932-38; individual practice, Detroit, 1938-41; partner Fulton & Donovan, Detroit, 1941-50, McClintock, Fulton, Donovan & Waterman, 1950-73, McClintock, Donovan, Carson & Roach, 1973-80, Donovan, Hammond, Carson, Ziegelman, Roach & Sotiroff, 1980-81, Donovan, Hammond, Ziegelman, Roach & Sotiroff, 1981—; dir. Bob-Lo Co., Detroit, Sabin Industries, Mich., Context Industries, Miami, Fla., Chase Devel. Corp., Hartford, Conn., W.H. Edgar & Son, Detroit, Zenith Labs, Inc., Northvale, N.J., Ryerson & Haynes, Inc., Jackson. Chmn. Italian Flood Relief Com., Detroit, 1966; chmn. Grosse Pointe War Meml. Assn., 1966-69; chmn. bd. Detroit Grand Opera Assn., Detroit Symphony Orch., Etruscan Found., Mich. Opera Theatre, David T. Chase Found.; mem. senate Stratford Shakespearean Fest. Found., Can.; mem. Met. Opera Assn. N.Y.; trustee Sheakespearean Drama Festival Found., Inc., N.Y.C.; bd. govs. Am. Mental Health Found. Recipient award merit Am. C. of C. for Italy, 1967, citation appreciation Greater Mich. Found., 1963; Frank W. Donovan Day in recognition cultural contbns. City of Detroit, 1963. Clubs: Detroit, Country of Detroit, Renaissance (Detroit); Grosse Pointe (Mich.); La Coquille (Palm Beach, Fla.). Home: 17170 E Jefferson Grosse Pointe MI 48230 Office: 400 Renaissance Center Suite 1100 Detroit MI 48243

DONOVAN, GERALD ALTON, univ. dean; b. Hartford, Conn., Feb. 10, 1925; s. Gerald Joseph and Alice Gertrude (Gleason) D.; m. Barbara Ann Hue, Feb. 1, 1948; children—Deborah E. (Mrs. Alan Abare), Clayton H., Bruce G. B.A., U. Conn., 1950, M.S., 1952; Ph.D., Iowa State U., 1955. Poultry nutritionist Charles Pfizer & Co., Inc., Terre Haute, Ind., 1955-60; prof., chmn. poultry sci. dept. U. Vt., 1960-66, asso. dir., asso. dean, 1966-73; dean Coll. Resource Devel., U. R.I., Kingston, 1973—, dir., 1975—; mem. U.S. AID/BIFAD Joint Research Council, 1979—. Contbr. articles to profl. jours. Bd. dirs. Vt. Community Coll., 1970-73. Served with USN, 1943-46. Mem. Am. Inst. Nutrition, Agrl. Research Inst., Assn. Agrl. Expt. Sta. Dirs., Sigma Xi, Alpha Zeta, Alpha Gamma Rho. Home: PO Box 122 Saunderstown RI 02874 Office: Coll Resource Devel U RI Kingston RI 02881

DONOVAN, HEDLEY WILLIAMS, journalist; b. Brainerd, Minn., May 24, 1914; s. Percy Williams and Alice (Dougan) D.; m. Dorothy Hannon, Oct. 18, 1941 (dec. 1978); children: Peter Williams, Helen Welles, Mark Vicars. A.B. magna cum laude, U. Minn., 1934; B.A. (Rhodes scholar), Oxford U., 1936; Litt.D. (hon.), Pomona Coll., Boston U., Mt. Holyoke Coll., L.H.D., Southwestern at Memphis, Rochester U., Transylvania U., LL.D., Carnegie-Mellon U., Lehigh U., Allegheny Coll. Reporter Washington Post, 1937-42; writer, editor Fortune mag., N.Y. C., 1945-51, asso. mng. editor, 1951-53, mng. editor, 1953-59; editorial dir. Time Inc., 1959-64, editor-in-chief, 1964-79, dir., 1962-79; sr. adv. to Pres. of U.S., 1979-80; fellow faculty of govt. Harvard U., 1980—; dir. Aerospace Corp. Trustee Carnegie Endowment for Internat. Peace, Ford Found., Nat. Center for Humanities, ASIA Soc. Served to lt. comdr. USNR, 1942-45. Recipient Outstanding Achievement award U. Minn. Alumni, 1956; Loeb Journalism award, 1978; Gallatin medal N.Y. U., 1979; hon. fellow Hertford Coll. Oxford (Eng.) U. Fellow Am. Acad. Arts and Scis.; mem. Council Fgn. Relations (dir. 1969-79), Phi Beta Kappa, Delta Upsilon. Clubs: University, Manhasset Bay Yacht, Century, Sands Point Golf; 1925 F St., Met. (Washington); St. Botolph (Boston). Home: 190 E 72d St New York NY 10021 also Harbor Rd Sands Point NY 11050 Office: Time and Life Bldg Rockefeller Center New York NY 10020

DONOVAN, JEROME FRANCIS, lawyer; b. Washington, Sept. 27, 1936; s. Jerome Francis and Charlotte (Lovekin) D.; m. Sharon Joy Bennett, Oct. 30, 1965; children: Bennett F., Garrett J., Anne C. B.A., Yale U., 1958; J.D., Columbia U., 1961. Bar: Ariz. 1964, D.C. 1969, U.S. Supreme Ct 1969. Asso. Evans, Kitchel & Jenckes, Phoenix, 1964-68; asst. dir. local coalitions div. Nat. Urban Coalition, Washington, 1968-69, spl. asst. to pres., 1970; exec. dir., counsel Commn. on Cities in the 70's, Washington, 1971; exec. dir. credentials com. Democratic Nat. Conv., dir. policy panels Dem. presdl. campaign, 1972; dir. programs 6th Internat. Conf. on World Peace through Law, Abidjan, Ivory Coast, 1973; sole practice, Washington, 1973-75; resident counsel Curtis, Mallet-Prevost, Colt & Mosle, Washington, 1975-77; partner firm Anderson & Pendleton, Washington, 1978-82; of counsel Chapman, Duff and Paul, Washington, 1983—; pres. Continental Africa Investors, Inc., Washington, 1982—. Editor: The State of the Cities, 1972. Served as 1st lt. U.S. Army, 1961-63. Mem. Am., Fed., D.C. bar assns., Am. Soc. Internat. Law, Am. Arbitration Assn., Phi Delta Phi. Roman Catholic. Clubs: Yale (N.Y.C.); Federal City (Washington). Home: 6114 Ramshorn Pl McLean VA 22101 Office: 1825 Eye St NW Washington DC 20006

DONOVAN, JOHN ANTHONY, bishop; b. Chatham, Ont., Can., Aug. 5, 1911; s. John J. and Mary C. (O'Rourke) D. B.A., Sacred Heart Sem., 1932; postgrad., N.A. Coll., Rome, 1936, J.C.L., Pontifical Athenaeum of Lateran, Rome, 1947; LL.D., U. Detroit, 1952. Ordained priest Roman Cath. Ch., 1935, domestic prelate, 1949; pastor St. Aloysius' Ch., Detroit, also chancellor Archdiocese of Detroit, 1951-58, St. Veronica's Ch., East Detroit, 1958-67; Titular Bishop of, Rhasus and Aux. Bishop of Detroit, 1954-67; vicar gen. Archdiocese of Detroit, 1959-67; bishop of, Toledo, 1967-81. Address: 4706 Whiteford Rd Toledo OH 43623

DONOVAN, JOHN CHAUNCEY, political science educator; b. N.Y.C., Feb. 9, 1920; s. Michael James and Myrtie (Tucker) D.; m. Beatrice Florence Witter, Sept. 9, 1947; children: Carey, Christine, Martha, John. A.B., Bates Coll., 1942; M.A., Harvard U., 1948, Ph.D., 1949. Teaching fellow Harvard U., 1946-49; mem. faculty Bates Coll., 1949-59, prof. govt., chmn. social sci. div., 1957-59; administrv., asst. to U.S. Senator Muskie, 1959-62; exec. asst. to sec. labor Wirtz, 1962-65; DeAlva Stanwood Alexander prof. govt. Bowdoin Coll., 1965—, chmn. dept. govt. and legal studies, 1967-69, 79—. Author: The Politics of Poverty, 1967, 2d edit., 1973, 3d edit., 1980, The Policy Makers, 1970, The Cold Warriors, 1974, Democracy at the Crossroads, 1978, (with R.E. Morgan and C.P. Potholm) American Politics: Directions of Change, Dynamics of Choice, 1979, The 1960's: Politics and Public Policy, 1980, (with Richard E. Morgan and Christian P. Potholm) People, Power and Politics, 1981; contbr. articles to profl. jours. Chmn. New Eng. Regional Manpower Adv. Com., 1965-69, Me. Bd. Arbitration and Conciliation, 1955-56; chmn. Me. Adv. Council on Vocational Edn., 1969-72; Chmn. Maine Democratic Com., 1957-58; candidate for U.S. Congress, 2d dist. Me., 1960; Overseer Bates Coll.; trustee U. Maine. Served with USNR, World War II; PTO. Mem. Am. Polit. Sci. Assn., New Eng. Polit. Sci. Assn. (pres. 1983-84), Phi Beta Kappa. Home: 56 Federal St Brunswick ME 04011

DONOVAN, JOSEPH LEO, educator; b. Boston, Jan. 23, 1936; s. Joseph J. and Helyn E. (Waible) D.; m. Joyce Farley, June 13, 1959; children: Joseph L., Jeffrey L., Julie A., John P., Jeremy F. B.S., Boston Coll., 1957; M.A., Framingham State Coll., 1981. Fire marshall McGregor Missle Range, Ft. Bliss, Tex., 1958-59; firefighter Hopkinton Fire Dept., Mass., 1962-67, lt., 1967-78; chief fire tng. Commonwealth of Mass., 1978-82; coordinator Mass. Fire Service in Emergency, 1979-82; supt. Nat. Fire Acad., Emmitsburg, Md., 1982—; cons. Mass. Fire Acad., 1973-78, U.S. Fire Adminstrn., 1978-81; chmn. State Dirs. Fire Tng., 1981-82; mem. adv. com. NFA Bd. Visitors, 1981-82; mem. Transport of Hazardous Materials Task Force subcom. Nat. Acad. Scis., 1984—. Lead author: MA 5 Year Fire T&E Plan, 1979; editor: Essentials of Firefighting, 1979, 83; contbr.: Ventilating Practices, 1981. Bd. dirs. Boy Scouts Am., Hopkinton, 1973; chmn. Bd. Water Commrs., 1978; mem. Gov.'s Arson Commn., Boston, 1979. Served to capt. U.S. Army, 1957-59. Recipient spl. commendation Gov. of Mass., 1982, Mass. Senate, 1982, Mass. Ho. of Reps., 1982, Everett Hudiberg award Internat. Fire Service Tng. Assn., 1984. Mem. Internat. Soc. Fire Service Instrs. (dir.), Internat. Fire Service Tng. Assn. (exec. bd.), Internat. Assn. Fire Chiefs, Fire Chiefs Assn. Mass., Nat. Fire Protection Assn. Republican. Roman Catholic. Lodges: Rotary; Kiwanis. Office: Nat Fire Acad 16825 S Seton Ave Emmitsburg MD 21727

DONOVAN, PAUL V., bishop; b. Bernard, Iowa, Sept. 1, 1924; s. John J. and Loretta (Carew) D. Student, St. Joseph Sem., Grand Rapids, Mich.; B.A., St. Gregory Sem., Cin., 1946; postgrad., Mt. St. Mary Sem. of West, Cin.; J.C.L., Pontifical Lateran U., Rome, 1957. Ordained priest Roman Catholic Ch., 1950; asst. pastor St. Mary Ch., Jackson, Mich., 1950-51; sec. to bishop of, Lansing, Mich.) and; adminstr. St. Peter Ch., Eaton Rapids, Mich., 1951-55; sec. to bishop, 1957-59; pastor Our Lady of Fatima Ch., Michigan Center, Mich. and; St. Rita Mission, Clark Lake, Mich., 1959-68; pastor St. Agnes Ch., Flint, Mich., 1968-71; bishop of Kalamazoo, 1971—; mem. liturgical commn. Diocese of Lansing, chmn., 1963; mem. Cath. Bd. Edn., Jackson and Hillsdale counties; mem. bishop's personnel com., priests' senate. Bd. dirs. Family Services and, Mich. Children's Aid. Office: 215 N Westnedge Ave PO Box 949 Kalamazoo MI 49005 *

DONOVAN, RAYMOND JAMES, sec. labor; b. Bayonne, N.J., Aug. 31, 1930; m. Catherine Sblendorio, 1957; children—Kenneth, Mary Ellen, Keith. B.A., Notre Dame Sem., New Orleans, 1952. With Am. Ins. Co., 1953-58; v.p. Schiavone Constrn. Co., Secaucus, N.J., 1959-71, exec. v.p., Seacaucus, N.J., 1971-81; sec. Dept. Labor, Washington, 1981—; mem. Cabinet Council on Commerce and Trade, Cabinet Council on Econ. Affairs and Human Resources. Chmn. lay bd. dirs. Shrine of St. Josephs, Stirling, N.J.; chmn. lay bd. advisors Missionary Servants of the Most Holy Trinity. Office: Dept Labor Office Sec 200 Constitution Ave NW Washington DC 20210

DONOVAN, RICHARD ARTHUR, manufacturing company executive; b. Bklyn., Dec. 23, 1927; s. Thomas C. and Ethel (Flanagan) D.; m. Eileen Karthaus, Oct. 6, 1951; children: Richard, Paul, Jeanne, Terence, Susan, John, Patricia, William. A.B., Fordham U., 1950. Spl. agt. FBI, 1951-59; personnel officer Litton Industries, Morris Plains, N.J., 1959-64; dir. indsl. relations Electronic Assos., Long Branch, N.J., 1964-67; v.p., employee relations Shoe Corp. Am., Columbus, Ohio, 1967-68; v.p. personnel NL Industries Inc. (formerly Nat. Lead Co.), N.Y.C., 1968-74, v.p. adminstrn., 1974-75, group v.p. pigments, 1975-76, exec. v.p., 1976-81; also dir.; pres. Wabash, Inc., Ind., 1980; also dir.; pres., chief exec. officer Kearney-Nat., Inc., N.Y.C., 1980—. Served with U.S. Army, 1946-47. Mem. Soc. Former FBI Agents, AMA, Am. Soc. Personnel Adminstrn. Home: 102 Ridge Rd Rumson NJ 07760 Office: Kearney-National Inc 200 Park Ave New York NY 10166

DONOVAN, ROBERT JOHN, retired journalist; b. Buffalo, Aug. 21, 1912; s. Michael J. and Katherine (Sullivan) D.; m. Martha Fisher, May 9, 1941 (dec.); children: Patricia, Peter, Amy; m. Gerry Van der Heuvel, Mar. 17, 1978. Litt.D. (hon.), Am. Internat. Coll., 1962, Stone hill Coll., 1983. Mem. staff Buffalo Courier-Express, 1933-37; with N.Y. Herald Tribune, 1937-63, on European edit., 1945, mem., Washington Bur., 1947-63, chief, 1957-63; chief Washington bur. Los Angeles Times, 1963-70, assoc. editor, Los Angeles, 1970-77; fellow Woodrow Wilson Internat. Center for Scholars, 1978-79; sr. fellow Woodrow Wilson Sch. Pub. and Internat. Affairs, Princeton, N.J., 1979-80; Ferris prof. journalism Princeton U., 1980-81. Author: The Assassins, 1955, Eisenhower: The Inside Story, 1956, (with Joseph W. Martin, Jr.) My First Fifty Years in Politics, 1960, PT 109: John F. Kennedy in World War II, 1961, The Future of the Republican Party, 1964, Conflict and Crisis: The Presidency of Harry S Truman, 1945-48,

1977, Tumultuous Years: The Presidency of Harry S Truman, 1949-53, 1982, Nemesis: Truman and Johnson in the Coils of War in Asia, 1984; also mag. articles. Served AUS, World War II; staff Stars and Stripes in Paris. Mem. White House Corrs. Assn. (pres. 1954). Clubs: Federal City (Washington); Gridiron. Home: 3031 Beechwood Ln Falls Church VA 22042

DONOVAN, THOMAS ROY, board of trade executive; b. Chgo., Sept. 13, 1937. B.A. in Bus. and Econs., Ill. Inst. Tech., 1972, M.P.A., 1975. Adminstrv. asst. to mayor City of Chgo., 1969-79; v.p., sec. Chgo. Bd. of Trade, 1979-81, exec. v.p., sec., 1981-82, pres., chief exec. officer, 1982—. Office: Chgo Bd Trade 141 W Jackson Blvd Chicago IL 60604

DONOVAN, TIMOTHY PAUL, historian; b. Terre Haute, Ind., Dec. 25, 1927; s. Harry Thomas and Gretchen Alma (Stakeman) D.; m. Eugenia Matella Trapp, June 1, 1950; children: Kevin, Rebecca, David, Richard. B.A., U. Okla., 1949, M.A., 1950, Ph.D., 1960. Instr. Okla. Mil. Acad., 1950-52, chmn. humanities div., 1952-57; teaching asst. U. Okla., 1957-60; asst. prof. history Tex. Tech. U., 1960-63, assoc. prof., 1963-68, prof., 1968-69, U. Ark., Fayetteville, 1969-76, chmn. dept. history, 1976—. Author: Henry Adams and Brooks Adams, 1961, Historical Thought in America: Postwar Patterns, 1973, The Governors of Arkansas, 1981. Recipient Disting Teaching award Standard Oil, 1968. Mem. Am. Hist. Assn., Orgn. Am. Historians, Popular Culture Assn., Ark. Hist. Assn., So. Hist. Assn., Phi Alpha Theta. Democrat. Roman Catholic. Home: 1503 Cedar St Fayetteville AR 72701 Office: Dept History U Ark Fayetteville AR 72701

DONOVAN, WARREN FRANCIS, food company executive; b. Westport, Mass., June 7, 1915; s. John E. and Lucy (Cummings) D.; m. Margaret E. Woods, Nov. 23, 1946; children: Paul Joseph, Sally Ann, Jay Christopher, James Richard. Grad. high sch. Lic. real estate agt.; notary public. With H. P. Hoods, Inc., 1940—, successive positions including mgr. Italian food div., dir. citrus div., exec. v.p., chief operating officer, also dir., now semi-ret.; now cons.; Bd. dirs. Milk Industry Found. Served with USAAF, 1941-45; lt. col. Res. ret. Decorated Air medal, Purple Heart, others. Mem. Res. Officers Assn. (service award), Mass. Milk Insps. Assn., Internat. Assn. Ice Cream Mfrs. Republican. Roman Catholic. Home: 5 Whittier Dr Acton MA 01720 Office: 500 Rutherford Ave Boston MA 02129

DOOB, JOSEPH LEO, mathematician, educator; b. Cin., Feb. 27, 1910; s. Leo and Mollie (Doerfler) D.; m. Elsie Haviland Field, June 26, 1931; children—Stephen, Peter, Deborah. B.A., Harvard U., 1930, M.A., 1931, Ph.D., 1932; D.Sc. (hon.), U. Ill., 1981. Faculty U. Ill., Urbana, 1935—, successively asso., asst. prof., asso. prof., 1935-45, prof. math., 1945—, now emeritus prof. Recipient Nat. Medal of Sci., 1979. Mem. Nat. Acad. Scis., Am. Acad. Arts and Scis., Acad. Scis. (Paris) (fgn. asso.). Home: 208 W High St Urbana IL 61801

DOOB, LEONARD WILLIAM, psychologist; b. N.Y.C., Mar. 3, 1909; s. William and Florence (Lewis) D.; m. Eveline Bates, Mar. 21, 1936; children—Christopher Bates, Anthony Newcomb, Nicholas Ellsworth. A.B., Dartmouth, 1929; A.M., Duke, 1930; postgrad., U. Frankfurt, Germany, 1930-32; Ph.D., Harvard, 1934. Asst. instr. psychology Duke, 1929-30; instr. sociology Dartmouth, 1932-33; mem. faculty Yale U., 1934-77, prof. psychology, 1950-77, also div. social scis., chmn. African studies, Sterling prof. emeritus psychology and sr. research scholar, 1977—. Home: Clark Rd Woodbridge CT 06525 Office: 2 Box 11 A Yale Sta New Haven CT 06520

DOODY, MARGARET ANNE, English educator; b. St. John, N.B., Can., Sept. 21, 1939; came to U.S., 1976; d. Hubert and Anne Ruth (Cornwall) D. B.A., Dalhousie U., Can., 1960, Lady Margaret Hall-Oxford (Eng.) U., 1962, M.A., 1965, D.Phil., 1968. Instr. English U. Victoria (B.C., Can.), 1962-64, asst. prof. English, 1968-69; lectr. Univ. Coll. Swansea (Wales), 1969-76; assoc. prof. English U. Calif.-Berkeley, 1976-80; prof. English dept. Princeton (N.J.) U., 1980—. Author: A Natural Passion: A Study of the Novels of Samuel Richardson, 1974; novel Aristotle Detective, 1978, The Alchemists, 1980. Guggenheim postdoctoral fellow, 1979. Episcopalian. Office: English Dept Princeton U Princeton NJ 08544

DOOHER, M(UREDACH) JOSEPH, editor, writer, pub. cons.; b. Ireland, Oct. 22, 1913; came to U.S., 1923, naturalized, 1938; s. James Francis and Mary Elizabeth (Nixon) D. Grad., St. Benedict's Coll. Prep. Sch., Newark, 1931. Editor Am. Mgmt. Assn., N.Y.C., 1937-56; exec. editor Dun's Rev., N.Y.C., 1956-61; editor indsl. and bus. books McGraw-Hill Book Co., 1961-71, cons. editor, 1971—. Editor: Rating Employee and Supervisory Performance, 1950, The A.M.A. Handbook of Wage and Salary Administration, 1950, The Supervisor's Management Guide, 1949, The Management Leader's Manual, 1947, The Development of Executive Talent, 1952, Effective Communication on the Job, 1956, Selection of Management Personnel, 1957; Author essays and verse in British and Am. periodicals. Mem. Indsl. Relations Research Assn. Republican. Roman Catholic. Home: 176 Grand Ave Rutherford NJ 07070 Office: McGraw-Hill Book Co 1221 Av of Americas New York City NY 10020

DOOKS, EDWARD EARL, news photographer; b. Cambridge, Mass., Oct. 26, 1941; s. Earl Joseph and Elsie May (Trevett) D.; m. Karen Ann Horn, June 12, 1965; children: David Edward, Susan Karen, Daniel Christopher. Student, Northeastern U., 1959-60, Franklin Inst., 1961-63. Cinematographer Acorn Films N.E., Inc., Boston, 1960-62; with Sta. WBZ-TV, Boston, 1962—; treas. Nat. Press Photographers Found., Inc., 1979—; lectr. news photography schs and news photo assns. Served with USAFR, 1964-70. Mem. Nat. Press Photographers Assn. (Pres.'s medal 1977, treas. 1978-82), Boston Press Photographers Assn. (treas. 1983—, named New Eng. Newsfilm Cameraman of Yr. 1964-67), Boston and Maine Railroad Hist. Soc. (life), Mystic Valley Rwy. Soc. Conglist. Club: Focal Point Camera (Lexington, Mass.). Office: 1170 Soldiers Field Rd Boston MA 02134

DOOLEN, PAUL DWIGHT, foundation executive, insurance company executive, consultant; b. Vernon, Ill., Feb. 24, 1905; s. Isham Willis and Rose (Arnold) D.; m. Martha Estine Lewis, Oct. 20, 1934; children: Mark Lorimer, Deborah Doolen Ittel. B.A., U. Ill., 1927; LL.B., Harvard U., 1931. Bar: Ill. 1932, U.S. Supreme Ct. 1946. Ptnr. Decker & Doolen, Waukegan, Ill., 1936-43; counsel, sales mgr. A.E. Staley & Co., Decatur, Ill., 1944-52; vice-chmn. Bankers Life & Casualty, Chgo., 1952-78, chmn. exec. com., pres., 1965-71, chmn. emeritus, 1978—; chmn. bd. John D. and Catherine T. MacArthur Found., Chgo., 1978—; pres., bd. chmn. Retirement Research Found., Park Ridge, Ill., 1978-80, bd. dirs., 1978—; chmn. exec. com., dir. Citizens Bank & Trust, Park Ridge, 1960-81. Chmn. Decatur-Macon County United Fund, Decatur, Ill., 1945-47; bd. dirs., chmn. aviation com. Ill. State C. of C., 1947-49; bd. dirs. Village of Palm Beach Gardens, Fla., 1958-61. Republican. Presbyterian. Clubs: Mount Dora Yacht (Fla.); Sapphire Valley Country (Sapphire, N.C.); Delta Tau Delta (Urbana, Ill.). Home: 2101 Overlook Dr Mount Dora FL 32757 Office: MacArthur Found 140 S Dearborn St Chicago IL 60603

DOOLEY, ARCH RICHARD, educator; b. Oklahoma City, Feb. 1, 1925; s. Archibald E. and Grace (Moore) D.; m. Patricia Folts, Sept. 5, 1953; children—Arch Richard, Christopher Folts. A.B., Yale, 1944; M.B.A., Harvard, 1950, D.C.S., 1960. Asst. prof. Oklahoma City U., 1946-47; asst. prof., asst. dean bus. U. N.C., 1950-54; mem. faculty Harvard Grad. Sch. Bus. Adminstrn., 1954—, prof., 1965—, Jesse Philips prof. mfg., 1969—; mem. vis. faculty Keio (Japan) U., U. Western Ont., Inst. Panamericano de Alta Dirección de Empresa, Mexico, Exec. Tng. Inst. Philippines, Singapore Mgmt. Inst., Instituto Centroamericano de Administración de Empresas, Nicaragua, U. de Carabobo, Venezuela; mem. adv. bd. Instituto Estudios Superiores Empresas, Spain; cons. to govt. and industry, 1952—. Author: Business Management Credit Bureaus, 1953, (with others) Casebooks in Production Management-Basic Problems, Concepts and Techniques, rev. edit, 1968, Production Operating Decisions in the Total Business Strategy, 1964, Operations Planning and Control, 1964, Wage Administration and Worker Productivity, 1964. Served as officer USNR, World War II. Mem. Acad. Mgmt., Beta Theta Pi. Home: 21 Summit Rd Lexington MA 02173 Office: Harvard Business Sch Soldiers Field Boston MA 02163

DOOLEY, DELMER JOHN, former foundation administrator; b. Ramona, S.D., Mar. 15, 1920; s. Frank M. and Theresa (DeRungs) D.; m. Thalia Elma Doty, June 12, 1952; children: Douglas John, Alan Patrick. B.S., S.D. State U., 1948; M.S., Colo. State U., 1952; Ed.D., U. Mo., 1964. Voca. agr. instr., Platte, S.D., 1948-53, Lakeview, Oreg., 1953-55; with Near East Found., 1955-83, exec. dir., 1964-83. Mem. exec. com. Am. Council Vol. Agys., 1965-83, treas, 1970-75, chmn., 1981-82; exec. bd. Morris-Sussex council Boy Scouts Am., 1968—, dist. vice chmn., 1967-69, dist. chmn., 1969-71, v.p., 1978—; Mem. com. on continuing edn. Hanover (N.J.) Public Schs.; bd. dirs. Musa Alami Found., 1982—. Served with USAAF, 1942-45. Decorated Air medal with clusters; Independence medal King Hussein of Jordan.; Awarded Silver Beaver Boy Scouts Am., 1972. Mem. Middle East Inst., Soc. Internat. Devel., Am. Legion, Alpha Tau Alpha, Phi Delta Kappa. Roman Catholic. Club: Rotarian. Home: 116 DeForest Ave East Hanover NJ 07936 Office: 29 Broadway New York NY 10006

DOOLEY, DONALD JOHN, pub. exec.; b. Des Moines, Aug. 16, 1921; s. Martin and Anne Marguerite (Barger) D.; m. Beverly Frederick, Dec. 21, 1955 (div. 1977); children—Nancy Elizabeth, Katherine Anne (dec.), Mary Bridget, Robert Frederick. B.A., State U. Iowa, 1947; postgrad., Drake U., 1949-50. Gen. Promotion and pub. relations mgr. Meredith Corp., Des Moines, 1953-59, dir. pub. relations, 1960-65; art and editorial dir. Better Homes and Gardens Books (Meredith Corp.), Des Moines, 1965-77, dir. editorial planning and devel., 1977—. Chmn. bd. adv. com. Sch. Vol. Program, Des Moines; steering com. Intercultural Affairs program to Desegregate Dist. Schs., 1975-77; treas. Iowa U. Parents Assn., 1977-79; bd. dirs. Iowa Cystic Fibrosis Found., 1979—, v.p., 1981—; trustee Citizens Scholarship Found. Am., 1976—, Iowa Freedom of Info. Council, 1977—; cons. White House Conf. on Families, 1981. Served with USAAF, 1942-46. Mem. Public Relations Soc. Am. (pres. chpt. 1969, dir. chpt. 1965—), ACLU, Sierra Club, Sigma Nu (comdr. chpt. 1946-47). Democrat. Home: 2727 Stanton St Des Moines IA 50321 Office: 1716 Locust St Des Moines IA 50336

DOOLEY, GEORGE ELIJAH, medical administrator; b. Hopland, Calif., Dec. 25, 1918; s. Franklin Wayne and Mary Catherine Dorathea (Hageman) D.; m. Helen Ursula Fitch, July 28, 1945; children—Jeffrey Earle, Jill (Mrs. Steven Robbat). B.S., St. Mary's Coll., Calif., 1939; M.S., George Washington U., 1966; postgrad., Nat. War Coll., 1960-61. Joined USMC, 1939, commd. 2d lt., 1940, designated Naval aviator, 1941, advanced through grades to brig. gen., 1966; served to, PTO, World War II, staff officer, Washington, 1957-60, comdg. officer, Hawaii, 1961-63, staff officer, Atlantic, 1963-65, chief of staff, Norfolk, Va., 1965-66; asst. dep. chief of staff Hdqrs., Washington, 1966-68; chief of staff 3d Marine Amphibious Force, Danang, Vietnam, 1968-70; comdg. gen. Landing Force Tng. Command, Pacific, 1970; ret., 1970; adminstr. Kensington Med. Group, San Diego, 1971—. Bd. dirs. Inst. for Burn Medicine, San Diego CHAD, San Diego.; adv. bd. Econ. Edn. Found., San Diego. Decorated D.S.M., Silver Star, Legion of Merit, D.F.C., Air medal, U.S.; Nat. Order 5th class; Gallantry cross with palm, Vietnam; Korean Chung Moo. Mem. Del Mar C. of C., Del Mar Civic Assn., Med. Group Mgmt. Assn., Navy League, Med. Adminstrs. Calif. Roman Catholic. Clubs: Rotarian., Del Mar Thoroughbred, La Jolla Beach and Tennis, Tambo D'Oro. Home: 2055 Seaview Del Mar CA 92014 Office: 4193 Adams Ave San Diego CA 92116

DOOLEY, PATRICK KIARAN, philosopher, educator; b. Fargo, N.D., June 23, 1942; s. Kiaran L. and Katharine M. (McDonald) D.; m. Nora Ann Householter, Dec. 27, 1969; children: Gregory, Hester, Mills. B.A., St. Paul Sem., 1964; M.A., U. Notre Dame, 1967, Ph.D., 1969. Instr. Stanley Clark Sch., South Bend, Ind., 1966-67, U. Notre Dame, 1967-68; asst. prof. St. Bonaventure U., N.Y., 1969-73, assoc. prof., 1973-74, prof. philosophy, 1977—, chmn. philosophy dept., 1970-77, 81—; vis. scholar Duke U., Durham, N.C., 1977; faculty rep. St. Bonaventure U. Senate Sch. Arts, 1971—, Univ. Fin. Com., 1975-77, chmn. faculty senate, 1977-81. Author: pragmatism as Humanism, 1975, (rev. edit) Pragmatism as Humanism, 1978, Pragmatism as Humanism: The Philosophy of William James, 1974; contbr. articles in philosophy, book reviews to profl. publs. U. Notre Dame scholar, 1965-67; U. Notre Dame teaching fellow, 1967-68; Schmitt. Found. fellow, 1968-69; Coll. Ctr. of Finger Lakes grantee Harvard U., summer, 1972; Council Philos. Studies grantee Calvin Coll., summer, 1973; NEH grantee Duke U., summer, 1975, U. Kans., 1978, U. Ill., 1981; St. Bonaventure U. Research grantee, spring, 1978, summers 1982, 83. Mem. Am. Philos. Assn., Am. Cath. Philos. Assn. (exec. com. 1973-74, regional pres. 1974-75), Soc. Advancement of Am. Philosophy. Democrat. Roman Catholic. Home: 61 South St Cuba NY 14727 Office: St. Bonaventure U. Box 7 Saint Bonaventure NY 14778

DOOLEY, RICHARD GORDON, insurance company executive; b. Salem, Mass., Aug. 5, 1929; s. Charles Augustus and Louise Mary (Foisy) D.; m. Bernadine Frances Daley, Apr. 7, 1956; children: Thomas, Paul, Richard, Gretchen, Charles. B.S., Northwestern U., Boston, 1951; M.B.A., U. Pa., 1955. Investment analyst Mass. Mut. Life Ins. Co., Springfield, 1955-69, investment exec., 1971—; investment mgr. Allstate Ins. Co., Northbrook, Ill., 1969-71. Office: Mass Mut Life Ins Co 1295 State St Springfield MA 01111

DOOLEY, THOMAS HENRY, banker; b. Cin., Jan. 29, 1931; s. Edward M. and Elfrieda M. (Mayer) D.; m. Patricia D. McCoy, Aug. 23, 1952; children—Roger, Dennis, Alyce, Kathleen, Jennifer, Thomas. B.B.A., U. Mich., 1954, M.B.A., 1954. C.P.A., Mich. Sr. acct. Peat, Marwick, Mitchell & Co., Detroit, 1956-63; 1st v.p., comptroller Am. Nat. Bank & Trust Co., Kalamazoo, 1963-68; v.p. adminstrn., controller Mfrs. Nat. Bank, Detroit, 1968-73; controller Mfrs. Nat. Corp., Detroit, 1973—, sr. v.p., 1977-80, exec. v.p., chief fin. officer, 1980-82, Calif. Fed. Savs. & Loan Assn., Los Angeles, 1982—. Served to 1st lt. AUS, 1954-56. Mem. Am. Inst. C.P.A.s, Bank Adminstrn. Inst., Fin. Execs. Inst., Mich. Assn. C.P.A.'s. Club: Forest Lake Country. Office: 5670 Wilshire Blvd Los Angeles CA 90036

DOOLEY, VINCENT JOSEPH, football coach; b. Mobile, Ala., Sept. 4, 1932; s. William Vincent and Nellie Agnes (Stauter) D.; m. Barbara Anne Meshad, Mar. 19, 1960; children: Deanna, Daniel, Denise, Derek. B.S., Auburn U., 1954, M.A. in History, 1963. Asst. football coach Auburn U. (Ala.), 1960, head freshman football coach, 1961-63; head football coach, athletic dir. U. Ga., Athens, 1964—. Chmn. Ga. State Easter Seals Soc. Served to 2d lt. USMC, 1954-56. Named NCAA Coach of Yr., 1980, S.E. Conf. Coach of Yr., U. Ga., 1964, 66, 68, 76, 78, 80, 81; winner nat. championship, 1980. Mem. Am. Football Coaches Assn. (trustee, past chmn. ethics com.). Office: University of Georgia Athletic Dept PO Box 1472 Athens GA 30613

DOOLIN, JOHN B., state supreme ct. justice; b. Alva, Okla., May 25, 1918; s. John B. and Leo M. (Museller) D.; m. Katherine E. Bruck, June 7, 1946; children—John William, Mary L. Doolin Trembley, Katherine, Carole and Colleen (twins), Martha. B.S. in Bus. Adminstrn, Okla. U., 1941, LL.B., 1947. Bar: Okla. bar 1942. Practiced in, Alva, 1947-53, Lawton, 1963-73; justice Okla. Supreme Ct., 1973—; mem. Okla. Hwy. Commn., 1959-63. Trustee Comanche County (Okla.) Meml. Hosp., 1967-73, chmn., 1968-73. Served to capt. AUS, 1941-45. Mem. Phi Delta Phi. *

DOOLITTLE, JAMES HAROLD, aviator, ins. co. exec.; b. Alameda, Cal., Dec. 14, 1896; s. Frank H. and Rosa C. (Shephard) D.; m. Josephine E. Daniels, Dec. 24, 1917; children—James H., John P. A.B., U. Calif., 1918 (1922); M.S., Mass. Inst. Tech., 1924, Sc.D., 1925. Aviator U.S. Army, 1917-30; resigned, 1930, maj.; teaching fellow aero. engrng. Mass. Inst. Tech., 1925; mgr. aviation dept. Shell Petroleum Corp., 1930-40; apptd. mem. Army AC Investigating Com. (Baker Bd.), 1934; apptd. maj. USAAF, 1940, lt. col. to maj. gen., 1942, lt. gen., 1944; comdr. (12th Air Force in), North Africa,, Okinawa, 1945, inactive duty, 1946-58, ret., 1959; v.p. Shell Oil Co., 1946-58, dir., 1946-67; chmn. bd. Space Tech. Labs., 1959-62; cons. TRW Systems, 1961-66, dir. parent co., 1961-69; dir. Mut. of Omaho Ins. Co. (and affiliates); trustee Aerospace Corp., 1963-69, vice chmn. bd. trustees, chmn. exec. com., 1965-69; Pres. Air Force Assn., 1946-47, chmn., 1948-49; apptd. chmn. Sec. War's Bd. on Enlisted Men-Officer Relationships; mem. NACA, 1948-56, chmn., 1956-58; adviser to Com. on Nat. Security Orgn. and Joint Congl. Aviation Policy Bd.; mem. adv. bd. Nat. Air Mus., Smithsonian Inst., 1956-65; chmn. Pres.'s Airport Commn., 1952, Pres.'s Task Group on Air Inspection, Stassen Disarmament Com., 1955, Pres.'s Bd. on Fgn. Intelligence, 1955-65, Air Force Sci. Adv. Bd., 1955-58; mem. Def. Sci. Bd., 1957-58, Pres.'s Sci. Adv. Com., 1957-58, Nat. Aeros. and Space Council, 1958. Contbr. sci., aero. articles to profl. jours. Decorated Congl. Medal of Honor, D.S.M. with oak leaf cluster, Silver Star, D.F.C. with two oak leaf clusters, Bronze Star, Air medal with three oak leaf clusters; Bolivian Order of Condor medal; Yon-Hwei Class III; grande officier French Legion d'Honneur, Croix de Guerre with palm; knight comdr. Order of the Bath; grande officer Order of Crown with Palm and Croix de Guerre with palm, both Belgium, 1948; Recipient Harmon Internat. Aviation award; winner Schneider Trophy Race, 1925; awarded Mackay trophy, 1926; Harmon trophy, 1930; winner Bendix Trophy Race, Burbank, Calif. to Cleve., 1931, Thompson Trophy Race, 258.68 miles per hr., 1932. Hon. fellow AIAA (pres. 1940, hon.), Royal Aero. Soc.; mem. Nat. Aero. Assn. Clubs: Explorers, Boone and Crockett, Bohemian, Wings, Lotos. Also set world's high speed record for landplanes, 1932. Home: 8545 Carmel Valley Rd Carmel CA 93923 Office: 1015 Cass St Monterey CA 93940

DOOLITTLE, JESSE WILLIAM, JR., lawyer; b. Wheaton, Ill., May 19, 1929; s. Jesse William and Selma Caroline (Schacht) D.; m. Annette Danforth Bush, May 5, 1962; children: Danforth Bush, Alice Walters. A.B., DePauw U., 1951; LL.B. magna cum laude, Harvard, 1954. Bar: D.C. 1954. Law clk. to U.S. Supreme Ct. Justice Felix Frankfurter, 1957-58; asso. firm Covington & Burling, Washington, 1958-61; asst. to solicitor gen. of U.S. Dept. Justice, Washington, 1961-63, 1st asst. civil div., 1963-66; gen. counsel Dept. Air Force, Washington, 1966-68, asst. sec. for manpower and res. affairs, 1968-69; partner firm Prather Seeger Doolittle & Farmer, Washington, 1969—. Mem.: Harvard Law Rev, 1952-54. Pres. bd. trustees Nat. Child Research Center, Washington, 1972-74; mem. bd. overseers' com. to visit ROTC programs Harvard, 1967-69; com. to visit Law Sch., 1969-75; mem. governing bd. Nat. Cathedral Sch. for Girls, Washington, 1979—, vice-chmn., 1981-82, chmn., 1982—. Served from pvt. to 1st lt. AUS, 1954-57. Recipient Career Service award Nat. Civil Service League, 1968, Exceptional Civilian Service award Dept. Air Force, 1969. Mem. Am. Bar Assn., Bar Assn. D.C. (chmn. coms.), Am. Law Inst., Harvard Law Sch. Assn. (council 1964-68), Harvard Law Rev. Assn. (bd. overseers 1967-72), Phi Beta Kappa, Delta Chi. Democrat. Episcopalian (sr. warden 1973-75, past vestryman). Clubs: Metropolitan, Chevy Chase. Home: 4238 50th St NW Washington DC 20016 Office: 1101 16th St NW Washington DC 20036

DOOLITTLE, ROBERT FREDERICK, lawyer; b. Oberlin, Ohio, June 14, 1902; s. Frederick Giraud and Maude (Tucker) D.; m. Gretchen Reller, Oct. 11, 1958. Grad., Ethical Culture Sch., N.Y.C., 1919; A.B. magna cum laude, Harvard, 1923; LL.B., 1930; LL.D., Youngstown State U., 1968. Bar: N.Y. State bar 1932, Ohio bar 1953. Asso. firm Taylor, Blanc, Capron & Marsh, N.Y.C., 1930-32, Cotton, Franklin, Wright & Gordon (name now Cahill, Gordon, Reindel), 1932-42; counsel for Baldwin Locomotive Works (name changed to Baldwin-Lima-Hamilton Corp., Dec. 1950), Phila., 1946-48, v.p., counsel, 1948-52; v.p. Baldwin Locomotive Sales Corp., Baldwin Locomotive Works of Can., Baldwin Locomotives Internat., Inc., 1948-52; asst. gen. counsel, asst. sec. Youngstown Sheet and Tube Co., O., 1952-59, gen. counsel, corp. sec., 1959-67, v.p., 1964-67, dir., 1967-69; counsel to law firm Baker, Hostetler & Patterson, Cleve., 1967—. Bd. dirs. World Affairs Council Phila., 1951-52; mem. Gov.'s Com. on Water Resources, Ohio, 1954-58; mem. adv. council Ohio Water Commn., 1966-67; chmn. adv. council task force on financing State Water Mgmt. Plan, 1966-67; mem. Gov.'s Com. Emergency Resource Planning, Ohio, 1966-67, Planning and Zoning Commn., Gates Mills, Ohio, 1970—; chmn. Charter Commn., 1972; Mem. Ohio Bd. Regents for Higher Edn., 1963—, vice chmn., 1966-77, chmn., 1977—; trustee, v.p. Arcadia Inst. Sci. Research; trustee, mem. exec. com. Cleve. Council on World Affairs. Served from maj. to lt. col. U.S. Army, 1942-44; assigned by War Dept. to Office Contract Settlement, Exec. Office Pres., 1944; Washington; disch., 1945; asst. gen. counsel, later gen. counsel Office Contract Settlement, 1945-46. Mem. Am. Judicature Soc., Am., N.Y. State, Ohio, Cleve. bar. assns., Ohio Mfrs. Assn. (trustee 1955-67, pres. 1965-67, exec. com. 1957—), Youngstown Symphony Soc. (dir. 1953-67), N.A.M. (edn. policy com.), Am. Iron and Steel Inst., Phi Beta Kappa, Phi Delta Phi. Conglist. Clubs: Youngstown Country; Merion Cricket (Haverford, Pa.); Merion Golf (Ardmore, Pa.); Rittenhouse (Phila.); Harvard (N.Y.C.); Chagrin Valley Hunt; Kirtland Country, Union (Cleve.). Home: Berkshire Rd Gates Mills OH 44040

DOOLITTLE, SIDNEY NEWING, retail executive; b. Binghamton, N.Y., Sept. 7, 1934; s. Raymond Luvurn and Helen Esther (Newing) D.; m. Barbara Mae Colsten, Sept. 12, 1954; children: Scott Sidney, Craig Francis, Sally Anne. A.A. in Advanced Mgmt, Harvard U., 1977. With Montgomery Ward & Co., 1955-83, dir. internat. ops., 1970-73, v.p., dir., 1972, corp. v.p., div. mgr. catalog mdse., Chgo., 1978-83; exec. v.p., mdse. mgr., dir. Warehouse Club, Inc., 1983—. Bd. dirs. Henrotin Hosp., Chgo., 1980-83. Mem. Mail Order Assn. Am. (chmn. bd. 1981-83), Chgo. Fgn. Relations Council. Presbyterian. Office: Warehouse Club Inc 7420 N Lehigh Niles IL 60648

DOORENBOS, NORMAN JOHN, university dean; b. Flint, Mich., May 13, 1928; s. Garrett Jake and Victoria (Manery) D.; m. Rose Lee Smith LeTourneau, Feb. 2, 1979; children: Beverly, Phillis, David

LeToruneau, Donna, Alice, Robin LeToruneau, Robert LeToruneau, Martha. B.S. in Chemistry, U. Mich., 1950; M.S. in Pharm. Chemistry, 1951, Ph.D., 1953. Reseearch chemist Ansco, Binghamton, N.Y., 1953-56; asst. prof., assoc. prof., prof. U. Md., Balt., 1956-65; prof. medicianal chemistry U. Miss., Oxford, 1965-77, prof., chmn. pharmacognosy, 1967-77; dean Coll. Sci., prof. physiology So. Ill. U., Carbondale, 1977—; dir. Marine Field Sta., Cayman Islands, 1970-74, Bitter End Field Sta., 1974—; cons. on drugs and toxins various ednl., prof., govt., indsl. groups. Contbr. articles to profl. jours.; patentee in field. Research grantee Mallinckrodt Chem. Works, Smith, Kline and French Lab., Merck, Sharp & Dohm, Sterling Winthrop Research Inst., Nat. Drug Co., Walker Labs., Penick Co., USDA, FDA, Nat. Marine Fisheries, Sea Grant Program, Century Am. Corp., Hokin Found., Fabik Found. Mem. Soc. for Econ. Botany, Am. Soc. Pharmacognosy, AAAS, Am. Pharm. Assn., Acad. Pharm. Scis., Am. Chem. Soc., Ill. Acad. Scis., Miss. Acad. Scis., Md. Acad. Scis., Assn. Island Marine Labs. of the Caribbean, Smithsonian Inst., Sigma Xi, Phi Lambda Upsilon, Rho Chi. Baptist. Office: College of Sci So Ill U Carbondale IL 62901

DORAIN, PAUL BRENDEL, chemist, coll. adminstr.; b. New Haven, Aug. 30, 1926; s. Hugh Alfred and Marion (Burritt) D.; m. Elsie Vega Ahlberg, Aug. 19, 1950; children—Melanie, Douglas. B.S., Yale, 1950; Ph.D., Ind. U., 1954. Postdoctoral fellow U. Chgo., 1954-56; solid state physicist Aero. Research Lab. USAF, Dayton, Ohio, 1956-58; mem. faculty Brandeis U., 1958-81, prof. chemistry, 1967-81, co-chmn. chemistry dept., 1970-72, chmn., 1972-75; acad. v.p. and dean of faculty Colby Coll., Waterville, Maine, 1981—; Tallman vis. prof. Bowdoin Coll., 1975. Author: Symmetry in Inorganic Chemistry, 1964. Vice pres. Norfolk Fellowship Found., 1968-73; founding mem. Laymen's Legislative League, 1967; Trustee Lowell Technol. Inst. Served with USNR, 1944-46. Mem. Am. Phys. Soc., Sigma Xi. Research optical and magnetic properties of solids, chem. reactions on surfaces

DORAIS, MARCEL, manufacturing company executive; b. Montreal, June 25, 1924; s. Honore and Albertine (Ladouceur) D.; children: Michel, Daniel, Anne. B.Sc. in Civil Engring., U. Montreal, 1948. V.p. constrn. Miron Ltd., Montreal, 1961-71; exec. v.p. Bell Asbestos Mines, Thetford Mines, Que., 1971, pres., chief exec. officer, Que., 1972-76, chmn. bd., chief exec. officer, 1976-82; pres., chief exec. officer Asbestos Corp., Thetford Mines, 1982—; dir. Thetford Indsl. Clinic, 1971—. Mem. Inst. Occupational and Environ. Health (dir.), Que. Asbestos Mining Assn. (dir.), Institut de Recherche et de Developpement sur Pamiante (dir.), Soc. Nationale de l' amiante (dir.), Centre Canadien d'information sur Pamiante (dir.). Roman Catholic. Club: St. Denis (Montreal). Home: 401 Lapierre St PO Box 577 Thetford Mines PQ Canada G6G 5T6 Office: Asbestos Corp Ltd 835 Mooney St Po Box 9 Thetford Mines PQ Canada G6G 5S1

DORAN, AMBROSE BENEDICT, mfg. co. exec.; b. N.Y.C., July 10, 1915; s. William T. and Johanna Ethel (Finotti) D.; m. Marjorie Westgate, Aug. 28, 1937; children—Marianne (Mrs. Robert Steinhacker), Linda (Mrs. William T. MacCary) (dec.), Patricia (Mrs. Fred Schaum), Kathleen. A.B., Dartmouth, 1937; M.B.A., Harvard, 1939. With Chatham Process Corp., 1939-40; asst. to v.p. Gen. Foods Corp., 1940-45; v.p. Thorsen Products Corp., 1945-55; (co. acquired by Union Camp Corp., 1956), gen. mgr. chem. div., 1958—, v.p. corp., 1964-74, sr. v.p., 1974—, dir., 1967—. Mem. dept. missions Episcopal Diocese of Newark, 1972-75; trustee Youth Consultation Service, chmn. devel. com.; trustee North Essex Devel. and Action Council, Inc., N.J. Theatre Found., Montclair Red Cross. Mem. Pulp Chems. Assn. (pres. 1960-62, 69-71), Fatty Acid Producers' Council (steering council). Episcopalian (sr. warden 1970-74). Home: 248 S Mountain Ave Montclair NJ 07042 Office: 1600 Valley Rd Wayne NJ 07470

DORAN, CHARLES EDWARD, textile mfg. co. exec.; b. Hartford, Conn., Mar. 31, 1928; s. Charles Edward and Josephine Catherine (Maher) D.; m. Anne Marie McGovern, May 18, 1957; children—Charles Francis, John Francis, Pamela Anne. B.A., Hamilton Coll., 1951; M.A., Yale, 1952. Trainee Gen. Elec. Co., 1953-56, financial mgmt. positions, 1956-65; asst. treas. Collins & Aikman Corp., N.Y.C., 1965-71, treas., 1971—; mem. adv. bd. Arkwright-Boston Ins. Co. Served with USNR, 1946-48. Mem. Financial Execs. Inst., Treasurers Group, Phi Beta Kappa, Chi Psi. Clubs: Yale, Williams (N.Y.C.). Home: 10 Hardscrabble Circle Armonk NY 10504 Office: 210 Madison Ave New York NY 10016

DORATI, ANTAL, composer, conductor; b. Budapest, Hungary, Apr. 9, 1906; came to U.S., 1941, naturalized, 1947; s. Alexander and Margit (Kunwald) D.; m. Klara Korody, 1929 (div.); 1 dau., Antonia; m. Ilse von Alpenheim, 1971. Student composition and piano, Acad. of Music, Budapest, diploma, 1924; student, U. Vienna, Austria, 1923-25; D.Mus., Macalester Coll., 1957; hon. doctorates, George Washington U., 1975, U. Md., 1976. Condr., Budapest Royal Opera House, 1924-28, Dresden State Opera, 1928-29, Munster State Opera, 1929-32, Ballet Russe de Monte Carlo, 1933-37; mus. dir. original Ballet Russe, 1938-40, Ballet Theatre, 1940-44; mus. dir., Dallas Symphony Orch., 1945-49, Mpls. Symphony Orch., 1949-60; chief condr., BBC Symphony Orch., London, 1962-66, Stockholm Philharmonic, 1966-74; music dir., Washington Nat. Symphony, 1969-77; sr. condr., Royal Philharmonic Orch., London, 1974-78; condr. laureate, Royal Philharmonic Orch., 1978-81; music dir., Detroit Symphony Orch., 1977-81, condr. laureate, 1981—; condr. laureate, Stockholm Symphony, 1981—; guest condr. all maj. orchestras, U.S., Europe, Latin Am., Australia; compositions include string quartet, quintet for oboe and strings, divertimento for small orchestra, Am. serenades for string orchestra, cello concerto The Way; cantata The Two Enchantments of Li Tai Pe; lyric scene for baritone and small orchestra Symphony; for large orch. Missa brevis; for mixed choir and percussion instruments Magdalena; ballet Madrigal Suite; chorus and orch. Chamber Music for Soprano and String Orchestra; night music for flute and small orch. Bartok Variations; piano solo The Voices; song cycle; ballet arrangements include Harvest Time; recs. for, Mercury Record Co., EMI, Philips, RCA-Victor, London-Decca. Decorated Royal Order of Vasa (Sweden); chevalier Ordre des Arts et Lettres (France); Order Arts and Letters (Austria). Mem. Royal Acad. Music London (hon.). Office: care Columbia Artists Mgmt 165 W 57th St New York NY 10019 *

DORCY, WILLIAM LEO, railroad executive; b. Sandstone, Minn., June 13, 1927; s. Frank A. and Irene A. (Gervais) D.; m. Gloria J. Aube, May 26, 1968; children: Mark W., Nadine F., Hollis M. A.B., U. Minn., 1951; grad., Transp. Inst., Northwestern U., 1958; M.S., N.D. State U., 1962. With Gt. No. Ry., 1943-62, train master, 1954-62; mgr. cost analysis Soo Line, 1963-69; mgr. new product devel., then dir. product devel. Ill. Central R.R., 1970-72; v.p. exec. dept., then v.p. mktg. M.K. and T. R.R., 1972-76; gen. mgr. Alaska R.R., Dept. Transp., Anchorage, 1976-79; v.p. acctg. M-K-T R.R., 1979—; dir. Tex. Am. Bank, Denison. Bd. dirs. Denison C. of C., N. Tex. Indsl. Devel. Corp.; mem. exec. bd. Texoma Valley council Boy Scouts Am. Served with USNR, 1945-46. Recipient award Fedn. Ry. Progress, 1958; Superior Achievement award Dept. Transp., 1979. Mem. Assn. Am. R.R.s (gen. com. acctg. div.). Clubs: Denison Rod and Gun, Tanglewood Country. Lodges: Rotary; Elks. Home: 1216 Lang St Denison TX 75020 Office: 104 E Main St Denison TX 75020

DORDAL, ERL, physician; b. Larimore, N.D., Sept. 22, 1927; s. Lars Andreas and Clara (Wegge) D.; m. Mildred Lorraine Reinke, June 14, 1952; children: Peter, Kristin, Andrew, Lisa. A.B., U. Chgo., 1952, M.D., 1956. Diplomate: Am. Bd. Internal Medicine. Intern U. Chgo. Hosps., 1956-57; resident LaCrosse (Wis.) Lutheran Hosp., 1957-58, U. Chgo., 1958-61, asst. prof. medicine, 1964-69; asso. prof. Northwestern U., 1970-77, chief sect. gastroenterology, 1970-76, clin. prof., 1977—; chief med. service VA Lakeside Hosp., 1974-76; practice medicine specializing in internal medicine and gastroenterology, Chgo., 1963—; mem. staff Columbus-Cuneo-Cabrini Med. Center, 1976—, v.p. internal medicine, 1976—; mem. staff Northwestern Meml. Hosp.; Trustee Augustana Hosp., 1972-74. Served with Signal Corps U.S. Army, 1946-48. Fellow A.C.P.; mem. Am. Assn. Study Liver Disease, Am. Gastroenterol. Assn., Chgo. Soc. Internal Medicine (sec.-treas. 1983-84). Lutheran. Club: Chgo. Lit. Home: 5649 S Woodlawn Ave Chicago IL 60637 Office: 2520 N Lakeview Ave Chicago IL 60614

DORDELMAN, WILLIAM FORSYTH, food company executive; b. Glen Ridge, N.J., Oct. 18, 1940; s. Wilbert E. and Dorothy F. (Forsyth) D.; m. Barbara Ann Gaddis, Sept. 16, 1959; children: Dorothy Ann, William Edward, Patricia Lynne, Lauren Forsyth. B.A. in Econs, U. Va., 1962; M.B.A., Harvard U., 1964. With Gen. Foods Corp., White Plains, N.Y., 1965—, advt. and merchandising mgr. Birdseye div., 1972-73, gen. mgr. main meal strategic bus. unit, 1973-77, v.p. corp., pres. Food Products div., 1977-80, corp. group v.p., 1980—; dir. Bailey & Alling Lumber Co. Bd. dirs. Cereal Inst., Mid-Fairfield Youth Hockey Assn., 1973-77, St. Vincent's Hosp. Mem. Am. Mgmt. Assn., Am. Mktg. Assn., Young Presidents Orgn. (bd. dirs. N.Y. chpt. 1982). Episcopalian. Clubs: Weeburn Country (Darien, Conn.); Westchester/Fairfield County, Harvard Bus. Sch. (dir. 1978—). Home: 9 Woodley Rd Darien CT 06820 Office: 250 North St White Plains NY 10605

DORE, FRED H., justice Wash. Supreme Ct.; b. Seattle, 1925; 4 children. B.A., Seattle U.; J.D., Georgetown U. Former mem. Wash. State Ho. of Reps., Wash. State Senate; judge Wash. Ct. Appeals, Seattle, 1977-81; asso. justice Wash. State Supreme Ct., Olympia, 1981—. Office: Temple of Justice Olympia WA 98504 *

DORE, STEPHEN EDWARD, JR., civil engineer; b. Providence, Apr. 1, 1918; s. Stephen Edward and Anna Caroline (Chace) D.; m. Evelyn Mae Andrews, Mar. 14, 1942; children: Linda Jane, Jeffrey Stephen, Sherrill Ann. B.S. in Engring, Brown U., 1940. Registered profl. engr., Conn., Maine, Mass., N.H., R.I.; registered land surveyor, Maine. Surveyor Met. Dist. Hartford County, Conn., 1940; engring. draftsman design dept. U.S. Navy, Quonset Point, R.I., 1940-42; draftsman R.I. Dept. Pub. Works, Providence, 1946; hydraulic engr. C.E., Providence, 1946; structural designer E.B. Badger Co., Boston, 1946-47; with Coffin & Richardson Inc. (Cons. Engrs.), Boston, 1947—, sr. project engr., 1958-62, v.p., chief engr., 1962-73, exec. v.p., 1973-79, pres., 1979-83, also dir. Treas. Cedarcrest Civic Assn., Canton, Mass., 1952-55. Served to capt. C.E. U.S. Army, 1942-46. Fellow ASCE, Cons. Engrs. Council; mem. ASTM, Am., New Eng. water works assns., Soc. Mil. Engrs., Boston Soc. Civil Engrs. Unitarian. Club: Blue Hills Tennis (Braintree, Mass.). Home: 33 Birchcroft Rd Canton MA 02021 Office: 87 Kilby St Boston MA 02109

DORE, VINCENT CYRIL, clergyman, coll. chancellor; b. New Haven, Jan. 31, 1900; s. John Joseph and Catherine Theresa (McMahon) D. A.B., Providence Coll., 1923, LL.D., 1945; A.M., Cath. U. Am., 1927; S.T.L., Dominican Inst. Theology, Washington, 1929; Ed.D., Suffolk U., 1952; LL.D., Bryant Coll., 1958, Brown U., Salve Regina Coll., 1964, Stonehill Coll., 1965, Albertus Magnus Coll., 1973; S.T.M., Rome, 1965; Pd.D., R.I. Coll., 1962, U. R.I., 1963. Joined Dominican Order, 1921; ordained priest Roman Catholic Ch., 1928; tchr. Aquinas High Sch., Columbus, Ohio; asst., acting chaplain Ohio State Penitentiary, 1929-31; prof. sociology Providence Coll., 1931-41, treas., 1941-45, dean of studies, 1945-57, v.p. charge acad. affairs, 1950-61, religious superior Dominican community, 1956-61, dean faculty, 1957-61, pres., 1961-65, chancellor, 1965—; Cons. indsl. and labor relations; mem. Dominican ednl. ann. conf. com., 1945-65; del. Coll. Entrance Exam. Bd., 1945-57. Mem. Minimum Wage Bd. for R.I. Retail Stores, 1940-41; chmn. Minimum Wage Bd. for R.I. Restaurants and Hotel Restaurants, 1941-50; arbiter R.I. Dept. Labor, 1938—; mem. R.I. Com. on Practical Nursing, 1955-65; mem. exec. bd. R.I. World Affairs Council, Urban League R.I., United Fund R.I., Progress for Providence, R.I. Council Community Services; mem. Com. of 100, R.I. White House Conf. Steering Com., 1956-57; industry council com. Am. Cath. Sociol. Soc., 1945—; mem. adv. com. on edn. handicapped children and youth U.S. Office Edn., 1964-67; v.p. United Fund Southeastern New Eng., 1969—; rep. R.I. Health Sci. Edn. Council, 1973-77; bd. dirs. Hosp. Service Corp. R.I., R.I. Health Facilities Planning Council, 1965-75, Research and Design Center, R.I. Group Health Assn., 1968—; also incorporator R.I. Group Health Assn.; mem. R.I. Soc. Prevention of Blindness; mem. citizens action council Gov.'s Com. on R.I. Adult Correctional Instns., 1972; trustee New Eng. Colls. Fund, 1961-65; mem. corp. R.I. Coll. Found., 1972—; rep. Providence Coll. to R.I. Health Sci. and Edn. Council, 1973-77. Recipient certificate Am. Arbitration Assn., 1944, White House Conf., 1950; certificate distinction Dept. War, A.S.T.P., World War II; U.S. Army Outstanding Civilian Service award, 1962; Georgetown U. 175th Anniversary medal honor, 1963; Pontifical Benemerenti medal, 1958; Roger Williams award for distinguished service Greater Providence C. of C., 1968; citation of honor Urban League R.I., 1971; mem. R.I. Heritage Hall Fame, 1971, Providence Coll. Athletic Hall of Fame, 1974. Mem. Am. Assn. Deans, Nat. Cath. Edn. Assn. (exec. bd.), New Eng. Assn. Colls. and Secondary Schs. (com. on instns. of higher learning 1947-51), Internat. Assn. U. Presidents, Eastern Assn. Deans, Newcomen Soc. N.Am., Group Health Assn. Am., Golden Friars Soc., Providence Coll. Alumni Assn., Delta Epsilon Sigma (nat. exec. com.), Alpha Epsilon Delta. Address: Providence Coll Providence RI 02918

DOREMUS, OGDEN, lawyer; b. Atlanta, Apr. 23, 1921; s. C. Estes and Mary (McAdory) D.; m. Carolyn Wooten Greene, Aug. 30, 1947; children: Celia Jane, Frank O., Dale Marie. B.A., Emory U., 1946, J.D., 1949. Bar: Ga. 1947. Asst. solicitor gen., Atlanta, 1947-49; partner firm Smith Field Doremus & Ringel, Atlanta, 1949-60, Falligant, Doremus and Karsman, Savannah, Ga., 1960-72, Doremus & Jones (P.C.), Metter, Ga., 1972—; prof. Woodrow Wilson Sch. Law, Atlanta, 1948-50. Editorial advisory bd.: Environ. Law, Reporter, 1969—. Mem. Atlanta City Council, 1950-53; mem. Savannah Govtl. Reorgn. Commn., 1960-61; adv. com. Nat. Coastal Zone Mgmt. Council, 1978—; Trustee Ga. Conservancy.; bd. dirs. Legal Environ. Assistance Found., 1983—. Served with USAAC, 1942-46; ETO. Named Young Man of Year Atlanta, 1951; recipient Thomas H. Gignilliat award Cultural Progress of Savannah, 1969. Mem. Am. Bar Assn. (chmn. environ. law com., gen. practice 1976-77), State Bar Ga. (chmn. ins. law sect. 1963-67, 77—), Savannah Bar Assn., Izaak Walton League (founder Ga chpt. 1950), Sierra Club (exec. com. Chattahoochee chpt. 1965—). Clubs: Savannah Golf, Chatham, Chatham Tennis; Willow Lake Country (Metter). Home: Route 2 Box 188A Metter GA 30439 Office: 11 S Rountree St PO Box 296 Metter GA 30439

DOREMUS, ROBERT HEWARD, educator; b. Denver, Sept. 16, 1928; s. Francis Heward and Elsie Marion (Segelke) D.; m. Germaine Briancon, Mar. 19, 1956; children—Marc Francis, Elaine, Carol, Natalie. B.S., U. Colo., 1950; M.S., U. Ill., 1951, Ph.D., 1953; Ph.D. (Fulbright fellow), U. Cambridge, Eng., 1956. Phys. chemist Gen. Electric Research and Devel. Center, Schenectady, 1956-71; N.Y. State prof. glass and ceramics Rensselaer Poly. Inst., Troy, N.Y., 1971—; cons. in field. Author: Glass Science, 1973; Co-editor: Growth and Perfection of Crystals, 1958; Contbr. articles to profl. jours. Bd. dirs. Phila. Luth. Sem., 1967-76. Fellow Am. Ceramic Soc.; mem. AAAS, Electrochem. Soc., Sigma Xi, Sigma Tau, Tau Beta Pi. Lutheran. Home: 1544 Keyes Ave Schenectady NY 12309 Office: Materials Dept Rensselaer Polytechnic Inst Troy NY 12181

DORER, FRED HAROLD, chemistry educator; b. Auburn, Calif., May 3, 1936; s. Fred H. and Mary E. (Fisher) D.; m. Marilyn Pearl Young, Sept. 6, 1958; children: Garrett Micael, Russell Kenneth. B.S., Calif. State U.-Long Beach, 1961; Ph.D., U. Wash., 1965; postgrad., U. Freiburg, (Germany), 1965-66. Research chemist Shell Devel. Co., Emeryville, Calif., 1966-67; prof. chemistry Calif. State U., Fullerton, 1967-75; assoc. program dir. chem. dynamics NSF, Washington, 1974-75; chmn., prof. chemistry San Francisco State U., 1975-81; dean natural scis. Sonoma State U., Rohnert Park, Calif., 1981-82, provost, v.p., 1982—. Contbr. articles to profl. jours. Served with USMC, 1954-57. Grantee Research Corp., 1968, NSF, 1969-75, Petroleum Research Fund, 1978, 80; fellow NSF, 1965. Mem. Am. Chem. Soc. Office: Sonoma State U Rohnert Park CA 94928

DORESCO, GEORGE DONALD, automobile parts manufacturing company executive; b. St. Catherines, Ont., Can., 1926; married. B.A., McMaster U., 1952. Chief plant acct. Dana Corp., Toledo, Ohio, 1947-65, mktg. mgr. Hayes Dana Ltd., 1947-65, plant mgr. drivetrain div., 1965-69, v.p. fin., treas., 1969-70, corp. controller, 1970-73, exec. v.p., gen. mgr. Hayes Dana Ltd., 1973-77, corp. v.p. light truck group, 1977-78, pres. Dana Vehicular, 1978-81, exec. v.p. parent co., 1981—, chmn. bd. Hayes Dana Inc., 1980—. Office: Dana Corp 4500 Dorr St Box 1000 Toledo OH 43697 *

DORETTI, ROBERT LEE, manufacturing company executive; b. Chgo., Nov. 24, 1942; s. Joseph and Sally (Benkawsky) D.; m. Carol Babek, June 18, 1966. B.S., So. Ill. U., 1967. With Xerox Corp., Chgo., 1967-68, Wang Labs, 1968—, sr. v.p. U.S. ops., Lowell, Mass., 1968—. Address: Wang Labs One Industrial Ave Lowell MA 01851

DORF, ERLING, geologist; b. Nysted, Nebr., July 19, 1905; s. Alfred T. and Thyra Axelsen (Dreier) D.; m. Ruth Kemmerer, Apr. 3, 1934; children—Thomas (dec.), Norman Kemmerer, Robert Erling, Martha Dreier. B.S., U. Chgo., 1925, Ph.D., 1930. Asst. instr. U. Chgo., 1926-27, fellow geology, 1928-30; instr. Princeton, 1926-3O, asst. prof., 1930-40, asso. prof., 1940-46, prof. geology, 1946-74, emeritus, 1974—, curator paleobotany, 1930-74, emeritus, 1974—; research asst. Carnegie Instn. of Washington, 1926-45; lectr. U. Pa., 1936-42, Princeton Adult Sch., 1964—; research curator Phila. Acad. Sci., 1936-46; prof. geology Wagner Free Inst. Sci., 1948-81; vis. lectr. Villanova U., 1963-67; vis. prof. Rutgers U., 1968-70, Fairleigh-Dickinson U., 1975; dir. NSF summer geol. conf., Mont., 1964-73; paleobot. cons. U.S. Nat. Mus.; chmn. com. on paleobotany NRC, 1941-46. Author: Pliocene Floras of California, 1933, Upper Cretaceous Floras of Rocky Mountain Region, 1942; Editor: Guidebook for Field Trips, Geol. Soc. Am., 1957; Bd. editors: Rev. Palaeobotany and Palynology, also Palaeogeography, Palaeoclimatology, Palaeoecology, 1968—; Contbr. articles to geol. and bot. jours. Bd. dirs. Princeton chpt. A.R.C., 1942-53, 60-66, vice chmn., 1964; nat. awards selection bd. Rec. for Blind, 1976—; mem. Princeton Twp. Bd. Health, 1960-76, Flood Control Com., 1976—, Environ. Com., 1977—, Environ. Design Rev. Com., 1977—; trustee Princeton Community Players, 1950-53, 56-58, Princeton Country Day Sch., 1946-56, Stony Brook-Millstone-Watersheds Assn., 1974-78; cons. Ednl. Testing Service, 1969-73; U.S. del. Indian Sci. Congress, 1953; sci. collaborator Nat. Park Service, 1954-58. Fellow AAAS (council 1947-57), Geol. Soc. Am., Paleontol. Soc. Am. (v.p. 1943), Bot. Soc. Am., N.J. Acad. Sci. (adv. council 1978—); mem. Nat. Assn. Geology Tchrs. (v.p. east sect. 1956-57, pres. 1957-58, Neil Miner award 1963, Ralph Digman award 1967), A.A.U.P., N.J. Geol. Soc., Internat., Am. assns. plant taxonomists, Yellowstone-Bighorn Research Assn. (council 1961—, pres. 1964-66, hon. life), Am. Inst. Biol. Scis., Am. Geol. Inst., Atlantic Coastal Plain Assn., Paleobot. Soc. India (hon.), Mont. Geol. Soc. (hon. life), Royal Danish Acad. Arts and Scis. (fgn.), Sigma Xi, Kappa Epsilon Pi, Alpha Tau Omega. Club: Nassau (pres. 1961). Home: 283 Mercer Rd Princeton NJ 08540 *Do you think of your life as merely a series of accidental events? Or is it actually being the right person, at the right place, at the right time? If the latter, recognize it when it occurs.*

DORF, PHILIP, public relations company executive; b. N.Y.C., Mar. 5, 1921; s. Max and Minnie (Siegelbaum) D.; m. Nathalie S. Bernstein, Mar. 30, 1947; children: Robert L., Lewis R., Margaret Sue. B.A., N.Y. U., 1942. Reporter, writer, editor United Press Assn., N.Y.C., 1946-56; account exec. pub. relations dept. N.W. Ayer & Son, Inc., N.Y.C., 1956-58; account supr. Tex. McCrary, Inc., N.Y.C., 1958-60; v.p. Rowland Co., Inc., 1960-63; sr. v.p., 1963-70; v.p. Harshe-Rotman & Druck, Inc. (pub. relations firm), N.Y.C., 1970-71, sr. v.p., 1971-73, exec. v.p., 1973-79, pres. eastern region, 1979-80; exec. v.p. Robert Marston & Assos., Inc., N.Y.C., 1980—. Served to capt. AUS, 1942-46. Decorated Silver Star, Bronze Star, Purple Heart. Mem. Pub. Relations Soc. Am., Nat. Investor Relations Inst., Overseas Press Club Am. Home: 500 E 77th St New York NY 10162 Office: 485 Madison Ave New York NY 10022

DORFMAN, ALLEN BERNARD, international management consultant; b. N.Y.C., Mar. 30, 1930; s. Harry and Jean (Schreiber) D.; m. Elaine Turbe, Jan. 9, 1955; children: Nancy Ann, Jeffrey David. B.B.A. summa cum laude, CCNY, 1952; postgrad. mgmt. studies, Harvard Bus. Sch., 1972. From mem. exec. tng. squad to sr. mgmt. R.H. Macy's, N.Y.C., 1954-67; asst. to gen. mdse. mgr., v.p., mem. mgmt. com. N.Y. div. Allied Stores Corp., N.Y.C., 1967-69; v.p., gen. mdse. mgr. hard and soft goods, mem. exec. com. Town & Country Full Line Discount Stores div. Lane Bryant Corp., N.Y.C., 1969-71; pres., dir. Nat. Bellas Hess Inc., Kansas City, Mo., 1971-73; corp. sr. v.p. and pres., chief exec. officer retail div. Jewelcor, Inc., N.Y.C., 1973-77; corp. v.p., dir. corp. ops., mem. exec. com. Vornado, Inc., Garfield, N.J., 1977-78; corp. pres., chief exec. officer Allen B. Dorfman Assocs., internat. mgmt. cons. to public, retail and fin. corps., 1978—; prof. Grad. Sch., L.I. U., evenings. Bd. dirs., exec. v.p. Am. Cancer Soc.; bd. dirs. Kings Point Civic Assn. Served with AUS, 1952-54. Recipient award Advt. Club N.Y., 1972, Torch of Liberty award Nat. Anti-Defamation League, 1975. Mem. Mass Retailing Inst., Nat. Retail Mchts. Assn., Nat. Assn. Catalog Showroom Merchandisers Inc., Adelphi Coll. Found., Boy Scouts Am., Boys Club, Philharmonic Assn., Police Athletic League, Beta Gamma Sigma, Eta Mu Pi, Sigma Alpha. Club: Wildwood Country (Kings Point, N.Y.) (pres., dir.). Patent pending zippered ice and roller skates. Home: 25 Canterbury Rd Great Neck NY 11021

DORFMAN, HENRY S., meat products company executive; b. 1924; married. With Sausage Mfg. Bus., 1944-49, Gen. Machines Co., 1949-50, Hudson Motor Car Co., 1950-51, B.M. Shindler Meats Co., 1951-52; chmn. bd., pres., chief exec. officer Frederick & Herrud Inc.,

Southfield, Mich., 1952—. Office: Frederick & Herrud Inc 18700 W Ten Mile Rd Southfield MI 48075

DORFMAN, ISAIAH S., lawyer; b. Kiev, Russia, Mar. 17, 1907; came to U.S., 1913, naturalized, 1931; s. Samuel and Ella (Kite) D.; m. Lillian Schley, Oct. 6, 1934; children: Paul, Tom, John. Ph.B., U. Chgo., 1927, J.D., 1931. Bar: Ill. 1931. Regional atty. Region 13, NLRB, Chgo., 1937-42, chief spl. litigation unit, Washington, 1942-43; chief analyst OSS, U.S. Govt., London, Eng., 1943-44; attaché U.S. legation, Stockholm, Sweden, 1944-45; formerly sr. partner, now of counsel Dorfman, Cohen, Laner & Muchin, Ltd. (and predecessor); instr. labor law Law Sch., Nat. Univ., Washington, 1942-43. Mem. Chgo. Bar Assn. (chmn. com. unauthorized practice law 1966-67), Ill. Bar Assn., ABA., B'nai B'rith. Jewish religion. Club: Standard (Chgo.). Home: 260 E Chestnut St Chicago IL 60611 Office: One IBM Plaza Chicago IL 60611

DORFMAN, LEON MONTE, chemist, educator; b. Winnipeg, Man., Can., June 9, 1922; came to U.S., 1947, naturalized, 1949; s. Gabriel and Dora (Gorin) D.; m. Lorraine Rose, Aug. 1, 1948; children: Gail Anne, Amy Rachel, David Alan. B.S., U. Man., 1944; M.A., U. Toronto, Ont., Can., 1945, Ph.D., 1947; Postdoctoral fellow, U. Rochester, 1947-49. Research asso. Gen. Electric Co., Schenectady, 1950- 57; sr. chemist Argonne (Ill.) Nat. Lab., 1957-64; prof. chemistry Ohio State U., Columbus, 1964—, chmn. chemistry dept., 1968-77; prof. chemistry U. Toronto, 1967; Vis. research scientist Hebrew U. of Jerusalem, 1969, Nat. Research Council Lab., Bologna, Italy, 1972; chmn. Gordon Conf. on Radiation Chemistry, 1966; cons. Westinghouse Research Lab., 1974-75. Author: (with M.S. Matheson) Pulse Radiolysis, 1969; Mem. editorial bd.: Jour. Phys. Chemistry, 1973-78, Radiation Effects, 1973—. Guggenheim fellow Royal Instn. Gt. Britain, 1972. Mem. Am. Chem. Soc. (Columbus Sect. award 1983), Am. Phys. Soc., Radiation Research Soc. Home: 2396 Southway Dr Columbus OH 43221

DORFMAN, MYRON HERBERT, petroleum engineer, educator; b. Shreveport, La., July 3, 1927; s. Samuel Yandell and Rose (Gold) D.; children: Shelley Fonda Dorfman Roberts, Cynthia Renee. B.S., U. Tex., 1950, M.S., 1972, Ph.D., 1975. Registered profl. engr., Tex. Geologist engr. Sklar Oil Co., Shreveport, 1950-56, mgr. prodn. and devel., 1957-59, partner, 1958-59; owner Dorfman Oil Properties, Shreveport, 1950-71, Austin, Tex., 1971—; prof. petroleum engring. U. Tex., Austin, 1976—, H.B. Harkins prof. petroleum engineering, 1980—, W.A. Moncrief Jr. Centennial chair in petroleum engring., 1983—, dir. Center Energy Studies, 1977—, chmn. dept. petroleum engring., 1978—; dir. Tex. Petroleum Research Commn., Tex. R.R. Commn., 1982—; disting. lectr. Soc. Petroleum Engrs. of AIME, 1978-79, disting. author, 1982—. Contbr. articles to profl. jours. Pres. Shreveport Community Council, 1966; bd. dirs. Gov.'s Com. Employment Handicapped, 1966-68, La. Youth Opportunity Center, Shreveport, 1966-71, ARC, Caddo Parish, La., 1964-71; pres. La. Mental Health Center, Shreveport, 1967. Served with USNR, 1945-46; PTO. Recipient medal State of Israel, 1963. Fellow Geol. Soc. Am.; mem. Am. Geophys. Union, Nat. Acad. Scis., Am. Assn. Petroleum Geologists, Soc. Profl. Well Log Analysts, AIME, Shreveport Geol. Soc., Petroleum Club Shreveport, Shreveport Jewish Fedn. (pres. 1967), Pi Epsilon Tau., Tau Beta Pi. Club: Shreveport Skeet (pres. 1964). Home: 7609 Valburn Dr Austin TX 78731 Office: Dept Petroleum Engring U Tex Austin TX 78712

DORFSMAN, LOUIS, broadcasting company executive; b. N.Y.C., Apr. 24, 1918; s. Sam and Mollie (Kruger) D.; m. Ann Hysa, Oct. 5, 1940; children: Elissa, Mitchell, Neil. B.F.A., Cooper Union, 1939. With CBS, 1946—, v.p. advt. and sales promotion, 1959-60, dir. advt. and sales promotion, 1960-64, dir. design, 1964-68, v.p. advt. and design, 1968, now sr. v.p., creative dir. mktg. communications and design.; Trustee Cooper Union Sch. Sci. and Art; bd. dirs. Internat. Design Conf., Aspen, Colo. (Emmy award 1979, 2 Clio awards for best television commls. and newspaper advertisements, Emmy award for opening titles 1980). Recipient Augustus St. Gaudens medal Cooper Union, 1963; 13 gold medals N.Y. Art Dirs. Club; gold medal Am. Inst. Graphic Arts, 1978; gold medal for best of year design Phila. Printing Club, 1962. Mem. N.Y. Art Dirs. Club (past pres., inducted Hall of Fame 1978), Am. Inst. Graphic Arts, Type Dirs. Club N.Y. Club: Century Assn. Home: 80 Station Rd Great Neck NY 11023 Office: CBS Inc 51 W 52d St New York NY 10019

DORGAN, BYRON LESLIE, congressman; b. Dickinson, N.D., May 14, 1942; s. Emmett P. and Dorothy (Bach) D.; children: Scott, Shelly. B.S. in Bus., U. N.D., 1964; M.B.A., U. Denver, 1966. Exec. devel. trainee Martin Marietta Corp., Denver, 1966-67; dep. tax commr., then tax commnr. State of N.D., 1967-80; mem. 97th-98th Congresses from N.D., mem. ways and means com.; instr. econs. Bismarck (N.D.) Jr. Coll., 1969-71; chmn. Multistate Tax Commn., 1972-74, Gov. N.D. Commn. Air Transp., 1973. Contbr. articles to profl. jours. Recipient Nat. Leadership award Office Gov. N.D., 1972. Mem. Nat. Assn. Tax Adminstrs. (exec. com. 1972-75). Office: US Ho of Reps Washington DC 20515

DORGAN, JOHN JOSEPH, JR., oil company executive; b. Providence, Sept. 1, 1923; s. John Joseph and Isabelle Regina (Carroll) D.; m. Cynthia Codrington, June 8, 1946; children: Carroll S., Elizabeth B., Peter M., John C. A.B., Harvard, 1944, M.B.A., 1948. Economist Continental Oil Co., 1948-52, asst. to pres., 1952-54, landman, 1954-56, dir. credit and ins., 1956-58, asst. treas., 1958-59, treas., 1958-64, coordinator plant foods, 1964-65, v.p., coordinator plant foods, 1965-68, v.p., gen. mgr. plant foods, 1968-69, v.p., gen. mgr. supply and transp., 1969-70, dir. supply and transp. Conoco, Europe/London, 1970-72; mng. dir. Raffinerie Belge de Petroles S.A., Belgium, 1972; v.p., treas. Occidental Petroleum Corp., 1972-75, exec. v.p. finance, 1975—; petroleum economist Petroleum Adminstrn. for Def., Washington, 1951-52; dir. Can. Occidental Petroleum, Quimica Hooker S.A. Served to lt. (j.g.) USNR, 1943-46. Mem. Am. Petroleum Inst. Clubs: Lansdowne (London); Harvard (treas. 1968-70), Links (N.Y.C.); Regency (Los Angeles). Home: 260 N Glenroy Ave Los Angeles CA 90049 Office: 10889 Wilshire Blvd Los Angeles CA 90049

DORIA, ANTHONY NOTARNICOLA, college dean; b. Savona, Italy, June 2, 1927; s. Vito Sante and Jolanda (Giampaolo) Notarnicola. M.B.A., Wharton Sch., U. Pa., 1953; LL.M. (equivalent), U. Paris, 1960; D.Jr., U. Rome, 1962. Prof. history, bus. and internat. law Community Coll. at Suffolk County, Selden, N.Y., 1960-65, L.I. U., Southampton, N.Y., 1964-65; founder, pres. Royalton Coll. Sch. Internat. Affairs, S. Royalton, Vt., 1965-72, dean, 1974—; founder, dean Vt. Law Sch., 1972-74; cons. internat. law and orgns.; panelist Am. Arbitration Assn.; mem. Vt. Gov.'s Commn. on Student Affairs, 1972-75. Author: Italy and the Free World, 1945, The Conquest of the Congo, 1947, Influences in the Making of Foreign Policy in the United States of America, Great Britain, and France, 1953, Introduction to International Law, 1976. Candidate for U.S. Senate, 1972. Served with underground resistance movement, World War II. Recipient Merit cert. UN; citation Boy Scouts Am., 1965. Mem. Am. Judicature Soc., Internat. Bar Assn., Internat. Law Assn., Am. Soc. Internat. Law, AAUP, Acad. Polit. Sci., Noble Assn. Chevaliers Pontificaux (life). Clubs: Elysee (Paris); Pen and Pencil. Home: The Royalton Inn South Royalton VT 05068 Office: Royal Coll Law Study Center South Royalton VT 05068

DORIA, VINCENT MARK, editor; b. Cin., Oct. 28, 1947; s. Vincent Joseph and Helen (Andio) D.; m. Suzanne Brissette, Nov. 8, 1980. B.A. in Journalism, Ohio State U., 1970. Sports writer Columbus (Ohio) Citizen-Jour., 1970-71; sports editor Ashtabula (Ohio) Star-Beacon, 1971-72; editor and sports writer, then asst. sports editor Phila. Inquirer, 1972-75; asst. sports editor Boston Globe, 1975-78, sports editor, 1978-82, asst. mng. editor/sports, 1982—. Mem. AP Sports Editors Assn. (chmn. exec. com. 1979-80, v.p. 1982-83, pres. 1983-84, award Best Sunday Sports Sect. 1980, award Best Sunday, Best Daily Sports Sect. 1981, 82), Baseball Writers Assn. Am. (Scarlet Quill award 1981). Home: 6 Louisburg Square S 150 Quincy Shore Dr Quincy MA 02171 Office: 135 Morrissey Blvd Boston MA 02107

DORIAN, NANCY CURRIER, educator; b. New Brunswick, N.J., NOv. 5, 1936; d. Donald Clayton and Edith (McEwen) D. B.A. summa cum laude, Conn. Coll. for Women, 1958; postgrad., Yale U., 1959-60; M.A., U. Mich., 1961, Ph.D. (Rackham fellow), 1965. Lectr. Bryn Mawr Coll., Pa., 1965-66, asst. prof. linguistics in German and antropology, 1966-72, assoc. prof., 1972-78, prof., 1978—, William R. Kenan Jr. prof., 1980—; vis. lectr. U. Pa., 1966, 70, U. Kiel, 1967-68. Author: East Sutherlan Gaelic, 1978, Language Death, 1981, Tyranny of Tide, 1983; contbr. articles to profl. jours. Fulbright scolar, W. Ger., 1958-59; NSF grantee, 1978-79. Mem. Linguistic Soc. Am., Internat. Linguistic Assn., N.E. (Folklore Soc.), Celtic Studies Assn., Scottish Oral History Group, An Comunn Gaidhealach, Phi Beta Kappa. Democrat. Unitarian. Office: Dept German and Anthropology Bryn Mawr College Bryn Mawr PA 19010

DORIS ANN (DORIS ANN SCHARFENBERG), producer, former broadcasting co. exec.; b. Newark, Feb. 24, 1917; d. Edgar Andrew and Anne E. Scharfenberg. A.B., Bucknell U., 1938; M.A. in Edn, N.Y. U., 1949; LL.D. (hon.), Muhlenberg U., 1962, H.H.D., Lafayette U., 1979. With NBC, N.Y.C., 1944-80, mgr. religious programs, producer and exec. producer, 1951-80; now instr. classes in TV, freelance TV producer. Producer programs including: art documentary The Prado, 1971; drama This Is My Son, 1977 (Emmy award); film/documentaries Continuing Creation, 1978 (2 Emmy awards), This Other Eden, 1979; (Recipient Emmy awards for Duty Bound 1973, A Determining Force 1976). Trustee Bucknell U. Ohio State U. awards; Christopher awards, 1958, 73; Gabriel awards, 1965, 66, 67, 68, 71; Freedom Found. awards, 1953, 56, 59, 60, 61, 62, 64, 67, 73; NCCJ awards, 1954, 56, 62; Gabriel Personal Achievement award, 1969; Abe Lincoln award, 1979. Home: 4407 Bellaire Dr S Fort Worth TX 76109

DORIUS, KERMIT PARRISH, architect; b. Salt Lake City, Aug. 2, 1926; s. Raymond E. and Claire Ford (Parrish) D.; m. Arlene Roehm, June 15, 1979; children: Lynn, Kristin, Mark. Student, U. Utah, 1943-44; B.Arch., U. Calif., Berkeley, 1950. Project architect Frederick Hodgdon (AIA), Newport Beach, Calif., 1954-57; prin. Brownell & Dorius, Corona Del Mar, Calif., 1957-59; pres. Kermit Dorius & Assos., Corona Del Mar, 1960—. Recipient Merit award Nat. Assn. Homebuilders/Pacific Coast Builders Conf.; Gold Nugget Awards, 1975, 76; Grand award (2), 1975; Archtl. award for excellence Nat. Assn. Homebuilders Sensible Growth, 1972; Merit award, 1976. Fellow AIA (Merit award Orange County chpt. 1959, pres. Orange County chpt. 1966-67, v.p. econ. affairs Calif. council 1975-76). Office: Kermit Dorius & Assos 1550 Bayside Dr Corona Del Mar CA 92625 *

DORKIN, FREDERIC EUGENE, lawyer; b. Bridgeport, Conn., Feb. 1, 1932; s. William and Selma (Kraus) D.; m. Harriette A. Garfinkel, June 14, 1959; children: Rosalyn Gail, David Ira, Deborah Ruth. A.B., Dartmouth Coll., 1953; LL.B., Duke U., 1956; LL.M., George Washington U., 1968. Bar: Conn. 1956. Atty. SEC, Washington, 1956-57; pvt. practice law, Bridgeport, 1960-61; asst. sec. CT Corp. System, N.Y.C., Washington, 1961-68; asso. counsel, asst. sec. Susquehanna Corp., Alexandria, Va., 1968-69; sec., counsel Microdot Inc., Greenwich, Conn., 1969-72; gen. counsel Boeing Computer Services, Inc., Morristown, N.J., 1972-78; corp. counsel Boeing Co., Seattle, 1978-82, sr. corp. counsel, 1982—. Served with JAGC, U.S. Army, 1957-60. Mem. ABA, Phi Delta Phi, Tau Epsilon Phi. Home: 8821 SE 55th Pl Mercer Island WA 98040 Office: PO Box 3707 Seattle WA 98124

DORLAND, GRAHAM, air freight company executive; b. 1941. Student, Ariz. State U. With Airborne Freight Corp., Seattle, 1965—, successively customer service mgr., dist. mgr., mgr. ops. gen. office, dir. personnel, dir. ops., 1965-73, v.p. div. IV, 1973-74, v.p. div. III, 1974-80, exec. v.p. airline div., 1980—; chmn., chief exec. officer Airborne Express. Office: Airborne Freight Corp 190 Queen Anne N Seattle WA 98111 *

DORMAN, ALBERT A., consulting engineer, architect; b. Phila., Apr. 30, 1926; s. William and Edith (Kleiman) D.; m. Joan Bettie Heiten, July 29, 1950; children: Laura Jane, Kenneth Joseph, Richard Coleman. B.S., Newark Coll. Engring., 1945; M.S., U. So. Calif., 1962. Registered profl. engr., Calif., N.Y., Ill., Oreg., Ariz., Hawaii, Pa., Nev., La.; registered architect, Calif., Oreg. City engr., mem. City Planning Commn., Lemoore, Calif., 1954-67, Corcoran, Calif., 1955-65; owner firm Albert A. Dorman, Hanford, Calif., 1954-66; v.p. Daniel, Mann, Johnson & Mendenhall, Los Angeles, 1967-73, dir., 1970—, exec. v.p., chief operating officer, 1973-74, pres., chief operating officer, 1974-77, pres., chief exec. officer, 1977—; pres., chmn. bd. dirs. Hanford Savs. & Loan Assn., 1963-72; pres. Hanford Service Co., Inc.; v.p., dir. Tristao Towers, Inc., 1958-62; dir. CHB Foods. Contbr. articles to profl. jours. Chmn. Kins County chpt. ARC, 1955-60; pres. Community Concerts Assn., 1962-64; mem. dean's council Sch. Architecture and Urban Planning, U. Calif., Los Angeles; commr. Oiland Gas div. Calif. Dept. Conservation, 1972-75; trustee City of Hope.; vice chmn. Los Angeles County Earthquake Fact-Finding Commn., 1980. Served with AUS, 1945-47. Recipient Civil Engring. Alumnus award U. So. Calif., 1976. Fellow ASCE (Harland Bartholomew award 1976), Inst. for Advancement of Engring. (Outstanding Engr. award 1980); mem. AIA, Am. Pub. Works Assn., Cons. Engrs. Assn. Calif. (bd. dirs. 1982-84), Am. Water Works Assn., Water Pollution Control Fedn., Los Angeles Area C. of C. (bd. dirs. 1983), Tau Beta Pi, Chi Epsilon. Clubs: Commonwealth (San Francisco); California (Los Angeles); Metropolitan (Washington); Kiwanis (pres. 1962). Home: 727 Brooktree Rd Pacific Palisades CA 90272 Office: 1 Park Plaza 3250 Wilshire Blvd Los Angeles CA 90010

DORMAN, LINNEAUS CUTHBERT, chemist; b. Orangeburg, S.C., June 28, 1935; s. John Albert and Georgia (Hammond) D.; m. Phae Louise Hubble, June 21, 1958; children: Evelyn Suzanne, John Albert III. B.S., Bradley U., 1956; Ph.D., Ind. U., 1961. Chemist No. Regional Lab., U.S. Dept. Agr., Peoria, Ill., summers 1956-59; research chemist Dow Chem. Co., Midland, Mich., 1960-68, research specialist, 1968-76, research assoc., 1976-83, assoc. scientist, 1983—; dir. Comml. Bank Midland, 1982—. Contbr. articles to profl. jours. Mem. Midland Commn. on Community Relations, 1963-73, vice-chmn., 1967; mem. Black Exec. Exchange Program, Urban League, 1971, 75; trustee Midland Found., 1980—; dir.-at-large Midland Ctr. for the Arts; bd. fellows Saginaw Valley State Coll., 1975—, v.p., 1981-83, pres., 1983—. Co-recipient Bond award Am. Oil Chemists Soc., 1960; recipient Central Research Inventor of Year award Dow Chem. Co., 1982. Mem. Nat. Orgn. Black Chemists and Chem. Engrs., AAAS, NAACP, Am. Chem. Soc. (sect. treas. 1966, sec. 1967, dir. 1968-70, councilor 1971-76, 80—), Midland Jaycees, Sigma Xi (chpt. treas. 1969, sec. 1970, pres. 1975), Phi Lambda Upsilon, Pi Kappa Delta, Omega Psi Phi. Mem. United Ch. of Christ. Clubs: Midland Rotary (sec. 1980-81, v.p. 1981-82), Midland Rotary (pres. 1982-83). Patentee in field. Home: 2506 Plymouth Midland MI 48640 Office: Dow Chemical Co 1712 Building Midland MI 48640

DORMAN, RICHARD FREDERICK, JR., association executive, consultant; b. Peoria, Ill., June 3, 1944; s. Richard Frederick and Pauline Elizabeth (Dryfus) D.; m. Jeri Sue Smallsreed (div. 1973); children: Richard F., Kevin M.; m. Anne Marie Carlton, May 28, 1976. Student, Franklin U., Columbus, Ohio, 1963-65, 68-69, New Sch. Social Reform, N.Y.C., 1979-80, U. Md., 1982. Field rep. Ohio Civil Service Employees Assn., Columbus, 1972-75; regional dir. St. Jude Children's Research Hosp., N.Y.C., 1975-80; exec. dir. Assembly Govtl. Employees, Washington, 1980—; ptnr. McIntosh & Dorman, Washington, 1982—. Founder, pres. Columbus Ind. Jr. High Football League, Ohio, 1970. Recipient Recognition for Contbn. to Women's Sports Ohio Ho. of Reps., 1975, 76. Mem. Am. Soc. Assn. Execs., Greater Washington Soc. Assn. Execs., Pub. Relations Soc. Am., Nat. Soc. Fund Raising Execs. Republican. Presbyterian. Office: Assembly of Govtl Employees 1730 Rhode Island Ave NW Washington DC 20036 *

DORMANN, HENRY O., corporation executive; b. N.Y.C., Mar. 5, 1932; s. Henry Maroni and Ivara (Soberg) D.; m. Alice Andreasen, Apr. 7, 1958; children—Kaari, Kristi. Chmn. bd. Nat. Enquirer, 1971-72; chmn. Internat. Bd. Indsl. Advisors, 1964—; pres., editor-in-chief S.I.P.A. News Service, N.Y.C., 1966—; chmn. bd. The Haitian Devel. Corp., 1969—, Sabador, Inc., Liberia, 1973—; pres. U.S. Tech. Devel. Co., 1969-70; pres., editor-in-chief Holiday Mag.; pres. editor-in-chief Leaders Mag., N.Y.C.; Mem. adv. council Joint Legis. Com. on Met. and Regional Areas Study N.Y. State, 1969-72; chmn. N.Y. State Assembly Council on Econ. Devel., 1972—. Mem. assn. bd. Mcht. Marine Acad., 1969—; founder Library Presdl. Papers, Inst. for Study of Presidency; trustee Am. U., Washington; active mem. internat. supreme council Order DeMolay. Served with USCG. Office: 59 E 54th St New York NY 10022

DORN, CHARLES MEEKER, art educator; b. Mpls., Jan. 17, 1927; s. Melville Wilkinson and Margaret (Meeker) D.; m. Virginia Josephine Coble, July 11, 1947; children: Mary Jan, Charles Meeker. B.A., M.A., George Peabody Coll. Tchrs., 1950; Ed.D., U. Tex., 1959. Asst. prof. art Union U., Jackson, Tenn., 1950-54; instr. art and edn. Memphis State U., 1954-57; lectr. edn. U. Tex., 1957-59; head art dept. Nat. Coll. Edn., Evanston, Ill., 1959-61; assoc. prof. art No. Ill. State U., 1961-62; exec. sec. Nat. Art Edn. Assn., Washington, 1962-70; prof., chmn. dept. art Calif. State U., Northridge, 1970-72; prof. creative arts Purdue U., Lafayette, Ind., 1972—, head dept., 1972-76. Served with AUS, 1945-46. Recipient 25th Anniversary award for disting. service Nat. Gallery Art, 1966; Disting. Service award NABA, 1979. Mem. Art Edn. Assn. Ind., Nat. Art Edn. Assn. (pres. 1975—, Disting. Service award 1979, Disting. fellow 1982), Internat. Soc. Edn. through Art, Phi Delta Kappa, Kappa Phi Kappa. Home: 220 Spring Valley Ln West Lafayette IN 47906 Office: Purdue U Lafayette IN 47907

DORN, EDWARD MERTON, poet, educator; b. Villa Grove, Ill., Apr. 2, 1929. Student, U. Ill., Black Mountain Coll. Vis. prof. Am. lit., Fulbright lectr. U. Essex, 1965-68; vis. poet U. Kans., 1968-69; mem. faculty Idaho State U., Northeastern Ill. U., U. Colo., 1977—. Author: What I See in the Maximus Poems, 1961, Hands Up!, 1964, Idaho Out, 1965, Geography, 1965, The North Atlantic Turbine, 1967, Twenty Four Love Songs, 1969, Recollections of Gran Apacheria, 1973, Some Business Recently Transacted in the White World, 1971, Gunslinger, Books I-IV, 1968-75, Collected Poems, 1975, 3d enlarged edit., 1984, Selected Poems, 1978, Captain Jack's Chaps, 1983. Nat. Endowment for Arts grantee, 1966, 68; D.H. Lawrence fellow, 1969. Office: Dept English Univ of Colo Boulder CO 80309

DORN, RUSSELL WILLIAM, JR., city adminstr.; b. Jersey City, July 1, 1946; s. Russell William and Catherine Veronica (O'Mara) D. B.A. in Govt. with honors, U. Ariz., 1968; M.P.A., Fairleigh Dickinson U., 1975. Mgmt. analyst budget div. Jersey City, 1972, asst. to bus. adminstrn. dept. adminstrn., 1972-73, sr. mgmt. analyst dept. public safety, 1973-74; prin. mgmt. analyst budget control office Hudson County, N.J., 1974-76, county adminstr., 1976-78; city mgr. City of Las Vegas, Nev., 1978—. Bd. dirs. United Way, 1976-77. Served to 1st lt. U.S. Army, 1970-71. Decorated Army Commendation medal; recipient Spl. Recognition award Alliance for Volunteerism, Mayor's Awards Program. Mem. Internat. City Mgmt. Assn. (asso.), VFW. Democrat. Roman Catholic. Home: 4216 Stonebridge Lane Las Vegas NV 89108 Office: 400 E Stewart Avenue Las Vegas NV 89101

DORN, WILLIAM JENNINGS BRYAN, polit. party ofcl., former congressman; b. Greenwood, S.C., Apr. 14, 1916; s. Thomas Elbert and Pearl (Griffith) D.; m. Millie Johnson; children—Briana Pearl Dorn Lawrence, Debbie Gail Dorn Pracht, Olivia Byrd Dorn Kennedy, William Jennings Bryan, Johnson Griffith. Ed. public schs., Greenwood; LL.D. (hon.), Lander Coll., 1965, Clemson U., 1970, Erskine Coll., 1973. Mem. S.C. Ho. of Reps., 1939-40, S.C. State Senate, 1940-42; mem. 80th, 82d to 93d U.S. Congresses from 3d S.C. Dist.; chmn. S.C. Democratic Party, 1980—; cattle and tree farmer; Disting. lectr. in politics U. S.C., Spartanburg. Vice chmn. steering com. Richard B. Russell Dam and Reservoir; mem. VA Com. on Memls. and Cemeteries, 1980—; Democratic nominee Gov. S.C., 1974; adv. bd. Nat. Fedn. Small Businesses; mem. Abbeville County Devel. Bd.; bd. dirs. Lander Coll. Found., Piedmont Tech. Coll. Found., Greenwood County Arts Council; bd. regents Leadership S.C.; mem. adv. bd. trustees North Greenville Coll. Served with USAAF, 1942-45; ETO. William Jennings Bryan Dorn VA Med. Center named in his honor. Mem. Am. Legion (state comdr. 1979), VFW, Air Force Assn., D.A.V., Amvets, S.C. Farm Bur. (dir.), Beef Producers Assn., S.C., Edgefield, Greenwood hist. assns., Pendleton Found. Hist. Preservation, S.C.V., Greenwood C. of C., Woodmen of World, Grange, S.C. Forestry Assn. (state dir.), Nat. Wild Turkey Fedn., Sigma Alpha Epsilon. Baptist. Clubs: Mason (Shriner), Rotarian, Moose. Address: RFD 1 Greenwood SC 29646 Office: Callison Hwy Greenwood SC 29646

DORNAN, ROBERT KENNETH, congressman; b. N.Y.C., Apr. 3, 1933; s. Harry Joseph and Gertrude Consuelo (McFadden) D.; m. Sallie Hansen, Apr. 16, 1955; children—Robin Marie, Robert Kenneth, II, Theresa Ann, Mark Douglas, Kathleen Regina. B.A. in History, Loyola U., Westchester, Calif., 1953. Nat. spokesman Citizens for Decency Through Law, 1973-76; mem. 95th-97th Congresses from 27th Calif. Dist. Host TV talk shows in, Los Angeles, 1967-70; host, producer: Robert K. Dornan Show, Los Angeles, 1970-73; Author film plays. Served to capt. as fighter pilot USAF, 1953-58. Decorated Commendation ribbon. Mem. AFTRA, VFW, Navy League, Air Force Assn. Republican. Roman Catholic. Club: K.C.

DORNBUSCH, SANFORD MAURICE, sociology and biology educator; b. N.Y.C., June 5, 1926; s. Meyer and Gertrude (Weisel) D.; m. Barbara Anne Farnham, Feb. 28, 1950; children: Jeffrey Neil, Steven Samuel. A.B., Syracuse U., 1948; M.A., U. Chgo., 1950, Ph.D., 1952. Instr. sociology Syracuse U., 1948-49, U. Ill., 1950-51, Ind. U., 1950- 52; research asso. U. Chgo., 1951-52; asst. prof. U. Wash., 1952-54, asso. prof., 1958-59; asst. prof. Harvard, 1955-58; head dept.

sociology Stanford U., 1959-64, prof., 1959—, Reed-Hodgson prof. human biology, 1978—, prof. edn., 1977—, asso. dean, 1961-62, dir. freshman seminars, 1967-69, chmn. senate acad. council, 1970-71, research asso., 1968—; vis. prof. sociology U. Ibadan, Nigeria, 1966-67; dep. dir. Stanford Center for Study of Youth Devel., 1980-83; cons. Social Sci. Research Council; mem. behavioral scis. fellowship panel NIH, 1961-67; editorial cons. Sociometry, 1957-60, Rev. Religious Research, 1980—, Devel. and Behavioral Pediatrics, 1983—. Author: A Primer of Social Statistics, 1955, Popular Religion, 1958, Evaluation and the Exercise of Authority, 1975, Toward Reform of Program Evaluation, 1980, Teacher Evaluative Standards and Student Effort, 1984; Cons. editor sociology, McGraw-Hill Book Co., 1958-62. Chmn. regional selection com. Woodrow Wilson Nat. Fellowship Found., 1963-66; founder Stanford-Midpeninsula Urban Coalition, 1968; mem. bd. maternal, child and family health NRC; mem. Pres.'s Commn. on Mental Health, Task Panel on Community Support Systems, 1977—; mem. evaluation task force Nat. Inst. Child Health and Human Devel., 1977—, mem. mental retardation research com., 1977-81; Bd. dirs. Urban Arts Found. Served as pvt. AUS, 1943-44; with USCG, 1944-45; with USNR, 1945-46. Grantee NSF, NIH, Ford Found., Russell Sage Found.; fellow Center Advanced Study Behavioral Scis., 1954-55; faculty research fellow Social Sci. Research Council, 1958-59; hon. univ. fellow U. Chgo., 1949-50. Fellow Am. Sociol. Assn. (chmn. methodology sect., social psychology sect.), African Studies Assn.; mem. A.A.U.P. (chpt. pres. 1968-69), Pacific Sociol. Assn. (pres. 1963-64), Am. Statis. Assn., Internat. Orgn. for Study Human Devel. (council 1970—), Soc. for Research in Child Devel. Home: 841 Pine Hill Rd Stanford CA 94305

DORNER, PETER PAUL, economist, educator; b. Luxemburg, Wis., Jan. 13, 1925; s. Peter and Monica (Altmann) D.; m. Lois Cathryn Hartnig, Dec. 26, 1950. B.S., U. Wis.-Madison, 1951; M.S., U. Tenn., Knoxville, 1953; Ph.D., Harvard U., 1959. Asst. prof. agrl. econs. U. Tenn., 1953-54; asst. prof. U. Wis.-Madison, 1954-56, assoc. prof., 1959-62, prof., 1962—, dir. Land Tenure Center, 1965-66, 68-71, chmn. dept. agrl. econs., 1972-76, dean internat. studies and programs, 1980—; prof. U. Chile, Santiago, 1963-65; sr. staff economist Pres.'s Council Econ. Advisors, Washington, 1967-68; Cons. UN, UN food, agrl. orgns., U.S. Govt., state govtl. agys. Author: Land Reform and Economic Development, 1972; Editor: Cooperative and Commune: Group Farming in the Economic Development of Agriculture, 1977, Resources and Development: Natural Resource Policies and Economic Development in an Interdependent World, 1980; Contbr. numerous articles to profl. jours., popular mags. Served with inf. U.S. Army, 1944-46. Mem. Am. Agrl. Econs. Assn., Am. Econ. Assn., AAUP. Home: 541 Woodside Terr Madison WI 53711

DORNFELD, ISAAC JOSEPH, airport mgr.; b. Bklyn., Oct. 31, 1924; s. Jacob and Anna (Cooperstock) D.; m. Muriel Brodsky, June 18, 1945; children—Robert, Howard, Nancy. B.C.E., Coll. City N.Y., 1947, B.Mech. Engring., 1953. Registered profl. engr., N.Y., N.J. With Port Authority, N.Y. and N.J., 1949—; asst. mgr., then mgr. plant and structures div. J.F. Kennedy Internat. Airport, 1963-73, gen. mgr. airport, 1973—. Served with AUS, 1943-46. Mem. Am. Assn. Airport Execs., Nat. Soc. Profl. Engrs., Queens C. of C. Club: Wings (N.Y.C.). Office: Bldg 141 Kennedy Internat Airport Jamaica NY 11430

DORNING, JOHN JOSEPH, nuclear engineering educator; b. Bronx, N.Y., Apr. 17, 1938; s. John Joseph and Sarah Cathrine (McCormack) D.; m. Helen Marie Driscoll, July 27, 1963; children: Michael, James, Denise. B.S. in Marine Engring., U.S. Mcht. Marine Acad., 1959; M.S. (AEC fellow), Columbia U., 1963, Ph.D., 1967. Marine engr. U.S. Mcht. Marine, 1960-62; asst. physicist Brookhaven Nat. Lab., Upton, N.Y., 1967-69, asso. physicist, 1969-70; asso. prof. nuclear engring. U. Ill., Urbana, 1970-75, prof., 1975—; NRC vis. prof. math. physics U. Bologna, Italy, 1975-76, 81; internat. prof. nuclear engring. Italian Ministry of Edn., 1981; physicist plasma theory group, div. magnetic fusion energy Lawrence Livermore (Calif.) Nat. Lab., 1977-78; cons. to U.S. nat. labs. and indsl. research labs., 1970—. Contbr. articles to various publs. Served as ensign USN, 1959-60. Fellow Am. Phys. Soc., Am. Nuclear Soc. (Mark Mills award 1967); mem. Soc. Indsl. and Applied Math., AAAS, N.Y. Acad. Scis., Sigma Xi. Office: Nuclear Engring Program Univ of Illinois 103 S Goodwin St Urbana IL 61801

DORNSBUSCH, RUDIGER, economics educator; b. Krefeld, Germany, June 8, 1942; came to U.S., 1967; s. Paul and Josefine (Buhner) Dornbusch. Lic., U. Geneva, 1966; Ph.D., U. Chgo., 1971. Asst. prof. econs. U. Chgo., 1971, U. Rochester, N.Y., 1972-73; assoc. prof. MIT, Cambridge, Mass., 1975-77, prof. econs., 1977—; advisor Inst. Internat. Econs., Washington, 1982—. Author: Open Economy Macro-economics, 1980, (with Stanley Fischer) Macroeconomics, 1977, Economics, 1983; co-editor: Jour. Internat. Econs., 1976-83; assoc. editor: Jour. Fin., 1979—. Fellow Guggenheim Found., 1979, Am. Acad. Arts and Scis., 1980, Econometric Soc., 1981. Office: Dept Econs Mass Inst Tech #52-357 Cambridge MA 02139

DORO, MARION ELIZABETH, political scientist, educator; b. Miami, Fla., Oct. 9, 1928; d. George and Alma (Carram) D. B.A., Fla. State U., 1951, M.A., 1952; Ph.D. (Bennett fellow), U. Pa., 1959. Instr. polit. sci. Wheaton Coll., Norton, Mass., 1958-60; Ford Found. Area Studies fellow U. London, Kenya, Africa, 1960-62; asst. prof. Conn. Coll., New London, 1962-65, assoc. prof., 1965-70, prof., 1970—, dir. grad. studies, 1975-79, chmn. dept. govt., 1981—. Editor: (with N. Stultz) Governing in Black Africa, 1970; mem. editorial bd.: African Studies Rev; contbr. articles and book revs. to profl. jours. Fulbright fellow Makere U., Kampala, Uganda, 1963-64; sr. research fellow Radcliffe Inst., Cambridge, Mass., 1968-69; vis. research fellow, Am. Philos. Soc. grantee East Africa Inst. Social Sci. Research, 1971-72; AAUW Am. fellow, sr. assoc. St. Anthony's Coll., Oxford U., 1977-78. Mem. Am. Polit. Sci. Assn., N.Eng. Polit. Sci. Assn. (chmn. status women com. 1972-75, exec. council 1973-75), Northeast Polit. Sci. Assn. (exec. council 1974-76), African Studies Assn. (dir. program nat. meetings 1976), AAUP, AAUW, Soc. Fellows Radcliffe Inst. (exec. council 1979—), Phi Beta Kappa, Phi Kappa Phi, Pi Sigma Alpha. Office: Conn Coll New London CT 06320

DORPAT, THEODORE LORENZ, psychoanalyst; b. Miles City, Mont., Mar. 25, 1925; s. Theodore Ertman and Eda (Christiansen) D.; m. Damaris Elisabeth Suttle, Aug. 11, 1972; 1 dau., Joanne Katherine. B.S., Whitworth Coll., 1948; M.D., U. Wash., 1952; grad., Seattle Psychoanalytic Inst., 1964. Resident in psychiatry Seattle VA Hosp., 1953-55, Cin. Gen. Hosp., 1955-56; instr. in psychiatry U. Wash., 1956-58, asst. prof. psychiatry, 1958-59, asso. prof., 1969-75, prof., 1976—; practice medicine specializing in psychiatry, Seattle, 1958-64, practice psychoanalysis, 1964; instr. Seattle Psychoanalytic Inst., 1966-71, tng. psychoanalyt, 1971—; chmn. Wash. Gov.'s Task Force for Commitment Law Reform; trustee Seattle Community Psychiat. Clinic; pres., trustee Seattle Psychoanalytic Inst. Contbr. numerous articles, revs. to profl. publs. Served to ensign USNR, 1943-46. Fellow Am. Psychiat. Assn.; m. Am. Psychoanalytic Assn., AMA, Seattle Psychoanalytic Soc. (sec.-treas. 1965-67, pres. 1972-73), AAAS, Alpha Omega Alpha, Sigma Xi. Home: 3815 46th Ave NE Seattle WA 98105 Office: 2271 NE 51st St Seattle WA 98105

DORR, JOHN A., JR., geologist, educator, researcher; b. Grosse Pointe Park, Mich., Oct. 25, 1922; s. John A. and Velma (Read) D.; m. Ruth Muriel Pritchett, Nov. 4, 1943; children: John A. III, James, Robin. B.S., U. Mich., 1947, M.S., 1949, Ph.D., 1951. Curator vertebrate paleontology Carnegie Mus., Pitts., 1951-52; prof. U. Mich., Ann Arbor, 1952—, chmn. geology dept., 1966-71, research assoc. Mus. Paleontology, 1952—, dir. Geol. Expdns., 1965-78, dir. Rocky Mountain Field Sta., 1978—. Author: (with Donald F. Eschman) Geology of Michigan, 1970; Contbr. articles to profl. jours. Fellow Geol. Soc. Am.; mem. Soc. Vertebrate Paleontology (past pres.), Paleontol. Soc., Mich. Acad. Sci., Sigma Xi, Phi Kappa Phi. Home: 3091 Warwick Rd Ann Arbor MI 48104

DORRA, HENRI, art historian, educator; b. Alexandria, Egypt, 1924; came to U.S., 1947, naturalized, 1953; s. Clement and Aimee (Castro) D.; m. Mary Lawrence Tonetti, 1965; children: Amy Lawrence, Helen Hyde. B.Sc. (Eng.), U. London, 1944; S.M., A.M., Harvard, 1950, Ph.D., 1953. Asst. dir. Corcoran Gallery Art, 1954-61, Phila. Mus. Art, 1961-62; exec. v.p. Art Assn. Indpls., 1962-63; faculty UCLA, 1963-65; prof. U. Calif., Santa Barbara, 1965—. Author: (with John Rewald) Georges Seurat, 1959, The American Muse, 1961, Art in Perspective, 1973; also articles. Trustee Santa Barbara Mus. Art. Recipient Bowdoin prize Harvard, 1948; student fellow Met. Mus. Art, 1951-52; Guggenheim fellow, 1978-79. Address: U Calif Dept Art History Santa Barbara CA 93106

DORRANCE, GEORGE MORRIS, JR., banker; b. Phila., Dec. 28, 1922; s. George Morris and Emily (Fox) D.; m. Carter Rogers; children: Mary Irwin, George Morris III. A.B., U. Pa., 1949, M.B.A., 1951. With Fed. Res. Bank, Phila., 1949-51; with Phila. Nat. Bank, 1951—, chmn., 1969—, also dir.; dir. Penn Va. Corp., R.R. Donnelly & Sons Co., Provident Mut. Life Ins. Co., Phila., Rohm and Haas Corp., Joh. Berenberg, Gossler & Co., Hamburg, Germany. Trustee U. Pa. Office: Phila Nat Bank Broad and Chestnut Sts Philadelphia PA 19101

DORRANCE, JOHN THOMPSON, JR., food processing executive; b. Cinnaminson, N.J., Feb. 7, 1919; s. John Thompson and Ethel (Mallinckrodt) D.; m. Diana R. Dripps, Apr. 26, 1979; children: John Thompson, III, Bennett, Mary Alice and Keith Bassett, Langdon Mannion.; stepchildren: Keith Bassett, Langdon Mannion, Robert D. Dripps, III, Susan Stauffer. Grad., St. George's School, Newport, R.I., 1937; A.B., Princeton, 1941. With Campbell Soup Co., 1946—, asst. treas., 1950, asst. to pres., 1955, chmn. bd., 1962—, also dir.; dir. Carter Hawley Hale Stores, Inc., Morgan Guaranty Trust Co. of N.Y., J.P. Morgan & Co., Inc.; trustee Penn Mut. Life Ins. Co. Trustee Princeton U. Served as capt. U.S. Army, World War II. Mem. Soc. Cin. Republican. Clubs: Union (N.Y.C.); Philadelphia, Rittenhouse, Union League, Racquet (Phila.); Gulph Mills (Pa.) Golf; Pine Valley (N.J.). Golf., Nat. Golf Links of Am. (Southampton, N.Y.). Home: Monk Rd Gladwyne PA 19035 Office: Campbell Pl Camden NJ 08101

DORRILL, WILLIAM FRANKLIN, college dean, political scientist, educator; b. Dallas, July 25, 1931; s. William Cumbie and Ruth (Esther Webb) D.; m. Martha Jeanne Brawley, Mar. 3, 1951; children: Jennifer Ruth, William Sidney, Rebecca Jeanne, Lisa Kathryn. B.A., Baylor U., 1952; M.A., U. Va., 1954; postgrad., Australian Nat. U., Canberra, 1954; Ph.D., Harvard U., 1972. Fgn. affairs anlayst U.S. Govt., Washington, 1961-63; polit. scientist RAND Corp., Santa Monica, Calif., 1963-67; project chmn., sr. staff mem. Research analysis Corp., McLean, Va., 1967-68; dir. Asian Studies Ctr., assoc. prof. polit. sci. U. Pitts, 1969-77, chmn. dept. East Asian langs. and lits., 1972-77; dean Coll.Arts and Sci., prof. polit. sci. Ohio U., Athens, 1977—; vis. lectr. Fgn. Service Inst., State Dept., Washington, 1962-80; mem. faculty coll. mgmt. program Carnegie-Mellon U. and Nat. Ctr. Higher Edn. Mgmt. Systems, summer 1980; vis. lectr. on univ. adminstrn. Chinese univs., 1980; program cons. La. Bd. Regents, Baton Rouge, summers 1982-83. Contbr. articles on East Asian politics and internat. relations to profl. jours., chpts. on Chinese politics and history to scholarly books. Mem. Athens County Bd. Mental Retardation and Devel. Disabilities, Ohio, 1982—. Recipient Disting. Achievement medal Baylor U., 1980; Fulbright scholar, 1954; Soc. for Values in Higher Edn. Kent fellow, 1957-58; Ford Found. fgn. area fellow, Taiwan, Hong Kong, 1959-61. Fellow Soc. for Values in Higher Edn.; mem. Am. Conf. Acad. Deans (vice chmn. 1981-82, chmn. 1982-83, bd. dirs.1980—), Assn. Asian Studies, Asia Soc. (adv. com. performing arts 1977—), Nat. Com. on U.S.-China Relations. Democrat. Presbyterian. Lodge: Rotary (Athens). Home: 17 Briarwood Dr Athens OH 45701 Office: Coll Arts and Scis Ohio U Athens OH 45701

DORRINGTON, KEITH JOHN, scientific laboratory executive, biochemistry educator; b. Tredegar, U.K., Oct. 26, 1939; s. Bruce and Wynne D.; children: Mark J., Jonathan P., Emma J. B.Sc. with honors, U. Sheffield, 1961, Ph.D., 1964, D.Sc., 1976. Sr. scientist MRC Molecular Pharmacology Unit, Cambridge (Eng.) U., 1968-70; asso. prof. biochemistry U. Toronto, Ont., Can., 1970-75, prof., 1975—, chmn. dept., 1977-82, assoc. dean medicine, 1978-82; v.p. research and tech. Connaught Labs. Ltd., Toronto, 1982—. Contbr. articles to profl. jours. Sir Henry Wellcome fellow, 1966-68; grantee Med. Research Council Can., 1970—; recipient Ayerst award Can. Biochem. Soc., 1977. Mem. Am. Assn. Immunologists, Am. Soc. Biol. Chemists, Brit. Soc. Immunology, Can. Soc. Immunology. Home: 43 Gloucester St Toronto ON M4Y 1L8 Canada Office: Connaught Research Inst 1755 Steeles Ave W Willowdale ON Canada M2R 3T4

DORRIS, MICHAEL ANTHONY, native American studies educator, university administrator; b. Dayton, Wash., Jan. 30, 1945; s. Jim and Mary Besy (Burkhardt) D.; m. Louise Erdrich, 1981; children: Reynold Abel, Jeffrey Sava, Madeline Hannah. B.A. magna cum laude, Georgetown U., 1967; M.Phil., Yale U., 1970. Grad. asst. Yale U., 1969-70; asst. prof. anthropology Johnston Coll., U. of Redlands, 1970-71; asst. prof. Franconia (N.H.) Coll., 1971-72; prof., chmn. dept. native Am. studies Dartmouth Coll., Hanover, N.H., 1972—, chmn. M.A. in Liberal Studies Program, 1983—; vis. asst. prof. U. N.H. Regional Center, 1973-74; Cons. Alaska State Operated Schs., 1973-74, Nat. Endowment for Humanities, 1976—. Author: Native Americans Today, 1975, Grandmother's Watch, 1975, Native Americans: 500 Years After, 1975; Editor: Viewpoint, 1967-68, Man in the Northeast, 1976, A Sourcebook for Native American Studies, 1977; Contbr. chpt.: Ency. Indians of the Americas, 1975; Mem. editorial bd.: Am. Indian Culture Center Jour, UCLA, 1974—, Suntracks, U. Ariz., 1978—; Contbr. articles to profl. jours. Danforth grad. fellow, 1967; Woodrow Wilson grad. fellow, 1967; NIMH fellow, 1970; grantee, 1971; Guggenheim fellow, 1978; Woodrow Wilson faculty fellow, 1980. Fellow Soc. Applied Anthropology, Soc. Values in Higher Edn.; mem. Am. Anthrop. Assn., AAUP, MLA (del. assembly 1975-78), AAAS, Council Anthropology and Edn., Nat. Congress Am. Indians, Nat. Indian Edn. Assn., Nat. Indian Youth Council, Alpha Sigma Nu, Explorers Club. Home: RFD 2 Cornish NH 03745 Office: Hinman Box 6152 Dartmouth Coll Hanover NH 03755

DORRITIE, JOHN FRANCIS, pharmaceutical advertising agency executive; b. N.Y.C., Feb. 26, 1934; s. George D. and Mary C. (Pollock) D.; m. Carol Kelley, July 23, 1960; children: George, Teresa, John, Carol Jean. B.S., Iona Coll., 1955. Product mgr., asst. advt. mgr. Sandoz Pharms., 1957-65; v.p. account services Sudler & Hennessey, Inc., 1965-68; founder, pres. Stat-Kit, Inc., 1968-69; exec. dir. Council for Interdisciplinary Communications in Medicine, N.Y.C., 1970; sr. v.p. Sudler & Hennessey, N.Y.C., 1970-77, exec. v.p., 1977-79; pres. Dorritie & Lyons Inc., 1979—; Bd. dirs. Inter, Lawrence, Kans. Served with U.S. Army, 1955-57. Mem. Am. Mktg. Assn., Pharm. Advt. Club, Midwest Pharm. Advt. Club, Soc. Advanced Med. Systems., AAAS, N.Y. Acad. Scis. Roman Catholic. Home: 8 Gable Rd New City NY 10956 Office: 655 3d Ave New York NY 10017

DORSCH, BERNARD JEROME, surety company executive; b. Chgo., Oct. 27, 1927; s. Bernard Peter and Ann (Jalloway) D.; m. Marilyn McSweeney, Sept. 9, 1950; children—Debra Lynn, Christine Marie, Mary Beth. B.A., Loyola U., Chgo., 1951. With Seaboard Surety Co., Chgo., 1952-65, mgr. to, 1965; v.p., dir. Capitol Transamerica Corp., Madison, Wis., 1965-68; with Fidelity & Deposit Co. of Md., Balt., 1968—, exec. v.p., dir., 1979—. Chmn. United Way Central Md., 1978. Served with U.S. Navy, 1944-46. Decorated Purple Heart. Mem. Am. Ins. Assn. (dir.), Surety Assn. Am. Republican. Roman Catholic. Clubs: Center, Balt. Country., Maryland. Home: 13410 Blythenia Rd Phoenix MD 21131 Office: 210 N Charles St Baltimore MD 21201

DORSEN, NORMAN, lawyer, educator; b. N.Y.C., Sept. 4, 1930; s. Arthur and Tanya (Stone) D.; m. Harriette Koffler, Nov. 25, 1965; children: Jennifer, Caroline Gail, Anne. B.A., Columbia U., 1950; LL.B. magna cum laude, Harvard, 1953; postgrad., London Sch. Econs., 1955-56; LL.D. (hon.), Ripon Coll., 1981. Bar: D.C. 1953, N.Y. 1954. Law clk. to judge U.S. Ct. Appeals, Boston, 1956-57; law clk. to Justice John Marshall Harlan U.S. Supreme Ct., Washington, 1957-58; asso. firm Dewey, Ballantine, Bushby, Palmer & Wood, N.Y.C., 1958-60; mem. faculty N.Y. U. Sch. Law, N.Y.C., 1961—, prof. law, 1961—, Stokes prof., 1981—, dir. Hays civil liberties program, 1961—; vis. prof. law London Sch. Econs., 1968, U. Calif., Berkeley, 1974-75, Harvard U., 1980, 83; cons. U.S. Commn. on Violence, 1968-69, Random House, 1969-73, B.B.C., 1969-73, U.S. Commn. on Social Security, 1979-80; exec. dir. spl. com. on courtroom conduct Assn. Bar N.Y.C., 1970-73; chmn. Com. for Pub. Justice, 1972-74; vice chmn. HEW sec.'s rev. panel on new drug regulation, 1975-76, chmn., 1976-77; mem. N.Y.C. Commn. on Status of Women, 1978-80. Author: (with others) Political and Civil Rights in U.S., 3d edit, 1967, 4th edit., Vol. I, 1976, Vol. II, 1979, Frontiers of Civil Liberties, 1968, Discrimination and Civil Rights, 1969, (with L. Friedman) Disorder in the Court, 1973; Editor: The Rights of Americans, 1971, (with S. Gillers) None of Your Business, 1974. Served to 1st Lt., JAGC U.S. Army, 1953-55. Mem. Am. Bar Assn. (chmn. com. free speech and press 1968-70), Am. Law Inst., ACLU (gen. counsel 1969-76, pres. 1976—, dir.), Phi Beta Kappa. Home: Central Park W New York NY 10023 Office: 40 Washington Sq S New York NY 10012

DORSETT, ANTHONY DREW (TONY), professional football player; b. Aliquippa, Pa., Apr. 7, 1954. Ed., U. Pitts. Profl. football player Dallas Cowboys, NFL, 1977—. Recipient Heisman Trophy, 1976; named to NFL All-Star Team, Sporting News, 1981, Coll. Player of Yr., Sporting News, 1976, Rookie of Yr., 1977; established NFL record for longest run from scrimmage (99 yds.), 1983. Office: care Dallas Cowboys 6116 N Central Expy Dallas TX 75206 *

DORSEY, BOB RAWLS, petroleum drilling co. exec.; b. Rockland, Tex., Aug. 27, 1912; s. Elias Leon and Lillie (Rawls) D.; m. Angelina Johnapelus, May 11, 1941; children—Michael Rawls, James Thomas, Ellen. B.S. in Chem. Engring, U. Tex., 1940; D.Sc. (hon.), U. Tampa, Fla., LL.D., Trio State Coll., Angola, Ind., Seoul Nat. U., Korea, Grove City (Pa.) Coll. Engr. Gulf Oil Corp., Port Arthur, Tex., 1940-48, coordinator mfg. dept., Pitts., 1955-58, adminstrv. v.p., 1958-60, sr. v.p., 1961, exec. v.p., 1962-65, pres., 1965-72, chmn. bd., chief exec. officer, 1972-76; also dir.; mgr. Gulf Refining Co., Puerto La Cruz, Venezuela, 1948-55; dir. Gearhart Ind., Inc., Superior Oil Co., Allegheny Internat. Industries, Inc., Corpus Christi Bank & Trust, 1st City Nat. Bank of Houston. Trustee U. Pitts.; mem. devel. bd. U. Tex. Recipient Distinguished Engring. Grad award U. Tex., 1965. Clubs: Duquesne, Rolling Rock (Pitts.); Ramada (Houston). Office: 2121 Sage Suite 321 Houston TX 77056

DORSEY, DOLORES FLORENCE, business executive; b. Buffalo, May 26, 1928; d. William G. and Florence R. D. B.S., Coll. St. Elizabeth, 1950. With Aerojet-Gen. Corp., 1953—, asst. to treas., El Monte, Calif., 1972-74, asst. treas., 1974-79, treas., 1979—. Mem. Cash Mgmt. Group San Diego (pres.), Fin. Execs. Inst. Republican. Roman Catholic. Club: Lomas Santa Fe Country. Office: 10300 N Torrey Pines Rd La Jolla CA 92037 *

DORSEY, FRANK JAMES, grocery company executive; b. Butte, Mont., Mar. 21, 1930; s. Franklyn Augustus and Theresa (Marron) D.; m. Betty Marie Elmborg, Jan. 7, 1956; children: Sheila Kaye, Kevin Frank. B.S., U.S. Naval Acad., 1954; M.B.A., Harvard U., 1962. Dir. indsl. engring. Avon Fashions, Inc., N.Y.C., 1970-72, v.p. ops., Newport News, Va., 1972-76, dir. facilities planning, N.Y.C., 1976-78; distbn. ctr. mgr. Lucky Stores, Inc., Vacaville, Calif., 1978-79, specialist distbn., Dublin, Calif., 1979-80, corp. v.p. warehousing and distbn., Dublin, 1980—. Served to 1st lt. USMC, 1954-58. Decorated Navy and Marine Corps. medal. Mem. Food Mktg. Inst., Pvt. Truck Council. Republican. Roman Catholic. Office: Lucky Stores Inc 6300 Clark Ave Dublin CA 94568

DORSEY, GRAY LANKFORD, educator; b. Hamilton, Mo., Feb. 16, 1918; s. Claude Purdue and Mary Alice (Lankford) D.; m. Jeanne DeVall, Jan. 1, 1942; 1 dau., Deborah DeVall. Student, Baker U., 1936-38; A.B. in Journalism, U. Kans., 1941; J.D., Yale, 1948, J.S.D., 1950. Bar: Mo. bar 1956. Editor, pub. Cameron (Mo.) Sun, 1940-42; mem. faculty Washington U., St. Louis, 1951—, Charles Nagel prof. jurisprudence and internat. law, 1962—; vis. prof. Nat. Taiwan U., also Soochow U., Taipei, Taiwan, 1952-53; lectr. philosophy U. Hawaii, summer 1959; fellow Center Advanced Study Behavioral Scis., Stanford, 1960-61; cons. antitrust law; cons. Nat. Endowment for Humanities.; Bd. dirs. Univ. Centers for Rational Alternatives; adv. bd. Ams. for Effective Law Enforcement; chmn. adv. com. on citizenship edn. Mo. Bar. Author publs. in fields of internat. law and legal and social philosophy. Served to lt. (s.g.) USCGR, 1942-46; to maj. U.S. Army Res., 1956-62. Fellow Am. Council Learned Socs. (1948-50); Mem. Am. Soc. Internat. Law, Internat. Assn. Philosophy of Law and Social Philosophy (pres. 1975-79), Am. Soc. Polit. and Legal Philosophy, Internat. Law Assn. Home: 8 Conway Springs Dr Chesterfield MO 63017 Office: Law Sch Washington U Saint Louis MO 63130

DORSEY, JOHN RUSSELL, journalist; b. Balt., Dec. 17, 1938; s. Charles Howard and Emma (Deputy) D. A.B., Harvard U., 1961. Mem. staff Balt. Sun, 1962-8, 83, Sunday Sun book rev. editor, 1967-69, Sunday Sun restaurant critic, 1971-81, Sunday Sun art critic, 1983. Author: (with James D. Dilts) A Guide to Baltimore Architecture, 1973, Mount Vernon Place, 1983; editor: On Mencken, 1980. Democrat. Episcopalian. Clubs: Maryland, 14 W. Hamilton St., Harvard (Balt.). Home: 1706 Park Ave Baltimore MD 21217 Office: Baltimore Sun Calvert and Centre Sts Baltimore MD 21203

DORSEY, JOHN WESLEY, JR., univ. adminstr., economist; b. Hagerstown, Md., June 13, 1936; s. John Wesley and Abbie Virginia (Wy) D.; 1 dau., Rachel Lynette. B.S., U. Md., 1958; cert., London Sch. Econs., 1959; M.A., Harvard U., 1962, Ph.D., 1964. Teaching fellow Harvard U., 1961, 62-63; asst. prof. econs. U. Md., 1963-66, asso. prof., dir., 1966-70, vice chancellor for adminstrv. affairs, College Park, 1970-77, acting chancellor, 1974-75, prof. econs., 1976—, chancellor, Baltimore County, 1977—; cons. to govt. Bd. dirs. Council on Econ. Edn. in Md., 1975—, Md. Employees Credit Union, 1975—. Rotary Found. scholar, 1958-59; Brookings research fellow, 1961-63. Mem. Am. Econs. Assn., Western Econs. Assn., Am. Assn. State Colls. and Univs., Am. Assn. Sch. Adminstrn., Am. Council on Edn., Baltimore County C. of C., Phi Beta Kappa, Phi Kappa Phi, Omicron Delta Kappa. Home: 11943 Old Columbia Pike Silver Spring MD 20904 Office: 5401 Wilkens Ave Catonsville MD 21228

DORSEY, PETER, lawyer; b. Mpls., Aug. 22, 1922; s. James Emmett and Mary (Toomey) D.; children: Sheila Dorsey Murphy, Cynthia Dorsey Kamesar, Justin, Sage. A.B., Harvard U., 1947, LL.B., 1949. Bar: Minn. 1949. With firm Dorsey & Whitney, and predecessors, Mpls., 1949—, jr. ptnr., 1956-59, gen. ptnr., 1959—; gen. counsel Minn. Twins Baseball Club, 1962—; v.p., bd. dirs. Cargill Found., 1979—; chmn. legal task force Urban Coalition Mpls., 1969-70. Bd. dirs. Minn. Theatre Co. Found., Guthrie Theatre, 1963-69; co-founder Legal Rights Center, 1971, bd. dirs., 1971-75, pres., 1971-72; bd. visitors U. Minn. Law Sch., 1983—. Served to 1st lt., inf. and airborne inf. U.S. Army, 1942-46. Mem. ACLU (pres. Minn. br. 1963-65, dir.), ABA; mem. Minn. Bar Assn., Hennepin County Bar Assn. Club: Minneapolis. Home: 1814 Mt Curve Ave Minneapolis MN 55403 also 743 Glenview Ln La Jolla CA 92037 Office: First Bank Pl E Minneapolis MN 55402

DORSEY, RAY, pub. relations exec.; b. Phila., July 29, 1913; s. Rudolph Raymond and Marjorie (Conner) D.; m. Bettie Arnette Brunn, Oct. 27, 1940; 1 son, Noel Michael. B.A., Dartmouth, 1936; M.S. in Journalism, Columbia, 1937. Gen. assignment and beat reporter Cleve. Plain Dealer, 1937-46, city hall reporter, 1946-56, polit. editor, 1956-63, asso. editor, editorial writer, 1964, chief editorial writer, editor editorial page, 1964-71; owner pub. relations bus., 1971—; Mem. 1967 Pulitzer Prize Journalism Jury. Chmn. Oceanside-Carlsbad br. Am. Cancer Soc., 1977-79. Mem. Am. Soc. Newspaper Editors, Alpha Sigma Phi. Home: 265 Stagecoach Rd Oceanside CA 92054

DORSEY, RHODA MARY, college president; b. Boston, Sept. 9, 1927; d. Thomas Francis and Hedwig (Hoge) D. B.A. magna cum laude, Smith Coll., 1949, LL.D., 1979; B.A., Cambridge (Eng.) U., 1951, M.A., 1954; Ph.D., U. Minn., 1956; LL.D., Nazareth Coll. Rochester, 1970; D.H.L., Mount St. Mary's Coll., 1976, Mount Vernon Coll., 1979, Coll. St. Catherine, 1983. Mem. faculty Goucher Coll., Towson, Md., 1954—, prof. history, 1965-68, dean, v.p., 1968-73, acting pres., 1973-74, pres., 1974—; lectr. history Loyola Coll., Balt., 1958-62, Johns Hopkins, 1960-61; mem. Md. Higher Edn. Supplemental Loan Authority, 1982—; dir. U.S. Fidelity & Guaranty Co., Balt., Chesapeake & Potomac Tel. Co. Md., Noxell Corp., First Nat. Bank Md. Bd. dirs. House of Good Shepherd, Am. Friends of Cambridge U., 1978—; mem. adv. com. Hewlett and Mellon Found. Liberal Arts Coll. Self-Renewal Program, 1979—; mem. Gov.'s Ad Hoc Bus. Adv. Council, 1980, So. Regional Edn. Bd., 1980—, Md.-D.C. Com. on Selection Rhodes Scholars, Lay Commn. Cath. Social Teaching, 1984; adv. com. Md. Historic Trust, "Md. Minutes" TV program. Recipient Outstanding Woman Mgr. of 1984 U. Balt. Women's Program in Mgmt. and WMAR-TV. Mem. Md. Ind. Coll. and Univ. Assn. (vice-chmn.), Assn. Governing Bds. of Univs. and Colls. (adv. council of presidents 1981—), Am. Council on Edn. (bd. dirs. 1981—), Middle States Assn. Colls. and Schs. Clubs: Smith, Hamilton St. (Balt.). Home: President's House Goucher Coll Towson MD 21204

DORSEY, THOMAS BROOKSHIER, media/communications executive; b. Keokuk, Iowa, Apr. 30, 1928; s. Frank Blinn and Johanna (Brookshier) D.; m. Helen Danner, June 30, 1951; children: Diana, Frank Blinn. Student, DePauw U., 1946-47, State U. Iowa, 1947-50. Corr., Des Moines Register, 1949-51; chief European corr. Times Pub. Co., 1954-56; nat. affairs editor Am. Weekend, Washington, 1956-57; editor, gen. mgr. N.Y. Herald Tribune News Service, 1957-59; v.p. Barnet & Reef Assos., Inc., N.Y.C., 1959-63; v.p., dir. internat. div. John Moynahan & Co., N.Y.C., 1963; dir., editor Newsday Spls. (syndicate) Newsday Inc., 1964-69; v.p., editor Chgo. Tribune-N.Y. News Syndicate, Inc., N.Y.C., 1969-74; sales mgr. Knight News Wire, 1972-74; dir., editor Los Angeles Times Syndicate, 1975-77; dir. Los Angeles Times/Washington Post News Service, 1975-77; chmn., chief exec. officer Dorsey Communications, Inc., Diana Prodns., Blinn Books, Los Angeles, 1977—; econ. devel. and pub. affairs counsel Govt. Eastern Nigeria, Nigerian Outlook newspaper, 1959-63; assoc. producer Adlai Stevenson Reports (ABC-TV), 1962-63. Served with USAF, 1951-54. Mem. Aviation/Space Writers Assn., Newspaper Comics Council, Internat. Radio and TV Soc., Internat. Platform Assn., Am. Film Inst., Sigma Delta Chi. Clubs: Nat. Press (Washington); Deadline (exec. bd. dir.). Home: 9239 Doheny Rd Los Angeles CA 90069 also Pink Sands Harbour Island Bahamas

DORSKY, STEPHEN MICHAEL, publishing company executive; b. Bangor, Maine, Nov. 7, 1947; s. Benjamin James and Priscilla (Raynes) D. Student, Rutgers U., 1966-70. Dir. sales Viking Penguin, San Francisco, N.Y.C., 1971-79; v.p. mktg. Holt Rinehart-CBS, N.Y.C., 1979-83; v.p., dir. mktg. Simon & Schuster, N.Y.C., 1983—. Mem. Am. Assn. Pubs. Office: Simon & Schuster Pubs 1230 Ave of Americas New York NY 10020

DORST, JOHN PHILLIPS, educator, physician; b. Cin., July 8, 1926; s. Stanley Elwood and Mary (Conway) D.; m. Marcia Louise Kinney, June 17, 1950; children—Stanley Kinney, Nancy, John Radcliffe, Margaret. Student, Princeton, 1944, 47-48, U. Cin., 1946, Pomona Coll., 1948-49; M.D., Cornell U., 1953. Rotating intern U. Iowa Hosps., 1953-54; resident in pathology Northwestern Hosp., Mpls., 1954; resident in radiology VA Hosp., Mpls., 1955, State U. Iowa Hosps., 1955-58; fellow in pediatric radiology U. Cin. Coll. Medicine, 1958-59, from asst. prof. to asso. prof. radiology, also from instr. to asst. prof. pediatrics, 1959-66; mem. faculty Johns Hopkins Med. Sch., 1966—, asso. prof. radiology, 1966-70, prof. radiology, 1970—, asso. prof. pediatrics, 1967-78, prof. pediatrics, 1978—; radiologist Johns Hopkins Hosp., 1966—; Vis. lectr. Armed Forces Inst. Pathology, 1968—; cons. NIH, 1969—, John F. Kennedy Inst., Balt., 1972—, Balt. City Hosps.; Bd. dirs. Howard County Gen. Hosp., 1977-80. Adv. editorial bd.: Radiology, 1973—. Served with U.S. Army, 1944-46. Fellow Am. Coll. Radiology; mem. Radiol. Soc. N.Am., Am. Roentgen Ray Soc., Soc. Pediatric Radiology (sec.-treas. 1973-76, pres. 1977-78), Md. Radiology Soc., Sigma Xi, Alpha Omega Alpha. Home: 10517 Catterskill Ct Columbia MD 21044

DORTCH, CARL RAYMOND, former association executive; b. nr. Madisonville, Ky., Sept. 14, 1914; s. Walter B. and Delia (Baldwin) D.; m. Anna Gale Greenland, Nov. 17, 1950; children: Walter A., David J. A.B., DePauw U., 1936, D.Public Service (hon.), 1979; M.A. in Pub. Adminstrn, U. Cin., 1938; LL.D. (hon.), Marian Coll., 1981. With Indpls. C. of C., 1936-79, asst. gen. mgr., 1950-62, gen. mgr., 1962-64, exec. v.p., 1964-75, pres., 1976-79; chmn. Ind. White River Park Devel. Commn.; dir. Midwest Nat. Bank. Bd. dirs. Indpls. chpt. ARC, Consortium for Urban Edn., Indpls. Ednl. TV, Greater Indpls. Progress Com., New Hope of Ind., Starlight Musicals, Center for Leadership Devel.; pres. United Fund Greater Indpls.; bd. advisers Christian Theol. Sem. Served as 1st lt. USAAF, 1943-45. Recipient John N. VanDerVries award U.S. C. of C., 1947, Distinguished Service award U.S. Jr. C. of C., 1949; named Man of Year Indpls. Times, 1956, Indpls. Press Club, 1978, Ind. Acad., 1979. Mem. Am. C. of C. Execs. (vice chmn., bd. dirs.), Ind. Commerce Execs. Assn. (past pres.), DePauw Alumni Assn., Edward Rector Alumni Assn. (past pres.). Presbyn. (elder). Clubs: Mason (33 deg.), Kiwanian., Indpls. Press, Indpls. Athletic, Meridian Hills Country (Indpls.). Home: 7031 Washington Blvd Indianapolis IN 46220 Office: 320 N Meridian St Indianapolis IN 46204

DORTON, JOSEPH LA DRUE, broadcasting executive; b. Apr. 27, 1941; m. Joan Anderson, Nov. 21, 1963; children: Kyle, Shelly, Wendy, Heather. B.S. in Mgmt, U. Utah, 1966; M.B.A., U. Chgo., 1972. Vice pres., gen. mgr. Sta. KMOR, Salt Lake City, 1968-69; sta. mgr. Sta. KIRO-FM, Seattle, 1969-70; pres., gen. mgr. Sta. WCLR, Chgo., 1970-74; v.p., chief exec. officer Calif. div. gen. mgr. Sta. KBIG/KBRT, Los Angeles, also Sta. KOIT, San Francisco, 1974-78; pres. Torbet Radio Inc. div. Bonneville Internat. Corp., N.Y.C., 1978-80, Gannett Radio div. Gannett Co., Inc., St. Louis, 1980—. Vice chmn. Stony Point council Boy Scouts Am., 1977; adviser Camp Cumorah Crest, Los Angeles, 1977. Recipient Disting. Sales award Sales and Mktg. Execs. Assn. Salt Lake City, 1966, 67; named Outstanding Salesman of Yr., 1968. Mem. So. Calif. Broadcasters Assn. Mormon. Home: 430 Herworth Dr Chesterfield MO 63017 Office: 10155 Corporate Sq Saint Louis MO 63132

DORVILLIER, WILLIAM JOSEPH, editor, pub.; b. North Adams, Mass., Apr. 24, 1908; s. Joseph and Aurise (Champagne) D.; m. Mary Elizabeth Johnson, Oct. 1, 1938; 1 son, William Clay. Student, N.Y.U. With North Adams Transcript; editor S. Am. desk A.P., N.Y.C.; then corr. A.P. and; U.P.I., Caribbean area; accredited war corr., World War II; editor Puerto Rico World Jour., 1940-43, 44-45, 56-57, Washington corr., 1945-53; founder Dorvillier News Letter (weekly bus. and econ. publ.), 1953, San Juan Star, 1959, editor, pub., 1959-67; pres., dir. Star Pub., editor, pub., 1959-67; past pres., dir. Star Pub. Corp.; chmn. bd. Dorvillier News Agy., Inc., 1953-79; ret., 1979; news dir. WAPA-TV, 1969-73. (Recipient Pulitzer prize for distinguished editorial writing 1961); Author: Workshop U.S.A., The Challenge of Puerto Rico, 1962. Mem. Sigma Delta Chi. Club: Nat. Press (Washington). Home: 35 Lawrence St Concord NH 03301 *Dissatisfaction has been the motivating influence in my life. Nothing I have ever done seemed quite good enough to me even when it had won the praise of professionals whose opinions I valued. I believe that the man or woman who can say that a personal creation, be it in the arts, science, professions or in business, is "the best", has nothing left but to take a quiet stroll on the Sea of Galilee.*

DORWEILER, JOHN P., political science educator; b. Guttenberg, Iowa, Sept. 1, 1926; s. John and Mary Amelia (Eggerth) D.; m. Evelyn Jean Greene, Nov. 28, 1958; children: Lynne Marie, Paul John. B.A., U. Iowa, 1948, M.A., 1949. Mem. faculty Loras Coll., Dubuque, Iowa, 1949—, prof., 1970—. Served with USNR, 1944-46. Home: 1870 Horizon Ct Dubuque IA 52001

DOSLAND, WILLIAM BUEHLER, lawyer; b. Chgo., Nov. 10, 1927; s. Goodwin Leroy and Beatrice Florence (Buehler) D.; m. Donna Mae Mathisen, Sept. 15, 1956; children: David William, Susan Elizabeth. B.A., Concordia Coll., 1949; J.D., U. Minn., 1954. Bar: Minn. 1954. Sr. partner firm Dosland, Dosland and Nordhougen, Moorhead, Minn., 1968—; gen. counsel, corp. sec. Am. Crystal Sugar Co., 1973—, No. Grain Co., 1975—; gen. counsel, dir. Am. Bank and Trust Co., 1969—. Regent U. Minn., 1979—; mem. Minn. State Senate, 1959-73. Served to capt. USNR, 1945-46, 51-53. Mem. Minn. State Bar Assn., Clay County Bar Assn. Republican. Lutheran. Clubs: Masons, Lions. Home: 3122 Rivershore Dr Moorhead MN 56560 Office: American Bank and Trust Co Bldg Moorhead MN 56560

DOSS, LAWRENCE PAUL, accounting firm executive; b. Cleve., June 16, 1927; s. Raymond Milton and Velma Lorraine (Kendall) D.; children: Paula, Lawrence, Lawry. Student, Ohio State U., 1947-49, Fenn Coll., 1949-51, Am. U., 1954; M.A. in Pub. Adminstrn, Nova U. With IRS, Detroit, 1949-70, dir. data center, 1967-70; coordinator decentralization program Detroit Pub. Schs., 1970-71; pres. Detroit Urban Coalition, New Detroit, Inc., 1971-77; partner Coopers & Lybrand, 1978—. Pres. Inner City Bus. Improvement Forum, Detroit, 1967-71; treas. Fed. Exec. Bd., Detroit, 1968-70; chmn. Mich. Neighborhood Edn. Authority, 1971-77; operating chmn. Mayor's Detroit Crime Task Force, 1976—; co-chmn. Move Detroit Forward, 1978—; mem. exec. com. Sch. Desegregation Monitoring Commn., 1976-78; bd. dirs., exec. com. Martin Luther King Center for Social Change; bd. dirs. New Detroit, Congl. Black Caucus, Am. Natural Resources, Inc.; trustee Hudson-Webber Founds., U. Detroit, United Found., Detroit; chmn. corp. urban affairs adv. council, mem. steering com. Nat. Urban Coalition; chmn. devel. commn. Black United Fund of Detroit.; mem. Mich. Commn. on Jobs and Econ. Devel.; chmn. fin. com. Wayne County Reorgn. Task Force; chmn. Coleman A. Young Found.; exec. vice chmn. D.C. Commn. on Crime and Justice, 1982—. Served with USNR, 1945-46. Recipient Meritorious Achievement award William A. Jump Found., 1964, U.S. Treasury Dept., 1964, Presdl. citation, 1964; named Citizen of the Year Omega Psi Phi, Detroit, 1974. Mem. Omega Psi Phi. Home: 651 Rivard Detroit MI 48207 Office: 400 Renaissance Center Detroit MI 48234

DOSTMAYER, PETER HOUSTON, congressman; b. N.Y.C., Sept. 27, 1946; s. John Houston and Julia Claiborne (Carson) Kostmayer; m. Pamela Jones Rosenberg, 1982; 2 stepdaus. B.A., Columbia U., 1971. Press sec. to atty. gen. State of Pa., 1972-73, dep. press sec. to gov., Harrisburg, 1973-76; mem. 95th-96th, 98th congresses from 8th Dist. Pa. Regional coordinator McGovern-Shriver campaign S.E. Pa., 1972. Democrat. Episcopalian. Office: Room 123 Cannon House Office Bldg Washington DC 20515

DOTEN, GEORGE WILLIAM, educator; b. Plymouth, Mass., Oct. 24, 1923; s. Everett Clifton and Edith (Wall) D.; m. Ramona Card, Sept. 5, 1948; children—Reed, Todd. B.S., U. Mass., 1948, M.S., 1950; Ph.D., Northwestern U., 1952. Asst. prof. psychology St. Lawrence U., Canton, N.Y., 1952-56; asso. social scientist RAND Corp., 1956-57; group head, human factor scientist System Devel. Corp., 1957-68; prof. psychology Trinity Coll., Hartford, Conn., 1968—, chmn. dept., 1968-75, 78-79. Sec. local troop Boy Scouts Am.; pres. Wetherfield (Conn.) Little League, 1971-72; mem. child advocacy center adv. com. Conn. Child Welfare Assn., 1972. Mem. Am., New Eng., Eastern psychol. assns., A.A.U.P., Am. Contract Bridge League, Sigma Xi. Home: 99 Meadow View Dr Wetherfield CT 06109 Office: Trinity Coll Hartford CT 06106

DOTSON, DONALD L., government official; b. Rutherford County, N.C., Oct. 8, 1938; s. Herman A. and Lottie E. (Hardin) D. A.B., U. N.C., 1960; J.D., Wake Forest U., Winston-Salem, N.C., 1968. Bar: N.C., Pa., U.S. Supreme Ct. Atty. NLRB, 1968-73, chmn., 1983—; labor counsel Westinghouse Electric Corp., 1973-75; labor atty. Western Electric Co., 1975-76; chief labor counsel Wheeling-Pitts. Steel Corp., 1976-81; asst. sec. labor, 1981-83. Served with USN, 1960-65. Mem. ABA. Republican. Episcopalian.

DOTSON, GEORGE STEPHEN, drilling company executive; b. Okemah, Okla., Dec. 25, 1940; s. Hilmer C. and Alma Lucille (McGee) D.; m. Phyllis A. Nickerson, Aug. 17, 1963; children: Sarah, Grant. B.S., M.I.T., 1963; M.B.A., Harvard U., 1970. Asst. to pres. Helmerich & Payne, Inc., Tulsa, 1970-73; v.p. Helmerich & Payne (Peru) Drilling Co., 1974-75, Helmerich & Payne Internat. Drilling Co., 1976-77, pres., chief operating officer, 1977—; v.p. drilling Helmerich & Payne, Inc., 1977—. Served to capt. U.S. Army, 1964-68. Decorated Bronze Star. Office: Helmerich & Payne Internat Drilling Co Utica at 21st Sts Tulsa OK 74114

DOTSON, JOHN LOUIS, JR., magazine editor; b. Paterson, N.J., Feb. 5, 1937; s. John Louis and Evelyn Elizabeth (Nelson) D.; m. Peggy Elaine Burnette, Apr. 4, 1959; children: John, Damon, Christopher, Brandon, Leslie. B.S., Temple U., 1958, Doctor of Journalism (hon.), 1981. Reporter Newark News, 1959-64; gen. assignment reporter Detroit Free Press, 1965; corr. Newsweek mag., Detroit, 1965-69, Los Angeles, 1969-70, bur. chief, 1970-75, news editor, N.Y.C., 1976-77, sr. editor, 1977—; asst. to exec. editor Philadelphia Inquirer, 1983—; bd. dirs. Inst. Journalism Edn., 1974—, treas., 1974-78, chmn., 1980—. Exec. editor, Michelle Clark Fellowship program Columbia U., 1974. Bd. visitors John S. Knight Fellowships Stanford U, 1983. Office: Newsweek Mag 444 Madison Ave New York NY 10022

DOTSON, ROBERT CHARLES, TV news correspondent; b. St. Louis, Oct. 3, 1946; s. William Henry and Dorothy (Bailey) D.; m. Linda Puckett, July 1, 1972; 1 dau., Amy Michelle. B.S. in Journalism and Polit. Sci., Kans. U., 1968; M.S. in TV, Syracuse U., 1969. Reporter, photographer, documentary producer KMBC-TV, Kansas City, Mo., 1967-68; WKY-TV, Oklahoma City, 1969-75, WKYC-TV, Cleve., 1975-77; network news corr. NBC News, Dallas, 1977-79; corr. Today Show, NBC, Prime Time Sunday, 1979-80, Atlanta, 1979—; vis. prof. journalism U. Okla., 1969-73. Documentaries include Through the Looking Glass Darkly, 1974 (Emmy award, RFK award), The Urban Reservation, 1975 (RFK award), Still Got Life To Go, 1972 (Emmy nomination), Smoke and Steel, 1973 (Emmy nomination), The Sunshine Child, 1982 (Emmy nomination). Mem. Sigma Delta Chi. Office: NBC News 100 Colony Sq 1175 Peachtree St Suite 300 Atlanta GA 30361

DOTT, ROBERT HENRY, JR., educator; b. Tulsa, June 2, 1929; s. Robert Henry and Esther Edgerton (Reed) D.; m. Nancy Maud Robertson, Feb. 1, 1951; children—James, Karen, Eric, Cynthia, Brian. Student, U. Okla., 1946-48; B.S., U. Mich., 1950, M.S., 1951; Ph.D. (AEC fellow), Columbia, 1955. Exploration geologist Humble Oil & Refining Co., Ariz., Oreg., Wash., 1954-56, So. Calif., 1958; mem. faculty U. Wis.-Madison, 1958—, prof. geology, 1966—, chmn. dept. geology and geophysics, 1974-77; vis. prof. U. Calif. at Berkeley, 1969; lectr. Tulsa U., 1969; NSF sci. faculty fellow Stanford U. and U.S. Geol. Survey, 1978, U. Colo., 1979; cons. Roan Selection Trust, Ltd., Zambia, 1967. Author: (with R.L. Batten) Evolution of the Earth, 1971, 3d edit., 1981; Contbr. articles on sedimentology, tectonics, geology of So. Andes and history of geology to profl. jours. Served to 1st lt. USAF, 1956-57. Recipient Outstanding Tchr. award Wis. Student Assn., 1969. Fellow Geol. Soc. Am.; mem. Am. Assn. Petroleum Geologists (Pres.'s award 1956), Soc. Econ. Paleontologists and Mineralogists (sec.-treas. 1968-70, v.p. 1972-73, pres. 1981-82), AAAS, Internat. Assn. Sedimentologists, Sigma Xi. Unitarian. Office: Dept Geology and Geophysics Univ Wisconsin Madison WI 53706 *To understand the earth's past, which no human was around to witness, has long seemed to me the most exciting challenge imaginable. It is like a great Sherlock Holmes mystery story.*

DOTTER, CHARLES THEODORE, radiology educator, researcher; b. Boston, June 14, 1920; s. John Maury and Rosalind (Allin) D.; m. Pamela Beattie, Sept. 30, 1944; children: Barbara Allin, Jeffrey Churchill, Jane Huntington. A.B., Duke U., 1941; M.D., Cornell U., 1944. Diplomate: Am. Bd. Radiology, 1950. Instr. medicine Cornell U. Med. Coll., N.Y.C., 1948-52, instr. radiology, 1948-51, asst. prof. radiology, 1951-52; mem. faculty Oreg. Health Scis. U., Portland, 1952—, now prof. radiology, chmn. dept.; cons. VA Hosp., Portland; mem. rev. bd. Nat. Heart and Lung Inst., 1965-68; mem. surg. drugs adv. com. FDA, 1974-77, chmn. com., 1977-78. Author: (with Israel Steinberg) Angiocardiography; contbr. over 300 articles to sci. jours.; author/producer 2 med. films. Served to lt. (j.g.) USNR, 1944-45; surgeon USMC, 1945-46; CBI. Recipient Gold medal Chgo. Med. Soc./Chgo. Radiol. Soc., 1981, Radiol. Soc. N.Am., 1981, Am. Coll. Radiology, 1983. Fellow Am. Coll. Angiology, Am. Coll. Radiology; mem. Am. Heart Assn., AMA, Am. Roentgen Ray Soc., Assn. Univ. Radiologists, Czechoslovak Med. Soc. (hon.), Internat. Cardiovascular Soc., Internat. Soc. Angiology, Multnomah County Med. Soc., Oreg. Heart Assn., Oreg. Radiol. Soc., Oreg. Med. Soc., Oreg. Thoracic Soc., Pacific N.W. Radiol. Soc., Radiol. Soc. N.Am., Soc. Chairmen Acad. Radiology Depts., Soc. Cardiovascular Radiology, Western Angiography Soc. Clubs: American Alpine, Mazamas (Portland). Office: 3181 SW Sam Jackson Park Rd Portland OR 97201

DOTTS, HAROLD WILLIAM, public relations executive; b. Corydon, Ia., May 7, 1904; s. William E. and Pauline (Goodell) D.; m. Evelyn Dosey, Oct. 10, 1931; children—Harold W., Robert D., Dorothy Catherine; m. Glady Carlisle, Dec. 26, 1965. A.B., Simpson Coll., 1926; postgrad., Harvard Bus. Sch., 1936. With Jewel Tea Co., Barrington, Ill., 1926-53, successively salesman, asst. mgr., br. and dist. mgr., asst. gen. sales mgr., gen. sales mgr. and v.p., 1942-53; pres. Stonegate China Co., 1953-62; exec. dir. Nat. Home Service Assn., 1962-68; with Knox Assos., Oak Brook, Ill., 1968-70; pub. relations dir. Northwest Trust & Savs. Bank, Arlington Heights, Ill., 1970-78. Dir. Northwest Community Hosp. Found., 1978—; Trustee Simpson Coll., Northwest Community Hosp. Mem. Am. Soc. Assn. Execs., Nat. Premium Sales Execs., Epsilon Sigma. Republican. Clubs: Chicago Sales Executives (pres. 1948-49), Nat. Sales Executive (dir. 1950-54), Economic). Home: 1015 S Highland Arlington Heights IL 60005 Office: 800 W Central Rd Arlington Heights IL *I have learned that job competition is easy when I select things that most people do not like to do and learn to do them so well that I enjoy doing them.*

DOTY, BENJAMIN EUGENE, army officer; b. Kellogg, Idaho, Mar. 24, 1931; s. Harvey Hammer and Anna Mary (Doubt) D.; m. Patricia M. Dyson, Sept. 5, 1954; children: Diana M., Craig A. B.A., U. Idaho, 1953; postgrad., Command and Gen. Staff Coll., 1965, Army War Coll., 1970; M.S., Shippensburg State Coll., 1972. Commd. 2d lt. U.S. Army, 1953, advanced through grades to maj. gen., 1981; served in, Vietnam, Europe; asst. div. comdr. 2d Armored Div., Ft. Hood, Tex., 1978-80; comdr. U.S. Army Combat Devel. Experimentation Command, Ft. Ord, Calif., 1980-81; comdg. gen. TRADOC Combined Arms Test Activity, Ft. Hood, 1981-83, U.S. Army Operational Test and Evaluation Agy., Falls Church, Va., 1983—. Decorated Legion of Merit, Bronze Star with oak leaf clusters, Air medal (2), others. Home: 8350 Wickham Rd Springfield VA 22152 Office: Comdg Gen US Army Operational Test and Evaluation Agy 5600 Columbia Pike Falls Church VA 22041

DOTY, DAVID SINGLETON, lawyer; b. Anoka, Minn., June 30, 1929. B.A., U. Minn., 1961, LL.B., 1961. Bar: Minn. 1961, U.S. Ct. Appeals (8th and 9th cirs.) 1976, U.S. Supreme Ct. 1982. V.p., dir. Popham, Haik, Schnobrich, Kaufman & Doty, Mpls., 1962—, pres.,

1977-79; instr. William Mitchell Coll. Law, Mpls., 1963-64; mem. com. public edn. and info. Minn. Supreme Ct., 1978-81. Trustee Mpls. Library Bd., 1969-79, Mpls. Found., 1976-83. Fellow ABA Found., Mem., Minn. Bar Assn. (gov. 1976-83, sec. 1980-83, pres.-elect 1983), Hennepin County Bar Assn. (pres. 1975-76), Am. Judicature Soc. Home: 23 Greenway Gables Minneapolis MN 55403 Office: 4344 IDS Center Minneapolis MN 55402

DOTY, DONALD D., banker; b. Independence, Kans., June 30, 1928; s. Laton L. and Dorothy (Russell) D.; m. Cheri F. Montgomery, June 14, 1952; children: John Scott, Susan Dorothy, Mark Montgomery. B.S., Okla. State U., 1950; postgrad., U. Wis. Grad. Sch. Banking, 1963. Rancher, nr. Bartlesville, Okla., 1950-53; with First Nat. Bank, Bartlesville, 1955—, asst. v.p., 1960-62, v.p., 1962-69, exec. v.p., 1969-76, pres., 1976—, also dir.; v.p., dir. Rocking D Land & Cattle Co., Bartlesville, New Camp Minerals, Inc., Wichita, Kan.; pres. First Bancshares, Inc., Bartlesville, 1974—; chmn. First Okla. Ventures Corp., Bartlesville.; Pres. Bartlesville Credit Bur., 1972—; pres. Bartlesville-Area Indsl. Devel. Co., 1970—. Chmn. trustees Jane Phillips Episcopal Meml. Med. Center, 1970—; trustee Washington County Indsl. Devel. Trust Authority, 1973-80, Frank Phillips Found., Bartlesville, 1975—. Served to capt. USAF, 1953-55. Recipient Disting. Service award Bartlesville, 1957. Mem. Bartlesville C. of C. (v.p., bd. dirs. 1965-81, pres. 1981-82), Sigma Alpha Epsilon. Republican. Episcopalian. Clubs: Masons, Shriners, Jesters, Rotary, Hillcrest Country (Bartlesville). Home: 1915 Hillcrest Dr Bartlesville OK 74003 Office: Box 999 Bartlesville OK 74003

DOTY, JAMES ROBERT, lawyer; b. Houston, May 14, 1940; s. Robert Earl and Vivian (Weaver) D.; m. Joan Richardson, June 10, 1972; children: Katherine Brooks, Robert, Daniel. B.A., Rice U., 1972; A.B., Oxford U., Eng., 1963; LL.B., Yale U., 1969. Bar: Tex. 1969. Ptnr. Baker & Botts, Houston, 1977—. Sr. warden Christ Ch. Cathedral; trustee Endowments Bd. Rhodes Scholar, 1962. Mem. Am. Law Inst., Houston Bar Assn., State Bar Tex., ABA. Office: 3000 One Shell Plaza Houston TX 77002

DOTY, JAY LOWELL, banker; b. Chgo., Nov. 1, 1938; s. James L. and Gertrude (Cywinski) D.; m. Susan G. Indridson, Sept. 8, 1967 (div.); 1 son, David Maves. B.S., Northwestern U., 1960; M.B.A., Harvard U., 1962. Vice pres. 1st Nat. Bank of Chgo., 1967-76; exec. v.p. Bank of Calif., San Francisco, 1976—. Served with U.S. Army, 1962-65. Mem. Am. Bankers Assn., Assn. Res. City Bankers, Robert Morris Assocs. Clubs: San Francisco Yacht, San Francisco Bay, Chgo. Yacht. Office: Bank of California 400 California St San Francisco CA 94104

DOUAIHY, SALIBA, artist; b. Ehden, Lebanon, Sept. 14, 1915; s. Anthony and Yasmin (Frangieh) D. One-man exhbns. include, Contemporaries Gallery, N.Y.C., 1966, Gallery One, Beirut, Lebanon, 1945-49, 71, 73, Livingston-Learmonth Gallery, N.Y.C., 1976, N.C. Mus. Art, Raleigh, 1978, group exhbns. include, Phila. Mus. Art, 1952, Guggenheim Mus., N.Y.C., 1967, Pa. Acad. Fine Arts, 1967, 68, Salon de Realites Nouvelles, Paris, 1973, Butler Inst. Am., Younstown, Ohio, 1974, Museo de Folkore Romano, Rome, Italy, 1977; represented in permanent collections, Akron Art Inst., Albright-Knox Art Gallery, Guggenheim Mus., Mus. Modern Art, N.Y.C., N.Y. U. Art Collection, Butler Inst. Am. Art, N.C. Mus. Art, Newark Mus., Syracuse U. (N.Y.). Recipient Medalia d'oro Accademia Italia delle arte, 1980. Mem. Artist Equity Assn. Vining Rd Windham NY 12496 also 74 Cornwall Gardens London England SW7

DOUB, WILLIAM OFFUTT, lawyer; b. Cumberland, Md., Sept. 3, 1931; s. Albert A. and Fannabelle (Offutt) D.; m. Mary Graham Boggs, Sept. 12, 1959; children: Joseph Peyton, Albert A., II. A.B., Washington and Jefferson Coll., 1953; LL.B., U. Md., 1956. Bar: Md. 1956, D.C. 1974. With law dept. B. & O. R.R., 1955-57; assoc. firm Bartlett Poe & Claggett, Balt., 1957-61; ptnr. firm Niles Barton & Wilmer, Balt., 1961-71; commr. AEC, 1971-74; ptnr. firm LeBoeuf, Lamb, Leiby & MacRae, Washington, 1974-77, Doub & Muntzing, 1977—; Chmn. Minimum Wage Commn., Balt., 1964-66; peoples' counsel Md. Pub. Service Commn., 1967-68, chmn., 1968-71; vice chmn. Washington Met. Area Transit Commn., 1968-71; mem. President's Air Quality Adv. Bd., 1970-71; mem. exec. adv. com. FPC, 1969-71, Nat. Gas Survey, 1975-78; pres. Great Lakes Conf. Pub. Utility Commrs., 1971; mem. nat. adv. bd. Am. Nat. Standards Inst., 1975-80; mem. Md. Adv. Com. Retardation, 1969-71. Mem. Adminstrv. Conf. U.S., 1973-75; chmn. U.S. nat. com. World Energy Conf., 1978-80, U.S. del., 1974, 77, 80, 83; mem. adv. groups Nat. Acad. Public Adminstrn., NSF; U.S. rep. So. States Energy Bd.; trustee Thomas Alva Edison Found.; bd. govs. Middle East Inst. Clubs: Metropolitan, City Tavern (Washington). Home: 6 Warde Ct Potomac MD 20854

DOUBET, EARL WESLEY, machinery co. exec.; b. Peoria, Ill., Aug. 13, 1926; s. Earl Wesley and Julia (Petzing) D.; m. Norma Mae Hill, Jan. 28, 1951; children—Earl Wesley III, Steven H. Diploma in Civil Engring, Oreg. State Coll., 1944; B.S.C., Bradley U., 1948; postgrad., Mass. Inst. Tech., 1966. Sales mgr. Caterpillar Tractor Co., Ltd., Glasgow, Scotland, 1959-61; European sales mgr. Caterpillar Overseas SA, Geneva, Switzerland, 1961-63, sales mgr., 1963-65; pres. Caterpillar Americas Co., Peoria, 1965-66; v.p. Towmotor Corp., Cleve., 1966-68, exec. v.p., 1968-70; mgr. new products Caterpillar Tractor Co., Peoria, 1970-71; mng. dir. lift truck operations Caterpillar Overseas S.A., Geneva, 1972-75; pres. Caterpillar Ams. Co., 1975—, Caterpillar Machinery Corp., Peoria, 1975—. Trustee Council of Ams. Served with AUS, World War II. Mem. Constrn. Machinery Mfrs. Assn. (chmn. fgn. ops. council), Nat. Alumni Assn. Bradley U. (dir.). Presbyn. Club: Mason (Shriner). Home: 323 E Morningside Dr Peoria IL 61614

DOUBLEDAY, NELSON, publisher, baseball exec. Grad., Princeton, 1954. With Doubleday & Co., Inc., 1954-56, 59—; now pres., chief exec. officer; chmn. bd., majority owner N.Y. Mets Baseball Team, 1980—. Served with USAF, 1956-59. Office: Doubleday & Co Inc 245 Park Ave New York NY 10167 *

DOUCE, WAYNE RICHARD, lawyer; b. Narka, Kans., Apr. 16, 1928; s. Jay Elwood and Elva Gertrude (Skipton) D.; m. Waneta Rose Biery, Aug. 28, 1949; children—Donald, Dwight, Denise. B.S., Kans. State U., 1949; J.D., U. Nebr., 1952. Bar: Nebr. 1952. Dep. city atty., City of Lincoln, Nebr., 1954-57, dept. atty. dept. ins., Lincoln, State of Nebr., 1957-61; mem. legal dept. Guarantee Mut. Life Co., Omaha, 1961—, sr. v.p., gen. counsel, dir., 1971—; Mem. Nebr. Hwy. Bond Commn., 1969-73. Trustee Nebr. Tax Research Council, Inc. Served with USAF, 1952-54. Mem. Omaha C. of C., Assn. Life Ins. Counsel, Am., Nebr., Omaha bar assns. Republican. Methodist. Club: Rotary. Home: 615 S 122d St Omaha NE 68154 Office: 8721 Indian Hills Dr Omaha NE 68114

DOUCE, WILLIAM CLARK, petroleum company executive; b. Kingman, Kans., Dec. 9, 1919; s. William Thew and Grace (Griswold) D.; m. Willene Brady Magruder, June 14, 1943; children: Terri Douce Springer, William Clark. B.S., U. Kans., 1942. With Phillips Petroleum Co., various locations, 1942—, mgr. chem. dept., 1966-69, sr. v.p., 1969-71, exec. v.p., from 1971, now pres., chief exec. officer, also dir.; dir. 1st Nat. Bank & Trust Co., Tulsa, 1st Nat. Bank, Bartlesville, Okla., Morrison-Knudson Co., Inc., Boise, Idaho. Trustee U. Tulsa, Jane Phillips Meml. Hosp. Center, Bartlesville, U. Kans. Endowment Assn.; bd. dirs. Nat. Council U.S.-China Trade, Philbrook Art Mus., Tulsa. Mem. NAM (dir.), Am. Petroleum Inst. (exec. com.), U. Kans. Alumni Assn. (pres. 1975), Bus. Roundtable, Nat. Petroleum Council, Council Fgn. Relations, Theta Tau, Phi Gamma Delta, Tau Beta Pi, Sigma Tau. Presbyterian. Club: Hillcrest Country (Bartlesville). Lodges: Masons; Shriners; Jesters. Office: Phillips Bldg Bartlesville OK 74004 *

DOUCETTE, JOSEPH JAMES, insurance company executive; b. Boston, Dec. 5, 1929; s. Joseph John and Helen Agnes (Lally) D.; m. Mary Louise Lillis, June 12, 1954; children: Bernadette, Mary Lou, Doucette Twomey, Joseph M., Sheila, Stephen, Therese, Paula. A.B. in Math., Boston Coll., 1951; M.Ed., Boston State Tchrs. Coll., 1952. Tchr. math. Boston Latin High Sch., 1952-53; instr. math. R.I. Sch. Design, Providence, 1957-59; actuarial fellow John Hancock Life Ins. Co., Boston, 1959-65; 2d v.p. New Eng. Life Ins. Co., Boston, 1965-71; sr. v.p. Union Mut. Life Ins. Co., Portland, Maine, 1971-83; v.p. Allstate Life Ins. Co., Northbrook, Ill., 1983—. Served to lt. USN, 1953-57. Fellow Soc. Actuaries; mem. Am. Acad. Actuaries. Republican. Roman Catholic. Home: 711 Oxbow Ln Barrington IL 60010 Office: Allstate Life Ins Co 60 Allstate Plaza Northbrook IL 60062

DOUD, WALLACE C., information systems executive; b. Bellingham, Wash., Feb. 25, 1925; s. Forest Roy and Florence (Pollock) D.; m. Marjorie K. Fenton, Oct. 25, 1949; children: Forrest J., Mary, Margaret, Barbara, Melissa, Michael, Karen; m. Janice F. Freudenberg, June 15, 1963 (dec. 1978); m. Jean A. Kennedy, Oct. 13, 1979. B.B.A., U. Wis., 1948; H.H.D. hon., Mercy Coll., 1983. With IBM, successively salesman, Milw., St. Paul, Detroit, then dir. patent relations, 1960-71, v.p. services staff, 1971-77, v.p. comml. and indsl. relations, Armonk, N.Y., 1977—; dir. Bank N.Y., White Plains. Chmn. Bd. Parks and Recreation White Plains, N.Y., 1983-84; chmn., pres. United Way, White Plains, N.Y., 1975-80. Recipient Youth Services B'nai B'rith, 1972, Medallion Westchester Community Coll., 1980. Republican. Presbyterian. Clubs: Whippoorwill (Armonk, N.Y.) (dir. 1984); Country of Fla. (Boynton Beach); Innisbrook Golf (Tarpon Springs, Fla.). Office: IBM Armonk NY *

DOUGAL, ARWIN ADELBERT, educator, electrical engineer; b. Dunlap, Iowa, Nov. 22, 1926; s. Adelbert Isaac and Goldya (White) D.; m. Margaret Jane McLennan, Sept. 3, 1951; children: Catherine Ann, Roger Adelbert, Leonard Harley, Laura Beth. B.S., Iowa State U., 1952; M.S., U. Ill., 1955, Ph.D., 1957. Registered profl. engr., Tex. Radio engr. Collins Radio Co., Cedar Rapids, Iowa, 1952; research asst., research asso., asst. prof., asso. prof. U. Ill., Urbana, 1952-61; prof., mem. grad. faculty, dir. labs. for electronics and related sci. research U. Tex., Austin, 1961-67, prof., 1969—; dir. Electronics Research Center, 1971-77, sec. grad. assembly, 1972-74; dir. Austron, Inc., 1977-82; asst. dir. def. research and engring. for research Office Sec. Def., Washington, 1967-69; cons. Tex. Instruments, Inc., Dallas, Gen. Dynamics Corp., Ft. Worth, U. Calif. Los Alamos Sci. Lab. Contbr. articles to profl. jours. Faculty sponsor U. Tex. Conservative Democrats Club, 1966-67; sr. mem. CAP, 1984—. Served with USAF, 1946-49. Recipient Teaching Excellence awards U. Tex. Students Assn., 1962, 63, Spl. award for outstanding service as program chmn. S.W. IEEE Conf. and Exhbn., 1967; Outstanding Grad. Adviser award Grad. Engring. Council, U. Tex., 1971; Disting. Advisor award Grad. Engring. Council, U. Tex., 1977, 84; Teaching Achievement award Grad. Engring. Council, U. Tex., 1977; Profl. Achievement citation in engring. Iowa State U. Alumni Assn., 1975. Fellow Am. Phys. Soc., IEEE (dir. 1980-81, Centennial medal 1984); mem. Am. Soc. Engring. Edn., Optical Soc. Am., Sigma Xi, Phi Kappa Phi, Tau Beta Pi, Eta Kappa Nu, Pi Mu Epsilon, Phi Eta Sigma. Presbyn. (elder). Club: Lakeway Yacht and Country. Home: 6115 Rickey Dr Austin TX 78731

DOUGAN, ROBERT ORMES, librarian; b. Ilford, Essex, Eng., Aug. 21, 1904; came to U.S., 1958, naturalized, 1964; s. Hugh and Rebecca (Ormes) D.; m. Olive Constant McMicken, Oct. 3, 1929 (dec. Jan. 1963); m. Margaret Truax Hunter, Jan. 21, 1964. Diploma librarianship, Univ. Coll., London, 1929; M.A., Trinity Coll., U. Dublin, Ireland, 1954; D.Lit., U. Redlands, 1974. Partime librarian Royal Hist. Soc., London, 1925-35; bibliog. research worker, cataloguer E.P. Goldschmidt and Co., Ltd., London, 1926-40; librarian Sandeman Pub. Library, Perth, Scotland, 1945-52; dep. librarian Trinity Coll., 1952-58; librarian Henry E. Huntington Library and Art Gallery, San Marino, Calif., 1958-72; lectr. for Foras Eireann, Dublin, 1955-58; organizer 2 Scottish book exhbns. Festival of Britain, 1950-51; Mem. Calif. Adv. Council Edn. Librarianship, 1962-65. Served to flight lt. RAF, 1941-45. Fellow Library Assn. U.K.; mem. Bibliog. Soc. U.K., A.L.A. (chmn. rare books sect. 1964-65), Internat. Bibliophile Assn. Presbyn. (elder). Club: Grolier. Collections of hist. photography in Met. Mus. Art, N.Y.C., Princeton U. Art Mus., Glasgow U. Library (Scotland). Home: 2663 Tallant Rd Apt N-293 Santa Barbara CA 93105

DOUGHERTY, CHARLES JOSEPH, utility executive; b. Clayton, Mo., Apr. 29, 1919; s. Harry J. and Loretto (Grace) D.; m. Suzanne L. Hamilton, May 1, 1943; children: Charles H., Mary Suzanne (Mrs. Thomas E. Helfrich), Amy Louise (Mrs. David R. Turissini). B.S.C., St. Louis U., 1941, LL.B., 1950. Bar: Mo. bar 1950. With Union Electric Co., St. Louis, 1941—, gen. counsel, 1964, exec. v.p., 1964-66, pres., 1966-80, dir., 1966—, chief exec. officer, 1968—, chmn. bd., 1980—; dir. Boatmen's Nat. Bank St. Louis, Boatman's Bancshares, Inc. Trustee Mo. Pub. Expenditure Survey, 1966—, Govtl. Research Inst., 1967-78; bd. dirs. Jr. Achievement Mississippi Valley, Inc., 1968—; mem. exec. bd. St. Louis Area Council Boy Scouts Am., 1966—; mem. pres.'s council St. Louis U.; exec. com. United Fund Greater St. Louis, Inc., 1967-77; bd. dirs. Municipal Theatre Assn., St. Louis, 1968—, Civic Center Redevel. Corp., 1970-81; chmn. Civic Center Redevel. Corp., 1975-81; vice chmn. parents council, bd. dirs. St. Mary's Coll., 1969-70, chmn., 1970-72. Served with USMCR, 1942-46. Recipient St. Louis U. Alumni Merit award, 1966. Mem. Am. Bar Assn., Mo. Bar, Bar Assn. St. Louis, C. of C. Met. St. Louis (dir. 1962-71, pres. 1970), Civic Progress, Inc., Nat. Assn. Electric Cos. (dir. 1968-71), Edison Electric Inst. (dir. 1968-71, 72-75, 80—, vice chmn. 1982-83, chmn. 1983-84), Assn. Edison Illuminating Cos. (exec. com. 1968-82, v.p. 1980, pres. 1981), Mo. Valley Elec. Assn. (exec. com. 1966-71), S.W. Electric Conf. (exec. com. 1969-71, 74-77), Atomic Indsl. Forum (dir. 1981—), Electric Power Research Inst. (dir. 1982—), Mo. C. of C. (dir. 1968-72), Alpha Sigma Nu. Clubs: St. Louis (dir. 1968-74), Old Warson Country (St. Louis); Stadium, Bogey, Noonday. Home: 18 Huntleigh Woods Saint Louis MO 63131 Office: PO Box 149 1901 Gratiot St Saint Louis MO 63166

DOUGHERTY, DANIEL JOSEPH, banker; b. Pitts., Aug. 28, 1931; s. Robert Joseph and Margaret Claire (McMahon) D.; m. Rose Marie Boyle, May 30, 1954; children—Dennis, Colleen, Mary, Daniel. B.A., Duquesne U., 1954. Advt. asst. Rockwell Mfg. Co., Pitts., 1957; asst. advt. mgr. Calgon Co., Pitts., 1958-62; account exec. Marsteller, Inc., Pitts., 1962-64; v.p. mktg. Pitts. Nat. Bank, 1964-74; v.p. mktg. Union Commerce Corp., Cleve., 1974—; exec. v.p. mktg. and retail banking Union Commerce Bank, Cleve., 1975—. Bd. dirs. Playhouse Sq. Assn., Downtown Bus. Council, Real Property Inventory Assn.; co-chmn. Cleve. Research Council. Served with USAF, 1954-57. Mem. Am. Mktg. Assn., Am. Banking Assn., Sales and Mktg. Execs. Assn., Bank Mktg. Assn., Bank Adminstrn. Inst. Clubs: Cleve. Athletic, Walden Coif, Communicators. Office: Union Commerce Bank Union Commerce Bldg Cleveland OH 44115

DOUGHERTY, DAVID MITCHELL, educator; b. Wilmington, Del., Aug. 6, 1903; s. George Myers and Jennie (Mitchell) D.; m. Edna M. Rettew, June 22, 1927 (dec. 1963); children: David M. Jr., Philip R.; m. Jean Bruere Jones, May 15, 1964. A.B., U. Del., 1925; A.M., Harvard U., 1927, Ph.D., 1932; student, U. Paris, 1923-24, 29. Tchr. Manlius (N.Y.) Sch., 1926-28; instr. French, MIT, 1929-30; instr. and tutor romance langs. Harvard U., 1929-31; asst. prof., assoc. prof., prof. romance langs. Clark U., 1931-46, chmn. dept., 1942-46, dir. A.S.T.P. unit, 1943-44, chmn. Acad. Council, 1943-45; dir. U. Del. Jr. Year Plan, Paris, 1939, Geneva, 1946-47; prof. romance langs. U. Ore., 1947-72, head dept. fgn. langs., 1947-64; dir. NDEA summer inst., Tours, France, 1961-68, exec. officer modern and classical langs. div., 1964-67, head dept. romance langs., 1967-69. Author: (with R. Picard and L. Wawrzyniak) Year Abroad, 1953, (with D. Hernried) Perspectives de la littérature française, 1961; Editor: (with E. B. Barnes) La Geste de Monglane, 1966, Le Galien de Chéltenham, 1981; Contbr. articles to ednl. jours., book revs. Trustee Episcopal Diocese of Oreg., 1973-76, v.p., 1974-76. Decorated Chevalier Legion of Honor, Medal of City of Tours, France). Mem. Modern Lang. Assn. Am., Medieval Acad. Am., Am. Assn. Tchrs. French (pres. 1966-70), Am. Assn. Tchrs. Spanish, Philol. Assn. Pacific Coast (pres. 1961-62), Société Rencesvals, Theta Chi. Episcopalian. Home: 2829 Central Blvd Eugene OR 97403

DOUGHERTY, DOUGLAS WAYNE, retail executive; b. Lemont, Ill., July 28, 1943; s. Wayne and Helen A. (Bancroft) D.; m. Shirley Darlene, Sept. 15, 1973; children: Beth Laurel, Erin Michelle. B.S., U. Dubuque, 1965; M.B.A., Kent State U., 1967. Fin. analyst Ford Motor Co., Detroit, 1967-70; fin. mgr. Dayton Hudson, Mpls., 1970-74, Copperweld Steel, Shelby, Ohio, 1975-76; group controller Cook United, Maple Heights, Ohio, 1976-78; v.p. May Dept. Stores, St. Louis, 1979-81; sr. v.p. Volume Shoe Corp., Topeka, 1982—. Lutheran. Office: Volume Shoe Corp 3231 E 6th St Topeka KS 66601

DOUGHERTY, GEORGE WIGHTON, publisher; b. Chgo., Aug. 7, 1921; s. Edward Hersey and Retta (Wighton) D.; m. Jeanette Trengove, June 12, 1964; children: Edward H., Barbara, Patricia Ann, David, Valerie, Michael George. Student, Columbia U., 1946-50. Printing and pub. salesman Dougherty Co., Inc., N.Y.C., 1946—, pres., 1950—; v.p. Bellak Color, Inc., Miami, Fla., 1968—; pres. Cycle Guide Publs., Inc., Compton, Calif., 1974—, Graphic Arts Cons. Co. Served to capt. USAAF, 1942-45; PTO. Decorated D.F.C., Air medal. Presbyterian. Clubs: Sleepy Hollow Country (Scarborough, N.Y.); Winged Foot Golf (Mamaroneck, N.Y.); Desert Island Country (Rancho Mirage, Calif.); La Quinta Hotel Golf (Calif.); N.Y. Athletic (N.Y.C.). Office: 770 Lexington Ave New York NY 10021

DOUGHERTY, JAMES DOUGLAS, lawyer; b. Baldwin, N.Y., Dec. 29, 1936; s. Thomas Francis and Jean May (Young) D.; m. Nancy Harrington Decker, Dec. 29, 1971. A.B., Dartmouth Coll., 1958; LL.B., Columbia U., 1963; A.M.P., Harvard Bus. Sch., 1983. Bar: N.Y. 1963. Asso. firm Hughes Hubbard & Reed, N.Y.C., 1963-69, Shea & Gould, 1969-71; asso. gen. counsel Supermarkets Gen. Corp., Woodbridge, N.J., 1971-72, sec., gen. counsel, 1972—, v.p., 1975-81, sr. v.p., 1981—; pres., dir. 132 E. 19th St., Inc., N.Y.C., 1964-78; lectr. Practising Law Inst., N.Y.C., 1970-74, Advanced Mgmt. Research, 1974-78. Served to lt. (j.g.) USNR, 1958-60. Mem. Am. Bar Assn., Assn. Bar City N.Y. (spl. com. on consumer affairs 1973-77, spl. com. electronic funds transfer 1976-79), Am. Soc. Corp. Secs. Clubs: Shelter Island Yacht., Metropolitan. Home: 132 E 19th St New York NY 10003 also Tuthills Hill Shelter Island NY 11964 Office: 301 Blair Rd Woodbridge NJ 07095

DOUGHERTY, JAMES THOMAS, indsl. co. exec., lawyer; b. Chgo., Aug. 31, 1935; s. Edward Warren and Edna Margaret (Macadory) D.; m. Rosemary Saballus, Nov. 21, 1959; children—Janet, Michael, Scott. B.S., DePaul U., 1957, J.D., 1960. Bar: Ill. bar 1960. Asso. firm Arnstein, Gluck & Lehr, Chgo., 1960-65; asst. gen. counsel Maremont Corp., Chgo., 1965-69, Rockwell Internat. Corp., Pitts., 1969-71; gen. counsel NVF Co., Yorklyn, Del., 1971-76, Sharon Steel Corp., 1971-76; v.p., gen. counsel, sec. Allegheny Internat., Inc., Pitts., 1976—. Bd. dirs. Sharon Indsl. Devel. Authority, 1972-76, Shenango Valley Charitable Capital Fund, 1972-75. Mem. Ill., Chgo. bar assns. Home: 120 Pheasant Dr Pittsburgh PA 15238 Office: Allegheny Internat Inc Two Oliver Plaza Pittsburgh PA 15222

DOUGHERTY, JOHN CHRYSOSTOM, III, lawyer; b. Beeville, Tex., May 3, 1915; s. John Chrysostom and Mary V. (Henderson) D.; m. Mary Ireland Graves, Apr. 18, 1942 (dec. July 1977); children: Mary Ireland, John Chrysostom IV; m. Bea Ann Smith, June 1978 (div. 1981); m. Sarah B. Randle, 1981. B.A., U. Tex., 1937; LL.B., Harvard, 1940; diploma, Inter-Am. Acad. Internat. and Comparative Law, Havana, Cuba, 1948. Bar: Tex. bar 1940. Atty. Hewit & Dougherty, Beeville, Tex., 1940-41; partner Graves & Dougherty, Austin, Tex., 1946-50, Graves, Dougherty & Greenhill, 1950-57, Graves, Dougherty & Gee, 1957-60, Graves, Dougherty, Gee & Hearon, 1961-66, Graves, Dougherty, Gee, Hearon, Moody & Garwood, 1966-73, Graves, Dougherty, Hearon, Moody & Garwood, 1973-79, Graves, Dougherty, Hearon & Moody, 1979—; spl. asst. atty. gen., 1949-50, Hon. French consul, Austin, 1971—, lectr. on tax, estate planning, probate code, community property problems.; dir. InterFirst Bank Austin, N.A.; Mem. Tex. Submerged Lands Adv. Com., 1963-72, Tex. Bus. and Commerce Code Adv. Com., 1964-66, Gov.'s Com. on Marine Resources, 1970-71, Gov.'s Planning Com. on Colorado River Basin Water Quality Mgmt. Study, 1972-73, Tex. Legis. Property Tax Com., 1973-75. Co-editor: Texas Appellate Practice, 1964, 2d edit., 1977; Contbr.: Bowe, Estate Planning and Taxation; Texas Lawyers Practice Guide, 1967, 71, How to Live and Die with Texas Probate, 1968, 3d edit., 1979, 4th edit., 1983, Texas Estate Administration, 1975, 78; Mem. bd. editors: Appellate Procedure in Tex., 1964, 2d edit., 1982; contbr. articles to legal jours. Bd. dirs. Grenville Clark Fund at Dartmouth Coll., 1976—; past bd. dirs. Advanced Religious Study Found., Holy Cross Hosp., Nat. Pollution Control Found.; trustee St. Stephen's Sch., Austin, U. Tex. Law Sch. Found., Austin. Served as capt. C.I.C. AUS, 1941-44; Judge Adv. Gen. Corps, 1944-46; now maj. Res. Decorated Medaille Française, France; Medaille d'honneur en Argent des Affairs Etrangeres, France. Fellow Tex. Bar Found., Am. Bar Found., Am. Coll. Probate Counsel, Am. Coll. Tax Counsel, Tex. State Bar Coll.; mem. Am. Arbitration Assn. (mem. nat. panel arbitrators 1958—), Inter-Am. Bar Assn., ABA (mem. Ho. Dels. 1982—), Travis County Bar Assn. (pres.-elect 1978, pres. 1979-80), State Bar Tex. (chmn. sect. taxation 1965-66, pres.-elect 1978, pres. 1979-80, chmn. State Bar Coll. Bd. 1983-84), Internat. Fgn. Law Assn., Am. Fgn. Law Assn., Am. Law Inst., Am. Soc. Internat. Law (exec. council 1959-62), World Assn. Lawyers, Internat. Acad. Estate and Trust Law, Cum Laude Soc., Phi Beta Kappa, Phi Eta Sigma, Beta Theta Pi (dir. Tex. Beta Students Aid Fund). Presbyterian. Lodge: Rotary. Home: 6 Green Lanes Austin TX 78703 Office: PO Box 98 Austin TX 78767

DOUGHERTY, JOHN JOSEPH, clergyman; b. Jersey City, Sept. 16, 1907; s. John J. and Christina (Farrell) D. A.B., Seton Hall U., 1930; student, U. Propaganda, Rome, 1930-32; S.T.L., Gregorian U., Rome, 1934, Pontifical Bibl. Inst., Rome, 1934-37, D.S.S., 1948; L.H.D. (hon.), U. Detroit, 1960; LL.D., Rutgers U., 1962, St. Peter's Coll., 1964, St. Ambrose Coll., 1964; L.H.D., Seton Hall U., 1969. Ordained priest Roman Cath. Ch., 1933, papal chamberlain, 1954, domestic prelate, 1958, titular bishop of Cotenna and auxiliary to archbishop of, Newark, 1963—; pastor St. Rose of Lima Ch., Short Hills, N.J., 1969-77; prof. sacred scriptures Immaculate Conception Sem., Darlington, N.J., 1937-59; radio broadcasting CBS, NBC, ABC, 1946—; TV broadcasting CBS, NBC, 1951—; regent Inst. Judaeo Christian Studies, Seton Hall U., 1954-59, pres. univ., 1959-69, scholar in residence, 1977—; mem. Vatican Commn. on Radio and TV, 1956-60, Vatican Com. on Peace Studies, 1972-76; chmn. World Conf. Religion and Peace, 1974—. Author: Searching the Scriptures, 1959. Bd. dirs. Cath. Bibl. Assn., 1957-59, UNDA (Internat. Assn. Cath. Radio and TV), 1956-59; mem. nat. council UNA-USA, 1977—; mem. Nat. Citizens Commn. Internat. Coop., 1965, Adv. Com. Edn. of the Deaf, 1966; vice chmn. com. of dept. internat. affairs U.S.C.C., 1969-74; trustee Council Religion and Internat. Affairs, 1971—, chmn., 1973-77. Decorated Star of Solidarity, Italy; recipient Freedoms Found. medal, 1953; award Cath. TV Arts, 1959; Ann. Americanism award B'nai B'rith, 1965; citation NCCJ, 1965. Address: Seton Hall U South Orange NJ 07079

DOUGHERTY, JUDE PATRICK, university dean; b. Chgo., July 21, 1930; s. Edward Timothy and Cecilia Anastasia (Loew) D.; m. Patricia Ann Regan, Dec. 28, 1957; children—Thomas, Michael, John, Paul. B.A., Cath. U. Am., 1954, M.A., 1955, Ph.D., 1960. Instr. Marquette U., 1957-58; instr. Bellarmine Coll., 1958-60, asst. prof., 1960-63, assoc. prof., 1963-66, Cath. U. Am., 1966-76, prof., 1976—, dean, 1967—; Vis. assoc. prof. Georgetown U., summer, 1965; vis. prof. Katholieke Universiteit te Leuven, Belgium, 1974-75. Author: Recent American Naturalism, 1960; co-author: Approaches to Morality, 1966; Editor: Theological Directions of the Ecumenical Movement, 1964, The Impact of Vatican II, 1966; editor: Rev. of Metaphysics, 1971—; gen. editor: Studies in Philosophy and the History of Philosophy, 1978—. Bd. advisers Franklin J. Matchette Found., 1971—; trustee Bellarmine Coll., 1972-75; mem. Pontifical Acad., St. Thomas, Rome, 1981—. Recipient William T. Miles award Bellarmine Coll., 1964. Mem. Am. Philos. Assn., Am. Cath. Philos. Assn. (pres. 1974-75), Metaphys. Soc. Am., Washington Philosophy Club (pres. 1968-69), Soc. for Philosophy Religion (pres. 1978-79), Metaphys. Soc. Am. (pres. 1983-84). Home: 9036 Rouen Ln Potomac MD 20854 Office: 620 Michigan Ave NE 112A McMahon Washington DC 20064

DOUGHERTY, PHILIP HUGH, journalist; b. N.Y.C., Dec. 21, 1923; s. Philip Hugh and Helen Flavia (O'Callaghan) D.; m. Dorothy Patt Tuomey, Jan. 15, 1953; children—Paul John, Peter Dyer, Margaret Dru. Student, Columbia U. Sch. Gen. Studies, 1947-51. With N.Y. Times, N.Y.C., 1943—, soc. reporter, 1950-63, gen. assignment reporter, 1963-66, advt. news columnist, 1966—. Served with Mil. Police U.S. Army, 1943-46. Roman Catholic. Office: 229 W 43d St New York NY 10036

DOUGHERTY, RICHARD, journalist, author; b. Bolivar, N.Y., Aug. 7, 1921; s. John Peter and Elizabeth (Crelly) D.; m. Cynthia Abbott, Apr. 23, 1966; 1 dau. by previous marriage, Lisa. A.B., Columbia, 1948. Reporter N.Y. Herald Tribune, 1948-51; press officer N.Y.C. Govt., 1951-56; corp. pub. relations counsel, 1956-60; nat. polit. writer Washington Bur., N.Y. Herald Tribune, 1964-66; N.Y. bur. chief Los Angeles Times, 1966-72; press sec. McGovern Presdl. Campaign, 1972; v.p. pub. affairs Met. Mus. Art, 1974—. Author: novels A Summer World, 1960, Duggan, 1962, The Commissioner, 1962, We Dance and Sing, 1971; non-fiction Goodbye, Mr. Christian: A Personal Account of McGovern's Rise and Fall, 1973; play Fair Game for Lovers, 1964. Served with USAAF, 1942-45. Democrat. Club: Century Assn. (N.Y.C.). Home: 168 E 74th St New York NY 10021

DOUGHERTY, ROBERT ANTHONY, manufacturing company executive; b. St. Louis, May 3, 1928; s. Joseph A. and Venita E. (Gretline) D.; m. Rosemary Schmertmann, Jan. 29, 1955; children: Kevin, Patrick, Michael, Mary Ann, Timothy. B.S. in Mech. Engring, U. Notre Dame, 1952. Registered profl. engr., Calif.; cert. mfg. engr. Sales engr. Robert R. Stephens Machinery Co., St. Louis, 1952-60, dist. mgr., 1961-72; pres. Dougherty & Assos., Prairie Village, Kans., 1972—. Served with U.S. Army, 1946-48. Recipient Productivity award Coll. and Univ. Mfg. Edn. Council, 1979; Outstanding Engring. Achievements award San Fernando Valley Engrs. Council, 1980. Mem. Am. Soc. for Metals, Soc. Mfg. Engrs. (pres. 1980-81, dir. 1971-82, Region 5 award of merit 1969). Roman Catholic. Clubs: Round Hill Bath and Tennis (pres. 1971), Hillcrest Country (v.p. 1982), Hillcrest Country (pres. 1983—). Office: PO Box 8149 Prairie Village KS 66208

DOUGHERTY, RUSSELL ELLIOTT, association executive, retired air force officer; b. Glasgow, Ky., Nov. 15, 1920; s. Ewell Walter and Bess (House) D.; m. m Geralee Shaaber, Apr. 26, 1943 (dec. Jan. 1978); children: Diane Ellen (Mrs. James R. Streicker), Mark Elliott, William Bryant; m. Barbara Brooks Lake, Sept. 1978. A.B., Western Ky. U., 1941; J.D., U. Louisville, 1948; grad., Nat. War Coll., 1960; LL.D., U. Akron, 1975, U. Nebr., 1976, U. Louisville, 1977; D.Sc., Westminster Coll., 1976. Bar: Ky. bar 1948. Also U.S. Supreme Ct.; commd. 2d. lt. USAAF, 1943; advanced through grades to gen. USAF, 1972; various staff and command assignments in Far East Air Forces, SAC, U.S. European Command, World War II; dir. European region Office of Sec. of Def., 1965-67; dep. chief of staff for plans and operations Hdqrs. USAF, 1970; comdr. 2d Air Force (Strategic Air Command), 1971; chief of staff Supreme Hdqrs. Allied Powers Europe, 1972-74; comdr.-in-chief Strategic Air Command and dir. U.S. Strategic Target Planning, 1974-77, ret., 1977; exec. dir. Air Force Assn., 1980—; dir. Inter North Inc., Aerospace Corp.; cons. Rand Corp.; mem. Def. Sci. Bd.; planned Operation Powerflight Mission, 1957; U.S. planner Stanleyville (Republic Congo) Rescue Operation, 1964. Bd. visitors Nat. Def. U.; bd. dirs. Atlantic Council of U.S., Falcon Found. Decorated D.S.M. USAF; 3), D.S.M. Dept. Def.; 2), Legion of Merit; 3), Bronze Star.; recipient Outstanding Alumnus award Western Ky. U., 1976, David Sarnoff award Armed Forces Communications and Electronics Assn., 1980, Gen. Thomas D. White Nat. Def. award U.S. Air Force Acad., 1983; named Man of Yr. Nat. Jewish Hosp., 1976, Los Angeles Philanthropic Soc.d, 1976. Mem. Ky. Bar Assn., Omicron Delta Kappa, Phi Alpha Delta, Lambda Chi Alpha. Home: Forest Hills 2359 S Queen St Arlington VA 22202 Office: 1750 Pennsylvania Ave NW Washington DC 20006

DOUGHERTY, WILLIAM JOHN, architect; b. Louisville, Ohio, Feb. 28, 1933; s. William A. and Maxine J. (Polen) D.; m. Helen T. Parker, Mar. 15, 1957; 1 son, William Reid. B.S. in Architecture, Ga. Inst. Tech., 1960. Prin. William J. Dougherty (architect), Atlanta, 1966-74; pres. Dougherty Assos. (P.C.), Atlanta, 1974-80, Dougherty, Fernandez, Marchant, Inc., 1980-82; prin. Wm. J. Dougherty, FAIA, 1982—; pres. Custom Structures, Inc., Atlanta, 1980—; prin. archtl. works include residential and comml. bldgs.; Del. community devel. citizens adv. com. Atlanta Regional Commn., 1973-75, chmn. land use task force, 1975; mem. Atlanta Zoning Rev. Bd., 1974-83, chmn., 1976-77; mem. Atlanta Mayor's Task Force for New Grand Mus. Park, 1975; mem. energy com. Atlanta Bd. Edn., 1976-77; bd. dirs. Druid Hills Arts Council, 1973-75, pres., 1972-73; trustee Ga. Conservancy, 1976-78, chmn. land use adv. com., 1973-74. Contbg. author: Land Use, 1974. Trustee Atlanta Outdoor Activity Center, 1976-82, vice chmn., 1979-82; trustee Arts Festival of Atlanta, 1968-69, pres., 1969-70. Served with U.S. Army, 1953-55. Fellow AIA (Ivan Allen Sr. award for service to community Atlanta chpt. 1975, pres. Atlanta chpt. 1977-78, commr. urban planning, housing, human relations and hist. preservations coms. 1975-76); mem. Ga. Planning Assn. Office: PO Box 9727 Atlanta GA 30319

DOUGLAS, BRUCE LEE, oral surgeon, public health administrator, educator; b. N.Y.C., July 14, 1925; s. William and Carrie (Basescu) D.; m. Veronica J. Ramsden; children: Clifford, Steven, Jennifer; m. Janet R. Douglas; 1 dau., Sarah. A.B., Princeton U., 1947; D.D.S., N.Y. U., 1948; postgrad. in oral surgery, Columbia U., 1951; M.A. in Edn, Columbia U., 1955; diploma in higher edn, Columbia U., 1957; M.P.H., U. Calif. at Berkeley, 1962. Diplomate: Am. Bd. Oral and Maxillofacial Surgery. Dental intern Queens Gen. Hosp., Jamaica, N.Y., 1948-49; oral surgery resident Queens Hosp. Center, Jamaica, 1953-54; practice oral surgery, Rego Park, N.Y., 1954-59, Fulbright prof., Japan, 1959-61; prof. oral medicine and community dentistry Colls. Dentistry and Medicine, U. Ill., 1962-72; prof. health adminstrn. Sch. Pub. Health, 1972—; prof. dental and oral surgery Rush Med. Coll., 1970-76; clin. prof. surgery Chgo. Med. Sch., 1979—; prof. Northwestern U., 1982—; chief dentistry and oral surgery Rush-Presbyn.-St. Luke's Med. Center, Chgo., 1968-75; dir. Office Dental Manpower Distbn., Ill. Dept. Pub. Health, 1975-76, chief div. dental health, 1976-77, chief health manpower devel., 1977-78; chief dept. dentistry Chgo. Center Hosp., 1978-81; chief sect. dentistry and oral surgery Grant Hosp. of Chgo.; pres. Chgo. Dental Group, Chgo., 1978—; dental columnist Chgo. Sun-Times, 1977-78; Fulbright prof. oral surgery Okayama (Japan) U. and Tokyo Med-Dental U., 1959-61; WHO cons. to U. Antioquia, Colombia, Nat. U. and U. Zulia, Venezuela, 1964-69, Mahidol U., Bangkok, Thailand, 1973, Gt. Britain, 1977; mem. transition team on health policy, chmn. com. on occupational health Mayor Harold Washington, 1983; cons. occupational health and safety Chgo. Dept. Health, 1983—. Author: Guide to Hospital Dental Procedure, 1964, Dental Care for Special Patient, 1966, Introduction to Hospital Dentistry, 1970; editor: Am. Assn. Hosp. Dentists, 1966-71; assoc. editor: Jour. Oral Surgery, 1959-67; Contbr. articles to profl. jours. Mem. Ill. Ho. of Reps., 11th Dist., 1971-72, 12th Dist., 1973-74; Bd. dirs. Chgo. Easter Seal Soc., Hemophilia Found., Infant Welfare Soc. Served with USNR, 1943-45; to lt. Dental Corps, 1951-53. Recipient William J. Gies Nat. Dental Editorial award, 1969, Best Legislator award Ind. Voters Ill., 1972, 74, numerous other legis. awards. Fellow Am. Pub. Health Assn., Internat. Coll. Dentists, Chgo. Inst. Medicine, Am. Dental Soc. Anesthesiology (past pres.); mem. ADA, Am. Assn. Hosp. Dentists (past pres.), Sigma Xi, Phi Delta Kappa, Omicron Kappa Upsilon. Home: 220 W Concord Ln Chicago IL 60614 *Achievement of a health professional degree can be the portal through which an educated person can pass to a fuller and richer life. My dental degree made it possible for me to broaden my involvement in the affairs of my community, my nation, and my world, and to serve individuals in need as well.*

DOUGLAS, BRYCE, pharmaceutical company executive; b. Glasgow, Scotland, Jan. 6, 1924; came to U.S., 1958; s. Alexander and Mary (Turner) D.; m. Joyce M. Flynn, Aug. 24, 1955; children: Alan David, Neal Malcolm, Iain Graham. B.Sc. with honors, Glasgow U., 1944; Ph.D. in Organic Chemistry, Edinburgh (Scotland) U., 1948. Chemotherapy researcher, research lab. Royal Coll. Physicians, Edinburgh, 1947-49; research asst. biol. chemistry Aberdeen (Scotland) U., 1949; research fellow in alkaloid chemistry NRC Can., Ottawa, 1949-51; research fellow dept. pharmacology Harvard U., 1952-53; research asso., lectr. Ind. U., Bloomington, 1953-56; vis. research asso. U. Malaya, Singapore, 1956-58; with Smith Kline & French Labs., Phila., 1956—, v.p. research and devel., 1971-80, pres. research and devel., 1980-81, v.p. sci. and tech., 1981—. Contbr. articles to profl. jours. Bd. dirs. Royal Soc. Medicine Found.; bd. overseers U. Pa. Sch. Dental Medicine; bd. mgrs. Franklin Inst. of Phila.; bd. dirs. Franklin Research Ctr., Bartol Found.; bd. dirs. Southeastern Pa. chpt. ARC. Fellow Royal Soc. Chemistry (U.K.), Coll. Physicians Phila.; mem. N.Y. Acad. Scis., AAAS, Am. Chem. Soc. Patentee in field. Home: Box 672 Kimberton PA 19442 Office: PO Box 7929 Philadelphia PA 19101

DOUGLAS, CATHLEEN CURRAN HEFFERNAN (MRS. WILLIAM O. DOUGLAS), widow of Supreme Ct. Justice, lawyer, conservationist; b. Apr. 30, 1943; d. Curtis V. and Mary (Curran) Heffernan; m. William O. Douglas. B.A., Am. U., 1969, J.D., 1972; LL.M., Georgetown Law Center, 1974. Active in work with urban problems, women's rights causes; currently partner firm Leva, Hawes, Symington, Martin & Oppenheimer, Washington. Inst. for Pub. Interest Representation fellow, 1974. Office: 815 Connecticut Ave NW Washington DC 20006

DOUGLAS, CHARLES FRANCIS, agronomist; b. Tucson, July 16, 1930; s. John and Viva Lee (Crum) D.; m. Betty Jean Morris, June 7, 1952; children: Sharon, Sandra. Student, Eastern Ill. U., 1948-50; B.S., U. Ill., Urbana, 1956, M.S., 1957; Ph.D., Purdue U., 1961. Research asst. U. Ill., Urbana, 1956-57; instr. Purdue U., Lafayette, Ind., 1957-61; ednl. rep. TVA, Muscle Shoals, Ala., 1961-63, Lafayette, Ind., 1963-65, sect. supr., Midwest, Middle Atlantic, New Eng. states, 1965-69; head dept. agronomy U. Ga. Coastal Plain Expt. Sta. at Tifton, 1969—; lectr. state fertilizer industry convs., 1963-69; mem. program planning com. Southeast Fluid Fertilizer Conf., 1977; demonstration plot co-chmn. Sunbelt Agrl. Exposition, 1978—; Mem. adv. com. Ga. Crop Improvement Assn., 1971—; chmn. peanut planning group U. Ga., 1971-75, mem. self-study com. on research Coll. Agr., 1970, mem. sr. faculty adv. com. Coll. Agr., 1982—, mem. Univ. Council, 1982—. Mem. com. to formulate and implement program for gifted children Tift County (Ga.) Schs., 1970-74; pres. Reddick Elementary Sch., PTO, 1979; bd. dirs. Tift Area Concert Assn., 1979, sec., 1980, 81; bd. dirs. Tift County Families in Action, 1981. Served with USAF, 1951-54. Mem. Am. Soc. Agronomy (So. rep. to establish nat. orgn. agrl. expt. farm mgrs. 1972-74, chmn. field research sta. suprs. 1975, pres. Ga. chpt. 1976, pub. relations com. 1977-79, chmn. 1979, dir. 1981-82, mem. Agronomic Service award com. 1983—), So. Assn. Agrl. Scientists (chmn. expt. sta. supts. 1972-73, dir. 1972-74), Field Research Sta. Suprs. (chmn. 1975), Ga. Plant Food Ednl. Soc. (program planning com. 1976). Methodist. Lodges: Lions (pres. Tifton 1978); Elk; Toastmaster (pres. Tifton 1971-72). Home: 802 Texas Dr Tifton GA 31794

DOUGLAS, CHARLES GWYNNE, III, state justice; b. Abington, Pa., Dec. 2, 1942; s. Charles Gwynne and Blanche Elizabeth (Graham) D.; children by previous marriage: Charles Gwynne IV, Thomas A. B.A., U. N.H., 1965; J.D., Boston U., 1968. Bar: N.H. bar 1968. Asso. firm McLane, Carleton, Graf, Greene & Brown, Manchester, N.H., 1968-70; partner firm Perkins, Douglas & Brock, Concord, N.H., 1970-74; legal counsel to gov. N.H., 1973-74; assoc. justice N.H. Superior Ct., 1974-76, N.H. Supreme Ct., 1977—; mem. faculty Am. Acad. Jud. Edn.; chmn. ct. tech. com. Appellate Judges Conf., 1981—. Contbr. articles to law jours. Alt. del. Republican Nat. Conv., 1972; chmn. N.H. Task Force on Child Abuse, 1977, N.H. Fair Trial-Free Press Com., 1979—. Served to maj. Army N.G., 1968—. Named Outstanding Young Man of Yr. N.H. Jaycees, 1977; recipient Pub. Service award N.H. Assn. Counties, 1979. Mem. N.H. Bar Assn., Am. Bar Assn. (chmn. judges' adv. com. to ethics com. 1979—), Phi Beta Kappa. Republican. Episcopalian. Office: Supreme Ct Bldg Concord NH 03301

DOUGLAS, DONALD STERLING, university official; b. Balt., June 11, 1935; s. George Anthony and Vera Elizabeth (Sterling) D.; m. Kari Stortebecker, Sept. 6, 1963; children—Kathryn Anne, Heather Elaine. A.B., Oberlin Coll., 1957; Ph.D., Duke U., 1963. Asst. prof. physiology Rutgers U., New Brunswick, N.J., 1962-65; asso. prof. biology George Washington U., Washington, 1965-70; dir. acad. devel. Governors State U., Park Forest South, Ill., 1970-73, prof., 1970-79, asst. dean, 1975-77, asso. dean, 1977-78, asso. v.p. research, 1978-79; provost, v.p. acad. affairs SUNY-, Brockport, N.Y., 1979-83; dean faculty, dean Grad. Sch. Southeastern Mass. U., North Dartmouth, 1983—. Contbr. articles to profl. jours. Mem. Regional Health Planning Agy., Will-Grundy-Kankakee Counties, Ill., 1974-76; mem., officer Park Forest South Plan Commn., 1973-75. Office: Adminstrn 312 Southeastern Mass U. North Dartmouth MA 02747

DOUGLAS, DONALD WILLS, JR., business executive; b. Washington, July 3, 1917; s. Donald Wills and Charlotte Marguerita (Ogg) D.; m. Molly McIntosh, May 1, 1939; children: Victoria, Holly; m. Jean Ashton, Aug. 17, 1950. Student, Stanford U., 1934-38. Engr. Douglas Aircraft Co., Inc., Santa Monica, Calif., 1939-43, chief flight test group, 1943-51, dir. contract adminstrn., 1948, in charge research labs. Santa Monica div., 1949, v.p. mil. sales, 1951-57, pres., 1957-67, Douglas Aircraft Co. div. McDonnell Douglas Corp. (merger Douglas Aircraft Co., Inc. and McDonnell Co.), 1967-68, v.p. and sr. v.p. adminstrn. parent co., 1967-71, also mem. exec. com., 1969-71; now dir.; chmn., pres. Douglas Aircraft Co., Can., Ltd., 1968-71; pres. Douglas Devel. Co., 1972-74; chmn. Capistrano Nat. Bank, 1975—, Biphase Energy Systems, Inc. (subs. Research-Cottrell, Inc.), 1977-80, 1980-81; chmn., chief exec. officer Douglas-Culbert-Orange-Riverside County Partners (DCOR Partners, Inc.), 1979-80; sr. cons. mktg. devel. Biphase Energy Systems subs. Transam. Delaval, Inc., 1982—; chmn. bd. Vuebotics Corp., 1982—; chmn. bd., dir. Aerotech Cons., Inc., 1982—; pres. Douglas Energy Co., 1981—; bus. cons., 1974—; dir. Hilton Hotels Corp., 1966—, Partners Real Estate, Inc., 1978—. Bd. dirs. Naval Aviation Mus. Assocs., Inc.; chmn. adv. com. Gt. Western council Boy Scouts Am., 1980—; chmn. Donald Douglas Mus. and Library, 1975—; trustee Air Force Mus. Assocs. Decorated chevalier Legion of Honor, France; officiale Order Merit, Republic of Itlay). Asso. fellow AIAA; mem. Aerospace Industries Assn. (bd. chmn. 1964), Nat. Def. Transp. Assn. (nat. v.p. 1958-63), Air Force Assn., Assn. U.S. Army, Navy League U.S. (life), Phi Gamma Delta. Home: 707 Brooktree Rd Pacific Palisades CA 90272

DOUGLAS, DWIGHT OLIVER, university administrator; b. Mt. Carmel, Ill., May 7, 1941; s. Dwight Oliver and Jeannette Elizabeth (Moyer) D.; m. Carol Jane Brunson, June 2, 1963; children: Terri, Stacy, Dana. B.S., Eastern Ill. U., 1962, M.S., 1966; D.Ed., U. Tenn., 1972. Asst. dir. residence halls U. Tenn., Knoxville, 1969-71, dir. residence halls, 1971-72; dir. housing U. Ga., Athens, 1972-74, dean student affairs, 1975-78, assoc. v.p. acad. affairs, 1978-80, v.p. student affairs, 1980—. Contbr. articles to profl. jours. Pres. PTA Council Clarke County, 1978, Gaines Sch. PTA, 1977-78. Mem. Nat. Assn. Student Personnel Adminstrs. (state dir. Ga. 1982-84), So. Assn. Coll. Student Affairs, Ga. Personnel Assn., Phi Delta Kappa, Kappa Delta Pi, Omicron Delta Kappa. Methodist. Club: Gridiron. Office: U Ga 201 Academic Bldg Athens GA 30602

DOUGLAS, HERBERT PAUL, JR., beverage co. exec.; b. Pitts., Mar. 9, 1922; s. Herbert Paul and Ilessa May (France) D.; m. Rozell Reid, Jan. 3, 1950; children—Barbara Joy, Herbert Paul III. B.S., U. Pitts., 1948, M.S., 1950. Sales rep. Pabst Brewing Co., So. Eastern states, 1950-58, dist. mgr., 1958-63; control states rep. Schieffelin & Co., N.Y.C., 1963-65, nat. spl. markets mgr., 1965-68, v.p. nat. spl. markets, 1968-83, v.p. urban market devel., 1983—; Lectr. West Chester Coll., Chester, Pa., 1972. Com. mem. Phila. chpt. Fight for Sight, 1974-75; chmn. Black Athletes Hall of Fame, 1974; mem. 1976 U.S. Olympic Com. Recipient Olympic medal for track and field, 1948; Beverage Industry award Urban League Guild, 1974; named Athlete of Yr., Pitts., 1948; inducted into Varsity Lettermen Club of Distinction U. Pitts., 1980. Mem. Sales Execs. Club of New York (mem. exec. bd.). Baptist. Club: Elk. Home: 407 Rices Mill Rd Wyncote PA 19095 Office: 30 Cooper Sq New York NY 10003

DOUGLAS, HERSCHEL LEWIS, physician, university dean; b. Sulphur, Okla., Feb. 10, 1935; s. Herschel E. and Evelyn (Lewis) D.; m. Constance R. Vaught, Dec. 29, 1968; children: Dane E., Craig S., Nicole. Student, U. Okla., 1953, Oklahoma City U., 1953-56; M.D., U. Okla., 1960. Diplomate: Am. Bd. Family Practice. Intern USPHS, New Orleans, 1960-61; practice medicine specializing in family practice, Lea County, N.Mex., 1961-65, 68-71; chief staff Lea Gen. Hosp., Lea County, 1964, 69, 70; active med. surg. staff, Lovington, N.Mex., 1961-71; active med.-surg. staff Bexar County Hosp. Dist., Tex., 1971-80, chief family practice service, 1973-80; pres. med.-dental staff, Tex., 1977-78; mem. staff dept. medicine St. Luke's Luth. Hosp., San Antonio, 1977-80; assoc. prof. dept. medicine U. Tex. Health Sci. Ctr., San Antonio, 1971-73, prof., chmn. dept. family practice, 1973-80, assoc. dean, clin. affairs, 1979-80, dir. family practice residency tng. program, 1973-78, clin. prof. Sch. Nursing, 1975-77; clin. prof. Coll. U. Tex. Pharmacy, Austin, 1976-80; prof. human ecology U. Tex. Sch. Pub. Health, Houston, 1980-81; dean Quillen-Dishner Coll. Medicine, East Tenn. State U., Johnson City, 1981—; cons. staff ambulatory care Audie Murphy VA Hosp., San San Antonio, 1974-80, Compas, Inc., 1974-75, Southwest Research Inst., San Antonio, 1979-80; adj. asst. prof. Trinity U., San Antonio, 1977-80. Contbr. articles on med. edn., health care, pub. health to profl.l jours. Served with USAID, 1965-68. Fellow Am. Acad. Family Physicians (dir. Alamo chpt. 1972-77, research com. 1978—); mem. Tex. Acad. Family Physicians (sci. program com. 1978—, liaison com. with med. schs. 1971—), Soc. Tchrs. Family Medicine (research com. 1976-78), Bexar County Med. Soc. (health careers com. 1979), Family Physicians Student Assn. (faculty adv. 1972—), AMA (physicians' Rcognition award 1970, 72, 76, 80), Tex. Med. Assn. (continuing edn. com. 1974—), Alpha Omega Alpha. Office: East Tenn State Quillen-Dishner Coll Medicine PO Box 23, 320A Johnson TN 37614

DOUGLAS, HOWARD EUGENE, ambassador-at-large; b. Wichita Falls, Tex., Oct. 5, 1940; s. Howard E. and Louise (Ridley) D.; m. Elisabeth Maria Douglas Weikert, June 29, 1967; children: Christopher James Eugene Weikert Douglas. B.A., U. Tex., 1963; Cert., U. Barcelona, Spain, 1961; M.A., Columbia U., 1966. Mgr. internat. planning Memorex Corp., Santa Clara, Calif., 1972-73, mgr. internat. product mktg., 1974-75, dir. internat. trade, 1975-80; sr. mem. policy staff Dept. State, Washington, 1981-82, U.S. ambassador-at-large, coordinator for refugee affairs, 1982—. Bd. dirs. Internat. Research and Exchange Bd.; v.p. Internat. Inst. Humanitarian Law, San Remo, Italy. Served to lt. USN, 1966-71. Mem. Asia Soc., Japan Soc., Tai Soc. Washington, Oriental Ceramic Soc. Republican. Episcopalian. Club: Princeton. Home: 9106 Steamview Ln Vienna VA 22180 Office: Dept State 2201 C St NW Washington DC 20520

DOUGLAS, JAMES, educator, engr.; b. Uvalde, Tex., Oct. 1, 1914; s. Raymond C. and Mae (Savage) D.; m. Sarah Maria Bisset, July 22, 1941; children—Sarah A., Susan E., Bonnie B., James A. B.S., U.S. Naval Acad., 1938; B.C.E., Rensselaer Poly. Inst., 1942; M.C.E., 1943; Ph.D., Stanford U., 1963. Registered profl. engr., D.C., Calif. Commd. ensign U.S. Navy, 1938, advanced through grades to capt., 1956; in charge constrn. (Cubi Point Naval Air Sta.), Philippines, 1951-54; dir. Seabee div. U.S. Navy, 1954-58; in charge constrn. (Antartic bases Internat. Geophys. Yr.), 1956-58, prof. constrn. engring., Stanford, 1963—; cons. constrn. engring. Stanford Research Inst., various corps., U.S. and fgn. govts., 1963—; chmn. com. constrn. mgmt. Transp. Research Bd., NRC, 1969-76. Author: Construction Equipment Policy, 1975, also numerous tech. articles. Active Boy Scouts Am., 1946—. Served with Armed Forces, World War II. Decorated Bronze Star; recipient Thomas Fitch Rowland prize ASCE, 1969, Constrn. Mgmt. award, 1975. Fellow ASCE (chmn. constrn. equipment com. 1960-65); mem. Tau Beta Pi, Sigma Xi, Chi Epsilon, Chi Phi. Republican. Episcopalian. Home: 768 Mayfield Ave Stanford CA 94305 Office: Stanford U Stanford CA 94305 *In retrospect I realize that the most important things in life are your friends and your relations with other people. Regardless of wealth or status, life cannot be wholly satisfactory without agreeable human relations, and these are not dependent on race, creed, color, age or sex but on the quality of the individuals.*

DOUGLAS, JAMES HOLLEY, state official; b. Springfield, Mass., June 21, 1951; s. Robert James and Cora Elizabeth (Holley) D.; m. Dorothy Foster, May 24, 1975; 1 son, Matthew James Douglas. A.B., Middlebury Coll., 1972. Gen. mgr. Credit Bur. of Middlebury, Vt., 1972-76; exec. dir. United Way of Addison County, 1976-79; exec. asst. to Gov. of Vt., 1979-80; sec. of state State of Vt., Montpelier, 1981—; mem. Vt. Ho. of Reps., 1973-79, majority leader, 1975-77, 77-79. Pres. United Way of Vt. Republican. Congregationalist. Lodge: Masons. Office: Pavilion Bldg Montpelier VT 05753 *

DOUGLAS, JAMES JARDINE, publisher; b. Edinburgh, Scotland, Mar. 26, 1924; emigrated to Can., 1954; s. Peter Jardine and Isabella Black (Br) D.; m. Muriel Ferguson; children: Diana, Christopher, Alan. Student, RAF Apprentice Sch., Cranwell, Eng., 1940-42, RAF Signals Officer Sch., 1949-51. Commd. leading airman RAF, 1942, advanced through grades to flight lt., 1950; photo reconnaissance, Burma and India, 1942-44, in Far East, 1944-45; staff officer RAF Coastal Command, 1952-54; ret., 1954, bookseller, Edinburgh, Scotland, 1946-49, electronics engr., 1954-57; pres. Douglas Agys., 1958-69, JJ Douglas Ltd., 1963-77, Douglas, David & Clarkes (pubs.), 1974—; Douglas & McIntyre Ltd., North Vancouver, B.C., Can., 1969-73; hotelier; farmer. Decorated Burma Star. Mem. Assn. Can. Pubs. (pres. 1975, 76, 83), B.C. Book Pubs. Assn. (founding pres. 1972-73). Office: Douglas & McIntyre Ltd 1615 Venable St Vancouver BC Canada V5L 2H1 *

DOUGLAS, JAMES NATHANIEL, astronomer, educator; b. Dallas, Aug. 14, 1935; s. Loyd and Nell (Curtis) D.; m. Charlotte Cummings, Aug. 30, 1956 (div. 1980); children—Neva Jean, James Loyd, Alan Nevins.; m. Elizabeth Gunn; 1 dau., Eleanore. B.S., Yale U., 1956, M.S., 1958, Ph.D., 1961. Instr. Yale U., 1960-61, asst. prof., 1961-65; asso. prof. astronomy U. Tex., Austin, 1965-71, prof., 1971—, dir.; mem. adv. panel for astronomy NSF, 1971-74. Contbr. articles to profl. jours. NSF fellow, 1959-60. Mem. Am. Astron. Soc., Internat. Astron. Union, Phi Beta Kappa. Home: 1300 Lorrain Austin TX 78703 Office: Dept Astronomy Univ of Tex Austin TX 78712

DOUGLAS, JOHN JEFFERSON, computer cons.; b. Cave-in-Rock, Ill., Oct. 14, 1935; s. Ulys J. and Rose Marie (Henry) D.; m. Monna Loy Nail, July 23, 1960; children—Kelley Jefferson, Kristen Neile. B.S. in Elec. Engring, Ariz. State U., 1965, M.S., 1969. Program dir. Series 6000, Honeywell/Gen. Electric Info. Systems Div., Phoenix, 1968-71; v.p., dir. mktg. services Courier Terminal Systems, Inc., Tempe, Ariz., 1971-74, v.p. ops., 1974-76, exec. v.p., 1976-78; v.p., gen. mgr. Computer Terminal Systems Ops., ITT Courier Terminal Systems, Inc., 1978-79, pres., 1979-80; computer cons., Paradise Valley, Ariz., 1980—; Mem. dean's adv. council Sch. Engring., Ariz. State U., Tempe, 1979; mem. Gov.'s Energy Conservation Com., 1979—. Served with USN, 1953-56. Home and Office: 3409 E Claremont Paradise Valley AZ 85253

DOUGLAS, KENNETH JAY, food company executive; b. Harbor Beach, Mich., Sept. 4, 1922; s. Harry Douglas and Xenia (Williamson) D.; m. Ann Elizabeth Schweizer, Aug. 17, 1946; children: Connie Ann, Andrew Jay. Student, U. Ill., 1940-41, 46-47; J.D., Chgo. Kent Coll. Law, 1950; grad., Advanced Mgmt. Program, Harvard, 1962. Bar: Ill. 1950, Ind. 1952. Spl. agt. FBI, 1950-54; dir. indsl. relations Dean Foods Co., 1954-64, v.p. finance and adminstrn., 1964-70, chmn. bd. dirs., chief exec. officer, 1970—; dir. Money Mart Assets, Inc., Cente Corp., Nat. Can Corp.; Bd. dirs., pres. mem. exec. com. Milk Industry Found. Trustee West Suburban Hosp., Oak Park, Ill. Served with USNR, 1944-46. Mem. Chgo. Bar Assn., Internat. Assn. Ice Cream Mfrs. (dir.), Phi Eta Sigma, Phi Delta Phi. Republican. Clubs: Chicago, Economic, Executives (Chgo.); Oak Park (Ill.); Country, River Forest Tennis, Steamboat Springs Country. Office: 3600 N River Rd Franklin Park IL 60131

DOUGLAS, KIRK, actor, motion picture producer; b. Amsterdam, N.Y., Dec. 9, 1918; s. Harry and Bryna (Sanglel) Danielovitch; m. Diana Dill (div. Feb. 1950); children—Michael, Joel; m. Anne Buydens, May 29, 1954; children—Peter, Eric Anthony. A.B., St. Lawrence U., 1938, D.F.A. (hon.), 1958; student, Am. Acad. Dramatic Arts, 1939-41. Appeared on: Broadway in Man Bites Dog; producer, star: Broadway play One Flew over the Cuckoo's Nest; motion pictures include The Man from Snowy River; producer, dir.: Posse; pres., Bryna Co.; producer actor: The Final Countdown; co-producer: One Flew Over the Cuckoo's Nest (Nominated for Acad. Award 1949, 52, 56, recipient N.Y. Film Critics award, also Hollywood Fgn. Press award 1956). Heart and Torch award Am. Heart Assn., 1956; Splendid Am. award of merit George Washington Carver Meml. Found., 1957; cited in Congl. Record for service as goodwill ambassador, 1964; Cecil B. DeMille award for contbns. in entertainment field, 1967; Presdl. Medal of Freedom, 1981. Mem. UN Assn. (dir. Los Angeles chpt.). Made State Dept.-USIA tours around world. Office: Bryna Co 141 El Camino Beverly Hills CA 90212

DOUGLAS, LESLIE, investment banker; b. Enon Valley, Pa., Mar. 14, 1914; s. Robert R. and Margaret M. (Mc Anlis) D.; m. Jean Wallace, Oct. 12, 1946; children—David, Ann and Joan (twins). B.S., Geneva Coll., Beaver Falls, Pa., 1935; M.B.A., Harvard U., 1937. Investment mgr. Royal Liverpool Group, N.Y.C., 1937-41; investment banker Folger Nolan Fleming Douglas, Inc., Washington, 1946—, v.p., 1955—; bd. govs. Assn. Stock Exchange Firms, 1969-72, Securities Industry Assn., 1972-75. Trustee Holton Arms Sch., Washington, Landon Sch., Washington, Vis. Nurses Assn., Washington. Served to lt. comdr. USN, 1941-46. Republican. Presbyterian. Clubs: Chevy Chase; Met. (Washington). Home: 4733 Woodway Ln Washington DC 20016 Office: 725 15th St NW Washington DC 20005

DOUGLAS, MARTIN, corporation executive; b. Milw., Nov. 20, 1935; m. Joan Grossman, June 13, 1959; children: Gloria, Donald, Susan. B.A., U. S.C., 1957; M.A., So. Methodist U., 1959. With Fingerhut Corp., Minnetonka, Minn., 1965-75, sr. v.p., 1973-75, Am. Can Co., 1975-81, exec. v.p., 1981—; dir. Fingerhut Corp. Trustee Blake Sch., Hopkins, Minn.; bd. govs. Children's Hosp., St. Paul;. Mem. NAM, Am. Packaging Inst., Mpls. C. of C. Office: Werik Bldg 84 S 6th St Suite 415 Minneapolis MN 55402

DOUGLAS, MARY TEW, anthropology and humanities educator; b. San Remo, Italy, Mar. 25, 1921; came to U.S., 1977; m. James Douglas, 1951; children: Janet, James, Philip. B.A., U. Oxford, Eng., 1943, M.A., 1947, B.Sc., 1948, Ph.D., 1951. Research fellow Internat. African Inst. for Fieldwork, Belgian Congo, 1949-50; lectr. anthropology Univ. Coll., London, 1951-62; reader U. London, 1963-70; prof. social anthropology Univ. Coll., London, 1971-78; dir. research on culture Russell Sage Found., N.Y.C., 1977-79; prof. depts. anthropology, history, lit. of religions Northwestern U., Evanston, Ill., 1981—. Author: Purity and Danger, 1966, Natural Symbols, 1970, Risk and Culture, 1982; author, editor: In The Active Voice, 1982, Essays in the Sociology of Perception, 1982. Home: 1738 Chicago Ave Evanston IL 60201 Office: Northwestern U 1940 Sheridan Rd Evanston IL 60201

DOUGLAS, MICHAEL KIRK, actor, film producer; b. New Brunswick, N.J., Sept. 25, 1944; s. Kirk and Diana D.; m. Diandra Mornell Luker, Mar. 20, 1977; 1 son, Cameron Morrell. B.A., U. Calif., Santa Barbara, 1967. Film appearances include: It's My Turn; film appearances include: Hail Heroll, 1969, Summertime, 1971, Napoleon and Samantha, 1972, Coma, 1978, Running, 1979, Star Chamber, 1983; appeared in: TV series Streets of San Francisco; producer: films The China Syndrome; film Romancing the Stone, 1984. Recipient Acad. award Best Film, One Flew Over the Cuckoo's Nest, Acad. Motion Picture Arts and Scis., 1975. Office: care Creative Artists Agy Inc 1888 Century Park E Suite 1400 Los Angeles CA 90067

DOUGLAS, MRS. WILLIAM O. *See* **DOUGLAS, CATHLEEN CURRAN HEFFERNAN**

DOUGLAS, PAUL LOUIS, state official; b. Sioux Falls, S.D., Sept. 19, 1927; s. Louis Paul and Victoria (Karavaselis) D. B.S., U. Nebr., 1951, J.D., 1953. Bar: Nebr. bar 1953. Individual practice law, Lincoln, 1953-56; with County Atty.'s Office, Lancaster County, Lincoln, 1956-74, chief dep. county atty., 1959-60, county atty., 1960-74; atty. gen., Nebr., Lincoln, 1975—. Served with USMC, 1945-47. Mem. Nebr., Lincoln bar assns., Nat. Assn. Attys. Gen., Midwest Attys. Gen. (chmn.), Am. Legion, Lincoln C. of C. Republican. Greek Orthodox. Clubs: Masons (32 deg.), Shriners, Order Eastern Star, Elks. Office: Dept Justice State Capital Room 2115 Lincoln NE 68509

DOUGLAS, PAUL WOLFF, natural resource company executive; b. Springfield, Mass., Sept. 12, 1926; s. Paul Howard and Dorothy (Wolff) D.; m. Colette Smith, Nov. 19, 1926; children: Philip LeBreton, Carolyn Jory, Christine Sanders, Paul Harding. A.B., Princeton, 1948; student, Leeds (Eng.) U., 1948. Dir. internal finance sect. ECA Mission to France, 1948-52; with Freeport Minerals Co., 1952—, exec., v.p., dir., 1970-75, pres., chmn. exec. com., 1975—; pres., chief exec. officer Freeport-McMoran Inc., 1981-83; chmn., chief exec. officer Pittston Co., 1984—; dir. Sulphur Export Corp., U.S. Trust Co., Philip Morris Inc.; Chmn. Community Planning Bd., N.Y.C., 1967-68. Served with USNR, 1944-46. Home: 25 Charlton St New York NY 10014 Office: 200 Park Ave Suite 4514 New York NY 10166

DOUGLAS, ROBERT ELLIS, lawyer; b. St. Joseph, Mo., Sept. 30, 1919; s. Richard Leroy and Edith Mary (Willis) D.; m. Jean M. Douglas, Jan. 30, 1942 (dec. June 1972); children—Linda Douglas Hardin, Maxwell (dec.); m. Alyce Douglas, Jan. 8, 1976; stepchildren—Casey Meyers, Molly Meyers. A.B., Westminster Coll., 1941; LL.B., U. Kans., 1947. Bar: Mo. bar 1947. Asso. firm. Brown, Douglas & Brown, St. Joseph, 1947-54, partner, 1954—; officer, dir. Kirkpatrick Jewelry Co., 1953-60; sec., dir. Civic Indsl. Assn., St. Joseph, 1961—, St. Joseph Indsl. Devel. Co., 1961—; dir. Star Blends, Inc. Bd. dirs. St. Joseph Indsl. Found., 1961—; bd. dirs. St. Joseph Symphony Soc., 1961-70, 76-79, pres., 1970-71; bd. dirs. Am. Lung Assn., 1963—, pres., 1977-78; trustee, regent Mo. Western State Coll., 1966-75. Served in U.S. Army, 1942-45. Fellow Am. Coll. Probate Counsel; mem. Am., Mo. bar assns., Am. Judicature Soc., Order of Coif, Phi Delta Theta, Phi Delta Phi. Republican. Presbyterian. Clubs: St. Joseph Country, Benton, St. Joseph Racquet, Elks. Home: 3 Hawthorn St Saint Joseph MO 64505 Office: Pioneer Bldg Suite 203-211 510 Francis St Saint Joseph MO 64501

DOUGLAS, ROBERT GORDON, JR., physician; b. N.Y.C., Apr. 17, 1934; s. Robert Gordon and Alice (Lewis) D.; m. Ann Castle Moses, Dec. 22, 1956; children: Robert Gordon, 3d, Timothy Stuart, Catherine Lewis. A.B., Princeton U., 1955; M.D., Cornell U., 1959. Diplomate: Am. Bd. Internal Medicine. Successively intern, asst. resident in internal medicine, resident N.Y. Hosp., 1959-61, 62-63; asst. resident Johns Hopkins Hosp., 1961-62; USPHS clin. assoc. clin. investigation Nat. Inst. Allergy and Infectious Disease, 1963-66; asst. prof., then assoc. prof. microbiology and medicine Baylor U. Coll. Medicine, Houston, 1966-70; mem. faculty U. Rochester (N.Y.) Sch. Medicine and Dentistry, 1970-82, prof. medicine and microbiology, 1974-82, head infectious disease unit, 1970-82, sr. assoc. dean edn., 1979-82; prof., chmn. dept. medicine Cornell U. Med. Coll., 1982—; physician in chief N.Y. Hosp., 1982—; cons. in field. Editor: Principles and Practices of Infectious Diseases, 1980, also numerous articles. Recipient Hawkins award Assn. Am. Publishers, 1980. Fellow A.C.P.; mem. Infectious Diseases Soc. Am., Am. Soc. Microbiology, Am. Soc. Clin. Investigation, Assn. Am. Physicians, Am. Clin. Climatol. Assn. Home: 1161 York Ave Apt 6J New York NY 10021 Office: Dept Medicine NY Hosp-Cornell Med Center 525 E 68th St New York NY 10021

DOUGLAS, ROD PETER, mining and smelting company executive; b. Ft. McLeod, Alta., Can., May 30, 1925; m. Irene Pinder; children: Steve, Susan, Cathy. B.Sc. in Mining Engring., U. Alta., 1948. With Cominco Ltd., 1948—, mgr. outside mines, B.C., 1966-73, asst. gen. mgr. western ops., 1974-75, group v.p., N.W.T., 1975-80, sr. v.p. ops., Vancouver, B.C., Can., 1980-83, exec. v.p., Vancouver, B.C., Can., 1983—; project engr. Cominco Am. Inc., Magmont, Mo., 1965-66; pres., chief exec. officer Pine Point Mines Ltd., Yellowknife, N.W.T., 1976—. Gov. Regent Coll., Vancouver. Mem. Can. Inst. Mining and Metallurgy, Assn. Profl. Engrs. B.C. Club: Terminal City (Vancouver). Office: Cominco Ltd 200 Granville St Vancouver BC Canada V6C 2R2

DOUGLAS, WALTER SPALDING, civil engineer; b. Cranford, N.J., Jan. 22, 1912; s. Walter Jules and Elizabeth Appleton (Spalding) D.; m. Jean Gairdner Moment, May 6, 1938; children—David, Joanne, Nancy. Grad., Phillips Exeter Acad., 1929; B.A., Dartmouth, 1933; M.S. in Civil Engring, Harvard, 1935. Structural steel detailer Nashville Bridge Co., 1935-37; asst. to chief engr. N.Y. World's Fair, Inc., 1937-39; asso. engr. Parsons, Brinckerhoff, Hall & Macdonald, N.Y., 1939-42, 46-52; partner Parsons, Brinckerhoff, Quade & Douglas, 1952—, sr. partner, chmn. bd., 1966-77. Prin. works include responsibility for design, constrn. mgmt. San Francisco Bay Area, Atlanta Rapid Transit System, Caracas, Venezuela; design Combat Operations Center, N.Am. Air Def., Colo., Toledo Port Authority Marine Terminal. Trustee Hillside Cemetery, Plainfield, N.J.; bd. govs. Muhlenberg Hosp., Plainfield, 1950—, pres., 1958-59; bd. dirs. Newport (R.I.) Hosp., 1977—. Served to lt. comdr. USNR, 1942-45. Recipient citation Engring. News-Record, 1966, Moles Assn. award for Outstanding Achievement in Constrn., 1970, hon. citation Newcomen Soc., 1975. Fellow ASCE (James Laurie prize 1969, named one of ten outstanding men in constrn. of last 50 years 1975); mem. Am. Inst. Cons. Engrs. (past v.p.), Soc. Am. Mil. Engrs., Nat. Acad. Engring. Clubs: Dartmouth (N.Y.C.); Conanicut Yacht (Jamestown, R.I.). Home: Route 1 Box 34M Beavertail Rd Jamestown RI 02835 Office: One Penn Plaza 250 W 34th St New York NY 10001

DOUGLAS, WILLIAM ERNEST, government executive; b. Charleston, S.C., Nov. 26, 1930; s. William Ernest and Helen A. (Fortune) D.; m. Nancy Anne Gibson, July 18, 1980. A.B., The Citadel, 1956; postgrad., U. S.C., 1956-59. Asst. dist. dir. Jackson dist. IRS, Miss., 1972-73, Atlanta dist. IRS, 1973-74; asst. regional commr. S.E. region IRS, Atlanta, 1974-78, dir. Regional Service Ctr., 1978-80; commr. Bur. Govt. Fin. Ops., Washington, 1980—. Served with U.S. Army, 1948-52. Home and office: 215 James Thurber Ct Falls Church VA 22046

DOUGLASS, BRUCE E., physician; b. Berwyn, Ill., Sept. 26, 1917; s. Frank Lionel and Helen Mary (Eccles) D.; m. Charlotte Maurer Natwick, Oct. 14, 1942; children: Jean N., Bruce G., John F. B.A., U. Wis., 1938, M.D., 1942; M.S. in Medicine, U. Minn., 1949. Intern Med. Coll. of Va., Richmond, 1942-43; resident in internal medicine Mayo Clinic, Rochester, Minn, 1947-50, mem. staff, 1949—, chmn. div. preventive medicine, 1962—, dir., 1976—; dir. Occupational Health Inst., Chgo., 1968—. Author: Anatomy of the Portal Vein and Its Tributaries, 1949, The Problem of Benign Bronchial Obstruction, 1954, Predicting Disease: Is It Possible?, 1971, Health Problems of Hospital Employees, 1971, Examining Healthy Persons: How and How Often?, 1980. Chmn. Rochester Music Bd., 1960-70; v.p. Minn. Zool. Soc., 1974-77. Served to capt. M.C. AUS, 1944-47. Fellow Am. Acad. Occupational Medicine, Am. Occupational Med. Assn. (pres. 1977-78, Meritorious Service award 1979); mem. AMA (Physician's Recognition award 1974-77, chmn. sect. council on preventive medicine 1978-80, del. for occupational med. to ho. of dels. 1978—), Minn. Med. Assn. (chmn. com. on public health edn. 1979), Ramazzini Soc., Assn. Tchrs. Preventive Medicine, Am. Coll. Preventive Medicine, Minn. Zool. Soc., Sigma Xi, Phi Kappa Phi, Sigma Phi, Nu Sigma Nu. Home: 6620 Buckthorn NW Rochester MN 55901 Office: Mayo Clinic Rochester MN 55905

DOUGLASS, CARL DEAN, govt. ofcl.; b. Little Rock, Apr. 27, 1925; s. Dennie and Elizabeth (Rives) D.; m. Vera Davis, Jan. 23, 1946; children—Joseph Dean, Katherine Elizabeth. B.S., Hendrix Coll., Conway, Ark., 1947; M.S. in Chemistry, U. Okla., 1949, Ph.D., 1952. From instr. to asso. prof. biochemistry U. Ark., 1952-59; chief nutrition research br. FDA, Washington, 1959-61; with NIH, Bethesda, Md., 1961—, asso. dir. statistics, analysis and research evaluation, div. research grants, 1970-71, dep. dir. div., 1971-76, dir., 1976—. Served with USNR, 1943-46. Fellow Oak Ridge Inst. Nuclear Studies, 1951-52. Fellow Am. Inst. Chemists, AAAS; mem. Am. Chem. Soc., Soc. Exptl. Biology and Medicine, Am. Inst. Nutrition, Am. Inst. Biol. Scis., Sigma Xi, Alpha Chi Sigma, Phi Lambda Upsilon. Home: 6310 Rockhurst Rd Bethesda MD 20817 Office: 9000 Rockville Pike Bethesda MD 20205

DOUGLASS, DAVID HOLMES, physicist; b. Bangor, Maine, Feb. 12, 1932; s. David Holmes and Helen Gertrude (Haley) D.; m. Eugenia Sepe, Mar. 14, 1981; children—Janet, James, Richard. B.S. in Physics, U. Maine., 1955, Ph.D., M.I.T., 1959. Research physicist Lincoln Lab., M.I.T., 1959-61, instr. physics, 1961-62; asst. prof. physics U. Chgo., 1962-65, asso. prof., 1965-67, prof., 1967-68, U. Rochester, 1968—; mem. ad hoc com. on gravitation physics NRC. Contbr. numerous articles on super conductivity, low temperature physics and gravitation to profl. jours.; editor: Superconductivity in d- and f- Band Metals, 1976, Measurements of Weak Force in Physics, 1977. Alfred P. Sloan fellow, 1962-66. Mem. Am. Assn. Physics Tchrs., AAAS, Am. Phys. Soc. Office: Dept Physics U Rochester Rochester NY 14627

DOUGLASS, FENNER, music educator; b. New London, Oct. 28, 1921; s. Walter Landon and Mildred (Fenner) D.; m. Jane Fetherlin, Aug. 25, 1951; children; Stephen, Emily, John. B.A., Oberlin Coll., 1942, B.Mus., 1943, M.Mus., 1948. Asst. prof. to prof. organ Oberlin Coll., Ohiho, 1946-74; prof. music Duke U., Durham, N.C., 1974—; dir. music St. Peter's Episcopal Ch., Cleve., 1957-74. Author: The Language of the French Classical Organ, 1969, Cavaille-Coll and the Musicians, 1980. Office: Dept Music Duke U Durham NC 27708

DOUGLASS, ROBERT ROYAL, banker, lawyer; b. Binghamton, N.Y., Oct. 16, 1931; s. Robert R. and Frances (Behan) D.; m. Linda Ann Luria, June 2, 1962; children: Robert Royal, Alexandra Brooke, Andrew. B.A. with distinction, Dartmouth Coll., 1953; LL.B., Cornell U., 1959. Bar: N.Y. Asso. Hinman, Howard & Kattell, 1959-64; 1st asst. counsel to Gov. N.Y. State, Albany, 1964-65, counsel to gov., 1965-70, sec. to gov., 1971-72; partner Milbank, Tweed, Hadley & McCloy, 1972-76; exec. v.p., gen. counsel Chase Manhattan Bank, N.Y.C., 1976-83, exec. v.p., 1983—; dir. Rockefeller Center, Inc.; chmn. Nelson Rockefeller's Campaign for Republican Nomination for Pres., 1968; commr. Port Authority of N.Y. State and N.J., 1972-76; trustee N.Y.C. Public Library, 1972—; bd. dirs., chmn. exec. com. Downtown-Lower Manhattan Assn., N.Y.C., 1973—; mem. vis. com. John F. Kennedy Sch. Govt., Harvard U., 1974-79; congl. liaison, counsel to Vice Pres. Rockefeller during Congl. Confirmation hearings, 1974; mem. N.Y. Landmarks Conservancy, 1977—. Bd. editors: N.Y. Law Jour. Served with M.C., U.S. Army, 1954-56. Recipient Wallace award Am.-Scottish Found., 1974. Mem. ABA, N.Y. State Bar Assn., Council Fgn. Relations. Roman Catholic. Clubs: Century Assn., at World Trade Center, Round Hill, Harbor. Office: Chase Manhattan Bank 1 Chase Manhattan Plaza New York NY 10081 *

DOURLET, ERNEST F., rubber and plastic products manufacturing executive; b. Lancaster, Ohio, 1924. B.S. Chem. Engring., W.Va. U.; postgrad., U. Pa. Wharton Sch. Pres. Cadillac Plastic & Chem. Co., 1957-71; exec. v.p. Dayco Corp., Dayton, Ohio, 1972-73, pres., chief operating officer, dir., 1973—; dir. Price Bros. Co., Winters Nat. Bank & Trust Co. Address: Dayco Corp 333 W 1st St Dayton OH 45402 *

DOUTT, RICHARD LEROY, entomologist, lawyer, educator; b. La Verne, Calif., Dec. 6, 1916; s. Mace and Adele (Bussey) D.; m. Lucinda Margaret Killian, Mar. 21, 1942 (dec.); children: Richard Jonathan, Jeffrey Thomas; m. Betty Mann, Apr. 20, 1979. B.S., U. Calif. at Berkeley, 1939, M.S., 1940, Ph.D., 1946; LL.B., San Francisco Law Sch., 1959, J.D., 1968. Bar: Calif. bar 1960. Faculty U. Calif. at Berkeley, 1946—, prof. entomology, 1960-75, prof. emeritus, 1975—, chmn. div. biol. control, 1964-69; acting dean Coll. Agrl. Scis., 1969-70; mem. firm Foley, Saler & Doutt, Albany, Calif., 1960-67; environ. counsel firm Henningson, Durham and Richardson, Santa Barbara, Calif., 1975-81; entomologist, Santa Barbara County, Calif., 1981-83. Contbr. articles to profl. jours. Served to lt. comdr. USNR, 1941-45. Fellow Calif. Acad. Scis.; mem. Entomol. Soc. Am., Calif. Bar, Sigma Xi. Democrat. Home: 1781 Glen Oaks Dr Santa Barbara CA 93108

DOUVAN, ELIZABETH, social psychologist, educator; b. South Bend, Ind., Nov. 3, 1926; d. John and Janet F. (Powers) Malcolm; m. Eugene Victor Douvan, Dec. 27, 1947; children—Thomas Alexander, Catherine Des Ormiers. A.B., Vassar Coll., 1946; M.A., U. Mich., 1948, Ph.D., 1951. Study dir. Survey Research Center, U. Mich., Ann Arbor, 1950-58, lectr. dept. psychology, 1951-61, asso. prof., 1961-65, Kellog prof. psychology, 1965—; also program dir. Inst. for Social Research, 1970—; cons. NIMH, NSF, various founds.; Mem. Ann Arbor Bd. Health, 1972-76. Author: The Adolescent Experience, 1966, Feminine Personality and Conflict, 1970, The Inner American, 1981, Mental Health in America, 1981; contbr. articles to profl. jours. Recipient various grants. Mem. Am. Psychol. Assn. (pres. div. 35 1970-71), AAAS, Am. Sociol. Assn., Assn. for Women in Psychology, Nat. Women's Studies Assn. Democrat. Office: Dept Psychology 580 Union Dr Ann Arbor MI 48109

DOVER, JAMES BURRELL, ins. co. exec.; b. Dawson, Ala., June 2, 1927; s. Doyle and Essie (Rucks) D.; m. Margaret Moody, Aug. 7, 1954; children—Suzanne, James, Donaldson. B.S., U. Ala., 1957. Chief examiner Ala. Ins. Dept., 1957-61; with Am. Amicable Life Ins. Co., Waco, Tex., 1961-80, asst. sec., 1965-69, sec., 1969-80, treas., 1976-80; sec., dir. U.S. Life Ins. Co., Waco, 1968-80, Alico Mgmt. Co., 1968-80; pres., dir. Officers Benefit Assn., Birmingham, Ala., 1980—. Served with USNR, 1950-52; Korea. Home: 4743 Marywood Circle Birmingham AL 35226 Office: Metroplex 2 Suite 204 Birmingham AL 35209

DOVRE, PAUL JOHN, college president; b. Minneota, Minn., Jan. 7, 1935; s. Nels E. and Inga (Borson) D.; m. Mardeth Bervig, June 3, 1958; children: Louise, Erik. B.A., Concordia Coll., Moorhead, Minn., 1958; M.A., Northwestern U., 1959, Ph.D., 1963; postgrad. (Rockefeller theol. fellow), Luther Theol. Sem., St. Paul, 1959-60. Instr. Northwestern U., 1962-63; mem. faculty Concordia Coll., 1963—, prof. speech communication, 1969—, chmn. dept. speech and drama, 1964-68, exec. v.p., then v.p. acad. affairs, 1969-70, 71-75, pres., 1975—; asst. to provost Central Mich. U., Mt. Pleasant, 1970-71; trustee, past dist. chmn. Nat. Debate Tournament. Author research papers. Bd. dirs. Fargo-Moorhead Symphony Orch., 1972-78, Tri-Coll. U., 1975—; bd. dirs., campaign chmn. Fargo-Moorhead United Way, 1977—; mem. adv. com. U. Minn. Health Scis., 1983—. Served with AUS, 1954-56. Mem. Midwestern Forensic Assn. (pres. 1967-69), Luth. Ednl. Conf. N.Am. (v.p. 1978-79), Luth. Ednl. Council N.Am. (pres. 1979-80), Pi Kappa Delta (past dist. gov.). Lutheran. Club: Moorhead Rotary. Office: Concordia Coll Moorhead MN 56560

DOW, DANIEL GOULD, educator; b. Ann Arbor, Mich., Apr. 26, 1930; s. William Gould and Edna Lois (Sontag) D.; m. Kathleen Mary Bond, June 19, 1954; children—Sarah, Suzanne, Jennifer, Gordon. B.S. in Engring, U. Mich., 1952, M.S., 1953; Ph.D., Stanford U., 1958. Asst. prof. elec. engring. Calif. Inst. Tech., Pasadena, 1958-61; with Varian Assos., Palo Alto, Calif., 1961-68; prof. U. Wash., Seattle, 1968—, chmn. dept. elec. engring., 1968-77; asso. dir. Applied Physics Lab., 1977-79; dir. Washington Energy Research Center, 1979-81; cons. Hughes Aircraft, Malibu, Calif., 1958-61, Varian Assos., 1968-71, Boeing Co., 1973-74, John Fluke Co., 1979—; mem. Adv. Group on Electron Devices, Microwave Working Group, 1965-76, Wash. Energy Policy Council, 1973-74; mem. subpanel on energy research Energy Research Adv. Bd., 1980; mem. panel on measurement services Nat. Acad. Scis.-Nat. Bur. Standards. Served to lt. USAF, 1953-55. Mem. IEEE. (sr. mem.). Home: 9620 NE 31st St Bellevue WA 98004

DOW, DOROTHY MINERVA, author; b. Lockport, Ill., Sept. 7, 1903; d. John Davis and Elizabeth (Gund) D.; m. James Edward Fitzgerald, Nov. 3, 1925. Ed. pub. high schs.; spl. work in English, U. Chgo.; student, Sch. Civics and Philanthrophy, Chgo. Author books.; Contbr.: verse and prose to Poetry Mag; also other mags. Recipient Maxwell Anderson award for play in blank verse Souvenir de la Malmaison (Leland Stanford Drama Festival), 1937. Home: 333 E Ontario St Apt 1601B Chicago IL 60611

DOW, FREDERICK WARREN, educator; b. Boston, Aug. 2, 1917; s. Frederick Vincent and Marcia (McMahon) D.; m. Patricia Rathbone, Oct. 2, 1943; children—Meryl (Mrs. Richard Wayne Brand), Frederick Warren, Bradford Rathbone, Martha Treleven (Mrs. Mark Herzog). B.S. in Chemistry, Boston Coll., 1940; M.S. in Physical Chemistry, U. Mass., 1942; A.M. in Ednl. Psychology, Yale, 1950; Ph.D. in U. Adminstrn, Yale, 1955. Various mgmt. positions Dow Chem. Co., 1950-67, mng. dir., France, 1963-66; gen. mgr. Latin Am., Pacific, Office of Asso. Cos., Midland, Mich., 1966-67; Hayes Healy prof. mktg. Grad. Sch. Bus., U. Notre Dame, 1967-77; Univ. prof. internat. mgmt. U.S. Internat. U., San Diego, 1977—; v.p. Kestrel Inc., N.Y.C.; Mem. sci. adv. com. Italian Ministry of Tourism. Served to maj. U.S. Army, 1942-46. Decorated Air medal, Bronze Star.; Sr. Fulbright scholar, Ecuador, 1973. Mem. Am. Chem. Soc., Sigma Xi, Phi Kappa Phi. Clubs: Union League (N.Y.C.); Travelers (Paris). Home: 5080 Carlsbad Blvd Carlsbad CA 92008 Office: College Business Administration US Internat U San Diego CA 92131

DOW, HERBERT HENRY, chemical company executive; b. Midland, Mich., Aug. 6, 1927; s. Willard Henry and Martha (Pratt) D.; m. Barbara Clarke, Sept. 16, 1951; children: Dana Dow Schuler, Willard Henry II, Pamela G. B.S., MIT, 1952; LL.D., Central Mich. U., 1972; H.H.D. (hon.), Saginaw Valley State Coll., 1975, D.Pub., Service Albion Coll., 1977. Mem. staff Midland div. Dow Chem. Co., 1952-54, mgr. fabric products, 1954-64, sec. exec. com., 1964—, corp. sec., 1968—, dir.; dir. Nat. Bank Detroit, NBD Bancorp. Inc., Detroit. Trustee Mich. Tech. U., Houghton, 1976—. Mem. Am. Soc. Corp. Secs. Office: Dow Chem Co 2030 Dow Center Midland MI 48640

DOW, JOHN PARKER, airline exec.; b. N.Y.C., Mar. 17, 1930; s. Henry John and Jane (Parker) D.; m. Janet Louise Lemme, Oct. 3, 1956; children—Jan, John Parker, Jeffrey, Judd, James. Student, U. Minn., Mpls., 1948-51. With Republic Airlines Inc. (and predecessor), Mpls., 1956—, sec., 1961—, v.p., 1967—; dir. Republic Energy, Inc. Served as pilot USAF, 1952-56. Mem. Quiet Birdmen. Episcopalian. Clubs: Minneapolis, Minikahda. Home: 26 Circle West Edina MN 55436 Office: 7500 Airline Dr Minneapolis MN 55450

DOW, WILBUR EGERTON, JR., lawyer; b. Bklyn., Aug. 5, 1906; s. Wilbur Egerton and Minnie Chloe (Oltman) D.; m. Ruth Elizabeth Paul, Sept. 2, 1931; children: William Paul, Lynn Elizabeth, Ruth Lee. Student, U. Wash., U. So. Calif.; LL.B., N.Y. U., 1934. Bar: N.Y. bar 1936. Specializing in admiralty, N.Y.C., 1936—; Mcht. marine license unlimited master; N.Y. harbor, Hudson River pilot; officer, dir. s.s. cos.; leader Dow Expdn. to Magnetic North Pole, 1954. Mem. Soc. Naval Architects and Marine Engrs., Maritime Law Assn., Am. Bar Assn., Marine Soc. City N.Y., Delta Tau Delta. Clubs: Down Town Assn. (N.Y.C.); Glens Falls Country (N.Y.); Plimsoll (New Orleans). Home and Office: Pine Point Lake George NY 12845 also 2340 ITM Bldg New Orleans LA 70130

DOW, WILLIAM GOULD, electrical engineer,, educator; b. Faribault, Minn., Sept. 30, 1895; s. James Jabez and Myra Amelia (Brown) D.; m. Edna Lois Sontag., Oct. 24, 1924 (dec. Feb. 1963); children—Daniel Gould, David Sontag; m. Katherine Bird Keene, Apr. 2, 1968; stepchildren—John S. Keene, Margaret Keene Hannan, Karen Keene Day. B.S., U. Minn., 1916, E.E., 1917; M.S.E., U. Mich., 1929; D.Sc. (hon.), U. Colo., 1980. Registered profl. engr., Mich. Diversified engring. and bus. experience, 1917-26; faculty, dept. elec. engring. U. Mich., Ann Arbor, 1926-65, prof. elec. engring., 1945-65, chmn. dept. elec. engring., 1958-64, prof. emeritus, 1966—; sr. research geophysicist Space Physics Research Lab., 1966-71; electronics cons. Nat. Bur. Standards, 1945-55; research staff Radio Research Lab., Harvard, 1943-45, assignment, U.K., winter 1944-45; sci. adv. com. Harry Diamond Labs., 1953-64; bus. mgr. Lang. Studies Abroad, Spain, summers, 1965-74; Mem. vacuum tube devel. com. NDRC, World War II; (European vacuum tube research survey), 1953, mem. rocket and satellite research panel, 1946-60; U.S. tech. panel on rocketry IGY, 1956-59; made world tour for space research and engring. edn. survey, 1969-70; Charter mem. bd. trustees Environmental Research Inst. Mich., 1972—. Author: Fundamentals of Engineering Electronics, 1937, rev. 1952, Very High Frequency Techniques (co-author), 2 vols, 1947; Contbr. tech. articles in field. Served as lt. C.E. U.S. Army, World War I. Recipient medal, award in elec. engring. edn. IEEE, 1963. Fellow IEEE (bd. editors 1941-54), Engring. Soc. Detroit, AAAS; mem. AAUP, Am. Phys. Soc., Am. Inst. Aeros. and Astronautics, Am. Geophys. Union, Nat., Mich. socs. profl. engrs., Am. Astronautical Soc., N.Y. Acad. Scis., Am. Soc. Engring. Edn., Am. Welding Soc., Nat. Electronics Conf. (dir. 1949-52, chmn. bd. 1951), Internat. Platform Assn., Sigma Xi, Tau Beta Pi, Eta Kappa Nu. Episcopalian. Clubs: Mason., Cosmos (Washington). Patentee trochoidal nuclear fusion system. Home: 915 Heatherway Ann Arbor MI 48104 *It has been my hope and prayer that I might always: Base decisions for action on my own judgements rather than on opinions of others; Live primarily in a world of people, rather than a world of dollars or of scientific or man-made laws; Always listen for the whistling of the winds of change, and so ever pursue the need to learn new skills of mind and hand, to keep up with the pace of change-for nothing is eternal but change-except that there remains eternal, ever, awareness of beauty, as in things seen and heard, and in graciousness of mind and spirit.*

DOWBEN, ROBERT MORRIS, physician, scientist; b. Phila., Apr. 6, 1927; s. Morris and Zena (Brown) D.; m. Carla Lurie, June 20, 1950; children—Peter Arnold, Jonathan Stuart, Susan Laurie. A.B., Haverford Coll., 1946; M.S., U. Chgo., 1947, M.D., 1949. Intern U. Chgo. Clinics, 1949-50; research fellow U. Oslo, 1950-51; fellow Johns Hopkins Hosp., 1951-52; resident in medicine U. Pa. Hosp., 1952-53; instr. medicine U. Pa. and dir. radiosotope unit VA Hosp., Phila., 1953-55; asst. prof. medicine Northwestern U. Med. Sch., 1957-62; asso. prof. biology M.I.T., 1962-68; lectr. medicine Harvard U. Med. Sch., 1962-68; prof. med. sci. Brown U., 1968-72; prof. biochemistry U. Bergen, Norway, 1972; prof. physiology and neurology, dir. grad. program in biophysics U. Tex. Health Sci. Center, Dallas, 1972—; cons. neurologist Children's, Scottish Rite, Presbyn., Baylor hosps., 1972—; Mem. corp. Haverford (Pa.) Coll., Marine Biol. Lab., Woods Hole, Mass.; bd. dirs. Greenhill Sch., Dallas, 1974-77. Author: Biol. Membranes, 1969, General Physiology, 1971, Cell Biology, 1972, also numerous articles; editor: Cell and Muscle Motility. Served to capt. M.C. USAF, 1955-57. Lalor fellow; recipient Disting. Service award Assn. Neuromuscular Diseases, 1964, Alumni Assn. U. Chgo., 1980. Mem. Am. Physiol. Soc., Am. Soc. Biol. Chemists, Am. Chem. Soc., Soc. Exptl. Biology and Medicine, Biophys. Soc., Soc. Clin. Investigation, Central Soc. Clin. Research, Mass. Med. Soc., Soc. Med. Soc., Dallas County Med. Soc., Tex. Med. Assn., Biochem. Soc. London, Faraday Soc. (London), Phi Beta Kappa, Sigma Xi. Quaker.

DOWD, DAVID JOSEPH, banker; b. Long Island City, N.Y., June 6, 1924; s. David Joseph and Elsie (Schaeffler) B.; m. Margaret Rapp; children—Laury, David, Patrick, Carol. B.S. in Bus. Adminstrn, N.Y. U., 1949. Asst. v.p. Irving Trust Co., N.Y.C., 1952-64; v.p. Franklin Nat. Bank, N.Y.C., 1964-66; sr. v.p. Security Nat. Bank, Huntington, N.Y., 1966-72; pres. Nassau Trust Co., Glen Cove, N.Y., 1972-75, Bankers Service Co., 1975—; pub. Long Island Financial Newsletter, 1976—; Dir. Randy Internat. Corp. Pres. Suffolk County council Boy Scouts Am., 1969-70; chmn. Suffolk Community Devel. Corp., 1973-74; Trustee Stony Brook Found., State U. N.Y., 1972. Served with USMCR, 1942-45, 51-52. Mem. N.Y. State Bankers Assn. (chmn. group VII 1972-75), L.I. Bankers Assn. (dir. 1969-74), Suffolk County Bankers Assn. (pres. 1971-72), Empire State C. of C. (dir. 1969-75). Box 1554 Shelter Island NY 11964

DOWD, MORGAN DANIEL, college dean, political science educator; b. Boston, Feb. 21, 1933; s. Joseph Francis and Marion Caroline (Calcari) D.; m. Dianne May Robichaud, Aug. 29, 1959; children: Megan Eileen, Sean Morgan, Colin Martin, Blaine Christopher, Roarke Terence. B.A. cum laude, St. Michael's Coll., 1955; J.D., Catholic U. Am., 1958; M.A., U. Mass., 1962, Ph.D., 1964. Instr. U. Maine, 1959-60, U. Mass., 1960-61; asst. prof. polit. sci. SUNY-Fredonia, 1963-67, assoc. prof., 1967-76, prof., 1976—, dean grad. studies and research, 1969-78, dean faculty for natural and social scis., 1978—; cons. Middle States Assn. Colls. and Univs., 1977—. Contbr. articles to law jours., 1956-78; co-editor: World Dictionary of Environmental Research Centers, 2d edit., 1974. Mem. Columbia U. Seminar on History of Legal and Polit. Theory, Torch Club, Delta Epsilon Sigma, Pi Sigma Alpha, Delta Theta Phi, Phi Eta Sigma. Democrat. Roman Catholic. Office: SUNY 803 Maytum Hall Fredonia NY 14063

DOWD, PETER JEROME, public relations executive; b. Bklyn., Oct. 5, 1942; s. Jerome Ambrose and Mary Agnes (Young) D.; m. Brenda Badura, Nov. 25, 1972; 1 dau., Kelly Ann. A.B., Fordham U., 1964. Reporter UPI, N.Y.C., 1964-66; account exec. Hill and Knowlton, N.Y.C., 1966-71, v.p., 1971-74, sr. v.p., mgr., 1974-78, mng. dir. Western region, 1978-80, exec. v.p., 1980; ptnr. Haley, Kiss & Dowd, Inc., Los Angeles, 1980—; v.p. Am. Med. Internat., 1983; instr. U. So. Calif., Calif. State U., Fullerton. Bd. dirs. Cath. Big Bros.; trustee Center for Non-profit Mgmt. Mem. Public Relations Soc. Am. (dir. Los Angeles chpt.), Town Hall West (v.p., dir.). Republican. Roman Catholic. Club: Jonathan (Los Angeles). Office: 405 Lexington Ave New York NY 10174

DOWD, THOMAS NATHAN, lawyer; b. Sioux City, Iowa, Mar. 29, 1917; s. Daniel Thornton and Eva (Willett) D.; m. Mary Catherine Majure, July 18, 1940; children—Margaret Majure, Catherine Eva. A.B., George Washington U., 1939, J.D. with distinction, 1942. Bar: D.C. bar 1942, Md. bar 1958. Also U.S. Supreme Ct.; with FBI, 1939-4O; practice in, Washington, 1942—; partner firm Pierson, Ball & Dowd (and predecessor), 1945-77, counsel, 1977—; dir. Potomac Valley Bank.; Operator horse and Angus cattle farm, 1958—. Served to maj. USMCR, 1942-46. Mem. Am., D.C., FCC bar assns., Phi Beta Kappa, Order of Coif, Phi Eta Sigma, Phi Delta Delta, Pi Kappa Alpha. Clubs: Metropolitan, Congressional Country (Washington); M.F.H., Potomac Hunt. Home: Inverness Farm 20700 Darnestown Rd Dickerson MD 20842 Office: Ring Bldg 1200 18th St NW Washington DC 20036

DOWDEN, CARROLL VINCENT, publishing company executive; b. Louisville, Apr. 9, 1933; s. Charles Merrill and Regina Celestine (Popham) D.; m. Eleanor Therese Dion, Nov. 24, 1956; children: Mark Vincent, Laura Anne, Amy Alexandra, Beth Regina. A.B., U. Notre Dame, 1955; M.S. in Journalism, Columbia U., 1960. Asst. financial editor Louisville Times, 1955-56; asso. editor Ind. U. News Bur., Bloomington, 1956-57; asst. financial editor Courier-Jour., Louisville, 1957-63; with Med. Econs. Co., Oradell, N.J., 1963—; gen. mgr. Drug Tropics mag., 1972-73; pub. Med. Econs. mag., 1973-77, exec. v.p. co., 1976-77, pres., 1977—, Next Pub. Co., N.Y.C., 1979-81; chmn. Washington legal com. Am. Bus. Press, 1979—; dir. bus. publs. audit Circulation, Inc., 1981—. Trustee Pascack Valley Hosp., Westwood, N.J., 1976-83, v.p. bd., 1978-80. Served to capt. U.S. Army, 1956, 61-62. Pulitzer traveling fellow Columbia U., 1960-61. Mem. Soc. Profl. Journalists. Club: Hackensack Golf (Oradell). Home: 27 Douglas Dr Hillsdale NJ 07642 Office: 680 Kinderkamack Rd Oradell NJ 07649

DOWDLE, JOHN WESLEY, JR., tobacco company executive; b. Rome, Ga., Mar. 8, 1926; s. John Wesley and Lucille (Field) D.; m. Virginia Louise Sandy, Nov. 23, 1950; children: John Wesley, Jason Earl, Merriman Lee Dowdle Miller. B.S., U.S. Mcht. Marine Acad., 1946; LL.B., U. S.C., 1952; LL.M., Georgetown U., 1955; S.J.D., 1958. Bar: S.C. bar 1951, N.C. bar 1961. Atty., chief counsel's office IRS, Washington, 1955-60; tax atty. R.J. Reynolds Tobacco Co., Winston-Salem, N.C., 1960-62, tax mgr., 1962-70, asst. sec., 1963-70, asst. treas., 1968-70; treas. R.J. Reynolds Industries, Inc., Winston-Salem, 1970-79, v.p., 1979—; dir. J.A. Jones Constrn. Co., Charlotte, N.C., Allendale Mut. Mem. N.C. Tax Study Commn., 1963-65; trustee Winston-Salem State U., 1973-76, N.C. Public Employee Deferred Compensation Plan, 1975-80, Fund Advancement N.C. Sch. Math. and Sci., 1981. Served with USNR, 1952-54. Mem. Nat. Investor Relations Inst., Fin. Execs. Inst. Republican. Episcopalian. Home: 2836 Fairmont Rd Winston-Salem NC 27106 Office: RJR World Hdqrs Winston-Salem NC 27102

DOWDS, JOHN JOSEPH, editor; b. Pitts., Feb. 4, 1938; s. Dennis Joseph and Marie Francis (Flynn) D.; m. Helen Ann Lahoski, Nov. 12, 1966; children: J. Brendan, Daniel Flynn. B.A., Duquesne U., 1965, M.Ed., 1975; cert. advanced study in info. sci., U. Pitts., 1983. Dir., gen. editor Duquesne U. Press, Pitts., 1966—; Mem. Soc. for Phenomenology and Existential Philosophy. Contbr. articles to profl. jours. Mem. Am. Soc. Info. Sci. Democrat. Roman Catholic. Home: 915 LaClair St Pittsburgh PA 15218 Office: 600 Forbes St Pittsburgh PA 15219

DOWDY, HOMER EARL, foundation executive; b. Flint, Mich., July 16, 1922; s. Homer Gilbert and Gladys Anna (Russell) D.; m. Nancy Elizabeth Showalter, June 14, 1947; children: Margaret Dowdy Pope, Rebecca Dowdy Johnson, Barbara Dowdy Wills, David A., Jennifer L., Susan J. A.B., Wheaton (Ill.) Coll., 1947; D.Pub. Service (hon.), U. Md., 1982. Editor, The Milepost, Ames, Iowa, 1947-48; reporter, then asst. city editor Flint Jour., 1948-62; freelance writer, 1962-63; mem. staff C.S. Mott Found., Flint, 1963—, v.p., 1970-80, sr. v.p. planning and dissemination, 1980—. Author: Christ's Withdoctor, 1963, The Bamboo Cross, 1964, Out of the Jaws of the Lion, 1965, Building a Christian Home, 1961, Christians Have Troubles, Too, 1968. Pres. Genesee County (Mich.) Parks and Recreation Commn., 1978; chmn. exec. com. Nat. Recreation and Park Assn., 1977; founding mem. Flint Area Conf., 1970; mem. nat. alumni bd. Wheaton Coll., 1980. Served with AUS, 1943-46. Recipient award Am. Polit. Sci. Assn., 1957, AP, 1961. Presbyterian. Clubs: Flint City, Univ. (Flint). Home: care Dick & Peggy Pope 229 S Lombard Oak Park IL 60302

DOWDY, JOHN WESLEY, clergyman, educator, mayor; b. Albertville, Ala., Jan. 7, 1912; s. Sherman and Beulah Bee (Strange) D.; m. Floy Weaver Thurston, Apr. 2, 1930; children—John Wesley, David, Floyd William, Paul Philip. A.B., Okla. Baptist U., 1934, D.D., 1960; Th.B., So. Bapt. Theol. Sem., Louisville, 1939, Th.M., 1940; Th.D., Central Baptist Theol. Sem., Kansas City, 1945; M.R.E., 1948. Ordained elder, ministry of Baptist Church, 1933, served pastorates in, Shawnee, Okla., 1933-34, Haskell, Okla., 1934-36, English, Ky., 1936-39, Wheatley, Ky., 1939-4O; asst. exec. sec. Ky. Baptist Gen. Assn., Louisville, 1940-43; asst. gen. supt. Mo. Baptist Gen. Assn., Kansas City, 1943-45; prof. systematic theology Central Baptist Theol. Sem., 1945-48; pres. S.W. Baptist Coll., Bolivar, Mo., 1948-61; pastor 1st Bapt. Ch., Guthrie, Okla., 1961—; mayor, City of Guthrie, 1977—; Moderator Central Bapt. Assn.; bd. dirs. Bapt. Gen. Conv. of Okla. Mem. Logan County Hosp., Assn.; chmn lay adv. bd. Alverno Heights Hosp.; chmn. Guthrie Human Relations Com.; Bd. dirs. United Community Chest Fund; trustee Okla. Bapt. U. Decorated Order Red Cross of Constantine. Mem. Order of Eastern Star, DeMolay Legion Honor (hon. life), Rotarian. Democrat. Club: Mason (33 deg., Shriner). Home: 410 E Mansur St Guthrie OK 73044

DOWDY, WAYNE, congressman; b. Fitzgerald, Ga., July 27, 1943; m. Susan Tenney; children: Dunbar, Charles, Eloise. B.A., Millsaps Coll., Jackson, Miss., 1965; LL.B., Jackson Sch. Law, 1968. Mayor, McComb, Miss., 1978-81, city judge, McComb, 1970-74; mem. 97th-98th congresses from 4th Dist. Miss. Pres. Pike County Indsl. Found.; past mem. state bd. Easter Seal Soc., United Way, Salvation Army. Mem. Am. Trial Lawyers Assn., Miss. Trial Lawyers Assn., Miss. Bar Assn., Pike County Bar Assn. Democrat. Methodist. Office: 210 Cannon House Office Bldg Washington DC 20515

DOWELL, ANTHONY JAMES, ballet dancer; b. London, Feb. 16, 1943; s. Arthur Henry and Catherine Ethel D. Studied with, June Hampshire; student, Royal Ballet Sch. Dancer Covent Garden Opera Ballet, 1960; dancer Royal Ballet, 1961-78, prin. dancer, 1966—; guest artist Am. Ballet Threatre, N.Y.C., 1977-79. Created: dance roles in ballets The Dream, 1964, Monotones, 1965, Jazz Calendar, 1968, Shadowplay, 1967, Enigma Variations, 1968, Meditation, 1971, Anastasia, 1971, Triad, 1972, Pavane, 1973, Manon, 1974, Four Schumann Pieces, 1975, A Month in the Country, 1976, Contre Dances, 1979; appeared in: film Valentino; guest artist: Nat. Ballet Can., 1979, 81. Comdr. Order Brit. Empire.; Recipient award Dance mag., 1972. Office: care Peter S. Diggins Assocs 133 W 71st St New York NY 10023 *

DOWELL, EARL HUGH, university dean, aerospace and mechanical engineering educator; b. Macomb, Ill., Nov. 16, 1937; s. Earl S. and Edna Bernice (Dean) D.; m. Lynn M. Cary, July 21, 1981; children: Marla Lorraine, Janice Lynelle, Michael Hugh. B.S., U. Ill., 1959; S.M., Mass. Inst. Tech., 1961, Sc.D., 1964. Research engr. Boeing Co., 1962-63; research asst. Mass. Inst. Tech., 1963-64, research engr., 1964, asst. prof., 1964-65; asst. prof. aerospace and mech. engring. Princeton U., 1964-68, asso. prof., 1968-72, prof., 1972-83, assoc. chmn., 1975-77, acting chmn., 1979; dean Sch. Engring. Duke U., Durham, N.C., 1983—; cons. to industry and govt. Author: Aeroelasticity of Plates and Shells, 1974, A Modern Course in Aeroelasticity, 1978; Assoc. editor: AIAA Jour, 1969-72; Contbr. articles to profl. jours. Chmn. N.J. Noise Control Council, 1972-76. Named outstanding young alumnus U. Ill. Sch. Aero. and Astronautical Engring., 1973, disting. alumnus, 1975. Assoc. fellow AIAA (Structures, Structural Dynamics and Material award 1980, v.p. publs. 1981-83). Mem. Acoustical Soc. Am., ASME, Am. Acad. Mechs. Home: duke univ school of engineering Durham NC 27706 Office: School of Engineering Duke University Durham NC *The pursuit of excellence is exciting; the achievement is sometimes anti-climatic* *

DOWELL, MICHAEL BRENDAN, chemist; b. N.Y.C., Nov. 18, 1942; s. William Henry and Anne Susan (Cannon) D.; m. Gail Elizabeth Renton, Mar. 16, 1968; children: Rebecca, Margaret. B.S., Fordham U., 1963; Ph.D., Pa. State U., 1967. Physicist U.S. Army Frankford Arsenal, Phila., 1967-69; research scientist Parma Tech.

Ctr., Union Carbide Corp., (Ohio), 1969-74, devel. mgr. carbon fiber applications, 1974-76, group leader metals and ceramics research, 1976-80, sr. group leader process research, 1980-82, mgr. market devel., 1982—. Contbr. articles to profl. jours. Chmn. 14th Congressional Dist. steering com. Common Cause, 1974-76; officer, trustee Hudson Montessori Assn., 1974-79. Served to capt. ordnance AUS, 1967-69. Mem. Am. Chem. Soc., Am. Phys. Soc., Am. Carbon Soc., Phi Lambda Upsilon. Roman Catholic. Home: 368 N Main St Hudson OH 44236 Office: PO Box 6087 Cleveland OH 44101

DOWGRAY, JOHN GRAY LAIRD, JR., educator, university official; b. Kansas City, Mo., Jan. 10, 1922; s. John Gray Laird and Mabel (Holmes) D.; m. Joanne Carol Fitzpatrick, Jan. 17, 1971; children by previous marriage: John Gray Laird III, Laurie Louise; stepchildren: Leana Kay Dooley, Kari Lynn Dooley. Student, Rockhurst Coll., 1939-41; A.B. with distinction in History, U. Kansas City, 1947; M.S., U. Wis., 1947; Ph.D. in History, U. Wis., 1956. Instr. history U. Mo. at Kansas City, 1952-56, asst. prof., 1956-59, asso. prof., 1959-63, prof., 1963-69, coordinator grad. studies, 1961-64, dean grad. studies, 1964-65, dean faculties, 1965-69; v.p. acad. affairs U. Tulsa, 1969-83, dir. info. services div., 1983—, Trustee prof. humanities, 1983—. Mem. Okla. Humanities Com., 1973-75, chmn., 1974-75; Bd. dirs. Okla. Osteo. Hosp., 1974—. Mem. Orgn. Am. Historians. Home: 6234 S 72d E Ave Tulsa OK 74133

DOWLEY, FRANCIS HOTHAM, art history educator; b. N.Y.C., Dec. 13, 1915; s. Francis Dwight and Helen Agnes (Blackburne) D. B.A. in Philosophy, Princeton U., 1936, M.A., U. Chgo., 1941, Ph.D., 1953. Instr. U. Chgo., 1949-53, asst. prof. art history, 1953-58, assoc. prof., 1959-73, prof., 1974—. Contbr. research publs. in art history. Served to lt. (j.g.) USN, 1943-46; Japan. Grantee Am. Council Learned Socs., Paris, 1947-48. Mem. Am. Soc. Eighteenth Century Studies (chmn. com. Best Article Prize 1972-75), Coll. Art Assn., Societe de L'Histoire de l'Art Francais, Art Inst. Chgo. Roman Catholic. Club: Quadrangle (Chgo.). Office: Dept Art U Chgo 5540 Greenwood Ave Chicago IL 60637

DOWLIN, KENNETH EVERETT, librarian; b. Wray, Colo., Mar. 11, 1941; s. Ross Everett and Fern Mae (Peterson) D.; m. Janice Marie Simmons, Mar. 11, 1961; children: Kevin Everett, Kristopher Everett. B.A., U. Colo., 1963, M.P.A., 1981; M.A., U. Denver, 1966. Bookmobile librarian, library asst. Adams County Public Library, Westminster, Colo., 1961-63; library asst. II Denver Public Library, 1962-64; head librarian Arvada (Colo.) Public Library, 1964-68; adminstrv. asst. Jefferson County (Colo.) Public Library, 1969; dir. Natrona County (Wyo.) Public Library, Casper, 1969-75, Pikes Peak Regional Library Dist., Colorado Springs, Colo., 1975—; instr. Casper Coll., 1971-73; chmn. Colo. Libraries in Coop., 1975-76, Colo. Ad-hoc Com. Networking, 1976; mem. Western Interstate Commn. Higher Edn. Library Network Task Force; past trustee Wyo. Dept. Library, Archives and History; mem. Library of Congress Commn. on Book of Future; bd. dirs. Satellite Library Info. Network; vis. instr. U. Denver, 1980, 81; Cons. in cable TV. Mem. adv. bd. for series on tech. WNET, N.Y.C., 1981—; bd. dirs. Citizens Goals for Colorado Springs, 1981—; bd. govs. Colo. Tech. Coll., 1982—. Served with USMCR, 1959-65. Mem. ALA (Hammond Inc. Library Award Jury 1968), ALA Library and Info. Tech. Assn. (lang. planning com. 1981-82, pres. 1983-84), Mountain Plains Library Assn., Colo. Library Assn. (pres. 1968-69), Denver Council Govts. (chmn. librarians com. 1966), Colo. Municipal League (chmn. librarians sect. 1967), Bibliog. Center Rocky Mountains (pres. 1972-74), Pikes Peak Area C. of C. (chmn. cultural affairs com. 1976-77). Home: 2477 N Circle Dr Colorado Springs CO 80909 Office: PO Box 1579 Colorado Springs CO 80901

DOWLING, JAMES HAMILTON, public realtions executive; b. Chgo., Oct. 20, 1931; s. Joseph Henry D. and Margaret (Hamilton) Dowlig; m. Julie Anne Pastor, Apr. 7, 1958; children: James Hamilton, Kenneth Edward, Tracy Anne. B.J., U. Mo., 1957. Writer, editor UPI, New Orleans, 1957, Newsweek, Atlanta and N.Y.C., 1958-59, AP, Chgo., NY, 1960-63; pub. relations staff Mobil Oil Corp., N.Y.C., 1963; with Burson-Marsteller Inc., 1964—, gen. mgr., N.Y.C., 1968-70, Chgo., 1970-75; pres. Burson-Marsteller, N.Y.C., 1975—. Mem. exec. com. Pres.'s Pvt. Sector Survey on Cost Control in Fed. Govt.; mem. devel. bd. Central Park Conservancy. Served with USMC, 1952-55. Li Found. fellow, 1957-58. Mem. Pub. Relations Soc. Am. Office: 866 3d Ave New York NY 10022 *

DOWLING, JOHN ELLIOTT, educator; b. Pawtucket, R.I., Aug. 31, 1935; s. Joseph Leo and Ruth W. (Tappan) D.; children by previous marriage: Christopher, Nicholas.; m. Judith Falco, Oct. 18, 1975; 1 dau., Alexandra. A.B., Harvard U., 1957, Ph.D., 1961; M.D. (hon.), U. Lund (Sweden), 1982. Asst. prof. biology Harvard U., 1961-64; prof. Harvard, 1971—; asso. prof. Johns Hopkins Sch. Medicine, 1964-71. Contbr. numerous articles on vision to profl. jours. Recipient ann. award N.E. Ophthal. Soc., 1979; award of merit Retina Research Found., 1981. Fellow Am. Acad. Arts, Scis., AAAS; mem. Assn. Research in Vision and Ophthalmology (Friedenwald medal 1970), Nat. Acad. Sci., Neurosci. Soc., Soc. Gen. Physiologists. Home: Master's Lodgings Leverett House 25 De Wolfe St Cambridge MA 02138 Office: Biol Labs Harvard U Cambridge MA 02138

DOWLING, JOSEPH ALBERT, historian; b. Dalmuir, Scotland, Nov. 10, 1926; came to U.S., 1940, naturalized, 1945; s. Joseph Albert and Maud Drury (Mitchell) D.; m. Sylvia Minkin, June 16, 1956; children—David, Kathryn, Juliet, Marc. A.B., Lincoln Meml. U., 1948; M.A., N.Y. U., 1951, Ph.D., 1958. Instr. English and history Shorter Coll., Rome, Ga., 1951-52; instr. cultural heritage Bates Coll., Lewiston, Maine, 1955-58; asst. prof. history Lehigh U., Bethlehem, Pa., 1958-61, asso. prof., 1961-67, prof., 1967-74, Distinguished prof., 1974—. Mem. Citizens Adv. Com. to Upper Milford Zoning Commn., 1970-72. Served with U.S. Army, 1945-46. Recipient Lindback award for distinguished teaching, 1966, Student award for outstanding teaching, 1967, Stabler award for disting. teaching, 1981, all from Lehigh U., Lehigh Yearbook dedication, 1973; Mellon Faculty Devel. grantee, 1977. Mem. Am. Hist. Assn., Am. Studies Assn., Orgn. Am. Historians, Eastern Community Coll. Social Sci. Assn. Democrat. Home: RD 1 Zionsville PA 18092 Office: Dept History Maginnes 9 Lehigh U Bethlehem PA 18018

DOWLING, PAUL THOMAS, steel company executive; b. St. Louis, Aug. 3, 1919; s. Thomas John and Cora Amanda (Wilson) D.; m. Eleanor Irene Heimberger, Sept. 20, 1941. B.S. in Metallurgy, Mo. Sch. of Mines, 1940, hon. degree, 1963, Dr. Engring. (hon.), 1976. Apprentice metallurgist Inland Steel Co., 1939-40; metallurgist Jones & Laughlin Steel Co., 1940-41, Granite City Steel, Ill., 1941; engr. in charge of ammunition component inspection St. Louis Ordnance Dist., 1941-44; with Nooter Corp., St. Louis, 1946—, pres., 1968-71, chief exec. officer, 1971—, chmn. bd., 1976—; dir. Merc. Bank Corp. Bd. dirs. Nat. Constrn. Employers Council, St. Louis Regional Commerce and Growth Assn.; Chmn. Jr. Achievement, St. Louis, mem. nat. bd.; Bd. dirs. United Way, St. Louis, St. Louis council Boy Scouts Am.; trustee Freedoms Found. at Valley Forge; chmn. chancellor's devel. council U. Mo., Rolla. Served with USNR, 1944-46. Recipient Spoehrer award Jr. Achievement, 1979. Mem. Nat. Assn. Constrn. Boilermaker Employers (pres., dir.), Mo. Soc. Profl. Engrs., Nat. Soc. Profl. Engrs., Steel Plate Fabricators Assn. (pres. 1974-76), AIME, Am. Petroleum Inst., Am. Soc. Metals, Tubular Exchanger Mfrs. Assn. (pres. 1971-72), Triangle Frat. (Outstanding Alumnus 1974). Presbyterian. Clubs: Mo. Athletic, Old Warson Country, St. Louis; Stadium; Petroleum (Houston); Carlton (Chgo.). Office: Nooter Corp PO Box 451 Saint Louis MO 63166

DOWLING, RODERICK ANTHONY, investment banker; b. N.Y.C., Dec. 29, 1940; s. John Joseph and Anne (Chisholm) D.; m. Lavinia Seibels, May 6, 1977; children: Lavinia Crosby, Roderick A.; children by previous marriage: Anne Chisholm, Katherine Burke. B.S., Fairfield U., 1962; J.D., Fordham U., 1965. Bar: N.Y. 1965, Ga. 1974. Assoc. Cahill, Gordon & Reindel, N.Y.C., 1965-72; v.p., gen. counsel U.S. Industries N.E. Corp., N.Y.C., 1972-73, Fugua Industries, Inc., Atlanta, 1973-81; v.p. Robinson Humphrey Inc., Atlanta, 1981—. Mem. Bar Assn. City N.Y., Am., Georgia, Atlanta bar assns., S.R. Clubs: University, Union, Capitol City, Lawyers. Home: 380 Argonne Atlanta GA 30305

DOWLING, THOMAS ALLAN, mathematics educator; b. Little Rock, Feb. 19, 1941; s. Charles and Esther (Jensen) D.; children: Debra Lynn, David Thomas. B.S., Creighton U., 1962; Ph.D., U. N.C., 1967. Research assoc. U. N.C.-Chapel Hill, 1967-69, asst. prof., 1969-72; assoc. prof. math. Ohio State U., Columbus, 1972-82, prof., 1982—; ops. researcher U.S. Govt., Patrick AFB, Fla., 1963-64; faculty fellow NASA at UCLA, Pasadena, summer 1968; conf. organizer U. N.C., 1967-70; cons. organizer Ohio State U., 1978-82. Editor: Combination Mathematics and its Applications, 1967-70; contbr. article to profl. jours.; discoverer: Dowling lattices. NSF grantee, 1972-79. Mem. Am. Math. Soc., Math. Assn. Am., AAUP. Democrat. Club: Ohio State U. faculty. Home: 200 Broadmeadows Blvd Apt 35 Columbus OH 43214 Office: Dept Math Ohio State Univ 231 W 18th Ave Columbus OH 43210

DOWNE, EDWARD R., JR., private investor. Founder Downe Communications, Inc. Home: 151 Ox Pasture Rd Southampton NY 11968

DOWNER, EUGENE DEBS, JR., editor, publisher; b. Stump Creek, Pa., Dec. 19, 1939; s. Eugene Debs and Vona (Weamer) D. B.A., Pa. State U., 1961. Asst. advt. dir. Bliss & Laughlin Industries, Oak Brook, Ill., 1964-66; mgr. pub. relations Nat. Can Corp., Chgo., 1966-67; Head Ski Co., Timonium, Md., 1967-68; pres. Osprey Enterprises, Jackson, Wyo., 1968-78; pub., editor Teton Mag., Jackson, 1969—; owner Teton Bookshops, also; Teton Bookshop Pub. Co., Jackson. Served with USCGR, 1961-62. Recipient Journalism award AMA, 1974, Wyo. State Hist. Soc., 1977. Mem. U.S. Ski Writers Assn. Republican. Methodist. Address: Box 1903 Jackson WY 83001

DOWNER, JOSEPH PLATT, oil company executive; b. Coblenz, Germany, July 11, 1922; s. John Walter and Gladys (Trevor) D.; m. Jannett Lord Tucker, Dec. 30, 1949; children—Jannett Trevor, William Tucker, John Ashton. B.S. cum laude, Harvard U., 1943, M.B.A., 1948. Asst. to v.p. for coordination and planning Continental Oil Co., 1948-52; mgr. oil dept. Wertheim & Co., Dallas and N.Y.C., 1952-59; with Sinclair Oil Corp., 1959-69, exec. v.p., 1968-69, chmn. finance com., 1966-69; also dir.; exec. v.p., dir. Atlantic Richfield Co., 1969-80, vice chmn., dir., 1980—; dir. Lockheed Corp., Burbank, Calif., Fiduciary Trust Co., N.Y.C., Community TV of So. Calif., Los Angeles. Trustee Los Angeles County Mus. Art., Com. Econ. Devel. Served to capt. AUS, 1943-46. Mem. Am. Petroleum Inst., Harvard U. Alumni Assn. (pres. 1983-84). Republican. Episcopalian. Clubs: Knickerbocker, Harvard (N.Y.C.); Army Navy (Washington); California (Los Angeles); Beach (Santa Monica, Calif.). Home: 605 Tigertail Rd Los Angeles CA 90049 Office: 515 S Flower St Los Angeles CA 90071

DOWNES, EDMUND WILLIAM, ret. newspaper exec.; b. Hartford, Conn., Oct. 23, 1920; s. William H. and Katherine L. (Delaney) D.; m. Mary Alice Moore, June 5, 1947; children—Donald W., Maryanne M., Elizabeth J. B.S., Hillyer Coll., Hartford, Conn., 1956. With Hartford Courant Co., 1952-80, pres., 1968-80, also dir.; dir. Conn. Bank and Trust Co., Hartford, Greater Hartford Corp.; Mem. Glastonbury (Conn.) Redevel. Agy. Bd. dirs. Jr. Achievement, Hartford, Hartford Courant Found., Eastern States Exposition; bd. corporators Hartford Hosp., Mt. Sinai Hosp. Served with USAAF, 1942-46. Mem. Conn. Daily Newspaper Assn.

DOWNES, EDWARD OLIN DAVENPORT, musicologist, critic, radio broadcaster; b. Boston, Aug. 12, 1911; s. Edwin Olin and Marian Amanda (Davenport) D.; m. Mildred Fowler Gignoux, Oct. 23, 1943 (div. Aug. 1954). Student, Columbia, 1929-30, Manhattan Sch. Music, 1930-32, U. Paris, France, 1932-33, U. Munich, Germany, 1932, 34-36, 38-39; Ph.D., Harvard, 1958. Asst. music critic N.Y. Post, 1936-38; music critic Boston Evening Transcript, 1939-41; commentator, asst. program mgr. radio sta. W67Ny, N.Y.C., 1941-42; intelligence analyst and editor OSS, Dept. State, also War Dept., 1943-46; program annotator, lectr. music Boston Mus. Fine Arts, 1946-50; lectr. music Wellesley Coll., 1948-49; prof. music history U. Minn., 1950-55, Ph.D. Grad. Ctr. Queens Coll. of CUNY, 1966-81, NYU, 1981—; asst. music critic N.Y. Times, 1955-58; quizmaster Met. Opera broadcasts, 1958—; program annotator N.Y. Philharmonic-Symphony Soc., 1960-74; lectr. music series Met. Mus. Art, 1960-66, 83—; lectr. Dialogue Series N.Y. Philharm., 1982—; faculty Master Classes Bayreuth (West Germany) Festival, 1959-65; intermission host N.Y. Philharmonic Symphony broadcasts, 1964-66, First Hearing Broadcast series, Sta. WQXR, N.Y.C., 1968—. Author: Adventures in Symphonic Music, 1943, Translator Verdi: The Man in His Letters, 1942; Editor: (with H.C. Robbins Landon) Temistocle, (opera by Christian Bach), 1965, (with others) Perspectives in Musicology, 1973, New York Philharmonic Guide to the Symphony, 1976; reprinted as Guide to Symphonic Music, 1981. Served with AUS, 1942-45. Mem. Am. Musicol. Soc. (council 1958-60, 69-71), Internat. Musicol. Soc., Am. Music Library Assn., Am. Council Learned Socs., Am. Soc. Theatre Research, Gesellschaft für Musikforschung., Società Italiana di Musicologia. Address: 1 W 72d St New York NY 10023

DOWNES, RACKSTRAW, artist; b. Pembury, Kent, Eng., Nov. 8, 1939; came to U.S., 1961; s Henry Alfred and Rosa Kathleen (Rackstraw) D. B.A., Cambridge U., 1961; M.F.A., Yale U., 1964. Asst. prof. U. Pa., Phila., 1967-78; mem.faculty Skowhegan Sch., Maine, 1975; mem. faculty N.Y. Studio Sch., N.Y.C., 1980-82; editor Fairfield Porter: Art in Its Own Terms, 1979; bd. govs. Skowhegan Sch. Painting and Sculpture, 1981—. Exhibited one man shows, Kornblee Gallery, (locat.) N.Y.C., 1972-82, Hirschl & Adler Modern, (locat.) N.Y.C., 1982—; group shows, San Antonio Mus., 1981, Pa. Acad., (locat.) Phila., Carnegie Internat., (locat.) Pitts., 1983; represented permanent collections, Whitney Mus. Am. Art, (locat.) N.Y.C., Hirschorn Mus., (locat.) Washington, Pa. Acad. Fine Art, (locat.) Phila., Mus. Art, Carnegie Inst., (loct.) Pitts., Corcoran Gallery Art, (locat.) Washington. Ingram Merrill fellow, 1974; grantee National Endowment for Arts, 1980; recipient creative artist's pub. service award State of N.Y., 1978.

DOWNEY, JAMES, univ. pres.; b. Winterton, Nfld., Can., Apr. 20, 1939; s. Ernest Fletcher and Mimy Ann (Andrews) D.; m. Laura Ann Parsons, July 25, 1964; children—Sarah Elizabeth, Geoffrey James. B.A., Meml. U. Nfld., 1962, B.Ed., 1963, M.A., 1964; Ph.D. (Rothermere fellow 1963-66), U. London, 1966. Mem. faculty Carleton U., Ottawa, 1966-80, prof. English, 1975, dean arts, then v.p., 1975-80, pres. pro tem, 1979; pres. U. N.B., Fredericton, 1980—. Author: The Eighteenth Century Pulpit, 1969; editor: Fearful Joy, 1974. Can. Council fellow, 1975-76. Home: 58 Waterloo Row Fredericton NB E3B 1Y9 Canada Office: Univ New Brunswick Fredericton NB E3B 5A3 Canada

DOWNEY, JOHN ALEXANDER, physician; b. Regina, Sask., Can., Sept. 16, 1930; came to U.S., 1954; s. John Stuart and Victoria (McKenzie) D.; children: Richard Stuart, Susan Elizabeth, Robert John, Jennifer Alison. B.Sc. in Medicine, U. Man., 1953, M.D., 1954; D.Phil., U. Oxford, Eng., 1962. Intern Vancouver Gen. Hosp., 1953-54; resident physician Columbia Presbyn. Med. Center, N.Y.C., 1954-56, 57-59; resident physician (jr. and sr.) Peter Bent Brigham Hosp., Boston, 1956-57, 59-60; research fellow Christ Ch., Oxford U., 1960-62; mem. faculty Columbia Coll. Phys. and Surg., 1962—, prof. rehab. medicine, 1967—, chmn. dept., 1974—; dir. rehab. medicine Blythdale Children's Hosp., Valhalla, N.Y.; vis. scientist dept. human physiology and pharmacology U. Adelaide, S. Australia. Office: 180 Fort Washington Ave New York NY 10032

DOWNEY, JOHN CHARLES, university dean, zoology educator; b. Eureka, Utah, Apr. 12, 1926; s. John Charles and Cleone (Owens) D.; m. Norine Margaret Simpson, June 25, 1949; children—John Charles III, Michael, Mary Ann, Dennis James, Patrick Joseph. B.S., U. Utah, 1949, M.S., 1950; Ph.D., U. Calif. at Davis, 1957. Faculty U. Utah, 1947-52, instr. biology, 1951-52; faculty U. Calif., Davis, 1952-56; asst. prof. zoology So. Ill. U., Carbondale, 1956-61, asso. prof., 1961-66, prof., 1966-68; prof., head dept. biology U. No. Iowa, Cedar Falls, 1968-81, dean, 1981—. Recipient research grants Am. Philos. Soc., 1959, NSF, 1959-61, 62, 64-66, 66-68. Mem. Soc. Study Evolution, Lepidopterists Found., Pacific Coast Entomologists Soc., Lepidopterists Soc. (sec. 1964-71), Soc. Systematic Zoologists (charter mem.), Entomologists Soc. Am., So. Calif., Ill., Iowa acads. scis., Sigma Xi, Phi Sigma, Phi Kappa Phi. Publs. on variation and evolution using insects, especially butterflies as the tool organism; studies of population dynamics showing how host-plants, parasites and symbiotic associations can influence evolution; studies on mimicry; sound prodn. in immature stages of butterflies; scan-electron microscope research on ultrastructure of integument. Home: 2425 Kaiser Ct Waterloo IA 50701 Office: U No Iowa Graduate College Cedar Falls IA 50613

DOWNEY, JOHN FRANCIS, lawyer; b. Sacramento, Dec. 31, 1914; s. Stephen W. and Persis (McIntire) D.; m. Betty Werner, Oct. 16, 1943; children—Barbara, Michael, Cynthia, David, Kathryn, Eve, Stephen, John, Richard, Thomas, Dennis. B.A., Stanford, 1936; LL.B., U. So. Calif., 1938. Bar: Calif. bar 1938. Practiced in, Visalia, 1938-39, fed. conciliation commr., Tulare County, Calif., 1939-40; partner Downey, Brand, Seymour & Rohwer, Sacramento, 1946—; tchr. McGeorge Coll. Law, 1946-47; Vice chmn. Calif. Capitol Bldg. Planning Commn., 1960-67; Mem. adv. bd. Sacramento State Coll., 1950—, chmn., 1967-70; mem. Human Relations Com., Sacramento County, 1963-68. Author: Doomstar, 1979. Chmn. chancellor's adv. council Calif. State Colls., 1974-76. Served to maj. C.E. AUS, 1940-45. Decorated Bronze Star medal with oak leaf cluster, Purple Heart. Fellow Am. Coll. Trial Lawyers, Am. Bar Found.; mem. Sacramento County Bar Assn. (pres. 1959), Sacramento Legal Aid Soc. (pres. 1956). Clubs: Rotarian (pres. Sacramento 1958, Paul Harris fellow 1980), Comstock (pres. 1974), Sacramento Univ. (pres. 1953). Home: 3850 W Land Park Dr Sacramento CA 95822 Office: 555 Capitol Mall Sacramento CA 95814

DOWNEY, JOHN WILHAM, composer, educator; b. Chgo., Oct. 5, 1927; s. James Bernard and Augustina (Haas) D.; m. Irusha Czuszak; children: Lydia, Marc. Docteur es Lettres (Ph.D.), U. Paris-Sorbonne, 1957; Prix de Composition (scholar), Paris Conservatory, 1956. Chmn. humanities dept. Mayfair Br., Chgo. City Coll., 1958-64; prof. theory and composition U. Wis., Milw., 1964—; instr. music theory De Paul U., Chgo., 1960-64, Roosevelt U., 1961; Bd. dirs. Rondel Arts Studio. Author: La Musique populaire dans l'Oeuvre de Bela Bartok, 1966; compositions include Cello Sonata; recorded, CRI label, 1968; Agort, woodwind quintet; recorded, Orion label, 1973; Adagio Lyrico: 2 pianos What If?; composer: for mixed choir, solo tympany and brass octet A Dolphin; voice and chamber ensemble Octet for Winds; recorded, Orion Label, 1974, Lydian Suite, 1975, String Quartet II, Gaspara Records, 1976, Crescendo, 1977, High Clouds and Soft Rain, 1977, The Edge of Space (Fantasy for Bassoon and Orchestra), Chandos Label, 1978; also electronic and computer music; resident artist, MacDowell Colony, summers 1971, 75-77, 82-83, fall 1978. Decorated chevalier de l'Ordre des Arts et Lettres, France; Fulbright Scholar, France, 1952-54, winter 1979; French Govt. scholar, 1954-55; teaching fellow, 1955-56; German Govt. teaching fellow, 1956-57; Copley Found. grantee, 1956-57, 57-58; recipient awards U. Wis., 1971, 73, 75, 77, 79, 83, Ford Found., 1976, Nat. Endowment Arts, 1977, 83; named Music Citizen of Yr. Civic Music Assn. of Milw., 1980. Mem. Am. Soc. Univ. Composers, Am. Music Center, ASCAP (awards 1974-82), Am. Fedn. Musicians, Wis. Contemporary Music Forum (founder, chmn. 1970—), Center 20th Century Studies, Phi Kappa Phi, Delta Omicron (nat. patron). Office: U Wis Sch Fine Arts-Music Milwaukee WI 53201 *Although styles change and vary with place and time, an artist's sincerity of purpose, depth of feeling, and intellectual finesse are values permeating most works of art regardless of time and fashion.*

DOWNEY, JUAN ANTONIO, artist; b. Santiago, Chile, May 11, 1940; came to U.S., 1965; s. David Gonzalo and Luisa Ester (Alvarado) D.; m. Marilys Belt, Feb. 25, 1969. B.Arch., Universidad Católica de Chile, 1961. Asst. prof. Pratt Inst. Sch. Arch.; artist-in-residence TV Lab., Sta. WNET, N.Y.C., 1978, Synapse, Syracuse U., 1979, WXXI, Rochester, N.Y., 1979. One-man shows, Galerie Jacqueline Ranson, Paris, 1968, Corcoran Gallery Art, Washington, 1969—, Howard Wise Gallery, N.Y.C., 1970—, Everson Mus. Art, Syracuse, N.Y., 1971-77, Center for Interam. Relations, N.Y.C., 1975, Anthology Film Archives, N.Y.C., 1976, Long Beach (Calif.) Mus., Whitney Mus., N.Y.C., 1976, 78, Mus. Contemporary Art, Houston, 1976, Museo de Arte Contemporáneo, Caracas, Venezuela, 1977, Galería Adler Castillo, Caracas, Univ. Art Mus., Berkeley, Calif., 1978, Leo Castelli Gallery, N.Y.C., Mandville Art Gallery, U. Calif., San Diego, 1979, Mandeville Art Gallery, La Jolla, Calif., The Kitchen, N.Y.C., 1980, group shows include, Venice Biennale, The Pluralist Decade, ICA, Phila., biennial exhbn., Whitney Mus., N.Y.C., TV appearances, N.Y.C., Chgo., Rochester, N.Y., Boston. Recipient Video award Rockefeller Found., 1981; Guggenheim fellow, 1971-76; Nat. Endowment for Arts grantee, 1980; N.Y. State Council Arts grantee, 1981; fellow M.I.T., 1973.

DOWNEY, MICHAEL PETER, public television executive; b. Springfield, Mass., Apr. 14, 1942; s. Mortimer Leo and Elizabeth Gertrude (Carlin) D.; m. Claudia West Allyn, Sept. 30, 1978; children: Sarah Carlin, Caitlin Stanford. B.S. in Broadcasting, Boston U., 1964. TV dir. Sta. WGBH, Boston, 1965-66, producer, dir., 1966-69, ops. mgr., 1969-76; dir. ops. Pub. Broadcasting Service, Washington, 1977-79, sr. v.p. Program adminstrn. and Info., 1979—; dir. Pub. Service Satellite Consortium, 1980-83. Bd. dirs. Kaiser-Georgetown Community Health Plan, 1980—, Boston's Fourth of July, Inc., 1976—. Served with USMCR, 1962. Recipient NET award for

Execellence as TV dir., 1968. Office: 475 L'Enfant Plaza SW Washington DC 20024

DOWNEY, MORTIMER LEO, III, municipal transportation authority executive; b. Springfield, Mass., Aug. 9, 1936; s. Mortimer L. and Elizabeth (Carlin) D.; m. Joyce Vander Meyden, Oct. 21, 1961; children: Stephen Michael, Christopher Sean. B.A., Yale U., 1958; M.P.A., N.Y. U., 1966. Various positions Port Authority, N.Y. and N.J., 1958-75, supr. rail public services, 1973-75; budget analyst Ho. of Reps., 1975-76; dep. undersec. Dept. Transp., Washington, 1977, asst. sec., 1977-81; asst. exec. dir. N.Y. Met. Transp. Authority, N.Y.C., 1981-83, dep. exec. dir., 1983—. Mem. Am. Soc. Public Adminstrn., Pi Sigma Alpha. Democrat. Roman Catholic. Club: Yale Sailing. Home: 218 Dalmeny Briarcliff Manor NY 10510 Office: MTA 347 Madison Ave New York NY 10017

DOWNEY, MORTON, co. exec.; b. Wallingford, Conn., Nov. 14, 1901; s. James Andrew and Elizabeth (Cox) D.; m. Ann Van Gerbig, Feb. 5, 1970. Decorated Grand Cross of Merit of Soverign Order of Malta. Roman Catholic. Clubs: Everglades, Bath and Tennis (Palm Beach). Address: care Arthur Stryker 65 Willets Rd Old Westbury NY 11568

DOWNEY, RICHARD KEITH, plant breeder; b. Saskatoon, Sask., Can., Jan. 26, 1927; s. Richard Albert and Alberta Georgina (Amy) D.; m. Edna Anne Brewer, Aug. 23, 1952; children—Debra Anne, Patricia Grace, Karen Elaine, Richard Douglas, Kevin Donald. B.S. in Agr, U. Sask., 1950, M.Sc., 1952; Ph.D., Cornell U., 1961. Research officer Agr. Can. Research Sta., Lethbridge, Alta., 1951-57, prin. research scientist, asst. dir., Saskatoon, 1958—; adj. prof. U. Sask., 1970—. Author numerous papers in field. Decorated officer Order Can., 1976; recipient Merit award Public Service Can., 1969, Queen's Silver Jubilee medal, 1977; co-recipient Royal Bank Can. award, 1975. Fellow Agrl. Inst. Can. (Grindley medal 1973), Royal Soc. Can.; mem. Can. Soc. Agronomy (pres. 1960-61), Sask. Inst. Agrologists (pres. 1967-68), Can. Seed Growers Assn. (chmn. plant breeders com. 1975—, chmn. policy com. 1978—), Am. Soc. Agronomy, Am. Oil Chemists Soc., Sigma Xi. Mem. United Ch. Can. Club: Nutana Rotary. Office: 107 Science Crescent Saskatoon SK S7N 0X2 Canada

DOWNEY, THOMAS JOSEPH, Congressman; b. Queens, N.Y., Jan. 28, 1949; s. Thomas Anthony and Norma Rita (Morgilla) D.; m. D. Chris Milanos, Dec. 1978; 1 dau., Lauren Katherine. B.S., Cornell U., 1970; postgrad., St. John's U. Law Sch., 1972; J.D., Am. U., 1980. With personnel dept. Macy's, N.Y.C., 1970-71; mem. 94th-98th Congresses from 2d N.Y. Dist., mem. ways and means budget com. Congl. SALT II adv., 1978-79; del. Democratic Nat. Conv., 1972; committeeman N.Y. State Dem. Com., 1972; mem. Suffolk County (N.Y.) Legislature, 1971-74. Mem. Sons of Italy. Methodist. Office: 303 Cannon House Office Bldg Washington DC 20515 *

DOWNIE, DANA, photographer; b. Pasadena, Cal., Sept. 9, 1948; d. Donald C. and Ruth E. (Crawford) D. A.A., Citrus Jr. Coll., 1968; B.S., Calif. State Poly. U., 1971. Free-lance photographer various studios, West Covina, Calif., 1964-71, various nat. aviation mags., 1965—; photographer J.A. Hawkins studio, Pasadena, 1965-75; chief photographer World Campus Afloat, Orange, Calif., 1968-69; reporter, photographer to six weekly newspapers of Bonita Pub. Co., Montclair, Calif., 1969-70, city editor, 1972; photographer San Gabriel Valley Tribune, 1971; staff photographer Press-Enterprise Co., Riverside, Calif., 1972-75, Des Moines Register, 1975-79; full-time free-lance photographer, 1979—. Active YWCA, Riverside, 1972-75. Recipient A.P. Photo Contest awards, 1974, 75; numerous Photo awards state and local photo contests. Mem. Nat., Calif., Iowa press photographers, Twin Counties Press Club. Home and Office: 1150 37th St Des Moines IA 50311

DOWNIE, LEONARD, JR., newspaper editor, author; b. Cleve., May 1, 1942; s. Leonard and Pearl Martha (Evenheimer) D.; m. Barbara Lindsey, July 15, 1960 (div. 1971); children: David Leonard, Scott Leonard; m. Geraldine Rebach, Aug. 15, 1971; children: Joshua Mark, Sarah Elizabeth. B.A., Ohio State U., 1964, M.A., 1965. Reporter, editor Washington Post, 1964-74, met. editor, 1974-79, London corr., 1979-82; nat. editor Washinton Post, 1982—. Author: Justice Denied, 1971, Mortgage on America, 1974, The New Muckrackers, 1976. Alicia Patterson Found. fellow, 1971-72; recipient Gavel award ABA, 1967, Front First Place award for newswriting Washington-Balt. Newspaper Guild, 1967, 68, award John Hancock Ins. Co., 1969. Office: Washington Post Co 1150 15th St NW Washington DC 20071

DOWNING, ALFRED ERIC, beverage company executive; b. Mount Elgin, Ont., Can., Feb. 28, 1923; s. Alfred Henry and Florence (Davis) D.; m. Elizabeth, June 26, 1948; children: Janet, Eric. B.A.Sc., U. Toronto, 1947. With Gooderham & Worts Ltd., Toronto, Ont., 1946, Corby Distilleries, Corbyville, Ont., 1947-50; with Hiram Walker & Sons Ltd., Walkerville, Ont., 1950—, v.p., 1967, Hiram Walker-Gooderham & Worts Ltd., 1972-76, sr. v.p., 1976-78, pres., 1978-84; pres., chief exec. officer, dir. Hiram Walker Resources Ltd., 1984—; dir. Corby Distilleries, Westinghouse, Can., Interprovincial Pipe Line Ltd., Liquid Carbonic, Can., Allendale Ins. Co. Served with Can. Navy, 1942-45. Mem. Assn. Profl. Engrs. Ont., Chem. Inst. Can. Clubs: Toronto, Windsor Yacht, Windsor Curling., Detroit Athletic. Office: Hiram Walker Resources Ltd PO Box 33 1 First Canadian Pl Toronto ON M5X 1A9 Canada

DOWNING, BRIAN THOMAS, business executive; b. Shalimar, Fla., Sept. 20, 1947; s. Robert James and Margaret Rita (O'Toole) D.; m. Carroll Ann Foote, Feb. 1, 1969; children: Christopher M., Kevin A. B.B.A., Ohio U., 1969; M.B.A., Fairleigh Dickinson U., 1981. Corp. banking officer Mellon Bank, N.A., Pitts., 1973-77; mgr. banking and investments Airco, Inc., Montvale, N.J., 1977-78, asst. treas., 1978-82; treas. The BOC Group, Inc. (formerly Airco, Inc., Montvale, 1982—. Served to capt. U.S. Army, 1969-73; Vietnam. Mem. Fin. Execs. Inst., Treas. Club N.Y., Beta Gamma Sigma, Phi Eta Sigma, Phi Kappa Phi. Office: BOC Group 85 Chestnut Ridge Rd Montvale NJ 07645

DOWNING, EVERETT RAPHAEL, architect, designer; b. New Orleans, Sept. 7, 1938; s. James Mitchell (Jr.) and Bertricia (Morris) D.; m. Adelle Marie Johnson, June, 1968; children: Yvette Rachel, Everett Raphael, Nicole Terese. B.S. in Indsl. Arts Edn., Xavier U., New Orleans, 1962, U. Colo., 1973. Tchr. indsl. arts Peabody High Sch., Alexandria, La., 1967-68, Hansville High Sch., La., 1968-69, J.B. Martin Jr. High Sch., Paradise, La., 1968-69, Baseline Jr. High Sch., Boulder, Colo., 1969-70; arthitect GSA, Denver, 1974-75; architect Heery & Heery Architects, Atlanta, 1974-75; project rep. Cimini-Meric Architects and Planners, New Orleans, 1975-77; sr. draftsman Roger-Nagel-Langhart, Denver, 1977-78, Craddock's Devel. Co., Lakewood, Colo., 1977-78, Ellerbie Assocs. Architects, New Orleans, 1978-79; draftsman Caudill-Rowelli-Scott, Houston, 1979-80; sr. draftsman, job. capt., archtl. designer Meurer-Serafini-Meurer Inc., Denver, 1980—; co-founder, organizer Urbtec Corp., 1980—. Works include Lake Buena Vista Shopping Ctr., Walt Disney World, Orlando, Fla., 1974, Hahnville Courthouse and Jail Facilities, 1976, housing facilities, Saudi Arabia, 1978, Sheridan Savs. & Loan and Office Bldg., Lakewood, 1980, expansion Meurer Serafini Meurer Cons. Office Bldg., Denver, 1980, Ponderosa Med. Office Bldg., Aurora, Colo., 1980, Savs. & Loan Bldg., Haxtun, Colo., 1980, Landmark Motor Motel, Metairie, La. Community rep., coordinator Vista Community Housing Project, Killona, La., 1968-69; community athletics coordinator summer programs, Killona, 1968, 78. Served with U.S. Army, 1962-65. Mem. AIA (assoc. mem.), Urban League Met. Denver, Constrn. Specifications Inst. (jr. mem.), Am. Mgmt. Assn. Democrat. Roman Catholic. Home: PO Box 533 Killona LA 70066

DOWNING, HENRY ABEL, shipping company executive; b. Lake Providence, La., July 19, 1923; s. Aucey N. and Thelma (Abel) D.; m. Betty Jo Griffen; children: Bobby G., Billie Jean Downing Russell; m. Sharon Fox; children: Lisa, Edward. Student, New London Maritime Sch., Conn. Gen. mgr. Gulf Oil Corp., Cynwyd, Pa., 1946-78; exec. v.p. Marine Transport Lines, N.Y.C., 1978—; dir. Internat. Cargo Gear Bur., N.Y.C., 1978—. Mem. Fedn. Am. Controlled Shipping (exec. com. 1978—), Maritime Assn. Port of N.Y. (bd. dirs. 1978—). Republican. Baptist. Home: 3 Highfield Ln Colts Neck NJ 07722 Office: Marine Transport Lines Inc 5 Hanover Sq New York NY 10004

DOWNING, JOAN FORMAN, editor; b. Mpls., Nov. 16, 1934; d. W. Chandler and Marie A. (Forster) Forman; children: Timothy Alan, Julie Marie, Christopher Alan. B.A., U. Wis., 1956. Editorial asst. Sci. Research Assos., Chgo., 1960-61, asst. editor, 1961-63, Children's Press div. Regensteiner Pub. Enterprises, Inc., Chgo., 1963-66, asso. editor, 1966-68, mng. editor, 1968-78, editor-in-chief, 1978-81, sr. editor, 1981—; dir. Chgo. Book Clinic, 1973-75, publicity chmn., 1973-74. Author: (with Eugene Baker) Workers Long Ago, 1968, Baseball Is Our Game, 1982, Junior CB Picture Dictionary, 1978; project editor: 15 vol. Young People's Story of Our Heritage, 1966 (Graphic Arts Council of Chgo. award), 20 vol. People of Destiny (Chgo. Book Clinic award 1967-68), 20 vol. Enchantment of South and Central America, 1968-70, 36 vol. Open Door Books, 1968, 42 vol. Enchantment of Africa, 1972-78, Hobbies for Everyone: Collecting Toy Trains, 1979 (Graphic Arts award Printing Industries Am.). Election judge, Cook County (Ill.), 1974—. Mem. Authors Guild, Authors League Am., Alpha Phi. Democrat. Home: 2414 Brown Ave Evanston IL 60201 Office: 1224 W Van Buren St Chicago IL 60607

DOWNING, ROBERT ALLAN, lawyer; b. Kenosha, Wis., Jan. 6, 1928; s. Leo Vertin and Mayme C. (Kennedy) D.; m. JoAnn C. Cramton, Apr. 17, 1951 (div. Sept. 1977); children: Robert A., Keven C., Tracey Elizabeth Downing Ballou, Gregory E.; m. Joan Govan, Oct. 29, 1977. B.S., U. Wis., 1950, J.D., 1956. Bar: Ill. 1956. Mem. Sidley & Austin, Chgo., 1956—. Served to lt. USN, 1950-53; Korea. Mem. ABA, Soc. Trial Lawyers Am. (bd. dirs. 1979-81), Chgo. Bar Assn., Ill. State Bar Assn., Seventh Circuit Bar Assn. Republican. Episcopalian. Clubs: Union League, Law, Legal, Midday (Chgo.). Office: Sidley & Austin One First Nat Plaza Chicago IL 60603

DOWNING, THOMAS NELMS, former congressman, lawyer; b. Newport News, Va., Feb. 1, 1919; s. Samuel and Lucille (Nelms) D.; m. Virginia Dickerson Martin, Feb. 17, 1947; children: Susan Nelms, Samuel Dickerson Martin. B.S., Va. Mil. Inst., 1940; LL.B., U. Va., 1947; LL.D., Coll. William and Mary, 1975. Bar: Va. bar 1947. Practiced in, Newport News, Hampton, Va.; substitute judge Municipal Ct., City of Warwick (now Newport News), 1953-58; mem. 86th-94th congresses from 1st Dist. Va.; mem. mcht. marine and fisheries com., sci. and tech. com., chmn. subcom. on mcht. marine, mem. subcom. space sci. and applications, mem. subcom. on energy, research and devel., subcom. on Panama Canal, chmn. select com. on Assignation; chmn. bd. dirs. TV Corp. Va., TV Corp. N.C.; dir. Atlantic Permanent Fed. Savs. and Loan Assn., C&P Telephone Co. Va.; mem. adv. bd. dirs. F&M Nat. Bank, Newport News. Sustaining mem. Peninsula council Boy Scouts Am.; trustee War Meml. Mus. Va., Newport News, Riverside Hosp., Newport News; bd. dirs. Mariner's Mus. Served to maj. Cav., 3d Army AUS, World War II. Decorated Silver Star; recipient Distinguished Virginian award Nat. Exchange Club, L. Mendel Rivers award Non-Commd. Officers Assn. U.S., 1975. Mem. Va. Bar Assn., Hampton Bar Assn., Newport News Bar Assn. (past pres.), Am. Legion (nat. distinguished guests com., Distinguished Service medal Dept. Va. 1975), V.F.W., Va. Firemen's Assn. (life), Assn. U.S. Army, Am. Soc. Golden Horseshoes (hon. life), Propeller Club U.S., U. Va., Va. Mil. Inst. alumni assns., Amvets (life), Mil. Order World Wars, 3d Cav. Group Vets. Assn., Res. Officers Assn., Nat. Assn. Suprs. Dept. Def. (hon.), Phi Theta Kappa (hon.). Democrat. Episcopalian (trustee). Clubs: Lion, Moose, Improved Order Red Men, Supreme Order Ahepa, Civitan (hon.), Saints and Sinners (hon.); James River Country (Newport News); Hampton Roads German. Home: 27 Indigo Dam Rd Newport News VA 23606 Office: Downing Conway & Beale 12482 Warwick Blvd Newport News VA 23606

DOWNS, ANTHONY, urban economist, real estate consultant; b. Evanston, Ill., Nov. 21, 1930; s. James Chesterfield and Florence Glassbrook (Finn) D.; m. Katherine Watson, Apr. 7, 1956; children: Katherine, Christine, Tony, Paul, Carol. B.A., Carleton Coll., 1952; M.A., Stanford U., 1956, Ph.D., 1956. With Real Estate Research Corp., Chgo., 1959-77, chmn. bd., 1973-77; asst. prof. econs. and polit. sci. U. Chgo., 1959-62; econ. cons. Rand Corp., Santa Monica, Calif., 1963-65; sr. fellow Brookings Instn., Washington, 1977—; dir. Urban Inst., Manpower Demonstration Research Corp., 1975-80, Standard Shares.; Dir. NAACP Legal and Ednl. Def. Fund, Inc.; mem. Nat. Commn. on Urban Problems, 1967-68; mem. adv. bd. Inst. for Research on Poverty, 1970-78; dir. Rush-Presbyn. St. Luke's Med. Center, Chgo., 1970-77. Author: An Economic Theory of Democracy, 1957, Inside Bureaucracy, 1967, Urban Problems and Prospects, 1970, 2d edit., 1976, Opening Up the Suburbs, 1973, Federal Housing Subsidies, 1973, Racism in America, 1970, Neighborhoods and Urban Development, 1981, Rental Housing in the 1980s, 1983; co-author: Urban Decline and the Future of the American Cities, 1982; co-editor: Do Housing Allowances Work, 1981. Served with USNR, 1956-59. Mem. Am. Econ. Assn., Phi Beta Kappa, Lambda Alpha. Democrat. Roman Catholic. Home: 8483 Portland Pl McLean VA 22102 Office: 1775 Massachusetts Ave NW Washington DC 20036

DOWNS, HARRY, highway construction company executive; b. Greene, Iowa, Mar. 8, 1932; s. Harry and Eugenie Elizabeth (Lucas) D.; m. Suzanne Lee Gilman, Aug. 28, 1954; children: Laura Lee, Rebecca Kyler, Stuart Gilman, Sarah Cushing. B.S., Iowa State U., 1952; LL.B., Harvard U., 1955. Bar: Conn. bar 1955, Mass. bar 1957, U.S. Supreme Ct. bar 1968. Asso. firm Marsh, Day & Calhoun, Bridgeport, Conn., 1955-56; atty. Warren Brothers Co. (now APAC Inc.), Atlanta, 1952—, gen. counsel, 1965—, corp. sec., 1966—, mem. exec. com., 1969—, v.p., 1970-83, sr. v.p., 1983—. Contbr. articles to profl. jours. Episcopalian (mem. com. to select bishop 1974-75, chmn. subcom. leadership needs 1974-75; del. diocesan conv. 1973-74, 74-75, 75-76, chmn. diocesan mut. ministry com. 1978—). Home: 445 Peachtree Battle Ave NW Atlanta GA 30305 Office: care APAC Inc 3340 Peachtree Rd NE Atlanta GA 30326

DOWNS, HUGH MALCOLM, radio and TV broadcaster; b. Akron, Ohio, Feb. 14, 1921; s. Milton Howard and Edith (Hick) D.; m. Ruth Shaheen, Feb. 20, 1944; children—Hugh Raymond, Deirdre Lynn. Student, Bluffton (Ohio) Coll., 1938-39, Wayne State U., 1940-41, Columbia, 1955-56. Staff announcer radio sta. WLOK, Lima, Ohio, 1939, program dir., 1939-40; staff announcer radio sta. WWJ, Detroit, 1940-42, NBC, Chgo., 1943-54; spl. cons. UN on refugee problems Middle East, 1961-64; cons. Center for Study Democratic Instns.; chmn. bd. Raylin Prodns., Inc., 1960—. Free-lance radio and TV broadcaster, 1954—; programs include Home Show, 1954-57, Sid Caesar's Hour, 1956-57, Concentration, 1958-68, Jack Paar show Tonight, 1957-62; host: Today Show, 1962-72, TV Mag. of Air 20/20, ABC; PBS daily series Over Easy. Pres. Nat. Space Inst.; chmn. U.S. com. for UNICEF. Address: care 20/20 ABC 1330 Ave of Americas New York NY 10019

DOWNS, JOHN EDWARD, lawyer; b. St. Joseph, Mo., May 12, 1917; s. William E. and Marguerite C. (Collins) D. J.D., U. Mo., 1940. Bar: Mo., U.S. Supreme Ct.; Lic. comml. pilot. Group atty. SEC, Washington, 1946-48; sr. partner firm Downs & Pierce, St. Joseph, 1948-77; U.S. rep. with rank minister to Internat. Civil Aviation Orgn., Montreal, Que., Can., 1977-82; of counsel Pope, Nichols, Hicks, St. Joseph, Mo., 1982—; pros. atty. Buchanan County, St. Joseph, 1950-54; mem. Mo. Ho. of Reps., 1954-56, Mo. Senate, 1958-68; polit. founder Mo. Western Coll., St. Joseph, pres. bd. trustees, 1975; guest lectr. internat. law M.I.T., McGill U. Served to lt. col. USMCR, 1941-45; PTO. Decorated D.F.C., Air medal (5). Mem. Am., Mo. bar assns., Am. Trial Lawyers Assn., Marine Corps Res. Officer Assn., ACLU. Democrat. Roman Catholic. Office: 2311 Strader Terr Saint Joseph MO 64503

DOWNS, ROBERT BINGHAM, librarian; b. Lenoir, N.C., May 25, 1903; s. John McLeod and Clara Catherine (Hartley) D.; m. Elizabeth Crooks, Aug. 17, 1929 (dec. Sept. 13, 1982); children: Clara Downs Keller, Mary Roberta Downs Andre.; m. Jane Bliss Wilson, Sept. 16, 1983. A.B., U. N.C., 1926, LL.D., 1949; B.S., Columbia U., 1927, M.S., 1929; Litt.D., Colby Coll., 1944; D.L.S., U. Toledo, 1953; L.H.D., Ohio State U., 1963, So. Ill. U., 1970; Litt.D., U. Ill., 1973. Asst. U. N.C. Library, 1922-26, N.Y. Pub. Library, 1927-29; librarian Colby Coll., Waterville, Maine, 1929-31; asst. librarian U. N.C., 1931-32, librarian and assoc. prof. library sci., 1932-34, librarian, prof., 1934-38; dir. libraries N.Y. U., 1938-43; dir. Library and Library Sch.; prof. library sci. U. Ill., Urbana, 1943-58, dean library adminstrn., 1958-71; assoc. Columbia Sch. Library Service, 1942-43; cons. Kabul U., Afghanistan, 1963; adviser U. Tunis, 1973; chmn. ALA Bd. on Resources Am. Libraries, 1939-42, 45-50; pres. Assn. Coll. and Reference Libraries, 1940-41; spl. cons. civil information and edn. sect. SCAP, Japan, 1948, 1950; vis. chief Union Catalog Div.; cons. in bibliography Library of Congress, 1949; adviser Nat. Library and Nat. U. Mexico, 1952; library adviser to Turkish Govt., 1955, 68, 71. Author: The Story of Books, 1935, Resources of Southern Libraries, 1938, Resources of New York City Libraries, 1942, Am. Library Resources, 1951-81, Books that Changed the World, 1956, 2d edit., 1978, Molders of the Modern Mind, 1961, Famous Books, Ancient and Medieval, 1964, Family Saga, 1958, Resources of North Carolina Libraries, 1965, How To Do Library Research, 1966, 2d edit. (with Clara D. Keller), 1975, Resources of Missouri Libraries, 1966, Resources of Canadian Academic and Research Libraries, 1967, Books That Changed America, 1970, Famous American Books, 1971, British Library Resources, 1973, Horace Mann, Champion of Public Schools, 1974, Books and History, 1974, Guide to Illinois Library Resources, 1974, Heinrich Pestalozzi, Father of Modern Pedagogy, 1975, Famous Books, 1975, Books That Changed the South, 1976, Henry Barnard, 1977, Friedrich Froebel, 1978, In Search of New Horizons, 1978, Australian and New Zealand Library Resources, 1979, British and Irish Library Resources, 1981, Landmarks in Science, 1982, (with others) Memorable Americans, 1983; editor: Library Specialization, 1941, Union Catalogs in the United States, 1942, Status of American College and University Librarians, 1958, The First Freedom, 1960, The Bear Went Over the Mountain, 1964, (with Frances B. Jenkins) Bibliography, Current State and Future Trends, 1967; Contbr. articles to library jours. Recipient Clarence Day award, 1963, Joseph W. Lippincott award, 1964; Centennial medal Syracuse U., 1970; Melvil Dewey award, 1974; decorated Order of Sacred Treasure (Japan); Guggenheim fellow, 1971-72; hon. adm. Tex. Navy, 1971. Mem. ALA (1st v.p. 1951-52, pres. 1952-53), Ill. Library Assn. (pres. 1955-56), Southeastern Library Assn., AAUP, Authors League Am., Phi Beta Kappa, Beta Phi Mu, Phi Kappa Phi. Democrat. Clubs: Dial, Caxton (Urbana). Lodge: Rotary (Urbana). Home: 708 W Pennsylvania Ave Urbana IL 61801 *The first requisite for success is to choose a career in complete harmony with one's interests and talents, preferably in a field where there are opportunities to benefit society. There are few callings in which such opportunities do not exist.*

DOWNS, WILBUR GEORGE, educator, physician; b. Perth Amboy, N.J., Aug. 7, 1913; s. James Cloyd and Mabel Lulu (Lehman) D.; m. Helen Hartley Geer; children: Helen (Mrs. Christian J. Haller III), Anne (Mrs. James A. Carroll), William M., Isabel (Mrs. Robert Warner); m. Dorothy Gardner, Feb. 10, 1973. A.B., Cornell U., 1935, M.D., 1938; M.P.H., Johns Hopkins U., 1941; M.A. (hon.), Yale, 1964. Diplomate: Am. Bd. Preventive Medicine. Mem. staff Rockefeller Found., 1941-61, asso. dir., 1961-71, dir. virus program, div. biomed. scis., 1961-71; prof. epidemiology Yale Med. Sch., 1964-71, clin. prof. epidemiology, 1973—; Mem. standing adv. com. Med. Research Brit. Caribbean, 1956-71; expert panel arthropod-borne viruses WHO, 1956—; commn. for malaria Armed Forces Epidemiological Bd., 1965-71. Bd. dirs. Hartley House, N.Y.C. Served with AUS, 1942-46. Mem. Am., Royal socs. tropical medicine and hygiene. Home: 10 Halstead Ln Branford CT 06405 Office: Yale Arbovirus Research Unit 60 College St New Haven CT 06510

DOWS, DAVID ALAN, educator; b. San Francisco, July 25, 1928; s. Samuel Randall and Rita M. (Bowers) D.; m. Wena Hunt Waldner, July 29, 1950; children—Janet Louise, Carol Marie, Joyce Ellen. B.S., U. Calif. at Berkeley, 1952, Ph.D., 1954. Instr. chemistry Cornell U., 1954-56; instr. U. So. Calif., Los Angeles, 1956-57, asst. prof., 1957-59, asso. prof., 1959-63, prof. chemistry, 1963—, chmn. dept., 1966-72; NATO prof., 1970. Contbr. articles profl. jours. NSF fellow, 1962-63. Fellow Chem. Soc. London; mem. Am. Chem. Soc., Am. Phys. Soc., Phi Beta Kappa. Office: U So Calif Chemistry University Park Los Angeles CA 90089

DOWSETT, ROBERT CHIPMAN, consulting actuary; b. Toronto, Ont., Can., June 27, 1929; s. Reginald Ernest and Jean Shillington (Rose) D.; m. Lois Eileen McHardy, June 28, 1950; children—David Robert, Mary Isabel, Carol Elizabeth. B.A., U. Toronto, 1950. With Crown Life Ins. Co., Toronto, 1950-82, v.p., actuary, 1969, exec. v.p., 1970, pres., dir., 1971-82, hon. dir., 1982—; cons. actuary, 1982—; dir. William M. Mercer Ltd., Can. Permanent Cos., Dofasco, Inc. Trustee McMichael Canadian Collection, 1980—; chmn. Council for Can. Unity, 1979-81; bd. dirs. Donwood Inst. Fellow Soc. Actuaries (bd. govs., past sec.), Can. Inst. Actuaries (pres. 1973-74); mem. Can. Life Ins. Assn. (pres. 1974-75), Health Ins. Assn. Am. (dir. 1976-79). Clubs: Donalda (Don Mills); Toronto. Home: 15 Caravan Dr Don Mills ON M3B 1M9 Canada Office: 1 First Canadian Pl PO Box 59-A Suite 5500 Toronto ON Canada M5X 1GS

DOXSEE, LAWRENCE EDWARD, corporate lawyer; b. Hartford, Conn., Mar. 23, 1934; s. Morley Irwin and Ella Alexandra Mills (McConkey) D.; children: Lawrence Edward, Andrew Bowen. B.A., Yale U., 1956; LL.B., Harvard U., 1959; LL.M., N.Y. U., 1964. Bar: Calif. 1960, Hawaii 1972. Asst. sec. Natomas Co., San Francisco, 1979-83; sec. Natomas Internat. Corp., San Francisco, 1979-83, corp.

lawyer, 1983—. Mem. ABA. Address: 350 Union St #610 San Francisco CA 94133

DOYEN, ROSS ORVILLE, state legislator; b. Rice, Kans., Oct. 1, 1926; s. Orville Girard and Millie Elda (Derby) D.; m. Judith Kay Elniff, Oct. 10, 1964; children: Cynthia, Angela. B.S., Kans. State U., 1950. Engaged in farming and ranching, Concordia, Kans.; mem. Kans. Ho. of Reps., 1958-68, Kans. Senate, 1968—, pres., 1975—, Nat. Conf. State Legislatures, 1981-82; bd. dirs. Kans. Advocacy and Protective Services Devel. Disabled; dir. 1st Bank and Trust Co., Concordia. Mem. Presdl. Adv. Com. Federalism, 1981; Adv. Commn. Intergovtl. Relations, 1981. Served with USNR, 1944-46. Recipient numerous public service awards. Mem. Council State Govts. Republican. Methodist. Lodge: Rotary. Office: Room 357 State Capitol Topeka KS 66612 *

DOYLE, ARTHUR JAMES, lawyer; b. Boston, June 19, 1923; s. M. Joseph and Grace M. (McPhee) D.; m. Glenda M. Luehring, Oct. 14, 1950; children: Teresa, Kevin, Kelley, Conaught, Briana, Michael, Brian, Christopher. J.D., Boston Coll., 1949. Bar: Mo. 1949, Mass. 1949. Asso. firm Johnson, Lucas, Graces & Fane, Kansas City, Mo., 1949-51, Spencer, Fane, Britt & Browne, Kansas City, 1951-57, partner, 1957-73; v.p., gen. counsel Kansas City Power & Light Co., 1973-77, dir., 1976—, exec. v.p., 1977-78, pres., 1978—; chief exec. officer, chmn. bd. KCPL, 1979—; dir. Bus. Men's Assurance Co. Am. Served to lt. (j.g.) USN, 1942-46. Mem. Mo. Bar Assn. (chmn. adminstrv. law sect. 1973-74, vice chmn. 1969—), Fed. Power Bar Assn., Mo. C. of C. (dir. 1968-70). Roman Catholic. Clubs: Kansas City, Mission Hills. *

DOYLE, CHARLOTTE LACKNER (MRS. JAMES J. DOYLE), psychology educator, writer; b. Vienna, Austria, June 25, 1937; came to U.S., 1939, naturalized, 1955; d. George and Mary (Meisel) Lackner; m. James J. Doyle, Aug. 20, 1959. B.A. summa cum laude (Woodrow Wilson fellow), Temple U., 1959; M.A., U. Mich., 1961, Ph.D. in Psychology, 1965. Teaching fellow U. Mich., 1962-64; instr., asst. prof. psychology Cornell U., 1964-66; prof. psychology Sarah Lawrence Coll., Bronxville, N.Y., 1966—. Author: (with W.J. McKeachie) Psychology, 1966, 70, (with McKeachie and M. Moffett), 1976; Contbr. articles to prof. publs. Mem. Am. Psychol. Assn., N.Y. Acad. Scis., Phi Beta Kappa. Home: 293 Bronxville Rd Bronxville NY 10708 *Here are the rules that I posted over my writing desk. 1. Keep your eye on the ball and your hand on the pencil. 2. You have permission to write it badly. 3. Beginnings are always difficult. 4. Don't pretend it is easy. 5. Don't be afraid. 6. Keep your eye on the ball and not on yourself. Sometimes I even remember to obey the rules.*

DOYLE, DANIEL MORAN, banker; b. Chgo., Apr. 28, 1929; s. Lawrence Joseph and Mary Margaret (Moran) D.; m. Martha Clare Rogers, Sept. 5, 1959; children: Martha Clare, Ann Rogers. A.B., U. Ill., 1956; grad., Stonier Grad. Sch. Banking, Rutgers U., 1963. With Fed. Res. Bank of Chgo., 1956-73, 75—, v.p., 1968-69, sr. v.p., mgr. Detroit br., 1969-73, 1st v.p., 1975—; mng. dir., bd. govs. Fed. Res. System, 1973-75. Served with U.S. Army, 1950-53. Decorated Bronze star. Mem. Phi Beta Kappa, Phi Alpha Theta, Phi Kappa Phi. Clubs: Bankers of Chgo., Econs. of Chgo. Office: 230 S LaSalle St Chicago IL 60690

DOYLE, DAVID KYTE, army officer; b. Pottsville, Pa., Dec. 8, 1931; s. L.T. and Emily L. (Belles) Alexander; m. Janet L. Colbourne, July 28, 1952; children: David K., Jeffrey A., Steven F. B.S., U. Md., 1963; M.S., U.S. Army Command and Gen. Staff Coll., 1966, George Washington U., 1972. Commd. 2d lt. U.S. Army, 1952, advanced through grades to maj. gen.; comdr. 3d Armored Cavalry Regiment, Ft. Bliss, Tex., util 1975; dep. to dir. of army staff Office of Army Chief of Staff, Washington, 1975-76; dep. comdg. gen. U.S. Armor Sch., Ft. Knox, 1977-78, asst. comdr., 1977-78; dep. comdg. gen. U.S. Armor Ctr., 1978-79; asst. comdt. U.S. Armor Shc., 1978-79; dep. comdg. gen. III Corps and Ft. Hood, Ft. Hood, Tex., from 1978; now maj. gen. DCSOPS FORSCOM, Ft. McPherson, Ga. Decorated Legion of Merit with 2 oak leaf clusters, Bronze Star, Air medal, Purple Heart. Office: Fort McPherson GA 30330

DOYLE, DONALD EDWARD, restaurant franchising company executive; b. Washington, Ind., Sept. 25, 1946; s. Christopher Wodrow and Marjorie E. (Williams) D.; m. Roberta Sue Sedletzeck, Dec. 17, 1966; children: Christopher, Mark, Ryan. B.S. in Math., Rose-Hulman Inst. Tech., 1968; M.B.A., Bowling Green State U., 1973. Mgr. strategic planning KFC Corp., Louisville, 1975-76, dir. strategic planning, 1977-78, v.p. strategic planning, 1978-79, v.p. mktg., 1980-81, sr. v.p. mktg and planning, 1981-82; pres. KFC Mgmt. Co., 1983—. Bd. dirs. Louisville Ballet, 1983—; mem. adv. com. KFC Bluegrass Festival U.S., 1981—; sect. chmn. Met. United Way, Louisville, 1983—. Roman Catholic. Home: 2530 Ransdell Ave Louisville KY 40204 Office: KCF Corp 1441 Gardiner Ln Louisville KY 40213

DOYLE, JAMES ALEXANDER, lawyer; b. Thedford, Neb., Jan. 19, 1904; s. John and Hattie (Beckhoff) D.; m. Amelia Brosius, June 9, 1927; children—James Alan, Katherine. Ph.B., Creighton U., 1924; LL.B., U. Nebr., 1933; LL.M., Harvard U., 1942. Bar: Nebr. bar. Ann. Supt. Thomas County High Sch., Thedford, Neb., 1927-30; law clerk to U.S. Circuit Judge, Omaha, 1933-35; prof. law U. Nebr., 1936-43; asst. reviser Nebr. Statute Commn., Lincoln, 1941-43; regional atty. U.S. Dept. of Agr., Lincoln, Nebr., 1943-44, Chgo., 1944-45; asso. solicitor, Washington, 1945-48; spl. cons. to solicitor on litigation, 1948; dean Creighton U. Sch. of Law, Omaha, Nebr., 1948-70, dean emeritus, prof. law, 1970—; also arbitrator in labor disputes. Fellow Harvard Law Sch., 1937-38; Former pres. Legal Aid Soc. Omaha, Inc. Contbr.: articles to Neb. Law Rev. Former mem. Am., Nebr. bar assns., Am. Arbitration Assn., Order of Coif, Phi Delta Phi, Alpha Sigma Nu. Roman Catholic. Club: Rotary. Home: 9468 Dewey Ave Omaha NE 68114

DOYLE, JAMES ALOYSIUS, assn. exec.; b. Pitts., Mar. 20, 1921; s. James A. and Anna Sophia (Holthaus) D.; m. Ethel Miriam Clancey, Oct. 3, 1943; children—John Kevin, Elizabeth Marie, Brian James, Peter Joseph, Thomas More Patrick. B.A., Queens Coll., N.Y.C., 1943. Editor, promotion mgr., circulation dir. Howes Pub. Co., Inc., N.Y.C., 1946-58; publicity chmn. Am. Assn. Textile Chemists and Colorists, 1955-58; exec. sec. Cath. Press Assn. U.S. and Can., 1958—. Served as master sgt. AUS, 1944-46; PTO; 1st lt., 1951-52; ETO. Mem. Internat. Cath. Union of Press (council), Alumni Assn. Queens Coll. (1st pres. 1946-47, dir. 1947-50, 77—). Home: 25 Gregory Ave Merrick NY 11566 Office: 119 N Park Ave Rockville Centre NY 11570

DOYLE, JAMES EDWARD, U.S. judge; b. Oshkosh, Wis., July 6, 1915; s. James Edward and Agnes (McCarthy) C.; m. Ruth Bachhuber, Aug. 10, 1940; children: Mary Eileen, James Edward, Catherine Margaret, Anne Malloy. A.B., U. Wis., 1937, LL.D. hon., 1983; LL.B., Columbia U., 1940. Bar: Wis. 1940. Also U.S. Supreme Ct.; atty. criminal div. Dept. Justice, 1940-41; law clk. to assoc. justice James F. Byrnes, U.S. Supreme Ct., 1941-42; cons. Office War Moblzn. and Reconversion, 1945; asst. to counselor State Dept., 1945-46; asst. U.S. atty., Madison, Wis., 1946-48; ptnr. LaFollette, Sinykin & Doyle, Madison, 1948-65; U.S. judge Western Dist. Wis., 1965-80, sr. judge, 1980—; lectr. U. Wis. Law Sch., 1951-53, 58; Mem. Jud. Conf. U.S., 1972-75. Bd. editors, Columbia Law Rev., 1938-40. Nat. co-chmn. Americans for Democratic Action, 1953-55; Chmn. Wis. Democratic Party, 1951-53; exec. dir. Nat. Stevenson for Pres. Com., 1960. Served to lt. USNR, 1942-45. Mem. Dane County Bar Assn. (pres. 1962-63). Office: US District Ct PO Box 591 Madison WI 53701

DOYLE, JAMES EDWIN (NED DOYLE), advt. exec.; b. N.Y.C., Oct. 23, 1902; s. William Joseph and Josephine (Huttenbrauch) D.; m. Helen Aisley; 1 son, Anthony Edwin; m. Marion E. Lance, May 26, 1945 (div. Jan. 1966); children—Michael Varian, Ellin Downey; m. Margaret Rivelli, Aug. 14, 1967 (div. June 1977). Student, Hamilton Coll., 1920-22; LL.B., Fordham U., 1931; LL.D., Hamilton Coll., 1977. Advt. mgr. Look mag., 1937-42; account exec., vp. Grey Advt. Agy., 1945-49; exec. v.p. Doyle Dane Bernbach (advt. agy.), N.Y.C., from 1949, formerly chmn. exec. com., now bd. dirs.; chmn. Simmons Market Research Bur., 1978; owner Floridians basketball team, 1970-72; Mem. bus. adv. com. on mgmt. improvement, State of N.Y. Trustee Hamilton Coll. Served as capt. USMC, 1942-45. Mem. Nat. Football League Alumni Assn. (hon.), Alpha Phi, Chi Psi. Clubs: Farmington Country (Charlottesville, Va.); Rockefeller Center Luncheon, Princeton (N.Y.C.). Home: 242 E 19th St New York City NY 10003 Office: 437 Madison Ave New York City NY 10022

DOYLE, JAMES LEONARD, bishop; b. Chatham, Ont., Can., June 20, 1929; s. Herbert Lawrence and Mary Josephine (Ennett) D. B.A., U. Western Ont., 1950; D.D., St. Peters Sem., London, 1954. Ordained priest Roman Catholic Ch.; then consecrated bishop; asso. rector St. Peter's Cathedral, London, Ont., 1954-60, rector, 1974-76; pastor Sacred Heart Ch., Windsor, Ont., 1960-66; prin. Brennan High Sch., Windsor, 1966-68; pastor Holy Name Ch., Windsor, 1968-74; bishop of, Peterborough, Ont., 1976—. Address: 350 Hunter St W Peterborough ON K9T 6Y8 Canada *

DOYLE, JAMES THOMAS, advertising agency executive; b. Detroit, July 14, 1933; s. Edmund Thomas and Mamie Irene (Wepplo) D.; m. Patricia Jean Godon, Nov. 29, 1958; children: Greg, Kerry, and Kevin (twins). B.S., Wayne State U., 1956. Account exec. J Walter Thompson Co., Detroit, 1956-64; account dir. McCann-Erickson Co., Detroit, 1964-66; advt.-mktg. mgr. Ford Motor Co., Dearborn, Mich., 1966-70; sr. v.p. mgmt. supr. Grey Advt., Detroit, 1970-75; pres. D'Arcy MacManus Masius, Bloomfield Hills, Mich., 1975—. City councilman City of Dearborn Heights, Mich., 1965-73, mayor pro-tem, Mich., 1967-73; trustee Oakwood Hosp. Named Outstanding Young Man City of Dearborn Heights, 1966; recipient Civic Service Ford Motor Co., 1966, 67, Pub. Service Mich. Cancer Found., 1982. Mem. Detroit Advt. Assn., Adcraft Club Detroit. Methodist. Clubs: Bloomfield Hills Country (Mich.); Dearborn Country; Renaissance (Detroit). Home: 26216 Sims Dr Dearborn Heights MI 48127 Office: D'Arcy MacManus Masius 1725 N Woodward Bloomfield Hills MI 48303

DOYLE, JOHN LAURENCE, manufacturing company executive; b. Whitestone, Devon, Eng., Sept. 7, 1931; came to U.S., 1953; s. John Edgcumbe and Grace Vera (Burd) D.; m. Judith Anne Nannizzi, Apr. 24, 1965; children: Jeffrey Michael, Peter John. B.S., Stanford U., 1956, M.S., 1959. Gen. mgr. AMD Hewlett Packard, Palo Alto, Calif., 1969-70; v.p., gen. mgr. Aerotherm, Sunnyvale, Calif., 1970-72; dir. corp. devel. Hewlett Packard, Palo Alto, 1972-76, v.p. personnel, 1976-81, v.p. research and devel., 1981—; dir. Hexcel, San Francisco, Verbatim, Sunnyvale. Chmn. bd. C.I.S. Adv. Com., Stanford, 1980—; bd. dirs. Urban Coalition, Stanford, 1978—; cabinet Calif. Poly. Inst., San Louis Obispo, 1980—. RAF, 1951-53. Office: Hewlett-Packard Co 1501 Page Mill Rd Palo Alto CA 94025

DOYLE, JOHN LAWRENCE, artist; b. Chgo., Mar. 14, 1939; s. John W. and Cecelia M. (Tarkowski) D.; children: Lynn, Sean, Morgan. B.A., Sch. of Art Inst. Chgo., 1962; M.A., No. Ill. U., 1967. Tchr. art Forest View High Sch., Arlington Heights, Ill., 1962-72. One-man shows of prints and/or paintings include, Denver Natural History Mus., Natural Am. Indian Mus., Spokane, Wash., Allen Galleries, Milw., U. N.D., U. S.D., Black Gallery, Taos, N.Mex., Vanderbilt U., Nashville, Tenn., Johns Hopkins U., Balt., Jockey Club Gallery, Miami, Fla., Harvard Med. Library, Lesch Gallery, Mpls., Clev. Clinic, Mayo Clinic, MGM Grand, Las Vegas, Yale U. Hosp., Now and Then Gallery, N.Y.C., Fine Print Unltd., Miami, Grand Gallery, Nev., Galerie Une, Puerto Vallarta, Mex., Welnetz Studio, Wis., Gallery G, Wichita, all 1981, group shows, latest being, Los Angeles County Mus., 1973, Taos (N.Mex.) Mcpl. Art Show, 1975, Colo. Womens Coll., Denver, Heritage West Gallery, Albuquerque, 1976, Art Wagon Gallery, Scottsdale, Ariz., 1977, Burpee Art Mus., Rockford, Ill., 1979; represented in permanent collections, Library of Congress, Washington, Art Inst. Chgo., Indpls., Mus. Art, Carnegie Inst., Pitts., Norton Gallery of Art, West Palm Beach, Fla., Birmingham (Ala.) Mus. Art, Columbus Mus. Fine Art, Columbus, Ohio, Fort Lauderdale (Fla.) Mus. Art, Miss. Art Mus., Jackson. Recipient Hon. Mention Internat. Printmakers, 1971; George Brown Travelling fellow, 1962. Address: PO Box 715 Burnsville NC 28714

DOYLE, JOSEPH, educator; b. Jersey City, Dec. 13, 1915; s. Joseph A. and Mary A. (Kelsey) D.; m. Alice Valentine Pulsifer, May 23, 1942 (div. 1970); children: Valentine, Allen Pulsifer; m. Katherine Sarah Ducharme, May 26, 1973. Grad., Newark Acad., 1933; A.B., Princeton, 1937; A.M., Columbia, 1941, Ph.D., 1952. Instr. French Peekskill Mil. Acad., 1938-39; asst. English Columbia, 1941-43, instr., 1947-48; asst. prof. English Washington and Jefferson Coll., 1948-50; dean prof. lit. Washington Coll., Chestertown, Md., 1953-58; acad. dean Am. Internat. Coll., Springfield, Mass., 1958-60; prof. English U. Hartford, 1960—, dean, 1960-66. Contbr. articles, poems to profl. jours. Served to lt. (s.g.) USNR, 1943-46. Mem. Eastern Assn. Deans (exec. com. 1956-58, v.p. 1958-59, pres. 1959-62), AAUP, Modern Lang. Assn., Coll. English Assn., Nat. Council Tchrs. English, Assn. Higher Edn. Unitarian. Home: 1564 Boulevard West Hartford CT 06107 Office: 200 Bloomfield Ave West Hartford CT 06117

DOYLE, JOSEPH ANTHONY, lawyer; b. N.Y.C., June 13, 1920; s. Joseph A. and Jane (Donahue) D.; m. Eugenie A. Fleri, Aug. 19, 1944; children: Christopher, Stephen, Eugenie, Jane, Richard. B.S., Georgetown U., 1941; LL.B., Columbia U., 1947. Assoc. Shearman & Sterling, N.Y.C., 1947-57, ptnr., 1957-79, 81—; asst. sec. for manpower, res. affairs and logistics U.S. Navy, Washington, 1979-81; dir. The Fuji Bank & Trust Co., N.Y.C., 1975-79, 81—. Served to lt. USNR, 1941-45. Decorated Navy Cross, D.F.C. with 3 gold stars, Air medal wiht 7 gold stars; recipient Disting. Pub. Service award Sec. of Navy, 1981. Mem. Assn. Bar City N.Y., N.Y. State Bar Assn., ABA. Democrat. Roman Catholic. Clubs: Broad St, Downtown Athletic (N.Y.C.); Metropolitan (Washington). Home: 32 Washington Sq W New York NY 10011 Office: 53 Wall St New York NY 10005

DOYLE, JOSEPH THEOBALD, physician, educator; b. Providence, June 11, 1918; s. Joseph Donald and Gertrude Harriet (Theobald) D.; m. Elizabeth Thompson, Dec. 26, 1944 (dec.); children: Shelagh Thompson, Michael Kedian; m. Joan Gleason Mastrianni, Dec. 29, 1976. A.B., Harvard U., 1939, M.D., 1943. Successively intern, asst. resident, chief resident in medicine Harvard Med. Service, Boston City Hosp., 1943-44, 47-49; Whitehead fellow in physiology, asst. in medicine and physiology Emory U. Med. Sch., 1950-52; asso. in medicine Duke U. Med. Sch., 1952; mem. faculty Albany (N.Y.) Med. Coll., 1952—, prof. medicine, head div. cardiology, 1961—, dir. cardiovascular health center, 1952—, head pvt. diagnostic clinic, 1957-82; cons. Albany VA Med. Center, 1962—. Author papers in field. Served as 1st lt. M.C. AUS, 1944-45. Fellow A.C.P., Am. Coll. Cardiology; mem. AMA, Am. Heart Assn. (chmn. council epidemiology 1969-71), Assn. Univ. Cardiologists, N.Y. Heart Assembly (pres. 1968-69), Med. Soc. County of Albany (pres. 1971-72). Presbyterian. Clubs: Ft. Orange, Schuyler Meadows. Home: 17 Lenox Ave Albany NY 12203 Office: Albany Med Coll Albany NY 12208

DOYLE, KATHERINE LEE LEE, research scientist, educator; b. Sacramento, Sept. 22, 1932; d. Maurice Omar and Lorena Augusta (Merrill) D.; m. F. Vincent Brecka, Jr., May 13, 1972. B.A. magna cum laude, Dominican Coll., San Rafael, 1954; M.A., Stanford U., 1961; Ph.D., Tulane U., 1971. Research asso. Stanford (Calif.) Med. Sch., 1958-62; asso. research specialist U. Calif. Med. Sch., San Francisco, 1962-67; instr. Tulane Med. Sch., New Orleans, 1967-70, asst. prof., 1970-72; adj. scientist Delta Regional Primate Center, Covington, La., 1967—; prof. U. Ark. Coll. Medicine, Little Rock, 1977—; acting chmn. Ob-Gyn, 1978; Bd. dirs., mem. exec. bd. Ark. Family Planning Council, 1977—, pres., 1979-80, 80-81; chmn. gov.'s task force for prevention of adolescent pregnancy, 1980—; cons. James Bowman Inc., 1977-78, Battelle Inst., 1977—, JWK Internat., Ark. Dept. Health, Ala. Dept. Health, Okla. Dept. Health, 1980, March of Dimes, 1980. Contbr. articles to profl. jours. Recipient Squibb award for outstanding research, 1963; Population Council grantee, 1963, 73; NIH grantee, 1969-72, 80-81. Mem. Am. Fertility Soc. (Rubin award 1962), Am. Assn. Planned Parenthood Physicians (program chmn. 1983), Am. Public Health Assn., Nat. Family Planning and Reproductive Health Forum, Am. Primatologic Soc., Soc. Study Reproduction, Am. Assn. Profs. Ob-Gyn. Roman Catholic. Home: 211 Gorgeous View Trail Little Rock AR 72210 Office: Dept Obstetrics and Gynecology U Ark Coll Medicine Little Rock AR 72203

DOYLE, KENNETH JOSEPH, lawyer, journalist; b. Troy, N.Y., Apr. 3, 1940; s. W. Kenneth and Sallie (Shea) D. B.A., Cath. U. Am., 1961, M.A., 1962; J.D., Albany Law Sch., 1978. Bar: N.Y. Ordained priest Roman Catholic Ch.; bur. chief Rome Office, Nat. Cath. News Service, 1981—. Recipient awards Nat. Cath. Press Assn., N.Y. State Press Assn. Home: 127 Elmgrove Ave Troy NY 12180 Office: Via dei Lucchesi 19 00187 Rome Italy

DOYLE, KEVIN JOHN, journalist; b. Fitzroy Harbour, Ont., Can., Feb. 6, 1943; s. John and Teresa Agnes (McHale) D.; m. Marion Helen Edmonds, June 26, 1970. B.A., U. Ottawa, 1965; M.Sc., London Sch. Econs., 1971. Ottawa parliamentary reporter Canadian Press, 1968-71, London corr., 1972-75, Washington corr., 1975-76; fgn. editor Maclean's mag., Toronto, Ont., 1976, nat. editor, 1976-77, mng. editor, 1977—. Home: 9 Birdsall Ave Toronto ON Canada Office: 481 University Ave Toronto ON M5W 1A7 Canada

DOYLE, MATHIAS FRANCIS, univ. pres.; b. Malone, N.Y., Nov. 18, 1933; s. Francis J. and Madeline L. (Donnelly) D. B.A., Siena Coll., 1955; M.A., Cath. U. Am., 1965; Ph.D., U. Notre Dame, 1968. Lectr. St. Francis Coll., Rye Beach, N.H., 1963-65; asso. prof. polit. sci. Siena Coll., Loudonville, N.Y., 1968-75; pres. St. Bonaventure (N.Y.) U., 1975—, also trustee. Contbr. articles periodicals. Trustee Siena Coll. Arthur Schmidt fellow, 1966-68. Mem. Am., Northeastern polit. sci. assns., Pi Gamma Mu, Delta Epsilon Sigma. Roman Catholic. Home: The Friary Saint Bonaventure NY 14778 Office: Saint Bonaventure University Saint Bonaventure NY 14778

DOYLE, MICHAEL, govt. ofcl.; b. Fall River, Mass., Sept. 19, 1941; s. Robert Augustus and Louise (Jackson) D.; m. Elisa Ernestine Falciglia, June 18, 1966; children—Allison, Lincoln. B.A., U. R.I., 1964, M.A., 1969; postgrad., Eagleton Inst. Politics, 1964-65, U. Pa., 1967-68. Mgmt. intern Econ. Devel. Adminstrn., Washington, 1969, policy analyst, 1970-73; spl. asst. to dep. asst. sec. for domestic commerce Dept. Commerce, 1973-76, acting dep. bur. dir., 1976, acting dep. asst. sec., 1977; exec. asst. to dep. sec. Commerce, 1977-80; dir. adminstrn. Internat. Trade Adminstrn., Dept. Commerce, 1980—. Mem. Am. Soc. Public Adminstrn. Home: 2026 Peppermint Ct Reston VA 22091 Office: Dept Commerce 14th and Constitution Ave Washington DC 20230

DOYLE, MORRIS MCKNIGHT, lawyer; b. Bishop, Cal., Jan. 4, 1909; s. Guy P. and Helen (McKnight) D.; m. Juliet H. Clapp, Sept. 15, 1934; children: Barbara Doyle Roupe, Thomas M. A.B., Stanford U., 1929; LL.B., Harvard U., 1932; L.H.D., Nat. Coll. Edn., 1965. Bar: Calif. 1932. Asso. McCutchen, Olney, Mannon & Greene; San Francisco, 1932-42; partner McCutchen, Thomas, Matthew, Griffiths & Greene, San Francisco, 1942-58, McCutchen, Doyle, Brown & Enersen, 1958—. Trustee Stanford U., 1959-79, pres. bd. trustees, 1962-65; trustee, chmn. James Irvine Found.; dir. Stanford Research Inst.; bd. overseers Hoover Instn. Fellow Am. Bar Found., Am. Coll. Trial Lawyers; mem. Am., Calif. San Francisco bar assns., Bar Assn. City N.Y., Am. Law Inst., Am. Judicature Soc. Clubs: Pacific Union, Bohemian, Commonwealth (San Francisco). Office: 3 Embarcadero Center San Francisco CA 94111

DOYLE, PATRICK JOHN, otolaryngologist; b. Moose Jaw, Sask., Can., Nov. 17, 1926; s. William E. and Bertha L. (Fisher) D.; m. Irene Strilchuk, May 21, 1949; children: Sharon, Patrick, Robert, Barbara, Joseph, Kathleen. B.Sc., U. Alta., 1947, M.D., 1949. Diplomate: Am. Bd. Otolaryngology. Intern U. B.C. Hosp., 1949-50; resident in medicine and pediatrics, 1950-51; resident in otolaryngology U. Oreg. Hosp., 1958-61; asst. prof., then asso. prof. U. Oreg. Med. Sch., 1965-70; mem. faculty U. B.C. Med. Sch., 1963—, prof. otolaryngology, 1972—, head dept., 1972—, program dir. residency tng. program, 1972—; head div. otolaryngology St. Paul's Hosp., mem. numerous nat. med. coms. Author numerous articles in field.; Mem. editorial bds. profl. jours. Fellow Royal Coll. Surgeons Can., Am. Laryngol., Rhinol., and Otol. Soc., Am. Acad. Facial, Plastic and Reconstructive Surgery, Am. Largyngol. Soc., Am. Acad. Otolaryngology-Head and Neck Surgery; mem. Can. Med. Assn., Vancouver Med. Assn., B.C. Med. Assn. (pres. oto-ophthal. div. 1973), Can. Otolaryngol. Soc. (sec. 1973-77), Pacific Coast Oto-Ophthal. Soc. (pres. 1977), Soc. Univ. Otolaryngologists, U. Oreg. Otolaryngology Alumni Assn. (pres. 1968-70), AMA, Centurion Club, Tinnitus Research Found. Roman Catholic. Office: 1081 Burrard St Vancouver BC Canada V6Z 1Y6

DOYLE, PATRICK JOHN, wholesale company executive; b. Chgo., Jan. 19, 1918; s. Patrick and Katherine (Moran) D.; m. Catherine Clarkson Thompson, Jan. 13, 1945; children: Sharon C., Cecelia E., Barbara L., Patrick John, Emily A., Jean M. Ph.B., Loyola U., Chgo., 1946. With McDade & Co., Inc. (catalog showroom), Carol Stream, Ill., 1950—, pres., 1959—, chmn. bd., 1959—; dir. United Security Ins. Co. Bd. dirs. St. Jude's Hosp., Memphis, 1979; mem. Back of the Yards Council, Chgo., 1980. Served with M.C. AUS, 1941-45. Recipient Humanitarian award Cardinal Cushing Sch. Exceptional Children, 1978; named B'nai B'rith Man of Year, 1977. Mem. Nat. Assn. Catalog Showrooms (dir.). Roman Catholic. Clubs: Boca Raton (Fla.); Irish Fellowship (Chgo.); K.C. Home: 601 Lake Hinsdale Dr Willowbrook IL 60514 Office: 505 E North Ave Carol Stream IL 60187

DOYLE, PATRICK LEE, insurance company executive; b. Pitts., July 17, 1929; s. Lee Patrick and Anne Louise (Stattmilller) D.; m. Ann Marie Yuhasz, Apr. 26, 1952; children: Robert Christopher, Patrick Brian, David Alan. B.A., Ohio State U., 1951. C.P.C.U., Am. Inst. Property Casualty Underwriters; C.L.U.; Assoc. in Risk Mgmt., Ins. Inst. Am. Life reins. mgr. Nationwide Ins. Cos., Columbus, Ohio, 1965-70, asst. to pres., 1970-79, v.p., adminstrv. asst. to pres., 1980-82, v.p. human resources, 1981-82, v.p. Office Gen. Chmn., 1982—; instr. Ohio State U., Columbus, 1969-82, Franklin U., 1973-82; mem. exam. com. C.P.C.U., Am. Inst. for Property and Liability Underwriters, Phila., 1980—; trustee Griffith Found. for Ins. Edn., Columbus, 1975—. Bd. dirs. Catholic Social Services, Columbus, 1981—; trustee Kinder Key, Columbus, 1973—. Mem. Ins. Inst. Am., Soc. C.P.C.U. (ednl. dir. 1965-72, Outstanding Educator award 1972), Soc. C.L.U., Soc. Ins. Research (dir. 1976-79), Gamma Iota Sigma. Republican. Roman Catholic. Home: 1919 Birkdale Dr Columbus OH 43232 Office: Nationwide Ins Cos 1 Nationwide Plaza Columbus OH 43216

DOYLE, RICHARD EDWARD, educator; b. Bklyn., Dec. 22, 1929; s. Walter Francis and Dorothy Helen (Brassell) D. A.B., Bellarmine Coll., 1953, Ph.L., 1954, M.A., 1955; S.T.B., Woodstock Coll., 1959, S.T.L., 1961; Ph.D., Cornell U., 1965. Joined S.J., 1947; ordained priest Roman Cath. Church, 1960; tchr. Xavier High Sch., N.Y.C., 1954-57; prof. Fordham U., N.Y.C., 1965—, chmn. classics dept., 1970-77; dean Grad. Sch. Arts and Sci., 1979, dean faculty, 1979—; prof. Santa Clara U., summer 1967; exec. com. Am. Acad. in Rome, 1974-77. Editor: Traditio; book rev. editor: Classical World; contbr. articles and revs. to publs. in field. Nat. Endowment for Humanities fellow, summer 1970; Fordham faculty fellow, 1974, 78-79. Mem. Am. Philol. Assn., Archaeol. Inst. Am. (exec. com. N.Y. Soc. 1974-79), Classical Assn. of Empire State, N.Y. Classical Club, Phi Beta Kappa, Phi Kappa Phi. Club: Cornell of N.Y. Office: Keating Hall Fordham University Bronx NY 10458 *I am grateful for my Jesuit training and education. It has afforded me an excellent background to deal with contemporary educational problems. The challenge of preparing undergraduate and graduate students for the twenty-first century is a very big one, and perhaps the most significant thing I can contribute to them is a sense of values and purpose in life.*

DOYLE, RICHARD JAMES, editor; b. Toronto, Ont., Can., Mar. 10, 1923; s. James Andrew and Lillian Gibson (Hilts) D.; m. Florence Chanda, Jan. 27, 1952; children: Kathleen Judith, Sean Gibson. City editor Chatham (Ont.) Daily News, 1940-51; mem. staff Globe and Mail, Toronto, 1951—, mng. editor, 1959-63, editor, 1963-78, editor-in-chief, 1978—. Author: Royal Story. Served with RCAF, World War II. *

DOYLE, ROBERT BATES, banker; b. Hyde Park, Mass., Feb. 13, 1916; s. George W. and Helen (Bates) D.; m. Mary Doris Freaney; children—Robert B., Judith Ann (Mrs. Gerard McCrory), Corinne Rita (Mrs. Paul Tierney). A.B., Harvard, 1938; grad., Stonier Grad. Sch. Banking, Rutgers U., 1961; postgrad., Columbia, 1964. Div. mgr. CIT Corp., Hartford, Conn., 1938-56; sr. v.p. Hartford Nat. Bank & Trust Co., 1956-75; exec. v.p. 1st Conn. Bancorp., Inc., 1975—; pres., dir. Pioneer Credit Corp. (subs. 1st Conn. Bancorp.), Hartford, 1978—; faculty U. Va., 1965—, Williams Coll. Grad. Sch. Banking, 1964—. Author: A Banker's Eye View of the Automobile Dealer, 1961. Dir. conv. and visitors bur. Greater Hartford C. of C.; trustee Grad. Sch. Consumer Banking U. Va.; corporator St. Francis Hosp., Hartford. Mem. Consumer Bankers Assn. Washington (dir). Home: 21 Midland Dr Avon CT 06001 Office: 101 Pearl St Hartford CT 06115

DOYLE, ROBERT EDWARD, educator; b. Valley Stream, N.Y., Dec. 25, 1929; s. John Joseph and Madeleine (Kappe) D. B.S., Iona Coll., 1951; M.S., N.Y.U., 1956, Ph.D., 1963. Tchr. math. West Hempstead (N.Y.) High Sch., 1955-57; asst. prof. Iona Coll., 1957-63, St. John's U., 1963-64, assoc. prof., 1964-67, prof. counselor edn., 1967—, chmn. dept. counselor edn., 1964-76, acting dean, 1972-74; cons. N.Y.C. Bd. Edn. Bd. Author: Career Patterns of Alumni of a Men's Liberal Arts College, 1963. Govs. Family Consultation Service Archdiocese of N.Y.; bd. advisors Episcopal Ch. Counseling Center, Great Neck, N.Y. Served with AUS, 1952-55. Mem. Assn. Religious and Value Issues in Counseling (pres. 1968-70), N.Y. State Assn. Counselor Educators and Suprs. (pres. 1969-70), Am. Psychol. Assn., N.Y. State Counselors Assn., Am. Assn. Counseling and Devel., Nat. Vocational Guidance Assn., Am. Sch. Counselors Assn., AAUP, Assn. Counselor Educators and Suprs., Am., N.Y. State rehab. counselors assns. Office: Saint John's U Jamaica NY 11439

DOYLE, WILFRED EMMETT, bishop; b. Calgary, Alta., Can., Feb. 18, 1913; s. John Joseph and Mary (O'Neill) D. B.A., U. Alta, 1935; D.C.L., U. Ottawa, Ont., Can., 1949. Ordained priest Roman Cath. Ch., 1938; chancellor Archdiocese Edmonton, Alta., Can., 1949-58; bishop, Nelson, B.C., Can., 1958—; Chmn. bd. govs. Notre Dame U., Nelson, 1963-74. Address: 813 Ward St Nelson BC V1L 1T4 Canada

DOYLE, WILLIAM DAVID, physicist; b. Boston, June 5, 1935; s. Philip Elisha and Marie (McDonald) D.; m. Carole Anne McIntire, Aug. 9, 1958; children: Deborah, Thomas, Jennifer, Michael. B.S., Boston Coll., 1957, M.S., 1959; Ph.D., Temple U., 1964. Research physicist Franklin Inst., Phila., 1959-64; dir. sold state tech. Sperry Univac, Blue Bell, Pa., 1964-79; vis. fellow U. York, Eng., 1970-71; mgr. Bubble Memory, Motorola, Inc., Tempe, Ariz., 1979—. Contbr. articles to various publs.; patentee in field. Fellow IEEE; mem. Magnetics Soc. IEEE (v.p. 1983), Am. Inst. Physics, Conf. Magnetism and Magnetic Materials (gen. chmn. 1967). Club: Enfield Soccer (Upper Dublin, Pa.) (pres. 1978-79). *

DOYLE, WILLIAM EDWARD, U.S. circuit judge; b. Denver, Feb. 5, 1911; s. William R. and Sarah (Harrington) D.; m. Helen Sherfey (div. Mar. 4, 1939); children—Michael J., Susan Kathleen. A.B., U. Colo. 1940, LL.D., 1977; J.D., George Washington U., 1937. Bar: Colo. bar 1938. Dep. dist. atty., Denver, 1938-41, pvt. practice, 1941-43, 46-58, dist. ct. judge, 1948-49, chief dep. dist. atty., 1948-52; justice Supreme Ct. Colo., 1959-61; U.S. dist. judge, Colo., 1961-71, U.S. circuit judge, Denver, 1971—; part-time tchr. law Westminister Coll. Law, 1946-56, U. Denver Coll. Law, 1956-68, adjunct prof., 1968—; vis. lectr. U. Colo., 1953, 81. Contbr. articles to legal jours. Served with AUS, 1943-45; ETO. Mem. Am., Colo., Denver (trustee) bar assns., Colo. Mental Health Assn., U.S. Jud. Conf. (chmn. magistrates com.), Order Coif, Order of St. Ives, Pi Sigma Alpha, Phi Alpha Delta. Democrat. Roman Catholic. Office: US Courthouse Denver CO 80294

DOYLE, WILLIAM THOMAS, educator, physicist; b. New Britain, Conn., Dec. 5, 1925; s. Thomas William and Kathleen (McConn) D.; m. Barbara May Grant, June 16, 1951; children—Peter, Jeffrey. Sc.B. in Physics, Brown U., 1951; M.A., Yale, 1952, Ph.D., 1955. Mem. faculty Dartmouth, 1955—, prof. physics, 1964—, chmn. dept., 1967-71. Served with USNR, 1943-46. NSF predoctoral fellow, 1953-54, 54-55; postdoctoral fellow, 1958-59. Mem. Am. Phys. Soc., A.A.A.S., Sigma Xi. Home: 6 Tyler Rd Hanover NH 03755

DOYLE, WILLIAM THOMAS, newspaperman, insurance company executive; b. Oakland, Calif., May 22, 1925; s. Albert Norman and Catherine (Stein) D.; m. Claire Louise Wogan, Sept. 1, 1946; children: Patrick, Lawrence, Brian, Carrie. B.Journalism, U. Nev., 1950. Reporter Richmond (Calif.) Independent, 1950-53; reporter Oakland Tribune, 1953-62, asst. state editor, 1962-64, telegraph editor, 1964-67, financial editor, 1967-79; editor San Francisco Bus. Jour., 1979-81; news dir. Fireman's Fund Ins. Cos., Novato, Calif., 1981—. Mem. editorial adv. bd.: Catholic Voice. Pres. Richmond Jr. C. of C., 1957-58; bd. dirs. Cath. Social Service Contra Costa County, Calif., 1959-62, Bay Area Coop. Edn. Clearing House, 1977—; mem. Richmond Schs. Citizens Adv. Com., 1969. Served with USAAF, 1943-45. Recipient award for best financial sect. daily newspaper Calif., Calif. Newspaper Pubs. Assn., 1968, 70, 72, 74; Knowland award for outstanding performance, 1972; Hughes fellow Rutgers U., 1969. Mem. Soc. Am. Bus. Writers, Marine Exchange San Francisco Bay Area, Sigma Delta Chi. Clubs: Contra Costa (Calif.); Press (Best News Story award 1965) (pres. 1956). Home: 2728 Del Monte Ave El Cerrito CA 94530 Office: 777 San Marin Dr Novato CA 94998

DOZA, LAWRENCE O., accountant, food company executive; b. Ste. Genevieve, Mo., June 6, 1938; m. Kenneth J. and Anna Mae D.; m. Lorraine M. Dickherber, July 9, 1960; children: Douglas, Jan, Dean. B.S. in Bus Adminstrn., U. Mo., 1962. Various positions to audit mgr. Price Waterhouse & Co., St. Louis, 1962-72; asst. gen. controller Borden Inc., Columbus, Ohio, 1972-74, gen. controller, 1974-77, v.p., gen. controller, 1977—. Mem. Fin. Execs. Inst. Republican. Roman Catholic. Clubs: Brookside Country, Columbus Athletic. Home: 4265 Reedbury Ln Columbus OH 43220 Office: Borden Inc 277 Park Ave New York NY 10172

DOZIER, CARROLL THOMAS, bishop; b. Richmond, Va., Aug. 18, 1911; s. Curtis M. and Rose A. (Conaty) D. A.B., Holy Cross Coll., 1932, LL.D. (hon.), 1973; postgrad., N.Am. Coll., Gregorian U., Rome. Ordained priest Roman Catholic Ch., 1937; curate St. Vincent's Ch., Newport News, Va., 1937-41, St. Joseph's Ch., Petersburg, 1941-45; dir. Soc. Propagandation of Faith, 1945-54; pastor Christ the King Ch., Norfolk, Va., 1954-71; first bishop of, Memphis, 1970—; mem. lay apostolate com., from 1972. Author pastoral letters. Named papal chamberlain, 1954, domestic prelate, 1962, proto. apost., 1967; Recipient Bill of Rights award ACLU, 1972; Cath. Human Relations award, Memphis, 1973. Address: 1325 Jefferson Ave Memphis TN 38104 *

DOZIER, WILLIAM, motion picture and TV executive; b. Omaha, Feb. 13, 1908; s. Robert C. and Emma (McElroy) D.; m. Katherine Foley, Sept. 14, 1929; 1 son, Robert J.; m. Joan Fontaine, May 2, 1946 (div. 1950); 1 dau., Deborah Leslie; m. Ann Rutherford, 1953. A.B., Creighton U., 1929. Rep. Berg-Allenberg, writers artists agy., 1935; head story and writing dept. Paramount Studios, Hollywood, Calif., 1941-44; prodn. exec. RKO-Radio Pictures, 1944-51, v.p. charge prodn., 1955-56; v.p. Universal-Internat. Pictures; producer Columbia Pictures, 1944-51; program exec. CBS, N.Y.C., 1951-55, exec. producer dramatic programs, 1955; v.p. charge programs Hollywood CBS-TV, 1957-59; v.p. charge prodn. Screen Gems, 1959-64; pres. Greenway Prodns., 1964—; prof. creative TV and drama Mt. St. Mary's Coll., West Los Angeles, Calif., 1972-78. Address: 826 Greenway Dr Beverly Hills CA 90210

DOZORETZ, LOUIS, mental hospital administrator; b. Bucharest, Rumania, Mar. 17, 1922; came to U.S., 1922, naturalized, 1928; s. Morris and Sonya (Fishman) D.; m. Bernice Fleischman, Jan. 6, 1940; children: Shari Lynne, Mark Jeremy, David Michael. Student, Coll. City N.Y., 1938-40; B.A., N.Y. U., 1943; M.D., Middlesex U., Waltham, Mass., 1947. Intern Gouverneur Hosp., N.Y.C., 1947-48; resident psychiatrist Buffalo State Hosp., 1948-51; sr. psychiatrist, 1951-53, supervising psychiatrist, 1953-58, Central Islip (N.Y.) State Hosp., 1958-61, clin. asst. dir., 1961-63, asso. dir., 1963-65; dir. Binghamton (N.Y.) Psychiat. Center, 1965—; asst. psychiatry U. Buffalo Sch. Medicine, 1956-59; Asso. examiner com. certification mental hosp. adminstrs. Am. Psychiat. Assn., 1966-69; chmn. area regional com. Mental Health and Retardation, 1968, mem. area com., 1968-74. Served with AUS, 1945-46. Mem. Am. Assn. Psychiat. Adminstrs. (treas. N.Y. State chpt. 1967-70), N.Y. State Med. Soc., Am. Psychiat. Assn. (certified mental hosp. adminstr.), Broome County Med. Soc., Am. Geriatrics Soc., AAAS, N.Y. Acad. Sci., Am. Profl. Practice Assn. Lodge: Rotary. Home: 425 Robinson St Binghamton NY 13901 Office: Binghamton State Hosp Binghamton NY 13901

DRABBLE, BERNARD JAMES, Canadian government official; b. Portsmouth, Eng., May 20, 1925; s. James C.W. and Mary Buchanan (Simpson) D. B.A., McGill U., 1947. With Bank of Can., Ottawa, Ont., 1947-81, dep. gov., 1974-81; exec. dir. for Can., Ireland, Jamaica IMF, Washington, 1974-81; asso. dep. minister Dept. Fin. Govt. Can., Ottawa, 1981—. Anglican. Office: 160 Elgin St Ottawa ON K1A 0G5 Canada

DRABBLE, MARGARET (MRS. CLIVE SWIFT), author; b. June 5, 1939; d. John Frederick and Kathleen Marie (Bloor) D.; m. Clive Swift, May 27, 1960 (dec. dissolved 1975); children—Adam, Rebecca, Joseph. B.A. with honors, Newnham Coll. Cambridge U., 1960. Author: novels A Summer Bird-Cage, 1963, The Garrick Year, 1964, The Millstone, 1965, Jerusalem the Golden, 1967, The Waterfall, 1969, The Needle's Eye, 1972, The Realms of Gold, 1975, The Ice Age, 1977, The Middle Ground, 1980; short stories Hassan's Tower, 1966, The Reunion, 1968, The Gifts of War, 1970; play Birds of Paradise, 1969; screenplay A Touch of Love, 1969; also: Wordsworth, 1966, Arnold Bennett, A Biography, 1974, For Queen and Country: Britain in the Victorian Age, 1978, A Writer's Britain, 1979; editor: The Gerius of Thomas Hardy, 1976. Recipient Rhys Meml. prize, 1966, Black Meml. prize, 1968, E.M. Forster award, 1973. Office: care AD Peters 10 Buckingham St London WC 2 England *

DRACHKOVITCH, MILORAD M., political science educator, author; b. Belgrade, Yugoslavia, Nov. 8, 1921; came to U.S., 1958, naturalized, 1965; s. Milorad and Jovanka (Milanovitch) D.; m. Helen Drachkovitch; children: Radoye, Alexandra. B.A. in Polit. Sci., U. Geneva, 1949, Ph.D., 1953. Dir. studies Coll. Europe, Bruges, Belgium, 1957-58; vis. asst. prof. polit. sci. U. Calif.-Berkeley, 1959-60; fellow Russian Research Center, Harvard U., 1960-61; sr. fellow and archivist Hoover Instn. War, Revolution and Peace, Stanford, Calif., 1961—. Author: Les socialismes français et allemand et le problème de la guerre, 1870-1914, 1953, De Karl Marx à Léon Blum, 1954, United States Aid to Yugoslavia and Poland, 1963, (with B. Lazitch) Lenin and the Comintern, vol. I, 1972, (also chpts. in books, articles in scholarly jours.); Editor: (with B. Lazitch) Comintern: Historical Highlights, 1966, Marxism in the Modern World, 1966, Marxist Ideology in the Contemporary World, 1966, Revolutionary Internationals, 1864-1943, 1966, Yearbook of International Communist Affairs, 1966, Fifty Years of Communism in Russia, 1968, East Central Europe: Yesterday-Today-Tomorrow, 1981. Mem. Am. Polit. Sci. Assn., Am. Assn. Advancement of Slavic Studies. Home: 1041 Cathcart Way Stanford CA 94305

DRACHLER, NORMAN, educator; b. Poland, May 20, 1912; (m), 1937; 3 children. B.A., Wayne State U., 1936, M.A., 1939; Ph.D., U. Mich., 1951, LL.D., 1972; Ed.D., No. Mich. U., 1970; LL.D., Eastern Mich. U., 1970. Tchr. Detroit Pub. Schs., 1936-46, asst. prin. elementary sch., 1946-53, prin., 1953-57; research dir. edn. Citizens Study Edn. Needs, 1957-59; exec. adminstrv. asst. Detroit Pub. Schs., 1959-61, asst. supt., 1961-66, acting supt., 1966-67, supt., 1967-71; dir. Inst. for Edn. Leadership, George Washington U., 1971-74; vis. prof. Stanford U., Calif., 1974—; cons. U.S. Office Edn., 1967—. Recipient Human Relations award U. Detroit, 1967; Human Right award Commn. Community Relations, 1967; Distinguished Alumnus award Wayne State U., 1969. Mem. Assn. Supervision and Curriculum Devel. (chmn. com. ethnic bias 1969-74), Nat. Assn. Temple Edn. (pres. 1957-59), Phi Kappa Phi. Office: 390 Hacienda Ct Los Altos CA 94022

DRACHMAN, DANIEL BRUCE, neurologist; b. N.Y.C., July 18, 1932; s. Julian Moses and Emily (Deitchman) D.; m. Jephta Piatigorsky, Aug. 28, 1960; children: Jonathan Gregor, Evan Bernard, Eric Edouard. A.B. summa cum laude (N.Y. State scholar), Columbia Coll., 1952; M.D. (N.Y. State Med. scholar), N.Y. U., 1956. Intern in internal medicine Beth Israel Hosp., Boston, 1956-57; asst. resident in neurology Harvard neurol. unit Boston City Hosp., 1957-58, resident in neurology, 1958-59; resident in neuropathology Harvard neurol. unit. and Mallory Inst. Pathology, 1959-60; teaching fellow in neurology Harvard U., 1957-60; clin. asso. Nat. Inst. Neurol. Diseases and Blindness, NIH, Bethesda, Md., 1960-62, research asso. lab. neuroanat. scis., 1962-63; asst. prof. neurology Tufts U., 1963-69; asso. prof. Johns Hopkins U., 1969-73, prof., 1974—; attending neurologist Johns Hopkins Hosp.; adv. bd. Multiple Sclerosis Soc., Myasthenia Gravis Found., Familial Dysautonomia Found.; clin. instr. Georgetown U., 1961-63. Clarinetist.; Author publs. on myasthenia gravis, muscular atrophy, muscular dystrophy, clubfoot, devel. disorders, neurology; editorial bd.: Muscle and Nerve jour. Research in neurol. and neuromuscular diseases. Served with USPHS, 1960-63. Recipient Founders' Day award N.Y. U., 1956; NIH grantee, 1963—; Muscular Dystrophy Assn. grantee, 1969—. Fellow Am. Acad. Neurology, N.Y. Acad. Scis.; mem. AAAS, Internat. Soc. Devel. Biology, Balt. Neurol. Soc., Phi Beta Kappa, Alpha Omega Alpha. Office: Dept Neurology Johns Hopkins U Sch Medicine 1721 E Madison St Baltimore MD 21205

DRACHMAN, DAVID ALEXANDER, neurologist; b. N.Y.C., July 18, 1932; s. Julian Moses and Emily (Drachman); m. Eleanor Betsy Derby, Nov. 26, 1959; children—Laura Jeanne, Jessica Gail, Douglas Emmet. A.B. with highest honors, Columbia U., 1952; M.D., N.Y. U., 1956. Diplomate: Am. Bd. Psychiatry and Neurology. Intern Duke U. Med. Center, 1956-57; resident in neurology Mass. Gen. Hosp., Boston, 1957-60; clin. asso. NIH, 1960-63; clin. instr. neurology Georgetown U. Med. Sch., 1961-63; mem. faculty Northwestern U. Med. Sch., 1963-77; dir. neurology clinics Duke U. Med. Center, 1963-77; prof. neurology Northwestern U. Med. Sch., 1971-77, asso. chmn. dept., 1972-75; attending physician Passavant Meml. Hosp., Chgo., 1964-72, Northwestern Meml. Hosp., 1972-77; prof. neurology, chmn. dept. U. Mass. Med. Center, 1977—; attending physician U. Mass. Med. Center, Worcester (Mass.) City Hosp., St. Vincent Hosp., Worcester; mem. med. adv. bd. Chgo. Multiple Sclerosis Soc., 1971-77, Mass. Multiple Sclerosis Soc., 1979—. Editorial bd.: Neurobiology of Aging, Archives of Neurology; contbr. articles to med. jours. Fellow Am. Acad. Neurology; mem. Am. Neurol. Assn., Alzheimer's Disease Assn. (Sci. adv. bd., trustee), AAAS, Am. Neurotology Soc., Assn. U. Profs. Neurology, Assn. Research Nervous and Mental Diseases, Mass. Assn. Neurology, N.Y. Acad. Scis., Chgo. Inst. Medicine, Boston Soc. Psychiatry and Neurology (pres.), Phi Beta Kappa, Sigma Xi, Alpha Omega Alpha. Home: 111 Barretts Mill Rd Concord MA 01742 Office: Dept Neurology Univ Mass Med Center 55 Lake Ave N Worcester MA 01605

DRACK, PAUL EDWARD, manufacturing company executive; b. Chgo., Nov. 18, 1928; m. Elaine Cheli; children: Kathy, Lisa. B.A., St. Mary's Coll., Winona, Minn., 1950; postgrad., Notre Dame U., 1960. Vice pres. Kawneer Co., Inc., Niles, Mich., 1973-74, group v.p., 1974-78, exec. v.p., 1978-79, pres., 1979—; group v.p. Alumax, Inc., San Mateo, Calif., 1982—. Served with USN, 1951-55. Office: Kawneer Co Inc 1105 N Front St Niles MI 49120 *

DRAEGER, WAYNE HAROLD, manufacturing company executive; b. Watertown, Wis., July 5, 1946; s. Harold A. and Dorothy L. (Wendt) D.; m. Bonnie Eileen Wendt, June 22, 1968; children: Eric Christopher, Kyle Douglas. B.A., Lawrence U., 1968; M.B.A., Dartmouth Coll., 1970. Fin. planning dir. Cummins Engine Co., Columbus, Ind., 1974-76, asst. controller, 1976-78, dir. 10 litre program, 1978-79, exec. dir. fin. adminstrn., 1979-81, v.p. fin. adminstrn., 1981-82, v.p. internat. affiliates, 1982—. Served to 1st lt. USAF, 1970-72. Office: PO Box 3005 Columbus IN 47201

DRAGO, RUSSELL STEPHEN, chemist, educator; b. Turners Falls, Mass., Nov. 5, 1928; s. Stephen R. and Lillian (Pucci) D.; m. Ruth Ann Burrill, Dec. 30, 1950; children: Patricia, Stephen, Paul, Robert. B.S., U. Mass., 1950; Ph.D., Ohio State U., 1954. Mem. faculty U. Ill., Urbana, 1955-82, prof. chemistry, 1965-82, U. Fla., Gainesville, 1982—. Author: (with T.L. Brown) Experiments in General Chemistry, 4th edit, 1977, Physical Methods in Chemistry, 1977, Prerequisites for College Chemistry, 1966, (with N.A. Matwiyoff) Acids and Bases, 1968, Qualitative Concepts from Quantum Chemistry, 1971, Organic Chemistry: A Short Introduction, 1972, (with N.A. Matwiyoff) Principles of Chemistry, 1974, 2d edit., 1977, Problem Solving in General Chemistry I, 1979; Contbr. articles profl. jours. Guggenheim fellow, 1973-74. Mem. Am. Chem. Soc. (award research inorganic chemistry 1969), Chem. Soc. (London). Home: 2281 NW 24th Ave Gainesville FL 32605 Office: 229 CRB U Fla Gainesville FL 32611

DRAGONE, ALLAN RUDOLPH, mfg. co. exec.; b. Melrose, Mass., 1926; (married). B.A., Middlebury, (Vt.) Coll., 1950; M.B.A., Harvard U., 1952. Mktg. sakes mgr. Champaion Paper Inc., 1959-60; v.p., gen. mgr. Standard Packaging Co., 1960-66; with Celanese Corp., N.Y.C., 1966—, corp. group v.p. domestic fibers, 1974-75, corp. exec. v.p. fibers group, 1975-80, corp. pres., chief operating officer, 1980—, also dir.; dir. Manhattan Life Ins. Co., Millhaven Galtex, Amcel Europe (S.A.), Celanse Can., Inc., Celanese Columbians, Celanese Mexicana, Celanese Venezolan. Office: Celanese Corp 1211 Ave Americas New York NY 10036 *

DRAGOO, DONALD WAYNE, research administrator, anthropologist; b. Indpls., Nov. 4, 1925; s. Calvin Ellsworth and Josephine (Coy) D.; m. Christine Worthington, Aug. 23, 1971; 1 son, Stephen W. A.B., Ind. U., 1948; M.A., U. N.Mex., 1949, postgrad., 1949-50; Ph.D., Ind. U., 1957. Archeologist Am. Found. Arabian Expdn., 1950-51; biochemist antiobiotic research and devel. Eli Lilly and Co., Indpls., 1951-52; archeologist Upper Ohio Valley Archaeol. Survey, Carnegie Mus., 1952-55, asst. curator sect. man, Pitts., 1956-59, assoc. curator, 1959-63, curator, 1963-77; head Anthropology Center, Butler, Pa., 1969-77; assoc. prof. anthropology U. Pitts., 1959-63, adj. research prof., 1971—; pres. Auctor Research, Inc., Gloucester, Va., 1980-82, dir., 1982—; pres. Inst. for Human History, Gloucester, Va., 1982—; dir. anthropology Environment Cons., Dallas, 1977-79. Author: Mounds for the Dead, 1962, Archaic Hunter, 1957; also numerous articles.; Editor: Archaeol. Newsletter, 1963—, Pandemia, 1982—; assoc. editor: Ethnology, 1962-63, Pa. Archaeologist, 1963—; asso. editor: Man in the Northeast, 1971—; collaborator: Abstracts of New World Archeology, 1965—; editorial chmn.: Annals of Carnegie Mus, 1967-68. Served with USNR, 1944-46. Fellow AAAS, Am. Anthrop. Assn.; mem. Am. Hist. Soc., Eastern States Archaeol. Fedn. (pres. 1970—), Soc. for Am. Archaeology, Am.

Indian Ethnohistoric Conf., Nat. Geog. Soc., Soc. Profl. Archaeologists, Soc. Archaeol. Scis., Am. Quaternary Assn. Home: PO Box 648 Gloucester VA 23061

DRAGOUMIS, PAUL, electric utility co. exec.; b. N.Y.C., Sept. 19, 1934; s. Andrew and Theologie D.; m. Maria William, Sept. 15, 1957; children—Ann Marie, Andrew Paul. B.S. in Elec. Engring, Poly. Inst. Bklyn., 1956; M.S. in Nuclear Engring, Internat. Sch. Nuclear Sci. and Engring., Argonne, Ill., 1959. Asst. v.p. Am. Electric Power Co., N.Y.C., 1956-70; mem. corp. exec. staff Allis Chalmers Corp., Milw., 1970-71; v.p. nuclear projects and fossil fuel supply group Potomac Electric Power Co., Washington, 1971-75; dir. nuclear affairs FEA, Washington, 1975-76; also exec. dir. Pres. Ford's Energy Resources Council; v.p. policy Potomac Electric Power Co., Washington, 1976-78, sr. v.p., 1978—; mem. mgmt. com. PJM Interconnection; exec. bd. Mid Atlantic Area council Nat. Electric Reliability Council. Trustee, mem. exec. com. Washington Opera, 1980—; trustee Greater Washington Research Center, 1978—; bd. dirs. Jr. Achievement Met. Washington, 1979—. Served with USN, 1956-57. Named U.S. Outstanding Young Elec. Engr. Eta Kappa Nu, 1964; Outstanding Young Man of Am. Jaycees, 1966. Mem. Edison Electric Inst., IEEE, Washington Bd. Trade, Md.-D.C. Utilities Assn. (pres.). Republican. Greek Orthodox. Clubs: City Tavern Assn., University (Washington). Office: 1900 Pennsylvania Ave NW Washington DC 20068

DRAGT, ALEXANDER JAMES, physicist; b. Lafayette, Ind., Apr. 7, 1936; s. Gerrit and Beulah (Westra) D.; m. Lavonne Ann Wolters, Nov. 28, 1957; children: Alison Ann, Alexander James, William David. A.B., Calvin Coll., 1958; Ph.D. in Physics (NSF fellow), U. Calif., Berkeley, 1964. Sr. scientist Lockheed Missiles & Space Corp., Palo Alto, Calif., 1961-62; staff scientist Aerospace Corp., Los Angeles, 1963; mem. Inst. Advanced Study, Princeton, N.J., 1963-65; asst. prof. physics U. Md., 1965-68, assoc. prof., 1968-74, prof., 1974—, chmn. dept. physics and astronomy, 1975-78; mem. vis. staff Los Alamos Sci. Lab., 1978-79, cons., 1979—. Fellow Am. Phys. Soc.; Mem. Am. Geophys. Union, AAAS, Am. Math. Soc. Mem. Christian Reformed Ch. Research in theoretical physics, applied math. Office: Dept Physics and Astronomy U Md College Park MD 20742

DRAIN, ALBERT STERLING, business consultant; b. Decatur, Tex., July 5, 1925; s. Albert S. and Bessie (Burk) D.; m. Mauvaline Joyce Beam, Apr. 18, 1946; children: Ronald Dale, Deborah Kay Drain Crawford. Student, Bellville (Ill.) Jr. Coll., Tex. Christian U., Iowa U., Milsaps Coll., Pittsburg (Kans.) Coll. With Armour & Co., 1945-79, regional mgr., Pitts., 1966-67, mgr. pork div., Chgo., 1967-68, fresh meats div. mgr., 1968-69, corporate v.p., 1968-75, exec. v.p., 1971-73, group v.p. food marketing div., 1973-75; pres. Armour Foods, 1975-79; also dir.; exec. v.p. for Iowa Beef Processors Inc., Dakota City, Nebr., 1979-80; group v.p. Greyhound Corp., Phoenix, 1977—; pres. Sterling Mktg. Inc. (ind. bus. cons. to meat industry), Phoenix, 1980—. Served with USNR, 1943-45. Baptist. Clubs: Masons, Shriners. Home and Office: 9515 N 47th St Phoenix AZ 85028

DRAINVILLE, GERARD, bishop; b. L'Isle-du-Pas, Que., Can., May 20, 1930. Ordained priest Roman Catholic Ch., 1953; ordained bishop of, Amos, Que., 1978—. Office: 450 Principale Nord Amos PQ J9T 2M1 Canada *

DRAKE, ALBERT ESTERN, statistics educator; b. Stamping Ground, Ky., June 12, 1927; s. John L and Dullia Zena (Humphrey) D.; m. Katherine Ashby, June 22, 1952; children: Alan Sanford, Paul Steven, Jane, Philip David. Student, Georgetown Coll., 1946-47; B.S., U. Ky., 1950, M.S., 1951; Ph.D., U. Ill., 1958; postgrad., N.C. State U., 1959, 63, U. Fla., 1960. Research asst. U. Ill., 1953-55, research asso., 1955-58; asso. prof. biometrics Auburn U., 1959-62, prof. and biometrician, 1962-63; dir. computer center W.Va. U., 1963-65, acting coordinator stats., 1965-66; prof. stats. U. Ala., 1966—, coordinator quantitative methods, 1966-72, acting head stats. and mgmt. sci., 1981; cons. in field. Contbr. articles to profl. jours., papers to profl. meetings. Bd. dirs. Little League, Auburn, 1961-63; active local council Boy Scouts Am., 1962-63, 66-67. Served with USMC, 1945-46. NSF grantee, 1959, 60, 63; Venture Fund grantee, 1975, 76, 81. Mem. Biometrics Soc., Am. Statis. Assn. (pres. Ala. chpt. 1972), Am. Inst. Decision Scis. (sec. 1973-74, council 1969-72, 75-77, editorial bd. 1969-72), Am. Agrl. Econs. Assn. Democrat. Home: 280 Woodland Hills Tuscaloosa AL 35405 Office: PO Box J U Ala University AL 35486

DRAKE, (BRYANT) STILLMAN, educator; b. Berkeley, Calif., Dec. 24, 1910; s. Bryant Stillman and Flora Ornis (Frickstad) D.; m. Eda Doreen Salzmann, Nov. 14, 1936; children: Mark Ernest, Daniel Lee; m. Lucille Daneri Jarrell, Feb. 22, 1950; m. Florence Selvin Casaroli, Apr. 1, 1967. A.B., U. Calif. at Berkeley, 1932, LL.D., 1968; LL.D. (hon.), U. Toronto, 1979. Vice pres. Calif. Municipal Statistics, San Francisco, 1934-41; finance cons. U.S. Def. Pub. Work, Los Angeles, 1941-42; regional statistician WPB, San Francisco, 1943-44; accountant Navy Price Adjustment Bd., San Francisco, 1944-45; municipal statistician Heller Bruce & Co., San Francisco, 1946-56; asst. v.p. govt. devel. Bank of P.R., San Juan, 1956-58; cons. municipal financing Blyth & Co., San Francisco, 1958-67; prof. history of sci. U. Toronto, Ont., Can., 1967-78, prof. emeritus, 1979—. Author: Discoveries and Opinions of Galileo, 1957, Galileo Studies, 1970, Galileo Against the Philosophers, 1976, Galileo At Work, 1978, Galileo, 1980, Cause, Experiment, and Science, 1981; translator: Dialogue, 1953, Mechanics, 1960, Assayer, 1960, Two New Sciences, 1974, Geometric and Military Compass, 1978. John Simon Guggenheim Meml. Found. fellow, 1971-72, 76-77. Fellow Am. Acad. Arts and Scis., Royal Soc. Can.; mem. Internat. Acad. History of Sci. Home: 219 Glen Rd Toronto ON M4W 2X2 Canada Office: 280 Huron St Toronto ON Canada *In both business and teaching, I have most respected plain language and avoidance of pretension. Experience has left me on the whole optimistic about everything but politics.*

DRAKE, CARL B., JR., insurance company executive; b. St. Paul, 1919; married. B.A., Yale U., 1941. With St. Paul Cos. Inc., St. Paul, 1941—, sec., 1960-63, asst. to pres., 1963-66, v.p., asst. to pres., 1966-68, exec. v.p., 1968-73, pres., chief exec. officer, 1973-78, chmn., chief exec. officer, 1978-82, chmn., pres., dir., 1982-83, chmn., 1983—; dir. St. Paul Fire and Marine Ins. Co., St. Paul Leasing Co., Postal Fin., St. Paul Title Ins. Corp., St. Paul Oil & Gas Corp., John Nuveen & Co. Inc., St. Paul Real Estate of Ill. Inc., Honeywell Inc., Western Life Ins. Co., St. Paul Life Ins. Co., St. Paul Land Resources Inc., St. Paul Properties Inc. Office: The St Paul Cos Inc 385 Washington St St Paul MN 55102 *

DRAKE, CHARLES GEORGE, neurosurgeon, educator; b. Windsor, Ont., Can., July 21, 1920. M.D., U. Western Ont., London, 1944, M.Sc., 1947; M.S., U. Toronto, 1956; D.Sc., Meml. U., St. John, Nfld., Can., 1973. Intern Toronto Gen. Hosp., 1944-45, resident div. neurosurgery, 1949-51, McLaughlin fellow, 1952-53; instr. physiology U. Western Ont., 1945-47; resident in surgery Victoria Hosp., London, Ont., 1948-49; clin. clk. Nat. Hosp., London, 1951; clin. fellow in neuropathology Banting Inst., Toronto, 1951-52; clin. prof. neurosurgery Victoria Hosp., 1952-69; prof., chmn. dept. clin. neurol. scis. Faculty of Medicine, U. Western Ont., 1969-74, prof., chmn. div. neurosurgery dept. clin. neurol. scis., 1969-74, prof., chmn. dept. surgery, 1974—. Mem. editorial bd.: Jour. Neurosurgery, 1967-74; chmn. bd., 1975-76. Decorated Order of Can.; recipient award Royal Bank of Can., 1983. Fellow Coll. Surgeons (South Africa) (hon.), Royal Coll. Surgeons Ireland, Royal Coll. Surgeons Edinburgh, Royal Australasian Coll. Surgeons; mem. Royal Coll. Physicians and Surgeons Can. (v.p. 1968-70, pres. 1971-73), Can. Council Hosp. Accreditation (chmn. council 1967-68), Am. Assn. Neurol. Surgeons (v.p. 1966-69, pres.-elect 1976, pres. 1977), A.C.S. (bd. regents 1975—), World Fedn. Neurosurg. Socs. (2d v.p. Eastern region 1976, pres. 1977-81), Am. Acad. Neurol. Surgeons (dir. 1968-70), S.W. Ont. Surg. Soc. (pres. 1968-70), Can. Assn. Clin. Surgeons (pres. 1973), James IV Assn. Surgeons Inc (sec.-treas. 1978—), Soc. Neurol. Surgeons (pres. 1980). Office: Univeristy Hosp 339 Windermere Rd London ON N6A 5A5 Canada

DRAKE, CHARLES LUM, geology educator; b. Ridgewood, N.J., July 13, 1924; s. Ervin Thayer and Elizabeth (Lum) D.; m. Martha Ann Churchill, June 24, 1950; children—Mary Aiken, Caroline Elizabeth, Susannah Churchill. B.S. in Engring, Princeton, 1948; Ph.D., Columbia, 1958. Research assoc. Lamont Geol. Obs. Columbia U., N.Y.C., 1948-56; sr. scientist Lamont Geol. Obs., 1956-58, acting asst. dir. Lamont Geol. Obs., 1963-65, became mem. faculty univ. Lamont Geol. Obs., 1958, prof. geology, chmn. dept. Lamont Geol. Obs., 1967-69; prof. dept. geology Dartmouth Coll., Hanover, N.H., 1969—, chmn. dept. geology, 1978-79, dean grad studies, assoc. dean sci. div., 1979—; mem. coms. Nat. Acad. Sci.; cons. NSF, 1964-82; mem. Nat. Adv. Com. on Oceans and Atmosphere, 1971-74; chmn. earth scis. div. NRC, 1973-76, mem. geophys. research bd., 1968-82. Trustee Village S. Nyack, N.Y., 1963-65, 66-69, dep. mayor, 1968-69. Served with AUS, 1943-46. NSF postdoctoral fellow, 1965-66. Mem. Internat. Council Sci. Unions (pres. interunion commn. on geodynamics 1970-75, chmn. U.S. Geodynamics com. 1970-78, chmn. U.S. nat. commn. geology 1979—), Am. Geophys. Union (pres.-elect 1982-84), AAAS, Am. Assn. Petroleum Geologists, Geol. Soc. Am. (pres. 1976-77), Geol. Soc. France (hon.), Seismol. Soc. Am., Royal Astron. Soc., Soc. Exploration Geophysicists, Marine Tech. Soc., Sigma Xi. Club: Cosmos. Home: RFD 1 East Thetford VT 05043

DRAKE, CHARLES WHITNEY, physicist; b. South Portland, Maine, Mar. 8, 1926; s. Charles Whitney and Katharine Gabrielle (O'Neill) D.; m. Ellen Tan, June 15, 1952; children—Judith Ellen, Robert Charles, Linda Ann. B.S., U. Maine, 1950; M.A., Conn. Wesleyan U., 1952; Ph.D., Yale U., 1958. Scientist Westinghouse Atomic Power Div., 1952-53; instr. Yale U., New Haven, 1957-60, asst. prof., 1960-66, research asso., 1966-69; asso. prof. Oreg. State U., 1966-74; prof., 1974—, chmn. dept. physics, 1976—; vis. prof. Oxford U. Clarendon Lab. and St. Peter's Coll., 1972-73, U. Tbingen (W.Ger.), 1982. Contbr. articles to profl. jours. Served with USNR, 1944-46. Recipient various fellowships and grants. Mem. Am. Phys. Soc., Am. Assn. Physics Tchrs., Sigma Xi, Tau Beta Pi, Sigma Pi Sigma. Home: 7330 NW Acorn Ridge Dr Corvallis OR 97330 Office: Dept Physics Oreg State U Corvallis OR 97331

DRAKE, DONALD CHARLES, journalist; b. N.Y.C., Jan. 12, 1935; s. Albert E. and Gloria (Walters) D.; m. Anne Bunting, Feb. 18, 1955 (div.); 1 dau., Valerie. Student, N.Y. U., 1953-56. Copy boy New York Herald Tribune, 1954-55; reporter Patent Trader, Mt. Kisco, N.Y., 1956-57, New Haven Register, 1957-58, Newsday, Garden City, N.Y., 1958-65; med. writer Phila. Inquirer, 1965—. Author: Medical School, 1978. Recipient Russell L. Cecil Writing award Arthritis Found., 1968, John S. Packard award Pa. Tb. and Health Soc., 1968, Howard W. Blakeslee awards Am. Heart Assn., 1969, 76, 81, Walter J. Donaldson awards Pa. Med. Soc., 1970, 71, Keystone Press awards, 1974-81, 83, Claude Bernard award Nat. Soc. for Med. Research, 1978, AP Mng. Editors award, Pa., 1978, 81, Robert Kennedy Journalism award, 1982, Robert F. Kennedy Journalism award, 1983, Grand prize Am. Psychiat. Assn., 1983, Morse award, 1982, others. Mem. Nat. Assn. Sci. Writers. Office: Phila Inquirer 400 N Broad St Philadelphia PA 19101 *Journalism would be much more worthwhile if its practitioners concerned themselves more with conveying the truth of events than just the facts. But that's much harder to do.*

DRAKE, ELIZABETH MERTZ, chemical engineering educator; b. N.Y.C., Dec. 20, 1936; d. John and Ruth (Johnson) Martin; m. Alvin William Drake, July 31, 1957; 1 son, Alan Lee. S.B. in Chem. Engring., MIT, 1958, Sc.D., 1966. Registered profl. engr., Mass. Staff engr. Arthur D. Little Inc., Cambridge, Mass., 1958-64, sr. staff, 1966-76, mgr. risk analysis, 1977-82, v.p. tech. risk mgmt., 1980-82; lectr. U. Calif.-Berkeley, 1971; vis. prof. MIT, Cambridge, 1973-74; chmn. chem. engring. dept. Northeastern U., Boston, 1982—; cons. Arthur D. Little, 1982—; corp. mgr. MIT, 1981—; mem. tech. pipeline safety standards com. U.S. Dept. Transp., 1980—. Contbr. articles to profl. jours.; inventor fractionation method and apparatus, 1972. Mem. Am. Inst. Chem. Engrs., AAAS, Am. Chem. Soc., Sigma Xi. Home: 30F Inman St Cambridge MA 02139

DRAKE, FRANK DONALD, astronomer; b. Chgo., May 28, 1930; s. Richard Carvel and Winifred Pearl (Thompson) D.; m. Amahl Z. Shakhashiri, Mar. 4, 1978; children: Nadia Meghann, Leila Marlyss; children by previous marriage: Stephen David, Richard Procter, Paul Robert. B. Engring. Physics, Cornell U., 1952; M.A., Harvard, 1956, Ph.D., 1958. Mem. Harvard Radio Astronomy Project, 1955-58; dir. Astron. Research Group, Ewen-Knight Corp., 1958; head telescope operations div. and sci. services div., radio studies Venus and Jupiter Nat. Radio Astronomy Obs., 1958-63; chief lunar and planetary scis. sect. Jet Propulsion Lab., 1963-64; assoc. prof. astronomy Cornell U., Ithaca, N.Y., 1964-66, prof., 1966—, Goldwin Smith prof. astronomy, 1976—, chmn. dept., 1968-71, assoc. dir. Center for Radiophysics and Space Research, 1965-74; dir. Arecibo Ionospheric Obs., 1966-68, Nat. Astronomy and Ionosphere Center, 1971-81; mem. NRC, 1969-71; adviser govt. coms. on space research and astronomy. Author: Intelligent Life in Space, 1962, Murmurs of Earth: The Voyager Interstellar Record, 1978; Editorial adv. bd.: World Book Ency. Vice-pres. CETI Found.; bd. dirs. Extrasolar Planetary Found. Mem. Am. Astron. Soc. (councillor, past chmn. div. planetary scis.), AAAS (past v.p., past chmn. astronomy sect.), Nat. Acad. Scis., Am. Acad. Arts Scis., Internat. Astron. Union (v.p. commn. on life in universe, vice chmn. U.S. nat. com.), Internat. Sci. Radio Union, Planetary Soc. (dir.), Sigma Xi, Tau Beta Pi. Club: Explorers. Organized pioneer search for extra-terrestrial life, project OZMA, 1960. Office: 422 Space Scis Bldg Cornell U Ithaca NY 14853

DRAKE, GEORGE ALBERT, college president, historian; b. Springfield, Mo., Feb. 25, 1934; s. George Bryant and Alberta (Stimpson) D.; m. Susan Martha Ratcliff, June 20, 1960; children: Christopher George, Cynthia May, Melanie Susan. A.B., Grinnell (Iowa) Coll., 1956; Fulbright scholar, U. Paris, 1956-57; A.B. (Rhodes scholar), Oxford U., 1959, M.A., 1963; B.D., U. Chgo., 1962, M.A., 1963, Ph.D. (Rockefeller fellow), 1965; LL.D. (hon.), Colorado Coll., 1980, Ripon Coll., 1982. Instr. history Grinnell (Iowa) Coll., 1960-61, pres., 1979—; asst. prof., assoc. prof., prof. history Colo. Coll., Colorado Springs, 1964-79, acting dean of Coll., 1967-68, dean, 1969-73. Trustee Grinnell Coll., 1970-79, Penrose Hosp., 1976-79, Grinnell Gen. Hosp., 1980—. NEH fellow, 1974. Mem. Am. Hist. Assn., Am. Ch. History Soc.

DRAKE, GEORGE LENTON, JR., research chemist; b. Georgiana, Ala., Mar. 16, 1923; s. George Lenton and Katie Lou (Lane) D.; m. Jeanette Woodruff Pickens, Sept. 10, 1949; children—George Lenton, III, Curtis Lee. B.S. in Chemistry, U. Ga., 1944, M.S., 1949. Chemist Cities Service Refining Corp., Lake Charles, La., 1944; asst. prof. chemistry U. Ga., 1949; research leader So. Regional Research Lab., Dept. Agr., New Orleans, 1949—. Author: Flame Resistant Cotton, 1971, Textile Flammability Handbook, 1974; also chpts. in books, articles. Leadership tng. chmn. New Orleans Area council Boy Scouts Am., 1972—. Served with AUS, 1944-46. Decorated Bronze Star, Army Commendation medal, Combat Inf. Badge.; Recipient Distinguished Service award Dept. Agr., 1964, Superior Service award, 1960, 64, 68, 69, 73, Certificate of Merit, 1963, 67; Civil Servant of Year award New Orleans Fed. Bus. Assn., 1962; Silver Beaver award Boy Scouts Am., 1968; Ednl. award, 1974. Mem. Am. Assn. Textile Chemists and Colorists (Olney medal 1976), Am. Chem. Soc. (Herty medal 1969), Fiber Soc., Internat. Brotherhood Magicians, Soc. Am. Magicians, Sigma Xi. Democrat. Baptist. Clubs: Zeus Carnival, Pistol, City Park Golf (New Orleans). Patentee in field. Home: 2009 Elizabeth Ave Metairie LA 70003 Office: 1100 Robert E Lee Blvd New Orleans LA 70179

DRAKE, HARRINGTON, business services and communications executive; b. Kansas City, Mo., Sept. 2, 1919; s. Embree and Orpha (Anderson) D.; m. Shirley Grant, Feb. 18, 1942; children: Ted G., Jeffrey, Anderson. B.A., Colgate U., 1941. With Reuben H. Donnelley Corp., N.Y.C., 1947-72, pres., prin. exec. officer, 1968-72; exec. v.p. Dun & Bradstreet, Inc., 1971-72; pres., chief operating officer The Dun & Bradstreet Corp., 1972-75, pres., 1975-81, chief exec. officer, 1975—, chmn., 1977—, also dir.; dir. Corinthian Broadcasting Corp., Irving Bank Corp., Irving Trust Co. Chmn. bd. trustees Colgate U. Clubs: Blind Brook (Port Chester, N.Y.); Cypress Point (Pebble Beach, Calif.); Links (N.Y.C.); Los Angeles Country, California (Los Angeles); Riverside Yacht (Conn.). Office: 299 Park Ave New York NY 10171

DRAKE, JOHN HAROLD, II, food company executive; b. Boston, Nov. 10, 1943; s. Robert Grant and Pleasantine (Wilson) D.; m. Linda Jean Lewis, July 16, 1964 (div. Feb. 1981); children: Tracy Lee, Joanna Grant. A.B., Dartmouth Coll., 1965; M.B.A., Harvard U., 1967. Account exec. Grey Advt., Inc., N.Y.C., 1967-70; v.p., account supr. Foote, Cone & Belding, N.Y.C., 1970-72; v.p. mktg., team sports Wilson Sporting Goods Co., River Grove, Ill., 1972-78; rep. dir. Pepsico (Japan) Ltd., Tokyo, 1978-79; v.p. internat. devel. Consol. Foods Corp., Chgo., 1979-83; pres., chief exec. officer Hollywood Brands, Inc. (subs. Consol. Foods Corp.), Centralia, Ill., 1983—. Clubs: University (Chgo.); Meadow Woods Country (Centralia). Home: 155 Harbor Dr 2109 Cicago IL 60601 Office: Hollywood Brands Inc 100 S Poplar Centralia IL 62801

DRAKE, JOHN WALTER, geneticist; b. Detroit, Feb. 10, 1932; s. John Alfred and Eleanor Bryan (Smith) D.; m. Pamela Elizabeth Grunau, Dec. 3, 1960; children: Juliet Anne, Jonathan Andrew Nicholas. B.S. magna cum laude, Yale U., 1954; Ph.D., Calif. Inst. Tech., 1958. Research asso., instr. microbiology U. Ill., Urbana, 1958-59, asst. prof., 1959-64, asso. prof., 1964-69, prof., 1969—, chmn. genetics program, 1969-75; chief lab. molecular genetics Nat. Inst. Environ. Health Scis., Research Triangle Park, N.C., 1977—; adj. prof. pathology U. N.C.; adj. prof. genetics Duke U. Author: Molecular Mechanisms of Mutation, 1970; editorial bd.: Genetics, 1982—. Fulbright fellow Weizmann Inst., Israel, 1957-58; Guggenheim fellow Lab. Molecular Biology, Cambridge, Eng., 1964-65; USPHS spl. fellow U. Edinburgh, Scotland, 1971-72. Mem. Genetics Soc. Am., Environ. Mutagen Soc. (pres. 1976-77). Research and pubis. in embryology, virology, genetics. Office: NIEHS Research Triangle Park NC 27709

DRAKE, JOHN WARREN, electronics engineering educator; b. Chgo., July 5, 1930; s. Robert Warren and Winifred Elizabeth (Bramhall) D.; m. Miriam Anna Engleman, Dec. 19, 1960; 1 son, Robert Warren. B.S., Rensselaer Poly. Inst., 1952; M.B.A., Harvard U., 1954, D.B.A., 1972. Research asso. Aero. Research Found., Cambridge, Mass., 1956-57; prin. United Research, Inc., Cambridge, 1957-61; v.p. Systems Analysis and Research Corp., Cambridge, 1961-69; prof., chmn. air transp. area Sch. Aeros. and Astronautics, Sch. Engring., Purdue U., 1972—, mem. president's council; cons. in field; mem. Transp. Research Bd. NRC. Author: The Administration of Transportation Modeling Projects, 1973. Served with U.S. Army, 1954-56. Mem. Transp. Research Forum, Inst. Mgmt. Sci., Air Transp. Research Internat. Forum (council), AIAA, Soc. Automotive Engrs. Club: University (Washington). Home: 1815 Woodland Ave West Lafayette IN 47906 Office: Sch of Aeronautics and Astronautics Purdue U West Lafayette IN 47907

DRAKE, OWEN BURTCH, advertising agency executive; b. N.Y.C., May 22, 1941; s. Owen Burtch Winters and Louise Harrison (Gwynn) D.; m. Joan Draper, Dec. 15, 1961 (div. July 1975); children: Burtch Winters, Frederic Malcolm; m. Deborah Edmonson, Jan. 8, 1977; 1 dau., Kelley Keresey. Student, U.Va., 1958-61. Sr. v.p. Dancer, Fitzgerald & Sample Inc., N.Y.C., 1974-78; pres. Dancer, Fitzgerald & Sample Inc., San Francisco, 1981—; dir. European area Life Savers Inc., London, 1978-80; sr. v.p. Foote, Cone & Belding, N.Y.C., 1981. Bd. dirs. San Francisco Zool. Soc., 1982—. Served with USMCR, 1959-65. Clubs: Racquet and Tennis (N.Y.C.); University (San Francisco); Rockaway Hunting (Cedarhurst, N.Y.); Lawrence Beach (Atlantic Beach, N.Y.); Coral Beach (Bermuda). Office: Dancer Fitzgerald Sample Inc 1010 Battery St San Francisco CA 94111

DRAKE, RICHARD MATTHEWS, educator; b. Albia, Iowa, May 25, 1906; s. Frank E. and Nellie (Mason) D.; m. Lillian M. Berg, June 26, 1929; children—Richard Matthews, Katharine. Student, Ft. Dodge (Iowa) Jr. Coll., 1924-25; B.S. in Math., Physics, Edn, U. Minn., 1928; M.A., Ph.D. in Math. Ednl. Psychology, Enl. Adminstrn., 1938. Instr. math. Antigo (Wis.) pub. schs., 1928-32; instr. edn., also chmn. math. dept. Lab. Sch., U. Minn., 1932-39; asst. prof. edn. U. Buffalo, 1939-42, asso. prof., 1942-44; co-ordinator inst. ASTRP, 1944-45, prof. edn., 1944-45; asst. dean Coll. Arts and Scis., also dir. tutorial instrn., 1948-54, acting dean students, 1949-50, dir. self appraisal, 1952-54; dir. Office Instl. Research, also prof. higher edn., 1954-55; vis. prof. edn. U. Minn., summer 1946-47; v.p., prof. higher edn. U. Kansas City, 1955-56, acting chancellor, 1956-57, chancellor, 1957-61; provost Fairleigh Dickinson U., 1962-71, prof. higher edn., 1972-74, cons., 1974—; cons. Ford Found. Fund for Advancement of Edn., 1961-62. Author: (with Harl R. Douglass and V.R. Walker) Survey Test in Plane Geometry, 1939, (with T.H. Fenske and A.W. Edson) Arithmetic in Agriculture, rev. edit, 1951, Self Appraisal of the College of Arts and Sciences, 1954; also numerous articles.; Contbr. to: Ency. Ednl. Research, 1950. Dir. Truman Library, 1958-61; trustee Camden (Maine) Pub. Library, 1976—. Recipient Distinguished Service award Fairleigh Dickinson U., 1974. Mem. Phi Delta Kappa, Sigma Nu. Home: One Trim St Camden ME 04843

DRAKE, ROBERT MORTIMER, JR., consulting engineer; b. Eagle Cliff, Ga., Dec. 13, 1920; s. Robert Mortimer and Elizabeth Margaret (Foushee) D.; m. Jane Mardelle Smith, Aug. 19, 1944; children—Dianne Elizabeth, Kevin Robert. B.S. in Mech. Engring, U. Ky., 1942, M.S., U. Calif. at Berkeley, 1946, Ph.D., 1950. Registered profl. engr., Calif., Ky. Asso. prof. mech. engring. U. Calif. at Berkeley, 1947-55; engine design cons. aircraft gas turbine div. Gen. Electric Co., 1954-56; prof. mech. engring., Princeton, 1956-63, chmn. dept., 1957-63; vis. prof. U. Ky., Lexington, 1964-65, prof. mech. engring, 1965-77, chmn.

dept. mech. engring., 1966-67; dean Coll. Engring., 1966-72, dir. office of research and engring. services, 1966-72, spl. asst. to pres., 1975-77; v.p. tech. Studebaker-Worthington, Inc., 1977-78; exec. v.p. Univ. Investments Co., Inc., 1978-79, pres., 1979; cons. engr., 1979—; v.p. research and devel. Combustion Engring. Inc., 1971-75; dir. Projectron, Inc.; Mem. Ky. State Bd. Registration Profl. Engrs., 1966-71; mem. Ky. Commn. on Coal Research, 1970-72, Ky. Commn. on Sci. and Tech., 1970-72; mem. adv. council Sch. Engring. U. Mass., 1973-75, Coll. Engring. U. Ky., 1971-76. Author: (with E.R.G. Eckert) Introduction to Transfer of Heat and Mass, 1950, Heat and Mass Transfer, 1959, Analysis of Heat and Mass Transfer, 1972, also numerous articles.; Cons. editor: McGraw Hill Book Co, 1958-66; editorial adv. bd.: Internat. Jour. Heat and Mass Transfer, 1960-70. Served to capt. USAAF, 1942-47. Fellow ASME (hon. mem.); mem. Nat. Acad. Engring., Sigma Xi, Tau Beta Pi, Pi Tau Sigma, Omicron Delta Kappa. Clubs: Lexington (Ky.); Country. Home: 648 Tally Rd Lexington KY 40502

DRAKE, STANLEY ALBERT, cartoonist; b. Bklyn., Nov. 9, 1921; s. Albert Edward and Josephine (Seaburry) D.; m. Elaine Moller, Dec. 6, 1976. Student, Art Students League, N.Y.C., 1938-39. Comml. artist, N.Y.C., 1947-53. Creator: comic strip The Heart of Juliet Jones, 1953—; illustrator: Golf Digest mag, 1969—, The Touch System for Better Golf, (Bob Toski), 1970; artist for, Kelly Green (Leonard Starr); adventure series Dargaud, Neuilly-Sur-Seine, France, 1980—. Served with U.S. Army, 1942-46. Mem. Nat. Cartoonists Soc. (Story Strip Cartoonist of Yr. award 1969, 70, 72), Artists and Writers Assn. (pres.). Office: 46 Post Rd E Westport CT 06880

DRAKE, SYLVIE (JURRAS DRAKE), theater critic; b. Alexandria, Egypt, Dec. 18, 1930; came to U.S., 1949, naturalized, 1952; d. Robert and Simonette (Barda) Franco; m. Kenneth K. Drake, Apr. 29, 1952 (div. Dec. 1972); children—Jessica, Robert I.; m. Ty Jurras, June 16, 1973. M. Theater Arts, Pasadena Playhouse, 1969. Free-lance TV writer, 1962-68; theater critic Canyon Crier, Los Angeles, 1968-72; theater critic, columnist Los Angeles Times, 1971—; free-lance travel writer, book reviewer; pres. Los Angeles Drama Critics Circle, 1979-81. Mem. Am. Theater Critics Assn. Office: Times-Mirror Sq Los Angeles CA 90053

DRAKE, WILLIAM DEPUE, educator; b. Evanston, Ill., Apr. 13, 1936; s. Charles Francis II and Helen (Depue) D.; m. Susan York, July 3, 1964; children—William Depue, Elizabeth Dean, Mark, Michael. B.S., U. Mich., 1959, M.B.A., 1960, Ph.D., 1964. Dep. exec. sec. Pres.'s Com. on Tech. Automation and Econ. Progress, 1965-66; asst. prof. Sch. Natural Resources, U. Mich., Ann Arbor, 1966-67, asso. prof., 1968-69, prof., 1970—, asso. dean for research, 1972-75; Cons., bd. mem. Consumers Union of U.S.A., 1966-71; chmn. Univ. Wide Ph.D. Program in Urban and Regional Planning, 1968-72; organizer Mich. Savs. & Loan Assn., chmn. bd., 1980—; mem. bldg. research adv. bd. NRC. Chmn. Ann Arbor Met. Transp. Authority, 1972-76; Sec., treas., trustee Community Systems Found., 1973-78, pres., 1978—, mem., Australasia. Mem. A.A.A.S., Ops. Research Soc. Am., Inst. Mgmt. Scis. Home: 1321 Brooklyn Ave Ann Arbor MI 48104

DRAKE, WILLIAM FRANK, JR., lawyer; b. St. Louis, Mar. 29, 1932; s. William Frank and Beatrice (Olmmstead) D.; m. Margaret Carkener Barnes, June 28, 1975; children by previous marriage: Stephen C., Peter O., Thomas W.; stepchildren: Stuart Barnes, Ashley Barnes. B.A., Principia Coll., 1954; LL.B., Yale U., 1957. Bar: Pa. 1958. Practice, Phila., 1958-68, practice in, Valley Forge, 1968—; mem. firm Montgomery, McCracken, Walker & Rhoads, 1958-68; sr. v.p., gen. counsel Alco Standard Corp., 1968-79, sr. v.p. adminstrn., 1979—. Served with U.S. Army, 1957-58. Mem. Am., Pa., Phila. bar assns. Christian Scientist. Clubs: Union League (Phila.); Merion Cricket (Haverford, Pa.). Office: Alco Standard Corp Valley Forge PA 19482

DRAKE, WILLIAM PLUMMER, manufacturing company executive; b. Bath, Maine, Jan. 18, 1913; s. Frederick Ellis and Henrietta Barker (Plummer) D.; m. Margaret Maynadier Hardcastle, June 19, 1937; children: James B., Margaret Drake Peckham, Anne Drake Mowat, Sally Plummer, William Plummer. Ed., Bowdoin Coll., 1936. With Pennwalt Corp. (formerly Pennsalt Chems. Corp.), 1934-78, successively student trainee, salesman, sales mgr. chem. specialities dept., asst. v.p., v.p. sales, v.p. and gen. mgr. indsl. chems. div., exec. v.p., dir., pres., chief exec. officer, 1955-69, chmn., chief exec. officer, 1969-71, pres., chmn., 1971-76, chmn., chief exec. officer, 1976-78, chmn. exec. com., dir., 1978-83; dir. Berwind Corp.; dir. rubber, chems. and drug. div. OPS, 1952. Bd. dirs. Phila. Orch. Assn.; trustee Bowdoin Coll. Mem. Psi Upsilon. Episcopalian. Clubs: Cruising of Am.; Union League, Bowdoin, Corinthian Yacht (Phila.). Home: Devon PA 19333 Office: Pennwalt Bldg Philadelphia PA 19102

DRAKE, WILLIAM WHITING, JR., aerospace company executive; b. N.Y.C., Sept. 7, 1922; s. William Drake and Heather (Goodwin) D.; m. Ruth Arlene Carey, Jan. 14, 1946; children: David Chisholm, Jonathan Carey, Pamela Jane. B.S., Principia Coll., Elsah, Ill., 1944; student, Harvard, 1946-47, Brown U., 1947-48. Mem. staff Mass. Inst. Tech., 1948-49, Los Alamos Sci. Lab., 1949-52; asst. to v.p. Europe Raytheon Co., Lexington, Mass., 1952-60; v.p. adminstrn., treas. Aerospace Corp., El Segundo, Calif., 1960-82, treas., 1982—. Bd. dirs. Region 4, Los Angeles area United Way, 1972-79; chmn. S.W. Los Angeles area United Crusade, 1966; exec. bd. Los Angeles area Boy Scouts Am., 1966—; trustee Wingrock Sch., Inc., Rolling Hills Estates, Calif., 1979-83; bd. dirs. Centinela Valley YMCA, 1983—. Served with USNR, 1943-45. Mem. Los Angeles C. of C. Home: 813 11th St Manhattan Beach CA 90266 Office: 2350 E El Segundo Blvd El Segundo CA 90245

DRAKE, WILLIS KIRK, company executive; b. LaCrosse, Wis., May 28, 1923; s. Donald and Signe (Giere) D.; m. Mildren Homola; children: Willis Kirk, Nancy J. B.S.A.E, Purdue U., 1947. Group v.p. Dataproducts Corp., Woodland Hills, Calif., 1969; pres., chmn. Data Card Corp., Minnetonka, Minn., 1969-80, chmn., chief exec. officer, 1980-81, chmn., 1981—; dir. First Trust Co., St. Paul, Kahler Corp., Rochester, Minn., Filmtec Corp., Edina, Minn., Dicomed Corp., Mpls., Confertech Internat., Denver. Chmn. Minn. Cooperation Office; bd. dirs. Minn. Bus. Partnership Project, Project Wellspring; regent U. Minn. Lt. j.g. USNR. Named to Minn. Bus. Hall of Fame. Clubs: Mpls., Edina Country. Home: 5704 Schaefer Rd Edina MN 55436 Office: Data Card Corp 11111 Bren Rd W Minnetonka MN 55434

DRANE, WALTER HARDING, publisher, business cons.; b. Clarksville, Tenn., Feb. 18, 1915; s. William McClure and Mary Stacker (Luckett) D.; m. Maud Carson Tucker, Aug. 30, 1941; children—Eleanor (Mrs. Harry Christensen), Roberta Drane Siegler, Walter Harding, Beverley (Mrs. Dennis Coughlin). A.B., U. of South, 1935; postgrad. in bus, Case-Western Res. U., 1936-38. Pres. Banks-Baldwin Law Pub. Co., Cleve., 1960-78, chmn., 1978—; also dir.; founder, pres. Walter H. Drane Co. (mcpl. code compilers and pubs.), Cleve., 1955—, chmn., 1960-75; profl. bus. cons., 1981—. Bd. dirs. Univ. Circle br. YMCA, Cleve., 1958-69, Christian Residences Found., 1979—; mem. adv. com. St. Lukes Hosp., Cleve., 1981—. Served with USN, 1940-45. Episcopalian. Home: 2312 Delamere Dr Cleveland Heights OH 44106 Office: 1904 Ansel Rd Cleveland OH 44106

DRANIAS, DEAN ANTHONY, financial corporation consultant; b. Chgo., Aug. 10, 1936; s. Anastasios K. and Helen (Sakellarakis) D.; m. Valerie C. Futris, May 24, 1970; 1 son, Patrick T. A.A., Wright Jr. Coll., 1956; B.S., Northwestern U., 1959. Registered rep. Paine Webber Jackson Curtis, Chgo., 1969-74; dir. chpt. services Bank Mktg. Assn., Chgo., 1974-75; dir. mktg. Comml. Nat. Bank, Chgo., 1975-76; ptnr., account div. mgr. Fin. Relations Bd., Chgo., 1976—. Author, editor: DeSoto Inc. Annual Reports, 1976, 82 (Bronze 1st Place award Fin. World Mag. 1977, 83), 1981 (1st. Place Award Nat. Assn. Investment Clubs 1982). Bd. dirs., interim pres. Summer Place Theater, Naperville, 1981—. Served with USAR, 1959-65. Recipient various awards Fin. World Mag., 1977-83, hon. mention Roalman awards Nat. Investor Relations Inst., 1980. Mem. Internat. Assn. Bus. Communicators, Pub. Relations Soc. Am. Greek Orthodox. Office: Fin Relations Bd 150 E Huron St Chicago IL 60611

DRAPEAU, JEAN, mayor of Montreal; b. Montreal, Que., Can., Feb. 18, 1916; s. J. N. and Berthe (Martineau) D.; m. Marie-Claire Boucher, June 26, 1945; 3 sons. Arts degree, U. Montreal, 1938, Lic. Soc., Econ. and Polit. Sci, 1937; student Faculty Law, 1938-41, U. Moncton, 1956, U. Montreal, 1964, McGill U., 1965, Boswell Inst. of Loyola U., New Orleans, 1966, Sir George Williams U., Laval U., 1967. Bar: Montreal bar 1943, apptd. Queen's counsel 1961. Began practice specializing in comml. and corp. law, became mayor Montreal for 1st time, 1954, re-elected, 1960, 62, 66, 70, 74, 78, 82; dir. BTM Internat. Founder Montreal Civic Party, 1960; sr. Can. rep. Internat. Bur. Exhbns., Paris, 1967—. Created companion Order Can., 1967; recipient Indsl. Devel. award Trade and Industry Dept. 10 Canadian Provinces, 1965; Gold medal Royal Archtl. Inst. Can., 1967; decorated companion Order of Can., commandeur Ordre de la Légion d'Honneur (France). Hon. mem. ABA, numerous other nat. and internat. orgns. Home: 5700 des Plaines Ave Montreal PQ H1T 2X1 Canada Office: City Hall: Montreal PQ Canada

DRAPER, EDGAR, psychiatrist, educator; b. St. Louis, Feb. 5, 1926; s. Neal McLain and Florence Mabel (Meyers) D.; m. Norma Jane Alexander, Mar. 16, 1949; children: Susan, Anne, Neal. B.A., Washington U., 1946; postgrad., Duke Div. Sch., 1946-47; B.D., Garrett Bibl. Inst., Northwestern U., 1949; M.D., Washington U., 1953; grad., Chgo. Inst. Psychoanalysis, 1966. Intern Washington U. Service City Hosp., St. Louis, 1953-54; resident U. Cin., 1954-55, 57-59; instr. U. Chgo., 1959-60, asst. prof., 1960-66, asso. prof., 1966-68, co-dir. psychiatry outpatient dept., 1966-68; prof. psychiatry U. Mich., 1968-75, dir. psychiat. resident edn., 1968-74, prof. postgrad. continuing edn., 1970-75; prof., chmn. dept. psychiatry U. Miss. Med. Center, Jackson, 1975—; cons. Bloomington (Ill.) Mental Health Center, 1962-68, Div. Children's Services, Springfield, Ill., 1965-68, Luth. Gen. Hosp., Chgo., 1968-70, VA Hosp., Ann Arbor, Mich., 1968-76, Peace Corps, 1970-71, VA hosps., Jackson and Biloxi, Miss., 1975—; cons. psychiatry edn. br. NIMH, 1975-77; examiner Am. Bd. Psychiatry and Neurology, 1970—; mem. Am. Psychiat. Assn. Consultation and Evaluation Service Bd., 1976-79; bd. dirs. Miss. Children's Home Soc., 1980—, Clin. Pastoral Edn., UNMC, 1980—. Editorial adv.: World Jour. Psychosynthesis, 1977—. Served with USPHS, 1955-57. Fellow Am. Psychiat. Assn. (chmn. com. on religion), Am. Coll. Psychiatry, So. Psychiat. Assn., Am. Soc. Psychoanalytic Physicians; mem. Miss. Psychiat. Assn. (pres. 1983), Miss. State Med. Soc., Central Med. Soc., Mich. Psychiat. Soc. (chmn. membership com. 1973-75), Internat. Assn. Suicide Prevention, Mich. Soc. Pastoral Care (dir. 1969-72), Soc. Sci. Study of Religion, So. Psychiat. Assn., Am. Assn. Chmn. Depts. of Psychiatry, Chgo. Psychoanalytic Soc., Acad. Religion and Mental Health (chmn. Chgo. chpt. 1966-67). Home: 2419 Lake Circle Dr Jackson MS 39211 Office: Univ Med Center 2500 N State St Jackson MS 39216

DRAPER, FREDA, opera and concert singer; b. Kansas City, Mo.; d. Frederick and Leila (Burleigh) Faulkner; m. Vernon Gerhardt, 1947. Student, Chgo. Mus. Coll.; studied voice, Edna Forsythe, Kansas City, Mo.; operatic work, Dino Bigalli, Chgo.; scholarship pupil, Mary Garden. Vocal faculty Northwestern U., 1941-44. Tour soloist, Ballet Russe de Monte Carlo, Chgo. Opera Co., 1937-42; sang: world premier Bride of Bagdad (winner Am. Opera Soc.'s 1st award 1940); with, Chgo. Opera Co., 1937-42; appeared as soloist with leading symphony orchs. U.S.; guest nat. radio programs; made seven months tour P.I. as soloist before armed forces, 1945; appeared in concert and opera on 3 continents, 1952-55; coached oratorio with, Chas. Baker, N.Y.C., light opera appearances, St. Louis Municipal Opera, Hollywood Prodns., Inc. Recipient Presdl. citation, Medal of Freedom, 1947; Hon. Dau. Mark Twain award for contbn. to Am. music. Hon. mem. Women's C. of C. Kansas City, Sigma Alpha Iota, Beta Sigma Phi (internat. hon.) *

DRAPER, JAMES (JIMMY) THOMAS, clergyman; b. Hartford, Ark., Oct. 10, 1935; s. James T. D.; m. Carol Ann Floyd, 1956; children: Randy, Bailey, Terri. B.A., Baylor U., 1957; B.D., Southwestern Bapt. Theol. Sem., M.Div.; hon. degree, Howard Payne U., Brownwood, Tex., Dallas Bapt. Coll.; D.D. hon., Campbell U., Buies Creek, N.C. Ordained to ministry Baptist Ch.; pastor Steel Hollow Bapt. Ch., Bryan, Tex., Iredell Bapt. Ch., Tex., Temple Bapt. Ch., Tyler, Tex., Univ. Park Bapt. Ch., San Antonio, Tex., Red Bridge Bapt. Ch., Kansas City, Mo., First So. Bapt. Ch., Del City, Okla.; assoc. pastor First Bapt. Ch., Dallas, pastor, Euless, Tex., 1975—; mem. adminstrv. com. Bapt. Gen. Conv., Tex., mem. exec. bd., mem. missions funding com., mem. exec. dir. search com.; pres. So. Bapt. Conv., 1982—, So. Baptist Conv. Pastors Conf., 1979—; trustee So. Bapt. Conv. Annuity Bd.; preacher numerous convs., confs. Contbr. articles to religious jours. Office: First Baptist Ch PO Box 400 Euless TX 76039

DRAPER, MORRIS, diplomat; b. Berkeley, Calif., Feb. 18, 1928; s. Morris and Anne Marie (Hanson) D.; m. Nancy Carol Moyer, Aug. 14, 1949 (div. 1981); children: Courtney Cathleen, Blair Alexander, Jonathan Morris; m. Roberta Hornig, Aug. 15, 1981. B.A., U. So. Calif., 1952; postgrad., Am. U. Beirut, 1959-61. Various positions U.S. Fgn. Service, Washington, Singapore, Amman, Jidda, 1955-70; counselor Am. Embassy, Ankara, Turkey, 1970-74; spl. asst. to sec. Dept. State, Washington, 1975-77, dep. asst. sec. of state, 1977-82, ambassador, 1982—, spl. Presdl. emissary to Middle East, 1982—. Served with U.S. Army, 1946-47. Decorated Order of Cedars of Lebanon, 1982. Mem. Phi Beta Kappa, Delta Tau Delta. Office: US Dept State 21st and Virginia Ave NW Washington DC 20520

DRAPER, NORMAN RICHARD, educator, statistician; b. Eng., Mar. 20, 1931; came to U.S., 1955; s. Norris and Helen (Draper). B.A., Cambridge (Eng.) U., 1954, M.A., 1958; Ph.D., U. N.C., 1958. Tech. officer, statistician plastics div. Imperial Chem. Industries, 1958-60; mem. Math. Research Center, U. Wis.-Madison, 1960-61, mem. faculty, 1961—, prof. statistics, 1966—, chmn., 1967-73; vis. prof. Imperial Coll., London, fall 1967, 68. Author: (with H. Smith) Applied Regression Analysis, 1966, 2d edit., 1981, (with G.E.P. Box) Evolutionary Operation, 1969, (with W. E. Lawrence) Probability: An Introductory Course, 1970. Fellow Royal Statis. Soc., Am. Statis. Assn., Inst. Math. Statistics, Am. Soc. Quality Control (lectr. 1963—); mem. Internat. Statis. Inst., Biometric Soc. Address: 1210 W Dayton St Madison WI 53706

DRAPER, THEODORE, author; b. Bklyn., Sept. 11, 1912; s. Samuel and Annie D.; son, Roger. B.S.S., Bklyn. Coll.; 1. Writer; cons. 20th Century Fund. Author: The Six Weeks' War, 1944, The Roots of American Communism, 1957, American Communism and Soviet Russia, 1960, Castro's Revolution: Myths and Realities, 1962, Castroism, Theory and Practice, 1965, Abuse of Power, 1967, Israel and World Politics, 1968, The Dominican Revolt, 1968, The Rediscovery of Black Nationalism, 1970, Present History, 1983; Contbr.: to magazines others. Fellow Am. Acad. Arts and Scis.; mem. Council on Fgn. Relations. Address: 35 Linwood Circle Princeton NJ 08540

DRAPER, VERDEN ROLLAND, accountant; b. St. Louis, Feb. 23, 1916; s. Neal McLain and Florence (Meyers) D.; m. Eileen Ogden, Aug. 18, 1940; children: Mallen, Eileen Ann, Cynthia, Patti, Verden. B.S., Washington U., St. Louis, 1938. With Price Waterhouse & Co. (C.P.A.s), St. Louis, 1938-51, Tulsa, 1951-55, Pitts., 1955-60, Buffalo, 1960—; mem. faculty Washington U., St. Louis U., U. Tulsa. Author: (with Robert H. Irving) Accounting Practices in the Petroleum Industry, 1958; contbr. articles profl. publs. Former pres. Better Bus. Bur. Western N.Y. Served with USNR, World War II. Mem. Am. Inst. C.P.A.s Mo., Okla., Pa., N.Y. State socs. C.P.A.s, Am. Accounting Assn., Buffalo Area C. of C. (treas., dir.), Beta Gamma Sigma, Omicron Delta Kappa, Delta Sigma Pi (Alumnae award 1938), Alpha Kappa Psi (hon.), Theta Xi. Presbyterian. Clubs: Buffalo Country (past treas., gov.), Buffalo). Home: 129 Greenaway Rd Eggertsville NY 14226 Office: 3600 Marine Midland Center Buffalo NY 14203

DRAPER, WILLIAM FRANKLIN, artist, portrait and landscape painter; b. Hopedale, Mass., Dec. 24, 1912; s. Clare Hill and Matilda Grace (Engman) D.; m. Barbara Cagiati, Oct. 7, 1944 (div. 1969); children: William Franklin, Francesca Cagiati Draper Linke, Margaret Joy. Student, Pomfret (Conn.) Sch., 1927-31, Harvard U., 1931-33, NAD, 1933-34, Grande Chaumiere, Paris, 1935, Art Student's League, N.Y.C., 1937. Instr. Art Students League N.Y., 1965-74. Exhibited, Nat. Gallery, Washington, Met. Mus., Nat. Portrait Gallery, NAD, Chgo. Art Inst., Inst. Modern Art, Mus. Fine Arts, Boston, Nat. Gallery, London; works include 3 murals, Bencroft Hall, U.S. Naval Acad.; portraits of numerous pub. figures John V. Lindsay; represented, Chrysler permanent collection, others; one man shows, N.Y.C., Boston, St. Louis, Palm Beach, Altanta. Served as lt. comdr., ofcl. combat artist USNR, 1942-46. Decorated Bronze star. Clubs: Harvard, Century Assn., Knickerbocker. Studio: 535 Park Ave New York NY 10021

DRAPER, WILLIAM HENRY, III, government official; b. White Plains, N.Y., Jan. 1, 1928; s. William Henry and Katherine (Baum) D.; m. Phyllis Culbertson, June 13, 1953; children: Rebecca, Polly, Timothy. B.A., Yale U., 1950; M.B.A., Harvard U., 1954. With Inland Steel Co., Chgo., 1954-59, Draper, Gaither & Anderson, Palo Alto, Calif., 1959-62; Founder Draper & Johnson Investment Co., Palo Alto, 1962-65; pres. Sutter Hill Capital Co., Palo Alto, 1965-70; founder, gen. ptnr. Sutter Hill Ventures, Palo Alto, 1970-81; now pres., chmn. Export-Import Bank U.S., Washington; dir. numerous firms. Chmn. bd. Calif. Assn. Am. Conservatory Theatre; bd. dirs. Population Crsis Com.; mem. adv. bd. Stanford Grad. Sch. Bus. Adminstrn.; nat. co-chmn. fin. com. George Bush for Pres., 1980; fund raiser Reagan-Bush campaign, 1980; dir., former chmn. Republican Alliance. Served with U.S. Army, 1951-52. Clubs: Palo Alto, Pacific Union., Bohemian, Met. Office: 811 Vermont Ave NW Washington DC 20571 *

DRAUS, FRANK JOHN, biochemistry educator; b. Dupont, Pa., Oct. 30, 1929; s. John and Helen (Gola) D.; m. Patricia Kagrise, Oct. 20, 1956; children: Julia, John, Peter, Elizabeth. B.S., Alliance (Pa.) Coll., 1951; M.S., Duquesne U., 1953, Ph.D., 1957. Mem. faculty U. Pitts. Sch. Dental Medicine, 1956—, prof. biochemistry, 1965—, head dept., 1966—, asst. dean acad. affairs, 1983—; exchange prof. U. Marseilles, France, 1972; Cons. to industry; temporary adviser WHO, 1969; Adv. mem. bd. trustees Alliance Coll., 1963—. Author articles in field. Recipient Distinguished Alumni award Alliance Coll., 1963. Fellow Am. Inst. Chemists; mem. Am. Chem. Soc., Internat. Assn. Dental Research, N.Y. Acad. Scis., A.A.A.S., Am. Dental Assn. (asso.), Alliance Coll. Alumni Assn. (pres. 1961-65, bd. dirs. 1965-70), Sigma Xi, Omicron Kappa Upsilon. Home: 1024 Dale Dr Pittsburgh PA 15220

DRAY, WILLIAM HERBERT, philosophy educator; b. Montreal, June 23, 1921; s. William John and Florence Edith (Jones) D.; m. Doris Kathleen Best, Sept. 18, 1943; children: Christopher Reid, Jane Elizabeth. B.A. in History, U. Toronto, 1949, Oxford U., 1951, M.A., 1955, D.Phil., 1956. Lectr. U. Toronto, 1953-55, asst. prof., asso. prof., 1956-63, prof., 1963-68, Trent U., 1968-76, chmn. dept. philosophy, 1968-73; prof. philosophy U. Ottawa, Ont., 1976—. Author: Laws and Explanation in History, 1957, Philosophy of History, 1964, Perspectives on History, 1980. Served with RCAF, 1941-46. Am. Council Learned Socs. fellow, 1960-61; Can. Council fellow, 1971-72, 78-79; Killam research fellow, 1980-81; Nat. Humanities Ctr. fellow, 1980-81. Fellow Royal Soc. Can.; mem. Can. Philos. Assn., Am. Philos. Assn., Can. Hist. Assn., Aristotelian Soc. Home: 166 Rodney Crescent Ottawa ON K1H 5J9 Canada Office: Dept Philosophy Univ of Ottawa Ottawa ON K1N 6N5 Canada

DRAYTON, WILLIAM, lawyer, management consultant; b. N.Y.C., June 15, 1943; s. William Astor and Joan (Bergere) D. B.A., Harvard, 1965; M.A. (Henry fellow), Oxford (Eng.) U., 1967; J.D., Yale, 1970. Bar: N.Y. State bar 1971, D.C. bar 1976. Cons. McKinsey and Co., Inc., N.Y.C., 1970-77, of counsel, 1982—; vis. assoc. prof. law Stanford, 1975-76; lectr. John F. Kennedy Sch. of Govt., Harvard; also dir. Harvard Regulatory Reform Group, 1976-77; cons. White House Domestic Council, 1977; asst. adminstr. for planning and mgmt. EPA, 1977-81; dir. Corp. for Fiscal Policy, 1971-75; founder, chmn. Yale Legis. Services. Contbr. articles in field to legal jours. Pres. Ams. in India for McGovern, 1972; mem. Carter-Mondale Policy Planning, 1976, Carter-Mondale Govt. Reorgn. Transition Group, 1976-77; pres. Soc. for Internat. Public Interest, 1980—; chmn. Am. Environ. Safety Council, 1981—; mem. Democratic Nat. Com. Com. energy and environment, 1982—. Mem. Am. Bar Assn., AAAS (mem. com. sci. pub. policy 1973-76), Council Fgn. Relations (mem. Working Group on Human Rights 1975-76), Friends India Soc. (chmn. 1974-75), Assn. Bar City N.Y., Phi Beta Kappa. Club: Yale (N.Y.). Home: 1200 N Nash St Arlington VA 22209 Office: 1521 New Hampshire Ave NW Washington DC 20036

DREBEN, BURTON SPENCER, educator, philosopher; b. Boston, Sept. 26, 1927; s. Robert and Florence (Levin) D.; m. Raya Spiegel, Mar. 26, 1950; children: Elizabeth Karen, Jonathan Stephen. B.A. summa cum laude, Harvard U., 1949; student, Oxford (Eng.) U., 1950-51. Instr. U. Chgo., 1955-56; mem. faculty Harvard U., 1956—, prof. philosophy, 1965—, Edgar Pierce prof. philosophy, 1982—, dean Grad. Sch. Arts and Scis., 1973-76, asso. dean faculty arts and scis., 1973-76, chmn. Soc. Fellows, 1976—. Author: (with Warren Goldfarb) The Decision Problem, 1979; Contbr. articles to profl. jours. Fulbright fellow, 1950-51; Guggenheim fellow, 1957-58. Fellow Am. Acad. Arts and Scis.; mem. Am. Math. Soc., Am. Philos. Assn., Assn. Symbolic Logic (editor jour. 1967-76, treas. 1973-78). Jewish. Office: Emerson Hall Harvard Univ Cambridge MA 02138

DREBEN, RAYA SPIEGEL, judge; b. Vienna, Austria, Dec. 3, 1927; came to U.S., 1928, naturalized, 1936; d. Shalom and Rose (Goldschmiedt) Spiegel; m. Burton S. Dreben, Mar. 26, 1950; children: Elizabeth, Jonathan. A.B. magna cum laude, Radcliffe Coll., 1949; LL.B. cum laude, Harvard U., 1954. Bar: Mass. 1957, U.S. Supreme Ct. 1960. Law clk. to Judge Bailey Aldrich, U.S. Dist. Ct. for Mass., 1954-55; Bigelow fellow and instr. U. Chgo. Law Sch., 1955-56; asso. Firm Palmer & Dodge, Boston, 1964-71, partner, 1971-79; assoc. justice Mass. Appeals Ct., Boston, 1979—; lectr. in copyright Harvard U. Law Sch., 1973-76. Trustee Radcliffe Coll., 1981—. Recipient 1st prize Nathan Burkan competition Harvard U. Law Sch., 1954, nat. winner, 1954. Mem. Am. Law Inst. (adv. on restatement, property), Am. Bar Assn. (chmn. com. on authors 1977-79), Am. Bar Found., Copyright Soc. U.S.A. (trustee 1973-76, editorial bd. bull. 1974—). Office: Appeals Ct Pemberton Sq Boston MA 02108

DREBIN, ALLAN RICHARD, business educator; b. Chgo., Mar. 17, 1936; s. Harry I. and Dorothy (Caplan) D.; m. Ellen Goldman, June 21, 1959; children: Donna Ann, Robert Andrew. B.B.A., U. Mich., 1957, M.B.A., 1958, Ph.D., 1962. C.P.A. Research fellow Fed. Res. Bank Chgo., 1959-60; asst. prof. UCLA, 1960-65; asso. prof. Cornell U., 1965-69; prof. accounting and info. systems Northwestern U., Evanston, Ill., 1969—, chmn. dept., 1975-79; prin. investigator, govtl. acctg. and fin. reporting research project Nat. Council Govtl. Acctg., 1979-82; vis. prof. Chulalongkorn U., Bangkok, Thailand, 1983. Author: Commercial Bank Earnings and Savings Accounts, 1963, Managerial Accounting, 1968, 3d edit., 1978, Financial Accounting, 1968, 3d edit., 1978, Advanced Accounting, 5th edit., 1982, Objectives of Accounting and Financial Reporting for Governmental Units, 1981. Mem. Am. Acctg. Assn., Am. Econ. Assn. Home: 2018 Orrington Ave Evanston IL 60201 Office: 2001 Sheridan Rd Evanston IL 60201

DREBUS, RICHARD WILLIAM, pharm. co. exec.; b. Oshkosh, Wis., Mar. 30, 1924; s. William and Frieda (Schmidt) D.; m. Hazel Redford, June 7, 1947; children—William R., John R., Kathryn L. B.S., U. Wis., 1947, M.S., 1949, Ph.D., 1952. Bus. trainee Marathon Paper Corp., Menasha, Wis., 1951-52; tng. mgr. Ansul Corp., Marinette, Wis., 1952-55, asst. to v.p., 1955-58, marketing mgr., 1958-60; dir. personnel devel. Mead Johnson & Co., Evansville, Ind., 1960-65, v.p. corporate planning, 1965-66, internat. pres., 1966-68; v.p. internat. div. Bristol-Myers Co. (merger Mead Johnson Internat. div. with Bristol-Myers Co. Internat. div.), N.Y.C., 1968-77, sr. v.p., 1977-78, v.p. parent co., 1978—. Served with inf. AUS, 1943-45. Decorated Combat Inf. Badge, Purple Heart, Bronze Star. Mem. Am. Psychol. Assn., N.Y. Acad. Scis., Phi Delta Kappa. Clubs: Fox River Hunting and Fishing, Silver Springs Country. Home: 16 Old Driftway Rd Wilton CT 06897 Office: 345 Park Ave New York NY 10022

DRECHSEL, EDWIN JARED, retired magazine editor; b. Bremen, Ger., Apr. 17, 1914; came to U.S., 1924, naturalized, 1935; s. William A. and Estelle Laura D.; m. Ilona Bolya, Aug. 12, 1972; children: John M., Barbara A. Grad., Dartmouth Coll., Amos Tuck Sch. Bus. Adminstrn., 1936. With Standard Oil Co., N.J., 1936-43; with U.S. News and World Report, 1943-79, regional editor, editorial ombudsman, San Francisco, 1976-79. Author shipping company histories and fleet lists, catalogs of ship mail postal markings. Former chmn. Reed Sch. Bd., Marin County, Calif.; former vestryman St. Stephen's Episcopal Ch., Belvedere, Calif.; former mayor, City of Belvedere. Club: San Francisco Press. Home: 170 Hillcrest Rd Berkeley CA 94705 Office: 601 California St San Francisco CA 94108

DRECKSEL, CALVIN OTIS, management consultant; b. Salt Lake City, Dec. 31, 1931; s. Carl Otto and Leona Vera (Chapman) D.; children—Debra, Linda, Paul. B.S., U. Utah, 1955. C.P.A., Utah. Pub. accountant Lincoln G. Kelly Co., Salt Lake City, 1955-59; dist. controller Modern Home Builders, Salt Lake City, 1959-61; sec.-treas. Edward L. Burton Co., Salt Lake City, 1961-63; exec. v.p., controller Skaggs Cos., Inc., Salt Lake City, 1963-82; v.p., controller Am. Stores Co., Salt Lake City, 1982-83; ptnr. Matson, Drecksel & Assocs. (restaurant mgmt. and mgmt. cons.), 1983—. Served with USAF, 1951-52. Club: Ft. Douglas-Hidden Valley Country. Home: 3620 E Oak Rim Way Salt Lake City UT 84109 Office: 310 Bearcat Dr Salt Lake City UT 84125

DREES, THOMAS CLAYTON, health care company executive; b. Detroit, Feb. 2, 1929; s. Clayton Henry and Mildred (Stevenson) D.; m. Elaine Hnath, Feb. 9, 1952; children: Danette, Clayton, Barry, Nancy. B.A. with honors, Coll. Holy Cross, 1951; M.B.A., Pacific Western U., 1979, Ph.D., 1980. With Spaulding Fibre Co., Inc., 1953-70, sales engr., N.Y.C., 1953-56, br. mgr., Toronto, Ont., Can., 1957-60, asst. to pres., Tonawanda, N.Y., 1960-63, sec., 1961-70, v.p. internat., 1963-66, exec. v.p., 1966-70; also dir., mem. exec. com.; mng. dir. Spauldings, Ltd., London, 1964-70, dir., 1963-70, chmn. bd. dirs., 1964-70; gen. mgr. Spaulding Fibre of Can., Ltd., Toronto, 1957-60, v.p., dir., 1957-70; pres., dir. La Fibre Vulcanisee Spaulding, Paris, 1964-70; v.p., dir. Mycalex Corp. Am., Clifton, N.J., 1967-70, Spaulding Norton, Inc., North Westchester, Conn., 1968-70; group v.p. Ipco Hosp. Supply Corp., 1970-72; pres., vice chmn. IVAC Corp., San Diego, 1972-73; v.p., gen. mgr. Abbott Labs., South Pasadena, Calif., 1973-78; v.p., dir. AMEC, Houston; pres., vice chmn. Alpha Therapeutic Corp., 1978—; dir. Green Cross Corp., Osak, Japan. Chmn. Sch. Bd.; mem. pres. council Holy Cross Coll.; bd. dirs. Hemophilia Found., Am. Blood Commn., Am. Blood Resources Assn., La Jolla Cancer Research Found.; mem. bus. adv. bd. U.S. Senate.; dir. president's adv. bd. Calif. State U.-Los Angeles; mem. exec. forum Calif. Inst. Tech.; trustee Thomas Aquinas Coll.; bd. dirs. Alliance Tech. Fund, Alliance Internat. Health Care Trust. Served from ensign to lt. (j.g.) USNR, 1951-53. Fellow Inst. Dirs.; mem. I.E.E.E., Nat. Sales Execs. Assn., Am. C. of C. Republican. Roman Catholic (bd. advisers). Clubs: Rotary, San Gabriel Country. Home: 784 Saint Katherine Dr Flintridge La Canada CA 91001 Office: 220 Pasadena Ave South Pasadena CA 91030

DREGER, RALPH MASON, psychologist, clergyman, educator; b. Chgo., Apr. 18, 1913; s. Emil H. and Clara P. (Mason) D.; m. Alice May Hill, Apr. 14, 1973; children by previous marriage: Philip Alan, Patricia Jean, David Herbert. A.B. cum laude, Wheaton Coll., 1935; M.Div. with distinction, Garrett-Evang. Theol. Sem., 1938; M.A., Northwestern U., 1939; Ph.D., U. So. Calif., 1950. Ordained to ministry United Methodist Ch., 1939; minister Meth. chs. in Rock River (Ill.) Conf., 1935-41, Calif.-Nev. Conf., 1941-46, So. Calif.-Ariz. Conf., 1946-48; tchr. psychology and lit. Adult Evening High Schs., Los Angeles, 1948; instr. psychology George Pepperdine U., Los Angeles, 1948-49; asst. prof. psychology Fla. State U., Tallahassee, 1949-56; dir. Child Guidance and Speech Correction Clinic, Jacksonville, Fla., 1956-60; prof. Jacksonville U., 1960-64, La. State U., 1964-83, prof. emeritus, 1983—; Psychol. examiner Lakeland Regional Personnel Com. Meth. Ch., 1954-64; psychol. cons. Fla. Annual Conf. Meth. Ch., 1956-64; mem. Fla. State Bd. Examiners Psychology, 1958-61; psychol. cons. Jackson Regional Personnel Com. Meth. Ch., 1964-75. Author: Fundamentals of Personality, 1962, Multivariate Personality Research, 1972; Co-editor: Comparative Studies of Blacks and Whites in U.S, 1973, Handbook of Modern Personality Theory, 1978; cons. editor: Jour. Abnormal Child Psychology, 1974—, Jour. Sci. Study of Religion, 1976-80, Multivariate Exptl. Clin. Research, 1978—, Jour. Psychology, 1979—; editor: The So. Psychologist, 1981—; mem. editorial bd.: Jour. Gen. Psychology, 1979—, Clinician's Research Digest, 1983—. Chmn. br. A.R.C., Clovis, Calif., 1943-46; mem. Citizens Adv. Com. on the Aged, 1960; chmn. Fla. Cooperating Council on Children and Youth, 1961-63; mem. La. adv. com. U.S. Civil Rights Commn., 1964-81; Bd. dirs. Fla. Council on Human Relations, 1956-64, pres., 1963; bd. dirs. La. Council on Human Relations, 1965—, pres., 1972-80; bd. dirs. So. Regional Council, 1964—, Wesley Found. and Uniting Campus Ministry La. State U., 1965-76; chmn. bd. Wesley Found. and Uniting Campus Ministry La. State U., 1969-70, 70-71. Fellow AAAS, Am. Psychol. Assn. (div. clin. psychology 1966—, div. psychologists interested in study religion 1980—), AAUP (sec. 1953-54); mem. Fla. Psychol. Assn. (chmn. standards and ethics com. 1954-55, 57-58, pres. 1959-60), La. Psychol. Assn. (exec. com. 1965-81, 83—), Southeastern Psychol. Assn. (pres. 1965-66), Southeastern Soc. for Multivariate Exptl. Psychology (chief exec. officer 1969-70), Soc. Research in Child Devel., Phi Beta Kappa, Sigma Xi, Sigma Pi Sigma. Home: 2106 Lee Dr Baton Rouge LA 70808

DREIER, DAVID TIMOTHY, congressman; b. Kansas City, Mo., July 5, 1952; s. H. Edward and Joyce D. B.A. cum, Claremont Men's Coll., 1973; M.A. in Am. Govt, Claremont Grad. Sch., 1975. Dir. corp. relations Claremont Men's Coll., 1975-79; dir. govt. affairs Indsl. Hydrocarbons, San Dimas, Calif., 1979-80; mem. 97th-98th Congresses from 35th Calif. Dist.; Mem. Calif. Republican Central Com. Mem. San Dimas C. of C., Congress for Protection Neighborhood Schs. Office: 410 Cannan House Office Bldg Washington DC 20515

DREIFKE, GERALD EDMOND, educator; b. St. Louis, June 21, 1918; s. Herman A. and Anna Margaret (Hollenbeck) D.; m. Lorraine Ann Feldhaus, June 9, 1951; children: Mark A., Matthew G., Laura Maria, Anne Marie. B.S., Washington U., 1948, M.S., 1948, D.Sc. (NSF fellow), 1961. Registered profl. engr., Mo. Layout man Curtiss-Wright Co., St. Louis, 1936-39, design engr., 1939-44; layout man Douglas Aircraft Co., 1939; instr. engring. St. Louis U., 1948-50, asst. prof., 1950-54, asso. prof. elec. engring., dir. grad. program elec. engring., 1954-61, prof. elec. engring., 1961-71; mgr. research and devel. Union Electric Co., 1971-77; cons., 1977—; vis. prof. physics U. Mo.-St. Louis, 1979—; cons. Emerson Electric Co., 1951-71, Monsanto Co., 1961-71; mem. tech. staff Bell Telephone Labs. N.J., summer 1963. Editor-in-chief: ISA Transactions, 1966—; Contbr. articles profl. jours. Mem. St. Louis County Bd. Elec. Examiners, Gov.'s Sci. Adv. Com. Mo. Served with USNR, 1944-45. Recipient certificate of merit WPB, 1942; research grants NSF, 1964, NASA, 1965, Monsanto Co., 1965-69; Nancy McNair-Ring Outstanding Faculty award St. Louis U. chpt. Gamma Pi Epsilon, 1965-66. Mem. Am. Soc. Engring. Edn. (past sec., com. chmn.), IEEE (past chmn. St. Louis sect.), Engrs. Club St. Louis (dir., com. chmn.), Mo. Soc. Profl. Engrs. (past pres. St. Louis chpt., Engr. of Yr. St. Louis chpt. 1977), St. Louis Elec. Bd. Trade, Sigma Xi, Tau Beta Pi, Eta Kappa Nu, Pi Mu Epsilon, Phi Eta Sigma. Home: 6 Westmoreland Pl St Louis MO 63108

DREILING, DAVID A., surgeon; b. N.Y.C., June 5, 1918; s. Louis and Rosalia (Lustic) D.; m. Muriel A. Oppenheimer, June 25, 1946; 1 son, David Arne. B.A., Cornell U., 1938; M.D., NYU, 1942. Diplomate: Am. Bd. Surgery. Prof. surgery Mt. Sinai Med. Ctr., N.Y.C., Alfred and Florence Gross prof. surgery; dir. Ctr. for Lab. Animal Sci., N.Y.C.; mem. staff Rockefeller Inst., Elmhurst Hosp.; mem. Bronx VA Hosp. Author: (with Janowitz and Perrier) Pancreatic Inflammatory Disease, 1964; editor: Am. Jour. Gastroenterology, Mt. Sinai Jour. Medicine. Recipient Jacobi medal, Copernicus medal. Mem. Am. Surg. Assn., ACS, Am. Gastroenterol. Assn., Am. Coll. Gastroenterology (disting. service award), N.Y. Surg. Soc. Democrat. Jewish. Office: The Mount Sinai Med Ctr 1 Gustave L Levy Pl New York NY 10029

DREIMANIS, ALEKSIS, geology educator; b. Valmiera, Latvia, Aug. 13, 1914; s. Peteris and Marta Eleonora (Leitis) D.; m. Anita Kana, Apr. 18, 1942; children: Mara Dreimanis Love, Aija Dreimanis Downing. Mag. rer. nat., Latvian U., 1938; D.Sc. (hon.), U. Waterloo, Ont., Can., 1969, U. Western Ont., 1980. Asst. to pvt. docent Latvian U., 1937-44; mil. geologist Latvian Legion, 1944-45; assoc. prof. geology Baltic U., Hamburg, W. Ger., 1946-48; mem. faculty U. Western Ont., London, Can., 1948—, prof. geology, 1964-80, prof. emeritus, 1980—; cons. in field. Asso. editor: Geosci. Can, 1976-78, Quaternary Sci. Revs, 1981—; contbr. articles to profl. jours. Fellow Royal Soc. Can.; Mem. Geol. Assn. Can., Geol. Soc. Am., Swedish Geol. Soc., German Quaternary Assn., Can. Quaternary Assn., Am. Quaternary Assn. (pres. 1981-83), Soc. Econ. Mineralogists and Paleontologists, Assn. Advancement Baltic Studies, Quaternary Research Assn., Latvian Nat. Fedn. Can. (chmn. council 1953-71), Latvian Cultural Found. (exec. com. 1973-77), London Latvian Soc. (pres. 1948—). Home: 287 Neville Dr London ON N6G 1C2 Canada Office: Geology Dept Univ Western Ont London ON N6A 5B7 Canada

DRELL, SIDNEY DAVID, physicist; b. Atlantic City, Sept. 13, 1926; s. Tulla and Rose (White) D.; m. Harriet Stainback, Mar. 22, 1952; children: Daniel White, Persis Sydney, Joanna Harriet. A.B., Princeton U., 1946; M.A., U. Ill., 1947, Ph.D., 1949, D.Sc. (hon.), 1981. Research asso. U. Ill., 1949-50; instr. physics Stanford, 1950-52, asso. prof., 1956-60, prof., 1960-63, Stanford Linear Accelerator Center, 1963—, Lewis M. Terman prof. and fellow, 1979—, dep. dir., exec. head theoretical physics, 1969—; research asso. Mass. Inst. Tech., 1952-53, asst. prof., 1953-56; vis. scientist Guggenheim fellow CERN Lab., Switzerland, 1961, U. Rome, 1972; vis. prof., Loeb lectr. Harvard, 1962, 70; vis. Schrodinger prof. theoretical physics U. Vienna, 1975; cons. Office Sci. and Tech., 1960-73, Office Sci. and Tech. Policy, 1977—, ACDA, 1969-81, Office Tech. Assessment U.S. Congress, 1975—, NSC, 1978-81; mem. high energy physics adv. panel Dept. Energy, 1973—, chmn., 1974-82, mem. energy research adv. bd., 1978-80; mem. Jason div. Inst. Def. Analyses, 1960-73; cons. div. SRI Internat., 1973—; Richtmyer lectr. to Am. Assn. Physics Tchrs., San Francisco, 1978; vis. fellow All Souls Coll., Oxford, 1979; Danz lectr. U. Wash., 1983. Author 3 books; contbr. articles to profl. jours. Trustee Inst. Advanced Study, Princeton, 1974—; bd. govs. Weizmann Inst. Sci., Rehovoth, Israel, 1970—; bd. dirs. Ann. Revs., Inc.; mem. Pres. Sci. Adv. Com., 1966-70. Recipient Ernest Orlando Lawrence Meml. award and medal for research in theoretical physics AEC, 1972; Alumni award for distinguished service in engring. U. Ill., 1973. Fellow Am. Phys. Soc. (Leo Szilard award for physics in the public interest 1980); mem. Nat. Acad. Scis., Am. Acad. Arts and Scis., Arms Control Assn. (dir. 1978—), Council on Fgn. Relations. Home: 570 Alvarado Row Stanford CA 94305 Office: SLAC PO Box 4349 Stanford CA 94305

DRELL, WILLIAM, chemical company executive; b. Chgo., Jan. 26, 1922; s. Hyman and Ida (Korey) D.; m. Ethel Hershenson, Feb. 7, 1943; children: Eric, Elizabeth, Eliot. B.A., UCLA, 1943, 1946, Ph.D., 1949; postdoctoral fellow, Calif. Inst. Tech., 1949-51. Chemist Shell Chem. Co., Los Angeles, 1944-46; instr. Los Angeles City Coll., 1946-47; research physiol. chemist UCLA Med. Sch., 1951-59, cons., 1959-62; with Calbiochem, La Jolla, Calif., 1959-81; pres. Calbiochem-Behring Corp., 1977-80, pres. Calbiochem. div., 1980-81. Author: (with Max S. Dunn) Experiments in Biochemistry, 1951; contbr. articles to profl. jours. Trustee Calif. Found. Biochem. Research, 1952—, Immaculate Heart Coll. Los Angeles, 1974-76, La Jolla Cancer Research Found., 1977—; mem. San Diego City Quality of Life Bd., 1978-81; mem. bd. overseers U. Calif., San Diego, 1979-81; dir. San Diego Econ. Devel. Corp., 1973-76, 81—. USPHS research fellow, 1947-49; established investigator Am. Heart Assn., 1954-59. Mem. Am. Chem. Soc. (chmn. San Diego br. 1977), Am. Soc. Biol. Chemistry, Biochem. Soc. London, Chem. Soc. London, Soc. Exptl. Biology and Medicine, Sigma Xi, Phi Lambda Upsilon. Patentee in chemistry and med. applications. Office: Valley Blvd Diego:

DRENDEL, FRANK MATTHEW, cable co. exec.; b. Paxton, Ill., Jan. 16, 1945; s. Nora and Odell (Drendel); m. Marilyn Beste, 1968; 1 son. B.S., No. Ill. U., 1970; postgrad., St. Louis U., 1973. Vice-pres., corp. mgr. Continental Transmission, St. Louis, 1969-72; v.p. ops. Cypress Communications, Los Angeles, 1972-73; pres., gen. mgr. Comm/Scope, Catawba, N.C., 1972-81, chmn., 1972—; pres., chief exec. officer Valtec Corp., West Boylston, Mass., 1977—, chmn., 1980—; exec. v.p. M/A-COM, Inc., Burlington, Mass., 1980—. Served with U.S. Army, 1968-74. Mem. Calif. Cable TV Assn. (past dir., asso. dir.), Nat. Cable TV Assn. (past dir.), C. of C. Presbyterian. Club: Lake Hickory Country. Home: Rural Route 10 Box FC-83 Hickory NC 28601 Office: Rural Route 1 Box 199A Catawba NC 28609

DRENNAN, G(EORGE) ELDON, utility company executive; b. Walla Walla, Wash., Mar. 22, 1921; s. George I. and Ella B. (Myrick) D.; m. Jane Nilsson, June 16, 1943 (dec. June 1976); children: Michael E., Barbara A. Student, Whitman Coll., 1938-39; B.S., Wash. State U., 1943; grad., Advanced Mgmt. Program, Harvard U., 1970. With Pacific Power & Light Co., Portland, Oreg., 1946—, v.p., 1971-74, sr. v.p., 1974-76, exec. v.p., 1976-79, pres., 1979-82, vice chmn. bd., 1982—. Served to lt. USNR, 1943-46. Clubs: Arlington, Univ., Portland Golf, Elks. Home: 1475 Cherry Crest Dr Lake Oswego OR 97034 Office: Pacific Power & Light Co 920 SW 6th Ave Portland OR 97204

DRENNAN, MERRILL WILLIAM, clergyman; b. Washington, Oct. 17, 1915; s. Milton William and Balbena (Altman) D.; m. Frances Emily Dunn, Apr. 26, 1937; children—Marilyn (Mrs. Louis E. Brus), Kathleen. B.C.S., Southeastern U., 1939; A.B., U. Md., 1950; M.Div., Westminster (now Wesley) Theol. Sem., 1953; D.D., Western Md. Coll., 1970. With banking dept. Am. Security and Trust Co., Washington, 1933-37; officer mgr. Brewood Engravers and Printers, Washington, 1937-42; spl. agt. FBI, 1942-48; ordained to ministry Methodist Ch., 1953; minister in, Ashton, Md., 1950-54, Rockville, Md., 1954-65; supt. Balt. Southeast Dist., 1965-67; sr. minister Met. Meml. United Meth. Ch., Washington, 1967-74; supt. Washington W. Dist., Balt. Conf., 1974-79, asso. council dir., 1979—; exec. com. Columbia Facilities Corp. Del. Northeastern Jurisdictional Conf. Meth. Ch., 1964, 68, 72, 76, 80, Gen. Conf. United Meth. Ch., Dallas, 1968, Atlanta, 1972, Portland, Oreg., 1976, Indpls., 1980. Home: 5681 Harpers Farm Rd Columbia MD 21044

DRENNEN, WILLIAM MILLER, U.S. judge; b. Jenkins, Ky., Mar. 1, 1914; s. Everett and Louise Bright (Miller) D.; m. Margaret Morton, Nov. 30, 1940; children—Margaret Penelope, William Miller, David Holmes, Dale Louise. B.S., Ohio State U., 1936, J.D., 1938. Bar: W.Va. bar 1939. Asst. to clk. Supreme Ct. of Ohio, 1937-38; law clk. to judge U.S. Dist. Ct., So. Dist. W.Va., 1938-40; with firm Jackson, Kelly, Holt & O'Farrell (and predecessor firms), 1940-58, partner, 1947-58; judge U.S. Tax Ct., Washington, 1958-80, 80—, chief judge, 1967-73. Former bd. dirs. Charleston Family Service, Meml. Hosp., Boy Scouts Am.; Mem. Charleston City Council, 1955-58. Served as lt. comdr. USN, 1942-45. Mem. Am., W.Va., Charleston bar assns., W.Va. Tax Inst. (past pres.). Republican. Episcopalian. Clubs: Chevy Chase (Md.); Metropolitan. Office: Tax Ct 400 2d St NW Washington DC 20217

DRENZ, CHARLES FRANCIS, army officer; b. Erie, Pa., Aug. 12, 1930; s. Frank and Rose Marie (Cummings) DiRienzo; m. Lillian P. Martin, Jan. 14, 1961; children—Susan Frances, Michael Staurt, Sandra Jeanne. B.S., Gannon U., 1953; M.S., Fla. Inst. Tech., 1973; postgrad., U. Pitts., 1980; grad., Command and Gen. Staff Coll., Air War Coll. Commd. officer U.S. Army, advanced through grades to brig. gen.; commdr. Corpus Christi (Tex.) Army Depot, 1977-79; project mgr. UH-60 Black Hawk, U.S. Army Devel. and Readiness Command, St. Louis, 1979-80; comdr. Def. Contract Adminstrn. Services, N.Y.C., 1980-81; dep. dir. Hdqrs. Def. Logistics Agy., Cameron Sta., Alexandria, Va., 1981-83; program mgr. Advanced Attack Helicopter, St. Louis, 1983—. Decorated Legion of Merit with 2 clusters, Bronze Star, Air medal with 8 clusters. Mem. Assn. U.S. Army, Army Aviation Assn. Am., Am. Def. Preparedness Assn., Am. Helicopter Assn., Nat Contract Mgmt. Assn., Ret. Officers Assn. Roman Catholic. Office: 4300 Goodfellow Blvd Saint Louis MO 63120

DRESCH, STEPHEN PAUL, economist; b. East St. Louis, Ill., Dec. 12, 1943; s. Lester Wilson Reuben and Leonore Marie (Steege) D.; m. Linda Carol Ness, May 18, 1963; children: Soren K., Stephanie Elizabeth, Phaedra Augusta, Karl Friedrick Johannes. A.B. Philosophy, Miami U., Oxford, Ohio, 1963; M.Phil. Econ., NSF fellow, Yale U., 1966, Ph.D., 1970. Mem. faculty dept. econs. Miami U., Oxford, Ohio, 1963-64; mem. Yale U., New Haven, Conn., 1966-67, South Conn. State Coll., New Haven, 1968-69, Rutgers U., New Brunswick, N.J., 1970; researcher Nat. Bur. Econ. Research, N.Y.C. and New Haven, 1969-77; cons. in residence Ford Found., N.Y.C., 1970-72; dir. reserch in econs. of higher edn. Yale U., 1972-75, chmn. Inst. for Demographic and Econ. Studies, 1975—; cons. in field. Author: Substituting a Value Added Tax for the Corporate Income Tax, 1977; contbr. articles to profl. jours. Mem. Instn. for Social and Policy Studies (Yale U. research affiliate), Am. Econ. Assn., AAAS, Fedn. of Am. Scientists. Libertarian. Mem. United Ch. Christ. Home: 100 McKinley Ave New Haven CT 06515 Office: Inst for Demographic and Econ Studies 210 Prospect St New Haven CT 06511

DRESCHER, JOHN MUMMAU, bishop, author; b. Manheim, Pa., Sept. 15, 1928; s. John L. and Anna (Mummau) D.; m. Betty Keener, Aug. 30, 1952; children: John Ronald, Sandra Kay, Rose Marie, Joseph Dean, David Carl. Student, Elizabethtown Coll., 1947-49; A.B., Eastern Mennonite Coll., 1951, Th.B., 1953; B.D., Goshen Bibl. Sem., 1954. Ordained to ministry Mennonite Ch., 1954; pastor (Crown Hill Mennonite Ch.), Rittman, Ohio, 1954-62, 1973-78, bishop, 1959-64; asst. moderator Mennonite Ch., 1967-69, moderator, 1969-71, bishop, 1959-64; writer, lectr., 1979—; mem. faculty Eastern Mennonite Sem., Harrisonburg, Va., 1979—; pres. Ohio Memmonite Mission Bd., 1956-62. Author: Meditations for the Newly Married, 1969, Blessings By Your Bedside, 1969, Heartbeats, 1970, Now is the Time to Love, 1970, Follow Me, 1971, In Grief's Lone Hour, 1971, May Your Marriage be a Happy One, 1971, Spirit Fruit, 1974, Talking It Over, 1975, I Lift My Eyes, 1976, Seven Things Children Need, 1976, The Way of the Cross and Resurrection, 1978, If I Were Starting My Family Again, 1979, For Better-For Worse, 1979, When Opposites Attract, 1980, What Should Parents Expect, 1980, Testimony of Triumph, 1980, When You Think You Are in Love, 1981, You Can Plan a Good Marriage, 1982, Why I am a Conscientious Objector, 1982; editor: Gospel Hearld, 1962-73; contbr. articles to mags. and jours.

DRESCHER, SEYMOUR, history educator, writer; b. N.Y.C., Feb. 20, 1934; s. Sidney and Eva Rita (Levine) D.; m. Ruth Lieberman, June 19, 1955; children: Michael, Jonathan, Karen. B.A., CCNY, 1955; M.S., U. Wis., 1956, Ph.D., 1960. Instr. history Harvard U.,

1960-62; asst. prof. U. Pitts., 1962-65, assoc. prof., 1965-69, prof., 1969—, chmn., 1980-83. Author: Toqueville and England, 1964, Dilemmas of Democracy, 1968, Econocide, 1977; creator film: Confrontation, Paris, 1968, 70. Fulbright scholar, 1957-58; Nat. Endowment for Humanities fellow, 1973-74; Guggenheim Found. fellow, 1977-78; Woodrow Wilson fellow, 1983—. Mem. Am. Hist. Soc., Tocqueville Soc., Soc. for French Hist. Studies (v.p. 1978-79). Home: 5550 Pocusset St Pittsburgh PA 15217 Office: Dept History U Pitts Pittsburgh PA 15260

DRESCHHOFF, GISELA AUGUSTE MARIE, physicist, educator; b. Moenchengladbach, Germany, Sept. 13, 1938; came to U.S., 1967, naturalized, 1976; d. Gustav Julius and Hildegard Friederieke (Krug) D. Ph.D., Tech. U. Braunschweig (Ger.), 1972. Staff scientist Fed. Inst. Physics and Tech. Ger., 1965-67; research assoc. Kans. Geol. Survey, Lawrence, 1971-72; vis. asst. prof. physics U. Kans., 1972-74; dep. dir. radiation physics lab. Space Tech. Ctr., 1972-78, assoc. dir., 1979—, adj. asst. prof. physics, 1974; assoc. program mgr. NSF, Washington, 1978-79. Patentee identification markings for gemstones. Named to Women's Hall of Fame, U. Kans., 1978; recipient Antarctic Service medal U.S.A., 1979. Mem. Am. Phys. Soc., Am. Geophys. Union, AAAS, Am. Polar Soc., Antarctican Soc., U.S. Naval Inst., Sigma Xi. Home: 2908 W 19th Lawrence KS 66044 Office: Space Tech Ctr 2291 Irving Hill Dr Lawrence KS 66045

DRESHER, JAMES T., manufacturing company executive; b. 1919. Self-employed fin. cons., to 1971; chmn. exec. com., dir. All Am. Industries, 1971-73; sr. v.p. fin., chief fin. officer Reed Tool Co., 1973-75; v.p., chief fin. officer Baker Internat. Corp., Orange, Calif., from 1975, now exec. v.p., chief fin. officer, dir. Office: Baker Internat Corp 500 City Pkwy West Box 5500 Orange CA 92667 *

DRESHER, WILLIAM HENRY, university dean; b. Phila., Mar. 15, 1930; s. Austin Conrad and Mildred Elizabeth (Leedom) D.; m. Ella Jane Batiste, Dec. 28, 1957; children—Elisabeth, Margaret. B.S. in Chem. Engring, Drexel Inst. Tech., 1953; Ph.D. in Metall. Engring, U. Utah, 1956. Research metallurgist Union Carbide Corp., Tuxedo and Tarrytown, N.Y., 1956-58, group leader, 1958-63, asst. dir. research, 1963-65, project mgr., 1965-71; prof. metall. engring., dean Coll. Mines, U. Ariz., Tucson, 1971-81; pres. Internat. Copper Research Assn., N.Y.C., 1981—; dir. Ariz. Bur. Geol. and Mine Tech. Mem. Am. Inst. Mining, Metall. and Petroleum Engrs., Am. Chem. Soc., Am. Soc. Engring. Edn., Mining and Metall. Soc. Am. (pres. 1983—), Sigma Xi, Sigma Pi Sigma. Home: 13 Singing Woods Rd Norwalk CT 06850

DRESSEL, EDWIN JACOB, marine contracting executive, civil engineer; b. New Orleans, Nov. 26, 1924; s. Noel Turner and Mary Claire (Brechtel) D.; m. Edith Martha Gaude, Jan. 5, 1952; 1 dau., Mary Edith. B.S.C.E., Southwestern La. Inst., 1950. Registered profl. engr., La. Surveyor La. Hwy. Dept., Lake Charles, 1950; engr. The Calif. Co., New Orleans, 1951-55; mgr. Hunt Tool Co., Harvey, La., 1955-59; v.p. Service Contracting Inc., Harvey, 1959-62; cons., New Orleans, 1962; v.p. McDermott Internat., Inc., New Orleans, 1962—. Patentee in field. Sgt. U.S. Army, 1942-45, 50-51; ETO. Mem. Am. Bur. Shipping (bd. mgrs.), Soc. Naval Architects and Marine Engrs. Democrat. Roman Catholic. Club: Petroleum (New Orleans). Office: McDermott Internat Inc 1010 Common St New Orleans LA 70112

DRESSEL, PAUL LEROY, educator; b. Youngstown, Ohio, Nov. 29, 1910; s. David Calvin and Aura Olive (Jacobs) D.; m. Wilma Frances Sackett, Sept. 16, 1933; children—Carol Ann, Linda Kathleen, Jeana Lynn. A.B., Wittenberg Coll., 1931, LL.D. (hon.), 1966; A.M., Mich. State Coll., 1934; Ph.D., U. Mich., 1939. From instr. to dir. counseling and chmn. bd. examiners Mich. State Coll., 1934-54; dir. coop. study evaluation gen. edn. Am. Council Edn., 1949-53; prof. univ. research Mich. State U., 1954—, dir., 1954-59, dir. instl. research, asst. provost, 1959-76, prof. univ. research, 1976-81; ret., 1981; Chmn. evaluation com. Nat. Sci. Tchrs. Assn., 1956-58; cons. Bd. Higher Edn., Mo. Synod, Lutheran Ch., 1959-75; mem. exec. bd. commn. on instns. higher edn. N. Central Assn., 1966-70, mem. commn. on research and service, 1970-76; cons. commn. scholars Ill. Bd. Higher Edn., 1966—; now chmn. commn.; cons. Okla. Consortium on Research Devel., 1968-70; chmn. com. gen. edn. Am. Assn. Higher Edn., 1953-54, v.p., dir., 1969-70, pres., 1970-71; chmn. com. on nontraditional study Fedn. Regional Accrediting Assns., 1972; cons. to colls. and univs. on problems of research and curriculum devel. Author: Comprehensive Examinations in a Program of General Education, 1949, Evaluation in the Basic College at Michigan State University, 1958, Evaluation in Higher Education, 1961, The Undergraduate Curriculum in Higher Education, 1963, College and University Curriculum, 1968, The Confidence Crisis, 1970, The World of Higher Education, 1971, Institutional Research in the University: A Handbook, 1971, Blueprint for Change: Doctoral Programs for College Teachers, 1972, Return to Responsibility, i972, Independent Study, 1973, Handbook of Academic Evaluation, 1976; Editor: The New Colleges: Toward An Appraisal, 1971, The Anatomy of Public Colleges, 1980, Improving Degree Programs, 1980, Administrative Leadership, 1981, On Teaching and Learning in College, 1982; editorial bd.: Jour. Higher Edn, 1969-72, Internat. Ency. Higher Edn, 1972—; publs. bd.: Assn. Instnl. Research, 1972—; editorial cons. bd.: Research in Higher Edn, 1972—; cons. editor: Jour. Exptl. Edn, 1972—. Home: 235 Maplewood Dr East Lansing MI 48823

DRESSELHAUS, MILDRED SPIEWAK, engineering educator; b. Bklyn., Nov. 11, 1930; d. Meyer and Ethel (Teichtheil) Spiewak; m. Gene F. Dresselhaus, May 25, 1958; children: Marianne, Carl Eric, Paul David, Eliot Michael. A.B., Hunter Coll., 1951, D.Sc. (hon.), 1982; Fulbright fellow, Cambridge (Eng.) U., 1951-52; A.M., Radcliffe Coll., 1953; Ph.D. in Physics, U. Chgo., 1958; D.Engring. (hon.), Worcester Poly. Inst., 1976, D.Sc., Smith Coll., 1980. NSF postdoctoral fellow Cornell U., 1958-60; mem. staff Lincoln Lab., MIT, 1960-67, prof. elec. engring., 1968—, asso. dept. head elec. engring., 1972-74; Abby Rockefeller Mauzé vis. prof. MIT, 1967-68, Abby Rockefeller Mauzé prof., 1973—, dir., 1977-83; vis. prof. dept. physics U. Campinas (Brazil), summer 1971, Technion, Israel Inst. Tech., Haifa, Israel, summer 1972, Nihon and Aoyama Gakuin Univs., Tokyo, summer 1973, IVIC, Caracas, Venezuela, summer 1977; mem. solid state scis. panel and com. NRC, 1973—; mem. exec. com. assembly of math. and phys. scis. Nat. Acad. Scis., 1975-78; chmn. steering com. of evaluation panels Nat. Bur. Standards, 1978-83. Contbr. articles to profl. jours. Named to Hunter Coll. Hall of Fame, 1972; recipient Alumnae medal Radcliffe Coll., 1973. Fellow Am. Phys. Soc. (chmn. nominating com. 1975, chmn. Buckley Prize com. 1977, v.p. 1982, pres.-elect 1983, pres. 1984), Am. Acad. Arts and Scis., IEEE; mem. Nat. Acad. Engring., Soc. Women Engrs. (Achievement award 1977); corr. mem. Brazilian Acad. Sci. Home: 147 Jason St Arlington MA 02174 Office: Mass Inst Tech Cambridge MA 02139

DRESSER, JESSE DALE, investor; b. San Diego, May 5, 1906; s. Charlwood Fessenden and Ora (Evans) D.; m. Mary A. Goldsworthy, June 9, 1934; children—Dennis T., Brian D., Linda A. Ed. pub. schs. Trainee Union Title Ins. Co., San Diego, 1926; sr. title examiner, chief title officer, v.p. So. Title & Trust Co., San Diego, 1927-51; v.p., chief title officer Security Title Ins. Co., San Diego, 1951-54; asst. to pres. San Diego Fed. Savs. & Loan Assn., 1954-55, v.p., sec., 1955-56, exec. v.p., dir., 1956-70; v.p., dir. Calif. Gen. Mortgage Service, Inc., 1967-70, San Diego Federated Ins. Agy., Inc., 1967-70; real estate investments, La Mesa, Calif., 1970—. Club: Kona Kai. Home: 3833 Acacia St Bonita CA 92002 Mailing Address: PO Box 418 Bonita CA 92002

DRESSER, PAUL ALTON, JR., paper and forest products executive; b. Corsicana, Tex., Apr. 20, 1942; s. Paul Alton and M. Elizabeth (Warren) D.; m. Judith J. Stewart, Mar. 23, 1968; 1 dau., Amanda Elizabeth. B.A. in History and Govt., Tex A&M U., 1964; M.B.A., Harvard U., 1970. Various mgmt. positions Badische Corp., Williamsburg, Va., 1970-75, asst. treas., 1976-78, treas., 1979-81; v.p. fin., chief fin. officer The Chesapeake Corp. of Va., West Point, 1981—; dir. Homecraft Corp., South Hill, Va. Bd. dirs. Williamsburg Community Hosp., 1979—, Coll. of William and Mary Sch. Bus Adminstrn. Sponsors, 1983; mem., past chmn. James City County Indsl. Devel. Authority, 1979—. Served to capt. U.S. Army, 1964-68. Named Disting. Mil. Grad. Tex. A&M U., 1964, Army aide to Pres. White House, 1967-68. Mem. Am. Paper Inst. (fin. com. 1982—). Club: Focus (Richmond). Home: 306 Buford Rd Williamsburg VA 23185 Office: Chesapeake Corp Va Hwy 30 West Point VA 23181

DRESSLER, DAVID CHARLES, manufacturing company executive; b. Cleve., June 21, 1928; s. Walter Carl and Beatrice (Albin) D.; m. Dorothea Walker, Dec. 22, 1950; children: David Charles, Bradley, Christopher. B.A., Yale U., 1950; grad., Advanced Mgmt. Program, Harvard Bus. Sch., 1973. With Armstrong Cork Co., 1950-51; with Martin Marietta Corp., 1953—, pres. Master Builders div., 1977-80, pres. Martin Marietta Chems. Co., 1979-81, corp. v.p., 1979-83, sr. corp. v.p., 1983—; pres. Master Builders Co. Ltd., Toronto, 1977-81, Martin Marietta Aluminum, 1982—. Served to capt. USMCR, 1951-53. Mem. Phi Beta Kappa. Episcopalian. Clubs: The Country, Harvard Bus. Sch. (Washington) (pres. 1983); Congressional. Office: 6801 Rockledge Dr Bethesda MD 20034

DRESSLER, ROBERT, building and agricultural products company executive; b. N.Y.C., May 5, 1925; s. Sam and Bertha (Dressler). B.S., Columbia U., 1946, M.S., 1948. Pres., chmn. bd., chief exec. officer, dir. Crown Industries, Inc., Tampa, Fla.; dir. RJ Fin., St. Petersburg, Fla., Infodata Systems, Pittsford, N.Y., S.E. Bank Tampa. Treas. Tampa Bay Area Research and Devel. Authority; chmn.-elect bd. govs. Fla. Orch.; mem. Pres.'s Council, U. South Fla., Tampa Com. on Fgn. Relations. Mem. IEEE, N.Y. Acad. Scis., Com. of 100. Office: Crown Industries Inc 3825 Henderson Blvd Tampa FL 33629

DRESSLER, ROBERT EUGENE, cons.; b. Evanston, Ill., Jan. 31, 1922; s. Eugene Francis and Hazel Margaret (Smith) D.; m. Marion E. Benken, Dec. 28, 1949 (div.); children—Heidi, Bruce, Wendy, Brian, Suzanne; m. Patricia P. Peden, May 28, 1976. B.A., Northwestern U., 1947, Mus.M., 1948. Faculty Shawnee Mission (Kans.) High Sch., 1948-49; free lance composer/arranger/condr., N.Y.C., 1949-50; faculty Jamestown (N.D.) Coll., 1950-53; faculty mem., dir. Glee Club U. Chgo., 1953-54; program mgr., producer/dir. WMAQ-TV (NBC), Chgo., 1954-61; dir. advt. and pub. relations Field Enterprises Ednl. Corp., Chgo., 1961-67; dir. Ampex Video Inst., Elk Grove, Ill., 1967-70; co-owner Dressler & Robinson, Chgo., 1970-72; gen. mgr. KOMU-TV; asso. prof. U. Mo. Sch. Journalism, 1972-74; pres. So. Ednl. Communications Assn., Columbia, S.C., 1974-76; cons. communications and edn., 1976—; Vis. prof. Northwestern U., 1955-56, Columbia Coll., Chgo., 1956. Bd. govs. Chgo. chpt. Acad. Television Arts and Scis., 1955-63. Served to lt. (j.g.) USNR, 1943-46. Mem. Phi Kappa Psi, Phi Mu Alpha Sinfonia. Presbyn. (dir. music 1966-72, 74—). Home: 52 Downing St Columbia SC 29209

DRESSNER, HOWARD ROY, found. exec., lawyer; b. N.Y.C., Feb. 14, 1919; s. Sol and Anna (Gross) D.; m. Sonia Segoda, Apr. 6, 1942; 1 son, Robert. B.S., N.Y. U., 1940; LL.B., Columbia U., 1948. With N.Y. U., 1948-64; successively instr. pub. speaking, asst. prof. pub. speaking, asst. v.p. devel.; dir. Albert Gallatin Assos., 1956-65; asst. to v.p. domestic programs Ford Found., 1964-67, sec. found., 1967-71, sec., gen. counsel found., 1971-76, v.p., gen. counsel, sec. found., 1976—. Co-author: Business Writing. Bd. dirs. Council on Founds. Candidate for N.Y. State Assembly, 1966. Served to maj. AUS, World War II. Decorated Bronze Star medal. Mem. Am. Bar Assn. (exempt orgns. com.), Assn. Bar City N.Y. (spl. com. on philanthropic orgns.). Home: 6 Peter Cooper Rd New York City NY 10010

DREW, CLIFFORD JAMES, educator; b. Eugene, Oreg., Mar. 9, 1943; s. Albert C. and Violet M. (Caskey) D. B.S. magna cum laude, Eastern Oreg. Coll., 1965; M.Ed., U.Ill., 1966; Ph.D. with honors, U. Oreg., 1968. Asst. prof. edn. Kent (Ohio) State U., 1968-69; asst. prof. dir. research and spl. edn. U. Tex., Austin, 1969-71; assoc. prof. spl. edn. U. Utah, Salt Lake City, 1971-76, prof., 1977—; asst. dean Grad. Sch. Edn., 1974-77, assoc. dean, 1977-79, prof. spl. edn. and ednl. psychology, 1979—; cons. HEW, 1969—; Bd. dirs. Far West Lab. Ednl. Research and Devel., San Francisco, 1974-80; mem. exec. bd. Salt Lake County Assn. Retarded Children, 1971-72; mem. adv. com. Mental Retardation Counseling Service, Tex. Dept. Mental Health Mental Retardation, 1969-70. Author: (with P. Chinn and D. Logan) Mental Retardation: A Life Cycle Approach, 2d edit, 1979, Introduction to Designing Research and Evaluation, 2d edit, 1980, (with M. Hardman and H. Bluhm) Mental Retardation: Social and Educational Perspectives, 1977, (with D. Gelfand and W. Jenson) Understanding Children's Behavior Disorders, 1982; numerous articles in field. NDEA fellow, 1965-66; U.S. Office Edn. fellow, 1966-68. Fellow Am. Assn. Mental Deficiency; mem. Am. Psychol. Assn., Am. Ednl. Research Assn., Council Exceptional Children. Office: Grad Sch Edn MBH 221 Univ of Utah Salt Lake City UT 84112

DREW, ELIZABETH HEINEMAN, editor; b. Evanston, Ill., Aug. 26, 1940; d. Ben Harlow and Marion Elizabeth (Heineman) D. B.A. cum laude, U. Wis., 1961. Sec. Doubleday & Co., Inc., N.Y.C., 1961-63, exec. sec., 1963-66, adminstrv. asst. to editor-in-chief, 1967-69, editorial asst. to editor-in-chief, 1969-71, asso. editor, 1971-73, editor, 1973-75, sr. editor, 1975-79, exec. editor, 1979—; mem. faculty Sch. Continuing Edn., N.Y. U.; Bd. dirs. Inst. Women's Wrongs; pres. Editors Lunch Group, 1976-77. Mem. AAP Internat. Freedom to Publish Com., Women's Media Group (treas. 1983-84), Internat. Platform Assn., Nat. Press Club, Internat. P.E.N., Kappa Alpha Theta. Democrat. Episcopalian. Office: 245 Park Ave New York NY 10017

DREW, ERNEST HAROLD, chemical company executive; b. Springfield, Mass., Apr. 15, 1937; s. Ernest L. and Marjorie E. (Canney) D.; 1 dau. by previous marriage: Karen; m. Mary T. Mayorga, Dec. 6, 1969; children: Linda, Leticia. B.S., Univ. Georgia, 1958, Ph.D., 1962; M.S., Univ. Ill., 1959. Sales mgr. resins Celanese Coatings Co., Louisville, 1971-74; v.p., gen. mgr. resins Celanese Specialty Co., Louisville, 1974-75; v.p. sales Celanese Chem. Co., N.Y.C.-Dallas, 1975-78, v.p. planning, Dallas, 1979-81; dir. strategic planning Celanese Corp., N.Y.C., 1981-82; pres., chief exec. officer Celanese Can. Inc., Montreal, Que., 1982—; dir. Bank Montreal Mortgage Corp., 1983—; mem. Can. adv. bd. Allendale Ins. Co., Montreal, 1982—. Served to capt. USAF, 1962-65. Woodrow Wilson fellow, 1958. Mem. Can. Textile Inst. (bd. dirs. 1982—), Can. Chem. Producer's Assn. (com. chmn. 1983—), Soc. Chem. Industry (bd. dirs. Can. sect. 1983), Am. Chem. Soc., Chem. Inst. Can., Phi Beta Kappa. Club: Mt.-Royal (Montreal). Home: 1250 Pine Ave W Apt 1140 Montreal PQ Canada H3G 2P5 Office: Celanese Can Inc 800 Dorchester Blvd W Montreal PQ Canada H3C 3K8

DREW, FRASER BRAGG ROBERT, English language educator; b. Randolph, Vt., June 23, 1913; s. George Albie and Hazel (Fraser) D. A.B., U. Vt., 1933; M.A., Duke U., 1935; Ph.D., U. Buffalo, 1952. Instr. Latin, Green Mt. Coll., Poultney, Vt., 1936-39; grad. asst. English, Syracuse U., 1939-41; instr. English, SUNY-Buffalo, 1945-47, asst. prof., 1947-52, prof., 1952-73, Disting. Teaching prof., 1973-83. Author: John Masefield's England, 1973; contbr. articles to profl. jours. Chmn. St. Patrick Scholarship Fund, Buffalo, 1969-79. Grantee SUNY Research Found., 1960-67; St. Patrick's scholar, 1967; recipient Disting. Alumnus award U. Vt., 1968, Irishman of Yr. award United Irish Socs. Western N.Y., 1970. Mem. Irish Am. Cultural Inst., Am. Com. Irish Studies, Acad. Am. Poets, Housman Soc., Ira Allen Soc., Millay Soc., Friends of Bailey Library, Phi Beta Kappa. Home: Tralee House 35 Danbury Ln Kenmore NY 14217

DREW, HOMER LEE, banker; b. Mayfield, Ky., Nov. 4, 1924; s. Hubert and Rhymon Ella (Riley) D.; m. Emma Jean Lutes, Sept. 10, 1949. B.A., U. Ky., 1951. Auditor Ky. Dept. Revenue, Frankfort, 1951-56; trust officer Security Trust Co., Lexington, Ky., 1956-69, v.p., trust officer and dir., 1959-61, First Security Bank, Lexington, 1961-73, exec. v.p., trust officer and dir., 1973—; dir. Clairborne Farms Inc., Paris, Ky. Curator and treas. Transylvania U., Lexington, 1965—; bd. dirs., treas. Henry Clay Found., Lexington, 1968—; bd. govs., treas. Frontier Nursing Service, Hyden, Ky., 1966—; trustee Good Samaritan Hosp., Lexington, 1968—. Served with USN, 1943-46; ETO. Democrat. Clubs: Rotary (Lexington); Lexington. Lodge: Mason (32 degree). Office: First Security Nat Bank and Trust One First Security Pl Lexington KY 40507

DREW, JAMES MULCRO, composer; b. St. Paul, Feb. 9, 1929; s. James Joseph and Gladys Jeanette (Drew) Mulcro; m. Gloria Kelly, Apr. 26, 1960; children: Drummond, Kelly Anne. Student, N.Y. Sch. Music, 1954-56; pupil of, Wallingford Riegger, 1956-59, Edgard Varese, 1956; M.A., Tulane U., 1964. Instr. composition and theory Northwestern U., 1965-67; vis. prof. Washington U., St. Louis, summer 1967; asst. prof. composition Yale, 1967-73; composer La. State U., Baton Rouge, 1973-75, Tangelwood, Lenox, Mass., 1973; music dir. Am. Music Theater, 1975—; sr. prof. Calif. State U., Fullerton, 1976-77; prof. U. Calif. at Los Angeles, 1977—. Composer: The Lute in the Attic, 1963, October Lights, 1969, Primero Libro de Referencia Laberinto, 1970, Metal Concert, 1971, Symphony No. 2, 1971, Chamber Symphony, 1972, Lux Incognitus, 1973, West Indian Lights, 1973, St Mark Concerto, 1973, Epitaphium pour Stravinsky, 1974, Cruxifixus Domini Christi, 1975, Songs of Death and Blue-light Dancing, 1975, Dance Steps and Fadeout Settings, 1975, Olde Lyme Sinfonia for Wind Orchestra, 1975, In Memorium: Mark Rothko, 1976, Orangethorpe Aria, 1976, Symphony No. 3, 1976; a stage work Five O'Clock Ladies, 1977-80; String Quartet No. 2, 1978, Pale Rider, 1978, All Saints' Chorales, 1978, Trio for the Firery Messengers, 1979, Cello Sonata, 1979, St. Dennis Variations, 1979, Sinfonia for Strings, 1979, Sonata for Violin and Piano, 1980, Purgatorium, 1980, Himself, The Devil, 1981, Open Closed Forms, 1982, An American Elegy, 1982, Becket: The Final Moments, 1983; works recorded on, TR Recs. Served with USNR, 1945-46. Recipient Panamericana prize Union Panamerica, 1974; electronic music grantee Northwestern U., 1965; Morse fellow, 1967-69; Calhoun fellow Yale, 1968-74; Guggenheim fellow, 1972-73; commd. by Fromm Music Found., 1973, Berkshire (Mass.) Music Center, 1973; N.Y. State Arts Council grantee, 1975; N.C. State Arts Council grantee, 1979-80; Durham Arts Council grantee, 1981. Mem. Am. Assn. Composers and Condrs., ASCAP (awards 1974-83). Address: care Theodore Presser Co Presser Pl Bryn Mawr PA 19010

DREW, KATHERINE FISCHER, history educator; b. Houston, Sept. 24, 1923; d. Herbert Herman and Martha (Holloway) Fischer; m. Ronald Farintön Drew, July 27, 1951. B.A., Rice Inst., 1944, M.A., 1945; Ph.D., Cornell U., 1950. Instr. history Rice U., 1946-48; asst. history Cornell U., 1948-50; mem. faculty Rice U., 1950—, prof. history, 1964—, Harris Masterson, Jr. prof. history, 1983—, chmn. dept. history, 1970-80, editor, 1967-81, acting dean humanities and social scis., 1973. Author: The Burgundian Code, 1949, Studies in Lombard Institutions, 1956, The Lombard Laws, 1973; Editor: Perspectives in Medieval History, 1963, The Barbarian Invasions, 1970; also articles.; bd. editors: Am. Hist. Rev., 1982-85; Contbr.: Life and Thought in The Middle Ages, 1967. Guggenheim fellow, 1959; Fulbright scholar, 1965; NEH Sr. fellow, 1974-75. Fellow Mediaeval Acad. Am. (mem. council 1974-77, del. to Am. Council Learned Socs. 1977-81); mem. Am. Hist. Assn. (council 1983-86), Internat. Soc. Study Rep. Instns., Am. Soc. Legal History, Phi Beta Kappa. Home: 509 Buckingham Houston TX 77024

DREW, PAUL, broadcasting consultant; b. Detroit, Mar. 10, 1935; s. Harry and Elizabeth (Schneider) Schlachman; m. Dove Ann Austin, Sept. 9, 1961. B.A., Wayne State U., Detroit, 1957. Disc jockey stas. in, Port Huron, Mich. and Atlanta, 1955-67; program dir. Sta. WQXI, Atlanta, 1966-67, Sta. CKLW, Detroit, 1967-68; program cons. Storer Broadcasting Co., Phila., 1968-69; program dir. RKO Radio stas. in, Detroit, San Francisco, Washington and Los Angeles, 1970-73, v.p. programming, 1973-77; pres. Paul Drew Enterprises, Los Angeles, 1977—, Red Carpet Prodns., 1978—, Real World Records, 1979, PAD Entertainment, Hollywood, Calif., 1980—; personal mgr. Pink Lady, outside Japan, 1978; partner Teawp/Teaspoon Music Pub. Co., 1978; chmn. Billboard Internat. Programming Conf., 1976; commr. Calif. Motion Picture Council. Del. Democratic Nat. Conv., 1976; mem. Dem. Nat. Com., Calif. Dem. Com., Dem. Nat. Fin. Council. Named DeeJay of Year Sixteen Mag., 1965; Program Dir. of Year Bill Gavin Report, 1967; recipient Superior Achievement award RKO Radio, 1973; also numerous gold records for contbs. toward million selling records. Mem. Nat. Acad. Rec. Arts. and Scis., Am. Advt. Fedn., Am. Film Inst., Hollywood Radio and TV Soc., Los Angeles World Affairs Council, Town Hall Calif., Japanese-Am. Citizens League., Japan Am. Soc. Clubs: Variety, Friars, Frat. of Friends, Music Center. Home: 2151 N Hobart Blvd Los Angeles CA 90027 Office: 1438 N Gower Hollywood CA 90028 *Don't make the same mistake once*

DREW, RUSSELL COOPER, physicist; b. Chgo., Aug. 16, 1931; s. Charles Cooper and Lucille Emma (Dezur) D.; m. Diane Marie Kent, Jan. 3, 1953; children: Cheryl (Mrs. Gerard Gebler), Christy (Mrs. Robert Sammis), Craig, Cynthia, Charles. B.S., U. Colo., 1953; postgrad., U.S. Naval Postgrad. Sch., 1957-58; Ph.D., Duke, 1961. Commd. ensign U.S. Navy, 1953, advanced through grades to capt., 1971; with Polaris Program-U.S.-U.K. negotiations on re-entry system and nuclear weapons, 1963-66; asst. to Pres.'s Sci. Adviser, 1966-72; staff dir. Pres.'s Space Task Group, sr. adviser on aerospace matters and telecommunications, 1966-72; head Office Naval Research (London Office), 1972-73; ret., 1973; dir. Sci. and Tech. Policy Office, NSF, Washington, 1973-76; exec. dir. office sci. and tech. Exec. Office of Pres., 1976-77; v.p. Systems Control, Inc., Arlington, Va., 1977-80; pres. Sci.-Tech. Corp., 1980—. Decorated Meritorious Service medal, Spl. Commendation-Cuban Missile Blockade.; Distinguished lectr. AIAA, 1968-70. Mem. IEEE (chmn. govt. activities council 1982-83), Sigma Xi, Sigma Pi Sigma. Lutheran (elder). Home: 701 Clear Spring Rd Great Falls VA 22066 Office: 701 Clear Spring Rd Great Falls VA 22066

DREW, WALTER HARLOW, paper manufacturing company executive; b. Chgo., Feb. 23, 1935; s. Ben Harlow and Marion Elizabeth (Heineman) D.; m. Garcia Ward McKenzie, June 27, 1959; children: Jeffrey, Martha. B.S., U. Wis.-Madison, 1957. Sales and sales mgmt. Kimberly-Clark Corp., Cleve. and Chgo., 1959-74, gen. mgmt., Wis., 1974-75, v.p., gen. mgr. paper div., Neenah, Wis., 1975-76, consumer products div. v.p., gen. sales mgr., 1976—, sr. v.p., 1980—; dir. Twin Cities Savs. and Loan. Bd. dirs. Camp Manitowish YMCA, 1983-86. Served as lt. USN, 1957-59. Republican. Episcopalian. Club: North Shore Golf (Menaha) (pres. 1983-85). Office: Kimberly Clark Corp 2100 Winchester Rd Neenah WI 54956

DREWER, MILTON LEE, JR., banker; b. Saxis, Va., Mar. 10, 1923; s. Milton Lee and Georgie (Seward) D.; m. Sarah Elizabeth Coshatt, Dec. 17, 1949; children: Milton Lee, III, Alan G., Carol Lynn, William D. B.A. in Econs. and Govt, Randolph-Macon Coll., 1949; M.A. in Sch. Adminstrn, U. Va., 1951. High sch. tchr., So. Va., 1952-57; head football coach, athletic dir. Coll. William and Mary, Williamsburg, Va., 1957-64; with First Am. Bank Va. (and predecessor), McLean, 1964—, pres., chief exec. officer, 1978—; dir. Va. Electric & Power Co.; mem. Gov. Va. Adv. Bd. Revenue Estimates, 1977-80, Gov. Va. Electricity Costs Commn. Bd. visitors Coll. William and Mary; trustee Va. Found. Ind. Colls.; bd. dirs. Arlington Hosp. Served with AUS. Mem. Am. Gas Assn. (banking adv. council), Va. Bankers Assn., Va. C. of C. (past pres.), Sigma Phi Epsilon, Omicron Delta Kappa. Methodist. Clubs: Washington Golf and Country (past pres.), Farmington Country (past pres.), Lago-Mar Country (past pres.). Office: 1970 Chain Bridge Rd McLean VA 22102 *

DREWES, WERNER, painter, graphic artist; b. Canig, Germany, July 27, 1899; came to U.S., 1925, naturalized, 1936; s. Georg and Martha (Schaefer) D.; m. Margaret Schrobsdorff, 1924 (dec. 1959); children: Harold, Wolfram, Bernard; m. Mary Lischer, 1960. Student, Bauhaus, Dessau, Germany, 1927. Traveled in Italy, Spain, S.Am., U.S., Japan, Korea, Russia, 1923-27; tchr. fine arts Columbia U., N.Y.C., 1937-40, Bklyn. Coll., 1945, Sch. of Design, Chgo., 1946, Washington U., St. Louis, 1947-65. Represented in collections in pub. libraries in, Newark, N.Y.C., Boston, Honolulu Acad., Yale and Washington U., art mus. in, St. Louis, art mus. in, Chgo., art mus. in, Bklyn., art mus. in, Phila., art mus. in, San Francisco, Fogg Mus., Boston, Mus. Modern Art, N.Y.C., Library of Congress, Washington, Victoria and Albert Mus., London, Nat. Gallery Am. Art, Nat. Gallery, Washington, Guggenheim Mus., Met. Mus., N.Y.C., and, others. Home: 11526 Links Dr Reston VA 22090

DREWNO, JOANNE META, foundation executive; b. Battle Creek, Mich., May 27, 1929; d. Lloyd Bernard and Martha Emma (Schumacher) Mason; m. Edward Laddie Drewno, July 17, 1954. Program sec. W.K. Kellogg Found., Battle Creek, 1948-67, adminstrv. asst. fellowships, 1968-70, asst. corp. sec., asst. office mgr., 1970-78, corp. sec., office mgr., 1978-82, v.p., corp. sec., 1982—. Bd. dirs. Big Bros.-Big Sisters, Battle Creek, 1980—. Mem. Battle Creek C. of C., Adminstrv. Mgmt. Soc. (dir. 1978—). Lutheran. Clubs: Altrusa (sec. 1974-76, dir. 1977—. Office: 400 North Ave Battle Creek MI 49016

DREWRY, GUY CARLETON, author; b. Stevensburg, Va., May 21, 1901; s. Rev. Samuel Richard and Julia Harriett (Pinckard) D.; m. Margaret Elizabeth McDonald, Apr. 2, 1942; children: Barbara Louise, Guy Carleton. Student pub. schs., Va. Asso. editor The Lyric, 1929-49; vis. lectr. English, Am. poetry Hollins College, 1952-53; instr. in creative writing U. Va. Extension Div. Contbr.: poetry to A Magazine of Verse also Voices; Work appears in: included in following anthologies Poetry Awards, 1949, 51, Proud Horns, 1933, The Sounding Summer, 1948, A Time of Turning, 1951, The Writhen Wood, 1953, Lyric Virginia Today, No. 2. The Best Poems of 1956, Cloud Above Clocktime, 1957, To Love That Well, 1975, (Winner The voices Award 1940, Poetry Awards prize for best book of poetry pub. in 1951); Editor: Southern Issue of Voices. Named Poet Laureate of Commonwealth of Va., 1970. Mem. Poetry Soc. Va. (pres. 1952- 55), Poetry Soc. of Am. (regional v.p.). Home: 2305 Maiden Lane SW Roanoke VA 24015 *In the places where we lived at the time of my early life there were few schools and no libraries. The only library in our house was burned down with the house when I was thirteen years old. The only poetry available to me was that in collected volumes of early American and British poets. Since I had no acquaintance with current poetry of that time, I had no way of becoming influenced by anything of the period. It is therefore a matter of fact that I had no influences prevailing upon me and that such distinction as I have managed to attain was due, rather than to the influence of others, to my sensitive reponse to the world of nature and the world of the Psyche surrounding me.*

DREWRY, JUDSON HARRELL, fertilizer and chemical company executive; b. Griffin, Ga., Nov. 19, 1928; s. Judson Harrell and Elizabeth (Harris) D.; m. Mary Emily Acree, Oct. 18, 1952; children: Libby, Lisa, Mimi, Jan. B.S. in Chemistry, U. Ga., 1949. Vice pres. Fla. ops. Internat. Minerals and Chem. Corp., Lakeland, 1975-76, sr. v.p. agrl. ops., Libertyville, Ill., 1976-78, sr. v.p., pres. fertilizer group, Northbrook, Ill., 1978-83, exec. v.p., 1983—; dir. Internat. Mineral and Chem. (Can.) Ltd., Toronto, Ont. Mem. Fertilizer Inst. (chmn. bd. 1982, dir. 1980-83), Internat. Fertilizer Industry (pres. N.Am., dir., v.p. fertilizers 1981-83), Potash and Phosphate Inst. (dir. 1979—). Roman Catholic. Home: 322 Island View Ln Barrington IL 60010 Office: Internat Minerals and Chem Corp 2315 Sander Rd Northbrook IL 60062

DREWRY, WILLIAM ALTON, civil engineer, educator; b. Dyess, Ark., Oct. 23, 1936; s. Charles Clarence and Cathleen (Ford) D.; m. Nancy Gray Miller, Jan. 4, 1981; children: by previous marriage: William Boyd, Bette Cathleen, Leslie Ann. Assoc. Sci., Ark. Poly. Coll., 1956; B.S. in Civil Engring., U. Ark., 1959, M.S., 1961; Ph.D., Stanford U., 1968. Registered profl. engr., Ark., Tenn., Va. Instr. U. Ark., Fayetteville, 1962-65, assoc. prof., 1965-68; research asst. Stanford U., Palo Alto, Calif., 1962-65; assoc. prof. dept. civil engring. U. Tenn., Knoxville, 1968-73, prof., 1973-76; prof., chmn. dept. civil engring. Old Dominion U., Norfolk, Va., 1976—; cons. numerous industries and govt. agys.; mem. sewerage adv. com. Va. State Water Control Bd., 1977—, State Dept. Health, Va., 1977—. Contbr. articles on wastewater treatment and environ. research to profl. jours. Mem. ASCE (pres. sect. 1983-84), Am. Soc. Engring. Edn., Nat. Soc. Profl. Engrs. (PEE bd. govs. 1978-81, 82—, trustee ednl. fund 1981—), Va. Soc. Profl. Engrs. (pres. Tidewater chpt. 1984-85), Engrs. Club Hampton Roads, Sigma Xi, Tau Beta Pi, Chi Epsilon. Office: Dept Civil Engring Old Dominion U Norfolk VA 23508

DREWS, HERBERT RICHARD, retail company executive; b. Mpls., May 3, 1924; s. Herbert H. and Zola (Howard) D.; m. Marlys Corinne Olson, Apr. 10, 1952; children: Pamela Kay, Richard Earl. B.S., U. Minn., 1948, J.D., 1950. Bar: Minn. 1950, U.S. Supreme Ct. Spl. agt. FBI, N.Y.C., 1950-52; atty. Walgreens, Chgo., 1952-56, asst. dir. employee relations, 1956-59, dir. employee relations, 1959-69, v.p. human resources, 1969-78, sr. v.p. human resources, 1978—; dir. Sanborn Hermanos, Mexico City; Mem. adv. com. Coll. Commerce and Bus. Adminstrn., U. Ill., Urbana, 1973—. Served with USAAF, 1943-46. Mem. Am. Mgmt. Assn. (human resources council), Am. Retail Fedn. (employee relations com.), Ill. C. of C., Fed. Bar Assn., Chgo. Crime Commn., Nat. Restaurant Assn., Phi Delta Theta, Phi Delta Phi. Republican. Lutheran. Clubs: Rotary, Econ., Exec. (Chgo.). Home: 62 Fox Trail Lincolnshire IL 60015 Office: 200 Wilmot Rd Deerfield IL 60015

DREWS, JOHN GEORGE, manufacturing executive; b. Wilmington, Del., Feb. 22, 1930; s. Hans and Anna K. (Stoffer) D.; children: Gary S., Ronald W., Thomas Jon. B.S. in Engring., USCG Acad., 1952; M.B.A., Harvard U., 1957. Fin. analyst Curtiss Wright Co., 1957-59; adminstrn. mgr. Raytheon Co., 1959-66; internat. controller, controller instrument group Varian Assos., 1966-71; v.p. fin., treas. Harrah's, Reno, 1971-77, exec. v.p. fin. and adminstrn., 1977-80; pres. Internat. Game Tech., Reno, 1980—; adj. faculty evening courses Grad. Sch. Bus. Northeastern U., 1965-66. Author: (with others) The Impact of High Temperature Technology, 1956. Mem. adv. bd. U. Nev.; adv. vocat. and tech. edn. State of Nev. Served with USCG, 1952-55. Mem. Assn. Corp. Growth. Home: 905 Juniper Hill Rd Reno NV 89509 Office: Internat Game Tech 520 S Rock Blvd Reno NV 89502

DREXLER, ARTHUR JUSTIN, museum director; b. N.Y.C., Mar. 13, 1925; s. Louis Alva and Claire (Tettelbaum) D. Student, Cooper Union Coll., 1942. Designer George Nelson Assos., N.Y.C., 1947-48; archtl. editor Interiors Mag., N.Y.C., 1948-50; curator dept. architecture and design Mus. Modern Art, N.Y.C., 1951-56, dir., 1956—; architect and exhibition designer Drexler & Henshell, N.Y.C.; trustee Inst. Architecture and Urban Studies, N.Y.C., chmn. bd. trustees, 1967-74; lectr. various univs. Author: The Architecture of Japan, 1955, Introduction to 20th Century Design from the Collection of the Museum of Modern Art, 1959, Ludwig Mies van der Rohe, 1960, The Drawings of Frank Lloyd Wright, 1962, Architecture of Skidmore, Owings & Merrill 1963-73, 1974; editor: Architecture of the Ecole des Beaux Arts, 1977. Served with C.E. U.S. Army, 1943-45. Recipient Medal for archtl. history Am. Inst. Architects, 1977. Fellow Soc. Arts Religion Contemporary Culture. Office: Mus of Modern Art 11 W 53d St New York NY 10019 *

DREXLER, FRED, insurance executive; b. Oakland, Calif., Nov. 17, 1915; s. Frederic I. and Jessie (Day) D.; m. Martha Jane Cunningham, Dec. 26, 1936; children: Kenneth, Roger Cunningham, Martha Drexler Spence. A.B., U. Redlands, 1936; J.D., Golden Gate U., 1947, LL.D., 1971. Bar: Calif. 1947. Editor Mill Valley (Calif.) Record, 1936-42; employee relations Marinship Corp., 1942-45; office mgr. Bechtel Corp., 1945-46; asst. to pres. Indsl. Indemnity Co., San Francisco, 1946-48, asst. sec., 1948-51, sec., 1951-56, sr. v.p., sec., 1956-67, exec. v.p., sec., 1967-68, pres., 1968-70, chmn. bd., chief exec. officer, 1970-76, chmn. exec. com., 1976-78, dir., 1957—; dir. Crum & Forster, Montgomery St. Income Securities, Inc.; mem. Calif. Workmen's Compensation Study Commn., 1963-65; sec.-treas. Calif. Workers Compensation Inst., 1968-70, pres., 1971-73, Pacific Ins. and Surety Conf., 1967-68. Pres. Marin (Calif.) United Fund, 1956; exec. bd. Marin council Boy Scouts Am., 1948-69, adv. bd., 1970—, mem. region 12 com., 1960-68, hon. mem., 1969—, mem. nat. exec. bd., 1973—; trustee Marin Country Day Sch., 1960-62, United Bay Area Crusade, 1968-73, Golden Gate U., 1957—; chmn. bd. Golden Gate U., 1968-70; bd. dirs. San Francisco Bay Area Council, 1972-76; trustee Pacific Med Center, 1974—, sec., 1979—; chmn. bd. Inst. Philos. Research, 1978—, trustee, 1973—; trustee World Affairs Council No. Calif., 1973-79. Recipient Silver Beaver, Silver Antelope awards Boy Scouts Am. Mem. Greater San Francisco C. of C. (dir. 1970-72), Calif. Bar Assn. Baptist. Clubs: Bankers (pres. 1976-78), Bohemian, Pacific Union (San Francisco); California (Los Angeles); Meadow (Marin, Calif.). Home: 1 Myrtle Ave Mill Valley CA 94941 Office: 255 California St San Francisco CA 94111

DREXLER, LLOYD, business executive; b. Chgo., 1918; (married). B.S., Northwestern U., 1939, M.A., 1941. Economist L.J. Sheridan & Co., 1946-49; pres., dir. South Shore Nat. Bank, 1950-52; partner Pioneer Auto Leasing System, 1952-55, Paulson, Drexler & Assos., 1952-55; vice chmn., chief exec. officer Am. Eagle Corp., 1962-65; partner No. Ill. Steel Co., 1946—; treas. Allied Products Co., 1964, 1964, v.p., sec., treas., mem. exec. com., 1964-68, exec. v.p., 1968-73, former pres., now chmn. exec. com., chief exec. officer, 1973—, also dir.; mem. exec. com. Victor Comptometer. Address: 10 S Riverside Plaza Chicago IL 60606 *

DREXLER, RICHARD ALLAN, manufacturing company executive; b. Chgo., May 16, 1947; s. Lloyd A. and Evelyn Violet (Kovaloff) D.; m. Dale Sue Hoffman, Sept. 4, 1971; children: Dan Lloyd, Jason Ian. B.S., Northwestern U., 1969, M.B.A., 1970. Staff v.p. Allied Products Corp., Chgo., 1973-75, sr. v.p. adminstrn., 1975-79, exec. v.p., chief fin. officer, adminstrv. officer, 1979-82, exec. v.p., chief operating officer, 1982, pres., chief operating officer, 1982—. Home: 2051 Clavey Rd Highland Park IL 60035 Office: Allied Products Corp 10 S Riverside Plaza Suite 2100 Chicago IL 60606

DREYER, JEROME LEE, trade assn. exec.; b. N.Y.C., Sept. 27, 1930; s. Murray and Blanche D.; children—Michael Lee, Suzanne Marie. B.S. in Journalism, 1952. Mgr. facilities Am. Mgmt. Assn., N.Y.C., 1956-60; dir. mem. programs Farm and Indsl. Equipment Inst., Chgo., 1960-62; dir. adminstrn. Council for Internat. Progress in Mgmt., N.Y.C., 1963; asst. to pres. Nat. Assn. Mut. Savs. Banks, N.Y.C., 1964-66; exec. v.p. Assn. Data Processing Service Orgns., Inc., Washington, 1967-79, pres., 1980—. Author: Office Management Handbook, 1972. Served with inf. U.S. Army, 1952-54. Mem. Am. Soc. Assn. Execs. Home: 6462 Rockshire St Alexandria VA 22310 Office: N 17th St:

DREYFUS, ALFRED STANLEY, rabbi; b. Youngstown, Ohio, Jan. 31, 1921; s. Marcel and Isabella (Mervis) D.; m. Marianne Cecilia Berlak, July 25, 1950; children—James Nathaniel, Richard Baeck. B.A., U. Cin., 1942; B. Hebrew Letters, Hebrew Union Coll., Cin., 1942, M. Hebrew Letters, 1946, Ph.D., 1951, D.D., 1971. Ordained rabbi; rabbi in, Terre Haute, Ind., 1951-56, Galveston, Tex., 1956-65, Union Temple, Bklyn., 1965-79; lectr. liturgy and commentaries N.Y. Sch., Hebrew Union Coll.-Jewish Inst. Religion, 1966—; dir. placement Rabbinical Placement Commn., 1979—; pres. Assembly Tex. Rabbis, 1962-63, Bklyn. Assn. Reform Rabbis, 1967-68, Bklyn. Bd. Rabbis, 1970-72; mem. governing body World Union Progressive Judaism, 1967—; bd. govs. N.Y. Bd. Rabbis, 1967—; co-chmn. Cath. Jewish Relations Com., Bklyn.-Queens Diocese, 1974-79; bd. dirs. Synagogue Council Am., 1968-72. Pres. Friends of Rosenberg Library, Galveston, 1961-62, bd. dirs., 1962-65; chmn. home service of Galveston chpt. ARC, 1956-65; vice chmn. Bklyn. chpt., 1973-79; hon. chmn. Bklyn. div. United Hosp. campaign, 1965-79. Served as chaplain AUS, 1953-55; lt. col. Res. ret. Mem. Central Conf. Am. Rabbis, Assn. Jewish Chaplains (pres. 1973-75), N.Y. Assn. Reform Rabbis (pres. 1975-77). Clubs: Masons (32 deg.), Shriners, Elks, B'nai B'rith; Unity (Bklyn.). Home: 9 Prospect Park W Brooklyn NY 11215 Office: 790 Madison Ave New York NY 10021

DREYFUS, GEORGE JOSEPH, musician; b. Boston, Mar. 14, 1920; s. Harry Frank and Bessie (Mindes) D.; m. Rita Gibson, Apr. 4, 1946; children—Laurence, Karen, Daniel. Certificate Applied Music, Boston Music Sch., 1948; student, Boston U., 1938-40. Violinist Nat. Youth Orch., Boston, 1938-41, Nat. Symphony Orch., Washington, 1946-48, Phila. Orch., 1953—; tchr. pub. sch., Brookline, Mass., 1948-53; violin tchr., orch. condr. Boston Music Sch., 1948-53; condr. Cherry Hill (N.J.) Community Symphony Orch., 1955—. Served with field arty. U.S. Army, 1942-46. Home: 1006 Kingston Dr Cherry Hill NJ 08034 Office: 1420 Locust St Philadelphia PA 19102

DREYFUS, LEE SHERMAN, former governor of Wisconsin; b. Milw., June 20, 1926; s. Woods Orlow and Clare (Bluett) D.; m. Joyce Mae Unke, Apr. 5, 1947; children: Susan Lynn Fosdick, Lee Sherman. B.A., U. Wis., 1949, M.A., 1952, Ph.D. in Communications, 1957; also hon. degrees. Radio actor Sta. WISN, Milw., 1933-49; instr. U. Wis., 1949-52; gen. mgr. Sta. WDET, Detroit, 1952-56; asst. prof. speech Wayne State U., asso. prof. speech, asso. dir. mass communications, 1952-62; gen. mgr. Sta. WHA-TV, Madison, Wis., 1962-65; dir. instructional resources U. Wis., 1965-67, prof. speech, chmn. radio-TV and films, 1962-67; pres., chancellor U. Wis.-Stevens Point, 1967-79; gov. State of Wis., Madison, 1979-83; former chmn. Nat. Army Adv. Panel on ROTC Affairs, Wis. Gov.'s Commn. on CATV; former chief of mission under Vietnam Contract for Higher Edn.-U. Wis.-Stevens Inc.; edn. adviser to sec. Army, 1970-73. Author: Televised Instruction, 1962, World's First Intercontinental Video Classroom Connection via Earlybird Satellite, 1965. Former bd. dirs. Sentry Ins. Found., Wis. Ballet Co., Wis. Fine Arts Found.; co-chmn. Nat. Am. Energy Week, 1981. Served with USNR, 1944-46. Recipient Pres.'s medallion Assn. U.S. Army, 1974. Mem. Am. Assn. State Colls. and Univs. (dir., mem. del. to Poland 1973, to Peking 1975), Nat. Assn. Ednl. Broadcasters (past dir.), Speech Assn. Am. (past chmn. radio-TV-film com.), Broadcast Pioneers Am., Nat. Govs. Assn. (past mem. exec. com., vice chmn. com. internat. trade and fgn. relations), Republican Govs. Assn. (policy com.), Midwest Govs. Assn. (vice chmn.), Am. Legion, Phi Beta Kappa, Phi Eta Sigma, Phi Kappa Phi, Phi Tau Phi, Kappa Sigma. Republican. Episcopalian. Club: Masons. Office: 440 Maple Bluff Rd Stevens Point WI 54481 *

DREYFUS, PIERRE MARC, neurologist, educator; b. Geneva, Switzerland, Oct. 14, 1923; came to U.S., 1941, naturalized, 1944; s. Paul Marc and Rosa (Wyler) D.; m. Dorothy R. Abrahams, July 5, 1947; children: Paul, Marc, Andrew Louis, Susan Ann. B.S., Tufts Coll., 1947; M.D., Columbia U., 1951. Diplomate: Am. Bd. Psychiatry and Neurology. Intern N.Y. Hosp.-Cornell U., 1951-52, resident, 1952-53, Mass. Gen. Hosp., 1953-55; asst. in neurology Harvard Med. Sch., 1958-59, instr. neurology, 1959-62, asso. in neurology, 1962-66, asst. prof. neurology, 1966-68; asso. neurologist Mass. Gen. Hosp., 1962-67, neurologist, 1967-68; prof., chmn. dept. neurology U. Calif., Davis, 1968-82, prof. neurology and pediatrics, 1982—; chief neurology U. Calif. at Davis Med. Center, 1968—; vis. prof. neurology 1st Med. Coll. and Hua Shan Hosp., Shanghai, China, 1980; mem. expert adv. panel WHO; U.S. del. to World Congress Neurology and World Fedn. Neurology; chmn. Conf. on Brain Research, 1981, 82. Editor: Western Jour. Medicine, 1971—, Internat. Jour. Vitamin Research, 1972—; corr. editor: Chinese Jour. Neurology and Psychology, 1981—; contbr. articles to profl. jours. Mem. Bd. of Health, Lincoln, Mass., 1962-68; bd. dirs. Sacramento Baroque Ensemble, Cambridge Soc. Early Music. Served with AUS, 1943-46. Mem. Am. Neurol. Assn. (councillor 1980-83), Royal Soc. Medicine, Soc. Neuroscis., Assn. Univ. Profs. Neurology, AMA, Calif. Med. Assn., Internat. Soc. Neurochemistry, Am. Inst. Nutrition, Am. Soc. Clin. Nutrition, N.Y. Acad. Scis., Am. Assn. Neuropathologists, Am. Acad. Neurology (1st v.p. 1975-77), Am. Med. Joggers Assn., Mex. Inst. Culture. Office: 4301 X St Sacramento CA 95817

DREYFUS, RAYNALD EUGENE, banker; b. Belfort, France, June 22, 1936; came to U.S., 1981; s. Marcel and Simone (Wolff) D.; m. Colette Leloir, July 2, 1965; children: Laurence, Nelly. Student, Centre d'Etudes Superieures de Banque, 1963; grad. advanced mgmt. program, Harvard U., 1961. Sub-mgr. Soc. Francaise de Banque et de Depot, Antwerp, Belgium, 1971; dep. gen. mgr. Societe General, Toyko, 1972, gen. mgr., 1974; pres. Societe General Can., Montreal, 1977-80; sr. v.p. European Am. Bank, N.Y.C., 1981, exec. v.p., 1982—; counsellor for fgn. trade French Govt., 1982; counsellor French Am. C. of C., U.S., 1981. Served with French Army, 1956-59. Decorated Commorative medal, Alegeria, 1959. Club: Canadian. Home: 26 Carriage House Ln Mamaroneck NY 10543 Office: 10 Hanover Sq New York NY 10015

DREYFUSS, JOHN ALAN, journalist; b. N.Y.C., Dec. 1, 1933; s. Henry and Doris (Marks) D.; m. Katharine Elizabeth Rich, June 28, 1958; children: Karen Elizabeth, James Henry, Kimberly Anne, Katharine Marks. B.S. in Biology, Boston U., 1959. Tchr. schs. in, Montclair, Pebble Beach and Los Olivos, Calif., 1959-63; reporter, editor San Luis Obispo (Calif.) Telegram Tribune, 1963-64; advt. salesman Ventura County (Calif.) Star-Free Press, 1964-66; mem. staff Los Angeles Times, 1966—, architecture and design critic, 1975-83, feature writer, 1984—. Served with AUS, 1953-55. Address: Los Angeles Times 145 S Spring St Los Angeles CA 90053

DREYFUSS, RICHARD STEPHAN, actor; b. N.Y.C., Oct. 29, 1947; s. Norman and Gerry D. Student, San Fernando Valley State Coll., 1965-67. Appeared in films: American Graffitti, 1972; Dillinger, 1973, The Apprenticeship of Duddy Kravitz, 1974, Jaws, 1975, Inserts, 1975, Close Encounters of the Third Kind, 1976, The Goodbye Girl, 1977, The Competition, 1980, Whose Life Is It Anyway?, 1981; theatrical appearances include: Julius Caesar, 1978; Othello, 1979; actor, producer: The Big Fix, 1978. Participant civil rights marches, lobbying for amnesty bills. Served alt. mil. duty Los Angeles County Gen. Hosp., 1969-71. Recipient Golden Globe award, 1978; Acad. award at best supporting actor in The Goodbye Girl, 1978. Mem. ACLU, Screen Actors Guild, Equity Assn., AFTRA, Motion Picture Acad. Arts and Scis. Office: care Mishkin Agy Inc 9255 Sunset Blvd Los Angeles CA 90069 *

DRICKAMER, HARRY GEORGE, chemistry educator; b. Cleve., Nov. 19, 1918; s. George Henry and Louise (Strempel) D.; m. Mae Elizabeth McFillen, Oct. 28, 1942; children: Lee Charles, Lynn Louise, Lowell Kurt, Margaret Ann, Priscilla. B.S., U. Mich., 1941, M.S., 1942, Ph.D., 1946. Chem. engr. Pan Am. Refining Corp., 1942-46; asst. prof. U. Ill. at Urbana, 1946-49, asso. prof., 1949-53, prof. phys. chemistry and chem. engring., 1953—. Recipient Bendix award, 1968; P.W. Bridgman award Internat. Assn. High Pressure Sci. and Tech., 1977; Guggenheim fellow, 1952; Michelson-Morley award Case Western Res. U., 1978. Fellow Am. Phys. Soc. (Buckley Solid State Physics award 1967), Am. Geophys. Union; mem. Nat. Acad. Engring., Am. Chem. Soc. (Ipatieff prize 1956, Langmuir award in chem. physics 1974), Am. Inst. Chemists (Chem. Pioneers award 1983), Am. Inst. Chem. Engrs. (Colburn award 1947, Alpha Chi Sigma award 1967, Walker award 1972), Faraday Soc., Nat. Acad. Scis., Am. Acad. Arts and Sci., Am. Philos. Soc., Center for Advanced Studies. Home: 304 E Pennsylvania St Urbana IL 61801

DRIEHAUS, ROBERT JOSEPH, financial company executive; b. Cin., Mar. 23, 1928; s. Leo A. and Julia (Normile) D.; m. Rita E. Spaccarelli, Jun. 24, 1953; children: Suzanne, Mary Beth, Barbara, Marilyn, Julia, Robert. B.S. in Bus. Adminstrn., Xavier U., Cin., 1950, M.B.A., 1959. Sec.-treas. Cin. Ins. Co., 1954—, dir.; fin. v.p. Cin. Fin. Corp., 1969—, dir.; v.p. CFC Investment Co., 1969—, dir.; sec.-treas. Queen City Indemnity, 1972—, dir.; sec. Life. Co. Cin., 1972—; dir. Life Ins. Co. Cin., 1972—. Mem. pres.'s adv. council Xavier U.; mem. Westwood Urban Redevel. Com., Cin. Served with U.S. Army, 1950-52. Democrat. Roman Catholic. Office: Cincinnati Fin Corp PO Box 14567 Cincinnati OH 45214

DRIEHUYS, LEONARDUS BASTIAAN, conductor; b. The Hague, Netherlands, Mar. 25, 1932; s. Bastiaan Leonardus and Maria Magdalena Driehuys-B.; m. Henrica Postma, Nov. 19, 1960; children—Nicolette, Bastiaan. Hon. degrees in oboe and piano, Royal Conservatory of Music, The Hague. Prin. oboe Netherlands Opera, Amsterdam, 1952-59, condr., 1959-65, Nederlandse Omroepstichting, 1965—; music dir. Het Gelders Orkest, Arnhem, 1970-74, Charlotte (N.C.) Symphony, 1977—. Served in Dutch Army. Recipient Fock medal for oboe playing. Club: Rotary (Charlotte). Home: 1016 Churchill Rd Davidson NC 28036 Office: 110 E 7 St Charlotte NC 28202

DRIGGS, CHARLES MULFORD, lawyer; b. East Cleveland, Ohio, Jan. 26, 1924; s. Karl Holcomb and Lila Vandeveer (Wilson) D.; m. Jean Ellen Johnson, Nov. 16, 1974; children: Ruth, Rachel, Carrie, Karl H. Charles M. B.S., Yale U., 1947, J.D., 1950. Bar: Ohio 1951. Assoc. Squire, Sanders & Dempsey, Cleve., 1950-64, ptnr., 1964—. Pres. Bratenahl Sch. Bd., Ohio, 1958-72; pres. bd. trustees Unity Ch. Mont Chalet, 1978—; mem. adv. council Cleve. Ctr. Theol. Edn., 1978—. Mem. ABA, Ohio Bar Assn., Bar Assn. Greater Cleve., Greater Cleve. Growth Assn., Cleve. Law Library Assn. (trustee 1977—), Ct. Nisi Prius, Citizens League Greater Cleve., Phi Delta Phi, Tau Beta Pi, Phi Gamma Delta. Home: 350 Wilson Mills Rd Chardon OH 44024 Office: Squire Sanders & Dempsey 1800 Huntington Bldg Cleveland OH 44115 *Any success I may have achieved I attribute to my continuing attempt to live and conduct my affairs in a manner that my family and friends may later reflect upon with pride.*

DRIGGS, DON WALLACE, educator; b. Phoenix, Sept. 26, 1924; s. Golden Kenneth and Maude (Macdonald) D.; m. Marilyn Louise Fisher, Sept. 5, 1953 (div.); children—Deborah, Pamela, Christopher. B.S., Brigham Young U., 1950; M.A., Harvard, 1955, Ph.D., 1956; Carnegie fellow, U. Mich., 1963-64. Instr., then asst. prof. U. Nev., Reno, 1956-61, asso. prof. polit. sci., 1965-68, prof., chmn. dept. polit. sci., 1968—; chmn. Faculty Senate, 1968-69; asst. prof., asso. prof., chmn. div. social scis. Stanislaus State Coll., 1961-63, asst. to pres., 1964-65. Author: The Consitution of the State of Nevada: A Commentary, 1961; co-author: The Nevada Constitution: Origin and Growth, 1980; Contbr.: Western Polit. Quar, 1957-71; asso. editor, 1970-72. Mem. platform com. Nev. State Democratic Conv., 1960, 68; mem. Nev. delegation Nat. Dem. Conv., 1968; Nev. commr. Western Interstate Commn. for Higher Edn., 1977—. Served with USAAF, 1943-46; Served with USAF, 1951-52. Decorated Air medal. Mem. Am. Polit. Sci. Assn., No. Calif. Polit. Sci. Assn. (exec. council 1968-70), Western Polit. Sci. Assn. (sec.-treas. 1966-69). Home: 945 Joshua Dr Reno NV 89509

DRIGGS, DOUGLAS HARMON, savings and loan association executive; b. Driggs, Idaho, Apr. 8, 1901; s. Don C. and May (Robison) D.; m. Effie Killian, Aug. 31, 1926; children: John Douglas, Lois, Gary Harmon, Anne. Sec. Western Savs. & Loan Assn., Phoenix, 1929-33, pres., 1933-65, chmn. bd., 1966-72, chmn. fin. com., 1975—; chmn. exec. com. Western Fin. Corp., Phoenix. Past pres., mem. adv. bd. Theodore Roosevelt council Boy Scouts Am.; Bd. dirs. Phoenix Symphony Assn., pres., 1971-73, vice chmn., 1974-75; mem. nat. adv. council Coll. Bus., Brigham Young U. Recipient Jessie Knight Indsl. Citizenship award Brigham Young U., 1977. Mem. Ch. of Jesus Christ of Latter-day Saints. Club: Rotarian (dist. gov. 1969-70). Home: 7610 Shadow Mountain Rd Paradise Valley AZ 85253 Office: 3443 N Central Ave Phoenix AZ 85012

DRIGGS, GARY HARMON, financial executive; b. Phoenix, July 13, 1934; s. Douglas H. and Effie (Killian) D.; m. Kay Taylor, June 9, 1959; children: Rebecca Taylor, Kimberly, Benjamin. Student, Stanford U., 1952-54; B.A., Brigham Young U., 1959; M.B.A., Ind. U., 1960, D.B.A., 1962. Faculty lectr. Ind. U., 1961-62; exec. v.p., economist Western Savs., Phoenix, 1962-73, pres., 1973—; chmn. bd. Romney Internat. Hotels, from 1976; lectr. Ariz. State U., 1962-67; pres. Western Fin. Corp., from 1976. Author: How to Reduce Risk in Apartment Lending, 1966. Active Boys Scouts Am.; mem. Ct. Commn. Maricopa County.; Chmn. City of Phoenix Sts. Adv. Bd., 1973—; pres. Ariz. Tomorrow; chmn. Gov.'s State Urban Lands Task Force; mem. Ariz. Commn. Nat. and Internat. Commerce. Named Outstanding Young Man of the Year in Ariz. Ariz. Jaycees, 1968, Phoenix Outstanding Young Man, 1969. Mem. Savs. and Loan League Ariz. (pres. 1972-73), Young Pres.'s Orgn. Republican. Mem. Ch. Jesus Christ of Latter-Day Saints. Club: Rotary. Office: 3443 N Central Ave Phoenix AZ 85012 *

DRIGGS, H. PERRY, JR., banker; b. N.Y.C., Oct. 25, 1936; s. H. Perry and Clara (Creer) D.; m. Mary Townsend, Sept. 5, 1970; children: Mark, Forest, Perry Townsend. B.A., Harvard, 1958, M.B.A., 1961; M.S., Northwestern U., 1959. With Mich. Bank N.A., Detroit, 1962, asst. v.p., 1965-67; sr. v.p. Mich. Nat. Bank, Lansing, 1967-70, sr. v.p., controller, 1970-79, pres., 1980—, chmn. bd., Grand Traverse, 1977—, Mich. Nat. Bank-North, Petoskey, 1980—; dir. Mich. Nat. Bank, Lansing, Mich. Nat. Leasing Corp., Mich. Air Travel Corp., Mich. Nat. Corp., Internat. Fin. Corp., N.Y.C.; Mem. applicant relations com. Harvard Bus. Sch., 1966—. Mem. Mich. Bldg. Commn., 1971—; Bd. dirs., pres. Lansing Symphony Orch.; adv. council Sch. Bus. Adminstrn., Central Mich. U.; treas., bd. dirs. Religious Heritage Am., Inc.; gen. chmn. United Way Lansing. Served with U.S. Army, 1961. Mem. Fin. Execs. Inst., Lansing C. of C., Alpha Pi Mu, Sigma Alpha Epsilon. Mem. Ch. of Jesus Christ of Latter-day Saints (missionary in Eng.). Clubs: Economic (Detroit); Walnut Hills Country; Little Harbor, Wequetonsing Golf (Harbor Springs, Mich.). Lodge: Rotary. Office: Mich Nat Bank 124 W Allegan St Lansing MI 48901

DRIGGS, JUNIUS ELMARION, savings and loan association executive; b. Driggs, Ida., June 28, 1907; s. Don Carlos and May (Robison) D.; m. Bernice Crouse, May 18, 1933; children: Don C., Sharon Driggs Hall, Deanna Driggs Hanson, Stephen C., Michael R. Ed. pub. schs. With Western Savs. & Loan Assn., Phoenix, 1931—, exec. v.p., 1955-64, pres., 1964-73, chmn. bd., 1973-82. Mem. Phoenix Human Relations Commn., 1964-69; chmn. Ariz. Heart Assn., 1961, Phoenix chpt. NCCJ, 1965-67; mem. at large bd. trustees, bd. govs. Phoenix chpt. NCCJ; adv. bd. Phoenix Salvation Army, 1965—, Roosevelt council Boy Scouts Am., 1956—. Mem. Ch. Jesus Christ of Latter-day Saints (regional rep. Council of Twelve 1967-74, pres. Ariz. temple 1975-80). Home: 1761 E Elmwood Mesa AZ 85203 Office: 3443 N Central Ave Phoenix AZ 85012

DRIGGS, ORVAL TRUMAN, JR., historian; b. Uvalde, Tex., Aug. 13, 1922; s. Orval Truman and Zeanette Idella (Perry) D. B.A., U. Ark., 1943, M.A., 1947; Ph.D. (George L. Harrison fellow 1950), U. Pa., 1950. Asst. prof. history Allegheny Coll., Meadville, Pa., 1952-57; prof., head dept. history Westminster Coll., Salt Lake City, 1957-63; prof. history U. Minn., Morris, 1963—, chmn. div. social sci., 1968-78. Author articles, abstracts in field. Chmn. Stevens County Democratic Farmer Labor Party Conv., 1968, 70, 72, 76, 78. Recipient Horace T. Morse-Amoco Teaching award U. Minn., 1967. Mem. AAUP, Am. Hist. Assn., Soc. French Hist. Studies, Soc. d'Histoire Moderne. Unitarian. Home: 530 E 4th St Morris MN 56267 Office: Social Sci Div Univ Minn Morris MN 56267

DRIKER, EUGENE, lawyer; b. Detroit, Feb. 24, 1937; s. Charles and Frances (Hoffman) D.; m. Elaine Carol Zeidman, June 17, 1959; children: Elissa Ruth, Stephen Joel. A.B., Wayne State U., 1958, J.D., 1961; LL.M., George Washington U., 1962. Bar: Mich. bar 1962. Trial atty. antitrust div. U.S. Dept. Justice, Washington, 1961-64; mem. firm Barris, Sott, Denn & Driker, Detroit, 1968—; lectr. law Wayne State U., Detroit, 1964-68. Commr. City of Detroit Bldg. Authority, 1974-79; mem. City of Detroit Bd. Police Commrs., 1979—83; chmn. Wayne State U. Law Sch. Fund, 1972-74; Bd. dirs. Jewish Vocat. Service and Community Workshop, 1983—, Detroit Symphony Orch., 1983—. Mem. Wayne State Law Sch. Alumni Assn. (pres. 1971-72). Clubs: Detroit, Renaissance. Home: 1525 Wellesley Dr Detroit MI 48203 Office: 2100 1st Fed Bldg Detroit MI 48226

DRIMMER, MELVIN, historian, educator; b. Bronx, N.Y., Nov. 2, 1934; s. Oscar and Natalie (Stessin) D.; m. Iris Alteres, June 26, 1959 (div. 1982); children: Alan Stessin, Barbara. B.A., CCNY, 1956; postgrad., Oxford U., summer 1957; Ph.D., U. Rochester, 1965; Ford postdoctoral fellow, Sch. Oriental and African Studies, U. London, 1966-67. Lectr., Hunter Coll., 1960-63; asst. prof. to prof., chmn. history dept. Spelman Coll., Atlanta H. Center, 1963-72; prof. Cleve. State U., 1972—, chmn. history dept., 1972-74; vis. asst. prof. NYU, summers 1965-66, vis. asso. prof., summer 1968; A. Lindsey O'Connor vis. prof. Am. instns. Colgate U., 1969-70; Lyceum vis. prof. Dillard U., 1977; research asso. DuBois Inst., Harvard U., 1981-83; exec. dir. Am. Forum Internat. Study; dir. numerous summer insts., Africa and Caribbean, 1968—; dir. NDEA Insts. in Black History, Spelman Coll., 1966, 68—; cons. Ford Found. Aspen Conf., 1970, Yale Danforth program, 1970, John Jay Coll., 1970, A. Philip Randolph Inst., 1970-72. Author: Black History, A Reappraisal, 1968; also articles. Bd. dirs. Karamu House, Cleve. Recipient Field Summer grants, 1964, 65, Atlanta U. research grant, 1966, Ford Humanities grant Colgate U., 1969-70; Dept. State grantee, 1975; Hayes-Fulbright grantee, 1976. Mem. Am. Hist. Assn., Assn. Study Afro-Am. Life and History, Phi Beta Kappa. Home: 2851 Hampton Rd Cleveland OH 44120 Office: Dept History Cleve State U Cleveland OH 44115 *I am a product of the great Civil Rights Revolution of the 1960's and very much influenced by the ideas and example of Martin Luther King. The example of Dr. King led me to think about the fact that one's life should not be passed in isolation or without commitment and that if you believed in your ideas, then you should act on them and take a stand as a man. Here I was teaching history and making value judgements on men and events without ever having participated in a historical movement myself. My involvement and commitment made me understand myself and the nature of history.*

DRINAN, ROBERT FREDERICK, lawyer, Congressman, educator, clergyman; b. Boston, Nov. 15, 1920; s. James Joseph and Ann Mary (Flanagan) D. A.B., Boston Coll., 1942, M.A., 1947; LL.B., Georgetown U., 1949, LL.M., 1950; Th.D., Gregorian U., Rome, 1954; study, Florence, Italy, 1954-55; LL.D., Worcester State Coll., 1970, L.I. U., 1970, R.I. Coll., 1971, St. Joseph's Coll., Phila., 1975, Syracuse U., 1977, Framingham (Mass.) State Coll., 1978, U. Santa Clara, 1980, Kenyon Coll., 1981, Lowell U., 1981, U. Bridgeport, 1981, Loyola U., Chgo., 1981, Gonzaga U., 1981. Bar: D.C. bar 1950, Mass. bar 1956, U.S. Supreme Ct. bar 1955. Entered S.J., 1942; ordained priest Roman Cath. Ch., 1953; asst. dean Boston Coll. Law Sch., 1955-56, dean, 1956-70; vis. prof. U. Tex. Law Sch., 1966-67; mem. 92d-96th congresses from 4th Dist. Mass.; mem. jud. com., govt. ops. com., house select com. on aging, chmn. subcom. on criminal justice; columnist Nat. Cath. Reporter, 1980; prof. Law Center, Georgetown U., Washington, 1981—; Chmn. adv. com. Mass. U.S. Commn. Civil Rights, 1962-70; mem. vis. com. Div. Sch., Harvard U., 1975-78; bd. dirs. Bread for the World; founder Nat. Interreligious Task Force on Soviet Jewry.; Mem. exec. com. Assn. Am. Law Schs. Author: Religion, the Courts and Public Policy, 1963, Democracy, Dissent and Disorder, 1969, Vietnam and Armageddon, 1970, Honor the Promise, America's Commitment to Israel, 1977, Beyond the Nuclear Freeze, 1983; Editor: The Right To Be Educated, 1968; editor-in-chief: Family Law Quar, 1967-70; corr. editor: nat. Cath. weekly America, 1958-70; Contbr. articles to jours. of opinion. Fellow Am. Acad. Arts and Scis.; mem. ABA, Mass. Bar Assn. (v.p. 1961), Boston Bar Assn., Am. Law Inst., Ams. for Democratic Action (v.p., pres. 1981—), NCCJ (nat. trustee), Common Cause (nat. governing bd. 1981—). Office: Georgetown U Law Center 600 New Jersey Ave NW Washington DC 20001

DRINKARD, DONALD, textile and floor covering company executive; b. Trenton, Mo., Mar. 29, 1919; s. Harry and Carrie (Kirk) D.; m. Helen C. Polson, Sept. 29, 1939; children: Judith C. (Mrs. Eugene A. Pearsall), Donald Dwight. Student, Kansas City (Mo.) Jr. Coll. With Fitts Dry Goods Co., Kansas City, Mo., 1937-53, v.p., gen. mgr., 1949-53, William R. Moore, Inc., Memphis, 1953-54, pres., 1954-58, pres., chmn. bd., 1958—; dir. Washington Industries, Inc., Nat. Commerce Bancorp., Nat. Bank Commerce, Memphis. Exec. com. Danny Thomas Memphis Classic; dir., past pres. Liberty Bowl Festival; past pres. Nat. Assn. Textile and Apparel Wholesalers, Memphis Cotton Carnival Assn., Memphis Cerebral Palsy Assn.; past chmn. Memphis and Shelby County Auditorium Commn.; mem. chancellor's roundtable U. Tenn. Med. Units; pres.'s council Memphis State U., Southwestern U.; Trustee William R. Moore Sch. Tech., Memphis U. Sch. Served to 1st lt. AUS, 1943-46. Mem. Memphis C. of C. (dir.). Club: Memphis Country (Memphis). Lodges: Masons; Shriners. Home: 578 Country Club Ln Memphis TN 38111 Office: 183 Monroe St Memphis TN 38101

DRINKWATER, ROBERT EDWARD, advt./mktg. exec.; b. Everett, Mass., Dec. 30, 1935; s. George Adolf and Claire Carre (Frederick) D.; m. Clare Lincoln Burns, June 24, 1961; 1 son, Robert Edward. B.S. in Bus. Adminstrn, Northeastern U., 1960; student, Boston Mus. Fine Arts Sch., 1955. Account exec. N.W. Ayer & Son, Inc., N.Y.C., 1963-65; sr. product mgr. Colgate-Palmolive Co., N.Y.C., 1965-69; mktg. mgr. Fragrance div. Revlon, Inc., N.Y.C., 1969-71; mgr. venture devel. Am. Cyanamid Co., Wayne, N.J., 1971-74; pres. The Walpert Co., Cherry Hill, N.J., 1974-76; dir. mktg. Ideal Toy Corp., Hollis, N.Y., 1976-77; v.p., mgmt. supr. C.T. Clyne Co., N.Y.C., 1977-80; pres., chief exec. officer Nat. Advt. Agy. Network, N.Y.C., 1980—. Bd. dirs. Bide-A-Wee Home Assn., Am. Humane Assn. Republican. Episcopalian. Clubs: Smoke Rise (N.J.); Bucks Harbor Yacht (South Brooksville, Me.). Home: 10 Brush Hill Rd Kinnelon NJ 07405 Office: 14 E 48th St New York NY 10017 *1) Above all, faith in God is the most important personal resource we have. (2) Very often, adversity proves to be opportunity in disguise. (3) The ability to anticipate, well in advance, is a key criterion for success.*

DRINNAN, ALAN JOHN, oral pathologist; b. Bristol, Eng., Apr. 6, 1932; came to U.S., 1962, naturalized, 1970; s. Leslie Cyril and Doris May (Porter) D.; m. Marguerite G. Bondolfi, Apr. 4, 1956; children: Michael James, Julia Mary. B.D.S., Bristol U., 1954, M.B.Ch.B., 1962; D.D.S., SUNY, 1964. Tutor oral surgery Bristol U., Eng., 1957-58; asst. prof. SUNY-Buffalo, 1964-68, assoc. prof., 1968-71, prof. dept. oral medicine, chmn., 1971—. Contbr. articles to numerous publs. Served to capt. Royal Army Dental Corps Brit. Army, 1955-57. Fulbright sr. scholar U. Melbourne, Australia, 1981. Mem. ADA, Am. Acad. Oral Pthology (pres.), Intenat. Assn. Dental Research. Home: 66 Chestnut Hill Ln Williamville NY 14221 Office: SUNY Farber 243 Dental Sch Buffalo NY 14214

DRINNON, RICHARD, history educator; b. Portland, Oreg., Jan. 4, 1925; s. John Henry and Emma (Tweed) D.; m. Anna Maria Faulise, Oct. 20, 1945; children: Donna Elizabeth, Jon Tweed. B.A. summa cum laude, Willamette U., 1950; M.A., U. Minn., 1951, Ph.D., 1957. Instr. humanities U. Minn., 1952-53, social sci., 1955-57; instr. Am. history U. Calif., 1957-58, asst. prof., 1958-61; Bruern fellow in Am. studies U. Leeds, 1961-63; faculty research fellow Social Sci. Research Council, 1963-64; asso. prof. history Hobart and William Smith Colls., 1964-66; chmn. dept. history Bucknell U., 1966-74, prof. history, 1974—; vis. prof. U. Paris, 1975. Author: Rebel in Paradise: a Biography of Emma Goldman, 1961, White Savage: The Case of John Dunn Hunter, 1972, Facing West: The Metaphysics of Indian-Hating and Empire-Building, 1980; Co-editor: Nowhere at Home: Letters from Exile of Emma Goldman and Alexander Berkman, 1974; Contbr. articles and revs. to profl. jours. and mags. Served with USNR, 1942-46. Nat. Endowment for Humanities sr. fellow, 1980-81. Mem. Am. Hist. Assn. Anarchist. Naturist. Office: Bucknell Univ Lewisburg PA 17837

DRISCHLER, ALVIN PAUL, government official; b. Milw., Apr. 1, 1947; s. Alvin Walter and Gertrude (Swenson) D.; m. Jill Cardoza, Aug. 28, 1971; children: Marlise, Lynsey, Alvin Paul. A.B., U. Calif.-Berkeley, 1969; M.A., Princeton U., 1971, Ph.D., 1973. With office of asst. sec. Dept. Def., Washington, 1971, Internat. Inst. Strategic Studies, London, 1971-72, Fgn. Policy Research Inst., Phila., 1972-73, Nat. Republican Senatorial Com., Washington, 1973-74, Senator Paul Laxalt, 1974-81; prin. dept. asst. sec. state for congl. relations, Washington, 1981—. Contbr. articles to profl. jours. U.S. Steel Found. fellow, 1969. Mem. Phi Beta Kappa. Lutheran. Home: 3420 Reedy Dr Annandale VA 22003 Office: Dept State 2201 C St NW Washington DC 20520

DRISCOLL, GLEN ROBERT, university president; b. Sligo, Ohio, Apr. 29, 1920; s. William Arthur and Jennie (Smith) D.; m. Dorothy Little, Nov. 9, 1941; children: David Arthur, Robert Earl, Nancy Lee Driscoll Husted; m. Emma McGlone, June 18, 1978; stepchildren: Todd Seeley, Brian Bolt. Student, DePauw U., 1938-41; A.B., U. Louisville, 1947, LL.D., 1973; M.A., U. Minn., 1949, Ph.D., 1952. From instr. to prof. history U. S.D., 1949-64; chmn. div. social scis., prof. history U. Mo. at St. Louis, 1964-65, dean arts and scis., dean, 1965-68, dean faculties, 1968-69, chancellor, 1969-72; pres. U. Toledo, 1972—; dir. 1st Nat. Bank of Toledo; Regional assoc. Am. Council Learned Socs., 1957-61; mem. regional bd. for Woodrow Wilson Fellowship Found., 1968, 69, 70. Bd. dirs. Toledo Symphony Orch., Found. for Ednl. Television, Toledo Mus. Art., Toledo Boys Club. Served with USAAF, 1942-46. Ford Found. fellow Harvard, 1955. Mem. Am. Hist. Assn., Soc. French Hist. Studies, Midwest Junto for History of Sci., Société d'Histoire Moderne, Am. Council on Edn. (com. on maj. problems in intercollegiate athletics), Am. Assn. State Colls. and Univs. (com. grad. studies), Am. Assn. Higher Edn., Toledo C. of C. (dir.). Home: 3425 W Bancroft St Toledo OH 43606 *Demonstrate a personal work ethic which goes beyond that expected from those to whom you administer. Develop an abundant self-confidence which always falls short of conceit. Know that listening is more self-enlightening than speaking. Remember that anyone has the capacity to do more. Practice occasional personal humility by asking, "How soon will I know as much as I do not know?"*

DRISCOLL, JOHN BRIAN, state official; b. Los Angeles, July 17, 1946; s. John Bryan and Ann Lorraine (Green) D.; m. Claudia Jo McMahon, June 7, 1969; children: Chanda Maureen, Tamara Jo. B.A., Gonzaga U., 1968; M.I.A., Columbia U., 1970; M.P.A., Harvard U., 1980; M.B.A., U. Mont., 1981. Mem. Mont. Ho. of Reps., 1972-80, house majority leader, 1976-77, speaker, 1977-78; public service commr. State of Mont., 1981—; smoke jumper U.S. Forest Service, 1968, 77; Coordinator Mont. Internat. Trade Commn., 1976; candidate U.S. Senate, 1978. Served with U.S. Army, 1970-72; Served with Mont. N.G., 1973-80. Democrat. Roman Catholic. Home: 533 Diehl Dr Helena MT 59601 Office: Pub Service Commn 2701 Prospect Helena MT 59601

DRISCOLL, JOHN GERARD, college president; b. N.Y.C., Apr. 17, 1933; s. John P. and Mary T. (Kennedy) D. B.S., Iona Coll., 1954; M.S., St. John's U., 1957; Ph.D., Columbia U., 1969; D.Sc., Coll. New Rochelle, 1971. Tchr. elem. schs. Rice High Sch., 1956-57, St. Joseph Sch., Antigua, 1957-61, Power Meml. Sch., 1961-65; prof. math. Iona Coll., New Rochelle, N.Y., 1965—, asst. to pres., 1969-71, pres., 1971—; vice-chmn. bd. trustees Commn. on Ind. Colls. and Univs.; dir. Nat. Bank of Westchester.; Trustee St. Joseph's Sem. and Sch. Theology, Yonkers, N.Y., Iona Coll., Westchester Arts Council. Bd. dirs. Drexel Burnham Scholarship Fund; chmn. Westchester County Pub. Utility Agy. Mem. World Trade Inst. Address: 715 North Ave New Rochelle NY 10801

DRISCOLL, JUSTIN ALBERT, bishop; b. Bernard, Ia., Sept. 30, 1920; s. William J. and Agnes (Healey) D. B.A., Loras Coll., Dubuque, Ia., 1942; postgrad., Cath. U. Am., 1945, Ph.D., 1952. Ordained priest Roman Cath. Ch., 1945; tchr. Loras Acad., Dubuque, 1945-48; sec. to Archbishop Rohlman, 1948-49, to Archbishop Binz, 1952-53; supt. schs., Dubuque, 1953-67; chaplain Mr. St. Francis Convent Motherhouse, Dubuque, 1954-67; pres. Loras Coll., 1967-70; bishop Diocese of Fargo, N.D., 1970—; Dir. Confraternity Christian Doctrine, Dubuque, 1953-67; moderator Council Women, Dubuque, 1953-67; Chmn. U.S. Cath. Sch. Supts. Assn. of U.S. Cath. Conf., 1966-67; mem. Ia. N. Central Sch. Com., 1957- 67. Author: We Pray for Our Priests, 1965, The Pastor and the School, 1966, With Faith and Vision: Schools of the Archdiocese of Dubuque, 1936-1966, 1967; Contbr. articles to profl. jours.; Mem. adv. bd.: Cath. Sch. Jour. Mem. Cath. Bus. Edn. Assn. (dir.), Alumni Assn. Theol. Coll. Cath. U. Am. (1st v.p. 1965—), Nat. Cath. Edn. Assn. (exec. bd.), K.C. (4 deg.). Address: 608 Broadway Fargo ND 58102

DRISCOLL, LEE FRANCIS, JR., diversified services company executive; b. Phila., July 27, 1926; s. Leon F. and Helen (Carroll) D.; m. Phoebe Albert, Dec. 30, 1959; children—Lee Francis III, Patrick McGill, Phoebe Poultney, Helen Louise. A.B., U. Pa., 1949, LL.B., 1953. Bar: Pa. bar 1954. Vice chmn., gen. counsel ARA Services, Inc.; dir. Rorer Group, Inc., First Pa. Corp., Blue Cross Greater Phila. Chmn. Phila. Com. of 70, 1960-62; pres. Phila. United Way, 1980-82; mem. exec. com. Greater Phila. Partnership; bd. mgrs. Pa. Hosp.; Dem. candidate for U.S. Congress, 1962. Served with inf. AUS, 1944-46, 50-51. Decorated Bronze Star. Mem. Am., Phila. bar assns., Sharswood Law Club, Zeta Psi. Roman Cath. Clubs: Union League, Philadelphia (Phila.). Home: Swedesford Rd Ambler PA 19002 Office: Independence Sq W Philadelphia PA 19106

DRISCOLL, ROBERT EDWARD, JR., lawyer, educator; b. Lead, S.D., Feb. 8, 1916; s. Robert Edward and Louise (Fearon) D.; m. Elinor Ash, Dec. 29, 1937; 1 son, Mike E. A.B., Stanford, 1937; J.D., U. Colo., 1942. Bar: S.D. bar 1942. Salesman Am. Colloid Co., Chgo., 1937-39; mem. Philip, Leedom & Driscoll, Rapid City, 1946-50, Kellar, Kellar & Driscoll, Lead, 1950-73; asst. gen. counsel Homestake Mining Co., Lead, 1950-73; ltd. pvt. practice with Driscoll, Mattson, Rachetto & Christenson, Deadwood, S.D., 1973—; prof. law U. S.D., Vermillion, 1975—; dir. First Nat Bank Black Hills, Belle Fourche Bentonite Products Co., Am. Colloid Co., Chgo., Rapid City, Bentonit Internat. G.m.B.H., Duisburg, Germany, Volclay Ltd., Wallsley, Eng.;

Mem. nat. adv. council Practising Law Inst.; mem. Spl. Pres.'s Com. Civil Rights Under Law; S.D. rep. Nat. Commn. Uniform Laws; mem. S.D. Bd. Pardons and Paroles, 1973—, Pres.'s Com. on Immigration Reform. Trustee Rocky Mountain Mineral Law Found., Am. Coll. Probate Council. Mem. Am. Bar Assn., Am. Bar Found., S.D. State Bar Commrs., State Bar S.D. (pres.). Republican. Home: PO Box 872 Lead SD 57754 *Integrity in business and personal life. Work discipline. Proper rest and relaxation. Reserve time for hobbies.*

DRISCOLL, ROBERT SWANTON, investment co. exec.; b. N.Y.C., Jan. 12, 1912; s. Clarence Uler and Elizabeth (Pinchbeck) D.; m. Jane Word, Sept. 30, 1936; children—Robert Swanton IV, Steven Word, David Christopher. A.B. with honors, Columbia, 1933. Investment counselor, 1934-40; with Research & Mgmt. Council, Inc. (subs. Lord, Abbett & Co.), 1941-47, v.p., 1942, pres., 1944; v.p. Lord, Abbett & Co., Inc., 1948, partner, 1949-64, 78-79; mng. partner, 1964-78, 79-80; v.p. Lord Abbett Income Fund, Inc., N.Y.C., 1949-61, exec. v.p., 1961-64, pres., chief exec. officer, 1964-80, dir., 1949—; pres., chief exec. officer Lord Abbett Developing Growth Fund, Inc., 1973-80, dir., 1973—; v.p. Affiliated Fund, Inc., N.Y.C., 1948-61, exec. v.p., 1961-64, pres., chief exec. officer, 1964-77, chmn., 1977-78, chmn., chief exec. officer, 1979-80, dir., 1948—; pres., chief exec. officer Lord, Abbett Bond-Debenture Fund, Inc., 1971-79, chmn., chief exec. officer, 1979-80; dir., 1971—; chmn. bd., pres. Am. Utility Shares, Inc. (merged into Lord Abbett Income Fund 1978), 1975-78; pres., chief exec. officer Lord Abbett Cash Res. Fund, Inc., 1979-80, dir., 1979—, Depository Trust Co., 1974-78, Whittaker, Clark & Daniels, Inc.; former mem. SEC rules com. Investment Co. Inst., also former mem. exec. com. and bd. govs. Commr. Washington Irving council Boy Scouts, 1951-61, pres., 1961-64, v.p., 1964—; trustee Securities Industry Found. for Econ. Edn. Former mem. Nat. Assn. Securities Dealers (long range planning com., com. on consumer affairs, past chmn. arbitration com., past gov.), Securities Industry Assn. (chmn. investment cos. com. 1977-78); mem. N.Y. Soc. Security Analysts, Amateur Fencers League (treas. 1947-52). Clubs: Fencers School (N.Y.C.) (pres. 1949-58, v.p. 1958—); Broad St. (N.Y.C.); Capitol Hill (Washington); Mount Kisco (N.Y.); Country. Mem. Olympic Fencing Com., 1947-52, nat. epée champion, 1943. Home: 345 Roaring Brook Rd Chappaqua NY 10514 Office: 63 Wall St New York NY 10005

DRISCOLL, SHIRLEY GRIFFITH, patholgist educator; b. Pittston, Pa., Feb. 8, 1923; d. William Edmund and Margaret Helen (Underwood) Griffith; m. John J. Driscoll, Sept. 18, 1948. A.B., U. Pa., 1945, M.D., 1949. Intern Mt. Auburn Hosp., Cambridge; resident Children's Hosp., Phila., Phila. Gen. Hosp., Peter Bent Brigham Hosp., Boston Lying-in Hosp., Free Hosp. for Women, Brookline, Mass.; pathologist Boston Lying-in Hosp., 1948-65, Boston Hosp. for Women, 1965-78, pathologist in chief, 1978-81; dir. women's and perinatal div. of pathology Brigham & Women Hosp. Harvard Med. Sch.; instr. pathology Harvard U., 1958-75, prof., 1975—. Author: (with Benirschke) Pathology of the Human Placenta, 1967. Mem. AAAS, Am. Med. Women's Assn., Teratology Soc., New Eng. Pediatric Pathology Group, Pediatric Pathology Club, Obstet. Soc. Boston, Mass. Med. Soc., New Eng. Soc. Pathology, Mass. Soc. Pathology, Am. Soc. Clin. Pathologists. Office: 75 Francis St Boston MA 02115

DRISCOLL, WALTER JOHN, banker; b. St. Paul, Mar. 20, 1929; s. Walter b. and Margaret L. (Weyerhaeuser) D.; m. Elizabeth M. Slade, Jan. 3, 1955; children: John B., William L., Elizabeth C., Margaret L. B.S., Yale U., 1951. Sales mgmt. Weyerhaeuser Co., Boston, 1954-64; exec. v.p. Rock Island Corp., St. Paul, 1964-73, pres., 1973—; chmn., dir. First Nat. Bank of, Palm Beach, Fla., 1978—, Dietzgen Corp., Des Plaines, Ill., 1973—; dir. St. Paul Cos. Inc., St. Paul, States Power Co., Mpls., Weyerhaeuser Co., Tacoma, Gould Inc., Rolling Meadows, Ill. Chmn. Northwest Area Found., St. Paul, Macalester Coll., St. Paul, 1969-72, Mpls. Inst. Arts. Served to capt. USMC, 1951-53; Korea. Republican. Presbyterian. Home: 357 Salem Church Rd Saint Paul MN 55118 Office: Rock Island Co 2100 First Nat Bank Bldg Saint Paul MN 55101

DRISCOLL, WILLIAM MICHAEL, corporation executive; b. Boston, Feb. 15, 1929; s. Edgar J. and Katharine (Rooney) D.; m. Catherine Moore, Sept. 12, 1959; children: William Michael, Sean Moore, Geoffrey Moore, David Moore. Student, Yale Comml. Execs. Sch., 1952-53. Exec. trainee F.W. Woolworth Co., 1946-50; sec. Retail Bd. Trade, Lawrence, Mass., 1950-52, Greater Lawrence C. of C., 1952-54; with Sales & Marketing Execs. Internat., N.Y.C., 1954-74, mng. dir., 1963-74; pres. Drivans Corp., Hastings-On-Hudson, N.Y., 1975—; dir. RJD Assocs., Inc., Westport, Conn., Griffin Leasing, Inc., Greenwich, Conn. Bd. counsellors Marymount Coll., Tarrytown, N.Y. Served with U.S. Army, 1954-56. Mem. Am. Marketing Assn., Am. Soc. Assn. Execs., Pi Sigma Epsilon. Clubs: Watch Hill Yacht (dir.), Misquamicut (Watch Hill, R.I.); Canadian, Metropolitan (N.Y.C.); Caledonian Curling (N.Y.). Address: 3 Fairmont Ave Hastings-on-Hudson NY 10706

DRISKILL, JOHN RAY, association executive; b. Tonkawa, Okla., Mar. 5, 1934; s. Bayne E. and Edna (Horton) D.; m. Dorothy Nace, Dec. 23, 1956; children: J. Bradley, Bryan D. B.S., Phillips Univ.; postgrad., Tex. Christian U., American Coll., Bryn Mawr, Pa. Agt. Bankers Life of Nebr., Fort Worth, 1961-63, asst. dir. tng., Lincoln, Nebr., 1963-67, dir. tng., 1967-73; supt. agys. Mass. Mut., Ins. Co., 1973-75, dir. agys., sr. officer, 1975-76; sr. v.p. Am. Soc. C.L.U.s, Bryn Mawr, Pa., 1976-79, exec. v.p., mng. dir., 1979—; mem., past chmn. Am. Soc. C.L.U.s Query Com. Served with U.S. Army, 1956-58. Republican. Presbyterian. Clubs: Merion Golf (Ardmore, Pa.); Union League (Phila.). Office: 270 Bryn Mawr Ave Bryn Mawr PA 19010

DRIVER, ALBERT WESTCOTT, JR., chain store executive; b. Bridgeport, Conn., Aug. 4, 1927; s. Albert W. and Bessie (Ferns) D.; m. Martha Lou Miller, Aug. 5, 1951; children: Martha, Sara. B.A., Yale, 1949; LL.B., U. Va., 1952. Bar: N.Y. 1952. Assoc. firm Cravath, Swaine & Moore, N.Y.C., 1952-60; with J.C. Penney Co., Inc., 1961—, sec., 1969—, v.p., 1974-81, gen. counsel, 1978—, sr. v.p., 1981—. Served with USNR, 1946. Mem. ABA (corp., banking and bus. law sect., mem. com. on corp. law depts., chmn. 1977-79, com. on audit inquiry responses, sect. planning rev. com., com. on corp. laws, com. on regulatory reform, com. on counsel responsibility and liability), N.Y. State Bar Assn. (exec. com. banking, corp. and bus. law sect., chmn. 1978-79, mem. bus. law com., chmn. 1977-78), Assn. Bar City N.Y. (chmn. com. on corp. law depts.), Nat. Retail Mchts. Assn. (mem. govt. and legal affairs com., chmn. 1977-79, mem. lawyers com., chmn. 1972-73). Home: PO Box 268 Allamuchy NJ 07820 Office: 1301 Ave of the Americas New York NY 10019

DRIVER, LOTTIE ELIZABETH, librarian; b. Newport News, Va., Dec. 6, 1918; d. James W. and Lottie (Williams) D. Student, Averett Coll., 1936-37; B.S., Mary Washington Coll. of U. Va., 1939; B.L.S., Coll. William and Mary, 1944. Band instr. Hampton (Va.) Sch. System, 1939-41; asst. librarian Newport News Pub. Library, 1941-47, librarian, 1947-69; asst. dir. Newport News Pub. Library System, 1969, dir., 1977-81; author book rev. column in Daily Press; library news reporter radio sta. WGH, 1959. Author articles for library supply house. Active United Fund. Recipient Community Service certificate Kiwanis Clubs Newport News, 1970; named Outstanding City Employee, 1970. Mem. ALA, Southeastern, Va. library assns., AAUW, P.E.O., DAR, Phi Theta Kappa, Alpha Phi Sigma. Baptist.

DRIVER, TOM FAW, theology educator, writer; b. Johnson City, Tenn., May 31, 1925; s. Leslie Rowles and Sarah (Broyles) D.; m. Anne L. Barstow, June 7, 1952; children: Katharine Anne, Paul Barstow, Susannah Ambrose. A.B., Duke U., 1950; M.Div., Union Theol. Sem., 1953; Ph.D., Columbia U., 1957; D.Litt., Denison U., 1970. Ordained to ministry Methodist Ch., 1951; dir. youth work Riverside Ch., N.Y.C., 1955-56; faculty Union Theol. Sem., N.Y.C., 1956—, Paul J. Tillich prof. theology and culture, 1973—; drama critic Christian Century, 1956-62, Sta. WBAI-FM, 1960-61, The Reporter, 1963-64; vis. assoc. prof. English Columbia U., 1964-65; vis. assoc. prof. religion Barnard Coll., 1965-66, Fordham U., 1967; cons. humanities and arts Coll. Old Westbury (N.Y.), 1970; William Evans vis. prof. religion U. Otago, N.Z., 1976; vis. prof. religion Vassar Coll., 1978, Montclair State Coll., 1981; vis. prof. English lit. Doshisha U., Kyoto, Japan, 1983. Author: liberetto for oratorio The Invisible Fire, 1957; The Sense of History in Greek and Shakespearean Drama, 1960, Jean Genet, 1966, Romantic Quest and Modern Query: A History of The Modern Theater, 1970, Patterns of Grace: Human Experience as Word of God, 1977, Christ in a Changing World: Toward an Ethical Christology, 1981; Editor: (with Robert Pack) Poems of Doubt and Belief, 1964; also articles. Bd. dirs. dept. worship and arts Nat. Council Chs., 1958- 63, Found. for Arts, Religion and Culture, 1963-67. Served with AUS, 1943-46. Kent fellow, 1953; Guggenheim fellow, 1962-63. Mem. Am. Acad. Religion, New Haven Theol. Group, Soc. Values in Higher Edn., AAUP, ACLU, Clergy and Laity Concerned, Phi Beta Kappa, Omicron Delta Kappa. Home: 606 W 122d St New York NY 10027

DRIVER, WILLIAM JOSEPH, lawyer, former government agency official; b. Rochester, N.Y., May 9, 1918; s. John J. and Bridget Anna (Farrell) D.; m. Marian R. McKay, Aug. 18, 1947; children: William Joseph, Kellie McKay. B.B.A., Niagara U., 1941; LL.B., George Washington U., 1952, M.A., 1965. Dir. compensation and pension service, VA, Washington, 1956-59, chief benefits dir., 1959-61, dep. adminstr. vets. affairs, 1961-65, adminstr. vets. affairs, 1965-69; pres. Mfg. Chemists Assn., 1969-78; practice law, Washington, 1978-79; commr. Social Security Adminstrn., Washington, 1980-81; Mem. Pres.'s Council Aging, 1965-69, Pres.'s Com. Employment Physically Handicapped, 1965-69, Pres.'s Com. on Health Manpower, 1967-69; chmn. Va. Gov.'s Bd. on Aging, 1981—. Served to lt. col. U.S. Army, 1941-45; Served to lt. col. U.S. Army, 1951-53. Decorated Legion of Merit, Bronze Star; Order Brit. Empire; Croix de Guerre, France; recipient Meritorious Service medal VA, 1957, Exceptional Service medal, 1960, Career Service award Nat. Civil Service League, 1964, Achievement award Soc. Advancement Mgmt., 1965; Alumni Achievement award George Washington U., 1967. Mem. D.C. Bar Assn. Home: 215 W Columbia St Falls Church VA 22046

DRIVER, WILLIAM RAYMOND, JR., banker; b. Germantown, Pa., Nov. 1907; s. William R. and Mary (Swift) D.; m. Charlotte I. Noyes, Apr. 9, 1937; children: Sarah J. Midgette, William R. III, Dorothy Q., Mary S., Emily N. A.B., Harvard, 1929, M.B.A., 1933; D. Music (hon.), New Eng. Conservatory Music, 1981. With Colo. Nat. Bank, 1930-31, Central Hanover Bank & Trust Co., N.Y.C., 1933-34; sec.-treas. 2 divs. Am. Pulp & Paper Assn., 1934-36; asst. cashier Bank of Manhattan Co., 1938-43, asst. v.p., 1943-46, v.p., 1946, Chase Manhattan Bank, 1946-60; partner Brown Bros. Harriman & Co., 1961—; corporator, hon. trustee Suffolk Franklin Savs. Bank. Incorporating mem. United Way of Mass. Bay; trustee New Eng. Conservatory of Music; life trustee, mem. exec. com., chmn. fin. com. Museum of Sci.; hon. trustee, corporator Northeastern U.; mem. corp. Mass. Gen. Hosp. Episcopalian. Clubs: Dedham Country and Polo; Harvard, Somerset, Commercial (Boston); The Country; Harvard (N.Y.C.). Home: 1184 South St Needham MA 02192 Office: 40 Water St Boston MA 02109

DROBILE, JAMES ALBERT, lawyer, chemical engineer; b. Germantown, Pa., Sept. 29, 1927; s. Albert William and Theresa (Janson) D.; m. Dorothy E. McGillicuddy, Oct. 8, 1955; children: Patricia Elizabeth, Margaret Theresa, James Albert, Mary Cornelia, Katharine Frances. B.S. in Chem. Engring, Villanova U., 1949, S.M., Mass. Inst. Tech., 1950; LL.B., Temple U., 1960. Bar: Pa. 1961, D.C. 1962; registered profl. engr. Pa. Various engring. positions, 1950-56; patent agt. then atty. Sun Oil Co., Phila., 1956-61; assoc., then partner firm Schnader, Harrison, Segal & Lewis, Phila., 1961—, mng. partner, 1968-71, exec. com., 1983—. Mem. adv. bd. lay trustees Villanova U., 1966-67, mem. devel. council, 1967-76, chmn. exec. bd., 1969-70, trustee, 1976—, chmn. nominating and by-laws com., mem. exec. com.; mem. ednl. council MIT, 1972-78; treas. Phila. Engring. Found., 1967—; mem. Radnor Twp. (Pa.) CSC, 1969—. Served with USNR, 1945-46. Recipient Morehouse award Villanova U., 1974, Alumni medal, 1974. Mem. ABA, Pa. Bar Assn. (spl. task force to rev. Pa. atty. gen. 1971), Phila. Bar Assn., Am. Patent Law Assn., Phila Patent Law Assn. (bd. govs. 1965-67, 80—, chmn. antitrust and misuse com. 1969-72, 76-77, sec. 1972-74, v.p. 1977-78, pres.-elect 1978-79, pres. 1979-80), Phila. Jr. Bar Assn. (exec. com. 1962-64), U.S. Trademark Assn. (chmn. state trademark com. 1977-79, dir. 1979—), Nat. Soc. Profl. Engrs., Pa. Soc. Profl. Engrs. (past dir., v.p. Phila. chpt.), Am. Inst. Chem. Engrs., Geog. Soc. Phila. (past bd. dirs., v.p. 1974-76, pres.-elect 1976-78, pres. 1978-81), Sigma Xi, Phi Alpha Delta, Sigma Nu, Tau Beta Pi. Roman Catholic. Clubs: Engrs. Phila (past pres., past bd. dirs.), Overbrook Golf, Urban, Union League (Phila.); Nat. Lawyers (Washington); Eagles Mere Country. Home: 401 Audubon Ave Wayne PA 19087 Office: 1600 Market St Suite 3600 Philadelphia PA 19103

DROESSLER, EARL GEORGE, meterologist; b. Dubuque, Iowa, Jan. 14, 1920; s. George Joseph and Mary Elizabeth (Steffes) D.; m. Virginia Kittridge Hastings, Sept. 17, 1944 (dec. Dec. 1947); 1 dau., Carol Joan; m. Carol Stoops, June 29, 1957; children: Maureen, Christopher, Mary Doran and Martha Gaylord (twins). A.B., Loras Coll., 1942, D.Sc., 1958; Naval Aerological Engr., U.S. Naval Post Grad. Sch., 1944; postgrad. (Fulbright fellow meterology), U. Oslo, 1950-51. Meterologist Office Naval Research, 1946-52; exec. dir., com. on geophysics and geography Office Asst. Sec. Def. (research and devel.), 1952-53, exec. sec. coordinating com. on gen. scis., 1954-58; program dir. atmospheric scis. program NSF, 1958-66; prof. atmospheric scis., v.p. research SUNY, Albany, 1966-71; prof. geoscis., adminstrv. dean for research N.C. State U. at Raleigh, 1971-79; dir. univ. affairs NOAA, Dept. Commerce, Washington, 1979—; mem. Oak Ridge Associated Univs. Council, 1974-79, bd. dirs., 1975-79, exec. com., 1978-79; Dept. Def. rep. U.S. adv. com. on weather control, 1953-57; mem. U.S. nat. com. IGY, 1955-64; vis. research fellow radio-physics div. CSIRO, Sydney, Australia, 1963-64; mem. N.C. Bd. Sci. and Tech., 1971-79, N.Am. Interstate Weather Modification Council, 1975-77; co-chmn. NSF Weather Modification Adv. Panel, 1975-77. Assoc. editor: Jour. Geophys. Research, 1966-68; exec. editor: Weatherwise, 1978—; contbr. articles to profl. jours. Trustee-at-large Univ. Corp. for Atmospheric Research, chmn. bd. trustees, 1969-73; trustee Dudley Obs., 1968-71, Triangle U. Center for Advanced Studies, Inc., 1976-79; bd. counselors Inst. on Man and Sci., 1974—; bd. govs. Research Triangle Inst., 1973-79, exec. com., 1975-79. Joined USN, 1942; commd. ensign, 1943; advanced through grades to lt. comdr., separated, 1947. Fellow Am. Geophys. Union, Am. Meterol. Soc. (councilor 1960-62, chmn. sci. and technol. activities commn. 1974-82, pres. 1983), AAAS; mem. Nat. Assn. State Univs. and Land-Grant Colls. (com. environ. and energy 1977-79), Sigma Xi, Delta Epsilon Sigma. Roman Catholic. Club: Cosmos (Washington). Office: NOAA Dept Commerce Washington DC 20230

DROGHEDA, EARL OF (MOORE CHARLES GARRETT PONSONBY), newspaperman; b. London, Eng., Apr. 23, 1910; s. Earl of Drogheda and Kathleen (Pelham-Burn) M.; m. Joan Carr, May 17, 1935; 1 son, Dermot (Viscount Moore). Student, Cambridge U., 1929-30. With Financial News, 1933, dir., 1938; following merger with Financial Times, became mng. dir. Financial Times, Ltd., 1945-71, chmn., 1971-75; chmn. Henry Sotheran Ltd., Clifton Nurseries Ltd.; dir. Economist Newspaper, Ltd. Chmn. Royal Opera House, Covent Garden, 1958-74, Royal Ballet Sch.; Asst. sec. Brit. Ministry of Prodn., 1941. Served as capt. Brit. Army, 1939. Mem. Inst. Dirs. (pres. 1975-76). Home: Parkside House Englefield Green Surrey SW 1 England

DROHAN, THOMAS H., investment management executive; b. Boston, Dec. 5, 1936. B.S., Holy Cross Coll., 1959; J.D., Suffolk U., 1967. Bar: Mass. 1967. Asst. clerk 1st U.S. Dist. Ct., So. Middlesex, Framingham, Mass., 1967-68; sole practice, Quincy, Mass., 1968-69; staff asst. John Hancock Mut. Life Ins. Co., Boston, 1969-74, legal cons., 1974-78; corp. sec. John Hancock Advisers, Inc., Boston, 1978-82, v.p., sec., 1982—. Club: Hingham Yacht (Mass.). Office: John Hancock Advisers Inc John Hancock Pl PO Box 111 Boston MA 02117

DROSDOFF, DANIEL AARON, wire service editor; b. Gainesville, Fla., Feb. 14, 1941; s. Matthew and Sarah (Max) D.; m. Maria Cecilia Bolognesi, Mar. 26, 1968; 1 son, David Joel. B.A., U. Wis., Madison, 1963, M.A. in History; M.S. in Journalism, Columbia U., 1965; Ph.D. in History, U. LaPlata, Argentina, 1973. Reporter Balt. Sun, 1965-67; news editor UPI, Buenos Aires, 1967-70, Brazil, 1970-73, cables desk editor, N.Y.C., 1973-75, Caribbean div. mgr., San Juan, P.R., 1975-80, news editor for Latin Am., N.Y.C., 1980-83, sr. editor for Latin Am., Buenos Aires, Argentina, 1983—. Author: The Government of Cows, 1972. Inter-Am. Press Assn. scholar, Argentina, 1967. Home: Federico Lacroze 2368 Segundo Piso 1426 Buenos Aires Argentina Office: United Press International Ave Belgrano 271 Primero Piso Buenos Aires Argentina

DROSSOS, ANGELO JOHN, investment company executive; b. San Antonio, Oct. 31, 1928; s. John Angelo and Demetra (Rigopoulos) D.; m. Lillie Fotenopulos, Dec. 4, 1960; children: Debra, John. Student, U. Tex., 1946-47, St. Mary's U., San Antonio, 1950, postgrad. in law, 1956-57. With Shearson, Hammill & Co. (merged with Shearson Hayden, Stone, Inc. 1974, now Dean Witter Reynolds, Inc.), San Antonio, 1963—; now sr. v.p. Dean Witter Reynolds, Inc.; pres. San Antonio Spurs; chmn. exec. com. SLM Corp. Chmn. bd. dirs. YMCA; pres. bd. dirs. St. Sophia Greek Orthodox Ch., San Antonio.; trustee St. Mary's U., San Antonio, 1983—. Served with U.S. Army, 1950-52. Mem. Nat. Basketball Assn. (dir., Exec. of Year 1978). Home: 7614 Woodhaven St San Antonio TX 78209 Office: 700 N St Mary's St Suite 412 San Antonio TX 78205 *Every failure or disaster will eventually be directly or indirectly responsible for a future success or accomplishment.*

DROTNING, JOHN EVAN, industrial relations specialist; b. N.Y.C., Jan. 20, 1932; s. Henry O. and Mary (Keating) D.; m. Charleen Ann Dorwald, June 20, 1959; children: Lucy E., Anne C., Sarah K., Henry O. Student, Cornell U., 1950-53; B.A., U. Rochester, 1958; M.B.A., U. Chgo., 1959, Ph.D., 1964. Asst. prof. indsl. relations SUNY, Buffalo, 1964-69, prof., 1969-72; prof. indsl. relations, asso. dean Sch. Indsl. and Labor Relations, Cornell U., 1972-76; prof. indsl. relations, head div. indsl. relations Sch. Mgmt., Case Western Res. U., 1976—; labor arbitrator, mediator, factfinder; vis. prof. indsl. mgmt. Krannert Grad. Sch., Purdue U., spring 1967; vis. prof. indsl. relations U. Wis., spring, 1971, U. Otago, N. Z., fall 1971. Served with U.S. Army, 1954-56. Mem. Nat. Acad. Arbitrators, Indsl. Relations Research Assn., Am. Arbitration Assn., Soc. for Profls. in Dispute Resolution. Clubs: Rockwell Springs Trout, Erie Yacht, Cleve. Racquet. Office: Sch Mgmt Case Western Res U Cleveland OH 44106

DROUIN, HUBERT E., association executive; b. Cornwall, Ont., Can., Oct. 21, 1942; s. Romeo Fabien and Laurette (Landriault) D.; m. Diane Drouin, July 8, 1967; 1 son, Paul. Ed., St. Patrick's Coll., Ottawa, Ont. Comml. asst. Bell Gen., Cornwall, 1965-69; mgr. bus. office Bell Can., Ottawa, 1969-71; exec. sec. Can. Lung Assn., Ottawa, 1971-79; exec. dir. Can. Dental Assn., Ottawa, 1979—; trustee Can. Fund for Dental Edn. Designer Can. Christmas Seal, 1975. Home: 2419 Wyndale Crescent Ottawa ON Canada K1H 8J2 Office: Can Dental Assn. 1815 Alta Vista Dr Ottawa ON Canada K1G 3Y6

DROUIN, MARIE-JOSEE, economist; b. Ottawa, Ont., Can., Sept. 11, 1949; d. Gaëtan and Anne D. B.A. in Econs, U. Que., Montreal, 1970; M.A., U. Ottawa, 1973. Fin. analyst Power Corp. Can. Ltd., 1969-70; spl. asst. to solicitor gen. Can., also to minister supply and services Govt. of Can., 1971-73; exec. dir. Hudson Inst. Can., Montreal, 1973—, Hudson Inst. Europe, 1983—; dir., mem. exec. com. Gen. Trust Can. Ltd.; bd. dirs. Social Sci. and Humanities Research Council Can.; mem. Communications Research Adv. Bd.; columnist The Gazette, Montreal; mem. bd. economists Maclean's; dir. Mediacom Ltd., L'Alliance Cie d'Assurance, Lise Watier Inc. Co-author: Canada Has a Future, 1978. Club: Forest and Stream (Dorval, Que.). Office: 666 Sherbrooke St W Suite 807 Montreal H3A 1E7 Canada

DROWN, GARY KIDD, life insurance company executive; b. Des Moines, Dec. 3, 1932; s. Hampton Kidd and Mary (Nicola) D.; m. Patricia Ann Walston Johnson, Nov. 30, 1968; children by previous marriage: Debra Sue, Catherine Louise, Paula Marie; stepdaus.—Bonnie Sue, Laura Jeanne. B.S. in Bus. Adminstrn. with gen. honors, Drake U., 1955; postgrad. bus. mgmt., Ohio State U., 1962-63. With Am. Asso. Ins. Cos., 1949-55; with Ohio Nat. Life Ins. Co., Cin., 1955-73; v.p. adminstrn. Indpls. Life Ins. Co., 1973—. Contbr. articles to profl. jours. Chmn. bd. pensions So. Ind. Conf., United Meth. Ch. Fellow Soc. Actuaries; mem. Am. Acad. Actuaries (enrolled actuary), Beta Gamma Sigma, Kappa Mu Epsilon, Omicron Delta Kappa, Delta Sigma Pi. Home: 18 Rolling Springs Ct Carmel IN 46032 Office: 2960 N Meridian St Indianapolis IN 46208

DROWOTA, FRANK F., justice Tenn. Supreme Ct.; b. Williamsburg, Ky., July 7, 1938; (married); 2 children. B.A., Vanderbilt U., 1960, J.D., 1965. Practice law, 1965-70; chancellor Tenn. Chancery Ct. Div. 7, 1970-74; judge Tenn. Ct. Appeals, Middle Tenn. Div., 1974-80; asso. justice Tenn. Supreme Ct., 1980—. Served with USN, 1960-62. Office: Supreme Ct Bldg 401 7th Ave N Nashville TN 37219

DROZ, HENRY, distribution company executive; b. Detroit, Sept. 26, 1926; s. Joseph and Katie (Zallman) D.; m. June Jacyno, May 31, 1959; 1 dau., Kathy Ann. B.A., Wayne State U., Detroit, 1950. Br. mgr. Decca Distbg. Corp., Detroit, 1952-54; pres. Arc Distbg. Co., Detroit, 1954-63; vice pres. Handleman Co., Detroit, 1963-72; v.p. Warner Elektra Atlantic Corp., Burbank, Calif., 1973-77, pres., 1977—. Pres. music chpt. City of Hope, 1978-80, trustee, 1979—, chmn. bd. Music chpt., 1980-82. Served with AUS, 1945-46. Mem.

Sigma Alpha Mu. Home: 4155 Alonzo Ave Encino CA 91316 Office: 111 N Hollywoodway Burbank CA 91505

DROZAK, FRANK, union executive. Student pubs. schs. Shipyard worker, Mobile, Ala.; organizer Port of Mobile, Seafarers Internat. Union, port agt. for union, Phila., from 1964, rep. West Coast, San Francisco, v.p., from 1965, v.p. in charge contracts, Camp Springs, Md., 1972—; pres. maritime trades dept. AFL-CIO and Seafarers Internat. Union N.Am., 1980—; mem. AFL-CIO Exec. Council; chmn. Gen. Pres. Offshore Com.; dir. Nat. Maritime Council; hon. chmn. Am. Trade Union Council for Histadrut; mem. labor adv. bd. Am. Income Life Ins. Co. Active United Way of Tri-State N.Y.; trustee Human Resources Devel. Inst.; nat. bd. dirs. A. Philip Randolph Inst. Office: Seafarers Internat Union 5201 Auth Way Camp Springs MD 20746 *

DRUCK, KALMAN BRESCHEL, public relations counselor; b. Scranton, Pa., Dec. 6, 1914; s. Jacob L. and Mabelle (Breschel) D.; m. Pearl Spiro, Nov. 26, 1936; children: Ellen Druck Mirtz, Nancy Druck Brassem. B.S. in Journalism, magna cum laude, Syracuse U., 1936. With Hearst Enterprises, 1936-39, Carl Byoir & Assos., 1939-59; pres. Harshe-Rotman & Druck, Inc., N.Y.C., 1960—, chmn. exec. com., 1973—, vice chmn., 1979; prin. Kalman B. Druck, Inc., 1981—; supr. courses public relations Baruch Sch. Bus., CCNY, 1939-55; mem. adv. com. schs. communications Syracuse U., Boston U. Bd. dirs. Union Am. Hebrew Congregations, 1956-71, N.Y. Fedn. Jewish Philanthropies, 1957-72, Freedoms Found. at Valley Forge; bd. govs. Am. Jewish Com.; mem. civilian public relations adv. com. U.S. Mil. Acad., West Point, N.Y.; trustee Found. Pub. Relations Research and Edn., 1981—. Named Public Relations Profl. of Year, 1966; recipient Disting. Alumnus Centennial medal Syracuse U., 1970. Mem. Public Relations Soc. Am. (pres. N.Y.C. 1953-55, nat. chmn. 1972, chmn. com. on profl. devel. 1979-80). Clubs: Quaker Ridge Golf (Scarsdale, N.Y.); Banyan (Palm Beach, Fla.). Home: 2780 S Ocean Blvd Palm Beach Fl 33480 2 Winding Brook Drive Larchmont NY 10538

DRUCKER, BERTRAM MORRIS, educator; b. N.Y.C., Oct. 6, 1919; s. Max and Ray (Friedberg) D. A.B., U. N.C., 1940, M.A., 1946, Ph.D., 1953. Instr. U. N.C., 1943-49; grad. fellow Oak Ridge Inst. Nuclear Studies, 1951-53; faculty Ga. Inst. Tech., 1953—, prof. math., 1962-80, prof. emeritus, 1980—; dir. Sch. Math., 1962-7O. Home: 392 Huntsman Way Marietta GA 30067

DRUCKER, DANIEL CHARLES, engineer, dean; b. N.Y.C., June 3, 1918; s. Moses Abraham and Henrietta (Weinstein) D.; m. Ann Bodin, Aug. l9, 1939; children: R. David, Mady. B.S., Columbia U., 1937, C.E., 1938, Ph.D., 1940; D.Engring. (hon.), Lehigh U., 1976, D.Sc. in Tech., Technion, Israel Inst. Tech., 1983. Instr. Cornell U., 194O-43; supr. Armour Research Found., Chgo., 1943-45; asst. prof. Ill. Tech., 1946-47; assoc. prof. Brown U., Providence, 1947-50, prof., 1950-64, L. Herbert Ballou Univ. prof., 1964-68, chmn. div. engring., 1953-59, chmn. phys. scis. council, 1960-63; dean Coll. Engring., U. Ill., Urbana, 1968—; Marburg lectr. ASTM, 1966; Mem., past chmn. U.S. Nat. Com. on Theoretical and Applied Mechanics; treas. Internat. Union Theoretical and Applied Mechanics, 1972-80, pres., 1980-84; mem. gen. com. Internat. Council Sci. Unions; past chmn. adv. com. for engring. NSF; hon. chmn. 3d SESA Internat. Congress on Exptl. Mechanics. Author: Introduction to Mechanics of Deformable Solids, 1967; Contbr. chpts. in tech. books, also tech. papers to mech. and sci. jours. Guggenheim fellow, 1960-61; NATO Sr. Sci. fellow, 1968; Fulbright travel grantee, 1968; Gustave Trasenster medal U. Liège, Belgium, 1979; Thomas Egleston medal Columbia U. Sch. Engring. and Applied Sci., 1978. Fellow ASME (chmn. applied mechanics div. 1963-64, v.p. policy bd. communications 1969-71, pres. 1973-74, Timoshenko medal 1983), Am. Acad. Mechanics (past pres.), Am. Acad. Arts and Scis. (mem. Midwest Council), AAAS (past chmn. sect. engring., mem. council 1980), Am. Inst. Aero. and Astronautical Scis. (asso. fellow), ASCE (von Karman medal 1966, past pres. New Eng. council, past pres. Providence sect., past chmn. exec. com. engring. mechanics div.); mem. Nat., R.I., Ill. socs. profl engrs., Soc. Exptl. Stress Analysis (hon.; past pres., W. M. Murray lectr. 1967, M.M. Frocht award 1971), Am. Technion Soc. (past pres. So. N.E. chpt.), Soc. of Rheology, Am. Soc. Engring. Edn. (charter fellow mem., past 1st v.p., past chmn. engring. coll. council, dir., pres. 1981-82, Lamme award 1967), Nat. Acad. Engring. (mem. com. on pub. engring. policy 1972-75), Nat. Acad. Scis. (chmn. subcom. on sci. unions, bd. internat. ops. and programs), Soc. Engring. Sci. (Wiliam Praeger medal 1982), Polish Acad. Scis. (fgn. mem.), Sigma Xi (past pres. Brown U. chpt.), Phi Kappa Phi, Tau Beta Pi, Pi Tau Sigma. Office: 106 Engring Hall U Ill 1308 W Green St Urbana IL 61801

DRUCKER, MIRIAM KOONTZ, psychologist, educator; b. Mechanicsburg, Pa., Feb. 3, 1925; (m), 1957. A.B., Dickinson Coll., 1947; M.A., Emory U., 1948; Ph.D., Peabody Coll., 1955. Counselor psychology Millsaps Coll., 1949-51; instr. Monticello Coll., 1951-52; asst. prof. psychology Agnes Scott Coll., Decatur, Ga., 1955-58, asso. prof., 1958-62, prof., 1962-80, Charles A. Dana prof., 1981—, former chmn. dept. psychology. Mem. Am. Psychol. Assn. Address: Dept Psychology Agnes Scott Coll Decatur GA 30030

DRUCKER, MORT, commercial artist; b. Bklyn., Mar. 22, 1929; s. Edward and Sarah (Spielvogel) D.; m. Barbara Hellerman, Aug. 28, 1948; children: Laurie Drucker Bachner, Melanie. Student public schs. Staff artist Nat. Periodicals, N.Y.C., 1948-51; freelance artist, 1951—. Artist for: Mad mag; artist: covers for Time mag; also nat. advt. agencies, TV commls. and movie posters. Recipient cert. merit Art Dirs. Club N.Y.; award excellence San Francisco Soc. Communicating Arts; Gold award, 1980. Mem. Graphic Artists Guild. Time covers in Nat. Portrait Gallery, Smithsonian Instn. Address: care Mad Mag 485 Madison Ave New York NY 10022 *

DRUCKER, PETER FERDINAND, writer, consultant, educator; b. Vienna, Austria, Nov. 19, 1909; came to U.S., 1937, naturalized, 1943; s. Adolph Bertram and Caroline D.; m. Doris Schmitz, Jan. 16, 1937; children: Kathleen Romola, J. Vincent, Cecily Anne, Joan Agatha. Grad., Gymnasium, Vienna, 1927; LL.D., U. Frankfurt, 1931; 14 hon. doctorates, U.S. and fgn. univs. Economist London Banking House, 1933-37; Am. adviser for Brit. banks, Am. corr. Brit. newspapers, 1937-42, cons. maj. bus. corps., U.S., 1940—; prof. philosophy, politics Bennington Coll., 1942-49; prof. mgmt. NYU, 1950-72, chmn. mgmt. area, 1957-62, disting. univ. lectr., 1972—; Clarke prof. social sci. Claremont Grad. Sch. (Calif.), 1971—; prof. dept art Pomona Coll., Calif., 1979—. Author: The End of Economic Man, 1939, The Future of Industrial Man, 1941, Concept of the Corporation, 1946, The New Society, 1950, Practice of Management, 1954, America's Next Twenty Years, 1957, The Landmarks of Tomorrow, 1959, Managing for Results, 1962, The Effective Executive, 1966, The Age of Discontinuity, 1969, Technology; Management and Society, 1970, Men, Ideas and Politics, 1971, Management: Tasks, Responsibilities, Practices, 1974, The Unseen Revolution: How Pension Fund Socialism Came to America, 1976, People and Performance, 1977, Management, An Overview, 1978, Adventures of a Bystander, 1979, Managing in Turbulent Times, 1980, Toward the Next Economics and Other Essays, 1981, The Changing World of the Executive, 1982; (fiction) The Last of All Possible Worlds, 1982, The Temptation to Dr. Good, 1984; producer: movie series The Effective Executive, 1969, Managing Discontinuity, 1971, The Manager and the Organization, 1977, Managing for Tomorrow, 1981. Recipient Parlin Meml. medal Am. Mktg. Assn., 1957; gold medal Internat. U. Social Studies, Rome, 1957; Wallace Clark Internat. Mgmt. medal, 1963; Hegemann medal, West Germany, 1966; Taylor Key Soc. for Advancement Mgmt., 1967; Presdl. citation NYU, 1969; CIOS Internat. Mgmt. gold medal, 1972. Fellow AAAS (council), Internat., Am. acads. mgmt., Brit. Inst. Mgmt. (hon.), Am. Acad. Arts and Scis.; mem. Soc. for History Tech. (pres. 1965-66), Nat. Acad. Pub. Adminstrn. (hon.).

DRUCKER, WILLIAM RICHARD, surgeon; b. Chgo., Apr. 5, 1922; s. Henry William and Mary Cathleen (Larzelere) D.; m. Barbara Ruth Victor, Sept. 27, 1947; children—John Michael, Robert Patrick, David Victor, Nancy Ann. B.S., Harvard, 1943; M.D., Johns Hopkins, 1946. Diplomate: Am. Bd. Surgery. Intern Johns Hopkins U., Balt., 1946-47; asst. resident in medicine Yale U. Sch. Medicine, New Haven, 1949-50; resident in surgery Case Western Reserve U. Sch. Medicine, Cleve., 1951-54, mem. faculty, 1954-66; prof., chmn. dept. surgery U. Toronto, 1966-72; surgeon-in-chief Toronto Gen. Hosp., 1966-72; prof. surgery, dean U. Va. Sch. Medicine, Charlottesville, 1972-77; prof., chmn. dept. surgery Med. Center, U. Rochester, N.Y., 1977—. Edit. bd.: Jour. Trauma; Contbr. profl. jours. Served with USNR, 1947-49. Markle scholar; Findlay scholar; A.C.S.-Royal Surgeons Can. fellow. Mem. Soc. for Exptl. Biology and Medicine, Central Soc. Clin. Research, Canadian Physiol. Soc., A.C.S., Am. Surg. Assn., Am. Assn. for Surgery of Trauma, Am. Fedn. for Clin. Research, Phi Beta Kappa, Alpha Omega Alpha. Research in nutrition in surg. patients, metabolic and physiol. changes in shock. Office: Dept Surgery Medical Center Univ Rochester Rochester NY 14642

DRUCKMAN, JACOB RAPHAEL, composer; b. Phila., June 26, 1928; s. Samuel and Miriam (Golder) D.; m. Muriel Helen Topaz, June 5, 1954; children—Karen, Daniel. B.S., Juilliard Sch. Music, 1954, M.S., 1956; student, Ecole Normale de Musique, Paris, 1954-55; studied composition with, Aaron Copland, Louis Gessensway, Peter Mennin, Vincent Persichetti, Bernard Wagenaar. Mem. faculty Juilliard Sch. Music, N.Y.C., 1956-72, Bard Coll., 1961-67; dir. Electronic Music Studio, Yale U. Sch. Music, 1971-72, Bklyn. Coll., 1972-76; prof. composition dept. Yale U. Sch. Music, 1976—; assoc. Columbia-Princeton Electronic Music Center, 1966—; composer-in-residence N.Y. Philharm., 1983—, artistic dir. Horizons '83, 1983. Composer music for: Joffrey City Center Ballet Co.'s Animus, 1969, Valentine, 1971; composer: Jackpot, 1973, Animus I, 1966, Animus II, 1968, Animus III, 1969, String Quarter no. 2, 1966, Incenters, 1968, Windows (orch.), 1972, Lamia, 1974, Mirage, 1976, Chiaroscuro, 1977, Viola Concerto, 1978, Aureole, 1979, Prism, 1980. Bd. dirs. Koussevitzky Found., 1972—, pres., 1980—; chmn. composer-librettist panel Nat. Endowment for Arts, 1980—. Recipient Soc. for Publ. Am. Music award, 1967; Am. Acad./Nat. Inst. Arts and Letters award, 1969; Pulitzer prize for Windows, 1972; citation in music Brandeis U. Creative Arts Commn., 1975; Fulbright grantee, 1954; Guggenheim grantee, 1957, 68; Juilliard String Quartet Commn. through LADO, 1966; Library of Congress, Koussevitzky Found. commn., 1969; Bicentennial Nat. Endowment Arts commn. St. Louis and Cleve. orchs., 1976; N.Y. Philharm. commn. for Viola Concerto, 1978; Aureole, 1979. Mem. Am. Acad. and Inst. Arts and Letters. Office: care Boosey and Hawkes Inc 24 W 57th St New York NY 10019

DRUHOT, THEODORE J(OSEPH), hospital admininntrator; b. Ft. Wayne, Ind., Aug. 13, 1934; s. Joseph John and Martha (Masters) D.; m. Shirley Miday, Aug. 10, 1957; children: John, Denise, Debra, Thomas, Michael, Peter. B.Sc., John Carroll U., 1956; M.B.A., Xavier U., Cin., 1961. Personnel dir. St. Joseph's Hosp., Ft. Wayne, 1958-65; coordinator adminstrv. affairs Hosp. Sisters of Third Order St. Francis, Springfield, Ill., 1965-75; exec. v.p. St. John's Hosp., Springfield, 1975—, bd. dirs., 1975—; bd. dirs. Catholic Care Ctr. Springfield, 1983—; corp. mem. Ill. Blue Cross, Chgo., 1982—. Mem. del. assembly Springfield-Sangamon County United Way, 1981—. Served to capt. U.S. Army, 1956-63. Recipient Disting. Service award Xavier U., 1982, Most Distng. Grad. Hosp. Adminstr. award Xavier U., 1961. Fellow Am. Coll. Hosp. Adminstrs.; mem. Springfield Central Area Devel. Assn. (bd. dirs. 1981—), Cath. Helath Assn. (bd. dirs. 1978-83, medal for Corp. Chmn. 1982), Ill. Hosp. Assn. (bd. dirs. 1983—, Pres.'s plaque 1977). Home: 34 Arabian Spur Springfield IL 62702 Office: Saint John's Hosp 800 E Carpenter St Springfield IL 62769

DRUMMOND, BRIAN P(AUL), business executive; b. Montreal, Que., Can., Feb. 17, 1931; s. Paul Cratherin and Elizabeth Petingill (Sise) D.; m. Althea Margaret McQuee, Oct. 28, 1950; children: Jeffrey Sise, Kim Ann, Willa McQueen. M.B.A, U. Western Ont. With Alcan Aluminum, Montreal, Que., Can., 1953-54, Alcan, Windsor, Ont., Can., 1954-56; with underwriting dept. Greenshields Inc., Montreal, 1958-64, br. mgr., Calgary, Alta., Can., 1964-66, mgr. corp. devel., Montreal, 1966-69, exec. v.p., 1969, pres., 1970-82; vice chmn. Richardson Greenshields of Can. Ltd., Montreal, 1982—; dir. ATCO Ltd., BP Tanker Fin. Can. Ltd., Mt. Bruno Assn. Ltd., Richardson Greenshields of Can Ltd., Trizec Corp. Ltd.; chmn. Montreal Exchange, gov. Dir. Centaur Theatre, Old Exchange Arts Found., Can. Council Christians and Jews; gov. Lower Can. Coll., Montreal Gen. Hosp.; mem. adv. com. Shc. Bus. Adminstrn., U. Western Ont. Mem. Investment Dealers Assn. Can. (past chmn.), Zeta Psi. Anglican. Clubs: Mt. Royal, St. James, Mt. Bruno Country, Montreal Badminton and Squash, Hillside Tennis. Home: 371 Metcalfe Ave Westmount PQ Canada H3Z 2J2 Office: 4 Place Ville Marie Montreal PQ Canada H3B 2E8

DRUMMOND, DONALD FRANCIS, educational administrator; b. Kalamazoo, Sept. 24, 1917; s. Merle Vaughn and Phyllis (DeWindt) D.; m. Elizabeth Ruth Biddle, Aug. 30, 1944; 1 son, Robert Ward. A.B., Western Mich. U., 1938; A.M., U. Mich., 1939, Ph.D., 1949. Instr., asst. prof. history U. Mich., Ann Arbor, 1948-57; prof. history SUNY-Geneseo, 1957-58; head dept. history and social scis. Eastern Mich. U., Ypsilanti, 1958-65, dean Coll. Arts and Scis., 1965-77, 79—, interim v.p. for acad. affairs, 1977-79. Author: Passing of American Neutrality, 1937-41, 1955; co-author: Five Centuries in America, 1964. Served with U.S. Army, 1941-45. Mem. Phi Beta Kappa, Phi Kappa Phi. Republican. Club: Forum (pres. 1971-72). Home: 1813 Waltham Dr Ann Arbor MI 48103 Office: Eastern Mich U Ypsilanti MI 48197

DRUMMOND, GARRY N., mining company executive. Chmn. Ala.-By-Products Corp., Birmingham. Office: Ala By-Products Corp Po Box 10246 Birmingham AL 35202§

DRUMMOND, GERARD KASPER, resource development company executive, lawyer; b. N.Y.C., Oct. 9, 1937; s. John Landells and Margaret Louise (Kasper) D.; m. Donna J. Mason, Sept. 14, 1957 (div. 1976); children: Alexander, Jane, Edmund. B.S., Cornell U., 1959, LL.B. with distinction, 1963. Bar: Oreg. 1963. Assoc. Davies, Biggs, Strayer, Stoel & Boley, Portland, Oreg., 1963-64; assoc., ptnr. Rives, Bonyhadi, Drummond & Smith, Portland, 1964-77; pres. Nerco, Inc., Portland, 1977—; mem. Corp. Policy Group Pacific Power & Light Co., 1979. Pres. Tri-County Met. Transit Dist., Portland, 1974—, bd. dirs., 1974—; mem. Oreg.-Korea Econ. Coop. Com., Portland, 1981—; trustee Reed Coll., Portland, 1982—; bd. dirs. Oreg. Contemporary Theatre, 1983—. 1st lt. USAR, 1959-67. Mem. ABA, Oreg. Bar Assn. Club: Arlington. Home: 1820 N Shore Rd Lake Oswego OR 97034 Office: Nerco Inc 111 SW Columbia St Portland OR 97201

DRUMMOND, IAN MACDONALD, economics educator, author; b. Vancouver, B.C., Can., June 4, 1933; s. George Finlayson and Laura (Milne) D. B.A., U. B.C., Vancouver, 1954; M.A., U. Toronto, Ont., Can., 1955; Ph.D., Yale U., 1959. Instr. Yale U., New Haven, Conn., 1958-60; lectr. U. Toronto, 1960-62, asst. prof. econs., 1962-65, assoc. prof., 1965-71, prof., 1971—, vice dean, 1982—; vis. prof. U. Edinburgh, Scotland, 1975-76; mem. acad. panel Social Scis. and Humanities Research Council, 1979-81. Author: Imperial Economic Policy, 1974, Economics, 1976, The Floating Pound and The Sterling Area, 1981; co-author: Canada Since 1945, 1981. Fellow Royal Soc. Can.; mem. Can. Econs. Soc. (council 1966-69, 80-83), Econ. History Soc., Econ. History Assn., Can. Hist. Assn. Liberal. Anglican. Office: U Toronto 150 Saint George St Toronto ONCanada M5S 1A1

DRUMMOND, JAMES EVERMAN, army officer; b. Stillwater, Okla., July 13, 1932; s. Garrett Bartlett and Frances Elizabeth (Rigdon) D.; m. Helen Wesley Hillman, Dec. 29, 1958; children—James Everman, Sarah Elizabeth. B.S., U.S. Mil. Acad., 1955; M.S., U. Ariz., 1962; postgrad., Army War Coll., 1975; M.A., Central Mich. U., 1982. Commd. 2d lt. U.S. Army, 1955, advanced through grades to maj. gen., served in Europe, Vietnam, Korea, comdr. III Corps Arty., 1979-81, dep. dir. Material Systems Analysis Activity, 1981-82, comdr. TCATA, Ft. Hood, Tex., 1983—; asst. prof. U.S. Mil. Acad., 1962-65. Decorated Legion of Merit with 2 oak leaf clusters, Bronze Star, Air medal, others. Mem. Assn. U.S. Army, Field Arty. Assn., Mil. Order World Wars, Assn. Grads. U.S. Mil. Acad. Presbyterian. Club: Masons. Office: TCATA Fort Hood TX 76544

DRUMMOND, SALLY HAZELET, artist; b. Evanston, Ill., June 4, 1924; d. Craig Potter and Frances (Gillam) Hazlet; m. F. Weichel Drummond, Mar. 25, 1961; 1 son, Craig Potter. Student, Rollins Coll., 1942-44; B.S., Coumbia, 1946; postgrad., Inst. Design, Chgo., 1949-50; M.A., U. Louisville, 1952. Exhibited in one-man shows at, Hadley Gallery, Louisville, 1952, Tanager Gallery, N.Y.C., 1955, 57, 60, Green Gallery, N.Y.C., 1962, Fishbach Gallery, N.Y.C., 1978, Aldrich Mus., Ridgefield, Conn., 1981, Merida Galleries, Louisville, 1982, Artists Space, N.Y.C., 1984; exhibited in group shows at, Am. embassy, Rome, 1953, Fgn. Artists Invitational, Bordighiera, Italy, Am. Artists Ann., 1960, Whitney Mus., N.Y.C., 1958-59, 64, Green Gallery, 1961, Mus. Modern Art, N.Y.C., 1963, Am. Inst. Arts and Letters, N.Y.C., 1982, retrospective exhbn. at, Corcoran Gallery, Washington, 1972; rep. permanent collections at, Mus. Modern Art, Whitney Mus., Met. Mus. Art, N.Y.C., Chase Manhattan Bank, N.Y.C., Speed Mus., Louisville, U. Iowa Mus. Art, Iowa City, Joseph H. Hirshorn, Greenwich, Conn., Hudsons Dept. Store, Detroit, AVCO Corp., Citizens Fidelity Bank and Trust Co., Louisville. Recipient Fulbright grant to Venice, 1952-53; Guggenheim fellow to France, 1967-68.

DRUMMOND, WINSLOW, lawyer; b. Phila., Jan. 29, 1933; s. Winslow Shaw and Dorothy (Moore) D.; m. Katherine Pace; children: Judith L., Kathryn W., Winslow Shaw II. 1A.B., Coll. of Wooster, Ohio, 1954; LL.B., Duke U., 1957. Bar: Ark. 1957, diplomate: Am. Bd. Trial Advocates. Since practiced in, Little Rock; mem. firm Wright, Lindsey & Jennings, 1957—, partner, 1962-83; ptnr. McMath Law Firm, 1982—; faculty Coll. of Advocacy, Hastings Coll. of Law, 1974-79, Nat. Inst. Trial Advocacy, 1979-81; chmn. com. on jury instrns. Ark. Supreme Ct., 1980—. Co-author: Arkansas Model Jury Instructions-Civil, 1965, 2d edit., 1974. Pres., bd. dirs. Urban League Greater Little Rock; bd. dirs. Little Rock Sch. Dist. Served with U.S. Army, 1957-58. Fellow Am. Coll. Trial Lawyers; mem. ABA, Ark. Bar Assn. (past chmn. exec. com., ho. of dels.), Pulaski County Bar Assn., Assn. Trial Lawyers Am., Am. Judicature Soc., Ark. Trial Lawyers Assn., Order of Coif, Phi Alpha Theta. Democrat. Presbyn. Home: 13001 Crabapple Pl Little Rock AR 72209 Office: 711 W 3d St Little Rock AR 72201

DRUMWRIGHT, JAMES ROBERT, banker, lawyer; b. Ripley, Tenn., June 16, 1929; s. Robert Lee and Alma (Chipman) D.; m. Elenita Milbank, Aug. 17, 1962; children: Elizabeth, Alexandra, Eliot. B.A. magna cum laude, Harvard U., 1951, LL.B., 1955; postgrad. (Fulbright scholar), U. London, 1951-52. Bar: Calif. 1955. Asst. legal counsel Bank of Am., San Francisco, 1955-62; adminstrn. officer Internat. Credit Adminstrn., 1962-64; asst. br. mgr. Bank of Am., Paris, 1964-67, br. mgr., Birmingham, Eng., 1967-68, v.p., asst. head European div., San Francisco, 1968-70, regional v.p. East Asia area office, Tokyo, 1970-74; sr. v.p., area gen. mgr. N.Y. corp. service office Bank of Am. Nat. Trust and Savs. Assn., N.Y.C., 1974-78; pres., chief exec. officer internat. banking subs. Bank of Am., N.Y., N.Y.C., 1974-78; pres., chief exec. officer, dir. Provident Nat. Bank, 1978-80; dir. Provident Nat. Corp., 1978-80; chief exec. officer U.S., Credit du Nord, 1982—. Bd. dirs. Greater Phila. Partnership, 1978-82, Pa. Ballet, 1978-81, Bryn Mawr Hosp., 1978-82, Pa. Economy League, 1978—; exec. com. Egypt-U.S. Bus. Council, 1975-78; mem. Can. U.S. Com., 1975-81; trustee Pa. Acad. Fine Arts, 1978-82. Mem. Council Fgn. Relations, Calif. State Bar, C. of C. U.S. (Can.-U.S. com. 1975-81). Clubs: Economic, Harvard, Links (N.Y.C.).

DRURY, ALLEN STUART, author; b. Houston, Sept. 2, 1918; s. Alden Monteith and Flora (Allen) D. B.A., Stanford U., 1939; Litt.D. (hon.), Rollins Coll., 1961. Editor Tulare (Calif.) Bee, 1940-41; county editor Bakersfield Californian, 1941-42; mem. Senate staff U.P.I., Washington, 1943-45; free lance corr., 1946; nation editor Pathfinder mag., 1947-53; nat. staff Washington Evening Star, 1953-54; mem. congl. staff N.Y. Times, 1954-59; polit. contbr. Reader's Digest, 1959-62. Author: Advise and Consent, 1959, A Shade of Difference, 1962, A Senate Journal, 1963, That Summer, 1965, Three Kids in A Cart, 1965, Capable of Honor, 1966, "A Very Strange Society,", 1967, Preserve and Protect, 1968, The Throne of Saturn, 1971, Courage and Hesitation, 1971, Come Nineveh, Come Tyre, 1973, The Promise of Joy, 1975, A God Against the Gods, 1976, Return to Thebes, 1976, Anna Hastings, 1977, Mark Coffin, U.S.S, 1979, Egypt: The Eternal Smile, 1980, The Hill of Summer, 1981, Decision, 1983, The Roads of Earth, 1984. Served with AUS, 1942-43. Recipient Pulitzer prize for fiction Advise and Consent, 1960. Mem. Sigma Delta Chi (nat. award for editorial writing 1941), Alpha Kappa Lambda. Clubs: Nat. Press, Cosmos, University (Washington); Bohemian (San Francisco). Address: care Doubleday & Co Inc 245 Park Ave New York NY 10167

DRURY, CHARLES EDWIN, indsl. exec.; b. Albany, Ill., Feb. 24, 1921; s. William B. and Mary E. (Ege) D.; m. Diana Amy Gardener, Apr. 13, 1946; children: Pamela Drury Kaspers, Charles E., Michael G., Deborah A. B.S. in Mech. Engring., U. Ill., 1949. Trainee central foundry div. Gen. Motors Corp., Danville, Ill., 1949-50; factory mgr. Saginaw (Mich.) malleable iron plant, 1955-56, works mgr. central foundry div., Saginaw, 1963-69; pres., chief operating officer Hayes-Albion Corp., Jackson, Mich., 1969-72, pres., chief exec. officer, 1972-83, chmn. bd., 1976—; dir. City Bank and Trust Co., Nat. Assn. Jackson. Trustee Albion (Mich.) Coll. Served to capt. C.E., AUS, 1942-46. Mem. Iron Castings Soc. (past dir.), Am. Foundrymen's Soc. (nat. dir. 1956-59, v.p. 1979-80, pres. 1980-81), Soc. Automotive Engrs. (past chmn. Mid-Mich. sect.), Mich. C. of C. (dir.), Mich. Srs. Golf Assn. Clubs: 300 of Republican Party, Country, Town (Jackson, Mich.). *

DRURY, CHARLES MILLS, Canadian offical; b. Westmount, Que., Can., May 17, 1912; s. Victor Montague and Pansy (Mills) D.; m. Jane Ferrier Counsell, Sept. 12, 1939 (dec.); children: Diana, Leith, Victor

Montague, Charles Gibbons. Student, Bishop Coll., Royal Mil. Coll.; B.Civil Law, McGill U.; postgrad., U. Paris; D.Sc., N.S. Tech. Coll. Bar: Que. Chief UNRRA Mission Govt. Can., Poland, 1945-47, civil servant, Ottawa, 1947-55; pres. Provincial Transport Co., Montreal, Que., Can., 1955-60; cabinet minister Govt. Can., Ottawa, Ont., 1963-76; chmn. Nat. Capital Commn., Ottawa, 1978—; spl. rep. constl. devel. Govt. Can., N.W. Territories, 1977-81. Pres. Bd. Trade, Montreal, U.N. Assn. Can., Can. Centenary Council; chmn. Can. Inst. Internat. Affairs, Montreal; mem. Parliament Can., Ottawa, 1962-78. Decorated Order of Can. Club: St. James (Montreal). Home: 71 Somerset St W Apt 1002 Ottawa ONCanada K2P 2G2 Office: Nat Capital Commn 161 Laurier St W Ottawa ONCanada K1P 6J6

DRURY, CHIPMAN HAZEN, insurance company executive; b. Montreal, Que., Can., July 15, 1917; s. Victor Montague and Pansy (Mills) D.; m. Dorothy Janet Dobell, Dec. 27, 1945; children: Sally, Penny, Pansy, Reid. Grad., Royal Mil. Coll., 1938; B.Chem. Engring., McGill U., 1939; M.B.A., Harvard, 1947. With Canadian Car Co., Ltd., Montreal, 1947-54, v.p. purchasing, 1952-54; v.p., mgr. Canadian Gen. Transit Co., Ltd., 1954-56, pres., mng. dir., 1956-63; exec. v.p. Dominion Steel & Coal Corp., Montreal, 1963-64; pres. Dosco Steel Ltd., 1964-68; chmn. bd. Avis Transport of Can., Ltd., 1968-73; also dir.; chmn. bd. Guardian Ins. Co. Can., Montreal, 1974-80, Montreal Life Ins. Co., 1974-80; pres., dir. Que. Industries, Ltd. Served to lt. col. Royal Canadian Arty., 1939-45. Mem. Newcomen Soc. N.Am., Montreal Bd. Trade, Engring. Inst. Can., Corp. Profl. Engrs. Que. Clubs: University, Canadian, Canadian Ry., Mt. Bruno Country. Office: Suite 446 1253 McGill College Ave Montreal PQ H3B 2Y5 Canada

DRURY, JOHN W., waste handling company executive; b. 1944. Pres., owner Lakeville San. Service, 1964-68; v.p. Atlas Disposal Service (acquired by Browing-Ferris Industries 1970), Houston, 1967-70; with Browing-Ferris Industries Inc., Houston, 1970—, exec. v.p. waste systems div., mem. mgmt. com., 1972-82, pres., chief operating officer, dir., 1983—. Office: Browning-Ferris Industies Inc 14701 St Marys Ln Houston TX 77079 *

DRURY, RALPH LEON, newspaper executive; b. Washington County, Ky., May 30, 1933; s. James E. and Susie (Griffey) D.; m. Doris Dean Clark, Aug. 27, 1949; children: Lawrence Wayne, Ronald Lee. B.S. in Physics, U. Louisville, 1961, M.S., 1962. Project engr. NASA Apollo Program, Huntsville, Ala., 1962-68; sr. project engr. Courier Jour. & Times, Louisville, 1968-71, dir. engring., 1971-77, v.p., dir. ops., 1977—. Mem. Sigma Xi, Sigma Pi Sigma, Phi Eta Sigma. Home: 1411 N Beckley Station Rd Louisville KY 40223 Office: Courier-Jornal and Louisville Times 525 W Broadway St Louisville KY 40202

DRURY, ROBERT EDWARD, lawyer; b. Detroit, May 19, 1916; s. John Francis and Theresa (Thomas) D.; m. Lois Lochridge, Oct. 16, 1944; children—Robert J., Diane L., Susan J. Student, Highland Park Jr. Coll., 1933-35; LL.B., J.D., U. Detroit, 1938. Bar: Mich. bar 1938. Practiced in, Detroit, 1938-42; investigator Air Force Intelligence, 1942-46; personnel dir. Chrysler Corp., 1946-52; v.p. mfg. Redmond Co., Owosso, Mich., 1952-61; group v.p. King-Seeley Thermos Co., Ann Arbor, Mich., 1961-72, sec., 1969-72; also dir.; of counsel Dobson, Griffin & Barense P.C., 1972—; dir. Bayport State Bank. Pres. County United Found., 1960-61; dir. A.R.C., 1954-60. Club: Rotarian. Home: 9030 Crescent Beach Rd Pigeon MI 48755

DRURY, THOMAS JOSEPH, bishop; b. County Sigo, Ireland, Jan. 4, 1908; s. Michael and Margaret (Lannon) D. Student, St. Benedict's Coll., Atchison, Kans., 1926-29; A.B., Kenrich Sem., 1931. Ordained priest Roman Catholic Ch., 1935; asst. and pastor (Sacred Heart Cathedral), 1935-45, pastor, Lubbock, Tex., 1956-61, bishop, 1961-65, consecrated, 1962, bishop, 1965—; Sec. of Matrimonial Ct., 1935, promotor of justice, from 1938, defender of the bond, 1939-; diocesan dir. Confraternity of Christian Doctrine, 1936, Soc. Propagation of the Faith, from 1936, Cath. Action, Holy Name Soc.; mem. bd. Diocesan Adminstrn., from 1938. Editor, bus. mgr.: Texas Panhandle Register, 1936-38. Chmn. Amarillo council Boy Scouts Am.; v.p. Amarillo Cath. Welfare Bur. Served to maj. Chaplains Corps, USAAF, 1945-47,; Served to maj. Chaplains Corps, USAF, 1949-55. Office: 620 Lipan St Corpus Christi TX 78401 *

DRVOTA, MOJMIR, cinema scientist, author; b. Prague, Czechoslovakia, Jan. 13, 1923; came to U.S., 1958, naturalized, 1963; s. Jan and Zdenka (Krejcikova) D.; m. Jana Kratochvilova, May 18, 1957; 1 dau., Monica. Student, Charles U., 1945-48; Ph.D., Palacky U., 1953; M.S., Columbia U., 1961. Stage dir. state theaters, Czechoslovakia, 1952-56; librarian Bklyn. Pub. Library, 1958-62; asst. prof. dramatic arts Columbia U., N.Y.C., 1962-69; asso. prof. cinema N.Y. U., N.Y.C., 1969-72; prof. cinema Ohio State U., Columbus, 1972—. Script writer, Czechoslovak State Film, Prague, 1948-52; Author: Short Stories, 1946; novels Boarding House for Artists, 1947, Solitaire, 1974, Triptych, 1980; The Constituents of Film Theory, 1973. Mem. Univ. Film Assn., AAUP, Phi Kappa Phi. Home: 2909 Asbury Dr Columbus OH 43221 Office: 156 W 19th Ave Columbus OH 43210 *Everything I stood for was defeated, everything I longed for remained unfulfilled. In the chasm thus rent I captured a glimpse of what is real and what only is, of what is an act of becoming and what is a mere activity. Henceforth, I made it my task to share in the linking effort of those individuals who communicate in the services of reality: the reality screened by objects into which we are situated.*

DRYBURGH, BRUCE SINCLAIR, cement mfg. co. exec.; b. Milw., Nov. 9, 1943; s. Walter S. and Jane E. (Erikson) D.; m. Nancy Surmacz, June 15, 1968; children—Audrey Jo, Jordon Bruce. B.B.A. in Ins, U. Wis., 1967; M.B.A. in Fin, 1968. Fin. planning and control analyst Jos. Schlitz Brewing Co., Milw., 1968-69, mgr. distbn. ops., 1969-70; asst. treas. Fairmont Foods Co., Omaha, 1970-72, Gen. Portland Inc., Dallas, 1972-74, dir. ops. planning, 1974-75, treas., 1975-78, v.p., treas., 1978—. Mem. Nat. Assn. Credit Mgrs., Am. Soc. Ins. Mgmt. Home: 2819 S Surrey St Carrollton TX 75006 Office: PO Box 324 Dallas TX 75221

DRYDEN, FRANKLIN BRIDGES, retired organization executive; b. Frankfort, Ky., June 11, 1915; s. Edwin C. and Edna (Bridges) D.; m. Dorothy Elvy Joyce, June 17, 1946; children: Steven Joyce, Susannah Dale. A.B., U. Ky., 1937. Mktg. specialist Dept. Agr., 1939-53; adminstrv. asst. to U.S. Senator Clements, 1953-57; staff asst. appropriation com. U.S. Senate, 1957-58, 62-64, dep. chief clk. rules and adminstrn. com., 1958-62; dep. dir. Office Emergency Planning. Exec. Office of Pres., 1964-66; asst. to pres. to sr. v.p. Tobacco Institute, 1966-80; sec.-treas. FBD Assos., Inc., 1980—; Exec. dir. Joint Congl. Inaugural Com., 1960-61. Served to capt., inf. AUS, 1942-46; PTO. Decorated Bronze Star, Combat Inf. badge. Mem. Phi Delta Theta. Clubs: Kiwanian., Internat., Capital Democratic (Washington). Home: 3800 N Fairfax Dr Arlington VA 22203

DRYDEN, MARTIN FRANCIS, JR., gas company executive; b. Baton Rouge, July 21, 1915; s. Martin Francis and Elizabeth (Mulvery) D.; m. Mary Mildren Franques, Mar. 9, 1941; children: Mary Frances, Ann Elizabeth. B.A., La. State U. Auditor Gen. Gas Corp., Baton Rouge, v.p., gen. mgr.; pres. Gas & Chems., Inc., Lafayette, La. and Memphis, 1962-69; sr. v.p. Empire Gas Corp., Lebanon, Mo., 1969, pres. Maj., Q.M.C. U.S. Army, 1940-46. Recipient Jefferson award. Mem. Nat. LP Gas Assn. (nat. dir. 1977—), Western LP Gas Assn. (dir. 1975—), Lebanon Area C. of C. (pres. 1981). Republican. Roman Catholic. Office: Empire Gas Corp 1700 Jefferson St S Lebanon MO 65536

DRYDEN, ROBERT EUGENE, lawyer; b. Chanute, Kans., Aug. 20, 1927; s. Calvin William and Mary Alfreda (Foley) D.; m. Jetta Rae Burger, Dec. 19, 1953; children: Lynn Marie, Thomas Calvin. A.A., City Coll., San Francisco, 1947; B.S., U. San Francisco, 1951, J.D., 1954. Bar: Calif. 1955, diplomate: Am. Bd. Trial Advs. Asso. Barfield, Barfield, Dryden & Ruane (and predecessor firm), San Francisco, 1954—, jr. partner, 1960-65, gen. partner, 1965—; lectr. continuing edn. of the bar, 1971-77. Served with USMCR, 1945-46. Fellow Am. Coll. Trial Lawyers; mem. ABA, San Francisco Bar Assn., State Bar Calif., Am. Judicature Soc., Assn. Def. Counsel (dir. 1968-71), Def. Research Inst., Internat. Assn. Ins. Counsel, Fedn. Ins. Counsel, Am. Arbitration Assn., U. San Francisco Law Soc. (mem. exec. com. 1970-72), U. San Francisco Alumni Assn. (bd. govs. 1977), Phi Alpha Delta. Home: 1320 Lasuen Dr Millbrae CA 94030 Office: Suite 3125 1 California St San Francisco CA 94111 *It is my firm belief that achievement of any goal that is worthy of attainment is not happenstance. If truly desired and sought after, industry, dedication, much hard work and faith in the moral principles that must guide your endeavors are mandatory. Without such effort, any good result is undeserved.*

DRYDEN, ROBERT LEWIS, computer services company executive; b. Winnfield, La., Sept. 24, 1933; s. Bernum D. and Gwen (Lewis) Alexander; m. Carole Sue Ebner, Oct. 21, 1956; children: Key Lynde, Sherry Michele, Susan Elaine. A.A.B., Hutchinson Jr. Coll., 1953; B.B.A., Wichita State U., 1959. Cert. data processor. Mktg. positions IBM, White Plains, N.Y., from 1959, dir. strategic planning, until 1980; exec. v.p. Boeing Computer Service Co., Bellevue, Wash., 1980-81; pres. Boeing Computer Services Co., 1981—. Div. chmn. United Way, Seattle, 1983; mem. adv. bd. Seattle Pacific U., 1983, Seattle U., 1982-83. U.S. Army, 1953-56. Mem. Data Processing Mgmt. Assn., Alpha Kappa Psi (sec. 1956-59). Republican. Episcopalian. Home: 14124 SE 44th Bellevue WA 98006 Office: Boeing Computer Service Co 2810 160th Ave SE Bellevue WA 98008

DRYER, DOUGLAS POOLE, emeritus philosophy educator; b. Toronto, Ont., Can., Nov. 27, 1915; s. William Poole and Mabel Elizabeth (McLeod) D.; m. Pegeen Synge, Mar. 22, 1946; children: Dagny, Matthew, Moira; m. Ellice Baird, May 29, 1965; 1 stepdau., Eleanor. A.B. magna cum laude, Harvard U., 1936, A.M., 1939, Ph.D., 1980. Instr. Union Coll., Schenectady, 1939-41; asst. Harvard Coll., 1943-45; lectr. Tufts Coll., 1944-45; lectr. philosophy U. Toronto, 1945-48, asst. prof., 1948-59, assoc. prof., 1959-63, prof., 1963-81, prof. emeritus, 1981—. Author: Kant's Solution for Verification in Metaphysics, 1966, Introduction to J.S. Mill, Essays on Ethics, Religion and Society, 1969. Fellow Royal Soc. Can.; mem. Am. Philos. Assn., Can. Philos. Assn. Clubs: Alpine of Can., Royal Scottish Country Dancing Soc. Home: 61 Lonsdale Rd Toronto ON M4V 1W4 Canada

DRYER, MURRAY, physicist; b. Bridgeport, Conn., Nov. 4, 1925; s. Sol and Sarah (Shapiro) D.; m. Geraldine Gray Goodsell, May 12, 1955; children: Steven Michael, Lisa Gray. Student, U. Conn., 1943-44; B.S., Stanford U., 1949, M.S., 1950; Ph.D., Tel-Aviv U., 1970. Research asst. NACA-NASA Ames Research Ctr., Calif., 1949; aero. research scientist NACA-NASA Lewis Research Ctr., Cleve., 1950-59; assoc. research scientist Martin Marietta Corp., Denver, 1959-65; chief interplanetary physics Space Environ. Lab., NOAA Environ. Research Labs., Boulder, Colo., 1965—; lectr. dept. aerospace engring. scis. U. Colo., 1963-76, dept. astrogeophysics, 1978—; vis. assoc. prof. dept. mech. engring. Colo. State U., 1966-67; mem. com. solar terrestrial research Nat. Acad. Sci., 1976-80. Author: (with others) Solar-Terrestrial Physics in the 1980's, 1981; editor: Solar Observations and Predictions of Solar Activity, 1972, Exploration of the Outer Solar System, 1976, Solar and Interplanetary Dynamics, 1980; spl. issue editor Space Sci. Revs., 1976; contbr. articles to profl. jours. Mem. Am. Phys. Soc., Am. Geophys. Union, AAAS, Sci. Com. Solar-Terrestrial Physics, Internat. Astron. Union, Com. Space Research, AIAA (Space Sci. award 1975), Sigma Xi. Office: Space Environment Lab Mail Code R-E-SE NOAA-ERL Boulder CO 80303

DRYNAN, JOHN JOSEPH, physician; b. Butte, Mont., Feb. 9, 1936; s. Arthur W. and Elsie C. (Bladen) D.; m. Rosalie May Sisich, July 2, 1960; children: Glenda, Deborah, Katherine, Stephanie, Timothy, Thomas, Jennifer. B.S., Carroll Coll., 1958; M.D., Loyola U., 1962. Intern Sacred Heart Hosp., Spokane, Wash., 1962-63, resident, 1963-66; practice medicine specializing in ob-gyn, Helena, Mont., 1966-80; dir. Mont. Dept. Health and Environ. Scis., Helena, Mont., 1981—; cons. staff St. Peter's Hosp., Helena, Mont., 1982—. Served to col. USNR, 1963—. Mem. Am. Pub. Health Soc., Mont. Med. Soc. Democrat. Roman Catholic. Club: Elks. Office: Dept Health and Environ Scis Mont Cogswell Bldg Helena MT 59601 *

DRYSDALE, DONALD SCOTT, sports broadcaster; b. Van Nuys, Calif., July 23, 1936; s. Scott Sumner and Verna Ruth (Ley) D.; m. Eula Eugenia Dubberly, Sept. 27, 1958; 1 dau., Kelly Eugenia. Student pub. schs., Van Nuys. Profl. baseball player Bklyn. and Los Angeles Dodgers, 1954-69; sports broadcaster Montreal Expos, 1970-71, Tex. Rangers, 1972, Calif. Angels, 1973-82, Chgo. White Sox and Sportsvision, 1982—, ABC Sports, N.Y.C., from 1978; runs tng. camp, Vero Beach, Fla. Served with U.S. Army, 1957-58. Recipient Cy Young award, 1962; named to Baseball Hall of Fame, 1984; mem. Nat. League All-Star Team, 9 times. Office: Sportsvision 875 N Michigan Ave Chicago IL 60611 *

DRZEWIENIECKI, WALTER MARIAN, historian, educator; b. Piotrkow Tryb, Poland, Dec. 14, 1914; came to U.S., 1950, naturalized, 1956; s. Edward and Zuzanna (Baranowska) D.; m. Zofia A. Wisniewski, June 10, 1945; 1 dau., Joanna E. B.S., Polish Mil. Acad., 1937; diploma, Brit. Army Staff Coll., 1943; B.S. in History, U. Wis. at Stevens Point, 1957; M.A., U. Chgo., 1958, Ph.D., 1963; postgrad., Russian Inst., Columbia U., 1965-66. Commd. 2d lt. Polish Army, 1937, advanced through grades to col., 1947, co. comdr., Corps and Army operation officer, div. chief of staff, service in, Poland; staff officer Polish Gen. Hdqrs., Middle East, Eng., Italy; ret. Polish Army, 1947; farmer, Can., 1947-50; farmer, also editor Polish lang. weekly Gwiazda Polarna, Stevens Point, Wis., 1954-57; asst. prof. history State U. Coll., Oswego, N.Y., 1959-63, asso. prof. history, Buffalo, 1963-66, prof., 1966-81, prof. emeritus, 1981—, chmn. East European and Slavic studies program, chmn. dept. history, 1969-71; vis. prof. Elizabeth Gaskell Coll., Manchester, Eng., 1975-76, dir. ethnic heritage studies program, 1980-81. Author: The German-Polish Frontier, 1959, Polonica Buffalonensis, 1976, Wrzesniowe wspomnienie podporucznika, 1978; Contbr. articles to profl. jours. Pres. Polish Cultural Found., Inc., 1965-71, v.p., 1971-74, pres., 1975—. Decorated Silver Cross Virtuti Militari, Order Polonia Restituta 2d class with star, Mil. Cross with 3 bars, Golden Cross of Merit with swords,, Silver Cross of Merit with swords, Mil. medal with 1 bar, Cross Monte Cassino, Underground Army Cross, all Poland, Croce al Valor Militare, Italy, Italy Star, Def. medal, war medal, Africa star, Britain, Royal Yugoslav War Cross, Yugoslavia; awarded hon. rank. of maj. gen. Polish Army, 1983; Recipient SUNY at Buffalo 125th Anniversary award, 1971; Creative Writing award Buffalo and Erie County Hist. Soc., 1975; 1st prize for memoirs Polish Acad. Scis., 1977. Mem. Polish Inst. Arts and Sci., Polish Am. Congress, J. Pilsudski Hist. Inst., Polish Inst. London, Polish-Am., Am. hist. assns., Polish Soc. Arts and Scis. Abroad (London), 1Am. Assn. Advancement Slavic Studies, Polish Nat. Alliance, Polish Army Vets. Assn., Polish Arts Club, Polish Gen. Staff Officers Assn., Nat. Ethnic Studies Assembly (v.p.). Home: 337 McKinley Ave Kenmore NY 14217 Office: SUNY Coll 1300 Elmwood Ave Buffalo NY 14222

D'SOUZA, ANTHONY FRANK, mechanical engineering educator, consultant, researcher; b. Bombay, India, May 9, 1921; came to U.S., 1958; s. Manuel Joseph and Laurentina (Ataide) D'S.; m. Cecilia Verdejo, Dec. 28, 1965; children: Geraldine, Raissa. B.E., U. Poona, India, 1954; M.S., U. Notre Dame, 1960; Ph.D., Purdue U., 1963. Jr. engr. Mahindra & Mahindra, Ltd., India, 1954-55; indsl. engr. Internat. Bus. Cons., India, 1955-57; trainee Ransome & Rapier, Ltd., Eng., 1957-58; teaching asst. U. Notre Dame, Ind., 1958-60; research asst. Purdue U., West Lafayette, Ind., 1960-63; from asst. prof. to prof. mech. engring. Ill. Inst. Tech., Chgo., 1963—; cons. Argonne Nat. Labs., 1973—, Par Enterprise, Inc., Fairfax, Va., 1980—. Author: Advanced Dynamics, 1983; contbr. articles to profl. jours. Research grantee NSF, 1963, 70, Dept. of Energy, 1978—, U.S. Air Force Office Sci. Research, 1977—, Assn. Am. R.R.s, 1980-82. Mem. ASME, Sigma Xi, Pi Tau Sigma. Roman Catholic. Home: 2244 W 110th St Chicago IL 60643 Office: Ill Inst Technology Mechanical Engring Dept Chicago IL 60616

DUALL, JOHN WILLIAM, retail company financial executive; b. Uniontown, Pa., Nov. 5, 1928; s. Stephen L. and Anna M. (Duranko) D.; m. Lesley A. Hall, Sept. 2, 1967; children: Stephen J., Elizabeth E. B.S., Temple U., 1956. Retail store controller Sears, Roebuck & Co., Phila., 1955-63; regional retail controller Montgomery Ward & Co., Chgo., 1964-69; sr. v.p., controller Levitz Furniture Corp., Pottstown, Pa., 1969—, dir., Pottstown, 1972—. Dir. United Way of Pottstown, 1973—. Served to 1st lt. U.S. Army, 1951-53. Office: Levitz Furniture Corp 212 High St Pottstown PA 19464

DUANE, MORRIS, lawyer; b. Phila., March 20, 1901; s. Russell and Mary Burnside Morris; m. Maud S. Harrison, June 11, 1927; children: Margaretta Sergeant, Russell. Student, Episcopal Acad., Phila., 1913-15, St. George's Sch., Newport, R.I., 1915-19; A.B., Harvard, 1923; postgrad., U. Pa. Law Sch., 1923-25; LL.B., Stetson U., 1927, LL.D., 1965, Bucknell U., 1967, LaSalle Coll., 1970, Drexel U., 1976; L.H.D., Women's Med. Coll. Pa., 1967; Litt.D., Beaver Coll., 1969. Engaged in gen. practice of law, Phila., 1927—; mem. firm Duane, Morris & Heckscher, 1931-79, of council, 1979—; former dir. Girard Trust Bank, Penn. Mut. Life Ins. Co., Phila. Saving Fund Soc., The Phila. Contributionship; and other corps., Ednl. Facilities Labs., Inc. Author: New Deal in Court, 1934; Contbr. articles to legal and other periodicals. Vice chmn. Cardinal's Com. to Study Phila. Catholic Schs., 1972; mem. Com. on Tri State Regional Devel., Pa., N.J., Del.; Bd. dirs., past co-chmn. Greater Phila. Movement; chmn. Phila. Adv. Council, 1974-77; bd. dirs. Univ. City Sci. Center, United Fund, 1955-69, Phila. Orch. Corp., 1976 Bicentennial Corp., 1967-71, Phila. Urban Coalition; pres., trustee Presser Found.; pres. bd. trustees Episcopal Acad., 1948-51; bd. dirs. Hosp. Survey Com., Phila., 1960-72, chmn., 1960-64, 72; chmn. Christian R. and Mary F. Lindback Found., 1955—; mem. Harvard Fund Council, 1949-55. Served from lt. to comdr. USNR, 1943-45; head materials and resources group, bur. aeros. U.S. Navy, 1944-45; rep. naval aviation on War Prodn. Bd. requirements com., Army and Navy munitions bd. exec. com., 1944-45; mem. Naval Air Res. Adv. Council (chmn.), 1947. Awarded Commendation Ribbon, 1945. Mem. Am. Philos. Soc., Am. Lawn Tennis Assn. (chmn. inter-collegiate com. 1928-33), Am., Pa., Phila. bar assns., Juristic Soc., Com. of Seventy (1938-46), Salvation Army (past mem. exec. bd., Phila.), Delta Psi. Republican. Episcopalian. Clubs: Philadelphia, Gulph Mills Golf, Legal (Phila.); Fly (Cambridge); Sharswood Law (U. Pa.). Home: 439 Garden Ln Bryn Mawr PA 19010 Office: One Franklin Plaza Philadelphia PA 19102

DUANE, THOMAS DAVID, ophthalmologist, educator; b. Peoria, Ill., Oct. 10, 1917; s. Joseph Francis and Alexa (Fischer) D.; m. Julia Ann McElhinney, Mar. 22, 1944; children: Alexa Duane Bresnan, Joseph McElhinney, Rachel Duane Lee, Andrew Thomas. B.S., Harvard U., 1939; M.D., Northwestern U., 1943, M.S., 1944; Ph.D., State U. Iowa, 1948. Diplomate: Am. Bd. Ophthalmology, Am. Bd. Preventive Medicine. Intern Evanston (Ill.) Hosp., 1943-44; resident ophthalmology U. Iowa, 1944-47, instr. physiology, 1947-49; practice medicine, specializing in ophthalmology, Bethlehem, Pa. and Phila., 1949—; instr. physiology U. Pa., 1952-56, instr. ophthalmology, 1958-62; prof. Jefferson Med. Coll., 1962—, chmn. ophthalmology, 1962-81; ophthalmologist-in-chief Wills Eye Hosp., 1973-81, cons. surgeon, 1981—; mem. Nat. Adv. Eye Council; cons. USN, 1958-74, NASA, 1966-74. Author: Ophthalmic Research; USA; Editor: Clinical Ophthalmology, 5 vols, 1976, Biomedical Foundations of Ophthalmology, 3 vols., 1982; Contbr. articles to profl. jours. Served to lt. USNR, 1950-53. Fellow A.C.S.; mem. Am. Bd. Ophthalmology, AMA (chmn. opthalmol. sect.), Am. Acad. Ophthalmology (councillor, residency rev. com.), Assn. Research Ophthalmology, Am. Ophthal. Soc. Home: Bedminster PA 18910 Office: 9th and Walnut Philadelphia PA 19107

DUBA, ARLO DEAN, educational administrator, theology educator; b. Brule County, S.D., Nov. 12, 1929; s. Frank Josef and Alvera Mae (Forman) D.; m. Doreen Elizabeth Eckles, June 18, 1954; children: Paul Douglas, Bruce Franklin, John David, Anne Elizabeth. B.A., U. Dubuque, 1952; B.D., Princeton Theol. Sem., 1955, Ph.D., 1960; postgrad., l'Institut Superieur de Liturgie, Paris, 1968-69. Chaplain, assoc. prof. religion Westminster Choir Coll., 1957-68; dir. chapel, dir. admissions Princeton Theol. Sem., 1969-82; dean, prof. worship U. Dubuque Theol. Sem., 1982—; mem. adminstrn. com. Presbyn. Office of Worship, 1979—. Author: (with Mary F. Carson) Praise God—Worship Through the Year, 1979, Principles of Protestant Worships (in Indonesian), 1980; composer musical settings for psalms, 1980-82. Mem. Liturg. Conf. (bd. dirs. 1978—, exec. com. 1979—), N. Am. Acad. Liturgy (charter mem., exec. bd. 1981-83), Societas Liturgica, Acad. Homiletics. Office: U Dubuque Theol Sem 2000 University Ave Dubuque IA 52001

DU BAIN, MYRON, diversified industry executive; b. Cleve., June 3, 1923; s. Edward D. and Elaine (Byrne) Du B.; m. Alice Elaine Hilliker, Sept. 30, 1944; children—Cynthia Lynn, Donald Aldous. B.A., U. Calif., Berkeley, 1943; grad. exec. program, Stanford Grad. Sch. Bus., 1967. Pres., chief exec. officer, dir. Amfac, Inc., San Francisco, 1983—; dir. Pacific Telephone Co., SRI Internat. Contbg. author: Property and Casualty Handbook, 1960, The Practical Lawyer, 1962. Chmn. bd. dirs. Bay Area Council; mem. adv. council Stanford U. Grad. Sch. Bus.; bd. dirs. San Francisco Opera, San Francisco Symphony; pres., trustee United Way of Bay Area; mem. nat. support council U.S. com. UNICEF; mem. industries adv. com. Advt. Council, Inc.; bd. dirs., past chmn. Invest-In-Am., Inc. Served as officer USNR, 1943-46, 50-52. Mem. Calif. Roundtable (dir.), Newcomen Soc. (chmn. No. Calif. com.). Republican. Episcopalian. Clubs: Bohemian, Pacific Union, Calif. Tennis (San Francisco); Links (N.Y.C.); Lagunitas Country; Coral Beach and Tennis (Bermuda). Office: 50 O'Farrell St San Francisco CA 94108

DU BAR, JULES RAMON, geologist, educator; b. Canton, Ohio, June 30, 1923; s. Joseph Adolphe and Inez Ismay (Simlar) DuB.; m. Susan Stokes Davidson, July 31, 1964; children—Nicole Mae, Scott Johnson. B.S., Kent State U., 1949; M.S., Oreg. State U., 1950; Ph.D., U. Kans., 1957. Instr. geology So. Ill. U., Carbondale, 1951-57; asso. prof. U. Houston, 1957-62, Duke U., Durham, N.C., 1962-64; with Esso Prodn. Research Co., Houston, 1964-67; prof. geology Morehead (Ky.) State U., 1967—, head dept. geosci., 1967-81; v.p. exploration Internat. Resource Devel. Corp., 1981-82; research scientist U. Tex. Bur. Econ. Geology, Austin, 1982—; vis. prof. U. N.C., Chapel Hill, 1963. Contbr. articles to profl. jours. Served with USCGR, 1942-46. NSF grantee, 1959-81; recipient Disting. Researcher medal Morehead State U., 1980. Fellow AAAS, Geol. Soc. Am., Explorers Club; mem. Am. Assn. Petroleum Geologists, Soc. Econ. Mineralogists and Paleontologists, Internat. Paleontol. Union. Home: 12600 Esplanade St Austin TX 78727

DUBBERLY, RONALD ALVAH, library director; b. Jacksonville, Fla., Oct. 25, 1942; s. Chester Alvah and Mary Margaret (Jessup) D.; m. Bonnie Rose Bazemore, June 15, 1963; children: Pamela Rose, Kenneth Alvah. B.A. in History, Jacksonville U., 1964; M.A. in L.S, Fla. State U., 1965. Reader's adviser asst. Jacksonville Pub. Library, 1961-64; reference librarian, br. librarian Baltimore County (Md.) Pub. Library, 1965-67, adminstrv. asst. to dir., 1967-69; dir. Sioux City (Iowa) Pub. Library, 1969-75, Seattle Pub. Library, 1975—; exec. bd. Md. Library Assn., 1969; cons. Iowa State Library, 1970-72; exec. bd. Iowa Library Assn., 1971-73, 75, chmn. legis. com., 1973-75; mem. Wash. Adv. Council Libraries, 1975-77; mem. exec. bd. Urban Libraries Council, 1981-83; chmn. public library principles task force PLA, 1980-82. Editorial bd.: Jour. Library Adminstrn, 1979—. Recipient Spl. Service award Iowa Library Assn., 1975. Mem. ALA (v.p., pres.-elect pub. library assn. 1976-78, pres. 1978-80), Pub. Library Assn. (goals, guidelines and standards com. 1982-84), Am. Library Trustee Assn. (bd. dirs. 1980-81), Wash. Library Assn., Pacific N.W. Library Assn. Club: Seattle Rotary. Home: 4115 NE 96th St Seattle WA 98115 Office: 1000 4th Ave Seattle WA 98104

DUBE, JEAN-EUDES, Canadian judge; b. Matapedia, Que., Can., Nov. 6, 1926; s. J. Albert and Flore (Poirier) D.; m. Noella Babin, June 25, 1956; children: Rachelle, Jean Francois. B.A., B.Ph., L.P.H., Ottawa U.; B.S. in Fgn. Service, Georgetown U.; B.C.L., U. N.B., LL.D., 1971; D.C.L., U. Moncton, 1973. Bar: apptd. Fed. Queen's counsel 1974, apptd. provincial Queen's counsel 1969. Alderman Campbellton City Council, 1959-63; mem. Canadian Ho. of Commons for Restigouche, N.B., 1962-75; minister vets. affairs, 1968-72, minister pub. works, 1972-74; justice trial div. Fed. Ct. Can., Ottawa, 1975—; judge Ct. Martial Appeal Can., 1975—; Pres. Can. NATO Parliamentary Assn., North Atlantic Assembly, 1967. Home: 1694 Playfair Dr Ottawa ON Canada Office: Supreme Ct Bldg Ottawa ON Canada

DUBE, JOHN, lawyer; b. Montreal, Que., Can., July 14, 1899; came to U.S., 1926, naturalized, 1945; s. Joseph Edmond and Marie Louise (Quintal) D.; m. Liliane Hibbert, 1981; 1 son by previous marriage, John Edmund. B.L., B.S., Montreal U., 1920, B.C.L., 1923; licentiate in Civil Law, Paris U., 1924; postgrad., U. Oxford, 1925. Bar: Montreal 1925, N.Y. 1945, apptd. king's counsel 1941, now Queen's counsel 1941, U.S. Supreme Ct. 1941, U.S. Treasury Dept 1941. Assoc. Coudert Bros., N.Y.C. and Paris office, 1926-32, Nice, France, 1933-40; practice, N.Y.C., 1945—; Past pres. Le Moulin Legumes Corp., Wilmington, Del.; past v.p. Bengue, Inc., Union City, N.J.; consul of Monaco, N.Y.C., 1949—; now consul gen.; dep. permanent observer for Monaco at UN, 1956-71, permanent observer, 1971—. Past trustee Soc. Rehab. Facially Disfigured. Decorated Comdr. Order of Grimaldi, Monaco). Mem. Union Interalliée (Paris), Assn. Bar City of N.Y., Am., Internat. bar assns., Am. Fgn. Law Assn., Am. Soc. Internat. Law, Soc. Fgn. Consuls, Société de Legislation Comparee, Confrerie des Chevaliers du Tastevin (comdr.). Clubs: Ardsley Country, Paris American, Rockefeller Center Luncheon, Sky (assoc.). Home: 340 E 64th St Apt 9U New York NY 10021

DUBERG, JOHN EDWARD, aero. engr.; b. N.Y.C., Nov. 30, 1917; s. Charles Augustus and Mary (Blake) D.; m. Mary Louise Andrews, June 11, 1943; children—Mary Jane, John Andrews. B.S. in Engring. Manhattan Coll., 1938; M.S., Va. Poly. Inst., 1940; Ph.D., U. Ill., 1948; grad., Fed. Exec. Inst., 1971. Engr. Cauldwell-Wingate Builders, N.Y.C., 1938-39; research asst. U. Ill., 1940-43; research engr. NASA, 1943-46; chief structures Langley Labs., NASA, Hampton, Va., 1948-56; research engr. Standard Oil Co. Ind., 1946-48; with Ford Aeros., Glendale, Calif., 1956-57; mem. faculty U. Ill., 1957-59; mem. staff Langley Research Center, NASA, 1959-79, assoc. dir., 1968-79; research prof. aeros. George Washington U., 1979—; dir. Joint Inst. Advanced Flight Scis., 1971-79; mem. materials adv. bd. Nat. Acad. Sci., 1950; mem. subcom. profl. and sci. manpower Dept. Labor, 1971; mem. indsl. adv. com. U. Va., 1978-80; president's adv. council Christopher Newport Coll., 1973-76, vice chmn., 1976; dir. Newport News Savs. & Loan Assn. Contbr. articles to profl. jours., chpts. to books. Trustee United Way Va. Peninsula, 1963—. Recipient Outstanding Leadership award NASA, 1977. Fellow AIAA (DeFlorez award 1977), AAAS; mem. Va. Acad. Scis., N.Y. Acad. Scis., Am. Soc. Engring. Edn. (dir.), Engrs. Club Peninsula Peninsula (pres. 1955), Soc. Engring. Scis. (dir.). Episcopalian. Clubs: James River Country, Rotary (pres. Newport News 1967-68). Home: 4 Museum Dr Newport News VA 23601 Office: GWU/JIAFS NASA Langley Research Center M/S 169 Hampton VA 23665

DUBERMAN, MARTIN BAUML, historian; b. N.Y.C., Aug. 6, 1930; s. Joseph M. and Josephine (Bauml) D. B.A., Yale U., 1952; M.A., Harvard U., 1953, Ph.D., 1957. Teaching fellow, Harvard U., 1955-57, instr. history, Yale U., 1957-61, Morse fellow, 1961-62; bicentennial preceptor, asst. prof. Princeton U., 1962-65, asso. prof., 1965-67, prof., 1967-71; Distinguished prof. Lehman Coll., City U. N.Y., 1971—. Author: Charles Frances Adams, 1807-1886, 1961 (Bancroft prize 1962), In White America (Vernon Rice award 1963-64), James Russell Lowell, 1967 (finalist Nat. Book award 1966), The Uncompleted Past, 1969, Black Mountain: An Exploration in Community, 1972; Editor, contbr.: Antislavery Vanguard, 1965; contbr.: Metaphors (play) in Collision Course, 1968, The Memory Bank; plays, 1970, The Recorder (play) in the Best Short Plays of 1970, 1971, The Colonial Dudes (play) in The Best Short Plays of 1972, 1973, Male Armor (plays) Selected Plays 1968-74, 1975, Visions of Kerouac, 1977. Mem. Am. Hist. Assn., Gay Acad. Union, Nat. Gay Task Force, Phi Beta Kappa. Address: 475 W 22 St New York NY 10011

DUBERSTEIN, KENNETH MARC, government official; b. Bklyn., Apr. 21, 1944; s. Aaron D. and Julie C. (Falb) D.; m. Marjorie Dee Parman, Mar. 21, 1970; 1 dau., Jennifer Darie. A.B. in Govt., Franklin and Marshall Coll., 1965; M.A. in Am. Polit. Dynamics, Am. U., 1967. Research asst. to Congressman Fred B. Rooney of Pa., 1965-66, to Senator Jacob K. Javits of N.Y., 1965-67, co-dir. campaign ops., N.Y.C., 1968; adminstrv. asst. to pres. Franklin and Marshall Coll., Lancaster, Pa., 1967-70; congl. liaison officer GSA, Washington, 1970-71, dep. dir. for congl. liaison, 1971-72, dir. congl. affairs, 1972-76; dep. under sec. legis. affairs Dept. Labor, Washington, 1976—. Mem. nat. adv. bd. Odyssey House Drug Rehab. Ctr.; Coll. chmn. Lancaster County United Fund, 1968; exec. com. Lancaster County Rep. Campaign Com., 1968; active campaign John Lindsay for Mayor, N.Y.C., Nelson Rockefeller for Gov., N.Y. Mem. Am. Coll. Pub. Relations Assn., Am. Alumni Council (ednl. fund-raising sch. 1969), Ripon Soc., Zeta Beta Tau (supreme council). Home: 2514 Lindley Terr Rockville MD 20850 Office: Legis Affairs Office 1600 Pennsylvania Ave NW Washington DC 20500

DUBES, GEORGE RICHARD, geneticist; b. Sioux City, Iowa, Oct. 12, 1926; s. George Wesley and Regina Eleanor (Kelleher) D.; m. Margaret Joanne Tumberger, July 25, 1964; children: George Richard, David Frank, Deanna Marie, Kenneth Wesley, Deborah Joanne, Keith Timothy. B.S., Iowa State U., 1949; Ph.D., Calif. Inst. Tech., 1953. Research assoc. McCollum-Pratt Inst. for Research in Micronutrient Elements, Johns Hopkins U., 1953-54; research assoc. sect. virus research dept. pediatrics U. Kans. Sch. Medicine, Kansas City, 1954-56, asst. prof., 1956-60, assoc. prof., 1960-64; head viral genetics Eppley Cancer Inst.-U. Nebr. Med. Ctr., Omaha, 1964-68, assoc. prof. dept. med. microbiology, 1964-81, prof., 1981—; vis. lectr. U. Baghdad, (Iraq), 1977, U. Mosul, 1977. Author: Methods for Transfecting Cells with Nucleic Acids of Animal Viruses; A Review, 1971; contbr. articles to sci. jours. Co-pres. Adams Sch. PTA, Omaha, 1976-77; mem. citizens adv. com. Omaha Pub. Schs., 1977-80. Served with AUS, 1945-46. Fellow AEC, 1951-52, Caltech McCallum, 1951-52; grantee Nat. Inst. Allergy and Infectious Diseases, 1966-69, NIH Gen. Research Support, 1964-72. Mem. Am. Assn. Cancer Research, AAAS, Am. Genetic Assn., Am. Inst. Biol. Scis., Am. Soc. Microbiology (pres. Missouri Valley br. 1983-84), Biometric Soc., Genetics Soc. Am., Nebr. Acad. Scis. (co-chmn. biol. and med. scis. sect. 1983—), N.Y. Acad. Scis., Sigma Xi. Home: 7515 Lawndale St Omaha NE 68134 Office: Dept Medical Microbiology U Nebr Coll Medicine 42d and Dewey Ave Omaha NE 68105

DUBES, RICHARD CHARLES, computer scientist; b. Chgo., Oct. 7, 1934; s. Charles M. and Evelyn G. D.; m. Marylyn Ann Doyle, Apr. 4, 1959; 1 dau., Jennifer. B.S.E.E., U. Ill., 1956; M.S., Mich. State U., 1959, Ph.D., 1962. Mem. tech. staff Hughes Aircraft Co., Culver City, Calif., 1956-57; asst. instr. elec. engring. dept. Mich. State U., East Lansing, 1957-61, instr., 1961-62, grad. fellow, 1962-63, asst. prof., 1963-66, asso. prof., 1966-70, prof. engring. research and computer sci., 1970—. Author: Theory of Applied Probability, 1970; asso. editor: Pattern Recognition, 1978—. Gen. Telephone grad. fellow, 1962. Mem. IEEE, Pattern Recognition Soc., Classification Soc., Sigma Xi. Roman Catholic. Home: 2677 Linden St East Lansing MI 48823 Office: 400 Computer Center Mich State U East Lansing MI 48824

DUBIN, ALVIN, chemist, educator; b. Russia, Jan. 23, 1914; came to U.S., 1923, naturalized, 1935; s. Solomon and Fanny (Beilly) D.; m. Gwennie Goldman, May 18, 1946 (dec. Oct. 1963); m. Beverley P. Barrow, Sept. 16, 1967. B.A., Bklyn. Coll., 1940, M.S., 1942. Diplomate: Am. Bd. Bio Analysts. Chief chem endocrinology Beth-El Hosp., Bklyn., 1938-42, asst. dir. labs., 1942-47; chief biochemist Cook County Hosp. and Hektoen Inst., Chg., 1947-53, dir. biochemistry, 1953-70, Hektoen Inst., 1953—; prof. clin. chemistry Cook County Grad. Sch. Medicine, Chgo., 1958—; asst. prof. dept. biochemistry U. Ill. Coll. Medicine, Chgo., 1960-70; asso. prof. dept. biochemistry Rush Med. Sch., Chgo., 1973-82, prof., 1982—; cons. clin chemistry Oak Forest (Ill.) Hosp., MacNeal Hosp., Berwyn, Ill.; cons. biol. div. Upjohn Pharm. Co., Kalamazoo; cons. Perkin-Elmer Inc. Chmn. Cook County Hosp. fund drive Combined Jewish Appeal. Fellow Nat. Acad. Clin. Biochemistry; mem. Am. Assn. Clin. Chemistry (pres. Chgo. 1955-57, chmn. 17th nat. meeting 1965), Soc. Exptl. Biology and Medicine, A.A.A.S., Am. Inst. Chemists, N.Y. Acad. Scis., Sigma Xi. Home: 6101 N Sheridan Rd E Chicago IL 60660 Office: 627 S Wood St Chicago IL 60612

DUBIN, ARTHUR DETMERS, architect; b. Chgo., Mar. 14, 1923; s. Henry and Anne (Green) D.; m. Lois Amtman, Mar. 10, 1951 (dec. Sept. 1980); children: Peter Arthur, Polly Louise; m. Phyllis Vollen Burman, Nov. 27, 1981; stepchildren: Garry Arthur, Jill Meredyth, David Yale, Eric Vollen. Student, Lake Forest Coll., 1943-44; B.Arch., U. Mich., 1949. Architect, partner Dubin & Dubin (architects and engrs.), Chgo., 1950-65, Dubin, Dubin & Black (architects and engrs.), 1965-66, Dubin, Dubin, Black & Moutoussamy, 1966-78, Dubin, Dubin & Moutoussamy, 1978—; v.p. DDBM, Inc. (constrn. mgmt. cons.), 1975—; v.p., dir. 7537 South Shore Dr. Corp., 7345 South Shore Dr. Corp.; mem. adv. Amtrak, 1972—; gen. partner 340 Wellington Assos., 1962-73; speaker at confs., U.S. and France.; Hon. research asso. Smithsonian Instn., 1975. Author: Some Classic Trains, 1964, More Classic Trains, 1974; author-editor, for N.Am., The Great Trains, 1973; Contbr. articles to mags., Archtl. works include, govtl. bldgs., rail transit stas. and transp. facilities, mil. installations, banks, indsl. plants, schs. and colls., hosps., housing and urban renewal planning. Chmn. Civic Beautification Com., Highland Park, Ill., 1965-74; mem. Bicentennial Commn. Highland Park, 1974-76, Ill. Commn. on High Speed Rail Transit, 1966-68, Met. Housing and Planning Council of Chgo., Nat. Council Archtl. Registration Bds., 1971—; Life mem. Art Inst., Chgo.; trustee NORTRAN, Des Plaines, Ill., 1980—. Served with inf. U.S. Army, 1943-46. Decorated Bronze Star with cluster, Purple Heart. Mem. A.I.A., Ill. Soc. Architects, Am. Pub. Transit Assn., Western Soc. Engrs., Railway and Locomotive Hist. Soc. (bd. dirs. 1960—), Train Collectors Assn. Clubs: Cliff Dwellers (bd. dirs. 1972-75), Builders (pres. 1970-71), Builders (bd. dirs. 1970—), Arts (Chgo.)). Home: 229 Park Ave Highland Park IL 60035 Office: 55 W Wacker Dr Chicago IL 60601 *

DUBIN, CHARLES LEONARD, judge; b. Hamilton, Ont., Can., Apr. 4, 1921; s. Harry and Ethel D.; m. Anne Ruth, Dec. 2, 1951. B.A., U. Toronto, Ont., 1941; LL.B., Osgoode Hall Law Sch., 1944. Bar: Ont. bar 1944, appointed Queen's Counsel 1952. Practiced in, Toronto, 1945-73; judge Ont. Supreme Ct. of Appeal, Toronto, 1973—; Royal commr. to inquire into air safety in Can., 1979; lectr. Osgoode Hall Law Sch., 1945-48. Home: 619 Avenue Rd Apt 1702 Toronto ON Canada M4V 2K6 Office: Osgoode Hall Toronto ON Canada

DUBIN, FRED STANLEY, mechanical engineer, energy consultant; b. Hartford, Conn., Jan. 31, 1914; s. Moses J. and Fannie C. (Siegal) D.; m. Sarah Vaughn, Jan. 31, 1969; children: Linda, John. B.S. in Mech. Engring, Carnegie Inst. of Tech., 1935; M.A. in Architecture, Pratt Inst., 1978. Registered profl. engr., N.Y., Conn., Calif., 24 other states, also P.R. Pres. Dubin Heating and Cooling Co., Hartford, 1936-42; mng. partner of Fred S. Dubin Associates, Rome; pres. Dubin-Bloome Associates (cons. engrs. and planners), N.Y.C. and Hartford, 1946—; vis. prof. Columbia U. Sch. Architecture, 1970-72; prof. U. So. Calif. Sch. Architecture, Los Angeles, 1967-69; guest lectr. Carnegie-Mellon U., Pitts., 1976; disting. prof. architecture U. Ark., 1980; guest lectr. various archtl. and engring. univs. in, U.S., 1960—, Europe, 1975—, cons. to various fed. and state govt. agencies, 1955—; cons. Ministry Mining and Energy, Jamaica, 1983. Author: Solar Energy Handbook, 1978; co-author: Energy Conservation in Buildings, 1978; contbr. numerous articles and reports on energy conservation and solar energy systems to profl. jours. and publs. Mem. planning team for City of Hartford Community Renewal Study, 1963; mem. advisory bd. Citizens for Clean Air, N.Y.C., 1973-75; advisory bd. Scientists Com. for Pub. Info., 1975—; adviser to Solar Energy Exhbn. Program, 1975—; lectr. on energy conservation and solar energy at various univs. in, Greece, France, Holland, Norway, Denmark, Sweden, 1975. Served to lt. comdr. USN, 1942-46. Named Engr. Who Has Made His Mark Engring. News Record, 1975. Fellow ASHRAE, Am. Cons. Engrs. Council (chmn. nat. energy com.), Scis. for Pub. Info.; mem. Am. Solar Energy Assn. (dir. 1980-83), New Eng. Solar Energy Assn. (dir. 1976—), Nat. Soc. Profl. Engrs., Nat. Acad. Engring. Democrat. Jewish. Home: 1 Seaside Pl East Norwalk CT Office: 42 W 39th St New York City NY 10019

DUBIN, HOWARD VICTOR, dermatologist; b. N.Y.C., Mar. 28, 1938; s. Meyer and Blanche D.; m. Patricia Sue Tucker, June 10, 1962; children—Douglas Scott, Kathryn Sue, David Andrew, Michael Stonier. A.B., Columbia U., 1958, M.D., 1962. Diplomate: Am. Bd. Dermatology, Am. Bd. Internal Medicine. Intern U. Mich., 1962-63, resident in internal medicine, 1963-64, resident in dermatology, 1968-70, asst. prof., 1970-72, asso. prof., 1972-75, clin. asso. prof., 1975-77, clin. prof., 1977—; resident in internal medicine Columbia-Presbyn. Med. Center, N.Y.C., 1966-68; practice medicine specializing in dermatology, Ann Arbor, Mich., 1970—. Contbr. articles to profl. jours. Trustee Greenhills Sch., Ann Arbor, 1979—, pres. bd. trustees, 1981—. Served with U.S. Army, 1964-66. Fellow A.C.P.; mem. Am. Acad. Dermatology, Soc. Investigative Dermatology, Dermatology Found., Mich. Dermatol. Soc., AMA, Mich. Med. Soc., Washtenaw County Med. Soc., Sigma Xi. Club: Rotary. Office: 3250 Plymouth Rd Ann Arbor MI 48105

DUBIN, MARTIN DAVID, architect; b. Chgo., Nov. 22, 1927; s. Henry and Anne (Green) D.; m. Joan Jankowsky, Sept. 6, 1953; children: Jan Anne, David Henry. B.S., U. Ill., 1950. Sr. project rep. Skidmore, Owings & Merrill, Chgo., 1956-58; gen. ptnr. Dubin & Dubin (Architects), Chgo., 1952-62; gen. partner Dubin, Dubin & Moutoussamy (Architects and Engrs.), Chgo., 1962—; lectr. dept. architecture U. Ill., Chgo., 1965—; trustee Inland Architect mag. Author: Architectural Supervision of Modern Buildings; contbr. articles to profl. jours. Mem. Appearance Rev. Commn. Highland Park, Ill., 1975-77; lay trustee St. Joseph's Home for the Elderly, Palatine, Ill. Fellow AIA (pres. Chgo. chpt. 1971, pres. Ill. council 1972-73); Mem. Art Inst. Chgo. (life friend), Peabody Mus. of Salem (Mass.) (life fellow), Maritime Mus. (life), Thomas Gilcrease Mus. Am. Art (life). Democrat. Jewish. Home: 239 Park Highland Park IL 60035 Office: 221 N LaSalle St Chicago IL 60601

DUBIN, MORTON DONALD, television commercial producer; b. N.Y.C., Sept. 1, 1931; s. Albert and Maria (Suskin) D.; m. Jean Brinning, Jan. 19, 1968; 1 son. Morton Donald. Student, NYU, 1949-50, CCNY, 1953-54. Prodn. asst. Screen Gems, Columbia Pictures, N.Y.C., 1953-54; producer Blou Advt. Agy., N.Y.C., 1954-55, Vidcam Pictures, Inc., 1955-59; v.p. sales M.P.O. Videotronics, Inc., N.Y.C., 1959-70; exec. v.p. Dirs. Circle, Inc., N.Y.C., 1970-74; pres. Iris Films-The Best People, N.Y.C., 1975—; v.p. Kaufman-Astoria Studies Inc., 1983—; speaker in field; mem. N.Y.C. Film, Theatre and Broadcasting Adv. Council, 1978—, Motion Picture and TV Joint Mgmt.-Labor Com. on U.S. Govt. Audio; chmn. Ad. Hoc Com. N.Y. State Motion Picture and TV Tax Reform, 1981, 82. Author pub.: The Videotape Glossary; contbr. articles to profl. jours. Aux. police insp. N.Y.C. Police Dept., 1978—. Recipient 11 Clio, Silver Bear Berlin Film Festival, 1964, Golden Reel Am. Cine Inst., 1964, Los Angeles Art Dirs. 2, Phoenix Grand Atlanta Film Festival, 1974, Effie 2, award of merit N.Y. Police Dept., 1969, 70, 78, 82, cert. of appreciation N.Y.C. Mayor's Office, 1970, award of commendation 3 FBI, Tokyo Art Dir.'s, 1974, others. Mem. Videotape Prodn. Assn. (chmn. bd.), Assn. Ind. Comml. Producers (East Coast dir.), Dirs Guild Am., U.S. Marine Corps Combat Corrs. Assn. Home: 63 W 83d St New York NY 10024 Office: Iris Films 236 E 46th St New York NY 11217

DUBIN, SETH HARRIS, lawyer; b. N.Y.C., July 1, 1933; s. Ralph and Sylvia Muriel (Rosenthal) D.; m. Dorothy Anne Bernstein, Apr. 16, 1961; children: Thomas I.H., Ellen R., Andrew R. Student, Columbia Coll., 1950-51; B.A., Amherst Coll., 1954; LL.B., Harvard, 1957. Bar: N.Y. 1957. Partner firm Satterlee & Stephens, N.Y.C.; dir. Plessey, Inc., Corp. Time-Sharing Services, WICAT Systems, Inc. Trustee Oxford U. Press; former trustee, treas. Millicent A. Rogers Meml. Mus., Taos, N.Mex.; former trustee, chmn. A Better Chance, Inc.; trustee, pres. N.Y. Hall of Sci.; past bd. overseers Hebrew Union Coll.-Jewish Inst. Religion. Recipient Eminent Service award Amherst Coll., 1977. Mem. Assn. Bar City N.Y., N.Y. State Bar Assn. Democrat. Jewish. Home: 875 Park Ave New York NY 10021 Office: 277 Park Ave New York NY 10017

DUBIN, WESLEY PAUL, television and radio executive; b. Chgo., Mar. 26, 1948; s. Bruno Wesley and Emily Helen (Chalmers) D.; m. Helene Yvonne Peters, Aug. 7, 1971; children: Rebecca, Barry, Gregory. B.A., U. Detroit, 1970. Sales planner ABC-TV Network, Chgo., 1970-73, dir. sales planning, 1974-75; mgr. network resources Needham, Harper & Steers, Inc., Chgo., 1975-81; sr. v.p., corp. dir. network TV and radio Needham, Harper & Steers U.S.A. Inc., Chgo., 1982—. Mem. Internat. Radio and TV Soc., Chgo. Broadcast Advt. Club. Roman Catholic. Home: 237 Leitch Ave La Grange IL 60525 Office: Needham Harper & Steers USA Inc 303 E Wackerr Dr Chicago IL 60601

DUBLIN, ARTHUR DETMERS, architect; b. Chgo., Mar. 14, 1923; s. Henry and Anne (Green) D.; m. Lois Amtman, Mar. 10, 1951 (dec. Sept. 1980); children: Peter Arthur, Polly Louise; m. Phyllis Vollen Burman, Nov. 27, 1981; stepchildren: Garry Arthur, Jill Mereydth, David Yale, Eric Vollen. Student, Lake Forest Coll., 1943-44; B.Arch., U. Mich., 1949. Architect, ptng. Dublin & Dublin, architects and engrs., Chgo., 1950-65, Dublin, Dublin & Black, architects and engrs., 1965-66, Dublin, Dublin Black & Moutoussamy, 1966-78, Dublin, Dublin & Moutoussamy, 1978—; v.p. DDBM, Inc., constrn. mgmt. cons., 1975—; v.p., dir. 7537 South Shore Dr. Corp., 7345 South Shore Dr. Corp.; gen. ptnr. 340 Wellington Assocs., 1962-73; mem. adv. bd. Amtrak, 1972, speaker at confs., U.S. and France, 1972; hon. research assoc. Smithsonian Instn., 1975; mem. Nat. Council Archtl. Registration Bds., 1971—. Author: Some Classic Trains, 1964, More Classic Trains, 1974; author-editor for N.Am.: The Great Trains, 1973; contbr. articles to mags.; archtl. works include govtl. bldgs., rail transit stas. and transp. facilities, mil. installations, banks, indsl. plants, schs. and colls., hosps., housing and urban renewal planning. Chmn. Civic Beautification Com., Highland Park, Ill., 1965-74; mem. Bicentenial Commn. Highland Park, 1974-76, Ill. Commn. on High Speed Rail Transit, 1966-68, Met. Housing and Planning Council Chgo.; trustee NORTRAN (transit dist.), Des Plaines, Ill., 1980—. Served with inf. U.S. Army, 1943-46. Decorated Bronze Star with cluster; deocrated Purple Heart. Mem. AIA, Ill. Soc. Architects, Am. Pub. Transit Assn., Western Soc. Engrs., Ry. and Locomotive Hist. Soc. (dir. 1960—), Train Collectors Assn., Art Inst. Chgo. (life mem.). Clubs: Cliff Dwellers (dir. 1972-75), Builders (pres. 1970-71), Builders (dir. 1970—), Arts (Chgo.)). Home: 229 Park Ave Highland Park IL 60035 Office: 55 W Wacker Dr Chicago IL 60601

DUBLIN, THOMAS DAVID, physician; b. N.Y.C., Jan. 18, 1912; s. Louis I. and Augusta (Salik) D.; m. Christina Macdonald Carlyle, June 3, 1939; children: Sarah Carlyle Dublin Slenczka, Barbara Dublin Van Cleve. A.B., Dartmouth Coll., 1932; M.D., Harvard, 1936; M.P.H., Johns Hopkins U., 1940, Dr.P.H., 1941. Diplomate: Nat Bd. Med. Examiners, Am. Bd. Preventive Medicine (dir. 1961-71, vice. chmn. for gen. preventive medicine 1965-71). Intern Boston City Hosp., 2d Harvard Med. Service, 1936-38; instr. preventive medicine Johns Hopkins Med. Sch., 1940-41; instr. preventive medicine and public health Albany Med. Coll., 1942; lectr. epidemiology DeLamar Inst. Pub. Health, Coll. Physicians and Surgeons, Columbia U., 1942-45; asso. prof. dept. preventive medicine and community health L.I. Coll. Medicine, Bklyn., 1942-43, prof. and exec. officer, 1943-48; epidemiologist Kingston Ave. Hosp., Bklyn., 1943-48; exec. dir. Nat. Health Council, 1948-53; med. cons. Nat. Found. for Infantile Paralysis, 1953-55; med. dir. USPHS, 1955-76, Community Services Programs, Office of Dir., NIH, Bethesda, Md., 1955-60; chief epidemiology and biometry br. Nat. Inst. Arthritis and Metabolic Diseases, Bethesda, 1960-66; research adviser, health service Office Tech. Coop. and Research, AID, 1966-68; dir. Office Health Manpower, HEW, 1968-70; program planning officer Bur. Health Manpower, Health Resources Adminstrn., 1970-72, spl. asst. dep. dir. bur., 1972-76; cons. health manpower supply and edn., 1976—; cons. div. med. edn. AMA and Coordinating Council on Med. Edn., 1976-78; cons. research and devel. Ednl. Commn. for Fgn. Med. Grads., 1978—; mem. expert adv. panel pub. health adminstrn. WHO, 1954-80; mem. Nat. Adv. Com. Epidemiology and Biometry, 1956-60; chmn. com. on cert. Am. Bd. Med. Specialists, 1972-77. Contbr. articles on internat. health and health manpower to profl. publs. Fellow Am. Pub. Health Assn. (governing council 1954-60, chmn. research policy com. 1957-60), Am. Coll. Preventive Medicine (regent 1973-76), N.Y. Acad. Medicine; mem. AMA, AAAS, Am. Epidemiol. Soc., Assn. Tchrs. Preventive Medicine (sec. 1944-48), Internat. Epidemiol. Assn., Delta Omega. Home: 2949 Garfield Terr NW Washington DC 20008 Office: 2938 Garfield St NW Washington DC 20008

DUBNER, RONALD, neurobiologist; b. N.Y.C., Oct. 12, 1934; s. Louis and Matilda (Fox) D.; m. Mary Ann Pollack, June 22, 1958; children: Susan R., Andrew D., Julia P. B.A., Columbia U., 1955, D.D.S., 1958; Ph.D., U. Mich., 1964. Intern USPHS Hosp., Balt., 1958-59; staff dentist Clin. Center, NIH, Bethesda, Md., 1959-61; research scientist Nat. Inst. Dental Research, NIH, 1961-68, chief neural mechanisms sect., 1968-73, chief neurobiology and anesthesiology br., 1973—; vis. scientist dept. anatomy Univ. Coll., London, 1970-71; vis. assoc. prof. Howard U., 1968-80. Co-author: Oral Facial Sensory and Motor Mechanisms, 1971, The Neural Basis of Oral and Facial Function, 1978, Oral-Facial Sensory and Motor Functions, 1981, Current Topics in Pain Research and Therapy, 1983; editorial bd.: Jour. Neurosci., 1980—, Jour. Dental Research, 1981—, Somatosensory Research, 1982—; contbr. articles to profl. jours., chpts. in books. Recipient Meritorious service medal USPHS, 1975, Birnberg Research Columbia U., 1981. Mem. Internat. Assn. Study of Pain (council 1975-81, v.p. 1981-84), Soc. Neurosci., Internat. Assn. Dental Research (pres. Neurosci. Group 1977), Am. Physiol. Soc., Am. Assn. Anatomists, AAAS, Am. Pain Sco. (dir. 1980-82), Omicron Kappa Upsilon. Office: NIH Bldg 30 Room B18 Bethesda MD 20205

DUBOFF, SAMUEL J., accountant; b. Bklyn., July 30, 1915; s. Jacob and Dora (Finkelstein) D.; m. Elizabeth E. Epstein, July 20, 1941; children: Judith A., Robert S., David B. B.B.A. cum laude, CCNY, 1934. With Seidman & Seidman (C.P.A.s), 1934-42; with S. D. Leidesdorf & Co., 1946-78, partner, 1957-78, Ernst & Whinney (formerly Ernst & Ernst), N.Y.C., 1978-79, cons., 1979—; dir. Lightolier, Inc.; former mem. N.Y. State Bd. C.P.A. Examiners. Past pres. Bd. Edn. Scarsdale; trustee Am. Jewish Com., Westchester, Community Service Soc. N.Y.; trustee, past chmn. bd. Better Bus. Bur. Met. N.Y.; trustee Council Better Bus. Burs., Burke Rehab. Center, White Plains, N.Y., Family Services of Westchester, Legal Aid Soc. of Westchester; past bd. dirs. N.Y. Conv. Bur.; bd. dirs. Scarsdale Found.; mem. adv. bd. Columbia U. Grad. Sch. Social Work; trustee, v.p. Com. for Modern Cts., Inc. Mem. Am. Inst. C.P.A.'s (council), N.Y. State Soc. C.P.A.'s (past v.p.; dir. and pres.), Beta Gamma Sigma, Beta Alpha Psi. Clubs: Quaker Ridge Golf; Town (Scarsdale) (past pres.). Home: 20 Barry Rd Scarsdale NY 10583 Office: 153 E 53d St New York NY 10022

DUBOFSKY, JEAN EBERHART, justice Colo. Supreme Ct.; m. Frank N. Dubofsky; children—Joshua, Matthew. B.A., Stanford U., 1964; LL.B., Harvard U., 1967. Bar: Colo. bar. Legis. asst. to U.S. Senator Walter F. Mondale, 1967-69; atty. Colo. Rural Legal Services, Boulder, 1969-72, Legal Aid Soc. Met. Denver, 1972-73; partner firm Kelly, Dubofsky, Haglund & Garnsey, Denver, 1973-75; dep. atty. gen., Colo., 1975-77; counsel Kelly, Haglund, Garnsey & Kahn, 1977-79; justice Colo. Supreme Ct., Denver, 1979—. Office: 430 State Judicial Bldg 2 E 14th Ave Denver CO 80203 *

DUBOIS, ALAN BEEKMAN, art museum administrator, curator; b. Forest Glen, N.Y., Dec. 14, 1935; s. Raymond Van Orden and Florence (Beekman) DuB.; m. Joan Edna Berger, Apr. 25, 1959; children: Dean, Ronald, Douglas, Jonathan. B.S. in Art Edu., SUNY-New Paltz, 1958; M.F.A. in Photography and Related Arts, Ind. U., 1966. Dir. Washington County Mus. Fine Arts, Hagerstown, Md, 1964-66; asst. dir. Mus. Fine Arts, St. Petersburg, Fla., 1966—. Deacon, elder Maximo Presbyterian Ch., St. Petersburg, 1969-80; elder Garden Crest Presbyn. Ch., 1981—. Nat. Endowment Arts fellow, 1972, 75. Mem. Coll. Art Assn., Am. Assn. Museums, Soc. Photog. Edn. (sec.-treas. S.E. div. 1976-81), Fla. Art Mus. Dirs. Assn., Southeastern Mus. Conf. Office: Museum Fine Arts 255 Beach Dr N Saint Petersburg FL 33701

DU BOIS, ARTHUR BROOKS, physiologist; b. N.Y.C., Nov. 21, 1923; s. Eugene Floyd and Rebeckah (Rutter) DuB.; m. Roberdeau Callery, June 21, 1950; children: Anne R., Brooks, James E.F. Student, Harvard U., 1941-43; M.D., Cornell U., 1946. Intern in medicine N.Y. Hosp., 1946-47; med. research fellow U. Rochester, 1949-51; asst. resident Peter Bent Brigham Hosp., Boston, 1951-52; asst. prof. to prof. physiology and medicine U. Pa., 1952-74; prof. epidemiology and physiology Yale U., 1974—; dir. John B. Pierce Found. Lab., 1974—. Author: The Lung, 1955, 62, Body Plethysmography, 1969; contbr. articles to profl. jours. Served with USNR, 1947-49. Recipient research career devel. award NIH, 1963-74. Mem. Am. Physiol. Soc., Am. Soc. Clin. Investigation, Assn. Am. Physicians, Undersea Med. Soc. Democrat. Clubs: Harvard, Cosmos. Home: 370 Livingston St New Haven CT 06511 Office: 290 Congress Ave New Haven CT 06519

DU BOIS, EDMUND LOUIS, operations analyst, retired army officer; b. Boston, Jan. 8, 1919; s. Bird Spencer and Pauline (Baldwin) DuB.; m. Ethel Raynor McDonald, Oct. 21, 1944 (div. Nov. 1983); children: Edmund Louis, John William, Laurence McDonald, Diane Catherine, Geoffrey Baldwin. B.S. in Civil Engring., U. Ill., 1941; M.S. in Phys. Scis., U. Chgo., 1948; grad., Army War Coll., 1962. Commd. 2d lt. U.S. Army, 1941, advanced through grades to brig. gen., 1967; served in PTO, World War II, assigned Joint Chiefs Staff, 1945-46, 62-65, 68-70, assigned Army Gen. Staff, 1955-58, assigned Armed Forces Spl. Weapons Project, Sandia (N.Mex.) Base, 1952-55, assigned SHAPE, 1958-61; Army Air Def., Seattle, 1965-67; assigned Joint Task Force 2, Sandia Base, 1967-68, comdg. gen. 6th region ARADCOM, Ft. Baker, Calif., 1970-71, ret., 1971; sr. ops. analyst Stanford Research Inst., Menlo Park, Calif., 1972-80; pres. Sipapu Inst., 1976-80, dir., 1980-83, cons., 1980—. Decorated D.S.M., Legion of Merit with 2 oak leaf clusters, Army Commendation medal with 2 oak leaf clusters. Mem. Explorers Club, Delta Tau Delta. Club: Commonwealth. Home: 850 Coleman Ave 3 Menlo Park CA 94025

DUBOIS, FRANK A., III, land and water resources official; b. Lynwood, Calif., May 29, 1947; s. Frank A. and Wanda Eileen (McCarey) DuB.; m. Sharon Rose Chesser; children: Frank Austin, Sevon Nichole. B.A., N.Mex. State U., 1973. Insp. N.Mex. State Govt., Albuquerque, 1973-74; legis. asst. U.S. Senate, Washington, 1974-75, spl. asst. field office, Las Cruces, N.Mex., 1976-79; agrl. programs specialist N.Mex., Las Cruces, 1979-81; spl. asst. to asst. sec. U.S. Dept. Interior, Washington, 1981, dep. asst. sec. land and water resources, 1981—. Mem. Soc. Range Mgmt., Soc. Am. Foresters. Republican. Home: 8009 Ferncliff Springfield VA 22153 Office: US Dept Interior Office of the Secretary 18th & C Sts NW Room 6610 Washington DC 20240

DU BOIS, JA'NET, actress; b. Phila., Aug. 5; m. Charles Bellinger (div.); children—Provat, Raj, Rani. Ed., Hunter Coll. Formerly factory worker, cosmetologist; taught in children's and community acting workshops. Wrote and acted in community theatre; Broadway appearances Nobody Loves an Albatross, Golden Boy, Raisin in the Sun; off-Broadway appearances The Reckoning, The Blacks; appeared in: Revolution, Los Angeles Music Center, The Hot L Baltimore, Los Angeles Music Center; now writes and directs at, Opus Four Theater Arts; motion picture appearances include A Piece of the Action, Diary of a Mad Housewife, Five on the Black Hand Side; appeared in: TV series Good Times, Love of Life; other TV appearances include Roots II, Shaft, Caribe, Kojak, Sanford and Son, J.T., A Beautiful Killing, Resolution of Mossie Way; singer and songwriter: including theme song on TV series The Jeffersons; Author: Maybe It's All in My Mind *

DUBOIS, JEAN-GUY, membert Canadian Parliament; b. Ste. Cecile-de-Levrard, Que., Can., Apr. 2, 1948; s. Paul-Emile and Mariette (Tousignant) D.; m. Pauline Boivin, Aug. 10, 1974; children: Andre, Yves, Eric. D.E.C., Sherbrooke U. (Que.), 1971, L.L.L., 1971. Bar: Que. 1973. Prof. adminstrn. and labor law Trois-Rivieres U., 1973-77; M.P. from Que. House of Commons, Ottawa, 1980—. Pres. Hockey Inter-Cities 2A, 1979-80; vice chmn. Beliveau-Perreault Golf Tournament, 1976-77; chmn. Bois-Francs Intermediary Hockey League, 1974-79, Indsl. Soft Ball League, 1974; organizer Hockey for Minors. Mem. Que. Bar Assn., Que. Liberal Caucus (vice chmn.). Mem. Liberal Party. Roman Catholic. Lodges: Optimist (vice chmn. 1977-78); K.C. Home: 25 Daveluy St Victoriaville PQ Canada G6P 8S6 Office: House of Commons 313 Confederation Bldg Ottawa ON Canada K1A oA6

DUBOIS, JOHN HARRY, plastics co. exec.; b. Clarion, Iowa, Sept. 18, 1903; s. John Harrison and Harriet (Warren) DuB.; m. Kathryn E. Peterson, June 17, 1933; children—John Harry, Helen Elizabeth DuBois Veltkamp. B.S., U. Minn., 1927. Plastics engr. Gen. Electric Co., Pittsfield, Mass., Chgo., Ft. Wayne, Ind., 1927-44; v.p. engring. Shaw Insulator Co., Irvington, N.J., 1944-50; with Plax Corp., Hartford, Conn., 1951; mgr. new product devel. Mycalex Corp. Am., Clifton, N.J., 1951-57; v.p. Tech. Art Plastics Co., 1958-66; pres. Molecular Dielectrics, Inc., Clifton, N.J., 1966-72; v.p. Mykroy Ceramics Co., 1972-74; propr. J. Harry DuBois Co., 1957—; gen. chmn. plastics adv. com. Smithsonian Instn.; dir. Delia Assos., Berkeley Heights, N.J., Glasflex Corp., Stirling, N.J., Arlington Plastics Co., Vt.; mem. Princeton Polymer Assos. Author: (with others) Plastics Product Design Engineering Handbook; tech. editor: Plastics Compounding. Charter mem. Plastics Hall of Fame, 1973.; Mem. Soc. Plastics Industry, Soc. Plastics Engrs. (Internat. award 1966), IEEE, Plastics Pioneers, Packaging Inst., Eta Kappa Nu. Home: Rt 10 Box 346 Morris Plains NJ 07950 Office: Box 346 Morris Plains NJ 07950 *You can not lose when you give more than you take.*

DU BOIS, PAUL ZINKHAN, library director; b. Ravenna, Ohio, Jan. 5, 1936; s. John Harold and Marie Eggleston (Miller) DuB.; m. Carol Ann Johnson, Aug. 15, 1959; children: Megan, Christopher. B.A., Hiram Coll., 1959; M.A. (Crawford scholar), Kent State U., 1960, Western Res. U., 1962, Ph.D., 1968. Library coordinator Mentor (Ohio) Pub. Sch. System, 1963-64; head librarian N.Y. State Hist. Assn., Cooperstown, 1964-69; asst. dir. Kent State U., 1969-72; dir. library, prof. media communications sci. Trenton (N.J.) State Coll., 1972—; v.p. DuBois Book Store, Inc., Kent; cons. N.Y. State Council on Arts, Nat. Am. Studies Faculty, NEH, Adirondack Mus., Historic Gainesville, Bucks County Hist. Soc., Inst. Mus. Services, N.J. and Pa. coms. on humanities, others; cons. and dealer antiquarian books; pres. N.J. Council State Coll. and Univ. Librarians, 1975-76; mem. N.J. Acad. Library Standards Task Force, 1983; mem. adv. bd. N.J. Musto Commn., 1979-80. Editor: Librarians' Choice, 1972—, Paul Leicester Ford, An American Man of Letters, 1977; contbr. articles and revs. to profl. jours. Recipient Hugo Alpers award Kent State U., 1960; fellow Seminar for Hist. Adminstrs., Colonial Williamsburg, 1963. Mem. ALA, Bibliog. Soc. Am., Nat. Trust Historic Preservation, Thoreau Soc., Beta Phi Mu, Phi Alpha Theta. Democrat. Presbyterian. Clubs: Rotary Internat., Trenton Torch (pres. 1975-76). Home: 29 Morningside Yardley PA 19067 Office: Box 940 Trenton NJ 08625

DU BOIS, PHILIP HUNTER, psychologist; b. Newburgh, N.Y., July 8, 1903; s. Henry Reynolds and Hattie Aletha (Clough) DuB.; m. Margaret Eloise Barclay, Dec. 27, 1936; 1 dau., Margaret (Mrs. Richard W. Watson). A.B., Union Coll., 1925; M.A., Columbia U., 1929, Ph.D., 1932. Diplomate: in counseling and guidance Am. Bd. Examiners in Profl. Psychology. Instr. English Am. U., Beirut, 1925-28; instr. psychology Columbia, 1930-33; intern psychology N.Y. State Psychiat. Inst. and Hosp., 1932-33; asst. prof. psychology Idaho State Coll., Pocatello, 1933-35; asst. prof., later asso. prof. and dir. bur. tests and records U. N.Mex., 1935-46; prof. Washington U., St. Louis, 1946-72, prof. emeritus, 1972—; dir. Psychol. Assos., 1958—, research psychologist, 1972—; test technician, later supr. N.Mex. Merit System Council, 1940-42; psychol. cons. Dept. Police St. Louis, 1947-77; cons. human resources research labs. Air Research and Devel. Command, 1951-54, U.S. VA, 1947-70; mem. panel on personnel, com. on human resources Research and Devel. Bd., Dept. Def., 1952-54; expert Air Force Personnel and Tng. Center, 1954-57; mem. panel on personnel and tng. Office Asst. Sec. Def. (research and devel.), 1954-57; cons. Cross-Cultural Research Project in Social Psychology, Cairo, summer 1954, USAF Sch. Aviation Medicine, 1955-58, U.S. Office Edn., 1963-67, University City (Mo.) Schs., 1963-66, Center for Nuclear Studies, Memphis State U., 1974—; Chmn. ETS Invitational Conf. on Testing Problems, 1969; Aviation psychologist USAAF, 1942-46, asst. dir., 1943, chief psychol. sect., 1943-44, chief publs. unit, psychol. sect., 1944-46. Author: Multivariate Correlational Analysis, 1957, An Introduction to Psychological Statistics, 1965, A History of Psychological Testing, 1970; Editor: A.A.F. Aviation Psychology Report 2, The Classification Program, 1947; Co-editor: monograph Research Strategies for Evaluating Training; Contbr. to profl. jours. Mem. AAAS, Am. Psychol. Assn. (pres. mil. div. 1954-55, pres. div. evaluation and measurement 1968-69), Mo. Psychol. Assn. (pres. 1954-55), Psychometric Soc. (past sec., past pres.), AAUP, Soc. Multivariate Exptl. Psychology., Nat. Council Measurement in Edn., Phi Beta Kappa, Sigma Xi, Phi Kappa Phi, Psi Upsilon. Home: 94 Aberdeen Pl Clayton MO 63105 Office: Dept of Psychology Washington U Saint Louis MO 63130 also 8201 Maryland Ave Clayton MO 63105

DU BOIS, RAOUL PENE, costume and set designer; b. N.Y.C., Nov. 29, 1914; s. Raoul George-Gontran Pene and Bessie (Hetherington) Du B. Designer sets for several prodns., Paris; 1st designs in N.Y.C. were costumes for Life Begins at 8:40, Winter Garden, 1934; since designer: Jumbo, 1935; 1st London design: Home and Beauty, 1937; designer: Broadway shows The Two Bouquets, Leave It to Me, The Ziefeld Follies, 1938, Du Barry Was a Lady, Too Many Girls, One for the Money, Aquacade, 1939, Two for the Show, Panama Hattie, Hold on to Your Hats, 1940, Liberty Jones, 1941, Carmen Jones, 1943, The Firebrand of Florence, Are You With It?, 1945, Heaven on Earth, Lend an Ear, 1948, Alive and Kicking, Call Me Madam, 1950, Make a Wish, 1951, New Faces of 1952, In Any Language, 1952, Wonderful Town, Maggie, Charley's Aunt, John Murray Anderson's Almanac, 1953, Mrs. Patterson, 1954, Plain and Fancy, The Vamp, 1955, Ziegeld Follies (sets and costumes for 3 different prodns.), Carmen Jones (costumes only), 1957, Gypsy (costumes only), 1959, Maurice Chevalier (decor and lighting), The Student Gypsy, 1963, PS I Love You, Royal Flush, 1964, Darling of the Day, 1968, double-bill Peter and the Wolf and Here and Now, Rondelay, 1969, No, No, Nanette, 1971, Rain, 1972; costumes and decor for Irene, 1973, Gypsy, London, 1973, N.Y.C., 1974, Doctor Jazz, 1975, Sugar Babies, 1979; costumes for Colette, Denver, 1982; designer for: Ballet Russe de Monte Carlo, Denver, 1982; designer films, 1941-45; films including Louisiana Purchase, Layd in the Dark, Dixie, also others. Recipient Tony award for Wonderful Town and No, No, Nanette. *

DU BOIS, WILLIAM PENE, author, illustrator; b. Nutley, N.J., May 9, 1916; s. Guy Pene and Florence (Sherman) duB.; m. Willa Kim; 1955. Student, Miss Barstow's Sch., N.Y.C., Lycée Hoche, Versailles, Lycée de Nice, France. Former corr.: Yank Mag; former art editor; designer: Paris Rev; author and illustrator: books for children including Elizabeth the Cow Ghost, 1936, The Twenty-One Balloons, 1947, Lion, 1956, Pretty Pretty Peggit Moffitt, 1968, Bear Circus, 1971, The Forbidden Forest, 1978. Served with AUS, 1941-45. Recipient Festival award N.Y. Herald Tribune, 1947, 56, Newberry medal, 1948, N.Y. Time award for illustration, 1971. Address: care Viking Press 625 Madison Ave New York NY 10022 *

DU BOSE, CHARLES, architect; b. Savannah, Ga., Aug. 16, 1908; s. Charles S. and Augusta (Wood) DuB.; m. Ruth Bogaty, Mar. 26, 1937; 1 dau., Pamela Barry (Mrs. Brian A. McIver). B.S. in Architecture, Ga. Inst. Tech., 1929; M. Arch., U. Pa., 1930; diploma, Fontainebleau, France, Sch. Fine Arts, summers 1928, 30. Pvt. practice architecture, N.Y.C., 1936-48, Hartford, Conn., 1958—; instr. archtl. design U. Pa., 1931; partner Frank Grad & Sons (architects and engrs.), Newark, 1948-56; pres. F.H. McGraw & Co. of Can., Montreal, Que., 1956-58; chmn. DuBose Assocs., Inc., Architects, Hartford, 1980—; AIA rep. on urban planning commn. Union Internationale des Architectes, del. assembly, Sofia, Bulgaria, 1972, Venice, 1975; rep. at UN.; AIA rep. Federacion Panamerica de Asociaciones de Arquitectos. Prin. works include Constitution Plaza, Hartford, Pratt and Whitney Aircraft, East Hartford, Conn., Founders Plaza, East Hartford, for, Phoenix Mut. Life Ins. Co., IBM Corp, Springfield, Mass., Hartford Nat. Bank & Trust Co, Conn. Bank & Trust Co, Travelers Ins. Co, Aetna Life & Casualty Co, U.S. Post Office, Hartford, U.S. VA, U.S. Navy, Air N.G, Monmouth Park Jockey Club, Oceanport, N.J., U.S. Air Force Bases in, France. Mem. Am. bd. trustees Ecoles d'Art Americaines, Fontainebleau, 1947—, pres., 1947-53, treas., 1953—. Winner internat. competition for design nat. capitol, Ecuador, 1946; awards of Merit for design AIA and U.S. Urban Renewal Adminstrn., 1964; honor awards Conn. chpt. AIA and; n. Bldg. Congress. Fellow AIA; mem. Am. Assn. Housing and Redevel. (mem. internat. com.), Sociedad Interamericana de Planificacion, Archtl. League N.Y., N.A.D., Chi Phi, Tau Sigma Delta. Clubs: Hartford, Hartford Golf. Home: 134 Woodrow St West Hartford CT 06107 Office: 49 Woodland St Hartford CT 06105

DUBOW, ARTHUR MYRON, business executive, lawyer; b. Chgo., Sept. 18, 1933; s. David and Matilda (Polter) D.; m. Isabella Goodrich Breckinridge, Mar. 2, 1962 (div. Dec. 1983); children: Charles Stewart, Alexandra Breckinridge. A.B., Harvard U., 1954, LL.B., 1957. Bar: N.Y. 1962. Asso. firm Webster Sheffield Fleischmann Hitchcock & Chrystie, N.Y.C., 1960-64; v.p., dir. Back Bay-Orient Enterprises, Inc., Boston, 1965-68, pres., 1968-76; pres., dir. Bayorient Holding Corp., Boston, 1969-76; pres. Korea Capital Corp., N.Y.C., 1968-76, Fortune Capital Ltd., Boston, 1979-84; pres., dir. Boston Co. Energy Advisers; dir. Sulpetro Can. Ltd., Calgary, Alta., 1966-76, chmn. exec. com., 1974-76; dir. Sulpetro Internat. Ltd., Dallas, 1973-76, chmn. exec. com., 1974-76; dir. Castle Convertible Fund, Inc., Spectra Fund, Inc., Back Bay-Orient Enterprises, Inc., Herald Prodns., Inc., Internat. Basic Economy Corp., 1977-80, Allegheny & Western Energy Corp., 1978-81, Calif. Energy Co., Devel. & Resources, Inc., 1977-80; fellow Center for Internat. Affairs, Harvard U., 1976-77. Mem. vis. com. dept. visual and environ. studies, dept. East Asian langs. and civilizations Harvard U.; bd. dirs. Inst. Ednl. Leadership, Sabre Found.; chmn. bd. dirs. Potomac Assocs., Inc., Washington; mem. nat. adv. com. on accreditation and instl. eligibility U.S. Dept. Edn.; co-chmn. New Am. Filmmakers' Series, Whitney Mus. Am. Art, N.Y.C., 1970-76; mem. adv. bd. Sch. Advanced Internat. Studies, Johns Hopkins U., 1980—; trustee Augustus St. Gaudens Meml., 1980—; mem. nat. fin. com. George Bush for Pres., 1980; mem. Council on Fgn. Relations. Clubs: Harvard of N.Y. and Boston., Tavern. Office: 1 Boston Place 3rd Floor Boston MA 02106

DU BRIDGE, LEE ALVIN, physicist; b. Terre Haute, Ind., Sept. 21, 1901; s. Frederick Alvin and Elizebeth Rebecca (Browne) DuB.; m. Doris May Koht, Sept. 1, 1925 (dec. Nov. 1973); children—Barbara (Mrs. David MacLeod), Richard Alvin; m. Arrola Bush Cole, Nov. 30, 1974. A.B., Cornell Coll., Iowa, 1922, Sc.D., 1940; A.M., U. Wis., 1924, Ph.D., 1926; Sc.D., Wesleyan U., 1946, Poly. Inst. Bklyn., 1946, Washington U., 1948, U. B.C., 1947, Occidental Coll., 1952, U. Md., 1955, Columbia, 1957, Ind. U., 1957, U. Wis., 1957, Pa. Mil. Coll., De Pauw U., 1962, Pomona Coll., Rockefeller Inst., Carnegie Inst. Tech., 1965, Syracuse U., 1969, Renssalaer Poly. Inst., 1970; LL.D., U. Calif., 1948, U. Rochester, 1953, U. So. Calif., 1957, Northwestern U., 1958, Loyola U. of Los Angeles, 1963, U. Notre Dame, 1967, Ill. Inst. Tech., 1967; L.H.D., Redlands U., 1958, U. Judaism, 1958; D.C.L., Union Coll., 1961. Asst. in physics U. Wis., 1922-25, instr., 1925-26; NRC fellow Calif. Inst. Tech., 1926-28; asst. prof. physics Washington U., St. Louis, 1928-33, asso. prof., 1933-34; prof. physics, chmn. dept. physics U. Rochester, 1934-46, dean faculty arts scis., 1938-41; investigator Nat. Def. Research Com.; dir. radiation lab. M.I.T., 1940-45; pres. Calif. Inst. Tech., 1946-69; pres. emeritus, 1970—; sci. adviser to Pres. U.S., 1969-70; Trustee Rand Corp., Santa Monica, Calif., 1948-61; mem. sci. adv. com. Gen. Motors, 1971-75; Mem. gen. adv. com. A.E.C., 1946-52; Naval Research Adv. Com., 1945-51, Air Force Sci. Adv. Bd., 1945-49; sci. advisor Weingart Found., 1979—; mem. Pres.'s Communications Policy Bd., 1950-51, Nat. Sci. Bd., 1950- 54, 58-64; chmn. sci. adv. com. Office Defense Moblzn., 1952-56. Author: (with A.L. Hughes) Photoelectric Phenomena, 1932, New Theories of Photoelectric Effect, 1935, Introduction to Space, 1960; Contbr. numerous sci. and ednl. articles to mags. Mem. Nat. Manpower Council, 1951-64, Nat. Adv. Health Council, 1960-61; mem. distinguished civilan service awards bd. U.S. Civil Service Commn., 1963-65; chmn. Greater Los Angeles Urban Coalition, 1968-69; mem. Pres.'s Air Quality Adv. Bd., 1968-69, Pres.'s Sci. Adv. Com., 1970-72; bd. dirs. Nat. Merit Scholarship Corp., 1963-69, Nat. Ednl. TV, N.Y., 1962-69; Trustee Mellon Inst., 1958-67, Rockefeller Found., 1956-67, Nutrition Found., 1952-63, Carnegie Endowment Internat. Peace, 1951-57, Community TV So. Calif., Los Angeles, 1962-69, Henry E.

Huntington Library and Art Gallery, 1962-69, Thomas Alva Edison Found., 1960-69, Pasadena Hall Sci., 1977-78. Recipient Research Corp. award, 1947; Medal for Merit, U.S., 1948; King's Medal for Service, Gt. Britain, 1946, Vannevar Bush award NSF, 1982—; Benjamin Franklin fellow Royal Soc. Arts. Fellow Am. Phys. Soc. (pres. 1947); mem. Nat. Acad. Sci., Am. Philos. Soc., A.A.A.S., Phi Beta Kappa, Sigma Pi Sigma, Sigma Xi, Tau Kappa Nu, Sigma Xi, Tau Kappa Alpha, Tau Beta Pi. Presbyn. Home: 1730 Homet Rd Pasadena CA 91106

DUBRIN, ANDREW JOHN, educator, author; b. N.Y.C., Mar. 3, 1935; s. Albert Edward and Louise Theresa (Walsh) D.; m. Drew, Douglas, Melanie. A.B., Hunter Coll., 1956; M.S., Purdue U., 1957; Ph.D., Mich. State U., 1960. Diplomate: Am. Bd. Profl. Psychology; cert. psychologist N.Y. state. Psychologist Data Systems div. IBM, Kingston, N.Y., 1962-63; teaching asst., part-time instr. Purdue U., West Lafayette, Ind., 1956-57, 1956-57; psychol. cons. Clark, Cooper, Field & Wohl, N.Y.C., 1963-64, Rohrer, Hibler & Replogle, 1964-70, ptnr., 1964-70; assoc. prof. Rochester (N.Y.) Inst. Tech., 1970-72, prof. behavioral sci., 1972—, dept. head mgmt. mktg. and mgmt. sci. faculty units, 1981—; mem. N.Y. State Bd. Psychology, 1979—; cons. lectr. in field. Author: The Practice of Managerial Psychology, 1972, Women in Transition, 1972, The Singles Game, 1973, Fundamentals of Organization Behavior; An Applied Perspective, 1974, Survival in the Sexist Jungle, 1974, The New Husbands and How To Become One, 1976, Casebook of Organizational Behavior, 1979, Human Relations: A Job Oriented Approach, 1978, Fundamentals of Organizational Behavior: An Applied Perspective, 2d edit., 1978, Winning at Office Politics, 1979; contbr. articles to profl. jours. Served to capt. U.S. Army, 1960-62. Mem. Am. Psychol. Assn. Home: 2100 Clover St Rochester NY 14618 Office: Rochester Inst Tech Coll of Bus Rochester NY 14623

DUBS, PATRICK CHRISTIAN, publisher; b. Paris, Jan. 18, 1947; U.S., 1978; s. Robert and Anne Marie D.; m. Catherine Claude Henry, Feb. 4, 1970; children—Vanessa, Olivier. Diplome de droit et scie. economiques, U. Paris, 1967. With Brit. European Airways, Paris, 1969; export dir. Hachette S.A., Paris, 1970-78; pres. Hachette Inc., N.Y.C., 1978—, Regents Pub. Co., Inc., 1980—; chmn. bd. Arista Corp., Concord, Calif. Mem. Am. Assn. Pubs., French-Am. C. of C. (councillor N.Y. chpt.). Roman Catholic. Club: Manursing Island (Rye). Office: 2 Park Ave New York NY 10016

DUBUC, SERGE, mathematics educator; b. Montreal, Que., Can., Apr. 16, 1939; s. Romuald and Fernande (Desmarchais) D.; m. Pierette Valois, June 3, 1962; children: Benoit, Martin, Jacinthe. B.Sc. in Math., U. Montreal, 1962, M.Sc., 1963, Ph.D., Cornell U., 1966. Asst. prof. math. U. Montreal, 1966-71, assoc. prof., 1973-76, 1976—, U. Sherbrooke, Que., Can., 1971-73. Author: Geometrie Plane, 1971, Problems d'Optimisation en Calcul de Probabilities, 1978; editor-in-chief: Annales de Sciences Mathematiques du Quebec, 1975-79; mng. editor, 1979-82. Ford Co. fellow, 1968-69; Can. Arts Council Killam fellow, 1975-76. Mem. Association Mathematique du Que. Roman Catholic. Office: Dept de Mathematiques et de Statistique Universite de Montreal 5620 Darlington St Monteal PQ Canada H3C 3J7

DUBY, PAUL FRANCOIS, metallurgical engineering educator; b. Brussels, Dec. 16, 1933; married, 1959; 3 children. Mech. and Elec. Engr., U. Brussels, 1956; Eng. Sc.D., Columbia U., 1962. Temporary research assoc. Ctr. Nuclear Sci., Brussels, 1957-58, Royal Mil. Sch., 1957-58; research assoc. mineral engr. Henry Krumb Sch. Mines, Columbia U., N.Y.C., 1961-63, mem. faculty, 1965—, prof. mineral engring., 1976—; asst. prof. metall. engring. U. Pa., 1963-65. Mem. AIME, Electrochem. Soc. Office: Dept Metal Engring Henry Kramb Sch Mines Columbia U New York NY 10027 *

DUCA, ALFRED MILTON, artist; b. Milton, Mass., July 9, 1920; s. Placido and Lavinia E. (Bianchi) D.; m. Linda M. Smalley, Jan. 1, 1948; children: David Riccardo, Richard Grant. Student, Pratt Inst., 1938-41, Boston Mus. Sch. Fine Arts, 1943-44. Pres., research dir. Polymer Tempera, Inc., Boston, 1950-57; program dir. Art Casting M.I.T., 1959-62; author-program dir. Gloucester Experiment, Mass., 1968—, Channel 1 youth programs, New Eng., 1977, nat. program dir., 1979—; vis. lectr. Boston U., 1957-58; vis. scholar M.I.T., 1962-68; mem. spl. investigative com. for establishment of Council for Arts and Humanities, Mass., 1966-70; mem. Nat. Policy Planning Com., Nat. Inst. Drug Abuse, 1974—; cons. White House Conf. on Children and Youth, 1970. Represented in permanent collections including, Addison Gallery Am. Art, Andover, Mass., Brandeis U., Boston U. Sch. Basic Studies, DeCordova Mus., Lincoln, Mass., Fogg Mus./Harvard Div. Sch., Munson Proctor Inst., Utica, N.Y., Worcester (Mass.) Art Mus.; maj. sculptural commissions include: Boston Tapestry, Prudential Bldg., Boston, 1960-68, Computersphere, J.F.K. Post Office, Boston, 1968, Greek Key, Project 57, Boston, 1968, Spiral Wave Standard Oil Ind, 1970, Mass. Artifact, McCormack Bldg., 1975. Subject of Smithsonian Archives Am. Art. Office: PO Box 15 Gloucester MA 01930

DUCANIS, ALEX JULIUS, educator; b. Pitts., Feb. 18, 1931; s. Alexander J. and Virginia (Vowinkel) D.; m. Natalie Jane Taylor, July 1, 1954. B.S., U. Pitts., 1953, M.Ed., 1954, Ed.D., 1961. Tchr. Lancaster (Pa.) Public Schs., 1956-58; lectr., adminstrv. asst. U. Pitts., 1959-61; research asso. div. research in higher edn. N.Y. State Edn. Dept., Albany, 1961-66; dir. instnl. research SUNY, Binghamton, 1966-69; project dir. Health Sci. Center Feasibility Study, 1967-68; asso. chmn. dept. higher edn. U. Pitts., 1969—, prof. edn. and health related professions, 1971—, dir., 1970-73, chmn. div. specialized profl. devel., 1973-75, dir. program higher edn., 1980—; cons. Coll. Entrance Exam. Bd., 1966-67, GEAR Corp., 1967, Broome County Social Planning Council, 1967-68 (dir. 1968), Broome County Med. Soc., 1968. Author: (with A.K. Golin) The Interdisciplinary Team: A Handbook for the Education of Exceptional Children, The Interdisciplinary Health Care Team (Book of Yr. award Am. Jour. Nursing 1981); Contbr. articles to ednl. jours. Chmn. dist. III regional adv. com. Statewide Rehab. Council, 1967-68; bd. dirs. N.Y.-Pa. Health Planning Council, Inc., 1968. Served with AUS, 1954-56. Mem. Am. Ednl. Research Assn., AAAS, Assn. Study Higher Edn., Am. Soc. Allied Health Professions, Am. Assn. Higher Edn., Am. Acad. Polit. and Social Sci., Assn. Instnl. Research, History Edn. Soc., Nat. Soc. Study Edn., Am. Public Health Assn., Phi Delta Kappa. Home: 230 N Craig St Pittsburgh PA 15213

DUCHAC, KENNETH FARNHAM, librarian; b. Antigo, Wis., Jan. 8, 1923; s. Carl O. and Alice Alberta (Farnham) D.; m. Gretchen Nommensen, May 12, 1944; children—Frederic Carl, John Nommensen. A.B., Carroll Coll., Waukesha, Wis., 1947; B.L.S., U. Chgo., 1947, postgrad. history, 1947-49. With Detroit Pub. Library, 1949-50; asst. dir. Decatur (Ill.) Pub. Library, 1950-53; dir. Kingsport (Tenn.) Pub. Library, 1953-57; cons. Wis. Free Library Commn., 1957-60, Md. Dept. Pub. Edn., 1960-68; dep. dir. Bklyn. Pub. Library, 1969-70, dir., 1970—; vis. prof. Pratt Inst., 1974-75; Dept. State cons. in, Jordan, 1960; cons. Pahlavi Nat. Library, Tehran, Iran; mem. N.Y. Commr. Edn.'s Com. on Libraries; trustee N.Y. Met. Reference and Research Library Agy., pres., 1980—. Chmn. Bklyn. Ednl. and Cultural Alliance, 1981—. Served with USNR, 1943-46. Mem. Am., N.Y. State library assns., L.I. Hist. Soc., Internat. Assn. Met. City Libraries (sec.-treas. 1974-77). Home: 245 Henry St Brooklyn Heights NY 11201 Office: Brooklyn Pub Library Grand Army Plaza Brooklyn NY 11238

DUCHIN, PETER OELRICHS, musician; b. N.Y.C., July 28, 1937; s. Edwin Frank and Marjorie (Oelrichs) D.; m. Cheray Zauderer, June 22, 1964; children: Jason Edwin, Courtnay Oelrichs, Colin Z., Malcolm. B.A. U., Yale U., 1958; student polit. scis. and music conservatory, Paris, 1957. Pres. Peter Duchin Orchs., 1963—. Bd. dirs. Greater N.Y. council Boy Scouts Am., Boys Harbor, Dance Theater Harlem, Internat. Med. Research Found., Am. Council on Arts, Am. Jazz Alliance; mem. council Yale U., 1974—; mem. N.Y. State Council on Arts, 1976—, Nat. Symphony Adv. Bd. Served with AUS, 1958-60. Clubs: Yale (N.Y.C.); Racquet and Tennis, Bedford Golf and Tennis, Stanley Rod and Gun. Office: care Willard Alexander Inc 660 Madison Ave New York NY 10021 *

DUCHOSSOIS, RICHARD LOUIS, manufacturing company executive; b. Chgo., Oct. 7, 1921; s. Alphonse Christopher and Erna (Hessler) D.; (widower); children: Craig J., Dayle, R. Bruce, Kimberly. Student, Washington and Lee U., 1940-42. With Thrall Car Mfg. Co., Chicago Hights, Ill., 1946—, pres., 1954-80, Duchossois/Thrall Group, 1980—, also chmn. bd.; chmn. bd. Chamberlain Mfg. Corp., Elmhurst, Ill., Transp. Corp. Am., Chicago Heights; dir. LaSalle Nat. Bank, Western Stoneware Co. Bd. dirs. Ry. Progress Inst. Served with AUS, 1942-46; ETO. Decorated Purple Heart with cluster, Bronze Star with clusters. Mem. Ill. Mfrs. Assn. (dir.), Chief Execs. Forum. Republican. Methodist. Club: Economic (Chgo.). Office: 26th and State Sts Chicago Heights IL 60411 *

DUCKERT, AUDREY ROSALIND, educator, lexicographer; b. Cottage Grove, Wis., Mar. 28, 1927; d. Harold William and Mabel Elina (Hoveland) D. B.S., U. Wis.-Madison, 1948, M.A., 1949; Ph.D., Radcliffe Coll., 1959. With editorial dept. G&C Merriam Co., Springfield, Mass., 1953-56; mem. faculty U. Mass., Amherst, 1959—, prof. English, 1972—; vis. prof. English Emory U., 1978. Co-author: A Method for Collecting Dialect, 1953; Co-editor: Handbook of the Linguistic Geography of New England, 2d edit, 1973, Lexicography in English, 1973; Contbr. papers and articles in field.; Asso. editor: Linguistic Atlas of the South and Middle Atlantic States, 1973—, Names, 1961-65; asso. dir.: Linguistic Atlas of the North Central States, 1975—; adv. bd.: Dictionary of Am. Regional English, 1965—; adj. editor, 1981—; cons.: Oxford English Dictionary, supplement II, 1968—. Sr. fellow in humanities Am. Council Learned Socs., 1973-74. Mem. Am. Dialect Soc. (pres. 1974), Am. Name Soc. (pres. 1971), Modern Humanities Research Assn., MLA, Medieval Acad. Am., Linguistic Soc. Am., N.Y. Acad. Scis., Am. Folklore Soc., Dictionary Soc. N.Am., Mass. Hort. Soc., Nat. Council Tchrs. English, Swift River Valley Hist. Soc. (librarian), Phi Beta Kappa. Presbyterian. Home: 1 Maplewood Terr Hadley MA 01035 Office: Dept English Univ Mass Amherst MA 01003 *I am a country woman, a worshipper of life—in language, in green and growing things.*

DUCKWORTH, HENRY EDMISON, univ. pres.; b. Brandon, Man., Can., Nov. 1, 1915; s. Henry Bruce and Ann (Edmison) D.; m. Katherine Jane McPherson, Nov. 21, 1942; children—Henry William, Jane (Mrs. Andrew Maksymiuk). B.A., U. Man., 1935, B.Sc., 1936, LL.D., 1978; Ph.D., U. Chgo., 1942; D.Sc., U. Ottawa, 1966, McMaster U., 1969, U. Laval, 1971, Mt. Allison U., 1971, U. N.B., 1972, Queen's U., 1978, U. Western Ont., 1979. Lectr. physics United Coll., Man., 1938-40; research scientist Nat. Research Council Can., 1942-45; asst. prof. physics U. Man., 1945-46; asso. prof. physics Wesleyan U., 1946-51; prof. physics McMaster U., 1951-65; v.p. U. Man., 1965-71; vis. prof. U. Laval, 1970-71; pres., vice-chancellor U. Winnipeg, 1971—; Mem. Nat. Research Council Can., 1961-67; mem. Def. Research Bd., 1965-71; chmn. Internat. Union Pure and Applied Physics commn. atomic masses and related constants, 1966-69; chmn. evaluation com. Communications Tech. Satellite, 1972-75; mem. Killam com. Canada Council, 1972-75, Can. Adv. Environ. Council, 1973-76, Sci. Council Can., 1973-77, Nat. Library Adv. Bd., 1974-79; pres. Assn. Univs. and Colls. of Can., 1976-77; mem. Natural Scis. and Engring. Research Council, 1978—; dir. Inst. for Research on Public Policy, 1978—; chmn. council Assn. Commonwealth Univs., 1978-79. Author: Mass Spectroscopy, 1958, Electricity and Magnetism, 1960, Little Men in the Unseen World, 1963. Recipient Nuffield Travelling fellowship; Can. Assn. Physicists medal; Royal Soc. Can. Tory medal; decorated officer Order of Can. Fellow Royal Soc. Can. (pres. 1971-72), Am. Phys. Soc.; mem. Canadian Assn. Physicists (pres. 1960-61). Mem. United Ch. Can. Clubs: Manitoba, Rotary. Home: 49 Oak St Winnipeg MB Canada

DUCKWORTH, T.A., insurance company executive; b. Albany, Mo., Mar. 26, 1912; s. Thomas Alexander and Sally (Edwards) D.; m. Edwina Nelson, July 12, 1941; children: Sally (Mrs. David P. Hansen), Celeste Nelson (Mrs. James Natwick), Jane Chilton (Mrs. Frank Grossman). Student, Central Coll., Fayette, Mo., 1930-33; LL.B., U. Mo., 1936. Bar: Mo., Wis. With Employers Ins. of Wausau, Wis., 1936—, sec., 1957-60, sr. v.p., sec., 1960-74, exec. v.p., 1974-75, pres., 1975-77, chmn., 1977-81, chmn. exec. com., 1981-84, dir. emeritus, 1984—. Mem. sr. council Wis. Lung Assn.; bd. dirs. The Leigh Yawkey Woodson Art Mus., Inc., Wausau; vice chmn. Wausau Hosps., Inc.; v.p. Daniel Storey Found., Wausau. Mem. Wausau Area C. of C. (past pres.), Delta Theta Phi, Phi Kappa Delta. Presbyterian (elder). Lodges: Masons; Shriners; Rotary. Home: 918 McIndoe St Wausau WI 54401 Office: 2000 Westwood Dr Wausau WI 54401

DUCKWORTH, WINSTON HOWARD, ceramic engr.; b. Greenfield, Ohio, Oct. 15, 1918; s. Benton Raymond and Carrie Lois (Schrock) D.; m. Clara Elizabeth Ayres, Dec. 15, 1941; children—Winston (dec.), Christopher. B.Chem. Engring., Ohio State U., 1940, M.S., 1941. Registered profl. engr., Ohio. With Battelle Meml. Inst., Columbus, Ohio, 1946—, research engr., 1946-48, asst. chief ceramic research, 1948-52, chief ceramic research, 1952-66, fellow, 1966—, dir., 1967-71, mem. research council, 1979—; Mem. Engrs. Joint Council, 1968—, trustee, 1975-77. Author: also numerous articles. Engineering Properties of Ceramics. Served with AUS, 1941-46; col. USAF; Ret. Fellow Am. Ceramic Soc. (Cramer award 1974, trustee 1968-74, v.p. 1976); mem. Nat. Inst. Ceramic Engrs. (pres. 1964, trustee 1963-74, permanent sec. 1978—), Can. Ceramic Soc., AAAS, Ohio Acad. Sci., Keramos, Sigma Xi. Home: 63 Brevoort Rd Columbus OH 43214 Office: 505 King Ave Columbus OH 43201

DUCOFF, HOWARD S., biologist, educator; b. N.Y.C., May 5, 1923; s. Dave and Tillie (Machinist) D.; m. Rose Hirsch, Aug. 25, 1946; children: Sandra, Barbara, Paul J., Laura. B.S., CCNY, 1942; Ph.D. in Physiology, U. Chgo., 1953. With Argonne (Ill.) Nat. Lab., 1946-63, asso. scientist, 1951-57, cons., 1957-63; faculty U. Ill., Urbana, 1957—, prof. physiology and biophysics, 1965—, prof. bioengring., 1973—; vis. scientist Lawrence Berkeley Lab. U. Calif., 1975-76; vis. investigator Sch. Biol. Sci., U. Sussex (Eng.), 1983-84; USPHS spl. fellow dept. zoology U. Cambridge, Eng., 1964-65. Editor: (with C. F. Ehret) Mitogenesis, 1959; Author articles. Served with AUS, 1943-46. Mem. Am. Soc. Cell. Biology, Am. Soc. Zoologists, Radiation Research Soc., Soc. Gen Physiologists, Soc. Invert. Pathologists, Sigma Xi. Home: 1516 W Charles St Champaign IL 61820 Office: 524 Burrill Hall 407 S Goodwin Ave Urbana IL 61801

DUCOMMUN, ALAN N., mfg. co. exec.; b. Alhambra, Calif., Mar. 20, 1916; s. Edmond F. and Lula Gladys (Morissey) D.; m. Shirley R. Rundquist, Oct. 16, 1964 (div. Feb. 1975); children—David and Ann (twins). B.A., Stanford U., 1940. Pres. Am. Metal Bearing Co., Garden Grove, Calif., 1961—. Served to 1st lt. USAF, 1942-45. Home: 3 Packsaddle Rd E Rolling Hills CA 90274 Office: Acacia Ave Grove:

DUCOMMUN, CHARLES EMIL, business executive; b. Los Angeles, Apr. 27, 1913; s. Emil C. and Bescelia (Shemwell) D.; m. Palmer Gross, June 15, 1949; children: Robert Constant, Electra Ducommun dePeyster. A.B., Stanford U., 1935; M.B.A. with distinction, Harvard U., 1942. With Ducommun Inc. (formerly Ducommun Metals & Supply Co.), Los Angeles, 1936—, dir., 1938—, sec., 1938-46, treas., 1946, v.p., treas., 1946-50, pres., 1950—, chmn., 1973-78, chmn. fin. com., 1978—; dir. Ducommun Realty Co., 1938-70, v.p., 1947-70; dir. Farmers & Merchants Nat. Bank of Los Angeles (merged with Security Pacific Nat. Bank 1957), Security Pacific Corp., Pacific Telephone and Telegraph Co.; adv. dir. Investment Co. Am.; mem. adv. com. internat. trade U.S. Dept. Commerce, 1957-60. Mem. Central City Com.; trustee Com. for Econ. Devel., 1958-76; mem. Los Angeles 200 Com., 1978—, Gov.'s Commn. on Calif. Small Bus., 1950-53, Rep. Nat. Finance Com., 1953-54; chmn. Rep. Finance Com. of Calif., 1953-54; del. Rep. Nat. Conv., 1960, 68; mem. Rep. State Central Com., 1953-56, 64-69; trustee Los Angeles County Mus. Art, 1960—, v.p., 1974-80, treas., 1980—; trustee So. Calif. Area Bldg. Funds; chmn. Stanford Cabinet, 1965-71; del. Japan Calif. Assn., 1965—; chmn. So. Calif., Invest-in-Am., 1969, now dir., mem.-at-large nat. adv. bd.; past chmn., now dir. Los Angeles Civic Light Opera Assn.; dir. Calif. Civic Light Opera Assn., 1979—; trustee Claremont Men's Coll., Stanford U., 1961-71; v.p. Stanford U., 1964-70; chmn. Los Angeles Bicentennial Student Art Competition, 1980-81; co-chmn. 1984 Olympics Youth Activities Commn., 1982—. Served as lt. USNR; aide to chief staff U.S. Fleet, 1942-46. Mem. Los Angeles C. of C. (chmn. fed. affairs com., pres. 1957, treas. 1958, dir. 1952-61), Harvard Bus. Sch. Alumni (exec. council 1953-57), Navy League U.S. (chpt. dir. 1955-60), Stanford Assos. (Gold Spike award 1980), Harvard Bus. Sch. (mem. overseers vis. com. 1962-68, 69-75, Statesman of Yr. So. Calif. 1975), Delta Kappa Epsilon. Clubs: Lincoln (pres. 1969, bd. govs. Office: 612 S Flower St Los Angeles CA 90017

DUDAN, PETER, ret. banker; b. Paterson, N.J., Mar. 30, 1920; s. Michael and Mary (Tuchty) D.; m. Jane Louise Fairchild, Apr. 10, 1948; children—Sandra (Mrs. Alfred T. Mahan IV), William Wade, Noel, Donald Michael. Grad., Phillips Acad., 1939; A.B., Amherst Coll., 1943; postgrad., Rutgers U., 1956-58. Asst. to div. sales mgr. U.S. Gypsum Co., Chgo., 1948-50; with Marine Midland Bank of Southeastern N.Y., Nyack, 1950-81, chmn. bd., chief exec. officer, 1971-81; dir. Kay Fries Chem. Co., Hackensack Water Co., Spring Valley Water Co., Marine Midland Municipals Co., Buffalo; exec. council Marine Midland Banks, Inc., Buffalo, cons., from 1975. Dir., v.p. Rockland County (N.Y.) Indsl. Devel. Com., 1962-67; mem. legislative com. Group VI, N.Y. State Bankers, 1968-71, nominating com., 1967—; dir., exec. com. Mid-Hudson Patterns for Progress, 1970—; chmn. Statewide Parks Adv. Com., 1971; lay mem. grievance com. 9th Jud. Dist. N.Y.; mem. Palisades Interstate Park Commn., 1971—, pres., 1977—; mem. Nyack Action Council, 1965-71; trustee Nyack Hosp.; mem. exec. com. Rockland County YMCA, bd. dirs., 1965-69. Served to lt. USNR, 1943-46. Mem. Rockland County Assn. (dir., v.p. 1967-71, pres. 1976-77), Nyack C. of C., Am. Arbitration Assn., Psi Upsilon. Republican. Episcopalian. Clubs: Rotarian (pres. Nyack 1969), Rockland (N.Y.) Country (pres. 1976-77). Home: 100 N Greenbush Rd West Nyack NY 10994

DUDDEN, ARTHUR POWER, educator, historian; b. Cleve., Oct. 26, 1921; s. Arthur Clifford and Kathleen (Bray) D.; m. Adrianne Churchill Onderdonk, June 5, 1965; 1 dau., Alexis B.; children by previous marriage: Kathleen (Mrs. James S. Andrasick), Candace L. A.B., Wayne State U., 1942; A.M., U. Mich., 1947, Ph.D., 1950. Faculty Bryn Mawr Coll., 1950—, prof. history, 1965—; instr. Coll. City N.Y., summer 1950; vis. asst. prof. Am. civilization U. Pa., 1953-54, ednl. coordinator spl. program Am. civilization, 1956, faculty, 1953-59, vis. asso. prof. history, summers 1958, 62-65, vis. prof. history, 1965-68; vis. asso. prof. Princeton, 1958-59, Haverford Coll., 1962-63; vis. prof. Trinity Coll., summer 1965; cons. Peace Corps, 1962-66; Mem. Bicentennial Com. on Internat. Confs. of Americanists, 1973-76; pres. Fulbright Assn. of Alumni, 1976-80, exec. dir., 1980—. Author: Teachers Manual to the American Republic, vols. I and II, 1959, 60, 70, Understanding the American Republic, vols. I and II, 1961, 70, Objective Tests, The American Republic, 1962, The Assault of Laughter, 1962, The United States of America: A Syllabus of American Studies, 2 vols, 1963, The Instructor's Guide to the United States, 3d edit, 1972, The Student's Guide to the United States, 2d edit, 1967, Joseph Fels and the Single Tax Movement, 1971, Pardon Us, Mr. President!, 1975; Editor: Woodrow Wilson and the World of Today, 1957; Compiler: International Directory of Specialists in American Studies, 1975. Served with USNR, 1942-45. Sr. Fulbright scholar, Denmark, 1959-60. Mem. Fellows Am. Studies (sec.-treas. 1957-59, pres. 1960-61), Am. Studies Assn. (treas. 1968, 72, exec. sec. 1969-72), Am. Hist. Assn., Orgn. Am. Historians (local arrangements chmn. Phila. 1969). Home: 829 Old Gulph Rd Bryn Mawr PA 19010

DUDDLES, CHARLES WELLER, food company executive; b. Cadillac, Mich., Mar. 31, 1940; s. Dwight Irving and Bertha (Taylor) D.; m. Judith Marie Robinson, June 23, 1962; children: Paul, Steven, Lisa. B.S., Ferris State Coll., 1961. C.P.A. Mich., Mo. Audit mgr. Price Waterhouse & Co., Battle Creek, Mich., 1961-72; mgr. gen. acctg. Ralston Purina Co., St. Louis, 1973-77, dir. spl. acctg. services, 1977-79; v.p., controllerr Foodmaker, Inc., San Diego, 1979-81, sr. v.p. fin. and adminstrn., 1981—. Chmn. bd. trustee First Presbyn. Ch., El Cajon, Calif., 1983. Mem. Fin. Execs. Inst., Nat. Assn. Accts., Am. Inst. C.P.A.s. Republican. Presbyterian. Club: Rotary (San Diego). Home: 1942 Hidden Mesa Rd El Cajon CA 92020 Office: Foodmaker Inc 9330 Balboa Ave San Diego CA 92123

DUDDY, FRANK EDWARD, JR., retired association executive; b. Poughkeepsie, N.Y., Sept. 26, 1917; s. Frank Edward and Neva Inez (Warfel) D.; m. Eleanor Lorraine Ibach, Dec. 25, 1940; children: Elizabeth Jean (Mrs. Richard H. Smith), Frank Edward III. B.A. cum laude, DePauw U., 1939, LL.D., 1959; A.M., Harvard, 1940, Ph.D. (Buckley scholar), 1942; Hum.D. Westminster Coll., Utah, 1968; LL.D., Ashland Coll., Ohio, 1973, Walsh Coll., 1976; L.H.D., Defiance Coll., Ohio, 1974. Instr. English, history Northeastern U., 1940-41; instr. history DePauw U., 1942; instr. humanities Stephens Coll., 1942-43; instr. history U.S. Naval Acad., 1946-48, asst. prof., 1948-51, assoc. prof., 1951-56; pres. Westminster Coll., Salt Lake City, 1956-63, Marietta (Ohio) Coll., 1963-73; also trustee ex-officio; pres. Assn. Ind. Colls. and Univs., Ohio, 1973-83; Pres., exec. dir. Intermountain Colls. Assn., 1958-63; Ohio rep. Task Force on Higher Edn., Appalachian Regional Commn., 1971-73; chmn. East Central Coll. Consortium, 1968-70; mem. adv. coms. on relations with pvt. instns. Ohio Bd. Regents and State Dept. Edn.; past chmn. Ohio Found. Ind. Colls.; mem. exec. com. Ind. Coll. Funds Am., 1970-73; sec.-treas. bd. dirs. Nat. Council Ind. Colls. and Univs., 1973-76. Contbr. articles to profl. publs. Sec.-treas. Ohio Energy Task Force, 1973-75; Bd. govs., chmn. pres. search com. Inst. European Studies, chmn. bd. govs., 1976—; bd. dirs. exec. com. Nat. Assn. Ind. Colls. and Univs., 1976-77; mem. Ohio Com. for Pub. Programs in Humanities, 1975-83. Served with USNR,

1943-46; now ret. lt. comdr. Res. Mem. Omicron Delta Kappa, Beta Theta Pi, Phi Mu Alpha, Alpha Phi Omega. Presbyn. (elder). Club: Mountain View Country (Greensboro, Vt.). Home: 2825 Northwood Rd Holladay UT 84117 Block House Hill Greensboro VT 05841

DUDEK, RICHARD ALBERT, engineering educator; b. Clarkson, Nebr., Sept. 3, 1926; s. Emil E. and Jennie (Indra) D.; m. Helen M. Staver, Dec. 19, 1954; children: Richard Emil, Rustin Max. B.S. in Mech. Engring, U. Nebr., 1950; M.S. in Indsl. Engring, U. Iowa, 1951, Ph.D., 1956. Plant indsl. engr. Fairmont Foods Co., Sioux City, Iowa, 1951-52, div. indsl. engr., Omaha, 1952-53; research asst. U. Iowa, 1953-54; asst. prof. mech. engring. U. Nebr., 1954-56; research asso. Sch. of Health Professions, also asso. prof. indsl. engring. U. Pitts., 1956-58; prof., head dept. indsl. engring. Tex. Tech U., Lubbock, 1958—; dir. Center of Biotech. and Human Performance, 1969-74, Horn Prof., 1970—; Tech. cons. industry, instns., religious orgns., hosps., 1951—; instr. TV courses. Dir. Found. Internat. Research and Devel., Lubbock, 1960-65. Contbr. to profl. jours. in field. Bd. dirs. South Plains chpt. Muscular Dystrophy Assn. Am., 1966-76, campaign chmn., 1968. Recipient Faculty Recognition award, 1978. Fellow Am. Inst. Indsl. Engrs. (pres. Great Plains chpt. 1960-61, chmn. nat. student chpt. 1961-63, ECPD guidance rep. 1965-68, research com. 1967-69, regional v.p. 1969-71, Appreciation award 1970, spl. service award 1971); mem. Council Indsl. Engring. Acad. Dept. Heads (asst. sec. 1980, sec. 1981-82, vice chmn. 1982-83, chmn. 1983-84), Am. Soc. Engring. Edn. (editor indsl. engring. div. 1965-66, sec. indsl. engring. div. 1966-67, vice chmn. 1967-68, chmn. 1968-69, chmn. planning com. of council of tech. divs. 1970-71, sec. council 1972-73), Inst. Mgmt. Sci., ASME, Human Factors Soc., Tech. Assessment Soc., Sigma Xi (pres. Tex. Tech. chpt. 1971-72), Phi Kappa Phi (chpt. pres. 1967), Pi Mu Epsilon, Pi Tau Sigma, Alpha Pi Mu, Tau Beta Pi. Home: 3707 46th St Lubbock TX 79413

DUDENHOEFFER, FRANK EDWARD, pediatrician; b. Cin., May 24, 1926; s. Frank Joseph and Norma (Simper) D.; m. Nina Genevieve Fincham, May 31, 1952; children: Ann Lynn, John Edward, Mary Jane, Thomas Martin, Susan Leigh. B.S., U. Cin., 1949, M.D., 1952. Intern Tripler Hosp., Honolulu, 1952-53; resident Children's Hosp., Los Angeles, 1954-56; practice medicine specializing in pediatrics, La Canada, Calif., 1956-78; med. dir. Hillside Center, Long Beach, Calif., 1978-80; mem. staff Children's Hosp., Los Angeles, 1954—, chmn. staff, 1979-81; mem. staff Verdugo Hills Hosp., Glendale, Calif., chmn. pediatric dept., 1974; mem. staff Huntington Meml. Hosp., Pasadena, Calif., Glendale Meml. and Glendale Adventist hosps., St. Joseph's Hosp., Burbank, Calif., Meml. Hosp., Long Beach; asst. clin. prof. pediatrics U. So. Calif., 1956-62, asso. clin. prof., 1962-71, clin. prof., 1971—; bd. dirs. Glendale Mental Health Clinic, 1957-61, Children's Hosp. Los Angeles, 1977—. Sec. edn. program Crescenta Canada YMCA, 1960-78; bd. dirs. La Canada Scholarship Found., 1972—. Served with USAAF, 1944-45; Served with U.S. Army, 1952-54; Korea. Fellow Am. Acad. Pediatrics (chmn. youth com. local chpt. 1966-80, mem. nat. adolescent com. 1977—, sec. sect. on adolescent medicine 1980—); mem. Southwestern, Los Angeles pediatric socs., AMA, Calif., Los Angeles med. assns., Los Angeles Physicians Art Soc., Am. Orthopsychiat. Assn., Los Angeles Physicians Art Soc. (art prizes 1974—), Am. Physicians Art Assn., U. Cin., Sigma Chi alumni assns. Republican. Roman Catholic. Club: Kiwanis. Office: 1346 Foothill Blvd La Canada CA 91011

DUDERSTADT, JAMES JOHNSON, university dean; b. Ft. Madison, Iowa, Dec. 5, 1942; s. Mack Henry and Katharine Sydney (Johnson) D.; m. Anne Marie, June 24, 1964; children: Susan Kay, Katharine Anne. B.Eng. with highest honors, Yale U., 1964; M.S. in Engring. Sci, Calif. Inst. Tech., 1965; Ph.D. in Engring. Sci. and Physics, Calif. Inst. Tech., 1967. Asst. prof. nuclear engring. U. Mich., 1969-72, asso. prof., 1972-76, prof., 1976-81, dean, 1981—; cons. in field. Author textbooks and; contbr. articles to profl. jours. AEC fellow, 1964-68. Fellow Am. Nuclear Soc., Mem. (Mark Mills award 1968), Am. Phys. Soc., AAAS, Sigma Xi, Tau Beta Pi. Office: Chrysler Ctr University of Michigan Ann Arbor MI 48109

DUDEWICZ, EDWARD JOHN, statistician; b. Jamaica, N.Y., Apr. 24, 1942; s. Edward George and Adele (Drula) D.; m. Patricia Anne Scott, July 6, 1963; children: Douglas, Robert, Carolyn. S.B., M.I.T., 1963; M.S., Cornell U., 1966, Ph.D., 1969. Asst. engr. AVCO Corp., Wilmington, Mass., 1963; asst. prof. stats. U. Rochester, 1967-72, asst. prof. biostats., 1971-72; assoc. prof. stats. Ohio State U., 1972-77, prof., 1977-82; prof. dept. math. Syracuse (N.Y.) U., 1982—, chmn. univ. stats. council, 1982—; chmn. grad. com. stats. and biostats. Ohio State U., 1973-75, 78-80; vis. scholar, vis. assoc. prof. Stanford U., 1976; vis. prof. U. Louvain, Belgium, 1979; cons. in field. Author: Introduction to Statistics and Probability, 1976, Solutions in Statistics and Probability, 1980, The Handbook of Random Number Generation and Testing, 1981, The Complete Categorized Guide to Statistical Selection and Ranking Procedures, 1982; editor: Statis. Theory and Method Abstracts, 1975-81, Am. Jour. Math. and Mgmt. Scis, 1979—, Stats. and Decisions, An Internat. Math. Jour. for Stochastic Methods and Models, 1982—; contbr. articles to profl. jours. Office Naval Research grantee, 1967-72, 79-82; U.S. Army grantee, 1972-74; NSF fellow, 1966-67; NATO grantee, 1978—; Nat. Cancer Inst. grantee, 1979-83. Fellow N.Y. Acad. Scis., Inst. Math. Stats., Am. Statis. Assn., Am. Soc. Quality Control, fellow (Jack Youden prize 1981); mem. Math. Assn. Am., AAUP, Japan Statis. Soc., Sigma Xi (research award Ohio State U. chpt. 1977), Phi Kappa Phi. Home: 20 Cross Rd DeWitt NY 13224 Office: Dept of Math Syracuse University Syracuse NY 13210 *When searching to make significant contributions to the theory of the field of mathematical statistics, I have always looked among the ideas and principles which are "self-evident" and accepted by most leaders of the field, and there have found a wealth of substantial improvement possible. In applications, one can trust the practitioner of statistics to tell you his needs; in theory, one can trust the theoretician to tell you how not to fill those needs. Being irreverent, I have avoided being irrelevant.*

DUDGEON, FARNHAM FRANCIS, editor; b. St. James, Minn., Feb. 16, 1912; s. Hugh G. and Mary Josephine (Nugent) D.; m. Gould Crook, July 6, 1937; children—Michael, Patrick, Timothy, Colleen. Student, St. John's U., 1928-29; B.S., U. N.D., 1934. Labor relations, investigative work N.D. state, fed. agencies, 1934-39; mem. editorial staff Western Newspaper Union, 1939-42, editor-in-chief, 1942-52; editor and pub. Feature Publs., Inc., 1952—. Contbr. weekly news analysis to 2,500 community newspapers, 1940-43. City commr., mayor pro tem, Frankfort, 1965-66, mayor, 1967. Mem. Sigma Delta Chi, Theta Chi, Phi Delta Kappa. Roman Catholic. Club: K.C. Home: 105 Dakota Rd Frankfort KY 40601 Office: McClure Bldg Suite 303A Frankfort KY 40601

DUDICK, MICHAEL JOSEPH, bishop; b. St. Clair, Pa., Feb. 24, 1917; s. John and Mary (Jurick) D. B.A., Ill. Benedictine Coll., Lisle, 1943; theol. studies, St. Procopius Sem., Lisle, 1943-45. Ordained priest Roman Cath. Ch., 1945; vice chancellor Exarchate of Pitts., 1946-55; chancellor Diocese of Passaic, N.J., 1963-68, bishop, 1968—; v.p. N.J. Coalition of Religious Leaders; cons. Roman Curia-Sacred Congregation Eastern Cath. Chs.; cons. ecumenical and interreligious com. Nat. Conf. Cath. Bishops. Bd. regents Seton Hall U., 1968—; mem. vis. com. Harvard U. Club: K.C. (4). Home: 324 Crestmont Rd Cedar Grove NJ 07009 Office: 101 Market St Passaic NJ 07055

DUDLEY, E. WALLER, lawyer; b. Alexandria, Va., Feb. 12, 1923; s. Luther H. and Katherine Carrol (Waller) D.; m. Letty Waugh; children: Carter, Waller, Luther. A.B., Washington and Lee U., 1943, LL.B., 1947. Bar: Va. 1947, D.C. 1982, U.S. Ct. Appeals (4th cir.) 1950, U.S. Supreme Ct. 1952. Sr. ptnr. Boothe, Prichard & Dudley, Alexandria, 1947—; dir. 1st Am. Bank Va. Trustee Washington and Lee U., Lexington, Va.; chmn. ARC, Alexandria, 1955-58, Alexandria Traffic Bd., 1954-57. Lt. j.g. USNR, 1943-46. Fellow Am. Coll. Trial Lawyers, Am. Bar Found.; mem. Va. Bar Assn. (past pres.), Alexandria Bar Assn. (past pres.), ABA. Episcopalian. Club: Kiwanis. Office: Boothe Prichard and Dudley 711 Princess St Alexandria VA 22313

DUDLEY, EDWARD, language educator; b. St. Paul, July 18, 1926; s. Edward Joseph and Ruth Esther (Grandquist) D.; m. Patricia Jane Hayes, Aug. 1, 1959; children: John, David. B.A. in English, U. Minn., 1949, M.A., 1951, Ph.D. in Spanish, 1963. Asst. prof. Spanish UCLA, 1963-70; dir. comparative lit. U. Pitts., 1972-74; chmn. dept. hispanic lang. and lit. UCLA, 1970-74; prof., chmn. Spanish, Italian and Protuguese SUNY-Buffalo, 1974-77, prof. Spanish and comparative lit., chmn. dept. modern lang. and lit., 1977-83, dir. Council on Internat. Studies, 1981—; cons. Nat. Endowment for Humanities, 1975—; reader SUNY Press, U. Calif. Press, U. Pitts. Press. Editor: (with others) El Cuento, 1967, (revised edit.) El Cuento, 1983, The Wild Man Within, 1972, American Attitudes Toward Foreign Language, 1983; co-editor: jour. Latin Am. Lit. Review, 1972-73; adv. editor, 1974-76. Served with USNR, 1944-46. NEH grantee, 1974. Mem. MLA, Conrad Soc. Am., Cervantes Soc. Am., Internat. Assn. Hispanists, Medieval Acad. Am., PEN. Home: 200 Rollingwood Williamsville NY 14221 Office: SUNY Dept Modern Langs and Lit Buffalo NY 14260

DUDLEY, EDWARD RICHARD, justice N.Y. Supreme Ct.; b. South Boston, Va., Mar. 11, 1911; s. Edward Richard and Nellie (Johnson) D.; m. Rae Olley, Jan. 31, 1942; 1 son, Edward D. B.S., Johnson C. Smith U., Charlotte, N.C., 1932; LL.B., St. Johns Sch. Law, Bklyn., 1941. Bar: N.Y. bar 1942. Asst. atty. gen., N.Y., 1942; asst. spl. counsel N.A.A.C.P., 1943-45, 1947-48; U.S. ambassador to, Liberia, 1948-53; judge Domestic Relations Ct., N.Y.C., 1955-60; borough pres., N.Y. County, 1960-65; justice N.Y. Supreme Ct. for 1st Jud. Dist., N.Y.C., 1965—, presiding justice, appellate term. Office: 60 Centre St New York NY 10007

DUDLEY, ELFORD SAMUEL, educator; b. Norfolk, Va., Oct. 17, 1923; s. Elford Samuel and Annabelle Lee (Warriner) D.; m. Eleanor Jeane Mulder, Aug. 9, 1947; children—David Michael, Sandra Lee. B.B.A., U. Mich., 1950, M.A., 1955, Ph.D., 1960; student, Norfolk div. William and Mary Va. Poly. Inst., 1941-43, 48, Hope Coll., 1943-44, Am. U., 1953. Tchr. Rufner Jr. High Sch., Norfolk, Va., 1951-52; exec. sec. United World Federalists, Ind., Mich., Ohio, 1952-54; speech instr. U. Mich., 1955-59; asst. prof. speech U. Ala., 1959-62; prof., head dept. communication Miss. State U., 1962—, dir. summer program academically talented students, 1965-82. Bd. dirs. Mississippians for Ednl. TV, pres., 1980-81. Served with AUS, World War II. Decorated Purple Heart, Bronze Star. Mem. Speech Communication Assn. (mem. legislative council 1970—), Assn. Communication Adminstrs., So. Speech Communication Assn. (pres. 1971), Miss. Speech Assn. (pres. 1964-66, 72-73), Miss. TV Council for Higher Edn. (chmn. 1968-81), Miss. Film Commn., Phi Kappa Phi, Pi Delta Kappa. Presbyn. (deacon 1968-72, elder 1973—). Home: 112 Seville Pl Starkville MS 39759 Office: Drawer PF Mississippi State MS 39762

DUDLEY, GEORGE AUSTIN, educator, architect, planning cons.; b. Pitts., Dec. 24, 1914; s. Samuel William and Mabel Eva (Allen) D.; children—George Bergin, Sally Jean, John Phillips, Samuel William III. B.A., Yale, 1936, B.F.A. in Arch, 1938, M.F.A. in City Planning, 1940. With Office Coordinator of Inter-Am. Affairs, 1941-45; dir. research Conn. Post War Planning Bd., 1944-45; with archtl. firm Harrison & Abramovitz, N.Y.C., 1945-48, 59-60; sec. internat. bd. design UN Hdqrs., 1945-46; pres. IBEC Housing Corp., 1948-59; cons. Internat. Devel. Adv. Bd., 1951; dir. N.Y. State Office Regional Devel.; also sec. Planning Coordination Bd. of Gov. Rockefeller, 1960-62; trustee N.Y. State U. Constrn. Fund; planning coordinator N.Y. State New South Mall Capital, 1962-65; dean Sch. Architecture, Rensselaer Poly. Inst., 1962-65; founding dean Sch. Architecture and Urban Planning, U. Calif. at Los Angeles, 1965-68; pres. N.Y. State Environ. Facilities Corp., 1967-72; chmn., chief exec. officer N.Y. State Council on Architecture, 1967-75; sr. cons. and phys. planning officer Kuwait Inst. Sci. Research, 1977-80; cons. master planning Saudi Arabian Nat. Center Sci. and Tech., Riyadh, 1980—, Amanat Al-Asima, Baghdad, Iraq, 1980—; lectr. USIS/ICA, Brazil, Venezuela, Trinidad, Honduras, Mexico, India, Singapore, Malaysia, Indonesia, S. Korea, Hong Kong, Japan; mem. U.S. del. UN Conf. Human Settlement, Vancouver, 1976. Contbg. editor: Architecture Plus. Trustee Inst. Architecture and Urban Studies, 1968-78; bd. dirs. AIA Found.; mem. overseers vis. com. Harvard Grad. Sch. Design, 1974-79; chmn. Yale Council Com. for Architecture and Art, 1970-75. Fellow AIA. Address: 121 W 15th St New York NY 10011

DUDLEY, GUILFORD, JR., insurance and oil executive, former ambassador; b. Nashville; s. Guilford and Anne (Dallas) D.; m. Jane Anderson; 1 dau., Trevania Dallas.; children by previous marriage: Guilford III, Robert Lusk. Student, Loomis Sch., Peabody Coll.; A.B., Vanderbilt U., 1929; LL.D. (hon.), Cumberland U., Tusculum U. Former pres., chmn. Life & Casualty Ins. Co. of Tenn., Nashville; vice-chmn. Ingram Corp., New Orleans; ambassador to, Denmark, 1969-72; dir. Am. Century Trust, Jacksonville, McDowell Enterprises Inc., 3d Nat. Bank, Nashville, Royal Trust Bank, Palm Beach. Author: The Skyline is a Promise. Chmn. Tenn. Republican Finance Com., 1964-69, 72—; mem. Congressional Awards Bd., Washington; Bd. dirs. Vanderbilt U., Ensworth Sch., Cumberland Coll. Recipient George Washington award Freedoms Found., 1967; named Nat. Salesman of Year Sales and Marketing Execs., 1965; Gold Good Citizen award SAR, 1965; Edward Potter Leadership award, 1978; Outstanding Citizenship award Nat. Football Hall of Fame, 1979; decorated Grand Cross Dannebrog, Denmark). Mem. Nat. Assn. Thorobred Breeders, Phi Delta Theta. Episcopalian. Clubs: Turf and Field, River (N.Y.C.); Nat. Steeple and Hunt; Hillsboro Hounds, Meadow, Bathing Corp. of Southampton (N.Y.); Everglades, Bath and Tennis, Seminole Golf (Palm Beach, Fla.). Home: 2201 Harding Pl Nashville TN 37215 also 1820 S Ocean Blvd Palm Beach FL 33480 Office: Life & Casualty Tower Nashville TN 37219

DUDLEY, JAMES HUDSON, lawyer; b. Comanche, Tex., July 10, 1939; s. Gail Paul and Editha Grace (Williams) D.; m. Margaret Elizabeth Goodwin, Apr. 26, 1975; 1 son, James Hudson Dudley. B.A., U. Tex., 1961, J.D., 1965. Bar: Tex. bar 1965. County atty., Comanche County, 1968-72; partner firm Sudderth, Woodley & Dudley, Comanche, 1973—; dir. Comanche Nat. Bank, Gore's, Inc. Bd. dirs., chmn. Central Tex. Mental Health Center, Tex. Retardation Center, Tex. Arts Alliance, Comanche County Hist. Commn., Comanche County Child Welfare Assn. Mem. Tex. Bar, ABA (grievance com. dist. 14B), 52d Jud. Dist. Bar Assn. (pres. 1976-77), Tex. Sheep and Goat Raisers Assn. (dir. 1969—), Friar Soc. Episcopalian (dir. mission bd. 1971-72, sr. warden 1967-70). Club: PAR Country. Home: 701 W Wright St Comanche TX 76442 Office: 109 W Grand Ave Comanche TX 76442 also 100 E Central Comanche TX 76442

DUDLEY, JONATHAN ELLWOOD, opera conductor, executive; b. Granville, Ohio, Sept. 1, 1940; s. Melvin John and Mabel Mary (Greiner) D. Student, Denison U., 1957-58, Boston U., 1958-61. Condr., music adminstr., Cin. Opera, 1967—; musical dir., Met. Opera Studio, N.Y.C., 1969-74; gen. dir., prin. condr., Omaha Opera Co., 1974-78; guest condr. throughout U.S. Mem. Sigma Alpha Epsilon. Office: care Artists Reps Inc 250 W 57th ST New York NY 10019 *

DUDLEY, PAUL V., bishop; b. Northfield, Minn., 1926; s. Edward Austin and Margaret Ann (Nolan) D. Student, Nazareth Coll., St. Paul Sem. Ordained priest Roman Cath. Ch., 1951; titular bishop of Ursona, aux. bishop of St. Paul-Mpls., 1977-78, bishop of, Sioux Falls, S.D., 1978—. Office: Chancery Office 423 N Duluth Ave Sioux Falls SD 57104 *

DUDLEY, RICHARD MANSFIELD, mathematician; b. East Cleveland, Ohio, July 28, 1938; s. Winston Mansfield and Charlotte Mae (Wheaton) D.; m. Elizabeth Allen Martin, June 3, 1978. A.B., Harvard U., 1959; Ph.D., Princeton U., 1962. Asst. prof. math. U. Calif., Berkeley, 1963-66; asso. prof. MIT, 1967-72, prof., 1972—. Editor: White Mountain Guide, 1979, Annals of Probability, 1979-81. Alfred P. Sloan Found. fellow, 1966-68. Mem. Am. Math. Soc., Inst. Math. Statistics, Sierra Club. Democrat. Home: 92 Lewis St Newton MA 02158 Office: Room 2-245 MIT Cambridge MA 02139

DUDLEY, ROBERT HAMILTON, state supreme court justice; b. Jonesboro, Ark., Nov. 18, 1933; s. Denver Layton and Helen (Paslay) D.; m. Sarah Wentzel, Apr. 2, 1954; children: Debbie, Kathy, Cindy, Bob. Student, George Washington U., 1952-54; J.D., U. Ark., 1958. Bar: Ark. 1958, U.S. Supreme Ct. 1959. Dep. pros. atty., Randolph County, Ark., 1958, spl. mcpl. judge, 1959; pros. atty. 16th Jud. Dist. Ark., 1965-70; chancery judge 3d Jud. Dist. Ark., 1971-80; justice Ark. Supreme Ct., Little Rock, 1981—. Dist. chmn. Boy Scouts Am., 1960; mem. Ark. State Crime Commn., 1970-80. Mem. Ark. Jud. Council (chmn. exec. com. 1978-79); Am. Bar Assn. Ark. Bar Assn., U. Ark. Alumni Assn. (dir. 1972-75). Democrat. Office: Justice Bldg Little Rock AR 72201

DUDLEY, ROBERT STANLEY, chemical industry executive; b. Shanghai, China, Oct. 18, 1925; s. Richard and Mona (Edwards) D.; m. Mary Stewart, Dec. 26, 1953; children: Jane, Moira, Jim, Shelagh. M.Sc., U. B.C., Can., 1951. With Can. Synthetic Rubber Ltd. (now Polysar Ltd.), Sarnia, Ont., Can., 1951—, devel. engr., copolymer process engr. tech. dept., 1952-55, supr. tech. devel., 1955-61, supr. planning and devel., 1961-65, mgr. bus. devel., 1964-68, gen. mgr. latex, 1968-69, v.p. European ops., 1969-71, group v.p. rubber and latex, 1971-79, exec. v.p. ops., 1979-81, pres., chief operating officer, dir., 1981—; dir. Petrosar Ltd. Mem. Can. Chem. Producers Assn. (bd. dirs.), Chem. Mfrs. Assn. U.S.A., Soc. Chem. Industry, Chem. Inst. Can., Can. Soc. Chem. Engrs., Profl. Engrs. Province Ont. Office: Office of Press Polysar Ltd 201 Front St N Sarnia ON Canada N7T 7V1 *

DUDLEY, RONALD G., food company executive; b. Sioux Falls, S.D., Dec. 26, 1939; s. Edward Francis and Lenore Sylvia (Hemeaur) D.; m. Patricia Schmitz, Aug. 1, 1963; children: Pamela, Kevin, Brian. B.S., Carneigie-Mellon U., 1962; postgrad., U. Pitts., 1962-64, U. Minn., 1966, 74; M.A. in Math., Duquesne U., 1966. Research engr. Jones & Laughlin Steel Corp., Pitts., 1962-65; with Gen. Mills., Mpls., 1966-75, gen. mgr., 1973-75; v.p. planning and tech. services Land O'Lakes, Inc., Mpls., 1975-78, group v.p. red meats, 1979-81, group v.p. commodities, 1981—; cons. Control Data Corp., 1968, Computer Sci. Corp., Palo Alto, Calif., 1968. Fund raiser Am. Cancer Soc.; asst. chmn. Wayzata Sch. Bd., Minn.; chmn., solicitor United Fund of Mpls.; advisor Mpls. Jr. Achievement. Mem. Nat. Assn. Corp. Planning, Assn. Corp. Growth. Republican. Roman Catholic. Home: 2605 Urbandale Ln Plymouth MN 55477 Office: Land O'Lakes Inc 4001 Lexington Ave N Arden Hills MN 55112

DUDLEY, TILFORD E., public affairs counsellor; b. Charleston, Ill., Apr. 21, 1907; s. Gerry Brown and Esther Wilhoit (Shoot) D.; m. Martha Fairchild Ward, Aug. 28, 1937; children: Donica Ward, Gerric Ward, Martha Fairchild. Ph.B. cum laude, Wesleyan U., 1928; LL.B., Harvard U., 1931; LL.D. (hon.), Eastern Ill. U., 1979. Bar: Ill. bar 1931. Gen. practice law, Aurora, Ill., 1931-34; chief legal sect. Land Program, Fed. Emergency Relief Adminstrn., 1934-35; chief land sect. Suburban Resettlement Adminstrn., 1935-37; chief land acquisition R.D.P., Nat. Parks Service, 1936-37; trial examiner NLRB, 1937-42; prin. mediation officer Nat. War Labor Bd., 1942-43, dir. disputes, 1943-44, prin. adminstrv. officer, 1944; asso. gen. counsel and Washington rep. United Packinghouse Workers Am., 1944-45; asst. to Sidney Hillman, chmn. CIO Polit. Action Com., 1945-46, asst. dir., 1946-55, AFL-CIO Com. on Polit. Edn., 1955-58; dir. AFL-CIO Speakers Bur., 1958-69, Washington office Council for Christian Social Action, United Ch. of Christ, 1969-75, pres. property mgmt. and maintenance, 1975—. Author: The Harvard Legal Aid Bureau, Its History and Purposes, 1930, Harvard Legal Aid Bureau, 1931, Digest of Decisions of National Labor Relations Board, Vol. 8, 1939, King for a Day, 1969, Poverty and Hunger, 1970, Need for a 30 Hour Week, 1975; Editor: The Washington Report, 1969-75. Chmn. of Citizens Council for D.C., 1962-67; Mem. exec. bd. div. Christian life and work and mem. gen. bd. Nat. Council Chs., 1954-57, 64, exec. bd. div. life and mission, 1965—; cons. 2d Assembly World Council Chs., 1954; Alt. mem. Dem. Nat. Com., 1948-68; del. Dem. Nat. Conv., 1948, 52, 60, 68; vice chmn. Dem. Central Com. for D.C., 1964-67, chmn., 1967-68; sec.-treas. Am. Com. on East-West Accord, 1983—. Mem. NAACP, Ams. for Democratic Action, Sigma Chi, Delta Sigma Rho. Methodist and Congregationalist. Club: Harvard (Washington). Home: 895 7th St Charleston IL 61920 2942 Macomb St NW Washington DC 20008

DUDMAN, RICHARD BEEBE, communications company executive, journalist; b. Centerville, Iowa, May 3, 1918; s. Virgil Ernest and Wilma (Beebe) D.; m. Helen Sloane, Mar. 14, 1948; children: Iris Janet Sloane, Martha Tod Howland. A.B., Stanford U., 1940; LL.D. (hon.), U. Mo., St. Louis, 1979. Reporter, photographer Oroville (Calif.) Mercury-Register, summer 1937; reporter Denver Post, 1946-49, St. Louis Post-Dispatch, 1949-53, mem. Washington bur., 1954-81, chief bur., 1969-81; chmn. bd., v.p. news Dudman Communications Corp., 1981—; mem. adv. com. Nieman Found. for Journalism, 1977-81. Author: Men of the Far Right, 1962, 40 Days with the Enemy, 1971, also articles. Trustee Washington Journalism Center, 1974—, Inst. Current World Affairs, 1983—. Served with USNR, 1942-45. Recipient award for reporting from Asia Overseas Press Club, 1972; Edward Weintal award for diplomatic corr., 1979; Mo. medal for Journalism, 1981; Nieman fellow Harvard, 1953-54. Clubs: Rotary (Ellsworth, Maine); Gridiron (Washington). Home: Southwest Harbor ME 04679 Office: WDEA Radio Ellsworth ME 04605

DUDOCK, BERNARD SAMUEL, biochemistry educator; b. N.Y.C., Nov. 17, 1939; s. Julius and Betty D. B.S., CCNY, 1961; Ph.D. in Chemistry, Pa. State U., 1966. NIH fellow dept. biochemistry Cornell U., 1966-68; asst. prof. biochemistry SUNY, Stony Brook, 1968-73, asso. prof., 1973-81, prof., 1981—, chmn. dept., 1978-81; vis. prof.

Weizmann Inst. Sci., Rehovot, Israel, 1974-75. Contbr. articles to profl. jours. Grantee in field; recipient NIH Research Career Devel. award, 1973-78. Mem. Am. Soc. Biol. Chemists, AAAS. Office: Department of Biochemistry SUNY Stony Brook NY 11794

DUDRICK, STANLEY JOHN, surgeon, educator; b. Nanticoke, Pa., Apr. 9, 1935; s. Stanley Francis and Stephania Mary (Jachimczak) D.; m. Theresa M. Keen, June 14, 1958; children: Susan Marie, Paul Stanley, Carolyn Mary, Stanley Jonathan, Holly Anne, Anne Theresa. B.S. cum laude, Franklin and Marshall Coll., 1957; M.D., U. Pa., 1961. Intern Hosp. of U. Pa., Phila., 1961-62, resident, 1962-67; practice medicine specializing in surgery, Phila., 1967-72, Houston, 1972—; chief surg. services Hermann Hosp., 1972-80; prof. surgery U. Tex. Med. Sch., Houston, 1972-82, clin. prof. surgery, 1982—, chmn. dept. surgery, 1972-80; cons. in surgery M.D. Anderson Hosp. and Tumor Inst., 1973—, cons. to pres., 1982—, clin. prof. surgery, 1982—; sr. cons. in surgery and medicine Tex. Inst. for Rehab. and Research, 1974—; Mem. Anatomical Bd. State of Tex., 1973-78; examiner Am. Bd. Surgery, 1974-78, bd. dirs., 1978—, also mem. or chmn. various coms.; Chmn. sci. adv. com. Tex. Med. Center Library, 1974; mem. food and nutrition bd. NRC-Nat. Acad. Scis., 1973-75; mem. sci. adv. com. Nat. Found. for Ileitis and Colitis. Editor: Manual of Surgical Nutrition, 1975, Manual of Preoperative and Postoperative Care, 1983; assoc. editor: Nutrition in Medicine, 1975—; editorial cons.: Jour. of Trauma, 1972-76; editorial bd.: Annals of Surgery, 1975—, Infusion, 1978—, Nutrition and Cancer, 1980—, Nutrition Support Services, 1980—, Jour. Clin. Surgery, 1980-83, Nutrition Research, 1981—, Intermed. Communications Nursing Services, 1981—; others.; Contbr. chpts. to books, articles to profl. jours. Bd. dirs. Found. for Children, Houston, Harris County unit Am. Cancer Soc. Decorated knight Order St. John of Jerusalem Knights Hopitaller; recipient VA citation for significant contbn. to med. care, 1970; Mead Johnson award for research in hosp. pharmacy, 1972; Seale Harris medal So. Med. Assn., 1973; AMA-Brookdale award in medicine, 1975; Great Texan award Nat. Found. Iletis and Colitis, 1975; Modern Medicine award, 1977; Disting. Alumnus citation Franklin and Marshall Coll., 1980; WHO, Houston, 1980, Stinchfield award Am. Acad. Orthopedic Surgery, 1981; nat. honoree Stanley J. Dudrick Surg. Soc., 1981; numerous others. Fellow ACS (vice chmn. pre and post operative com. 1975, gov. 1979—, com. on med. motion pictures 1981-84), Philippine Coll. Surgeons (hon.), Am. Coll. Nutrition (Grace A. Goldsmith award 1982); mem. AMA (council on food and nutrition 1971-76, exec. com. 1975-76, council on sci. affairs 1976-81, Goldberger award in clin. nutrition 1970), Am. Surg. Assn., Am. Pediatric Surg. Assn. (hon.), Am. Soc. Nutritional Support Services (bd. dirs. 1982—, pres.-elect 1983), Soc. Univ. Surgeons (exec. council 1974-78), Assn. for Acad. Surgery (founders group), Internat. Soc. Parenteral Nutrition (exec. council 1975—, pres. 1978-81), Houston Gastroent. Soc., Tex. Surg. Soc., Tex. Med. Assn. (com. nutrition and food resources), Harris County Med. Soc., Am. Radium Soc., Am. Soc. Parenteral and Enteral Nutrition (pres. 1977, bd. advs. 1978—, chmn. bd. advisers 1978, Vars award 1982), Am. Gastroent. Assn., Soc. Surg. Oncology, James Ewing Soc., Ravdin-Rhoads Surg. Assn., Excelsior Surg. Soc. (Edward D. Churchill lectr. 1981), Soc. Surg. Chairmen, So. Surg. Assn., Southwestern Surg. Congress, Southeastern Surg. Congress, Surg. Biology Club II, Western Surg. Soc., Halsted Soc., Allen O. Whipple Surg., Soc. Am. Inst. Nutrition, Soc. Clin. Surgery, Am. Soc. Clin. Investigation, Soc. for Surgery of Alimentary Tract, Am. Trauma Soc. (founders group), Am. Assn. for Surgery of Trauma, Soc. Clin. Surgery, Am. Soc. Clin. Nutrition, Am. Burn Assn., AAAS, AAUP, Phi Beta Kappa, Sigma Xi, Alpha Omega Alpha. (sec.-treas. Houston chpt. 1982-83). Club: Houston Doctors (gov. 1973-75). Inventor of new technique of intravenous feeding. Home: 527 Saddlewood St Houston TX 77024 Office: St Luke's Episcopal Hosp PO Box 20269 Houston TX 77225

DUDROW, LOUIS ALBERT, banker; b. New Windsor, Md., May 11, 1924; s. LeRoy Andrew and Mabel (Geiman) D.; m. Nancy Leonie Dangoisse, July 24, 1948 (dec. Apr. 1958); children: Patricia, Richard, Caryn; m. Thelma Jean Allin, July 11, 1959 (div. Jan. 1977); children: Elizabeth, Jennifer; m. Margaret Watson Alan, Mar. 12, 1977 (div. Nov. 1979); m. Mara Donovan Lang, Feb. 9, 1980. A.B., Denison U., 1945. With Union Trust Co. Md., Balt., 1948—, treas., 1958-69, 72-83, sec., 1960-72, v.p., 1969—; v.p., treas. Union Trust Bancorp, Balt., 1972-83. Trustee Balt. Employees Retirement System, 1972-79. Served to lt. USNR, 1946, 50-53. Democrat. Presbyterian. Home: 4503 Roland Ave Baltimore MD 21210 Office: Union Trust Co PO Box 1077 Baltimore MD 21203

DUE, JEAN MARGARET, agrl. economist; b. Peterborough, Ont., Can., Sept. 19, 1921; d. Allan B. and Katherine Jean (Calder) Mann; m. John F. Due, Aug. 18, 1950; children—Allan Malcolm, Kevin John Burritt. B.Com., U. Toronto, 1946; M.S., U. Ill., 1, 950, Ph.D., 1953. Economist Dept. Agr., Ottawa, Ont., 1946-49; research asso. in home econs. U. Ill., 1959-61, vis. prof., 1965-70, prof. dept. agr. econs., 1970—. Contbr. articles to profl. jours. Mem. bd. United Ch. for World Ministries, 1977—. Mem. African Studies Assn., Am. Econ. Assn., Am. Agrl. Econs. Assn., Can. African Assn., Internat. Assn. Agrl. Econs. Home: 808 Dodds Dr Champaign IL 61820 Office: 311MH Univ Illinois Urbana IL 61801

DUE, JOHN FITZGERALD, educator, economist; b. Hayward, Cal., July 11, 1915; s. Jackson Angelo and Emmarene (Hurd) D.; m. Margaret Jean Mann, Aug. 18, 1950; children: Allan, Kevin. A.B., U. Calif., Berkeley, 1935, Ph.D., 1939; A.M., George Washington U., 1936. Instr. U. Utah, 1939-42, asst. prof., 1945-48; economist Treasury Dept., 1942; faculty U. Ill., 1948—, prof. econs., 1951—, chmn. dept., 1963-67, 71-72, acting dean, 1976. Author: Taxation and Economic Development in Tropical Africa, 1963, Indirect Taxation in Developing Economies, 1970, Sales Taxation: State and Local Structure and Operation, 1983; co-author: The Electric Interurban Railway in America, 1960, Rails to The Ochoco Country-The City of Prineville Railway, 1968, Government Finance, 7th edit, 1981, Rails to the Mid Columbia Wheatlands, 1979. Served with USMCR, 1942-45. Mem. Am. Econ. Assn., Nat. Tax Assn., Phi Beta Kappa. Home: 808 Dodds Dr Champaign IL 61820 Office: Com W Univ Ill Champaign IL 61820

DUECY, CHARLES MICHAEL, lawyer; b. Everett, Wash., Oct. 16, 1912; s. Patrick Rowan and Marie (Maecker) D.; m. Gratia Sanborn Riesche, Oct. 16, 1940; children: Charles Michael, Gratia (Mrs. Jimmy R. Evans), Margaret Theresa, Robert Riesche. Student, U. Wash., 1929-34, Stanford U., 1954-55; J.D., U. Ariz., 1957. Bar: Ariz. 1957. Sec.-treas. Coos Head Timber Co., Coos Bay, Oreg., 1945-50, Menasha Plywood Co., Coos Bay, 1948-54; pres. Menasha Sales Co., Chgo., 1952-54; sec.-treas. Builders Mortgage & Trust Co., 1954-77; practice law Scottsdale; sr. partner Duecy, Moore, Robinson & Bennett, 1957-84, of counsel, 1984—; dir. Columbia Riverlog Scaling & Grading Bur., 1948-52; mem. Pulp, Paper, Lumber and Plywood Labor Relations Com., 1948-52; spl. counsel state atty. gen. on city annexation work, 1962-64. Author: Odd Adventures of the Electrical Pussy Cat, 1964; contbr. articles to profl. jours. Chmn. Gov.'s Com. on Alcoholism, 1966-68; counsel Legal Aid Soc. juvenile work, 1964—, Retarded Children's Assn., 1960—; mem. Compensation Fund Investment Com. of Ariz., 1976-83; bd. dirs. Scottsdale Meml. Hosp. Served to lt. USNR, 1942-46; ETO. Mem. Internat. Bar Conf., ABA (chmn. forest resources com., vice chmn. membership com., chmn. subcom. on legislative devel., all of natural resources sect.), Internat. Bar Assn. (co-chmn. Am. law com. of com. on creditors rights, insolvency, liquidation and reorgn.), Ariz. Bar Assn., Am. Soc. Internat. Law, Am. Judicature Soc., Phi Delta Phi, Phi Delta Theta. Democrat. Episcopalian. Home: 4229 E Desert Crest Dr Scottsdale AZ 85253 also Bahia de San Carlos Guaymas Sonora Mexico Office: 3740 Civic Center Plaza Scottsdale AZ 85251

DUELL, DANIEL PAUL, ballet dancer; b. Rochester, N.Y., Aug. 17, 1952; s. Seth Joseph and Ellen Catharine (Newton) D. Diploma, Profl. Children's Sch., N.Y.C., 1970; scholarship student, Sch. Am. Ballet, 1969-72. Mem. faculty Akron (Ohio) Ballet Co., Dayton (Ohio) Ballet Co., Upper Montclair (N.J.) Acad. Dance. Mem., N.Y.C. Ballet, 1972—; soloist, 1977—; prin. dancer, 1979—. Mem. Sch. Am. Ballet Assn. Office: NYC Ballet Columbus Ave at 62d St New York NY 10023 *All of us know all we need to know. We but need to reach and manifest our inner knowledge to achieve self-realization.*

DUEMLING, ROBERT WERNER, diplomat; b. Ann Arbor, Mich., Feb. 8, 1929; s. Werner William and Anne (Lindemulder) D.; m. Louisa Copeland Biddle, May 15, 1982. B.A., Yale U., 1950, M.A., 1953; student, Cambridge U., Eng., 1950-51. Joined fgn. service Dept. State, Washington, 1957, with, 1957-60, 66-70, Am. embassy, Rome, 1960-63, Kuala Lumpur, 1963-65, Tokyo, 1970-74; U.S. consul, Kuching, Malaysia, 1965-66; exec. asst. to dep. sec. state Dept. State, Washington, 1974-76; dep. chief of mission with rank of minister Am. embassy, Ottawa, Ont., Can., 1976; U.S. ambassador, to Paramaribo Suriname. USN, 1953-57. Henry fellow, 1950-51. Office: Am Embassy Raramaribo Surinam Dept State Washington DC 20520

DUENAS, CRISTOBAL CAMACHO, judge; b. Agana, Guam, Sept. 12, 1920; s. Jose Castro and Concepcion Martinez (Camacho) D.; m. Juanita Castro Calvo, May 8, 1954; children—Christopher, Therese, Vincent, Zerlina, Joanna, Richard, David. Student, Aquinas Coll., Grand Rapids, Mich., 1946-48; A.B., U. Mich., 1950, J.D., 1952. Bar: Guam bar 1952. Asst. atty. gen. Dept. of Law, Govt. of Guam, Agana, 1952-57; dir. dept. of Land Mgmt. Govt. Guam, Agana, 1957-60; judge Island Ct. of Guam, Agana, 1960-69, U.S. Dist. Ct. for Guam, 1969—. Mem. ABA, Guam Bar Assn. (v.p. 1966-67), Am. Judicature Soc. Club: K.C. Office: 6th Floor Pacific News Bldg PO Box DC Agana GU 96910 *

DUENSING, DAVID L., food processing company executive; b. 1922; married. Student, Wright Jr. Coll., 1940, U. Fla., 1942. With Armour & Co., Phoenix, 1946-77, 80—, various advt. and mktg. positions, 1946-60; v.p., dir. mktg. Armour Grocery Products Co., 1960-68; pres. Armour-Dial Inc. subs. (name changed from Armour Grocery Products Co. 1968, 1964-68; exec. v.p. Armour & Co., 1977—; pres. Armour-Dial Inc., 1977—; dir. DeSoto Inc., Wayne-Gossard Corp. Served to 1st lt. USAF; 1942-46. Office: Armour & Co 111 W Clarendon St Greyhound Tower Phoenix AZ 85077

DUERINCK, LOUIS T., railroad executive; b. Chgo., Aug. 1, 1929; s. Aloys L. and Thais E. (De Backer) D.; m. Patricia A. Bird, June 27, 1953; children: Louis M., Kathleen M., Kevin F., Mark V., Lynn P., Brian T., Paul S. Student, U. Notre Dame, 1947-48; LL.B., DePaul U., Chgo., 1952. Bar: Ill. 1952. Commerce atty. N.Y. Central R.R., Chgo., 1955-65; gen. atty. Nat. Ry. Labor Conf., Chgo., 1967-68; with C&NW Ry. Co., Chgo., 1965-67, 68—, sr. v.p. law and real estate, 1979-83, sr. v.p. traffic, 1983—, also dir. Served with AUS, 1952-55. Mem. ABA, ICC Practitioners Assn., Ill. Bar Assn., Chgo. Ry. Club. Roman Catholic. Clubs: Glen Oak Country; Tower, Met. (Chgo.). Home: 1061 Fairview Ave Lombard IL 60148 Office: 165 N Canal St Chicago IL 60606

DUERR, HERMAN GEORGE, magazine editor, art director; b. Nagold, Germany, June 24, 1931; came to U.S., 1949, naturalized, 1975; s. Adolf Gustav and Wilhelmine Dorothea (Walz) Durr; m. Shirley Yvonne Jones, June 29, 1957; children: Suzanne, Steffan, Krista. B.F.A., Wayne State U., 1958. Publs. designer Ceco Pub. Co., Warren, Mich., 1958-60; art dir. Am. Youth mag., 1960-67, Friends mag., 1967—, exec. editor, 1978—; v.p. Ceco Pub. Co., 1981—. Served with U.S. Army, 1952-55. Office: 30400 Van Dyke Warren MI 48093

DUERRE, JOHN ARDEN, microbial physiologist, biochemist; b. Webster, S.D., Aug. 21, 1930; s. Dewey H. and Stella M. (Barber) D.; m. Benna Bee Harris, June 16, 1957; children: Gail, Dawn, Arden. B.S., S.D. State U., 1952, M.S. (Lederle fellow), 1956; Ph.D., U. Minn., 1960. Research asso., AEC fellow Argonne (Ill.) Nat. Lab., 1960-61; research bacteriologist NIH Rocky Mountain Lab., Hamilton, Mont., 1961-63; asst. prof. microbiology U. N.D. Med. Sch., 1963-65, assoc. prof., 1965-71, prof. microbiology, 1971—; vis. scientist neuropsychiat. research unit Research Council Lab., Carshalton, Surrey, Eng., 1969-70. Contbr. numerous articles to profl. publs. Chmn. Grand Forks County (N.D.) Wildlife Fedn., 1965-67, 77-78, Grand Forks chpt. Ducks Unltd., 1970, 77-78; dist. dir. N.D. Wildlife Fedn., 1976-77. Served with U.S. Army, 1953-55. Recipient Career Devel. award NIH, 1965-75; NIH grantee, 1966, 71-83; NSF grantee, 1963-71. Mem. N.Y. Acad. Scis., N.D. Acad. Scis., Am. Soc. Microbiologists, Fedn. Am. Socs. Exptl. Biology, Henrici Soc., Sigma Xi (Outstanding Research award 1977). Clubs: Grand Forks Curling, Grand Forks Gun. Lodge: Elks. Home: 918 N 26th St Grand Forks ND 58201 Office U ND Med Sch Grand Forks ND 58202

DUESENBERG, RICHARD WILLIAM, lawyer; b. St. Louis, Dec. 10, 1930; s. John August) Hugo and Edna Marie (Warmann) D.; m. Phyllis Evelyn Buehner, Aug. 7, 1955; children: Karen, Daryl, Mark, David. B.A., Valparaiso U., 1951, J.D., 1953; LL.M., Yale U., 1956. Bar: Mo. 1953. Prof. law N.Y. U. Sch. Law, N.Y.C., 1956-62, dir., 1960-62; sr. atty. Monsanto Co., St. Louis, 1963-70, asst. gen. counsel, asst. sec., 1975-77, sr. v.p., sec., gen. counsel, 1977—; dir. law Monsanto Textiles Co., St. Louis, 1971-75; corp. sec. Fisher Controls Co., Marshalltown, Iowa, 1969-71, Olympia Industries Inc., Spartanburg, S.C., 1974-75; vis. prof. law U. Mo., 1970-71; faculty Banking Sch., S. La. State U., 1967-83; mem. legal adv. com. Chem. Mfrs. Assn., Washington, NAM. Author: (with Lawrence P. King) Sales and Bulk Transfers Under the Uniform Commercial Code, 2 vols, 1966, rev., 1984, New York Law of Contracts, 3 vols, 1964, Missouri Forms and Practice Under the Uniform Commercial Code, 2 vols, 1966; Editor: Ann. Survey of Am. Law, N.Y. U., 1961-62; Mem. bd. contbg. editors and advisors: Corp. Law Rev, 1977—; Contbr. articles to law revs., jours. Bd. dirs. Luth. Med. Center, St. Louis, 1973-82, Luth. Charities Assn., St. Louis, 1984—; vice chmn. Luth. Med. Center, 1975-80; bd. dirs. Valparaiso U., 1977—, chmn. bd. visitors Law Sch., 1966—; bd. dirs. Bach Soc. St. Louis, 1965—, pres., 1973-77; adv. council Southwestern Legal Found., Dallas, 1977—; mem. lawyers adv. council NAM, Washington, 1980; mem. Adminstrv. Conf. of U.S., 1980; mem. legal adv. com. N.Y. Stock Exchange, 1983—; mem. corp. law dept. adv. council Practising Law Inst., 1982. Served with U.S. Army, 1953-55. Named Disting. Alumnus Valparaiso U., 1976. Mem. Am. Law Inst., Luth. Acad. Scholarship, Am. Arbitration Assn. (nat. panel arbitrators 1960), ABA (chmn. com. uniform comml. code 1976-79, council sect. corp., banking and bus. law 1979-83, sec. 1983-84), Mo. Bar Assn., St. Louis Bar Assn., Internat. Bar Assn., Assn. Gen. Counsel, Am. Soc. Corp. Secs. (securities com., bd. dirs. 1983—), Am. Judicature Soc., Order of Coif. Lutheran. Home: 9124 Glencrest Dr Saint Louis MO 63126 Office: Monsanto Co 800 N Lindbergh Blvd Saint Louis MO 63166

DUESENBERRY, JAMES STEMBLE, economist; b. July 18, 1918; m. Margaret. A.B., U. Mich., 1939, A.M., 1941, Ph.D., 1948. Teaching fellow U. Mich., 1939-41; research fellow Social Sci. Research Council, 1941; instr. M.I.T., 1946; teaching fellow Harvrd U., Cambridge, Mass., 1946-48, asst. prof. econs., 1948-53, asso. prof., 1953-57, prof. econs., 1957—, chmn., 1972-77; Fulbright fellow Cambridge (Eng.) U., 1954-55; Ford research prof., 1958-59; mem. Pres.'s Council Econ. Advisors, 1966-68; chmn. bd. dirs. Fed. Res. Bank of Boston, 1969-74. Author: Income Saving and the Theory of Consumer Behavior, 1949, Business Cycles and Economic Growth, 1957, (with Lee E. Preston) Cases and Problems in Economics, 1960, Money and Credit: Impact and Control, 1964, (with Barry Bosworth and Andrew S. Carron) Capital Needs in the Seventies, 1975, (with T. Mayer, Robert Aliber) Money, Banking and the Economy, 1981; contbr. articles to profl. jours. Served with USAF, 1942-45. Home: 25 Fairmont St Belmont MA 02178 Office: Dept Econs Harvard U Littauer Center Cambridge MA 02128

DUFF, CLOYD EDGAR, timpanist; b. Marietta, Ohio, Sept. 26, 1915; s. Clarence Edgar and Mattie (Sielaff) D.; m. Margaret Kapp, Oct. 26, 1940; children: Jonathan, Barbara. Diploma, Curtis Inst. Music, Phila., 1938. Head timpani and percussion dept. Cleve. Inst. Music, 1950-81, Baldwin-Wallace Coll., 1950-63, Oberlin Conservatory Music, 1955-68, Aspen Festival, 1966, Blossom Music Festival, 1968—. Timpanist, Indpls. Symphony Orch., 1938-42, Cleve. Orch., 1942-81; artist-in-residence, Colo. State U., 1982, 83; Timpanist, Robin Hood Dell Orch., Phila., summers 1938-50; percussionist, Stokowski All Am. Youth Orch., S.Am. tour, 1940; timpanist, U.S. tour, 1941. Named to Percussive Arts Soc. Hall of Fame, 1977. Mem. Pi Kappa Lambda. Home: Ponderocks Rt 1 Livermore CO 80536

DUFF, DANIEL VINCENT, former mayor, former insurance company executive; b. N.Y.C., Sept. 22, 1916; s. Daniel Vincent and Marie V. (Salzer) D.; m. Priscilla J. Booth, Sept. 3, 1942; children—Daniel V., David, R. Michael, William, Priscilla, Paul John, Carolyn, Elizabeth, Stephen. A.B. cum laude, Fordham U., 1937. With Equitable Life Assurance Soc., N.Y.C., 1937-78, asst. v.p., 1965-69, 2d v.p., 1969-70, v.p., 1970-78; ret., 1978; trustee Village of Garden City, 1973—, dep. mayor, 1977-79, mayor, 1979-81. Trustee Library Bd. Garden City, 1965-68, chmn., 1968-73. Mem. Internat. Claims Assn. Republican. Roman Catholic. Club: Garden City Golf. Home: 39 Prospect Ave Garden City NY 11530

DUFF, FRATIS LEE, ret. air force officer, physician; b. Randlett, Okla., July 7, 1910; s. George E. and Mae E. (McNeill) D.; m. Beryl Hilborne, Sept. 18, 1937; children—Dennis E., Randolph L. B.S. in Chemistry, U. Okla., 1933, M.D. with honors, 1939; M.P.H., Johns Hopkins, 1950, D.P.H., 1953; grad. various service schs. Diplomate: Am. Bd. Preventive Medicine. Intern Colo. Gen. Hosp., 1939-40; commd. 1st lt., M.C. USAAF, 1940; advanced through grades to brig. gen. USAF, 1963; various assignments, U.S., Egypt and Japan, 1940-48, chief profl. services br., Japan, 1948-49; prof. mil. sci. and tactics Johns Hopkins, 1949-51; chief preventive medicine div. Surgeon's Gen. Office, USAF, 1951-53; comdr. (Gunter br. Sch. Aviation Medicine), 1953-59, dep. surgeon, Weisbaden, Germany, 1959-62, command surgeon, Andrews AFB, Md., 1962-63, Langley AFB, Va., 1964-68; ret.; dir. planning Tex. Dept. Health, 1968-69, dep. commr. for program planning, 1969-73, dep. commr., 1973-75; dir. Tex. Dept. Health Resources, Austin, 1975-77; commr. health Tex. Dept. Health, 1977-80. Author articles. Decorated Legion of Merit with 2 oak leaf clusters; recipient certificate of achievement Surgeon Gen. USAF, 1962. Home: 4211 Lostridge Dr Austin TX 78731

DUFF, GEORGE ALEXANDER, association executive; b. Detroit, Nov. 13, 1931; s. Robert Hugh and Marion (Rocke) D.; m. Marilyn Marie Stostad, Aug. 31, 1954; children: Brian, Doreen, Bruce, Laura. B.S., Wayne State U., 1956. Regional distbn. rep. Minute Maid Frozen Foods, 1956-58; with Greater Detroit C. of C., 1958-68, exec. v.p., 1967-68, Seattle C. of C., from 1968; now pres. Seattle C. of C. Pres. Inst. for Puget Sound Needs. Served with U.S. Army, 1952-54. Mem. Am. C. of C. Execs. (chmn.-elect), Wash. C. of C. Execs. (past pres.). Clubs: Rainier, Rotary (past dir.). Office: 1200 One Union Sq Seattle WA 98101

DUFF, GEORGE FRANCIS DENTON, mathematician; b. Toronto, Ont., Can., July 28, 1926; s. George Henry and Laura (Denton) D.; m. Mary Elaine Wood, June 16, 1951; children—Valerie, John, Catherine, Janet, George. B.A., Toronto U., 1948, M.A., 1949; Ph.D., Princeton U., 1951. Instr. M.I.T., 1951-52; asst. prof. U. Toronto, 1952-57, asso. prof., 1957-61, prof. math., 1961—. Editor: Can. Jour. Math, 1957-61, 78-81. Fellow Royal Soc. Can.; mem. Can. Math. Soc. (pres. 1971-73). Office: Dept Math Univ of Toronto Toronto ON M5S 1A1 Canada

DUFF, HOWARD, actor; b. Bremerton, Wash., Nov. 24, 1917; m. Ida Lupino. Student, Repertory Playhouse, Seattle. With, Sta.-KOMO, 1935; originating the role of Sam Spade: films include Brute Force, 1947, Naked City, 1948, Shakedown, 1950, While the City Sleeps, 1956, Boy's Night Out, 1962, The Late Show, 1977, A Wedding, 1978, Kramer vs. Kramer, 1980, Double Negative, 1980, Oh God!, Book II, 1980, East of Eden, 1981; appeared in: TV series Mr. Adams and Eve, 1956-57, Dante, 1960-61, Felony Squad, 1966-68, Flamingo Road, 1980—; other TV appearances include Lou Grant, Combat, The Rogues, Name of the Game, Police Story, Medical Center, Kung Fu, Mannix. Served with U.S. Army, 1941-45. Office: care Press Dept 30 Rockefeller Plaza New York NY 10020 *

DUFF, JAMES GEORGE, automobile company executive; b. Pittsburg, Kans., Jan. 27, 1938; s. James George and Camilla (Vinardi) D.; m. Linda Louise Beeman, June 24, 1961 (div.); children: Michele, Mark, Melissa. B.S. with distinction, U. Kans., 1960, M.B.A., 1961. With Ford Motor Co., Dearborn, Mich., 1962—, various positions fin. staff, 1962-69; dir. product, profit, price, warranty Ford of Europe, 1972-73; controller Ford Div., 1974-76, controller car ops., 1976, controller car product devel., 1976-80; exec. v.p. Ford Motor Credit Co., 1980—, also dir.; dir. Am. Rd. Ins. Co., Ford Life Ins. Co., Vista Life Ins. Co., Vista Ins. Co., Am. Rd. Services Co., Ford Consumer Credit Co. Mem. adv. bd. Sch. Bus., U. Kans., 1980—. Home: 411 S Woodward Apt 703 Birmingham MI 48011 Office: Ford Motor Credit Co American Rd Dearborn MI 48121

DUFF, JAMES HENRY, music director; b. Pitts., Oct. 11, 1943; s. James Sylvester and Virginia (Henry) D.; m. Sally Kathryn Tredwell, Sept. 14, 1963; children: Abigail Margaret, Jessica Lauren. B.A., Washington and Jefferson Coll., 1965; M.A., U. Mass., 1970. Teaching asst. U. Mass., Amherst, 1965-66; dir. Mus. of Hudson Highlands, Cornwall-on-Hudson, N.Y., 1966-73, trustee, 1973-76; dir. Brandywine River Mus., Chadds Ford, Pa., 1973—; exec. dir. Brandywine Conservancy, Chadds Ford, 1976—; cons. N.Y. State Council on the Arts, 1970-72; panel mem. Pa. Council on Arts, 1976-79, 83. Author Not for Publication, Landscapes, Still Lifes and Portraits by N.C. Wyeth, The Western World of N.C. Wyeth; Contbr. articles on mus. programs to profl. jours. Served with AUS, 1967-69. Mem. N.E. Museums Conf. (pres.), Assn. Art Mus. Dirs. (council.),

Am. Assn. Museums. (accreditation vis. com.). Home: PO Box 297 Chadds Ford PA 19317 Office: PO Box 141 Chadds Ford PA 19317

DUFF, JOHN BERNARD, state education official, former university president; b. Orange, N.J., July 1, 1931; s. John Bernard and Mary Evelyn (Cunningham) D.; m. Helen Mezzanotti, Oct. 8, 1955; children: Michael, Maureen, Patricia, John, Robert, Emily Anne. B.S., Fordham U., 1953; M.A., Seton Hall U., 1958; Ph.D., Columbia, 1964. Sales rep. Remington-Rand Corp., 1955-57, dist. mgr., 1957-60; faculty Seton Hall U., 1960-70, prof. history, 1968-70, acad. v.p., 1970-71, exec. v.p., acad. v.p., 1971-72, provost, acad. v.p., 1972-76; pres. U. Lowell, Mass., 1976-81; chancellor of higher edn., State of Mass., 1981—; cons. Essex County Youth and Econ. Rehab. Commn., Office Econ. Opportunity, Newark, N.J., 1966-67; mem. Gov.'s Commn. to Study Capital Punishment, 1972-73; chmn. bd. dirs. Mass. Corp. Ednl. Telecommunications, 1983—; dir. Mass. Tech. Park Corp., Bay State Skills Corp. Author: The Irish in the United States, 1971, also articles.; Editor: (with others) The Structure of American History, 1970, (with P.M. Mitchell) The Nat Turner Rebellion: The Historical Event and the Modern Controversy, 1971, (with L. Greene) Slavery: Its Origin and Legacy, 1975. Democratic candidate to U.S. Congress, 1968; mem. State Bd. Edn., 1981—; chmn. Livingston Town Democratic Com., 1972—; bd. dirs. Merrimack Regional Theatre, 1981—, Mass. Higher Edn. Assistance Corp., 1981—; trustee Essex County Coll., 1966-70, Mass. Community Coll. System., St. John's Prep. Sch., Danvers, Mass.; chmn. Lowell Hist. Preservation Commn., 1979—; mem. adv. bd. Wang Inst., 1979—; mem. nat. adv. com. on accreditation and indsl. eligibility U.S. Dept. Edn., 1981-82. Served with U.S. Army, 1953-55. Mem. Am. Hist. Assn., Orgn. Am. Historians, AAUP, Acad. Polit. Sci., Am. Catholic Hist. Assn., Am. Assn. State Colls. and Univs. (chmn. cultural affairs com. 1979—), Immigration History Research Group. Club: K.C. Home: 124 Mansur St Lowell MA 01852 Office: One Ashburton Pl Boston MA 02108

DUFF, JOHN EWING, sculptor; b. Lafayette, Ind., Dec. 2, 1943; s. John Ewing and Ruth (Miller) D. B.F.A., San Francisco Art Inst., 1967. Exhbns. include, Whitney Museum, N.Y.C., 1969, 81, David Whitney Gallery, N.Y.C., 1970, 71, Irving Blum Gallery, Los Angeles, 1972, John Bernard Meyers Gallery, N.Y.C., 1972, 73, Willard Gallery, N.Y.C., 1975, 76, 77, 78, one-man show, Margo Leavin Gallery, Los Angeles, 1981; represented in public collections, including, Inst. Contemporary Art, Boston, Kaiser Wilhelm Mus., Krefeld, W. Ger., Mus. Modern Art, N.Y.C. Recipient Theodoren award Guggenheim Mus., 1977; award Am. Acad. and Inst. Arts and Letters, 1981; John Simon Guggenheim fellow, 1979-80. Home and office: 7 Doyers St New York NY 10013

DUFF, RAYMOND STANLEY, pediatrics educator; b. Hodgdon, Maine, Nov. 2, 1923; s. Maurice Cameron and Ruth Myrtle (Barton) D.; m. G. Joyce London, Nov. 28, 1945; children: Jane, Carole, Lori. B.S., U. Maine, 1948; M.D., Yale U., 1952, M.P.H., 1959. Diplomate: Am. Bd. Pediatrics. Intern Yale-New Haven Hosp., 1952-53, resident in pediatrics, 1953-55; dir. med. services New Haven Health Dept., 1955-56; instr. pediatrics and pub. health Yale U., New Haven, 1956-60, asst. prof., 1960-67, assoc. prof., 1967-78, prof. pediatrics, 1978—; advisor Louise Mellen Fellowship in Intensive Care Nursing, Cleve., 1978-83. Author: Sickness and Society, 1968; contbr. articles on moral and ethical issues in health care to profl. jours., chpts. in books. Mem. Woodbridge Democratic Town Com., 1972-75. Served to 2d lt. F.A. AUS, 1943-46. HEW research grantee, 1958-65; research grantee Robert Wood Johnson Found., 1973-79; Alpha Omega Alpha vis. prof., U. Hawaii, 1978. Fellow Am. Acad. Pediatrics; mem. AAAS, Am. Sociol. Assn. Home: 259 Newton Rd Woodbridge CT 06525 Office: Yale U Sch of Medicine 333 Cedar St New Haven CT 06510

DUFF, WILLIAM LEROY, JR., educator; b. Oakland, Calif., Sept. 14, 1938; s. William Leroy and Edna Francis (Gunderson) D.; m. Arline M. Wight, Sept. 1, 1962; children—Susan M., William Leroy III. B.A., Calif. State U.-, San Francisco, 1963, postgrad., 1963-64; M.S.Sc., Nat. Econs. Inst., U. Stockholm, 1965; Ph.D., UCLA, 1969. Research assoc. C.F. Kettering Found., 1967-69; asst. JOBS program Nat. Alliance Businessmen, 1969-70; prof., assoc. dean Sch. Bus., U. No. Colo., Greeley, 1970—, dir., 1972-75, chmn. faculty senate, 1981-82; on leave as UN adviser to Govt. of Swaziland, 1975-77; cons. in field.; Mem. exec. bd., bd. dirs. Economia de Aztlan Econ. Devel. Corp. Contbr. articles to profl. jours. Mem. Greeley Planning Commn., 1972-75, chmn., 1974-75. Served with AUS, 1958-60. Mem. Assn. Univ. Burs. Bus. and Econ. Research, Am. Ednl. Research Assn., Acad. Internat. Bus., AAUP, Urban and Regional Info. Systems Assn. Home: 1614 Lakeside Dr Greeley CO 80631 Office: Sch Bus U No Colo Greeley CO 80631

DUFFEY, DONALD CRAEGH, educator; b. Winchester, Va., Feb. 9, 1931; s. Hugh Sisson and Vera (Lynch) D.; m. Elizabeth Mallard, Aug. 25, 1965. B.S., Va. Poly. Inst., 1953; M.S., Rice U., 1955; Ph.D., Ga. Inst. Tech., 1959. Fellow Pa. State U., 1959-60; asst. prof. chemistry Miss. State U., 1960-62, asso. prof., 1962-67, prof., 1967—; vis. prof. U. Cin., 1968, Max-Planck Inst., 1968, U. Utah, 1979, U. Va., 1980; Oak Ridge Associated Univs. faculty research participant Morgantown Energy Tech. Center, 1978. Contbr. articles in field to profl. jours. Mem. Am. Chem. Soc., Sigma Xi, Phi Kappa Phi. Office: PO Box 35 Mississippi State U State College MS 39762

DUFFEY, JOSEPH DANIEL, university chancellor; b. Huntington, W.Va., July 1, 1932; s. Joseph I. and Ruth (Wilson) D.; m. Anne Wexler, 1974; children: Michael, David. A.B., Marshall U., Huntington, 1954; S.T.M., Yale U., 1964; B.D., Andover Newton Theol. Sch., 1957; Ph.D., Hartford Sem. Found., 1969; L.H.D., CUNY, 1978, U. Cin., 1978; Litt.D., Dickinson Coll., Pa., 1978, Centre Coll., Ky., 1977, Gonzaga U., Ky., 1980; LL.D., Monmouth Coll., 1980, CCNY, Amherst Coll., Bethany Coll., Austin Coll., Alderson-Broadus Coll., Adelphi U., Central Fla. Asst. prof. Hartford (Conn.) Sem., 1960-63; assoc. prof. and dir. Center for Urban Studies, 1965-70; fellow Harvard U. Kennedy Sch. Govt., 1971; adj. prof. and fellow Calhoun Coll., Yale U., 1971-73; exec. officer AAUP, 1974-76; asst. sec. for edn. and cultural affairs Dept. State, 1977; chmn. NEH, 1977-81; chancellor U. Mass., Amherst, 1982—; mem. U.S. del. 20th and 21st Gen Confs., UNESCO, 1978, 80; dir. Bay Bank of Springfield (Mass.). Contbr. numerous articles to profl. jours. Bd. dirs. Woodrow Wilson Internat. Center for Scholars, East-West Center, Western Mass. Area Devel. Corp., Jewish Theol. Sem. Library; del. Democratic Nat. Conv., 1968, 72; Dem. candidate for U.S. Senate from Conn., 1970. Rockefeller fellow, 1966-68; decorated Order of Leopold IV, Belgium). Mem. Council on Fgn. Relations. Clubs: Yale, Cosmos, Fed. City (Washington); Colony. Address: U Mass Amherst Office of the Chancellor Amherst MA 01003

DUFFEY, PAUL ANDREWS, bishop; b. Brownsville, Tenn., Dec. 13, 1920; s. George Henderson and Julia Griffin (McKissack) D.; m. Anna Louise Calhoun, June 20, 1944; children: Melanie Duffey Hutto Jr., Paul Andrews. Student, U. Ala., 1938-40; A.B., Birmingham-So. Coll., 1942, D.D., 1966; B.D., Vanderbilt U., 1945. Ordained to ministry as deacon United Meth. Ch., 1944, elder, 1946; pastor Chapel Hill Ch., Tenn., 1944-46, Abbeville, Ala., 1946-50, Marion, Ala., 1950-54, Dexter Ave United Meth. Ch., Montgomery, Ala., 1954-61, First Ch., Pensacola, Fla., 1961-66, Dothan, Ala., 1966-70, Montgomery, Ala., 1970-76; supt. Montgomery dist. United Meth. Ch., from 1976, mem. jud. council, from 1976; bishop United Meth. Ch., Lexington, Ky. Chmn. community council United Appeal, 1974; trustee Birmingham-So. Coll., 1956-73, chmn. bd., 1956-73, trustee, 1976—. Office: United Meth Ch PO Box 5107 Lexington KY 40505

DUFFIELD, PETER R., government and business consultant; b. Montreal, Que., Can., Mar. 23, 1938; s. Alfred R. and Elsie C. (Wallis) D.; m. Martha Richardson, May 11; children: Andrew, Benjamin. B. Chem. Engring. with honors, McGill U., 1959; student Ecole du Louvre, U. Paris, 1960, Goethe Instut, Munich, 1960, Universidad de Mendendez, Pelayo, Spain, 1960. With Dupont Can., Inc., Westmount, Que., 1960-82, mgr. floor coverings, 1972-76, mgr. woven polyolefins, 1976-77, v.p. Fibres Group, officer, 1978-82; pres. Peter R. Duffield and Assocs., Westmount, 1983—; dir. Advanced Dynamics Corp., Centraide. Alderman City of Westmount, 1983; mem. Can. Council, 1979; active Centaur Theatre, Mus. Fine Arts, Nat. Theatre Sch., Can. Club; gov. Montreal Gen. Hosp., Douglas Hosp.; bd. dirs. Westmount Liberal Assn.; vice chmn. Selwyn House Endowment Fund; echanson Le Commanderie de Bordeaux. Mem. Chem. Inst. Can., Can. Soc. Chem. Engrs., Can. Inst. Internat. Affairs (vice chmn.). Liberal. Anglican. Clubs: Montreal Badminton and Squash, Univ. of Montreal (mem. council), Hillside Tennis). Home: 132 Clandeboye Ave Westmount PQ Canada H3Z 1Z1 Office: Peter R Duffield and Assocs Inc 1 Westmount Sq Wesmount PQ Canada H3Z 2P9

DUFFIN, JOHN HENRY, educator; b. Easton, Pa., June 18, 1919; s. George Thomas and Agatha (Rose) D. B.Ch.E., Lehigh U., 1940; Ph.D., U. Cal. at Berkeley, 1959. Research chemist High Explosives Lab., Hercules Powder Co., Kenvil, N.J., 1940-42, Bacchus, Utah, 1942-44; shift supr., tech. adviser Tenn. Eastman Corp., Oak Ridge, 1944-46; research engr. Allied Chem. and Dye Corp., Buffalo, 1946-52, research engring. supr., 1949-52; sr. research engr. Battelle Meml. Inst., Columbus, O., 1952-54; teaching asst U. Cal. at Berkeley, 1954-57, instr., 1957-59; asst. prof. chem. engring., dir. Computer Center San Jose State Coll., 1959-62; asso. prof. chem. engring. Naval Postgrad. Sch., Monterey, Cal., 1962-66, prof., 1966—, chmn. dept. material sci. and chemistry, 1969-72; cons. Naval Air Rework Facility, San Diego, 1972—. Contbr. articles sci. jours. Fellow Am. Inst. Chemists; mem. Am. Inst. Chem. Engrs., N.Y. Acad. Scis., Sigma Xi. Home: 6170 Brookdale Dr Carmel CA 93923 Office: US Naval Postgrad Sch Code 62 DN Monterey CA 93940

DUFFIN, RICHARD JAMES, mathematician, educator; b. Chgo., Oct. 13, 1909; s. Daniel and Mary (Curran) D.; m. Carolyn Jeanne Hartman, July 19, 1947; children—Virginia Mae, Martha Jane. B.S. in Engring, U. Ill., 1932, Ph.D. in Physics, 1935. Teaching asst. physics U. Ill., 1935, asso. math., 1941-42; instr. math. Purdue U., 1936-41; physicist terrestrial magnetism Carnegie Instn. Wash., 1942-46; faculty Carnegie-Mellon U., 1946—, prof. math., 1948-70, Univ. prof. math. scis., 1970—; vis. prof. Purdue U., 1949, Inst. Advanced Studies, Dublin, Ireland, 1959; dir. spl. research applied math. Duke, 1958; distinguished vis. prof. engring. U. State N.Y. at Stony Brook, 1967; distinguished vis. prof. math. Tex. A. and M. U., 1968; cons. in field, 1956—. Co-author: Geometric Programming, 1967; Mem. editorial bds. jours. in field. Recipient von Neumann theory prize Ops. Research Soc. Am., 1982. Mem. Nat. Acad. Scis., Am. Acad. Arts and Scis., Am. Math. Soc., Soc. Indsl. and Applied Math. (nat. lectr. 1961, 64, 76), Nat. Philosophy Soc., Sigma Xi, Tau Beta Pi, Triangle. Home: 424 S Linden Ave Pittsburgh PA 15208

DUFFY, EARL GAVIN, hotel exec.; b. Boston, Oct. 11, 1926; s. William Emmett and Mary Irene (Costello) D.; m. Bernice Rose MacMaster, Feb. 14, 1948; children—Earl Gavin, Joan Irene, Mark Charles, Neil William, Lynn Anne. Student public schs., Boston. In various hotel positions, Boston, 1941-52; sales mgr. Somerset Hotel, Boston, 1952-56; eastern sales mgr. Hotel Corp. Am., Boston, 1956-59, asst. nat. sales mgr., 1959-61, nat. sales mgr., 1961-64; v.p., gen. mgr. Hotel America, Houston, 1964-67, Hartford, Conn., 1967-69, Royal Sonesta Hotel, New Orleans, 1969-71, Soneta Beach Hotel, Key Biscayne, Fla., 1971-76, Boston Park Plaza Hotel, 1977-80; pres. Earl G. Duffy & Assos., 1981—; guest lectr. Cornell U., 1961, U. Houston, 1965, Wash. State U., 1966, Fla. Internat. U., 1971-76; pres. Greater Hartford Conv. and Visitor's Bur., 1969. Chmn. div. bus. and industry Harris County (Tex.) March of Dimes, 1964-67; pres. New Orleans Jazz Festival, 1970-71. Served with USN, 1943-46. Recipient Golden Host award Wash. State U., 1964. Mem. Skal Club, Am. Hotel and Motel Assn., Hotel Sales Mgmt. Assn. Internat., Greater Boston Hotel and Motor Inn Assn., Mass. Hotel and Motel Assn., New Eng. Innkeepers Assn., Boston Exec. Club. Roman Catholic. Club: Rotary. Home and Office: 345 W Enid Dr Key Biscayne FL 33149 *There is no question in my mind that anyone who wants to "make it" in America can do so.*

DUFFY, EDWARD WILLIAM, manufacturing company executive; b. LaSalle, Ill., Sept. 25, 1919; s. Edward J. and Margaret (Brunick) D.; m. Rosemary G. Dee, June 28, 1941; 1 dau., Jill Anne. Grad., LaSalle-Peru Jr. Coll., 1938; student, Loyola U., Chgo.; also exec. devel. program, Cornell U. Research chemist, 1941-45, engaged in sales, mdsg. and sales mgr., 1945—; v.p. U.S. Gypsum Co., 1963-69, exec. v.p., 1969-71, pres., 1971-81, vice-chmn., 1981-83, chmn., chief exec. officer, 1983—, dir., 1969—; dir. Harnischfeges Corp., Am. Nat. Bank & Trust Co., Chgo., W. W. Grainger Co., Inc., UNR Corp., Walter E. Heller Corp., BPB Industries Ltd., London. Home: 1815 W Ridgewood Ln Glenview IL 60025 Office: 101 S Wacker Dr Chicago IL 60606

DUFFY, FRANCIS RAMON, sociology educator; b. Phila., Mar. 26, 1915; s. John J. and Anna (Rodgers) D. B.A., Holy Ghost Coll., 1938; B.D., St. Mary's Coll., 1942; M.A., Cath. U., 1944; Ph.D., U. Pitts., 1955. Ordained priest Roman Catholic Ch., 1941; asst. prof. sociology Duquesne U., 1943-50, prof., chmn. dept., from 1953; now dir. St. Joseph's House, Phila.; chaplain Juvenile Ct. Allegheny County, 1947-68; instr. Pitts. Police Acad., 1956-68, Army Officer Career Course; cons. Pitts. Behavior Clinic, Pa. Gov.'s Justice Commn.; also med. dept. Gulf Oil Corp.; producer radio series. Smoking intervention specialist, div. research Lankenau Hosp., Phila. Author: Title System in Nigeria, 1944, Study of Male White Delinquents in Pittsburgh, 1955, Social Psychology of Growing Up, Juvenile Delinquency, Personal and Social Adjustment, Teen Age Accommodation, Social Deviation, Hypnosis. Mem. adv. bd. Nazareth Acad.; bd. dirs. Duquesne U. Served as maj., chaplain U.S. Army, 1950-52; ret. col. Res. Decorated Legion of Merit, D.S.M. Fellow Royal Anthrop. Assn. Gt. Britain and Ireland; mem. Am., Pa. sociol. socs., Phila. Soc. Clin. Hypnosis (bd. govs.), Am. Soc. Clin. Hypnosis, Pa. Chiefs Police Assn., AAUP; corr. asso. Royal Coll. Psychiatry. Clubs: Knights of Equity., KC. Address: St Joseph's House 8101 Cresco Ave Philadelphia PA 19136

DUFFY, HUGH GAVIN, govt. ofcl., lawyer; b. Boston, Aug. 11, 1938; s. Walter James and Margaret Theresa (McCarthy) D. B.S. cum laude, Boston Coll., 1959, J.D., 1962. Bar: D.C. bar 1964. Counsel subcom. manpower, compensation, health and safety U.S. Ho. of Reps., 1976, asso. counsel com. edn. and labor, 1977-80, staff dir., gen. counsel com. house adminstrn., 1980—. Mem. D.C. Bar Assn. Democrat. Home: 2039 37th St NW Washington DC 20007 Office: US Capitol Bldg Room H-331 Washington DC 20515

DUFFY, JACQUES WAYNE, engineering educator; b. Nimes, France, July 1, 1922; s. Edward F. and Eveline (Lagier) D.; m. Angeline Coultas, June 17, 1950; children: Jacqueline, Philip, Paul. A.B., Columbia U., 1947, B.S., 1948, M.S., 1949, Ph.D., 1957; D.Sc. (hon.), U. Nantes, France, 1980. Mem. research dept. Grumman Aircraft Engring. Corp., 1950-52; research asst. Columbia U., 1952-54; prof. engring. Brown U., 1954—, chmn. Center for Biomed. Engring., 1969-72; editorial adv. bd. Inst. Sci. Info., 1970—. Served with AUS, 1943-46. Guggenheim fellow Cambridge (Eng.) U., 1964-65; Engring. Found. fellow, 1978-79. Fellow ASME; mem. ASTM, Soc. Exptl. Stress Analysis, Am. Soc. Metals. Home: 71 Lorraine Ave Providence RI 02906 Office: Div Engring Brown U Providence RI 02912

DUFFY, JAMES EDSON, broadcasting co. exec.; b. Decatur, Ill., Apr. 2, 1926; s. Harold Francis and Corinne (Longenbaugh) D.; m. Betty Jane Zuehsow, Feb. 7, 1947; m. Deanna Lund, Aug. 29, 1980; children—Jay Edson, Marcia Elizabeth, Corinne. B.A., Beloit Coll., 1949, LL.D. (hon.), 1974. Reporter Beloit Daily News, also Rockford (Ill.) Morning Star, 1947-49; announcer-sportscaster Sta. WBNB, Beloit, 1948-49; publicity writer ABC (radio and TV), Chgo., 1949-51, asst. publicity dir. central div., 1951-52, advt. and promotion dir. div., 1952-53, account exec. radio network central div., 1953-55, TV network central div., 1955-57, sales mgr. radio network central div., 1957-60, nat. dir. sales radio network, 1960-61, exec. v.p. radio network, 1962-63; v.p. in charge TV network sales dept. 1963-70; pres. ABC TV Network, N.Y.C., 1970—. Co-chmn. Nat. Asthma Center, 1976. Recipient Communicator of Yr. award Sales and Mktg. Execs. Internat., 1974, Golden 44 award Los Angeles C. of C., 1977; named Ill. State Broadcaster of Yr., 1978. Mem. Broadcast Advt. Club Chgo., Sales Exec. Club N.Y., Internat. Radio and TV Soc., Advt. Council, Inc. (dir.), Bedside Networks (bd. advs.), Internat. Radio and TV Founds. (past dir.), Leukemia Soc. N.Y. (past chmn.), Boy Scouts Am. (past program chmn.), Ill. Jr. C. of C. (past pres. and state dir.). Office: ABC TV Network 1330 Ave of Americas New York NY 10019

DUFFY, JAMES EDWARD, history and literature educator; b. Elkton, Md., May 1, 1923; s. Edward H. and Sara (Whitlock) D.; m. Lillian Chase Johnson, Oct. 26, 1944 (div. 1976); children: David Livingstone, Amanda Chase, Priscilla Kingsley; m. Paula Stapleton Barker, Aug. 22, 1976; children: Sarah Zinha Harrison, Anna Victoria Stapleton. A.B., U. N.C., 1944; A.M., U. San Carlos de Guatemala, 1947; Ph.D., Harvard, 1952. Instr. U. N.C., 1945-46; dir. acad. course Guatemalan-Am. Inst., 1946, dir. inst., 1947-48; teaching fellow Harvard, 1948-51; faculty Brandeis U., 1951—, now prof. history and lit.; founder, mng. dir. Crossroads Press, 1977-81; cons. State Dept., Council Fgn. Relations, Brookings Inst. Author: Shipwreck and Empire, 1955, Portuguese Africa, 1959, (with Robert Manners) Africa Speaks, 1961, Portugal in Africa, 1962, The Portuguese African Territories, 1961, A Question of Slavery, 1967, Internat. Directory Africanist Scholars and Specialists, 1979, Internat. Directory of Third World Scholars and Specialists, 1981; also articles. Ford fellow, 1955-56; Bollingen fellow, 1962-63; Social Sci. Research Council fellow, 1962-63; NSF fellow, 1962-63; Rockefeller fellow, 1964; Guggenheim fellow, 1966; Social Sci. Research fellow, 1971-72. Mem. African Studies Assn. (pres. 1967-68, exec. sec. 1969-80), Phi Beta Kappa. Home: 58 Old Mystic St Arlington MA 02174 Office: Dept of Romance Lit Brandeis Univ Waltham MA 02154

DUFFY, JAMES HENRY, lawyer; b. Lowville, N.Y., Feb. 3, 1934; s. William Christopher and Phyllis Catherine (Rofinot) D.; m. Martha McDowell, May 25, 1968. A.B., Princeton U., 1956; LL.B., Harvard U., 1959. Bar: N.Y. 1960. Assoc. Cravath, Swaine & Moore, N.Y.C., 1959-67, ptnr., 1968—. Author: Domestic Affairs: American Programs and Priorities, 1979. Mem. Mayor's Commn. Cultural Affairs, 1981—; bd. dirs. Nat. Corp. Fund for Dance, Inc., 1981—. Mem. Council Fgn. Relations, ABA, N.Y. State Bar Assn., Assn. Bar City N.Y. Democrat. Roman Catholic. Clubs: Wall Street, Century Assn. (N.Y.C.). Office: One Chase Manhattan Plaza New York NY 10005

DUFFY, JOHN, history educator; b. Barrow-in-Furness, Eng., Mar. 27, 1915; came to U.S., 1928; m. Florence Corinne Cook, 1942; 2 children. B.A., La. State Normal Coll., 1941; M.A., La. State U., 1944; Ph.D. in History, UCLA, 1946. Asst. prof. Northwestern State Coll., 1949-53; from asst. prof. to assoc. prof. history La. State U., 1953-60; from assoc. prof. to prof. pub. health history Grad. Sch. Pub. Health, U. Pitts., 1960-65; prof. history med. Coll. Arts and Sci. and Sch. Medicine, Tulane U., 1965-72; Priscilla Alden Burke prof. history U. Md., College Park, 1972—; cons. N.Y.C. Health Dept., 1963-69; mem. hist. life sci. study sect. NIH, 1967-70, chmn., 1970-71, cons., 1971—; interim editor Am. Hist. Rev., 1975. Author: Epidemics in Colonial America, 1953, (2 vols.) Rudolph Matas History of Medicine in Louisiana, 1958-62, Sword of Pestilence, the New Orleans Yellow Fever Epidemic of 1853, 1966, A History of Public Health in New York City, 1625-1866, 1968, A History of Public Health in New York City, 1866-1966, 1974, The Healers, the Rise of the Medical Establishment, 1976; co-author: Social Welfare in Transition, 1966; editor: Ventures in World Health, The Memoirs of Fred Lowe Soper, 1977. Ford Found. fellow, 1951-52. Mem. Am. Hist. Assn., Am. Assn. Hist. Medicine (pres. 1976-78), Orgn. Am. Historians, Southern Hist. Assn., Am. Inst. Hist. Pharmacy. Office: Dept History U Md College Park MD 20742

DUFFY, JOHN LESTER, pathologist; b. Huntington, N.Y., Jan. 26, 1927; s. Lester Maurice and Mildred (Aitken) D.; m. Katherine Dann Smyth, June 21, 1952; children: Mary, Sarah, John. A.B., Columbia U., 1948; M.D., N.Y. Med. Coll., 1952. Diplomate: Am Bd. Pathology, Nat. Bd. Med. Examiners. Intern Nassau County Med. Center (formerly Meadowbrook Hosp.), East Meadow, N.Y., 1952-53, resident, 1953-58, assoc. dir. med. tech. program, asso. chmn. dept. pathology and labs.; practice medicine specializing in pathology, East Meadow, 1959—; asst. clin. prof. pathology N.Y. Med. Coll., 1966-70, clin. assoc. prof. pathology, 1970-71; asso. prof. pathology SUNY, Stony Brook, 1971-79, prof. pathology, 1979—. Served to capt. M.C. AUS, 1955-57. Fellow Coll. Am. Pathologists; Fellow Am. Soc. Clin. Pathologists, Nassau Acad. Medicine; mem. AMA, N.Y. State, Nassau County med. socs., N.Y. State Assn. Public Health Labs., Internat. Acad. Pathology, N.Y. Acad. Scis., Internat. Soc. Nephrologists. Research in renal diseases. Office: Nassau County Med Center East Meadow NY 11554

DUFFY, KEVIN THOMAS, federal judge; b. N.Y.C., Jan. 10, 1933; s. Patrick John and Mary (McGarrell) D.; m. Irene Krumeich, Nov. 9, 1957; children: Kevin Thomas, Irene Moira, Gavin Edward, Patrick Giles. A.B., Fordham Coll., 1954, J.D., 1958. Bar: N.Y. 1958. Clk. to chief circuit judge, N.Y.C., 1955-58; asst. chief criminal div. U.S. Atty.'s Office, N.Y.C., 1958-61; asso. Whitman, Ransom & Coulson, N.Y.C., 1961-66; partner Gordon & Gordon, N.Y.C., 1966-69; regional adminstr. SEC, N.Y.C., 1969-72; judge U.S. Dist. Ct. So. Dist. N.Y., 1972—; adj. prof. securities law Bklyn. Law Sch., 1975-80; prof. trial advocacy NYU, 1982—. Recipient Achievement in Law award Fordham Coll. Alumni Assn., 1976. Mem. N.Y. State, Westchester County bar assns., Assn. Bar N.Y.C., Fed. Bar Council (trustee 1970-72), Fordham Law Sch. Alumni Assn. (trustee 1969—). Clubs: Adventurers, Merchants (N.Y.C.). Home: 1436 Roosevelt Ave Pelham Manor NY 10803 Office: US Courthouse Foley Sq New York NY 10007

DUFFY, MICHAEL PETER, hospital administrator; b. Newark, Mar. 28, 1939; s. Howard Francis and Agnes (Keogan) D.; m. Dorothy Ann Finan, Feb. 27, 1960; children: Debra Marie, Michael Peter, Mark John, Matthew Joseph. B.A., Kean Coll., Newark State Coll., 1962; hosp. mgmt. cert., Rutgers U., 1972, cert. nursing home adminstrn., 1974; M.P.A., Fairleigh Dickinson U., 1976. Lic. nursing home adminstr., 1973. Tchr. Newark Sch. System, 1962-67; supt. Essex County Geriatrics Center, Belleville, N.J., 1974—; div. dir. Essex County Hosp. Center, Cedar Grove, N.J., 1973—. Mem. Essex County Heart Assn., 1975, trustee, 1975-76. Fellow Am. Coll. Nursing Home Adminstrs.; mem. Am. Hosp. Assn., Am. Coll. Hosp. Adminstrs.; Mem. Greater Essex Hosp. Council, N.J. Hosp. Assn., Sigma Theta Chi. Home: 22 Fairview Ave Box 966 Cedar Grove NJ 07009 Office: 125 Fairview Ave Cedar Grove NJ 07009

DUFFY, PATRICK, actor; b. Townsend, Mont., Mar. 17, 1949; m. Carlyn; 2 sons. Attended, U. Wash. Former actor-in-residence, State of Wash.; with various state-funded groups; acted off-Broadway; taught mime and movement classes in summer camp, Seattle; appeared in plays with, San Diego Shakespeare Festival, 1975; TV movies Hurricane, Enola Gay, Cry for the Strangers; star: TV series The Man From Atlantic, 1977-78, Dallas, 1978—; other TV appearances include The Last of Mrs. Lincoln. Office: care CBS Entertainment 51 W 52d St New York NY 10019 *

DUFFY, ROBERT ALOYSIUS, aeronautical engineer; b. Buck Run, Pa., Sept. 9, 1921; s. Joseph Albert and Jane Veronica (Archer) D.; m. Elizabeth Reed Orr, Aug. 19, 1945; children: Michael Gordon, Barclay Robert, Marian Orr, Judith Elizabeth, Patricia Archer. B.S. in Aero. Engring, Ga. Inst. Tech., 1951. Commd. 2d lt. U.S. Army, 1942; commd. U.S. Air Force, advanced through grades to brig. gen, 1967; service in, C.Z., Morocco, Algeria, Tunisia, Sicily, Italy, Vietnam; vice comdr. USAF Space and Missile Systems Orgn., Los Angeles, 1970-71; ret., 1971; v.p., dir. Draper Lab. div. M.I.T., Cambridge, Mass., 1971-73; pres., dir., chief exec. officer Charles Stark Draper Lab., Inc., 1973—; chmn. USAF-NOAA weather satellite program rev. Dept Def.-NASA, 1972; chmn Fed. Contract Research Center Task Force, Dept. Def., 1975; mem. indsl. and profl. adv. council Pa. State U. Sch. Engring., 1979—. Contbr. articles to profl. jours. Decorated Disting. Service medal, Legion of Merit; recipient Thomas D. White award Nat. Geog. Soc., 1970. Fellow AIAA; mem. Nat. Acad. Engring., Inst. Navigation (Thurlow award 1964, pres. 1976-77), Air Force Assn., U.S. Naval Inst. Clubs: Algonquin (Boston); Concord Country. Home: 115 Indian Pipe Ln Concord MA 01742 Office: 555 Technology Sq Cambridge MA 02139

DUFNER, MAX, educator; b. Davos-Platz, Switzerland, June 17, 1920; came to U.S., 1926, naturalized, 1952; s. William and Béatrice Philomène (Collin) D.; m. Marguerite Little, Aug. 30, 1951; children: Margaret Beatrice, Christina Marie, Thomas William. A.A., Grand Rapids Jr. Coll., 1940; A.B., U. Mo., 1942; M.A., U. Ill., 1947, Ph.D., 1951. Instr. German U. Ky., Lexington, 1947, U. Ill., Urbana, 1951-52; instr. German U. Mich., Ann Arbor, 1952-56, asst. prof. German, 1956-61, assoc. prof. German, 1961-69; prof. German U. Ariz., Tucson, 1969—, head dept., 1969-77; resident dir. Wayne State U. Jr. Year Program, Freiburg, Germany, 1962-63. Editor: (with V.C. Hubbs) German Essays: Vol. I, Aufklärung, Vol. II, Goethe, Vol. III, Schiller, Vol. IV, Romanticism, 1964. Served with AUS, 1942-46. Mem. MLA, Am. Assn. Tchrs. of German, Lessing Soc., Goethe Soc. N.Am., Western Assn. for German Studies, AAUP, Phi Beta Kappa, Phi Kappa Phi, Delta Phi Alpha. Home: 8440 E Kent Pl Tucson AZ 85710

DUFOUR, VAL (ALBERT VALERY DUFOUR), actor; b. New Orleans, Feb. 5, 1927; s. Albert Valery and Cleotile (Brouillette) D. B.A., La. State U., 1949; M.A., Cath. U. Am., 1952. Appeared in: Broadway plays High Button Shoes, 1950, Mister Roberts, 1951, The Grass Harp, 1952, South Pacific, 1953, Media, 1953, Abe's Irish Rose, 1954; appeared in: films The Lonely Night, 1952, The Undead, 1957, Ben Hur, 1957, King of Kings, 1957, Land of Plenty, 1960, She-God, 1961; appears in role of John Wyatt: television series Search for Tomorrow, 1972— (Recipient Emmy award 1977). Roman Catholic. Office: CBS 51 W 52d St New York NY 10019 *I live only for my art, which is sad.*

DUFRESNE, ARMAND ALPHEE, JR., state justice; b. Auburn, Maine, Jan. 17, 1909; s. Armand and Emelina (Couture) D.; m. Colette M. Thibault, Oct. 5, 1939; children: Louise M., Pauline J., Carmen D. A.B., U. Montreal, 1930; LL.B., Boston Coll., 1935; LL.D. (hon.), U. Maine-Orono, 1973. Bar: Maine 1936. Since practiced in Lewiston, corp. counsel, Lewiston, 1937-38, asst. county atty., Androscoggin County, 1939-40, county atty., 1941-44, judge of probate, 1945-56; justice Superior Ct. Maine, 1956-65, Supreme Jud. Ct. Maine, 1965-70, chief justice, 1970-77, active ret. justice, 1977—; mem. Jud. Council Maine, 1954-65, 70-77. Named Laureatus Alumnus, Association des Anciens, Séminaire de Sherbrooke (Que., Can.), 1975. Mem. Am., Maine, Androscoggin County bar assns. Home: 12 Sylvan Ave Lewiston ME 04240 Office: Supreme Ct Maine Auburn ME 04210

DUGAL, LOUIS PAUL, univ. dean; b. Quebec City, Que., Can., Oct. 1, 1911; s. Arthur J. and Jeanne (Bolduc) D.; m. Marie Necker, May 24, 1937; children—Monique Dugal Oaks, Lise Dugal Audet, Michel. B.Sc., Laval U., 1933, M.Sc., 1935; Ph.D., U. Pa., 1939; LL.D. (hon.), U. Toronto, 1965, Concordia U., 1975, U. Ottawa, 1978. From asst. to prof. biology U. Montreal, 1935-45; prof. physiology Laval U., 1945-56; prof. biology, dean Faculty Sci., U. Ottawa, 1956-66, vice dean medicine, 1966—; vice rector U. Sherbrooke, 1967—, prof. emeritus, 1976—; mem. bd. NRC Can., 1942-48, Def. Research Bd., 1955-58, Med. Research Council, 1964-65. Contbr. articles to profl. jours. Decorated Order Brit. Empire; laureate French Acad. Sci. Fellow Royal Soc. Can., Am., Can. physiol. socs. Home: 340 de la Corniche St St Nicolas Levis PQ G0S 2Z0 Canada

DUGAN, DENNIS JOSEPH, accounting company executive; b. Omaha, Mar. 21, 1939; s. Gerald C. and Wilma B. D.; children: Timothy, Thomas, Erin, Molly. B.S. in Math, Creighton U., 1962; Ph.D. in Econs., Brown U., 1966. Assoc. prof. econs. Notre Dame U., 1966-70, chmn. dept. econs., 1970-74; chief economist GAO, Washington, 1974-81; dir. econ. studies Coopers & Lybrand, N.Y.C., 1981—; adj. prof. Am. U. Author: Perspectives on Poverty, 1973; contbr. articles to publs. in field. Commr. Mt. Vernon Youth Athletic Assn., 1979-80. Woodrow Wilson fellow, 1965-66; NSF fellow, 1965; Brookings Instn. fellow, 1968-69. Mem. Am. Econ. Assn., Econometric Soc., Nat. Assn. Bus. Economists, Phi Beta Kappa. Roman Catholic. Office: 1251 Ave of Americas New York NY 10020

DUGAN, DONOVAN PAUL, pipe line co. exec.; b. Morgantown, W. Va., Oct. 23, 1907; s. Joshua Fleming and Grace Gertrude (Hildebr) D.; m. Mary Kelley Fisher, Feb. 15, 1934; children—Dorothy Dale, Don Paul. Student engring., W. Va. U., 1929-31. Jr. engr. U.S. Army Engrs., 1926-28, 30; engr., insp. Ariz. Hwy. Dept., 1928-29; with Tuscarora Pipe Line Co., Ltd., Harrisburg, Pa., after 1931, supt., 1944-50, v.p., 1950-59, pres., 1959-61, also mem. bd. mgrs.; supt. Dixie Pipeline Co., Columbia, S.C.; then mgr. of the Eastern div.; part owner Petroleum Engineering Italiana, Rome; pipeline cons. B.P. Barber & Assos., Columbia; head petroleum sect. NATO, Paris, France, 1957-59. Mem. Pa. Engrs. Soc., Am. Petroleum Inst., Assn. Oil Pipelines. Republican. Methodist. Club: West Shore Country (Camp Hill). Home: 5306 Lakeshore Dr Columbia SC 29206

DUGAN, EDWARD FRANCIS, investment banker; b. Jersey City, July 3, 1934; s. Edward F. and Anna V. D.; m. June D. Hulings, June 28, 1958 (div. 1981); children—Jamie, Edward, Kirsten. B.S., St. Peter's Coll., Jersey City, 1958; M.B.A., N.Y. U., 1961. With Smith Barney & Co., N.Y.C., 1961-75; pres. Warburg Paribas Becker, Inc., N.Y.C., 1975-78; mng. dir. Blyth Eastman Paine Webber, Inc., N.Y.C., 1978—. Served as officer USAR, 1959-61. Club: Bond (N.Y.C.). Office: 1221 Ave of Americas New York NY 10020

DUGAN, HUGH PATRICK, civil engr.; b. Louisville, Colo., Apr. 15, 1914; s. Walter Hugh and Christine (Zurick) D.; m. Alice L. Pennock, May 19, 1938; 1 dau., Michele Diane Kennedy. B.S. in Civil and Irrigation Engring, Colo. State U., 1936. Registered profl. engr., Cal., Colo. With Bur. Reclamation, Dept. Interior, 1936—, asst. chief devel. engr., 1954-59, regional dir., 1959-63, 1963-67, chief project investigations, 1967-69; chmn., U.S. commr. Upper Colorado River Commn., 1969—; civil engr., adviser World Bank, 1969-71; cons. engr. water resource devel., 1971—. Mem. Federal Exec. Bd. Denver, Central Bd. Civil Service Examiners; mem. U.S. nat. com. on large dams Internat. Commn. Irrigation and Drainage. Served to lt. USNR, World War II. Mem. Nat. Soc. Profl. Engrs., Internat. Commn. Large Dams, Chi Epsilon. Address: 3541 Montclair Rd Shingle Springs CA 95682

DUGAN, JOHN LESLIE, JR., foundation executive; b. Phila., Nov. 6, 1921; s. John Leslie and Ellen May (Reid) D.; m. Barbara McClelland Day, Dec. 21, 1946; children: Barbara Nicholas, Geoffrey McClelland, Sara Ellen. B.S., Swarthmore Coll., 1943; postgrad., Harvard U., 1947-48; M.B.A., U. Pa., 1950. Instr. Swarthmore Coll., 1946-47, U. Pa., 1948-50; cons. Booz, Allen and Hamilton, 1951-55; asst. to pres. Grace Nat. Bank, N.Y.C., 1955-58; treas. Underwood Corp., N.Y.C., 1958-60; v.p. fin. Chicopee div. Johnson & Johnson, New Brunswick, N.J., 1960-75; dir., adminstr. Robert Wood Johnson Found., Princeton, N.J., 1975-77; exec. v.p. Am. Diabetes Assn., Inc., N.Y.C., 1977-80; exec. dir. Fin. Analysts Fedn., N.Y.C., 1981—, The Greenwall Found., 1981—; adj. prof. mgmt. St. Peter's Coll., 1975-81. Committeeman Millburn Twp., N.J., 1975-79, commr. fin. and welfare, 1976-79; vestryman, warden, lay reader Christ Ch. in Short Hills, N.J. Served to lt. comdr. USNR, 1943-46. Mem. Fin. Execs. Inst., Tau Beta Pi. Republican. Clubs: Univ., Baltusrol Golf, Short Hills. Home: 5 Hillside Ave Short Hills NJ 07078 Office: 1211 Ave of Americas New York NY 10036

DUGAN, JOHN MICHAEL, steel co. exec.; b. Springfield, Ohio, Aug. 30, 1909; s. John M. and Rosanna (Brady) D. A.B., Wittenberg U., 1933; B. Metall. Engring., Ohio State U., 1937. Registered profl. engr., Ohio. Various metall. positions Ohio Steel Foundry Co., Lima, Ohio, 1937-55, v.p., 1955-67; also dir.; v.p. research Blaw-Knox Co., Pitts., 1967—; dir. Aceros Tepeyac (S.A.), Mexico City, 1973—. Author: Roll Specifications for Continuous Rod Mill Strip Mill, 1965, Development of Roll Specifications for Modern Strip Mill, 1970, Factors Which Influence Roll Specifications, 1978. Trustee St. Rita's Hosp., Lima, 1962-72; pres. United Fund, Lima, 1964-66. Recipient Disting. Alumnus award Coll. Engring., Ohio State U., 1970. Mem. AIME, Assn. Iron and Steel Engrs., Am. Welding Soc., Steel Founders Soc., Am. Soc. Engring. Edn., Nat. Soc. Profl. Engrs., Pitts. Athletic Assn., Alpha Tau Omega. Roman Catholic. Clubs: Springfield Country, Pitts. Field, K.C. Patentee in field, including metal casting method. Office: One Oliver Plaza Pittsburgh PA 15222

DUGAN, PATRICK RAYMOND, microbiologist, university dean; b. Syracuse, N.Y., Dec. 14, 1931; s. Francis Patrick and Joan Irma (Clause) D.; m. Patricia Ann Murray, Sept. 22, 1956; children: Susan Eileen, Craig Patrick, Wendy Shawn, Carolyn Paige. B.S., Syracuse U., 1956, M.S., 1959, Ph.D., 1964. Asso. research scientist Syracuse U. Research Corp., 1956-63; mem. faculty Ohio State U., Columbus, 1964—, asso. prof., 1968-70, prof., chmn. dept. microbiology, 1970-73, acting dean, 1978-79, dean, 1979—. Author: Biochemical Ecology of Water Pollution, 1972. Trustee, Columbus Zool. Assn. and Zoo, 1982—. Fellow Am. Acad. Microbiology; mem. Am. Soc. Microbiology (Ohio pres. 1968-70), A.A.A.S., Soc. Indsl. Microbiology, Water Pollution Control Fedn., Ohio Acad. Sci., Sigma Xi. Club: Creichton. Home: 466 Haymore Ave Worthington OH 43085 Office: Dept Microbiology Ohio State U Columbus OH 43210

DUGAN, RICHARD TAYLOR, telephone company executive; b. Newark, Jan. 23, 1919; s. Fred Taylor and Ethel Charity (Burroughs) D.; m. Marion Higgins, Feb. 21, 1942; children: Richard W., William B., Nancy F. A.B. in Sci, Montclair State Coll., 1940; postgrad., Williams Coll., 1956, Columbia U., 1961. Tchr. sci. and math. high schs., N.J., 1940-42, civil service radio engring. instr., 1942-43; with AT&T, 1946—; v.p. Cin. Bell Inc., 1973, pres., 1974—, chmn., chief exec. officer, 1983—; dir. Multimedia Inc., Cin., The Central Bancorp, Union Central Life Ins. Co., Sencorp., West Shell Inc. Bd. dirs. Cin. Children's Hosp., Xavier U., Cin., Cin. United Appeal, Cin. Salvation Army, Nat. Council Alcoholism. Served with USAAF, 1943-46. Mem. Ohio C. of C. (dir.). Clubs: Bankers, Queen City, Cin. Country, Hundred, Comml., Recess (Cin.). Office: 201 E 4th St Cincinnati OH 45202

DUGAN, ROBERT PERRY, JR., minister, religious organization administrator; b. Morristown, N.J., Jan. 19, 1932; s. Robert P. and Marion Frances (Sahrbeck) D.; m. Marilyn I. Wertz, Aug. 8, 1953; children: Robert Perry, Cheryl. A.B., Wheaton Coll., 1953; M. Div., Fuller Theol. Sem., 1956, postgrad., 1956-57. Ordained to ministry Conservative Baptist Assn. Am., 1957; minister of youth ch., Bloomfield, N.J., 1957-58, pastor, Rochester, N.H., 1959-63, Elmhurst, Ill., 1963-69, Trinity Baptist Ch., Wheat Ridge, Colo., 1970-75; chaplain Senate of State of Colo., 1974-75; pres. Conservative Baptist Assn. Am., 1973-76; v.p. Rockmont Coll., Lakewood, Colo., 1976-78; dir. Office of Pub. Affairs, Nat. Assn. Evangelicals, Washington, 1978—; bd. dirs. Conservative Baptist Theol. Sem., Denver.; Bd. dirs. Rockmont Coll., Denver. Editor: monthly newsletter NAE Washington Insight. Candidate for U.S. Congress, 1976; mem. ethics adv. bd. USIA, 1982—. Home: 1712 Paisley Blue Ct Vienna VA 22180 Office: 1430 K St NW Washington DC 20005

DUGAS, LOUIS, JR., lawyer; b. Beaumont, Tex., Dec. 12, 1928; s. Louis and Loney (Duron) D.; m. Frances Elizabeth Tuley, Feb. 3, 1956; children: Mary Hester Dugas Kinard, Kerry Beth Dugas Davidson, Louis Claiborne, Evin Garner, Reagan Taylor Alton. A.A., Lamar Jr. Coll., 1950; B.B.A., U. Tex., 1955, LL.B., 1960. Bar: Tex. 1960. Justice of peace, Orange County, Tex., 1963, practicing atty., 1960-68; spl. counsel D.C. com. U.S. Ho. of Reps., 1967; dist. atty., Orange County, 1968—; instr. govt. and Tex. history Lamar U., 1970-72; columnist Opportunity Valley News. Bd. dirs. Orange Little Theater, 1964-66, 79—; bd. dirs. Friends of Arts of Lamar U., v.p., 1983; rep. Tex. Legislature, 1954-60; tchr. Cajun French Orange City Parks and Recreation Dept., 1980-81. Served with USMC, 1950-52. Mem. Tex. Bar Assn. (sec., dir. criminal law and procedure sect. 1970,72), Orange County Bar Assn. (pres. 1979), Orange County Hist. Soc. (pres. 1974-76), Nat. Assn. Criminal Def. Lawyers, Tex. Assn. Criminal Def. Lawyers (dir. 1976—, 2d v.p. 1982, 1st v.p. 1983), Tex. Assn. Bd. Cert. Specialists in Criminal Law (v.p. 1982, pres. 1983), Les Acadiens (founder 1980), Tex. Criminal Def. Lawyers (sec.-treas. 1981), Tex. Assn. Bd.-Cert. Specialists in Criminal Law (sec.-treas. 1981), VFW, Phi Alpha Delta. Democrat. Methodist. Club: Optimist (Orange). Home: 1802 16th St Orange TX 77630 Office: 1804 16th St Orange TX 77630

DUGGAN, ANDREW, actor; b. Franklin, Ind., Dec. 28, 1923; s. Edward Dean and Annette (Beach) D.; m. Elizabeth Logue, Sept. 20, 1953; children—Richard, Nancy, Melissa. B.A., Ind. U., 1943. Broadway appearances include Dream Girl, 1946, The Innocents, 1949, Rose Tattoo, 1952, Paint Your Wagon, 1952, Gently Does It, 71953, Anniversary Waltz, 1954, Fragile Fox, 1955, Third Best Sport, 1957; film appearances include Patterns, 1954, Decision at Sundown, 1957, The Bravados, 1958, Merrill's Marauders, 1962, Chapman Report, 1962, Seven Days in May, 1965, The Glory Guys, 1968, In Like Flint, 1969, Incredible Mr. Limpet, 1962, Secret War of Harry Frigg, 1970, Bone, 1972, It's Alive, 1974, The Bears and I, 1974, Skin Game, 1975; TV films include The Last Angry Man, 1974, Two on a Bench, 1972, The Pueblo, 1974, The Missiles of October, 1975, Tail Gunner Joe, 1978, Backstairs at the Whitehouse, 1979, Fire in the Sky, 1979, Overboard, 1979; numerous appearances on TV series, 1950—. Served with USAAF, 1943-46.

DUGGAN, DENNIS MICHAEL, newspaper editor; b. Detroit, Oct. 12, 1927; s. Michael and Anne (Judge) D.; (divorced); 7 dau., Nancy Ellen. A.B., Wayne U., Detroit, 1952. Wall St. columnist N.Y. Herald Tribune, 1960-61; asst. real estate editor N.Y. Times, 1961-62; fin. writer N.Y. Daily News, 1967; sr. editor, N.Y. bur. chief Newsday, 1973—. Mem. Inner Circle, Soc. Silurians. Home: 235 W 11th St New York NY 10014 Office: 1500 Broadway New York NY 10036

DUGGAN, HERBERT GARRISON, engineer; b. Knoxville, Tenn., Jan. 25, 1919; s. Claude Vernon and Fannie Mae (Garrison) D.; m. Lilian Kathryn Calafati, June 5, 1948. B.S.M.E., U. Tenn., 1943, postgrad., 1950-53. Registered profl. engr., Tenn. Mech. engr. Buick Motor Div., Flint, Mich., 1943-44; mech. engr. Union Carbide-Oak Ridge Nat. Lab., 1946-48, design group leader, 1948-55, head, nuclear equipment design dept., 1955-74; supt. mech. design engring. Union Carbide. Y-12 Plant, 1974-79; project mgr. Union Carbide-ORGDP, 1979—; tech. adviser Info. Center for Nuclear Standards, 1971—. Contbr. articles to profl. lit. Served to lt. (j.g.) USNR, 1944-46; PTO. Fellow ASME (v.p. 1969-71), Am. Nuclear Soc. (chmn. remote systems tech. div. 1964-65); mem. Nat. Soc. Profl. Engrs., Am. Soc. Engring. Mgmt. Club: Elks. Instrumental in devel. remote handling techniques for nuclear industry. Home: 126 Grandcove Ln Oak Ridge TN 37830 Office: Union Carbide Corp PO Box P Oak Ridge TN 37830

DUGGAN, JEROME TIMOTHY, utilities exec.; b. Kansas City, Mo., Oct. 30, 1914; s. Jerry F. and Claire (Aaron) D.; m. Dorothy Blanche Castle, May 4, 1940; children—Jerome Castle, Dorothy Lucinda Kobusch. A.B., U. Mo., 1936, LL.B., 1938. Bar: Mo. bar 1938. With Hook & Thomas, Kansas City, 1938-4O; city counselor, Kansas City, 1940-42; regional rationing atty. OPA, 1942-43; mem. firm Gage, Hillix & Phelps, 1946-50; gen. counsel Gas Service Co. Kansas City, Mo., 1950-68, v.p., dir., 1956-64, exec. v.p., dir., gen. counsel, 1964-68, pres., dir., 1968-78, chmn. bd. dirs., 1978-79; dir. Commerce Bank, Kansas City.; Mem. Gov's. Adv. Commn. on Indsl. Devel., 1961—; chmn. Kansas City Housing Authority, 1947-5O; dir. Indsl. Council Kansas City, 1951-55; mem. Indsl. Devel. Commn., Kansas City, 1959—, Municipal Service Commn., 1955-56. Bd. dirs. Citizens Regional Planning Council, Downtown Inc., Kansas City Indsl. Found.; pres. bd. dirs. Asso. Inustries of Mo., 1970—; Trustee, pres. Research Hosp. and Med. Center, 1970-71; trustee Mo. Pub. Expenditure Survey, Midwest Research Inst., Jacob Loose Fund.; bd. regents Rockhurst Coll. Served as lt. USNR, World War II. Mem. Mo. Bar Assn., Am. Gas Assn. (dir.), Am. Royal Assn. (bd. govs.), Kans. Assn. Commerce and Industry (dir.), Sigma Nu, Phi Delta Phi. Clubs: Kansas City (pres. 1976-77), Mission Hills Country.). Home: 11215 Holly St Kansas City MO 64114 Office: 2460 Pershing Rd Kansas City MO 64108

DUGGAN, JOHN JOSEPH, oil company executive, lawyer; b. Dubuque, Iowa, Dec. 11, 1935; s. Donald Lloyd and Oliva E. (McGinnis) D.; m. Karen A. Cole, Feb. 24, 1962; children: Dainel Joseph, Kristen Kay, Kelly Ann. B.A., U. Iowa, 1959, LL.B., 1962. Bar: Iowa 1963, Fla. 1970. Dir. indsl. relations Amerada Hess Corp., Woodbridge, N.J., 1972-76, v.p. labor relations, 1976—. Served with U.S. Army, 1954-56; Korea. Republican. Roman Catholic. Home: 2 Birch Dr Basking Ridge NJ 07920 Office: Amerada Hess Corp 1 Hess Plaza Woodbridge NJ 07095

DUGGAN, JOHN MICHAEL, college president; b. Bridgeport, Conn., June 8, 1928; s. John Hanley and Mary (Dixon) D.; m. Claire Keenan, June 2, 1951; children: Michael, Christopher, Paul, Timothy, John. A.B., Coll. of Holy Cross, 1950; M.A., Yale, 1955, Ph.D., 1957. Instr. Canterbury Sch., New Milford, Conn., 1950-51, U. Bridgeport, 1951-53; asst. dean of freshmen Yale, 1953-57; dir. guidance services Coll. Entrance Exam. Bd., 1957-60, dir. program devel., 1960-63, v.p., 1963-68; v.p. student affairs prof. psychology Vassar, 1968-75; pres. St. Mary's Coll., Notre Dame, Ind., 1975—; mem. fin. com. (Coll. Bd.), 1979—; dir. Am. Nat. Bank & Trust Co. Bd. dirs. Meml. Hosp. South Bend, Ind., 1980, South Bend Symphony, 1978, Ind. Colls. and Univs. of Ind., 1977—, Stanley Clark Sch., 1977—. Mem. Assn. Cath. Colls. and Univs. (dir. 1979—). Club: Univ. (N.Y.C.). Address: Office of Pres St Mary's Coll Notre Dame IN 46556

DUGGAN, TIMOTHY JOHN, educator, philosopher; b. Worcester, Mass., Feb. 20, 1928; s. Timothy John and Esther (McDermott) D.; m. Joan Lamoureux, Aug. 23, 1951; children—Theresa Elizabeth, Timothy John, Christine Frances. A.B., Brown U., 1952, A.M., 1953, Ph.D., 1957; M.A., Harvard, 1954, Dartmouth, 1969. Faculty Dartmouth, 1957—, prof. philosophy, 1968—, chmn. dept., 1963-67, 74-79, asso. dean faculty, 1980—. Editor: The Philosophical Works of Thomas Reid, 1969. Served with USAAF, 1946-48. Mem. Am. Philos. Assn. Home: 2 Spencer Rd Hanover NH 03755

DUGGER, EDWIN ELLSWORTH, composer, educator; b. Poplar Bluff, Mo., Mar. 21, 1940; s. Harrison Elsworth and Esther Leona (Scowden) D.; m. Kathryn Lou Hake, Feb. 2, 1963; 1 son, Alan Keith. B.M., Oberlin Conservatory Music, 1962; M.F.A., Princeton U., 1964. Lectr. Oberlin Coll. Conservatory Music, 1965-67; assoc. prof. U. Calif., Berkeley, 1967—. Composer: Intermezzi, 1969, Divisions of Time, 1961, Music for Synthesizer and Six Instruments, 1965-66, Adieu, 1972, Abwesenheiten und Wiedersehen, 1971, Matsukaze, 1976, Fantasy for Piano, 1977, Variations and Adagio, 1979, Septet, 1980. Guggenheim fellow; recipient Naumburg award. Mem. Broadcast Music. Office: Department of Music University of California Berkeley CA 94720 *

DUGGER, GORDON LESLIE, aeronautical engineer; b. Winter Haven, Fla., Nov. 13, 1923; s. Herman Leslie and Beulah (McCormick) D.; m. Mary Louise Kennedy, Apr. 8, 1945; children: George Leslie, Mary Susan Dugger Hansen, Barbara Ann Dugger Thornton. B.S. in Chem. Engring., U. Fla., 1944, M.S., 1947; Ph.D., Case Inst. Tech., 1953. Aero. research scientist Lewis Flight Propulsion Lab., NACA, Cleve., 1947-54; supr. chem. processing Fla. Research

Sta., Internat. Minerals & Chem. Corp., Mulberry, 1954-57; supr. External Ramjets Project, Johns Hopkins Applied Physics Lab., Laurel, Md., 1957-63, supr. hypersonic propulsion group, 1963-73, asst. supr. aeros. div., 1973-78, supr., 1978—. Editor-in-chief: Jour. of Spacecraft and Rockets, 1964-70; contbr. articles profl. jours. Served with C.E., AUS, 1944-46. Recipient Engring. Scis. award Washington Acad. Scis., 1964, Silver medal Combustion Inst., 1970. Fellow AIAA (v.p. publs. 1971-74), AAAS (mem. council 1971-74); mem. Am. Solar Energy Soc., Combustion Inst., Sigma Xi, Sigma Tau, Phi Kappa Phi. Republican. Methodist. Home: 1023 Kathryn Rd Silver Spring MD 20904 Office: Johns Hopkins Rd Laurel MD 20810

DUGGER, RONNIE E., writer, publisher; b. Chgo., Apr. 16, 1930; s. W.L. and Mary (King) D.; m. Jean Williams, June 13, 1951 (div. 1978); children—Gary McGregor, Celia Williams.; m. Patricia Blake, June 29, 1982. B.A., U. Tex., 1950, postgrad., 1954; student, Oxford U., 1951-52. Journalist Tex. newspapers, 1947-52; asst. to exec. dir. Nat. Security Tng. Commn., Washington, 1952-54; editor Tex. Observer, 1954-61, 63-65, 81, pub., 1965—; Rockefeller fellow, 1969; Research fellow Inst. Indsl. Relations, U. Calif. at Los Angeles, 1969-70; vis. prof. communications Hampshire Coll., 1976; George Miller vis. prof. English U. Ill. at Urbana, 1976; vis. prof. English U. Va., 1977; fellow Woodrow Wilson Internat. Ctr. for Scholars, 1983-84. Author: Dark Star; Hiroshima Reconsidered in the Life of Claude Eatherly of Lincoln Park, Texas, 1967, Our Invaded Universities, Form, Reform, and New Starts, A Nonfiction Play for Five Stages, 1974, The Politician: The Life and Times of Lyndon Johnson, 1982, On Reagan, The Man & His Presidency, 1983; Editor: Three Men in Texas, Bedichek, Webb and Dobie, 1967; Contbr. articles to mags., jours. Nat. Endowment for Humanities fellow, 1978. Mem. Authors Guild, ACLU (nat. adv. council), P.E.N., San Antonio Conservation Soc., Tex. Inst. Letters, Philos. Soc. Tex. Home: PO Box 1466 Austin TX 76767 Office: 600 W 7th Austin TX 78701

DUGGER, WILLIE MACK, JR., botany educator; b. Adel, Ga., July 28, 1919; s. Willie Mack and Kate (Hendry) D.; m. Dot Towler, June 12, 1946; children: Thomas, Lucinda. B.S., U. Ga., 1941; M.S., U. Wis., 1942; Ph.D., N.C. State Coll., 1950. Asst. prof. botany U. Ga., 1946; asst. prof. plant physiology U. Md., 1950-55; asso. prof. plant physiology U. Fla., 1955-60; faculty U. Cal. at Riverside, 1960—, prof. botany, chmn. dept. life sci., 1963-68, dean, 1968-74, asso. dir., 1971-81, dean, 1974-81, prof. botany, 1981—. Served to capt. U.S. Army, 1942-46. Mem. Am. Soc. Plant Physiology, Am. Inst. Biol. Scis., A.A.A.S., Sigma Xi, Phi Kappa Phi, Alpha Zeta, Gamma Sigma Delta. Home: 780 N University Dr Riverside CA 92507

DUGMORE, EDWARD, painter; b. Hartford, Conn., Feb. 20, 1915; s. Walter and Ellen (Spragg) D.; m. Edith Oslund, Aug. 20, 1938; 1 dau., Linda Carol. One-man exhbns. include, Stable Gallery, N.Y.C., 1953, 54, 56, Holland-Goldowsky Gallery, Chgo., 1959, Howard Wise Gallery, N.Y.C., 1960, 61, 63, Des Moines Art Center, 1972; group exhbns. include Pitts. Internat. Exhbn. of Contemporary Painting, Carnegie Inst., 1955, Am. Abstract Expressionists and Imagists, Guggenheim Mus., 1961, 65th Ann, Art Inst. Chgo., 1962 (M.V. Kohnstamm award), Painting and Sculpture in Calif.-The Modern Era, San Francisco Mus. Art, 1976-77, Group Show, Nat. Art Collection, Washington, 1975; represented in permanent collections, Albright-Knox Art Gallery, Buffalo, Walker Art Center, Mpls., Des Moines Art Center, Weatherspoon Art Gallery, Greensboro, N.C., Kresge Art Center, E. Lansing, Mich., Ciba-Geigy Corp., N.Y.C., Mobil Oil Corp., Arlington, Va. Served with USMC, 1943-44. Recipient award Am. Acad. and Inst. Arts and Letters, 1980; grantee Nat. Endowment Arts, 1976; Guggenheim fellow, 1966-67. Address: 118 W 27th St New York NY 10001

DUGOFF, HOWARD JAY, government official; b. Yonkers, N.Y., Nov. 23, 1936; s. Benjamin and Bessie (Ettinger) D.; m. Sandra N. Karp, Dec. 25, 1958; children: Lorraine, Richard, Julie. M.E., Stevens Inst. Tech., 1958, M.S. in Physics, 1960. Research engr. Davidson Lab.-Stevens Inst. Tech., Hoboken, N.J., 1959-67, Hwy. Safety Research Inst.-U. Mich., Ann Arbor, 1967-71; chief research-analysis br. U.S. Army Tank Automotive Command, Warren, Mich., 1971-74; assoc. adminstr. Nat. Hwy. Traffic Safety Adminstrn.-U.S. Dept. Transp., Washington, 1974-77, dep. adminstr., 1977-79, research and spl. adminstr., 1979-84, Sci. and tech. advisor to sec. transp., 1984—; mem. U.S. Radiation Policy Council, 1979-80; mem. exec. policy bd. Alaska Natural Gas Transp. System, 1979—; U.S. rep. European council of Ministers of Transport, Paris, 1979. Curtiss-Wright Corp. fellow, 1959; recipient U.S. Army Research & Devel. award, 1973; named Meritorious Fed. Exec. Pres. of U.S., 1980. Mem. Soc. Automotive Engrs. (dir. 1977). Home: 11404 Grundy Ct Potomac MD 20854 Office: Dept Transp 400 7th St SW Washington DC 20590 *I find a request to write on the subject "Thoughts on my life" thoroughly intimidating. After some consideration, and in all due immodesty, I've decided to try to record a "thought" about my approach to my work. The essence of that approach is a real commitment to the interests of the organization for which I work. I come by that commitment, which I've felt in every job I've ever had, not through intellectual or moral conviction, but by instinct. And the instinct serves me well. I've enjoyed personal gratification and success as by-products of my efforts thus motivated, to a degree far greater than I believe I could achieve by directly pursuing personal goals.*

DUGUAY, MARTIN ROBERT, psychiatrist, educator; b. Montreal, Que., Can., Dec. 12, 1934; s. Joseph Gerard and Blance (Rioux) D.; m. Marie Saucier, June 11, 1959; children: Marie-Halene, Etienne, Jean-Christope, Angelique, Jeanne. B.S., U. Paris, 1953; M.D., U. Montreal, 1959. Intern L'Hotel-Dieu, Montreal, 1959-60, clin. supr. med. students, residents, mem. staff, 1974—, psychiatrist-in-chief, 1978—; resident in psychiatry Payne Whitney Clinic Cornell U., N.Y.C., 1960-63; resident in child psychiatry la Salpetrie Hosp., Paris, 1963-64, chief of service, coordinator of med. students, 1966-74, pres., 1973; psychiat. expert Que. Workman Compensation Bd.; asst. prof. psychiatry U. Montreal, 1966-73, assoc. prof., 1974—; mem. test com. Royal Coll. Can.; examiner in psychiatry Royal Coll. Physicians, Surgeons of Can. Author: (with Henri Ellenberger) Precis Pratique de Psychiatrie; contbr. articles to profl. jours. Mem. Que. Psychiat. Assn. (sec. 1967-70), Can. Psychiat. Assn. (pres. 1980), Am. Psychiat. Assn. Home: 44 Maplewood Ave Outremont 915 Montreal PQ Canada

DUGUNDJI, JOHN, aero. engr.; b. N.Y.C., Oct. 25, 1925; s. Basile and Rosa (Finale) D.; m. Wraye Polkey, July 25, 1965; children—Elenna Rose, Elisa Anthe. B.A.E., N.Y. U., 1944; M.S. in Aero. Engring, M.I.T., 1948, Sc.D., 1951. Research engr. Grumman Aircraft Co., Bethpage, N.Y., 1948-49; dynamics engr. Republic Aviation Corp., Farmingdale, N.Y., 1951-56; research asso. M.I.T., 1956-57, asst. prof. aero. engring., 1957-62, asso. prof., 1962-70, prof., 1970—. Served with USN, 1944-46. Mem. AIAA, Sigma Xi, Tau Beta Pi. Greek Orthodox. Home: 39 Albert Ave Belmont MA 02178 Office: Dept Aeros and Astronautics MIT Cambridge MA 02139

DUHAMEL, PIERRE ALBERT, educator; b. Putnam, Conn., Feb. 6, 1920; s. Albert and Rose (Comeau) D.; m. Helen L. Stowell, Sept. 4, 1943; 1 dau., Mary Elizabeth. A.B., Holy Cross Coll., 1941; M.A., Boston Coll., 1942; Ph.D., U. Wis., 1945. Prof. U. Chgo., 1945-49; prof. English Boston Coll., 1949—, Philomatheia prof., 1954—; vis. prof. U. Wis., 1947, 49; lit. editor Boston Herald Am., 1965—; Mem. Pulitzer Prize Jury, 1967-74, Nat. Book Awards Jury, 1973-74, Am. Book Awards, 1980, 81; Nat. Endowment for Humanities lectr. Boston Pub. Library, 1976; Mem. adv. bd. Assumption Coll., 1958—. Moderator: TV program I've Been Reading, 1956-63; Author: Essays in American Catholic Tradition, 1960, Rhetoric, 1962, Persuasive Prose, 1963, Principles of Rhetoric, 1964, Literature: Form and Function, 1965, After Strange Fruit, 1980, also weekly columns, essays, book revs. Mem. AAUP (chpt. pres. 1949-56), Shakespeare Soc., Nat. Conf. Tchrs. English. Club: Tavern. Home: Saddle Ridge Rd Dover MA 02030 Office: Boston Coll Chestnut Hill MA 02167

DUHL, LEONARD J., psychiatrist, educator; b. N.Y.C., May 24, 1926; s. Louis and Rose (Josefsberg) D.; m. Lisa Shippee; children: Pamela, Nina, David, Susan, Haydée. B.A., Columbia U., 1945; M.D., Albany Med. Coll., 1948; postgrad., Washington Psychoanalytic Inst., 1956-64. Diplomate: Am. Bd. Psychiatry and Neurology (examiner 1977—). Intern Jewish Hosp., Bklyn., 1948-49; with USPHS, 1951-53, 54-72, Med. dir., 1954-72; fellow Menninger Sch. Psychiatry, resident psychiatry Winter VA Hosp., Topeka, 1949-51, 53-54; med. dir., asst. health officer Contra Costa County (Calif.) Health Dept., 1951-53; dir. study psychosocial and statis. aspects of Tb USPHS, 1951-53; psychiatrist profl. services br. NIMH, 1954-64, chief office planning, 1964-66, chmn. com. psychol. variables as related to mental health, 1959-68; spl. asst. to sec. HUD, 1966-68; cons. Peace Corps, 1961-68; assoc. psychiatry George Washington Med. Sch., 1961-63, asst. clin. prof., 1963-68, assoc. prof., 1966-68; prof. public health and urban social policy Coll. Environ. Design and Sch. Pub. Health, U. Calif. at Berkeley, 1968—, dir. dual degree program in health and med. scis., 1971-77; clin. prof. psychiatry U. Calif. at San Francisco, 1969—; pvt. practice psychiatry, Berkeley; pres. Human Dimensions, Inc., 1981—; chmn. Mayor's Task Force on Health, Washington, 1969; research adv. com. NIE, 1974-78; mem. Kans. com. White House Conf. on Children and Youth, 1950; mem. sci. adv. council Calif. Legislature, 1970—, sr. cons. Assembly Office of Research, 1981—; cons. Commonweal, others. Author: Approaches to Research in Mental Retardation, 1959, The Urban Condition, 1963, (with R.L. Leopold) Mental Health and Urban Social Policy, 1969, Making Whole Health for a New Epoch, 1980; assoc. editor medicine and psychiat. sects.: Am. Jour. Mental Deficiency, 1957-61; bd. editors: Volunteer's Digest, 1965-70, (with R.L. Leopold) Trans-Action mag, 1965-70, Jour. Community Psychology, 1974—, Jour. Community Mental Health, 1974—, Jour. Mental Health Consultation and Edn, 1978—, Jour. Prevention, 1978—; contbr. (with R.L. Leopold) articles to tech. lit. Bd. dirs. Calif. Sch. Profl. Psychology, 1977—, Epoch B Found., La Jolla, 1977—; trustee Robert F. Kennedy Found., 1971—; bd. dirs. Touch for Health Found., Pasadena, 1977—, Citizens Policy Center, San Francisco, 1975—, Magic Mountain Sch., 1971-78, New World Alliance, 1980—, Books Unltd. Coop., 1980-82. Rosenberg Found. grantee, San Francisco, 1951-53. Fellow Am. Psychiat. Assn. (chmn. com. on poverty 1963, chmn. com. preventive psychiatry 1964, chmn. com. energy issues 1983—), Am. Coll. Psychiatry, Am. Orthopsychiat. Assn. (sec. 1964-66); mem. No. Calif. Psychiat. Soc., Am. Assn. Mental Deficiency (councilor 1959-63, editorial bd. Jour. 1957-60), Group Advancement Psychiatry (chmn. com. preventive psychiatry 1962-66). Office: Sch Public Health Warren Hall U Calif Berkeley CA 94720 639 Cragmont Ave Berkeley CA 94708

DUHME, H(ERMAN) RICHARD, JR., sculptor, educator; b. St. Louis, May 31, 1914; s. Herman Richard and Ruth Frances (Leggat) D.; m. Carol Louise McCarthy, Apr. 9, 1947; children: David W., Benton Roblee (dec. 1971), Ann Duhme Welker, Warren L. Student, Pa. Acad. Fine Arts, 1932-38, U. Pa., 1934, Am. Sch. Classical Studies, Athens, Greece, 1951; B.F.A., Washington U., St. Louis, 1953. Prof. sculpture Washington U., St. Louis, 1947-82, prof. emerits, 1982—; head sculpture dept. Chautauqua Instn. Summer Sch., 1953—, Syracuse U. Chautauqua Center, 1953-69. Served with USAAF, 1942-46. Decorated Bronze Stars. Fellow Nat. Sculpture Soc.; mem. Allied Artists Am. Clubs: St. Louis Country, Univ. Home: 8 Edgewood Rd Saint Louis MO 63124 Office: Washington U Saint Louis MO 63130 *I feel that an artist's life and work is of no importance unless it touches those around him and gives pleasure, help, or increased knowledge and enrichment in so doing. I have tried to remember this in creating my sculpture and in my contacts with my students.*

DUIGNAN, PETER JAMES, historian, curator; b. San Francisco, Aug. 6, 1926; s. Peter James and Delia (Conway) D.; m. Frances Sharpe, Aug. 13, 1949; children—Kathleen, Patricia, Peter, Frances, Rose Marie, Sheila Marie. B.S. cum laude, U. San Francisco, 1951; Ph.D., Stanford, 1960. Instr., Western civilization Stanford, 1955-57, 59-60, curator African collections, 1966—; mem. staff Hoover Instn., Stanford, 1959—, exec. sec., 1963-65, dir. African program, 1965—, also Stella W. and Ira S. Lillick African curator. Author: (with L.H. Gann) White Settlers in Tropical Africa, 1962, (with C. Clendenen and R. Collins) United States and Africa, 1865-1900, 1966, (with L. H. Gann) Burden of Empire: An Appraisal of Colonialism in Africa, 1967, Handbook of American Resources for African Studies, 1967, Colonialism in Africa, 5 vols, 1969-75, Africa and the World, 1972, Why South Africa Will Survive, 1981, North Africa and the Middle East, 1981; Editor: African Studies Bull. of African Studies Assn, 1965-66, Guide to Research and Reference Material on Africa, 1971, The United States in the 1980's, 1980. Served with U.S. Army, 1944-46. Ford Found. fellow, Africa, 1957-59; Rockefeller Found. fellow, 1963-64; Nat. Def. Edn. Act fellow, 1963; Guggenheim fellow, 1973. Fellow African Studies Assn. (chmn. libraries com. 1960-63, bd. dirs. 1965-68); mem. Assn. Research Libraries (chmn. subcom. Africa 1965-67), Am. Hist. Assn., N.A.A.C.P., Am. Civil Liberties Union. Roman Catholic. Home: 939 Casanueva Pl Stanford CA 94305

DUKAKIS, MICHAEL STANLEY, governor of Massachusettes; b. Boston, Nov. 3, 1933; s. Panos and Euterpe (Boukis) D. B.A., Swarthmore Coll., 1955; LL.B., Harvard U., 1960. Bar: Mass. 1960. Mem. firm. Hill and Barlow, Boston, 1960-74; gov. State of Mass., Boston, 1975-79, 83—. Mem. Mass. Ho. of Reps., 1962-70. Mem. Phi Beta Kappa. Office: Office of Gov Room 360 State House Boston MA 02133

DUKAS, PETER, educator, mgmt. cons.; b. Lewiston, Maine, Apr. 7, 1919; s. Peter and Katherine (Bezantakos) D.; m. Aphrodite Dukas, June 22, 1950; 1 son, Stephen Peter. B.S., U. Chgo., 1950, M.S.A., 1951. Ops. analyst Brass Rail, N.Y.C., 1951-52; mgr. Mid City Enterprises, N.Y.C., 1953-54, Prince of Wales Hotel, Can., 1958; mgmt. cons., pres. Manco Assos., Inc., Tallahassee, 1958—; prof., dir. Sch. Hotel and Restaurant Mgmt., Fla. State U., 1954—; real estate broker, 1980—; Bd. dirs. Nat. Council Hotel and Restaurant Edn. Author: Hotel Front Office Management, 1957, 3d rev. edit., 1970, How To Operate a Restaurant, 1960, How To Organize and Operate a Profitable Restaurant, 1971, Planning Profits in the Food and Lodging Industry, 1975, Guide to Profitable Bar Management, 1975, also articles. Dir. Greek Orthodox Community, Tallahassee, 1961, pres. Ahepa Patmos chpt., dist. gov., 1961; Sec. Ahepa Ednl. Found. Bd. Served with USMCR, 1942-46. Recipient numerous awards from motel and restaurant assns. Mem. Internat. Soc. Food Service Cons.'s, AAUP, Am. Hellenic Ednl. Progressive Assn. (dir.), Beta Gamma Sigma. Home: 504 Driftwood Ave Daytona Beach FL 32018 *We are our own worst enemy. The real values of life, like the rain, falls equally on everyone. Unfortunately, some remain parched because of the waterproof defenses they themselves have created, many are moistened and comforted for a brief period and a few are saturated. The underlying cause of success is not working harder or working smarter, nor is it a matter of good or bad luck; in all instances of substantial achievement of personal values, the inner attitude one has about himself and his fellow human beings is the determining factor. Without love and affection for himself and others, an individual life becomes a meaningless, desolate, and arid voyage. No matter how pure the liquid poured, the soiled container discharges waste.*

DUKE, ANGIER BIDDLE, foundation executive, former diplomat; b. N.Y.C., Nov. 30, 1915; s. Angier Buchanan and Cordelia (Biddle) D.; m. Robin Chandler Lynn, May 12, 1962; 1 son, Angier Biddle; children by previous marriage: A. St. George B., Maria-Luisa B. Duke de Peyster, Dario B. Student, Yale U., 1934-37; LL.D., Iona Coll., 1957, Duke U., 1969; L.H.D., L.I. U., 1967. Pres. Duke Internat. Corp., N.Y.C., 1945-48; apptd. 2d sec. U.S. Fgn. Service, 1949; with Am. embassy, Buenos Aires, Argentina, 1949, spl. asst. to ambassador, Madrid, 1951; U.S. ambassador to, El Salvador, 1952-53; v.p. CARE, 1958-60; pres. Am. Immigration and Citizenship Com., 1960-64; chief of protocol White House and Dept. State, 1961-65; ambassador to, Spain, 1965-68; chief of protocol Dept. State, 1968; ambassador to, Denmark, 1968-69, commr. civic affairs and pub. events, N.Y.C., 1973-76; chmn. N.Y.C. Dem. Com., 1976-77; pres. The Spanish Inst., N.Y.C., 1977-79, chmn., 1983—, N.Y. State Council on Ethnic Affairs, 1978-79; pres. Nat. Com. on Am. Fgn. Policy, Inc., N.Y.C., 1978-79; ambassador to, Morocco, 1979-81; chmn. U.S.-Japan Found., N.Y.C., 1981—; spl. adv. The Aspen Inst., Colo., 1981—; Pres. Internat. Rescue Com., 1954-60; chmn. Dem. State Com. Nationalities and Intergroup Relations, 1960, Appeal of Conscience Found., 1974—; pres.'s assoc. Duke U. Commr. L.I. State Park, 1955-61; trustee L.I. U., 1981—; chmn. World Affairs Council L.I., 1981—. Served from pvt. to maj. AUS, 1940-45; officer in charge Paris sect. Air Transport Command, 1945. Decorated by govts. Gt. Britain, France, Spain, Haiti, Sweden, Greece and Denmark. Mem. Council Fgn. Relations, Fgn. Policy Assn. (dir.), Fgn. Service Assn., The Pilgrims, SAR, Soc. Colonial Wars. Clubs: Brook, River, Racquet and Tennis (N.Y.C.); Travellers (Paris); Buck's (London). Address: US Japan Found 560 Lexington Ave New York NY 10022

DUKE, ANNA MARIE *See* **ASTIN, PATTY DUKE**

DUKE, DONALD NORMAN, publisher; b. Los Angeles, Apr. 1, 1929; s. Roger V. and Mabel (Weineger) D. B.A. in Ednl. Psychology, Colo. Coll., 1951. Comml. photographer, Colorado Springs, Colo., 1951-53; pub. relations Gen. Petroleum, Los Angeles, 1954-55; agt. Gen. S.S. Corp., Ltd., 1956-57; asst. mgr. retail advt., sales promotion Mobil Oil Co., 1958-63; pub. Golden West Books, Alhambra, Calif., 1964—; dir. Pacific R.R. Publs., Inc., Athletic Press.; Pub. relations cons. Santa Fe Ry., 1960-70. Author: The Pacific Electric—A History of Southern California Railroading, 1958, Southern Pacific Steam Locomotives, 1962, Santa Fe. . Steel Rails to California, 1963, Night Train, 1961, American Narrow Gauge, 1978; editor: Water Trails West, 1977. Recipient Spur award for Trails of the Iron Horse Western Writers Am., 1975. Mem. Ry. and Locomotive Hist. Soc. (dir. 1944—), Western History Assn., Newcomen Soc., Lexington Group of Western Historians, Western Writers Am., P.E.N. Internat. (v.p. 1975-77), Authors Guild Am., Book Pubs. Assn. So. Calif. (dir. 1968-77), Cal. Writers Guild (dir. 1976-77), Calif. Book Pubs. Assn. (dir. 1976-77), Westerners Internat. (editor Branding Iron 1971-80), Hist. Soc. So. Calif. (dir. 1972-75), Kappa Sigma (lit. editor Caduceus 1968-80). Home: PO Box 80250 San Marino CA 91108 Office: 525 N Electric St Alhambra CA 91801

DUKE, DOUGLAS, educator; b. Phila., Aug. 7, 1923; s. Samuel and Anne (Klein) D.; m. Helen May Squires, Apr. 20, 1944; children—Kathleen (Mrs. Arnold P. Deutsch), Jeanne M. B.A., U. Cal. at Berkeley, 1947; Ph.D., U. Chgo., 1950. Asst. prof. U. N.C., Chapel Hill, 1950-51; asso. prof. U. Fla., Gainesville, 1952-54; prof. astronomy U. Miami, Coral Gables, Fla., 1965—; sr. research engr. Gen. Dynamics, San Diego, 1955-57; scientist RCA, Cape Kennedy, Fla., 1957-59; mem. tech. staff Inst. Def. Analysis, Washington, 1959-62; staff scientist to v.p. Research Autonetics div. N.Am. Aviation Corp., Anaheim, Cal., 1962-64; dir. Systems Analysis Corp., Satellite Beach, Fla., 1969—; Bd. dirs. Friends of Physics, Miami. Served from pvt. to 1st lt. USAAF, 1943-46. Fellow A.A.A.S.; mem. Am. Astron. Soc., Astron. Soc. Pacific. Research in interstellar matter, visual binary stars, ground photography of fgn. space vehicles, atmospheric optics and radar meteorology, statistics and time series analysis. Home: 5900 SW 63d Ct Miami FL 33143 Office: Dept of Physics University of Miami Coral Gables FL 33124

DUKE, EMANUEL, lawyer; b. Buffalo, Sept. 4, 1916; s. Harry and Ida (Malek) D.; m. Shirley F. Martin, May 28, 1969; children by previous marriage: Cathy E., James L. B.A., Cornell U., 1937, LL.B., 1939. Bar: N.Y. 1939. Since practiced in, Buffalo; partner firm Saperston, Wiltse, Duke, Day & Wilson (and predecessors), 1949-70; sr. partner firm Duke, Holzman, Yaeger & Radlin (and predecessors), 1970—; dir. Mader Corp. Bd. mem.-at-large Jewish Fedn. Buffalo, 1948-61, 63-70; mem. bd. Jewish Family Service, 1963-70; mem. bd. govs. Am. Jewish Com., Buffalo, 1963-68. Served to lt. USNR, 1941-45. Mem. Am., N.Y. State, Erie County bar assns., Erie County Trial Lawyers Assn., Sigma Alpha Mu., B'nai B'rith (pres. lodge 1953-54, chmn. Buffalo council 1955). Jewish. Club: Westwood Country (Williamsville, N.Y.) (dir.). Home: 306 Forestview Dr Williamsville NY 14221 Office: 2410 Main Place Tower Buffalo NY 14202

DUKE, HAROLD BENJAMIN, JR., business executive; b. Washington, Iowa, Jan. 11, 1922; s. Harold Benjamin and Nordica (Wells) D.; m. Maud Barnard Banks, June 11, 1949; children: James Lenox, Harold Benjamin III, Peter Wells, Lester Perrin, Charles Banks. B.A., Williams Coll., 1943. With Gates Corp., Denver, 1946—, mem. exec. com., 1959—, v.p., 1960-73, exec. v.p., 1973-83, pres., 1983—, also dir.; dir. subs. cos. Gates Corp.; dir. A-Bar-A Ranches, Gates Energy Products, Gates Data Products, Gates Land Co., Gates Learjet, Vail Assos., Inc., Colo., 1965—, chmn. bd., 1983—. Mem. Denver Com. on Fgn. Relations, 1967—; Bd. dirs. Boys Clubs of Denver, 1960—; pres., trustee Denver Country Day Sch., Englewood, Colo., 1958-71; trustee Social Sci. Found., U. Denver, 1967-75, pres., 1972-75; trustee Denver Pub. Library Found., 1974—, pres., 1976-79. Served with U.S. Army, 1943-45. Decorated Bronze Star medal, Purple Heart. Republican. Clubs: University, Mile High, Denver Country, Country of Colo., Castle Pines. Office: PO Box 5887 Denver CO 80217

DUKE, JOHN MURRAY, mineralogist; b. Montreal, Que., Can., Jan. 3, 1947; s. Nelson Harold and R. Eileen (Crane) D.; m. Sally Munnell, Apr. 12, 1975; children: James Harold, Jennifer Frances. B.Sc., McGill U., 1968, M.Sc. (NRC scholar), 1971; Ph.D. (fellow), U. Conn., 1974. NRC postdoctoral fellow U. Toronto, 1974-76; econ. mineralogist Geol. Survey Can., Ottawa, Ont., 1976—; Exec. sec. Mineral. Assn. Can., 1978—, head mineral deposits, geology sect., 1983—. Editorial bd.: Econ. Geology, 1983—; contbr. articles to profl. jours. Fellow Geol. Assn. Can. Research in genesis of magmatic ores of nickel, platinum and chromium. Home: 10 Chimo Dr Kanata ON K2L 1A4 Canada Office: 601 Booth St Ottawa ON K1A 0E8 Canada

DUKE, RICHARD DE LA BARRE, urban planner; b. Washington, Dec. 19, 1930; s. James Paul and Florence Hilda (De La Barre) D.; m. Marie Alice Myers, Aug. 27, 1955; children—Kathryn, Paul, Michele,

Lynda, Lorraine, Richard. B.S., U. Md., 1952, Mich. State U., 1954; M.Urban Planning (Land Econs. Found. award), Mich. State U., 1956; Ph.D. (Schoen-Rene award, Samuel Trask Dana grantee, NSF faculty fellow), U. Mich., Ann Arbor, 1964. Dir. environ. simulation lab. U. Mich., 1967-73, prof. urban and regional planning, 1956—, chmn. urban planning program, 1976-82; bd. dirs. Housing Renovation, Lansing, Mich., 1969-72; lectr. over 50 univs. Author: (with Cathy S. Greenblat) Gaming/Simulation: Ratioale; Design; Use, 1974, Gaming: The Future's Language, 1974, Metropolis: The Urban Systems Game, 1975, Game Generating Games for Community and Classroom, 1979, Principles and Practices of Gaming-Simulation, 1981, (with Ingolf Stahl) Game-Simulation for Applied Public Policy - The International Experience, 1982; also monographs and articles; editorial bd. profl. jours. Bd. dirs. Community Systems Found., Ann Arbor, 1962-71. Served to 1st lt., C.E. AUS, 1952-56. Fulbright scholar, W.Ger., 1969; fellow Netherland Inst. Advanced Study, Wassenar, 1973-74. Mem. Am. Planning Assn., Internat. Simulation and Gaming Assn., Nat. Assn. Simulation and Gaming. Home: 321 Parklake Ave Ann Arbor MI 48103 Office: 2155 Art and Architecture Bldg U Mich Ann Arbor MI 48109

DUKE, ROBERT DOMINICK, mineral company executive; b. Goshen, N.Y., Oct. 14, 1928; s. Robert DeWitt and Elma Christina (Dominick) D.; m. Jeannette Parham, Apr. 24, 1954; children: Katherine Campbell, Robert Dominick, Peter Benjamin DeWitt, Lois Christina. B.A., Va. Mil. Inst., 1947; LL.B., Yale U., 1950; M.B.A., U. Pa., 1952. Bar: N.Y. 1950. With Cravath, Swaine & Moore, N.Y.C., 1951-52, 54-64, Freeport-McMoRan Inc. (and predecessors Freeport Minerals Co. and Freeport Sulphur Co.), 1964—, sec., 1965-67, v.p., 1967-73, gen. counsel, 1970—, sr. v.p., 1973—; dir. Freeport Indonesia, Inc., Freeport Queensland Nickel, Inc. Served as 1st lt. JAGC, U.S. Army, 1952-54. Mem. Assn. Bar City N.Y., Am., N.Y. State bar assns. Presbyterian. Clubs: Yale, Sky (N.Y.C.); Wilton Riding, Silvermine Golf. Home: 67 Ridgefield Rd Wilton CT 06897 Office: 200 Park Ave New York NY 10166

DUKE, STEVEN BARRY, legal educator; b. Mesa, Ariz., July 31, 1934; s. Alton and Elaine (Altman) D.; m. Janet Truax, Aug. 29, 1956; children: Glenn, Warren, Alison, Sally. B.S., Ariz. State U., 1956; J.D., U. Ariz., 1959; LL.M., Yale U., 1961. Bar: Ariz. 1959. Law clk. to Supreme Ct. Justice Douglas, 1959; grad. fellow Yale Law Sch., 1960, mem. faculty, 1961—, prof. law, 1966—, Law of Sci. and Tech. prof., 1982—; vis. prof. U. Calif.-Berkeley, 1965, Hastings Coll. Law, 1981; Bd. dirs. New Haven Legal Assistance Assn., 1968-70; cons. Commn. to Revise Fed. Criminal Code; mem. Conn. Commn. on Medicolegal Investigations, 1976—. Contbr. profl. jours.; Editor-in-chief: Ariz. Law Rev. Mem. Woodbridge (Conn.) Bd. Edn., 1970-72; mem. Woodbridge Democratic Town Com., 1967-72. Mem. Nat. Assn. Criminal Def. Lawyers, Am. Trial Lawyers, Am. Civil Liberties Union, Phi Kappa Phi, Alpha Tau Omega. Home: 250 Grandview Ave Hamden CT 06514 Office: 401A Yale Station New Haven CT 06520

DUKE, WAYNE, athletic adminstr.; b. Burlington, Iowa, Nov. 9, 1928; s. Herald M. and Mildred (Lavine) D.; m. Martha Buesch, June 11, 1950; children—Dan Wayne, Sarah Jane. B.A., State U. Iowa, 1950. Sports information dir. State Coll. Iowa, 1950-51, U. Colo., 1951-52; asst. to dir. Nat. Collegiate Athletic Assn., Kansas City, Mo., 1952-63; commr. Big Eight Conf., Kansas City, 1963-71, Big Ten Athletic Conf., 1971—; Nat. Collegiate Athletic Assn.-NBC television pub. relations liaison officer, N.Y.C., 1957. Office: Big 10 Athletic Conf 1111 Plaza Dr Schaumburg IL 60195

DUKEMINIER, JESSE, legal educator; b. West Point, Miss., Aug. 12, 1925; s. Jesse J. and Lucile (Weems) D. A.B., Harvard U., 1948; LL.B., Yale U., 1951. Bar: N.Y. 1952, Ky. 1957. Practice in, N.Y.C., 1951-53; asst. prof. law U. Minn., 1954-55; prof. law U. Ky., 1955-63, UCLA, 1963—; vis. prof. U. Chgo., 1959, U. Miss., 1958; adv. Calif. Law Revision Commn. Author: Perpetuities Law in Action, 1962, Family Wealth Transactions, 2d edit, 1978, Summary of the Law of Future Interests, 2d edit, 1979, Property, 1981, Summary of the Law of Property, 11th edit, 1981; also numerous articles. Served with inf. AUS, 1943-45. Mem. Am. Bar Assn., Phi Beta Kappa. Home: 630 Burk Pl Beverly Hills CA 90210

DUKER, BRACK WILLIAM, oil company executive; b. Qunicy, Ill., Apr. 26, 1939; s. William Theodore and Ariel (McHan) D.; m. Elizabeth Brubaker, Sept. 21, 1968; children: Emily Elizabeth, Nancy Lee, Barbara Jane. B.S., U. Ill.-Chgo., 1961, M.B.A., 1962. Audit mgr. Price Waterhouse & Co., Chgo., 1963-70; dir. fin. services Heizer Corp., Chgo., 1970-72; v.p., controller Magnavox Co., Ft. Wayne, Ind., 1972-76; controller Atlantic Richfield Co., Los Angeles, 1976-77, v.p., controller, 1977-81, v.p. corp. planning, 1981—; dir. Looart Press Inc., Colorado Springs, Colo., 1980—. Served with U.S. Army, 1962-63. Mem. Fin. Execs. Inst., Planning Execs. Inst., Am. Inst. C.P.A.s, Am. Acctg. Assn., Assn. Corp. Growth. Office: Atlantic Richfield Co 515 S Flower St Los Angeles CA 90071

DUKES, DAVID VIRGIL, government finance official; b. Longview, Wash., July 13, 1932; s. Eldridge O. D. and Darrel Rebecca (Booth) Sullivan; 5 children. B.S., Husson Coll., Bangor, Maine, 1957; M.P.A., U. Wash., 1970. Auditor GAO, Denver, 1957-60; auditor AEC, San Francisco, 1960-62; price analyst Gen. Electric Missile and Space Vehicle Dept., Phila., 1962-63; auditor AEC, Boston, 1963-66; accountant NASA, Washington, 1966-67; systems acct. HEW, Washington, 1967-70, budget analyst, 1971-73; dep. asst. sec. fin. HHS, 1974—. Served with USNR, 1952-54. Lutheran. Home: PO Box 15416 Arlington VA 22215 Office: Dept HHS 200 Independence Ave SW Washington DC 20201

DUKES, HARRY LUTHER, JR., army officer; b. Newberry, S.C., Oct. 29, 1928; s. Harry Luther and Willie Elizabeth (Whitten) D.; m. Shirley Blanche West, Mar. 18, 1956; children: Lisa Carol Dukes Nishikawa, Kimberly Lynn. B.A. in Textile Mfg., Clemson U., 1952; M.S. in Textile Engring., Ga. Inst. Tech., 1957; postgrad., Northwestern U., Chgo., 1978. Commd. 2d lt. U.S. Army, 1952, advanced through grades to maj. gen., 1980; chief of staff Troop Support Command, St. Louis, 1973-75; comdr. quartermaster brigade, Fort Lee, Va., 1975-77; dep. chief of staff logistic Army Tng. and Doctrine Command, Ft. Monroe, Va., 1977-79; comdg. gen. Army and Air Force Exchange Service, Munich, West Germany, 1979-81, Army Quartermaster Ctr., Ft. Lee, 1981—, quartermaster gen., 1981—. Club: Masons. Home: 1 Normandy Rd Fort Lee VA 23801 Office: Army Quartermaster Ctr Fort Lee VA 23801

DUKES, THADDEUS A., heavy machinery manufacturing company executive. Exec. v.p. Ingersoll-Rand Co., Woodcliff Lake, N.J. Office: Ingersoll-Rand Co 200 Chestnut Ridge Rd Woodcliff Lake NJ 07675§

DUKLER, ABRAHAM EMANUEL, chemical engineer; b. Newark, Jan. 5, 1925; s. Louis and Netty (Charles) D.; children—Martin Alan, Ellen Leah, Malcolm Stephen. B.S., Yale U., 1945; M.S., U. Del., 1950, Ph.D., 1951. Devel. engr. Rohm & Haas Co., Phila., 1945-48; research engr. Shell Oil Co., Houston, 1950-52; mem. faculty dept. chem. engring. U. Houston, 1952—, prof., 1963—, chmn. dept., 1967-73, dean engring., 1976-83; dir. State of Tex. Energy Council, 1973-75; cons. U.S. Nuclear Regulatory Commn., Brookhaven Nat. Lab., Shell Devel. Co., Exxon, others. Contbr. chpts. to books, articles to profl. jours. Recipient Research award Alpha Chi Sigma, 1974. Fellow Am. Inst. Chem. Engrs., Nat. Acad. Engring., Am. Soc. Engring. Edn. (research lectureship award 1976); mem. Am. Inst. Chem. Engrs., ASME, AAAS, Am. Chem. Soc., AAUP, Sigma Xi, Tau Beta Pi. Office: Coll of Engring Univ of Houston Houston TX 77004

DULAI, SURJIT SINGH, humanities educator, critic; b. Danubyo, Lower Burma, Burman, Nov. 6, 1930; came to U.S., 1960, naturalized, 1968; s. Milkha Singh and Udham (Kaur) D.; m. Carolyn Ann Shirrell, Dec. 27, 1965; children: Gareth Singh, Sushil Kaur. B.A., Panjab U., Solan, India, 1950, M.A., 1959; Ph.D., Mich. State U., 1965. Lectr. English Panjab U., Chandigarh, India, 1954-59; asst. prof. English L.I.U., Bklyn., 1965-66; asst. prof. humanities Mich. State U., East Lansing, 1966-70, assoc. prof., 1970-74, prof., 1974—, chmn. dept. humanities, 1981—. Contbr. articles on lit. criticism to profl. jours.; editor: Jour. South Asian Lit., 1968—. Fulbright fellow, India, 1970-71. Mem. Assn. Asian Studies, Research Com. on Punjab, Soc. Internat. Devel. Home: 14823 Woodbury Rd Haslett MI 48840 Office: Dept Humanities Mich State U. 503 S Kedzie Hall East Lansing MI 48824

DULAN, HAROLD ANDREW, educator, former ins. co. exec.; b. Bridgeton, N.J., June 28, 1911; s. Thomas Francis and Mamie (Corson) D.; m. Bess Gunn, May 31, 1946; children: Susan Matilda Dulan Hall, Kathleen Dulan Burke, Elizabeth Ann Dulan Sexton. B.B.A., U. Tex., 1936, M.B.A., 1937, Ph.D., 1945; postgrad., Harvard, summer 1955, U. Chgo., Beloit, Wis., 1956, 63. C.P.A., Tex., Ark. Mem. faculty Tex. A&M Coll., 1938-42; pub. accountant, Dallas, 1941-46; financial economist Fed. Res. Bank, Dallas, 1944-46; faculty Dallas Coll., So. Meth. U., 1945; pvt. investment counsellor, 1938—; prof., former head dept. finance U. Ark., Fayetteville, 1946—; co-founder Participating Annuity Life Ins. Co., Fayetteville, 1954, chmn. investment com., v.p., pres., chmn. bd., 1954-68; financial cons. Argentine bus. concern, Buenos Aires, summer 1953; lectr., moderator Southwestern Bell Telephone Co. Mgmt. Seminars, Galveston, Tex., 1956-58, Hot Springs, Ark., 1958; conferee Conf. Savs. and Residential Financing Savs. and Loan League, Chgo., 1958; mem. Financial Analysts Fedn. European Econ. Conf. Tour, 1964; dir. First Ark. Devel. Finance Corp.; fellow N.Y. Fin. Dist., 1950; mem. chancellor's council U. Tex.; mem. Ark. Econ. Devel. Study Commn., 1975-76; condr. econ. study of capital formation, Australia, Orient, 1971, of high level inflation, Brazil, Argentina, Chile, 1975, of econ. growth and monetary aspects of Circum-Pacific capital formation in, Singapore, Indonesia and Malaysia, 1980. Contbr. articles to profl. jours. Commr. Tex. Centennial Statehood, 1946; commr., vice chmn. Gov.'s Commn. Status of Women for Ark., 1964-65. Mem. Am. Inst. C.P.A.'s, Am. Inst. Chartered Financial Analysts (past mem. council examiners), Nat. Assn. Bus. Economists, N.Y. Soc. Security Analysts, Am. Finance Assn., Southwestern Social Sci. Assn. (past pres. finance sect.), Ark. Soc. C.P.A.'s, Fayetteville C. of C., Beta Gamma Sigma, Beta Alpha Psi, Sigma Iota Epsilon. Methodist. Clubs: Country of Austin, Fayetteville Country. Lodge: Rotary. Home: 1500 Clark St Fayetteville AR 72701

DULANY, ELIZABETH GJELSNESS, univ. press adminstr.; b. Charleston, S.C., Mar. 11, 1931; d. Rudolph Hjalmar and Ruth Elizabeth (Weaver) Gjelsness; m. Donelson Edwin Dulany, Mar. 19, 1955; 1 son, Christopher Daniel. B.A., Bryn Mawr Coll., 1952. Proofreader, editor Books in Print, R.R. Bowker Co., N.Y.C., summers 1948-51, mng. editor, summer 1952; med. sec., editor dept. pediatrics U. Mich. Hosp., Ann Arbor, 1953-54; editorial asst. E.P. Dutton & Co., N.Y.C., 1954-55, U. Ill. Press, Champaign, 1956-59, asst. to editor, 1959-60, asst. editor, 1960-67, asso. editor, 1967-72, mng. editor, 1972—. Democrat. Episcopalian. Home: 73 Greencroft Champaign IL 61820 Office: U Ill Press 54 E Gregory St Champaign IL 61820

DULBECCO, RENATO, biologist, educator; b. Catanzaro, Italy, Feb. 22, 1914; came to U.S., 1947, naturalized, 1953; s. Leonardo and Maria (Virdia) D.; m. Gulseppina Salvo, June 1, 1940 (div. 1963); children: Peter Leonard, Maria Vittoria; m. Maureen Muir; 1 dau., Fiona Linsey. M.D., U. Torino, Italy, 1936; D.Sc. (hon.), Yale U., 1968, Vrije Universiteit, Brussels, 1978; LL.D., U. Glasgow, Scotland, 1970. Asst. U. Torino, 1940-47; research asso. Ind. U., 1947-49; sr. research fellow Calif. Inst. Tech., 1949-52, asso. prof., then prof. biology, 1952-63; sr. fellow Salk Inst. Biol. Studies, San Diego, 1963-71; asst. dir. research Imperial Cancer Research Fund, London, 1971-74, dep. dir. research, 1974-77; disting. research prof. Salk Inst., La Jolla, Calif., 1977—; prof. pathology and medicine U. Calif. at San Diego Med. Sch., La Jolla, 1977-81, mem. Cancer Ctr.,; vis. prof. Royal Soc. Great Britain, 1963-64, Leeuwenhoek lectr., 1974; Clowes Meml. lectr., Atlantic City, 1961; Harvey lectr. Harvey Soc., 1967; Dunham lectr. Harvard U., 1972; 11th Marjory Stephenson Meml. lectr., London, 1973, Harden lectr., Wye, Eng., 1973, Am. Soc. for Microbiology lectr., Los Angeles, 1979; Mem. Calif. Cancer Adv. Council, 1963-67; adv. bd. Roche Inst., N.J., 1968-71, Inst. Immunology, Basel, Switzerland, 1969—; chmn. sr. council Internat. Assn. Breast Cancer Research, 1980—; pres., trustee Am.-Italian Found. for Cancer Research. Trustee LaJolla Country Day Sch. Recipient John Scott award City Phila., 1958; Kimball award Conf. Pub. Health Lab. Dirs., 1959; Albert and Mary Lasker Basic Med. Research award, 1964; Howard Taylor Ricketts award, 1965; Paul Ehrlich-Ludwig Darmstaedter prize, 1967; Horwitz prize Columbia U., 1973; with David Baltimore and Howard Martin Temin Nobel prize in medicine, 1975; Targa d'oro Villa San Giovanni, 1978; Mandel Gold medal Czechoslovak Acad. Scis., 1982; named Man of Yr., London, 1975; Italian Am. of Yr. San Diego County, Calif., 1978; hon. citizen City of Imperia (Italy), 1983; Guggenheim and Fulbright fellow, 1957-58; decorated grand ufficiale Italian Republic, 1981; hon. founder Hebrew U., 1981. Mem. Nat. Acad. Scis. (Selman A. Waksman award 1974), Am. Acad. Arts and Scis., Am. Assn. Cancer Research, Internat. Physicians for Prevention Nuclear War, Accademia Nazionale dei Lincei (fgn.), Accademia Ligure di Scienze e Lettre (hon.), Royal Soc. (fgn. mem.). Club: Athenaeum. (London). Home: 7525 Hillside Dr La Jolla CA 92037 Office: Salk Inst PO Box 85800 San Diego CA 92138

DULIN, JACQUES MATAGNE (JAMES DULIN), lawyer, cons., mineral development company executive; b. Toledo, Nov. 23, 1934; s. James Harvey and Renee Henriette (Lienard) D. B.S. in Biochemistry (Laverne Noyes scholar 1952-55, DuPont fellow 1956-57), U. Chgo., 1957; J.D. with honors, George Washington U., 1966. Bar: Va. 1966, Ill. 1967; Master in Accounting U.S. Dist. Ct. No. Dist. Ill., 1973-74. Tchr. physics New Trier Township High Sch., Winnetka, Ill., 1959-62; patent examiner U.S. Patent Office, Washington, 1962-64; law clk., tech. advisor to late Hon. I. Jack Martin, Judge U.S. Ct. Customs and Patent Appeals, Washington, 1964-66; pres. firm Dulin & Assocs., Ltd. (and predecessor firm), Chgo., 1978—; chmn. exec. com. Indsl. Resources Inc., Chgo., 1972—, also dir.; pres. Exchange Info. Systems Internat., Inc., Chgo, 1983—; v.p., gen. counsel Scantic Internat. Inc., Chgo., 1983—, also dir.; adj. prof. intellectual property div. John Marshall Law Sch., Chgo.; speaker in field. Author: Teacher: Law and the Arts; Research editor: George Washington U. Law Rev, 1965-66; columnist: Law and the Arts, Creative Communicator, 1977—; Contbr. articles to profl. jours. Mem. Bd. Police Commrs., Deerfield, Ill., 1969-71. Recipient Nathan Burkan Meml. Copyright award ASCAP, 1964, Van Vleck Moot Ct. award, 1964. Mem. Am., Va., Ill., Chgo. bar assns., Lawyers for Creative Arts, Patent Law Assn. Chgo., Am. Arbitration Assn. (nat. panel arbitrators, nat. panel patent arbitrators), Order of Coif. Club: Union League (Chgo.). Inventor, patentee in air, water pollution control. Home: 2448 Pomona Ln Wilmette IL 60091 Office: 208 S LaSalle St Chicago IL 60604 *A man's character is his destiny.*

DULIN, JOHN P., bank executive; b. 1925. With First Tenn. Nat. Corp., Memphis, 1950—, now pres., dir. Office: First Tenn Nat Corp 165 Madison Ave Box 84 Memphis TN 38101

DULL, CARL AREY, JR., corporate executive; b. Winston-Salem, N.C., Jan. 5, 1918; s. Carl Arey and Nora Mae (Alspaugh) D.; m. Mary Chitwood Cooper, June 15, 1946; children: Donna Dull Hurt, Sybil Jane Dull Edwards, Keith R. B.S. in Bus. Adminstrn. cum laude, Wake Forest U., 1939. Realtor, ins. agt., Winston-Salem, 1939-41; with Integon Corp., Winston-Salem, 1946—, v.p., asst. treas., 1970-79, pres., chief exec. officer, 1979—, also chmn. all subs.; Mem. Winston-Salem Housing Authority. Trustee Salem Acad. and Coll., 1969-77, Denmark Loan Fund of Winston-Forest U., from 1965, N.C. Council Econ. Edn., 1976—. Served to lt. comdr. USNR, 1941-46. Mem. N.C. Fin. Analysts Soc., Winston-Salem C. of C. (dir. 1976-78). Democrat. Mem. Moravian Ch. Clubs: Forsyth Country, Rotary, Deacon. Office: 500 W 5th St Winston-Salem NC 27159 *

DULLEA, GERARD JOHN, chess assn. exec.; b. Boston, May 24, 1943; s. Walter A. and Edna R. (Barthel) D.; m. Ervene F. Gulley, July 10, 1976. A.B., Boston Coll., 1965; M.A., Lehigh U., 1967; Ph.D., Syracuse U., 1975. Grad. asst. Lehigh U., Bethlehem, Pa., 1965-67; part time English instr. Syracuse (N.Y.) U., 1967-70; instr., asst. prof. English U. Maine, Orono, 1970-76; part time instr. Bloomsburg (Pa.) State Coll., 1976-77; pvt. practice cabinetmaker, 1977-78; asst. staff dir. U.S. Chess Fedn., New Windsor, N.Y., 1978-79, exec. dir., 1979—. Home: 27 Oxford Rd New Windsor NY 12550 Office: 186 Route 9W New Windsor NY 12550

DULLEA, KEIR, actor; b. Cleve., May 30, 1936; s. Robert and Margaret (Ruttan) D.; m. Margo Bennett (div.); m. Susan Coe, 1971. Grad., Neighborhood Playhouse. Appeared in: motion pictures The Hoodlum Priest, 1961, David and Lisa, 1962 (best male performance San Francisco Film Festival 1962), Thin Red Line, 1964, The Naked Hours, Mail Order Bride, 1964, Bunny Lake is Missing, 1965, Madame X, 1966, The Fox, 1968, 2001: A Space Odyssey, 1968, De Sade, 1969, Paperback Hero, 1973, Devil in the Brain, 1972, Pope Joan, 1972, Paul and Michelle, 1974, Black Christmas, 1975, Welcolm to Blood City, 1977, Full Circle, 1977, Leopard in the Snow, 1978; appeared on: Broadway in Dr. Cook's Garden, 1967, Butterflies Are Free, 1969-70, Cat on a Hot Tin Roof, 1974, P.S. Your Cat is Dead, 1975; acted in: TV shows including Law and Order, 1976, Legend of the Golden Gun, 1978. Address: care Phil Gersh Agency Inc 232 N Canon Dr Beverly Hills CA 90210 *

DULLES, AVERY, clergyman; b. Auburn, N.Y., Aug. 24, 1918; s. John Foster and Janet Pomeroy (Avery) D. A.B., Harvard U., 1940, postgrad. in law, 1940-41; Ph.L., Woodstock Coll., 1951, S.T.L., 1957; S.T.D., Pontifical Gregorian U., Rome, 1960; LL.D., St. Joseph's Coll., Phila., 1969, Iona Coll., New Rochelle, N.Y., 1980; L.H.D., Georgetown U., 1977, Creighton U., 1983; Th.D., U. Detroit, 1978; D.D., St. Anselm Coll., Manchester, N.H., 1981. Joined S.J., 1946; ordained priest Roman Catholic Ch., 1956; tchr. philosophy Fordham U., 1951-53; mem. faculty Woodstock Coll., N.Y.C., 1960-74, prof. theology, 1969-74, Cath. U. Am., Washington, 1974—; Gasson chair in theology Boston Coll., 1981-82; vis. lectr. Fordham U., 1970, Weston Coll., Cambridge, Mass., 1971, Union Theol. Sem., N.Y.C., 1971-74, Princeton Theol. Sem., 1972, Pontifical Gregorian U., 1973, Episc. Theol. Sem., Alexandria, Va., 1975, Luth. Sem. Pa., 1978; Martin C. D'Arcy lectr. Campion Hall, Oxford U., Eng., 1983; fellow Woodrow Wilson Internat. Center for Scholars, 1977; mem. commn. on Christian unity Archdiocese of Balt., 1962-70, Cath. Commn. on Intellectual and Cultural Affairs, 1967—, Cath. Bishops' Adv. Council, 1969-75; consultor to Papal Secretariat for Dialogue with Non-Believers, 1966-73. Author: Princeps Concordiae, 1941, A Testimonial to Grace, 1946, (with others) Introductory Metaphysics, 1955, Apologetics and the Biblical Christ, 1963, The Dimensions of the Church, 1967, Revelation and the Quest for Unity, 1968, Revelation Theology: A History, 1969, Spirit, Faith, and Church, 1970, The Survival of Dogma, 1971 (Christopher award 1972), A History of Apologetics, 1971, Models of the Church, 1974, Church Membership as a Catholic and Ecumenical Problem, 1974, The Resilient Church, 1977, A Church to Believe In, 1982, Models of Revelation, 1983; assoc. editor for: ecumenism Concilium, 1963—; contbr.: column Theology for Today to America, 1967-68; (with others) also articles to theol. publs. Bd. dirs. Georgetown U., 1966-68, Woodstock Theol. Center, 1974-79; bd. consultors Gustave Weigel Soc., 1966—; trustee Fordham U., 1969-72; acad. council Irish Sch. Ecumenics, 1971-78. Served to lt. USNR, 1942-46. Decorated Croix de Guerre, France; recipient Cardinal Spellman award for distinguished achievement in theology, 1970. Mem. Cath. Theol. Soc. Am. (dir. 1970-72, 74-77, v.p. 1974-75, pres. 1975-76), Am. Theol. Soc. (v.p. 1977-78, pres. 1978-79), Phi Beta Kappa. Address: Caldwell Hall Catholic U Am Washington DC 20064

DULLES, ELEANOR LANSING, diplomatic consultant, retired diplomat, educator; b. Watertown, N.Y., June 1, 1895; d. Allen Macy and Edith (Foster) D.; m. David Blondheim, Dec. 9, 1932 (dec. 1934); children: David Dulles, Ann Dulles Joor. A.B. (1st New Eng. scholar), Bryn Mawr Coll., 1917, A.M. (fellow labor and indsl. economics), 1920; student, London Sch. Econs., 1921-22; A.M., Radcliffe Coll., 1924, Ph.D., 1926; Faculté de Droit, U. Paris, 1925-27; LL.D., Wilson Coll., 1950, Western Coll., 1957; Dr. honoris causa, Free U. Berlin, 1957; LL.D., Mt. Holyoke Coll., 1962; Dr. Litt., Duke U., 1965, Mt. Vernon Coll., 1975, Clarkson Coll., 1979. Relief and reconstrn. Shurtleff Meml. Relief at Paris, 1917; relief work Am. Friends Service Com., 1918-19; asst. personnel mgr. Am. Tube & Stamping Co., Bridgeport, Conn., 1920-21; employment mgr. S. Glemby, N.Y.C., 1920-21; research assoc. Harvard and Radcliffe Bur. Research, France, 1925-27, Switzerland, 1930-32; tchr. Simmons Coll., Boston, 1924-25, 27-28; asst. prof. Bryn Mawr Coll., 1928-30, lectr., 1932-36; research assoc. U. Pa., 1932-36; chief finance div. Social Security Bd., Washington, 1936-42; economist Bd. Economic Warfare, 1942; economic officer Dept. State, 1942-45; fin. attaché, Vienna, Austria, 1945-49; Western European div. Dept. State, 1949-51; with Nat. Prodn. Authority, Dept. Commerce, 1951-52; spl. asst. Office of German Affairs, Dept. State, 1952-59; spl. asst. info. and research Dept. State, 1959-62, ret.; lectr., vis. prof. Duke U., 1962- 63; prof. Georgetown U., 1963-71; with Center for Strategic Studies, Washington, 1964-67; research fellow Hoover Inst., Stanford, 1967-68; cons. Dept. State, 1970—, Youth for Understanding, Ann Arbor, Mich., 1969-73; Mem. Geneva Conf. on Investment Social Security Funds, 1938; rep. U.S. Govt. on Bretton Woods Conf. on IMF, 1944; Investigated unemployment ins. Pres. Hoover's Com., 1931. Author: The French Franc, 1928, The Bank for International Settlements at Work, 1932, Depression and Reconstruction, 1934, The Dollar, The Franc and Inflation, 1933; monograph The Evolution of Reparation Ideas, 1932; John Foster Dulles, The Last Year, 1963, Détente, Cold War Strategies in Transition, 1965, Dominican Action, 1965—, Intervention or Cooperation, 1966, Berlin: The Wall Is Not Forever, 1967, American Foreign Policy in the Making, 1968, One Germany or

Two The Struggle at The Heart of Europe, 1970, The Wall: A Tragedy in Three Acts, 1972, Eleanor Lansing Dulles—Chances of a Lifetime, a Memoir, 1980; contbr. articles on social security, monetary policy investment, etc. Decorated Grand Cross of Merit Fed. Republic Germany.; Recipient Distinguished Achievement award Radcliffe Coll., 1955; Carl Schurz plaque, 1957; Ernst Reuter plaque City of West Berlin, 1959; citation for distinction Bryn Mawr Coll., 1960. Mem. P.E.N., Phi Beta Kappa. Clubs: Cosmopolitan (N.Y.C.); Henderson Harbor Yacht; Internat. (Washington). Home: 3900 Watson Pl Bldg B Washington DC 20016

DULUDE, DONALD OWEN, electric company executive; b. Bay City, Mich., Oct. 13, 1928; s. Owen P. and Bertranda L. (Lalonde) D.; m. Dorothy A. Atkinson, Feb. 21, 1980; 1 son, Timothy Donald. B.S. in Mech. Engring., U. Mich., 1950. Design engr. Bay City Shovels, Inc., 1950-57; mech. engr. Kuhlman Electric Co., Birmingham, Mich., 1957-60; ptnr. Barribeau-Dulude & Assoc., Inc., Birmingham, 1960-68; pres., gen. mgr. Quality Spring Products, Inc. subsidiary Kuhlman Corp., Coldwater, Mich., 1968-72, dir.; pres., dir. Kuhlman Corp.; dir. Wolverine Aluminum Corp. Patentee in field. Bd. dirs. Howe Mil. Sch. Fathers Assn., Ind. Served with U.S. Army, 1953-55. Mem. Spring Mfrs. Inst. (nat. dir.), Mich. Spring Mfrs. Assn. (pres. 1972-76), Detroit Engring. Soc., Battle Creek Engring. Soc., Oakland Hills C. of C. Roman Catholic. Club: Detroit Athletic. Lodge: Elks. Address: 2565 W Maple Rd Troy MI 48084

DULUDE, RICHARD, glass manufacturing company executive; b. Dunbarton, N.H., Apr. 20, 1933; s. Joseph Phillip and Anna (Lenz) D.; m. Jean Anne MacDonald, Sept. 11, 1954; children—Jeffrey, Jonathan, Joel. B.M.E., Syracuse (N.Y.) U., 1954; postgrad., M.I.T., 1969. With Allis Chalmers Mfg. Co., Milw., 1954-55; with Corning Glass Works, N.Y., 1957—, v.p., gen. mgr. tech. products div., 1972-75, v.p., gen. mgr. European ops., 1975-78; pres. Corning Europe, 1978-80, sr. v.p., dir. parent co., also dir. mktg. and bus. devel., 1980-83, pres. Telecom & Electronics Group, 1983—; dir. Optical Fibers S.A., France, Optical Fibers Ltd., U.K., Fibre Optique, France, Corning Internat. Corp., Siecor Corp., Seicor GmbH, W.Ger.; mem. adv. council Sch. Engring., Clarkson Coll. Tech.; trustee Clarkson Coll.; mem. engring. adv. bd. Syracuse U. Bd. dirs. Corning YMCA.; Past bd. dirs. Better Vision Inst., N.Y.C., Am. Sch., Paris, Am. Hosp., Paris, Am. C. of C., Paris. Served to 1st lt. AUS, 1955-57. Mem. Optical Soc. Am., Illuminating Engring. Soc., Nat. Ski Patrol Svstem (past bd. dirs.). Club: Travellers (Paris). Patentee combination space lighting, heating and ventilation fixture. Home: RD 2 Spencer Hill Corning NY Office: Corning Glass Works Corning NY 14831

DUMA, RICHARD JOSEPH, physician, researcher, educator; b. Bethlehem, Pa., Apr. 2, 1933; s. Joseph Anthony and Helen Veronica (Bartek) D.; m. Mary Alyce Fridley, Apr. 18, 1957; 1 son, Scott. B.A., Va. Poly. Inst., 1955; M.D., U. Va., 1959; Ph.D., Va. Commonwealth U.-Med. Coll. Va., 1978. Diplomate: Am. Bd. Internal Medicine. Intern, then resident in medicine U. Ala. Med. Center, Birmingham, 1959-60, 62-65; research fellow Harvard U. Med. Sch.-Mass. Gen. Hosp., 1965-67; mem. faculty Med. Coll. Va., Richmond, 1967—, prof. medicine, 1975—, prof. pathology, 1975—, prof. microbiology, 1977—, chmn. div. infectious diseases, 1974—; mem. U.S. Pharmacopeia Adv. Panel on Hosp. Practices, 1971—, chmn. subcom. research, 1976—; v.p. bd. dirs. Nat. Found. Infections Diseases, 1973-75, pres., 1975—. Served with M.C. USNR, 1960-62. Mem. Am. Fedn. Clin. Research, Am. Soc. Microbiology, Va. Soc. Microbiology, A.C.P., Am. Soc. Internal Medicine, Va. Soc. Internal Medicine, Richmond Soc. Internal Medicine, Infectious Disease Soc. Am., AAAS, So. Soc. Clin. Investigation, Am. Thoracic Soc., Royal Soc. Medicine, Med. Soc. Va., Richmond Acad. Medicine, Sigma Xi, Tau Beta Pi. Home: 2410 Castlebridge Rd Midlothian VA 23113 Office: Med Coll Va PO Box 92 Richmond VA 23219

DUMAINE, FREDERIC C., holding company executive; b. m. Margaret Williams, Oct. 9, 1926; children: Frederic C. III, Dudley B., Ruth (Mrs. G. E. Brooking, Jr.). Chmn. exec. com., dir. Amoskeag Co.; dir. Bangor & Aroostook R.R. Co., Fanny Farmer Candy Shops, Inc.; chmn. exec. com., dir. Fieldcrest Mills, Inc.; dir. Westville Homes Corp. Office: Prudential Center Suite 4500 Boston MA 02199 *

DUMARESQ, JOHN EDWARD, lawyer; b. Guernsey Channel Islands, Eng., Aug. 16, 1913; came to U.S., 1924, naturalized, 1942; s. James Edward and Helen (Gilfillan) D.; m. Eleanor Merrell Clark, Sept. 14, 1946; children—Peter John, Thomas Alan, Philip Clark. B.A., Columbia U., 1935, B.S., 1936, M.S., 1937; LL.B., N.Y. U., 1941. Bar: N.Y. bar 1942. Mem. firm Brumbaugh, Graves, Donohue & Raymond, N.Y.C., 1937-48, partner, 1948—; Mem. Columbia U. Engring. Council, 1966—. Trustee North Shore Hosp., Manhasset, N.Y., 1972. Served to capt. AUS, 1943-46. Mem. Am., City N.Y. bar assns., Am., N.Y. patent law assns., I.E.E.E., Sigma Xi, Theta Tau. Home: 214 Manor Rd Douglaston NY 11363 Office: 30 Rockefeller Plaza New York NY 10112

DUMAS, LAWRENCE, lawyer; b. Talladega, Ala., Oct. 12, 1908; s. William Lawrence and Mary (Hicks) D.; m. Donald Berry, Dec. 4, 1940; children—Aleta McDonald Dumas Schanbacher, Lawrence, William Berry, John Hicks. A.B. summa cum laude, Davidson Coll., 1929; J.D., Harvard U., 1932; LL.M., George Washington U., 1933; J.D., Georgetown U., 1935. Bar: Ala. bar 1932, D.C. bar 1933. Atty. Fed. Farm Bd. and PWA, 1932-36; practice in, Birmingham, Ala., 1936-43, 44—, atty. OPA, asst. U.S. atty., 1943-44; mem. firm Cabaniss, Johnston, Gardner, Dumas & O'Neal; mem. Ala. Constn. Commn., 1970-77, Indsl. Securities Adv. Council, 1975-78. Contbr. articles to legal jours. Mem. Ala. Ho. of Reps., 1947-55, Ala. Senate, 1959-66; chmn. Ala. Legis. Council, 1955, 63; Chmn. adv. bd. local Salvation Army; trustee Carraway Meth. Med. Center. Mem. Am. Judicature Soc., Ala. Bar Found., ABA (Ala. chmn. jr. bar conf. 1947), Ala. Bar Assn., Birmingham Bar Assn. Methodist (ofcl. bd.). Clubs: Masons, Shriners (potentate Zamora temple 1967), Birmingham Exchange (pres. 1958-59). Home: 3251 Dell Rd Birmingham AL 35223 Office: First Nat Southern Natural Bldg Birmingham AL 35203

DUMAS, RHETAUGH ETHELDRA GRAVES, nursing school dean; b. Natchez, Miss., Nov. 26, 1928; d. Rhetaugh Graves and Josephine (Clemmons) Graves) Bell; m. A.W. Dumas, Jr., Dec. 25, 1950; 1 dau., Adrienne. B.S. in Nursing, Dillard U., 1951; M.S. in Psychiat. Nursing, Yale U., 1961; Ph.D. in Social Psychology, Union Grad. Sch. 1, Union for Experimenting Colls. and Univs., Yellow Springs, Ohio, 1975; also various other courses; D.Public Service (hon.), Simmons Coll., 1976, U. Cin., 1981. Instr. Dillard U., 1957-59, 61; research asst., instr. Sch. Nursing, Yale U., 1962-65, asst. prof. nursing, 1965-66, assoc. prof. nursing, 1966-72, chmn. dept. psychiat. nursing, 1972; dir. nursing Conn. Mental Health Center, Yale-New Haven Med. Center, 1966-72; chief psychiat. nursing edn. br. Div. Manpower and Tng. Programs, NIMH, Rockville, Md., 1972-75, dep. dir. Div. Manpower and Tng. Programs, 1976-79; dep. dir. NIMH, 1979-81; dean U. Mich. Sch. Nursing, 1981—; dir. Group Relations Confs. in Tavistock Model; cons., speaker, panelist in field; fellow Helen Hadley Hall, Yale U., 1972, Branford Coll., 1972; dir. Community Health Care Center Plan, New Haven, 1969-72. Author profl. monographs; contbr. articles to profl. publs.; editorial bd.: Community Mental Health Rev, 1977-79, Jour. Personality and Social Systems, 1978-81. Bd. dirs. Afro Am. Center, Yale U., 1968-72; mem. New Haven Bd. Edn., 1968-71, New Haven City Demonstrations Agy., 1968-70, Human Relations Council New Haven, 1961-63. Named Disting. Alumna Dillard U., 1966; recipient various awards, including cert. Honor NAACP, 1970, Disting. Alumnae award Yale U. Sch. Nursing, 1976, award for outstanding achievement and service in field mental health D.C. chpt. Assn. Black Psychologists, 1980. Fellow A.K. Rice Inst., Am. Coll. Mental Health Adminstrs. (founding); mem. Am. Nurses Assn., Am. Acad. Nursing, Nat. Black Nurses Assn., Am. Public Health Assn., Urban League, NAACP, Sigma Theta Tau, Delta Sigma Theta. Office: 1335 Catherine St Ann Arbor MI 48109

DUMBAULD, EDWARD, judge; b. Uniontown, Pa., Oct. 26, 1905; s. Horatio S. and Lissa Grace (MacBurney) D.; m. Mary Ellen Whelpley, Jan. 1, 1941. A.B., Princeton U., 1926; LL.B., Harvard U., 1929, LL.M., 1930; Dr. Law, U. Leyden, Netherlands, 1932; LL.D. hon., Findlay Coll., 1981. Bar: Mem. Pa., D.C., U.S. Supreme Ct. bars. Practitioner before ICC, FCC (other adminstrn. agys.); former spl. asst. to atty. gen. U.S., Washington; (charge of litigation under acts regulating transp. and communications); judge Ct. Common Pleas Fayette County, 1957-61; U.S. dist. judge Western Dist. Pa., 1961—; sec. Am. Soc. Internat. Law, 1948-78. Author: Interim Measures of Protection in International Controversies, 1932, Thomas Jefferson, American Tourist, 1946, The Declaration of Independence and What It Means Today, 1950, The Political Writings of Thomas Jefferson, 1955, The Bill of Rights and What It Means Today, 1957, The Constitution of the United States, 1964, Sayings of Jesus, 1967, Life and Legal Writings of Hugo Grotius, 1969, Thomas Jefferson and the Law, 1978. Democratic county chmn., Fayette County, 1934-36; del. Dem. Nat. Conv., Phila., 1936. Mem. Pa. Bar Assn. (chmn. com. on lawyers referral service). Presbyn. Club: Cosmos (Washington). Lodge: Kiwanis (pres. Uniontown 1955). Office: US Court House Pittsburgh PA 15219

DUMETT, CLEMENT WALLACE, JR., oil co. exec.; b. Tacoma, Dec. 30, 1927; s. Clement Wallace and Dilma (Arnold) D.; m. Carolyn Jane Coulthurst, Mar. 9, 1957; children: Daniel, Joanne, Patricia. B.Sc. in Petroleum Engring, Stanford U., 1951. With Union Oil Co. Calif., 1951-55; with Union Oil Co. Can., 1955—, v.p. exploration, then v.p. prodn., 1967-75, pres., Calgary, Alta., Can., 1975—; dir. Peace Pipe Line Ltd. Served with AUS, 1946-47. Mem. Canadian Petroleum Assn. (dir.), Petroleum Soc., Soc. Petroleum Engrs. Mem. Anglican Ch. Clubs: Petroleum, Golf and Country (Calgary); Canyon Meadows Golf and Country. Home: 443 Scarboro Ave SW Calgary AB T3C 2H7 Canada Office: PO Box 999 Calgary AB T2P 2K6 Canada

DUMKE, GLENN S., university and college chancellor emeritus; b. Green Bay, Wis., May 5, 1917; s. William F. and Marjorie S. (Schroeder) D.; m. Dorothy Deane Robison, Feb. 3, 1945. A.B., Occidental Coll., 1938, M.A., 1939, LL.D., 1960; Ph.D., U. Calif., 1942; H.L.D., U. Redlands, 1962, Hebrew Union Coll., 1968, Windham Coll., 1969; LL.D., U. Bridgeport, 1963, Transylvania Coll., 1968, Pepperdine Coll., 1969, Our Lady of the Lake U., 1977, Dickinson State Coll., 1978, Calif. State U., 1982. Teaching asst. U. Calif. at Los Angeles, 1940-41; instr. history Occidental Coll., 1940-43, asst. prof., 1943-46, asso. prof., 1947-50, prof. history, 1950, Norman Bridge prof. Hispanic Am. history, 1954, dean faculty, 1950-57; pres. San Francisco State Coll., 1957-61; vice chancellor acad. affairs Calif. State Colls., 1961-62; chancellor Calif. State Univ. and Colls., 1962-82; pres. Inst. for Contemporary Studies, 1982—; dir. Barclays Bank of Calif., Olga Co.; 1st chmn. Calif. Council Econ. Edn., 1968—; past mem. exec. com., chmn. Western Interstate Commn. for Higher Edn.; Mem. founding bd. Civilian/Mil. Inst., USAF Acad. Found.; chmn. bd. Econ. Lit. Council Calif.; former mem. exec. com., chmn. fin. com. Council on Postsecondary Accreditation; former trustee Community TV So. Calif.-KCET; past mem. exec. com. Calif. Council for Humanities in Pub. Policy, 1974-77; chmn. Calif. Selection Com. for Rhodes Scholarships, 1966; former mem. com. on state relations Am. Assn. State Colls. and Univs.; bd. visitors USAF Air U.; past mem. bd. visitors USAF Acad.; bd. commrs. Nat. Commn. on Accrediting, 1959-65, 70-74; bd. dirs. Am. Council Edn., 1967-68; trustee Calif. Industry-Edn. Council. Author: The Boom of the Eighties in Southern California, 1944, Mexican Gold Trail, 1945, (with Dr. Osgood Hardy) A History of the Pacific Area in Modern Times, 1949, (under name Glenn Pierce) The Tyrant of Bagdad, 1955, (under name Jordan Allen) Cavern of Silver, 1982; Co-author, editor: (under name Glenn Pierce) From Wilderness to Empire: A History of California, 1959; Contbr. articles to profl. and popular pubs. Alt. del. Republican nat. conv., 13th dist. Calif., 1948 Alt. del. Republican nat. conv., 24th dist. Calif., 1952; trustee emeritus U. Redlands. Research fellow Huntington Library, 1943-45; Haynes Found. grantee, 1943. Mem. Los Angeles World Affairs Council (dir.), Calif. Hist. Soc., Joint Council Econ. Edn. (dir. 1969—), Western Coll. Assn. (past chmn. membership and standards com.), Am. Mgmt. Assn. (dir. 1970-73, 74-77, 79—), Inst. Internat. Edn. (West Coast adv. bd. 1972—), Calif. C. of C. (dir.), Phi Beta Kappa (hon. councilor alumni assn.). Methodist. Clubs: Los Angeles, Bohemian, Commonwealth, Town Hall, Long Beach Rotary, Va. Country; Univ. (San Francisco). Home: 16332 Meadow Ridge Rd Encino CA 91436 Office: 260 California St San Francisco CA 94111

DUMM, DEMETRIUS ROBERT, priest, educator; b. Carrolltown, Pa., Oct. 1, 1923; s. Gordon Hildebert and Esther Frances (Kirsch) D. B.A., St. Vincent Coll., Latrobe, Pa., 1945; S.T.D., Collegio di Sant'Anselmo, Rome, 1950; postgrad., Ecole Biblique Française, Jerusalem, 1950-52; S.S.L., Pontifical Bibl. Commn., Rome, 1952. Joined Order of St. Benedict, Roman Catholic Ch., 1943, ordained priest, 1947; mem. faculty St. Vincent Sem., 1952—, prof. N.T., 1952—, rector, 1963-80; master of novices St. Vincent Archabbey, 1980—. Author articles in field; contbr.: Jerome Bibl. Commentary. Mem. Soc. Bibl. Lit., Cath. Bibl. Assn. Am., East. Coast Rectors Conf. (past pres.). Address: St Vincent Archabbey Latrobe PA 15650 *If I have acquired any wisdom from my experience, it has been mainly through the ministry of other good people. They have helped me to see opportunity and promise rather than threat in the often ambiguous situations of life. Now, as my human abilities begin to decline with age, my faith indicates that the greatest promise of all is hidden in that ambiguous future where my Creator has reserved it for me.*

DUMONT, ROBERT CRAIG, employment cons.; b. Marlboro, Mass., Nov. 28, 1934; s. Raymond Montmigny and Barbara (Craig) D.; m. Susanne Storm, Aug. 23, 1958; children—Robert Craig, Storm, Anthony Chase. A.B., Dartmouth Coll., 1956. With New Eng. Life Ins. Co., Boston, 1957-80, v.p. personnel and equal opportunity, 1979; adminstrv. asst. to gov. of Mass., 1973-74; pres. Dumont, Kiradjieff & Moriarty (employment cons.), Boston, 1981—. Trustee St. Mark's Sch., 1976—; deacon Pilgrim United Ch. of Christ, Southborough, Mass., 1978—; selectman Town of Southborough, 1968-74; chmn. Southborough Republican Town Com., 1977-80; pres. Boston Jr. C. of C., 1959-60. Mem. Am. Soc. Personnel Adminstrn. Home: 15 Latisquama Rd Southborough MA 01772 Office: 79 Milk St Boston MA 02109

DUMONT, W. HUNT, U.S. attorney; b. Easton, Pa., Aug. 12, 1941. B.A., Lafayette Coll., 1963; LL.B., Seton Hall U., 1967. Bar: N.J. 1967. Assoc. firm Stryker, Tams & Dill, 1967-69; asst. U.S. atty. Dist. of N.J., 1969-71; mem. firm Robinson, Wayne & Greenberg, Newark, 1971-81; U.S. atty. for N.J., Newark, 1981—. Mem. ABA, N.J. State Bar Assn., Essex County Bar Assn., Assn. Fed. Bar of State N.J. Office: US Atty for NJ Room 502 Federal Bldg 970 Broad St Newark NJ 07102 *

DUMOUCHEL, PAUL, archbishop; b. Winnipeg, Man., Can., Sept. 19, 1911; s. Joseph and Josephine D. Grad., St. Boniface (Man.) Coll., 1930; student, U. Man., 1929-300, Sem. Lebret, Sask., Can., 1931-36. Ordained priest Roman Cath. Ch., 1936; missionary to Indians of Man., 1936-50, retreat master, 1940-50, sch. prin., 1950-55, bishop of, Keewatin, Can., 1955-67, 1st archbishop, Le Pas, 1967—. Author: Saulteux Grammar, 1942. Address: 108 1st St W The Pas MB Canada

DUMOVICH, LORETTA, real estate and transportation company executive; b. Kansas City, Kans., Sept. 29, 1930; d. Michael Nicholas and Frances Barbara (Horvat) D. Student public schs., Kansas City. Lic. real estate broker, Kans., Mo. Pres., dir. Columbia Properties, Inc., Kansas City, Mo., 1969—; v.p., corp. sec., dir. Riss Internat. Corp., Kansas City, 1950—; dir., v.p., corp. sec. Republic Industries, Inc., Kansas City, 1969—; dir. Grandview Bank & Trust Co., Grandview, Mo., 1969—, mem. trust dept. exec. com.; dir., corp. sec. Dominion Bancqueshares Ltd., Riss Transp. Co., Riss. Intermodal Corp., Profl. Driving Acad., Inc., World Leasing, Inc. Mem. Kansas City (Mo.) Real Estate Bd., Bldg. Owners and Mgrs. Assn. of Kansas City (Mo.), Terminal Properties Exchange (founding mem.), Am. Royal Assn. (gov.). Office: 215 W Pershing Rd Kansas City MO 64108

DUNATHAN, HARMON CRAIG, university dean; b. Celina, Ohio, July 25, 1932; s. Harry V. and Mildred B. (Greek) D.; m. Katy Mary Dragati, Mar. 15, 1956; children: Christine, Susan, Amy, Andrea. B.A., Ohio Wesleyan U., 1954; M.S., Yale U., 1956, Ph.D., 1958. Mem. faculty Haverford (Pa.) Coll., 1957-75, assoc. prof. chemistry, 1964-70, prof., 1970-75; provost, dean faculty Hobart and William Smith Colls., Geneva, N.Y., 1975-84, acting pres., 1978-79; dean faculty Hampshire Coll., 1984—. Office: Hampshire Coll Amherst MA 01002

DUNAWAY, FAYE, actress; b. Bascom, Fla., Jan. 14, 1941; d. John D.; m. Peter Wolf, Aug. 7, 1974. Student, U. Fla., Boston U. An original mem., Lincoln Center Repertory Co.; appeared in: off-Broadway Hogan's Goat; played Bonnie in: motion picture Bonnie and Clyde, 1967; appeared in: motion pictures Oklahoma Crude, 1973, Chinatown, 1974, Three Days of the Condor, 1975, Network, 1976 (Acad. award), The Voyage of the Damned, 1976, The Eyes of Laura Mars, 1978, The Champ, 1979, The First Deadly Sin, 1980, Mommie Dearest, 1981, The Wicked Lady, 1982; others; TV movie Evita Peron, 1981; play The Curse of an Aching Heart, 1982. Recipient Most Promising Newcomer Award Brit. Film Acad., 1968. Address: care William Morris Agency 151 El Camino Beverly Hills CA 90212 *

DUNBAR, BYRON HERBERT, lawyer, legal educator; b. Three Forks, Mont., June 8, 1927; s. Bryon B. and Georgette (Walsh) D.; m. Margaret Jo Lovelace, Dec. 23, 1948; children: Lynn Dunbar Ryerson, Michael, Patrick, Lisa. J.D., U. Mont., 1952. Bar: Mont. 1952. Spl. agt. FBI, 1952-79; pros. atty., Bozeman, Mont., 1979-80; legal cons. Mont. Law Enforcement Acad., 1980-81; U.S. atty., Billings, Mont., 1981—; chief legal instr. Mont. Law Enforcement Acad., 1966-79; legal instr. Mont. Supreme Ct., Helena, 1980—. Served to lt. U.S. Mcht. Marine, 1944-47. Mem. Mont. Bar Assn., Gallatin County Bar Assn., Yellowstone County Bar Assn. Lodges: Elks; Bozeman Rotary. Home: 1400 Poly Dr Suite 2A Billings MT 59101 Office: U S Attorneys Office 310 N 26th St Billing MT 59103

DUNBAR, CHARLES EDWARD, III, lawyer; b. New Orleans, Apr. 19, 1926; s. Charles Edward and Ethelyn (Legendre) D.; m. Marguerite Stephanie Dinkins, July 23, 1959; children: Ladd Dinkins, Charles Edward IV, Ethelyn Legendre, George Bauer II. B.A., Tulane U., 1949, LL.B., 1951. Bar: La. 1951. Since practiced, New Orleans; partner firm Phelps, Dunbar, Marks, Claverie & Sims, 1955—. Mem. citizens adv. com. Bur. Child Welfare, New Orleans, 1955-62, chmn., 1961; citizens adv. com. Juvenile Ct. New Orleans, 1960-65, chmn., 1964; charter mem. Information Council Americas, bd. dirs., 1964-68; Del. Republican Nat. Conv., 1968, 72, 76; Presdl. elector, 1980; mem. La. Rep. state central com., Orleans Parish Rep. exec. com.; finance chmn. New Orleans Rep. party, 1969; Bd. dirs. La. Civil Service League, 1960—, vice chmn., 1964-69; pres., 1970; bd. govs. Tulane U. Med. Center.; bd. dirs. Internat. House, New Orleans. Served with USNR, 1944-46. Mem. Fed., Am., La., New Orleans bar assns., Maritime Law Assn. U.S., Southeastern Admiralty Law Inst., Assn. Average Adjustors, Am. Legion, Phi Beta Kappa, Delta Kappa Epsilon, Phi Delta Phi. Roman Catholic. Clubs: Boston, La., Stratford, Round Table, International House (New Orleans). Home: 411 Fairway Dr New Orleans LA 70124 Office: Hibernia Bldg New Orleans LA 70112

DUNBAR, ISOBEL MOIRA, glaciologist; b. Edinburgh, Scotland, Feb. 3, 1918; d. William and Elizabeth Mary (Robertson) D. B.A., Oxford U., 1939, M.A., 1948. With div. earth sci. Can. Def. Research Bd., Ottawa, Ont., 1947-78, dir. earth scis. div., 1975-77, sr. scientist, 1977-78; mem. Can. Environ. Adv. Council, 1972-78. Contbr. articles to profl. jours. Recipient Centennial award Can. Meteorol. Service, 1971; Massey medal Royal Can. Geog. Soc., 1972; Decorated Order of Can., 1976. Fellow Royal Soc. Can., Arctic Inst. N. Am. (gov. 1966-69), Royal Can. Geog. Soc. (dir. 1974—); mem. Internat. Glaciological Soc. Home: Rural Route 1 Dunrobin ON K0A 1T0 Canada

DUNBAR, JOHN BURTON, dentist, govt. ofcl.; b. Birmingham, Ala., June 24, 1929; s. Collis Burton and Unavay (Gandy) D.; m. Ruby F. Berry, June 29, 1953; 1 dau., Inga. Student, Birmingham-So. Coll., 1947-49, A.B., 1957; D.M.D., U. Ala., 1953; M.P.H., Tulane U., 1959, Dr.P.H., 1963. Pvt. practice dentistry, Birmingham, 1953-54; instr. clin. dentistry U. Ala. Sch. Dentistry, 1953-54, trainee in epidemiology div. oral medicine and oral surgery, 1956-58, co-dir. study oral health in Iceland, asso. dir. Grad. Program in Epidemiology, asst. prof. dentistry, 1961-64, asst. to v.p. for devel., 1964-65; asso. prof. epidemiology and biometry, asst. dean Med. Coll. Ala. and U. Ala. Sch. Dentistry, coordinator research grants for, interim dir., 1965-67; prof. dentistry, coordinator research grants for newly established U. Ala. in Birmingham, 1965-67; dir. Center for Urban Studies, 1969-70, v.p. student and community affairs, 1970-74, v.p. for adminstrn., 1974-76; spl. asst. office of Prevention, Edn. and Control Nat. Heart, Lung and Blood Inst., 1976—; jr. cons. U. Ky. Med. Sch., 1958; asst. dir. Ariz. Med. Sch. Study, Phoenix, 1960-61; demographer Mountain States Med. Edn. Study, 1963-64; program dir. Health Scis. Advancement Award div., research facilities and resources NIH, 1967-68; chief program projects br. Nat. Heart Inst., 1968-69. Author articles. Pres. Jefferson County Com. for Econ. Opportunity, 1967, exec. com., chmn. projects planning com., 1969; mem. Mayor's Council on Youth Opportunity, 1969; v.p. Positive Maturity, Inc., 1972, pres., 1973-75; vice chmn. Mayor's Manpower Area Planning Council, 1973; Bd. dirs. Met. YMCA, 1971-74, Birmingham Symphony, 1974-76, Birmingham Area chpt. A.R.C., 1975-76. Served with USAF, 1954-56. Fellow Am. Pub. Health Assn.; mem. Ala. Acad. Sci., Phi Beta Kappa, Sigma Xi, Omicron Kappa Upsilon, Delta Omega. Home: 21 Buckspark Ct Potomac MD 20854 Office: Fed Bldg Room 4CO8 Bethesda MD 20205

DUNBAR, JOHN RAINE, emeritus English educator; b. Eugene, Oreg., May 21, 1911; s. Harry Aurelius and Lu Mae (Renshaw) D.; m. Virginia J. Esterly, 1938; 1 dau., Judy Dunbar Jacobson. B.A., U.

Oreg., Eugene, 1932, M.A., 1936; Ph.D., Harvard U., 1947. Head dept. English Pendleton (Oreg.) Sr. High Sch., 1936-39; instr. English Tufts Coll., Medford, Mass., 1942-43, Ga. Inst. Tech., 1943-46; asst. prof. Miami U., Oxford, Ohio, 1946-47; mem. faculty Claremont McKenna Coll. (Calif.), 1947—; prof. English McKenna Coll. (Calif.), 1957-77, Josephine Olp Weeks prof., 1970-77, prof. emeritus, 1977—, chmn. dept. langs. and lit., 1971-74, chmn. humanities program, 1951-54, 55-57, 60-65; prof. English Claremont Grad. Sch., 1957—; Fulbright lectr. Åbo Acad. and Turun Yliopisto, Turko/Åbo, Finland, 1956-57, U. Vienna, 1965-66, U. Delhi, 1969-70; vis. lectr. U. Uppsala, Sweden, 1956; USIS lectr., Nepal, 1969; dir. regional seminar 19th century Am. lit. All North Indian Univs., 1969; participant numerous seminars, including DuPont, 1958. Author: The Paxton Papers, 1957, The Combat at the Barrier, 1967; also articles, revs., curriculum material. Mem. Watts Tower Com., Los Angeles, 1950-60. Recipient medal Finnish Govt., 1957. Mem. Am. Studies Assn. (sec. So. Calif. 1958-60), Phi Beta Kappa, Phi Kappa Phi. Address: 457 Willamette Ln Claremont CA 91711

DUNBAR, LESLIE WALLACE, writer, consultant; b. Lewisburg, W.Va., Jan. 27, 1921; s. Marion Leslie and Minnie Lee (Crickenberger) D.; m. Peggy Rawls, July 5, 1942; children: Linda Dunbar Kravitz, Anthony Paul. M.A., Cornell U., 1946, Ph.D., 1948. Asst. prof. polit. sci. Emory U., Atlanta, 1948-51; chief community affairs Savannah River plant AEC, Aiken, S.C., 1951-54; asst. prof. polit. sci. Mt. Holyoke Coll., 1955-58; dir. research So. Regional Council, Atlanta, 1958-61, exec. dir., 1961-65; exec. dir., sec. Field Found., N.Y.C., 1965-80; vis. prof. polit. sci. U. Ariz., 1981; cons. Fund for Peace, Nat. Urban League, 1980-82; co-dir. William O. Douglas Inquiry of Fund for Peace, 1982-83. Author: A Republic of Equals, 1966; co-author, editor: Minority Report, 1984. Bd. dirs. Eleanor Roosevelt Inst., 1976—, Field Found., 1978-80, Children's Found., 1980—; pres. Children's Found., 1982—; Bd. dirs. Minority Rights Group, N.Y.C., 1980—, Nation Inst., 1980—; pres. Nation Inst., 1980-84; bd. dirs. Ctr. Nat. Security Studies, 1980—; Bd. dirs. Amnesty Internat., 1984—; Bd. of dirs. Village of Pelham (N.Y.) Library Bd., 1980—, pres., 1982—. Guggenheim fellow, 1954-55; United Negro Coll. Fund scholar-at-large, 1984-85. Home: 56 Benedict Pl Pelham NY 10803

DUNBAR, MAXWELL JOHN, educator, oceanographer; b. Edinburgh, Scotland, Sept. 19, 1914; s. William and Elizabeth (Robertson) D.; m. Joan Jackson, Aug. 1, 1945; children: Douglas, William; m. Nancy Wosstroff, Dec. 14, 1960; children: Elisabeth, Andrew, Christine, Robyn. B.A., Oxford (Eng.) U., 1937, M.A., 1939; Ph.D., McGill U., 1941. Mem. faculty McGill U., Montreal, 1946—, prof., 1959—; also chmn. dept. marine sci., dir. Marine Sci. Center; dir. Eastern Arctic Investigations, Can., 1947-55. Author: Eastern Arctic Waters, 1951, Ecological Development in Polar Regions, 1968, Environment and Good Sense, 1971; Contbr. articles profl. jours. Guggenheim fellow, Denmark, 1952-53; recipient Bruce medal Royal Soc. Edinburgh, 1950; Fry medal Can. Soc. Zoologists, 1979. Fellow Royal Soc. Can., Linnaean Soc. London, Arctic Inst. N.Am. (gov., past chmn., recipient Fellows award 1973). Home: 488 Strathcona Ave Westmount PQ H3Y 2X1 Canada

DUNBAR, ROBERT STANDISH, JR., coll. dean; b. Providence, Nov. 30, 1921; s. Robert Standish and Lucie (Lowell) D.; m. Mary Agnes O'Grady, Dec. 8, 1941; children—Robert Standish, Barbara Louise (Mrs. John R. Fields). B.S., U. R.I., 1949; Ph.D., Cornell U., 1952. Mem. faculty W.Va. U., 1952—, prof. statistics, expt. sta. statistician, 1957-63, chmn. dept. animal and vet. sci., 1963-64, dean, 1964-74, prof. animal sci., 1974—. Served with U.S. Army, 1942-46. Mem. Gamma Sigma Delta, Alpha Zeta, Phi Kappa Phi. Home: 313 Simpson St Morgantown WV 26505

DUNBAR, WALLACE HUNTINGTON, manufacturing company executive; b. N.Y.C., Dec. 17, 1931; s. Duncan and Marion (Eaton) D.; m. Ellen Thomas, June 13, 1953; children: Wallace Huntington, Thomas, Martha, Laura, Sarah, Jonathan. A.B., Denison U., 1953; M.B.A., Ind. U., 1954. Accountant Gen. Electric Co., N.Y.C., 1954-55; with Thomas Industries, Inc., Louisville, 1957-81, financial v.p., 1962-72, chmn. bd., chief exec. officer, 1972-79, cons., 1979-81; chmn. bd. Trojan Luggage Co., Memphis, 1981—; dir. Preway Inc., Wisconsin Rapids, Wis., Liberty Nat. Bank and Trust Co., Louisville. Bd. dirs. Honey Locust Found., 1959—, Dunbar Found., 1967—; trustee Denison U., Granville, Ohio, Spalding Coll., Louisville. Served with AUS, 1955-57. Mem. Phi Delta Theta. Club: Harmony Landing Country. Lodge: Rotary. Home: 5 River Hill Rd Louisville KY 40207 Office: 9213 US Hwy 42 Prospect KY 40059

DUNCALF, DERYCK, anesthesiologist; b. York, Eng., Nov. 14, 1926; came to U.S., 1956; s. Hubert Claude and Anne Elizabeth D.; m. Mira Novakovic, July 23, 1978; children: Richard Michael, Tamara. M.B., Ch.B., U. Leeds, 1950. Diplomate: Am. Bd. Anesthesiology. Resident in anesthesia St. James Hosp. and Gen. Infirmary, Leeds, 1950-54, Cardiff Royal Infirmary (Wales), 1954-56; fellow Faculty of Anaesthetists Royal Coll. Physicians and Surgeons, 1954; fellow in anesthesiology Mercy Hosp., Pitts., 1956-57, Montreal Children's Hosp. (Que., Can.), 1958-59; staff anesthesiologist Kings County Hosp., Bklyn., 1959-62, Montefiore Med. Center, Bronx, 1962—, chmn. dept. anesthesiology, 1975—; prof. anesthesiology Albert Einstein Coll. Medicine, Bronx, 1971—; cons. Wyckoff Heights Hosp., Bklyn., 1966—. Author: (with D.H. Rhodes) Anesthesia in Clinic Ophthalmolgy, 1963; contbr. articles to profl.jours. Fellow Am. Coll. Anesthesiologists; mem. AMA, Am. Soc. Anesthesiologists, N.Y. State Soc. Anesthesiologists, Assn. Anaesthesists Gt. Britain and Ireland, Internat. Anesthesia Research Soc., Pan Am. Med. Assn. (diplomate and hon. life mem. sect. on anesthesiology), AAAS, N.Y. Acad. Sci., N.Y. Soc. Acute Med. Care, Assn. Advancement of Med. Instrumentation, N.Y. Acad. Medicine, Assn. Univ. Anesthetists, Scandinavian Soc. Anaesthesiologists, Nat. Fire Protection Assn., Am. Soc. Regional Anesthesia, Internat. Assn. Study of Pain, Am. Pain Soc., Ecuatoriana de Anesthesiologia (hon.). Home: 33 Ferncliff Rd Cos Cob CT 06807 Office: Montefiore Med Center 111 E 210th St Bronx NY 10467

DUNCAN, A. BAKER, investment banker; b. Waco, Tex., Dec. 29, 1927; s. A. Baker and Frances (Higginbotham) D.; m. Sally P. Witt, Jan. 31, 1953; children: Addison Baker III, Richard Witt, Andrew Prescott. Grad., Woodberry Forest (Va.) Sch., 1945; B.A., Yale, 1949; M.A., U. Tex., 1952. Master Hill Sch., Pottstown, Pa., 1949-51; partner Rotan Mosle & Co. (investment bankers), Houston, 1953-61; headmaster Woodberry Forest Sch., 1962-70; sr. v.p., dir. Rotan Mosle Inc., 1970-78; pres. Duncan-Smith Co., 1978—. Chmn. bd. San Antonio Mus. Assn.; mem. devel. bd. U. Tex.; bd. dirs. Trinity U.; trustee S.W. Research Inst. bd. Mem. Chi Psi. Democrat. Episcopalian (vestryman). Home: 410 Elizabeth Rd San Antonio TX 78209 Office: 262 Losoya San Antonio TX 78205

DUNCAN, ALASTAIR ROBERT CAMPBELL, educator; b. Scotland, July 12, 1915; s. Leslie and Jean (Anderson) D.; m. Francoise Pellissier, June 11, 1938; children—Alain, Gregor, Colin. M.A. with 1st class honors in Philosophy, U. Edinburgh, Scotland, 1936; postgrad., Marburg U., Germany, 1936-37; D.Litt., Lakehead U., 1979. Lectr. U. London, Eng., 1938-39; lectr., dir. studies U. Edinburgh, 1945-49; chmn. dept. philosophy Queen's U., Kingston, Ont., Can., 1949-80, prof. emeritus, 1980—, dean faculty of arts and sci., 1959-64; vis. Truax prof. Hamilton Coll., 1974. Author: Practical Reason and Morality, 1957, Moral Philosophy, 1965, also articles on philosophy, edn., decision making and Dante.; Translator: (Vleeschauwer) Development of Kantian Thought, 1962. Served with Brit. Army, 1939-45. Ferguson scholar, 1938. Mem. Royal Inst. Philosophy, Aristotelian Soc., Mind Assn., Canadian Philos. Assn. (pres. 1960-61, 66-67), Dante Soc. N. Am. Club: Kingston Yacht. Home: 68 Kensington Ave Kingston ON Canada

DUNCAN, BUELL GARD, JR., banker; b. Orlando, Fla., July 31, 1928; s. Buell Gard and Elizabeth Phillips (Parks) D.; m. Patricia Ann Jones, Mar. 25, 1952; children: Buell Gard III, Patricia Ann, Allan Griffin, Nancy Elizabeth. B.A., Emory U., 1950; postgrad., BMA Sch. Bank Mktg., 1959. With Sun First Nat. Bank (name now Sun Bank, N.A.), Orlando, 1953—, asst. cashier, 1956-60, asst. v.p., 1960-61, v.p., 1961-68, sr. v.p., 1968-72, exec. v.p., 1972-75, pres., 1975-76, chmn. bd., chief exec. officer, 1977—, also dir.; exec. v.p. Sun Banks of Fla., N.A.; dir. Sun Univ. of Jacksonville, Nat. Standard Life Ins. Co., Orlando. Bd. dirs. United Way of Orange County, Fla., 1966—, pres., 1973; chmn. Downtown Devel. Bd.; treas., dir. Central Fla. Blood Bank, 1962—; active Valencia Community Coll. Found.; mem. bd. advs. U. Central Fla.; mem. Com. of 100 of Orange County. Served with USAF, 1951-53. Mem. Fla. Bankers Assn. (chmn. group V), Bank Mktg. Assn. (pres. 1971-72), Fla. C. of C. (v.p. econ. devel.), Orlando C. of C. (pres. 1970-71), Navy League (dir. central Fla. council 1969—), Fla. Blue Key, Phi Delta Theta. Clubs: Kiwanian., Country of Orlando (pres., dir.), Citrus, Univ. (Orlando). Office: Sun First Nat Bank 200 S Orange Ave Orlando FL 32802 *

DUNCAN, CARL PORTER, educator; b. Presque Isle, Maine, Dec. 27, 1921; s. Beecher Henry and Vivian (Howlett) D.; m. Marie Castaldi, July 10, 1948. B.A., U. Maine, 1942; M.A., Brown U., 1945, Ph.D., 1947. Instr. psychology Brown U., 1943-45; asst. prof. psychology Northwestern U., 1947-51, asso. prof., 1952-59, prof., 1960—. Author: Elementary Statistics, rev. edit, 1967, Human Thinking, 1967, Human Memory, 1972; Contbr. numerous articles sci. jours. Served with U.S. Army, 1942-43. Mem. Midwestern Psychol. Assn. (pres. 1965-66), Am. Psychol. Assn., Soc. Exptl. Psychologists, AAAS (v.p. 1973-74), Sigma Xi. Office: Dept Psychology Northwestern U Evanston IL 60201

DUNCAN, CHARLES HOWARD, educator; b. Tarentum, Pa., Jan. 11, 1924; s. James Boyd and A. Elizabeth (Wilson) D.; m. Mary Jane Ferrier, Nov. 23, 1954; children—Betsy Ann, Laurel Ann. B.S., Indiana (Pa.) U., 1950; M.Ed., U. Pitts., 1954, Ed.D., 1959; Litt.D. (hon.), Geneva Theol. Coll., 1979. Asst. dir. Franklin Comml. Coll., Connellsville, Pa., 1950-52; tchr. Butler (Pa.) Sr. High Sch., 1952-54; instr. U. Pitts., 1954-59; prof. Indiana (Pa.) U., 1959-65, Eastern Mich. U., Ypsilanti, 1965—, former head dept. bus. edn. Author: (with Lessenberry and Wanous) College Typewriting, 1964, 69, 74, 80; Services editor typewriting: Business Education Forum, 1968—. Vol. instr. Wayne County Econ. Opportunity Com.; lay chairperson 9th dist. Mich. Synod Lutheran Ch. in Am., 1977; trustee Geneva Theol. Coll., Maggie Valley, N.C., 1979—. Served with USNR, 1943-47. Recipient certificate of appreciation Wayne County Econ. Opportunity Com., 1968. Mem. Nat. Bus. Edn. Assn., Eastern Bus. Edn. Assn., Tri-State Bus. Edn. Assn., Pa. Bus. Edn. Assn. (past treas.), Mich. Bus. Edn. Assn. (past publicity dir.), Delta Pi Epsilon. Home: 2245 Valley Dr Ypsilanti MI 48197

DUNCAN, CHARLES TIGNOR, lawyer; b. Washington, Oct. 31, 1924; s. Robert Todd and Nancy Gladys (Jackson) D.; m. Dorothy Adelena Thrasher, July 31, 1947 (dec. Dec. 1972); 1 son, Charles Todd. B.A., Dartmouth Coll., 1947; J.D., Harvard U., 1950. Bar: N.Y. 1951, D.C. 1953, Md. 1955, U.S. Supreme Ct. 1954; FAA licensed comml. pilot, instrument rating. Assoc. firm Rosenman, Goldmark, Colin & Kaye, N.Y.C., 1950-53; partner firm Reeves, Robinson & Duncan, Washington, 1953-60; prin. asst. U.S. atty., Washington, 1961-65; gen. counsel U.S. Equal Employment Opportunity Commn., Washington, 1965-66; corp. counsel, D.C., 1966-70, acting dir. pub. safety, 1969; partner firm Epstein, Friedman, Duncan & Medalie, Washington, 1970-74; dean, prof. law Sch. Law Howard U., 1974-78; partner firm Peabody, Lambert & Meyers, Washington, 1978—; dir. Eastman Kodak Co., Procter & Gamble, TRW, Inc. Trustee Northfield Mt. Hermon Sch., NAACP Legal Def. and Edn. Fund. Served with USNR, 1944-46. Recipient Distinguished Service award D.C. Bar, 1974. Fellow Am. Bar Found.; mem. ABA, Nat. Bar Assn., D.C. Bar Unified (Pub. Service award 1974, pres. 1973-74), Phi Beta Kappa, Alpha Phi Alpha, Sigma Pi Phi, Delta Theta Phi. Democrat. Clubs: Masons (32 deg.), Burning Tree (Bethesda, Md.)). Active participant in preparation and presentation of sch. desegregation cases before U.S. Supreme Ct., 1953-55. Home: 1812 Upshur St NW Washington DC 20011

DUNCAN, CHARLES WILLIAM, JR., investor, former government official; b. Houston, Sept. 9, 1926; s. Charles William and Mary Lillian (House) D.; m. Thetis Anne Smith, June 10, 1957; children: Charles William III, Mary Anne. B.S. in Chem. Engring., Rice U., 1947; postgrad. mgmt., U. Tex., 1948-49. Roustabout, chem. engr. Humble Oil & Refining Co., 1947; with Duncan Foods Co., Houston, 1948-64, adminstrv. v.p., 1957-58, pres., chmn. adv. bd., 1958-64; pres. Coca-Cola Co. Food Div., Houston, 1964-67; chmn. Coca-Cola Europe, 1967-70; exec. v.p. Coca-Cola Co., Atlanta, 1970-71, pres., 1971-74; chmn. bd., dir. Rotan Mosle Fin. Corp., Houston, 1974-77; dep. sec. Dept. Def., Washington, 1977-79; sec. Dept. Energy, Washington, 1979-81; dir. Coca-Cola Co., Am. Express, Tex. Eastern Corp., Tex. Commerce Bancshares, Inc., United Technologies Inc.; Chmn. bd. trustees Rice U.; trustee Brookings Instn. Served with USAAF, 1944-46. Mem. Sigma Alpha Epsilon, Sigma Iota Epsilon, Council Fgn. Relations. Methodist. Clubs: Houston Country, River Oaks Country, Allegro (Houston). Home: 9 Briarwood Ct Houston TX 77019 Office: PO Box 4394 Houston TX 77210

DUNCAN, CLARENCE AVERY, JR., savings and loan association executive; b. LaGrange, Ga., Jan. 28, 1917; s. Clarence Avery and Maude (Borders) D.; m. Lucy Carolyn Watson, Nov. 14, 1981; children: John Davis, David Ray, Lea Ann, Lucy Carroll, Dempsey Snead, Melanie Ann. Student, San Angelo Jr. Coll. (Tex.), 1935-37, U. Tex., 1937-39. With Farm & Home Savs. Assn., Nevada, Mo., 1945—, v.p., 1950-56, pres., dir., 1956-84, also chmn. bd., 1968—. Mem. U.S. Savs. and Loan League (pres. 1966). Episcopalian. Club: Rotarian. Home: 102 Country Club Dr Nevada MO 64772 Office: care Farm & Home Savings Assn 221 W Cherry St PO Box 1893 Nevada MO 64772

DUNCAN, CYNTHIA BERYL, university library administrator; b. Madison, Pa., Apr. 26, 1932; d. Andrew and Harriet (Morris) D. B.S., California (Pa.) State Coll., 1953; M.Litt., U. Pitts., 1958; M.S., Fla. State U., 1965; Ph.D. (fellow), Ind. U., 1973. Tchr., Gateway Union Sch., Monroeville, Pa., 1953-64; instr. Fla. State U., 1965, spl. librarian, 1966, acting librarian, 1967; asso. prof. library sci. Mansfield (Pa.) State Coll., 1966-67, Winthrop Coll., Rock Hill, S.C., 1967-70; adj. prof. library sci. Ind. State U., 1972; prof. library sci., dir. Sandel Library, N.E. La. U., 1973-76; dean library services Old Dominion U., Norfolk, Va., 1976—; adj. lectr. library sci. Cath. U. Am., 1979-80; dir. SOLINET, 1982-83; mem. OCLC Users Council, 1981-83. Mem. ALA (chmn. com. 1984), La. Library Assn., Va. Library Assn. (chmn. coll./univ. sect. 1980-81), Assn. Am. Library Schs. Office: University Library Old Dominion Univ Norfolk VA 23508

DUNCAN, DAVID DOUGLAS, photojournalist, author; b. Kansas City, Mo., Jan. 23, 1916; s. Kenneth Stockwell and Florence (Watson) D.; m. Leila Khanki, Sept. 20, 1947 (div. 1962); m. Sheila Macauley, July 13, 1962. Student archaeology, U. Ariz., 1935; B.A. in Zoology and Spanish, U. Miami, Fla., 1938. Free-lance photojournalist, 1938-39; photographer Am. Mus.-Michael Lerner expdns., 1940-41; Chile-Peru coordinator Interam. affairs, Mexico/Central Am., 1941-42, Life mag. photographer, 1946-56, self-employed as photojournalist in, Europe, Mid-East, Africa, Asia and Africa, 1956—; photo-corr. Life mag. and ABC-TV, Vietnam, 1967-68. Photographed Presdl. Convs. at Miami Beach and Chgo. for NBC-TV, 1968; exhibited retrospective one-man photog. exhbns., William Rockhill Nelson Gallery Art, Kansas City, Mo., 1971, Whitney Mus. Am. Art, N.Y.C., 1972; Author: This is War!, 1951, The Private World of Pablo Picasso, 1958, The Kremlin, 1960, Picasso's Picassos, 1961, Yankee Nomad, 1966, I Protest!, 1968, Self-Portrait: U.S.A, 1969, War Without Heroes, 1970, Portfolio, 1972, Prismatics: Exploring a New World, 1973, Goodbye Picasso, 1974, The Silent Studio, 1976, Magic Worlds of Fantasy, 1978, The Fragile Miracle of Martin Gray, 1979, Viva Picasso: A Centennial Celebration, 1980, The World of Allah, 1982, New York/New York: masterworks of a street peddler, 1984. Served with USMCR, 1943-46; PTO. Decorated Legion of Merit, D.F.C. (2), Air medal (4), Purple Heart; recipient U.S. Camera Gold award, 1950; Overseas Press Club award, 1951, 52; Robert Capa Gold medal, 1968. Address: Castellaras Mouans-Sartoux 06370 France

DUNCAN, DONAL BAKER, software company executive; b. Altus, Okla., May 16, 1925; s. Luther Hendrix and Blanche (Baker) D.; m. Lavon Elaine Johnson, July 24, 1946; children: David W., Brent B., Debbie, Dwight R. Student, Stanford U., 1942-43; B.S., Calif. Inst. Tech., 1945, Ph.D., 1951. Engring. mgr. N. Am. Aviation, Downey, Calif., 1950-59; asst. gen. mgr. aeronutronic div. Ford Motor Co., Newport Beach, Calif., 1959-66; v.p. Litton Industries, Woodland Hills, Calif., 1966-68, Singer Co., N.Y.C., 1968-74, Varian Assocs., Inc., Palo Alto, Calif., 1974-82, dir., 1980-82, mem. office of pres., 1979-82; pres., chief exec. officer Gilchrist Software Corp., Irvine, Calif., 1982—; dir. Benson (S.A.), Paris; mem. sci. adv. bd. U.S. Air Force, 1968-72. Mem. Newport Beach Sch. Bd., 1964-65; pres. Newport-Mesa Unified Sch. Bd., 1965-66. Served with USNR, 1943-46. Mem. AIAA, IEEE, Navy League, Air Force Assn., Assn. U.S. Army, Sigma Xi, Tau Beta Pi, Sigma Alpha Epsilon. Patentee in field. Home: 10 Mapache Ct Portola Valley CA 94025 Office: 2212 Dupont Ave Irvine CA

DUNCAN, DONALD, educator; b. Marietta, Minn., Jan. 31, 1903; s. Henry and Clara (Olson) D.; m. Margaret Aileen Eberts, Sept. 18, 1924; children—Mary Jeanne (Mrs. Ronald Arthur Welsh), Margaret Caroline (Mrs. Nester Paul Arceneaux), Kathleen Elizabeth (Mrs. William Moten Edwards). B.A., Carleton Coll., Northfield, Minn., 1923; M.A., U. Minn., 1927, Ph.D., 1929. Asst. prof. anatomy U. Utah, 1929-30; asst. prof. anatomy U. Buffalo, 1930-32, prof., head dept., 1942-43; prof. La. State U., 1943-46; asso. prof. anatomy U. Tex. Med. Br., 1932-42, prof., chmn. dept., 1946-68, Ashbel Smith prof. anatomy, 1968—, asso. dean grad. studies, 1952-69; vis. prof. anatomy Stanford, 1975, 76, 79; Mem. adv. com. med. student research NIH, 1961-63, anat. tng., 1960-65; chmn. expert adv. panel chiropractic and naturopathy USPHS, 1968. Editor: Am. Jour. Anatomy, 1960-68; Contbr. articles profl. jours. Recipient Henry Gray award for distinguished service in anatomy, 1971. Mem. Tex. Acad. Sci. (pres. 1962), Am. Assn. Anatomy (pres. 1967), Phi Beta Kappa, Sigma Xi, Nu Sigma Nu, Alpha Omega Alpha. Episcopalian. Home: 2706 Pinewood Terr Austin TX 78757

DUNCAN, DONALD PENDLETON, educator; b. Joliet, Ill., Feb. 24, 1916; s. Kenneth Whitney and Nettie (Pendleton) D.; m. Dymer Mercein Benzie, July 6, 1956; children: Kenneth Houlton, Nancy Susan, Debra Mercein. Student, North Park Coll., 1934-35, Mich. Coll. Mining and Tech., summer 1935; B.S.F., U. Mich., 1937, M.S., 1939; Ph.D., U. Minn.; 1951. Shelter-belt asst. U.S. Forest Service, Meade, Kans., 1939-40, jr. forester, Harrison, Ark. and Brooklyn, Miss., 1940-41; instr. Kans. State Coll., Manhattan, 1941-42, extension forester, 1946-47; instr., asst. prof., asso. prof. U. Minn., St. Paul, 1947-59, prof., 1959-65, asst. dir., 1964-65; dir. Sch. Forestry, Fisheries and Wildlife, U. Mo., Columbia, 1965—; forester Coop. Research-Sci. and Edn. Adminstrn., U.S. Dept. Agr., Washington, 1980-81; cons. Minn. Natural Resources Council, 1961-63, Coop. State Research Service, 1969, Fgn. Area Fellowship Program, 1969, 70, Council Grad. Schs., 1970, Ohio State U., 1975, Duke U., 1975, U. Ky., 1976, U. Fla., 1979, TVA, 1979, U. Ark., 1980, U. Tenn., 1984; vis. scientist NSF, 1965, 68, 69, 72; mem. Nat. Coop. Forestry Research Adv. Bd., 1967-74; exec. bd. Assn. State Coll. and U. Forestry Research orgns., 1967-68, v.p., 1975-76, pres., 1977-78; chmn. Council Forestry Sch. Exec., 1970-71, Com. on Forestry Accreditation, 1970-74. Dist. chmn. Boy Scouts Am., 1969-71. Served with AUS, 1942-45. Decorated Bronze Star, Purple Heart. Fellow AAAS, Soc. Am. Foresters (past sect. chmn. and sec.-treas., chmn. recreation and edn. div., chmn. com. on ednl. policies); mem. Am. Forestry Assn., Ecol. Soc. Am., Wildlife Soc., Forest Products Research Soc. (sect. exec. bd.), Forest History Soc. (past dir.), Mo. Acad. Sci., Audubon Soc. (past chpt. chmn.), Sigma Xi, Gamma Alpha, Xi Sigma Pi, Phi Sigma, Gamma Sigma Delta. Presbyn. (elder). Research in forest ecology, forest influences and outdoor recreation. Home: 209 W Brandon Rd Columbia MO 65201
If other commitments permit, when opportunities arise to assume important responsibilities, assume them—but stay consistently within your limitations. Importance is measured by the magnitude of the contribution to one's fellows. The importance of any particular responsibility changes over time and the good judgment to distinguish at any given time between the important and the less important is paramount.

DUNCAN, DONALD WILLIAM, lawyer; b. Baldwin, Md., May 18, 1932; s. William Rush and Mary Alice (MacBlane) D.; m. Patricia A. Conner, Mar. 4, 1983; children: David, Lisa, Jeffrey, Mark. A.A., U. Balt., 1956, J.D., 1960. Bar: Md. bar 1960. Asso. Haynie & McFerrin, C.P.A., Balt., 1956-61; controller H.C. Weiskettel Co., Balt., 1961-62; v.p. adminstrn., sec., dir. Balt. Aircoil Co., Inc., 1962—; dir. Md. Blue Cross, Inc. Served with USAF, 1951-55. Mem. Am. Bar Assn., Md. Bar Assn., Fin. Execs. Inst., Am. Inst. C.P.A.'s. Republican. Presbyterian. Club: Turf Valley Country. Office: Baltimore Aircoil Co Inc PO Box 7322 Baltimore MD 21227

DUNCAN, FRANCIS, government official, historian; b. Oak Park, Ill., July 12, 1922; s. Fred B. and Olive (Whitney) D.; m. Frances M. Mergus, Aug. 16, 1947; children: Evan, April. B.A., Ohio Wesleyan U., 1944; M.A., U. Chgo., 1947, Ph.D., 1954. Instr. history Wayne State U., Detroit, 1947-50; civilian employee Office of Intelligence, USAF, Washington, 1950-57; analyst Office of Controller, AEC, Washington, 1957-62, asst. historian, 1962-74; asso. historian div. naval reactors ERDA, 1974-77; historian div. naval reactors Dept. Energy, 1977—. Author: (with Richard G. Hewlett) Atomic Shield, 1969, Nuclear Navy 1946-62, 1974; Author articles in naval history; Contbr. to encys. Served with USNR, 1943-46. Recipient David D. Lloyd Prize in History, 1970. Mem. U.S. Naval Inst., Am. Hist. Assn., Orgn. Am. Historians, Soc. for History in the Fed. Govt., AAAS. Home: 9209

Ewing Dr Bethesda MD 20817 Office: Dept Energy Washington DC 20585

DUNCAN, GEORGE H., broadcasting company executive; b. N.Y.C., Aug. 26, 1931; m. Mary Joan Murphy, Feb. 15, 1958; children: Keith, Kathryn, Patricia. Student, Hofstra Coll., 1949-50; B.A. in Govt, Cornell U., 1955. Sales engr. Dewey and Almy Chem. div. W.R. Grace Co., Cambridge, Mass., 1955-56; account exec. Avery-Knodel, Inc., N.Y.C., 1956-58; with Metromedia, Inc., N.Y.C., 1958—; account exec. Sta. WNEW, 1958-66; v.p., gen. mgr. Sta. WNEW-FM, 1966-69; pres. Metromedia Stereo, 1969-71; exec. v.p. Metromedia Radio, 1971-72, pres., 1972-80; v.p. ops. Metromedia, Inc., 1980-82, pres., dir., 1982—; bd. dirs. Radio Advt. Bur. Mem. council Cornell U. Served with USMCR, 1950-51. Mem. Internat. Radio TV Soc., Phi Gamma Delta. Club: Cornell. Home: 15 Overlook Rd Scarsdale NY 10583 Office: Metromedia Inc One Harmon Plaza Secaucus NJ 07094

DUNCAN, HEARST RANDOLPH, lawyer; b. Center Junction, Iowa, Aug. 28, 1905; s. John Edgar and Maude (Stingley) D.; m. Louise Ezell, June 16, 1932; children—Barbara Jean, Hearst R. Student, Lenox Coll., 1922-24; A.B., George Washington U., 1928, J.D., 1931. Bar: Iowa bar 1931. Partner Duncan, Jones, Riley & Finley, Des Moines; state's atty., Mitchell County, Iowa, 1932-34, spl. asst. atty. gen., State Iowa, 1937; Iowa atty. C., M., St.P & Pacific R.R. Fellow Am. Coll. Trial Lawyers; mem. Nat. Assn. R.R. Trial Counsel (UN nat. legacies com.), ABA, Iowa Bar Assn. (past pres.), Order of Coif, Delta Sigma Rho. Home: 726 54th St Des Moines IA 50312 Office: Equitable Bldg Des Moines IA 50309

DUNCAN, JAMES HERBERT CAVANAUGH, banker; b. Madison, Wis., June 13, 1925; s. Dorman L. and Marie (Cavanaugh) D.; m. Colleen Patricia Cloney, Sept. 14, 1946; children—James H., John P., Gary T., Phillip K., Katherine M., Thomas M., Mark J. Duncan. Student, Western Mich. U., 1950; grad., Sch. Fin. Pub. Relations, Northwestern U., 1954, Grad. Sch. Banking, U. Wis., 1962. Assoc. with First Nat. Bank & Trust Co., Kalamazoo, 1950—, sr. v.p., 1964-65, exec. v.p., 1965-69, pres., 1969-76, chmn. bd., 1976-79; pres., chief exec. officer 1st Nat. Fin. Corp., Kalamazoo, 1971-78; chmn., chief exec. officer First of Am. Bank Corp., 1978—; dir. First of Am. Bank, Lansing, Mich., Royal Oak, Mich., Ann Arbor, Mich., Detroit, Detroit br. Fed. Res. Bank of Chgo.; former mem. nat. adv. council Conf. State Bank Suprs., 1977-80. Author articles in field. Gen. campaign chmn. Kalamazoo Community Chest, 1958, pres., 1964; mem. exec. com. Operation Action Upper Peninsula, 1975—; pres. Constance Brown Hearing Center, Kalamazoo, 1960; chmn. Kalamazoo chpt. ARC, 1967; mem., chmn. pres.'s council Nazareth Coll., Kalamazoo, 1966-71; trustee, pres. Lift Found., Kalamazoo, 1967-70; trustee Citizens Research Council Mich., 1980—, W.E. Upjohn Inst., 1971—, Borgess Med. Center, 1979—, Western Mich. U. Found.; pres. Western Mich. U. Found., 1982—; bd. dirs. Jobs for Mich. Grads. Served to 2d lt., inf. AUS, World War II. Decorated Bronze Star with oak leaf cluster, Purple Heart with oak leaf cluster, Combat Inf. badge. Mem. Am. Bankers Assn. (governing council 1975-79, Mich. v.p. 1976-77, dir. 1977-79, mem. edn. policy and devel. council 1975-79, chmn. 1977-79), Mich. Bankers Assn. (pres. 1972-73), Charge Account Bankers Assn. (pres. 1957), Nat. Alliance Businessmen (chmn. Southeastern Mich. metro 1975-76). Clubs: Kiwanis (pres. Kalamazoo 1964), Kalamazoo Country, Park (Kalamazoo) (pres. 1970). Home: 1806 Greenbrier Dr Kalamazoo MI 49008 Office: 108 E Michigan Ave Kalamazoo MI 49006

DUNCAN, JAMES RUSSELL, industrial executive; b. Tucson, Apr. 17, 1917; s. Bradford and Mattielee (Josey) D.; m. Mimi Galloway; children: Joanne, Robert, Lance. Student, U. Ariz., U. Wis. Extension, Milw. Vice pres., gen. mgr. Peerless Machine Co., Racine, Wis., 1940-45; gen. mgr. Moore Machinery Co., Los Angeles, 1945-46; sec.-treas. McCulloch Motors Corp., Los Angeles, 1946-48; chief of capital goods ECA Mission to Italy, 1948-50; indsl. cons., Italy, 1950-52; pres. Electric Sprayit Co. (and subs.), Sheboygan, Wis., 1952-53; asst. to pres. Stewart-Warner Corp. (cons.), Chgo., 1954-55; v.p. Misco Corp., also Consol. Founderies & Mfg., Chgo., 1955-57; chmn., pres., dir. Mpls.-Moline Co., Hopkins, Minn., 1957-60; cons., dir. Bowser, Inc., 1960-62, United Board & Carton Corp., 1960-62; chmn. bd., chief exec. officer, treas. Steego Corp. (formerly Sterling Precision Corp.), 1962—; chmn. bd. Resource Exploration, Inc., Shreveport, La., Milw. Western Corp., Milw. Recipient Recognition award U. Ariz. Clubs: Memphis Country, Memphis Hunt and Polo, Delray (Fla.) Beach Yacht; Everglades, Bath and Tennis (Palm Beach, Fla.). Office: Suite 900 319 Clematis St West Palm Beach FL 33401 *

DUNCAN, JAMES WENDELL, state legislator; b. Muscatine, Iowa, May 4, 1942; s. Paul Revere and Hazel Jeanette (Brayton) D.; m. Charlotte Marvin, June 30, 1981; children—James, Desiree, Michelle, Derek, Jon, Marc, Caron. B.S., Ill. State U., 1965; M.B.A., Oreg. State U., 1970. Instr. Sheldon Jackson Coll., Sitka, Alaska, 1968-70; instr. Juneau-Douglas Community Coll., 1970-73; supr. office ops. Alaska Dept. Revenue, 1972-74; controller T-H Regional Housing Authority, 1974-78; mem. Alaska Ho. of Reps., 1974—, chmn. legis. budget and audit com., 1979-80, speaker, 1981—. Assemblyman City and Borough of Juneau, 1972-74. Democrat. Presbyterian. *

DUNCAN, JOHN BONNER, consultant; b. Springfield, Ky., Feb. 6, 1910; s. Samuel E. and Lena Bell (Jordan) D.; m. Edith L. West, July 2, 1938 (dec. Mar. 1O, 1966); children—John Bonner, Joan West; m. B. Dolores Berry, Aug. 14, 1969; children—Jay Berry. A.B., Howard U., 1934; scholarship student, Grad. Sch. Philosophy, 1933-35, Grad. Sch. Law, 1935-38; LL.B., Terrell Law Sch., Washington, 1938. Bar: Md. bar 1941. With Dept. of Interior, 1934-41; atty. Bituminous Coal Commn., 1942-43; atty., then sr. atty. solid fuels br. OPA, 1943-46; sr. atty., atty.-adviser Office Housing Expediter, 1947-49; sr. atty. research sect., law div. HHFA, 1949-52; recorder deeds, D.C., 1952-61, commr., 1961-67, asst. to sec. interior for urban relations, 1967-69; gen. cons., pres. Housing Devel. Assos., Washington, 1969—. Author: New Dimension Bidding in Contract Bridge, 1963. Vice pres. Nat. Capital area Nat. Council Chs.; sponsor Club of All Nations; Bd. dirs. Nat. Capital area United Givers Fund; bd. dirs., chmn. personnel com. Nat. Capital area Big Bros.; trustee Barney Neighborhood House. Recipient Afro-Am. Newspaper award, 1950; citation Pitts.-Courier, 1951, Chgo. Defender, 1955; ann. award D.C. Fedn. Civic Assns., 1952, 62; award Washington Urban League, 1959; Brotherhood award Nat. Conf. Christians and Jews, 1961; award for community service Am. Legion, 1962, Nat. Assn. Colored Womens Clubs, 1962, Nat. Capital area Council of Chs., 1962, others.; award Man of Year Met. Wash. Bd. Trade, 1978. Mem. A.M.E. Zion Ch. Home: 307 Yoakum Pkwy Apt 3-325 Alexandria VA 22304

DUNCAN, JOHN JAMES, congressman; b. Scott County, Tenn., Mar. 24, 1919; married; 4 children. Asst. state atty. gen., 1947-56, dir. law, Knoxville, Tenn., 1956- 59, mayor, 1959-64; mem. 89th to 98th Congresses, 2d Dist. Tenn. Pres. Knoxville Profl. Baseball Club, 1956-59; past pres. So. Baseball League. Served with AUS, 1942-45. Mem. Am., Tenn., Knoxville bar assns., Am. Legion (comdr. Tenn. 1954), VFW. Republican. Presbyterian. Address: House Office Bldg Washington DC 20515

DUNCAN, JOHN LAPSLEY, manufacturing company executive; b. Nashville, Dec. 16, 1933; s. Ruel Laverne and Lorene (Ellis) D.; m. Patricia Louise Cogburn, Aug. 27, 1955; children: Sharon Gayle, John Lapsley, Ruel Laverne, II, Thomas Ellis. B.S. in Mech. Engring., U. S.C., 1960. Sales mgr. So. die casting div. Arwood Corp., 1966-69; v.p. mfg. and engring., power tool div., then dir. corp. bus. analysis Singer Co., 1969-78; pres., chief operating officer Murray Mfg. Co., Brentwood, Tenn., 1978-82; pres. Motor Products div. Singer Co., Pickens, S.C., 1982—. Served with AUS, 1953-56. Mem. Outdoor Power Equipment Inst., Power Tool Inst. (dir.). Republican. Mem. Christian Ch. (Disciples of Christ). Office: PO Box 35 Pickens SC 29671

DUNCAN, JOSEPH WAYMAN, business economist; b. Cambridge, Ohio, Dec. 2, 1936; s. George Wendall and Elizabeth (Fuller) D.; m. Janice Elaine Grouveia, Aug. 19, 1961; children: Jeffrey Wayman, James Wendall. B.S. in Mech. Engring, Case Inst. Tech., 1958; M.B.A., Harvard U., 1960; Ph.D., Ohio State U., 1970. Economist Battelle Meml. Inst., Columbus, Ohio, 1961-68, coordinator urban affairs, 1969-73; dep. asst. sec. for econ. policy Dept. Commerce, Washington, 1968-69; dep. assoc. dir. Office Mgmt. and Budget, Washington, 1974-78; dir. Office Fed. Statis. Policy and Standards, Dept. Commerce, Washington, 1978-81; asst. adminstr. for statis. policy Office of Info. and Regulatory Affairs, Office of Mgmt. and Budget, Washington, 1981; corp. economist and chief statistician Dun & Bradstreet Corp., 1982—; chmn. coordination bd. OAS Com. on Improvement of Nat. Statistics, 1975-79; U.S. rep., chmn. UN Statis. Commn., 1981—. Author books, also numerous articles in field. Fellow Am. Statis. Assn.; mem. Nat. Economists Club (pres. 1979, chmn.), Internat. Statis. Inst., Nat. Assn. Bus. Economists. Home: 39 Sturges Hwy Westport CT 06880

DUNCAN, KENT WHITNEY, retired banker; b. Quincy, Ill., Feb. 13, 1915; s. Laurance Morgan and Margaret (Kent) D.; m. Deuel Rowan, Jan. 13, 1946; children: Cole Rowan, Sarah Whitney. B.A., Grinnell Coll., 1936; postgrad., U. Wis., 1947-49, U. Ind., 1954-55. With Harris Trust & Savs. Bank, Chgo., 1936-80, v.p., 1958-68, sr. v.p., 1968-73, exec. v.p., 1973-80; also dir.; exec. v.p., dir. Harris Bankcorp Inc., 1974-80; dir. Consolidated Papers, Inc., Wisconsin Rapids, Wis. Mem. exec. bd. Chgo. council Boy Scouts Am., 1954-80, mem. nat. council, 1970-80; Trustee Ravinia Festival Assn., chmn., 1979-81. Served to lt. col. C.E. U.S. Army, 1941-46. Clubs: Tequesta Country (Fla.); Chicago, Mid-America (Chgo.); Westmoreland Country (Wilmette, Ill.). Home: 595 Elm St Winnetka IL 60093 Office: 111 W Monroe St Chicago IL 60603

DUNCAN, LOUIS CHARLES, manufacturing company executive; b. Kokomo, Ind., Feb. 20, 1913; s. John P. and Nellie C. (Stevens) D.; m. Marguerite Dewees, Sept. 3, 1934 (dec. Aug. 1968); children: Carole (Mrs. William Kuehn), Craig; m. Eileen Hastings, Apr. 26, 1969. B.A., Ind. U., 1933; LL.D. (hon.), Buena Vista Coll. Ret. vice chmn. Household Internat., Chgo.; chmn. bd. Sealy Inc., Chgo., 1978—; chmn. East West Capital Corp.; dir. CAM-OR Corp., Indpls., East West Mut. Stock Corp., A.I. Corp., Lexicon Corp., Denver. Bd. dirs. Am. Heart Assn.; mem. adv. council U. Ill.; bd. dirs. Ill. Council Econ. Edn. Served as field dir. ARC, World War II. Recipient Disting. Service award Nat. Consumer Finance Assn., 1970. Mem. Chgo. Commerce and Industry Assn., Mid-Am. Com., English Speaking Union, Chgo. Council Fgn. Relations. Presbyterian (elder). Clubs: Union League, Mid-Am., Executives, Economic (Chgo.); Hinsdale Golf (Ill.).; Army Navy (Washington). Home: #5 Oak Brook Club Dr Oak Brook IL 60521 Office: 525 W Monroe St Chicago IL 60601

DUNCAN, MCLEAN KENNEDY, legal educator; b. 1942. B.A., Harvard U., 1964; LL.B., Yale U., 1970. Law clk. Justice Potter Stewart U.S. Supreme Ct., Washington, 1970-71; now prof. Harvard U Law Sch., Cambridge, Mass.; past note and comment editor Yale Law Jour. Office: Harvard U Law Sch Cambridge MA 02138

DUNCAN, MARGARET CAROLINE, physician; b. Salt Lake City, June 9, 1930; d. Donald and Margaret Aileen (Eberts) D.; m. N. Paul Arceneaux, Dec. 26, 1958; children—David Paul, Eleanor Anne, Stephen Louis, Andre. B.A., U. Tex., 1952, M.D., 1955. Intern Kings County Hosp., Seattle, 1955-56; resident in pediatrics John Sealy Hosp., Galveston, Tex., 1956-58; resident in neurology Charity Hosp., New Orleans, 1958-60; fellow child neurology Johns Hopkins Hosp., 1960-61; mem. faculty La. State U. Med. Center, New Orleans, 1961—, prof. neurology and pediatrics, 1973—. Chmn. La. Com. Epilespy and Cerebral Palsy, 1976-79. Fellow Am. Acad. Neurology, Am. Acad. Pediatrics; mem. Child Neurology Soc., Profs. Child Neurology, Am. Assn. Mental Deficiency, Alpha Omega Alpha. Episcopalian. Office: 1542 Tulane Ave New Orleans LA 70112

DUNCAN, PAUL R., giftware company executive; b. Selmer, Tenn., Oct. 25, 1940; s. William T. and Buna M. D.; m. Margery Ann Trigg, Apr. 15, 1942; children: Kenneth S., Amy E. A.B., Dartmouth Coll., 1962, M.B.A., 1963. C.P.A., Mass., Ohio. With Ernst & Whinney (C.P.A.), Boston and Cleve., 1964-80, partner, until 1980; sr. v.p. fin., chief fin. officer, treas. Towle Mfg. Co., Boston, 1980-82, pres., treas., 1982—. Served with USAR, 1963-64. Mem. Fin. Execs. Inst., Am. Inst. C.P.A.s, Nat. Assn. Accts. Clubs: Harvard (Boston); Nashawtuc Country. Office: 144 Addison St Boston MA 02128

DUNCAN, POPE ALEXANDER, college president; b. Glasgow, Ky., Sept. 8, 1920; s. Pope Alexander and Mabel (Roberts) D.; m. Margaret Flexer, June 30, 1943; children—Mary Margaret Jones, Annie Laurie Kelly, Katherine Maxwell. B.S., U. Ga., 1940, M.S., 1941; Th.M., So. Bapt. Theol. Sem., 1944, Ph.D., 1947; postgrad., U. Zurich, 1960-61. Instr. physics U. Ga., 1940-41; fellow So. Bapt. Theol. Sem., 1944-45; dir. religious activities Mercer U., 1945-46, Roberts prof. ch. history, 1948-49; prof. religion Stetson U., 1946-48, 49-53; prof. ch. history Southeastern Bapt. Theol. Sem., 1953-63; dean Brunswick Coll., 1964; pres. South Ga. Coll., Douglas, 1964-68; v.p. Ga. So. Coll., Statesboro, 1968-71, pres., 1971-77, Stetson U., DeLand, Fla., 1977—. Author: Our Baptist Story, 1958, The Pilgrimage of Christianity, 1965, Hanserd Knollys, 1965. Pres. Wake Forest Civic Club, 1959-60, Ga. Assn. Colls., 1968-69; pres. Coastal Empire council Boy Scouts Am., 1973-74; chmn. council of presidents So. Consortium for Internat. Edn., Inc., 1974-75; mem. commn. on colls. So. Assn. Colls. and Schs., 1978-82; bd. dirs. Fla. Assn. Colls. and Univs., 1978—, v.p., 1981-82, pres., 1982-83; bd. dirs. Fla. Endowment for Humanities, 1978; chmn. pres.'s council Ind. Colls. and Univs. Fla., 1982—; chmn. Fla. Ind. Colls. Fund, 1980-81; mem. exec. com. So. Univ. Conf., 1981—. Mem. Am. Hist. Assn., Am. Soc. Ch. History, Douglas Coffee County C. of C. (dir. 1966-68), DeLand (Fla.) C. of C. (dir. 1978-81), Nat. Assn. Ind. Colls. and Univs. (dir. 1979-83), Phi Beta Kappa, Omicron Delta Kappa, Phi Kappa Phi, Phi Delta Kappa, Kappa Delta Pi, Pi Mu Epsilon, Phi Eta Sigma, Sigma Phi Sigma. Democrat. Baptist. Lodges: Rotary (dir. 1965-66, 70-72, pres. 1967-68).

DUNCAN, ROBERT EDWARD, poet; b. Oakland, Calif., Jan. 7, 1919; s. Edward Howard and Marguerite (Wesley) D. Student, U. Calif., Berkeley, 1936-38, 48-50. Editor Exptl. Rev., 1938-40, Phoenix, Berkeley Miscellany, 1948-49; tchr. Black Mountain Coll., N.C., 1956. Author: Selected Poems, 1959, The Opening of the Field, 1960, Roots and Branches, 1964, A Book of Resemblances, Poems, 1950-53, Of the War: Passages 22-27, 1966, The Years as Catches, First Poems 1939-46, 1966, Bending the Bow, 1967, Selected Poems 1940-50, 1968, Derivations, Selected Poems 1950-56, 1968, Tribunals, Passages 31-35, 1970, Dante, 1974. Recipient Civic and Arts Found. prize Union League, 1957; Harriet Monroe Meml. prize Poetry mag., 1961; Lovinson prize, 1961; grantee Nat. Endowment Arts, 1966-67; Guggenheim fellow, 1963 *

DUNCAN, ROBERT MORTON, judge; b. Urbana, Ohio, Aug. 24, 1927; s. Benjamin A. and Kathleen Wanda (Brown) D.; m. Shirley A. Thomas; children—Linn, Robert, Harriet Theresa. B.S., Ohio State U., 1948, J.D., 1952. Bar: Ohio bar 1952. Atty. examiner Ohio Bur. Workmen's Compensation, 1959-60; asst. city atty., Columbus, Ohio, 1960-61, chief counsel to atty. gen. Ohio, 1965-66; judge Franklin County Municipal Ct., 1966-69; justice Ohio Supreme Ct., 1969-71; judge U.S. Ct. Mil. Appeals, from 1971, chief judge, 1974; now judge U.S. Dist. Ct. Ohio, Columbus.; Mem. President's Commn. White House Fellows, 1970-74. Mem. Am., Fed., Ohio, Columbus bar assns. Office: US Courthouse Columbus OH 43215

DUNCAN, SANDY, actress; b. Henderson, Tex., Feb. 20, 1946; d. Mancil Ray and Sylvian Wynne (Scott) D. Studied dance at, Lon Morris Coll. Stage debut in The King and I, at State Fair Music Hall, Dallas, 1958; N.Y. stage debut in The Music Man, 1965; stage appearances include The Boyfriend (Outer Critics Circle award, N.Y. Drama Desk award), Ceremony of Innocence, (Theater World award), Your Own Thing, The Music Box, Love Is a Time of Day, Peter Pan; starred in: TV series Funny Face, 1971, The Sandy Duncan Show, 1972; appeared in: TV mini-series Roots, 1977; other TV appearances include The Flip Wilson Show; film appearances include The Cat From Outer Space, Million Dollar Duck, Star Spangled Girl. Recipient Gold medal Photoplay, 1971, Golden Apple award, 1971. Office: care Wm Morris Agy 151 El Camino Beverly Hills CA 90212 *

DUNCAN, VERNE ALLEN, state education official; b. McMinnville, Oreg., Apr. 6, 1934; s. Charles Kenneth and S. La Verne (Robbins) D.; m. Donna Rose Nichols, July 11, 1964; children—Annette Marie, Christine Lauree. B.A., Idaho State U., 1960, M.Ed., 1964; Ph.D., U. Oreg., 1968; M.B.A., U. Portland, 1976. Tchr. Butte County (Idaho) Pub. Schs., 1954-56, prin., 1958-63, supt. schs., 1963-66; research asst. U. Oreg., 1966-68, asst. prof. ednl. adminstrn., 1968-70; supt. Clackamas County (Oreg.) Intermediate Edn. Dist., 1970-75; supt. pub. instruction, State of Oreg., 1975—; mem. Nat. Adv. Council on Internat. Studies; mem. commn. on ednl. credits and credentials Am. Council on Edn.; mem. Edn. Commn. of States. Author numerous articles on ednl. adminstrn. Trustee Marylurst Coll.; bd. dirs. Oreg. Hist. Soc.; mem. Oreg. Gov's. Mgmt. Council, Gov's. State Job Tng. Coordinating Council; Mem. Idaho Ho. of Reps., 1962-65, chmn. econ. affairs com.; mem. interim com. Oreg. Legis. Assembly Improvements Com. Served with U.S. Army, 1956-58. Mem. Am. Assn. Sch. Adminstrs., Council Chief State Sch. Officers, Res. Officers Assn., Phi Delta Kappa (Educator-Statesman of Yr. award 1977). Republican. Presbyterian. Home: 16911 SE River Rd Milwaukie OR 97222 Office: State Capitol Salem OR 97310

DUNCAN-PETERS, STEPHEN JAMES, corp. exec., ret. fgn. service officer; b. N.Y.C., Mar. 13, 1915; s. James and Olga (Manarolis) Duncan-P.; m. Helen Politis, Feb. 11, 1945; children—Stephanie, Gregory. B.S. in Econs, Columbia, 1953. Sect. chief First Nat. City Bank N.Y., 1945-52; treas. Angyra (seaman's aid soc.), N.Y.C., 1952; jointed U.S. Fgn. Service, 1954; operations officer Refugee Relief Program, Salonika and Athens, Greece, 1954-56; econ. and comml. officer, Tripoli, Libya, 1957-61; sect. chief Africa div. Dept. Commerce, Washington, 1961-63; comml. attache, Helsinki, Finland; dir. U.S. Trade Center for Scandinavia, 1966-69; comml. attache, Stockholm, Sweden, 1966-69; dep. dir. Africa div. Dept. Commerce, 1970-71; counsellor for comml. affairs Am. embassy, New Delhi, India, 1971-75; ret., 1975; v.p. Horace H. Smith (Internat.), Inc., Arlington, Va., 1976, pres., 1976—. Served with Canadian Army, 1940-42; Served with AUS, 1942-45. Decorated Purple Heart. Mem. Black Watch Assn., Am. Fgn. Service Assn., Mil. Order Purple Heart. Home: 8209 Scotch Bend Way Potomac MD 20854

DUNCOMBE, RAYNOR LOCKWOOD, astronomer; b. Bronxville, N.Y., Mar. 3, 1917; s. Frederic Howe and Mabel Louise (Taylor) D.; m. Julena Theodora Steinheider, Jan. 29, 1948; 1 son, Raynor B. B.A., Wesleyan U., Middletown, Conn., 1940; M.A., State U. Iowa, 1941; Ph.D., Yale U., 1956. Astronomer U.S. Naval Obs., Washington, 1942-62; dir. Nautical Almanac Office, 1963-75; prof. aerospace sci. U. Tex., Austin, 1976—; research asso. Yale U. Obs., 1948-49; lectr. dynamical astronomy U. Md., 1963, Yale Summer Inst., 1959-70, Office Naval Research Summer Inst. in Orbital Mechanics, 1971, NATO Advanced Study Inst., 1972; cons. orbital mechanics Projects Vanguard, Mercury, Gemini, Apollo, USN Space Surveillance System; mem. NASA space scis. steering com., NASA research adv. panel in applied math., 1967; adviser Internat. Com. on Weights and Measures, Internat. Radio Consultative Com., Internat. Telecommunications Union; mem. Nat. Acad.-NRC astronomy survey com., 1970-72. Author: Motion of Venus, 1958, Coordinates of Ceres, Pallas, Juno and Vesta, 1969; editor: (with V.G. Szebehely) Methods in Celestial Mechanics, 1966, Dynamics of the Solar System, 1979; asso. editor: Fundamentals of Cosmic Physics, 1971; exec. editor: Celestial Mechanics, 1977—; contbr. articles to profl. jours. Recipient Superior Achievement award Inst. Navigation, 1967. Fellow Royal Astron. Soc., AAAS (sect. chmn.); asso. fellow AIAA; mem. Internat. Astron. Union (pres. com. on ephemerides), Am. Astron. Soc. (chmn. div. dynamical astronomy 1970), Inst. Navigation (councillor 1960-64, v.p. 1964-66, pres. 1966-67, Hays award 1975), ASME (sponsor applied mechanics div. 1968-70), Internat. Assn. Insts. Nav. (v.p.), Assn. Computing Machinery, Sigma Xi. Club: Nat. Aviation (Washington). Home: 1804 Vance Circle Austin TX 78701 Office: Dept Aerospace Engring U Tex Austin TX 78712

DUNDES, JULES, educator; b. N.Y.C., Sept. 12, 1913; s. Leopold and Ida (August) D.; m. Frances Becker, July 31, 1937; children—Leslie Weir, Suresa. B.S., Columbia, 1933. Sports reporter N.Y. Post, 1929-34; copywriter Hallee Co., 1934-36; promotion copywriter CBS, 1936-40; advt. and sales promotion mgr. WCBS, N.Y.C., 1940-49; dir. sales and advt. KCBS, San Francisco, 1949-55, mgr., 1955-56, gen. mgr., 1961-67; v.p. advt., sales promotion CBS Radio, 1956, v.p. charge sta. adminstrn., 1956-61; v.p., gen. mgr. KCBS, 1961-67; lectr. in communication Stanford U., 1967—; dir. Stanford Mass Media Inst., 1972—. Chmn. communications com. San Francisco Human Rights Commn.; Bd. dirs., pres. Cerebral Palsy Assn. Mem. San Francisco Radio Broadcasters Assn. (pres.), Cal. Broadcasters Assn. (chmn. bd.), Radio Pioneers, Sigma Delta Chi. Home: 38 Rossi Ave San Francisco CA 94118 Office: Stanford U Stanford CA 94305

DUNE, STEVE C., lawyer; b. Vithkuqi, Korea, Albania, June 15, 1931; s. Costa Pappas and Evanthia (Vangel) D.; m. Irene Duff Boudreau, Sept. 4, 1955; children: Michelle Anna, Christopher Michael. A.B., Clark U., 1953; J.D., NYU, 1956. Bar: N.Y. 1957. Law clk. U.S. Ct. Appeals 1st Cir., 1956-57; assoc. firm Cadwalader, Wickersham & Taft, N.Y.C., 1957-65, ptnr., 1965—. Trustee Clark U., Worcester, Mass., 1974—, vice-chmn. bd. trustee, Worcester, Mass., 1980—, chmn. presdl. search com., Worcester, Mass., 1983-84. Root-Tilden scholar, 1953-56. Mem. ABA, N.Y. State Bar Assn., Fed. Bar Council, N.Y. County Lawyers Assn., Assn. Bar City N.Y. (admiralty com. 1976-79), Maritime Law Assn. U.S. (marine fin. com. 1980—),

Phi Beta Kappa. Club: India House. Office: Cadwalader Wickersham & Taft 1 Wall St New York NY 10005

DUNEA, GEORGE, physician; b. Craiova, Rumania, June 1, 1933; came to U.S., 1964; s. Charles L. and Gerda (Low) D.; m. Mary Mills Barr, 1969; 1 dau., Melanie; stepchildren—Mary Louise, John Barr. M.D., U. Sydney, Australia, 1957. Diplomate: Am. Bd. Internal Medicine. Intern Royal North Shore Hosp., Sydney, 1958-59; resident in internal medicine, Australia and Eng., 1959-63; fellow in nephrology Cleve. Clinic, Presbyn.-St. Luke's Hosp., Chgo., 1964-66; practice internal medicine, specializing in nephrology, Chgo., 1972—; attending physician Cook County Hosp., Chgo., 1966—, dir. dept. nephrology-hypertension, 1969—; prof. medicine U. Health Scis.-Chgo. Med. Sch., 1973—; vis. prof. medicine Rush Med. Coll., 1976—. Contbr. chpts. to books, articles to profl. publs. Fellow A.C.P., Royal Coll. Physicians (London, Edinburgh); mem. AMA, Am. Soc. Nephrology, Brit. Med. Assn., Soc. Med. History. Home: 222 E Chestnut St Chicago IL 60611 Office: 1835 W Harrison St Chicago IL 60612

DUNFEE, THOMAS WYLIE, legal educator; b. Huntington, W.Va., Nov. 15, 1941; s. Wylie Ray and Chloe Edith (Wylie) D.; m. Dorothy Jane Taylor, Aug. 26, 1967; children: John Wylie, Jennifer Sue, Shannon Elizabeth. A.B., Marshall U., 1963; J.D., N.Y. U., 1966, LL.M., 1969. Bar: W.Va. 1966. Instr. N.Y. Inst. Tech., 1965-68; asst. prof. Ill. State U., Normal, 1968-70, Ohio State U., Columbus, 1970-72, asso. prof., 1972-74; asso. prof. legal studies Wharton Sch., U. Pa., Phila., 1974-79, prof., 1979—, Kolodny prof. social responsiblity, 1982—, chmn. dept. legal studies and public mgmt., 1980—; vis. prof. U. Newcastle (Australia), 1981; cons. AT&T, Western Electric Co., Business and Its Legal Environment, 1983, Nat. Tire Dealers and Retreaders Assn., U.S. Dept. Commerce. Author: Antitrust and Trade Regulation, 1977, Modern Business Law, 1979; contbr. articles to profl. jours.; editor in chief: Am. Bus. Law Jour, 1976-79. Nat. Endowment Humanities grantee, 1977-78. Mem. Am. Bar Assn., Am. Bus. Law Assn. Republican. Home: 517 Arthur Dr Cherry Hill NJ 08003 Office: Wharton Sch U Pa Philadelphia PA 19104

DUNFORD, MAX PATTERSON, biology educator; b. Bloomington, Idaho, June 17, 1930; s. George Osmond and Venna (Patterson) D.; m. Katie Pearl Thornhill, Sept. 1, 1954; children: Mark L., Steven O., Keith M., Thomas M., Karen, Allen R. A.S., Snow Coll., 1950; B.S., Brigham Young U., 1954, M.S., 1958; Ph.D., U. Calif., Davis, 1962. Faculty U. Calif., Santa Barbara, 1961-62, Mills Coll., Oakland, Calif., 1962-63; faculty biology dept. N.Mex. State U., Las Cruces, 1963—, now prof. biology. Contbr. articles to profl. jours. Served with U.S. Army, 1954-56. NSF grantee, 1966-68, 75, 77, 78, 79, 81. Fellow AAAS (exec. officer Southwestern and Rocky Mountain div. 1973-78, pres. SWARM 1981-82, mem. council, com. for council affairs 1973-79); mem. Bot. Soc. Am., Am. Genetic Assn. Mem. Ch. of Jesus Christ of Latter-day Saints. Home: 205 Capri Rd Las Cruces NM 88005

DUNGAN, MALCOLM THON, lawyer; b. Butler County, Kans., Mar. 17, 1922; s. Quintin Randolph and Henrietta Mathilde (Blumer) D.; m. Nancy Murray Traverso, Feb. 7, 1950; children: Nicholas William Fitz-Randolph, Sally Murray. A.A., Bartlesville Jr. Coll., 1941; B.A., Stanford U., 1947, LL.B., 1948. Bar: Calif. 1949, U.S Supreme Ct. 1958. Assoc. Brobeck, Phleger & Harrison, San Francisco, 1949-58, ptnr., 1958—. Contbr. articles to legal jours. Served to 1st lt. USMCR, 1942-46; PTO. Decorated Air medal, D.F.C. Fellow Am. Bar Found.; mem. Am Law Inst., ABA. Republican. Episcopalian. Clubs: Bohemian, Presidio Golf (San Francisco). Office: Brobeck Phleger Harrison One Market Plaza San Francisco CA 94105

DUNHAM, AUDIAN D., retail company executive; b. Albuquerque, May 15, 1941; s. William Dale and Evelyn Elaine (Ward) D.; m. Jane P. Mercer, June 15, 1963 (div. Nov. 1983); 1 son, Jerin Joseph. B.S., Rollins Coll., 1968; postgrad., Fla. Inst. Tech., 1968. Personnel supr. Boeing Co., Seattle, 1966-69; mgr. mgmt. devel. and tng. Xerox Corp., Rochester, N.Y., 1969-77; prin. Harbridge House, Inc., Boston, 1977-79; dir. mgmt. devel. Rockwell Internat., Pitts., 1979-80; v.p. orgn. and exec. devel. Federated Dept. Stores, Cin., 1980—; dir. Assessment Design Inc., Orlando, Fla.; pres., cons. Dunham & Assocs., Cin., 1981—. Contbg. editor: The Shelby Directories, 1979, 80. Mem. Am. Mgmt. Assn., Human Resource Planning Soc., Am. Soc. Tng and Devel., Am. Soc. Personnel Adminstrn. Republican. Office: Federated Dept Stores 7 W 7th Cincinnati OH 45202

DUNHAM, CORYDON BUSHNELL, broadcasting executive, lawyer; b. Yonkers, N.Y., Nov. 14, 1927; s. Corydon Busnhell and Marion (Howe) D.; m. Janet Burke, Oct. 29, 1966; children: Corydon B. III, Christopher B. B.A., Bowdoin Coll., 1948; LL.B., Harvard U., 1951. Bar: N.Y. Assoc. Cahill, Gordon, Reindel & Ohl, N.Y.C., 1951-65; asst. gen. atty. NBC Inc., N.Y.C., 1965-68, v.p., gen. counsel, 1971-76, exec. v.p., gen. counsel, 1976—. Bd. dirs. United Way, Greenwich, Conn., 1981. Served to 2d lt. Arty AUS, 1944-46; Japan. Mem. ABA, Fed. Communications Bar Assn., Am. Arbitration Assn. (dir.), Assn. Bar City N.Y. Episcopalian. Clubs: Harvard (N.Y.C.); Riverside Yacht (Conn.). Office: NBC Inc 30 Rockefeller Plaza New York NY 10020

DUNHAM, DONALD CARL, UN ofcl.; b. Columbus, Ohio, Aug. 30, 1908; s. Ray Stanley and Agnes (Jordan) D.; m. Florence Atkins Ross. Ph.B., Yale, 1930; Ph.D., U. Bucharest, 51948; postgrad., Harvard Grad. Sch., 1939-40. Am. Fgn. Service officer, 1931-39, vice consul, Berlin, Germany, 1931-32, Hong Kong, 1932-35, Athens, Greece, 1935-38, Aden, Arabia, 1939, N.Y. State WPA mus. supr., 1940; adminstrv. asst. Met. Mus. Art, N.Y.C., 1941-42; dir. East and West Assn., 1942; initiated and promoted repeal of Chinese Exclusion Act, 1942-43; editor financial research program Nat. Bur. Econ. Research, 1943-45; lectr. internat. affairs Cooper Union, 1945; asst. cable editor Life mag., 1945-46; UNESCO relations officer Dept. State, 1946-47; pub. affairs officer, Bucharest, Rumania, 1947-50, Bern, Switzerland, 1950-52, Office U.S. Polit. Adviser; also dir. pub. information office Allied Mil. Govt., Trieste, F.T.T., 1952-55; dir. planning Am. Com. for Liberation, 1955-61; adj. asso. prof. Fordham U., 1962; dir. pub. services U.S. Mission to UN, 1962-68; rep. UN Devel. Program, UNICEF and Office UN High Commr. for Refugees, Australia, New Zealand and Papua New Guinea, 1968-71; ofcl. UN Inst. Tng. and Research, N.Y.C., 1971—. Author: Envoy Unextraordinary, 1944, Rumanian Profile, 1948, Kremlin Target: USA, 1961, Zone of Violence, 1962; Contbr. articles to various publs. Mem. Explorers Club, Delta Kappa Epsilon. Club: Dutch Treat. Home: 270 Riverside Dr New York NY 10025 Office: RCLO United Nations New York NY 10017

DUNHAM, MENEVE, college president; b. Dubuque, Iowa, Dec. 28, 1930; d. Walter Edgar and Kathryn Mae (Babcock) D. B.A., Clarke Coll., 1955; Mus.M., DePaul U., 1963; Ph.D., U. Mich., 1969. Mem. faculty Clarke Coll., Dubuque, 1962-71, asst. to pres., 1972-73, pres., 1977-83; v.p. devel. Mt. Mercy Coll., 1983; Am. Council Edn. fellow Claremont (Calif.) Colls., 1971-72; asst. dean Newcomb Coll., Tulane U., New Orleans, 1973-76, acting assoc. dean, 1976-77. Editor: Vivaldi Cantatas, 2 vols, 1979. Bd. dirs. Cedar Rapids Symphony Orch., Jr. Achievement, Profl. Women's Network; budget rev. United Way of Eastern Iowa. Nat. Endowment for Humanities grantee, summer 1970. Mem. Am. Musicol. Soc., NOW, AAUW, Phi Delta Kappa. *

DUNHAM, ROY HENRY, mech. engr.; b. Nixa, Mo., Aug. 29, 1923; s. Leslie Ward and Lois Delena D.; m. Helen Marie Wagner, Mar. 19, 1944; children—Sara Lynne, Michael Roy, Merrily Frances, Richard Alan. B.S.M.E., U. Mo., Rolla, 1947. Instr. in mech. engring. U. Ala., 1949-50; with TVA, Knoxville, 1950-80, dir. div. engring. design, 1973-79, mgr. div. engring. design, 1979-80; mgr. engring. Bechtel Energy Corp., Memphis, 1980—. Served with AC U.S. Army, 1943-45; ETO, NATOUSA. Decorated Air medal with oak leaf cluster. Mem. ASME, Tenn. Soc. Profl. Engrs., Nat. Soc. Profl. Engrs. Methodist. Office: 889 Ridge Lake Blvd Memphis TN 38119

DUNHAM, WOLCOTT BALESTIER, JR., lawyer; b. N.Y.C., Sept. 14, 1943; s. Wolcott Balestier and Isabel Caroline (Bosworth) D.; m. Joan Findlay, Jan. 26, 1974; children: Mary Findlay, James Wolcott. B.A. magna cum laude, Harvard U., 1965, LL.B. cum laude, 1968. Bar: N.Y. 1969. Vol. VISTA, 1968-69; assoc. Debevoise & Plimpton and predecessor Debevoise, Plimpton, Lyons & Gates, N.Y.C., 1969-76, ptnr., 1977—; exec. dir. N.Y. State Exec. Adv. Commn. on Ins. Industry Regulatory Reform, 1982. Contbr. articles to profl. jours. Sec., treas., trustee Fund for Astrophys. Research, N.Y.C., 1970—; bd. dirs. UN Assn. N.Y.C., 1973-79, vice chmn., 1975-79; bd. dirs. Neighborhood Coalition for Shelter, Inc., 1983—. Mem. ABA (chmn. com. on ins. sect. adminstrv. law 1979-83), Assn. Bar City N.Y. (com. on ins. 1981—), Union Internationale des Avocats, Am. Soc. Internat. Law, Harvard Law Sch. Assn. N.Y.C. (dir. 1978-81). Episcopalian. Office: Debevoise & Plimpton 875 3d Ave New York NY 10022

DUNHILL, JOHN STOKES, banker; b. Toronto, Ont., Can., Jan. 25, 1920; s. Reginald O. and Dorothy (McCune) D. B.A., Princeton U., 1941. With Harris Trust & Savs. Bank, Chgo., 1941-80, sr. v.p., 1975-80. Served to 1st lt. AUS, 1942-46. Club: University (Chgo.). Home: 175 E Delaware Pl Chicago IL 60611

DUNHILL, ROBERT, advertising direct mail executive; b. Los Angeles, Sept. 28, 1929; s. Herbert G. and Irma (Meyer) Odza; m. Joan Scheer, Dec. 19, 1952; children: Andrew, Candy, Cindy. B.S., Adelphi Coll., 1952; M.S., N.Y. U., 1954. Prin. Dunhill Internat. List Co., Inc., N.Y.C., 1948—, pres., chmn., 1975—. Served with USNR, 1955-57. Mem. Direct Mktg. Assn., Am. Mgmt. Assn., Ft. Lauderdale C. of C., U.S. Tennis Assn. Republican. Clubs: Fla. Direct Mktg., Inverrary Tennis Assn., N.Y. Direct Mktg. (N.Y.C.); Inverrary Racquet. Home: 4560 NW 70th Ave Lauderhill FL 33319 Office: Dunhill Internat List Co Inc 2430 W Oakland Park Blvd Fort Lauderdale FL 33311

DUNIWAY, BENJAMIN CUSHING, U.S. judge; b. Stanford, Calif., Nov. 21, 1907; s. Clyde A. and Caroline M. (Cushing) D.; m. Ruth Mason, Oct. 28, 1933; children—Anne (Mrs. Anne Barker), Carolyn (Mrs. Edward P. Hoffman), John M. B.A., Carleton Coll., 1928, LL.D., 1981; LL.B., Stanford, 1931; B.A. (Rhodes scholar), Oxford U., 1933, M.A., 1964. Bar: Calif. bar 1931. Practice in, San Francisco, 1933-42, 47-59; partner firm Cushing, Cullinan, Duniway & Gorrill, 1947-59; regional atty. OPA, San Francisco, 1942-45, regional adminstr., 1945-47, asst. to adminstr., Washington, 1945; justice Dist. Ct. Appeals, 1st Appellate Dist. Calif., San Francisco, 1959-61; U.S. circuit judge 9th Circuit Ct. Appeals, 1961-76, sr. judge, 1976—; judge Temp. Emergency Ct. Appeals U.S., 1979—; mem. com. trial practice and techniques Jud. Conf. U.S., 1969-74, mem. com. jud. stats., 1970-76; dir. Schlage Lock Co., 1951-59. Author: (with C.J. Vernier) American Family Laws, Vol. II, 1932. Chmn. Gov.'s Commn. Met. Area Problems, 1958-59; pres. Community Chest San Francisco, 1956-57, Calif. Conf. Social Work, 1950, Family Service Agy. San Francisco, 1950-51, Urban League San Francisco, 1952; Trustee Carleton Coll., 1958-71, Stanford, 1962-72; trustee James D. Phelan Found., 1957-71, pres., 1969-71; trustee Rosenberg Found., 1960-75, pres., 1964, 68-70; bd. dirs. Legal Aid Soc. San Francisco, 1955-70, Family and Children's Agy. San Francisco, 1948-51; life gov. Mill Life Sch., Eng., 1933—. Recipient Presdl. Cert. of Merit, 1947. Mem. Am. Bar Assn., Am. Judicature Soc., Am. Law Inst., Conf. Calif. Judges, Bar Assn. San Francisco (treas. 1958, sec. 1959), Soc. Calif. Pioneers, World Affairs Council San Francisco, Order of Coif, Phi Beta Kappa, Delta Smiga Rho. Clubs: Chit Chat, Commercial (San Francisco). Home: 1330 University Dr Menlo Park CA 94025 Office: PO Box 547 San Francisco CA 94101

DUNKAK, JOHN HENRY, III, forest products industry executive; b. Bklyn., Oct. 17, 1922; s. John Henry and Grace Margaret (Brinkman) D.; m. Phyllis Jean Marble, Feb. 9, 1946; children: Barbara Ann Dunkak Mills, Carol C. Dunkak Clark, Jan L., Lynn E. B.Chem. Engring., Rensselaer Poly. Inst., 1951, M.Chem. Engring., 1952. Research engr. Gen. Electric Co., Schenectady, 1951; project engr. Ketchikan Pulp Co., Alaska, 1952-54; gen. supt. Puget Sound Pulp & Timber Co., Bellingham, Wash., 1954-63; v.p. Belling Ham div. Ga.-Pacific Corp., 1968-82, sr. v.p. western pulp and paper, Portland, Oreg., 1982—; dir. Puget Sound Power & Light Co., Horizon Mut. Savs. Bank. Bd. dirs. Washington Pulp and Paper Found., 1968—, pres., 1972-74; bd. dirs. St. Luke's Hosp., 1968-77, Jr. Achievement, Inc., 1967-71, Whatcom County Health Services, 1962-68; deacon 1st Congregational Ch., 1964—. Served with USN, 1943-46. Mem. Am. Inst. Chem. Engrs., TAPPI, Air Pollution Control Assn., N.W. Pulp and Paper Assn. (trustee 1965—, pres. 1976-77), Assn. Wash. Bus. (bd. dirs. 1973—), Portland C. of C. (bd. dirs.), Whatcom County Devel. Council (bd. dirs. 1973—, pres. 1978), Sigma Xi. Republican. Clubs: Bellingham Yacht, Bellingham Golf and Country, Waverly Country. Home: 3476 Devonshire Lake Oswego OR 97034 Office: 900 SW 5th Ave Portland OR 97204

DUNKEL, WILBUR DWIGHT, educator, author; b. Elwood, Ind., Feb. 15, 1901; s. Joel Ambrose and Lulu Dell (Baker) D.; m. Georgia Osborn, Aug. 29, 1925; children—Patricia Ann, Robert Osborn. A.B., Ind. U., 1922; A.M., Harvard, 1923; Ph.D., U. Chgo., 1925. Fellow in English U. Chgo., 1923-25; mem. faculty U. Rochester, 1925-66, prof. English, 1947-66, Roswell S. Burrows prof. English, 1934-66, prof. emeritus, 1966—, chmn. dept., 1958-60; vis. prof. English U. Hull, Eng., 1955-56. Author: The Dramatic Technique of Thomas Middleton, 1926, Sir Arthur Pinero, 1941, William Lambarde Elizabethan Jurist, 1536-1601, 1965; also newspaper column Literature and Life, 1942-45; Mem. editorial bd.: Theology Today; reviewer: U.S. Quar. Book List; Contbr. edn. and religious jours. Fellow Folger Shakespeare Library, 1960-61. Mem. Modern Lang. Assn., Council Tchrs. English, Coll. English Assn., Am. Assn. U. Profs., Soc. Theatre Research (London), Beta Theta Pi. Republican. Presbyn. Club: Mountain View Country (Greensboro, Vt.). Home: 1570 East Ave Rochester NY 14610

DUNKELBERGER, HARRY EDWARD, JR., lawyer; b. Los Angeles, Apr. 16, 1930; s. Harry Edward and Helen G. (Black) D.; m. Jean Anne Driscoll, June 14, 1958; children: Anne, Amy, Teddy, Sarah, Emily. B.A., Yale U., 1954, J.D., 1957. Bar: D.C. Assoc. Covington & Burling, Washington, 1957-66, ptnr., 1966—. Articles and book rev. editor: Yale Law Jour., 1956-57; contbr. articles to legal jours. Served with USMC, 1950-52. Mem. ABA, D.C. Bar Assn., Order of Coif, Phi Beta Kappa. Democrat. Clubs: Met., City Tavern (Washington). Home: 4712 Jamestown Rd Bethesda MD 20816 Office: PO Box 7566 Washington DC 20044

DUNKERTON, THOMAS HUDSON, advertising agency executive; b. Detroit, May 26, 1926; s. Orrun Esbond and Robina Mowat (Leask) D.; m. Sherline Ruth Grimes, June 4, 1949; children—Robin, Elizabeth, Richard, Peter. B.S. in Mktg, N.Y. U., 1948, postgrad., 1948-49. Jr. asso. A.S. Bennett Assos., N.Y.C., 1947-49; market analyst Nabisco, N.Y.C., 1950; research supr. Compton Advt., Inc., N.Y.C., 1950-55; market research mgr. Vick Chem. Co., N.Y.C., 1955-61; research dir., dir. mktg. services Compton Advt., Inc., N.Y.C., 1961-64, sr. v.p., mgmt. dir., 1964—, also dir.; bd. dirs. Advt. Research Found., 1970-79. Mem. Briarcliff Manor (N.Y.) Bd. Edn., 1975—, pres., 1977-78, 82-83. Served with USAAF, 1944-45. Mem. Am. Mktg. Assn., Copy Research Council, Market Research Council, Advt. Research Commn., Gideons Internat. Mem. Community Bible Ch. Club: World Trade (N.Y.C.). Home: 48 Central Dr W Briarcliff Manor NY 10510 Office: 625 Madison Ave New York NY 10022

DUNKLAU, RUPERT LOUIS, investment consultant; b. Arlington, Nebr., May 19, 1927; s. Louis Z. and Amelia S. (Gnuse) D.; m. Ruth Eggert, June 4, 1950; children: Paul, Janet. B.S., U. Nebr., 1950; Litt.D. (hon.), Concordia Coll., St. Paul, 1982. Exec. v.p. Valmont Industries, Inc., Valley, Nebr., 1950-73; dir. Fremont Nat. Bank, Nebr., 1968—, Nebr. Savs. & Loan Assn. Bd. dirs. Midland Lutheran Coll., Community Chest, Meml. Hosp. Dodge County, Fremont, Luth. Ch.-Mo. Synod, St. Louis, Concordia Pub. House, St. Louis, Valparaiso (Ind.) U. Served with USNR, 1945. Republican. Club: Rotarian. Home: 2146 Phelps Ave Fremont NE 68025 Office: 1900 E Military PO Box 256 Fremont NE 68025

DUNKLE, WILLIAM FREDERICK, JR., clergyman; b. McAlester, Okla., May 16, 1911; s. William F. and Nell (Munn) D.; m. Olga Carolyn Watson, June 12, 1936; children—Amelia Ann (Mrs. B.W. Libby), William Frederick III, Zillah Beth. A.B., U. Fla., 1934; B.D., Emory U., 1936; Th.M., Union Theol. Sem., 1948; D.D., Am. U., 1951; LL.D., McMurray Coll., 1968. Ordained to ministry Meth. Ch., 1937; pastor, Pinecastle and Conway, Fla., 1936, Fernandina, 1936-41, Jacksonville, Fla., 1941-44, Barton Heights Ch., Richmond, Va., 1944-48, Grace Meth. Ch., Wilmington, Del., 1948-66; sr. minister Wilmette (Ill.) Trinity Parish Ch., 1966-76, Greenwood (Fla.) Ch., 1976—; prof. polity, vis. lectr. Crozer Theol. Sem., Chester, Pa., 1958-59; vis. prof. liturgical theology Garrett Theol. Sem., Evanston, Ill., 1969-73; Chaplain Va. Senate, 1946; exchange minister, London, 1950; rep. Am. Methodism World Meth. Conf., Oxford U., 1951, Oslo, 1961, London, 1966, Dublin, 1976; speaker Chgo. Sunday Evening Club; mem. commn. on worship Gen. Conf. Meth. Ch., 1940-46, sec., 1964-68, v.p., 1968-74; mem. bd. evangelism Fla. Conf. Meth. Ch., 1940-42, Peninsula Conf., 1950, pres. bd. Christian edn., 1960-64, trustee, 1960-66; del. Meth. Gen. Conf., 1964, Northeastern Jurisdictional Conf., 1960, 64; sec. com. Episcopacy, 1964; sec. Nat. Commn. on Worship Meth. Ch., 1964-72; mem. editorial council Meth. Story; mem. adv. com. Meth. Ch. Sch. Curriculum. Author: Church Year Values for Evangelical Churches, 1959, The Office of a Methodist Steward, 1963; Editor: Companion to the Methodist Book of Worship, 1970, Splendor of God's Glory, 1978; contbr. articles to religious publs. Del. White House Conf. on Children and Youth, 1950; adv. bd. Del. Youth Services Commn., Del. Commn. on Aging; mem. clergy adv. council Wesley Theol. Sem., Washington; mem.-at-large Nat. council Boy Scouts Am., 1950-60; mem. bd. Del-Mar-Va. council, 1950-60, N.E. Ill. council, 1970-74, Goodwill Industries, 1950-60; chmn. Wesley Found., U. Del., Washington Coll., 1956-60; mem. Bd. Ministerial Tng., 1967-75, Meth. Student Center Northwestern U., 1967-70, Meth. Bd. of Homes and Services, 1974, Bd. Edn. No. Ill. Meth. Conf., 1967-70; Trustee Meth. Found. No. Ill., 1968—, Wesley Coll., Drew U., Madison, N.J., Am. U. Recipient Order of Merit Nat. council Boy Scouts, 1956, Silver Beaver award, 1962. Mem. Nat. Council Chs., Del. Council Chs. (pres. 1959-60), Wilmington Council Chs. (pres. 1956-58), Hymn Soc. Am., Phi Delta Theta. Clubs: Mason (32 deg., Del. grand chaplain 1955-56), Rotarian., Lincoln of Delaware, University, Torch; Union League (Chgo.); Michigan Shores, Westmoreland Country, University of Evanston. Home: 100 Kelson Ave Marianna FL 32446

DUNLAP, CONNIE, librarian; b. Lansing, Mich., Sept. 9, 1924; d. Frederick Arthur and Laura May (Robinson) Robson; m. Robert Bruce Dunlap, Aug. 9, 1947. A.B., U. Mich., 1946, A.M. in Library Sci, 1952. Head acquisitions dept., then head grad. library U. Mich. Library, 1961-75, dep. asso. dir., 1972-75; univ. librarian Duke U., 1975-80; cons., 1980—. Authors articles in field, chpts. in books. Forewoman Grand Jury U.S. Dist. Ct. 13th Dist. Mich., 1967-68. Recipient Disting. Alumnus award U. Mich. Sch Library Sci., 1977. Mem. ALA (council 1974-83, exec. bd. 1978-83, pres. resources and tech. services div. 1972-73), Assn. Coll. and Research Libraries (pres. 1976-77), Assn. Research Libraries (bd. dirs. 1976-80, pres. 1979-80), AAUP. Address: 1570 Westfield St Ann Arbor MI 48103

DUNLAP, E. T., state ednl. adminstr.; b. Cravens, Okla., Dec. 19, 1914; s. C.C. and Ida (McWhirter) D.; m. Opal O. Jones, June 3, 1934; 1 son, E. Tom. B.S., Southeastern Okla. State U., 1940; M.S., Okla. State U., 1942, Ed.D., 1956; LL.D. (hon.), Oklahoma City U., 1962, John Brown U., 1968, Oral Roberts U., 1979, Pepperdine U., 1979. Tchr., prin. Latimer County (Okla.) Schs., 1936-38, supt. schs., 1938-42; high sch. insp. Okla. Dept. Edn., 1942-45; supt. schs. Red Oak (Okla.) Schs., 1945-52; pres. Eastern Okla. State Coll., 1952-61; chancellor Okla. System Higher Edn., Oklahoma City, 1961—; mem. steering com. Edn. Commn. of the States, 1978—, exec. com., 1979—, treas., 1979—; mem. numerous other profl. bds., commns.; chmn. bd. dirs. Fed. Student Loan Mktg. Assn. Author: books and monographs, including History of Legal Controls of Public Higher Education in Oklahoma, 1956; contbr. numerous articles to profl. publs. Mem. Okla. Ho. of Reps., chmn. edn. com., 1947-51; mem. Gov.'s Cabinet, 1979—; mem. exec. com. Last Frontier council Boy Scouts Am.; mem. Wesley Methodist Ch., Oklahoma City. Recipient cert. achievement Hdqrs. U.S. Army, Europe and 7th Army, 1972, Disting. Public Service award Okla. Coll. Osteo. Medicine and Surgery, 1974, Med. Ambassador award U. Okla. Health Scis. Center and Okla. Med. Assn., 1968; commendation in Senate Concurrent Resolution Number 89 Okla. Legislature, 1976; named to Okla. State U. Alumni Hall of Fame, 1977; Henry G. Bennett Disting. Service award Okla. State U., 1980, Edn. Commn. of States, 1980, State Higher Edn. Exec. Officers Assn., 1980; named to Okla. Hall of Fame, 1981. Mem. Okla. Edn. Assn. (dir. 1945-48), NEA, Okla. Assn. Sch. Adminstrs., Am. Assn. Sch. Adminstrs., Am. Assn. Higher Edn., Nat. Soc. Study Edn., Okla. Polit. Sci. Assn., Okla. Hist. Soc., State Higher Edn. Exec. Officers Assn. (pres. 1966-67, chmn. budget and fin. com. 1974-75, chmn. planning bd. of inservice edn. project 1974—), Okla. State Dental Assn. (hon.), Phi Delta Kappa, Pi Kappa Alpha. Democrat. Clubs: Lions (pres. local club 1964-65), Men's Dinner of Oklahoma City, Masons, Shriners, Jesters, Grotto. Home: 5304 Stonewall Dr Oklahoma City OK 73111 Office: Okla State Regents for Higher Edn 500 Edn Bldg State Capitol Complex Oklahoma City OK 73105

DUNLAP, GEORGE WESLEY, elec. engr.; b. Gardnerville, Nev., Apr. 13, 1911; s. Fred Sherwin and Rhoda (Early) D.; m. Alice Catherine Lloyd, Mar. 2, 1935 (dec. Nov. 1966); children—Barbara Rae, George Wesley, John Frederick, James Lloyd; m. Maude Harnden Gray, Apr. 20, 1968; stepson, Christopher G. Gray. A.B., Stanford, 1931, E.E., 1933, Ph.D., 1936. Registered profl. engr. With Gen. Electric Co., Schenectady, 1935-76, student engr., 1935-36; elec.

engr. high voltage and impulse sect. Gen. Engring. Lab., 1936-45; asst. div. engr. high voltage and nucleonics div. Gen. Engring. & Cons. Lab., 1945-51, div. engr., 1951-53, mgr. instrument and nuclear radiation engring. services, 1953-55, mgr. engring. physics and analysis lab., 1955-61, sr. engr., 1961-66; cons. engr. Research and Devel. Center, 1966-76, ret.; pvt. cons., 1976—; vis. Webster prof. elec. engring. Mass. Inst. Tech., 1955-56. Contbr. tech. jours. Recipient Harris J. Ryan High Voltage Research fellowship, 1932-35; Alfred Noble prize, 1943. Fellow IEEE (life); mem. Am. Phys. Soc., Am. Nuclear Soc., N.Y. State Soc. Profl. Engrs., Sigma Xi, Tau Beta Pi. Home and Office: 1970 Village Road Schenectady NY 12309

DUNLAP, JAMES LAPHAM, petroleum company executive; b. Bakersfield, Calif., Aug. 20, 1937. B.S. in Petroleum Engring, U. Okla., 1961; M.B.A., Columbia U., 1963. Asst. to pres. Texaco, Inc., White Plains, N.Y., N.Y.C., 1974-76, asst. to pres., gen. mgr. corp. services, 1976-77, gen. mgr. personnel and corp. services, Harrison, N.Y., 1977-79, gen. mgr. Latin Am., Coral Gables, Fla., 1979, v.p., Harrison, 1980—, vice chmn., London, 1983—. Mem. Soc. Petroleum Engrs.

DUNLAP, MARJORIE SNYDER, nursing educator; b. Kansas City, Mo., Dec. 7, 1917; d. Carl R. and Alice (Cleary) Snyder; divorced. B.A., U. Mo., 1949; diploma, Washington U. Sch. Nursing, St. Louis, 1942; M. Personnel Service, U. Colo., 1947; student, U. Chgo., spring 1951; Ed.D., U. So. Calif., 1959. Staff nurse Vis. Nurse Assn. Mo., 1942-43; instr. St. Luke's Hosp. Sch. Nursing, Kansas City, Mo., 1943-45, clin. instr., Denver, 1945-46; ednl. dir. Presbyn. Hosp. Sch. Nursing, Denver, 1946-48; mem. faculty U. Colo. Sch. Nursing, 1948-55, asso. prof. nursing dir. nursing service adminstrn. project, 1951-55; nursing service cons. Hawthorne (Calif.) Community Hosp., 1955-56; vis. asst. prof. U. Calif. Sch. Nursing at Los Angeles, 1956-57, mem. faculty, 1957-66, asso. prof., 1963-66; prof., dean Sch. Nursing, U. Hawaii, 1966-69; dean Sch. Nursing, U. Calif., San Francisco, 1969-76, prof., 1966-82; cons. in field. Contbr. articles, monographs to profl. jours. Rocky Mountain Soroptomist fellow, 1954-55. Mem. Am. Nurses Assn. (chmn. EACT sect. 1953-54), Hawaii Nurses Assn. (pres. 1967-69), Nat. League Nursing, Nat. Honor Soc., Phi Kappa Phi, Sigma Theta Tau. Club: Toast Mistress (Inglewood, Calif.). Home: 951 Holly Ave Rohnert Park CA 94928

DUNLAP, PAUL DAVID, banker; b. Douglas, Nebr., Nov. 15, 1930; s. Maynard W. and Helen A. (Jobes) D.; m. Jackaline Baldwin, Mar. 3, 1975; children: Daniel, Kathi, Robert, Thomas. LL.B., U. Nebr., 1956. Pres. Houghton State Bank, Red Oak, Iowa, 1961—; pres. Hawkeye Bancorp., Des Moines, 1968—; mem. faculty Colo. Sch. Banking, Boulder.; bd. dirs. Internat. Fin. Conf. Served with USN, 1952-54. Mem. Nebr. Bar Assn., Iowa Bar Assn. Republican. Presbyterian. Office: Stephens Bldg 7th Locust Des Moines IA 50305

DUNLAP, RICHARD FREEMAN, ry. exec.; b. Roanoke, Va., Mar. 24, 1922; s. Albert Christian and Helen (Meals) D.; m. Marie Fallwell, Nov. 22, 1946; children: Richard Freeman, Anne Fallwell Dunlap Kanady. Ed., Hampden Sydney Coll., 1939-42. With N.&W. Ry., 1942—, asst. trainmaster, Portsmouth, Ohio, 1953-54, Williamson, W.Va., 1954-55, trainmaster, Portsmouth, 1955-56, asst. supt., Norfolk, Va., 1956-57, supt., Crewe, Va., 1957-58, Bluefield, W.Va., 1958-60, gen. supt., Roanoke, 1960-62, regional mgr. Eastern region, 1962-64, gen. mgr. Lake region, Cleve., 1964-65, asst. v.p. ops., 1965-66, v.p. ops., 1966-73, sr. v.p. ops., 1973-80, exec. v.p., 1980-82, pres., 1982—; chief exec. officer, dir. Norfolk, Franklin & Danville Ry. Co.; pres., dir. C.W. Ry., Lake Erie & Fort Wayne R.R. Co., Lorain & W.Va., R.R. Co., Wheeling & Lake Erie Ry. Co.; v.p., dir. Va. Holding Corp.; dir. Belt Ry. Co. of Chgo., High Point, Thomasville & Denton R.R., Lake Erie Dock Co., Norfolk & Portsmouth Belt Line R.R. Co., Pocahontas Land Corp., Toledo Terminal R.R. Co., Terminal R.R. Assn. St. Louis, Wabash R.R. Co., Dereco, Ill. Terminal R.R., Winston-Salem Southbound Ry. Co., Winston-Salem Terminal Co., Winston Land Corp.; mem. adv. bd. First Nat. Exchange Bank of Va., Roanoke; dir., mem. exec. com. Dominion Bankshares Corp.; asso., regional So. exec. reservist Nat. Def. Exec. Res. Bd. dirs. Community Hosp. Roanoke Valley, Inc.; bd. dirs., exec. com. Western Va. Found. for Arts and Scis.; bd. dirs. Roanoke Symphony Soc.; mem. Roanoke Valley War Meml. Com. Served to capt. inf. AUS, 1942-46. Decorated Silver Star, Bronze Star, Purple Heart, Combat Infantryman's badge. Mem. Assn. Am. R.R.'s (past chmn. gen. com. operating-transp. div.), Am. Ry. Engrs. Soc., Ohio, Va., Roanoke chambers commerce, Kappa Alpha Frat. Episcopalian. Clubs: Shenandoah, Little Scorpions, Roanoke, German. Home: 323 Cassell Ln SW Roanoke VA 24014 Office: 8 N Jefferson St Roanoke VA 24042

DUNLAP, WILLIAM CRAWFORD, physicist; b. Denver, July 21, 1918; s. William Crawford and Helen (Kiester) D.; m. Ellen Hebrew, Mar. 22, 1940; 1 dau., Nancy. B.S., U. N.M., 1938; Ph.D., U. Calif. at Berkeley, 1943. Asst. physicist Dept. Agr., 1942-45; research asso., research lab. Gen. Electric Co., 1945-55, cons. physicist electronics lab., 1955-56; supr. solid state research, research lab. Bendix Corp., 1956-58; dir. solid state electronic research Raytheon Co., 1958-64; asst. dir. electronic components research Electronics Research Center, NASA, Cambridge, Mass., 1964-68, dir. research, 1968-70; sci. adviser to dir. U.S. Transp. Systems Center, Cambridge, 1970-75; pres. W.C. Dunlap & Co., 1975—. Author: An Introduction to Semiconductors, 1957; Editor-in-chief: Solid State Electronics, 1959—. Fellow I.E.E.E. (dir. 1966-68, dir. region I 1966-68), Am. Phys. Soc., Am. Inst. Aeros. and Astronautics (asso.); mem. Sigma Xi, Phi Kappa Phi. Spl. research transistor prodn. techniques in alloying, diffusion, epitaxy. Patentee in field. Home: 126 Prince St West Newton MA 02165

DUNLAP, WILLIAM DEWAYNE, JR., advertising agency executive; b. Austin, Minn., Apr. 8, 1938; s. William D. and Evelyn (Hummel) D.; m. Lois Mary Apple, Sept. 23, 1961; children: Kristin, Leslie, Brenda. B.A., Carleton Coll., 1960. Dir. mktg. Procter & Gamble, Cin., 1960-69; asst. postmaster gen. U.S. Postal Service, Washington, 1970-75; pres. MCA Advt., Westport, Conn., 1976-81; pres., chief exec. officer Campbell-Mithun Inc., Mpls., 1981—; chmn. postmaster gen.'s customer council U.S. Postal Service, Washington, 1971-75, chmn. stamp adv. council, 1972-75. Mem. Nat. Republican Leadership council Republic Eagles, Reagan Adv. Group. Recipient Superior Achievement award U.S. Postal Service, 1975. Lutheran. Home: 1000 Willow Dr S Wayzata MN 55391 Office: Campbell-Mithun Inc 1000 Northstar Ctr Minneapolis MN 55402

DUNLAVEY, DEAN CARL, lawyer; b. Waterloo, Iowa, Oct. 31, 1925; s. Ralph Earnest and Lou Emma (Caffall) D.; m. Dorian Brown, Sept. 8, 1948; children: Dudley Ralph, Dean Geoffrey, Dana Charles. B.S., Harvard U., 1949, LL.M., 1956; Ph.D., U. Calif., Berkeley, 1952, LL.B., 1955. Bar: Calif. 1956. Assoc. firm Gibson, Dunn & Crutcher, Los Angeles, 1956-61, partner, 1962—. Served to capt. AUS, 1943-45. Mem. Calif. State Bar, Am. Coll. Trial Lawyers. Republican. Home: 3255 Parkhurst Rolling Hills CA 90274 Office: 333 S Grand Ave Los Angeles CA 90071

DUNLEAVY, GARETH WINTHROP, educator; b. Willimantic, Conn., Feb. 24, 1923; s. Henry J. and Mabel (Hobbs) D.; m. Elizabeth Anne Lucas, May 31, 1947 (div.); children: Gweneth Anne, Stephen Arthur; m. Janet Frank Egleson, July 25, 1971; 1 stepchild, Karen Rande. A.B., Clark U., 1947; M.A., Brown U., 1949; Ph.D., Northwestern U., 1952. Asst. prof. to prof. English, U. Wis.-Milw., 1956-63, prof. English and comparative lit., 1975—, chmn. dept. English, 1964-67, asso. dean, 1967-68, coordinator grad. studies in English, 1970-72, faculty, 1982; vis. prof. English, U. Ill., 1978. Author: Colum's Other Island: The Irish at Lindisfarne, 1960, Douglas Hyde, 1974, (with Janet E. Dunleavy) The O'Conor Papers, 1977; contbr.: Old Ireland, 1965, Art and Age of Geoffrey Chaucer, 1967, George Moore in Perspective, 1983. Served with U.S. Army, 1943-45; ETO. Decorated Purple Heart.; Am. Irish Found. grantee, 1973, 74; Am. Council Learned Socs. grantee, 1972; Am. Philos. Soc. grantee, 1971, 73, 80, 81; Fromkin Research grantee, 1976; Guggenheim fellow, 1983. Mem. MLA, Mediaeval Acad., Am., Com. for Irish Studies, Internat. Assn. Study Anglo-Irish Lit., AAUP, Phi Beta Kappa, Phi Kappa Phi. Office: Dept English U Wis-Milwaukee Milwaukee WI 53201

DUNLEAVY, RICHARD MICHAEL, naval officer; b. Everett, Mass., Apr. 25, 1933; s. John Francis and Bridget Agnes (Gallagher) D.; m. Sibyl Evelyn Blair, Aug. 15, 1959; children: Richard M., Mark B., Matthew C., David P. B.S., Boston Coll., 1955. Commd. ensign U.S. Navy, 1955; advanced through grades to rear admiral, 1981; served with USS Kitty Hawk, 1974-76, USS Ponchatoula, 1978-79, USS Coral Sea, 1979-81; comdr.-in-chief Pacific rep., Philippines, 1981-82; dir. Aviation Manpower & Tng. Div. and Carrier and Air Sta. Programs Div. (OPNAV), Washington, 1982—. Recipient John Paul Jones award Navy League, 1975, Henry M. Jackson award, 1974; decorated 8 Air medals, Navy Commendation medal, Navy Achievement medal, Legion of Merit. Home: 4340 Ashford Ln Fairfax VA 22032 Office: Chief Naval Ops Dir Carrier Programs Dir Aviation Manpower and Tng Navy Dept Washington DC 20350

DUNLEAVY, ROSEMARY, ballet dancer; b. N.Y.C.; d. John Francis and Lucy (Wavrik) D. Grad., High Sch. Performing Arts, N.Y.C. Ballet dancer N.Y.C. Ballet, 1961-71; asst. ballet master, 1968-83, ballet mistress, 1983—. Office: New York City Ballet Lincoln Center New York NY 10023

DUNLOP, BECKY NORTON, White House official; b. Columbus, Ohio, Oct. 2, 1951; d. Carl Jack and Helen Louise (Betow) Norton; m. George Smith Dunlop, Sept. 17, 1977. B.S. in Polit. Sci., Miami U., Oxford, Ohio, 1973. Asst. exec. dir., cons. to bd. Am. Conservation Union, Washington, 1973-80; pres. Century Communications, Washington, 1977-81; assoc. dir. Presdl. personnel White House, Washington, 1981, dep. dir. Presdl. personnel, 1981-82, spl. asst. to Pres., dir. Office of Cabinet Affairs, 1982-83, dep. asst. to Pres. for Presdl. personnel, 1983—; chmn. Interagency Com. on Women's Bus. Enterprise, Washington, 1983—. Active Reagan campaigns, Washington, 1976, 80; bd. dirs. Ranaissance Women, Washington, 1983—. Republican. Baptist. Home: 2816 S Joyce St Arlington VA 22202 Office: White House 1600 Pennsylvania Ave Washington DC 2050

DUNLOP, GEORGE RODGERS, surgeon; b. St. Peter, Minn., Mar. 31, 1906; s. George Crawford and Pearl (Rodgers) D.; m. Barbara Wallace, Apr. 3, 1939; children: Susan Dunlop Roberts, Madora Dunlop Matava. B.S., U. Cin., 1927; M.D., Harvard U., 1931. Diplomate: Am. Bd. Surgery. Intern Cin. Gen. Hosp., 1931-32; asst. resident in surgery N.Y. Hosp.-Cornell Med. Center, 1932-35; resident in surgery Worcester (Mass.) City Hosp., 1935-36; practice medicine specializing in surgery, 1935—; sr. surgeon, past chief surgery Worcester Meml. Hosp.; prof. surgery U. Mass. Med. Sch.; dir., past chmn. Mass. Blue Shield; bd. dirs., past chmn. bd. Nat. Assn. Blue Shield Plans; past dir. Med. Indemnity Am.; bd. commrs. Joint Commn. Accreditation Hosps.; mem. Pres.'s Commn. for Study of Ethical Problems in Medicine and Biomed. and Behavioral Research. Bd. dirs., past chmn. Mass. div. Am. Cancer Soc., also, Worcester Found. Exptl. Biology; past bd. dirs. Bancroft Sch., Worcester Boys' Club, Community Chest. Served to lt. comdr. M.C. USNR, 1942-45. Fellow A.C.S. (past pres.), Royal Australasian Coll. Surgeons (hon.); mem. AMA, New Eng. Surg. Soc. (past pres.), New Eng. Cancer Soc., Northwestern Med. Soc. (past pres.), Boston Surg. Soc., Soc. Surgery Alimentary Tract (founder), Am. Surg. Assn., Pan Am. Med. Assn. Club: Worcester. Home: 54 Massachusetts Ave Worcester MA 01602 Office: 65 Elm St Worcester MA 01609

DUNLOP, JOHN THOMAS, economics educator, former sec. labor; b. Placerville, Calif., July 5, 1914; s. John W. and Antonia (Forni) D.; m. Dorothy Webb, July 6, 1937; children—John Barrett, Beverly Claire, Thomas Frederick. A.B., U. Calif., 1935; Ph.D., 1939; LL.D., U. Chgo., 1968, U. Pa., 1976. Acting instr. Stanford, 1936-37; instr. Harvard, 1938-45, asso. prof. econs., 1945-50, prof. econs., 1950—, Lamont U. prof., 1970—, dean, 1970-73; Served as vice chmn. Boston Regional War Labor Bd., 1944-45; chmn. Nat. Joint Bd. for Settlement of Jurisdictional Disputes in bldg. and constrn. industry, 1948-57; Cons. Office Econ. Stblzn., 1945-47, NLRB, 1948-52, Atomic Energy Labor Panel, 1948-53; Mem. bd. inquiry Bituminous Coal Industry, 1950; pub. mem. WSB, 1950-52; mem. Emergency Bd., 1954-55, 60, 66, Presdl. Railroad Commn., 1960-62, Missile Sites Labor Commn., 1961-67, Pres.'s Com. Equal Employment Opportunity, 1964-65; impartial chmn. constrn. Industry Joint Conf., 1959-68; dir. Cost of Living Council, 1973-74; sec. labor, 1975-76; chmn. Pay Adv. Com., 1979-80. Author: Wage Determination and Trade Unions, 1944, Collective Bargaining; Principles and Cases, 1949, Industrial Relations Systems, 1958, (with D. C. Bok) Labor and the American Community, 1970, The Lessons of Wage and Price Controls, 1977, Business and Public Policy, 1980; Editor: Wertheim Series in Industrial Relations, 1945—. Mem. Am. Acad. Arts and Scis., Am. Philos. Soc., Nat. Acad. Arbitrators. Home: 509 Pleasant St Belmont MA 02178 Office: 208 Littauer Ctr Harvard Cambridge MA 02138

DUNLOP, RICHARD GALBRAITH, retail company executive; b. Phila., Nov. 24, 1942; s. Robert Galbraith and Emma (Brownback) D.; m. Kathleen Sittig, Aug. 11, 1967; children: Robert, Allison Suzanne. B.A. in Econs., Trinity Coll., 1965; M.B.A. in Fin., U. Pa., 1968. Asst. controller Acme Markets Inc., Phila., 1974-75, controller, 1975-80; v.p., asst. to chmn. Am. Stores Co., Salt Lake City, 1980-81, v.p., sec., Salt Lake Co., 1981-82, exec. v.p., sec., Salt Lake City, 1982-83; vice chmn. bd., treas., 1983—. Republican. Presbyterian. Club: Ft. Douglas (Salt Lake City). Home: 609 N Perrys Hollow Rd Salt Lake City UT 84102 Office: American Stores Co 709 E South Temple Salt Lake City UT 84102

DUNLOP, ROBERT GALBRAITH, petroleum exec.; b. Boston, July 2, 1909; s. James B. and Caroline (Cowan) D.; m. Emma L. Brownback, Dec. 4, 1937; children—Barbara E. (Mrs. Robert P. Hauptfuhrer), Richard G. B.S., U. Pa., 1931. C.P.A., Pa. Asso. with Barrow, Wade, Guthrie & Co., 1931-33; dir. Sun Co., Radnor; dir. The Glenmede Trust Co. Trustee U. Pa. Mem. Sigma Phi Epsilon, Beta Gamma Sigma. Republican. Presbyterian. Home: 1062 Rock Creed Rd Bryn Mawr PA 19010 Office: 100 Matsonford Rd Radnor PA 19087

DUNLOP, ROBERT HUGH, veterinarian, educator; b. London, Apr. 16, 1929; U.S., 1980; s. Hugh Alexander and Kathleen Mary (Hibberd) D.; m. Josephine Mary Helyer, Oct. 4, 1958; children: Robert Hugo, Tasha Jane, Lachlan Stuart, Karma Jo, Boadie Waid, Pytt Andrew. Cert. agr., Royal Agr. Coll., 1947; D.V.M., Ont. Vet. Coll., 1956; Ph.D., U. Minn., 1961. Research fellow, instr. Coll. Vet. Medicine, U. Minn., St. Paul, 1956-61, dean coll., 1980—; clin. pathologist Wickham Labs., Wickham, Hampshire, U.K., 1961-62; asso. prof. pharmacology N.Y. State Coll. Vet. Medicine, Cornell U., Ithaca, 1962-65; prof., head dept. physiol. scis. W. Coll. Vet. Medicine, U. Sask., Saskatoon, Can., 1965-71; dean faculty vet. sci. Makerere U., Kampala, Uganda, 1971-73; dean Sch. Vet. Studies, Murdoch (W. Australia) U., 1973-80. Contbr. articles to profl. jours.; editor: (with M. Brin) Chemistry and Metabolism of L- and D- Lactic Acids, 1965, Can. Vet. Jour., 1969, 70, (with H.W. Moon) Resistance to Infectious Disease, 1970. Mem. program com. Prospect 2000 Conf., Perth, W. Australia, 1979. Fellow Am. Acad. Vet. Pharmacology and Therapeutics; mem. AVMA, Minn. Vet. Med. Assn., Australian Coll. Vet. Scientists, Research Workers in Animal Disease, Brit. Vet. Assn., Australian Vet. Assn., Council Agrl. Sci. and Tech., Assn. Am. Vet. Med. Colls., Royal Coll. Vet. Surgeons, Phi Zeta, Gamma Sigma Delta. Episcopalian. Home: 2137 Folwell St Saint Paul MN 55108 Office: 1365 Gortner Ave Saint Paul MN 55108

DUNMIRE, WILLIAM WERDEN, national parks adminstrator; b. Alameda, Calif., Feb. 24, 1930; s. Samuel P. Dumire and Margaret L. (Dickinson) D.; m. Marjorie S. Schoder, June 14, 1954 (div. 1972); children: Glenn E., Peter P.; m. Evangeline L. Blinn, Oct. 17, 1972. B.A., U. Calif., 1954, M.A., 1957. Chief park naturalist Nat. Park Service, Badlands Nat. Monument, S.D., 1961-63, Isle Royale Nat. Park, Mich., 1963-66, Yellowstone Nat. Park, Wyo., 1968-72; chief interpretation Nat. Park Service, Washington, 1973-77; supt. Couleee Dam NRA, Washington, 1977-81, Carlsbad Caverns/Guadalupe Mountains Nat. Parks, Carlsbad, N.Mex., 1981—. Bd. dirs. United Way, Carlsbad, 1981—, div. chmn., Carlsbad, 1983-84. Served to cpl. U.S. Army, 1954-56. Recipient Meritorious Service award U.S. Dept. Interior, 1973, Spl. Achievement award Nat. Park Service, 1976, Pres.'s award United Way, 1983. Mem. Carlsbad C. of C. (hon. dir. 1981—). Clubs: Am. Alpine, Sierra, Wilderness Soc., Rotary Internat. Home: 1412 W Orchard Ln Carlsbad MN 88220 Office: Nat Park Service 3225 National Parks Hwy Carlsbad MN 88220

DUNMORE, CHARLOTTE JEANETTE, social worker, educator; b. Phila., Nov. 16, 1926; d. Charles and Georgia (White) D. B.S., U. Pa., 1949; M.S.W., Columbia U., 1954; Ph.D., Brandeis U., 1968. Social worker Ch. Home Soc., Boston, 1954-57; supr. foster care and adoption Boston Children's Aide Soc., 1957-62; research worker Episcopal Community Services, Phila., 1962-64; asso. prof. Simmons Coll. Sch. Social Work, Boston, 1967-76; prof. Sch. Social Work, U. Pitts., 1976—; cons. Atlanta U. Sch. Social Work, 1973-75, Boston Model Cities Program, 1970; vis. research scholar UCLA, 1975, Radcliffe Coll., 1972. Author: bibliographies Black Americans, 1970, Black Children and Their Families, 1975. NIMH fellow, 1964; Research Scientist award, 1971-76; recipient Cabot award, 1969. Mem. Council Social Work Edn. (accreditation commn.), Nat. Assn. Social Workers, Nat. Assn. Cert. Social Workers, Nat. Assn. Black Social Workers, AAUP. Office: 2317CL Univ Pitts Pittsburgh PA 15260

DUNN, ALBERT WILKERSON, rubber co. exec.; b. Durham, N.C., Mar. 2, 1921; s. William Burwell and Maude (Wilkerson) D.; m. Jane Ballard, Oct. 23, 1943; children—Robert R., Stephen R., Christie A. (Mrs. C.D. Miller). A.B., Duke U., 1943. Prodn. supervision trainee Goodyear Tire & Rubber Co., Akron, Ohio, 1946-47, with pub. relations dept., 1947-48, mgr. aviation products div., Dayton, Ohio, 1948-55, aviation products mil. coordinator, Akron, 1955-57; mgr. aviation products div. Goodyear Internat. Corp., Akron, 1957-59, sales dir., 1959-61, v.p., gen. mgr., 1961-71, mng. dir., 1971-78; pres., chief exec. officer, dir. (Goodyear Can., Inc.), Toronto, Ont., 1978—; dir. Seiberling Can., Inc., Kelly-Springfield Can., Inc., Hallmark Auto-Centres, Inc.; past chmn. Tire Mfrs. Conf. (South African). Past pres. Am. Sch. Bd., Manila, Am. C. of C., Manila; past dir. Manila Rotary Club. Served to 1st lt. USAAF, World War II. Decorated Air medal with 3 oak leaf clusters, D.F.C. Mem. Soc. Automotive Engrs. Club: Mississauga Golf and Country. *

DUNN, ANDREW FLETCHER, physicist; b. Sydney, N.S., Can., Jan. 17, 1922; s. Harold Stuart and Tomasina Marion (Fletcher) D.; m. Xenia Mills Reid, Feb. 9, 1943 (dec. June 15, 1982); children: Marion Elizabeth, John Andrew. B.Sc., Dalhousie U., Halifax, N.S., Can., 1942, M.Sc., 1947; Ph.D., U. Toronto, 1950. With electricity sect., div. physics Nat. Research Council Can., Ottawa, 1950—, head electricity sect., 1971-80, co-head elec. and time standards sect., 1981—; pres. Dunn Constrn. Co., Baddeck, N.S., 1964-70, dir., 1948-70. Contbr. articles to profl. jours. Nat. chmn. Boy Scouts Can., 1969-70. Served to capt. Royal Can. Arty., 1942-45. Fellow IEEE; mem. Assn. Profl. Engrs. Ont., Canadian Assn. Physicists. Home: 734 Eastbourne Ave Ottawa ON K1K 0H7 Canada Office: Nat Research Council Montreal Rd Ottawa ON K1A 0R6 Canada *The person who's paid to continue to do the work he enjoys is fortunate; when that work is beneficial to the community he is doubly fortunate. I consider myself doubly fortunate.*

DUNN, ARNOLD SAMUEL, biochemistry educator; b. Rochester, N.Y., Jan. 31, 1929; s. Alexander and Dora (Cohen) D.; m. Doris Ruth Frankel, Sept. 14, 1952; children: Jonathan Alexander, David Hillel. B.S., George Washington U., 1950; Ph.D., U. Pa., 1955. Research assoc. Michael Reese Hosp. Research Inst., Chgo., 1955-56; asst. prof. NYU Sch. Medicine, N.Y.C., 1956-62; vis. prof. Weizmann Inst. Sci., Rehovot, Israel, 1972-73, 83-84; prof. molecular biology U. So. Calif., Los Angeles, 1962—, dir. molecular biology, 1982—. Contbr. articles to profl. jours.; mem. editorial bd.: Am. Jour. Physiology, 1979—, Analytical Biochemistry, 1980—. Recipient award for Teaching Excellence U. So. Calif., 1969, award for Research Excellence U. So. Calif., 1972, Raubenheimer award, 1981; UPSHS fellow, 1972, 83; Meyerhoff fellow Weizmann Inst. Sci., 1983. Mem. Am. Physiol. Soc., Am. Soc. Biol. Chemists, Endocrine Soc. Office: U So Calif University Park Los Angeles CA 90089

DUNN, CHARLES T., banker; b. Phila., Apr. 9, 1930; s. Charles A. and Helen (Courts) D.; m. Barbara Helen Long, Sept. 4, 1954; children—Kathleen, Patricia, Charles, Barbara Ann, Rosemary, Carolyn Marie. B.S., St. Joseph's Coll., Phila.; M.B.A., U. Pa. With Fed. Res. Tng. Program, Phila., 1953-55; with Heritage Bank N.A., Cherry Hill, N.J., 1955—, now sr. v.p. Vice pres. Pa./N.J./Del. Council; trustee So. N.J. Devel. Council, United Fund. Served to capt. USMCR, 1951-53. Mem. Camden Jr. C. of C. (past pres.). Club: Rotarian. Home: 127 Dumas Rd Cherry Hill NJ 08003 Office: One Executive Campus Cherry Hill NJ 08034

DUNN, CHARLES WILLIAM, educator, author; b. Arbuthnott, Scotland, Nov. 30, 1915; came to U.S., 1928, naturalized, 1961; s. Peter Alexander and Alberta Mary Margaret (Freeman) D.; m. Patricia Campbell, June 21, 1941 (dec. 1973); children: Deirdre, Peter Arthur; m. Elaine Heller, Oct. 25, 1974; 1 son, Alexander Joseph. B.A. with honors, McMaster U., 1938; A.M., Harvard, 1939, Ph.D., 1948. Asst. in English Harvard, 1939-40, tutor, 1940-41; instr. humanities Stephens Coll., 1941-42; instr. English Cornell U., 1943-46; instr. then asso. prof. English Univ. Coll., U. Toronto, 1946-56; prof. English N.Y. U., 1956-63; prof. Celtic langs. and lits., chmn. dept. Harvard, 1963—, master of Quincy House, 1966-81, Margaret Brooks Robinson prof. Celtic langs. and lits., 1967—; Taft lectr. U. Cin., 1956. Author: Highland Settler: A Portrait of the Scottish Gael in Nova Scotia, 1953, corrected reprint, 1968, The Foundling and the Werwolf: A Study of Guillaume de Palerne, 1960 (Chgo. Folklore prize 1960); Editor: A

Chaucer Reader, 1952, History of the Kings of Britain (Geoffrey of Monmouth), 1958, Chronicles (Froissart), 1961, Romance of the Rose, 1962, Lays of Courtly Love, 1963, (with Edward Byrnes) Middle English Literature, 1973; Contbr. articles, revs. to profl. jours. Dexter fellow, N.S., summer 1941; Rockefeller fellow, N.S., 1942-43; Nuffield fellow, Dublin, Edinburgh and Aberystwyth, 1954-55; Guggenheim fellow, Scotland, Wales and Brittany, 1962-63; recipient Canada award Fedn. Gaelic Socs., 1955. Fellow Am. Acad. Arts and Sci.; mem. Am. Folklore Soc., Modern Lang. Assn., Irish Texts Soc., Mediaeval Acad. Am., Early English Text Soc., Royal Scottish Country Dance Soc., St. Andrews Soc. N.Y., Comunn Gaidhealach (Scotland), Celtic Union Edinburgh (hon. pres. 1963—), Scots' Charitable Soc. Boston, Commanderie de Bordeaux à Boston (Maître). Clubs: Tavern, Somerset, Odd Volumes (Boston); Harvard (N.Y.C.); Scottish Arts (Edinburgh). Home: 25 Longfellow Rd Cambridge MA 02138

DUNN, CLARK ALLAN, civil engr., educator; b. Stichney, S.D., Sept. 9, 1901; s. Wilfred E. and Elizabeth (Batcheldor) D.; m. Mary Eveland, Sept. 6, 1928; children—Kenneth A., Gerald L. B.S., U. Wis., 1923; M.S., Okla. A. and M. Coll., 1934, C.E., 1936; Ph.D. (McMullen fellow), Cornell U., 1941. Registered profl. engr., Okla. Engr., bridge div. S.D. Hwy. Commn., 1923-27; asso. with J.E. Kirkham (cons. engr.), Pierre, S.D., 1927; constrn. engr. bridge div. Ark. Hwy. Dept., 1927-29; staff mem. Coll. Engring., Okla. State U., Stillwater, 1929—, prof. civil engring., 1941—, dir. engring. research, 1945-66, asso. dean engring., 1966—; Cons. Observer Task Force Frigid Operations, Fairbanks, Alaska, 1947; mem adv. mem. Okla. Planning and Resources Bd., 1948; chmn. Master Planning Bd., Stillwater, 1950; observer Air Force Operation Cool Sch., Newfoundland. Greenland, Alaska, Can., 1959. Fellow AAAS; mem. ASCE (past pres. Okla. sect.), Am. Soc. for Engring. Edn., Nat. Soc. Profl. Engrs. (nat. dir. 1951-55, v.p. 1955-57, pres. 1958-59), Okla. Soc. Profl. Engrs. (past pres.), Sigma Tau, Chi Epsilon, Phi Alpha Theta, Tau Beta Pi, Phi Kappa Phi. Methodist. Home: 2119 W University Ave Stillwater OK 74074

DUNN, DANIEL FRANCIS, state official; b. Natick, Mass., May 26, 1928; s. John M. and Mary (Murphy) D.; m. Isabel Maureen Burns, June 18, 1952; children: Maureen Dunn Harvey, Daniel Francis, Kathleen Dunn Lockhart, Patricia Elaine. A.B., Harvard U., 1950; J.D., Boston Coll., 1953. Bar: Mass. 1953. Spl. agt. FBI, Cleve., Atlanta, Pitts., 1956-79; commr. Pa. State Police, Harrisburg, 1979—. Served with CIC, AUS, 1945-48. Mem. FBI Ex-Agts., Internat. Chiefs of Police Assn., Pa. Chiefs of Police Assn. Roman Catholic. Office: 1800 Elmerton Ave Harrisburg PA 17109

DUNN, DAVID E., geological consultant; b. Dallas, Oct. 13, 1935; s. Nelson E. and Lamoine (Kellett) Dunn N.; m. Gretchen Yost, Jan. 24, 1958; 1 son, Dusty Peter. B.S. in Geology, So. Meth. U., 1957, M.S., 1959; Ph.D., U. Tex., 1964. Cert. profl. geologist. Instr. geology U. Tex., Austin, 1960-61; asst. prof. geology Tex. Tech. Inst., Lubbock, 1962-63, U. N.C., Chapel Hill, 1963-66, assoc. prof., 1967-73, prof., 1973-79; dean coll. sci. U. New Orleans, 1979—; cons. various legal firms, N.C., 1967-79, Pennzoil, Houston, 1980—, Amoco, Tulsa, 1982—; chmn. La. Univs. Marine Consort, Baton Rouge, 1981-83. Co-author: A Characterization of Faults in the Appalachian Foldbelt, 1980; contbr. chpt. to book, articles to sci. jours. Fund-raiser numerous candidates, Chapel Hill, 1969-75. Fellow Geol. Soc. Am. (chmn. structure and tectonics div. 1983); mem. Am. Geophys. Union, AAAS, Am. Inst. Profl. Geologists, Carolina Geol. Soc. (chmn. 1968-69). Office: Coll Scis U New Orleans-Lakefront New Orleans LA 71048

DUNN, EDWARD CLARE, former army officer; b. White Lake, S.D., Feb. 28, 1913; s. Peter George and Catherine (Hanten) D.; m. Jane Ellen Grace, June 15, 1940; children—Peter, Michael, John, Patrick. B.S., U.S. Mil. Acad., 1936; M.A., Harvard, 1950; grad., Army Command and Staff Coll., 1951, Army War Coll., 1955. Commd. 2d lt. U.S. Army, 1936, advanced through grades to maj. gen., 1965; troop officer, 1935-42, comdr. battalion and regt., 1943-45, instr., 1946-50, various staff and command assignments in, U.S., Turkey, S. Vietnam, 1951-61, dep. comdt., 1963-64, chief staff, 1964-65, 1965-68. Author: USAA: Life Story of a Business Cooperative, 1970; Co-author: Dawn at PM, 1983; also articles. Decorated Distinguished Service medal, also the; Legion of Merit; Joint Services Commendation medal; Bronze Star; Army Commendation medal (2); Croix de Guerre with palm, France). Mem. United Services Automobile Assn. (bd. dirs. 1965-68, mem. exec. com. San Antonio 1967-68), Assn. U.S. Army (past chpt. v.p.). Club: Ft. Leavenworth Hunt (Kans.) (past pres.). Home: 123 Brandon Dr E San Antonio TX 78209 *As a soldier, I fought for the country I believe in. As a writer, I can only write about people and institutions in which I believe.*

DUNN, EDWARD K., JR., investment banker; b. Balt., May 20, 1935; s. Edward K. and Anne (Butler) D.; m. Janet Evans, June 14, 1958; children: J. Holliday, Edward K., Peter C. A.B., Princeton U., 1958; M.B.A., Harvard U., 1960. C.F.A., Inst. Chartered Fin. Analysts, 1966. Securities analyst Robert Garrett & Sons, Balt., 1960-64, various positions, 1964-73, pres., 1973-74; gen. ptnr. Alex Brown & Sons, Balt., 1974—; dir. Provident Savs. Bank, Green Mt. Cemetery. Chmn., pres. Johns Hopkins Hosp. Endowment Fund, 1976—; pres. Hopkins Assocs., 1982—; trustee Johns Hopkins Hosp., Evergreen House Found., Robert Garrett Fund for Surg. Treatment for Children, Family and Children's Soc. Balt., Garrison Forest Sch., Thomas Nilson Sanitarium, Transit Action Group. Democrat. Roman Catholic. Home: Vesper Hill 7315 W Bellona Ave Baltimore MD 21212 Office: 135 E Baltimore St Baltimore MD 21202

DUNN, ELWOOD, clergyman; b. Grant County, Ind., Jan. 8, 1906; s. Sylvester M. and Ida Belle (Ferrell) D. B.S.L. cum laude, Butler U., 1929, M.Div., Christian Theol. Sem., 1941; postgrad., Wayne State U.; grad. student, Mich. State U. Ordained to ministry Christian Ch., 1926; minister in, Palestine, Ind., 1926-30, Etna Green, Ind., 1926-36, Medaryville, Ind., 1936-39, N. Salem, Ind., 1939-43, Wabash, Ind., 1943-46, Pontiac, Mich., 1946-49; gen. sec. Mich. Christian Endeavor Union, Detroit, 1948—; v.p. Leadership Tng., Inc., 1952-55; minister Ferndale (Mich.) Christian Ch., 1962—; asst. dir. Neighborhood Youth Corps, Pontiac, 1967, dir., 1967-73; Mgr. div. manpower Oakland Livingston Human Serves Agy., 1973-78; Mem. Ind. youth work com. Christian Ch., 1936-40, chmn. Mich. youth work com., 1947-49; pres. Ministerial Assn., Wabash, 1943-44; v.p. Great Lakes region Internat. Soc. Christian Endeavor, 1951-55, 1955-61, chmn. youth work com., 1955-67, mem. exec. com., 1955—, pres., 1967-71; trustee World's Christian Endeavor Union. Co-author: Training for Service Senior High Department, 1966. Mem. Mayor Pontiac Com. Youth Opportunity, 1968-71, Avondale Area Youth Guidance Com., 1968-71; chmn. Oakland County Youth Assistance Com., 1971—. Recipient scholastic honors award dept. Christian doctrine Butler U., 1929. Mem. Theta Phi. Club: Exchange (Disting. Service award 1982). Home: 640 3d St Pontiac MI 48055 Office: 3201 Hilton Rd Ferndale MI 48220

DUNN, FLOYD, biophysicist, bioengineer, educator; b. Kansas City, Mo., Apr. 14, 1924; s. Louis and Ida (Leibtag) D.; m. Elsa Tanya Levine, June 11, 1950; children: Andrea Susan, Louis Brook. Student, Kansas City Jr. Coll., 1941-42, Tex. A. and M. U., 1943; B.S., U. Ill., Urbana, 1949, M.S., 1951, Ph.D., 1956. Research asso. elec. engring. U. Ill., Urbana, 1954-57, research asst. prof. elec. engring., 1957-61, asso. prof. elec. engring. and biophysics, 1961-65, prof., 1965—, prof. elec. engring., biophysics and bioengring., 1972—, dir. bioacoustics research lab., 1976—, chmn. bioengring. faculty, 1978-82; vis. prof. dept. microbiology Univ. Coll., Cardiff, Wales, 1968-69; vis. sr. scientist Inst. Cancer Research, Sutton, Surrey, Eng., 1975-76, 82-83; vis. prof. Inst. Chest Diseases and Cancer, Tohoku U., Sendai, Japan; mem. radiation study sect. NIH, 1976-81; steering com. NSF Workshop on Interaction of Ultrasound and Biol. Tissues, 1971-72; chmn. WHO working group on health aspects of exposure to ultrasound radiation, London, 1976; mem. tech. elec. products radiation standards com. FDA, 1974-76. Editorial bd.: Ultrasonic Imaging, others; manuscript reviewer: Jour. Phys. Chemistry, Jour. Acoustical Soc. Am., IEEE Transactions, others; Contbr. articles on biophys. acoustics to profl. jours. Trustee Hensley Twp., Ill., 1980-81. Served with AUS, 1943-46. NIH Spl. Research fellow Univ. Coll., Cardiff, 1968-69; Am. Cancer Soc.-Eleanor Roosevelt-Internat. Cancer fellow, 1975-76, 82-83; Fulbright Fellow, 1982-83; Japan Soc. for Promotion of Sci. Fellow, 1982. Fellow Acoustical Soc. Am. (asso. editor Jour., v.p. 1981-82), Am. Inst. Ultrasound in Medicine, IEEE, Inst. Acoustics (U.K.); mem. Am. Inst. Physics, Biophys. Soc., Nat. Acad. Engring., AAAS, Sigma Xi, Sigma Tau, Eta Kappa Nu, Tau Beta Pi, Pi Mu Epsilon, Phi Sigma. Home: Rural Route 3 Box 295 Champaign IL 61820 Office: Bioacoustics Research Lab U Ill 1406 W Green St Urbana IL 61801 *Excellent, dedicated and understanding teachers, bright and energetic students, and a single-mindedness to see a problem to solution are the ingredients for a modicum of success.*

DUNN, FRANCIS G., state justice; b. Scenic, S.D., Nov. 12, 1913; s. Thomas B. and Mary L. D.; m. Betty, Jan. 3, 1942; children—David, Rebecca, Tom, Carol. LL.B., U. S.D., 1937; M.A., George Washington U. Bar: S.D. bar 1937. Practice law, Madison, S.D., to 1941; former sec. to U.S. Senator W.J. Bulow; trial atty. Dept. Justice, Washington, 1946-50; asst. U.S. atty. for, S.D., 1950-54; asso. firm Doyle, Mahoney & Dunn, Sioux Falls, S.D., 1954-56; judge Sioux Falls Municipal Ct., 1956-59, S.D. Circuit Ct., 1959-73; justice S.D. Supreme Ct., 1973—, chief justice, 1974-78. Office: SD Supreme Ct State Capitol Pierre SD 57501

DUNN, FRANCIS JOHN, bishop; b. Elkader, Iowa, Mar. 22, 1922; s. Peter A. and Josephine (Feeney) D. B.A., Loras Coll., Dubuque, Iowa, 1944; degree in philosophy, Kenrick Sem., St. Louis, 1948; J.C.L., Angelicum U., Rome, Italy, 1960. Ordained priest Roman Cath. Ch., 1948; asst. pastor in, Iowa, 1948-56; asst. chancellor Archdiocese Dubuque, 1956-60, chancellor, 1960—, aux. bishop, 1969—; vicar gen. Archdiocese of Dubuque, 1969—; pastor St. Joseph's Ch., 1969-76; dir. Family Life Program Archdiocese Dubuque, 1956-69, Cemetery Assn., 1960-69. Trustee United Fund Dubuque; trustee Divine Word Coll., Epworth, Iowa; com. mem. N.Am. Coll., Louvain, Belgium; bd. dirs. N.E. Iowa council Boy Scouts Am.; Episcopal moderator Worldwide Marriage Encounter. Mem. Nat. Council Cath. Bishops (mem. edn. com., pro life activities com.), Dubuque C. of C., Cath. Order Foresters. Club: K.C. (4 deg.). Home: 1227 Blackhawk Dr Dubuque IA 52001

DUNN, H. STEWART, JR., lawyer; b. Pitts., July 9, 1929; s. H. Stewart and Marie (Galvin) D.; m. Martha J. Hoovler (dec. Sept. 1975); children—Christopher T., Anthony S., Timothy P.; m. Loti Kennedy, Aug. 3, 1978. A.B., Yale U., 1951; LL.B. magna cum laude, Harvard U., 1954. Bar: D.C. bar 1954, U.S. Supreme Ct. bar 1960. Asso. firm Ivins, Phillips & Barker, Washington, 1957-61, partner, 1962—; adj. prof. Georgetown U. Law Center, 1976—; chmn. U.S. Com. Selection Jud. Officers. Bd. editors: Harvard Law Rev, 1953-54. Mem. Am. Bar Assn. Office: 1700 Pennsylvania Ave NW Washington DC 20006

DUNN, HARRY LIPPINCOTT, lawyer; b. Santa Barbara, Calif., Feb. 24, 1894; s. Ebenezer Pedrick and Margaret Ann (Robinson) D.; m. Louise Dodge Reding, Feb. 7, 1925 (dec. 1952); children—Peter Reding, Priscilla (Mrs. Priscilla D. Flynn); m. Katharine Tilt McCay, Feb. 3, 1955 (dec. 1976). A.B., U. Calif., 1915; postgrad., Columbia Law Sch., 1915-16, Harvard, 1919-21. Bar: N.Y. State bar 1922, Calif. bar 1925. Asso. firm Cravath, Henderson, Leffingwell & de Gersdorff, N.Y.C., 1921-24, O'Melveny & Myers, Los Angeles, 1924-27, partner firm, 1927-68, counsel, 1968—. Trustee Claremont U. Center. Served Commn. for Relief in Belgium, 1916-17; with Am. Field Service, 1917; France; 1st lt., 6th F.A., 1st Div. AEF, 1917-19; with Am. Relief Adminstrn. in Poland, 1919. Mem. Am., Los Angeles bar assns., Am. Bar Found., Los Angeles C. of C., Harvard Law Sch. Assn. (past v.p.), Friends of Claremont Colls. (past pres.), Los Angeles World Affairs Council (past v.p., Phi Delta Theta.). Republican. Clubs: California (Los Angeles); Annandale Golf, Harvard, Zamorano, Twilight, Valley Hunt (Pasadena, Calif.). Home: 1360 Hillcrest Ave Pasadena CA 91106 Office: 400 S Hope St Los Angeles CA 90071

DUNN, HELEN ASHLEY, nurse, univ. dean; b. Muskogee, Okla., Nov. 22, 1925; d. Alvin Homer and Mary Marie (Smyser) Ashley; m. James B. Dunn, Aug. 31, 1947; children—Alice Jean Dunn Samson, Theresa Jan Dunn Ashton. Diploma, Sparks Meml. Hosp. Sch. Nursing, 1947; B.S., U. Houston, 1958; M.P.H., Tulane U., 1963, D.P.H., 1974. Staff nurse U. Ark. Infirmary, 1947; relief supr. Sparks Meml. Hosp., Fort Smith, Ark., 1947; pvt. duty nurse, Fayetteville, Ark., 1947-48; nurse VA Hosp., Fayetteville, 1948-49, Shell Refinery, Deer Park, Tex., 1950, physician's office, Houston, 1951-52, Tex. Children's Hosp., 1954-58; sch. nurse Houston Ind. Sch. Dist., 1958-61; instr. Mather's Sch. Nursing, New Orleans, 1963-65, SE La. Hosp., 1965-67; asst. prof. Southeastern La. U., 1967-71, Nicholls State U., 1971; sch. nurse, cons. Orleans Parish Sch. Bd., 1971-72; faculty La. State U. Med. Center Sch. Nursing, New Orleans, 1971—, acting dean, 1976-77, dean, 1977—; teaching asst. Tulane U., 1972-74; coordinator State of La. Health and Social Rehab. Services Adminstrn., 1974; workshop cons. U. So. Miss., 1974. Mem. implementation com. New Orleans Area/Bayou River Health Systems Agy., 1973—, bd. dirs., 1978—; mem. State of La. Nurse Stipend Com., 1977—; bd. dirs. Tchefuncta Club Estates; mem. adminstrv. bd. First United Meth. Ch. Mem. Am. Nurses Assn., La. State Nurses Assn., Fla. Parishes Dist. Nurses Assn., S. La. League Nursing, Nat. League Nursing, Am. Assn. Colls. Nursing, La. State U. Med. Center Sch. Nursing Alumni Assn. (hon.), Delta Omega. Home: 45 Riverdale Dr Covington LA 70433 Office: La State U Med Center Sch Nursing 420 S Prieur St New Orleans LA 70112

DUNN, HORTON, JR., organic chemist; b. Coleman, Tex., Sept. 3, 1929; s. Horton and Lora Dean (Bryant) D. B.A. summa cum laude, Hardin-Simmons U., 1951; M.S., Case Western Res. U., 1975, Ph.D., 1979. Research chemist Lubrizol Corp., Cleve., 1953-70, dir. tech. info. ctr., 1970-79, supr. research div., 1980—; chmn. bd., bus. mgr. Isotopics, Cleve., 1964-67, editor, 1961-63. Contbr. articles to profl. jours.; patentee (in field). Mem. Am. Chem. Soc. (chpt. treas. 1968-70), Am. Soc. for Info. Sci. (chpt. pres. 1973-74), AAAS, Beta Phi Mu, Alpha Chi. Home: 530 Sycamore Dr Cleveland OH 44132 Office: 29400 Lakeland Blvd Wickliffe OH 44092

DUNN, JAMES JOSEPH, mag. pub.; b. N.Y.C., July 22, 1920; s. James A. and Mary A. (Kelly) D.; m. Elinor M. Hargesheimer, Aug. 30, 1943; children—Patricia Ann, Kevin James, Gregory John, Sean David, Christopher Kelly. B.B.A., Manhattan Coll., 1941. With McCall Corp., 1946-50; with Time, Inc., 1950-66, advt. dir., N.Y.C., 1961-66; pub., v.p. Forbes, Inc., 1966—. Bd. dirs. Salvation Army; trustee Manhattan Coll. Served to lt. comdr. USNR, 1941-46. Mem. Mag. Pubs. Assn. (dir.). Clubs: Blind Brook, Winged Foot Golf, Laurel Valley. Home: Glenville Rd Greenwich CT 06830 Office: 60 Fifth Ave New York NY 10011

DUNN, JAMES ROBERT, geologist; b. Sacramento, Oct. 18, 1921; s. Walter Ray and Frances (Latta) D.; m. Marjorie Ralph, Nov. 17, 1946 (div. 1970); children—Marsha, Brian, David, Sheldon; m. Nancy Berry Smyth, Oct. 24, 1970. A.B., U. Calif. at Berkeley, 1943, Ph.D., 1950. Asst. prof. Rensselaer Poly. Inst., 1950-55, asso. prof., 1955-65, prof., 1965-70, adj. prof., 1970-75; pvt. practice as geologic cons. various state agys. and to firms including Ind. Cement Co., Atlantic Cement, Houdaille Industries, Peckham Industries, N.Y. State U. Constrn. Fund; pres. James R. Dunn & Assos., Inc., 1960-70, chmn. bd., 1971-72, Dunn Geosci. Corp., 1972—; geologic cons., Latham, N.Y. Contbr. articles profl. jours. Fellow Geol. Soc. Am.; mem. AIME, Am. Inst. Prof. Geologists (v.p. 1969, pres.-elect 1979, pres. 1980, pres. Found. 1981), Assn. Engring. Geologists, Am. Concrete Inst., ASTM, Am. Inst. Planners, Empire State Concrete and Aggregate Producers Assn. (asso.), Pa. Sand and Gravel Assn. (asso.), Soc. Econ. Geologists, Nat. Sand and Gravel Assn. (asso.), Nat. Crushed Stone Assn. (asso.; dir. 1981), N.Y. Crushed Stone Assn., Sigma Xi, Phi Kappa Tau. Home: Mountain View Dr Averill Park NY 12018 Office: 5 Northway Ln N Latham NY 12110

DUNN, JIM, Congressman; b. Detroit, July 21, 1943; s. James Whitney and Pauline D.; m. Gayle Lynn Yerkey; children—Jeffrey, Julie, Kate. B.A. in Bus. Adminstrn, Mich. State U., 1967. Partner Dunn & Fairmont (constrn. co.), East Lansing, Mich., 1967—; mem. 97th Congress from 6th Mich. Dist., mem. sci. and tech. com., com. on vets. affairs; mem. Mich.'s Small Bus. Adv. Council. Chmn. Greater Lansing (Mich.) Council, Internat. Yr. of Disabled Persons; mem. Lansing Council on Arts, N.E.-Midwest Coalition, Congl. Auto Caucus, Congl. Solar Coalition. Mem. Nat. Home Bldg. Assn., Mich. Home Bldg. Assn., Mich. C. of C., Lansing C. of C. Republican. Episcopalian.

DUNN, JOHN JOSEPH, JR., advertising executive; b. Yonkers, N.Y., July 2, 1937; s. John Joseph and Anna Mary (Griggs) D.; m. Katherine Marie Ender, Nov. 14, 1959; children: Barbara, Michael, Thomas, Brian. B.A., Iona Coll., 1961. Media trainee-account exec. Dancer-Fitzgerald & Sample Inc., N.Y.C., 1955-60, v.p. account supr., 1960-73; v.p., accoutn supr. Waring & La Rosa, N.Y.C., 1974-77; v.p. mktg. Knickerbocker Toy Co., N.Y.C., 1977-79; sr. v.p., account dir. McCann-Erickson Inc., N.Y.C., 1979—; dir. tng. program McCann U., N.Y.C., 1982—. Vice-chmn. Zoning Bd. Adjustment, Dumont, N.J., 1975—; mgr. farm div. Dumont Little League, 1970—. Lodge: K.C. Home: 13 Blanche Ct Dumont NJ 07628 Office: McCann-Erickson Inc 485 Lexington Ave New York NY 10017

DUNN, JOHN MICHAEL, association executive; b. Los Angeles, July 22, 1927; s. John Michael and Mary Janet (Murphy) D.; m. Mary Frances Hobbs, Nov. 17, 1950; children: Alan Michael, Neal Patrick. A.B., Harvard U., 1948; M. Pub. Adminstrn., Princeton U., 1959, M.A., 1960, Ph.D., 1961; grad., Nat. War Coll., 1967. Commd. 2d lt. U.S. Army, 1949, advanced through grades to maj. gen., 1971; personal asst. ambassador to, Vietnam, 1963-64, asst. to v.p. of U.S., 1969-74; exec. dir. Council Internat. Econ. Policy, Office of Pres., 1974-76; pres. Can Mfrs. Inst., Washington, 1976—. Contbr. articles, reviews to profl. and popular jours. Decorated D.S.M., Legion of Merit, Silver Star, Bronze Star, Purple Heart; numerous fgn. decorations, including; Knights of Malta; Knights of Saint Denis. Mem. Pi Eta. Clubs: Pisces, Federal City, Capitol Hill, 1925 F Street. Home: 2707 N Nelson St Arlington VA 22207 Office: Can Mfrs Inst 1625 Massachusetts Ave NW Washington DC 20036

DUNN, LEO JAMES, obstetrician, gynecologist, educator; b. Trenton, N.J., May 23, 1931; s. Augustine Leo and Molly (McDaid) D.; m. Betty Beatrice Buchanan, Aug. 28, 1954; children: Laurie, Cary. A.B., Hofstra U., 1952; M.D., Columbia U., 1956. Diplomate: Am. Bd. Ob-Gyn. Intern Cin. Gen. Hosp., 1956-57; resident Sloane Hosp for Women, Columbia-Presbyn. Med. Ctr., 1957-62; asst. prof. ob-gyn U. Iowa Coll. Medicine, Iowa City, 1962-65, assoc. prof. ob-gyn, 1965-67; prof., chmn. dept. Med. Coll. Va., Richmond, 1967—; bd. dirs. Am. Bd. Ob-Gyn, 1975—, pres., 1982—; mem. Nat. Bd. Med. Examiners, 1979-83. Recipient Silver medal as disting. alumnus Columbia U. Coll. Physicians and Surgeons, 1967; Markle scholar, 1963. Fellow Am. Coll. Ob-Gyn (dist. v.p. 1976-78); mem. Soc. Gynecol. Oncology (chmn. program com., v.p.), Am. Assn. Ob-Gyn (council 1975-79, pres. found. 1980-82, trustee 1975-82), Va. Ob-Gyn Soc. (pres. 1981-82), Phi Beta Kappa. Office: Dept Ob-Gyn Med Coll Va 1100 E Marshall St Richmond VA 23298

DUNN, MARVIN IRVIN, physician; b. Topeka, Dec. 21, 1927; s. Louis and Ida (Leibtag) D.; m. Maureen Cohen, Mar. 10, 1956; children—Jonathan Louis, Marilyn Paulette. B.A., U. Kans., 1950, M.D., 1954. Intern USPHS, San Francisco, 1954-55; resident U. Kans., 1955-58, fellow, 1958-59, instr. medicine, 1958-60, asso. in medicine, 1960-62, asst. prof. medicine, 1962-65, asso. prof., 1965-70, prof., 1970—, Franklin E. Murphy Disting. prof., 1978—; dir. Cardiovascular Lab.; head sect. Cardiovascular Disease Med. Center, 1963—, dean, 1980—; cons. USAF, 1971—. Author: Translator Deductive and Polyparametric Electrocardiography, 1970, (with others) Clinical Vectorcardiography and Electrocardiography, 2d edit, 1977; editorial bd.: Am. Jour. Cardiology, 1970—, Catheterization and Cardiovascular Diagnosis, 1980—; editorial cons.: Chest, 1980—, Practical Cardiology, 1980—; cons., reviewer: Griffith Resource Library, 1980—. Bd. dirs. Hebrew Acad. Jewish Geriatric and Convalescent Center, Beth Shalom Synagogue. Served with AUS, 1946-47. Fellow A.C.P., Am. Coll. Chest Physicians (dir.; gov. State of Kans.), Am. Coll. Cardiology, Am. Heart Assn.; mem. Am. Physicians Fellowship (dir.), Univ. Cardiologists, Alpha Omega Alpha, Phi Chi. Home: 3205 Tomahawk Rd Shawnee Mission KS 66208 Office: 39th and Rainbow St Kansas City KS 66103 *My small modicum of success was achieved by hard work, dedication to a single goal, and an application of total energy in achieving this goal. Open-mindedness, imaginativeness, and fair play have helped to make the road easier.*

DUNN, MARY MAPLES, historian, coll. dean; b. Sturgeon Bay, Wis., Apr. 6, 1931; d. Frederic Arthur and Eva (Moore) Maples; m. Richard S. Dunn, Sept. 3, 1960; children—Rebecca Cofrin, Cecilia Elizabeth. B.A., Coll. William and Mary, Williamsburg, Va., 1954; M.A., Bryn Mawr Coll., 1956, Ph.D., 1959. Faculty Bryn Mawr Coll., 1958—, prof. history, 1974—, acting dean, 1978-79, dean, 1980—. Author: William Penn: Politics and Conscience, 1967; Editor: Political Essay on the Kingdom of New Spain (Alexander von Humboldt), 1972, (with Richard S. Dunn) Papers of William Penn, 1979-80. Recipient Lindbeck Found. award distinguished teaching, 1969; Fellow Inst. Advanced Study Princeton U., 1974. Mem. Berkshire Conf. Women Historians (pres. 1973-75), Coordinating Com. Women Hist. Profession (pres. 1975-77), Am. Hist. Assn., Inst. Early Am. History and Culture (chmn. adv. council 1977-80), Phi Beta Kappa. Office: Office of Dean Taylor Hall Bryn Mawr Coll Bryn Mawr PA 19010

DUNN, MIGNON, mezzo-soprano; b. Memphis; m. Kurt Klippstaller, July 1972. Studied in, Memphis; pupil of, Karin Branzell, Armen Boyajian, Mrs. Hardesty Johnson; Dr. Music (hon.), Southwestern at Memphis. Debut at Town Hall with, Little Orch. Soc., 1954, debut in, New Orleans as, Carmen, 1955; debut at, N.Y.C. Opera as, Carmen, 1956; debut with Met. Opera; as nurse in: Boris Godunoff, 1958, debut Arena DiVerona, Italy, 1970, Covent Garden, Eng., 1973; appeared with maj. opera cos., throughout Europe and U.S., including, Paris Opera, Vienna State Opera, Hamburg State Opera; numerous roles including Judith in: Bartok's Bluebeard's Castle; Azucena in: Verdi's Il Trovatore; Dalila in: Saint Saens' Samson et Dalila; Carmen in: Bizet's Carmen; Marina in: also entire Wagnerian repertoire of mezzo-soprano roles Mussorgsky's Boris Godunov; recitalist also recs. for, Angel Records. Recipient Bethoven prize, Memphis; Exptl. Opera Theatre Am. award, 1955. Address: care Columbia Artists Mgmt Inc 165 W 57th St New York NY 10019 *

DUNN, NORMAN SAMUEL, business executive; b. Woonsocket, R.I., Sept. 17, 1921; s. Israel M. and Ida (Mayerson) D.; m. Mildred M. Michaels, Aug. 31, 1975; 1 son, by previous marriage, Jeffrey Mark. Ph.B. cum laude, Providence Coll., 1942. Purchasing agt. Uniroyal Inc., Conn., 1942-48; pres. Emerson Textile Co., Chelsea, Mass., 1948-64; exec. v.p., treas. Chelsea Industries Inc., 1964—; chmn. bd. Am. Shacks Inc., 1982—; dir. NFA Corp. Mem. Two Ten Nat. Found. Clubs: Belmont Country (Mass.); Rockrimmon Country (Stamford, Conn.). Home: Bayberry Way Pound Ridge NY 10576 Office: 181 Spencer Ave Chelsea MA 02150

DUNN, PARKER SOUTHERLAND, chemical company consultant; b. Portsmouth, Ohio, Aug. 25, 1910; s. Joseph Sidney and Florence (Bowen) D.; m. Mayde Smith, July 15, 1939; children: Joseph Smith, Dwight James. B.Chem. Engring., Ohio State U., 1930; M.S., MIT, 1931. Tech. asst. Mead Corp., Chillicothe, Ohio, 1930-32; foreman Columbia Southern Corp., Barberton, Ohio, 1932-33, asst. plant supt., Corpus Christi, Tex., 1934-38, tech. dir., 1938-41; research dir. Potash Co. Am., Carlsbad, N.Mex., 1941-46, resident mgr., 1946-51; asst. v.p. Am. Potash & Chem. Corp., Trona, Calif., 1951-52, v.p., Trona, 1952-55, Los Angeles, 1955-63, dir., 1958-71, pres., 1963-69, chmn. bd., 1969-71; v.p. Kerr McGee Corp., 1968-73, cons., 1975—; v.p. Kerr McGee Nuclear Corp., 1974-75; v.p., dir. Am. Lithium Chems. Co., 1959-64, San Antonio Chem. Co., 1957-75. Recipient Benjamin Garver Lamme engring. medal Ohio State U., 1966. Mem. Am. Inst. Chem. Engrs., AIME. Anglican. Clubs: Greens Country, Beacon (Oklahoma City). Home: 3332 Quail Creek Rd Oklahoma City OK 73120 Office: Kerr McGee Center Oklahoma City OK 73102

DUNN, RICHARD BRANDNER, solar astronomer; b. Balt, Dec. 14, 1927; s. Halbert Louis and Katherine (Brandner) D.; m. Alice Jane Biggam, July 21, 1951. B.M.E., U. Minn., 1949; M.S., 1950; Ph.D., Harvard U., 1961. Solar astronomer Sacramento Peak Obs., Sunspot, N.Mex., 1953—, acting dir., 1975-76. Served with U.S. Army, 1945-46. Mem. Am. Astron. Soc. Designer vacuum solar telescope, 1969. Home: 4015 Cholla Las Cruces NM 88001 Office: Sacramento Peak Observatory Sunspot NM 88349

DUNN, RICHARD JOHN, English educator; b. Pitts., June 8, 1938; s. John and Esther (Goe) D.; m. Virginia L. Dick, June 17, 1961; children: Richard, Susan, Catherine. B.A., Allegheny Coll., Meadville, Pa., 1960; M.A., Western Res. U., 1961, Ph.D., 1964. Asst. prof. English U.S. Air Force Acad., Colorado Springs, Colo., 1964-67; from asst. prof. to prof. English U. Wash., Seattle, 1967-82, dean summer quarter, 1980-82, chmn. dept. English, 1982—. Author: David Copperfield: An Annotated Bibliography, 1981; editor: The English Novel: Checklist of Twentiety Century Criticism, 1976, Jane Eyre: Critical Edition, 1971. Huntington Library fellow, 1983; named to Allegheny Coll. Athletic Hall of Fame, 1981. Mem. MLA, Dickens Soc. (pres. 1981-82), Dickens Fellowship. Office: Dept English U Wash Seattle WA 98195

DUNN, ROBERT EARL, lawyer; b. Grand Rapids, Mich., June 27, 1921; s. Ralph Orace and Luella Mary (McKay) D.; m. Doris Koehler, Dec. 29, 1977; children: Juliana Irene, William Robert. B.S. in Chemistry, Mich. State U., 1942; LL.B., U. Mich., 1950. Bar: Mich. 1951. Supr. ordnance plant Hercules Powder Co., 1942-43; pilot plant researcher Phillips Petroleum Co., 1943-46; pvt. practice, Grand Rapids, 1950-51; agt. FBI, 1951-52; patent atty. Phillips Petroleum Co., 1953-55; with BASF Wyandotte Corp., Parsipanny, N.J., 1955—, gen. counsel, corp. sec., 1969—. Mem. ABA, Am. Patent Law Assn., Assn. Corp. Counsel N.J., State Bar Mich. Office: BASF Wyandotte Corp 100 Cherry Hill Rd Parsippany NJ 07054

DUNN, ROBERT FRANCIS, naval officer; b. Chgo., June 15, 1928; s. Joseph Earl and Frances Madeline (Wilberding) D.; m. Annette Brown, Dec. 29, 1953; children: Carol, Diane. B.S., U.S. Naval Acad., 1951; M.S., U.S. Naval Postgrad. Sch., 1964. Commd. ensign U.S. Navy, 1951, advanced through grades to rear adm., 1976; naval aviator, Atlantic and Pacific, 1953-67; comdg. officer Amphibious Commandship, Mt. Whitney, 1973-74, Aircraft Carrier Saratoga, 1974-76; comdr. Naval Safety Center, Norfolk, Va., 1976-78, Carrier Group Eight, 1978-80, Naval Mil. Personnel Command, Washington, 1980-82. Decorated Silver Star (2), D.F.C. (2), others. Mem. U.S. Naval Inst., Assn. Naval Aviation., Naval Acad. Alumni, Naval Res. Assn., Naval Enlisted Res. Assn., Naval Aviation Mus. Found. Episcopalian. Home: 8854 Glenridge Ct Vienna VA 22180 Office: Chief Naval Reserve Washington DC 20350

DUNN, ROBERT JOSEPH, advt. agy. exec.; b. Orange, N.J., Sept. 7, 1941; s. Robert Joseph and Marie Grace (Breidt) D.; m. Phyllis Ann Kearney, June 13, 1964; children—Robert, James, Kevin, Matthew. B.A., Georgetown U., 1963. Vice pres. J. Walter Thompson Co., N.Y.C., 1965-77; sr. v.p. Doyle Dane Bernbach, Inc., N.Y.C., 1977—. Bd. dirs. Research Inst. Hearing and Balance Disorders. Served to 1st lt. USAR, 1963-65. Decorated Army Commendation medal; recipient Internat. TV and Film Festival award, 1979; Clio award, 1980; Gold medal N.Y. Art Dirs. Club, 1980; Bronze medal, 1980. Republican. Roman Catholic. Club: Apawamis (Rye). Home: 57 Osborn Rd Rye NY 10580 Office: 437 Madison Ave New York NY 10022

DUNN, SAMUEL WATSON, educator, former college dean; b. Vanderbilt, Pa., Aug. 24, 1918; s. Arthur Collins and Mary (Everett) D.; m. Elizabeth Carson Schick, Dec. 30, 1949; children: Mary Elizabeth, Eloise Schick. A.B., Harvard U., 1943, M.B.A., 1946; Ph.D., U. Ill., 1951. Instr. bus. adminstrn. U. Western Ont., London, 1946-47; asst. prof. bus. adminstrn. U. Pitts., 1947-49; research asst. U. Ill., Urbana, 1949-51, prof., head dept. advt., 1966-77; asst. prof. to prof. U. Wis., 1951-66; dean Coll. Bus. and Pub. Adminstrn., U. Mo., Columbia, 1977-80, prof. mktg. and journalism, 1980—; with Young & Rubicam, N.Y.C., 1957, Norman, Craig & Kummel, 1958, Leo Burnett Co., 1962; vis. Fulbright lectr. École Supérieure de Commerce, Lyons, France, 1959-60; chmn. Internat. Advt. Assn. Seminars, Lisbon (Portugal), Luanda (Angola), and Laurencö Marques, Mozambique, 1972, Nat. Conf. Univ. Tchrs. Advt., 1971; research projects, lectr. numerous fgn. countries. Author: Advertising Copy and Communication, 1956, International Handbook of Advertising, 1964, Advertising: Its Role in Modern Marketing, 5th edit, 1982, How Fifteen Transnational Corporations Manage Public Affairs, 1979, International Advertising and Marketing, 1979, also articles. Served with AUS, 1943-46. Recipient research grants Office Naval Research, 1964-66, Am. Assn. Advt. Agys. Ednl. Found., 1968-72, Marsteller Found., 1972-73, 75-76, Stanford Research Inst., 1974-75. Mem. Am. Mktg. Assn., Assn. Edn. in Journalism, Am. Acad. Advt. (pres. 1970-72), Acad. Internat. Bus., Kappa Tau Alpha., Beta Gamma Sigma, Alpha Kappa Psi. Presbyterian. Clubs: Rotary, Columbia Country. Home: 117 W Burnam Rd Columbia MO 65201 Office: 319 Middlebush Hall U Mo Columbia MO 65211

DUNN, THEODORE FRANKLIN, advt. exec.; b. N.Y.C., July 9, 1926; s. Irving and Anne (Hartman) D.; m. Lenore Feldhuhn, June 20, 1948 (div. Mar. 1969); children: Meryl (Mrs. Robert Hammond), Marjorie, Gary, Laurence; m. Susan Sloves Renoir, Aug. 18. 1978. B.A., George Washington U., 1948, M.A., 1950; Ph.D., Am. U., 1958. Research psychologist Dept. Army, 1950-57; account research supr. Kenyon & Eckhardt, Inc., N.Y.C., 1957-60; dir. communication research, v.p. Ted Bates Advt., N.Y.C., 1960-64; v.p., dir. research Kenyon & Eckhardt, Inc., 1964-69; also dir.; sr. v.p., dir. research services Benton & Bowles, Inc., N.Y.C., 1969-83, also dir.; pres. Dunn & David Inc., N.Y.C., 1983—; adj. asso. prof. Baruch Coll., N.Y.C., 1970-71; Bd. dirs. Advt. Research Found., 1979—, vice chmn., 1980, chmn., 1981-82. Served with AUS, 1944-46. Fellow Am. Psychol. Assn. (pres. consumer psychology div. 1972-73, council of reps. 1976-79); mem. Am. Assn. Advt. Agys. (chmn. research com. 1971-73), Am. Marketing Assn. (pres. N.Y. 1975-76), Am. Assn. Pub. Opinion Research, Copy Research Council (sec., treas. 1977-78, pres. 1978-79), Market Research Council. Home: 19 E 88th St New York NY 10028 Office: 164 Madison Ave New York NY 10016

DUNN, WALTER SCOTT, JR., mus. dir.; b. Detroit, Apr. 5, 1928; s. Walter Scott and Minnie (Van Lahr) D.; m. Jean Wendeberg, July 11, 1959. B.A., U. Durham, Eng., 1951; M.A., Wayne State U., 1953; Ph.D., U. Wis., 1971. Curator indsl. history Detroit Hist. Mus., 1952-56; chief curator State Hist. Soc. Wis., Madison, 1956-63; dir. Buffalo and Erie County Hist. Soc., 1963-78, Des Moines Center Sci. and Industry, 1978—. Author: Western Commerce 1760-1774, 1971, Second Front Now, 1943, 80. Served with AUS, 1946-47. Mem. Am. Assn. State and Local History, Am. Assn. Museums. Home: 510 NE 8th St Ankeny IA 50021 Office: 4500 Grand Ave Greenwood Ashworth Park Des Moines IA 50312 *Improvement of human and spiritual well-being can be achieved on a continuing, more vertical curve, only if we refuse to accept the status quo.*

DUNN, WARREN HOWARD, brewery exec.; b. Omaha, Sept. 25, 1934; s. John Ralph and Frances (Liddell) D.; m. Nancy Ann Nolan, July 2, 1955; children—Kathleen, Erin, Theresa, Maureen. B.S. in Bus. Adminstrn, Creighton U., Omaha, 1956, J.D., 1958. Bar: Nebr. bar 1958, Wis. bar 1967. Claims adjuster U.S. Fidelity & Guarantee Co., Omaha, 1958-59; spl. agt. FBI, 1959-66; with Miller Brewing Co., Milw., 1966—, v.p., gen. counsel, 1973—. Mem. Am. Bar Assn., Wis. Bar Assn., Nebr. Bar Assn., Milw. Bar Assn. Office: 3939 W Highland Blvd Milwaukee WI 53208

DUNN, WESLEY JOHN, dental educator; b. Toronto, Ont., Can., May 21, 1924; s. John James and Grace Eleanor (Bryan) D.; m. Jean Mildred Nicholls, Nov. 6, 1948; children: Steven, Brian, Bruce. D.D.S., U. Toronto, 1947. Individual practice dentistry, Toronto, 1947-55; editor Jour. Canadian Dental Assn., 1953-58; registrar, sec.-treas. Royal Coll. Dental Surgeons, Ont., 1956-65; dean Faculty Dentistry, U. Western Ont., London, 1965-82, prof. community dentistry, 1965—; Chmn. Ont. Council Univ. Health Scis., 1973-75; charter mem. Ont. Council Health, 1966-71; weekly dental columnist Toronto Star, 1972-74; Pres. Assn. Can. Faculties of Dentistry, 1976-78. Bd. dirs. Women's Coll. Hosp., Toronto, 1960-65, London YM-YWCA, 1966-70, United Community Services London, 1968-71. Fellow Am. Coll. Dentists, Royal Coll. Dentists Can. (hon.); mem. London Dist. Dental Soc., Ont. Dental Assn., Can. Dental Assn. (chmn. council edn. 1968-71). Home: 134 Wychwood Park London ON N6G 1R7 Canada

DUNN, WILLIAM GERARD, mag. pub. exec.; b. Pittsfield, Mass., June 9, 1925; s. William F. and Loretta F. (Kelly) D.; m. Marjorie A. Stenzel, May 24, 1952; children—Kathleen, Patricia, Nancy. B.A. in English, U. Mass., 1950, hon. D.Public Service, 1981. Mktg. trainee Life mag., 1951-52; salesman Haywood Pub. Co., 1952-59; nat. sales mgr. McCalls mag., 1959-68; v.p. mktg. Mag. Pub. Assn., N.Y.C., 1969-72; asst. v.p. Fawcett Publs., N.Y.C., 1972-74; v.p. advt. U.S. News & World Report, Washington, 1974-78, pub., 1978—, also dir. Served with USMCR, 1943-46. Office: U S News & World Report 2300 N St NW Washington DC 20037 also 45 Rockefeller Plaza New York NY 10020

DUNN, WILLIAM L., publishing executive; b. Des Moines, Jan. 13, 1936; s. William L. and Gladys (Gray) D.; m. Roberta E. Johnson, Nov. 3, 1960; children: Suzanne Lynne, Kara Lisa, Kristin Lisel, William Christopher. B.A., Drake U., 1961, postgrad., 1962. With Des Moines Register and Tribune, 1953-61; asst. prodn. mgr. Dow Jones & Co., Inc., Chgo., 1961, prodn. mgr., Chicopee, Mass., 1963-65, nat. prodn. mgr., Princeton, N.J., 1969-72, bus. mgr., mem. mgmt. com., 1972-75, v.p., bus. mgr., 1975-77, v.p., gen. mgr., 1977-80, pres/pub. Info. Services Group, pres. Operating Services Group, 1980—; dir. Dow Jones News Retrieval Service, Inc., Dow Jones Newsprint Co., Inc., D.J. Va. Co., Inc., Nat. Delivery Service, Extel Corp., Teleprinter Leasing Corp. Mem. Phi Beta Kappa, Alpha Tau Omega, Phi Eta Sigma. Office: Post Office Box 300 Princeton NJ 08540

DUNNAHOO, TERRY (MRS. THOMAS WILLIAM DUNNAHOO), author, editor; b. Fall River, Mass., Dec. 8, 1927; d. Joseph Alfred and Emma Marie (Dolbec) Janson; m. Thomas William Dunnahoo, Sept. 18, 1954; children: Kim, Sean, Kelly. Student, Fall River Bus. Inst., 1948-49. Sec. Fall River Bus. Inst., 1949-51, Edwin Macy, Fall River, 1951-52; land title researcher U.S. Navy, Guam, 1952-54; escrow officer S.W. Escrow Co., Inglewood, Calif., 1954-55; instr. Pasadena (Calif.) City Coll., 1971, 73, Pepperdine U., Los Angeles, 1971, So. Mass. U., Dartmouth, 1973, UCLA, 1976—; children's book editor, book reviewer W. Coast Rev. Books, 1977—; book reviewer Los Angeles Herald-Examiner, 1980—; story cons. Asselin Prodns., Inc. Author: Nellie Bly, 1970, Annie Sullivan, 1970, Emily Dunning, 1970, Before the Supreme Court—The Story of Belva Ann Lockwood, 1974 (So. Calif. Council on Lit. for Children and Young People award 1975), Who Cares About Espie Sanchez?, 1975, This Is Espie Sanchez, 1976, Who Needs Espie Sanchez?, 1977, (pseudonym Margaret Terry) Last of April, 1982. Mem. So. Calif. Council Lit. for Children and Young People, 1970—. Mem. Authors Guild Am., Calif. Writers Guild (membership com. 1973-74, dir. 1974-78), PEN (exec. bd. 1972-77, pres. Los Angeles Center 1975-77), Book Publicists So. Calif., Women in Film, Soc. Children's Book Writers. Home: 4061 Tropico Way Los Angeles CA 90065

DUNNE, JAMES ARTHUR, space scientist; b. N.Y.C., Mar. 5, 1934; s. Arthur James and Anna Cecelia (McCarthy) D.; m. Janet Keller, July 7, 1979; children: Michael, Sean, Eric James. B.A. magna cum laude, Hofstra U., 1955; M.A., Columbia U., 1957, Ph.D., 1960. Geologist Texaco Inc., Houston, 1958-59; chief physicist Philips Electronic Instruments, Mt. Vernon, N.Y., 1960-64, prin. scientist, 1967-68; sr. scientist Jet Propulsion Lab., Pasadena, Calif., 1964-67; project scientist Mariner Venus-Mercury, 1970-74; ocean expts. mgr. SEASAT-A Project, 1974-80, Office Tech. and Space Program Devel., 1980-83, Project Galileo, 1983—. Contbr. articles to profl. jours. Served with U.S. Army, 1957-58. Mem. AAAS, Sigma Xi. Home: 110 El Nido Ave Pasadena CA 91107 Office: Jet Propulsion Lab 4800 Oak Grove Dr Pasadena CA 91109

DUNNE, JOHN GREGORY, author; b. Hartford, Conn., May 25, 1932; s. Richard Edwin and Dorothy (Burns) D.; m. Joan Didion, Jan. 30, 1964; 1 adopted dau, Quintana Roo. B.A., Princeton U., 1954. Writer, editor Time mag., N.Y.C. Columnist: (with Joan Didion) Points West, Saturday Evening Post, 1967-69, The Coast, Esquire mag., 1976-77; author: books, including Delano" The Story of the California Grape Strike, 1967, The Studio, 1969, Vegas: A Memoir of a Dark Season, 1974, True Confessions, 1977, Quintana and Friends, 1978, Dutch Shea, Jr., 1982; (with Joan Didion) screenplay Panic in Needle Park, 1971, Play It As It Lays, 1972, True Confessions, 1981; contbr. articles to mags., including, Nat. Rev., New Republic, New York, Atlantic Monthly. Served with U.S. Army. Office: care Lynne Nesbit Internat Creative Mgmt 40 W 57th St New York NY 10019 *

DUNNE, JOHN HENRY, labor union official; b. Chgo., Sept. 28, 1928; s. Adeline D.; m. Ann Dunne, 1962; 5 children. Student, Ill. Inst. Tech., 1946-50, Loyola U., 1952-53, Harvard U., 1959. Field rep. United Hatters, Cap, and Millinery Workers Internat. Union, 1959-62; organizer Internat. Fedn. Profl. and Tech. Engrs., Silver Spring, Md., 1962-67, internat. sec.-treas., dir., 1967—. Served with U.S. Army, 1950-52. Office: Internat Fedn Profl and Tech Engrs 818 Roeder Rd Suite 702 Silver Spring MD 20910 *

DUNNE, PHILIP, writer, dir.; b. N.Y.C., Feb. 11, 1908; s. Finley Peter and Margaret (Abbott) D.; m. Amanda Duff, July 15, 1939; children—Miranda, Philippa, Jessica. Student, Harvard U., 1925-29. Bd. govs. Motion Picture Acad. Arts and Scis., 1946-48; Pres. bd. trustees Verde Valley Sch., Sedona, Ariz.; Chief prodn. bur. motion pictures OWI (overseas br.), 1942-45. Writer, dir., producer motion pictures, 1932—; writer: The Count of Monte Cristo, 1934, The Rains Came, 1939, Stanley and Livingstone, 1940, How Green Was My Valley, 1941, The Late George Apley, 1946, The Ghost and Mrs. Muir, 1947, Pinky, 1950, David and Bathsheba, 1951, The Agony and the Ecstasy, 1965; producer, dir.: Prince of Players, 1955; writer, producer, dir.: The View From Pompey's Head, 1956; writer, dir.: Ten North Frederick, 1958, Blue Denim, 1961, Blindfold, 1965; dir.: Lisa, 1963; Author: Mr. Dooley Remembers, 1963, Take Two-A Life in Movies and Politics, 1980; co-author: stage play Mr. Dooley's America, 1976; contbr.: short stories to New Yorker mag. Mem. Writers Guild Am. (Laurel award 1962, Valentine Davies award 1974), Dirs. Guild Am., Screen Producers Guild, Screen Writers Guild (v.p. 1938-40), Dramatists Guild. Home: 24708 Pacific Coast Hwy Malibu CA 90265

DUNNE, THOMAS LEO, editor, author; b. Providence, July 30, 1946; s. Leo Thomas and Cecilia Elizabeth (Manning) D.; m. Mary Morabito, July 7, 1969. A.B., Brown U., 1968; M.A., Columbia U., 1969, M. Phil., 1972. Articles editor Avant-Garde mag., N.Y.C., 1968; dir. coll. dept. Penguin Books, N.Y.C., 1969-71; exec. editor, trade div. St. Martin's Press, N.Y.C., 1971—. Author: history Ellis Island, 1971; novel The Scourge, 1979; humor The One Minute Lover, 1983. NIMH fellow, 1969-73. Mem. Book League N.Y. Democrat. Home: 25 Worthen Way Chappaqua NY 10514 Office: St Martin's Press Inc 175 Fifth Ave New York NY 10010

DUNNELL, ROBERT CHESTER, archaeologist, educator; b. Wheeling, W.Va., Dec. 4, 1942; s. Arthur and Kathryn (McCarter) D.; m. Mary Jewett Davidson, June 4, 1966. B.A., U. Ky., 1964; Ph.D. (Woodrow Wilson fellow, Univ. fellow), Yale U., 1967. Asst. prof. anthropology U. Wash., Seattle, 1967-71, asso. prof., 1971-74, prof., 1974—, chmn. dept. anthropology, 1973—; prin. investigator Nat. Park Service contracts, U.S. Army Corps Engrs. contracts; adj. curator N.Am. archaeology Burke Meml. Wash. State Mus., 1971—; mem. sci. com. Wash. Archaeol. Research Center, 1975—; adj. prof. Quaternary Research Center, 1976—; council from Anthropology to Quaternary Research Center Adv. Council, 1976—. Mem. editorial bd.: Advances in Archaeological Theory and Method, 1977—. Fellow Am. Anthrop. Assn., N.Y. Acad. Sci.; mem. Classification Soc., Soc. for Am. Archaeology, AAAS, Am. Soc. for Conservation Archaeology. Office: Dept Anthropology U Wash Seattle WA 98195

DUNNIGAN, FRANK JOSEPH, publishing company executive; b. Westport, Conn., Dec. 15, 1914; s. Francis P. and Kathryn (Grossmann) D.; m. Teresa L. Razete, Aug. 13, 1966. A.A., Jr. Coll. Conn., 1934; B.S., N.Y. U., 1940; L.H.D. (hon.), U. Bridgeport, 1976. Acct. Consol. Edison Co., N.Y.C., 1934-37; with Prentice-Hall, Inc., Englewood Cliffs, N.J., 1937—, exec. v.p., 1965-71, pres., chief exec. officer, 1971-80, chmn. bd., chief exec. officer, 1980-83, chmn. bd., 1983—, also dir. Trustee Pren-Hall Found. Served to capt. AUS, 1941-46. Recipient Madden Meml. award N.Y. U., 1980. Mem. Newcomen Soc., Phi Theta Kappa. Club: Manor (Mt. Pocono, Pa.). Home: 1500 Palisade Ave Fort Lee NJ 07024 Office: Prentice-Hall Sylvan Av Englewood Cliffs NJ 07631

DUNNIGAN, T. KEVIN, elec. and electronics mfg. co. exec.; b. 1938; (married). B.A. in Commerce, Loyola U., 1971. With Can. elec. distbg. co., prior to 1962; with Thomas & Betts Corps., Raitan, N.J., 1962—, pres., 1974-78, corp. exec. v.p. electronics, 1978-80, pres., chief operating officer, also dir. Office: Thomas & Betts Corp 820 Route 202 Raritan NJ 08869 *

DUNNIGAN, THOMAS JOHN, government official; b. Canton, Ohio, May 22, 1921; s. John Michael and Josephine Leona (Beck) D.; m. Rae Marie Fox; children: Michael, John, Ralph, Leo, Claudia. A.B., John Carroll U., 1943; M.A., George Washington U., 1967. Fgn. service officer in, Berlin, 1946-50, London, 1950-54, Manila, 1955-56, Hong Kong, 1956-57; assigned Dept. of State, 1957-61, 65-69, 81—, Nat. War Coll., 1961-62, 62-65; polit. counselor, The Hague, 1969-72, dep. chief mission, Copenhagen, Denmark, 1972-75, Tel Aviv, Israel, 1975-77; diplomat-in-residence Centre Coll., Danville, Ky., 1977-78; dep. chief mission, The Hague, 1978-81, dep. U.S. rep. to OAS, 1983—. Served with AUS, 1943-46. Mem. Am. Fgn. Service Assn. Home: 2801 Park Center Dr Alexandria VA Office: ARA/OAS Washington DC

DUNNING, THOMAS EARL, newspaper editor; b. Lamasco, Ky., Nov. 2, 1944; s. Floyd Bowman and Tylene Elizabeth (Garrett) D.; m. Judy Davis, Feb. 28, 1981; 1 son, Thomas Matthew. B.A., U. Evansville (Ind.), 1967. Sportwriter The Evansville Press, 1962-67; city editor The Evansville Courier, 1970-76; Sunday editor The Knoxville News-Sentinal (Tenn.), 1976-77; asst. mng. editor The Cin. Post, 1977-81, mng. editor, 1981—. Bd. dirs. The Mental Health Assn., Cin., 1982, Leadership Cin., 1981-83. Served with USCG, 1967-70. Recipient 1st place Sportswriter award Ind. Collegiate Press Assn., 1964, 1st place newspaper layout award Press Club of Evansville, 1975. Mem. UPI (dir. Ohio Adv. Council 1983-84, recipient 1st place newspaper design award 1979, 3d v.p. 1983-84). Episcopalian. Club: Maketewah Country (Cin.). Home: 1315 Park Ridge Pl Cincinnati OH 45208 Office: The Cin Post 800 Broadway St Cincinnati OH 45202

DUNNOCK, MILDRED, actress; b. Balt. A.B., Goucher Coll.; M.A., Columbia. Made profl.: debut in Life Begins, N.Y.C., 1932; toured with, Katharine Cornell in, Herod and Marianne, 1938; with, George M. Cohan in, Madam, Will You Walk?, 1941; in: The Corn is Green, 1942; appeared in: Richard III, N.Y.C., 1943, Only the Heart, 1944, Foolish Notion, 1945, Another Part of the Forest, 1946, The Hallams, 1948, The Leading Lady, 1948, Death of a Salesman, 1949, Pride's Crossing, 1950; film version The Corn is Green, 1945, Child of Fortune, Love Me Tender, 1956, Baby Doll, 1956, Nun's Story, 1959, Story on Page One, 1960, Farewell Eugene, Butterfield 8, 1960, Sweet Bird of Youth, 1962, Seven Women, 1965, Barefoot in The Park, 1967, What Ever Happened to Aunt Alice?, 1969, Dragonfly, 1976; N.Y. stage play The Cantilevered Terrace, 1962, Traveller Without Luggage, 1964 (Recipient TV award 1955). Address: 888 7th St New York NY 10019 *

DUNOYER, PHILIPPE, petroleum industry executive; b. Paris, May 3, 1930; s. Bernard and Suzanne (De Mones) D.; m. Cynthia Troxell, Apr. 4, 1956; children: Cecilia, Louis, François, Jean. Grad. Engr., École Polytechnique, Paris, 1951; Certificate of Geology, U. Montpellier, France, 1952; postgrad. in geophysics, Colo. Sch. Mines, 1952-53, U. Calif., Los Angeles, 1953-54; postgrad. exec. program, Stanford U., 1970. With Compagnie Française des Petroles and Affiliates, 1954—, mgr. operational planning, coordinator, Paris, 1972-75; chmn. bd., pres., chief exec. officer Total Petroleum (N.Am.) Ltd.; chmn., pres., chief exec. officer Total Petroleum, Inc., Denver and; Calgary, Alta., Can., 1975—. Trustee Alma Coll., 1976. Served with French Army, 1953-54. Mem. Am. Petroleum Inst. (dir.), French Assn. Oil Industry Profls. (chmn. econ. com. 1968-71). Roman Catholic. Home: 2000 E 12th Ave Box 22 Denver CO 80206 Office: Total Petroleum (NAm) Ltd 999 18th St Suite 2201 PO Box 500 Denver CO 80201 639 5th Ave SW Calgary AB T2P 0M9 Canada

DUNPHY, DONAL, pediatrician, educator; b. Northampton, Mass., Feb. 24, 1917; s. Michael and Catherine (Duggan) D.; children—Karen, Christine, Michael, Colin. B.A., Holy Cross Coll., Worcester, Mass., 1939; M.D., Yale U., 1944. Diplomate: Nat. Bd. Pediatrics, Am. Bd. Pediatrics (mem.), Am. Bd. Family Practice (dir. 1976-81). Intern New Haven Gen. Hosp., 1943-45, resident, 1945-46; instr. pediatrics Yale Sch. Medicine, 1947-50; attending physician Bridgeport (Conn.) Gen. Hosp., 1950-53; pvt. practice medicine, specializing in pediatrics, Stratford, Conn., 1950-53; asso. pediatrics dept. U. Buffalo, 1955-56, asst. prof., 1956-59, asso. prof., 1959-61; prof., chmn. dept. pediatrics U. Iowa, 1961-73; prof. pediatrics Sch. Medicine, U. N.C., 1973—, acting chmn. dept. family medicine, 1975-76; dir. outpatient dept. Grace New Haven Hosp., 1947-50, Buffalo Children's Hosp., 1955-61; dir., co-investigator Child Devel. Program NINDB Collaborative Project, 1958-61, cons. to project, 1960-61. Served to capt. U.S. Army, 1953-55; ETO. Mem. Am. Acad. Pediatrics, Am. Pediatric Soc., Midwest Soc. Pediatric Research, N.Y. Acad. Sci., AAUP. Office: Dept Pediatrics U NC Sch Medicine Chapel Hill NC 27514

DUNPHY, T.J. DERMOT, manufacturing company executive; b. Dublin, Ireland, Apr. 15, 1932; came to U.S., 1954, naturalized, 1962; s. Phillip Augustine and Marion (Moore) D.; m. Joan Steinhardt, July 5, 1974; children: Deirdre Louise, Madeleine Gay, Shannon Beth. M.A., Oxford (Eng.) U., 1954; M.B.A., Harvard U., 1956. With Air Conditioning div. Westinghouse Electric Corp., Staunton, Va., 1956-61, mgr. mktg. services, 1961; pres. Custom-Made Paper Bag Co. (and subsidiaries), Long Island City, N.Y., 1961-70; pres., chief exec. officer Sealed Air Corp., Saddle Brook, N.J., 1971—, also dir.; dir. Potdevin Machine Co. (and subsidiaries), Teterboro, N.J., Loctite Corp., Newington, Conn. Mem. Young Presidents Orgn. (past chmn. chmn.). Clubs: Harvard, Harvard Bus. Sch. (N.Y.C.) (past pres.). Office: Park 80 Plaza East Saddle Brook NJ 07662 *

DUNSIRE, PETER KENNETH, fin. co. exec.; b. Man., Can., Mar. 1, 1932; s. Robert Anderson and Margaret (Kinnear) D.; m. Nancy Suzanne Hilts, Feb. 10, 1979; children—Robert Kenneth, Barbara Lynn. Student, U. B.C., Can. With AVCO Corp., from 1961; sr. v.p. AVCO Fin. Services; chmn. bd. Am. Benefit Plan Adminstrs. subs.; now pres. Carte Blanche Corp. *

DUNSKY, MENAHEM, advertising agency executive, communications consultant; b. Montreal, Que., Can., July 5, 1930; s. Simsom and Esther (Stilman) D.; m. Liliane Spector, Apr. 11, 1960 (div. 1975); children: Ron Abraham, Ilan Isaac, Dan David Gil. Teaching diploma, Jewish Tchrs. Sem., Montreal, 1948; B.A., Concordia U., Montreal, 1952; M.A., NYU, 1954; cert. of graduation, Parsons Sch. Design, 1956. Tchr. Jewish People's Schs., Montreal, 1948-52; asst. art dir. L.W. Frohlich Advt., N.Y.C., 1956-58; creative dir. Gordon, Lewinson Advt., Tel Aviv, Israel, 1958-59; lectr. art history Saidye Bronfman Cultural Centre, Montreal, 1960-63; pres. Dunsky Advt. Ltd., Westmount, Que., Can., 1960—; cons. Govt. of Man., Winnipeg, 1970-77, Govt. of Sask., Regina, 1971-82, Govt. of B.C., Victoria, 1972-75; panelist pub. symposium Politics and the Media, 1980. Chmn. bd. Saidye Bronfman Cultural Centre, 1969-70; officer Jewish People's Sch. System, Montreal, 1982—; chmn. edn. com. Bialik High Sch., Montreal, 1981—, chmn. personnel com., Montreal, 1983—; exec. mem. YM/YWHA, Montreal, 1969-71. Mem. Trans Can. Advt. Agy. Network-Toronto (founding mem.), Trans. Can. Advt. Agy. Network-Toronto (dir. 1962—), Trans Can. Advt. Agy. Network-Toronto (pres. 1965), Inst. Can. Advt.-Toronto (dir. 1972-75, chmn. profl. com. 1974-75), Advt. Agy. Council Que. (founding mem., exec. com. 1969-75). Jewish. Home: 4 Forden Ave Westmount PQ Canada H3Y 2Y7 Office: Dunsky Advt Ltd 1310 Greene Ave Westmount PQ Canada H3Z 2B2 *The extent to which one manages to meld the pursuit of one's career interests with considerations of a broader social nature has always served me as a principal concern. As well, I have tried to keep career considerations from diminishing the time and quality of attention which family and self deserve and require.*

DUNSMORE, BARRIE, television news correspondent; b. Sask., Can. Ed., Regina Coll. Formerly reporter and news anchorman various Can. TV and radio Stas.; gen. assignment corr. ABC-TV News, 1965-66, corr. Paris bur., 1966-68, chief Mediterranean bur., 1968-74; host Can. TV program W-5, 1974-75; mil. affairs corr. ABC News, 1975-76, diplomatic corr., 1976—, also chief corr., El Salvador, 1981. Office: ABC News 7 W 66th St New York NY 10023 *

DUNSON, WILLIAM ALBERT, biology educator; b. Cedartown, Ga., Dec. 17, 1941; s. James Blake and Eleanor (Adams) D.; m. Margaret E. Kvashay, Aug. 19, 1963; children: Mary Elizabeth, William Albert, David Brian. B.S. in Zoology with honors, Yale U., 1962; M.S. (teaching fellow 1962-63), U. Mich., 1964, Ph.D., 1965. Mem. faculty Pa. State U., University Park, 1965—, prof. biology, 1974—; adj. prof. biology U. Miami; chief scientist various internat. oceanographic expdns.; collaborator Everglades Nat. Park. Author: The Biology of Sea Snakes, 1975; 75 research papers. Queen fellow marine sci. Australia, 1972; hon. Fulbright fellow, 1972; NSF grantee, 1967—. Mem. Am. Physiol. Soc., AAAS, Soc. Study Amphibians and Reptiles (editorial bd. jour.), Am. Soc. Ichthyologists and Herpetologists, Herpetologists League, Fla. Acad. Sci. Home: 575 Brittany Dr State College PA 16801 Office: Pa State U 208 Mueller Bldg University Park PA 16802

DUNST, LAURENCE DAVID, advertising executive; b. N.Y.C., Feb. 21, 1941; s. Philip R. and Mae (Fruchthendler) D.; m. Diane Gordon, Dec. 22, 1962; children: Lee Gordon, Melissa Susan. B.A., Syracuse U., 1961. Advt. copywriter R.H. Macy & Co., 1961-63; with Daniel & Charles, N.Y.C., 1963—; pres. Laurence, Charles & Free, Inc., 1969—. Mem. Young Pres.'s Orgn. Home: 41 Huntting Ln East Hampton NY 11937 Office: 261 Madison Ave New York NY 10016

DUNSTON, ALFRED GILBERT, JR., bishop; b. Coinjock, N.C., June 25, 1915; s. Alfred Gilbert and Cora Lee (Charity) D.; m. Permilla Rollins Flack, June 18, 1940 (div. 1947); children—Carol Dunston Goodrich, Aingred Dunston James, Armayne Dunston Pratt. A.B., Livinstone Coll., 1938; student, Drew U., 1938-39, 41-42. Ordained elder African Methodist Episcopal Zion Ch., 1938, now minister; consecrated bishop; pastor chs., Advance, N.C., 1936, Thomasville, N.C., 1937-38, Atlantic City, 1941-43, Summit, N.J., 1946-48, Knoxville, Tenn., 1948-52, Wesley A.M.E. Zion Ch., Phila., 1952-63, Mother A.M.E. Zion Ch., N.Y.C., 1963-64; prof. Black Ch. History Inst. for Black Ministries, 1971—; bishop 4th Episc. area A.M.E. Zion Ch., Phila. Author: Black Man in Old Testament and Its World. Mem. Alpha Phi Alpha. Home: PO Box 19788 Philadelphia PA 19143 *

DUNTEMAN, GEORGE HENRY, psychologist; b. Little Falls, N.Y., Sept. 10, 1935; s. George Henry and Bertha Ernestine (Bollman) D.; m. Rosarie Ann Brandfino, Apr. 20, 1963; children: George Eric, Elizabeth Ann. B.A., St. Lawrence U., 1957; M.S., Iowa State U., 1959; Ph.D., La. State U., 1962. Grad. research asst. La. State U., Baton Rouge, 1959-62; asst. prof. U. Rochester Coll. Bus. Adminstrn., N.Y., 1962-63; research psychologist U.S. Army Personnel Research Office, Washington, 1963-64; assoc. prof. U. Fla., Gainesville, 1964-67; research project dir. Ednl. Testing Service, Princeton, N.J., 1967-69; chief sicentist Research Triangle Inst., Research Triangle Park, N.C., 1969—; NSF grant application reviewer. Author: Introduction to Linear Models, 1984, Introduction to Multivariate Analysis, 1984; editorial bd.: Ednl. and Psychol. Measurements; author, contbg. author numerous presentations, articles for profl. jours., policy reports to govt. agys. Recipient Profl. Devel. award Research Triangle Inst., 1977. Mem. Acad. Mgmt., Sigma Xi, Psi Chi, Sigma Alpha Epsilon. Home: 332 Wesley Dr ChapelHill NC 27514 Office: Research Triangle Institute PO Box 12194 Research Triangle Park NC 27514

DUNWIDDIE, CHARLOTTE, sculptor; b. Strasbourg, France, June 19, 1907. Student, Acad. Fine Arts, Berlin, Mariano Benlliure, Madrid, Alberto Lagos, Buenos Aires, Argentina. Nat. Academician. Editorial bd.: Nat. Sculpture Rev; One-woman shows, Kennedy Galleries, N.Y.C., Salon de Bellas Artes, Buenos Aires, Nat. Horse Show, Madison Sq. Garden, N.Y.C., Aqueduct Racetrack, N.Y.C., Pimlico Racetrack, Balt., Nat. Arts Club, N.Y.C., group shows include, NAD, N.Y.C., Nat. Sculpture Soc., N.Y.C., Allied Artists Am., N.Y.C., Am. Artists Profl. League, N.Y.C., Hudson Valley Art Assn., Pen and Brush, N.Y.C.; represented in permanent collections including, Mus. Brookgreen Gardens, Myrtle Beach, S.C., Marine Corps Mus., Washington, Mus. Am. Art, New Britain, Conn., O'Bannon Hall, USMC, Quantico, Va., Sem. of Redemptorist Fathers, Suffield, Conn., Ch. of Good Shepherd, Lima, Peru, Nuncio Palace, Lima, also pvt. collections. (Recipient numerous awards including 15 gold medals.). Fellow Allied Artists, Nat. Sculpture Soc. (pres. 1982—), Royal Soc. Arts (London); mem. Am. Artists Profl. League, Pen and Brush (pres. 1964-68). Club: Cosmopolitan.

DUNWODY, WILLIAM ELLIOTT, JR., lawyer; b. Jacksonville, Fla., Dec. 17, 1910; s. William Elliott and Reba (Williams) D.; m. Sara Jane Evans, June 8, 1940; children: Carolyn Dale, William Elliott III. LL.B., U. Fla., 1933. Bar: Fla. 1933. Practice in, Miami, 1935—; of counsel firm Mershon, Sawyer, Johnston, Dunwody & Cole, 1946—. Home: 1049 Malaga Ave Coral Gables FL 33134 Office: 1600 Southeast Bank Bldg Miami FL 33131

DUNWOODY, ROBERT CECIL, investment banker; b. Kings County, N.Y., Oct. 18, 1933; s. Cecil and Gertrude Ann (Moore) D.; m. Margaret Gordon Harmon, Nov. 16, 1958; children—Laura, William, Sean. B.B.A. cum laude, Baruch Sch. Bus., 1954. Account exec. Merrill Lynch, Pierce, Fenner & Smith, N.Y.C.; from br. mgr. to group v.p. E.I. duPont & Co., Rochester, N.Y., Boston and N.Y.C.; sr. v.p. sales, dep. dir. br. office group, dir. Paine, Webber, Jackson & Curtis Inc., N.Y.C.; gen. ptnr. Boettcher & Co., Boettcher Western Properties; dir. Cashfund, Paine Webber Income Properties.; mem. exec. com., pres. R.C. Dunwoody, Inc. Served with AUS, 1955-57. Republican. Clubs: Short Hills Racquets; Union League (N.Y.C.); Canoe Brook Country, Masons. Home: 23219 Shinglecreek Road Golden Co 80401 Office: Boettcher & Co 828 17th St Denver CO

DUNWORTH, JOHN, superintendent of schools; b. Los Angeles, Jan. 6, 1924; s. Charles William and Alice (Morris) D.; m. Lavona Anita Walden, July 7, 1956. B.A., U. Calif.-Berkeley, 1949, M.A., 1953; Ed.D., U. So. Calif., 1959. Spl. edn. cons. pub. schs. San Diego (Calif.) County, 1949-51; speech therapist Walnut Creek (Calif.) Sch. Dist., 1952-54; tchr., vice prin., prin. Torrance (Calif.) Unified Sch. Dist., 1954-59; asst. supt. Lawndale (Calif.) Sch. Dist., 1959-62; supt. schs. Beaumont (Calif.) Unified Sch. Dist., 1962-64; supt. dependents schs. Dept. Def., Pacific and Far East, 1964-66; dean Tchrs. Coll. Ball State U., Muncie, Ind., 1966-73; pres. George Peabody Coll. for Tchrs., Nashville, 1974-79; dean Coll. Edn., U. West Fla., Pensacola, 1979-82; supt. Santa Ana (Calif.) Unified Sch. Dist., 1982—; lectr. U. Redlands, 1963, U. Hawaii, 1965, U. So. Calif., 1968; del. World Conf. on Edn., Switzerland, 1975; commr. Ind. Sch. Fund Commn., 1969-73. Author: (with E. Stoops) Classroom Discipline, 1958, (with T. Drysdale) Millions of People, 1965, Kindergarten Overseas, 1967, (with L. Dunworth and E. Stoops) Kindergarten Overseas; bimonthly periodical Discipline, 1962—. Bd. dirs. Am. Council on Edn., 1974-75, Nashville Symphony, 1975-79, Tenn. Council Econ. Edn., 1976-79, Aerospace Edn. Found., 1981—; pres. Beaumont C. of C., 1963-64. Served with U.S. Maritime Service, 1943-46. Recipient Service award Los Angeles Community Chest, 1961, Distinguished Am. Educators medal Freedoms Found., Valley Forge, 1960, U.S. Sec. Def. medal for outstanding pub. service, 1976. Mem. Ind. Assn. Colls. for Tchr. Edn. (pres. 1970-71), Am. Assn. Sch. Adminstrs., Council Ednl. Facility Planners (dir. 1969-72), So. Assn. Colls. and Schs. (commn. on colls.), Am. Assn. Colls. for Tchr. Edn. (pres. 1975-76). Episcopalian. Club: Cosmos (Washington). Office: Santa Ana Unified Sch Dist 1405 French St Santa Ana CA 92701

DUPEE, PAUL RICH, JR., business executive; b. Boston, May 11, 1943; s. Paul Rich and Marilyn (Mayo) D.; m. Martha Perrone, Feb. 28, 1970 (div.). A.B., Brown U., 1967. Vice pres. Integrated Resources, Inc., N.Y.C., 1970-72; dir., sr. v.p. NASCO Internat., Inc., Ft. Atkinson, Wis., 1972-73; v.p. Gulf & Western Industries, N.Y.C., 1973-82; pres. Providence Capitol Corp., N.Y.C., 1982—; chmn. Capitol Life Ins. Co., Denver, Providence Washington Ins. Co., Providence Capitol Life Assurance, Ltd., London. Home: 1120 5th Ave New York NY 10028 Office: Providence Capitol Corp 499 Park Ave New York NY 10022

DU PEN, EVERETT GEORGE, sculptor, educator; b. San Francisco, June 12, 1912; s. George E. and Novelle (Freeman) DuP.; m. Charlotte Canada Nicks, July 1, 1939; children: Stuart, Destia, Novelle, William, Ninia, Marguerite. Student, U. So. Calif., 1931-33, Chouinard Art Sch., Los Angeles, summer 1932, Harvard Sch. Architecture, summer 1933; B.F.A. (scholar), Yale, 1937, 1937-38. Teaching fellow Carnegie Inst. Tech. Sch. Art, 1939-39; teaching asst. sculpture Washington U. Sch. Art, St. Louis, 1939-42; marine draftsman and loftsman Sausalito Shipbldg. Corp., Calif., 1942-45; instr. sculpture U. Wash. Sch. Art, Seattle, 1945-47, asst. prof., 1947-54, asso. prof. sculpture, 1954-60, prof. art, 1960-82, prof. emeritus, 1982—, chmn. sculpture div. One man exhbns., Bon Marche Nat. Gallery, Seattle, 1970, Fred Cole Gallery, Seattle, 1973, Pacific Luth. U., Tacoma, 1975; one man exhbns., Wash. Mut. Savs. Bank, Seattle, 1979-80; exhibited, Prix de Rome Exhbn., Grand Central Gallery, N.Y.C., 1935-37, 39, St. Louis Mus. Ann., 1939-42, N.A.D., N.Y.C., 1943, 49, 53-55, 57-58, Seattle Art Mus. Ann., 1945-59, Pa. Acad. Art, Phila., 1950-52, 55-58, Ecclesiastical Sculpture competition, 1950, Sculpture Center, N.Y.C., 1951, 53, 54, Pa. Acad. Fine Arts, 1954-58, Detroit Mus. Art, 1958, N.W. Inst. Sculpture, San Francisco Art Assn., 1959, Mainstreams, 1972, Marietta Coll.; Creator garden figures and portrait heads, small bronze, terra cotta, hardwood sculptures, archtl. medallions, sculpture panels for comml. bldgs. and theatres, figures and wood carvings various chs., relief panels, U. Wash. campus, 1946, 83, bronze fountain, Wash. State Library, Olympia, 1959; Du Pen Fountain; bronze fountain, Coliseum Century 21, Seattle World's Fair, 2 walnut screens, Municipal Bldg., Seattle, 8 large sculpture commns. Seattle chs., 1957-64; wood carving Risen Christ, St. Pius X Cath. Ch., Montlake Terrace, Wash., 1983; Bronze Figure, Edmonds, Wash., 1983-84, bronze sculpture of Charles Odegaard, Pres. U. Wash., 1973, pvt. commns. Mem. U. Wash. Senate, 1952-55, exec. com., 1954-55; v.p. Allied Arts Movement for Seattle; mem. Seattle Municipal Art Commn., 1958-63. Recipient Saltus gold medal NAD, 1954, 1st prize for sculpture Bellevue (Washington) Arts and Crafts Fair, 1957; U. Wash. research grantee for creative sculpture, 1953-54. Fellow Nat. Sculpture Soc. (hon. mention Henry Herring competition); mem. Artists Equity Assn. (bd. Seattle chpt.), Nat. Acad. Design, Puget Sound N.W. Painters Group (bd.), N.W. Inst. Sculpture (pres. 1957), Allied Artists Am., U. Wash. Research Soc. Home: 1231 20th Ave E Seattle WA 98112

DUPIES, DONALD ALBERT, civil engineer, consultant; b. Waukegan, Ill., Apr. 17, 1934; s. Renie Bernard and Catherine Marie (Dowe) D.; m. Margaret T. McKibbin, Sept. 29, 1962; children: Mark, Patrick, Peggy, Colleen. B.C.E., Marquette U., 1957. Registered profl. engr., Wis., Ill. With Howard, Needles, Tammen & Bergendoff, Milw., 1959—, office engr., 1969-71, engr. in charge, 1971-74, assoc., 1974-79, cons. engr., ptnr., 1980—. Bd. dirs. Centurions of St. Joseph Hosp., Milw., 1971-76; cubmaster Milw. County council Boy Scouts Am., 1973-75. Served with C.E. U.S. Army, 1957-59. Mem. ASCE, Wis. Assn. Mfg. and Commerce, Wis. Council for Transp. Info., Engrs. and Scientists of Milw., Inst. Transp. Engrs., Ma. Mgmt. Assn., Internat. Bridge, Tunnel and Turnpike Assn., Bicentennial Engring., Sci. and Tech. Exposition and Conf. Council, Am. Pub. Works Assn., Water Pollution Control Fedn., Transp. Research Bd., Assn. Wis. Planners, Marquette U. Engring. Alumni Assn. (dir. Milw. 1976—), Tau Beta Pi, Chi Epsilon. Roman Catholic. Home: 4733 N Cumberland Blvd Whitefish Bay WI 53211 Office: Howard Needles Tammen & Bergendoff 6815 W Capitol Dr Milwaukee WI 53216

DUPLANTIER, ADRIAN GUY, federal judge; b. New Orleans, Mar. 5, 1929; s. F. Robert and Amelie (Rivet) D.; m. Sally Thomas, July 15, 1951; children: Adrian G., David L., Thomas, Jeanne M., Louise M., John C. J.D. cum laude, Loyola U., New Orleans, 1949. Bar: La. bar 1950, U.S. Supreme Ct 1954. Practiced law, New Orleans, 1950-74; judge Civil Dist. Ct. Parish of Orleans, 1974-78, U.S. Dist. Ct., New Orleans, 1978—; part-time prof. code of civil procedure Loyola U., 1951—, lectr. dental jurisprudence, 1960-67, lectr. English dept., 1948-50; mem. La. State Senate, 1960-74; 1st asst. dist. atty., New Orleans, 1954-56. Editorial bd.: Loyola Law Rev, 1947-48; editor-in-chief, 1948-49. Del. Democratic Nat. Conv., 1964; pres. Associated Cath. Charities New Orleans, Social Welfare Planning Council Greater New Orleans; mem. adv. bd. St. Mary's Dominican Coll., 1970-71, Ursuline Acad., 1968-73, Mt. Carmel Acad., 1965-69; chmn. pres.'s adv. council Jesuit High Sch., 1979—; active Assn. Retarded Children, Cystic Fibrosis Found. Recipient Meritorious award New Orleans Assn. Retarded Children, 1965; Gov.'s Cert. of Merit, 1970. Mem. Am. Bar Assn. (award 1960), La. Bar Assn., New Orleans Bar Assn., Order of Coif, Alpha Sigma Nu. Office: Chambers C-205 500 Camp St New Orleans LA 70130

DUPONT, EDWARD B., avation service and sales company executive. Chmn. Atlantic Aviation Corp., Wilmington, Del. Office: Atlantic Aviation Corp Wilmington DE§

DU PONT, PIERRE SAMUEL, IV, governor of Delaware; b. Wilmington, Del., Jan. 22, 1935; s. Pierre Samuel and Jane (Holcomb) du P.; m. Elise Ravenel Wood, 1957; children: Elise, Pierre, Benjamin, Eleuthere. Grad., Phillips Exeter Acad., 1952; B.S. M.E., Princeton U., 1956; LL.B., Harvard U., 1963. Bar: Del. 1964. Mem. staff Photo Products Dept., E.I. duPont Co.; mem. Del. Ho. of Reps., 1968-70; mem.-at-large 92d to 94th Congresses from Del.; gov., State of Del., 1977—. Served with USNR, 1957-60. Republican. Office: Legislative Hall Dover DE 19901

DU PONT, ROBERT L., JR., physician; b. Toledo, Mar. 25, 1936; s. Robert Louis and Martha Ireton (Lancashire) DuP.; m. Helen Gayden Spink, July 14, 1962; children: Elizabeth, Caroline. B.A., Emory U., 1958; M.D., Harvard U., 1963. Diplomate: Am. Bd. Psychiatry and Neurology. Intern Western Res. U., 1963-64; resident in psychiatry Harvard Med. Sch., 1964-66; clin. asso. NIH, 1966-68; research psychiatrist, acting asso. dir. for community services D.C. Dept. Corrections, Washington, 1968-70; practice medicine specializing in psychiatry, 1968—; adminstr. Narcotics Treatment Adminstrn., D.C. Dept. Human Resources, 1970-73; acting adminstr. Alcohol, Drug Abuse and Mental Health Adminstrn., HEW, Rockville, Md., 1974; dir. Nat. Inst. on Drug Abuse, HEW, Rockville, 1973-78, Spl. Action Office for Drug Abuse Prevention, Exec. Office Pres., Washington, 1973-75; pres. Inst. for Behavior and Health Inc., 1978—, Am. Council for Drug Edn., 1980—; U.S. del. UN Commn. on Narcotic Drugs, 1973-78; mem. Coordinating Council on Juvenile Justice and Delinquency Prevention, Dept. Justice, 1974-78; assoc. clin. prof. psychiatry and behavioral scis. George Washington Med. Sch., 1972-80; clin. prof. psychiatry Georgetown U. Med. Sch., 1980—; vis. assoc. clin. prof. psychiatry Harvard U. Med. Sch., 1978—; dir. Ctr. Behavioral Medicine, 1978—; v.p. Bensinger, DuPont Assocs., Inc, 1983—. Contbr. articles in fields of drug abuse, criminology and mental health to profl. jours.; appearances on: Good Morning America, ABC-TV, 1978-80. Bd. dirs. Washington Soc. for Performing Arts, 1972-76; mem. adv. com. Washington Jr. League, 1972-76. Served to surgeon (maj.) USPHS, 1966-68. Fellow Am. Psychiat. Assn.; mem. Washington Psychiat. Soc., World Psychiat. Assn., Pan Am. Med. Assn., Phobia Soc. Am. (pres. 1982—). Home: 8708 Susanna Ln Chevy Chase MD 20815 Office: 6191 Executive Blvd Rockville MD 20852 *Serious human problems such as drug dependence, phobias, and eating disorders are too often overlooked and underestimated by those who do not have them. They can be overcome by the comprehensive application of biological and psychological treatments with the support of others suffering from similar problems and with the active involvement of the family. The key to real, lasting recovery is hard work and courage which is an inspiration, not only to other sufferers, but* *to everyone whose life is touched by these painful, crippling and potentially life threatening disorders.*

DUPONT, TODD F., mathematics educator; b. Houston, Aug. 29, 1942; s. T.F. and Nan D.; m. Judy Smith, Aug. 20, 1964; children: Michelle, Todd K. B.A., Rice U., 1963, Ph.D., 1968. Research mathematician Esso Prodn. Research, Houston, 1968; instr. U. Chgo., 1968-69, asst. prof., 1969-72, assoc. prof., 1972-75, prof. math., 1975—; prin., officer, dir. Dupont-Rachford Engring. Math. Co., Houston, 1969—. Assoc. editor: Math. of Computation, SIAM Jour., others; contbr. articles to profl. jours. Mem. Am. Math. Soc., Soc. Indsl. and Applied Math., AAAS. Home: 1335 E Park Pl Chicago IL 60637 Office: Dept Math U Chicago 5734 University St Chicago IL 60637

DUPRAS, MAURICE, Canadian government official, insurance broker; b. St. Jerome, Que., Can., Sept. 13, 1923; s. Louis and Germaine (Desormeaux) D.; m. Marcelle Plouffe, Sept. 10, 1951; children: Louis, Carole, Elyse. Mem. House of Commons, 1970—, sec. to Minister of Energy, Mines and Resources, 1976, sec. of state for external affairs, 1977, chmn. com. veterans affairs; pvt. practice ins. broker. Pres. Canadian Red Cross, St. Jerome. Served with RCAF, 1942-45. Mem. C. of C., Air Cadet League. Address: La Marquise Mont-Gabriel PQ Canada J0R 1R0 *

DU PRÉ, JACQUELINE, violoncellist; b. 1945. Ed., London Cello Sch.; pupil of, William Pleeth at Guildhall Sch.; Music, of, Paul Tortelier, Paris, France, Rostropovich, Moscow, USSR; D.Litt. (hon.), U. Salford, 1978, D.Music, U. London, 1979, U. Sheffield, 1980. Now tchr. music, London. Rec. artist for, Angel Records. (Decorated Order Brit. Empire), Angel Records. (recipient Suggia Internat. Cello award 1956), Angel Records. (Guildhall Sch. of Music fellow 1975); Made debut at, Wigmore Hall, London, 1961; soloist with prin. orchs. and condrs. in, Eng., Europe, U.S. and Eastern Europe. Fellow Royal Coll. Music; hon. fellow Royal Acad. Music. Address: care Harold Holt Ltd 134 Wigmore St London England W1

DUPRÉ, LOUIS, philosopher, educator; b. Veerle, Belgium; came to U.S., 1958, naturalized, 1966; s. Clement and Francisca (Verlinden) D. Ph.D., U. Louvain, Belgium. From asst. prof. to prof. philosophy Georgetown U., 1959-73; T. Lawrason Riggs prof. philosophy of religion Yale U., 1973—. Author: Kierkegaard as Theologian (also in Dutch), 1963, The Philosophical Foundations of Marxism, 1966, Dutch edit., 1970, The Other Dimension, 1972, French edit., 1977, Transcendent Selfhood, 1976, Dutch edit., 1981, A Dubious Heritage, 1977, The Deeper Life, 1981, Marx's Social Critique of Culture, 1983; also articles. Mem. Am. Cath. Philos. Assn. (pres. 1971), Hegel Soc. Am. (pres. 1972-73). Roman Catholic. Home: 67 N Racebrook Rd Woodbridge CT 06525 Office: 320 Temple St New Haven CT 06520

DUPREE, ANDERSON HUNTER, historian, educator; b. Hillsboro, Tex., Jan. 29, 1921; s. George W. and Sarah (Hunter) D.; m. Marguerite Louise Arnold, July 18, 1946; children: Marguerite Wright, Anderson Hunter. A.B. summa cum laude, Oberlin Coll., 1942; A.M., Harvard U., 1947, Ph.D., 1952. Asst. prof. Tex. Tech. U., 1950-52; research fellow Gray Herbarium, Harvard U., 1952-54, 55-56, 81—; vis. asst. prof. U. Calif., Berkeley, 1956-58, from assoc. prof. to prof., 1958-68, asst. to chancellor, 1960-62, dir. Bancrof Library, 1965-66; George L. Littlefield prof. Am. history Brown U., Providence, 1968-81, emeritus, 1981—; scholar-in-residence So. Oreg. State Coll., 1983; vis. prof. history of sci. U. Minn., 1984; cons. com. sci. and public policy Nat. Acad. Sci., 1963-64; mem. history adv. com. NASA, 1963-73, AEC, 1967-74; mem. panel on sci. and tech. U.S. Ho. of Reps. Com. on Sci. and Astronautics, 1969-73; project dir. on grants NSF, 1953-55, 61-68; mem. Smithsonian Council, 1975—; cons. in field. Author: Science in the Federal Government, 1957, Asa Gray, 1959; Editor: Darwiniana, 1963, Science and the Emergence of Modern America, 1963. Served to lt. USNR, 1942-46. Recipient Presdl. award N.Y. Acad. Scis., 1976; fellow Center Advanced Study Behavioral Scis., 1967-68, Nat. Humanities Center, 1978-79. Fellow AAAS, Am. Acad. Arts and Scis. (sec. 1973-76); mem. Am. Hist. Assn., History of Sci. Soc., Soc. History of Tech., Phi Beta Kappa. Congregationalist. Club: Cosmos. Home: 114 Morris Ave Providence RI 02906

DUPREE, FRANKLIN TAYLOR, JR., judge; b. Angier, N.C., Oct. 8, 1913; s. Franklin T. and Elizabeth Mason (Wells) D.; m. Rosalyn Adcock, Dec. 30, 1939; children: Elizabeth Rosalyn, Nancy Alice (Mrs. Philip R. Miller, Jr.). A.B., U. N.C. at Chapel Hill, 1933, LL.B., 1936. Bar: N.C. 1936. Practiced in, Angier, 1936-39; asso. firm A.J. Fletcher, Raleigh, N.C., 1939-48; practiced in, Raleigh, 1948-52; partner firm Dupree, Weaver, Horton, Cockman & Alvis (and predecessor firm), Raleigh, 1952-70; judge U.S. Dist. Ct. (ea. dist.) N.C., Raleigh, 1971—. Mem. Wake County (N.C.) Bd. Elections, 1961-67; chmn. Wake County Republican Com., 1967-70; mem. N.C. Rep. Exec. Com., 1968-70. Served to lt. USNR, 1943-46. Mem. Am., N.C., Wake County bar assns., Am. Judicature Soc. Baptist. Clubs: Elk, Lion., Carolina Country, Stag. Home: 713 Westwood Dr Raleigh NC 27607 Office: PO Box 27585 Raleigh NC 27611

DUPREE, LOUIS BENJAMIN, anthropologist; b. Greenville, N.C., Aug. 23, 1925; s. Chauncey Leary and Luna Emily (Tripp) D.; m. Nancy Marie Shakuntala Hatch, Feb. 20, 1966; children by previous marriage: Duggie, Louis F.R., Sally. A.B. cum laude, Harvard U., 1949, A.M., 1953, Ph.D., 1955. Asst. prof. Air U., Maxwell AFB, Ala., 1954-57, assoc. prof., 1957; assoc. prof. anthopology Pa. State U., 1957-66, adj. prof., 1966—; dir. Archaeol. Mission in Afghanistan, 1959-78; rep. Am. univs. field staff, Afghanistan, Pakistan, Soviet Central Asia, 1959-83; faculty asso. Columbia U. Seminar in Archaeol. of Eastern Mediterranean, East Europe, Near East, 1967—; vis. lectr. Kabul U., 1962, 64-66, U. Chgo., 1968; Disting. prof. U. Md., 1981, Mary Washington Coll., 1981, U. Nebr., 1980; vis. prof. Woodrow Wilson Sch., Princeton U., 1983-84, U.S. Mil Acad., 1984-85; mem. Near and Middle Eastern com. of Social Sci. Research Council, N.Y., 1958-59; mem. commn. of Govt. Afghanistan for Japanese Archaeology Exhbn., 1963; Archaeol. Inst. Am. rep., People's Republic of China, 1978; mem. Eisenhower Exchange Fellowship Com. for Afghanistan, 1971; mem. adv. bd. Afghanistan Freedom Orgn.; trustee Am. Friends of Afghanistan, Afghan Relief Com.; mem. adv. council Com. for a Free Afghanistan; corr. World Paper, Boston, 1979—. Author: 13 books including Afghanistan, 1973, 2d edit., 1978, paperback edit., 1980; editor: (with L. Albert) Afghanistan in the 1970's, 1974; G. S. Robertson's Kafirs of the Hindu Kush (1896), 1974, The First Russo-Afghan War: 1979—?, 1982; contbr. articles to profl. jours. Served with USNR, 1943-44; Served with AUS, 1944-47. Decorated Air Force Commendation medal for meritorious civilian service; Am. Philos. Soc. grantee, 1964-66; Social Sci. Research Council grantee, 1964-65; NSF grantee, 1969-70; Heinze Found. grantee, 1970-71; NEH grantee, 1972-73; Wenner-Gren Found. grantee, 1959-60, 65, 78-80; Am. Council Learned Socs. fellow King's Coll., Cambridge, Eng., 1972-73; Ford Found. grantee, 1982-83. Fellow Am. Anthrop. Assn. (com. ethics 1966), AAAS, Soc. Applied Anthropology, Am. Oriental Soc., Am. Geog. Soc., Am. Ethnol. Soc., Soc. Am. Archaeology; mem. Soc. Afghan Studies (founding), Archaeol. Inst. Am., Royal Soc. Asian Affairs, N.C. Archaeol. Soc., Societe Prehistorique Française, Brit. Inst. Persian Studies, Soc. World War I Aero Historians, Explorers Club, Friends of Nat. Army Mus. (U.K.), Gamma Alpha. Club: Harvard Travellers. Office: Princeton U Princeton NJ 08544

DUPREY, JOHN PAUL, photographer; b. Bronxville, N.Y., Aug. 8, 1927; s. Paul T. and Florence C. D.; m. Ruth Lois West, Aug. 14, 1948; children: Diane, James, Janet, Daniel, Dennis, Jean, Jacqueline, Jerilyn. Student pub. schs., N.Y.C. Copy boy N.Y. Daily News, N.Y.C., 1946-51, photographer, 1951-71, chief photographer, 1971-77, photog. mgr., 1978—; judge photog. contests; lectr. in field. Served with USN, 1944-46. Recipient numerous awards. Mem. N.Y., Nat. press photographers assns., Photog. Adminstrs. Club. Roman Catholic. Home: 113 Lynn St Harrington Park NJ 07640 Office: 220 E 42d St New York NY 10017

DUPREY, WILSON GILLILAND, librarian; b. Van Wert, Ohio, June 21, 1924; s. Rei and Berneace (Gilliland) D. Student, Ohio State U., 1942-44; B.A., George Washington U., 1946; M.S., Columbia U., 1949. Reference asst. Stanford U. Library, 1949-51, with rare book room, 1951-53; reference asst. prints div. N.Y. Pub. Library, 1953-66; curator map and print room N.Y. Hist. Soc., N.Y.C., 1966-74; dir. Brumback Library, Van Wert, 1976—. Picture researcher: Kunitz & Colby European Authors, 1000-1900, 1967, Ewen Great Composers, 1300-1900, 1966, Ewen Popular American Composers, 1962; author: introduction The Cabinet of Natural History and American Rural Sports, 1973. Mem. L.I. Hist. Soc., Van Wert County Hist. Soc., Walters Art Gallery (Balt.), Constitution Island Assn., Toledo Mus. Art. Republican. Methodist. Club: Men's Garden Am. Home: Route 2 Box 28 Van Wert OH 45891

DUPUIS, ROBERT NEWELL, chemist, mgmt. cons.; b. Indpls., June 4, 1910; s. Arthur J. and Veronica (Cox) DuP.; m. Eleanor Thomsen, June 29, 1935; children—Robert Thomsen, Eleanor Joan. A.B., U. Ill., 1931; Ph.D. in Organic Chemistry, N.Y. U., 1934. Research chemist Miner Labs., Chgo., 1935-45, asst. dir., 1945-47; research and devel. mgr. S.C. Johnson & Son, Inc., 1947-52; dir. research and devel. Philip Morris, Inc., Richmond, Va., 1952-55, v.p. research, 1955-60, dir., 1957-63; v.p. tech. Gen. Foods Corp., 1960-67; mgmt. cons., 1968—. Editor: Research Management, 1967-70; Contbr. to patent lit., sci. publs. Trustee Sunnyside Presbyterian Home, Harrisonburg, Va. Mem. Am. Chem. Soc., Phi Beta Kappa, Sigma Xi, Alpha Chi Sigma. Clubs: Chemists (Chgo., N.Y.C.); Downtown (Richmond). Home: 3902 Exeter Rd Richmond VA 23221

DUPUIS, VICTOR LIONEL, educator; b. Chgo., Oct. 30, 1934; s. Edward G. and LaVerne Ann (Brown) D.; m. Mary Jean Miles, Aug. 11, 1956; children: Mary Catherine, Victor Edward, Elizabeth Ann. B.S., Northwestern U., 1956; M.A., Am. U., 1961; Ph.D., Purdue U., 1965. Tchr. jr. high sch., Arlington, Va., 1956-61; tchr. Klondike Sch. Dist., West Lafayette, Ind., 1961-63, curriculum dir., 1962-63; grad. instr. Purdue U., West Lafayette, 1963-65, curriculum dir., 1962-63, grad. instr., West Lafayette, 1963-65; asst. prof. No. Ill. U., DeKalb, 1965-67, Pa. State U., 1967-70, assoc. prof. curriculum, 1970-74, prof. edn., 1974—, also chmn. curriculum and supervision, 1971—; cons. to various pvt. and public schs., state depts. edn. Native Am. programs. Author: (with others) Introduction to the Foundations of American Education, 1966, Introductory Readings in the Foundations of American Education, 1966, Resource Booklet and Overhead Transparency Masters for the Foundations of American Education, 1966, An Introduction to the Foundations of American Education, 1969, rev. 5th edit., 1982, Foundations of American Education: Readings, 1969, rev. 5th edit., 1982, Resurce Booklet: Foundations of American Education, 1970, rev. 5th edit., 1982; also articles on nat., state jours. Chmn. Patton Twp. (Pa.) Park Bd., 1969-70, Patton Twp. Planning Commn., 1971-73; Democratic precinct committeeman Patton Twp., 1971-76, chmn., twp. supr., 1973—. Served to 2d lt. inf. U.S. Army, 1957-59. Mem. Am. Ednl. Research Assn., Assn. Supervision and Curriculum Devel., AAUP, Nat. Congress Parents and Tchrs., Phi Delta Kappa. Home: Rural Route 1 Box 417 Bellefonte PA 16823 Office: Coll Edn Pa State U University Park PA 16802

DUPUY, FRANK RUSSELL, JR., mag. pub.; b. San Antonio, Jan. 30, 1907; s. Frank Russell and Sarah (Tankersley) D.; m. Nancy Jane McGinley, Oct. 24, 1954; children—Sarah Anne, Frank Russell III. Student, Washington and Lee U., 1924-25. Advt. rep. Los Angeles Examiner, 1930-41; asst. to pub. Good Housekeeping mag., 1946-59; advt. dir. Popular Mechanics, 1960-62; v.p., pub. Cosmopolitan mag., N.Y.C., 1962—. Served with AUS, 1942-46. Home: 45 E 72d St New York City NY 10021 Office: 959 8th Ave New York City NY 10019

DUPUY, HOWARD MOORE, JR., lawyer; b. Portland, Oreg., Mar. 15, 1929; s. Howard Moore and Lola (Dunham) D.; m. Anne Irene Hanna, Aug. 26, 1950; children—Loanne Kay, Brent Moore. B.A., U. Portland, 1951; postgrad., Willamette U., Salem, Oreg., 1951; LL.B., Lewis and Clark Coll., 1956. Bar: Oreg. bar 1956. Since practiced in, Portland; asso. Green, Richardson, Green & Griswold, 1956; partner Morton & Dupuy, 1957-67, Buell, Black & Dupuy (and predecessor firm), 1968—. Mem. fin. com. Oreg. Republican Central Com., 1962. Served with AUS, 1946-47. Mem. Am., Oreg., Multnomah County bar assns., Am. Arbitration Assn. (nat. panel arbitrators), Portland C. of C. Club: Aero of Oreg. (Portland). Home: 16116 NE Stanton St Portland OR 97230 Office: 421 SW Fifth Ave Suite 202 Mead Bldg Portland OR 97204

DUPUY, JAMES ROBERT, life insurance company executive; b. Teague, Tex., Mar. 20, 1940; s. Dwight Leldon and Juliet (Beauchamp) DuP.; m. Judith Ann Almon, July 15, 1978; children: Claire, Miles. B.A., U. Tex., 1962. Actuarial asst. Am. Nat. Ins. Co., Galveston, Tex., 1964-67; assoc. actuary Protective Life, Birmingham, Ala., 1967-70; v.p., actuary southwestern Life Ins. Co., Dallas, 1970-74; exec. v.p. adminstrn. Southwestern Life Ins. Co., Dallas, 1974—. Fellow Soc. Actuaries, Life Office Mgmt. Assn.; mem. Actuaries Club of Southwest (pres.). Republican. Club: Royal Oaks Country (Dallas). Office: Southwestern Life Ins Co 1807 Ross Ave Dallas TX 75201

DUPUY, TREVOR NEVITT, historian, research executive; b. S.I., N.Y., May 3, 1916; s. Richard Ernest and Laura (Nevitt) D.; m. Jonna Sløk Bjerggaard, Oct. 16, 1968 (dec. Apr. 1982); 1 dau., Signe Sløk; children (by previous marriage): Trevor Nevitt, Richard Ernest II, George McVicar, Laura Nevitt, Charles Geissbuhler, Mirande Elisabeth, Arnold Geissbuhler, Fielding Davis. Student, St. Peter's Coll., 1933-34; B.S., U.S. Mil. Acad., 1938; grad., Joint Services Staff Coll., Latimer, Eng., 1948-49; student, Harvard Grad. Sch. Pub. Adminstrn., 1953-54. Commd. 2d lt. U.S. Army, 1938, advanced through grades to col., 1953; prof. mil. sci. and tactics Harvard, 1952-56, mem. original faculty Def. Studies program, 1954-56; dir. mil. history program Ohio State U., 1956, 57; ret., 1958; vis. prof. internat. relations program Rangoon (Burma) U., 1959-60; mem. internat. studies div. Inst. Def. Analyses, 1960-62; pres., exec. dir., bd. dirs. Hist. Evaluation and Research Orgn., 1962—; pres. bd. dirs. T.N. Dupuy Assos., Inc., 1971-83, Data Memory Systems, Inc., 1983—. Author: (with R.E. Dupuy) To The Colors, 1942, Faithful and True, 1949, (with R.E. Dupuy) Military Heritage of America, 2d edit., 1984, Campaigns of the French Revolution and of Napoleon, 1956, (with R.E. Dupuy) Brave Men and Great Captains, 1960, Compact History of the Civil War, 1960 (Fletcher Pratt award), Civil War Land Battles, 1960, Civil War Naval Actions, 1961, Military History of World War II, 19 vols, 1962-65, (with R.E. Dupuy) Compact History of the Revolutionary War, 1963, Military History of World War I, 12 vols, 1967, The Battle of Austerlitz, 1968, Modern Libraries for Modern Colleges: Research Strategies for Design and Development, 1968, Ferment in College Libraries: The Impact of Information Technology, 1968, Military History of the Chinese Civil War, 1969, (with R.E. Dupuy) Encyclopedia of Military History, 3d edit, 1984, Military Lives, 12 vols, 1969, (with Grace P. Hayes) Revolutionary War Naval Battles, 1970, (with Gay M. Hammerman) Revolutionary War Land Battles, 1970; editor, contbr.: Holidays, 1965, (with John A. Andrews and Grace P. Hayes) Almanac of World Military Power, 1970, 72, 74, 80, (with Gay M. Hammerman) Documentary History of Arms Control and Disarmament, 1973, People and Events of the American Revolution, 1974, (with R.E. Dupuy) An Outline History of the American Revolution, 1975, A Genius for War: The German Army and General Staff, 1807-1945, 1977, Numbers, Prediction and War, 1978, Elusive Victory: The Arab-Israeli Wars, 1947-1974, 1978, The Evolution of Weapons and Warfare, 1980, (with Paul Martell) Great Battles of the Eastern Front, 1982, A Theory of Combat, 1984. Trustee Coll. Potomac. Decorated Legion of Merit, Bronze Star with combat V, Air medal; Brit. Distinguished Service Order; Chinese Nat. Govt. Cloud and Banner (2 grades). Mem. Am. Hist. Assn., Am. Mil. Inst. (pres. 1958-59), Assn. U.S. Army, Internat. Inst. Strategic Studies, U.S. Naval Inst. Home: 3816 N Tazewell St Arlington VA 22207 Office: 8316 Arlington Blvd Fairfax VA 22031

DUQUEMIN, GORDON JAMES, former army officer; b. Milw., Jan. 3, 1924; s. Charles H. and Ethel Maud (Kimber) D.; m. Patricia Jones, Apr. 5, 1949; children: Peter James, David Patrick, Margaret Kimber. Student, U. Wis., 1942-44; B.S., U.S. Mil. Acad., 1947; M.S. in Internat. Relations, George Washington U., 1966. Commd. 2d lt. U.S. Army, 1947, advanced through grades to maj. gen., 1972; bn. comdr. 2d Bn., 4th Inf. Div., Vietnam, 1966-67; brigade exec. officer 2d Brigade, 4th Inf. Div., Vietnam, 1967, brigade comdr., 1968-69; exec. officer plans and policies directorate Office of Joint Chief of Staffs, Washington, 1967-68; div. chief of staff 4th Inf. Div., Vietnam, 1969; dep. sr. adviser to comdg. gen. II Corps, Tactical Zone, Vietnam, 1969-70; dep. comdg. gen. U.S. Army Tng. Center, Inf., Ft. Jackson, S.C., 1970-71; asst. dept. chief of staff for individual tng. Continental Army Command, Ft. Monroe, Va., 1971-72, spl. asst. to chief of staff, 1972-73; comdr. 1st Inf. Div., Ft. Riley, Kans., 1973-74; dep. chief of staff for ops. U.S. Army Forces Command, Ft. McPherson, Ga., 1974-76; dep. chief of staff ops. U.S. Army Europe and 7th Army, Heidelberg, Germany, 1976-79; comdr. U.S. Army Readiness Regiona IV, Ft. Gillem, Ga., 1979-81; ret., 1981; program gen. mgr. to modernize Saudi Arabian N.G. Vinnell Corp. Decorated D.S.M., Silver Star with 2 oak leaf clusters, Legion of Merit with 2 oak leaf clusters, D.F.C., Bronze Star medal with 3 oak leaf clusters, Air medal with 16 oak leaf clusters, Joint Services Commendation medal, Army Commendation medal, Purple Heart. Home: 255 10th Fairway Roswell GA 30076

DUR, PHILIP FRANCIS, educator, ret. fgn. service officer; b. St. Louis, June 30, 1914; s. Alphonse and Sarah (Ralston) D.; m. Elena Delgado, June 30, 1942; children: Elena (Mrs. Philip A. Morris), Philip, Stansbury, Carmen (Mrs. Norman B. Conley, Jr.), Jacqueline (Mrs. James Chase Sheppard), John. A.B., Harvard U., 1935, Ph.D., 1941; postgrad., Fgn. Service Inst., 1961. Consul, pub. affairs officer, Lyon, France, 1948-51; chief Office Pub. Affairs, Office U.S. High Commr. for Germany, Bonn, 1951-52; consul, exec. officer, Bremen, Germany, 1952-53; comml. controls officer Mil. Security Bd., Coblenz, Germany, 1953-54; consul, Colon, Panama, 1954-55, Yokohama, Japan, 1955-58; pub. affairs adviser Dept. State, 1958-61; consul, Nagoya, Japan, 1961-65; Jefferson Caffery prof. polit. sci. U. Southwestern La., Lafayette, 1965—, faculty senate, 1969—; adviser Council for Devel. of French in La., 1968—; mem. U. Southwestern La. Found., 1969-71; pres. France-Amerique de la Louisiane Acadienne, 1970-72; resident dir. La. Consortium Colls. and Univs., Montpellier, France, 1976-77; organizer, exchange prof. La. Center for Studies, U. Paul Valéry, Montpellier. Served to lt. comdr. USNR, 1942-46. Decorated Acad. Palms (France); recipient Nat. Medal of Honor DAR, 1983. Mem. Am. Fgn. Service Assn., Soc. Historians Am. Fgn. Relations, Phi Beta Kappa. Home: 517 Woodvale Ave Lafayette LA 70501

DURACK, DAVID TULLOCH, physician; b. Perth, Australia, Dec. 18, 1944; s. Reginald Wyndham and Grace Enid (Tulloch) D.; m. Carmen Elizabeth Prosser, July 25, 1970; children: Jeremy, Kimberley, Sonya, Justin. M.B., B.S., U. Western Australia, 1969; D.Phil., Oxford U., Eng., 1973. Cert. internal medicine Royal Coll. Physicians U.K., diplomate: Am. Bd. Internal Medicine. Chief resident medicine, asst. prof. medicine U. Wash., Seattle, 1975-77; chief infectious diseases Duke U., Durham, N.C., 1977—, prof. medicine and microbiology, 1982—. Contbr. articles to profl. jours. Rhodes scholar, 1969; NIH grantee, 1980; R.J. Reynolds Co. grantee, 1983. Fellow Royal Coll. Physicians U.K.; mem. ACP, Royal Australasian Coll. Physicians, Infectious Diseases Soc. Am., Am. Fedn. Clin. Research. Presbyterian. Office: Duke U Med Center Durham NC 27710

DURAN, SERVET AHMET, engring. educator; b. Kutahya, Turkey, Jan. 2, 1920; came to U.S., 1939, naturalized, 1959; s. H. Muammer and Asiye (Rifat) D.; m. Martha Tucker, May 4, 1946; children—Meliha Sue, Frederick Rifat, Michael Halis. B.S., Mo. Sch. Mines and Metallurgy, 1943; A.M., Stanford, 1945, Engr. Phys. Metallurgy, 1946, Ph.D., 1963. Teaching asst. Stanford, 1946, vis. asso. prof. materials sci., 1956-58; instr. Wash. State U., Pullman, 1947-49, asst. prof. metallurgy, 1949-53, asso. prof., 1953-61, prof., 1961—, chmn. metallurgy dept., 1959-70, head metals research sect., 1960-66; research metallurgist Kaiser Aluminum & Chem. Corp., 1954; cons. Middle East Tech. U., Ankara, Turkey, 1969. Contbr. articles profl. jours. Bd. dirs. Pullman Concert Assn. Mem. Metall. Soc. of Am. Inst. Mining, Metall. and Petroleum Engrs., Am. Soc. for Metals (chmn. Inland Empire chpt. 1953), Am. Soc. Engring. Edn. (chmn. materials div. 1965-66), Sigma Xi, Sigma Tau, Alpha Sigma Mu. Home: SE 250 Derby St Pullman WA 99163

DURAND, HARVEY STOWE, food and drug retail executive; b. Detroit, Sept. 6, 1941; s. John Ralph and Dorothy (Vale) Kissinger; m. Paula Susan Neitz, June 18, 1966; children: Tammy, John, Erik. B.A. in Geology, U. Ariz., Tucson, 1963, M.S., 1966. Geologist Heinrichs Geoexploration, Tucson, 1965-67; various positions Osco Drug (Jewel Co.), Oakbrook, Ill., 1967-71, dist. mgr., 1971-74; v.p. ops. Turnstyle (Jewel Co.), Oakbrook, Ill., 1974-78, Payless Drug Co., Oakbrook, CA., 1978-80; v.p. drug sales Albertson's Inc., Boise, Idaho, 1980—. Cubmaster Cub Scouts Boy Scouts Am., Boise, 1982-83. Republican. Presbyterian. Office: Albertsons Inc 250 Parkcenter Bldg Boise ID 83726

DURAND, LOYAL, III, educator, physicist; b. Madison, Wis., May 19, 1931; s. Loyal and Dorothy (Lee) D.; m. Wesley Ann Travis, Dec. 22, 1954 (div.); children—Travis Loyal, Timothy Bartlett, Christopher Alan; m. Bernice Black, Oct. 18, 1970. B.S., Yale, 1953, M.S., 1954, Ph.D., 1957. Mem. Inst. Advanced Study, Princeton, 1957-59, 75; research physicist Brookhaven Nat. Lab., 1959-61; asst. prof. physics Yale, 1961-65; prof. physics U. Wis., Madison, 1965—, chmn. dept., 1969-71; vis. prof. U. Colo., summer 1960; mem. policy adv. com. Nat. Accelerator Lab., 1969-72, mem. long range planning com., 1973-75; chmn. exec. com. Aspen Center for Physics, 1968-76, pres., 1972-76; also trustee; cons. Los Alamos Sci. Lab., 1975—, mem. vis. staff, 1976, Fermi Nat. Accelerator Lab., 1982-83. Asso. editor: Jour. Math. Physics, 1973-76; Contbr. articles to profl. jours. Mem. Am. Phys. Soc.,

Am. Math. Soc., AAAS, Sigma Xi. Spl. research theory elementary particles, high energy physics, applied math. Home: Deer Run Route 1 Cross Plains WI 53528

DURANT, FREDERICK CLARK, III, consultant; b. Ardmore, Pa., Dec. 31, 1916; s. Frederick Clark, Jr. and Cornelia Allen (Howel) D.; m. Carolyn Griscom Jones, Oct. 4, 1947; children: Derek C. (dec.), Carolyn M., William C., Stephen H. B.S. in Chem. Engring, Lehigh U., 1939; postgrad., Phila. Mus. Sch. Indsl. Arts, 1946-47. Registered profl. engr., D.C., Mass. Engr. E.I. duPont de Nemours & Co., Inc., 1939-41; rocket engr. Bell Aircraft Corp., 1947-48; dir. engring. Naval Air Rocket Test Sta., 1948-51; cons., Washington, 1952-53; mem. sr. staff Arthur D. Little, Inc., 1954-57; dir. Maynard Ordnance Test Sta., 1954-55; exec. asst. to dir. Avco-Everett Research Lab., 1957-59; dir. pub. and govt. relations, research and advanced devel. div. Avco Corp., Wilmington, Mass., 1959-61; sr. rep. Bell Aerosystems Co., Washington, 1961-64; asst. dir. and head astronautics dept. Nat. Air and Space Mus., Smithsonian Instn., Washington, 1964-80; cons., 1980—; dir. Nat. Space Inst., Washington, 1982—; participant ann. congresses Internat. Astronautical Fedn., 1951—, pres., 1953-56; mem. organizing com. Project Orbiter, 1954. Author: First Steps toward Space, 1975, Worlds Beyond: The Art of Chesley Bonestell, 1983; Contbg. editor: Missiles and Rockets, 1956-58; contbr. to: Funk & Wagnalls Year Book; contbr.: space terms Am. Heritage Dictionary; Ency. Brit. Served to comdr. as naval aviator USNR, 1941-46,48-52. Recipient spl. medal L'Assn. Pour l'Encouragement de l'Aeronautique et de l'Astronautique, 1963, Charles A. Lindbergh award Smithsonian Instn., 1976, hon. 6 Dan Karate-Do, Japan, 1978. Fellow Am. Astronautical Soc., AIAA, Am. Rocket Soc. (pres. 1953); mem. Internat. Acad. Astronautics, Nat. Space Club (gov. 1961), Mat. Space Club (Disting. Service award 1982); hon. fellow or mem. numerous fgn. rocket and space flight socs. Club: Cosmos. Home: 109 Grafton St Chevy Chase MD 20815

DURANT, JOHN RIDGEWAY, physician; b. Ann Arbor, Mich., July 29, 1930; s. Thomas Morton and Jean Margaret (deVries) D.; m. Marlene Hamlin, June 28, 1974; children: Christine Joy, Thomas Arthur, Michele Grace, Jennifer Margaret. B.A., Swarthmore (Pa.) Coll., 1952; M.D., Temple U., Phila., 1956. Diplomate: Am. Bd. Internal Medicine. Intern, then jr. asst. resident in medicine Hartford (Conn.) Hosp., 1956-58; resident in medicine Temple U. Med. Center, 1960-62; spl. fellow med. neoplasia Meml. Hosp. for Cancer and Allied Diseases, N.Y.C., 1962-63; Am. Cancer Soc. advanced clin. fellow Temple U. Health Scis. Center, 1964-67, instr., then asst. prof. medicine, 1963-67; clin. assoc. chemotherapy Moss Rehab. Hosp., Phila., 1964-67; research assoc. Fels Research Inst., Phila., 1965-67; mem. faculty U. Ala. Med. Center, Birmingham, 1968-82, prof. medicine, dir. comprehensive cancer center, 1970-82, prof. radiation oncology, 1978-82, chmn. Southeastern coop. cancer study group at univ., 1975-82, Disting. faculty lectr., 1980; pres. Fox Chase Cancer Ctr., Phila., 1982—; chmn. coop. group exec. com. Nat. Cancer Inst., NIH, 1977-82, chmn. coop. group chairmen, 1979-82; cons. VA Hosp., Tuskegee, Ala., 1970-82; exec. com. Birmingham chpt. ARC, 1972-77. Editorial bd.: Cancer Clin. Trials, 1979-82; assoc. editor, 1982—; Editorial bd.: Med. and Pediatric Oncology, 1979-82; editorial adv. bd.: Oncology News, 1975—; contbr. numerous articles to med. jours. Served as officer M.C. USNR, 1958-60. Fellow A.C.P., Coll. Physicians Phila.; mem. Am. Cancer Soc. (vice chmn. advanced clin. fellowship com. 1974-76, mem. instl. research grant com. 1979-82, pres. Ala. div. 1973-75, 77-79), Am. Soc. Clin. Oncology (dir. 1979—), Am. Assn. Cancer Research (pres.-elect 1982-83), Am. Radium Soc. (2d v.p. 1977-79), Assn. Am. Cancer Insts. (dir. 1978—, pres. 1982-83), Assn. Community Cancer Centers (dir. 1979-81), Am. Soc. Clin. Oncology (chmn. public relations com. 1976-79), A.C.S., James Ewing Soc., Southeastern Cancer Research Assn. (pres. 1976—), AMA, Am. Fedn. Clin. Research, Am. Assn. Cancer Edn., Med. Assn. Ala., Jefferson County Med. Assn., AAAS, Am. Soc. Hematology, Alpha Omega Alpha. Presbyterian. Office: Fox Chase Cancer Ctr 7701 Burholme St Philadelphia PA 19111

DURBIN, ENOCH JOB, engineering educator; b. N.Y.C., Sept. 6, 1922; s. David and Ida (Deutsch) D.; m. Marilyn Lehman, Sept. 15, 1945; 3 children. B.S., CCNY, 1943; M.S., Rensselaer Poly. Inst., 1947. Research scientist NACA, Langley, Va., 1947-51; sr. mem. tech. staff n. Am. Aviation, Downey, Calif., 1951-54; prof. aero-mech. sci. Princeton U., 1954—, sr. research asso., 1954-58, dir. instrumentation and control lab., 1954—; founder, dir. Center Alt. Fueling of Combustion Engines, U. B.C., 1980—; cons. European and U.S. auto industry. Author: Methane-fuel for the Future, 1982; Gen. editor, contbg. author: Flight Test Manual, 1964. Mem. Princeton Borough Council, 1965-68; pres. Unitarian Ch. Princeton, 1975-77. Served with U.S. Army, 1943-46. Fellow AAAS, Instrument Soc. Am.; mem. Internat. Symposium on Automotive Tech. and Automation, Sigma Xi. Patentee tennis racket, ion mass flow meter. Home: 246 Western Way Princeton NJ 08540 Office: Dept Mech and Aerospace Engring Princeton U Engring Quadrangle Princeton NJ 08544

DURBIN, RICHARD JOSEPH, Congressman; b. East St. Louis, Ill., Nov. 21, 1944; s. William and Ann D.; m. Loretta Schaefer, June 24, 1967; children: Christine, Paul, Jennifer. B.S. in Econs., Georgetown U., 1966, J.D., 1969. Bar: Ill. 1969. Chief legal counsel Lt. Gov. Paul Simon of Ill., 1969; mem. staff minority leader Ill. Senate, 1972-77, parliamentarian, 1969-77; practice law, 1969—; mem. 98th Congress from 20th Dist. Ill.; assoc. prof. med. humanities So. Ill. U., 1978—. Campaign worker Sen. Paul Douglas of Ill., 1966; staff Office Ill. Dept. Bus. and Econ. Devel., Washington; candidate for Ill. Lt. Gov., 1978; staff alt. Pres.'s State Planning Council, 1980; advisor Am. Council Young Polit. Leaders, 1981; mem. YMCA Ann. Membership Roundup, YMCA Bldg. Drive, Pony World Series; bd. dirs. Cath. Charities, United Way of Springfield, Old Capitol Art Fair, Springfield Youth Soccer; mem. Sch. Dist. 1986 Referendum Com., Springfield NAACP. Democrat. Roman Catholic. Office: 417 Cannon House Office Bldg Washington DC 20515

DURBIN, RICHARD LOUIS, health planning administrator; b. Millersport, Ohio, Aug. 28, 1928; s. Clark Babe and Mabel (Bushee) D.; m. Carolyn Bohrer, Mar. 18, 1955; children: Richard Louis, Margot Jane, Melissa Durbin Bushee. B.A., Ohio State U., 1949; M.B.A., U. Chgo., 1956; M.P.A., U. Ariz., 1969; postgrad., Pace Coll., 1973, U. Tex. Sch. Pub. Health, 1977—. Research chemist Battelle Meml. Inst., Columbus, Ohio, 1949-50; sales rep. Am. Cyanamid Co., N.Y.C., 1953-54; adminstrv. asst. Lancaster (Ohio)-Fairfield Hosp., 1954; adminstrv. resident Gary (Ind.) Meth. Hosp., 1955-56; asst. adminstr. City of Memphis Hosps., 1956-58, asso. adminstr., 1958-60; dir. outpatient and profl. services Presbyn.-St. Luke's Hosp., Chgo., 1960-61; asso. dir. grad. program in hosp. adminstrn., faculty U. Chgo. Grad. Sch. Bus., 1961-62; exec. sec. Am. Assn. Univ. Programs in Hosp. Adminstrn., 1960-62; asso. prof. bus. adminstrn. Temple U., 1967-69, prof. mgmt., 1969-70, founder, dir. grad. program in health care adminstrn., 1967-70, exec. dir., 1966-70, Lubbock County Dist. Hosp., Lubbock, Tex., 1970-71; now cons.; v.p. Coll. Medicine and Dentistry N.J., 1971-75; also v.p. Acad. Health Center; asst. prof. N.J. Med. Sch., 1973-75; chief adminstr. Harris County Hosp. Dist., Houston, 1975—; pres. D & H Enterprises, Durbin Internat.; project dir., chief planner, exec. dir. Newark Comprehensive Health Plan, 1974; cons. div. hosp. and med. facilities HEW, 1967—, mem. design adv. group, mem. nat. rev. com., cons. exptl. health systems, 1971-73; cons. Nat. Commn. on Productivity, U.S. Bur. Prisons, 1968—; mem. Hosp. Devel., Inc., N.J. Gov.'s Correctional Health Service Investigations Com.; mem. adv. bd. Comprenetics, Inc., 1967—; mem. steering commn. Tucson Hosp. and Health Planning Commn., 1962—, Asso. Hosp. Services Ariz., 1963-64; treas. Ariz. League Nursing, 1963-64. Author: A Statistical Methodology of Evaluating a Medical Staff, 1961, New Ideas and Concepts in Outpatient Management, 1963, (with others) Ivory Tower to Workshop, 1964, Ambulatory Care Development, 1966, (with W.H. Springall) Organization and Administration of Health Care, 2d edit, 1974, (with Springall, P. High) Manual for Hospital Program and Performance Budgeting at the Operating Level, 1968, (with G. Connor) Design of a City-Wide HMO, 1974; cons. editor: Hosp. Topics; editor: The Forum, What's Going On—Hospital Topics; editorial adv. bd.: Physician Weekly; contbr.: articles to profl. jours. Mem. Phila. Crime Commn., 1967—; bd. dirs. Ariz. Blue Cross.; mem. Tex. Indigent Care Task Force. Served to lt. USNR, 1945-46, 50-53. Recipient editorial award Hosp. Mgmt. mag., 1961, 63, 65; cert. of merit Gov. Ariz., 1967, 68. Fellow Am. Coll. Hosp. Adminstrs.; mem. Houston C. of C. (health com.), Nat. Assn. Public Hosps. (dir.), Am. Chem. Soc., Nat. Assn. Clinic Mgrs., Am. Hosp. Assn. (council public hosps.), Pa. Hosp. Assn., So. Ariz. Hosp. Council (pres. 1963), Am. Criminology Soc., Am. Soc. Pub. Adminstrn., AIM, Internat. Hosp. Fedn., Am. Mgmt. Assn. (Excellence award 1968), AAUP, Sigma Xi, Sigma Alpha Epsilon. Presbyterian (deacon). Clubs: Tucson Press (life), Rotary, Quadrangle (U. Chgo.), Buckeye Lake Yacht; Columbian Yacht (Chgo.); Headliners (Austin, Tex.); Hillcrest Country, Houston Yacht; Army-Navy Capitol Hill (Washington); Pa. Soc. Home: 7222 Northampton Way Houston TX 77055 Office: 726 Gillette St Houston TX 77006 *Each man must not only carry his own load, but share in the carrying of all or part of others.*

DURDEN, CHARLES DENNIS, manufacturing company executive; b. Atlanta, Jan. 13, 1930; s. Cecil and Helen (Adams) D.; m. Diana Widrig, Feb. 11, 1955; children: Thomas, Merideth, Sarah, Matthew. B.S., Ga. Inst. Tech., 1951; M.A., U. Wash., Seattle, 1953, Ph.D., 1955. Cons. Larry Smith and Co., Washington, 1955-59, 60-62; dep. gen. mgr. Charles Center Project, Balt., 1959-60; exec. dir. Downtown Devel. Com., Cin., 1962-67; operating v.p. Federated Dept. Stores, Cin., 1967-75; v.p., dir. corp. public affairs, sec. internat. adv. bd. R.J. Reynolds Industries, Inc., Winston-Salem, N.C., 1975—; adj. assoc. prof. Yale U., 1961-67. Vice chmn. Ohio Commn. Local Govt. Service, 1972-73; mem. Ohio Energy Adv. Council, 1974-75; sec. N.C. Council Mgmt. and Devel., 1978—; mem. N.C. Commn. on Edn. for Econ. Devel., 1983-84. Recipient award of excellence Urban Land Inst., 1980. Mem. Public Affairs Council (dir.). Episcopalian. Home: Route 3 5945 Arden Dr Clemmons NC 27012 Office: RJRI World Hdqrs Reynolds Blvd Winston-Salem NC 27102

DURDEN, ROBERT FRANKLIN, history educator; b. Twin City, Ga., May 10, 1925; s. Virgil Edward and Mildred Frances (Donaldson) D.; m. Anne Dudley Oller, Sept. 3, 1952; children: Marie, Mildred Frances. A.B., Emory U., 1947, M.A., 1948, D.Litt. (hon.), 1981; M.A., Princeton, 1950, Ph.D., 1952. Asst. instr. Princeton (N.J.) U., 1950-52; mem. faculty Duke U., Durham, N.C., 1952—, asso. prof. history, 1960-65, prof., 1965—, chmn., 1974-80; Fulbright prof., Bologna, Italy, 1965-66, Melbourne, Australia, 1980; James Pinkney Harrison prof. Coll. William and Mary, Williamsburg, Va., 1970-71. Author: James S. Pike, 1957, Reconstruction Bonds and Twentieth Century Politics, 1962, Climax of Populism, 1965, The Gray and the Black, 1972, The Dukes of Durham 1865-1929, 1975, (with J. Crow) Maverick Republican in the Old North State, 1977; Editor: Prostrate State (James S. Pike), 1968. Served to lt. (j.g.) USNR, 1943-46. Mem. Am. Hist. Assn., Orgn. Am. Historians, So. Hist. Assn., Hist. Soc. N.C., AAUP. Home: 2532 Wrightwood Ave Durham NC 27705

DURELL, ANN, publisher; b. Belleplain, N.J., Sept. 20, 1930; d. Thomas J. and Marian (Dudley) D.; m. James T. McCrory, May 8, 1982. B.A., Mt. Holyoke Coll., 1952. Editor-in-chief Jr. Literary Guild, N.Y.C., 1960-62; children's book editor Holt, Rinehart & Winston, N.Y.C., 1962-69; pub., v.p. children's books E.P. Dutton, Inc., N.Y.C., 1969—. Author: Holly River Secret, 1956, My Heart's in the Highlands, 1957. Mem. ALA, Children's Book Council (pres.), Nat. Council Tchrs. English. Democrat. Presbyterian. Club: Naval and Mil. (London).

DUREN, PETER LARKIN, educator, mathematician; b. New Orleans, Apr. 30, 1935; s. William and Mary (Hardesty) D.; m. Grace Olcott Adkins, June 15, 1957; children: Elizabeth Adkins, William Larkin. A.B. cum laude (scholar), Harvard U., 1956; Ph.D. (Ramo-Wooldridge Corp. fellow, NSF fellow), M.I.T., 1960. Instr. Stanford, 1960-62; asst. prof. U. Mich., 1962-66, assoc. prof., 1966-69, prof. math., 1969—; temporary mem. Inst. Advanced Study, 1968-69; vis. scholar U. London, also U. Paris, 1964-65; vis. lectr. Technion, Haifa, Israel, 1975; vis. scholar U. Paris-Sud, 1982-83, Mittag-Leffler Inst., Djursholm, Sweden, 1983, E.T.H., Zurich, 1983; prin. lectr. NATO Instructional Conf. on Complex Analysis, Durham, Eng., 1979; mem. regional confs. panel Conf. Bd. Math. Scis., 1979-82. Author: Theory of Hp Spaces, 1970, Univalent Functions, 1983; also articles.; Mng. editor: Mich. Math. Jour, 1976-77; editorial bd.: Complex Variables: Theory and Application, 1981—. Sloan Found. fellow, 1964-66. Mem. Am. Math. Soc. (assoc. editor procs. 1973-75, chmn. com. on teaching loads and class size 1975-78, invited address 1976), London Math. Soc., AAUP, Math. Assn. Am. (gov. 1979-82). Home: 1225 Baldwin Ave Ann Arbor MI 48104

DURENBERGER, DAVID FERDINAND, U.S. senator; b. St. Cloud, Minn., Aug. 19, 1934; s. George G. and Isabelle M. (Cebulla) D.; m. Gilda Beth (Penny) Baran, Sept. 4, 1971; children by previous marriage: Charles, David, Michael, Daniel. B.A. cum laude in Polit. Sci, St. Johns U., 1955; J.D., U. Minn., 1959. Bar: Minn. bar 1959. Mem. firm LeVander, Gillen, Miller & Durenberger, South St. Paul, 1959-66; exec. sec. to Gov. Harold LeVander, 1967-71; counsel for legal and community affairs, corporate sec. H.B. Fuller Co., St. Paul, 1971-78; mem. U.S. Senate from Minn., 1978—. Co-chmn. NAIA Football Bowl Playoff, 1963; div. chmn. United Fund of South St. Paul, 1965; chmn. citizens sect. Minn. Recreation and Park Assn., 1971-72; mem. South St. Paul Parks and Recreation Commn., 1971-72; chmn. Metro Council Open Space Adv. Bd., 1972-74; commr. Murphy-Hanrehan Park Bd., 1973-75; chmn. Save Open Space Now, 1974, Close-Up Found. Minn., 1975-76, Social Investment Task Force, Project Responsibility, 1974-76, Spl. Service div. St. Paul Area United Way, 1973-76; chmn. bd. commrs. Hennepin County Park Res. Dist.; vice chmn. Met. Parks and Open Space Bd.; exec. vice chmn. Gov.'s Commn. on Arts; exec. dir. Minn. Constl. Study Commn., Supreme Ct. Adv. Com. on Jud. Responsibility; pres. Burroughs Sch. PTA, Mpls.; chmn. Dakota County Young Republican League, 1963-64; dir., legal counsel Minn. Young Rep. League, 1964-65; co-chmn. State Young Rep. League, 1965; del. State Rep. Conv., 1966, 68, 70, 72; first vice chmn. 1st Dist. Rep. Party, 1970-72; vice chmn. 13th ward Rep. Party Mpls., 1973-74; bd. dirs. Met. Parks Found., Pub. Service Options, Inc., St. Louis Park AAU Swim Club, Minn. Landmarks, 1971-73, Pub. Affairs Leadership and Mgmt. Tng., Inc., 1973-75, U. Minn. YMCA, 1973-75, Community Planning Orgn., Inc., St. Paul, 1973-76, Project Environment Found., 1974-75, Urban Lab., Inc., 1975, Nat. Recreation and Park Assn., Within the System, Inc., 1976—; trustee Children's Health Center and Hosp., Inc., Mpls.; mem. exec. com. Nat. Center for Vol. Action, Minn. Charities Rev. Council. Served as 2d lt. U.S. Army, 1955-56; as capt. Res., 1957-63. Named Outstanding Young Man in South St. Paul, 1964, One of Ten Outstanding Young Men in Minn., 1965. Mem. Am., Minn., 1st Dist. bar assns., Corp. Counsel Assn., St. Johns U. Alumni Assn. (pres. Twin Cities chpt. 1963-65, nat. pres. 1971-73), Mpls., St. Paul Area chambers commerce, Gamma Eta Gamma (chancellor 1958-59, v.p. Alumni Assn. 1965-75). Roman Catholic. Club: K.C. Home: 7732 Canal Ct McLean VA 22101 *I believe that faith in God gives meaning and purpose to human life. Each of us has God-given talents which are best used in service to mankind. We can go beyond those perceived abilities to reach seemingly impossible goals, so long as we believe we can each make a difference.*

DURFEE, HAROLD ALLEN, philosophy educator; b. Bennington, Vt., May 21, 1920; s. Lynn Stanton and Ethel (Foster) D.; m. Doris Graver, Aug. 10, 1944; children: Peter Allen, Gary Robert. Ph.B., U. Vt., 1941; B.D., Yale U., 1944; Ph.D., Columbia U., 1951; postgrad., Harvard U., 1954-55, U. Oxford, 1968-69, 76. Ordained to ministry Presbyn. Ch., 1944; chmn. dept. philosophy Park Coll., Parkville, Mo., 1946-55; asso. prof. philosophy Am. U., Washington, 1955-57, chmn. dept. philosophy and religion, 1957-73, William Frazer McDowell prof. philosophy, 1957—; faculty Forum on Psychiatry and Humanities, Washington Sch. Psychiatry, 1979—; dir. seminar contemporary European philosophy, 1963; exchange prof. Cath. U. Am., 1972; pres. Mo. Philos. Assn., 1953-54. Author: (with Harold E. Davis) The Teaching oi Philosophy in Universities of the United States, 1965; editor: Analytic Philosophy and Phenomenology, 1976; co-editor, contbr.: Explanation: New Directions in Philosophy, 1973; asso. editor, contbr.: Psychiatry and The Humanities, Vol. II, Thought, Consciousness and Reality, 1977, Vol. V, Kierkegaard's Truth: The Disclosure of the Self, 1981. Trustee Washington Consortium of Univs., 1970—. Fund for Advancement Edn. fellow, 1954-55. Mem. Am. Philos. Assn., Metaphys. Soc. Am., Am. Acad. Religion, Internat. Soc. Metaphysics, Internat. Phenomenological Research Soc., AAUP, Washington Philosophy Club (pres. 1961-62), Kappa Sigma, Phi Kappa Phi. Home: 12405 St James Rd Rockville MD 20850 Office: Am U Washington DC 20016

DURFEY, ROBERT WALKER, consultant; b. Oak Park, Ill., Feb. 7, 1925; s. George Jackson and Cornelia Needles (Walker) D.; m. Sally McCracken, Oct. 22, 1955; children—Robert Walker, Margaret, Rebecca. B.S., USCG Acad., 1948; M.S. in Internat. Affairs, George Washington U., 1968. Commd. ensign USCG, 1948, advanced through grades to rear adm., 1974; chief Office of Personnel, Hdqrs. USCG, Washington, 1974-76; comdr. (7th Coast Guard Dist.), Miami, Fla., 1976-79, ret., 1979, cons. marine affairs and cargo security, 1979—. Decorated Legion of Merit, Bronze Star (3). Episcopalian. Address: 17503 SW 74th Ct Miami FL 33157

DURGIN, DON, publishing company and broadcasting executive; b. Chgo., Sept. 24, 1924; s. William Ryerson and Ada Cleveland (Emmett) D. A.B. summa cum laude, Princeton U., 1947; LL.B., N.Y. U., 1954. Asst. research account supr. Foote, Cone & Belding, N.Y.C., 1947, asst. account exec., 1948; features and filler editor Pageant mag., 1948-49; asst. to advt. and promotion mgr., spot sales div. NBC, 1949-51; presentation writer ABC, 1951-53, mgr., tv spot sales devel., 1953; mgr. tv sales devel. ABC-TV Network, 1954; dir. research and sales devel. ABC Radio and TV Networks, 1954; v.p. charge ABC Radio Network, 1955-57; v.p. sales planning, tv network sales NBC, 1957, v.p., nat. sales mgr., 1958-59, v.p. charge sales, 1959-65; pres. NBC-TV Network, N.Y.C., 1966-73; exec. v.p. NBC, 1973-75; pres. McCaffrey & McCall, Inc., N.Y.C., 1975-76; exec. v.p. Dun & Bradstreet Corp., N.Y.C., 1977-82, v.p. mktg. services, 1982—. Served as 1st lt. USAAF, 1943-45. Club: Univ. (N.Y.C.). Home: Box 264 Mill Neck NY 11765 Office: Dun & Bradstreet Corp 299 Park Ave New York NY 10171

DURGIN, FRANK ALBERT, JR., economics educator; b. Lynn, Mass., Dec. 8, 1923; s. Frank Albert and Dorothy (Smith) D.; m. Barbara Louise Ann Bright, Feb. 12, 1952 (div. Jan. 1983); children—Stephen, Brian, Peter, Katie. B.A., Tufts U., 1949; doctorate and licence en droit, U. Toulouse, 1956. With U.S. Dept. Def., 1956-57; lectr. U. Md., 1957-59; with USIA, 1959-60; asst. prof. Babson Inst., Babson Park, Md., 1960-64; prof. econs. U. So. Maine, Portland, 1964—. Contbr. articles to profl. jours. Served with USAF, 1943-46. Decorated Air Medal (2).; Recipient Disting. Service award USIA, 1960; Ford Found. faculty research grantee, 1964. Mem. Assn. Comparative Econ. Studies, Am. Assn. Advancement Slavic Studies, Maine Econ. Soc. (v.p. 1983-84), Phi Kappa Phi. Home: 21 Deering St Portland ME 04101 Office: 96 Falmouth St Portland ME 04103

DURGIN, RICHARD LINWOOD, manufacturing executive; b. York, Maine, Feb. 19, 1926; s. Harold Linwood and Sarah (Norton) D.; m. Mary Cunningham, Aug. 11, 1979. B.S. with distinction, U. Rochester, 1947. Gear engr. Gleason Works, Rochester, N.Y., 1947-52; gear lab. engr. Chrysler Corp., Detroit, 1952-55; gear mfr. engr. Ill. Gear (div. Wallace Murray Corp.), Chgo., 1955-61, v.p. sales, 1961-69, v.p., gen. mgr., 1969-77; group v.p. Wallace Murray Corp., N.Y.C., 1977-79, exec. v.p., 1979-80, pres., chief exec. officer, 1980-83; sr. exec. v.p. Household Mfg. Inc., Prospect Heights, IL, 1983—. Served with USNR, 1944-46. Mem. ASME, Soc. Automotive Engrs., Am. Gear Mfrs. Assn., Newcomen Soc., Tau Beta Pi. Republican. Methodist. Clubs: Masons, Elks. Home: 2340 Dorina Dr Northfield IL 60093

DURHAM, CHRISTINE MEADERS, justice Supreme Court Utah; b. Los Angeles, Aug. 3, 1945; d. William Anderson and Louis (Christensen) Meaders; m. George Homer Durham II, Dec. 29, 1966; children: Jennifer, Meghan, Troy, Melinda, Isaac. A.B., Wellesley Coll., 1967; J.D., Duke U., 1971. Bar: N.C. 1971, Utah 1974. Sole practice law, Durham, N.C., 1971-73; instr. legal medicine Duke U., Durham, 1971-73; adj. prof. law Brigham Young U., Provo, Utah, 1973-78; ptnr. Johnson, Durham & Moxley, Salt Lake City, 1974-78; judge Utah Dist. Ct., 1978-82; justice Utah Sup. Ct., 1982—; faculty Nat. Jud. coll., Reno, 1983. Mem. Nat. Assn. Women Judges (v.p. 1983), ABA, Utah Bar Assn. Mormon. Home: 1702 Yale Ave Salt Lake City UT 84108 Office: Utah Supreme Court 332 State Capital Salt Lake City UT 84114

DURHAM, CLARENCE RAY, banker; b. Pineville, Ky., Sept. 1, 1930; s. James M. and Mattie (Lefevers) D.; m. Shelby Frances Wilburn, Aug. 18, 1956; children—Linda Rae, James Shelby. B.S., Eastern Ky. U., 1957. Agt. Internal Revenue Service, Louisville, 1957-65, spl. agt., criminal investigator, 1965-67; with Liberty Nat. Bank & Trust Co., Louisville, 1967—, mgr. accounting dept., 1968, comptroller, 1969-74, chief fin. officer, 1974—, sr. auditor, 1980—, also treas. Bd. dirs., treas. Anchorage Civic Club. Served with USN, 1950-54. Mem. Nat. Assn. Accountants (past asso. dir.), Bank Adminstrn. Inst., Fin. Execs. Inst. (treas., dir.). Home: 2407 Anchor Way Anchorage KY 40223 Office: 416 W Jefferson St Louisville KY 40202

DURHAM, GEORGE HOMER, educator, ch. exec.; b. Parowan, Utah, Feb. 4, 1911; s. George Henry and Mary Ellen (Marsden) D.; m. Eudora Widtsoe, June 20, 1936; children—Carolyn, Doralee (Mrs. R.H. Madsen), George. A.B., U. Utah, 1932; Ph.D., U. Calif. at Los Angeles, 1939; LL.D., Ariz. State U., 1971, Ind. State U., 1976, State Coll. So. Utah, U. Utah, 1977; D. Pub. Service, Brigham Young U., 1975. Finance div. mgr. Zion's Coop. Merc. Inst., Salt Lake City, 1935-

36; fellow, asst. U. Calif., Los Angeles, 1937-39, vis. prof., summer 1950; polit. sci. dept. Utah State Coll., 1939-42, Swarthmore Coll., 1942-43, U. Utah, 1944-60; dir. Inst. Govt., U. Utah, 1946-53, head polit. sci. dept., 1948-53, v.p. univ., 1953-60; pres. Ariz. State U., 1960-69; Utah commr. higher edn., Salt Lake City, 1969-76; research prof. U. Utah, 1976-77; mng. dir. hist. dept. Ch. of Jesus Christ of Latter-day Saints, 1977—; Mem. Western Interstate Commn. for Higher Edn., 1955-60, 69-76; mem. Ariz. State Bd. Edn., 1960-66; mem. U.S. nat. commn. for UNESCO, 1955-57,59; cons., current affairs analyst KTVT, Intermountain TV Corp., Salt Lake City, 1956-58; mem. lang. adv. devel. bd. U.S. Office Edn., 1959-63; mem. Air Force ROTC adv. panel to sec. air force, 1961-64, Army ROTC Panel, 1968-70; adviser Army Command and Gen. Staff Coll., 1970-73; mem. Bd. Fgn. Scholarships, 1963-66; Bd. dirs. Am. Council on Edn., 1967-70, Ari. Acad., 1964-69, Phoenix Symphony, 1961-69; adv. bd. Utah Symphony, 1969—, Am. Grad. Sch. Internat. Mgmt. Author: Joseph Smith: Prophet-Statesman, 1944, The Adminstration of Higher Education in Montana, 1958, other monographs.; Contbg. editor: The Improvement Era, 1946-70. Mem. world-wide exec. com. Sunday schs. Ch. of Jesus Christ of Latter-day Saints, 1971-73; pres. Salt Lake Central stake, 1973-76; regional rep. Council of 12, 1976-77; mem. First Quorum of the Seventy, 1977—. Mem. Am. Polit. Sci. Assn. (exec. council 1949-51), Western Polit. Sci. Assn. (pres. 1948), Am. Soc. Pub. Adminstrn. (council 1949-51, v.p. 1952, pres. 1959-60), Nat. Acad. Pub. Adminstrn., Pi Gamma Mu, Pi Sigma Alpha, Phi Kappa Phi. Clubs: Timpanogos, Windsor. Home: 515 S 10th E Salt Lake City UT 84102 Office: 50 E North Temple St Salt Lake City UT 84150

DURHAM, JOHN HENDRICK, investment company executive; b. Amsterdam, Netherlands, Aug. 7, 1937; came to U.S., 1939, naturalized, 1945; s. Jules Henry and Lulu (Kirchhof) D.; m. Carol Ann Rohrbach, Dec. 22, 1962; children: Christine, John Paul. A.B. in Econs., Queens Coll., 1959; M.B.A. in Fin, Wharton Sch., U. Pa., 1961. With Del. Mgmt. Co., Phila., 1960—, exec. v.p. policy, 1974—; pres. Del. Group Mut. Funds, 1977—, Del. Investment Advisers, 1975—. Trustee Germantown Acad. Mem. Fin. Analysts Phila. (past dir., past pres.), Investment Co. Inst. Mem. United Ch. Christ. Club: Union League. Home: Wood Spring Rd Gwynedd Valley PA 19437 Office: 10 Penn Center Philadelphia PA 19103

DURHAM, NORMAN NEVILL, scientist, educator; b. Ranger, Tex., Feb. 14, 1927; s. Harold H. and Bernice (Griffith) D.; m. Jane Harriet Stovall, July 26, 1952; children—Susan Lynne, Janet Anne, Diane Elizabeth, Linda Jane. B.S., N. Tex. State U., 1949, M.S., 1951; Ph.D., U. Tex., 1954. Student instr., research asst. N. Tex. State U., Denton, 1947-51; research asso., teaching asst. U. Tex., 1951-54; faculty dept. microbiology Okla. State U., Stillwater, 1954-66, prof., 1961-66, dean, prof. microbiology, 1967—; dir. Water Research Center; cons. biol. scis. communication project NASA, 1963—; vis. lectr. U. Okla. Sch. Medicine, 1963, Kans. State Tchrs. Coll., 1963, 65; program dir. molecular biology and cellular genetics U.S. AEC, 1966-67; evaluation team Nat. Council Accreditation Tchr. Edn., 1968—; mem. manpower adv. com. U.S. Office Edn., 1973—; mem. tech. adv. com. Fed. Energy Adminstrn., 1974—. Contbr. articles profl. publs. Served with USNR, 1944-45. Recipient Coll. Arts and Scis. award, 1963, Distinguished Alumni citation N. Tex. State U., 1970. Fellow Am. Acad. Microbiology, Okla. Acad. Sci. (pres. 1974-75); mem. Am. Soc. Microbiology (councilor 1961-65), Biochem. Soc., Soc. Gen. Microbiology, AAAS, AAUP, Stillwater C. of C. (pres. 1975), Sigma Xi, Pi Kappa Alpha, Phi Delta Kappa, Beta Beta Beta, Phi Kappa Phi. Presbyn. (elder). Clubs: Elk, Kiwanian. Home: Route 5 Box 138 Stillwater OK 74074

DURHAM, ROBERT LEWIS, architect; b. Seattle, Apr. 28, 1912; s. William Worth and Abbie May (McNett) D.; m. Dorothy Evelyn Wyatt, May 14, 1935 (dec. Nov. 1935); m. Marjorie Ruth Moser, Sept. 19, 1936; children: David Robert, Gail Maureen Durham Philippson, Catherine Louise Durham Lonheim, Jennifer Ann Durham Jerde. Student, Coll. Puget Sound, 1930-31; B.Arch. cum laude, U. Wash., 1936. Draftsman B. Dudley Stuart (Architect), Seattle, 1936-38; cost engr. FHA, 1938-41; partner Stuart & Durham (Architects), Seattle, 1941-51, Robert L. Durham & Assos., 1951-54, Durham, Anderson & Freed (Architects), 1954-74, pres., 1974-77; cons. HDR Inc. (Architects), 1977—; Mem. Bldg. Code Adv. Commn. City Seattle, Seattle Planning Commn., 1969—; mem. Seattle Municipal Art Commn., 1955-65, chmn., 1957-59; com. worship and arts Nat. Council Chs.; chmn. cultural arts com. Century 21 Expn., Seattle, 1958-62; speaker art, architecture. Prin. works include Constrn. Center, Seattle, Downtown YWCA, student union Seattle Pacific Coll, Evergreen State Coll. Library, Fidelity Savs. & Loan Assn. Recipient honor award for various chs. Ch. Archtl. Guild Am., 1952, 55, 57, 59, 60, 64; honor awards Wash. chpt. AIA, 52, 59, 54, 56; award for S.W. Br. Library, Seattle, AIA-ALA, 1964. Fellow AIA (past pres. Washington, nat. pres. 1967-68, bursar Coll. Fellows 1976-78, vice chancellor Coll. Fellows 1978-79, chancellor 1979-80, Kemper award 1981); hon. fellow Royal Archtl. Inst. Can., Mexican, Peruvian socs. architects; mem. Ch. Archtl. Guild Am. (v.p. 1963-65, dir), Seattle C. of C., Tau Sigma Delta. Congregationalist. Club: Seattle Engrs. Home: 900 University St Apt 3-V Seattle WA 98101 Office: 1100 Eastlake E Seattle WA 98109

DURIEUX, CAROLINE WOGAN, artist, educator; b. New Orleans, Jan. 22, 1896; d. Charles N. and Anna Lovisa (Spelman) Wogan; m. Pierre Durieux, Apr. 14, 1920 (dec.); 1 son, Charles Wogan. B.A., Newcomb Coll., 1917; student, Pa. Acad. Design, 1919-20; M.A., La. State U., 1949. Faculty Newcomb Coll., 1918, asst. prof. painting, drawing, art anatomy, 1938-43; faculty Arts and Crafts Club Art Sch., 1921; cons. Fed. Art Project of La., 1938-43; instr. painting, drawing La. State U., 1943-45, asst. prof. graphic art, drawing, 1945-50, asso. prof., 1950-55, prof., 1955-64, prof. emeritus, 1964—. Illustrator: New Orleans City Guide, 1938, Gumbo YaYa, 1945, Mardi Gras Day, 1948, Caroline Durieux, 45 lithographs and drawings, 1949, Caroline Durieux Lithographs from the 30s and 40s, 1977, others.; lithographs, drawing reproduced numerous newspapers, mags., U.S., Mex. and Cuba, 1934—, one-man shows, Galleria Central, Mexico City, Marie Sterner Gallery, Delgado Mus., New Orleans, Va. Mus. Fine Arts, Richmond, Witte Mus., San Antonio, Houston Mus. Fine Arts, Univ. Mus., Tulsa, U. Fla., Fine Arts Club of Chgo., Burlington (Vt.) Mus., U. Ga., U. Ala., Carnegie Library, Atlanta, La. State U., Newcomb Coll., Centenary Coll., Shreveport, others; prints shown in nat. exhibits, Met. Mus., N.Y.C., Phila. Mus. Fine Arts, Nat. Acad. Design, others; works represented in permanent collections, Mus. Modern Art, N.Y.C., Phila. Mus. Fine Arts, Library Congress Print Collection, N.Y. Pub. Library Print Collection, IBM Collection, N.Y.C., Biblioteque Nationale, Paris, Brooks Meml. Gallery, Memphis, Smithsonian Instn., Rosenwald collection, Historic New Orleans collection, others. (Recipient graphic prize Delgado Mus. 1944), Historic New Orleans collection, others. (purchase prize Library Congress Print Collection 1944, 46-52), Historic New Orleans collection, others. (fifty prints of year award Am. Inst. Graphic Art 1944). Mem. Baton Rouge Gallery. Developer electron process for production of prints (with Dr. Harry and Naomi Wheeler), color process for electron prints (with Dr. Olen Nance), cliches verres in color

DURIG, JAMES ROBERT, college dean; b. Washington, Pa., Apr. 30, 1935; s. and Roberta Wilda Mounts; m. Kathryn Marlene Sprowls, Sept. 1, 1955; children: Douglas Tybor, Bryan Robert, Stacey Ann. B.A., Washington and Jefferson Coll., 1958, D.Sc. (hon.), 1979; Ph.D., M.I.T., 1962. Asst. prof. chemistry U. S.C., Columbia, 1962-65, asso. prof., 1965-68, prof., 1968—, Ednl. Found. prof. chemistry, 1970-73, dean, 1973—. Editor: Vibrational Spectra and Structure, 10 vols, 1972—, Jour. Raman Spectroscopy, 1979—; mem. editorial bd.: Jour. Molecular Structure, 1972—; contbr. articles to profl. jours. Served with Chem. Corps U.S. Army, 1963-64. Recipient Russell award U.S.C., 1968; Alexander von Humboldt Sr. Scientist award, W. Ger., 1976. Mem. Am. Chem. Soc. (So. Chemist award Memphis sect. 1976, Charles A. Stone award S.E. Piedmont sect. 1975), Am. Phys. Soc., Soc. for Applied Spectroscopy (Pitts. sect. award 1981), Coblentz Soc. (mem. governing bd. 1972-76, pres. 1974-76, award for outstanding research in molecular spectroscopy 1970), Internat. Union Pure and Applied Chemistry (chmn. sub-commn. on infrared and Raman spectroscopy 1975—, mem. commn. molecular spectra and structure 1978—, sec. 1981—), Blue Key Soc., Phi Beta Kappa (pres. Alapha chpt. S.C. 1970), Sigma Xi, Phi Lambda Upsilon. Presbyterian. Home: 3815 Fernleaf Rd Columbia SC 29206 Office: Coll Sci and Math U SC Columbia SC 29208 *Everything has a lighthearted side which is sometimes difficult to recognize. Never lose your sense of humor*

DURKAN, MICHAEL JOSEPH, college librarian; b. Louisburgh, County Mayo, Ireland, Aug. 11, 1925; came to U.S., 1958, naturalized, 1971; s. Michael Thomas and Mary B. (O'Malley) D.; m. Yvonne Marie Walsh, Jan. 13, 1958; children: Ciaran P., Maeve B., Michael C., Niall T. B.A., St. Patrick's Coll., Maynooth, 1949; diploma in L.S, Univ. Coll., Dublin, 1950. Asst. librarian Longford/Westmeath County Library, 1956-57; librarian USIA, Dublin, Ireland, 1950-56; tech. services librarian, asst. librarian Wesleyan U., Middletown, Conn., 1958-76; coll. librarian Swarthmore (Pa.) Coll., 1976—; instr. Anglo-Irish lit. Wesleyan U. and; Swarthmore Coll. Author: (with R. Ayling) Sean O'Casey: A Bibliography, 1978; contbr. articles on Anglo-Irish lit. and library adminstrn. to profl. publs. Mem. community services com. Middletown Public Library; mem. Del. County Library adv. bd., Nether Providence Athletic Assn. Mem. Bibliog. Soc. Am., Library Assn. Ireland, Am. Com. for Irish Studies, Irish Studies Center, Balch Inst., Philobiblon Club (Phila.). Democrat. Roman Catholic. Office: McCabe Library Swarthmore College Swarthmore PA 19081 *

DURLAND, JACK RAYMOND, art gallery executive; b. Taylor, Tex., Sept. 21, 1916; s. Den D. and Percy (Langrill) D.; m. June Kathryn Cain, Feb. 5, 1937; children: Jack Raymond, Diane Elizabeth. LL.B., U. Okla., 1941. Bar: Okla. 1941. Spl. agt. FBI, 1942-46; pvt. practice law, Oklahoma City, 1946-50; asst. to pres. Cain's Coffee Co., Oklahoma City, 1950-52, pres., 1952-82, Gallery at Nichols Hills Inc., Oklahoma City, 1982—; Chmn. bd. Nat. Coffee Assn., 1961-62. Bd. dirs. Met. YMCA, Oklahoma City, Oklahoma City C. of C. Mem. ABA; Mem. Okla. Bar Assn. Home: 1620 Queenstown Rd Oklahoma City OK 73116 Office: 6460 Avondale Oklahoma City OK 73116

DURN, RAYMOND JOSEPH, lawyer; b. Cleve., Nov. 28, 1925; s. Joseph Frank and Mary (Spenko) D.; m. Emmy Reboly, June 5, 1954; children: David, Sarah, Tamara. B.A., Harvard U., 1950, LL.B., 1953. Bar: Ohio 1953, U.S. Dist. Ct. Ohio 1954, U.S. Ct. Appeals 6th cir. 1974. Assoc. Jones, Day, Reavis & Pogue, Cleve., 1953-60, ptnr., 1960—. Trustee Cleve. Neighborhood Health Services, Inc., 1969—, Chester Twp., Ohio, 1972-75; mem. Chester Twp. Bd. Zoning Appeals, Ohio, 1969-72. Serves with USAAF, 1944-46. Mem. Ohio Bar Assn., Cleve. Bar Assn. Democrat. Unitarian. Club: City (Cleve.). Home: 13088 W Geauga Tr Chesterland OH 44026 Office: Jones Day Reavis & Pogue 1700 Huntington Bldg Cleveland OH 44115

DURNING, CHARLES, actor; b. Highland Falls, N.Y., Feb. 28, 1923; m. Mary Ann Amelio, 1974. Attended, Columbia U., N.Y. U. Former boxer, cab driver, waiter, ironworker, constrn. worker, elevator operator. Profl. theatre debut with nat. co. of: The Andersonville Trial, 1960; since 1962 has appeared in: Measure for Measure, King John, Chronicles of Henry IV, N.Y. Shakespeare Festival; stage appearances include That Championship Season (Drama Desk award 1972), The Boom Boom Room, The Child Buyer, Drat! The Cat!, Lemon Sky, The Comedy of Errors, The Au Pair Man, Knock Knock, others; movie appearances include The Final Countdown, The Sting, Front Page, North Dallas Forty, Muppet Movie, Die Laughing; appeared in: TV films, including The Trial of Chaplain Jensen, The Connection, Switch, Stonestreet, The Cop and the Kid; TV series Captains and the Kings; other TV appearances include The Queen of the Stardust Ballroom, High Chapparral, The Defenders, Madigan, All in the Family. Served with U.S. Army. Office: care Jack Fields and Assos 9255 Sunset Blvd Suite 1105 Los Angeles CA 90069 *

DURONI, CHARLES EUGENE, food company executive; b. McCune, Kans., Apr. 9, 1933; s. Charley S. and Dorothy M. D.; m. Charlene D. White, Feb. 18, 1978; children: Renee, Ashley, Michelle, Lance. B.S., U. Kans., 1955; LL.B., U. Wis., 1962. Bar: Wis. 1962, Pa. 1979, U.S. Supreme ct. 1979, U.S. Dist. Ct. (mid. dist.) Pa. 1980. Staff counsel Rockwell Internat. Co., Pitts., 1964-68; sr. atty. H.J. Heinz Co., Pitts., 1968-77; sr. assoc. counsel, asst. gen. counsel Hershey (Pa.) Foods Corp., 1977-79, v.p., gen. counsel, 1979—; bd. dirs. U.S. Trademark Assn., 1972-76. Served with USAF, 1955-59. Mem. ABA, Wis. Bar Assn., Pa. Bar Assn., Dauphin County Bar Assn., Sigma Chi, Phi Delta Phi. Club: Met. (N.Y.C.). Office: 100 Mansion Rd E Hershey PA 17033 *Of the highest importance in the legal and business world is the exercise of conservative, but imaginative, good judgment, acceptable to the environment, consistently exercised with a sensitivity to others.*

DURR, JOHN W., distribution company executive; b. Montgomery, Ala., Feb. 17, 1931; s. James Judkins and Ann Elia (Garrett) D.; m. Patricia Powers Collins, Sept. 22, 1956; children: James Judkins II, Lucy Powers. B.S., U. Ala., 1955. Exec. v.p. Durr-Fillauer Med., Inc., Montgomery, Ala., 1972—. Served to cpl U.S. Army, 1951-53. Presbyterian. Home: 305 Gatsby Dr Montgomery AL 36106 Office: Durr-Fillauer Med Inc 218 Commerce St Montgomery AL 36104

DURRANI, SAJJAD HAIDAR, aerospace scientist; b. Jalalpur, Pakistan, Aug. 27, 1928; came to U.S., 1959, naturalized, 1966; s. Inayat Ullah and Hameedah Khanum D.; m. Brita Katarina Yasmin Portin, May 21, 1959; children: Zarina, Amina, Arif. B.A., Govt. Coll., Lahore, Pakistan, 1946; B.Sc. in Elec. Engring. with honors, Engring. Coll. Lahore, 1949; M.Sc.Tech., Coll. Tech., Manchester, Eng., 1953; Sc.D., U. N.Mex., 1962. Lectr., asst. prof. Engring. Coll., Lahore, 1949-59; instr., research asso. U. N.Mex., Albuquerque, 1959-62; sr. engr. Gen. Electric Co., Lynchburg, Va., 1962-64; prof., chmn. dept. elec. engring. Engring. U. Lahore, 1964-65; asso. prof. Kans. State U., Manhattan, 1965-66; sr. engr. RCA Space Center, Hightstown, N.J., 1966-68; staff scientist, br. mgr. COMSAT Labs., Clarksburg, Md., 1968-73; sr. scientist Ops. Research, Inc., Silver Spring, Md., 1973-74; sr. engr. NASA-Goddard Space Flight Center, Greenbelt, Md., 1974-79, mgr. for system planning, tracking and data relay satellite system, 1981—; sr. communications scientist NASA Hdqrs., Washington, 1979-81; vis. prof. U. Md., 1972; instr. George Washington U., 1980-82; mem. Engring. Manpower Commn., Assn. Engring. Socs., 1981—. Mem. editorial bd.: COMSAT Tech. Rev, 1972, IEEE Spectrum, 1975-78. Pres. Muslim Community Center, Silver Spring, 1976-82. Recipient spl. achievement award NASA, 1977, 78. Fellow IEEE (gov. IEEE Aerospace and Electronic Systems Soc. 1977—, pres. 1982-83, Outstanding Mem. region 2 1982), Washington Acad. Scis., AIAA (asso.). Office: NASA GSFC Code 800.1 Greenbelt MD 20832

DURRANT, GEOFFREY HUGH, emeritus educator; b. Pilsley, Eng., July 27, 1913; s. John and Charlotte (Atkinson) D.; m. Barbara Joan Altson, June 2, 1942; children—John Guy, Catherine Jane. B.A., Cambridge (Eng.) U., 1932-35; diploma in edn, London U., 1935-36; student, Tuebingen (W. Ger.) U., 1937-39. Prof., English U. Natal, South Africa, 1945-60; head dept. English; prof. U. Man., Can., Winnipeg, 1961-66; prof. emeritus U. B.C., Can., Vancouver, master tchr., 1973. Author: William Wordsworth, 1969, Wordsworth and the Great System, 1970. Served with South African Armed Forces, 1940-44. Carnegie fellow, 1960; Killam sr. fellow, 1976. Fellow Royal Soc. Can.; mem. Assn. Can. Univ. Tchrs. English. Anglican. Home: 3994 W 34th Ave Vancouver BC V6N 2L5 Canada Office: U BC Vancouver BC V6T 1W5 Canada

DURRELL, RICHARD J., publisher; b. Mpls., July 22, 1925; s. Royal S. and Dorothy Ann (Jones) D.; m. Jacquelyn C. Durrell, Apr. 22, 1949; children: Piper, Robyn, Kerry, Bradford, B. Alexander. B.A., U. Minn., 1948. Order clk. Lowe & Campbell div. Wilson Sporting Goods, Mpls., 1949; newsstand circulation rep. Time Inc., Mpls., 1949-51, corp. trainee, retail rep., Mpls. and Dallas, 1951-52, adv. sales rep. Life Mag., Mpls. and N.Y.C., 1952-59; account exec. Grey Advt.-Young & Rubicam, N.Y.C., 1959-62; adv. sales rep. Life Mag. Time Inc., N.Y.C., 1962-64; N.Y. mgr. Life Mag. Grey Advt.-Young & Rubicam, 1964-67, assoc. advt. sales dir. Life Mag., 1967-70, asst. pub. Life Mag., 1970-72, asst. pub., advt. sales dir. Life Mag., 1972, pub. People Mag., N.Y.C., 1973—. Trustee Northland Coll. Served with USMC, 1943-46. Recipient cert. exec. program U. Calif., Berkeley, 1968. Mem. Am. Advt. Fedn. (dir. Washington 1980), Mag. Pubs. Assn. (mktg. com. 1974-83, mem. Kelley Award com. 1983). Clubs: Country Club Fairfield (Conn.); Nat. Golf Links (Southampton, N.Y.); Hemisphere (N.Y.C.). Home: 206 Salt Meadow Rd Fairfield CT 06430 Office: Time Inc 1271 Ave of the Americas New York NY 10020

DURRENBERGER, ROBERT WARREN, educator, climatologist; b. Perham, Minn., Oct. 2, 1918; s. John George and Mary Angela (Weibeler) D.; m. Bernadine Ann Stiegel, July 15, 1946; children: Daniel Joseph, Mary Ann. B.S., Moorhead State Coll., 1940, Calif. Inst. Tech., 1941; M.S. in Geography, U. Wis., 1949, Ph.D., U. Calif. at Los Angeles, 1955. Jr. exec. R.S. Bacon Veneer Co., Chgo., 1945-47; instr. U. Ky., 1948-49; asst. prof., chmn. dept. geography Los Angeles State Coll., 1949-58; asso. prof., prof., chmn. dept. geography San Fernando Valley State Coll., 1958-61, coordinator grad. studies, 1961-63, prof. geography, 1964-65, 66-70; asso. dean acad. planning Calif. State Coll., 1963-64; vis. prof. U. Calif. at Los Angeles, 1965-66; prof. Ariz. State U., Tempe, 1970—, dir., mem. solar energy com.; state climatologist, State of Ariz., 1973-79; mem. Gov.'s Adv. Commn. Ariz. Environment, Ariz. Water Resources Com.; cons. agrl. climatology Libyan Arab Republic; participant numerous seminars, cons. in field. Author: Patterns on the Land, 1957, The Geography of California, 1959, Sources of Information About California, 1961, California and the Western States, 1963; film California's Natural Regions, 1963; California-the Last Frontier, 1969, California: Its People, Its Problems, Its Prospects, 1971, Geographical Research and Writing, 1971, Dictionary of the Environmental Sciences, 1973, Climatological Map of Arizona, 1976, Solar Radiation and Sunshine Data for the Southwestern United States, 1976, A Cloud Atlas of the United States, 1976, Arizona and the Southwest—An Atlas of Climate and Solar Energy; contbg. author: Regions of the United States, 1972, Reader's Encyclopedia of the American West, 1977; editor: Directory of Climatologists, Physical Enviroment Vol., U.S.-Mexico-Borderland Atlas; contbg. editor: World Book Ency; Contbr. articles to profl. jours., encys., chpt. to book. Served to maj. USAAF, 1940-45. Recipient Distinguished Alumni award Moorhead State U., 1977. Mem. Am. Meteorol. Soc., Assn. Am. Geographers, Assn. Pacific Coast Geographers (pres.), Internat. Solar Energy Soc. (exec. bd. solar radiation div.), Am. Assn. State Climatologists (pres.), Am. Water Resources Assn., Blue Key, Sigma Xi. Roman Catholic. Home: 6233 E Catalina St Scottsdale AZ 85251

DURRENBERGER, WILLIAM JOHN, retired army officer, investment consultant; b. Wadena, Minn., Mar. 15, 1917; s. John George and Mary Angela (Weibeler) D.; m. Alma Mary Pagliai, Jan. 3, 1947; children: William John, Robert Scott, Philip Michael. Student, U. Minn., 1935-40, Brit. Coll. Mil. Sci., 1943; B.S., U. Md., 1951; M.B.A., Syracuse U., 1954; grad., Indsl. Coll. Armed Forces, 1960. Commd. 2d lt. U.S. Army, 1939, advanced through grades to maj. gen., 1968; chief logistics plan div. (UN Command), Korea, 1960-61, dep. comdr. Ordnance Weapons Command, Ill., 1962, comdg. officer Springfield (Mass.) Armory, 1963-65, comdg. gen. Army Tank Automotive Center, Warren, Mich., 1965-66, comdg. gen. U.S. Army Weapons Command, Rock Island, Ill., 1966-68, dep. chief of staff Logistics; acting chief staff U.S. Army, Pacific, 1968-70; ret., 1970; dir. Des Moines/Polk County (Iowa) Met. Criminal Justice Center, 1971-73; asst. v.p. ednl. services Drake U., 1971-81; bus. cons., 1981—; profl. asso. Mitchell & Mitchell Economists, 1979-82. Author over 100 tech. intelligence reports on Brit. and German combat vehicles and weapons, 1943-46. Decorated D.S.M. with oak leaf cluster, Bronze Star, Army Commendation medal with oak leaf cluster. Mem. Assn. U.S. Army (nat. v.p. for Iowa), Cath. League Religious and Civil Rights, Am. Legion, VFW, DAV, Ret. Officers Assn., Porsche Club Am. Roman Catholic. Club: Oakmoor Racquet. Home: 2708 Lynner Dr Des Moines IA 50310

DURRETT, JAMES FRAZER, JR., lawyer; b. Atlanta, Mar. 23, 1931; s. James Frazer and Cora Frazer (Morton) D.; m. Lucretia McPherson, June 9, 1956; children: James Frazer III, William McPherson, Lucretia Heston, Thomas Ratcliffe. A.B., Emory U., 1952; postgrad., Princeton U., 1952-53; LL.B. cum laude, Harvard U., 1956. Bar: Ga. 1955. Partner firm Alston & Bird (and predecessor firm), Atlanta, 1956—; adj. prof. Emory U. Law Sch., 1961-77. Trustee Student Aid Found.; bd. govs. Ga. Assn. for Pastoral Care, 1978—. Fellow Am. Coll. Probate Counsel; mem. Am. Law Inst. (adv. estate and gift tax project, restatement, second, property), Am. Bar Assn., Ga. Bar Assn., Atlanta Bar Assn., Lawyers Club of Atlanta, Atlanta Tax Forum (dir.). Presbyterian. Clubs: Capital City; Harvard, Georgian, World Trade (Atlanta). Home: 3483 Ridgewood Rd NW Atlanta GA 30327 Office: Citizens & Southern National Bank Bldg Atlanta GA 30335

DURSLAG, MELVIN, author, newspaper columnist; b. Chgo., Apr. 29, 1921; s. William and Frieda (Berliner) D.; m. Lorayne Jane Sweet, Nov. 21, 1948; children—Ivy, William, James. B.A., U. So. Calif., 1943. Reporter, feature writer Los Angeles Examiner, 1938-43, reporter, 1946-53; columnist Los Angeles Examiner and Herald-Examiner, 1953—; syndicated by King Features Syndicate, Hearst News Service, free-lance writer, 1950—; contbg. editor TV Guide. Bd. dirs. Sch. Journalism, U. So. Calif., Los Angeles Press Club Welfare Found. Served with USAAF, 1943-46; CBI. Decorated Bronze Star (5); recipient Nat. Headliners award, 1960. Mem. Sigma Delta Chi, Kappa Tau Alpha. Home: 523 Dalehurst Ave Los Angeles CA 90024 Office: 1111 S Broadway Los Angeles CA 90054

DURYEA, PERRY BELMONT, JR., business executive; b. East Hampton, N.Y., Oct. 18, 1921; s. Perry Belmont and Jane (Stewart) D.; m. Elizabeth Ann Weed, Apr. 4, 1944; children—Lynn, Perry Belmont III. B.A., Colgate U., 1942; LL.D., Dowling Coll., 1963, Southampton Coll., 1968; L.H.D. (hon.), Sienna Coll., 1972. Mem. N.Y. State Assembly, 1960-78, minority leader, 1966-68, speaker of assembly, 1969-74, minority leader, 1975-78; chmn. Perry B. Duryea and Son, Inc., Montauk, N.Y., 1950-78, v.p., 1978—; vice chmn. Beker Industries, Greenwich, Conn., 1979—, also dir.; trustee Seamen's Bank for Savs. Mem. N.Y. State Republican Com., 1965-78; del. Rep. Nat. Conv., 1972, 76. Served to lt. comdr. USN, 1943-46. Recipient Disting. Alumni award Colgate U., 1972; Pres.'s Disting. Service award SUNY, Buffalo, 1972. Presbyterian. Club: Masons. Home: Old Montauk Hwy Montauk NY 11954 Office: Tuthill Rd Montauk NY 11954

DURYEE, A. WILBUR, ret. physician; b. North Hackensack, N.J., July 5, 1899; s. Abram and Margaret (Clarke) D.; m. Helen Deborah Moore; children—A. Wilbur, Deborah Jane, Mary Ellen. B.Sc., Rutgers Coll., 1921; M.D., Columbia, 1925. Intern N.Y. Postgrad. Hosp., 1925-28; formerly attending physician Univ. Hosp., Bellevue Hosp., N.Y.C.; formerly cons. Samaritan Bklyn., Prospect Heights, Englewood, St. Claire hosps.; formerly prof. clin. medicine N.Y. U. Served as pvt. U.S. Army, World War I. Mem. Am. Heart Assn. (exec. com.; dir.; v.p. 1959), N.Y. Heart Assn. (pres.), Am. Therapeutic Soc. (pres. 1947), Am. Acad. Compensation Medicine (pres. 1955), Phi Beta Kappa. Club: University (N.Y.C.). Home: Box 188 Quaker Hill Pawling NY 12564

DUSCHA, JULIUS CARL, journalist; b. St. Paul, Nov. 4, 1924; s. Julius William and Anna (Perlowski) D.; m. Priscilla Ann McBride, Aug. 17, 1946; children: Fred C., Steve D., Suzanne, Sally Jean. Student, U. Minn., 1943-47; A.B., Am. U., 1951; postgrad. (Nieman fellow), Harvard U., 1955-56. Reporter St. Paul Pioneer Press, 1943-47; publicist Democratic Nat. Com., 1948, 52; writer Labor's League for Polit. Edn., AFL, 1949-52, Internat. Assn. Machinist, 1952-53; editorial writer Lindsay-Schaub Newspapers, Ill., 1954-58; nat. affairs reporter Washington Post, 1958-66; asso. dir. Profl. Journalism Fellowships Program, Stanford U., 1966-68; dir. Washington Journalism Center, 1968—; columnist, lectr., bd. Sci. Service. Author: Taxpayer's Hayride: The Farm Problem from the New Deal to the Billie Sol Estes Case, 1964, Arms, Money and Politics, 1965, The Campus Press, 1973; contbr.: articles to mags. including Washingtonian, Changing Times. Recipient award for distinguished Washington corr. Sigma Delta Chi, 1961. Mem. Kappa Sigma, Nat. Press Club. Club: Cosmos (Washington). Home: 3421 Raymond St Chevy Chase MD 20015 Office: 2401 Virginia Ave NW Washington DC 20037

DUSEBERG, HORST WILLI ALBERT, banker; b. Frankfurt/Main, Ger., Apr. 11, 1934; came to U.S., 1965; s. Karl and Anna Maria (Rebmann) D.; m. France H. Mellet, Mar. 28, 1963. Student German schs. Fgn. exchange trader Dresdner Bank, Frankfurt, 1951-60; with fgn. exchange and money desk First Nat. City Bank, Frankfurt, 1960-63; Euromoney Market specialist Soc. Generale, Paris, 1963-65, charge fgn. exchange and money desk br., N.Y.C., 1965-69, asst. mgr. br., 1969-71; v.p., then sr. v.p. charge fgn. exchange dept. European Am. Bank, N.Y.C., 1972-79, treas., exec. v.p. charge treasury div., 1979—. Clubs: N.Y. Athletic, India House (N.Y.C.). Home: Boldwyck House Rural Route 2 Box 558 Califon NJ 07830 Office: 77 Water St New York NY 10015

DUSENBERY, WALTER CONDIT, sculptor; b. Alameda, Calif., Sept. 21, 1939; s. Walter A. and Allegra V. (McIlrath) D.; m. Janet Stayton, Jan. 3, 1969. Student, San Francisco Art Inst., 1961; M.F.A., Calif. Coll. Arts and Crafts, Oakland, 1969. Instr. U. Calif. Extension-San Francisco, 1967-69; vis. sculptor Grad. Sch. Design-Harvard U., Cambridge, Mass., 1979—. Exhibitor one-man shows, Laumeir Internat. Sculpture Park, St. Louis, 1983, Va. Commonwealth U., Richmond, Harvard U. Grad. Sch. Design, 1982, Nassau County Mus. Fine Art, Roslyn, N.Y., 1981, Hamilton Gallery Contemporary Art, N.Y.C., 1978, 80, represented in permanent collections, Carnegie Inst., Pitts., Columbus (Ohio) Mus. Art, Commune of Glostrup, Denmark, Solomon R. Guggenheim Mus., N.Y.C., Huntington (W. Va.) Galleries, Met. Mus. Art, N.Y.C., San Francisco Mus. Modern Art, U. N.Mex. Mus., Albuquerque; author: The Story of the Bed, 1970. Creative Artists Program Service fellow, N.Y.C., 1980; Nat. Endowment for the Arts fellow, 1980. Home: 216 Lafayette St New York NY 10012

DU SHANE, JAMES WILLIAM, physician, educator; b. Madison, Ind., Apr. 17, 1912; s. Donald and Harriette Graham (McLell) DuS.; m. Mary Margaret Hill, May 7, 1939; children: Mary Margaret, James Anderson. A.B., DePauw U., 1933; M.D., Yale U., 1937. Diplomate: Am. Bd. Pediatrics (chmn. sub-bd. cardiology 1961-66). Intern Yale-New Haven Hosp., 1937-38, resident pediatrics, 1938-39; resident Children's Meml. Hosp., Chgo., 1939-42; pvt. practice pediatrics, Evanston, Ill., 1942-44; instr. Northwestern U. Med. Sch., 1942-44; mem. staff Mayo Clinic, 1946—, head sect. pediatrics, 1957-69, mem. bd. govs., 1961-73; prof. pediatrics Mayo Found., U. Minn., 1960—. Contbr. articles to med. jours. Trustee Mayo Found., 1967-73. Served to lt. USNR, 1944-46. Mem. AMA, Am. Acad. Pediatrics (founding chmn. cardiology sect. 1958), Am. Coll. Chest Physicians, Am. Pediatric Soc., Am. Heart Assn. (chmn. council rheumatic fever and congenital heart disease 1960-62), Alpha Omega Alpha, Phi Kappa Psi. Home: 600 4th St SW Rochester MN 55902 Office: Mayo Clinic Rochester MN 55901

DUSSAULT, JOSEPH HECTOR ANDRE, publisher; b. Montreal, Que., Can., Feb. 5, 1916; s. Joseph Charles Hector and Alice (Dupuis) D.; m. Lucile Archambault, May 8, 1954; children: Michel, Philippe, Jean Louis, François. B.A., Coll. Brebeuf, Montreal, 1936; LL.B., U. Montreal, 1939. Bar: Called to Que. bar. Partner Les Editions Varietes, Montreal, 1940-52; pres. Librairie Dussault, Montreal, 1952—, Librairie Garneau, 1977—; pres. Editions du Renouveau Pedagogique Inc., Montreal, 1965—, Editions Mirabel, 1970, Diffusion du Livre Mirabel, 1981. Roman Catholic. Home: 475 Mitchell St Mt Royal PQ H3R 1L3 Canada Office: 8925 St Laurent Blvd Montreal PQ H2N 1M5 Canada

DUSSEAU, JOHN LAFONTAINE, writer, pub. co. exec.; b. Phila., July 4, 1912; s. Thomas LaFontaine and Amelia (McClure) D.; m. Sheila Sloane, July 1, 1980. B.A., Haverford Coll., 1934; M.A., Duke U., 1935. Prodn. mgr. W.B. Saunders Co., Phila., 1945-50, mng. editor, 1950-56, editor-in-chief, 1956-77, sr. editor, 1977—, also v.p. Home: 609 Fox Fields Rd Bryn Mawr PA 19010 Office: W Washington Square Philadelphia PA 19105

DUSTAN, HARRIET PEARSON, physician; b. Craftsbury Common, Vt., Sept. 16, 1920; d. William Lyon and Helen (Paterson) D. B.S., U. Vt., 1942, M.D., 1944, D.Sc. (hon.), 1977, Cleve. State U., 1978. Diplomate: Am. Bd. Internal Medicine (residency rev. com. internal medicine). Intern Mary Fletcher Hosp., Burlington, Vt., 1944-45; resident in internal medicine Royale Victoria Hosp., Montreal, 1945; research fellow, then mem. asst. staff research div. Cleve. Clinic, 1948-55, mem. staff research div., 1955-77, vice chmn. research div., 1971-77; dir. Cardiovascular Research and Tng. Center, U. Ala. Med. Center, Birmingham, 1977—; mem. adv. council Nat. Heart and Lung Inst., 1972-76. Contbr. articles to med. jours. Recipient Distinguished Service award U. Vt. Med. Alumni Assn., 1973; Distinguished Achievement award Modern Medicine mag., 1976. Master A.C.P.; mem. Am. Heart Assn. (pres. 1976-77), Am. Soc. Clin. Investigation, Assn. Am. Physicians, Central Soc. Clin. Research, Council High Blood Pressure Research. Office: Univ Ala Univ Station Birmingham AL 35294

DUSTHIMER, THOMAS LEE, banker; b. Danville, Ill, Dec. 27, 1934; s. William V. and Elizabeth D.; m. Louis V. Young, Apr. 29, 1961; children: Lynn, Diane, Jill. B.S.A. in Fin., Ind. U., 1957, M.B.A., 1958; postgrad., Wis. Sch. Banking, 1963-65. Sr. v.p. Am. Fletcher Nat. Bank, Indpls., 1969; pres., dir. Mark Twain Bancshares, Inc., St. Louis, 1969-70; pres., chief exec. officer, dir. Miami Beach First Nat. bank, Fla., 1970-72, Coral Gables First Nat. bank, 1972-73; pres. First Nat. Bank, Elkhart, Ind., 1973—; chmn. First Nat Bank, Elkhart, Ind., 1981—. Bd. dirs., fin. com. chmn. Elkhart Gen. Hosp., 1975; mem. pres.'s adv. council Goshen Coll., Ind., 1975—; trustee YMCA Endowment Trust Commn., Elkhart, 1976—; county campaign chmn. United Way, Elkhart, 1976—; vice chmn. Notre Dame Campaign, Elkhart, 1977; mem. Richard Lugar's Personal Adv. Council, Indpls., 1981; chmn. Enterprise Zone Commn., Indpls., 1981—; fund drive chmn. Am. Heart Assn., 1983—; mem. Ind. Toll Fin. Authority, 1983—. Served to 1st lt. U.S. Army, 1958-59; served with USAR, 1959-66. Recipient 1st $1MM United Way award, 1976, Others Salvation Army, 1978, Outstanding Service Urban League, 1979, Man of Yr. Am. Heart Assn., 1982, Community Service Elkhart NAACP, 1983. Mem. Ind. Bankers Assn. (dir. 1981-82), Am. Bankers Assn. (banking adv. 1980-82), Fla. bankers Assn. (dir. 1972-73). Roman Catholic. Clubs: Columbia (Indpls.); Elcona Country (Elkhart) (dir. 1973); Ind. Soc. (Chgo.)). Office: First Nat Bank 301 S Main St Elkhart IN 46515

DUSTIN, ALAN GRANT, ry. exec.; b. Rouses Point, N.Y., May 31, 1929; s. Grant A. and Edith (Hyde) D.; m. Elsie C. Namer, June 25, 1953; children—Diane E., Carol J., Alan K., Sandra J. With Del. & Hudson Ry., 1947-68, asst. to pres. and gen. mgr., 1964-68; asst. to v.p. ops. and maintenance Erie Lackawanna Ry., Cleve., 1968-69, div. supt., Scranton, Pa., 1969-70; v.p. Bangor & Aroostock R.R., 1970-71, exec. v.p., 1971-73; chmn. bd. Pittsburg and Shawmut R.R., 1971-73; exec. v.p. Boston and Maine Corp., North Billerica, Mass., 1973-74, pres., chief exec., chief operating officer, 1974—. Served with U.S. Army, 1949-51. Mem. Assn. Railroad Supts., Mass. Railroad Assn. (pres.), Nat. Freight Traffic Assn., New Eng. Council, Transp. Assn. Am., New Eng. Railroad Club. Home: 67 Bear Hill Rd Merrimac MA 01860 Office: Boston and Maine Corp Iron Horse Park North Billerica MA 01862

DUSTO, FREDERICK RELEE, business executive; b. Highland Park, Ill., June 23, 1928; s. Frederick R. and Clara A. (Hunn) D.; m. Betty L. Campbell, June 14, 1952; children: Bradley P., Timothy L., Matthew A. B.S.E.E., Purdue U., 1951; postgrad., Northwestern U., 1953. With Motorola, Inc., 1951-59, ACF Industries, 1959-61, Veeder Industries, 1961-70, v.p. mktg., until 1970; with Harvey Hubbell, Inc., Orange, Conn., 1970—, pres., 1980—, chief exec. officer, 1983—, also dir.; dir. Lukens, Inc., Coatsville, Pa. Trustee St. Vincent Hosp. Served with USN, 1946-48. Republican. Roman Catholic. Clubs: Brooklawn Country, Houndslake Country. Home: 870 Mine Hill Fairfield CT 06430 Office: 584 Derby Milford Orange CT 06477

DUTCHER, PHILLIP CHARLES, health care administrator; b. Flint, Mich., Sept. 22, 1950; s. Doris Lucille (Holt) D.; m. Diane Eileen Myers, Apr. 21, 1979; children: Brent David, Lindsey Leigh. B.I.A., Gen. Motors Inst., 1972; M.B.A., U. Mich., 1974, M.H.S.A., 1980. Prodn. supr. Buick Motor Div. Gen. Motors Corp., Flint, Mich., 1974-75; installation dir. Hosp. Computer Ctr., Flint, 1975-76; asst. to dir. Hurley Med. Ctr., Flint, 1976-77, asst. dir., 1977-80, assoc. dir., 1980, acting hosp. dir., 1980-81, dir., 1981—. Bd. dirs. ARC, Flint, 1982—; vice chmn. bd. trustees and bd. dirs. Greater Flint Area Hosp. Assembly; vice chmn. bd. dirs. Greater Flint HMO. Mem. Mich. Hosp. Assn. (task force on teaching hosps. shared services subcom). Lodge: Rotary. Office: Hurley Med Ctr 1 Hurley Plaza Flint MI 48502

DUTCHER, RUSSELL RICHARDSON, geology educator; b. Bklyn., Oct. 28, 1927; s. Edwin Brown and Belle (Richardson) D.; m. Linda A. Flucekinger; children: Russell Richardson, Jan Elizabeth. B.A., U. Conn., 1951; M.S., U. Mass., 1953; Ph.D, Pa. State U., 1960. Cert. profl. geologist, Maine. Instr. in geology U. Mass., Amherst, 1952-53; research asst., research assoc. Pa. State U., University Park, 1954-63, asst. prof., research assoc., 1963-66, assoc. prof., 1966-70; prof. geology, dept. chmn. So. Ill. U., Carbondale, 1970-83; acting dean Coll. Sci., So. Ill. U., Carbondale, 1983—. Editor: Profl. Geologist, 1979-82, Internat. Jour. Coal Geology, 1980—. Mem. energy com. Greater Egypt Regional Planning Commn.; mem. coal panel Ill. Energy Resources Commn. Fellow Geol. Soc. Am.; mem. Am. Assn. Petroleum Geologists (sect. pres. 1984), AIME, Am. Inst. Profl. Geologists (nat. exec. com. 1979-82), Yellowstone-Bighorn Research Assn. (pres.). Home: Box 128 Carbondale IL 62901 Office: Coll Sci Ill U Neckers 162A Carbondale IL 62901

DUTIL, MARCEL E., business executive; b. St. Georges de Beauce, Que., Can., Aug. 17, 1942; s. Roger and Gilberte (Lacroix) D.; m. Helen Giguere, Feb. 1, 1964; children: Marc, Marie, Charles, Sophie. Doctorate hon., Faculty of Commerce, Laval U., 1978, 1983. Plant mgr. Canam Steel Works Inc., St. Gedeon de Beauce, 1963-66, gen. mgr., 1966-73; pres., chief exec. officer Canam Manac Inc., St. Georges de Beauce, Que., Can., 1973—; chmn. bd. Canam Steel Works Inc., 1966—, Manac Inc., 1966—, Canam Steel Corp., Boston, 1973—, Biltrite Furniture Mfg. Ltd., Montreal, 1980—, Treco Internat. Inc., Que., 1981—; adminstr. Banque Nationale du Canada, 1981—, Maritime Life Assurance Co., 1980—, Compagnie d'Assurance du Quebec, 1982—. Named Man of Month Revue Commerce, 1978. Mem. Young Presidents Orgn. Office: Canam Manac Inc 11535 1st Ave 7th Floor St Georges de Beauce PQ Canada G5Y 2C7

DUTOIT, CHARLES, conductor; b. Lausanne, Switzerland, Oct. 7, 1936. Studied at, Conservatory of Lausanne, Acad. Music, Geneva, Academia Musicale Chigiana, Siena, Conservatory Benedetto Marcello, Venice, Italy; attended session in conducting, Berkshire Music Center, Tanglewood, Mass. Formerly violinist with, Lausanne Chamber Orch.; debut as condr. with, Bern (Switzerland) Symphony Orch., 1963; conducting: Stravinsky's Le Sacre du Primtemps; condr. and asst. music dir., Bern Symphony Orch., 1964; later music dir.; condr. and artistic dir., Radio-Zurich (Switzerland) Orch., 1967; also guest condr., Vienna Opera; appointed regular condr., Goteborg (Sweden) Orch., in 1975; music dir., condr., Montreal (Que., Can.) Symphony Orch., 1977—; guest condr., S. Am., S. Africa, Japan, Australia, Eng., U.S., Can. and, Israel.; rec., Deutsche Gramophon Decca, Erato, CBS, Decca/London. Office: care Montreal Symphony Orch Place de Arts 200 de Maisonneuve Blvd W Montreal PQ Canada

DUTRO, JOHN THOMAS, JR., geologist, paleontologist; b. Columbus, Ohio, May 20, 1923; s. John Thomas and Dorothy Durstine (Smith) D.; m. Nancy Ann Pence, Jan. 2, 1948; children: Sarah Dutro Cormier, Christopher, Susan. B.A., Oberlin Coll., 1948; M.S., Yale U., 1950, Ph.D., 1953. Geologist, U.S. Geol. Survey, 1948—, chief paleontology and stratigraphy br., 1962-68, mem. geologic names com., 1962—; research asso. Smithsonian Instn., 1962—; vis. lectr. Am. U., 1957-59, George Washington U., 1962-63; mem. geology panel Bd. Civil Service Examiners, 1958-65; dir., field trip chmn. 9th Internat. Carboniferous Congress, 1979. Active PTA, 1959-69, Boy Scouts Am., 1963-66, Fairlington Players, 1965-75. Served with USAAF, 1943-46. Recipient Superior Accomplishment award U.S. Geol. Survey, 1954; Sterling fellow, 1949. Fellow Arctic Inst. N.Am.; mem. Am. Geol. Inst. (vis. geoscientist 1961-67, dir., sec.-treas. 1965-71), Geol. Soc. Am. (asso. editor 1974-82), Paleontol. Soc., Paleontol. Assn., AAAS (sec. sect. E), Paleontol. Research Instn., Internat. Paleontol. Assn., Paleontol. Soc. Washington (pres. 1955-56), Geol. Soc. Washington (sec. 1959-60, pres. 1978), Sigma Xi. Democrat. Clubs: Pick and Hammer, Cosmos, Yale (Washington). Research and publs. on Paleozoic biostratigraphy and biogeography of Arctic regions. Home: 5173 Fulton St NW Washington DC 20016 Office: US Nat Museum Washington DC 20560

DUTT, JAMES L., food company executive. B.A., Washburn U., 1950; M.B.A., U. Dayton, 1966. With Beatrice Foods Co., Kans., from 1947, mgr. dairy plant, Dayton, from 1961, various mktg. and mgmt. positions, then exec. v.p. dairy and soft drink divs., 1974, dir. internat. dairy ops., 1974, pres. internat. food ops., Chgo., from 1975, exec. v.p., 1975-77, pres., 1977—, chief operating officer, 1977—, chief exec. officer, 1979—, also dir.; dir. various corps. including GATX Corp., McDermott Internat. Bd. dirs. Art Inst. Chgo., Lyric Opera Chgo., Chgo. Council on Fgn. Relations. Mem. Grocery Mfrs. Am. (dir.), Nat. 4-H Council. Office: Beatrice Foods Co 2 N LaSalle St Chicago IL 60602

DUTTA, SISIR KAMAL, educator; b. Bengal, India, Aug. 28, 1928; came to U.S., 1956, naturalized, 1974; s. Krishna K. and Satyabati (Chanda) D.; m. Minati Roy, July 1, 1955; children: Mahasweta, Basabi. M.S., Kans. State U., 1958, Ph.D., 1960. Dir., chief research officer Nat. Pineapple Research Inst., Malaysia, 1961-64; research assoc. Rice U., 1964-65; asst. prof. biology Tex. So. U., Houston, 1965-66; chmn. div. sci. and math., assoc. prof. biology Jarvis Christian Coll., 1966-67; prof. molecular genetics dept. botany Howard U., 1967—; cons. pineapple industries, Formosa, Philippines, Malaysia, various univs.; collaborator Pasteur Inst., Carnegie Instn.; lectr. Univs., U.S. and abroad. Contbr. articles to profl. jours. Vis. scientist Rockefeller U., 1968-69, Pasteur Inst., Paris, 1974-75, NIH, Bethesda, Md., 1974-75. Grantee NSF, Dept. Energy, NIH, Olin Found., EPA, Research Corp. N.Y., Anna Fuller Fund., USNR. Mem. AAAS, Indian Sci. Congress, Genetics Soc. Am., AAUP, Am. Mycol. Soc., Am. Soc. Environ. Mutagen, Sigma Xi, Beta Kappa Chi. Home: 8841 Tuckerman Ln Potomac MD 20854 Office: Dept Botany Howard U Washington DC 20059

DUTTON, CLARENCE BENJAMIN, lawyer; b. Pitts., May 31, 1917; s. Clarence Benjamin and Lillian (King) D.; m. Marian Jane Stevens, June 21, 1941; children: Victoria Lynn, Barbara King. B.S. with distinction, Ind. U., 1938, LL.B. with high distinction, 1940, LL.D., 1970. Bar: Ind. 1940. Instr. bus. law Ind. U. Sch. Bus., 1940-41; atty. E.I. duPont de Nemours & Co., Inc., Wilmington, Del., 1941-43; asst. prof. law Ind. U. Sch. Law, 1946-47; pvt. practice, Indpls., 1947—; dir. Sarkes Tarzian, Inc., Huber Hunt & Nichols, Inc., Paul Harris Stores, Inc., Central Supply Co., J L Realty, Inc.; mem. Ind. Jud. Study Commn., 1965-74; mem. regional adv. group Ind. U. Sch. Medicine, 1966-75; mem., sec. Ind. Civil Code Study Commn., 1967-73; mem. Ind. Commn. on Uniform State Laws, 1970—, chmn., 1980—. Author: (bus. law sect.) Chemical Business Handbook, 1954; contbr. articles to profl. jours. Bd. dirs. Found. Ind. U. Sch. Bus., Found. Econ. and Bus. Studies; bd. visitors Ind. U. Sch. Law, 1971—, chmn., 1974-75. Served to comdr. USNR, 1943-45. Mem. ABA (ho. dels. 1960-62, Mem., state del. 1967-72, chmn. gen. practice sect. 1971-72, gov. 1971-74), Ind. Bar Assn. (bd. mgrs. 1957-63, pres. 1961-62), Indpls. Bar Assn. (v.p. 1957), Ind. Soc. Chgo. Republican. Presbyn. Clubs: Lawyers (pres. 1959-60), Indianapolis Country (pres. 1955), Columbia, Woodstock (Indpls.); Ponte Vedra (Fla.); Wilderness Country (Naples, Fla.). Home: 1402 W 52d St Indianapolis IN 46208 Office: 710 Century 36 S Pennsylvania St Indianapolis IN 46204

DUTTON, FREDERIC BOOTH, chemist, educator; b. Cleve., Dec. 24, 1906; s. Charles Frederic and Elma (Booth) D.; m. Faith Kedzie; children—James Kedzie, Diane Hope (Mrs. John B. Haney). A.B., Oberlin Coll., 1928, A.M., 1932; Ph.D., Western Res. U., 1937. Instr. chemistry Baldwin-Wallace Coll., 1931-34, asst. prof., 1934-39, asso. prof., 1941-47; instr. Yale, 1939-40; prof. Olivet Coll., 1941; instr. Cleve. Coll., Western Res. U., 1938-39, summer 1939; asso. prof. chemistry Mich. State U., East Lansing, 1947-50, prof., 1950—, head sci. and math. teaching center, 1957-66; dean Lyman Briggs Coll., 1967-73, cons. to provost, 1973-76; Program dir. NSF, 1964-65. Fellow AAAS (sect. sec. 1964-67, sect. chmn., v.p. 1970); mem. Am. Chem. Soc. (sec. Cleve. 1943-46, treas. div. chem. edn. 1952-54, chmn. Mich. U. sect. 1949—), Nat. Assn. Research Sci. Teaching (pres. 1964-65), Nat. Higher Edn. Assn., Northeastern Ohio Chemistry Tchrs. Orgn. (pres. 1939, 4O, 42), Mich. Sci. Tchrs. Assn. (pres. 1963-64), Nat. Sci. Tchrs. Assn., NEA, Sigma Xi, Alpha Chi Sigma. Home: 931 Wick Ct East Lansing MI 48823

DUTTON, FREDERICK GARY, lawyer; b. Julesburg, Colo., June 16, 1923; s. F.G. and Lucy Elizabeth (Parker) D.; m. Nancy Dutton. B.A. with honors, U. Calif. at Berkeley, 1946; LL.B. (bd. editors Law Rev.), Stanford, 1949. Bar: Calif. 1949. With firm Kirkbride, Wilson, Harzfeld & Wallace, San Mateo, Calif., 1949-50; 1st asst. counsel So. Counties Gas Co. Calif., 1952-56; chief asst. atty. gen., Calif., 1957-58; exec. sec. to gov. Calif., 1959-60; spl. asst. to Pres. Kennedy, 1961; asst. sec. of state for congl. relations, 1962-64; with firm Dutton, Zumas & Wise (and predecessors), 1965-76; firm Dutton & Dutton, 1979—; corp. practice law, 1977-78; exec. dir. Robert F. Kennedy Meml. Found., 1978-70; Editor Los Angeles Bar mag., 1955; spl. counsel judiciary com. Calif. Senate, 1956-57; So. Calif. chmn. Stevenson presdl. campaign, 1956; Calif. campaign chmn. Brown for Gov., 1958; dep. nat. chmn. Citizens for Kennedy and Johnson campaign, 1960; exec. dir. platform com. Democratic Nat. Conv., 1964; dir. research and planning nat. Dem. presdl. campaign, 1964, in charge Senator Robert F. Kennedy's travel campaign in primaries, 1968, mem. Dem. delegation selection (reform) com., 1969-72; aide to Senator George McGovern, 1972; organizing dir. John F. Kennedy Meml. Library Oral History Project, 1964-65. Contbr. legal jours., mags.; Author: Changing Sources of Power: American Politics in the 1970's, 1971, Election Guide for 1972, 1972. Bd. dirs. Center for Community Devel. and, Citizens Adv. Com., 1969-70; Am. U. Cairo, 1983—; bd. regents U. Calif., 1962-78. Served with inf. AUS, World War II; prisoner of war; Germany; served with Judge Adv. Gen. Corps, Korean Emergency; Japan. Decorated Bronze Star, Purple Heart, Combat Inf. Badge. Mem. Fed. Bar Assn., State Bar Calif., Delta Tau Delta. Address: Suite 801 1140 Connecticut Ave NW Washington DC 20036

DUTTON, JOHN ALTNOW, meteorologist; b. Detroit, Sept. 11, 1936; s. Carl Evans and Velma (Altnow) D.; m. Frances Elizabeth Andrews, Jan. 13, 1962; children—Christopher Evan, John Andrews, Jan Frederik. B.S., U. Wis., 1958; M.S., 1959; Ph.D., 1962. Mem. faculty Pa. State U., University Park, 1965—, assoc. prof. meteorology, 1968-71, prof., 1971—, head dept. meteorology, 1981—; expert aero. system div. USAF, 1965-71; vis. scientist Riso Research

Establishment, Roskilde, Denmark, 1971-72, summer 1975, 78-79; vis. prof. Tech. U., Denmark, 1978-79. Author: The Ceaseless Wind: An Introduction to the Theory of Atmospheric Motion, 1976; assoc. editor: Meteorol. Monographs, 1973-79; editor, 1979—; contbr. articles to profl. jours. Trustee Univ. Corp. for Atmospheric Research, 1974-81, sec., 1977, treas., 1978-79, vice-chmn., 1980—; Mem. bd. atmospheric scis. and climate Nat. Acad. Scis., 1982—; mem. space and earth scis. adv. com. NASA, 1982—. Served with USAF, 1962-65. Fellow Am. Meteorol. Soc.; mem. Math. Assn. Am., Soc. Indsl. and Applied Math., Sigma Xi, Phi Kappa Phi, Theta Delta Chi. Home: 447 Nimitz Ave State College PA 16801 Office: 503 Walker Bldg University Park PA 16802

DUTTON, JOHN COATSWORTH, consulting engineer; b. Chgo., Mar. 8, 1918; s. Henry Post and Lulu Mae (Broceus) D.; m. Elizabeth Lillian Ahlen, Aug. 24, 1941; children: John Coastworth, Anne, Louise, Sally Elizabeth. B.S.E. with honors, Swarthmore Coll., 1939; M.S. in Elec. Engring., Rensselear Poly. Inst., 1950. Registered profl. engr., Ga. Mass. With Gen. Electric Co., 1952—, supr. transformer engring. design, Pittsfield, Mass., Rome, Ga., acting mgr. computer application project dept., 1956-59, mgr. advanced product engring., 1956-62, mgr. advance devel. engring., 1962-71, mgr. transformer tech. program, research and devel. ctr., Schenectady, 1971-73, cons. engr. standards, medium trans. dept., Rome, Ga., 1973—. Patentee in field. Chmn. Carnegie Library Bd., Rome, Ga., 1962. Served to lt. USNR, 1942-45. Fellow IEEE; mem. Elfun Soc., Internat. Electrotech Commn. Tech. Com. (U.S. tech. advisor), Sigma Tau. Lodge: Kiwanis. *

DUTTON, JOHN EDGAR, librarian; b. Lethbridge, Alta., Can., Aug. 30, 1924; s. Edgar Evans and Hannah Eleanor (Turner) D.; m. Helen Irene, Nov. 28, 1945; children: Corinne Eleanor, Carolyn Ann, Dianne Lillian. B.A. with honors in History, U. Alta., Can., 1950; B.L.Sc., U. Toronto, Ont., Can., 1951. Librarian U. Alta. Library, Edmonton, Can., 1951-53; chief librarian Lethbridge Pub. Library, Alta., 1953-63, North York Pub. Library, Toronto, Ont., Can., 1963-77; city librarian Winnipeg Pub. Library, Man., Can., 1977-79; dir., sec.-treas. Calgary Pub. Library, Can., 1979—. Contbr. articles to profl. jours. and encys. Served with RCAF, 1943-46. Mem. Library Assn. Alta. (pres. 1962), Can. Library Assn. (2d v.p.), Ont. Library Assn. (pres. 1969-70), Nat. Library Adv. Bd. Progressive Conservative. Mem. United Ch. of Canada. Office: Calgary Pub Library 616 MacLeod Terr SE Calgary AB Canada T2G 2M2 *

DUTTON, JOHN MAYNARD, financial executive; b. Phila., May 17, 1942; s. John W. and Emilie S. D.; m. Robin Ellen Cook, Sept. 6, 1980; children: John Allen, Lauren Stanfield, Elisabeth Meyers. A.B., Brown U., 1964; M.B.A., U. Pa., 1966. Dir. securities research Estabrook & Co., Boston, 1966-71; v.p. Moseley, Hallgarten, Estabrook & Weedon, Inc., Boston, 1971-75; dir., exec. v.p. Am. Med. Internat., Inc., Beverly Hills, Calif., 1975-81; pres., chief exec. officer Corsair Asset Mgmt., Inc., Los Angeles, 1981—; chmn. bd. Berton Group, Inc., 1983—. Mem. Boston Soc. Security Analysts, Fedn. Am. Hosps. Office: 6167 Bristol Pkwy Culver City CA 90230

DUTTON, ROBERT EDWARD, JR., medical educator; b. Milford, N.H., Aug. 11, 1924; s. Robert Edward and Mildred Beatrice (Prior) D.; m. Cynthia Baldwin, June 15, 1958; children: Elizabeth Helen, Leila Baldwin. Student, Gettysburg Coll., 1942-43, The Citadel, 1943-44, Johns Hopkins U., 1944-45; M.D., Med. Coll. Va., 1949. Intern Boston City Hosp., 1950-51, resident, 1953-54, SUNY, Syracuse, 1954-56, instr. medicine, 1956-59; asst. prof. environ. medicine and medicine Johns Hopkins U., 1964-68; asso. prof. physiology Albany Med. Coll., Union U., 1968-74, asso. prof. medicine, 1970-77, prof. physiology, 1974—, prof. medicine, 1977—, also cons. trauma research unit, 1971—; prof. biomed. engring. Rensselaer Poly. Inst., 1972—; cons. pulmonary div. VA hosps., 1968-69. Contbr. articles to profl. jours. Served with AUS, 1943-46; Served with USAF, 1951-53. Nat. Heart Inst. postdoctoral fellow, 1959-61. Mem. Am. Physiol. Soc., Am. Thoracic Soc. (pres. Eastern sect.), Internat. Union Physiol. Scis., Am. Fedn. Clin. Research, Johns Hopkins Med. and Surg. Assn., Sigma Xi (pres. SUNY-Albany chpt. 1983-84), Sigma Zeta. Office: Albany Med Coll Albany NY 12208

DUTTON, ROBERT WILBUR, electrical engineering educator; b. Eugene, Oreg., Mar. 24, 1944; s. Wilbur H. and Roberta (Holden) D.; m. Mary Lou Allen, June 6, 1976; 1 son, Jordan. B.S., U. Calif.-Berkeley, 1966, M.S., 1967, Ph.D., 1970. Acting asst. prof. elec. engring. U. Calif.-Berkeley, 1970-71; mem. tech. staff Bell labs., Homdel, N.J., 1973, Hewlett-Packard, Palo Alto, Calif., 1975, IBM Reserach, Yorktown Heights, N.Y., 1977; prof. elec. engring. Stanford U., 1971—. Author computer programs. NSF fellow, 1967-70; NATO fellow, 1975. Fellow IEEE (chmn. prize paper com. 1982). Office: Stanford U 204 AFL Bldg Stanford CA 94305

DUTTON, WILLIAM LAWRENCE, international relations educator, former diplomat; b. Cedar Rapids, Iowa, Mar. 15, 1929; s. William Lawrence and Louise (Crousez) D.; m. Jane Johnston, Sept. 29, 1956; children: Anne, Samuel, Susan. B.A., Grinnell Coll., 1951; M.A., Georgetown U., 1959; postgrad., Rand Inst. Policy Analysis, 1971-72. Diplomat Dept. State U.S.A., W. Ger., Japan, 1957-83, head Europe Community Desk, Washington, 1972-75; dean. Sch. Area Studies Fgn. Service Inst., Washington, 1975-78; consul gen., Osaka, Kobe, Japan, 1979-83; prof. Kyoto U. Fgn. Studies, Japan, 1983—. Served with U.S. Army, 1951-54. Mem. Phi Beta Kappa. Home: Higashi Nada-ku Motoyama Kitamachi 6-10-13 Kobe Japan 658 Office: Kyoto U Fgn Studies Ukyo-Ku 6 Saiin Kasame-cho Kyoto Japan 616

DUTTON, WILMER COFFMAN, JR., city planner; b. Ridgewood, N.J., Aug. 28, 1920; s. Wilmer C. and Florence (Bardsley) D.; m. Ann Pickells, July 29, 1949 (div. 1954); 1 son, Christopher; m. Frances Wilson Zerbst, Nov. 22, 1957; children—Sharon, Janet, Karen. A.B., Dartmouth, 1942; postgrad., U. N.C., 1947, 48. Asst. dir. planning, Greensboro, N.C., 1949-50; sr. planner Chgo. Housing Authority, 1950-51; dir. planning Cook County Housing Authority, 1951-53, Charleston County (S.C.) Planning Bd., 1954-57; exec. dir. Am. Inst. Planners, Washington, 1958-63; dir. Nat. Capital Planning Commn., Washington, 1963-65; chmn. Md.-Nat. Capital Park and Planning Commn., 1965-71, 74—, planning adviser, 1965-66, 71-74, 79—. Chmn. Nat. Com. Urban Life, 1963-65; chmn. Prince George's dist. Boy Scouts Am., 1969-72. Served to 1st lt. AUS, 1942-46. Mem. Am. Inst. Cert. Planners (treas. Chgo. region 1953-54, pres. S.E. 1955-56), Nat. Assn. Housing Ofcls., Am. Planning Assn., Piping and Marching Soc., Lower Chalmers St., Md. Assn. County Planning Ofcls. (pres. 1970), Upper Marlboro C. of C. (pres. 1981—). Episcopalian. Clubs: Rotary, Dartmouth of Washington (exec. com. 1976—). Home: 8210 McClure Rd Upper Marlboro MD 20772 Office: 5415 Water St Upper Marlboro MD 20772

DUVAL, ALBERT FRANK, paper company executive; b. Holyoke, Mass., Oct. 31, 1920; s. Albert Frank and Lena (Potvin) D.; m. Mary Tague, Apr. 12, 1947; children: Denise, Richard, Nanette, Robert, Carolyn, Michele, Kathleen. B.A., Amherst Coll., 1943. Mgr. Calif. div. U.S. Envelope Co., 1946-52, sales mgr., 1952-55, v.p. sales, 1955-60, pres., 1960; v.p. Hammermill Paper Co., Erie, Pa., 1960-69, sr. v.p., 1969, pres., 1970—, chief exec. officer, 1971—, chmn., 1983—, also dir.; dir. Milton Bradley Co., Springfield, Mass., Pennbancorp., Erie, Nat. Fuel Gas, N.Y.C. Trustee Mercyhurst Coll.; trustee St. Vincent's Hosp., chmn., 1976. Served with USAAF, 1944-46; ETO. Mem. Envelope Mfrs. Assn. (pres. 1963-65), Am. Paper Inst. (chmn. 1976). Club: Kahkwa (Erie) (pres. 1969—). Home: 6521 W Fair Oaks Circle Fairview PA 16415 Office: E Lake Rd Erie PA 16512

DUVAL, DANIEL WEBSTER, manufacturing company executive; b. Cin., May 27, 1936; s. Harry A. and Wilda (Webster) D.; m. Sue Ann Howard, July 20, 1962; children: Laurie Ann, Paula Lee, Christopher Webster. B.A., U. Cin., 1960. With Midland-Ross, 1960—, v.p. staff elec. products div., Cleve., 1976-78, group v.p., 1979-81, exec. v.p., 1981-83, pres., chief operating officer, 1983—. Bd. dirs. St. Luke's Hosp.; pres. Civitan Found. Ariz., 1973-74; trustee Gilmour Acad. Served with AUS, 1954-56. Mem. Nat. Elec. Mfrs. Assn. Republican. Roman Catholic. Clubs: Chagrin Valley Racquet, Hillbrook, Firestone Country, Chagrin Valley Country. Patentee container coupling mechanism. Home: 14821 River Glen Dr Novelty OH 44072 Office: 20600 Chagrin Blvd Cleveland OH 44122

DU VAL, PHILIP LIVINGSTON ROLLIN, advertising sales exec.; b. N.Y.C., Apr. 6, 1920; s. Clive Livingston and Augusta (Lynde) DuV.; m. Barbara V. Wheeler, Dec. 27, 1952 (div. Nov. 1968); children—Philip L.R. II, Alexandra Lynde; m. Janis Locke Lee, Feb. 1, 1969. B.A., Yale U., 1943. Salesman Bates Fabrics Co., N.Y.C., 1946-51; asst. sales mgr. William Skinner & Sons, N.Y.C., 1953-54; category mgr. The New Yorker mag., N.Y.C., 1955-57; exec. v.p., mgr. sales and advt. Gordon Ford Sales Co., N.Y.C., 1957-59; with Harper-Atlantic Sales Co., N.Y.C., 1959—, exec. v.p., 1965-68, pres., 1968-76; asso. pub. Quest/77 Mag., 1977-79; mktg. dir. N.Y. Times Sunday Mag., 1979—; chmn. bd. Yale Alumni Publs., Inc., New Haven, 1969-72; Vice pres. Nat. Inst. Social Scis., 1971-79, chmn., 1979-82; bd. mgrs. St. Andrews Soc. N.Y., N.Y.C., 1969-72. Officer New Canaan Vol. Fire Co. 1, 1958-82, chmn. fire commrs., 1974-82; chmn. zoning bd. appeals, Town New Canaan, 1960-72; mem. nat. exec. com. Purnell Sch., Pottersville, N.J., 1970-75; bd. dirs. Am.-Scottish Found., 1970—, Publishers Info. Bur., 1973-79, Save the Children Fedn., 1977-82. Served to comdr. USNR, 1942-46, 51-52. Decorated Bronze Star with valor clasp. Mem. Elihu Soc. (Yale), Mag. Publishers Assn. (mktg. com. 1974-79). Republican. Presbyterian (elder). Clubs: Yale, Pilgrims (N.Y.C.); New Canaan Country. Home: 388 Brushy Ridge New Canaan CT 06840 Office: care NY Times 229 W 43d St New York NY 10036

DUVAL, ROBERT, steel fabrication and construction company executive; b. Bronx, N.Y., June 23, 1937; s. Jack Leon and Cornelia (Gerry) D.; m. Harriet Elin, June 4, 1960; children: Stacey R., Jennifer E. B.S., Cornell U., 1959; LL.B., St. Johns U., 1967. Bar: N.Y. 1968, Pa. 1976, U.S. Supreme Ct. 1971. Asso. firm Hart & Hume, N.Y.C., 1967-69, Kelley, Drye & Warren, 1969-72, Gates & Laber, 1972-75; mem. law dept. Westinghouse Electric Corp., Pitts., 1976-78; gen. counsel, sec. Pitts.-Des Moines Co., Pitts., 1978—; sec., gen. counsel PDM Internat. Ltd. Served with U.S. Army, 1961. Mem. Am. Bar Assn., N.Y. Bar Assn., Am. Arbitration Assn. (arbitrator). Home: 1350 Old Meadow Rd Pittsburgh PA 15241 Office: Pittsburgh-Des Moines Co 3400 Grand Ave Neville Island Pittsburgh PA 15225

DUVALL, JOSEPH MICHAEL, dermatologist; b. Ste. Genevieve, Mo., May 14, 1948; s. Orville Henry and Odile Genevieve (Naeger) D.; m. Carolyn Marie Lutkewitte, Aug. 14, 1971; children: Joseph, Sarah, John, Elizabeth. B.A., U. Mo., 1970, M.D., 1974.. Intern U. Mo. Med. Ctr., Columbia, 1974-75, fellow in dermatology, 1975-78; dir. div. dermatology St. Louis U. Sch. Medicine, 1980—, St. John's Mercy Med. Ctr., 1982—. Fellow Am. Acad. Dermatology. Republican. Roman Catholic. Office: St Johns Mercy Med Ctr 621 S New Ballas Rd Saint Louis MO 63141 *

DUVALL, ROBERT, actor; b. San Diego, 1931; s. William Howard D. Grad., Principia Coll., Ill.; student, Neighborhood Playhouse, N.Y. Film appearances To Kill a Mockingbird, 1963, Captain Newman, M.D, 1964, The Chase, 1965, Countdown, 1968, The Detective, 1968, Bullitt, 1968, True Grit, 1969, The Rain People, 1969, M*A*S*H, 1970, The Revolutionary, 1970, THX-1138, 1971, Lawman, 1971, The Godfather (N.Y. Film Critics award Best Supporting Actor), 1972 (nominee Acad. award), Tomorrow, 1972, The Great Northfield, Minnesota Raid, 1972, Joe Kidd, 1972, Lady Ice, 1973, Badge 373, 1973, The Outfit, 1974, The Conversation, 1974, The Godfather Part II, 1974, Breakout, 1975, The Killer Elite, 1975, Network, 1976, The Seven Per Cent Solution, 1976, The Eagle Has Landed, 1977, The Greatest, 1977, The Betsy, 1978, Apocalypse Now, 1979, The Great Santini, 1980 (Acad. award nominee for best actor 1981), True Confessions, 1981, The Pursuit of D.B. Cooper, 1981, Tender Mercies, 1983 (Acad. award for best actor 1984), Angelo My Love, 1983, The Natural, 1984; dir.: We're Not the Jet Set, 1977; stage appearances include A View from the Bridge, 1965 (Obie award), Wait Until Dark, 1966, American Buffalo, 1977; appeared in: TV miniseries Ike, 1979 (Recipient Golden Globe award, Brit. Acad. award, award Nat. Assn. Theatre Owners, Acad. award nomination.). Office: care Creative Artists Agy 1888 Century Park E Suite 1400 Los Angeles CA 90067 *

DUVALL, ROBERT F., university president. Pres. Pacific U., Forest Grove, Oreg. Office: Pacific U 2043 College Way Forest Grove OR 97116

DUVALL, SHELLEY, actress; b. Houston, 1949; d. Robert and Bobby D. Film debut in Brewster McCloud, 1970; other films include McCabe and Mrs. Miller, 1971, Thieves Like Us, 1974, Nashville, 1975, Buffalo Bill and the Indians, 1976, Three Women, 1977 (Cannes Film Festival Best Actress award), Annie Hall, 1977, Time Bandits, 1981, Bernice Bobs Her Hair, Public Broadcasting System, 1977, Popeye, 1979, The Shining, 1980; exec. producer (Showtime pay TV), Faerie Tale Theatre, 1983—. Office: care CAA 1888 Century Park East Suite 1400 Los Angeles CA 90067 *

DUVICK, DONALD NELSON, plant breeder; b. Sandwich, Ill., Dec. 18, 1924; s. Nelson Daniel and Florence Henrietta (Appel) D.; m. Selma Elizabeth Nelson, Sept. 10, 1950; children: Daniel, Jonathan, Randa. B.S., U. Ill., 1948; Ph.D., Washington U., St. Louis, 1951. With Pioneer Hi-Bred Internat., Inc., Johnston, Iowa, 1951—, corn breeding coordinator, 1965-71, dir. corn breeding dept., 1971-75, dir. plant breeding div. Eastern and So. div., 1975—, co. dir., 1982—; lectr. in field. Author articles on genetics and plant breeding, developmental anatomy and cytology, cytoplasmic inheritance, quantititive genetics.; Assoc. editor: Plant Physiology, 1977-78. Pres. Johnston Consol. Sch. Bd., 1965-67. Served with AUS, 1943-46. Pioneer Hi-Bred fellow U. London, 1968. Fellow Crop Sci. Soc. Am.; mem. Bot. Soc. Am., Genetics Soc. Am., Am. Soc. Plant Physiologists, N.Y. Acad. Scis., AAAS, Am. Soc. Agromomy, Crop Sci. Soc. Am., Am. Seed Trade Assn., Council Agrl. Sci. and Tech. Democrat. Mem. United Ch. Christ. Home: 6837 NW Beaver Dr Johnston IA 50131 Office: 7301 NW 62d Ave Johnston IA 50131

DUVIN, ROBERT PHILLIP, lawyer; b. Evansville, Ind., May 18, 1937; s. Louis and Henrietta (Hamburg) D.; m. Darlene Chmiel, Aug. 23, 1961; children: Scott A., Marc A., Louis A. B.A. with honors, Ind. U., 1958, J.D. with highest honors, 1961, LL.M., Columbia U., 1963. Bar: Ohio 1964. Since practiced in, Cleve.; pres. Duvin, Flinker & Cahn (L.P.A.), 1972—; lectr. law schs.; labor adviser corps., cities and hosps. Contbr. to books and legal jours.; bd. editors: Ind. Law Jour., 1961, Columbia Law Rev., 1963. Served with AUS, 1961-62. Mem. Am., Fed., Ohio, Cleve. bar assns. Jewish. Club: Cleve. Racquet. Home: 2775 S Park Blvd Shaker Heights OH 44120 Office: Duvin Flinker & Cahn 1400 Citizens Federal Tower 2000 E 9th St Cleveland OH 44115

DUWEZ, POL EDGARD, educator; b. Mons, Belgium, Dec. 11, 1907; s. Arthur and Jeanne (Delcourt) D.; m. Nera Faisse, Sept. 4, 1935; 1 dau., Nadine. Metall.E., Sch. Mines, Mons, 1932; D.Sc., U. Brussels, 1933, Calif. Inst. Tech., 1935. Instr., prof. Sch. Mines, Mons, 1935-40; research engr. Calif. Inst. Tech., Pasadena, 941-45, chief materials sect. jet propulsion lab., 1945-54, asso. prof. materials sci., 1947-52, prof., 1952-78, prof. emeritus, 1978; Campbell Meml. lectr., 1967; mem. sci. adv. bd. to chief of staff USAF, 1945-55. Contbr. articles to profl. jours. Recipient Charles B. Dudley award ASTM, 1951; Francis J. Clamer medal Franklin Inst., 1968; Gov. Cornez prize, Belgium, 1973; Paul Lebeau medal French Soc. for High Temperature, 1974; Heyn medal Deutsche Gesellschaft für Metallkunde, 1981; W. Hume-Rothery award Metall. Soc. of AIME, 1981. Fellow AIME (C.H. Mathewson Gold medal 1964), Am. Soc. Metals (Albert Sauveur Achievement medal 1973); mem. Nat. Acad. Scis., Nat. Acad. Engring., Am. Ceramic Soc., Am. Acad. Arts and Scis., Am. Phys. Soc. (internat. prize for new materials 1980), AAAS, Brit. Inst. Metals, Société Francaise des Ingenieurs Civils, Sigma Xi. Home: 1535 Oakdale St Pasadena CA 91106

DVORAK, HAROLD F., pathologist, educator; b. Milw., June 20, 1937; s. Harold J. and Laura (Fisher) D.; m. Ann Marie Tompkins, June 13, 1962; children: John, Laura, Jane. A.B., Princeton U., 1958; M.D., Harvard U., 1963. Diplomate: Am. Bd. Pathology. Paratice medicine specializing in pathology, Boston; asst. prof. pathology Harvard U. Med. Sch., Boston, assoc. prof., prof., Mallinckrodt prof. pathology, 1979—; mem. staff Mass. Gen. Hosp., asst. pathologist, 1969-75, assoc. pathologist, 1975-78, head immunopathology unit, 1976-80, chief dept. pathology, 1979—; mem. study sect. pathology NIH, 1978-82, Am. Canver Soc., N.Y.C., 1982—; chmn. merit rev. bd. immunology VA, Washington, 1982—. Served to lt. comdr. USPHS, 1965-67. Mem. Am. Assn. Pathologists, Sm. Assn. Immunologists, Am. Acad. Sci., Internat. Acad. Pathology, Pluto Club, Collegium Internat. Allergologieum, Phi Beta Kappa, Sigma Xi, Alpha Omega Alpha. Home: 27 Mason Rd Newton Center MA 12159 Office: Beth Israel Hosp 330 Brookline Ave Boston MA 02115

DVORCHAK, THOMAS EDWARD, financial executive; b. Westfield, Mass., Jan. 14, 1933; s. Michael Edward and Josephine M. D.; m. Eleanor Elizabeth Achillich, Nov. 10, 1962; children: Gary, Mark, Paula. B.S. in Acctg., Am. Internat. Coll., 1960. C.P.A., N.Y. Sr. acct. Arthur Young & Co., N.Y.C., 1960-65; subs. controller Northwest Industries, Chgo., 1965-68, fin mgr., 1968-70; v.p., corp. controller Bandag Inc., Muscatine, Iowa, 1971-78, sr. v.p., chief fin. officer, 1978—. Bd. dirs. YMCA, Muscatine, 1981-83. Served with USN, 1950-53. Mem. Am. Inst. C.P.A.s, N.Y. State Soc. Pub. Accts. Republican. Roman Catholic. Club: Geneva Country (pres 1979-80). Office: Bandag Inc Bandag Center Muscatine IA 52761

DWASS, MEYER, mathematician, educator; b. New Haven, Conn., Apr. 9, 1923; s. Israel and Golda (Haz) D.; m. Shirley Labowitz, May 29, 1949; children—Golda, Emily, Michael, Claudia. B.A., George Washington U., 1949; M.A., Columbia U., 1950; Ph.D., U.N.C., 1952. Statistician U.S. Census Bur., Suitland, Md., 1948-50; asst. prof. math. Northwestern U., Evanston, Ill., 1952-58, asso. prof., 1958-60, prof., 1960—, chmn. dept. math., 1978-81; dir. Center for Statistics and Probability, 1975—. Author: First Steps in Probability, 1967, Probability and Statistics, 1970. Served with AUS, 1943-46. Fellow Inst. Math. Stats.; mem. Am. Math. Soc., Am. Statis. Assn., Inst. Math. Stats., Soc. Indsl. and Applied Math., Phi Beta Kappa. Home: 814 Lincoln St Evanston IL 60201 Office: Dept Math Northwestern U Evanston IL 60201

DWEK, CYRIL S., banker; b. Kobe, Japan, Nov. 9, 1936; s. Nessim S. and Alice (Stambouli) D.; children: Nevil, Alicia. B.S., Wharton Sch., U. Pa., 1958. With Trade Devel. Bank, Geneva, Switzerland, 1962-65; with Republic Nat. Bank of N.Y., 1966—, dir., 1967—, exec. v.p., 1973—, vice chmn., 1983—; dir. Republic N.Y. Corp., 1974—, vice chmn., 1983—; Bd. advisers Brazilian Inst. Bus. Programs, Pace U. Mem. Brazilian Am. C. of C. (dir.). Club: Racing Club de France (Paris). Office: 452 Fifth Ave New York NY 10018

DWIGHT, DONALD RATHBUN, newspaper publisher; b. Holyoke, Mass., Mar. 26, 1931; s. William and Dorothy Elizabeth (Rathbun) D.; m. Susan Newton Russell, Aug. 9, 1952; children: Dorothy Campbell, Laura Newton, Eleanor Addison, Arthur Ryan, Stuart Russell.; m. Nancy John Sinnott, Dec. 18, 1982. A.B., Princeton U., 1953; D.Sc. (hon.), U. Lowell, Mass., 1974. Reporter, asst. to pub. Holyoke Transcript-Telegram, 1955-63, assoc. pub., 1966-69; asso. commnr. Mass. Dept. Pub. Works, 1963-66; commr. adminstrn. Commonwealth Mass., 1969-70, lt. gov., 1971-75; assoc. pub., v.p. Mpls. Star and Tribune, 1975-76, pub., sr. v.p., 1976-81; exec. v.p., pres., pub. Star & Tribune Newspapers, 1981-82; exec. v.p., dir. Cowles Media Co., 1981-82; chmn. bd. Newspapers of New Eng., Inc., 1982—; dir. Recorder Pub. Co., Greenfield, Mass., Prospect Group, Inc. Mem. Town Meeting, South Hadley, Mass., 1957-69; chmn. Guthrie Theatre Found., 1972-82, bd. dirs., 1976-82; bd. dirs. Mpls. Soc. Fine Arts, 1976—; trustee Twin Cities Pub. TV, 1976—, Mpls. Downtown Council, 1977—. Served to lt. USMCR, 1953-55. Mem. Am. Newspaper Pubs. Assn., Sigma Delta Chi. Republican. Episcopalian. Clubs: Minneapolis, Minn. Press; Princeton (N.Y.C.). Home: 1941 Penn Ave South Minneapolis MN 55405

DWIGHT, JAMES SCUTT, JR., accounting firm executive; b. Pasadena, Calif., Mar. 9, 1934; s. James Scutt and Natalie (Phelps) D.; m. Elsa Fae Hardy, Dec. 27, 1953; children: Catherine, Janet, Dianne, James Scutt III. Student, Pomona Coll., 1951-53; B.S., U. So. Calif., 1956. C.P.A., Calif., D.C., N.C., La. With Deloitte Haskins & Sells (C.P.A.'s), Los Angeles, 1955-59; controller Sunkist Growers, Inc., Los Angeles, 1959-66; chief dep. dir. fin., State of Calif., 1966-72; asso. dir. Office Mgmt. and Budget, Exec. Office Pres., Washington, 1972-73; adminstr. Social and Rehab. Service, HEW, 1973-75; partner govtl. affairs Deloitte Haskins & Sells (C.P.A.s), Washington, 1975—; dir. Calif. Pub. Employees Retirement System, 1967-72, Calif. State Tchrs. Retirement System, 1967-72; alt. mem. Calif. Franchise Tax Bd., 1967-72, Calif. State Lands Commn., 1967-72, Calif. Toll Bridge Authority, 1967-72; alt. dir. San Francisco Port Authority, 1970-72; lectr. Fed. Exec. Inst., Charlottesville, Va., 1972-78, MFOA Career Devel. Center, 1979-81. Bd. dirs., v.p. Los Angeles Jr. C. of C., 1962-66; bd. dirs. Red. Shield Youth Center, 1963-66, United Black Fund D.C., 1977—; mem. D.C. Mayor's Adv. Panel, 1977; bd. dirs. Nat. Inst. Public Mgmt., 1981; chmn. Pres.'s Commn. on Hostage Compensation, 1981; mem. transition team on budget Office of Pres.-elect, 1981; bd. govs. govt. relations com. United Way of Am., 1981; trustee Meridian House, 1982—; mem. Cabinet Council Work Group on Federalism, 1982; pvt. citizen mem. Adv. Commn. on Intergovtl. Relations, 1983—. Recipient Outstanding Young Man award U.S. Jaycees, 1966. Mem. Am. Inst. C.P.A.s (fed. govt. exec. com.), D.C. Soc. C.P.A.s. Clubs: Washington Golf and Country, Federal City (Washington). Home: 4109 N River St

Arlington VA 22207 Office: Met Sq Suite 700 655 15th St NW Washington DC 20005

DWINGER, PHILIP, educator, university dean; b. The Hague, The Netherlands, Sept. 25, 1914; came to U.S., 1956; s. Aron and Geline (van Dam) D. Ph.D. in Math, U. Leiden, The Netherlands, 1938. Tchr. Lyceum, The Netherlands, 1937-52; prof. math., head dept. U. Indonesia, 1952-56; prof. Purdue U., 1956-62, Tech. U. Delft, The Netherlands, 1962-65, U. Ill. at Chgo. Circle, 1965—, head dept. math., 1975-79, dean, 1979—; vis. prof. U. Hamburg, W. Germany, 1960, Calif. Inst. Tech., 1971, U. Amsterdam, Netherlands, 1972, Technol. U., Darmstadt, West Germany, summer 1974; vis. mathematician Math. Assn. Am., 1966—. Author: Introduction to Boolean Algebras, 1961, (with R. Balbes) Distributive Lattices, 1974; also research papers in lattice theory and universal algebra. Mem. Math. Assn. Am., Am. Math. Soc., Royal Netherlands Acad. Scis. and Letters (corr.), Math. Assn. The Netherlands, Sigma Xi., Phi Kappa Phi. Home: 505 N Lake Shore Dr Chicago IL 60611

DWORETZKY, MURRAY, physician, educator; b. N.Y.C., Aug. 18, 1917; s. Samuel and Frieda (Newhoff) D.; m. Barbara Ratner, June 11, 1943; children: Thomas Alan, Joan Mara. B.A., U. Pa., 1938; M.D., SUNY, Coll. Medicine, N.Y.C., 1942; M.S. in medicine, U. Minn., 1950. Diplomate: Am. Bd. Internal Medicine, Am. Bd. Allergy and Immunology (founding mem., dir. 1971-74), Pan Am. Med. Assn. Intern City Hosp., N.Y.C., 1942-43, asst. resident pathology, 1943, fellow in pathology, 1946-47; resident pathology U. Chgo., 1947-48; fellow in medicine Mayo Found., Rochester, Minn., 1948-50; practice medicine, specializing in internal medicine and allergy, N.Y.C., 1951—; asst. physician N.Y. Hosp., 1951, physician, 951-56, asst. attending physician, 1956-61, asso. attending, 1961-66, attending physician, 1966—, physician-in-charge Allergy Clinic, 1961—; asst. in medicine Cornell U. Med. Coll., 1951-52, instr. medicine, 1952-56, clin. asst. prof., 1956-61, clin. asst. prof. pub. health, 1957-62, clin. asso. prof. medicine, 1961-66, clin. prof. medicine, 1966—; attending physician Manhattan Eye, Ear and Throat Hosp., 1953-62; Med. dir.-at-large Asthma-Allergy Found. Am., 1963-64, bd. dirs., 1964-78, mem. exec. com., 1964-77. Contbr. articles to profl. jours. Served to capt., M.C. AUS, 1943-46. Fellow Am. Acad. Allergy (past pres.), N.Y. Acad. Medicine, A.C.P.; mem. N.Y. County Med. Soc., N.Y. Allergy Soc. (past pres.), Soc. Exptl. Biology and Medicine, Harvey Soc., Am. Fedn. Clin. Research, AMA (chmn. allergy sect. council 1973-77, mem. residency rev. com. for allergy and immunology 1979—), Am. Assn. Immunologists, Sigma Xi. Home: 21 E 87th St New York NY 10028 Office: 115 E 61st St New York NY 10021

DWORK, BERNARD M., mathematics educator. Eugene Higgins Prof. Maths. Princeton U., Princeton, N.J. Office: Dept Maths Princeton U Princeton NJ 08544

DWORKIN, HOWARD JERRY, nuclear physician, educator; b. Bklyn., Oct. 29, 1932; s. Joseph Henry and Molly M. (Hodas) D.; m. Carole Joan Meyer, July 5, 1955; children: Rhonda Fran, Steven Irving, Paul J. B.S. in Chem. Engring., Worcester Poly. Inst., 1955; M.D., Albany Med. Coll., 1959; M.S. in Radiation Biology, U. Mich., 1965. Intern Albany Hosp., (N.Y.), 1959-60; resident Rochester Gen. Hosp., (N.Y.), 1960-62, U. Mich. Hosps., 1962-64, asst. coordinator nuclear medicine unit, 1963-66, instr., 1965-66; asst. prof. medicine U. Toronto, Ont., Can., 1966, assoc. prof., 1967; head dept. nuclear medicine Princess Margaret Hosp., Toronto, 1967; head nuclear medicine sect., radiology Nat. Naval Med. Ctr., Bethesda, Md., 1967-69; dir. sch. nuclear medicine tech. William Beaumont Hosp., Royal Oak, Mich., 1969—, chief dept. nuclear medicine, 1969—, dir. nuclear medicine resident tng. program, 1970—; clin. asst. prof. dept. medicine Wayne State U. Med. Sch., Detroit, 1970—; asst. clin. prof. dept. radiology Mich. State U., East Lansing, 1976—; clin. prof. med. physics Ctr. for Health Scis., Oakland U., Rochester, Mich., 1977—; treas. Am. Bd. Nuclear Medicine. Author: (with N. Aspin and R.G. Baker) Clinical Use of Isotopes in the Physics of Radiology, 1969, Part Two, Clinical Prodedures in Radioisotope Laboratory Procedures, 1969; contbr. articles and chpts. to med. jours. and texts; patentee radioactive labeled protein material process and apparatus. Served with USN, 1967-69. Fellow ACP; mem. Soc. Nuclear Medicine (trustee 1973-81, v.p. 1982-83), Am. Fedn. Clin. Research, Am. Thyroid Assn., Endocrine Soc., AMA, Am. Coll. Nuclear Physicians (sec. 1974-77, pres. 1978-79). Office: Dept Nuclear Medicine William Beaumont Hosp Royal Oak MI 48072

DWORKIN, MARTIN, microbiologist; b. N.Y.C., Dec. 3, 1927; s. Hyman Bernard and Pauline (Herstein) D.; m. Nomi Rees Buda, Feb. 2, 1957; children—Jessica Sarah, Hanna Beth. B.A., Ind. U., 1951; Ph.D. (NSF predoctoral fellow), U. Tex., Austin, 1955. NIH research fellow U. Calif., Berkeley, 1955-57, vis. prof., summers 1958-60; asst. prof. microbiology Ind. U. Med. Sch., 1957-61, asso. prof., 1961-62, U. Minn., 1962-69, prof., 1969—; vis. prof. U. Wash., summer 1965, Stanford U., 1978-79; vis. scholar Oxford (Eng.) U., 1970-71; Found. for Microbiology lectr., 1973-74, 76-77, 81-82. Contbr. numerous articles, revs. to profl. publs.; editorial bd.: Jour. Bacteriology, 1967-74, Ann. Revs. Microbiology, 1975-79. Alt. del. Democratic Nat. Conv., 1968; mem. Minn. Dem. Farm Labor Central Com., 1969-70. Served with U.S. Army, 1946-48. Recipient Career Devel. award NIH, 1963-68, 68-73; John Simon Guggenheim fellow, 1978-79. Mem. Am. Soc. Microbiology (vice chmn. div. gen. microbiology 1977-78, chmn. 1978-79, div. councillor 1980-82), Soc. Gen. Microbiology (Eng.). Home: 2123 W Hoyt Ave Saint Paul MN 55108 Office: Microbiology Dept U Minn Minneapolis MN 55455

DWORKIN, ROGER BARNETT, legal educator; b. Cin., Jan. 19, 1943. A.B., Princeton U., 1963; J.D., Stanford U., 1966. Bar: Calif. 1967. Assoc. Hewitt, Klitgaard & Sharkey, San Diego, 1966-68; asst. prof. law Ind. U., Bloomington, 1968-71, assoc. prof., 1971-74, prof., 1974—; vis. prof. biomed. history U. Wash. Sch. Medicine, 1974-75, summer 1976, 77, 79; vis. prof. U. Va. Sch. Law, 1978-79. Mem. Soc. for Health and Human Values, Inst Society Ethics and Life Scis. (assoc.), AAAS, Order of Coif, Phi Beta Kappa, Phi Delta Phi. Office: Ind U Sch Law Bloomington IN 47405

DWORKIN, SAMUEL FRANKLIN, psychologist, dentist; b. Freedom, Ohio, Sept. 26, 1933; s. Louis and Minnie (Katz) D.; m. Mona Mae Moskowitz, Dec. 23, 1956; children: Adam, Ted. B.S., CCNY, 1954; D.D.S., NYU, 1958, Ph.D., 1969. Practice dentistry, N.Y.C., 1959-65, Nat. Inst. Dental Research spl. fellow, 1965-69; asst. prof. dept. preventive dentistry and community health N.Y. U. Coll. Dentistry, 1969-70; asso. prof. div. preventive dentistry, dir. office of edn. and behavioral research Columbia U. Sch. Dental and Oral Surgery, 1970-74; prof. oral surgery, asso. dean acad. affairs U. Wash. Sch. Dentistry, Seattle, 1974-77, adj. prof. psychiatry and behavioral sci., 1974—, dir. psychophysiologic liaison clinic dept. psychiatry and behavioral scis., 1978—; cons. ADA, Nat. Inst. Dental Research, Am. Dental Hygiene Assn. Cons. editor: Jour. Dental Edn, 1976—, Jour. Dental Research, 1976—; guest editor: Jour. Preventive Dentistry, 1977; Contbr. articles to profl. jours. Co-founder, pres. League of Parents of Hearing Impaired Infants, N.Y.C., 1966-70; v.p. N.Y. State Parents of Hearing Impaired Children, 1970-74; adv. council Lexington Sch. of Deaf, N.Y.C., 1970-74; bd. dirs. Seattle Pro-Musica, 1977—, v.p., 1978-81. NIH grantee, 1979-86. Mem. ADA (council dental health edn., council nat. bd. exams. 1974-79), AAAS, Am. Assn. Dental Schs., Am. Psychol. Assn., Assn. Behavioral Scis. in Med. Edn., Behavioral Scientists in Dental Research, Internat. Assn. Study of Pain, Am. Pain Soc., Internat. Soc. Clin. and Exptl. Hypnosis. Office: Dept Psychiatry U Wash Seattle WA 98195

DWORKIN, SIDNEY, business executive; b. Detroit; (married). B.A., Wayne State U., 1942. Partner Dworkin Boone & Gross, 1950-66; indsl. acct., 1966; with Revco D S Inc., Twinsburg, Ohio, 1966—, now pres., chief exec. officer, dir. Office: Revco DS Inc 1925 Enterprise Parkway Twinsburg OH 44087 *

DWORSKY, DANIEL LEONARD, architect; b. Mpls., Oct. 4, 1927; s. Lewis and Ida (Fineberg) D.; m. Sylvia Ann Taylor, Aug. 10, 1957; children: Douglas, Laurie, Nancy. B.Arch., U. Mich., 1950. Practice architecture as Dworsky Assocs., Los Angeles, 1953—; design critic, lectr. arch. UCLA, 1983, 84. (Recipient Design citation Progressive Arch. mag. 1967, Gov. Calif. award 1966, 3 Los Angeles Grand Prix awards So. Calif. AIA and City of Los Angeles 1967); Prin. works include Angelus Plaza Elderly Housing, Los Angeles, 1981, Ontario (Calif.) City Hall, 1980, CBS Exec. Office Bldg, North Hollywood, Calif., 1970, U. Calif. at Los Angeles Stadium, 1969, Fed. Res. Bank Bldg., Los Angeles, U. Mich. Crisler Arena at Ann Arbor, 1968, Dominguez Hills State U. Theatre, 1977, Ventura County Govt. Center, 1979, Lloyds Bank Ops. Ctr., Los Angeles, 1980, The Park Office Bldgs., Los Angeles, 1980, Skyline Condominiums, Los Angeles, 1982, Northrop Electronics Hdqrs., Los Angeles, 1983, Hewlett-Packard Region Office, North Hollywood, 1984. Fellow AIA (20 awards So. Calif. chpt., including 11 honor awards; Nat. honor award 1974, 1968-69, merit award Calif. chpt. 1984). Home: 9225 Nightingale Dr Los Angeles CA 90069 Office: 2029 Century Park E Suite 350 Los Angeles CA 90067

DWYER, BERNARD JAMES, congressman; b. Perth Amboy, N.J., Jan. 24, 1921; s. Daniel F. and Alice (Zehrer) D.; m. Lilyan Sudzina, 1944; 1 dau., Pamela Dwyer Stockton. Student, Rutgers U. Ins. broker, owner Fraser Brothers, Edison, N.J.; mem. 97th-98th Congresses from 15th Dist. N.J.; Mem. City Council, Edison, N.J., 1958-69, mayor, 1969-73; mem. N.J. Senate, 1974-80, majority leader, 1979-80. Trustee J.F.K. Med. Center. Served with USN, 1940-45. Mem. VFW, Am. Legion, Edison C. of C. Roman Catholic. Clubs: K.C., Elks. Office: 404 Cannon House Office Bldg Washington DC 20515 *

DWYER, GREGG ALLAN, lawyer; b. Indpls., Dec. 9, 1943; s. Thomas I. and Doris (Hart) D.; m. Patareka Korbly, May 28, 1966; children: Christopher, Amy, Susan. B.A., Marian Coll., 1966; J.D., Ind. U., 1970. Bar: Ind. 1970. Fin. analyst The Buehler Corp., Indpls., 1966-70; atty. Stokely-Van Camp, Inc., Indpls., 1970-71; sec., v.p., gen. counsel Duracell, Inc., Bethel, Conn., 1971—. Mem. Am. Corp. Counsel Assn., Am., Ind. bar assns. Roman Catholic. Home: 2 Taylor Dr New Fairfield CT 06812 Office: Berkshire Indsl Park Bethel CT 06801

DWYER, JAMES BERNARD, III, investment banker; b. Erie, Pa., May 3, 1943; s. James B. and Margaret E. (Quinn) D.; m. Laura Lawrence, Apr. 10, 1977; 1 son, James Bernard, IV. B.B.A., U. Nortre Dame, 1965; M.B.A., Columbia U., 1970. C.P.A., N.Y. Vice pres. Kidder, Peabody, N.Y.C., 1970-76; sr. v.p. Shearson Loeb Rhoades, N.Y.C., 1976-80, Donaldson, Lufkin & Jenrette, 1980—; exec. v.p. Assn. for Corp. Growth, Chgo., 1983—. Pres. 1060 Owners, Inc., N.Y.C., 1980-83; treas. N.Y. Com. for Young Audiences, N.Y.C., 1979-81. Recipient T.W. McMahon award for leadership Columbia Grad. Sch. Bus., 1970. Mem. Am. Inst. C.P.A.s, Assn. for Corp. Growth (pres. chpt. 1981-82), Columbia Bus. Sch. Alumni Assn. (pres. 1980-81). Roman Catholic. Club: Weshampton Country. Home: 940 Park Ave New York NY 10028 Office: 140 Broadway New York NY 10005

DWYER, JOHN DUNCAN, biology educator; b. Newark, Apr. 26, 1915; s. William Charles and Elizabeth (MacIsaac) D.; m. Marie Rita Rozelle, Sept. 8, 1942; children: John Duncan, Joseph, James, Jerome. A.B., St. Peters Coll., 1936; M.S., Fordham U., 1938, Ph.D., 1941. Tchr. St. Francis Coll., Bklyn., 1941-42, Union U., 1942-48, Siena Coll., 1948-53; faculty St. Louis U., 1953—, prof. biology, 1959—, chmn. dept., 1953-63, bot. cons. forensic medicine, 1975—; research assoc. Mo. Bot. Garden, 1954—; curator S.Am. Phanerogams, 1964—; Cons. floristics of Panama U.S. AID, summers 1962-63, U.S. Army Tropic Test Center, Panama, 1965, Middle Am., OAS, Guatemala, 1970; in NCCJ. Grantee Danforth Found., NSF, Nat. Acad. Scis., Nat. Geog. Soc. Mem. Am. Inst. Biol. Scis., Am. Soc. Plant Taxonomists, Bot. Soc. Am., Torrey Bot. Club, AAAS, Mo. Acad. Sci. (pres. 1964-65), Internat. Assn. Plant Taxonomy, AAUP, Sigma Xi (chpt. pres 1968, Scientist of Yr award 1980). Home: 526 Oakwood St Webster Groves MO 63119 Office: 221 N Grand St Saint Louis MO 63103

DWYER, JOHN J., lawyer; b. Gary, Ind., 1917; (married). A.B., De Pauw U., 1939; LL.B., Harvard U., 1944. Bar: bar. With Oglebay Norton Co., 1946-83, v.p., sec., gen. counsel, 1946-67, exec. v.p., 1967-70, pres., chief exec. officer, 1970-82, vice chmn. bd., 1982—, also dir.; ptnr. Thompson, Hine and Flory, 1983—; dir. Acme-Cleve. Corp., AmeriTrust Corp., Atlas Corp., Diamond Crystal Salt Co., Higbee Co. Address: 1100 National City Bank Bldg Cleveland OH 44114

DWYER, ROBERT BUDD, treasurer Pennsylvania; b. St. Charles, Mo., Nov. 21, 1939; s. Robert M. and Alice M. (Budd) D.; m. Joanne M. Grappy, Aug. 23, 1963; children—Robert Ross, Dyan Danuta. B.A., Allegheny Coll., 1961, M.A., 1963; J.D., Dickinson Sch. Law. Asst. alumni sec. Allegheny Coll., Meadville, Pa., 1967-75; mem. Pa. Ho. of Reps., 1965-70, Pa. Senate, 1971-81; treas., State of Pa., 1981—; of counsel Culbertson Weiss Schetroma & Schug, Meadville, 1981—. Del. Republican Nat. Conv., 1976. Named Pa. Conservationist of Year, 1972, 78. Mem. NEA, Nat. Assn. State Treas.'s. Clubs: Eagles, Elks. Home: 26 Locust Ave Hershey PA 17033 Office: Room 129 Finance Bldg Harrisburg PA 17120

DWYER, VIRGINIA ALICE, telephone company executive; b. N.Y.C., May 11, 1921; d. Harold Arthur and Alice Marie (Cullen) D. A.B., U. Rochester, 1943; M.A., N.Y. U., 1953. With Western Electric Co., N.Y.C., 1943-75, chief economist, dir. acctg. research, 1972-75; asst. treas. AT&T, N.Y.C., 1975-79, v.p., treas., 1979—; dir. Centennial Ins. Co., Borden Co., AT&T Internat.; trustee (Atlantic Cos.). Trustee U. Rochester, 1979—, Com. for Econ. Devel., 1978—; Com. for Econ. Devel. YWCA, N.Y.C., 1979—. Recipient Econ. Equity award Women's Equity Action League, 1980. Mem. Telephone Pioneers Am., Fin. Execs. Inst., Treasurers Club, Am. Econ. Assn., Nat. Assn. Bus. Economists, Conf. Bus. Economists, Am. Fin. Assn., Nat. Economists Club, Downtown Economists Luncheon Group N.Y. Office: 195 Broadway New York NY 10007

DWYER-DOBBIN, MARY ALICE, TV programmer; b. St. Louis, Dec. 22, 1942; d. Paul Authur and Mary Albertina (Goessling) Dwyer; m. Leon Dobbin, July 29, 1973. B.A. in Speech and Drama, Webster (Mo.) Coll., 1963; M.F.A. in Theatre, Catholic U. Am., 1967. Chmn. speech and drama dept. St. Joseph's Acad., St. Louis, 1963-65; asst. to producer Bob Stewart Prodns., N.Y.C., 1968-70; producer Rankin-Bass Prodns., N.Y.C., 1970-73; mgr. daytime programs, then dir. children's programs ABC-TV, 1974-77; dir. daytime and children's programs, then v.p. children's programs NBC-TV, 1977-81; v.p. programming Hearst/ABC Video Services Inc., N.Y.C., 1981—. Recipient TV Critics Circle award for children's programming, 1977, AWRT/Good Housekeeping mag. award children's programming, 1979, Action for Children's TV award, 1981. Mem. Nat. Acad. TV Arts and Scis. Office: 555 5th Ave New York NY 10020

DWYRE, WILLIAM RAYMOND, army officer, pathologist; b. Elgin, Ont., Can., Dec. 18, 1926; came to U.S., 1952, naturalized, 1960; s. John Herbert and Margaret Elizabeth D.; m. Georgia M. Bailey, June 21, 1952. B.S., U. Ottawa, 1948, M.D., 1952; D.J., U. London, 1968. Diplomate: Am. Bd. Anat. Pathology, Am. Bd. Clin. Pathology. Rotating intern, then resident in surgery U. Vt. Hosps., 1952-56; resident in surg. pathology Sacred Heart Hosp., Allentown, Pa., 1956; resident in pathology Fitzsimons Gen. Hosp., Aurora, Colo., 1963-65; fellow in forensic pathology London Hosp., 1968; commd. capt. M.C. U.S. Army, 1957, advanced through grades to brig. gen., 1977; service in, Pakistan and Europe, dep. dir. Armed Forces Inst. Pathology, Washington, 1976-77, comdg. gen. Madigan Army Med. Center, Tacoma, 1977-80, comdg. gen. Fitzsimons Army Med. Center, 1980—; assoc. clin. prof. pathology U. Colo. Med. Sch., 1966-70; mem. dean's com. U. Wash. Med. Sch., Seattle, 1978; clin. prof. Uniformed Services U. Health Scis., 1977; cons. in field. Co-author: Textbook of Pathology, 1969; Contbr. articles to profl. jours. Decorated Army Commendation medal, Navy Commendation medal, Joint Services Commendation medal, Meritorious Service medal (2), D.S.M. Fellow Coll. Am. Pathologists (chmn. govtl. pathology sect. 1970-77), Am. Soc. Clin. Pathologists, Assn. Mil. Surgeons, Am. Acad. Med. Dirs.; mem. AMA, Am. Coll. Physician Executives, Internat. Acad. Pathology, Assn. U.S. Army, N.W. Soc. Pathologists, Denver C. of C., Aurora C. of C. Club: Rotary. Home: Quarters 1 Fitzsimons Army Med Center Aurora CO 80045

DYAL, WILLIAM M., JR., foundation executive; b. Austin, Tex., May 13, 1928; s. William M. and Mildred Eleanor (Taylor) D.; m. Edith Colvin, May. 6, 1950; children: Kathy Lynn Dyal Schwab, Deborah Irene, Maria Lisa. A.B., Baylor U., 1949; Th.M., So. Theol. Sem., 1953. With Fgn. Mission Bd., Costa Rica, Guatemala and Argentina, 1953-62; dir. orgn. Christian Life Commn., 1962-66; dir. Peace Corps, Colombia, 1966-69, regional dir., N. Africa, Near East and S. Asia, 1969-71; pres. Inter-Am. Found., Rosslyn, Va., 1971-80; advisor to pres. Ford Found., N.Y.C., 1980-81; pres. Am. Field Service Internat./Intercultural Programs, N.Y.C., 1981—. Author: Its Worth Your Life, 1967, Un Desafio al Discipulado, 1970, also articles. Recipient Santander Gold medal, Colombia, 1968; Woodrow Wilson sr. fellow, 1975—. Office: AFS Internatl Inter-cultural Programs 313 E 43d St New York NY 10017

DYATT, BETTY MARIE, mut. fund exec.; b. Denver, Mar. 3, 1924; d. Andrew and Olive (Burnap) D. B.S. in Commerce, U. Denver, 1945, LL.B. cum laude, 1947. Bar: Colo. bar 1947. Law clk. Justice Mortimer Stone, Supreme Ct. Colo., Denver, 1946; pvt. practice, Colo., 1947—; counsel Bank Stock Fund, Inc., 1965-70, pres., 1970-76; v.p., sec., dir., counsel, registered prin. First Colo. Investments, Inc., Colorado Springs, 1966—; exec. v.p., sec., dir., house counsel Ramah, Ltd., Colorado Springs, 1966—; v.p., dir., counsel Silver Prince Mines, 1969—, Napolean Mines, 1969—, Elements Refining Corp., 1969—; vis. prof. Colo. Coll., 1977—. Mem. adv. council Pikes Peak Community Coll., 1969—, Family Counseling Service, 1959—, Inst. Internat. Edn., 1960—, League Women Voters, 1957—. Mem. El Paso County, Colo., Am. bar assns., AAUW. Home: 1082-C Frontmore Rd Colorado Springs CO 80904 Office: 607 Exchange Nat Bank Bldg Colorado Springs CO 80903

DYBECK, ALFRED CHARLES, assn. exec.; b. Camden, Del., Nov. 16, 1928; s. George L. and Freda (Alexander) D.; m. Leah Anne Pestell, June 28, 1952; 1 son, Alfred Arthur. Student, Emmanuel Missionary Coll., 1946-49; B.A., George Washington U., 1955, J.D., 1958. Bar: Va. bar 1958. Field atty. NLRB, Pitts., 1958-63, supervising atty., 1963-65, asst. regional atty., Milw., 1965; asso. chmn. bd. arbitration United Steelworkers Am. and; U.S. Steel Corp., Pitts., 1965-78, chmn. bd. arbitration, 1979—; exec. sec. Nat. Acad. Arbitrators, 1971-77. Served with AUS, 1951-53. Mem. Order Coif. Home: 1235 Cardinal Dr Pittsburgh PA 15243 Office: Bd Arbitration 530 Oliver Bldg Pittsburgh PA 15222

DYCHE, DAVID BENNETT, JR., consultant; b. Port Chester, N.Y., July 23, 1932; s. David B. and Julia H. D.; m. Mary J. Moorman, Apr. 28, 1956; children—David B. III, Williard H. A.B., Dartmouth Coll., 1954; M.B.A., Wharton Sch., U. Pa., 1958. Chartered fin. analyst. With J.P. Morgan & Co., and Morgan Guaranty Trust Co., N.Y.C., 1958-81; sr. cons. Arthur D. Little, Inc., 1981—. Served with U.S. Army, 1954-56. Mem. N.Am. Soc. Corp. Planning, N.Y. Soc. Security Analysts. Home: 162 Julian St Rye NY 10580 Office: 405 Lexington Ave New York NY 10174

DYCK, ARTHUR JAMES, ethicist, educator; b. Saskatoon, Sask., Can., Apr. 27, 1932; s. Jacob Peter and Mary (Zacharias) D.; m. Sylvia Willms, Sept. 2, 1952; children—Sandra Lynn and Cynthia Ann (twins). B.A., Tabor Coll., 1953; M.A., U. Kans., 1958, 1959; Ph.D., Harvard, 1966. Research asst. psychology U. Kans., 1957-60; spl. lectr. philosophy U. Sask., 1964-65; asst. prof. social ethics Harvard Div. Sch. and, 1965-69; Mary B. Saltonstall prof., 1969—, Co-dir., 1971—, mem., 1965—. Author: On Human Care: An Introduction to Ethics, 1977; Editor: (with S.J. Reiser, W.J. Curran) Ethics in Medicine, 1977; asso. editor: Jour. Religious Ethics; editorial bd.: Linacre Quar; Contbr. articles to profl. jours. Mem. Am. Soc. Christian Ethics, Am. Acad. Religion, Population Assn. Am., Sociêté Européenne de Culture, Inter-Univ. Seminar on Armed Forces and Soc., Phi Beta Kappa. Congregationalist. Home: RFD 1 Box 236A Alton NH 03809 Office: 45 Francis Ave Cambridge MA 02138 *I do not measure success apart from what moral principles require of me. To do my chosen scholarly work honestly, fairly, enthusiastically, and in ways that contribute, however modestly, to learning, knowledge and social justice is success. The most important measures of success are the increase of love for others and for the divine power that makes the moral life possible on earth. This is true in my family as well as in my vocation.*

DYCK, GEORGE, medical educator; b. Hague, Sask., Can., July 25, 1937; came to U.S., 1965; s. John and Mary (Janzen) D.; m. Edna Margaret Krueger, June 27, 1959; children: Brian Edward, Janine Louise, Stanley George, Jonathan Jay. Student, U. Sask., 1955-56; B. Christian Edn., Can. Mennonite Bible Coll., 1959; M.D., U. Man., 1964; postgrad., Menninger Sch. Psychiatry, 1965-68. Diplomate: Am. Bd. Psychiatry and Neurology, Royal Coll. Physicians and Surgeons (Can.) in Psychiatry. Fellow community psychiatry Prairie View Mental Health Center, Newton, Kans., 1968-70, clin. dir. tri-county services, 1970-73; prof. U. Kans., Wichita, 1973—, chmn. dept. psychiatry, 1973-80; med. dir. Prairie View, Inc., 1980—. Bd. dirs. Mennonite Mut. Aid, Goshen, Ind., 1973—, Mid-Kans. Community Action Program, 1970-73, Wichita Council Drug Abuse, 1974-76. Fellow Am. Psychiat. Assn. (pres. Kans. dist. br. 1982-84); mem. AMA, Kans. Med. Soc. Mennonite. Home: 1505 Hillcrest Rd Newton KS 67114 Office: 1901 E 1st St Newton KS 67114

DYCK, MARTIN, literary theoretician, educator; b. Grunfeld, Russia, Jan. 16, 1927; came to U.S., 1956; s. Martin and Helene (Peters) D.; m. Marie Wiens, June 12, 1949; children—Vernon George M., Victor Herbert M., Martin Christopher C. and Ingrid Rose Marie (twins). Abitur, Gisela Gymnasium für Jungen, Munich, Germany, 1947; B.A. with double honours in German Lit. and Pure Math, U. Man., Can., 1953; M.A. in German and Math, U. Man., Can., 1954, Ph.D., U. Cin., 1956. Asst. prof. German and Russian Mass. Inst. Tech., 1956-58; from asst. prof. to prof. German U. Mich., 1958-65; prof. German and humanities Mass. Inst. Tech., Cambridge, 1965—. Author: Novalis and Mathematics, 2d edit, 1969, Die Gedichte Schillers, 1967, also numerous articles.; Mem. editorial bd.: Historia Mathematica, 1973-76. Guggenheim fellow, 1961-62; fellow Am. Council Learned Socs., 1961-62; Taft Meml. fellow, 1954-56; Isbister, McLean scholar, U. Man. travelling fellow, 1952-55; Am. Philos. Soc. grantee, Germany, 1969. Mem. MLA (del. assembly 1979-81), NE MLA, Am. Soc. Eighteenth Century Studies, Modern Humanities Research Assn., Internat. Vereinigung für germanische Sprach und Literaturwissenschaft, History of Sci. Soc., Freies Deutsches Hochstift Goethehaus (Frankfurt am Main), AAUP, Kafka Soc. Am., Lessing Soc. Mennonite and Congregationalist. Home: PO Box 281 Cambridge MA 02238 Office: Mass Inst Tech Cambridge MA 02139 *To taste-and-test the poetry-and-algebra of man-against-matter.*

DYCK, WALTER PETER, physician; b. Winkler, Man., Can., 1935. M.D., U. Kans., 1961. Diplomate: Am. Bd. Internal Medicine. Intern Henry Ford Hosp., Detroit, 1961-62, resident in internal medicine, 1962-63, 65-66; research fellow gastroenterology U. Zurich, Switzerland, 1963-64; fellow enzymology research U. Toronto, Ont., Can., 1964-65; fellow gastroenterology Mt. Sinai Sch. Medicine, N.Y.C., 1966-68; mem. sr. staff Scott and White Clinic, Temple, Tex., 1968—, chmn. dept. research, 1969-72, dir. div. gastroenterology, 1972—; prof. medicine, dir. div. gastroenterology Tex. A&M Coll. Medicine, 1978—; Mem. gen. medicine study sect. A NIH, 1973-77. Fellow A.C.P.; mem. Am. Fedn. Clin. Research, Am. Gastroenterology Assn., AMA, Am. Physiol. Soc., So. Soc. Clin. Investigation, Soc. for Exptl. Biology and Medicine. Address: Scott and White Clinic Temple TX 76501

DYCKMAN, THOMAS RICHARD, accounting educator; b. Detroit, Feb. 25, 1932; s. Clovis E. and Wildarene A. (Andrus) D.; m. Alice Ann Pletta, Nov. 14, 1955; children: Daniel, James, Linda, David. B.A., U. Mich., 1954, M.B.A., 1955, Ph.D., 1961. Asst. prof. acctg. U. Calif., Berkeley, 1961-64; asso. prof. Cornell U., Ithaca, N.Y., 1964-68, prof., 1968—, Ann Whitney Olin prof. bus., 1978—; cons. Fin. Acctg. Standards Bd., IBM, GTE. Author: Statistical Decision Theory, 1968, Algebra and Calculus for Business, 1975, Fundamental Statistics for Business and Economics, 1977, Managerial Cost Accounting, 3d edit, 1978, Efficient Capital Markets, 1977, Cases in Financial Accounting, 2d edit., 1980. Served with USNR, 1955-58. Recipient Gold medal award Am. Inst. C.P.A.s, 1966, 78. Mem. Am. Acctg. Assn. (pres. 1981-82). Home: 402 Winthrop Dr Ithaca NY 14850 Office: Malott Hall Cornell Univ Ithaca NY 14853

DYE, BRADFORD JOHNSON, JR., lieutenant governor Mississippi; b. Tallahatchie County, Miss., Dec. 20, 1933; married; 3 children. B.B.A., LL.B., U. Miss. Bar: Miss 1959. Practiced law, Grenada, Miss., 1959-61, later in Jackson, Miss.; mem. Miss. Ho. of Reps., 1960-64, Miss. Senate, 1964-68; dir. Agrl. and Indsl. Bd., 1968-71; treas., State of Miss., 1972-76, lt. gov., 1980—; formerly served with U.S. Senate Judiciary Com. Staff; pres. Jackson Fed. Savs. Assn., 1976-79. Mem. Pi Kappa Alpha. Methodist. Office: Office Lt Gov New Capitol Bldg Jackson MS 39205 *

DYE, KENNETH MALCOLM, Canadian government official; b. Vancouver, B.C., Can., Jan. 16, 1936; s. Allan Edward and Mabel Elizabeth (Elrick) D.; m. Frances Marion Johnson, Dec. 13, 1958; children: Elizabeth, Georgia, Lesleigh, Marion, James, Kenneth. Auditor Frederick Field & Co. (name later changed to Campbell Sharp), Vancouver, B.S., Can.; pftnr. Campbell Sharp, Chartered Accts., Vancouver, Can., 1968-81; ptnr. Pannel Kerr Forster Campbell Sharp mgmt. cons.; auditor gen. Can., Ottawa, 1981—. Served with RCAF, 1954-57. Fellow Inst. Chartered Accts. B.C. (pres. 1979-80), Inst. Chartered Accts. Ont.; mem. Inst. Chartered Accts. Yukon, Inst. Chartered Accts. N.W.T., Ordre des comptables agrees du Que. Anglican. Clubs: Country; Rideau (Ottawa); Hollyburn Country; University (Vancouver). Home: 1907 Highland Terr Ottawa ON Canada K1H 5A5 Ofice: Office Auditor Gen 240 Sparks St Ottawa ON Canada K1A 0G6

DYE, PAUL, golf course design company executive; b. Urbana, Ohio, Dec. 29, 1925; s. Paul Francis and Elizabeth (Johnson) D.; m. Alice O'Neal, Feb. 2, 1950; children: Perry O'Neal, Paul Burke. Student, Rollins Coll. Pres. Dornach Co., Gulf Stream, Fla. Served with U.S. Army. Mem. Am. Soc. Golf Course Architects. Office: Dornoch Corp 3247 Polo Dr Delray Beach FL 33444 *

DYE, SHERMAN, lawyer; b. Portland, Oreg., Nov. 18, 1915; s. Trafton M. and Mary (Ward) D.; m. Jean Forsythe, Dec. 22, 1939; children—Peter S., Kathleen, Richard F., Alice, William T., Mary H. A.B., Oberlin Coll., 1937; LL.B., Case Western Res. U., 1940. Bar: Ohio bar 1940, U.S. Supreme Ct. bar 1972. Jr. atty. SEC, Washington, 1940-41; law clk. Tax Ct. U.S., Washington, 1941-42; asso. mem. firm Baker, Hostetler & Patterson, Cleve., 1942-51; partner firm Baker & Hostetler, Cleve., 1952—. Trustee, chmn. First Bapt. Ch. Greater Cleve.; trustee, treas. Am. Cancer Soc., Cleve.; trustee PACE Assn. Served with USAF, 1945. Mem. Am. Bar Assn., Ohio Bar Assn., Cleve. Bar Assn. (trustee 1954-57), Soc. Benchers, Order of Coif, Phi Delta Phi. Republican. Baptist. Club: Union. Home: 12700 Lake Ave Lakewood OH 44107 Office: 3200 National City Center Cleveland OH 44114

DYE, THOMAS ROY, political science educator; b. Pitts., Dec. 16, 1935; s. James Clair and Marguerite Ann (Dewan) D.; m. Joan Grace Wohleber, June 29, 1957; children: Roy Thomas, Cheryl Price. B.A., Pa. State U., 1957, M.A., 1959; Ph.D., U. Pa., 1961. Asst. prof. polit. sci. U. Wis., Madison, 1962-63; asso. prof., head dept. polit. sci. U. Ga., Athens, 1963-68; prof., chmn. dept. govt. Fla. State U., Tallahassee, 1968-78, dir. policy scis., 1978—; vis. prof. polit. studies Bar Ilan U., Israel, 1972, U. Ariz., 1976. Author: Politics, Economics and the Public, 1966, Politics in States and Communities, 1969, 5th edit., 1984, The Irony of Democracy, 1970, 6th edit., 1984, The Politics of Equality, 1971, Understanding Public Policy, 1972, 4th edit., 1980, Power and Society, 1975, 3d edit., 1983, Who's Running America?, 1976, Policy Analysis, 1976, Who's Running America?-The Carter Years, 1979, Determinants of Public Policy, 1980, Who's Running America? - The Reagan Years, 1983, Politics in the Media Age, 1983. Served to 1st lt. USAF, 1961-62. Mem. Am. Polit. Sci. Assn. (sec. 1969-72), So. Polit. Sci. Assn. (v.p. 1974-75, pres. 1976-77), Phi Beta Kappa, Omicron Delta Kappa. Club: Bay Point Yacht and Country (Panama City). Home: 2321 Killarney Way Tallahassee FL 32308 Office: Dept of Govt Fla State Univ Tallahassee FL 32306

DYEN, ISIDORE, educator, linguistic scientist; b. Phila., Aug. 16, 1913; s. Jacob and Dena (Bryzell) D.; m. Edith Brenner, June 11, 1939 (dec. 1976); children—Doris Jane, Mark Ross. B.A., U. Pa., 1933, M.A., 1934, Ph.D. in Indo-European Linguistics, 1939; postgrad. Slavic, Columbia, 1938-39, Yale, 1939-40. Faculty Yale, 1942—; prof. Malayan langs., 1957—, prof. Malayopolynesian and comparative linguistics, 1958-73, prof. comparative linguistics and Austronesian langs., 1973—, dir. grad. studies Indic and Far Eastern langs. and lit., 1960-62, Indic and Southeast Asia, 1960-66, dir. grad. studies linguistics, 1966-68; Linguist Coordinated Investigation Micronesian Anthropology, Truk, 1947, Sci. Investigation Micronesia, Yap, 1949; vis. prof. U. Padjadjaran, Bandung, 1960-61, U. Auckland, summer 1969, Australian Nat. U., fall 1971, U. Philippines, spring 1972, Inst. Study of Langs. and Cultures of Asia and Africa, Tokyo U. for Fgn. Langs., 1982-83; coordinator linguistics sect. 10th Pacific Sci. Congress, Honolulu, 1961; asso. prof. U. Chgo. Linguistic Soc.'s Summer Inst., 1955; prof. U. Mich. Linguistic Soc. Summer Inst., 1957; dir. SE Asia Linguistics Program, 28th Internat. Congress Orientalists, Canberra, 1971; organizing com. Conf. Genetic Lexicostatistics, New Haven, 1971; organizer 1st Eastern Conf. Austronesian Linguistics, New Haven, 1973; adv. com. 1st Internat. Conf. Comparative Austronesian Linguistics, Honolulu, 1974. Author: Spoken Malay, 2 vols, 1945, The Proto-Malayo-Polynesian Laryngeals, 1953, A Lexicostatistical Classification of the Austronesian Languages, 1965, A Sketch of Trukese Grammar, 1965, A Descriptive Indonesian Grammar, 1967, Beginning Indonesian, 4 vols, 1967, Lexicostatistics in Genetic Linguistics: Proc. of Yale Conf, 1973, (with David Aberle) Lexical Reconstruction: The Case of the Athapaskan Kinship System, 1974, Linguistic Subgrouping and Lexicostatistics, 1975, (with Guy Jucquois) Lexicostatistics in Genetic Linguistics II, 1976. Research fellow Slavic Am. Council Learned Socs., 1938-40; Guggenheim fellow, 1949, 64; Tri-Instl. Pacific Program grantee, 1956-57; NSF grantee, 1960-77. Mem. Linguistic Soc. Am., Am. Oriental Soc. (v.p. 1965-66), Am. Anthrop. Assn., Current Anthropology, Société de Linguistique de Paris, Koninklijk Instituut voor Taal-, Land-, en Volkenkunde, New Haven Oriental Club (pres. 1963-64, 74-76). Office: Hall Grad Studies Yale Univ New Haven CT 06520 *My aim has been to further linguistic science, particularly in comparative linguistics, by research in both Austronesian and Indoeuropean languages. In large part my work has been devoted to combining traditional and mathematico-statistical methods to improve subgrouping procedures. The different interlocking roles of theory, hypothesis, and methodology have been kept to the fore throughout. I hope my research will develop strong evidence regarding the Austronesian homeland.*

DYER, ALEXANDER PATRICK, indsl. gas mfg. co. exec.; b. Santa Rosa, Calif., Aug. 30, 1932; s. John Alexander and Amie Marie (Moore) D.; m. Shirley Aiken Shine, Dec. 11, 1954; children—David P., Steven S. (dec.). B.S. in Engring, U.S. Mil. Acad., 1954; M.B.A., Harvard U., 1959. With Humble Oil Co., 1959-63; with Air Products and Chems., Inc., 1963—, No. area mgr., then pres. indsl. gas div., Allentown, Pa., 1966-78, corp. v.p., 1969-78, group v.p. gas products, 1978—; v.p. Catalytic Enterprises Ltd.; dir. Air Products S.A. (Pty.) Ltd. Bd. dirs. Historic Bethelem, Pa., St. Luke's Hosp., Bethelehem, WLC-TV, Channel 39; exec. bd. Minsi Trails council Boy Scouts Am. Served with U.S. Army, 1954-57. Mem. Compressed Gas Assn. (chmn., dir.), Internat. Oxygen Mfrs. Assn. (pres., dir.). Presbyterian. Club: Saucon Valley Country. Home: Apple Tree Ln RD 4 Bethlehem PA 18015 Office: PO Box 538 Allentown PA 18017

DYER, DAVID WILLIAM, federal judge; b. Columbus, Ohio, June 28, 1910; s. Joseph H. and Nelle (Peters) C.; m. Helen Hannah., June 28, 1932 (dec.); children—David William, Hannah; m. Mary Elsie Ring, Apr. 29, 1978. Student, Ohio State U., 1932; LL.B., John B. Stetson Coll. Law, 1933. Bar: Fla bar 1933. Ptnr. firm Batchelor & Dyer, 1934-42, Smathers, Thompson & Dyer, 1945-61; judge U.S. Dist. Ct., So. Dist. Fla., 1961-66, chief judge, 1962-66; judge U.S. Court of Appeals, 5th Circuit, 1966-80, U.S. Court of Appeals, 11th Circuit, 1980—. Served to maj., judge adv. gen. dept. AUS, 1942-45. Mem. Fla. Bar (exec. com. 1957-59), Maritime Law Assn. U.S. (exec. com. 1957-59), Dade County Bar Assn. (pres. 1955-56), Sigma Chi. Home: 200 Ocean Lane Dr Key Biscayne FL 33149 Office: US PO and Court House PO Box 012319 Miami FL 33101 *

DYER, IRBY LLOYD, lawyer; b. Pecos, Tex., Aug. 26, 1916; s. Freeman Irby and Katie (Lloyd) D.; children—Irby III (dec.), Deborah Frances Dyer Gutting; m. Margaret Pondrom Wilson, 1979. Student, Schreiner Inst., 1934-36, U. Tex., 1936-40. Bar: Tex. bar 1940. Asso. firm Hubbard & Kerr, Pecos, 1940-42; partner firm Turpin, Smith, Dyer & Saxe, Midland, Tex., 1945—; Gen. counsel, mem. exec. com., dir. Central Airlines Inc., Ft. Worth, 1963-68; pres. DST Exploration Corp., Midland, 1957—, White Sands Oil & Gas Corp., Midland and Corpus Christi, 1960-72; gen. counsel, dir. Petroleum Exploration & Devel. Funds, Inc., Midland, Tex., 1967—. Chmn. A.R.C., Midland County, 1948. Served with USAAF, 1942-45. Decorated Bronze Star, Air medal. Mem. ABA, Tex. Bar Assn., Midland County Bar Assn. (past pres.), Midland Jr. C. of C. (past pres.). Presbyn. Clubs: Midland Petroleum, Midland Country. Home: PO Box 913 Midland TX 79701 Office: First Nat Bank Bldg Midland TX 79701

DYER, JAMES SIMPSON, management educator, consultant; b. Brownsboro, Tex., May 7, 1943; s. Melvin J. and Lucille (Simpson) D.; m. Jonanna Perry, Dec. 18, 1965; children: James Perry, Jeffery Hubbard. B.A., U. Tex., 1965, Ph.D., 1969. Prof. UCLA, 1969-78, U. Tex., Austin, 1978—, chmn. dept. mgmt., 1982—. Mem. Ops. Research Soc. Am., Inst. Mgmt. Sci., Phi Beta Kappa, Beta Gamma Sigma, Phi Kappa Phi.

DYER, JOHN MARTIN, lawyer, marketing educator; b. St. Louis, Feb. 27, 1920; s. George L. and Katharine (Dobson) D.; m. Emily Ramsay Young, Aug. 9, 1947; children: Katherine, Susan, Patricia Ann, Theresa, Carolyn. A.B., St. Louis U., 1941; J.D., U. Miami, Fla., 1951; M.B.A., U. Pa., 1953. Bar: Fla. 1951, U.S. Supreme Ct. 1966. Practiced in, Miami, 1951—; assoc. prof. mktg. U. Miami, 1958-59, prof., 1969—, acting chmn. dept. mktg., 1968-69, chmn. mktg. dept., 1982—; speaker, cons. in field; dir. Atlas Sewing Centers Inc., 1960; vis. prof. U. Del., 1969, 70, Distinguished vis. prof., 1969; lectr. Universidad Nacional, Leon, Nicaragua, 1959; Distinguished vis. prof. San Francisco State U., summer 1975; mem. adv. bd. Internat. Bank of Miami, 1971-75; dir. U.S. Govt. Securities Fund, Inc., Fla. Mut. Ins. Co.; mem. Fla. Dist. Export Expansion Council, 1971, 73-75, 76-77, 81-82; dir. subcom. for Latin Am. U.S. Senate Interstate and Fgn. Commerce Com. Staff, 1960; mem. Southeastern World Trade Group, U.S. Dept. Commerce, 1957; trustee Center for Internat. Bus., Dallas, 1976—; ednl. cons. Nat. Assn. Credit Mgmt., S. Fla., 1977; editor conf. reports, program dir. various internat. trade seminars; dir. Rayne Internat., Inc. Contbg. author: Marketing in Latin America, 1960; author: United States-Latin American Trade and Financial Relations, 1961, (with F. C. Dyer) Export Financing, 1963, Bureaucracy vs. Creativity: The Dilemma of Modern Leadership, 1965, The Enjoyment of Management, 1971, Guidelines to Operating in Latin America, 1970, International Finance Law and Marketing, 1976, 4th edit., 1980; contbr. articles, revs. to profl. jours.; cons. editor: Industria Turistica, 1972—; contbg. editor: Wall Street Rev. of Books. Speaker platform com. Nat. Republican Conv., 1968; bd. dirs. Goodwill Industries, Inc., Miami, 1977—, mem. adv. bd., 1978—; hon. advisor World Trade Council of Palm Beach County, 1982. Named hon. vice consul Govt. Guatamala, 1959; recipient Phi Sigma Phi award for achievement in fgn. commerce Propeller Club U.S., 1954, Forum on Finance award Am. Securities Assn., 1954, N.Y. Stock Exchange Faculty fellow, 1954, Bus. Week plaque U. Miami, 1972, Iron County cert. of appreciation, 1980; Arrow U. Miami, 1970; certificate of appreciation student chpt. Alpha Kappa Phi, 1971; First Pres's. award Am. Grad. Sch. Internat. Mgmt., 1975; Gold Key City of Coral Gables, Fla.; Met.-Dade County cert. of appreciation, 1980; Internat. Mktg. award Fla. Exporters and Importers Assn, 1983. Mem. Acad. Mktg. Scis., Am. Inst. Fgn. Trade (asso.), Fla., Fed. bar assns., Am. Fgn. Law Assn., Am. Mktg. Assn., Serra Club of Miami (2d v.p. 1969), Assn. Edn. Internat. Bus., Acad. Mktg. Sci., Nat. Airlines Three Coast Club, Internat. Exec. Service Corps, Am. Arbitration Assn., Fla. Internat. Devel. Adv. Council, Sales and Mktg. Execs. Miami (hon.), Travelers Aid Soc. Dade County (Fla.) (1st v.p. 1971), Beta Gamma Sigma, Lambda Chi Alpha, Alpha Kappa Psi, Phi Alpha Delta. Clubs: Coral Gables Country, Racquet. Home: 7701 SW 52d Ct Miami FL 33143 Office: Box 248147 U Miami Coral Gables FL 33124

DYER, SISTER MARY CELESTINE, hospital executive; b. Santa Barbara, Calif., Nov. 30, 1915; d. Edward E. and Myrtle E. D. A.B., Coll. of Holy Names, Oakland, Calif., 1943; M.A., Cath. U. Am., Washington, 1952. Joined Sisters of Mercy, 1933; secondary sch. prin. St. Joseph High Sch., Sacramento, 1945-56, Bishop Armstrong High Sch., 1956-62, Mercy High Sch., Carmichael, Calif., 1968-72; dean Coll. of Our Lady of Mercy, Auburn, Calif., 1963-68; coordinator of schs. Sisters of Mercy, Auburn, 1968-72; pres. Mercy Hosps. of Sacramento, 1975-82; dir. Mercy Hosp. of Redding (Calif.) Inc., 1962-82, vice chmn., 1970-80; dir. Cath. Social Services of Diocese of Sacramento, 1976-82; mem. Diocesan Council Cath. Charities, 1982—; mem. adv. council Calif. Health Facilities Commn., 1979-83; mem. Greater Sacramento Area Hosp. Arbitration Bd. Mem. Cath. Health Assn. U.S., Calif. Hosp. Assn., Calif. Assn. Cath. Hosps. (dir., pres. 1980-81), Sacramento-Sierra Hosp. Assn. Democrat. Roman Catholic. Home: 6555 Coyle Ave Carmichael CA 95608 Office: 3 Parkcenter Dr Sacramento CA 95825

DYER, ROBERT BRUCE, manufacturing company executive; b. Tulia, Tex., Feb. 17, 1937; s. Claud Bruce and Beulah Francis (Hall) D.; m.; children: Kathryn F., R. Scott, Steven J. B.S. in Indsl. Engring, Tex. Tech U., 1960; M.B.A., U. Pa., 1965. Planning analyst Exxon Corp., Houston, 1965-66; with Cooper Industries, Inc., Houston, 1967—, Controller C/B So. div., 1967-69, Corp. sr. coordinator ops. planning and analysis, 1970-72, asst. controller ops., 1972-73, dir. ops. analysis, 1973-74, dir. planning and analysis, then v.p. planning and analysis, 1974-80, sr. v.p. planning and devel., 1980—; dir. MESBIC Fin. Corp. of Houston. Bd. dirs. Tex. Opera Theatre, Houston-Harris County chpt. ARC, 1977-81; vice chmn. Greater Houston area chpt. ARC, 1983—. Served to Capt. USAF, 1961-63. Mem. N.Am. Soc. Corp. Planning, Fin. Execs. Inst., Assn. Corp. Growth. Clubs: The Houstonian, Lakeside Country (Houston). Address: PO Box 4446 Houston TX 77210

DYER, WAYNE WALTER, author, psychologist, radio and television personality; b. Detroit, May 10, 1940; s. Melvin L. and Hazel I. (Vollick) D.; m. Susan Elizabeth Casselman, Mar. 2, 1974; 1 dau., Tracy Lynn. B.S., Wayne State U., 1965, M.S. in Counseling and Ednl. Psychology, 1966, Ed.D. in Counseling and Psychology, 1970. Tchr. and counselor Pershing High Sch., Detroit, 1965-67; instr. counselor edn. Wayne State U., Detroit, summer, 1970, 71, 72, 73; dir. guidance and counseling Mercy High Sch., Farmington, Mich., 1967-71; staff cons. and trainer guidance and sch. psychol. personnel Half Hollow Sch. Dist., Huntington, N.Y., 1973-75; staff cons. Drug Info. and Service Center, N.Y., 1972-74, Herman Kiefer Hosp., Detroit, 1974-75; mem. teaching faculty North Shore U. Hosp. (div. of Cornell U. Med. Coll.), Manhasset, N.Y., 1974-75; pvt. practice counseling and psychotherapy, Huntington, N.Y., 1973—; asst. prof. counselor edn. St. John's U., Jamaica, N.Y., 1971-74; asso. prof., 1974-77. Over 4000 appearances on TV and radio shows and programs including Phil Donohue Show, Tonight Show, Dinah Shore Show, Merv Griffin Show, Mike Douglas Show, Good Morning America, Canada A.M., David Susskind Show, numerous other talk shows in every state; radio host for: Kathryn Crosby Show, San Francisco, At Your Service program, Sta. KMOX, St. Louis.; Author: (with John Vriend) Counseling Effectively in Groups, 1973, Counseling Techniques That Work, 1974, 2d edit., 1977, Group Counseling for Personal Mastery, 1980, Your Erroneous Zones, 1976 (Literary Guild selection, Psychology Today Book Club selection, also 4 others), Pulling Your Own Strings, 1977, 1978 (Lit. Guild main selection, also 6 others), The Sky's the Limit, 1980 (Lit. Guild selection); novel Gifts from Eykis, 1983; cassette tape series The Wit & Wisdom of Dr. Wayne W. Dyer, 1977, How To Be a No-Limit Person, 1981; contbr. chpts. on counseling to books on psychology, numerous articles on psychology to popular mags. and articles on counseling to profl. jours.; producer tape recordings on counseling techniques; audio cassette program Secrets of the Universe. Served with USN, 1958-62. Named Disting. Alumni of Yr. Wayne State U.

DYER, WILLIAM ALLAN, JR., newspaper executive; b. Providence, Oct. 23, 1902; s. William Allan and Clara (Spink) D.; m. Marian Elizabeth Blumer, Aug. 9, 1934; children: Allan H., William E. B.Ph., Brown U., 1924; LL.D. (hon.), Ind. U., 1977, H.L.D., Butler U., 1983. Reporter Syracuse (N.Y.) Jour., 1923; various advt. positions Syracuse Post-Standard, 1925-41; v.p., gen. mgr. Star Pub. Co., Indpls., 1944-49, Indpls. Newspapers, Inc., 1949-74, pres., 1975—, Muncie Newspapers, Inc., 1975—; dir. Central Newspapers, Inc., Indpls., 1949—, exec. v.p., 1964-73; N.Y.C. dir Met. Sunday Newspapers, 1951-75, pres., 1969-75; dir. Am. Newspaper Pubs. Assn.; bur. advt., 1963-69, Research Inst., 1955-64, pres., 1963-64, Central Newspapers Found. Indpls., 1969—. Mem. exec. com. United Fund Indpls., 1954-77, pres., 1970, chmn. bd., 1971; v.p. Community Service Council, Indpls., 1967-68; trustee Brown U., 1952-59; pres. Indpls. Community Hosp. Found., 1976-83, hon. bd. dirs., 1983—; pres. Goodwill Industries Found., 1980—; bd. dirs., v.p. Ind. Symphony Soc. Served to lt. comdr. USNR, 1941-44. Recipient Brown Bear award Brown U., 1968; Torch of Truth award Advt. Club, 1975; Silver medal Am. Advt. Fedn., 1971. Mem. Better Bus. Bur. Indpls. (dir. 1950—, pres. 1958, 65), Nat. Better Bus. Bur. (dir. 1950-70), Council Better Bus. Burs. (dir. 1970-78, 80—), Indpls. C. of C. (dir. 1967—, v.p. 1970-73), Am. Newspaper Pubs. Assn. (labor relations com. 1953-63), Indpls. Advt. Club (dir. 1952-54, pres. 1952-53), Indpls. Community Hosp. (dir. 1952-54, 66-69, v.p. 1954). Clubs: Brown U. Ind. (sec. 1946-52, pres. 1952-54. Home: 401 Buckingham Dr Indianapolis IN 46208 Office: 307 N Pennsylvania Ave Indianapolis IN 46204

DYESS, BOBBY DALE, lawyer; b. Waxahachie, Tex., Jan. 27, 1935; s. Robert Olin and Rubie Lee (Odom) D.; m. Janet Lee Hassell, Jan. 30, 1960 (dec. 1973); children—Robert Dale, Jonathan David, Julianna Whitfield; m. Sharon Erwin Saylor, June 6, 1974. B.A., N. Tex. State U., Denton, 1956; J.D., So. Methodist U., 1959. Bar: Tex. 1959. Since practiced in, Dallas; partner firm Elliott, Churchill, Hansen, Dyess & Maxfield, 1965—, DeHay & Blanchard, 1983—; chmn. bd. Rainbow Sound, Inc., 1975—; dir. Combined Am. Ins. Co. Editor: Bests, Life and Health Ins. Edit., 1973—. Bd. mgmt. East Dallas YMCA, 1970, 76, campaign chmn., 1976, chmn. bd. mgmt., 1977-79; chief Indian Guides, 1971; sponsor The 500 Inc., 1978; chmn. Cub Scout pack com. Boy Scouts Am., 1970. Served with USAF, 1960-63. Mem. Am., Tex., Dallas bar assns., Am. Arbitration Assn. (comml. panel 1978—), Am. Counsel Assn. (membership chmn. 1976, dir. 1977-78, pres. 1979-80), Historic Preservation League, Scribes, Am. Assn.

Legal Writers (pres. 1975, dir. 1976). Methodist (chmn. bd. stewards 1974-75, stewardship chmn. 1978, trustee 1971-72). Club: Lakewood Country. Home: 6808 Meadow Lake Circle Dallas TX 75214 Office: 2300 S Tower Plaza of the Americas Dallas TX 75201

DYESS, WILLIAM JENNINGS, diplomat; b. Troy, Ala., Aug. 1, 1929; s. Thomas J. and Mae G. D.; m. Mary Elizabeth Awad Dyess, Apr. 23, 1965; 1 son, Chandler Jefferson Thomas. Student, U. Mo., 1947-48; B.A., U. Ala., 1950, M.A., 1951; postgrad., Oxford U., 1951-52, Syracuse U., 1952-53, 56-57. Commd. fgn. service officer, 1958; polit. officer Am. Embassy, Belgrade, 1961-63, Copenhagen, 1963-65, Moscow, 1966-68; chief Liaison U.S. Mission, Berlin, 1968-70; officer-in-charge Czechoslovak affairs, 1970-72, chief U.S.-Soviet bilateral relations, 1973-75; dir. public affairs Office Plans and Mgmt., Dept. State, Washington, 1975-77; dep. asst. sec. State Bur. Public Affairs, 1977-80, asst. sec. State, 1980-81; ambassador to, Netherlands, 1981—. Mem. Am. Fgn. Service Assn., Phi Beta Kappa. Baptist. Address: US Embassy Lange Voorhout The Hague Netherlands

DYHOUSE, HENRY NORVAL, lawyer; b. Miami, Fla., Oct. 26, 1945; s. Ruel N. and Ruby F. (Schult) D.; m. Janice Sue Roberts, Mar. 30, 1968; 1 son, Thomas Edward. B.A., U. Mo., 1967; M.B.A., Loyola U., Chgo., 1971, J.D., 1974. Bar: Ill. 1974, Mo. 1979. Atty. SEC, Chgo., 1974-78; spl. asst. U.S. atty. Dept. Justice, Milw., 1977-78; atty. Farmland Industries Inc., Kansas City, Mo., 1978—, sec., 1981—. Mem. Fire and Police Commn., Matteson, Ill., 1976-78. Served to 1st lt. U.S. Army, 1968-70. Recipient Curators award U. Mo. Bd. Curators, 1963; Charles Evans scholar Evans Scholars Found., 1963. Mem. ABA, Ill. Bar Assn., Mo. Bar Assn., Matteson Jaycees. Presbyterian. Home: 4009 NE 59th St Gladstone MO 64119 Office: Farmland Industries Inc 3315 N Oak Tafficway Kansas City MO 64116

DYK, ROBERT PEDER, journalist; b. Oakland, Calif., Mar. 6, 1937; s. Robert and Marirose (Donahue) D.; m. Susan Francesca Scott, Aug. 1976 (dec. 1983); children: Thomas Karl, Mary Eloise Gabrielle. Student, Colo. Coll., Colorado Springs. News dir. Sta. KAPP, Redondo Beach, Calif., 1962-64; producer-editor-writer stas. KMPC-KTLA, Los Angeles, 1964-65, sta. KABC-TV, 1965-72; reporter CBS Radio News, London, 1972-78, ABC Radio News, 1978-79, staff TV fgn. corr., 1979—. Served with U.S. Army, 1960-62. Recipient award Acad. TV Arts and Scis., 1971; K.P. Nat. scholar, 1955. Mem. Am. Corrs. Assn. London, Sigma Delta Chi (Disting. Service award 1979), Soc. Calif. Pioneers. Office: ABC News 8 Carburton St London W1 England

DYKE, CHARLES WILLIAM, army officer; b. Covington, Ga., July 28, 1935; s. John William and Chessie Belle (Burke) D.; m. Nancy Jeanne Bearg, June 22, 1980; children by previous marriage: Michael A., Eva J., Charles M., Robert W. B.A. in History, U. So. Miss., 1963; M.Mil. Arts and Sci., Command and Gen. Staff Coll., 1967; M.A. in Internat. Relations, George Washington U., 1968; postgrad., U.S. Army War Coll., 1970-71, Shippenburg State Coll., 1970-71. Served as enlisted man U.S. Army, 1954-55, commd. 2d lt., 1955, advanced through grades to maj. gen., 1980, exec. officer 1st Brigade, 101st Airborne Div., Vietnam, 1968, comdr. 2d Bn., 327th Inf., 1968-69, G1, later G3 101st Airborne Div., 1969-70, exec. asst. Ops. Directorate J3 Orgn. Joint Chief of Staff, Washington, 1971-72, asst. sec. of gen. staff Office Chief of Staff, 1972-73, mil. asst., later exec. to sec. of army, 1973-75, comdr. 1st Brigade, 101st Ariborne Div., Ft. Campbell, Ky., 1975-76, asst. div. comdr. 3d Inf. Div., W. Ger., 1976, exec. to supreme allied comdr. for Europe, Belgium, 1977-78; vice dir. J3 joint staff, later dir. internat. standardization (NATO) Hdqrs. Dept. Army, 1978-79; vice dir. joint staff Orgn. Joint Chiefs of Staff, Pentagon, Washington, 1979-82; dep. chief staff for ops. U.S. Army, Europe, 1982-83, comdg. gen. 8th Inf. Div. (Mech.), 1982—. Decorated Silver Star with oak leaf cluster, Legion of Merit with three oak leaf clusters, Bronze Star with V (3 awards), Def. Superior Service medal, Joint Service Commendation medal, Army Commendation medal with four oak leaf clusters, Air medal (19), Purple Heart. Mem. Assn. U.S. Army, 101st Airborne Div. Assn., Am. Def. Preparedness Assn., Army Aviation Assn. Am., Nat. Security Indsl. Assn., Pen and Sword Assn., Nat. Beta Club, Pi Gamma Mu, Phi Alpha Theta. Home: 1464 Kirby Rd McLean VA 22101 Office: 8th Inf Div (Mech) APO New York NY 09111

DYKE, JAMES TRESTER, building materials distributing company executive; b. Ft. Smith, Ark., June 4, 1937; s. Francis Willard and Virginia Lee (Benton) D.; m. Helen Lanier Porter, Oct. 11, 1967; children: Merritt, Simmons, Rob, Greg, Jim, Jonathan. B.A., U. Ark., 1959; LL.B., J.D., Yale U., 1962. Bar: Ark. 1962. Assoc. Warner, Warner, Ragon & Smith, Ft. Smith, 1962-65; pres. Dyke Industries, Inc., Little Rock, 1965-78, chmn. bd., chief exec. officer, 1979—; of counsel Wright, Lindsey & Jennings, Little Rock, 1983—; exec. dir. Ark. Dept. Econ. Devel., 1979-80; dir. Union Nat. Bank, Little Rock. Pres. Ark. Arts Center, 1964-65, Ark. Arts Center Found., 1979-81; sec. Metrocentre Improvement Dist., 1973-81, 82—, chmn., 1983—; v.p. Ark. Children's Hosp., 1979-81, pres., 1982. Mem. ABA, Ark. Bar Assn. Episcopalian. Clubs: Country of Little Rock, Memphis Country; Yale (N.Y.C.). Home: 18 Edgehill Rd Little Rock AR 72207 Office: 309 Center St Little Rock AR 72201

DYKEMA, JOHN RUSSEL, lawyer; b. Washington, June 1, 1918; s. Raymond Kryn and Margery (Russel) D.; m. Rosemary McDonald, June 21, 1950; children—Mary McDonald, John Russel, Peter Kryn. A.B., Princeton, 1940; J.D., U. Mich., 1947. Bar: Mich. bar 1947. Asso. firm Dykema, Gossett, Spencer, Goodnow & Trigg (and predecessor), Detroit, 1947-48, 49-51, 53-58, mem. firm, 1958—; law clk. to Justice Murphy, U.S. Supreme Ct., 1948-49; corp. and securities commr., Mich., 1951-53. Trustee Western Mich. U., 1964-80, chmn., 1976-77. Served with USNR, 1941-45. Mem. State Bar Mich., Am., Detroit bar Assns. Home: 260 Stephens Rd Grosse Pointe Farms MI 48236 Office: 35th Floor 400 Renaissance Center Detroit MI 48243

DYKEN, MARK LEWIS, neurologist, educator; b. Laramie, Wyo., Aug. 26, 1928; s. Mark L. and Thelma Violet (Achenbach) D.; m. Beverly All, June 8, 1951; children: Betsy Lynn, Mark Eric, Julie Suzanne, Amy Luise, Andrew Christopher, Gregory Allen. B.S. in Anatomy and Physiology, Ind. U., 1951, M.D., 1954. Diplomate: Am. Bd. Psychiatry and Neurology. Intern Indpls. Gen. Hosp., 1954-55; resident in neurology Ind. U. Med. Center, 1955-58; clin. dir., dir. research New Castle (Ind.) State Hosp., 1958-61; asst. dept. neurology Ind. U., 1958-61, asso. prof. neurology, 1964-69, prof., 1969—, chmn. dept. neurology, 1971—; dir. Ind. U. Cerebrovascular Disease Center, 1966—; chmn. profl. adv. council Nat. Easter Seal Soc.; cons., chmn. panel on rev. neurol. devices subcom. FDA. Contbr. numerous articles on topics including cerebral vascular disease, blood flow, epilepsy, electroencephalography, muscle disease, to profl. jours. Served with U.S. Army, 1946-48. Recipient numerous grants in cerebrovascular disease. Fellow A.C.P.; mem. AMA, Am. Assn. Univ. Profs. Neurology, Epilepsy Found. Am., Stroke Council Am. Heart Assn., Ind. Neurol. Assn. (charter pres. 1966-68), Am. Acad. Neurology, Am. Neurol. Assn., Sigma Xi, Alpha Omega Alpha. Home: 7406 W 92d St Zionsville IN 46077 Office: Dept Neurology 125 Emerson Hall Ind U Sch Medicine 545 Barnhill Dr Indianapolis IN 46223

DYKES, ARCHIE REECE, financial services; b. Rogersville, Tenn., Jan. 20, 1931; s. Claude Reed and Rose (Quillen) D.; m. Nancy Jane Haun, May 29, 1953; children: John Reece, Thomas Mack. B.S. cum laude, East Tenn. State U., 1952; M.A., E. Tenn. State U., 1956; Ed.D., U. Tenn., 1959. Prin., Church Hill (Tenn.) High Sch., 1955-58; supt. Greeneville (Tenn.) Schs., 1959-62; prof. edn., dir. U. Tenn. Center for Advanced Grad. Study in Edn., Memphis State U., 1962-66; chancellor U. Tenn. at Martin, 1967-71, at Knoxville, 1971-73, U. Kans., 1973-80; pres., chief exec. officer Security Benefit Group of Cos., Topeka, 1980—; also dir. Security Benefit Life Ins. Co.; dir. Esmark, 1st Nat. Bank Kansas City (Mo.), First Nat. Bank Topeka, Fleming Cos. Inc. Author: School Board and Superintendent, 1965, Faculty Participation in Academic Decision Making, 1968. Vice chmn. Commn. on Operation U.S. Senate, 1975-76; mem. Nat. Adv. Council Edn. Professions Devel., 1975-76; trustee Truman Library Inst., 1973-80, Menninger Found., 1982—, Nelson Art Gallery, 1973-80; chmn. bd. trustees U. Mid-Am., 1978-79; mem. adv. commn. U.S. Army Command. and Gen. Staff Coll., 1974-79, chmn., 1978-79; mem. consultative bd. regents U. Qatar, 1979-80; mem. Bd. Regents State of Kans., 1982—. Ford Found. fellow, 1957-59; Am. Council on Edn. postdoctoral fellow U. Ill., 1966-67; named Outstanding Alumnus, E. Tenn. State U., 1970. Mem. Tenn. Coll. Assn. (pres. 1969-70), Am. Council Life Ins. (dir. 1981—), Nat. Assn. State Univs. and Land Grant Colls. (council pres. 1971-80), Newcomen Soc. N.Am., Kans. Assn. Commerce and Industry (dir. 1975-82), Phi Kappa Phi. Home: 2329 Mayfair Pl Topeka KS 66611 Office: 700 Harrison St Topeka KS 66636

DYKES, JAMES EDGAR, former business educator; b. Wetumpka, Ala., Aug. 11, 1919; s. Reuben Owen and Sunie (Cannon) D.; m. Mary Jane Roth, Nov. 28, 1942; children: Stephen Van, Michael James. Student, Washington U., St. Louis, 1939-41; B.A., Auburn U., 1947; M.B.A., Tex. Tech. U.l, 1953. Advt. mgr. Nolin Mfg. Co., Montgomery, Ala.l, 1947-79; copywriter Craig & Webster, advt. agy., Lubbock, Tex., 1952-53; instr. Fla. State U., Tallahassee, 1948-50; asst. prof. Tex. Tech. U., Lubbock, 1950-53; prof., head advt. sequence William Allen White Sch. Journalism, U. Kans., Lawrence, 1953-73; prof. Sch. Bus. and Commerce, Troy State U., Ala., 1973-82; free-lance creative and cons. work in advt. Author: (with others) Principles of Advertising, 1963. Served with USMCR, 1943-45. Fellow Newspaper Advt. Execs. Assn., 1962, Am. Assn. Advt. Agys., 1965. Mem. Am. Acad. Advt. (pres. 1965), Assn. Edn. in Journalism (chmn. advt. div. 1968), Assn. Indsl. Advertisers. Methodist. Lodge: Kiwanis. Home: 22 Cathy Pl West Panama City Beach FL 32407

DYKES, JEFFERSON CHENOWTH, author; b. Dallas, July 20, 1900; s. George Richard and Melrose (Chenowth) D.; m. Martha Lewin Read, Aug. 1, 1923; 1 dau., Martha Ann. B.S., Texas A&M Coll., 1921; postgrad., Colo. Agrl. Coll., 1924-29. Tchr. vocation agr., Stephenville and McAllen, Tex., 1921-29; prof. agrl. edn. Texas A&M Coll., 1929-35; erosion specialist Soil Conservation Service, Dept. Agr., Lindale, Tex., 1935, chief erosion control practices div., asst. regional conservator, Ft. Worth, 1936-42, asst. chief, 1942-50, dept. chief, 1950-53, asst. adminstr. field services, 1953-63, dep. adminstr. field services, 1963-65; western Americana dealer, 1965—. Author: Billy the Kid: Bibliography Of a Legend, 1952, American Guide Series-A Bibliographic Check List, 1966, (with O.C. Fisher) King Fisher, 1966, Rangers All, 1969, Four Sheriffs of Lincoln County, 1969, My Dobie Collection, 1971, (with J. Frank Dobie) 44 Range Country Books, 1972, 44 More Range Country Books, 1972, Russell Roundup, 1972, Fifty Great Western Illustrators, 1975 (Western Heritage Wrangler award 1976); introduction Custer in Periodicals (John M. Carroll), 1975; Western High Spots, 1977, I Had All the Fun, 1978, The True Life of Billy the Kid, 1980, Collecting Range Life Literature, 1982; also articles, chpts. in books, revs. in mags. and profl. jours.; Editor: Great Western Indian Fights, 1960, On the Border with Mackenzie, 1962, The West of the Texas Kid, 1962, Trans-Missouri Stock Raising, 1962, Cow Dust and Saddle Leather, 1968, 44 Range Country Books (J. Frankie Dobie), 1944, 44 More Range Country Books, 1973; co-editor: Flat Top Ranch: A Grassland Venture, 1957; asso. editor: Brand Book, 1950—; Cons.: Cowboys and Cattle Country, 1962. Pres. Friends of Tex. A&M U. Library, 1979. Fellow Soil Conservation Soc. Am. (council); mem. Western Writers Am., Range Soc. Am., Westerners Internat. (pres. 1980, 81), Antiquarian Booksellers Assn. Am. Home: 4511 Guilford Rd College Park MD 20740 Office: Western Books Box 38 College Park MD 20740

DYKHOUSE, DAVID JAY, lawyer; b. Charlotte, Mich., Oct. 2, 1936; s. Jay and Mary (Carland) D.; m. Caroline Dow, June 15, 1963; children: Mary Catherine, David J., Jr., Jay Douglas. B.A. with highest honors, Rutgers U., 1958; J.D., U. Mich., 1962. Bar: Mich. 1962. Asso. firm Honigman, Miller, Schwartz & Cohn, Detroit, 1962-65; dept. dir. Mich. Dept. Commerce, Lansing, 1965-66, Mich. commr. ins., 1966-69; legal adviser to Gov. Mich., 1969; partner firm Dykhouse & Wise, Detroit, 1970—; Adj. prof. law Wayne State U., Detroit, 1970—; chmn. Mich. adminstrv. law commn.; cons. HUD, 1970-71, N.Y. Urban Devel. Corp., 1971-72, Mich. Housing Authority, 1970-72, N.Y. Ins. Dept., 1970-75. Author: Construction Surety Bonds - Their Adequacy and Availability, 1970, Cases and Materials on Regulated Industries, 1972; Contbr. articles to profl. jours. Woodrow Wilson fellow, 1958-59. Mem. Mich., Am., Detroit bar assns., Phi Beta Kappa. Republican. Presbyn. Clubs: Detroit Athletic, Prismatic, Sons of Whiskey Rebellion (Detroit); Bay View Boat (Mich.); Players (N.Y.C.). Office: 11th Floor Buhl Bldg Detroit MI 48226

DYKSTRA, DANIEL JAMES, lawyer, educator; b. Fremont, Mich., Feb. 25, 1916; s. John D. and Elizabeth (Grotemat) D.; m. Lily M. Salay, Aug. 1, 1942; children: Daniel James, Ann Marie. B.S., Wis. State U.-River Falls, 1938; LL.B. (Rockefeller research fellow), U. Wis., 1948, S.J.D., 1950. Bar: Wis. 1948, Utah 1952. Asst. prof. law Drake U., 1948-49; faculty U. Utah Coll. Law, 1949-52, 52-66, prof. law, 1952-66, dean coll., 1954-61, acad. v.p., 1961-63; prof. law U. Calif. at Davis, 1966—, dean, 1971-74; atty. OPS, 1952; Vis. prof. U. Minn., summer 1950, U. Wis., summers 1957, 58; Fulbright prof. U. Melbourne, Australia, 1959; Frederick William Reynolds lectr. U. Utah, 1959. Author: monograph Right Most Valued by Civilized Man, 1959. Served with USNR, 1942-45. Recipient Distinguished Alumnus award Wis. State U., River Falls, 1970. Mem. Am., Utah, Wis. bar assns., Nat. Acad. Arbitrators, Am. Law Inst., Order of Coif. Home: 3024 Country Club Dr El Macero CA 95618 Office: Sch Law U Calif Davis CA 95616

DYKSTRA, FRANCIS EARL, real estate co. exec.; b. Pella, Iowa, Nov. 3, 1905; s. John F. and Josephine (Thomassen) D.; m. Virginia Warner, Jan. 18, 1936. B.C.S., Drake U., 1927. Field rep. Stern Fin. Co., Des Moines, 1927-28; br. mgr. Midwest Comml. Credit Co., Sioux City and Mason City, Iowa, 1928-29; with Interstate Fin. Corp., Dubuque, Iowa, 1929-42, br. mgr., Madison, Wis., 1931-42; alien property custodian U.S. Govt., N.Y.C., 1942-44; with Thorp Fin. Corp., Wis., 1944-54; v.p. Marathon Fin. Corp. (subs. Thorp Fin. Corp.), Wausau, Wis., 1948-54; pres. Rock Fin. Co., Green Bay, Wis., 1954-61; with Sunrise Golf Devel. Corp. (and affiliated cos.), Fla., 1961—, pres., 1965—, Pub. Utilities Corp., 1965-69, Uniflow Gas Co., Inc., 1965-73; dir. Plantation 1st Nat. Bank, 1968—, mem. exec. com., 1973—; dir. Landmark Bank of Sunrise, 1974—, chmn. bd., 1974-77; dir., chmn. audit com. Landmark 1st Nat. Bank of Ft. Lauderdale. Mem. city council Sunrise, 1961-66. Mem. Wis. Assn. Fin. Cos. (past pres.), Wis. Consumer Fin. Assn. (past dir.), Am. Fin. Conf. (dir.), Am. Indsl. Bankers Assn., Greater Plantation C. of C. (past dir.), Sunrise C. of C. (founder, past chmn.), Delta Sigma Pi, Tau Kappa Epsilon. Clubs: Elks, Rotary. Home: Apt 4M Plaza South 4280 Galt Ocean Dr Fort Lauderdale FL 33308 Office: 1096 Sunset Strip Sunrise FL 33313 *Refine a good idea and it will produce results that dwarf original expectations.*

DYKSTRA, ROBERT ROZEBOOM, history educator; b. Ames, Iowa, Aug. 29, 1930; s. Bernard Ryer and Lucy Ruth (Dykstra) Rozeboom; m. Fritzen Ellen Hinman, Dec. 19, 1952 (div. 1979); children: Michael Jack, Terry Jones, Robert Dirk, Eugene Ryer; m. Jo Ann Manfra, Aug. 2, 1980. Student, Iowa State Coll., 1948; B.A., U. Iowa, 1953, M.A., 1959, Ph.D., 1964. Asst. prof. history U. N.Mex., Albuquerque, 1965-67; asso. prof. history U. Nebr., Lincoln, 1967-68, U. Iowa, Iowa City, 1968-73, prof., 1973-81; Jour. editor (Civil War History), 1962-65; prof. history and pub. policy SUNY at Albany, 1981—; Charles Warren fellow Harvard U., 1978-79; Western history cons. Time-Life Books, 1972; project cons. Wichita Hist. Mus. Assn., 1979-80; external examiner U. Waikato, Hamilton, N.Z., 1979-80. Author: The Cattle Towns, 1968; editorial bd.: Am. Studies, 1980-81, Upper Midwest History, 1981—; Contbr. numerous articles to profl. publs. Mem. Iowa Rev. Com., Historic Preservation Program, Nat. Park Service, 1971-81; editorial cons. Annals of Iowa, 1978—. Served with U.S. Army, 1953-57. Recipient Western Heritage award for outstanding Western non-fiction book of 1968 Nat. Cowboy Hall of Fame, 1969; Social Sci. Research Council fellow, 1961-62. Fellow Soc. Am. Historians (judge Parkman prize competition 1982-83); mem. Agrl. History Soc. (Everett Eugene Edwards Meml. award 1961, exec. com. 1958-79), Iowa Hist. Soc. (curator, trustee 1973-80), Kans. Hist. Soc., Orgn. Am. Historians (editorial bd. Jour. Am. History 1979—), Social Sci. History Assn. (regional vice chmn. 1975-76, chmn. nominating com. 1977). Home: 75-7 Park Ave Worcester MA 01605

DYKSTRA, VERGIL HOMER, College administrator; b. Harrison, S.D., Feb. 1, 1925; s. Broer Doekeles and Nellie (Schippers) D.; m. Shirley Margaret Leslie, June 9, 1949 (div. July 1978); children—Leslie Fran, Lynne Meredith, Craig David, Kevin Scott; m. Wanda Rappaport, Feb. 10, 1980. B.A. summa cum laude, Hope Coll., 1949; M.A., U. Wis., 1950, Ph.D., 1953. Instr. philosophy U. Cin., 1953-54; instr. philosophy U. Oreg., 1954-56, asst. prof., 1957-60, asso. prof., 1960-61; vis. lectr. philosophy U. Wis., 1956-57; postdoctoral fellow U. Mich., 1961-62; asso. dean Harpur Coll., 1962-64; dean adminstrn. State U. N.Y. at Binghamton, 1964-65, v.p. adminstrn., 1965-69, prof. philosophy, 1969-73; pres. George Mason U., Fairfax, Va., 1973-77; ednl. cons., 1977-78; adminstrv. v.p. Montgomery Coll., Rockville, Md., 1978—. Contbr. articles to profl. jours. Served with USNR, 1943-46. Mem. Am. Philos. Assn., Am. Assn. Higher Edn., Am. Soc. Public Adminstrn. Home: 11563 Maple Ridge Rd Reston VA 22090 Office: Montgomery Coll 51 Mannakee St Rockville MD 20850

DYKSTRA, WILLIAM HENRY, corp. exec.; b. Boston, May 4, 1928; s. Harry Martin and Margaret Louise (Pierce) D.; m. Carol Alden Clement, Oct. 18, 1959; children—Mark, Nancy, Amy. B.S. in Bus. Adminstrn, Boston U., 1950; grad., Advanced Mgmt. Program, Harvard, 1965. C.P.A., Mass. Accountant Lybrand, Ross Bros. & Montgomery Co., Boston, 1950-55; auditor USM Corp., Boston, 1955-63, asst. treas., 1963-69, treas., 1969-77; with Reed and Barton Corp., Taunton, Mass., 1977—, v.p., treas., 1978—; v.p. East Boston Savs. Bank, 1974—, mem. bd. investment. Mem. Braintree Town Meeting, 1962—, Braintree Housing Authority, 1965—; commr. Braintree Trust Fund, 1972—; chmn. Braintree Republican Town Com., 1964-68; Bd. dirs. Industries Mass., 1971—; trustee Wentworth Inst. and Coll., Boston, 1970-77. Served with AUS, 1945-47. Mem. Am. Inst. C.P.A.'s, Fin. Execs. Inst. Club: Rotary. Home: 346 Tremont St Braintree MA 02184 Office: 144 Britannia St Taunton MA 02780

DYLAN, BOB, singer, composer; b. Duluth, Minn., May 24, 1941. Student, U. Minn., 1960; self-taught on guitar, piano, autoharp, harmonica; Mus.D. (hon.), Princeton U., 1970. Albums include The Free Wheelin' Bob Dylan, Bringing It All Back Home, Highway 61 Revisited, Blonde on Blonde, Nshville Skyline, Self Portrait, New Morning, Dylan, Planet Waves, Before the Flood, Hard Rain, Street Legal, Slow Train Coming, In, 1960—; appearances in movies Renaldo and Clara, 1978; composer: numerous songs including Blowin' in the Wind, Like a Rolling Stone, Lay, Lady, Lay, Forever Young and Gotta Serve Somebody; albums include The Free Wheelin' Bob Dylan, Bringing It All Back Home, Highway 61 Revisited, Blonde on Blonde, Nashville Skyline, Self Portrait, New Morning, Dylan, Planet Waves, Before the Flood, Hard Rain, Street Legal, Slow Train Coming,; Author: numerous publs. including Tarantula, 1966, 71; Writings and Drawings by Bob Dylan, 1973, The Songs of Bob Dylan from 1966-1975, 1976. Devised and popularized folk-rock. Office: PO Box 870 Cooper Station New York NY 10276

DYM, CLIVE LIONEL, engineering educator; b. Leeds, Eng., July 15, 1942; came to U.S., 1949, naturalized, 1954; s. Isaac and Anna (Hochmann) D.; children: Jordana, Miriam. B.C.E., Cooper Union, 1962; M.S., Poly. Inst. Bklyn., 1964; Ph.D., Stanford U., 1967. Asst. prof. SUNY, Buffalo, 1966-69; asso. professorial lectr. George Washington U., Washington, 1969; research staff Inst. Def. Analyses, Arlington, Va., 1969-70; asso. prof. Carnegie-Mellon U., Pitts., 1970-74; vis. asso. prof. TECHNION, Israel, 1971; sr. scientist Bolt Beranek and Newman, Inc., Cambridge, Mass., 1974-77; prof., head civil engring. dept. U. Mass., Amherst, 1977—; vis. sr. research fellow Inst. Sound and Vibration Research, U. Southampton, Eng., 1973; vis. scientist Xerox PARC, 1983; vis. prof. civil engring. Stanford U., 1983, MIT, 1984; cons. Bell Aerospace Co., 1967-69, Dravo Corp., 1970-71, Salem Corp., 1972, Gen. Analytics Inc., 1972, ORI, Inc., 1979, BBN Inc., 1979. Editorial bds.: Jour. of Sound and Vibration; author: (with I.H. Shames) Solid Mechanics: A Variational Approach, 1973, Introduction to the Theory of Shells, 1974, Stability Theory and Its Applications to Structural Mechanics, 1974, (with A. Kalnins) Vibration: Beams, Plates, and Shells, 1977, (With E.S. Ivey) Principles of Mathematical Modeling, 1980, (with I.H. Shames) Energy and Finite Element Methods in Structural Mechanics, 1983; contbr. (with I.H. Shanes) articles and tech. reports to profl. publs. NATO sr. fellow in sci., 1973. Fellow Acoustical Soc. Am., ASME, ASCE (Walter L. Huber research prize 1980); mem. AAAS, Inst. Noise Control Engring. Jewish. Office: Civil Engineering Dept U Mass Amherst MA 01003

DYMALLY, MERVYN MALCOLM, congressman; b. Trinidad, W.I., May 12, 1926; s. Hamid A. and Andreid S. (Richardson) D.; m. Alice M. Gueno; children: Mark, Lynn. B.A., Calif. State U., Los Angeles, 1954, M.A., 1970; LL.D. (hon.), U. W. Los Angeles, 1970; Ph.D. in Human Behavior, U.S. Internat. U., 1978; J.D. (hon.), Lincoln U., Sacramento, 1975, Ph.D., Shaw U., N.C. Lectr. Whittler and Claremont colls.; mem. Calif. Assembly, 1962-66, Calif. Senate, 1967-74; lt. gov., Calif., 1975-79; mem. 97th Congress from 31st Calif. Dist.; Mem. Calif. adv. com. U.S. Civil Rights Commn., 1964; pres. Caribbean Action Lobby. Author: Black Politician-His Struggle for Power. Trustee Shaw U.; bd. govs. Joint Ctr. Polit. Studies. Mem. AAUP, Am. Acad. Polit. Sci., Am. Polit. Acad., Phi Kappa Phi Honor Soc. Address: US Ho of Reps Washington DC 20515

DYMOND, LEWIS WANDELL, lawyer; b. Lansing, Mich., June 28, 1920; s. Lewis Wandell and Irene (Parker) D.; m. Betty Louise Blood,

Sept. 6, 1942; children: Lewis W., Jean Ann; m. Joann Surrey, Sept. 3, 1966; 1 son, Steven Henry. J.D. cum laude, U. Miami, 1956. Bar: Fla. 1957. With Nat. Airlines, Inc., Miami, Fla., 1938-62, mechanic, agt., sta. mgr., flight dispatcher, ops. mgr., pilot, v.p. ops., maintenance and engring., 1955-62; pres., chief exec. officer, dir. Frontier Airlines, 1962-69; dir. Trust Bank, Miami. Mem. Com. of 100, Miami. Mem. U. Miami Alumni Club, Phi Kappa Phi, Phi Alpha Delta. Clubs: Mason (32, Shriner), Union League (N.Y.C.); Cherry Hills Country, Denver, Petroleum of Denver; Garden of the Gods (Colorado Springs, Colo.); Surf, Miami, Palm Bay (Miami, Fla.); La Gorce Country (Miami Beach, Fla.) (dir.). Office: Taylor Brion Buker and Greene 1111 S Bayshore Dr Miami FL 33131

DYMSZA, WILLIAM ALEXANDER, educator; b. Cambridge, Mass., Aug. 2, 1922; s. Alexander and Mary (Lucas) D.; m. Begona Lamana, May 20, 1957; children: Christina, Madeline. A.B., Pa. State U., 1943; M.B.A., U. Pa., 1948, Ph.D. (UN fellow), 1951. Asst. prof. econs. Boston Coll., Newton, Mass., 1948-51; chief economist Office Price Stablzn., Boston, 1951-52; asst. econ. commr. U.S. Econ. Mission to Vietnam, Cambodia and Laos, 1952-55; lectr. internat. econs. U. Md. in Germany, Eng. and France, 1955-58; asso. prof. Grad. Sch. Bus. Adminstrn., Rutger U., Newark, 1958-64, prof. internat. bus., 1965—, founder, dir., 1966-70; organizer Mktg. Mgmt. Confs. in, Belgrade, Yugoslavia, Bucharest, Rumania, summer 1970; vis. prof. Econ. Research Center and Sch. Bus. Adminstrn., U. Hawaii, 1964-65; vis. prof. internat. econs. Naval War Coll., Newport, R.I., 1966-67; staff mem., sr. adviser trade devel. UN Econ. Commn. for Latin Am., Santiago, Chile, 1970-72; del. bus. and econ. devel. confs.; adviser Hawaii Dept. Planning and Econ. Devel., 1965, N.J. Dept. Econ. Devel., 1962-68, Dept. Commerce, 1962-69; advisor internat. investment OECD Devel. Center, Paris, 1979—; cons., lectr. World Trade Inst., World Trade Center, N.Y.C., 1972-74; rapporteur Internat. Conf. Mgmt. in 21st Century, Paris, 1980; guest lectr. Indian Inst. Econs., U. Osmania, 1975, univs. Madrid, Barcelona, Poly. U. Spain, U. Alexandria, Egypt, Tel Aviv and Hebrew Univs., Israel, 1979, OAS Meetings, Rio de Janeiro, summer 1982; staff mem. UN Tng. Program on Negotiation and Regulation Fgn. Investments for Asian countries, New Delhi, 1975; mem. internat. adv. council state of N.J., 1974-82; adv. UN Centre on Transnat. Corps., 1978-81; mem. N.J. Gov.'s Task Force on Export Policy, 1979. Author: Foreign Trade Zones and International Business, 1963, Multinational Management Strategy, 1972, also Japanese, Spanish, Portuguese, French edits, East-West Trade: Type of Business Arrangement, 1974, Technology Transfer By Multinational Firms to Developing Countries, 1978, Joint Ventures by Transnational Corporations, 1979; editor-in-chief: Jour. Internat. Bus. Studies, 1975—; mem. adv. bd.: Soviet and Eastern European Trade, 1973—; contbr. articles to profl. jours. Served with USMCR, 1943-46. Ford Found. faculty fellow Mass. Inst. Tech., 1959. Mem. Acad. Internat. Bus., Am. Econ. Assn., Center for Inter-Am. Relations, AAUP, Phi Beta Kappa, Beta Gamma Sigma. Home: 73 Martin Rd Livingston NJ 07039 Office: 92 New St Newark NJ 07102

DYNES, RUSSELL ROWE, sociologist; b. Dundalk, Ont., Can., Oct. 2, 1923; s. Oliver Wesley and Carlotta Lillian (Rowe) D.; m. Susan M. Swan, July 26, 1947; children: Russell Rowe, Patrick, Gregory, Jon Kurt. B.A., U. Tenn., 1948, M.A., 1950; Ph.D., Ohio State U., 1954. Instr. U. Tenn., 1948-50; mem. faculty Ohio State U., Columbus, 1952-77, prof. sociology, 1965-77, chmn. dept. sociology, 1974-77; chmn. dept. of sociology U. Del., 1982—; co-dir. Disaster Research Center Ohio State U., 1964-77; exec. officer Am. Sociol. Assn., Washington, 1977-82; pres. Disaster Research Services Inc., 1972-77; Sr. Fulbright lectr. Ain Shams U., United Arab Republic, 1964-65; Fulbright lectr. Center for Advanced Study in Sociology, U. Delhi, India, 1972; mem. staff Arab State Centre for Edn. in Community Devel., UNESCO, Sirs-ellayyan, United Arab Republic, 1964-65; asso. Danforth Found., 1956. Author: Social Problems: Dissensus and Deviation in an Industrial Society, 1964, Deviance: Studies in the Process of Stigmatization and Societal Reaction, 1969, Organized Behavior in Disaster, 1970, Social Movements, Violence and Change: The May Movement in Curacao, 1975, Deviance: Definition, Management, Treatment, 1975, Applied Sociology, 1983; asso. editor: Rev. of Religious Research, 1968-76. Mem. Mayor's Faculty Com., Columbus, 1967-68; mem. adv. com. Com. on Internat. Exchange of Persons, 1970-71; mem. spl. adv. com. emergency housing NRC-Nat. Acad. Scis., 1972, chmn. com. internat. disaster assistance, 1976-79; dir. emergency preparedness task force President's Commn. on Accident at Three Mile Island, 1979; hon. mem. faculty Def. Civil Preparedness Staff Coll., 1973; cons. Fed. Disaster Assistance Agy., 1978—; trustee Wesley Found., 1958—, treas., 1961-63. Served with U.S. Army, 1942-45. Mem. Am. Sociol. Assn. (com. internat. cooperation 1968—, chmn. com. on coms. 1975), Religious Research Assn., North Central Sociol. Soc. (past pres.), Internat. Sociol. Assn., AAUP (dir. Ohio State chpt. 1970-71), AAAS, Soc. for Sci. Study Religion (treas. 1976-79), Am. Research Center in Egypt. Methodist. Home: 346 S College Ave Newark DE 19711 Office: U Del 322 Smith Hall Newark DE 19716

DYRUD, JARL EDVARD, psychiatrist; b. Maddock, N.D., Oct. 20, 1921; s. Jens Bernard and Lena Bertina (Engebretson) D.; m. Rose Hildreth Bullard, Aug. 22, 1952; children: Jarl Edvard, Anne Hildreth, Christine Maria. A.B., Concordia Coll., 1942; M.D., Johns Hopkins U., 1945. Intern Johns Hopkins U., Balt., 1945-46; resident in psychiatry Chestnut Lodge, Rockville, Md., 1949-51; resident, USPHS fellow Spring Grove State Hosp., 1952-53; mem. psychiat. staff Chestnut Lodge, 1951-52, 53-56, dir. research, 1967-68; research asso., prin. investigator Inst. Behavioral Research, 1963-68; asso. prof. psychiatry U. Chgo., 1968-71, prof., 1971—, asso. dean faculty, 1978-81; bd. dirs. Chestnut Lodge Research Inst. Contbr. articles to profl. jours. Served with USNR, 1946-48. John Nuveen lectr. Div. Sch., U. Chgo., 1978. Fellow Am. Psychiat. Assn.; mem. Ill. Psychiat. Soc., Chgo. Psychoanal6tic Soc., Am. Psychoanalytic Assn., Internat. Psychoanalytic Assn., AAAS, Am. Soc. Adolescent Psychiatry, Soc. Psychotherapy Research, Sigma Xi. Republican. Episcopalian. Home: 5728 Woodlawn Ave Chicago IL 60637 Office: 5841 Maryland Ave. Chicago IL 60637 8 S Michigan Chicago IL 60603

DYSART, BENJAMIN CLAY, III, environmental engineer, educator, conservationist; b. Columbia, Tenn., Feb. 12, 1940; s. Benjamin Clay and Kathryne Virginia (Thompson) D.; m. Virginia Carole Livesay, Sept. 3, 1960. B.Engring in Civil Engring., Vanderbilt U., 1961, M.S. in San. Engring., 1964; Ph.D. in Civil Engring., Ga. Inst. Tech., 1969. Staff engr. Union Carbide Corp., Columbia, Tenn., 1961-,62, 64-65; teaching fellow dept. civil engring. Vanderbilt U., Nashville, 1962-64; san. engr. P.A. Krenkel P.E., Nashville, 1963; instr. U. Tenn. Nashville Ctr., 1963, 65; Fed. Water Pollution Control Adminstrn. trainee Ga. Inst. Tech., Atlanta, 1965-67, grad. research asst., 1967-68; asst. prof. Clemson U., S.C., 1968-70, assoc. prof., 1970-75, prof., 1976—, McQueen Quattlebaum prof. engring., 1982-83; George A. Miller lectr. U. Ill., 1984; mem. directorate S.C. Water Resources Research Inst., Clemson U., S.C., 1968-75; dir. water resources engring. grad. program Clemson U., S.C., 1972-75; sci. advisor for civil works Office Sec. of Army, Washington, 1975-76; mem. EPA Sci. Adv. Bd., 1983—; sec. appointee Outer Continental Shelf Adv. Bd. and OCS Sci. Com. Dept. Interior, 1979-82; mem. S.C. Environ. Quality Control Adv. Com., 1980—, chmn., 1980-81; mem. Sci. Panel to Rev. Interagy. Research on Impact of Oil Pollution NOAA, Dept. Commerce, 1980; mem. Nuclear Energy Ctr. Environ. Task Force Dept. Energy-So. States Energy Bd., 1978-81; mem. Nonpoint Source Pollutant Task Force EPA, 1979-80; mem. civil works adv. com. Office Sec. Army-Young Pres's Orgn., 1975-76; mem. S.C. Heritage Adv. Bd. S.C. Wildlife Marine Resources Dept., 1974-76; cons., advisor on environ. protection and water resources matters to industry and govt. agys., 1969—. Contbr. articles on math. modeling in water quality and environ. mgmt. to profl. jours.; author numerous profl. papers, reports. Trustee Nat. Wildlife Fedn. Endowment, Inc., 1983—. Recipient Tribute of Appreciation for Disting. Service EPA, 1981, McQueen Quattlebaum Engring. Faculty Achievement award Clemson U., 1982, Roland P. McClamroch lectr. N.C. Ednl. Found., 1976, Order of Palmetto Gov. S.C., 1984. Mem. Nat. Wildlife Fedn. (bd. dirs. 1974—, mem. exec. com. 1976—, v.p. 1978-83, pres., chmn. bd. 1983—), Am. Geophys. Union, ASCE, Assn. Environ. Engring. Profs. (bd. dirs. 1978-83, pres., chmn. bd. 1981-82), Water Pollution Control Fedn., S.C. Wildlife Fedn. (bd. dirs. 1969—, pres. 1973-74, S.C. Wildlife Conservationist of Yr 1979), SAR, Sigma Xi, Chi Epsilon, Omega Rho, Sigma Nu. Methodist. Club: Cotillion. Lodge: Masons. Home: 8 Holiday Ave E Clemson SC 29631 Office: Environ Systems Engring Dept 401 Rhodes Research Ctr Clemson U Clemson SC 29631

DYSART, DAVID DUNCAN, insurance company executive; b. Columbia, Mo., June 5, 1928; s. Searcy Barnett and Katherine Elizabeth (Lewis) D.; m. Mary Elizabeth Nistendirk, Mar. 6, 1948; children: Mary Lynn Burrell, Nancy Lee Johnson, Pamela Sue Eisenberg, Elizabeth Ann Aubrey. Student, U. Mo., 1945-46. Staff mgr. Nat. Life and Accident Ins. Co., Columbia, 1948-55; regional dir. Kansas City Life Ins. Co., 1956-68, v.p., dir. agys., 1969-76, sr. v.p. mktg., 1976-80, exec. v.p., 1980—, also dir.; dir. Sunset Life Am., Olympia, Wash., Nat. Res. Life Ins. Co., Topeka, Kans. Mem. Life Ins. Mgmt. and Research Assn. (bd. dirs. 1976-79), Nat. Assn. Life Underwriters. Republican. Lodge: Elks. Home: 633 W 68th Terr Kansas City MO 64113 Office: Kansas City Life Ins Co 3520 Broadway Kansas City MO 64111

DYSINGER, PAUL WILLIAM, physician, educator; b. Burns, Tenn., May 24, 1927; s. Paul Clair and Mary Edith (Martin) D.; m. Yvonne Minchin, May 11, 1958; children: Edwin, Wayne, John, Janelle. B.A., So. Missionary Coll., 1951; M.D., Coll. Med. Evangelists, 1955; M.P.H., Harvard, 1962. Diplomate: Nat. Bd. Med. Examiners, Am. Bd. Preventive Medicine. Intern, Washington, 1955-56; sr. asst. surgeon USPHS; with Blackfeet Indians in Mont., Navajos of Ariz., 1956-58; physician, med. adviser Am. embassy, PhnomPenh, Cambodia, 1958-60; research asso. dept. preventive medicine Loma Linda (Calif.) U. (formerly Coll. Med. Evangelists), 1960—, dir. field sta., Western Tanganyika, 1962-64, adminstrv. asst. div. pub. health, 1964-67, asst. to dean, chmn. dept. tropical health, 1967-69, asst. dean for acad. affairs and internat. health Sch. Pub. Health, 1969-71, asso. dean for acad. affairs, 1971-79, prof. internat. health, 1971—, dir. prev. med. residency, 1983—; WHO fellow, Somalia, Ethiopia, India, Nepal, Burma, 1969; mother and child health cons. Ministry of Health, Tanzania, 1978-80; med. cons. Dept. Vocat. Rehab., Riverside, Calif., 1982—; med. dir. Village Health Program, Punjab, Pakistan, 1980-81, tchr., cons., S.Am. and Caribbean, 1981-83. Contbr. articles to med. publs. Fellow Royal Soc. Tropical Medicine and Hygiene, Am. Pub. Health Assn.; mem. So. Calif. Pub. Health Assn., Calif. Acad. Preventive Medicine., Nat. Council for Internat. Health, Adventist Internat. Med. Soc. (pres. 1983-84). Seventh-day Adventist. Home: 39290 Oak Glen Rd Yucaipa CA 92399

DYSON, ALLAN JUDGE, librarian; b. Lawrence, Mass., Mar. 28, 1942; s. Raymond Magan and Hilda D. B.A. in Govt, Harvard U., 1964; M.S. in L.S, Simmons Coll., 1968. Asst. to dir. Columbia U. Libraries, N.Y.C., 1968-71; head Moffitt Undergrad. Library, U. Calif., Berkeley, 1971-79; univ. librarian U. Calif., Santa Cruz, 1979—. Editor: Coll. and Research Libraries News, 1973-74; chmn. editorial bd.: Choice mag, 1978-80; adv. bd.: Ency. Buying Guide, 1976—. Served to lt. U.S. Army, 1964-66. Decorated Army Commendation medal; Council on Library Resources fellow, 1973-74. Mem. ALA, Assn. Coll. and Research Libraries, Librarians Assn. U. Calif. (pres. 1976), ACLU, Sierra Club. Home: 1719 Escalona Dr Santa Cruz CA 95060 Office: McHenry Library U Calif Santa Cruz CA 95064

DYSON, CHARLES HENRY, manufacturing company executive; b. N.Y.C., Aug. 2, 1909; s. Martin Lawrence and Lillian (Patterson) D.; m. Margaret Macgregor, Aug. 8, 1941; children: John Stuart, Robert Richard, Anne Elizabeth, Peter L. B.B.A., Pace U., 1930, D.C.S. (hon.), 1965; LL.D., N.Y. Law Sch., 1973. C.P.A., N.Y. With Price, Waterhouse & Co. (C.P.A.'s), N.Y.C., 1932-41; exec. v.p., dir. Textron, Inc., 1946-49; v.p., mem. exec. com., dir. Burlington Mills Corp., 1949-51; cons. to nat. cos., 1951-54; chmn. bd. Dyson-Kissner-Moran Corp., N.Y.C., 1954—; dir., chmn. bd. Wallace-Murray Corp., N.Y.C., Esterline Corp., Conn.; Spl. cons. to sec. war, Washington, 1941; rep. U.S. Treasury Dept., IMF, Bretton Woods (N.H.) Conf., 1944. Hon. trustee Hosp. for Spl. Surgery; former trustee N.Y. Law Sch.; chmn. bd. Westchester Med. Center Found.; chmn. emeritus bd. trustees Pace U.; bd. dirs. Common Cause; mem. council Rockefeller U. Served to col. USAAF, World War II. Decorated D.S.M.; comdr. Order of Brit. Empire. Mem. Pace Alumni Assn. Clubs: Burning Tree, Union League, Brook., Union. Home: 71 E 71st St New York NY 10021 Office: 230 Park Ave New York NY 10017

DYSON, FREEMAN JOHN, physicist; b. Crowthorne, Eng., Dec. 15, 1923; s. George and Mildred Lucy (Atkey) D.; m. Verena Haefeli-Huber, Aug. 11, 1950 (div. 1958); children—Esther, George; m. Imme Jung, Nov. 21, 1958; children—Dorothy, Emily, Miriam, Rebecca. B.A., Cambridge U., 1945. Operations research R.A.F. Bomber Command, 1943-45; fellow Trinity Coll., Cambridge U., Eng., 1946-49; Commonwealth fellow Cornell U., Princeton, 1947-49; prof. physics Cornell U., 1951-53; prof. Inst. Advanced Study, Princeton, 1953—. Author: Disturbing the Universe, 1979. Fellow Royal Soc. London; mem. Am. Phys. Soc., Nat. Acad. Scis. Home: 105 Battle Rd Circle Princeton NJ 08540

DYSON, ROBERT HARRIS, museum director, archaeologist; b. York, Pa., Aug. 2, 1927; s. Robert and Harriet Myrtle (Duck) D. A.B., Harvard Coll., 1950; Ph.D., Harvard U., 1966; A.M. (hon.), U. Pa., 1971. Asst. curator, prof. U. Pa. Mus., Phila., 1955-62, assoc. curator, prof., 1962-67, curator, prof., 1967—, dean faculty arts and scis., 1979-82, dir. mus., 1982—, field dir. Iran expdn., 1956-77; dir. Mus. Council Phila., 1982—. Bd. dirs. World Affairs Council, Phila., 1982—, Phila. Art Alliance, 1982—; chmn. vis. com. dept. anthropology Harvard U., 1983—; vice chmn. Columbia U. seminar in archaeology; hon. trustee Am. Inst. Iranian Studies, 1975-78, 79-82, pres., 1968; trustee Brit. Sch. Archaeology Iraq, Brit. Sch. Archaeology Persian Studies in Tehran. Served as yeoman USN, 1945-46; PTO. Decorated Chevalier des Arts et Lettre France, 1962. Fellow Am. Acad. Arts and Scis., Am. Anthropology Assn., Soc. Fellows Harvard U., Am. Inst. Archaeology (pres. 1977-80), Deutschen Archaeology Inst. (corr.). Home: 302 S 2d St Philadelphia PA 19106 Office: Univ Museum 33d and Spruce Sts Philadelphia PA 19104

DYSON, ROY PATRICK, Congressman; b. Gt. Mills, Md., Nov. 15, 1948; s. LeRoy Benedict and Virginia (Meise) D. Student, U. Md., U. Balt. Legis. asst. to Agrl.-Labor Subcom., Washington, 1973-74; mem. Md. Ho. of Dels., 1974-80, Electoral Coll., 1976; del. Dem. Nat. Issues Confs., 1978; mem. U.S. House of Reps., from 1st Dist. of Md. Mem. Isaac Walton League, Md. Farm Bur. Democrat. Roman Catholic. Clubs: K.C., Elks, Moose. Address: Room 224 Congl House Office Bldg Washington DC 20515

DYSTEL, OSCAR, publishing company executive; b. N.Y.C., Oct. 31, 1912; s. Jacob and Rose (Pintoff) D.; m. Marion Deitler, Oct. 2, 1938; children: Jane Dee, John Jay. B.C.S., N.Y. U., 1935; M.B.A., Harvard U., 1937. Circulation mgr. Sports Illus. and Am. Golfer, 1937; circulation, promotion mgr. Esquire and Coronet mags., Chgo., 1938-40; circulation mgr. Coronet mag., 1940, editor, 1940-42, 44-48; mng. editor Collier's, 1948-49; exec. staff Cowles Mags., Inc., 1949-51; editorial adviser Parents Inst., Inc., 1951-54; pres. Bantam Books, Inc., N.Y.C., 1954-78, chmn., chief exec. officer, 1978-80; pres. Oscar Dystel & Ptnrs., 1982—; cons., 1980-82. Editor of: U.S.A. Mag; pub.: OWI, 1942-43; Author: Analysis of Paid and Controlled Circulation Among Business Papers, 1938. Mem. Rockefeller U. Council; bd. dirs. Nat. Multiple Sclerosis Soc.; chmn. MS Read-A-Thon Program; mem. adv. council Center Strategic and Internat. Studies. Engaged in psychol. warfare ops. Allied Force Hdqrs., 1943-44; MTO. Decorated medal of Freedom, 1946; Brandeis U. fellow. Mem. N.Y. U. Alumni Assn. Clubs: City Athletic, Harvard (N.Y.C.); Dutch Treat. Home: Pine Ln Rye NY 10580 Office: 630 Fifth Ave New York NY 10111

DYYON, FRAZIER (LEROY FRAZIER), artist; b. Fort Myers, Fla., May 2, 1946; s. and Sallie Frazier Williams. Lectr., Westside Community Ctr., N.Y.C., 1971, Case Western Res. U., 1983. Group exhbns. include, Cleve. Top Artists, Intown Club, Cleve., 1969, Art Inst. Akron, 1969-70, Mus. Modern Art, N.Y.C., 1970, Whitney Mus. Annual, 1972, one-man show, Case Western Res. U., 1983; represented in permanent collections, Mus. Modern Art, N.Y.C., Whitney Mus. Am. Art, N.Y.C., Case Western Res. U., Larry Aldrich Mus., Conn., various pvt. collections. (Recipient Montalbano award 1979). Printmaker's Workshop Scholar, 1982. Address: 155 W 73d St New York NY 10023 *Success is a love for your work. Art gives man dignity and the armor of hope.*

DZIEWANOWSKI, MARIAN KAMIL, history educator; b. Zhytomir, Russia, June 27, 1913; came to U.S., 1947, naturalized, 1953; s. Kamil Antoni and Zofia (Kamienska) D.; m. Ada Karczewska, Oct. 4, 1946; children: Barbara, Jan. M.Law, Warsaw U. (Poland), 1937; diploma, Warsaw French Inst., 1937; M.A., Harvard U., 1948, Ph.D., 1951. Research fellow Russian Research Center, Harvard U., 1949-52; research asso. Center Internat. Studies, MIT, 1952-53; prof. history Boston Coll., 1954-65; Ford exchange prof., Poland, 1958, exchange scholar, USSR, 1960; vis. prof. Brown U., Providence, 1961-62, 68; prof. history Boston U., 1965-78, U. Wis., Milw., 1979—; asso. Russian Research Center, Harvard U., 1960-68; vis. prof. European Inst., Florence, Italy, 1979. Commentator,, BBC, London, 1942-44; author: The Communist Party of Poland, 1959, 76, Joseph Pilsudski: A European Federalist, 1969, Poland in the 20th Century, 1977, 80, A History of Soviet Russia, 1979, 80; co-author 22 other books.; editor: The Russian Revolution, 1970; contbr. articles to scholarly jours. Served as lt. Polish Army, 1939-46; Polish, French campaigns; mil. asst. attaché, 1944; Washington. Decorated Polish Cross of Valor (two). Fellow Am. Philos. Soc.; mem. Am. Hist. Assn., Am. Assn. Advancement Slavic Studies, Polish Inst. Arts and Scis. in Am. Home: 3352 N Hackett Ave Milwaukee WI 53211

DZIEWONSKI, ADAM MARIAN, earth science educator; b. Lwow, Poland, Nov. 15, 1936; came to U.S., 1965; s. Jane Roman and Jadwiga (Smulikowska) D.; m. Sybil W. McDonald, Nov. 15, 1967. M.S., U. Warsaw, Poland, 1961; D.Tech. Sci., Acad. Mines and Metallurgy, Cracow, Poland, 1965; M.S., Harvard U., 1976. Research assoc. S.W. Ctr. Advancement Studies, Richardson, Tex., 1965-69; asst. prof. U. Tex.-Dallas, 1969-72; assoc. prof. geology Harvard U., Cambridge, Mass., 1972-76, prof. geology, 1976—, chmn. dept., 1982—; Disting. Fairchild scholar Calif. Inst. Tech., Pasadena, 1983-84; chmn. panel movement measurements Nat. Acad. Scis., 1979-81. Contbr. articles to profl. jours. NSF grantee, 1969-73. Fellow Am. Geophys. Union; mem. Seismol. Soc. Am., Soc. Exploration Geophysicists. Roman Catholic. Office: Dept Geol Sci Harvard U 20 Oxford St Cambridge MA 02138 *

DZIUBA, HENRY FRANK, educator; b. Detroit, Feb. 16, 1918; s. Frank and Anna (Jarzynka) D.; m. Stella Madeline Walush, May 28, 1948; children—Kenneth John, Denise Susan. D.D.S., U. Detroit, 1942. With U. Detroit Sch. Dentistry, 1945—, coordinator clinics, 1962-63, prof. prosthetics, 1962—, asst. dean, 1962-66, dean, 1967, asso. dean clin. affairs, 1977—. Recipient inter-prof. award Advocates, 1967, Prestigious Tower award, 1976; named Alumnus of Yr. U. Detroit, 1975. Fellow Am., Internat. colls. dentists; mem. Am. Prosthodontic Soc., Detroit Dist. Dental Soc., Am., Mich. dental assns., Am. Assn. Dental Schs., Am. Pub. Health Assn., Omicron Kappa Upsilon, Psi Omega. Home: 250 Claremont St Dearborn MI 48124 Office: 2985 E Jefferson St Detroit MI 48207

EACKER, EDWARD WILCOX, utility exec.; b. Cambridge, Mass., Feb. 29, 1928; s. Earl Herkimer and Eleanor Eaton (Bailey) E.; m. Eleanor Baskerville Zehmer, May 2, 1953; children—Elizabeth Carmon, Edward Kennedy, Eugenia Prentiss. B.S., Mass. Inst. Tech., 1948. With Liberty Mut. Ins. Co., 1948-50, W.C. Gilman & Co. (cons. engrs.), N.Y.C., 1950-51; with L.I. Lighting Co., Mineola, N.Y., 1953—, treas., 1974—. Served with USNR, 1951-52. Mem. Am. Gas Assn. Republican. Episcopalian. Home: 22 Smith St Glen Head NY 11545 Office: 250 Old Country Rd Mineola NY 11501

EADE, GEORGE JAMES, retired air force officer, research executive; b. Lockney, Tex., Oct. 27, 1921; s. George William and Isabel Theresa (Barnd) E.; m. Colette Eliane Cachelin, May 18, 1946; children: George Walter, Helen Marie-Louise (Mrs. Jean Oesch), Anne Catherine Eade Pullen, Christine Colette, Dominique Frances. Student, Woodrow Wilson Coll., Chgo., 1939-41, Ill. Inst. Tech., 1941-42. Commd. 2d lt. USAAF, 1942; advanced through grades to gen. USAF, 1971; chief current operations br. Hdqrs. SAC, 1952-56, dep. dir. operations Hdqrs. 7th Air Div., Eng., 1956-58, dir. operations 4238 Strategic Wing, Barksdale AFB, La., 1958-59, dep. comdr. for operations 4238 Strategic Wing, 1959-60, vice comdr. 4238 Strategic Wing, 1960, comdr. 4238 Strategic Wing, 1961, comdr. 7th Bombardment Wing, Carswell AFB, Tex., 1961-63, chief safety div. Hdqrs. SAC, Offutt AFB, Neb., 1963-65, chief control div. Hdqrs. SAC, 1965-66, dir. command control Hdqrs. SAC, 1966-67, dir. operations plans DCS/Operations, 1967-70; dir. plans, dep. chief of staff plans and operations Hdqrs. USAF, Washington, 1970-71, asst. dep. chief of staff, 1971-72, dep. chief staff, 1972-73; (DCINC U.S. European Command), Stuttgart, Germany, 1973-75; chmn. U.S. sect. Mil. Coordinating Com. U.S.-Can.; USAF rep. Sec. Def. Blue Ribbon Action Com.; ret., 1975; v.p., dir. European ops. R & D Assocs., Munich, Germany, 1975—. Pres. Catholic Edn. Assn., Omaha, 1968-70. Decorated D.S.M., Legion of Merit, Air Force Commendation medal with two oak leaf clusters, U.S.; Order Merit, France). Mem. Air Force Assn., Order of Daedalians. Home: 35 Nikolausstrasse 8137 Farchach-Berg 2 Federal Republic of Germany Office: R & D Assocs 8000 Munich 90 Reichenhallerstrasse 8 Federal Republic of Germany *Establish some general goals and lay plans to reach them. Neither be capricious nor struggle doggedly toward a goal no longer of interest. Above all follow your own plan, not what someone plans for you. The ultimate objective is to make a contribution to mankind and be happy in* *the process of so doing. Putting the two together is to discover the art of living.*

EADES, JAMES BEVERLY, JR., aeronautical engineer; b. Bluefield, W.Va., July 22, 1923; s. James Beverly and Harriet Beulah (Smith) E.; m. Sara M. Porterfield, Dec. 20, 1950; children: Sara Leslie, Beverly Anne, James Christian. Student, Bluefield Coll., 1940-42; B.S. in Aero. Engring., Va. Poly. Inst., 1944; M.S. in Applied Mechanics, Va. Poly. Inst., 1949, Ph.D., 1958. Registered profl. engr., Va., W.Va. Asst. prof. aero. engring. Va. Poly. Inst., 1947-50, asst. prof., research asso. aero. engring., 1953-58, prof. aero. engring., 1958-60, 60-67, head aerospace engring., 1961-67; aero. research scientist NACA, Langley Research Center, Langley Field, Va., 1958, 59, Naval Ordnance Lab., Silver Spring, Md., 1960, 63-69; research asso. Nat. Acad. Scis., Goddard Space Flight Center, NASA, Greenbelt, Md., 1967-69; with Analytical Mechanics Assos., Inc., Seabrook, Md., 1969-77; sr. staff scientist Bus. and Technol. Systems, Inc., Seabrook, 1977-81, prin. scientist, 1979-81; v.p., prin. scientist Engring. and Science Assocs., Inc., 1981—; dir. Conf. Lunar Explorations, 1962. Asst. exec. editor: Celestial Mechanics Jour., 1969-75. Served to lt. USNR, World War II, 1951-53; comdr. Ret. Res. Assoc. fellow AIAA (chmn. Blue Ridge sect. 1964, profl. edn. com. 1969-75); mem. Celestial Mechanics Inst. (v.p.), Am. Astronautics Soc., Va. Acad. Sci. (sec. engring. sect. 1961, chmn. sect. 1962, mem. council, chmn. space sci. and tech. sect. 1968), Sigma Xi, Sigma Gamma Tau, Tau Beta Pi. Club: Mason. Home: 1603 Peacock Ln Silver Spring MD 20904 Office: 6110 Executive Blvd Rockville MD 20852

EADES, LUIS ERIC, artist; b. Madrid, June 25, 1923; U.S., 1949, naturalized, 1967; s. Alwyn Turley and Luisa (Olmedo) E.; m. Ursula Jean Lambert, Dec. 27, 1957; children—Peter Luis, Helen Elisabeth. Student, Bath (Eng.) Sch. Art, 1940-42, London U. Slade Sch., 1947-48, Nat. Poly. Inst. Mex., 1948-49; B.A. summa cum laude, U. Ky., 1952. Instr., then asst. prof. U. Tex., 1954-61; faculty fine arts dept. U. Colo., Boulder, 1961—, prof., 1970—. Exhibited one-man shows, Carlin Galleries, Fort Worth, Tex., 1968, 71, 74, 77, 80, Janet Nessler Gallery, N.Y.C., 1960, 64, Carson/Sapiro Gallery, Denver, 1979, group shows include, Mus Modern Art, N.Y.C., 1962, A.F.A., N.Y.C., 1970; represented in permanent collections, Whitney Mus. Am. Art, N.Y.C., Dallas Mus. Fine Arts. Served with Brit. Intelligence Corps, 1943-45. U. Tex. research grantee, 1960; U. Colo. grantee, 1966, 72, 78. Mem. Phi Beta Kappa. Roman Catholic. Home: 1627 5th St Boulder CO 80302 Office: Fine Arts Dept U Colo Boulder CO 80309

EADS, GEORGE CURTIS, economics educator; b. Clarkesville, Tex., Aug. 20, 1942; s. Delbert Curtis and Eliza Mae (Hicks) E.; m. Margaret Helen Hall, Nov. 17, 1973; children: Geoffrey Thomas, Katherine Elizabeth. B.A., U. Colo., 1964; M.A., Yale U., 1965; M.Phil., 1967; Ph.D., Yale U., 1968. Asst. prof. econs. Harvard U., Cambridge, Mass., 1966-69, Princeton U., 1969-71; spl. asst. antitrust div. Dept. Justice, Washington, 1971-72; assoc. prof. George Washington U., Washington, 1972-74; asst. dir. Council Wage and Price Stability, Washington, 1974-75; exec. dir. Nat. Commn. Supplies and Shortages, Washington, 1975-77; economist, research program dir. Rand Corp., Santa Monica, Calif., 1977-79, 81; mem. Pres.'s Council Advisors, Washington, 1979-81; prof. Sch. Pub. Affairs, U. Md., College Park, 1981—. Author: The Local Service Airline Experiment, 1972. Mem. Am. Econ. Assn. Democrat. Home: 3718 Harrison St NW Washington DC 20015 Office: 1218 Lefrak Hall School of Public Affairs University of Maryland College Park MD 20742

EADS, ORA WILBERT, clergyman, ch. ofcl.; b. Mill Spring, Mo., Jan. 2, 1914; s. John Harrison and Effie Ellen (Borders) E.; m. Mary Ivaree Cochran, Mar. 25, 1944; children—Ora Wilbert, Wayne B., Carol Vernice, Janet Karen and Janice Inez (twins). J.D., John Marshall Law Sch., Atlanta, 1940, LL.M., 1941; postgrad., Sch. Theology, St. Lawrence U., Canton, N.Y., 1947-48. Bar: Ga. bar 1940. Practiced in, Atlanta, 1940-46; ordained to ministry Christian Congregation, Inc., 1946; parish minister, Sampson County, N.C., 1948-52, evangelist, Charlotte, N.C., 1952-61; gen. supt. Christian Congregation, Inc., 1961—. Author numerous books of poetry, 1967—. Address: 804 W Hemlock St LaFollette TN 37766

EADY, CAROL MURPHY (MRS. KARL ERNEST EADY), medical association administrator; b. Cleve., Dec. 3, 1918; d. Alfred John and Beatrice B. (Winternitz) Murphy; m. Karl Ernest Eady, July 7, 1945. Diploma, St. Luke's Hosp. Sch. Nursing, Cleve., 1940; B.S. magna cum laude, Baldwin-Wallace Coll., 1943; M.S. in Adminstrn. in Schs. of Nursing, Western Res. U., (now Case Western Res. U.), 1955. Dir. edn. Elyria (Ohio) Meml. Hosp. Sch. Nursing, 1952-57; dir. nursing edn. Mt. Sinai Hosp. Sch. Nursing, Cleve., 1957-62, Michael Reese Hosp. Sch. Nursing, Chgo., 1962-73; coordinator of nursing component Area Health Edn. System, U. Ill., Chgo., 1973-77; asst. dir. dept. health manpower AMA, Chgo., 1977-81, dir. office of related health professions, 1981—; Vice pres. Chgo. Video Nursing, 1966-68; mem. project grants rev. com. Nurse Tng. Act USPHS, 1966-70. Fellow Inst. Medicine Chgo.; mem. Nat. League Nursing (vice chmn. bd. rev. for diploma programs in nursing 1964-68, 3d v.p. 1969-71, pres. 1973-75), Ill. League Nursing (pres. 1978-82). Republican. Lutheran. Home: 1115 S Seminary Ave Park Ridge IL 60068 Office: AMA 535 N Dearborn Chicago IL 60610

EAGEN, MICHAEL JOHN, state chief justice; b. Jermyn, Pa., May 9, 1907; s. Michael J. and Sarah (Nallin) E.; m. Helen Fitzsimmons, June 27, 1935; children—Helen Marie (Mrs. Thomas J. Foley), Michael John Jr., Jeremiah William, James. B.A., St. Thomas Coll., (now U. Scranton), Scranton, Pa., 1927; student, Harvard Law Sch., 1927-28; LL.D. (hon.), U. Scranton, 1955, Dickinson Sch. Law, 1977; D.H.L., St. Joseph's Coll., 1978. Bar: Pa. bar 1931. Pvt. practice, 1931-41, dist. atty., Lackawanna County, 1934-41, judge ct. common pleas, 1942-59; justice Supreme Ct. Pa., 1960-77, chief justice, 1977-80. Pres. Coll. of Presdl. Electors of Pa., 1940, Lackawanna United Fund, 1955-59. Decorated knight Equestrian Order Holy Sepulchre; recipient Golden Deeds award Exchange Club of Scranton, 1950, Americanism award B'nai B'rith, 1969, award for outstanding community service Friendly Sons of St. Patrick of Lackawanna, Scranton-Dunmore Community Chest award, 1944, award ARC, 1944, Lackawanna United Fund award, 1958, award Am. Legion, 1959, Distinguished Pa. award, 1978. Mem. Am., Pa., Lackawanna County bar assns., Am. Law Inst. Clubs: Elk (past local exalted ruler), Moose.). Home: 711 Taylor Ave Scranton PA 18510

EAGER, HENRY IDE, state judge; b. Hopkinsville, Ky., July 16, 1895; s. Ben F. and Carrie (Downer) E.; 1 son, Henry G. (dec.). Student, U. Wash., 1913-14; J.D., U. Mich., 1920. Bar: Mo. bar 1920. Mem. firm Blackmar, Eager. Swanson, Midgley & Jones, Kansas City, 1920-55; judge Supreme Ct. Mo., 1955-68, spl. commr., 1969—; Mem. Bd. Law Examiners., 1946-54. Served from 2d to 1st lt. 34th Inf., 7th Div. U.S. Army, 1917-19. Mem. ABA, Mo. Bar Assn. (gov., chmn. appellate practice com.), Kansas City Bar Assn., Lawyers Assn. Kansas City, Delta Theta Phi. Baptist. Home: 2323 W Main St Jefferson City MO 65101 Office: Supreme Court Bldg Jefferson City MO 65101

EAGER, JOHN HOWARD, III, banker; b. Balt., Oct. 1, 1928; s. Auville and Clara (Murray) E.; m. Elizabeth Hartley, Nov. 23, 1948 (div. Mar. 14, 1981); children: Elizabeth, John Howard IV.; m. Nina Miller, Oct. 18, 1981. Student pvt. sch., Kent, Conn. With Warfield-Dorsey Co., 1950-53, Hedwin Corp., 1953-56; with Md. Nat. Bank, Balt., 1956—, asst. cashier, 1960-63, asst. v.p., 1963-65, v.p., 1965—, cashier, 1975—; v.p., sec. Md. Nat. Corp., Balt., 1975—; pres. Manab Properties, Balt., 1969—; sec.-treas. Ten Light Street Corp., Balt., 1966—; dir. Mann & Parker Lumber Co.; pres. Chesapeake Amphibious Aircraft, Inc., Balt., 1970—. Asst. sec. Md. Nat. Found.; bd. dirs. Balt. Symphony Orch.; sec., bd. dirs. Harriet Lane Home. Club: Maryland. Home: 12130 Harford Rd Glen Arm MD 21057 Office: PO Box 987 Baltimore MD 21203

EAGLE, HARRY, physician, dean; b. N.Y.C., July 13, 1905; s. Louis and Sadie (Kushnoy) E.; m. Hope Whaley, Aug. 31, 1928; 1 dau., Kay Whaley (Mrs. Robert B. Kyle, Jr.). A.B., Johns Hopkins U., 1923, M.D., 1927; M.S. (hon.), Yale U., 1948, D.Sc., Wayne State U., 1965, Duke U., 1981, Rockefeller U., 1982. Intern, asst. and instr. medicine Johns Hopkins, 1927-32; asst. and asso. prof. bacteriology U. Pa., 1933-36; commd. officer USPHS, 1936-61; dir. Venereal Disease Research Lab., Johns Hopkins Hosp., 1936-46, Lab. Exptl. Therapeutics, Johns Hopkins Sch. Hygiene and Pub. Health, 1946-48, adj. prof. bacteriology, 1946-47; sci. dir. research br. Nat. Cancer Inst., 1947-49; chief sect. exptl. therapeutics Nat. Inst. Allergy and Infectious Diseases, NIH, 1949-58, chief, 1959-61; prof., dept. cell biology Albert Einstein Coll. Medicine, 1961-70, chmn. div. biol. scis., 1968-70, asso. dean for sci. affairs, 1970-72, 74-—, dir. cancer research center, 1972—, Univ. prof., 1971—. Author: Laboratory Diagnosis of Syphilis, 1937, papers relating to immunology, blood coagulation, chemotherapy antibiotics and tissue culture. Recipient Eli Lilly Co. bronze medal, 1936; Presdl. Certificate Merit, 1948; Borden award Assn. Am. Med. Colls., 1965; Albert Einstein Commemorative award, 1968; N.Y. Acad. Medicine award, 1970; Modern Medicine award, 1972; Louisa Gross Horwitz prize, 1973; Sidney Farber Med. Research award, 1974; Hon. Alumnus award Albert Einstein Coll. Med., 1976; Hubert H. Humphrey Cancer Research Ctr. award, 1982; elected to Johns Hopkins Soc. Scholars. Mem. Nat. Acad. Scis., Am. Acad. Arts and Scis., Am. Soc. Biol. Chem., Soc. Am. Microbiologists (past pres.), Soc. Clin. Investigation, Assn. Am. Physicians, Am. Assn. Immunologists (pres. 1964-65), Soc. Exptl. Biology and Medicine (pres. 1963-65), Am. Soc. Cell Biology, Am. Assn. for Cancer Research. Home: 370 Orienta Ave Mamaroneck NY 10543 Office: Albert Einstein Coll Medicine EastChester Rd and Morris Park Ave New York NY 10461

EAGLEBURGER, LAWRENCE SIDNEY, consultant, former ambassador; b. Milw., Aug. 1, 1930; s. Leon Sidney and Helen (Van Ornum) E.; m. Marlene Ann Heinemann, Apr. 23, 1966; 1 son by previous marriage, Lawrence Scott; children: Lawrence Andrew, Lawrence Jason. Student, Central State Coll., Stevens Point, Wis., 1948-50; B.S., U. Wis., 1952, M.S., 1957. Teaching asst. U. Wis., 1956-57; joined U.S. Fgn. Service, 1957; 3d sec., Tegucigalpa, Honduras, 1957-59; assigned State Dept., 1959-62, 65-66; 2d sec., Belgrade, Yugoslavia, 1962-65; mem. staff NSC, 1966-67; spl. asst. under sec. State Dept., 1967-69; exec. asst. to asst. to Pres. for nat. security affairs, 1969; polit. adviser, counselor for polit. affairs U.S. Mission to NATO, Brussels, Belgium, 1969-71; dep. asst. sec. Dept. Def., 1971-73, dep. asst. to Pres. for nat. security ops., 1973; exec. asst. to sec. state, 1973-75, dep. undersec. state for mgmt., exec. asst. to sec. state, 1975-77, ambassador to Yugoslavia, Belgrade, 1977-81; asst. sec. for European affairs Dept. State, 1981-82, undersec. for polit. affairs, from 1982; pres. Kissinger Assos., Inc., N.Y.C., 1984—; dir. ITT Corp. Vice chmn. 7th Dist. Young Republicans Wis., 1950-51; mem. Wis. Young Rep. Exec. Com., 1949-51. Served to 1st lt. AUS, 1952-54. Recipient Disting. Civilian Service medal Dept. Def., 1973; President's award for distinguished fed. civilian service, 1977. Mem. Alpha Sigma Phi. Office: Kissinger Assocs Inc 55 E 52nd St New York NY 10055

EAGLES, SIDNEY SMITH, JR., lawyer, judge; b. Asheville, N.C., Aug. 5, 1939; s. Sidney Smith and Mildred Truman (Brite) E.; m. Rachel Phillips, May 22, 1965; children: Virginia Brite, Margaret Phillips. B.A., Wake Forest U., 1961, J.D., 1964. Bar: N.C. 1964. Mem. staff Office Atty. Gen. N.C., 1967-77, spl. dep. atty. gen., 1975-77, chief spl. prosecutor's div., 1973-76; chmn. N.C. del. Nat. Conf. Commrs. Uniform State Laws, 1969-76, vice chmn. legis. com., 1973—; counsel to speaker N.C. Ho. of Reps., 1977-80; adj. prof. Campbell U. Sch. Law, 1977-80, 84—. Author articles; co-author legal formbook. Vice pres., dir. Raleigh Jaycees, 1969-73; mem. Senatorial Dist. Dem. Com., 1979-81; bd. elders, chmn. bd. deacons Hillyer Meml. Christian Ch., 1980-81; bd. dirs. Wake County (N.C.) Symphony Soc., 1980-81, Wake County Women's Aid. Served with USAF, 1964-67; col. Res. Decorated Air Force Commendation medal, Meritorious Service medal; travel grantee N.C. Justice Found., Eng., 1971. Mem. ABA, N.C. Bar Assn., Wake County Bar Assn. (chmn. exec. com. 1975), N.C. Acad. Trial Lawyers, Am. Law Inst., N.C. State Bar, N.C. Criminal Code Commn. Democrat. Club: Raleigh Kiwanis. Office: PO Box 2211 Raleigh NC 27602

EAGLES, STUART ERNEST, business executive; b. Saint John, N.B., Can., July 29, 1929; s. Ernest Lyle and Evelyn Gertrude (Feltmate) E.; m. Margaret Anne Gulliver, Sept. 20, 1952; children: James Stuart, Patricia Anne, Mark Edward. B.Sc., Acadia U., 1949. With stats. dept. Can. Pacific, 1949-62, asst. to v.p., 1962; asst. to pres. Can. Pacific Investments, 1964-68, v.p. Eastern region, 1969; res. Can. Pacific Enterprises Ltd., Calgary, Alta., Can.; chmn., pres., chief exec. officer Marathon Realty Co. Ltd., 1970—; dir. Marathon U.S. Holdings Inc., Mrathon Aviation Terminals Ltd., Baker Commodities Inc., Can. Pacific Enterprises (U.S.) Inc., Canborough Corp., Canborough Ltd., CanPac Agriproducts Ltd., Chateau Ins. Co., MICC Investments Ltd., Mortgage Ins. Co. of Can., Processed Minerals Inc., Syracuse China Corp. Bd. govs., exec. com. Acadia U.; trustee, v.p. Can. Com. Internat. Council Shopping Ctrs.; pres. Can. Inst. Pub. Real Estate Cos. Mem. Ont. Bus. Adv. Council. Clubs: National (v.p., bd. dirs.), Canadian). Office: Office of Pres Can Pacific Enterprises Ltd 125 9th Ave SE Calgary AB Canada T2G 0P6 *

EAGLESON, PETER STURGES, educator, hydrologist; b. Phila., Feb. 27, 1928; s. William Boal and Helen (Sturges) E.; m. Marguerite Anne Partridge, May 28, 1949 (div.); children: Helen Marie, Peter Sturges, Jeffrey Partridge; m. Beverly Grossmann Rich, Dec. 27, 1974. B.S. in Civil Engring, Lehigh U., 1949, M.S., 1952; Sc.D., MIT, 1956. Jr. engr. George B. Mebus (cons. engr.), Glenside, Pa., 1950-51; teaching asst. Lehigh U., 1951-52; research asst. Mass. Inst. Tech., 1952-54; mem. faculty MIT, 1954—, prof. civil engring., 1965—, head dept. civil engring., 1970-75; vis. asso. Calif. Inst. Tech., 1975-76; Fulbright sr. research scholar Commonwealth Sci. and Indsl. Research Orgn., Canberra, Australia, 1966-67. Author: (with others) Estuary and Coastline Hydrodynamics, 1966, Dynamic Hydrology, 1970. Served to 2d lt. C.E. AUS, 1949-50. Recipient Desmond Fitzgerald medal, 1959, Clemens Herschel prize, 1965; both Boston Soc. Civil Engrs.; research prize Am. Soc. C.E., 1963. Fellow Am. Geophys. Union (Robert E. Horton award 1979); mem. Nat. Acad. Engring. Office: Dept Civil Engring Room 48-335 Mass Inst Tech Cambridge MA 02139

EAGLESON, WILLIAM BOAL, JR., banker; b. Phila., Dec. 10, 1925; s. William Boal and Helen (Sturges) E.; m. Catherine West McLean, May 28, 1960; children: Elizabeth West, John McLean. B.S., Lehigh U., 1949; M.B.A., U. Pa., 1951. With Fed. Res. Bank Phila., 1949-51; investment officer Girard Bank, Phila., 1951-61, v.p., 1961, exec. v.p., 1967; pres., dir. Girard Co., Girard Bank, 1970-80, chmn. bd., 1974—; trustee Penn Mut. Life Ins. Co.; dir. Anchor Hocking Corp., Gen. Accident Ins. Co. Am., Pvt. Investment Co. for Asia, Phila. Port Corp., Pennwalt Corp. Mem. Phila. City Planning Commn., 1972-73; Trustee Acad. Natural Scis. Phila., 1967-75, Lehigh U.; bd. dirs. Phila. Orch. Assn. Served with USNR, 1944-46. Mem. Assn. Res. City Bankers, Am. Philos. Soc., Phi Beta Kappa. Episcopalian. Clubs: Econ. (N.Y.C.); Racquet, Phila. (Phila.). Home: Jaffrey Rd Malvern PA 19355 Office: Girard Bank One Girard Plaza Philadelphia PA 19101

EAGLETON, LEE CHANDLER, chemical engineer, educator; b. Vallejo, Calif., July 27, 1923; s. William L. and Mary Louise (Chandler) E.; m. Mary E. Stewart, Feb. 21, 1953; children: James C., William L., Elizabeth L. S.B., MIT, 1946, S.M., 1947; D.Eng., Yale U., 1950. Research asso. Columbia U., 1950-51; devel. engr. Rohm & Haas Co., Phila., 1951-56; lectr. Drexel Inst. Tech., 1954, U. Pa., Phila., 1954-55, asso. prof., 1956-65, prof., 1966-69; prof. head dept. chem. engring. Pa. State U., 1970—; cons. Rohm & Haas, 1956-74, Inst. for Def. Analyses, 1961-63, Martin Marietta Co., 1970-72, 74. Served with AUS, 1942-46. Fellow Am. Inst. Chem. Engrs. (dir. 1980-82); mem. Am. Soc. Engring. Edn. (chmn. chem. engring. div. 1970-71), Am. Chem. Soc., AAUP. Home: 445 Cricklewood Dr State College PA 16801 Office: 160 Fenske Lab Pa State U University Park PA 16802

EAGLETON, RICHARD ERNEST, judge; b. Peoria, Ill., June 29, 1930; s. William Lester and Mary Louise (Chandler) E.; m. Elizabeth Louise Waterman, Jan. 31, 1953; children: David Pierce, Margaret Waters. B.A., Yale U., 1952; LL.B., U. Ill., 1958. Bar: Ill. 1958. Practice law, Peoria, 1958-61, 69-70; asst. U.S. atty. So. Dist. Ill., 1961-64, U.S. atty., 1965-69; 1st asst. state's atty., Peoria, 1964-65; circuit judge 10th Ill. Circuit, 1970—, chief judge, 1979-82; mem. com. criminal justice programs Ill. Supreme Ct., 1969-82, also mem. com. on jud. info. systems, 1979-82; mem. edn. com. Ill. Jud. Conf., 1978-80, mem. criminal jury instrns. com., 1982—; mem. Peoria Criminal Justice Commn., 1969-73, Ill. Law Enforcement Commn., 1973-77, Ill. Criminal Justice Info. Authority, 1983—. Bd. dirs. Peoria Mental Health Clinic, 1959-65, treas., 1964; Democratic candidate Ill. circuit judge, 1963. Served with USN, 1952-55; capt. Res. Recipient Ill. Gov.'s Criminal Justice award, 1972. Mem. ABA (nat. dir. crime control project 1969-70, crisis in jails com. 1982—), Ill. Bar Assn. (chmn. criminal law sect. 1969-70, chmn. jud. adminstrn. sect. 1974-75, council bench and bar sect. 1983—), Peoria County Bar Assn. (sec. treas. 1962-65), Phi Gamma Delta, Phi Delta Phi. Baptist. Clubs: Masons, Country (Peoria). Home: 1610 W Moss Ave Peoria IL 61606

EAGLETON, ROBERT DON, physics educator; b. Ladonia, Tex., Aug. 19, 1937; s. Winslow Frank and Bertha Mae (Hidler) E.; m. Barbara Francis Eagleton, Aug. 17, 1963; children: David, Jonathan, Jennifer, Elizabeth. B.S., Abilene Christian Coll., 1959; M.S., Okla. State U., 1962, Ph.D., 1968. Mem. faculty dept. physics Calif. State Poly. U., Pomona, 1968—, prof. physics., 1978—. Served with USNR, 1962-65. NDEA fellow, 1959-62. Mem. Am. Assn. Physics Tchrs., Sigma Xi. Democrat. Home: 1572 N Mountain Ave Claremont CA 91711 Office: 3801 W Temple Ave Pomona CA 91768

EAGLETON, THOMAS FRANCIS, senator; b. St. Louis, Sept. 4, 1929; s. Mark David and Zitta Louise (Swanson) E.; m. Barbara Ann Smith, Jan. 20, 1956; children: Terence, Christin. B.A. cum laude, Amherst Coll., 1950, LL.B., Harvard U., 1953. Bar: Mo. bar 1953. Since practiced in, St. Louis; partner firm Eagleton & Eagleton; circuit atty., St. Louis, 1957-60; Atty. gen. State of Mo., 1960, lt. gov., 1964-68; mem. U.S. Senate from Mo., 1968—. Served with USNR, 1948-49. Office: SD-197 Dirksen Senate Office Bldg Washington DC 20510

EAGLSTEIN, WILLIAM HOWARD, dermatologist, educator; b. Kansas City, Mo., Mar. 27, 1940; s. Max A. and Mildred (Bernstein) E.; m. Janet Strickland, Aug. 23, 1979. M.D., U. Mo., 1965. Intern Kings County (N.Y.) Hosp., 1965-66; resident U. Miami, 1966-69, prof. dermatology, 1971-80; prof., chmn. dept. dermatology U. Pitts., 1980—; chmn. dermatologic adv. com. FDA, 1983—. Author: Office Techniques for Diagnosing Skin Diseases, 1978; asso. editor: Jour. Dermatology and Related Allergies, 1978-80. Served with USN, 1969-71. Fellow Am. Bd. Dermatology; mem. Am. Acad. Dermtology, Soc. Investigative Dermatology, Am. Dermatol. Assn., AMA. Jewish. Office: Univ Health Center 3601 5th Ave Pittsburgh PA 15213

EAKER, IRA, publisher; b. N.Y.C., Jan. 14, 1922; s. Samuel and Hannah (Conner) E.; m. Lee Eisenberg, Nov. 24, 1946; children—Sherry Ellen, Dean Ross. Ed., Coll. City N.Y. Advt. sales rep. John Morris Chanin Orgn., N.Y.C., 1946-48; advt. mgr. Show Bus. Weekly, N.Y.C., 1948-60; founder, pub., advt. dir. Back Stage Publs., N.Y.C., 1960—. Served with F.A. AUS, 1943-46; ETO. Clubs: Friars, Woodcrest, K.P. Home: 15 72 216th St Bayside NY 11360 Office: 330 W 42d St New York NY 10036

EAKIN, THOMAS CAPPER, sports promotion executive; b. New Castle, Pa., Dec. 16, 1933; s. Frederick William and Beatrice (Capper) E.; m. Brenda Lee Andrews, Oct. 21, 1961; children: Thomas Andrews, Scott Frederick. B.A. in History, Denison U., 1956. Life ins. cons. Northwestern Mut. Life Ins. Co., Cleve., 1959-67; regional dir. sales Empire Life Ins. Co. Ohio, 1967-68; dist. mgr. Putman Pub. Co., Cleve., 1968-69; regional bus. mgr. Chilton Pub. Co., Cleve., 1969-70; dist. mgr. Hitchcock Pub. Co., Cleve., 1970-72; founder, pres. Golf Internat. 100 Club, Shaker Heights, Ohio, 1970—; founder, pres., dir. Cy Young Mus., 1975-80; pres. TCE Enterprises, Shaker Heights, Ohio, 1973—; founder, pres. Ohio Baseball Hall of Fame, 1976—, Ohio Baseball Hall of Fame Celebration, 1977-79, Ohio Baseball Hall of Fame and Mus., 1980—; founder, chmn. Ohio Baseball Hall of Fame Golf Invitational, 1980—; dir. New Hope Records; trustee Newcomerstown Sports Corp., 1975-80; Founder, nat. chmn. Cy Young Centennial, 1967; founder, nat. chmn. Cy Young Golf Invitational, 1967-79; mem. adv. bd. Cleve. Indian Old Timers Com., 1966-67, Portage County Sports Hall of Fame (Ohio), 1983—; hon. dir. Tuscarawas County (Ohio) Old Timers Baseball Assn., 1972—, commendation, 1970; Ohio exec. sponsor chmn. World Golf Hall of Fame, Pinehurst, N.C., 1979—. Fund drive rep. Boy Scouts Am., Cleve., 1959-60, United Appeal, 1959-63, Heart Fund, 1963-64; mem. Cleve. Council Corrections, 1971-73; mem. adv. bd. Cuyahoga Hills Boys Sch., Warrensville Heights, Ohio, 1971—, Camp Hope, Warrrensville Twp., 1973—, Fitness Evaluation Services, Inc., 1977-79, Interact Club of Twinsburg (Ohio), 1981—; founder, bd. dirs. TRY (Target/Reach Youth), 1971—, Interact Club Shaker Heights, 1971—; mem. exec. com. Tuscarawas County Am. Revolution Bicentennial Commn., 1974-76; trustee Tuscarawas County Hist. Soc., 1978-81; bd. dirs. Shaker Hts. Youth Center, 1975, Tuscarawas Valley Tourist Assn., 1979-81, Buckeye Tourist Assn., 1979-80; mem. adv. bd. Ohio Racquetball Assn., 1981-82. Served with AUS, 1956-58. Recipient commendation awards Cy Young Centennial Com., 1967, Tuscarawas County C. of C., 1967, Sporting News, 1968, Gov. James A. Rhodes, Ohio, 1968, 75, 78, Gov. John J. Gilligan, Ohio, 1972, Newcomerstown (Ohio) C. of C., 1967; Outstanding Contbn. to Baseball award baseball commr. William Eckert, 1967; Sport Service award Sport mag., 1969; Civic Service award Cuyahoga Hills Boys Sch., 1970; citation of merit La. Stadium and Expn. Dist., 1972; Presdl. commendation Richard M. Nixon, 1973; Distinguished Service award Camp Hope, 1974;

Founder's award Interact Club Shaker Heights, 1974; Gov.'s award for community action State of Ohio, 1974; award of achievement Ohio Assn. Hist. Socs., 1975; Chief Newawatowes award Newcomerstown C. of C., 1975; Proclamation award, Thomas C. Eakin Day City of Cleve., 1974; Outstanding Alumnus award Phi Delta Theta Alumni Club, Cleve., 1975; commendation Ohio Am. Revolution Bicentennial Adv. Commn., 1976; certificate of merit Tuscarawas County Am. Revolution Bicentennial Commn., 1976; commendation Ohio Senate, 1976, 79; Presdl. commendation Pres. Ford, 1977; Appreciation award Am. Revolution Bicentennial Adminstrn., 1977; Cert. of Merit State of La., 1978; Commendation Ohio Ho. of Reps., 1978; Gov.'s award State of Ohio, 1978; named Hon. Citizen City of New Orleans, 1978; Founder's Award TRY, 1979; named to Chautauqua Sports Hall of Fame (N.Y.), 1983, hon. bd. dirs., 1982—. Fellow Intercontinental Biog. Assn.; fellow Am. Biog. Inst.; mem. Tuscarawas County Hist. Soc. (trustee 1978-81), Shaker Hist. Soc. (trustee 1980-82), Internat. Platform Assn., English Speaking Union, Denison U. Cleve. Men's Club (v.p. 1964-65), Phi Delta Theta (pres. Cleve. alumni club 1970, Appreciation award 1971, dir. 1971-75, exec. com. nat. Lou Gehrig award com. 1975—, trustee Ohio Iota chpt. 1979-82). Baptist (mem. bd. 1966-69). Clubs: Rotary (pres. Shaker Heights 1970-71, founder and chmn. club's internat. student exchange program U.S. and Can. 1965-70), Rotary (Outstanding Young Rotarian award 1962), Rotary (founder, chmn. Henry G. Duchscherer Meml. award com. 1971), Rotary (trustee V. Blakeman Qua Scholarship Fund 1972-73), Wahoo (dir. 1975-77); Executive (Woodmere, Ohio); PGA Nat. Golf (Palm Beach Gardens, Fla.) (internat. mem.); Legend Lake Golf (Chardon, Ohio)). Address: 2729 Shelley Rd Shaker Heights OH 44122

EALUM, JAMES MAURICE, diplomat; b. Altus, Okla., Dec. 30, 1930; s. Elbert Leon and Harriet Opal (Haigwood) Ealum H.; m. Shirley Lou McKinney, June 13, 1953; children: Sydney Ann, James Holland. B.A., U. Okla., 1953; M.A., Harvard U., 1957. Commd. fgn. service officer Dept. State; served Am. embassy, Tel Aviv, 1958-62, Moscow, 1965-67, chief consular sect., Tehran, Iran, 1967-70; with Dept. State, Washington, 1970-80; consul gen., Dhahran, Saudi Arabia, 1980-83; dir. Office Iranian affairs Dept. State, Washington, 1983—. Served to lt. (j.g.) USNR, 1953-55; Far East. Office: Dept State 22d and Ct St Washington DC 20520 *

EALY, DONALD RAE, corp. exec.; b. Altus, Okla., Apr. 18, 1928; s. Elzah LeRoy and Lalah Rae (Byerly) E.; m. Cynthia Howland Pike, Dec. 14, 1952; children—Elizabeth, Dennis, Jonathan, Richard. B.A., Long Beach (Calif.) State Coll., 1953; postgrad., U. So. Calif., 1958. Various mgmt. positions Firestone Tire & Rubber Co., 1951-60; with ITT Corp., 1960—; dir. adminstrn., v.p. ITT Europe, 1971-75; v.p. ITT Corp.; dir. adminstrn. ITT Europe, Brussels, 1977—; v.p. Internat. Standard Electric Co. Served with U.S. Army, 1946-48. Club: Shriners. Office: 480 Ave Louise Brussels B-1050 Belgium

EALY, LAWRENCE ORR, author, educator; b. Ocean City, N.J., Sept. 17, 1915; s. Vance Lawrie Orr and Nelle Gray (Rohm) E.; m. Margaret A. Scott, Aug. 10, 1942 (dec. 1945); 1 son, Grant Haertter. A.B., Temple U., 1934; LL.B., U. Pa., 1937, M.A., 1947, Ph.D., 1951; Litt.D., Rider Coll., 1982; student, Navy Supply Corps Sch., Grad. Sch. Bus. Adminstrn., Harvard, 1941. Bar: Ohio bar 1938, Pa. bar 1941. Pvt. practice law, Steubenville, Ohio and, Phila., 1938-41; instr. history Temple U., 1947-51, asst. prof., 1951-54, asso. prof., 1954-58; lectr. Naval Res. Officers Sch., 1956-57, Rutgers U., 1954-55; Ernest J. King prof. history Naval War Coll., Newport, R.I., 1958-59; provost, dean of faculties, prof. history Hobart Coll., William Smith Coll., 1959-62; dean, prof. history and govt. Rider Coll., Trenton, N.J., 1962-66, v.p. coll., 1966-70. Author: Under the Puppet's Crown, 1939, Tacony Farm, 1942, Republic of Panama in World Affairs, 1951, reprinted, 1971, Yanqui Politics and the Isthmian Canal, 1971; Mem. bd.: Am. Jour. Legal History, 1957—. Mem. Pa. Citizens Com. for Eisenhower, 1952; Trustee Temple U. Alumni Fund Council, 1947-51, Ednl. Found. of Alpha Chi Rho, 1956-57. Served from ensign to comdr. USNR, 1941-46. Recipient Christian R. and Mary F. Lindbach award, 1973. Mem. Pa., Phila. bar assns., Ret. Officers Assn., Pa. Soc. N.Y., Am. Legion, Phi Beta Kappa, Phi Alpha Theta, Pi Gamma Mu, Delta Sigma Pi, Alpha Chi Rho, Pi Delta Epsilon. Republican. Episcopalian. Clubs: Elk., Torch (Trenton, N.J.) (pres. 1966-67); Pa. Soc. N.Y.). Home: 2103 Central Ave Ocean City NJ 08226 *My life was shaped by dedicated and loving parents who came from a Colonial American heritage. They taught me to love and appreciate my country and to understand the good citizen's mission and duty to serve in its interests whenever called upon to do so. Whatever success and honor came to me simply flowed out of a lifetime spent in dedication to that ideal. I found my opportunities in professional activity which was always related to public or quasi-public service.*

EALY, ROBERT PHILLIP, educator; b. Kay County, Okla., July 6, 1914; s. Charles Gustav and Annie Emily (Johnson) E.; m. Carol Lavina Smith, May 29, 1939. B.S., Okla. State U., 1941; M.S., Kans. State U., 1946; Ph.D., La. State U., 1955. Landscape nurseryman Paul's Garden, Blackwell, Okla., 1932-37; teaching asst. Kans. State U., 1941-42; asst. prof. horticulture Okla. State U., 1946-55, assoc. prof., 1955-58, prof., 1958-61; prof., head dept. horticulture Kans. State U., Manhattan, 1961-63, prof., head dept. horticulture and landscape architecture, 1963-66, prof. landscape architecture, 1966-82, prof. emeritus, 1982—, head dept., 1966-79, assoc. dean, 1967-74; cons. landscape architect, 1947—; mem., sec. Kans. State Registration Bd. Landscape Architects, 1968-76. Contbg. author: Elements of Planting Design, 1975, Designing with Plants, 1982. Mem. environ. concerns com., City of Manhattan. Served with AUS, 1942-46. Fellow Am. Soc. Landscape Architects (pres. Mo. Valley chpt., trustee); mem. Council Landscape Archtl. Registration Bds. (nat. sec. 1972-74), Internat. Fedn. Landscape Architects, Assn. Kans. Landscape Architects, Kans. State Hort. Soc., Sigma Xi, Alpha Zeta, Phi Kappa Phi, Phi Sigma, Tau Sigma Delta. Presbyterian. Home: 1925 Vermont St Manhattan KS 66502 Office: Dept Landscape Architecture Kans State U Manhattan KS 66506

EAMER, RICHARD KEITH, health care company executive, lawyer; b. Long Beach, Calif., Feb. 13, 1928; s. George Pierce and Lillian (Newell) E.; m. Eileen Laughlin, Sept. 1, 1951; children—Brian Keith, Erin Maureen. B.S. in Acctg, U. So. Calif., 1955, LL.B., 1959. Bar: Calif. 1960; C.P.A., Calif. Acct. L. H. Penney & Co. (C.P.A.s), 1956-59; asso. firm Ervin, Cohen & Jessup, Beverly Hills, Calif., 1959-63; partner firm Eamer, Bell and Bedrosian, Beverly Hills, 1963-69; chmn. bd., chief exec. officer Nat. Med. Enterprises, Inc., Los Angeles, 1969—, also dir.; dir. Union Oil Co. Calif., Imperial Bank. Mem. Am. Bar Assn., Am. Inst. C.P.A.s, Calif. Bar Assn., Los Angeles County Bar Assn. Republican. Clubs: Bel Air Country, Bel Air Bay, California. Office: 11620 Wilshire Blvd Los Angeles CA 90025

EAMES, EARL WARD, JR., UN ofcl., mgmt. cons., bus. exec.; b. Morris, Minn., Oct. 22, 1923; s. Earl Ward and Camilla (Hendricks) E.; m. Anyes de Horst, June 26, 1954; children—Elizabeth Anne, Earl Ward III, Erik Michael, Christopher Paul. Student, U. Minn., 1941; S.B., Mass. Inst. Tech., 1949. Vice pres., then pres., dir. Consultants Inc., Boston and Amsterdam, Netherlands, 1949-54; prodn. specialist Found. Productivity Research, Helsinki, Finland, 1955-57; pres. Gen. Mgmt. Assos., Boston, 1957-63; sr. asso. Cresap, McCormick & Paget, N.Y.C., 1963-66; v.p. ops. Council Internat. Progress in Mgmt., N.Y.C., 1966, pres., chief exec. officer, dir., 1967-69; v.p., dir. Reed, Cuff & Becker, N.Y.C., 1970-73; sr. asso. Wilmer Wright Assos., 1973-78; vis. prof. and mgmt. consultancy expert UNIDO, U. Ife, Nigeria, 1978-80; adv. on small-scale industry World Bank, 1980—; Royal Danish consul for New Eng., 1952-55; lectr. internat. econs. Fisher Coll., 1954-55, 60-63; Mem. Gov. Com. Refugees, 1961—; chmn. trustees Nat. Service Secretariat, 1966—; rep. Internat. Council for Sci. Mgmt. to ECOSOC, 1967—; mem. internat. exec. programs Ind. U. Grad. Sch. Bus., 1967—; mem. ednl. council Mass. Inst. Tech., 1974—. Author: Estimation of Managerial and Technical Personnel Requirements in the Pulp and Paper Industry, 1968; Contbr. to: Training Managers: The International Guide, 1969, University Involvement in Industrial Development, 1979. Treas. New Eng. Opera Theatre, 1958-63; mem. com. Friends of N.Y. Philharmonic, 1967—; corporate mem. Vols. for Internat. Tech. Assistance, 1967—. Served with USNR, 1942-46. Mem. Acad. of Mgmt. Republican. Lutheran. Clubs: M.I.T. Alumni (Washington); Staff (U. Ife). Home: 439 15th St NE Washington DC 20002

EAMES, HERBERT HOWELL, JR., corp. exec.; b. Keene, N.H., Aug. 2, 1934; s. Herbert Howell and Mary Caroline (Shaffer) E.; m. Pamela Hodgdon Phillips, Aug. 16, 1958; children—Elisabeth Mary, Stephen David, Peter Howell. Grad., Valley Forge Mil. Acad., 1953; B.A., Tufts U., 1961; M.B.A., St. John's U., 1971. Budget analyst Nestle Co., Inc., White Plains, N.Y., 1960-64; financial analyst McCall Corp., 1964-65; controller McCall Information Service Co., Dayton, Ohio, 1965-68; asst. controller Bristol-Myers Co., N.Y.C., 1968-70, controller, 1970-72, v.p. systems and controls, 1972-77; v.p., controller F.W. Woolworth Co., N.Y.C., 1977-80; exec. v.p. JWT Group, Inc., 1980—; dir. Firemen's Fund, Am. Life Ins. Co. N.Y. Bd. bus. advisers Empire State Found. Liberal Arts Colls. Served with USMC, 1953-57. Mem. Financial Execs. Inst., Controllers Inst. Am., Nat. Assn. Accountants, Zeta Psi.

EAMES, RAY, designer; b. Sacramento; d. Alexander Kaiser and Edna Mary (Evans) Burr; m. Charles Eames, June 20, 1941; 1 dau., Lucia Eames Demetrios. Student of painting, with Hans Hofmann, 1933-39; M.A. hon., May F. Bennett Sch., 1960, D.F.A., Art Ctr. Coll. Design, 1977, U. Cin., 1978. Designer (with Charles Eames), 1941-78; free-lance designer, Venice, Calif., 1978—; co-founder basic design course for beginning architecture, U. Calif.-Berkeley, 1953; contbr. to books, exhbns.,furniture, films. Co-recipient 1st One Man Shoe of Furniture Mus. Modern Art, 1946, First Ann. Kaufmann Internat. Design Award, 1960, Emmy award, 1960, First Domus Obelisk award, 1963. Mem. Am. Abstract Artists (founding), Alliance Graphique Internationale, Am. Council for Arts in Edn. (arts, and Ams. panel 1975—), Acad. Motion Picture Arts and Scis., AIA (hon. assoc. So. Calif. chpt.). Office: 901 Washington Blvd Venice CA 90291

EAMES, WILMER BALLOU, dental educator; b. Kansas City, Mo., May 8, 1914; s. Prescott W. and Alice (Ballou) E.; m. Elma Elaine Bitter, July 2, 1939; children: Douglas, Alice Eames Lillian. D.D.S., K.C.-Western Dental Coll., Kansas City, Mo., 1939. Practice dentistry, Grand Junction, Colo., 1939-41, Denver, 1945-47, Glenwood Springs, Colo., 1947-61; prof. operative dentistry Northwestern U. Dental Sch., 1961-67, asso. dean, 1964-67; prof. operative dentistry, dir. div. applied dental materials Emory U. Sch. Dentistry, 1967-79, prof. emeritus, 1979—; vis. prof. U. Colo., 1980—; lectr. dental materials; research and publs. Served to maj., Dental Corps, USAAF, 1941-45. Recipient Albert L. Borish award Acad. Gen. Dentistry, 1983, Outstanding Contbns. award Colo. Dental Assn., 1982, Alumnus of Yr. award U. Mo.-Kansas City, 1983, Hinman Disting. Service medallion City of Atlanta, 1981, Jerome and Dorothy Schweitzer Research award Greater N.Y. Acad. Prosthodontics, 1979; named Dentist of Yr., Colo. Acad. Gen. Dentistry, 1982; others. Fellow Am., Internat. colls. dentists, Ga. Dental Assn.; mem. Internat. Assn. Dental Research, ADA, Am. Acad. Restorative Dentistry, Acad. Operative Dentistry (Hollenback Meml. prize 1979), Sigma Xi, Omicron Kappa Upsilon. Developed technique for preparation of 1 1 ratio dental amalgam. Home: Apt 501 14390 E Marina Dr Aurora CO 80014 *If the premise for an idea or a plan is reasonable and sound, unrelenting determination will almost certainly assure the unbounded fulfillment of any objective.*

EANES, JOSEPH CABEL, JR., surety company executive; b. Long Island, N.Y., Mar. 2, 1935; s. Joseph Cabel and Mae (McCormick) E.; m. Carolyn Williams, Sept. 3, 1955; children—Deborah L., J.C. Eanes, III, Rebekah L. B.S., U. Richmond, 1958. Spl. agt. Fidelity and Deposit Co. of Md., Richmond, 1958-62, in charge, 1962-67, asst. mgr. Richmond br., 1967-71, exec. asst. home office, 1971-73, v.p. mktg. and adminstrn., 1973-78, sr. v.p. underwriting, claims, reinsurance, legal and trade assns., 1978-79, exec. v.p., 1979-81, pres., chief operating officer, 1981—, also dir. Mem. Surety Assn. Am. (mem. exec. com.), Am. Ins. Assn. (mem. fidelity and surety com.). Methodist. Clubs: Center (Balt.); Maryland. Home: 8 Galetree Ct Cockeysville MD 21030 Office: 611 Fidelity Bldg Baltimore MD 21201

EAPEN, THOMAS, internist, gastroenterologist, educator; b. Quilon, Kerala, India, Aug. 27, 1939; came to U.S., 1973; s. Koithodathil and Kochettu Mary (Kuruvilla) E.; m. Anne Mathew, July 4, 1966; 1 son, Rohan. M.B.B.S., Christian Med. Coll., Vellore, India, 1963; M.D., Kerala U., India, 1966. Diplomate: Am. Bd. Internal Medicine. Asst. prof. medicine Stanley Med. Coll., Madras, India, 1966-70; lectr. in medicine (part-time) U. Adelaide (South Australia), 1970-73; asst. prof. medicine N.Y. Med. Coll., N.Y.C., 1973-77, assoc. prof., 1977-79; prof. medicine Quillen-Dishner Coll. Medicine/East Tenn. State U., Johnson City, 1979—, chief div. gastroenterology, 1979—. Contbr. articles to med. jours. Fellow ACP, Am. Coll. Gastroenterology, Royal Australasian Coll. Physician, Royal Coll. Physicians Can. Home: 709 Wilmar St Johnson City TN 37601 Office: Div Gastroenterology Quilen-Dishner Coll Medicine Johnson City TN 37614

EARDLEY, RICHARD ROY, mayor of Boise (Idaho); b. Denver, Dec. 23, 1928; s. Walter B. and Pearl (Wessels) E.; m. Patricia L. Engum, May 28, 1950; children: Rick, Randall, Ronald. Student, Eastern Oreg. Coll., 1947-48. Reporter Democrat Herald, Baker, Oreg., 1951-52; news dir. Sta. KBKR, Baker, 1952-55; sports editor Idaho Statesman, Boise, 1955-59; news dir. Sta. KBOI-Radio-TV, Boise, 1959-73; mem. Boise City Council, 1970-74; mayor, City of Boise, 1974—. Office: Office of Mayor City Hall PO Box 500 Boise ID 83702 *

EARHART, EILEEN MAGIE, educator; b. Hamilton, Ohio, Oct. 21, 1928; d. Andrew J. and Martha (Waldorf) Magie; m. Paul G. Earhart; children: Anthony G., Bruce P., Daniel T. B.S., Miami U., Oxford, Ohio, 1950; M.A. in Adminstrn. and Ednl. Services, Mich. State U., 1962; Ph.D. in Edn., Mich. State U., 1969; H.H.D. (hon.), Miami U., Oxford, Ohio, 1980. Tchr. home econs. W. Alexandria (Ohio) Schs., 1950-51; elementary tchr. Waterford Twp. Schs., Pontiac, Mich., 1958-65, reading specialist, 1965-67; prof., chmn. family and child ecology dept. Mich. State U., East Lansing, 1968—. Author: Attention and Classification Training Curriculum; contbr. chpts. to profl. books. Mem. adv. bd. Lansing Com. on Children's TV; bd. dirs. Women's Resource Center, Grand Rapids, Mich. Mem. Soc. Research in Child Devel., AAUW, Nat. Assn. Edn. Young Children, Assn. Childhood Edn. Internat., Am. Home Econs. Assn., Mich. Home Econs. Assn. (pres. 1980-82), Am. Ednl. Research Assn., Internat. Reading Assn., Assn. Supervision and Curriculum Devel., Am. Vocat. Assn., Phi Kappa Phi, Omicron Nu, Delta Kappa Gamma. Home: 2030 Tamarack Dr Okemos MI 48864 Office: Family and Child Ecology Dept Coll Human Ecology Michigan State U East Lansing MI 48824

EARL, ANTHONY SCULLY, governor of Wisconsin; b. Lansing, Mich., Apr. 12, 1936; s. Russell K. and Ethlynne Julia (Scully) E.; m. Sheila Rose Coyle, Aug. 11, 1962; children: Julia, Anne, Mary, Catherine. B.S., Mich. State U.; J.D., U. Chgo. Bar: Wis., Minn. Asst. dist. atty. Marathon Co., Wausau, Wis., 1965-66; city atty. City of Wausau, 1966-69; mem. Wis. Assembly, Madison, 1969-74; mem. firm Crooks, Low & Earl, 1969-74; sec. Wis. Dept. Adminstrn., Madison, 1974-75, Dept. Nat. Resources, 1975-80; v.p. firm Foley & Lardner, Madison, 1980-82; gov. State of Wis., Madison, 1983—. Served as lt. USN, 1962-65. Democrat. Roman Catholic. Office: State Capitol PO Box 7863 Madison WI 53707

EARL, GERALD ERICKSON, oil co. exec.; b. Logan, Utah, Mar. 10, 1930; s. Ernest G. and Vernetta (Erickson) E.; m. JoAn Williamson, Aug. 6, 1976; children—Brian, Michael; stepchildren—Mark Goodnight, John Goodnight, Matthew Goodnight. B.S. in Petroleum Refining Engring, U. Tulsa, 1959. With Universal Oil Products Co., 1959-68; tech. adviser Sunray-DX Oil Co., Tulsa, 1968-70; managerial positions Champlin Petroleum Co., Ft. Worth and Houston, 1970-78; gen. mgr. mfg. Commonwealth Oil Refining, Ponce, P.R., 1978-79, v.p. mfg., 1979-81, sr. v.p., 1981—; v.p., dir. Pipelines P.R. Served with USN, 1948-52. Mem. Am. Petroleum Inst., Am. Inst. Chem. Engrs. Republican. Mormon. Address: 8626 Tesoro Dr San Antonio TX 78217

EARL, LEWIS HAROLD, consulting economist, lawyer; b. Guthrie, Tex., Dec. 17, 1918; s. Henry W. and Ruth (O'Neal) E.; m. Patricia Miller, Mar. 5, 1943 (dec. Jan. 1973); children: William Lee, Patricia Lewise, Robert Charles, James Michael; m. Meade Randolph Loomis, July 1, 1977 (div. May 1979); m. Maxine Durrett Marks, Jan. 31, 1981. B.A., Tex. Technol. Coll., 1939; student, U. Tex., 1939-40, Am. U., 1941-42; J.D., Georgetown U., 1950. Bar: D.C. 1950, U.S. Supreme Ct. 1972, Tex. 1983. With Bur. Labor Statistics, Dept. Labor, 1940-42, 46-54; industry, commodity economist NPA Dept. Commerce, 1951-53; productivity specialist, economist, program analyst, asst. program officer U.S. Tech. Cooperation Program in Brazil, 1953-57, program officer, Argentina, 1957-59, El Salvador, 1959-61; internat. relations officer AID, Washington, 1961-63; chief internat. research Office Manpower Automation and Tng., U.S. Dept. Labor, Washington, 1963-65; chief Fgn. manpower program staff Office Manpower Policy, Evaluation and Research, Dept. Labor, 1965-70; U.S. del. 8th meeting Am. mem. states ILO, 1966, U.S. del. to chem. industries com., 1969; tech. dir. Seminar for Ministry Labor Tng. Coordinators, OAS, Mexico City, Mexico, 1970; asst. dir. for program devel. for Human Resources U. Houston, 1970-75; manpower planning officer Gulf Coast CAMPS Secretariat, Mayor's Office, City of Houston, 1970-74; cons. Tex. Gov.'s Office Policy Coordination, Austin, 1974; asso. dir. human resources program, instr. econs. U. Mo.-Columbia, 1975-78; expert cons. Human Resources Devel., Bur. Internat. Labor Affairs, U.S. Dept. Labor and UN Devel. Program for Egypt, 1978-80; staff adv. Am. Productivity Center, Houston, 1980—; expert cons. UN Indsl. Devel. Orgn., Cairo, Egypt, 1981—; lectr. Coll. Bus. Adminstrn. Tex. Tech U., 1982-83. Served as lt. USNR, 1942-46. Mem. Acad. Polit. Sci., Am. Acad. Polit. and Social Soc., Soc. for Internat. Devel., Nat. Planning Assn., Am. Soc. for Tng. and Devel., Nat. Economist Club, Houston Personnel Assn., Indsl. Research Assn., Am. Statis. Assn., Alpha Chi, Omicron Delta Epsilon, Pi Sigma Alpha., Sigma Iota Epsilon. Home: 601 W Main St Post TX 79356 Office: 1929 Stoney Brook Houston TX 77063 *I believe that individuals will make the right decisions if they have full and adequate information and facts, and therefore, I have sought to find the truth that will make men free.*

EARLE, ARTHUR PERCIVAL, textile executive; b. Montreal, Que., Can., Apr. 23, 1922; s. Arthur Percival and Bernadette (Gosselin) E.; m. Muriel Elizabeth Vining, June 1, 1946; children: Arthur Percival, Richard John, Janet Elizabeth. B.E.E., McGill U., Montreal, 1949; M.M.P., Harvard U., 1957. Registered profl. engr., Que., Ont. With Shawinigan Water & Power Co., 1949-63, asst. mgr. prodn. and plant, 1949-63; with Dominion Textile Inc., Montreal, 1963—, group v.p., then group v.p. subs., 1970-78, sr. v.p. ops. services, 1978—; past pres. Lana Knit Ltd., Fireside Fabrics Ltd., Fiber-World Ltd., Elpee Yarns Ltd., Jaro Ltd., Esmond Mills Ltd.; past chmn. Penmans Ltd.; bd. dirs. Ecole de Technologie Superieure, U. Que., 1978—; pres. Montreal Bd. Trade, 1980-81. Served with RCAF, 1941-45. Mem. IEEE (past sect. chmn.), Order Engrs. Que., Assn. Profl. Engrs. Ont., Engring. Inst. Can., Am. Textile Managerial Engring. Soc., Que. C. of C. (pres. 1983-84). Conservative. Anglican. Clubs: Royal Montreal Golf, Montreal Amateur Athletic Assn., Thistle Curling (pres. 1974-75), Mt. Stephen). Office: 1950 Sherbrooke St W Montreal PQ H3H 1E7 Canada

EARLE, CLIFFORD JOHN, JR., mathematician; b. Racine, Wis., Nov. 3, 1935; s. Clifford John and Anne Elizabeth (Griffith) E.; m. Elizabeth Joan Deutsch, Dec. 27, 1960; children—Rebecca Ann, Susan Deborah. B.A., Swarthmore Coll., 1957; M.A., Harvard U., 1958, Ph.D., 1962. Instr. Harvard U., 1962-63, vis. lectr., 1968-69; mem. Inst. for Advanced Study, Princeton, N.J., 1963-65, 81; asst. prof. Cornell U., Ithaca, N.Y., 1965-66, asso. prof., 1966-69, prof., 1969—, chmn. dept. math., 1976-79; vis. prof. U. Warwick, 1967; vis. lectr. Inst. Mittag-Leffler, 1972. Asso. editor: Duke Math. Jour, 1973-79; Contbr. articles to math. research jours. John Simon Guggenheim Meml. fellow, 1974-75. Mem. Am. Math. Soc. Home: 314 Elmwood Ave Ithaca NY 14850 Office: Dept Mathematics Cornell Univ Ithaca NY 14853

EARLE, DAVID PRINCE, JR., educator, physician; b. Englewood, N.J., May 23, 1910; s. David Prince and Paula (Benner) E.; m. Elizabeth Temple Ingraham, June 27, 1936; children—David Prince III, Paul Winthrop, Kevin Campbell, Charles Benner. A.B., Princeton, 1933; M.D., Columbia, 1937, Sc.D. in Medicine, 1942. Intern St. Luke's Hosp., N.Y.C., 1937-39; resident Columbia Univ. Research Service, Goldwater Meml. Hosp., N.Y.C., 1939-41; research asso. N.Y. U. Service, 1939-41; dir. N.Y. U. Research Service, 1947-48; asst. prof. medicine, then asso. prof. N.Y. U. Coll. Medicine, 1943-54; prof. medicine Northwestern U. Med. Sch., 1954-78, emeritus, 1978—, chmn. dept., 1965-73; chmn. dept. research Chgo. Wesley Meml. Hosp., 1960-69, attending physician, 1969-73, Bellevue Hosp., N.Y.C., 1948-54, Passavant Meml. Hosp., Chgo., 1954-73, Northwestern Meml. Hosp., 1973-78, sr. attending physician, 1978—; Sec. clin. testing panel, bd. coordination antimalarial studies NRC, 1943-45; mem. medicine test com. Nat. Bd. Med. Examiners, 1956-60, chmn., 1960; mem. cardiovascular study sect. NIH, 1958-61, mem. diabetes and metabolism tng. com., 1964-67, chmn., 1966-67, chmn. urology tng. com., 1967-68, mem. nat. adv. arthritis and metabolic diseases council, 1970-73, mem. artificial kidney and chronic uremia rev. com., 1970-75; mem. ad hoc group clin. and preclin. pharmacology Walter Reed Army Inst. Research, 1967-76, chmn., 1976; mem. sci. adv. bd. Nat. Kidney Found., 1965-68, Ill Kidney Found., 1966—, chmn., 1969-70, chmn. nat. med. adv. council, 1969-70; mem. malaria commn. Armed Forces Epidemiological Bd., 1966-73; chmn. Internat. Com. Nomenclature and Nosology of Renal Disease. Author articles, chpts. in books in field.; Editor: Jour. Chronic Diseases, 1966-81; editorial bd.: Clin. Pharmacology and Therapeutics, 1967-73; adv. bd.:

Internat. Dictionary Medicine and Biology, 1976—; Editorial bd.: Cardiovascular Medicine, 1976-79. Fellow A.A.A.S., A.C.P. (master, rep. residency rev. com. internal medicine 1961-65); mem. Am. Heart Assn. (dir. 1962-65, chmn. council circulation 1963-65), Ill. Heart Assn., Chgo. Heart Assn. (dir.) (1966-69), Central Soc. Clin. Research (pres. 1964-65), Am. Soc. Clin. Investigation (editorial com. 1952-57), Assn. Am. Physicians, Am. Physiol. Soc., Am. Clin. and Climatological Assn. (councilor 1970-73, pres. 1978), Soc. Exptl. Biology and Medicine, A.M.A., Chgo. Soc. Internal Medicine (pres. 1967-68), Am. Soc. Nephrology (founding mem.), Internat. Soc. Nephrology (exec. com. 1975—), Assn. Former Chairmen of Medicine (pres. 1980), Alpha Omega Alpha. Club: Indian Hill (Winnetka, Ill.). Home: 764 Locust Winnetka IL 60093 Office: 303 E Chicago Ave Chicago IL 60611

EARLE, HARRY WOODWARD, printing company executive; b. Norwalk, Conn., June 17, 1924; s. Harry W. and Rose Lillian (Agnew) E.; m. Barbara Aymar, Dec. 14, 1944; children: David, Penrhyn, John, Gordon, Barbara. B.A., Williams Coll., 1946. Vice-pres. mktg. McCall Printing Co., McCall Corp., N.Y.C., 1946-66; group v.p. consumer products div. Arcata Nat. Corp., Menlo Park, Calif., 1966-74; v.p. W.A. Krueger Co., N.Y.C., 1979—; chmn. bd., pres., chief exec. officer George Banta Co., Menasha, Wis., 1976—; dir. Nash Engring. Co., Norwalk, Conn., Menasha Corp., Wis., Security Fin. Services, Sheboygan, Wis. Bd. selectman, Darien, Conn., 1949-62, chmn. bd. fin., 1962-66, mem. police commn., 1976-78. Served with USAAF, 1942-45. Decorated D.F.C., 3 air medals. Home: 1071 Brighton Dr Menasha WI 54952 Office: Curtis Reed Plaza Menasha WI 54952

EARLE, KENNETH MARTIN, neuropathologist; b. Jacksonville, Tex., Dec. 29, 1919; s. Allen and Flora Lois (Martin) E.; m. Mary Ellen Sammons, Mar. 12, 1944; children: Mary, Katherine, Thomas Hugh. B.A., Rice U., 1942; M.D., U. Tex., 1945; M.Sc., McGill U., 1951. Diplomate: Am. Bd. Pathology (cons. for neuropathology 1965-76); Certified Med. Technologist, 1940; Certified Radiol. Technician, 1941. Rotating intern John Sealy Hosp., 1945-46; resident gen. surgery U.S. Naval Hosp., San Diego, 1947-48; fellow neuroanatomy and neuropathology Montreal Neurol. Inst., McGill U., 1949-51; fellow pathology Pathol. Inst., 1951-52; instr. pathology U. Calif. Sch. Medicine, Los Angeles; also sr. resident tng. VA Hosp., Los Angeles and VA Hosp., Long Beach, Calif., 1952-53; mem. faculty U. Tex. Sch. Medicine, 1953-62, prof. pathology, 1960-62, dean medicine, 1959-62; chief neuropathology Armed Forces Inst. Pathology, Washington, 1962-74, 77-79; assoc. chmn. Center for Advanced Pathology; and chmn. neuropathology dept., 1974-76, 78-79; exec. dir. Am. Registry of Pathology, Inc., 1980-82; asst. exec. for medical affairs Our Lady of Lourdes Regional Med. Ctr., Lafayette, La., 1983—; prof., chmn. dept. pathology Uniformed Services U. of Health Scis., Bethesda, 1976-77, acting chmn., 1977-79; professorial lectr. George Washington U., 1962—; clin. prof. pathology U. Tex. Med. Br., also Georgetown U., 1973-76. Contbr. articles to profl. jours. Served to lt. (j.g.) M.C. USNR, 1943-45, 46-49. Recipient Meritorious Civilian Service award Dept. Army, 1967, also Exceptional Civilian Service award, 1968. Mem. Am. Assn. Pathologists, Washington Soc. Pathologists, Am. Assn. Neuropathologists (pres. 1966-67), Internat. Soc. Neuropathology (project sec. 1970-78, pres. VIII internat. congress), Internat. Acad. Pathology (sec.-gen. 1976 internat. congress), Internat. Acad. Pathologists (internat. sec. 1978—, v.p. U.S.-Can. div. 1978-79, pres.-elect 1979-80, pres. 1980-81), alumni assns. Rice Inst., U. Tex. Sch. Medicine, Alpha Omega Alpha. Presbyterian. Club: Masons (32 deg.). Office: Our Lady of Lourdes Regional Med. Ctr. Lafayette LA 70502

EARLE, RALPH, III, lawyer; b. Byrn Mawr, Pa., Sept. 26, 1928; s. George Howard and Huberta (Potter) E.; m. Eleanor Forbes Owens, Nov. 29, 1952; children: Eleanor F., Ralph, Duncan O., Amanda W., Caroline E. A.B., Harvard U., 1950, LL.B., 1955. Bar: Mass. 1955, Pa. 1957, D.C. 1980. Law clk. U.S. Dist. Ct., 1955-56; assoc., then ptnr. Morgan, Lewis Bockius, Phila., 1956-68, 72-73; prin. dep. asst. sec. internat. security affairs U.S. Dept. Def., Washington, 1968-69; def. advisor U.S. mission to NATO, 1969-72; ACDA rep. to SALT, 1973-77, ambassdor, alt. chmn. U.S. del, 1977-78, chmn., 1978-80, spl. rep. for arms control and disarmament negotiations, 1977-80; ptnr. Earle and Greene & Co., Stamford, Conn., 1982-83, Baker & Daniels, Washington, 1983—; dir. ACDA, 1980-81, Provident Nat. Bank, Phila. Bd. mgrs. Phila. Zool. Soc.; mem. Phila. Com. of Seventy, 1965-68, chmn. mcpl. affairs subcom., 1967; bd. mgrs. Overbrook Sch. Blind, Pa., 1964-69; pres., bd. dirs. Easter Seal Soc., Phila., 1966-68. Served with AUS, 1950-52. Mem. Am. Law Inst. Clubs: Philadelphia; Metropolitan (Washington); Harvard (Phila.) (pres. 1967-68). Office: Baker & Daniels 1920 N St NW Suite 600 Washington DC 20036

EARLE, RICHARD MILLAR, advertising agency executive; b. Cohasset, Mass., Mar. 7, 1932; s. Roland Deming and Helen Frances (Millar) E.; m. Patricia Norah Kane, Mar. 17, 1960; children: Melissa, Carol. B.A., Amherst Coll., 1953. Producer, dir. Sta. WBZ-TV, Boston, 1957-59; producer Carousel Theatre, Framingham, Mass., 1959-61; TV producer Benton & Bowles, Inc., N.Y.C., 1961-63, Doyle, Dane Bernbach, 1963-65; v.p., creative supr. Grey Advt., N.Y.C., 1965-73; v.p., dir. creative services Marsteller, Inc., N.Y.C., 1973-75; v.p., assoc. creative dir. Rumrill-Hoyt, Inc., N.Y.C., 1975-78; sr. v.p., creative dir. Compton Advt., Inc., N.Y.C., 1978—, also dir. Contbr. articles on drug abuse to profl. jours. Pres. Nat. Coordinating Council on Drug Edn., Washington, 1972-73, chmn., Washington, 1973-74. Served to lt. USNR, 1954-57. Recipient Lion D'Or Internat. Festival Advt. Film, 1970. Home: 38 W 95th St New York NY 10025 Office: Compton Advt Inc 625 Madison Ave New York NY 10022

EARLE, VICTOR MONTAGNE, III, lawyer; b. N.Y.C., June 13, 1933; s. Victor Montagne and Marian Jeanette (Litonius) E.; m. Lois MacKennan, Dec. 28, 1955 (div. Jan. 1980); children: Jane Stewart, Susan Elizabeth, Anne McCallum. A.B., Williams Coll., 1954; LL.B., Columbia U., 1959. Bar: N.Y. 1960, U.S. Supreme Ct. 1963. Law clk. to Hon. Leonard P. Moore U.S. Ct. Appeals 2d Circuit, 1959-60; assoc. firm Cravath, Swaine & Moore, N.Y.C., 1960-68; gen. counsel Peat, Marwick, Mitchell & Co., N.Y.C., 1968—, Peat, Marwick Internat., 1978—; lectr. constl. and corp. law issues, U.S. and abroad. Contbr. articles to profl. jours. and popular mags. Served with U.S. Army, 1954-56. Mem. Am. Bar Assn., N.Y. State Bar Assn., Internat. Bar Assn., Assn. Bar City N.Y., Am. Law Inst., Lawyers Com. Civil Rights under Law (trustee), Legal Aid Soc. (dir.), Fund for Modern Cts. (dir.). Office: 345 Park Ave New York NY 10154

EARLE, WILLIAM ALEXANDER, II, philosopher; b. Saginaw, Mich., Feb. 18, 1919; s. James Hudson and Elsie (Goeschel) E. B.A., U. Chgo., 1941, Ph.D., 1951; Docteur de l'Universite, U. Aix-Marseilles, France, 1948. Mem. faculty Northwestern U., 1948—, prof. philosophy, 1961—; vis. lectr. Yale U., 1956, Harvard U., 1959. Author: Objectivity, 1956, Autobiographical Consciousness, 1972, Public Sorrows and Private Pleasures, 1976, Mystical Reason, 1981, Evanescence, 1984; co-author: Christianity and Existentialism, 1963. Served to 1st lt. AUS, 1941-45. Rockefeller fellow, 1947-48; Carnegie grantee, 1965-66. Mem. Am. Philos. Soc., Soc. Phenomenology and Existential Philosophy, Hegel Soc., Am. Aesthetics Soc., Am. Metaphys. Soc. Home: 1237 Jarvis Ave Chicago IL 60626 Office: 1818 Hinman Ave Evanston IL 60201

EARLES, WILLIAM EUGENE, corporation executive; b. New Orleans, May 9, 1928; s. John Henry and Beatrice (Hughes) E.; m. Joan Ann Sturdivant, Aug. 14, 1954 (div. 1976); children: William H., Glenn A., Janet L.; m. Kathleen Zoie Daigle, Feb. 17, 1976; 1 stepson, Jerry J. Rock III. Student, Southeastern La. Coll., 1948-49, Southwestern La. Inst., 1949-51. Draftsman Austin Co., Freeport, Tex., 1951-52, J.F. Pritchard & Co., New Orleans, 1952-54; sr. v.p. McDermott, Inc., New Orleans, 1954—, dir., 1975-80. Served with USMC, 1946-47. Mem. Am. Welding Soc. (dir., Morgan City chpt.), Am. Soc. Mill. Engrs. (adv. bd. Atchalafaya chpt. 1977-81), Am. Petroleum Inst., Morgan City C. of C. (dir. 1980-81). Clubs: Morgan City Petroleum (pres. 1975-76, dir. 1977-81. Lodge: Lions (past dir.). Home: 2 Chateau Margaux Ct Kenner LA 70065 Office: McDermott Inc PO Box 60035 New Orleans LA 60035

EARLEY, ERNEST BENTON, educator, plant physiologist; b. Orangesburg, S.C., Dec. 19, 1906; s. Thomas Edward and Gussie Hydrick (Bair) E.; m. Liberty Mundo, Aug. 17, 1931; children—Carol Ann (Mrs. Edward L. Hanson), Thomas David. B.S. in Agronomy, Clemson U., 1928; M.S., Va. Poly. Inst., 1929; Ph.D., U. Ill., 1941. Asst. agronomy U. Ill. at Urbana, 1929-37; asst. agronomist Regional Soybean Lab., Bur. Plant Industries, Soils and Agrl. Engring., Dept. Agr., 1937-44; mem. faculty U. Ill. at Urbana, 1944—, prof. agronomy, 1955-75, prof. emeritus, 1975—. Active local Boy Scouts Am. Mem. Am. Soc. Agronomy, Am. Soc. Plant Physiologists, Sigma Xi, Phi Sigma, Gamma Sigma Delta. Presbyn. Home: 1102 S Garfield St Urbana IL 61801

EARLEY, JAMES STAINFORTH, educator, economist; b. Valley City, N.D., Oct. 16, 1908; s. James Jerome and May (Macgowan) E.; m. Emily Hornblower, June 19, 1939; children—Dorothy, Susan and Jerome (twins); m. Elizabeth Blankinship Pohle, Apr. 22, 1961. A.B., Antioch Coll., 1932; M.A., U. Wis., 1934, Ph.D., 1939; student, U. London, Eng., 1936-37. Mem. faculty U. Wis., 1937-67, prof. econs., 1947-67, chmn. dept., 1962-65; chmn. dept. econs. U. Calif. at Riverside, 1967-70, prof. econs., 1967—, dean, 1970-73, acting dean, 1981-82; vis. prof. Yale, 1953-54, U. Hawaii, 1963, Athens Grad. Sch. Econs., U. Manchester, 1966, U. Philippines, 1965; Economist, then sr. economist with Nat. Def. Adv. Commn., OPA, 1940-45; adviser Brit. Commonwealth affairs State Dept., 1945; mem. Com. Internat. Exchange Persons, 1953-57, Univs.-Nat. Bur. Com. Econ. Research, 1951-67; dir. quality credit program Nat. Bur. Econ. Research, 1960-76. Author: British Wartime Price Administration, 2d edit. 1944, Economic Theory in Review, 1950, Pricing for Profit and Growth, 2d edit, 1962, Home Mortgage Delinquency and Foreclosure, 1970, also articles. Trustee Antioch Coll., 1949-52. Ford Found. fellow, 1957-60. Mem. Am. Econ. Assn., Midwest Econ. Assn. (1st v.p. 1955-56), Western Econ. Assn., Am. Finance Assn., Royal Econ. Soc. Home: 393 Two Trees Rd Riverside CA 92507 Office: Univ of Calif-Riverside Riverside CA 92521

EARLEY, JEROME ANTHONY, manufacturing company executive; b. Pitts., Feb. 26, 1924; Vincent M. and Hilda Maria (O'Neill) E.; m. Mary Jane Bell, Sept. 1, 1951; children: Daniel, Margaret, Robert, Thomas, Richard. B.S. in Bus. Adminstrn, U. Pitts., 1948, LL.B., 1950. Bar: Pa. bar 1950. Gen. atty. to v.p. corp. devel. Rockwell Mfg. Co., Pitts., 1953-73, staff v.p. strategic planning, 1973-75, staff v.p. corp. devel., 1975; v.p. corp. devel. Rockwell Internat., 1975—; dir. Babcock Lumber Co., Airway Industries. Bd. dirs. Greater Pitts. Guild for Blind, Three Rivers Tng. Orch. Assn.; trustee Seton Hill Coll., Greensburg, Pa. Mem. Am. Bar Assn., Allegheny County Bar Assn. Office: Rockwell Internat 600 Grant St Pittsburgh PA 15219

EARLL, JERRY MILLER, internist, educator; b. Hawarden, Iowa, Aug. 15, 1928; s. Harry Ezra and Magdalene Anna (Miller) E.; m. Faith Anne Allbaugh, Sept. 13, 1956; children: Leslie Anne, Nikki Lee, Holly Magdalene. B.S., U. Nebr., 1950; M.D., U. Iowa, 1958; postgrad., U. Calif., 1965-66. Diplomate: Am. Bd. Internal Medicine, Am. Bd. Endocrinology, Am. Bd. Nuclear Medicine. Commd. 2d lt. U.S. Army, 1951, advanced through grades to col., 1972; intern Letterman Gen. Hosp., San Francisco, 1958, resident in internal medicine, 1959-62; chief endocrinology and metabolism William Beaumont Gen. Hosp., El Paso, 1963-69, Tripler Gen. Hosp., Honolulu, 1965-69, Walter Reed Army Inst. Research and Walter Reed Army Hosp., Washington, 1969-76; chief dept. medicine Walter Reed Army Hosp., 1976—; cons. endocrinology Office Surgeon Gen.; asso. prof. medicine U. Hawaii, 1967-69; clin. prof. medicine Georgetown U., 1970-79; prof. medicine, vice chmn. dept. medicine Uniformed Services Univ. Health Scis., Washington, 1977-79; prof. and chief Div. Medicine, Georgetown U. and Hosp., Washington, 1979—. Decorated Legion of Merit, Army Commendation medal, Meritorious Service medal. Fellow ACP; mem. Am. Fedn. Clin. Research, Am. Diabetes Assn., Endocrine Soc., N.Y. Diabetes Assn., Assn. Mil. Surgeons, Nat. Acad. Sci. Research and publs. on pituitary and thyroid physiology. Home: 8529 Brickyard Rd Potomac MD 20854 Office: Georgetown U Hosp 3800 Reservoir Rd NW Washington DC 20007

EARLY, JACK DENT, trade association executive; b. Florence, S.C., Feb. 28, 1929; s. Thomas Patrick and Corean Elsie (Dent) E.; m. Annie Wood, Jan. 30, 1954; children: Sharon K., Jack Dent, David E. B.S., Clemson U., 1953, M.S., 1954; Ph.D., N.C. State U., 1958. Research entomologist Monsanto Co., St. Louis, 1958-68, mgr. govt. relations, Washington, 1968-75; v.p., dir. regulatory affairs Nat. Agrl. Chems. Assn., Washington, 1975-76, pres., 1976—. Served to 2d lt. U.S. Army, 1957-58. Mem. Am. Soc. Assn. Execs. Clubs: Univ., Capitol Hill (Washington). Office: Nat Agrl Chems Assn 1155 15th St NW Washington DC 20005

EARLY, JACK JONES, insurance company executive; b. Corbin, Ky., Apr. 12, 1925; s. Joseph M. and Lela (Jones) E.; m. Nancye Bruce Whaley, June 1, 1952; children: Lela Katherine, Judith Ann, Laura Hattie. A.B., Union Coll., Barbourville, Ky., 1948; M.A., U. Ky., 1953, Ed.D. (So. scholar 1955-56), 1956; B.D., Coll. of Bible, Lexington, Ky., 1956; D.D., Wesley Coll., Grand Forks, N.D., 1961; LL.D., Parsons Coll., 1962, Iowa Wesleyan Coll., 1972; Litt.D., Dakota Wesleyan U., 1969; L.H.D., Union Coll., Barbourville, Ky., 1979; D.Adminstrn., Cumberland Coll., 1981. Ordained to ministry Methodist Ch., 1954; pastor Rockhold Circuit, Ky., 1943-44, Craig's Chapel and Laurel Circuit, London, Ky., 1944-47, Trinity Ch., Oak Ridge, summer 1945, Hindman Ch., Ky., 1947-52; dean of men Hindman Settlement Sch., 1948-51; asso. pastor Park Ch., Lexington, Ky., 1952-54; asst. to pres., dean Athens (Ala.) Coll., 1954- 55; v.p., dean of coll. Iowa Wesleyan Coll., Mt. Pleasant, 1956-58; pres. Dakota Wesleyan U., 1958-69, Pfeiffer Coll., Misenheimer, N.C., 1969-71; exec. dir. Am. Bankers Assn., Washington, 1971-73; pres. Limestone Coll., Gaffney, S.C., 1973-79; exec. dir. edn. Combined Ins. Co. Am., Chgo., 1979-82, v.p., exec. dir. edn. and communications, 1982—; dir. 1st Nat. Bank of Northbrook (Ill.). Active Boy Scouts Am.; mem. pres.' adv. council North Park Coll.; mem. Felician adv. bd. Felician Coll.; mem. Ky. Ho. of Reps., 1952-54; bd. dirs. S.D. Found. Pvt. Colls., S.D. Meth. Found., Ctr. for Citizenship Edn., YMCA, Motivational Inst., Mid-Am. chpt. ARC, 1980—, W. Clement and Jessie V. Stone Found., Northbrook Symphony Orch. Recipient Spoke award Mitchell Jr. C. of C., 1959, Distinguished Service award, 1960; Distinguished Service award S.D. Jr. C. of C., 1960, Gaffney Jaycees, 1979; named Outstanding Former Kentuckian, 1963; Hon. fellow Wroxton Coll., Oxfordshire, Eng. Mem. Jr. C. of C. (dir. 1959), C. of C., Blue Key, Kappa Delta Pi, Phi Delta Kappa (dir. Northwestern U. 1980—), Kappa Phi Kappa, Alpha Psi Omega, Theta Phi, Pi Tau Chi. Republican. Club: Rotary (pres. Northbrook). Home: 2833 Manor Dr Northbrook IL 60062 Office: Combined Ins Co Am 707 Skokie Blvd Northbrook IL 60062

EARLY, JAMES, univ. dean; b. Worcester, Mass., Apr. 19, 1923; s. Edward and Rose Helena (Shea) E.; m. Ann Marie McKenny, Aug. 20, 1949; children—Mark, Edward, Joanne. B.A., Bowdoin Coll., 1947; M.A., Harvard, 1949, Ph.D., 1953. Instr. Yale, New Haven, 1953-57; asst. prof. Vassar Coll., Poughkeepsie, N.Y., 1957-64; asso. prof. So. Methodist U., Dallas, 1964-67, prof., 1968—, chmn. English dept., 1968-71, asso. dean, 1971-74, dean, dean of faculties, 1974—; vis. prof. Stanford, 1967; Pres. S.W. Conf. Humanities Consortium. Author: Romanticism and American Architecture, 1965, The Making of Go Down, Moses, 1972. Served with USAAF, 1943; Served with AUS, 1943-46. Mem. MLA, Coll. Art Assn., ACLU, Tex. Inst. Letters, Colophon. Home: 7015 Lake Shore Dr Dallas TX 75214

EARLY, JAMES MICHAEL, semiconductor company executive; b. Syracuse, N.Y., July 25, 1922; s. Frank J. and Rhoda Gray E.; m. Mary Agnes Valentine, Dec. 28, 1948; children—Mary, Kathleen, Joan Early Farrell, Rhoda Early Alexander, Maureen Early Mathews, James, Margaret Mary. B.S., N.Y. Coll. Forestry, Syracuse, N.Y., 1943; M.S., Ohio State U., 1948, Ph.D., 1951. Instr., research asso. Ohio State U., Columbus, 1946-51; dir. lab. Bell Telephone Labs., Murray Hill, N.J., 1951-64, Allentown, Pa., 1964-69; research and devel. dir. Fairchild Camera and Instrument Corp., Palo Alto, Calif., 1969—. Served with U.S. Army, 1943-45. Fellow IEEE (recipient J.J. Ebers award IEEE Electron Device Soc. 1979); mem. AAAS, Am. Phys. Soc., Electrochem. Soc., Internat. Platform Assn. Roman Catholic. Club: Palo Alto (Calif.) Yacht. Home: 740 Center Dr Palo Alto CA 94301 Office: 4001 Miranda Ave Palo Alto CA 94304

EARLY, JOSEPH DANIEL, congressman; b. Worcester, Mass., Jan. 31, 1933; s. George F. and Mary V. (Lally) E.; m. Marilyn Powers, Apr. 7, 1956; children—Joseph D., Mark, Colleen, Maureen, Lynn, Sean, Eileen, Patrick. B.S. in Bus. Adminstrn, Coll. of Holy Cross, 1955; LL.D., Central New Eng. Coll. Tech., 1975. Tchr. St. John's Prep. Sch., Shrewsbury, Mass., 1962-65; tchr., coach David Prouty High Sch., Spencer, Mass., 1959-63; mem. Mass. Ho. of Reps., 1963-74, vice-chmn., 1973-74; mem. 94th-7th Congresses from 3d Mass. Dist.,; mem. exec. com. Democratic Nat. Congressional Com. Served as ensign USN, 1955-57. Roman Catholic. Office: 2349 Rayburn House Office Bldg Washington DC 20515 also 34 Mechanic St Worcester MA 01608 *

EARLY, WILLIAM JAMES, educational administrator; b. Holyoke, Mass., Mar. 22, 1921; s. John J. and Mary Leah (LaPointe) E.; m. Clare Patricia Milacki, June 8, 1946; children: Patricia, John, Kathleen, Marilyn. B.S., U. Toledo, 1946; M.A., U. Mich., 1949; Ph.D., Mich. State U., 1963. Tchr. social studies and English, Bedford High Sch., Temperance, Mich., 1946-54; supt. schs. Deerfield (Mich.) Pub. Schs., 1954-57, Fenton (Mich.) Area Pub. Schs., 1957-63, Rochester (Mich.) Community Schs., 1963-66, Flint (Mich.) Community Schs., 1966-73, West Irondequoit Central Sch. Dist., Rochester, N.Y., 1973—; Cons. HEW Vocational Dept.; mem. faculty Nat. Acad. for Sch. Execs.; prof. edn. Corpus Christi State U. (Tex.), 1983. Mem. exec. com. Otetiana council Boy Scouts Am.; bd. govs. Mott Inter-Univ. Clin. Preparation Program; mem. nominations bd. Armed Service Acad. Served with USMCR, 1942-45. Decorated Silver Star, Purple Heart. Mem. Nat. Sch. Pub. Relations Assn., Am. Assn. Sch. Adminstrs. (past chmn. fed. policy and legis. com.), Phi Delta Kappa. Clubs: Kiwanis, Crystal Downs Golf (Frankfort, Mich.); Pharoahs Country (Corpus Christi). Home: 113 S Shore Rd Frankfort MI Home: 4600 Ocean Dr Corpus Christi TX 78412 Office: 6300 Ocean Dr Corpus Christi TX 78412

EARNEST, JACK EDWARD, lawyer; b. Dallas, June 18, 1928; s. William Hubert and Uma Mae (Jolly) E.; m. Billie Jo Young, Aug. 1, 1953; children: Laura Ellen, Jack Edward. Student (Founders scholar), Vanderbilt U., 1944-46; B.B.A., So. Methodist U., 1948, LL.B., 1952; postgrad., Stanford U., summer 1967. Bar: N.Y. 1962, Tex. 1952, U.S. Supreme Ct. 1952. With Mobil Oil Corp., 1946-79, v.p. natural gas N. Am., Houston, 1970-76, v.p. natural gas (worldwide), N.Y.C., 1976-79; pres., chief operating officer Transcontinental Gas Pipe Line Corp., Houston, 1979-80; sr. v.p., gen. counsel Tex. Eastern Corp., Houston, 1981-83. Mem. Southeastern Gas Assn., So. Gas Assn. (dir.), Interstate Natural Gas Assn. Am. (dir.), Am. Bar Assn., Natural Gas Supply Assn. (chmn. 1979). Methodist. Clubs: Jesters, Wee Burn Country, Univ. of Houston, Ramada. Office: 4600 Post Oak Pl Houston TX 77027

EARNHARDT, RALPH (DALE EARNHARDT), race acr driver; b. Concord, N.C., Apr. 29; s. Ralph Lee and Martha King (Coleman) E.; m. Teresa Dianne Houston, Nov. 14, 1982; children by previous marriage: Kerry Dale, Kelley King, Ralph Dale. Lic. race car driver Automobile Competition Com. for U.S.; lic. gold driver Nat. Assn. Stock Car Auto Racing. Late model sportsman driver NASCAR, Daytona Beach, Fla., 1974-78, Winston Cup Grand Nat. driver, 1979—. Hon. mem. Chgo. Boys Club, 1981—; dir. youth services Stonewall Jackson Sch., 1979. Named Rookie of Yr. Grand Nat. Rcing, 1979, Winston Cup Grand Nat. Champion, 1980, runner up as Pro Athlete of Yr. in Carolinas Charlotte Athletic Club, 1980. Home and Office: Route 8 Box 463 Mooresville NC 28115 *Positive attitude and steadfast goals.*

EARNHART, DON BRADY, foundation executive; b. Marion, Ind., Aug. 5, 1925; s. Don A. and Bernice (Brady) E.; m. Suzanne Kersting, Aug. 5, 1950; children: Elizabeth Ann, Susan, Stephen. B.S., Ind. U., 1949. C.P.A., Ind. With Ernst & Ernst (C.P.A.s), Indpls., 1949-53; with Inland Container Corp., Indpls., 1953-72, asst. treas., 1957-60, sec., asst. treas., 1961-64, sec.-treas., 1965-67, v.p., treas., 1968-72; adminstrv. trustee, sec.-treas. Krannert Charitable Trust, 1973—; dir. Indpls. Life Ins. Co., First Nat. Bancorp, New Castle, Ind., Pendleton Banking Co., Data Chem. Inc., State Bank of Lapel, Ind.; trustee, pres. Ind.-Fla. Realty Trust. Former mem. adv. bd. Ind. U.-Purdue U. at Indpls.; mem. Community Service Council Met. Indpls.; chmn. edn. study team Ind. Gov.'s Economy Program, 1969; Trustee, chmn. finance com. Ind. Central U.; trustee, past treas. Indpls. Mus. Art; former bd. dirs., treas. Indpls. Met. YMCA; former bd. dirs. Jr. Achievement, Indpls., Indpls. Symphony Orch., Greater Indpls. Progress Com.; bd. dirs. Ind. U. Found. Served with U.S. Mcht. Marine, 1943-46. Designated Sagamore of Wabash by Gov. Ind., 1969. Mem. Ind. Assn. C.P.A.s (past dir., sec.), Indpls. C. of C. (past dir.), Ind. U. Sch. Bus. Alumni Assn. (past exec. council). Club: Columbia (Indpls.). Home: 7275 Lakeside Dr Indianapolis IN 46278

EARTHMAN, WILLIAM FLETCHER, banker; b. Nashville, Jan. 21, 1926; s. William Fletcher and Georgia (Bell) E.; m. Alice Warfield Tyne, June 24, 1950 (div. 1966); children: William Fletcher III, Thomas, Elizabeth, John Christopher Burch; m. Dorothy Ann Bartlett, Sept 7, 1968; 1 dau., Catherine C. Student, Cornell U., 1944-45; B.S., U.S. Mil. Acad., 1949. With Commerce Union Bank, Nashville, 1954—, pres., 1961-72, chmn. exec. com., dir., 1972—, chmn. bd., chief exec. officer, 1976-83; chmn. bd., chief exec. officer Tenn. Valley Bancorp, Inc. (now Commerce Union Corp.), 1972-83; chmn. exec. com., dir. Commerce Union Corp., 1983—. Commd. 2d lt. U.S. Army,

1949; advanced through grades to capt., 1954; ret., 1954; capt. Res. Mem. Am. Bankers Assn., Tenn. Bankers Assn. Clubs: Belle Meade Country (Nashville); River (N.Y.C.). Office: Commerce Union Bank One Commerce Pl Nashville TN 37219

EASH, MAURICE JAMES, univ. adminstr.; b. Fulton County, Ind., Dec. 20, 1928; s. Edward A. and Gertrude Ethel (Barkman) E.; m. Edith Syrjala, July 3, 1981. B.Sc., Manchester Coll., 1950; M.A., Ohio State U., 1955; Ed.D., Columbia U., 1959. Mem. faculty Ball State U., 1959-65, Hunter Coll., City U. N.Y., 1965-69; mem. faculty U. Ill., Chgo., 1969—, now dean Coll. Edn., prof. urban edn. Contbr. articles profl. publs. Served with AUS, 1950-52. Mem. AAAS, N.Y. Acad. Scis., Phi Delta Kappa. Office: College of Education Box 4348 University of Illinois Chicago Circle Chicago IL 60680

EASLEY, JOHN ALLEN, JR., educator; b. Manning, S.C., Jan. 15, 1922; s. John Allen and Eleanor Martin (Robertson) E.; m. Elizabeth Fumiko Fujioka, Aug. 15, 1948; children—Allen Ken, Robert Fumio, David Fumitaka, John Makoto. B.S. in Physics, Wake Forest Coll., 1943; M.Ed. in Sci. Edn, U. Hawaii, 1952; Ph.D., Harvard, 1955. Radio engr. dept. terrestrial magnetism Carnegie Inst., Washington, Baffin Island, Hawaii, 1942-46; prin. Marshall Islands Intermediate Sch., 1949-50; instr. sci. edn. U. Hawaii, 1950-52, asst. prof. sci., 1955-60, asso. prof., 1960-62, acad. chmn., 1960-61; asso. prof. edn. U. Ill., Urbana, 1962-67, prof. secondary edn., 1967-69, prof. tchr. edn., 1969—, chmn. com. on culture and cognition, 1975-76, 1982—, dir., 1977-82; cons. Peace Corps, 1961-62, UNESCO, 1970; mem. Bur. Ednl. Research, 1979-82; chmn. research adv. Com. CEMREL Aesthetics Edn. Program, 1978-81; Chmn. strategy com. United Commn. Campus Christian Ministries Ill., 1969-70; mem. adv. bd. Center for Ednl. Research and Evaluation, Boulder, Colo. Author: (with Maurice Tatsuoka) Scientific Thought: Cases from Classical Physics, 1968, (with Robert E. Stake and others) Case Studies in Science Education, 1978, (with J. Gallagher) Piaget and Education, 1978. Danforth asso., 1969—. Fellow AAAS; mem. AAUP, Jean Piaget Soc. (mem. internat. bd. advisers 1974-78), Nat. Assn. Research in Sci. Teaching (exec. bd. 1979-82), Nat. Council Tchrs. Math., Internat. Group for Psychology of Math. Edn., Am. Ednl. Research Assn., Sch. Sci. and Math. Assn., Phi Delta Kappa. Mem. United Ch. of Christ. Home: 1406 W Green St Champaign IL 61821 Office: 260 B Bldg 1310 S 6th St U Ill Champaign IL 61820

EASLEY, MACK, retired chief justice New Mexico Supreme Court; b. Akins, Okla., Oct. 14, 1916; s. John Robert and Mary Ellen (Duggins) E.; m. Loyce Anna Rogers, Nov. 17, 1939; children: June, Roger. Student, Northeastern Okla. State Coll., 1935-39; LL.B., U. Okla., 1947. Bar: N.Mex. 1948. Practiced law, Hobbs, 1948-74, asst. dist. atty., Lea County, 1949-50; mem. N.Mex. Ho. of Reps., 1951-52, 55-62, speaker, 1959-60; lt. gov., State of N.Mex., 1963-66; mem. N.Mex. Senate, 1967-70, majority whip, 1969-70; judge 5th Dist. Ct. N.Mex., 1974-76; justice N.Mex. Supreme Ct., 1976-82, chief justice, 1981-82; chmn. N.Mex. Legis. Council, 1960, N.Mex. Jud. Conf., 1978-79, N.Mex. Democratic Conv., 1960, 69, 70, 72; mem. Nat. Dem. Charter Commn., 1973-74; dir. Nat. Lt. Govs. Conf., 1966. Served with USAAF, 1942-46. Mem. ABA., N.Mex. Bar Assn., Lea County Bar Assn. (pres. 1950), N.Mex. Judges Assn. (pres. 1979-80), VFW, Am. Legion. Presbyterian. Club: Lions. Office: 218 Montezuma St Santa Fe NM 87501

EASLICK, DAVID KENNETH, telephone co. exec.; b. Jackson, Mich., Jan. 10, 1921; s. Kenneth Alexander and Mercie Marie (VanAken) E.; m. Lucy Thomas Barnwell, Dec. 16, 1943; children—David Kenneth, Susan Blair, Anne Barnwell. A.B., U. Mich., 1942, postgrad., 1945-46; postgrad., George Washington U., 1946-47, Am. U., 1947; D.B.A., Eastern Mich. U., 1981; Sloan fellow, Mass. Inst. Tech., 1954-55; LL.D. (hon.), Butler U., 1972. With Mich. Bell Telephone Co., 1948-63, exec. asst., 1958-59, asst. v.p. labor relations, 1959-60, v.p. personnel, 1960-63; asst. v.p. AT&T, 1963; v.p. ops. Ind. Bell Telephone Co., 1963-70, pres., 1970-72, dir.; v.p. human resources devel. dept. AT&T, 1972-73; pres., dir. Mich. Bell Telephone Co., Detroit, 1973-83, chmn. bd., 1983—; dir. Am. United Life Ins. Co., Circle Income, Inc., Nat. Bank Detroit, Nat. Detroit Corp., Blue Cross/Blue Shield, Sealed Power Corp. Active Boy Scouts Am.; bd. dirs. Internat. Freedom Festival, United Found. Served to maj. AUS, 1942-45. Decorated Silver Star, Bronze Star with oak leaf cluster, Presdl. citation with cluster; Croix de Guerre, France). Mem. Soc. Sloan Fellows, Phi Kappa Psi. Episcopalian (vestryman). Clubs: Detroit, Econ. Detroit. Home: 2401 Gulf Shore Blvd N Naples FL 33940 Office: Room 818 444 Michigan Ave Detroit MI 48226

EASON, ROBERT GASTON, educator; b. Bells, Tenn., May 15, 1924; s. William Bryant and Noba (Proctor) E.; m. Dorothy Jean Goodner, Sept. 5, 1952; children—Robert Gregory, Linda Joan. B.A., U. Mo., 1950, M.A., 1952, Ph.D., 1956. Postdoctoral fellow physiology U. Calif. at Los Angeles, 1956-57; research psychologist Navy Electronics Lab., San Diego, 1957-67; asst. prof. San Diego State Coll., 1960-63, asso. prof., 1963-66, prof., 1966-67; Elizabeth Rosenthal Excellence Fund prof. U. N.C.-Greensboro, 1967-80. Served with USAAF, 1943-46. Mem. Am., Southeastern psychol. assns., AAAS, Psychonomic Soc., Soc. for Neurosci., Soc. Psychophysiol. Research, Sigma Xi. Home: 115 Falkener Dr Greensboro NC 27410

EASSON, WILLIAM MCALPINE, psychiatrist; b. Evanston, Ill., July 3, 1931; s. Alexander and Anne Meldrum (Watson) E.; m. Gwendolyn Bowen, May 31, 1958; children: Anne, Jane, David, Michael. M.B., Ch.B., U. Aberdeen, Scotland, 1954, M.D., 1967. Fellow in medicine and psychiatry Mayo Clinic, Rochester, Minn., 1956-59; resident in psychiatry U. Sask., 1959-60, instr. psychiatry, 1959-61; fellow in child psychiatry Menninger Clinic, Topeka, 1961-63, staff child psychiatrist, 1963-67; prof. psychiatry, chmn. dept. Med. Coll. Ohio, Toledo, 1967-72; prof., dir. div. child and adolescent psychiatry U. Minn. Med. Sch., Mpls., 1972-74; prof. psychiatry, head dept. La. State U. Med. Center, New Orleans, 1974—; vis. prof. U. Garyounis Med. Sch., Benghazi, Libya, 1979; prof. Sch. Grad. Studies, U. Riyadh, Saudi Arabia, 1980-81; U.S.-USSR health scientist, Moscow and Leningrad. Author: The Severely Disturbed Adolescent, 1969, The Dying Child, 2d edit, 1981, Psychiatry Examination Review, 3d edit, 1982, Psychiatry Patient Management Review, 1977; editor: Jour. Clin. Psychiatry, 1977-80. Carnegie fellow, 1956-58; Anderson fellow, 1956-58; WHO fellow, 1976. Fellow Am. Psychiat. Assn., Am. Orthopsychiat. Assn., Royal Coll. Psychiatry. Home: 5218 St Charles Ave New Orleans LA 70115 Office: Dept Psychiatry La State U Med Center 1542 Tulane Ave New Orleans LA 70112

EAST, CHARLES E., writer, editor; b. Shelby, Miss., Dec. 11, 1924; s. Elmo M. and Mabel (Gradolph) E.; m. Sarah Simmons, 1948; 1 son, Charles E. B.A., La. State U., 1948, M.A., 1962. Editorial asst. Collier's mag., N.Y.C., 1948-49; reporter, then Sunday mag. editor Morning Advocate, Baton Rouge, 1949-55; staff writer, then asst. city editor State-Times, Baton Rouge, 1955-62; editor, then asst. dir., then asso. dir. La. State U. Press, Baton Rouge, 1962-70, dir., 1970-75; freelance writer, editor, 1975-80; asst. dir. and editor U. Ga. Press, Athens, 1980—. Author: Where the Music Was, 1965, (with Elemore Morgan) The Face of Louisiana, 1969, Baton Rouge: A Civil War Album, 1977; Contbr. articles to mags. Mem. La. Bicentennial Commn., 1971-72. Recipient Henry H. Bellamann award, 1965. Mem. La. Geneal. and Hist. Soc. (past editor Geneal. Register; founder, charter mem.), Kappa Alpha, Phi Kappa Phi, Phi Eta Sigma. Home: 330 Snapfinger Dr Athens GA 30605 Office: U Ga Press Terrell Hall Athens GA 30602

EAST, F. HOWARD, paper company executive; b. Muncie, Ind., Dec. 25, 1937; s. F. Harold and Esther (Hall) E.; m. Lynn A. Haskett; children: Kim L., Kathy A. B.S., Ball State U., 1960, M.S., 1960. C.P.A., Ind. Mgmt. cons. Ernst & Whinney, Indpls., 1960-65; controller, v.p. fin. Bell Fibre Products, Marion, Ind., 1965-78, exec. v.p., 1978-80, pres., 1980—; dir. Am. Bank and Trust Co., Marion; c.p., dir. Marion Nat. Corp., 1972—; v.p., dir. Menominee Paper Co., Mich., 1973—. Mem. adv. com. Marion Coll., 1979—; pres. Marion Easter Pageant, 1981—; treas., bd. dirs. Marion Gen. Hosp., 1978—; bd. dirs. YMCA, Marion, 1978-80, Jr. Achievement, Marion, 1972—; mem. Marion Redevel. Com., 1978-80. Mem. Am. Inst. C.P.A.s, Ind. C.P.A. Soc., Pres.'s Assn., Fin. Execs. Inst., Am. Mgmt. Assn., Nat. Assn. Accts., Marion C. of C. Republican. Clubs: Mecca; Mesingomesia Country (Marion). Lodges: Masons; Shriners. Home: 916 W Sydney Ln Marion IN 46952 Office: Bell Fibre Products Corp 3102 S Boots St Marion IN 46952

EAST, JOHN PORTER, U.S. senator; b. Springfield, Ill., May 5, 1931; s. Laurence J. and Virginia (Porter) E.; m. Priscilla Sherk, Sept. 26, 1953; children—Kathryn, Martha. B.A. in Polit. Sci, Earlham Coll., 1953; LL.B., U. Ill., 1959; M.A. in Polit. Sci, U. Fla., 1962, Ph.D., 1964. Bar: Fla. bar 1959. Prof. polit. sci. E. Carolina U., Greenville, N.C., 1964-80; mem. U.S. Senate from N.C., 1980—; Del. to Republican Nat. Conv., 1976, 80, nat. committeeman, 1976—. Author: Council-Manager Government: The Political Thought of Its Founder, Richard S. Childs, 1965; contbr. numerous articles on American polit. thought to scholarly jours., book revs. in field to lit. jours.; mem. editorial bd.: Polit. Sci. Reviewer, 1970—, Modern Age, 1975—. Served to lt. USMC, 1953-55. Nat. Def. fellow, 1961-64. Mem. Am. Polit. Sci. Assn., Fla. Bar Assn., So. Polit. Sci. Assn., Am. Legion, Phi Beta Kappa. Republican. Methodist. Home: 5901 Mount Eagle Dr Apt 1418 Alexandria VA 22303 Office: US Senate Washington DC 20510 *There is no one road to success; however, the best approach generally is to know one's interests and talents and to vigorously pursue them.*

EAST, RICHARD CLAYTON, real estate appraiser; b. Memphis, Dec. 19, 1921; s. Thomas Franklin and Bessie (Andrews) E.; m. Mary Kathryn Wiggins, July 13, 1945; children—Richard Clayton, Robert A., Carol E. B.S., Memphis State Coll., 1943; LL.B., So. Law U., Memphis, 1942. Mortgage loan rep. Gen. Am. Life Ins. Co., Memphis, 1946-48, Oklahoma City, 1948-51; real estate mgr. Safeway Stores, Inc., Oklahoma City, 1951-53; appraiser Continental Fed. Savs. & Loan Assn., 1953-66, pres., 1966-75; ret., 1975, real estate appraiser, Oklahoma City, 1975—. Served to lt. (j.g.) USNR, 1943-46. Mem. Oklahoma City C. of C. (dir. 1966), Oklahoma City Bd. Realtors (v.p. 1963), Soc. Real Estate Appraisers (internat. v.p. 1966), Am. Inst. Real Estate Appraisers. Methodist. Clubs: Oklahoma City Kiwanis (v.p. 1969), Oak Tree Golf.). Home: 2804 NW 61st St Oklahoma City OK 73112 Office: 2630 C NW Expressway Oklahoma City OK 73112

EAST, WILLIAM G., fed. judge; b. Le Compton, Kans., Apr. 25, 1908; s. William G. and Bertha Mary (Waterbury) E.; m. Louise Frances Wilhelm, Feb. 21, 1933; 1 dau., Sara Elizabeth East Coit. B.A., U. Oreg., 1931, J.D., 1932. Bar: Oreg. bar 1932. Pvt. practice law, Eugene, Oreg., 1932-42, 46-49; partner firm Harris, Bryson & East, 1941-42; city atty., City of Eugene, 1946-47; gen. counsel Eugene Water Bd., 1946-49; circuit judge 2d Jud. Dist. Oreg., 1949-55; U.S. dist. judge Dist. Oreg., 1955-67, U.S. sr. dist. judge for, 1967—. Served with inf. AUS, 1942-46; ETO. Mem. ABA, Oreg. Bar Assn (past mem. bd. govs., bd. bar examiners), Am. Judicature Soc. (dir. from Oreg.), Oreg. Assn. Circuit Judges (past pres.), Eugene Round Table (past pres.), Delta Tau Delta, Phi Delta Phi. Conglist. Clubs: Mason, Elk., Multnomah Athletic (Portland, Oreg.). Home: PO Box 747 Neskowin OR 97149 Office: 1065 High St Eugene OR 97401 *Select a person whom you admire for his integrity, faithfulness to home and work, intellectual honesty, and understanding of man. Then endeavor to emulate him throughout your life's efforts.*

EASTBURN, DAVID PLUMB, economic consultant, retired banker; b. Doylestown, Pa., Jan. 9, 1921; s. Arthur Moses and Marie (Plumb) E.; m. Phyllis Ann Groff, June 25, 1949; children: David Rodman, Stephen Frazier, Susan Barbara, Laurie Ann. A.B., Amherst Coll., 1942; M.A., U. Pa., 1945, Ph.D., 1957. With Fed. Res. Bank of Phila., 1942-81, pres., 1970-81, ret., 1981; dir. Vanguard Group, Gen. Accident Group, United Med. Corp.; trustee Penn Mut. Life Ins. Co.; instr. U. Pa., summer 1945, spring 1947. Author: The Federal Reserve on Record, 1965; Editor: Men, Money and Policy, 1970; Contbr. articles to profl. jours. Pres. Phila. Orch. Assn., 1978—. Mem. Am. Philos. Soc. Home: 75 Short Rd Doylestown PA 18901

EASTER, GEORGE CORDELL, financial executive; b. Spokane, Wash., Sept. 8, 1934; s. Charles Harold and Mary Frances (Cordell) E.; m. Sarah Lovell Jones, Sept. 7, 1957; children: Sally, George, Jennifer. A.B., Princeton U., 1956; LL.B., George Washington U., 1961; M.B.A., Harvard U., 1962. Mgr. internat. investments Am. and Fgn. Power Co., N.Y.C., 1962-68; v.p., treas. Waltham Industries Corp., N.Y.C., 1968-71; v.p. fin. Church and Dwight Co., Inc., Piscataway, N.J., 1971-79; v.p., treas. Assoc. Dry Goods Corp., N.Y.C., 1979—. Served to lt. (j.g.) USNR; 1957-60. Unitarian. Clubs: Harvard Bus. Sch., Union League; Princeton (N.Y.C.). Office: Associated Dry Goods Corp 417 Fifth Ave New York NY 10016

EASTERBROOK, JAMES ARTHUR, psychology educator; b. Spooner, Minn., Apr. 10, 1923; s. William James and Bertha Lillian (Amorde) E.; m. Margaret Pamela Edith Evans, Nov. 19, 1944; children: Christine, Anthony, Pamela, Laurence, Margaret. B.A. with honors, Queen's U., Kingston, Ont., Can., 1949, M.A. (J. McBeth Milligan fellow), 1954; Ph.D., U. London, Eng., 1963. Mem. Canadian Def. Research Sci. Service, Churchill, Man., Edmonton, Alta., Halifax, N.S., 1950-57; research psychologist Burden Neurol. Inst., Bristol, Eng., 1959-61; mem. faculty medicine U. Alta. at Edmonton, 1961-67; prof. psychology U. N.B. at Fredericton, 1967—; mem. N.B. Bd. Examiners in Psychology, 1973-79. Served with RCAF, 1941-45. Mem. Brit. Psychol. Soc. Home: 180 Dunns Crossing Rd Fredericton NB Canada E3B 2A6

EASTERDAY, BERNARD CARLYLE, veterinary medicine educator; b. Hillsdale, Mich., Sept. 16, 1929; s. Harley B. and Alberta M. (Bodenbender) E. D.V.M., Mich. State U., 1952; M.S., U. Wis., 1958, Ph.D., 1961. Diplomate: Am. Coll. Veterinary Microbiology. Pvt. practice veterinary medicine, Hillsdale, Mich., 1952; veterinarian U.S. Dept. Def., Frederick, Md., 1955-61; assoc. prof. to prof. veterinary medicine U. Wis.-Madison, 1961-83, dean Sch. Vet. Medicine, 1979—; mem., chmn. com. animal health Nat. Acad. Sci.-NRC, Washington, 1980-83; mem. tech. adv. com. Binat. Agrl. Research and Devel., Bet-Deagn, Israel, 1982-84; mem. expert adv. panel on zoonoses WHO, Geneva, 1978-84. Served to 1st lt. V.C. U.S. Army, 1952-54. Recipient Disting. Alumnus award Coll. Vet. Medicine, Mich. State U., 1975; named Wis. Veterinarian of Yr. Wis. Vet. Med. Assn., 1980. Mem. AVMA, Am. Assn. Vet. Med. Colls., Am. Assn. Avian Pathologists. Lodge: Rotary (Madison). Office: Sch Vet Medicine 2015 Linden Dr W Madison WI 53706

EASTERLING, CRAWFORD ALAN, JR., naval officer; b. Nashville, June 29, 1928; s. Crawford Alan and Lucille Story E.; m. Beverly Sherburne, Feb. 10, 1956; children: Crawford Alan, Karen Lynn. B.E.E., Rensselaer Poly. Inst., 1951; M.S., MIT, 1964, Engr. Aeros. and Astronautics, 1964. Commd. ensign U.S. Navy, 1951, advanced through grades to rear adm., 1977, comdg. officer fighter squadrons 13 and 124 USS Concord and USS Frank D. Roosevelt, 1974-76; exec. asst. to asst. sec. for research and devel. Dept. Navy, 1972-73, dir. command and control and info. systems, Washington, 1977-79, comdr. Carrier Group, from 1979; now comdr. Naval Air Force US Pacific Fleet, San Diego. Decorated Legion of Merit with 2 gold stars. Office: NAS North Island San Diego CA 92135

EASTERLING, WILLIAM EWART, JR., obstetrician, gynecologist; b. Raleigh, N.C., Oct. 8, 1930; s. William Ewart and Hannah Montgomery E.; m. Mary Ellyn Royer, June 7, 1952; children—William E., David R., John Wyatt, Robert Bryan, Jeffrey T. A.B., Duke U., 1952; M.D., U. N.C., 1956. Intern N.C. Meml. Hosp., 1956-57, resident in ob-gyn, 1957-61; instr. ob-gyn U. N.C. Sch. Medicine, 1960-61, asst. prof., 1964-67, asso. prof., 1967-72, prof., 1972—, asst. dean, 1974-76, asso. dean, 1976-77, vice dean, 1977-81, asso. dean clin. affairs, 1981—; chief staff N.C. Meml. Hosp., Chapel Hill, 1974—; mem. Council on Resident Edn. in Ob-gyn, 1972-80, chmn., 1978-80. Contbr. chpts. to textbooks; contbr. articles to profl. jours. Bd. dirs. Episcopal Home for Aging; bd. dirs. N.C. div. Am. Cancer Soc., chmn., 1976-77, pres., 1977-78. Served to capt. M.C. USAF, 1961-63; USPHS trainee, 1963-64. Mem. Am. Coll. Obstetricians and Gynecologists, Am. Assn. Obstetricians and Gynecologists, Assn. Profs. in Gynecology and Obstetrics, Endocrine Soc., Soc. Gynecol. Investigation. Home: Route 2 105 Stoneridge Dr Chapel Hill NC 27514 Office: Dept Ob-Gyn 4027 Old Clinic Bldg U NC Sch Medicine Chapel Hill NC 27514

EASTERLY, EMBREE KLINE, banker; b. Watson, La., Mar. 10, 1919; s. Isaac Dwight and Elma (Underwood) E.; m. Ruth Breaud, July 19, 1940; children: Robert, Richard, James, Sharon. Pres. Capital Bank & Trust Co., Baton Rouge, 1960-81, chief exec. officer, 1960-81, 1981—. Active civic and polit. orgns.; mem. U.S. Savs. Bonds Program, U.S. Treasury Dept. Served USMC, 1944-45; PTO. Mem. Ind. Bankers Assn. Am. (pres. 1974-76), Am. Bankers Assn. (exec. com. comml. lending div.), La. Bankers Assn., La. Ind. Bankers Assn. (founding dir.), Baton Rouge C. of C. (past dir.), U.S. C. of C. Democrat. Methodist. Clubs: Baton Rouge Country (Baton Rouge); Baton Rouge City (pres.), Sherwood Forest Country (pres. founding dir.). Home: 1371 Ashbourne Dr Baton Rouge LA 80815 Office: Capital Bank & Trust Co PO Box 2710 Baton Rouge LA 70821

EASTERWOOD, HENRY LEWIS, artist; b. Villa Rica, Ga., Oct. 29, 1934; s. Clyde Harris and Lois (Bently) E. B.F.A., Memphis Acad. Arts, 1958; student, Royal Tapestry Mfr., Madrid, Spain, 1965, Wverij de Uil, Amsterdam, Netherlands, 1965. Asso. prof. art Memphis Acad. Arts, 1959—; chmn. textile dept. Haystack Mountain Sch. Crafts, Deer Isle, Maine, 1966. One-man exhbns. include, Memphis Acad. Arts, 1964, Group Gallery, Jacksonville, Fla., 1967, Louisville Art Center, 1966, Brooks Meml. Gallery Art, Memphis, 1968, Fairweather Hardin Gallery, Chgo., 1970, Miss. Art Assn., 1971, group exhbns. include, Mus. Contemporary Art, N.Y.C., 1964, 66, America House, N.Y.C., 1965-70, Ark. Arts Center, 1966-68, Tulane U., Norfolk (Va.) Mus. Arts and Scis., 1968, St. Paul Mus., 1969, 61, 63; represented in permanent collections, Memphis Acad. Arts, Brooks Meml. Gallery, Tenn. Collection Crafts, also pvt. collections.; tapestry commns. include, Gov. and Mrs. Winthrop Rockefeller, 1965, Virgin Gorda for Lawrence Rockefeller, 1965, St. Anne's Ch., Bartlett, Tenn., 1969, First Am. Nat. Bank, also Worthen Bank and Trust Co., Little Rock, Mayo Clinic, 1970, Tupperware Internat. for Edward Durrell Stone, architect, 1971, Memphis Meml. Park, 1974, Jones, Day, Reavis and Pogue, Washington, 1975, Vanderbilt U. Surratt Commons, 1974, Goldsmith Civic Garden Center, Memphis, 1975, Commerce Union Bank, Chattanooga, 1976, Lewis State Bank, Tallahassee, Fed. Home Loan Bank Bd., Washington, 1978. Mem. adv. panel crafts Tenn. Arts Commn., 1969-70; mem. Fed. Home Bank Bd., 1978. Named An Outstanding Young Man in Am., 1966; recipient Craftsmanship award A.I.A., 1969. Mem. Am. Craftsmen's Council (rep. of Tenn. 1963-65, Nat. Merist award 1966). Home: 694 N Trezevant St Memphis TN 38112

EASTHAM, JEROME FIELDS, educator, physician; b. Daytona, Fla., Sept. 22, 1924; s. Jerome Folger and Polly (Fields) E.; m. Laura Telford Newton, Dec. 20, 1949; children—Jerome Fields, Edward D., Grace, Katherine, David G. B.S., U. Ky., 1948; Ph.D., U. Cal. at Berkeley, 1951; M.D., U. Tenn., 1973. Fellow U. London, 1952; fellow U. Wis., 1953; prof. U. Tenn., 1954—; instr. in internal medicine; cons. Chemetron Corp., Lithium Corp., Union Carbide Nuclear Corp. Served with AUS, 1942-45. Mem. Am. Chem. Soc., Chem. Soc. (London), A.A.U.P., A.A.A.S., A.M.A., Phi Beta Kappa, Sigma Xi. Research chemistry steroids, phys. organic chemistry, organometallic chemistry. Home: 7841 Ramsgate Dr Knoxville TN 37919

EASTHAM, THOMAS, press secretary; b. Attelboro, Mass., Aug. 21, 1923; s. John M. and Margaret (Marsden) E.; m. Berenice J. Hirsch, Oct. 12, 1946; children: Scott Thomas, Todd Robert. Student English, Northwestern U., 1946-52. With Chgo. American, 1945-56, asst. Sunday editor, 1953-54, feature writer, 1954-56; news editor San Francisco Call Bull., 1956-62, exec. editor, 1962-65; exec. editor, then D.C. bur. chief San Francisco Examiner, 1965-82; press sec. to mayor of San Francisco, 1982—. Served with USMC, 1941-45. Mem. Am. Soc. Newspaper Editors, Inter-Am. Press Assn., Am., Internat. press insts., White House Corrs. Assn., Nat. Press Club, Sigma Delta Chi. Home: 555 Laurel Ave San Mateo CA 94401 Office: Mayor's Office City Hall Rm 200 San Francisco CA 94102

EASTHAM, WILLIAM KENNETH, chemical company executive; b. Mineola, N.Y., Dec. 30, 1917; s. William and Alice (Watson) E.; m. Dorothy Brush, Mar. 25, 1942 (dec. Dec. 1979); children: Gale Eastham Shadrick, Nancy Eastham Kaydo; m. Robin J. Ehrlich, Nov. 6, 1980. Student, Am. Inst. Banking, 1936-38, NYU, 1946-48; grad. Advanced Mgmt. Program, Harvard U., 1954. Teller Am. Bank for Savs., N.Y.C., 1935-39; asst. advt. mgr. Whitehall Pharm. div. Am. Home Products Co., N.Y.C., 1945-51; brand mgr. Soap div., advt. mgr. Good Luck div.; advt. mgr. Pepsodent div. Lever Bros. Co., N.Y.C., 1951-59; asst. to pres. Am. Home Products Co.; exec. v.p. div. Boyle Midway, 1959-64; v.p. div. household products S.C. Johnson & Son, Inc., Racine, Wis., 1964-67, exec. v.p. U.S. ops., 1967-71, exec. v.p. U.S. and European ops., 1971-72, pres., chief operating officer, 1972-79, pres., chief exec. officer, 1979-80, vice chmn., 1980—, also dir.; dir. Meredith Corp.; chmn. bd. Heritage Nat. Bank of Racine. Bd. dirs. Racine Zool. Soc. Served with U.S. Army, 1940-45. Mem. C. of C. U.S. (dir.), Vets. of 7th Regt. Clubs: Racine Country, Burning Tree; Metropolitan (Washington). Office: 4061 N Main St Racine WI 53402

EASTIN, KEITH E., lawyer; b. Lorain, Ohio, Jan. 716, 1940; s. Keith Ernest and Jane E. (Heimer) E. A.B., U. Cin., 1963, M.B.A., 1964; J.D., U. Chgo., 1967. Bar: Ill. 1967, Tex. 1974, Calif. 1975, U.S. Supreme Ct. 1975. Atty. Vedder, Price, Kaufman & Kammholz, Chgo., 1967-73; v.p., sec., gen. counsel, Nat. Convenience Stores, Inc., Houston, 1973-77; partner Payne, Eastin & Widmer, Houston, 1977-83; assoc. solicitor U.S. Dept. Interior, 1983—; dir. Nat. Money

Orders, Inc., Feast & Co., Inc., Kempco Petroleum Co., Bertman Drilling Co., Pacific Options, Inc., Del Rey Food Services, Inc., Stratford Feedyards, Inc. Mem. Am., Ill., Tex. bar assns., State Bar Calif., Beta Gamma Sigma, Phi Delta Phi, Beta Theta Pi. Club: University (Houston).

EASTLAKE, WILLIAM DERRY, author; b. N.Y.C., July 14, 1917; s. Gordon and Charlotte (Bradley) E. Student, Alliance Française, Paris, 1948-50; LL.D., U. Albuquerque, 1970. Lectr. U. N.Mex., 1967-68, U. So. Calif., 1968-69, U. Ariz., 1969-71, U.S. Mil. Acad., 1975. Writer in residence, Knox Coll., Galesburg, Ill., 1967; Author: novels Go in Beauty, 1955, The Bronc People, 1958, Portrait of an Artist with Twenty-Six Horses, 1963, Castle Keep, 1965, The Bamboo Bed, 1969, Dancers in the Scalp House, 1975, The Long Naked Descent Into Boston, 1977; poems and essays A Child's Garden of Verses for the Revolution, 1970; corr. in Vietnam for The Nation mag; author stories pub. in 40 anthologies and textbooks, 1 screen play, 13 fgn. lang. editions.; Contbr.: stories to Harper's, Atlantic Monthly, Ms., Evergreen Rev., numerous others. Served with inf. AUS, World War II; ETO. Decorated Bronze Star; recipient Les Lettres Nouvelles award for best fgn. novel pub. in France, 1972; Ford Found. grantee, 1963; Rockefeller Found. grantee, 1966, 67; subject of spring 1983 issue Rev. Contemporary Fiction. Mem. Writers Guild, Author's Guild, PEN, AAUP. Address: 15 Coy Rd Bisbee AZ 85603

EASTLAND, JAMES O., former U.S. Senator, lawyer; b. Doddsville, Miss., Nov. 28, 1904; s. Woods Caperton and Alma (Austin) E.; m. Elizabeth Coleman, July 6, 1932; children: Nell, Anne, Sue, Woods Eugene. Student, U. Miss., 1922-24, Vanderbilt U., 1925-26, U. Ala., 1926-27; LL.D. (hon.), Miss. Coll., 1971. Bar: Miss. 1927. Practiced law, Forest, Miss., Sunflower County, after 1934; mem. Miss. Ho. of Reps., 1928-32; apptd. to U.S. Senate to fill vacancy, June-Sept. 1941; U.S. Senator from Miss., 1943-78; pres. protem U.S. Senate, 1972-78, chmn. judiciary com., 1956-78, former mem. agr. and forestry com., Democratic policy com., commn. on art and antiquities. Democrat. Office: Ruleville MS 38771 *

EASTLICK, JOHN TAYLOR, librarian; b. Norris, Mont., Apr. 28, 1912; s. Jack T. and Stella Mae (Tate) E. A.B., Ariz. State Tchrs. Coll., 1934; B.L.S., U. Denver, 1940; M.A., Colo. State Coll. Edn., 1939. Instr. English, speech dramatics Yuma (Ariz.) Union High Sch., 1934-38; librarian U. Wis., Wis. High Sch., Madison, 1940-42; instr. library sci. Mich. State Coll., East Lansing, summers 1940, 41, Wash. State Coll., Pullman, summer 1942; chief library div. VA, Denver, 1946-48; instr. hosp. and med. library coll. librarianship U. Denver, 1946-50, prof. librarianship, 1969-76, asso. dean, 1976-79, prof. emeritus, 1979—; cons. to Sec. of Army (instructing Japanese educators in reorgn. Japanese ednl. system), Japan, 1948-49; circulation dept. Denver Pub. Library, 1939-40, asst. to librarian, 1948-51, librarian, 1951-61, 62-69; asst. state supt. edn. for library services, State Hawaii, 1962; mem. U.S.A.-Mex. Bi-lateral Com. on Edn. and Tng., 1976—; Dir. Adult Edn. Council, Denver; chmn. finance com., asst. treas. Bibliog. Center for Research, Rocky Mountain Region, 1949-51, treas., 1951-65; Mem. adv. com. U.S. Office of Edn., 1956-57. Author: (with Robert Steuart) Library Management, 1976, 2d edit., 1981; Editor: Changing Environment in Libraries, 1971. Served as capt. USAAF, 1942- 46. Mem. A.L.A. (pres. pub. libraries div. 1956-57, com. architecture and bldgs. 1949-51, 2d v.p. 1959-60, mem. com. on accreditation 1971-76), Colo. Library Assn. (exec. bd.), Denver Dist. Library Assn. (pres. 1950-51), Ariz. State Library Assn. (pres. 1937), Alpha Psi Omega, Phi Delta Kappa. Club: City (Denver). Home: 3914 E Evans Ave Denver CO 80210

EASTMAN, ALBERT THEODORE, clergyman; b. San Mateo, Calif., Nov. 20, 1928; s. Carl John and Inette (Nordeen) E.; m. Sarah Virginia Tice, June 13, 1953; children: Sarah, Anne, Andrew. B.A., Harvard Coll., 1950; M.Div., Va. Theol. Sem., 1953, D.D., 1983; L.H.D., Episcopal Theol. Sem. Southwest, 1982. Ordained priest Episcopal Ch., 1954; vicar Trinity Ch., Gonzales, Calif., 1953-56; exec. sec. Overseas Mission Soc., Washington, 1956-68; cons. House Bishops, Washington, 1968; rector Ch. of Mediator, Allentown, Pa., 1969-73, St. Alban's Ch., Washington, 1973-82; bishop coadjutor Episcopal Diocese Md., Balt., 1982—; co-chmn. Aglican-Roman Cath. Consultation, 1983—. Author: Christian Responsibilty in One World, 1965, Chosen and Sent, 1971, The Baptizing Community, 1982. Vis. fellow Episcopal Theol. Seminary Southwest, 1963; Scholar-in residence Coll. Preachers, 1981. Fellow Coll. Preachers. Democrat. Episcopalian. Home: 3601 N Charles St Baltimore MD 21218 Office: Episcopal Diocese Md 105 W Monument St Baltimore MD 21201

EASTMAN, DEAN ERIC, physicist; b. Oxford, Wis., Jan. 21, 1940; s. Eric and Mildred (Benson) E.; m. Ella Mae Staley, Aug. 18, 1979. B.S.E.E., M.I.T., 1962, M.S.E.E., 1963, Ph.D.E.E., 1965. Research staff mem. IBM, Yorktown Heights, N.Y., 1963-74, IBM fellow, 1974—, mgr. surface physics and photoemission, 1972—. Contbr. numerous articles on solid state physics to profl. jours. Fellow Am. Phys. Soc. (Oliver C. Buckley prize 1980, councilor at large), Nat. Acad. Scis. Home: 806 Pines Bridge Rd Ossining NY 10562 Office: IBM T J Watson Research Center Yorktown Heights NY 10598

EASTMAN, HARLAND HORACE, former fgn. service officer; b. Springvale, Me., Apr. 14, 1929; s. Harland Horace and Bernice Maud (Haley) E.; m. Nancy Lee Emery, July 12, 1958; children—Eliza Witham, Stephen Emery, Mohamed-Said. A.B., Colby Coll., 1951; A.M., Fletcher Sch. Law and Diplomacy, 1952; student, London Sch. Econs., 1952-53. Teacher Kent's Hill (Me.) Sch., 1953; with U.S. Fgn. Service, State Dept., 1955-79, Washington, 1955-57, 66-71, NATO, 1957-60, Paris, 1960-62, Saigon, 1962-64, Cotonou, Dahomey, 1964-66, consulate, Liverpool, Eng., 1971-74, consul gen., Tel Aviv, Israel, 1974-75, Tangier, Morocco, 1975-79, ret., 1979. Author: The Eastmans of Tamworth, New Hampshire, 1964. Served with AUS, 1953-55. Rotary Found. fellow, 1952-53. Mem. Me. Hist. Soc., New Eng. Hist. Geneal. Soc., Phi Beta Kappa. Baptist. Clubs: Rotarian., Lyceum (Liverpool). Home: 66 Main St Springvale ME 04083

EASTMAN, HARRY CLAUDE MACCOLL, economic educator; b. Vancouver, C., July 29, 1923; s. Samuel Mack and Antonia (Larribe) E.; m. Sheila Baldwin MacQueen, July 10, 1949; children: Julia, Alice, Harriet. B.A., U. Toronto, 1947; A.M., U. Chgo., 1949, Ph.D., 1952. Instr. Duke U., 1949-52; mem. faculty dept. econs. U. Toronto, 1953—, prof. econs., 1961—, v.p. research and planning, registrar, 1977-81. Contbr. articles to profl. jours. Served with RCAF, 1943-45. Fellow Royal Soc. Can.; mem. Can. Econs. Assn. (pres. 1971-72), Internat. Econs. Assn. (council 1962-81, exec. com. 1968-74), Can. Polit. Sci. Assn., Am. Econ. Assn., Royal Econ. Assn., Société canadienne de science économique. Home: 41 Hawthorn Ave Toronto ON M4W 2Z1 Canada Office: Univ of Toronto Dept Econs Toronto ON M5S 1A1 Canada

EASTMAN, JOHN RICHARD, manufacturing company executive; b. Ottawa, Ohio, Sept. 28, 1917; s. Herbert Parrett and Marie (Brown) E.; m. Hope Ruth, June 12, 1943; 1 dau., Janet Ruth. B.A., Ohio State U., Columbus, 1939, LL.B., 1941. Bar: Ohio 1941. With firm Eastman, Stichter, Smith & Bergman, Toledo, 1941-42, 46-75, ptnr., 1950-75; sr. v.p., gen. counsel Sheller-Globe Corp., Toledo, 1975-77, pres., 1977-82, vice chmn., 1982—; lectr. Coll. Law, U. Toledo, 1954-55. Bd. dirs. United Way, 1978-82, 84—. Served with USNR, 1942-46. Decorated Purple Heart. Mem. ABA., Ohio Bar Assn., Lucas County Bar Assn. (pres. 1960), Toledo Bar Assn. (exec. com. 1963-69), Am. Judicature Soc., Internat. Assn. Ins. Counsel, Am. Coll. Trial Lawyers, Toledo C. of C. (chmn. elect 1984). Methodist. Clubs: Exchange, Toledo, Toledo Country, Belmont Country (Toledo). Lodge: Masons (Toledo). Home: 415 E 5th St Perrysburg OH 43551 Office: 1505 Jefferson Ave Toledo OH 43624

EASTMAN, LESTER FUESS, elec. engr., educator; b. Utica, N.Y., May 21, 1928; s. Howard Socrates and Mayme Lois (Fuess) E.; m. Anne Marie Gardner, Dec. 22, 1948; children—David Joel, Daniel Gardner, Laurie Suzanne. B.E.E., Cornell U., 1953, M.S., 1955, Ph.D., 1957. Instr. Cornell U., Ithaca, N.Y., 1954-56, asst. prof., 1957-60, asso. prof., 1960-66, prof. elec. engring., 1966—, founder, dir. joint services electronics program and research lab., 1979—; founding mem. Nat. Research and Resource Facility for Submicron Structures, 1977—; laborator Chalmers Tech. U., Gothenburg, Sweden, 1960-61; mem. tech. staff RCA Research Lab., 1964-65; founder, pres. Cayuga Assos., Ithaca, 1971-72; mem. tech. staff M.I.T. Lincoln Lab., Lexington, Mass., 1978-79; dir. Cornell Research Found., 1974—; cons. to industry. Guest editor IEEE transactions, 1967, 78; Contbr. articles to profl. jours. Served with USN, 1946-48. Sperry Gyroscope fellow, 1953-54; Gen. Electric fellow, 1956-57. Fellow IEEE; mem. Sigma Xi, Eta Kappa Nu, Tau Beta Pi, Phi Kappa Phi. Presbyterian. Patentee in field. Home: 61 Burdick Hill Rd Ithaca NY 14850 Office: 425 Phillips Hall Cornell Univ Ithaca NY 14853

EASTMAN, RICHARD MORSE, educator; b. Locust Valley, N.Y., Aug. 20, 1916; s. Elmer Fred and Lilla (Morse) E.; m. Vivian Clare Bolger, Nov. 14, 1942; children: Patricia, Susan, Julie. B.A., Oberlin Coll., 1937; student, Yale U., 1937-39; M.A., U. Chgo., 1949, Ph.D. with honors, 1952. Instr. English North Central Coll., 1946-49, asst. prof., 1949-52, asso. prof., 1952-55, prof., 1955-70, chmn., 1952-70, chmn. humanities div., 1961-70, dir. Summer Sch., 1961-67, dean faculty, v.p. acad. affairs, 1961-67, 70-76, chmn. gen. studies, 1961-67, 76—; pres. North Central Conf. on Summer Schs., 1968. Author: A Guide to the Novel, 1965, Style, 1970, 3d edit., 1984; contbr. articles on critical theory, modern fiction and drama to profl., scholastic and lit. jours. Pres., Naperville (Ill.) Human Relations Council, 1966-68. Served to maj. AUS, 1941-46. Mem. Nat. Council Tchrs. English. Home: 961 E Porter Ave Naperville IL 60540

EASTMAN, WILLIAM DON, publishing exec.; b. Arlington, Oreg., Jan. 18, 1931; s. Harrison Cyrus and Helen Margaret (Myers) E.; m. Caroline Aldrich Lanford, July 1, 1972; children—Caroline Sherman, Bronwen Shama. B.A., U. Wash., 1958. Coll. travel Ginn & Co., Boston, 1962-63; field editor Blaisdell Pub. Co., N.Y.C., 1963-64, editor, 1964-65, Macmillan Co., N.Y.C., 1965-69, exec. editor, 1969-71; editor-in-chief Harper & Row, Pubs., Inc., N.Y.C., 1971-72, editorial dir., 1972-76; dir. Harpers Coll. Press, 1976-77, SUNY Press, Albany, 1978—. Served with USNR, 1953-54. Home: Hayes Rd Castleton-on-Hudson NY 12033 Office: State Univ Plaza Albany NY 12246

EASTON, ANTHONY TERRENCE, telecommunications executive; b. Balt., Sept. 6, 1947; s. Anthony and Margaret Leona (Koutz) E.; m. Susan Lentz, July 2, 1970. B.S., Johns Hopkins U., 1969; M.S., Am. U., 1972. Customer system designer Info. Services Div., Gen. Electric Co., Washington, 1968; engr. simulation team Manned Space Flight Network simulation team Apollo Project, NASA, Washington, 1970-71; lectr., mgmt. of tech. Am. U., Washington, 1972-74; asst. dir. computer sci. dept. Strayer Coll., Washington, 1971-73; network dir. Internat. Corp. Networks, ICM Ltd., London, 1973-76; pres. Internat. Communications Mgmt., Inc., San Francisco, 1976-78, Technology Mktg. Analysis Corp., 1978-80; chmn. bd. Nat. Entertainment TV, Inc., 1980-82; pres. Am. Internat. Telephone Corp., 1982—; dir. Internat. Bus. Bank, San Francisco, Island TV Corp.; prof. mgmt., chmn. grad. dept. telecommunications mgmt. studies Golden Gate U., 1976—. Author: Executive Telecommunications Handbook, 1977; co-author: Telecommunications: An Interdisciplinary Survey, 1979, The Home Satellite TV Book: How to Put the World in Your Backyard, 1981, The Satellite TV Handbook, 1983, The Under $800 Computer Buyer's Guide, 1984. Mem. Explorers Club, IEEE, AAUP, World Future Soc., Am. Radio Relay League, Nat. Soc. Profl. Engrs., Engrs. Club of San Francisco., Bankers Club of San Francisco. Club: Los Angeles Athletic. Office: 559 Pacific Ave Suite 32 San Francisco CA 94133

EASTON, DAVID, political science educator; b. Toronto, Ont., Can., June 24, 1917; came to U.S., 1943; m. Sylvia Isobel Victoria Johnstone; 1 son, Stephen Talbot. B.A., U. Toronto, 1939, M.A., 1943; Ph.D., Harvard U., 1947; LL.D., McMaster U., 1970, Kalamazoo Coll., 1972. Teaching fellow Harvard, 1944-47; asst. prof. U. Chgo., 1947-53, asso. prof., 1953-55, prof., 1955—, now Andrew MacLeish Distinguished Service prof.; exec. com. Inter-Univ. Consortium for Polit. Research, 1962-64; chmn. com. information behavioral scis. div. Nat. Acad. Sci.-NRC, 1968-70; fellow Center for Advanced Study in Behavioral Scis., Stanford, 1957-58; cons. Brookings Instn., 1955, Mental Health Research Inst., U. Mich., 1955-56, Royal Commn. on Bilingualism and Biculturalism, Can., 1964-66; Ford prof., 1960-61. Author: The Political System, 1953, A Framework for Political Analysis, 1965, A Systems Analysis of Political Life, 1965; co-author: Children in the Political System, 1969; Editor: Varieties of Political Theory, 1966; Bd. editors: Jour. Polit. Methodology, Youth and Soc., Internat. Polit. Sci. Abstracts; bd. editors: Behavioral Sci. Fellow Am. Acad. Arts and Scis. (mem. council 1975—, chmn. research and planning com. 1979-82, exec. bd. 1979—), Acad. Ind. Scholars (trustee, chmn. 1979-81), Royal Soc. Can. (com. on higher edn. 1978-80); mem. Am. Polit. Sci. Assn. (mem. council 1964-66, pres. 1968-69, chmn. com. on sci. information exchange 1972), Internat. Com. Social Sci. Documentation (pres. 1969-71). Office: Dept Polit Sci Univ Chicago Chicago IL 60637

EASTON, GLENN HANSON, JR., management and insurance consultant, federal official; b. N.Y.C., Mar. 11; s. Glenn Herman and Cornelia Blanchard (Hanson) E.; m. Jeanne Milhall, June 15, 1944; children: Jeanne, Glenn Hanson III, Michelle, Carol. Assoc. in Bus. Adminstrn., U. Pa., 1949, B.A. in Econs., 1950; M.B.A., NYU, 1959. CLU, Am. Coll. Life Underwriters. Various positions to asst. traffic mgr. Keystone Shipping Co., Phila., 1940-54; various positions to mgr. transp. econs. div. Standard-Vacuum Oil Co., White Plains, N.Y., 1954-59; various positions to cons. to pres. S.R. Guggenheim Found., N.Y.C., 1959—; pres. Glenn Easton & Assocs. (mgmt. and ins. consultants), Port Chester, N.Y., 1970—; polit. appointee U.S. Dept. Labor, Washington, 1982—; assoc. prof. mgmt. L.I. U., Brookville, N.Y., 1971-72. Candidate for Republican nomination for congressman from 24th dist. N.Y., 1972, 74, 80; pres. local Rep. Club, 1973-74; mem. Westchester County Rep. Com., 1972-83; Rep., Conservative and Ind. candidate for supr. Town of Rye, N.Y., 1973, 75, 79, 81, Rep. candidate for councilman, 1977; vice-chmn. Ind. Conservative Caucus, Westchester, 1977-83; exec. v.p. bd. trustees New York-Phoenix Schs. Design, 1968-74. Served with USNR, 1943-46; PTO; Served with USNR, 1950-54, 70; PTO; comdr. Res. Mem. Soc. Naval Architects and Marine Engrs. (life), Pa. Jr. C. of C. (1948-57), C. of C., Naval Res. Assn. (life mem.; v.p. Westchester chpt.), Militia Assn. N.Y. (life), Westchester Organ Soc. (v.p.), Pi Gamma Mu, Sigma Kappa Phi, Phi Delta Theta. Clubs: Masons, Shriners, Kiwanis, Elk. *Much hard work, a desire for knowledge, great integrity, persistence, enthusiasm, determination, and some vision are essential ingredients in the success formula. In addition, successful leaders must never shrink from responsibility! While it helps to be lucky, to have friends in the right places, or to be in the right place at the right time, it is more important in a man's quest for success to deal honestly and fairly with one's fellowman in order that when material success is achieved peace of mind and happiness come with it.*

EASTON, JOHN DONALD, neurologist, educator; b. Saskatoon, Sask., Can., Apr. 1, 1938; s. John and Winnifred J. (Small) E.; m. Carol Anne May, Jan. 31, 1960; children—Erin Kathleen, John Hendry, Murray Raymond. B.S., Wash. State U., 1960; M.D., U. Wash., 1964. Intern and resident in neurology Cornell Med. Center, N.Y. Hosp., N.Y.C., 1964-68; asst. prof., asso. prof. neurosci. U. Calif., San Diego, 1970-74; asso. and prof. medicine (neurology) So. Ill. U., Springfield, 1974-77; prof., chmn. dept. neurology Health Scis. Center U. Mo., Columbia, 1977—. Asso. editor: (Stein) textbook Internal Medicine; editorial bds.: Missouri Medicine. Served with USN, 1968-70. Fellow Am. Acad. Neurology, Stroke Council-Am. Heart Assn. (exec. com.); mem. Assn. Univ. Profs. of Neurology (exec. com.), AMA. Home: Univ of Texas Health Science Center Div of Neurology 7703 Floyd Curl Drive San Antonio TX 78284

EASTON, JOHN EDWARD, multi-industry executive; b. Oelwein, Iowa, May 20, 1935; s. William Howard and Irene (Burke) E.; m. Audrey M. Erdmann, Sept. 5, 1960; children: Anne, Betsy, John, Sarah, Susan. B.S.C., U. Iowa, 1959, M.A. in Acctg., 1961. C.P.A. Mgr. Price Waterhouse & Co., Mpls., 1961-69; asst. treas. Internat. Multifoods, Mpls., 1970-71; v.p. fin. MoAmCo, Mpls., 1971-74; ptnr. Peat, Marwick, Mitchell, Chgo. and St. Louis, 1974-82; v.p. tax Tenneco, Inc., Houston, 1982—. Mem. adv. council bd. U. Tex., Austin, 1982—. Mem. Petroleum Inst., Am. Inst. C.P.A.s. Republican. Roman Catholic. Clubs: Houston; Chevaliers Tastevin (St. Louis). Home: 46 Williamsburg Ln Houston TX 77024 Office: Tenneco Inc 1010 Milan St Houston TX 77002

EASTON, JOHN JAY, JR., state govt. ofcl.; b. San Francisco, June 16, 1943; s. John Jay and Julia (Crawford) E. B.S., U. Colo., 1964; J.D., Georgetown U., 1970. Bar: Va. bar 1970, Vt. bar 1971. Mktg. rep. Gen. Dynamics Corp., Washington, 1968-70; asso. firm Paterson, Gibson, Noble & Brownell, Montpelier, Vt., 1970-72; partner firm Davison & Easton, Stowe, Vt., 1972-75; asst. atty. gen., chief consumer protection Office Vt. Atty. Gen., 1975-78; dir. div. rate setting Vt. Agy. Human Services, 1978-80; atty. gen., State of Vt., 1981—; Mem. product safety adv. council U.S. Consumer Product Safety Com., 1977-79. Mem. Vt. Natural Resources Council, 1976—. Served to capt. USAF, 1964-68. Mem. Am. Bar Assn. (ho. of dels. 1979—), Vt. Bar Assn. (del. 1980—, chmn. coms. 1974-78, bd. mgrs. 1973-75), Am. Legion, VFW. Republican. Episcopalian. Club: Rotary. Home: Barba Dr Stowe VT 05672 Office: 109 State St Montpelier VT 05602

EASTON, LOYD DAVID, educator; b. Rockford, Ill., July 29, 1915; s. Boyd J. and Elda (Holden) E.; m. Millison K. Shedd, June 14, 1942 (dec.); children—David, Carol, Judith; m. Martha Hutchison, Nov. 28, 1963; stepchildren—Martha Hutchison (Mrs. Anderson), Anne Hutchison (Mrs. Lundin). A.B., DePauw U., 1937; M.A., Boston U., 1939, Ph.D., 1942; postgrad., Harvard, 1941-42, Glasgow U., 1946. Borden Bowne fellow Boston U., 1939-40; instr. to asso. prof. philosophy Ohio Wesleyan U., 1946-54, chmn. dept. philosophy, 1952-76, found. prof. philosophy, 1955—, Trumbull Duvall prof. philosophy, 1978-80, prof. emeritus, 1980—; vis. prof. Ohio State U., summer 1957; vis. prof. philosophy religion Meth. Theol. Sch. in Ohio, 1960-61; Kent fellow Soc. for Values in Higher Edn., 1940—. Author: Ethics, Policy and Social Ends, 1955, Hegel's First American Followers, The Ohio Hegelians, 1967; Co-editor, co-translator: Writings of the Young Marx on Philosophy and Society, 1967; editor: with introduction Philosophical Analysis and Human Welfare by Dickinson S. Miller, 1975; Contbr. articles to profl. jours. Served with AUS, 1942-46. Recipient grant-in-aid Am. Council Learned Socs., 1961-62, Am. Assn. for State and Local History, 1963; Nat. Endowment for Humanities fellow, 1976. Mem. AAUP (nat. council 1960-63), Am.Philos. Assn., Ohio Philos. Assn. (pres. 1964-67), ACLU, Phi Beta Kappa, Omicron Delta Chi. Methodist. Home: 998 Braumiller Rd Delaware OH 43015

EASTON, ROBERT (OLNEY), author, environmentalist; b. July 4, 1915; s. Robert Eastman and Ethel (Olney) E.; m. Jane Faust, Sept. 24, 1940; children: Joan Easton Lentz, Katherine Easton Renga, Ellen Easton Brumfiel, Jane. Student, Stanford U., 1933-34, postgrad., 1938-39; B.S., Harvard U., 1938; M.A., U. Calif.-Santa Barbara, 1960. Ranch hand, day laborer, mag. editor, 1939-42; co-pub., editor Lampasas Dispatch, Tex., 1946-50; instr. English Santa Barbara City Coll., 1959-65; writing and pub. cons. U.S. Naval Civil Engring. Lab., Port Hueneme, Calif., 1961-69. Author: The Happy Man, 1943, (with Mackenzie Brown) Lord of Beasts, 1961, (with Jay Monaghan and others) The Book of the American West, 1963, The Hearing, 1964, (with Dick Smith) California Condor: Vanishing American, 1964, Max Brand: The Big Westerner, 1970, Black Tide: The Santa Barbara Oil Spill and Its Consequences, 1972, Guns, Gold and Caravans, 1978, China Caravans: An American Adventurer in Old China, 1982, This Promised Land, 1982; editor: Max Brand's Best Stories, 1967; co-editor: Bullying the Moqui (Charles F. Lummis), 1968; contbr. stories and articles to mags., including Atlantic and N.Y. Times mag., also chpts. to books. Co-chmn. Com. for Santa Barbara; trustee Santa Barbara Mus. Natural History. Served to 1st lt., F.A., Tank Destroyer Command, inf. U.S. Army, 1942-46. A creator Sisquoi Sanctuary for Calif. condor, 1937, also first wilderness area established under Nat. Wilderness Act, Los Padres Nat. Forest, Calif., 1968. Home: 2222 Las Canoas Rd Santa Barbara CA 93105 Office: care Dorothy Olding Harold Ober Assocs 40 E 49th St New York NY 10017

EASTON, WILLIAM HEYDEN, educator; b. Bedford, Ind., Jan. 14, 1916; s. Harry Thomas and Katharine (Gillen) E.; m. Phoebe Jane Beall, Aug. 10, 1940; children—Phoebe Beall, Robert Bruce, Katharine Louise. B.S., George Washington U., 1937, M.A., 1938; Ph.D., U. Chgo., 1940. With Nat. Park Service, summers 1936, 37, Ark. Geol. Survey, summer 1939, U. Hawaii, summer 1962; with Ill. Geol. Survey, 1940-44; mem. faculty U. So. Calif., 1946—, prof. geology, 1951-81, prof. emeritus, 1981—, chmn. dept., 1963-67, acting chmn. dept. French and Italian, 1975-76; with U.S. Geol. Survey, 1952-53; cons. geologist, 1950—. Author: Invertebrate Paleontology, 1960, also articles. Served with USNR, 1944-46. Recipient Publ. award Assn. Engring. Geologists, 1973, Raubenheimer Disting. Faculty award U. So. Calif., 1980; Guggenheim fellow, 1959-60. Fellow Geol. Soc. Am. (chmn. Cordilleran sect. 1965), So. Calif. Acad. Sci.; mem. Am. Assn. Petroleum Geologists (Distinguished lectr. 1955), Paleontol. Soc. (pres. West Coast br. 1950, pres. 1969), Soc. Econ. Paleontologists and Mineralogists (pres. Pacific sect. 1955), Coconut Island Inst., Sigma Xi (Outstanding Service award 1981), Phi Beta Kappa, Phi Kappa Phi, Sigma Gamma Epsilon. Home: 3818 Bowsprit Circle Westlake Village CA 91361 Office: Dept Geological Sciences Univ Southern Calif University Park Los Angeles CA 90089

EASTWOOD, CLINT, actor, director; b. San Francisco, May 31. Ed., Oakland Tech. High Sch., Los Angeles City Coll. Worked as lumberjack in Oreg. before being drafted into the Army; Mem. Nat.

Council Arts, 1973. Starred in: TV series Rawhide, 7 1/2 yrs; motion pictures include: A Fistful of Dollars, 1967, For a Few Dollars More, 1967, The Witches, The Good, The Bad and the Ugly, 1967, Paint Your Wagon, 1969, Hang 'Em High, 1968, Coogan's Bluff, 1968, Where Eagles Dare, 1969, Two Mules for Sister Sara, 1970, Kelly's Heroes, 1970, Beguiled, 1971, Play Misty for Me (also dir.), 1971, Dirty Harry, 1972, Joe Kidd, 1972, High Plains Drifter, 1973, Magnum Force, 1973, Breezy (also dir.), 1973, Thunderbolt and Lightfoot, 1974, The Eiger Sanction, 1975, The Enforcer, 1976, The Gauntlet, 1977, Every Which Way But Loose, 1978, Escape from Alcatraz, 1979, Bronco Billy (also dir.), 1980, Any Which Way You Can, 1980; dir., actor, producer: Firefox, 1982, Honky Tonk Man, 1982, Sudden Impact, 1983. Address: Warner Bros Studio 4000 Warner Blvd Burbank CA 91522

EASTWOOD, CLYDE WILLIAM, food co. exec.; b. Newport News, Va., May 5, 1943; s. Clyde McLaughlin and Edith A. (Craddock) E.; m. Sally Sue Jones, Dec. 26, 1975; children—Cliff, Elizabeth. Bar: Va. bar 1968, also N.Y 1968, Nebr. bars 1968. With Touche Ross & Co. (C.P.A.'s), N.Y.C., 1968; with firm Brown, Wood, Ivy, Mitchell & Petty, N.Y.C., 1971-73; partner firm Wright & Eastwood, Lincoln, Nebr., 1973-76; exec. v.p. Spencer Foods, Inc., Iowa, 1976—. Served to 1st lt. AUS, 1969-70. Decorated Distinguished Service award; recipient Outstanding Bus. and Econs. award Delta Sigma Pi, 1965. Mem. Am., N.Y., Nebr. bar assns. Republican. Methodist. Club: Spencer Country. Home: 1111 W 8th St Spencer IA 51301

EASTWOOD, DOUGLAS WILLIAM, anesthesiologist; b. Ellsworth, Wis., Sept. 17, 1918; s. Frederick William and Maud (Holmes) E.; m. Ruth E. Beitel, June 12, 1943; children—William Ashley, Mary Ruth, Robert Douglas, James Edward. Student, Washington and Jefferson Coll., 1936-37; A.B., Coe Coll., 1940; M.D., U. Iowa, 1943, M.S., 1949. Diplomate: Am. Bd. Anesthesiology. Intern Receiving Hosp., Detroit, 1944, asst. resident internal medicine, 1944-45; asst. resident anesthesiology U. Iowa Coll. Medicine, 1947-48, resident anesthesiology, 1948-49, instr. anesthesiology, 1949-50, asso. anesthesiology, 1950, asso. prof. div. anesthesiology, 1954-55; instr. dept. internal medicine Wayne U., 1944-45; asst. prof., chief div. anesthesiology Washington U. Sch. Medicine, 1950-54; chmn. dept. anesthesiology U. Va. Hosp., 1955-71; prof. anesthesiology Case Western Res. U., 1972—, also asso. prof. med. edn., dir. program devel. in medicine. Served as capt. AUS, 1945-47. Fellow Am. Coll. of Anesthesiologists; mem. Am. Soc. Anesthesiologists, A.M.A., Internat. Anesthesia Research Soc., Assn. U. Anesthetists, Am. Assn. U. Profs., Sigma Xi. Home: 3630 Mt Laurel Cleveland Heights OH 44121 Office: Sch Medicine Case Western Res U Cleveland OH 44106

EASTWOOD, GREGORY LINDSAY, medical educator; b. Detroit, July 28, 1940; s. William Inwood and Kathryn (Bradley) E.; m. Lynn Marshall, June 19, 1964; children: Kristen, Lauren, Kara. A.B., Albion Coll., 1962; M.D., Case-Western Res. U., 1966. Diplomate: Am. Bd. Internal Medicine, Am. Bd. Gastroenterology. Intern Hosp. U. Pa., 1966-67, resident in internal medicine, 1967-70; asst. prof. medicine Harvard U., Boston, 1974-77; assoc. prof. medicine U. Mass., Worcester, 1977-82, prof., 1982—, dir. gastroenterology, 1977—. Fellow ACP; mem. Am. Gastroent. Assn., New Eng. Endoscopy Soc. (pres. 1983-84). Office: University of Massachusetts Medical Sch 55 Lake Ave N Worcester MA 01605

EASUM, DONALD B., inst. exec.; b. Ind., Aug. 27, 1923; m. Augusta Pentecost. B.A., U. Wis., 1947; M.P.A., Princeton, 1950, M.A., 1950, Ph.D., 1953. Tchr., 1947-48, newspaper reporter, 1949, independent research, London, 1950-51, Buenos Aires, 1951-52; with Dept. State, 1953; econ.-labor officer, Managua, 1955-57, cons., econ. officer, Djakarta, 1957-59; fgn. affairs officer State Dept., 1959-61; det. dep. exec. sec. ICA, 1961, AID, 1961-62, exec. sec., 1962-63; polit. officer, Dakar, Gambia, Port Guinea, 1963-66, counsellor, dep. chief mission, Niamey, 1966-68; detailed to Sr. Sem in Fgn. Policy, Fgn. Service Inst., 1968-69; dir. Interdept. Group Staff Bur. Inter-Am. Affairs, Nat. Security Council, 1969-71; ambassador E. and P. to Upper Volta, Ouagadougou, 1971-74, asst. sec. state for African affairs, 1974-75, ambassador E. and P. to Nigeria, 1975-79; pres. African-Am. Inst., N.Y.C., 1979—. Served with AUS, 1942-46. Address: African-Am Inst 833 United Nations Plaza New York NY 10017

EATON, ALLEN OBER, lawyer; b. Waterford, N.Y., May 28, 1910; s. Arthur Chester and Ethel (Obear) E.; m. Marjorie Eisenwinter, Sept. 8, 1934; 1 dau., Barbara (Mrs. Kent Neilson). B.S., U. Vt., 1932; LL.B., Harvard, 1935. Bar: Mass. 1935. Practiced in, Boston, 1935—; with Ropes & Gray (and predecessor firm), 1935—, partner, 1944-83, of counsel, 1983—; Dir., adv. council Central Vt. Pub. Service Corp.; trustee Winchester Savs. Bank. Trustee U. Vt., 1970-76, chmn. bd. trustees, 1975-76. Mem. Am., Mass., Boston bar assns., Sigma Phi. Conglist. Clubs: Union (Boston); Winchester (Mass.) Country. Office: 225 Franklin St Boston MA 02110

EATON, ALVIN KANE, contracting co. exec.; b. Chgo., Jan. 4, 1928; s. William J. and Zicel (Rubenstein) E.; m. Arlene Udell, June 20, 1948; children—Nancy, David, Alice. B.S., Ill. Inst. Tech., 1948. Elec. engr. Tuttle & Kift, Chgo., 1948-49; plant engr. W.F. Hall Printing Co., Chgo., 1949-51; treas. Culberg Asbestos & Cork Co., Chgo., 1951-61; dir., founder Brand Insulations, Inc., Chgo., 1961-76, pres., 1976—; dir. Small Bus. Mgmt. Investors, Inc. Club: Twin Orchard Country (Long Grove, Ill.). Home: 7141 N Kedzie Ave Apt 215 Chicago IL 60645 Office: 1420 Renaissance Dr Park Ridge IL 60068

EATON, BERRIEN CLARK, lawyer, author; b. Chgo., Feb. 12, 1919; s. Berrien Clark and Gladys (Hambleton) E.; m. Donna K. Priestwood; children: Theodore Hambleton, Ann Berrien. Student, Williams Coll., 1936-38; B.S., U. Va., 1940, LL.B., 1948, J.D., 1970. Bar: Mich. 1948, Ariz. 1969, Ga. 1971. Practiced in, Detroit, 1948-69, Phoenix, 1969—; assoc. Miller, Canfield, Paddock & Stone, 1948-58, partner, 1958-69; mem. Leibsohn, Eaton, Gooding & Romley, P.C., 1971-79; partner Gray, Plant, Mooty, Mooty & Bennett, Phoenix, 1979-80; mem. firm Eaton, Lazarus & Dodge, Ltd., 1981—; instr. Wayne State U. Law Sch., 1954-69; prof. U. Ga. Law Sch., 1970-71; lectr. at law Ariz. State U. Coll. Law, 1970-71. Author: Professional Corporations and Associations, 6 vols., updated annually; co-author: tax newsletter Veba Report; Editorial bd.: jour. Estate Planning; Contbr. articles to profl. jours. Served to capt. F.A., AUS, 1941-46. Decorated Bronze Star; named hon. Ky. Col. Fellow Am. Assn. Probate Counsel, Am. Coll. Probate Counsel; mem. ABA. (com. chmn. tax sect.); Mem. Mich. Bar Assn. (past chmn. tax sect.), Detroit Bar Assn. (past chmn. tax sect.), Ariz. Bar Assn. (chmn. tax sect.), Ga. Bar Assn., AAUP, Valley Estate Planning Council, Western Pension Conf., Am. Coll. Tax Counsel (regent), Am. Law Inst. (program chmn.), Newcomen Soc. N.Am., Order of Coif, Kappa Alpha. Episcopalian. Clubs: Paradise Valley Country, Waweatonong. Home: 7239 N Mockingbird Ln Paradise Valley AZ 85253 Office: 5050 N 40th St Suite 108 Phoenix AZ 85018

EATON, CHARLES EDWARD, educator, author; b. Winston-Salem, N.C., June 25, 1916; s. Oscar Benjamin and Mary Gaston (Hough) E.; m. Isabel Patterson, Aug. 16, 1950. Student, Duke, 1932-33; A.B., U. N.C., 1936; postgrad., Princeton, 1936-37; M.A., Harvard, 1940. Instr. English U. Mo., 1940-42; prof. creative writing U. N.C., 1946-51; Am. vice-consul, Rio de Janeiro, Brazil, 1942-46. Author: poems The Bright Plain, 1942, The Shadow of the Swimmer, 1951, The Greenhouse in the Garden, 1956, Countermoves, 1963, On the Edge of the Knife, 1970, The Man in the Green Chair, 1977, Colophon of the Rover, 1980, In the Land of the Thing King, 1983; art criticism Karl Knaths: Five Decades of Painting, 1973, Robert Broderson: Paintings and Graphics, 1975; short stories Write Me from Rio, 1959, The Girl from Ipanema, 1972, The Case of the Missing Photographs, 1978; Contbr. to: anthologies Best American Short Stories, 1952, American Literature: Readings and Critiques, 1961, Epoch Anthology, 1968, Best Poems of the Year, 1965, 68, 69, 70, 74, 75, O. Henry Prize Stories, 1972, New Southern Poets, 1975, The Poet in Washington, 1977, Contemporary Poetry of North Carolina, 1977, Contemporary Southern Poetry, 1979, Anthology of Magazine Verse, 1980, 81. Recipient Ridgely Torrence Meml. award, 1951; Gertrude Boatwright Harris award, 1954; Ariz. Quar. award, 1956, 82; Roanoke-Chowan Poetry Cup, 1970; Oscar Arnold Young Meml. award, 1971; Golden Rose award New Eng. Poetry Club, 1972; Alice Fay di Castagnola award Poetry Soc. Am., 1974; Ariz. Quar. award, 1977, 79; Arvon Found. award, London, 1981; Fellow Bread Loaf Writers Conf., 1941; fellow Boulder Writers Conf., 1942. Mem. Am. Acad. Poets, Poetry Soc. Am., New Eng. Poetry Club, N.C. Poetry Soc., N.C. Art Soc., Phi Beta Kappa, Sigma Nu. Address: 808 Greenwood Rd Chapel Hill NC 27514 *I believe in the world seen through a temperament, and I am certain that it is always the main task of the writer to give us his personal vision of reality, objectively and subjectively explored.*

EATON, CHARLES LUTHER, transportation and energy company executive; b. Radford, Va., Jan. 21, 1932; s. Crozier Anderson and Margaret Sue (Munsey) E.; m. Mary Jo Kinder, Sept. 15, 1951; children: Cathi, Charles, Steve, Ted, Patty. B.S. in Accounting-Bus. Adminstrn, Va. Poly. Inst., 1953. Various supervisory and mgmt. positions. Gen. Electric Co., 1954-75, mgr. telecommunications and info. processing ops., Schenectady, N.Y., 1966-69, gen. mgr. telecommunications products dept., Lynchburg, Va., 1969-75; v.p. fin. and adminstrn. Union Pacific Corp., Rocky Mountain Energy Co., Denver, 1976-79, v.p. strategic planning, 1979—; also sr. v.p. planning and external affairs Union Pacific Corp. Mem. Adv. Council Coll. Bus., Va. Poly. Inst. Office: 345 Park Ave New York NY 10154

EATON, CONRAD PAUL, librarian; b. Seattle, Mar. 18, 1941; s. Paul J. and Helen Cecilia (Sartori) E.; m. Leslie Eileen Pearce, July 3, 1965; children—Alicia Marie, John Paul, Mara Terese, David Michael, Brian Conrad, Christopher Louis. B.A., Seattle U., 1963; M.L.S., U. Wash., 1965. Spl. recruit Library of Congress, Washington, 1965-66, subject cataloger, 1966, tech. asst., 1966-68, asst. field dir., New Delhi, 1968-71; chief tech. services br. State Dept. Library, Washington, 1971-73, librarian, 1973—. Served with AUS, 1963-64. Home: 2710 Belleview Ave Cheverly MD 20785 Office: State Dept Library Washington DC 20520

EATON, FRANCIS HOMER, food co. exec.; b. Honolulu, Sept. 10, 1934; s. Francis Homer and Zaderine Margaret (Lindemann) E.; m. Evelyn Jenney, Aug. 1, 1959; children—Rebecca Ann, Barbara True. B.S.E. magna cum laude, Princeton U., 1956; M.B.A., Harvard U., 1962. With Castle & Cooke (and subs.'s), Honolulu, 1962—; cannery supr. and supt. Dole Co., 1962-72, plant mgr., 1966-71, regional mgr., 1972; Far East regional mgr. Castle & Cooke Foods, Manila, 1972-73, C.Am. regional mgr., Honduras and Guatemala, 1974-75; v.p. seafood prodn. Castle & Cooke, San Francisco, 1975-76, v.p. and gen. mgr. salmon/shellfish products group, 1977-79, v.p., gen. mgr. tuna products group, 1979-81, exec. v.p., 1981—, pres., 1981—. Served in USN, 1956-62. Mem. Nat. Food Processors Assn. (dir.), Sigma Xi. Republican. Unitarian. Clubs: Peninsula Golf and Country, Princeton No. Calif. Office: 50 California St San Francisco CA 94111

EATON, GEORGE HOWARD, banker; b. Placerville, Calif., Apr. 12, 1935; s. George Howard and Catherine (Winslow) E.; m. Dawn Brown, May 13, 1978; children: Renee, Daphne, Howard; 1 stepson, Todd. B.A. in E. Asian Studies, U. Oreg., 1962. Asst. cashier Bank Am., Calif. and S.E. Asia, 1964-67; with money market dept. Odlum Brown and T.B. Read, Vancouver, B.C., 1967-69; with Bank B.C., Vancouver, 1969-74, exec. v.p., 1973-74; exec. v.p., chief operating officer First City Fin. Corp., Vancouver, 1974-76; chmn., chief exec. officer Can. Comml. Bank, Edmonton, Alta., 1976—; chmn. CCB Mortgage Investment Corp., BB & E Corp.; dir. Fin. Life Ins. Co. Ltd., Cancom Mgmt. Ltd. Served with USAF, 1956-60. Mem. Can. Bankers Assn. (exec. council), Can. Council Christians and Jews. Clubs: Edmonton, Royal Vancouver Yacht, Santa Barbara (Calif.) Yacht. Office: 1801 CCB Tower Edmonton Centre Edmonton AB T5J 0H8 Canada

EATON, GORDON PRYOR, university administrator, geologist; b. Dayton, Ohio, Mar. 9, 1929; s. Colman and Dorothy (Pryor) E.; m. Virginia Anne Gregory, June 12, 1951; children: Gretchen Maria, Gregory Mathieu. B.A., Wesleyan U., 1951; M.S. (Standard Oil fellow), Calif. Inst. Tech., 1953, Ph.D., 1957. Instr. geology Wesleyan U., Middletown, Conn., 1955-57, asst. prof., 1957-59, U. Calif., Riverside, 1959-63, assoc. prof., 1963-67, chmn. dept. geol. sci., 1965-67; with U.S. Geol. Survey, 1963-65, 67—; dep. chief Office Geochemistry Geophysics, Washington, 1972-74, project chief geothermal geophysics, Denver, 1974-76; scientist-in-charge Hawaiian Volcano Obs., 1976-78, asso. chief geologist, Reston, Va., 1978-81; dean Coll. Geoscis. Tex. A&M U., 1981-83, provost, v.p. acad. affairs, 1983—. Contbr. articles to profl. jours.; Mem. editorial bd.: Jour. Volcanology and Geothermal Research, 1976-78. NSF grantee, 1955-59. Fellow Geol. Soc. Am.; mem. AAAS, Am. Geophys. Union, Soc. Exploration Geophysicists, Hawaii Natural History Assn. (dir. 1976-78). Club: Rotary. Home: 201 Pershing Ave College Station TX 77840 Office: Office of Dean Coll Geoscis Tex A and M U College Station TX 77843

EATON, HAVEN MCCRILLIS, communications company executive; b. Youngstown, Ohio, Sept. 26, 1926; s. Gordon Forest and Elsie Marie (Werts) E.; m. Mary Ellen Lyman, Mar. 23, 1946; children: Haven McCrillis, John G., Laura M., Kathryn A. B.B.A., Western Res. U., 1947; J.D., Duquesne U., 1959. Bar: Pa. 1959. Clerical asst. Pitts. Steel Co., 1947-48; v.p., sec.-treas. Kenn Buick, Inc., Pitts., 1949-58; v.p., gen. mgr. S.H. Motors, Pitts., 1958-59; salesman Terryphone Corp., Pitts., 1959-60, asst. sec., Harrisburg, Pa., 1960-61, sec., 1961-62, treas., 1962-63, v.p., Camp Hill, Pa., 1963-64; v.p., chief counsel, sec., dir. ITT Terryphone Corp., Harrisburg, 1964—; asso. firm Kirkpatrick Pomeroy, Lockhart and Johnson, Pitts., 1959-60. Maj., CAP USAF. Mem. Am. Bar Assn., Fed. Bar Assn., Pa. Bar Assn. (chmn. sect. corp. banking and bus. law), Dauphin County Bar Assn., N. Am. Telephone Assn. (dir., mem. exec. com. 1973—), Air Force Assn. (state v.p. 1971-73, pres. Olmsted chpt. 1973-74), Nat. Rifle Assn., Am. Mgmt. Assn., Am. Ordnance Assn., Pa. C. of C., Harrisburg Area C. of C., Pa. Econ. League (chmn. Harrisburg Area com. 1982-84), U.S. Power Squadron, Am. Security Council, Omicron Delta Kappa, Phi Gamma Delta. Republican. Unitarian. Clubs: Masons, Shriners; Rotary, Tuesday (Harrisburg). Office: 300 E Park Dr Harrisburg PA 17111

EATON, HENRY FELIX, public relations executive; b. Cleve., Nov. 30, 1925; s. Henry F. and Stella (Simon) E.; m. Barbara Feder, Aug. 28, 1950; children: Deborah, Richard, David, Susan. B.A., U. Chgo., 1947. Asst. advt. mgr. Kromex Corp., Cleve., 1947-48; editor Material Handling Engring. mag., Cleve., 1948-52; chmn., chief exec. officer Dix & Eaton, Inc., Cleve., 1952—. Vice pres. adv. bd. trustees Notre Dame Coll. Ohio, Cleve.; exec. com. bd. trustees Playhouse Sq. Found., Cleve.; trustee Hawker Sch., Cleve., Cleve. Council Ind. Schs. Served with AUS, 1944-46. Mem. Pub. Relations Soc. Am. (counselors sect.), Nat. Investor Relations Inst. Clubs: Union, Cleve. Athletic, Cleve. Racquet, Oakwood Country. Home: 23690 Letchworth Rd Beachwood OH 44122 Office: The 1010 Euclid Bldg Cleveland OH 44115

EATON, JOE O., judge; b. Monticello, Fla., Apr. 2, 1920; s. Robert Lewis and Mamie (Gireadeau) E. A.B., Presbyn. Coll., 1941, LL.D. (hon.), 1979; LL.B., U. Fla., 1948. Practiced in, Miami, Fla., 1948-51, 55-59, asst. state atty., Dade County, Fla., 1953, circuit judge, Miami, 1954-55, 59-67; mem. Fla. Senate, 1956-59; mem. law firm Eaton & Achor, Miami, 1955-58, Sams, Anderson, Eaton & Alper, 1958-59; judge U.S. Dist. Ct. for So. Dist. Fla., 1967—, chief judge, 1983—; Instr. law U. Miami Coll. Law, 1954-56. Served with USAAF, 1941-45; Served with USAF, 1951-52. Decorated D.F.C., Air medal. Methodist. Club: Kiwanian. Office: US Dist Ct PO Box 014941 Miami FL 33101

EATON, JOSEPH W., sociology educator; b. Nuremburg, Germany, Sept. 28, 1919; s. Jacob and Flora (Wechsler) E.; m. Helen Goodman, June 8, 1947; children: David, Seth, Debra, Jonathan. B.S., Cornell U., 1940; Ph.D., Columbia U., 1948. Faculty Wayne State U., Detroit, 1947-56; lectr., then vis. prof. Sch. Social Welfare, U. Calif. at Los Angeles, 1956-60; prof. social work research U. Pitts., 1960-70, dir. advanced program, 1966-69, prof. sociology in pub. health and social work research, 1970-73, Sch. Pub. and Internat. Affairs, 1974—; Russell Sage Found. vis. prof. Western Res. U., 1953-56, cons., 1958-59; project dir. Conf. on Social Welfare Consequences of Migration and Residential Movement, 1969; dir. instn. bldg. program Interuniv. Research Consortium, 1966-71; curriculum cons., later dir. social work and social adminstrn. program U. Haifa, Israel, 1970-74; USICA cons., lectr., Africa, 1979, Sweden, W.Ger., Romania, 1982, Fulbright lectr. and cons., 1979, Nat. Acad. Scis. guest scholar in, Poland and German Democratic Republic, 1980. Author: (with Saul M. Katz) Research Guide on Cooperative Group Farming, 1942, Exploring Tomorrow's Agriculture, 1943, (with Albert Mayer) Man's Capacity to Reproduce, 1954, (with Robert J. Weil) Culture and Mental Disorders, 1955, (with Kenneth Polk) Measuring Delinquency, 1961, Stone Walls Not a Prison Make: The Anatomy of Planned Adminstrative Change, 1962, Prisons in Israel, 1964, (with Michael Chen) Influencing the Youth Culture: A Study of Youth Organization in Israel, 1970, The Rurban Village, 1980, Can Business Save South Africa, 1980; also chpts. in books, articles.; Editor: (with Michael Chen) Institution Building and Development, 1972. Served with AUS, 1941-46. Faculty Research fellow Social Sci. Research Council, 1962. Mem. Nat. Assn. Social Workers (chmn. research council 1968-71), Internat. Assn. Social Psychiatry (mem. council 1969—), Am. Sociol. Assn. Home: 2208 Beechwood Blvd Pittsburgh PA 15217 Office: 3 E 38 Forbes Quadrangle Univ Pitts Pittsburgh PA 15260

EATON, LEONARD JAMES, JR., banker; b. N.Y.C., Sept. 18, 1934; s. Leonard James and Alice Edna (Leach) E.; m. Patricia Pride, Nov. 30, 1957; children: Leslie, Pamela, Alexander. B.A., Cornell U., 1956; postgrad., Harvard, 1971. With First Nat. City Bank, N.Y.C., 1956-71; exec. v.p. Bank of Okla. N.A. (formerly Nat. Bank of Tulsa), 1972-73, pres., 1973-78, chmn. bd., chief exec. officer, 1978—, also dir.; chmn. bd., chief exec. officer dir. Banc Okla. Corp. Bd. dirs. Downtown Tulsa Unltd.; trustee Lew Wentz Found., Hillcrest Med. Center, U. Tulsa.; vice chmn. Univ. Ctr. at Tulsa Found. Mem. Young Pres.'s Orgn., Tulsa C. of C. (dir.). Home: 1530 E 27th St Tulsa OK 74114 Office: PO Box 2300 Tulsa OK 74192

EATON, LEWIS SWIFT, savings and loan executive; b. San Francisco, Aug. 10, 1919; s. Edwin M. and Gertrude (Swift) E.; m. Virginia Stammer, Apr. 21, 1950; children: William L., Joan E., John W. B.A., Stanford U., 1942. With Guarantee Savs. & Loan Assn., Fresno, Calif., 1946—, v.p., 1950-56, pres., 1956—, also chmn. bd.; dir. Fed. Home Loan Bank, San Francisco, 1964-70, MGIC Investment Corp., Milw., Pacific Gas & Electric Corp. Pres. Fresno Zool. Soc., 1967-68; Mem. Fresno City Bd. Edn., 1958-66; pres., 1959-62; Chmn. bd. govs. Fresno Regional Found., 1972-79; Trustee Fresno Community Hosp., 1965-81, Fresno State Coll. Found., 1969—, Jr. Achievement, 1951—, Calif. Mus. Found., 1970—; mem. adv. bd. Fresno State Coll., 1965-75; chmn. bd. dirs. Fresno Met. Mus., 1980—; Chmn. Nat. Parks Adv. Bd. Western Region, 1972-79. Served to capt. 77th Inf. Div. AUS, 1942-46. Mem. Calif. Savs. and Loan League (pres. 1959-60), U.S. Savs. and Loan League (pres. 1970-71), Calif. C. of C. (dir. 1977—), C. of C. Fresno City and County (pres. 1967), Yosemite Natural History Assn. (dir. 1977-79), Stanford Alumni Assn. (pres. 1975-76), Beta Gamma Sigma, Lambda Alpha. Home: 4115 N Van Ness Blvd Fresno CA 93704 Office: 1177 Fulton Mall Fresno CA 93721

EATON, MERRILL THOMAS, psychiatrist, educator; b. Howard County, Ind., June 25, 1920; s. Merrill Thomas and Dorothy (Whiteman) E.; m. Louise Foster, Dec. 23, 1942; children: Deirdre Ann, Thomas Anthony, David Foster. A.B., Ind. U., Bloomington, 1941, M.D., 1944. Diplomate: Am. Bd. Psychiatry. Intern St. Elizabeth's Hosp., Washington, 1944-45; resident Sheppard and Enoch Pratt Hosp., Towson, Md., 1948-49; practice medicine, specializing in psychiatry, Kansas City, Kans., 1949-60, Omaha, 1960—; dir. Nebr. Psychiat. Inst., 1968—; assoc. in psychiatry Kans. U. Sch. Medicine, 1949-50, asst. prof., 1951-54, assoc. prof., 1954-60; assoc. prof. psychiatry U. Nebr. Coll. Medicine, 1960-63, prof., 1963—, chmn. dept. psychiatry, 1968—. Author: Psychiatry, 1967, 4th edit., 1981, (with David Kentsmith) Treating Sexual Problems in Medical Practice, 1979. Served to capt. U.S. Army, 1945-47. Fellow A.C.P., Am. Psychiat. Assn.; mem. Am. Assn. Chmn. Depts. Psychiatry, Assn. Am. Med. Colls., Group for Advancement Psychiatry (chmn. com. on mental health services 1970-73, chmn. publ. bd. 1976-83), Nebr. Med. Assn., Nebr. Psychiat. Soc. (pres. 1973-75). Office: 602 S 45th St Omaha NE 68106

EATON, MORRIS LEROY, statistics educator; b. Sacramento, Aug. 10, 1939; s. Franklin LeRoy and Dorothy Evelyn (Ward) E.; m. Marcia Mae Muelder, Aug. 13, 1964; 1 son, Dennis Owen. B.S., U. Wash., 1961; M.S., Stanford U., 1963, Ph.D., 1966. Research assoc. Stanford U., 1966; asst. prof. stats. U. Chgo., 1966-70, assoc. prof., 1970-71; vis. prof. U. Copenhagen, 1971-72; asso. prof. theoretical stats. U. Minn., 1972-73, prof., 1973—, chmn. dept. theoretical stats., 1978-81. Author: Multivariate Statistical Analysis, 1972, Multivariate Statistics: A Vector Space Approach, 1983; asso. editor: Annals Stats, 1978-83. Population Council grantee, 1969-70; NSF grantee, 1972-84. Fellow Inst. Math. Stats., Am. Stats. Assn. (assoc. editor Jour. Am. Stats. Assn. 1970-72). Home: 33 Park Ln Minneapolis MN 55416 Office: 206 Church St Vincent Hall 270 Minneapolis MN 55455

EATON, ROBERT JAMES, automotive company executive; b. Buena Vista, Colo., Feb. 13, 1940; s. Eugene Hiram and Mildred Inez (Stokes) E.; m. Cornelia Cae Drake, June 28, 1964; children: Scott C., Matthew D. B.S.M.E., U. Kans., 1963. Exec. engr. engring. staff Gen. Motors Corp., Warren, Mich., 1974-75, chief engr. small family car project Chevrolet div., 1975-76, chief engr. corp. car programs engring. staff, 1976-79, asst. chief Oldsmobile div., Lansing, Mich., 1979-82, dir.

reliability, 1982, v.p. advanced product and mfg. engring. staff, Lansing, Detroit, 1982—. Mem. Soc. Automotive Engrs. (tech. bd. 1983—, chmn. nat. congress 1984), Engring. Soc. Detroit. Home: 920 Sandhurst Bloomfield Hills MI 48013 Office: Gen Motors Corp GM Tech Center Twelve Mile and Mound Rds Warren MI 48090

EATON, SAMUEL DICKINSON, international business consultant, former fgn. service officer; b. Plymouth, N.Y., Feb. 13, 1923; s. Harry W. and Nellie L. (Bernhard) E.; m. Mercedes Herrera, Feb. 16, 1949. A.B., Drew U., 1947; student, Columbia, 1947, Fletcher Sch. Law and Diplomacy, 1952-53. Third sec. Am. embassy, La Paz, Bolivia, 1948-50, 2d sec., Rio de Janeiro, 1950-52, Bangkok, Thailand, 1953-55; chief financial stablzn. br., div. internat. finance Dept. State, 1955-59; chief econ. sect. Am. embassy, Bogota, Colombia, 1959-65; also dep. dir. AID mission, 1962-65; dep. dir. N. Coast Am. Republic Affairs Dept. State, 1965-66; spl. asst. to asst. sec. Am. Republic Affairs, 1966-67; at Nat. War Coll., 1967-68; dir. AID Mission to Peru, 1968-69; dep. chief mission Am. embassy, Quito, Ecuador, 1969-70; mem. planning and coordination Staff Dept. State, 1970-74; dep. chief mission Am. embassy, Madrid, Spain, 1974-78; diplomat-in-residence, vis. prof. govt. Mills Coll., 1978-79; dep. asst. sec. state for Latin Am. affairs, 1979-81; internat. bus. cons., 1981—. Author: The Forces of Freedom in Spain, 1974-79: A Personal Account, 1981. Served as 2d lt. USAAF, 1945-46. Recipient Superior Honor award U.S. Dept. State, 1980, Alumni Achievement award Drew U., 1982. Address: 4995 Glenbrook Rd NW Washington DC 20016

EATON, WILLIAM JAMES, newspaperman; b. Chgo., Dec. 9, 1930; s. Wlliam Millar and Rose (Ellenbast) E.; m. Marilynn Myers, Sept. 6, 1952 (div. Sept. 24, 1980); children: Susan, Sally Ann. B.S., Northwestern U., 1951, M.S., 1952. With City News Bur., Chgo., 1952-53; with U.P.I., Washington, 1955-66; corr. Washington Bur. Chgo. Daily News, 1966-76, Knight-Ridder Newspapers, 1977-78, Los Angeles Times, 1978—; chmn. standing com. corrs. U.S. Capitol Press Gallery, 1973. Author: (with Frank Cormier) Reuther, 1970. Served with AUS, 1953-55. Recipient Sidney Hillman award, 1970, Pulitzer prize for nat. reporting, 1970; Nieman fellow Harvard, 1962-63. Club: Washington Press (pres. 1976-77). Office: 1 Hunamun Rd New Delhi India

EATON, WILLIAM MELLON, lawyer; b. N.Y.C., Oct. 5, 1924; s. Ernest Risley and Carolyn (Mellon) E.; m. Elizabeth Waring Witsell, Dec. 21, 1956; children: Carolyn, Alexander, Sarah, Lisa. B.S., Duke, 1945; J.D., Harvard, 1949. Bar: N.Y. 1949, U.S. Supreme Ct. 1961. Since practiced in, N.Y.C.; asso. firm White & Case, 1949-60; mem. firm Hardy, Peal, Rawlings, Werner & Maxwell, 1960-65; sr. partner firm Eaton & Van Winkle (specializing bank, corp., estate and trust law and litigation), 1965-—; pres. BT Capital Corp., SBIC of Bankers Trust, 1972-80, now dir.; dir. N.Y. Corp. Trustee, executor pvt. estates; dir. various corps. and founds.; Trustee Skowhegan Sch. Painting and Sculpture, Hartford Family Fund, other charitable orgns.; asst. sec., ofcl. adviser U.S.-Japan Found.; sec. Moroccan Am. Found.; chmn. investment com. N.Y. State Bar Found., 1974-81, now fellow. Served with USNR, 1943-46; PTO. Mem. Internat. Bar Assn., ABA. (chmn. com. investment securities 1969-73, now mem.), N.Y. State Bar Assn. (chmn. investment com.), Assn. Bar City N.Y., N.Y. County Lawyers Assn., Soc. Colonial Wars (chancellor Gen. Soc. 1978—), St. Nicholas Soc. (gov. 1965-68), Pilgrims. Episcopalian. Clubs: Union, Pinnacle (N.Y.C.) (pres.); Anglers; Profile (N.H.); French Alpine, Appalachian Mountain, others. Office: 600 3d Ave New York NY 10016

EAVES, JAMES CLIFTON, mathematician; b. Hillside, Ky., June 26, 1912; s. John Ridley and Agnes (Williams) E.; m. Maona Shinkle, Aug. 20, 1938; children: James Clifton, Mona Jane. A.B., U. Ky., 1935, M.A. (Haggen fellow), 1941; Ph.D., U. N.C., 1949. Tchr., Hillside, 1932-35; math. tchr., asst. athletic coach, debate coach Pineville (Ky.) City High Sch., 1935-37; math. tchr. Morton Jr. High Sch., Henry Clay High Sch., Lexington, Ky., 1937-40; grad. asst. U. Ky., 1941-42, instr., 1942-43, 46, prof., 1954, head dept. math. and astronomy, 1954-63, prof. math., 1963-67; Centennial prof. math. W. Va. U., 1967—; research cons., dir. Inst. Consultants Math., Statistics and Patent Law, 1956—; part-time instr. U. N.C., 1947-49; asst. prof. U. Ala., 1949-50; asso. prof. Ala. Poly. Inst., 1950-51, research asso. prof., 1951-52; prof., research asso. Auburn Research Found., 1952-53, prof., adminstrv. asst. dept. math., 1953-54; Dir. Ky. Space Flight Program in Math. and Astronomy. NASA. Author: (with W. V. Parker) Matrices, 1954, (with A.J. Robinson) An Introduction to Euclidean Geometry, 1955, (with T.J. Pignani) Digital Computer Programing, 1959, Mathematics of Finance and Business, 1960, Trigonometry for Self Study and Review, 1976, Geometry, An Appreciation Offering, 1976, A Development of Trigonometry As It Was, As It Is, 1976, (with Maona S. Eaves) Metric Notes, 1976; Gen. editor: College Algebra and Basic Set Theory, 1963; Contbr. research articles profl. math. jours.; author feature articles on astronomy. Scoutmaster, Pineville, Ky. Served as lt. USNR, 1943-46. Fellow AAAS; mem. Ky. Assn. Colls. and Secondary Schools (pres. math sect. 1957, 64), Ky. Soc. for Promotion Useful Knowledge, Math. Assn. Am. (lectr. Ky. sect. 1955-57, sec.-treas. 1960-66, chmn. 1959, 63, chmn. Allegheny Mountain sect. Pa.-W. Va. 1971-73), Am. Math. Soc., AAUP, Ala. Assn. Coll. Tchrs. Maths. (pres. 1953-54), Newcomen Soc. N.Am., Sigma Xi, Phi Delta Kappa (sec., Meritorious Service award), Pi Mu Epsilon (nat. councilor gen. 1960-63, nat. pres. 1967-73, C.C. MacDuffee award of excellence for disting. service to math.), Mu Alpha Theta (nat. pres. 1959-62, Disting. Leadership award for internat. officers), Alpha Nu (state pres.). Clubs: Kiwanis, Bluegrass (Lexington). Patentee dial setting mechanism, buckle protector, design for award Key. Home: Hermit's Holler 1493 Van Voorhis Rd Morgantown WV 26505

EAVES, RONALD WELDON, computer scientist, educator; b. Beaumont, Calif., Aug. 28, 1937; s. Riley Weldon and Ruth (Marshall) E.; m. Betty L. Eaves; children by previous marriage: Christopher, David, Erin. B.A., San Jose State U., 1959, M.A., 1962; Ph.D., UCLA, 1976. Cert. data processor. Tchr. math. jr. high sch., San Jose, Calif., 1960-62; tchr. sci. Fullerton Jr. Coll., 1962-65; systems engr. Honeywell, Inc., Los Angeles, 1965-68; prof. info. systems Calif. State Poly. U., Pomona, 1968—, chmn. dept., 1972-76; prin. lectr. computing sci. Hong Kong Poly., 1979-80. Asst. treas. Hosp. Chaplains Ministry of Am., Inc., Fullerton, 1968-78; bd. dirs. Calif. Ednl. Computing Consortium. NSF fellow, 1973. Mem. Assn. Computing Machinery, Electronic Data Processing Auditors Assn. Office: 3801 W Temple Ave Pomona CA 91768

EBACHER, ROGER, bishop; b. Amos, Que., Can., Oct. 6, 1936. Ordained priest Roman Cath. Ch., 1961; ordained bishop of, Hauterive, Que., 1979. Office: 639 Rue de Bretagne CP 10 Hauterive PQ G5C 1X2 Canada *

EBAUGH, FRANKLIN GESSFORD, JR., physician, dean medical school; b. Phila., Dec. 25, 1921; s. Franklin G. and Dorothy (Reese) E.; children: Sandra D., Patricia S., Jeanette H. B.A. magna cum laude, Dartmouth Coll., 1944; M.D., Cornell U., 1946. Intern, then resident N.Y. Hosp., 1946-50; research fellow physiology Cornell U. Med. Coll., 1948; research fellow Evans Meml. Hosp., Boston U. Med. Sch., 1950-53; surgeon USPHS, 1953-55; asso. prof. clin. pathology, also asso. dir. labs. Dartmouth Med. Sch. and Mary Hitchcock Meml. Hosp., 1955-64; dean Boston U. Sch. Medicine, 1964-69; prof. medicine U. Utah, 1969-72, dean, 1969-71; asso. dean, prof. medicine Stanford U. Med. Sch., 1972—; mem. staff Evans Meml. Hosp., 1964-69; vis. physician Boston City Hosp., 1965-69; chmn. Boston VA Hosp. deans com., 1965-69, Salt Lake City VA deans com., 1969-71; chief of staff VA Hosp., Palo Alto, Calif., 1972—; Cons. council health professions constrn. facilities USPHS, 1965-70; mem. study sect. tng. grants USPHS-NIH, 1960-64; mem. study sect. program projects grants NIH-Nat. Inst. Neurol. Diseases and Blindness, 1965-69. Author articles, contbr. to books in field. Mem. Am. Soc. Clin. Investigation, Am. Acad. Arts and Scis., A.C.P., Am. Coll. Pathologists, Am. Soc. Hematology (exec. com. 1965-69), Am. Assn. Med. Coll. (exec. council 1967-69), Nat. Assn. VA Chiefs of Staff (pres. 1976), Phi Beta Kappa, Sigma Xi, Alpha Omega Alpha, Delta Tau Delta, Nu Sigma Nu. Home: 420 Gerona Rd Stanford CA 94305

EBB, FRED, lyricist, librettist; b. N.Y.C., Apr. 8, 1936; s. Harry and Anna Evelyn (Gritz) E. B.A., NYU, 1955; M.A. in English Lit., Columbia U., 1957; Hon. Degree in Theatre Arts, Emerson U., 1975. Lectr. in field. Author: Plays Flora, The Red Menace, 1963; Cabaret, 1965, Zorba, 1966, The Happy Time, 1968, Girls, 1971, Chicago, 1974, The Act, 1977, Woman of the Year, 1981; TV shows Liza with A Z, 1967, Ole Blue Eyes is Back, 1972, Gypsy in My Soul, 1976, Goldie and Liza Together, 1980, Baryshnikov on Broadway, 1980; motion pictures Cabaret, 1970, Funny Lady, 1973, Lucky Lady, 1976, New York, New York, 1977. Recipient Tony award N.Y. Theatres and Producers, 1967, 81, Drama Desk award N.Y. Drama Critics Circle, 1967, 68, Outer Circle award Orgn. Writers on Theatre, 1968, 69, George Foster Peabody award Grady Sch. Journalism, U. Ga., 1972, Drama Critics Circle award, 1967, Image award NAACP, 1973, Achievement award B'nai B'rith, 1967, Christopher award Catholic Socs., 1976; named to Songwriters' Hall of Fame, 1983. Mem. Dramatists Guild, Equity, Nat. Acad. TV Arts and Scis. (Emmy award 1972, 75, 76), Am. Guild Authors and Composers, Acad. Motion Picture Arts and Scis.

EBBERT, ARTHUR, JR., univ. dean; b. Wheeling, W.Va., Aug. 25, 1922; s. Arthur and Margaret (Henning) E. B.A., U. Va., 1944, M.D., 1946; M.A. (hon.), Yale U., 1971. Intern, then asst. resident in internal medicine U. Va. Hosp., 1946-51, resident in med. service, 1951-52; instr. internal medicine, asst. to dean U. Va. Med. Sch., 1952-53; mem. faculty Yale U. Med. Sch., 1953—, prof. clin. medicine, 1971—, prof. medicine, 1978—, dep. dean, 1974—. Editor: Yale Medicine, 1966—. Served as officer M.C. AUS, 1947-49. Mem. Assn. Am. Med. Colls., Conn. Med. Soc., New Haven County Med. Assn., Beaumont Med. Club, Alpha Omega Alpha. Office: 333 Cedar St PO Box 3333 New Haven CT 06510

EBBOTT, RALPH DENISON, mfg. co. exec.; b. Edgerton, Wis., Apr. 8, 1927; s. Elmer Thomas and Anne Louise (Moss) E.; m. Elizabeth Adams, July 23, 1950; children—Andrew Denison, Douglas Martin, Alison Ann, Kendrick Alan. B.B.A., U. Wis., 1948, M.B.A., 1949. C.P.A., Minn. Jr. acct. Arthur Andersen & Co., N.Y.C., 1949-51, sr. acct., Mpls., 1954-55; with Minn. Mining & Mfg. Co., St. Paul, 1955—, v.p. mgmt. info., 1974-77, v.p., treas., 1977—; dir. Eastern Heights State Bank. Served with USAF, 1951-53. Mem. Am. Inst. C.P.A.'s, Fin. Execs. Inst. Republican. Mem. United Ch. of Christ. Club: Jesters. Home: 409 Birchwood Ave White Bear Lake MN 55110 Office: 220 3M Center Saint Paul MN 55144

EBBS, JOHN DALE, English educator; b. Carbondale, Ill., Sept. 26, 1925; s. Charles and Dora (Fox) E.; m. Dorothy Ruth Churchwell, Mar. 14, 1953; children: Laura Ebbs Benjamin, Charles Curtis. A.B., U. N.C.- Chapel Hill, 1948; M.A., U. N.C.-Chapel Hill, 1949, Ph.D., 1958. Tchr. English Clinton (N.C.) High Sch., 1949-50; instr. English Tex. A&M U., 1950-54; grad. instr. English U. N.C., Chapel Hill, 1955-58; assoc. prof. English High Point (N.C.) Coll., 1958-59; asst. prof. Tex. A&M U., College Station, 1959-60; assoc. prof. E. Carolina U., Greenville, N.C., 1960-63, prof. English, 1963—, dir. Pockets of Excellence project, 1973—; supr. English for State N.C., 1966-67; vis. prof. English U. Nebr., Lincoln, 1967-68. Author: The Principle of Poetic Justice Illustrated in Restoration Tragedy, 1973, Manual of Style for Research Writing, 1976, rev. edit., 1980; editor: Early Methodism in Greenville, North Carolina: A History of the Jarvis Memorial United Methodist Church, 1979; contbr. articles, revs. to state, nat. jours. Treas. Jarvis Meml. United Meth. Ch., 1984—. Served with USAAF, 1943-45. Decorated D.F.C. Air Medal with five oak leaf clusters; named Outstanding Tchr. E. Carolina U., 1978; grantee to Eng. Z Smith Reynolds Found., 1973. Mem. MLA, Mediaeval Acad., Am. Council Tchrs. English, Nat. Council Tchrs. English, NEA, N.C. Assn. Educators, Phi Delta Kappa. Democrat. Methodist. Club: Exchange (Greenville, N.C.). Home: 1202 Drexel Ln Greenville NC 27834 Office: E 5thSt Greenville NC 27834

EBEID, RUSSELL JOSEPH, business executive; b. Detroit, Feb. 9, 1940; s. Joseph Zahour and Theresa (Salamie) E.; m. Carolee M. Cram, Feb. 14, 1961; children: Kevin, Evon, Carrie, Scott. B.E.E., Gen. Motors Inst., 1963; M.S. in Indsl. Engring., Wayne State U., 1969. Registered profl. engr., Mich. Sr. mech. engr. Gen. Motors Corp., Detroit, 1968-70; maintenance supt. Guardian Industries Corp., Carleton, Mich., 1970-71, plant engr., 1971-73, prodn. mgr., 1973-78, plant mgr., Kingsburg, Calif., 1978-81, group v.p., 1981—; mng. dir. Luxguard S.A., Luxembourg, 1982—. Author: Instrumentation of Welding, 1963. Decorated knight Order of Merit Luxembourg; recipient Employee of Yr. for Corp. award Guardian Industries Corp., 1979. Roman Catholic. Home: 3761 W Alluvial Fresno CA 93711 Office: Guardian Industries Corp 11535 E Mountain View Kingsburg CA 93631

EBEL, MARVIN EMERSON, educator, physicist; b. Waterloo, Iowa, Sept. 23, 1930; s. Louis August and Emily (Mussett) E.; m. Barbara Ann Schuck, July 22, 1960; children—Frederick Louis, Charles August, Elizabeth Ann, Katherine Susan. Student, Iowa State Tchrs. Coll., 1946-47; B.S., Iowa State Coll., 1950, M.S., 1952, Ph.D., 1953. NSF postdoctoral fellow Inst. Theoretical Physics, Copenhagen, Denmark, 1953-54; mem. faculty Yale, 1954-57, U. Wis., 1957—, prof. physics, 1965—, asso. dean, 1976—; cons. Los Alamos Sci. Lab., 1959-72. Sloan fellow, 1957-61. Fellow Am. Phys. Soc.; mem. Sigma Xi. Home: 910 Hampshire Pl Madison WI 53711

EBERHARDT, JOHN FOWLER, lawyer; b. Salina, Kans., Oct. 14, 1910; s. John J. and Mary Grace (Fowler) E.; m. Rebecca Jane Butts, Nov. 11, 1939; 1 dau., Gail. A.B., U. Kans., 1932; LL.B., Harvard, 1935. Bar: Kans. 1935. Since practiced in, Wichita; asso. Foulston, Siefkin, Powers & Eberhardt (and predecessors), 1935-38, partner, 1938—; gen. counsel The Coleman Co., Inc. Asso. editor: Kans. Bar Jour, 1939-41; editor-in-chief, 1942-43; contbr. articles to profl. jours. Vice pres., dir. Kans. Found. for Blind, Inc., 1955—; chmn. bd. trustees Inst. Logopedics, Inc., Endowment Trust, 1958-73; trustee Epworth Assembly, 1960-66, Kans. U. Endowment Assn., 1970—, Inst. Logopedics, Inc., 1975-77; mem. adv. council Kans. Community Jr. Colls., 1965-68; adv. trustee Mid-Am. All-Indian Center, 1970—; bd. regents State Kans., 1965-69, chmn., 1967-68; chmn. athletic bd. U. Kans., 1970-76. Served to lt. USNR, 1943-46; PTO. Mem. Am., Kans. bar assns., Kans. U. Alumni Assn. (trustee 1963-65), Beta Theta Pi. Methodist. Club: Rotary. Home: 1349 Cardington Ct Wichita KS 67212 Office: 700 Fourth Financial Center Wichita KS 67202

EBERHARDT, JULIAN STANLEY, transportation company executive; b. Chgo., Feb. 2, 1940; s. Andrew and Alice E.; m. Diane Louise Frey, June 16, 1963; children: Eric, Paul, Sara. B.S., Northwestern U., 1963, M.S., 1965. Indsl. engr. Chgo., Burlington & Quincy R.R., Chgo., 1965-69; project mgr. Chgo. & Northwestern Transp. Co., Chgo., 1970-72, dir. indsl. engring., 1972-73, asst. v.p., corp. indsl. engr., 1973-78, v.p. planning, 1978—. Precinct co-capt. New Trier Republican Orgn., 1972-82, precinct capt., 1982—; pres. Wilmette Hockey Assn., 1980-82. Mem. Am. Inst. Indsl. Engrs., Am. Assn. R.R.'s. Home: 1121 Chestnut St Wilmette IL 60091 Office: One North Western Ctr Chicago IL 60606 *

EBERHART, JOHN CAROL, fed. govt. sci. ofcl.; b. Lima, Ohio, Dec. 26, 1907; s. Frank and Morna (Davis) E.; m. Sylvia Rothman, Feb. 8, 1937; 1 son, Jonathan. B.A., U. Oreg., 1929; M.A., Northwestern U., 1931, Ph.D., 1934. Instr., asst. prof. psychology Northwestern U., 1936-43; tng. specialist, chief research grants and fellowships br. NIMH, Bethesda, Md., 1947-54, dir. instramural research, 1961-81; sr. adviser, dep. dir. sci. NIH, 1981—. Exec. asso. Commonwealth Fund, N.Y.C., 1954-61; Bd. dirs. Found. for Advanced Edn. in Scis., 1962—. Served to lt. USNR, 1943-46. Decorated Bronze Star medal; Social Sci. Research Council fellow, 1940-41, 46; recipient Superior Service award HEW, 1965, Disting. Service award, 1969, Career Civil Service award Nat. Civil Service League, 1974, Presdl. Meritorious Exec. Rank award, 1980. Mem. Am. Psychol. Assn. (Harold H. Hildreth Meml. award 1968), Soc. for Neurosci., Assn. for Research in Nervous and Mental Disease, Am. Psychopath. Assn., Phi Beta Kappa, Sigma Xi. Club: Cosmos (Washington). Home: 7935 Deepwell Dr Bethesda MD 20817 Office: NIH Room 101 NIH Bldg 1 9000 Rockville Pike Bethesda MD 20205

EBERHART, MARY ANN PETESIE, wholesale company executive; b. Baton Rouge, Aug. 20, 1940; d. Wilford Malvern and Mary Gordon (Davidson) E. B.S., McNeese State U., 1963. With United Service Warehouse, Inc., Baton Rouge, 1963-82, v.p., 1974-82, sales mgr., 1979-82; v.p. United Engine Service, Baton Rouge, 1980-82, pres., 1983—, gen. mgr., 1981—. Mem. Women's Profl. Assn. (v.p. 1978-83, Worlds Champion Cutting Horse 1971), Automotive Wholesalers Assn. La. (chmn. fin. com.), McNeese State U. Alumni Assn., Delta Zeta. Democrat. Episcopalian. Home: 3770 Stumberg Ln Baton Rouge LA 70816 Office: PO Box 3076 Baton Rouge LA 70821 Office: 13521 S Choctaw St Baton Rouge LA 70815 *I have always tried to pattern my goals and my life after my father. I only wish he could have lived to see that his teaching was successful.*

EBERHART, MIGNON GOOD, author; b. Lincoln, Nebr.; d. William Thomas and Margaret Hill (Bruffey) Good; m. Alanson C. Eberhart, Dec. 29, 1923 (div.) (; remarried), 1948 (dec.); m. John P. Hazen Perry, 1946 (dec.). Student, Nebr. Wesleyan U., 1917-20, D.Litt. (hon.), 1935. Author: The Patient in Room 18, 1929, rev. edit., 1972, Five Passengers from Lisbon, 1946, Another Woman's House, 1947, House of Storm, 1949, Hunt With the Hounds, 1950, Never Look Back, 1951, Dead Man's Plans, 1952, Unknown Quantity, 1953, Man Missing, 1954, Post Mark Murder, 1956, Another Man's Murder, 1958, Melora, 1959, Jury of One, 1960, The Cup, the Blade or the Gun, 1961, Enemy in the House, 1962, Run Scared, 1963, Call After Midnight, 1964, R.S.V.P. Murder, 1965, Witness at Large, 1966, Woman on the Roof, 1967, Message from Hong Kong, 1968, El Rancho Rio, 1970, Hangman's Whip, 1971, Glass Slipper, 1971, Cases of Susan Dare, 1971, Chiffon Scarf, 1971, From This Dark Stairway, 1972, Hasty Wedding, 1972, The House on the Roof, 1972, Murder by an Aristocrat, 1972, The Mystery of Huntings End, 1972, Two Little Rich Girls, 1973, Murder in Waiting, 1973, Danger Money, 1974, Wolf in Man's Clothing, 1974, Unidentified Woman, 1975, Fair Warning, 1975, Family Fortune, 1976, The Man Next Door, 1976, The White Dress, 1976, With This Ring, 1976, Nine O'Clock Tide, 1978, The Bayou Road, 1979, Casa Madnone, 1980, Family Affair, 1981, Next of Kin, 1982, The Patien in Cabin C, 1983; also short stories.; Contbr. to mags. Mem. Mystery Writers Am. (grand masters award), Authors League Am., P.E.N., Art Club, Alpha Gamma Delta. Club: Indian Harbor Yacht (Greenwich, Conn.). Office: care Popular Library 1515 Broadway New York NY 10036

EBERHART, RICHARD, poet; b. Austin, Minn., Apr. 5, 1904; s. Alpha LaRue and Lena (Lowenstein) E.; m. Helen Elizabeth Butcher, Aug. 29, 1941; children: Richard Butcher, Margaret Ghormley. Student, U. Minn., 1922-23; A.B., Dartmouth Coll., 1926, Litt.D., 1954; B.A., Cambridge U., 1929, M.A., 1933; student grad. sch. arts and sci., Harvard U., 1932-33; Litt.D., Skidmore Coll., 1966, Coll. Wooster, 1969, Colgate U., 1974; D.H.L., Franklin Pierce Coll., 1978. Tutor son of King Prajadhipok of Siam, 1930-31; master English, St. Mark's Sch., Southborough, Mass., 1933-41; tchr. English, Cambridge Sch., Kendal Green, Mass., 1941-42; vis. prof. English, poet in residence U. Wash., 1952-53; prof. English, U. Conn., 1953-54; Wheaton vis. prof. English, poet in residence Wheaton Coll., 1954-55; resident fellow (prof.) in creative writing and Christian Gauss lectr. Princeton U., 1955-56; prof. English, poet in residence Dartmouth Coll., 1956—, Class of 1925 prof., 1968-71, emeritus, 1970—; disting. vis. prof. U. Fla., Gainesville, spring 1974, vis. prof., 1975—; adj. prof. Columbia U., spring 1975; Regents' prof. U. Calif.-Davis, fall 1975; with Butcher Polish Co., Boston, 1946—, v.p., 1952, hon., 1958, also dir.; mem. Yaddo Corp., 1955—, dir., 1964—; cons. in poetry Library of Congress, 1959-61, hon. cons. in Am. letters, 1963-69; Founder, first pres. The Poets' Theater, Inc., Cambridge, Mass., 1951; hon. pres. 3d World Congress Poets, Balt., 1976; Mem. adv. com. on arts Nat. Cultural Center, 1959—. Author: A Bravery of Earth, 1930, Reading the Spirit, 1936-37, Song and Idea, 1940, 42, Poems New and Selected, 1944, Burr Oaks, 1947, Brotherhood of Men, 1949, An Herb Basket, 1950, Selected Poems, 1951, Undercliff: Poems, 1946-53, Great Praises, 1957, Collected Poems, 1930-60, 1960, Collected Verse Plays, 1962, The Quarry, 1964, Selected Poems, 1965, Thirty One Sonnets, 1967, Shifts of Being, 1968, Fields of Grace, 1972, Poems to Poets, 1976, Collected Poems, 1930-1976, 1976, To Eberhart from Ginsberg, 1976, Of Poetry and Poets, Criticism, 1979, Survivors, 1979, Ways of Light, 1980, Four Poems, New Hampshire/Nine Poems, 1980, Festschrift Richard Eberhart: A Celebration, 1980, Chocorua, Florida Poems, 1981, The Long Reach, 1984; verse drama The Visionary Farms (produced Fogg Art Mus., 1952, The Playhouse, U. Wash., 1953, Inst. Contemporary Arts, Washington, 1957); Editor: (with Selden Rodman) War and the Poet, 1945, recs. for Caedmon, Library Congress, Yale Recs., London Poetry Internat. 73. Served from lt. to lt. comdr. USNR, 1942-46. Recipient Guarantors prize Poetry mag., 1946, Harriet Monroe Meml. prize, 1950; The Golden Rose, N.E. Poetry Soc., 1950; Shelley Meml. prize Poetry Soc. Am., 1951; 1000 grant Nat. Inst. Arts and Letters, 1955; Harriet Monroe Poetry award, 1955; Bollingen prize, 1962; Pulitzer prize, 1966; Nat. Book award, 1977; President's medallion U. Fla., 1977; Nat. Poetry Day award N.Y. Quar., 1980; Sarah Josepha Hale award Newport (N.H.) Library, 1982; named Poet Laureate of N.H., 1979; Acad. Am. Poets fellow, 1969; Richard Eberhart Day proclaimed by Gov. R.I., 1982, Dartmouth Coll., 1982. Mem. Am. Acad. and Inst. Arts and Letters, Nat. Acad. Arts and Scis., Poetry Soc. Am. (hon. pres. 1972—), Phi Beta Kappa (hon.). Clubs: Century (N.Y.); Buck Harbor Yacht (Maine); Signet, Harvard. Home: 5 Webster Terr Hanover NH 03755 *Poetry is a recognition of man's estate and of his fate, and ultimately poetry is praise.*

EBERLE, CHARLES EDWARD, consumer products company executive; b. St. Louis, Mar. 20, 1928; s. Charles Edward and Hazel (Williams) E.; m. Nancy Ellen Paddock, Aug. 1, 1953; children: Charles Edward, Richard Clay, Julia Lee. B.S. in Chem. Engring., Washington U., St. Louis, 1949. Prodn. mgr. Procter & Gamble, St. Louis, 1949-55, plant mgr., Lexington, Ky., 1955-57, St. Louis, 1957-60, Sacramento, 1960-64, mgr. mfg., Cin., 1964-79, v.p. mfg., 1979—. Vice pres. bd. trustees Children's Hosp. Med. Ctr., Cin., 1975—; mem. Cin. Council on World Affairs, 1979—. Served with U.S. Army, 1951-52. Recipient Engring. Alumni Achievement award Washington U., 1977. Republican. Clubs: Queen City, Indian Hill. Office: PO Box 599 Cincinnati OH 45201

EBERLE, ROBERT WILLIAM, sales company executive; b. Albuquerque, Aug. 18, 1931; s. James Herman and Belt Ann (Vencil) E.; m. Deborah; children by previous marriage—Janine, Michelle. B.A., U. So. Calif., 1957, also postgrad. Vice pres. Dempsey-Tegeler & Co., Inc., Los Angeles, 1960-66; exec. v.p., treas., dir. Denny's Restaurants, Inc., La Mirada, Calif., 1966-69, pres., chief exec. officer, 1969-72; chmn., chief exec. officer William Flagg's Restaurants, Commerce, Calif., 1972-78; exec. v.p. Winston Tire Co., Burbank, Calif., 1976-80; chmn., chief exec. officer Direct Sales Tire Co., 1982—. Served with USNR, 1952-54. Mem. U. So. Calif. Commerce Assos., Delta Tau Delta. Home: 1615 Emerald Bay Laguna Beach CA 92651 Home: 21789 Cabrini Blvd Golden CO 80401 Office: 9251 E 104th Ave Henderson CO 80640

EBERLE, ROLF ARTHUR, educator; b. Aarau, Switzerland, Feb. 7, 1931; s. Arthur and Aline (Wagner) E.; m. Helen I. Guard, Dec. 6, 1958; children—Janet C., Monic G., Julia L. A.B., UCLA, 1969, M.A., 1964, Ph.D., 1966. Asst. prof. Kans. State U., 1965-67; asst. prof. U. Rochester, 1967-69, asso. prof., 1969-75, prof., 1975—. Author: Nominalistic Systems, 1970. Woodrow Wilson fellow, 1960-61. Mem. Am. Philos. Assn., Philos. Sci. Assn., Phi Beta Kappa. Office: Dept Philosophy U Rochester Rochester NY 14627 *

EBERLE, WILLIAM DENMAN, business executive; b. Boise, Idaho, June 5, 1923; s. J. Louis and Clare (Holcomb) E.; m. Jean Cilista Quick, Sept. 20, 1947; children—Jeffrey Louis, William David, Francis Quick, Cilista Clare. B.A., Stanford, 1945; M.B.A., Harvard, 1947, LL.B., 1949. Bar: Idaho 1950. Partner firm Richards, Haga & Eberle, Boise, 1950-60; mem. Idaho Ho. of Reps. from Ada County, 1953-63, majority leader, 1957, minority leader, 1959, speaker, 1961; dir. Boise Cascade Corp., 1952-68, sec., 1960-65, v.p., 1961-66; pres., chmn., dir. Am. Standard, Inc., N.Y.C., 1966-71; Pres.'s spl. rep. for trade negotiations, Washington, 1971-75; exec. dir. Cabinet Council on Internat. Econ. Policy, 1974-75; mem. Pres.'s Econ. Policy Bd., 1974-75; pres., chief exec. officer Motor Vehicle Mfrs. Assn., 1975-77; chmn. EBCO Inc., Holders Capital Corp.; pres. Manchester Assocs. Ltd., Kans. Refined Helium Co.; dir. Mitchell Energy & Devel. Corp., Ampco-Pitts. Corp., Geosource Inc., Fraser Paper, Inc. Chmn. Idaho Republican Finance Com., 1961-66; mem. Nat. Rep. Finance Com., 1961-66; Trustee Stanford U., 1970-80, Com. for Econ. Devel., UN Assn., Atlantic Council. Served to lt. USNR, 1944-46. Mem. Council Fgn. Relations, Am. Bar Assn., Idaho Bar Assn., Internat. C. of C. (vice chmn. U.S. Council). Episcopalian. Clubs: University, River (N.Y.C.); Metropolitan (Washington). Home: 36 Masconomo St Manchester MA 01944 Office: 53 Mt Vernon St Boston MA 02108

EBERLEIN, PATRICIA JAMES, mathematician, computer scientist, educator; b. Washington, July 15, 1925; d. William Stubbs and Rose Ramsay James; m. Wentzle Ruml, 1944; m. Elroy Wells, 1946; m. William Eberlein, June 23, 1956; children: Patrick, Kathy, Michael, Sarah, Robert, Mary, Kris. B.S., U. Chgo., 1944; Ph.D., Mich. State U., 1955. Asst. prof. Wayne State U., 1955-56; with electronic computer project Inst. for Advanced Study, 1956-57; asst. prof. bus. adminstrn., asst. dir. computer center U. Rochester, 1957-67; asso. prof. math. and computer sci. SUNY-Buffalo, Amherst, 1967-75, prof. computer sci., 1975—, chmn. dept., 1981—. Treas. Soc. of Friends, Rochester, 1970-76. Mem. Am. Math. Soc., Assn. Computing Machinery, AAAS, Soc. Indsl. and Applied Math. (council 1971-77, chmn. vis. lectureship program 1977-80), Assn. Women in Math., IEEE Computer Soc. Office: Dept Computer Sci SUNY-Buffalo 4226 Ridge Lea Amherst NY 14226

EBERLEIN, WILLIAM FREDERICK, mathematician, emeritus educator; b. Shawano, Wis., June 25, 1917; s. Michael Gustave and Lora Elizabeth (Rather) E.; m. Mary Barry, May 29, 1943 (div. Jan. 1952); children—Patrick, Kathryn, Michael, Robert; m. Patricia James, June 23, 1956 (div. Sept. 1976); 1 dau., Kristen. A.B., Harvard U., 1938, Ph.D., 1942; M.A., U. Wis., 1939. Instr. Purdue U., 1946, U. Mich., 1946-47; mem. Inst. for Advanced Study, Princeton, N.J., 1947-48; asst. prof. U. Wis., Madison, 1948-54, asso. prof., 1954-55; vis. prof. Wayne U., Detroit, 1955-56; mem. Courant Inst., NYU, N.Y.C., 1956-57; prof. math. U. Rochester (N.Y.), 1957-82, prof. emeritus, 1982—. Contbr. articles to profl. jours. Mem. Democratic Com., Rochester, 1958-60. Served with USNR, 1942-46. Office Naval Research grantee, 1957-62; NSF grantee, 1962-69. Mem. Am. Math. Soc., Math. Assn. Am. Club: Harvard (Rochester). Home: 250 Crosman Terr Rochester NY 14620 Office: Math Dept U Rochester Rochester NY 14627

EBERLY, JOSEPH HENRY, physics educator, consultant; b. Carlisle, Pa., Oct. 19, 1935; s. Norman McKinley and Mary Weigle (Keeny) E.; m. Shirley Warren Smith; children: Rebecca Leas, Virginia Westcott, Lynn Elizabeth. B.S., Pa. State U., 1957; Ph.D., Stanford U., 1962. Prof. physics U. Rochester (N.Y.), 1976-79, prof. physics and optics, 1979—; vis. fellow Joint Inst. for Lab. Astrophysics and Nat. Bur. Standards, Boulder, Colo., 1977-78; adv. editor for physics John Wiley Pubs., N.Y.C., 1975—; cons. U.S. Dept. Energy, 1974—, Battelle Labs., Durham, N.C., 1974—. Author: Optical Resonance and Two-Level Atoms, 1975; editor: Multiphoton Bibliography, 1970—; auhtor: Multiphoton Processes, 1978. Sci. and Engring. Research Council vis. fellow physics dept. London Imperial Coll. and Tech., 1983. Fellow Am. Phys. Soc., Optical Soc. Am. Club: C.V. Tummer Soc. (founding mem.).

EBERLY, RALPH DUNBAR, English educator; b. Norfolk, Va., Mar. 5, 1917; s. Ralph Hubly and Roberta (Hyslop) E.; m. Mary Katherine Causey, Mar. 22, 1940 (div.); children: Deirdre Lashgari, R. Stephens Eberly, Clark R.; m. Marlis Lehi Stegemann, Feb. 18, 1943. A.B. with final honors, U. Va., 1939; Ph.D., U. Mich., 1953. Instr., asst. prof. English Purdue U., West Lafayette, Ind., 1946-55, assoc. prof., 1955-67; asst. prof. English North Tex. State U., Denton; disting. prof. English U. Ark., Little Rock, 1967—. Auhtor: Moonfire, 1976. Served to lt. (j.g.) USNR, 1944-46. Home: 12 Broadmoor Dr Little Rock AR 72204 Office: English Dept U Ark 33d St and University Ave Little Rock AR 72204

EBERSOLE, ALVA VERNON, Spanish language educator; b. Liberal, Kans., June 27, 1919; s. Alva Vernon and Eleanor Lucia (Cash) E.; m. Carmen Iranzo, Sept. 24, 1949. B.A., Mexico City Coll., 1949; M.A., Kans. U., 1951, Ph.D., 1957. Asst. instr. Spanish Kans. U., 1952-57; instr. U. Ill., Champaign-Urbana, 1957-59; asst. prof., then asso. prof. U. Mass., Amherst, 1959-62; prof. Spanish, head dept. Adelphi U., Garden City, N.Y., 1962-68; prof. Spanish U. N.C., Chapel Hill, 1968—. Author: Jose de Cañizares, dramaturgo olvidado, 1975, Perspectivas de la comedia, 1978, Disquiciciones sobre el Burlador de Sevilla, 1980, Santos Díez Gonzales Censor, 1982, Los sainetes de Ramón de la Cruz: Nuevo examen, 1983; Editor: (J.R. de Alarcón) El Texedor de Segovia, 1974, La verdad sospechosa, 1976, (Lope de Vega) Las ferias de Madrid, 1977, (Pedro Ciruelo) Reprobación de las supersticiones y hechicerías, 1978, Hispanófila, 1957—, Estudios de Hispanófila, 1962—; co-editor: Albatros ediciones-Hispanofila, 1978—. Served with USMC, 1937-41; Served with USNR, 1944-45. Kenan fellow, 1979. Mem. AAUP, Am. Assn. Tchrs. Spanish and Portuguese (chpt. pres. 1973-74), Sigma Delta Pi, Pi Delta Phi. Office: Dept Romance Langs U NC Chapel Hill NC 27514

EBERSOLE, MARK CHESTER, coll. pres.; b. Hershey, Pa., Nov. 3, 1921; s. Benjamin W.S. and Mary (Patrick) E.; m. Dorothy Baugher, June 26, 1943; children—Philip B., Stephen B. B.S., Elizabethtown (Pa.) Coll., 1943, LL.D., 1969; B.D., Crozer Theol. Sem., 1946; M.A., U. Pa., 1948; Ph.D., Columbia, 1952. UNRRA relief adminstr., Europe, 1946-47; asst. prof. religion and philosophy Elmira Coll., 1952-53; faculty Bucknell U., 1953-69, prof. religion, chmn. dept., chaplain of univ., 1958-61, asst. dean univ., 1961; dean Coll. Arts and Scis., 1961-62, v.p. acad. affairs, 1961-68, univ. provost, 1968-69; project specialist, spl. projects in edn. Ford Found., 1967-69, program adviser, 1969-71; dean Grad. Sch.; asso. v.p. for acad. affairs Temple U., 1971-77; pres. Elizabethtown (Pa.) Coll., 1977—. Author: Christian Faith and Man's Religion, 1961, also articles. J.P. Crozer Found. fellow, 1949-51. Mem. Pa. Soc., Cliosophic Soc., Delta Upsilon, Delta Sigma Rho, Tau Kappa Alpha, Omicron Delta Kappa, Phi Eta Sigma. Home: 307 College Ave Elizabethtown PA 17022

EBERSOLE, WILLIAM GLENN, newspaper publisher; b. Arcadia, Fla., Sept. 30, 1924; s. Glenn Robert and Dora (Pelot) E.; m. Wanda Edleweiss Cowart, Aug. 6, 1950; children—Glenda Ray, William James. B.A. in Journalism, U. Fla., 1949, M.A., 1957. With Arcadia, weekly, part-time 1939-42; with Gainesville (Fla.) Sun, 1948—, v.p., then gen. mgr., 1964-71, pub., 1971—; exec. v.p. N.Y. Times Affiliated Newspaper Group, 1975-81. Bd. dirs. Gainesville Boy's Club, Gainesville United Way, Univ. United Methodist Ch., Gainesville; past pres. J.J. Finley Sch. PTA, Gainesville. Served as pilot USAAF, 1943-46; PTO. Decorated D.F.C., Air medal with 3 oak leaf clusters. Mem. Internat. Newspaper Advt. Execs. Assn., Am. Newspaper Pubs. Assn., Nat. Newspaper Assn., So. Newspaper Pubs. Assn., Fla. Newspaper Advt. Execs. Assn. (pres. 1960-61), Fla. Press Assn. (past v.p., dir.), Gainesville Area C. of C. (past v.p., dir.). Clubs: Univ. City, Kiwanis. Home: 1424 NW 14th Ave Gainesville FL 32605 101 Office: SE 2d Pl: Gainesville FL 32602

EBERT, CARROLL E., retail executive; b. 1924. B.B.A., U. Wis., 1949. With Touche, Ross & Co., chgo., 1960-66; v.p. fin. and ops. T.A. Chapman Co., 1966-67; v.p., treas., dir. Wieboldt Stores, Chgo., 1968-72; v.p. Carson Pirie Scott & Co., Chgo., 1972-74, v.p. fin., treas., 1974-79, exec. v.p. fin.and adminstrn., 1979-80, pres., 1980—, chmn. bd., 1981—; dir. Carson Internat., Inc. Mem. bd. edn. State of Ill. Office: Carson Pirie Scott & Co 1 S State St Chicago IL 60063 *

EBERT, JAMES DAVID, research biologist; b. Bentleyville, Pa., Dec. 11, 1921; s. Alva Charles and Anna Frances (Brundege) E.; m. Alma Christine Goodwin, Apr. 19, 1946; children—Frances Diane, David Brian, Rebecca Susan. A.B., Washington and Jefferson Coll., 1942, Sc.D., 1969; Ph.D., Johns Hopkins, 1950; Sc.D., Yale, 1973, Ind. U., 1975; LL.D., Moravian Coll., 1979. Jr. instr. biology Johns Hopkins, 1946-49, Adam T. Bruce fellow biology, 1949-50, hon. prof. biology, 1956—, hon. prof. embryology, 1956—; instr. biology Mass. Inst. Tech., 1950-51; asst. prof. zoology Ind. U., 1951-54, asso. prof., 1954-56, Patten vis. prof., 1963; dir. dept. embryology Carnegie Instn. of Washington, 1956-76, pres., 1978—; vis. scientist med. dept. Brookhaven Nat. Lab., 1953-54; Philips vis. prof. Haverford Coll., 1961; instr. in charge embryology tng. program Marine Biol. Lab., summers 1962-66, trustee, 1964—, pres., 1970-78, dir., 1970-75, 77-78; mem. Commn. on Undergrad. Edn. in Biol. Scis., 1963-66; mem. vis. com. for biol. and phys. scis. Western Res. U., 1964-68; Mem. panels on morphogenesis and biology of neoplasia of com. on growth NRC, 1954-56; mem. adv. panel on genetic and developmental biology NSF, 1955-56, mem. divisional com. for biology and medicine, 1962-66, mem. univ. sci. devel. panel, 1965-70, adv. com. for instl. devel., 1970-72; mem. panel basic biol. research in aging Am. Inst. Biol. Sci., 1957-60; mem. panel on cell biology NIH, USPHS, 1958-62, mem. child health and human devel. tng. com., 1963-66; mem. bd. sci. counselors Nat. Cancer Inst., 1967-71, Nat. Inst. Child Health, 1973-77; mem. Com. on Scholarly Communication with People's Republic of China, 1978-81; mem. vis. com. to dept. biology Mass. Inst. Tech., 1959-68; mem. vis. com. biology Harvard, 1969-75, Princeton, 1970-76; chmn. bd. sci. overseers Jackson Lab., 1976-80; mem. Inst. Medicine. Author: (with others) The Chick Embryo in Biological Research, 1952, Molecular Events in Differentiation Related to Specificity of Cell Type, 1955, Aspects of Synthesis and Order in Growth, 1955, Interacting Systems in Development, 2d edit, 1970, Biology, 1973, Mechanisms of Cell Change, 1979; Mem. editorial bd.: Abstracts of Human Developmental Biology; editor: Oceanus; Contbr. articles to profl. jours. Trustee Jackson Lab. Served as lt. USNR, 1942-46. Decorated Purple Heart. Fellow AAAS (v.p. med. scis. 1964), Am. Acad. Arts and Scis., Internat. Soc. Developmental Biology; mem. Nat. Acad. Scis. (chmn. assembly life scis. 1973-77, v.p. 1981—), Am. Philos. Soc., Royal Soc. Medicine London (affiliate), Am. Inst. Biol. Scis. (pres. 1963, Pres.'s medal 1972), Am. Soc. Naturalists, Am. Soc. Zoologists (pres. 1970), Soc. Study Growth and Devel. (pres. 1957-58), Phi Beta Kappa, Sigma Xi, Phi Sigma. Home: 2101 Connecticut Ave NW Washington DC 20008 Office: Carnegie Instn 1530 P St NW Washington DC 20005

EBERT, JOYCE ANNE, actress; b. Homestead, Pa., June 26, 1933; d. John Leib and Bertha Louise (Freidel) Womack; m. Arvin Bragin Brown, Nov. 2, 1969. B.A., Carnegie Mellon U., 1955; pupil of, Uta Hagen, Lee Strasberg. Mem. Washington Arena Theatre, 1960, Williamstown (Mass.) Summer Theatre, 1961-63, 65-69, 71, 73, The Long Wharf Theatre, New Haven, 1967—. Appeared in: The Tempest, Stratford, Conn., 1960, Mark Taper Forum, 1966; off-Broadway appearances include Hamlet, 1961, Trojan Women (Clarence Derwent award Actors Equity 1964), 1964 (Obie award 1964), Andromache, 1963-64, The National Health, 1974; Broadway appearances include Solitaire, Double Solitaire, 1970 (award Variety mag. 1970), The Shadow Box, 1977 (Drama Desk nomination 1977), Watch on the Rhine, 1979; appearance at, Lincoln Center in, Tartuffe, 1964-65; TV plays include The Widowing of Mrs. Holyrode, 1973, Forget-Me-Not Lane, 1975; appearance in: Ah, Wilderness, 1976, Blessings, 1978, James at 16, 1978. Address: care Long Wharf Theatre 222 Sargent Dr at Conn Turnpike Exit 46 New Haven CT 06511

EBERT, LEONARD TODD, savs. bank exec.; b. Collingswood, N.J., Apr. 17, 1920; s. Raymond M. and Ethel M. (Todd) E.; m. Shirley Pfeil, June 22, 1963; children—Douglas, Cynthia, Todd.; grad., Rutgers U. Grad. Sch. Banking, 1954. With Phila. Saving Fund Soc., 1937—, comptroller, 1955-66, sr. v.p., 1966-71, vice chmn., 1971-79, pres., 1979—, trustee, 1971—; bd. dirs. Pa. Savs. League, Mut. Instns. Nat. Transfer System; instr. Grad. Sch. Savs. Banking, 1965-72. Bd. dirs. Med. Coll. Pa., 1971—, Phila. div. Am. Cancer Soc., 1976—. Served with U.S. Army, 1942-45. Mem. Fin. Execs. Inst. Republican. Office: 1212 Market St Philadelphia PA 19107 *

EBERT, LYNN JOHN, educator; b. Sandusky, Ohio, Apr. 17, 1920; s. Harry and Wilma (Yerges) E.; m. Mary Kathryn Schmitt, May 22, 1943; children—Mary Lynne (Mrs. James Pesto), Patricia Marie, Richard John, Timothy Edward. B.S. in Metall. Engring, Case Inst. Tech., 1941, M.S., 1943, Ph.D., 1954. From research asst. to sr. research asso. Case Inst. Tech., 1941-53, mem. faculty, 1953—, prof. metallurgy, 1964—, acting head dept., 1965-66; cons. in field, 1947—. Author: Aluminum Casting Alloys, 1948, Significant Properties of Cold Worked Steels, 1955, also articles. Mem. Cleve. Tech. Socs. Council (bd. govs. 1958- 63), Am. Soc. Metals (pres. Cleve. 1947-68, mem. nat. com. 1963-68), Am. Inst. Mining and Metall. Engring. (pres. Cleve. 1965-66, mem. nat. com. 1961-64), Sigma Xi, Tau Beta Pi, Phi Kappa. Republican. Roman Catholic. Home: 104 E 197th St Euclid OH 44119 Office: University Circle 10900 Euclid Ave Cleveland OH 44106

EBERT, PAUL ALLEN, educator, surgeon; b. Columbus, Ohio, Aug. 11, 1932; s. George R. and Evelyn M. (Court) E.; m. Louise Joyce Parks, Sept. 4, 1954; children—Leslie Ann, Michael Dean, Julie Ellen. B.S., Ohio State U., 1954, M.D., 1958. Diplomate: Am. Bd. Surgery, Am. Bd. Thoracic Surgery. Intern in surgery Johns Hopkins Hosp., Balt., 1958-59, asst. resident surgeon, 1959-60, 62-65, chief resident surgeon, 1965-66; sr. asst. surgeon Clinic of Surgery, Nat. Heart Inst., USPHS, Bethesda, Md., 1960-62; asst. prof. surgery Duke Med. Center, Durham, N.C., 1966-68, asso. prof., 1968-71; prof., chmn. dept. surgery Cornell U. Med. Coll., 1971-74; Johnson & Johnson prof., 1972; prof., chmn. dept. surgery U. Calif. at San Francisco Med. Sch., 1974—; surgeon-in-chief N.Y. Hosp., 1971-74. Mem. editorial bd.: Jour. of Surg. Research, 1970—, Surgery, 1970—, Am. Jour. of Surgery, 1971—; Contbr. articles profl. jours. Nat. Cancer Inst. postdoctoral fellow Johns Hopkins Hosp., 1962-63; Mead Johnson scholar A.C.S., Johns Hopkins Hosp., 1964; Markle scholar Duke U. Med. Center, 1967. Mem. Am. Surg. Assn., Am. Med. Assn., Assn. for Acad. Surgery, Am. Heart Assn., A.C.S., Internat. Cardiovascular Soc., Soc. Univ. Surgeons, Soc. for Vascular Surgery, Am. Coll. Cardiology, Am. Assn. Thoracic Surgery, Internat. Soc. Surgery (N.Am. chpt.), Alpha Omega Alpha. Home: 314 Woodland Rd Kentfield CA 94904 Office: Dept Surgery U Calif San Francisco CA 94143

EBERT, RICHARD VINCENT, physician, educator; b. St. Paul, Oct. 25, 1912; s. Michael Higgins and Lilian (Gilbertson) E.; m. Shirley Fairburn Ebert, June 1947; children—Michael, Richard, Susan, Constance, Robert H. B.A., U. Chgo., 1933, M.D., 1937. Intern Boston City Hosp., 1937-39; resident in medicine Peter Bent Brigham Hosp., Boston, 1937-41; chief VA Hosp., Mpls., 1946-52; prof. medicine U. Minn., 1947-53; chief VA Research Hosp., Chgo., 1953-54; prof. medicine Northwestern U., Chgo., 1953-54; chmn. dept. medicine, prof. U. Ark. Sch. Medicine, Little Rock, 1954-66, Disting. prof. medicine, 1978—; staff physician VA Med. Center, Little Rock, 1978—; chmn. dept. medicine, prof. U. Minn. Med. Sch., Mpls., 1966-78; mem. Nat. Heart and Lung Council, 1965-71; chmn. Am. Bd. Internal Medicine, 1971. Contbr. chpts. to med. textbooks, articles to med. jours. Served with M.C. AUS, 1941-45. Decorated Bronze star. Master A.C.P.; mem. Am. Soc. Clin. Investigation (pres. 1958), Assn. Am. Physicians. Home: 6 Lake Vista Rd Roland AR 72135 Office: VA Hosp 300 Roosevelt Rd Little Rock AR

EBERT, ROBERT ALVIN, lawyer, retired airline executive; b. Mpls., Oct. 13, 1915; s. Alvin C. and Caroline (Reutelsterz) B.; m. Trudy M. O'Leary, Feb. 8, 1947; children: Kathryn Hilger, Richard Friess. Student, U. Minn., 1933-35; J.D. cum laude, St. Paul Coll. Law, 1939. Bar: Minn. 1939, U.S. Supreme Ct. 1939. Practiced in, Brainerd, until 1942; with Dept. Justice, 1942-43, Northwest Airlines, Inc., 1943-76, v.p. personnel, 1960-76; practiced law in, St. Paul, 1976—; personnel cons. Mem. Am., Minn., Ramsey County bar assns. Club: Rotary. Home and office: 1164 Edgcumbe Rd Saint Paul MN 55105

EBERT, ROBERT HIGGINS, physician, educator; b. Mpls., Sept. 10, 1914; s. Michael and Lilian (Gilbertson) E.; m. Emily Hirsch, June 17, 1939; children: John, Elizabeth Ebert Schmidt-Nowara, Thomas. B.S., U. Chgo., 1936, M.D., 1942; D.Phil., Oxford U., 1939; A.M. (hon.), Harvard U., 1964; D.Sc. (hon.), Northeastern U., 1968, U. Md., 1970, Notre Dame U., 1977, N.Y. Med. Coll., 1983; LL.D. (hon.), U. Toronto, 1970; D.H.L. (hon.), Rush Med. Coll., 1974. Intern, asst. resident medicine Boston City Hosp., 1942-44; successively asst., instr., asst. prof., asso. prof. medicine U. Chgo., 1946-55, prof., 1955-56; Hanna Payne prof. medicine Western Res. U., 1956-58, John H. Hord prof. medicine, 1958-64; dir. medicine Univ. Hosps., 1956-64; Jackson prof. clin. medicine Harvard U., 1964-65, prof. medicine, 1965—, dean Med. Sch., 1965-77, dean faculty of medicine, 1965-77; head Harvard dept. medicine Mass. Gen. Hosp., 1964-65; pres. Harvard Med. Center, 1965-77, Harvard Community Health Plan, 1968-72, chmn. bd., 1972—; examiner Am. Bd. Internal Medicine, 1961-64; vice chmn. President's Biomed. Research Panel, 1975-76; dir. Squibb Corp.; trustee Rockefeller Found., 1966-77, Population Council, 1966—, chmn. bd., 1978—; mem. tech. bd. Milbank Meml. Fund, 1966—, pres., 1978—; mem. Nat. Adv. Commn. on Health Manpower, 1966-67; mem. vis. com. on coll. U. Chgo., 1967-70; bd. regents Nat. Library Medicine, 1967-71, chmn., 1970-71; mem. bd. visitors U. Pa. Sch. Medicine, 1968-71; mem. adv. com. to dir. NIH, 1968-71; trustee Meharry Med. Coll., 1969-74, Barnard Coll., 1977—, Mt. Sinai Med. Center, 1981—; chmn. bd. overseers Dartmouth Med. Sch., 1983—. Served to lt. USNR, 1944-46. Recipient Alumni Achievement medal U. Chgo., 1968, also Disting. Service award, 1962; Rhodes scholar, 1936-39; Markle scholar, 1948. Fellow ACP, Am. Pub. Health Assn., Am. Acad. Arts and Scis.; mem. Am. Soc. Clin. Investigation, Am. Thoracic Soc. (chmn. com. med. research 1955, pres. 1961-62), Am. Clin. and Climatol. Assn., Assn. Am. Physicians (recorder 1962-66, councillor 1966, pres. 1972-73), AMA, Mass. Med. Soc., Phi Beta Kappa, Sigma Xi, Delta Kappa Epsilon, Alpha Omega Alpha, Omicron Kappa Upsilon (hon.), Kappa Pi Eta. Clubs: Century, Harvard (N.Y.C.). Home: 29 Sergeant St Princeton NJ 08540 Office: 1E 75th St New York NY 10021

EBERT, ROGER JOSEPH, film critic; b. Urbana, Ill., June 18, 1942; s. Walter H. and Annabel (Stumm) E. B.S., U. Ill., 1964; grad. student, U. Cape Town, South Africa, U. Ill., U. Chgo. Editor Daily Illini, 1963-64; pres. U.S. Student Press Assn., 1963-64; staff writer News-Gazette, Champaign-Urbana, Ill., 1958-66; film critic Chgo. Sun-Times, 1967—, US mag., 1978-79, NBC TV News, Chgo., 1980-83; pres. Ebert Co., Ltd., 1981—; instr. English Chgo. City Coll., 1967-68; lectr. film criticism, fine arts program U. Chgo., 1969—; lectr. film Columbia Coll., Chgo., 1973-74, 77-80; cons. Nat. Endowments for Arts and Humanities, 1972-77; juror film festivals. Co-host: Sneak Previews TV show, PBS, 1977-82, At the Movies TV show, syndicated, 1982—; broadcaster: Movie news, ABC Radio, 1982—; Author: An Illini Century, 1967, Beyond the Valley of the Dolls, 1970, Beyond Narrative: The Future of the Feature Film, 1978. Recipient award Overseas Press Club, 1963, Chgo. Headline Club, 1963, Chgo. Newspaper Guild, 1973, Pulitzer prize, 1975, Emmy award, 1979; Rotary fellow, 1965. Mem. Am. Newspaper Guild, Writers Guild Am. West, Nat. Soc. Film Critics, Sigma Delta Chi, Phi Delta Theta. Clubs:

Arts, Cliff Dwellers (Chgo.). Home: 2114 N Cleveland Chicago IL 60614 Office: 401 N Wabash Ave Chicago IL 60611 *Keep it simple.*

EBERT, SCOTT WARD, naval officer; b. Long Beach, Calif., May 13, 1931; s. Hilan V. and Alda Martine (Ward) E.; m. Catherine Ann Ward, June 6, 1953; children: Scott Ward, Charles H., Lee G., Karl W. B.S. in Elec. Engring., U.S. Naval Acad., 1953; M.B.A., U.S. Naval Postgrad. Sch., Monterey, Calif., 1963. Commd. ensign U.S. Navy, 1953, advanced through grades to rear adm., 1981; Served on U.S.S. Briareus, 1953; supply officer U.S.S. Richard E. Kraus, 1954-56, Naval Ammunition Depot, Earle, N.J., 1956-58, Naval Support Activity, Nice, France, 1958-60, U.S.S. Luce, 1963-65; dep. dir. provisioning, allowance, load list div. Naval Supply Hdqrs. Systems Command, Washington, 1965-68; supply systems mgmt. officer, ships supply readiness officer Comdr. Service Force-Pacific, Honolulu, 1968-71; dir. inventory control dept., dir. material dept. Naval Supply Center, San Diego, 1971-74, chief Vietnamese Navy Supply Support Br., Office Def. Attache, Saigon, 1974-75, dir. weapons systems support group, exec. officer Navy Ships Parts Control Center, Mechanicsburg, Pa., 1975-78, comdg. officer Naval Supply Depot Subic Bay, Philippines, 1978-80, asst. chief of staff, logistics readiness/fleet supply officer Comdr. in Chief U.S. Atlantic Fleet, Norfolk, Va., 1980-81, comdg. officer Naval Supply Center, Norfolk, 1981—. Decorated Legion of Merit with 2 gold stars, Vietnamese Navy D.S.M. Republican. Clubs: American Bugatti, Bugatti Owners, Masons. Home: 431 Dillingham Blvd Norfolk VA 23511 Office: Comdg Officer Naval Supply Center Norfolk VA 23512

EBLEN, GEORGE THOMAS (TOM EBLEN), journalist; b. St. Joseph, Mo., Nov. 1, 1936; s. George Clarence and Mary Irene (McLain) E.; m. Jean Kygar, June 5, 1966; children—Courtney Allison, Matthew Vaughn. B.J., U. Mo., 1958. Copy editor Amarillo (Tex.) Daily News, 1959-60; reporter Kansas City (Mo.) Star, 1960, copy editor, 1960-65, asst. city editor, 1965-70, city editor, 1970-75, mng. editor, 1975-78, mng. editor for adminstrn., 1978-79; Gannett Found. profl. in residence William Allen White Sch. of Journalism, U. Kans., Lawrence, 1979-80; editor and gen. mgr. Fort Scott (Kans.) Tribune, 1980—. Editor: Asso. Press Mng. Editor News, 1977-79; chmn.: communications com. Mo. Alumnus mag, 1978-81. Mem. Asso. Press Mng. Editors (dir. 1977-79), Sigma Delta Chi. Methodist. Club: Carriage. Home: Route 5 Fort Scott KS 66701 Office: 6 E Wall St Fort Scott KS 66701

EBNER, KURT EWALD, biochemistry educator; b. New Westminster, B.C., Can., Mar. 30, 1931; s. Sebastian Alois and Martha (Gmundner) E.; m. Dorothy Colleen Reader, May 4, 1957; children: Roger, Michael, Colleen, Paul. B.S.A., U. B.C., 1955, M.S.A., 1957; Ph.D., U. Ill., 1960; postdoctoral, U. Reading, Eng., 1960-61, U. Minn., 1961-62. Mem. faculty Okla. State U., Stillwater, 1962-74, prof. biochemistry, 1969-71, Regents prof., 1971-74; chmn. dept. biochemistry U. Kans. Med. Center, Kansas City, 1974—. Can. Overseas Postdoctoral fellow, 1960; recipient NIH Career Devel. award, 1969, Borden award Am. Chem. Soc., 1969; Okla. State U. Sigma Xi lectr., 1970. Mem. AAAS, Am. Chem. Soc., Am. Soc. Biol. Chemistry, Soc. Complex Carbohydrates, Sigma Xi, Phi Kappa Phi, Gamma Sigma Delta. Presbyn. (elder). Home: 7210 W 101st Terr Overland Park KS 66212 Office: Dept of Biochemistry U Kans Med Center Kansas City KS 66103

EBY, CECIL DEGROTTE, educator, writer; b. Charles Town, W.Va., Aug. 1, 1927; s. Cecil and Ellen (Turner) E.; children: Clare Virginia, Lillian Turner. A.B., Shepherd Coll., 1950; M.A., Northwestern U., 1951; Ph.D., U. Pa., 1958. Instr., then asst. prof. English High Point Coll., 1955-57; asst. prof., then asso. prof. Madison Coll., 1957-60; mem. faculty Washington and Lee U., 1960-65; prof. U. Mich., 1965—; prof. English, chmn. dept. U. Miss., University, 1975-76; Fulbright prof. Am. lit. U. Salamanca, Spain, 1962-63; Fulbright prof. Am. studies U. Valencia, 1967-68; Fulbright prof. Am. lit. U. Budapest, 1981. Author: Porte Crayon: The Life of David H. Strother, 1960, The Siege of the Alcazar, 1965, (translations in Italian, German, Finnish, Dutch, Portuguese) Between the Bullet and the Lie: American Volunteers in the Spanish Civil War, 1969 (transl. in Spanish), That Disgraceful Affair: The Black Hawk War, 1973; Editor: The Old South Illustrated, 1959, A Virginia Yankee in the Civil War, 1961. Served with USNR, 1945-46. Rackham Research grantee, 1967, 71, 77, 79. Mem. Alpha Psi Omega, Pi Kappa Phi, Sigma Tau Delta. Democrat. Episcopalian. Office: Haven Hall U Mich Ann Arbor MI 48104

EBY, HAROLD IRAM, mfg. co. exec.; b. Kitchener, Ont., Can., Feb. 6, 1925; s. Hiram and Ida (Snider) E.; m. Agnes, Sept. 25, 1976. Accountant Electrohome Ltd., Kitchener, 1945-53, controller, 1953-65, sec., treas., 1965—. Served with RCAF, 1940-45. Mem. Fin. Execs. Inst., Canadian Mfrs. Assn., Exec. Inst. Clubs: Gyro, RCAF 404th Wing. Home: 592 Sugarbush Dr Waterloo ON N2K 1Z8 Canada Office: 809 Wellington St E Kitchener ON Canada

EBY, HELEN MARIE, planning research company executive; b. Indpls., July 19, 1933; d. Robert Killian and Florence Charlotte (Hamilton) E. B.A., Hanover Coll., 1955. Paraprofl. asst./sec. firm Gibson, Dunn & Crutcher, Los Angeles, 1958-68; asst. sec., supr. legal dept. Whittaker Corp., Los Angeles, 1968-71; mgr. legal dept., legal coordinator with outside law firms Planning Research Corp., McLean, Va., 1971-79, corp. sec., 1974—; asst. instr. Dale Carnegie Course, 1964-66. Recipient Disting. Service award Dale Carnegie. Mem. Am. Soc. Corp. Secs. Office: 1500 Planning Research Dr McLean VA 22102

EBY, JOHN CLIFTON, JR., construction company executive; b. Curtis, Ark., Aug. 28, 1937; s. John Clifton and Miriam Louise (Thomas) E.; m. Judith Ellen Boorman, Mar. 10, 1962; children: Jennifer, John Clifton III, Susannah. B.S. in Mech. Engring., U. Cin., 1960; postgrad., Harvard U., 1973. Mgr. engring. A.E. Anderson Constrn., Buffalo, 1962-67; v.p. A.E. Anderson Ltd., Burlington, Ont., Can., 1967-72; v.p. constrn. Anoco Inc., Buffalo, 1972-77, BMI Inc., Carnegie, Pa., 1977-79; pres., chief exec. officer Furnco Constrn. Corp., Lancaster, N.Y., 1979—; dir. Nat. Maintenance Agreement Policy Com., Washington, 1982—, mgmt. mem., 1973-82. Moderator South Hills Community Bapt. Ch., Upper St. Clair Pa., 1980-82. 2d lt. U.S. Army, 1961. Mem. Nat. Erectors Assn. (dir. 1975—), Am. Iron and Steel Inst. Republican. Club: Park Country (Buffalo). Office: Furnco Constrn Corp 3815 Walden Ave Lancaster NY 14086

EBY, MARGARETTE FINK, university administrator, musician; b. Detroit, Feb. 8, 1931; d. Christian Gotthilf and Martha Frieda (Noack) Fink; m. Stewart Leon Eby, Aug. 25, 1950; children: Dayle Marlene, Mark Douglas, Jonathan Stewart, Margaret Lynn. Student, Wheaton Coll. (Ill.), 1947-49; B.A., Wayne State U., 1955, M.A., 1962; Ph.D., U. Mich., 1971. Prof. music U. Mich., Dearborn, 1972-77, chmn. dept. humanities, 1975-77; dean Coll. Humanities and Fine Arts U. No. Iowa, Cedar Falls, 1977-81; provost, vice chancellor U. Mich., Flint, 1981-83, spl. asst. to chancellor, 1983—; pres. Flint Community Cultural Festivals, 1983—; cons., evaluator Nort Central Assn. Colls. and Schs., Chgo., 1982—; dir. Flint Inst. Music, 1981-83, Waterloo-Cedar Falls Symphony Orch., 1979-81; artistic dir. Fair Lane Music Guild, Dearborn, 1973-77; piano and harpsichord recitalist, Mich., Wis., Iowa. Chmn. U. Mich.-Flint United Way, 1982; regent Wartburg Coll., Waverly, Iowa, 1980—. Rackham research grantee, 1968; fellow Inst. Adminstrv. Advancement, Ford Found. and Carnegie Corp., 1975. Mem. Am. Assn. Higher Edn. Home: 1400 E Kearsley Gatehouse Flint MI 48503 Office: Univ of Michigan 303 E Kearsley Flint MI 48502

EBY, MARTIN KELLER, JR., construction company executive; b. Wichita Falls, Tex., Apr. 19, 1934; s. Martin and A. Pauline (Kimbell) E.; m. Melodee Stanley, Aug. 20, 1955; children: Stanley, Suzanna, David. B.S. in Civil Engring, Kans. State U., 1956. Registered profl. engr., Kan. With Martin K. Eby Constrn. Co., Inc., Wichita, Kan., 1956—, engr., project mgr., v.p., 1956-67, pres., 1967—; dir. First Nat. Bank in Wichita, 1981-83, Kans. Assoc. Gen. Contractors, Topeka, 1965-68; mem. engring. adv. council Kans. State U., Maanhattan, 1970-83. Bd. dirs. Veritas Found., Wichita, 1981-83; mem. Wichita Mayor's Econ. Analysis Panel, Wichita, 1982-83; chmn. Constrn. Industry Polit. Action Com. of Kans., Topeka, 1978. Mem. Kans. Engring. Soc., Nat. Soc. Profl. Engrs., ASCE, Wichita Profl. Engring. Soc., Young Pres. Orgn. (chmn. 1975-76). Methodist. Home: 1440 N Gatewood Apt 37 Wichita KS 67206 Office: Martin Eby Constrn Co Inc 610 N Main Wichita KS 67203

ECCLES, SPENCER FOX, banker; b. Ogden, Utah, Aug. 24, 1934; s. Spencer Stoddard and Hope (Fox) E.; m. Cleone Emily Peterson, July 21, 1958; children: Clista Hope, Lisa Ellen, Katherine Ann, Spencer Peterson. B.S., U. Utah, 1956; M.A., Columbia U., 1959. Trainee First Nat. City Bank, N.Y.C., 1959-60; with First Security Bank of Utah, Salt Lake City, 1960-61, First Security Bank of Idaho, Boise, 1961-70; exec. v.p. First Security Corp. Salt Lake City, 1970-75, pres., 1975—, chief operating officer, 1980-82, chmn. bd., chief exec. officer, 1982—, also dir.; dir. Union Pacific Corp., Amalgamated Sugar Co., Anderson Lumber Co., Zions Corp., Merc. Instn., Aubrey G. Lanston & Co., Inc.; mem. adv. council U. Utah Bus. Coll. Served to 1st lt. U.S. Army. Mem. Am. Bankers Assn., Assn. Bank Holding Cos., Assn. Res. City Bankers, Young Pres. Orgn. Clubs: Salt Lake Country, Alta, Arid. Office: First Security Corp 79 S Main St PO Box 30006 Salt Lake City UT 84125 *

ECHELMAN, SHIRLEY T., librarian, assn. exec.; b. Omaha, Oct. 7, 1934; d. Nathan W. and Rose (Ricks) Gimple; m. Elliott J. Echelman, Oct. 3, 1964. Student, U. Wis., 1952-54; B.Sc., U. Nebr., 1956; M.L.S., Rutgers U., 1966. Librarian BEA Asso., Inc., N.Y.C., 1960-65; research librarian Chem. Bank, N.Y.C., 1966-70, asst. sec., chief librarian, 1971-74, asst. v.p., 1974-78; exec. dir. Med. Library Assn., Chgo., 1979-81, Assn. Research Libraries, 1981—; lectr. Rutgers U. Grad. Sch. Library Sci., 1970-71; mem. adv. com. White House Conf. on Libraries and Info. Services, 1979. Contbr. articles to profl. jours. Trustee Pub. Affairs Info. Service, Inc., N.Y.C., 1972—; bd. regents Nat. Library Medicine, 1981—. Mem. ALA, Spl. Libraries Assn. (v.p. N.Y. chpt. 1968-70, chmn. bus. and fin. div. 1971-72, div. liaison officer 1972-74, chmn. div. cabinet 1975-76, pres. 1977-78), Pi Gamma Mu, Beta Phi Mu, Archons of Colophon. Office: 1527 New Hampshire Ave NW Washington DC 20036

ECK, JOHN EDGAR, lawyer, public accountant; b. Gastonia, N.C., Oct. 20, 1923; s. John Edgar and Elizabeth (McDermott) E.; m. Jeanne Rice, June 18, 1945 (dec. Feb. 1982); children: Vincent, Francis. B.S., U.S. Mcht. Marine Acad., 1944; J.D., U. S.C., 1950. Bar: S.C. 1950, N.C. 1950; C.P.A., N.C. Ptnr. Eck & Eck, C.P.A.s, Gastonia, 1946-58; ptnr. firm Garland & Eck, Attys., Gastonia, 1958-62; gen. counsel Akers Motor Lines, Gastonia, 1962-66; v.p., gen., counsel Greenwood Mills Inc. (S.C.), 1966—; dir. Greenwood Motor Lines, Central Trust Co., Ninety Six Mfg. Co. Trustee The Self Found., Greenwood, 1968—. Served to lt. USNR, 1944-46. Mem. ABA, S.C. Bar Assn., N.C. Bar Assn. Democrat. Roman Catholic. Club: Rotary (Greenwood). Home: 219 Forest Dr W Greenwood SC 29646 Office: Greenwood Mills Inc 104 Maxwell Ave Greenwood SC 29648

ECKARDT, ARTHUR ROY, emeritus religious studies educator; b. Bklyn., Aug. 8, 1918; s. Frederick William and Anna (Fitts) E.; m. Alice Eliza Lyons, Sept. 2, 1944; children—Paula Jean, Stephen Robert. B.A., Bklyn. Coll., 1942; M.Div., Yale, 1944; Ph.D., Columbia-Union Theol. Sem., 1947; L.H.D., Hebrew Union Coll.-Jewish Inst. Religion, 1969. Ordained to ministry United Methodist Ch., 1944; asst. prof. religion Lawrence Coll., 1947-50, Duke, 1950-51; asso. prof., head dept. religion studies Lehigh U., Bethlehem, Pa., 1951-56, prof., chmn. dept., 1956-80, prof. emeritus, 1980—; vis. prof. dept. Jewish studies CCNY, 1973; vis. scholar Oxford Centre for Postgrad. Hebrew Studies, 1982-83. Author: Christianity and the Children of Israel, 1948, The Surge of Piety in America, 1958, Elder and Younger Brothers, 1967, 73, (with Alice L. Eckardt) Encounter with Israel, 1970, Your People, My People, 1974, Long Night's Journey into Day, 1982; editor: The Theologian at Work, 1968, Christianity in Israel, 1971, Jour. of Am. Acad. Religion, 1961-69; Contbr. articles to profl. jours. Vice pres. Christians Concerned for Israel; bd. dirs. Nat. Com. on Am. Fgn. Policy; sponsor Am. Profs. for Peace in Middle East; spl. cons. Pres.'s Commn. on Holocaust, 1979. Recipient Distinguished Alumnus award Bklyn. Coll., 1963; with wife) Human Relations award Am. Jewish Commn., 1971; Jabotinsky medal, 1980; Fellow Harvard U. Fund For Advancement Edn., 1955-56; Lilly fellow U. Cambridge, 1963-64; fellow Nat. Found. for Jewish Culture, 1968-69; Rockefeller Found. humanities fellow U. Tübingen, Hebrew U. of Jerusalem, 1975-76. Mem. Am. Acad. Religion (past pres.), Am. Soc. Christian Ethics, Phi Beta Kappa, Pi Gamma Mu. Research in Middle East, Europe. Home: Beverly Hill Rd Box 619A Coopersburg PA 18036 Office: Lehigh U Bethlehem PA 18015

ECKART, DENNIS EDWARD, congressman; b. Cleve., Apr. 6, 1950; s. Edward Joseph and Mary E.; m. Sandra Jean Pestotnik; 1 son, Edward John. B.S., Xavier U., 1971; LL.B., Cleveland John Marshall Law Sch., 1974. Mem. Ohio Ho. of Reps., 1975-80; chmn. Cuyahoga County del., 1979-80; mem. 97th-98th Congresses from 11th Ohio Dist. Nat. v.p. Slovene Nat. Benefit Soc. Office: 1221 Longworth Bldg Washington DC 20515 24700 Chagrin Blvd Beachwood OH 44122

ECKAUS, RICHARD SAMUEL, economist, educator; b. Kansas City, Mo., Apr. 30, 1926; s. Julius and Bessie (Finklestein) E.; 1 dau., Susan L. B.S., Iowa State Coll., 1946; M.A., Washington U., St. Louis, 1948; Ph.D., Mass. Inst. Tech., 1954. Instr., asst. prof., asso. prof. Brandeis U., 1951-62; research assoc. Center For Internat. Studies, Mass. Inst. Tech., Cambridge, 1954-61, asso. prof., prof., 1962—, Ford internat. prof., 1977—; mem. Bd. Econ. Advisers to Gov. Mass., 1963-65; cons. OECD, AID, IBRD., govts. of Jamaica, Portugal, Egypt, Sri Lanka and Mexico. Author: (with K. Parikh) Planning for Growth, 1968; Editor: (with J. Bhagwati) Foreign Aid, 1970, Development and Planning, 1973, Basic Economics, 1972, Estimating the Returns to Education, 1973, Appropriate Technologies for Developing Countries, 1976. Served with USNR, 1944-46. Guggenheim and Social Sci. Research Council fellow, 1962; Ford Found. Faculty fellow, 1965. Mem. Am. Econ. Assn., Econometric Soc. Home: 4 Blanchard Rd Cambridge MA 02138 Office: Mass Inst Tech Cambridge MA 02139

ECKBO, GARRETT, landscape architect, urban designer; b. Cooperstown, N.Y., Nov. 28, 1910; s. Axel and Theodora (Munn) E.; m. Arline Williams, Sept. 17, 1937; children: Marilyn Kweskin, Alison Peper. B.S., U. Calif., Berkeley, 1935; M. Landscape Architecture, Harvard U., 1938. Landscape architect Armstrong Nurseries, Ontario, Calif., 1935-36, Farm Security Adminstrn., U.S. Dept. Agr., San Francisco, 1939-42; pvt. practice landscape architecture, San Francisco, 1942-46, 65—, Los Angeles, 1946-65; vis. lectr. landscape architecture U. So. Calif., 1948-56; prof. landscape architecture U. Calif., Berkeley, 1965-78, chmn. dept. landscape architecture, 1965-69. Author: Landscape for Living, 1950, The Art of Home Landscaping, 1956, Urban Landscape Design, 1965, The Landscape We See, 1969, Home Landscape, 1978, Public Landscape, 1978. Recipient numerous awards including; Calif. Gov.'s award for Union Bank Sq., Los Angeles, 1966; AIA citation for excellence in community architecture for Fresno (Calif.) Mall, 1965; Am. Soc. Landscape Architects medal, 1975; merit award for Shelby Farms, Memphis, 1976; spl. award for U. N.Mex.; honor award for Tucson Community Center, 1978; certificate of achievement in publ. and writing Harvard U. Dept. Landscape Architecture, 1976. Fellow Am. Soc. Landscape Architects, Am. Inst. Interior Designers (hon.); mem. Inst. Cons. Planners, Internat. Fedn. Landscape Architects, Internat. Shade Tree Conf. (hon.), NAD (assoc.), World Soc. for Ekistics. Home and Office: 1006 Cragmont Ave Berkeley CA 94708 *My fundamental focus has been on the qualitative nature of relations between people and environment; between construction and open space; between architecture and nature; and between development and conservation. The environmental response of the American people during the last ten years has exceeded our profession's wildest dreams.*

ECKDAHL, DONALD EDWARD, management consultant; b. Los Angeles, Apr. 29, 1924; s. Edward Bernhard and Esther Amelia (Nystrom) E.; m. Barbara D. Crease, May 1, 1981; children by previous marriage: Karin, Robert. B.S.E.E., U. So. Calif., 1944, M.S.E.E., 1949. Project engr. Northrop Aircraft Corp., Hawthorne, Calif., 1946-50; founder, v.p. ops. Computer Research Corp., Hawthorne, 1950-53; v.p., gen. mgr. data processing div. Nat. Cash Register Corp., Hawthorne, 1953-70; sr. v.p. engring. and mfg. group NCR Corp., Dayton, Ohio, 1970-81, ret., 1981; sr. v.p. McCray, Shriver, Eckdahl and Assocs., Inc., Los Angeles, 1982—. Served with USNR, 1943-46. Mem. IEEE, Assn. Computing Machinery. Republican. Lutheran. Address: 4643 Tam O'Shanter Dr Westlake Village CA 91362

ECKEL, EDWIN BUTT, geologist; b. Washington, Jan. 27, 1906; s. Edwin Clarence and Julia Egerton (Dibblee) E.; m. LaCharles Quarles Goodman, Apr. 22, 1931 (dec. Apr. 13, 1983); children: Edwin Goodman, Charles Richard (dec.), Robert Roman. B.S., Lafayette Coll., 1928; M.S. (fellow), U. Ariz., 1930. Geologist U.S. Geol. Survey, 1930-67, chief engring. geology br., 1945-61, chief spl. projects br., 1962-67, research geologist, part-time 1968—; editor bull. Geol. Soc. Am., Boulder, Colo., 1968-71, exec. sec., 1970-74; Chmn. landslide com. Hwy. Research Bd., 1950-62; tech. adviser Paraguay, 1952; mem. com. Alaska earthquake Nat. Acad. Sci., 1964-71. Author, editor numerous books and reports on ore deposits, engring. geology, history of geology; Contbr. articles to profl. jours. Recipient medallion of merit U. Ariz., 1960; Distinguished Service award Dept. Interior, 1965. Fellow Geol. Soc. Am., Mineral. Soc. Am.; mem. Soc. Econ. Geologists, Assn. Engring. Geologists (hon.), Assn. Earth Sci. Editors (hon.), Geol. Soc. London (hon.), Colo. Sci. Soc. (hon.), N.Mex. Geol. Soc. (hon.), Colo. Engring. Council (hon.), Sigma Xi, Phi Kappa Phi, Delta Upsilon. Home: 1109 S High St Denver CO 80210 Office: US Geol Survey Federal Center Denver CO 80225

ECKELMAN, WILLIAM CHARLES, chemist; b. Houston, July 30, 1941; married; 2 children. B.S. in Chemistry, St. Louis U., 1963; M.A., Washington U., St. Louis, 1966, Ph.D., 1968. Group research and devel. leader Mallinckrodt Nuclear, St. Louis, 1968-69; assoc. chemist Brookhaven Nat. Lab., Upton, N.Y., 1969-72; asst. prof. radiology George Washington U. Med. Ctr., 1972-74, assoc. prof., 1974-77, prof., chief radiopharm. chemistry sect., radioassay sect., 1972-83, dir. radiol. sci. grad. program, 1972-83; research assoc. Georgetown U. Med. Ctr., Washington, 1972—; research collaborator Brookhaven Nat. Lab.-Armed Forces Radiobiology Research Inst., 1972—; mem. diagnostic radiology study sect. NIH (Nat. Inst. Health), Bethesda, Md., 1982—, head chemistry sect. dept. nuclear medicine, 1983—. Contbr. articles to profl. jours. Wheeler fellow Washington U., 1966-68. Mem. Am. Chem. Soc., Soc. Nuclear Medicine, AAAS, Mideastern Radioassay Soc., Clin. Radioassay Soc. Home: 2 Harvard Ct Rockville MD 20850 Office: Dept Nuclear Medicine NIH Clin Ctr Bldg 10 Bethesda MD 20205

ECKELMANN, FRANK DONALD, educator; b. Englewood, N.J., May 25, 1929; s. Herman J. and Rosa (Schwarz) E.; m. Beverly Jean Roberts, June 20, 1953; children—Frank Donald, Susan Diane. B.S., Wheaton Coll., 1951; M.S., Columbia, 1954, Ph.D., 1956. Postdoctoral appointment geochemistry Columbia, 1956-57; asst. prof. Brown U., 1957-60, asso. prof., 1960-64, prof., 1964-78, chmn. dept. geol. scis., 1961-68, dean coll., 1968-71; prof., head dept. geology U. Ga., Athens, 1978-81; prof., dean Coll. Arts and Scis., George Mason U., Fairfax, Va., 1981—. Contbr. articles profl. publs. Fellow Geol. Soc. Am., Mineral. Soc. Am.; mem. Geochem. Soc., Am. Geophys. Union, Nat. Assn. Geology Tchrs., Yellowstone-Bighorn Research Assn., Sigma Xi. Address: Coll Arts and Scis George Mason U 4400 University Dr Fairfax VA 22030

ECKELMANN, GEORGE WILLIAM, pharmaceutical company executive; b. St. Louis, June 27, 1931; s. George Lewis and Helen Mae (Waters) E.; m. Susan Catherine O'Leary, Jan. 28, 1956; children: Ellen, George, Edward, David, Daniel. B.S., St. Louis U., 1956. With Hoechst Pharms., Cin. and Somerville, N.J., 1956-74, v.p. sales, mktg., 1968-70, exec. v.p., 1970-74; pres. Hoechst-Roussel Pharms., Inc., Somerville, 1974—, chief exec. officer, 1980—; group v.p. Health Care Group, including Hoechst-Roussel Pharms., Inc., Calbiochem-Behring Div., Animal Health Div., Agrl. Div., Pharm. Prodn. Div. Am. Hoechst Corp., 1982—; chmn., chief exec. officer Calbiochem.-Behring Corp. (subs.), 1980-82, head, animal health div. of parent co., 1979-82. Active in formation Advanced Coronary Treatment Found., 1971; gen. campaign chmn. Somerset County Heart Assn., 1979. Served with USAF, 1952-54. Mem. Nat. Pharm. Council (chmn. bd. 1979, exec. com. 1974—), Animal Health Inst. (dir. 1979-82), Pharm. Mfrs. Assn. (mktg. exec. com. 1980-83). Home: 366 Ridge Rd Watchung NJ 07060 Office: Hoechst-Roussel Pharms Inc Route 202-206 North Somerville NJ 08876

ECKELMANN, WALTER ROBERT, petroleum company executive; b. Englewood, N.J., May 25, 1929; s. Herman John and Rosa (Schwarz) E.; m. Barbara Burda, Aug. 25, 1951; children—Robert, Carol, Bryan. B.S., Wheaton Coll., 1951; M.A., Columbia U., 1953, Ph.D., 1956. Various tech. mgmt. positions Exxon Corp., Houston, 1957-72; pres., dir. Esso Prodn. Research Co., Houston, 1972-75; ops. mgr. Exxon USA, Houston, 1975-76; dir. Esso Australia, Sydney, 1976-78; dep. mgr. sci. and tech. Exxon Corp., N.Y.C., 1978-83; sr. v.p. tech. Sohio Petroleum Co, Houston, 1983—. Mem. AAAS, Am. Assn. Petroleum Geologists, Am. Chem. Soc., Am. Petroleum Inst., Am. Geophys. Union, N.Y. Acad. Scis., Am. Geophys. Soc., Indsl. Research Inst., Sigma Xi. Office: One Lincoln Ctr 5400 LBJ Freeway Suite 1200 LB 25 Dallas TX 75240

ECKELS, THEODORE W., pharmaceutical and hospital supply company executive; b. N.Y.C., 1916. With Ethicon, Inc., prior to 1966, Howmet Corp., 1966-70; pres. Howmedica, Inc., N.Y.C., 1970—, chief exec. officer, 1974—; v.p. Pfizer, Inc., N.Y.C., 1975—. Office: Howmedica Inc 235 E 42d St New York NY 10017 *

ECKENFELDER, WILLIAM WESLEY, JR., environmental engineer; b. N.Y.C., Nov. 15, 1926; m. Kathy Hurley; children—Larry, Janice, Jennifer. B.C.E., Manhattan Coll., 1946; M.S., Pa. State U., 1948; M.C.E., N.Y. U., 1954. From instr. to assoc. prof. civil engring. Manhattan Coll., 1951-65; prof. civil engring. U. Tex., Austin, 1965-69; disting. prof. environ. and water resources engring. Vanderbilt U., 1970—; also exec. dir. Center Environ. Quality Mgmt.; cons. in field. Author: Water Quality Management, 1970; co-author: Water Pollution Control, 1970, Process Design Techniques for Industrial Waste Treatment, 1974; Contbr. articles profl. publs. Recipient Indsl. Wastes medal Fedn. Sewage and Indsl. Waste Assn., 1957, Kenneth Allen award N.Y. State Sewage and Indsl. Waste Assn., 1957, SOCMA gold medal, 1974, Thomas Camp medal Water Pollution Control Fedn., 1981; research fellow N.C. State Coll., 1947, Pa. State U., 1948. Fellow Instn. Public Health Engrs., Am. Inst. Chemists; mem. Internat. Assn. Water Pollution Research (hon.), Water Pollution Control Fedn., Am. Chem. Soc., ASCE, Am. Soc. Engring. Edn., Am. Inst. Chem. Engrs., Instn. Public Health Engrs., Instn. Sewage Purification, N.Y. Acad. Scis., TAPPI, Sigma Xi, Chi Epsilon. Office: Center Environ Quality Mgmt Vanderbilt U Nashville TN 37235 *In 1945 Environmental Engineering provided a new and challenging field. The opportunity presented itself to make a significant contribution to an emerging science: Water pollution control with a close integration between technology and society. To be a part of the development of this field has been a constant challenge and satisfaction.*

ECKENHOFF, JAMES EDWARD, physician, educator; b. Easton, Md., Apr. 2, 1915; s. George L. and Ada (Ferguson) E.; m. Bonnie Lee Youngerman, June 4, 1938 (div. Jan. 1973); children: Edward Alvin, James Benjamin, Walter Leroy, Roderic George; m. Jane M. Mackey, Sept. 22, 1973. B.S., U. Ky., 1937; M.D., U. Pa., 1941; D.Sc., Transylvania U., 1970. Diplomate: Am. Bd. Anesthesiology (bd. dirs. 1965-73, pres. 1972-73). Intern Good Samaritan Hosp., Lexington, Ky., 1941-42; Harrison fellow anesthesia U. Pa., 1945-48, mem. faculty, 1948-65, prof. anesthesiology, 1955-65; physician anesthetist Hosp. U. Pa., 1948-65; prof. anesthesia Northwestern U. Med. Sch., Chgo., 1966—, chmn. dept., 1966-70, dean, 1970-83; pres. McGaw Med. Center, 1980—; Fellow faculty anesthesia, also Hunterian prof. Royal Coll. Surgeons.; chief anesthesia Passavant Meml. Hosp., Chgo., 1966-70; chmn. anesthesia Chgo. Wesley Hosp., 1966-70; cons. VA Research Hosp., Childrens Hosp., Chgo., 1966—; surgeon gen. U.S. Navy, 1964—; Mem. surgery study sect. NIH, 1962-66, anesthesia tng. com., 1966-70; vis. prof. Australian and New Zealand Soc. Anesthetists, 1968, South African Soc. Anesthetists, 1970; dir. Nat. Bd. Med. Examiners, 1975—, treas., 1979-83. Author: (with others) Introduction to Anesthesia, 6th edit, 1982, Anesthesia from Colonial Times, 1966, also numerous articles.; Editor: Science and Practice in Anesthesia, 1965, (with J. Beal) Intensive and Recovery Room Care, 1969, Jour. Anesthesiology, 1958-62, Yearbook of Anesthesia, 1970-81, Controversy in Anesthesiology, 1979. Trustee Evanston Hosp., 1972-83, Rehab. Inst. Chgo., 1972-83, Northwestern Meml. Hosp., 1973—, Children's Meml. Hosp., 1977—, Ill. Hosp. Assn., 1983—. Served to capt. M.C. AUS, 1942-45; ETO. Commonwealth Fund fellow Queen Victoria Hosp., East Grinstead, Eng., 1961-62. Fellow Inst. Medicine Chgo., A.C.P.; mem. Australian, New Zealand, South African socs. anesthesiologists, Soc. Acad. Anesthesia Chairmen (pres. 1967-68), Soc. Med. Consultants to Armed Forces, Am. Soc. Anesthesiologists (Disting. Service award 1981, Ralph Waters award 1984), AMA, Assn. Univ. Anesthetists (pres. 1962), Am. Assn. U. Profs., Ill. Council Med. Deans (pres. 1973-74), Chgo., Ill. med. socs., Am. Physicians Art Assn., Am. Physiol. Soc. Home: Stokelea 8601 N State Rd 39 La Porte IN 46350 Office: 339 E Chicago Ave Chicago IL 60611

ECKER, ALLAN BENJAMIN, lawyer, corporation executive; b. N.Y.C., 1921; s. Samuel and Frances (Schuman) E.; m. Elizabeth Jane Rice, May 19, 1956; children—David Rice (dec.), Sarah Rice. B.A., Harvard U., 1941, LL.B., 1953. Ptnr. firm Sidamon-Eristoff, Morrison, Warren, & Ecker, N.Y.C.; sec., dir., mem. exec. com. Warner Communications Inc. Mem. ABA, Assn. Bar of City of N.Y. Clubs: Coffee House, Overseas Press, Harvard of N.Y. Home: 133 E 94th St New York NY 10028 Office: 551 Fifth Ave Room 800 New York NY 10176

ECKERMAN, JEROME, physicist; b. Bklyn., Nov. 18, 1925; s. Louis and Helen E.; m. Nicki Tolstoi, Dec. 18, 1948; children: Teresa Rose, Stephan David, Lisa Beth. B.S., Worcester Poly. Inst., 1948; M.S., Catholic U. Am., 1956, Ph.D., 1958. Instrument research scientist NACA, Hampton, Va., 1948-50; research physicist Naval Ordnance Lab., White Oak, Md., 1950-59; chief, applied physics sect. Avco Corp., Wilmington, Mass., 1959-68; research physicist NASA Electronics Research Center, Cambridge, Mass., 1968-70; chief, microwave sensor br. Goddard Space Flight Center, Greenbelt, Md., 1970-72; program mgr. Systems Planning Corp., 1982—. Contbr. tech. articles to profl. jours. Served with USAF, 1943-45. Recipient Meritorious Civilian Service award, 1956, Sustained Superior Performance award, 1970, Superior Achievement award, 1975. Sr. mem. IEEE (v.p., pres. Geosci. Electronics Soc.); mem. Am. Phys. Soc., Am. Meteorol. Soc., Sigma Xi. Jewish. Home: 11817 Hunting Ridge Ct Potomac MD 20854 Office: NASA/Goddard Space Flight Center Greenbelt MD 20771

ECKERSON, DONALD ALFRED, aerospace company executive; b. Salinas, Calif., June 21, 1934; s George Donald and Angela (Steinmeyer) E.; m Louise Jeanette Pomo, Dec. 26, 1955; children: David, Jennifer. A.A., Hartnell Coll., 1954; B.S., U. Calif.-Berkeley, 1961, M.B.A., 1962. With Controllers Office, Ford Motor Co., Newport Beach, Calif., 1962-66; plant controller Ford Motor Co, Newport Beach, Calif., 1966-69; mem. community relations com. Ford Motor Co., Los Angeles, 1966-69; div. controller Menasco Inc., Burbank, Calif., 1969-74, dir. planning, 1974-77; div. pres. Colt Industries, Burbank, 1977—. Mem. cons. Parks and Recreation Com., Tustin, Calif., 1965. Served to lt. USN, 1954-58. Mem. Am. Mgmt. Assn., Aerospace Industries Assn. Republican. Roman Catholic. Clubs: North Ranch Country; Westlake tennis (Westlake Village); Verdugo (Glendale, Calif.). Home: 2255 Kelmscott Ct Westlake Village CA 91361 Office: Colt Industries Menasco Overhaul Div 26 E Providence Ave Burbank CA 91502

ECKERT, ALLAN W., author; b. Buffalo, Jan. 30, 1931; s. Edward Russell and Ruth Rose (Roth) E.; (div. 1975); children: Joseph Matthew, Julie Anne; m. Nancy Dent, 1978. Student, U. Dayton, 1951-52, Ohio State U., 1953-54. Formerly reporter, columnist Dayton Jour. Herald; also asso. editor N.C.R. News, Dayton; free-lance writer, 1960—; cons. LaSalle Extension U., Chgo. Writer: numerous TV scripts for NBC's Wild Kingdom; created courses article and short story writing, Writer's Digest; Author: The Great Auk, 1963, A Time of Terror, 1965, The Silent Sky, 1965, Wild Season, 1967, The Frontiersmen, 1967, Bayou Backwaters, 1967, The Crossbreed, 1968, Blue Jacket, 1968, The King Snake, 1968, The Dreaming Tree, 1968, Wilderness Empire, 1968, In Search of a Whale, 1969, The Conquerors, 1970, Incident at Hawk's Hill, 1971, The Court-Martial of Daniel Boone, 1973, The Owls of North America, 1973, The HAB Theory, 1976, The Wilderness War, 1978, The Wading Birds of North America, 1979, Savage Journey, 1979, Song of the Wild, 1980, Whatizzit?, 1981, Gateway to Empire, 1982, Johnny Logan: Shawnee Spy, 1982, The Dark Green Tunnel, 1983, The Scarlet Mansion, 1985; outdoor drama Tecumseh, 1971; screenplay Kentucky Pioneers, 1969, The Legend of Koo-Tan, 1971; 200 TV scripts for Wild Kingdom; also numerous articles, short stories, poetry. Trustee Dayton Museum Natural History, 1963-65; Founder, chmn. bd. Lemon Bay Conservancy, Englewood, Fla. Served with USAF, 1948-52. Recipient Ohioana Book award, 1968; Best Book award Friends of Am. Writers, 1968; Emmy award outstanding program achievement Nat. Acad. TV Arts and Scis., 1968-69; Newbury-Caldecott Honor Book award, 1972; George G. Stone/Claremont Colls. Recognition of Merit, 1974; Austrian Juvenile Book of Yr. award, 1976; nominated five times for Pulitizer prize; Allan W. Eckert Collection established at Mugar Meml. Library Boston U., 1965. Life mem. Dayton Soc. Natural History. Office: Don Congdon Assocs Inc 177 E 70th St New York NY 10021

ECKERT, ERNST R. G., emeritus mechanical engineering educator; b. Prague, Czechoslovakia, Sept. 13, 1904; came to U.S., 1945, naturalized, 1955; s. Georg and Margarete (Pfrogner) E.; m. Josefine Binder, Jan. 30, 1931; children: Rosemarie Christa Eckert Koehler, Elke, Karin Eckert Winter, Dieter. Diploma Ing., German Inst. Tech., Prague, 1927, Dr.Ing., 1931; Dr. habil., Inst. Technology, Danzig, 1938; Dozent, Inst. of Technol., Braunschweig, Germany, 1940; hon. doctorates, Inst. Tech., Munich, 1968, Purdue U., 1968, U. Manchester, Eng., 1968, U. Notre Dame, 1970, Poly. Inst. Romania, Jassy, 1973. Registered profl. engr., Minn. Chief engr., lectr. Inst. Technology, Danzig, 1934-38; sect. chief thermodynamics Aero. Research Inst., Braunschweig, 1938-45; prof., dir. Inst. Technology, Prague, 1943-45; cons. USAF, 1945-49, Lewis Flight Propulsion Lab., NASA, 1949-51; prof. mech. engring. dept. U. Minn., 1951-73, dir. thermodynamics and heat transfer and of heat transfer lab., 1955-73, Regents' prof. emeritus mech. engring., 1966-73; former vis. prof. Purdue U.; cons. Gen. Electric Co.; former cons. Trane Co.; U.S. rep. aerodynamics panel Internat. Com. Flame Radiation. Author: Introduction to the Transfer of Heat and Mass, 1950, 2d edit., 1959, Heat and Mass Transfer, (translated by J.F. Gross), 1963; others in German and Russian, (with Goldstein) Measurement Techniques in Heat Transfer, 1970, 2d edit., 1976, (with Drake) Analysis of Heat and Mass Transfer, 1972; Chmn. hon. editorial adv. bd.: Internat. Jour. Heat and Mass Transfer; Editor: Thermal Sciences series, Wadsworth Pub. Co., Belmont, Cal.; editor: Thermo and Fluid Dynamics; co-chmn. adv. editorial bd.: Heat Transfer-Japanese Research; co-editor: Energy Developments in Japan; chmn. hon. editorial adv. bd.: Letters in Heat and Mass Transfer; editorial adv. bd.: Numerical Heat Transfer; Contbr. articles to sci. mags. Mem. Nat. Commn. Fire Prevention and Control, 1970-73. Recipient Max Jacob Meml. award, 1961, Distinguished Teaching award U. Minn., 1965, Western Electric Fund award, 1965, Gold medal French Inst. Energy and Fuel, 1967, Vincent Bendix award, 1972; Alexander von Humboldt U.S. Sr. Scientist award, 1980, A.V. Luikov medal, 1979; research fellow Japan Soc. Promotion Sci., 1982. Fellow N.Y. Acad. Scis., AIAA; mem. Am. Soc. Engring. Edn. (hon.), Wissenschaftliche Gesellschaft für Luft and Raumfahrt, Sigma Xi, Pi Tau Sigma, Tau Beta Pi. Home: 60 W Wentworth Ave W St Paul MN 55118 Office: U Minn Minneapolis MN 55455

ECKERT, FRED JAMES, ambassador, advertising company executive; b. Rochester, N.Y., May 6, 1941; s. Fred James and Veronica Ann (Costello) E.; m. Karen Frances Laughlin, Aug. 7, 1964; children: Douglas, Brian, Cynthia. B.A., N. Tex. State U., 1964; postgrad., NYU, 1965-66, New Sch. for Social Research, 1965-66. Asst. dir. mass communications Catholic Fgn. Mission Soc. Am., Maryknoll, N.Y., 1964-65; pub. relations exec. Gen. Foods Corp., White Plains, N.Y., 1965-67; account exec. Rumrill-Hoyt, Inc., Rochester, N.Y., 1967-69; chief exec. Town of Greece, N.Y., Rochester, 1970-72; pres. Eckert Assocs. Advt. Agy., Rochester, N.Y., 1973-81, Eckert-Hogan-Newell, Inc. Advt. Agy., 1981; mem. N.Y. State Senate, 1973-82; U.S. ambassador to Fiji (also accredited to Kiribata, Tonga, Tuvalu), 1982—; U.S. rep. S. Pacific Commn. Meeting, Noumea, New Caledonia, 1982; adv. to numerous orgns. Editor: What's So Funny, Padre?, 1965; contbr. articles to nat. mags. Del. Republican Nat. Conv., Kansas City, Mo., 1976 del. Republican Nat. Conv., Detroit, 1980; internat. del. Africa Am. Council fo Youung Polit. Leaders (Sudan, Kenya, Tanzania, Nigeria, Liberia), 1977; mem. nat. adv. bd. Reagan for Pres. Com., Washington, 1980; campaign advt. cons. to several congressmen. Recipient local awards from town govt. and state senate services; named state legislator of yr. Nat. Right-To-Work Com., 1981. Roman Catholic. Clubs: Senate (Albany, N.Y.); Fiji Golf, Fiji Art (Suva). Home: 101 Sherri Ann Ln Rochester NY 14626 Office: Am Embassy Suva Fiji

ECKERT, RALPH JOHN, insurance company executive; b. Milw., Mar. 12, 1929; John C. and Vlasta (Stauber) E.; m. Greta M. Allen, July 11, 1953; children: Maura, Peter, Thomas, Karen, Edward. B.S., U. Wis., 1951. With Benefit Trust Life Ins.Co., Chgo., 1954—, pres., chief exec. officer, 1971-72; chmn. bd. Benefit Trust Life Ins. Co., 1972—, pres., 1972-82, also dir.; pres. Ill. Life Ins. Council. Served with AUS, 1951-53. Fellow Soc. Actuaries; mem. Am. Acad. Actuaries, Chgo. Actuarial Club (pres. 1965). Lutheran. Clubs: Masons; Michigan Shores (Wilmette, Ill.); Cedar Lake Yacht (Slinger, Wis.). Office: 1771 W Howard St Chicago IL 60626 *

ECKERT, ROBERT RAY, newspaper pub.; b. Binghamton, N.Y., Mar. 15, 1920; s. Clarence Calvin and Agnes Rosella (Malseed) E.; m. Geane Louise Martin, June 12, 1948; children—Kathleen, John, David. B.A., Yale U., 1946. Reporter, editor Ottaway Newspapers, 1937-41; editor, pub. Vestal (N.Y.) News, 1947-54; with Gannett Newspapers, 1955-76, pub., Elmira, Binghamton, N.Y., Hartford, Conn., dir. ops., Rochester, N.Y.; pub. Internat. Herald Tribune, Paris, France, 1976-79; pub., v.p. Balt. News-American, 1979—; dir. Security Mut. Life Ins. Co. Served with USNR, 1941-46. Mem. Am. Newspaper Pubs. Assn., Md.-Del.-D.C. Press Assn. Presbyterian. Clubs: Econ. (N.Y.C.); Balt. Country, Center, Merchants. *

ECKERT, ROGER E(ARL), chemical engineering educator; b. Lakewood, Ohio, Aug. 8, 1926; s. Elmer George and Elsie V. (Schwede) E.; children: Roger Earl, Rhonda Carol, Robyn Claire. B.S., Princeton U., 1948; M.S., U. Ill., 1949, Ph.D., 1951. Process devel. engr., indsl. and biochems. dept. E.I. duPont de Nemours & Co., Inc., Wilmington, Del., 1951-64, math. cons., 1956-60, sr. research engr., engring. research lab. and elastomers chems. dept., 1960-64; assoc. prof. Purdue U., West Lafayette, Ind., 1964-73; asst. head Sch. Chem. Engring., 1970-75, prof. chem. engring., 1973—; vis. prof. U. Colo., 1971, U. Wis., 1981; Am. Soc. Engring. Edn.-NASA faculty fellow Case Western Res. U. and Lewis Research Center, 1966-67. Contbr. tech. articles to profl. jours. Served with U.S. Army, 1946-47. Mem. Am. Inst. Chem. Engrs., Phi Beta Kappa, Sigma Xi, Phi Lambda Upsilon, Pi Mu Epsilon, Alpha Chi Sigma. Presbyterian. Home: 153 Indian Rock Dr West Lafayette IN 47906 Office: Sch Chem Engring Purdue U West Lafayette IN 47906

ECKES, ALFRED EDWARD, JR., government official; b. North Conway, N.H., July 11, 1942; s. Alfred Edward and Virginia (Marshall) E. B.A., Washington and Lee U., 1964; M.A., Fletcher Sch. of Law and Diplomacy, Tufts U., Medford, Mass., 1966; Ph.D., U. Tex., 1969. Asst. prof. history Ohio State U., 1969-75, assoc. prof., 1975-79; exec. dir. House Republican Conf., U.S. Ho. of Reps., 1979-81; commr. U.S. Internat. Trade Commn., Washington, 1981—, chmn., 1982—. Author: A Search for Solvency: Bretton Woods and the International Monetary System, 1941-71, 1975, The U.S. and the Global Struggle for Minerals, 1979, (with Eugene Roseboom) A History of Presidential Election: From George Washington to Jimmy Carter, 1979; editor: edtorial page Columbus (Ohio) Dispatch 1977-79. Fulbright fellow, 1964-65. Mem. Soc. Historians of Am. Fgn. Relations, Orgn. Am. Historians, Phi Beta Kappa. Clubs: Capital Hill; Army Navy (Washington). Home: 1050 N Royal St Alexandria VA 22314 Office: US International Trade Commn 701 E St NW Washington DC 20436

ECKHARDT, AUGUST GOTTLIEB, educator; b. Sylvan, Wis., Aug. 8, 1917; s. Levi and Euphemia (Hall) E.; m. Catherine Louise Henderson, June 26, 1942; children—James Henderson, Patricia Kay. Student, Nebr. State U. at Kearney, 1935-37; B.A., U. Wis., 1939, LL.M., 1946, S.J.D., 1951; LL.B., George Washington U., 1942. Bar: D.C. bar 1941, Wis. bar 1946, Ariz. bar 1974. Practice in, Merrill, Wis., 1946-47, 50-52; asst. prof. law George Washington U., 1947-49; prof. law U. Wis.-Madison, 1954-72, U. Ariz., Tucson, 1972—; dir. Continuing Legal Edn. Wis., 1954-58, 63-67; Labor arbitrator, 1955—. Author: Workbook for Wisconsin Estate Planners, 1961. Served with USNR, 1942-46. Mem. Am. Bar Assn., State Bar Wis., State Bar Ariz. Home: 2002 E 3d St Tucson AZ 85719

ECKHARDT, CRAIG JON, chemistry educator; b. Rapid City, S.D., June 26, 1940; s. Reuben H. and Hilda W. (Craig) E. B.A. magna cum laude, U. Colo., 1962; M.S., Yale U., 1964, Ph.D., 1967. Asst. prof. chemistry U. Nebr., Lincoln, 1967-72, assoc. prof., 1972-78, prof., 1978—; cons., mem. adv. panel, condensed matter scis. div. materials research NSF, 1976-79. NIH predoctoral fellow, 1964-67; Yale predoctoral fellow, 1967; John Simon Guggenheim fellow, 1979-80; German Acad. Exchange fellow; NSF grantee, 1974—; Dept. Energy grantee, 1979—; Petroleum Research Fund-Am. Chem. Soc. grantee, 1968-72; Research Corp. grantee, 1971-74. Mem. Am. Phys. Soc., Am. Assn. Physics Tchrs., Optical Soc. Am., Am. Chem. Soc., Royal Chemistry Soc., Phi Beta Kappa, Sigma Xi. Office: Dept Chemistry U Nebr Lincoln NE 68588

ECKHARDT, RICHARD DALE, physician, educator; b. DeKalb, Ill., June 24, 1918; s. William George and Eva Luella (Alverson) E.; m. Catherine Shevchuk, Aug. 4, 1946; children: Dale Eva (Mrs. Richard Paul Jacobi), Catherine Elena (Mrs. Steven Alan Bartholow), Jane Ellen (Mrs. Ronald Keith McMullen), Barbara Ann. A.B., U. Ill., 1940; M.D., Harvard, 1943. Diplomate: Am. Bd. Internal Medicine. Intern Boston City Hosp., 1944, resident, 1944-46; research fellow Thorndike Meml. Lab., 1946-49; mem. faculty Harvard Med. Sch., 1944-49, U. Ill. Coll. Medicine, 1957-58, U. Iowa Coll. Medicine, 1949-57, 58—; mem. staff Boston City Hosp., 1944-49, Research and Ednl. Hosps., Chgo., 1957-58, Univ. Hosps., Iowa City, 1949-57, 58—, VA Hosps., Chgo., 1957-58, Iowa City, 1952-57, 58—; asst. chief med. services VA Hosps. U. Iowa Coll. Medicine, 1952-57, chief, 1957-68, chief of staff, 1968-80; asst. dean VA Hosp. Affairs, 1968-80, now prof. emeritus dept. internal medicine.; Civilian dir. Hepatitis Survey Group U.S. Army Hosp., Kyoto, Japan, 1952. Contbr. articles profl. jours. Served from lt. (j.g.) to lt. comdr. M.C. USNR, 1946, 53-55. USPHS Postdoctoral Research fellow Thorndike Meml. Lab., Boston City Hosp., 1948-49. Fellow A.C.P.; mem. Am. Fedn. for Clin. Research, Am. Assn. for Study Liver Disease, Central Soc. for Clin. Research, Central Clin. Research Club. Home: 1675 Ridge Rd Iowa City IA 52240

ECKHARDT, WILLIAM RUDOLF, III, lawyer; b. Houston, Dec. 14, 1915; s. William Rudolf and Ura (Link) E.; m. Elra Hodges, Oct. 11, 1940; 1 son, Donald Kent. B.A., Rice Inst., 1937; LL.B., U. Tex., 1940. Bar: Tex. 1940. Asst. U.S. atty. Dept. Justice, So. Dist. Tex., 1940-44, 46-52; assoc. McGregor & Sewell, Houston, 1952-56, Vinson & Elkins, 1956—. Served to lt. (j.g.) USN, 1944-46. Fellow Am. Coll. Trial Lawyers; mem. ABA, Tex. Bar Assn., Maritime Law Assn., Tex. Def. Attys. Assn., Chancellors, Order of Coif, Phi Delta Phi, Chi Phi. Republican. Baptist. Clubs: Houst; Inns of Ct. (Houston). Home: 25 Robin Lake Ln Houston TX 77024

ECKHART, MYRON, JR., marine engineer; b. South Bend, Ind., Mar. 29, 1923; s Myron Lester and Neva (Whitmer) E.; m. Joan Elizabeth Daniels, June 29, 1946; children: Joan Theresa, Michael Thomas, Jeri Ann. B.S., U.S. Naval Acad., 1945, M.I.T., 1949, M.S., George Washington U., 1967. Commd. ensign U.S. Navy, 1945, advanced through grades to capt., 1966; stationed at (Norfold (Va.) Naval Shipyard), 1950-55, project officer Regulus Missilie, 1955-60; chmn. elec. sci. U.S. Naval Acad., 1962-65; dir. ship design div. (Hdqrs.), 1967-70, ret., 1970; mgr. engring., marine systems div. Rockwell Internat., Anaheim, Calif., 1970-75, chief scientist, 1975—. Contbr. articles to profl. jours. Mem. Soc. Naval Architects and Marine Engrs., Am. Soc. Naval Engrs., Am. Def. Preparedness Assn., U.S. Naval Inst. Patentee fourier synthesis of complex waveforms; ship designs include Nimitz aircraft carriers, Trident strategic submarines, Los Angeles class submarines. Home: 1211 Belle Vista Dr Alexandria VA 22307 Office: 1745 Jefferson Davis Hwy Arlington VA 22202 *Success depends upon figuring out the price associated with each of one's goals, and then being willing to pay that price with no assurance of reward.*

ECKLER, JOHN ALFRED, lawyer; b. Elyria, Ohio, July 2, 1913; s. Frank Roy and Ida Jean (Phipps) E.; m. Mary Emily Rickey, Dec. 21, 1936; children: Rickey, Jenne, Molly. A.B., Ohio Wesleyan U., 1935; J.D., U. Chgo., 1939. Bar: Ill. 1939, Ohio 1945. With Gen. Electric Co., Schenectady, 1935-36; asso. Knapp, Allen & Cushing, Chgo., 1939-43; adminstrv. asst. to Senator John W. Bricker, Washington, 1947-49; practiced in, Columbus, Ohio, 1946—; partner firm Bricker and Eckler, 1954—; Mem. Ohio Bd. Bar Examiners, 1954-59; chmn. Nat. Conf. Bar Examiners, 1958—, chmn. standing com. on multi-state bar exam., 1968-74; chmn. Fed. Bar Exam. Com., 1975—. Contbr.: articles U. Chgo. Law Rev; others. Pres. Upper Arlington Civic Assn., 1952; active in United Appeals; mem. bd. health City Upper Arlington, 1956-70; Mem. chmn. bd. trustees Ohio Wesleyan U., 1958—; trustee, chmn. bd. World Neighbors, Inc., 1952—. Served as lt. USNR, World War II. Fellow Am. Bar Found., Ohio State Bar Found. (pres. 1977-79), Am. Coll. Trial Lawyers; mem. Am. Judicature Soc. (bd. dirs. 1977-79), ABA (chmn. spl. com. ct. congestion 1958-60, mem. ho. of dels. 1960-69, assembly del. to ho. of dels. 1977-82), Ohio Bar Assn., Columbus Bar Assn. (pres., bd. govs.), Am. Legion, Ohio Wesleyan U. Alumni Assn. (pres. 1958-60), Phi Beta Kappa, Omicron Delta Kappa, Delta Sigma Rho, Phi Delta Theta, Order of Coif. Methodist. Clubs: Mason (33), University, Scioto Country, Torch (pres. 1955), Kit Kat (pres. 1972-73), Rotary (Columbus) (bd.). Office: 100 E Broad St Columbus OH 43215

ECKLES, LUCIUS ELKANAH, physician; b. Eskridge, Kans., Jan. 15, 1905; s. William Thomas and Nellie (Kingman) E.; m. Josephine E. Meier, Nov. 1, 1959; children—Lucius Elkanah, Peter N., Amey. A.B, U. Kans., 1927; M.D., Harvard, 1931. Diplomate: Am. Bd. Pediatrics. Intern, then resident Childrens Med. Center, Boston, 1931-35; practice medicine specializing in pediatrics, Topeka, 1935-42, 46-62; med. dir. Waimano Tng. Sch. and Hosp., Pearl City, Hawaii, 1962-72; asso. clin. prof. pediatrics Med. Sch. U. Hawaii, 1966—; Pres. Kans. Bd. Health,

1950. Served to comdr., M.C. USNR, 1942-46. Mem. Sigma Chi. Address: 129 Valley Dr Santa Fe NM 87501

ECKLEY, GRACE ESTER, educator; b. Alliance, Ohio, Nov. 30, 1932; d. Clyde L. and Wilma Agnes (Hahn) Williamson; m. Wilton Eckley, Sept. 12, 1954; children—Douglas, Stephen, Timothy. B.A., Mount Union Coll., 1955; M.A., Case Western Res. U., 1964; Ph.D., Kent State U., 1970. Instr. English Simpson Coll., Indianola, Iowa, 1965-68; prof. dept. English Drake U., Des Moines, 1968—. Author: Benedict Kiely, 1972, Edna O'Brien, 1974, (with Michael Begnal) Narrator and Character in Finnegans Wake, 1974; contbr. articles to profl. jours. Mem. AAUW. Home: 529 Waterbury Circle Des Moines IA 50312 Office: Drake U Des Moines IA 50311

ECKLEY, ROBERT SPENCE, college president; b. Kankakee, Ill., Sept. 4, 1921; s. George Alva and Mary (Spence) E.; m. Nell Mann, Mar. 28, 1947; children—Robert George, Jane Ann, Paul Nelson, Rebecca Helen. B.S., Bradley U., 1942; M.B.A., U. Minn., 1943; M.A., Harvard, 1948, Ph.D., 1949. Asst. prof. econs. U. Kans., Lawrence, 1949-51; indsl. economist Fed. Res. Bank of Kansas City, Mo., 1951-54; mgr. bus. econs. dept. Caterpillar Tractor Co., Peoria, Ill., 1954-68; pres. Ill. Wesleyan U., Bloomington, 1968—; Dir. State Farm Mutual Automobile Ins. Co., Central Ill. Pub. Service Co. Contbr. articles to profl. publs. First v.p. Ill. Council of Churches, 1968-70; Trustee Meth. Med. Center Ill., 1968-80. Served to lt. (j.g.) USCGR, 1943-46. Recipient Phi Kappa Phi Alumni award Bradley U., 1966, Distinguished Alumni award, 1972. Mem. Am. Econ. Assn., Nat. Assn. Bus. Economists, Am. Statis. Assn. Methodist. Home: 1201 N Park St Bloomington IL 61701

ECKLEY, WILTON EARL, JR., humanities educator; b. Alliance, Ohio, June 25, 1929; s. Wilton Earl and Louise (Bert) E.; m. Grace Ester Williamson, Sept. 12, 1954; children: Douglas, Stephen, Timothy. B.A., Mt. Union Coll., 1952; M.A., Pa. State U., 1955; Ph.D., Case Western Reserve U., 1965; John Hay fellow, Yale U., 1961-62. Chmn. English Euclid (Ohio) Sr. High Sch., 1955-63; dir. tchr. tng. Hollins Coll., 1963-65; prof. English Drake U., 1965—, chmn. dept. English, 1965-80; Fulbright prof. Am. lit. U., Ljubljana, Yugoslavia, 1972-73, U. Veliko, Turnouski, Bulgaria, 1981-82. Author: A Guide to E.E. Cummings, 1970, A Checklist of E.E. Cummings, 1970, Harriette Arnow, 1974, T.S. Stribling, 1975, Herbert Hoover, 1980, The American Circus, 1983. Coe fellow Am. Studies, 1957—. Mem. Modern Lang. Assn., Circus Hist. Soc., Phi Kappa Tau. Home: 529 Waterbury Circle Des Moines IA 50312

ECKLUND, LEROY A., hospital administrator; b. West Palm Beach, Fla., June 14, 1930; s. Leslie Olaf and Elsie Marie (Leisner) E.; m. Alma Marie Gromer, June 15, 1963; children: Marilyn, Kristin, Ann, Lars. B.A., U. Chgo., 1951; M.D., Northwestern U., 1956. Intern Chgo. Wesley Meml. Hosp., 1957; resident Inst. Pa. Hosp., 1958, 59, 62; dir. Mendota State Hosp., Madison, Wis., 1962-81, med. dir., 1981—; asst. clin. prof. U. Wis., 1962—. Active local mental health and health planning groups. Served to capt. USAF, 1960-61. Fellow Am. Psychiat. Assn. (Hubbs award com.); mem. Wis. Psychiat. Assn., State Med. Soc. Wis., Dane County Med. Soc., Am. Deafness and Rehab. Assn. Club: Rotary. Home: 3501 Memorial Dr Madison WI 53704 Office: 301 Troy Dr Madison WI 53704

ECKMAN, DAVID WALTER, lawyer; b. Ogden, Utah, Oct. 23, 1942; s. Walter and Ann-Marie Pauline (Nelson) E.; m. Laurie Alden Waters, Aug. 28, 1965; children: Christian Davidson, Catherine Marie. Student, Rice U., 1960-61; B.A. with honors, U. Tex., Austin, 1964; J.D. (Sam D. Hanna scholar), U. Tex., Austin, 1967. Bar: Tex. 1967, Calif. 1976, U.S. Dist. Ct. (so. dist.) Tex. 1983, U.S. Ct. Appeals (5th Cir.) 1983. With Exxon Co., U.S.A. div. Exxon Corp., 1967-78, mem. Prudhoe Bay Law Task Force, Houston and Los Angeles, 1974-75, counsel Pacific Region, Los Angeles, 1975-77, counsel hdqrs., Houston, 1977-78; gen. counsel Natomas N.Am. Inc., Houston, 1978, v.p.-legal, corp. chief legal counsel, 1978-82; sole practice, Houston, 1982—. Vestryman, dir. Christian edn. All Saints Episcopal Ch., Corpus Christi, 1968-70; leader adult study St. Mark's Episcopal Ch., Houston, 1971-74; v.p. St. Mark's Sch. PTO, Houston, 1981-82; lay reader St. John the Divine Episc. Ch., Houston, 1982—, leader adult study, Houston, 1983—; mem. St. Patrick's Sch. Bd., Thousand Oaks, Calif., 1976-77; pres. Houston Youth Soccer Assn., 1979-81, bd. dirs., 1979-83; pres. Neartown Soccer Club, 1980-83; v.p. Old Braeswood Civic Assn., 1982—. Recipient Am. Jurisprudence award in antitrust law U. Tex., 1967. Mem. Tex. State Bar, Calif. State Bar, ABA, Houston Bar Assn., Lambda Chi Alpha, Phi Delta Phi. Office: 1900 W Loop S Suite 1000 Houston TX 77027

ECKMAN, FERN MARJA, journalist; b. N.Y.C., Aug. 27; d. Isidor Peter and Zara Nettie (Sloate) Friedman; m. Irving Eckman, June 21, 1957. B.A., N.Y. U., 1957. Reporter N.Y. Post, 1944-78; assigned to UN, 1945-49, 60-65. Contbg. editor: McCall's Working Mother, 1981—; feature writer for nat. publs.; Author: The Furious Passage of James Baldwin, 1967. Recipient George Polk Meml. award for distinguished met. reporting, 1951, 55; Page One award for community service N.Y. Newspaper Guild, 1955, for best feature reporting, 1961; citation for community service Council Puerto Rican and Spanish-Am. Orgns., 1955; Lasker award for med. journalism, 1960; Front Page award for distinguished feature writing, News Women's Club N.Y., 1949, 51, 56, 64; for distinguished series (co-recipient), 1970; Cultural News award Newspaper Reporters Assn., N.Y.C., 1967; Empire State award for excellence in med. reporting, 1968. Home: Stones 53 Ferriss Estate Rd New Milford CT 06776 also 749 West End Ave New York NY 10025

ECKMAN, JAMES RUSSELL, medical editor, technical historian; b. Sioux City, Iowa, Apr. 25, 1908; s. James Abram and Katherine Russell (Letts) E.; m. Frances Elizabeth Kadlec, June 12, 1937. B.A., U. Minn., 1932; M.A., Georgetown U., 1944, Ph.D., 1946. Asst. editor Jour.-Lancet (med. jour.), Mpls., 1934-38; mem. sect. publs. Mayo Clinic, Rochester, Minn., 1938—, press officer, 1948-65, sr. cons. sect. publs., 1965—; asst. prof. history medicine Mayo Found., U. Minn., 1960-73; hist. editor Printing Impressions, 1960-72; owner Doomsday Press, Rochester, 1939—; cons. Assn. Med. Illustrators, 1965. Author: Jerome Cardan, 1946, Sterling P. Rounds and His Printers Cabinet, 1962, The Heritage of the Printer, Vol 1, 1965; also articles on hist. research tech. aspects printing methods.; Editor: (Sterling P. Rounds) Among the Craft: Notes by the Way, 1968; editor, annotator: History of Typefounding in the United States (David Bruce), 1981. Bd. dirs. Rochester (Minn.) Civic Theatre, 1967. Served to capt. AUS, 1943-45. Mem. Mediaeval Acad. Am., Am. Inst. Graphic Arts, Soc. Typographic Arts Chgo., Gutenberg Gesellschaft (Mainz, Germany), Minn. Hist. Soc. (exec. council 1973), Omlsted County Hist. Soc. (sec. 1955-65), Printing Hist. Soc. (Eng.), Sigma Xi, Sigma Delta Chi, Phi Alpha Theta, Chi Phi. Clubs: Grolier, Typophiles (N.Y.C.); Press (Mpls.); Ampersand (Mpls.-St. Paul). Home: 921 8th Ave SW Rochester MN 55902 Office: 200 1st St SW Rochester MN 55905

ECKMAN, JOHN WHILEY, business executive; b. Forest Hills, N.Y., July 20, 1919; s. Samuel Whiley and Anna (Wolfram) E.; children: Alison Elizabeth, Stephen Keyler. Student, Yale U., 1937-38; B.S., U. Pa., 1943; H.H.D. (hon.), Pa. Coll. Podiatric Medicine, 1979, LL.D., Phila Coll. Pharmacy and Sci., 1981. With Smith Kline & French Labs., Inc., Phila., 1947-52; v.p. Thomas Leeming & Co., Inc., N.Y.C., 1952-62; exec. v.p., dir. Rorer Group Inc. (and predecessors), Ft. Washington, Pa., 1962-70, pres., 1970-80, chmn. bd., 1976—; chmn. Fed. Res. Bank Phila., 1977-81; also dir.; dir. Provident Mut. Life Ins. Co., 1976—, Betz Labs., Inc., 1979-80. Life trustee U. Pa.; bd. mgrs. Wistar Inst. Anatomy and Biology, 1968—, pres., 1975-84; bd. dirs. World Affairs Council, 1978—, Community Home Health Services Phila., 1979-81, Greater Phila. First Corp., 1982—, Phila. Urban Coalition, 1973-83, Greater Phila. Urban Affairs, 1976—; co-chmn. Greater Phila. Urban Affairs, 1982—; bd. dirs. Univ. City Sci. Center, 1974—; trustee Phila. Area United Way, 1974—, gen. chmn., 1984—. Served from ensign to lt. USNR, 1943-46. Fellow N.Y. Acad. Sci.; mem. Pharm. Advt. Club (pres. 1960), Pharm. Mfrs. Assn. (dir. 1975—, chmn. 1981), Greater Phila. C. of C. (dir. 1972-83), Hist. Soc. Pa. (pres. 1980—), AAAS, Acad. Scis. at Phila., Am. Acad. Polit. and Social Sci., Pa. Soc., Wharton Sch. Alumni Assn (dir. 1966-68, pres. 1968-70), Phila. Com. on Fgn. Relations, S.R., St. Andrews Soc., Sigma Chi (Significant Sig award 1981), Beta Gamma Sigma. Presbyterian. Clubs: Union League, Phila. Cricket, Sunday Breakfast, U. Pa. Faculty, Rittenhouse (Phila.); Nantucket (Mass.); Yacht; Yale, Economic (N.Y.C.); Rodney Square (Wilmington). Home: 611 W Mermaid Ln Philadelphia PA 19118 Office: 500 Virginia Dr Fort Washington PA 19034

ECKSEL, MEYER M., publisher; b. Phila., July 21, 1925; s. Isadore and Fannie (Klimoff) E.; m. Irma Belle Berke, Feb. 7, 1947; children: Robert, Irene. Cert. mktg., B.A. in Mktg. and Advt., Wharton Sch., U. Pa., 1947; student, Rutgers U., 1948, Harvard Grad. Sch. Bus., 1949; M.B.A., Hamilton State U., 1959. With R.H. Donnelley Corp., Phila., 1950-58, Ames Pub. Co., 1958-70, A&E Advt. Assos., Inc., 1970-72; pub. Indsl. Machinery News, Noticias de Maquinaria Industrial, Canadian Machinery News, Industrial Machinery Focus, Shop & Factory, Fast Reply Service, Southfield, Mich., 1972—; pres. IMN div. subs. Hearst Bus. Media Corp. (IMN Index/Directory, Metalworking Buyer's Guide); lectr. telephone mktg., 1959—. Pub: Serial Number Reference Book for Metalworking Machinery, 7th edit., 1978, How To Buy Metalworking Machinery and Equipment, 1977, Machinery Checklists, 1978; author: The Why and How of Industrial Direct Mail, 1975. Pres. Franklin Woods Assn., Birmingham, Mich., 1974-76. Served with AUS, 1942-46. Decorated Silver Star, Purple Heart; named Man of Year, Phila. Indsl. Advertisers Assn., 1965. Mem. Adcrafters Club Detroit, Direct Mail Assn. Club: Mason. Home: 4635 Pickering Rd Birmingham MI 48010 Office: 29516 Southfield Rd Southfield MI 48076

ECKSTEIN, JOHN WILLIAM, physician, educator; b. Central City, Iowa, Nov. 23, 1923; s. John William and Alice (Ellsworth) E.; m. Imogene O'Brien, June 16, 1947; children—John Alan, Charles William, Margaret Ann, Thomas Cody, Steven Gregory. B.S., Loras Coll., 1946; M.D., U. Iowa, 1950. Asst. prof. internal medicine U. Iowa, Iowa City, 1956-60, asso. prof., 1960-65, prof., 1965—; asso. dean VA Hosp. affairs, 1969-70, dean coll. medicine, 1970—; Chmn. cardiovascular study sect. NIH, 1970-72, Nat. Heart, Lung and Blood Adv. Council, 1974-78; gen. research support rev. com. NIH, 1980—. Author papers and abstracts. Served with USAAF, 1943-45. Rockefeller Found. postdoctoral fellow, 1953-54; Am. Heart Assn. Research fellow, 1954-55; Nat. Heart Inst. spl. research fellow, 1955-56; Am. Heart Assn. established investigator, 1958-63; recipient USPHS Research Career award, 1963-70. Mem. Am. Heart Assn. (v.p. 1969, chmn. council on circulation 1969-71, pres. 1978-79), AMA (mem. health policy agenda panel 1983—), Am. Fedn. Clin. Research (chmn. Midwestern sect. 1965), Central Soc. Clin. Research (sec.-treas. 1965-70, pres. 1973-74), Am. Soc. Clin. Investigation, Am. Clin. and Climatol. Assn., Assn. Am. Physicians, Assn. Am. Med. Colls. (exec. council 1981-82, adminstrv. bd. 1980-82). Home: 1415 William White Blvd Iowa City IA 52240 Office: 120-CMAB-Coll Medicine Univ of Iowa Iowa City IA 52242

ECKSTINE, BILLY (WILLIAM CLARENCE ECKSTINE), singer; b. Pitts., July 8, 1914. Student, Howard U. Night club singer, emcee, Buffalo, Detroit; then, Club de Lisa, Chgo.; vocalist, Earl Hines Band, 1939-43; night club soloist, 1943; with, Budd Johnson, organized band featuring bop music, 1944; orch. leader; singer; trombone player; popular ballad singer, 1948—, also jazz music; numerous appearances include, Mill Run Theatre, Niles, Ill.; appeared: motion picture Let's Do It Again, 1975; now with, Enterprise Records; recs. include Prime of My Life, 1963, For the Love of Ivy, My Way, 1967, Senior Soul, Stormy, Feel the Warm, If She Walked Into My Life, The Legendary Big Band of Billy Eckstine-Together, The Soul Sessions (vol. 6 Newport in New York, 1972. Address: care Redbeard Presents Ltd 1061 E Flamingo Rd # 7 Las Vegas NV 89109 *

ECONOMAKI, CHRIS CONSTANTINE (CHRISTOPHER ECONOMAKI), publisher, editor; b. Bklyn., Oct. 15, 1920; s. Christopher C. and Gladys Toomey (Burt) E.; m. Alvera H. Tomljanovic, May 29, 1946; children: Christine, Corinne. Student, Drake U. Sales rep. Divco Corp., 1946-49; editor, pub. Nat. Speed Sport News newspaper; pres. Kay Pub. Co., Ridgewood, N.J., 1949—; Color commentator Wide World of Sports ABC-TV, 1961-83, CBS-TV Sports, 1984—. Served with AUS, 1942-46; ETO. Recipient Henry McLemore award for excellence in broadcast journalism, 1973; Ken Purdy award Internat. Motor Press Assn., 1978; Patrick Jacquemart award for service to motorsports, 1983. Mem. Am. Assn. Auto Racing Writers and Broadcasters (pres. 1969-71). Home: Wood Hollow Ridgewood NJ 07450 Office: 30 Oak St Box 608 Ridgewood NJ 07451

ECONOMOS, GEORGE THEMISTOCLES, educator, physician; b. N. Epiros, Greece, Feb. 2, 1922; came to U.S., 1950, naturalized, 1959; s. Themistocles G. and Fotini (Papinghi) E.; m. Stavroula Perdikis, Sept. 6, 1959; children—Demetra, Gregory, Themis. B.S., M.D., U. Athens, 1949; M.D., U. Vt., 1954. Intern medicine George Washington U. Hosp., 1954-55, fellow medicine, 1959-60; asst. resident medicine D.C. Gen. Hosp., 1955-56, sr. resident medicine, 1958-59; med. dir. Children's Center D.C., 1960—; pvt. practice diagnostic medicine and consultations, 1960—; mem. faculty George Washington U. Med. Sch., 1960—, asst. clin. prof. medicine, 1964—; spl. research mental retardation. Served to capt., M.C. AUS, 1956-58. Mem. Am., So. med. assns., D.C., So. med. socs., Am. Assn. Med. Supts., Assn. Mil. Surgeons, Am. Rheumatism Assn., Am. Heart Assn., Am. Soc. Internal Medicine, Am. Geriatrics Soc., D.C. Internal Medicine Soc., Vt. State Soc., U. Vt. Med. Alumni Assn., Am. Hellenic Edn. Progressive Assn., Pan Epirotan Soc. U.S., Nu Sigma Nu. Home: 7513 Arrowwood Rd Bethesda MD 20817 Office: 2141 K St NW Washington DC 20037

ECONOMOS, JAMES PETER, lawyer, traffic court and law consultant; b. Chgo., Feb. 18, 1908; s. Peter D. and Eugenia G. (Sikokis) E.; m. Eleanore R. McCann, July 17, 1943; 1 son, Peter L.; m. 2d Jessica Gavrilovich, Aug. 7, 1979; stepchildren: G. Raymond Gavery, Georgina Spielke. B.S. in Acctg., U. Ill., 1930, J.D., 1931; H.H.D., Lewis U., 1979. Bar: Ill. 1931, U.S. Dist. Ct. (no dist.) Ill. 1933, U.S. Supreme Ct. 1944. Assoc. Reeda & Peace, Chgo., 1931-37; ptnr. Reeda, Peace, Bopp & Economos, Chgo., 1937-47, Economos and Reeda, 1947-80; sole practice, Chgo., 1980—; dir. Nat. Safety Council, 1966-77, v.p., 1968-77; chmn. Nat. Commn. Alcohol and Drugs, 1959-61, Ill. Sec. State Traffic Safety Adv. Council, 1972-80, vice chmn., 1980—; sec. Dr. William M. Scholl Found., 1947-80, exec. dir., 1972-80. Preparer studies of 48 city, county and state cts., 1952-72; contbr. numerous book chpts., jour. articles on traffic courts, safety and law. Bd. dirs. Viterbo Coll., LaCross, Wis., 1980—, Lewis U., Romeoville, Ill., 1979—; mem. audit com. Loyola U., Chgo. Recipient Paul Gray Hoffman award Automotive Safety Found., 1971, dist. service award, traffic conf. Nat. Safety Council, 1972, Pope John XXIII Dist. Service award Viterbo Coll., 1981, St. LaSalle award St. Mary's Coll., 1981, Glenn R. Winters award Am. Judges Assn., 1982. Fellow Am. Bar Found., Inst. Jud. Adminstrn.; mem. ABA (asst. sec. 1948-52, ho of dels. 1942-44, chmn. various confs., exec. dir. traffic ct. program 1942-72), Chgo. Bar Assn., Ill. State Bar Assn., Am. Judicature Soc., Am. Judges Assn. (law 1960-79), Delta Theta Phi. Republican. Greek Orthodox. Clubs: University, Legal, Mid-Day. Lodges: Rotary One; Shriners; K.T. Address: Suite 1000 303 E Wacker Dr Chicago IL 60601

ECROYD, LAWRENCE GERALD, association executive; b. Montreal, Que., Can., Sept. 14, 1918; s. George Smith and Marie (Guibord) E.; m. Dorothy Gertrude Howson, Dec. 26, 1949; children: Lynn (Mrs. Thomas Egan), Claire (Mrs. Lawrence Northway), Beverly (Mrs. Glen Brown), Bruce. Intermediate cert., U. London, Eng., 1960; M.B.A., Fla. Atlantic U., 1972. B.C. mgr. Can. C. of C., Vancouver, 1946-53; exec. dir. Mitchell Press Ltd., Vancouver, 1953-61; exec. v.p. Travel Industry Assn. Can., Ottawa, Ont., 1961-73; pres. Can. Inst. Plumbing and Heating, Toronto, 1973—. Served to lt. comdr. Royal Can. Navy, 1941-45. Recipient Bota award tourism, 1973. Mem. Am. Soc. Assn. Execs. (Merit award 1971, Cert. Assn. Exec. 1974), Inst. Assn. Execs. (Can.). Home: Unit 4 24 La Rose Ave Weston ON M9P 1A5 Canada Office: 5468 Dundas St W Islington ON M9B 6E3 Canada

EDDISON, JOHN CORBIN, economist; b. N.Y.C., Nov. 4, 1919; s. William Barton and Mary (Corbin) E.; m. Elizabeth Owsley Bole, Feb. 10, 1951; children: Jonathan B., Elizabeth O., Martha C. Grad., St. Paul's Sch., 1938; A.B., Cornell U., 1942, M.S., 1948; Ph.D., Mass. Inst. Tech., 1955. Personnel asst. E.I. duPont de Nemours & Co., 1947-48; indsl. engr. Campbell Soup Co., 1949-51; indsl. adviser EDA, San Juan, P.R., 1955-56; asst. to rep. in, Burma, Ford Found., 1956-57; econ. adviser to Govt. W. Pakistan, Harvard Adv. Group, Lahore, 1958-61, to; Pakistan Planning Commn., Karachi, 1961-63; dep. dir. AID mission to Bolivia, La Paz, 1963-65, Central Am. affairs Dept. State, Washington, 1965-68; dir. Near East affairs AID, 1968-69; econ. adviser to planning dept. Govt. Colombia, Harvard U. Devel. Adv. Service, Bogota, 1969-71, asso. dir., Cambridge, Mass., 1971-74, Harvard Inst. for Internat. Devel., Cambridge, 1974-80; exec. v.p. and treas. Warner-Eddison Assos., Inc., Cambridge, 1980—. Author papers, reports. Selectman City of Lexington (Mass.), 1984—. Served to capt. C.E. AUS, 1942-46. Overseas fellow Ford Found., 1953-54. Mem. Soc. Internat. Devel., Am. Civil Liberties Union, Am. Econ. Assn., Alpha Delta Phi. Episcopalian. Home: 20 Nickerson Rd Lexington MA 02173 Office: 186 Alewife Brook Pkwy Cambridge MA 02138

EDDLEMAN, ELVIA ETHERIDGE, JR., physician; b. Birmingham, Ala., Oct. 20, 1922; m. Stella R. Eddleman; 1 son, John Steven. B.S., Howard Coll., 1944; M.D., Emory U., 1948. Diplomate: Am. Bd. Internal Medicine. Intern Grady Meml. Hosp., Atlanta, 1948-49; asst. resident internal medicine Parkland Hosp., Dallas, 1949-50; research fellow medicine Med. Coll. Ala., Birmingham, 1952-53, research fellow, instr., 1953-54, asst. prof. medicine, 1954-57, asso. prof., 1957-62; asst. chief med. service, chief cardiovascular sect. VA Hosp., Birmingham, 1954-57, acting chief med. service, 1957, chief, 1957-62, asso. chief staff for research, 1954-81; prof. medicine U. Ala. Sch. Medicine, Birmingham, 1962-81, prof. emeritus, 1981—, asso. prof. physiology and biophysics, 1966—; mem. panel study sect. Nat. Heart and Lung Inst., 1971-72. Contbg. author: Methods in Medical Research, 1958, Clinical Cardiopulmonary Physiology, 1960, The Heart, 1978, Principles of Internal Medicine, 1966; contbr. articles to profl. jours. Fellow ACP, Am. Coll. Cardiology; mem. Ala. Heart Assn. (pres. 1967-68), Am. Heart Assn., Ballistocardiograph Research Soc., Birmingham Soc. Internists, Jefferson County Med. Soc., Laennec Cardiovascular Sound Group, Med. Assn. Ala., So. Soc. Clin. Investigation, Sigma Xi, Alpha Omega Alpha. Address: 4209 Mountaindale Rd Birmingham AL 35213

EDDLEMAN, WILLIAM ROSEMAN, lawyer; b. Shelby, N.C., May 21, 1913; s. William Peter and Nellie Holland (Roseman) E.; m. Ruth Carolyn Phelps, Aug. 31, 1952 (dec. Aug. 1966); 1 son, William Lammers; m. Elizabeth Dorothy Carp, Nov. 1, 1966. Student, U. N.C., 1930-34, Pace Inst., 1934-35, Washington Coll. Law, 1935-37; LL.B., Gonzaga U., 1939; Licenciado en Derecho, Nat. U. Mex., 1968. Bar: Wash. 1939, U.S. Supreme Ct. 1945, Mexico 1968, Tex. 1972. Mem. firm Eddleman & Wheeler, Seattle, 1946-64, Perez, Verdia, Eddleman, 1963-64; with Parker Sch. Internat. Law, Columbia, 1964; Facultad de Derecho Nat. U. Mex., 1964-67; mem. firm Carp & Eddleman, Dallas, 1972—, Bufete-Eddleman, Mex., 1968-81; del. Internat. Bar Assn. meeting, Mexico, 1964, Inter-Am. Bar Assn. meeting, 1944. Author: Legal Aspects of LAFTA, 1967, Full Faith and Credit in Federal Systems, 1968, Conflicts—Private International Law, 1969, Legal Aspects Current Latin American Integration and Development, 1979. Exec. bd. Chief Seattle council Boy Scouts Am., 1959-61; Republican dist. leader, 1949-52, mem. Rep. exec. com., 1950-52. Mem. Inter-Am. Bar Assn. (chmn. com. legal aspects devel. and integration 1978—, council 1981—), Internat. Bar Assn., ABA (nat. chmn. younger lawyers 1948-49, ho. of dels. 1949-50), Wash. Bar Assn. (chmn. war readjustment and traffic ct. coms. 1944-46), Dallas Bar Assn. (internat. com. 1974-80), Tex. Bar Assn. (lawyer referral com. 1981), Whitman County Bar Assn. (pres. 1943-44), Fedn. Ins. Counsel (v.p. 1960-61), Comml. Law League Am. (pres. 1961-62), Selden Soc., SAR (pres. Dallas chpt. 1981, state chancellor 1982-83). Episcopalian (vestryman). Clubs: Odd Fellows (sovereign grand rep. 1954), Lions (dir. 1963-64), Spokane; College (Seattle). Home: 7149 Northaven Dallas TX 75230 Office: 4014 Republic Nat Bank Tower Dallas TX 75201 *The rewards of life arise from faith, service and loyalty. The law recognizes justice can only be achieved by strong advocacy and equality.*

EDDY, BOB, writer, cons., educator; b. Lake Benton, Minn., Jan. 24, 1917; s. Charles W. and Nona (Kimball) E.; m. Corinne Brandon, May 13, 1939 (div. Mar. 1974); children—Bob II, Kay, Brandon, Jane, David. A.B. summa cum laude, U. Minn., 1940, M.A., 1948; student Japanese lang, U. Mich., 1944; Nieman fellow, Harvard, 1951. Copyreader St. Paul Pioneer Press, 1939-40, asst. city editor, 1941-43, 46, telegraph editor, 1947-51; editorial writer Mpls. Star, 1940-41; copydesk editor St. Paul Dispatch, 1952-56, mng. editor, 1957-62; editorial writer Dispatch and Pioneer Press, 1957; asst. to pub. Hartford (Conn.) Courant, 1962-68, editor, 1966—, also pub., 1968-74; Past lectr. Northeastern U., Boston, U. Minn. Sch. Journalism; vis. asso. prof. journalism U. Nebr. at Omaha, 1975-76, S.I. Newhouse Sch. Journalism, Syracuse U., 1976-78. Contbr. articles to popular and profl. mags. Incorporator Hartford, St. Francis hosps., Hartford Public Library, Inst. of Living; trustee Hartford Coll. for Women, Soc. for Savs.; mem. adv. bd. Greater Hartford Salvation Army. Served with AUS, 1943-46. Recipient Distinguished Alumnus award U. Minn., 1976; Ogden Reid fellow, Europe, 1956; Fulbright lectr., India, summer 1975. Mem. Soc. Profl. Journalists, Phi Beta Kappa. Episcopalian. Club: Twentieth Century. Home: 74 S Hollister Way Glastonbury CT 06033

EDDY, CHARLES P(HILLIPS), corporation official; b. Westfield, N.J., Apr. 2, 1941; s. Charles P. and Maria Ines (Cabanellas) E.; m. Brenda Broz, June 15, 1968; children—Charles Matthew, William Broz, Marisa Larose. B.A., U. Colo., 1963; J.D., Cornell U., 1970. Bar: Calif. bar 1971. Atty.-adv. Office of Solicitor, Dept. Interior, Washington, 1970-72; project counsel Ford Found. Energy Policy Project, Washington, 1972-74; sr. staff mem. for energy programs Pres.'s Council on Environ. Quality, Washington, 1974-77; dep. asst. sec. for energy and minerals Dept. Interior, Washington, 1977-80; dir. environ. Programs Tosco Corp., 1980—; mem. various faculties, adv. groups; participant Dept. Interior Solicitor's Office Honors Program, 1970. Author: (with Baldwin) A Time To Choose, 1974, Environment and Conservation in Energy R and D, 1976; contbr. articles to profl. jours. Served with USN, 1963-67. Decorated Bronze Star with V, Navy Commendation medal with V, U.S.; Vietnamese Cross. Office: Tosco Corp 10100 Santa Monica Blvd Los Angeles CA 90067

EDDY, DARLENE MATHIS, educator, poet; b. Elkhart, Ind., Mar. 19, 1937; d. William Eugene and Fern (Paulmer) Mathis; m. Spencer Livingston Eddy, Jr., May 23, 1964 (dec. May 1971). B.A., Goshen Coll., 1959; M.A., Rutgers U., 1961, Ph.D., 1967. Instr., lectr. Douglass Coll. and Rutgers U., 1962-64, 66-67; asst. prof. English Ball State U., Muncie, Ind., 1967-70, asso. prof., 1971-75, prof., 1975—. Author: The Worlds of King Lear, 1968, Leaf Threads, Wind Rhymes, 1983, Weathering, 1983; contbr.: articles to English Lang. Notes; others; poetry to others. Recipient numerous research, creative teaching and creative arts grants; Woodrow Wilson Nat. fellow, 1959-62; Rutgers U. grad. honors fellow, 1964-65. Mem. Nat. Council Tchrs. of English, MLA, AAUP, Melville Soc., Shakespeare Assn., DAR. Home: 1409 W Cardinal St Muncie IN 47303 Office: 207B English Ball State Univ Muncie IN 47303

EDDY, DON, artist; b. Long Beach, Calif., Nov. 4, 1944; s. Myron and Ruth (Chase) Eddy K.; m. Nancy Walker, June 12, 1967 (div. 1976); 1 dau., Sarah. B.F.A., U. Hawaii, 1967, M.F.A., 1969. Artist, N.Y.C. Exhibited one man shows, Galerie Petit, (locat.) Paris, 1973, Nancy Hoffman Gallery, (locat.) N.Y.C., 1974, 76, 79, 83, Molly Barnes Gallery, (locat.) Los Angeles, 1970, 71, French & Co., (locat.) N.Y.C., 1971, group shows, (locat.) U.S. and Europe; represented permanent collections, Akron Art Inst., Cleve. Mus. Art, Fogg Art Mus. Harvard U., Utrecht Mus., (locat.) (Belgium), Toledo Mus. Art, Whitney Mus. Am. Art, others.

EDDY, DONALD DAVIS, English language educator; b. Norfolk, Va., Apr. 19, 1929; s. Clarence Ford and Rebekah (Proctor Davis) E.; m. Edith Ann Quattlebaum, Dec. 20, 1954; children: Edith Evelyn, Elizabeth Nelson. B.A., Dartmouth Coll., 1951; Ph.D., U. Chgo.; M.A. (Munby fellow), Cambridge (Eng.) U., 1978. Mem. faculty Cornell U., Ithaca, N.Y., 1961—, now prof. English, head dept. rare books. Works include A Bibliography of John Brown, 1971, Samuel Johnson: Book Reviewer in the Literary Magazine, 1979. Served with USN, 1952-55. Mem. MLA, Bibliog. Soc., Oxford Bibliog. Soc., Cambridge Bibliog. Soc., Bibliog. Soc. Am., Bibliog. Soc. U. Va. Episcopalian. Clubs: Grolier; Athenaeum (London); The Johnsonians. Home: 240 Renwick Dr Ithaca NY 14850 Office: Dept English Cornell U Ithaca NY 14853

EDDY, EDWARD DANFORTH, university president; b. Saratoga Springs, N.Y., May 10, 1921; s. Edward Danforth and Martha (Henning) E.; m. Mary Allerton Schurman, June 23, 1949; children: Edward Danforth III, Mary Isabel, Catherine Schurman, David Henning. B.A., Cornell U., 1944, Ph.D., 1956; M.Div., Yale U., 1946; LL.D., Thiel Coll., 1962; Dr.Lit., Duquesne U., 1966; Litt.D., St. Vincent Coll., 1967; LL.D., U. N.H., 1967; L.H.D., Keuka Coll., 1968, Chatham Coll., 1977, Juniata Coll., 1980. Asso. dir. interfaith office Cornell U., 1946-49; asst. to pres., instr. English, U. N.H., 1949-54, acting pres., 1954-55, v.p., provost, 1955-60; dir. Nat. Study of Character Influence in Edn., 1957-58; pres. Chatham Coll., Pitts., 1960-77; provost Pa. State U., University Park, 1977-83; pres. U. R.I., Kingston, 1983—. Author: Colleges for Our Land and Time, 1957, The College Influence on Student Character, 1959, (with others) The Public Schools and the Public, 1969; contbr. articles to nat., ednl. jours. Trustee, mem. exec. com. Wheaton Coll.; trustee St. Vincent Coll.; mem. exec. bd. HERS-Mid-Atlantic. Named one of 10 outstanding young men U.S. Jr. C. of C., 1955; recipient Disting. Service awards U. Buffalo, Pitts. Pub. Schs., All Pa. Coll. Alumni Assn.; Nat. Brotherhood award NCCJ. Mem. Pa. Soc., Newcomen Soc., Omicron Delta Kappa, Sigma Phi, Phi Delta Kappa. Clubs: University (N.Y.C.); Hope, Dunes. Home: 56 Upper College Rd Kingston RI 02881 Office: Office of the Pres Univ RI Kingston RI 02881

EDDY, GEORGE AMOS, educator; b. Unity, Sask., Can., June 8, 1928; s. Wilbur Lorne and Myrl Ruth (Phillips) E.; m. Margaret Roberta Follis, Aug. 5, 1950; children—Michael, Kathleen, Terrance, Jacqueline, Daniel. B.A., U. B.C., 1950; M.A., U. Toronto, 1951; Ph.D., McGill U., 1963. With Canadian Meteorol. Service, Edmonton, Alta., 1951-57, Montreal, Que., 1957-63; asst. prof. U. Tex., Austin, 1963-67, asso. prof., 1967-68; prof. meteorology and environmental design U. Okla., Norman, 1968—; pres. Amos Eddy, Inc.; founder, dir. Okla Climatological Survey; state climatologist for, Okla. Contbr. articles to profl. jours. Mem. N.Y. Acad. Scis. (life). Home: 318 Royal Oak Dr Norman OK 73069

EDDY, JOHN PAUL, educator; b. Glencoe, Minn., Jan. 18, 1932; m. Elizabeth Ann Hobe, May 17, 1958; children—John Mark, Mary Elizabeth, Matthew Edwin Paul, Michael John. B.S., U. Minn., 1954; M.Div., Garrett Evang. Theol. Sem., 1959; M.A., Northwestern U., 1960; Ph.D., So. Ill. U., 1968. Research dir. Central Mindanao Rural Center, Cotabato, Philippines, 1954; ordained to ministry United Methodist Ch., 1957; minister Greenwood Meth. Ch., Rockford, Minn., 1955, Woodstock, Ill., 1958-60; asso. minister Barry Meml. Ch., Chgo., 1956-57; program dir. Wesley Found., Pa. State U., 1957-58; dir. Wesley Found., Mankato (Minn.) State Coll., 1960-65; exchange prof. Rust Coll., 1963; minister Hope Chapel, Colp, Ill., 1966-68; asst. to dean Coll. Edn. So. Ill. U., Carbondale, 1966, asso. dir. coll. exchange program, 1966-67, Baker fellow, 1966-68, instr. philosophy resident dir., 1967-68; dean students, asst. prof. philosophy Johnson State Coll., 1968-69; asso. prof. edn., dir. tchr. edn., acting dean students, coll. counselor N.Mex. Inst. Mining and Tech., Socorro, 1969-70; adj. prof. edn. U. Albuquerque, 1970; prof. edn. Loyola U., Chgo., 1970—; Ednl. cons., lectr., del. various state, nat. and internat. confs.; cons., Chgo., Gary bds. edn., HEW Regional Drug Center; fed. program auditor HEW. Author: Comparison of the Characteristics and Activities of Religious Personnel Employed in Selected Four Year State Colleges and Universities in the United States, 1969, Religious Affairs in Church Related Colleges, 1971, College Student Personnel Development, Administration, and Counseling, 1977; co-author: Action and Careers in a New Age, 1973, The Teacher and the Drug Scene, 1973, Career Education Primer for Educators, 1975; film World Educators and Peace Education in Schools and Society, 1973; cassette tape Counseling and Education on Drugs in the Schools, 1973; Editor: Education and Ethical Inquiry, 1969, Principles of Marketing, 1972; editorial bd.: World Circulation Newsletter of Internat. Assn. Educators for World Peace; Contbr. to: Unistar, 1970, also articles, chpts. to profl. publs. Chmn. North Central Evaluation of Holy Trinity High Sch., Chgo. Served with N.G., 1964-65. Recipient service citation Mankato United Fund, 1965, Service citation Minn. Valley Council Boy Scouts Am., 1965; others.; NASA fellow, 1970; NIMH fellow, 1972. Mem. Am. Philos. Assn., Philosophy of Edn. Soc., Nat. Soc. Profs. Edn., Am. Personnel and Guidance Assn. (past chmn. peace commn., C. Gilbert Wrenn award), Nat. Assn. Student Personnel Adminstrs., Assn. Coordination Univ. Religious Affairs, Ill. Coll. Personnel Assn. (senator), Internat. Assn. Educators for World Peace (past world pres.), Soc. World Service Fedn. (v.p.), World Peace Acad. (v.p.), Alpha Zeta, Phi Delta Kappa, Kappa Delta Pi, Phi Kappa Phi, numerous others. Home: 1320 Heather Ln Denton TX 76201 Office: Coll Education North Tex State U Denton TX 76203

EDDY, WILLIAM CRAWFORD, TV engr.; b. Saratoga Springs, N.Y., Aug. 28, 1902; s. William Daniel and Ethel (Thomas) E.; m. Christine Woolridge, July 11, 1927; children—Nancy Jane (Mrs. George McClure), William Crawford, Dianna Kay (Mrs. Lucas Schuyler Van Orden). Student, N.Y. Mil. Acad., 1917-21; B.S., U.S. Naval Acad., 1926. Registered profl. engr., Ind. Employed Farnsworth TV, Phila., 1934-36, NBC-TV, N.Y.C., 1936-49; dir. TV sta. WBKB, Chgo., 1940-48; former chmn. bd., pres. TV Assos. of Ind., Inc.; cartoonist Ann. Mpls.-Honeywell Calendar, 1935—; cons. TV sta. installation, microwave network planning, installation, design, devel. equipment for TV studios, design, devel. audio-visual equipment. Author: Television, the Eyes of Tomorrow, 1945, A Little Humor Now and Then, 1956, Back to the Drawing Board, 1962; co-author: Wartime Refresher in Mathematics, 1943. Served with U.S. Navy, 1936-34; comdg. officer radar tng. USN Radio Chgo., 1942-45; ret. as capt. Decorated Legion of Merit Navy).; Recipient Ann. Achievement award Nat. Assn. Radio and TV Broadcasters, 1947. Mem. Soc. Motion Picture and TV Engrs., Soc. Mil. Engrs., U.S. Naval Acad. Alumni Assn., Soc. Tv Pioneers. Club: Army-Navy. Home: 2711 E Michigan Blvd Michigan City IN 46360

EDEL, ABRAHAM, philosophy educator; b. Pitts., Dec. 6, 1908; s. Simon and Fannie (Malamud) E.; m. May Mandelbaum, Jan. 30, 1934 (dec. May 1964); children: Matthew, Deborah; m. Elizabeth Flower, May 11, 1973. B.A., McGill U., 1927, M.A., 1928; B.A., Oxford U., 1930; Ph.D., Columbia U., 1934. Mem. dept. philosophy Coll. City N.Y., 1931-73, prof. emeritus philosophy, 1973—; Distinguished prof. philosophy City U. N.Y. Grad. Sch., 1970-73, emeritus, 1973—; research prof. philosophy U. Pa., 1974—; Vis. appointments Columbia, U. Calif., Berkeley, Swarthmore Coll., U. Pa., Western Res. U., SUNY Downstate Med. Center; others. Author: The Theory and Practice of Philosophy, 1946, Ethical Judgment, 1955, Science and the Structure of Ethics, 1961, Method in Ethical Theory, 1963, Aristotle, 1967, (with May Edel) Anthropology and Ethics, 1959, Analyzing Concepts in Social Science, 1979, Exploring Fact & Value, 1980, Aristotle and his Philosophy, 1982. Assoc. Nat. Humanities Center, 1978-79; sr. fellow Center for Dewey Studies, 1981-82. Recipient Butler Silver medal Columbia, 1959; Guggenheim fellow, 1944-45; Rockefeller Found. grantee, 1952-53; NSF grantee; 1959-60. Mem. Am. Philos. Assn. (v.p. Eastern div. 1972), Metaphys. Soc. Am., Am. Soc. Polit. and Legal Philosophy, Internat. Assn. Philosophy Law and Social Philosophy (v.p. Am. sect. 1971-73, pres. 1973-75), Philosophy Edn. Soc. Office: 305 Logan Hall/CN Univ of Pa Philadelphia PA 19104

EDEL, (JOSEPH) LEON, author, educator; b. Pitts., Sept. 9, 1907; s. Simon and Fannie (Malamud) E.; m. Roberta Roberts, Dec. 2, 1950 (div. 1979); m. Marjorie P. Sinclair, May 30, 1980. M.A., McGill U., 1928, Litt.D., 1963; Litt.D., U. Paris, Sorbonne, 1932, Union Coll., 1963, U. Sask., 1982. Writer, journalist, 1932-43; vis. prof. N.Y. U., 1950-52, assoc. prof. English, 1953-54, prof. English, 1955-66, Henry James prof. English and Am. letters, 1966-73, emeritus, 1973; citizens prof. English U. Hawaii, 1971-78, emeritus, 1978—; mem. faculty Harvard U., summer 1952; Centenary vis. prof. U. Toronto, 1967; Gauss seminar lectr. Princeton U., 1952-53; vis. prof. Ind. U., 1954-55, U. Hawaii, summer 1955, 69-70; Alexander lectr. U. Toronto, 1956; Westminster Abbey address Henry James Meml., 1976; vis. prof. Harvard U., 1959-60, Center Advanced Study, Wesleyan U., 1965; vis. fellow Australian Nat. U., 1976; Bollingen Found. fellow, 1958-61. Author: Henry James: Les années dramatiques, 1932, James Joyce: The Last Journey, 1947, Life of Henry James, 5 vols. (Untried Years, 1953, Conquest of London, Middle Years, 1962, Treacherous Years, 1969, The Master, 1972), The Psychological Novel, 1955, Literary Biography, 1957, (with E.K. Brown) Willa Cather, 1953, (with Dan H. Laurence) Bibliography of Henry James, 1957, Bloomsbury: A House of Lions, 1979, Stuff of Sleep and Dreams, 1982, Edmund Wilson: The Forties, 1983; Editor: The Ghostly Tales of Henry James, 1949, Stories of the Supernatural, 1970, The Complete Plays of Henry James, 1949, Selected Fiction of Henry James, 1953, Selected Letters of Henry James, 1955, The Future of the Novel, 1956, The American Essays of Henry James, 1956, (with Gordon N. Ray) Henry James and H.G. Wells, 1958, The Complete Tales of Henry James, 12 vols, 1963-65, The Bodley Head Henry James, 11 Vols, 1967-74, The Diary of Alice James, 1964, H.D. Thoreau, 1970, Letters of Henry James, 4 vols., 1974-84, Edmund Wilson Papers, 1972, The Devils and Canon Barham, 1974, The Twenties, 1975, The Thirties, 1980, The Forties, 1982; adv. editor: Studies in American Fiction. Mem. adv. com. edn. Met. Mus. Centenary, 1969-70; mem. ednl. adv. com. Guggenheim Found., 1967-80. Served as lt. AUS, World War II; dir. Press Agy., 1945-47; U.S. zone Germany. Decorated Bronze Star; recipient Pulitzer prize in biography, 1963; Nat. Book award for non-fiction, 1963; medal of lit. Nat. Arts Club, 1981; Nat. Inst. Arts and Letters grantee, 1959; elected to Am. Acad. Arts and Letters, 1972; Gold medal for biography Acad.-Inst., 1976; Hawaii Writers award, 1977; Guggenheim fellow, 1936-38, 65-66; Nat. Endowment for Humanities grantee, 1974-77. Fellow Am. Acad. Arts and Scis., Royal Soc. Lit. (Eng.); mem. Nat. Inst. Arts and Letters (sec. 1965-67), W.A. White Psychoanalytic Soc. (hon.), Am. Acad. Psychoanalysis (hon.), Soc. Authors (Eng.), Authors Guild (mem. council, pres. 1969-71), P.E.N. (pres. Am. Center 1957-59), Hawaii Lit. Arts Council (pres. 1978-79), Modern Humanities Research Assn., Soc. Am. Historians. Clubs: Century (N.Y.C.); Athenaeum (London); Outrigger Canoe (Honolulu). Office: Dept English Univ Hawaii 1733 Donaghho Rd Honolulu HI 96822 *There is, in reality, only one school: the school of experience. I have been a student in it all my life.*

EDELCUP, NORMAN SCOTT, bank holding company executive; b. Chgo., May 8, 1935; s. Irving L. and Pauline (Bolz) E. B.S. in Bus. Adminstrn, Northwestern U., 1957. C.P.A., Fla., Ill. Sr. accountant Arthur Andersen & Co., Chgo., 1957-62; sec.-treas. Acme Printing Ink Co., Chgo., 1962-65; accountant, asst. to chmn. Commonwealth Edison Co., Chgo., 1965-68; sr. v.p., vice-chmn. bd. Keller Industries, Miami, Fla., 1968-76; v.p., treas. Avatar Holdings (formerly GAC Corp.), 1976-80, exec. v.p., treas., Chief fin. officer, dir., mem. exec. com., 1980-83; pres., treas., dir. Avatar Properties Inc. (formerly GAC Properties, Inc.), 1976-83, Avatar Properties Credit (formerly GAC Properties Credit, Inc.), 1976-83; vice chmn., chief operating officer Nat. Banking Corp. Fla., Miami; chmn. treas. Scroll Casual Inc.; chmn. Fla. Powder Coatings, Inc.; dir. Nat. Bank Fla., LLC Corp. Served with AUS, 1958-60. Mem. Am., Fla., Ill. insts. C.P.A.s, Fin. Execs. Inst., Greater Miami C. of C. (trustee 1979—). Home: 244 Atlantic Isle North Miami Beach FL 33160 Office: 3550 N Biscayne Blvd Miami FL 33137

EDELIN, KENNETH CARLTON, physician; b. Washington, Mar. 31, 1939; s. Benedict and Ruby (Goodwin) E.; m. Barbara Evans, Aug. 5, 1978; children: Kenneth Carlton, Kimberly Cybele, Joseph Evans, Corinne Ruby Elizabeth. B.A., Columbia Coll., 1961; M.D., Meharry Med. Coll., 1967. Intern Wright-Patterson AFB Hosp., Ohio, 1967-68; resident Boston City Hosp., 1971-74; instr. ob-gyn sch. Medicine, Boston U., 1974-76, asst. prof., 1976, asso. prof., 1977-78, prof. ob-gyn, dept. chmn., 1978—; asst. dir. ob-gyn Boston City Hosp., 1974-76, asso. dir., 1977-78, dir., 1978—; gynecologist-in-chief Univ. Hosp., 1978—; med. dir. Boston Family Planning Project. Served to capt. USAF, 1968-71. Fellow Am. Coll. Obstetricians and Gynecologists, Obstetrical Soc. Boston; mem. Planned Parenthood Fedn. Am. (vice chmn.), Nat. Med. Assn., New Eng. Med. Soc., AAAS, Am. Fertility Soc., Am. Pub. Health Assn., Assn. Profs. Ob-Gyn, Assn. Gynecologist Laparoscopists, Sigma Pi Phi. Office: 720 Harrison Ave Boston MA 02118

EDELMAN, ALVIN, lawyer; b. Chgo., Dec. 12, 1916; s. Leon and Sally (Kramer) E.; m. Rose Marie Slossy, Sept. 22, 1940; children—Marilyn Frances Edelman Snyder, Stephen D., Leon F. B.S. in Law, Northwestern U., 1938, J.D., 1940. Bar: Ill. bar 1940. Since practiced in, Chgo.; pres. firm Edelman & Rappaport, Chartered, and (predecessors), 1973—; gen. counsel Internat. Coll. Surgeons. Contbr. articles to profl. jours. Lectr. Internat. Museum Surg. Sci. and Hall of Fame; chmn. wills and gifts com. Medinah Temple of Masonic Shrine, Chgo., 1975-79; pres. Lawyers Shrine Club of Medinah Temple, 1971-73. Fellow Am. Coll. Probate Counsel; mem. ABA, Ill. Bar Assn., Chgo. Bar Assn. (chmn. grievance com. 1971-72), Phi Beta Kappa (pres. Chgo. area assn. 1975—), Phi Beta Kappa Assos. (v.p. East Central Dist. 1979—). Clubs: Monroe, Elks (Chgo.) (past exalted ruler). Home: 1100 Oak Ridge Dr Glencoe IL 60022 Office: 1 N LaSalle St Chicago IL 60602

EDELMAN, ARTHUR JAY, leather company executive; b. N.Y.C., July 19, 1925; s. Samuel and Beatrice (Edelman) E.; m. Theodora Joffe, May 28, 1950; children: Samuel, Sally, Antonia, David, Mary Elizabeth, John George. B.A., Sarah Lawrence Coll., 1950. With Fleming-Joffe Ltd., N.Y.C., 1951—, pres., 1963—; pres. Fleming-Joffe Jentra Ltd., 1973—; chmn. bd. Lighthouse Footwear, Inc., N.Y.C., 1978—; pres. Capezio Internat., Saddle Room Inc. Actor: appearing in the Big People, 1947, Nativity, 1948. Served with USNR, 1942-45. Recipient Mercury award Nat. Shoe Retailers Assn., 1963, Coty award Am. Fashion Critics, 1963; Neiman Marcus award, 1965. Home: Spring Valley Rd Ridgefield CT 06877 Office: 1 Rowan St Danbury CT 06810

EDELMAN, DANIEL JOSEPH, public relations counsel; b. N.Y.C., July 3, 1920; s. Selig and Selma (Pfeiffer) E.; m. Ruth Rozumoff, Sept. 3, 1953; children: Richard, Renee, John. Grad., Columbia Coll., 1940; postgrad., Columbia U., 1941. Reporter Poughkeepsie (N.Y.) newspapers, U.P.I., 1941-42; news writer CBS, 1946-47; staff mem. Edward Gottlieb & Assocs., 1947; pub. relations dir. Toni Co., Chgo., 1948-52; founder Daniel J. Edelman, Inc., Chgo., also Denver, Houston, Los Angeles, Miami, N.Y.C., St. Louis, Washington, London, Frankfurt, Dublin, Hong Kong, 1952—. Chmn. Chgo. chpt. Young Pres.'s Orgn., 1963; chmn. parents council Phillips Exeter Acad., 1972; chmn. vis. com. U. Chgo. Library, 1976; Bd. dirs. Ill. Children's Home and Aid Soc.; chmn. sustaining fellows individual campaign Chgo. Art Inst., 1982. Served to 2d lt. AUS, 1942-46; ETO. Recipient 11 Silver Anvils. Mem. Pub. Relations Soc. Am. (past chmn. counselor sect.), Publicity Club Chgo., Phi Beta Kappa, Zeta Beta Tau. Jewish. Clubs: Chgo., Standard, Harmonie. Home: 1301 N Astor St Chicago IL 60610 Office: 221 N La Salle St Chicago IL 60601

EDELMAN, GERALD MAURICE, biochemist; b. N.Y.C., July 1, 1929; s. Edward and Anna (Freedman) E.; m. Maxine Morrison, June 11, 1950; children: Eric, David, Judith. B.S., Ursinus Coll., 1950, Sc.D., 1974; M.D., U. Pa., 1954, D.Sc., 1973; Ph.D., Rockefeller U., 1960; M.D. (hon.), U. Siena, Italy, 1974; D.Sc., Gustavus Adolphus Coll., 1975; Sc.D., Williams Coll., 1976. Med. house officer Mass. Gen. Hosp., 1954-55; asst. physician hosp. of Rockefeller U., 1957-60, mem. faculty, 1960—, assoc. dean grad. studies, 1963-66, prof., 1966-74, Vincent Astor Distinguished prof., 1974—; Mem. biophysics and biophys. chemistry study sect. NIH, 1964-67; mem. Sci. Council, Center for Theoretical Studies, 1970-72; assoc., sci. chmn. Neurosciences Research Program, 1980—, dir. Neuroscis. Inst., 1981—; mem. adv. bd. Basel Inst. Immunology, 1970-77, chmn., 1975-77; non-resident fellow, trustee Salk Inst.; bd. overseers Faculty Arts and Scis., U. Pa., 1976-83; trustee, mem. adv. com. Carnegie Inst., Washington. Bd. govs. Weizmann Inst. Sci.; trustee Rockefeller Bros. Fund., 1972-82. Served to capt. M.C. AUS, 1955-57. Recipient Spencer Morris award U. Pa., 1954; Ann. Alumni award Ursinus Coll., 1969; Nobel prize for physiology or medicine, 1972; Albert Einstein Commemorative award Yeshiva U., 1974; Buchman Meml. award Calif. Inst. Tech., 1975; Rabbi Shai Shacknai meml. prize Hebrew U.-Hadassah Med. Sch., Jerusalem, 1977. Fellow N.Y. Acad. Scis., N.Y. Acad. Medicine; mem. Am. Philos. Soc., Am. Soc. Biol. Chemists, Am. Assn. Immunologists, Genetics Soc. Am., Harvey Soc. (pres. 1975-76, Am. Chem. Soc., Eli Lilly award biol. chemistry 1965), AAAS, Am. Acad. Arts and Scis., Nat. Acad. Sci., Am. Soc. Cell Biology, Acad. Scis. of Inst. France (fgn.), Japanese Biochem. Soc. (hon.), Pharm. Soc. Japan (hon.), Soc. Developmental Biology, Council Fgn. Relations, Sigma Xi, Alpha Omega Alpha. Research structure of antibodies, molecular and devel. biology.

EDELMAN, HAROLD, architect; b. N.Y.C., Aug. 4, 1923; s. Joseph S. and Rose (Kaminsky) E.; m. Judith Hochberg, Dec. 26, 1947; children: Marc, Joshua. B.Arch., Cornell U., 1943; certificate civil engring, Stanford U.; student, Ecole des Beaux Arts, Paris, 1951. Asso. Huson Jackson, 1951-58; pvt. practice architecture, 1958-60; partner firm Edelman & Salzman, N.Y.C., 1960-79, Edelman Partnership (Architects), 1979—; asso. prof. architecture Pratt Inst., 1952-62; lectr. design Columbia, 1952-53; vis. lectr. urban design and architecture New Sch. Pa. State U. Served with AUS, 1943-46. Recipient spl. Brunner award A.I.A., 1960, 61, citation in house alteration, 1961; Bard 1st honor award for excellence in civic architecture and urban design City Club N.Y., 1969; Bard award of merit, 1975; residential design award A.I.A., 1969; award for design excellence HUD, 1970; Honor award N.Y. State Assn. Architects-AIA, 1975; 1st prize Nat. Trust Historic Preservation in U.S., 1975; Preservation honor Nat. Trust Historic Preservation in U.S., 1983; Bard award for merit in architecture and urban design, 1982; cert. of merit Mcpl. Art Soc. N.Y., 1983; Pub. Service award Settlement Housing Fund, 1983. Fellow AIA. Home: 13 Bank St New York NY 10014 Office: 434 6th Ave New York NY 10011

EDELMAN, HARRY ROLLINGS, III, engineering and construction company executive; b. Pitts., Aug. 16, 1928; s. Harry Rollings, Jr. and Marian A. (Crooks) E.; m. Nancy Jane McCune, Aug. 26, 1950; children: Lisa, Harry Rollings, IV, John Reed, Amy Lou. B.S., U. Pitts., 1950. With Heyl & Patterson, Inc. (contracting engrs.), Pitts., 1950—, exec. v.p., 1960-65, pres., gen. mgr., 1965-77, chmn. bd., pres., chief exec. officer, 1977—, also dir.; dir. Dedert Corp., Thermal Processes, Inc., Heyl & Patterson Internat., Inc., Heylpat Engrs. Pty. Ltd.; treas. Met. Broadcasting Co. Pitts. Author papers in engring., constrn., religion and mgmt. Bd. dirs. Allegheny Gen. Hosp.; past pres. Christian Assn. S.W. Pa.; vice chmn. Presbyn. Assn. Aging, Allegheny Singer Research Inst.; past chmn. Vocat. Rehab. Center Allegheny County. Served with AUS, 1952-54. Mem. AIME, World Bus. Council, Chief Execs. Orgn. Clubs: Duquesne, Pitts. Field,

University (Pitts.); Masons. Office: 250 Park West Dr PO Box 36 Pittsburgh PA 15230

EDELMAN, HENDRIK, university librarian; b. Wageningen, Netherlands, Nov. 27, 1937; U.S., 1967; s. Cornelis Hendrik and Johanna (van Werkhoven) E.; children: Stijn Willem, Mark Bastiaan, Kees Maarten. M.L.S., George Peabody Coll., 1969. With Martinus Nijhoff (Pubs. & Booksellers), Netherlands, 1958-65, D. Reidel Pub. Co., 1965-67; univ. bibliographer Vanderbilt U., 1967-70; asst. dir. Cornell U. Libraries, Ithaca, N.Y., 1970-78; univ. librarian, prof. library and info. studies Rutgers-State U. N.J., New Brunswick, 1979—; dir. Cornell Mellon Project for Collection Devel. and Mgmt., 1978-79; bd. dirs. Book Industry Study Group, 1977—; editorial, mktg. cons. Am., European pubs. (booksellers); acad. library cons. Author: Dutch-American Bibliography, 1693-1794, 1974; contbr. articles, revs. to profl. jours. Mem. ALA, N.J. Library Assn. (award 1983), Bibliog. Soc. Am., Am. Antiquarian Soc., Beta Phi Mu. Office: Rutgers U Library New Brunswick NJ 08903

EDELMAN, ISIDORE SAMUEL, educator, scientist; b. N.Y.C., July 24, 1920; s. Abraham and Fannie (Thaler) E.; children: Arthur, Susan, Joseph, Ann. B.A., Ind. U., 1941, M.D., 1944. Intern, Greenpoint Hosp., Bklyn., 1944-45; resident Montefiore Hosp., Bronx, N.Y., 1947-49; postdoctoral research fellow Harvard Med. Sch., 1949-52; prof. medicine and physiology U. Calif.-San Francisco, 1960-67, prof. biophysics, 1969-78, Samuel Neider Research prof. medicine, 1967-78; Robert Wood Johnson, Jr. prof., chmn. biochemistry Coll. Physicians and Surgeons Columbia U., 1978—; Harry T. Dozor vis. prof. biochemistry Ben-Gurion U., Beer Sheva, Israel, 1980; mem. research career awards com. Nat. Inst. Gen. Med. Sci., NIH, 1969-72; bd. sci. counselors Nat. Heart, Lung and Blood Inst., 1978-82; mem. U.S. nat. com. Internat. Union Pure and Applied Biophysics, 1971-73. Editor: Ann. Revs. Physiology; editorial bd.: Current Topics in Membranes and Transport, Jour. Membrane Biology. Served to capt. AUS, 1945-47. Mem. Assn. Am. Physicians, Am. Acad. Arts and Scis., Am. Physiol. Soc., Inst. Medicine of Nat. Acad. Scis., Am. Soc. Clin. Investigation, Biophys. Soc. (council 1974-77), Soc. Gen. Physiology, Western Soc. Clin. Research, Am. Soc. Biol. Chemistry, Endocrine Soc. (publs. com. 1974-77, council 1979—), Western Assn. Physicians, Harvey Soc. Research transport solutes and water across cell membranes; molecular mechanisms in actions of adrenal, posterior pituitary and thyroid hormones. Dept Biochem Coll Physicians & Surgeons Columbia U 630 W 168th St New York NY 10032

EDELMAN, JOEL, medical center executive; b. Chgo., Mar. 24, 1931; s. Maurice B. and Ethel J. (Newman) E.; m. Beth L. Sommers, July 31, 1955; children: Peter J., Ann Elizabeth, Deborah S. B.A. in Spl. Edn., U. Mich., 1952; J.D., DePaul U., 1960. Bar: Ill. 1961. Program dir. Chgo. Heart Assn., 1955-61; staff atty. Michael Reese Hosp. and Med. Center, Chgo., 1961-70, exec. v.p., 1971-73; dir. Ill. Dept. Pub. Aid, 1973-74; exec. dir. Ill. Legis. Adv. Com. on Pub. Aid, 1974-77; pres. Rose Med. Center, Denver, 1979—; assoc. prof. Grad. Sch. Mgmt., Northwestern U.; dir. office legal affairs Am. Hosp. Assn., 1970. Contbr. articles to profl. jours. Served with AUS, 1955. Mem. Soc. Hosp. Attys. (charter). Home: 3156 S Hills Ct Denver CO 80210 Office: 4636 E 9th Ave Denver CO 80220

EDELMAN, JUDITH HOCHBERG, architect; b. Bklyn., Sept. 16, 1923; d. Abraham and Frances (Israel) Hochberg; m. Harold Edelman, Dec. 26, 1947; children: Marc, Joshua. Student, Conn. Coll., 1940-41, NYU, 1941-42; B.Arch., Columbia U., 1946. Designer, drafter Huson Jackson, N.Y.C., 1948-58; Schermerhorn traveling fellow Mcpl. Art Soc., N.Y.C., 1950; pvt. practice architecture, 1958-60; partner Edelman & Salzman, N.Y.C., 1960-79, Edelman Partnership (Architects), 1979—; adj. prof. Sch. Architecture, City U. N.Y., 1972-76; vis. lectr. urban renewal New Sch., 1968; vis. lectr. Washington U., St. Louis, 1974, U. Oreg., 1974, Mass. Inst. Tech., 1975, City U. N.Y. Grad. Program Environ. Psychology, 1975, Pa. State U., City U. N.Y. Grad. Program Environ. Psychology, 1977, Rensselaer Poly Inst., 1977, Columbia U., 1979; First Claire Watson Forrest Meml. lectr. U. Oreg., U. Calif.-Berkeley, U. So. Calif., 1982. Major archtl. works include: Restoration of St. Mark's Ch. in the Bowery, N.Y.C., 1970-82, Two Bridges Urban Renewal Area Housing, 1970-84, Jennings Hall Sr. Citizens Housing, Bklyn., 1980, Goddard Riverside Elderly Housing and Community Ctr., N.Y.C., 1983. Recipient Bard 1st honor award City Club N.Y., 1969, Bard award of merit, 1975, 82; Residential Design award A.I.A., 1969; award for design excellence HUD, 1970; Honor award N.Y. State Assn. Architects-AIA, 1975; 1st prize Nat. Trust Historic Preservation, 1975; Honor award Nat. Trust Historic Preservation, 1983; art. of merit Mcpl. Art Soc. N.Y., 1983; Pub. Service award Settlement Service award, 1983. Fellow AIA (dir. N.Y. chpt., chmn. commn. archtl. edn. 1971-73, chmn. nat. task force on women in architecture 1974-75, v.p. N.Y. chpt. 1975-77, chmn. ethics com. 1975-77); mem. Alliance of Women in Architecture (founding mem., mem. steering com. 1972-74), Architects for Social Responsibility (exec. com. 1982—), Columbia Archtl. Alumni Assn. (dir. 1968-71). Home: 13 Bank St New York NY 10014 Office: 434 6th Ave New York NY 10011

EDELMAN, MARIAN WRIGHT (MRS. PETER B. EDELMAN), lawyer; b. Bennettsville, S.C., June 6, 1939; d. Arthur J. and Maggie (Bowen) Wright; m. Peter B. Edelman, July 14, 1968; children: Joshua, Jonah, Ezra. Merrill scholar, univs. Paris, Geneva, 1958-59; B.A., Spelman Coll., 1960; LL.B. (J.H. Whitney fellow 1960-61), Yale, 1963,; M.A.; LL.D., Smith Coll., 1969, Lowell Tech. U., 1975, Williams Coll., 1978; D.H.L., Lesley Coll., 1975, Russell Sage Coll., 1978, Syracuse U., 1979, Coll. New Rochelle, 1979, Swarthmore Coll., 1980, SUNY at Old Westbury, 1981, Northeastern U., 1981, Bard Coll., 1982, U. Mass., 1983, Hunter Coll., U. So. Maine, SUNY-Albany, 1984. Bar: D.C., Miss., Mass. Staff atty. NAACP Legal Def. and Edn. Fund, Inc., N.Y.C., 1963-64, dir., Jackson, Miss., 1964-68; Congl. and fed. liaison Poor People's Campaign, summer 1968; partner Washington Research Project of So. Center for Pub. Policy, 1968-73; dir. Harvard U. Center for Law and Edn., 1971-73; pres. Children's Def. Fund, 1973—. Mem. exec. com. Student Non-Violent Coordinating Com., 1961-63; mem. adv. council Martin Luther King, Jr. Meml. Library; mem. adv. bd. Hampshire Coll.; mem. Presdl. Commn. on Missing in Action, 1977, Presdl. Commn. on Internat. Yr. of Child, 1979, Presdl. Comm. on Agenda for 80's, 1980; bd. dirs. Center for Law and Social Policy, Eleanor Roosevelt Inst., Nat. Office for Rights of the Indigent, NAACP Legal Def. and Ednl. Fund; trustee, chmn. bd. Spelman Coll., Atlanta, Arts, Edn. and Ams., Carnegie Council on Children, 1972-77, Martin Luther King, Jr. Meml. Center, Nat. Council Children and TV; mem. Yale U. Corp., 1971-77, German Marshall Fund Found., Aetna Found. Named an Outstanding Young Woman of Am., 1966; recipient Mademoiselle mag. award, 1965, Louise Waterman Wise award, 1970; Washington of Yr. award, 1979; Whitney M. Young award, 1979; Profl. of Yr. award Black Enterprise, 1979; Leadership award Nat. Women's Polit. Caucus, 1980; Black Womens Forum award, 1980; medalist Columbia Tchrs. Coll., 1984. Mem. Council Fgn. Relations.; Hon. fellow U. Pa. Law Sch. (1969). Address: 122 C St NW Washington DC 20001

EDELMAN, MARK LESLIE, government official; b. St. Louis, June 27, 1943; s. Marvin and Ruth Faye (Goldstein) E.; m. Nancy M. Wasell, May 12, 1973. A.B., Oberlin Coll., Ohio, 1965; portgrad., George Washington U., 1965-66. Budget analyst USIA, Washington, 1965-67; researcher Planning Research Corp., Washington, 1968; budget examiner Office Mgmt. and Budget, Washington, 1968-72; budget dir. State of Mo., Jefferson City, 1973-76; legis. asst. U.S. Senate, Washington, 1977-81; dep. asst. sec. U.S. Dept. State, Washington, 1981—. Mem. exec. bd. Washington Oberlin Alumni Assn., 1966-72; class v.p. Oberlin Coll., 1982—. Republican. Office: Dept State 2201 C St NW Washington DC 20520

EDELMAN, MURRAY JACOB, political science educator; b. Nanticoke, Pa., Nov. 5, 1919; s. Kalman and Sadie (Wiesenberg) E.; m. Bacia Stepner, June 15, 1952; children: Lauren Beatrice, Judith Sybil, Sarah Miriam. B.A., Bucknell U., 1941; M.A., U. Chgo., 1942; Ph.D., U. Ill., 1948. Mem. faculty U. Ill., 1948-66, prof. polit. sci., 1958-65, chmn. dept. polit. sci., 1965-66; prof. polit. sci. U. Wis., 1966—, George Herbert Mead prof., 1972—. Author: The Licensing of Radio Services in the United States, 1927-47, 1950, National Economic Planning by Collective Bargaining, 1954, (with R.W. Fleming) The Politics of Wage-Price Decisions: A Four Country Analysis, 1965, The Symbolic Uses of Politics, 1964, Politics as Symbolic Action: Mass Arousal and Quiescence, 1971, Political Language, 1977. Served with USAAF, 1942-45. Guggenheim fellow, 1962-63, 83-84; Fulbright grantee, Austria, 1952, Italy, 1956; NEH sr. fellow, 1974-75. Home: 1824 Vilas Ave Madison WI 53711

EDELMAN, PETER BENJAMIN, lawyer; b. Mpls., Jan. 9, 1938; s. Hyman and Miriam Hazel (Lieberman) E.; m. Marian Elizabeth Wright, July 14, 1968; children: Joshua, Jonah, Ezra. A.B., Harvard U., 1958, LL.B., 1961. Bar: N.Y. 1962, D.C. 1979. Law clk. Judge Henry J. Friendly, N.Y.C., 1961-62, Justice Arthur J. Goldberg, Washington, 1962-63; spl. asst. to asst. atty. gen. John Douglas Dept. Justice, Washington, 1963-64; legis. asst. to Sen. Robert F. Kennedy, Washington, 1964-68; asso. dir. Robert F. Kennedy Meml., Washington, 1969-70, bd. dirs., 1970—; staff dir. Pres.'s Com. on the Future of U. Mass., Boston, 1971, v.p. univ. policy, 1972-75; dir. N.Y. State Div. Youth, Albany, 1975-79; partner firm Foley, Lardner, Hollabaugh & Jacobs, Washington, 1979-82; prof. law Georgetown U. Law Ctr., Washington, 1982—; lectr. MIT, 1972-75; issues dir presdl. campaign Senator Edward M Kennedy, 1980. Chmn. bd. New World Found., 1983—; vice chmn. bd. Ctr. for Community Change, 1983—; v.p. Nat. Child Labor Com., 1982—; mem. exec. com. Ctr. for Youth Services, 1982—, Washington Lawyers Com. for Civil Rights Under Law, 1981—. Served with Air N.G., 1963. Ford Found. travel-study grantee, 1968. Democrat. Jewish religion. Home: 3208 Newark St NW Washington DC 20008 Office: 600 New Jersey Ave NW Washington DC 20001

EDELMANN, CHESTER MONROE, JR., pediatrician, medical school dean; b. N.Y.C., Dec. 26, 1930; s. Chester Monroe and Nannette L. (Goodhart) E.; m. Norma M. Glehs, June 28, 1953; children—John Stephen, Christopher Matthew, Kathy Jeanne. A.B., Columbia Coll., 1951; postgrad., Washington U. Sch. Medicine, St. Louis, 1951-53; M.D., Cornell U., 1955. Diplomate: Am. Bd. Pediatrics. Intern N.Y. Hosp., N.Y.C., 1955-56; resident in pediatrics Bronx (N.Y.) Mcpl. Hosp. Center, 1956-57, chief resident in pediatrics, 1957-58, asst. attending pediatrician, 1959-67, asso. attending pediatrician, 1967-70, attending pediatrician, 1970—, dir. pediatrics, 1973-80, pres. med. bd., 1978-80; postdoctoral fellow in pediatric nephrology Albert Einstein Coll. Medicine, 1958-59, 61-63, asst. instr., 1958-59, instr., 1959-62, asst. prof. pediatrics, 1962-67, assoc. prof., 1967-70, prof., 1970—, dir. div. pediatric nephrology, 1963-73, chmn. dept. pediatrics, 1973-80, asso. dean, 1980—; attending pediatrician Hosp. Albert Einstein Coll. Medicine, 1966—; mem. staff Montefiore Hosp., N.Y.C., 1970—, Lincoln Hosp., 1970-78; mem. med. adv. bd. Kidney Found. N.Y., 1969—; Joseph S. Wall Meml. lectr. Children's Hosp. D.C., 1973; Amberg-Helmholz lectr. Mayo Clinic, 1975; Daniel C. Darrow lectr. U. Kans. Med. Center, 1980; Stary White lectr. Emory U., 1981; Samuel W. Clausen lectr. U. Rochester Sch. Medicine and Dentistry, 1982. Editor, contbg. author: Pediatric Kidney Disease, 1978; editorial bd.: Pediatrics, 1973-79, The Kidney, 1974-76, Kidney Internat, 1975-78, Renal Physiology, 1977—; assoc. editor: Pediatric Research, 1973—; contbr. articles to profl. publs. Served to lt. comdr. USN, 1959-61. Recipient Research Career Devel. award NIH, 1963-69, Career Scientist award Health Research Council City N.Y., 1969-72, E. Mead Johnson award Am. Acad. Pediatrics, 1972, Tech., Sci. and Med. award Assn. Am. Pubs. for Pediatric Kidney Disease, 1978. Mem. AAAS, Am. Acad. Pediatrics, Harvey Soc., Am. Physiol. Soc., Am. Fedn. Clin. Research, Bronx Pediatric Soc., N.Y. Acad. Sci., Am. Inst. Biol. Scis., Am. Heart Assn., N.Y. Acad. Medicine, Soc. Pediatric Research (council 1970-73), Soc. Exptl. Biology and Medicine, Internat. Soc. Nephrology, Am. Soc. Nephrology, Am. Soc. Pediatric Nephrology (pres. 1975-76), Am. Pediatric Soc., N.Y. Soc. Nephrology, Am. Soc. Clin. Investigation, Internat. Pediatric Nephrology Assn. (asst. sec. 1974-77). Democrat. Lutheran. Office: 1300 Morris Park Ave Bronx NY 10461

EDELSON, ALAN MARTIN, neurophysiologist, med. publisher; b. N.Y.C., Mar. 17, 1937; s. H. Edward and Jean (Malsman) E.; m. Carol M. Herman, Jan. 21, 1959; children—Richard, Helena. B.S., U. Rochester, 1959; M.S., Columbia U., 1964, Ph.D., 1972. Founder, publisher Raven Press (med. publishers), N.Y.C., 1964—; research postdoctoral fellow dept. neurology Coll. Physicians and Surgeons Columbia U., 1972-73. Mem. N.Y. Acad. Sci., AAAS, Am. Chem. Soc., Internat. Soc. Neurochemistry, Phi Beta Kappa, Sigma Xi. Office: Raven Press 1140 Ave of the Americas New York NY 10036

EDELSON, BURTON IRVING, communications engineer; b. N.Y.C., July 31, 1926; s. Samuel and Margaret (Raff) E.; m. Betty Frances Goad, Aug. 30, 1952; children: Stephen, John, Daniel. B.S., U.S. Naval Acad., 1947; M.S., Yale U., 1954, Ph.D., 1960. Registered profl. engr., Ohio. Officer, U.S. Navy, 1947-67; with Communications Satellite Corp., Washington, 1968-82; dir. Comsat Labs., Clarksburg, Md., 1973-79, v.p. systems, 1979-82; assoc. adminstr. space sci. and applications NASA Hdqrs., Washington, 1982—. Contbr. articles to profl. jours. Decorated Legion of Merit; recipient Howe Research medal, 1963. Fellow AIAA, AAAS, IEEE. Clubs: Army Navy, Cosmos (Washington); Yale (N.Y.C.). Home: 116 Hesketh St Chevy Chase MD 20815 Office: Space Science and Applications NASA Washington DC 20546

EDELSON, MARSHALL, psychiatry educator, psychoanalyst; b. Chgo., May 31, 1928; s. George I. E. and Ida (Bernstein) Riskind; m. Zelda Sarah Toll, Dec. 27, 1952; children: Jonathan Toll, Rebecca Jo, David Jan. Ph.B., U. Chgo., 1946, Ph.D., 1954, M.D., 1955; A.B., Stanford U., 1949; M.A. hon., Yale U., 1976. Diplomate: Nat. Bd. Med. Examiners. Intern Presbyterian Hosp., Chgo., 1955-56; resident in psychiatry Sheppard and Enoch Pratt Hosp., Towson, Md., 1956-59; asst. prof. psychiatry U. Okla., Oklahoma City, 1961-63; staff psychiatrist Austen Riggs Ctr., Stockbridge, Mass., 1964-68; assoc. prof. psychiatry Yale U., New Haven, 1968-76, dir. edn., dept. psychiatry, 1973—, prof. psychiatry, 1976—; ednl. cons. Western New Eng. Inst. Psychanalysis, 1973—. Author: Sociotherapy and Psychotherapy, 1970, The Idea of a Mental Illness, 1971, Languages and Interpretation in Psychoanalysis, 1975, Hypothesis and Evidence in Psychoanalysis, 1984. Served to capt. U.S. Army, 1959-61. NIMH Career Tchr. fellow, 1962; recipient Heinz Hartmann N.Y. Psychoanalytic Inst., 1973. Fellow Am. Psychiat. Assn.; mem. Am. Psychoanalytic Assn. (cert.), Internat. Psychoanalytic Assn., Western New Eng. Inst. Psychoanalysis and Psychoanalytic Soc., Ctr. Advanced Psychoanalytic Studies, AMA. Office: Yale U Sch Medicine Dept Psychiatry 25 Park St GB 617 New Haven CT 06519

EDELSTEIN, DAVID NORTHON, federal judge; b. N.Y.C., Feb. 16, 1910; s. Benjamin and Dora (Mancher) E.; m. Florence Koch, Feb. 18, 1940; children—Jonathan H., Jeffrey M. B.S., M.A., LL.B., Fordham U. Bar: N.Y. State bar. Practiced in, N.Y.C.; atty. claims div. U.S. Dept. Justice, 1944; asst. U.S. atty. So. Dist. N.Y., 1945-47, spl. asst. to atty. gen. in charge lands div., 1947-48, asst. atty. gen. in charge customs div., 1948-51; judge U.S. Dist. Ct. So. Dist. N.Y., 1951—, chief judge, 1971-80; former elected mem. Jud. Conf. U.S., chmn. rules com., 1982—; rep. Nat. Conf. Fed. Trial Judges; also mem. exec. and program coms.; assisted Pres.'s Temp. Commn. on Employee Loyalty, chmn. preparation of report, 1946; mem. legis. com. Attys. Gen. Conf. on Crime, 1950; former mem. steering com. N.Y. Fed. Exec. Bd.; former mem. planning commn. Met. Conf. Chief Judges; founder student litigation tng. program So. Dist. N.Y.; mem. com. courtroom facilities Jud. Adminstrv. Div.; mem. White Plains Courthouse Com., 1983—; mem. nat. adv. bd. Ctr. for the Study of the Presidency. Fellow Am. Bar Found.; mem. Fed. Bar Assn. (past pres. Empire chpt., past nat. del., past mem. jud. selection com., past alt. del. ho. of dels. for Fed. Bar Assn.), Am. Bar Assn. (mem. spl. com. to survey legal needs 1971-77, mem. speedy trial planning group, mem. subcom. on planning for Dist. Cts.), Maritime Lawyers Assn. (jud. mem.), Am. Trial Lawyers Assn. (hon.), Nat. Lawyers Club (hon.), Lawyers Assn. Textile Industry (1st hon. mem.), Phi Delta Phi (hon.). Office: US Courthouse Foley Sq New York NY 10007

EDELSTEIN, JEROME MELVIN, librarian; b. Balt., July 31, 1924; s. Joseph and Irene (Schwartz) E.; m. Eleanor Rockwell, Nov. 5, 1950; children: Paul Rockwell, Nathaniel Benson. A.B. cum laude (teaching fellow 1946-49), Johns Hopkins U., 1947, postgrad., 1947-49; M.L.S., U. Mich., 1953; Italian Govt. fellow, Fulbright grantee, U. Florence, Italy, 1949-50. Reference librarian rare book div. Library of Congress, 1955-62; bibliographer Medieval and Renaissance studies UCLA, 1962-64; librarian spl. collections N.Y. U., 1964-66; humanities bibliographer, lectr. bibliography UCLA, 1966-72; chief librarian Nat. Gallery Art, Washington, 1972—; lectr. rare book librarianship Cath. U. Am., Washington, 1975—. Author: A Bibliographical Checklist of Thornton Wilder, 1959; editor, contbr.: A Garland for Jake Zeitlin, 1967, The Library of Don Cameron Allen, 1968, Wallace Stevens: A Descriptive Bibliography, 1974; contbr. articles, revs. to profl. jours. Pres. trustees Crossroads Sch., Santa Monica, Calif., 1970-72, hon. mem. bd. trustees ex officio, 1972—. Served with AUS, 1943-46. Mem. Am. Antiquarian Soc., Bibliog. Soc. Am. (notes editor 1964-81), Bibliog. Soc. London, Bibliog. Soc. U. Va., Assn. Internat. de Bibliophilie, Wallace Stevens Soc. (cons. editor jour. 1976—), Am. Printing History Assn., Art Libraries Soc. N. Am., Jargon Soc. (dir. 1976—), Phi Beta Kappa. Clubs: Grolier, Century Assn. (N.Y.C.); Cosmos (Washington); Rounce and Coffin (Los Angeles). Home: 3421 34th Pl NW Washington DC 20016 Office: Nat Gallery Art Washington DC 20565

EDELSTEIN, RICHARD MALVIN, physicist, educator; b. Los Angeles, May 28, 1930; s. Maurice Samuel and Sally (Fronenberg) E.; m. Ruth Whiteman, Aug. 7, 1955; children: Daniel C., Amy C., Elizabeth. B.A., Pomona Coll., 1951; Ph.D., Columbia U., 1960. Research physicist Carnegie-Mellon U., Pitts, 1960-62, asst. prof., Pitts., 1962-65; assoc. prof., 1965-69, prof., 1969—; assoc. dean Mellon Coll. Sci., 1978-81; vis. fellow Weizmann Inst. Sci, Rehovot, Israel, 1970-71; Karl T. Compton vis. prof. Israel Inst. Tech., Technion, Haifa, 1980; vis. scientist Stanford Linear Accelerator Ctr., 1982-83. Follow Am. Phys. Soc.; mem. AAAS, Phi Beta Kappa, Sigma Xi. Democrat. Jewish. Home: 133 S Linden Ave Pittsburgh PA 15208 Office: Carneigie-Mellon U. 5000 Forbes Ave Pittsburgh PA 15213

EDEN, BARBARA JEAN, actress; b. Tucson; d. Harrison Connor and Alice Mary (Franklin) Huffman; m. Charles Donald Fegert, Sept. 3, 1977; 1 son, Matthew Michael Ansara. Student, San Francisco City Coll., San Francisco Conservatory of Music, Elizabeth Holloway Sch. of Theatre. Pres. Mi-Bar Productions; dir. Security First Nat. Bank of Chgo. Films include Voyage to the Bottom of the Sea, 1961, Five Weeks in a Balloon, 1962, Wonderful World of the Brothers Grimm, 1963, Seven Faces of Dr. Lao, 1964, Harper Valley PTA, 1978, also The Brass Bottle, Ride the Wild Surf, The New Interns; TV debut: on series West Point, 1956; numerous other TV appearances; starred: in TV series I Dream of Jeannie, 1965-69, Harper Valley P.T.A., 1980-82; appeared: in several TV movies, including The Feminist and the Fuzz, 1971, Guess Who's Sleeping in My Bed, 1973, The Stranger Within, 1974, Let's Switch, 1975, How to Break Up a Happy Divorce, 1976; also stage and club appearances. Office: care Plant-Cohen Co 9777 Wilshire Blvd Beverly Hills CA 90212 *My life has been blessed with good friends, a wonderful family and a productive profession. I hope I have contributed to the world at least a small measure of the joy that has been afforded me.*

EDEN, CHARLES HENRY, lawyer; b. Boston, Apr. 14, 1895; s. Charles H. and Evelyn (MacLellan) E.; m. Harriet E. Carpenter, 1924 (div. 1949); children: Harriet E. Eden Powell, Charles H. Student, N.Y. Mil. Acad., 1907-10, Moses Brown Sch., Providence, 1910-14, Brown U., 1914-17; J.D., Harvard U., 1922. Bar: R.I. 1923, Mass. 1927. Practiced law, Providence, 1923-83, town solicitor, Coventry, R.I., 1928-30; asst. U.S. atty. Dist. R.I., 1930-33; co-founder, dir., sec. Fram Corp., East Providence, R.I., 1932-43. Alderman City of Providence, 1939-40; mem. Gov.'s Commn. to Revise Election Laws, 1939-40; chmn. Willkie for Pres. Com. of R.I., 1940; mem. Republican State Central Com. R.I., 1942-52, 54-60, chmn., 1952-54; del. Rep. Nat. Conv., 1960; Rep. candidate U.S. Congress, 1942, for mayor of Providence, 1946; mem. Eisenhower for Pres. Club, 1952, Rep. Nat. Com., 1952-54; chmn. R.I. Goldwater for Pres. Com., 1964, Conservative Com. of R.I., 1965. Served with R.I. N.G., Mexican Border, 1916; Served with AEF, 1917-19; Served with AUS, 1943-44. Recipient R.I. Conservative of Year award Young Americans for Freedom, 1965. Mem. Am., R.I. bar assns., Am. Judicature Soc. Clubs: Young Republicans Providence (pres. 1937-38), Republican R.I. (pres. 1940-41). Home: 895 Gilbert Stuart Rd Saunderstown RI 02874

EDEN, LEE SMYTHE, broadcasting executive; b. Memphis, Sept. 13, 1937; s. Lee S. and Helen (Harris) E.; m. Ann Wheaton Graff, Apr. 6, 1974; children: Elizabeth Graff, Kate Smythe; 1 dau. from previous marriage, Meredith Napier. A.B., Columbia Coll., 1959. Asst. to chmn. Post-Newsweek Stas., Washington, 1969-71; program dir. sta. WPLG-TV, Miami, Fla., 1971-73; exec. v.p. Telcom Assns., N.Y.C., 1973-74; v.p. Corinthian Broadcasting, N.Y.C., 1974-80; chmn., pres. TVS TV Network, N.Y.C., 1980—. Served with U.S. Army, 1961-63. Republican. Episcopalian. Clubs: Siwanoy Country (Bronxville); City Tavern (Washington). Home: 139 Hampshire Rd Bronxville NY 10708 Office: TVS TV Network 475 Fifth Ave New York NY 10016

EDEN, MURRAY, electrical engineer, emeritus educator; b. Bklyn., Aug. 17, 1920; s. Emanuel and Rae (Taran) Edelstein; m. Patricia Warnock, Sept. 16, 1962; stepchildren—Shirley Eden Seawell, John W. Hartle; children by previous marriage—Abigail, Susanna, Mark D. B.S., Coll. City N.Y., 1939; M.S., U. Md., 1944, Ph.D., 1951. Physic. chemist Nat. Bur. Standards, 1943-49; biophysicist Nat. Cancer Inst., 1949-53; spl. fellow math. USPHS, Princeton, 1953-55; biophysicist

Nat. Heart Inst., 1955-59; prof. elec. engring. MIT, 1959-79, prof. emeritus, 1979—; adj. prof. elec. engring. Johns Hopkins U., 1979-81; guest prof. Ecole Federale Polytechnique de Lausanne (Switzerland), 1983; chief bioengring. and instrumentation br. NIH, 1976—; lectr. preventive medicine Harvard Med. Sch., 1960-74, Am. U., 1949-50; cons. for research to dir. gen. WHO, 1963-74. Author: (with David Rutstein) Engineering and Living Systems, 1970; Editor: (with Paul Kolers) Recognizing Patterns, 1968, (with John W. Boretos) Contemporary Biomaterials for clinical Care, 1983; editor-in-chief: Information and Control, 1961—; editor: Methods of Information in Medicine, 1961—; mem. editorial bd.: Med. Research Engring, 1964—; adv. editorial bd.: Linguistic Inquiry, 1970—. Chmn. U.S. Nat. Com. Engring. in Medicine and Biology. Fellow IEEE (chmn, adminstrv. com. group engring. in medicine and biology 1964-66); mem. Am. Physiol. Soc., Biophys. Soc. Home: 8900 Oneida Ln Bethesda MD 20817

EDENFIELD, BERRY AVANT, judge; b. Bulloch County, Ga., Aug. 2, 1934; s. Perry and Vera E.; m. Vida Melvis Bryant, Aug. 3, 1963. B.B.A. U. Ga, 1956; LL.B., 1958. Bar: Ga. 1958. Partner firm Allen, Edenfield, Brown & Wright (and predecessors), Statesboro, Ga., 1958-78; judge U.S. Dist. Ct., So. Dist., Ga., 1978—. Chmn. Statesboro Regional Library, Savannah.; mem. Ga. Senate, 1965-66. Served with Army N.G., 1957-63. Office: PO Box 9865 Savannah GA 31412

EDENS, DONALD KEITH, oil company executive; b. Salt Lake City, Aug. 3, 1928; s. Roger Edward and Elsie Vera (Johnson) E.; m. Elizabeth Adele Mays, Dec. 29, 1950; children: Karen Elizabeth, Donald Edward, Douglas Mays. B.S. in Bus. Adminstrn, U. Utah, 1951. With Phillips Petroleum Co., 1953-72; mng. dir. Phillips Petroleum Ltd., London, 1964-68; v.p. Coastal States Gas Corp., Houston, 1972-74; pres., chief exec. officer Union Petroleum Corp., Revere, Mass., 1974-78; sr. v.p. Oasis Petroleum Corp., also, pres. Gulf Coast and Eastern region, Houston, 1979-82; v.p. Barrick Petroleum Corp., Toronto, Ont., Canada, 1983—, Barrick Petroleum (USA) Inc., Houston, 1983—. Served with AUS, 1946-48; Served with USAAF, 1951-53. Recipient Chmn.'s Cup award Phillips Petroleum Co., 1971. Mem. Soc. Automotive Engrs., Am. Mgmt. Assn., Am. Soc. Lubrication Engrs., Am. Petroleum Inst., 25 Yr. Club of Petroleum Industry, UN Assn., Beta Theta Pi. Clubs: Champions Golf, Houston. Lodge: Masons. Home: 6110 Rolling Water Houston TX 77069

EDENS, HENRY HARMAN, lawyer; b. Clio, S.C., Mar. 31, 1909; s. Jefferson Davis and Anna (Walser) E.; m. Jane Mason Gibbes, Nov. 25, 1933; children—Jane Mason (Mrs. William C. Hawley), Henry Harman, Anne Walser (Mrs. Tom Evins). Grad., Blue Ridge Sch. for Boys, Hendersonville, N.C., 1927; A.B., U. S.C., 1931. Bar: S.C. bar 1934, also U.S., S.C. supreme cts., U.S. Dist. Ct., U.S. Ct. Appeals, U.S. Ct. Claims 1934. Asst. U.S. atty. Eastern Dist., S.C., 1937-49; spl. circuit judge, 1955; counsel U.S. Senate Com. for Investigation Govt. Employee Security Program, 1955. Pres. Heart of Columbia Motel, Inc., Midlands Devel. Co.; pres. Edenwood Water Co., Inc., Cayce, S.C. Permanent mem. Fed. Jud. Conf., 4th Circuit. Mem. Internat. Acad. Trial Lawyers, Am. Trial Lawyers Assn., S.C. Bar Assn. (pres. 1959-60), Kappa Alpha, Omicron Delta Kappa. Home: 700 Sweetbriar Columbia SC 29205 Office: PO Box 11580: Columbia SC 29211

EDENS, ROBERT LUTHER, JR., advertising executive; b. Bartlesville, Okla.; s. Robert Luther and Mona (Bates) E.; children—Stephanie Edens Wilson, Robert Luther III. Grad., Woodberry Forest Sch.; B.A. cum laude, Yale. With Hicks & Greist, 1951-54; copy chief, then v.p. Warwick & Legler, 1954-62; v.p., creative dir. Leo Burnett Co., 1962-66, corp. dir., 1963-66; v.p., creative dir. J. Walter Thompson Co., 1966-67, exec. v.p., mgr. Chgo. office, 1967—, mem. exec. com., dir., 1968-71; pres. Robert L. Edens Co., Chgo., 1972-79; dir. internat. advt. Gen. Foods, 1980—; dir. Nat. Blvd. Bank, Chgo., Domingo Reyes, Inc., Spalding Bates & Co., Seward, Whitlock & Co. Sect. chmn. Chgo. Crusade of Mercy, 1969. Mem. Am. Assn. Advt. Agys. (chmn. Chgo. 1970-71), Chi Phi. Clubs: Casino, Racquet, Commonwealth, Yale (Chgo.); Indian Hill (Winnetka); Yale (N.Y.C.); Sleepy Hollow Country (Westchester, N.Y.); Shoreacres (Lake Bluff, Ill.); DeLand (Fla.); Country. Home: 100 Indian Hill Rd Winnetka IL 60093 Office: 250 North St White Plains NY 10625

EDER, GEORGE JACKSON, lawyer, economist; b. N.Y.C., Sept. 5, 1900; m. Marceline Gray, June 14, 1927 (dec. 1971); children: Donald Gray, Richard Gray, Luisa Gray, Elizabeth McCulloch. Student, Columbia U., 1919, Am. Inst. Banking, 1921-22; B.S. in Econs., Nat. U., Washington, 1928, LL.B., 1928; auditor, Universidad Nacional, Buenos Aires, 1937-43; J.D., George Washington U., 1968. Asst. mgr. fgn. dept. Battery Park Nat. Bank, N.Y.C., 1920-23; mgr. Three Mountain Coffee Corp., San Jose, Costa Rica, 1926; chief Latin Am. sect. U.S. Bur. Fgn. and Domestic Commerce, 1926-32; mgr. internat. securities div. Standard Stats. Co., 1932-37; mgr. Pan Am. Mgmt. Corp., Buenos Aires, 1937-39; asst. gen. atty. ITT, N.Y.C., Buenos Aires, 1935-61; mng. partner Empresas Interamericanas, 1955—; dir. subs. IT&T Corp.; sr. editor World Tax Series Harvard Law Sch., 1961-63; mem. faculty Grad. Sch. Bus. Adminstrn. U. Mich., 1963-67; econ. and legal adv. to govts., Cuba, 1930, Colombia, 1931, Chile, 1935-37, Argentina, 1946-47, Bolivia, 1956-57; founder, exec. dir. Nat. Monetary Stabilization Council of Bolivia, 1956-57. Author: Current Trends in Argentine Trade, 1931, Taxation in Colombia, 1963, Inflation and Development in Latin America, 1968, What's Behind Inflation and How to Beat It, 1979, 80; author romantic novels under nom de plume Jackson Reed.; Contbr. articles to profl. jours. Served to sgt. U.S. Army, World War I; lt. USAR. Mem. Am. Bar Assn., Am. Econ. Assn., InterAm. Bar Assn. Address: 4545 Connecticut Ave Washington DC 20008

EDER, HOWARD ABRAM, physician; b. Milw., Sept. 23, 1917; s. Samuel and Rebecca (Abram) E.; m. Barbara Straus, July 15, 1954; children—Rebecca, Susan, Michael. A.B., U. Wis., 1938; M.D., Harvard U., 1942, M.P.H., 1945. Intern Peter Bent Brigham Hosp., Boston, 1942-43, asst. resident, 1943-44; research fellow in medicine Harvard Med. Sch., 1943-44, research fellow in biochemistry, 1945-46; asst. in medicine, asst. physician Rockefeller U. Hosp., 1946-50; asst. prof. medicine Cornell U. Med. Coll., N.Y.C., 1950-53; mem. staff Nat. Heart Inst., Bethesda, Md., 1953-55; asso. prof. medicine State U. N.Y., Downstate Med. Coll., Bklyn., 1955-57, Albert Einstein Coll. Medicine, 1957-60, prof., 1960—; vis. prof. St. Marys Hosp. Med. Sch., London, 1965-66; chmn. lipid metabolism adv. com. Nat. Heart, Lung and Blood Inst., 1978-80. Editorial bd.: Am. Jour. Physiology, 1968-71, 79-82, Jour. Lipid Research, 1964—, Am. Jour. Medicine, 1976-80. Mem. Assn. Am. Physicians, Am. Soc. Clin. Investigation, Am. Soc. Biol. Chemists, Am. Physiol. Soc., Royal Soc. Medicine, Biochem. Soc. London, Soc. Exptl. Biology and Medicine, N.Y. Acad. Medicine, Am. Heart Assn., Interurban Clin. Club (pres. 1971-72), Phi Beta Kappa, Alpha Omega Alpha. Home: 4683 Waldo Ave New York NY 10471 Office: Albert Einstein Coll Medicine 1300 Morris Park Ave New York NY 10461

EDERSHEIM, MAURITS ERNST, investment banker; b. Amsterdam, May 22, 1918; U.S., 1939, naturalized, 1942; s. Samuel and Ella Edersheim-Levenbach E.; m. Claire Kantyff, May 6, 1963; children: Leo, Arthur, Steven, Terri, Ellen, Judith, Peggy. Student, Ecole de Scis. Politiques, Paris, 1937-38. Mem. firm Herzfeld & Stern, N.Y.C., 1939-42; owner Stern & Co., N.Y.C., 1945-50; with Drexel Burnham & Co., Inc. (now Drexel Burnham Lambert Group Inc.), N.Y.C., 1950—, dep. chmn., 1950—; dir. United Nat. Corp., FGH Credit Corp., Netherlands Am. Amity Trust; chmn. bd. Worldwide Spl. Fund, Worldwide Securities Fund. Served with OSS, 1942-45. Mem. Netherlands Am. Community Assocs. Inc. (pres.). Clubs: Netherlands, Sunningdale Country, Harmonie. Home: 927 Fifth Ave New York NY 10021 Office: Drexel Burnham Lambert Inc 60 Broad St New York NY 10004

EDES, NIK BRUCE, lawyer; b. Chgo., Nov. 11, 1943; s. Samuel and Claire I. (Rosen) E.; children: Jeremy Isaac, Matthew Nathan. A.B., U. Pa., 1965; J.D., U. Mich., 1968. Bar: D.C. 1968. Atty. div. labor relations and civil rights Office of Solicitor U.S. Dept. Labor, Washington, 1968-69; legis. asst. to Senator Harrison A. Williams, Jr. of N.J., Washington, 1969-70; spl. counsel U.S. Senate Com. on Labor and Pub. Welfare, Washington, 1970-77; dep. under sec. for legislation and intergovtl. relations Dept. Labor, Washington, 1977-81; ptnr. Feder & Edes, Washington, 1981—. Home: 1616 Manchester Ln NW Washington DC

EDEY, MAITLAND ARMSTRONG, writer; b. N.Y.C., Feb. 13, 1910; s. Alfred and Marion H. (Armstrong) E.; m. Helen Winthrop Kellogg, Apr. 24, 1934; children: Maitland Armstrong, Winthrop K., Beatrice W., Marion B. A.B., Princeton U., 1932. Editorial assoc. various book pub. cos., 1933-41. Editor: Life mag, 1946-56; free-lance writer mag. articles, 1957-60; editor: Time-Life Books, N.Y.C., 1960-66; editor-in-chief, 1966-72; free-lance writer books and mag. articles, 1972—; Author: American Songbirds, 1941, American Waterbirds, 1942, (with F. Clark Howell) Early Man, 1965, The Cats of Africa, 1968, The Northeast Coast, 1972, The Missing Link, 1973, The Sea Traders, 1974, The Lost World of the Aegean, 1975, Great Photo Essays from Life, 1978, (with D.C. Johanson) Lucy: The Beginnings of Humankind, 1981 (Am. Book award for best book on sci. subject 1982); contbr. articles on wildlife, sea adventure and anthropology to popular mags. Mayor Village of Upper Brookville, N.Y., 1956-60; chmn. Council Old Westbury Coll., SUNY, 1968-73; bd. dirs. N.Y. Philharm. Symphony, 1952-75, Putney (Vt.) Sch., 1957-75, Conservation Found., Washington, 1966—, Scudder Spl. Fund, 1967—, Felix Neck Wildlife Sanctuary, Martha's Vineyard, Mass., 1975—, Sheriff's Meadow Found., Martha's Vineyard, 1978—. Served with USAAF, 1942-46. Decorated Legion of Merit; recipient Disting. Service medal Coll. Old Westbury, 1981. Mem. Author's Guild Am., Am. Ornithologists Union. Clubs: Century Assn., Coffee House (N.Y.). Crew mem. of Mayflower replica which sailed across Atlantic, 1957.

EDGAR, JAMES, secretary of state Illinois; b. Vinita, Okla., July 22, 1946; m. Brenda Smith; children: Brad, Elizabeth. Grad., Eastern Ill. U., 1968; postgrad., U. Ill., Sangamon State U., 1971-74. Legis. intern pres. pro tem Ill. Senate, 1968; key asst. to speaker ho. Ill. Ho. of Reps., 1972-73; aide to pres. Ill. Senate, 1974, to Ho. minority leader, 1976; mem. Ill. Ho. of Reps., from 1977; dir. legis. affairs Ill. Gov., 1979-80; sec. state, State of Ill., 1981—. Precinct committeeman, treas. Coles County Republican Com., 1974; dir. state service Nat. Conf. State Legislatures, 1975, 76; mem. Ill. Ho. Rep. Campaign Com., 1977-79. Mem. Coles County Hist. Soc. (pres. 1976-79). Baptist. Office: State Capitol Bldg Springfield IL

EDGAR, ROBERT WILLIAM, Congressman, clergyman; b. Phila., May 29, 1943; s. Leroy Raymond and Marion Louise (Fish) E.; m. Merle Louise Deaver, Aug. 29, 1964; children: Robert William, Thomas David, Andrew John. B.A. in History and Religion, Lycoming Coll., 1965; M.Div., Drew U., 1968; cert. in pastoral psychiatry, Hahnemann Med. Coll. and Hosp., 1969. Ordained to ministry Methodist Ch., 1968; pastor chs., Pa., 1961-71, Lansdowne (Pa.) United Meth. Ch., 1973-74; mem. 94th-98th congresses from 7th Dist. Pa.; mem. pub. works and transp. com. on its subcoms.; econ. devel., water resources, surface transp.; mem. vets. affairs com.; exec. com. for house environ. study group; mem. House Select Com. Assassinations, 1977-78; Chmn. N.E.-Midwest Congressional Coalition; mem. Police-Clergy Unit, Phila., 1968-71; co-dir., funding coordinator People's Emergency Center, Phila., 1971-74; United Protestant chaplain Drexel U., 1971-74. Organizer, first pres. Human Relations Com. of East Falls, Phila., 1968-71; vice-chmn. Emergency Housing Com., Phila., 1973. Recipient Most Effective Mem. Congress award Nat. Com. for Effective Congress, 1978; Outstanding Young Man award Pa. Jaycees, 1978; Conservation award Sierra Club, 1978; Disting. Conservation award Am. Rivers Council, 1979; Bread for World awards, 1979; Smaller Mfrs. Council award, 1980. Democrat. Office: 2352 Rayburn House Office Bldg Washington DC 20515 *

EDGAR, THOMAS FLYNN, chemical engineering educator; b. Bartlesville, Okla., Apr. 17, 1945; s. Maurice Russell and Natalie (Flynn) E.; m. Donna Jean Proffitt, July 15, 1967; children: Rebecca, Jeffrey. B.S. in Chem. Engring., U. Kans., 1967, Ph.D., Princeton U., 1971. Registered profl. engr., Tex. Process engr. Conoco, Balt., 1968-69; prof. chem. engring. U. Tex., Austin, 1971—, U. Calif., Berkeley, 1978; pres. CACHE Corp., Salt Lake City, Utah, 1981-84; 2d v.p. CAST Div. Am. Inst. Chem. Engring., N.Y.C., 1984; mem. editorial bd. Am. Inst. Chem. Engring. Jour., N.Y.C., 1983—; dir. Am. Automatic Control Council, Pitts. Author: Coal Processing and Pollution Control, 1983; co-author: Real Time Computing, 1982; editor: Chemical Process Control, 1981; jours. Coordinator Northwest YMCA Soccer League, Austin, 1982-84. Mem. Am. Inst. Chem. Engrs. (Outstanding Counselor award 1974), Am Inst. Chem. Engrs. (Colburn award 1980), Soc. Petroleum Engrs., Tau Beta Pi, Phi Lambda Upsilon, Omicron Delta Kappa. Democrat. Methodist.

EDGAR, WALTER BELLINGRATH, historian; b. Mobile, Ala., Dec. 10, 1943; s. Charles Ernest, Jr. and Amelia Lyon (Moore) E.; m. Elizabeth Giles, Aug. 6, 1966; children: Eliza, Amelia. A.B., Davidson Coll., (N.C.), 1965; M.A., U. S.C., 1967, Ph.D., 1969. Hist. editor com. hist. research S.C. Ho. of Reps., 1972-74; asst. prof., assoc. prof., history U. S.C., Columbia, 1974—, dir. Inst. So. Studies, 1980—; sec. Hist. Columbia Found., 1975-77, pres., 1977-78. Co-author: The GOvernor's Mansion of the Palmetto State, 1979; editor: The Letterbook of Robert Pringle, 1972, A Southern Renascence Man: Views of Robert Penn Warren, 1984; compiler: The Biographical Directory of the South Carolina House of Representatives: Vol. 1, Session Lists. 1692-1973, 1974, Vol. II, the Commons House of Assembly, 1692-1775, 1977. Pres. Friends County Library, 1981-82; vestryman Trinity Episcopal Cathedral, Columbia, 1977-80. Served to capt. U.S. Army, 1969-71; lt.col. Res. Decorated Bronze Star, Meritorious Service medal, Army Commendation medal; recipient Disting. Achievement award Hist. Columbia Found., 1981; fellow Nat. Hist. Publs. Commn., 1971-72. Mem. Orgn. Am. Historians, So. Hist. Assn., S.C. Hist. Assn. (exec. council 1979—, pres. 1982-83), South Carolinians Soc. (exec. council 1979—). Lodge: Kiwanis. Home: 1731 Hollywood Dr Columbia SC 29205 Office: Inst So Studies U SC Columbia SC 29208

EDGAR, WILLIAM JOHN, philosphy educator; b. Charlottesville, Va., Jan. 20, 1933; s. William John and Frances (Ring) E.; m. Stacey Lynn Walter, June 20, 1962; children: Michael Kent, Stephen Scott, Elizabeth Ann, Chandra Lynn. B.S., Cornell U., 1959; M.A., Syracuse U., 1966, Ph.D., 1972. Systems analyst Advanced Eletronics Ctr., Ithaca, N.Y., 1959-62, Electronics Lab., Syracuse, N.Y., 1962-65; asst. prof. philosophy SUNY-Geneseo, 1969-74, assoc. prof., 1974-79, disting. teaching prof., chmn. dept., 1979—. Author: Evidence, 1980, The Problem Solver's Guide to Logic, 1983; contbr. articles to profl. jours. Served to 1st lt. U.S. Army, 1952-56. Fellow NDEA Title IV Syracuse U., 1965-68; mem. Am. Philos. Assn, Albany, 1974,76. Home: 5722 Logan Rd RD 1 Mount Morris NY 14510 Office: Dept Philosophy SUNY Geneseo NY 14454

EDGE, BILLY LEE, civil engineer, educator; b. Yorktown, Va., June 19, 1942; s. Henry and Viola Louise (Honeycutt) E.; m. Rebecca Jane Douglas, Dec. 14, 1963; children: Karen Leigh, Mark Douglas, William Scott. B.S.C.E., Va. Poly. Inst., 1964, M.S.C.E., 1966; Ph.D. in Civil Engring., Ga. Inst. Tech., 1969. Registered profl. engr., S.C. Surveying instr. Macomb County Community Coll., Warren, Mich., 1970; sr. coastal engr. Dames & Moore, Bethesda, Md., 1978-80; prof. civil engring. Clemson (S.C.) U., 1970-82; sr. engr., pres., chmn. bd. Cubit Engring. Ltd., Clemson, 1980—; affiliate marine scientist S.C. Marine Resources Ctr.; gen. chlmn. Coastal Zone, 1980; vice chmn. shoreline erosion adv. panel to chief corps engrs., 1975-80; mem. S.C. Boundary Commn.; chmn. symposia. Editor conf. proceedings; contbr. articles to profl. jours. Served to capt. C.E. AUS, 1964-70. Named Marksman of Yr. Engring. News Record, 1979; recipient Wellington prize internat. transp., 1983. Mem. Am. Shore and Beach Preservation Assn. (dir.), Am. Geophys. Union, ASCE (exec. com. waterways, harbors and coastal engring. div. 1974-79, sec. Coastal Engring. Research Council), Internat. Assn. Gt. Lakes Research, Internat. Assn. Hydraulic Research, Marine Tech. Soc., Am. Orchid Soc., Athletics Congress, Am. Road Runners Assn., Sigma Xi, Chi Epsilon. Office: Cubit Engring Ltd Suite 311 207 E Bay St Charleston SC 29401

EDGE, CHARLES GEOFFREY, Canadian government official; b. Wilmslow, Eng., Aug. 8, 1920; s. Charles Edmund and Dorothy Adelaide (Potts) E.; m. Madeline Tarrant, May 25, 1940; children: Christine Jeffery, Jennifer Doyle. B.Sc. with honours in Econs., U. London. Various positions Chemcell and (related cos. and subsidiaries), 1964-69; mem. Nat. Energy Bd., Can., 1971-75, assoc. vice chmn., 1975-78, vice chmn., 1978-80, chmn., 1980—. Author: Appraisal of Capital Expenditures, 1959, 64, 81; co-author: The Impact of Systems and Computers on Management and the Accountant, 1966. Served with Royal Arty., 1939-45. Fellow Royal Statis. Soc., Inst. Statisticians, Soc. Mgmt. Accts. Can. Home: 333 Chapel St Apt 806 Ottawa ON Canada K1N 8Y8 Office: 473 Albert St Ottawa ON Canada K1A 0E5

EDGE, HAROLD LEE, manufacturing executive; b. Houston, Feb. 4, 1933; s. Monroe Lee and Aline (Daigle) E.; m. D. Geraldine Morgan, June 9, 1956; children: Cynthia Ann, Michael Lee, Stephen Douglas. B.S. in Elec. Engring., Tex. A&M U., 1955, 1956. Dir. fin. Houston ops. Philco Ford, 1964-69; v.p. fin. microelectronics div. Rockwell Internat., Anaheim, Calif., 1969-73, v.p., gen. mgr., 1973-75, v.p. aerospace and electronics bus. devel., Dallas, 1975-78, corp. v.p. strategic planning, Pitts., 1978—. Served with U.S. Army, 1956. Mem. Am. Mgmt. Assn., Am. Inst. Indsl. Engrs., N. Am. Soc. Corp. Planning, IEEE. Office: 600 Grant St Pittsburgh PA 15219 *We are only stewards of the material blessings God has provided, and He alone will judge if we have used well that which has been trusted to us.*

EDGE, LAWRENCE LOTT, real estate executive; b. Atlanta, Aug. 11, 1945; s. Lawrence Lott E. and Sarah Simms (Edge) Fletcher; m. Dawne Daniel, Sept. 5, 1970; children: Nancy, Sallie, Laura. B.S., Yale U., 1967; M.B.A., Harvard U., 1969. Mkt. research asst. C. & S. Nat. Bank, Atlanta, 1965; asst. to pres. Consol. Equities Corp., Atlanta, 1967-68, dir. devel., 1969-70, treas., dir., 1971-73, exec. v.p., dir., 1974-80, pres., chief operating officer, dir., 1980—; v.p., dir. CECOR, IMR; chmn. bd. Am. Reservation Systems Inc., Realty Capital Corp. Elder, Sunday sch. tchr. First Presbyterian Ch., Atlanta, pres. Men of Ch., Atlanta, 1977, stewardship chmn., Atlanta, 1981-82; bd. vistors Presbyn. Coll.; assoc. staff Campus Crusade for Christ, 1969—; bd. dirs. Lay Involvement for Evangelism, 1979—. Clubs: Harvard Bus. Sch., Yale of Ga.; Piedmont Driving (Atlanta). Home: 3219 Rockingham Dr NW Atlanta GA 30327 Office: Consolidated Equities Corp 1280 W Peachtree St NW Atlanta GA 60367

EDGE, ROBERT LANEER, retired air force officer; b. Los Angeles, Sept. 8, 1925; s. Dan and Mary Gertrude (Baker) E.; m. Mary Catherine Boyce, Mar. 14, 1945; children—Rebecca (Mrs. Teddy Roberts), Jeffrey Glenn, Claudia Mary (Mrs. Scott Martin). A.A., Armstrong Coll., Savannah, Ga., 1958; B.Gen. Edn., Omaha U., 1961; M.S. in Elec. Engring, Stanford, 1964; grad., Advanced Mgmt. Program, Harvard, 1968. Joined USAAF, 1943, commd. 2d lt., 1945; advanced through grades to maj. gen. USAF, 1974; participant (Crossroads Project, 1st Pacific atom bomb tests), CIC spl. agt., 1946-48, bomber pilot, 1950-59, project officer, program dir. 1st automation Hdqrs.., comdr., dep. for plans and programs Hdqrs., dep. dir., then dir., Washington, 1974-75, asst. chief staff for communications and computer resources, 1975-77, ret., 1977; cons. def. industry; ex-offico mem. U.S. Mil. Communications-Electronics Bd., U.S. Communications Security Bd., 1974-75. Cub Scout pack com. chmn. Boy Scouts Am., Offutt AFB, Neb., 1960. Mem. Armed Forces Communications-Electronics Assn. (nat. v.p.), Order of Daedalians. Club: Mason (32 deg.).

EDGELL, ROBERT LOUIS, publisher; b. Port Huron, Mich., Aug. 2, 1922; s. Carl Robert and Faye Alberta (Neikirk) E.; m. Yvonne Richardson de Clairmont, Nov. 10, 1981; children: Robin, Douglas, Sarah, Deborah, Jane. B.S., Mich. State U., 1944. With Young Am. Pub., N.Y.C., 1946-48; founder, prin. Robert Edgell & Assos., N.Y.C., 1948-51; (merged into Davidson Pub. Co., 1951-62, then into Ojibway Press, Inc. (exec. v.p.), 1962-68, purchased by Harcourt Brace Jovanovich, 1968); various positions Harcourt Brace Jovanovich, 1968-76; pres. Harcourt Brace Jovanovich Publs., 1977, chmn., 1977—, sr. v.p. bus. publs. and broadcasting group, 1977-78, exec. v.p., pres. and head gen. books, mags. and broadcasting group, 1978—, also dir.; chmn. Communications and Service Inc., Am. Bus. Press; dir. Sea World, Inc., Am. Bus. Press, Inc., Bus. Publs. Audit of Circulation, Inc. Mem. Pubs.'s Adv. Com., Instl. Food Service Mfrs. Am., Nat. Assn. Food Equipment Mfrs., Soc. Am. Magicians. Office: Harcourt Brace Jovanovich Publs 7500 Old Oak Blvd Cleveland OH 44130 *

EDGELL, WALTER FRANCIS, educator; b. Kokomo, Ind., July 26, 1916; s. Marshall Hall and Lucretia (Farnsworth) E.; m. Rene DaValle, Feb. 14, 1937; children—Marshall Hall, Richard Garrett, Colleen Francis, Geraldine Ann. B.Sc., U. Calif. at Berkeley, 1939; postgrad., U. Minn., 1939-40; M.Sc., U. Iowa, 1941; Ph.D., Harvard U., 1943. Austin teaching fellow Harvard U., 1943; instr. U. Iowa, 1944-47, asso. prof. chemistry, 1947-49; prof. Purdue U., 1949—; cons. Philips Petroleum Co., Oak Ridge Nat. Labs., U.S. Naval Weapons Center. Editorial bd.: Jour. Applied Spectroscopy; Contbr. profl. jours. Trustee Serra Club, Lafayette Diocese. Recipient Research award Iowa Acad. Sci., 1947; Frank Martin Teaching award, 1976; Guggenheim fellow, 1957. Mem. Am. Chem. Soc., Soc. Applied Spectroscopy, Coblentz Soc., Am. Chem. Soc. (chmn. Iowa 1947, chmn. Purdue U. 1952), Alpha Chi Sigma. Home: 2507 Oswego Ln Lafayette IN 47907

EDGERLY, WILLIAM SKELTON, banker; b. Lewiston, Maine, Feb. 18, 1927; s. Stuart and Florence (Skelton) E.; m. Lois Stiles, June 12, 1948; children: Leonard Stuart, Stephanie Lois. B.S. in Econs. and Engring, Mass. Inst. Tech., 1949; M.B.A., Harvard U., 1955. With Eastman Kodak Co., 1949-50; with Cabot Corp., Boston, 1952-75, treas., 1960-63, v.p., 1963-66; v.p., gen. mgr. (Oxides div.), 1967-68, fin. v.p., 1969-75; also dir.; pres., dir. State St. Boston Corp., 1975—, chmn. bd., 1976—, Boston Housing Partnership Inc.; mem. fed. adv. council Fed. Res. Bd., Washington. Trustee Comm. Econ. Devel.; Trustee, overseer Children's Hosp. Med. Center, Boston; bd. dirs., pres. Jobs for Mass.; mem. corp. devel. com., also corp. vis. coms. on econs. and Sloan Sch. Mgmt., M.I.T.; mem. corp. Northeastern U.; dir. Boston Pvt. Industry Council, Nat. Alliance Bus., Boston.; chmn. New Eng. region Nat. Alliance Bus., Boston. Served with USNR, 1945-46, 50-52. Mem. Boston Econ. Club, Mass. Inst. Tech. Alumni Assn. (pres. 1973-74), Greater Boston C. of C. (dir.), Mass. Bus. Round Table, Mus. Sci., Harvard Bus. Sch. Assn., Harvard Musical Assn. Clubs: Somerset, Cambridge Boat, Univ. Home: 32 Highland St Cambridge MA 02138 Office: 225 Franklin St Boston MA 02101

EDGERTON, HAROLD EUGENE, educator, elec. engr.; b. Fremont, Nebr., Apr. 6, 1903; s. Frank Eugene and Mary Nettie (Coe) C.; m. Esther May Garrett, Feb. 25, 1928; children—Mary Louise, William Eugene, Robert Frank. B.S., U. Nebr., 1925, Dr.Engring. (hon.), 1948; M.Sc., Mass. Inst. Tech., 1927, D.Sc., 1931; LL.D. (hon.), Doane Coll., 1969, U. S.C., 1969. Elec. engr. Nebr. Light & Power Co., 1920-25, Gen. Electric Co., 1925-26; Inst. prof. emeritus Mass. Inst. Tech. Author: (with James R. Killian, Jr.) Moments of Vision, 1979, Electronic Flash, Strobe, 1979, also numerous tech. articles. Recipient medal Royal Photog. Soc.; Gold medal Nat. Geog. Soc.; Modern Pioneer award; Potts medal Franklin Inst.; Albert A. Michelson medal, 1969. Fellow I.E.E.E., Am. Inst. Elec. Engrs., Soc. Motion Pictures and TV Engrs., Royal Soc. Gt. Britain; mem. Nat. Acad. Scis., Nat. Acad. Engrs., Marine Tech. Soc., Sigma Xi, Eta Kappa Nu, Sigma Tau. Republican. Conglist. Club: Mason. Inventor of stroboscopic high-speed motion and still photography apparatus; designer underwater camera and high-resolution sonar equipment. Home: 100 Memorial Dr Cambridge MA 02142 Office: MIT Room 4-405 Cambridge MA 02139

EDGERTON, MILLS FOX, JR., foreign language educator; b. Hartford, Conn., June 11, 1931; s. Mills Fox and Miriam (Reynolds) E.; m. Marianne Simonson, Dec. 27, 1957; children: Michael, Nicholas. B.A., U. Conn., 1953; student, U. Nac. Autónoma de México, Mexico City, 1951; A.M., Princeton, 1955, Ph.D., 1960. Instr. Romance langs. Princeton, 1957, Rutgers U., 1957-60; assoc. prof., chmn. dept. Spanish Bucknell U., Lewisburg, Pa., 1960-66, prof., 1966—, chmn. dept. modern langs., lit. and linguistics, 1968-74; dir. Univ. Press, 1976—, Middlebury Coll. Grad. Sch. Spanish in Spain, Madrid, 1971-72, Middlebury Coll. Intensive Lang. Program, 1973, Grad. Sch. Spanish, Middlebury Coll., 1980-81. Contbr. profl. jours.; author poetry in Spanish and Italian. Chmn. Northeast Conf. on Teaching Fgn. Langs., 1972, Spanish Com for Grad. Record Exams, 1965-69. Recipient Lindback award for distinguished teaching, 1971; Alexander von Humboldt Found. grantee, 1961; Am. Philos. Soc. grantee, 1962. Mem. Modern Lang. Assn. Roman Catholic. Home: 136 Saint George St Lewisburg PA 17837

EDGERTON, MILTON THOMAS, JR., reconstructive and hand surgeon, educator; b. Atlanta, July 14, 1921; s. Milton Thomas and Elizabeth (Roddick) E.; m. Patricia Jane Jones, June 30, 1945; children: Bradford Wheatly, William Alton, Sandra Roddick, Diane Miller. B.A., Emory U., 1941; M.D., Johns Hopkins U., 1944. Diplomate: Am. Bd. Surgery, Am. Bd. Plastic Surgery (mem. tripartite residency rev. com. in plastic surgery 1963-70, bd. examiners 1964-70, vice chmn. 1969-70). Intern Barnes Hosp., St. Louis, 1944-45; instr. surgery Johns Hopkins Hosp., 1947-49, plastic surgeon-in-charge, 1951-70; mem. faculty surgery Johns Hopkins Sch. Medicine, 1947-70, asso. prof. surgery, 1953-62; prof. plastic surgery Johns Hopkins U., 1962-70; prof. plastic surgery, chmn. dept. plastic and maxillo-facial surgery U. Va., Charlottesville, 1970—; plastic surgeon in chief U. Va. Med. Center, 1970—; pvt. practice medicine, specializing in reconstructive and hand surgery, 1945—; vis. prof. plastic and reconstructive surgery Christian Med. Coll., Vellore, India, 1962, Rochester (N.Y.) U., 1966, Washington U., St. Louis, 1968, U. Chgo., 1969, Ohio State U., Columbus, 1970, U. Tex., Galveston, 1971, Harvard U., 1978, 81, Colo. U., 1979, Washington U., 1980, UCLA, 1980; Thuss prof. Vanderbilt U., 1977; cons. VA Hosp., Balt., 1953—, Salem, Va., 1970—, Nat. Clin. Center, NIH, 1954—, Balt. City Hosps., 1956-70, Children's Hosp., Balt., 1965-70, Good Samaritan Hosp., 1968-70, Walter Reed Army Hosp., 1965-73, cons. emeritus, 1973—; adv. bd. Medico, 1963—; mem. State of Va. Med. Malpractice Rev. Panel; mem. surgery study sect. NIH, 1967—; founder Acad. Adv. Council Plastic Surgery. Asso. editor: Jour. Plastic and Reconstructive Surgery, 1963-72, Transplantation Jour., 1961-68; mem. internat. editorial bd. Plastic Surgery div.: Exerpta; editor: (with R. Tanzer) Symposium on Reconstruction of the Auricle, 1974; contbr. numerous articles med. publs. and textbooks. Trustee Lake Placid Ednl. Found., W. Alton Jones Cell Sci. Center, N.Y., Ednl. Found. Soc. Plastic and Reconstructive Surgery. Served to capt. M.C., AUS, 1945-47. Decorated Cert. of Merit; recipient Dow Corning award for outstanding contbns. to plastic surgery, 1975, Ethicon Achievement award for Contbns. in Wound Healing, 1976. Fellow ACS (bd. govs. 1962-71, sr. mem. cancer com. 1975—, grad. com. on edn. 1973—, sr. mem. cancer com. 1975); mem. Am. Soc. Plastic and Reconstructive Surgery (trustee 1974—, Nat. award for sci. merit 1974, traveling prof. 1976, mem. ad hoc com. competency in plastic surgery 1976—), Am. Assn. Plastic Surgeons (pres. 1973-74, legis. rep. to Council Acad. Socs. 1976—, Clinician of Yr. award 1980), Soc. Head and Neck Surgeons (founder), Internat. Soc. Aesthetic Plastic Surgery, Soc. Univ. Surgeons, AMA, Am. Assn. Cleft Palate Rehab., Plastic Surgery Research Council (founder), Harry Benjamin Internat. Gender Dysphoria Assn. (pres.-elect 1983-85), Pan Am. Med. Assn. (pres.), Instn. Nuclear Engrs. (med. sect.), AAUP, Assn. for Advancement Med. Instrumentation, Transplantation Soc. (chmn. and founder coordinating com. acad. affairs in plastic surgery 1975—), Am. Soc. Surgery of the Hand, Am., So. surg. assns., Med. and Chirurg. Faculty State of Md., Balt. Med. Soc., Albemarle County Med. Soc., Am. Psychosomatic Soc., Nat. Acad. Scis., Nat. Soc. Med. Research, Internat. Soc. Plastic and Reconstructive Surgery, Am. Soc. Aesthetic Surgery, Soc. Biomaterials (founder), Internat. Soc. Aesthetic Surgeons, Internat. Soc. Capillary and Blood Research, Japanese Soc. Plastic and Reconstructive Surgeons (hon.), Phi Beta Kappa, Eta Sigma Psi. Clubs: Hamilton Street, Elkridge (Balt.); Lake Placid (N.Y.); Farmington Hunt, Farmington Country (Charlottesville, Va.); Lyford Cay (New Providence Island). Home: Timbercreek Farm Route 5 Box 339 Charlottesville VA 22901 Office: Dept Plastic Surgery U Va Med Center Charlottesville VA 22908

EDGERTON, NORMAN EDWARD, bus. exec.; b. Raleigh, N.C., June 14, 1898; s. Noah Edward and Alma (Wynne) E.; m. Mishew Rogers, Feb. 9, 1929; 1 dau., Mishew Ellen (Mrs. Mishew Edgerton Smith). Student, Duke U., 1917-19. Founder Raleigh Bonded Warehouse, Inc., 1923, pres., 1923—. Hon. mem. N.C. Conf. Meth. Bd. Publ. Inc.; Former chmn. com. on improvement state care of mental patients 1st chmn., N.C. Hosps. Bd. Control.; Trustee emeritus Duke U.; former trustee Eastern Carolina Sch. Boys. Mem. Raleigh C. of C. (past pres.), Raleigh YMCA (past pres.), Duke U. General Alumni Assn. (past pres.), S.A.R., Am. Legion, Omicron Delta Kappa, Pi Kappa Alpha. Clubs: Mason (Shriner, past potentate), Kiwanian (past pres.), Carolina Country.). Home: Tatton Hall Oberlin Rd Raleigh NC 27608 Office: Box 6158 Raleigh NC 27608 *Knowing that God must be first, I constantly use prayer in seeking His help and guidance which I have bountifully received. With integrity a "must," I realize a good name is rather to be chosen than great riches. When considering actions that I may take, it is my endeavor that they harm no one and hope that by the example that I set, others will be helped and lives saved.*

EDGERTON, SAMUEL YOUNGS, JR., art historian, educator; b. Cleve., Sept. 30, 1926; s. Samuel Youngs and Mary (Martineau) E.; m. Dorothy W. Dugan, June 2, 1951; children—Perky, Samuel Youngs III, Mary. A.B., U. Pa., 1950, M.F.A., 1956, M.A., 1960, Ph.D., 1965. Prof., chmn. dept. art history Boston U., 1964-80; prof., dir. grad. program in art history Williams Coll., Williamstown, Mass., 1980—; Fulbright Exchange tchr. to, Germany, 1957-58; mem. Inst. for Advanced Study, Princeton, N.J., 1967-68. Author: The Renaissance Rediscovery of Linear Perspective, 1975. Nat. Endowment for Humanities grantee, 1967, 70-71; fellow Villa I Tatti, Florence, Italy, 1971-72; Am. Council Learned Socs. fellow, 1977; Guggenheim fellow, 1977-78. Mem. Coll. Art Assn., Renaissance Soc. Am. Home: 163 Park St Williamstown MA 01267 Office: Sterling and Francine Clark Art Inst Box 8 Williamstown MA 07267

EDGERTON, WILLIAM B(ENBOW), foreign language educator; b. Winston-Salem, N.C., Mar. 11, 1914; s. Paul Clifton and Annie Maud (Benbow) E.; m. Jewell Mock Conrad, June 6, 1935; children: Susan, David. B.A., Guilford Coll., 1934; M.A., Haverford Coll., 1935; Ph.D., Columbia U., 1954. Tchr. French. German, Spanish, English in secondary schs., U.S. and France, 1935-39; faculty French and Spanish Guilford Coll., 1939-47; faculty Russian lit. Pa. State U., University Park, 1950-56, U. Mich., Ann Arbor, 1954-55, Columbia U., N.Y.C., 1956-58; prof. Slavic langs. and lits. Ind. U., Bloomington, 1958—, chmn. Slavic dept., 1958-65, 69-73, acting dir. Russian and European Inst., 1981-82; cons. Ford Found., 1952-61; mem. joint com. on Slavic studies Am. Council Learned Socs., 1951-62; chmn. joint com. on Slavic studies Am. council Learned Socs., 1958-61. Gen. editor: Columbia Dictionary of Modern European Literature, 1980; translator, editor: Satirical Stories of Nikolai Leskov, 1969; editor: Ind. Slavic Studies, III, 1963, Ind. Slavic Studies, IV, 1967, Am. Contributions to the Fifth Internat. Congress of Slavists, 1963; contbr. articles to profl. jours. Bd. dirs. Am. Friends Service Com., 1956-59; trustee Guilford Coll., 1969—; mem. vis. com. for Slavic Studies Harvard U., 1967-77; mem. adv. com. Nat. Humanities Ctr., 1978—. Recipient Josef Dobrovsky medal Czechoslovak Acad. Sci., 1968; Am. Council Learned Socs. fellow, 1948-50; Guggenheim fellow, 1963-64. Mem. MLA (exec. council 1962-65), Am. Assn. Advancement Slavic Studies (pres. 1961), Internat. Comparative Lit. Assn. Democrat. Quaker. Home: 1801 E Maxwell Ln Bloomington IN 47401 Office: Ballantine 502 Ind U Bloomington IN 47405

EDGETT, WILLIAM MALOY, lawyer, labor arbitrator; b. Balt., Feb. 26, 1926; s. Eugene Albert and Priscilla Ruff (Streett) E.; m. Bronwen Winifred Reese, Nov. 25, 1950. A.A., Towson State Coll., 1949; B.A., U. Md., 1951, J.D., 1959; LL.M., Georgetown U., 1970. Bar: Md. bar 1959. Asst. personnel mgr. Am. Sugar Refining Co., Balt., 1951-55; supr. indsl. relations Westinghouse Electric Co., Balt., 1955-61; sr. labor relations specialist Martin Co., Balt., 1961-64; asst. mgr. indsl. relations Md. Shipbuilding and Drydock Co., Balt., 1964-67; pvt. practice law, 1967—; Asst. prof. Towson State U., 1971-72. Mem. Md. Commn. Nursing, 1974-76; chmn. pub. law bds. Nat. Mediation Bd., 1971—; neutral mem. Nat. R.R. Adjustment Bd., 1971—. Served to staff sgt. USAAF, 1944-46. Mem. Nat. Acad. Arbitrators, Am. Arbitration Assn., Am., Md. State bar assns., Roster Arbitrators Fed. Mediation and Conciliation Service. Home: 3 Beechmere Ln Cockeysville MD 21030 Office: 8651 Baltimore Nat Pike Ellicott City MD 21043

EDICK, GLENN ELLIS, former agricultural company executive; b. Columbia Center, N.Y., Feb. 8, 1918; s. Ellis and Mary (Salesman) E.; m. Janet Palmer, Sept. 23, 1939; children: Dolores (Mrs. John Puit), Darleen (Mrs. Dale Statucki). B.S. in Agr, Cornell U., 1940. With Grange League Fedn., 1940-64; with Agway, Inc., DeWitt, N.Y., 1964-82, v.p. prodn., 1968-72, group v.p., 1972-82; pres. United Coops., Alliance, Ohio, 1962-65, Allied Seed Co., 1962-72; v.p. Select Seeds, Fort Wayne, Ind., 1963-72; chmn. bd. Am. Feed Mfrs., 1972-74; dir. Am. Agriculturist, 1974—, Voluntary Devel. Corp.; trustee Adv. Com. on Overseas Cooperative Devel., Agrl. Cooperative Devel. Internat. Pres. Dryden Central Sch. Bd., 1954-64; Trustee, pres. N.Y. State 4-H Found.; chmn. Grad. Inst. Coop. Leadership, 1979-80, Am. Inst. Cooperation, 1979—. Mem. U.S. (mem. agr. com.), N.Y. State Empire chambers commerce. Club: Mason (32 deg.). Home: 4672 Ridge Rd Cazenovia NY 13035 Office: 333 Butternut Dr DeWitt NY 13214

EDIDIN, MICHAEL AARON, educator; b. Chgo., Mar. 31, 1939; s. Alex and Zelda (Tenner) E.; m. Ruth Glicenstein, June 25, 1964; children—Avram, Dan. B.Sc., U. Chgo., 1960; Ph.D., London U., 1963. NSF postdoctoral fellow Weizmann Inst., Rehovoth, Israel, 1963-64; Am. Heart Assn. fellow Harvard Med. Sch., 1964-66; asst. prof. dept. biology Johns Hopkins U., Balt., 1966-71, asso. prof., 1971-75, prof., 1975—; cons. NIH, NSF. Editor: (with M.H. Johnson) Immunobiology of Gametes, 1977; Mem. editorial bd.: Jour. Immunology, 1977-82, Jour. Reproductive Immunology, 1978—, Immunogenetics, 1974-78, Jour. Supramolecular Structure, 1979—. Recipient K.S. Cole award Am. Biophys. Soc., 1979; Meyerhoff fellow, 1981. Mem. AAAS, Am. Soc. Cell Biology, Am. Assn. Immunologists, Phi Beta Kappa. Jewish. Office: Biology Dept Johns Hopkins U Charles and 34th Sts Baltimore MD 21218

EDIE, JAMES M., educator; b. Grand Forks, N.D., Nov. 3, 1927; s. Albert Mayo and Elizabeth (Murphy) E.; m. Carolyn Andervont, July 16, 1960. B.A., St. John's U., 1949; Ph.D., U. Louvain, Belgium, 1958. Asst. prof. philosophy Hobart and William Smith Colls., 1959-61; asst. prof. philosophy Northwestern U., 1961-65, asso. prof., 1965-70, prof., 1970—, chmn. dept., 1969-77; gen. editor Northwestern U. Studies in Phenomenology and Existential Philosophy, 1963—. Author: (with others) Christianity and Existentialism, 1963, Speaking and Meaning: The Phenomenology of Language, 1976; Co-editor: Russian Philosophy, 1965; editor: An Invitation to Phenomenology, 1965, Phenomenology in America, 1967, New Essays in Phenomenology, 1969. Am. Council Learned Socs. grantee, 1967, 1973. Mem. Am. Philos. Assn., Soc. Phenomenology and Existential Philosophy, Am. Aesthetics Assn., Metaphys. Soc. Am. Home: 3950 N Lake Shore Dr Chicago IL 60613 Office: Dept Philosophy Northwestern U Evanston IL 60201

EDIGER, NICHOLAS MARTIN, resource co. exec.; b. Winnipeg, Man., Can., June 25, 1928; s. Nicholas and Anna (Hamm) E.; m. Elizabeth D. Cattley, Sept. 18, 1973; 1 dau., Julia Anne. B.Sc., U. Man., 1950. Positions in exploration, prodn. and corp. planning Gulf Oil Corp., 1950-74; v.p., chief exec. Gulf Minerals Can. Ltd., Toronto, Ont., 1974; chmn., pres., chief exec. officer Eldorado Nuclear Ltd., Ottawa, Ont., 1974-81; pres., chief exec. Eldorado Aviation Ltd., Ottawa, 1974—; chmn. chief exec. officer Eldor Resources, Ottawa, 1978—. Mem. Canadian Nuclear Assn. (exec. dir.), Uranium Inst. London (exec. dir.), Mining Assn. Can. (dir.), Am. Assn. Petroleum Geologists. Clubs: Rideau (Ottawa); Engrs. (Toronto); Glencoe (Calgary, Alta.). Home: 20 Crichton St Ottawa ON K1M 1V4 Canada Office: 255 Albert St Ottawa ON K1P 6A9 Canada

EDIGER, ROBERT IKE, botanist, educator; b. Hutchinson, Kans., Apr. 2, 1937; s. Peter F. and Martha (Friesen) E.; m. Patricia L. Dickerson, Feb. 7, 1981; children: Madeline, Maureen, Alan, Shelly. B.A., Bethel Coll., 1959; M.S., Emporia State U., 1964; Ph.D., Kans. State U., 1967. Tchr. public schs., Ford, Kans., 1959-62, Hays, Kans., 1962-63; teaching and research asst. Kans. State U., 1964-67; asst. prof. dept. biol. scis. Calif. State U., Chico, 1967-71, asso. prof., 1971-74, prof., 1975—, chmn. dept. biol. scis., 1974-77, dir.Eagle Lake field sta., 1967-73. Mem. Am. Soc. Plant Taxonomists, Internat. Assn. Plant Taxonomy, Orgn. Biol. Field Stas. (pres. 1975), Calif. Bot. Soc., Calif. Native Plant Soc. Methodist. Home: 2940 San Verbena Way Chico CA 95926 Office: Dept Biol Scis Chico CA 95929

EDINGER, LEWIS JOACHIM, political science educator; b. Frankfort, Germany, Feb. 1, 1922; came to U.S., 1936; s. Mark A. and Dora (Meyer) E.; m. Hanni Blumenfeld, Sept. 11, 1950; children: Monica Ruth, Susan Yvonne. A.B., Wabash Coll., 1943; Ph.D., Columbia U., 1951. Instr. NYU, 1947-49; vis. asst. prof. Sweet Briar Coll., 1950-51; vis. lectr. Vassar Coll., 1951-52; vis. asst. prof. U. N.C., 1952-53; assoc. prof. Air War Coll., 1953-57; asst. prof.to prof. Mich. State U., East Lansing, 1957-63; Fulbright prof. Free U. Berlin, 1959-60; prof. Washington U., St. Louis, 1963-67; research assoc. Yale U., New Haven, 1964-65; fulbright prof. U. Bonn, 1964-65; prof. govt. and mem. Inst. Western Europe, Columbia U., N.Y.C., 1969-71; co-adj. prof. Rutgers U., 1975; disting. Fulbright prof. U. Bonn, 1980-81; vis. fellow Nuffield Coll., Oxford U., 1981; fellow Brookdale Inst. Aging and Human Devel., Columbia U., 1981—; assoc. dir. Bur. Applied Social Research, Columbia U., 1969-71, dep. adminstr. polit. sci., 1972-73, dir. grad. studies in comparative politics, 1974-76. Author: Foreign Policy in World Politics, 1958, 61, 67, 72, Kurt Schumacher: A Study in Personality and Political Behavior, 1965, France, Germany, and the Western Alliance, 1967, Political Leadership in Industrialized Societies, 1967, Politics in Germany, 1968, Politics in West Germany, 1977, Comparative Politics Today, 1980; contbr. articles to profl. jours.; mem. editorial bd.: Comparative Politics, Polit. Sci. Quar. Ford Found. fellow, 1956-57; Social Sci. Research Council grantee, 1958, 59-63; NSF grantee, 1971-73; Guggenheim Found. fellow, 1973-74. Mem. AAUP. Home: 83 Lefurgy Ave Dobbs Ferry NY 10522 Office: Columbia Univ 420 W 118th St New York NY 10027

EDINGER, LOIS VIRGINIA, educator; b. Thomasville, N.C., Apr. 17, 1925; d. William Paul and Essie (Byerly) E. A.B., Meredith Coll., 1945; M.Ed., U. N.C., 1959, Ph.D., 1964. Tchr. Thomasville High Sch., 1945-46; tchr. history, North Wilkesboro, 1946-47; youth dir. St. John's Bapt. Ch., Charlotte, N.C., 1947-49; tchr. social studies, Whiteville, N.C., 1949-57; studio tchr. U.S. history N.C. In-Sch. TV project, Chapel Hill, 1957-60; instr. tchr. edn. U. N.C.-Chapel Hill, 1960-62; asst. prof. U. N.C.-Greensboro, 1962-65, asso. prof., 1965-71, prof., 1971—; del. World Confedn. Orgns. Teaching Profession, 1959-61, 64-65, chmn. U.S. del., 1965; mem. Gov.'s. Commn. Ednl. TV, 1962-64; tech. cons. edn. theory SEARCH; cons. N.C. In-Sch. TV; coordinator UNESCO Associated Schs. Project in N.C. Author: (with Nelson) Leadership Training for Directors of Group Seminars Abroad; editor: Teaching: Your Career, 1954-55, (with Houts and Meyer) Education in the 80's: Curricular Challenges, 1981; contbr. articles to profl. jours. Trustee, mem. exec. com. Meredith Coll., 1976-80; deacon Baptist Ch. Recipient N.C. Prin. award, 1965; O. Max Gardner award U. N.C., 1966; Disting. Alumnae award Meredith Coll., 1975; Distinguished Woman award N.C. Fedn. Women's Clubs, 1977. Mem. NEA (pres. 1964-65, recipient H. Councill Trenholm award 1974), N.C. Edn. Assn. (pres. 1960, pres. div. classroom tchrs. 1954-55), Nat., N.C. councils social studies, N.C. Hist. and Lit. Soc., Assn. Supervision and Curriculum Devel., Asia Soc. (adv. com. edn. programs), Delta Kappa Gamma. Home: 2409 Berkley Pl Greensboro NC 27403

EDINGTON, ROBERT SHERARD, lawyer, state senator; b. Mobile, Ala., Nov. 18, 1929; s. David Henry and Cornelia (Owen) E.; m. Patricia Gentry, June 2, 1962; children: Sherard Caffey, Virginia Ellen. B.A. in History with distinction, Southwestern at Memphis, 1950; J.D., U. Ala., 1956. Bar: Ala. bar 1956. Since practiced in, Mobile; asso. Caffey, Gallalee & Caffey, 1956-59; prin. Robert S. Edington (P.A.); consul of Guatemala at Mobile, 1959—; chmn. Consular Corps of Mobile, 1965; atty. gen. Internat. Consular Acad.; Mem. Ala. Ho. of Reps., 1962-70, Ala. Senate, 1970-74; Apptd. to U.S.S. Ala. Battleship Commn., 1963; Sec. Ala.-Guatemala Partners for Alliance, 1968. Del. Democratic Nat. Conv., 1968, 80; adv. bd. Bishop State Coll., Spring Hill Meml. Hosp.; dist. chmn. Boy Scouts Am. Served with USNR, 1951-55; comdr. Res. Recipient Distinguished Service award Ala. Hist. Commn., 1970; Ala. Commendation medal, 1970. Mem. Am., Inter-Am. bar assns., Mobile Jr. C. of C. (past v.p.), Am. Legion, V.F.W., Navy League U.S. (past pres. Ala., nat. dir.), Mobile C. of C., Mobile Carnival Assn., English-Speaking Union (pres. Mobile), Alpha Tau Omega, Phi Delta Phi, Omicron Delta Kappa. Presbyn. (elder). Club: Kiwanian. Home: 1220 Selma St Mobile AL 36602 Office: 551 Church St Mobile AL 36602

EDINGTON, ROBERT VAN, university administrator; b. Burns City, Ind., July 19, 1935; s. Guy Franklin and Nancy (Banks) E.; m. Ann Beach, July 18, 1959; children: Ellen, Russell, Garrett. AA., Vallejo Community Coll., 1955; B.A. in Internat. Relations, San Francisco State Coll., 1957; M.A. in Polit. Sci, U. Wash., 1963; Ph.D., 1968. Student activities advisor Office Dean Students, Sacramento State Coll., 1959-62; chmn. internat. studies James Madison Coll., Mich. State U., East Lansing, 1971-74; assoc. dean coll. Liberal Arts Idaho State U., Pocatello, 1975-76, dean Coll. Liberal Arts, 1976-83; provost, acad. v.p. Clarion U. of Pa., 1983—. Author: The Recruiting and Retention of Students: Handbook for an Experimental Program, 1979; contbr. articles to profl. jours. Rep. for higher edn. State of Idaho Profl. Standards Commn., 1979-84; co-founder Pocatello Forward; lay leader, edn. com. Pocatello United Meth. Ch., 1979-80; active local polit. campaigns. NSF fellow, 1967-68; Dept. State Scholar-Diplomat fellow, 1970; recipient numerous grants. Mem. Am. Assn. Univ. Adminstrs. (regional coordinator); mem. Am. Polit. Sci. Assn., Assn. for Asian Studies, Council Colls. Arts and Scis., Rocky Mountain Deans Assn., Western Polit. Sci. Assn., English Speaking Union, Friends of Idaho Mus. Natural History, Phi Kappa Phi. Republican. Club: Clarion Rotary. Office: Clarion U of Pa Clarion PA 16214

EDISON, ALLEN RAY, elec. engr., educator; b. Plainview, Nebr., Sept. 21, 1926; s. Arthur and Lela (Johnson) E.; m. Betty Jean Broer, Dec. 27, 1949; children—Karl Arthur, Kathryn Johannah. B.S., U. Nebr., 1950, M.S., 1957; D.Sc., U. N.M., 1962. Engr. Silas Mason Co., Burlington, Iowa, 1950-53; instr. U. Nebr., Lincoln, 1953-57, prof. elec. engring., 1957—, chmn. dept. elec. engring., 1964-70. Served with USNR, 1944-46. Mem. I.E.E.E. (past sect. chmn.), Sigma Xi, Sigma Tau, Eta Kappa Nu. Home: 511 S 54th St Lincoln NE 68510 Office: 1400 R St Lincoln NE 68588

EDISON, BERNARD ALAN, retail apparel company executive; b. Atlanta, 1928; s. Irving and Beatrice (Chanin) E.; m. Marilyn S. Wewers, Apr. 26, 1975. A.B., Harvard U., 1949, M.B.A., 1951. With

Edison Bros. Stores Inc., St. Louis, 1951—, asst. v.p., 1957-58, v.p. leased depts., 1958-67, v.p., asst. treas., 1967-68, pres., 1968—, also dir.; dir. Gen. Am. Life Ins. Co., Mercantile Trust Co., Mercantile Bancorp. Office: Edison Bros Stores Inc 400 Washington Ave St Louis MO 63102

EDISON, JULIAN IRVING, retail chain executive; b. St. Louis, May 12, 1929; s. Mark A. and Ida (Edison) E.; m. Hope Rabb, Jan. 4, 1949; children: Mark, Aaron. A.B., Harvard U., 1951, M.B.A., 1953. Dir. Edison Bros. Stores, Inc., St. Louis, 1965—, chmn. bd., 1974—; dir. Boatmen's Bancshares, Inc., Boatmen's Nat. Bank St. Louis, The Stop and Shop Cos., Inc., Boston. Bd. dirs. Barnes Hosp., St. Louis. Served to 1st lt. AUS, 1953-55. Clubs: Westwood Country, Mo. Athletic. Home: 16 Dromara Rd Saint Louis MO 63124 Office: 400 Washington Ave Saint Louis MO 63102

EDISON, ROBERT DONALD, insurance company executive; b. Lakeland, Fla., May 18, 1922; s. Donald E. and Helen Ruth (Cederstrom) E.; m. Jane Porter, Aug. 18, 1946; children: Pamela Jane, Nancy Louise. B.A., U. Iowa, 1946, M.A., 1948. With Hawkeye-Security Ins. Co., Des Moines, 1948—, pres., 1969-77, dir., 1965—; with United Security Ins. Co., Des Moines, 1964—, pres., 1969-77, dir., 1964—; v.p. Fin. Security Group, Inc., Washington, 1971-75, pres., 1975—, also dir.; pres., dir. Northeastern Ins. Co., 1974—; sr. v.p. Internat. Bank, Washington, 1974—; dir. IB Credit Corp., Bankers Security Life Ins. Soc., Internat. Risks, Inc., Ins. Co. Africa; bd. dirs. Iowa Ins. Guaranty Assn., 1970-76, Internat. Ins. Seminars, 1972. Gen. chmn. Greater Des Moines United Way, 1972; bd. dirs. Des Moines Jr. Achievement, 1965-76, Des Moines C. of C., 1969-76, Des Moines Art Center, 1972-76. Served with USNR, 1943-46. Republican. Presbyterian. Clubs: Des Moines, Univ., Congressional Country. Office: Internat Bank 1701 Pennsylvania Ave NW Washington DC 20006 *

EDLER, RICHARD BRUCE, advertising agency executive; b. Chgo., Nov. 23, 1943; s. Francis and Kathryn (Merryweather) E. B.A. in English, U. Iowa, 1965, M.A. in Bus., 1969. Copywriter Gen. Electric Co., Schenectady, 1965-67; brand mgr. Procter & Gamble Co., Cin., 1969-74; sr. v.p. Ketchum Communications, San Francisco, 1974-81; pres. Doyle Dane Bernbach, Los Angeles, 1981—. Home: 1621 Via Barcelona Palos Verdes Estates CA 90274

EDLEY, CHRISTOPHER FAIRFIELD, association executive; b. Charleston, W. Va., Jan. 1, 1928; s. Phillip and Helen (Penn) E.; m. Zaida Coles, Sept. 2, 1950; children: Christpher F., Judith Coles. A.B., Howard U., 1949; LL.B., Harvard U., 1953; LL.D., Swarthmore Coll., 1976; L.H.D., Rust Coll., 1975. Bar: Mass. 1953, Pa. 1954. Asst. dist. atty., Phila., 1954-56; ptnr. Moore, Lightfoot and Edley, 1956-60; chief adminstrn. justice div. U.S. Commn. Civil Rights, 1960; regional counsel Fed. Housing and Home Fin. (now HUD), 1961-63; program officer in charge govt. and law Ford Found., 1963-73; pres. United Negro Coll. Fund., Inc., 1973—; dir. Am. Airlines., A & P Co., Bowery Savs. Bank. Active numerous civic and charitable orgns. including bd. dirs. Internat. House, NAACP, Legal Def. Fund, Center Nat. Policy Rev., Citizens Research Found., Nat. Com. Against Discrimination in Housing, Nat. Adv. Council Minorities in Engring.; mem. vis. com. Harvard Law Sch. Served with U.S. Army, 1946-47, 50-51. Recipient Howard U. Alumni award, 1959, Congl. award, Disting. Service award Phila. Commn. Human Relations, 1966; named Humanitarian Father of Year, 1974, numerous others. Mem. Am., Nat., Mass., Pa. bar assns., Assn. Bar City N.Y. Home: 90 Vaughn Ave New Rochelle NY 10801 Office: 500 E 62d St New York NY 10021

EDLUND, MILTON CARL, physicist, educator; b. Jamestown, N.Y., Dec. 13, 1924. B.S., M.S., U. Mich., 1948, Ph.D., 1966. Physicist reactor physics, gaseous diffusion plant, 1948-49, Oak Ridge Nat. Lab., 1949-50; physicist, lectr. Sch. Reactor Tech., 1950-51, sr. physicist and sect. chief, 1953-55; mgr. devel. dept. Babcock & Wilcox Co., 1955-65, asst. mgr. atomic energy div., 1965-66; prof. U. Mich., 1966-67; planning cons. AEC, 1967-68; exec. v.p. Nuclear Assurance Corp., Atlanta, 1968-70; chmn. nuclear engring. Va. Poly. Inst. and State U., Blacksburg, 1970-74; dir. Center for Energy Research, 1974-78, prof. nuclear engring., 1978—; Vis. lectr. Swedish Atomic Energy Com., 1953. Author: (with S. Glasstone) Elements of Nuclear Reactor Theory, 1952, (with J. Fried) Desalting Technology, 1971. Recipient Ernest Orlando Lawrence award, 1965. Fellow Am. Nuclear Soc.; mem. Nat. Acad. Engring. Spl. research neutron diffusion, nuclear reactor design, energy policy analysis. Address: 302 Neil St Blacksburg VA 24060

EDLY, ALAN JOHN, food company executive; b. N.Y.C., June 22, 1935; s. Alexander John and Grace Catherine (Hauss) E. A.B. magna cum laude, Holy Cross Coll., 1957; M.B.A., N.Y. U., 1963. C.P.A., N.Y. Staff acct. Arthur Andersen & Co., N.Y.C., 1957-65; controller Gibbs & Co., N.Y.C., 1966-68; mgr. corp. acctg. Am. Maize-Products Co., N.Y.C., 1968-71, controller, 1971-74, fin. v.p., 1974—, also dir. Served with AUS, 1957. Mem. Am. Inst. C.P.A.s, N.Y. State Soc. C.P.A.s. Home: 81-02 Courtland Ave Stamford CT Office: Am Maize-Products Co 41 Harbor Plaza Dr Stamford CT 06904

EDMAN, JOHN RICHARD, automotive executive; b. Brighton, Mich., Oct. 14, 1927; s. Martin Wagner and Elizabeth Statira (Jacobs) E.; m. Betty Jean Bailey, Aug. 12, 1951; children: Jill, Thomas, Jody, Tracy, Julie, John. B.B.A., U. Mich., 1950, M.B.A., 1951. Comptroller, Terex div. Gen. Motors, 1966-69, comptroller Packard Electric div., 1969-71; comptroller Gen. Motors Can., 1971-72, AC Spark Plug div. Gen. Motors, 1972-74; asst. comptroller Gen. Motors Corp., 1974-75, treas., 1975-78, v.p. fin., 1978—. Served with U.S. Army, 1946-47. Mem. Fin. Execs. Inst., Nat. Assn. Accts. Republican. Presbyterian. Clubs: Detroit Athletic (Detroit); Presidents (U. Mich.); Bloomfield Hills (Mich.). Home: 5175 Winlane Bloomfield Hills MI 48013 Office: 3044 W Grand Blvd Detroit MI 48202

EDMISTEN, RUFUS LIGH, attorney general North Carolina; b. Boone, N.C., July 12, 1941; s. Walter F. and Nell (Hollar) E.; m. Martha Jane Moretz, Aug. 3, 1963; 1 dau., Martha Rebecca. B.A., U. N.C., 1963; J.D. with honors, George Washington U., 1967. Bar: D.C., N.C. Counsel Judiciary Subcom. on Constl. Rights, U.S. Senate, Washington, 1967-69, chief counsel and staff dir. Judiciary Subcom. on Separation of Powers, 1969-74, chief dep. counsel Select Com. on Presdl. Campaign Activities, 1973-74; atty. gen. State of N.C., Raleigh, 1974—. Served with U.S. Army, 1966-67. Recipient Wildlife Conservation award, Watauga County, N.C., 1962, Good Govt. award State of N.C., 1969. Mem. Am., Fed., D.C., N.C. bar assns. Democrat. Baptist. Club: Masons. Office: Dept Justice PO Box 629 Raleigh NC 27602 *

EDMISTER, RICHARD RILEY, lawyer, engring. and constrn. co. exec.; b. Columbus, Ohio, Apr. 19, 1939; s. William K. and Elizabeth (R.) E.; m. Michaeleen A. Ziobro, Nov. 19, 1966; children—Whitney B., Bradley K. B.S. in M.E, Ohio State U., 1962; J.D., Georgetown U., 1966. Bar: Ohio bar 1967, D.C. bar 1967, U.S. Ct. Claims 1967, U.S. Supreme Ct. bar 1970; Registered profl. engr., Ohio. Contract adminstr. Washington Metro Transit Authority, 1967-69; asst. gen. counsel Morrison-Knudsen Co., Inc., Boise, Idaho, 1969-72; gen. counsel, sec. The H.K. Ferguson Co., Cleve., 1972—. Mem. Am. Arbitration Assn. (arbitrator), Nat. Constructors Com. of Gen. Counsels (chmn. 1978-79). Office: 1 Erieview Plaza Cleveland OH 44114

EDMISTON, MARK MORTON, b. Yonkers, N.Y., July 9, 1943; s. Marcus Morton and Josephine (Brown) E.; m. Lisa Mary Pustorino, Aug. 28, 1965; children: Ann Kathleen, Laura Mary. B.A., Wesleyan U., 1966. Circulation mgr. Life mag., N.Y.C., until 1969, circulation and mktg. dir., Tokyo, 1969-70; circulation dir. Saturday Rev., Inc., 1971-73; circulation dir. internat. edits. Newsweek, Inc., 1973-76, pub., 1976-78, pres., 1978-79, corp. exec. v.p., 1979-81, chmn. and pres., 1981—. Trustee Wesleyan U., 1983—. Mem. Japan Soc., Mag. Pub. Assn. (dir.), Internat. Advt. Assn. Office: 444 Madison Ave New York NY 10022

EDMOND, JOHN MARMION, chemistry educator. Prof. marine chemistry MIT, Cambridge. Office: Mass Inst Tech Cambridge MA02139

EDMONDS, ANNE CAREY, librarian; b. Penang, Malaysia, Dec. 19, 1924; d. William John and Nell (Carey) E. Student, U. Reading, Eng., 1942-44; B.A., Barnard Coll., 1948; M.S. in L.S, Columbia U., 1950; M.A., Johns Hopkins U., 1959; postgrad., Western Res. U., 1960-61. With War Damage Commn., London, Eng., 1944-46; children's asst. Enoch Pratt Free Library, Balt., 1948-49; reference librarian Sch. Bus. Adminstrn., CCNY., 1950-51; reference librarian, then asst. librarian readers' services Goucher Coll., Balt., 1951-60; exchange reference librarian European services library BBC, London, 1955; instr. Sch. L.S., Syracuse U., summer 1960; librarian Douglass Coll., Rutgers U., New Brunswick, N.J., 1961-64, instr., summer 1962, fall 1963; librarian Mt. Holyoke Coll., 1964—; vis. librarian U. North, Turfloop, South Africa, 1976-77; mem. library vis. com. Wheaton Coll., Norton, Mass., 1978—; Mem. South Hadley (Mass.) Bicentennial Com., 1975-76; mem. accreditation teams Middle States Assn. Colls. and Secondary Schs., 1963—; bd. dirs. U.S. Book Exchange, 1973-76, 80-83; exec. com. New Eng. Library Info. Network, 1974-76, 79—, chmn., 1982—; mem. Adv. Commn. Historic Deerfield, 1975-81. Mem. ALA, Am. Hist. Assn., Assn. Coll. Research Libraries (pres. 1970-71, chmn. constn. and bylaws com. New Eng. chpt. 1975-76, pres. New Eng. chpt. 1983-84), AAUP, AAUW. Home: 79 Cold Hill Granby MA 01033

EDMONDS, FRANK NORMAN, JR., astronomer, educator; b. Mpls., Sept. 2, 1919; s. Frank Norman and Irene (Radcliffe) E.; m. Joan Mary McKinney, Mar. 24, 1945; children—Cynthia Ann Edmonds Torkelson, Christopher Norman. A.B., Princeton, 1941; Ph.D., U. Chgo., 1950. Asst. prof. astronomy U. Mo.-Columbia, 1950-52; mem. faculty U. Tex., Austin, 1952—, asso. prof. astronomy, 1958-65, prof., 1965—; Mem. naval adv. com. astronomy NRC, 1958-61, chmn., 1960-61. Served to capt. AUS, 1941-45; Served to capt. USAAF, 1945-46. Guggenheim fellow, 1962-63. Mem. Internat. Astronom. Union, Am. Astron. Soc., Sigma Xi. Home: 3005 Wade Ave Austin TX 78703

EDMONDS, GEORGE P., corporation executive; b. Boston, Mass., 1905. Ed., Mass. Inst. Tech. Dir. Wilmington Trust Co.; dir., mem. fin. com. E.I. duPont de Nemours & Co.; dir. Continental Am. Life Ins. Co. Home: 920 Westover Rd Westover Hills Wilmington DE 19807 Office: Wilmington Trust Co Wilmington DE 19890

EDMONDS, THOMAS ANDREW, law school dean; b. Jackson, Miss., July 5, 1938. B.A., Miss. Coll., 1962; LL.B., Duke U., 1965. Bar: Fla. 1965, Va. 1981. Pvt. practice law, Orlando, Fla., 1965-66; assoc. prof. law U. Miss., Oxford, 1966-70; assoc. prof.law Fla. State U., Tallahassee, 1970-74, prof., 1974-77; dean Sch. Law, U. Richmond (Va.), 1977—; vis. assoc. prof. Duke U., 1968-69; prof. McGeorge Sch. Law U. Pacific, 1975-76. Served with USMC, 1957-60. Office: U Richmond T C Williams Sch of Law Richmond VA 23173

EDMONDS, WALTER DUMAUX, author; b. Boonville, N.Y., July 15, 1903; s. Walter Dumaux and Sarah (May) E.; m. Eleanor Livingston Stetson, 1930; children: Peter B., Eleanor D., Sarah M.; m. Katharine Baker-Carr, 1956. A.B., Harvard U., 1926; Litt.D., Union Coll., 1936, Rutgers U., 1940, Colgate U., 1947, Harvard U., 1952. Mem. bd. overseers Harvard, 1945-50; pres., pub. Harvard Alumni Bull., 1957-66, dir., 1966-73. Author: latest books In the Hands of the Senecas, 1947, The Wedding Journey, 1947, Cadmus Henry, 1949, Mr. Benedict's Lion, 1950, They Fought with What They Had, 1951, Corporal Bess, 1952, The Boyds of Black River, 1953, Hound Dog Moses and the Promised Land, 1954, Uncle Ben's Whale, 1955, They Had A Horse, 1962, Three Stalwarts, 1962, The Musket and the Cross, 1968, Time To Go House, 1969, Seven American Stories, 1970, Wolf Hunt, 1970, Beaver Valley, 1971, The Story of Richard Storm, 1973, Bert Breen's Barn, 1975 (Nat. Book award 1976), The Night Raider, 1980; Contbr.: fiction to Sat. Eve. Post; others. Mem. Am. Acad. Arts and Scis., Phi Beta Kappa. Club: Saint Botolph's (Boston). Home: 27 River St Concord MA 01742

EDMONDSON, FRANK K., astronomer; b. Milw., Aug. 1, 1912; s. Clarence Edward and Marie (Kelley) E.; m. Margaret Russell, Nov. 24, 1934; children: Margaret Jean, Frank K. Jr. A.B., Ind. U., 1933, A.M., 1934; Ph.D., Harvard U., 1937. Lawrence fellow Lowell Obs., 1933-34, research asst., 1934-35; Agassiz fellow Harvard Obs., 1935-36, asst., 1936-37; instr. astronomy Ind. U., Bloomington, 1937-4O, asst. prof., 1940-45, asso. prof., 1945-48, prof., 1949-83, prof. emeritus, 1983—, dir. Kirkwood Obs., 1945-83; dir. Goethe Link Obs., 1948-78, chmn. astronomy dept., 1944-78; research asso. McDonald Obs., 1944—; Observations of asteroids in cooperation with Internat. Astron. Union's Minor Plant Center; program dir. for astronomy NSF, 1956-57; acting dir. Cerro Tololo Inter-Am. Obs., 1966; lectr. astron. socs. Contbr. numerous papers to Am., Brit., German astron. jours. Decorated Order of Merit, Chile, 1964; recipient Meritorious Pub. Service award NSF, 1983. Fellow AAAS (chmn. sect. D, v.p. 1962); mem. Assn. Univs. Research in Astronomy (pres. 1962-65, dir. 1957-83), Can. Astron. Soc., Am. Astron. Soc. (treas. 1954-75), Astron. Soc. Pacific, Internat. Astron. Union (chmn. U.S. nat. com. 1963-64, v.p. commn. minor planets, comets and satellites 1967-70, pres. 1970-73), Ind. Acad. Science, Am. Mus. Natural History (corr. mem.), Explorers Club, Phi Beta Kappa, Sigma Xi. Home: 716 S Woodlawn Ave Bloomington IN 47401

EDMONDSON, HUGH ALLEN, physician; b. Maysville, Ark., Jan. 3, 1906; s. James Turner and Julia Ann (Phillips) E.; m. Dorothy E. Mossman, July 14, 1930; children: Hugh Allen, James Paul, Marian Ann, Marjorie Jean. A.B., U. Okla., 1926; M.D., U. Chgo., 1931; LL.D. (hon.), U. So. Calif., 1977. Instr. pathology U. So. Calif. Med. Sch., 1938-41, asst. prof. pathology, 1941-43, asso. prof., 1943-48, prof., 1948—, head dept., 1951-72; dir. labs. and pathology Los Angeles County-U. So. Calif. Med. Center, 1968-72; attending staff Los Angeles County Hosp., 1939—. Contbr. articles med. publs. Trustee Estelle Doheny Eye Found., 1971—, pres. bd., 1972—; chmn. bd. Estelle Doheny Eye Hosp., 1983—; trustee Eisenhower Med. Center, Palm Desert, Calif., 1974—. Recipient Profl. Achievement award U. Chgo. Alumni Assn., 1979. Fellow A.C.P.; mem. AMA (chmn. sect. pathology and physiology 1963-64), Coll. Am. Pathologists, Gastroent. Assn., Cal. Med. Assn. (past chmn. sec. pathology sect.), Am. Assn. Pathologists and Bacteriologists, Am. Soc. Clin. Pathologists, Internat. Acad. Pathology (council 1960-63), Sigma Xi, Sigma Alpha Epsilon, Nu Sigma Nu. Club: Valley Hunt (Pasadena). Home: 1411 Circle Dr San Marino CA 91108 Office: 1200 N State St Los Angeles CA 90033

EDMONDSON, JAMES WILLIAM (JAY EDMONDSON), insurance company executive; b. Artesia, Calif., July 1, 1930; s. Edward Vernon and Doris LaVerna (Holsington) E.; m. Susanne Martin, Sept. 5, 1953; children: Susan, John. B.A., U. Calif.-Berkeley, 1952. V.p. State Farm Ins. Cos., Bloomington, Ill., 1954—. Chmn. Human Relations Com., Normal, Ill., 1975-76; bd. dirs. United Way, McLean County, Ill., 1981—, Blomington-Normal Symphony, 1977—. Recipient Hardy prize Ins. Inst. Am., 1960. Republican. Roman Catholic. Office: State Farm Ins Cos One State Farm Plaza Bloomington IL 61701

EDMONDSON, JEANNETTE B., sec. state Okla.; b. Muskogee, Okla., June 6, 1925; d. A. Chapman and Georgia (Shutt) Bartleson; m. J. Howard Edmondson, May 15, 1946 (dec.); children—James H. (dec.), Jeanne E. Watkins, Patricia E. Zimmer. B.A., U. Okla., 1946. Sec. of state State of Okla., Oklahoma City, 1979—. Chmn. bd. Okla. affiliate Am. Heart Assn., 1979. Democrat. Methodist. Office: Office of Sec of State 101 State Capitol Oklahoma City OK 73105

EDMONDSON, JOHN RICHARD, pharmaceutical manufacturer; b. N.Y.C., Mar. 1, 1927; s. Richard Emil and Josephine (Schroeter) E.; m. Rozanne Hume, Oct. 30, 1954; children: Lisa M., Kate H., Timothy H., Nicholas D., Julia N. A.B., Georgetown U., 1950; LL.B., Columbia, 1953. Bar: N.Y. bar 1953. Asso. atty. Winthrop, Stimson, Putnam & Roberts, N.Y.C., 1953-59; with Bristol-Myers Co., N.Y.C., 1959—, asst. sec., 1960-69, sec., 1969—, v.p., 1974-80, gen. counsel, 1977—, sr. v.p., 1980—. Served with AUS, 1945-47. Mem. Assn. Bar City N.Y. Clubs: University (N.Y.C.); Lake Waramaug Country (New Preston, Conn.). Home: 60 E 96th St New York NY 10028 Office: 345 Park Ave New York NY 10022

EDMONDSON, KEITH HENRY, chem. co. exec.; b. Wheaton, Ill., May 16, 1924; s. Edwin Ray and Mildred Lorraine (Henry) E.; m. Peggy Eleanor Wood, Sept. 22, 1945; children—Robert Earl, Kris E., John David, Keith Clark. B.S., Purdue U., 1948, M.S., 1949. With Upjohn Co., Kalamazoo, Mich., 1949—, exec. v.p. internat. div., 1962-67, v.p., gen. mgr. chem. div., 1967—. Mem. Kalamazoo Bd. Edn., 1958-62, pres., 1962. Served to 1st lt. USAAF, 1942-45. Decorated D.F.C. with oak leaf cluster, Air medal with 6 oak leaf clusters. Mem. Internat. Isocyanate Inst. (pres. 1976), Kalamazoo C. of C. (v.p. 1973), Kalamazoo Mgmt. Assn. (pres. 1957), Am. Inst. Chem. Engrs., Am. Chem. Soc., Tau Beta Pi, Sigma Xi, Phi Lambda Upsilon. Republican. Methodist. Home: 2033 Saxonia Ln Kalamazoo MI 49008 Office: 7000 Portage Rd Kalamazoo MI 49001

EDMONDSON, W(ALLACE) THOMAS, limnologist, educator; b. Milw., Apr. 24, 1916; s. Clarence Edward and Marie (Kelley) E.; m. Yvette Hardman, Sept. 26, 1941. B.S., Yale U., 1938, Ph.D., 1942; postgrad., U. Wis., 1938-39. Research assoc. Am. Mus. Natural History, 1942-43, Woods Hole Oceanographic Instn., 1943-46; lectr. biology Harvard U., 1946-49; faculty U. Wash., Seattle, 1949—, prof., 1957—. Editor: Freshwater Biology (Ward and Whipple), 2d edit, 1959; contbr. articles to profl. jours. NSF sr. postdoctoral fellow, Italy, Eng. and Sweden, 1959-60; recipient Einar Naumann-August Thienemann Medal Internat. Assn. Theoretical and Applied Limnology, 1980. Mem. Nat. Acad. Scis., Am. Micros. Soc., Nat. Acad. Scis. (Cottrell award 1973), AAAS, Am. Soc. Limnology and Oceanography, Internat. Assn. Limnology, Am. Soc. Naturalists, Phycol. Soc. Am., Ecol. Soc. Am. (Disting. Ecologist award 1983). Office: Dept Zoology U Wash Seattle WA 98195

EDMONDSON, WILLIAM BROCKWAY, foreign service officer; b. St. Joseph, Mo., Feb. 6, 1927; s. Harold and Anna Laura (Sherman) E.; m. Donna Elizabeth Kiechel, Oct. 6, 1951; children: Barbara Elizabeth, Paul William. A.B. with high distinction, U. Nebr., 1950; M.A., Fletcher Sch. Law and Diplomacy, 1951; student African area studies, Northwestern U., 1957-58. Joined U.S. Fgn. Service, 1952; fgn. affairs officer Bur. UN Affairs, State Dept., 1951-52; adviser U.S. delegation 11th session UN Trusteeship Council, 1952; vice consul Dar es Salaam, Tanganyika, 1952-55; 3d sec., then 2d sec. embassy, Bern, Switzerland, 1955-57; research analyst, then acting chief W. Africa div. Office Research and Analysis for Africa, State Dept., 1958-61; 2d sec., then 1st sec. and consul, polit. sect. chief embassy, Accra, Ghana, 1961-64; officer charge Ghanaian affairs Bur. African Affairs, State Dept., 1964-65; counselor of embassy, dep. chief of mission, Lusaka, Zambia, 1965-68, chargé d'affaires ad interim, 1968-69; assigned Nat. War Coll., 1969-70; dep. dir. African programs Bur. Ednl. and Cultural Affairs, Dept. State, 1970, dir., 1971-74; minister-counselor, dep. chief mission Am. embassy, Pretoria, South Africa, 1974-76; dep. asst. sec. for African affairs State Dept., 1976-78; ambassador to South Africa, Pretoria, 1978-81; fgn. service officer Dept. State, Washington, 1981, now dep. insp. gen. Served to 1st lt. AUS, 1944-48. Fellow African Studies Assn.; mem. Am. Fgn. Service Assn., Phi Beta Kappa. Address: Dept State 2201 C St NW Washington DC 20520 *Persistent hard work, sincerity, broad intellectual curiosity and a strong touch of idealism in striving for a better world are qualities I admire and try to emulate.* *

EDMONSON, DAN HUTCHESON, Marketing executive; b. Baskerville, Va., Nov. 12, 1916; s. Haynie Stokes and Nell (Jones) E.; m. Johnnie Naron, Mar. 9, 1947; children: Robert Stokes, Joan. B.A., Coll. William and Mary, 1937. Store mgr. Firestone Tire & Rubber Co., Richmond, Va., 1938-42; sales v.p. Mass. Mohair Plush Co., N.Y.C., 1947-55; v.p., sales mgr. Kroeher Mfg. Co., Naperville, Ill., 1955-62, v.p., gen. sales mgr., 1962-75, dir. sales, 1964-69, exec. v.p. marketing, 1969-73, exec. v.p. corporate devel., 1973-75, dir., 1962-80; v.p., gen. mgr. Kroehler S.W., Dallas, 1975-80; pres. Fairway Mktg. Co., Dallas, 1980—; dir. Hickerson Oil Co.; Petx Petroleum Co. Served as lt. USNR, 1942-46. Recipient Sports Illustrated silver anniversary award, 1961; named to William and Mary Athletic Hall of Fame, 1975. Mem. Coll. William and Mary Alumni Assn. (mem. bd. 1971-75). Methodist. Clubs: Glen Oak Country (Glen Ellyn, Ill.); Northwood (Dallas). Home: 5122 Spring Meadow Dr Dallas TX 75229

EDMONSON, MUNRO STERLING, educator, anthropologist; b. Nogales, Ariz., May 18, 1924; s. Everett Sterling and Lillian (Munro) E.; m. Barbara Bay Wedemeyer, Aug. 1, 1953; children—Evelyn Mila, Ann Munro, Sallie Ross. B.A., Harvard, 1945, M.A., 1948, Ph.D., 1952. Instr. Washington U., St. Louis, 1951; mem. faculty Tulane U., New Orleans, 1951—, prof. anthropology, 1960—; Vis. prof. U. de San Carlos, Quezaltenango, Guatemala, 1960-61, Purdue U., 1964, Harvard, 1965-66. Author: Los Manitos, 1957, Status Terminology and Social Structure of North American Indians, 1958, (with others) The Eighth Generation, 1959, Quiche-English Dictionary, 1965, Lore, 1971, The Book of Counsel, 1971, The Ancient Future of the Maya, 1981. Served to lt. (j.g.) USNR, 1944-46. Fellow, Am. Anthrop. Assn.; mem. AAAS, AAUP, Am. Ethnol. Soc. (pres. 1965-66), So. Anthrop. Soc. Address: Tulane Univ Coll Arts and Scis Dept Anthropology New Orleans LA 70118

EDMONSTON, WILLIAM EDWARD, JR., psychology educator; b. Balt., Nov. 20, 1931; s. William Edward and Helen (Mallonee) E.; m. Nellie Jane Kerley, Aug. 3, 1957; children—Kathryn Nell, Rebecca

Jane, Owen William. B.A., Johns Hopkins U., 1952; M.A., U. Ala., 1956; Ph.D., U. Ky., 1960. Diplomate: Am. Bd. Psychol. Hypnosis. Instr., asst. prof. Washington U., St. Louis, 1960-64; mem. faculty Colgate U., Hamilton, N.Y., 1964—, dir. neurosci. program, 1972—, prof. psychology, 1973—, chmn. dept. psychology, 1971-81; Gast prof. U. Erlanger, Nürnberg, W. Ger., 1982. Author: Hypnosis and Relaxation: Modern Verification of an Old Equation; Editor: Am. Jour. Clin. Hypnosis, 1968-76; contbr. articles to profl. jours. Served with U.S. Army, 1952-54. Recipient Bernard E. Gorton award, 1961; Sloan Found. fellow, 1967, 69; sr. fellow U. Wash., 1971; USPHS grantee, 1964-65; Fulbright fellow, 1982. Fellow AAAS, Am. Psychol. Assn., Am. Soc. Clin. Hypnosis, Internat. Soc. Clin. and Exptl. Hypnosis; mem. N.Y. Acad. Scis., Eastern Psychol. Assn., Soc. Neurosci., Am. Psychopathol. Assn., Sigma Xi. Home: 30 Maple Ave Hamilton NY 13346 Office: Dept Psychology Colgate U Hamilton NY 13346 *By being born to intelligent parents, I started with the genetic potential for success and was reared in a social atmosphere in which hard work, honesty, thrift and accomplishment were highly regarded. I later recognized perseverance, even in the face of apparent failure, and a compulsive attention to (but not an obsession with) details as fundamental to accomplishment. Perseverance is by far the most regnant, for without tenacity one's genetic potential and early social learnings will lie fallow.*

EDMUNDS, JANE CLARA, editor; b. Chgo., Mar. 16, 1922; d. John Carson and Clara (Kummerow) Carrigan; m. William T. Dean, Aug. 30, 1947 (div. 1953); 1 son, John Charles; Edmund S. Kopacz, Sept. 24, 1955 (div. 1973); children: Christine Ellen, Jan Carson. B.Ph. in Chemistry, Northwestern U., 1947. Chemist Mars Inc., Oak Park, Ill., 1942-47; with Maujer Pub. Co., St. Joseph, Mich., 1953-58, 69-74; asst. editor women's pages rewrite desk News-Palladium, Benton Harbor, Mich., 1967-68; free lance journalist, St. Joseph, 1959-68; sr. editor Cons. Engr. Mag. Tech. Pub. Co., Barrington, Ill., 1975-77, exec. editor, 1977-82, editorial dir., 1983—. Chmn. Berrien County (Mich.) Nat. Found. March of Dimes, 1968; mem. campaign com. Rep. Party, 1954. Recipient award Bausch & Lomb, 1940, Nat. Found. Service, 1969; grantee AID, 1979. Assoc. fellow Soc. Tech. Communication (chmn. St. Joseph chpt. 1972, Disting. Tech. Communication awards); mem. Am. Soc. Bus. Press Editors (past bd. mem.), Constrn. Writers Assn. (past dir.), Smithsonian Instn., Barrington Assocs., Field Mus. Assocs. Republican. Episcopalian. Office: Tech Pub Co 1301 S Grove Ave Barrington IL 60010

EDMUNDS, PALMER DANIEL, lawyer, educator; b. Terre Haute, Ill., Oct. 29, 1890; s. Amos and Mary Ann (Campbell) E.; m. Margaret Burton, June 29, 1932 (dec. 1964); m. Sarah Shepard Brown, 1970. A.B., Knox Coll., 1912, LL.D., 1945; LL.B., Harvard U., 1915; LL.D., John Marshall Law Sch., 1973, Piedmont Coll., 1975. Bar: Ill. bar 1915. Since practiced in, Chgo.; dir., counsel Ill. Service Recognition Bd., 1922-25; mem. firm Dodd, Matheny & Edmunds, 1925-29; commr. Supreme Ct. Ill., 1929-32; mem. Dodd & Edmunds, Chgo., 1932-58; lectr. conflict of laws and Ill. practice John Marshall Law Sch., Chgo., 1926-58, prof. law, 1958—, lectr. fed. practice, 1938-58; dir. Lawyers Inst.; vis. prof. law Knox Coll., 1944-57; compliance commr. WPB and Civilian Prodn. Adminstrn., 1944-47; hearing commr. NPA, 1951-53. Author: (with W. F. Dodd) Illinois Appellate Procedure, 1929, Edmunds Common Law Forms, 1931, Illinois Civil Practice Forms, 1933, Edmunds Federal Rules of Civil Procedure, 1938, Cyclopedia of Federal Procedure Forms, 1939, Law and Civilization, 1959; co-author: Encyclopedia of Federal Procedure, 2d edit, 1944, Edmunds Conflict of Laws, 1948; Editor, compiler: Jones Illinois Statutes Annotated, vols. 18-22, 24. Charter mem. World Peace Through Law Center.; Trustee John Marshall Law Sch.; Past comdr. Black Hawk Post, Am. Legion, Chgo.; past historian Dept. of Ill. First lt. A.E.F., 1917-19; capt. O.R.C. Mem. Am. Polit. Sci. Assn., Am. Acad. Polit. and Social Sci., Fgn. Policy Assn., Am., Ill., Chgo., Internat. bar assns., India Soc. Internat. Law, Ill. Hist. Soc., S.A.R., Nat. Sojourners, Am. Bantam Assn., Sebright Club Am., 40 and 8, Soc. of 28th Div., Com. for Continuation Congl. Christian Chs. U.S., Phi Gamma Delta, Delta Sigma Rho. Democrat. Conglist. Clubs: Mason, Elk., Harvard (Chgo.). Home and Office: Gilman IL 60938 *Life is a continuing process of adjustment to the environment—physical and social—in which one finds himself. The individual lives under constant prssures, some good and some bad. Each person is born with a desire to achieve a satisfying life. What constitutes such a life is purely subjective. Each achieves his aim as he recognizes and by-passes diversionary courses and chooses those which lead to the end he seeks. Our Creator has equipped each person with a free soul and fortified that soul with powers of reason and conscience to make the choice. Satisfaction is promoted in greatest measure by cultivation of and reliance upon those powers.*

EDMUNDS, ROBERT LARRY, textile co. exec.; b. Pell City, Ala., Dec. 19, 1930; s. Jesse Thomas and Eunice (Bain) E.; m. Sara Ann Peters, June 8, 1952; children—Melanie Jane, Mary Catherine, Robert Larry. B.S. in Bus. Adminstrn, Auburn U., 1952. With Avondale Mills, Sylacauga, Ala., 1954—, gen. auditor, 1963- 64, sec., 1964-72, v.p., sec., 1972—. Baptist. Home: 20 Lake Louise Dr Sylacauga AL 35150 Office: Avondale Mills Avondale Ave Sylacauga AL 35150

EDMUNDS, STAHRL WILLIAM, former university dean and official, educator; b. Cambridge, Minn., May 15, 1917; s. Adoniran W. and Axeline (Holmgren) E.; m. Amy Margaret Klein, Aug. 17, 1940; children: Dewey Edmunds, Laura (Mrs. Robert Newman), Rollin. B.B.A. with distinction, U. Minn., 1939, M.A., 1941. Exec. asst. to pres. Northwestern Nat. Life Ins. Co., 1945-53; economist McGraw-Hill Pub. Co., also Nat. City Bank, N.Y.C., 1953-55, Ford Motor Co., 1955-58; marketing dir. Hughes Aircraft Co., 1959-65; indsl. devel. adviser Govt. of Ecuador of State Dept., 1966-67; vice chancellor U. Calif. at Riverside, 1967-69, dean, 1969—; Mem. research com. U. S. C. of C., 1953-55; mem. Tech. Adv. Com. Econ. Devel. Calif., 1961-65; mem. sci. adv. com. to Calif. Assembly, 1970—. Author articles in field. Bd. dirs. Riverside Community Hosp., 1968-70. Served to lt. (s.g.) USNR, 1941-45. Mem. Am. Econ. Assn., Am. Mktg. Assn. Home: 1921 Arroyo Dr Riverside CA 92506

EDRIS, PAUL MILBURN, clergyman; b. Spring Creek Twp., Iowa, July 28, 1909; s. Frank Milburn and Carrie Edith (Nichol) E.; m. Jane Alice Glascock, Sept. 8, 1930; children: James Edwin, Robert Paul. A.B., Maryville (Tenn.) Coll., 1932, D.D., 1957; B.D., Louisville Presbyn. Sem., 1935. Ordained to ministry Presbyterian Ch., 1935; pastor chs. in, Ky., 1935-39; pastor First Presbyn. Ch., Daytona Beach, Fla., 1939-75; moderator Presbytery St. Johns, Fla., 1955, Synod Fla., 1956-57, Gen. Assembly Presbyn. Ch. in U.S., 1975-76, chmn. operational bd. mission bd., 1976—; trustee Fla. Presbyn. Coll. (now Eckerd Coll.), 1958-77; bd. dirs. Columbia Theol. Sem., 1974-75, 77-79. Contbr. ch. publs. Mem. Daytona Beach Interracial Adv. Bd., 1953-70; pres. Daytona Beach YMCA, 1941-46. Democrat. Club: Daytona Beach Rotary (past pres.). Address: 301 Morningside Ave Daytona Beach FL 32018 *The quality of human life is determined not by "success", whatever that is interpreted to mean, not by ease and comfort of living, but by significance. That person is a happy person who feels that his/her life is significant.*

EDSALL, KENNETH RICHARD, utility exec.; b. Des Moines, Dec. 6, 1926; s. Irving K. and Irene (Wupper) E.; m. Arlene Wilson; children—Diane Fuller, Claudia Anne. A.B., U. Wichita, 1949; LL.B., U. So. Calif., 1956. Bar: Calif. bar 1957. Atty. firm Best, Best & Krieger, Riverside, Calif., 1957-59, Calif. Electric Power Co., Rialto, 1959-63; atty. Pacific Lighting Corp., Los Angeles, 1963-75, v.p., sec., gen. counsel, 1975—. Served with AUS, 1944-46. Mem. Am. Gas Assn., Pacific Coast Gas Assn., Am., Fed. Energy Bar Assn., Los Angeles County Bar Assn., Am. Gas Assn., Am. Soc. Corporate Secs., State Bar Calif., Conf. Calif. Pub. Utility Counsel, Phi Alpha Delta. Club: Jonathan (Los Angeles). Office: 810 S Flower St Los Angeles CA 90017

EDSON, SANDRA JENE, association executive; b. Gothenburg, Nebr., May 10, 1948; d. Darwin Elmer and Eunice Eileen (Anderson) E. B.S. in Bus. Adminstrn., U. Denver, 1972. C.P.A., Colo. Ptnr. Thomas A. Ward & Co., C.P.A.s, Denver, 1972-80; v.p. Fleming Assn., Denver, 1980-82; exec. dir. Am. Soc. Quality Control, Milw., 1982—. Pres. Mental Health Assn. Colo., 1982. Named Vol. of Yr. Mental Health Assn. Colo., 1977. Mem. Colo. Soc. C.P.A.s (dir. 1980-82), Am. Soc. Assn. Execs., Am. Ins. C.P.A.s. Office: Am Soc Quality Control 230 W Wells St 7000 Milwaukee WI 53203

EDSON, WILLIAM ALDEN, electrical engineer; b. Burchard, Nebr., Oct. 30, 1912; s. William Henry and Pearl (Montgomery) E.; m. Saralou Peterson, Aug. 23, 1942; children: Judith Lynne, Margaret Jane, Carolyn Louise. B.S. (Summerfield scholar), U. Kans., 1934, M.S., 1935; D.Sc. (Gordon McKay scholar), Harvard U., 1937. Mem. tech. staff Bell Telephone Labs., Inc., N.Y.C., 1937-41, supr., 1943-45; asst. prof. elec. engring. Ill. Inst. Tech., Chgo., 1941-43; prof. physics Ga. Inst. Tech., Atlanta, 1945-46, prof. elec. engring., 1946-51, dir. sch. elec. engring., 1951-52; vis. prof., research asso. Stanford U., 1952-56, cons. prof., 1956; mgr. Klystron sub-sect. Gen. Electric Microwave Lab., Palo Alto, Calif., 1955-61; v.p., dir. research Electromagnetic Tech. Corp., Palo Alto, 1961-62, pres., 1962-70; sr. scientist Vidar Corp., Mountain View, Calif., 1970—71; asst. dir. Radio Physics Lab., SRI Internat., Menlo Park, Calif., 1971-77, staff scientist, 1977—; cons. high frequency sect. Nat. Bur. Standards, 1951-64; dir. Western Electronic Show and Conv., 1975-79. Author: (with Robert I. Sarbacher) Hyper and Ultra-High Frequency Engineering, 1943, Vacuum-Tube Oscillators, 1953. Fellow IEEE (chmn. San Francisco sect. 1963-64, com. standards piezoelectricity 1950—); mem. Am. Phys. Soc., Sigma Xi, Tau Beta Pi, Sigma Tau, Phi Kappa Phi, Eta Kappa Nu, Pi Mu Epsilion. Home: 25346 La Loma Dr Los Altos Hills CA 94022 Office: 333 Ravenswood Ave Menlo Park CA 94025

EDWARD, JOHN THOMAS, chemist, educator; b. London, Mar. 23, 1919; s. John William and Jessie Christina (Simpson) E. (parents Can. citizens); m. Deirdre Mary Waldron, Mar. 21, 1953; children: John Valentine, Jeremy Bryan, Julian Kevin. B.S., McGill U., Montreal, Que., Can., 1939, Ph.D., 1942; D.Phil., Oxford U., Eng., 1949; M.A., Dublin U., Ireland, 1955, Sc.D., 1971. Postdoctoral fellow Iowa State U., 1942-43; research scientist div. explosives NRC Can., Ottawa, Ont., 1943-45; lectr. U. Man., Can., 1946-47; Imperial Chem. Industries research fellow U. Birmingham, Eng., 1949-52; lectr. Trinity Coll., Dublin U., 1952-56; mem. faculty McGill U., 1956—, asst. prof. chemistry, 1957-61, assoc. prof., 1961-66, prof., 1966—, MacDonald prof. chemistry, 1973—. Contbr. articles to profl. publs. Fellow Royal Soc. Can., Chem. Inst. Can.; mem. Am. Chem. Soc., Order Chemists Que., AAAS. Home: 51 Chesterfield Montreal PQ Canada H3Y 2M4 Office: Dept Chemistry McGill U 801 Sherbrooke St W Montreal PQ Canada H3A 2K6

EDWARDS, ALFRED LEROY, economist; b. Key West, Fla., Aug. 9, 1920; s. Eddie E. and Kathleen L. E.; m. Willie Mae Lewis, June 4, 1949; children—Beryl L., Alfred Leroy. B.S., Livingstone Coll., Salisbury, N.C., 1948; M.A., U. Mich., 1949; Ph.D., U. Iowa, 1957. Spl. asst. to commnr. Consumer Product Safety Commn., Washington, 1973-74; dep. asst. sec. agr., 1963-74; asst. prof. econs. Mich. State U., East Lansing, 1957-60, prof., 1974—, dir. research, 1974—; econ. advisor to, Nigeria, 1960-62; mem. adv. com. equal opportunity Dept. Agr., 1979; dir. Security Bankcorp., Southgate, Mich.; cons. in field. Trustee Western Mich. U. Served with USAAF, 1943-46. Postdoctoral fellow Ford Found., 1957, U. Mich., 1958; Danforth Faculty fellow, 1956. Mem. Am. Econs. Assn., Nat. Econs. Assn. Presbyterian. Office: Grad Sch Bus Adminstrn Univ Mich Ann Arbor MI 48109

EDWARDS, ARTHUR ANDERSON, mech. engr.; b. Bklyn., Sept. 18, 1926; s. Arthur Caldwell and Alice (Anderson) E.; m. Beulah Schwarcz, June 8, 1973; children—Lisa, Julie. B.S.M.E., Duke U., 1947. Engr. Krey and Hunt (Cons. Engrs.), N.Y.C., 1947-57, partner, 1957-67; prin. Arthur A. Edwards (Cons. Engr.), N.Y.C., 1967—; pres. Edwards and Zuck (P.C.), N.Y.C., 1976—. Served to lt. j.g. USNR, 1944-47. Fellow Am. Cons. Engrs. Council; mem. Am. Arbitration Assn., Am. Soc. Heating Refrigeration Air Conditioning Engrs., ASME, Nat. Soc. Profl. Engrs., N.Y. Assn. Cons. Engrs. (pres. 1968-70), Soc. Am. Mil. Engrs. Episcopalian. Home: 420 E 51st St New York NY 10022 Office: 330 W 42d St New York NY 10036

EDWARDS, BENJAMIN FRANKLIN, III, investment banker; b. St. Louis, Oct. 26, 1931; s. Presley William and Virginia (Barker) E.; m. Joan Moberly, June 13, 1953; children: Scott P., Benjamin Franklin IV, Pamela M. Edwards Bunn, Susan B. B.A., Princeton U., 1953. With A.G. Edwards & Sons, Inc., St. Louis, 1956—, pres., 1967—, chmn., 1983—; dir. Jefferson Bank and Trust Co., Psychol. Assocs., Helig-Meyers, Inc. Bd. dirs. Inroads. Served with USNR, 1953-56. Mem. Investment Bankers Assn. (gov. 1968—), Securities Industry Assn. (gov. 1974—, chmn. 1980—), Mo. Hist. Soc. (dir.). Presbyterian. Clubs: Noonday, Old Warson Country (St. Louis); Bogey. Home: 9846 Old Warson Rd Saint Louis MO 63124 Office: One N Jefferson Saint Louis MO 63103

EDWARDS, BLAKE, film director; b. Tulsa, July 26, 1922; m. Julie Andrews. Ed. high sch. Writer: radio shows Line-Up; writer-creator: radio show Richard Diamond; creator: TV show Mr. Lucky; co-producer, writer: film Panhandle, Stampede; writer: mus. version Notorious Landlady; writer-dir.: movies This Happy Feeling; dir.: films The Carey Treatment; producer, co-writer, dir.: Gunn; co-writer, dir.: The Great Race; producer, co-writer, dir.: The Pink Pather Strikes Again; producer, dir.: Experiment in Terror; producer, dir., writer: 10, S.O.B., Victor/Victoria, The Trial of the Pink Panther; writer, dir., co-producer: Wild Rovers, Curse of the Pink Panther, The Man Who Loved Women. Served with USCGR, World War II. Office: care Dirs Guild Am 7950 W Sunset Blvd Hollywood CA 90046 *

EDWARDS, BRYAN C., gas company executive. Chmn. AMOCO Gas Co., Chgo. Office: AMOCO Gas Co 200 E Randolph Chicago IL 60601

EDWARDS, CHARLES CORNELL, physician, research administrator; b. Overton, Nebr., Sept. 16, 1923; s. Charles Busby and Lillian Margaret (Arendt) E.; m. Sue Cowles Kruidenier, June 24, 1945; children: Timothy, Charles Cornell, Nancy, David. Student, Princeton U., 1941-43; B.A., U. Colo., 1945, M.D., 1948; M.S., U. Minn., 1956; L.L.D. (hon.), Phila. Coll. Pharmacy and Sci., L.H.D., Pa. Coll. Podiatry. Diplomate: Am. Bd. Surgery. Intern St. Mary's Hosp., Mpls., 1948-49; resident surgery Mayo Found., 1950-56; pvt. practice medicine specializing in surgery, Des Moines, 1956-61; mem. surg. staff Georgetown U., Washington, 1961-62; also cons. USPHS; dir. div. socio-econ. activities A.M.A., Chgo., 1963-67; v.p., mng. officer health and sci. affairs Booz, Allen & Hamilton, 1967-69; commr. FDA, Washington, 1969-73; asst. sec. for health HEW, Washington, 1973-75; sr. v.p., dir. Becton, Dickinson & Co., 1975-77; pres. Scripps Clinic and Research Found., La Jolla, Calif., 1977—; Mem. health adv. com. Princeton; mem. health econ. com. Leonard R. Davis Inst., U. Pa.; adj. prof. surgery Cornell U. Med. Center; mem. nat. policy bd. Modern Medicine; bd. dirs. World Rehab. Found., Huntingdon (Eng.) Research Ctr.; former pres. Nat. Health Council; trustee Centenary Coll. for Women, Caneer Inst. N.J.; adj. prof. surgery Cornell U. Med. Center; trustee-at-large Nat. Kidney Found.; adv. com. Robert Wood Johnson Found. Program for Prepaid Managed Health Care; overseers com. Harvard U.; mem. policy adv. com. Nat. Bd. Med. Examiners; mem. com. on technology and internat. econ. and trade issues NRC; Nat. Acad Engring., 1980—. Served to lt. M.C. USNR, 1942-46. Fellow A.C.S.; mem. AMA, Soc. Med. Adminstrs., U.S. Pharmacopeia 11360, Inst. Critical Care Medicine, Am. Pharm. Assn. (hon.), Chgo. Gynecol. Soc. (hon.), Acad. Pharm. Scis., Am. Hosp. Assn., San Diego C. of C. (dir.), Food and Drug Law Inst., Am. Pub. Health Assn., Health Policy Adv. Group. Clubs: University (Washington); Chevy Chase, Princeton La Jolla Country. Office: Keeney Park 10666 N Torrey Pines Rd La Jolla CA 92037

EDWARDS, CHARLES EDWARD, business administration educator; b. Charleston, S.C., July 19, 1930; s. Edward and Elizabeth (Orr) E.; m. Carol Latimer Little, Apr. 28, 1951; children: Mary Lynn, Charles Edward, Betty Ann, John Orr. B.S., Ga. Inst. Tech., 1952, M.S., 1953; Ph.D., U. N.C., Chapel Hill, 1961. Part time instr. Ga. Inst. Tech., Atlanta, 1952-53, U. N.C., Chapel Hill, 1955-58; asst. prof. U. S.C., Columbia, 1959-63, assoc. prof., 1963-68, prof. bus. adminstrn., 1968—; dir. Child Centers, Inc., Columbus, Ga. Author: Dynamics of the U.S. Automobile Industry, 1965; contbr. articles to profl. jours. Served with USAF, 1953-55. Faculty fellow for advanced research and study So. Fellowship Fund, 1958-59; Ford. Found. regional seminar in econs., summer 1962. Mem. Am. Fin. Assn., Fin. Mgmt. Assn., Soc. History of Tech., So. Fin. Assn. Presbyterian. Home: 4615 Limestone St Columbia SC 29206 Office: U SC Columbia SC 29208

EDWARDS, CHARLES ELVIN, mfg. co. exec.; b. Ridgeway, N.C., Oct. 31, 1928; s. Clyde Raymond and Elizabeth Lorena (Hayes) E.; m. Linda Williams, June 14, 1950; children—Charles Elvin, Brenda Kay. B.S., N.C. State U.; postgrad., Syracuse U., 1975. Engr., mgr. tech. services Dayco Co., N.C. and Ohio, 1950-67; plant mgr. 3 Rivers Rubber Co., 1967-69; with Bandag, Inc., Muscatine, Iowa, 1969—, now pres., chief exec. officer. Served with USAF. Mem. ASME, Am. Mfrs. Assn. Republican. Methodist. Clubs: Mason, Elks. Patentee in field. Office: Bandag Inc Bandag Center Muscatine IA 52761 *

EDWARDS, CHARLES HAYDEN, railroad exec.; b. Louisville, June 24, 1924; s. James P. and Margaret (Wathen) E.; m. Sara Hulette Cummins, June 7, 1958; children—Richard Wathen, Cecilia Barber. A.B., Harvard, 1948; LL.B., U. Va., 1951. Bar: Ky. bar 1951. Asst. city atty., Louisville, 1952-57, pvt. practice law, 1957-58; with L. & N. R.R., 1958—, sec., gen. atty., 1965-66, sec., treas., 1967—, v.p., 1972—; also v.p. and corp. sec. all corps. comprising The Family Lines Rail System. Trustee Aquinas Prep. Sch., 1965-67; campaign chmn. Louisville Fund for Arts, 1973, pres., 1974. Mem. Am., Ky., Louisville bar assns., Assn. Am. R.R. (chmn. treasury div.). Democrat. Roman Catholic. Clubs: Louisville Country, Tavern (pres. 1970), Filson; River Valley (Louisville) (pres. 1973-74); Harmony Landing Country (Goshen, Ky.)). Home: 465 Lightfoot Rd Louisville KY 40207 Office: 908 W Broadway Louisville KY 40201

EDWARDS, CHARLES MUNDY, JR., management consultant, former university dean; b. Richmond, Va., Nov. 2, 1903; s. Charles Mundy and Lelia Le Moyne (Gahagan) E.; m. Nancy Blow Rawls, Apr. 2, 1931 (dec. Nov. 1968); children—Charles M. III, Richard Franklin; m. Marie Elizabeth Flannery, Oct. 10, 1969. B.S. in Bus. Adminstrn, U. Richmond, 1925, LL.D. (hon.), 1963; M.S. in Retailing, N.Y. U., 1930, D.C.S., 1936. Instr. English, head track coach Staunton Mil. Acad., Va., 1925-29; with mgmt. div. James McCreery & Co., N.Y.C., 1929-30; merchandising and sales promotion exec. Frederick Loeser & Co., Bklyn., 1930-31; with Inst. Retail Mgmt. N.Y. U., 1930—, successively lectr., instr., asst. prof., asso. prof., prof., 1943-63, Mchts. Council prof. retail mgmt., 1964-70, dean, 1946-70, sr. dean univ., 1959-70, dean emeritus, prof. emeritus, 1970—; cons. retailers and mfrs., 1936—; sr. v.p. Search Assos., Inc., Summit, N.J.; dir. Russ Togs, Inc., Concord Fabrics, Inc., Old Deerfield Fabrics, Inc. Author: (with William H. Howard) Retail Advertising and Sales Promotion, 1936, rev. edit., 1943, 3d edit, (with Russell A. Brown), 1959, 4th edit, (with Carl F. Lebowitz), 1981, The Retail Advertising Budget, 1950, rev. edit., 1952; Editor: The Retailing Series, 1946-63; chmn. editorial bd.: Jour. Retailing, 1946-73. Served from 2d lt. to capt., CAC U.S. Army Res., 1924-37; organizer, dir. Army Exchange Service Sch.; ETO; with assimilated rank col., 1945. Decorated chevalier Ordre Du Merité Commercial, France; recipient Gold medal for distinguished service to retailing Nat. Retail Mchts. Assn., 1958, named One of All-Time Greats in retail sales promotion, 1969; named to Retail Advt. Hall of Fame, 1958; named to Retail Educators Hall of Fame, 1981. Mem. Nat. Retail Mchts. Assn. (dir. 1951-53), Am. Marketing Assn., Am. Collegiate Retailing Assn. (founding mem., pres. 1948-49), Kappa Alpha, Omicron Delta Kappa, Eta Mu Pi, Alpha Delta Sigma. Methodist. Home: 65 Hobart Ave Summit NJ 07901 Office: Tisch Hall Washington Sq New York NY 10003

EDWARDS, DON, congressman; b. San Jose, Calif., Jan. 6, 1915; s. Leonard P. and Clara (Donlon) E.; children—Leonard P., Samuel D., Bruce H., Thomas C., William D. A.B., Stanford, 1936; student, Law Sch., 1936-38. Agt. FBI, 1940-41; mem. 88th-93d congresses from 9th Calif. Dist., 94th-97th congresses from 10th Calif. Dist.; Nat. chmn. Americans for Democratic Action, 1965—. Served to lt. USNR, 1941-45. Democrat. Unitarian. Office: House Office Bldg Washington DC 20515

EDWARDS, DONALD KENNETH, mechanical engineer, educator; b. Richmond, Calif., Oct. 11, 1932; s. Samuel Harrison and Georgette Marie (Bas) E.; m. Nathalie Beatrice Snow, Oct. 11, 1955; children: Victoria Ann, Richard Earl. B.S. with highest honors in Mech. Engring., U. Calif.-, Berkeley, 1954, M.S. in Mech. Engring., 1956, Ph.D., 1959. Thermodynamics engr. missile systems div. Lockheed Aircraft Co., Palo Alto, Calif., 1958-59; asst. prof. engring. UCLA, 1959-63, assoc. prof., 1963-68, prof., 1968-81, chmn. dept. chem., nuclear and thermal engring., 1975-78; prof. U. Calif.-Irvine, 1981—, chmn. dept. mech. engring, 1982; dir., chmn. bd. Gier Dunkle Instruments, Inc., 1963-66. Author: (with others) Transfer Processes, 1973, 2d edit., 1979; Assoc. editor: ASME Jour. Heat Transfer, 1975-80, Solar Energy, 1982—; contbr. articles to profl. jours. Fellow ASME (Heat Transfer Meml. award 1973); Mem. Optical Soc. Am., Internat. Solar Energy Soc., AIAA (first Thermophysics award 1976), Phi Beta Kappa, Sigma Xi, Pi Tau Sigma, Tau Beta Pi. Office: Mechanical Engring Dept Univ of California Irvine Irvine CA 92717 *

EDWARDS, DONALD MERVIN, educator; b. Tracy, Minn., Apr. 16, 1938; s. Mervin B. and Helen L. (Halstenrud) E.; m. Judith Lee Wilson, Aug. 8, 1964; children: John, Joel, Jeffrey, Mary. B.S., S.D. State U., 1960, M.S., 1961; Ph.D. in Agrl. Engring, Purdue U., 1966. Registered profl. engr., Nebr. With Soil Conservation Service, U.S. Dept. Agr., Marshall, Minn., 1957-62; teaching, research asst. S.D.

State U. and Purdue U., 1960-66; asso. prof. agrl. engring. U. Nebr. at Lincoln, 1966-71, prof., 1971-80; asst. dean Coll. Engring. and Tech., 1970-73; asso. dean, dir. Engring. Research Center, 1973-80; dir. Energy Research and Devel. Center, 1976-80; prof. and chmn. dept. agrl. engring Mich. State U., East Lansing, 1980—; collaborator, cons. to numerous industries and agys., 1966—; mem. Engring Accreditation Commn. of Accreditation Bd for Engring. and Tech. Contbr. numerous articles on irrigation, water pollution, remote sensing, energy, engring. edn. to profl. jours. Active Boy Scouts Am., Am. Field Service, 4-H; bd. dirs. Nat. Safety Council; mem. adv. bd. local sch.; past chmn. bd. dirs. Lincoln Transp. System.; mem. Christian edn. com. East Lansing Trinity Ch. Mem. Profl. Engrs. Nebr. (v.p. 1976-77), Mich. Soc. Profl. Engrs. (nat. dir.), Nat. Soc. Profl. Engrs., AAAS, Am. Soc. Agrl. Engrs. (nat. dir. profl. dept. 1977-79), Nat. Assn. Coll. Tchrs. Agr., Internat. Water Resources Assn., Sigma Xi, Alpha Gamma Rho. Clubs: Farmhouse, Triangle. Home: 4557 Arrow Head Rd Okemos MI 48864

EDWARDS, DOUGLAS, radio, television news reporter; b. Ada, Okla., July 14, 1917; s. Tony and Alice (Donaldson) E.; m. Sara Byrd, Aug. 29, 1939; children: Lynn Alice, Robert Anthony, Donna Claire; m. May H. Dunbar, May 10, 1966. Student, U. Ala., 1934-35, Emory U., 1936, U. Ga., 1937-38. Jr. announcer radio sta. WHET, Troy, Ala., 1932-35; mem. radio news staff radio sta. WSB, Atlanta and Atlanta Jour., 1935-38; news reporter radio sta. WXYZ, Detroit, 1938-42; fgn. corr., Britain, France, Germany, Middle East, 1945-46, anchored 1st CBS-TV polit. conv. gavel-to-gavel coverage, 1948. Features Report to the Nation, CBS, N.Y.C., 1942-45; feature World News Round Up and TV News, since 1946. Recipient Peabody award for news, 1955. Mem. Radio-TV Corrs. Assn., Washington Assn. Radio and TV Analysts, Sigma Delta Chi. Clubs: Field (New Canaan, Conn.); Overseas Press (N.Y.C.). Office: Columbia Broadcasting System 51 W 52d St New York NY 10019 *

EDWARDS, EDWARD EVERETT, emeritus finance educator; b. Bloomfield, Ind., July 15, 1908; s. Lewis Baker and Alta Ethel (Terrell) E.; m. Louise Robinson, Sept. 2, 1933; children: Robert Alan, Margaret Louise. B.S., Ind. U., 1928, M.S., 1934. Methods investigator Western Electric Co., 1928-31; statistician Ind. Dept. Financial Instns., 1933-36; Ind. dir. Nat. Youth Adminstrn., 1935- 36; asst. prof. Ind. U., Bloomington, 1936-41, asso. prof., 1941-48, prof. finance, 1948-62, Fred T. Greene prof. finance, 1962-73, prof. finance emeritus, 1973—; asso. dir. Grad. Sch. Savs. and Loan, 1946-62; v.p. Bus. and Real Estate Trends, Inc., 1949—; cons. to chmn. Fed. Home Loan Bank Bd., 1961-62, 82-83; dir. Irwin Union Bank, Columbus, Ind., 1963-81, Gt. N.W. Fed. Savs. and Loan Assn.; vis. prof. Ariz. State U., 1968-69, 80; adv. com. 1950 and 1960 Census of Housing; cons. White House, Sec. Def., Sec. Army, 1948-50, FDIC, 1964-65, Commn. Fin. Structure and Regulation, 1970-72; dir. Fed. Home Loan Bank Indpls., 1963-64. Cons. editor: MGIC newsletter, 1968-76. Served from capt. to lt. col. finance dept. AUS, 1942-46. Recipient Disting. Alumnus award Ind. U., 1982. Mem. Am. Finance Assn. (sec.-treas. 1947-51, pres. 1952), Am. Econ. Assn., Beta Gamma Sigma, Delta Sigma Pi. Democrat. Methodist. Home: 2608 E 2d St Bloomington IN 47401

EDWARDS, EDWIN WASHINGTON, lawyer, governor of Louisiana; b. Marksville, La., Aug. 7, 1927; s. Clarence W. and Agnes (Brouillette) E.; m. Elaine Schwartzenburg, Apr. 5, 1949; children: Anna Edwards Edmonds, Victoria Elaine Edwards Arledge, Stephen Randolph, David Edwin. J.D., La. State U., 1949. Bar: La. 1949. Practiced in, Crowley, La., 1949—, Baton Rouge, La., 1980—; sr. partner firm Edwards, Edwards & Broadhurst; mem. Crowley City Council, 1954-62, La. Senate from 35th dist., 1964-66; mem. 89th-92d Congresses from 7th La. dist.; gov. State of La., 1972-80, 84—; Chmn. Interstate Oil Compact Commn., Ozarks Regional Commn., So. Govs.' Conf., So. Regional Energy Adv. Bd. Served with USNR, World War II. Mem. Internat. Rice Festival, Greater Crowley C. of C., Crowley Indsl. Found., Am. Legion. Democrat. Roman Catholic. Club: Lion. Office: 15919 Highland Rd Baton Rouge LA 70810

EDWARDS, ELLEN JOY, book editor; b. Norwich, Conn., Jan. 26, 1954; d. John Owen and Marilyn Joy (McGinniss) E. B.A. in English summa cum laude, Drew U., 1977. Editorial asst. Dell Pub., N.Y.C., 1978-80, asst. editor, 1980-81; assoc. editor Berkeley Pub. Group, N.Y.C., 1981-82, sr. editor Second Chance at Love series, 1982—. Office: 7 Berkeley Publishing Group 200 Madison Ave New York NY 10016

EDWARDS, ERNEST PRESTON, biologist; b. Landour, India, Sept. 25, 1919; s. Preston Hampton and Mabel (Griffith) E.; m. Mabel Jean Thacher, Apr. 9, 1955. B.A., U. Va., 1940; M.A., Cornell U., 1941, Ph.D., 1949. Instr. zoology U. Ky., 1949-50; civilian employe U.S. Army Chem. Corps, Camp Detrick, Md., 1952-54; asst. prof. biology Hanover Coll., 1955; screen tour lectr. Nat. Audubon Soc., 1955-59; assoc. dir. Houston Museum Natural History, 1957-60; prof. biology U. of Pacific, 1960-65; prof. Sweet Briar Coll., 1965—, Duberg prof. ecology, 1978—. Author: Finding Birds in Mexico, 2d edit, 1968, (with Horace Loftin) Finding Birds in Panama, 1971, A Field Guide to the Birds of Mexico, 1972, A Coded List of Birds of the World, 1974, A Coded Workbook of Birds of the World, Vol. I: Non-Passerines, 1982. Served with USAAF, 1942-44; Chem. Corps U.S. Army, 1945-46, 51-52. Mem. Am. Ornithologists Union, Wilson Ornithol. Soc., Cooper Ornithol. Soc., Va. Soc. Ornithology, Phi Beta Kappa, Sigma Xi. Democrat. Presbyterian. Office: Sweet Briar Coll Sweet Briar VA 24595

EDWARDS, ESTHER, rec., film, entertainment co. exec.; b. Oconee, Ga., Apr. 25; d. Berry and Bertha Ida (Fuller) Gordy; m. George H. Edwards, Apr. 12, 1951; 1 son (by previous marriage), Robert Bullock. Ed., Howard U., Wayne State U. Sr. v.p., sec., dir. Motown Record Corp., Detroit, 1959—; sec., dir. Jobete Music Pub. Co., Inc., 1959—; sr. v.p., corporate sec. Motown Industries, Hollywood, Calif. and; Detroit, 1973—; dir. Bank of the Commonwealth, 1972-79. Bd. dirs. Detroit Econ. Growth Corp.; exec. dir. Gordy Found., 1968—; chmn. Wayne County Democratic Women's Com., 1956; Mich. del.-at-large Dem. Nat. Conv., 1960; bd. dirs. Martin Luther King Center for Social Change. Mem. Greater Detroit C. of C. (treas., exec. bd. 1973-79), Central Bus. Dist. Assn. Detroit (v.p. exec. bd.), Met. Detroit Conv. and Visitors Bur. (v.p. exec. bd.), Econ. Club Detroit (dir.), African Am. Heritage Assn. (founder/chmn.), Alpha Kappa Alpha, Gamma Phi Delta. Office: Motown Industries 2648 W Grand Blvd Detroit MI 48208 also 6255 Sunset Blvd Hollywood CA 90028 *I accredit my accomplishments to keeping an open mind, thoroughly evaluating and re-evaluating any offer or situation before making a decision; taking advantage of every offered opportunity that provides an education or broadens my experiences; assuming responsibility while remaining goal-oriented; setting priorities; promoting harmony and unity; performing to the ultimate of my ability.*

EDWARDS, GEORGE ALVA, physician, educator; b. Killeen, Tex., Oct. 19, 1916; s. John Clem and Maude May (Lam) E.; m. Winnie Belle Landes, Jan. 23, 1946; children—Karen Leigh, David Glen. B.A., Howard Payne Coll., 1939; postgrad., N. Tex. State Coll., 1946; M.D., U. Tex., Southwestern Med. Sch., 1950. Intern Johns Hopkins Hosp., Balt., 1950-51, resident, 1952-53, Duke Hosp., Durham, N.C., 1951-52, Firmin Desloge Hosp., St. Louis, 1953-54; asst. chief med. service VA, St. Louis, 1954-55; chief med. service, VA Hosp., McKinney, Tex., 1955-59, Pitts., 1959-66; asst. chief med. service VA Hosp., Dallas, 1966-68, chief of staff, 1972—, chief med. service, Cin., 1968-72; asst. prof. U. Tex., Southwestern Med. Sch., Dallas, 1955-59, asso. prof., 1966-68, prof. medicine, 1972—, asst. dean, 1973—; asso. prof. U. Pitts., 1959-66; prof. medicine U. Cin., 1968-72. Served with USAAF, 1940-46. Decorated Air medal. Fellow A.C.P.; mem. Alpha Omega Alpha. Baptist. Home: 3630 Granada Ave Dallas TX 75205 Office: 4500 S Lancaster Rd Dallas TX 75216

EDWARDS, GEORGE CLIFTON, JR., judge; b. Dallas, Aug. 6, 1914; s. George Clifton and Octavia (Nichols) E.; m. Margaret McConnell, Apr. 10, 1939; children: George Clifton III, James McConnell. B.A., So. Meth. U., 1933; M.A., Harvard U., 1934; J.D., Detroit Coll. Law, 1949. Bar: Mich. 1944. Coll. sec. League Indsl. Democracy, 1934-35; prodn. worker Kelsey Hayes Wheel Co., 1936; rep. UAW-CIO, 1937, dir. welfare dept., 1938-39; dir., sec. Detroit Housing Commn., 1940-41; mem. Detroit Common Council, 1941-49, pres., 1945-49; with firm Edwards & Bohn, Detroit, 1946-50, Rothe, Marston, Edwards and Bohn, 1950-51; probate judge charge Wayne County Juvenile Ct., 1951-54; judge Jud. Circuit, Wayne County, 1954-56; justice Supreme Ct., Mich., 1956-62; commr. of police, City Detroit, 1962-63; judge U.S. Ct. Appeals 6th Circuit, 1963—, chief judge, 1979—; chmn. com. adminstrn. criminal laws Jud. Conf. U.S., 1966-70; mem. Nat. Com. Reform of Fed. Criminal Laws, 1967-71. Author: The Police on the Urban Frontier, 1968, (with others) The Law of Criminal Correction, 1963, Pioneer-at-Law, 1974; also articles on crime and delinquency. Chmn. S.E. Mich. Cancer Crusade, 1950-51; chmn. 13th Congressional Dist. Democratic party Wayne County, 1950-51. Served from pvt. to lt., inf. AUS, 1943-46. Recipient award for community work for social progress Workmen's Circle, 1949; award for community work for civil rights St. Cyprian's Episcopal Ch., 1950; Americanism award Jewish War Vets., 1953; award for outstanding achievement juvenile rehab. VFW, 1953; St. Peter's medal for outstanding service to youth St. Peter's Episcopal Ch., Detroit, 1956; August Vollmer award Am. Soc. Criminology, 1966; Judiciary award Assn. Fed. Investigators, 1971. Mem. VFW, Am. Legion, Am., Mich., Detroit bar assns., Nat. Council Judges, Nat. Council Crime and Delinquency, Am. Law Inst., Phi Beta Kappa, Kappa Sigma. Democrat. Episcopalian. Club: Masons. Home: 4057 Egbert Cincinnati OH 45220 Office: US Courthouse Cincinnati OH 45202

EDWARDS, GEORGE KENT, lawyer; b. Ogden, Utah, Oct. 3, 1939; s. George and S. Ruth (Engelke) E.; m. Patricia Ann Brown, Sept. 16, 1972; children: Scott M., Stacey R., Mark D. B.A., Occidental Coll., 1961; J.D., U. Calif. at Berkeley, 1964. Bar: Calif. 1965, Alaska 1966. Legislative counsel Alaska Legislature, 1964-66; partner firm Stevens, Savage, Holland, Erwin & Edwards, Anchorage, 1966-67; dep. atty. gen., Alaska, 1967-68, atty. gen., 1968-70; U.S. atty. Dist. Alaska, 1971-77; individual legal practice, 1977-81; partner firm Hartig Rhodes Norman Mahoney & Edwards, Anchorage, 1981—; mem. Nat. Conf. Commrs. Uniform State Laws, 1968-70; chmn. Gov. Alaska Planning Council Adminstrn. Criminal Justice, 1968-70; guest lectr. bus. law U. Alaska, 1981-82; guest editorial columnist Anchorage Times, 1982—. Pres. Greater Anchorage Area Young Republicans, 1967; orgn. chmn. Southcentral Alaska Rep. Commn., 1966-67; pres. Lake Otis PTA, 1975-76; pres. bd. dirs. Miss Alaska Scholarship Pageant, 1980—; bd. dirs. Anchorage Crime Stoppers, 1981—; pres. Common Sense Alaska, 1982—. Mem. Am., Calif., Alaska bar assns., Nat. Assn. Attys. Gen., Phi Delta Phi, Sigma Alpha Epsilon (Outstanding Sr. award Calif. Epsilon chpt. 1961). Home: 2113 Duke Dr Anchorage AK 99504 Office: Suite 102 717 K St Anchorage AK 99501

EDWARDS, GILBERT FRANKLIN, educator, sociologist; b. Charleton, S.C., June 2, 1915; s. Gilbert Franklin and Bertha (Allen) E.; m. Peggy Jarvis Park, Sept. 8, 1946; 1 dau., Donalee Marie. A.B., Fisk U., 1936; Ph.D., U. Chgo., 1952. Tchr. social studies Fessenden (Fla.) Acad., 1937-39; mem. faculty Howard U., Washington, 1941—, prof. sociology, 1960—; Vis. tchr. Washington U., St. Louis, summer 1954, Harvard, summer 1967, 68; cons. in field, 1961—; Pub. mem. Nat. Capital Planning Commn., 1965-71. Author: The Negro Professional Class, 1959; Editor: E. Franklin Frazier on Race Relations, 1968. Mem. Am. Sociol. Assn., White House Hist. Assn. (dir. 1979—), Eastern Social Soc., Population Assn. Am., Phi Beta Kappa (alumni mem.). Home: 4643 16th St NW Washington DC 20011

EDWARDS, GLENN THOMAS, history educator; b. Portland, Oreg., June 14, 1931; s. Glenn Thomas E. and Marie Ann (Cheska) McMullen; m. Nannette Wilhelmina, June 15, 1957; children: Randall Thomas, Stephanie Lynn. B.A., Willamette U., 1953; M.A., U. Oreg., 1960, Ph.D., 1963. Asst. prof. San Jose State U., 1962-64, Whitman Coll., Walla Walla, Wash., 1964-68, assoc. prof., 1968-75, prof., 1976—; cons. photography Wash. State Hist. Soc., 1980; cons. TV documentary Yakima Valley Mus. on William O. Douglas, Yakima, Wash., 1981-82; trustee Wash. Commn. of Humanities, Olympia, 1981—. Contbr. articles to profl. jours. Mem. pub. edn. adv. com. State Supt. of Pub. Instrn., Olympia, 1975-78; mem. bd. curators Wash. State Hist. Soc., 1983. Served with U.S. Army, 1954-56. Grantee Am Philos. Soc., 1971. Mem. Am. Hist. Assn., Orgn. Am. Historians, So. Hist. Assn., Oreg. Hist. Soc. Congregationalist. Office: Whitman Coll Walla Walla WA 99362

EDWARDS, HAROLD MILLS, lawyer, govt. ofcl.; b. Anson County, N.C., Nov. 20, 1930; s. William H. and Bertha (Baucom) E. B.S., Wake Forest U., 1953, LL.B., 1959. Bar: N.C. bar 1959. Practice law, Charlotte, N.C., 1959-75; chief legis. counsel to Senator Robert Morgan, Washington, 1975-76; U.S. atty., Western Dist. N.C., 1977-81, practice law, Charlotte, 1981—; judge Charlotte Municipal Ct., 1964-68; Mem. N.C. Bd. Alcoholic Control, 1970-73. Home: 5680C Grand Canal Way Charlotte NC 28226 Office: 900 Law Bldg Charlotte NC 28202

EDWARDS, HAROLD MORTIMER, mathematics educator; b. Champaign, Ill., Aug. 6, 1936; s. Harold Mortimer and Marian Bell (Scarlett) E.; m. Betty Rollin, Jan. 21, 1979. B.A., U. Wis., 1956; M.A., Columbia U., 1957; Ph.D., Harvard U., 1961. Instr. Harvard U., 1961-62; research assoc. Columbia U., 1962-63, asst. prof., 1963-66, N.Y. U., N.Y.C., 1966-69, assoc. prof., 1969-79, prof. math., 1979—; vis. sr. lectr. Australian Nat. U., 1971. Author: Advanced Calculus, 1969, Riemann's Zeta Function, 1974, Fermat's Last Theorem, 1977, Galois Theory, 1984. Guggenheim fellow, 1981-82. Mem. Am. Math. Soc. (Steele prize 1980), Math. Assn. Am., N.Y. Acad. Scis. Home: 24 W 55th St New York NY 10019 Office: 251 Mercer St New York NY 10012

EDWARDS, HARRY LEON, ins. co. exec.; b. Lafayette, Ga., June 12, 1921; s. William Fred and Hattie Mae (Harrison) E.; m. Mary Louise Hamm, Jan. 21, 1944; children—Thomas W. Edwards, Richard M. Edwards, Linda A. Edwards Johnson. Student, Berea Coll., 1939-41, George Washington U., 1942. Mgr. sales promotion Black Hills Power & Light Co., Rapid City, S.D., 1948-63; pres. Stockman Nat. Life Ins. Co., Rapid City, 1963-69; pres., dir. Nat. Western Life Ins. Co., Austin, Tex., 1969—, Comml. Adjusters, Inc., 1970—; sec., dir. Galvez Offshore Inc., 1976—. Bd. govs. Tex. Arts Alliance; chmn. bd. trustees St. Edwards U. Served with USMC, 1943-48. Mem. Austin C. of C., Nat. Assn. Life Underwriters, Life Office Mgmt. Assn. Republican. Roman Catholic. Clubs: Balcones Country, Lost Creek, Headliners, Capital, Austin, Elks. Home: 8707 Silverhill Ln Austin TX 78759 Office: 850 E Anderson Ln Austin TX 78776

EDWARDS, HARRY T., judge; b. N.Y.C., Nov. 3, 1940; m. Ila Hayes; children: Brent, Michelle. B.S., Cornell U., 1962; J.D., U. Mich., 1965. Assoc. firm Seyfarth, Shaw, Fairweather & Geraldson, Chgo., 1965-70; prof. law U. Mich., 1970-76, 77-80; vis. prof. law Harvard U., 1975-76, prof., 1976-77, part-time lectr. law, 1980—; now judge U.S. Ct. Appeals, Washington; vis. prof. Free U. Brussels, 1974; dir. AMTRAK, 1977-80, chmn. bd., 1979-80; disting. lectr. law Duke U., 1983—; Mem. Adminstrv. Conf. of U.S., 1976-80. Co-author: Labor Relations Law in the Public Sector, 1975, 79, Lawyer as a Negotiator, 1977, Collective Bargaining and Labor Arbitration, 1979, Higher Education and the Law, 1979. Mem. Nat. Acad. Arbitrators (dir. 1975-80, v.p. 1978-80), Am. Arbitration Assn. (dir. 1979-80), Am. Bar Assn. (sec. sect. labor law 1976-77), Indsl. Relations Research Assn., Order of Coif. Office: US Courthouse 3d and Constitution NW Washington DC 20001

EDWARDS, HERBERT MARTELL, civil engineer; b. Brockville, Ont., Can., Dec. 16, 1921; s. Walter Martell and Pauline Agnes E.; m. Jayne Ann Westburg, Nov. 3, 1945; children: Douglas, Barbara, Peter. B.S. in Civil Engring., Queen's U., Kingston, Ont., 1944; M.S.C.E., Purdue U., 1954. With Can. Vickers Aircraft Div., Montreal, Que., 1944, Douglas Aircraft, Santa Monica, Calif., 1944-45, Canadair, Ltd., Montreal, 1945; successively lectr. civil engring., asst. prof., assoc. prof., acting dean, assoc. dean Queens U., Kingston, from 1946, prof., head civil engring. dep., 1975—. Editorial bd.: RTAC Forum, 1976; contbr. articles to tech. jours. Research grantee Ont. Dept. Hwys., NRC Can. Mem. Assn. Profl. Engrs. Ont., Can. Soc. Civil Engrs., Engring. Inst. Can., Inst. Transp. Engrs. (dir. Dist. 7), Ont. Traffic Conf. (life), Roads and Transp. Assn. Can., Transp. Research Bd. Anglican. Home: 39 Lakeland Point Dr Kingston ON Canada K7L 4E8 Office: Ellis Hall Queens U Kingston ON Canada K7L 3N6

EDWARDS, HORACE BURTON, oil pipeline company executive; b. Tuscaloosa, Ala., May 20, 1925; s. Burton and A.B. (Bryant) E.; m. Patsy M. Carter, Sept. 11, 1948 (div.); children: Adrienne, Paul, David, Michael. B.S. in Naval Sci., Marquette U., 1947, B.S.M.E., 1948; M.B.A. in Fin. Mgmt, Iona Coll., 1972; L.D.H. (hon.), Tex. So. U., 1982. Registered profl. engr., Wis., Kans. Various engring. positions Allis Chalmers, 1948-52, Gen. Motors, 1952-56, Conrac, 1956-63, Northrop, 1963-71; with Atlantic Richfield Co., 1967-80, mgr. planning/evaluation, N.Y.C., 1976-79, v.p. planning/control, Los Angeles, 1979-80; pres., chmn., chief exec. officer ARCO Pipe Line Co., Independence, Kans., 1980—; v.p., dir. Independence Industries, Inc., 1981—; mem. adv. bd. Energy Bur.; mem. adv. com. Energy and Environ. Law Sect., Nat. Bar Assn. Pres. bd. dirs. Jr. Achievement, Independence, 1980—; trustee Kans. Council Econ. Edn., Topeka, 1981—, Leadership Independence, 1984-85. Recipient Marquette U. Dist. Engring. Alumnus award, 1984. Mem. Am. Petroleum Inst., Assn. Oil Pipelines (exec. com.), Am. Assn. Blacks in Energy (bd. dirs.), Kans. Chamber Commerce and Industry (trustee Leadership Kans. 1983, dir. 1983—). Clubs: Independence Country, Petroleum of Tulsa. Lodges: Rotary; Elks. Office: ARCO Pipe Line Co ARCO Bldg Independence KS 67301

EDWARDS, HOWARD DAWSON, business executive, physicist; b. Athens, Ga., Dec. 11, 1923; s. Howard Thomas and Inez (Glenn) E.; m. Mary Lemon, Mar. 10, 1961; children: David, Jerry, David Bradley (stepson), Kathy. B.S., U. Ga., 1944; Ph.D. in Physics, Duke, 1950. Chief atmospheric energy br. Air Force Cambridge Research Labs., Bedford, Mass., 1949-55; operations research scientist Lockheed Aircraft Corp., Marietta, Ga., 1956-58; faculty Ga. Inst. Tech., Atlanta, 1959-82, prof. aerospace engring., 1965-82; dir. Aerospace Environment Lab., 1963-75; Pres. SIR-Atlanta, Inc., 1963—. Contbr. articles profl. jours. Mem. Ga. Acad. Sci. (pres. 1966). Home: 365 Amberidge Trail Atlanta GA 30328

EDWARDS, HOWARD LEE, petroleum company executive; b. Baker, Oreg., June 10, 1931; s. Elmer L. and Bernice (Stringham) E.; m. Carolyn Bagley, Mar. 19, 1954; children: Bryant B., H. McKay, Mitchell L., Paul S. B.S., Brigham Young U., 1955; postgrad., Stanford U., 1955-56, U. Utah, 1956-57; J.D., George Washington U., 1959. Bar: Utah 1959, Colo. 1981, Alaska 1982. Legal asst., atty. Office of Dir., Bur. Land Mgmt., Washington, Office of Solicitor, U.S. Dept. Interior, Salt Lake City, 1957-61; partner Van Cott, Bagley, Cornwall & McCarthy, Salt Lake City, 1961-68; asst. gen. counsel Anaconda Co., N.Y.C., 1968, asst. to chmn. bd., 1969, v.p., sec., 1970-77; gen. atty. Atlantic Richfield Co., Denver, 1977-82, Anchorage, 1982—. Trustee Rocky Mountain Mineral Law Found.; nat. adv. council Brigham Young U. Sch Mgmt.; bd. visitors J. Reuben Clark Law Sch.; bd. dirs. Anchorage Civic Opera. Mem. Am., Utah bar assns., Am. Mining Congress (chmn. pub. lands com.), Council on Fgn. Relations, Brigham Young U. Alumni Assn. (dir., pres. 1980-81). Republican. Mem. Ch. of Jesus Christ of Latter-day Saints. Club: Tower (Anchorage). Lodge: Rotary. Home: 2448 Loussac Dr Anchorage AK 99503

EDWARDS, JACK, congressman; b. Birmingham, Ala., Sept. 20, 1928; s. William Jackson and Sue (Fuhrman) E.; m. Jolane Vander Sys, Jan. 30, 1954; children: Susan Lane, Richard Arnold. B.S. in Commerce and Bus. Adminstrn, U. Ala., 1952, LL.B., 1954. Bar: Ala. 1954, D.C. 1983. Practice law, Mobile, 1954-58; gen. atty. G., M. & O. R.R., 1958-64; mem. 89th-98th congresses from 1st Dist. Ala.; mem. com. appropriations; vice chmn. House Republican Conf. Served with USMC, 1946-48, 50-51. Mem. ABA, Ala. Bar Assn., Mobile Bar Assn. (sec. 1956), Mobile Jr. Bar Assn. (pres. 1957), Mobile Jr. C. of C. (pres. 1961-62), Kappa Alpha (pres. 1951-53), Omicron Delta Kappa. Presbyterian. (elder). Office: House Office Bldg Washington DC 20515

EDWARDS, JACK DONALD, political scientist, college dean; b. Stanley, N.D., Feb. 9, 1933; s. Leroy and Winnie Mae (Burlingame) E.; m. Edith Peatross Rogers, Sept. 6, 1958; children: David, Stan, Allison. B.A., Macalester Coll., 1955; LL.B., Harvard U., 1958; Ph.D. in Polit. Sci, Vanderbilt U., 1966. Asst. prof. polit. sci. U. Nev., Reno, 1961-62; asst. prof. govt. Coll. William and Mary, Williamsburg, Va., 1962-65, asso. prof., 1966-73, prof., 1973—, dean, 1974-81; asst. prof. polit. sci. Grinnell (Iowa) Coll., 1965-66; Mem. James City County Bd. Suprs., 1972—, chmn., 1974, 78, 80; pres. Va. Assn. Counties, 1977-78; mem. exec. com. Va. Mcpl. League, 1982—. Recipient Thomas Jefferson award Coll. William and Mary, 1977. Mem. Am. Polit. Sci. Assn., So. Polit. Sci. Assn., AAUP. Democrat. Home: 114 Stanley Dr Williamsburg VA 23185 Office: Coll William and Mary Williamsburg VA 23185

EDWARDS, JAMES BENJAMIN, accountant, educator; b. Atlanta, Apr. 27, 1935; s. James T. and Louis F. (McEachern) E.; m. Virginia Ann Reagin, Feb. 21, 1958; children: James Benjamin II, Chad Reagin, Calli Ann, Judy Clair. B.B.A. Earhart Found. scholar, U. Ga., 1958, M.B.A., 1962, Ph.D. Ernst and Ernst fellow, 1971. C.P.A., Tenn., Ga., S.C.; cert. mgmt. acct.; cert. internal auditor; cert. data processor. Controller Better Maid Dairy Products, Inc., Athens, Ga., 1958-62; semi-sr. acct. Max M. Cuba & Co., Atlanta, 1962-63; ptnr. Wilson, Edwards and Swang, accts., Nashville, 1964-68, Q.F. Lester & Co.,

Athens, 1967-68; instr. U. Ga., Athens, 1966-71; prof. acctg. U. S.C., Columbia, 1971—, bus. Partnership Found. fellow; instr. staff tng. program local C.P.A. firms, Nashville, 1963-66. Contbr. articles on mgmt. acctg. to profl publs. Coach Little League Baseball, Columbia, 1972—; bd. dirs. Atlanta Bible Camp, Inc., Ga. Christian Found., Inc.; pres. Ga. Christian Found., Inc., 1968-69. Recipient 6 nat. awards for contbns. to acctg. lit. Mem. Am. Acctg. Assn., Am. Inst. C.P.A.s, Inst. Internal Auditors, Planning Execs. Inst. (asst. editor nat. mag. 1971-77), Am. Inst. Decision Scis. (v.p. Southeastern sect. 1975-76), Am. Mgmt. Assn., Nat. Assn. Accts. (pres. Columbia chpt. 1973-74, nat. research com. 1974-75, nat. edn. com. 1977-80, nat. dir. 1875-77, pres. Carolinas council 1976, nat. v.p. 1980-81), S.C. Soc. C.P.A.s, S.C. Assn. Acctg. Instrs. (founding pres. 1972-73), Omicron Delta Epsilon, Beta Alpha Psi, Delta Sigma Pi, Sigma Chi. Mem. Ch. of Christ. Clubs: Five Points Optimist of Athens, Spring Valley Band Boosters. Home: 9842 Windsor Lake Blvd Columbia SC 29206 Office: U SC Coll Bus Adminstrn Columbia SC 29208

EDWARDS, JAMES BURROWS, cabinet officer, unversity president, former president; b. Hawthorne, Fla., June 24, 1927; s. O.M. E.; m. Ann Norris Darlington, Sept. 1951; children: James Burrows, Catharine Edwards Darlington. H.H.D., Francis Marion Coll., 1978; B.S., Coll. of Charleston, S.C., 1950, Litt.D., 1975; D.M.D., U. Louisville, 1955; LL.D., U. S.C., 1975, Bob Jones U., 1976, The Citadel, 1977. Diplomate: Am. Bd. Oral and Surgery. Deck officer Alcoa S.S. Co., 1950-51; intern Grad. Med. Sch., U. Pa., 1957-58; oral surgery resident Henry Ford Hosp., Detroit, 1958-60; practice dentistry, specializing in oral surgery; gov. S.C., 1975-78; sec. Dept. Energy, Washington, 1981-82; pres. Med. U. S.C., Charleston, 1982—; dir. 1st Nat. Bank of S.C.; Burris ChemCo, S.C. Dental Assn.; rep. Gov.'s Statewide Com. for Comprehensive Health Care Planning, 1968-72; mem. Fed. Hosp. Council, 1969-73; chmn. subcom. nuclear energy Nat. Govs. Assn., 1978. Mem. Charleston council Navy League of U.S.; chmn. Charleston County Republican Com., 1964-69; del. Nat. Rep. Conv., 1968, 72, 76; chmn. First Congl. Dist. Rep. Com., 1970-71, Rep. Steering Com. for Charleston County; mem. S.C. Statewide Rep. Steering Com., S.C. Senate from Charleston-Georgetown Dist., 1972-74; former mem. bd. dirs. Coastal Carolina council Boy Scouts Am.; trustee Charleston County Hosp., Greater Charleston YMCA, Coll. Prep. Sch., Charleston; bd. dirs. Baker Hosp., Harry Frank Guggenheim Found. Served with U.S. Maritime Service, 1944-47; to lt. Dental Corps USN, 1955-57; res., 1957-67. Fellow Am., Internat. colls. dentists; mem. Am. Dental Assn. (del. ann. session 1972), S.C. Dental Assn., Charleston (pres. 1974—), Coastal Dist. (past pres.) dental socs., Chalmers J. Lyons Acad. Oral Surgery, Internat. Soc. Oral Surgeons, Am.Soc. Oral Surgeons, Southeastern Soc. Oral Surgeons, S.C. Soc. Oral Surgeons (past pres.), Brit. Assn. Oral Surgeons, Fedn. Dentaire Internationale, Oral Surgery Polit. Action Com. (founder, chmn., dir. 1971-73), Delta Sigma Delta, Pi Kappa Phi, Omicron Delta Kappa, Phi Delta. Club: Masons. Address: Medical Univ of South Carolina 80 Barre Charleston SC 29401

EDWARDS, JAMES COOK, investment counselor; b. N.Y.C., Aug. 4, 1923; s. James A. and Edith (Cook) E.; m. Sally Matson, Apr. 21, 1951; children—James Cook, Anne Matson. B.A., Yale U., 1945; LL.B., Columbia U., 1949. Bar: N.Y. bar 1949. V.p., sec., dir. Douglas T. Johnston & Co., Inc., N.Y.C., 1949-78; pres., dir. Millan House, Inc., 1965-72; v.p., dir. Johnston Mut. Fund, Inc., 1956-66; pres., dir. James C. Edwards & Co., Inc., N.Y.C., 1978—; Mem. E. Hampton (N.Y.) Zoning Bd. Appeal, 1962-64. Trustee, v.p. Buckley Sch. Served with AUS, 1943-45. Decorated Air medal with 8 oak leaf clusters. Presbyn. Clubs: Maidstone (Union) (past pres., gov.); Yale (N.Y.C.); Triton (Can.); Fish and Game. Home: 115 E 67 St New York NY 10021 Office: 805 3d Ave New York NY 10022

EDWARDS, JAMES DONALD, accounting educator; b. Ellisville, Miss., Nov. 12. 1926; s. Thomas Terrell and Rietha Mae (Cranford) E.; m. Clara Florence Maestri, Aug. 16, 1947; 1 son, James Donald. B.S., La. State U., 1949; M.B.A., U. Denver, 1950; Ph.D., U. Tex., 1953. Instr., grad. asst. U. Denver, 1949-50, U. Tex., 1950-51; instr. accounting Mich. State U., 1951-53, asst. prof., 1953-55, asso. prof., 1955-57, prof., 1957-71, acting head dept., 1957-58, head dept. accounting and financial adminstrn., 1958-71, acting asso. dean, 1960; dean (Sch. Bus. Adminstrn.), Grad. Sch. Bus. Adminstrn., U. Minn., 1971-72; J.M. Tull prof. acctg. Sch. Acctg., U. Ga., Athens, 1972—; formerly with Touche, Ross, Bailey & Smart, C.P.A.s; mem. Pub. Rev. Bd. Arthur Andersen & Co., 1974-82, Ga. Bd. Accountancy, 1978—; chmn. Ga. State Bd. Accountancy, 1982; vis. scholar Nuffield Coll., Oxford (Eng.) U., 1979-80; Mem. nat. research com. U.S. Bus. Edn. Assn. and Research Found.; Trustee, sec. Financial Accounting Found. Author: History of Public Accounting in the United States, 1978, (co-author) Elementary Accounting, 1956, Intermediate Accounting, 1958, Administrative Control and Executive Action, Contributions of Four Accounting Pioneers, Preparation for the Professional CPA Examination, 2 vols, Financial and Management Accounting-A Programmed Text, vol. 1-2, 1970, 2d edit., 1971, vol. 4, 1978, (with Hermanson and Salmonson) Accounting Principles, 1980, Survey of Basic Accounting, 2d edit, 1981, Accounting Education: Problems and Prospects, The Accounting Cycle, The Modern Accountants' Handbook, 1976, (with Bergold) Career Accounting; Editor: Jour. Accountancy; hon. mem. editorial adv. bd. Am. Biog. Inst.; co-editor: The Managerial and Cost Accountant's Handbook, 1979; Contbr. articles to profl. publs. Mem. Am. Acctg. Assn. (v.p. 1964, pres. 1970-71, chmn. C.P.A. exam. com., nominations com. 1980, Acctg. Educator of Year 1975), Am. Inst. C.P.A.s (dir. 1979-83), Ga. Assn. C.P.A.s, Am. Fin. Assn., Bank Adminstrn. Inst. (bd. regents 1975-81, exam. com.), Nat. Assn. Accountants (v.p., asso. dir. publs., chpt. pres., nat. dir. 1962-63, chmn. research planning com., chmn. research grants com., mem. mgmt. acctg. practices com. 1977—), Commn. on Study Objectives of Financial Statements, Omicron Delta Kappa, Phi Kappa Phi, Beta Gamma Sigma, Beta Alpha Psi (outstanding accountant award), Delta Sigma Pi. Club: Mason. Home: 325 St George Dr Athens GA 30606

EDWARDS, JEROME, lawyer; b. N.Y.C., July 5, 1912; s. Philip and Anna (Hollinger) E.; m. Mildred Kahn, Dec. 7, 1941; children—Susan, Bruce (dec.). B.S., NYU, 1931, J.D., 1933. Bar: N.Y. State 1934, Calif. 1975. Asso. firm T.J. Lesser, 1934-36; pvt. practice, N.Y.C., 1936-42; sr. partner Phillips, Nizer, Benjamin, Krim & Ballon, N.Y.C., 1942-64; v.p., gen. counsel 20th Century Fox Film Corp., N.Y.C. and Los Angeles, 1962-77; of counsel firm Kaplan, Livingston, Goodwin, Berkowitz & Selvin, Beverly Hills, Calif., 1977-81, Musick, Peeler & Garrett, Los Angeles, 1982—. Mem. N.Y. County Lawyers Assn., Am. Bar Assn., Calif. Bar Assn., Fed. Bar Council, Am. Arbitration Assn. (nat. panel). Home: 1221 Ocean Ave Santa Monica CA 90401 Office: One Wilshire Boulevard Los Angeles CA 90017

EDWARDS, JESSE EFREM, physician, educator; b. Hyde Park, Mass., July 14, 1911; s. Max and Nellie (Gordon) E.; m. Marjorie Helen Brooks, Nov. 12, 1952; children—Ellen Ann, Brooks Sayre. B.S., Tufts Coll., 1932, M.D., 1935. Diplomate Am. Bd. Med. Examiners, Am. Bd. Pathology. Resident Mallory Inst. Pathology, Boston, 1935-36, asst., 1937-40; intern Albany (N.Y.) Hosp., 1936-37; instr. pathology Boston U., 1938; instr. pathology, bacteriology, surgery Tufts Med. Coll., 1939-40; research fellow Nat. Cancer Inst. USPHS, 1940-42; cons. sect. pathologic anatomy Mayo Clinic, 1946-60; asst. prof. grad. sch. U. Minn., Mpls., 1946-51, asso. prof., 1951-54, prof. pathologic anatomy, 1954-60, clin. prof. med. sch., prof. pathology grad. sch., 1960—; chief pathologist. Chas. T. Miller Hosp., St. Paul, 1960—; cons. pathologist Hennepin County Hosp., Mpls., 1964—; cons. dept. medicine Mpls. Vets. Hosp., 1966—; cons. pathologist St. Paul Ramsey Hosp., 1967—; prof. med. tech. Macalester Coll., St. Paul, 1960-67; pres. World Congress Pediatric Cardiology, 1980; Mem. pathology study sect. USPHS, 1957-62; civilian cons. surgeon gen. AUS, 1947-69. Author: Atlas Acquired Diseases of Heart and Great Vessels, 1961, (with T.J. Dry and others) Congenital Anomalies of the Heart and Great Vessels, 1948, (with others) An Atlas of Congenital Anomalies of the Heart and Great Vessels, 1954, (with R.S. Fontana) Congenital Cardiac Disease, 1962, (with J.R. Stewart, O. Kincaid) An Atlas of Vascular Rings and Related Malformations of the Aortic System, 1963, (with C.A. Wagenvoort, D. Heath) Pathology of Pulmonary Vasculature, 1963, (with others) Correlation of Pathologic Anatomy and Angiocardiography, 1965, Coronary Arterial Variations in the Normal Heart and in Congenital Heart Disease, 1975, Coronary Heart Disease, 1976; Editor: Circulation; Contbr. articles to profl. jours. Served from capt. to lt. col. M.C. AUS, 1942-46. Recipient Distinguished Tchr. award Minn. Med. Found., 1974; Gold Heart award Am. Heart Assn., 1970; Gifted Tchr. award Am. Coll. Cardiology, 1977. Mem. Soc. Exptl. Biology and Medicine, Am. Heart Assn. (pres. 1967-68), Minn. Heart Assn. (pres. 1962-63), Internat. Acad. Pathology (pres. 1955-56), Am. Assn. Pathologists and Bacteriologists, Coll. Am. Pathologists, Am. Soc. Exptl. Pathology, Am., Minn. med. assns., Sigma Xi, Alpha Omega Alpha. Home: 1565 Edgcumbe Rd St Paul MN 55116 Office: United Hosp St Paul MN 55102

EDWARDS, JOHN ALLEN, mfg. co. exec.; b. Chgo., Dec. 22, 1917; s. Thomas Michael and Pearl (McCorkel) E.; m. Ruth S. Anderson, June 13, 1942; children—Michael K., Patricia L. Grad., Northwestern U., 1948. With Continental Ill. Nat. Bank & Trust Co., Chgo., 1936-40; acct., mgr., asst. controller, treas. Liquid Carbonic Corp., Chgo., 1940-53, treas., comptroller, 1953-56, v.p., comptroller, 1956-61, exec. v.p., 1961-63, pres., 1963—; vice chmn. bd. Houston Natural Gas Corp.; dir. Liquid Carbonic Corp., Liquid Carbonic Inc., Can.; Mem. adv. com. Forty Plus of Chgo., 1971—. Served to maj. USAF, 1941-45. Mem. Compressed Gas Assn. (exec. bd.), Econ. Club Chgo., Chgo. Council Fgn. Relations, Execs. Club Chgo., Ill. C. of C., Newcomen Soc., Delta Mu Delta. Clubs: Flossmoor Country, Union League, Chgo. Athletic Assn. Home: 809 Bruce St Flossmoor IL 60422 Office: 135 S LaSalle St Chicago IL 60603

EDWARDS, JOHN HAMILTON, educator; b. San Francisco, Oct. 16, 1922; s. Henry William and Hilda (Chew) E.; m. Dixie Swaren, July 14, 1947; children—Gregory William, John Steven, Mark Hamilton. B.A., U. Calif. at Berkeley, 1947, Ph.D., 1952; M.A., Columbia, 1948. Instr. English U. Calif. at Berkeley, 1952-54, asst. prof., 1954-59, asst. to v.p., 1959-60; mem. faculty San Francisco State U., 1960—, prof., 1964—, exec. v.p., 1970-72; lectr. ednl. TV KRON-TV, San Francisco, 1962-67. Author: Annotated Index to the Cantos of Ezra Pound, 1957, 71; Editor: The Pound Newsletter, 1954-56. Trustee Lone Mountain Coll., San Francisco, 1968-72; bd. dirs. Am. Civil Liberties Union, No. Calif., 1966-72. Served with OSS AUS, 1944-46. Recipient James D. Phelan award for arts, 1954, Am. Philos. Soc. research awards, 1954, 55. Mem. Modern Lang. Assn., Philol. Assn. Pacific Coast. Home: 1290 Monterey Blvd San Francisco CA 94127

EDWARDS, JOHN RALPH, chemist, educator; b. Streator, Ill., Feb. 27, 1937; s. Ralph E. and Ruth M. (Wilson) E.; m. Margaret E. Smith, July 15, 1961; children: Peter J., Sharon E., Susan D. B.S., Ill. Wesleyan U., 1959; Ph.D., U. Ill., 1964. NIH postdoctoral fellow Tufts U, Boston, 1964-66; asst. prof. chemistry Villanova U., Pa., 1966-73, assoc. prof., 1973-80, prof., chmn. chemistry dept., 1980—. Contbr. articles to profl. jours. Bd. dirs. Indian Rights Assn.; active Boy Scouts Am. NIH grantee, 1970-76. Mem. Am. Soc. Biol. Chemists, Am. Soc. Microbiology, Am. Chem. Soc., U.S. Orienteering Fedn., Sigma Xi, Phi Kappa Phi. Office: Chemistry Dept Villanova U Villanova PA 19085

EDWARDS, JOHN S., orch. mgr.; b. St. Louis, 1912. A.B., U. N.C., 1930; M.A., Harvard U., 1932; D.Musical Arts (hon.), Cleve. Inst. Music, 1978, L.H.D., DePaul U., 1979. Began as music reviewer St. Louis Globe-Democrat; staff St. Louis Symphony Orch.; later mgr.; formerly bus. mgr. Los Angeles Philharmonic Orch., also Hollywood Bowl; asst. mgr. Pitts. Symphony Orch., 1945-48; mgr. Balt. Symphony Orch., Washington Nat. Symphony Orch., 1948-55, Pitts. Symphony Orch., 1955-67, Chgo. Symphony Orch., 1967—, exec. v.p., 1975; Past mem. adv. com. Nat. Cultural Center, Washington, Commonwealth Pa. Council on Arts.; Bd. dirs. Am. Symphony Orch. League, Vienna, Va., past pres., chmn. bd., 1968-73; charter mem. Chgo. Council on Fine Arts, 1978—. Recipient Gold Baton award Am. Symphony Orch. League, 1975. Office: Chgo Symphony Orch 220 S Michigan Ave Chicago IL 60604

EDWARDS, JOSEPH CASTRO, physician; b. Springfield, Mo., Dec. 24, 1909; s. Lyman Paul and Lela (Bedell) E.; m. Virginia Moser, Jan. 8, 1942; children: Virginia Lee, Joseph Byron, Jonathan Paul. A.B., U. Okla., 1930; M.D., Harvard, 1934. Diplomate Am. Bd. Internal Medicine. Tutorial fellow cardiology Dr. Paul D. White Mass. Gen. Hosp., 1934; intern Springfield (Mass.) Hosp., 1935; house physician med. service Barnes Hosp., 1936-37; Stroud fellow, resident Pa. Hosp., Phila., 1937-38; Eli Lilly fellow on pneumonia research Washington U. Med. Sch., St. Louis, 1939, Smith Kline and French fellow in hypertension, 1940, instr. clin. medicine, 1939-60, asst. prof. clin. medicine, 1960—, cons. clinics and div. gerontology; asst. physician Barnes Hosp.; vis. physician St. Louis City Hosp.; mem. staff Deaconess Hosp.; mem. cons. staff St. Joseph Hosp., St. Louis; cardiologist, dir. high blood pressure clinic St. Luke's Hosp.; area med. cons. hearings and appeals div. U.S. Social Security Adminstrn.; med. cons. R.R. Retirement Bd.; cardiovascular cons. div. gerontology Washington U. Sch. Medicine, St. Louis.; med. cons. Fifth Army U.S.A., Chgo. Author: Hypertensive Disease and Clinical Management, 1959, Management of Hypertensive Disease, 1960; also chpt. in Drugs of Choice, 1959, others; Cons. bd.: Folia Clinica Internacional, Barcelona, Spain.; Contbr. articles to profl. Jours. Bd. dirs. Boys Town, Mo.; former bd. dirs. Speech and Hearing Soc. St. Louis; pres. Doctors Med. Found., St. Louis, 1964; mem. steering com. U.S. Senatorial Bus. Adv. Bd., 1981—. Served as lt. col., M.C. AUS. Decorated Legion of Merit. Fellow A.C.P., Am. Coll. Cardiology (gov. Mo. 1962-65), Royal Soc. Medicine (London); mem. Miss. Valley Med. Soc. (pres. 1958), St. Louis Med. Soc. (pres. 1970), Am. Heart Assn., Mo. Heart Assn. (dir.), St. Louis Heart Assn., St. Louis Cardiac Club (dir.), Central Soc. Clin. Research, A.M.A. (cons. council on drugs), So. Med. Assn., Am. Diabetes Assn., Endocrine Soc., Am. Therapeutic Soc. (v.p. 1961, treas. 1962), Constantinian Soc. (pres. 1978), Paul Dudley White Soc., Soc. for Acad. Achievement (mem. adv. and editorial bd.), S.A.R., Phi Beta Kappa, Alpha Omega Alpha. Methodist (ofcl. bd.). Clubs: Skeet and Trap, Internists, University (St. Louis); Marshland Duck. Home: 610 W Polo Dr Saint Louis MO 63105 Office: Queeny Tower 4989 Barnes Hospital Plaza Saint Louis MO 63110

EDWARDS, JOSEPH DANIEL, JR., educator; b. Alexandria, La., Nov. 25, 1924; s. Joseph Daniel and Florence Coral (Hoell) E.; m. Eunice Ray Rike, July 16, 1960; 1 dau., Laurésia Catharine. B.S. with spl. distinction, La. Coll., 1944; M.A., U. Tex., 1948, Ph.D., 1950; postdoctoral, U. Ill., 1950-51. Chemist Fercleve Corp., Oak Ridge, 1944, U.S. Naval Research Lab., Washington, 1945; prin. sci. VA Research Lab., Baylor U. Coll. Medicine, Houston, 1951-58; also asso. prof.; asso. prof. chemistry Clemson (S.C.) U., 1959; asso. prof. Lamar U., Beaumont, Tex., 1960-65, prof., 1965-67; prof., head dept. chemistry U. Southwestern La., Lafayette, 1967-72, prof., 1972—. Synthesis of Gossypol, 1958, Necic acids, 1964-67. Robert A. Welch Found. grantee, 1961-67. Fellow Chem. Soc. (London); mem. Am. Chem. Soc., Phytochem. Soc. N.Am., Sigma Xi, Phi Lambda Upsilon, Alpha Chi (Distinguished Alumnus). Research in positional selectivity and reactivity of acylating agts.; the importance of free radical oxidative coupling to form complex phenols in biosynthetic processes; the preparation of a platinum hydrogenation catalyst of high and reproducibile activity. Home: 401 Brentwood Blvd Lafayette LA 70503

EDWARDS, JOSHUA LEROY, physician, educator; b. Jasper, Fla., Aug. 9, 1918; s. Harry L. and Julia B. (Miller) E.; m. Jeane Perrin, July 7, 1953; children—Julia E., Jean A., Joshua Leroy III. B.S., U. Fla., 1939; M.D., Tulane U., 1943. Diplomate: Am. Bd. Pathology. Intern Bapt. Hosp., New Orleans, 1943-44; practice medicine, Lake City, Fla., 1946-48; resident pathology Touro Infirmary, New Orleans, 1948-49; asst. resident lab. pathology N.E. Deaconess Hosp., Boston, 1949-50, chief resident pathology, 1950-51; teaching fellow pathology Harvard Med. Sch., 1950-51; instr. pathology Duke Sch. Medicine, 1951-52, asso. pathology, 1951-52; asst. pathology and microbiology; Rockefeller Inst. Med. Research, 1953-55; prof. pathology, chmn. dept. U. Fla. Coll. Medicine, 1955-67; prof. pathology, dir. combined degree program in med. scis. Ind. U., Bloomington, 1967-69; prof., chmn. dept. pathology Ind. U. Med. Center, Indpls., 1969—. Contbr. articles to profl. jours. Served with M.C. AUS, 1944-46. Fellow Coll. Am. Pathologists; mem. Internat. Acad. Pathology, AAAS, N.Y., Fla., Ind. acads. sci., Am. Assn. Pathology, Tissue Culture Assn., Reticuloendothelial Soc., Am., Fla., Ind. med. assns., Am. Soc. Clin. Pathologists, Am. Soc. Cell Biology, Phi Beta Kappa, Sigma Xi, Alpha Omega Alpha. Home: 7601 Morningside Dr Indianapolis IN 46240

EDWARDS, JULIA SPALDING, journalist; b. Louisville, Oct. 6, 1920; d. James P. and Margaret (Wathen) E. B.A., Barnard Coll., 1940; M.S., Columbia, 1942. Postgrad. internat. relations, 1966; Reporter Balt. Sun, 1942-44; re-writeman Chgo. Daily News, 1944-45; corr. to Frankfurt bur. chief Stars and Stripes, Germany, 1946-48; Washington corr. Pulliam Newspapers, 1949-50; editor USIA, Washington, Tokyo, 1951-52; mng. editor Worldwide Press Ser., N.Y.C., 1953-54; pub. info. dir. Research Inst. Am., 1955-56; ind. fgn. corr., writer, editor, N.Y.C., 1957-67; chief World Affairs Bur., Washington, 1968—; corr. news agys., mags., Korea, Vietnam, Germany, Japan, China, more than 100 others. Author: The Occupiers, 1967. Mem. Nat. Press Club, Overseas Press Club (chmn. Washington 1969-73), Am. Newspaper Women's Club, Author's Guild. Address: 2801 New Mexico Ave NW Apt 1110 Washington DC 20007

EDWARDS, JULIUS HOWARD, orgn. exec.; b. Petersburg, Tenn., Jan. 10, 1914; s. Claude Hardison and Ella (Sowell) E.; m. Jane Paschall, June 21, 1939; children—Beverly Ann, Paula Jane, Jan Howard. Grad., David Lipscomb Coll., Nashville, 1936. With Nashville Pure Milk Co., 1936-42; Consol. Vultee Aircraft Corp., 1942-45; purchasing agt. V-M Corp., Benton Harbor, Mich., 1945-46, mgr. cost accounting, 1946-47, asst. gen. mgr., 1947-62, 66-71, dir., 1962-71; exec. dir. Area Resources Improvement Council, Benton Harbor, Mich., 1971—; gen. mgr. Fairplain Engring., Inc., 1979—; Dep. dir. USOM to Korea, 1962-64; dir. AID Indonesia, 1964-65, dep. dir., Vietnam, 1965-66; exec. dir. Area Resources Improvement Council, 1971-78. Active Berrien United Way. Mem. bd. Berrien County Dept. Social Services., Twin Cities Area C. of C. Clubs: Rotarian., Berrien Hills Country. Home: 1304 Seneca St Benton Harbor MI 49022 Office: 777 Riverview Dr Benton Harbor MI 49022
An acceptable citizen must prove he can be a constructive force in his family initially, and if so, he can contribute to his church, to his community, and to his nation. I cling to the idea that you must contribute to every environment and people those things that make them better because you touched them.

EDWARDS, LESTER RICHARD, publishing company executive; b. LaCrosse, Wis., Aug. 10, 1890; s. Julius Augustus and Olive (Spicer) E.; m. Caroline K. Steckhahn, Sept. 1, 1915; children: Jean Olive (Mrs. Dale E. Graham), Betty Lou (Mrs. Kenneth R. Hall), Charlotte Helen (Mrs. Harlan L.R. Anderson), Joyce Lillian (Mrs. Charles K. Test). M.E., Ill. Inst. Tech., Chgo., 1912. Partner Edwards & Daley, Elkhorn, Wis., 1906-11; salesman, sales mgr. Aeroshade Co., Waukesha, 1912-17; mgr. P. Hohenadel Jr. Canning Co., Janesville, 1919-22; pres. Garden Canning Co., also Fairview Farms Co., Evansville, 1922-25; asst. to pres. Kieckhefer Container Co., Milw., 1925-29, sec.-treas., 1925-35; also officer subsidiary, affiliated firms; sec.-treas., sales and prodn. mgr. Eddy Paper Corp., Chgo., 1930-35; pres., treas., dir., gen. mgr. Northeastern Container Corp., Bradford, Pa., 1935-56; v.p., dir. Nat. Container Corp., N.Y.C., 1943-56, pres., 1956-57; also v.p., dir. 6 subsidiaries; v.p., dir. Marinette, Tomahawk & Western R.R. Co., 1946-56; pres., dir. Bradford Publs., Inc., 1943—, Hotel Emery Corp., Bradford, 1944-64, Sta. WESB, 1946—, Port Allegany Corp., 1947-62, Urell, Inc., Tioga, Pa., 1953-60, Travel Network, Inc., Susquehanna Chem. Co., 1955-70, Penn Capital Corp., 1959-66; v.p. Owens-Ill. Glass Co., 1956-60; gen. mgr. Forest Products div., 1956-60; pres. Orchard Apts., Inc., Bradford, 1952—, Warren Apts., Inc., 1952-54; v.p. Condor Corp.; v.p., dir. Nat. Bottle Corp., 1960-81, Star City Glass Co., 1960-81, Top Line Corp., 1967—, Allegheny Bradford Corp., 1969—; partner Smith Ins. Agy., 1950-74, Kane Pub. Co., 1957-80; pres., dir. Smith Realty Co., Inc., 1972—, Spirit Pub. Co., 1972—, Carmi Times Pub. Co., 1974—; chmn. bd. Producers Bank and Trust Co., 1948-54; dir. Bradford Pipe and Supply Co., Whitewater Canning Co. Humbird Canning Co., Wis. Pres., dir. McKean County chpt. Am. Cancer Soc., 1939-56, dir. Pa. div., 1955—, pres., 1959-60, nat. del.-dir., 1962-64, life dir. Pa. div., mem. exec. com., 1963-64; v.p., dir. Bradford U.S.O.; trustee YMCA; bd. dirs. Nat. Edn. and Research Inst., Tb and Health Soc.; chmn. bd. dirs. Bradford Hosp., 1945-55. Served as ensign USNR, 1917-19. Mem. Pa. C. of C., Bradford C. of C. (U.S. councilor, past pres.), Am. Legion, 40 and 8, Pa. Soc. (N.Y.C.), Newcomen Soc. N.Am. Presbyn. Clubs: Mason (32 deg., Shriner), Elk, Rotarian (past pres.), Bradford. Home: Hedgehog Rd Bradford PA 16701 Office: Box 36 Bradford PA 16701

EDWARDS, LOUIS WARD, JR., diversified manufacturing company executive; b. Detroit, July 22, 1936; s. Louis Ward and Sally (Tryke) E.; m. Juanita Krause, Dec. 28, 1963; children: Louis Ward III, Preston Stephen, Alisa Macall. B.A., Albion Coll., 1958. Mgr. Price Waterhouse & Co. (C.P.A.'s), Milw., 1958-67; treas. Fuqua Industries, Inc., Atlanta, 1967-72; v.p. Ivy Corp., Atlanta, 1972-83; treas., dir. Fabco-Air, Inc., Gainesville, Fla., 1981—; v.p., dir. Moore-Handley, Inc., Birmingham, 1981—; partner Edwards-Harvey Organ Co., Atlanta.; Bd. dirs. Druid Hills Civic Assn. C.P.A., Wis. Mem. Am. Inst. C.P.A.s, Ga. Soc. C.P.A.s, Tax Execs. Inst. (treas. 1971).

Republican. Home: 1156 Lullwater Rd Atlanta GA 30307 Office: Equitable Bldg Atlanta GA 30303

EDWARDS, MALCOLM LAUREN, lawyer; b. Raymond, Wash., Feb. 28, 1932; s. Malcolm Best and Frances Sarah (Simpson) E.; m. Lois L. Grady, Jan. 3, 1981; children: Michael, Victor, Malcolm R., Ruth, Matthew, Heide, Susan. B.A., Wash. State U., 1954; LL.B., U. Wash., 1957; postgrad., U. Wis., 1958-59. Bar: Wash. 1958, U.S. Dist. Ct. (we. dist.) Wash. 1960, U.S. Dist. Ct. (ea. dist.-Wash.) 1960, U.S. Ct. Appeals (9th cir.) 1961, U.S. Tax Ct. 1965, U.S. Supreme Ct. 1967, U.S. Ct. Appeals (5th cir.) 1979. Instr. law U. Nebr., 1957-58, U. Wash., Seattle, 1959-60; sole practice, Seattle, 1959-61; ptnr. Culp, Dwyer, Gutterson & Edwards, Seattle, 1961-64; prin. Edwards & Barbieri, and predecessor firms, Seattle, 1964—; sec., mem. exec. com. Bd. for Jud. Edn., Wash. State Jud. Council. Contbr. articles on appellate advocacy to profl. jours. Recipient Order of Barristers award U. wash. Law Sch., 1980. Fellow Am. Bar Found.; mem. ABA, Wash. State Bar Assn., Wash. State Trial Lawyers Assn., Assn. Trial Lawyers Am. Office: Edwards & Barbieri 3701 Bank of Calif Ctr Seattle WA 98164

EDWARDS, MARVIN H. MICKEY, Congressman; b. Cleve., July 12, 1937; s. Edward A. and Rosalie (Miller) E.; m. Lisa Reagan. B.J., Okla. U., 1958; J.D., Oklahoma City U., 1969. Dir. pub. relations Beals Advt. Agy., Oklahoma City, 1964-68; editor Pvt. Practice mag., 1968-73; spl. legis. cons. Republican Steering Com., Washington, 1973-74; tchr. law and journalism Oklahoma City U., 81975-76; mem. 95th-98th Congresses Congresses from 5th Okla. Dist., House Appropriations com. (various subcoms.); asst. House Rep. whip; vice chmn. Nat. Rep. Congressional Com.; organizer, supr. congressional adv. com. to Reagan presdl. campaign.; Chmn. Am. Conservative Union. Editor: Muskogee (Okla.) Daily Phoenix, 1958-59; reporter, editor: Oklahoma City Times, 1959-63; Author: Hazardous to Your Health, 1972, Behind Energy Lines, 1983. Recipient Freedom Founds. medal (3); named Outstanding Young Man Am., 1973. Mem. Sigma Delta Chi, Phi Delta Phi. Clubs: Masons (32 deg.), Kiwanis.). *

EDWARDS, RALPH LIVINGSTON, TV and radio producer, entertainer; b. Merino, Colo.; s. Henry Livingstone and Minnie Mae (Browns) E.; m. Barbara Jean Sheldon, Sept. 19, 1939; children—Christine Allison, Gary Livingstone, Lauren Avery. A.B., U. Calif., 1935; LL.D. (hon.), Pepperdine U., Alice Lloyd Coll., L.H.D., St. Mary of the Plains Coll. Radio writer, actor, producer, announcer: Sta. KROW, Oakland, Calif., 1929-35, Sta. KSFO, Oakland and San Francisco, Sta. KFRC, San Francisco, 1935-36; announcer, CBS, N.Y.C., 1936-38, 45 weekly radio shows, CBS and NBC, N.Y.C., 1938-40; originator, producer, master of ceremonies: Mr. Hush and Walking Man charity contests radio, 1940-54; originator, master ceremonies: radio show Truth or Consequences; creating: Am. Heart Assn. Nationally; master of ceremonies: radio show This Is Your Life, 1948-50; producer, master of ceremonies creator: NBC-TV show This is Your Life, 1952-61, 70-73; master of ceremonies: TV Ralph Edwards Show, NBC, 1952—; producer, creator: TV and radio Place the Face, CBS-TV; creator, producer: NBC-TV show It Could Be You, 1956-61; TV show About Faces, 1959, End of the Rainbow, 1960, Wide Country, 1961, Who in the World, 1962, Woody Woodbury Show, 1969, Name That Tune, 1974-81, The Cross Wits, 1975-81, Knockout, 1977; exec. producer: The People's Court, 1981; also actor for, RKO Pictures; also actor: movies including 7 Days Leave, 1945; also actor for: Radio Stars on Parade, 1947, Bamboo Blonde, 1948, Beat the Band, 1949; (1st recipient Carbon Mike award Pacific Pioneer Broadcasters, 3 Emmy awards). Nat. crusade chmn. Am. Cancer Soc.; chmn. Nat. Easter Seal Soc., 1973. Recipient Eisenhower award (highest E bond salesman award of Treasury Dept.), 1946; seat of Sierra County, N.Mex.; named Truth or Consequences; named Alumnus of Year U. Calif., 1965. Mem. Berkeley Fellows U. Calif., Robert Gordon Sproul Assn. (founder, chmn. 1965-66). Presbyn. Clubs: Bohemian (San Francisco); Los Angeles Country, Los Angeles 100. Office: 1717 N Highland Ave Hollywood CA 90028

EDWARDS, RALPH M., librarian; b. Shelley, Idaho, Apr. 17, 1933; s. Edward William and Maude Estella (Munsee) E.; m. WinifredWylie, Dec. 25, 1969; children: Dylan, Nathan, Stephen. B.A., U. Wash., 1957, M.Library, 1960; D.L.S., U. Calif.-Berkeley, 1971. Librarian N.Y. Pub. Library, N.Y.C., 1960-61; catalog librarian U. Ill. Library, Urbana, 1961-62; br. librarian Multnomah County Library, Portland, Oreg., 1964-67; asst. prof. Western Mich. U., Kalamazoo, 1970-74; chief of the Central Library Dallas Pub. Library, 1975-81; city librarian Phoenix Pub. Library, 1981—; accrediting team site visitor for library schs. ALA Com. on University Libraries, 1975. Author: Role of the Beginning Librarian in Univeristy Libraries, 1975. U. Calif. doctoral fellow, 1967-70; library mgmt. internship Council on Library Resources, 1974-75. Mem. ALA, Ariz. Library Assn., Assn. Coll. and Research Libraries. Democrat. Home: 4839 E Mulberry Dr Phoenix AZ 85018 Office: 12 E McDowell Rd Phoenix AZ 85004 *Knowledge and better understanding have always been strong drives in my life. The choice of a career in libraries was a logical and happy consequence. My major challenge and goal now is to convince more people of the value to our society of great libraries.*

EDWARDS, RICHARD, art history educator; b. Auburn, N.Y., Dec. 30, 1916; s. Deane and Margaret J. (Dulles) E.; m. Vee Tsung Ling, Mar. 31, 1947; children: Margaret Dulles, Jean, Richard Lawrence, Edith Foster. B.A., Princeton U., 1939; M.A., Harvard U., 1942, Ph.D., 1953. Instr. Boston U., 1953-54; asst. prof. Brandeis U., Waltham, Mass., 1954-56; assoc. prof. Washington U., St. Louis, 1956-60; prof. history of art U. Mich., Ann Arbor, 1960—, chmn. dept., 1969-73. Author: The Field of Stones, 1962, Liti, 1967, The Painting of Tao-chi, 1967, The Art of Wen-Cheng-ming, 1978. Mem. Assn. Asian Studies, Mid-Am. Coll. Art Assn. Home: 1327 Brooklyn St Ann Arbor MI 48104 Office: History of Art Dept U Mich Ann Arbor MI 48109

EDWARDS, RICHARD AMBROSE, lawyer, insurance company executive; b. Roachdale, Ind., May 10, 1922; s. Ralph A. and Bess May (McCampbell) E.; children—Craig Richard, Barbara F. A.B., Ind. U., 1947; LL.B. Harvard U, 1949; Ph.D. (Curtis fellow), Columbia U., 1952. Bar: Ind. bar, U.S. Supreme Ct. bar 1954. Instr. Rutgers U., 1949-51; asso. prof. pub. law and govt. Lafayette Coll., 1952-56; dir. research U.S. Commn. on Govt. Security, Washington, 1956-57; asst. dir. legislative research Columbia Law Sch., N.Y.C., 1957-58; Asso. gen. counsel Health Ins. Assn. Am., N.Y.C., 1958-66; v.p. head public relations dept. Assos. Investment Co., South Bend, Ind., 1966-68; v.p., head govt. and industry relations dept. Met. Life Inst. Co., N.Y.C., now sr. v.p. Author: (with N.T. Dowling) American Constitutional Law, 1954; editor: Index Digest of State Constitutions, 1958. Trustee Nat. Mcpl. League. Served to capt. U.S. Army, World War II; Korea. Decorated Bronze Star. Mem. Am. Bar Assn., Assn. Life Ins. Counsel, Phi Beta Kappa. Republican. Presbyterian. Home: 431 E 20th St Apt 7B New York NY 10010 Office: 1 Madison Ave New York NY 10010

EDWARDS, ROBERT HAZARD, college president; b. London, May 26, 1935; s. Arthur Robinson and Marjorie Hazard (Mayes) E. (father Am. citizen); m. Ellen Ramsay Turnbull, Sept. 10, 1966; children: Elizabeth, Daphne, Nicholas. A.B., Princeton U., 1957; B.A., Cambridge (Eng.) U., 1959, M.A. (hon.), 1977; LL.B., Harvard U., 1961. Bar: Fed. 1961. Ford Found. fellow in, Africa, 1961-63; with UN polit. affairs Dept. State, 1963-65, Ford Found., 1965-77; rep. for Pakistan, 1968-72; head Middle East and Africa, 1973-77; pres. Carleton Coll., Northfield, Minn., 1977—; dir. Gt. No. Ins. Co., 1st Nat. Bank Mpls.; Bd. dirs. Gen. Service Found.; bd. overseers U. Minn. Sch. Mgmt.; mem. adv. com. African-Am. Inst.; trustee Deerfield (Mass.) Acad., Sci. Mus. of Minn. Mem. Council Fgn. Relations N.Y.C. Home: 217 Union St Northfield MN 55057 Office: Carleton Coll Northfield MN 55057

EDWARDS, ROBERT M., lawyer, banker; b. Columbus, Ohio, Apr. 17, 1931; s Robert H. and Iola (Knolbauch) E.; m Joyce Finley, Mar. 5, 1961; children: Susan, Daniel. J.D., Ohio State U., 1955, B.S.B.A., 1955. Bar: Ohio 1955, N.Y. 1982. Ptnr. Teaford, Bernard & Edwards, Columbus, 1959-63; securities trust officer Ohio Treasury Dept., Columbus, 1963-65; asst. supt. banks State of Ohio, Columbus, 1965-67, supt. banks, 1967-71; sr. v.p. BancOhio Corp., Columbus, 1971-81; counsel, sec. 1st. Empire State Corp., Buffalo, 1982—; v.p., council, sec. Mfrs. & Traders Trust Co., subs., 1982—. Bd. visitors Ohio U. Coll. Sch., 1977-81; paralegal adv. council Hilbert Coll., Hamburg, N.Y., 1983; pres. Buckeye Republican Club, 1964. Served to 1st lt. USAF, 1955-57. Named Hon. Ky. Col.; recipient Dist. Service Aladdin Shrine, 1971, Meritorious Service Columbus Bar Assn., 1981. Mem. Am. Bankers Assn. (legis. liason com.), Erie County Bar Assn., N.Y. State Bar Assn. Methodist. Clubs: Worthington Hills Country, West Columbus Optimist (pres. 1964), Shriners, Transit Valley Country. Office: 1st Empire State Corp One M & T Plaza Buffalo NY 14240

EDWARDS, ROBERT RANDLE, legal educator; b. 1934. A.B., Harvard U., 1956, A.M., 1964, J.D., 1964. Bar: D.C. 1965. Atty., Office of Gen. Counsel HUD, Washington, 1966; research assoc Harvard U., 1967-73, acting dir. East Asian Legal Studies, 1971-72, assoc. dir. East Asian Legal Studies, 1972-73; lectr. history Boston U., 1968-70, lectr. law, 1969-73; assoc. prof. law Columbia U., N.Y.C., 1973-79, prof., 1979—. Mem. Assn. Asian Studies, Am. Fgn. Law Assn., Japanese Am. Soc. Office: Columbia U Law Sch 435 W 116th St New York NY 10027

EDWARDS, RYAN HAYES, baritone; b. Columbia, S.C., Aug. 5, 1941; s. William Munroe and Dorothy LeGrande (Sawyer) Faucett; m. Leila Scelonge Cain, Dec. 24, 1979; children: Geoffrey C., Trevor B. Mus.B., U. Tex., 1964; Mus.M., Tex. Christian U., 1971. Scholar, Juilliard Am. Opera Center, N.Y.C., 1968-71; debut, N.Y.C. Opera, 1971, Hollywood Bowl, 1973, New York Philharmonic, 1971, Los Angeles Philharmonic, San Francisco Opera Co., 1975, Miami Opera Co., 1976, Boston Opera, Teatro del Liceo, Barcelona, 1973, Royal Festival Hall, London, 1974, 75, Met. Opera Co., 1976; radio debut, O.R.T.F., Paris, 1973-74; assoc. prof. voice-opera, Northwestern U., Evanston, Ill. Rockefeller grantee, 1968-69; Nat. Opera Inst. grantee, 1970-72; Edwin H. Mosler Found. grantee, 1970-74; William Mathews Sullivan Mus. Found. grantee, 1971-72. Mem. Am. Guild Musical Artists, Actors Equity, Phi Mu Alpha, Lambda Chi Alpha. Winner San Angelo Symphony competition, 1967, Nat. Radio Auditions for Acad. Vocal Arts, Phila., 1964-65, Internat. Verdi competition, Bussetto, Italy, 1971. Office: care Robert Lombardo Assocs 61 W 62d St New York NY 10023 *I am a totally American trained and prepared artist. Hopefully this fact will be of inspiration to other young American singers who, for too many years, have had to try to impress European smaller companies before becoming worthy to have any sort of career here in their own country. America is finally coming to acknowledge its own native operatic talent.*

EDWARDS, STEVE, physics educator; b. Quincy, Fla., June 16, 1930; s. Steve and Sarah Frances (Ryan) E.; m. Helen Wallace Carothers, Dec. 17, 1964; children: Ashley Lynn, Leigh Holladay. B.S., Fla. State U., 1952, M.S., 1954; Ph.D. (Gen. Motors fellow), Johns Hopkins, 1960. Grad. asst. Fla. State U. at Tallahassee, 1952-55, asst. prof. physics, 1960-65, asso. prof., 1965-69, prof., 1969—, asso. chmn. physics, 1965-73, chmn. physics, 1973-79, pres. faculty senate, 1983-84, chmn. athletic bd., 1980; jr. instr. Johns Hopkins, 1955-57; bd. dirs. Recon, Inc., Tallahassee, 1960-65, staff coms., 1965-70. Author: Lectures on the Theory of Direct Reactions, 1961, General Physics, 1968, Physics-A Discovery Approach, 1971; also articles. Recipient Coyle E. Moore award Fla. State U., 1965. Mem. Am. Assn. Physics Tchrs., Am. Phys. Soc. (chmn. Southeastern sect. 1982-83), Order De Molay (chevalier degree 1949, legion of honor 1963), Sigma Xi, Sigma Pi Sigma (zone supr. southeastern U.S. 1962-65), Gamma Alpha, Kappa Sigma, Phi Mu Alpha Sinfonia, Omicron Delta Kappa, Order Omega. Democrat. Episcopalian. Home: 5026 Barfield Rd Tallahassee FL 32308

EDWARDS, THOMAS ROBERT, JR., educator; b. Findlay, Ohio, Oct. 12, 1928; s. Thomas Robert and Helen Louise (Havighurst) E.; m. Nancy Mathis, Sept. 3, 1957; children—Sarah Louise, John Morgan. B.A., Amherst, 1950; M.A. (Am. Council Learned Socs. fellow), Harvard, 1951, Ph.D., 1956. Instr. to asso. prof. English U. Calif., Riverside, 1956-64; asso. prof. English Rutgers U., New Brunswick, N.J., 1964-66, prof., 1966—; chmn. New Brunswick dept. English, 1973-79; lit. critic; journalist; dir. Continental Land and Fur Co., 1976—. Author: This Dark Estate: A Reading of Pope, 1963, Imagination and Power, 1971; exec. editor: Raritan: A Quar. Rev, 1980—. Trustee Hartridge Sch., 1972-76, Wardlaw-Hartridge Sch., 1976—. Rutgers research fellow, 1967-68; Guggenheim fellow, 1972-73. Mem. Modern Lang. Assn., P.E.N., Phi Beta Kappa, Phi Gamma Delta. Club: Century Assn. Home: 1240 Rahway Rd Plainfield NJ 07060

EDWARDS, WALLACE WINFIELD, automotive company executive; b. Pontiac, Mich., May 9, 1922; s. David W. and Ruby M. (Nutting) E.; m. Jean Austin Wolfe, Aug. 24, 1944; children: Ronald W., Gary R., Ann E. B.S. in Mech. Engring, Gen. Motors Inst., 1949, M.B.A., 1966. With GMC Truck & Coach div. Gen. Motors Corp., Pontiac, Mich., 1940—, truck service mgr., 1961-62, head engine design, 1962-64, dir. reliability, 1964-66, dir. prodn. control and purchasing, 1966-70, dir. engring., 1970-78; dir. Worldwide Truck Project Center, Warren, Mich., 1978-80; gen. dir. Worldwide Truck and Transp. Sys. Center, 1980—; v.p. G.M.O.D.C., 1980-81; group mgr. small and light truck and van ops. Truck and Bus. Group, Gen. Motors Corp., 1981-82, mgr. internat. staff, 1982—. Past pres., mem. exec. com., mem. nat. council Boy Scouts Am.; mem. devel. com. St. Joseph Mercy Hosp. Served with USNR, 1944-46. Mem. Soc. Automotive Engrs., Engring. Soc. Detroit, Def. Preparedness Assn., Am. Security Council, Tau Beta Pi, Beta Gamma Sigma. Office: Gen Motors Tech Center Warren MI 48090

EDWARDS, WALTER MEAYERS, editor, photographer; b. Leigh-on-Sea, Essex, Eng., July 21, 1908; came to U.S., 1930, naturalized, 1936; s. Walter James and Lillian Emma (Meayers) E.; m. Mary Woodward Worrall, Feb. 11, 1937. Student, Lindisfarne Coll., Westcliff, Essex, Eng., 1917-26. Staff Paris bur. N.Y. Times-Wide World Photos, 1926-27; with Topical Press Agy., London, 1927-29, Harris & Ewing, photographers, Washington, 1930-31; sec.-treas. Pioneer Air Transport Operators Assn., N.Y.C., Washington, 1931-33. Illustrations staff, Nat. Geog. mag., 1933-54; illustrations editor, 1955-58; fgn. editorial staff, 1958-62; chief pictorial research div., 1963-73; Author of articles; contbr.: color photographs for Great American Deserts, 1972, 3America's Beginnings, 1974. Recipient Americanism medal D.A.R., 1968; Picture of the Year in mag. sports N.P.P.A., 1969, 72. Christian Scientist. Clubs: Mason., Explorers (N.Y.C.); Sierra (San Francisco). Home: PO Box 1631 Sedona AZ 86336

EDWARDS, WARD, educator, psychologist; b. Morristown, N.J., Apr. 5, 1927; s. Corwin D. and Janet W. (Ferriss) E.; m. Silvia Callegari, Dec. 12, 1970; children: Tara, Page. B.A., Swarthmore Coll., 1947; M.A., Harvard U., 1950, Ph.D., 1952. Instr. Johns Hopkins U., 1951-54; with Personnel and Tng. Research Center, USAF, Denver, 1954-56, San Antonio, 1956-58; research psychologist U. Mich., 1958-63, prof. psychology, 1963-73, head Engring. Psychology Lab., 1963-73; asso. dir. Hwy. Safety Research Inst., 1970-73; prof. psychology and indsl. engring., dir. Social Sci. Research Inst., U. So. Calif., 1973—; cons. in field. Author: (with J. Robert Newman) Multiattribute Evaluation, 1982; editor: (with A. Tversky) Decision Making: Selected Readings, 1967; Contbr.: Ency Social Scis, 1968. Served with USNR, 1945-46. Mem. Am., Western psychol. assns., Psychonomic Soc., Soc. Med. Decision-Making, Ops. Research Soc. Am. (council, spl. interest group on decision analysis), Sigma Xi. Address: Social Science Research Inst U Southern California Los Angeles CA 90089

EDWARDS, WAYNE FORREST, paper company executive; b. St. Louis, Dec. 30, 1934; s. Forrest M. and Irma (Muecke) E.; m. Cela Ann Williams, June 14, 1958; children: Laura, Sally. B.S. in Bus. Adminstrn, Washington U., St. Louis, 1957, M.B.A., 1958; Ph.D., St. Louis U., 1965. With Crown Zellerbach Corp., San Francisco, 1957—, group controller, containers and packaging, 1973-76; v.p. fin., v.p. for Latin Am. Crown Zellerbach Internat., 1977-82, v.p. subs. and affiliates, 1982—; instr. M.B.A. program U. South Fla., 1961-65. Trustee Pacific Sch. Religion. Served with U.S. Army, 1954-56. Office: 1 Bush St San Francisco CA 94119

EDWARDS, WILBUR SHIELDS, publishing company executive; b. Charlotte, N.C., July 25, 1916; s. William James and Amy (Shields) E.; m. Jane Holman, Mar. 16, 1940; children: Ashton S., William J., Alisa Carroll. B.A., Davidson Coll., 1937, Yale Div. Sch., 1938. With CBS, 1938-56; account exec. WBT, Charlotte, N.C., 1938-40, WCBS, N.Y., 1940-42, CBS radio sales, 1942-45; western sales mgr. CBS Radio Sales, Chgo., 1945-48; asst. gen mgr. WEEI, Boston, 1948-50; dir. KNX, Los Angeles, 1950-51; gen mgr. KNXT, Los Angeles, 1951-52; gen. sales mgr. CBS Films, N.Y.C., 1952-56; v.p. Ency. Brit. Films, Inc., 1956-62; exec. v.p. Ency. Brit. Ednl. Corp., 1965-71; pres., dir. F.E. Compton & Co., 1962-65, chmn., chief exec. officer, 1971-73; pres., dir. Electronic Pub. Inc., 1974-77; pres., chief exec. officer, dir. Magna Systems Inc., 1978—. Bd. dirs. Presbyn. Home, Evanston, Ill., David C. Cook Found. Presbyn. (elder, stated clk.). Club: Barrington Hills Country. Home: Route 2 Box 95 Barrington IL 60010

EDWARDS, WILLIAM CLEVELAND, investor; b. Los Angeles, Sept. 9, 1928; s. Leland Tabor and Katharine Louise (Knauf) E.; m. Bette Cree, Mar. 13, 1954 (dec.); children: William Leland, Cree Adams, Paul Cleveland, Katharine Ruth; stepchildren: Kristin Elizabeth Gray, Katherine Virginia Gray; m. Barbara Haag Gray, Aug. 6, 1983. B.S. in Petroleum Engring, Stanford U., 1951; M.B.A., Harvard U., 1953. Engr. Standard Oil of Calif., Los Angeles Basin, 1953-56, San Francisco, 1956-59; investment counselor, v.p. Lionel D. Edie & Co., San Francisco, 1959-68; venture capital investor, partner Bryan and Edwards, San Francisco, 1968—; gen. ptnr. Ritter Ptnrs., Banner Ptnrs.; dir., chmn. bd. Acurex Corp., Mountain View, Calif.; dir. Avantek, Santa Clara, Calif., Hambrecht & Quist, San Francisco, Sea Tek, Imperial Automation, Inc., Summit Info. Systems, Therma Wave, Inc., Boole & Babbage, Sunnyvale, Calif.; assoc. Ctr. for Econ. Policy Research; Trustee emeritus Deerfield (Mass.) Acad., 1974-79; trustee Scripps Coll., 1979—; mem. adv. council SBA, 1964-65; founding mem. bd. dirs. Opportunity Capital Corp., San Francisco. Mem. Fin. Analysts Fedn, Nat. Venture Capital Assn. (bd. dirs. 1981—), Western Assn. Venture Capitalists (pres. 1973-74, 80-81). Clubs: Pacific Union, Bohemian, Cypress Point, Menlo Country., Spyglass Hill. Office: 3000 Sand Hill Rd Bldg 2 Suite 260 Menlo Park CA 94025

EDWARDS, WILLIAM FOSTER, oil and gas company executive; b. N.Y.C., Mar. 9, 1946; s. William F. and Catherine (Eyring) E.; m. Kathleen Harrington, June 19, 1970; children: Rebecca, David, Jennifer, William. B.A. in Math, U. Utah, 1970; M.B.A., Northwestern U., 1972. C.P.A., Calif., Utah. Mem. staff Arthur Andersen & Co. (C.P.A.'s), San Francisco, 1972-75; treas., v.p. Mountain Fuel Supply Co., Salt Lake City, 1975—. Mem. Am. Inst. C.P.A.s. Republican. Mormon. Home: 4195 Adonis Dr Salt Lake City UT 84117 Office: 180 East 1st South Salt Lake City UT 84139

EDWARDS, WILLIAM HENRY, hotel executive; b. Muskegon, Mich., 1917. B.A., U. Mich., 1939. Asst. mgr. Grand Hotel, Mackinac Island, Mich., 1937-39, William Penn Hotel, Pitts., 1939-42; sales mgr. Statler Hotel, Detroit, 1945-54; asst. gen. sales mgr. Hilton Hotels Corp., 1954-57; resident mgr. Statler Hilton Hotel, Detroit, 1957-61; sales mgr. Palmer House Co., Chgo., 1961-66, v.p., mgr., 1966-67, v.p., gen. mgr., 1967-68; v.p. Chgo. div. Hilton Hotels Corp., 1968-70, sr. v.p., 1970-71, corp. exec. v.p. ops., pres. Hilton Hotels div., 1971—, mng. dir. Palmer House Co., 1971—, also dir.; dir. Lloyds Bank Calif. Mem. Nat. Restaurant Assn. (dir.), Am. Hotel and Motel Assn. (chmn. energy task force). Office: Hilton Hotels Corp 9880 Wilshire Blvd Beverly Hills CA 90210 *

EDWARDS, WILLIAM JAMES, broadcasting executive; b. Birmingham, Ala., Mar. 30, 1915; s. Perron Austin and Eugenia (Evans) E.; m. Julia M. Stacey, May 15, 1937; children: Julia Beverly, Linda J. Edwards Riley. Student, Birmingham-Southern Coll., 1934-37. Announcer, Sta. WBRC, Birmingham, 1933-34; program dir. Sta. WMBR, Jacksonville, Fla., 1934; announcer Sta. WLW, Cin., 1938; comml. mgr. Storer Broadcasting, Fairmont, W.Va., 1939-42; news commentator Sta. KMTR (now KLAC), Hollywood, Calif., 1944-45; exec. Sta. WIBC, Indpls., 1942-44; founder, pres. Lake Huron Broadcasting Corp., Saginaw, Mich., 1947—; pres. G.C.C. Communications of Houston, Inc., Suncoast Stereo Corp., St. Petersburg, Fla.; (Stas. KRBE-FM & AM, Houston, WQYK, Tampa-St. Petersburg); dir. Design Craftsmen, Inc., Midland, Mich.; Co-chmn. Saginaw chpt. ARC, 1951, gen. fund chmn., 1952. Pres. Saginaw Symphony Orch. Assn., 1954, United Fund Saginaw County, 1960-62, Saginaw Community Chest, 1960-62; chmn. YWCA Adv. com., 1955-68; mem. Saginaw Library Commn., 1952-70, Am. Council United Funds, 1965-66; bd. of fellows Saginaw Valley State Coll., 1968-75; trustee Alvin M. Bentley Found., Owosso, Mich., 1969—. Served with Armed Forces Radio Service USN, 1945-46. Recipient Disting. Service award Jaycees, 1951; named Saginaw Man of Yr., 1950. Mem. Nat. Assn. Broadcasters. Republican. Methodist. Clubs: Saginaw Country, Saginaw; Feather Sound Country (Clearwater, Fla.); Old Port Yacht (North Palm Beach, Fla.); JDM Country, U.S. Navy League (chpt. dir.), Masons, Shriners, Rotary of Saginaw (pres. 1959-60). Home: 100 Lakeshore Dr North Palm Beach FL 33408 Office: 840 US Hwy One North Palm Beach FL 33408

EDWARDS, WILLIAM STERLING, III, cardiovascular surgeon; b. Birmingham, Ala., July 23, 1920; s. William Sterling, Jr. and Elizabeth Alabama (Wyman) E.; m. Ann Rohrer Dudley, July 13, 1946; children—Bruce Sterling, Peter Dudley, Katherine Wyman, Benjamin

Wyman. B.S., Va. Mil. Inst., 1942; M.D., U. Pa., 1945. Diplomate: Am. Bd. Surgery, Am. Bd. Thoracic Surgery (dir. 1973-79). Intern, then resident in surgery Mass. Gen. Hosp., Boston, 1945-52; from instr. to prof. surgery Med. Coll. Ala., 1952-69; prof., chief div. cardio thoracic surgery U. N.Mex. Med. Sch., Albuquerque, 1969-74, prof., chmn. dept. surgery, 1974—. Served to capt. M.C. AUS, 1946-48. Fellow A.C.S.; mem. Am. Surg. Assn., Soc. Vascular Surgery (pres. 1970), Internat. Cardiovascular Soc. (pres. N. Am. chpt. 1978), Am. Thoracic Soc., Soc. Thoracic Surgeons, So. Surg. Assn., Western Surg. Assn. Episcopalian. Devel. 1st prefabricated and corrugated cloth arterial graft for human use. Home: 250 Spring Creek Pl NE Albuquerque NM 87122 Office: Dept Surgery Univ New Mexico Med Sch Albuquerque NM 87106

EEK, NATHANIEL SISSON, university dean; b. Maryville, Mo., Oct. 16, 1927; s. Lauris Martin and Donna (Sisson) E.; m. Patricia Ann Fulton, May 10, 1952; children: Robert, Konrad, Erik. A.B., U. Chgo., 1948; B.S., Northwestern U., 1950, M.A., 1954; Ph.D., Ohio State U., 1959. Dir. studio theatre U. Kans., Lawrence, 1954-57; asst. prof. speech Mich. State U., East Lansing, 1959-62; dir. Sch. Drama, U. Okla., Norman, 1962-75; dean Coll. Fine Arts, 1976—. Author: Touring Manual, 1965; contbg. author: Ency. Edn., 1971; columnist: Musings, 1979—. Mem. adv. panel Okla. State Arts Council, 1966—; mem. Okla. Summer Arts Inst. Served with USNR, 1946; with AUS, 1951-53. Mem. Internat. Assn. Theatres for Children and Young People (pres. internat. group 1972-75), Children's Theatre Conf. (dir. 1965-67), Am. Theatre Assn. (treas. 1981—), Nat. Theatre Conf., Southwest Theatre Conf., U.S. Inst. Theatre Tech., Okla. Community Theatre Assn., Alliance for the Arts in Edn. (v.p. 1979-81), Internat. Conf. Fine Arts Deans (exec. com. 1982-84), Nat. Assn. Schs., Univs. and Land Grant Colls. (arts commn. 1982-84). Republican. Episcopalian. Home: 734 McCall Dr Norman OK 73069

EEKMAN, THOMAS ADAM, educator, Slavist; b. Middelharnis, Holland, May 20, 1923; came to U.S., 1966; s. Thomas Adam and Anna (de Kruyff) E.; m. Tine de Jong, May 2, 1946; children: Menno, Roeland, Ivo, Milja. M.A., U. Amsterdam, 1946, Ph.D., 1951. Research asst. Russian Inst., Amsterdam U., 1948-55, lectr. Slavic langs. at univ., 1955-60, asst. prof., 1960-66; vis. prof. U. Calif. at Los Angeles, 1960-61, prof. Slavic langs., 1966—, chmn. dept., 1968-72. Author: The Realm of Rime, A Study of Rime in the Poetry of the Slavs, 1974, Thirty Years of Yugoslav Literature, 1945-1975, 1978; contbr. to profl. jours.; editor: Anton Cechov, 1860-1960, 1960, (with A. Kadic) Juraj Krizanic (1618-1683) Russophile and Ecumenic Visionary, 1976, (with P. Debreczeny) Chekhov's Art of Writing, a Collection of Critical Essays, 1978, (with H. Birnbaum) Fiction and Drama in Eastern Europe, Evolution and Experiment in the Postwar Period, 1980, (with D.S. Worth) Russian Poetics, 1983, Calif. Slavic Studies, 1972—, (with D.S. Worth) Russian Poetics, 1983. Decorated Order Yugoslav Flag, 1964; recipient Martinus Nijhoff prize, 1981. Mem. Western Slavic Assn., Philol. Assn. Pacific Coast (pres. 1971), Assn. Internationale des Langues et Litteratures Slaves. Humanist. Office: 115 Kinsey Hall Slavic Dept U Calif Los Angeles CA 90024

EELKEMA, ROBERT CAMERON, physician, community medicine educator; b. Mankato, Minn., Sept. 24, 1930; s. H.H. and Ruth E.; m. Virginia Kieseau, Aug., 1973; children: Susan, Barbara, Katie, Jennifer, Emily, Robbie, Rienk; stepchildren: Scott, Cindy, Wade, Chad. B.S., U. Minn., 1954, D.V.M., 1956, post grad. in Epidemiology, 1969; B.S. in Medicine, U. N.D., 1959; M.D., U. Wash., 1961; M.P.H., U. Calif.-Berkeley, 1968. Diplomate: Am. Bd. Preventive Medicine, Am. Bd. Family Practice, Nat. Bd. Med. Examiners. Pvt. practice vet. medicine, Valley City, N.D., 1956-57; intern USPHS Hosp., Seattle, 1961-62; epidemic intelligence service Communicable Disease Center, USPHS, Atlanta, 1962-64; instr. physiology U. N.D. Sch. Medicine, Grand Forks, 1964-65, prof. pub. health and preventive medicine, 1965—, asst. coordinator Med. Edn. for Nat. Def., 1965-66, prof., chmn. dept. community medicine, 1968—, dir. Area Health Edn. Center, 1972-74, chmn. med. ops. com., 1972-73, prin. investigator, med. dir. Family nurse practitioner program, dept. community medicine, 1974—; dir. Drayton Project U. N.D. Sch. Medicine, Grand Forks, 1975; student health physician U. N.D., 1964-67; epidemiologic cons. N.D. State Dept. Health, 1964—; chmn. Fogaty Workshop on Physician Extenders John E. Fogarty Internat. Ctr., Bethesda, Md., 1973—; mem. Internat. Network for Mid-Level Health Manpower, Sch. Medicine and Pub. Health, U. Hawaii, 1977—; cons. State Health Dept. Grant Devel. for Sch. Nurse Practitioners, Robert Wood Johnson Found., 1978—, Grant Devel. for Emergency Room Nurse Practitioners, Old West Region, 1978—; mem. exec. bd. dirs. Internat. Health Soc., 1978—; monitor for fed. ct. concerning Grafton State Sch., 1981—; cons. Ministry of Health, Liberia, 1979. Contbr. articles to profl. jours. Noyes scholar, 1954-56; recipient Ralph Leigh award in physiology, 1959, Mary Wilson stipend, 1960-61; WHO fellow, Norway, Sweden, Germany Holland, 1974; recipient Physician's Recognition award, 1979, Presdl. medal for Service to Mankind, 1980. Mem. Assn. Tchrs. Preventive Medicine, Am. Pub. Health Assn. (epidemiology sect.), AMA, Am. Coll. Preventive Medicine, Internat. Soc. for Edn. in Health Scis., Greater Grand Forks Inter-Agy. Forum (pres. 1970-72). Home: RR1 Box 123A Grand Forks ND 58201 Office: Univ ND Med School 221 S 4th St Grand Forks ND 58201

EELLS, JOHN SHEPARD, JR., retired educator; b. San Francisco, Mar. 31, 1906; s. John Shepard and Marion (Coffin) E.; m. Juliet Guion Oakes, July 30, 1938; children: Guion Oakes, Marion Coffin. B.A., Yale U., 1928; LL.B., J.D., Stanford U., 1931; M.A., U. Calif., 1939, Ph.D., 1943. Bar: Calif. 1932. Assoc. Orrick, Palmer & Dahlquist, San Francisco, 1931-35; faculty mem. Thacher Sch., 1935-38, Pomona Coll., 1943-44, U. Chgo., 1944-45; prof. English Beloit Coll., 1945-55, Winthrop Coll., 1955-71, disting. prof., 1967—; chmn. honors council, 1960-71, Faculty rep. on bd. trustees, 1970, cons. to pres., 1971-73. Author: Telling Time, The Touchstones of Matthew Arnold; Contbr. to: Atlantic Monthly; Contbr.: works Kenyon Rev., others. Pres. Nat. Collegiate Honors Council, 1970-71. Mem. MLA, State Bar Calif., Am. Soc. Psychical Research, Phi Beta Kappa, Phi Kappa Phi. Clubs: Elizabethan (Yale), Rock Hill Country. Home: 623 Meadowbrook Ln Rock Hill SC 29730

EELLS, RICHARD, found. exec., educator; b. Cashmere, Wash., Aug. 5, 1917; s. Fred K. and Sophia (Fox) E. A.B., Whitman Coll., 1940, LL.D., 1982; M.A., Princeton, 1942. Fellow Library of Congress, 1945-46, chief div. aeros., 1946-50, Guggenheim chair aeros., 1949-50; field dir. Near East Coll. Assos., 1950-52; ednl. cons. Gen. Electric Co., N.Y.C., 1952-53, mgr. pub. relations research, 1953-56, mgr. pub. policy research, 1956-60; founder, pres. Richard Eells and Assos. Inc., 1961—; sr. researcher Grad. Sch. Bus., Columbia, N.Y.C., 1959-60, adj. prof., 1960—; dir., editor Studies of the Modern Corp., 1964—, mem. nat. devel. bd., 1974—, counselor to dean, 1975—, spl. adviser to pres., 1977—; ct.-apptd. observer U.S. Ct., Berlin, 1979; John M. Olin Disting. Lectr. Berry Coll., 1980; cons., adviser IBM, Gen. Electric Co., Kaiser Cos., Rockefeller Bros. Fund, Com. for Econ. Devel., Continental Group, Ashland Oil Co.; Mem. adv. research bd. Nat. Merit Scholarship Corp., 1957-59; pres. Found. Study Human Orgn.; trustee Arkville Erpf Fund, 1962-82, also sec. and treas.; dir. Midgard Found. Author: Corporation Giving in a Free Society, 1956, The Meaning of Modern Business: An Introduction to the Philosophy of Large Corporate Enterprise, 1960, (with Clarence Walton) Conceptual Foundations of Business, 1961, 3d edit., 1974 (McKinsey Found. Acad. Mgmt. award), The Business System: Readings in Ideas and Concepts, 1967, Man in the City of the Future, 1968, The Government of Corporations, 1962, The Corporation and the Arts, 1967, (with Kenneth G. Patrick) Education and the Business Dollar, 1969, Global Corporations: The Emerging System of World Economic Power, 2d edit, 1976, (with Neil H. Jacoby and Peter Nehemkis) Bribery and Extortion in World Business, 1977, International Business Philanthropy, 1979, The Political Crisis of the Enterprise System, 1980; author: (with Peter Nehemkis) Corporate Intelligence and Espionage, 1984. Trustee New Eng. Conservatory Music, 1974-78; trustee, v.p., treas. Weatherhead Found.; bd. overseers Whitman Coll.; bd. founders Acad. Gerontol. Edn. and Devel. Served with USAAF, 1943-45. Alfred P. Sloan Found., grantee, 1956; Rockefeller Found. grantee, 1963. Mem. The Pilgrims, Phi Beta Kappa. Episcopalian. Clubs: Metropolitan (N.Y.C.); Church; Cosmos (Washington). Home: 251 E 51st St New York NY 10022

EFFERSON, JOHN NORMAN, university chancellor; b. Holden, La., Nov. 18, 1912; s. Whitney H. and Gladys (Musselman) E.; m. Ruth Mansinger, Dec. 22, 1939; children: John W., Elizabeth, Sarah A. Undergrad. B.S., La. State U., 1934; M.S., Cornell U., 1936, Ph.D., 1938. Instr. agronomy La. State U., Baton Rouge, 1932-33, prof. agrl. econs., research economist, 1938-54, dir. agr. expt. sta., 1954-56; dean Coll. Agr., 1956—, now chancellor; instr. vocat. agr., Welsh, La., 1933-34; research asst. agrl. econs. Cornell U., 1935-38, vis. prof. agrl. econs., 1940-41; agr. tour, study in, Europe, 1938; internat. commodity specialist rice and sugar Dept. Agr., 1948, 49; food studies 45 countries, Asia, Africa, Europe, C.Am., S.Am., lectr. internat. problems, 1948-51; econs. cons. Govt. Venezuela.; Mem. postwar planning com. Nat. Land Grant Colls.; mem. Pres. Kennedy's task force on agrl. policy, 1961; board cons. Rockefeller Found., mem. found.'s study of diversification in, Malaya, 1962, agr., Venezuela, 1963; cons. AID, El Salvador, 1964, Agrl. adviser in, Brit. Guiana, 1965; Spl. cons. studies agrl. devel. in, Colombia and Venezuela, Ford Found., 1964; Aid study of N.E. Thailand, 1965, Ford Found. study edn. in, Malaysia, 1966, Nat. Acad. Sci. Com. on P.R., 1966, Ford Found. study agr. edn., Philippines, 1967, study rice marketing, Pakistan, 1968-71, AID study agr., Nicaragua, 1967, Jamaica, 1968-75, Pakistan, 1970-73, India, 1970-74, Ghana, 1974, Nigeria, Liberia and Senegal, 1979, Sri Lanka, Thailand and Jamaica, 1980; cons. Ford Found., Israel, 1976, Govt. Nicaragua, 1977, Govt. Malaysia, 1977, Ford Found. in, Philippines, Thailand, Pakistan and Bangladesh, 1978, Senegal, Nigeria, Jamaica, 1980, others; mem. Pres. Reagan's Task Force to Thailand. Author: Principles of Farm Accounting, 1942, Farm Management, 1942, Farm Records and Accounts, 1949, The Principles of Farm Management, 1952, The Production and Marketing of Rice, 1954, also expt. sta. bulls., research circulars.; Contbr. articles to profl. jours. Trustee Agrl. Devel. Council, Rockefeller Bros. panel on econs. and social policy. Mem. Am. Farm Econ. Assn., Pres.'s Export Council, Internat. Assn. Agrl. Economists, Am. Sugar Technologist Assn., Phi Kappa Phi, Alpha Zeta, Alpha Tau Alpha. Home: 5804 Boone Dr Baton Rouge LA 70808

EFFINGER, CECIL, educator, composer; b. Colorado Springs, Colo., July 22, 1914; s. Stanley Smith and Lucy (Graves) E.; m. Corinne Ann Lindberg, June 14, 1968; children (by previous marriage): Elizabeth Effinger (Mrs. Ted Baker), Gove Effinger. A.B. in Math, Colo. Coll., 1935, Mus.D. (hon.), 1959. Instr. math. Colorado Springs High Sch., 1936; instr. music Colo. Coll., 1936-41, asst. prof., 1946-48; instr. music Colo. Sch. for Blind, 1939-41; 1st oboist Denver Symphony, 1937-41; music editor Denver Post, 1946-48; asso. prof. music U. Colo., Boulder, 1948-56, prof., 1956-81, prof. emeritus and composer-in-residence, 1981—, faculty research lectr., 1955, faculty fellow, 1969-70; pres. Music Print Corp. Composer: numerous compositions, 1937—, more important being Little Symphony No. 1, 1945, Symphony No. 5, 1958, Cello Suite, 1945, Quartet No. 5, 1963, Symphony for Chorus and Orchestra, 1952, The Glorious Day is Here, 1955, Set of Three for Chorus and Brass, 1961, Four Pastorales for Oboe and Chorus, 1962, Cyrano de Bergerac; opera, 1965; The Invisible Fire, 1957, Paul of Tarsus, 1968, The St. Luke Christmas Story, 1953, A Cantata for Easter, 1971, Concerto for Violin and Chamber Orchestra, 1974, Capriccio for Orch, 1975, Fantasy for Piano and Voices, 1980, Ten Miniatures for Piano, 1982, Landscape II for Orchestra, 1983. Served with USAAF, 1941-46. Presser scholar, 1931; Cooke Daniel lectr. Denver Art Mus., 1957; recipient Stoval prize in composition Am. Conservatory, Fontainbleau, France, 1939, Naumburg Recording award, 1959; Gov.'s award in arts and humanities, 1971; U. Colo. medal, 1981. Mem. A.S.C.A.P., Am. Fedn. Musicians, Sigma Chi, Tau Beta Sigma, Phi Mu Alpha, Pi Kappa Lambda, Delta Omicron. Inventor Musicwriter; Open-end Typewriter; designer Tempowatch. Home: 2620 Lafayette Dr Boulder CO 80303 *To know and have respect for your own living self opens the door so that you may know and love your fellow man and know and do God's will - as best your gifts will let you.*

EFORO, JOHN FRANCIS, financial officer; b. N.Y.C., June 30, 1930; s. John J. and Rose (Lo Trianti) E.; m. Tina Liggio, Dec. 23, 1956; children—Joanne, Carla, John C. B.A. in Econs, CCNY, 1952, Am. Inst. Banking, 1953-55. Asst. v.p. ops. Nat. Bank of N.Am., N.Y.C., 1958-69; v.p., comptroller United Mut. Savs. Bank, N.Y.C., 1969-82; comptroller, chief fin. officer State of N.Y. Mortgage Agy., N.Y.C., 1982—; officer, dir. Joint Computer Center, Inc., 1974—. Home: 53 Sprague Rd Scarsdale NY 10583 Office: 260 Madison Ave New York NY 10016

EFRON, BRADLEY, educator; b. St. Paul, May 24, 1938; s. Miles Jack and Esther (Kaufman) E.; m. Gael Guerin, July 1969 (div.); 1 son, Miles James. B.S. in Math., Calif. Inst. Tech., 1960; Ph.D., Stanford U., 1964. Asst. and assoc. prof. stats. Stanford U., Calif., 1965-72, chmn. dept. stats., 1976-79, chmn. math. scis., 1982—, prof. stats., 1972—; statis. cons. Alza Corp., 1970—, Rand Corp., 1966—. Author: Bootstrap Methods, 1982, Biostatistics Casebook, 1980. MacArthur Found. fellow, 1983; named Outstanding Statistician of the Yr. Chgo. Statis. Assn., 1981; Walk and Rietz Lectr. Inst. Math. Stats., 1977, 81. Fellow Inst. Math. Stats., Am. Statis. Assn.; mem. Internat. Statis. Assn. Democrat. Office: Dept Statistics Sequoia Hall Stanford CA 94305

EFRON, SAMUEL, lawyer; b. Lansford, Pa., May 6, 1915; s. Abraham and Rose (Kaduchin) E.; m. Hope Bachrach Newman, Apr. 5, 1941; children: Marc Fred, Eric Michael. B.A., Lehigh U., 1935; LL.B., Harvard U., 1938. Bar: Pa. 1938, D.C. 1949, N.Y. 1967. Atty. forms and regulations div., also registration div. SEC, 1939-40; Office Solicitor Dept. Labor, 1940-42; asst. chief real and personal property sect. Office Alien Property Custodian, 1942-43; chief debt claims sect., also asst. chief claims br. Office Alien Property, Dept. Justice, 1946-51; asst. gen. counsel internat. affairs Dept. Def., 1951-53, cons., 1953-54; partner firm Surrey, Karasik, Gould & Efron, Washington, 1954-61; exec. v.p. Parsons & Whittemore, Inc., N.Y.C., 1961-68; now partner Arent, Fox, Kintner, Plotkin & Kahn, Washington.; Trustee Meridian House Internat. Author: Creditors Claims Under the Trading with the Enemy Act, 1948, Foreign Taxes on United States Expenditures, 1954, Offshore Procurement and Industrial Mobilization, 1955, The Operation of Investment Incentive Laws with Emphasis on the U.S.A. and Mexico, 1977. Served to lt. USNR, 1943-46. Decorated Order of the Lion of Finland 1st class. Mem. Am., Fed., Inter-Am. bar assns., Am. Soc. Internat. Law, Assn. Bar City N.Y., Bar Assn. D.C., Phi Beta Kappa. Clubs: Army-Navy, Capitol Hill, Cosmos, Harvard, Internat., Nat. Press, University, Fed. Bar (Washington); Harvard, Lehigh, Lotos (N.Y.C.). Home: 3537 Ordway St NW Washington DC 20016 Office: 1050 Connecticut Ave NW Washington DC 20036

EFROYMSON, ROBERT ABRAHAM, investment company executive; b. Indpls., Sept. 27, 1905; s. Gustave Aaron and Mamie (Wallenstein) E.; m. Shirley Green, Mar. 20, 1977; children by previous marriage: Gustave A., Daniel R., Mary Ann Efroymson Stein. Student, Butler U., 1922-23, LL.B. (hon.), 1969; A.B., Harvard U., 1926, LL.B., 1929. Bar: Ind. bar 1930. Practiced law, Indpls., 1929-42; pres. Real Silk Hosiery Mills, Inc., Indpls., 1946—; v.p., dir. Occidental Realty Co.; dir. Ind. Nat. Bank, Ind. Nat. Corp., Lincoln Nat. Life Ins. Co., Lincoln Nat. Corp. Trustee Indpls. Found., 1946—; pres. William E. English Found., Indpls., 1959—; bd. dirs. Jewish Welfare Fedn., Indpls. Served to capt. USAAF, 1942-45. Mem. Ind. Acad. Jewish. Clubs: Indpls. Athletic, Broadmoor Country. Office: 445 N Pennsylvania St 908 Indianapolis IN 46204

EGAN, EILEEN MARY, college president; b. Boston, Jan. 11, 1925; d. Eugene O. and Mary B. (Condon) E. A.B., Spalding Coll., 1956; M.A., Cath. U. Am., 1963, Ph.D. (Bd. Trustees scholar), 1966; J.D., U. Louisville, 1981. Bar: Ky. 1981. Joined Sisters of Charity of Nazareth, Roman Catholic Ch., 1944; tchr. secondary schs., Wakefield, Mass., 1956-60, Memphis, 1960-62; mem. faculty English dept. Cath. U. Am., Washington, 1963-66; chmn. dept. English, Spalding Coll., Louisville, 1966-67, v.p., 1968-69, pres., 1969—; prof. U. Louisville Law Sch., 1982-83; adminstrv. intern Smith Coll., Northampton, Mass., 1967-68; mem. Ky. State Commn. on Higher Edn., 1969-72, 75-77; chmn. Louisville br. Fed. Res. Bank, 1981. Exec. bd. Old Ky. Home council Boy Scouts Am., 1976—; mem. bishop's pastoral council Archdiocese of Louisville, 1975-78; mem. Louisville Com. Fgn. Relations, 1978—; chmn. open spaces adv. com. City of Louisville, 1976—; bd. dirs. Met. United Way, 1976-80; bd. dirs. chpt. NCCJ, 1973—; bd. dirs. Better Bus. Bur. Greater Louisville, 1974-79, v.p., 1975-79; bd. dirs. St. Joseph Infirmary, 1970-71, trustee, 1971-76, chmn. bd. trustees, 1975-76; mem. community audit com. Jefferson County Bd. Edn., 1980—; trustee Ky. Ind. Coll. Found., 1970—; bd. dirs. Kentuckiana Metroversity, 1972—, exec. com., 1977—, chmn. exec. com., 1982—. Recipient Equality award Louisville Urban League, 1978, award Phi Delta Kappa, 1979; Blanche B. Ottenheimer award Louisville Jewish Community Center, 1978; Brotherhood award NCCJ, 1979; Inst. Internat. Edn. fellow, 1963. Mem. Am. Assn. Higher Edn., So. Assn. Colls. and Schs., Nat. Cath. Edn. Assn. (exec. com. 1973-76), Louisville C. of C. (public edn. com. 1978—, dir. 1982—), English Speaking Union, AAUW. Democrat. Home: 2511 River Bend Louisville KY 40206 Office: 851 S 4th St Louisville KY 40203

EGAN, FRANK T., writer, editor; b. N.Y.C., May 1, 1933; s. Frank X. and Ann M. (Hatton) E.; m. Helen Birmingham, June 5, 1954; children—Patricia, Thomas, Barbara, Richard, Maureen. Student, Drexel Inst. Tech., 1955-56, N.Y. U., 1956-60. Editor, Mc-Graw-Hill Pub. Co., N.Y.C., 1956-65, Hayden Pub. Co., Rochelle Park, N.J., 1965-71, Cahners Pub. Co., Boston, 1971-76, United Tech. Publs., Garden City, N.Y., 1976—; Author: Ideas for Design, 1970. Served with USN, 1951-55. Home: 1 Birchwood Ct Mineola NY 11501 Office: United Tech Publs 645 Stewart Ave Garden City NY 11530

EGAN, JOSEPH GILBERT, lawyer; b. Chgo., Oct. 7, 1923; s. Gilbert and Mary (Leech) E.; m. Carolyn Hegwood, Mar. 15, 1945; children: Michael J., Alexandra Egan. A.B., U. Mich., 1948, J.D., 1950. Bar: Ill. 1950. Atty. Lord, Bissell & Brook, Chgo., 1950-55; jr. atty. Quaker Oats Co., Chgo., 1955-64, atty., 1964-72, counsel, 1972-77; v.p. trade regulation 2, Chgo., 1977-80, v.p., gen. corp. counsel, 1980—. Bd. dirs. Chgo. Crime Commn., 1983; advisor Chgo. United Profl. Services Com., 1978—. Served to 1st lt., inf. U.S. Army, 1942-46. Decorated Silver Star, Purple Heart. Mem. ABA, Ill. Bar Assn., Chgo. Bar Assn. Club: Mid-America. Home: 175 E Delaware Pl Apt 6115 Chicago IL 60611 Office: 345 Merchandise Mart Chicago IL 60654

EGAN, KEVIN P., service company executive; b. Evanston, Ill., Sept. 27, 1943; s. Charles N. and Margaret (Hubsch) E.; m. Pamela T. Egan, Jan. 6, 1966; children: Jennifer, Zachary, Patrick. B.A., Parson Coll., 1965. Mktg. rep. 3M Co., St. Paul, 1965-69; dir. European ops. Transam Computer Co., London, 1969-72; v.p. Little Rapids Corp., Green Bay, Wis., 1972-75; pres. Mailhouse Inc., Mpls., 1983—; sr. v.p. Manpower Internat., Milw., 1975—; dir. Sault News Printing, 1977—, Snow Goose, Inc., Milw., 1978—. Bd. dirs. Boys Club of Am., Green Bay, 1972-75. Mem. Nat. Railroad Mus., Milw. Art Inst., Nat. Assn. Advt. Distributors, Health Equip. Mfrs. Assn., Am. Paper Inst. Republican. Roman Catholic. Clubs: Milwaukee Yacht (fleet capt.); Milwaukee Athletic. Office: 5301 N Ironwood Rd Milwaukee WI 53201

EGAN, MICHAEL JOSEPH, lawyer; b. Savannah, Ga., Aug. 8, 1926; s. Michael Joseph and Elise (Robider) E.; m. Donna Cole, Apr. 4, 1951; children: Moira Elizabeth, Michael Joseph, Donna, Cole, Roby, John Patrick. B.A., Yale U., 1950; LL.B., Harvard U., 1955. Bar: Ga., D.C. Asso. firm Sutherland, Asbill & Brennan, Atlanta, 1955-61, partner, 1961-77, 79—; mem. Ga. Ho. of Reps., 1966-77, minority leader, 1971-77; asso. atty. gen. U.S. Dept. Justice, Washington, 1977-79. Served with U.S. Army, 1945-47, 50-52. Mem. Am., Atlanta bar assns., State Bar Ga., Atlanta Lawyers Club, Am. Law Inst., Am. Coll. Probate Counsel. Republican. Roman Catholic. Home: 97 Brighton Rd NE Atlanta GA 30309 Office: 3100 First Atlanta Tower Atlanta GA 30383 1666 K St NW Washington DC 20006

EGAN, RICHARD LEO, medical association executive; b. Omaha, Dec. 27, 1917; s. George Leo and Mary V. (Shearer) E.; m. Alice Larsen, May 1, 1943; children: Katherine Ruth, Richard George. B.S. in Medicine, Creighton U., 1938; M.D., 1940. Mem. faculty Creighton U. Sch. Medicine, Omaha, 1941-71, assoc. prof. medicine, 1953- 69, prof. medicine, 1969-71, dean, 1959-70, asst. to pres. for health scis., 1970-71; asst. dir. dept. undergrad. med. edn. A.M.A., Chgo., 1971-75, dir., 1975-76, dir. div. ednl. standards and evaluation, 1976-82, dir. div. med. edn., 1982—, sec. council med. edn., 1976—; Mem. exec. com. health council United Community Services, Omaha, 1956-66, chmn., 1958-60; Mem. med. adv. bd. Salvation Army Central Territory, 1971—. Recipient Cert. of Merit U.S. Navy, 1966. Fellow Inst. Medicine Chgo.; mem. Am. Heart Assn. (dir. 1962-68, Award of Merit 1972), Nebr. Heart Assn. (bd. dirs., exec. com. 1957-70, sec. 1958, pres. 1960-61), Am. Med. Assn., Nebr. Med. Assn. (ho. dels. 1954-71), Ill. Med. Assn., Assn. Am. Med. Colls., Am. Assn. History of Medicine, Health Planning Council of Midlands (mem. exec. com. adv. council 1969-71), U.S. Catholic Conf. (mem. com. health affairs 1969-71), Alpha Omega Alpha. Home: 323 Cottage Ave Glen Ellyn IL 60137

EGAN, ROBERT LEE, physician, educator; b. Morrilton, Ark., May 9, 1920; s. Philip Kearny and Camilla (Roach) E.; m. Mary Alice Vetterly, Oct. 27, 1950; children—Kathleen Louise, Deborah Ann, Cheryl Lynn, Melissa Jean, Patricia Lea. Student, Coll. of Ozarks, Clarksville, Ark., 1935-39; M.D., U. Pitts., 1950. Diplomate: Am. Bd. Radiology. Intern U.S. Naval Hosp., Portsmouth, Va., 1950-51; resident Jefferson Med. Coll. Hosp., Phila., 1953-55; practice medicine specializing in radiology, Houston, 1955-62, Indpls., 1962-64, Atlanta, 1964—; asso. radiologist diagnostic radiology U. Tex. M.D. Anderson Hosp. and Tumor Inst., Houston, 1961-62; chief sect. exptl. diagnostic radiology M.D. Anderson Hosp., 1961-62; radiologist dept. radiology Methodist Hosp. of Ind., Indpls., 1962-65; chief mammography sect. Emory U., Atlanta, 1965—, asso. prof. radiology, 1965-68, prof., 1968—. Author: Mammography, 1964, 72, Technologist Guide to Mammography, 1968, Egan's Data on Mammography and Breast Cancer, 1972. Served to lt. (j.g.) USNR, 1937-38, 44-46, 50-51. Fellow Am. Coll. Radiology; mem. AMA, Fulton County Med. Soc., Radiol. Soc. N.Am., Ga. Radiol. Soc., Am. Roentgen Ray Soc., Ewings Soc. Home: RD 10 Box 44 Cumming GA 30130

EGAN, ROGER EDWARD, publishing consultant; b. N.Y.C., Jan. 26, 1921; s. William Joseph and Josephine (Anderson) E.; m. Grace Dorothy Olsen, Sept. 3, 1949; children: Roger Emmett, Gregory J., David C., Mary Jo, Laura G. A.B. cum laude, St. Francis Coll., 1949; M.A., NYU, 1954. Chmn. English dept. St. Francis Prep. Sch., 1948-53; gen. mgr. Silver-Burdett Co. (subsidiary Time, Inc.), N.Y.C., 1958-67; pres. L.W. Singer Co. (subsidiary Random House), N.Y.C., 1967-70; dir. Random House Pub. Co., 1967-70; editorial dir. McGraw Hill Book Co., N.Y.C., 1970-73, gen. mgr. sch. div., 1973-76; publishing cons., 1977-78, 82—; v.p. McKnight Pub. Co., Bloomington, Ill., 1978-82; lectr. English Coll. St. Elizabeth's, 1958-63; Mem. N.Y. State Youth Bd., 1949-53. Mng. editor sch. books, Doubleday Book Co., N.Y.C., 1953-58; Editor numerous books for use in elem., secondary schs., colls. Served with AUS, 1942-45. Decorated Bronze Star. Roman Catholic (chmn. edn. comn. parish, 1970-71, mem. com. lay advisers to Council Am. Bishops, 1967-71). Home: 1103 Hollyridge Circle Bloomington IL 61701

EGAN, SYLVIA, hosp. adminstr.; b. Oshkosh, Wis., Sept. 15, 1930; d. Edward James and Dorothy Loretta (Loewen) E. B.S.N., U. Marquette, 1956; postgrad., Wayne State U., 1969; B.S., Okla. Bapt. U., 1978; M.S.A., Notre Dame U., 1981. Joined Congregation of Sisters of Sorrowful Mother, Roman Catholic Ch., 1949; nurse Mercy Hosp. Sch. Nursing, Oshkosh, 1952-54, night supr., 1954-55; med. supr. Mercy Hosp., Oshkosh, 1956-57; instr. St. John's Hosp. Sch. Nursing, Tulsa, 1957-63; dir. St. Mary's Hosp. Sch. Practical Nursing, Roswell, N.Mex., 1963-65; dir. novices, Tulsa Province, Sisters of Sorrowful Mother, 1965-69, provincial adminstr., 1970-78; pres. Franciscan Villa, Broken Arrow, Okla., 1978-79; pres., chief exec. officer St. Francis Hosp., Wichita, Kans., 1979—; del. renewal chpt. Sisters of the Sorrowful Mother, Milw., 1967-68, 69, chmn. formation com., Tulsa Province, 1968, chpt. del. to, Rome, 1970, 74, 78; internat. chmn. Centenary Com., Germany, 1980; Bd. dirs. ARC, 1981—. Mem. Am. Coll. Hosp. Adminstrs., Kans. Hosp. Assn., Cath. Health Assn., Kan. Cath. Health Conf., Med. Edn. Assos. (v.p. 1980-81), Kans. Assn. Commerce and Industry. Republican. Club: Notre Dame Alumnae. Address: 929 N Saint Francis St Wichita KS 67214

EGAN, VINCENT JOSEPH, journalist; b. Toronto, Ont., Can., July 23, 1921; s. James Aloysius and Margaret (Ahearn) E.; m. Margaret Mary Maley, Apr. 23, 1962. B.A., U. Toronto, 1951; M. B.A., 1955. Asst. editor Financial Post, Toronto, 1952-61; asst. to pres. Toronto Stock Exchange, 1961-62. Financial columnist: Globe and Mail, Toronto, 1962-68; financial editor: Toronto Telegram, 1968-71; bus. columnist: Thomson Newspapers, 1972—; Author: Making Money In The Market, 1955. Served with RoyalCan. Navy, 1942-46. Decorated Victory medal; Can. Vol. Service medal. Roman Catholic. Club: Ticker (Toronto). Home: 50 Rolph Rd Toronto ON Canada Office: 65 Queen St W Toronto ON Canada

EGAN, WESLEY WILLIAM, ambassador; b. Madison, Wis., Jan. 21, 1946; s. Wesley William and Ruth (Skeuse) E.; m. Virginia Warren, Aug. 15, 1967; children: Wesley Matthew, Kimberley Katherine. B.A. with honors, U. N.C., 1968. Vice consul Am. Consulate Gen., Durban, South Africa, 1972-74; spl. asst. to sec. state Dept. State Washington, 1974-77; 1st sec. Am. embassy, Portugal, 1977-79, dep. chief mission, Republic Zambia, 1979-82; ambassador to Republic of Guinea-Bissau, 1983—. Mem. Am. Fgn. Service Assn.; life mem. U. N.C. Alumni Assn. Republican. Episcopalian.

EGBERT, EMERSON CHARLES, publisher; b. Los Angeles, Nov. 30, 1924; s. Charles Barnes and Ethel Annette (Feader) E.; m. Kathryn Eleanor Tressel, Apr. 6, 1947; children—Susan Ann, John Charles, James Emerson, Michael Warren, Patricia Ann. Ed., Pasadena Jr. Coll., Woodbury Bus. Coll. Distbn. mgr. Newsstand Distbrs., 1947-49; dist. sales mgr. So. Calif., Pocket Books, Inc., 1949-59, sales mgr. Eastern div., 1959-61, v.p., circulation dir., 1961-71; pres. Pocket Books Distbn. Corp., N.Y.C., 1971-81; sr. v.p. Silhouette Books div. Simon & Schuster, 1981—. Past dist. commr. Boy Scouts Am.; bd. dirs. 25 Year Club. Served with USNR, 1942-45. Decorated D.F.C., Air Medal with 4 oak leaf clusters. Mem. Ind. Newsstand Circulation Execs. Assn. (past chmn.), Internat. Periodical Distbrs. Am. (chmn.), Bur. Ind. Pubs. and Distbrs. (past chmn. book com.), Anti-Defamation League. Republican. Home: 28 Lexington St Rockville Centre NY 11570 Office: 1230 Ave of Americas New York NY 10020

EGBERT, RICHARD COOK, banker; b. N.Y.C., June23, 1927; s. Lester D. and Beatrice (Cook) E.; m. Anne Merrill Becker, Sept. 11, 1954; children: Allison Huntting, Anne Merrill, Richard Cook. B.A., Yale U., 1950. With Chase Nat. Bank, 1950-53; with Estabrook & Co., N.Y.C., 1954-68, partner, 1963-68; v.p. Spencer Trask & Co., Inc. (and successor cos.), N.Y.C., 1968-79, Bankers Trust Co., 1979—; Mem. Blue Hill Troupe, Ltd., N.Y.C., 1951—, pres., 1961-62; v.p., dir. 1030 Fifth Ave. Corp., 1968-72. Trustee, former treas. and chmn. finance com. W. Side Day Nursery, N.Y.C., 1957—; adv. bd. Nat. Choral Council, 1981—. Served with USNR, 1945-46. Mem. Soc. Colonial Wars, St. Nicholas Soc. N.Y., Pilgrims U.S., Chi Phi. Presbyn. (past deacon). Club: Bond (N.Y.C.). Home: 270 Old Church Rd Greenwich CT 06830 Office: 280 Park Ave New York NY 10017

EGDAHL, RICHARD HARRISON, medical educator; b. Eau Claire, Wis., Dec. 13, 1926; s. Harry I. and Rebecca (Ball) E.;, Mar. 3, 1953; children: Scott, David, Bruce, Julie. M.D., Harvard U., 1950; Ph.D., U. Minn., 1957. Intern U. Minn. Hosp., 1950-51, resident, 1956-57; prof. surgery Med. Coll. Va., 1957-64; prof., chmn. surgery Boston U. Med. Center, 1964-73, dir., 1973—; also acad. v.p. for health affairs, dir. Center for Industry and Health Care, Boston U.; Chmn. VA and Nat. Inst. Gen. Med. Scis.; surg. tng. commn., 1971-72; sr. cons. Pres.'s Adv. Council Mgmt. Improvement and Nat. Center Health Services, 1971-73; chmn. surg. A study sect. NIH. Editor: Comprehensive Manuals of Surgical Specialties; editorial bd.: Surgery, New Eng. Jour. Medicine, World Jour. Surgery. Bd. dirs. Med. Found. Served to lt. USNR, 1952-55. Mem. Soc. Univ. Surgeons (pres. 1970-71), A.C.S., Am. Physiol. Soc., Am. Soc. Clin. Investigation, Am. Surg. Assn. (1st v.p. 1980), Boston Surg. Soc. (pres. 1977), Endocrine Soc. (CIBA award 1961), Inst. Medicine Nat. Acad. Scis., Internat. Assn. Endocrine Surgeons (pres. 1981-83), Phi Beta Kappa, Alpha Omega Alpha. Clubs: The Brookline Country, Cosmos, Algonquin, Union., Badminton and Tennis. Home: 333 Commonwealth Ave Apt 23 Boston MA 02115 Office: 720 Harrison Ave Boston MA 02118

EGEBERG, ROGER OLAF, physician; b. Chgo., Nov. 13, 1903; s. Hans Olaf and Ulrikka Rostrup (Nielsen) E.; m. Margaret McEchron Chahoon, Sept. 5, 1929; children: Dagny (Mrs. William Hancock), Sarah (Mrs. Robert Beauchamp), Roger Olaf, Karen (Mrs. Richard Warmer). B.A., Cornell U., 1925; M.D., Northwestern U., 1929. Diplomate: Am. Bd. Internal Medicine. Intern Wesley Hosp., Chgo., 1928-29; resident Passavant Meml. Hosp., 1929-30, Univ. Hosp., Ann Arbor, Mich., 1930-32; practice medicine, specializing in internal medicine, Cleve., 1932-42; chief med. service VA Hosp., Los Angeles, 1946-56; med. dir. Los Angeles County Hosp., 1956-59, Los Angeles County Dept. Charities, 1958-64; mem. staff Los Angeles County Gen. Hosp., Rancho Los Amigos Hosp., Downey, Calif., Olive View (Calif.) Hosp.; clin. prof. medicine U. Calif. at Los Angeles, 1948-64, Coll. Med. Evangelists, 1956-64; prof. medicine U. So. Calif., 1956-69, dean Sch. Medicine, 1964-69, now prof. emeritus Sch. Medicine, 1964-69, adj. prof. Ctr. for Gerontology; asst. sec. for health and sci. affairs HEW, 1969-71, spl. asst. to sec. for health policy, 1971-77, spl. asst. for health edn., 1976-77, spl. cons. to pres. for health affairs, 1971-77, chief med. officer, 1977-78; dir. office Profl. and Sci. Affairs, Health Care Financing Adminstrn., from 1978; now sr. scholar in residence Inst. Medicine, Nat. Acad. Scis.; mem. Calif. Bd. Pub. Health, 1961-67, pres., 1964-67; chmn. Gov. Calif. Com. Study Med. Care and Health in Calif., 1959-60, Pres.'s Panel Narcotics Addiction, 1962, Pres.'s Adv. Commn. Narcotic and Drug Abuse, 1963, Nat. Adv. Cancer Council, 1964-67; mem. spl. med. adv. group to VA, 1965—; chmn. Calif. regional planning programs, 1967—; co-chmn. U.S.-USSR Joint Com. for Health Cooperation, 1972—. Chmn. med. adv. com. Los Angeles chpt. Planned Parenthood-World Population Assn., 1965—; mem. bd. Calif. div. Am. Cancer Soc., 1959—. Served to col., M.C. AUS, 1942-46. Decorated Bronze Star, Legion of Merit; St. Olaf's medal, Norway). Master A.C.P.; mem. A.M.A., Calif., Los Angeles County med. assns., Am. Clin. and Climatol. Assn., Calif. Soc. Internal Medicine, Western Assn. Physicians, Pacific Interurban Club, Alpha Omega Alpha. Spl. research ecology of coccidioides Immitis. Address: Inst Medicine 2101 Constitution Ave Suite JH 716 Washington DC 20418

EGEKVIST, W. SOREN, corp. cons., educator; b. Mpls., Dec. 9, 1918; s. Soren Andersen and Lillian (Anderson) E.; m. Margaret Stang, Oct. 21, 1948. A.B., Carleton Coll., 1941; M.B.A., Harvard, 1943; postgrad., Sch. Mil. Govt., U. Va., 1944, U. Chgo., 1945, 51; LL.D., Jamestown Coll., 1975. Chief economist U.S. Civil Service, also chief price control and rationing div. GHQ-SCAP, Tokyo, Japan, 1945-47; partner Robert Heller & Assos., Cleve., 1948-52; asst. to pres. J. Kayser Co., N.Y.C., 1952-55; v.p., gen. mgr. Munsingwear, Inc., Mpls., 1955-58; pres., dir. Sorenco, Inc., Mpls., 1958—; mng. dir. PORSA Systems; interim pres. Jamestown (N.D.) Coll., 1974-76, prof. history, 1976—, hon. chancellor, 1978—, also trustee; consul gen., Japan, Mpls., 1976—; del. FAO-UN, India, 1947. Author: Economic Stabilization Plan for Japan, 1947, Legislation for Economic Stabilization Board, 1947, Economic Controls During Occupation of Japan, 1952. Bd. dirs. Twin City area Internat. Exec. Service Corps; recipient citation for distinguished service, 1970; trustee Jamestown Med. Found., 1975—, Bishop Whipple Schs., 1976-79. Served to capt. AUS, 1943-46. Decorated Legion of Merit; recipient Meritorious Civilian Service medal War Dept., 1947. Mem. Japan Soc. Minn. (pres. 1975, chmn. bd. 1977—), Newcomen Soc., U.S. C. of C. (exec. res. 1958-68), Beta Gamma Sigma. Clubs: Mason (32 deg., Shriner, Jester), Rotarian., Harvard Bus. Sch. (pres. 1962-63), Minneapolis Skylight, Six O'clock, Torske Klubben, Interlachen Country (gov. 1963-69), Minneapolis (Mpls.)). Office: 5316 Dundee Rd Edina MN 55436

EGEN, RICHARD BELL, health care company executive; b. Hastings, Nebr., July 28, 1938; s. Lothar Fredrick and Ruth Pauline (Ellis) E.; m. Donna Diane Lambert, Aug. 18, 1962; children: Richard Bell, Elizabeth. P.E., Colo. Sch. Mines, 1960; M.I.A., Yale U., 1965. Engr. Atlantic Richfield Co., 1963; cons. McKinsey & Co., 1965-73; dir. planning Baxter Travenol Labs., Inc., Deerfield, Ill., 1974—, dir. Can. ops., 1974-75, pres. med. products div., 1976-82, exec. v.p. Europe, 1982-83; pres. European div. Travenol Internat. Services, Inc., 1983—. Served with C.E. USAR, 1961-62. Home: Ave de la Petite Espinette 9A Brussels 1180 Belgium Office: 130 La Hulpe Brussels Belgium

EGENSTEINER, DONALD THOMAS, advertising agency executive; b. N.Y.C., May 1, 1932; s. Clifford Frederick and Mae (Dietz) E.; m. Virginia E. Andersen, Oct. 7, 1956; children: Erik Donald, Eva Beth, Lynne Marie. B.F.A., Pratt Inst., 1954. Art dir. Young & Rubicam, Inc., N.Y.C., 1954-61, v.p., asso. creative dir., 1961-70, sr. v.p. creative dir., Detroit, 1970-72, sr. v.p. group creative dir., N.Y.C., 1972-80, sr. v.p., dir. comml. TV prodn., 1981—; sr. v.p., worldwide creative dir. Marsteller, Inc., N.Y.C., 1980-81. Served with U.S. Army, 1954-56. Mem. N.Y. Art Dirs. Club. Presbyterian. Home: 99 Fox Ridge Rd Stamford CT 06903 Office: 285 Madison Ave New York NY 10017

EGER, JOSEPH, conductor, music director; b. Hartford, Conn., July 9, 1925; s. Abraham and Clara (Ellovich) E. Grad., Curtis Inst., Berkshire Music Center; studied with, Monteux, Stokowski, Steinberg, Lert, Rudolf, Kahne. Faculty Aspen (Colo.) Music Festival, 1952-57, Peabody Conservatory, 1962-65, New Sch., 1971-72; creator Harlem Music Project (published by Schirmer's, Consol. Music Pubs.); condr. seminar Smithsonian Instn., 1979; faculty, dir. internat. concert/seminar Salzburg Seminars, 1980. First horn, N.Y., Los Angeles, Israel philharmonics, other maj. orchs.; solo rec. artist, RCA Victor, motion picture, TV, radio recs.; French horn soloist, 1956, world concert tours; lectr.; music dir., Eger Players; founder, condr., Camera Concerti Chamber Orch., 1958, Westside Symphony Orch., 1961, N.Y. Orch. Soc., 1963-73; condr., Midland (Mich.) Symphony, 1962-64; guest condr., Royal Philharmonic, London Philharmonic, New Philharmonia, Sinfonia of London, Pitts., Cin., Balt., Am. symphony orchs., Vienna Radio Orch., Dessoff Choir, Haifa, others; condr.: Town Hall series, 1962-63, Carnegie Hall, 1964-71, Philharmonic Hall, 1965-72, Young People and Teenage Concerts; asso. condr. to, Leopold Stokowski, 1967-70; condr. rec. for, Life mag., 1966, Westminster Record Co., 1967; music dir., Indian Hill, 1967, N.Y. Symphony Premiere Performance, 1968, N.Y. Concertante; condr., Athens Festival; founder, music dir., Symphony of N.Y.; founder, Crossover; founder, dir., Aware, N.Y., 1971-74, Internat. Yoga Symphony, Canada, N.Y., 1973; music dir., Symphony for UN, 1975—, UN Singers, 1975, Bklyn. Heights Symphony, 1978-82; composed score for film Carolina, 1970; recorded: albums Joseph Eger Retrospective Series, 1978; condr. concert series, UN, Apr. 1980; Contbg. author: UNESCO Cultures; contbr.: guest editorial Newsweek mag, Sept. 1980, Christian Sci. Monitor, July 1981, N.Y. Times, Apr. 1982; Editor: Citibank AWARE Playbill. Served to staff sgt. USAAF. Recipient N.Y.C. Mayor's award, 1975. Mem. Nat. Assn. Am. Condrs. and Composers (program chmn. 1965-67), Acad. Ind. Scholars. Home: 40 W 67th St New York NY 10023

EGERTON, JOHN WALDEN, author; b. Atlanta, June 14, 1935; s. William Graham and Rebecca Crenshaw (White) E.; m. Ann Elizabeth Bleidt, June 6, 1957; children: Brooks Bleidt, March White. Student, Western Ky. State Coll., 1953-54; B.A., U. Ky., 1958, M.A., 1960. With pub. relations dept. U. Ky., 1958-60; dir. pub. info. U. South Fla., 1960-65. Staff writer, So. Edn. Report mag., 1965-69, Race Relations Reporter mag, 1969-71; contbg. editor, 1973-74; free lance writer, Nashville, 1971—; journalist in residence, Va. Poly. Inst. and State U., Blacksburg, 1977-78; contbg. editor: Saturday Rev. of Edn, 1972-73, So. Voices, 1974-75; Author: A Mind to Stay Here, 1970, The Americanization of Dixie, 1974, Visions of Utopia, 1977, Nashville: The Faces of Two Centuries, 1979, Generations, 1983; contbr. articles to mags. Served with AUS, 1954-56. Address: 4014 Copeland Dr Nashville TN 37215

EGERTSON, DARRELL JERLOW, financial exec.; b. Albert Lea, Minn., Nov. 29, 1933; s. Ernest Sigfred and Ardis (Jerlow) E.; m. Helga Oberzaucher, Sept. 29, 1959; children—Kurt Darrell, Eric Sven. B.A. in Bus. Adminstrn, Augsburg Coll., 1955; postgrad., U. Minn., 1958-59. With Apache Corp., Mpls., 1960—, corp. accountant, 1963-65, chief accounting officer, 1965-67, controller, 1967-80, v.p., 1977-80, exec. v.p., 1980—. Republican precinct chmn.; bd. regents Augsburg Coll., Mpls., 1980—; trustee, treas. Nat. Found. Philanthropy, 1981—. Served with AUS, 1956-57. Mem. Fin. Execs. Inst., Am. Inst. Corp. Controllers, Mpls. C. of C. Lutheran. Home: 509 S Blake Rd Edina MN 55343 Office: Foshay Tower Minneapolis MN 55402

EGETH, HOWARD ELLIOTT, psychologist, educator; b. Newark, Feb. 15, 1940; s. Elias Louis and Lillian (Horn) E.; m. Sylvia Marcy Frank, Aug. 17, 1969; children—Jill Deborah, Marc Jonathan. A.B., Rutgers U., 1961; Ph.D., U. Mich., 1966. Asst. prof. psychology Johns Hopkins U., Balt., 1965-70, asso. prof., 1970-73. prof., 1973—. Author: (with S.H. Hulse and J.E. Deese) The Psychology of Learning, 1975, 80; cons. editor: Perception and Psychophysics, 1972—. Mem. Am. Psychol. Assn., Psychonomic Soc., Am. Psychology-Law Soc., Sigma Xi. Home: 11405 Belfield Rd Owings Mills MD 21117 Office: Dept Psychology Johns Hopkins U Baltimore MD 21218

EGGAN, FRED RUSSELL, anthropology educator; b. Seattle, Sept. 12, 1906; s. Alfred Julius and Olive M. (Smith) E.; m. Dorothy Way, Aug. 9, 1938 (dec. 1965); m. Joan Rosenfels, June 29, 1969. Ph.B., U. Chgo., 1927, A.M., 1928, Ph.D., 1933; M.A., Oxford U., 1970. Research asso. in Philippine ethnology U. Chgo., 1934-35, instr. anthropology, 1935-40, asst. prof., 1940-42, asso. prof., 1942-48, prof., 1948-74, chmn. dept., 1948-52, 61-63, dir. Philippine studies program, 1953—, Harold H. Swift Disting. Service prof., 1963-74, prof. emeritus, 1974—; Morgan lectr. U. Rochester, 1964; Frazer lectr. Cambridge, 1971; vis. fellow All Souls Coll., Oxford U., 1970; vis. prof. U. Calif., Santa Cruz, winter 1976; Weatherhead research scholar Sch. Am. Research, Santa Fe, 1979-80; ofcl. U.S. del. 8th Pacific Sci. Congress, Manila, 1953, 9th, Bangkok, 1957, 10th, Honolulu, 1961, 11th, Tokyo, 1966, 13th, Vancouver, B.C., Can., 1975; mem. Pres.'s Com. on Scientists and Engrs., 1956-57; chmn. bd. Human Relations Area Files, Inc., 1964-67; research asso. Lab. Anthropology, Santa Fe, 1964—; adv. com. social scis. NSF, 1961-62; hon. cons. Bernice P. Bishop Mus., Honolulu; mem. Commn. Coll. Geography, 1965-67; councillor Smithsonian Instn., 1966-78; mem. adv. bd. Desert Research Inst., U. Nev.; bd. dirs. Founds. Fund for Research Psychiatry, 1967-69; mem. Pacific Sci. Bd., 1968—. Author: Social Organization of the Western Pueblos, 1950, The American Indian, 1966; Editor: Social Anthropology of North American Tribes, 1937, enlarged edit., 1955; supr.: Handbook on the Philippines, 4 vols., 1956; Supr.: Essays in Social Anthropology and Ethnology, 1975; mem. sr. adv. com.: Ency. Brit., 1953—; editorial bd.: Science, 1968-70. Trustee Mus. of American Indian, Heye Found., 1981—. Served as capt. AUS, 1943; dir. Civil Affairs Tng. Sch. for Far East, U. Chgo., 1943-45. Fulbright research scholar, Philippines, 1949-50; Guggenheim fellow, 1953; fellow Center for Advanced Study in Behavioral Scis., Stanford, 1958-59; recipient Viking Fund medal and award, 1956; hon. curator Chgo. Natural History Mus., 1962—. Fellow Royal Anthrop. Inst. (hon.), Brit. Acad. (corr.), Human Relations Area Files (hon.), AAAS; mem. Nat. Acad. Scis. (mem. com. on scis. and pub. policy 1965-67, mem. council 1967-70), Assn. Asian Studies (dir. 1966-68), Am. Anthrop. Assn. (pres. 1953, Memoirs editor 1960-64), Am. Philos. Soc. (council 1983—), Am. Acad. Arts and Scis. (council 1981—), Am. Ethnol. Soc., NRC (chmn. com. Asian anthropology 1952-53), Social Sci. Research Council (chmn. bd. 1953-56), Phi Beta Kappa, Sigma Xi, Tau Kappa Epsilon. Club: Quadrangle. Home: 5752 S Harper Ave Chicago IL 60637 Office: 1126 E 59th St Chicago IL 60637

EGGAR, SAMANTHA (VICTORIA LOUISE SAMANTHA MARIE ELIZABETH THERESE EGGAR), actress; b. London, Eng., Mar. 5, 1939; m. Tom Stern (div.); 2 children. Student, Webber-Douglas Dramatic Sch., London; student, Slade Sch. Art. Films include The Wild and the Willing, 1961, Dr. Crippen, 1962, Doctor in Distress, 1963, Psyche 59, 1963, The Collector, 1964, Walk, Don't Run, 1965, Return from the Ashes, 1965, Doctor Doolittle, 1967, The Molly Maguires, 1969, The Lady in the Car, 1970, Walking Stick, 1969, Light at the Edge of the World, 1972, The Seven Per Cent Solution, 1976, Why Shoot the Teacher, Blood City, The Brood, The Uncanny, Curtains, French Kiss, Macabre, The Exterminator; appeared: TV series Anna and the King, 1972; also appearances in series Fantasy Island, Love Boat, Hart to Hart, Family; TV movies The Killer Who Wouldn't Die, 1976, Ziegfield: The Man and His Women, 1978, The Hope Diamond. Recipient Acting award for The Collector Cannes Film Festival, 1965; Golden Globe award, 1966. Address: care Phil Gersh Agy Inn 222 N Canon Dr Beverly Hills CA 90210

EGGEN, DONALD TRIPP, physics educator; b. Hemet, Calif., Feb. 11, 1922; s. Albert William and Iris (Tripp) E.; m. Frances Allison Dibelka, Aug. 30, 1942; children—Joan (Mrs. John E. Barber), Eric Carl, Norman Richard, Alan William. A.B., Whittier Coll., 1943; student, Pa. State Coll., 1943-44; Ph.D., Ohio State U., 1948. Physicist, technician electromagnetic separation of U-235 process devel. Tenn. Eastman Corp., Oak Ridge, 1944-46; research asst. nuclear physics Ohio State U., 1946-48; fast reactor program mgr., research specialist Atomics Internat., Canoga Park, Calif., 1949-66; program sect. mgr. liquid metal fast breeder reactor Argonne (Ill.) Nat. Lab., 1966-68, cons., 1968—; prof. nuclear engring., dir. energy engring. Northwestern U., 1968—; cons. Gen. Atomics, 1973, GAO, 1975-77; on acad. leave Cabri project, Cadarache, France, 1978-79. Contbr. articles to sci. jours. Active Boy Scouts Am. NIH fellow, 1947-48. Fellow Am. Nuclear Soc. (chmn., mem. exec. com. Chgo. sect. 1968-74, exec. com. nuclear reactor safety div. 1974-77, chmn. spl. publ. com. 1970-77, dir. 1977-80); mem. Am. Phys. Soc., AAAS, Am. Soc. Engring. Edn. Lutheran (v.p. 1970-73, deacon 1954-75). Home: 2025 Sherman Ave Evanston IL 60201

EGGER, GEORGE EDWARD, corporate director; b. St. Louis, July 9, 1905; s. George Edward and Drussie Lee (Logan) E.; m. Helen Alexander, Nov. 30, 1933; 1 son, Douglas Alexander. A.B., Washington U., St. Louis, 1925. Sales exec. Gen. Foods, Inc. and Best Foods, Inc., 1925-35; v.p. Jefferson Island Salt Co., 1935-41, Harold H. Clapp, Inc., 1941-44; v.p., dir. George Washington Coffee Co., 1941-44; v.p. Reynolds Metals Co., Richmond, Va., 1944-47; pres. Morton Frozen Foods, Inc., 1950-58; pres., dir. WLKY-TV, Louisville, 1961-68; chmn. bd. Loma Linda Corp., Orlando, Fla.; adv. dir. Louisville Investment Co. Chmn. guarantors fund com. Louisville Park Theatrical Assn., 1952-54; bd. dirs. Washington U., St. Louis, 1962-65, Norton Children's Hosp., Louisville, 1968-72, Ky. Council on Econ. Edn., 1979—; chmn. Ky. State Racing Commn., 1968-72; vis. com. U. Louisville Med. Sch., 1976; mem. exec. bd. Boy Scouts Am., Old Ky. Home Council, 1980—. Mem. Ky. C. of C. (dir. 1955-56), Ky. Thoroughbred Breeders Assn. (pres. 1971-72), Sigma Chi. Episcopalian. Clubs: Wynn-Stay, Pendennis, Filson, Louisville Country, River Valley (Louisville); Owl Creek Country (Anchorage, Ky). Home: 12409 Osage Rd Anchorage KY 40223 also Greenhaven Ln Prospect KY Office: Starks Bldg Louisville KY 40202

EGGER, ROSCOE L., JR., government official; b. Jackson, Mich., Sept. 19, 1920; s. Roscoe L. and Harriette L. (Youngs) E.; m. Betty Slattery; children—Gabrielle, Antoinette Egger Taylor. B.A., Ind. U., 1942; LL.B., George Washington U., 1950. With GAO, 1946-48; pvt. practice acctg., 1948-50, individual practice law, 1950-56; with Office of Govt. Service, Price Waterhouse, 1956-81; commr. IRS, Washington, 1981—. Mem. Commn. on Adminstrv. Rev. Ho. of Reps.; chmn. bd. Nat. Cathedral Sch. for Girls, 1974-76; chmn. bd. dirs. Wolf Trap Assos.; bd. dirs., mem. exec. com. Wolf Trap Found. Served with U.S. Army, 1943-46. Mem. Am. Inst. C.P.A.s, Am. Bar Assn., D.C. Bar Assn., U.S. C. of C. (dir.). Republican. Episcopalian. Clubs: Metropolitan, Columbia Country, Farmington Country (Charlottesville, Va.); Federal City. Home: 8101 Connecticut Ave #C-509 Chevy Chase MD 20815 Office: 1111 Constitution Ave Washington DC 20224

EGGERS, DAVID FRANK, JR., educator; b. Oak Park, Ill., July 8, 1922; s. David Frank and Anne Elizabeth (Anderson) E.; m. Vera Ethel Dalton, Jan. 23, 1945; children—Daniel David, Richard Carl, Ann Mabel. B.S., U. Ill., 1943; Ph.D., U. Minn., 1951. Chemist Tenn. Eastman Corp., Oak Ridge, 1944-47; mem. faculty U. Wash., Seattle, 1950—, asso. prof. chemistry, 1956-63, prof., 1963—; Cons. Jet Propulsion Lab., Pasadena, Calif., 1966. Author: (with Gregory, Halsey, Rabinovitch) Physical Chemistry, 1964; Contbr. profl. jours. Com. chmn. Chief Seattle council Boy Scouts Am., 1956-64. Recipient research grants USAF, NSF, Petroleum Research Fund. Mem. Am. Chem. Soc., Optical Soc. Am., Sigma Xi. Presbyn. Home: 6011 26th Ave NE Seattle WA 98115

EGGERS, ERNEST RUSSELL, management consultant; b. 1931; (married). B.A., Wesleyan U., 1953; B.A., M.A. (Rhodes scholar), Oxford U., Eng., 1955. Bus. economist McGraw-Hill Corp., 1956-58; European Common Market expert Chase-Manhattan Bank, 1958-65; v.p. Chase Manhattan Overseas Banking Corp., 1965-68, Bendix Corp., Detroit, 1968; pres. Bendix Internat., 1970-74, Loctite Corp., Newington, Conn., 1974-80, chief exec. officer, 1977-80; pres., chief exec. officer DNA Science Inc., N.Y.C., 1981; dir. Perkin-Elmer Corp., Conn. Gen. Mut. Funds (CIGNA Corp.), Cambridge Bio Sci. Corp., Signum Micro Systems, Xenogen Inc., Polycell Inc. Home and Office: 900 5th Ave New York NY 10021

EGGERS, MELVIN ARNOLD, educational administrator, economist; b. Ft. Wayne, Ind., Feb. 21, 1916; s. Frederick Carl and Minnie (Kiel) E.; m. Mildred Grace Chenoweth, Apr. 5, 1941; children: Nancy Louise, William David, Richard Melvin. A.B., Ind. U., 1940, A.M., 1941; Ph.D., Yale U., 1950; LL.D., Nazareth Coll., 1981. Clk. Peoples Trust & Savs. Co., Ft. Wayne, 1934-38; instr. econs., Yale, 1947-50; mem. faculty Syracuse U., 1950-70, prof. econs., 1963-70, chmn. dept., 1960-70, vice chancellor for acad. affairs, also provost, 1970-71, chancellor, 1971—, also pres.; Dir. Key Banks, Inc., Key Trust Co., Key Banks of Central N.Y., Empire Airlines, Inc.; Mem. faculty Pacific Coast Banking Sch., 1955-70; cons. financial instns. Bd. dirs. Urban League of Onandaga County, Inc.; mem. Commn. on Ind. Colls. and Univs.; mem. exec. com. N.Y. State Edn. Commrs. Adv. Council on Post-Secondary Edn. Served to lt. USNR, 1942-46. Mem. Assn. Am. Univs., Nat. Assn. Ind. Colls. and Univs., Am. Council on Edn.; Mem. Assn. Colls. and Univs. of N.Y. State, Phi Beta Kappa. Office: Office of Chancellor Syracuse Univ Syracuse NY 13210 *

EGGERT, GERAL GORDON, american history educator; b. Berrien County, Mich., Apr. 12, 1926; s. Gordon De Witt and Marguerite (Inman) E.; m. Hean Higgins, June 20, 1953; children: Michael Leroy, Susan Dian, Christine Elizabeth. B.A., Western Mich. U., 1949; M.A., U. Mich., 1951, Ph.D., 1960. Tchr. social studies secondary pub. sch., Battle Creek, Mich., 1949-54; instr. history U. Md., College Park, 1957-60; asst. prof. history Bowling Green State U., Ohio, 1960-65; asst. prof. Am. history Pa. State U., University Park, 1965-67, assoc. prof., 1967-72, prof., 1972—, head dept., 1980—. Author: Railroad Labor Disputes, 1967, Richard Olney, 1974, Steelmasters and Labor Reform, 1981. Served with U.S. Army, 1946-47. Mem. Am. Hist. Assn., Orgn. Am. Historians, Pa. Hist. Assn. Home: 517 Nimitz Ave State College PA 16801 Office: 601 Liberal Arts Tower Pa State U University Park PA 16801

EGGERT, ROBERT JOHN, economist; b. Little Rock, Dec. 11, 1913; s. John and Eleanora (Fritz) Lapp; m. Elizabeth Bauer, Nov. 28, 1935; children: Robert John, Richard F., James E. B.S., U. Ill., 1935, M.S., 1936; candidate in philosophy, U. Minn., 1938. Research analyst Bur. Agrl. Econs., U.S. Dept. Agr., Urbana, Ill., 1935; prin. marketing specialist War Meat Bd., Chgo., 1943; research analyst, U. Ill., 1935-36, U. Minn., 1936-38, asst. prof. econs., Kans. State Coll., 1938-41; asst. dir. marketing Am. Meat Inst., Chgo., 1941-43, economist, asso. dir., 1943-50; mgr. dept. marketing research Ford div. Ford Motor Co., Dearborn, Mich., 1951-53, mgr. program planning, 1953-54, mgr. bus. research, 1954-57, mgr. marketing research marketing staff, 1957-61, mgr. marketing research, 1961-64, mgr. internat. marketing research marketing staff, 1964-65, mgr. overseas marketing research planning, 1965-66, mgr. marketing research, 1966-67; dir. agribus. programs Mich. State U., 1967-68; staff v.p. econ. and marketing research RCA Corp., N.Y.C., 1968-73, staff v.p., chief economist, 1974-76; pres., chief economist Eggert Econ. Enterprises, Inc., Sedona, Ariz., 1976—; lectr. marketing U. Chgo., 1947-49; adj. prof. bus. forecasting No. Ariz. U., 1976—; mem. econ. adv. bd. U.S. Dept. Commerce, 1969-71, mem. census adv. com., 1975—; mem. panel econ. advisers Congl. Budget Office, 1975-76. Contbr. articles to profl. lit.; editor: monthly Blue Chip Econ. Indicators, 1975-79, Blue Chip Fin. Forecasts; co-editor: Blue Chip Econ. World Scan. Mem. Ariz. Econ. Estimates Commn., 1978—. Recipient Econ. Forecast award Chgo. chpt. Am. Statis. Assn., 1950, 60, 68; Seer of Yr. award Harvard Bus. Sch. Indsl. Econs., 1973. Mem. Council Internat. Marketing Research and Planning Dirs. (chmn. 1965-66), Am. Marketing Assn. (dir., v.p. 1949-50, pres. Chgo. chpt. 1947-48, v.p. marketing mgmt. div. 1972-73, nat. pres. 1974-75), Am. Statis. Assn. (chmn. bus. and econ. statistics sect. 1957—, pres. Chgo. chpt. 1948-49), Fed. Statistics Users Conf. (chmn. trustees 1960-61), Conf. Bus. Economists (chmn. 1973-74), Nat. Assn. Bus. Economists (council 1969-72), Ariz. Econ. Roundtable, Am. Econs. Assn., Am. Quarter Horse Assn. (dir. 1966-73), Alpha Zeta. Republican. Mem. Ch. of Red Rocks. Club: Poco Diablo Country. Home: Schnebly Hill Rd PO Box 1569 Sedona AZ 86336 Office: Sedonan-South Bldg Suite E Jordon Rd PO Box 1569 Sedona AZ 86336 *Have always strived to be a person of greater value. My modest success has resulted largely from the manifold contribution of others. In fact, the only true measure of my accomplishments will unfold in the future. What the future will be is difficult to foretell, but it always has been a challenge to maximize productivity and to look ahead, and to dream of things that never were and say—why not!"*

EGGERTSEN, CLAUDE ANDREW, educator; b. Thistle, Utah, Feb. 25, 1909; s. Claude E. and Helen El Deva (Blackett) E.; m. Nita Wakefield, June 3, 1931; children: Sheary Jill (Mrs. Virgil F. Fairbanks), Claude Wakefield, John Hale. A.B., Brigham Young U., 1930, M.A., 1933; postgrad., Stanford U., 1931; Ph.D., U. Minn., 1939. Tchr. Carbon County (Utah) Sch. Dist., 1931-34; mem. faculty U. Minn., 1934-39, instr. edn., 1935-39; mem. faculty U. Mich., Ann Arbor, 1939-79, prof. edn., 1953-79, emeritus prof. edn., 1979—, dir. program comparative edn., 1959-79, dir. internat. edn. projects, 1966-79, chmn. social founds., 1952-62, 68-75; Gerald H. Rega prof. comparative and internat. edn. Kent (Ohio) State U., 1980—; vis. faculty mem. Brigham Young U., 1935, U. Colo., 1937, Ohio State U., 1948, San Jose Coll., 1955, UCLA, 1951; hon. vis. prof. U. Sheffield, Eng., 1958, 62; vis. prof. edn., India, 1962, 64; vis. prof. Utah State U.; vis. scholar U. Kyoto, Japan; lectr. comparative edn. U. Hiroshima, U. Kyushu, both Japan, Chinese U. of Hong Kong, summer 1980. Contbr. articles to jours., chpts. to books.; Editor: Studies in the History of Higher Education in Michigan, 1950, Studies in the History of the School of Education, The University of Michigan, 1955, History of Education Jour, 1950-60, Notes and Abstracts in American and International Education, 1962. Chmn. bd. trustees Inter-Univ. Internat. Tchr. Edn. Council.; mem. planning com. Ann Arbor Council Chs., 1979-81, chmn., 1982-83. Served to lt. (s.g.) USNR, 1944-46. Decorated Bronze Star medal. Fellow Philosophy Edn. Soc., John Dewey Soc.; mem. Nat. Soc. Coll. Tchrs. (sec. 1948-60, co-chmn. history edn. sect. 1948-50), Comparative Edn. Soc. (exec. com. 1959-61, pres. 1963-64), History Edn. Soc., Am. Ednl. Research Assn., UN Assn. of U.S.A. (pres. Mich. div. 1966-70), Phi Delta Kappa, Phi Kappa Phi, Tau Kappa Alpha, Theta Alpha Phi. Home: 1044 Ferdon Rd Ann Arbor MI 48104

EGGLETON, ARTHUR C., mayor of Toronto; b. Toronto; 1 dau., Stephanie. Mem. Toronto City Council, 1969-81; served as pres. and dep. mayor 2 terms; mayor City of Toronto, 1981—; chmn. Liaison Com., Ont. Municipal leaders, 1975; dir. Can. Nat. Exhbn.; pres. Non-Profit Housing Corp.; mem. Toronto Hydro Commn. Office: City Hall Toronto ON Canada M5H 2N2 *

EGINTON, CHARLES THEODORE, surgeon, educator; b. Staples, Minn., 1914; m. Sally Eginton; children—William C., Julie Ann, Mark Theodore, C. William, Nancy Elizabeth. B.A., Macalester Coll.; M.B. with distinction, U. Minn., 1938, M.D., 1939, M.S. in Surgery, 1942. Diplomate: Am. Bd. Surgery. Intern Ancker Hosp., St. Paul, 1938-39; fellow in surgery Mayo Found., Rochester, Minn., 1939-42; asst. in surgery Mayo Clinic, 1941-42; chief surg. service VA Hosp., Fargo, N.D., 1967-71, chief of staff, 1971-78, chief surg. services, 1978—; clin. prof. surgery U. N.D., 1970—; adj. prof. pharmacy N.D. State U., 1970—. Served to maj., M.C. AUS, 1942-46. Fellow A.C.S., Internat. Coll. Surgeons; mem. AMA, Phi Beta Kappa, Alpha Omega Alpha. Home: 509 N Shore Dr Detroit Lakes MN 56501 Office: VA Center Fargo ND 58102

EGINTON, WARREN WILLIAM, federal judge; b. Bklyn., Feb. 16, 1924. A.B., Princeton U., 1948; LL.B., Yale U., 1951. Bar: N.Y. 1952, Conn. 1954. Assoc. Donovan Leisure Newton & Irvine, N.Y.C., summer 1950, Davis Polk & Wardwell, 1951-53; ptnr. Cummings & Lockwood, Stamford, Conn., 1954-79; judge U.S. Dist. Ct., Bridgeport, Conn., 1979—. Mem. Am. Judicature Soc., ABA, Am. Bar Found., Conn. Bar Assn., Am. Soc. Internat. Law, Fgn. Policy Assn. Office: US Courthouse 915 Lafayette Blvd Bridgeport CT 06604

EGLER, FREDERICK NORTON, lawyer; b. Pitts., May 27, 1922; s. Frederick N. and Agnes (Norton) E. B.A., Duquesne U., 1943; J.D., U. Pitts., 1947. Bar: Pa. 1948. Mem. Egler, Anstandig, Garrett & Riley, Pitts., 1950—. Chmn. bd. dirs. Allegheny County San. Authority, Pitts., 1974-79. Fellow Am. Law Inst., Am. Coll. Trail Lawyers, Internat. Acad. Trial Lawyers; mem. Internat. Assn. Ins. Counsel, Acad. Trial Lawyers Allegheny County, ABA, Pa. Bar Assn., Allegheny County Bar Assn. Office: Egler Anstandig Garrett & Rile 428 Forbes Ave Pittsburgh PA 15219

EGLESON, JIM (JAMES DOWNEY), artist; b. Capelton, Que., Can., Mar. 12, 1907; s. James Ernest Aiken and Edith Thompson (Downey) E.; m. Nancy Cardozo, Nov. 26, 1938 (div. 1953); children—Nicholas Michael, Jan Ernest; m. Janet Frank, Aug. 7, 1959 (div. 1961). B.S., Swarthmore Coll., 1929; postgrad., Mass. Inst. Tech., 1929-30. Engr. N.Y. Telephone Co., N.Y.C., 1930-33; apprentice, asst. to Orozco, Guadalajara, Mexico, 1935-36; instr. etching Silvermine Guild Artists, 1972—. Co-founder (with Jacqueline Bernard), Parents Without Partners, Inc., N.Y.C., 1957; 1st pres., 1957-59; Author: (with Janet Frank Egleson) Parents Without Partners, 1961; fresco series executed at, Swarthmore Coll., 1936-38, one-man shows, New Britain (Conn.) Mus. Am. Art, 1976, Silvermine Guild Artists, New Canaan, Conn., 1973, 79, Lyman Allyn Mus., New London, Conn., 1975, Oreck Gallery, New Orleans, 1979; represented by, Asso. Am. Artists, N.Y.C., 1971—; exhibited group shows, Weyhe Galleries, N.Y.C., 1971, N.A.D., 1968, 69, 70, 71 (prize 73, 76), Soc. Am. Graphic Artists, Kennedy Galleries, N.Y.C., 1971, 73, Silvermine Nat. Print Exhbn., 1968, 70, 76, 80, Conn. Acad. Fine Arts, Wadsworth Atheneum, Hartford, Conn., 1970, 71, 72, 74, 77, Conn. Printmakers, Bridgeport, 1975; represented in permanent collections, Print Collection N.Y. Pub. Library, New Britain Mus. Am. Art, Addison Gallery Am. Art, Andover, Mass., Met. Mus. Art, N.Y.C., others; News artist, CBS-TV, 1948-50; graphic artist, sci. illustrator: Scientific American mag, McGraw-Hill Books, Fortune, Sci. and Tech, 1946—. Served to lt. (s.g.) USNR, 1942-46. Recipient prize New Haven Festival Arts, 1968, Anonymous prize N.A.D., 1972, 1st prize graphics Cooperstown (N.Y.) Art Assn., 1970, New Canaan Outdoor Ann., 1972. Mem. Conn. Acad. Fine Arts, Silvermine Guild Artists, Soc. Am. Graphic Artists. Home and studio: 22 Dock Rd South Norwalk CT 06854

EGUCHI, YASU, artist; b. Japan, Nov. 30, 1938; came to U.S., 1967; s. Chihaku and Kiku (Koga) E.; m. Anita Phillips, Feb. 24, 1968. Student, Horie Art Acad., Japan, 1958-65. Exhibited exhbns., Tolyo Mus. Art, 1963, 66, Santa Barbara Mus. Art, Calif., 1972, 73, 74, Everson Mus. Art, Syracuse, N.Y., 1980, Nat. Acad. Design, N.Y.C., 1980-83, one-man shows, Austin Gallery, Scottsdale, Ariz., 1968-83, Greyston Galleries, Cambria, Calif., 1969, 70, 72, Copenhagen Galleries, Calif., 1970-78, Charles and Emma Frye Art Mus., Seattle, 1974, Hammer Galleries, N.Y.C., 1977, 79, 81, City of Heidenheim, W. Ger., 1980, Artique Ltd., Anchorage, 1981-83, pub. and pvt. collections, Voith Gmbh, W. Ger., City of Giengen and City of Heidenheim, W. Ger.; represented, Deer Valley, Utah, Hunter Resources, Santa Barbara, Am. Embassy, Paris, Charles and Emma Frye Art Mus., Seattle, Nat. Acad. Design, N.Y.C.; author: Der Brenz Entlang, 1980; contbr. to jours in field. Active Guide Dogs for the Blind, San Raphael, Calif., 1976, City of Santa Barbara Arts Council, 1979, The Eye Bank for Sight Restoration, N.Y., 1981, Anchorage Arts Council, 1981. Recipient Selective artist award Yokohama Citizen Gallery, 1965, Artist of Yr. award Santa Barbara Arts Council, 1979, Hon. Citizen award City of Heidenheim, 1980, The Adolph and Clara Obrig prize Nat. Acad. Design, 1983. Home: PO Box 30206 Santa Barbara CA 93130

EHINGER, CHARLES E., aircraft company executive; b. Huntington, Ind., Dec. 2, 1928; s. Norbert Aloysius and Ruth (Smith) E.; m. Dorothy Mary Kender, Apr. 28, 1962; children—Suzanne Marie, Beverly Ann. B.S. in Bus. Adminstrn, U. Ind., 1950. C.P.A., Ind. Financial analyst Ford Motor Co., Dearborn, Mich., 1950-56; asst. div. controller Curtiss-Wright Corp., Caldwell, N.J., 1959-63, div. controller, 1963-64, asst. corporate controller, 1964-65, asst. gen. mgr., 1965-66, gen. mgr., 1966-68, exec. dir., 1968-69, v.p. corporate services staff, 1970-71, sr. v.p., 1971-74, exec. v.p., 1974—; v.p., treas. Dorr-Oliver Inc., Stamford, Conn., 1969—, also dir.; dir. Dorr Oliver Inc., Lynch Corp., N.J. Bank N.Am., Greater Jersey Bancorp., Cenco Corp. Mem. Ind. U. Alumni Assn., Alpha Kappa Psi, Beta Gamma Sigma (round table). Clubs: Nat. Aviation, Tuxedo (Washington). Home: 35 Cider Hill Upper Saddle River NJ 07458 Office: Passaic Ct Wood-Ridge NJ 07075

EHINGER, ROBERT FRANCIS, public relations executive; b. Saco, Maine, Mar. 7, 1920; s. George and Ruth (Francis) E.; m. Mary Joan Weisz, Dec. 11, 1948; children: Elizabeth W., Ruth Ellen, Robert Francis, John Anthony. B.A., Dartmouth Coll., 1943. With Western Electric Co., 1946—, mgr., 1965-68, dir. community relations and pub. affairs, N.Y.C., 1968-70, sec., treas., 1971-73, v.p. pub. relations, 1973-77, sec., v.p. pub. relations, 1977-82; asst. v.p. pub. relations AT&T, 1982—. Pres. Summit Lay Com. on Edn., 1964-65. Served with USNR, 1943-46. Mem. Pub. Relations Soc. Am., Pub. Affairs Council, N.Y. C. of C., Delta Tau Delta. Episcopalian. Home: 41 Sweetbriar Rd Summit NJ 07901 Office: 195 Broadway New York NY 10007

EHLE, JOHN MARSDEN, JR., author; b. Asheville, N.C., Dec. 13, 1925; s. John M. and Gladys (Starnes) E.; m. Gail Oliver, Aug. 30, 1952 (div. Apr. 1967); m. Rosemary Harris, Oct. 22, 1967; 1 dau., Jennifer Anne. B.A., U. N.C., 1949, M.A., 1953. Faculty U. N.C., Chapel Hill, 1951-63; spl. asst. to Gov. Terry Sanford, Raleigh, N.C., 1963-64; program officer Ford Found., N.Y.C., 1964-65; spl. cons. Duke U., 1976—. Author: novels Move Over, Mountain, 1957, Kingstree Island, 1959, Lion on the Hearth, 1961, The Land Breakers, 1964, The Road, 1967, Time of Drums, 1970, The Journey of August King, 1971, The Changing of the Guard, 1975, The Winter People, 1981; biographies The Free Men, 1965 (Mayflower Soc. cup), The Survivor, 1968, Shepherd of the Streets, 1960; non-fiction The Cheeses and Wines of England and France, with Notes on Irish Whisky, 1972; plays American Adventure; broadcast, 1954-56; pub. also, in several fgn. countries. Mem. U.S. Nat. Commn. for UNESCO, 1965-68, White House Group for Domestic Affairs, 1964-66, Nat. Council Humanities, 1966-70; exec. com. Nat. Book Com., N.Y.C., 1972-75, N.C. Sch. of Arts Found., Winston-Salem, 1970-75; bd. dirs. Inst. Outdoor Drama, U. N.C., Chapel Hill, N.C. Sch. Sci. and Math., Durham, Penland (N.C.) Sch. Crafts. Served with inf. AUS, 1944-46. Recipient Walter Raleigh prize, 1964, 67, 70, 75, State of N.C. award for Lit., 1972; Gov.'s award for disting. meritorious service, 1978; Lillian Smith prize, 1982. Mem. Authors League, P.E.N. Democrat. Methodist. Club: Century (N.Y.C.). Home: 125 Westview Dr NW Winston-Salem NC 27104 Office: care Candida Donadio 111 W 57th St New York NY 10019

EHLERS, JOSEPH HENRY, civil engineer, lawyer; b. Hartford, Conn., Dec. 31, 1892; s. C. Julius and Caroline T. (Sauer) E.; m. Marcellite Edwards Hardy, Feb. 15, 1945 (dec. Apr. 1964). B.S., Trinity Coll., 1914; M.S. in Civil Engring, U. Calif., 1915; M.C.E., Cornell U., 1916. Registered profl. engr., D.C. Chief insp. for Modjeski & Angier, Pitts., 1919; prof. structural engring. Pei Yang U., China, 1920-24; constrn. engr. Asia Devel. Co. on diversion of Yellow River, 1923; U.S. trade commr. on earthquake reconstrn. and tech. devel. of Japan, 1926-30, acting comml. attache Am. embassy, Tokyo, 1929; tech. dir. Nat. Conf. on Constrn., Washington, 1931-33; asst. to dep. adminstr. Fed. Emergency Adminstrn. Pub. Works, Washington, 1933-38; chief cons. engring. div. Fed. Works Agy. (War Pub. Works Program), 1942-46; cons. engr., atty., Washington, 1946—; exec. dir. Nat. Conf. on Pub. Works, 1955-56; san. engring. dir. USPHS Res. Corps, ret.; asst. commr. tech. services Urban Renewal Adminstrn., Washington, 1955-58; housing coordinator ICA, Yemen, 1960-61; cons. UN, 1962-63; tech. adviser Govt. of Iraq Ministry Works at Baghdad. Author: Letters of Travel, 1965, Far Horizons-The Travel Diary of An Engineer, 1966; Editor: Jour. Chinese and Am. Engrs. Assn, 1923-24; Contbr. articles to profl. mags. Mem. organizing com., del. World Engring. Congress, Tokyo, 1929; chmn. adv. com. engrs. U.S. Civil Service Commn., 1950-57; pres. Joseph H. Ehlers Found., Russellville, Ky., 1971. Decorated Order Brilliant Star, China).; Recipient medal for excellence Trinity Coll., 1974; Founder's gold medal Phi Tau Phi, Scholastic Honor Soc. China; award Washington Soc. Engrs., 1982. Fellow ASCE (Washington reg. 1949-55, sec. city planning div.); mem. Inter-Am. Bar Assn., D.C. Bar Assn. (com. Internat. law), D.C. Soc. Prof. Engrs. (dir.), AIA (hon.), Explorers Club. Club: University (Washington). Lodge: Rotary. Address: 4000 Cathedral Ave Washington DC 20016

EHLERS, KATHRYN HAWES (MRS. JAMES D. GABLER), physician; b. Richmond Hill, N.Y., Aug. 22, 1931; d. Albert and Edna (Hawes) E.; m. James D. Gabler, Dec. 5, 1959; children—Jennifer K., Emily E. A.B., Bryn Mawr Coll., 1953; M.D., Cornell U., 1957. Diplomate: Am. Bd. Pediatrics, Am. Bd. Pediatric Cardiology. Intern N.Y. Hosp., 1957-58, asst. resident pediatrics, 1958-60; fellow in pediatric cardiology Cornell U. Med. Coll., N.Y.C., 1960-64, instr. pediatrics, 1964-66, asst. prof., 1966-70, asso. prof. pediatrics, 1970-75, prof., 1975—; practice medicine specializing in pediatric cardiology, N.Y.C., 1958—. Contbr. articles to profl. jours. Research trainee N.Y. Heart Assn., 1960-62, Am. Heart Assn., 1962-64. Fellow Am. Coll. Cardiology; mem. N.Y. Heart Assn., Am. Heart Assn., Harvey Soc., Am. Pediatric Soc., Am. Acad. Pediatrics, Alpha Omega Alpha. Home: 1035 Park Ave New York NY 10028 Office: 525 E 68th St New York NY 10021

EHLERS, WAYNE HENRY, educator, state legislator; b. Bellingham, Wash., Nov. 25, 1938; s. Fritz and Maxine (Teller) E.; children: Jefry Spencer, Marcus Evans. B.A., B.S., Western Wash. U., 1960; M.A., U. Denver, 1967. Tchr. Tacoma Sch. Dist., 1960-61, Sedro-Woolley Sch. Dist., (Wash.), 1961-64, Lake Stevens Sch. Dist., 1964-66; prof. Pacific Luth. U., Tacoma, 1968-81; librarian Franklin Pierce Sch. Dist., Tacoma, 1967—; mem. Wash. Ho. of Reps, 1983—; minority leader Wash. Ho. of Reps., 1981-83, speaker of house, 1983—. Served with USMCR, 1956. Named Legislator of Yr. Wash. VFW, 1977, Disting. Alumnus Western Wash. U., 1979, Newsmaker of Tomorrow Pierce county, Wash., 1983. Mem. NEA, Wash. Edn. Assn. Democrat. Office: Speakers Office Legislative Bldg Olympia WA 98504

EHLERT, JOHN AMBROSE, publisher; b. Albany, Minn., July 20, 1945; s. Melvin George and Helen Mary (Borgerding) E.; m. s. Katherine Allison Myers, Nov. 23, 1969; children: Adam Christopher, Zachary John. B.A., St. Mary's Coll., Winona, Minn., 1967. Founder, pub., pres. JAE Communications, Inc., Wayzata, Minn., 1976-80; pub., pres. Winter Sports Publ. Inc., Milw., 1980—; speaker, cons. in field. Mng. editor, editor, Snow Sports Publ., Mpls., 1970-75. Mem. Minnetonka Beach (Minn.) City Council, 1976-78, mayor, 1978-79. Served with USMCR, 1967-69. Mem. Internat. Snowmobile Industry Assn. (Journalism awards 1974-79). Republican. Roman Catholic. Clubs: Minnesota Press; Lafayette (Minnetonka Beach). Home: 1785 Concordia St Wayzata MN 55391 Office: 715 Florida Ave S Minneapolis MN 55426

EHMANN, DEE E., commerical airline executive; b. Batavia, N.Y., Jan. 16, 1926; s. William Carl and Norma (Snyder) E.; m. Joan Wening, Dec. 12, 1957; children: Abigail, Martha. Student, Hobart Coll., Monmouth Coll., U. Iowa, U. Buffalo. Cert air transport pilot, FAA; cert. airline dispatcher, FAA. First officer Am. Airlines, Buffalo, 1951-55, capt., 1st officer, N.Y.C., 1955-60, capt., Buffalo, 1960-65, supt. flying, 1965-70, base mgr. flight, San Francisco, 1970-75, v.p. flight, Ft. Worth, 1975—; dir. Tex. Commerce Bank. Ensign USNR, 1943-47; lt. USNR, 1952-52. Recipient Fellowship award Orgn. of Black Airline Pilots, 1978. Mem. Confederate Air Force (col.), Allied

Pilots Assn. (council chmn. 1963-66), Exptl. Aircraft Assn., Assn. Naval Aviation. Republican. Clubs: Century (Ft. Worth); Aero of Buffalo, Quiet Birdmen. Lodges: Internat. Order of Characters; Grey Eagles. Home: 3712 Briarhaven Ln Bedrord TX 76021 Office: Am Airlines Inc PO Box 61616 MD4G06 Dallas-Fort Worth Airport TX 75261

EHMANN, FRANK A., hospital supply company executive; b. Chgo., 1933; married. B.A., Northwestern U., 1955. With Am. Hosp. Supply Corp., Evanston, Ill., 1957—, pres. Am. Health Facilities, 1970-71, pres. Am. Hosp. Supply div., Evanston, Ill., 1971-73, corp. v.p., pres. dental and pharm. groups, 1973-74, corp. v.p., pres. hosp. group, 1974-78; exec. v.p., pres. hosp. and pharm. bus. Am. Hospital Supply Corp., Evanston, Ill., 1978-80; v.p. hosp. bus. Am. Hosp. Supply Corp., Evanston, Ill., 1980—, dir., 1983—. Office: American Hospital Supply Corp 1 American Plaza Evanston IL 60201

EHMANN, WILLIAM DONALD, educator; b. Madison, Wis., Feb. 7, 1931; s. William F. and Victoria V. (Koperske) E.; m. Nancy M. Gallagher, July 16, 1955; children—William J., John M., James T., Kathleen E. B.S., U. Wis., 1952, M.S., 1954; Ph.D., Carnegie Inst. Tech., 1957. NRC-NSF research asso. Argonne Nat. Lab., Ill., 1957-58; mem. faculty U. Ky., Lexington, 1958—, asso. prof. chemistry, 1963-66, prof., 1966—, chmn. dept., dir. grad. studies, 1972-76, Coll. Arts and Scis. Disting. prof., 1968-69, univ. research prof., 1977-78, asso. dean for research, 1980—; vis. prof. Ariz. State U., Tempe, 1969, Fla. State U., Tallahassee, 1972; cons. Argonne Nat. Lab., 1958-67; Research dir. project AEC, 1960-71, Agr. Dept., 1968-70, NASA, 1968-77, NIH, 1977-80. Contbr. articles to profl. jours. Fulbright scholar, hon. fellow Australian Nat. U. Inst. Advanced Studies, Canberra, 1964-65. Fellow A.A.A.S., Meteoritical Soc.; mem. Am. Chem. Soc. (chmn. Lexington sect. 1963-64), Ky. Acad. Scis. (bd. dirs. 1964-67, Disting. Ky. Scientist award 1982), Soc. for Environmental Geochemistry and Health, Internat. Assn. Geochemistry and Cosmochemistry, Sigma Xi, Phi Lambda Upsilon, Phi Eta Sigma, Phi Kappa Theta. Roman Catholic. Research in chemistry of meteorites, moon, human brain and activation analysis. Analyst 1st moon samples. Home: 769 Zandale Dr Lexington KY 40502

EHRE, EDWARD, editor; b. Rochester, N.Y., June 4, 1905; s. Abraham and Mollie (Karpf) E.; m. Gertrude Siltzbach, Dec. 1934; children—Steven, Paul. B.A., U. Rochester, 1932; M.A., Columbia, 1935; postgrad., Adelphi Coll., 1945-46, Hofstra Coll., 1951-52. Tchr. English Manasquan (N.J.) Pub. Schs., 1935-38; tchr. English and drama Port Washington (N.Y.) Pub. Schs., 1939-71. Co-editor: Best Sports Stories, E.P. Dutton Co., N.Y.C., 1944—; Author: book and lyrics Fit for a King; author: Sportsman's Guide to Space Travel, 1960. Violinist Rochester Civic Orch., 1928-29, N.J. Philharmonic, 1936-38. Mem. N.E.A., N.Y. State Tchrs. Assn. Home: 1315 Westport Ln Sarasota FL 33580 also Birch Rd Canaan CT 06018 *Being a teacher by profession, I sought to bring through literature various aspects of life to my students. I now know that I brought most benefit to myself.*

EHRE, VICTOR TYNDALL, ins. co. exec.; b. Boston, July 25, 1913; s. Victor H. and Ethel (Woods) E.; m. Allison DeWolfe, Aug. 20, 1938; children: Victor Tyndall, Donald DeWolfe. B.S. cum laude, Wharton Sch., U. Pa., 1935; H.H.D., Springfield Coll. With Travelers Ins. Co., 1935-38, Kemper Orgn., 1938-55; with Buffalo Ins. Co., 1955-64, pres., 1956-64; pres., chief exec. officer Utica Mut. Ins. Co., N.Y., 1964—, chmn. bd., chief exec. officer, 1970—, chmn., 1979—, also dir.; vice chmn., dir. Graphic Arts Mut. Ins. Co.; chmn. bd., chief exec. officer, dir. Utica Nat. Life Ins. Co.; chmn. bd. UNI-Service Credit Corp., UNI-Service Leasing Co., Inc., UNI-Service Risk Mgmt. Corp., Available Funds, Inc., UNI-Service Ops. Corp.; trustee Adirondack Ry. Corp.; dir. Security Mut. Life Ins. Co. N.Y., Marine Midland Bank-Central, UNI-Service Excess Facilities, Inc., Republic Franklin Ins. Co.; past chmn. Bus. Council of N.Y. State, Inc.; governing com., past chmn. Improved Risk Mutuals. Bd. dirs., dir., adv. bd. State Traffic Council N.Y.; dir., past 1st pres. Western N.Y. Traffic Safety Council; bd. dirs. Central N.Y. Community Arts Council, Utica Found., Mid-Atlantic Legal Found.; vice chmn. Concerned Citizens for the Arts; adv. com. Nat. Alliance Businessmen; chmn. N.Y. State adv. bd. Future Bus. Leaders Am.; past pres. Civic Mus. Soc. Utica, Utica Bus. Opportunities Corp.; founder Operation Sunshine; pres. United Arts Fund of Mohawk Valley; mem. N.Y. Gov.'s Statewide Com. Children and Youth; past chmn. Region II Boy Scouts Am.; also mem. exec. bd. Nat. council; bd. dirs., exec. bd. Upper Mohawk council; mem. U. Pa. Alumni Clubs Adv. Council; pres., past chmn. Atlantic Coast Hockey League; chmn. N.Y. Gov.'s Project Rev. Com.; mem. Nat. Venture in Mission, Episcopal Ch.; trustee State Univ. N.Y. Coll. Tech., Hobart and William Smith Colls. Served to lt. (s.g.) USNR, 1943-46. Recipient Award of Merit Gov. Rockefeller of N.Y., 1965; named Indsl. Man of Year, 1968, Ins. Man of Year, 1971; recipient Rotarian Citizen's award, 1969; Alumni award merit U. Pa., 1977; Presdl. award Nat. Assn. Mut. Ins. Cos., 1979. Mem. Greater Utica C. of C. (dir.), Am. Arbitration Assn. (dir.), U. Pa. Alumni Club Western N.Y. (past pres.). Episcopalian (warden). Clubs: Mason (vice chmn. home bldg. fund com.), Fort Schuyler (Utica); Yahnundasis (New Hartford, N.Y.); Lake Placid; India House (N.Y.C.). Home: 1730 Sherman Dr Utica NY 13501 Office: PO Box 530 Utica NY 13503 *I think that the thing that has guided me the most through life is the combination of the Cub Scout and Boy Scout mottos of the Boy Scouts of America. "Be prepared and do your best."*

EHREN, CHARLES ALEXANDER, JR., lawyer, educator; b. N.Y.C., Dec. 13, 1932; s. Charles Alexander and Alma Elise (Holmstrom) E.; m. Joan Anne Bansemer, Sept. 4, 1954. A.B., Columbia U., 1954, J.D., 1956. Bar: N.Y. bar 1956. Asso. firm LeBoeuf, Lamb and Leiby, N.Y.C., 1958-67; Reginald Heber Smith fellow U. Pa. Sch. Law at Legal Aid Soc. of Westchester County (N.Y.), White Plains, 1967-68, dir. soc., 1975-77; dir. curriculum Nat. Inst. Edn. in Law and Poverty, Northwestern U., 1968-70; asso. prof. law U. Denver, 1970-74, prof., 1974-75; dean, prof. Pace U. Sch. Law, 1975-76; vis. scholar Columbia U. Sch. Law, 1976-77; dean Valparaiso U. Sch. Law, 1977-82, prof., 1977—; trustee Ind. Continuing Legal Edn. Found., Ind. Bar Found., 1977-82; dir. Westchester Legal Services, 1975-77. Author: (with others) Electricity and the Environment, The Reform of Legal Institutions, 1972. Served with U.S. Army, 1956-58. Mem. Ind. State Bar Assn. (ho. of dels. 1977-82), Assn. Bar City N.Y. (exec. dir. spl. com. on electric power and environment 1971-73), ABA, N.Y. State Bar Assn., Fed. Bar Assn., Fed. Energy Bar Assn., Soc. Am. Law Tchrs., Acad. Polit. Sci. Democrat. Lutheran. Office: Valparaiso U Sch Law Valparaiso IN 46383

EHRENBERG, EDWARD, manufacturing company executive; b. N.Y.C., Aug. 24, 1930; s. Meyer and Bessie (Purkin) E.; m. Lenore Kaufman, June 19, 1955; children—Ellen, Roger. B.S., N.Y. U., 1956; M.B.A., Wharton Sch., U. Pa., 1958. With Ford Motor Co., Dearborn, Mich., 1957-70, mgr. service ops., 1966-70; pres. West Ford, Inc., Xerox Corp., Rochester, N.Y., 1970-78; with Internat. Harvester Co., Chgo., 1978—, group v.p. fin. services, mktg., 1980-81, dir. devel. planning, 1978—; pres. Harco Leasing, 1979-80. Served with USAF, 1950-54. Home: 1098 Mt Pleasant Rd Winnetka IL 60093

EHRENBERG, JOHN MICHAEL, JR., motion picture equipment company executive; b. Chgo., Sept. 28, 1937; s. John Michael and Ann (Gairing) E. B.S. in Mech. Engring., Northwestern U., 1960; postgrad., Chgo.-Kent Coll. Law., 1962-64, Northwestern U. Grad. Sch. Bus. Adminstrn., 1964-66. Mng. engring. Profl. Equipment dev. Bell & Howell, Lincolnwood, Ill., 1966-70, mgr. product planning, 1970-72, dir. mktg., 1971-73, gen. mgr., 1973-79, pres., 1979-83, BHP, Inc., Bell & Howell, 1983—. Fellow Soc. Motion Picture and TV Engrs. (gov. 1975-80); mem. Brit. Kinematograph Sound and TV Soc., Assn. Cinema and Video Labs. Republican. Lutheran. Home: 912 Michigan Ave Evanston IL 60202 Office: BHP Inc 7100 McCormick Rd Lincolnwood IL 60645

EHRENFELD, JOHN HENRY, grocery co. exec.; b. Sharpsburg, Pa., July 25, 1917; s. Charles and Mary (Conlon) E.; m. Florence Maxwell, Feb. 14, 1941; children—Barbara, Carol, Robert. B.A., U. Pitts., 1939. With Libby, McNeill & Libby, 1940-69, v.p. co., 1961-69, gen. mgr. canned meat div., 1953-69, v.p. sales, Chgo., 1966-69; v.p., gen. mgr. Western div., mgr. corporated bd. dirs.; v.p. marketing Tootsie Roll Ind., Chgo., 1969-72; v.p., gen. mgr. Household Grocery Products div. Alberto Culver Co., 1972—; Mem. Cling Peach Adv. Bd. Mem. Nat. Meat Canners Assn. (pres. 1959-61, dir. 1956-61), Canners League of Calif. (dir.), San Francisco C. of C. (dir.). Club: Lion. Home: 3543 Willow St Flossmoor IL 60422

EHRENHAFT, JOHANN LEO, surgeon; b. Vienna, Austria, Oct. 10, 1915; came to U.S., 1934, naturalized, 1939; s. Felix and Olga (Steindler) E.; m. Jean Lovett, Oct. 17, 1953; 1 son, John Bruce. Student, U. Vienna, 1933-34; M.D., U. Iowa, 1938. Diplomate: Am. Bd. Surgery. Intern Johns Hopkins Hosp., 1938-39, Halsted fellow in surgery, 1939-40; resident surgery U. Iowa, 1940-42, 45-47, instr., 1947-48, asso., 1948-49, asst. prof., 1949-51, asso. prof., 1951-53, prof. surgery, 1953—; fellow in thoracic surgery Barnes Hosp., St. Louis, 1948-49; chmn. div. thoracic surgery U. Iowa Hosps., Iowa City, 1949—; Mem. Council on Cardiovascular Surgery, Am. Heart Assn., 1952—, Bd. Thoracic Surgery, Inc., 1966—. Editorial bd.: Annals Thoracic Surgery, 1964—; Contbr. articles on thoracic and cardiovascular surgery to med. jours. Served to maj. AUS, 1942-46. Fellow A.C.S.; mem. AMA, Am. Surg. Assn., Am. Assn. Thoracic Surgery, Am. Heart Assn., Soc. U. Surgeons, Am., Central, Pan-Am. surg. assns., Am. Coll. Chest Physicians (past regent), Internat. Cardiovascular Soc., Soc. Thoracic Surgeons, Soc. Vascular Surgery, Société Internationale de Chirugie, Sigma Xi, Alpha Omega Alpha. Home: 325 Beldon Ave Iowa City IA 52240

EHRENHAFT, PETER DAVID, lawyer; b. Vienna, Austria, Aug. 16, 1933; came to U.S., 1940, naturalized, 1945; s. Bruno B. and Ann J. (Polacek) E.; m. Charlotte Kennedy, May 4, 1958; children: Elizabeth Ann, James Bruno, Daniel Parker. A.B. with honors, Columbia U., 1954, LL.B. and M.I.A., Schs. Law and Internat. Affairs, 1957. Bar: N.Y. 1958, D.C. 1961. Motions law clk. to U.S. Ct. Appeals, D.C. Circuit, 1957-58; sr. law clk. to Chief Justice U.S. Supreme Ct., 1961-62; assoc. firm Cox, Langford & Brown, Washington, 1962-66, partner, 1966-68; ptnr. firm Fried, Frank, Harris, Shriver & Kampelman, Washington, 1968-77; dep. asst. sec., spl. counsel for tariff affairs Dept. Treasury, Washington, 1977-79; ptnr. firm Hughes, Hubbard & Reed, Washington, 1980-83, Bryan, Cave, McPheeters & McRoberts, 1984—; professorial lectr. in law George Washington U., 1965-72; mem. faculty Salzburg (Austria) Seminar in Am. Studies Law Session, 1973; lectr. in law U. Pa., 1980—; mem. Fed. Jud. Center Study Group on Workload of Supreme Ct., 1971-74. Contbr. articles, revs., mainly on internat. trade or arbitration, to law jours.; mem. adv. bd.: Jour. Law and Policy in Internat. Bus, 1967—, Patent, Trademark and Copyright Jour., 1970—; editorial bd.: Internat. Legal Materials, 1977—. Pres. bd. trustees Nat. Child Research Center, Washington, 1976-77. Served with USAF, 1958-61. Recipient Reginald Harmon award USAF, 1977, Exceptional Service medal Dept. Treasury, 1979. Mem. Am. Law Inst., ABA (council internat. law sect. 1983—, co-chmn. internat. trade com. 1983—), Am. Soc. Internat. Law, Washington Fgn. Law Soc. (bd. govs. 1982—). Home: 2932 Garfield Terr NW Washington DC 20008 Office: Suite 1000 1015 15th St NW Washington DC 20005

EHRENKRANZ, JOEL S., lawyer; b. Newark, Mar. 25, 1935; s. George J. and Hilda (Schreiber) E.; m. Anne Bick, June 9, 1963; children: Alissa, John, Jeanne. B.S. in Econs., U. Pa., 1956, M.B.A., 1957; LL.B., NYU, 1961, LL.M. in Taxation, 1964. Bar: N.Y. 1961; C.P.A., N.Y. Accountant Peat, Marwick, Mitchell & Co., N.Y.C., 1957-62; sr. ptnr. Ehrenkranz, Ehrenkranz & Schultz, Attys. at Law, N.Y.C., 1962—. Trustee, mem. distbn. com. Fedn. Jewish Philanthropies, N.Y.C., 1974-82; trustee United Jewish Appeal/Fedn. Jewish Philanthropies, N.Y.C., 1979—, Jewish Communal Fund, N.Y.C., 1982—, Archives Am. Art, N.Y.C., 1973—; trustee, v.p. Whitney Mus. Am. Art, N.Y.C., 1975—; exec. com. Council of Friends NYU Inst. Fine Arts, 1982; mem. adv. com. of fin. com. Wharton Sch. of U. Pa., 1982—; trustee, mem. exec. com., chmn. patient care com. Mt. Sinai Med. Ctr., N.Y.C., 1982—. Mem. ABA, Am. Inst. C.P.A.s, Estate Planning Council N.Y. Clubs: Board Room, Harmonie (N.Y.C.); Century (White Plains, N.Y.). Home: 4 E 72d St New York NY 10021 also Keller Ln North Salem NY 10560 Office: 375 Park Ave New York NY 10152

EHRENPREIS, IRVIN, educator; b. N.Y.C., June 9, 1920; s. Louis and Edith (Lipman) E.; m. Anne Willard Henry, Aug. 19, 1961 (dec. 1978); 1 son, David Henry; m. Mary Louise Kemp, 1983. B.A., CCNY, 1938; M.A., Columbia U., 1939, Ph.D., 1944; Docteur Honoris Causa, U. Besançon, France, 1965. With dept. English, Ind. U., 1945-65, prof., 1961-65; prof. English, U. Va., 1965—, Commonwealth prof. English, 1967-75, Linden Kent prof. English, 1975—; vis. prof. Brandeis U., 1961, Harvard Summer Sch., 1962, U. Minn. Summer Sch., 1960, U. Wash. Summer Sch., 1964, U. Münster (Ger.), summer 1983; Beckman prof. U. Calif., Berkeley, spring 1978; seminar leader Folger Inst., fall 1981; vis. fellow All Souls Coll., Oxford (Eng.) U., 1981-82; vis. research fellow Merton Coll., Oxford (Eng.) U., 1968. Author: The Types Approach to Literature, 1945, The Personality of Jonathan Swift, 1958, Swift, Vol. I, 1962, Vol. II, 1967, Vol. III, 1983, Fielding: Tom Jones, 1964, Wallace Stevens: A Critical Anthology, 1972, Literary Meaning and Augustan Values, 1974, Acts of Implication, 1980; co-editor: J. Swift, Prose Works, VIII, 1953, XIV, 1968; contbr. N.Y. Rev. of Books. Fulbright fellow Oxford (Eng.) U., 1949-50; Guggenheim fellow, 1955-56, 62-63; Am. Council Learned Socs. fellow, 1958-59; NEH sr. fellow, 1967-68. Fellow Am. Acad. Arts and Scis. Office: Dept English Univ Va Charlottesville VA 22903

EHRENPREIS, SEYMOUR, pharmacology educator; b. N.Y.C., June 20, 1927; s. William and Ethel (Balk) E.; m. Bella R. Goodman, June 30, 1953; children: Mark, Eli, Ira. B.S., CCNY, 1949; Ph.D., NYU, 1954. Mem. faculty dept. pharmacology Chgo. Med. Sch., now prof., chmn. pharmacology; grants reviewer NSF, 1977-83, March of Dimes, 1983. Editor: Neurosciences Research, vols. 1-5, 1967-75, Revs. of Neurosci., vols. 1-3, 1974-77, Methods in Narcotics Research, 1974, Degradation of Endogenous Opoids, 1983; mem. editorial bd.: Jour. Medicinal Chemistry, 1969-72. Served with USN, 1945-46. Recipient Meritorious Service award Coll. Pharm. Sci., Columbia U., 1976, Parker award Chgo. Med. Sch., 1981, Vis. Prof. award Japan Soc. Promotion Sci., 1974. Fellow N.Y. Acad. Sci. (chmn. cholinergic mechanisms conf. 1966), Am. Inst. Chemists, AAAS; mem. Am. Soc. Pharmacology and Exptl. Therapeutics, Sigma Xi. Office: Univ Health Sci Chgo Med Sch 333 Green Bay Rd North Chicago IL 60041

EHRENREICH, BARBARA, author; b. Butte, Mont., Aug. 26, 1941; d. Ben Howes and Isabelle (Oxley) Alexander; m. John H. Ehrenreich, Aug. 6, 1966; children: Rosa, Benjamin. B.A., Reed Coll., 1963; Ph.D., Rockefeller U., 1968. Editor Health Policy Adv. Ctr., N.Y.C., 1969-70; asst. prof. SUNY-Old Westbury, 1971-74; freelance writer, lectr.; vis. fellow N.Y. Inst. Humanities, N.Y.C., 1980—; editor Seven Days mag., N.Y.C., 1974—. Author: For Her Own Good: 150 Years of the Experts' Advice to Women, 1978, (with Deirdre English) The American Health Empire, 1970, (with John Ehrenreich) Witches, Midwives and Nurses: A History of Women Healers, 1972, (with D. English) Complaints and Disorders: The Sexual Politics of Sickness, 1973. Recipient award Nat. Mag., 1980. Mem. PEN, Soc. Study of Social Problems, Health Right. Home: 9 Devine Ave Syosset NY 11791 Office: 19 Univ Pl New York NY 10003

EHRENREICH, HENRY, physicist, educator; b. Frankfurt, Germany, May 11, 1928; came to U.S., 1940, naturalized, 1946; s. Nathan and Frieda (Rosenstein) E.; m. Tema P. Hasnas, Feb. 1, 1953; children—Paul, Beth-Ida, Robert. A.B., Cornell U., 1950, Ph.D., 1955; student, Columbia, 1950-51; M.A. (hon.), Harvard, 1963. Theoretical physicist Gen. Electric Research Lab., Schenectady, 1955-63; vis. lectr. Harvard, 1960-61, Gordon McKay prof. applied physics, 1963—, Clowes prof. Sci., 1982—; vis. prof. Brandeis U., 1969, U. Paris, 1969, U. Pa., 1976; mem. Materials Research Council, 1972—; sec. solid state commn. Internat. Union Pure and Applied Physics, 1978-81; mem. solar photovoltaic energy adv. com. Dept. Energy, 1980-83. Contbr. to profl. jours.; Bd. editors: Phys. Rev, 1965-67; co-editor: Solid State Physics, 1966—. Fellow Am. Phys. Soc. (chmn. div. solid state physics 1969, chmn. study group on solar energy 1977-81), Am. Acad. Arts and Scis., AAAS; mem. Phi Beta Kappa, Sigma Xi. Office: Pierce Hall Harvard Univ Cambridge MA 02138

EHRENSBERGER, RAY, emeritus university chancellor; b. Indpls., Dec. 7, 1907; s. Edward H. and Elizabeth (M. Peetz) E.; m. Helen L. Myers, Sept. 21, 1939; children: Betty Ann, Ray. A.B., Wabash Coll., 1929; A.M., Butler U., 1930; fellow, Syracuse U., 1935-36, Ph.D., 1937; grad. student, Ind. U., U. Wis.; LL.D. (hon.), Wabash Coll., 1966. Instr. speech Doane Coll., 1930-32; head speech dept. Franklin Coll., 1932-35; asso. prof. speech U. Md., 1936-39, prof., chmn. dept. speech and dramatic art, 1939-52, dir., Heidelberg, Germany, 1949-50, dean, 1952-59, 1959-70, chancellor, 1970-75, chancellor emeritus, 1975—; dir. Bi-nat. Center, Dept. of State, Ankara, Turkey, 1951-52. Author: (with Elaine Pagel) A Notebook for Public Speaking, 1946. Recipient Exceptional Service award U.S. Air Force, Distinguished Civilian Service medal Dept. Def., Distinguished Pub. Service medal U.S. Army. Mem. Speech Assn. Am., Phi Delta Kappa, Phi Kappa Phi, Sigma Chi, Omicron Delta Kappa, Delta Sigma Rho, Tau Kappa Alpha, Blue Key. Club: Rotary. Home: 4608 Harvard Rd College Park MD 20740

EHRHARD, EDWARD ROWLAND, manufacturing executive; b. Newark, Sept. 23, 1922; s. Julius and Grace (Hurtt) E.; m. Kathryn M. Pringle, Apr. 22, 1944; children—Pamela Grace, Deborah Lynn. A. Mech.Engring., Newark Coll. Engring., 1949. With Monroe Calculating Machine Co.; div. Litton Industries, Orange, N.J., 1941-59, asst. chief engr., 1957-59; with Automatic Switch Co., Florham Park, N.J., 1969—, pres., 1978—, dir., 1976—; adv. com. Am. Stock Exchange, 1980—. Served with USN, 1944-46. Mem. Nat. Elec. Mfrs. Assn. (bd. govs.), Nat. Fluid Power Assn., Fluid Power Inst., Am. Refrigeration Inst., N.J. C. of C. (bd. dirs.). Republican. Roman Catholic. Clubs: Canoe Brook Country (Summit, N.J.); Seaview Country (Abesecon, N.J.). Office: Hanover Rd Florham Park NJ 07932

EHRHARDT, GEORGE, JR., banker; b. Rockville Centre, N.Y., July 17, 1933; s. George and Helen B. (Scharff) E.; m. Edith A. Carlisle, Sept. 24, 1960; children: George R., David B. B.A., Hobart Coll., 1954; certificate in banking, Rutgers U., 1967. With First Nat. City Bank of N.Y., 1958-60, Colonial Bank, Waterbury, Conn., 1960—, sr. v.p., 1969-76, pres., 1976—; v.p. Colonial Bancorp, Inc., 1970-79, exec. v.p., 1979-81, pres., 1981—; dir. Colbanc Realty Corp., 1973—, Policy Advancing Corp., Platt Bros. Corp.; mem. bankers adv. council to Am. Gas Assn., 1979—; chmn. Conn. Pub. Expenditures Council. Active Waterbury chpt. ARC; trustee Waterbury Hosp., 1980—. Served to 1st lt. USAF, 1954-57. Mem. Am. Inst. Banking, Financial Execs. Inst., Bank Adminstrn. Inst. (chmn. 1978-79), Conn. Bankers Assn., Waterbury C. of C. (past chmn., dir. 1969—). Conglist. Clubs: Mason., Country of Waterbury, Waterbury. Office: Colonial Bank 81 W Main St Waterbury CT 06720

EHRHART, CARL YARKERS, former college administrator; b. Lebanon, Pa., May 11, 1918; s. Oliver Tillman and Edna (Yarkers) E.; m. Geraldine May Baldwin, Sept. 8, 1945; children: Carole Lynne, Constance Sue, Anne Baldwin Ehrhart Bocian. A.B., Lebanon Valley Coll., 1940; M.Div., United Theol. Sem., 1943; Ph.D., Yale, 1954. Prof. philosophy Lebanon Valley Coll., 1947-60, dean coll., prof. philosophy, 1960-67, v.p., dean coll., 1967-80, v.p., asst. to pres., 1980-83. Bd. dirs. Met. Collegiate Ctr., Germantown, Pa.; trustee United Theol. Sem., Dayton, Ohio. Methodist. Home: 643 E Queen St Annville PA 17003

EHRICH, ROBERT WILLIAM, anthropologist, archaeologist, retired educator; b. N.Y.C., Apr. 23, 1908; s. William Joseph and Adelaide (Price) E.; m. Ann Marie Hoskin, Mar. 12, 1937; children—Judith, Holly Ann (Mrs. Gerald M. Henderson). B.A., Harvard, 1931, M.A., 1933, Ph.D., 1946. Archaeol. excavations and anthropometry in Iraq, 1929-30, Czechoslovakia, 1929-31, 60-61, Yugoslavia, 1932-33, 69, 70, Turkey, 1934-39, Saratoga (N.Y.) Battlefield, 1940-42; mem. faculty Bklyn. Coll. of City U. N.Y., 1947-73, prof. anthropology, 1963-73, chmn. dept., 1965-71, exec. officer anthropology City U., 1966-68; research asso. Peabody Mus., Harvard, 1972—, Archeol. Inst., Bklyn. Coll., 1973—; Mem. adv. panel anthropology NSF, 1962-64; fgn. currency program Smithsonian Instn., 1965-70. Author: (with E. Pleslova-Stikova) Homolka, an Eneolithic Site in Bohemia, 1968; also articles.; Editor, contbr.: Relative Chronologies in Old World Archaeology, 1954, Chronologies in Old World Archeology, 1965; area editor for: Council Old World Archaeology, 1956—. Served to capt. USMCR, 1943-45. Decorated Bronze Star; Rockefeller fellow, 1946-47. Fellow Am. Anthrop. Assn. (exec. bd. 1960-62, ethics com. 1970-72); mem. Internat. Union Prehistoric and Protohistoric Scis. (permanent council 1962-76), Soc. Am. Archaeology, Archaeol. Soc. Yugoslavia (hon.), German Archaeol. Inst. (corr.). Home: Upper Troy Rd Fitzwilliam NH 03447

EHRICKE, KRAFFT ARNOLD, space engineer; b. Berlin, Germany, Mar. 24, 1917; came to U.S., 1947, naturalized, 1955; s. Arnold F. and Ruth (Konietzko) E.; m. Ingeborg Mattull, Jan. 16, 1945; children: Krista, Astrid, Doris. M.S. in Aero. Eng, Tech. U., Berlin, 1942, courses atomic physics and celestial mechanics, 1941-42; L.H.D., Nat. Tchrs. Coll., Evanston, Ill., 1961. Devel. engr. V-2 propulsion system, Peenemuende, Germany, 1942-45; jet propulsion engr. Dept. Army, Ft. Bliss, Tex., 1947-50; chief gasdynamics sect. Army Ballistic Missile Center, Redstone Arsenal, Ala., 1950-52; preliminary design engr. Bell Aircraft Corp., 1952-54; with Convair div. Gen. Dynamics Corp., 1954-65, design specialist, 1954-55, chief design and systems analysis, 1956-57; asst. to tech. dir. Convair-Astronautics, 1957-58, originator, also program dir. Centaur space vehicle, 1958-62, dir. advanced studies dept., 1962-65; asst. div. dir. astrionics div. N.Am. Aviation, Autonetics div., Anaheim, Calif., 1965-68; chief scientist space systems and applications space div. N.Am. Rockwell Corp., Downey, Calif., 1968-73; exec. adviser N.Am. space ops. Rockwell Internat. Corp., 1973-76, mgr., 1976-77; founder, pres. Space Global Co., 1977—. Author: Space Flight, Vol. I, Environment and Celestial Mechanics, 1959, Vol. II, Dynamics, 1961, (with E.A. Miller) Exploring the Planets, 1969, Beyond Earth, 1971, Cosmic Engineering (in Russian); numerous articles. Recipient 1st Guenther Loeser medal for best paper (The Satelloid) presented during 6th Internat. Astronautical Congress Internat. Astronautical Fedn., 1956, G. Edward Pendray award Am. Rocket Soc., 1961, Astronautics award, 1957, I.B. Laskowitz award N.Y. Acad. Scis., 1972; named to Internat. Aerospace Hall of Fame, 1966. Fellow Am. Inst. Aeros. and Astronautics, Brit. Interplanetary Soc., Deutsche Ges. f. Weltraumforschg. (pres. 1942-43); mem. Internat. Acad. Astronautics. Introduced microwave reflector concept for long-distance power transmission, 1972, Lunar Slide Lander Concept, 1977. Home: 845 Lamplight Dr LaJolla CA 92037 *Learn, but never become imprisoned by what you have been taught. Think, but never become a prisoner of your own thoughts. Be sensitive beyond your own sphere, but retain a non-negotiable core of your self. Deal with life's bitter realities, but retain awareness of the unending wonders of your universe. In short, keep the balance, baby, and remember always: there are no limits to growth, only to multiplication.*

EHRLICH, AMY, editor, writer; b. N.Y.C., July 24, 1942; d. Max and Doris (Rubenstein) E.; 1 son, Joss. Student, Bennington Coll., Vt., 1960-63, 64-65. Roving editor Family Circle Mag., N.Y.C., 1975-76; sr. editor Dial Books for Young Readers, N.Y.C., 1977-82, exec. editor, 1982—. Author: children's book Zeek Silver Moon, 1972 (named Best Book of Yr. 1972); children's books Leo, Zack and Emmie (named booklist reviewers choice Sch. Library Jour. 1981); children's book others; reteller: The Snow Queen, 1982, others. Office: Dial Books for Young Readers 2 Park Ave New York NY 10016

EHRLICH, BERNARD HERBERT, lawyer, assn. exec.; b. Washington, Apr. 3, 1927; s. Samuel Zachary and Elsie (Klein) E.; m. Edna Kraft, June 17, 1951; children—Vivian Rose, Beverly Denise, Brenda Susan, Lisa Jean. A.B., George Washington U., 1946, LL.B., 1949, J.D., M.A., 1950. Bar: D.C. bar 1949. Since practiced in, Washington, gen. counsel numerous corps., industries, 1949—; mgr., gen. counsel Inst. Indsl. Launderers, Washington, 1949—; counsel Nat. Home Study Council, Nat. Assn. Trade and Tech. Schs., Nat. Assn. Cosmetology Schs.; adv. panel employee recruitment and job devel. U.S. C. of C., 1967—. Served with USN, 1943-45. Recipient service plaque Am. Inst. Launderers, 1966, Nat. Assn. Trade and Tech. Schs., 1967, Nat. Home Study Council, 1970. Mem. Am. Bar Assn., Bar Assn. D.C., Am. Soc. Internat. Law, Am. Hist. Assn., Am. Soc. Assn. Execs., Soc. Am. Travel Writers, Am. Polit. Sci. Assn., Phi Beta Kappa, Nu Beta Epsilon, Phi Delta Pi. Jewish. Home: 507 Bonifant St Silver Spring MD 20910 Office: 2000 L St NW Washington DC 20036

EHRLICH, CLIFFORD JOHN, hotel executive; b. N.Y.C., Nov. 17, 1938; s. Joseph George and Eugenia Marie (Rybacky) E.; m. Patricia Marie Stankunas, June 20, 1964; children: Susan, Brian, Scott. B.A. in Econs., Brown U., 1960; J.D., Boston Coll., 1965. With Monsanto Co., 1960-73, personnel supt., Miamisburg, Ohio, 1969-73; dir. labor relations, then v.p. employee relations Marriott Corp., Washington, 1973-78, sr. v.p. human resources, 1978—. Bd. dirs. Jr. Achievement of Washington. Served with USAFR, 1962. Mem. Conf. Board (orgn. planning council 1981—), Council Personnel Officers Hospitality Industry (pres. 1981-82), Com. on Labor Law Equity, U.S.C. of C. (labor law com.). Home: 9128 Vendome Dr Bethesda MD 20817 Office: Marriott Corp Marriott Dr Washington DC 20058

EHRLICH, EDWARD NORMAN, physician, educator; b. Detroit, Sept. 20, 1928; s. Adolph and Faye (Cashdan) E.; m. Rosanne Mitshkun, Sept. 3, 1961; children—Lisa, Joel, Janet. B.S., YU. Mich., 1948, M.D., 1952. Instr. dept. medicine U. Chgo., 1960-61, asst. prof., 1961-68, asso. prof., 1968-73, prof., 1973-74; prof., asso. chmn. dept. medicine U. Wis.-Madison, 1974—. Contbr. articles to med. jours. Served with U.S. Navy, 1955-57. Recipient USPHS career devel. award, 1964. Mem. AAAS, Am. Fedn. Clin. Research, Madison Acad. Internat. Medicine (pres. 1980—), Am. Polar Soc., Central Clin. Research Club (v.p. 1980—), Central Soc. Clin. Research, Endocrine Soc., Soc. Gynecologic Investigation. Home: 113 Island Dr Madison WI 53705 Office: 202 S Park St Madison WI 53715

EHRLICH, GEORGE EDWARD, physician; b. Vienna, Austria, July 18, 1928; came to U.S., 1938, naturalized, 1944; s. Edward and Irene (Elling) E.; m. Gail S. Abrams, Mar. 30, 1968; children: Charles Edward, Steven L. Abrams, Rebecca Ann Abrams. A.B. cum laude, Harvard U., 1948; M.B., M.D., Chgo. Med. Sch., 1952. Intern Michael Reese Hosp., Chgo., 1952; resident Francis Delafield Hosp., N.Y.C., 1955, Beth Israel Hosp., Boston, 1956, New Eng. Center Hosp., 1957; fellow rheumatology NIH, Bethesda, Md., 1958, Hosp. for Spl. Surgery, N.Y.C., 1959-61, asst. attending physician, 1960-64; spl. fellow Sloan Kettering Inst., 1960-61; instr. medicine Cornell U., 1960-64; dir. Arthritis Center, chief rheumatology Albert Einstein Med. Center and Moss Rehab. Hosp., Phila., 1964-80; asst. prof. medicine Temple U., 1964-67, asso. prof. medicine, 1967-72, prof. medicine, 1972-80, asso. prof. rehab. medicine, 1964-74, prof., 1974-80; vis. lectr. U. Pa., 1964-80; prof. medicine, dir. div. rheumatology Hahnemann Med. Coll. and Hosp., Phila., 1980—; cons. in field. Author: Differential Diagnosis of Rheumatoid Arthritis, 1972, Oculocutaneous Manifestations of Rheumatic Diseases, 1973, Total Management of the Arthritic Patient, 1973, Rehabilitation Management of Rheumatic Conditions, 1980, (with J. Fries) Prognosis, 1981, (with H.E. Paulus) Controversies in the Clinical Evaluation of Analgesic-Anti-Inflammatory-Antirheumatic Drugs, 1981; editor: Jour. Albert Einstein Med. Center, 1966-71, Arthritis and Rheumatic Diseases Abstracts, 1968-71; editorial bd.: Inflammation, 1974—, Psychosomatics, 1977—, Sexual Medicine Today, 1977—; contbr. articles to profl. jours. Pres. Eastern Pa. chpt. Arthritis Found., 1970-72; mem. Phila. Mayor's Sci. and Tech. Adv. Council, 1972—; chmn. ad hoc adv. com. Bur. Drugs, FDA, 1971. Served to comdr. M.C. USNR, 1953-55; Res., to 1978. Recipient citations City Phila., 1969, 74, Distinguished Alumnus award Chgo. Med. Sch., 1969; decorated Cavaliere Order of Star of Italian Solidarity. Fellow A.C.P., Royal Soc. Tropical Medicine, N.Y. Acad. Medicine, Am. Geriatric Soc., Phila. Coll. Physicians, Am. Coll. Clin. Pharmacology; mem. Am. Soc. Clin. Therapeutics, Am. Coll. Rehab., Acad. Sci., AMA (editorial bd. Jour. 1972—), Am. Fedn. Clin. Research, Am. Soc. Human Genetics, Assn. Mil. Surgeons (Philip Hench award 1971), Am. Rheumatism Assn. (com. for publ. Arthritis and Rheumatism 1977-79, editorial bd. 1980—), Am. Med. Writers Assn., Brit. Assn. Rheumatology and Rehab. (overseas mem., edit. bd. 1979—), Alpha Omega Alpha. Clubs: Harvard (Boston, N.Y.C., Phila.); Harvard Faculty. Home: 2223 Delancey Pl Philadelphia PA 19103 Office: Hahnemann Med Coll and Hosp 230 N Broad St Philadelphia PA 19102 *Respect for the ideas of others, but ultimately responsible for my own ideas, thus, a liberal philosophy in a conservative setting. Like Brecht's Galileo, I should like to be remembered as a lover of old wines and new ideas.*

EHRLICH, GERTRUDE, mathematics educator; b. Vienna, Austria, Jan. 7, 1923; came to U.S., 1939, naturalized, 1945; d. Josef and Charlotte (Kobak) E. B.S., Ga. Coll., 1943; M.A., U. N.C., 1945; Ph.D., U. Tenn., 1953. Instr. Oglethorpe U., Atlanta, 1946-50; grad. asst. U. Tenn., Knoxville, 1950-53; instr. U. Md., College Park, 1953-56, asst. prof., 1956-62, assoc. prof., 1962-69, prof. math., 1969—; chmn. U. Md. Math. Competition, 1979-82. Author: (with L.W. Cohen) Structure of the Real Number System, 1963, (with J.K. Goldhaber) Algebra, 1970; Assoc. editor: classroom notes Am. Math. Monthly, 1963-66; Asso. editor (with J.K. Goldhaber) research papers in ring theory. Recipient Disting. Alumna award Ga. Coll., 1970. Mem. AAUP, Am. Math. Soc., Math. Assn. Am., Sigma Xi, Phi Kappa Phi. Home: 6702 Wells Pkwy University Park MD 20782 Office: Math Dept U Md College Park MD 20742

EHRLICH, GRANT C(ONKLIN), corporation executive; b. Chgo., Aug. 16, 1916; s. Howard and Jenese (Conklin) E.; m. Gretchen Woerz, Sept. 14, 1940; children: Galen Matthews, Gretel Stephens. B.S. in Adm. Engrng. and mech. Engrng., Cornell U., 1938. Sales and engrng. mgr. New Eng. Tape Co., Hudson, Mass., 1938-44; pres. Resin Industries, Inc., Santa Barbara, Calif., 1944-56, Industrial de Resinas. S.A., Mexico City, 1953—; chmn. Templock Corp., Carpinteria, Calif., 1977—; chmn., chief exec. officer Flow General Inc., McLean, Va., 1983—; dir. Diversion Dynamics, Inc., Santa Barbara, Gen. Research Corp.-Flow Gen., Inc. Chmn. Young Republicans of Calif., 1950. Club: Valley Club of Montecito (treas., dir. 1980-82). Office: Flow General Inc 7655 Old Springhouse Rd McLean VA 22102

EHRLICH, IRA ROBERT, mechanical engineering educator; b. Washington, Sept. 1, 1926; s. Abraham Moses and Anna (Garonzik) E.; m. Sheila Lenor Kaminsky, June 11, 1950; children: Richard Mark, Heather Maureen. B.S., U.S. Mil. Acad., 1950; M.S., Purdue U., 1956; Ph.D., U. Mich., 1960; M.S. (hon.), Stevens Inst. Tech., 1982. Registered profl. engr., Mich., N.J. Supr. ITT, Paramus, N.J., 1960-62; mgr. transp. research group Stevens Inst. Tech., Hoboken, N.J., 1962-74, dean research, 1974—, head dept. mech. engrng., 1979—; chmn. sci. adv. com. U.S. Army Tank-Automotive Research and Devel. Command; cons. to industry; mem. N.J. Motor Vehicle Insp. Sta. Rev. Commn., chmn. safety com., 1977—. Asso. editor: Tire Sci. and Tech, 1972—. Served to capt. U.S. Army, 1950-60. Themis grantee, 1967-71. Mem. Internat. Soc. Terrain-Vehicle Systems (gen. sec. 1967-78, v.p. 1978-81, pres. 1981—), Soc. Automotive Engrs. (chmn. spl. purpose vehicle com.), ASME, U.S. Armor Assn., Am. Def. Preparedness Assn., Nat. Assn. Profl. Engrs. Jewish. Club: B'nai B'rith (chpt. pres. 1967-68). Home: 859 Columbus Dr Teaneck NJ 07666 Office: Castle Point Station Hoboken NJ 07030 *1) Never conduct an experiment without a theory with which to compare, 2) When policy does not provide direction, never ask permission. Someone may say, "No." 3) Make the most of your scraps of time.*

EHRLICH, MORTON, airline exec.; b. N.Y.C., Dec. 1, 1934; s. Milton and Anne (Tannenbaum) E.; m. Rosalind, Feb. 7, 1960; children—Bruce, Ellen, Wendy. B.B.A. cum laude, City Coll. N.Y., 1960; Ph.D. in Economics (Ford Found. fellow), Brown U., 1965. Economist Fed. Res. Bank of N.Y., 1965-67, Nat. Indsl. Conf. Bd., N.Y.C., 1967-68; v.p. Eastern Airlines, Miami, Fla., 1968-76, sr. v.p. planning, 1976—, also dir.; dir. Eastern Airlines (S.A.), IBM World Trade Ams./Far East Corp. Author: Discretionary Income, 1967, A Weekly Index of Business Activity, 1967, U.S. Foreign Trade, 1968, Computer Application in the Allocation of Airline Resources, 1975, An Integrated System for Airline Planning and Management Information, 1977. Trustee U. Miami; bd. dirs. Nat. Bur. Econ. Research. Served with U.S. Army, 1953-56. Mem. Am. Econ. Assn., Nat. Assn. Bus. Economists, Econ. Soc. South Fla. (dir.), Downtown Econs. Clubs: New York, U.S. C. of C. Home: 7541 SW 114th St Miami FL 33156 Office: Eastern Airlines Miami Internat Airport Miami FL 33148

EHRLICH, PAUL, chemist, educator; b. Vienna, Austria, Feb. 26, 1923; came to U.S., 1940, naturalized, 1944; s. Jacob and Irma (Hutter) E.; m. Celia Lesley, Apr. 16, 1949; children—Daniel, James, Catherine, Margot, Paul R. B.S., Queens Coll., 1944; M.S., U. Wis., 1948, Ph.D., 1951. Phys. chemist Nat. Bur. Standards, Washington, 1951-53; postdoctoral fellow Harvard, 1953-54; research chemist, scientist Monsanto Co., Springfield, Mass. and St. Louis, 1955-67; asso. prof., prof. State U. N.Y. at Buffalo, 1967—. Mem. editorial bd.: Jour. Macromolecular Sci, 1966-81; Contbr. articles profl. jours. Served with AUS, 1944-46. Recipient Research grants NSF, 1968, 72, 75, 77, 79; Am. Chem. Soc., 1968. Mem. Am. Chem. Soc., Am. Phys. Soc., Am. Inst. Chem. Engrs., AAAS. Home: 49 Ivyhurst Rd Buffalo NY 14226 Office: SUNY at Buffalo Amherst NY 14260

EHRLICH, PAUL RALPH, biology educator; b. Phila., May 29, 1932; s. William and Ruth (Rosenberg) E.; m. Anne Fitzhugh Howland, Dec. 18, 1955; 1 dau., Lisa Marie. A.B., U. Pa., 1953; A.M., U. Kans., 1955, Ph.D., 1957. Research assoc. U. Kans., Lawrence, 1958-59; asst. prof. biol. scis. Stanford, 1959-62, asso. prof., 1962-66, prof., 1966—, Bing prof. population studies, 1976—, dir. grad. study dept. biol. scis., 1966-69, 1974-76; cons. Behavioral Research Labs., 1963-67; cons. biology, editor in population biology McGraw Hill Book Co., N.Y.C., 1964—. Author: How to Know the Butterflies, 1961, Process of Evolution, 1963, Principles of Modern Biology, 1968, Population Bomb, 1968, 2d edit., 1971, Population, Resources, Environment: Issues In Human Ecology, 1970, 2d edit., 1972, How to Be a Survivor, 1971, Global Ecology: Readings Toward a Rational Strategy for Man, 1971, Man and the Ecosphere, 1971, Introductory Biology, 1973, Human Ecology: Problems and Solutions, 1973, Ark II: Social Response to Environmental Imperatives, 1974, The End of Affluence: A Blueprint for the Future, 1974, Biology and Society, 1976, Race Bomb, 1977, Ecoscience: Population, Resources, Environment, 1977, The Golden Door: International Migration, Mexico, and the U.S, 1979, Extinction: The Causes and Consequences of the Disappearance of Species, 1981; contbr. articles to profl. jours. Fellow Calif. Acad. Scis., Am. Acad. Arts and Scis.; mem. Soc. for Study Evolution, Soc. Systematic Zoology, Am. Soc. Naturalists, Lepidopterists Soc., Am. Mus. Natural History (hon. life mem.). Address: Biological Scis Stanford U Stanford CA 94305

EHRLICH, RICHARD, bacteriologist; b. Bedzin, Poland, Jan. 19, 1924; came to U.S., 1949, naturalized, 1952; s. Jacob and Gela E.; m. June Beinhorn, June 2, 1950; children: Glenn J., Jeffrey P. M.S., Tech. U. Munich, W. Ger., 1948, Ph.D., 1949. Lab. dir. Am. Butter Inst., Chgo., 1949-52; bacteriologist I.I.T. Research Inst., Chgo., 1952-57, supr. biol. research, then assoc. dir. life scis. research, 1957-63, dir. life sci. research, 1963-77, v.p. life scis. research, 1977—; mem. NOX subcom. NRC-Nat. Acad. Scis., 1975; mem. rev. com. air quality criteria EPA, 1970. Mem. editorial bd.: Advances in Modern Environ. Toxicology; Author papers in field. Mem. Air Pollution Control Assn., Am. Soc. Microbiology, AAAS, N.Y. Acad. Sci., Soc. Occupational and Environ. Health, Am. Public Health Assn., Soc. Française de la Tuberculose and Maladies Respiratoires (fgn. asso.), Sigma Xi. Home: 4857 Davis St Skokie IL 60077 Office: IIT Research Inst 10 W 35th St Chicago IL 60616

EHRLICH, S(AUL) PAUL, JR., physician, former government official; b. Mpls., May 4, 1932; s. Sol P. and Dorothy E. (Fiterman) E.; m. Geraldine McKenna, June 20, 1959; children: Susan P., Paula J., Jill M. B.A., U. Minn., 1953, B.S., 1955, M.D., 1957; M.P.H., U. Calif., 1961. Diplomate: Am. Bd. Preventive Medicine. Intern USPHS Hosp., S.I., N.Y., 1958; resident epidemiology U. Calif., 1961-63; mem. grants and tng. br. Nat. Heart Inst., Bethesda, Md., 1959-60; chief field and tng. sta. div. chronic diseases Heart Disease Control Program, San Francisco, 1961-65, asst. chief program devel., Arlington, Va., 1966-67; dep. chief Heart Disease Control Program of Nat. Center Chronic Disease Control, Arlington, 1967; asso. dir. bilateral programs Office Internat. Health of USPHS, Washington, 1967; dep. dir. Office of Internat. Health, Office of Sec., HEW, Washington, 1968-69, acting dir., 1969-70, dir., 1970-77; also acting surgeon gen. USPHS, 1973-77, dep. surgeon gen., 1976-77; v.p. Am. Insts. Research, Washington, 1978-79; dep. dir. Pan Am. Health Orgn., Washington, 1979-83; lectr. epidemiology U. Calif.; clin. asso. prof. community medicine and internat. health Georgetown U.; adj. prof. internat. health U. Tex.; U.S. rep. exec. bd. WHO, 1969-72, 73-76, chmn., 1972. Contbr. articles to profl. jours. Bd. regents Uniformed Services U. Health Scis. Served to lt. USCG, 1958-59. Fellow Am. Coll. Preventive Medicine, Am. Pub. Health Assn., Am. Heart Assn.; mem. AMA, AAAS, Am. Geriatrics Soc., Assn. Mil. Surgeons (pres. 1977), Internat. Epidemiol. Assn., D.C. Pub. Health Assn. Home: 6512 Lakeview Dr Falls Church VA 22041 Office: 525 23d St NW Washington DC 20037

EHRLICH, THOMAS, university administrator, law educator; b. Cambridge, Mass., Mar. 4, 1934; s. William and Evelyn (Seltzer) E.; m. Ellen Rome, June 18, 1957; children—David, Elizabeth, Paul. A.B., Harvard, 1956, LL.B., 1959; LL.D. (hon.), Villanova U., 1979, Notre Dame U., 1980. Bar: Wis. bar 1959. Law clk. Judge Learned Hand U.S. Ct. Appeals 2d Circuit, 1959-60; spl. asst. to legal adviser Dept. State, 1962-64, spl. asst. to under-sec., 1964-65; asso. prof. law Stanford, 1965-68, prof., 1968-75, also dean, 1971-75, Richard E. Lang dean and prof., 1973-75; pres. Legal Services Corp., Washington, 1976-79; dir. Internat. Devel. Coop. Agy., Washington, 1979-81; provost, prof. law U. Pa., Phila., 1981—. Author: (with Abram Chayes and Andreas F. Lowenfeld) The International Legal Process, 3 vols, 1968, (with Herbert L. Packer) New Directions in Legal Education, 1972, International Crises and the Role of Law, Cyprus, 1958-67, 1974; Editor: (with Geoffrey C. Hazard, Jr.) Going to Law School?, 1975. Office: Office of Provost 102 College Hall/CO U Pa Philadelphia PA 19104

EHRLICHMAN, JOHN DANIEL, author, radio and TV commentator, former asst. to Pres.; b. Tacoma, Mar. 20, 1925; s. Rudolph I. and Lillian C. (Danielson) E.; m. Christy McLaurine, Nov. 3, 1978; children: Peter, Jan, Thomas, Jody, Robert, Michael. B.A., UCLA, 1948; J.D., Stanford U., 1951. Bar: Calif. 1951-75, Wash. State 1952-75. Partner firm Hullin, Ehrlichman, Roberts & Hodge, Seattle, 1952-68; dir. conv. activities, tour dir. Nixon for Pres. campaign, 1968; counsel to Pres. Nixon, 1969; asst. to Pres. for domestic affairs, also exec. dir. staff Domestic Council, Washington, 1969-73; Mem. Fed. Property Rev. Bd., 1970-73, Pres.'s Council Internat. Econ. Policy, 1971-73. Radio and TV commentator, MBS, 1978-80; Author: The Company, 1976, The Whole Truth, 1979, Witness to Power, 1982; contbr. to periodicals. Served with AUS, 1943-45; ETO. Decorated Air medal with clusters D.F.C. Mem. Kappa Sigma. Office: PO Box 5559 Santa Fe NM 87502

EHRLING, ROBERT F., real estate company executive; b. N.Y.C., Dec. 7, 1939; s. John Robert and Kathleen (Clarke) E.; m. Cheryl M. Vogt, Aug. 6, 1966; children: Michael, John, Robert. B.S., Fordham U., 1961; M.B.A., St. John's U., 1967. Dir. Levitt & Sons Inc., N.Y.C., 1968-72; v.p. Larwin Group, Beverly Hills, Calif., 1973-74; various positions Gen. Devel. Corp., Miami, Fla., 1974-80, pres., 1980—. Vice-pres. Big Bros.-Big Sisters, Miami, 1982-83; chmn. Gov.'s Adv. Council-H.R.S., Fla., 1982; panel chmn. United Way of Miami, 1982. Roman Catholic. Home: 14600 SW 79th Ct Miami FL 33158 Office: Gen Devel Corp 1111 S Bayshore Dr Miami FL 33131

EHRLING, SIXTEN, orchestra conductor; b. Malmö, Sweden, Apr. 3, 1918; came to U.S., 1963; s. Gunnar and Emilia (Lundgren) E.; m. Gunnel Lindgren, Sept. 19, 1947; children: Elisabeth, Ann-Charlotte. Student, Royal High Sch. Music, Stockholm, 1936-40. Head conducting and orch. dept. Juilliard Sch., N.Y.C., 1973—. Condr., Royal Opera House, Stockholm, 1940-53; prin. condr., music dir., 1953-60; condr., music dir., Detroit Symphony Orch., 1963-73; mus. advisor, prin. guest condr., Denver Symphony, 1978—; guest condr., Met. Opera, N.Y.C., U.S., Europe, Japan, Australia. Home: Park Ten 10 W 66th St New York NY 10023 Office: Juilliard School Lincoln Center New York NY 10023

EHRMAN, JOACHIM BENEDICT, mathematics educator; b. Nuremberg, Germany, Nov. 12, 1929; emigrated to U.S., 1938, naturalized, 1943; s. Fritz Sally and Ilse (Benedict) E.; m. Gloria Jeanette Gould, Jan. 24, 1961; 1 son, Carl David. A.B., U. Pa., 1948; A.M., Princeton, 1949, Ph.D., 1954. Research physicist N.Am. Aviation, Inc., Downey, Calif., 1951-53; instr. physics Yale, 1954-55; research physicist U.S. Naval Research Lab., Washington, 1955-68; prof. dept. applied math. U. Western Ont., Can., London, 1968—; asso. prof. physics George Washington U., 1956-57; lectr. U. Md., 1963-64; vis. research staff Plasma Physics Lab., Princeton, 1975-76. Contbr. profl. jours. Mem. Am. Phys. Soc., Sigma Xi, Phi Beta Kappa, Pi Mu Epsilon. Jewish Religion. Office: Dept Applied Math U Western Ontario London ON N6A 5B9 Canada

EHRMAN, JOSEPH S., lawyer; b. Milw., Mar. 28, 1931; s. Joseph S. and Pauline (Breslauer) E.; m. Hazel Hope Justus, June 16, 1962; children: Douglas Spencer, Robert Russell. B.S. in Econs. with highest distinction, U. Minn., 1953; J.D. cum laude, Harvard U., 1956, LL.M., 1957. Assoc. Sidley & Austin, Chgo., 1957-66, ptnr., 1966—; mem. inquiry bd. Atty. Registration and Disciplinary Commn., State of Ill., Chgo., 1973-78. Vice pres., dir. Chgo. Commons Assn., 1964-68; bd. dirs., bd. atty. Montessori Sch., Lake Forest, Ill., 1980—; chmn. solictations com. Harvard Law Sch., Chgo. Fellow Am. Coll. Investment Counsel; mem. Legal Club Chgo. (past dir.), Law Club Chgo., ABA, Chgo. Bar Assn. Clubs: Union League; Mid-Day (Chgo.); Winter (Lake Forest). Home: 321 N Ahwahnee Rd Lake Forest IL 60045 Office: Sidley & Austin One 1st National Plaza Chicago IL 60603

EHRMAN, LEE, natural sciences educator; b. N.Y.C., May 25, 1935. B.S., Queens Coll., 1956; M.S., Columbia U., 1957, Ph.D. in Genetics, 1959. Mem. faculty Barnard Coll., 1956-58; postdoctoral fellow in genetics Columbia U., N.Y.C., 1959-61, assoc. seminar on population biology, 1981; mem. faculty SUNY-Purchase, 1980—, prof. div. natural scis., 1972—; mem. spl. study sect. NIH, NIMH, 1979-80; vis. prof. U. Miami, Coral Gables, Fla., 1981; coordinator, panelist workshops, programs in field. Author: Behavior Genetics and Evolution, 2d edit., 1981; assoc. editor: Evolution; assoc. editor for genetics and cytology: Am. Midland Naturalist; co-editotr: Behavior Genetics; assoc. editor, exec. com.: Am. Naturalists, 1977—. Recipient Lit. Soc. Found. medal in German, 1956, chancellor's award for excellence in teaching SUNY, 1977; Shirley Farr postdoctoral fellow, 1961-62; USPHS postdoctoral fellow, 1959-61; faculty exchange scholar, 1974-81; NSF grantee, 1979—. Fellow AAAS, Inst. Soc. Ethics and Life Scis; mem. AAUW, Am. Soc. Naturalists (v.p. 1982—), Behavior Genetics Assn. (pres. 1978), Phi Beta Kappa, Sigma Xi. Home: 2 Jennifer Ln Rye Brook NY 10573 Office: Div Natural Scis SUNY Purchase NY 10577

EHRNSCHWENDER, ARTHUR ROBERT, utility company executive; b. Cin., Oct. 3, 1922; s. Arthur Michael and Lydia Carol (Widmer) E.; m. Grace Scholl Popplewell, Oct. 19, 1983; children: Barry N., Scott A. M.E., U. Cin., 1948, B.S. in Commerce, 1959; M.B.A., Xavier U., 1959; D. Tech. Letters (hon.), Cin. Tech. Coll., 1980. Registered profl. engr., Ohio, Ky. Field engr. SKF Bearing Co., Cin., 1948-49; Chevrolet field rep. Gen. MotorsCorp., Cin., 1949-50; with Cin. Gas and Electric Co., 1952—, now sr. v.p.; chmn. Thrift Savs. & Loan., cin.; v.p., dir. Highway Rental Co., Cin., 1970—; dir. Jetcom Inc., Cin., OKI Supply Co., KDI Corp. Past pres. Goodwill Industries, Cin., 1961-82; trustee Cin. Assn. for blind, 1965-82, Hamilton county YWCA, 1974-82; chmn. bd. trustees Deaconess Hosp., Cin., 1970-82. Served to capt. U.S. Army, 1943-46, 1950-52. Decorated Bronze Star, 1952; named Disting. Alumnus U. Cin., 1974. Mem. Soc. Automotive Engrs. (sect. chmn.), Engring. Soc. Cin., Edison Electric Inst. (div. chmn.), Am. Gas Assn. (sect. chmn.). Republican. Presbyterian. Clubs: Queen city, Cincinnati Country. Lodges: Masons; Scottish Rite; Shriners; Royal Order of Jesters. Home: 5161 Salem Hills Ln Cincinnati OH 45230 Office: The Cin Gas & Electric Co 4th and Masin Sts Cincinnati OH 45202

EIBEN, ROBERT MICHAEL, pediatric neurologist, educator; b. Cleve., July 12, 1922; s. Michael Albert and Frances Carlysle (Gedeon) E.; children: Daniel F., Christopher J., Thomas M., Mary, Charles G., Elizabeth A. B.S., Western Res. U., 1944, M.D., 1946. Diplomate: Am. Bd. Pediatrics. Intern medicine Univ. Hosp., Cleve., 1946-47; asst. resident pediatrics and contagious diseases City Hosp., Cleve., 1947, asst. med. dir. div. contagious diseases, 1949-50, visitant in pediatrics, 1949-50, acting dir. dept. pediatrics and contagious diseases, 1950-52; asst. resident pediatrics Babies and Children's Hosp., Cleve., 1948, clin. fellow pediatrics, 1948-49; practice medicine, specializing in pediatrics, Cleve., 1949—; asst. dir. dept. pediatrics and contagious diseases Cleve. Met. Gen. Hosp., 1952-60; med. dir. Respiratory Care and Rehab. Center, 1954-60, pres. med. staff, 1958-60, pediatric neurologist, 1963—, acting med. dir. comprehensive care program, 1966-67, med. dir., 1968-73, mem. med. exec. com., 1974-76, acting dir. dept. pediatrics, 1979—; USPHS fellow in neurology U. Wash., 1960-63; acting chief, sect. on clin. investigations and therapeutics Developmental and Metabolic Neurology br. Nat. Inst. Neurol. and Communicative Disorders and Strokes, NIH, Bethesda, Md., 1976-77; clin. instr. pediatrics Western Res. U., 1949-50, instr. pediatrics, 1950-51, asst. clin. prof., 1951-54, asst. prof., 1954-65, asst. prof. neurology, 1964-72, asso. prof. pediatrics, 1965-75, asso. prof. neurology, 1972—, prof. pediatrics, 1975—; cons., project site visitor Nat. Found. Birth Defects Center Programs, 1961-66; mem. adv. com. on grants to train dentists to care for handicapped Robert Wood Johnson Found., 1975—. Trustee St. Anthony's Children's Village; chmn. adv. com. Genetics Center, Western Res. U. Recipient Presdl. award Internat. Poliomyelitis Congress, Geneva, 1957. Mem. Am. Acad. Pediatrics, Am. Acad. Neurology, Am. Soc. Human Genetics, Am. Pediatric Soc., Am. Epilepsy Soc., Ohio Med. Assn., No. Ohio Pediatric Soc., No. Ohio Neurol. Soc., Cleve. Acad. Medicine, Cuyahoga County Med. Soc., Innominatum Soc., Pasteur Club, Child Neurology Soc. (chmn. tng. program com. 1976-77, pres.-elect 1982—, sec.-treas. 1978—), Case Western Res. U. Med. Alumni Assn. (pres. 1979). Home: 2 Oakshore Dr Bratenahl OH 44108 Office: Cleve Met Gen Hosp Cleveland OH 44109

EIBERGER, CARL FREDERICK, II, lawyer; b. Denver, Jan. 17, 1931; s. Carl Frederick and Madeleine Anastasia (Ries) E.; children: Eileen, Carl, Mary, James. B.S. magna cum laude in Chemistry, Notre Dame U., 1952, J.D., 1954; M.B.A., Denver U., 1959. Bar: Mich. 1954, Colo. 1954, U.S. Fed. Ct. 1954. Since practiced in Denver area; partner DeMuth & Eiberger, 1964-79; sr. partner Eiberger, Stacy and Smith, 1979—; mem. Colo. Gov's. Adv. Council to Dept. Labor and Employment, 1966—; mem. faculty Nat. Practising Law Inst., 1970. Chmn. bd. Colo. Assn. Commerce and Industry, 1979-84; mem. Gov.'s Labor Mgmt. Conf., 1977—. Served with AUS, 1955-57. Recipient Disting. Service award Denver Jaycees, 1966. Mem. Am. Arbitration Assn. (arbitrator), Colo. Bar Assn. (gov. 1971-75), Denver Bar Assn. (chmn. com. on econs. law practice 1968), Notre Dame Law Assn. (dir.). Clubs: Rolling Hills Country; Denver Athletic, Notre Dame (Denver) (dir. 1958—). Home: 14330 Farview Ln Golden CO 80401 Office: 2390 Cadillac Bldg 410 17th St Denver CO 80202

EIBERSON, HAROLD, librarian; b. N.Y.C., Sept. 5, 1913; s. Joseph and Rose (Davis) Eibeshutz; m. Rosalyn K. Feinberg, Aug. 25, 1940; children—Jeffrey, Linda. B.S., City Coll. N.Y., 1933; M.A., Columbia U., 1936, B.L.S., 1937. Mem. staff Baruch Sch. Library City Coll. N.Y. (now Bernard M. Baruch Coll.), N.Y.C., 1933—, prof. library, chief librarian, 1968—; adj. lectr. polit. sci. Baruch Sch., 1946-73, asst. prof. library, 1965-66, asso. prof., 1966-70, prof., 1971—; mem. Inst. N.Y. Area Studies, 1956-60. Author: Sources for the Study of the New York Area, 1960. Mem. ALA, Library Assn. City Colls. N.Y. (pres. 1943-46), N.Y. Library Club (sec. 1951-54). Home: 22708 57th Rd Oakland Gardens NY 11364 Office: 156 E 25th St New York City NY 10010

EICHELBAUM, STANLEY, journalist; b. N.Y.C., Oct. 5, 1926; s. Sam and Rebecca (Rosen) E. B.A. magna cum laude, Coll. City N.Y., 1947; M.A., Columbia U., 1968; Certificat d'Etudes, Sorbonne, Paris, 1949. Editorial researcher, reporter New Yorker Mag., N.Y.C., 1949-58; with San Francisco Examiner, 1958-79, drama editor, critic plays and movies, 1961-79; entertainment critic, plays and movies KQED-TV, San Francisco, 1979—; lectr. on arts, various colls., univs., clubs, 1961—; Mem. selections com. San Francisco Internat. Film Festival, 1962-65; instr. workshop in critical writing U. Calif. Extension, San Francisco, 1968—; mem. program San Francisco Art Inst., 1968-70. Painter exhbt. in group show, Forum Gallery, N.Y.C., 1955-56; Contbr. articles to mags. Mem. Calif. Hist. Soc., Am. Theatre Critics Assn., Phi Beta Kappa. Home: 515 Kansas St San Francisco CA 94107

EICHELBERGER, ROBERT JOHN, government research and development administrator; b. Washington, Pa., Apr. 10, 1921; s. John Eugene and Dorothy Louise (Failinger) E.; m. Estella Ann Westcott, May 14, 1943; children: William J., Charles R., Sara Jane Eichelberger Hans, Mary Ann. A.B., Washington and Jefferson Coll., 1942; M.S., Carnegie Inst. Tech., 1948, Ph.D., 1954. Research supr. Carnegie Inst. Tech., 1943-55; chief detonation physics br. U.S. Army Ballistic Research Labs., Aberdeen Proving Ground, Md., 1955-62, asso. tech. dir. labs., 1962-67, dir. labs., 1967—; asso. tech. dir. U.S. Army Armament Research and Devel. Command., 1976-80; lectr. in field. Contbr. articles to profl. publs. Recipient Disting. Civilian Service award Dept. Def., 1977; Exceptional Civilian Service award Dept. Army, 1971; Research and Devel. Achievement award, 1961, 71, Presdl. meritorious exec. award, 1982, Crozier prize Am. Def. Preparedness Agy., 1984. Mem. Am. Phys. Soc., Nat. Council Advancement Research (dir.), AAAS, Soc. Natural Philosophy, Am. Def. Preparedness Assn. (cons.), Assn. U.S. Army, Combustion Inst. Democrat. Presbyterian. Home: 409 W Catherine St Bel Air MD 21014 Office: Ballistic Research Lab Aberdeen Proving Ground MD 21005

EICHENBERG, FRITZ, artist, writer, educator; b. Cologne, Germany, Oct. 24, 1901; came to U.S., 1933, naturalized, 1941; s. Siegfried and Ida (Marcus) E.; m. Mary Altmann, 1926 (dec. 1937); 1 dau., Suzanne; m. Margaret Ladenburg, 1941 (div. 1965); 1 son, Timothy; m. Antonie Schulze-Forster, 1975. Student, Sch. Applied Arts, Cologne, 1916-20, State Acad. Graphic Arts, Leipzig, 1921-23; D.F.A., Southeastern Mass. U., 1972, U. R.I., 1974, Pratt Inst., Bklyn., 1976, Calif. Coll. Arts and Crafts, 1978; D.H.L., Marymount Coll., 1984. With art dept. New Sch. for Social Research, 1935-41; mem. Pennell Fund com. Library of Congress, 1962-68; prof. art, chmn. dept. graphic art Pratt Inst., 1956-63; prof. U. R.I., 1966-71, chmn. dept. art, 1966-69; founder, dir. emeritus Pratt Graphic Art Center; mem. art faculty Albertus Magnus Coll., 1972-73; also lectr. Staff artist and illustrator for German mags. and newspapers, 1926-33; illustrator numerous book classics with wood engravings and lithographs, works in ann. print exhbns.; represented by prints and drawings in major collections, U.S., also abroad; exhibited numerous one man shows, including, AAA Galleries, N.Y., 1967, 77, Boston Public Library, Impressions Gallery, Boston, 1976; retrospective exhbn., Klingspor Mus., Offenbach am Main, Germany, 1974; (Yale U. established archives of his work 1978); author: Art and Faith, 1952, The Art of the Print, Masterpieces, History and Techniques, 1976; author-illustrator: Ape in a Cape, 1952, Dancing in the Moon, 1955; illustrator-translator: Erasmus In Praise of Folly, 1972; author-illustrator: The Wood and the Graver, 1977, Endangered Species and other Fables with a Twist, 1979 (nominated for Nat. Book Award 1980), The Adventures of Simplicissimus, 1981, Dance of Death, 1983; editor, founder: Artist's Proof Ann, 1961-72. Recipient Silver medal Ltd. Editions Club, 1954, Purchase prizes Library of Congress Print Exhibit, 1943-54; S.F.B. Morse medal NAD, 1973; R.I. Gov.'s AA award, 1981; Pennell medal Pa. Acad., 1944; J.D.R. III Fund grantee, 1968; 1st prize Prints, NAD, 1946. Fellow Royal Soc. Arts (corr.); mem. Soc. Am. Graphic Artists, NAD. Mem. Soc. of Friends. Home: 142 Oakwood Dr Peace Dale RI 02883 *I want to be remembered as an artist with a social conscience who loves his fellowmen regardless of sex, creed or race, and through his work and his actions has tried to serve peace in the world.*

EICHENWALD, HEINZ FELIX, physician; b. Switzerland, Mar. 3, 1926; came to U.S., 1936, naturalized, 1945; s. Ernst M. and Stella E.; m. Elva C. MacDonald, Nov. 7, 1951; children—Kathryn S., Eric C., Kurt A. B.A. in Biochem. Scis. magna cum laude with highest honors, Harvard U., 1946; M.D., Cornell U., 1950. Successively intern, sr. asst. resident, sr. resident pediatrician N.Y. Hosp., 1950-51; asst. in pediatrics Cornell U. Med. Sch., 1951-53, instr., then asst. prof., 1955-58, asso. prof., then prof. pediatrics, 1958-64; USPHS instr. pediatrics Emory U. Med. Sch., 1953-55; also vis. physician Grady and Crawford Long hosps., both Atlanta; mem. staff N.Y. Hosp., 1958-65, attending pediatrician, 1963-65; vis. asst. prof. Albert Einstein Med. Sch., 1956-58; cons. Hosp. Spl. Surgery, N.Y.C., 1956-64, Patterson (N.J.) Gen. Hosp., 1958-64; prof. pediatrics, chmn. dept. U. Tex. Southwestern Med. Sch., Dallas, 1964—; chief-of-staff Children's Med. Center, Dallas, 1964—; chief pediatrics Parkland Meml. Hosp., Dallas, 1964—; cons. St. Paul, Irving Community, Presbyn. hosps., all Dallas; chief hepatitis investigation unit, epidemiology br. USPHS, 1954-55; Richard Bruce Miller lectr. Harvard U. Med. Sch., 1960; lectr. Columbia U. Tchrs. Coll., 1960-64; chmn. Internat. Research Confs. Mental Retardation, 1965-66; chmn. panel anti-infectives Nat. Acad. Scis.-NRC, 1966-69; vis. prof. U. Saigon Med. Sch., 1968-72; Vanuxem lectr. Princeton U., 1970; bd. dirs. Dallas Free Clinic, 1970-74, Children's Devel. Center, Dallas, 1974—; mem. bd. maternal and child health NIH, 1974-78; cons. in field, mem. numerous profl. coms. Author numerous articles in field; asso. edito: Pediatric Therapt, 1974; mem. editorial bds. profl. jours. Bd. dirs., chmn. exec. com. Lamplighter Sch., Dallas, 1971—; bd. dirs. Winston Sch., Dallas, 1974. Recipient Career Research award NIH, 1963-65, Alexander von Humboldt prize Fed. Republic Ger., 1979, Weinstein-Goldeson award United Cerebral Palsy Found., 1980; Markle scholar med. sci., 1953. Mem. Harvey Soc., Soc. Pediatric Research, Am. Pediatric Soc., Infectious Disease Soc. Am., N.Y. Acad. Scis., Tex. Pediatric Soc., Phi Beta Kappa, Sigma Xi, Alpha Omega Alpha. Office: 5323 Harry Hines Blvd Dallas TX 75235

EICHER, GEORGE JOHN, aquatic biologist; b. Bremerton, Wash., Aug. 27, 1916; s. George John and Caroline Agnes (Wolfer) E.; m. Patricia Jane Davies, Feb. 17, 1951; children: George C., Kenneth. Student, Wash. State U., 1938; B.S., Oreg. State U., 1941. Research party leader in Alaska U.S. Bur. Fisheries, 1939-41; fish biologist Ariz. Game and Fish Commn., 1943-47; charge salmon research in Western Alaska U.S. Fish and Wildlife Service, 1947-56; chief aquatic biologist Gen. Electric Co., Portland, Oreg., 1956-72, mgr. dept. environ. services, 1972-78; pres. Eicher Assos., Inc., Portland, 1978—; cons. in field, 1958—; Mem. Gov. Oreg. Outdoor Recreation Council, 1960—; sci. bd. cons. demonstration grants water quality and pollution control HEW, 1963—; adviser fisheries Nat. Izaak Walton League Am., 1960-65; mem. U.S. Com. on Large Dams. Free-lance writer, 1941-43; patentee turbine fish screen. Fellow Am. Inst. Fishery Research Biologists, Internat. Acad. Fishery Sci.; mem. Am. Fisheries Soc. (pres. 1965), Assn. Power Biologists (pres. 1958-60), Wildlife Soc., Explorers Club, Am. Soc. Limnology and Oceanography, Am. Inst. Biol. Scis., Pacific Fishery Biologists (sec. 1950), U.S. C. of C. (nat. resources com.), Portland C. of C. (chmn. recreational and natural resources com. 1962, chmn. water standards com. 1966-70), Sigma Chi.

EICHHORN, FREDERICK FOLTZ, JR., lawyer; b. Gary, Ind., Oct. 16, 1930; s. Fredreick Foltz and Adele D. (DeLano) E.; m. Julia Abel, Aug. 27, 1955; children: Jill, Thomas, Timothy, Linda. B.S., Ind. U., 1952, J.D., 1957. Bar: Ind. 1957, U.S. Ct. Appeals (7th cir.) 1957, U.S. Dist. Ct. (no dist.) Ind. 1957, U.S. Supreme Ct. 1973. Assoc. Eichhorn, Eichhorn & Link, and predecessor firm, Hammond, Ind., 1961-63, ptnr., 1963—; sr. ptnr. Eichhorn, Eichhorn & Link and predecessor firm, 1977—. Bd. dirs. Gary Housing Authority, 1972-75, United Fund, Planned Parenthood, Gary Police Civil Service Commn., 1975-82; bd. dirs., founder Miller Citizens Com., 1971; mem. Ind. Sesquicentennial Commn. Served with USAF, 1952-54. Fellow Am. Bar Found.; mem. Ind. Bar Assn. (inst. chmn. white collar crime 1979), Am. Gas. Assn. (state rate litigation com. 1982, regulation of gas supplies com., state regulatory matters com.), Midwest Gas Assn. (legal affairs sect. 1982), Phi Delta Phi, Delta Tau Delta. Clubs: Columbia, University (Indpls.). Office: 5243 Hohman Ave Hammond IN 46230

EICHHORN, GEORGE CARL, found. exec.; b. Norfolk, Va., Apr. 8, 1901; s. George Jacob and Katherine Elizabeth (Marburger) E.; m. Hermene Wharton Warlick, Aug. 2, 1926; children—Charles Richard, Mary Louise Eichhorn Simons. Student pub. schs., Greensboro, N.C. City clk., treas. City of Greensboro, 1924-37; with Richardson-Merrell Inc. (formerly Vick Chem. Co.), Wilton, Conn., 1937-66, pres., 1951-63, corp. v.p. for mfg., 1964-66, ret., 1966; asst. to pres. Smith Richardson Found., Inc., Greensboro, 1967-70, asst. sec.-treas., 1970-74, adminstrv. v.p., treas., 1974-81, trustee, 1974—. Bd. dirs. United Arts Council, Greensboro, 1966-76, pres., 1968-70; bd. dirs. Greensboro Preservation Soc., 1971-78; trustee Bus. Found. N.C., Chapel Hill, 1959-71, Excellence Fund, U. N.C., Greensboro, 1966—; bd. visitors Guilford Coll., Greensboro, 1968-74; sr. warden Holy Trinity Episcopal Ch., Greensboro, 1949-51. Clubs: Rotary (pres. 1952-53), Greensboro Country (Greensboro)). Home: 1504 Kirkpatrick Pl Greensboro NC 27408

EICHHORN, GUNTHER LOUIS, chemist; b. Frankfurt am Main, Germany, Feb. 8, 1927; s. Fritz David and Else Regina (Weiss) E.; m. Lotti Neuhaus, June 25, 1964; children: David Mark, Sharon Julie. A.B. in Chemistry, U. Louisville, 1947; M.S., U. Ill., 1948, Ph.D., 1950. Asst. prof., then asso. prof. chemistry La. State U., 1950-57; commd. officer USPHS, 1954-57; asso. prof. chemistry Georgetown U., 1957-58; guest scientist Naval Med. Research Inst., 1957-58; chief sect. molecular biology Gerontology Research Center, Nat. Inst. Aging, NIH, Balt., 1958-78, chief lab. cellular and molecular biology and head sect. inorganic biochemistry, 1978—; pres. Nat. Inst. Child Health and Human Devel. Assembly Scientists, 1972-73; mem. panel nickel NRC, 1974; distinguished lectr. Mich. State U., 1972; Watkins vis. prof. Wichita State U., 1983; condr. seminars, lectr. in field. Editor: Inorganic Biochemistry, 1973; co-editor: Advances in Inorganic Biochemistry, 1978—; mem. editorial bds. profl. jours.; Author papers in field. Gen. Aniline and Film Co. grantee, 1949; postdoctoral fellow Ohio State U., summers 1951, 52; recipient Woodcock medal U. Louisville, 1947; Md. Chemist award, 1978; NIH Dir.'s award, 1979; Sr. Exec. Service bonus award, 1982. Fellow AAAS, Am. Inst. Chemists, Gerontol. Soc. (fin. com. 1980-82, research and edn. com. 1982—); mem. Am. Chem. Soc., N.Y. Acad. Scis., Am. Inst. Biol. Chemists, Biophys. Soc. Home: 6703 97th Ave Seabrook MD 20801 Office: Gerontology Research Center NIH Baltimore City Hosps Baltimore MD 21224

EICHHORN, HENRICH KARL, astronomer, educator, consultant; b. Vienna, Austria, Nov. 30, 1927; came to U.S., 1956, naturalized, 1963; s Heinrich and Johanna (Augustin) E.; m, 1952 (div. 1977); children: Luitgard, Edelgard, Armgard, Heinrich; m Eva Marakova, Apr. 9, 1977. Dr. Phil., U. Vienna, Vienna, Austria, 1949, Wissenschaftliche Hilfskraft, 1951-56, Hochschulassistent, 1956. Asst. prof. astronomy Georgetown U., Washington, 1956-59; assoc. prof. Wesleyan U., Middletown, Conn., 1959-64; prof., chmn. dept. astronomy U. South Fla., Tampa, 1964-79; prof. astronomy U. Fla., Gainesville, 1975—, chmn. dept. astronomy, 1979—; cons. in field; vis. prof. U. Vienna, 1971, Yale U., New Haven, 1976; astronome adjoint Observatoire de l'Universite Louis Pasteur, Strasbourg, France, 1977. Author: Astronomy of Star Positions, 1974; researcher numerous publs. in field, 1950—; editor: Conference on Photographic Astrometric Technique, 1971. Named Hon. prof. U. Graz, Austria, 1977, Brit. Council scholar, Glasgow, Scotland, 1951-52; Nat. Acad. Sci. OEEC fellow U. Va., Charlottesville, 1954-56; NSF grantee, 1956—; NASA grantee, 1965—; named U. South Fla. Disting scholar, 1979; grantee U.S. govt. agys. Mem. Internat. Astron. Union (v.p. Commn. 24 1976-79), Internat. Astrpn. Union (pres. Commn. 24 1979-82), Am. Astron. Soc. (vice chmn. div. dynamical astronomy 1979-80, chmn. div. dynamical astronomy 1980-81). Office: Dept Astronomy U Fla 211 Space Sci Bldg Gainesville FL 32611

EICHHORN, ROGER, university dean; b. Slayton, Minn., Apr. 1, 1931; s. Irvin George and Myrtle Edna (Jones) E.; m. Patricia Ann Lachowitzer, Aug. 23, 1952; children—Kevin, Elise, Stacy, Lynn, Gregg. B.S. in Elec. Engring, U. Minn., 1953, M.S. in Mech. Engring, 1955, Ph.D., 1959. Instr. U. Minn. at Mpls., 1955-59; asst. prof. Princeton, 1959-61, asso. prof., 1961-67; prof., chmn. mech. engring. U. Ky. at Lexington, 1967-75, acting dean, 1975-76, dean, 1979-82, asso. dean research, 1976-78; prof., dean U. Houston, 1982—; cons. Intertech Corp., Princeton, N.J., 1964-72, Pratt & Whitney Aircraft Corp., Hartford, Conn., 1969-75, IBM, Lexington, 1971-72; with summer vis. faculty program Sandia Corp., Albuquerque, 1968; vis. prof. Imperial Coll., London, 1974, Assiut U., Egypt, Jan. 1979. Mem. hon. bd. editors: Internat. Jour. Heat and Mass Transfer, 1970-82, Jour. Math. and Phys. Scis, 1974—; tech. editor: Jour. Heat Transfer, 1975-80; Contbr. articles profl. jours. Bd. dirs. U. Ky. Research Found., 1969-82, Internat. Book Project. Recipient Sang award U. Ky., 1972; NSF sci. faculty fellow Imperial Coll., London, 1963-64; Fulbright scholar, Guayaquil, Ecuador, summer 1976. Fellow ASME (Heat Transfer Div. Meml. award 1983—); mem. Am. Inst. Aeros. and Astronautics, AAAS, Am. Soc. Engring. Edn., Sigma Xi. Research in area of heat transfer and fluid mechanics with specialization in natural convection, turbulent boundary layers, mass transfer, multiphase flow. Home: 3542 Sun Valley Houston TX 77025

EICHMAN, PETER LIEBERT, physician, educator; b. Phila., Nov. 18, 1925; s. Edward A. and Frances (Liebert) E.; m. Phyllis Kettelhon, Dec. 12, 1959; children—Mary Katherine, Elizabeth Louise, Susan Lynn, Erich Liebert, Philip John. B.S., St. Joseph's Coll., Phila., 1945; M.D., Jefferson Med. Coll., Phila., 1949. Diplomate: Am. Bd. Psychiatry and Neurology, Am. Bd. Internal Medicine. Intern Fitzgerald-Mercy Hosp., Lansdowne, Pa., 1949-50; fellow, resident hepatic and metabolic diseases Walter Reed Army Hosp., 1950-51; infectious diseases Jefferson Med. Coll., 1951-52; medicine and neurology Mayo Found., 1952-54; neuropsychiatry U. Wis. Hosp., Madison, 1954-55; mem. faculty U. Wis. Med. Sch. and Univs. Hosps., 1955-, asst. dean clin. affairs, 1965, prof. medicine and neurology, dean, also dir., 1965-72, prof. neurology, 1973—; dep. dir. Bur. Health Manpower Edn. NIH, Dept. Health, Edn., Welfare, 1972-73; acting dir. Bur. Health Resource Devel., 1973. Mem. A.C.P., A.M.A., Am. Acad. Neurology, Dane County Med. Soc. Home: 1801 Camelot Dr Madison WI 53705

EICHNER, HANS, German language and literature educator; b. Vienna, Austria, Oct. 30, 1921; emigrated to Can., 1950; s. Alexander and Valerie (Ungar) E.; m. Joan M. Partridge, May 29, 1957; children: Jane Elizabeth, James Alexander. B.A., U. London, 1944, 1946; Ph.D., 1949; LL.D., Queen's U., 1974. Asst. lectr. Bedford Coll. London, 1948-50; mem. faculty Queens U., Kingston, Ont., Can., 1950-67, assoc. prof., 1956-62, prof., 1962-67; chmn. grad. dept. German U. Toronto, Ont., Can., 1967-72, prof., 1967—, chmn. dept. German, 1975—; hon. prof. humanities U. Calgary, Alta., Can., 1978—. Author: Thomas Mann, 1953, 61, Four German Authors, 1964, Friedrich Schlegel, 1970; Editor: Literary Notebooks (Friedrich Schlegel), 1957, Critical Edition of F. Schlegel Works, vols 2-6, 16, 1959-81, Romantic: The European History of a Word, 1972. Recipient Goethe Inst. medal, 1973; Nuffield Found. fellow, 1952-53; Can. Council sr. fellow, 1959-60; McLaughlin Research prof., 1965-66. Fellow Royal Soc. Can.; mem. Modern Lang. Assn., Can. Assn. U. Tchrs. of German (pres. 1976-78). Club: Boulevard. Home: 12 Hopperton Dr Willowdale ON Canada Office: Dept German U Toronto Toronto M5S 1A1 ON Canada

EICHORN, JOHN FREDERICK GERARD, JR., utility executive; b. Boston, Mar. 3, 1924; s. John Frederick Gerard and Hazel (Morris) E.; m. Mary Louise MacIsaac, Oct. 11, 1952; children: Christine Louise, Elisabeth Anne (dec.), Ellen Marie. B.S. in Mech. Engring, U. Maine, 1949; postgrad., Northeastern U., 1963-64. Registered profl. engr., Mass. With New Eng. Elec. System (various locations), 1949-71; v.p., regional exec. New Eng. System (Mass. Electric div.), North Andover, Mass., 1968-71; exec. v.p. Eastern Utilities Assos., Boston, 1971-72, pres., chief exec. officer, 1972—, also trustee; pres., dir. Montaup Electric Co., Somerset, Mass., 1971—, EUA Service Corp., Boston, 1971—; chmn., dir. Blackstone Valley Electric Co., Lincoln, R.I., 1971—, Eastern Edison Co., Mass., 1971—; dir. Yankee Atomic Power Co., Rowe, Mass., Conn. Yankee Atomic Power Co., Haddem Neck, Conn., Maine Yankee Atomic Power Co., Wiscasett, Vt. Yankee Nuclear Power Corp., Vernon.; Chmn. exec. com. New Eng. Power Pool. Served with AUS, 1942-45. Mem. Edison Electric Inst. (dir.), Electric Council New Eng. (dir.). Clubs: Algonquin, Fed. (Boston). Office: One Liberty Sq PO Box 2333 Boston MA 02107

EICKHOFF, HAROLD W., college president. Pres. Trenton (N.J.) State Coll. Office: Trenton State Coll Hillwood Lakes Trenton NJ 08625

EICKHOFF, MARGARET KATHRYN, economist; b. Sedalia, Mo., Apr. 11, 1939; s. Leo E. and Magdalene (Piatt) E.; m. A. James Smith, Jr., Mar. 9, 1973. Contract writer Group Ins. Mut. of N.Y., N.Y.C., 1960-61; research asst. Van Alstyne, Neol & Co., N.Y.C., 1961-62; economist Townsend-Greenspan & Co., Inc., N.Y.C., 1962—, dir., 1964—, treas., 1966—, v.p., 1972-80, exec. v.p., 1980—; bd. dirs. N.Y. Futures Exchange, 1979-82; exec. dir. Econalyst, 1979—; dir. Tenneco, Inc., Upjohn Co., Interpace Corp., Townsend-Greenspan & Co., Inc.; mem. econ. adv. bd. U.S. Dept. Commerce. Mem. alumni devel. council U. Mo., 1976-78; mem. adv. com. Pace U. Fellow Nat. Assn. Bus. Economists (pres. 1980-81, exec. com., governing council 1967-73); mem. Am. Fin. Assn., Am. Econ. Assn., Econ. Club N.Y., Conf. Bus. Economists, Bus. Economists Council, Women's Econ. Roundtable. Office: 1 New York Plaza New York NY 10004

EICKHOFF, THEODORE CARL, physician; b. Cleve., Sept. 13, 1931; s. Theodore Henry and Clara (Strassen) E.; m. Margaret Heinecke, Aug. 24, 1952; children: Stephen, Mark, Philip. B.A., Valparaiso U., 1953; M.D., Case Western Res. U., 1957. Diplomate: Am. Bd. Internal Medicine. Intern, then resident Harvard Med. Services, Boston City Hosp., 1957-59; fellow in medicine Harvard Med. Sch.-Boston City Hosp., 1961-64; epidemiologist Center for Disease Control, 1964-67; head div. infectious disease U. Colo. Med. Center, 1967-80, vice chmn. dept. medicine, 1976—; dir. internal medicine Presbyn./St. Luke's Med. Ctr.; dir. medicine Denver Gen. Hosp., 1978-81; cons. FDA, Centers for Disease Control, Am. Hosp. Assn. Contbr. articles to med. jours. Served with USPHS, 1959-67. Mem. Am. Fedn. Clin. Research, ACP, Am. Soc. Clin. Investigation, Assn. Am. Physicians, Infectious Diseases Soc. Am. (sec. 1978-82, pres. 1983-84), Am. Epidemiol. Soc. (sec.-treas. 1978-82). Home: 15 S Franklin Circle Littleton CO 80121

EIDENBERG, EUGENE, political scientist; b. N.Y.C., Oct. 5, 1939; s. Nathan and Eve E. B.A. with honors, U. Wis., Madison, 1961; M.A., Northwestern U., 1963, Ph.D., 1966. Mem. polit. sci. faculty U. Minn., Mpls., 1965-72, v.p. adminstrn., 1972; vice chancellor U. Ill., Chgo., 1972-77; dep. mayor, Mpls., 1968-70; dep. undersec. HEW, Washington, 1977-78; dep. asst. to pres., dep. sec. to Cabinet, Washington, 1978-79, asst. to pres., sec. to, 1979-80; dir. Democratic Nat. Com., Washington, 1981-82; sr. v.p. MCI Communications Corp., 1982—; chmn. Ill. Law Enforcement Commn., 1974-77; mem. nat. adv. com. Am. Bar Assn. Com. on Citizenship Edn., 1979—. Bd. dirs. Mpls. Urban Coalition, 1969-70; mem. governing bd. Mpls. OEO, 1969-70. Recipient Disting. Service award U. Ill. Alumni Assn., 1978; fellow Inst. Politics, JFK Sch. Govt., Harvard U., 1981. Mem. Am. Polit. Sci. Assn. (Congressional fellow 1964-65). Democrat. Jewish. Office: 1133 19th St NW Washington DC 20036

EIDMAN, KRAFT WARNER, lawyer; b. Liberty Hill, Tex., Jan. 17, 1912; s. Kraft H. and Vera (Bates) E.; m. Julia Mary Bell, Aug. 31, 1940; children: Kraft Gregory, Dan Kelly, John Bates. Student, Rice U., 1929-30; A.B., U. Tex., 1935, LL.B., 1935. Bar: Tex. 1935. Since practiced in Houston; sr. partner Fulbright & Jaworski (and predecessors), 1947—; lectr. law sci. insts., medico-legal insts., state bar meetings.; v.p., dir. Def. Research Inst.; mem. centennial commn. U. Tex. Editor: Ins. Counsel Jour., 1961-63; contbr. articles to legal jours. Life trustee, pres. U. Tex. Law Sch. Found.; trustee, past chmn. U. Tex. Health Sci. Center Found. at Houston; mem. exec. com., chancellor's council U. Tex.; former trustee, mem. exec. com. Inst. Rehab. and Research; bd. dirs. Tex. Med. Ctr., Houston, Houston chpt. ARC; trustee M.D. Anderson Found. Served to lt. comdr. USNR, 1942-45. Named Disting. Alumnus, U. Tex., 1978. Fellow Am. Coll. Trial Lawyers (regent 1972-76, pres. elect 1976-77, pres. 1977-78), Am., Tex. bar founds.; mem. Anglo-Am. Exchange, Am. Counsel Assn., ABA (vice chmn. trial tactics coms.), Tex. Bar Assn. (chmn. tort and compensation law), Houston Bar Assn. (pres. 1960-61), Internat. Assn. Ins. Counsel (exec. com. 1957-60, 51-66, pres. 1964-65), Houston C. of C., U. Tex. Law Sch. Alumni Assn. (pres., Disting. Alumnus 1980), T Assn., Chancellors, Friar Soc. Democrat. Roman Catholic. Clubs: KC, Kiwanis (pres. S.W. Houston 1958), Houston, Colonneh, Houston Country, Briar (pres. 1952), Chaparral (Dallas); Lakeway Country, University, Capitol, Tarry House (Austin). Home: 5559 Sugar Hill Houston TX 77056 Office: Bank of Southwest Bldg Houston TX 77002

EIDSON, RICHARD IRWIN, savings and loan association executive; b. Columbus, Ohio, Jan. 1, 1931; s. Willard Cole and Helen (Irwin) E.; 1 dau., Ann S. Student, Miami U., Oxford, Ohio, 1950-51, Ohio State U., 1952-53. With Mid-America Fed. Savs. & Loan (formerly First Fed. Savs. & Loan Assns.), Columbus, 1953—, dir., 1958—, pres., 1964—, chmn. bd., 1976—; pres., chmn. bd. 1st Capital Devel. Corp., 1976—. Past mem. adv. bd. St. Anthony Hosp., Columbus; trustee alumni bd. Columbus Acad., 1978-81; trustee, chmn. loan com. Columbus Neighborhood Housing Services, 1982—; trustee Central Ohio chpt. Leukemia Soc. Am. Mem. Nat. League Insured Savs. Assns. (dir. 1965-79, exec. com. 1970-71), World Bus. Council, Nat. Savs. and Loan League (dir. 1965, 81-83, exec. com. 1982-83), Mid-Ohio Savs. and Loan League (sec.-treas. 1978-79, v.p. 1979-80, pres. 1980-81, dir. 1978—), Young Pres.'s Orgn., Phi Kappa Psi., Delta Kappa Upsilon. Clubs: Pres.'s Ohio State U., Columbus Country, Columbus. Home: 328 Fairway Circle Columbus OH 43213 Office: 2450 E Main St Columbus OH 43209

EIDSON, WILLIAM WHELAN, physicist, educator; b. Indpls., July 22, 1935; s. Alonzo Duncan and Gertrude (Whelan) E.; m. Janis Fischer, Feb. 23, 1974; children—William Benjamin, Duncan McBrayer, Christy Lorene. B.S., Tulane U., 1957; M.S., Ind. U., 1959, Ph.D. (NSF fellow), 1961. Mem. faculty Ind. U., Bloomington, 1961-67, asso. prof. physics, 1966-67; prof., chmn. dept. physics U. Mo., St. Louis, 1967-72; prof., head dept. physics and atmospheric sci. Drexel U., Phila., 1972—. Mem. Am. Phys. Soc., Am. Assn. Physics Tchrs., A.A.A.S., I.E.E.E., Sigma Xi, Sigma Pi Sigma. Home: 950 Conestoga Rd Rosemont Bryn Mawr PA 19010 Office: Dept Physics and Atmospheric Sci Drexel U Philadelphia PA 19104

EIDT, CLARENCE MARTIN, JR., research/development executive; b. Natchez, Miss., Feb. 4, 1935; s. Clarence Martin and Mary Ernestine (Breithaupt) E.; m. Rosa Lee Simonton, Jan. 26, 1957; children: Brian D., Kevin E., Leslie A. B.S., La. State U., 1956, M.S., 1962. Registered profl. engr., La. With Esso Research Labs., Baton Rouge, La., 1956-72, 73-76, sect. head, process devel., 1963-67, asst. dir. process devel., 1968-72; mgr. Exxon Research and Devel. Labs., 1973-76; asst. gen. mgr. petroleum dept. Exxon Research and Engring. Co., Florham Park, N.J., 1972-73, gen. mgr. petroleum dept., 1980-83, v.p. petroleum and synthetic fuels, 1983—; mgr. regional planning logistics dept. Exxon Corp., N.Y.C., 1976-78, mgr. corp. planning coordination, corp. planning dept., 1978-80. Mem. Am. Inst. Chem. Engrs., Am. Petroleum Inst.; mem. Soc. Automobile Engrs. Patentee in field. Home: 3 Huron Dr Chatham NJ 07928 Office: 1251 Ave of the Americas New York NY 10020

EIGEL, EDWIN GEORGE, JR., mathematics educator; b. St. Louis, June 4, 1932; s. Edwin George and Catherine (Rohan) E.; m. Marcia Jeanne Duffy, May 30, 1959; children: Edwin George III, Mary Marcia. B.S., MIT, 1954; postgrad., U. Marburg, Germany, 1954-55; Ph.D., St. Louis U., 1961. Lectr. math. George Washington U., 1961; asst. prof. math. St. Louis U., 1961-64, asso. prof., 1964-69, asst. to dean Grad. Sch., 1965-67, prof., 1969-79, dean Grad. Sch., 1967-71, asso. acad. v.p., 1971-72, acad. v.p., 1972-79, exec. v.p., 1973; asso. prof. math. U. Bridgeport, Conn., 1979-82, prof., 1982—, v.p. acad. affairs, 1979—, provost, 1981—; Danforth asso., 1964—. Commr. McDonnell Planetarium, St. Louis, 1972-79; mem. Conn. Disting. Citizens Task Force on Quality Teaching, 1982-83. Served to 1st lt. AUS, 1959-61. Mem. Am. Math. Soc., Math. Assn. Am., Mo. Acad. Sci., Phi Beta Kappa, Sigma Xi, Pi Mu Epsilon, Phi Kappa Phi. Research in math. applications of computers. Home: 33 Pepperbush Ln Fairfield CT 06430

EIGENBRODT, HAROLD JOHN, educator; b. Peoria, Ill., June 19, 1928; s. Harold John and Mildred Geneva (Hixson) E. B.A., N. Central Coll., 1949; B.D., Yale, 1952, M.A., 1955, Ph.D., 1960; postgrad. (Lilly fellow), Oxford (Eng.) U., 1964-65. Instr. Berkeley Div. Sch., New Haven, 1954-55; instr. Yale Div. Sch., 1955-56; faculty DePauw U., Greencastle, Ind., 1957—, prof. religion, 1970—; staff Westcott House, Cambridge U., 1979; ordained priest Episcopal Ch., 1958. Ford Found. fellow, 1970, 72. Fellow Soc. for Religion in Higher Edn.; mem. Am. Acad. Religion, Soc. Bibl. Lit. Home: 606 E Walnut St Greencastle IN 46135

EIGER, NORMAN NATHAN, circuit court judge; b. Chgo., Aug. 6, 1903; s. Isaac and Rachel (Brender) E.; m. Leona Wolan, Dec. 31, 1935; children: Lawrence H., Rodney I. J.D., De Paul U., 1924. Bar: Ill. 1924. Mem. exec. staff, capital stock tax assessor Ill. Tax Commn., 1932-36; asst. to corp. counsel City Chgo., 1936-47; chmn. Ill. Bd. Rev., Dept. of Labor, 1948-52; judge Municipal Ct., Chgo., 1952-64, Circuit Ct., Cook County, Ill., Chgo., 1964—; adj. clin. prof. DePaul U. Law Sch.; Past v.p. Coll. Jewish Studies; now hon. trustee; arbitrator, mem. panel Am. Assn. Arbitrators; mem. panel arbitrators Fed. Mediation and Conciliation Service; lectr. groups; past v.p. Adult Edn. Council Met. Chgo.; exec. sec. Patriotic Found. Chgo. Past chmn. lawyers div. Chgo. Combined Jewish Appeal; past co-chmn. Conciliation Commn., Chgo. Fedn., United Am. Hebrew Congregations; past v.p. Bd. Jewish Edn., now hon. life trustee; hon. life trustee K.A.M. Isaiah Israel Congregation. Served with USCGR, World War II. Mem. Ill., Chgo. bar assns., Decalogue Soc. Lawyers (financial sec.), Ill. Judges Assn. (past pres., chmn. ann. conv. 1972-77, chmn. emeritus 1977-83, dir. emeritus), Nu Beta Epsilon (past grand chancellor), Alpha Epsilon Pi (hon.). Mem. B'nai B'rith (past v.p. Chgo. Council, past pres. Jackson Park Lodge, mem. awards com. Youth Orgn.). Home: 505 N Lake Shore Dr Chicago IL 60611

EIGNER, RICHARD MARTIN, lawyer; b. Swampscott, Mass., July 7, 1929; s. Israel and Bessie (Polansky) E.; m. Beverly Israel, Dec. 25, 1964; children: David, Danielle. A.B., Dartmouth Coll., 1951; J.D., Harvard U., 1954. Bar: Calif. 1955, Mass. 1956. Ptnr. Pillsbury, Madison & Sutro, San Francisco, 1965—; cons. Internat. Tax Project, Am. Law Inst., 1981—. Mem. Internat. Tax Planning Assn., Internat. Fiscal Assn. Jewish. Home: 2955 Piedmont Ave Berkeley CA 94705 Office: Pillsbury Madison & Sutro 225 Bush St San Francisco CA 94104

EIHUSEN VIRGIL R., manufacturing company executive; b. Hastings, Nebr., June 11, 1930; s. George E. and Minnie (Henrickus) Eihusen; m. Margarette Luebbe (dec.); children: Libby Eihusen Henry, Robert, Teresa Eihusen Rank. Grad., high sch. Founder Chief Industries Inc., Grand Island, Nebr., 1956, chmn. bd., chief exec. officer, 1956—; dir. Commerce Group Inc., Overland, Overland Nat. Bank. Mem. Grand Island City Council, 1968-72; bd. dirs. Nebr. Ind. Coll. Found.; pres. (past) Grand Island Indsl. Found. Named Diplomat of Yr. Nebr. Dept. Econ. Devel., 1973. Mem. U.S. C. of C. (dir., Boss of Yr. 1969), Nebr. Assn. Commerce and Industry (past. pres.), Am. Mgmt. Assn., Nebr. Diplomats (past pres.). Republican. Lutheran. Clubs: Riverside Golf, Platt-Deutsche. Lodges: Elks; Shriners. Home: 717 Stagecoach Rd Grand Island NE 68801 Office: Chief Industries Inc Old West Hwy 30 Grand Island NE 68801

EIKENBERRY, KENNETH OTTO, lawyer; b. Wenatchee, Wash., June 29, 1932; s. Otto Kenneth and Florence Estelle E.; m. Beverly Jane Hall, Dec. 21, 1963. B.A. in Polit. Sci., Wash. State U., 1954; LL.B., U. Wash., 1959. Bar: Wash. 1959. Spl. agt. FBI, 1960-62; dep. pros. atty., King County (Wash.), Seattle, 1962-67; with firm Clinton, Andersen, Fleck & Glein, Seattle, 1967-73; staff atty. King County Council, 1974-77; chmn. Wash. Republican party, 1977-80; atty. gen. State of Wash., 1981—; judge pro tem Seattle Mcpl. Ct., 1979-80; mem. Pres.'s Task Force on Victims of Crime. Chmn., King County Rep. Conv., 1974, 78; mem. Wash. Ho. of Reps., 1970-74. Served with AUS, 1954-56. Named Legislator of Year, Young Americans for Freedom/Wash. Conservative Union, 1974, Rep. Man of Year, Young Men's Rep. Club King County, 1979. Mem. Wash. Bar Assn., Western Conf. Attys.-Gen. (chmn.), Soc. Former Spl. Agts. FBI, Internat. Footprint Assn., Delta Theta Phi, Alpha Tau Omega. Clubs: Elks, Kiwanis, Olympia Goose and Duck. Office: Temple of Justice Olympia WA 98504

EIKERENKOETTER, FREDERICK JOSEPH, II (REVEREND IKE), evangelist, educator, lecturer; b. Ridgeland, S.C., June 1, 1935; s. Frederick Joseph and Rema Estelle (Matthews) E.; m. Eula Mae Dent, Feb. 7, 1964; 1 son, Xavier Frederick III. B.Th., Am. Bible Coll., 1956; D.Sc. of Living, Sci. of Living Inst., 1971. Founder, pres. United Christian Evangelist Assn., 1962—, United Ch. Sci. of Living Inst., 1969—, Rev. Ike Found., 1973—; vis. lectr. dept. psychiatry Harvard Med. Sch., May 1973, U. Ala., Jan. 1975, Atlanta U. Center, Nov. 1975; vis. lectr. dept. sociology Rice U., 1977. Served with chaplain sect. USAF, 1956-58. Recipient World Service award for outstanding contributions to mankind Prince Hall Masons, 1975. Founder of the Science of Living philosophy, church and inst. Office: 4140 Broadway New York NY 10033 *

EILBER, JANET SUSAN, dancer, singer, actress; b. Detroit, July 27, 1951; d. Charles Routledge and Carol Virginia (Brown) E. B.F.A., Juilliard Sch., 1973. Tchr. dance Nat. Music Camp, 1970, 72. Choreographer, performer, Dance Mobile, 1969-72, Young Audiences, 1972; prin. dancer, Martha Graham Dance Co., 1972-80; guest artist, Joffrey Ballet, 1978, Am. Dance Machine, 1978—; leading role: in Broadway musicals Swing, 1980, Dancin', 1980; featured: in movie Who's Life Is It, Anyway?, 1981; title role: in TV movie This is Kate Bennett, 1981; Roles created by Graham for Eilber Hester Prynne in The Scarlet Letter, 1975, Night in Lucifer, Mary Queen of Scotts in Episodes, Young Love in Shadows, Cleopatra in Frescoes; roles performed with Graham Lilith; narrator in Owl and The Pussycat; invited to perform at, White House, 1976, 79. Office: care ICM Artists 40 W 57th St New York NY 10019 *

EILBRACHT, LEE PAUL, association executive; b. St. Louis, Mar. 22, 1924; s. Winfield Charles and Viola Ann (Nixon) E.; m. Euline Dallas Wilson, June 29, 1967; children: Kurt, Ellen, Ann Carey, Deborah Flack, Douglas Wilson. B.S., U. Ill., 1947. Profl. baseball player, 1947-52; mgr. profl. teams Chgo. Cubs. Orgn., 1948-52; head baseball coach U. Ill., Champaign, 1952-78; exec. dir. Am. Baseball Coaches Assn., Champaign, 1978—; asst. prof. Coll. Phys. Edn., U. Ill., Champaign, 1955-70; mem. U.S. Olympic Baseball Com. Author: Baseball, 1972; editor: Research in Baseball, 1971, Clinic Notes, Am. Assn. Coll. Baseball Coaches, 1962—; editorial bd.: Collegiate Baseball, 1961—. Mem. City of Champaign Recreation Bd., 1960-66. Served with U.S. Army, 1943-45; ETO. Recipient Lefty Gomez award Wilson Sporting Goods Co., 1972; 500 Victory award U.S. Baseball Fedn., 1978; named Coach of Yr. Coach and Athlete mag., 1972; elected to Baseball Coaches Hall of Fame, 1979. Mem. U.S. Baseball Fedn., Coll. Baseball Writers Assn., Am. Assn. Coll. Baseball Coaches. Club: Champaign Country. Home: 605 Hamilton Dr Champaign IL 61820 *Hard work, a competitive spirit, dedication and loyalty to vocation along with a loving and supportive wife make for a happy and successful career.*

EILTS, HERMANN FREDERICK, international relations educator; b. Weissenfels Saale, Germany, Mar. 23, 1922; came to U.S., 1926, naturalized, 1930; s. Friedrich Alex and Meta Dorothea (Prûser) E.; m. Helen Josephine Brew, June 12, 1948; children—Conrad Marshall, Frederick Lowell. B.A., Ursinus Coll., 1942, LL.D., 1960; M.A., Johns Hopkins, 1947; student Arabic, Near East area, Dept. State Fgn. Service Inst. and U. Pa., 1950-51. Fgn. service officer, 1947—, 3d sec., vice consul, Tehran, Iran, 1947-48, Jidda, Saudi Arabia, 1948-50, consul, prin. officer, Aden, Arabia, 1951-53, also 2d sec., consul, Sana, Yemen, 1951-53, 2d sec., consul, chief polit. sect., Baghdad, Iraq, 1954-56; officer-in-charge Baghdad Pact affairs (CENTO) Dept. State, Washington, 1957-59, Arabian Peninsula Affairs, 1959-61; detailed Nat. War Coll., Ft. McNair, 1961-62; 1st sec. Am. embassy, London, Eng., 1962-64, counsellor, dep. chief of mission, Tripoli, Libya, 1964-65; U.S. ambassador to Saudi Arabia, 1965-70; diplomatic adviser U.S. Army War Coll., Carlisle Barracks, Pa., 1970-73; ambassador to Egypt, 1973-79; disting. univ. prof. internat. relations Boston U., 1979—, chmn. dept. polit. sci., 1979—, dir. Ctr. Internat. Relations, 1979—. Served as 1st lt. with Mil. Intelligence AUS, 1942-45. Decorated Purple Heart, Bronze Star; recipient Arthur Flemming award for govt. service, 1958; Disting. Civilian Honor award Dept. Army, 1972; Disting. Honor award Dept. State, 1979; Joseph C. Wilson award, 1979. Fellow Royal Geog. Soc., Royal Asiatic Soc.; mem. Am. Fgn. Service Assn., Middle East Inst., Royal Central Asian Soc. Mem. Evang. and Reformed Ch. Address: Ctr Internat Relations Boston U 152 Bay State Rd Boston MA 02215

EIMICKE, VICTOR W(ILLIAM), publishing co. exec.; b. N.Y.C., Feb. 4, 1925; s. Victor H. and Anna (Gille) E.; m. Maxine Howard Thome, Aug. 6, 1955; children: Laura Suzanne, Alicia Karen. A.B., N.Y. U., 1945, M.A., 1946, Ph.D., 1951. Lectr. N.Y. U., 1945-47, Bklyn. Coll., 1946-49; dir. audio visual dept. Coll. City N.Y., 1947-53; asst. prof. Pace Coll., 1953-56; v.p. Inst. Human Research in Industry, N.Y.C., 1947-48; pres. V.W. Eimicke Assos. Inc., N.Y.C., 1951—, V.W. Eimicke Ltd., Peterborough, Can., 1978—; chmn. Eimicke Assos. Ltd., London, 1956-69; pres. Action Aids, Inc., N.Y.C., 1969-73, Laurel Office Aids, Inc., 1969-73, Action List Services, Inc., Yonkers, N.Y., 1976-80, Eimicke Pub. Co., Yonkers, 1976-78, Geschaeftsfuehrer, Enuelo-Formulare GmbH, Krefeld, Ger., 1978—; dir. New England Grocer Supply Co., Worcester, Mass., 1964-68, Nathan's Famous, Inc., N.Y.C., 1974-79, Wetson's, Inc., 1975-79. Pres. bd. trustees Halsted Sch., Yonkers, 1969-74; bd. govs. Lawrence Hosp., Bronxville, N.Y., 1971-74; bd. dirs. Internat. Christian U. Found., Japan, 1972—; trustee Hope Coll., Holland, Mich., 1976—, chmn. bd. trustees, 1978—. Mem. Am., Eastern, N.Y. State, Westchester psychol. assns., Nat. Inst. Social Scis., Phi Beta Kappa, Kappa Delta Pi, Phi Delta Kappa. Mem. Ref. Ch. (elder, mem. consistory 1968—; asso. chmn., treas., dir. Laymen's Nat. Bible Com. 1969—, pres. 1982). Clubs: Am. Yacht (Rye, N.Y.); Met., Met. Opera, Union League, Univ. (N.Y.C.); Siwanoy Country (Bronxville); Lake Placid (N.Y.). Home: 20 Hereford Rd Bronxville NY 10708 Office: 35 E Grassy Sprain Rd Yonkers NY 10710

EINHORN, ARTHUR, importing company executive; b. Newark, June 24, 1934; s. Morris and Anna (Schwartz) E.; m. Judith B. Evans, Aug. 7, 1960; children: Laura, Amy. B.S., Fairfield U., 1959; M.B.A., U. Pa., 1965. Bus. mgr. Cable TV div. Triangle Publs., Phila., 1966-68; asst. to treas. Vikoa, Inc., Hoboken, N.J., 1968-69, treas., 1969-71, pres. Cable TV div., 1971-75; owner, pres. Triangle, Inc., 1975—. Home: 51 Fernwood Ln Roslyn NY 11576

EINHORN, EDWARD (EDDIE) MARTIN, professional baseball team executive; b. Paterson, N.J., Jan. 3, 1936; s. Harold Benjamin and Mae (Lippman) E.; m. Ann Magdelene Pelachik, Apr. 24, 1962; children: Jennifer, Jeffrey. A.B., U. Pa., 1957; J.D., Northwestern U., 1960. Radio sports announcer Sta.-WXPN, Phila., 1954-57; founder, pres. Midwestern Sports Network, Chgo., 1957-61, TV sports Inc. (name changed to TVS 1968, became subs. Corinthian Broadcasting Corp. 1973), N.Y.C., 1961-65, pres., chief exec. officer, 1965-78; exec. producer CBS Sports, N.Y.C., from 1978; now pres. Chgo. White Sox; dir. Corinthian Broadcasting Corp., 1973-77. Editor-in-chief: Jour. Air Law and Sci., 1959-60, Northwestern Jour. Criminal Law Sci., 1958-60. Recipient Honor award Namismith Basketball Hall of Fame, 1973, Merit award Nat. Assn. Basketball Coaches, 1973, Victor award City of Hope, 1974. Mem. Nat. Acad. Radio, TV Arts and Scis., Internat. Radio, TV Soc., Nat. Assn. TV Program Execs., Nat. Assn. Coll. Dirs., Nat. Assn. Basketball Coaches. Office: care Chgo White Sox Dan Ryan at 35th St Chicago IL 60616

EINHORN, EDWARD MARTIN, profl. baseball club exec.; b. 2. Paterson, N.J., Jan. 3, 1936; s. Harold Benjamin and Mae (Lippman) E.; m. Ann Magdelene Pelachik, Apr. 24, 1962; children—Jennifer, Jeffrey. A.B., U. Pa., 1957; J.D., Northwestern U., 1960. Radio sports announcer Sta. WXPN, Phila., 1954-57; founder, pres. Midwestern Sports Network, Chgo., 1957-61, TV Sports Inc. (name changed to TVS 1968, became subs. of Corinthian Broadcasting Corp. 1973), N.Y.C., 1961-65, pres., chief exec. officer, 1965-78; exec. producer CBS Sports, N.Y.C., 1978-81; pres., chief operating officer, co-gen. partner Chgo. White Sox Baseball Club, 1981—; dir. Corinthian Broadcasting Corp., 1973-77. Editor-in-chief: Jour. Air Law and Sci, 1959-60, Northwestern Jour. Criminal Law, Sci, 1958-60. Recipient Honor award Namismith Basketball Hall of Fame, 1973, Merit award Nat. Assn. Basketball Coaches, 1973, Victor award City of Hope, 1974. Mem. Nat. Acad. Radio, TV Arts and Scis., Internat. Radio, TV Soc., Nat. Assn. TV Program Execs., Nat. Assn. Coll. Dirs., Nat. Assn. Basketball Coaches. Home: 160 E Pearson Chicago IL Office: Comiskey Park Dan Ryan at 35th St Chicago IL 60616

EINHORN, HERBERT ARTHUR, lawyer; b. N.Y.C., Feb. 5, 1913; s. William and Sadie (Reich) E.; m. Roslyn Appel, Feb. 11, 1940; children: Eric Stanley, Diane Margery. A.B. cum laude, Ohio U., 1933; LL.B., Columbia U., 1935; LL.D., Ohio U., 1982. Bar: N.Y. 1935. Pvt. practice, N.Y.C., 1935-38, 41-43; sr. counsel N.Y. State Ins. Fund, 1938-40, spl. counsel, 1940-41; asst. atty. gen., N.Y., 1943-46; partner Aranow, Brodsky, Bohlinger, Einhorn & Alter (and predecessor), N.Y.C., 1946-79; atty. fellow, cons. SEC, Washington, 1979-81; spl. counsel Cadwalader, Wickersham & Taft, N.Y.C., 1983—; lectr. Law Jour. Seminars, Am. Mfrs. Assn., Practicing Law Inst., Law Sch. N.Y. U. Author: (with Edward R. Aranow) Proxy Contests for Corporate Control, 1957, rev. edit., 1968, Tender Offers for Corporate Control, 1973, Development in Tender Offers for Corporate Control, 1977; also contbr. articles to profl. jours. Chmn. bd. dirs. Camp Loyaltown, 1962-79; mem. trustees acad. of Ohio U., Athens, 1966—. Served with arty.

AUS, World War II; capt. N.Y. N.G. Res. Recipient Ohio U. Alumni award for achievement in field of corp. law, 1980. Mem. Am., N.Y. State bar assns., Fed. Bar Council, N.Y. County Lawyers Assn., Assn. Bar City N.Y., D.C. Bar Assn., Columbia Law Sch. Alumni Assn. (dir. 1968-71), Assn. Ex-mems. Squadron A. Club: Capitol Hill (Washington). Home: 550-A Heritage Village Southbury CT 06488

EINHORN, HILLEL JASON, educator; b. Bklyn., June 12, 1941; s. Sonny T. and Lulu (Perleman) E.; m. Susan Bernice Michaels, June 16, 1966. B.A., Bklyn. Coll., 1964, M.A., 1966; Ph.D., Wayne State U., 1969. Asst. prof. behavior scis. U. Chgo., 1969-71, asso. prof., 1973-76, prof., 1976—; dir. Center Decision Research, 1977—; vis. asst. prof. Carnegie Mellon U., Pitts., 1971-72; vis. prof. Hebrew U., Jerusalem, Israel, 1977-78, Lady Davis vis. prof, Jerusalem, 1980; panel mem. NSF, 1981—. Contbr. articles to profl. jours.; Edit. bd.: Organizational Behavior and Human Performance, 1970—. Mem. bd. human resources Naval Research Advisory Com. Grantee NIMH, 970, Spencer Found., 1972-74, Ill. Dept. Mental Health, 1977-79; Grantee Office Naval Research, 1979-82. Fellow Am. Psychol. Assn.; Mem. Am. Statis. Assn., N.Y. Acad. Scis., Sigma Xi, Psi Chi. Home: 5217 University Ave S Chicago IL 60615

EINHORN, STEVEN GARY, investment banker; b. Newark, Nov. 28, 1948; s. Jack and Sally (Broden) E.; m. Shelley Fredericks, June 1, 1974; children: Stacy, Eric. A.B., Rutgers U., 1970; M.S. (NSF grantee), U. Ill., 1972. Investment mgr. Prudential Ins. Co., Newark, 1972-77; vice chmn. investment policy com. Goldman, Sachs & Co., N.Y.C., 1977—. Mem. N.Y. Soc. Security Analysts, Investment Tech. Symposium N.Y. Office: 85 Broad St New York NY 10004

EINKAUF, OSCAR ERNEST, JR., corporate executive; b. San Antonio, Sept. 14, 1924; s. Oscar Ernest and Ruby (Crowell) E.; m. Eunice Mary Armstrong, June 9, 1952; children: Oscar Ernest III, Robert Benson. B.B.A. in Accounting, U. Tex., 1949. Accountant Rodgers, Chorpening & Jungmann, San Antonio, 1949-57, Johnston Testers, Inc., Houston, 1957-59; controller Houston Oil Field Materials Co., Inc., 1959-63; staff asst. to v.p. finance Sinclair Oil & Gas Co., Tulsa, 1963-64; v.p. Internat. Systems & Controls Corp., Houston, 1964-66; controller Black, Sivalls & Bryson, Inc., Kansas City, Mo., 1964-66; controller, mgr. Bank of Southwest Nat. Assn., Houston, 1966-71; sr. v.p., sec., treas. S.W. Bancshares, Inc., Houston, 1970—. Mem. Am. Inst. C.P.A.s, Tex. Soc. C.P.A.s, Delta Chi. Baptist. Home: 13315 Westport Ln Houston TX 77079 Office: PO Box 2629 Southwest Bancshares Inc Houston TX 77252

EINSIDLER, FREDERICK ROY, transportation company executive; b. N.Y.C., 1925. B.S., U.S. Mil. Acad., 1947; grad. in Mech. and Auto Engring., U. Mich. Commd. 2d lt. U.S. Army, 1947, resigned, 1953; with Am. Machine & Foundry Co., 1953-59; pres., chief operating officer Cons. & Designers Inc., 1959-68; with Butler Internat., Inc., Montvale, N.J., 1972—, pres., 1972—, also dir., chief exec. officer; vice chmn., chief exec. officer Butler Aviation Internat.; chmn., chief exec. officer Butler Tech. Services Inc.; chmn. Internat. Transport Inc.; dir. Aeronca, Inc. Mem. Am. Def. Preparedness Assn., AIAA, Nat. Assn. Corp. Dirs., Newcomen Soc. Am., Wings Club (v.p., bd. dirs.). Lodge: Masons. Office: Butler Internat 110 Summit Ave Montvale NJ 07645

EINSMAN, HAROLD, consumer goods company executive; b. Hamburg, Ger., Mar. 21, 1934; s. Kurt E. Einsmann and Henny (Cords) E.; m. Elke Prinke, Sept. 22, 1968; children: Kerstin, Jens. Diploma KFM, Hamburg and Heidelberg U., 1956; M.B.A., U. Fla., 1958, Ph.D. in Bus. Adminstrn., Econs. and Law, 1960. With advt. and copy depts., brand mgr. Proctor & Gamble, Ger., 1961-68, country mgr., Austria, 1968-72, mktg. dir., Belgium and Holland, 1975-78, v.p., No. Europe, France Gt. Britain, Belgium and Holland, 1979—. Office: Procter & Gamble 100 Temselaan 1820 Strombek-Brussels Belgium

EINSPRUCH, NORMAN GERALD, university dean; b. N.Y.C., June 27, 1932; s. Adolph and Mala (Goldblatt) E.; m. Edith Melnick, Dec. 20, 1953; children—Eric, Andrew, Franklin. B.A. in Physics, Rice U., 1953, M.S., U. Colo., 1955; Ph.D. in Applied Math, Brown U., 1959. Mem. tech. staff, central research labs. Tex. Instruments, Inc., Dallas, 1959-62, mgr. electron transport physics br., central research labs., 1962-68, dir. advanced tech. lab., central research labs., 1968-69, dir. tech., chem. materials div., 1969-72, dir. central research labs., 1972-75, asst. v.p., 1975-77, mgr. corp. devel., 1975-76, mgr. tech., consumer products, 1976-77; prof. dept. elec. engring. and computer sci. Coll. Engring. U. Miami, Coral Gables, Fla., 1977—; dean Sch. Engring. and Architecture, U. Miami (Sch. Engring. and Architecture), 1977—; chmn. panel on thin film microstructure sci. and tech. NRC, 1978-79; dir. Ogden Corp. Editor: Microstructure Science and Engineering, Vols. I and II, 1981; Vols. III, IV and V, 1982, Vol. VI, 1983; Editor: series VLSI Electronics: Microstructure Science; Contbr. articles to profl. jours. Fellow Am. Phys. Soc., Acoustical Soc. Am., IEEE, AAAS; mem. Am. Inst. Indsl. Engrs., Am. Soc. Engring. Edn., Sigma Xi, Tau Beta Pi, Eta Kappa Nu, Phi Kappa Phi, Alpha Pi Mu, Tau Sigma Delta., On icron Delta Kappa. Home: 1415 Trillo Ave Coral Gables FL 33146 Office: U Miami Coll Engring PO Box 248294 Coral Gables FL 33124

EINSTEIN, CLIFFORD JAY, advt. exec.; b. Los Angeles, May 4, 1939; s. Harry and Thelma (Bernstein) E.; m. Madeline Mandel, Jan. 28, 1962; children: Harold Jay, Karen Holly. A.B. in English, UCLA, 1961. Writer Norman, Craig & Kummel, N.Y.C., 1961-62, Foote, Cone & Belding, Los Angeles, 1962-64; partner Silverman & Einstein, Los Angeles, 1965-67; vice chmn., creative dir. Dailey & Assos., Los Angeles, 1968—, also dir.; dir. Campaign '80, advt. agy. Reagan for Pres., 1980; lectr. various colls. Producer: play Whatever Happened to Georgie Tapps?, Los Angeles and San Francisco, 1980; (Clio award for best comml. music 1973). Mem. Los Angeles-Aukland Sister City Com.; bd. trustees Crossroads Sch. for Arts and Scis. Served with U.S. Army, 1957. Recipient Am. Advt. award as Best in West, 1968, 73, 79; Clio award for best radio comml.; Internat. Broadcast pub. service award, 1970; Sweepstakes award Los Angeles Advt. Club, 1974, 78; Nat. Addy award for best campaign, 1979; named Creative Dir. of the West Adweek Poll. Mem. AFTRA, ASCAP, Screen Actors Guild., Dirs. Guild Am. Home: 11940 Brentwood Grove Los Angeles CA 90049 Office: 3055 Wilshire Blvd Los Angeles CA 90010

EINSWEILER, ROBERT CHARLES, urban planning consultant; b. Freeport, Ill., Dec. 2, 1929; s. Frank L. and Emma Irene (Wachlin) E.; m. Cornelia Robb Downs, Jan. 6, 1956; children: Kevin Frank, Lee Downs, Sheila Strand. B.S. in Archtl. Engring, U. Ill., 1953, M.S. in City Planning, 1958. Asso. city planner, Syracuse, N.Y., 1958-59; transp. planner Twin Cities Met. Planning Commn., St. Paul, 1959-61, chief met. studies div., 1961-65, dir. planning, 1966-67, Twin Cities Met. Council, St. Paul, 1967-71; planning cons. Robert C. Einsweiler, Inc., Mpls., 1971—; cons. World Bank, Dept. HUD, Nat. Commn. on Water Quality, Dept. Interior, U.S. EPA, U.S. Econ. Devel. Adminstrn.; adviser U.S. Office Mgmt. and Budget; lectr. in planning U. Minn., 1963-65, 72-79, prof., dir. planning program, 1979—. Mem. bd. adv. editors: Urban Ecology; Contbr. articles profl. jours. Trustee Center for Study Noise in Soc.; chmn. dirs. Am. Land Forum, 1979—; bd. dirs. Center for Environ. Conflict Resolution, Mpls., 1979—. Served from 2d lt. to 1st lt., C.E. AUS, 1953-55. Univ. fellow, 1957-58. Mem. Am. Inst. Planners (gov. 1968-71, pres. 1973-75), Am. Planning Assn. (pres. 1983-84), Am. Soc. Planning Ofcls., Am. Inst. Cert. Planners, Urban Land Inst., World Future Soc., Internat. Fedn. for Housing and Planning, Gargoyle, Alpha Rho Chi, Lambda Alpha, Tau Beta Pi. Unitarian-Universalist (trustee). Home: 1226 W Minnehaha Pkwy Minneapolis MN 55419 Office: 267 19th Ave S Minneapolis MN 55455

EIRICH, FREDERICK ROLAND, educator, chemist; b. Vienna, Austria, May 23, 1905; came to U.S., 1947, naturalized, 1953; s. Otto George and Hermine (Perlhefter) E.; m. Maria Dorothea Dehne, Feb. 1, 1936; children-Ursula D., Richard S. Moeller, Susan H. Ph.D., U. Vienna, 1929, Dr. Phil. habil., 1938; M.A., U. Cambridge, Eng., 1939. Research asso., lectr. U. Vienna, 1934- 38, U. Cambridge, 1939-47; mem. faculty Poly. Inst., Bklyn., 1948—, prof., 1952—; distinguished prof., 1969—, dean research, 1967-70; vis. prof. U. Uppsala, 1950; Unilever prof. U. Bristol, 1965; cons. Govt. Com. Chems., Plastics and Rubber Industry. Author, editor numerous books and research papers. Recipient A. Humboldt Found. award, 1980. Fellow N.Y. Acad. Sci. (chmn. chem. sect. 1952-53), Faraday Soc., Internat. Inst. Fracture Mechanics (hon.); mem. Am. Chem. Soc. (chmn. colloid div. 1960, Distinguished Service award 1975, Merit award Rubber Div. 1978), AAAS (chmn., councillor Gordon Confs. 1959-65), Soc. Rheology (pres. 1972-73), Am. Phys. Soc. (gov. bd. 1970-74), Sigma Xi (research award 1970). Home: 22 Deerfield Ave Tuckahoe NY 10707 Office: 333 Jay St Brooklyn NY 11201

EISAMAN, JOSIAH REAMER, III, advertising executive; b. Pitts., Oct. 9, 1924; s. Josiah Reamer and Anne (Soule) E.; m. Karren Lee Johnson, Mar. 9, 1968; children: George Preston, Cynthia Anne, Elizabeth Soule, Kari Jo, Liv Anna. B.A., Dartmouth Coll., 1947. Asst. advt. mgr. Reliance Life Ins. Co., Pitts., 1948; chmn. bd. Eisaman, Johns & Laws Advt., Inc., Los Angeles, 1949—. Asso. editor: Bull. Index mag., Pitts., 1947-48. Served with USNR, 1944-46. Republican. Presbyterian. Club: Mulholland Tennis. Address: 6255 Sunset Blvd Los Angeles CA 90028

EISBERG, ROBERT MARTIN, physics educator; b. Kansas City, Mo., July 1, 1928; s. Jacob Louis and Betty Rae (Slotkin) E.; m. Lila Mae Nommensen, Aug. 29, 1951; 1 dau., Joann. B.S., U. Ill., 1949; Ph.D., U. Calif.-Berkeley, 1953. Research asso. Brookhaven Nat. Lab., Upton, N.Y., 1953-55; research asso. U. Minn.-Mpls., 1955-56, asst. prof., 1957-59, asso. prof., 1959-60; physicist Cavendish Lab., Cambridge, Eng., 1956-57, Ka-Ken Lab., Tokyo, 1960-61, Cyclotron Lab., Buenos Aires, Argentina, 1962, Rutherford Lab., Harwell, Eng., 1965, Conseil Européen Recherche Nucleaire Lab., Geneva, 1969, Flinders U., Adelaide, Australia, 1972, U. Surrey, Guildford, Eng., 1978; asso. prof. physics U. Calif.-Santa Barbara, 1961-62, prof. physics, 1963—; cons. Los Alamos Sci. Lab., 1970-72, Ednl. Testing Service, Princeton, N.J., 1968-72, 74-76. Author: Fundamentals of Modern Physics, 1961, (with Robert Resnick) Quantum Physics, 1974, Applied Mathematical Physics, 1976, (with Wendell Hyde) Countdown, 1978, (with Lawrence Lerner) Physics: Foundations and Applications, Vols. I and II, 1981, (with Herbert Peckham) Numerical Calculation Supplement, 1981; editorial adviser, John Wiley & Sons, Inc., N.Y.C., 1965-74; cons. editor, McGraw-Hill Book Co., N.Y.C., 1976—; contbr. numerous articles profl. jours. Bd. dirs. Los Alamos Meson Physics Facility Users, Inc., 1973-75. Guggenheim fellow, 1960-61; Fulbright research fellow, 1960-61; Fulbright-Hays fellow, 1970. Fellow Am. Phys. Soc.; mem. Am. Assn. Physics Tchrs. Club: U. Calif. Faculty (dir. 1967-69). Home: 1400 Dover Rd Santa Barbara CA 93103

EISCH, JOHN JOSEPH, chemist; b. Milw., Nov. 5, 1930; s. Frank Joseph and Gladys (Riordan) E.; m. Joan Terese Scheuerell, Sept. 5, 1953; children: Margaret (dec.), Karla, Paula, Joseph, Amelia. B.S. summa cum laude, Marquette U., 1952; Ph.D. (Procter and Gamble fellow 1955, Union Carbide fellow 1956), Iowa State U., 1956. Postdoctoral fellow Max Planck Inst. für Kohlenforschung, Mülheim, Germany, 1956-57; research asso. European Research Assos., Brussels, 1957; faculty St. Louis U., 1957-59, U. Mich., 1959-63, Catholic U. Am., Washington, 1963-72; chmn. dept. chemistry State U. N.Y., Binghamton, 1972-78, prof., 1972—; cons. to bus., 1964—, Brookhaven Nat. Lab., 1978—, Stauffer Chem. Co., 1979—. Author: The Chemistry of Organometallic Compounds, 1967, (with R. B. King) Organometallic Syntheses, Vol. I, 1965, Vol. II, 1981. Mem. Am. Chem. Soc., Am. Inst. Chemists, Sigma Xi, Phi Lambda Upsilon, Phi Kappa Phi. Research and publs. on the synthesis and properties of organometallic compounds (those with carbon-metal bonds) and heterocycles, with emphasis on the kinetics and stereochemistry of carbon-metal bond and hydrogen-metal bond additions to olefins, acetylenes; radical-anion, halogenation, nonbenzenoid aromatic studies. Home: 2501 Lynnhurst Dr Vestal NY 13850 Office: Dept Chemistry U NY Binghamton NY 13901

EISELE, DONN FULTON, investment counselor, former astronaut; b. Columbus, Ohio, June 23, 1930; s. Herman E. and June (Davisson) E.; m. Susan H. Hearn, Aug. 2, 1969; children: Melinda Sue, Donn Hamilton, Jon, Kristin, Andrew. B.S., U.S. Naval Acad., 1952; M.S. in Astronautics, USAF Inst. Tech., 1960. Commd. 2d lt. USAF, 1953, advanced through grades to col.; assigned, Rapid City, S.D., 1953-55, Wheelus AFB, Libya, 1955-58; missile systems engr., Wright-Patterson AFB, Ohio, 1960-61; student test pilot Aerospace Research Pilot Sch., Edwards AFB, Calif., 1962; exptl. flight test officer, Kirtland AFB, N.Mex., 1962-63; astronaut NASA Manned Spacecraft Center, Houston, 1964-70, command module pilot Apollo Seven, 11-day maiden Apollo flight, 1968, backup crew mem.; tech. cons. Langley Research Center, Hampton, Va., 1970-72; ret. USAF, 1972; dir. Peace Corps, Bangkok, Thailand, 1972-74; dir. sales Eastern U.S. Marion Power Shovel Co., 1975-79; exec. v.p. Trans Carib Air, 1979-80; v.p. investments Drexel Burnham Lambert, Lauderhill, Fla., 1980-81; v.p. instl. and pvt. accounts Oppenheimer & Co., Ft. Lauderdale, Fla., 1981—. Decorated D.F.C., Legion of Merit; recipient Exceptional Service medal NASA, Diplome de Record FAI; Haley Astronautics award.; TV Emmy award. Fellow Am. Astronautical Soc., Explorers Club; mem. Soc. Exptl. Test Pilots, AFTRA, Tau Beta Pi.

EISELE, GARNETT THOMAS, judge; b. Hot Springs, Ark., Nov. 3, 1923; s. Garnett Martin and Mary (Martin) E.; m. Kathryn Freygang, June 24, 1950; children: Wendell A., Garnett Martin II, Kathryn M., Jean E. Student, U. Fla., 1940-42, Ind. U., 1942-43; A.B., Washington U., 1947; LL.B., Harvard U., 1950, LL.M., 1951. Bar: Ark. Practiced in, Hot Springs, 1951-52, Little Rock, 1953-69; asso. firm Wootten, Land and Matthews, 1951-52, Owens, McHaney, Lofton & McHaney, 1956-60; asst. U.S. atty., Little Rock, 1953-55, individual practice, 1961-69; U.S. dist. judge Eastern Dist. Ark., 1970—, chief judge, 1975—; Legal adviser to gov. Ark., 1966-69. Del. Ark. 7th Constl. Conv., 1969-70; Trustee U. Ark., 1969-70. Served with AUS, 1943-46; ETO. Mem. Am., Ark., Pulaski County bar assns., Am. Judicature Soc., Am. Law Inst. Office: PO Box 3684 Little Rock AR 72203 *

EISEMAN, BEN, educator, surgeon; b. St. Louis, Nov. 2, 1917; s. Frederick B. and Justine (Godchaux) E.; m. Mary Harding, Dec. 22, 1945; children: Jane, John, Lucy, Andrew. B.A., Yale, 1939; M.D., Harvard, 1943. Diplomate: Am. Bd. Thoracic Surgery, Am. Bd. Surgery. Surg. intern Mass. Gen. Hosp., Boston, 1943; surg. resident Barnes Hosp., St. Louis, 1946-50; instr., then asst. prof. surgery Washington U. Med. Sch., St. Louis, 1950-53; asso. prof., then prof. surgery U. Colo. Med. Sch., 1953-61; prof., chmn. dept. surgery U. Ky. Med. Sch., 1961-67; prof. surgery U. Colo., Denver, 1967—; dir. dept. surgery Denver Gen. Hosp., 1967-77; chmn. dept. surgery Rose Med. Center, 1977—; vis. prof. surgery, Thailand, 1950, 51, 53, Burma, 1951, Singapore, 1960, Sweden, 1975, E.Ger., Australia, 1976, Japan, Indonesia, Costa Rica, 1977, Iran, Turkey, Israel, Sweden, Finland, 1978; Disting. vis. prof. Royal Soc. Medicine, Eng., 1979, Chile, 1980, South Africa, 1981; mem. surg. com. Nat. Bd. Med. Examiners; mem. surg. study sect. com. on trauma USPHS-NRC; mem. exam. com. Am. Bd. Surgery, 1964—; cons. surgeon gen. USN, Vietnam, 1966, 68. Editorial bd.: Am. Surgery, Gastroenterology; Author articles in field. Trustee, chmn. Kent-Denver Country Day Sch., 1967-73; trustee Denver Pub. Library, 1974—, Colo. Outward Bound, 1969—; chmn. bd. trustees Colo. Outward Bound, 1980—. Served to lt. (s.g.) M.C.; Served to lt. (s.g.) USNR, 1943-46; rear adm. Res. Recipient Certificate of Merit U.S. Navy, 1969. Mem. ACS (com. internat. relations, forum com., post operative care com., com. on issues, v. p. 1983-84), Am. Surg. Assn. (v.p. 1982-83), Soc. Univ. Surgeons, Am. Thoracic Assn., Soc. Clin. Surgery, Am. Gastroent. Assn., Soc. Vascular Surgery, Internat. Surg. Soc., Internat. Cardiovascular Soc. Home: 3 Village Rd Englewood CO 80110 Office: Dept Surgery U Colo Med Sch 4200 E 9th Ave Denver CO 80220

EISEMAN, WILLIAM CLIFFORD, banker; b. Troy, N.Y., Jan. 3, 1924; s. Norman William and Sara Elizabeth (Clifford) E.; m. Jane Robbins McKee, June 30, 1951; children: Susan Eiseman MacPherson, Elizabeth Eiseman Emmons, Hope Holmes, William Stuart. A.B., Union Coll., Schenectady, 1945; M.B.A., Harvard U., 1949. With Morgan Guaranty Trust Co., N.Y.C., 1949—, sr. v.p. personnel adminstrn., 1970—; dir. John Wiley & Sons, Inc., New Yorker Mag. Inc. Served with AUS, 1942-45. Republican. Presbyterian. Address: Morgan Guaranty Trust Co 23 Wall St New York NY 10015

EISEN, HENRY, pharmaceutics educator; b. Bklyn., Dec. 18, 1921; s. Irving and Dorothy (Wilchins) E.; (married). B.S., St. John's U., 1949; M.S., Rutgers U., 1951; Ph.D. (Am. Found. Pharm. Edn. fellow), U. Conn., 1954. Mem. faculty St. John's U., Jamaica, N.Y., 1954—, prof. pharmaceutics, chmn. dept., 1961—, chmn. dept., 1961-76, 79-83; cons. pharm. industry, 1958—. Served with AUS, 1942-46. Mem. Am. Pharm. Assn., Acad. Pharm. Scis., Sigma Xi, Rho Chi.

EISEN, LEONARD, distribution company executive; b. Toronto, Ont., Can., Oct. 14, 1934; s. Harry Mandle and Anne Miriam E.; m. Merle Faye Dover, June 18, 1958; children: Rhonda Lynn, Beth Francis. C.A., Inst. Chartered Accts. Ont., 1957; B.A., York U., 1977. Mgr. corp. fin. Vise, Rumack, Seigel, Kurtz & Co. (Chartered Accts.), Toronto, 1960-63; partner Bernard C. Kurtz & Co. (Chartered Accts.), Toronto, 1963-64; v.p. fin. and adminstrn. WIMCO Steel Sales Co. Ltd., Toronto, 1964-68, Toronto Iron Works Ltd., 1965-68; with Oshawa Group Ltd., Toronto, 1968—, asst. treas., 1970-74, treas., 1974—. Mem. Inst. Chartered Accts. Ont. (chmn. tax com.), Order Chartered Accts. Que., Nat. Assn. Accts., Tax Execs. Inst., Toronto Cash Mgmt. Soc. (pres., dir.). Office: 302 The East Mall Islington ON Canada M9B 6B8

EISENBERG, ADI, chemist; b. Breslau, Germany, Feb. 18, 1935; emigrated to U.S., 1951; s. Oscar and Helene E.; m. Sandra M. Kloner, June 9, 1957; 1 son, Elliot. B.Sc., Worcester Poly. Inst., 1957; M.A., Princeton U., 1959, Ph.D., 1960. Postdoctoral fellow U. Basel, Switzerland, 1961-62; asst. prof. chemistry UCLA, 1962-67; asso. prof. chemistry McGill U., Montreal, Que., Can., 1967-74, prof., 1975—; cons. in field. Author 3 books in field; contbr. articles to profl. jours. NATO fellow, 1961-62. Fellow Am. Phys. Soc. (chmn. div. high polymer physics 1975-76); mem. Am. Chem. Soc., Chem. Inst. Can., Sigma Xi. Patentee in field. Office: 801 Sherbrooke St W Montreal PQ H3A 2K6 Canada

EISENBERG, ALAN, association executive; b. N.Y.C., Apr. 15, 1935; s. Arthur and Mollie (Novak) E.; m. Rebecca Cooper, July 14, 1972 (div. May 19, 1980); m. 2d Claire Copley, May 23, 1982; 1 dau., Mollie Copley. A.B., U. Mich., 1956; LL.B., NYU, 1959. Bar: N.Y., Va., D.C. Assoc. Booth. Lipton & Lipton, N.Y.C., 1960, Hirson & Bertini, 1960-64; atty. NLRB, Washington and Chgo., 1964-68; assoc. Seligman & Seligman, N.Y.C., 1968-72; ptnr. Eisenberg & Paul, Arlington, Va., 1972-81; exec. sec. Actors Equity Assn., N.Y.C., 1982—; vis. prof. theatre adminstrn. Yale U. Sch. Drama, New Haven. Served with AUS, 1959. Office: Actors Equity Association 165 W 46th St New York NY 10036

EISENBERG, DAVID SAMUEL, chemistry educator; b. Chgo., Mar. 15, 1939; s. George and Ruth E.; m. Lucy Tuchman, Aug. 25, 1963; children: Jenny, Nell. A.B., Harvard U., 1961; Phil.D., Oxford U., Eng., 1964. NSF postdoctoral fellow Princeton U., 1964-66; research fellow chemistry Calif. Inst. Tech., Pasadena, 1966-69; asst. prof. UCLA, 1968-71, asoc. prof., 1971-76, prof. chemistry, biochemistry, 1976—, assoc. dir. Molecular Biology Inst., 1981—. Author: (with W. Kauzmann) Structure and Properties of Water, 1969, (with D.M. Crothers) Psysical Chemistry with Applications in the Life Sciences, 1979. Mem. adv. council chemistry dept. Princeton U., 1984—; chmn. Citizens for West Los Angeles Veloway, 1977—; bd. dirs. Westlake Sch., 1983—. Recipient Disting. Teaching award USPHS, 1975; Rhodes scholar, 1961-64; USPHS Career Devel. awardee, 1972-77. Mem. Am. Soc. Biol. Chemists; Mem. Am. Crystallographic Assn., Biophys. Soc. (councillor 1977-80). Office: Dept Chemistry-Biochemistry UCLA Los Angeles CA 90024

EISENBERG, DONALD HARVEY, hospital administrator; b. Tampa, Fla., Oct. 17, 1928; s. David and Toba (Moss) E.; m. Brenda Bernowitz, Nov. 28, 1960; children: Cindy, Lawrence, Robert. A.B., Bklyn. Coll., 1949; M.P.A., NYU, 1970. Assoc. dir. Mt. Sinai Hosp., N.Y.C., 1961-71; exec. v.p. N.Y.C. Health & Hosp. Corp., 1971-74; exec. dir. Nassau County Med. Center, East Meadow, N.Y., 1974—; clin. prof. community medicine SUNY, Stony Brook; bd. dirs. L.I. council Am. Cancer Soc.; mem. adv. council N.Y. State Senate Com. on Health. Active Big Bros./Sisters of L.I. Served with U.S. Army, 1950-52. Recipient Disting. Contbn. award L.I. chpt. Am. Soc. Public Adminstrn., 1977. Mem. Am. Coll. Hosp. Adminstrs., Hosp. Assn. N.Y. State Hosp. Soc. N.Y. Home and Office: 2201 Hempstead Turnpike East Meadow NY 11554

EISENBERG, JAMES, beef processing company executive; b. Chgo., Apr. 17, 1930; s. Sam and Celia E.; m. Elin Ladany, Aug. 5, 1955; 1 son, Steven Jamie. B.A., Carlton Coll., 1952. Western sales mgr. Eisenberg Originals, Chgo., 1952-55; with Vienna Sausage Mfg. Co., Chgo., 1956—, v.p., sec., 1964-73, exec. v.p., 1973-78, pres., chief exec. officer, 1978—; dir. Food Internat. Japan, Tokyo. Clubs: Northmoor Country., Standard. Office: 2501 N Damen Ave Chicago IL 60647

EISENBERG, JEROME CECIL, lawyer; b. Newark, Dec. 31, 1905; s. Herman and Esther (Sheps) E.; m. Isabelle R. Roemer, Mar. 8, 1942 (div. May 1974); children—Peter R., Mary; m. Meg Wohlberg, June 14, 1974. Student, Columbia, 1925-27; LL.B., N.J. Law Sch., 1925. Bar: N.J. bar 1927. Since practiced in, Newark; partner Clapp & Eisenberg, 1959—; Hearing commr. OPA, 1943. Sec., Lawyers Non-Partisan Com. for Constl. Revision, 1943-44; pres. West Orange Citizens Charter Assn., 1961-62; Trustee Far Brook Sch., Short Hills, N.J., pres., 1954-58. Mem. Am., N.J., Essex County bar assns., Am.

Judicature Soc. Clubs: N.J. Automobile (pres. 1972-73, trustee. Home: 124 E 30th St New York NY 10016 Office: 80 Park Plaza Newark NJ 07102

EISENBERG, JOHN MEYER, physician, educator; b. Atlanta, Sept. 24, 1946; s. Irvin and Roslyn Furchgott (Karesh) E. A.B. magna cum laude, Princeton U., 1968; M.D., Washington U., 1972; M.B.A. with distinction, U. Pa., 1976. Resident in medicine Hosp. of U. Pa., 1972-75, fellow, 1975-77; assoc. dir. med. affairs Nat. Health Care Mgmt. Center, 1976-78; asst. prof. medicine U. Pa., Phila., 1976-78, Sol Katz asst. prof. gen. medicine, 1978-81, Sol Katz assoc. prof., 1981—, chief sect. gen. medicine, 1978—; cons. Bur. Radiol. Health, 1979—, Bur. Health Standards and Quality Assurance, 1978—, Nat. Center for Health Services Research, 1981—; chmn. primary care com. Mayor's Commn. on Health in the Eighties, 1982-83. Editor: The Physicians Practice, 1980; mem. editorial bd.: Med. Decision Making; contbr. articles in field to profl. jours. Robert Wood Johnson Found. clin. scholar, 1974-77. Fellow ACP (mem. health professions subcom. 1982—), Phila. Coll. Physicians; mem. Soc. Research and Edn. in Primary Care Internal Medicine (sec.-treas. 1978-80, pres. 1982-83), Soc. Med. Decision Making (v.p. 1980-81), Assn. Program Dirs. Internal Medicine, Am. Public Health Assn., Am. Fedn. Clin. Research. Office: 3 Silverstein Pavilion Hosp U Pa 3400 Spruce St Philadelphia PA 19104

EISENBERG, KENNETH SAWYER, restoration expert; b. Newark, Dec. 30, 1932; s. William C. and Elsie G. (Greenfield) E.; m. Rica Miller, Aug. 15, 1965. B.S., N.Y. U., 1954, LL.B., 1961. Pioneered in devel. plans for hist. restoration programs Universal Engring., Newark, 1961-69; founder Universal Restoration, Inc., numerous locations, 1967, pres., chmn. bd., 1969-75; pres. Preservation Tech. Group, Ltd., 1975—; Cons. restoration tech. Gen. Services Adminstrn. on Renwick restoration, Jackson Pl. Row Houses rehab., The Pentagon, all Washington, Escanaba-Carnegie Library, Escanaba, Mich., Pioneer Courthouse restoration, Portland, Oreg., Peale Mus., Balt., Old San Francisco Mint restoration, Old Ben Franklin Sta. P.O., Washington, Field Mus. of Natural History, Chgo.; cons. restoration projects Nat. Park Service (including Castle Clinton Nat. Monument), Battery Park, N.Y., Grant's Tomb, N.Y.C., Lincoln Meml., Washington; cons. N.Y.C. Landmarks Commn., Calif. State Capitol Bldg. restoration, Sacramento, Internat. Center for Preservation, Rome, Italy, No. Ind., Minn. hist. socs., Va. Hist. Landmarks Commn., Turkish Ministry Culture, Ankara, Office Architect Hist. Monuments, Paris, France, Danish Royal Acad. Art, Copenhagen, Office Cultural Patrimony, Santo Domingo, Dominican Republic, Centre Experimental de Recherches et d'Etudes du Batiment et des Travaux Publics, Saint-Remy-Les-Chevreuse, France, UNESCO, Paris. Served to lt. USAF, 1955-57. Mem. Nat. Trust for Historic Preservation (cons.), Nat. Capital Hist. Soc. (cons.), Assn. for Preservation Tech., Soc. for Preservation Ancient Bldgs. (cons., London, Eng.), Internat. Platform Assn., ASTM, Constrn. Specifications Inst., Internat. Wine and Food Soc., Internat. Fund for Monuments (Venice com.), Confrerie de la Chaine des Rotisseurs. Club: International (Washington). Inventor Permo Bond/Dekosit Process for re-creating stone, 1963; Dekosit II Process for preserving ancient wood, stone and metal, 1973. Office: 1700 K St Washington DC 20006 *It is my intent to encourage those who seek to preserve, restore, and use significant architectural works for the benefit of all. The past works of man assist him in interpreting the present and securing his future. Fusing the disciplines of art with those of technology has given those dedicated to that pursuit the means to attain their goal. If, in working to protect the symbols of a heritage, I am able to leave what I have touched more secure than when I first encountered it, my purpose will be successful.*

EISENBERG, LEE B., editor, author; b. Phila., July 22, 1946; s. George M. and Eve (Blonsky) E. A.B. cum laude, U. Pa., 1968; M.A., Annenberg Sch. Communications, Phila., 1970. With Esquire mag., N.Y.C., 1970—, mng. editor, 1975-76, editor, 1976-78, 84—, v.p., 1981-84; founding partner Eisenberg, McCall & Okrent, Inc. (book producers), N.Y.C., 1978-81; co-dir. Rice U. Pub. Program, 1979; instr. journalism N.Y. U., 1974-75; playwright Actors theater of Louisville, 1983; cons. N.Y. Times Co., 1977, Warner Bros., 1978. Co-author: Sneaky Feats, 1975, More Sneaky Feats, 1976; author: Atlantic City, 1979; editor: The Ultimate Fishing Book, 1981. Recipient One-Man Show award Art Dirs. Club, N.Y.C., 1974. Mem. Am. Soc. Mag. Editors, Authors Guild. Club: Theodore Gordon Flyfishers (N.Y.C.).

EISENBERG, LEON, child psychiatrist; b. Phila., Aug. 8, 1922; s. Morris and and Elizabeth (Sabreen) E.; m. Ruth Harriet Bleier, June 11, 1948 (div. 1967); children: Mark Philip, Kathy Bleier; m. Carola Blitzman Guttmacher, Aug. 31, 1967; children: Laurence, Alan. A.B., U. Pa., 1944, M.D., 1946; M.A. (hon.), Harvard, 1967, D.Sc., U. Manchester, Eng., 1973. Diplomate: in child psychiatry and psychiatry Am. Bd. Psychiatry and Neurology. Intern Mt. Sinai Hosp., N.Y.C., 1946-47; instr. physiology U. Pa., 1947-48; resident psychiatry Sheppard-Pratt Hosp., Towson, Md., 1950-52; with Johns Hopkins, 1952-67; prof. child psychiatry Med. Sch., 1961-67; psychiatrist-in-charge children's psychiat. service Harriet Lane Home, 1958-67; prof. psychiatry Harvard Med. Sch., 1967—, Maude and Lillian Presley prof. psychiatry, 1975-80, chmn. exec. com. dept. psychiatry, 1973-80, Maude and Lillian Presley prof. social medicine and chmn. dept. social medicine and health policy, 1980—; psychiatrist-in-chief Mass. Gen. Hosp., 1967-74, mem. bd. consultation, 1974—; sr. asso. in psychiatry Children's Hosp., Boston, 1974—; psychiat. cons. Crownsville (Md.) State Hosp., 1954-58, Rosewood State Tng. Sch., Owings Mills, Md., 1957-60, Balt. City Hosp., 1959-62, Children's Guild, Balt., 1954-61; cons. Sinai Hosp., Balt., 1963-67; Mapother-Lewis ann. lectr. Maudsley Hosp., London, 1977; Baan Meml. lectr. Netherlands Psychiat. Soc., Amsterdam, 1978; Royal Soc. Medicine vis. prof., London, 1983; Mem. subcom. psychiat. nomenclature, com. vital statistics USPHS; chmn. WHO Conf. Developmental Regulation, 1964-67; mem. Joint Commn. Mental Health of Children; cons. Office Mental Health, World Health Assn., 1974—; mem. adv. com. to dir. NIH, 1977-80. Editor: Am. Jour. Orthopsychiatry, 1963-73; editorial bd.: Medicine and Psychiatry. Served to capt. M.C.; Served to capt. AUS, 1948-50. Theobald Smith award Albany Med. Coll., 1979; Recipient Orton award Orton Soc., 1980. Fellow Am. Psychiat. Assn. (trustee 1973-76), Am. Orthopsychiat. Assn., A.A.A.S., Soc. Research Child Devel.; mem. Inst. Medicine of Nat. Acad. Scis. (council 1975-77, program and membership coms. 1979-82), AAUP (past pres. Johns Hopkins), Am. Acad. Pediatrics (Aldrich award 1980), Am. Pediatric Soc., Assn. Research Nervous and Mental Disease, Am. Psychopath. Assn., Md. Psychiat. Soc. (past pres.), Am. Acad. Arts and Scis., Psychiat. Research Soc. (past pres.), Soc. Neurosci., Mass. Med. Soc., Greek Soc. Neurology and Psychiatry (hon.), Johns Hopkins Soc. Scholars, Phi Beta Kappa (chpt. pres.), Sigma Xi, Alpha Omega Alpha. Home: 9 Clement Circle Cambridge MA 02138 Office: Dept Social Medicine and Health Policy Harvard Med Sch Boston MA 02115

EISENBERG, M. MICHAEL, educator, physician; b. N.Y.C., Jan. 27, 1931; s. George Herman and Dorothy (Rosenfeld) E.; children—Elyse Debra, Ellen Beth, Andrea Carla. A.B. cum laude, N.Y. U., 1952, M.D., Harvard, 1956. Diplomate: Am. Bd. Surgery. Surg. intern Peter Bent Brigham Hosp., Boston, 1956; surg. resident New Haven Med. Center, 1960; asst. prof. surgery, then asso. prof. U. Fla. Med. Sch., 1962-68; prof. surgery U. Minn. Med. Sch., Mpls., 1968-81; also chief gastrointestinal surgery; chief surgery Mt. Sinai Hosp., Mpls., 1968-75; cons. VA, Northwestern hosps.; sr. investigator NIH, 1968—; dir. surgery L.I. Coll. Hosp.; and prof. surgery, vice-chmn. dept. SUNY Downstate, 1981—. Author: Ulcers, 1978; Contbr. articles to med. jours. Mem. budget panel United Fund Mpls. Served with M.C.; Served with AUS, 1958-60. Fellow A.C.S.; mem. Am. Surg. Assn., Soc. Univ. Surgeons, Internat. Soc. Surgery, Am. Physiol. Soc., Am. Gastroent. Assn., Soc. Surgery Alimentary Tract, Soc. Exptl. Biology and Medicine, Internat. Coll. Surgery Digestive Diseases (pres. 1977, 78), Phi Beta Kappa, Alpha Omega Alpha. Home: 63 E 79 St New York NY 10021

EISENBERG, MARVIN, art history educator; b. Phila., Aug. 19, 1922; s. Frank and Rosalie (Julius) E. B.A., U. Pa., 1943; M.F.A., Princeton, 1949, Ph.D., 1954. Mem. faculty U. Mich., Ann Arbor, 1949—, prof. art history, also chmn. dept., 1960-69, collegiate prof., 1974-75; mem. Inst. for Advanced Study, Princeton, N.J., 1970; vis. prof. Stanford U., 1973; Mem. adv. com. Center for Advanced Study in Visual Arts, Nat. Gallery, Washington; mem. vis. com. dept. fine arts, Harvard U., 1975-81, Freer Gallery Art, Washington. Contbr. articles on early Italian painting to profl. jours. Served with AUS, 1944-46. Guggenheim fellow, 1959; recipient Star of Solidarity II, Italy, 1961. Mem. Coll. Art Assn. Am. (dir. 1965-70, v.p. 1966-67, pres. 1968-69, mem. Meiss Fund com.), Royal Soc. Arts (Benjamin Franklin fellow), Phi Beta Kappa, Phi Kappa Phi. Home: 2200 Fuller Rd Apt 1201 Ann Arbor MI 48105

EISENBERG, MELVIN A., legal educator. A.B., Columbia U., 1956; LL.B., Harvard U., 1959. Bar: N.Y. 1960. Assoc. firm Kay Scholer Fierman Hays & Handler, 1959-63, 64-66; asst. counsel Pres.'s Commn. on Assassination of Pres. Kennedy, 1964; asst. corp. counsel City of N.Y., 1966; acting prof. U. Calif.-Berkeley, 1966-69, prof. law, 1969—; vis. prof. Harvard U., 1969-70; counsel Mayor's Task Force on Reorgn. N.Y.C. Govt., 1966; mem. Mayor's Task Force on N.Y.C. Transp. Reorgn., 1966, Mayor's Task Force on Mcpl. Collective Bargaining. Mem.: Harvard Law Rev.; author: (with D. Fuller) Legal Process: Basic Contract Law, 1972, The Structure of the Corporation, 1977, (with Cary) Cases and Materials on Corporation, 1980. Pres. Queen's Child Guidance Ctr., 1963-66. Guggenheim fellow, 1971-72. Mem. Phi Beta Kappa. Office: U Calif Law Sch 225 Boalt Hall Berkeley CA 94720

EISENBERG, MEYER, lawyer; b. Bklyn., Dec. 15, 1931; s. Samuel and Bella (Fishman) E.; m. Carolyn Schoen, Dec. 25, 1954; children—Julie S., Ellen M. B.A., Bklyn. Coll., 1953; LL.B., Columbia U., 1958. Bar: N.Y. State bar 1960, D.C. bar 1970, U.S. Supreme Ct. bar 1963. Law clk. to Chief Justice William McAllister, Supreme Ct. Oreg., Salem, 1958-59; atty. SEC, Washington, 1959-70, counsel spl. study securities markets, 1962-64, asst. gen. counsel, 1966-68, exec. asst. to chmn., 1968-69, asso. gen. counsel, 1969-70; with firm Lawler, Kent & Eisenberg, Washington, 1970-79, Rosenman, Colin, Freund, Lewis & Cohen, 1980—; cons. in field; adj. prof. law George Washington U., 1972-75; exec. com. Securities Law Inst., U. Calif. Contbr. articles to profl. publs. Mem. Md. Commn. Aid to Non-Public Schs., 1968-70; chmn. Nat. Law Commn., Internat. Affairs Commn.; mem. nat. exec. com. Anti-Defamation League, B'nai B'rith; pres. dist. 5 B'nai B'rith., 1982-83. Mem. ABA (chmn. com. on devels. in investment services), Fed. Bar Assn. (chmn. securities law com.), Am. Law Inst. Office: 1300 19th St NW Washington DC 20036

EISENBERG, NORMAN, editor, writer; b. Bklyn., Dec. 5, 1921; s. Abraham S. and Rose (Hyman) E.; m. Phoebe Ruth Rosenberg, Feb. 22; 1953. A.B., Bklyn. Coll., 1947; postgrad., Columbia U., 1947-49. Asst. editor Radio-TV Service Dealer mag., N.Y.C., 1953-54; advt. mgr. Fisher Radio, N.Y.C., 1954; asso. editor, feature editor Popular Electronics, N.Y.C., 1954-57; asso. editor Consumer Reports, Mt. Vernon, N.Y., 1957-58; editor Maco Mag. Corp., N.Y.C., 1958-60; tech. editor, audio-video editor, exec. editor High Fidelity mag., Great Barrington, Mass., 1960-75; editor-in-chief Stereo, Stereo Internat., Great Barrington, 1968-75; editorial bd. Modern Recording and Music, N.Y.C., 1975-82; columnist stereo-hi-fi Washington Post, 1971—; contbg. editor Ovation, N.Y.C., 1980—. Author: HIFI, 1959, Hi Fi Stereo Kits, 1961, Stereo, 1968, The New World of Audio, 1982; Contbr. articles to mags., annuals, anthologies. Served with AUS, 1942-46. Mem. Soc. Audio Cons. (mem. certification bd.), Audio Engring. Soc. Address: Nielsen Ln Stockbridge MA 01262

EISENBERG, PHILLIP, consulting engineer; b. Detroit, Nov. 6, 1919; s. Morris and Ida (Blaizovsky) E.; m. Edith S. Rosenbaum, Nov. 21, 1942; children: Elyse, Jean. B.S., Wayne State U., 1941; postgrad., U. Iowa, 1942; C.E., Calif. Inst. Tech., 1948. Instr. U. Iowa, Iowa City, 1941-42; head research br. David Taylor Model Basin, Navy Dept., Carderock, Md., 1942-44, 46-53; pres. Hydronautics, Inc., Laurel, Md., 1959-74, 78-82, chmn. exec. com., Washington, 1974-82, also dir.; pvt. cons., 1982—; Mem. bd. cons. Iowa Inst. Hydraulic Research, 1954-56, 59-61; mem. Md. Ocean Sci. Com., 1969-70; mem. sea grant adv. panel NOAA, 1969-76; Mem. vis. com. ocean engring. MIT, 1974—; mem. Marine Bd., Maritime Transp. Research Bd., NRC; bd. dirs. Am. Bur. Shipping. Contbr. articles to publs. in field. Served to lt. (j.g.) USNR, 1944-47. Recipient Meritorious Civilian award U.S. Navy, 1944, Distinguished Alumni award Wayne State U., 1958; tech. achievement award ASME, 1959; Gold medal Nat. Acad. Scis., 1974. Fellow Royal Inst. Naval Architects, ASME, Soc. Naval Architects and Marine Engrs. (pres. 1973-74, hon. mem. gold medal 1972), Marine Tech. Soc. (pres. 1976, recipient Lockheed award for ocean sci. and engring. 1980); mem. Nat. Acad. Engring., Am. Inst. Aeros. and Astronautics, Am. Phys. Soc., Am. Inst. Physics, Acoust. Soc. Am. Club: Cosmos (Washington). Patentee in field. Home: 6402 Tulsa Ln Bethesda MD 20034

EISENBERG, RICHARD S., chemistry educator; b. N.Y.C., Feb. 12, 1943; s. Paul and Norma (Frommer) E.; m. Marcia Landau, Wug. 6, 1966; children: Alan, Robert. A.B., Columbia U., 1963, M.A., 1964, Ph.D., 1967. Asst. prof. chemistry Brown U., Providence, 1967-71, assoc. prof., 1971-73; assoc. prof. chemistry U. Rochester (N.Y.), 1973-76, prof., 1976—; vis. scuebtust Calif. Inst. Tech., 1977-78; vis. scholar Cambridge (Eng.) U., 1978; cons. SOHIO, Cleve., 1982—, Eastman Kodak, Rochester, 1982. Contbr. numerous articles on chemistry to profl. jours.; mem. editorial adv. bd.: Jour. Am. Chem. Soc., 1982—. Alfred P. Sloan fellow, 1972-74; Guggenheim fellow, 1977-78. Mem. Am. Chem. Soc. (chmn. organometallic subdiv. inorganic div. 1982), Chem. Soc., Am. Crystallographic Assn. Home: 175 Parkwood Ave Rochester NY 14620 Office: Dept Chemistry U Rochester River Campus Rochester NY 14627

EISENBERG, ROBERT SHIM, physiologist, educator; b. Bklyn., Apr. 25, 1942; s. Harold Jerome and Lucille Ruth E.; m. Brenda Russell, July 11, 1964; children: Benjamin, Emily, Jill Anna, Sally. A.B. summa cum laude, Harvard U., 1962; Ph.D., Univ. Coll. London, 1965. Assoc. dept. physiology Duke U., 1965-68; asst. prof. to prof. dept. physiology U. Calif., Los Angeles, 1968-76; chmn., Bard prof. dept. physiology Rush U., Chgo., 1976—; mem., then chmn. physiology study sect. NIH, 1979—. Grantee NIH, 1969—, NSF, 1968-77, Muscular Dystrophy Assn., 1969—; also grantee heart assns. Mem. Biophys. Soc. (council, exec. com. 1983—), Am. Physiol. Soc., Soc. Gen. Physiology (council 1983—), Am. Soc. Cell Biology, Neurosci. and Physiol. Soc. (London) (assoc.), Chgo. Soc. Neurosci. (pres. 1983-84), Soc. Indsl. and Applied Math., Inst. Strategic Studies (London), Am. Math. Soc. Home: 720 Keystone St River Forest IL 60305 Office: 1750 W Harrison St Chicago IL 60612

EISENBERG, STEPHEN PAUL DAVID, lawyer; b. Chgo., July 16, 1944; s. Morris and Esther (Greenberg) E.; m. Susan Irene Sair, July 4, 1968; children—Morris Robert, Jamie Sharon. B.A., Washington U., St. Louis, 1966; J.D., DePaul U., 1969. Bar: Ill. bar 1969. Asso. firm Upton, Conklin & Leahy, Chgo., 1969-72; partner firm Conklin, Leahy & Eisenberg, Chgo., 1972-79, firm Leahy & Eisenberg, Ltd., 1979—. Chmn. Ill. Adv. Com. on Arson Prevention; mem. Gov. Thompson's Arson Adv. Bd. Mem. Internat. Assn. Arson Investigators. Clubs: Union League of Chicago, Idlewild Country. Home: 1822 Western Ave Flossmoor IL 60422 Office: 29 S LaSalle St Chicago IL 60603

EISENBERGER, GARY D., publisher; b. Lancaster, Pa., May 18, 1934; s. Kervin V. and Ruth E. (Hunchberger) E.; m. Gail M. Compton, July 11, 1981; children by previous marriage: Johanna L., Jennifer L. B.S. in Sci., Lebanon Valley Coll., Annville, Pa., 1958. Mem. adj. faculty Franklin and Marshall Coll., Lancaster, Pa., 1958-60; with Charles E. Merrill Pub. Co. (div. Bell & Howell Co.), Columbus, Ohio, 1960—, v.p., then sr. v.p. adminstrn., 1969-72, pres., 1972—, corp. v.p., 1982—. Trustee Children's Hosp., Columbus, 1975-76, mem. devel. bd., 1973—, chmn. membership com., 1978—. Served with USNR, 1952-54. Mem. Assn. Am. Pubs. (exec. com. sch. div. 1977—, chmn. 1979-80, dir. 1979-81). Episcopalian. Clubs: Rotary (chmn. youth service com. 1977-78), City (Columbus)). Home: 411 Mainsail Dr Westerville OH 43081 Office: 936 Eastwind Dr Westerville OH 43081

EISENBRAUN, EDMUND JULIUS JOHANNES, educator; b. Wewela, S.D., Dec. 10, 1920; s. Julius and Elizabeth (Hermann) E.; m. Joyce Marie Abrahamson, Aug. 20, 1949; children—Ellen, Greta, Ann. B.S., U. Wis., 1950, M.S., 1951, Ph.D. (Carbide and Carbon Chem. Co. fellow), 1955. Research chemist Monsanto Chem. Co., Dayton, Ohio, 1955-56; postdoctoral research fellow chemistry Wayne State U., Detroit, 1956-59; sr. research asso. Stanford, 1959-61; dir. research Aldrich Chem. Co., Milw., 1961-62; prof. chemistry, dir. research project Am. Petroleum Inst. Okla. State U., Stillwater, 1962—, Regents prof., 1975—. Contbr. articles to profl. jours. Served with AUS, 1941-46; NATOUSA; Served with AUS; MTO. Mem. Am. Chem. Soc., Chem. Soc. London, Sigma Xi, Phi Lambda Upsilon. Home: 1102 Graham Dr Stillwater OK 74074

EISENBUD, MERRIL, environmental scientist; b. N.Y.C., Mar. 18, 1915; s. Kalman and Leonora (Kopaloff) E.; m. Irma Onish, Jan. 22, 1939; children—Elliott, Michael, Fredrick. B.S. in Elec. Engring, N.Y. U., 1936; Sc.D. (hon.), Fairleigh Dickinson U., 1960; D.H.C., Catholic U., Rio de Janiero. Diplomate: Am. Acad. Environ. Engrs. Indsl. hygienist Liberty Mut. Ins. Co., 1936-47; asso. prof. indsl. medicine Sch. Medicine, N.Y. U., 1945-55, adj. prof., 1956-59, prof. environ. medicine, dir. lab. environ. studies, 1959—; adminstr. N.Y.C. EPA, 1968-70; dir. health and safety lab. AEC, 1947-59; mem. Nat. Commn. on Radiation Protection and Measurements, 1965—, dir., 1971-76; mem. expert panel on radiation hazards WHO, 1956—; mem. N.Y. State Health Adv. Council, 1975-80. Author: Environmental Radioactivity, 2d edit, 1973, Environment, Technology, and Health, 1979. Bd. dirs. Blue Cross-Blue Shield Greater N.Y., 1968-75; bd. mgrs. State Community Aid Assn.; mem. adv. council Electric Power Research Inst. Recipient Gold medal AEC, 1974; Hermann Biggs medal N.Y. State Pub. Health Assn.; Arthur Holly Compton award Am. Nuclear Soc.; Power-Life award Am. Inst. Elec. and Electronic Engrs. Fellow AAAS, N.Y. Acad. Scis. (hon. life mem., gov., v.p. 1979-80), N.Y. Acad. Medicine; mem. Nat. Acad. Engring., Health Physics Soc. (pres. 1965-66), Am. Indsl. Hygiene Assn., Radiation Research Soc., Am. Bd. Health Physics. Clubs: Cosmos (Washington); Explorers, Century (N.Y.C.). Home: PO Box 837 Tuxedo NY 10987 Office: NYU Med Center Tuxedo NY 10987

EISENHART, CHARLES ROBERT, coll. pres.; b. Binghamton, N.Y., Mar. 12, 1912; s. John A. and Nellie (Van Patten) E.; m. Judith Annabel Russell, Aug. 31, 1935; children-Charles Robert, Judith Annabel, John Brainard. Ph.B., Muhlenberg Coll., 1933; M.A., SUNY at Albany, 1940; Ed.D., Columbia U., 1954; H.D., Defiance Coll., 1961. Tchr. rural schs., 1934-35, tchr., Harpursville, N.Y., 1935-37, Johnson City, N.Y., 1937-43; asso. prof., dean men Hartwick Coll., 1946-54; dean Jacksonville (Fla.) U., 1954-56, Defiance Coll., 1956-61; pres. Adirondack Community Coll., Glens Falls, N.Y., 1961-78; Ohio del. White House Conf. Aging, 1961; chmn. Defiance County Com. Problems of Aging, 1959-61; del. state conv.; mem. Balance of State Adv. Council N.Y. State. Bd. dirs. Hyde Art Collection, Tri-County United Way; councilman Town of Queensbury; exec. bd. Mohican council Boy Scouts Am. Served with AUS; World War II; col. USAF Res.; ret. Mem. Phi Sigma Kappa, Phi Sigma Iota, Kappa Phi Kappa, Phi Delta Kappa. Home: 238 Bay St Glens Falls NY 12801 *The major part of joy comes from energetic and dedicated service—to God and man and to those institutions which have been the strength of man's struggle to escape from savagery.*

EISENHAUER, HARRY MACDONALD, lawyer; b. Lower LaHave, N.S., Can., July 9, 1920; s. John Archibald and Lillian Maxwell (Adams) E.; m. Ruth Louise Paterson, Sept. 23, 1963; children by previous marriage—John, David, Janice. LL.B., Dalhousie U., Halifax, N.S., 1948. Bar: N.S. bar 1948. Trust officer, br. mgr. Eastern Trust Co., Calgary, Alta., Can., 1948-57; counsel, sec. Hudson's Bay Oil & Gas Co. Ltd., Calgary, 1958-59; mem. then mgr. law dept. Dome Petroleum Ltd., Calgary, 1959-75, corporate sec., 1973—. Served to maj. Can. Army, 1940-45. Mem. Can. Bar Assn., N.S. Barristers Soc. Liberal. Presbyterian. Clubs: Canyon Meadows Golf and Country, Ranchmen's (Calgary). Home: 23 Bay View Dr SW Calgary AB T2V 3N7 Canada Office: Dome Petroleum Ltd Dome Tower 333 7th Ave SW Calgary AB T2P 2Z1 Canada

EISENHOWER, JOHN SHELDON DOUD, former U.S. ambassador; b. Denver, Aug. 3, 1922; s. Dwight David (34th Pres. of U.S.) and Mamie (Doud) E.; m. Barbara Jean Thompson, June 10, 1947; children: Dwight David II, Barbara Anne (Senora de Echavarria), Susan Elaine (Mrs. Mahon), Mary Jean (Mrs. DeYoung.). B.S., U.S. Mil. Acad., 1944; M.A. in English Lit, Columbia, 1950. Commd. 2d lt. U.S. Army, 1944, advanced through grades to lt. col., 1963; assigned Army of Occupation, Europe, 1945-47, Korean War, 1952-53, Army Gen. Staff, 1957-58, White House Staff, 1958-61; resigned, 1963; brig. gen. USAR, 1974; engaged in writing, 1965-69, U.S. ambassador to, Belgium, 1969-71; cons. to the Pres.; also chmn. Interagency Classification Review Com., 1972-73; chmn. bd. Academy Life Ins. Co., Valley Forge, Pa.; Mem. adv. council Nat. Archives, 1974-77; chmn. President's Adv. Com. on Refugees, 1975. Author: The Bitter Woods, 1969, Strictly Personal, 1974; editor: Letters to Mamie, 1978, Allies, 1982. Trustee Eisenhower Fellowships; mem. diplomatic council Pres.'s People-to-People Sports Com.; bd. govs. USO; trustee Alumni Fedn. Columbia U., Authors Guild, Authors League Am. Decorated Legion of Merit, Bronze Star medal, Combat Inf. badge; grand cross Order of Crown, Belgium; Chungmu Distinguished Service medal, Korea). Mem. Explorers Club, Internat. Platform Assn. Clubs: Capitol Hill, Army-Navy Country. Home: PO Box 278 Kimberton PA 19442

EISENMAN, ALVIN, educator, graphic designer; b. DuBois, Pa., June 18, 1921; s. Alvin and Janice (Neiman) E.; m. Hope Greer, Nov. 12, 1942; children: Susan S. Eisenman Restino, James H., Sara S. A.B. Dartmouth Coll, 1943; M.A. (hon.), Yale U., 1961. Mgr. design dept. McGraw-Hill Book Co., 1945-50; typographer Yale U. Press, 1950-60; lectr. graphic arts Sch. Fine Arts Yale U., 1950-52, chief critic Sch. Architecture and Design, 1953-56, asso. prof. graphic arts, 1956-61, prof. graphic design, 1961-79, Street prof. painting and design, 1979—, fellow Pierson Coll., 1951—; corr. prof. Royal Coll. Art, London, 1982—; Mellon prof. graphic design Cooper Union, 1978; typog. adviser Morgan Guaranty Trust Co., 1959-82. Pres. bd. trustees Barlow Sch., Amenia, N.Y., 1963-68; trustee Hartford Art Sch., 1983—. Mem. Am. Inst. Graphic Arts (pres. 1960-63). Club: Double Crown (hon.). Home: 163 Carrington Rd Rural Route 2 Bethany CT 06525 Office: Yale U Sch Art Yale Sta New Haven CT 06520

EISENMAN, PETER DAVID, architect, educator; b. Newark, Aug. 11, 1932; s. Herschel I. and Sylvia H. (Heller) E.; m. Elizabeth Henderson, July 20, 1963; children: Julia, Nicholas. B.Arch. (Charles G. Sands Meml. medal 1955), Cornell U., 1955; M.S. in Architecture (Alumni tuition scholar 1959, William Kinne fellow 1960-61), Columbia U., 1960; M.A., Cambridge (Eng.) U., 1962, Ph.D., 1963. Prin. firm Eisenman/Robertson Architects, N.Y.C., 1980—; founder Inst. Architecture and Urban Studies, N.Y.C., 1967, dir., 1967-82; mem. faculty Cambridge U., 1960-63, Princeton U., 1965-67, Cooper Union, 1970—, adj. prof., 1975—; architect-in-residence Am. Acad. Rome, 1976; Kea prof. U. Md., 1978; Charlotte Davenport prof. Yale U., 1980; Arthur Rotch prof. Harvard U., 1982—. Editor: Oppositions Books 1982—, House X Rizzoli 1982—; prin. works include pvt. residences, Princeton, N.J., Hardwick, Vt., Lakeville and, Cornwall, Conn., 1968-76; Cummins Engine Co., Madison, Housing Koch-Friedrichstrasse, Berlin. Served with U.S. Army, 1955-57. Fellow Graham Found., 1966; Guggenheim Found., 1976; grantee Princeton U., 1964, 66; recipient Arnold W. Brunner Meml. prize in architecture Am. Acad. and Inst. Arts and Letters, 1984. Fellow AIA; mem. Archtl. League N.Y. (v.p. 1970), Conf. Architects Study Environ. (co-founder 1964). Club: Century Assn. (N.Y.C.). Office: 560 Fifth Ave New York NY 10036

EISENMENGER, ROBERT WALTZ, banker; b. N.Y.C., June 30, 1926; s. Walter S. and Emily (Brenner) E.; m. Carolyn Lois Shaver, Oct. 11, 1952; children—Anne Waltz, Katherine Carol, Lisa Ellen. B.A., Amherst Coll., 1949; M.F., Yale, 1951; M.P.A. (Conservation fellow), Harvard, 1955; Ph.D. in Econs. (Littauer fellow), Harvard, 1964. Asst. forester Dept. Interior, Eugene, Oreg., 1951-52, forest economist, Portland, Oreg., 1952-53, forester, Salem, Oreg., 1953-54; economist Fed. Res. Bank, Boston, 1955-63, dir. research, 1963—, v.p., 1965-68, sr. v.p., 1969—; lectr. Wellesley Coll., 1969; vis. lectr. Yale U., 1977; lectr. Inst. of Politics, Harvard U., 1980. Author: The Dynamics of Growth in New England's Economy 1870-1964, 1967. Mem. town meeting Town of Natick, Mass., 1964—, planning bd., 1973-79, chmn., 1980—; mem. New Eng. Bd. Higher Edn., 1970-72, vice chmn., 1972-74, chmn., 1974—; mem. Yale U. Council com. to Sch. Forestry and Environmental Studies, 1972—; Trustee New Eng. Natural Resources Center, 1971—, clk., 1973-74, treas., 1974—; trustee Bacon Free Pub. Library. Served with USNR, 1944-46. Mem. Nat. Assn. Bus. Economists, Boston Econ. Club (pres. 1972), Am. Econ. Assn. Club: Amherst (Boston). Home: 92 Woodland St Natick MA 01760 Office: Fed Reserve Bank Boston 600 Atlantic Ave Boston MA 02106

EISENPREIS, ALFRED, advertising and marketing executive; b. Vienna, Austria, June 16, 1924; came to U.S., 1939, naturalized, 1942; s. Zygmunt and Claire (Silberman-Günsberg) E.; 1 son, Steven. A.B., St. Thomas Coll., 1943; M.A., N.Y. Sch. Social Research, 1974. Exec. Pomeroy's Inc. (dept. store), Wilkes-Barre, Pa., 1943-57; with Allied Stores Corp., N.Y.C., 1957-74, v.p. planning and research, 1963-69, v.p. mktg., 1970-74; adminstr. Econ. Devel. Adminstrn. City of N.Y., 1974-76; v.p. Newspaper Advt. Bur., 1977—; dir. Henchy & Assocs., N.Y.C., 1982—; spl. cons. N.Y. C. of C., Econ. Devel. Council N.Y.C., 1976; mem. faculty Grad. Sch. Mgmt. and Urban Professions, New Sch. Social Research, 1975—, mem. adv. coms. on manpower and tourism programs, 1975—; Mem. policy com. City of N.Y., 1974-76; pres. N.Y.C. Indsl. Devel. Corp., 1974-76; mem. Port Devel. Council N.Y., 1974-76; vice chmn. Interagy. Rail Com., 1975; steering com. Westside Hwy., 1974-76; dir. N.Y.C. Indsl. Devel. Agy., 1974-76; chmn. Retail Research Inst., 1963-68; mem. com. dept. store statistics Fed. Res. System, 1960-65; chmn. adv. com. Center Econ. Projections, Nat. Planning Assn., 1963-68; mem. dept. urban research Nat. Acad. Scis., 1964-69; cons. U.S. Dept. Commerce, 1965-69; dir. Greater Jamaica Devel. Com., 1965-68; trustee Fed. Statis. Users Conf., 1965-67, N.Y. Met. Regional Statis. Center, 1965-67; mem. Census Adv. Com., 1966-68, 72-74; mem. nat. mktg. adv. com. U.S. Dept. Commerce, 1968-72; cons. Office of Emergency Preparedness-Fed. Emergency Mgmt. Agy., 1966—; mem. Nat. Def. Exec. Res., 1966—, Nat. Mgmt. Council Mktg. Edn., chmn., 1972, 79-81; mem. Nat. Bus. Council on Consumer Interests, 1972-73. Author: The Changing Consumer, 1961, Organization for Multi-Unit Stores, 1962, Evaluation of Retail Store Location Research, 1965, Retail Marketing, 1981. Trustee Wilkes Coll., Wilkes Barre, Pa., 1968-74, Reece Sch., N.Y.C., 1968-72; trustee, exec. com. Union Am. Hebrew Congregations, 1970-81; trustee French and Polyclinic Med. Sch. and Health Center, N.Y.C., 1972-73, Pub. Devel. Corp., 1974-76; bd. dirs. N.Y.C. Conv. Center, 1974-76, N.Y.C. Conv. and Visitors Bur., 1974-76, Nat. Found. Jewish Culture, 1974—; treas. Nat. Found. Jewish Culture, 1977—; adv. com. N.Y. Pub. Library, 1968-74; bd. dirs. Nat. Council for Urban Econ. Devel., 1975-76; trustee Emanu-El Congregation, N.Y.C., 1968—; mem. exec. com. N.Y.C. chpt. Am. Jewish Com., 1976—; mem. adv. com. Inst. Internat. Edn., N.Y.C.; mem. N.Y.C. Jewish Community Relations Council, 1976-78; mem. president's council Sch. Social Work, N.Y. U., 1977-80; v.p. Joyce Theater Found., N.Y.C., 1980—; exec. council Am. Jewish Hist. Assn., 1983—. Mem. Forecasters Club N.Y. (pres. 1973-74), Am. Statis. Assn., Am. Econ. Assn., Am. Mktg. Assn., Nat. Retail Mchts. Assn. (dir. 1963-72, exec. com. 1968-72, v.p. 1970), Am. Retail Fedn. (dir., exec. com. 1968-72), N.Y. Acad. Scis., Retail Research Soc. (hon.), Newcomen Soc., Regional Plan Assn. N.Y.C. (com. 2d regional plan), Internat. Newspaper Advt. Execs. Clubs: Grolier, Univ. (N.Y.C.). Home: 40 E 83d St New York NY 10028 Office: 485 Lexington Ave New York NY 10017

EISENSTADT, ABRAHAM S., history educator; b. N.Y.C., June 18, 1920. Ph.D., Columbia U., 1955. Lectr. Bklyn. Coll., 1950-56, instr., 1956-60, asst. prof., 1961-63, assoc. prof., 1964-67, prof. history, 1968—; Fulbright prof. Am. history and Am. studies Sch. Advanced Internat. Studies, John Hopkins U., Bologna, Italy, 1962-63; lectr. Council for Am. studies seminar, Rome, 1963; panelist, cons. div. research grants Nat. Endowment Humanities, 1979—; mem. nat. screening com. Fulbright-Hays Grants for Study in U.K., 1974-76; chmn. acad. seminars com. City U. Acad. Scis. and Humanities, 1979—; bd. dirs., 1979—; founder, dir. Bklyn. Coll. Hist. Manuscripts Collection, 1960-66. Author: Charles M. Andrews: A Study in American Historial Writing, 1956; co-author: Beyond Watergate: Problems of Corruption in American History, 1979; editor: American History: Recent Interpretations, 2 vols, 1962, 2d edit., 1969, The Craft of American History, 2 vols, 1966; series editor: (with John Hope Franklin) The Crowell Davidson Series in American History, 1967—, Pitman Major Issues in American History Series, 1971-72; Contbr. articles to profl. jours., chpts. to books. NEH fellow, 1982-83. Mem. Orgn. Am. Historians, Am. Hist. Assn., Am. Studies Assn., Conf. Brit. Studies, Columbia U. Seminar in Am. Civilization. Home: 567 1st St Brooklyn NY 11215 Office: Dept History Bklyn Coll Bedford Ave and Ave H Brooklyn NY 11210

EISENSTAEDT, ALFRED, photojournalist; b. Dirschau, Germany, Dec. 6, 1898; came to U.S., 1935; s. Joseph and Regina (Schoen) E.; m. Alma Kathy Kaye, 1949. Grad., Hohenzollern Gymnasium, Berlin. Spl. photo reporter Pacific and Atlantic Photos, Berlin office, 1929-35; (this firm taken over with unchanged activities by A.P., 1931); staff photographer Life mag., 1936—. Author: Witness to Our Time, 1966, The Eye of Eisenstaedt, 1968, Martha's Vineyard, 1970, Witness to Nature, Wimbledon: A Celebration, People, Eisenstaedt's Album, Eisenstaedt's Guide to Photography, 1978, Eisenstaedt-Germany, 1980, Eisenstaedt-Aberdeen, 1984. Named Photographer of Year Ency. Brit. and; U. Mo., 1951; recipient Culture prize in photography German Soc. for Photography, Cologne, 1962; achievement award Photog. Soc. Am.; Lifetime Achievement in Photography award Am. Soc. Mag. Photographers, 1978. Work has covered outstanding events and persons throughout the world. A pioneer in introduction of candid camera technique into news reporting. Office: Time Inc Rockefeller Center New York NY 10020

EISENSTEIN, ELIZABETH LEWISOHN, historian, educator; b. N.Y.C., Oct. 11, 1923; d. Sam A. and Margaret V. (Seligman) Lewisohn; m. Julian Calvert Eisenstein, May 30, 1948; children: Margaret, John (dec.), Edward. A.B. (History prize; Belle Skinner fellow), Vassar Coll., 1944; M.A., Radcliffe Coll., 1947, Ph.D., 1953; Litt. D. (hon.), Mt. Holyoke Coll., 1979. From lectr. to adj. prof history Am. U., Washington, 1959-79; Alice Freeman Palmer prof. history U. Mich., Ann Arbor, 1975—; scholar-in-residence Rockefeller Found. Center, Bellagio, Italy, June 1977; mem. vis. com. dept. history Harvard U., 1975-81, vice-chmn., 1979-81; dir. Ecole des Hautes Etudes en Sciences Sociales, Paris, 1982; guest speaker, participant confs. and seminars; I. Beam vis. prof. U. Iowa, 1980; Mead-Swing lectr. Oberlin Coll., 1980; first resident cons. Center for the Book, Library of Congress, Washington, 1979; mem. Council of Scholars, 1980—. Author: The First Professional Revolutionist: F. M. Buonarroti, 1959, The Printing Press as an Agent of Change, 1979 paperback edit., 2 vols., 1980 (Phi Beta Kappa Ralph Waldo Emerson prize 1980); Editorial bd.: Jour. Modern History, 1973-76, 83—, Revs. in European History, 1973—, Jour. Library History, 1979—, Eighteenth Century Studies, 1981—; Contbr. articles to profl. jours., chpts. to books. Nat. Endowment for Humanities fellow, 1977; Guggenheim fellow, 1982; Fellow Center Advanced Studies in Behavioral Scis., 1982-83. Fellow Am. Acad. Arts and Scis., Royal Hist. Soc.; mem. Soc. French Hist. Studies (v.p. 1970, mem. program com. 1974), Am. Soc. 18th Century Studies (nominating com. 1971), Soc. 18th Century Studies (v.p. 1974-75, 75-76), Soc. 16th Century Studies, Am. Hist. Assn. (com. on coms. 1970-72, chmn. Modern European sect. 1981, council 1982—), Renaissance Soc. Am. (council 1973-76), Am. Antiquarian Soc. (exec. com., adv. bd. 1984—), Phi Beta Kappa. Office: Dept History U Mich Ann Arbor MI 48109

EISENSTEIN, IRA, rabbi; b. N.Y.C., Nov. 26, 1906; s. Isaac and Sadie (Luxenberg) E.; m. Judith Kaplan, June 10, 1934; children: Miriam Rachel, Ann Nehamah Johnson. A.B., Columbia U., 1927, Ph.D., 1941; Rabbi, Jewish Theol. Sem. Am., 1931, D.D., 1958. Exec. dir. Soc. for Advancement of Judaism, 1930-31, asst. leader, 1931-33, asso. leader, 1933-45, leader, 1945-54; rabbi Anshe Emet Synagogue, Chgo., 1954-59; asso. chmn. editorial bd. The Reconstructionist, 1935-59, editor, 1959-83; pres. Reconstructionist Rabbinical Coll., 1968-81, pres. emeritus, 1981—; vis. prof. homiletics Jewish Theol. Sem., 1951. Author: Creative Judaism, 1936, Ethics of Tolerance, 1941, Judaism Under Freedom, 1956, What We Mean by Religion, 1958; Co-editor: Guide to Jewish Ritual, 1963, The Daily Prayer Book, New Haggadah Sabbath Prayer Book, High Holiday Prayerbook; editor: Varieties of Jewish Belief, Mordecai M. Kaplan: An Evaluation. Pres. Jewish Reconstructionist Found., 1959-80, hon. pres., 1980—. Mem. Rabbinical Assembly Am. (pres. 1952-54). Home: 17 DeLisio Ln Woodstock NY 12498

EISENSTEIN, JULIAN CALVERT, educator, physicist; b. Warrenton, Mo., Apr. 3, 1921; s. Otto and Nell (Calvert) E.; m. Elizabeth Lewisohn, May 30, 1948; children—Margaret, John, Edward. B.S., Harvard, 1941, M.A., 1942, Ph.D., 1948. Instr. U. Wis., 1948-52; Nat. Research fellow Oxford, 1952-53; asst. prof., asso. prof. Pa. State U., 1953-57; physicist Nat. Bur. Standards, Washington, 1957-66; prof. George Washington U., Washington, 1966—. Contbr. articles profl. jours. Pres., trustee Washington Gallery Modern Art, 1961-65. Fellow Am. Phys. Soc.; mem. Phi Beta Kappa, Sigma Xi. Club: Cosmos (Washington). Home: 82 Kalorama Circle NW Washington DC 20008

EISENSTEIN, ROBERT ALAN, physicist, educator; b. St. Louis, July 17, 1942; s. Albert Bernard and Barbara (Oppenhaim) E.; m. Karlyn Ennis Kirby, Jan. 22, 1967; children: Daniel James, William Alan. A.B., Oberlin Coll., 1964; M.S., Yale U., Ph.D., 1968. Postdoctoral fellow Weizman Inst. Sci., Rehovot, Israel, 1968-70; prof. physics Carneigie-Mellon U., Pitts., 1970—; mem. NSF Com. for Physics, 1979-82. Researcher elementary particle and nuclear physics; contbr. articles to sci. publs. Active Am. Jewish Com. Recipient Ryan Teaching award Carnegie-Mellon U., 1979. Mem. Am. Phys. Soc., Sigma Xi. Home: 5824 Northumberland Pittsburgh PA 15213 Office: Dept Physics Carnegie-Mellon U Pittsburgh PA 15213

EISENTEIN, TOBY K., microbiology educator; b. Phila., Sept. 15, 1942; d. Edward and Sylvia (Mandel) Karet; m. Bruce A. Eisenstein, Sept. 8, 1963; children: Eric, Andrew, Ilana. B.A., Wellesley Coll., 1964; Ph.D., Bryn Mawr, 1969. Instr. Med. Sch. Temple U., Phila., 1969-71, asst. prof., 1971-79, assoc. profl. microbiology Med. Sch., 1979—; mem. bacteriology and mycology study sect. NIH, 1976-80. Contbr. articles to profl. jours. NIH fellow, 1965-69; USPHS grantee, 1971—. Mem. Am. Soc. Microbiology (pres. elect E.Pa. br.), AAAS, Reticuloendothelial Soc., Sigma Xi. Office: Dept Microbiology and Immunology Temple Univ Med Sch Philadelphia PA 19140

EISERLING, FREDERICK ALLEN, microbiologist, educator; b. San Diego, May 8, 1938; s. Allen Frederick and Nancy Lucille (Simpson) E.; m. Monica Runeling, Dec. 9, 1963 (div. 1981); children: Erik Robert, Ingrid Monica; m. Judith Ann Lengyel, Nov. 20, 1983. B.A., UCLA, 1959, Ph.D., 1964. Postdoctoral U. Geneva, 1964-66; asst. prof. UCLA, from 1966, assoc. prof., to 1981, prof., chmn. dept. microbiology, 1981—; cons. USPHS, NSF, Washington, 1968-83. Contbr. articles to sci. jours. Research grantee NIH, NSF. Mem. Am. Soc. Microbiology (chmn. 1983), Am. Soc. Virology, AAAS, Fedn. Am. Scientists. Office: UCLA Dept Microbiology Los Angeles CA 90024 *

EISLER, COLIN TOBIAS, art historian, curator; b. Hamburg, Germany, Mar. 17, 1931; came to U.S., 1940, naturalized, 1946; s. George Bernard and Kate Minden (Basseches) E.; m. Benita J. Blitzer, 1960; 1 dau., Rachel. Ed., Yale U., 1952; postgrad. (Henry fellow), Magdalen Coll., Oxford (Eng.) U., 1952-53; Ph.D., Harvard U., 1956. Instr. art Yale U., 1955-56, asst. prof., 1956-57, curator dept. print and drawings, 1955-57; fellow Saybrook Coll.; mem. faculty Harvard U., summer 1956, N.Y. U. Inst. Fine Arts, 1958-60, asst. prof., 1960-65, asso. prof., 1965-77, Robert Lehman prof. art, 1977—; research curator paintings dept. Met. Museum Art, N.Y.C., 1958-60; mem. vis. com. Smith Coll. Art Mus., Cooper Hewitt Prints and Drawings Dept.; Bd. dirs. Drawing Center, Archtl. History Found.; v.p. Am. Friends of Israel Mus.; sec. Nat. Com. History of Art; exec. mem. Comité International pour l'histoire de l'art; fellow Inst. Advanced Study, 1957-58. Author: Early Netherlandish Painting in New England Collections, 1960, The Seeing Hand, 1975, Non-Italian Paintings from the Samuel M. Kress Collection, 1976, The Master of the Unicorn, 1979, Sculptors' Drawings Over Five Centuries, 1981; Editorial bd.: Studia Neerlandica, 1976—, Jour. Jewish Art, 1979—. Vice pres. Jewish Peace Fellowship, N.Y.C; vis. com. Wellesley Coll. Art Mus., 1984. Commn. Relief Belge fellow, 1953, 55; Ford fellow, 1959; Guggenheim fellow, 1960-61; Nat. Endowment for Humanities sr. fellow, 1972-73; Am. Council Learned Socs. fellow, 1979; Delmas fellow, 1980; Kress travel grantee. Mem. Coll. Art Assn. (dir. 1958-61, editorial bd. 1978—). Clubs: Elizabethan, Century Assn. (house art com.). Office: NYU Inst Fine Arts 1 E 78th St New York NY 10021

EISLEY, JOE GRIFFIN, aerospace engineering educator; b. Wapakoneta, Ohio, Apr. 7, 1928; s. Harold Samuel and Velma (Griffin) E.; m. Marilyn Ethel Fleck, June 9, 1956; children: Paul Edward, Susan Elaine. B.S., St Louis U., 1951; M.S., Calif. Inst. Tech., 1952, Ph.D., 1956. Stress analyst N.Am. Aviation Inc., Downey, Calif., 1952, Douglas Aircraft Co., El Segundo, Calif., 1953; asst. prof. aerospace engring. U. Mich., 1956-60, assoc. prof., 1960-65, prof., 1965—, assoc. dean, 1967-81, spl. asst. to dean, 1981—, dir. Computer Aided Engring. Lab., 1980—; cons. various indsl. firms and sci. insts., Gen. Motors Corp., 1983. Author articles on flutter, vibration, nonlinear mechanics, flight mechanics, engring. edn. Served with AUS, 1946-47. NSF Sci. Faculty fellow Swiss Fed. Inst. Tech., 1962-63; recipient Alumni Merit award St. Louis U., 1970. Mem. AIAA, Am. Soc. Engring. Edn. (chmn. North Central sect. 1973), ASME, Soc. Automotive Engrs., Computer and Automated Systems Assn. of Soc. Mfg. Engrs., Sigma Xi, Tau Beta Pi. Home: 2632 Park Ridge Dr Ann Arbor MI 48103

EISNER, ELLIOT WAYNE, art educator; b. Chgo., Mar. 10, 1933; s. Louis and Eva E.; m. Eleanor Ann Rose, Jan. 6, 1957; children: Steven, Linda. B.A., Roosevelt U., 1954; M.S. in Art Edn, Ill. Inst. Tech., 1955; M.A. in Edn, U. Chgo., 1958, Ph.D., 1962. Tchr. art Carl Schurz High Sch., Chgo., 1956-58; instr. Sch. Art, Ohio State U., 1960-61; asst. prof. edn. U. Chgo., 1961-65; asso. prof. Sch. Edn. and dept. art Stanford U., 1965-70, prof., 1970—. Author: books including Educating Artistic Vision, 1972, The Educational Imagination: On the Design and Evaluation of School Programs, 1979, Cognition and Curriculum, 1982. Trustee Community Sch. Music and Art, 1976-82, Castilleja Sch., Palo Alto, Calif., 1977-78. Guggenheim fellow, 1969-70; Fulbright scholar, 1978. Mem. AAUP (pres. Stanford chpt. 1975-76), Nat. Art Edn. Assn. (pres. 1977-79), Assn. Supervision and Curriculum Devel., Am. Ednl. Research Assn. (v.p. div. B 1981-83). Home: 820 Tolman Dr Stanford CA 94305 Office: Sch Edn Stanford Univ Stanford CA 94305

EISNER, HOWARD, consulting company executive; b. N.Y.C., Aug. 8, 1935; s. Samuel and Mary (Isser) E.; m. Joan Knopfer, Feb. 9, 1957; children: Seth Eric, Susan Rachel, Oren David. B.E.E., CCNY, 1957; M.S., Columbia U., 1958; D.Sc., George Washington U., 1966. Teaching asst. Columbia U., 1957; lectr. dept. physics Bklyn. Coll., 1957-59; lectr. George Washington U., from 1961, asst. professorial lectr., until 1967; with ORI, Inc., Silver Spring, Md., 1959—, v.p., 1968-71, exec. v.p., 1971—, also dir. Contbr. articles in field. Fellow N.Y. Acad. Scis.; mem. IEEE, Ops. Research Soc. Am., Inst. Mgmt. Sci., AIAA, Tau Beta Pi, Eta Kappa Nu. Office: 1400 Spring St Silver Spring MD 20910 *

EISNER, JANET MARGARET, coll. pres.; b. Boston, Oct. 10, 1940; d. Eldon and Ada (Martin) E. A.B., Emmanuel Coll., 1963; M.A., Boston Coll., 1969; Ph.D., U. Mich., 1975. Joined Sisters of Notre Dame de Namur, Roman Catholic Ch.; asst. dir. admissions Emmanuel Coll., Boston, 1966-67, dir. admissions, 1967-71; dir. Emmanuel Coll. and City of Boston Pairings, 1976-78, asst. prof. English, 1976-78, chmn. dept., 1977-78, acting pres., 1978-79, pres., 1979—; lectr., teaching asst. U. Mich., 1971-73; mem. Mass. Bd. Regents, Mass. Bd. Regional Community Colls., until 1981. Trustee Trinity Coll. Rackham prize fellow; Ford Found. fellow. Mem. Assn. Cath. Colls. and Univs., New Eng. Enrollment Planning Council, Women's Coll. Coalition, Assn. Governing Bds., Am. Council Edn. Home: 37 Castleton St Jamaica Plain MA 02130 Office: 400 The Fenway Boston MA 02115

EISNER, MARVIN MICHAEL, distribution company executive; b. Detroit, Feb. 16, 1938; s. Harry and Gold (Linn) E.; m. Gail Leon, June 14, 1959; 1 son, Alan. B.B.S. in Acctg, Wayne State U., Detroit, 960. Controller bag div. Union Camp Corp., 1971-74; v.p., chief fin. officer Am. Optical Co., Southbridge, Mass., 1974-76; v.p. fin. consumer products group Warner-Lambert Co., Morris Plains, N.J., 1977-80; sr. v.p., chief fin. officer Home Ins. Co., N.Y.C., 1980-81; also dir.; exec. v.p. Arrow Electronic Inc., Farmingdale, N.J., 1981—; dir. Home Indemnity Co., City Ins. Co., Home Ins. Co. Ind., Home Ins. Co. Ill. Mem. Am. Mgmt. Assn., Am. Inst. C.P.A.'s. Home: 58 Hewlett Ln Port Washington NJ 11050 Office: 900 Broad Hollow Rd Farmingdale NJ 11735

EISNER, MICHAEL DAMMAN, motion picture company executive; b. N.Y.C., 1942; married. B.A., Denison U. Began career in programming dept. CBS; asst. to nat. programming dir. ABC, 1966-68, mgr. spls. and talent, dir. program devel.-East Coast, 1968-71, v.p. daytime programming, 1971-75, v.p. program planning and devel., 1975-76, sr. v.p. prime time prodn. and devel., 1976; pres., chief operating officer Paramount Pictures, 1976—. Office: Paramount Pictures 1 Gulf and Western Plaza New York NY 10023 *

EISNER, ROBERT, economics educator; b. N.Y.C., Jan. 17, 1922; s. Harry and Mary (Goldberg) E.; m. Edith Avery Chelimer, June 30, 1946; children: Mary Eisner Eccles, Emily. B.S.S., Coll. City N.Y., 1940; M.A., Columbia, 1942; Ph.D., Johns Hopkins, 1951; postgrad., U. Paris, 1945-46. Economist, statistician U.S. Govt., 1941-42, 46-47; instr. to asst. prof. econs. U. Ill., 1950-52; from asst. prof. to prof. econs. Northwestern U., 1952—, William R. Kenan prof., 1974—, chmn. econs. dept., 1964-67, 74-76; also sr. research asso. Nat. Bur. Econ. Research, 1969-78; econ. cons.; vis. distinguished prof. State U. N.Y., Binghamton, 1971; Chmn. exec. com. Conf. Research in Income and Wealth, 1967-68; mem. Conf. Bd. Econ. Forum, 1974—. Author: Factors in Business Investment. Bd. editors Am. Econ. Review, 1966-68; asso. editor: Rev. Econs. and Statistics, 1973—; Contbr. articles to profl. jours. Mem. McGovern Econ. Adv. Group, 1971-72; Trustee Roycemore Sch., 1969—. Served to capt. F.A.; Served to capt. F.A. AUS, 1942-46. Guggenheim fellow, 1960; fellow Center Advanced Study in Behavior Scis., 1968. Fellow Econometric Soc., Am. Acad. Arts and Scis.; mem. Am. Econ. Assn. (exec. com. 1971-73, v.p. 1977), Midwest Econ. Assn. (pres.-elect 1981-82, pres. 1982-83), Social Sci. Research Council (bd. dirs., exec. com. 1977-79), Phi Beta Kappa. Home: 800 Lincoln St Evanston IL 60201

EISNER, THOMAS, biologist, educator; b. Berlin, June 25, 1929; s. Hans Edouard and Margarete (Heil) E.; m. Maria Lobell, June 10, 1952; children: Yvonne, Vivian, Christina. B.A., Harvard U., 1951, Ph.D., 1955; D.Sc. hon., U. Wurzburg, W. Ger., 1982, U. Zurich, Switzerland, 1983. Postdoctoral fellow Harvard U., 1955-57; asst. prof. biology Cornell U., Ithaca, N.Y., 1957-62, assoc. prof., 1962-65, prof., 1965-76, Jacob Gould Schurman prof. biology, 1976—; vis. scientist dept. entomology Sch. Agr., Wageningen, Netherlands, 1964-65; vis. scientist Smithsonian Tropical Research Lab., Barro Colorado Island, C.Z., 1968; sr. vis. scientist Max Planck Inst. für Verhaltensphysiologie, Seewisen, W. Ger., 1971, Div. Entomology, Canberra, Australia, 1972-73; Rand fellow Marine Biol. Labs., Woods Hole, Mass., 1974; vis. research prof. U. Fla., Gainesville, 1977-78; vis. prof. Stanford U., 1979-80, U. Zurich, 1980-81. Co-author: Animal Adaptation, 1964, Life on Earth, 1973, and 3 other books.; Mem. editorial bd.: Sci, 1970-71, Am. Naturalist, 1970-71, Jour. Comparative Physiology, 1974-80, Chem. Ecology, 1974—, Cornell Rev, 1976-77, Behavioral Ecology and Sociobiology, 1976—, Sci. Yr. World Books, 1979—; contbr. articles to profl. jours. Guggenheim fellow, 1964-65, 72-73; Recipient Newcomb Cleveland prize AAAS, 1967; Founder's Meml. award Entomol. Soc. Am., 1969, Archie F. Carr medal, 1983. Fellow Explorers Club, AAAS (chmn. sect. biology 1979—, mem. com. for sci. freedom and responsibility 1980—), Am. Acad. Arts and Scis., Royal Soc. Arts; mem. Nat. Acad. Sci., Zero Population Growth (dir. 1969-70), Nat. Audubon Soc. (dir. 1970-75), Nature Conservancy (nat. council 1969-74), Fedn. Am. Scientists (mem. council 1977-81). Office: Dept Neurobiology and Behavior W347 Mudd Hall Cornell U Ithaca NY 14853 *I am a naturalist, interested primarily in field exploration and discovery. My research deals with the behavior and ecology of insects, and with the photographic and cinematographic documentation of little-known aspects of the life of these animals. My chief goal in life is to relate my findings to the cause of wildlife and wilderness preservation, to which I am fiercely devoted.*

EISNER, WILL, publishing company executive; b. N.Y.C., Mar.6, 1917; s. Samuel and Fannie (Ingber) E.; m. Ann Louise Weingarten, June 15, 1950; children: John David, Alice Carol (dec.). Student, Art Student's League, N.Y.C., 1935. Pres. Am. Visuals Corp., 1949—, N.Am. Newspaper Alliance, 1962-64, Ednl. Supplements Corp., 1965-72; exec. v.p. Koster-Dana Corp., 1962-64; chmn. bd. Croft Ednl. Services Corp., 1972—; Mem. faculty Sch. Visual Arts, N.Y.C., 1973. Author, cartoonist syndicated newspaper feature: The Spirit, 1940-52; pub.: Eisner-Arnold Comic Group, 1940-46; editor: U.S. Army Ordnance, 1942-45; (Recipient award as comic book artist of yr. Nat. Cartoonist Soc., N.Y. 1967, Best Artist award 1968-69, ann. award for quality of art in comic books Soc. Comic Art Research 1968, Internat. Cartoonist award Angouleme, France 1974); Author: America's Combat Weapons, 1960, America's Space Vehicles, 1961, Contract with God, Gleeful Guides Series, Life on Another Planet, 1982, Big City, 1983; newspaper feature Odd Facts. Bd. dirs. Westchester (N.Y.) Philharmonic. Club: Princeton (N.Y.C.). Home and office: 8333 W McNag Rd Suite 114 Tamarac FL 33321

EISWERTH, BARRY NEIL, architect, educator; b. Williamsport, Pa., Sept. 16, 1942; s. Eugene Lewis and Mary Jane (Winters) E.; m. Anne Caroline Essl, Apr. 8, 1967; children: Jason, Brendan. B.Arch., Pa. State U.-University Park, 1965. Registered architect, Pa. Assoc. H2L2 Architects/Planners, Phila., 1967-77, ptnr., 1977—; pres. H2L2 Design Co., Phila., 1980—; asst. prof. archtl. design Drexel U., 1975-81; mem. faculty, thesis advisor Phila. Coll. Art. Archtl. works include, Children's Hosp., Phila., bldgs. Phila. '76 Bicentennial, Phila. Bourse Bldg., Cypress Sq. Townhouse Complex Phila. (recipient Design award Old Phila. Devel. Corp.). Trustee curator Phila. City Inst.; trustee St. Peter's Sch., Phila. Recipient awards for archtl. designs. Mem. AIA, Pa. Soc. Architects, Nat. Acad. Design. Democrat. Roman Catholic. Club: Rittenhouse (Phila.). Home: 270 S 3d St Philadelphia PA 19106 Office: H2L2 Architects/Planners 714 Market St Philadelphia PA 19106

EISZNER, JAMES RICHARD, food products company executive; b. Chgo., Aug. 12, 1927; s. William Henry and Gertrude (Peifer) E.; m. Joyce Carolyn Holland, Oct. 14, 1950; children: James Richard, Timothy John. Student, Drake U., 1945; B.S., U. Ill., 1950; Ph.D., U. Chgo., 1952. Chemist Standard Oil Co. (Ind.), Whiting, 1952-54; market analyst Indoil Chem. Co., Chgo., 1954-57; dir. market devel. Amoco Chems. Co., Chgo., 1957-63; v.p. mktg. Ott Chem. Co., Muskegon, Mich., 1963-65, exec. v.p., 1965-66, pres., 1967-70; also dir.; sr. v.p. indsl. div. CPC Internat. Inc., Englewood Cliffs, N.J., 1970-71, pres., 1971-76, v.p. parent co., 1971-76; dir. CPC Internat., Inc., 1975—; exec. v.p., chief adminstrv. officer CPC Internat. Inc., 1977-79, pres., chief operating officer, 1979—; mem. Chgo. Bd. Trade, 1971-80. Bd. dirs. Muskegon Area Econ. Planning and Devel. Assn., 1967-70. Served with AUS, 1946-47. Mem. Comml. Devel. Assn., Corn Refiners Assn. (dir. 1971-83, chmn. bd. 1981-82). Republican. Presbyterian. Clubs: Univ., Econ., Sky (N.Y.C.); Knickerbocker Country (Tenafly, N.J.); Seaview Country (Absecon, N.J.). Home: 24 Kennedy Rd Cresskill NJ 07626 Office: CPC Internat Inc International Plaza PO Box 8000 Englewood Cliffs NJ 07632

EITEL, KARL EMIL, hotel executive; b. Chgo., Dec. 26, 1928; s. Karl F. and Suzanne (Schmidt) E.; m. Mary Ann Lease, June 16, 1951; children: Richard, Susan, Janet. Student, Trinity Coll., 1946-48; B.S., Mich. State U., 1951. Room clk. St. Anthony Hotel, San Antonio, 1951-52; with Cosmopolitan Hotel, Denver, 1952-58, exec. asst. mgr., 1954-58, Sir Francis Drake Hotel, San Francisco, 1958-61; mgr. Broadmoor Hotel, Colorado Springs, Colo., 1961-66, exec. v.p., mng. dir., 1966-81; pres., dir. Broadmoor Hotel Inc., 1981—; chmn. bd., dir. Broadmoor Mgmt. Co.; dir. First Nat. Bank Colorado Springs; dir., mem. exec. com. Affiliated Bank Shares Colo.; dir. Garden City Co., Manitou and Pikes Peak Ry. Co. Vice pres. Colo. Visitors Bur.; trustee El Pomar Found. Mem. Am. Hotel and Motel Assn. (dir.), Colo.-Wyo. Hotel and Motel Assn., Hotel Greeters Am., Colorado Springs C. of C., Hotel Sales Mgmt. Assn., Inter-Am. Hotel Assn., Nat. Assn. Travel Orgns. Clubs, U.S. Tennis Lawn Assn., Navy League U.S., Assn. U.S. Army, Colo.-Wyo. Restaurant Assn., Sigma Nu. Mem. Community Ch. Clubs: Broadmoor Golf (dir.), Broadmoor Ski, Cheyenne Mountain Country, Country of Colo., Rio Verde (Ariz.) Country. Home: 15 Thayer Rd Colorado Springs CO 80906 Office: The Broadmoor Hotel Colorado Springs CO 80906

EITEMAN, WILFORD J., economics educator, author; b. Rock Island, Ill., Feb. 13, 1902; s. Wilford Lee and Elida (Palmer) E.; m. Sylvia F. Chmelik, June 15, 1927; children: David Kurt, Dean Spencer. B.M., Chgo. Mus. Coll., 1922; A.B., Ohio Wesleyan U., 1926, M.A., 1928; Ph.D., Ohio State U., 1931. Instr. econs. Ohio Wesleyan U., 1926-28; prof. acctg. Miami-Jacobs Coll., 1928-29; asst. instr. econs. Ohio State U., 1929-31; prof. econs. Albion Coll., 1931-37; Social Science Research Council fellow, 1932-33; asst. prof. econs. Duke U., 1937-44, asso. prof., 1945-46; asso. prof. finance Sch. Bus. Adminstrn., Rutgers U., 1946-47; prof. finance U. Mich., 1947—; vis. prof. econs. U. Ceylon, 1954-55; economist zinc, tin and lead div. OPA, 1942, territorial price exec., Alaska, 1942-1943; instr. Army Univ. Center, Biarritz, France, 1945-46; ednl. adviser European Productive Agy., Paris, 1959-60; Carnegie vis. prof. finance U. Hawaii, 1964; vis. prof. finance U. Fla., 1968, Ariz. State U., 1970; staff mem. Twentieth Century Fund Inc., stock market investigation, 1933-34; chmn. econs. sect. Mich. Acad. Arts, Scis. and Letters, 1937-38; mem. State Mich. Pension Com., 1969-74. Co-author: Stock Market Control, 1934, The Security Markets, 1935; author: Corporation Finance, 1948, Price Determination, Theory and Practice, 1949, Graphic Budgets, 1949, (with Frank Smith) Investment Advice for Professional Men, 1951, (with others) Essays in Business Finance, 1951, (with C. S. Davidson) The Lease, 1951, Personal Finance and Investment, 1952, Business Forecasting, 1954, Essentials of Accounting Theory, 1961, Price Determination by Oligopolists, 1961, (with D.S. Eiteman) Common Stock Values and Yields, 1962, (with D.K. Eiteman) The Stock Market, 4th edit., 1966, World Leading Stock Exchanges, 1966, Perfect Competition vs. Competitive Activity, 1966, (with S.C. Eiteman) Nine Leading Stock Exchanges, 1968, Causes and Cures of Depression, 1970; contbr. articles to profl. jours. Mem. Am. Econ. Assn., Delta Sigma Pi, Beta Gamma Sigma, Phi Mu Alpha, Delta Sigma Phi. Home: 8400 Vamo Rd Sarasota FL 33581 Office: Sch Bus U Mich Ann Arbor MI 48105 *In my youth I decided that the welfare of society would advance fastest if everyone would draw conclusions by the application of strictly logical reasoning to carefully observed facts entirely divorced from pre-conceived ideas stemming from tradition or fractional experience. I have tried to keep my writing and teaching consistent with this principle. I have also aimed to make complex things simple rather simple things complex.*

EITZEN, DAVID STANLEY, sociologist, educator; b. Glendale, Calif., Aug. 4, 1934; s. David Donald and Amanda Emma (Heidebrecht) E.; m. Florine Kay Voran, May 29, 1956; children: Keith, Michael, Kelly. A.B. in History, Bethel Coll., 1956; M.S., Emporia State U., 1962; M.A. in Sociology, U. Kans., 1966, Ph.D., 1968. Recreational therapist Menninger Found., Topeka, Kans., 1956-58; tchr. Galva (Kans.) High Sch., 1958-60, Turner (Kans.) High Sch., 1960-65; asst. prof. sociology U. Kans., 1968-72, asso. prof., 1972-74; prof. sociology Colo. State U., Ft. Collins, 1974—. Author: Social Structure and Social Problems, 1974, Sociology of American Sport, 1978, In Conflict and Order: Understanding Society, 1978, Sport in Contemporary Society, 1979, Social Problems, 1980, Elite Deviance, 1981; Editor: Social Sci. Jour, 1978—; Contbr. articles to profl. jours. NDEA fellow, 1965-67. Mem. Internat. Sociol. Assn., Am. Sociol. Assn., Midwest Sociol. Soc., Soc. Study Social Problems, Western Social Sci. Assn., Southwestern Social Sci. Assn., Internat. Com. for Sociology Sport., N.Am. Soc. for Sociology Sport. Democrat. Mennonite. Home: 1756 Concord Dr Fort Collins CO 80526 Office: Dept Sociology Colo State U Fort Collins CO 80523

EIZENSTAT, STUART E., lawyer, former White House staff mem.; b. Chgo., Jan. 15, 1943; m. Fran; children—Jay, Brian. A.B. cum laude, U. N.C., 1964; LL.B., Harvard U., 1967. Bar: Ga. 1967, D.C. 1981. Mem. White House staff, 1967-68; mem. nat. campaign staff Hubert H. Humphrey, 1968; law clk. U.S. Dist. Ct. No. Dist. Ga., 1968-70; partner firm Powell, Goldstein, Frazer & Murphy, Washington, 1970-77, 81—; adj. lectr. John F. Kennedy Sch. Govt., Harvard U., 1981—; asst. to Pres. U.S. for domestic affairs and policy, 77-81, dir. Domestic Policy Staff, 1977-81; mem. Energy Coordinating Council, Econ. Policy Group, 1977-81; dir. Hercules, Inc. Contbr. articles to profl. jours. Vice-pres. Jewish Publ. Soc., 1981—; chmn. Inst. U.S. Jewish-Israeli Relations; Bd. dirs. Woodrow Wilson Center for Internat. Scholars, 1978—, Nat. Jewish Conf. Center, 1981—, Washington Jewish Community Center, 1981—; mem. exec. com. Center for Dem. Policy. Mem. Am., Atlanta, D.C. bar assns., Am. Judicature Soc., Phi Beta Kappa, Phi Eta Sigma. Democrat. Jewish. Office: 1110 Vermont Ave NW Washington DC 20005

EKAIREB, HUSKEL, pharmaceutical company executive; b. Penang, Malaya, Jan. 14, 1917; s. Raymond and Rose (Ellis) E.; m. Hannah, Apr. 7, 1946; children: Jason, Louis. With Sterling Products Internat., Inc., 1940-48, Merck N.Am., 1948-54, regional sales dir. Far East, 1952-53; with Merck Sharp & Dohme Internat., Rahway, N.J., 1954—, sr. v.p. internat. div., 1967-68, exec. v.p., 1969-70, pres. internat. div., 1970-74, sr. v.p. Merck, pres. MSDI, 1975-76, exec. v.p. Merck, pres. MSDI, 1977, exec. v.p. Merck, 1977—, also dir. Mem. Far East Am. Council, Internat. Council Conf. Bd., Asia Soc., Nat. Fgn. Trade Council. Home: 983 Park Ave New York NY 10028 Office: 126 E Rahway NJ 07065

EKBERG, CARL EDWIN, JR., civil engineering educator; b. Mpls., Oct. 28, 1920; s. Carl Edwin and Ruth Elizabeth (Olin) E.; m. Dorothy Heley, May 25, 1944; children: Carl Edwin III, Gretchen Heley, Janet Heley, Thomas William. B. Civil Engring, U. Minn., 1943; M.S., 1947, Ph.D., 1954. Registered civil and structural engr., Minn., Iowa. Instr. math. and mechanics U. Minn., 1946-51; structural engr. M., St. P. & S.Ste.M. R.R., summers, 1948-51; asst. prof. civil engring. N.D. State U., 1951-53; asst. prof., asso. prof. civil engring. Lehigh U., 1953-59; prof. civil engring., head dept. Iowa State U., 1959—; Dir. Univ. Bank & Trust Co., Ames. Author articles in field. Served as lt. (j.g.) USNR, 1943-46. Fellow ASCE, Am. Concrete Inst.; mem. Nat. Soc. Profl. Engrs., Iowa Engring. Soc., Am. Soc. Engring. Edn., Am. Ry. Engring. Assn., Sigma Xi, Tau Beta Pi, Chi Epsilon, Phi Kappa Phi. Club: Rotarian. Home: 420 E 20th St Ames IA 50010

EKEBLAD, FREDERICK ALFRED, management consultant; b. Providence, Sept. 6, 1917; s. Carl Alfred and Eva (MacCrea) E.; m. Dorothy L. Sebbens, June 9, 1942; children—Steven Frederick, Russell Alfred, Louise Elizabeth. A.B., Brown U., 1938, M.A., 1941; Ph.D., Northwestern U., 1947. Sales research L. Bamberger & Co., 1938-39; faculty Northwestern U., 1941-66, prof. bus. statistics, 1962-66, chmn. dept., 1958-66; dean Coll. Bus. Adminstrn., U. Bridgeport, Conn., 1966-73, William Benton prof. mgmt. scis., 1973-77, cons., 1977—; Mem. Full Employment Com., Chgo., 1963-65. Author: The Statistical Method in Business, 1962. Counselor Evanston YMCA, 1957-59; coach Evanston Little League, 1957-58. Mem. Am. Statis. Assn. (editorial collaborator 1956, v.p. Chgo. chpt. 1961-65, pres. 1965-66), Am. Econ. Assn. (chmn. election com. 1964), Acad. Mgmt., Bridgeport Area C. of C. (v.p., dir. 1972-73), Phi Beta Kappa, Beta Gamma Sigma. Club: Black Hall. Home: 13 Point Rd Niantic CT 06357

EKEBLAD, RAYMOND EDWIN, manufacturing company executive; b. Providence, Aug. 18, 1921; s. Jennings Edwin and Ethelda Louise (Mack) E.; m. Elena A. Betancourt, Apr. 18, 1953; children: Eric, Diane. Student, Lehigh U., 1939-40; B.S., NYU, 1949, M.B.A., 1951. With Western Electric Co. and subs. (now AT&T Techs., Inc.), 1940—; asst. sec. Western Electric Co. and subs., 1977-81, asst. treas. parent co., 1969-77, sec., 1977—, treas., 1981—; treas. subs. Nassau Recycle Corp., Tottenville, S.I., N.Y., 1969-77; asst. sec. Teletype Corp., 1977-1981. Bd. dirs. Jr. Achievement Kansas City, 1962-64; bd. dirs., pres. Nassau Suffolk chpt. Am. Lung Assn., Counseling Service of L.I. Council Chs.; v.p. L.I. Council Chs.; bd. pensions United Presbyn. Ch. U.S.A. Served to capt. AUS, 1943-46. Mem. Telephone Pioneers Am. (pres. Thayer chpt.). Presbyn. (elder). Clubs: Nassau Country.; Plantation Golf and Country (Venice, Fla.). Home: 19 Edwards Ln Glen Cove NY 11542 Office: 222 Broadway New York NY 10038

EKELUND, JOHN JOSEPH, naval officer; b. Washington, Jan. 19, 1928; s. Kenneth Oscar and Marjorie (Buscher) E.; m. Lynn Marie Schumacher, May 3, 1952; children—John Joseph, Christopher P., Terri L., Peter L., Tracy A., Patricia M., C. Kent. B.S., U.S. Naval Acad., 1949; M.S. in Systems Analysis, U. Rochester, N.Y., 1969. Commd. ensign U.S. Navy, 1949, advanced through grades to rear adm., 1976; service in, Korea and Vietnam; chief staff Naval Forces, Vietnam, 1972-73; comdr. guided missile cruiser U.S.S. Albany, 1973-75; dean Naval War Coll., 1975-76; dep. dir. naval edn. and tng. Office Chief Naval Ops., Washington, 1976-77; nat. intelligence officer CIA, 1977-78; comdr. U.S. South Atlantic Force, 1978-80; supt. Naval Postgrad. Sch., Monterey, Calif., 1980—. Decorated Legion of Merit, Meritorious Service medal, Joint Commendation medal. Mem. U.S. Naval Acad. Alumni Assn., U.S. Naval Inst. Devel. math. treatment of modern submarine torpedo fire control, 1956. Home: Quarters A Naval Postgrad Sch Monterey CA 93940 Office: california maritime academy p o box 1372 vallejo CA 94590

EKIRCH, ARTHUR ALPHONSE, JR., historian, educator; b. N.Y.C., Dec. 15, 1915; s. Arthur Alphonse and Louise Elizabeth (Borgstede) E.; m. Dorothy Gustafson, Aug. 24, 1940; children: Cheryl Nancy, Caryl Jocelyn, Arthur Roger. B.A., Dartmouth Coll., 1937; M.A., Columbia U., 1938, Ph.D., 1943. Instr. history Conn. Coll., 1942, Bklyn. Coll., 1942-43, Hofstra U., 1946-47; asst. prof. to prof. Am. U., 1947-65; prof. history SUNY, Albany, 1965—. Author: Decline of American Liberalism, 1955, Civilian and the Military, 1956, Progressivism in America, 1974, others. Guggenheim fellow; Volker Fund fellow. Mem. Am. Hist. Assn., Orgn. Am. Historians, Phi Beta Kappa. Home: 24 Tierney Dr Delmar NY 12054 Office: Dept History SUNY-Albany 1400 Washington Ave Albany NY 12222

EKLUND, DONALD ARTHUR, trade assn. exec.; b. Galesburg, Ill., Oct. 31, 1929; s. Carl Arthur and Oral Fern (McCann) E.; m. Gloria May Peterzen, Apr. 6, 1952; children—Michael Lee, Julie Anne, David Alan, Barbara Lynne. B.S., Ill. State U., 1955, M.S., 1959. Tchr. high sch., Manito, Ill., 1955-57, Knoxville, Ill., 1957-58, Princeton, Ill., 1958-65; with Litton Ednl. Publishing, Inc., N.Y.C., 1965-79; nat. sales mgr. McCormick-Mathers Div., 1969-71, v.p., 1971-72, exec. v.p., 1972-74, pres., 1974-78, Am. Book Co. div., 1975-78, v.p., dir. corp. devel. parent co., 1978-79; pres. Eklund Assos., 1979-81; v.p. Assn. Am. Publishers, N.Y.C., 1981—. Served with U.S. Marine Corps, 1951-53. Mem. Assn. Am. Publishers, Profl. Bookmen Am. Republican. Lutheran. Club: Ramsey Golf and Country. Home: 191 Nottingham Rd Ramsey NJ 07446 One Park Ave New York NY 10016

EKLUND, GORDON STEWART, writer; b. Seattle, July 24, 1945; s. Alfred James and DeLois (Stewart) E.; m. Dianna Jean Mylarski, Mar. 12, 1969; 1 son, Jeremy Clark. Student, Contra Costa Coll., 1973-75. Free-lance writer, El Cerrito, Calif., 1969—; novels include: The Eclipse of Dawn, 1971, Beyond the Resurrection, 1973, All Times Possible, 1974, The Grayspace Beast, 1976, If the Stars Are Gods, 1977; contbr. short stories to Analog, Fantasy and Sci. Fiction and Galaxy mags. Served with USAF, 1963-67. Mem. Sci. Fiction Writers Am. (Nebula award 1975). Home: 6305 East D St Tacoma WA 98403

EKMAN, ANDERS LUNDIN, banker; b. Tampa, Fla., Nov. 14, 1919; s. P. G. and Olga C. (Lundin) E.; m. Winifred E. Parham, Oct. 6, 1951; 1 dau., Holly Ekman Holt. Student public schs. With Holtsinger Motor Co., 1936-64, gen. mgr., to 1964; with First Nat. Bank of Fla./First Fla. Banks, Inc., Tampa, 1965-80; exec. v.p. First Fla. Banks, Inc.; former pres., former vice chmn., now chmn. First Nat. Bank of Fla.; also dir.; chmn. Lee County Bank, Ft. Myers, Fla.; dir. Nat. Bank of Collier County, Marco Island, Fla., Inter City Nat. Bank, Bradenton, Fla., First Nat. Bank, Plant City, Fla., Lakeland, Fla., First Am. Bank, Pensacola, Fla. Served to capt. USAAF, 1941-45. Decorated D.F.C., Bronze Star, Air medal with 3 oak leaf clusters, Naval Commendation plaque; recipient numerous citations and mgmt. awards. Mem. Fla. Assn. Registered Bank Holding Cos., Tampa Exec. Club (pres.), Greater Tampa C. of C. Methodist. Clubs: Tampa Yacht and, Country, Tower (Tampa). Office: PO Box 1810 Tampa FL 33601 *

EKSTROM, NORRIS KENNETH, machinery company executive; b. Kiron, Iowa, Nov. 4, 1927; s. John Edwin and Anna Catherine (Ogren) E.; m. Genevieve Lydia Schwartz, May 25, 1963. B.A., Gustavus Adolphus Coll., St. Peter, Minn., 1949; C.P.A., Northwestern U., Chgo., 1958; postgrad., U. Chgo., 1958-59. Accountant, internal auditor, plant controller Link-Belt Co., Chgo., 1949-61; asst. to v.p., controller Bucyrus-Erie Co., South Milwaukee, Wis., 1961, plant mgr., Erie, Pa., 1961-62, controller, South Milwaukee, 1962-66, v.p., controller, 1966-68, v.p. fin., treas., controller, dir., 1968-75, v.p. fin., treas., dir., 1975-78, chmn., dir., chief exec. officer, 1978—; chmn. bd., pres., dir. Bucyrus Disc, Inc.; chmn. bd., dir. Bucyrus-Erie Co. of Can., Ltd., Bucyrus (Africa) Proprietary, Ltd., Bucyrus (Australia) Proprietary, Ltd., Brad Foote Gear Works, Inc., Pitts. Gear Co., Bucyrus Internat., Inc.; pres., dir. Bucyrus-Erie Found.; dir. Ruston-Bucyrus, Lincoln, Eng., W.H. Brady Co., Milw. Mem. Greater Milw. Com. on Community Devel.; mem. adv. council U. Wis. Sch. Bus. Adminstrn., Milw. Recipient Disting. Alumni citation Gustavus Adolphus Coll., 1978. Clubs: Milwaukee, Milw. Country, University (Milw.); Knollwood Country (Lake Forest, Ill.); University (N.Y.C.); Bent Pine (Vero Beach, Fla.). Office: Bucyrus-Erie Co 1100 Milwaukee Ave South Milwaukee WI 53172

EKSTROM, WILLIAM FERDINAND, college administrator; b. Rockford, Ill., June 14, 1912; s. Anton Ivar and Mabel Elizabeth (Mattoon) E. B.A., U. Ill., 1935, M.A., 1936, Ph.D., 1947. Indsl. adminstr. Harvard, 1943; Instr. English, U. Ill., 1946-47; asst. prof. English U. Louisville, 1947-51, assoc. prof. English, 1951-56, head dept., 1955-67, prof. English, 1956-82, v.p. acad. affairs, 1967-72, acting pres., 1972-73, 80-81, exec. v.p., 1973-80, 81-82, exec. v.p., prof. emeritus, 1982—; cons. U. Louisville, Bellarmine Coll., 1982—; Mem. curriculum study com. Commonwealth of Ky. Pub. Edn. Comm., 1961. Author: Toward Better English, 1940, Guide to Composition, 1953. Bd. dirs. Louisville Presbyn., Sem., Met. Louisville YMCA; chmn. bd. dirs. Kentuckiana Metroversity, 1978—. Served with USAAF, 1943-45; instr. Chinese Air Force. Mem. AAUP (pres. Ky. conf. 1955-56), Ky. Council Tchrs. English, Arts in Louisville Assn., Modern Lang. Assn., Coll. English Assn., Nat. Council Tchrs. English, Am. Studies Assn. (pres. Ky.-Tenn. 1961-62), Modern Humanities Research Assn., English-Speaking Union, Newcomen Soc., Phi Beta Kappa, Phi Kappa Phi, Lambda Chi Alpha. Presbyn. Club: Jefferson. Home: 1611-3F Spring Dr Louisville KY 40205

ELAM, ALBERT RICHARD, JR., media educator, broadcaster, publisher; b. Pecos, Tex., Oct. 11, 1928; s. Albert Richard and Lena (Young) E.; m. Maxine Smith, June 1950 (dec. 1973); children: Sheryl, Cynthia, Michaella, Kelson; m. Margaret Abel, June 4, 1977. A.B., U. Tex.-Austin, 1950; M.A., U. Tex.-Austin, 1968; Ph.D., U. N.C., 1972. Reporter Abilen (Tex.) Reporter-News, 1950-52; v.p. Elam Trucking, Abilene, 1952-60, Elam Drilling Mud, 1952-60; pres./owner KPAR-TV, Abilene-Sweetwater, 1960-66; dir. England Transfer & Storage, Abilene, 1958—, Sta. KXGC-FM/El Campo, Tex., 1968—, Sta. KULP-AM, El Campo, 1968—, El Campo Leader-News, 1968—, Whatron (Tex.) Jour., 1976—; prof. radio, TV and motion pictures U. N.C., Chaepl Hill, 1977—. Active Chisholm Trail council Boy Scouts Am., Abilene, 1966; coordinator Tower for Senate relection, Austin, 1966. Served to lt. comdr. USNR, 1964-73. Recipient Silver Beaver award Boy Scouts Am., 1966. Mem. Nat. Broadcast Editorial Assn. (assoc. dir.), Radio and TV News Dirs., Sigma Delta Chi. Home: 916

Kings Hill Rd Chapel Hill NC 27514 Office: 204A Swain Hall Univ NC Chapel Hill NC 28514

ELAM, HARPER JOHNSTON, III, textile company executive, lawyer; b. Greensboro, N.C., Sept. 30, 1926; s. Harper Johnston and Elizabeth (Martin) E.; m. Mary Carolyn Glendinning, Aug. 30, 1947; children: George Martin, John Claibourne, Erin Patricia. B.S. in Commerce, U. N.C., 1950, J.D., 1952; grad. exec. program., Grad. Sch. Bus. Adminstrn., U. Va., 1967. Bar: N.C. 1952, U.S. Supreme Ct. 1957. Asst. prof. pub. law and govt. U. N.C., Chapel Hill, 1952-54; asst. to city atty., Greensboro, 1954-57, city atty., 1957-61; corp. counsel, asst. sec. Cone Mills Corp., Greensboro, 1961-68, gen. counsel, 1968—, v.p., 1980—; dir. First Peoples Savs. and Loan Assn.; lectr. Inst. Govt., U. N.C., 1954—; mem. U. N.C. Law Found. Council, 1961—, Greensboro City Council, 1965-73, mayor pro-tem, 1967-69, 71-73, mayor, 1969-71. Bd. dirs. Better Bus. Bur. Central N.C.; pres. sponsor trustees U. Va. Grad. Sch. Bus.; chmn. Process Gas Consumers Group. Served with USNR, 1944-46; Served with USNR, PTO; now comdr. Res. ret. Recipient Bancroft-Whitney award in constl. law U. N.C. Law Sch., 1952. Mem. U. N.C. Law Alumni Assn. (past pres.), Am. Mgmt. Assn. (seminar chmn. 1962—), Nat. Inst. Mcpl. Law Officers (past treas.), Am., N.C. bar assns., Lawyers Assn. Textile Industry (past pres.), N.C. League Municipalities (past pres.), Textile Lawyers Assn. (past pres., bd. govs.), Internat. Fedn. Indsl. Energy Consumers (U.S. dir. 1982—), Greensboro C. of C. (dir.), Phi Delta Theta, Phi Delta Phi. Presbyterian (deacon). Clubs: Masons, Greensboro Country, Greensboro City, Odd Fellows; Farmington Country (Charlottesville, Va.); Capital City (Raleigh, N.C.). Home: 110 S Park Dr Greensboro NC 27401 Office: 1201 Maple St Greensboro NC 27405 *I believe in: individual responsibility for one's thoughts and deeds, and for living by a moral code; devotion to one's spouse and children; dedication to a productive career; service to one's community.*

ELAM, JACK, actor; b. Miami, Ariz., Nov. 13, 1916; m. Margaret, 1961; 3 children. Attended jr. colls. in, Modesto, Calif. Worked as bookkeeper, acct., ind. auditor, until 1947; including work as controller for Hopalong Cassidy movies. Movie debut in The Sundowners, 1950; subsequently appeared in numerous movies, including Vera Cruz, Gunfight at the OK Corral, The Comancheros, Firecreek, Once Upon a Time in the West, Support Your Local Sheriff, Rio Lobo, Support Your Local Gunfighter, Rawhide, The Villain, Baby Face Nelson, Hannie Calder, Grayeagle, Hot Lead and Cold Feet, The Norsemen, The Apple Dumpling Gang Rides Again; appeared on TV series The Dakotas, 1963, Temple Houston, 1963-64, The Texas Wheelers, 1974-75, Struck By Lightning, 1979, The Villain, 1979; other TV appearances include Lacy and the Mississippi Queen, Gunsmoke, Huckleberry Finn, How the West Was Won, Black Beauty, The Ransom of Red Chief, The Daughters of Joshua Cabe. Served with USN, World War II. Office: care Contemporary-Korman Artists Ltd Comtemporary Artists Bldg 132 Lasky Dr Beverly Hills CA 90212 *

ELAM, JAMES O., physician; b. Austin, Tex., May 31, 1918; s. William Nile and Hallie Mae (Hedgpeth) E.; m. Elinor Mae Foster, Oct. 20, 1946; children: Michael, JoAnne, Peter, Susan, David. A.B., U. Tex., 1942; M.D., John Hopkins, 1945; postgrad., U. Minn., 1946-47, Washington U., St. Louis, 1947-48, State U. Iowa, 1949-51. Diplomate: Am. Bd. Anesthesiology. Intern Bethesda (Md.) Naval Hosp., 1945-46, Barnes Hosp., St. Louis, 1947-48; resident anesthesiology State U. Iowa, 1949-51; asst. prof. anesthesia Washington U. Sch. Medicine, 1951-53; dir. dept. anesthesia Roswell Park Meml. Inst., Buffalo, 1953-63; prof., chmn. dept. anesthesiology U. Mo., Kansas City, 1964-66; prof. anesthesiology, U. Chgo., 1966-81; clin. prof. anesthesiology Southwestern Med. Sch., U. Tex., Dallas, 1981—; contractor, cons. U.S. Army Office Surgeon Gen., 1954-70. Author: (with J.R. Jude) Fundamentals of Cardiopulmonary Resuscitation, 1965; asso. editor: Advances in Cardiopulmonary Resuscitation, 1977. Served to maj., M.C. AUS, 1953-55. Recipient Albion O. Berstein award N.Y. State Med. Soc., 1962. Fellow Am. Coll. Anesthesiologists, A.M.A., Ill. State Med. Soc., Tex. Soc. Anesthesiologists. Research in resuscitation and anesthesia. Home: 1822 Canelo St Dallas TX 75232

ELAM, LESLIE ALBERT, assn. exec.; b. Balt., May 12, 1938; s. Albert and Mary (Walker) E.; m. Judith Anne Clark, Apr. 4, 1964; children—Jennifer Helen, Jeffrey Walker. B.A., Lehman Coll., City U. N.Y., 1973. Editor J.J. Augustin, Inc. Pub., Locust Valley, N.Y., 1958-61; editorial asst. Am. Numis. Soc., N.Y.C., 1963-66, editor, 1966—, adminstrv. officer, 1966-69, sec., 1969—, dir., 1972—. Editor: Am. Numis. Soc. Museum Notes, 1966—. Served with; AUS, 1961-63. Mem. Phi Beta Kappa. Home: Old Post Rd Route 35 South Salem NY 10590 Office: Broadway at 155th St New York NY 10032

ELAM, LLOYD CHARLES, college chancellor, physician; b. Little Rock, Oct. 27, 1928; s. Harry and Ruth (Davis) E.; m. Clara Carpenter, Feb. 16, 1957; children: Gloria, Laurie. B.S., Roosevelt U., 1950; M.D. U. Wash. 1957. Intern U. Ill. Hosp., 1957-58; resident in psychiatry U. Chgo. Hosp., 1957-61; instr. psychiatry U. Chgo., 1961; instr. psychiatry, staff psychiatrist Billings Hosp., Chgo., 1961; mem. staff dept. psychiatry George W. Hubbard Hosp., Nashville, 1961; asst. prof. psychiatry Meharry Med. Coll., Nashville, 1961-63, prof., 1963-68, chmn. dept. psychiatry, 1961-66, interim dean Med. Sch., 1966-68, pres., 1968-81, chancellor, 1981—; dir. Kraft Inc., Glenview, Ill., Merck & Co., Rahway, N.J. Contbr. articles to profl. jours. Mem. nat. adv. council John F. Kennedy Center for Research on Edn. and Human Devel., Peabody Coll.; mem. council Nashville U. Center; mem. nat. adv. council Children's Television Workshop, 1971; mem. nat. adv. council mental health NIMH; vice chmn. Tenn. Health Planning Council, 1973; Trustee Fisk U.; bd. dirs. Communiversity, Nashville Pub. Television Council, Mass. Gen. Hosp., Alfred P. Sloan Found. Served with AUS, 1950-52. Recipient Eleanor Roosevelt Key Roosevelt U., 1972; Bus. and Profl. Leader of Yr. award Religious Heritage of Am., 1974. Fellow Am. Psychiat. Assn. (mem. profl. standards com. Tenn. br.); mem. A.M.A., Nat. Med. Assn., Pan Am. Med. Assn., Tenn. Med. Assn., Nashville Acad. Medicine, Vol. State Med. Assn., R.F. Boyd Med. Soc., Am. Coll. Psychiatrists, Inst. Medicine, Nashville Area C. of C. (chmn. health com. 1972-74), Frontiers of Am. Internat., Group for Advancement of Psychiatry, Nashville Mental Health Assn. (dir. 1963-66), Tenn. Council Pvt. Colls. (mem. exec. com. 1973-74), Alpha Omega Alpha, Omega Psi Chi. Office: Office of Chancellor Meharry Med Coll 1005 18th Ave N Nashville TN 37208 *

ELBAUM, MELVIN, advertising agency executive; b. N.Y.C., May 9, 1934; s. Herman and Rose L. (Cohen) E.; m. Linda Susan Mufson, May 26, 1963; 1 son, Laurence Bradford. B.B.A., Baruch Sch. Bus. and Public Adminstrn., 1956. Product mgr. Lever Bros., 1960-63, Armour Dial Co., 1963-65; account exec. Ted Bates & Co., N.Y.C., 1965-66, account supr., 1966-67, account dir., 1968-72, exec. v.p. client services, 1977—. Bd. dirs. Goodwill Industries of Am., Inc., 1982—. Served with U.S. Navy, 1956-60. Office: Ted Bates & Co Inc 1515 Broadway New York NY 10036

EL-BAZ, FAROUK, corporate executive; b. Zagazig, Egypt, Jan. 2, 1938; came to U.S., 1960, naturalized, 1970; s. El-Sayed Mohammed and Zahia Abul-Ata (Hammouda) El-B.; m. Catherine Patricia O'Leary, 1963; children—Monira, Soraya, Karima, Fairouz. B.Sc., Ain Shams U., 1958; M.S., U. Mo., 1961; Ph.D., U. Mo. and Mass. Inst. Tech., 1964. Demonstrator geology dept. Assiut U., Egypt, 1958-60; lectr. Mineralogy-Petrography Inst., U. Heidelberg, Ger., 1964-65; geologist exploration dept. Pan Am.-UAR Oil Co., Egypt, 1966; supr. lunar exploration Bellcomm and Bell Telephone Labs., Washington, 1967-72; research dir. Center for Earth and Planetary Studies, Nat. Air and Space Mus., Smithsonian Instn., Washington, 1973-82; v.p. internat. devel. Itek Optical Systems, Litton Industries, Lexington, Mass., 1982—; cons. geology; prof. geology and geophysics U. Utah, 1975-77; prof. geology Ain Shams U., Egypt, 1976-81; sci. adviser Pres. Anwar Sadat of Egypt, 1978—. Author or co-author: Say It in Arabic, 1968, Coprolites: An Annotated Bibliography, 1968, Glossory of Mining Geology, 1970, The Moon as Viewed by Lunar Orbiter, 1970, Astronaut Observations from the Apollo-Soyuz Mission, 1977, Apollo Over the Moon: A View from Orbit, 1978, Egypt As Seen by Landsat, 1979, Apollo-Soyuz Test Project Summary Science Report: Earth Observations and Photography, 1979; Author: Desert Landforms of Southwest Egypt: A basis for Comparison with Mars, 1982; Author or co-author also articles. Decorated Order of Merit 1st class, Egypt; recipient certificate merit U.S. Bur. Mines, 1961, Exceptional Sci. Achievement medal NASA, 1971, Alumni Achievement award U. Mo., 1972, Honor citation Assn. Arab-Am. U. Grads., 1973. Fellow Royal Astron. Soc., Geol. Soc. Am. (certificate commendation 1973); mem. AAAS, Sigma Xi. Clubs: Explorers., University. Office: Itek Optical Systems 10 Maquire Rd Lexington MA 02173

ELBERG, DARRYL GERALD, publisher, educator; b. N.Y.C., July 21, 1944; s. Irving and Pearl (Bernstein) E.; m. Judith Oliff, May 28, 1967; children: Meredith Fahn, Shana Alyse. B.A., CCNY, 1967. Tchr. N.Y.C. Bd. Edn., 1967—; also pres., exec. editor For Srs. Only Mag., Sr. Publs., Ltd., N.Y.C., 1969—; pres., exec. editor For Grads Only. Ford Found. grantee, 1969. Mem. Fraternity of Emile. Democrat. Jewish. Home: 6 Meadow Ln New City NY 10956

ELBERG, SANFORD SAMUEL, university administrator; b. San Francisco, Dec. 1, 1913; s. Solomon and Elizabeth (Levene) E.; m. Sylvia Marans, July 11, 1943; children: Cassandra, Graeme. A.B., U. Calif., 1934, Ph.D., 1938; L.H.D. (hon.), Hebrew Union Coll., 1967. Instr. Wash. State Coll., also San Francisco City Coll., 1940-41; instr. U. Calif., 1941-46, asst. prof. bacteriology, 1946-47, assoc. prof., 1947-52, prof., 1952—, prof. med. microbiology and immunology, 1966-78, vice chmn. dept., 1949-52, chmn. dept. bacteriology, 1952-57, dean grad. div., 1961-78, prof. emeritus, dean emeritus, 1978—, acting provost Profl. Schs. and Colls., 1984; dir. U. Calif. Study Ctr., London; assoc. dir. Edn. Abroad Program U. Calif., 1982-83; acting dir. Naval Biol. Lab., 1956-57; John Simon Guggenheim fellow, 1957-58; with WHO and Guggenheim Found., Spain, 1957; cons. chief Office Naval Research, 1950-55; chmn. bd. Grad. Record Exam., 1975-76; mem. adv. panel Naval Biol. Lab., 1952-69; cons. Naval Radiol. Def. Lab., 1951-57; mem. expert panel brucellosis WHO-FAO, UN; mem. Armed Forces Epidemiology Bd., Commn. Radiation, Infection, 1965-70; F.G. Novy lectr. U. Mich., 1964; mem. adv. com. Pan Am. Zoonosis Center, Argentina, 1970-78; mem. com. animal health NRC-Nat. Acad. Sci., 1977—. Author papers on immunology, infectious diseases, cellular immunity. Served from 1st lt. to major AUS, 1942-46. Fellow AAAS, Am. Acad. Microbiology, Am. Assn. Immunologists, Soc. Am. Bacteriologists, Western Assn. Grad. Schs. (v.p. 1972-73), pres. (1973-74), Assn. Grad. Schs. (pres. 1965-66), Council Grad. Schs. U.S.A. (chmn. 1976), Am. Council Edn., Sigma Xi, Phi Beta Kappa, Delta Omega, Phi Sigma. Club: Cosmos (Washington). Home: 1066 Park Hills Rd Berkeley CA 94708

ELBERSON, ELWOOD L., food company executive; b. Ft. Wayne, Ind., May 30, 1918; s. Carl L. and Selma (Strasser) E.; m. Jean D. Pressler, Apr. 28, 1938; children: Tom L., Terry S., Karen Elberson Tubbs, Carol Elberson Sutherland, Michael D., Mary J. Elberson Hetz. Student, Ind. U. Extension Sch., 1936-40. Mem. sales staff Kuhner Packing Co., Ft. Wayne, 1936-43; mem. gen. acctg. dept. Gen. Electric Co., Ft. Wayne, 1943-44; sec.-treas. Dinner Bell Foods Inc., Defiance, Ohio, 1944-60, exec. v.p., 1960-68, pres., 1968—, chief exec. officer, 1968—, also chmn., dir.; dir. Browns Baker, State Bank & Trust Co., Toledo Edison Co., Bettcher Industries. Councilman City of Defiance, 1954-56; trustee Defiance Coll.; pres. bd. dirs. United Fund; bd. dirs. Defiance Hosp.; chmn. bd. 4 County Tech. Sch., Ohio. Mem. Am. Meat Inst. (bd. dirs. 1964—), Defiance C. of C. (bd. dirs. 1956-59, pres. 1958). Home: 731 E High St Defiance OH 43512 Office: Dinner Bell Foods W High St PO Drawer 388 Defiance OH 43512

ELBERSON, ROBERT EVANS, food industry executive; b. Winston-Salem, N.C., Nov. 9, 1928; m. Helen Hanes; children: Nancy Ann, Charles Evans II. Grad., Choate Sch., 1946; B.S. in Engring, Princeton U., 1950; M.B.A., Harvard U., 1952. Mgmt. trainee Hanes Hosiery Mills Co., Winston-Salem, 1954-56, office mgr., 1956-62, sec., 1959-62, v.p. mfg., 1962-65, mem. exec. com., dir., 1963-65, v.p. planning Hanes Corp., 1965-68, pres. hosiery div., v.p. corp., 1968-72, pres., chief exec. officer, 1972-79, dir., 1972-79, Consol. Foods Corp., 1979—; exec. v.p. CFC, 1979-82, vice chmn., 1982-83, pres., chief operating officer, 1983—; trustee Salem Acad. and Coll., Winston-Salem., 1980—. Bd. visitors Babcock Grad. Sch. Mgmt., Wake Forest U., 1977-83. Served as lt. USAF, 1952-54. Home: Chicago IL Office: Consolidated Foods Corp Three First National Plaza Chicago IL 60602

ELDER, ELDON, stage designer, theatre consultant; b. Atchison, Kans., Mar. 17, 1924; s. Clifford Phillips and Signe (Larsen) E. B.S., Emporia State Coll., 1944; postgrad., U. Denver, 1947; M.F.A., Yale U., 1958. Critic in stage design Yale U., New Haven, 1954, U. Denver, 1964-65; asst. prof. stage design Bklyn. Coll., CUNY, 1956-66, assoc. prof., 1966-69, prof., 1969-75; pres. Eldon Elder Assocs., N.Y.C., 1975—; theatre designer/cons. Theatre Projects Cons., N.Y.C., 1982—; participant cultural exchange tour Dept. State, USSR, Poland, 1965; vis. critic U. Ga., 1979; guest prof. design U. Ohio, 1979. Scene, costume, lighting designer for over 250 plays, operas, TV prodns., including Broadway, Off Broadway prodns., Delacorte Theatre, N.Y.C.; scene designer for numerous plays, operas, TV prodns., including Broadway, Off Broadway prodns., Am. Shakespeare Festival, Stratford, Conn.; scene, costume, lighting designer, Santa Fe Opera Co., Seattle Repertory Theatre, Center Stage, Balt., Long Wharf Theatre, New Haven, Alliance Theatre, Atlanta; theatre cons., Bininger Performing Arts Ctr., Eckard Coll., St. Petersburg, Fla., Theatre Devel. Project, Southeast Alaska, 42d Street Redevel. Project, N.Y.C.; scene, costume, lighting designer one man show, Performing Arts Mus., Lincoln Ctr., N.Y.C., 1978; group shows Contemporary Stage Design-U.S.A., N.Y.C., Washington, Prague, Czechoslovakia, 1975; author: Will It Make a Theatre, 1979; catalogue Eldon Elder: Designs for the Theatre, 1978. Served to lt. (j.g.) USNR, 1945-47; PTO. Guggenheim fellow, Greece, Italy, 1963; Ford Found. grantee, 1960. Mem. U.S. Inst. Theatre Tech. (bd. dirs. 1956), United Scenic Artists (cert.). Office: Eldon Elder Assocs 27 W 67th St New York NY 10023

ELDER, FRED KINGSLEY, JR., physicist, educator; b. Coronado, Calif., Oct. 19, 1921; s. Fred and Ethel S. (Tait) E.; m. Elinor Jean Goertz, July 5, 1947; children: Nancy Elisabeth Elder Backus, Jessie Custer Elder James, Jacqueline Lesesne Elder Shafer, Elinor Tait Elder Powell, Lydia Jean Elder Archer, Robert Abraham, Mary Grace, John Philip. B.S. in Physics, U. N.C., 1941, M.S., Yale U., 1943, Ph.D., 1947. Instr., Yale U., 1943-44; instr. U. Pa., 1947-49; asst. prof. U. Wyo., 1949-50; sr. physicist applied physics lab. Johns Hopkins U., 1950-53; assoc. prof. physics Wabash Coll., Crawfordsville, Ind., 1953-55; prof., chmn. physics dept. and div. natural scis. and math. Belhaven Coll., Jackson, Miss., 1955-59; research physicist U.S. Naval Ordnance Lab., White Oak, Md., summers 1957-59; head research br. antisubmarine warfare lab. U.S. Naval Air Devel. Center, Johnsville, Pa., 1959-65; prof. physics Rochester (N.Y.) Inst. Tech., 1965—, head dept., 1965-72. Scoutmaster, Nat. Capital Area council Boy Scouts Am., 1950-53; Scoutmaster Central Indiana council, 1953-55; trustee Westminster Theol. Sem., Phila., 1960—, sec. bd. trustees, 1981-83, mem. exec. com., 1965-78, sec. bd., 1981-83; trustee Presbyn. Guardian Pub. Corp., 1958-79; trustee, mem. exec. com. Presbyn. Jour. Corp., 1979—, mem. exec. com., 1979—; mem. various denominational bds.; coms. gen. assembly Orthodox Presbyn. Ch., 1952—; trustee Great Commn. Publs., 1976—. Served to lt. comdr. USNR, 1944-46; physicist U.S. Naval Research Lab.; Washington. Mem. Am. Assn. Physics Tchrs. (vice chmn. N.Y. State sect. 1976-78, chmn. 1978-82), Netherlands, Am. phys. socs., Am. Geophys. Union, Franklin Inst., U.S. Naval Inst., Phi Beta Kappa, Phi Kappa Phi, Sigma Pi Sigma, Sigma Xi. Orthodox Presbyn. (ruling elder 1952—). Research, publs. on physics of fluids. Home: 341 Barrington St Rochester NY 14607 Office: Rochester Inst Tech Rochester NY 14623

ELDER, JAMES LANPHERE, lawyer; b. Hanover, Ill., Mar. 21, 1914; s. Frank Ray and Frances Mae (Lanphere) E.; m. Frances Emily Wagner, Jan. 27, 1950; children—James Lanphere, William Paddack, Suzanne DuVal. B.A., Hampden-Sydney Coll., 1936; LL.B., Harvard U., 1939. Bar: Pa. bar 1940, Ohio bar 1941. Asso. firm Taft, Stettinius & Hollister, Cin., 1942-49; partner firm Nieman, Aug, Elder & Jacobs (and predecessor), 1949—; prof. Salmon P. Chase Coll. Law, 1952-60, Cin. Law Sch., 1961; lectr. Ohio Bar Legal Edn. Program. Author: Elder's Revision Stearns on Suretyship, 1951. Founding mem. Greater Cin. Found., 1963-76, chmn. distbn. com., 1969-70; elder Seventh Presbyn. Ch., Cin. Served with U.S. Army, 1942-44. Fellow Am. Bar Found., Ohio State Bar Found. (trustee 1980—); mem. Am. Bar Assn., Ohio Bar Assn. (chmn. sect. real property 1966-68, mem. exec. com. 1975-77), Cin. Bar Assn. (exec. com. 1958-68, pres. 1966-67). Republican. Clubs: Cin. Univ. (bd. govs. 1960-66), Harvard (Cin.) (pres. 1979-80). Home: 5 Dexter Pl Cincinnati OH 45206 Office: 1000 Atlas Bank Bldg Cincinnati OH 45202

ELDER, JEAN KATHERINE, government official; b. Virginia, Minn., May 30, 1941; d. Clarence Adrian and Katherine C. (Miltich) Samuelson. B.S., U. Mich., 1963, A.M., 1966, Ph.D., 1969. Tchr. 5th grade Ypsilanti Pub. Schs., Mich., 1963-64; tech. educable mentally retarded Quantico Marine Corps Dependent Sch., Va., 1964-65; dir. remedial reading program Iron Mountain Pub. Schs., Mich., 1966; research asst. U. Mich., 1966-69; asst. prof. spl. edn. Ind. U., Bloomington, 1969-71; dir. delinquency modifiaction through edn. project Marquette-Alger Intermediate Sch. Dist.-Marquette County Probate Ct., Mich., 1971-72; asst. prof. edn. No. Mich. U., Marquette, 1972-76, assoc. prof., 1977-78, coordinator Title IX, 1975-76; project dir., assoc. scientist Specialist Office Three, Wis. Research and Devel. Ctr. for Cognitive Learning, U. Wis., Madison, 1976-77; assoc. prof. med. edn. Coll. Human Medicine, Mich. State U., 1978-81; commr. Adminstrn. of Devel. Disabilities, Washington, 1981—; cons. in field. Author: (with others) Planning Individualized Education Programs in Special Education, 1977; contbr. articles to profl. jours. Mem. bd. Child and Family Service Upper Peninsula Mich.; mem. Press's Com. on Mental Retardation, 1976-79. U.S. Office Edn. Fellow, 1966-69. Fellow Am. Assn. Mental Deficiency; mem. Am. Assn. Edn. Severely (Profoundly Handicapped), Assn. Retarded Citizens U.S., Council Exceptional Children, AAUW, Pi Lambda Theta, Phi Delta Kappa, Delta Kappa Gamma. Lutheran. Club: Zonta. Home: 7375 Hallcrest Dr McLean VA 22102 Office: Administration on Developmental Disabilities 200 Independence Ave SW Washington DC 20201

ELDER, JOHN THOMPSON, JR., pharmacologist, educator; b. Fall River, Mass., June 30, 1927; s. John Thompson and Jessie (Holland) E.; m. Barbara Jane Carson, Dec. 31, 1958; children: Bruce, Janet. B.S., Mass. Coll. Pharmacy, 1953, M.S., 1955; Ph.D., U. Wash., Seattle, 1959. Instr., then asst. prof. pharmacology U. Wash. Med. Sch., 1956-65; mem. faculty Creighton U. Med. Sch., Omaha, 1965—, prof. pharmacology, 1974—; cons. editor W.H. Freeman Co., Nebr. Commn. Drugs, 1972-80; leader workshops. Author papers in field. Served with USNR, 1945-47. Grantee NMH Health Careers Opportunity Program. Mem. Am. Soc. Pharmacology and, Exptl. Therapeutics, Western Pharmacology Soc. Democrat. Episcopalian. Home: 1910 N 58th St Omaha NE 68104 Office: 2500 California St Omaha NE 68178

ELDER, JOSEPH WALTER, educator, sociologist; b. Kermanshah, Iran, July 25, 1930; s. John and Ruth Deborah (Roche) E.; m. Joann Arlene Finley, Aug. 4, 1951; children: Shonti Rebecca, John Arthur, Edward Byers. B.A., Oberlin Coll., 1951, M.A., 1954; Ph.D., Harvard, 1959. Tchr. Am. Coll. High Sch., Oberlin Shansi Meml. Assn., Madurai, South India, 1951-53; instr. Oberlin (Ohio) Coll., 1959-61; from asst. prof. to prof. sociology and South Asian studies U. Wis.-Madison, 1961—; coordinator Coll. Year in India program, 1962—, Coll. Yr. in Nepal program, 1982—; Cons. Ford Found., Peace Corps, Danforth Found., Smithsonian Instn., Nat. Endowment for Humanities. Co-author: A Compassionate Peace, 1982; Editor: Lectures in Indian Civilization, 1970, Chapters in Indian Civilization vols. I and II, 1970, Planned Resettlement in Nepal's Terai, 1976; dir. 14 documentary films on South Asia, 1974-83. Trustee Oberlin Coll., 1970-82, Oberlin Shansi Meml. Assn., 1964-68; bd. dirs. Am. Inst. Pakistan Studies, 1973-82, Am. Friends Service Com., 1968-73; mem. corp. Am. Friends Service Com., 1973—; bd. dirs. Quaker Housing Inc., 1970—, pres., 1970-73; mem. U.S. Nat. Commn. for UNESCO, 1976-81, chmn. permanent com. on social scis., 1978-81; sr. social sci. adv. U.S. del. to UNESCO Gen. Conf., 1980. Recipient Harbison Teaching award, 1966; Steiger Teaching award, 1976.; Assn. Indians in Am. Honor award, 1984. Fellow Am. Inst. Indian Studies, Center for Advanced Studies at Wesleyan U.; mem. Am. Sociol. Assn., Assn. Asian Studies, South Asia Regional Council (chmn. 1970-71); chmn. South Asia Council (1980-83, dir. 1969-72, 80-83); Mem. Soc. of Friends. Home: 1112 Grant St Madison WI 53711

ELDER, LONNE, III, playwright; b. Americus, Ga., Dec. 26, 1931; m. Judith Ann Johnson, 1969; 2 children. Attended, Yale U. Sch. Drama, 1965-67. Formerly dockworker, waiter, profl. gambler. Author plays: Ceremonies in Dark Old Men, 1965, Charades on East 4th St, 1967; screenplays Sounder, 1972, Melinda, 1972, Sounder, Park II; coordinator, Negro Ensemble Co., N.Y.C., 1967-69; writer, Talent Assos., N.Y.C., 1968; producer, Cinema Center Films, Hollywood, Calif., 1969-70, Universal Pictures, Hollywood, 1970-71, Radnitz/Mattel Prodns., Hollywood, 1971, Talent Assos., Hollywood, MGM, Columbia Pictures, Hollywood, 1972; stage appearances include A Raisin in the Sun, 1959, Days of Absence, 1965. Served with U.S. Army. Recipient Stanley Drama award, 1965, Am. Nat. Theatre Acad. award, 1967, Outer Circle award, 1970. Office: 12237 La Maida St North Hollywood CA 91607 *

ELDER, REX ALFRED, civil engineer; b. Pa., Oct. 4, 1917; s. George Alfred and Harriet Jane (White) E.; m. Janet Stevens Alger, Aug. 10, 1940; children: John A., Carol S., Susan A., William P. B.S. in Civil

Engring, Carnegie Inst. Tech., 1940; M.S., Oreg. State Coll., 1942. Hydraulic engr. TVA, Norris, Tenn., 1942-48, dir. hydraulic lab., 1948-61, dir. engring. lab., 1961-73; engring. mgr. Bechtel Civil & Minerals Inc., San Francisco, 1973—. Contbr. numerous articles on hydraulic structures, reservoir stratification and water quality, hydraulic research and hydraulic machinery to profl. jours. Served with USN, 1945-46. Fellow ASCE (James Laurie prize 1949); mem. Nat. Acad. Engring., ASME, Internat. Assn. Hydraulic Research, Permanent Internat. Assn. Nav. Congresses. Home: 2180 Vistazo E Tiburon CA 94920 Office: PO Box 3965 San Francisco CA 94119

ELDER, ROBERT LEE, golfer; b. Dallas, July 14, 1934; s. Charles and Sadie E.; m. Rose Lorraine Harper, July 18, 1966. H.H.D. (hon.), Daniel Hale Williams U. Profl. golfer appearing in tournaments sponsored by United Golf Assn., 1961-67, Profl. Golfers Assn., 1967—; founder Lee Elder Celebrity Pro-Am Golf Classic, 1970—; pres. Lee Elder Enterprises. Founder Lee Elder Scholarship Found.; Promoter Summer Youth Golf Devel. Programs, Washington; mem. nat. adv. bd. Goodwill Industries Am.; bd. dirs. Met. Washington Police Boys Club. Served with U.S. Army, 1959-61. Recipient Charles Bartlett award Golf Writers Am., 1977; Herman A. English Humanitarian award City of Los Angeles, 1977; A.G. Gaston Business of Year Nat. Bus. League, 1978; named Goodwill Ambassador to Africa, U.S. Dept. State, 1972; inducted into Washington Hall Stars, 1979. Mem. NAACP (life), Profl. Golfers Assn. Am. (dir.). Episcopalian. Club: Masons. Winning tournaments include Nigerian Open, 1971, Monsanto Open, 1974, Houston Open, 1976, Milw. Open, 1978, Westchester Classic, 1978; First black golfer to qualify for Ryder Cup Golf Team, 1979. Office: care Lee Elder Enterprises 1725 K St NW Suite 1201 Washington DC 20006

ELDER, SAMUEL ADAMS, educator; b. Balt., July 13, 1929; s. Fred Kingsley and Ethel (Tait) E.; m. Sylvia Maynard, Jan. 1, 1955; children—Susan Spottiswoode (Mrs. Lawrence E. Erikson), Sheila Jean (Mrs. Daniel L. Korzep), Sarah Maynard, Sandra Louise, Sharon Elisabeth. B.S., Hampden-Sydney Coll., 1950; Sc.M., Brown U., 1953, Ph.D., 1956. Sr. staff physicist Johns Hopkins Applied Physics Lab., Silver Spring, Md., 1956-64; asso. prof. physics U.S. Naval Acad., 1964-68, prof., 1968—; Mem. computer policy bd. USN, 1968-76, chmn., 1973-74. Composer: Random Afternoon, 1969. Pres. bd. dirs. Annapolis Area Christian Sch. Soc., 1974. Mem. Acoustical Soc. Am. (chmn. Washington chpt. 1969-70, mem. tech. com. on mus. acoustics 1970-76), Am. Assn. Physics Tchrs., Catgut Acoustical Soc., Phi Beta Kappa, Sigma Xi. Republican. Presbyn. (elder). Research and publs. in aeroacoustics, non-linear acoustics, musical acoustics, optical pyrometry, computer-aided education. Home: 308 Halsey Rd Annapolis MD 21401

ELDER, STANLEY DAVID, steel co. exec.; b. Montreal, Que., Can., Oct. 18, 1924; s. James and Helen Georgina (Hood) E.; m. Fay Higginbottom, Sept. 3, 1949; children—Susan, Douglas, Carol, Ken. Student, McGill U., 1945-49. Auditor Stevenson, Walker, Knowlers, C.A., Montreal, 1945-50; with Consol. Paper Corp., Ltd., Montreal, 1950-57, treas., 1960-64, controller, 1964-65, v.p. fin., 1965-67; also dir.; v.p. fin. and mgmt. service Consol. Bathurst, Ltd., Montreal, 1967-71; sec. treas. Westeel-Rosco Ltd., Toronto, Ont., Canada, 1973-76, v.p., 1974—, sec., 1976—, also dir. and v.p. all subs. cos. Served with RCAF, 1943-45. Fellow Chartered Inst. Secs., Chartered Accountants Assn. Ont., Fin. Exec. Inst. Clubs: York Downs Golf and Country, National (Toronto). Home: 4 Donwoods Grove Toronto ON M4N 2X5 Canada Office: 1 Atlantic Ave Toronto ON M6K 1X7 Canada

ELDER, STEWART TAYLOR, dentist, retired naval officer; b. Darlington, Pa., Aug. 6, 1917; s. William Carl and Olive Gertrude (Taylor) E.; m. Loretta Tersa Vitio, Apr. 23, 1946; children: Donna Lou, Susan Loretta. B.S., Mt. Union Coll., 1940; D.D.S., Ohio State U., 1945; postgrad., Naval Dental Sch., Nat. Naval Med. Center, Bethesda, Md., 1952-53. With Deming Pump Co., Salem, Ohio, 1935-36, prodn. mgr., 1940-42; commd. lt. (j.g.) U.S. Navy, 1945; advanced through grades to capt. Dental Corps, 1960; prosthetics officer 50th Field Hosp., Paris, 1946-47; asst. dental officer Norfolk Naval Shipyard, Portsmouth, Va., 1948-50, U.S.S. Wisconsin, 1950-52; postgrad. resident in prosthodontics Naval Weapons Plant, Washington, 1953-54; prosthetics officer Norfolk Naval Shipyard, Portsmouth, 1954-55, 57-60; dental officer, prosthetics officer U.S.S. Vulcan, 1955-57; prosthetics officer, exec. officer Naval Dental Clinic, Guantanamo Bay, Cuba, 1960-62; prosthetics officer Naval Dental Clinic Marine Corps Base, Camp Pendleton, Calif., 1962-66; comdg. officer 11th Dental Co., Republic of Vietnam, 1966-67; chief dental service Naval Hosp., Camp Pendleton, 1967-71; exec. officer Naval Dental Clinic, Washington, 1971-73, comdg. officer, 1973-75, Naval Regional Dental Center, Washington, 1975-76, Nat. Naval Dental Center, Bethesda, Md., 1976-79; lectr., instr. Navy Dental Corps Continuing Edn. Program, 1963—, Dental Intern and Postdoctoral Fellowship Programs, 1967—; practice gen. dentistry, Salem, Ohio, 1947-48, lectr. and condr. clinics in field. Mem. Tri Service Utilization Lab. Com. Mem. ADA, Am. Prosthodontic Soc., Am. Assn. Dental Schs., Internat. Gnathological Congress, Fedn. Prosthodontic Orgns., Internat. Assn. Dental Research (asso.), Internat. Coll. Dentists, Nat. Capitol Prosthodontic Study Club, Am. Assn. Dental Research, Ohio State Dental Alumni., Am. Soc. Ret. Dentists (pres.). Home: 2201 Embassy Dr West Palm Beach FL 33401

ELDER, WILLIAM HANNA, zoology educator; b. Oak Park, Ill., Dec. 24, 1913; s. Robert A. and Margaret (Hanna) E.; m. Nina Leopold, Sept. 20, 1941; children—Nina, Patricia; m. Glennis Martin, Mar. 31, 1973. B.S., U. Wis., 1936, Ph.M., 1938, Ph.D., 1942. Game technician Ill. Natural History Survey, 1941-43; toxicologist Nat. Def. Research Com., U. Chgo., 1943-45; asst. prof. zoology U. Mo., Columbia, 1945-47, asso. prof., 1948-51, prof., 1952-54, chmn. dept. zoology, 1950-53, William Rucker prof., 1954—; Sabbatical year study in, Europe, 1953. Guggenheim Found. fellow for research in Hawaii, 1956-57; Fulbright fellow for research, Rhodesia, 1965-66; NSF grantee for elephant research, Zambia, 1967-68. Mem. Nature Conservancy (pres. Mo. 1959, 68), Soc. Mammalogists, Wildlife Soc. (editorial bd. 1956—), Wilson Ornithol. Soc., Phi Beta Kappa, Sigma Xi, Gamma Alpha. Home: 2105 Rock Quarry Rd Columbia MO 65201

ELDERFIELD, JOHN, art historian, museum curator; b. Yorkshire, Eng., Apr. 25, 1943; s. Henry and Rhoda May (Risbrough) E.; m. Joyce Davey, Jan. 9, 1965; children: Matthew, Jonathan. Student, U. Manchester, 1961-62; B.A. with honors, U. Leeds, 1966, M.Phil.; with distinction, 1970; Ph.D., U. London, 1975. Lectr. art history Winchester Sch. Art, 1966-70; Harkness fellow Yale U., 1970-72; lectr. art history U. Leeds, 1973-75; curator painting and sculpture Mus. Modern Art, N.Y.C., 1975—, dir. dept. drawings, 1979—; adj. prof. art history Hunter Coll. Author: Morris Louis, 1974, Hugo Ball: The Flight Out of Time, 1975, Fauvism and Its Affinities, 1976, European Master Paintings, 1976, Matisse, 1978, The Cut-outs of Henri Matisse, 1978, The Masterworks of Edvard Munch, 1979, New Work on Paper, 1981. Guggenheim fellow, 1972-73. Fellow Royal Soc. Arts; mem. Internat. Assn. Art Critics. Office: 11 W 53d St New York NY 10019

ELDERKIN, CHARLES EDWIN, meteorologist; b. Seattle, Aug. 6, 1930; s. Andrew Charles and Hilda Olena E.; m. Mary DuPriest, May 28, 1959; 1 son, Christopher Charles. B.S., U. Wash., 1953, Ph.D., 1966. Meteorologist Gen. Electric Co., 1959-65; mgr. atmospheric physics sect. Battelle Pacific N.W. Lab., Battelle Meml. Inst., Richland, Wash., 1965-72, asso. mgr. atmospheric scis. dept., 1972-79, program mgr. wind characteristics program element of fed. wind energy program, 1976-79, mgr. atmospheric scis. dept., 1979-82, assoc. mgr. geoscis. research and engring. dept., 1982—; mem. field obs. adv. panel Nat. Center Atmospheric Research. Served with USAF, 1954-55. Recipient E.O. Lawrence award U.S. Energy Research and Devel. Adminstrn., 1975. Mem. Am. Meteorol. Soc. (chmn. com. atmospheric turbulence and diffusion 1972), Sigma Xi. Home: 531 Holly St Richland WA 99352 Office: Battelle Pacific NW Labs Battelle Blvd Richland WA 99352

ELDERKIN, DAVID MACDUFF, lawyer; b. Cedar Rapids, Iowa, Nov. 5, 1913; s. Amos Arthur and Elisebeth M. (MacDuff) E.; m. Frances M. Elderkin, Aug. 14, 1937; children: David A., Kenton W. B.A., State U. Iowa, 1935, J.D. cum laude, 1937. Bar: Iowa 1937, U.S. Dist. Ct. (no. dist.) Iowa 1937, U.S. Dist. Ct. (so. dist.) Iowa 1937, U.S. Ct. Appeals (8th cir.) 1950. Ptnr. J.D. Locher (Jr.), 1937-43, Barnes, Wadsworth, Elderkin, Locher & Pirine, 1946-69, Wadsworth, Elderkin, Pirnie & von Lacum, 1969-78, Elderkin, Pirnie, von Lackum & Elderkin, Cedar Rapids,, Iowa, 1978—; trial prosecutor Linn County, Iowa, 1946-52; dir. copley Press, Inc.; mem. adv. com. on Rules of Civil Procedure and Evidence Iowa Supreme Ct.; lectr. seminars, profl. assns. U. Iowa Sch. Law. Assoc. editor: Trial Practice Handbook, 1973; contbr. articles to profl. jours. Capt. USMCR, World War II. Fellow Am. Coll. Trial Lawyers (state chmn. 1980), Am. Bar Found.; mem. Iowa Bar Assn. (adv. mem. bd. govs., past pres.), Linn County Bar Assn. (adv. bd. govs., past pres.), Iowa Acad. Trial Lawyers (pres., past gov.), ABA, Am. Soc. Hosp. Attys., Iowa Def. Council, Am. Judicature Sco., JAG Assn. U.S. Presbyterian. Home: 3420 Random Rd Cedar Rapids IA 52403 Office: Elderkin, Pirnie, von Lackum & Elderkin 619 Highey Bldg Cedar Rapids IA 52406

ELDERKIN, EDWIN JUDGE, lawyer; b. Missoula, Mont., Oct. 25, 1932; s. Emerson W. and Valma (Judge) E.; m. Marie F. Fletcher, June 20, 1954; children: Susan, Michael. B.S., U. Oregon, 1954; LL.B., U. Calif.-Berkeley, 1959. Bar: Calif. 1960. Assoc. and ptnr. Brobeck, Phleger & Harrison, San Francisco, 1959—; lectr. in field. Served to maj. U.S. Army, 1954-67. Fellow Am. Coll. Trial Lawyers, Am. Bar Found.; mem. ABA. Clubs: World Trade (San Francisco); Orinda (Calif.) Country. Office: Brobeck Phleger & Harrison One Market Plaza San Francisco CA 94105

ELDERSVELD, SAMUEL JAMES, political science educator; b. Kalamazoo, Mar. 29, 1917; s. Samuel P. and Minnie (Kooiman) E.; children: Lucy Angeline, Samuel Keith. A.B., Calvin Coll., Grand Rapids, Mich., 1938; Ph.D., U. Mich., 1946. Mem. faculty U. Mich., Ann Arbor, 1946—, prof. polit. sci., 1957—, chmn. dept., 1964-70; Mayor of Ann Arbor, 1957-59. Author: Political Parties: A Behavioral Analysis (Woodrow Wilson Found. award), 1964 1965; also articles. Served to lt. USNR, 1942-46. Mem. Am. Polit. Sci. Assn. Democrat. Episcopalian. Home: 3653 Larchmont Dr Ann Arbor MI 48105

ELDRED, GERALD MARCUS, theatre administrator; b. Cambridge, Ont., Can., Oct. 5, 1934; s. Albert Harold and Ethel Emily Hope (Bardwell) E.; m. Marjorie Christine Kidd, Aug. 4, 1956; 1 son, Peter Marcus. Diploma, Nat. Theatre Sch., Montreal, 1965. Adminstr. Nat. Ballet Can., Toronto, 1972-79; adminstrv. dir., acad. prin. Nat. Ballet Sch., Toronto, 1979-82; exec. dir. Stratford Festival, (Ont.), 1982—; cons. in field. Stage producer, dir., adminstr., Canadian Players, Toronto, 1965-66, Man. Theatre Centre, Winnipeg, 1966-72, Shaw Festival, Niagara-on-the-Lake., Ont., 1967, Expo '67, Montreal, Rainbow Stage, Winnipeg, 1968, Kawartha Summer Festival, Lindsay, Ont., 1966; producer commd. opera for, Nat. Arts Centre, Ottawa, 1969—. Mem. Canadian Actors Equity Assn., Assn. Cultural Execs., Can. Council (adv. arts panel 1970-72, dir. touring office). Home: 89 Elm Ave Toronto ON M4W 1N9 Canada Office: PO Box 520 Stratford ON Canada

ELDRED, KENNETH MCKECHNIE, acoustical consultant; b. Springfield, Mass., Nov. 25, 1929; s. Robert Mosley and Jean McKechnie (Ashton) E.; m. Helene Barbara Koerting Fischer, May 31, 1957; 1 dau., Heidi Jean. B.S., MIT, 1950, postgrad., 1951-53; postgrad., UCLA, 1960-63. Engr. in charge vibration and sound lab. Boston Naval Shipyard, 1951-54; supervisory physicist, chief phys. acoustics sect. U.S. Air Force, Wright Field, Ohio, 1956-57; v.p., cons. acoustics Western Electro-Acoustics Labs., Los Angeles, 1957-63; v.p., tech. dir. sci. services and systems group Wyle Labs., El Segundo, Calif., 1963-73; v.p., dir. div. environ. and noise control tech. Bolt Beranek and Newman Inc., Cambridge, Mass., 1973-77, prin. cons., 1977-81; dir. Ken Eldred Engring.; mem. exec. standards council Am. Nat. Standards Inst., 1979—, vice-chmn., 1981—, bd. dirs., 1983—; mem., past chmn. Acoustical Standards Bd.; mem. com. hearing, bioacoustics and biomedics NRC, 1963—. Served with USAF, 1954-56. Fellow Acoustical Soc. Am. (chmn. coordinating com. environ. acoustics), Nat. Acad. Engring., Inst. Noise Control Engring. (pres. 1976), Inst. Environ. Scis. (chmn. tech. com. on acoustics 1963-71), Soc. Automotive Engrs., Soc. Naval Architects and Marine Engrs., U.S. Yacht Racing Union. Home: 722 Annursnac Hill Rd Concord MA 01742 Office: PO Box 1037 Concord MA 01742

ELDREDGE, CHARLES CHILD, III, museum director; b. Boston, Apr. 12, 1944; s. Henry and Priscilla Marion (Bateson) E.; m. Jane Allen MacDougal, June 11, 1966; children: Henry Gifford, Janann Bateson. B.A., Amherst Coll., 1966; Ph.D., U. Minn., 1971. Curator asst. Minn. Hist. Soc., St. Paul, 1966-68; mem. edn. dept. (Mpls. Inst. Arts), 1967-69; teaching asso. art history U. Minn., 1968-70; asst. prof. art history, curator collections Spencer Mus. Art, U. Kans., Lawrence, 1970-71, dir. mus., 1971-82, asso. prof., 1974-80, prof., 1980-82; dir. Nat. Mus. Am. Art, Washington, 1982—; trustee Watkins Community Mus., Lawrence, 1972 76. Author: monograph Ward Lockwood, 1894-1963, 1974; American Imagination and Symbolist Painting, 1979, Charles Walter Stetson, Color and Fantasy, 1982; gen. editor: The Register of The Museum of Art, 1971-82; editor, Mus. News column Art Jour., 1979-81; editorial bd., Am. Studies, 1974-77. Vis. mus. scholar Nat. Collection Fine Arts, Smithsonian Instn., 1979; Fulbright scholar, N.Z., 1983. Mem. Assn. Art Mus. Dirs. (treas. 1981-82), Coll. Art Assn. Am., Am. Assn. Museums. Office: Nat Mus Am Art Smithsonian Instn Washington DC 20560

ELDREDGE, HANFORD WENTWORTH, city planning educator; b. Bklyn., Oct. 16, 1909; s. Hanford W. and (Taylor) E.; m. Diana Younger, Apr. 21, 1947; children: James Wentworth, Alan Wentworth. A.B., Dartmouth Coll., 1931; Ph.D., Yale U., 1935. Instr. sociology Dartmouth Coll., 1935-39, asst. prof., 1939-49, prof., 1949-74, chmn. dept. sociology, 1953-57, 65-68, chmn. internat. relations program, 1959-62, chmn. city planning and urban studies program, 1959-65; guest lectr. Royal Archtl. Assn. London, Yale U., U. Pa., U. N.C., MIT, Cornell U.; vis. lectr. on city planning Harvard, 1963; vis. prof. city planning U. Calif.-Berkeley, 1967; vis. prof. city and regional planning Harvard U., 1974; orgns. analyst Dept. Justice, 1942; intelligence officer Dept. State, 1942; cons. Exec. Office of Pres., 1956; guest lectr. NATO Def. Coll., Paris, 1955-60, Institut des Hautes Études de Defense Nationale, 1960, Fuehrungs Akademie der Bundeswehr, Hamburg, 1960, USAF Acad., 1961, Ecole de Guerre, Brussels, 1962; faculty Salzburg Seminar in Am. Studies, 1965. Author: (with F.E. Merrill) Culture and Society, 1952, The Second American Revolution, 1964; editor: Taming Megalopolis, 1967; Editor: World Capitals, 1975; contbr. to Studies in the Science of Society, 1937. Trustee Outboard Bound, Inc. Served with USAAF, 1942-45. Decorated Bronze Star medal; recipient cert. of appreciation CIA, 1982. Mem. Am. Sociol. Soc., Am. Soc. Planning Ofcls., Am. Inst. Planners, AAUP, Beta Theta Pi. Clubs: Wianno, Brook; American (London). Home: Tarn House Norwich VT 05055

ELDREDGE, JOSEPH LIPPINCOTT, architect; b. South Bend, Ind., Jan. 13, 1924; s. Donald Herbert and Elsie (Lippincott) E.; m. Joan Marie Wohlenberg, Feb. 11, 1950; children: Peter Ames, Stephen Sperry. A.B., Harvard U., 1945, M.Arch., 1949. Partner Brigham & Eldredge, Boston, 1957-58; Ptnr. Strickland, Brigham & Eldredge, 1958-69; Partner Brigham, Eldredge, Limon & Hussey, 1970-75; pvt. practice architecture, Boston and Martha's Vineyard, 1975—; dir. Mass. Roadside Council, 1964; chmn. Beacon Hill Archtl. Commn., 1967-77. Author: Architecture/Boston, 1976; Editor: Architecture: New England, 1975, Marketplace Life, 1976-77; archtl. critic, Boston Globe, 1964-66; Important works include J.F. Kennedy Post Office, Boston, Brookline Hosp. (Mass.); archtl. critic: Chilmark (Mass.) Post Office, Edgartown (Mass.) Waterfront Complex, Edgartown Restoration of Whaling Ch; restoration and additions The Vineyard Gazette. Pres. Beacon Hill Civic Assn., 1962-64; cons. Park Plaza Civic Adv. Com., 1972-73; bd. dirs. Neighborhood Assn. of Back Bay, 1969-75; trustee Boston Arts Festival, 1956-64, mem. exec. com., 1967-68. Served to lt. (j.g.) USNR, 1943-46; ETO. Fellow AIA (chmn. New Eng. Regional Conf. 1972); mem. Mass. Assn. Architects (exec. com. 1971-72), Boston Soc. Architects (pres. 1973-74). Clubs: Harvard Lampoon, Hasty Pudding. Home and Office: Box 1833 Vineyard Haven MA 02568

ELDREDGE, WILLIAM AUGUSTUS, JR., lawyer; b. Memphis, July 21, 1925; s. William Augustus and Lucile (Crews) E.; m. Lee Campbell, Aug. 4, 1951; children: Michael Charles, Elizabeth Lee, William Augustus III. LL.B., U. Ark., 1949, J.D., 1969. Bar: Ark. 1949. Practiced in, Little Rock, 1949—; partner Friday, Eldredge & Clark (and predecessor firm), 1953—; vol. instr. legal medicine U. Ark. Sch. Medicine, 1954—; clin. prof. med. jurisprudence U. Ark., 1976—; asst. gen. atty. Mo. Pacific R.R. for state of Ark. Chmn. city and county campaign March of Dimes, 1959-61; chmn. Pulaski County chpt. Nat. Found., 1961-62. Served with USNR, 1944-46; 1st lt. JAG Corps U.S. Army, 1951-53. Recipient Little Rock Kappa Sigma Disting. Alumni award, 1965; U. Ark. Coll. Medicine Disting. Service award, 1978. Fellow Ark. Bar Found. (patron); mem. Am. Coll. Trial Lawyers, ABA, Ark. Bar Assn., Pulaski County Bar Assn. (past pres.), Fedn. Ins. Counsel, Def. Research Inst., Blue Key, Kappa Sigma, Delta Theta Phi. Methodist. Home: 6608 Granada St Little Rock AR 72205 Office: 200 First Commercial Bldg Little Rock AR 72201

ELDRIDGE, CARL WALLACE, real estate consultant; b. Seattle, Aug. 24, 1923; s. Clark Henry and Eleanor (Niles) E.; m. Norma Jeanette Zabriskie; children from previous marriage: Susan Carol (Mrs. Harry J. Repstad), George Earl. Student, U. Wash., 1941. Purchasing agt. Met. Constrn. Co., Seattle, 1946-47; gen. mgr. mortgage loan and real estate investment dept. Prudential Ins. Co. of Am., Seattle, Portland, Oreg., Newark and Los Angeles, 1947-64; sr. v.p., trustee Wash. Mut. Savs. Bank, Seattle, 1964-72, exec. v.p., 1972, pres., 1973—, chmn., 1981—. Served with USNR, 1943-46; PTO. Mem. Seattle Mortgage Bankers Assn. (past pres.), Mortgage Bankers Assn. Am., Nat. Assn. Mut. Savs. Banks. Republican. Presbyterian. Club: Rainier (Seattle). Home: 231 98th Ave NE Bellevue WA 98004 Office: 1101 2d Ave Seattle WA 98101

ELDRIDGE, DOUGLAS HILTON, economist; b. Lewistown, Mont., Apr. 12, 1916; s. Harry Hilton and Elsie (Hobensack) E.; m. Clara E. Young, June 8, 1940; children—Douglas Alan, Maurice Paul. B.A., U. Wash., (1937), M.B.A., 1941; M.A., U. Chgo., 1948, Ph.D., 1949. Research asst. Wash. State Tax Commn., Olympia, 1939-41; fiscal economist U.S. Dept. Treasury, Washington, 1949-62, chief tax analysis staff, 1957-62; prof. public fin. Claremont (Calif.) Men's Colls. and Claremont Grad. Sch., 1962-65; v.p., exec. sec. Nat. Bur. Econ. Research, N.Y.C., 1965-78; economist Scarborough, N.Y., 1978—; cons. in field. Contbr. articles to profl. jours. Served to lt. USNR, 1942-46. Social Sci. Research Council fellow, 1947-49. Mem. Am. Econ. Assn., Nat. Assn. Bus. Economists, Nat. Tax Assn., Tax Inst. Am., Phi Beta Kappa, Beta Gamma Sigma. Home: 24 Creighton Ln Scarborough NY 10510

ELDRIDGE, JOHN COLE, judge; b. Balt., Nov. 3, 1933; s. Arthur Clement and Bertha Jean (Klitch) E.; m. Dayne S. Worsham, July 15, 1961; children—Kathryn Chandler, John Cole. B.A., Harvard U., 1955; LL.B., U. Md., 1959. Bar: Md. bar 1960, D.C. bar 1961. Law clk. to chief judge U.S. Ct. Appeals 4th Circuit, 1959-61; trial atty. appellate sect., civil div. Dept. Justice, 1961-67, asst. chief appellate sect., 1967-69; chief legis. officer, counsel Staff of Gov. of Md., 1969-74; asso. judge Ct. Appeals Md., Annapolis, 1974—; Chmn. Md. Adv. Bd. Correction, 1969-70; dir. Annapolis Fine Arts Found., 1974-77. Mem. Anne Arundel County Bar Assn. Democrat. Methodist. Clubs: Nat. Lawyers, Annapolis Yacht. Home: 231 Riverside Dr Annapolis MD 21401 Office: Court of Appeals 361 Rowe Blvd Annapolis MD 21401

ELDRIDGE, LARRY (WILLIAM LAWRENCE ELDRIDGE), newspaperman; b. Phila., Sept. 15, 1932; s. William Stauffer and Irene Elizabeth (Dougherty) E.; m. Joyce Meckling, Sept. 6, 1952 (div. 1966); children—William Lawrence, Janice Lynn, Scott Richard; m. Joyce Pearlswig Leffler, Aug. 23, 1970; children—Nicole Elizabeth, Ross Gregory, Robin Natalie. B.A., U. Pa., 1958. Sports clk. Phila. Inquirer, 1953-59; asst. dir. pub. relations Colby Coll., 1959-60; newsman AP, Portland, Maine and Boston, 1960-71; sports columnist Christian Sci. Monitor, Boston, 1971-75, sports editor, 1975—. Contbr. articles to, Reader's Digest, Sports Illustrated, Sporting News; chess columnist, Me. Sunday Telegram; work included in Best Sports Stories, 1976. Mem. Baseball Writers Assn. Am. (dir. Boston chpt.), U.S. Ski Writers Assn., Profl. Hockey Writers Assn., U.S. Chess Fedn., AAU, Sigma Delta Chi. Winner several chess tournaments. Home: 36 Wedgewood Rd West Newton MA 02165 Office: 1 Norway St Boston MA 02115

ELDRIDGE, ROBERT HUYCK, financial consultant; b. N.Y.C., Mar. 13, 1938; s. William A. and Barbara F. (Jones) E.; m. Elisabeth B. Palmer, Sept. 11, 1965; children: Daniel H., Cynthia B. B.A. magna cum laude, Harvard U., 1961; M.S., MIT, 1966. Corporate finance Kuhn Loeb & Co., N.Y.C., 1969-71; exec. v.p. Ocean Protein Corp., N.Y.C., 1972-73; treas. Brascan, Ltd., Toronto, Ont., Can., 1973-79; fin. cons., 1980—; pres. Lands of Bible Archaeology Found., Toronto, 1977—. Author: (with J.W. Lowe and E. Jaramillo) La Palma Africana en Colombia, 1967. Served with USMC 1959. Mass. Inst. Tech. fellow, 1966-69. Presbyterian. Clubs: A.D. (Cambridge, Mass.); York (Toronto); Knickerbocker (N.Y.C.). Home: 24 Castle Frank Crescent Toronto ON M4W 3A3 Canada Office: Bata Internat 59 Wynford Dr Don Mills ON M3C 1K3 Canada

ELDRIDGE, ROY, jazz musician; b. Pitts., Jan. 30, 1911; s. Alexander and Blanche (Oakes) E.; m. Viola Lee Fong, Jan. 24, 1936; 1 dau.,

Carole Elizabeth. Student high sch., Pitts. Drummer; trumpeter began profl. career with, Greater Sheesley Shows, carnival, 1927, played with, Chocolate Dandies, Teddy Hill, Mckinney's Cotton Pickers, Fletcher Henderson Band, organized own band, later joined, Gene Krupa, 1941, Benny Goodman, 1950, Count Basie, 1966; with, Jazz at the Philharmonic, 1945-51, on tour of Europe, 1949-51; tours individually and with various groups; recording artist for Murcury Records. Recipient Citation of Merit Muscular Dystrophy Assn.; awards Down Beat mag., Westinghouse Trophy award, others; named to Downbeat Hall Fame, 1971. Presbyterian. Address: care Pablo Records Inc 451 N Canon Dr Beverly Hills CA 90210 *

ELEFANTE, MICHAEL BARRETT, lawyer; b. Ft. Wayne, Ind., Feb. 15, 1944; s. Michael Alfred and Jean Lytton (Harris) E.; m. Louise Sawyer; children: Mark Barrett, Amy Lytton. A.B., Syracuse U., 1965; postgrad., Harvard U., 1965-66, J.D., 1969. Bar: Mass. bar 1969. Law clk. Hon. Raymond S. Wilkins, Chief Justice Supreme Judicial Ct., Mass., 1969-70; ptnr. firm Hemenway and Barnes, Boston, 1976—; dir. Greater Boston Legal Services, Inc., 1972—, Civil Liberties Union Mass., 1978—. Mem. Am. Law Inst., Boston Bar Assn. Episcopalian. Office: 60 State St Boston MA 02109

ELEGANT, ROBERT SAMPSON, journalist, author; b. N.Y.C., Mar. 7, 1928; s. Louis and Lillie Rebecca (Sampson) E.; m. Moira Clarissa Brady, Apr. 16, 1956; children: Victoria Ann, Simon David Brady. A.B., U. Pa., 1946; diploma proficiency, Inst. Far Eastern Langs. and Lit., Yale U., 1948; M.A. in Chinese and Japanese, Columbia U., 1950; M.S. in Journalism, Columbia, 1951. Far East corr. Overseas News Agy., 1951-52; war corr. Internat. News Service, Korea, 1953; corr. in Singapore CBS; N.Am. Newspaper Alliance, also, MCGraw-Hill News Service, 1954-55; South Asian corr., chief New Delhi (India) bur. Newsweek mag., 1956-57, Southeast Asian corr., chief Hong Kong bur., 1958-61, chief Central European bur., Bonn (Germany) bur., 1962-64; chief Hong Kong bur. Los Angeles Times, 1965-69, fgn. affairs columnist, Munich, 1970-72, Hong Kong, 1973-76; author, 1977—; vis. prof. U. S.C., 1976; lectr. in field, 1964—. Author: China's Red Masters, 1951, The Dragon's Seed, 1959, The Center of the World, 1964, rev. 1968, Mao's Great Revolution, 1971, Mao vs. Chiang, 1972, The Great Cities: Hong Kong, 1977; novels A Kind of Treason, 1966, The Seeking, 1969, Dynasty, 1977, Manchu, 1980, Mandarin, 1983; also numerous articles. Served with AUS, 1946-48. Pulitzer Travelling fellow, 1951-52; fellow Ford Found., 1954-55; research fellow Am. Enterprise Inst. Pub. Policy Research, 1977-79; citation best mag. reporting from abroad Overseas Press Club, 1962, award for best interpretation of fgn. affairs, 1967, 69, 72; Edgar Allan Poe award Mystery Writers Am., 1967; Sigma Delta Chi award, 1967; Columbia Journalism Alumni award, 1970. Mem. Asia Soc., Authors League, Phi Beta Kappa. Clubs: Hong Kong Foreign Correspondents (pres. 1960), Royal Hong Kong Yacht (Lansdowne (London). Address: Manor House Middle Green near Langley Berkshire England

ELEY, LOMMEN DONALD, lawyer; b. Des Plaines, Ill., Sept. 14, 1908; s. Ning and Sarah (Lommen) E.; m. Lee House, Dec. 19, 1944; children—William, Janet, David. Ph.B., Yale, 1929; J.D., U. Chgo., 1932. Bar: Ill. bar 1932. Partner firm Eley, Koch & Rusher, 1961, Eley & Koch, Chgo., 1971—; dir. North Fed. Savs. & Loan Assn., Chgo. Served with AUS, 1942-46. Mem. Chgo., Ill., Am. bar assns. Clubs: Lion, Elk, Mason., Union League (Chgo.); Park Ridge (Ill.) Country. Home: 1595 Ashland Ave Des Plaines IL 60016 Office: 127 N Dearborn Chicago IL 60602

ELEY, LYNN W., educator; b. Zearing, Iowa, Oct. 23, 1925; s. Wilbur Charles and Myrtle (Wolford) E.; m. Elizabeth Sherwood Hill, Aug. 25, 1950 (div. 1970); children—Thomas Wendell, David Matthew, Mary Sherwood; m. Janet Burdy, Aug. 26, 1971; children—Benjamin Charles, Margaret Burdy. B.A., Harvard U., 1949; M.A., U. Iowa, 1951; Ph.D., 1952. Orgn. and methods analyst Dept. Agr., Washington, 1952-55; research assoc., supr. Lansing Office, Inst. Pub. Adminstrn., 1955-58; assoc. dir. Extension Service; assoc. prof. polit. sci. U. Mich., 1959-64; dean Sch. Continuing Edn., and Summer Sch.; assoc. prof. polit. sci. Washington U., St. Louis, 1964-68; asst. chancellor U. Wis.-, Milw., 1968-72; prof. polit. sci. dept. govt. affairs U. Wis.-Extension, 1972—; editorial asst. com. on appropriations U.S. Ho. of Reps., 1953; instr. U.S. Dept. Agr. Grad. Sch., 1954-55; mayor City of Mequon (Wis.), 1980—. Author: The Executive Reorganization Plan: A Survey of State Experience, 1967, The Regionalization of Business Services in the Agricultural Research Service, 1967, Local Ombudsmen in America, 1973, An Ombudsman for Milwaukee?, 1974; with others Representation of the Poor in Milwaukee's War on Poverty, 1977, A Guide to Citizen Participation in Government: Administrative Rule Making, 1979, 80; Sr. editor: The Politics of Fair-Housing Legislation: State and Local Case Studies, 1968; mem. editorial bd.: Pub. Adminstrn. Rev, 1969-72. Sec. Gov.'s Adv. Com. Reorgn. State Govt. Mich., 1958-62; city councilman Ann Arbor, Mich., 1961-63; mem. Milw. Model Cities Policy Commn., 1970-75; bd. dirs. Wis. Congress on Aging, 1979-82. Served with USNR, 1944-46. Ellis L. Phillips Found. Postdoctoral intern in acad. adminstrn., 1963-64. Mem. Nat. Council of Sr. Citizens Inc. Home: 11417 N Spring Ave Mequon WI 53092 Office: Bolton 640 Univ Wis-Milw Milwaukee WI 53201 *The capacity to adapt affirmatively to conditions of change in one's life situation not only through childhood, but throughout adulthood, seems to me the essential ingredient in successful living.*

ELFELT, JAMES SIDLE, naval officer; b. Mpls., Dec. 28, 1929; s. Lawrence DeHuff and Helen McGuire E.; m. Sally Dahm, Nov. 26, 1955; children: Elizabeth Ann, Helen Suzanne, James Sidle, Cordelia Ann. B.B.A., U. Minn., 1951; M.A., Stanford U., 1959, George Washington U., 1966. Commd. USN, advanced through grades to rear admiral; 2d div. officer, 1951; communications officer (USS Shannon), 1952-53, chief staff officer, comdr., 1953-54, comdg. officer, 1955-56, with automatic data processing, 1956-58, missile officer, 1959-61, exec. officer, 1961-63, distbn. officer, 1963-65, comdg. officer, 1966-67, exec. officer, 1967-69, strategic plans officer, 1970-73, comdg. officer, Naples, Italy, 1973-75, internat. affairs officer, 1975-76, Navy mem., 1976-79, dep. chief of staff for plans, policy, and intelligence, 1979-81, comdr., 1981-82, exec. officer, staff, 1982—. Decorated Legion of Merit; Bronze Star. Republican. Roman Catholic. Home: 85 Floridastrasse Patch Barracks Vaihingen Federal Republic Germany Office: Box 612 EUCOM J-3 APO New York NY 09128

ELFENBEIN, MICKEY, corp. exec.; b. Estevan, Can., Sept. 29, 1947; s. Archie and Sophie E.; m. son, Mark Bradley. B.Commerce (honors), U. Man., (1970). Exec. v.p., dir. K-tel Internat. Inc., Mpls., 1973—. Office: 1670 Inkster Blvd Winnipeg MB R2X 2W8 Canada

ELFERS, WILLIAM, investment company director; b. N.Y.C., June 6, 1918; s. Herman and Katherine (Evers) E.; m. Ann Rice, Dec. 8, 1944; children: William Rice, Joanne (Mrs. Richard M. Haughton), Jane Fuller (Mrs. Herbert C. Muther III). Student, Hotchkiss Sch., 1933-37; B.A., Princeton U., 1941; M.B.A., Harvard U., 1943. Advt. mgr. Modern Materials Handling, Boston, 1946-47; staff asso. Am. Research and Devel. Corp., Boston, 1947-50, asst. v.p., 1950-52, v.p., 1952-65; gen. partner Greylock and Co., Boston, 1965-79, Greylock Investors and Co., 1973-76, ltd. partner, 1977—; pres. Greylock Mgmt. Corp., Boston, 1965-76, chmn. exec. com., 1977—; dir. Conrac Corp., N.Y.C., Hartford Fire Ins. Co., ITT, N.Y.C., Shipley Co. Inc., Newton, Mass., Westvaco Corp., N.Y.C., DBS, Inc., Randolph, Mass.; corporator Provident Inst. Savs. Inc., Boston. Trustee Northeastern U., Boston; bd. dirs. Sherman Fairchild Found., Inc.; trustee emeritus Hotchkiss Sch., Lakeville, Conn. Served to lt. USNR, 1943-46. Episcopalian. Clubs: Commercial, Algonquin (Boston); Longwood Cricket (Chestnut Hill, Mass.); Wianno (Mass.); Princeton, River (N.Y.C.); Wellesley (Mass.) Country. Home: 70 Greylock Rd Wellesley Hills MA 02181 Office: One Federal St Boston MA 02110

ELFIN, MEL, mag. editor; b. Bklyn., July 18, 1929; s. Joseph and Bess (Margolis) E.; m. Margery Lesser, June 21, 1953; children—David, Dana. A.B., Syracuse U., 1951; M.A., Harvard, 1952; student, New Sch. Social Research, 1955-58. Copywriter Marvin and Leonard, advt., Boston, 1953-54; successively reporter, travel editor, asst. city editor L.I. Daily Press, Jamaica, N.Y., 1954-58; mem. staff Newsweek mag., 1958—, gen. editor, 1964-65; chief Washington bur., 1965—; TV panelist; cons. Ednl. Facilities Lab., N.Y.C. Author: (with others) Bricks and Mortarboards, 1963; also articles. Served as officer SAC; Served as officer USAF, 1952-53. Recipient George Polk Meml. award reporting, 1957, N.Y. Newspaper Guild Page One award, 1957; award Edn. Writers Assn., 1966. Mem. White House Corr. Assn., World Press Inst. (adv. bd.), Phi Beta Kappa. Clubs: International, Press, Federal City (Washington). Home: 2804 29th St NW Washington DC 20008 Office: 1750 Pennsylvania Ave NW Washington DC 20006

ELFRIG, DAVID ERIC, ophthalmologist, educator; b. Oak Park, Ill., Jan. 4, 1935. B.A., Carleton Coll., Northfield, Minn., 1956; M.D., Johns Hopkins U., 1960.. Mem. liason service Phipps Psychiat. Clinic, Johns Hopkins U. Hosp., Balt., 1957, mem. dept. pathology, 1958; mem. dog lab. dept. surgery Phipps, Psychiat. Clinic, Johns Hopkins U. Hosp., Balt., 1959-60; intern, asst. resident Halsted Surg. Service Phipps Psychiat. Clinic, Johns Hopkins U. Hosp., Balt., 1960-62, resident in ophthalmology Wilmer Eye Isnt., 1964-67; retinal fellow Jules Stein Eye Inst., UCLA, 1967-68; asst. prof. dept. ophthalmology U. Ky. Sch. Medicine, Lexington, 1968-70, U. Minn. Sch. Medicine, Mpls., 1970-73, assoc. prof., 1973-77; prof. dept. ophthalmology U. N.C. Sch. Medicine, Chapel Hill, 1977—, Sterling A. Barrett prof., 1980—, chmn. dept. ophthalmology, 1977—. Contbr. articles to profl. jours.; lectr. to profl. confs. Served with M.C. USNR, 1962-64. Recipient Schwentker Medal for research Johns Hopkins U., 1967. Fellow ACS; mem. Am. Acad. Ophthalmology, AMA, Assn. Research in Vision and Ophthalmology, Assn. Univ. Profs. in Ophthalmology, Durham-Orange County Med. Soc., Johns Hopkins Med. and Surg. Assn., N.C. Med. Soc., N.C. Soc. of Ophthalmolgy Inc., Research to Prevent Blindness Inc., Retina Soc., So. Med. Assn., Soc. Eye Surgeons, Order Ky. Cols., Mensa. Home: Route 7 Durham NC 27707 Office: Dept Opthalmology 617 Clinical Scis 229H Chapel Hill NC 27514

ELFVIN, JOHN THOMAS, judge; b. Montour Falls, N.Y., June 30, 1917; s. John Arthur and Lillian Ruth (Dorning) E.; m. Peggy Pierce, Oct. 1, 1949. B.E.E., Cornell U., 1942; J.D., Georgetown U., 1947. Bar: D.C. 1948, N.Y. 1949. Confidential clk. to U.S. Circuit Ct. Judge E. Barrett Prettyman, 1947-48; asst. U.S. atty. Western Dist. N.Y., Buffalo, 1955-58, U.S. atty, 1972-75; with firm Cravath, Swaine & Moore, N.Y.C., 1948-51, Dudley, Stowe & Sawyer, Buffalo, 1951-55, Lansdowne, Horning Elfvin, 1958-69, 70-72; justice N.Y. Supreme Ct., 1969; judge U.S. Dist. Ct. for Western Dist. N.Y., Buffalo, 1975—; Mem. bd. suprs. Erie County, N.Y., 1962-65, mem. bd. ethics, 1971-74, chmn., 1971-72; mem., minority leader Buffalo Common Council Delaware Dist., 1966-69; trustee Buffalo Assn. Blind. Mem. Harvard Law Assn., Engring. Soc. Buffalo (pres. 1958-59), Tech. Socs. Niagara Frontier (pres. 1960-61), Phi Kappa Tau, Delta Sigma Chi. Republican. Clubs: Cornell (pres. 1957-58); City, Buffalo Country, Saturn (Buffalo). Office: 609 US Courthouse Buffalo NY 14202 *

ELGART, LARRY, orchestra leader; b. New London, Conn., Mar. 20, 1922; s. Arthur M. and Bessie (Aisman) E.; m. Lynn Walzer, June 28, 1963; children by previous marriage: Brock, Brad. Altosaxophonist; formed, Les and Larry Elgart Orch., 1947; rec. artist for, Decca, RCA, Victor, MGM, Columbia records. Recipient Billboard award for outstanding achievement in recorded music, 1959, Downbeat Most Played Band award Disco Jockey poll, 1959; nomination Nat. Acad. Rec. Arts and Scis., 1959, Downbeat, Cashbox and Billboards awards in popularity polls, Gold record album for Hooked on Swing, 1982.

ELGART, MERVYN L., dermatologist; b. Bklyn., Aug. 12, 1933; s. Jacob and Sally R. E.; m. Sheila Ruth Cliff, June 13, 1954; children—Brian, George, Paul, Adam, James. A.B., Bklyn. Coll., 1953; M.D., Cornell U., 1957. Intern Buffalo Gen. Hosp., 1957-58; resident in dermatology Walter Reed Gen. Hosp., Washington, 1960-63; chief dermatology Andrews AFB Hosp., Washington, 1964-66; mem. faculty George Washington U. Med. Sch., 1967—, prof. dermatology, 1974—, chmn. dept., 1975—, prof. child health and devel., 1972—. Served as officer M.C. USAF, 1958-66. Fellow Am. Acad. Dermatology; mem. AMA, So. Med. Assn., Med. Soc. D.C., Soc. Investigative Dermatology, Internat. Soc. Dermatology, Washington Dermatol. Soc., Phi Beta Kappa, Alpha Omega Alpha. Roman Catholic. Office: 2150 Pennsylvania Ave NW Washington DC 20037

ELGART, STEVEN J., business executive; b. Phila., Aug. 12, 1947. B.Sc.; cum laude, Wharton Sch., U. Pa., 1969; postgrad., Yale U., 1969-71. Co-founder, v.p., chief fin. officer Chase Econometric Assos., Inc., Bala Cynwyd, Pa., 1971-79, also dir.; v.p. Chase Manhattan Bank, N.Y.C., 1979-80; chmn. Wistar Corp., N.Y.C., 1980—, also dir.; dir. Managistics, Inc., Computer Power, Inc., Chase World Info. Corp. Author: The Effects of Credit Rationing on Manufacturing Industries, 1969. Recipient Joseph Warner Yardly award econs., others; Yale U. fellow. Mem. Am. Econ. Assn., Nat. Assn. Bus. Economists, N.Y. Assn. Bus. Economists. Club: Nat. Economists (Washington). Home: 45 W 10th St New York NY 10011

ELGEE, NEIL JOHNSON, physician; b. Oxford, N.S., Can., Apr. 3, 1926; came to U.S., 1946, naturalized, 1955; s. William Harris and Lucile (Nevers) E.; m. Leona Victoria Karlsson, Aug. 18, 1951; children—Joan, Susan, Laurie, Steve, Karen. B.Sc., U. N.B., Can., 1946; M.D., U. Rochester, 1950. Intern Peter Bent Brigham Hosp., Boston, 1950-51; resident Strong Meml. Hosp., Rochester, N.Y., 1951-52; fellow in endocrinology U. Wash., 1952-54, clin. prof. medicine, 1968—; resident in medicine Harborview Med. Center, Seattle, 1954-55; practice medicine specializing in endocrinology, Seattle, 1957—; mem. staff Swedish Med. Center, Harborview Med. Center, Seattle. Served as capt. USAF, 1955-57. Mem. A.C.P. (gov. for Wash. and Alaska 1965-71, regent 1974-78), Endocrine Soc., Inst. Medicine. Home: 3621 72d Ave SE Mercer Island WA 98040 Office: 1221 Madison St Seattle WA 98104

ELIADE, MIRCEA, historian, author; b. Bucharest, Romania, Mar. 9, 1907; s. Gheorghe and Ioana (Stonenescu) E.; m. Georgette C. Cottescu, Jan. 9, 1950. M.A., U. Bucharest, 1928, Ph.D., 1932; student, U. Calcutta, 1928-31. Asso. prof. faculty letters Bucharest U., 1933-39; vis. prof. Ecole des Hautes Etudes, Sorbonne, Paris, 1946-48; Haskell lectr. U. Chgo., 1956, vis. prof. history religion, 1956-57, prof., 1958—, Swell L. Avery distinguished service prof., 1963—; lectr. univs. Rome, Lund, Marburg, Munich, Frankfurt, Strasbourg, Padua; cultural attache Romanian legation, London, Eng., 1940-41, cultural conseiller, Lisbon, Portugal, 1941-44; Dir. Zalmoxis Revue des études religieuses, Paris, Bucharest, 1938-42; pres. Centre Roumain de Recherches, Paris, 1950-55. Author: Yoga, 1936, Techniques du Yoga, 1948, Traité d'Histoire des Religions, 1949, Le Chamanisme, 1951, Images et Symboles, 1952, The Myth of the Eternal Return, 1954, Forêt Interdite, 1954, Forgerons et Alchimistes, 1956, Patterns in Comparative Religions, 1958, Birth and Rebirth, 1958, Myths, Dreams and Mysteries, 1959, Images and Symbols, 1960, The Forge and the Crucible, 1962, Myth and Reality, 1963, Shamanism, 1964, The One and the Two, 1965, From Primitives to Zen, 1967, The Quest, 1969, Zalmoxis, the Vanishing God, 1972, Australian Religions, 1973, Occultism, Witchcraft and Cultural Fashions, 1976, No Souvenirs, 1977, The Forbidden Forest, 1978, A History of Religious Ideas, vol. 1, 1979. Mem. Am. Soc. for Study Religion (pres. 1963-67), Romanian Writers Soc. (Sec. 1937), Société Asiatique, Frobenius Institut. Address: Swift Hall U Chgo Divinity Sch 5711 woodlawn ave Chicago IL 60637 *

ELIAS, HAROLD JOHN, artist, educator; b. Cleve., Mar. 12, 1920; s. John H. and Rose F. (Schmillmenn) E.; m. Marian L. Mark, Apr. 6, 1947; children: Dennis H., David B. Student, DePaul U., 1948-50; B.F.A., Sch. of Art Inst. Chgo., 1950, M.F.A., 1961; postgrad., Mich. State U., 1958-60, U. Mich., 1959; Ph.D. (hon.), Hamilton State U., 1972. Asst. dir. Hackley Art Gallery, Muskegon, Mich., 1952-57, instr., 1952-56; instr. drawing, ceramics and painting Muskego (Mich.) Community Coll., 1952-57; head indsl. art dept. Clark Equipment Co., Benton Harbor, Mich., 1957-67; mem. faculty dep art Lake Michigan Coll., Benton Harbor, 1964-67, Kilgore (Tex. Coll.), 1969-72; mktg. services supr. Stemco Mfg. Co., Longview, Tex., 1971-72; dir. corporate communications Wellman Industries Inc., Longview, 1972-74; mgr. advt. and mktg. service R.G. LeTourneau Inc., Longview, 1967-71; mem. faculty art LeTourneau Coll., Longview, 1974-75; asst. prof. art Ambassador Coll., Big Sandy, Tex., 1973-77; pres. Indsl. Illustrated, Longview, 1977-80; mem. faculty art Stephen F. Austin State U., Nacogdoches, Tex., 1977-78, Kilgore Coll., Longview Center, 1978-80; instr. drawing and painting Tarrant County Jr. Coll., Fort Worth, Tex., 1980—; asst. art creative dir. Radio Shack/Tandy Corp., Fort Worth, Tex., 1980; lectr. and demonstrator Grumbacher and Winsor & Newton Cos., 1976-80. Designer sets, Muskegon Community Theatre, 1952-54; Numerous one-man shows of paintings, 1950—, latest being: travelling exhbn., U.S. Army Commands, 1976-78; travelling exhbn. Art in Embassies Program, U.S. State Dept., (1977-79); numerous others; represented in permanent collections, Ill. State Mus., Springfield U. Idaho, Moscow, Upjohn Collection, Kalamazoo, Mich., U. Ill., Champaign, Massillon (Ohio) Mus. Mem. Mich. Council on Arts, 1964-65; Chmn. public relations com. East Tex. council Boy Scouts Am., 1968-70, bd. dirs. Longhorn council, 1983—; mem. Tex. Commn. on Arts and Humanities, 1970-77; regional dir. Art Week, 1964-65; chmn. Fine Arts Festival of Southwestern Mich., 1961; bd. dirs. Longview United Fund, 1971-72. Served with USAF, 1941-45. Recipient numerous awards. Mem. Tex. Fine Arts Assn., Arts Council of Fort Worth and Tarrant County (mem. govt. and advt. coms. 1980-81), Coll. Art Assn. Am., Artists Equity. Home: 6008 Westridge Ln 512 Fort Worth TX 76116 Office: 1400 One Tandy Center Fort Worth TX 76102

ELIAS, JULIUS ANTONY, philosophy educator, university dean; b. London, May 25, 1925; U.S., 1952; s. Max and Annie (Gershon) E.; m. Wilma Weyns, July 8, 1952 (dec. 1982); children: Edmund, Christopher, Anthony. B.S., Columbia U., 1955, A.M., 1958, Ph.D., 1963. Lectr. philosophy CCNY, 1960-63, asst. prof., 1963-68, assoc. prof., 1968-72, prof., 1972-74; prof.philosophy, dean U. Conn., 1974—. Author: Schiller's Naive and Sentimental Poetry, 1968, Plato's Defence of Poetry, 1983. Mem. academic freedom com. ACLU, 1972—. Recipient CCNY 125th Anniversary medal, 1972; Woodrow Wilson fellow, 1955-56; Columbia U. Pres. fellow, 1958-59. Mem. Am. Philos. Assn., Am. Soc. Aesthetics, AAUP. Home: 35 Dog Ln Storrs CT 06268 Office: U Conn S-98 Storrs CT 06268

ELIAS, PAUL S., mktg. co. exec.; b. Chgo., July 5, 1926; s. Maurice I. and Ethel (Tieger) E.; m. Jennie Lee Feldschreiber, June 28, 1953; children—Eric David, Stephen Mark, Daniel Avrum. B.S., Northwestern U. Sch. Bus., 1950; hon. degree, N.Y. U. Sch. Continuing Edn., 1972. Buyer Mandel Bros., Chgo., 1950-53; salesman Internat. Latex Corp., Chgo., 1953-56; v.p. Hy Zeiger & Co., Milw., 1957-59; exec. v.p. K-Promotions, Inc., Milw., 1959—; dir. Windsor Group, Milw. Officer, dir. Milw. Jewish Community Center; pres. regional bd. Anti-Defamation League. Served with USAAF, 1945-46. Mem. Nat. Premium Sales Execs., Direct Mail Advt. Assn., Premium Advt. Assn. Am. Jewish. Developer inflight mail order mktg. programs for airlines. Home: 9201 N Broadmoor Rd Bayside WI 53217 Office: 3825 W Green Tree Rd Milwaukee WI 53209 *

ELIAS, ROBERT HENRY, educator, writer; b. N.Y.C., Sept. 17, 1914; s. Henry Hart and Edna Weil (Bernhard) E.; m. Helen Beatrice Larson, June 13, 1947; children—Jonathan Hart, Abigail, Sara, Eben Lars. A.B., Williams Coll., 1936; A.M., Columbia, (1937); Ph.D., U. Pa., 1948. Instr. English, asst. history U. Pa., 1942-45; instr. English Cornell U., Ithaca, N.Y., 1945-49, asst. prof., then asso. prof. English, 1949-59, prof., 1959-68, Ernest I. White prof. Am. studies, 1959-64, also chmn. com. Am. studies, 1959-64, 66-67, 75-78, sec. faculty, 1965-68, Goldwin Smith prof. English literature and Am. studies, 1968-80, emeritus, 1980—; Fulbright-Hays lectr. U. Toulouse, France, 1963-64, Centre d'Etudes Anglaises et Nord-americaines, Pau, France, 1968; lectr., mem. corp. Nathan Mayhew Seminars of Martha's Vineyard, 1980—; Mem. West Tisbury (Mass.) Hist. Commn., 1981—. Author: Theodore Dreiser: Apostle of Nature, 1949, rev. edit., 1970, Entangling Alliances with None, 1973; Editor: (Charles Francis Adams, Jr. and Henry Adams) Chapters of Erie, 1956, Letters of Theodore Dreiser, 1959; co-editor: Letters of Thomas Attwood Digges, 1982; Asso. editor: Epoch, 1947-54; Contbr. articles to numerous periodicals. Harrison fellow U. Pa., 1941-42; Ford Found. fellow, 1952-53. Mem. Am. Studies Assn. (co-founder N.Y. State 1951), Modern Lang. Assn. Home: Music St Gen Delivery West Tisbury MA 02575

ELIAS, ROSALIND, mezzo-soprano; b. Lowell, Mass., Mar. 13, 1931; d. Salem and Shelahuy Rose (Namy) E.; m. Zuhayr Moghrabi. Student, New Eng. Conservatory Music, also in Italy. Debut with Boris Goldowsky, Boston, 1948; appeared, San Carlo Opera, Naples, Italy; debut, Met. Opera Co., 1954; originated role of Erika in, Samuel Barber's opera Vanessa; TV and concert artist; recs. for, RCA, Columbia records. Mem. Sigma Alpha Iota. Office: care Columbia Artists Mgmt Inc 165 W 57th St New York NY 10019 *

ELIAS, SAMY E. G., transit authority executive; b. Cairo, June 28, 1930; U.S., 1956, naturalized, 1964; s. Elias Girgis and Ehia N. (Kassabgy) E.; m. Janice Lee Craig, Aug. 21, 1960; children: Mona Lee, Tresa Jean, Cecilia Ruth. B.S., Cairo U., 1955; M.S., Tex. A&M U., 1958; Ph.D., Okla. State U., 1960. Grad. asst. Tex. A&M U., College Station, 1957-58; grad. asst. Okla. State U., Stillwater, 1958-60; asst. prof., indsl. engring. Kans. State U., Manhattan, 1960-61; exec. asst. to chmn. bd. Orgn. of Mil. Factories, Egypt, 1961-62; asso. prof. indsl. engring. Kans. State U., 1962-65; assoc. prof. indsl. engring. W.Va. U., Morgantown, 1965-67, prof., 1967-79, chmn. dept. indsl. engring., 1969-76, spl. asst. to univ. pres. for personal rapid transit, 1970-77, Claude Worthington Benedum prof. transp., 1976-82; dir. Harley O. Staggers Nat. Transp. Center, 1980-82; dir. transit engring. and safety Washington Met. Area Transit Authority, 1982—;

cons. Kansas City Transit, N.Y. Transit Authority, N.Y. Transit Authority Police Dept., Omaha Transit Co., Cin. Transit Co., W.C. Gilman & Co., Inc., Brown Engring., Transp. and Distbn. Assos., PRC Harris, Arab Petroleum Consultants, Urban Transp. Devel. Corp., also others. Recipient Americanism medal DAR, 1977. Fellow Chartered Inst. Transp. Engring.; mem. Am. Inst. Indsl. Engrs. (Transp. and Distbn. award 1979), Soc. Am. Value Engrs., Am. Soc. Engring. Edn. (chmn. indsl. engring. div. 1972-73), Soc. for Computer Simulation, Nat. Soc. Propl. Engrs., W.Va. Soc. Profl. Engrs. Episcopalian. Home: 6152 Kellogg Dr McLean VA 22101 Office: Washington MetArea Transit Authority 600 5th St NW Washington DC 20001

ELIASON, FRANS ROBERT, insurance company executive; b. Wahoo, Nebr., Apr. 9, 1929; s. Bernard Emanuel and Yerda Elvira (Magnusson) E.; m. Eleanor Jane Lesnak, Dec. 28, 1957; children: Kent, Cinda. Student, Luther Jr. Coll., 1946-48; B.B.A., U. Minn., 1950. Asst. v.p. Northwestern Nat. Ins. Co., Milw., 1963-64, v.p., 1964-72, exec. v.p., 1972-73, pres., 1973-75, chmn. bd., 1975—; also dir.; pres. NN Corp., 1979-80; pres., chief operating officer Armco Ins. Group, 1980-81, pres., chief exec. officer, 1981-84, vice chmn. bd., 1984—; dir. First Wis. Corp. Bd. dirs. United Performing Arts Fund; bd. dirs. Milw. County council Boy Scouts Am. Served to lt. USNR, 1951-55. Mem. Soc. CPCUs, Am. Inst. Property and Liability Underwriters (trustee). Clubs: Milwaukee, Westmoor Country., Milw. Country. Home: 2695 Woodhill Ct Brookfield WI 53005 Office: 731 N Jackson St Milwaukee WI 53201

ELIASON, NORMAN ELLSWORTH, educator; b. Glenwood, Minn., Mar. 12, 1907; s. Andrew and Marie (Sagvold) E.; m. Dorothy Haskins, Aug. 23, 1930. A.B., Luther Coll., Decorah, Ia., 1927; A.M., U. Ia., 1931; Ph.D., Johns Hopkins, 1936; Litt.D., Luther Coll., 1967. Prin. high sch., Charter Oak, Ia., 1927-28; instr. English Luther Coll., 1928-29, U. Neb., 1929-32; instr., asst. prof. Ind. U., 1932-37; prof. English U. Fla., 1937-46, U. N.C., Chapel Hill, 1946-66, Kenan prof., 1966—; research at the Linguistic Inst., Mich., 1936, U. Oslo, summer 1939; vis. prof. U. Ia., summer 1952, U. Innsbruck, Austria, 1956, King's Coll., U. London, 1962, Columbia, summer 1964, U. Wash., 1965, Harvard, 1966, Stanford, 1968. Author: Tar Heel Talk: An Historical Study of the English Language in North Carolina to 1860, 1956, The Language of Chaucer's Poetry, 1972, English Essays Literary and Linquistic, 1975; Co-author: The effect of Stress upon Vowel Quantity, 1939; Co-editor: Ideas and Models, 1935, Studies in Heroic Legend and Current Speech, 1959, Aelfric's First Series of Catholic Homilies, 1966; Asst. editor So. Folklore Quar., 1937-47; adv. editor Am. Speech, 1939-40, 60-61; co-editor: Anglistica, 1964—; Contbr. articles and revs. to profl. jours. Served from lt. (j.g.) to lt. comdr. USNR, 1942-46. Guggenheim fellow, 1951-52; sr. fellow Southeastern Inst. Medieval and Renaissance Studies, 1969. Mem. Am. Dialect Soc. (exec. com. 1956-60), Acad. Literary Studies, Linguistic Soc. Am. (exec. com. 1940), Modern Lang. Assn. (chmn. practical phonetics group 1937-39, sec. exptl. phonetics group 1942-44, sec. Old English group 1954, chmn. 1955, sec. English sect. 1960, chmn. 1961), Medieval Acad. Am., Internat. Assn. U. Profs. English (mem. cons. com. 1956-71, v.p. 1971-74), N.C. Folklore Soc. Democrat. Episcopalian. Home: 186 Carol Woods Chapel Hill NC 27514

ELIASSEN, ROLF, environmental engineer, emeritus educator; b. N.Y.C., Feb. 22, 1911; s. Olaf and Effie (Albrethsen) E.; m. Mary F. Hulick, Dec. 12, 1941; children: Thomas R., James H. B.S., Mass. Inst. Tech., 1932, M.S., 1933, Sc.D., 1935. Design engr. J.N. Chester Engrs., Pitts., 1935-36; san. engr. Dorr Co., Inc., Chgo., Los Angeles, 1936-39; asst. prof. civil engring. Ill. Inst. Tech., 1939-40; assoc. prof. san. engring. NYU, 1940-42, prof., 1946-49; design engr. Parsons, Klapp, Brinckerhoff & Douglas, N.Y.C., 1941; chmn. civil engring. dept. Biarritz Am. U., France, 1945; prof. san. engring., dir. Sedgwick Labs San. Sci., Mass. Inst. Tech., cons. engr., 1949-60, acting head dept. civil engring., 1960-61; prof. civil engring. Stanford U., 1961-73; now Silas H. Palmer prof. civil engring. emeritus; partner Metcalf & Eddy, Inc. (cons. engrs.), Palo Alto, Calif., also Boston, 1961-73, chmn. bd., 1973—; dir. Multisonics, Inc., Ramtek Corp.; cons. IAEA, WHO, UN, Exec. Office Pres. of U.S., Calif. Dept. Water Resources, Fed. Power Commn., U.S. Senate Com. on Pub. Works; mem. gen. adv. com. AEC, 1970-75. Contbr. articles to tech. jours. Served to lt. col., C.E. AUS, 1942-46; ETO. Mem. Am. Acad. Arts and Sci., ASCE (hon.), Nat. Acad. Engring., Am. Water Works Assn., Sigma Xi, Tau Beta Pi. Conglist. Home: 850 Webster St Apt 318 Palo Alto CA 94301 Office: Coll Engring Stanford U Stanford CA 94305 also 1029 Corporation Way Box 10-046 Palo Alto CA 94303

ELICK, JOHN WILLIAM, anthropology educator, field researcher; b. Enid, Okla., Feb. 21, 1919; s. James Granville and Anna Laura (Hestwood) E.; m. Marjorie Edith Rickard, Feb. 19, 1942; children: John, Kathleen. B.A., La Sierra Coll., Riverside, Calif., 1951; postgrad., Seventh-Day Adventist Sem., Washington, 1955, Inst. Ethnology, Lima, Peru, 1957; M.A., UCLA, 1965; Ph.D. with distinction, UCLA, 1969. Dir. Nevati Mission, Ucayali Dist., Peru, 1951-59; pres. Upper Amazon Mission, Iquitos, Peru, 1959-61, Inca Union Mission, Lima, 1961-63; mem. faculty Loma Linda U., Riverside, Calif., 1964—, prof. anthropology, 1973—; assoc. dir. Inst. World Mission, Andrew U., Berrien Springs, Mich., 1982—. Field research grantee Latin Am. Ctr. UCLA, Eastern Peru, 1967, Loma Linda U., Lebanon, Jordan, 1973, 74, Marshall Islands, 1981, Brit. Mus., 1974, Gen. Conf. Seventh-day Adventists, Caribbean, 1982. Fellow Royal Anthrop. Inst. Gt. Britain and Ireland, Am. Anthrop. Assn., AAAS; mem. Soc. Applied Anthropology, Assn. Adventist Beheavioral Scientists, Sigma Xi. Home: 11657 Doverwood Dr Riverside CA 92505 Office: Loma Linda U Riverside CA 92515

ELICKER, PAUL H., corporate executive; b. N.Y.C., 1923. B.A., Yale U., 1943; M.B.A., Harvard U., 1948. With Ford Motor Co., 1949-51, Mckinsey & Co., 1952-56; with S C M Corp., 1956—, v.p. fin., 1958-70, exec. v.p., 1970-72, chmn., pres., chief exec. officer, 1972—, also dir. Home: 2704 Long Ridge Rd Stamford CT 06903 Office: SCM Corp 299 Park Ave New York NY 10171 *

ELIE, JEAN ANDRÉ, investment banker; b. Montreal, Que., Can., Oct. 8, 1943; s. Jean-Paul and Violet (Trempe) E.; m. Josée Langevin. B.A., Coll. Jean de Brébeuf, 1962; B.C.L., McGill U., 1965; M.B.A., U. Western Ont., 1968. Bar: Que. bar 1966. With Rolland Inc., Montreal, 1968-81, sec., 1974-81, counsel, 1974-81, v.p. planning, 1978-81; dir. corp. services Burns Fry Lte., Montreal, 1981—. Bd. dirs. Montreal Symphony Orch. Mem. Canadian Bar Assn. Roman Catholic. Clubs: St. Denis, Tennis Saint-Laurent. Home: 2250 Dunkirk Rd Mount Royal PQ H3R 3K8 Canada Office: 1 Pl Ville Marie Suite 1712 Montreal PQ H3B 2C1 Canada

ELIEL, ERNEST LUDWIG, educator, chemist; b. Cologne, Germany, Dec. 28, 1921; came to U.S., 1946, naturalized, 1951; s. Oskar and Luise (Tietz) E.; m. Eva Schwarz, Dec. 23, 1949; children—Ruth Louise, Carol Susan. Student, U. Edinburgh, (1939-40), Scotland; D.Phys.-Chem. Sci., U. Havana, Cuba, 1946; Ph.D., U. Ill., 1948. Mem. faculty U. Notre Dame, South Bend, Ind., 1948-72, prof. chemistry, 1960-72, head dept., 1964-66; W.R. Kenan Jr. prof. chemistry U. N.C., Chapel Hill, 1972—; Le Bel Centennial lectr., Paris, 1974; Benjamin Rush lectr. U. Pa., Phila., 1978; Sir C.V. Raman vis. prof. U. Madras, India, 1981. Author: Stereochemistry of Carbon Compounds, 1962, Conformational Analysis, 1965, Elements of Stereochemistry, 1969; Co-editor: Topics in Stereochemistry, Vols. I-XII, 1967-80. Pres. Internat. Relations Council, St. Joseph Valley, 1961-63. NSF sr. research fellow Harvard, 1958; Calif. Inst. Tech., 1958-59; E.T.H., Zurich, Switzerland, 1967-68; Recipient Coll. Tchrs. award Mfg. Chemists Assn., 1965; Morley medal Cleve. sect. Am. Chem. Soc., 1965; Laurent Lavoisier medal French Chem. Soc., 1968; Guggenheim fellow Stanford, Princeton U., 1975-76. Mem. Nat. Acad. Scis., Am. Acad. Arts and Scis., Am. Chem. Soc. (chmn. St. Joseph Valley sect. 1960, councillor 1965-73, 75—, chmn. com. publs. 1972, 76-78), AAAS, Chem. Soc. London, AAUP (chpt. pres. 1971-72, 78-79), Sigma Xi (chpt. pres. 1968-69), Phi Lambda Upsilon, Phi Kappa Phi. Home: 725 Kenmore Rd Chapel Hill NC 27514

ELIEL, LEONARD PAUL, educator, physician; b. Los Angeles, Sept. 14, 1914; s. Paul and Harriet Stewart (Judd) E.; m. Marjorie Blake, Jan. 14, 1943; children—Alan, Suzanne. B.S., Harvard, 1936, M.D., 1940. Diplomate: Am. Bd. Internal Medicine. Intern Mass. Gen. Hosp., Boston, 1940-42; med. officer Pan Am. Airways, Accra, Africa and N.Y.C., 1942-44; head cancer research sect. Okla. Med. Research Found., Oklahoma City, 1951-64, dir. research, 1956-59, exec. dir., 1959-65, v.p., also dir. research, 1965-70; asso. dir., U. Okla. Health Scis. Center, Oklahoma City, 1970, interim exec. v.p., 1970-71, exec. v.p., dir., 1971-73; asso. chief staff for research VA Hosp., American Lake, Wash., 1974—, Prof. medicine U. Okla. Sch. Medicine, 1966-74, head endocrinology sect., 1973-74; vis. prof. U. Wash. Dept. Medicine, Seattle, 1969-70, clin. prof. medicine, 1974-77, prof. medicine, 1977—; chmn. clin. cancer tng. com. Nat. Cancer Inst., 1969-71. Contbr. abstracts, articles to med., sci. jours. Pres. Oklahoma City Symphony Soc., 1968-69. Served with USNR, 1944-46. Research fellow pediatrics Harvard Med. Sch., 1946-47; Milton fellow, 1947-48; Damon Runyan Sr. Clin. Research fellow Sloan-Kettering Inst., 1949-51. Fellow A.C.P.; mem. Am. Clin. and Climatol. Assn., Am. Fedn. Clin. Research, A.M.A., Am. Soc. Clin. Investigation, Endocrine Soc., Alpha Omega Alpha. Home: 4234 Soundview Dr W Tacoma WA 98466 Office: VA Med Center Tacoma WA 98493

ELIKANN, LAWRENCE S. (LARRY ELIKANN), TV and film dir.; b. N.Y.C., July 4, 1923; s. Harry and Sadye (Trause) E.; m. Corinne Schuman; Dec. 6, 1947; children—JoAnne Jarrin, Jill Barad. B.A., Bklyn. Coll., 1943; E.E., Walter Harvey Coll., 1948. Tech. dir. NBC-TV, N.Y.C., 1948-64; comml. dir. VPI-TV, N.Y.C., 1964-66, Filmex-TV, 1966-68, Plus two TV, 1968-70. Free-lance TV and film dir., 1970—; (Recipient Emmy award Nat. Acad. TV Arts and Scis. 1973-76, 77, 78, 79, Christopher award 1972-76, 78, Media award Ohio Film Festival 1977, Chgo. Internat. Film Festival award 1977, Internat. Film and TV Festival of N.Y. award 1977, Dir. of Yr. award Am. Center Films for Children 1978). Served with Signal Corps U.S. Army, 1943-46. Mem. Dirs. Guild Am., Am. Film Inst., Nat. Acad. TV Arts and Scis. (gov. 1961-63). Home and office: 100 S DoHeny Dr Los Angeles CA 90048

ELINSON, JACK, sociology educator; b. N.Y.C., June 30, 1917; s. Sam and Rebeccah (Block) E.; m. May Gomberg, July 5, 1941; children: Richard, Elaine, Mitchell, Robert. B.S., CCNY, 1937; M.A., George Washington U., 1946, Ph.D., 1954. Social sci. analyst Dept. Def., Washington, 1942-51; sr. study dir. Nat. Opinion Research Center, 1951-56; asst. prof. sociology U. Chgo., 1954-56; asso. prof. adminstrv. medicine Columbia U., N.Y.C., 1956-64, prof. adminstrv. medicine, 1964-68, prof. sociomed. scis. and sociology, 1968—; Service fellow Nat. Center Health Stats., 1977-81; vis. prof. behavioral scis. U. Toronto, 1969-77; dir. program evaluation dept. patient care Harlem Hosp. Ctr., 1966-71; Bd. dirs. Med. and Health Research Assn., N.Y.C., Bergen County, N.J.; Tb and Health Assn.; mem. adminstrv. bd. Bur. Applied Social Research, Columbia U. Author: (with R. E. Trussell) Chronic Illness in a Rural Area, 1959, (with E. Padilla and M. Perkins) Public Image of Mental Health Services; editor: (with A.E. Siegmann) Sociomedical Health Indicators, (with A. Mooney and A. Siegmann) Health Goals and Health Indicators: Policy, Planning and Evaluation. Fellow Am. Sociol. Assn. (chmn. med. sociology), AAAS, Am. Assn. Public Opinion Research (pres. 1979-80), Am. Public Health Assn.; mem. Inst. of Medicine, Nat. Acad. Sci., N.Y.C. Public Health Assn. (dir.). Office: 60 Haven Ave New York NY 10032

ELION, GERTRUDE BELLE, research scientist, pharmacology educator; b. N.Y.C., Jan. 23, 1918; d. Robert and Bertha (Cohen) E. A.B., Hunter Coll., 1937; M.S., N.Y. U., 1941; D.Sc. (hon.), George Washington U., 1969, U. Mich., 1983, D.M.S., Brown U., 1969. Lab. asst. biochemistry N.Y. Hosp. Sch. Nursing, 1937; research asst. in organic chemistry Denver Chem. Mfg. Co., N.Y.C., 1938-39; tchr. chemistry and physics N.Y.C. secondary schs., 1940-42; food analyst Quaker Maid Co., Bklyn., 1942-43; research asst. in organic synthesis Johnson & Johnson, New Brunswick, N.J., 1943-44; biochemist Wellcome Research Labs., Tuckahoe, N.Y., 1944-50, sr. research chemist, 1950—; asst. to asso. research dir., 1955-62, asst. to the research dir., 1963-66, head exptl. therapy, 1966-83, sci. emeritus, 1983—; adj. prof. pharmacology and exptl. medicine Duke U., 1970, research prof. pharmacology, 1983—; adj. prof. pharmacology U. N.C., Chapel Hill, 1973; cons. USPHS, 1960-64; Chmn. Gordon Conf. on Coenzymes and Metabolic Pathways, 1966; mem. bd. sci. counselors Nat. Cancer Inst., 1980-84; mem. council Am. Cancer Soc., 1983—. Contbr. articles to profl. jours. Recipient Garvan medal, 1968; Pres.'s medal Hunter Coll., 1970; Disting. Chemist award N.C. Inst. Chemists, 1981; Judd award Meml. Sloan-Kettering Cancer Ctr., 1983; named to Hunter Coll. Hall Fame, 1973. Fellow N.Y. Acad. Scis.; mem. Am. Chem. Soc., AAAS, Chem. Soc. (London), Am. Soc. Biol. Chemists, Am. Assn. Cancer Research (bd. dirs. 1981, 83, pres. 1983-84, Cain award 1984), Am. Soc. Hematology, Transplantation Soc., Am. Soc. Pharmacology and Exptl. Therapeutics. Patentee in field. Home: 1 Banbury Ln Chapel Hill NC 27514 Office: 3030 Cornwallis Rd Research Triangle Park NC 27709

ELIOT, ALEXANDER, author, critic, historian; b. Cambridge, Mass., Apr. 28, 1919; s. Samuel Atkins, Jr. and Ethel (Cook) E.; m. Jane Winslow Knapp, May 3, 1952; children: May Rose, Jefferson, Winslow. Student, Black Mountain Coll., 1936-38, Boston Mus. Sch., 1938-39. Dir., Pinkney St. Artists Alliance, Boston, 1940-41; asst. to producer March of Time newsreel, 1941-42; asst. dir. films OWI, 1942-43; editor films (Coordinator Inter-Am. Affairs), 1943-45; art editor Time mag., 1945-60; prof. emeritus program Hampshire Coll., 1977. Contbr.: Travel & Leisure; author: Proud Youth, 1953, Three Hundred Years of American Painting, 1957, Sight and Insight, 1959, Earth, Air, Fire and Water, 1962, Greece, 1963, Love Play, 1966, Creatures of Arcadia, 1967, Socrates, 1967; film The Secret of Michelangelo, Every Man's Dream, 1968; A Concise History of Greece, 1972, Myths, 1976, Zen Edge, 1979. Guggenheim fellow, 1960; Japan Found. fellow, 1975. Fellow Internat. Inst. Arts and Letters; mem. PEN, Authors Guild, Free Lance Council, Soc. Am. Travel Writers, Northampton (Mass.) Hist. Commn., Northampton Arts Council. Clubs: Century Assn., Dutch Treat (N.Y.C.); Bay State Writers. Home: 12 Hampton Terr Northampton MA 01060 Office: c/o Sterling Lord Agency 660 Madison Ave New York NY 10021 *The moon, the planets, pass around my heart. The sun shines into me, and in me as well. Yet what am I? A goose-pimpled crazy on a skewed glass bicycle, continually crashing into scribbled walls. And this moment, this being is the thing.*

ELIOT, LUCY CARTER, artist; b. N.Y.C., May 8, 1913; d. Ellsworth and Lucy Carter (Byrd) E. B.A., Vassar Coll., 1935; postgrad., Art Students League, 1935-40. Tchr. painting and drawing Red Cross Bronx Vets. Hosp., N.Y.C., 1950, 51. Exhibited one-woman shows, Rochester Meml. Art Gallery, 1946, Cazenovia Coll., 1942, 47, 62, Syracuse Mus. Fine Arts, 1947, Wells Coll., 1953, Ft. Schuyler Club, Utica, N.Y., 1971, nat. shows, Pa. Acad. Fine Arts, Phila., 1946, 48, 49, 50, 52, 54, Corcoran Biennial, Washington, 1947, 51, Va. Biennial, Richmond, 1948, NAD, N.Y.C., 1971, 78. Bd. dirs. Artists Tech. Research Inst., 1975-79. Recipient First prize Rochester Meml. Art Gallery, 1946, Purchase prize Munson-Williams-Proctor Inst., 1949, Painting of Industry award Silvermine Guild, 1957, 1st prize in oils Cooperstown Art Assn., 1978. Mem. N.Y. Artists Equity, N.Y. Soc. Women Artists (pres. 1973-75), Audubon Artists (dir. oil. 1983—). Episcopalian. Clubs: Cazenovia (N.Y.); Cosmopolitan (N.Y.C.). Home: 131 E 66th St New York NY 10021 *I feel that there has been slow but fairly steady improvement in my work as each painting has constituted a learning process (offering a better chance for the next.) I hope to be able to continue working for some time to come, as I have the same feeling now that I have had over the years: that I am just beginning to paint.*

ELIOT, ROBERT SALIM, physician; b. Oak Park, Ill., Mar. 8, 1929; s. Salim and Ruth (Buffington) Elia; m. Phyllis Allman, June 15, 1957; children: William Robert, Susan Elaine. Student, Northwestern U., 1947-48; B.S., U. N.Mex., 1952; M.D., U. Colo., 1955. Intern Northwestern U., Evanston, Ill., 1955-56; resident U. Colo., Denver, 1956-58, fellow cardiology, 1958-60; trainee cardiovascular pathology U. Minn., St. Paul-Mpls., 1962-63, instr., 1963-65, asst. prof., 1965-67; mem. faculty U. Fla., Gainesville, 1967-72, prof. medicine, 1969-72; chief div. cardiology VA Hosp., 1970-72; prof. medicine, dir. Cardiovascular Center U. Nebr. Med. Ctr., Omaha, 1972—, dir. div. cardiology, 1972-80, 1972-80, chmn. dept. preventive and stress medicine, 1981—; med. dir. Internat. Stress Found., 1977—; cardiol. cons. Cape Kennedy, 1971-77; cons. Kellogg Found., 1978; chmn. Nat. Goals and Objectives for Stress Mgmt. for Surgeon Gen. U.S., 1980—; nat. and internat. lectr. med. and sci. topics. Pres. Alachua County Heart Div., 1969, 70; bd. dirs. Am. Inst. Stress, 1980—; mem. adv. bd. stress and cardiovascular research center Eckerd Coll., St. Petersburg, Fla., 1980—; chmn. Bethesda Conf. Com. on Prevention of Coronary Disease in the Occupational Setting, 1980-81; cons., lectr. in field to corps., pub. and profl. orgns. Author: Stress and the Major Cardiovascular Disorders; editor: Cardiac Emergencies; editorial bd.: Heart and Lung; creator ednl. TV series: Heartline to Health; Contbr. profl. jours. Served to capt. AUS, 1960-62. Recipient grants USPHS, VA, Fla. Heart Assn., various pvt. sources. Fellow A.C.P., Clin. Council Am. Heart Assn., Am. Coll. Cardiology (mem. continuing edn. com., Mountain States coordinator for continuing edn., mem. long range planning com., mem. exec. com. gov. Nebr., vice chmn. bd. govs. 1976-77, chmn. bd. govs. 1977-78, trustee 1977-83, chmn. liaison com. to Am. Acad. Family Physicians), N.Y. Acad. Scis.; mem. AMA, Nebr. Med. Assn., Central Soc. Clin. Investigation, Biophysical Soc., Acad. Behavioral Medicine Research (charter), Soc. Behavioral Medicine (charter), Interstate Postgrad. Med. Assembly (pres. 1982), Alpha Omega Alpha, Phi Sigma, Phi Rho Sigma. Research on effects of changes in blood-oxygen transport and their role in producing or in treating heart disease, mechanisms causing heart attacks, role of stress in heart disease. Home: 405 Ridgewood Dr Bellevue NE 68005

ELIOT, THEODORE LYMAN, JR., university dean; b. N.Y.C., Jan. 24, 1928; s. Theodore Lyman and Martha Williams (Bigelow) E.; m. Patricia F. Peters, Apr. 14, 1951; children: Sarah Winslow, Theodore Lyman III, Wendy Peters, Peter Bigelow. B.A., Harvard, 1948, M.P.A., 1956; LL.D., U. Nebr., Omaha, 1975. Vice consul, 3d sec. Am. embassy, Colombo, Ceylon, 1950-52; U.S. info. and cultural officer, Germany, 1953-55; 2d sec. Am. embassy, Moscow, 1956-58; spl. asst. to under sec. of state, 1959-61, to sec. treasury, 1961-62, 1st sec. Am. embassy, Tehran, Iran, 1963-66; country dir. for Iran Dept. State, 1966-69, exec. sec., also spl. asst. to sec. of state, 1969-73; ambassador to Afghanistan, 1973-78; insp. gen. Fgn. Service Dept. State, Washington, 1978; dean Fletcher Sch. Law and Diplomacy, Tufts U., Medford, Mass., 1979—; adviser U.S. del. to meeting Inter-Am. Devel. Bank, Rio de Janeiro, 1961, NATO meeting, Paris, 1961, others.; dir. Raytheon Co. Mem. Am. Fgn. Service Assn. (vice chmn. bd. dirs. 1967-69, pres. 1970-72), Council Fgn. Relations, Inst. Fgn. Policy Analysis (dir.), World Peace Found. (trustee). Clubs: Cosmos, Somerset. Address: Fletcher Sch Law and Diplomacy Tufts U Medford MA 02155

ELISAR, PATRICIA GARSIDE, publishing executive; b. Albany, Ga., Jan. 10, 1934; d. George Lyons and Anne Lillian (Miller) Garside; m. Rene Elisar, 1978 (dec. 1981); children: Matthew Raymond Fitch, Katherine, Scott Elisar. B.A., Ohio U., Athens, 1978. Sec., Argus Camera Co., Ann Arbor, Mich., 1954-56; sec., research asst. U. Pa., 1956-60; adminstrv. asst. chemistry Yale U., 1960-66; sales and bus. mgr., then asst. dir. Ohio U., Athens, 1966-73, dir., 1973—, N.Am. distbn. U. Singapore Press, Gadja Mada U. Press, Indonesia, Ohio U. Press/Swallow Press, 1979—; mem. Mayor Athens Adv. Com. Waste Reclamation, 1974—, Univ. Library Adv. Com., 1980—; bd. dirs. Friends of Ohio U. Library, 1980—, pres., 1981. Recipient commendation Athens City Council, 1974. Mem. League Women Voters (editor local newsletter 1966-67, chmn. local environ. com. 1967-69). Home: 58 Fairview Ave Athens OH 45701 Office: Ohio Univ Press Athens OH 45701

ELISCU, FRANK, sculptor; b. N.Y.C., July 13, 1912; s. Charles Henry and Florence (Kane) E.; m. Mildred Norman, May 3, 1942; 1 dau., Norma (Mrs. Francis Banas, Jr.). Student, Beaux Arts Inst. Design, Pratt Inst., 1930-33. Author: Direct Wax Sculpture; One-man exhbn. sculpture, Mexico, 1955, works represented, Bookgreen Gardens, S.C., portrait busts, Aero. Hall of Fame, other works, Stevens Inst., Cornell Med. Sch., Olin Hall, N.Y., Heismann Meml. Trophy, Naiad; fountain figure, N.Y.C., Heroic; Atoms for Peace figure, Ventura, Cal., Headley Mus., (The Astronauts), Lexington, Ky., Steuben Glass Co., (Noah), St. Christopher's Chapel, (St. Christopher), N.Y.C., Soc. Medallists, (Sea Treasures); designer: Presdl. Eagle for Oval Room, White House, also reverse side of ofcl. inaugural medal, 1974; other works include Chase of the Sea Urchin, Sarasota, Fla., 1980, Holocast, Orlando, Fla., 1981, Bronze Grille, James Madison, Library of Congress, Washington, 1981 (Recipient Edith S. Moore prize for sculpture 1948), Library of Congress, Washington (Bennet prize Nat. Sculpture Soc.), Library of Congress, Washington (Henry Hering award 1960). Fellow Sculpture Soc. (pres. 1967-70); mem. Archtl. League N.Y. (v.p. sculpture, silver medal 1958), Sculpture Center N.Y., Nat. Academician. Address: 4707 Ocean Blvd Sarasota FL 33581

ELISHA, WALTER Y., textile manufacturing company executive; b. 1932; married. Student, Wabash (Ind.) Coll., Harvard U. Sch. Bus. Vice chmn. bd., dir. Jewel Cos., 1965-80; chmn., pres., chief exec. officer Springs Mills Inc., Ft. Mill, S.C. Office: Springs Industries Inc PO Box 70 205 N White St Fort Mill SC 29715 *

ELIZABETH II (ALEXANDRA MARY ELIZABETH II), Her Majesty Queen Elizabeth II, Queen of U.K. of Gt. Britain and No. Ireland, and her other realms and Tys., head of the Commonwealth, defender of the faith; b. Apr. 21, 1926; d. King George VI and Queen

Elizabeth; m. Prince Philip, Duke of Edinburgh, Nov. 20, 1947; children—Charles Philip Arthur George, Anne Elizabeth Alice Louise, Andrew Albert Christian Edward, Edward Antony Richard Louis. Succeeded to throne following death of father, Feb. 6, 1952. Crowned Queen, June 2, 1953. Address: Buckingham Palace London SW 1 England *

ELIZONDO, HECTOR, actor; b. N.Y.C., Dec. 22, 1936; s. Martin Echevarria and Carmen Medina (Reyes) E.; m. Carolee Campbell, Apr. 13, 1969; 1 son, Rodd. Student, CCNY, 1955-56. Actor: plays Steambath, 1970 (OBIE award), Prisoner of Second Avenue, 1974, Sly Fox (Dr. Desk-Nun award), Medal of Honor Rag, American Playhouse; movie American Gigolo, 1979. Mem. Amnesty Internat. Roman Catholic.

ELKAN, GERALD HUGH, microbiologist, educator; b. Berlin, Aug. 3, 1929; s. George Herman and Eva Joan (Karger) E. A.B., Brigham Young U., Provo, Utah, 1951; M.S., Pa. State U., 1955; Ph.D., Va. Poly. Inst. and State U., Blacksburg, 1959. Mem. faculty N.C. State U., Raleigh, 1958—, prof. microbiology, 1969—, asst. univ. dean research, 1976-79; dir. N.C. Jr. Acad. Sci., 1973-76; chmn. N.C. High Sch. Sci. Fairs, 1973-74. Author articles in field, chpts. in books. Pres. Wake County (N.C.) Young Democratic Clubs, 1969; mem. N.C. Dem. Exec. Com., 1970-74, N.C. Water Control Council, 1970-76, N.C. Energy Com., 1973-74. Served with AUS, 1951-53, col. Res. Recipient Outstanding Teaching award N.C. State U., 1972; Fulbright scholar, Sweden, 1963-64; Fulbright Research scholar, Venezuela, 1980-81; grantee NSF, NIH, Dept. Agr., Am. Soybean Assn., Dept. State. Fellow Am. Acad. Microbiology; mem. AAAS, Can. Bacteriology Soc., Am. Acad. Biology, Soc. Gen. Microbiology, Netherlands Soc. Microbiology, World Acad. Arts and Scis., AAUP, N.C. Bacteriology Soc. (pres. 1968), N.C. Acad. Sci. (exec. sec. 1976-80), Antique Automobile Club Am., Res. Officers Assn., Sigma Xi (nat. dir. 1973-74, 76-83, Research award 1965), Phi Kappa Phi, Phi Sigma, Sigma Alpha Mu, Gamma Sigma Delta. Club: B'nai B'rith. Office: Dept Microbiology NC State U Raleigh NC 27650

ELKEN, JOHN HAYNES, ins. co. exec.; b. Mayville, N.D., Dec. 29, 1926; s. Guy L. and Gladys (Haynes) E.; m. Colleen LaMae Bakke, July 6, 1947; children—Eric Mikkel, Ann Louise. B.S., Stanford, 1949; M.S., U. Mich., 1950. With Bankers Life Co., 1950—, 2d v.p. underwriting, 1968-70, v.p., 1970-74, sr. v.p., 1974—. Served with USNR, 1944-46. Asso. Soc. Actuaries; mem. Acad. Actuaries. Conglist. (trustee 1963-67). Clubs: Des Moines, Des Moines Golf and Country (dir. 1969-71). Home: 124 53d St Des Moines IA 50312 Office: 711 High St Des Moines IA 50307

ELKES, TERRENCE ALLEN, corporation executive; b. N.Y.C., Apr. 28, 1934; s. Sidney and Beatrice (Sachnin) E.; m. Ruth Jerkowsky, June 14, 1959; children: Steven Andrew, David Adam, Daniel Arthur. B.A. cum laude, CCNY, 1955; J.D., U. Mich., 1958. Bar: N.Y. 1959. Atty. Prentice Hall, Inc., 1958-59; counsel internat. div. Norwich Pharmacal Co., 1959-65; corp. counsel Parsons & Whittemore, Inc., 1965-72; also v.p., sec.; corp. counsel Black Clawson Co., 1965-72; treas. Prince Albert Pulp Co. Ltd., 1966-72; v.p., sec., gen. counsel, dir. Viacom Internat., Inc., N.Y.C., 1972-76, exec. v.p., 1976-78, pres., 1978—, chief exec. officer, 1984—. Mem. Am., N.Y. State, N.Y. City bar assns. Home: 60 Stratford Ln Hastings-on-Hudson NY 10706 Office: 1211 Ave of Americas New York NY 10036

ELKHADEM, SAAD ELDIN AMIN, educator, author, editor, publisher; b. Cairo, Egypt, May 12, 1932; emigrated to Can., 1968, naturalized, 1974; s. Amin Saad and Zahra Amin (Tharwat) E.; m. Madiha Mahmoud, July 16, 1962; 1 dau., Sherifa. Ph.D., U. Vienna, 1961. Press attache Egyptian Govt., Berne, 1962-65; dir. Office for Cultural Relations, Cairo, 1965-67; asst. prof. U. N.D., Grand Forks, 1967-68; asso. prof. German U. N.B., Fredericton, 1968-74, prof., chmn. dept. comparative lit., 1974—. Author: Sechs Essays ueber den deutschen Roman, 1969, Ajniha Min Rasas, 1972, Zur Geschichte des deutschen Romans, 1974, Tajarib Laylah Wahidah, 1975, Dictionary of Literary Terms, 1976, The York Press Style manual, From Travels of the Egyptian Odysseus, 1979; Editor: Internat. Fiction Rev, 1974—; editor, gen. mgr.: York Press; Contbr. articles to profl. jours. Can. Council grantee, 1974-75. Mem. Modern Lang. Assn., Internat. Fiction Assn. (pres.), Am., Canadian Assn. Univ. Tchrs. Home: 96 Meadow Green Ct Fredericton NB Canada Office: Dept German and Russian University New Brunswick Fredericton NB Canada *The more the creative mind is separated from the suffering man, the more perfection the artist can attain in his work! My principles will never prevent me from living freely without restrictions. Principles are slavery. The determination not to adopt any values is a principle in itself.*

ELKIN, MILTON, educator, physician; b. Boston, Feb. 24, 1916; s. Philip and Rose (Dexter) E.; m. Gloria King, Nov. 12, 1943; children: Philip, Karen, Laura. A.B., Harvard, 1937; M.D., Harvard U., 1941. Diplomate: Am. Bd. Radiology (trustee 1983—). Asso. radiologist Peter Bent Brigham Hosp., Boston, 1951-52; dir. radiology Cambridge (Mass.) City Hosp.; asst. radiologist New Eng. Med. Center, Boston, 1952-53; asso. radiologist Cedars of Lebanon Hosp., Los Angeles, 1953-54; prof., chmn. dept. radiology Albert Einstein Coll. Medicine, Yeshiva U., N.Y.C., 1954—; dir. radiology Bronx Municipal Hosp. Center, N.Y.C., 1954—; Spl. cons. radiology tng. com. Nat. Inst. Gen. Med. Scis., NIH, USPHS, 1966-70; cons. Gen. Med. Research Program-Project Com., 1970-72; radiology rep. to Council Med. Splty. Socs., 1976-81. Author: Radiology of the Urinary System, 1980; Contbr. articles to profl. jours. Fellow Am. Coll. Radiology (bd. chancellors 1970-76, gold medal 1977); mem. AMA, Harvard Med. Soc., Am. Roentgen Ray Soc., Radiol. Soc. N.Am. (dir. 1975—, chmn. bd. 1978-79, pres. 1980-81), Assn. Univ. Radiologists, N.Y. Roentgen Soc. (pres.). Home: 13 Kingston Rd Scarsdale NY 10583 Office: 1300 Morris Park Ave New York NY 10461

ELKIN, STANLEY LAWRENCE, author, literature educator; b. N.Y.C., May 11, 1930; s. Philip and Zelda (Feldman) E.; m. Joan Marion Jacobson, Feb. 1, 1953; children: Philip Aaron, Bernard Edward, Molly Ann. A.B., U. Ill., 1952, M.A., 1953, Ph.D., 1961. Faculty Washington U., St. Louis, 1960; prof. Am. lit., 1969—, Merl Kling prof. modern letters, 1983—; vis. lectr. Smith Coll., 1964-65; vis. prof. U. Calif. at Santa Barbara, 1967, U. Wis. at Milw., 1969, U. Iowa, 1974, Yale U., 1975, Boston U., 1976. Author: Boswell, 1964, Criers and Kibitzers, Kibitzers and Criers, 1966, A Bad Man, 1967, The Dick Gibson Show, 1971; Editor: Stories from The Sixties, 1971, The Making of Ashenden, 1972, Searches and Seizures, 1973, The Franchiser, 1976, The Living End, 1979, Best American Short Stories of 1980, 1980, Stanley Elkin's Greatest Hits, 1980, George Mills, 1982. Served with AUS, 1955-57. Recipient Humor prize Paris Rev., 1965; Longview Found. award, 1962; Guggenheim fellow, 1966-67; Rockefeller grantee, 1968-69; Nat. Endowment for Humanities grantee, 1972; Am. Acad. and Nat. Inst. Arts and Letters award, 1974; Richard and Hinda Rosenthal award, 1980; So. Rev. award for short fiction, 1981; Nat. Book Critics Circle award, 1982. Mem. Am. Acad. Arts and Letters, Nat. Inst. Arts and Letters. Home: 225 Westgate University City MO 63130 Office: Duncker Hall Washington Univ Saint Louis MO 63130

ELKIND, DAVID, educator; b. Detroit, Mar. 11. 1931; s. Peter and Betsy (Nelson) E.; m. Sally Faye Malinsky, Dec. 21, 1960 (div.); children: Paul Steven, Robert Edward, Eric Allen.; m. Nina C. Lide W. Ingrao, Nov. 25, 1982. B.A., UCLA, 1952, Ph.D., 1955. Diplomate: Am. Bd. Profl. Examiners in Psychology. Research asst. to David Rapaport, Austen Riggs Center, Stockbridge, Mass., 1956-57; staff psychologist Beth Israel Hosp., Boston, 1957-59; asst. prof. Wheaton Coll., Norton, Mass., 1959-61; asst. prof. med. psychology U. Calif. Med. Sch., Los Angeles, 1961-62; assoc. prof., dir. Child Study Center, U. Denver, 1962-66; prof., dir. grad. tng. in developmental psychology, dept. psychology U. Rochester, N.Y., 1966-78; chmn. Eliot Pearson dept. child study Tufts U., Medford, Mass., 1978—; research dir. World of Inquiry Evaluation-NSF, 1970; project dir. Tng. of Early Childhood Specialists, U.S. Office Edn., 1970; psychol. cons. VA, 1962-74, Rochester Mental Health Center, 1966-74, Rochester Family Ct., 1967-73; headmaster Mt. Hope Sch., Rochester, 1974-77. Author: (with H.J. Flavell) Studies in Cognitive Development, 1969, Children and Adolescents, 1974, A Sympathetic Understanding of the Child, 1974, (with I. Weiner) Child Development: A Core Approach, 1972, (with others) Psychology: An Introduction, 1973, Child Development and Education, 1976, (with D. Hetzel) Readings in Human Development: Contemporary Perspectives, (with Weiner) Development of the Child, 1978, The Child's Reality: Three Developmental Themes, 1978, The Child and Society, 1979, The Hurried Child, 1982, All Grown Up and No Place to Go, 1984. NSF Sr. Postdoctoral fellow, Geneva, 1964-65. Fellow Am. Psychol. Assn., AAAS. Home: 1600 Massachusetts Ave #805 Cambridge MA 02138 Office: Tufts U Medford MA 02155

ELKIND, MORTIMER MURRAY, biophysicist; b. Bklyn., Oct. 25, 1922; s. Samuel and Yetta (Lubarsky) E.; m. Karla Annikki Holst, Jan. 27, 1960; children—Sean Thomas, Samuel Scott, Jonathan Harald. B.M.E., Cooper Union, 1943; M.M.E., Poly. Inst. Bklyn., 1949; M.S. in Elec. Engring, Mass. Inst. Tech., 1951; Ph.D. in Physics, Mass. Inst. Tech., 1953. Asst. project engr. Wyssmont Co., N.Y.C., 1943; project engr. Safe Flight Instrument Corp., White Plains, N.Y., 1946-47; head instrumentation sect. Sloan Kettering Inst. Cancer Research, 1947-49; physicist Nat. Cancer Inst. on assignment to Mass. Inst. Tech., 1949-53; on assignment to Donner Lab., U. Calif. at Berkeley, 1953-54; physicist Lab. Physiology, Nat. Cancer Inst., Bethesda, Md., 1954-67, sr. research physicist, 1967-69; sr. biophysicist biology dept. Brookhaven Nat. Lab., Upton, L.I., N.Y., 1969-73; guest scientist MRC exptl. radiopathology unit Hammersmith Hosp., London, 1971-73; sr. biophysicist, div. biol. and med. research Argonne (Ill.) Nat. Lab., 1973-76, asst. dir., 1976-78, head mammalian cell biology group, 1978-81; prof. radiology U. Chgo., 1973-81; chmn. dept. radiology and radiation biology Colo. State U., 1981—; Mem. radiation study sect. NIH, 1962-66, molecular biology study sect., 1970-71; mem. developmental therapeutics com. Nat. Cancer Inst., 1975—. Author monograph. Served with USNR, 1944-46. Recipient E.O. Lawrence award AEC, 1967; Superior Service award HEW, 1969; L.H. Gray medal Internat. Com. Radiation Units and Measurements, 1977; E.W. Bertner award M.D. Anderson Hosp. and Tumor Inst., 1979; A.W. Erskine award Radiol. Soc. N. Am., 1980; Nat. Cancer Inst. Spl. fellow, 1972-74. Mem. AAAS, Biophys. Soc., Radiation Research Soc. (council 1965-66, asso. editor jour. 1965-68, pres.-elect 1980—), Tissue Culture Assn., Am. Assn. Cancer Research (asso. editor jour. 1980—), Sigma Xi, Tau Beta Pi. Office: Dept Radiology and Radiation Biology Colo State U Fort Collins CO 80523

ELKINS, BETTYE SWALES, lawyer; b. San Antonio, Apr. 3, 1941; d. Franklin Easterby and Eddy Bernice (Henderson) Swales; m. Aubrey Christian Elkins, Jr., June 3, 1962; children: Duncan Christian, Ellen Vivian. B.J., U. Tex.-Austin, 1962; J.D., U. Mich., 1970. Bar: Mich. 1971, U.S. Supreme Ct. 1975. Assoc. firm Dykema, Gossett, Spencer, Goodnow & Trigg, Detroit, 1971-78, ptnr., Ann Arbor, 1978—; asst. prof. law U. Toledo, 1973-74; vis. lectr. U. Mich.; adj. asst. prof. Wayne State U., 1978-80. Bd. dirs. Met. Hosp., Detroit, Hospice of Washtenaw, Ann Arbor, Ann Arbor Art Assn., 1978-82; trustee Greenhills Sch., Ann Arbor, 1981—. Mem. ABA, Mich. Bar Assn., Am. Soc. Hosp. Attys., Am. Soc. Law and Medicine, Mich. Soc. Hosp. Attys. Democrat. Presbyterian. Home: 3791 Waldenwood Dr Ann Arbor MI 48105 Office: 206 S 5th Ave 300 Fed Ctr Bldg Ann Arbor MI 48105

ELKINS, FRANCIS CLARK, history educator, university official; b. Scranton, Ark., Feb. 24, 1923; s. Frank and Auby (Moore) E.; m. Norma Trice, Aug. 18, 1946; 1 dau., Annette. B.A., State Coll. Ark., 1943; M.A., U. Ark., 1947; Ph.D., Syracuse U., 1953. From instr. to prof., chmn. div. social sci. Henderson State Coll., Arkadelphia, Ark., 1946-61; pres. Chadron (Nebr.) State Coll., 1961-67, N.E. Mo. State Coll., Kirksville, 1967-69; coordinator Univ. Coll., Ark State U., 1969-70, v.p. instrn., 1970-78, v.p. univ. relations, 1979-80; v.p. univ. relations and devel. No. Ariz. U., Flaggstaff, 1980-83, prof. history, 1980—, president's coordinator univ. relations, 1983—; Mem. exec. com. Rocky Mountain Edn. Lab., 1965-67; examiner North Central Assn. Colls. and Schs.; examiner, cons. Nat. Council Accreditation Tchr. Edn., chmn. visitation and appraisal com., 1963-68; mem. Nebr. Ednl. TV Council Higher Edn., 1966-67, Ark. Council Econ. Edn., 1970-81. Mem. adv. council Mo. 4-H Found., 1968-69; mem. Ark. Adv. Council on Career Edn.; bd. dirs. United Way, 1980—. Served with USAAF, 1943-45. Decorated D.F.C., Air medal with four oak leaf clusters. Mem. Am. Assn. Colls. Tchr. Edn. (dir. 1968-71, state liaison rep. 1974-77), Asso. Orgns. Tchr. Edn. (adv. council), N.E.A. (life), Ark. Edn. Assn. (life), C. of C. (dir. 1980—), Phi Delta Kappa, Kappa Delta Pi, Phi Alpha Theta, Alpha Chi, Phi Kappa Phi, Sigma Tau Gamma, Sigma Nu. Methodist. Clubs: Elk, Rotarian. Home: 800 W University Heights Dr S Flagstaff AZ 86001 Office: Exec Center No Ariz U Flagstaff AZ 86011

ELKINS, GLEN RAY, service company executive; b. Winnsboro, La., May 23, 1933; s. Ceicel Herbert and Edna Mae (Luallen) E.; m. Irene Kay Hildebrand, Aug. 25, 1951; children: Steven Breen, Douglas Charles, Karen Anne, Michael Glen. A.A. in Indsl. Mgmt, Coll. San Mateo, 1958. Successively mgr. production control, mgr. logistics, plant mgr., asst. v.p. ops. Aircraft Engring. and Maintenance Co. (Aemco), 1957-64; successively mgr. field ops., v.p. ops., exec. v.p., now pres. Internat. Atlas Services Co., Princeton, N.J., 1964—; sr. v.p. Atlas Corp., Princeton; chmn., chief exec. officer, dir. Global Assocs.; pres. Global Assocs. Internat. Ltd. Area chmn. Easter Seals drive, 1974. Served with USN, 1950-54. Mem. Nat. Mgmt. Assn., Electronic Industries Assn. Clubs: Beden Brook Country., Sequoya Country, Round Hill Country, Lakeview. Lodge: Rotary. Home: 198 Bolla Ave Alamo CA 94507 Office: 2010 Webster St Suite 300 Oakland CA 94612

ELKINS, HILLARD, producer; b. N.Y.C., Oct. 18, 1929; s. Max and Rachel (Kaplan) E.; m. Judith Wilson, Oct. 5, 1976; children—John, Daniel Hillard. B.A., N.Y. U., 1953. Exec. William Morris Agy., 1949-50; exec. v.p. Gen. Artists Corp., 1952-53; pres. Hillard Elkins Mgmt., 1953-60, Elkins Prodns. Internat. Corp., N.Y.C., 1960—, Elkins Prodns. Ltd., 1972—, Hillard Elkins Entertainment Corp., 1974—, Media Mix Prodns. Inc., 1979—. Producer: films A Dolls House, 1972 (Outer Critics award), Alice's Restaurant, 1969 (Film Daily award), A New Leaf, 1971, Oh! Calcutta!, 1972, Richard Pryor Live in Concert, 1978; theatre plays Golden Boy, 1967, Oh! Calcutta!, 1970, A Doll's House, 1973, A Streetcar Named Desire, 1974, Carte Blanche, 1976, A Doll's House, 1972, The Rothschilds, 1972 (Tony award nomination for best mus.), Oh! Calcutta, 1969, Golden Boy, 1964, Hedda Gabler, 1972, Broadway South African Season, 1974 (Tony award nomination for best play), Kings and Clowns, London; The Travelling Music Show, London; producer: theatre plays Stop the World, N.Y.C., An Evening With Quentin Crisp, N.Y.C. and Los Angeles, 1978, Georgia Brown and Friends, Los Angeles. Served with AUS, 1950-52. Mem. Dramatists Guild, League New York Theatres. Address: 1357 Schuyler Rd Beverly Hills CA 90210

ELKINS, JAMES ANDERSON, JR., banker; b. Galveston, Tex., Mar. 24, 1919; s. James Anderson and Isabel (Mitchell) E.; m. Margaret Wiess, Nov. 24, 1945; children—Elise, James Anderson III, Leslie K. B.A., Princeton, 1941. With First City Nat. Bank, Houston, 1941—, v.p., 1946-50, pres., 1950; now chmn. bd.; chmn. bd. First City Bancorp., Tex.; dir. Cameron Iron Works, Inc., Freeport Minerals, Inc., N.Y.C., Eastern Airlines, Hill Samuel Group, Ltd., Am. Gen. Ins. Co., Houston. Trustee Tex. Children's Hosp., Baylor U. Coll. Medicine. Episcopalian. Home: 101 Farish Circle Houston TX 77024 Office: First City Nat Bank Houston TX 77001

ELKINS, JAMES ANDREW, JR., lawyer; b. Little Rock, Jan. 24, 1940; s. James Andrew and Doris (O'Neal) E.; m. Martha Lee Allen, Nov. 11, 1963; children: James Andrew, Allen Lee, Martha Lee. A.B., U. South, 1962; J.D., U. Ga., 1965. Bar: Ga. 1965. Assoc. Roberts and Thornton, Columbus, Ga., 1965-69, Roberts, Elkins & Kilpatrick, Columbus, 1969-71, Grogan, Jones & Layfield, 1971-72; sole practice, Columbus, 1972-73; ptnr. Elkins & Flournoy, P.C., Columbus, 1973-83, Elkins & Gemmette, P.C., 1983—. Bd. dirs. Pioneer Little League Columbus, Inc., 1977-79, sec., 1978-79; mem. Com. on Drug Abuse Control, 1971-75. Mem. Am. Trial Lawyers Assn., Ga. Trial Lawyers Assn., Ga. Assn. Criminal Def. Lawyers, State Bar. Ga., Chattahooche Bar Assn., Nat. Orgn. Social Security Claimants Reps. Republican. Episcopalian. Club: Columbus Lawyers. Home: 6130 Canterbury Dr Columbus GA 31909 Office: PO Box 1736 Columbus GA 31902

ELKINS, LLOYD EDWIN, petroleum engineer, energy consultant; b. Golden, Colo., Apr. 1, 1912; s. Edwin and Beulah M. (Feitch) E.; m. Virginia L. Crosby, May 27, 1934; children: Marylou, Barbara Lee, Lloyd Edwin. Petroleum Engr., Colo. Sch.Mines, 1934; Ph.D. in Sci, Coll. Ozarks. With Amoco Prodn. Co., 1934-77; successively field engr., petroleum engr. Tulsa gen. office, sr. petroleum engr., petroleum engring. supr., asst. chief prodn. engr., chief prodn. engr., chief engr. prodn. dept., prodn. research mgr. oil and gas prodn. Amoco Products Co., 1949-77; energy cons., 1977—. Contbr. articles to profl. jours. Named to Engring. Hall of Fame Okla. State U., 1961; recipient Distinguished Service medal Colo. Sch. Mines, 1961; named to Engring. Hall of Fame U. Tulsa. Mem. Am. Assn. Petroleum Geologists, Am. Petroleum Inst. (chmn. mid-continent dist. div. prodn. 1948-49, chmn. adv. com fundamental research on occurrence and recovery petroleum 1941), Am. Inst. Mining, Metall, and Petroleum Engrs. (hon., v.p. 1953-59, pres. 1962, Anthony F. Lucas gold medal 1966), Nat. Acad. Engring., Tulsa Geol. Soc., Australian Inst. Mining and Metallurgy (hon.). Methodist. Clubs: Engineers (pres. 1950-51), Petroleum, Tulsa Country (Tulsa). Home: 2806 E 27th St Tulsa OK 74114 Office: PO Box 4758 Tulsa OK 74159

ELKINS, STANLEY MAURICE, historian, educator; b. Boston, Apr. 27, 1925; s. Frank and Frances (Reiner) E.; m. Dorothy Adele Lamken, June 22, 1947; children: Susan Roselyn, Robert Joel, Barbara Marion, Sara Ann. A.B., Harvard, 1949; M.A., Columbia, 1951, Ph.D., 1959. Tchr. Fieldston Sch., N.Y.C., 1951-54; asst. prof. history U. Chgo., 1955-60; faculty Smith Coll., Northampton, Mass., 1960—, prof. history, 1964-69, Sydenham Clark Parsons prof. history, 1969—; fellow Inst. for Advanced Study, 1970-71, 76-77. Author: Slavery: A Problem in American Institutional and Intellectual Life, 1959. Served with AUS, 1943-46. Social Sci. Research Council fellow, 1963-64; Rockefeller fellow, 1954-55; Guggenheim fellow, 1976-77. Mem. Orgn. Am. Historians, Am. Jewish Hist. Soc., Am. Hist. Assn. Home: 17 Kensington Ave Northampton MA 01060

ELKO, NICHOLAS THOMAS, clergyman; b. Donora, Pa., Dec. 14, 1909; s. John and Mary (Vazur) E. B.A., Duquesne U., 1931, LL.D., 1958; M.Theology, Byzantine Cath. Sem., Uzhorod, Czechoslovakia, 1935; L.H.D., Stuebenville Coll., 1960; Litt.D., St. Vincent Coll., Latrobe, Pa., 1962. Ordained priest Roman Cath. Ch., 1934; consecrated bishop, 1955; bishop Byzantine Cath. Diocese of Pitts., 1955-67; named archbishop Oriental Congregation, Rome, 1967; head liturgical commn., ordaining prelate Byzantine Rite Vatican, 1967-71; aux. archbishop of Cin., vicar gen., 1971—; Bd. visitors Thomas Aquinas Coll., Ojai, Calif.; bd. dirs. Athenaeum of Ohio, Cin.; spiritual dir. Cath. Physicians Guild; chmn. Archbishop Elko Found., Dayton, Ohio. Mem. Newcomen Soc., Veneration Soc. Sanctity (spiritual dir.), Internat. Orgn. More Agrl. Prodn. Address: 2300 S Smithville Rd Dayton OH 45420

ELKOURI, FRANK, legal educator; b. Byron, Okla., Sept. 3, 1921; s. David and Adel (Elkouri) E.; m. Edna Anne Asper, Aug. 26, 1956. B.A., U. Okla., 1943, LL.B., 1947; LL.M., U. Mich., 1948, S.J.D., 1951. Bar: Okla. 1947. Mem. firm Quinlan & Elkouri, Oklahoma City, 1948-49, 50-51; atty. Nat. Wage Stablzn. Bd., Washington and Dallas, 1951-52; mem. faculty Coll. Law U. Okla., Norman, 1952—; now George Lynn Cross research prof.; Adviser to Office Pres. U. Okla., 1952-57; exec. reservist U.S. Labor Dept., 1963—; arbitrator, labor-mgmt. disputes, 1948—; spl. justice Okla. Supreme Ct., 1967; vis. prof. Law Sch. U. Mich., 1961. Author: (with Edna Asper Elkouri) How Arbitration Works, 1952, 60, 73; Contbr. to profl. jours. Mem. Okla. Gov.'s Spl. Adv. Com. on Workmen's Compensation, 1975. Served to 2d lt. F.A. AUS, 1943-44. W.W. Cook fellow, 1947-48. Mem. Okla. Bar Assn., Nat. Acad. Arbitrators, Am. Arbitration Assn. (Whitney North Seymour arbitration medal 1980), Order Coif, Phi Beta Kappa, Phi Eta Sigma. Home: 1001 Whispering Pines Dr Norman OK 73069

ELKS, HAZEL HULBERT (MRS. DAVID ELKS), librarian; b. Franklin, N.J., June 16, 1916; d. Harry C. and Hazel (Ball) Hulbert; m. David L. Elks, July 6, 1957. Student, Library Sch., Trenton State Coll., summer 1938; extension student, Rutgers U. With Elizabeth (N.J.) Pub. Library, 1941—, librarian, 1946-49, personnel dir., 1949-62, dir. library, 1962—. Trustee Elizabeth League Women Voters, 1959-62, Elizabeth YWCA, 1960-62; mem. exec. bd. Elizabeth Bicentennial Com., 1975-76; Vis. Nurse and Health Service Union County, 1977—; mem. citizen advisory bd. Elizabeth Bd. Edn., 1976—; bd. mgrs. Egenolf Nursery, 1980; chmn. scholarship com. Soroptimist Found., 1980; vol. Meml. Hosp., Union, N.J., 1980; mem. Elizabeth Mcht.'s Com., 1980. Mem. N.J. Library Assn. (chmn. fed. relations com. 1965—). Home: 1389 Vauxhall Rd Union NJ 07083 Office: 11 S Broad St Elizabeth NJ 07202

ELKUS, HOWARD F., architect; b. San Francisco, Apr. 12, 1938; s. Eugene S. and Felice (Kahn) E.; m. Lorna W. Elkus, Apr. 25, 1971. B.S. in M.E., Stanford U., 1959; M.Arch. with distinction, Harvard U., 1963. Registered architect, Calif., Mass., Wis., Fla., Tex., Ohio. Vice pres., prin. The Architects Collaborative, 1962—, Fry Drew & Ptnrs., London, 1961, Wilsey, Ham & Blair, San Mateo, Calif., 1960, A.B. Atomenergi, Stockholm, 1958, Wagner & Martinez, Palo Alto, Calif., 1957. Archtl. works include, Copley Pl., Boston, GSIS Hdqrs. and Fin. Ctr., Manila, Philippines, Johnson Wax Hdqrs. Complex expansion, Racine, Wis., AIA Hdqrs., Washington. Recipient Prestressed Concrete Inst. award, 1983, The Concrete Industry Bd. Spl.

Recognition, 1983, citation Engring. News Record, 1982, Constrn. Man of Yr. award, 1982, White House citation for contbn. to energy efficient environment, 1983, Passive Solar Design award, 1982, Owens-Corning Energy Conservation award, 1982, others. Fellow AIA; mem. Mass. Assn. Architects, Boston Soc. Architects, Boston Archtl. Ctr., Urban Land Inst. Address: The Architects Collaborative Inc 46 Brattle St Cambridge MA 02138

ELKUS, RICHARD J., financial co. exec.; b. San Francisco, May 12, 1910; s. Eugene S. and Miriam (Meyerfeld) E.; m. Ruth Kahn, Mar. 23, 1933; children—Richard J., Peter K. Pres. Mangrum Holbrook & Elkus, San Francisco, 1939-48, First Nat. Bank San Mateo County, Redwood City, Calif., 1950-55; exec. v.p. Wells Fargo Bank, San Francisco, 1955-56, dir., 1955-60; pres. U.S. Leasing Corp., San Francisco, 1960-64, chmn. bd. dirs., 1964-69; former chmn. bd. Ampex Corp., Redwood City; dir. Merc. Credit Co., London, Barclays Bank Calif.; past mem. commn. legislation and taxation Calif. Bankers Assn. Author: Alamos: A Philosophy in Living, 1965. Chmn. San Francisco Bay Area council Sequoia chpt. ARC, San Mateo County Charter Revision Commn.; bd. govs. Smaller War Plants Corp., World War II; also mem. Coordinating Council, San Francisco; mem. Prodn. Urgency Com, Manpower Priorities Com., U.S. nat. commn. for UNESCO, Pres.'s Commn. on Mental Retardation; hon. chmn. Richard J. Elkus Youth Ranch; mem. Com. of 25, Palm Springs, Calif.; Bd. dirs. San Francisco Boy Scouts Am., Children's Health Council, Meml. Blood Bank, Vis. Nurses Assn., Coro Found., Golden Gate chpt. ARC, Mental Research Inst.; bd. regents Coll. Notre Dame; bd. govs. United Crusade San Francisco. Mem. San Mateo County Hist. Soc. (dir.), Am. Horse Shows Assn. (dir.), Am. Hackney Horse Soc. Clubs: St. Francis Yacht (chmn. bd.), Family, Commonwealth (San Francisco); Sequoia (Redwood City) (pres.); Racquet, O'Donnel Golf. Office: PO Box 432 Redwood City CA 94064

ELLEDGE, SCOTT BOWEN, educator; b. Pitts., Jan. 7, 1914; s. Harvey Gerald and Eva (Bowen) E.; m. Liane von Krolikiewicz, Feb. 15, 1950. A.B., Oberlin Coll., 1935; A.M., Cornell U., 1936, Ph.D., 1941. Instr. English Purdue U., 1936-38, 39-40, Cornell U., 1941-45, Harvard, 1945-47; asso. prof. English Carleton Coll., Northfield, Minn., 1947-52, chmn. dept., 1951-62, prof., 1952-62; prof. English Cornell U., Ithaca, N.Y., 1962—; co-founder Salzburg (Austria) Seminar in Am. Studies, 1947. Editor: Eighteenth Century Critical Essays, 1961, The Continental Model, 1960, Lycidas (Milton), 1966, Paradise Lost (Milton), 1975, E.B. White: A Biography, 1984; Contbr. articles to ednl. jours. Me. AAUP, Modern Lang. Assn., Phi Kappa Phi. Home: 107 Overlook Rd Ithaca NY 14850

ELLEGOOD, DONALD RUSSELL, publishing exec.; b. Lawton, Okla., June 21, 1924; s. Claude Jennings and Iva Claire (Richards) E.; m. Bettie Jane Dixon, Dec. 11, 1947; children—Elizabeth Nemi, Francis Hunter, Kyle Richards, Sarah Helen. B.A., U. Okla., 1948, M.A., 1950. Asst. editor U. Okla. Press, 1950-51; editor Johns Hopkins Press, 1951-54; dir. La. State U. Press, 1954-63, U. Wash. Press, Seattle, 1963—. Contbr. articles to profl. jours. Served to 1st lt. USAAF, 1943-46. Decorated Air medal, D.F.C. Mem. Am. Univ. Pubs. Group London (dir.), Am. Assn. Univ. Presses (pres.), Phi Beta Kappa. Home: 17852 49th Pl NE Seattle WA 98155 Office: U Wash Press Seattle WA 98105

ELLENBERG, MAX, physician, medical educator; b. N.Y.C., Jan. 29, 1911; s. Philip and Sarah (Yablon) E.; m. Mary M. Lemon, Dec. 1, 1942; children: Richard Dennis, William Arthur. B.S., CUNY, 1931; M.D., NYU, 1935. Diplomate: Am. Bd. Internal Medicine. Intern Mt. Sinai Hosp., N.Y.C., 1931-34; resident in medicine, 1935-38, research asst. in chemistry, 1940-51, chief diagnostic clinic, 1951-55, attending physician for diabetes, 1969—; instr. medicine Columbia U. Coll. Physicians and Surgeons, 1940-52; clin. prof. medicine Mt. Sinai Med. Center, 1970—. Editor: Diabetes Mellitus, Theory and Practice, 1970, 3d edit., 1983; contbr. numerous articles to med. jours. Served to lt. col. M.C. AUS, 1942-46. Recipient Prof. Frank Meml. award Turkish Diabetes Assn., 1978. Mem. Am. Diabetes Assn. (pres. 1974-75, dir. 1972—, Banting medal 1975), Internat. Diabetes Fedn., A.C.P., Am. Soc. Internal Medicine, Am. Med. Writers Assn., Internat. Soc. Internal Medicine, AMA, N.Y. Acad. Scis. (chmn. sect. bio-medicine 1979—), N.Y. Diabetes Assn. (pres. 1964-65, dir. 1950—), Mt. Sinai Alumni Assn. (pres. 1962-63, Abraham Jacobi medallion 1964). Jewish. Club: Waccabuc Country. Office: 936 Fifth Ave New York NY 10021

ELLENBERGER, JACK STUART, law librarian; b. Lamar, Colo., Sept. 5, 1930; s. Emmert C. and Ruby F. (Overstreet) E. B.S., Georgetown U., 1957; M.L.S., Columbia U., 1959. Law librarian HEW, 1957; librarian Carter, Ledyard & Milburn, N.Y.C., 1957-60, Jones, Day, Reavis & Pogue (and predecessor firm), Cleve., 1960, Bar Assn. of D.C., Washington, 1961-63, Covington & Burling, 1963-78, Shearman & Sterling, N.Y.C., 1978—. Editor: (with Mahar) Legislative History of the Securities Act of 1933 and the Securities Exchange Act of 1934, 1973. Served with USAF, 1951-54. Mem. Am. Assn. Law Libraries (pres. 1976-77), Spl. Libraries Assn. Office: Shearman & Sterling 53 Wall St New York NY 10005

ELLENBOGEN, GEORGE, educator; b. Montreal, Que., Can., Nov. 19, 1934; came to U.S., 1966; s. Moses and Jenny (Borenstein) E.; m. Karia Doris Feinzig, Dec. 18, 1960; children: Sara Rachel, Adam. B.A., McGill U., Montreal, 1955; M.A., U. Montreal, 1962; Ph.D., Tufts U., 1969. Mem. faculty Bentley Coll., Waltham, Mass., 1965—, prof. English, 1980—, chmn. dept., 1980—; poetry editor Boston Today, 1978-81. Author: Winds of Unreason, 1957, The Nights Unstones, 1971; also articles, numerous poems to mags. Mem. AAUP, MLA, Coll. English Assn., Nat. Council Tchrs. of English. Home: 22 Lewis Rd Belmont MA 02178 Office: Bentley Coll Waltham MA 02154

ELLENBOGEN, MILTON JOSEPH, editor; b. N.Y.C., Mar. 18, 1935; s. Jacob and Edith (Horowitz) E.; m. Linda Letich, Mar. 11, 1973; 1 son, Michael Joseph. Tech. degree, Mondell Inst. Maths., 1957, RCA Inst. Electronics, 1959; B.A. in English Lit, Queens Coll., 1974, M.A., 1977. Electronics technician IBM Corp., Endicott, N.Y., 1959-60; tech. writer Coastal Publs., N.Y.C., 1960-65, Grumman Aerospace Corp., Beth Page, N.Y., 1965-69; asso. editor Elec. Equipment Mag. (published by Sutton Pub. Co.), White Plains, N.Y., 1969-71, editor, 1971-82; mng. editor Indsl. Distbn. Mag. (published by Morgan-Grampian Pub. Co.), N.Y.C., 1982—. Contbr. short stories to popular mags. Served with USN, 1952-56; Korea. Mem. Am. Bus. Press, Mystery Writers Am., Nat. Writers Club (pres. N.Y. chpt. 1964-66), Alliance Française. Democrat. Club: Overseas Press. Home: 20 Daniels Pl White Plains NY 10604

ELLER, CHARLES HOWE, physician; b. Bloomington, Ind., June 5, 1904; s. Charles Asbury and Alice Belle (Howe) E.; m. Jacqueline Marie Rousseau, Dec. 1933; children—Patricia Ann, Mary Jacqueline. A.B., Stanford, 1927; M.D., U. Colo., 1930; Dr. P.H., Johns Hopkins, 1934. Diplomate: American Bd. Preventive Medicine and Pub. Health. Health officer, Valencia and Bernalillo countries, N.M., 1931-34, health officer, Charlottesville, Va., 1934-35; asso. prof. preventive medicine U. Va. Med. Sch., 1934-35; asst. dir., later dir. rural health Va. Health Dept., 1935-37; dir. Eastern health dist., Balt., 1937-46; asso. prof. pub. health adminstrn. Johns Hopkins Sch. Hygiene, 1937-46; dir. health, Richmond, Va., 1946-49, Louisville, also Jefferson County, Ky., 1949-55; asso. prof. preventive medicine Med. Coll. Va., 1946-49; prof., chmn. dept. community health U. Louisville, 1949-59; commr. health, St. Louis County, Mo., 1959-73; prof. pub. health Washington U. Sch. Medicine, 1959-75; ret., 1975; Bd. dirs. Louisville Rehab. Center.; Cons. NIH, 1951-55, 57-59; exec. dir. Health Delivery Systems, Inc., St. Louis, from 1973-75; spl. cons. commn. Research Assos., N.Y.C., 1955—; former asso. area med. dir. United Mine Workers's Welfare and Retirement Fund; cons. preventive medicine, Ft. Knox, 1958; mem. task force Nat. Commn. Community Health Services, 1963; mem. Mo. Adv. Council for Comprehensive Health Planning, 1968—. Fellow Am. Pub. Health Assn. (gov. 1962-65 67-70, exec. bd. 1970-73), Am. Coll. Preventative Medicine; mem. Am., Mo. med. assns., St. Louis County Med. Soc. (past pres.), Mo. Pub. Health Assn. (past pres.). Address: El Castillo Apts 515 250 E Alameda St Santa Fe NM 87501

ELLER, JOHN CLINTON, hosp. exec.; b. Salem, Va., Sept. 25, 1916; s. Christian Emery and Rebecca Martha (Henry) E.; m. Jessie Mae Conner, June 9, 1943 (dec. Jan. 6, 1978); children—John Thomas, Michael Conner; m. Leona Z. Row, Dec. 24, 1979. A.B., Bridgewater (Va.) Coll., 1941; M.Div., Bethany Theol. Sem., 1948; M.S. in Hosp. Adminstrn, Northwestern U., 1952. Tchr., Fincastle, Va., 1939-40; prin. Cloverdale (Va.) Elementary Sch., 1941-42; ordained to ministry Ch. of Brethren, 1936; pastor in, Crab Orchard, W.Va., 1942-44; with Bethany Brethren Hosp., Chgo., 1945-66, chaplain, 1945-50, asst. adminstr., 1950-52, adminstr., 1952-64, exec. dir., 1964-66, Am. Protestant Hosp. Assn., Chgo., 1966-73; dir. planned giving Swedish Covenant Hosp., Chgo., 1973—; Bd. dirs. Chgo. Hosp. Council, 1954-66, pres., 1959-61; bd. dirs. Ill. Hosp. Assn., 1962-65, Sears, Roebuck YMCA, Chgo., 1958-66. Mem. Am. Protestant Hosp. Assn. (dir. 1958, pres. 1965), Am. Coll. Hosp. Adminstrs., Brethren Health and Welfare Assn. (pres. 1954-57, 68-69, sec. 1964-66), Coll. Chaplains, Am. Protestant Hosp. Assn., Am. Hosp. Assn., Nat. Soc. Fund Raising Execs., AM. Assn. Hosp. Devel., Nat. Geog. Soc., Am. Audubon Soc., Nat. Parks Assn., Nat. Wildlife Fedn. Club: Torch. Home: 315 Constitution Ave NE Washington DC 20002 Office: 5145 N California Ave Chicago IL 60625

ELLERBEE, LINDA, broadcast journalist; b. Bryan, Tex., Aug. 15, 1944. Ed., Vanderbilt U. Newscaster, disc jockey Sta. WVON, Chgo., 1964-67; program dir. Sta. KSJO, San Francisco, 1967-68; reporter Sta. KJNO and AP, Juneau, Alaska, 1969-72, Sta. KHOU-TV, Dallas, 1972-73, Sta. WCBS-TV, N.Y.C., 1973-76; Washington corr. NBC News, 1975-78; co-anchor Weekend, NBC News, NBC-TV, 1978-80; reporter NBC Nightly News, 1980-82; co-anchor NBC News Overnight, 1982—. Office: NBC News 30 Rockefeller Plaza New York NY 10020 *

ELLERY, JOHN BLAISE, state official; b. N.Y.C., Feb. 3, 1920; s. William Hoyt and Thea (Kavanagh) E.; m. Ellen Jane Savacool, Sept. 21, 1946; children: Thea Jane, Martha Ann, Sarah Savacool, John Blaise, Jessica Joyce. A.B., Hamilton Coll., 1948; M.A., U. Colo., 1950; Ph.D., U. Wis., 1954. Instr. U. Colo., 1948-50; asst. prof. U. Iowa, 1952-56; asso. prof. Wayne State U., 1957-61; prof., chmn. dept. English East Tenn. State U., Johnson City, 1961-66; sr. lectr. Njala U. Coll., West Africa, 1966-68; asst. to chancellor U. Wis., Stevens Point, 1968-74, vice chancellor, 1974-80, acting chancellor, 1978-79, dean Coll. Natural Resources, 1970-72, dir. Ednl. Media Center, 1980-82; sec. of state Wis. Dept. Vet. Affairs, 1982—; Mem. Wis. Gov.'s Commn. on Edn., 1969; v.p. Wis.-Nicaragua Partners of Ams., 1979-80, pres., 1980-81, bd. dirs., exec. com., 1978—. Works include John Stuart Mill, 1964, Linguistic Impedance and Dialect Interference Among Certain African Tribes, 1970; also short stories, articles; contbg. author: Essays on Language and Literature, 1969. Served to ensign USNR, 1938-41; with inf. AUS, 1941-45; col. Army N.G. Decorated Silver Star, Bronze Star with oak leaf cluster, Purple Heart with oak leaf cluster, Conspicuous Service Cross; Croix de Guerre; Medaille Militaire Fourragere; recipient U.S. Army patriotic civilian service award. Mem. Ret. Officers Assn., Res. Officers Assn., Assn. of U.S. Army, Sigma Phi Epsilon, Sigma Tau Delta, Eta Sigma Phi. Office: 77 N Dickinson St Madison WI 53702 *As a soldier, sailor, and sometime scholar, I have learned to place my confidence in personal commitment rather than statistical probabilities, and to accept the fact that criticism will vary in direct proportion to the distance from the point of responsibility.*

ELLETT, ALAN SIDNEY, real estate devl. co. exec.; b. Seven Kings, Essex, Eng., Jan. 6, 1930; s. Sidney Walter and May (Fowler) E.; m. Moira Aileen Mills, Oct. 6, 1951; children—Denise, Michelle, Wayne. B.Sc. in Bldg. Constrn, 1951; also M.B.A. Mng. dir. Gilbert Ash Structures, 1960-68; dir., gen. mgr. Lyon Group (real estate), 1968-70; mng. dir. (pres.) Gilbert Ash Ltd., 1970-72; dir. Bovis Ltd., chief exec., 1972-74; pres., chmn. bd. Forest City Dillon, Inc., 1974—; exec. v.p., dir. Forest City Enterprises, Inc., Cleve., 1974—. Contbr. articles to profl. jours. Fellow Inst. Builders, Inst. Mktg., Inst. Dirs.; mem. Brit. Inst. Mgmt. Mem. Conservative Party. Mem. Ch. of Eng. Club: 21 (London). Home: The Meridian Suite 1701 12550 Lake Ave Lakewood OH 44107 Office: 10800 Brookpark Rd Cleveland OH 44130

ELLIN, MARVIN, lawyer; b. Balt., Mar. 6, 1923; s. Morris and Goldie (Rosen) E.; m. Stella J. Granto, Aug. 2, 1948; children: Morris, Raymond, Elisa. LL.B., U. Balt., 1953. Bar: Md. 1953, U.S. Supreme Ct. 1953. Practice law, Balt., 1953—; mem. firm Ellin & Baker, 1957—; specialist in med. malpractice law; cons. med./legal trial matters lectr. ACS, U. Md. Law Sch., U. Balt. Law Sch., Md. Bar Assn., Bar Assn. Balt. City. Writer; producer ct. dramatizations featured on various TV and radio stas., Balt. Fellow Internat. Acad. Trial Lawyers. Home: 13414 Longnecker Rd Glyndon MD 21071 Office: 1101 Saint Paul St Baltimore MD 21202

ELLIN, STANLEY BERNARD, author; b. Bklyn., Oct. 6, 1916; s. Louis William and Rose (Mandel) E.; m. Jeanne Michael, Nov. 23, 1937; 1 dau., Susan Ellin Brown. B.A., Bklyn. Coll., 1936. Author: novels Dreadful Summit, 1948, The Key to Nicholas Street, 1952, The Eighth Circle, 1958, The Winter After This Summer, 1960, The Panama Portrait, 1962, House of Cards, 1967, The Valentine Estate, 1968, The Bind, 1970, Mirror, Mirror on the Wall, 1972, Stronghold, 1974, The Luxembourg Run, 1977, Star Light, Star Bright, 1979, The Dark Fantastic, 1983, Very Old Money, 1985; short story collections include Mystery Stories, 1956, The Blessington Method, 1964, The Specialty of the House, 1980. Served with U.S. Army, 1945-46. Recipient Edgar Allan Poe awards, 1954, 56, 58, Grandmaster award Mystery Writers Am., 1981, Grand Prix, France, 1975, Foley/Burnett award, 1960. Mem. Mystery Writers Am., Crime Writers Assn. Eng., PEN Am. Ctr., Authors League, Authors Guild. Quaker. Address: c/o Curtis Brown Ltd 575 Madison Ave New York NY 10022

ELLINGHAUS, WILLIAM M., communications executive; b. Balt., Apr. 19, 1922; m. Erlaine Dietrich, May 30, 1942; children: Marcia A. Barone, Eric J., Douglas A., Barbara E. Gurne, Raymond W., Mark D., Christopher C., Jonathan P. Grad. high sch.; LL.D., Iona Coll., 1974, Pace U., 1976, St. John's U., 1976, Poly. Inst. N.Y., 1976, W.Va. Wesleyan Coll., 1981; L.H.D., Manhattan Coll., 1975, Union Coll., 1982; D.B.A., Curry Coll., 1978; D.Sc. (hon.), Washington Coll., 1979, N.Y. U., 1981. With Bell System, 1940—; comml. mgr. Chesapeake & Potomac Telephone Co. Md., Balt., 1950-51; pub. office mgr. Chesapeake & Potomac Telephone Co. Va., Norfolk, 1951-52, dist. comml. mgr., Culpeper, 1952-55; gen. comml. supr. Chesapeake & Potomac Telephone Co. W.Va., Charleston, 1955-57, div. comml. mgr., 1957, gen. accounting supr., 1957-58, comptroller, 1958-60, v.p., dir., 1960-62; v.p. accounts Chesapeake & Potomac Telephone Cos., Washington, 1962, v.p. personnel, 1962-65; asst. v.p. planning AT&T, N.Y.C., 1965-66, v.p. mktg. and rate plans, 1967-70, exec. v.p., 1970, vice chmn. bd., 1976-79, pres., 1979—, dir., 1976—; pres. N.Y. Telephone Co., 1970-76; dir. Bankers Trust Co., Internat. Paper Co., J.C. Penney Co., Inc., Bristol Myers Co., Armstrong World Industries, Inc., AVCO Co. Trustee St. John's U.; bd. dirs. Greater N.Y. council Boy Scouts Am., United Fund Greater N.Y.; mem. N.Y. Blood Center; bd. govs. United Way Am. Served with USNR, 1943-45. Mem. Am. Soc. Corp. Execs., N.Y. Chamber Commerce and Industry (vice chmn.), Sovereign Order Knights of Malta, Equestrian Order Holy Sepulchre of Jerusalem. Clubs: Rehoboth Beach Country (Del.); Union League, Siwanoy Country (N.Y.C.). Home: 55 Crows Nest Rd Bronxville NY 10708 Office: 195 Broadway New York NY 10007

ELLINGSON, STEVE, newspaper exec.; b. Havana, N.D., Oct. 6, 1910; s. Stephen and Florence (Young) E.; m. Lois Lawson, Feb. 22, 1958. B.S., U. Minn., 1932. Credit mgr. Bullocks, Los Angeles, 1935-41; spl. investigator Western Def. Command, Fourth Army, 1941-42; syndicated newspaper columnist, 1942—; pres. U-B Newspaper Syndicate, Cathedral City, Calif., 1947—. Bd. dirs. Valley Youth Found. Mem. Los Angeles Press Club, Phi Sigma Kappa. Club: Mason. Home and office: 464 Cerritos Way Cathedral City CA 92234

ELLINGTON, CHARLES RONALD, lawyer, educator; b. Cuthbert, Ga., Sept. 3, 1941; s. Charles Bartlett and Annie Claire (Moore) E.; m. Jean Alice Spencer, Apr. 29, 1967; children—Gregory Spencer, Alicia Nicole. A.B. summa cum laude, Emory U., 1963; LL.B., U. Va., 1966; LL.M., Harvard U., 1978. Bar: Ga. bar 1967, D.C. bar 1967. Asso. firm Sutherland, Asbill and Brennan, Atlanta, 1966-69; mem. law faculty U. Ga. Sch. Law, 1969—, prof. law, 1977—; on leave as scholar in residence U.S. Dept. Justice, Washington, 1979-80. Harvard U. fellow in law and humanities, 1973-74; Woodrow Wilson fellow, 1963. Mem. Am. Law Inst., Am. Judicature Soc. Home: 135 Beaver Trail Athens GA 30605 Office: Univ Ga Sch Law Athens GA 30602

ELLINGTON, MERCER KENNEDY, trumpeter, conductor, composer; b. Washington, Mar. 11, 1919; s. Edward Kennedy (Duke) and Edna (Thompson) E.; children: Mercedes, Edward, Gaye, Ralph, Paul. Attended, Columbia, Juilliard Sch. Music, N.Y. U. Radio commentator WLIB, N.Y.C., 1962-65. Leader of own band, until 1949; road mgr., trumpeter, Cootie Williams Orch., 1954; gen. asst. to, Duke Ellington, 1955-59; trumpeter, mgr. band, Duke Ellington Orch., 1965-74; leader orch., 1974—; Composer: (with Duke Ellington) The Three Black Kings; author: (with Stanley Dance) Duke Ellington in Person: an Intimate Memoir, 1978. Served with AUS, World War II. Office: care Willard Alexander 660 Madison Ave New York NY 10021

ELLINGWOOD, BRUCE RUSSELL, structural engineering researcher; b. Evanston, Ill., Oct. 11, 1944; s. Robert W. and Carolyn L. (Ehmen) E.; m. Lois J. Drager, June 7, 1969; 1 son, Geoffrey D. B.S.C.E., U. Ill., Urbana, 1968, M.S.C.E., 1969, Ph.D., 1972. Structural engr. Naval Ship Research and Devel. Ctr., Bethesda, Md., 1972-75; research structural engr. Ctr. Bldg. Tech., Nat. Bur. Standards, Washington, 1975—; lectr., cons. Contbr. articles to profl. jours. Recipient Dural Research prize U. Ill., 1968, Nat. Capital award for Engring. Achievement D.C. Joint Council Engring. and Archtl. Socs., 1980, Walter L. Huber prize ASCE, 1980, Silver medal U.S. Dept. Commerce, 1980. Mem. ASCE, ASTM, Am. Nat. Standards Inst., Am. Inst. Steel Constrn., Sigma Xi, Chi Epsilon. Presbyterian. Office: Nat Bur Standards Washington DC 20234

ELLINGWOOD, HERBERT E., government official; b. Ordway, Colo., Mar. 5, 1931; married; 2 children. B.A., Yale U., 1953; LL.B., Stanford U., 1960. Bar: Calif. Dep. asst. atty. Alameda County, (Calif.), 1960-66; legis. advocate for law and legis. coms. Dist. Attys. and Peace Officers Assn., 1966-69; legal affairs sec. to gov. State of Calif., 1969-74, spl. asst. to atty. gen., 1975-79; ptnr. Caldwell and Toms, Sacramento, 1979-81; dep. counsel to Pres., Washington, 1982—. Served with U.S. Army, 1953-56. Office: Merit Systems Protection Bd Office of the Chairman 1120 Vermont Ave NW Washington DC 20419 *

ELLINS, MYRA HARRIET, lawyer; b. Newark, July 4, 1938; d. Benjamin Victor and Alice Cohen; m. Lynn J. Ellins, May 13, 1960; children: Bradley, Rachel Starr. B.A. cum laude, Barnard Coll., Columbia U., 1960; J.D., U. Colo., 1975. Bar: Colo. 1975. Clk. to judge Colo. Ct. Appeals, 1975-76; staff atty., assoc. gen. counsel then gen. counsel Monfort of Colo., Inc., Greeley, 1976—, v.p., sec., 1980—; grad. asst. Ctr. Labor Edn. and Research, U. Colo., 1975. Republican committeewoman, 1979-80. Mem. ABA, Colo. Bar Assn., Weld County Bar Assn., Colo. Assn. Corp. Counsels. Jewish. Office: Monfort of Colo Inc PO Box G Greeley CO 80632

ELLIOT, DAVID CLEPHAN, history educator; b. Larkhall, Scotland, Sept. 17, 1917; came to U.S., 1947, naturalized, 1954; s. John James and Edith Emily (Bell) E.; m. Nancy Franelle Haskins, Dec. 3, 1945; children: Enid Frances, John Clephan, Nancy Elizabeth. M.A., St. Andrews U., 1939; A.M., Harvard U., 1948, Ph.D., 1951; M.A., Oxford U., 1956, postgrad. (Ford fellow), 1956-57. With Indian Civil Service, 1941-47; teaching fellow Harvard U., 1948-50; asst. prof. history Calif. Inst. Tech., Pasadena, 1950-53, asso. prof., 1953-60, prof., 1960—, chmn., 1965-67, exec. officer for humanities and social scis., 1967-71. Trustee Westridge Sch., 1970—, pres., 1976-78. Served with Royal Arty., 1940. NATO fellow, 1980. Mem. Am. Hist. Assn., Internat. Inst. for Strategic Studies (London), Los Angeles Com. on Fgn. Relations, Inst. of Current World Affairs (gov. 1964-70, chmn. 1969-70, trustee 1979-82). Home: 1251 Inverness Dr Pasadena CA 91103 Office: Calif Inst Tech Div Humanities and Social Scis 1201 E California Blvd Pasadena CA 91125

ELLIOT, DAVID HAWKSLEY, geologist; b. Chilwell, Eng., May 22, 1936; came to U.S., 1966; m. Ann Elliot, 1963. B.A., Cambridge U., 1959; Ph.D., Birmingham U., 1965. Mem. faculty Ohio State U., Columbus, 1969—, prof. dept. geology and mineralogy, 1979—, dir. Inst. Polar Studies, 1973—. Mem. Geol. Soc. Am., Geol. Soc. London, Ohio Acad. Sci., Sigma Xi. Office: Inst Polar Studies Ohio State U Columbus OH 43210

ELLIOT, IRWIN (WIN ELLIOT), sports commentator; b. Chelsea, Mass., May 7, 1915; s. I. Michael and Susan Miriam Shalek; m. Rita A. Barry, Nov. 3, 1951; children: Richard, Peter, Sue Ann, Michael, Robert, Marilyn, Patricia, Kathy, Douglas, Charles. A.B., U. Mich., 1937. Announcer Sta. WMEX, Boston, 1937-39; news, sports editor Sta. WFBR, Balt., 1939-40; announcer NBC, Washington, 1940, ABC Radio Network, 1940. Free lance sports emcee, announcer all networks, 1941—; including sports commentator, CBS Radio Network-World Series-Racing Triple Crown, Superbowl-NFL; weekly CBS programs All Am. Futrity-yearly; play by play all major sports, all major networks and, Northside Prodns., Inc. Mem. rep. Town Meeting, Westport, Conn. Served with U.S. Maritime Service, 1939-41. Recipient Eclipse award for excellence in thorobred racing reporting, 1971, 76, Disting. Citizen award Football Hall of Fame, Ga.

Broadcasting award as sportsman of year. Mem. AFTRA, Screen Actors Guild. Clubs: Patterson Country (Fairfield, Conn.); U. Mich. M. *

ELLIOT, JAMES LUDLOW, astronomer; b. Columbus, Ohio, June 17, 1943; s. James Ludlow and Doris Belle (Eckfeld) E.; m. Elaine Kasparian, Nov. 24, 1967; children—Lyn, Martha. S.B., M.I.T., 1965, S.M., 1965; A.M., Harvard U., 1967, Ph.D., 1972. Research asso. Cornell U., Ithaca, N.Y., 1972-74, sr. research asso., 1974-77, asst. prof. astronomy, 1977-78; asso. prof. astronomy M.I.T., Cambridge, 1978—; dir. George R. Wallace Jr. Astrophys. Obs., 1978—. Recipient medal for exceptional sci. achievement NASA, 1977; NSF fellow, 1965-71. Mem. Am. Astron. Soc., Internat. Internat. Astron. Union. Discovered rings of Uranus, 1977. Home: 27 Forest St Wellesley MA 02181 Office: Bldg 54-422A MIT Cambridge MA 02139

ELLIOT, JARED, diversified company executive; b. Albany, N.Y., Oct. 15, 1928; s. Henry Melvin and Gladys Dolores (Richter) E.; m. Janet Eleanor Malott, Sept. 15, 1951; children: Michael B., Lynn Elliot Hancock, Blake R., Jared. B.C.E., Yale U., 1950; M.B.A., Stanford U., 1955. Mgr. electronic data processing and mfg. scheduling Lenkurt Electric Co. Inc., San Carlos, Calif., 1955-58; sec., treas. Spectracoat Inc., San Carlos, 1958-61; mng. asso. mgmt. services dept. Arthur Young & Co., San Francisco, 1961-69; v.p. Tex. Gas Resources Corp., Owensboro, Ky., 1969—, treas., 1979—. Bd. dirs. United Way, Owensboro, 1969-80, pres., 1972; bd. dirs. Community Concert Assn., Owensboro, 1974-77. Served with USN, 1950-53. Republican. Office: 3800 Frederica St Owensboro KY 42301

ELLIOT, JEFFREY M., political science educator, author; b. Los Angeles, June 14, 1947; s. Gene and Harriet (Sobsey) E. B.A., U. So. Calif., 1969, M.A., 1970; D.Arts in History, Carnegie-Mellon U., 1976; Ed.D., Laurence U., 1976; D.Arts in Govt., Claremont Grad. Sch., 1978. Research asst. U. So. Calif., 1969-70; instr. polit. sci. Glendale Coll., 1970-72, Cerritos Coll., 1970-72; asst. prof. history and polit. sci. U. Alaska-Anchorage Community Coll., 1973-74; asst. prof. history and polit. sci., dean curriculum Miami-Dade Community Coll., 1974-76; asst. prof. polit. sci. Va. Wesleyan Coll., Norfolk, 1978-79; sr. curriculum specialist Edn. Devel. Center, Newton, Mass., 1979-81; assoc. prof. polit. sci. N.C. Central U., 1981—; asso. editor Community Coll. Social Sci. Jour., 1974-80. Author: 36 books, including Keys to Economic Understanding, 1976, Science Fiction Voices, 1979, Literary Voices, 1980, Analytical Congressional Directory, 1981, Deathman Pass Me By: Two Years on Death Row, 1982, Tempest in a Teapot: The Falkland Islands War, 1983, Black Voices: The Politics of Race, 1983, The Presidential-Congressional Political Dictionary, 1983; contbr. 400 articles and revs. to profl. and popular jours.; contbg. editor: Negro History Bull., 1976-80, West Coast Writers' Conspiracy, 1978-80. Mem. community services adv. council Miami (Fla.) Community Services, 1974-76; mem. Los Angeles Mayor's Adv. Com., 1971-72; speechwriter, research asst., campaign strategist U.S. Sen. Howard W. Cannon of Nev., 1969—; cons. Calif. Clean Environment Act, 1970-72. Recipient Fair Enterprise Medallion award, 1965; Outstanding Polit. Sci. Scholar citation, 1970; Outstanding Tchr. award, 1971; Outstanding Am. Educator citation, 1975; Distinguished Service Through Community Effort award, 1976. Mem. Community Coll. Social Sci. Assn. (dir. 1970-77, pres. 1975-77), So. Assn. Colls. and Schs. (accreditation team 1974-76), AAUP, Am. Polit. Sci. Assn., Assn. Supervision and Curriculum Devel., Nat. Council for Social Studies, Rocky Mountain Social Sci. Assn., Am. Hist. Assn., Pi Sigma Alpha, Phi Delta Kappa. Home: 1419 Barliff Pl Durham NC 27712 Office: Dept Polit Sci NC Central U Durham NC 27707 *I have attempted to live those ideals which inspire me to fight for a more humane world—love, honor, courage, integrity, and truth. I have also taken to heart the wisdom of the prophets who implore us to live and love as though life and love were one. Although this is a difficult and frustrating task, it is the only way to live. And finally, I have come to recognize that what matters most, after everything is said, are people-close family and friends who reach out and say in a host of ways, "I care."*

ELLIOT, JOHN T., filmmaker, artist. Student Acad. Fine Arts, France, 1947-50, NYU, 1951-54, 1958-59. Pres. Graphics for Industry, Englewood, N.J., 1968—; spl. cons. AT&T, Bell Labs., NASA, Nova, Ltd., Xerox, others; guest lectr. NYU; head film dept. Art Ctr. No. N.J. Designer, producer TV shows, commls., motion pictures; group shows Knickerbocker Artists, 1979, Copley Soc., Boston, 1979, Illustrators XX Internat., 1978, Pastel Soc. Am., 1977, 78, 79, N.Y. Advt. Club, 1963, Volkswagon World Hdqrs., Englewood Cliffs, N.J., 1976, Washington Sq. Art Show, 1959, Salmagundi Club, 1981, 82, Lever House, 1982, Lincoln Ctr., N.Y.C., 1982; represented: permanent collections Naumkeag, Trustees of Reservations, State of Mass. Mus., Chesterwood Mus., Stockbridge, Mass., Vassar Alumnae Art Collectors League, Wharton Sch. Fin., U. Pa. Alumni Investment Group, Nat. Trust Historic Preservation, Met. Mus. Art, N.Y.C., Fogg Art Mus., Harvard U., Nat. Collection Fine Arts, Smithsonian Instn., Detroit Mus. Art.; paintings for children's books Children's Bible, Children's Day mag., Children's Almanac, The Legend of John Henry, Alexander Hamilton. Recipient 1st prize Cannes Film Festival, 1965, 72, Gold award N.Y. Internat. Film Festival, 1973, Grand award, 1975, Spl. award for best film in cinemascope, 1970, Chris award, 1970, Gold medal Freedom Found., 1970, Cine award, 1965, 75, Chgo. Film Festival award, 1973, Best Still Life Pastel Soc. Am., Nat. Arts Club, 1979, Liskin award, 1981, Van Kreugher Meml. award for paster, 1982. Mem. Soc. Illustrators, Pastel Soc. Am. (dir. 1979-81, v.p. 1982—), Salmagundi Club. Office: Graphics for Industry Box 544 Tenafly NJ 07670

ELLIOT, R LANCE, trade association executive; b. Chillicothe, Ohio, Aug. 1, 1943; s. Kennety Leroy and Ethel Miriam (Kinsley) E.; m. Susan Jeanne Ames, Aug. 24, 1968; children: Jocelyn, Amy, Peter. A.B., MacMurray Coll., 1967; J.D., Georgetown U., 1977. Bar: D.C. 1977. Tchr. Sch. Dist. 6, Waverly, Ill., 1968-69; dir. pub. relations Urban Land Inst., Washington, 1969-71; exec. dir., treas. Nat. Bowling Council, Washington, 1971—. Mem. ABA, Am. Soc. Assn. Execs., Greater Washington Soc. Assn. Execs. Episcopalian. Office: Nat Bowling Council 1919 Pennsylvania Ave 504 Washington DC 20006

ELLIOT, ROBERT M., furniture company executive. With Levitz Furniture Corp., 1914—, chmn., chief exec. officer, 1983—. Office: Levitz Furniture Corp 1317 NW 167th St Miami FL 33169§

ELLIOT, WIN *See* **ELLIOT, IRWIN**

ELLIOTT, ALBERT RANDLE, retired college president; b. St. Louis County, Mo., Jan. 10, 1914; s. Thomas Barrett and Olinda (Hoevel) E.; m. Gwendolyn Stager Crawford, Jan. 28, 1948; 1 dau., Dawn. A.B., Westminster Coll., 1935; LL.D., 1962; A.M., Harvard U., 1938, Ph.D., 1949. Teaching asst. depts. govt. Harvard U. and Radcliffe Coll., 1936-39; research assoc. Fgn. Policy Assn., 1939-41; adminstrv. assoc. Inst. Internat. Edn., N.Y.C., 1941-43; dir. Counsel and Guidance Center for Fgn. Students in U.S., Washington, 1943-45, administr. Washington Bur., 1946-47; econ. analyst U.S. Strategic Bombing Survey, Eng. and Germany, 1945; chief reports officer Office Mil. Govt. for Germany, Berlin, 1945-46; London corr. McGraw-Hill World News, 1947-48; exec. dir. Greer Sch., Hope Farm, Dutchess County, N.Y., 1949-61; pres. Hood Coll., 1961-71, Bay Path Jr. Coll., Longmeadow, Mass., 1971-79, trustee, 1971-80, mem. adv. council, 1980—. Author: Spain After Civil War, 1940, The Resources and Trade of Central America, 1941, (with others) The United States at War, 1942, The Institute of International Education, 1919-44, 1944; Editor (with others) numerous govt. reports; contbr. articles to periodicals. Exec. bd. Dutchess County council Boy Scouts Am., 1950-61, Pioneer Valley council, 1972-79; mem. nat. council Boy Scouts Am., 1953-58; mem. Md. State Com. for Fulbright Scholarships, 1967-71. Rockefeller Found. research fellow, 1939-41; Recipient alumni achievement award Westminster Coll., 1980. Mem. Council World Affairs (vice chmn. Dutchess County 1955-61, dir. Conn. Valley 1972-79), Council Fgn. Relations, Am. Polit. Sci. Assn., Acad. Polit. Sci., Assn. Ind. Colls in Md. (dir. 1961-71, pres. 1964-66), Am. Acad. Polit. and Social Sci., Am. Mus. Nat. History, Md. Ind. Coll. and Univ. Assn. (sec.-treas. 1970-71), Nat. Council Ind. Jr. Colls. (dir. 1976-79), Springfield Adult Edn. Council (exec. com., v.p. 1976-79), Omicron Delta Kappa, Pi Kappa Delta, Beta Theta Pi. Republican. Episcopalian (vestryman). Clubs: Rotarian., Harvard (N.Y.C.); Millbrook (N.Y.) Golf and Tennis; Colony, Century (Springfield, Mass.); Pioneer Valley Racquet (Agawam, Mass.). Home: Hickory Heath Chestnut Ridge Rd RD 2 Box 198 Millbrook NY 12545

ELLIOTT, ANSON WRIGHT, banker; b. New Orleans, Aug. 9, 1935; s. Anson E. and Edna Jo (Wright) E.; m. Jane Rader; children: Michael, Stephen, David. B.A., Princeton U., 1957; M.A., La. State U., 1964. With Whitney Nat. Bank, New Orleans, 1961-62; exec. v.p. NAM, Washington, 1964-74, The Chase Manhattan Bank N.A., N.Y.C., 1974—. Pres. Broxville Sch. Bd. Edn., 1983; bd. dirs. South Street Seaport Mus., N.Y.C., 1983. Served to capt. USMCR, 1958-62. Mem. Manhattan Inst. Policy Research (dir. 1980-83), Economic Club N.Y. Republican. Clubs: Knickerbocker, Princeton, Siwanoy Country. Home: 1 Beechwood Rd New York NY 10708 Office: The Chase Manhattan Bank NA 1 Chase Manhattan Plaza New York NY 10081

ELLIOTT, BENJAMIN PAUL, architect; b. Washington, Dec. 27, 1920; s. Benjamin Sargent and Marguerite (Plenckner) E.; m. Mary Dickenson, July 22, 1943; children: Paul Charles, Sara. B.Arch., Catholic U. Am., 1948. Pvt. practice architecture, Silver Spring, Md., 1950-81; pres. Duane, Elliott & Assocs. (P.A., Architects and Planners), Rockville, Md., 1981—; Chmn. Washington Regional Conf. Religious Arch., 1966; bd. dirs., hon. chmn. Nat. Conf. Religious Arch., Washington, 1968-70. Publisher: Potomac Valley Architect, 1957-59; publisher, bus. mgr.: Faith & Form, 1966-71. Pres. West Montgomery Citizens Assn., 1962-63; chmn. trustees Potomac Elem. Sch., 1963-69. Served with AUS, 1942-45. Recipient Distinguished Service award Potomac Valley chpt. A.I.A., 1970; spl. citation Guild for Religious Architecture, 1971; E.B. Morris Distinguished Service award, 1975; Masonry Inst. award, 1976, 79, 82; citation Combined Chambers of Commerce, Montgomery County, 1980. Fellow A.I.A. (sec. Md. div. 1952-57, mem. nat. com. religious architecture 1963-66, pres. chpt. 1957-58, chmn. com. on bylaws Potomac Valley chpt. of Md. 1965-76); mem. Md. Soc. Architects (sec.-treas. 1975-78). Episcopalian (vestryman 1956-59, 65-68, jr. warden 1968-69). Home: 11000 Dobbins Dr Potomac MD 20854 Office: 100 Park Ave Rockville MD 20850

ELLIOTT, BRUCE ALAN, bus. exec.; b. Wabasso, Minn., Apr. 23, 1934; s. Howard William and Marcella (Wittwer) E.; m. Wendy L. Bebout, Nov. 27, 1957; children—Brian Keith, Bradley Kent, Beth Kathleen, Brent Kevin, Katrina Diane, Kyle Darren. B.S. in Acctg, U. So. Calif., 1960. Sr. acct. Purex Corp., Lakewood, Calif., 1961-67, v.p. auditing, 1975—; Commr. Orange County Jr. All Am. Football Assn., 1976—. Served with U.S. Army, 1953-56. Mem. Inst. Internal Auditors. Republican. Office: 5101 Clark Ave Lakewood CA 90712

ELLIOTT, BYRON KAUFFMAN, lawyer, business executive; b. Indpls., May 5, 1899; s. William Frederick and Effie (Marquardt) E.; m. Helen Alice Heissler, July 15, 1938 (dec. 1973); children: Barbara (Mrs. John D. Niles), Kent, David. A.B. cum laude, Ind. U., 1920, LL.D., 1955; LL.B., Harvard, 1923; L.H.D., Northeastern U., 1971. Bar: Ind. 1921. Began practice in, Indpls., asst. atty. gen., Ind., 1925; elected judge Superior Ct., Indpls., 1926-29; pres. Curtiss Flying Service of Ind., 1927-29; mgr., gen. counsel Am. Life Conv., 1929-34; pres. Am. Service Bur., 1929-33, chmn. bd., 1933-34; with John Hancock Mut. Life Ins. Co., 1934-69, gen. counsel, 1936, v.p., gen. counsel, 1937-47, exec. v.p., 1947-57, pres., 1957-65, chmn. fin. com., 1961-69, chmn. bd., 1963-69; trustee Provident Instn. Savs., 1950-70; dir. Arthur D. Little Co., 1949-69, Pullman Co., 1950-64, Am. Research and Devel. Co., 1952-70, 1st Nat. Bank of Boston, 1960-69, Boston Edison Co., 1961-69. Author booklets, articles ins. law. Mem. Nat. Commn. Coop. Edn.; trustee Wellesley Coll., 1951-69, Ind. Coll. Funds Am., Boston Mus. Sci., 1952-70, Fed. City Council, Washington, Tufts Civic Edn. Center, French Library in Boston, Hosp. Research and Edn. Trust Am. Hosp. Assn., 1960-69; bd. overseers Boston Symphony Orch.; chmn. bd. trustees, chmn. corp. Northeastern U., 1960-72; bd. dirs. Ind. U. Found., World Wildlife Fund, 1964-70, Boston Opera Assn., World Affairs Council Boston, 1950-68; nat. chmn. Ind. U. Sesquicentenniel Fund, 1970; gen. chmn. United Fund Greater Boston, 1960; bd. advisers Nat. Fund for Med. Edn.; chmn. devel. fund Cape Cod Conservatory of Music and Art, 1975-79; mem. corp. Peter Bent Brigham Hosp. Served as 2d lt. CAC, World War I. Fellow Am. Acad. Arts and Scis.; mem. Am. Bar Assn., Am. Law Inst. (life), Am. Judicature Soc., Council Fgn. Relations, Assn. Life Ins. Counsel (pres. 1949-50), Mass. Charitable Fire Soc., Mass. Com. Catholics, Protestants and Jews (exec. com. 1957-60), Inst. Life Ins. (dir., chmn. 1965-66), Am. Legion, Mil. Order Loyal Legion, Pilgrims, S.A.R., Gen. Soc. Colonical Wars, Bostonian Soc., U.S. C. of C. (mem. task force on econ. growth), Ind. Pioneers, Scribes, Beta Theta Pi, Sigma Delta Chi, Sigma Delta Kappa. Republican. Presbyn. Clubs: Commercial (pres. 1950-52), Harvard, Brookline Country, Algonquin, St. Botolph (Boston); Tavern (Chgo.); Woodstock, Columbia, Dramatic (Indpls.). Lodge: Masons. Home: 780 Boylston St Apt 23-I Boston MA 02199 Office: 200 Berkeley St Boston MA 02117

ELLIOTT, CARL HARTLEY, univ. pres.; b. Columbus, Ind., Mar. 21, 1922; s. Herschel B. and Hazel (Hartley) E.; m. Elizabeth Schmitt, July 8, 1945; children: Prudence, Lisa, Linda, Nancy. A.B., Ind. U., 1946, M.B.A., 1947; Ph.D., Purdue U., 1952. Jr. mgmt. cons. Dillard E. Bird Assos., Cin., 1947-48; asst. prof. psychology Miami U., Oxford, Ohio, 1948-51; asso. prof. Purdue U., Hammond, Ind., 1952-55, dean, dir., Hammond, 1959-74, chancellor, 1974; employee relations mgr. East Chicago Refinery (Ind.), Socony Mobil Oil Co., Inc., 1955-57, supr. selection and placement, N.Y.C., 1957-59; pres. Tri-State U., Angola, Ind., 1974—; dir. No. Ind. Pub. Service Co., Angola State Bank, Angola Indsl. Growth Inc. Adviser Lake County Community Devel. Com., 1965-74, Lake County Econ. Opportunity Council, 1965-71; pres. Lake County Econ. Opportunity Council, 1965; v.p. N.W. Ind. chpt. A.R.C., 1968-70, Gt. Lakes Health and Edn. Found., 1968-76; Mem. citizens bd. St. Margaret Hosp., 1966-74, chmn., 1974; bd. dirs. Purdue Calumet Devel. Found., 1964-76, pres., 1973-76; bd. dirs. N.W. Ind. United Fund, 1970-73, v.p., 1970-72; pres. NWI Research, Inc., 1970-72; bd. dirs. Lake Area United Way, 1973-74, Indiana Forum, 1976-79; sec. exec. com. Associated Colls. Ind., 1978-80; exec. com. Ind. Conf. Higher Edn., 1978-80; bd. dirs. Ind. Colls. and Univs. of Ind., 1979-81, vice chmn., 1981. Served with USAAF, 1942-46. Fellow Am. Psychol. Assn.; mem. Midwest Psychol. Assn., Soc. for Advancement Mgmt. (pres. Calumet chpt. 1964-65), Assn. Continuing Higher Edn. (dir. 1969-75, pres. 1973-74), Angola Area C. of C. (dir. 1978-81), Sigma Xi, Beta Gamma Sigma, Delta Mu Delta, Delta Sigma Pi, Kappa Kappa Psi, Psi Chi, Phi Eta Sigma, Alpha Sigma Lambda. Methodist. Lodges: Masons (33 deg.); Rotary (pres. Hammond 1972-73). Home: 520 E Gale St Angola IN 46703 *I believe that all one's actions must be based on a strong sense of morality and personal integrity. It is important to be honest and straightforward. Communication with others must be open and forthright, with the recognition of both our own dependence on others and the consequences of our behavior. Working with and through others magnifies our own actions and is the only real road to accomplishment.*

ELLIOTT, DANIEL WHITACRE, educator, surgeon; b. Greenville, Ohio, Aug. 5, 1922; s. James Scott and LaVirge (Whitacre) E.; m. Elizabeth Lucille Wolff, Aug. 11, 1961; children: James Calvin, Lisa Ann. Student, Ohio State U., 1942-43, M.Med. Sci., 1956; M.D., Yale, 1949. Diplomate: Am. Bd. Surgery. Intern surgery Columbia Presbyn. Hosp., N.Y.C., 1949-50; surgery resident Ohio State U. Hosp., 1951, 53-57; mem. faculty Ohio State U. Sch. Medicine, 1957-64; prof. surgery U. Pitts. Sch. Medicine, 1965-76; Chief surgery Pitts. VA Hosp., Pitts., 1971-76; staff Presbyn., Western Pa., Shadyside, Children's hosps., Pitts., to 1976; mem. staff Kettering Meml., Miami Valley, Good Samaritan, St. Elizabeth's, VA hosps., all Dayton, Ohio; chmn. dept. surgery Wright State U. Sch. Medicine, 1976—. Editorial bd.: Am. Surgeon, Am. Jour. Surgery; Contbr. numerous articles to profl. jours. Served with AUS, 1943-45; as capt. M.C. USAF, 1951-53. Fellow A.C.S.; mem. Am., Central, Western, Internat. surg. assns., Am. Burn Assn., Soc. Univ. Surgeons, Am. Gastroenterology Assn., Soc. Surgery Alimentary Tract, Sigma Xi., Alpha Kappa Kappa, Alpha Omega Alpha. Home: 701 Murrell Dr Kettering OH 45429 Office: Wright State Univ Sch Medicine Box 927 Dayton OH 45401

ELLIOTT, DONALD HARRISON, lawyer; b. N.Y.C., Aug. 20, 1932; s. Harrison Sackett and Grace (Loucks) E.; m. Barbara Ann Burton, Sept. 1, 1956; children—Steven Burton, Drew Harrison, Douglas Warren. B.A., Carleton Coll., 1954; LL.B., N.Y. U., 1957. Bar: N.Y. State bar 1958. Since practiced in, N.Y.C.; assoc. firm Webster, Sheffield, Fleischman, Hitchcock & Crystie, 1957-59, 61-65; asst. counsel N.Y. State Commn. Investigation, 1959-61; counsel to Mayor John Lindsay, N.Y.C., 1966; chmn. N.Y.C. Planning Commn., 1966-73; ptnr. firm Webster and Sheffield, 1973—; mem. Met. Transp. Authority, 1968-78; mem. N.Y.C. Health and Hosps. Corp., 1973-78. Chmn. bd. dirs. L.I. U., 1975—, N.Y. Urban Coalition, 1975—. Mem. Assn. Bar City N.Y. Home: 118 Pierrepont St Brooklyn NY 11201 Office: 1 Rockefeller Plaza New York NY 10020

ELLIOTT, EDDIE MAYES, college president; b. Grain Valley, Mo., Sept. 12, 1938; s. Franklin E. and Edna Mae (Rowe) E.; m. Sandra Temple, Nov. 23, 1960; children: Glenn, Gregg, Grant. A.B., William Jewell Coll., 1960; M.A., Columbia U., 1964; Ed.D., U. No. Colo., 1969. Tchr. Harrisonville High Sch., Mo., 1960-61, Excelsior Springs Pub. Schs., 1961-63, The Trinity Sch., N.Y.C., 1963-64; mem. faculty dept. phys. edn. CCNY, 1964-65; chmn. athletics, coach Mo. Valley Coll., Marshall, 1965-71; v.p. Wayne State Coll., Nebr., 1975-82, pres., 1982—; assoc. Ctr. for Planned Change, 1975-82; mem. adv. bd., bd. dirs. Nebr. Council on Econ. Edn., 1977-83; bd. incorporators Higher Edn. Strategic Planning Inst., 1981—. Named outstanding faculty mem. Wayne State Coll., 1973; recipient Cecil R. Martin award William Jewell Coll., 1960. Mem. Am. Assn. Higher Edn., Am. Assn. Acad. Deans, AAUP, Am. Coll. Sports Medicine, Wayne C. of C., Assn. Health, Phys. Edn. and Recreation, N. Central Assn. Evaluation Teams, Nat. Council Accreditation of Tchrs., Am. Assn. State Colls. and Univs. Home: 1204 Crescent Dr Wayne NE 68787 Office: Wayne State Coll Wayne NE 68787

ELLIOTT, EDWARD, investment executive, financial planner; b. Madison, Wis., Jan. 11, 1915; s. Edward C. and Elizabeth (Nowland) E.; m. Letitia Ord, Feb. 20, 1943 (div. Aug. 1955); children: Emily, Ord; m. Melita Uihlein, Jan. 1, 1958; 1 dau., Deborah. B.S. in Mech. Engring, Purdue U., 1936. Engr. Gen. Electric Co., Schenectady, 1936-37; engr. Pressed Steel Tank Co., Milw., 1937-38, N.Y.C., 1939-41, dist. sales mgr., Cleve., 1946-48, N.Y.C., 1949-54, sales mgr., Milw., 1954-58; v.p. sales Cambridge Co. div. Carrier Corp., Lowell, Mass., 1958-59; mgr. indsl. and med. sales Liquid Carbonic div. Gen. Dynamics Corp., Chgo., 1959-61; v.p. Haywood Pub. Co., Chgo., 1961-63; pres. Omnibus, Inc., Chgo., 1963-67; gen. sales mgr. Resistoflex Corp., Roseland, N.J., 1967-68; investment exec. Shearson, Hammill & Co., Inc., Chgo., 1968-74; v.p. McCormick & Co., Inc., 1974-75; now v.p. Paine Webber, Inc., Naples, Fla., 1975—. Bd. govs. Purdue U. Found. Served with USAAF, 1941-46. Decorated officer Order Brit. Empire. Mem. ASME, Air Force Assn., Inst. Cert. Fin. Planners, Internat. Assn. Fin. Planning, Phi Delta Theta. Republican. Episcopalian. Clubs: Mid-Day, Racquet (Chgo.); Shore Acres Golf (Lake Bluff, Ill.); Onwentsia (Lake Forest, Ill.); Milwaukee Country, University (Milw.); Chenequa Country (Hartland); Lake (Oconomowoc, Wis.); Army-Navy Country (Arlington, Va.); Lafayette (Ind.) Country; Coral Beach (Paget Bermuda); Royal Poinciana Golf, Hole-in-Wall Golf, Naples Yacht, Naples Olympiad, Naples Athletic, Rotary (Naples). Home: 1285 Gulf Shore Blvd N Naples FL 33940 Office: Paine Webber Inc 1400 Gulf Shore Blvd N Naples FL 33940

ELLIOTT, EDWARD PROCTER, architect; b. Warrington, Eng.; came to U.S., 1939, naturalized, 1951; s. Arthur Spencer and Ethel Gertrude (Musket) E.; m. Cynthia Jean Heideman, June 7, 1958; children by former marriage: Stewart, Edward, Lauren, Eleanor. B.Arch. with honors, Liverpool U., Eng., 1939; fellow in City Planning, Cranbrook Acad. Art, Mich., 1939-40. Chief designer Eero Saarinen & Assos. (architects), Bloomfield Hills, Mich., 1945-50; partner Elliott & Dworski, Birmingham, Mich., 1950-57; planning supr. Knoll Assos., Inc., 1951-57; partner Knorr-Elliott & Assos., San Francisco, 1957—, Lane-Knorr-Elliott, Anchorage, Alaska, 1972—; supervising architect Bechtel Power Corp., Gaithersburg, Md., 1974—; Mem. Nat. Council Archtl. Registration Bds.; Asso. Mich. Acad. Sci. Arts and Letters, 1957. Served to lt. comdr. Royal Canadian Navy, 1940-45. Recipient AIA awards, 1953, 56, 59, 63, Nat. Gold medal Exhbn., N.Y., 1962, award of excellence Am. Inst. Steel, 1963, Nat. award U. Alaska, 1967, Top Ten awards Comml. Indsl. Bldgs., 1968, Environmental award, San Francisco, 1972. Mem. Royal Inst. Brit. Architects, AIA, Archtl. Research Group of Ottawa, Can. Home: 38 Deer Park Ave San Rafael CA 94901 Office: Bechtel Power Corp San Francisco CA 94119

ELLIOTT, ELEANOR THOMAS, foundation executive, civic leader; b. N.Y.C., Apr. 26, 1926; d. James A. and Dorothy Q. (Read) Thomas; m. John Elliott, Jr., July 27, 1956. B.A., Barnard Coll., 1948. Asso. editor Vogue mag., 1948-52; asst. dir. research and speech writing div. N.Y. State Republican Com., 1952; social sec. to Sec. of State and Mrs. John Foster Dulles, 1952-55; dir. James Weldon Johnson Community Centers, N.Y.C., 1955-60, Celanese Corp., INA Life Ins. Co. of N.Y. Author: Glamour Magazine Party Book, 1966. Trustee Barnard Coll., 1959—, chmn. bd., 1973-76; bd. dirs. Maternity Center Assn., 1960-70, pres., 1965-69; bd. govs. N.Y. Hosp., 1970—, v.p., 1979—; bd. dirs. Found. for Child Devel., N.Y.C., 1969—, chmn., N.Y.C., 1972-79, chmn., 1973—; bd. dirs. United Way Greater N.Y., 1977—, NOW Legal Def. and Edn. Fund, 1983—, Catalyst Inc., 1978-83, Am. Women's Econ. Devel. Corp., 1980—, Woodrow Wilson Nat. Fellowship Found, 1983—. Recipient Alumni medal Columbia U.,

1977, medal of distinction Barnard Coll., 1979. Mem. NOW, Nat. Women's Polit. Caucus. Republican. Episcopalian. Club: Colony (N.Y.C.). Home: 1035 Fifth Ave New York NY 10028

ELLIOTT, EMORY BERNARD, english educator, educational adminstrator; b. Balt., Oct. 30, 1942; s. Emory Bernard and Virginia L. (Ulbrick) E.; m. Georgia Ann Caroll, May 14, 1966; children: Scott, Mark, Matthew, Laura, Constance. A.B., Loyola Coll., Balt., 1964; M.A., Bowling Green State U., 1966; Ph.D., U. Ill., 1972. Instr. Cameron Coll., Lawton, Okla., 1966-67, U.S. Mil Acad., West Point, N.Y., 1967-69; asst. prof. to English Princeton U., N.J., 1972—, chmn. Am. studies program, 1976—, master Lee D. Butler Coll., 1982—; writing cons. Bell Labs., Holmdel, N.J., 1975-79, RCA, Princeton, 1980-81; edn. cons. Western Electric Corp. Edn. Ctr., Hopewell, N.J., 1974-79. Author: Power and the Pulpit in Puritan New England, 1975, Puritan Influences in American Literature, 1979, Revolutionary Writers: Literature and Authority in the New Rupublic, 1982, Cambridge History of American Literature, vol. 1, 1983; editor: Dictionary of Literary Biography, 3 vols., 1606-1910, 1983-84; mem. editorial bd.: Am. Quar., 1976-80; mem. adv. com.: Gale Bibliography of Am. Lit., 1981—. Served to capt. U.S. Army, 1966-69. Fellow Nat. Humanities Ctr., 1979-80, Guggenheim Found., 1976, Am. Council Learned Socs., 1973, Woodrow Wilson Found, 1971-72; preceptor Princeton U., 1975-78. Mem. MLA (chmn. Early Am. lit. div.). Office: Dept. English Princeton Univ Princeton NJ 08544

ELLIOTT, FRANK ABERCROMBIE, physician; b. Cape Town, S. Africa, Dec. 18, 1910; s. Arthur Abercrombie and Kathleen (Gosslin) E.; m. Betty Kathleen Elkington, Oct. 31, 1940; children—Sally Dawn, Gillian Kathleen Elliott Andrew; m. Gwladys Hopkins Marvel, 1970. M.B., Ch.B., U. Cape Town, 1936. Intern Groote Schuur Hosp., Cape Town, 1936; resident Nat. Heart Hosp., London, 1937, Queen Sq. Hosp., 1938; practice medicine specializing in neurology, London, 1945-59, Phila., 1959—; mem. staff Pa. Hosp., Phila., dir. neurology, 1959-73; prof. neurology U. Pa., Phila., 1964—; dir. Elliott Neurol. Center, 1975—; neurologist Charing Cross Hosp., London, 1947-59. Author: Clinical Neurology, 1964, 71; contbr. articles to profl. jours. Served to lt. col. Brit. Army, 1942-47. Fellow Royal Coll. Physicians, A.C.P., Acad. Neurology; mem. Brit. Neurol. Assn., Assn. Brit. Physicians, Internat. Soc. Internal Medicine. Club: Philadelphian. Home: 232 Philip Pl Philadelphia PA 19106

ELLIOTT, FRANK NELSON, college president; b. Dunkirk, N.Y., Mar. 18, 1926; s. Warren D. and Ima M. (Wilson) E.; m. Mary Elizabeth Neish, July 26, 1952; children: Robert Frank (dec.), Susan Marie, Ann Neish. B.A. cum laude with dept. honors, Alfred U., 1949, LL.D., 1972; M.A., Ohio U., 1950; Ph.D., U. Wis., 1956. Grad. asst. Ohio U., 1949-50; Draper fellow Wis. Hist. Soc., 1951-52, field rep., field supr., 1952-56; curator history, asst. prof. history Mich. State U., 1956-61; asso. dean Sch. Gen. Studies, Columbia U., 1961-64, acting dean, 1964; dir. div. arts and scis. State U. N.Y. Coll. at Cortland, 1964-65, acting dean, 1965-66; v.p. Hofstra U., Hempstead, N.Y., 1966-69; pres. Rider Coll., Lawrenceville, N.J., 1969—; dir. New Trenton Corp., Colonial Savs. & Loan, Roselle Park, N.J., Goodall Rubber Co. Contbr. articles to profl. jours. Mem. adv. council N.J. State Library, 1972—; Bd. dirs. N.J. Council for Humanities, 1972-76, Mercer Hosp., Freedoms Found., Valley Forge; trustee Alfred U., 1964-69. Served with AUS, 1944-46; PTO. Mem. Am. Assn. State and Local History (council 1960-62), Mich. Hist. Soc. (trustee 1959-61, award for TV lectures 1960), Mercer County C. of C. (dir. 1975—). Presbyterian (elder). Home: 2064 Lawrenceville Rd Lawrenceville NJ 08648

ELLIOTT, FRANK WALLACE, lawyer, foundation executive; b. Cotulla, Tex., June 25, 1930; s. Frank Wallace and Eunice Marie (Akin) E.; m. Winona Trent, July 3, 1954 (dec. 1981); 1 dau., Harriet Lindsey. Student, N.Mex. Mil. Inst., 1947-49; B.A., U. Tex., 1951, LL.B., 1957. Bar: Tex. 1957. Asst. atty. gen., State of Tex., 1957; briefing atty. Supreme Ct. Tex., 1957-58; prof. U. Tex. Law Sch., 1958-77; dean, prof. law Tex. Tech U. Sch. Law, 1977-80; pres. Southwestern Legal Found., 1980—; parliamentarian Tex. Senate, 1969-73; dir. research Tex. Constl. Revision Commn., 1973. Author: Texas Judicial Process, 2d edit, 1977, Texas Trial and Appellate Practice, 2d edit, 1974, Cases on Evidence, 1980, West's Texas Forms, 16 vols, 1977—. Served with U.S. Army, 1951-53, 73-74. Decorated Purple Heart, Meritorious Service medal, Army Commendation medal. Mem. Am. Bar Assn., State Bar Tex., Judge Advs. Assn., Am. Judicature Soc., Am. Bar Found., Tex. Bar Found., Am. Law Inst. Home: 7710 Scotia Dr Dallas TX 75248 Office: PO Box 707 Richardson TX 75080

ELLIOTT, GROVER SAGER, textile executive; b. Danville, Va., June 15, 1940; s. Claude H. and Sadie Mae (Bradley) E.; m. Pauline M. Smith, Sept. 8, 1971; 1 son, Steven. B.S. in Accounting, Va. Poly. Inst., 1964; M.B.A., Furman U., 1973; postgrad. program for mgmt. devel., Harvard U., 1973. With Dan River, Inc., 1964—, internal auditor, Danville, Va., 1964-65, fin. analyst, 1965-68; mgr. banking dept., Greenville, S.C., 1968-71, asst. treas., 1971-75, treas., 1975-81, v.p., treas., 1981-82, v.p. fin., chief fin. officer, 1982—; instr. bus. Furman U., Greenville. Advisor Jr. Achievement, 1975; treas. Greenville County United Way, 1978. Mem. Nat. Assn. Accountants (v.p. 1977-78, pres. 1979-80), Greenville C. of C. (fin. com. 1977). Presbyterian. Club: Pleasantburg Rotary (sec., treas. 1976—). Office: Box 2424 Danville VA 24541 Home: 134 Berman Dr Danville VA 24540

ELLIOTT, HOWARD CLYDE, JR., educator; b. Birmingham, Sept. 21, 1924; s. Howard Clyde and Charlotte Augusta (Smith) E.; m. Mary Claire Baker, Apr. 24, 1958; children—Ann BeAyre, Catherine Claire and Ellen Clyde (twins). B.S., Birmingham So. Coll., 1948; M.S., U. Ala., 1951, Ph.D., 1956. Asso. prof. chemistry U. Ala., Birmingham, 1959-64, prof. chemistry, 1965—, clin. asso. prof. dept. medicine, 1972—, asso. chmn. natural sci. and math., 1968-69, vol. research prof. chemistry, 1970—; asso. Casey, Lohmann & Elliott, Birmingham, 1969—; biochemistry cons. Bapt. Hosp. Labs., 1955-64. Contbr. articles sci. jours. Served with M.C. AUS, 1943-46. Recipient Kimble Nat. Med. Tech. award, 1961. Mem. Am. Assn. Clin. Chemists (chmn. S.E. sect. 1968-69), Soc. Exptl. Biology and Medicine, Am. Diabetes Assn., Am. Chem. Soc., Sigma Xi. Presbyn. (elder). Clubs: Vestavia Country, The Club (Birmingham). Home: 4260 Sharpsburg Dr Birmingham AL 35213

ELLIOTT, JAMES HEYER, museum dir.; b. Medford, Oreg., Feb. 19, 1924; s. Bert R. and Marguerite E. (Heyer) E.; m. Judith Ann Algar, Apr. 23, 1966 (div.); children—Arabel Joan, Jakob Maxwell. B.A., Willamette U., Salem, Oreg., 1947, D.F.A. (hon.), 1978; A.M., Harvard U., 1949. James Rogers Rich fellow Harvard U., 1949-50; Fulbright grantee, Paris, 1951-52; art critic European edit. N.Y. Herald-Tribune, 1952-53; curator, acting dir. Walker Art Center, Mpls., 1953-56; asst. chief curator, curator modern art Los Angeles County Mus. Art, 1956-63, chief curator, 1964-66; dir. Wadsworth Atheneum, Hartford, Conn., 1966-76, Univ. Art Mus., Berkeley, Calif., 1976—; adj. prof. Hunter Coll., N.Y.C., 1968, U. Calif., Berkeley, 1976—; commr. Conn. Commn. Arts, 1970-76; fellow Trumbull Coll., Yale U., 1971-75; mem. museum arts panel Nat. Endowment Arts, 1974-77; bd. dirs. San Francisco Art Inst., 1980—. Author: Bonnard and His Environment, 1964. Served with USNR, 1943-46. Mem. Internat. Council Museums, Am. Assn. Museums, Coll. Art Assn., Assn. Art Mus. Dirs. (sec., trustee 1980—), Artists Space N.Y. (dir. 1980—). Club: Arts (Berkeley). Home: PO Box 4848 Berkeley CA 94704 Office: 2626 Bancroft Way Berkeley CA 94720

ELLIOTT, JAMES ROBERT, Judge; b. Gainesville, Ga., Jan. 1, 1910; s. Thomas M. and Mamie Lucille (Glenn) E.; m. Brownie C. Buck, Aug. 3, 1949; children: Susan G., James Robert. Ph.B., Emory U., 1930, LL.B., 1934. Bar: Ga. 1934. Practiced law, Columbus, Ga., 1934-62; judge U.S. Dist. Ct. for Middle Dist. Ga., Columbus, 1962—; Mem. Ga. Ho. of Reps., 1937-43, 47-49; Democratic nat. committeeman, 1948-56. Served as lt. USNR, 1943-46; PTO. Mem. Ga. Bar Assn., Lambda Chi Alpha, Phi Delta Phi, Omicron Delta Kappa. Lodge: Kiwanis. Home: 2612 Carson Dr Columbus GA 31906 Office: PO Box 2017 Columbus GA 31902

ELLIOTT, JOHN FRANK, engineering educator; b. St. Paul, July 31, 1920; s. Stowe E. and Helen (Grube) E.; m. Frances Pendleton, May 4, 1946; children: William S., Dorothy E. Sempolinski. B.S., U. Minn., 1942; Sc.D., MIT, 1949. Phys. chemist Fundamental Research Lab. U.S. Steel Corp., Kearny, N.J., 1949-51; research metallurgist Inland Steel Co., East Chicago, Ind., 1951-54, asst. supt. quality control, 1954-55; asso. prof. dept. metallurgy MIT, Cambridge, 1955-60, prof. metallurgy dept. materials sci. and engring., 1960—; now AISI Disting. prof.; dir. MIT (Mining and Mineral Resources Research Inst.), 1978—. Author: Thermochemistry for Steelmaking, vol. I, 1960, vol. II 1963, Steelmaking: The Chipman Conference, 1965; editor: The Physical Chemistry of Steelmaking, 1958; contbr. articles to profl. jours. Served to lt. comdr. USNR, 1942-46. Guggenheim fellow, 1965; Disting. mem. Iron and Steel Soc., 1976. Fellow Metall. Soc., AIME (hon. mem. 1982;, Douglas Gold medal 1976, Howe Meml. lectr. 1963, extractive metallurgy lectr. 1975), Am. Soc. Metals (White disting. teaching award 1971), Am. Inst. Chem. Engrs.; mem. Nat. Acad. Engring., Am. Acad. Arts and Scis., Metals Soc. (Gt. Britain), Iron and Steel Inst. Japan (hon.), Can. Inst. Mining and Metallurgy, Venezuelan Soc. Mining and Metall. Engrs. (hon.), Société Française de Métallurgie (hon.), AAAS, Sigma Xi, Tau Beta Pi. Home: 118 Arlington St Winchester MA 01890 Office: 77 Massachusetts Ave Cambridge MA 02139

ELLIOTT, JOHN MICHAEL, lawyer; b. Girardville, Pa., July 8, 1941; s. John T. and Clair C. E.; m. Jane L. Dalton, Aug. 25, 1944; children: John P., Heather D., Kirwan B., Kyle M. A.B. in Econs. magna cum laude, St. Vincent Coll., 1963; LL.B. cum laude, Georgetown U., 1966. Bar: Pa. 1966, U.S. Dist. Ct. (ea. dist.) Pa. 1967, U.S. Ct. Appeals (3d cir.) 1967, U.S. Supreme Ct. 1968. Sr. ptnr. Dilworth, Paxson, Kalish & Kauffman, Phila., 1970—; mem. Phila. Coal Rail Task Force, Rockefeller Commn., White Ho. Coal Adv. Commn.; bd. dirs. James A. Finnegan Fellowship Found., Irish Ednl. Devel. Found. Inc.; mem. Pa. Citizens Adv. Council Dept. Environ Resources, 1970-78, chmn. urban com.; mem. environ quality bd. Commonwealth of Pa., 1970-78; commr. Del. River Port Authority; mem. Phila. City Planning Commn., 1970-75, Del. Valley Citizens Council for Clean Air.; mem. Disciplinary Bd. Supereme Ct. Pa., 1982, chmn. rules com. Contbr. articles to profl. jours. Williston research fellow, 1965. Mem. ABA, Pa. Bar Assn. (del. 1983, task force on civil ct. rules), Pa. Bar. Inst. (couse planner, faculty), Am. Law Inst. (ABA appellate practice program), Nat. Inst. Trial Advocacy (lectr.), Fed. Bar Assn., Phila Bar Assn. (environ. quality com.), Nat. Lawyers Com. for Civil Rights Under Law, Braehon Law Soc., NCCP (co chmn. chpt.), Friendly Sons of St. Patrick (co chmn. chpt.), Irish Soc. Phila, Pa. Hist. Soc., Chestnut Hill Community Assn., John Buchan Soc. Edinborough, Mil. History Soc. Ireland. Home: 8112 St Martins Ln Philadelphia PA 19118 Office: Dilworth Paxson Kalish & Kauffman 2600 Fidelity Bldg Philadelphia PA 19109

ELLIOTT, JOHN, JR., advertising agency executive; b. N.Y.C., Jan. 25, 1921; s. John and Audrey Neilson (Osborn) E.; m. Eleanor Lansing Thomas, July 27, 1956. A.B., Harvard U., 1942. Copywriter Batten, Barton, Durstine & Osborn, 1945-49, account exec., 1949-60, v.p., 1956-60, dir., 1958-60; sr. v.p., dir. Ogilvy, Benson & Mather, 1960-65; chmn. Ogilvy & Mather (U.S.), N.Y.C., 1965-75, Ogilvy & Mather Internat., 1975-82; dir. Fireman's Fund Am. Life Ins. Co. N.Y., 1972-82. Trustee, pres. Alumni Assn. Browning Sch., 1950-60; trustee St. Paul's Sch., 1978-81, Internat. House, 1967—, N.Y. Zool. Soc., 1979—; bd. dirs. Park Assn., N.Y.C., 1956-60; bd. dirs., v.p. Mus. City of N.Y., 1956-65; gen. chmn Red Cross Campaign for Mems. and Funds, N.Y.C., 1970-71; TV advisor Rep. Party, 1950-53; bd. overseers Meml. Sloan-Kettering Cancer Care Center; pres. Scottish Nat. Trust Golden Jubilee Found., 1980—; mem. President's Adv. Council Pvt. Sector Initiatives, 1983—. Served with USMC, 1942-45. Mem. Am. Assn. Advt. Agys. (chmn. 1974-75), Advt. Council (dir. 1972—, vice chmn. 1979—). Clubs: Bedford Golf and Tennis; Harvard (N.Y.C.). Office: 2 E 48th St New York NY 10017

ELLIOTT, JOSEPH GORDON, JR., retired newspaper executive; b. Milford, Del., Apr. 28, 1914; s. Joseph Gordon and Mary Bess (Shaw) E.; (widower). Student, Graphic Sketch Club, 1931-36, Pa. Acad. Fine Arts, 1947, 82. Artist Phila. Public Ledger, 1935-36; mem. staff Phila. Bull., 1936—, asst. bus. mgr., 1955-71, v.p. personnel, 1971-75, v.p., bus. mgr., 1975-81; dir. Donohue-Charlevoix, Inc. Served with AUS, 1941-46. Mem. Am. Newspaper Pubs. Assn. Republican. Presbyterian. Clubs: Union League (Phila.); Barnegat Light Yacht. Home: 18 Haddonfield Commons Haddonfield NJ 08033

ELLIOTT, LARRY PAUL, cardiac radiologist; b. Manhattan, Kans., Oct. 16, 1931; s. Leonard Paul and Mary Elizabeth (Myers) E.; m. Betty Lou Hawkins, June 23, 1956; children—Laurie Lou, Mary Elizabeth, Larry Paul. B.S., U. Fla., 1954; M.D., U. Tenn., 1957. Intern John Gaston Hosp., Memphis, 1957-58; resident in pediatrics and pediatric cardiology U. Fla. Hosp., 1958-61; resident in cardiac pathology and cardiovascular radiology U. Minn. Hosp., 1961-65; asso. prof. cardiac radiology Washington U. Med. Sch., St. Louis, 1966-67; prof. cardiac radiology U. Fla. Med. Sch., 1967-76; prof. radiology, dir. div. cardiac radiology U. Ala. Med. Sch., Birmingham, 1976-81; prof., chmn. dept. radiology Georgetown U. Sch. Medicine, 1981—. Author: The X-Ray Diagnosis Heart Disease, 1968, 79; editor: Radiology, 1967—, Cardiovascular and Interventional Radiology, 1979—; contbr. articles to med. jours. Grantee cardiac radiology Nat. Heart Inst., 1968-76, Allied Health Profl. Act, 1970—. Fellow N.Am. Soc. Cardiac Radiology (pres. 1977-78), Am. Coll. Cardiology; mem. Radiol. Soc. N.Am., Soc. Cardiac Angiography, Am. Heart Assn. Home: 4420 Hadfield Ln Washington DC 20007 Office: 3800 Reservoir Rd NW Washington DC 20007 *In my own success, I have found 5 key ingredients. (1) A mentor who ignited the switch or literally turned me on. (2) Superb training, especially in sound fundamental principles. (3) An obsessive enthusiasm, a prime feature I look for in all postgraduate students. (4) An element of discipline, which has prevented succumbing to the siren song of private practice. (5) Reward, the only fountain of youth that exists - a close association with each generation of students.*

ELLIOTT, LAWRENCE, writer; b. Bklyn., Jan. 18, 1924; s. Samuel and Gussie (Goldsmith) Edelstein; m. Gisèle Kayser, July 1969; 1 son Nicholas, children by previous marriage: Jain, Elizabeth, Barbara. B.S.S., City Coll. N.Y., 1950. Asso. editor Coronet mag., 1948-54; free-lance writer, 1954-62; staff writer Reader's Digest, 1962—, European corr., 1968-69, 78—, roving editor, 1971—. Author: A Little Girl's Gift, 1963, George Washington Carver: The Man Who Overcame, 1966, (with James Huntington) On the Edge of Nowhere, 1966, (with Senator Daniel K. Inouye) Journey to Washington, 1967, The Legacy of Tom Dooley, 1969, I Will Be Called John, 1973, The Long Hunter: A Biography of Daniel Boone, 1976, The Last Insurgent: The Life of Fiorello H. LaGuardia, 1982, Little Flower: The Life and Times of Fiorello LaGuardia, 1983. Served to 1st lt. AUS, 1942-46. Recipient Freedoms Found. award, 1951, Alaska Press Club Award, 1966, German Jugendbuchpreis, 1970. Clubs: Overseas Press (N.Y.C.); Anglo-Am. Press of Paris., Authors Guild. Address: Reader's Digest 16 rue Washington 75016 Paris France

ELLIOTT, LEE ANN, federal election commissioner; b. St. Louis, June 26, 1927; d. Ernest Silvester and Ida May (Davis) Layton; m. William Jerome Elliott, Sept. 22, 1956; 1 son, William Jay. B.A., U. Ill., 1949. Cert. assn. exec. Legis. asst. AMA, Chgo., 1951-62; assoc. exec. dir. Am. Med. Polit. Action Com., Chgo., 1962-79; v.p. Bishop, Bryant and Accocs., Chgo., 1979-81; mem. Fed. Election Commn., Washington, 1981—. V.p. Skokie Caucus Party (Ill.), 1973—; mem. Thompson for Gov. Com., 1978, Senator Percy Adv. Com., 1978, Porter for Congress Com., 1982, Young for Congress Com., 1978. Recipient Excellence in Pub. Affairs award NAM, 1979. Mem. Am. Soc. Assn. Execs., Am. Assn. Polit Cons. (bd. 1975-81), Chgo. Area Pub. Affairs Group (pres. 1972), U.S. C. of C., Alpha Delta Pi. Republican. Home: 1425 Lamon Ave Skokie IL 60077 Office: Fed Election Commission 1325 K St NW Washington DC 20463

ELLIOTT, LLOYD HARTMAN, university president; b. Clay County, W.Va., May 21, 1918; s. John and Belva (Stone) E.; m. Evelyn Elder, Aug. 25, 1936; children: Lloyd Gene, Patricia Ann. A.B., Glenville State Coll., 1937; M.A., W.Va. U., 1939, LL.D., 1967; Ed.D., U. Colo., 1948; LL.D., U. N.H., 1963, Colby Coll., 1965, Concord Coll., 1966, U. Maine, 1969, Husson Coll., 1970, Georgetown U., 1971. Tchr. pub. sch., Widen, W.Va., 1937-39, elem., high sch. prin., 1939-42; instr. U. Colo., summer 1947; asst. supt. Boulder pub. sch., 1947-48; vis. prof. U. Tex., 1948; asst. prof. edn. Cornell U., 1948-50, assoc. prof. edn., 1950-54, dir. summer session, 1953-58, prof. edn., 1954, exec. asst. to pres., 1956-58; pres. U. Maine, 1958-65, George Washington U., 1965—; dir. Bell Atlantic, Am. Security Trust Co., Acacia Mut. Life Ins. Co., Woodward & Lothrop Corp.; cons. curriculum N.C. Survey Pub. Edn., 1950-51; Bd. dirs. Consortium Washington Univs. Contbr. articles profl. publs. Mem. Nat. Geog. Soc. (trustee), Am. Council on Edn. (sec. 1967), Phi Kappa Phi, Phi Delta Kappa. Club: Cosmos. Home: 2330 Tracy Pl NW Washington DC 20008

ELLIOTT, OSBORN, univ. dean, former editor; b. N.Y.C., Oct. 25, 1924; s. John and Audrey N. (Osborn) E.; m. Deirdre M. Spencer, May 8, 1948 (div. Dec. 1972); children: Diana, Cynthia, Dorinda; m. Inger McCabe, Oct. 20, 1973; stepchildren: Kari, Alexander, Marit. Grad., St. Paul's Sch., 1942; A.B., Harvard U., 1946; L.H.D., Mich. State U., 1972. Reporter N.Y. Jour. Commerce, 1946-49; contbg. editor Time mag., 1949-52, asso. editor, 1952-55; sr. bus. editor Newsweek, 1955-59, mng. editor, 1959-61, editor, 1961-69, 72-75, editor-in-chief, vice chmn., 1970, pres., 1971, chief exec. officer, 1971-76, chmn. bd., 1972-76, editor-in-chief, 1975-76; former dir. Washington Post Co.; dep. mayor econ. devel., City of N.Y., 1976-77; dean Grad. Sch. Journalism, Columbia U., N.Y.C., 1979—, pub. Columbia Journalism Rev., 1982—. Author: Men At the Top, 1959, The World of Oz, 1980; Editor: The Negro Revolution in America, 1964. Chmn. N.Y.C. Indsl. and Comml. Incentive Bd., 1976-77; co-chmn. N.Y.C. Bus. Mktg. Corp., 1976-77; mem. N.Y.C. Indsl. Devel. Bd., 1976-77; bd. overseers Harvard Coll., 1965-71; trustee N.Y. Pub. Library, 1968-72, 77-79, St. Paul's Sch., 1969-73, Am. Mus. Natural History, 1958-80, Asia Soc., Carnegie Endowment for Internat. Peace; chmn. bd. dirs. Citizens Com. for N.Y.C., 1975-79. Served with USNR, 1944-46. Fellow Am. Acad. Arts and Scis.; mem. Council Fgn. Relations. Clubs: Harvard, Century Assn., Coffee House (N.Y.C.). Office: Journalism Bldg Columbia U New York NY 10027

ELLIOTT, PETER R., athletic orgn. exec.; b. Bloomington, Ill., Sept. 29, 1926; s. Joseph Norman and Alice (Marquis) E.; m. s. Joan Connaught Slater, June 14, 1949; children: Bruce Norman, David Lawrence. B.A., U. Mich., 1949. Asst. football coach Oreg. State U., 1949-50, U. Okla., 1951-55; head football coach Nebr. U., 1956, U. Calif., Berkeley, 1957-59, U. Ill., 1960-66, U. Miami, Fla., 1973-74, dir. athletics, 1974-78; asst. football coach St. Louis Cardinals, 1978; exec. dir. Pro Football Hall of Fame, Canton, Ohio, 1979—. Served with USNR, 1944-45. Named Region 8 Coach of Year, 1958, Region 5, 1963; (both Am. Football Coaches Assn.).; named to Mich. Sports Hall of Fame, 1983. Mem. Am. Football Coaches Assn. Presbyterian. Home: 3003 Dunbarton St Canton OH 44708 Office: 2121 Harrison St Canton OH 44708

ELLIOTT, PHILIP CLARKSON, educator, artist; b. Mpls., Dec. 5, 1903; s. Charles Burke and Edith (Winslow) E.; m. Virginia Isobel Cuthbert, June 8, 1935. Student, U. Minn., 1921-23; B.F.A., Yale U., 1926; Chaloner fellow for European study, 1929-33. Asst. prof. fine art U. Pitts., 1934-41; dir. Albright Art Sch., U. Buffalo, 1941—; prof., dir. dept. art SUNY-Buffalo, prof. emeritus, 1974—. Exhibited paintings, Mus. Modern Art, Phila. Acad., Carnegie Internat., Albright Art Gallery, Whtney Mus. Am. Art, Met. Mus., Albright-Knox Gallery, Butler Art Inst. Ann., Syracuse (N.Y.) State Expn., Three Rivers Art Festival, W. N.Y. Art Exhbns., Charles Burchfield Center, State U. N.Y. at Buffalo, N.Y. State Mus. Travelling Exhbn., Kenan Art Center, Lockport, N.Y., Gallery Without Walls, Buffalo, Westmoreland County Mus. Art, Greensburg, Pa., 1981; represented permanent collection, Albright-Knox Gallery, Charles Burchfield Center, Newark Mus., also, numerous pvt. collections. Recipient Distinguished Faculty fellowship U. State N.Y., 1967. Mem. Buffalo Fine Arts Acad. (hon. life), Patteran Artists. Democrat. Episcopalian. Home: 1240 Delaware Ave Apt 114 Buffalo NY 14209

ELLIOTT, R. KEITH, specialty chemical company executive; b. Abbeville, S.C., Feb. 25, 1942; s. Bridwell Douglas and Sara (Broome) E.; m. Geraldine Louise Tobia, July 30, 1966; children: M. Lance, Chad L. B.S., U. S.C.-Columbia, 1964; M.B.A., U. S.C-Columbia, 1965. With E.I. duPont de Nemours, Wilmington, Del., 1965-69, Mine Safety Appliances Co., Pitts., 1969-74; asst. treas. The Carborundum Co.(acquired by Kennecott Corp., 1978), Niagra Falls, N.Y., 1975-77; treas. The Carborundum Co. (acquired by Kennecott Corp., 1978), Niagra Falls, N.Y., 1977-79; asst. treas. Kennecott Corp., Stamford, Conn., 1979-80, v.p., treas, 1980-81; v.p., treas. Engelhard Corp., Edison, N.J., 1981—. Cons. City Mgmt. Adv. Bd., Niagra Falls, N.Y., 1976-79. Served with AUS, 1966-72. Mem. Fin. Execs. Inst., Nat. Assn. Corp. Treas., Machinery and Allied Products Inst. (mem. fin. council). Home: 18 Shrewsbury Dr Rumson NJ 07760 Office: Engelhard Corp 33 Wood Ave S Menlo Park CN40 NJ Edison 08818

ELLIOTT, ROBBINS LEONARD, association executive; b. Can., Aug. 12, 1920; s. Malcolm Robertson and Jean Steadman (Haley) E.; m. Myfanwy Esther Millward, Sept. 9, 1950; children: Michael, Wendy, Ruth, Robbins. B.A., Acadia U., 1941; M.A. in Econs., U. Toronto, 1947. With Can. Fed. Govt., Ottawa, 1947-58, 63-76; exec. dir. Royal Archtl. Inst. Can., Ottawa, 1958-63, exec. v.p., 1976-81; pres. Robbins Elliott Assos. Ltd., Ottawa, 1981-83; exec. dir. Can. Housing Design Council, 1983—. Trustee Ottawa Bd. Edn., 1974-76;

vice-chmn. Ont. Heritage Found.; dir. Ont. Bicentennial Adv. Commn. Served to capt. Can. Army, World War II. Fellow Royal Soc. Arts; mem. Archaeol. Inst. Am. Mem. Progressive Conservative Party. Baptist. Club: Rideau (Ottawa). Home: 2325 Georgina Dr Ottawa ON K2B 7M4 Canada Office: 172 L'Esplanada Laurier 171 Bank St Ottawa ON K2P 1N5 Canada

ELLIOTT, ROBERT B., comedian; b. Boston, Mar. 26, 1923; m. Jane Underwood, Sept., 1943 (div.); m. Lee Knight, June 1954; children: Colony, Shannon, Amy, Robert, Christopher. Student, Feagin Sch. of Drama and Radio, N.Y.C. Mem.: comedy team Bob and Ray, 1946—; appeared on daily radio program, Sta. WHDH, Boston, 1946-51, nat. daily radio program, NBC, 1951, 56-73; NBC radio program Moniter, 1952-56; appeared in various other radio programs, NBC, ABC, Mut. Broadcasting System; appeared on: Broadway in Bob and Ray: The Two and Only, 1970; appeared in: film Cold Turkey, 1971; (Recipient George Foster Peabody awards 1952, 57); Author: (with Ray Gouldin) Write If You Get Work, 1976. Served with AUS, 1943-46; ETO. Address: care Random House Inc 201 E 50th St New York NY 10022 *

ELLIOTT, RONNIE (MRS. JOHN PAUL KNAPP), artist; b. N.Y.C., Dec. 16, 1916; m. John Paul Knapp, Oct. 16, 1940. Student, N.Y. U., Hunter Coll., Art Students League. One-woman shows, Delphic Gallery, N.Y.C., 1937, 42, Grand Central Moderns, N.Y.C., 1947, 64, Norlyst Gallery, N.Y.C., 1948, Carlebach Gallery, N.Y.C., Raymond Creuze Gallery, Paris, Collette Allendy Gallery, Paris, 1952, Granville Gallery, N.Y.C., 1964, Rose Fried Gallery, N.Y.C., 1956, 57, 58, 67, Andre Zarre Gallery, N.Y.C., 1975-77, Polo Gallery, Washington, 1976, St. Peter's Coll., Jersey City, Nardin Gallery, N.Y.C., 1979, others, group shows include, Pa. Acad., 1933, Met. Mus., N.Y.C., 1942, Art of This Century, Peggy Guggenheim Gallery, N.Y.C., 1943, 44, 45, Mus. Modern Art, 1948, Musée des Arts Decorative, Louvre, Paris, 1964, St. Etienne Musée, France, Annely-Juda Fine Arts, London, 1972, Galerie Liatowitsch, Basel, Switzerland, Galleria Milano, Italy, 1972, U. Tex. Art Mus., Austin, 1973, Annely-Juda Fine Arts, London; represented in permanent collections, Mus. Modern Art, N.Y.C., Whitney Mus., N.Y.C., N.Y.U., N.Y. Hosp., Balt. Mus., Carnegie Inst. Tech., Pitts., Musée d'art et d'industrie, St. Etienne, France, Farnsworth Mus., Wellesley (Mass.) Coll., Andrew Dickson White Mus., Cornell U., Birla Acad. Art and Culture, Calcutta, India, Finch Coll. Mus., N.Y. Chase Manhattan Bank, Ciba-Geigy Corp., N.Y., Boston Mus. Art, Corcoran Gallery Art, Washington, Neuberger Mus., SUNY at Purchase, also numerous pvt. collections. Studio: 68 E 7th St New York NY 10003

ELLIOTT, R(OY) FRASER, holding and management company executive, lawyer; b. Ottawa, Ont., Can., Nov. 25, 1921. B.Comm., Queen's U., Kingston, Ont., Can., 1943; grad., Osgoode Hall Law Sch., 1946, Harvard U. Sch. Bus. Adminstrn., 1947. Bar: Ont. 1946, Que. 1948; created queen's counsel. Ptnr. Stikeman, Elliott, Robarts & Bowman, Toronto, Ont., Stikeman, Elliott, Tamaki, Mercier & Robb, Toronto; chmn. CAE Industries Ltd., Toronto, Standard Paper Box Ltd.; v.p., dir. Custom Concrete Ltd.; dir. Montreal Shipping Co., Ltd., Can. Imperial Bank Commerce, New Providence Devel. Co. Ltd., Frank W. Horner Ltd., Can. Cement Lafarge Ltd.; lectr. co. law McGill U., Montreal,, Que.,, Can., 1951-51. Contbg. author, editor: Que. Corp. Manual, 1948-53; co-editor: Doing Business in Canada. Mem. Montreal Bar Assn., Can. Bar Assn., Law Soc. Upper Can. Office: Suite 4950 Commerce Ct W Toronto ON Canada

ELLIOTT, THOMAS MICHAEL, professional association executive, educator, consultant; b. Evansville, Ind., Aug. 4, 1942; s. Thomas Ira and Pauline (Dawson) E.; m. Susan M. Spiers, July 8, 1967 (div. Aug. 1975); 1 son, Christopher Michael; m. Loretta S. Glaze, Jan. 28, 1976. A.B. in Zoology, Ind. U., 1965, M.S. in Higher Edn., 1967, Ed.D., 1970. Asst. to pres. Purdue U., West Lafayette, Ind., 1972-73, asst. provost, 1973-74; exec. dir. Nat. Commn. United Methodist Higher Edn., Nashville, 1974-77; dep. commr. Mo. Dept. Higher Edn., Jefferson City, 1977-79; exec. dir. Ark. Dept. Higher Edn., Little Rock, 1979-82, IEEE Computer Soc., Silver Springs, Md., 1982—; ptnr. Planning Mgmt. Services Group, Washington, 1976—; cons. numerous colls. and univs. Author: Computer Simulation System, 1975; contbr. articles to profl. jours. Bd. dirs., mem. exec. com. So. Regional Edn. Bd., Atlanta, 1980-82; mem. Cabinet of Gov. Bill Clinton and Gov. Frank White, State of Ark., 1979-82. Mem. Am. Assn. Higher Edn., Soc. Coll. and Univ. Planning, Assn. Instnl. Research, IEEE Computer Soc., State Higher Edn. Exec. Officers Assn., Am. Soc. Assn. Execs. Home: 2021 Kalorama Rd NW Apt 2 Washington DC 20009 Office: IEEE Computer Soc 1109 Spring St Suite 300 Silver Spring MD 20910

ELLIOTT, WARREN G., lawyer; b. Pueblo, Colo., Jan. 3, 1927; s. Wallace Ford and Hazel (Ellsworth) E.; m. Martha McCabe, June 20, 1953; children: Mark, Winthrop, Carolyn, Byron. Student, U. Nebr., 1944-45, U. Colo., 1947-49, A.B., 1973; LL.B., U. Mich., 1952. Bar: Colo. 1952, Conn. 1976, D.C. bar 1978. Asst. city mgr., city atty., Pueblo, 1952-55; adminstrv. asst., legislative counsel U.S. Senator Gordon Allott, 1956-61; asst. gen. counsel Life Ins. Assn. Am., Washington, 1961-68; gen. counsel Aetna Life & Casualty Co., Hartford, Conn., 1968-78; mem. firm Hedrick & Lane, Washington, 1978-79, Nossaman, Guthner, Knox & Elliott, 1979—. Corporator Hartford Hosp., St. Francis Hosp., Inst. for Living. Served with USAAF, 1944-46. Mem. Am., Fed. bar assns., Greater Hartford C. of C., Congl. Club Greater Hartford, Phi Gamma Delta, Phi Alpha Delta. Club: University (Washington). Home: 2700 N St NW Washington DC 20007 Office: 1140 19th St NW Washington DC 20036

ELLIOTT, WILLIAM MICHAEL, manufacturing company executive; b. Leavenworth, Kans., Apr. 18, 1934; s. James E. and Grace M. E.; m. Maria Esther Vega; children: Carmen Marissa, Stephanie Lynn. B.A. (Victor Wilson scholar 1957-59), U. Mo., Kansas City, 1959, J.D., 1962. Bar: Mo. 1962, Mich. 1965, Calif. 1968, Md. 1975, D.C. 1975. Counsel Mobil Oil Co., Mich. and Calif., 1962-68; gen. counsel, sec. Martin Marietta Aluminum Co., Calif. and Md., 1968-77; sec. Martin Marietta Corp., N.Y. and Md., 1974-77; sr. v.p., gen. counsel Northrop Corp., Los Angeles, 1977—; speaker in field. Served with USMC, 1953-56. Mem. U.S. Supreme Ct. Bar, ABA, State Bar Calif., Mich. Bar Assn., Mo. Bar Assn., Md. Bar Assn., D.C. Bar Assn., Los Angeles County Bar Assn., Century City Bar Assn. Address: Northrop Corp 1840 Century Park E Los Angeles CA 90067

ELLIOTT-SMITH, PAUL HENRY, marketing consultant; b. N.Y.C., Nov. 13, 1919; s. Henry Paul and Helen Felecia (Ruby) E-S.; m. Cecily Gardiner, July 1, 1941; children: Christie, Deirdre; m. Alta Jo Douglas, 1963; 1 dau., Elise Suzanne. B.S., Fordham U., 1942. Copywriter Breese Assos., Inc., N.Y.C., 1942-47; exec. v.p. Breese, Enloe & Elliott-Smith, Inc., N.Y.C., 1947-51; product dir. Gen. Foods Corp., N.Y.C., 1951-53, mgr. operations new products/acquisitions dept., 1953-57; dir. advt. Warner Lambert Pharm. Co., Morris Plains, N.J., 1958-59; dir. new products, 1959-60; exec. v.p. Morse Internat., Inc., N.Y.C., 1961, pres., 1962-66; exec. v.p., gen. mgr. Gaynor & Ducas, Inc., N.Y.C., 1967-74; chmn. S.A. Mktg. Co., 1975—; sr. partner Paul Elliott-Smith & Co., 1975—; dir. Communications Corp. Am., N.Y.C. Bd. dirs. Dwight D. Eisenhower Inst. for Stroke Research, N.Y.C.; trustee Hillcrest Gen. Hosp., N.Y.C. Served with AUS, 1942-45; ETO. Mem. Copy Research Council N.Y.C. Club: University (N.Y.C.). Home: 1009 Park Ave New York NY 10028 Office: 200 Park Ave New York NY 10017

ELLIS, ALBERT, clinical psychologist, educator, author; b. Pitts., Sept. 27, 1913; s. Henry Oscar and Hettie (Hanigbaum) E.; m. Rhoda Winter, May 26, 1956. B.B.A., CCNY, 1934; M.A., Columbia U., 1943, Ph.D., 1947. Diplomate: Am. Bd. Profl. Psychology; in clin. hypnosis Am. Bd. Psychol. Hypnosis. Free-lance writer, 1934-38; personnel mgr. Distinctive Creations, 1938-48; sr. clin. psychologist N.J. State Hosp., Greystone Park, 1948-49; instr. psychology Rutgers U., 1948-49, adj. prof., 1971—; inst. psychology N.Y. U., 1949; adj. prof. Union Grad. Sch., 1971-77, U.S. Internat. U., 1974-80, Pittsburg State U., 1978—; chief psychologist N.J. State Diagnostic Center, Menlo Park, 1949-50, N.J. Dept. Instns. and Agys., Trenton, 1950-52; pvt. practice psychotherapy and marriage and family therapy, N.Y.C., 1943-68; exec. dir. Inst. for Rational-Emotive Therapy, N.Y.C., 1959—; Cons. clin. psychology VA, 1961-67. Author: An Introduction to the Principles of Scientific Psychoanalysis, 1950, The Folklore of Sex, 1951, (with A.P. Pillay) Sex, Society and the Individual, 1953, The American Sexual Tragedy, 1954, Sex Life of the American Woman and, the Kinsey Report, 1954, New Approaches to Psychotherapy Techniques, 1955, (with Ralph Brancale) The Psychology of Sex Offenders, 1956, How to Live With a Neurotic, 1957, Sex Without Guilt, 1958, What Is Psychotherapy?, 1959, The Place of Values in the Practice of Psychotherapy, 1959, The Art and Science of Love, 1960, (with Robert A. Harper) Creative Marriage, 1961, (with R.A. Harper) A Guide to Rational Living, 1961, (with Albert Abarbanel) The Encyclopedia of Sexual Behavior, 1961, Reason and Emotion in Psychotherapy, 1962, The Intelligent Woman's Guide to Manhunting, 1963, If This Be Sexual Heresy, 1963, Sex and the Single Man, 1963, The Origins and the Development of the Incest Taboo, 1963, Nymphomania, A Study of the Over-Sexed Woman, 1964, Homosexuality, 1965, Suppressed: Seven Key Essays Publishers Dared Not Print, 1965, The Case for Sexual Liberty, 1965, The Search for Sexual Enjoyment, 1966, (with others) How to Prevent Your Child From Becoming a Neurotic Adult, 1966, (with Roger O. Conway) The Art of Erotic Seduction, 1967, Is Objectivism a Religion?, 1968, (with John M. Gullo) Murder and Assassination, 1971, (with others) Growth Through Reason, 1971, Executive Leadership: A Rational Approach, 1972, The Civilized Couple's Guide to Extramarital Adventure, 1972, How to Master Your Fear of Flying, 1972, The Sensuous Person: Critique and Corrections, 1972, (with others) Sex and Sex Education: A Bibliography, 1972, Humanistic Psychotherapy: The Rational-Emotive Approach, 1973, (with Robert A. Harper) A New Guide to Rational Living, 1975, Sex and the Liberated Man, 1976, How to Live With—and Without—Anger, 1977, (with Russell Grieger) Handbook of Rational-Emotive Therapy, 1977, (with W. Knaus) Overcoming Procrastination, 1977, (with E. Abrahms) Brief Psychotherapy in Medical and Health Practice, 1978, (with J.M. Whiteley) Theoretical and Empirical Foundations of Rational-Emotive Therapy, 1979, The Intelligent Woman's Guide to Dating and Mating, 1979, (with I. Becker) A Guide to Personal Happiness, 1982, Rational-Emotive Therapy and Cognitive Behavior Therapy, 1984, (with M. Bernard) Rational-Emotive Approaches to the Problems of Childhood, 1984. Fellow Am. Psychol. Assn. (pres. div. cons. psychology 1961-62, exec. com. div. psychotherapy 1969-73, council of reps. 1963-64, 72-74), AAAS, Am. Assn. Marriage and Family Therapists (exec. com. 1957-59), Soc. Sci. Study Sex (exec. com. 1957-68, pres. 1960-62), Am. Orthopsychiat. Assn., Am. Sociol. Assn., Am. Assn. Applied Anthropology; mem. N.Y. Assn. Clin. Psychologists in Pvt. Practice (chmn. 1952-54), N.Y. Joint Council Psychologists on Legislation (exec. com. 1951-53), Am. Group Psychotherapy Assn., Am. Acad. Psychotherapists (mem. exec. com. 1954-64, v.p. 1962-64), Mensa, Am. Assn. Advancement Psychotherapy, N.Y. State Psychol. Assn., Soc. Exptl. and Clin. Hypnosis. Office: 45 E 65th St New York NY 10021 *I now see that I have given up any addiction to MUSTurbation many years ago—to thinking that I must do well; that others must treat me considerately or fairly; and that the world must provide me with the things I want easily and quickly. I now almost always think that it would be better or nicer if I did well, others treated me fairly, or the world proved easy and pleasant. But it doesn't have to turn out those ways—and that makes quite a difference!*

ELLIS, ANTHONY THORNTON, venture capitalist; b. Eminence, Ky., Feb. 26, 1929; s. Anthony Thornton and Georgiana (Swinney) E.; m. Jane Canning, Nov. 10, 1956; children: Susan, Winnifred, David. B.S., U. Calif., Berkeley, 1951; M.B.A., Harvard U., 1956; grad. exec. program, Stanford U., 1971; advanced profl. cert. in acctg., NYU Grad. Sch. Bus., 1974. Asst. cashier First Nat. City Bank, N.Y.C., 1958-60, asst. v.p., 1960-62, v.p., 1962-70; treas. Kennecott Copper Corp., N.Y.C., 1970-76, v.p. fin., 1976-78, v.p., treas., 1978-79; exec. v.p. Am. Security Bank N.A., Washington, 1979-81; gen. ptnr. Pacific Venture Ptnrs., Menlo Park, Calif., 1982—. Bd. dirs., mem. exec. com. ARC. Served to lt. (j.g.) USN, 1951-54. Mem. Beta Theta Pi. Republican. Clubs: Harvard (N.Y.C.); Bronxville (N.Y.) Field; Univ. (Washington). Home: 1404 35th St NW Washington DC 20007 Office: 3000 Sand Hill Rd Menlo Park CA 94025

ELLIS, BILLY JOE, retired air force officer; b. De Quincy, La., Dec. 11, 1928; s. Nolan Price and Lillian Doris (Isdale) E.; m. Barbara Hope Higginbotham, Feb. 9, 1952; children—Elaine, Mark, Kevin, Christopher, Yvonne, Adele, John, Brian. B.S., U.S. Mil. Acad., 1951; M.S. in Bus. Adminstrn, George Washington U., 1964. Commd. 2d lt. U.S. Air Force, 1951, advanced through grades to maj. gen., 1973; fighter pilot, Korea, 1952-53, fighter gunnery instr., 1953-55; pilot Air Force Thunderbirds, 1955-57; air officer comdg. 5th Squadron, Air Force Acad., 1957-60; fighter pilot, Germany, 1960-63; assigned Hdqrs. Tactical Air Command, 1964-67; dir. ops. 388 Tactical Fighter Wing, Thailand, 1968-69; asst. for gen. officer matters Pentagon, Washington, 1969-71; div. comdr. SAC, Mich., 1972, Thailand, 1973, dep. chief of staff, personnel, Offutt AFB, Nebr., 1973-74, dep. chief of staff-ops., 1974-75; dir. ops. Hdqrs. U.S. Air Force, Washington, 1975-76, dep. insp. gen., 1976-77; dep. chief of staff ops. TAC, Langley AFB, Va., 1977-79; vice comdr. 9th Air Force, Shaw AFB, S.C., 1979-81, ret., 1981. Decorated D.S.M. with oak leaf cluster, Legion of Merit with cluster, D.F.C. with 2 oak leaf clusters, Air medal with 11 oak leaf clusters, Air Force Commendation medal. Mem. Air Force Assn., Order of Daedalions. Home: Route 3 Box 278 Sumter SC 29150

ELLIS, BRENT E., Baritone; b. Kansas City, Mo., June 20, 1946; s. John Waldo and Marcella (Grimes) E.; m. Linda Jean Phillips (div.); m. Whitney Ann Burnett (div.); 1 son, Burnett Grimes. Student, Edna Forsythe, 1962-65, Mme. Marian Freschl, 1965-71, Daniel Ferro, 1971—, Juilliard Sch. Music, 1965-67, 70-72. Performed with, Chgo. Lyric Opera, 1974, San Francisco Opera, 1974-78, Hamburg (W. Ger.) Staatsopera, 1977-79, Glyndebourne Festival Opera, 1977, 78, Nat. Arts Center, Ottawa, Ont., Can., 1976, Scottish Nat. Opera, Glasgow, 1979, 80, 84, Met. Opera, N.Y.C., 1979-84, Can. Opera Co., Toronto, Ont., 1979, Houston Grand Opera, 1972-81, Boston Opera, 1975-83, Washington Opera Soc., 1966, 79, N.Y.C. Opera, 1973, Phila. Lyric Opera, Seattle Opera Assn., 1975, Wexford (Ireland) Festival, 1972, Aspen (Colo.) Music Festival, 1972, 77, 83, Welsh Nat. Opera, 1979, Santa Fe (N.Mex.) Opera, 1972-82, Newport (Mass.) Music Festival, 1972, 73, Balt. Opera, 1979, Pitts. Opera, New Orleans Opera Assn., 1978, London Philharm., Toronto Symphony, 1979, 83, Chgo. Symphony, 1980, Mich. Opera Theatre, Detroit, 1976, 79, Omaha Opera, 1975, 76, TriCities Symphony, Ohio, 1975, San Francisco Symphony, 1974, 79, 81, N.J. Symphony, Newark, 1974, Houston Symphony, Nat. Symphony Orch. N.Y., 1971, 72, Minn. Orch., Mpls., 1971, N.Y.C. Opera, 1973, 79-81, many others. (Nat. Opera grantee 1972, Bori grantee Met. Opera 1972); (recipient Young Artist of Yr. award Mus. Am. 1973, winner WGN Auditions of Air 1973, Montreal Internat. Competition 1973). Named Artist of Year Greater Miami Opera Assn., 1982; Sullivan grantee, 1972; Bagby Found. grantee, 1972; Martha Baird Rockefeller grantee, 1975. Office: care Columbia Artists Mgmt Inc 165 W 57th St New York NY 10019

ELLIS, C. DOUGLAS, linguistics educator; b. Shawville, Que., Can., Dec. 6, 1923; s. John David and Ada Belle (Higgins) E.; m., June 6, 1953; children: Marilyn Joan, John Douglas. B.A., McGill U., 1944, Ph.D., 1954; M.A., U. Toronto, 1946; Lincentiate in Sacred Theology, Trinity Coll., Toronto, 1948; M.A., Yale U., 1949; B.A., Cambridge U., 1951. Asst. prof. dept. anthropoogy (U. Toronto), 1959-63; assoc. prof. dept. classics McGill U., Montreal, 1963-67, vice dean humanities div. Faculty Arts, 1964-68, prof. linguistics, 1967—, dept. chmn., 1972—; invited prof., cons. equipe professionelle U. Que. Chicoutini. Author: Spoken Cree, part 1, rev. edit. 1983, (with A. Schachter and J.G. Griffith) Ancient Greek: A Structural Programme, 1973; contbr. articles to profl. publs. Mem. Linguistic Soc. Am., Can. Linguistics Assn. Orthodox Ch. Am. Office: 1001 Sherbrooke St W Montreal PQ Canada H3A 1G5

ELLIS, CALVERT N., former college president; b. Zion City, Ill., Apr. 16, 1904; s. Charles Calvert and Emma Read (Nyce) E.; m. Elizabeth Olier Wertz, June 18, 1929; children: Elizabeth Anne, David Wertz. A.B., Juniata Coll., Huntingdon, Pa., 1923, LL.D., 1963; B.Th., M.A., Princeton, 1927; Ph.D., Yale U., 1932; D.D., Bethany Bibl. Sem., 1950; LL.D., Manchester Coll., 1956, Bridgewater Coll., 1965. Instr. Lewistown (Pa.) High Sch., 1923-24, Wilson Coll., Chambersburg, Pa., 1927-28; asst. prof., prof. bibl. studies and philosophy Juniata Coll., Huntingdon, Pa., 1931-43, pres., 1943-68, pres. emeritus, 1968—; mgr. D.M. Wertz Orchards, Waynesboro, Pa., 1940-60; chmn. bd. Penn Central Nat. Bank, Huntingdon, 1978—; Mem. adv. com. AID, 1966-69; cons. higher edn., 1968—. Author: The Conception of Revelation in the Dialectic Theology, 1932. Trustee J.C. Blair Hosp., Huntingdon, 1945-65; chmn. Gen. Brotherhood Bd., Elgin, Ill., 1948-54, 66-67; adv. com. higher edn. Edn. Compact States, 1966-68; adviser Com. on Edn. and Labor, Ho. of Reps., 1944-47, chmn. commn. on legislation, Assn. Am. Colls., 1961-64; chmn. bd. Assn. Am. Colls., 1969. Mem. Middle States Assn. Colls. and Secondary Schs. (pres. 1965). Church of the Brethren. Clubs: Skytop (Pa.); University, Pitts. (Sarasota, Fla.). Lodge: Rotary. Home: Route 4 Box 43 Huntingdon PA 16652

ELLIS, CHARLES CALVERT, corporate executive; b. Balt., Feb. 2, 1919; s. Luke and Olivia (Kelley) E.; m. Jean Ella Good, Dec. 29, 1942; children: Charles Calvert III, Pauline Olivia, Nancy Ruth, Richard James. A.B., Juniata Coll., Huntingdon, Pa., 1940, LL.D., 1981; M.B.A., Harvard, 1942. With Armstrong Cork Co., 1946-52, plant controller, Beaver Falls, Pa., 1949-52; with Ford Motor Co., 1952-59, regional fin. exec., internat. div., Latin Am., 1958-59, dir., 1958-59; controller Kordite Corp., 1959-62; with Philco Ford Corp., 1962-65, controller consumer products div., 1964-65; with Irving Trust Co., N.Y.C., 1965—, sr. v.p., comptroller, 1966-69, exec. v.p., 1969—; asst. treas. Charter N.Y. Corp., 1966-69, sr. v.p., treas., 1969—; sr. v.p. fin. RCA Corp., 1972-80, exec. v.p. long-range fin. planning, 1980—; Disting. lectr. Georgetown U. Sch. Bus. Adminstrn., Washington; chmn. RCA Internat. Ltd., RCA Internat. Devel. Corp.; pres. RCA Disc Corp.; dir. Random House, RCA Globcom, Hertz, RCA Ltd., U.K., Banquet Foods, RCA Americom, So. Gen. Internat. Fund, Coronet, USLIFE Income Fund, Optelicom, Inc., Fred F. French Investment Co.; tchr. extension U. Mich., 1956-59; Chmn. acctg. and fin. com. Nat. Flexible Packaging Assn., 1961-62; chmn. acctg. and tax com. N.Y. Clearing House, 1968-69; mem. Fin. Acctg. Standards Adv. Council, 1980—. Trustee Juniata Coll., 1966—, chmn., 1979; chmn. Pro Musicis Found. Served to lt. USNR, 1942-46. Home: Box 203 Waterford VA 22190 Office: Georgetowm U. Sch. Bus. Adminstrn. Washington DC 20057

ELLIS, DAVID MALDWYN, history educator; b. Utica, N.Y., Oct. 14, 1914; s. Samuel and Margaret Brymer (Jones) E.; m. Carolyn Crawford, June 20, 1953. B.A., Hamilton Coll., 1938; M.A., Cornell U., Ithaca, N.Y., 1939, Ph.D., 1942. Instr. history U. Vt., 1942-44; asst. prof. history Cornell U., Ithaca, N.Y., 1944; faculty Hamilton Coll., 1946-80, P.V. Rogers prof. history, 1957—, also chmn. history dept., 1968-78; pres. N.Y. Assn. Am. Studies. Author: Landlords and Farmers in the Hudson-Mohawk Region 1790-1850, 1946; co-author: A History of New York State, 1967; Co-author: New York the Empire State, 5th edit., 1980, New York: State and City, 1979, The Upper Mohawk Country. An Illustrated History of Greater Utica, 1982; also articles; gen. editor: The Frontier in American Development, 1969. Fellow N.Y. State Hist. Assn. (trustee); mem. Am. Hist. Assn., Orgn. Am. Historians, Am. Studies Assn. (exec. bd.), Phi Beta Kappa. Presbyterian. Home: 250 College Hill Clinton NY 13323

ELLIS, DAVID WERTZ, college president; b. Huntingdon, Pa., Feb. 8, 1936; s. Calvert Nice and Elizabeth Oller (Wertz) E.; m. Marion Elizabeth Schmitt, June 24, 1961; children: Kathryn Dana, Lorna Beth, Audrey Heather. B.A. with honors in Chemistry, Haverford Coll., 1958; Ph.D. in Chemistry, MIT, 1962; LL.D. (hon.), Lehigh U., 1979, D.Sc., Susquehanna U., 1982. Asst. prof. chemistry U. N.H., 1962-67, asso. prof., 1967-78, acting asst. dean Grad. Sch., 1967, asst. dean Coll. of Tech., 1968, asso. acad. v.p., 1968-71, vice provost acad. affairs, 1971-77, v.p. acad. affairs, 1977-78; pres. Lafayette Coll., Easton, Pa., 1978—; dir. Easton Nat. Bank and Trust Co., Elderhostel, Mchts. Bancorp. Author: (with others) Calculations of Analytical Chemistry, 7th edit., 1971; contbr. articles to profl. jours. Mem. long range planning com. Oyster River Coop Sch. Dist., 1966-68. Dupont fellow, 1960-61. Mem. AAAS, Am. Chem. Soc. Mem. United Ch. of Christ. Clubs: Northampton County; Pomfret (Easton, Pa.); University (N.Y.C.); Rittenhouse (Phila.). Home: 515 College Ave Easton PA 18042 Office: Lafayette Coll Easton PA 18042

ELLIS, DON EDWIN, educator; b. Ames, Iowa, Apr. 8, 1908; s. Charles Elmer and Bertha Helen (Fraker) E.; m. Helen Margaret Watkins, Dec. 29, 1928; 1 dau., Carol Don Ellis Montague. A.B., Nebr. Central Coll., 1928, B.S., 1929; M.S., La. State U., 1932; Ph.D., U. N.C., 1945. Sci. tchr. Juniata (Nebr.) High Sch., 1929-31; research asst. La. State U., 1931-33; asst. pathologist div. forest pathology U.S. Dept. Agr., Ariz., N.Mex., 1934-40; faculty N.C. State U., Raleigh, 1940—, prof., 1950—, head, dept. plant pathology, 1954-73, prof. emeritus, 1973—; Visited agrl. areas and research installations in, Mexico, Guatemala, 1962, Venezuela, 1966, Colombia, Panama, 1970, plant pathology cons., Peru, Servicio de Investigacion y Promocion Agraria, Universidad Agraria, N.C. State Agr. Mission to Peru, 1963, 66, 70. Contbr. articles to sci. publs. Mem. A.A.A.S., Am. Phytopath. Soc. (pres. So. div. 1962, mem. council 1957-59, chmn. com. on awards and honors 1960-63, v.p. 1967-68, pres. 1969-70, award of merit Caribbean div. 1972, rep. to A.A.A.S. 1971-73, 74-76), Am. Inst. Biol. Scis., Mycol. Soc. Am., Assn. Tropical Biology, Internat. Soc. for Plant Pathology, N.C. Acad. Sci., Sigma Xi, Gamma Sigma Delta (Merit award 1970-71). Home: 324 Shepherd Raleigh NC 27607

ELLIS, DONALD EDWIN, physicist; b. San Diego, Feb. 20, 1939; s. Mack Donald and Dorothy C. (Brown) E.; m. Georgianne R. Boyle, May 1965; children—Peter, Ryan, Alexander. B.S., M.I.T., 1961, M.S., 1964, Ph.D., 1966. Asst. prof. physics U. Fla., Gainesville, 1966-68; mem. faculty Northwestern U., 1968—, prof. physics and chemistry, 1976—. Mem. Am. Phys. Soc., Am. Chem. Soc. Address: Dept Physics and Astronomy Northwestern Univ Evanston IL 60201

ELLIS, DONALD HOWARD, real estate investment company executive; b. Long Beach, Calif., Feb. 9, 1931; s. Carl O. and Reta (Cooper) J.; m. Mary Elin Gomes, Aug. 12, 1953; children: Mark, Lisa. A.A., Pasadena City Coll., 1951; B.S., UCLA, 1953. SRS, Nat. Assn. Realtors, 1982. Account exec. Univac div. Sperry Rand Co., Los Angeles, 1956-63; dir. research Financial Sec., Inc., Los Angeles, 1963-65, dir., 1965-66; pres. Property Research Corp., Los Angeles, 1965—; exec. v.p., dir. Property Research Financial Corp., 1971, Ellis & Lane, Inc., 1971—; Tchr. computer programming Los Angeles Met. Coll., 1963-64; Bd. govs. Real Estate Securities Inst. div. Nat. Assn. Realtors, 1972-77. Served with USNR, 1953-55. Mem. Nat. Assn. Security Dealers. Home: 30851 Greens East Dr Laguna Niguel CA 92677 Office: 635 Camino de los Mares San Clemente CA 92672

ELLIS, E. FRANK, govt. ofcl.; b. Pitts., Apr. 23, 1918; s. Almer E. and Sallie T. E.; m. Welcome Mae, Nov. 1945; children—Frank, Shirley Ellis MacCarther, Sally Ellis Fletcher. Student, U. Mich., 1935-37, Boston U., 1938-40; M.D., Meharry Med. Coll., 1944; M.P.H., U. Mich., 1968. Former mem. faculty Case Western Res. U. Sch. Medicine, U. Mo. Sch. Medicine, Northwestern U. Sch. Medicine, U. Mich. Sch. Public Health; med. cons. Mo. Dept. Public Health and Welfare; dir. ambulatory services, asst. adminstr. Kansas City Gen. Hosp., 1961-67; dir. Cleve. Dept. Health and Welfare, 1967-71; regional health adminstr. USPHS, Chgo., 1971—. Bd. dirs. ARC, Mo. Assn. Social Welfare. Served to maj. U.S. Army. Mem. Am. Pub. Health Assn. (pres.), U. Mich. Sch. Pub. Health Alumni Assn. (chmn. bd. govs.), Omega Psi Phi. Office: 34th Floor 300 S Wacker Dr Chicago IL 60606

ELLIS, ELLIOT FREDERIC, physician; b. Englewood, N.J., Apr. 7, 1929; s. Melvin William and Florence (Germain) E.; m. Jann Elizabeth Netter, Oct. 16, 1955; children—Michael, John, Nancy, Andrew. A.B., Kenyon Coll., 1950; M.D., Western Res. U., 1954. Intern. Lenox Hill Hosp., N.Y.C., 1954-55; resident Babies Hosp., Columbia-Presbyn. Med. Center, N.Y.C., 1957-59; fellow Children's Asthma Research Inst. and Hosp., Denver, 1962-63; fellow dept. pediatrics U. Fla. Coll. Medicine, Gainesville, 1963-66; asst. prof. pediatrics U. Colo., 1966-69, asso. prof., 1970-74; chief pediatric allergy, immunology Nat. Jewish Hosp. and Research Center, Denver, 1970-74; prof. pediatrics SUNY, Buffalo, 1974—, chmn., 1975—; pediatrician-in-chief Children's Hosp., Buffalo, 1975—, acting dir., 1976-77, dir. clin. research center and div. allergy-immunology, 1974-76. Contbr. articles to med. jours. Served with USAF, 1955-62. Recipient Bela Schick award Am. Coll. Allergists, 1964. Mem. Soc. Pediatric Research, Am. Acad. Pediatrics, Am. Acad. Allergy, Am. Assn. Immunologists, Am. Coll. Allergists. Office: 219 Bryant St Buffalo NY 14222

ELLIS, ELMO ISRAEL, broadcasting executive; b. Birmingham, Ala., Nov. 11, 1918; s. Samuel B. and Bertha F. (Seletz) Israel; m. Ruth M. Ballinger, Dec. 26, 1944; children: Janet Faye, William Bryan. A.B., U. Ala., 1940; M.A., Emory U., 1948; postgrad., Am. Mgmt. Assn., 1959, Emory U., 1965. Dir. publicity, prodn. mgr. Sta. WSB-AM-FM, Atlanta, 1940-42, dir. scripts and prodn., 1947—; prodn. mgr. WSB-TV, 1948-52; mgr. programming WSB-AM-FM, 1952-63, v.p., gen. mgr., 1963—; v.p. Cox Broadcasting Corp., 1969-82; chmn. Radio Advt. Bur.; syndicated radio commentator Meredith Broadcasting Co.; past chmn. NAFMB, NBC Radio Affiliates; past chmn. radio code bd. Nat. Assn. Broadcasters; dir. Mut. Broadcasting System Affiliates; mem. nat. adv. bd. Am. Women in Radio and TV, 1981-82. Writer-producer network radio programs, NBC, ABC, CBS and Mut. Broadcasting System, 1942-46; author: Business and the Media, 1978, Exploring Mental Health Parameters, Vol. III, 1980; columnist: Marietta (Ga.) Daily Jour. and Neighbor newspapers. Radio-TV rep. Nat. Heart Assn., 1969; adv. bd. Consumer Credit Services Greater Atlanta; mem. adv. com. N.W. Ga., Girl Scouts U.S.A.; mem. Atlanta area council Boy Scouts Am.; bd. dirs. Friends of Library Emory U.; pres. Ga. Safety Council, 1981-82; chmn. S.E. regional adv. bd. Anti-Defamation League, B'nai B'rith, mem. nat. adv. commn., 1983; mem. adv. council Ga. State U. Sch. Bus. Adminstrn.; chmn. Atlanta Christmas Seals Drive, 1977, 78; asst. to dir. Democratic Nat. Convs., 1952, 56, 60, 64; bd. dirs. Jr. Achievement Greater Atlanta, Multiple Sclerosis, Arthritis Found., Parents Anonymous, Am. Jewish Com., Gerontology Ctr. of Ga. State U.; trustee Oglethorpe U.; mem. visitors bd. Emory U.; chmn. Ga. Easter Seal Celebrity Telethon, 1980, Jewish Nat. Fund Telethon, 1983; active numerous other civic and charitable orgns. Served to capt. USAAF, 1942-46. Recipient Silver Medal award Atlanta Advt. Club, 1965; Peabody award, 1966; Alfred P. Sloan award, 1966; Sch. Bell award Ga. Edn. Assn., 1967; named Citizen of Year, Ga. Assn. Broadcasters, 1965, Southeastern Father of Yr., 1978; recipient Disting. 20-year Service award ARC, 1968; Abraham Lincoln awards So. Baptist Radio-TV Commn., 1972, 77; Silver Beaver award Boy Scouts Am., 1972; Pioneer Broadcaster Ga. award Di Gamma Kappa, 1972; Meritorious Service award Am. Heart Assn., 1970; Disting. Alumnus award U. Ala., 1971; Gavin Disting. Broadcaster award, 1972; Disting. Service award Nat. Safety Council, 1973; George Washington Honor medal and Disting. Service award Freedom's Found., 1973; Abe Goldstein award Anti-Defamation League, 1975; Gold Boot award March of Dimes, 1975; George Erwin award Ga. Assn. Realtors, 1975, 76, 77, 78; Humanitarian award Nat. Jewish Hosp., 1979; Big Drop award Red Cross, 1979; Operation Lifesaver award Ga. Safety Council, 1979; named Gavin Mgr. of Year, 1971. Mem. Ga. Assn. Broadcasters (past pres.), Emory U., U. Ala. alumni assns., Ga. C. of C., Phi Beta Kappa, Sigma Delta Chi, Omicron Delta Kappa. Clubs: Standard, Commerce, B'nai B'rith (bd. dirs.), Atlanta Broadcast Executives, Atlanta Press. Home: 6345 Aberdeen Dr NE Atlanta GA 30328 Office: Sta WSB-AM-FM 1601 W Peachtree St NE Atlanta GA 30309 *In the dawning days of man's arrival on this planet, he became aware of the desirability of peace and the blessings of brotherly love. He has not ceased to yearn for both, although he has shown little disposition to make either one a reality. Nevertheless, man's highest aspirations have not changed. His hope is to be better than he his, and his dream is to make his world a better place. The simple and basic guidelines for achieving these goals are at our fingertips.*

ELLIS, FLOYD EARL, oil company executive; b. Cheyenne, Wyo., Mar. 9, 1933; s. Earl O. and Erma (Richmond) E.; m. Valerie Diane Picard, Dec. 28, 1954; children: Valerie Ann, Marley Jo, David Kipp. B.S., U. Wyo., 1955; M.S., MIT, 1970. Registered profl. engr., Tex. Engr. trainee Conoco Inc., Thermopolis, Wyo., 1955-56, petroleum engr., Termopolis, Wyo., 1956-66; chief petroleum engr. Conoco, Houston, 1966-69; v.p. prodn. Conoco Inc., Houston, 1975—. Served to 1st lt. U.S. Army, 1957. Mem. Soc. Petroleum Engrs., Nat. Ocean Industries Assn. (bd. dirs. 1977), Am. Petroleum Inst. Republican. Episcopalian. Clubs: Petroleum, Pine Forest Country. Lodge: Elks. Office: Conoco Inc 5 Greenway Plaza E Houston TX 77252

ELLIS, FRANK HALE, educator; b. Chgo., Jan. 18, 1916; s. Frank Hale and Gay (Shepherd) E.; m. Constance Dimock, Dec. 20, 1940; 1 dau., Gay. B.S., Northwestern U., 1939; Ph.D., Yale, 1948. Mem. faculty U. Buffalo, 1941-42; mem. faculty Yale, 1945-51, asst. prof. English lit., 1950-51; with Dept. State, Washington, 1951-54; mem. faculty Smith Coll., 1958—, prof. English lit., 1966—, Mary Augusta Jordan prof. English lit., 1974—. Author: Swift's Discourse, 1967, Twentieth Century Interpretations of Robinson Crusoe, 1969, Poems on Affairs of State, 1697-1714, 2 vols., 1970, 75; Contbr. articles to profl. jours. Served with AUS, 1942-45; ETO and PTO. Decorated Bronze Star medal.; Morse fellow, 1950-51; Huntington Library fellow, 1975. Mem. Cum Laude Soc., Conn. Acad. Arts and Scis., Modern Lang. Assn., Phi Beta Kappa. Clubs: Elizabethan, Lawn (New Haven). Home: 146 Elm St Northampton MA 01060

ELLIS, FRANKLIN HENRY, JR., educator, surgeon; b. Washington, Sept. 20, 1920; s. Franklin Henry and Katherine (McClintock) E.; m. Mary Jane Walsh, Dec. 2, 1978; children: Katherine de Saulles (Mrs. Robert Manoff), Elizabeth Dunston, Franklin Henry III, Margot McClintock (Mrs. Hugh Starkey), Laura Lawson, Marie-Armide Longer, Hedrick Watson, Michael Garrison. A.B., Yale U., 1941; M.D., Columbia U., 1944; Ph.D. in Surgery, U. Minn., 1951. Diplomate: Am. Bd. Surgery, Am. Bd. Thoracic Surgery. Intern Bellevue Hosp., N.Y.C., 1944-45; fellow surgery Mayo Clinic, 1945-46, 48-52, fellow thoracic surgery, 1952-53, asst. to surg. staff, 1952-53, cons. surgery, 1953-70; mem. faculty Mayo Grad. Sch. Medicine, 1952-70, prof. surgery, 1964-70, chmn. thoracic surg. sect., 1966-70; chief cardiovascular surgery Lahey Clinic Found., Boston, 1970-75, chmn. dept. thoracic and cardiovascular surgery, 1975—, New Eng. Deaconess Hosp., Boston, 1971—; Lectr. surgery Harvard Med. Sch., 1970-74, asso. clin. prof. surgery, 1974-80, clin. prof. surgery, 1980—. Served with USNR, 1946-48. Mem. Am. Assn. Thoracic Surgery, A.C.S., Am. Heart Assn., A.M.A. (Billings Gold medal 1955), Am., Central surg. assns., Internat. Cardiovascular Soc., Internat. Soc. Surgery, Boston, New Eng. surg. socs., Soc. Clin. Surgery, Soc. U. Surgeons, Soc. Vascular Surgery (pres. 1971), Soc. Thoracic Surgeons (pres. 1977), Phi Beta Kappa, Sigma Xi, Alpha Omega Alpha. Home: 21 Fairmount St Brookline MA 02146 Office: Lahey Clinic Med Center 41 Mall Rd Box 541 Burlington MA 01805

ELLIS, FRED WILSON, pharmacology educator; b. Heath Springs, S.C., Apr. 24, 1914; s. George Dixon and Mary Jane (Hammond) E.; m. Elizabeth Ervin Landrum, Aug. 6, 1940; children: Barbara (Mrs. Glenn E. Minah), Marybeth, Frances (Mrs. Alan Segar), Frieda (Mrs. Lawrence G. Norris). B.S., U. S.C., 1936; postgrad., Yale U., 1936-37; M.S., U. Fla., 1938; Ph.D., U. Md., 1941; cert. in medicine, U. N.C., 1948; M.D., Duke, 1952. Asso. pharmacology Jefferson Med. Coll., 1942-44; faculty pharmacology U. N.C. Sch. Medicine, Chapel Hill, 1944—, prof., 1964—; Vis. prof. pharmacology U. Ky. Med. Center; cons. Research Triangle Inst., N.C.; Mem. sci. adv. council Distilled Spirits Council U.S., Washington, 1973—; mem. peer rev. bd. Nat. Council on Alcoholism, N.Y.C., 1973—; mem. N.C. Alcoholism Research Authority, 1974—, vice-chmn., 1978—; mem. psychopharmacology study sect. NIH. Contbr. articles to sci. jours. Vice-chmn. Chapel Hill Bd. Edn., 1961-63, mem., 1963-67. Postdoctoral fellow U. Md. Sch. Medicine, 1941-42; research grantee Nat. Inst. Alcohol Abuse and Alcoholism, 1977—, Nat. Found. March of Dimes, 1977-79. Mem. AMA (cons. council pharmacy, chemistry, drugs), AAAS, Soc. Exptl. Biology and Medicine (sec. Southeastern sect. 1958-62), Am. Soc. Pharmacology and Exptl. Therapeutics, Research Soc. on Alcoholism (constn. com. 1979, chmn. membership com. 1980, chmn. fetal alcohol study group 1983, 84), Sigma Xi. Home: 805 Old Mill Rd Chapel Hill NC 27514

ELLIS, GEORGE FITZALLEN, JR., energy services company executive; b. Salisbury, N.C., May 4, 1923; s. George F. and Lena (Ramsay) E.; m. Rachael Trexler, Oct. 27, 1945; children: Susan Ellis Snyder, George F. B.S., U.S. Naval Acad., 1944; M.S., Rensselaer Poly. Inst., 1957. Commd. ensign U.S. Navy, 1944, advanced through grades to rear adm., 1972; comdr. South Atlantic Force, U.S. Atlantic Fleet, 1975-76; staff supreme Allied Command Europe, 1974-75; ret. U.S. Navy, 1976; dir. internat. bus. Babcock & Wilcos, Lynchburg, Va., 1976-78, dir. govt. relations, Washington, 1978-79; v.p. govt. ops. McDermott Internat., Inc., Washington, 1979—. Trustee Am. U., 1982—, Ch. of the Covenant, Arlington, Va., 1981—. Decorated Legio of Merit with 3 clusters. Mem. Nat. Fgn. Trade Council (dir.), Am. Nuclear Soc., Am. Soc. Naval Engrs., Iron and Steel Inst., Washington Indsl. Roundtable. Clubs: Internat., Army-Navy, Capitol Hill, Metropolitan (Washington); Army-Navy Country. Home: 3687 N Nelson St Arlington VA 22207 Office: 1735 Eye St NW Washington DC 20006

ELLIS, GEORGE HATHAWAY, banker, economist; b. Orono, Maine, Jan. 29, 1920; s. Milton and Carrie (White) E.; m. Sylvia Poor, Aug. 18, 1946; children: Rebecca Anne, George Milton, Randall Poor, Deborah Josephine. B.A., U. Maine, 1941, LL.D., 1962; M.A., Harvard, 1948, Ph.D., 1950; LL.D., Nasson Coll., 1961, Bates Coll., 1968, U. Mass., 1968; D.C.S. (hon.), Western New Eng. Coll., 1968. Teaching fellow econs. Harvard, 1948-49; asst. prof. U. Me., 1949-51; indsl. economist Fed. Res. Bank Boston, 1951-53, dir. research, 1953-57, v.p., dir. research, 1957-61, pres., 1961-68, Keystone Custodian Funds, Inc., 1968-74, chief exec. officer, 1970-74; pres. Home Savs. Bank Boston, 1975—; chmn., dir. Central Maine Power Co.; dir. Mut. Instn. Nat. Transfer System, Inc.; chmn., dir. Savs. Mgmt. Computer Corp. Mem. com. on N.E. economy Pres.'s Council Econ. Advisers, 1950-51; dir. research com. N.E., NPA, 1951-55; econ. adviser N.E. Gov.'s Com. Pub. Transp., 1955-57; research com. chmn. Greater Boston Econ. Study Com., 1957-61; chmn. New Eng. Econ. Research Found., 1962-70; bd. govs. Investment Co. Inst., 1972-74; mem. Mass. Task Force on Capital Formation for Econ. Devel.; Trustee, pres. Mass. Congl. Fund, Mass Samaritan Corp.; trustee United Ch. of Christ Pension Bds., Econ. Edn. Council Mass.; bd. dirs. Mass. Higher Edn. Assistance Corp., New Eng. Edn. Loan Mktg. Corp., Savs. Bank Assn. Mass.; corporator Univ. Hosp. Served from 2d lt. to maj. AUS, 1941-45. Mem. Am. Acad. Arts and Scis., New Eng. Council, Phi Beta Kappa, Phi Kappa Phi, Beta Gamma Sigma (nat. honoree). Conglist. Clubs: Commercial Merchants, Economic (Boston); Wellesley. Home: 177 Benvenue St Wellesley MA 02181 Office: 69 Tremont St Boston MA 02108

ELLIS, GEORGE RICHARD, museum adminstrator; b. Birmingham, Ala., Dec. 9, 1937; s. Richard Paul and Dorsie (Gibbs) E.; m. Sherroll Edward, June 20, 1961 (dec. 1973); m. Nancy Enderson, Aug. 27, 1975; 1 son, Joshua. B.A., U. Chgo., 1959, M.F.A., 1961; postgrad., UCLA, 1971. Art supr. Jefferson County Schs., Birmingham, 1962-64; asst. dir. Birmingham Mus. Art, 1964-66, UCLA Mus. Cultural History, 1971-81, assoc. dir., 1981-82; dir. Honolulu Acad. Arts, 1981—. Author various works on non-western art, 1971—. Recipient Ralph Altman award UCLA, 1968, Outstanding Achievement award UCLA, 1980; fellow Kress Found., 1971. Mem. Assn. Art Mus. Dirs., Am. Assn. Mus., Los Angeles Ethnic Arts Council (hon.). Club: Pacific (Honolulu). Office: Honolulu Academy of Arts 900 S Beretania St Honolulu HI 96822

ELLIS, HAROLD BERNARD, electrical engineer; b. Havre, Mont., Dec. 31, 1917; s. Arthur Thomas and Ammie Lillian (Smith) E.; m. Virginia Joan Adams, May 18, 1944; children: Mary Virginia Ellis Avvenire, Nancy Jeanne Ellis Hughes, Susan Catheleen Ellis Weber, Stephen Randolph. B.S. in Elec. Engring, Wash. State U., 1941; M.S. in Civil Engring, Mass. Inst. Tech., 1947; Ph.D., Iowa State U., 1963. Registered profl. engr., Tex. Commd. 2d lt. C.E. U.S. Army, 1941, advanced through grades to lt. col., 1951; assigned 47th Engrs. Regt., PTO, World War II; staff officer, bn. and group comdr. 417th Engr. Brigade, Korea, 1952-53; staff officer Aviation Engr. Force, Wolters AFB, Tex., 1953-55; asso. prof. mil. sci. and tactics Army R.O.T.C., Iowa State U., Ames, 1955-59; dep. comdr. for depot operation U.S. Army Gen. Depot, Chinon, France, 1959-62; ret., 1962; prof. civil engring. and constrn. tech., head dept. engring. tech. Iowa State U., 1962-73; dir. personnel devel. Black & Veatch, Cons. Engrs., Kansas City, Mo., 1973-79; asso. prof. civil engring. U. Mo., Kansas City, 1979-80; cons. AID Summer Sci. Inst., Chandigahr, India, 1966; year-in-industry prof. engring. dept. E.I. duPont de Nemours & Co., Inc., Wilmington, Del., 1969-70. Pres. Ames Zoning Adjustment Bd., 1969. Decorated Bronze Star, Purple Heart. Mem. ASCE (mem. subcom. tech. and accreditation 1978-80), Accreditation Bd. for Engring. and Tech. (mem. engring. tech. com. 1973-78), Alpha Tau Omega, Sigma Tau, Phi Kappa Phi, Sigma Delta Psi, Scabbard and Blade. Office: 8501 Ensley Pl Leawood KS 66206

ELLIS, HARRY BEARSE, journalist; b. Springfield, Mass., Dec. 9, 1921; s. Harry Dutton and Helen (Bearse) E.; m. Ann Sherman Michelson, June 25, 1949; 1 son, Andrew Bearse. B.A., Wesleyan U., Middletown, Conn., 1947, L.H.D., 1959. With Christian Sci. Monitor, Boston, 1947—, Middle East corr., 1952-54, Mediterranean corr., 1958-60, chief, 1961-64, staff corr., Germany, 1964-72, sr. econs. corr., Washington, 1972—; tv, radio commentary BBC, NBC, PBS, Westinghouse Broadcasting Corp., CBS, Voice of Am., Nat. Pub. Radio.; Lectr. fgn. affairs. Author: Heritage of the Desert, 1956, Israel and the Middle East, 1957, The Arabs, 1958, Challenge in the Middle East, 1960, The Common Market, 1965, Ideals and Ideologies, Communism, Socialism, and Capitalism, 1968, The Dilemma of Israel, 1970, Israel: One Land, Two Peoples, 1972; Contbg. author: The United States and the Middle East, 1964, Reporting on Business and the Economy, 1980. Served as 2d lt. AUS, 1943-45. Decorated Bronze Star medal, Combat Inf. Badge. Mem. Authors Guild, Authors League, Phi Beta Kappa. Home: 13107 Parkridge Circle Fort Washington MD 20744 Office: 910 16th St NW Washington DC 20006

ELLIS, HARRY MCPHEE, Canadian provincial official, company official; b. Vancouver, C., Can., Jan. 12, 1923; s. and Sarah (McPhee) E.; m. Doreen N. Lewis, June 13, 1953; children: Gary, Richard, Wendy, Nancy. B.Sc., U. B.C., 1945; M.Sc., Calif. Inst. Tech., 1948, Ph.D., 1951. Mgr. engring. div. B.C. Hydro and Power Authority, Surrey, 1970-73, mgr. system engring., 1973-75, dir. research and devel., 1975—; vice chmn. B.C. Research Council; chmn. study com. 38-system analysis and techniques Internat. Conf. Large High Voltage Electric Systems. Fellow IEEE; mem. B.C. Sci. Council (dir. 1980). Office: 12388 88th Ave Surrey BC Canada V3W 7R7

ELLIS, HENRY CARLTON, psychologist, educator; b. Bern New, N.C., Oct. 23, 1927; s. Henry Afford and Frances Lee (Mays) E.; m. Florence Pettyjohn, Aug. 24, 1957; children: Joan, Diane Elizabeth, John Weldon. B.S., Coll. William and Mary, 1951; M.A., Emory U., 1952; Ph.D. (Van Blarcom fellow), Washington U., 1958. Asst. prof. psychology U. N.Mex., Albuquerque, 1957-62, assoc. prof., 1962-67, prof. psychology, 1967—, chmn. dept., 1975—; v.p. Gen. Programmed Teaching Corp., 1960-62; mem. vis. faculty Washington U., St. Louis, 1963-67; vis. prof. psychology U. Calif.-Berkeley, 1971, U. Hawaii, 1977; disting. vis. prof. U.S. Air Force Med. Ctr., Lackland AFB, Tex., 1978; chmn. Nat. Council Grad. Depts. Psychology, 1977-79, bd. dirs., 1976-81. Author: The Transfer of Learning, 1965, Fundamentals of Human Learning and Cognition, 1972, Fundamentals of Human Learning, Memory and Cognition, 1978, (with Bennett, Daniels and Rickert) Psychology of Learning and Memory, 1979, (with Hunt) Fundamentals of Human Memory and Cognition, 1983; editorial bd.: Jour. Exptl. Psychology, 1967-74, Jour. Exptl Psychology: Human Learning and Memory, 1974-76, Perception and Psychophysics, 1971-78; contbr. articles to profl. jours. Served with USAAF, 1946-47. Fellow Am. Psychol. Assn. (council reps. 1980-81, 83-86, Fellow, edn. and tng. bd. 1981-84, chmn. 1984); mem. Psychonomic Soc., AAAS, Sigma Xi, Phi Kappa Phi. Methodist. Clubs: Albuquerque Tennis, Twenty-One; Cosmos (Washington). Office: Dept Psychology U New Mexico Albuquerque NM 87131 *Part of wisdom is the ability to recognize one's own weaknesses as well as strengths and yet maintain an optimistic view of life's possibilities; a strong achievement orientation coupled with the willingness to assist others is always important.*

ELLIS, HOWARD WOODROW, evangelist, clergyman, artist, author; b. Linton, Ind., Feb. 19, 1914; s. Lee and Effie (Walraven) E.; m. Susanna Goldsmith, Aug. 27, 1942; children: Patricia Sue Ellis Beebe, Mary Lou Ellis Bardwell. Student, Washington Sch. Art, 1930-31, Art Inst. Chgo., 1944-45, Am. Art Acad., 1945-46; A.B., U. Evansville, 1943; H.H.D. hon., U. Evansville, 1962; B.D., Garrett Theol. Sem., 1946, Th.M., 1973; postgrad., Peabody Coll., 1959-60, U. Tenn.-Nashville. Ordained to ministry United Methodist Ch., 1943; approved leader and evangelist, United Christian Ashram movement. Mem. nat. staff Gen. Bd. Evangelists, Meth. Ch., Nashville, 1946-66; pastor Central Avenue Meth. Ch., Indpls., 1966-68, Main Street United Meth. Ch., Boonville, Ind., 1968-74, Wall Street United Meth. Ch., Jeffersonville, Ind., 1974-80, Gobin United Meth. Ch., 1978-82; condr. evangelist missions to, Sweden, Norway, Denmark, Finland, 1957, 59, 82, Mex., 1961, 65, Korea, 1961, Gt. Britain, 1982, India, 1984, also throughout U.S.,. Exhibited paintings in group shows, Nashville Fine Arts Festival, 1959, 60, 61, Tenn. State Fair, Nashville, 1959-66, painting in group shows, Smithsonian Instn., Washington, 1960, paintings in group shows, U. Evansville, Ind., 1960, Ohio U., Athens, Ewah U., Seoul, 1962, Inst. Mexican-Am. Cultural Relations, Mexico City, Doshisha U., Kyoto, Japan, Nat. Convocation Meth. Youth, Purdue U., West Layayette, Ind., 1964, Concordia Sem., St. Louis, Augustana Coll., Mpls., 1965, Valparaiso U., Ind., 1966, Bethany Theol. Sch., Mpls., 1971, Garrett Theol. Sem., Evanston, Ill., 1972, Evang. Theol. Sem., Naperville, Ill.; retrospective show, North United Meth. Ch., Indpls., 1967, represented in permanent collections, U. Evansville, Parthenon Gallery, Nashville, Upper Room Mus., Nashville; author: Sallman Interpretations, 1944, The Witnessing Fellowship, 1961, Evangelism for Teen-Agers for a New Day, rev. edit., 1966, The Last Supper, 1963, (with Kenneth Reed) Encounter Diaglog in Art, 1966; author, illustrator: How To Draw and Speak, 1961, He Took the Cup, 1961; author: (with T. McEachern) Youth Evangelism, New Reflections, 1963, An Artist Looks at Jesus, 1984, Art with a Message, 1984, The Marks of a Christian, 1984; also others; contbr. articles and art to numerous publs. Home: 605 Anderson St Greencastle IN 46135

ELLIS, JAMES REED, lawyer; b. Oakland, Calif., Aug. 5, 1921; s. Floyd E. and Hazel (Reed) E.; m. Mary Lou Earling, Nov. 18, 1944 (dec.); children: Robert Lee, Judith Ann (dec.), Lynn Earling, Steven Reed. B.S., Yale, 1942; J.D., U. Wash., 1948; LL.D., Lewis and Clark U., 1968, Seattle U., 1981. Bar: Wash. 1949, D.C. 1971. Partner firm Preston, Thorgrimson, Horwitz, Starin & Ellis, 1952-69; Preston, Thorgrimson, Starin, Ellis & Holman, Seattle, 1969-72, Preston, Thorgrimson, Ellis, Holman & Fletcher, 1972-79; sr. partner firm Preston, Thorgrimson, Ellis & Holman, 1979—; dep. pros. atty., King County, 1952—; gen. counsel Municipality of Met. Seattle, 1958-79. Mem. Nat. Water Commn., 1970-73; mem. urban transp. adv. council U.S. Dept. Transp., 1970-71; mem. Wash. Planning Adv. Council,

1965-72; pres. Forward Thrust Inc., 1966-73; chmn. Mayors Com. on Rapid Transit, 1964-65; Trustee Ford Found., 1970-82, mem. exec. com., 1978-82; bd. regents U. Wash., 1965-77, pres., 1972-73; trustee Resources for the Future, 1983—; mem. council Nat. Municipal League, 1968-76, v.p., 1972-76, 83—; chmn. Save our Local Farmlands Com., 1978-79, King County Farmlands Adv. Com., 1980-82; pres. Friends of Freeway Park, 1976—; bd. dirs. Nat. Park and Recreation Assn., 1979-82, Wash. State Conv. and Trade Ctr., 1982—; also vice chmn, chmn. design com. Wash. State Conv. and Trade Ctr. Served to 1st lt. USAAF, 1943-46. Recipient Bellevue First Citizen award, 1968, Seattle First Citizen award, 1968, Nat. Conservation award Am. Motors, 1968, Distinguished Service award Wash. State Dept. Parks and Recreation, 1968, Distinguished Citizen award Nat. Municipal League, 1969, King County Distinguished Citizen award, 1970, La Guardia award Center N.Y.C. Affairs, 1975, Environ. Quality award EPA, 1977, Am. Inst. for Public Service award, 1974, U. Wash. Recognition award, 1981. Fellow Am. Bar Found.; Mem. ABA (ho. dels. 1978-82, past chmn. urban, state and local govt. law sect.), Wash. Bar Assn., Seattle Bar Assn., D.C. Bar Assn., Am. Judicature Soc., Acad. Public Adminstrn., Council on Fgn. Relations, Municipal League Seattle and King County (past pres.), Order of Hosp. of St. John of Jerusalem, AIA (hon.), Order of Coif (hon.), Phi Delta Phi, Phi Gamma Delta. Club: Rainier (Seattle). Home: 903 SE Shoreland Dr Bellevue WA 98004 Office: IBM Bldg Seattle WA 98101

ELLIS, JAMES THORNTON, automobile credit co. exec.; b. Anderson, Ind., Aug. 8, 1928; s. Clinton Hugh and Jesse Helen (Harrison) E.; m. Anna Marie Nordholt, May 10, 1952. B.S. in Edn, Ind. U., 1955. With Gen. Motors Acceptance Corp., 1951—, asst. mgr. staff adminstrn. dept., N.Y.C., 1970-74, treas., 1974—. Served with AUS, 1952-54. Republican. Presbyterian. Clubs: Meadowbrook Country, Innisbrook Golf and Country. Home: 41490 Woodridge Ct Northville MI 48167 Office: 3044 W Grand Blvd Detroit MI 48202

ELLIS, JAMES WATSON, univ. dean; b. Uruguaiana, Brazil, Aug. 16, 1927; s. James Elijah and Frances (Watson) E.; m. Betty Jane Brock, Aug. 4, 1951; children—Cynthia Ann Ellis Pendergrass, Wendy Sue, Marcia Lynn. A.B., Wofford Coll., 1948; M.S., Tulane U., 1951, Ph.D. in Math, 1952. Asst. prof., asso. prof. math. Fla. State U., 1952-58; faculty La. State U. in New Orleans (now U. New Orleans 1974), 1958—, prof. math., chmn. dept., 1961-64, prof. math., dean jr. div., 1964—. Chmn. colls. and univs. div. New Orleans United Fund drive, 1967-68. Served with AUS, 1953-55. AEC Predoctoral fellow, 1949-52. Mem. Am. Math. Soc., Math. Assn. Am., Phi Beta Kappa, Sigma Xi. Methodist. Home: 2328 Lark St New Orleans LA 70122

ELLIS, JOHN, educational administrator; b. Amherst, Ohio, Sept. 15, 1929; s. Edward Pierson and Jean (Scott) E.; m. Carolyn Elizabeth Collier, Dec. 29, 1951; children: Linda Ellis Wieand, Jeanine Fay, Jeanette Kay Ellis Hale, John Edward. B.S., Bowling Green State U., 1953; M.A., Case-Western Res. U., 1958; Ed.D., Harvard U., 1964. Tchr. pub. schs., Lorain, Ohio, 1953-54, prin., 1957-61, asst. supt. schs., Massillon, Ohio, 1963-64, supt. schs., 1964-66, Lakewood, Ohio, 1966-71, Columbus, Ohio, 1971-77; adj. prof. ednl. adminstrn. Ohio State U., 1971-77; exec. dep. commr. edn. U.S. Office Edn., Washington, 1977-80; supt. schs., Austin, Tex., 1980—. Served with USAF, 1947-49, 54-57. Recipient Silver medal Arnold Air Soc., 1952, Phi Delta Kappa Book award Harvard U., 1964, Massillon Young Man of Year award, 1965; named to Saturday Rev. Honor Roll, 1977. Mem. Phi Delta Kappa, Pi Kappa Alpha, Phi Alpha Theta, Kappa Delta Pi, Gamma Theta Upsilon. Presbyterian (elder). Club: Rotary. Home: 7007 One Oak Rd Austin TX 78749 Office: 6100 Guadalupe Austin TX 78752

ELLIS, JOHN MARTIN, university dean; b. London, May 31, 1936; U.S., 1966, naturalized, 1972; s. John Albert and Emily (Silvey) E.; m. Barbara Stephanie Rhoades, June 28, 1978; children: J. Richard, Andrew W., Katherine M., Jill E. B.A. with 1st class honours, U. London, 1959, Ph.D., 1965. Tutorial asst. German Univ. Coll., Wales, Aberystwyth, 1959-60; asst. lectr. U. Leicester, Eng., 1960-63; asst. prof. U. Alta., Edmonton, Can., 1963-66; mem. faculty U. Calif., Santa Cruz, 1966—, prof. German, 1970—, dean grad. div., 1977—; vis. prof. U. Kent, Canterbury, Eng., 1970-71. Author: Schiller's Kalliasbriefe and the Study of His Aesthetic Theory, 1969, Kleist's Prinz Friedrich von Homburg: A Critical Study, 1970, Narration in the German Novelle, 1974, The Theory of Literary Criticism: A Logical Analysis, 1974, Heinrich von Kleist: Studies in the Character and Meaning of His Writings, 1979, One Fairy Story Too Many: The Brothers Grimm and Their Tales, 1983. Served with Brit. Army, 1954-56. Fellow Guggenheim Found., 1970-71, Nat. Endowment Humanities, 1975-76. Mem. MLA, Am. Assn. Tchrs. German, AAUP, Kleist Gesellschaft, English Goethe Soc., Internat. Assn. Germanic Studies. Office: Crown Coll Univ of Calif Santa Cruz CA 95060

ELLIS, JOHN TRACY, clergyman, educator; b. Seneca, Ill., July 30, 1905; s. Elmer Lucian and Ida Cecilia (Murphy) E. A.B., St. Viator Coll., 1927; A.M., Cath. U. Am., 1928, Ph.D., 1930, Litt.D. (hon.), 1978; student, Sulpician Sem., Washington, 1934-38; D.H.L., Mt. Mary Coll., 1954; LL.D., U. Notre Dame, 1957, Belmont Abbey Coll., 1960, Fordham U., 1972; Litt.D. (hon.), Loyola Coll., Balt., 1960, U. Portland, 1969, U. Fla., 1973, Marquette U., 1974, St. Vincent Coll., 1979. Ordained priest Roman Catholic Ch., 1938; prof. history St. Viator Coll., 1930-32, Coll. St. Teresa, 1932-34; instr. history Cath. U. Am., 1938-41, asst. prof., 1941-43, asso. prof., 1943-47, prof. ch. history, 1947-64, vis. prof., 1976—; prof. ch. history U. San Francisco, 1964-76; professorial lectr. ch. history Cath. U. Am., 1977—; vis. prof. Brown U., 1967, U. Notre Dame, 1970, Grad. Theol. Union, Berkeley, Calif., 1970-71, Gregorian U., Rome, Italy, 1974-75, Angelicum U., Rome, 1976; cons. com. for observance bicentennial Nat. Conf. Cath. Bishops, 1973-76. Author: Anti-Papal Legislation in Mediaeval England, 1066-1377, 1930, Cardinal Consalvi and Anglo-Papal Relations, 1814-1824, 1942, The Formative Years of the Catholic University of America, 1946, The Life of James Cardinal Gibbons, Archbishop of Baltimore, 1834-1921, 2 vols, 1952, American Catholicism, 1956, rev. edit., 1969, Documents of American Catholic History, 1956, rev. edit., 1962, 67, American Catholics and the Intellectual Life, 1956, A Guide to American Catholic History, 1959, John Lancaster Spalding, First Bishop of Peoria, American Educator, 1962, Perspectives in American Catholicism, 1963, Catholics in Colonial America, 1965, A Committment to Truth, 1966, Essays in Seminary Education, 1967; Editor, contbr.: The Catholic Priest in the United States: Historical Investigations, 1971; mng. editor: Cath. Hist. Rev, 1941-63; adv. editor, 1963—. Domestic prelate of Pope Pius XII, 1955; recipient John Gilmary Shea prize, 1956; Golden Jubilee medal St. Mary's Dominican Coll., New Orleans, 1960; Campion award Catholic Book Club, 1965; Bene Merenti medal Cath. U. Am., 1961; Research and Scholarship award Alumni Assn. Cath. U. Am., 1969; Laetare medal, 1978. Fellow Am. Benedictine Acad. (1969); Mem. Am. Cath. Hist. Assn. (pres. 1969), Am. Hist. Assn., Am. Soc. Ch. History (pres. 1969), Phi Beta Kappa (hon.), Delta Epsilon Sigma (hon.), Phi Alpha Theta (hon.). Address: Catholic University of America Washington DC 20064

ELLIS, JOHN W., utility co. exec.; b. Seattle, Sept. 14, 1928; s. Floyd E. and Hazel (Reed) R.; m. Doris Stearns, Sept. 1, 1953; children: Thomas R., John Barbara, Jim. B.S., U. Wash., 1952, J.D., 1953. Bar: Wash. State bar 1953. With firm Perkins, Coie, Stone, Olsen & Williams, Seattle, 1953-70; with Puget Sound Power & Light Co., Bellevue, Wash., 1970—, exec. v.p., 1973-76, pres., chief exec. officer, 1976, also dir.; chmn. Seattle br. Fed. Res. Bank of San Francisco, 1981; dir. Wash. Mut. Savs. Bank, Seattle, SAFECO Corp.; mem. Wash. Gov's. Spl. Com. Energy Curtailment, 1973-74; chmn. Pacific N.W. Utilities Coordinating Com., 1976-82. Pres. Bellevue Boys' Club, 1969-71; mem. exec. dirs. Seattle-King County Boys' Club, 1972-75; bd. dirs. Overlake Hosp., Bellevue, 1974—, United Way King County, 1977—, Seattle Sci. Found., 1977—, Seattle Sailing Found., Evergreen Safety Council, 1981, Assn. Wash. Bus., 1980-81, Wash. State Bus. Round Table, 1983. Served with AUS, 1950-52. Mem. Am., Wash., King County (Wash.) bar assns., Nat. Assn. Elec. Cos. (dir. 1977-79), Edison Electric Inst. (dir. 1978-80, exec. com. 1982), Assn. Edison Illuminating Cos. (exec. com. 1979-81), Seattle C. of C. (dir. 1980—), Phi Gamma Delta, Phi Delta Phi. Clubs: Rainier (sec. 1972), Seattle Yacht, Corinthian Yacht (Seattle); Meydenbauer Bay Yacht (Bellevue). Home: 901 SE Shoreland Dr Bellevue WA 98004 Office: Puget Power Bldg Bellevue WA 98009

ELLIS, JOSEPH JOHN MICHAEL, III, educator; b. Washington, July 18, 1943; s. Joseph J. and Jeanette H. (Sigafoose) E.; m. Antonia Woods, June 20, 1970; children: Peter, Scott. B.A., William and Mary Coll., 1965; M.A. (Woodrow Wilson fellow 1965-66), Yale U., 1967, Ph.D., 1969. Asst. prof. U.S. Mil. Acad., West Point, N.Y., 1969-72; asst. prof. Mount Holyoke Coll., South Hadley, Mass., 1972-75, asso. prof., 1975-79, prof. history, 1979—, dean, 1980—, acting pres., 1984—. Author: The New England Mind in Transition, 1972, School for Soldiers: West Point and the Profession of Arms, 1974, After the Revolution, 1979. Mem. exec. com. Mass. Found. for Humanities, 1978-81. Served to capt. U.S. Army, 1969-72. Nat. Endowment for Humanities fellow, 1976-77. Mem. Am. Hist. Assn., Inst. Early Am. History and Culture, Nat. Humanities Faculty, Phi Beta Kappa. Home: 15 Ashfield Ln South Hadley MA 01075 Office: Dean of Faculty Mount Holyoke Coll South Hadley MA 01075

ELLIS, JOSEPH N., distribution company executive; b. Tenn., Oct. 19, 1928; s. Richard M. and Pearl A. (Fuqua) E.; m. Barbara Harpster, Sept. 17, 1955; 1 dau., Patricia Anne. B.S., Northwestern U., 1954. Co-founder LaSalle-Deitch Co., Inc. div. N.Am. Phillips Corp., Elkhart, Ind., 1963, exec. v.p., 1969-72, pres., chief exec. officer, 1972—. Served with U.S. Army, 1950-52. Home: 54400 Old Bedford Trail Mishawaka IN 46544 Office: LaSalle-Deitch Co Inc 640 Inudstrial Pkwy Elkhart IN 46515

ELLIS, KENT, educator, radiologist; b. Grand Rapids, Mich., June 22, 1921; s. Luther Edward and Dorothy (Groman) E.; m. Barbara Janet Koehler, June 10, 1950; children—Stephen Mark, Karen, Kent Bradford. B.S., Yale, 1942, M.D., 1950. Diplomate: Am. Bd. Radiology. Intern Walter Reed Army Hosp., Washington, 1950-51; resident radiology Columbia Presbyn. Med. Center, 1952-54, attending radiologist, 1955-69; prof. radiology Columbia Coll. Physicians and Surgeons, 1958—; Cons. USPHS, Yale Med. Sch., Inter-Soc. Commn. for Heart Disease Resources, N.Y. Heart Assn. Contbr. articles to profl. jours. Served to lt. USNR, 1943-46. Fellow Am. Coll. Radiology, Radiol. Soc. N.Am.; mem. Med. Soc. State N.Y. (chmn. sect. radiology 1968-69), Assn. U. Radiologists, AAUP, N.Am. Soc. Cardiac Radiology (v.p. 1975-76, pres. 1976—), N.Y. Roentgen Soc. (v.p. 1974-75, pres. 1975—), Fleischner Soc. (sec. 1977—, sec. 1977-80, pres. 1981-82), Am. Heart Assn. (chmn. council on cardiovascular radiology 1980-82, dir. 1980—), Am. Roentgen Ray Soc., St. Anthony Hall. Presbyterian. Home: 226 Chestnut St Englewood NJ 07631 Office: 622 W 168th St New York NY 10032

ELLIS, LAURENCE BREWSTER, cardiologist; b. Monson, Mass., Nov. 14, 1902; s. Fred Warren and Martha (Alvord) E.; m. Alice Whiting, Sept. 14, 1934; children—Isabel (Mrs. Charles Kurzon), Deborah (Mrs. Llewellyn Bigelow), Priscilla Ellis Crabtree. A.B. cum laude, Harvard, 1922, M.D., 1926. Intern Mass. Gen. Hosp., Boston, 1926-28; resident Thorndike Meml. Lab. Boston City Hosp., 1928-32; practice medicine specializing in cardiology, Boston, 1928—; teaching, research Harvard Med. Sch., 1928-72; now clin. prof. medicine emeritus; mem. staff Thorndike Meml. Lab., Boston City Hosp., 1928-72; now hon. physician. Pres. Postgrad. Med. Inst., 1953-58; cons. to numerous hosps. Contbr. articles to profl. jours. Served from lt. col. to col., M.C. AUS, 1943-45. Fellow A.C.P., Am. Coll. Cardiology; mem. Mass. Med. Soc. (v.p. 1965-66), Assn. U. Cardiologists (pres. 1962-63), Am. Heart Assn., New Eng. Heart Assn. (pres. 1948-49), Mass. Heart Assn. (pres. 1948-49), N.E. Cardiovascular Soc. (pres. 1949-50), Assn. Am. Physicians, Am. Clin. and Climatol. Assn., Am. Soc. Clin. Investigation, Soc. Med. Cons. to Armed Forces, Sigma Xi, Alpha Omega Alpha. Clubs: St. Botolph; Harvard (Boston). Lectureship named for him Harvard Med. Sch., 1962. Home: 24 Francis Ave Cambridge MA 02138 Office: 319 Longwood Ave Boston MA 02115

ELLIS, LAWRENCE DOBSON, physician; b. Pitts., Oct. 11, 1932; s. Robert S. and Elizabeth (Dobson) E.; m. Jacqueline Coogan, June 8, 1954; children: Christine, Thomas, Holly Anne, Jerome. B.S., U. Notre Dame, 1954; M.D., U. Pitts., 1958. Diplomate: Am. Bd. Internal Medicine. Intern in internal medicine U. Pitts. Health Center Hosps., 1958-59; resident in internal medicine Presbyn.-Univ. Hosp., Pitts., 1959-60, 62-63, fellow in hematology, 1963-64; practice medicine specializing in internal medicine, hematology and oncology, Pitts., 1964—; clin. asst. prof. medicine U. Pitts., 1966-71; clin. assoc. prof. U. Pitts, 1971-81; clin. prof. U. Pitts., 1981—; mem. active staff Presbyn.-Univ. Hosp., sec., treas. med. staff, 1972-76, v.p. med. staff, 1976-78, pres., 1978—; mem. cons. staff Forbes Hosp. System, Pitts., 1964—, Divine Providence Hosp., 1964—, Shadyside Hosp., 1964—, Allegheny County Bd. Health, 1976—; bd. commrs. Health Edn. Ctr., Pitts., 1976—. Contbr. articles to profl. jours., chpts. to med. books. Trustee Leukemia Soc. Am., 1972—, chmn. profl. edn., 1973—; trustee Presbyn.-Univ. Hosp., 1981—. Served to lt. M.C. USN, 1960-62. Recipient Frederick M. Jacob Physician Merit Allegheny County Med. Soc., 1981, John J. Kenny Leukemia Soc. Am., 1981. Fellow ACP; mem. Pa. Med. Soc. (del. 1974—), Allegheny County Med. Soc. (pres. 1976, chmn. bd. 1977, dir. 1970—), Pitts. Acad. Medicine, Royal Soc. Medicine, N.Y. Acad. Scis., AMA, Am. Soc. Hematology, Leukemia Soc. Am. (exec. com. 1978—), Med. Alumni Assn. U. Pitts. (pres. 1979-80), Alpha Omega Alpha. Republican. Roman Catholic. Clubs: Pitts. Field, Seaview Country, Univ. Office: 3600 Forbes Ave Iroquois Bldg Ste 305 Pittsburgh PA 15213

ELLIS, MICHAEL, theatrical producer; b. Phila., Oct. 25, 1917; s. Alexander and Mollie (Fein) Abrahamson; m. Neva Patterson, Mar. 22, 1953 (div.); m. Mary Elizabeth Walker, May 10, 1958; children: Sandra, Gordon, Thomas. Student, U. Grenoble, 1937, Sorbonne, 1937-38; B.A., Dartmouth Coll., 1939; M.A. in English, Drew U., 1973. Owner, operator Bucks County (Pa.) Playhouse (now State Theatre Pa. 1959), 1954-64; mng. dir. Parker Playhouse, Ft. Lauderdale, Fla., 1973-76; founder with wife Package Center and One of a Kind, Delray Beach, 1975—. Actor, stage mgr. Broadway shows; producer five (with James Russo) Broadway shows, 1948-53; producer: Come Blow Your Horn, (with William Hammerstein), 1961, The Advocate, (with William Hammerstein), 1963, The Beauty Part, 1962, Absence of a Cello, (with Jeff Britton), 1964, The Paisley Convertible, 1967, The Girl in the Freudian Slip, 1967; off Broadway Sweet Eros and Witness, 1968, Ceremonies in Dark Old Men, 1969, Who's Happy Now?, (with Samuel Bronstein), 1969; (with Elliot Martin) Angela, 1969. Mem. adv. bd. Hopkins Center, Dartmouth Coll.; trustee Solebury Sch., 1967-70; pres. Delray Beach Tennis Center, 1976-77. Mem. Internat. Brotherhood Magicians., Soc. Am. Magicians, Magic Circle, Magic Castle. Club: Dutch Treat. Home: 963 Eve St Delray Beach FL 33444

ELLIS, NEWTON CASS, industrial engineering educator; b. Paris, Tex., Aug. 2, 1934; s. Woodrow W. and Evelyn (Cass) E.; m. Mary Lucille Kettrick, July 16, 1954; children: Lori Luann, Jon Michael. B.S., Baylor U., Waco, Tex., 1956; M.S., Tex. Christian U., 1962, Ph.D. (NSF fellow 1964), 1964. Registered profl. engr., Tex.; cert. safety profl.; cert. psychologist. With payroll dept. Temco Aircraft Corp., Grand Prairie, Tex., 1956-61; research asst. Inst. Behavior Research, Ft. Worth, 1961-62; teaching asst. Tex. Christian U., Ft. Worth, 1962-63; human factors engr. astronautics div. LTV, Inc., Dallas, 1961-65, sr. engr. aeronautics div., 1968-69; lectr. U. Tex., Arlington, 1964-69; exec. v.p., sr. scientist Life Scis., Inc., Ft. Worth, 1965-68; mem. faculty Tex. A&M U., College Station, 1969—, prof. indsl. engring., 1975—, head dept., 1975—; div. head Tex. Transp. Inst., 1975-76; bd. dirs. Tex. Occupational Safety and Health Center; cons. in field. Contbr. articles to profl. jours. Recipient Outstanding Teaching award Tex. A&M U., 1970; Student Engrs. Council grantee, 1975-77. Fellow Human Factors Soc. (editorial bd. jours.); sr. mem. Am. Inst. Indsl. Engrs.; mem. Nat. Soc. Profl. Engrs. (dir. Tex. chpt. 1980-82), Transp. Research Bd. Baptist. Club: Lions (pres. College Station 1978-79). Home: 3702 Oak Ridge St Bryan TX 77801 Office: Dept Indsl Engring Tex A&M U College Station TX 77803

ELLIS, BROTHER PATRICK (H.J. ELLIS), university president; b. Balt., Nov. 17, 1928; s. Harry James and Elizabeth Alida (Evert) E. A.B., Cath. U. Am., 1951; A.M., U. Pa., 1954, Ph.D., 1960; postgrad., Barry Coll., 1963-64, Institut Catholique, Paris, 1958. Joined Brothers of Christian Schs., 1946; tchr. English dept. West Cath. High Sch. for Boys, Phila., 1951-60, chmn. English dept., 1956-58, guidance dir., 1959-60; dir. practice teaching, sch. prin. St. Gabriel's Hall, Phoenixville, Pa., summers 1960-61, 65-66; asst. prof. English La Salle U., Phila., 1960-62, assoc. prof., 1968-73, prof., 1973—, dir. housing, 1961-62, dir. honors program, 1964-69, dir. devel., v.p., 1969-76, pres., 1977—; prin. La Salle High Sch., Miami, Fla., 1962-64. Condr.: series for How To Read Gt. Books, U. of the Air, WFIL-TV, Phila., 1961, 65; Contbr. articles to profl. publs. Trustee Manhattan Coll., N.Y.C., St. Mary's Coll., Minn.; bd. dirs. Greater Phila. 1st Corp., Urban Affairs Partnership; chmn. Assn. Cath. Colls. and Univs.; bd. dirs. Phila. Community Leadership Seminars, World Affairs Council Phila., Phila.-N.J. region NCCJ. Recipient Lindback Award for distinguished teaching LaSalle Coll., Phila., 1965. Mem. Assn. Higher Edn., Pa. Assn. Colls. and Univs. (exec. com.), Phi Beta Kappa. Home and Office: La Salle U 20th and Olney Ave Philadelphia PA 19141

ELLIS, PERRY EDWIN, fashion designer; b. Mar. 3, 1940; s. Edwin L. and Winifred (Roundtree) E. B.A., Coll. William and Mary, 1961; M.R., NYU, 1963. Buyer Miller & Rhoads, Richmond, Va., 1963-67. Design dir., John Meyer Co., Norwich, Conn., 1967-74; designer, Portfolio, Vera Cos., N.Y.C., 1974-79; pres., designer, Perry Ellis Co., N.Y.C., 1979—. Served with USCG, 1961-62. Recipient Neiman-Marcus award, 1979, Winnie award Am. Fashion Critics, 1979, Mens Fashion award Council Fashion Designers of Am., 1983, Coty Hall of Fame Citation, 1984; inducted into Coty Hall of Fame, 1984; named Outstanding U.S. Designer, Cutty Sark Men's Fashion awards, 1984. Office: 575 7th Ave New York NY 10018 *Proportion is everything in life—Health, love, career. Balance them well.*

ELLIS, RICHARD STEPHENS, archaeology educator, field archaeologist, researcher, consultant; b. Detroit, Dec. 16, 1934; s. Seth Wiley and Mildred Elizabeth (Hill) E.; m. Maria DeJong, Dec. 28, 1964; 1 son, Seth Stephens. B.A. in History, Wabash Coll., Crawfordsville, Ind., 1956; M.A. in Near Eastern Archaeology, U. Chgo., 1960, Ph.D., 1965. Acting instr. near eastern archaeology Yale U., 1964-65, asst. prof., 1967-70, assoc. prof., 1970-74; vis. prof. Bryn Mawr (Pa.) Coll., 1973-74, assoc. prof., 1974-81, prof., 1981—, dir. Gritille Project, 1980—; mem. vis. com. Near Eastern dept. Met. Mus. Art, N.Y.C., 1967—; ann. prof. Baghdad Am. Schs. Oriental Research, 1967-68; field work, Turkey, 1959, 81—, Iran, 1959, 67, Iraq, 1967, 68. Author: Foundation Deposits in Ancient Mesopotamia, 1968, A Bibliograph of Mesopotamian Archaeological Sites, 1972; mem. edit. bd.: Bulletin of Am. Schs. of Oriental Research, 1967-68; contbr. articles to profl. jours. Served with U.S. Army, 1960-62. Morse J. Faculty fellow Yale U., 1967-68; Am. Council Learned Socs. fellow, 1977-78. Mem. Am. Oriental Soc., Archaeol. Inst. Am. (pres. New Haven Soc. 1971-73), Phila. Soc. (1978-80), Am. Anthrop. Assn., Soc. for History of Tech., Brit. Sch. Archaeology in Iraq. Presbyterian. Home: 33 St Paul's Rd Ardmore PA 19003 Office: Bryn Mawr Coll Bryn Mawr PA 19010

ELLIS, ROBERT ARTHUR, sociology educator; b. Hudson, N.Y., May 31, 1926; s. Lawrence Louis and Jean (Hudson) E.; m. Dorothy Caryle Godin, Aug. 31, 1950; children: Roger Morgan, Robert A. B.A. in Psychology, Yale U., 1952, M.A. in Sociology, 1953, Ph.D. (Ford Found. fellow), 1956. Instr. to asst. prof. U. So. Calif., 1955-57; asst. prof. Stanford U., 1957-60; asso. prof. U. Oreg., Eugene, 1960-65, prof., dir. Center for Research in Occupational Planning, 1965-70; prof., head dept. sociology U. Md., College Park, 1970-72; prof. sociology, head dept. U. Ga., Athens, 1972-81, acting chmn. div. social scis., 1977-78, Franklin prof. sociology, 1981—; vis. asst. prof. Mich. State U., summer 1959; mem. adv. com. on population stats. U.S. Census, 1972-74. Book rev. editor: Am. Sociol. Rev., 1960-62; asso. editor: Estudios Sociologia, 1960-62, Sociology of Edn., 1972-75; adv. bd.: Jour. Human Resources, 1965-73; bd. editors, U. Ga. Press, 1973-76. Served from pvt. to 2d lt. AUS, 1946-48. Grantee Social Sci. Research Council, Office Edn., NIMH. Mem. Am. Sociol. Assn. (exec. council, sect. on sociology edn. 1963-66, mem. com. on nominations 1971), Pacific Sociol. Assn. (sec.-treas. 1964-67), So. Sociol. Soc. Home: 545 Milledge Circle Athens GA 30606

ELLIS, ROBERT LESLIE, building products executive; b. Johnstown, Pa., Aug. 17, 1921; s. Caradoc and Sarah H. (Davies) E.; m. Margaret Elizabeth Middleton, June 17, 1944; children: Robert Leslie, Daniel Middleton. B.A., Pa. State U., 1942. With Armstrong World Industries, Inc. (formerly Armstrong Cork Co.), Lancaster, Pa., 1944—, controller, 1965-66, controller, dir. mgmt. information, 1966-76, v.p., 1968-76, sr. v.p. mgmt. info., 1976-79, group v.p. mgmt. info., 1979—. Bd. dirs., past pres. Lancaster County Mental Health Assn.; bd. dirs. Lancaster Symphony Orch., 1965-67; trustee Lancaster Theol. Sem., 1979-83; regent Inst. Mgmt. Acctg., 1979-82, chmn. bd. regents, 1980-82. Served with AUS, 1942-44. Recipient Alumni Achievement award Coll. Bus. Adminstrn., Pa. State U., 1977. Mem. Fin. Execs. Inst., Nat. Assn. Accts. (pres. Lancaster 1961-62, nat. dir. 1964—, nat. v.p. 1967-68, exec. com. 1967, nat. pres. 1977-78), Inst. Mgmt. (dir. Lancaster 1964-67, pres. 1967-68), Phi Eta Sigma, Pi Gamma Mu, Beta Alpha Psi. Republican. Presbyterian (elder). Clubs: Masons (past officer), Optimists, Hamilton (Lancaster). Home: 2508 Butter Rd Lancaster PA 17601 Office: Armstrong World Industries Inc Lancaster PA 17604

ELLIS, ROBERT WILLIAM, JR., engineer; b. Richmond, Va., Oct. 16, 1939; s. Robert William and Odessa (Thompson) E.; m. Donna Lee Bell, Mar. 22, 1960; children: Robert William III, Richard

Berkeley, John Stephen, Donna Elaine. B.S., Va. Poly. Inst., 1962, M.S., 1963, Ph.D., 1966. Registered profl. engr., Fla., Mich. Materials engr., engr. Polysci. div. Litton Industries, Blacksburg, Va., 1962-63; Nat. Def. Edn. Act fellow engring. Va. Poly. Inst., 1962-65; asst. prof. engring. U. South Fla., Tampa, 1965-66, assoc. prof., 1967-68, asst. dean engring., 1969-71, asst. v.p. acad. affairs, 1971-72; dean Sch. Tech., Fla. Internat. U., Miami, 1972-78, 1972-74, provost North Miami campus, 1977; exec. v.p. Detroit Inst. Tech., 1978-80, pres., 1980-81; sr. engr. U.S. Army Tank Automotive Research and Devel. Center, Warren, Mich., 1981—; lectr. mech. engring. Lawrence Inst. Tech., 1981—; vice chmn. Fla. Engrs. in Edn., 1978; cons. in field; tech. adv. bd. Fla. Solar Energy Center. Pack master Tampa council Boy Scouts Am.; mem. economy task force Met. Dade County Planning Adv. Bd.; bd. dirs. State U. System Inst. Oceanography. Recipient Nat. Faculty Service award Nat. Univ. Extension Assn., 1977. NASA fellow (1969); Mem. Am. Soc. Metals, Am. Soc. Engring. Edn. (chmn. southeastern sect. tech. div. 1976, bd. dirs. coll. industry council 1975-78, chmn. div. on relations with industry 1980-81), Engrs. Council for Profl. Devel. (visitors com.), Nat. Soc. Profl. Engrs. (vice chmn. Central region profl. engrs. in edn.), Fla. Engring. Soc., Mich. Soc. Profl. Engrs., Greater Miami C. of C., Sigma Xi, Omicron Delta Kappa, Phi Kappa Phi, Sigma Pi Sigma, Tau Beta Pi, Sigma Lambda Chi, Alpha Sigma Mu. Home: 35945 Fredericksburg Farmington Hills MI 48018 Office: Lawrence Institute of Technology Southfield MI 48075

ELLIS, ROY GILMORE, educator; b. Peterborough, South Australia, July 10, 1906; s. Howard and Mary (Gilmore) E.; m. Constance Ferguson, June 29, 1935; children—Paul Gilmore, Brian Gilbert. D.D.S., U. Toronto, 1929, B.Sc.D., 1930, M.Sc.D., 1942, LL.D., 1975; LL.D., U. Western Ont., 1968; D.D.Sc., U. Adelaide, S. Australia, 1972. Faculty U. Toronto, 1931—, prof. operative dentistry, 1945-70, dean faculty dentistry, until 1970; chmn. Health Scis. Council, 1970-72. Author: Classification and Treatment of Injuries to the Teeth of Children, 1945. Fellow dental surgery Royal Coll. Surgeons, Royal Coll. Dentists Can. (hon.); mem. Ont. Dental Assn., Toronto Acad. Dentistry (hon. life). Home: 426 Glencairn Ave Toronto ON M5N-1V5 Canada

ELLIS, RUDOLPH LAWRENCE, insurance company executive; b. N.Y.C., Mar. 27, 1911; s. August and Alice (Lamoureaux) E.; m. Lois Dale Bankenship, Apr. 18, 1947; children: Rudolph Lawrence, Douglas Hassell. With Union Labor Life Ins. Co., N.Y.C., 1928—, v.p., group adminstr., 1950-56, exec. v.p., 1956-68, pres., 1969-79, cons., 1979—, dir., mem. fin. and investment com., 1969—. Mem. Life Ins. Council, Health Ins. Assn. Am., Conf. Bd. Home: 35 Kerry Ln Chappaqua NY 10514 Office: 111 Massachusetts Ave Washington DC 20001

ELLIS, SPENCER PERCY, former state official, landscape architect; b. Joaquin, Tex., Dec. 17, 1923; s. Nathan Percy and Audrey (Cole) E.; m. Frances Pierce Schulter, Apr. 1, 1977. B.S. in Architecture, Tex. A&M U., 1943, M.Landscape Architecture, 1948. Supt. parks City of Corpus Christi, 1948-54; dir. parks and recreation City of Wichita Falls, Tex., 1954-63; dir. forests and parks State of Md., Annapolis, 1963-71; asst. sec. Md. Dept. Natural Resources, Annapolis, 1971-83; Md. Gov.'s rep. Public Land Law Rev. Commn.; mem. Appalachian Nat. Trail Adv. Council; state liaison officer Dept. Interior; mem. Susquehanna River Study Group, Chesapeake Bay Task Force (C.E.), Chesapeake and Delaware Canal Master Plan Team, Potomac Nat. River Group, Nat. Park Service, Islands Task Force, Bur. Outdoor Recreation, Adv. Commn. on Potomac River Basin, Adv. Com. on Susquehanna River; sec. Md. Bd. Landscape Architects; chmn. Md. Scenic Rivers Rev. Bd.; mem. Md. Bicentennial Commn., Md. Mine Land Reclamation Com., Md. Scenic Beauty Commn., Md. Soil Conservation Com., Md. Interagency Task Force on Outdoor Edn., Md. Rural Safety Commn., Md. Pesticide Commn. Designer various state and mcpl. parks, sub-divs., golf courses; contbr.: articles to Landscape Architecture, Parks and Recreation. Pres. Md. Fedn. of Art, Inc., 1965-69, YMCA of Anne Arundel County, Md., 1966-68, Woods Landing Community Service Assn., 1980-84; bd. dirs. Patuxent 4-H Found., 1965—. Served with U.S. Army, 1943-47. Decorated D.S.M., Silver Star, Legion of Merit, Bronze Star with V device, Army Commendation medal, Purple Heart; recipient Disting. Service award Am. Inst. Park Execs., 1964. Fellow Am. Acad. Park Adminstrn., Am. Soc. Landscape Architects (pres. S.W. chpt. 1961-63, Md. chpt. 1978-79, trustee 1974-78, 79-80, nat. treas. 1976-77, nat. v.p. 1977-78, sec.-treas. council of fellows 1980-82, chmn. 1983-85); mem. Am. Recreation Soc., Nat. Assn. State Outdoor Recreation Liaison Officers (pres. 1971-72), Am. Inst. Park Mgmt. (fellow mem.), Nat. Recreation and Parks Assn. (Meritorious Service award 1966), Am. Park and Recreation Soc., Nat. Soc. Park Resources. Democrat. Clubs: Bay Hills Golf (charter), Watergate Village Yacht (founder), Annapolis Yacht, Rotary. Office: 570 Foxpaw Trail Annapolis MD 21401

ELLIS, STEPHEN BARRY, retail executive; b. Bklyn., July 29, 1940; s. Joseph and Sarah (Blumensien) E.; m. Myra D. Richman, May 23, 1943; children: Marc, Robin. B.B.A., Pace U., 1963. Dept. head Lerner Shops, N.Y.C., 1963-75; v.p. Brooks Fashion Stores Inc., N.Y.C., 1975-78, exec. v.p. mdse. planning and distbn., 1978—; dir. Midtown Antiques. V.p. East Bay Reform Temple, Bellmore, N.Y. Served with U.S. Army, 1962-63. Mem. Pi Sigma Epsilon. Home: 2755 Ellen Rd Bellmore NY 117010 Office: Brooks Fashion Stores Inc 370 7th Ave New York NY 10001

ELLIS, SYDNEY, scientist, educator; b. Boston, Apr. 20, 1917; s. George I. and Sarah (Gaull) E.; m. Marion Gardner, Oct. 8, 1942; children—Jeanne (Mrs. Richard P. Jaffe), Richard Jay. B.S., Boston U., 1938, M.A., 1939, Ph.D., 1941. Fellow, then asst. Harvard Med. Sch., 1941-44; asst. prof. Duke Sch. Medicine, 1946-49; asso. prof. Temple U. Sch. Medicine, 1949-57; prof. pharmacology, chmn. dept. Woman's Med. Coll. Pa., 1957-67; prof. pharmacology U. Tex. Med. Br., Galveston, 1967-80, chmn. dept., 1967-77; dep. dir. div. drug biology FDA, 1980—; vis. prof. U. Paris Inst. Pharmacology, 1972; vis. scientist div. drug biology FDA, 1979-80; cons. in field; mem. pet study sect. NIH, 1960-64, med. chem. B study sect., 1964-68; mem. Nat. Bd. Med. Examiners, 1964-68. Served to capt. AUS, 1944-46. Recipient Lindback Found. award distinguished teaching, 1964; named to Collegium of Distinguished Alumni Boston U., 1974. Mem. Am. Soc. Pharmacology (councilor 1967-70, sec.-treas. 1976-79), Am. Chem. Soc., Soc. Exptl. Biology and Medicine, AAAS, N.Y. Acad. Sci., AAUP, Sigma Xi (pres. Temple U. chpt. 1957). Home: 4601 N Park Ave Chevy Chase MD 20815

ELLIS, WILLIAM BEN, utility executive; b. Vicksburg, Miss., July 4, 1940; s. Conrad Ben and Viola Elizabeth (Stigall) E.; children: Bradford, Katherine, Emily, Ben. B.S., Carnegie-Mellon U., 1962; Ph.D. (NSF fellow), U. Md., 1966; postgrad., La. State U., 1966, Am. U., 1968. Research asst. Olin Mathieson Chem. Corp., West Monroe, La., 1958, Comml. Solvents Corp., Sterlington, La., 1959; engr. Procter & Gamble Co., Cin., 1961; process engr. Standard Oil N.J., Baton Rouge, 1962-67; asso. McKinsey & Co., Inc., Washington, 1960-75, prin., 1975-76, exec. v.p., chief fin. officer, 1976-78, pres., chief fin. officer, 1978-80, pres., chief operating officer, 1980-83; trustee N.E. Utilities, Hartford, Conn., 1977—; also chmn., dir. subsidiaries; chmn., dir. Conn. Yankee Atomic Power Co.; chmn., dir. Nuclear Electric Ins. Ltd.; pres., dir. Conn. Econ. Devel. Corp.; chmn., chief exec. officer Northeast Utilities and subs., 1983—; dir. CBT Corp., Emhart Corp. Bd. dirs. United Way of Capital Area, 1979-84, Hartford Stage Co., 1977—, Hartford Hosp., 1980—; elector Wadsworth Atheneum, Hartford, 1977—; corporator St. Francis Hosp. and Med. Center, Hartford, 1977—, Inst. of Living, Hartford, 1978—. Served with U.S. Army, 1967-79. Mem. Edison Electric Inst., Atomic Indsl. Forum, Conn. Bus. and Industry Assn. (dir. 1978—), Greater Hartford C. of C. (dir. 1978—). Office: PO Box 270 Hartford CT 06141

ELLIS, WILLIAM HAROLD, former naval officer; b. Rossmoyne, Ohio, Jan. 2, 1925; s. William Engelage and Norma Belle (Rose) E.; m. Irene Harriet Werner, May 15, 1947; children: Susan, William, Cynthia. Student, U. Cin., 1942-43, Ohio State U., 1948-50; A.B., George Washington U., 1960, M.S., 1967. Commd. ensign U.S. Navy, 1945, advanced through grades to rear adm., 1973; comdr. Carrier Air Wing 21, 1965-66; comdg. officer USS Raleigh, 1970-71; comdr. Amphibious Squadron 3, 1972-73, Amphibious Group 2, 1973-75, Naval Safety Center, 1975-76, Naval Base Norfolk, Va.; comdt. 5th Naval Dist., 1976-78. Bd. dirs., exec. com. Navy YMCA, Norfolk; mem. Mayor's Citizens Adv. Com.; mem. exec. bd. Norfolk Council Boy Scouts Am.; bd. dirs. Norfolk United Way; chmn. Norfolk Combined Fed. campaign, 1976-77. Decorated D.S.M., D.F.C., Bronze Star, Air Medal, Legion of Merit. Mem. Hampton Roads Maritime Assn. (dir.), Navy League U.S., Assn. Naval Aviation. Republican. Methodist. Club: Masons. Home: PO Box 935 Pinehurst NC 28374

ELLIS, WILLIAM LEIGH, former govt. ofcl.; b. Petoskey, Mich., Jan. 26, 1908; s. William E. and Gertrude May (Webb) E.; m. Norma Foster, Nov. 16, 1935; children—William L., Amy Foster (Mrs. Pierre Conhagen). A.B., Hillsdale (Mich.) Coll., 1929; LL.B., George Washington U., 1933, LL.M., 1936. Bar: Mich. bar 1935. With State Dept., TVA, 1930-35; atty. GAO, 1935-45, asst. to comptroller gen., 1945-49, chief of investigations, 1949-55; trial atty. Fed. Energy Regulatory Commn., 1955-57, hearing examiner, adminstrv. law judge, 1960-80; dep. dir. Adminstrv. Office U.S. Cts., 1957-60; lectr. law George Washington U., 1942-52. Mem. Fed. Bar Assn. (pres. 1952-53), Mason. Club: Cosmos. Home: 3419 Q St Washington DC 20007

ELLIS, WILLIS HILL, lawyer, educator; b. Detroit, Aug. 30, 1927; s. Seth Wiley and Mildred (Hill) 6E.; m. Gwyneth Fair Saylors, July 7, 1977; 1 stepson, Kevin Saylors; children by previous marriage—Richard Wiley, Jennifer Jean, Scott Mabry. A.B., Wabash Coll., 1951; J.D., Ind. U., 1954. Bar: Ind. bar 1954. Practice law, Indpls., 1954-59; teaching fellow Harvard Law Sch., 1960-61; asst. prof. U. Denver, 1961-64, assoc. prof., 1964-65, U. N.Mex. Coll. Law, Albuquerque, 1965-68, prof. law, 1968—; vis. holder, chair natural resources law Faculty Law U. Calgary (Alta., Can.), 1983. Contbr. chpts. to books, articles to profl. jours. Trustee Rocky Mountain Mineral Law Found. Mem. Am. Bar Assn. Home: 8 Lakeshore Dr NE Albuquerque NM 87112 Office: U NMex Law Sch 1117 Stanford NE Albuquerque NM 87131

ELLISON, CYRIL LEE, publisher; b. N.Y.C., Dec. 11, 1916; s. John and Rose (Arnott) E.; m. Anne N. Nottonson, June 4, 1942. Vice pres., advt. dir. Watson-Guptill Publs. and Am. Artist mag., 1939-69; exec. v.p. Communication Channels, Inc., N.Y.C., 1971-79; pub. Fence Industry, 1970—, Pension World, Trusts and Estates mags., 1973-81, Nat. Real Estate Investor, 1974-78, Shopping Center World, 1974-78. Pres. Westbury Hebrew Congregation, 1954, chmn. bd. trustees, 1955. Served with USAAF, 1942-46; PTO. Named Gray-Russo Advt. Man of Year, 1954. Mem. Am. Legion (comdr. advt. men's post 1954-64). Home: 390-5th Avenue New York NY 10018 Office: 461 8th Ave New York NY 10001

ELLISON, DAVID ERNEST, banker; b. Tacoma, Aug. 15, 1921; s. Herbert Ray and Vena (Norris) E.; m. Diane Morris, Dec. 23, 1946; children—Dava Rae, Darlene, Dayle Gwen, Drew Mitchell. Student, Whitman Coll., 1940, U. Wash., 1945-46; J.D., U. Mont., 1948. Bar: Wash. bar 1948. Hearing examiner Wash. Dept. Pub. Utilities, 1948-49; with Seattle-1st Nat. Bank, 1950-79, sr. v.p., mgr. trust div., 1969-79; pres. Laird, Norton Trust Co., Seattle, 1979—; former tchr. Pacific Coast Banking Sch. Pres. Seattle Found., 1979-80. Served to capt. USAAF, 1941-45. Mem. Am., Mont., Wash. bar assns., Am. Bankers Assn., Corporate Trustees Assn. Wash. (past pres.). Home: 3655 Evergreen Point Rd Bellevue WA 98004 Office: Laird Norton Trust Co 13th Floor Norton Bldg Seattle WA 98104

ELLISON, FRED PITTMAN, foreign language educator; b. Denton, Tex., Jan. 11, 1922; s. Lee Monroe and Hixie (Pittman) E.; m. Adeline Frances Story, June 20, 1947; children: Carol, Thomas, Jamie, Cynthia, John. B.A., U. Tex., 1941; M.A., U. Calif., Berkeley, 1948, Ph.D., 1952. Translator, spl. agt. FBI, 1941-44; assoc. prof. Spanish and Portuguese U. Ill., 1952-61; prof. Spanish and Portuguese U. Tex., 1961—, dir. Lang. and Area Center Latin Am. Studies, 1962-64, assoc. dean, 1970-73; cons. in field, 1952—. Author: Brazil's New Novel, 1954, (with others) Development and Evaluation of Methods and Materials to Facilitate Foreign Language Instruction in Elementary Schools, 1963; coordinator: Modern Portuguese, rev. edit, 1971. Mem. joint com. Latin Am. Studies, Social Sci. Research Council-Am. Council Learned Socs., 1960-65. Served to lt. (j.g.) USNR, 1944-46. NDEA grantee, 1960-62; OAS fellow to Brazil, 1962. Mem. MLA, Academia Brasileira Letras (life, corr.), Instituto de Catedráticos de Literatura Ibero-americana, Am. Assn. Tchrs. Spanish and Portuguese (chmn. Portuguese lang. devel. group 1964-67, chmn. task force to promote Portuguese studies in U.S. 1974-79), Academia Brasileira de Letras (corr. mem.). Home: 2907 Townes Ln Austin TX 78703

ELLISON, HARLAN JAY, author; b. Cleve., May 27, 1934; s. Louis Laverne and Serita (Rosenthal) E.; m. Charlotte Stein, 1956 (div. 1959); m. Billie Joyce Sanders, 1961 (div. 1962); m. Lory Patrick, 1965 (div. 1965); m. Lori Horwitz, 1976 (div. 1976). Student, Ohio State U., 1953-55. A founder Cleve. Sci.-Fiction Soc., 1950; pub. mag. Sci.-Fantasy Bull. (later retitled Dimensions); editor Rogue Mag., Chgo., 1959-60, Regency Books, 1960-61; lectr. colls. and univs.; book critic Los Angeles Times, 1969-82; editorial commentator Canadian Broadcasting Co., 1972-78; pres. Kilimanjaro Corp., 1979—; instr. Clarion Writers Workshop, Mich. State U., 1969-77. Actor, Cleve. Playhouse, part time 1944-49; script writer: television series Logan's Run; others, 1962-77; writer 7: scripts for Burke's Law; creator (under pseudonym Cordwainer Bird): The Starlost, NBC-TV series; scenarist: 2-hour NBC spl. The Tigers Are Loose, 1974-75; writer: motion pictures The Dream Merchants, The Oscar, Nick the Greek, Best by Far, Harlan Ellison's Movie; adaptations Robot, 1978; scenarist: Bug Jack Barron, 1982-83; writer: Nebula winning novella-into-film A Boy and His Dog, 1975 (Hugo award for film adaptation 1976); Author: 39 books including Web of the City, 1958; The Sound of a Scythe, 1960, Gentleman Junkie, 1961, Memos from Purgatory, 1961, Spider Kiss, 1961, Ellison Wonderland, 1962, Paingod (translated into French, Japanese, German, Spanish), 1965, I Have No Mouth & I Must Scream (translated into Japanese, French, Italian, Spanish, German), 1967, From the Land of Fear, 1967, Love Ain't Nothing But Sex Misspelled, 1968, The Beast that Shouted Love at the Heart of the World, 1969, Over the Edge, 1970, Alone Against Tomorrow, 1971, Partners in Wonder, 1971, Approaching Oblivion, 1974, Deathbird Stories, 1975, No Doors, No Windows, 1976, Strange Wine, 1978, All The Lies That Are My Life, 1980, Shatterday, 1980, Stalking the Nightmare, 1982; Editor, compiler: anthology Dangerous Visions (transls. French, German, Japanese, Italian, Spanish, U.K. edits.), 1967, Again, Dangerous Visions, 1972; editor: Medea: Harlan's World, 1985; author 4 books on juvenile delinquency; writer: weekly television column The Glass Teat, Los Angeles Free Press, 1968-71, pub. in 2 vols., 1970, 75; weekly column Harlan Ellison Hornbook, Los Angeles Free Press, 1972-73, An Edge in My Voice, Future Life, 1980-81, Los Angeles Weekly, 1982-83, pub. in 1 volume, 1984; Creator: (with Larry Brody) weekly series The Dark Forces, NBC-TV, 1972; (with Ben Bova) series Brillo, ABC-TV, 1974; Creator, editor: Harlan Ellison Discovery Series of 1st novels for, Pyramid Books, 1973-77. Served with AUS, 1957-59. Recipient Hugo awards World Sci.-Fiction Conv., 1965, (2) 67, 68, 73, 74, 75, 77; Spl. Achievement awards, 1968, 72; Certificate of merit Trieste Film Festival, 1970; Edgar Allan Poe award Mystery Writers Am., 1974; George Méliès awards for cinematic achievement, 1972, 73; Jupiter award Instrs. Sci. Fiction in Higher Edn., 1974, 77; award for journalism PEN Internat., 1982. Mem. Writers Guild Am. (Most Outstanding Scripts awards 1965, 67, 74, screen bd., mem. West council 1971-72), Sci. Fiction Writers Am. (co-founder, Nebula awards 1965, 69, 77, v.p. 1965-66). Address: 3484 Coy Dr Sherman Oaks CA 91423 *It is madness for an artist in our time to take himself or herself seriously. The work, yes, of course; take that seriously. But oneself? Never! For a writer in these lunatic years it is best to think of oneself, at best, as a gadfly, an ally of no one and nothing, save the purity of the work. And realizing this, one must, of necessity, develop a love-hate relationship with the human race. One must become a humane elitist goading even the dullest to try to paint the Sistine Chapel ceiling.*

ELLISON, HERBERT JAY, educator; b. Portland, Oreg., Oct. 3, 1929; s. Benjamin F. and Esther (Anderson) E.; m. Alberta M. Moore, June 13, 1952; children: Valery, Pamela. B.A., U. Wash., 1951, M.A., 1952; Ph.D. (Fulbright fellow), U. London, 1955. Instr. history U. Wash., 1955-56; asst. prof. history U. Okla., 1956-62; asso. prof. history, chmn. Slavic studies program U. Kans., 1962-67, dir. NDEA Lang. and Area Center Slavic Studies, 1965-67, prof., 1965-68, asso. dean faculties internat. programs, 1967-68; prof. history, Russian and Eastern European studies U. Wash., 1968—, dir. div. internat. programs, 1968-72, vice provost for ednl. devel., 1969-72, dir. Inst. Comparative and Fgn. Area Studies, 1973-78, chmn. Russian and East European studies, 1979—; sec. Kennan Inst. Advanced Russian Studies, Washington, 1983—. Author: History of Russia, 1964, Sino-Soviet Conflict, 1982, Soviet Policy toward Western Europe, 1983; contbr. articles to profl. jours. Mem. AAUP, Am. Hist. Assn., Am. Assn. Advancement of Slavic Studies (v.p.). Home: 2828 Wisconsin Ave NW Washington DC 20007 Office: Kennan Inst Woodrow Wilson Ctr Smithsonian Instn Bldg Washington DC 20560

ELLISON, JAMES OLIVER, judge; b. St. Louis, Jan. 11, 1929; s. Jack and Mary (Patton) E.; m. Joan Roberts Ellison, June 7, 1950; 1 son, Scott. Student, U. Mo., Columbia, 1946-48; B.A., U. Okla., 1951, LL.B., 1951. Bar: Okla. Individual practice, Red Fork, Okla., 1953-55; partner Boone, Ellison & Smith, Davis & Minter, 1955-79; judge U.S. Dist. Ct. No. Dist. Okla., Tulsa, 1979—. Trustee Hillcrest Med. Center, Institution Programs, Inc.; elder Southminster Presbyterian Ch. Served to capt., inf. AUS, 1951-53. Mem. ABA, Okla. Bar Assn., Tulsa County Bar Assn., Alpha Tau Omega. Office: US Courthouse 333 W 4th St Tulsa OK 74103 *

ELLISON, LORIN BRUCE, consultant; b. Chgo., Jan. 5, 1932; s. Edward L. and Bertha A. (Hoverson) E.; m. Beverley A. Burtar, July 24, 1953; children—Richard, Glen, Kirk, Kevin. B.S. in Bus. Adminstrn, Drake U., 1954. C.P.A., Ill. Auditor Arthur Andersen & Co., Chgo., 1957-62; mem. corporate staff, div. controller Interlake Steel Co., Chgo., 1962-65; v.p. finance, chief fin. officer, sec., div. pres. Tappan Co., Mansfield, Ohio, 1965-77; asso. cons. A.T. Kearney, Inc., Cleve., 1978-80; corp. controller, v.p. fin., chief fin. officer, v.p. bus. systems Bausch & Lomb, Rochester, N.Y., 1980—. Mem. Fin. Execs. Inst. Home: 550 Beech Dr Mansfield OH 44906

ELLISON, NICHOLAS HOWELL, literary agent; b. N.Y.C., Mar. 18, 1946; s. William and Virginia (Howell) Soskin; children: Gustave Nicholas, Catherine Hannah. B.A., Boston U., 1969. Sr. editor Thomas Y. Crowell Pub. Co., N.Y.C., 1972-76; sr. editor Harper & Row Pubs., N.Y.C., 1976-79; editor-in-chief Delacorte Press, N.Y.C., 1979-81; pres. Edward Acton, Inc., N.Y.C., 1981—, Nicholas Ellison, Inc., 1983—; prof. writing Fairfield U., 1980—; dir. Verreaux Enterprises. Editor numerous books. Pres. Bell Island Assn., Rowayton, Conn., 1972. Recipient Outstanding Achievement award Folio Mgmt. Tng. Seminars, 1979. Congregationalist. Club: Shore and Country (Norwalk, Conn.). Home: 92 Mather Rd Stamford CT 06903 Office: 825 3d Ave New York NY 10017

ELLISON, RALPH (WALDO), writer; b. Oklahoma City, Mar. 1, 1914; s. Lewis Alfred and Ida (Millsap) E.; m. Fanny McConnell, July, 1946. Student, Tuskegee Inst., 1933-36; Ph.D. in Humane Letters (hon.), 1963; Litt.D., Rutgers U., 1966, U. Mich., 1967, Williams Coll., 1970; L.I. U., Coll. William and Mary, 1972, Wake Forest U., 1974, Harvard U., 1974; L.H.D., Grinnell Coll., 1967, Adelphi U., 1971. Participant N.Y.C. Writer's Project; lectr. Am. Negro culture, folklore, creative writing N.Y. U., Columbia U., Fisk U., Antioch Coll., Princeton U., Bennington Coll., others; tchr. Russian, Am. lit. Bard Coll., Annandale-on-Hudson, N.Y., 1958-61; Alexander White vis. prof. U. Chgo., 1961; vis. prof. writing Rutgers U., 1962-64; Albert Schweitzer prof. humanities N.Y. U., 1970-79; Hon. cons. in Am. letters Library of Congress, 1966-72; mem. Carnegie Commn. Ednl. TV, 1966-67; vis. fellow Am. studies Yale U., 1966. Author: Invisible Man, 1952 (Nat. Book award 1953, Nat. newspaper pubs. Russwurm award 1953), Shadow & Act; essays, 1964; Editorial bd.: Am. Scholar, 1966-69; Contbr. short stories, articles, book revs. to pop., profl. mags., 1939—. Trustee John F. Kennedy Center Performing Arts, 1967-77, New Sch. Social Research, Bennington Coll., Colonial Williamsburg Found.; nat. adv. council Hampshire Coll.; bd. dirs. Asso. Council Arts. Served with U.S. Mcht. Marine, 1943-45. Decorated chevalier Ordre et Lettres, France; Medal of Freedom, U.S.; Ralph Ellison Br. Library, Oklahoma City, named in his honor, 1975; Rosenwald fellow, 1945; Nat. Am. Acad. Arts and Letters fellow, Rome, 1955-57. Mem. Am. Acad. Arts and Letters, PEN, Nat. Council Arts, Am. Acad. Arts and Scis., Inst. Jazz Studies (bd. advisers), Nat. Inst. Arts and Letters (chmn. lit. grants com. 1964-67). Club: Century. *

ELLISON, ROBERT GORDON, thoracic-cardiac surgeon; b. Millen, Ga., Dec. 4, 1916; m. Lois Taylor, Feb. 11, 1945; children—Robert Gordon, Gregory, Mark, James, John. A.B., Vanderbilt U., 1939; M.D., Med. Coll. Ga., 1943. Diplomate Am. Bd. Surgery, Am. Bd. Thoracic Surgery (chmn. 1979-81). Intern, resident in gen. surgery Univ. Hosp., Augusta, Ga., 1943-46, resident in thoracic-cardiac surgery, 1947-48, resident in pathology, 1949; resident in cardiopulmonary physiology Bellevue Hosp., N.Y.C., 1948; mem. faculty Med. Coll. Ga., 1947—, chief sect. thoracic surgery, 1955—, prof. surgery, 1959—, Charbonnier prof. surgery, 1973—; mem. surgery study sect. NIH, 1969-73; com. cardiovascular disease Ga. Regional Med. Program, 1971-74; cons. area hosps. Author 1 book, chpts. and, papers in field.; Editorial bd.: Annals Thoracic Surgery, 1965-79. Fellow A.C.S. (chmn. local credentials com. 1968-73, gov. 1973-78), Am. Coll. Chest Physicians, Am. Coll. Cardiology (past gov.), Southeastern Surg. Congress; mem. Am. Thoracic Soc. (councilor 1963-66), Soc. Thoracic Surgeons (pres. 1971, historian 1973—), Thoracic Surgery Dirs. Assn. (exec. com., chmn. in-tng. exam. com. 1976-78), AMA, Soc. Univ. Surgeons, Am. Assn. Thoracic Surgery, Am. Surg. Assn., Am. Physiol. Soc., Am. Soc. Artificial Internal Organs, So. Thoracic Surg. Assn. (pres. 1963-64), So. Surg. Assn., So. Soc. Clin. Investigation, Ga. Heart Assn. (pres. 1974-75), Ga. Thoracic Soc. (pres. 1965-66), Ga. Tb Assn. (pres. 1959), Med. Assn. Ga., Ga. Surg. Soc., Richmond County Med. Soc. (v.p. 1968), Richmond County Heart Assn. (trustee 1970—), Augusta Area Tb Assn. (pres. 1954), Augusta Coll. Alumni Assn. (trustee 1969-73, Most Outstanding Alumnus award 1962), Alpha Omega Alpha, Sigma Psi. Methodist. Address: Med Coll Ga Augusta GA 30912

ELLISON, SAMUEL PORTER, JR., geologist, educator; b. Kansas City, Mo., July 1, 1914; s. Samuel Porter and Mary Frances (Edwards) E.; m. Dorothy Mabel Cannady, June 9, 1949; children: Samuel David, John Robert, Stephen Paul. Student, Jr. Coll. Kansas City, 1930-31; A.B. with honors, U. Kansas City, 1936; A.M. (Gregory fellow), U. Mo., 1938, Ph.D., 1940. Instr. geology U. Mo. Sch. Mines and Metallurgy, 1939-43; asst. prof. U. Md. Sch. Mines and Metallurgy, 1943-44; ranger, naturalist Yellowstone Nat. Parks, Wyo., summer 1941; jr. geologist, asst. geologist U.S. Geol. Survey, Washington, summers 1941-44; geologist Stanolind Oil & Gas Co., Midland, Tex., 1944-47, dist. geologist, Wichita Falls, 1947-48; prof. geol. sci. U. Tex., 1948-79, Alexander Deussen prof. energy, 1972-79, prof. emeritus, 1979—, chmn. dept. geology, 1952-62, acting dean, 1970-71, dean, 1971-73; geol. cons. Shell Oil Co., Casper, Wyo., summers 1953-56; cons. John A Jackson., Dallas, 1957, Humble Oil & Refining Co., Houston, 1959-64, Esso Prodn. Research Co., 1964-76, Republic Gypsum Co., 1979—, Alpine Resources, 1980—; vis. prof. geology U. Sao Paulo, Brazil, 1976. Contbr. articles to profl. jours. Fulbright sr. research fellow, Germany, 1970. Fellow Geol. Soc. Am. (councilor), Paleontol. Soc., AAAS; mem. Am. Assn. Petroleum Geologists (v.p. 1972-73, distinguished service award 1977, hon. life mem.), Soc. Econ. Paleontologists and Mineralogists (sec.-treas. 1954-58, pres. 1959, hon. mem.), Am. Inst. Mining and Metall Engrs., Nat. Assn. Geology Tchrs. (v.p. 1964-64, pres. 1964-65), W. Tex. Geol. Soc., Tex. Acad. Sci., Am. Inst. Profl. Geologists (pres. Tex. sect. 1969), U. Tex. Geology Found. (hon. life mem. council), C.H. Pander Soc. (medal for excellence in conodont research 1977). Methodist. Home: 5948 Highland Hills Dr Austin TX 78731

ELLISON, SOLON ARTHUR, educator; b. N.Y.C., July 13, 1922; s. Nathan and Frieda (Bierner) E.; m. Rose Ruth Tarr, Dec. 27, 1946; children—Judith Ann, Susan Joan. B.S., Coll. City N.Y., 1942; D.D.S., Columbia, 1946, Ph.D., 1958. Mem. faculty Coll. Physicians and Surgeons, Columbia, 1951-62, asst. prof. microbiology, 1958-62, asso. prof., 1962; asso. prof. oral biology Sch. Dentistry, State U. N.Y. at Buffalo, 1962-64, prof., chmn. dept., 1964-77, asso. dean, 1977-78; prof. dentistry and microbiology Sch. Dental and Oral Surgery, Columbia U., N.Y.C., 1978—; mem. dental study sect. USPHS, 1965-69. Contbr. articles to profl. jours. Served with AUS, 1943-44, 46-48. Univ. fellow Columbia, 1948-50; Office of Naval Research grantee, 1958-67; USPHS grantee, 1956—. Fellow Am. Coll. Dentists; mem. Am. Assn. Immunologists, Am. Soc. Microbiology, Internat. Assn. Dental Research. Home: 231 N Woodland St Englewood NJ 07631 Office:

ELLMANN, WILLIAM MARSHALL, lawyer; b. Highland Park, Mich., Mar. 23, 1921; s. James I. and Jeannette (Barsook) E.; m. Sheila Estelle Frenkel, Nov. 1, 1953; children: Douglas S., Carol E., Robert L. Student, Occidental Coll., 1939-40; A.B., U. Mich., 1946; LL.B., Wayne State U., 1951. Bar: Mich. 1951. Practiced in, Detroit, 1951—; ptnr. firm Ellmann & Ellmann, 1970—; Spl. com. atty. gen. Mich. to study use state troops in emergencies, 1964-65; mem. exec. com. Inst. Continuing Legal Edn., 1964-68; mem. Mich. Employment Relations Commn., 1973—, chmn., 1983—; commr. Mackinac Island State Park Commn., 1979—, chmn., 1983—. Served with USAAF, 1942-46. Fellow Am. Bar Found.; mem. Am. Arbitration Assn., Nat. Acad. Arbitrators, Am. Bar Assn. (ho. of dels. 1969-72), Detroit Bar Assn. (vice chmn. pub. relations com. 1959), State Bar Mich. (commr. 1959-69, pres. 1966-67), Practicing Law Inst. (adv. council 1969-70, spl. asst. atty. gen. 1970—), State Bar Mich. (co.-chmn. com. on qualification jud. candidates 1970-78, mem. Detroit News secret witness panel 1983), Sigma Nu Phi. Home: 28000 Weymouth Farmington MI 48018 Office: 1465 Penobscot Bldg Detroit MI

ELLSBERG, DANIEL, writer, lectr., former govt. ofcl., polit. activist; b. Chgo., Apr. 7, 1931; s. Harry E.; m. Carol Cummings, 1951 (div.); children—Robert, Mary; m. Patricia Marx, Aug. 8, 1970; 1 son, Michael Gabriel. B.A. in Econs. summa cum laude, Harvard, 1952, M.A., 1953, Ph.D., 1962; postgrad. (Woodrow Wilson fellow), Cambridge U., Eng., 1952. With Rand Corp., Santa Monica, Calif., 1959-64, 67-70; spl. asst. to asst. sec. def. for internat. security affairs, 1964-65; sr. liaison officer Am. embassy, South Vietnam, 1965-66; asst. to dep. U.S. ambassador to South Vietnam, Saigon, 1967; sr. research asso. Mass. Inst. Tech. Center for Internat. Studies, 1970-72; Cons. strategic nuclear war planning and nuclear command and control Office Sec. Def., White House, Dept. State, 1959-64, 1962; cons. interagy. study crisis decision-making Dept. State, 1964; cons. to spl. asst. for nat. security affairs on Vietnam options and Nat. Security Study Memo 1, 1968-69; mem. McNamara study group History of U.S. Decision-making in Vietnam, 1945-68; (Pentagon papers), 1967-69. Author: Papers on the War, 1972; Contbr.: articles to profl. jours. including Quar. Jour. Econs, Am. Econs. Rev. Served with USMCR, 1954-57. Jr. fellow Soc. Fellows, Harvard U., 1957-59; Recipient Pi Sigma Alpha award Am. Polit. Sci. Assn., 1971; Spl. Freedom of Speech award Ams. for Democratic Action, 1972; Tom Paine award Nat. Emergency Civil Liberties Com., 1971; Am. Peace award Bus. Execs. Move for Peace, 1971; with Andrei Sakharov Eleanor Roosevelt Peace award SANE, 1974; Gandhi Peace award, 1976. Mem. Council Fgn. Relations, War Resisters League, Phi Beta Kappa. Provided Pentagon Papers to Senate Fgn. Relations Com., 1969, later for publ. to N.Y. Times, 1971; consequent criminal charges conspiracy, theft, violation Espionage Act dismissed, 1973. Address: 90 Norwood Ave Kensington CA 94707

ELLSWORTH, ARTHUR WHITNEY, publisher; b. N.Y.C., May 31, 1936; s. Duncan Steuart and Esther Bowes (Stevens) E.; m. Sarah Bingham, Oct. 11, 1958 (div. 1965); 1 son, Barry; m. Priscilla Wear, July 1, 1967; children: Joshua, Nina. B.A., Harvard U., 1958. Editorial assoc. Atlantic, 1959-63; pub. N.Y. Rev. Books, 1963—. Chmn. bd. trustees Harvard Adv.; pres. bd. dirs. Ellsworth Meml. Clinic, Chester Vt; mem. internat. exec. com. Amnesty Internat. Served with AUS, 1958-59. Office: 250 W 57th St New York NY 10107

ELLSWORTH, FRANK L., college president; b. Wooster, Ohio, May 20, 1943; s. Clayton Sumner and Frances (Fuller) E.; 1 dau., Kirstin Lynne. B.A., Western Res. Coll., 1965; M.Ed., Pa. State U., 1967; M.A., Columbia U., 1969; Ph.D., U. Chgo., 1976. Asst. dir. devel. Columbia Law Sch., 1968-70; dir. spl. projects, prof. lit. Sarah Lawrence Coll., N.Y., 1971; asst. dean Law Sch., U. Chgo., 1971-79, instr. social sci. collegiate div., 1975-79; pres. Pitzer Coll., Claremont, Calif., 1979—, also prof. polit. sci., 1979—. Author: Law on the Midway, 1977, Student Activism in American Higher Education; contbr. articles to profl. jours. Mem. vis. coms. Western Res. Coll.; trustee Southwestern Coll. Law; pres. bd. dirs. Los Angeles Ballet; bd. dirs., v.p. Ind. Colls. So. Calif.; bd. fellows Claremont Univ. Center. Recipient Disting. Young Alumnus award Case Western Res. U., 1981. Mem. Assn. Ind. Colls. and Univs. (bd. dirs.), Am. Hist. Assn., Friends Huntington Library, History Edn. Soc., Council for Advancement of Secondary Edn., Young Pres.'s Orgn. Clubs: Arts (Chgo.); University (Los Angeles and Claremont); Zamorano (Los Angeles). Office: 1050 Mills Ave Claremont CA 91711

ELLSWORTH, L. JAMES, holding company executive. Exec. v.p. Dean Witter Reynolds Orgn., Inc., San Francisco. Office: Dean Writer Reynolds Orgn Inc 45 Montgomery St San Francisco CA 94106§

ELLSWORTH, LUCIUS FULLER, university dean, history educator; b. Wooster, Ohio, July 6, 1941; s. Clayton Sumner and Frances Lindemuth (Fuller) E.; m. Linda Diane Vollmar, July 3, 1969. B.A. with high honors, Coll. of Wooster, 1963; M.A. Andelot fellow, U. Del., 1966; Ph.D. Rovensky fellow, U. Del., 1971. Acting coordinator Hagley Grad. program U. Del., 1968-69, adj. instr. history, 1968-69; vis. honors prof. Villanova U., Pa., 1968; asst. prof. history U. West Fla., Pensacola, 1969-74, assoc. prof., 1974-78, prof., 1978—, provost Alpha Coll., 1975-79, dean Coll. Arts and Scis., 1979—; grant proposal reviewer NEH, 1975, 76, 77; cons. to div. history Sec. of State, State of Fla., 1977; cons. N.Y. State Dept. Edn., 1969, Pensacola Jr. Coll., 1970, Chipla Jr. Coll., 1973; mem. Task Force on Research and Service State U. System, Fla., 1975-76; bd. dirs. Fla. Endowment for Humanities, 1983—. Author: (with Brooke Hindle) Technology in Early America, 1966, The American Leather Industry, 1969, The Americanization of the Gulf Coast, 1803-1850, 1972; atuhor: Traditionalism and Change: The New York Tanning Industry in the Nineteenth Century, 1975; author: (with L.V. Ellsworth) The Deep Water of City, 1982. Chmn. Escambia County Bicentennial Festival Com., Fla., 1972-75; bd. dirs. Fla. Inst. Govt., 1980—. Am. Council on Edn. fellow, 1975-76; Nat. Trust for Hist. Preservation grantee, 1975; Fla. Endowment for Humanities Project grantee, 1978. Mem. Orgn. Am. Historians, Am. Hist. Assn., Econ. History Assn., Agrl. History Soc. (Edwards award 1969), Soc. for History of Tech., Am. Assn. Higher Edn., Fla. Hist. Soc. (dir. 1979—, mem. Arthur Thompson Meml. award com. 1974, 78, pres.-elect 1984—), Phi Alpha Theta, Phi Kappa Phi. Democrat. Presbyterian. Home: 8680 Scenic Hwy #7 Pensacola FL 32514 Office: U West Fla Pensacola FL 32514

ELLSWORTH, ROBERT FRED, investment firm executive; b. Lawrence, Kans., June 11, 1926; s. W. Fred and Lucile (Rarig) E.; m. Vivian Esther Sies, Nov. 10, 1956; children: Robert William, Ann Elizabeth. B.S., U. Kans., 1945; J.D., U. Mich., 1949. Bar: D.C., Mass., Kans., U.S. Supreme Ct. bars. Mem. 87th to 89th Congresses from 2d and 3d Dist., Kans., 1961-67; asst. to Pres. of U.S., Washington, 1969; U.S. ambassador to NATO, 1969-71; gen. partner Lazard Freres & Co., N.Y.C., 1971-74; asst. sec. for internat. security affairs U.S. Dept. Def., Washington, 1974-75, dep. sec. Def., 1976-77; pres. Robert Ellsworth & Co., Inc., Washington. Lay reader Episcopal Ch. Served with USNR, 1944-46, 50-53. Recipient Presdl. Nat. Security medal, 1977. Mem. Council Fgn. Relations, Internat. Inst. Strategic Studies (vice chmn. council), Atlantic Council U.S. (dir.), Atlantic Inst. (gov.). Home: 24020 Old Hundred Rd Dickerson MD 20842 Office: 1616 H St NW Washington DC 20006

ELLSWORTH, ROBERT MALCOLM, ophthalmologist, educator; b. Wilkes-Barre, Pa., Feb. 6, 1928; s. Elijah Martyn and Laura Eva (Carey) E.; m. Grace A. Foster, Aug. 6, 1955; children: Robert Malcolm, Jr., Laura. B.A., Princeton U., 1949; M.D., Columbia U., 1952. Asso. prof. ophthalmology Columbia U., from 1958; asso. attending ophthalmologist Presbyn. Hosp., N.Y.C., to 1979; prof. ophthalmology Cornell U. Med. Coll., N.Y.C., 1979—; attending ophthalmologist N.Y. Hosp., N.Y.C. Served with USMC, 1953-55. Mem. N.Y. Ophthal. Soc., Am. Ophthal. Soc., Am. Assn. Ophthalmologists, Pan Am. Assn. Ophthalmologists, Eye Study Club, Retina Soc., French Ophthalmology Soc., Australian Ophthalmology Soc., N.Z. Ophthalmology Soc. Republican. Methodist. Clubs: Princeton, Knickerbocker Country, Campfire, Mason. Home: 232 Lydecker St Englewood NJ 07631 Office: 515 E 71st St New York NY 10021

ELLSWORTH, SAMUEL GEORGE, educator, historian; b. Safford, Ariz., June 19, 1916; s. James Clarence and Julia (Claridge) E.; m. Maria Smith, Oct. 24, 1942; children—Stephen George, Mark Addison. B.S., Utah State Agrl. Coll., 1941; M.A., U. Calif. at Berkeley, 1947, Ph.D., 1951. Tchr. pub. schs., Bunkerville, Nev., 1941-42; teaching asst. U. Calif. at Davis and Berkeley, 1948-50; faculty Utah State U., Logan, 1951—, asst. prof. history, 1951-54, asso. prof., 1954-63, prof., 1963—, head dept., 1966-69; vis. prof. W.Va. U., 1954, Brigham Young U., 1956. Author books, articles on Utah and Mormon history.; Editor: Western Hist. Quar, 1969-79. Served with AUS, 1942-46. Faculty Honor lectr. humanities Faculty Assn., 1959; named Prof. of Year, 1965. Fellow Utah State Hist. Soc.; mem. Am., Western, Mormon history assns., Orgn. Am. Historians, Cache Valley Hist. Soc. (officer 1951-56, pres. 1954-56), Am. Assn. for State and Local History (award merit 1974), Phi Kappa Phi, Phi Alpha Theta. Home: 496 N 3d East Logan UT 84321

ELLWOOD, ROBERT SCOTT, JR., educator; b. Normal, Ill., July 17, 1933; s. Robert Scott and Knola Lorraine (Shanks) E.; m. Gracia Fay Bouwman, Aug. 28, 1965; children: Richard, Fay Elanor. B.A., U. Colo., 1954; M.Div., Berkeley Div. Sch., 1957; M.A. U. Chgo, 1965; Ph.D., 1967. Ordained priest Episcopal Ch., 1957; pastor ch., Central City, Nebr., 1957-60; chaplain USNR, 1961-62; asst. prof. religion U. So. Calif., 1967-71, assoc. prof., 1971-75, prof., 1975—, Bishop Bashford prof. Oriental studies, 1977—, dir. East Asian Studies Center, 1977-81. Author: Religious and Spiritual Groups in Modern America, 1973, One Way: The Jesus Movement and Its Meaning, 1973, The Feast of Kingship, 1973, The Eagle and the Rising Sun, 1974, Many Peoples, Many Faiths, 1976, Words of the World's Religions, 1977, Introducing Religion, 1978, Readings in Religion, 1978, Alternative Altars, 1979, Mysticism and Religion, 1980, Invitation to Japanese Civilization, 1980. Mem. Am. Acad. Religion, Assn. Asian Studies. Home: 2011 Rose Villa St Pasadena CA 91107 Office: U So Calif Sch Religion University Park Los Angeles CA 90089

ELMAGHRABY, SALAH ELDIN, indsl. engr., educator; b. Fayoum, Egypt, Oct. 21, 1927; s. Abdel Fattah and Leila (Orabi) E.; m. Amina Ishac, July 9, 1964; children—Leila, Wedad, Karima. B.Sc. in Mech. Engring, Cairo U., 1948; M.Sc. in Indsl. Engring, Ohio State U., 1955, Ph.D., Cornell U., 1958. Engr. Fgn. Inspection Office of Egyptian State Railways, 1949-54; research asst. Cornell U., 1955-58; research leader Western Electric Co. Research Center, Princeton, N.J., 1958-62; vis. asso. prof. Yale U., 1967, asso. prof., 1962-67; prof., dir. grad. program in ops. research N.C. State U., Raleigh, 1967—. Author: Activity Networks, 1977; co-editor: Handbook of Operations Research, 1978. Recipient Disting. research award Am. Inst. Indsl. Engrs., 1970, research div. award, 1980. Mem. Ops. Research Soc. Am., Inst. Mgmt. Sci., Am. Inst. Indsl. Engrs., AAUP. Home: 124 Perquimans Dr Raleigh NC 27619 Office: Grad Program in Ops Research Box 5511 NC State U Raleigh NC 27650

ELMAN, PHILIP, lawyer; b. Paterson, N.J., Mar. 14, 1918; s. Jacob and Anne (Nirenberg) E.; m. Ella M. Shalit, Dec. 21, 1947; children: Joseph, Peter, Anthony. A.B., CCNY, 1936; LL.B., Harvard U., 1939. Bar: N.Y. 1940, D.C. 1948. Law clk. to Judge Magruder, U.S. Ct. Appeals, Boston, 1939-40; atty. FCC, 1940-41; law clk. to Supreme Ct. Justice Frankfurter, 1941-43; asst. chmn. Office Fgn. Econ. Coordination, State Dept., 1943-44; asst. to solicitor gen. U.S., 1944-61; legal adviser Mil. Govt. U.S., Berlin, 1945-46; commr. FTC, 1961-70; of counsel Wald, Harkrader & Ross, 1971—; prof. law Georgetown U. Law Center, Washington, 1970-76, U. Hawaii, Honolulu, 1982—. Editor: Of Law and Men (papers of Felix Frankfurter), 1956; mem. staff: Harvard Law Rev. Recipient Rockefeller Pub. Service award, 1967. Mem. Am. Law Inst., Phi Beta Kappa. Home: 6719 Brigadoon Dr Bethesda MD 20817 Office: 1300 19th St NW Washington DC 20036

ELMENDORF, WILLIAM WELCOME, educator; b. Victoria, C., Can., Sept. 10, 1912; s. William Judson and Mary (Johnson) E.; m. Eleanor Gerlough, Oct. 12, 1940; children: William John, Anthony Daniel. B.A., U. Wash., 1934, M.A., 1935; Ph.D., U. Calif. at Berkeley, 1949. Teaching asst. U. Calif. at Berkeley, 1940-42; instr., then asst. prof. anthropology U. Wash., 1946-57; teaching asso. Northwestern U., 1950-51; lectr., then asso. prof. Wash. State U., 1957-65; mem. faculty U. Wis., 1963—, prof. anthropology, 1964-81, prof. emeritus, 1981—; profl. cons. Skokomish Indian Claims Case, 1956. Author: The Structure of Twana Culture, 1960, kokomish and Other Coast Salish Tales, 1961, Lexical and Cultural Change in Yukian, 1968. Served to capt. AUS, 1942-46, 51-52. Fellow Am. Anthrop. Assn., Am. Ethnol. Soc.; mem. Linguistic Soc. Am., Central States Anthrop. Soc., Northwest Anthrop. Conf. (pres. 1958), Sigma Xi. Home: 1309 Redwood Ln Davis CA 95616

ELMER, WILLIAM MORRIS, retired pipe line executive; b. Rochelle, Ill., Apr. 25, 1915; s. Gertis Dresser and Josephine (Morris) E.; m. Ruth Alexander, July 9, 1939; children: Ruth Ann, William A. Student, Lyons Twp. (Ill.) Jr. Coll., 1934; B.A., U. Ill., 1936. Accounting mgr. Arthur Andersen & Co., 1936-46; sr. v.p. Tex. Gas Transmission Corp., 1946-57, exec. v.p., 1957, pres., 1957-68, chmn. bd., chief exec. officer, 1968-78, chmn. bd., 1978-80; pres. Tex. Gas Exploration Corp., 1953-58, chmn., until 1980; dir. emeritus CSX Corp. Served as lt. comdr. USNR, 1942-46. Mem. Ill. Soc. C.P.A.s, Interstate Natural Gas Assn., Am., Am. Gas Assn., Am. Petroleum Inst. Club: Mason. Home: PO Box 349 Point Clear AL 36564 Office: 102 Fairhope Ave Fairhope AL 36532

ELMES, DAVID GORDON, psychologist; b. Newton, Mass., Feb. 13, 1942; s. Leslie and Ruth (Adams) E.; m. Anne Louise Lawrence, June 7, 1963; children: Matthew David, Jennifer Anne. B.A., U. Va., 1964; M.A., U.Va., 1966; Ph.D., U. Va., 1967. Mgmt. trainee C & P of Va., 1963; asst. prof. Washington and Lee U., Lexington, Va., 1967-71, assoc. prof., 1971-74, prof., 1975—; research assoc. Human Performance Center, U. Mich., 1973-74. Author: Readings in Experimental Psychology, 1978, Methods in Experimental Psychology, 1981; contbr. articles in field to profl. jours. Bd. dirs. Rockbridge Mental Health Clinic, 1968-73; ofcl., coach Little League Baseball and Basketball, 1969-77. Mem. Psychonomic Soc., Va. Acad. Sci. Home: 3 Westside Ct Lexington VA 24450 Office: Washington and Lee U Lexington VA 24450

ELMORE, EDWARD WHITEHEAD, lawyer; b. Lawrenceville, Va., July 15, 1938; s. Thomas Milton and Mary Norfleet (Whitehead) E.; m. Gail Harmon, Aug. 10, 1968; children: Mary Jennifer, Edward Whitehead. B.A., U. Va.-Charlottesville, 1959, J.D., 1962. Bar: Va. 1962. Assoc. firm Hunton & Williams, Richmond, Va., 1965-69; staff atty. Ethyl Corp., Richmond, 1969-78, asst. gen. counsel, 1978-79, gen. counsel, 1979-80, gen. counsel., sec., 1980-83, v.p., gen. counsel, sec., 1983—. Served to capt. AUS, 1962-65. Decorated Army Commendation medal. Mem. ABA, Va. Bar Assn., Internat. Bar Assn., Va. State Bar, Am. Soc. Corp. Secs., Raven Soc., Phi Beta Kappa. Home: 2901 W Bridgstock Rd Midlothian VA 23113 Office: Ethyl Corp 330 W 4th St Richmond VA 23219

ELMORE, JAMES WALTER, architect, university dean; b. Lincoln, Nebr., Sept. 5, 1917; s. Harry Douglas and Marie Clare (Minor) E.; m. Mary Ann Davidson, Sept. 6, 1947; children: James Davidson, Margaret Kay. A.B., U. Nebr., 1938; M.S. in Architecture, Columbia U., 1948. Mem. faculty Ariz. State U., 1949—, prof. architecture, 1959—, founding dean Coll. of Architecture,, 1964-74; cons. architect, 1956—. Trustee Heard Museum, Phoenix, 1968-79; bd. dirs. Valley Forward Assn., Phoenix, 1969—; bd. dirs. Central Ariz. chpt. Ariz. Hist. Soc., 1973—; bd. dirs. Ariz. Architects Found., 1978—, Rio Salado Devel. Dist., 1980—. Served to col., C.E. U.S. Army, 1940-46. Decorated Bronze Star. Fellow AIA; mem. Ariz. Acad. Home: 6229 N 29th Pl Phoenix AZ 85016 Office: Coll of Architecture Ariz State U Tempe AZ 85287

ELMORE, STANCLIFF CHURCHILL, lawyer; b. Washington, Sept. 6, 1921; s. John Archer and Doris Ernestine (Churchill) E.; m. Betty Buchanan, June 12, 1948; children—Stancliff Churchill, Maralyn Ann. Student, Washington and Lee U., 1939-42; LL.B., George Washington U., 1950. Bar: D.C. bar 1950, Md. bar 1960. Counsel U.S. Ho. of Reps. Appropriations Com., subcoms. mil., public works, 1952-53; partner firm Lambert, Furlow, Elmore & Heidenberger, Washington, 1961-79, Williams, Myers and Quiggle, Washington and Montgomery County, Md., 1979—; gen. counsel Southeastern U.; legal counsel, lawyer mem. D.C. Real Estate Commn., 1966-74. Served with AUS, 1942-46. Mem. Am. Law Inst. Republican. Episcopalian. Club: Chevy Chase. Home: 5142 Tilden St NW Washington DC 20016 Office: 900 Brawner Bldg 888 17th St NW Washington DC 20006

ELMORE, WALTER A., electrical engineer, consultant; b. Bartlett, Tenn., Oct. 2, 1925; s. Walter Alcon and Lucille (Tapp) E.; m. Jane Ann Huey, June 3, 1950; children: Robin, Jamie, Laura. B.S. in Elec. Engring., U. Tenn., 1948. Registered profl. engr., Fla. With cons. engring. sect., relay instrument div. Westinghouse Electric Co., Newark, 1951-79, Coral Springs, Fla., 1979—. Author: Applied Protective Relaying, 1976. Fellow IEEE (chmn. power system relaying com. 1983-84); mem. Tau Beta Pi, Eta Kappa Nu, Phi Kappa Phi. Republican. Home: 2435 NW 115th Dr Coral Springs FL 33065 *

ELMS, JAMES CORNELIUS, IV, aerospace and energy consultant; b. East Orange, N.J., May 16, 1916; s. James Cornelius and Iva Marguerite (Corwin) E.; m. Patricia Marguerite Pafford, Jan. 4, 1942; children: Christopher Michael, Suzanne, Francesca, Deborah. B.S. in Physics, Calif. Inst. Tech., 1948, M.A., UCLA, 1950. Registered profl. engr., Calif. Stress analyst Consol. Aircraft Corp., San Diego, 1940-42; chief devel. engr. G.M. Giannini & Co., Pasadena, Calif., 1948-49; research asso. in geophysics UCLA, 1949-50; mgr. dept. armament systems, div. autonetics N.Am. Aviation Co., Downey, Calif., 1950-57; mgr. dept. avionics Martin Co., Denver, 1957-59; exec. v.p. Crosley div. AVCO Corp., Cin., 1959-60; gen. ops. mgr. aeronutronic div. Ford Motor Co., Newport Beach, Calif., 1960-63; dep. dir. Manned Spacecraft Center NASA, Houston, 1963-64, dep. assoc. adminstr. for manned space flight Manned Spacecraft Center, Washington, 1965-66, dir. Electronics Research Ctr., Cambridge, Mass., 1966-70, cons. to adminstr.; as dep. dir. Space Shuttle Assessment Team, Washington, 1975; corp. v.p., gen. mgr. div. space and info. systems Raytheon, Sudbury, Mass., 1964-65; dir. Trans. Systems Center, Dept. Transp., Cambridge, 1970-74; cons. to adminstr. ERDA, 1975-77; cons. to mgmt. of aerospace and energy cos., Newport Beach, 1975-81; cons. to adminstr. NASA, 1981—; mem. space systems com. space adv. council NASA, 1970-77. Served to capt. USAAF, 1942-46. Recipient Spl. award NASA, 1964, Exceptional Service medal, 1969, Outstanding Leadership medal, 1970; Sec.'s award for meritorious service Dept. Transp., 1974. Fellow IEEE, AIAA (asso.); mem. Nat. Acad. Engring., Am. Phys. Soc., Air Force Assn., Assos. of Calif. Inst. Tech., Res. Officers Assn., Soaring Soc. Am., Aircraft Owners and Pilot's Assn., Explorers Club. Episcopalian. Club: Balboa Yacht. Patentee instrumentation, computers, radars and mechanisms. Home and Office: 112 Kings Pl Newport Beach CA 92663

ELMSLIE, KENWARD GRAY, author; b. N.Y.C., Apr. 27, 1929; s. William Gray and Constance Helen (Pulitzer) E. B.A., Harvard U., 1950. Pres. Z Press Inc., Calais, Vt., 1973—. Author: poetry The Champ, 1968, Album, 1969, Circus Nerves, 1971, Motor Disturbance, 1971, The Orchid Stories, 1972, Tropicalism, 1976, The Alphabet Work, 1977, Communications Equipment, 1979, Moving Right Along, 1980, Bimbo Dirt, 1981; opera libretto Lizzie Borden, 1966; Miss Julie, 1966; musical plays The Grass Harp, 1971; The Sweet Bye & Bye, 1973, The Seagull, 1974, Washington Square, 1976, The Three Sisters, 1979; Lola, 1982; Author: play City Junket, 1978; album rec.: Lizzie Borden, 1967, The Sweet Bye and Bye, 1973, The Glass Harp, 1973, Highlights from Miss Julie, 1980, Rare Meat, 1980, Kenwald Emslie Visited, 1981; panelist librettist-composer program play, NEA, 1973-75; Editor: Z, 1973, ZZ, 1974, ZZZ, 1974, ZZZZ, 1975, ZZZZZ, 1976, ZZZZZZ, 1977, Miltie is a Hackie, 1973, Mobile Homes, 1979, Tulsa Kid, 1980. Recipient Frank O'Hara Poetry award O'Hara Found., 1971, Librettist award Nat. Endowment for Arts, 1978; Ford Found. grantee, 1965, 66. Mem. ASCAP, Authors League, Dramatists Guild. Address: Poets Corner Calais VT 05648

ELORRIAGA, JOHN A., banker; b. Jordan Valley, Oreg., 1923. A.A., Boise (Idaho) Jr. Coll., 1949; B.B.A., U. Oreg., 1951; M.B.A., U. Pitts., 1953; postgrad., Pacific Coast Sch. Banking, 1959. Exec. trainee U.S. Nat. Bank of Oreg., 1951-66, v.p., loan officer, 1966-72, pres., 1972-74, chmn. bd., dir., 1974; pres., chmn. bd., chief exec. officer, dir. U.S. Bancorp., Portland, Oreg.; exec. v.p. Evans Products Co., 1967-70; pres. Columbia Corp., 1970-72; dir. Pacific Northwest Bell Telephone Co. Bd. dirs. Blue Cross and Blue Shield of Oreg., Oreg. Shakespearean Festival Assn., St. Vincent Hosp. and Med. Center, U. Oreg. Devel. Fund; mem. adv. council Sch. Bus., Boise State U.; mem. bus. adv. council Coll. Bus. Adminstrn., U. Oreg.; mem. bd. commrs. Port of Portland; bd. regents U. Portland; bd. cons. Goodwill Industries Oreg. Served with USAAF, 1944-46. Office: c/o US Bancorp 309 SW 6th Ave Portland OR 97208

ELROD, BEN MOODY, college executive; b. Rison, Ark., Oct. 13, 1930; s. Benjamin Searcy and Frances Othello (Sadler) E.; m. Betty Lou Warren, Aug. 7, 1951; children: Cynthia Lou, William Searcy. B.A., Ouachita Baptist U., 1952; Th.D., Southwestern Bapt. Theol. Sem., 1960; Ed.D., Ind. U., 1976. Ordained to ministry Baptist Ch., 1950; pastor First Bapt. Ch., Atkins, Ark., 1951-53, Tioga, Tex., 1955-57, Marlow, Okla., 1957-60, South Side Bapt. Ch., Pine Bluff, Ark., 1960-63; v.p. for devel. Ouachita Bapt. U., 1963-68, 70-78; pres. Oakland City Coll., 1968-70, Georgetown (Ky.) Coll., 1978-83, Ind. Colls. of Ark., 1983—; vis. lectr. in field; cons. higher edn. Contbr. articles to religion jours. Page U.S. Ho. of Reps., 1946-47; trustee Clark County (Ark.) Hosp., 1973-77, chmn., 1975-77; trustee Ark. Bapt. Med. System, 1978. Mem. Am. Assn. Higher Edn., Internat. Platform Assn., Bapt. Public Relations Assn., Phi Delta Kappa. Democrat. Home: 3 Cedar Creek Ct North Little Rock AR 72116 Office: Ind Colls of Ark 1 Riverfront Pl Suite 610 North Little Rock AR 72114

ELROD, HAROLD GLENN, educator; b. Manchester, N.H., Nov. 19, 1918; s. Harold Glenn and Marion Gladys (Fritz) E.; m. Ruth Allison Starr, Mar. 28, 1942; children—Joanne Hilton, Carolyn Ann, Harold Glenn III. B.Sc., M.I.T., 1942; M.A., Harvard U., 1947, Ph.D., 1949. Registered profl. engr., Ohio. Research engr. (Babcock & Wilcox Research), Alliance, Ohio, 1949-52; asst. prof. Case-Western Res. U., Cleve., 1952-55; asso. prof. Columbia U., N.Y.C., 1955-57, prof. engring. sci., 1957-61, 62—; prof. Mich. State U., East Lansing, 1961-62. Contbr. articles in field to profl. jours. Mem. ASME, AIAA, Sigma Xi. Republican. Unitarian. Home: 61 Nannahagan Rd Pleasantville NY 10570 Office: Columbia U Mech Engring Dept Mudd Bldg New York NY 10027

EL SAFFAR, RUTH SNODGRASS, Spanish language educator; b. N.Y.C., June 12, 1941; d. John Tabb and Ruth (Wheelwright) Snodgrass; m. Zuhair M. El Saffar, Apr. 11, 1965; children: Ali, Dena, Amir. B.A., Colo. Coll., 1962; Ph.D., Johns Hopkins U., 1966. Instr. Spanish, Johns Hopkins U., Balt., 1963-65; instr. English, Univ. Coll. Baghdad, 1966-67; asst. prof. Spanish, U. Md.-Baltimore County, 1967-68; asst. prof. U. Ill.-Chgo., 1968-73; asso. prof. U. Ill., 1973-78, prof., 1978-83, research prof. Spanish, 1983—; dir. summer seminar on Spanish Golden Age lit. NEH, 1979, 82. Author: Novel to Romance: A Study of Cervantes's Novelas Ejemplares, 1974, Distance and Control in Don Quixote, 1975, Cervantes's Casamiento engañoso and Coloquio de los perros, 1976, Beyond Fiction, 1983, 1984; adv. bd.: PMLA; editorial bd.: Cervantes. Woodrow Wilson fellow, 1962; Nat. Endowment for Humanities fellow, 1970-71; Guggenheim fellow, 1975-76; Danforth asso., 1973-79; Am. Council Learned Socs. grantee, 1978; Newberry Library fellow, 1982. Mem. MLA (exec. council 1974-78, commn. on future of the profession 1980-82, exec. com. div. on Spanish Golden Age poetry and prose 1977-82), Am. Assn. Tchrs. Spanish and Portuguese, Midwest MLA, Cervantes Soc. Am. (exec. com. 1979-82). Home: 7811 Greenfield River Forest IL 60305 Office: Dept Spanish U Ill Chgo Circle Chicago IL 60680 *I was encouraged from my earliest years to understand that I could do anything I set my mind to. My father took an active role in stimulating my academic ambitions, and my mother always reminded me to give my best effort in all things. That parental orientation carried me solidly through the first three decades of my life. I have since learned that in addition to knowledge, determination, and ambition, a truly successful life requires love, an active realization of one's unfolding in spirit, devotion, and humility. These are the deeper foundations on which the remainder of one's life must be built.*

ELSAS, LOUIS JACOB, II, physician; b. Atlanta, Feb. 10, 1937; s. Herbert R. and Edith (Levy) E.; m. Nancy Terrell, July 15, 1961; children: Nancy Louise, Margaret Edith, Louis Jacob, III. B.A., Harvard U., 1958; M.D., U. Va., 1962. Diplomate: Am. Bd. Internal Medicine, Am. Bd. Med. Genetics. Intern Yale-New Haven Hosp., 1962-63, resident in internal medicine, 1963-65; NIH postdoctoral fellow in med. genetics Yale U., 1965-68, from instr. to asst. prof. sect. genetics, dept. medicine and pediatrics, 1968-70; mem. faculty Emory U. Med. Sch., 1970—, prof. pediatrics and biochemistry, 1977—, dir. med. genetics, 1970—; dir. Ga. Comprehensive Genetic System, 1978; vis. prof. Japan Soc. Promotion Sci., 1976; Bd. dirs. Patch, Inc., 1975—. Author papers in field. Recipient Research Career Devel. award NIH, 1972-77, John Horsley Meml. prize U. Va. Med. Sch., 1972; named hon. citizen, Interlaken, Switzerland, 1980. Fellow Am. Acad. Pediatrics; mem. Soc. Inherited Metabolic Disorders (founding pres.), Am. Soc. Clin. Investigation, Soc. Pediatric Research, Am. Soc. Biol. Chemistry, Am. Soc. Human Genetics, Soc. Study Inborn Errors Metabolism, Atlanta Clin. Soc., Atlanta Genetic Soc., Sigma Xi (past chpt. pres.). Clubs: Emory U. Faculty, Druid Hills Golf, Civitan (Humanitarian award 1979). Home: 858 Oakdale Rd Atlanta GA 30307 Office: Emory U PO Drawer AM Atlanta GA 30322 *The successful biomedical scientist must develop a personal balance between science and humanism; innovation and application; learning and teaching. This goal can be met if one starts at an early age and continues as a student of fundamental science; is curious and tests central dogma; uses truth and the scientific method as standards of conduct and is sympathetic to the needs of individuals and society.*

ELSASSER, WALTER MAURICE, physicist, educator; b. Mannheim, Germany, Mar. 20, 1904; came to U.S., 1936, naturalized, 1940; s. Moritz and Johanna (Masius) E.; m. Margaret Trahey, July 17, 1937; children—Barbara, William; m. Suzanne Rosenfeld, June 24, 1964. Ph.D., U. Goettingen, Germany, 1927. Instr. U. Frankfurt, Germany, 1930-33; research fellow Sorbonne, Paris, 1933-36, Calif. Inst. Tech., 1936-41; war research on radar U.S. Signal Corps and RCA Labs., 1941-47; prof. physics U. Pa., 1947-50, U. Utah, 1950-56, U. Calif. at La Jolla, 1956-62; chmn. dept. physics U. N.Mex., Alburquerque, 1960-61; prof. geophysics, dept. geology Princeton, 1962-68; research prof. U. Md., College Park, 1968-74; adj. prof. dept. earth and planetary sci. Johns Hopkins, 1975—. Author: theory of earth's magnetic field The Physical Foundation of Biology, 1958; Atom and Organism, 1966; theory of earth's magnetic field The Chief Abstractions of Biology, 1975, Memoirs of a Physicist in the Atomic Age, 1978. Recipient Gauss medal W. Ger., 1977. Fellow Am. Phys. Soc., Am. Geophys. Union (Bowie medal 1959, Fleming medal 1971); mem. Nat. Acad. Sci. Home: 500 W University Pkwy Apt 7E Baltimore MD 21210

ELSBERG, MILTON LEONARD, drug company executive; b. Balt., Sept. 29, 1912; s. Simon and Ida (Levy) E.; m. Rita Kahn, Sept. 13, 1936; 1 son, Stuart Michael. Ph.G., U. Md., 1931. Disc jockey radio sta. WCBM, Balt., 1930; clk. Lober Bros., N.Y.C., 1932; pharmacist Nat. Press Pharmacy, Washington, 1933; mgr. So. Drug Co., Washington, 1935-37; partner Drug Fair, Washington, 1938-40, pres., chief exec. officer, 1940-81, ret., 1981; dir., mem. exec. com. Riggs Nat. Bank, Washington. Bd. dirs. Better Bus. Bur. Met. Washington, Greater Nat. Capital com., Kauffman Camp for Boys and Girls, Fed. City Council, Brand Names Found.; trustee Boys Club Washington, United Jewish Appeal Greater Washington; nat. trustee, chmn. drive Eleanor Roosevelt Inst. Cancer Research.; Mem. pres.'s council Brandeis U. Recipient award of achievement Advt. Club, 1958; Brand Name Retailers of Year awards for chains in U.S., Can., 1958, 64. Mem. Washington Bd. Trade, Nat. Assn. Real Estate Bds., Bd. Affiliated Drug Stores, Nat. Assn. Chain Drug Stores, Washington Bd. Realtors, D.C. C. of C. Clubs: Variety, Saints and Sinners, Advertising, Internat., Georgetown (Washington); Woodmont Country (Rockville, Md.). Home: Shoreham W 2700 Calvert St NW Washington DC 20008 also 2100 Ocean Blvd Palm Beach FL 33480 Office: 1120 Connecticut Ave Washington DC

ELSBERG, STUART MICHAEL, business consultant, video producer; b. Washington, Feb. 2, 1939; s. Milton Leonard and Rita Ann (Kahn) E.; m. Margery Ann Merkin, Aug. 29, 1965; children: Andrew Marc, Jonathan Simon, Daniel Harry. B.A., Cornell U., 1960; J.D., Georgetown U., 1963. Bar: D.C. 1964. With Drug Fair, Inc., Alexandria, Va., 1953-81, dir., 1961-81, asst. dir. statistics and analysis, 1963-66, asst. dir. merchandising, 1966-72, sec., 1968-73, mdse. mgr., 1972-75, v.p., 1973-75, sr. v.p., 1975-81; of counsel firm Kaufmann, Glosser & Greenburg, 1981-83; now bus. cons., video producer; founder Elsberg Assos., Retail Counselors, 1981; pres. Drug Fair D.C., 1969-81, Active Casuals Inc., 1977-81; adv. bd. Riggs Nat. Bank, 1977—. Mem. personnel policies forum Bur. Nat. Affairs, 1965-67; mem. businessmen's com. Washington Nat. Symphony, 1968-70; mem. Cabin John Park Vol. Fire Dept., 1969—, pres., 1975—; bd. dirs. Jr. Achievement Met. D.C., 1973—, v.p., 1974-75, pres., 1976, chmn. bd., 1977; chmn. bd. Eastern regional council, 1978—; trustee, bd. dirs. Potomac Conservation Found., 1971-78; bd. dirs. Washington Performing Arts Soc., 1973-79, Children's Hosp. Nat. Med. Center, 1977—; exec. adv. bd. Nat. Alliance Business, 1979-81; mem. Washington Bd. Trade, 1978—; vice chmn. Retail Bur. Washington Bd. of Trade, 1981—; Appointee Montgomery County Drug Abuse Adv. Council, 1981—; mem. Washington Area bd. Jewish Nat. Fund, 1981—, sr. v.p., mem. nat. leadership council, 1983. Mem. Potomac C. of C. (chmn. 1971), D.C. Bar Assn., Affiliated Chain Drug Stores (dir. 1970-81, exec. com. 1972-75, sec. 1972, v.p. 1973, chmn. bd. 1974), Nat. Bus. Leadership Conf. (sponsoring com. 1977), Pi Epsilon Delta, Phi Delta Phi, Tau Delta Phi. Jewish (dir. congregation brotherhood 1967-70, mem. adminstrv. com. 1969, bldg. com. 1978-81, fine arts com. 1979-82). Clubs: Rhode River Boat, Shearwater Sailing, Severn River Yacht (Annapolis, Md.); Woodmont Country. Home: 10305 Garden Way Potomac MD 20854 Office: 4400 Jenifer St NW Suite 325 Washington DC 20015

ELSBREE, JOHN FRANCIS, banker; b. Methuen, Mass., Apr. 19, 1912; s. Leslie Francis and Beatrice (Roberts) E.; m. Ida Letitia Brooks, Aug. 13, 1938; children: Janet Elaine Elsbree Amoling, John Francis, Marjorie Evelyn Elsbree Evans, David Brooks, Ruth Elizabeth Elsbree Newman. Student, Harvard U., 1928-30, Am. Inst. Banking, 1933-45, Stonier Grad. Sch. Banking, 1955-57. With Webster & Atlas Nat. Bank, Boston, 1930-48, auditor, 1945-48; asst. auditor Rockland-Atlas Nat. Bank, Boston, 1948-51, auditor, 1951-57, asst. v.p., 1957-61, State St. Bank & Trust Co., Boston, 1961-62, v.p., 1962-75, sr. v.p., 1975-77, gen. auditor, 1964-77; v.p., gen. auditor State St. Boston Corp., 1970-74, sr. v.p., gen. auditor, 1974-77; past lectr. Am. Inst. Banking, Northwestern U.; lectr. No. New Eng. Sch. Banking, NABAC Sch. at U. Wis. Author: Social, Economic and Political Causes and Effects of Commercial Bank Mergers, 1957; contbr. articles to profl. publs. Treas. Boston Latin Sch. Assn., 1955-77, asst. treas., 1977—. Semi-finalist Am. Inst. Banking Nat. Debate Contest, 1950, 53, 54. Mem. Bank Officers Assn. Boston, Am. Inst. Banking (past asso. councilman, nat. debate chmn.), Inst. Internal Auditors (dir. New Eng. chpt., past chpt. pres.), Bank Adminstrn. Inst. (past pres. Boston chpt., state, dist. dir. 1970-71, Chmn. bd. regents). Episcopalian. Home: 56 Brooks St Brighton Boston MA 02135 *Keep striving!*

ELSEN, ALBERT EDWARD, art history educator; b. N.Y.C., Oct. 11, 1927; s. Albert George and Julia Louise (Huseman) E.; m. Patricia Morgan Kline, July 7, 1951; children: Matthew, Nancy, Katherine. A.B., Columbia, 1949, M.A., 1951, Ph.D., 1955; D.F.A. (hon.), Dickinson Coll., 1980. Asst. prof. art history Carleton Coll., Northfield, Minn., 1952-58; asso. prof. Ind. U., Bloomington, 1958-62, prof., 1963-68; prof. art history Stanford U., 1968—, Walter A. Haas prof. art history, 1976—. Author: Rodin's Gates of Hell, 1960, Purposes of Art, 1962, 2d edit., 1968, 3d edit., 1974, 4th edit., 1981, Rodin, 1963, The Partial Figure in Modern Sculpture, From Rodin to 1969, Seymour Lipton, 1970, The Sculpture of Henri Matisse, 1971, Paul Jenkins, 1973, Origins of Modern Sculpture: Pioneers and Premises, 1974, (with John Merryman) Law, Ethics and the Visual Arts, 1979, Modern European Sculpture 1918-1945, 1979, In Rodin's Studio, 1980; editor, contbr.: Rodin Rediscovered, 1981. Served to sgt. maj. AUS, 1945-46; ETO. Fulbright fellow, 1949-50; Guggenheim fellow, 1966-67; Nat. Endowment for Humanities sr. fellow, 1973-74. Mem. Coll. Art Assn. (dir. 1966-70, pres. 1974-76), AAUP, Authors Guild. Home: 10 Peter Coutts Circle Stanford CA 94305

ELSEN, SHELDON HOWARD, lawyer; b. Pitts., May 12, 1928; m. Gerri Sharfman, 1952; children: Susan Rachel, Jonathan Charles. A.B., Princeton U., 1950; A.M., Harvard U., 1952, J.D., 1958. Bar: N.Y. 1959, U.S. Supreme Ct. 1971. Mem. firm Orans, Elsen & Lupert, N.Y.C., 1965—; adj. prof. law Columbia Law Sch., 1969—; chief counsel N.Y. Moreland Act Commn., 1975-76; asst. U.S. atty. So. Dist. N.Y., 1960-64; cons. Pres's. Commn. Law Enforcement Adminstrn. Justice, 1967; mem. faculty Nat. Inst. Trial Advocacy, 1973. Contbr. articles to legal jours. Mem. Am. Law Inst., Assn. Bar City N.Y. (chmn. com. on fed. legislation 1969-72, mem. com. on judiciary 1972-75), Phi Beta Kappa. Home: 50 Fenimore Rd Scarsdale NY 10583 Office: 1 Rockefeller Plaza New York NY 10020

ELSEY, GEORGE MCKEE, former association executive; b. Palo Alto, Calif., Feb. 5, 1918; s. Howard McKee and Ethel May (Daniels) E.; m. Sally Phelps Bradley, Dec. 15, 1951; children: Anne Bradley (Mrs. Roger Kranz), Howard McKee. A.B., Princeton U., 1939; A.M., Harvard U., 1940; L.H.D., Am. Internat. Coll., 1982. Mem. staff White House, 1947-53; with ARC, 1953-61, v.p., 1958-61; with various divs. Pullman Inc., 1961-65, asst. to chmn. and pres., 1966-70; pres. Am. Nat. Red Cross, 1970-82; dir. Security Storage Co., Perpetual Am. Bank F.S.B. Pres. Meridian House Found., Washington, 1961-66, vice chmn., 1967-68, counselor, 1971—; mem. Nat. Archives Adv. Council, 1974-79; trustee George C. Marshall Research Found., 1973—, Brookings Instn., 1971-83, Harry S. Truman Library Inst., 1973—; trustee emeritus Nat. Trust Historic Preservation, 1976—. Served to comdr. USN, 1941-47. Decorated Legion of Merit; Order Brit. Empire; medals from Red Cross socs., Finland, Korea, Greece, Netherlands, W. Ger. and Can.; Recipient Distinguished Pub. Service medal Dept. Def. Mem. Columbia Hist. Soc., AAAS, Nat. Geog. Soc. (trustee 1977—), White House Hist. Assn. (dir. 1979—), Phi Beta Kappa. Presbyterian (ruling elder). Clubs: Princeton (N.Y.); Metropolitan, City Tavern Assn. (Washington). Home: 2201 King Pl NW Washington DC 20007 Office: 17th and D Sts NW Washington DC 20006

ELSILA, DAVID AUGUST, editor; b. Detroit, Feb. 2, 1939; s. Edward J. and Sylvia (Mikkola) E.; m. Kathlyn Deutch, July 17, 1965; children: Mikael, Jamie and Kari (twins). B.A., Eastern Mich. U., 1960, postgrad., 1962. Tchr. pub. schs., Livonia, Mich., 1960-64; editor-in-chief Livonia Observer, 1964-65; dir. publs., editor Am. Tchr., also; Changing Edn., Am. Fedn. Tchrs., Washington, 1965-76; mng. editor UAW Solidarity, UAW, 1976—; editor ofcl. publs. ACLU, Ill., Mich., 1964-67; del. Greater Washington Central Labor Council, AFL-CIO. Co-author: Union Town: A Labor History Guide to Detroit, 1980. Recipient Page 1 award Chgo. Newspaper Guild, 1967, Washington-Balt. Newspaper Guild, 1970, 71, 72, 73, 1st awards in Journalism Internat. Labor Press Assn., 1968, 69, 72, 73, 75, 76, Ednl. Press Assn. Am., 1968, 69, 70, 71, 72, 73, 75, 76, 82, 83. Mem. Washington-Balt. Newspaper Guild (mem. exec. bd. 1970-71), Ednl. Press Assn. Am. (pres. Washington chpt. 1971), Internat. Labor Communications Assn. (v.p. 1983—), ACLU, Phi Delta Kappa. Home: 1411 Three Mile Dr Grosse Pointe Park MI 48230 Office: 8000 E Jefferson Ave Detroit MI 48214

ELSING, WILLIAM TADDES, lawyer; b. Bisbee, Ariz., May 8, 1910; s. Morris J. and Celestine (Marks) E.; m. Ferol Cox, May 29, 1941. Student, Stanford, 1928, U. Calif. at Berkeley, 1929; J.D., U. Ariz., 1933. Bar: Ariz. bar 1933, Calif. bar 1946. Practiced in, Prescott, Ariz., 1933-38, Phoenix, 1938—. Chmn. bd. govs. Ariz. Dept. Mineral Resources, 1969-76. Served with CIC AUS, 1942-45. Mem. Am., Calif., Ariz., Maricopa County bar assns., Soc. Mining Engrs., Am. Inst. Mining, Metall. and Petroleum Engrs., AAAS, Phi Delta Phi. Republican. Presbyn. Office: Suite 1010 34 W Monroe St Phoenix AZ 85003

ELSMAN, JAMES LEONARD, JR., lawyer; b. Kalamazoo, Sept. 10, 1936; s. James Leonard and Dorothy Isabell (Pierce) E.; m. Janice Marie Wilczewski, Aug. 6, 1960; children—Stephanie, James Leonard III. B.A., U. Mich., 1958, J.D., 1962; postgrad., Harvard Div. Sch., 1958-59. Bar: Mich. bar 1963. Clk. Mich. Atty. Gen.'s Office, Lansing, 1961; atty. legal dept. Chrysler Corp., Detroit, 1962-64; founding partner Elsman, Young, O'Rourke, Bruno & Bunn, Birmingham, 1964—. Author: novel The Seekers, 1962; screenplay, 1976, 200 Candles for Whom?, 1973; Contbr.: articles to profl. jours. 200 Candles for Whom?; Composer: 200 Candles for Whom?, 1976, 1974. Mem. Regional Export Expansion Council, 1966-73, Mich. Partners for Alliance for Progress, 1969—; Candidate U.S. Senate, 1966, 76, U.S. Ho. of Reps., 1970. Rockefeller Brothers Found. fellow Harvard Div. Sch., 1969. Mem. Econ. Club Detroit, Council on Fgn. Relations, World Peace Through Law Center, Am. Soc. Internat. Law, Am. Bar Assn. Democrat. Mem. Christian Ch. Clubs: Rotarian., Bloomfield Open Hunt; Presidents (U. Mich.); Circumnavigators. Home: 4811 Burnley Dr Bloomfield Hills MI 48013 Office: 635 Elm St Birmingham MI 48011

ELSNER, LARRY EDWARD, educator; b. Gooding, Idaho, Dec. 12, 1930; s. George Stewart and Thelma (Fulkerson) E.; m. Yoko Yamakawa, June, 1960; 1 dau., Tami Ione. Student, U. Idaho, 1948-51; B.S., Utah State U., 1957; M.F.A. in Sculpture, Columbia U., 1958. Mem. faculty dept. art Utah State U., Logan, 1960—, now prof. Served with USN, 1953-55. Mem. Am. Craftsmen's Council, Utah Designer Craftsmen, Coll. Art Assn. Buddhist. Office: Art Dept Utah State U Logan UT 84322

ELSNER, SIDNEY EDGAR, journalist; b. Cleve., May 30, 1919; s. Sidney Edgar and Charlotte (Sill) E.; m. Jean Helen Leaf, June 8, 1947; children: David M., Lawrence B., Michael C. B.S., Ohio State U., 1941. Sports editor Washington Court House (Ohio) Record-Herald, 1941-42; reporter Springfield (Ohio) Daily News, 1942; copy editor Columbus (Ohio) Citizen, 1942-43; reporter, copy editor, asst. city editor, state editor, day city editor, met. editor, asso. editor/editorial writer Cleve. Plain Dealer, 1943-84; attended City Editors Seminar, Am. Press Inst. at Columbia, 1960. Recipient Best News Reporting award Cleve. Newspaper Guild, 1950, 54. Mem. Workmens Circle, Sigma Delta Chi (pres. Cleve. chpt. 1972-73). Jewish. Clubs: Cleve. City (chmn. forum com. 1967-68, trustee 1980-83. Office: 1801 Superior Ave NE Cleveland OH 44114

ELSON, ALEX, lawyer, legal educator; b. nr. Kiev, Russia, Apr. 17, 1905; came to U.S., 1906, naturalized, 1913; s. Jacob and Rebecca (Brodsky) E.; m. Miriam Almond, July 6, 1933; children: Jacova Silverthorne, Karen O'Neil. Ph.B., U. Chgo., 1925, J.D., 1928. Bar: Ill. 1928. Bill drafter Legislative Reference Bur., Springfield, Ill., 1929; atty. Legal Aid Bur., Chgo., 1929-34; asso. atty. Tolman, Chandler & Dickinson, 1934-38; regional atty. Wage-Hour Div., Chgo., 1938-41; regional atty., asst. gen. counsel OPA, 1941-45; lectr. U. Chgo., intermittently 1933-48, Yale Law Sch., 1946, seminar-labor relations Northwestern U. Sch. Law, 1961-65; seminar constl. law Ariz U., 1971. Author: Civil Practice Forms, 1934; co-author: Civil Practice Forms, Illinois-Federal, 1952, rev., 1965; contbr.: articles to profl. jours., also to Ency. Brit. Former pub. mem. Regional War Labor Bd.; former chmn. Chgo. Rent Commn.; pres. Fund for Justice, 1972-76; vice chmn. Ill. div. ACLU; former vice chmn. Ill. Commn. on Children; former chmn. Bd. Mental Health Commrs. State Ill., 1960-69; v.p. Law in Am. Soc. Found.; cons. Ford Found., 1963-68; bd. dirs. Hull House Assn., 1955-65. Fellow Am. Bar Found.; mem. ABA, Ill. Bar Assn.,

Chgo. Bar Assn. (bd. mgrs.), Am. Law Inst., Nat. Acad. Arbitrators (v.p. 1983—), Inst. Psychoanalysis (pres. 1976-79). Home: 5642 Dorchester Ave Chicago IL 60637 Office: 55 E Monroe St Chicago IL 60603

ELSON, CHARLES, educator, stage designer; b. Chgo., Sept. 5, 1909; s. Jacob and Rebecca (Brodsky) E.; m. Diana Rivers, Aug. 12, 1938; 1 dau., Alexandra. Student, Hull House Little Theatre, Chgo., 1914-32, U. Ill., 1929-30; Ph.B., U. Chgo., 1932; D.F.A., Yale, 1935. Instr. U. Iowa, art dir., 1935-36; asso. prof. U. Okla., art. dir. Univ. theatre, 1937-43; civilian design engr. tng. aid USNR, 1943-45; prof. Hunter Coll., dir. Theatre Workshop, 1948-69, prof. emeritus, 1974—; vis. lectr. stage design, dept. drama Yale, 1950-51; vis. critic stage lighting Yale Sch. Drama, 1964-67, vis. prof. design, 1967-69; doctoral faculty CUNY, now prof. emeritus; Fulbright lectr., India, 1959-60; Mem. design com. Internat. Theater Inst. U.S.A.; western theater del. 3d Asian Symposium Arts, Seoul, Korea, 1974; U.S. Dept. State specalist S.E. Asia, 1974. Art dir., stage lighting dir., WPA Fed. Theatre Project, Los Angeles, 1936-37; art dir., Ogunquit (Maine) Summer Theatre, 1939-41, 45; design asst. Broadway plays, operas, 1945-47; stage designer, 1947—; first N.Y. prodn. Twelfth Night; designed, lighted: settings for plays, operas, ballets including Kiss Me Kate, London, Music In The Air, Deep Blue Sea, Lohengrin, The Flying Dutchman, His and Hers, Don Giovanni, Norma, Champagne Complex, The Lovers, Compulsion, Blue Denim, Troilus and Cressida, Henry IV, Richard II, Wildcat, Photo Finish, Dialogues of the Carmelites; exhbns., City Center Gallery, U. Conn., 1955—; editor: Stage Design Throughout the World, Brussels), vol. 1, 1956, vol. 2, 1964. Bd. dirs. North Castle Citizens Council, North Castle Hist. Soc.; chmn. bd. dirs. The Family; chmn. North Castle Bicentennial July 4th Commn.; pres. bd. trustees North Castle Pub. Library. Recipient Nat. award for outstanding contbn. U.S. Inst. Theatre Design and Tech., 1981. Fellow Internat. Inst. Arts and Letters; mem. United Scenic Artists Am. Clubs: Century Assn., Yale. Am. Home: 1 Faraway Ln Armonk Village NY 10504

ELSON, EDWARD ELLIOTT, distribution/retail executive; b. Bklyn., Mar. 8, 1934; s. Harry and Esther (Cohn); m. Suzanne Goodman, Aug. 24, 1957; children: Charles Myer, Louis Goodman, Harry Elson II. Grad., Phillips Acad., 1952; B.A. with honors in Polit. Sci, U. Va., 1956; J.D., Emory U., 1959. With Atlanta News Agy., Inc., 1959—, pres., 1961-82, chmn., 1982—; pres. Airport News Corp., Atlanta, 1961—, Elson's, Atlanta, Atlantic, 1963-82; chmn. Elson's, Atlanta, 1963-82; mem. publ. com. Commentary Mag., 1967—, chmn., 1975-80; chmn. Gordon County Bank, 1979-83; dir. Citizens and So. Ga. Corp., 1978—, W. H. Smith and Son, (USA) Holdings, Inc. Bd. govs. Am. Jewish Com., 1966—, trustee, 1977—, v.p., 1982-84, treas., 1984; bd. dirs. So. Regional Council, 1966—; mem. Presdl. Commn. on Obscenity and Pornography, 1967-71; mem. pres.'s council Brandeis U., 1967; bd. visitors U. Va., 1984—; mem. City of Atlanta Fund Appeals Rev. Bd., 1971-73; v.p. Muscular Dystrophy Assn. Am., 1972-73; mem. corp. 1973-74; mem. Atlanta-Fulton County Recreation Authority, 1973-80, vice chmn., 1975-80; bd. visitors Clark Coll., 1973—, chmn., 1982—; mem. alumni council Phillips Acad., Andover, Mass., 1973-76; mem. pres.'s council Agnes Scott Coll., 1973—, chmn., 1975—; trustee Talladega Coll., 1973—, U. Mid-Am., 1979-82; fellow Brandeis U., 1979—; chmn. Ga. Adv. Com. to U.S. Commn. Civil Rights, 1974-82; mem. Ga. Adv. Commn. Civil Rights, 1974—; bd. dirs. Reading Is Fundamental, 1975—, Atlanta Urban League, 1978-79; chmn. adv. bd. Southeastern Center for Contemporary Art, 1976—; mem. Nat. Adv. Commn. Pub. Edn. and Desegregation, 1976-77; chmn. bd. Nat. Pub. Radio, 1977-80; chmn. So. Regional Adv. Com. to U.S. Commn. Civil Rights, 1978; mem. presdl. del. returning Crown of St. Stephen to Hungary, 1978. Recipient Robert B. Downs award Grad. Sch. Library Sci., U. Ill., 1971; Human Relations award Am. Jewish Com., 1975; Nat. Pub. Radio's Disting. Service award, 1979; Inst. Human Relations award Inst. Human Relations award, 1982. Mem. Ga. Bar Assn., Atlantic Coast Ind. Distbrs. Assn. (dir. 1963-76), L.Q.C., Lamar Soc. (v.p. 1973-74, chmn. bd. 1974—), Jewish Publ. Soc. (trustee 1974-82), Am. Jewish Hist. Soc. (exec. com. 1980—, v.p. 1982—), U. Va. Alumni Assn. (bd. mgrs. 1982-84). Democrat. Jewish. Clubs: Commerce, Standard Town and Country (Atlanta); Farmington Country (Charlottesville, Va.). Home: 65 Valley Rd NW Atlanta GA 30305 Office: 4070 Shirley Dr SW Atlanta GA 30336

ELSON, JOHN, legal educator; b. 1943. A.B., Harvard U., 1964, J.D., 1967; M.A., U. Chgo., 1968. Bar: Ill. 1967. Staff lawyer Mandel Legal Aid Clinic, U. Chgo., 1971-75; assoc. prof. Northwestern U. Law Sch., Chgo., 1976-79, prof., 1979—. Office: Northwestern U Law Sch 357 E Chicago Ave Chicago IL 60611

ELSON, JOHN ALBERT, geology educator; b. Kiating, China, Mar. 2, 1923; s. Albert Joseph and Evelyn Amelia (Hockey) E.; m. Jeanne Bridgman Hickey, Jan. 4, 1957,; children—Sarah Bridgman, Rebecca Anne Wood. B.Sc., U. Western Ont., 1945; M.Sc., McMaster U., 1947; Ph.D., Yale, 1956. Lectr. McMaster U., Hamilton, Ont., Can., 1945-46; geologist Geol. Survey Can., Ottawa, Ont., 1946-56; faculty McGill U., Montreal, Que., Can., 1956—, prof., 1968—, chmn. dept. geol. scis., 1974-75; Cons. geologist, 1956-67. Fellow Geol. Soc. Am., Geol. Assn. Can.; mem. AAAS, Am. Soc. Photogrammetry, Glaciological Soc., Am. Quaternary Assn., NRC Can. (asso. com. for quaternary research 1971-74), Can. Quaternary Assn., Sigma Xi. Home: 467 Clarke Ave Montreal PQ H3y 3c5 Canada

ELSTER, SAMUEL KASE, medical educator, college dean, physician; b. N.Y.C., Dec. 6, 1922; s. Morris and Rebecca (Post) E.; m. Maxine Lefkowitz, June 17, 1945; children: Charles, Amy. B.S., CCNY, 1942; M.D., NYU, 1946. Diplomate: Am. Bd. Internal Medicine. Intern Mt. Sinai Hosp., 1946-47, resident, 1950-52; asst. in pathology NYU Sch. Medicine, N.Y.C., 1947-48; instr. medicine Columbia U. Coll. Physicians and Surgeons, N.Y.C., 1959-66; clin. prof. medicine Mount Sinai Sch. Medicine, CUNY, N.Y.C., 1974—; dean Page and William Black Postgrad. Sch., Mount Sinai Sch. Medicine, CUNY, N.Y.C., 1976—, dean continuous edn., 1981—. Contbr. articles in field to profl. jours. Mem., pres. bd. edn., Tenafly, N.J., 1968-73. Served to capt., M.C. U.S. Army; 1948-50. Fellow Am. Coll. Cardiology, ACP, N.Y. Acad. Medicine; Mem. Am. Heart Assn. (mem. council in clin. cardiology), Assn. Am. Med. Colls. Democrat. Jewish. Office: Page and William Black Postgrad Sch Mount Sinai Sch Medicine 1 Gustav Levy Pl New York NY 10029

ELSTON, LLOYD WARREN, confectionery company executive; b. Lewistown, Pa., May 5, 1926; s. Clair Mortimer and Irene (Brickwood) E.; m. Dorothea Kazanjian, June 22, 1949; children: Calvin Warren, Lynn Butler, Richard Lloyd. B.A. in Indsl. Administrn., Yale, 1949; LL.D., Babson Coll., 1973. Asst. engring. dept. Collins Co., Collinsville, Conn., 1949-50; with Peter Paul Cadbury, Inc., 1950—, exec. v.p., 1962-65, pres., 1966—, chief exec. officer, 1971-82, sr. v.p. parent co. Cadbury Schweppes, Inc., 1982—; dir. Reymond Baking Co., Waterbury, Raymond Industries, Inc., Middletown, Conn. Trustee Naugatuck YMCA; treas., trustee Calvin K. Kazanjian Econs. Found. Served with USNR, 1944-46. Mem. Naugatuck C. of C., Nat. Confectioners Assn. (chmn. 1976—). Club: Masons. Home: Cleft Rock Ln Woodbridge CT 06525 Office: Cadbury Schweppes Inc 1200 High Ridge Park Stamford CT 06905

ELTERICH, JOACHIM GUSTAV, agricultural economics educator; b. Dresden, Germany, May 22, 1930; came to U.S., 1958, naturalized, 1973; m. Martha Munson Slagel, June 17, 1961; children: Stafan, Karin, Christian. Diploma in sci. agr., Rheinr-Friedr Wilhelms U., 1956; M.S. in Agrl. Econs., U. Ky., 1960, Ph.D., Mich. State U., 1964. Research asst. dept. agrl. econs. U. Ky., Lexington, 1958-60, Mich. State U., Lansing, 1960-64; research assoc. Inst. for Agrl. Econs. U. Bonn, W.Ger., 1964-67; prof. agrl. econs. U. Del., Newark, 1967—; cons. Ford Found., 1976, Minimum Wage Commn., 1980-81, AID, 1976—; del. Dept. Labor, 1980-83; vis. prof. U. Kiel, W.Ger., 1974. Contbr. numerous articles to profl. jours.; mem. editorial bd.: N.E. Jour. Agrl. Econs., 1967-83. Mem. Am. Agrl. Econs. Assn., Am. Econs. Assn., N.E. Agrl. Econs. Council, Internat. Assn. Agrl. Economists, Sigma Xi, Gamma Sigma Delta, Phi Kappa Phi. Episcopalian. Home: 145 Timberline Dr Newark DE 19711 Office: Dept Agrl Econs U Del Newark DE 19711

ELTING, EVERETT E., advertising agency executive; b. N.Y.C., Feb. 14, 1936; emigrated to Can., 1976, naturalized, 1979; s. Everett Ely and Louise E.; m. Judith Lass, June 19, 1960; children—Lynn, Elizabeth. B.A., Trinity Coll., Hartford, Conn., 1958. Account mgr. Grey Advt., Inc., N.Y.C., 1964-67; group product mgr. Chesebrough-Ponds, Inc., N.Y.C., 1968-72; v.p. mktg. Norton Simon Communications, Inc., N.Y.C., 1972-74; mng. dir. Sara, S.A.R.L., Lisbon, Portugal, 1975; also dir.; exec. v.p., gen. mgr., chief operating officer Grey Advt. Ltd., Toronto, Ont., Can., 1976-80, pres., chief operating officer, dir., 1980—; dir. Grey Ronalds Smith Ltd. Bd. dirs. Children's Aid Soc. Met. Toronto, Children's Aid Soc. Met. Toronto Found. Served to lt. USAF, 1958-62. Home: 62 Wellesley St W Toronto ON M5S 2X3 Canada Office: 1075 Bay St Toronto ON M5S 2B1 Canada

ELTON, ROBERT MOFFAT, army officer; b. Cleve., Sept. 13, 1932; s. Frederick Moffat and Ruth Aldrich E.; m. Marilyn Fairchild, Dec. 23, 1954; children: Carin Leigh, Richard Moffat. B.S., U.S. Mil. Acad., 1954; M.S., U. Va., 1963. Commd. 2d lt. U.S. Army, 1954, advanced through grades to lt. gen.; asst. prof. physics U.S. Mil. Acad., West Point, N.Y., 1964-67; comdr., staff officer 101st Airborne Div., Vietnam, 1967-68, 82d Ajrborne Div., 1971-74; chief of staff, asst. div. comdr. 3d Infantry Div., 1975-78; dir. officer personnel mgmt. directorate Mil. Personnel Center, 1978-79, comdr., 1980-81; comdg. gen. 9th Inf. Div., Ft. Lewis, Wash., 1981-83; dep. chief of staff for personnel Dept. Army, Washington, 1983—. Decorated Bronze Star, Air medal (7). Mem. Assn. U.S. Army, Assn. Grads. U.S. Mil. Acad., Am. Amateur Racquetball Assn. Office: Dep Chief of Staff for Personnel Dept Army Washington DC 20310

ELVERUM, HARVARD DEA, manufacturing company executive; b. Howard Lake, Minn., Jan. 20, 1925; s. Horace Hagen and Zelda Marie E.; m. Joan Anita Tjomsland, Jan. 25, 1947; children: Jacklyn, Dana, Anne. B.B.A., U. Minn., 1949. Vice-pres. ops. Residential div. Honeywell, Mpls., 1964-70, v.p., gen. mgr. Test Instruments div., Denver, 1970-72; pres. Honeywell Europe, Brussels, 1972-77; group v.p. Components Group Honeywell, Mpls., 1977-83, exec. v.p. Control Products, 1983—. Served with USAF, 1943-46. Clubs: Minikahda, Masons, Shriners. Home: 6101 Waterford Ct Edina MN 55436 Office: Honeywell Plaza Minneapolis MN 55408

EL-WAKIL, MOHAMED, nuclear engineering educator; b. Alexandria, Egypt, Mar. 9, 1921; came to U.S., 1946, naturalized, 1959; s. Mohamed and Tafida El-W.; m. Tatiana Pronin, Oct. 29, 1950 (div. 1975); children: Fred W., Leila J.; m. Betty Wass, June 1980. B.S., Cairo U., 1943; M.S., U. Wis., 1947, Ph.D., 1949. Lectr. U. Alexandria, 1950-52; research asso. U. Wis.-Madison, 1954-55, asst. prof., 1955-57, asso. prof., 1957-61, prof. mech. and nuclear engring., 1961—; asst. prof. U. Minn., 1954-55. Author: Nuclear Power Engineering, 1962, Nuclear Heat Transport, 1971, Japanese transl., 1972, Nuclear Energy Conversion, 1971, Japanese transl., 1977; also articles. Recipient award for meritorious paper ASME, 1952; Western Electric award for excellence in instrn. of engrs. Am. Soc. Engring. Edn., 1969; Disting. Teaching award nuclear engring. div., 1971; Benjamin Smith Reynolds award U. Wis., 1970; Fulbright scholar, 1966, 78. Fellow Am. Nuclear Soc. (Arthur Holly Compton award 1979); mem. ASME, Am. Soc. for Engring. Edn., Assn. Egyptian-Am. Scholars (pres. 1975—), Sigma Xi, Tau Beta Pi, Pi Tau Sigma. Club: Rotary. Home: 1010 Edgehill Dr Madison WI 53705

ELWELL, HARRY HOWARD, JR., educator; b. El Dorado, Kans., July 1, 1921; s. Harry Howard and Margaret Leona (Rutan) E.; m. Betty Beverly Stayton, May 24, 1947 (div. Nov. 1968); children: Beverly Ann, Scott Merriman, James Weldon.; m. Caroline Wilson Tucker, Nov. 24, 1972 (div. Apr. 6, 1982). B.B.A., U. Tex., Austin, 1947, M.B.A., 1949; Ph.D., U. Ill., Urbana, 1960. FCC licensed amateur radio operator, 1949. Instr. mgmt. U. Tex., 1946-50; asst. prof., head dept. mgmt. U. Wichita, Kans., 1956-57; instr. mktg. U. Ill., 1957-60; asso. prof. mktg. and mgmt. Fla. State U., 1960-67; prof. Tex. Tech. Coll., 1967-69, Memphis State U., 1969—, dir. grad. studies, 1972-75; cons. in field. Sec.-treas. Portwood Motor Co. Inc., Brownfield, Tex., 1952-56; office mgr. McAdoo Chevrolet Co., Seagraves, Tex., 1950-52; mem. staff CAP Aerospace Edn. Workshops Fla. A. and M. U., 1966-67; sr. grad. asst. Dale Carnegie Courses Brickell Inst. Leadership Tng., Memphis, 1971-72; participant numerous confs., meetings. Author: F.S. U. Executive Decision Game I, 1964, (with Patricia Walton Custead) Computer Users Reference Ency. With a Glossary of Terminology, 1967, Reference Manual For the 5-D Executive Decision Game, 1970, Multivariate Analysis for Business Problems; contbg. author: Emergency Resources Management Plan, 1965; Staff writer, War Coll of Air U., 1961-63; editor: Store Arrangement and Display, 1961; Contbr. articles to revs. and profl. jours. Chmn. Gaines County Democratic Del. Tex. State Conv., 1952. Served with USAAF, 1942-45; lt. col. Res. ret. Council for Instrn. grantee, 1964, 66; Research Council grantee, 1965, 65-66, 66-67; Tex. Bus. Adminstrn. Research grantee, 1967-68; Memphis State U. Coll. Bus. Adminstrn. grantee, 1969-70, 70; Memphis State U. Faculty grantee, 1972, 76-77. Mem. Am., So. mktg. assns., Am. Inst. Decision Scis., Nat. Assn. Purchasing Agts., Beta Gamma Sigma, Sigma Iota Epsilon, Alpha Iota Delta. Episcopalian (vestryman 1970-71, licensed lay reader 1970—). Clubs: Mason (K.T., 32 deg.), Rotarian (editor Rota Vista 1951-52). Established math. stages of product life cycle, 1967; discovered statis. test for probability calibration of linear discriminent function boundary, 1970. Home: 244 Conlee Pl Memphis TN 38111

ELWELL, RICHARD RHEA, editor; b. Waterloo, Iowa, Feb. 6, 1926; s. Harold Rhea and Edith Rebecca (Foster) E.; m. Susan Elizabeth Black, Dec. 5, 1964; children: Martin, Wimburn; children by previous marriage: David Rhea, John Joseph, Peter Geofferey, Robert Paul. Student, Drake U., 1946-48, Stanford U., 1949-50. Reporter, San Francisco News, 1950-52; fin. editor San Francisco Daily Comml. News, 1952-55; West Coast editor McGraw-Hill Petroleum Publs., Los Angeles, 1955-57; writer public affairs Ramo-Wooldridge Corp., Los Angeles, 1957-61; evaluator Peace Corps, Washington, 1961-65, dir., Niger, 1966-68; editor OEO, Washington, 1965-66; chief Washington office U.S. Research and Devel., 1969-71; info. officer U.S. Office Edn., Washington, 1971-79; editor Am. Edn. mag. Dept. Edn., 1979-81; info. officer U.S. Dept. Edn., 1981—. Served with U.S. Army, 1943-46. Decorated Purple Heart. Mem. Am. Fedn. Govt. Employees. Democrat. Home: 7103 Fulton St Chevy Chase MD 20015 Office: 400 Maryland Ave Washington DC 20202

ELWORTHY, ROBERT WILLIAM, French horn player; b. Elmhurst, Ill., May 30, 1929; s. Robert William and Florence Marie (Hediger) E.; m. Maxine Sutherland, Sept. 6, 1959; children: Karen Ann, Brian Robert. Mus.B., Northwestern U., 1951; Mus.M., Eastman Sch. Music, 1952. Assoc. prof. horn Oberlin (Ohio) Conservatory, 1964-65; prof. music Ind. U., Bloomington, 1977—; mem. faculty Loyola U., New Orleans, 1955-60, Carleton Coll., Northfield, Minn., 1960-61, U. Minn., Mpls., 1970-77, U. Wis., Eau Claire, 1972-73. Prin. horn, Norfolk (Va.) Symphony, 1952-54, New Orleans Symphony and Opera, 1955-60, Mpls. Symphony Orch., 1960-64, St. Paul Chamber Orch., N.C. Symphony, 1961, Nat. Symphony Mex.; prin. horn, Minn. Orch., Mpls., 1965-77, orchestral recs. on Mercury and Vox; prin. horn, mem. faculty, Brevard (N.C.) Music Center, summers 1954-59, Santa Fe Opera, summers 1960—. Served with U.S. Army, 1952-54. Mem. Internat. Horn Soc., Phi Mu Alpha Sinfonia, Phi Eta Sigma, Pi Kappa Lambda. Home: 2962 Ramble Rd W Bloomington IN 47401 Office: Sch Music Ind U Bloomington IN 47401

ELY, CHARLES AUBREY, anatomist; b. Washington, Pa., Dec. 11, 1913; s. Charles A. and Lida M. (Iams) E. A.B., Washington (Pa.) and Jefferson Coll., 1936; M.S., U. Hawaii, 1940; Ph.D., U. Wis., 1948. Mem. faculty Columbia U. Coll. Physicians and Surgeons, 1948—, prof. anatomy, 1975—. Grantee Damon Runyon Fund, NIH, Am. Cancer Soc. Mem. Am. Physiol. Soc., Endocrine Soc., Am. Assn. Cancer Research, Soc. Study Exptl. Biology and Medicine, Am. Assn. Anatomists, AAAS, N.Y. Acad. Sci., Harvey Soc., Sigma Xi. Office: 630 W 168th St New York NY 10032

ELY, JOHN HART, lawyer, university dean; b. N.Y.C., Dec. 3, 1938; s. John H. and Martha Foster (Coyle) E.; children: John Duff, Robert Allan Duff. A.B. summa cum laude, Princeton U., 1960; LL.B. magna cum laude, Yale U., 1963; M.A. (hon.), 1971, Harvard U., 1973. Bar: D.C. 1965, Calif. 1967. Atty. Warren Commn., 1964; law clk. to Chief Justice Warren, 1964-65; Fulbright scholar London Sch. Econs., 1965-66; atty. Defenders, Inc., San Diego, 1966-68; asso. prof., then prof. law Yale U. Law Sch., 1968-73; mem. faculty Harvard U. Law Sch., 1973-1982, Ralph S. Tyler, Jr. prof. constl. law, 1981-1982; Richard E. Lang prof. law Stanford U. Law Sch., Calif., 1982—, dean, 1982—; gen. counsel U.S. Dept. Transp., 1975-76. Author: Democracy and Distrust, 1980. Served with USAR, 1963-69. Fellow Woodrow Wilson Internat. Center scholars (1978-79), Am. Acad. Arts and Scis. Office: Stanford U Law Sch Stanford CA 94305

ELY, JOSEPH BUELL, II, corporate executive; b. Boston, Nov. 5, 1938; s. Richard and Louise (Ludwick) E.; m. Barbara Kurzina, Aug. 5, 1967; children: Joseph Buell, III, Christina, Peter Douglas, Sarah Ann. B.S., Boston U., 1965, Ph.D., 1981. Dir. Amoskeag Co., Boston, 1977—, pres., chief exec. officer, 1978—; dir. Fieldcrest Mills, Inc., Eden, N.C., 1976—, chmn. bd., 1982—; chmn., chief exec. officer, also dir. Fanny Farmer Candy Shops, Inc., Bedford, Mass., 1980-84, also dir.; chmn., chief exec. officer Bangor & Aroostook R.R. Co., Bangor, Maine, Westville Homes corp., 1974—, also dir. Office: Amoskeag Co Suite 4500 Prudential Center Boston MA 02199

ELY, PAUL C., JR., electronics company executive; b. McKeesport, Pa., Feb. 18, 1932; s. Paul C. and Jean C. E.; m. Barbara Sheiry, Apr. 3, 1953; children: Paul C., Glenn E. B.S. in Engring. Physics, Lehigh U., 1953; M.S. in Elec. Engring, Stanford U., 1964. Research and devel. engr. Sperry Rand Corp., Great Neck, N.Y. and Clearwater, Fla., 1953-62; research and devel. sect. mgr., engring. mgr. microwave div. Hewlett-Packard Co., Palo Alto, Calif., 1962-73, gen. mgr. data systems div., 1973-74, gen. mgr. computer group, 1974-76, v.p., 1976-80, exec. v.p., 1980—. Chmn. Cupertino United Fund, 1976, Bay Area Sci. Fair, 1969; mem. Calif. Econ. Devel. Commn., 1976. Mem. IEEE. Office: 3000 Hanover St Palo Alto CA 94303

ELY, THOMAS SHARPLESS, physician; b. Phila., Sept. 26, 1924; s. Frederic Gilbert and Ruthanna (Sharpless) E.; m. Carol Elsa Kruse, June 23, 1945; children—John, Carolyn, Elizabeth (Mrs. George L. O'Brien), Richard, Douglas. M.D., Georgetown U., 1948; M.S. in Occupational Medicine, U. Rochester, 1963. Diplomate: Am. Bd. Preventive Medicine. Intern U.S. Naval Hosp., Bethesda, Md., 1948-49; asst. chief med. br. AEC, Washington, 1956-58, chief health protection br., 1958-61; resident, U. Rochester, 1961-63; with health, safety and human factors lab. Eastman Kodak Co., Rochester, N.Y., 1963—, supr. environ. health services, 1969-72, asst. dir., 1972—; clin. asst. prof. preventive medicine and community health U. Rochester Med. Sch., 1966-83. Assoc. editor: Jour. Occupational Medicine, 1963-76; Contbr. articles to profl. jours. Mem. Genesee Region Health Planning Council, 1971-74. Served to comdr. M.C. USNR, 1943-46, 48-56. Mem. Am. Occupational Med. Assn. (pres. 1973-74), Am. Acad. Occupational Medicine. Home: 464 Smith Rd Pittsford NY 14534 Office: Eastman Kodak Co Rochester NY 14650

ELY, WALTER RALEIGH, JR., judge; b. Baird, Tex., June 24, 1913; s. Walter Raleigh and Lucy Ann (McCoy) E.; m. Billie Bernice Gambill, Oct. 27, 1937; 1 son, William Raleigh; m. 2d, Ruby Ilene Walters, Sept. 18, 1945; 1945. A.B., U. Tex., 1935, LL.B., 1935; LL.M., U. So. Calif., 1949, LL.D., 1973. Bar: Tex. bar 1935, Calif. bar 1945. Gen. practice, Abilene, Tex., 1935-39, asst. atty. gen., Tex., 1939-40; judge U.S. Ct. Appeals, 9th Circuit, 1964—; Mem. exec. com. Calif. Conf. State Bar Dels., 1957-60; spl. counsel U.S. Senate, 1955. Contbr. articles to profl. jours. Bd. dirs. Los Angeles County Bar Found., Travel Program for Fgn. Diplomats. Served with USMCR, 1941-44. Decorated Silver Star medal. Fellow Am. Coll. Trial Lawyers; mem. Am., Tex. bar founds., ABA (ho. of dels. 1961-64), Los Angeles County Bar Assn. (pres. 1962), Marine Corps Res. Officers Assn. (hon. life), VFW, Order of Coif, Phi Delta Phi, Delta Kappa Epsilon. Methodist. Clubs: Mason (Shriner, K.T.), Los Angeles, Athletic, Chancery (Los Angeles); Lakeside Golf of Hollywood; Navy Golf Course (Los Alamitos, Calif.). Office: 1621 US Courthouse 312 N Spring St Los Angeles CA 90012

ELYN, MARK, opera singer, educator; b. Seattle, Feb. 4, 1932; s. Isadore and Goldie E.; m. Jaclyn Rendall. Student, U. Wash., 1948-51, Seattle U., 1951-52; student of Robert Weede. Debut, N.Y.C. Opera, 1956; leading roles, San Francisco Opera, NBC Opera, Phila. Lyric Opera; leading bass, Cologne, Munich, Hamburg, Stuttgart, Vienna, Monte Carlo, Geneva, Barcelona; roles include: Don Giovanni, Sarastro in The Magic Flute, Philip II in Don Carlo, Figaro in The Marriage of Figaro; prof. music, U. Ill., Urbana, 1977—. Mem. Am. Guild Mus. Artists, Deutsche Buehnengenossenschaft, Nat. Assn. Tchrs. of Singing. Home: 2305 Burlison Dr Urbana IL 61801 Office: 207 Smith Hall Univ Ill Urbana IL 61801

ELZINGA, DONALD JACK, industrial engineering researcher, educator; b. Coupeville, Wash., Jan. 16, 1939; s. Martin Jay and Phyllis Margaret (Dickson) E.; m. Marley Ann Plomer, July 18, 1962 (div. 1981); children; Erik, Bruce, Mark; m. Virginia Collins, Aug. 14, 1981. B.E. in Chem. Engring., U. Wash., 1960, M.S., Northwestern U., 1965, Ph.D., 1968. Vol. Peace Corps, Colombia, 1961-63; asst. prof. chem. enging. Johns Hopkins U., Balt., 1967-68, asst. prof. ops. research, 1972-73, assoc. prof., 1973-79, research scientist, 1978-79; prof. indsl. and system engring., chmn. dept. indsl. and system engring.

U. Fla., Gainesville, 1979—; cons. in field. Standard Oil Co. fellow, 1965-67. Mem. Ops. Research Soc. Am., Math Programming Soc., Inst. Indsl. Engrs. (regional pres. 1982-83), Sigma Xi, Tau Beta Pi. Home: 1819 SW 81st St Gainesville FL 32607 Office: Dept Indsl and System Engring 303 Weil Hall Gainesville FL 32611

EMANUEL, HERBERT LEON, former air force officer, association executive; b. Pittsfield, Mass., June 17, 1930; s. Leon and Moira (Haskins) E.; m. Barbara Ann Urbanek, July 4, 1953. B.A., U. Mass., 1952; M.B.A., George Washington U., 1963; postgrad., Armed Forces Staff Coll., Indsl. Coll. Armed Forces. Commd. 2nd lt. U.S. Air Force, 1952, advanced through grades to maj. gen., 1979—; cadet activities officer, spl. asst. to commandant of cadets U.S. Air Force Acad., Colo., 1958-62; personnel officer, personnel plans Hdqrs. PACAF, 1971-72, dir. personnel plans, 1973-76; vice comdr. Air Force Personnel Center, 1976-79; dir. personnel programs Hdqrs. USAF, Washington, 1979-81, asst. dep. chief of staff, manpower and personnel, 1981; commandant Air Force Inst. Tech., Def. Inst. Security, until 1983; ret., 1983; v.p. personnel United Services Automobile Assn., San Antonio, 1983—. Active Boy Scouts Am., 1940-45. Decorated Legion of Merit with oak leaf cluster, Bronze Star, D.S.M., Air Force Commendation medal with oak leaf cluster, Meritorious Service medal, Army Commendation medal. Mem. Air Force Assn., Kappa Sigma.

EMANUEL, IRVIN, medical administrator, educator; b. Balt., Oct. 9, 1926; s. David and Dora (Hollander) E.; m. Patricia Mae Tharp, June 18, 1960; children—Gina Marie, Melissa Pauline. B.S., Rutgers U., 1951; M.A., U. Ariz., 1956; M.D., U. Rochester, 1960; M.S., U. Wash., 1966. Asst. prof. anthropology, asst. dir. U.S. Air Force anthropology project Antioch Coll., Yellow Springs, Ohio, 1953-55; anthropologist Aerospace Med. Lab., Dayton, Ohio, 1955-56, cons., 1956-60; intern Cleve. Met. Gen. Hosp., 1960-61; resident U. Wash., Seattle, 1961-62; sr. fellow depts. preventive medicine and pediatrics, 1962-66, asst. prof. depts. epidemiology, internat. health and pediatrics, 1966-70, assoc. prof., 1970-74, prof. epidemiology and pediatrics, 1974—, dir., 1973—; guest investigator U.S. Naval Med. Research Unit 2, Taipei, Taiwan, 1964-66; mem. Harvard Peabody Mus. Solomon Islands Expdn., 1966; Bd. dirs. Am. Assn. U. Affiliated Programs for Developmentally Disabled, 1977-80. Contbr. articles on phys. anthropology, pediatrics and epidemiology to profl. jours. Served with USNR, 1945-46. Recipient award Spl. Act Service Air Research Devel. Command USAF, 1961; Nat. Inst. Child Health and Human Devel. research career devel. awardee, 1966-71. Mem. Am. Pub. Health Assn., Soc. Epidemiol. Research, Am. Assn. Mental Deficiency, Internat. Epidemiol. Assn., Teratology Soc., Am. Epidemiol. Soc., Phi Beta Kappa. Home: 4230 137th Ave NE Bellevue WA 98005 Office: Child Devel and Mental Retardation Center WJ-10 U Wash Seattle WA 98195

EMANUELSON, JAMES ROBERT, insurance company executive; b. Hammond, Ind., Sept. 12, 1931; s. Clarence Harry and Ethel Janet (Anderson) E.; m. Dolores Patricia Fordyce, Aug. 10, 1957; children: James Robert, John Thomas, Karen Lynn. B.S., Denison U., 1953. With Midland Mut. Life Ins. Co., Columbus, Ohio, 1953-67, mgr. gen. accounting, 1957-62, dir. cost accounting, 1962-67; with Columbus Mut. Life Ins. Co., 1967—, comptroller, 1969—, apptd. v.p., 1970-76, v.p., elected officer, 1976—. Mem. Ins. Accounting and Statis. Assn. (chpt. pres. 1966-67), Life Office Mgmt. Assn. (mem. intercompany fin. rev. com. 1972-82, chmn. com. 1978-82, mem. fin. planning and control council 1978—, cost acctg. com. 1982—), Sigma Chi. Republican. Home: 4530 Reed Rd Columbus OH 43220 Office: 303 E Broad St Columbus OH 43216

EMBERSON, RICHARD MAURY, physicist, consultant; b. Columbia, Mo., Apr. 2, 1914; s. Richard Huff and Lulu (Guthrie) E.; m. Virginia Nicoll, Aug. 23, 1947; children: Cynthia Emberson Irvine, Richard M., Margaret Ann, Heather V. A.B., U. Mo., 1931, M.A., 1932, Ph.D., 1936. Bemis fellow Harvard Coll. Obs., 1936-38; instr. U. Pitts., 1939-40; staff Radiation Lab. M.I.T., 1941-46; staff Naval Research Lab., Washington, 1946, Research and Devel. Bd. Dept. Def., 1947-51; asst. to pres., asst. sec. Asso. Univ. Inc., N.Y.C., 1951-62; staff dir. tech. activities IEEE, N.Y.C., 1963-77, gen. mgr., exec. dir., 1977-79; cons., 1980—. Contbr. articles to profl. jours. Fellow Am. Phys. Soc., IEEE; mem. Am. Assn. Physics Tchrs., Am. Astronomy Soc., N.Y. Acad. Sci., AAAS, Sigma Xi. Home: 3588 Spring Blvd Eugene OR 97405

EMBLETON, TONY FREDERICK WALLACE, Canadian government official; b. Hornchurch, Essex, Eng., Oct. 1, 1929; emigrated to Can., 1952; s. Frederick William Howard and Lucy Violet Muriel (Wallace) E.; m. Eileen Loraine Blackall, Nov. 14, 1953; 1 dau., Sheila. B.Sc. with honours, U. London, 1950, Ph.D. in Physics, 1952, D.Sc., 1964. Postdoctoral fellow NRC, Ottawa, Ont., Can., 1952-53, asst. research officer, 1954-57, asso. research officer, 1957-62, sr. research officer, 1962-74, prin. research officer, 1974—; vis. lectr. U. Ottawa, 1959-69, Mass. Inst. Tech., 1964, 67, 72; John Wiley Jones award lectr. Rochester Inst. Tech., 1976; adj. prof. Carleton U., 1977—. Contbr. articles to profl. jours. Mem. Rockcliffe Park Pub. Sch. Bd., 1966-69; Bd. dirs. Youth Sci. Found., 1967-72. Recipient Arch T. Coldwell award Soc. Automotive Engrs., 1974. Fellow Acoustical Soc. Am. (asso. editor Jour., mem. exec. council, v.p. 1977-78, pres. 1980-81, Biennial award 1964), Royal Soc. Can. (hon. treas. 1982—); mem. Can. Acoustical Assn. (founding sec. 1961-64, founding editor Jour. 1971-74). Patentee in field. Home: 26 Birch Ave Ottawa ON Canada K1K 3G6 Office: Montreal Rd Ottawa ON Canada K1A OS1

EMBREE, AINSLIE THOMAS, history educator; b. N.S., Can., Jan. 1, 1921; came to U.S., 1958, naturalized, 1965; s. Ira Thomas and Margaret (Langley) E.; m. Suzanne Helene Harpole, May 24, 1947; children: Ralph Thomas, Margaret Louise. B.A., Dalhousie U., Halifax, N.S., 1941; B.D., Pine Hill Theol. Sem., Halifax, 1946; M.A., Union Theol. Sem., 1947, Columbia U., 1955, Ph.D., 1960; LL.D. hon., Juniata Coll., 1982. Prof. history Indore (India) Christian Coll., 1948-58, lectr., 1958; asst. prof., assoc. prof. history Columbia U., 1958-69, prof., 1972-78; assoc. dean Sch. Internat. Affairs, 1972-78, chmn., 1982—, on leave, 1978-80; prof. Duke U., 1969-72; counsellor for cultural affairs Am. embassy, New Delhi, 1978-80; cons. in field. Author: Charles Grant and British Rule in India, 1962, India, 1967, India's Search for National Identity, 1971; editor: The Hindu Tradition, 1966, Alberuni's India, 1971, (with others) Pakistan's Western Borderlands, 1978. Served with RCAF, 1942-45. Can. Council fellow, 1953-54; Am. Council Learned Socs. fellow, 1967; Am. Inst. Indian Studies fellow, 1968-69; Nat. Endowment for Humanities fellow, 1977. Mem. Council Fgn. Relations, Assn. Asian Studies (pres. 1982-83), Am. Oriental Soc., Am. Hist. Soc., Am. Inst. Indian Studies (pres. 1970-73). Home: 54 Morningside Dr New York NY 10025 Office: Dept History Columbia U New York NY 10027

EMBREE, LARRY JONATHAN, physician; b. Magnolia, Ark., Oct. 3, 1932; s. Lon J. and Maude (Laramore) E.; m. Gertrude Mead Schenck, Sept. 23, 1961; children: Gertrude Mead, Laurence Jonathan, Robert Cumming Schenck, Katherine Cutler. B.S., M.D., U. Ark., Little Rock, 1957. Diplomate: Am. Bd. Psychiatry and Neurology (invited examiner 1976—). Intern, then resident in medicine Peter Bent Brigham Hosp., Boston, 1957-59; research asso. Nat. Inst. Neurol. Diseases and Blindness, 1959-61; resident in neurology Mass. Gen. Hosp., Boston, 1961-64; spl. research fellow Nat. Inst. Neurol. Diseases and Blindness, U. Göteborg, Sweden, 1964-67; instr., then asst. prof. Harvard Med. Sch., 1967-74; prof. neurology and pathology, head dept. neurology La. State U. Med. Center, Shreveport, 1974—; cons. Schumpert Med. Center, Brentwood Hosp., N.W. La. State Sch., VA hosps.; mem. test com. Nat. Bd. Med. Examiners, 1979—, chmn., 1982—. Contbr. articles to med. jours. Grantee Nat. Inst. Neurol. Diseases and Blindness, 1968-74, Magale Found., 1976-83, VA, 1979-83. Mem. Internat. Soc. Neurochemistry, Am. Soc. Neurochemistry, Am. Acad. Neurology, Am. Assn. Neuropathologists, AMA, Soc. Neurosci., Assn. Univ. Profs. Neurology, La. Med. Soc., Shreveport Med. Soc. (dir. 1979—, program chmn. 1980), La. Epilepsy Assn. (dir. 1978-79), Epilepsy Assn. N.W. La. (dir. 1979-80). Methodist. Clubs: Harvard (Boston and N.Y.C.); Atlanta Deer (Magnolia); Univ. (Shreveport). Home: 540 Oneonta St Shreveport LA 71106 Office: PO Box 33932 Shreveport LA 71130

EMBRY, WAYNE RICHARD, basketball executive; b. Springfield, Ohio, Mar. 26, 1937; s. Floyd and Anna Elizabeth (Gardner) E.; m. Theresa Jackson, June 6, 1959; children: Deborah, Jill, Wayne Richard. B.S., Miami U., 1958. Profl. basketball player Cin. Royals, 1958-66, Boston Celtics, 1966-68; basketball player Milw. Bucks, 1968-69, gen. mgr., after 1972, v.p., 1974—; Dir. Recreation City, Boston, 1969-70. Trustee Basketball Hall of Fame. Office: care Milw Bucks 901 N 4th St Milwaukee WI 53203 *

EMCH, ARNOLD FREDERICK, management consultant; b. Manhattan, Kans., Nov. 3, 1899; s. Arnold and Hilda (Walters) E.; m. Minna Libman, July 22, 1927 (dec. Sept. 1958); m. Eleanore Merckens, June 30, 1960; children:Arnold Devere, Frederick Bolebec. A.B., U. Ill., 1925, A.M., 1926; postgrad., U. Chgo., 1930; Ph.D., Harvard, 1934. Pres. Emch Constrn. Co., Wichita, Kans., 1920-22; regional dir. Tambly & Brown Co., Chgo., 1926-29; exec. dir. Chgo. Hosp. Council, 1936-39; assoc. dir. Am. Hosp. Assn., 1939-42, U. Chgo. Inst. for Hosp. Adminstrn., 1939-42; mgr. Booz, Allen & Hamilton, mgmt. consultants, Chgo., 1942-48, partner, 1948-60, ret.; cons. corp., 1960—, pvt. and personal mgmt. cons.; pres. North End Water Co., Colo., 1964-67, sec.-treas., 1967-83; dir. mgmt. cons. Calif.-Time Petroleum Corp., 1967-70; pres. Glory Ranch Arabian Stables, 1966—; sec.-treas. Eagle Rock Ranches, 1971—. Author: Crowded Years, Uncommon Letters to a Son, Life, Love, and Logic; Contbr. articles to various jours. Trustee William Alanson White Psychiat. Found., Washington, 1945-46, v.p., 1947, pres., 1948-52; dir. Washington Sch. Psychiatry, 1946-56, Mental Health Soc. Greater Chgo., 1958-59, Council on Hosp. Planning and Resources Devel. State Colo., 1961-77. Served in AEF, 1918-19; France; comdr. USNR; mgmt. cons. to Navy Surg. Gen., 1942-45; hon. cons. Navy Surg. Gen., 1945—. Mem. Am. Philos. Assn., AAAS, Shakespearean Authorship Soc., English Cocker Spaniel Club Am., Chi Psi. Clubs: Harvard, University (Chgo.); Colo. Arabian Horse. Address: Glory Ranch Devil's Gulch Rd Estes Park CO 80517

EMCH, GERARD GUSTAV, mathematics and physics educator; b. Geneva, July 21, 1936; U.S., 1964; s. Martial Desire and Violette Marie (Cornaglia) E.; m. Antoinette S. Deriaz, July 25, 1959; children: Florence Christiane, Rene-Didier Guillaume. Ph.D., U. Geneva, 1963. Asst. in theoreticial physics. U.Geneva, 1959-63, chef des travux in math. physics, 1963-64; research assoc. dept. applied math. U.Md., 1965-66; asst. prof. math. and physics U. Rochester, N.Y., 1966-71, assoc. prof., 1971-78, prof., 1978—; vis. prof. U. Nijmegen; vis.prof. U. Brussels; vis. prof. EPF-Lausanne, U. Bielefeld, U. Geneva, U. Sao Paulo. Author: Algebraic Methods in Statistical Mechanics and Quantum Field Theory, 1972; contbr. chpts., numerous articles to profl. publs. Mem. Am. Phys. Soc., Am. Math. Soc., Am. Math. Assn., N.Y. Acad. Scis., AAUP. Presbyterian. Office: Depts Math and Physics U Rochester Rochester NY 14627

EMERICH, DONALD WARREN, educator; b. Schuylkill Haven, Pa., July 12, 1920; s. Edward Robert and Minie (Beck) E.; m. Evelyn Freda Graulich, Sept. 24, 1943; children—Douglas William, Dwight Edward, David Graulich. B.S. in Chem. Engring, Pa. State U., 1942; Ph.D. in Chemistry, Ohio State U., 1951. Research and devel. Hercules, Inc., Parlin, N.J., 1942-43; prodn. supr. Badger Ordnance Works, Baraboo, Wis., 1943-45; research and devel. U.S. Vanadium Corp., Niagara Falls, N.Y., 1945-47; instr. Kan. State U., Manhattan, 1951-53, asst. prof., 1953-54; asso. prof. Centenary Coll., Shreveport, La., 1954-58, prof., 1958-60; asso. prof. Miss. State U., 1960-62, acting head chemistry dept., 1964-66, 80-81, prof. chemistry, 1962—, head dept., 1966-76; sec. Starkville-Miss. State U. Symphony Assn., 1975-78. Violinist, Miss. State Coll. Women-Community Orch., 1963-65; violinist, Starkville-Miss. State U. Symphony Orch., 1969—. Mem. Am. Chem. Soc. (newsletter editor Miss. sect. 1976-79), Sigma Xi, Tau Beta Pi, Sigma Tau, Phi Lambda Upsilon, Pi Mu Epsilon, Phi Kappa Phi. Home: 2007 Pin Oak Dr Starkville MS 39759 Office: Box CH Miss State Univ Mississippi State MS 39762

EMERSON, ALICE FREY, college president; b. Durham, N.C., Oct. 26, 1931; d. Alexander Hamilton and Alice (Hubbard) Frey; (div.)children: Rebecca, Peter. A.B., Vassar Coll., 1953; Ph.D., Bryn Mawr Coll., 1964. Tchr., Newton (Mass.) High Sch., 1956-58; mem. faculty Bryn Mawr (Pa.) Coll., 1961-64, U. Pa., Phila., 1966-75, asst. prof. polit. sci., 1966-75, dean of women, 1966-69, dean of students, 1969-75; pres. Wheaton Coll., Norton, Mass., 1975—; dir. Bank of Boston Corp., Bank of Boston, Boston; trustee Penn Mut. Life Ins. Co.; adv. bd. HERS Mid-America. Mem. adv. bd. Com. for Nat. Security, 1982—; bd. dirs. Corp. for Public/Pvt. Ventures, 1978-82; pres. New Eng. Colls. Fund, 1978-80; trustee Vassar Coll., 1977—, Sturdy Meml. Hosp., 1977—; mem. exec. com. Women's Coll. Coalition, 1980—; mem. Mayor's Adv. Bd., Attleboro, Mass., 1984—. Mem. New Eng. Concerns Group, Am. Polit. Sci. Assn., AAUP, Am. Council Edn. (commn. on leadership devel. 1979-82, com. on collegiate athletics 1979—, nominating com. 1980-82), Assn. Am. Colls. (dir. 1984—), Council Fgn. Relations (dir. 1983—). Home: 28 E Main St Norton MA 02766 Office: Office of Pres Wheaton Coll Norton MA 02766

EMERSON, DANIEL EVERETT, telephone co. exec.; b. Passaic, N.J., Oct. 22, 1924; s. Daniel T. and Jennie (VanBeveren) E.; m. Patricia Thorston, June 14, 1947; children—Patricia Sue Nancy Ellen, Pamela Thorston. B.E.E., Cornell U., 1949; postgrad., George Washington U., Boston U., N.Y. U., 1951-56, Dartmouth Coll., 1956, U. Pa., 1959-60. With A.T.&T., 1949—, v.p. fed. relations, 1968-74; v.p. network ops. N.Y. Telephone, N.Y.C., 1974-75, v.p. ops. analysis and methods, 1975-76, exec. v.p. corp. devel., dir., 1976—; dir. First Fed. Savs. and Loan Assn., Rochester (N.Y.). Mem. bus. adv. council Religion In Am. Life; dir. trustee YMCA of Greater N.Y.; former trustee, pres. Kent Pl. Sch., Summit, N.J.; pres. State Traffic Safety Council; mem. univ. council, bus. adv. council Sch. Bus. and Public Adminstrn., Cornell U. Served to 1st lt. USAAF, 1943-45. Decorated Air medal. Mem. U.S. C. of C. (communications com. 1972-74), German Am. C. of C. (dir.), Tau Beta Pi, Eta Kappa Nu, Theta Xi. Club: Canoe Brook Country (Summit). Office: 1095 Ave of Americas New York NY 10036

EMERSON, DAVID WINTHROP, coll. dean; b. Littleton, Mass., Mar. 13, 1928; s. Leon Ware and Alice Sophia (Howe) E.; m. Margaret Shirley Armstrong, Sept. 4, 1954; children—Richard R., Eric H., Ellen N. A.B., Dartmouth Coll., 1952; M.S. in Chemistry, U. Mich., 1954, Ph.D., 1958. Research chemist Shell Oil Co., Houston and N.Y.C., 1957-63; mem. faculty U. Mich., Dearborn, 1963-81, prof. chemistry, 1969-81, dean, 1979-81, Coll. Sci., Math. and Engring., U. Nev., Las Vegas, 1981—. Served with AUS, 1946-47, 50-51. Mem. Am. Chem. Soc., Chem. Soc. London, AAAS, AAUP, Sigma Xi. Home: 4513 La Roca Circle Las Vegas NV 89121 Office: 4505 S Maryland Pkwy Las Vegas NV 89154

EMERSON, FREDERICK GEORGE, service company executive; b. Quincy, Mass., Dec. 6, 1933; s. George Bliss and Mildred Louella (Hynes) E.; m. Marion Orr Stewart, June 10, 1961; children: Elizabeth Lynn, David George. B.A. with honors in Philosophy, U. Va., 1955, J.D., 1960. Sec., counsel Commonwealth Gas Corp., N.Y.C., 1960-67; asst. sec. The Greyhound Corp. (and subs. cos.), Phoenix, 1967-77, sec., 1977—. Bd. dirs. Inst. Cultural Affairs Ariz., 1971—, Lupus Found. Phoenix, 1980—, Friendly House, Inc., 1974-78. Served to 1st lt. Transp. Corps, U.S. Army, 1955-57. Mem. Am. Soc. Corp. Secs., Va. State Bar Assn. Office: Greyhound Corp 111 W Clarendon Ave Phoenix AZ 85077

EMERSON, GLADYS ANDERSON, biochemist, nutritionist; b. Caldwell, Kans., July 1, 1903; d. Otis Anderson and Louise (Williams) Anderson. A.B., B.S., U. Sci. and Arts Okla., 1925; M.A., Stanford, 1926; Ph.D., U. Calif. at Berkeley, 1932; postgrad., U. Göttingen, 1932-33. Teaching asst. U. Sci. and Arts, Okla., 1923-25; asst. Stanford, 1925-26; research asso. Inst. Exptl. Biology, U. Calif. at Berkeley, 1933-42; vis. lectr. pharmacology med. sch. U. Calif. at San Francisco, 1945; research asso. Sloan-Kettering Inst. Cancer Research, 1950-53; head dept., animal nutrition Merck Inst. Therapeutic Research, Rahway, N.J., 1942-56; dir. nutrition Merck, Sharp & Dohme Research Labs., 1956-57; Marie Curie lectr. Pa. State U., 1951; research lectr. Iowa State U., 1952; prof., chmn. dept. home econs. U. Calif. at Los Angeles, 1957-61, prof. nutrition, 1961-70, prof. emeritus, 1970—; head div. nutrition Sch. Pub. Health, 1961-69; vis. lectr. biochemistry and nutrition U. Nebr., 1958; lectr. univs., sci. and profl. socs., Japan, 1964, 65, 67, 70, 75; engaged in research OSRD, 1943-45; mem. liaison and sci. adv. bd. Q.M. Food and Container Inst., 1949-50; food and nutrition research com. NRC, 1952; mem. Food and Nutrition Bd., 1959-64, mem. com. dietary allowances, 1960-64; exec. council Am. Bd. Nutrition, 1959-68; panelist Rensselaer Poly. Inst. indsl. council, 1955; mem. U.S. nat. com. Internat. Union Nutrition Scientists, 1958-62; organizing com. 5th Internat. Congress Nutrition, 1961; vice chmn. panel on new foods White House Conf. on Food, Nutrition and Health, 1969; del. confs. in field; instr. trainees Peace Corps, 1962, 63, 64. Author articles to books and sci. jours.; Asso. editor: Jour. Nutrition, 1952-56. Mem. State Nutrition Com., 1966-69, Calif. Nutrition Council, 1971—, So. Calif. Com. on Food and Nutrition, 1973—; sponsor Calif. Freedom from Hunger Com., 1966-70, sci. adviser, 1970-74; mem. sci. bd. Meals for Millions, 1970-79, hon. trustee, 1979—, mem. nominating com. nutrition program com., 1977; expert witness FDA, FTC, 1972-76; mem. So. Calif. com. ONA-U.S.A., 1974-76; chmn. So. Calif. com. WHO, 1973-75; Mem. bd. So. Calif. Friends Soochow U., 1970—; mem. Los Angeles Interagy. Disaster Com., 1976. Recipient Garvan medal Am. Chem. Soc., 1952; named to Okla. Hall Fame, 1943, to; Univ. Scis. and Arts Okla., 1972. Fellow Am. Inst. Chemists, A.A.A.S., N.Y. Acad. Scis., Am. Pub. Health Assn., Am. Inst. Nutrition (councillor 1952-55, chmn. membership com. 1964, fellows com. 1975-78, history of nutrition com. 1976-78); mem. Am. Chem. Soc. (chmn. women's service com. 1953-58), Am. Soc. Biol. Chemists, Soc. Exptl. Biology and Medicine, Gordon Research Conf. (chmn. vitamins and metabolism 1952, vice chmn. 1951), Pan Am. Med. Assn. (nutrition council 1959-60), UN Assn. So. Calif. (mem. council 1974—, v.p. community relations and edn. 1976-78), Los Angeles World Affairs Council, Town Hall of Calif., Sigma Xi, Delta Omega (nat. pres. 1971-72), Sigma Delta Epsilon, Iota Sigma Pi (nat. v.p. 1945-51, nat. pres. 1951-57, nat. hon. mem.). Co-isolator Vitamin E, 1936. Home: 319 Amalfi Dr Santa Monica CA 90402 Office: Sch of Public Health U Calif at Los Angeles Los Angeles CA 90024

EMERSON, GORDON EDWARD, JR., real estate executive; b. Medford, Mass., Nov. 2, 1916; s. Gordon Edward and Helen I. (Long) E.; m. Margaret Jones, Mar. 17, 1945; children—David A., Christopher J., Jonathan S. A.B., Middlebury (Vt.) Coll., 1940; grad. Advanced Mgmt. Program, Harvard, U., 1963; postgrad., Aspen Inst. Humanistic Studies, 1968. With John Hancock Mut. Life Ins. Co., Boston, 1940-70, sr. v.p. mortgages and real estate, 1968-70; pres. John Hancock Realty Co., 1966-70; exec. v.p. Cabot, Cabot & Forbes Co., Boston, 1970-76; chmn. bd., mng. trustee Bay Colony Property Co., Boston, 1971—; chmn. Bay Fin. Corp., 1980—; dir. Diversified Mortgage Investors, Inc.; chmn. Mass. Housing Fin. Agy., 1967-77, Mass. Home Mortgage Fin. Agy., 1972-77. Author articles in field. Chmn. Boston Mcpl. Research Bur., 1976-79, Rockport (Mass.) Sch. Com., 1956-66; mem. Lynnfield (Mass.) Sch. Com., 1948-49. Served with USCGR, 1941-45. Mem. United Ch. Christ. Home: Highland Rd RFD Box 395 South Hampton NH 03827 Office: 2 Faneuil Hall Marketplace Boston MA 02109

EMERSON, HORACE MANN, III, ret. r.r. exec.; b. Wilmington, N.C., Jan. 22, 1914; s. Horace Mann Jr. and Laura Placida (Clark) E.; m. Susan LeRoy Carr, June 1, 1943; children: Susan C. Emerson Bancks, Laura C. Emerson Taylor. Student pub. and pvt. schs., Sumter, Columbia, S.C. Clk. A.C.L. R.R., Wilmington, N.C., 1934-47, gen. agt., Jacksonville, Fla., 1947-51, asst. gen. freight agt., Wilmington, 1952-57, asst. treas., 1957-58, treas., Wilmington and Jacksonville, 1958-61, asst. v.p. traffic, 1961-67; sr. asst. v.p. traffic Seaboard Coast Line R.R. Co., Jacksonville, 1967-68, v.p. freight traffic, 1968-73, sr. v.p., 1973-76; also dir.; sr. v.p. traffic SCL Industries, 1973-76; ret., 1976; sr. v.p., dir. Louisville & Nashville R.R.; chief traffic officer Ga. R.R., A. & W.P. R.R., W. Ry. of A., C.C. & O. R.R., 1973-76; past dir. Central R.R. Co. S.C., Columbia, Newberry & Laurens R.R., Seacoast Transp. Co., S.C. Pacific Ry. Co. Served to capt. AUS, 1942-46, 51-52. Mem. Assn. ICC Practitioners, Nat. Freight Traffic Assn., Fla. Traffic Assn., N.Y. Traffic Club, Jacksonville Area C. of C., SCV, Order of Stars and Bars, Tenn. Squires. Republican. Episcopalian (mem. vestry 1970-73). Clubs: Timuquana Country, River, Meninak, Ponte Vedra, 200, St. Johns Dinner. (Jacksonville). Home: 2970 Saint Johns Ave Jacksonville FL 32205

EMERSON, J. MARTIN, union ofcl.; b. Washington, Aug. 12, 1912; s. Harry Pliny and Roberta Estelle (Johnson) E.; m. Reva Emerson, 1944; children—Sharon Emerson Decker, Jay Martin. Student public schs., Washington. Sec. local 161-170 Am. Fedn. Musicians, Washington, 1950-75, mem. internat. exec. bd., 1966—, internat. sec.-treas., 1975—; pub., editor-in-chief Internat. Musician; v.p. Interam. Fedn. Entertainment Workers. Bd. dirs. Wolf Trap Farm Park, Va. Clubs: Masons, Elks. Office: 1500 Broadway New York NY 10036 *

EMERSON, PAUL CARLTON, assn. exec.; b. Biddeford, Maine, July 21, 1923; s. James E. and Clara (Macomber) E.; m. Marion G. Tanner; 1 dau., Beverly Ann. Student, Grove City Coll., 1942-43. Exec. dir. Portland (Maine) Vets. Service Center, 1945-46; field mgr. Maine State C. of C., Portland, 1946-47, exec. mgr., 1947-68, exec. v.p., 1968-75, pres., 1975—. Mem. Maine Com. Youth Opportunities, 1960—, Maine Com. Aging, 1960—, Maine Com. Vocat. Edn., 1958—, Maine Adv. Council Higher Edn., 1966, Can.-U.S. Commn. U.S. C. of C.,

1967-81; founder (with others) Maine World Trade Council; mem. regional export expansion council U.S. Dept. Commerce, 1969—; mem. Gov.'s Task Force on Maine Environment, 1969—; chmn. Maine Hwy. Users Conf.; Bd. dirs. Vacation Travel Council Maine; trustee, pres. Osteo. Hosp. Maine, 1969—, Maine Council Econ. Edn. Served to 1st lt. USAAF, 1943-45; lt. col. Res.; ret. Mem. Am. Assn. C. of C. Execs., New Eng. Assn. C. of C. Execs., Maine Assn. C. of C. Execs. (founder, treas.). Club: Cumberland (Portland) (exec. com.). Home: Spurwink Ave Cape Elizabeth ME 04107 Office: 477 Congress St Portland ME 04111

EMERSON, THOMAS EDWARD, JR., cardiovascular physiologist, educator; b. Wilson, Okla., Feb. 3, 1935; s. Thomas Edward and Dovie Beatrice (Tuck) E.; m. Joan Mac Evans, Dec. 24, 1955 (div. Jan. 1982); children: Thomas E. III, Keli D., Lea G. B.S. in Zoology, Okla. U., 1958; M.S. in Med. Physiology, U. Alta. (Can.), 1961, Ph.D., U. Okla., 1964. Research physiologist Civil Aeromed. Research Inst., Oklahoma City, 1961-65; asst. prof. depts. physiology and surgery Okla. U., 1965-66; asso. prof. physiology Mich. State U., 1966-73, prof., 1973-83; prin. scientist physiology research dept., exptl. therapeutics R&D div. Cutter group Miles Labs., Inc., Berkeley, Calif., 1983—. Contbg. author: Shock and Hypotension: Pathogenesis and Treatment, 1965, Bradykinin, Kallidinand Kallikrein, 1970, The Fundamental Mechanisms of Shock, 1972, Cerebral Circulation and Metabolism, 1975, The Cerebral Vessel Wall, 1976; contbr. articles to profl. jours. Coach, Okemas Little League Football, 1968-70, Pop Warner Little League Football, East Lansing, Mich., 1971-75; pres. Donley P.T.O., East Lansing, 1969-71; cubmaster Cub Scouts Am., East Lansing, 1967-70; instr. first aid ARC, East Lansing, 1975-82; asst. coach Girls Softball, Okemas, 1970—. Served to 2d lt., inf. AUS, 1958-59. Mem. Am. Physiol. Soc., Am. Heart Assn., Am. Fedn. Clin. Research, Shock Soc., Soc. Exptl. Biology and Medicine, Medicine, Circulation Group, Nat. Ski Patrol System, Lansing, Schuss Mountain ski patrols, Sigma Xi, Beta Theta Pi, Phi Sigma. Methodist (dir.). Clubs: Lansing (Mich.); Ski, Okla. U. Letterman., Research in bacterial shock, brain blood flow regulation and circulatory shock: mechanisms of pathology and treatment. Home: 981 Regal Rd Berkeley CA 94708 Office: Cutter Group Miles Labs Berkeley CA 94701

EMERSON, THOMAS IRWIN, lawyer; b. Passaic, N.J., July 12, 1907; s. Luther Lee and Wilhelmina (Runft) E.; m. Bertha R. Paret, Oct. 9, 1934 (dec. 1958); Joan Paret, Robert Madden, Luther Lee; m. Ruth B. Calvin, May 27, 1960. A.B., Yale, 1928, LL.B., 1931, M.A., 1946; LL.D., U. Pa., 1976, Amherst Coll., 1976. Bar: N.Y. bar 1932. Assoc. with law firm Engelhard, Pollak, Pitcher & Stern, N.Y.C., 1931-33; asst. counsel Nat. Recovery Adminstrn., 1933-34; prin. atty. NLRB, 1934-36, asst. gen. counsel, then asso. gen. counsel, 1937-40; prin. atty. Social Security Bd., 1936-37; spl. asst. to atty. gen. U.S. Dept. Justice, 1940-41; asso. gen. counsel OPA, 1941-43, dep. adminstr. for enforcement, 1943-45; gen. counsel Office of Econ. Stblzn., 1945, Office War Moblzn. and Reconversion, 1945-46; prof. law Yale, 1946—, Lines prof. law, 1955; vis. prof. London Sch. Econs. Polit. Sci., 1953-54, Brookings Instn., 1960-61. Author: (with David Haber and Norman Dorsen) Political and Civil Rights in the United States, 1952, 4th edit., 1976, Toward a General Theory of the First Amendment, 1966, The System of Freedom of Expression, 1970; Contbr. to profl. periodicals. Guggenheim fellow, 1953; Fulbright fellow, Japan, 1974-75. Mem. Nat. Lawyers Guild (pres. 1950-51). Home: 2271 Ridge Rd North Haven CT 06473 Office: Yale Law Sch New Haven CT 06520

EMERSON, WILLIAM, congressman; b. St. Louis, Jan. 1, 1938; s. Norvell Preston and Marie (Reinemer) E.; m. Jo Ann Hermann, June 21, 1975; children: Victoria Marie, Elizabeth, Abigail. B.A., Westminster Coll., 1959; LL.B., U. Balt., 1964. Mem. congressional staffs, 1961-70; dir. govt. relations Fairchild Industries, Germantown, Md., 1970-74; dir. public affairs INGAA, Washington, 1974-75; exec. asst. to chmn. Fed. Election Commn., 1975; dir. fed. relations TRW, Inc., Washington, 1975-79; public affairs cons., 1980; mem. 94th-98th congresses from 10th Dist. Mo. Served to capt. USAF. Republican. Presbyterian. Office: 418 Cannon House Office Bldg Washington DC 20515 *

EMERSON, WILLIAM ALLEN, stockbroker; b. Columbia, Tenn., July 13, 1921; s. Henry Houston and Mabel N. (Allen) E.; m. Jane Stannard, Oct. 5, 1944; children: Marshal Henry, Shelley, Stacey, Kimberly. A.A., St. Petersburg Jr. Coll., 1941; B.S. in Bus. Adminstrn, U. Fla., 1946. With Merrill Lynch, Pierce, Fenner & Smith, Inc., 1947—, dir. gen. services div., N.Y.C., 1968-72, Southeast regional dir., corp. dir., Atlanta, 1972-81, sr. v.p., nat. sales dir., 1981—; vice chmn. bd. Oglethorpe Corp., N.Y.C., 1981—; Bd. dirs. Oglethorpe U., Atlanta; mem. pres. council Columbia Theol. Sem., Atlanta. Served with USMC, 1942-45. Republican. Presbyterian. Clubs: Capital City, Commerce, St. Petersburg Yacht, Biltmore Forest Country, Gate City Masons. Home: 45 W 60th St New York NY 10023 Office: 165 Broadway New York NY 10080 *I believe that what you give away returns to bless you in many ways, and that what you have left becomes more than before the gift.*

EMERSON, WILLIAM HARRY, oil company executive; b. Rochester, N.Y., Jan. 13, 1928; s. William Canfield and Alice Sarah (Adams) E.; m. Jane Anne Epple, Dec. 27, 1956; children: Elizabeth Anne, Carolyn Jane. B.A., Cornell U., 1951, LL.B., 1956. Bar: Ill. 1974. Atty. Standard Oil Co., Ind., 1956—; sec., dir. Amoco Gas Co., 1979—. Pres., dir. Undercraft Montessori Sch., Tulsa, 1965-67, Tulsa Figure Skating Club, 1969; bd. dirs. Lake Forest Found. for Historic Preservation, Ill., 1983—. Served to 1st lt. AUS, 1945, 52. Home: 593 Greenvale Rd Lake Forest IL 60045 Office: 200 E Randolph Dr Chicago IL 60601

EMERSON, WILLIAM KEITH, zoologist; b. San Diego, May 1, 1925; s. Horace P. and Vera (Vaught) E. A.B., Calif. State U.-San Diego, 1948; M.S., U. So. Calif., 1950; Ph.D., U. Calif.-Berkeley, 1956. Paleontologist U. Calif. Mus. Paleontology, Berkeley, 1951-55; asst. curator invertebrates Am. Mus. Natural History, 1955-61, asso. curator, 1961-66, curator, 1966—, chmn. dept. living invertebrates, 1960-74; research asso. San Diego Natural History Mus., 1962—; Leader, Puritan expdn. to Western Mexico Am. Mus. Natural History, 1957; mem. Belvedere Expdn. to Gulf of Calif., 1962. Author: (with M.K. Jacobson) Shells of the New York City Area, 1961, Wonders of the World of Shells: Sea, Land and Fresh-Water, 1971, American Museum of Natural History Guide to Shells, 1976, Wonders of Starfish, 1977, (with Andreas Feininger) Shells, 1972, (with Arnold Ross) Wonders of Barnacles, 1974; Contbr. papers to profl. jours. Fellow AAAS; mem. Calif. Acad. Scis., Am. Malacological Union (pres. 1961-62, mem. council 1963—), Western Soc. Malacologists (pres. 1968-69, mem. council 1970-72), Paleontology Soc., Soc. Systematic Zoology (mem. council 1960-63, 70-72), Paleontol. Research Instn., San Diego Soc. Nat. History, Cal. Malacozool. Soc., Blue Key, Sigma Xi, Sigma Phi Epsilon. Home: 10 East End Ave New York NY 10021 Office: Am Mus Natural History Central Park W at 79th St New York NY 10024

EMERSON, WILLIAM RICHARD, librarian; b. Little Rock, May 17, 1923; s. Harry A. and Estella M. (Baldridge) E.; m. Barbara Lang Clogher Woodriff, Nov. 27, 1967; stepchildren—Carol Woodriff Quillen, Anne Clogher Woodriff. B.A., Yale, 1948; D. Phil., Oxford (Eng.) U., 1952. From instr. to asst. prof. history Yale, 1951-63; asst. to pres. Hollins (Va.) Coll., 1964-69; dir. div. research grants Nat. Endowment for Humanities, Washington, 1969-74; dir. Franklin D. Roosevelt Library, Hyde Park, N.Y., 1974—; cons. manpower Dept. Def., 1963-69. Served with USAAF, 1942-45. Office: Franklin D Roosevelt Library and Museum Old Albany Post Rd Hyde Park NY 12538

EMERY, ALBERT WALDRON, JR., advt. agy. exec.; b. Denver, Jan. 15, 1923; s. Albert Waldron and Margaret (Grimson) E.; m. Lucille E. Eye, Oct. 22, 1948; children—Linden, Lisa, Thomas Alan, Courtney. Student, DePauw U., 1943-44; B.S., U. Va., 1948. Sales promotion asst. Westinghouse Electric Corp., 1948-50, advt. account rep., 1950-53; div. mgr. Gen. Products Advt., 1953-54, Indsl. Products Advt., 1954-55; account exec. Harris D. McKinney, Inc., Phila., 1955-56, v.p., account supr., 1956-59, exec. v.p., 1960-62, pres., 1962—, chmn. bd., 1964—. Served with USNR, 1940-46. Mem. Franklin Inst., Sigma Chi. Clubs: Poor Richard, Virginia, Union League (Phila.); Tucson Nat. Golf. Home: 305 Pine St Philadelphia PA 19106 Office: Independence Mall West 411 N 20th St Philadelphia PA 19130

EMERY, ALDEN HAYES, JR., educator; b. Pitts., May 2, 1925; s. Alden Hayes and Dorothy (Radde) E.; m. Verna Elizabeth Murphy, Mar. 1, 1952; children—Janice Elaine, Gregg Alden. B.S., Pa. State U., 1947; M.S., Mass. Inst. Tech., 1949; Ph.D., U. Ill., 1955. Chem. engr. E.I. duPont de Nemours & Co., Wilmington, Del., 1949-52; asst. prof. Sch. Chem. Engring., Purdue U., Lafayette, Ind., 1954-58, asso. prof., 1958-64, prof., 1964—. Served with USNR, 1944-45. Fulbright scholar, 1967. Mem. Am. Inst. Chem. Engrs., Am. Chem. Soc., Am. Soc. Microbiology, Soc. Indsl. Microbiology, AAAS, AAUP. Office: Dept Chem Engring Purdue U Lafayette IN 47907

EMERY, EDWIN, journalist, educator; b. Chino, Calif., May 14, 1914; s. William E. and Laura A. (Miller) E.; m. Mary Margaret McNevin, Dec. 28, 1935; children: Michael Charles, Laurel Christine, Alison Clare. B.A., U. Calif., Berkeley, 1935, Ph.D., 1943. Mem. editorial staff San Francisco Examiner, 1935-36; asst. editor Calif. Monthly mag., 1936-41, mng. editor, 1941-43; lectr. journalism U. Calif., Berkeley, 1938-41; staff writer, war desk editor and bur. chief UP, San Francisco, 1943-45; lectr. journalism and mass communication U. Minn., 1945-46, asst. prof., 1946-50, asso. prof., 1950-54, prof., 1954—, dir. grad. study, 1973-79; vis. prof. journalism and mass communication U. Wash., Seattle, 1959, Nat. Chengchi U., Taiwan, 1972-73, U. de Navarra, Spain, 1973, Nanyang U., Singapore, 1979-80; vis. scholar Moscow State U., 1971; Fulbright vis. lectr., Afghanistan, 1973, USIS lectr., Asia, Europe, 1972-73, 79-80; cons. UNESCO, various publishers, 1954—; editorial writer St. Paul Pioneer Press and Dispatch, summers, 1946-54. Author: The Press and America: An Interpretative History of the Mass Media, 1954, 2d edit., 5th edit. with Michael Emery, 1984, History of the American Newspaper Publishers Assn, 1950, (with P.H. Ault) Reporting the News, 1959, (with P.H. Ault and W.K. Agee) Introduction to Mass Communications, 1960, Perspectives on Mass Communications, 1982, Reporting and Writing the News, 1983; editor: Journalism Quar. research jour, 1964-73; editorial bd.: Journalism Quar, 1973—, Journalism History, 1973—. Mem. Citizens League of Mpls., 1960—; mem. exec. com. Democratic-Farmer-Labor party, 1948-50. Guggenheim fellow, 1959-60. Mem. Assn. Edn. in Journalism (pres. 1974-75, Bleyer award 1980), Soc. Profl. Journalists (Nat. Disting. Teaching award 1980), Newspaper Guild, Internat. Press Inst., Internat. Assn. for Mass Communication Research, Am. Soc. of Newspaper Editors (mem. edn. com. 1965-68), A.P. Mng. Editors Assn. (mem. research com. 1970-72), Public Relations Soc. Am. (pres. Minn. chpt. 1956), AAUP, Minn. Hist. Soc., Minn. Press Club, Singapore Press Club, Minn. Soc. Fine Arts, UN Assn. of Minn., Minn. Public TV, Sigma Delta Chi (Research award 1950, 54), Phi Beta Kappa, Phi Alpha Theta, Kappa Tau Alpha, Phi Kappa Tau, Pi Delta Epsilon. Democrat. Club: U. Minn. Campus. Home: 2524 Seabury Ave S Minneapolis MN 55406 Office: 108 Murphy Hall Univ Minn Minneapolis MN 55455

EMERY, JOHN COLVIN, JR., air freight company executive; b. Madison, Wis., July 14, 1924; s. John Colvin and Janet (Millar) E.; m. Frances Toomy, May 28, 1960; children: John Colvin III, Susan Farlow, Ann Louise, Michael William, Patricia Millar. Student, Dartmouth, 1942-43. With United Airlines, 1944-45, Nat. Airlines, 1945-46; with Emery Air Freight Corp., Wilton, Conn., 1946—, v.p. sales, 1956-62, exec. v.p., 1963-68, pres., 1968—, also dir.; dir. Cluett, Peabody & Co., Inc., N.Y.C., Gen. Housewares, Stamford, Conn., Pitney Bowes, Inc., Stamford. Served with A.C. USNR, 1943-44. Mem. Sales Execs. Club N.Y. (pres. 1967-69, dir. 1963—), Nat. Def. Transp. Assn. (life). Episcopalian (vestry). Clubs: Wee Burn Country (Darien, Conn.); Wings (N.Y.C.) (pres. 1980-81). Office: Emery Air Freight Corp Wilton CT 06897

EMERY, KENNETH ORRIS, marine geologist; b. Swift Current, Sask., Can., June 6, 1914; s. Clifford Almon and Agnes (Baird) E.; m. Caroline Roberta Alexander, Oct. 3, 1941; children—Barbara Kathryn Emery Alvarado, Charlet Adelia Emery Shave. Student, N. Tex. Agrl. Coll., 1933-35; B.S., U. Ill., 1937, Ph.D., 1941. Staff Ill. State Geol. Survey, Urbana, 1941-43; staff div. war research U. Calif., San Diego, 1943-45; asso. marine geologist, prof. geology U. So. Calif., Los Angeles, 1945-62; marine geologist Woods Hole (Mass.) Oceanographic Inst., 1962-75, Henry Bryant Bigelow oceanographer, 1975-79, emeritus, 1979—; mem. U.S. Geol. Survey, Los Angeles, 1945-58. Author: books including Sea Off Southern California, 1960, Oceanography in a Coastal Pond, 1967, (with E. Uchupi) Western North Atlantic, 1972; contbr. numerous articles to profl. jours. Guggenheim fellow, 1959; recipient Shepard prize for marine geology Soc. Econ. Paleontologists and Mineralogists, 1969; Outstanding Alumnus award U. Tex. at Arlington, 1969; Prince Albert de Monaco medal U. Paris, 1971; Compass Distinguished Achievement award Marine Tech. Soc., 1974; Rosenstiel-AAAS award in oceanographic sci., 1974; Illini Achievement award U. Ill., 1977. Fellow Am. Geophys. Union; mem. Am. Assn. Petroleum Geologists, Geol. Soc. Am., Soc. Econ. Paleontologists and Mineralogists, Nat. Acad. Scis., Am. Acad. Arts and Scis., China Acad. Sci., Swedish Royal Acad. Sci. Home: 74 Ransom Rd Falmouth MA 02540 Office: Woods Hole Oceanographic Inst Woods Hole MA 02543

EMERY, SHERMAN RAYMOND, editor; b. Eliot, Maine, Mar. 19, 1924; s. John Lord and Manie (Goodwin) E. B.A. magna cum laude, Boston U., 1949; M.A., Columbia, 1952. Mem. staff Interior Design mag., N.Y.C., 1952—, asso. editor, 1952-62, editor, 1962-83, editorial cons., 1983—. Editor: Styled for Living, 1984. Served with USAAF, 1942-46. Home: 230 E 79th St New York NY 10021 Office: 850 3d Ave New York NY 10022

EMIL, SISTER MARY (SISTER MARY EMIL PENET), educator; b. Detroit, Aug. 8, 1916; d. Emil Louis and Nellie (Houben) Penet. A.B., Marygrove Coll., Detroit, 1936; student, U. Detroit Law Sch., 1936-37; Ph.D., St. Louis U., 1951; LL.D., Marquette U., 1957, St. Mary Coll., Notre Dame, Ind., 1959, U. Notre Dame, 1959, Seattle U., 1960; D.Ped., St. John's U., 1959; D.Litt. (hon.), DePaul U., 1964. Joined Sisters of Immaculate Heart of Mary, 1937; tchr., Monroe, Mich., Detroit, Akron, Ohio, 1939-47; instr., then asst. prof. philosophy Marygrove Coll., Detroit, 1951-56, asso. prof., 1957, pres., 1961-68; dir. Edn. Research Center, 1968-69; postdoctoral research, writing and translation in social philosophy St. Louis U. and Gregorian Inst., Rome, Italy, 1969-72; vis. prof. moral theology St. John's Provincial Sem., Plymouth, Mich., 1974-75; asso. prof. Weston Coll., Cambridge, Mass., 1975-81, St. Vincent's Sem., Boynton Beach, Fla., 1981—; Mem. staff Nat. Cath. Ednl. Assn., Washington, 1957-61; nat. chmn. Sister Formation Conf., 1953-57, exec. sec., 1957-60, community cons., dir. spl. projects, 1960-61; dir. Everett (Wash.) Curriculum Workshop, 1956; mem. tchr. edn. com. New Horizons Project, Nat. Commn. Tchr. Edn. and Profl. Standards, 1960-61; curriculum cons. Seattle U., spring 1960; staff Marquette U. Curriculum Workshop, 1958-61; mem. Nat. Commn. on Presdl. Scholars, 1969-74; mem. adv. bd. com. on Cath. edn. Archdiocese of N.Y., 1968; mem. higher edn. adv. com. Commn. on States, 1968-69. Author: Property and Right in Representative Catholic Moralists of the 13th to 17th Centuries, 1950; also numerous articles.; Editorial bd.: Cath. Youth Ency, 1960—; adv. bd.: Sponsa Regis, 1959-65; chmn. editorial bd.: Jour. Tchr. Edn, 1968-69; editorial bd.: Cath. Sch. Jour, 1968-70. Trustee Marywood Coll., Scranton, Pa., 1968-69; Mem. nat. bd. dirs. Citizens for Ednl. Freedom, 1968. Fund Advancement Edn. grantee, 1956; recipient St. John Baptist de la Salle medal Manhattan Coll., 1957; Alumni Merit award St. Louis U., 1957; Ursula Laurus media Ursuline Coll., Cleve., 1960; Centennial Medallion award Wayne State U., 1967; Elizabeth Seton medal Marillac Coll., 1968; Merit award Nat. Cath. Edn. Assn., 1970. Mem. Assn. Am. Colls. (mem. commn. on coll. and soc. 1965-66, chmn. com. on profl. accreditation 1965-68), Am. Assn. Colls. for Tchr. Edn. (exec. com. 1965-68), Nat. Cath. Ednl. Assn. (chmn. survey dept. tchr. edn. sect. coll. and univ. dept. 1952, sec. Midwest coll. and univ. dept. 1955, v.p. coll. and univ. dept. 1966-67), Religious Edn. Assn. (dir. 1957—), Nat. Council for Accreditation Tchr. Edn. (visitation and appraisal com. 1964-66, exec. com. 1965-68), Council Coop. Tchr. Edn. (exec. com. 1958-60). Address: St Vincent's Seminary Military Trail PO Box 460 Boynton Beach FL 33435

EMILIANI, CESARE, educator; b. Bologna, Italy, Dec. 8, 1922; came to U.S., 1948; s. Luigi and Maria (Manfredini) E.; m. Rosita Manzanares, June 26, 1951; children—Sandra, Mario. D.Geology, U. Bologna, 1945; Ph.D. in Geology, U. Chgo., 1950. Geologist Soc. Idrocarburi Nazionali, Florence, Italy, 1946-48; research asso. U. Chgo., 1950-56; faculty U. Miami (Fla.), 1957—, prof. geology, 1963—, chmn. dept. geology, 1967—. Fellow AAAS, Am. Geophys. Union; mem. Sigma Xi. Research on oxygen isotopic analysis of pelagic microfossils from deep-sea sediment cores. Home: 151 Edgewater Dr Coral Gables FL 33133 Office: Dept Geology U Miami Coral Gables FL 33124

EMILITA, MARIA BERNADETTE, advertising agency executive; b. Passic, N.J., Aug. 28, 1945; d. Chester J. and Sophia H. (Zawadzki) Lewandowski; m. Charles Peter Emilita, Dec. 19, 1970; 1 dau., Amy. B.A., Skidmore Coll., 1966. With J. Walter Thompson U.S.A., Inc., N.Y.C., 1966—, creative dir., 1979—. Home: 174 Terrace Ave Hasbrouck Heights NJ 07604 Office: J Walter Thompson USA Inc 466 Lexington Ave New York NY 10017

EMINIAN, SARKIS JOSEPH, advt. exec.; b. Cleve., Mar. 9, 1926; m. Joanne, Feb. 20, 1960; children—David, Robert, Karen. B.A., Western Res. U., 1954. Sales corr., adminstrv. asst. Tremco Mfg., Cleve., 1954-60; copywriter, copy chief, creative dir., retail advt. mgr. Glidden-Durkee, Cleve., 1960-69; account exec. Griswold Eshleman Co., Cleve., 1969-80, v.p., asso. creative dir., to, 1980; v.p. merchandising Hesselbart & Mitten, Fairlawn, Ohio, 1980—. Served with USNR, 1944-46. Recipient Communication Gold award, 1978, 79, Andy award, 1979, CSCA Silver medal, 1978, 79, 80. Mem. Premium Advt. Assn. Am., Cleve. Advt. Club. Home: 7419 Amber Ln Brecksville OH 44141 Office: 2680 W Market St Fairlawn OH

EMKEN, ROBERT ALLAN, diversified company executive; b. Portland, Oreg., June 13, 1929; s. Cecil Wheeler and Grace (Hill) E.; m. Constance Cook, May 1, 1954; children: Judith, Janice, Robert A. B.S., U. Md., 1951; M.A., George Washington U., 1957. Staff accountant Stoy, Malone & Co., Washington, 1956-58; comptroller R.J. Reynolds Tobacco Co., Winston-Salem, N.C., 1958-70, R.J. Reynolds Industries, Winston-Salem, 1970-75; exec. v.p. Sea-Land Service subsidiary, Edison, N.J., 1975-79; v.p. fin. and adminstrn. R.J. Reynolds Tobacco Co., Winston-Salem, N.C., 1979-83, exec. v.p. fin. and adminstrn., 1983—. Served with USCGR, 1951-54. Mem. Am. Inst. C.P.A.s, Find. Execs. Inst., Nat. Assn. Accountants. Home: 305 Banbury Rd Winston-Salem NC 27104 Office: RJ Reynolds Tobacco Co Winston-Salem NC 27102

EMLEN, STEPHEN THOMPSON, zoology educator; b. Sacramento, Aug. 21, 1940; s. John Thompson and Virginia (Merritt) E.; m. Natalie Jean Demong, June 29, 1973; children: Douglas John, Katharine Merritt. B.A. with distinction, Swarthmore Coll., 1962; M.S., U. Mich., 1964, Ph.D., 1966. Asst. prof. animal behavior Cornell U., 1966-70, asso. prof., 1970-76, prof., 1976—; bd. dirs. Cornell Lab. Ornithology. John Simon Guggenheim fellow, 1973; Nat. Geog. Soc. fellow, 1973, 75. Fellow AAAS, Am. Ornithologists Union, Deutschen Ornithologen-Gesellschaft (corr.); fellow Animal Behavior Soc.; mem. Brit. Ornithologists Union, Am. Soc. Naturalists, Cooper Ornithol. Soc., Wilson Ornithol. Soc., Ecol. Soc. Am. Home: 45 Lone Oak Rd Ithaca NY 14850 Office: Neurobiology and Behavior Cornell U Ithaca NY 14853

EMMANUEL, MICHEL GEORGE, lawyer; b. Clearwater, Fla., May 16, 1918; s. George M. and Alexandra (Damianakes) E.; m. Betty Boring, Dec. 19, 1942; children: George Michel II, Martha Alexandra. B.S., U. Fla., 1940, LL.B., 1948; LL.M., N.Y. U., 1949. Bar: Fla. 1948. Research fellow NYU, N.Y.C., 1948-49; partner Mabry, Reaves, Carlton, Fields & Ward, Tampa, 1951-63; mem. firm Carlton, Fields, Ward, Emmanuel, Smith & Cutler, 1963—, now pres., head tax dept.; mem. adv. com., lectr. N.Y. U. Tax Inst.; lectr. Estate Planning Inst. U. Miami. Contbr. articles to profl. jours. and yachting mags. Bd. dirs., past pres. Hillsborough County Crime Commn.; chmn. Mayor's Com. on Juvenile Delinquency; bd. dirs. Anclote Found., U. of S. Fla. Found., U. Tampa, Saunders Found., Fla. Hist. Soc., Univ. Community Hosp., Fla. Yacht Club Council, United Fund, Tampa Improvement Found., Fales Com., U.S. Naval Acad. Served to comdr. USNR, World War II. Decorated D.F.C., Air medal with 2 stars, Purple Heart; recipient Gov.'s award for distinguished service to State of Fla. Fellow Am. Coll. Probate Counsel, Am. Coll. Tax Counsel; mem. Am., Hillsborough County, Tampa bar assns., D.C. Bar, Fla. Bar (past chmn. tax sect.), Am. Judicature Soc., Tampa C. of C. (past pres.), U.S. C. of C. (taxation com.), Ancient and Secret Order of Quiet Birdmen, Sigma Chi, Phi Delta Phi. Episcopalian. Clubs: Rotarian (past pres.), Ye Mystic Krewe of Gasparilla (past king), University (past pres.), Tampa Executives, Tampa Yacht and Country, Tower (Tampa); Tampa, Gainesville (Fla.) Golf and Country. Home: 2806 Terrace Dr Tampa FL 33609 also Kritonos 9 Aegina Greece Office: NCNB Nat Bank Bldg Tampa FL 33602

EMMERICH, ANDRE, art dealer, author, lecturer; b. Frankfurt, Germany, Oct. 11, 1924; came to U.S., 1940; s Hugo and Lily (Marx) E.; m Constance R. Marantz, Aug. 25, 1958; Adam Oliver, Tobias David Hugo, Noah Nicholas. B.A., Oberlin Coll., 1944. Writer, editor Time-Life Internat., N.Y.C., 1944-53, N.Y. Herald Tribune, 1944-53,

Realities, Paris, 1944-53; pres. Andre Emmerich Gallery, Inc., N.Y.C., Zurich, 1954—; trustee Triangle Artists' Workshop, Pine Plains, N.Y., 1983. Author: Art before Columbus, 1963, Sweat of the Sun and Tears of the Moon, 1965. Mem. Art Dealers Assn. Am. (dir. 1966, pres. 1972-74), Am. Assn. Dealers in Ancient, Oriental and Primitive Art (dir. 1972—). Jewish. Club: Century Assn. (N.Y.C.). Office: Andre Emmerich Gallery Inc 41 E 57th St New York NY 10022

EMMERICH, KAROL DENISE, retail company executive; b. St. Louis, Nov. 21, 1948; d. George Robert and Dorothy (May) Van Houten; m. Richard James, Oct. 18, 1969; 1 son, James Andrew. B.A., Northwestern U., 1969; M.B.A., Stanford U., 1971. Nat. div. account officer Bank of Am., San Francisco, 1971-72; fin. analyst Dayton Hudson Corp., Mpls., 1972-73, sr. fin. analyst, 1973-74, mgr. short term financing, 1974-76, asst. treas., 1976-79, treas., 1979—, v.p., 1980—. Bd. dirs. CHART., Minn. Council Econ. Edn., Walk-In Counseling Ctr., Dayton Hudson Found. Mem. Fin. Execs. Inst., Stanford Bus. Sch. Assn., Minn. Women's Econ. Roundtable. Club: Minneapolis. Home: 7302 Claredon Dr Edina MN 55435 Office: 777 Nicollet Mall Minneapolis MN 55402

EMMERT, RICHARD EUGENE, chemical company executive; b. Iowa City, Iowa, Feb. 23, 1929; s. Frank Thomas and Okie Leona (Seydel) E.; m. Marilyn Ruth Marner, June 19, 1949; children: Debra Sue, Andrea Gale Mazzuca, Lisa Alison. B.S., U. Iowa, 1951; M.S., U. Del., 1952, Ph.D., 1954. Dir. research and devel. pigmentsdept. E.I. du Pont de Nemours & Co., Wilmington, Del., 1973-74, dir. instruments products, 1975-76, dir. electronic products, 1977-78, gen. mgr. textile fibers, 1979-80, v.p. planning, 1981—. Author: Absorption and Extraction, 1963. Bd. dirs. Mid Center, Wilmington, Del., 1981—; mem. adv. bd. U. Calif.-Berkeley, 1975—, U. Iowa, Iowa City, 1973-79; mem. bd. overseers N.J. Inst. Tech., Newark, 1974-76; vice chmn. Stanton (Del.) Sch. Bd., 1960-63. Served with U.S. Army; 1954-56. Mem. Am. Inst. Chem. Engrs., Am. Chem. Soc. Republican. Office: EI du Pont de Nemours & Co 1007 Market St Wilmington DE 19898

EMMETT, JOHN LESTER, physicist; b. Rochester, Minn., July 20, 1939; s. John Lester and Erma (Blood) E.; m. Terry K. Sweitzer, Mar. 21, 1965; 1 son, Geoffrey John. B.S., Calif. Inst. Tech., Pasadena, 1961; Ph.D., Stanford U., 1967. Cons. Lawrence Radiation Lab., Livermore, Calif., 1963-66; cons., dir. research and devel. PEK Labs., Sunnyvale, Calif., 1963-67; cons. MHD pumped laser systems Stanford Research Inst., Menlo Park, Calif., 1965; head laser physics br. Naval Research Lab., Washington, 1969-72; leader Y div. Lawrence Livermore Lab., 1972-75, asso. dir. lasers, 1975—; cons. in field, 1962—. Author papers in field. Recipient E.O. Lawrence award Dept. Energy, 1978. Fellow Am. Phys. Soc.; mem. Sigma Xi. Office: Lawrence Livermore Nat Lab PO Box 5508 L-488 Livermore CA 94550

EMMETT, MARTIN FREDERICK CHEERE, food company executive; b. Johannesburg, South Africa, Aug. 30, 1934; s. Cecil Frederick Cheere and Thelma Marie (Ford) E.; m. Alice Ellen Lavers, Aug. 18, 1956; children: Karen Ann, Robert Martin Cheere, Susan Marie. B.Sc.M.E., U. Witwatersrand, Johannesburg, 1957; M.B.A., Queens U., Kingston, Ont., Can., 1962. Vice pres. consumer products ALCAN Aluminum Co., Montreal, Que., Can., 1962-72; v.p., gen. mgr. beverage div. Standard Brands Ltd., Montreal, 1972-73, pres., chief exec. officer, 1973-76; sr. v.p., group exec. Standard Brands Inc., N.Y.C., 1976-79, pres., chief operating officer, dir., 1980-81; pres., chief exec. officer Internat. Standard Brands Inc., N.Y.C., 1976-79; sr. exec. v.p., dir. Nabisco Brands Inc., N.Y.C., 1981-83, now dir.; dir. Swift Ind. Corp., Chgo., Swift Ind. Packing Co., Burns Fry Ltd., Burns Fry & Timmons, Inc. Mem. Young Pres. Orgn., Assn. Profl. Engrs. Ont. Clubs: Brook, various golf clubs. Home: Frost Rd Greenwich CT 06830 Office: 625 Madison Ave New York NY 10022

EMMONS, C.S., lawyer; b. 1908; m. Mildred Emmons; children—David, Terence, Patrick (dec.), Michael, Karen. A.B., LL.B., Willamette U., Oreg. Bar: Oreg. bar 1931. Now mem. firm Emmons, Kyle Kropp & Kryger, Albany, Oreg. Mem. Aba, Oreg. bar assn. (past pres.). Address: 507 S Washington Albany OR 97321

EMMONS, ROBERT JOHN, corporate executive; b. Trenton, N.J., Sept. 18, 1934; s. Charles John and Ruth Marie (Heilhecker) E.; m. Christine Young Bebb, July 13, 1980; children: Bradley Thomas, Cathy Lynne, Christopher Robert. A.B. in Econs, U. Mich., 1956, M.B.A., 1960, J.D., 1964. Vice-pres. Baskin-Robbins Co., Burbank, Calif., 1964-68; pres. United Rent-All, Los Angeles, 1968-69, Master Host Internat., 1969-71; prof. Grad. Sch. Bus., U. So. Calif., 1971-82; pres. LTI Corp., Monterey, Calif., 1982-84; pres., chief exec. officer, dir. Thriftimart, 1984—; dir., Fotomat, OPCON, Probe Systems Co. Author: The American Franchise Revolution, 1970; poetry Other Places, Other Times, 1974, Love and Other Minor Tragedies, 1980. Mem. Am. Mktg. Assn., European Mktg. Assn., Am. Econ. Assn., AAUP, Beta Gamma Sigma, Pi Kappa Alpha. Clubs: Calif. Yacht (Los Angeles); Hawaii Yacht (Honolulu); Montecito Country (Santa Barbara, Calif.); Monterey Peninsula Yacht. Office: 396 Las Alturas Rd Santa Barbara CA 90006

EMONT, MILTON DAVID, educator; b. Paterson, N.J., Apr. 11, 1923; s. George and Rose (Hoffspiegel) E.; m. Marietta Gruenbaum, Jan. 29, 1950; children—Carl Denis, George Daniel. B.A., Montclair State Coll., 1943; postgrad., U. Cin., 1944, Sorbonne, Paris, 1945, U. Grenoble, France, 1951-52; A.M., Middlebury Coll., 1948; Ph.D., U. Wis., 1958. Telegraph operator airline communications Trans World Airline Co., Orly Field, Paris, 1946-47; tchr. Vets. Evening High Sch., Jersey City, 1948-49; teaching asst. U. Wis., Madison, 1949-51, 52-54; faculty Denison U., Granville, Ohio, 1954—, prof. French, 1965—, chmn. dept. modern langs., 1970-74. Served with AUS, 1943-46. Fulbright scholar, 1951-52; Markham traveling fellow, 1960-61. Mem. Modern Lang. Assn., Am. Assn. Tchrs. of French. Home: 101 Mount Parnassus PO Box 363 Granville OH 43023

EMOREY, HOWARD OMER, hwy. trailer co. exec., automotive supplier; b. Royal Oak, Mich., Mar. 22, 1928; s. Edward O. and Grace (Crissman) E.; m. Elmer B. Bell, June 9, 1951; children—Kathryn, Martha, Lee. B.A., Mich. State U., 1951. C.P.A., Mich. Jr. accountant to audit mgr. Price Waterhouse & Co., Detroit, 1951-66; with Fruehauf Corp., Detroit, 1966—, mgr. fin. planning, 1966-69, treas., 1969—; Mem. Mich. State U. Annual Detroit Mgmt. Conf. Com., 1967-72. Served as p.f.c. AUS, 1946-48. Mem. Am. Inst. C.P.A.'s, Mich. Assn. C.P.A.'s, Fin. Execs. Inst., Mich. State U. Bus. Alumni Assn. (dir. 1973—, pres. 1978). Methodist (chmn. adminstrv. bd.). Clubs: Rotarian, Red Run Golf (Royal Oak, Mich.) (dir.). Home: 2321 Hunt Club Dr Bloomfield Hills MI 48013 Office: 10900 Harper Ave Detroit MI 48232

EMORY, MEADE, lawyer; b. Seattle, Feb. 26, 1931; s. DeWolfe and Marion (Burton) E.; m. Deborah Carley, Apr. 30, 1959; children: Ann, Campbell, Elizabeth. A.B., George Washington U., 1954, LL.B., 1957; LL.M. in Taxation, Boston U., 1963. Bar: D.C. bar 1958, Wash. bar 1958, Iowa bar 1966. Trial atty. IRS, Boston, 1961-64; teaching fellow N.Y.U. Sch. Law, 1964-65; mem. faculty U. Iowa Sch. Law, 1965-70; legislation atty. Joint Com. on Taxation, U.S. Congress, 1970-72; mem. faculty U. Calif. Sch. Law, Davis, 1972-75; asst. to commr. IRS, 1975-77; ptnr. firm LeSourd & Patten, Seattle, 1978—. Co-author: Federal Income Taxation of Corporations and Shareholders-Forms, 1981; bd. editors: Jour. Taxation. Trustee Seattle Symphony Orch., 1978—; bd. dirs. Cornish Inst. Art, Seattle, 1979—. Recipient Commr.'s award IRS, 1976. Mem. Am. Bar Assn. Clubs: Rainier, Seattle Tennis, Univ. (Seattle); Cosmos (Washington).

EMRICH, RAYMOND JAY, physicist, educator; b. Denver, Nov. 30, 1917; s. Jay Leroy and Lola Mary (Baker) E.; m. Carolyn Sarah Schleicher, Sept. 4, 1942; children: Fredrica Lucile Smith, Lynn Margaret Roller. A.B., Princeton U., 1938, A.M., Ph.D., 1946; Henry fellow, Cambridge (Eng.) U., 1938-39; postgrad., Cornell U., 1939-40. Physicist Nat. Def. Research Com., Princeton, 1941-46; faculty Lehigh U., Bethlehem, Pa., 1946—, prof. physics, 1955—, chmn. dept. physics, 1956-68, prin. investigator shock tube research program, 1948-74, microscopic fluctuations and small particle transport project, 1968-75; Cons. Sandia Corp., 1954-55, Los Alamos Sci. Lab., 1961-62; vis. scientist Ernst Mach Inst., Germany, 1968; Nat. Acad. Scis. exchange visitor Novosibirsk, 1970-71, Minsk, USSR, 1979; vis. prof. Ruhr U., Bochum, Ger., spring 1980. Contbr. articles to profl. jours.; Editor and contbr.: Methods of Experimental Physics, Vol. 18 Fluid Dynamics; Editorial bd.: Physics of Fluids, 1958-60, Experiments in Fluids, 1983—; asso. editor: Phys. Rev. Letters, 1974-79. Fellow Am. Phys. Soc. (chmn. div. fluid dynamics 1967, div. councilor 1967-71), AAAS; mem. Am. Assn. Physics Tchrs., Am. Soc. Engring. Edn. (chmn. physics div. 1963-65), Franklin Inst. (com. on sci. and arts 1960—, chmn. 1976), Sigma Xi, Tau Beta Pi. Episcopalian. Home: 517 7th Ave Bethlehem PA 18018

EMRICK, TERRY LAMAR, automotive equipment company executive; b. Bowling Green, Ohio, Aug. 24, 1935; s. Everett Dale and Lois (Fry) E.; m. Alma Faye Adams, July 3, 1953; children—Jacquelyn, Kelly. B.S., Bowling Green State U., 1957. Jr. acct., supr. tax dept. Ernst & Ernst, C.P.A.'s, Toledo, 1957-64; tax mgr., asst. controller, corporate controller and v.p., cons. Champion Spark Plug Co., Toledo, 1964—; owner tax cons. service, 1967-72. Mem. Perrysburg Sch. Bd., 1972-75; bd. dirs., treas. Toledo Zool. Soc., 1978-82. Mem. Tax Forum (pres. 1970-71), Ohio Soc. C.P.A.s, Fin. Execs. Inst. (dir., pres. Toledo chpt.), Alliance Ch. (treas.). Home: 29592 Shelbourne Rd Perrysburg OH 43551 Office: 900 Upton Ave Toledo OH 43661

ENARSON, HAROLD L., emeritus university president; b. Villisca, Iowa, May 24, 1919; s. John and Hulda (Thorson) E.; m. Audrey Pitt, June 7, 1942; children: Merlyn Pitt Prentice, Elaine Pitt Hering, Lisa Pitt Kraxberger. B.A., U. N.Mex., 1940, L.H.D., 1981; M.A., Stanford U., 1946; Ph.D., Am. U., 1951; L.H.D., Kent State U., 1972, U. Detroit, 1975, Ohio State U., 1981; D.P.S., Bethany Coll., 1975; LL.D., Miami U., Oxford, Ohio, 1978, U. Akron, 1981, Central State U., 1981. Teaching asst., research asst. Stanford U., 1940-41, asst. prof., 1949-50; examiner Bur. Budget, Washington, 1942-43, 46-49; asst. prof. Whittier Coll., 1949; exec. sec. Steel Industry Bd., summer 1949; cons. Nat. Security Resources Bd., summer 1950; spl. asst. White House, Washington, 1950-52; pub. mem. WSB, 1952-53; asst. dir. commerce, City Phila., 1953, exec. sec. mayor, Phila., 1954; exec. dir. Western Interstate Commn. Higher Edn., 1954-60, sr. advisor, 1981—; adminstrv. v.p. U. N.Mex., 1960-61, acad. v.p., 1961-66, past project dir.; Internships in Latin Am.; pres. Cleve. State U., 1966-72, Ohio State U., Columbus, 1972-81, pres. emeritus, 1981—; Carl Hatch chair pub. adminstrn. U. N.Mex., 1982-83; Cons. on utilization coll. teaching resources project Fund for Advancement Edn., 1957-58; Carnegie Corp. adminstrs. fellowship, 1958, mem. surgeon gen.'s cons. group on med. manpower, 1960; cons. Ford Found., Egypt, 1960, AID, 1965; dir. edn. services Office Human Resources and Social Devel., 1963-64; mem. nat. adv. health council USPHS, 1964-68, mem. task force on reorgn., 1967; mem. com. to evaluate health relationships; mem. rural area devel. com. U.S. Dept. Agr., 1962-63; cons. Ford Found., C.Am., summers 1961-63; mem. com. internat. edn. Am. Assn. Colls. for Tchr. Edn., 1967-69; mem. com. on internat. edn. Coll. Entrance Exam. Bd., 1967-70; mem. adv. council on developing instns. U.S. Office Edn., 1968-71; mem. Nat. Com. on U.S.-China Relations, 1976—, Nat. Commn. for Coop. Edn., 1968-78; mem. task force on grad. edn. Edn. Commn. of States, 1973-75, task force on state policy and pvt. higher edn., 1976-77; mem. Nat. Dental Research Council, 1958-62; mem. adv. com. U.S. Army Command and Gen. Staff Coll., 1975-78; mem. Kellogg Found. Task Force on Centers for Advanced Studies in Health Adminstrn., 1975-77, Ohio Citizens' Council for Health and Welfare, 1975-77; Bd. visitors Air U., 1968-70; trustee Griffith Found. for Ins. Edn.; bd. dirs., mem. planning com. Nat. Center for Higher Edn. Mgmt. Systems, 1976-79, Council for Fin. Aid to Edn., 1977—; panelist nat. identification program for advancement women in higher edn. Am. Council on Edn., 1977-80, mem. commn. on internat. edn., 1965-67; past mem. commn. on acad. affairs, mem. council overseas liaison com., 1977-80, bd. dirs., 1970-73, 79-82; mem. nat. model task force analysis and planning for improved distbn. of nursing personnel and services project Western Interstate Commn. for Higher Edn., 1975-77; Mem. Midwest regional adv. bd. Inst. Internat. Edn., 1978—; Chmn. Council of Pres.'s Midwest Univs. Consortium for Internat. Activities, Inc., 1979-80; chmn. Inter-Univ. Council of Ohio, 1979-80. Trustee Am. Coll. Testing Program, 1979-82; mem. Nat. Council on Ednl. Research, 1980-81; mem. nat. sponsors com. Council for Internat. Exchange of Scholars, 1981—; co-chmn. Com. on Future of SUNY, 1984. Served with inf. AUS, 1943-46. Mem. Am. Polit. Sci. Assn., Am. Soc. Pub. Adminstrn. (mem. com. on higher edn. and govt. relations), Nat. Assn. State Univs. and Land-Grant Colls. (chmn. internat affairs com., mem. com. on financing higher edn., commn. on arts and scis. 1978, assn. chmn. 1980-81), Council of Presidents (chmn. 1978-79, mem. exec. com. 1978—), Nat. Acad. Pub. Adminstrn., Assn. Urban Univs. (pres. 1971-72), Assn. Am. Univs. (health policy joint com. 1978—, rep. council on postsecondary accreditation 1978—), Univs. Research Assn., Inc. (exec. com. 1979—), Ohio C. of C., Columbus C. of C. (dir.). Club: Rotary. Home: 2994 Nogales Ct Boulder CO 80301 Office: PO Drawer P Boulder CO 80302

ENBERG, DICK, sportscaster; m. Barbara. Grad., Central Mich. U., 1957; Ph.D. in Health Sci, Ind. U., 1961. Formerly assoc. prof., asst. baseball coach Calif. State U., Northridge; sportscaster, 1965—; with NBC Sports, 1975—. Co-producer: The Way It Was, Public Broadcasting System (Emmy award). Recipient Calif. Sportscaster of Yr. award Nat. Sportscasters and Sportswriters Assn., 1967, 68, 70, 73, Nat. Sportscaster of Yr. award, 1979, 80, 81, Emmy award for outstanding personality in play-by-play category, 1981. Office: care NBC Sports 30 Rockefeller Plaza New York NY 10020

ENDAHL, LOWELL JEROME, electric cooperative executive; b. Jerauld County, S.D., July 2, 1922; s. John Martin and Olga A. (Bunde) E.; m. Vronna Belle Lee, Oct. 16, 1948; children: John Raymond and Jay Jerome (twins), Mark Arnold. B.S. in Agrl. Engring., S.D. State U. Power use adviser Tri-County Electric Assn., Plankinton, S.D., 1948-51; mgr. power use dept. Sioux Valley Empire Electric, Colman, S.D., 1951-54; mgr., mem. services Nat. Rural Electric Coop. Assn., Washington, 1954-75, mgr. energy research and devel., 1975—; U.S. rep. UN Working Party on Rural Electrification, Belgium and Netherlands, 1968; cons. Internat. Program div. NRECA, Ecuador and Colombia, 1969, cons. internat. program div., Vietnam, 1970. Columnist: Rural Electrification, 1975—. Pres. Luther Pl. Meml. Ch., Washington, 1976-78. Capt. USMC, 1943-46; PTO. Fellow Am. Soc. Agrl. Engrs. (chmn. EPP div. 1873-74, George W. Kable Electrification award 1983, vice-chmn. editorial bd. Agrl. Engr. 1981-82, past pres. Md.-D.C. chpt.). Office: Nat Rural Electric C-op Assn 1800 Massachusetts Ave NW Washington DC 20036

ENDERS, JOHN FRANKLIN, virologist, emeritus educator; b. West Hartford, Conn., Feb. 10, 1897; s. John Ostrom and Harriet Goulden (Whitmore) E.; m. Sarah Frances Bennett, Sept. 17, 1927 (dec.); children: John Ostrom II, Sarah; m. Carolyn Keane, May 12, 1951; 1 stepson, William Edmund Keane. A.B., Yale U., 1920, Sc.D. hon., 1953; M.A., Harvard U., 1922, Ph.D., 1930, Sc.D., 1956; Sc.D., Trinity Coll., 1955, Northwestern U., 1956, Western Res. U., 1958, Tufts U., 1960; LL.D., Tulane U., 1958; L.H.D., Hartford U., 1960; D.Sc., Jefferson Med. Coll., 1962, U. Pa., 1964, U. Ibadan, 1968, Oxford U., 1975, Duke U., 1976. Asst. dept. bacteriology and immunology Harvard U., 1929-30, instr., 1930-32, faculty instr., 1932-35, asst. prof., 1935-42, assoc. prof., 1942-56, prof., 1956-62, Univ. prof., 1962-67, emeritus Univ. prof. bacteriology and immunology, 1967—; civilian cons. on epidemic diseases to Sec. of War, 1942-46; mem. Commn. on viral Infections Armed Forces Epidemiol. Bd.; mem. sci. adv. bd. (Armed Forces Inst. Pathology); chief research div. infectious diseases Children's Hosp., Boston, 1947-80, chief virus research unit, cons. virology. Author: (with Hans Zinsser and Leroy D. Fothergill) Immunity: Principles and Application in Medicine and Public Health, 1939; editorial bd.: Jour. Immunology, Jour. Bacteriology, Jour. Virology, others. Lt. (j.g.) Naval Res., 1917-20. Decorated comdr. Order Nat. de la Republic de Haute Volta; recipient Passano Found. award for culturing poliomyelitis viruses in living tissues, 1953, Lasker award, 1954, Kimball award, 1954, Nobel prize in medicine and physiology, 1954, Kyer award USPHS, Chapin medal, 1955, Bruce award ACP, 1956, Cameron prize U. Edinburgh, 1961, Howard Taylor Ricketts Meml. award U. Chgo., 1962, New Eng. Israel Freedom award, 1962, Diesel Gold medal, 1962, Robert Koch medal, Germany, 1962, Sci. Achievement award AMA, 1963, Presdl. medal of Freedom, 1963. Fellow Am. Acad. Arts and Scis.; mem. Nat. Acad. Scis., Harvey Soc., Am. Philos. Soc., Soc. Gen. Microbiology (hon), Soc. Am. Bacteriologists, Am. Assn. Immunologists (pres. 1952-53), Soc. Exptl. Biology and Medicine, Am. Pub. Health Assn., AAAS, Sigma Xi, Aplha Omega Alpha; assoc. mem. Mass. Med. Soc.; fgn. mem. Royal Soc.; hon. mem. Academie des Sciences de l'Institut de France. Home: 64 Colbourne Crescent Brookline MA 02146

ENDERS, THOMAS OSTROM, diplomat; b. Hartford, Conn., Nov. 28, 1931; s. Ostrom and Alice Dudley (Talcott) E.; m. Gaetana Elena Mathilde Costanza Marchegiano, June 6, 1955; children: Domitilla Elena, Alice Talcott, Claire Whitmore, Ostrom. B.A., Yale U., 1953; Docteur de l'Universite, U. Paris, 1955; M.A., Harvard U., 1957. Joined U.S. Fgn. Service, 1958; assigned, Washington, 1958-60, 63-69, Stockholm, 1961-63; spl. asst. to under sec. for polit. affairs Dept. State, 1966-68, dep. asst. sec. internat. monetary affairs, 1968-69; dep. chief mission, Belgrade, 1969-70, Phnom Penh, 1970-73, chargé d'affaires, 1973-74; asst. sec. econ. and bus. affairs Dept. State, Washington, 1974-76; ambassador to Can., 1976-79, ambassador to European Communities, Brussels, 1979-81; asst. sec. inter-Am. affairs Dept. State, 1981-83; ambassador to Spain, 1983—. Recipient Arthur S. Flemming award, 1969. Office: US Embassy in Spain APO NY 09285

ENDERVELT, JEFFREY KENNETH, diversified company executive; b. Bklyn., May 5, 1941; s. David S. and Belle (Slavitsky) E.; m. Polly Bergern, 1982. Student, Bklyn. Coll., 1963; LL.B., U. Balt., 1967. Bar: Md. 1968, N.Y. 1972. Sole practice, N.Y.C, 1967-74; legis. counsel Rep. John M. Murphy of S.I., 1968-69; adminstrv. counsel Stanley Steingut, speaker of the Assembly, Albany, N.Y., 1969-70; asst. atty. Michael Industries, Inc., N.Y.C., 1972-73; gen. counsel Michael Industries, Inc, N.Y.CV., 1973; chmn. bd. pres., chief exec. officer Michael Industries Inc., N.Y.C, 1974—; vice chmn. bd. Lehigh Valley Industries, Inc., N.Y.C., 1980-82, chmn. bd., 1982—. Exec. com. Nat. Com. on Am. Fgn. Policy, 1975; bd. dirs. Bklyn. Acad. Music, 1980—. Mem. Md. Bar Assn., N.Y. Bar Assn., Young Pres. Orgn., Young Men's Philanthropic League. Office: Lehigh Valley Industries Inc 200 E 42d St New York NY 100107

ENDICK, KENNETH J., computer co. exec.; b. N.Y.C., Sept. 29, 1942; s. Irving R. and Rae (Pievko) E.; (div.)children—Alysia J., Carrie J. B.A., Queens Coll., 1963; J.D., Fordham U., 1966. Bar: N.Y. bar 1967. Corp. counsel, asst. sec. Radolph Computer Corp., Greenwich, Conn., 1968-73; sec., gen. counsel DPF Inc., Hartsdale, N.Y., 1973—; arbitrator Am. Arbitration Assn. Mem. Am. Soc. Corp. Secs., Am. Bar Assn., Computer Law Assn., N.Y. State Bar Assn., Westchester County Bar Assn. Democrat. Jewish. *

ENDICOTT, WILLIAM F., journalist; b. Harrodsburg, Ky., Aug. 26, 1935; s. William O. and Evelyn E.; m. Mary Frances Thomas, Dec. 27, 1956; children: Gene, Fran, Greg. Student, Am. U., 1955; B.A. in Polit. Sci, Transylvania U., 1957. With Lexington (Ky.) Leader, 1957; sports writer Louisville Courier-Jour., 1958-62; reporter Tulare (Calif.) Advance-Register, 1963; reporter, city editor Modesto (Calif.) Bee, 1963-66; city editor Sacramento Union, 1966-67; with Los Angeles Times, 1968—, now Sacramento Bur. chief. Served with USMCR, 1957-58. Recipient various journalism awards Disting. Alumnus award Transylvania U., 1980. Episcopalian. Office: 1121 L St Suite 200 Sacramento CA 95814

ENDLEMAN, ROBERT, sociologist, psychotherapist, educator; b. Sudbury, Ont., Can., Oct. 2, 1923; came to U.S., 1946, naturalized, 1957; s. Harry Max and Rose (Cherin) E.; m. Moselle Galbraith, 1961 (div. 1964); 1 dau., Julie. B.A., U. Toronto, 1946; M.A., U. Wis., 1947; Ph.D., Harvard, 1955; grad. postdoctoral psychoanalytic program, N.Y. U. Instr. social scis. U. Minn., 1949-51; asst. prof. sociology State U. N.Y., 1951-52; research sociologist U. Chgo., 1952-54; instr. to asst. prof. sociology U. Ill., Chgo., 1953-57; asst. prof. sociology Hofstra Coll., 1957-58; asso. prof. social sci. State U. N.Y., Oyster Bay, 1958-61; asso. prof. sociology Adelphi U., 1961-64, prof., 1964—, chmn. dept. sociology, 1963-69; Vis. prof. sociology McGill U., 1970, U. Haifa (Israel), Spring 1984; pvt. practice psychotherapy, N.Y.C. Co-author: Human Reactions to Disaster, 1954; author: Personality and Social Life, 1967, Culture and Personality Dynamics, 1971, Psyche and Society, 1981; assoc. editor: Jour. Psychoanalytical Anthropology. Recipient Clement Staff award Psychoanalytic Rev., 1966. Mem. Internat., Am. sociol. assns., Eastern Sociol. Soc., Am. Anthrop. Assn., Am. Psychol. Assn., Soc. for Study Social Problems, Psychoanalytic Soc. N.Y. U. Postdoctoral Program. Home: 595 West End Ave New York NY 10024 Office: Adelphi Univ Garden City NY 11530 also 595 West End Ave New York NY 10024

ENDRIES, JOHN MICHAEL, utility exec.; b. New Berlin, N.Y., Sept. 10, 1942; s. Norton Leo and Alice (Simons) E.; m. Anne Jones, Sept. 9, 1967; children—Carrie Anne, John Michael. B.B.A. in Acctg, U. Notre Dame, 1964. C.P.A., N.Y. Audit mgr. Price Waterhouse & Co. (C.P.A.'s), Syracuse, N.Y., 1964-73; asst. to v.p. fin., then v.p., controller Niagara Mohawk Power Corp., Syracuse, 1973-80, sr. v.p., 1980—. Mem. Am. Inst. C.P.A.'s, Edison Electric Inst., Fin. Execs. Inst. (dir., past pres. Syracuse chpt.), N.Y. State Soc. C.P.A.'s. Home: 8518 Equestrian Ridge Manlius NY 13104 Office: 300 Erie Blvd W Syracuse NY 13202

ENELL, JOHN WARREN, Association executive, educator; b. N.Y.C., June 24, 1919; s. William Howard and Cristabel (Baumann) E.; m. Anna Louise Lefferts, June 4, 1949; children: Margaret Ann, Janet Ellen, Kathryn Laurel, Mark William. B.S., U. Pa., 1940, M.E., 1948; M.Adminstrv. Engring., N.Y. U., 1947, D.Eng. Sci., 1949. Test engr., asst. project engr., sr. exptl. engr. Wright Aero. Corp. div. Curtiss-Wright Corp., Paterson, N.J., 1940-45; research asst. to prof. mgmt. engring. N.Y. U., 1946-58; dir. info. service and surveys Am. Mgmt. Assn., 1954-61, dir. research, 1961-66, v.p. for research, 1967—; mem. U.S. Mut. Security Adminstrn. mission to Italy, 1952-53; dir. research Am. Found. Mgmt. Research, 1961-67, v.p., 1970-73; mem. AID mission to, Vietnam, 1972, IESC missions to, Greece, 1973, to; Colombia, 1978. Author: Are Your Findings Trustworthy?, 1950, (with others) Quality Control Handbook, 1951, Production Handbook, 1972, (with G.H. Haas) Setting Standards for Executive Performance, 1960; editorial bd.: Jour. Indsl. Engring. Trustee Wayne Pub. Library; mem. adv. bd. N.Y. U., N.J. Inst. Tech., Bradley U., Adelphi U. Fellow Am. Inst. Indsl. Engrs. (nat. v.p. 1966-68, nat. pres. 1968-69); mem. Acad. Mgmt., Am. Mgmt. Assn., Am. Assn. Engring. Socs. (sec.-treas. 1980), ASME, Am. Soc. Quality Control, Am. Statis. Assn., Council on the Continuing Edn. Unit (v.p. 1977-80, pres. 1980-82), Engrs. Council Profl. Devel. (dir., nat. treas. 1973-77), Engrs. Joint Council (nat. treas. 1979), Inst. Cert. Profl. Mgrs. (bd. regents 1981—), Sigma Xi, Alpha Pi Mu. Home: 165 Lake Dr W Packanack Lake Wayne NJ 07470 Office: 135 W 50th St New York NY 10020

ENELOW, ALLEN JAY, psychiatrist, educator; b. Pitts., Jan. 15, 1922; s. Isadore M. and Rose (Kasdan) E.; m. Mary Cleveland, July 21, 1946 (div. Sept. 1965); children: David, James, Susan, Margaret, Patience, Abigail; m. Sheila Kearns, Oct. 1, 1966 (div. 1983); stepchildren: Lauren, Lisa. A.B., W.Va. U., 1942; M.D., U. Louisville, 1944. Intern Michael Reese Hosp., Chgo., 1944-45; resident psychiatry Winter VA Hosp., Topeka, 1947-49; mem. staff Menninger Found. and Asso. Hosps., 1947-52; practice medicine specializing in psychiatry, Beverly Hills, Calif., 1952-58, Pacific Palisades, Calif., 1956-64; faculty U. So. Calif., Los Angeles, 1960-67; prof., chmn. dept. psychiatry Mich. State U., East Lansing, 1967-72; prof. psychiatry U. of Pacific, 1972-78; chmn. dept. psychiatry Pacific Med. Center, San Francisco, 1972-82; clin. prof. psychiatry U. Calif., 1977-82, U. So. Calif., 1982—; cons. NIMH, VA, others. Author: Psychiatry in the Practice of Medicine, 1966, Interviewing and Patient Care, 1972, 2d edit., 1979, Elements of Psychotherapy, 1977; Contbr. numerous articles to profl. jours. Served with M.C. AUS, 1945-47. Fellow Am. Psychiat. Assn., ACP; mem. AMA (chmn. sect. nervous and mental disease 1967-68). Home: 2001 Santa Monica Blvd Santa Monica CA 90404

ENERSEN, BURNHAM, lawyer; b. Lamberton, Minn., Nov. 17, 1905; s. Albert H. and Ethel (Rice) E.; m. Nina H. Wallace, July 21, 1935; children: Richard W., Elizabeth. A.B., Carleton Coll., 1927, L.H.D., 1974; LL.B., Harvard U., 1930. Bar: Calif. 1931. Assoc. McCutchen, Doyle, Brown & Enersen, San Francisco, 1930-43, ptnr., 1943-78, counsel, 1978—; dir. Pomfret Estates, Inc.; Chmn. Gov.'s Com. Water Lawyers, 1957; mem. Calif. Jud. Council, 1960-64; vice chmn. Calif. Constn. Revision Commn., 1964-75; mem. com. to rev. Calif. Master Plan for Higher Edn., 1971-72. Mem. Calif. Citizens Commn. for Tort Reform, 1976-77; chmn. Assn. Calif. Tort Reform, 1979-83; mem. Calif. Postsecondary Edn. Com., 1974-78; pres. United Bay Area Crusade, 1962, United Crusades of Calif., 1969-71; trustee Mills Coll., 1972-82, chmn., 1976-80. Fellow Am. Bar Found.; mem. Am. Judicature Soc., ABA (ho. of dels. 1970-76), State Bar Calif. (pres. 1960), Bar Assn. San Francisco (pres. 1955), Bar Assn. City N.Y., Am. Law Inst., Calif. C. of C. (dir. 1962-78, pres. 1971), Calif. Hist. Soc. (dir. 1976-78, 83—). Clubs: Bohemian, Pacific-Union, Commercial (pres. 1966), Commonwealth Calif., San Francisco Golf, Cypress Point. Home: 40 Arguello Blvd San Francisco CA 94118 Office: 3 Embarcadero Center San Francisco CA 94111

ENERSEN, LAWRENCE ALBERT, architect; b. Lamberton, Minn., July 5, 1909; s. Albert Hovesoe and Ethel (Rice) E.; m. Eleanore Cullinan Vail, Nov. 23, 1939; children—David, Stephen, Philip. A.B., Carleton Coll., 1931; M.L.A., Harvard, 1935, 1936-37; D.F.A. (hon.), Doane Coll., 1980. Designer, draftsman Olmsted Bros., Brookline, Mass., 1937-38; instr. U. Mich., 1939-42; asst. prof. Harvard, 1942-43; prof. U. N.C., 1947-52; prin. firm Clark & Enersen, Lincoln, Nebr., 1946-72, treas., 1972—; Mem. Lincoln Center Devel. Assn., 1960—, Lincoln Housing Authority, 1966-68; sec. Capitol Murals Commn., 1960—; chmn. Mayor's Com. on Urban Design, 1969—; co-chmn. C.E. Adv. Com. in Environmental Planning, 1967—; mem. Gov.'s Com. on Employment Handicapped, 1972—. Co-chmn. Better Lincoln Com., 1957-59; pres. Lincoln Arts Council, 1966-68; mem. exec. com. Arbor Day Found., 1971—; Adv. bd. St. Elizabeth Hosp., 1960-71. Served with USNR, 1943-46. Recipient Conservationist award Lower Platte S. Natural Resource Dist., 1974; Disting. Service medal Kiwanis Club, 1977; Gov.'s Art award, 1979. Fellow AIA, Am. Soc. Landscape Architects; mem. Nebr. Bd. Landscape Architects. Clubs: Mason. Clubs, Sertoma, University, Torch. Home: 2346 Harwood St Lincoln NE 68502 Office: 600 NBC Bldg Lincoln NE 68508

ENFIELD, CLIFTON WILLIS, lawyer; b. Watertown, N.Y., Nov. 26, 1918; s. George Hyson and Anna Murel (Humerick) E.; m. Mary Verone Sullivan, Feb. 14, 1948; children—Douglas George, Brian Michael. B.S. in Textiles, N.C. State Coll., 1938; J.D., U. Va., 1948. Bar: Oreg. bar 1948, Md. bar 1959. Sales rep. Textiles Distbrs., Inc., Thomasville, N.C., 1938-39; cloth prodn. mgr. E.M. Holt Plaid Mills div. Burlington Mills, Inc., N.C., 1939-40; asst. atty. gen., State of Oreg., 1948-56; asst. counsel Oreg. Hwy. Commn., 1948-51, chief counsel, 1951-56; gen. counsel Bur. Pub. Rds. Dept. Commerce, 1956-61; minority counsel Com. Pub. Works Transp. of U.S. Ho. of Reps., Washington, 1961-77; legis. cons., 1977—. Contbr. articles to hwy., legal publs. Served from 2d lt. to lt. col., inf. AUS, 1940-46. Mem. Oreg., Md. bar assns., Am. Rd. Builders Assn., Nat. Acad. Sci., Am. Right of Way Assn., Delta Theta Phi, Sigma Tau Sigma, Order Coif. Presbyn. Home and Office: 350 South Shore Dr Osprey FL 33559

ENFIELD, FRANKLIN D., geneticist; b. Woolstock, Iowa, Dec. 26, 1933; s. Clyde and Anna Mary (Wernet) E.; m. Maxine Ann Miller, Aug. 14, 1955; children—Mark, Marsha, Kathy. B.S., Iowa State U., 1955; M.S., Okla. State U., 1957; Ph.D., U. Minn., 1960. Asst. prof. U. Minn., Mpls., 1960-65, asso. prof., 1965-70, prof. genetics, 1970—, dir. grad. studies in genetics, 1971-76. Contbr. sci. articles to profl. jours. USPHS and NSF grantee, 1963—; Genetics Soc. travel grantee to USSR, 1978. Mem. Am. Soc. Animal Sci., Genetics Soc. Am., AAAS, Sigma Xi, Phi Kappa Phi, Gamma Sigma Delta, Alpha Zeta, Phi Eta Sigma. Lutheran. Home: 8400 Manning Ave N Stillwater MN 55082 Office: 254 BioScience Center U Minn Saint Paul MN 55108

ENGBRETSON, WILLIAM EARL, educator; b. Milw., Oct. 9, 1926; s. Earl Wilfred and Frances Cecelia (Sears) E.; m. Catherine Ann Sampe, Aug. 23, 1947 (div. 1972); children: Kristine Marie, Jan Earl, Gregg William; m. Barbara A. Morton, Dec. 16, 1978. A.B., Western Mich. U., 1947; M.A., Mich. State U., 1950; Ph.D., Northwestern U., 1955. Tchr. social studies Portage Twp. High Sch., Portage Center, Mich., 1948; grad. asst. basic coll. Mich. State U., 1948-49; county welfare agt., juvenile ct. referee, Ingham County, Mich., 1949-50, elementary sch. tchr., Glencoe, Ill., 1950-53; lectr. edn. Roosevelt U., Chgo., 1952-53, asso. prof., 1953-54; asst. prof., then asso. prof. edn. Western Mich. U., Kalamazoo, 1954-57; vis. assoc. prof. U. Fla., 1957; assoc. sec. Am. Assn. Colls. Tchr. Edn., 1957-59; prof. edn., asst. to pres. Kans. State Tchrs. Coll., Emporia, 1959-60; prof. edn., dean Sch. Edn. Ind. State U., Terre Haute, 1960-66; prof. higher edn. U. Denver, 1966-68, Temple U., Phila., 1968-69; prof. higher edn., pres. Governors State U., Park Forest South, Ill., 1969-76; prof. Union Grad. Sch., 1976—; pres. Am. Sch. Mgmt., Kenosha, Wis., 1977—; project dir. TRUST, Inc., Chgo., 1979-81, Nat. Center for Health Edn., San Rafael, Calif., 1981—; mem. Am. Assn. Colls. Tchr. Edn.-AID study team, Pakistan, 1964; cons. colls., univs., pub. schs., founds., govt. agys. Asso. C.F.K., Ltd.; dir. 1st Bank Park Forest South. Contbr. profl. jours. Bd. dirs. Union for Experimenting Colls. and Univs., Coll. St. Francis, St. Anthony's Hosp., Martin Center Coll. Served with USNR, 1944-46. Recipient Disting. Alumni Western Mich. U., 1965. Fellow AAAS (life); mem. NEA (life), Am. Edn. Research Assn., Am. Assn. Sch. Adminstrs., Alliance Advancement Health Edn., Am. Assn. Higher Edn. (life), Am. Pub. Health Assn., Am. Assn. Coll. Tchr. Edn. (pres. 1968-69), Am. Sch. Health Assn., Am. Assn. State Colls. and Univs. (mem. coms.), Am. Coll. Health Assn., NAACP, Urban League, ACLU (life), AAUP, World Future Soc., Phi Delta Kappa, Kappa Delta Pi. Home: 888 6th St Petaluma CA 94952 *Education is the key to the solution of mankind's problems...everything else is transitory.*

ENGDAHL, GORDON WILLIAM, human resources consultant; b. Chgo., Dec. 15, 1920; s. Knut and Clara (Nilson) E.; m. Phyllis Ester Hallen, Aug. 26, 1944; children: Patricia Engdahl Sailhamer, Judith Engdahl Howlin, Steven. B.S. in chem. Engring., U. Ill., 1943; postgrad. in bus. adminstrn., U. Minn., 1961-62. With 3M Co., St. Paul, 1943-83, dir. new bus. devel., 1968-72, v.p. indsl. specialties div., 1973-80, v.p. human resources, 1980-83; chem. tech. com. Pressure Sensitive Tape Council, 1961-62; mem. Midwest Human Resources Network, Chgo., 1981-83. Bd. dirs. Send-Internat., Detroit, 1946-83, Sister Kenny Inst. of Abbot Northwestern Hosp., Mpls., 1982-83. Served to lt. (j.g.) USN, 1944-46; PTO. Republican. Club: White Bear Yacht (White Bear Lake, Minn.). Office: 3M Co 3M Ctr Saint Paul MN 55101

ENGDAHL, JAMES CAMERER, lawyer; b. Geneseo, Ill., Mar. 11, 1918; s. Victor E. and Edith (Young) E.; m. Joyce R. Stringer, Aug. 3, 1947; children—Victor, James, David. A.B., Stanford U., 1940, J.D., 1943. Bar: Calif., Ariz. bars 1946. Practice in, Phoenix, 1946—; partner firm Engdahl, Jerman, Butler & Estep, 1958—; dir. Heritage Life Ins. Co., Sun State Savs. & Loan Assn. Mem. Phoenix Planning Commn., 1960-63, vice chmn., 1963; mem. Phoenix Sts. Adv. Com., 1960-77; bd. dirs. First Meth. Found., Phoenix, 1954—, pres., 1965-73; trustee Sch. Theology, Claremont, Calif., 1961-75. Served with AUS, 1943-46. Mem. state bars Ariz., Calif., Am. Bar Assn. Home: 6135 N 38th St Paradise Valley AZ 85253 Office: 1421 E Thomas Rd Phoenix AZ 85014

ENGDAHL, RICHARD BOTT, mechanical engineer; b. Elgin, Ill., Apr. 16, 1914; s. Walter Frederick and Emma Mae (Bott) E.; m. Helen Keller Klaas, Nov. 21, 1940; children: Karen Louise, Eric Klaas. B.S., Bucknell U., 1936; M.S., U. Ill., 1938. Diplomate: Am. Acad. Environ Engrs. Research asst. dept. mech. engring. U. Ill., 1938-40, instr., 1940-41; research engr. Battelle Meml. Inst., Columbus, Ohio, 1941-46, chief, 1947-60, sr. project leader, after 1960-76, semi-ret., 1976; cons. WHO, Malaysia, 1979-80, China, 1981, IESC, Turkey, 1980. Contbr. chpts. to sci. texts. Recipient Distinguished Service awards Bucknell Alumni Assn., 1972; U. Ill. Coll. Engring., 1976; Chambers award Air Pollution Control Assn., 1976; Nichols award ASME, 1976. Fellow ASME, AAAS, Am. Soc. Heating, Refrigeration and Air Conditioning Engrs.; mem. Air Pollution Control Assn.; Am. Meteorol. Soc., Sigma Xi, Tau Beta Pi, Pi Mu Epsilon. Home: 1750 W 1st Ave Columbus OH 43212 Office: 505 King Ave Columbus OH 43201

ENGDAHL, WALTER ARNOLD, banker, corporate lawyer; b. N.Y.C., May 16, 1938; s. Walter E. and Lillian I. (Nelson) E.; m. Sandra E. Young, July 24, 1965; children: Linda Elizabeth, Lauren Kristine. B.S., Cornell U., 1964; J.D., U. Ill., 1969; LL.M. in Taxation, U. Miami, 1977. Bar: N.Y. 1969, Fla. 1973. Assoc. firm Wilkie Farr & Gallagher, N.Y.C., 1969-73; Tylander, deClaire & Van Kleeck, Boca Raton, Fla., 1973-78; gen. counsel Gulfstream Banks, Inc., Boca Raton, 1978-83; corp. counsel Sensormatic Electronics Corp., Boca Raton, 1983—. Served with AUS, 1956-57. Mem. Am. Bar Assn., Fla. State Bar, N.Y. State Bar Assn., S. Palm Beach County Bar Assn. Home: 1920 SW 67th Terr Plantation FL 33317 Office: 1150 Broken Sound Pkwy NW Boca Raton FL 33431

ENGEBRETSEN, ARDEN BERNT, lawyer, chemical company executive; b. San Francisco, Dec. 2, 1931; s. Ray and Zina (Rice) E.; m. Joye Eleanore Allen, Aug. 25, 1953; children—James Ray, Arden Allen, Steven Brent, William Curtis, Thomas Quinn, Bryan Charles. B.S., U. Utah, 1953, J.D., 1955. Bar: Utah bar 1956, Del. bar 1969. Legis. asst. to Gov. of Utah, 1958 and after; also asst. atty. gen. State of Utah; adminstrv. asst. Hercules, Inc., Bacchus, Utah, 1959, counsel, Wilmington, Del., 1968-71, sr. counsel, 1971-74, asst. treas., 1974-75, treas., 1975—, v.p., 1977-83, divisional v.p., dir., 1983—; dir. Girard Bank of Del. Served with USAF, 1955-58. Mem. Am., Del., Utah bar assns. Republican. Mormon. Home: 100 Havernill Ln Centerville DE 19807 Office: Hercules Plaza Wilmington DE 19899

ENGEBRETSON, MILTON BENJAMIN, clergyman; b. Grand Forks, N.D., Dec. 29, 1920; s. Hans Emil and Anna Sophie (Huss) E.; m. Esther Rhoda Hollenbeck, Dec. 12, 1945; children—Jon Philip, Donn Norman. B.A., U. Wash., 1950; grad., North Park Theol. Sem., Chgo., 1954, D.D., 1975; D.D., Seattle Pacific U., 1967. Ordained to ministry Evang. Covenant Ch., 1956; pastor Stotler Mission Covenant Ch., Osage City, Kans., 1951-52, Mission Covenant Ch., Mankato, Minn., 1954-57, Elim Covenant Ch., Mpls., 1957-62; exec. sec. Evang. Covenant Ch. Am., 1962-67, pres., 1967—; conf. chmn. meeting U.S. Church Leaders, 1972-79; pres. Internat. Fedn. Free Evang. Chs., 1979. Served with USAAF, 1942-45. Decorated comdr. Royal Order Polar Star, Sweden, 1974. Club: Union League (Chgo.). Home: 6607 N Lightfoot St Chicago IL 60646 Office: 5101 N Francisco Ave Chicago IL 60625

ENGEL, ALBERT JOSEPH, judge; b. Lake City, Mich., Mar. 21, 1924; s. Albert Joseph and Bertha (Bielby) E.; m. Eloise Ruth Bull, Oct. 18, 1952; children: Albert Joseph, Katherine Ann, James Robert, Mary Elizabeth. Student, U. Md., 1941-42; A.B., U. Mich., 1948, LL.B., 1950. Bar: Mich. 1951. Ptnr. firm Engle & Engel, Muskegon, Mich., 1952-67; judge Mich. Circuit Ct., 1967-71; judge U.S. Dist. Ct. Western Dist. Mich., 1971-74; circuit judge U.S. Ct. Appeals, 6th Circuit, Grand Rapids, Mich., 1974—. Served with AUS, 1943-46; ETO. Fellow Am. Bar Found.; mem. Am., Fed., Cin., Grand Rapids bar assns., Am. Judicature Soc., Am. Legion, Phi Sigma Kappa, Phi Delta Phi. Episcopalian. Clubs: Rotary, Grand Rapids Torch. Home: 7287 Denison Dr SE Grand Rapids MI 49506 Office: 640 Fed Bldg Grand Rapids MI 49503 *

ENGEL, ANDREW GEORGE, neurologist; b. Budapest, Hungary, July 12, 1930; s. Alexander and Alice Julia (Gluck) E.; m. Nancy Jean Brombacher, Aug. 15, 1958; children: Lloyd William, Andrew George, Mary Jean. B.Sc., McGill U., 1953; M.D., 1955. Diplomate: Am. Bd. Internal Medicine, Am. Bd. Psychiatry and Neurology. Intern Phila. Gen. Hosp., 1955-56; sr. asst. surgeon, clin. asso. USPHS, NIH, Bethesda, Md., 1958-59; fellow in neuropathology Columbia U., N.Y.C., 1962-64; with Mayo Clinic, 1956-57, 60-62; cons., 1965—; prof. neurology Mayo Med. Sch., Rochester, Minn., 1973—; mem. sci. adv. com. Muscular Dystrophy Assn., 1973—; mem. rev. com. NIH, 1977-81. Mem. editorial bd.: Neurology, 1973-77, Annals of Neurology, 1978—, Muscle and Nerve, 1978—, Jour. Neuropathology, 1981-83; Contbr. articles to profl. jours. Served with USPHS, 1957-59. Mem. Am. Acad. Neurology, Am. Neurol. Assn., Am. Assn. Neuropathologists, Am. Soc. Cell Biology, Soc. Neuroscis., AAAS. Home: 2027 Lenwood Dr Rochester MN 55901 Office: 200 SW 1st St Rochester MN 55901

ENGEL, BERNARD THEODORE, psychologist; b. Chgo., Apr. 18, 1928; s. Marvin I. and Hannah (Hollander) E.; m. Rae Goldberg, Mar. 10, 1951; children: Sandra E., Jeffrey P., Lauren C. B.A., UCLA, 1954, Ph.D., 1956. Cert. biofeedback, 1981. Jr. research psychologist UCLA, 1956; research psychologist Inst. Psychosomatic and Psychiatric. Research and Tng., Michael Reese Hosp., Chgo., 1957-58; lectr. med. psychology, mem. sr. staff Cardiovascular Research Inst., U. Calif. Sch. Medicine, San Francisco, 1959-67; chief lab. behavioral scis., chief psychophysiology sect. Gerontology Research Center, Nat. Inst. Aging, NIH, Balt., 1967—; assoc. prof. behavioral biology Johns Hopkins Sch. Medicine, Balt., 1970-82, prof., 1982—. Contbr. 100 articles to sci. jours. Served in U.S. Army, 1950-52. Recipient award Pavlovian Soc., 1979. Fellow AAAS, Gerontol. Sci.; mem. Soc. Psychophysiol. Research (pres. 1970-71), Biofeedback Soc. (pres. 1981-82), Am. Psychosomatic Soc. (sec.-treas. 1981—), Pavlovian Soc., Internat. Coll. Psychosomatic Medicine, Soc. Behavioral Medicine, Acad. Behavioral Medicine Research, Sigma Xi. Home: 106 Welford Rd Lutherville MD 21093 Office: Balt City Hosp Gerontology Research Ctr Baltimore MD 21224

ENGEL, CHARLES ROBERT, chemistry educator; b. Vienna, Austria, Jan. 28, 1922; s. Jean and Lucie (Fuchs) E.; m. Edith H. Braillard, Aug. 6, 1951; children: Lucie Tatiana Engel Berthoud, Christiane Simonne, Engel Vaillancourt, Francis Pierre, Marc Robert. B.A., U. Grenoble, 1941; M.Sc., Swiss Fed. Inst. Tech., Zurich, 1947, D.Sc., 1951; State-D.Sc., U. Paris, 1970. Research fellow, asst. Swiss Fed. Inst. Tech., Zurich, 1948-51; asst. prof. med. research Collip Med. Research Lab. U. Western Ont., London, 1951-55, asso. prof. med. research, 1955-58, hon. spl. lectr. chemist, dept. chemistry, 1951-58; prof. chemistry Laval U., Quebec, Que., 1958—; vis. prof. Inst. de Chimie des Substances Naturelles CNRS, Gif-sur-Yvette, France, 1966-67. Editorial bd.: Steroids, 1964—; hon. editorial bd.: Current Abstracts of Chemistry, 1971-72, Index Chemicus, 1971-72; mem. editorial adv. bd.: Can. Jour. Chemistry, 1974. Lt. for Can.-Que., Equestrian Order of Holy Sepulchre of Jerusalem, 1970—; bd. dirs. Cath. Culture Center, London, Ont. Decorated comdr. Equestrian Order of Holy Sepulchre of Jerusalem, 1964, comdr. with star, 1970, knight grand cross, 1973; medal Austrian Ministry of Edn. Fellow Chem. Inst. Can. (chmn. organic div. 1965-66, exec. med. div. 1968—), Royal Chem. Soc. (London); mem. Am., Swiss, French chem. socs., Canadian Biochem. Soc., N.Y. Acad. Scis., Order Chemists Que. Office: Dept Chemistry Laval U Quebec PQ G1K 7P4 Canada

ENGEL, EVA JOHANNA, educator; b. Dortmund, Germany, Aug. 18, 1919; came to U.S., 1968; d. Stefan and Margarete (Litten) E.; m. Albert E. Holland, June 12, 1970. B.A. with honours, U. London, Eng., 1941; M.A., Cambridge (Eng.) U., 1955; Ph.D., Cornell U., 1954. Teaching fellow Cornell U., 1952-54; research fellow, asst. lectr. Girton Coll., Cambridge U., 1955; lectr. Keele (Eng.) U., 1960; vis. prof. Boston U., 1967-68; prof. German lit. Wellesley Coll., 1968—; vis. prof. Harvard U., summer 1970, Herzog August Bibliothek, 1980-81. Author: C.P. Moritz, 1954, Schulmeisterlein Wutz, 1961, German Narrative Prose, 1965; editor: Mendelssohn Jubilaeumausgabe IV, 1977, VI. 2, 1981. Sr. fellow Nat. Endowment for Humanities, 1976; Inst. fellow Radcliffe Inst., Harvard, 1976-77. Mem. Lessing Akademie, Lessing Soc., Modern Lang. Assn., Am. Soc. for 18th Century Studies, Gesellschaft für Erforschung des 18th Jahrhunderts. Home: 83 Leighton Ave Wellesley MA 02181

ENGEL, GEORGIA BRIGHT, actress; b. Washington, July 28, 1948; d. Benjamin Franklin and Ruth Caroline (Hendron) E. B.A. in Drama, U. Hawaii, 1969. Appeared in: Lend an Ear, Equity Liberty Theatre, 1969; as Minnie Fay in: Hello Dolly, Broadway, 1970; off-Broadway appearance in House of Blue Leaves, 1971; film appearance in Taking Off, 1970; TV appearances include role of; Georgette in: Mary Tyler Moore Show, 1972-77; Mitzi in: Betty White Show, 1977, The Good Time Girls, 1980. Mem. Actors Equity Union, Screen Actors Guild, AFTRA. Christian Scientist. Office: care Arcara Bauman & Heller 850 7th Ave Suite 1201 New York NY 10019 *

ENGEL, JOSEPH HENRY, mathematician, operations research analyst; b. N.Y.C., May 15, 1922; s. Arthur and Jennie (Gotthilf) E.; m. Beverly Rosenblum, May 2, 1943; children: Wendy, Eric, David. B.S. (Tremaine gift), CCNY, 1942; postgrad., Yale, 1946; M.A., U. Wis., 1947; Ph.D., 1949. With Operations Evaluation Group, Center Naval Analyses, 1949-67, dir., 1962-65; asst. chief scientist Center Naval Analyses, 1965-67; dir. planning research and services Communications Satellite Corp., 1967-71; prof. systems engring. dept. U. Ill., Chgo. Circle, 1971-79, head dept., 1971-77; chief math. analysis div. Nat. Center for Stats. and Analysis, U.S. Dept. Transp., 1979-81; chief ops. research div. Nat. Bur. Standards, 1981—; Chmn. NATO Adv. Panel on Operational Research, 1970-73, NATO Spl. Program Panel on Systems Sci., 1973-74. Contbr. articles; Asso. editor: Operations Research, 1963-67; editorial adv. bd.: Computers and Operations Research, 1974—. Served to 1st lt. USAAF, 1942-46. Decorated D.F.C. Fellow AAAS. Mem. Am. Math. Soc., Am. Inst. Indsl. Engrs. (sr.), Mil. Operations Research Soc., Operations Research Soc. Am. (sec. 1964-66, pres. 1968), Sigma Xi, Pi Mu Epsilon, Omega Rho (founding, v.p. 1976-78, pres. 1978-80). Home: 7311 Broxburn Ct Bethesda MD 20817 Office: Ops Research Div Nat Bur Standards Washington DC 20234 *My life derives from Earth, and to Earth will return. My knowledge comes from man, and it must serve man. Wherever man goes, there may Truth be found. Seek truth, so man and Earth may thrive.*

ENGEL, LYLE KENYON, book producer; b. N.Y.C., May 12, 1915; s. George Shandor and Beatrice (Michaels) E.; m. Gertrude Warshaw; 1 son, George S.; m. Marjorie Helen Ray, June 14, 1975. Student, N.Y. U., N.Y. Coll. Music. Editor, pub. Song Hits mag., 1938-49; ind. promotion cons., 1950-52; pres., exec. producer Book Creations Inc., Canaan, N.Y., 1973-83, chmn. bd., 1984—. Originator, producer series: Nick Carter-Killmaster, 1962, Richard Blade, 1968; creator: Fred Astaire Dance Book, 1961, Pearl S. Buck's Fairy Tales of the Orient, 1963, Pearl S. Buck's People of Japan, 1964, Pearl S. Buck's Oriental Cook Book, 1965, Pearl S. Buck's Story Bible, 1965, Pearl S. Buck's Book of Christmas, 1971, Kent Family Chronicles, 1973, Creole Surgeon, 1975, Windhaven, 1976, Roselynde Chronicles, 1976, Oakhurst, 1977, Eve, 1977, Inheritors of the Storm, 1977, Wagons West, 1977, The Australians, 1977, White Indian, 1978, Children of the Lion, 1979, Heiress, 1979, Royal Dynasty, 1979, Saga of the Southwest, 1979, American Patriot, 1980, The Centurions, 1980, Rakehell Dynasty, 1980, Northwest Territory, 1982, Yankee, 1982, Stagecoach, 1982, Daimyō, 1983, Taming of the West, 1983, Worldshakers, 1983, Haakon, The Viking, 1984, Terminal Transfer,

1984; originator term book producer; promoted original: Today Show, 1950; creator: The Song from Moulin Rouge, 1952. Recipient Best of Industry award Direct Mail Advt. Assn., 1952. Mem. ASCAP, Broadcast Music. Address: Book Creations Inc Canaan NY 12029 *Creating good entertainment in book form for the American public has become the high point in my business career as well as in my lifestyle.*

ENGEL, MARIAN RUTH, novelist; b. Toronto, Ont., Can., May 24, 1933; d. Frederick Searle and Mary Elizabeth (Fletcher) Passmore; children—William and Charlotte (twins). B.A., McMaster U., 1955; M.A., McGill U., 1957. Tchr. Mont. State U., Missoula, 1957-58, The Study, Montreal, Que., Can., 1958-60, St. John's Sch., Nicosia, Cyprus, 1962-63; writer-in-residence U. Alta., Edmonton, Can., 1977-78, U. Toronto, 1980-81. Free-lance writer: novels include No Clouds of Glory, 1968, The Honeyman Festival, 1970, Monodromos, 1974, Joanne, 1975, Inside the Easter Egg, 1975, Bear, 1976, The Glassy Sea, 1978, The Year of the Child, 1981, Islands of Canada, 1981; books for children include Adventure at Moon Bay Towers, 1975, My Name Is Not Odessa Yar Rev, 1977; contbr.: short stories and articles to numerous mags. and newspapers including N.Y. Times Book Rev; (Recipient Gov. Gens. award for Best Novel in English in Can. for Bear 1976). Trustee Toronto Pub. Library Bd., 1974-77; mem. Toronto Book Prize com., 1974-77. Mem. Assn. Canadian TV Radio Artists, Writers Union Can. Mem. New Democratic Party. Home: 70 Marchmount Rd Toronto ON M6G 2A9 Canada

ENGEL, PAUL BERNARD, lawyer; b. Balt., Feb. 6, 1926; s. Robert and Ida (L) E.; m. Lorraine Goodman, Sept. 7, 1947; children—Seena Engel Kling, Cindy Engel Dubansky, Lon Craig. A.A., U. Balt., 1947, LL.D., 1950. Bar: Md. bar 1950, D.C. bar 1950. Since practiced in, Balt. Served with AUS, 1944-45. Mem. Am., Balt. bar assns., Md. Plaintiffs Bar Assn. Clubs: Masons, Bonnie View Country (dir.). Home: 3409 Deep Willow Rd Baltimore MD 21208 Office: 222 St Paul Pl Suite 302 Baltimore MD 21202

ENGEL, RALPH, manufacturers association executive; b. Balt., Mar. 19, 1934; s. William and Anna G. E.; m. Patricia R. Kahn, June 21, 1959; children—William, Steven. P.D. in Pharmacy, U. Md., 1956, J.D., 1966. Bar: N.Y. bar 1966. Gen. practice pharmacy, Balt., 1956-66; counsel, dir. regulatory affairs Purdue Frederick Co., Yonkers, N.Y., 1966-69; dir. Nat. Health Care Council, Washington, 1970-74; pres. Chem. Specialties Mfrs. Assn., Washington, 1974—, Chem-Spec Ins. Ltd.; adj. prof. adminstrn. U. Md.; mem. pesticide policy advisory com. EPA; vice chmn. ISAC 7 com. Dept. Commerce; mem. com. environ. carcinogens Nat. Cancer Inst. Contbr. articles in field to mgmt. and tech. jours. Recipient Merck award Chemistry, 1956; L.S. Williams award Pharmacology, 1956. Fellow Am. Soc. Pharmacy Law; mem. Am. Soc. Assn. Execs., U.S. C. of C. Clubs: Capitol Hill, Univ. Home: 13621 Middlevale Ln Silver Spring MD 20906 Office: 1001 Connecticut Ave NW Washington DC 20036

ENGEL, ROBERT GEHRELS, banker; b. Teaneck, N.J., Feb. 7, 1932; s. Daniel Currie and Margaret Mary (Sweeney) E.; m. Jane Virginia Coe, June 20, 1953; children—Jennifer Margaret, Robert Andrew, Elizabeth Hunter. A.B., Cornell U., 1953; postgrad., Columbia U. Grad. Sch. Bus., 1956-58. Sales engr. Corning Glass Works, N.Y., 1953-55; with Morgan Guaranty Trust, N.Y.C., 1957—, sr. v.p., 1971-78, exec. v.p., treas., 1978—; dir. Diamond Crystal Salt Co., Raychem Corp. Trustee Cornell U.; mem. Bergen County (N.J.) Republican Com., HoHoKus (N.J.) Bd. Edn. Served with CIC AUS, 1955-57. Mem. Psi Upsilon. Episcopalian. Clubs: Union League, Laurel Valley Golf, Hackensack Golf. Home: 80 Wearimus Rd HoHoKus NJ 07423 Office: 23 Wall St New York NY 10015

ENGEL, THEODORE ALBERT, chair manufacturing company executive; b. Allegan, Mich., July 15, 1924; s. Albert Howard and Lola Belle (Miller) E.; m. Judith A. Visscher, Fed. 20, 1953; children: Ann Marie Engel Basile, Mary Elizabeth Engel Knierim, Theodore A. Sutdent, Saugatuck pub. schs., Mich. Cert. mfg. engr. Furniture finisher Baker Furniture Co., Holland, Mich., 1946-59; foreman Brammer Mfg. Co., Davenport, Iowa, 1959-66; tech. service rep. Lilly Indsl. Coatings, Indpls., 1966-67; finishing supt. La-Z-Boy Chair Co., Monroe, Mich., 1967-81, also corp. finishing and poly supt. and quality control mgr., v.p., gen. mgr., Dayton, Tenn., 1981—. Trustee Douglas Village Bd., Mich., 1958-59; mem. Mich. State Democratic Com., 1957-58; bd. dirs. Little League, Bettendorf, Iowa, 1965. Served to sgt. U.S. Army, 1943-46. Mem. Assn. Finishing Processes (dir. 1979-80), Dayton C. of C. (dir.), Rhea County Vocat. Edn. Dept. (adv. bd.), Pvt. Industry Council Rhea County. Lutheran. Clubs: Nat. Rifle Assn., Ducks Unltd., Sertoma (dir.). Office: La-Z-Boy Tennessee PO Box 457 Dayton TN 37321

ENGEL, WILLIAM FREMONT, state official; b. N.Y.C., June 23, 1930; s. Abraham Lisman and Hattye (Kaufman) E.; m. Sharon Ruth Moyers, May 18, 1954; 1 dau., Laurie Anne. B.S. in Journalism, U. Nev., Reno, 1957. Public info. officer Nev. Hwy. Dept., Carson City, 1957-74, exec. asst. to hwy. engr., 1974-79; adj. gen. State of Nev., 1979—; v.p. Fed. Exec. Council. Asso. editor: Nev. mag, 1955-61. V.p. council ARC; bd. dirs. Nev. Area Council Boy Scouts Am. Served with inf. AUS, 1953-55. Decorated Legion of Merit, Meritorious Service medal. Mem. Adj. Gens. Assn., N.G. Assn. U.S., Nev. N.G. Assn. Democrat. Clubs: Rotary (dir., treas.), Capital (Carson City); Elks. Home: 3350 Idlewild Dr Reno NV 89509 Office: 2525 S Carson St Carson City NV 89701

ENGEL, WILLIAM KING, neurologist, educator; b. St. Louis, Nov. 19, 1930; s. William Ernst and Opal (King) E.; m. Valerie Askanas; children: W. Keith, Peter J., Bradford C., Eve M. B.A., Johns Hopkins U., 1951; M.D., C.M., McGill U., 1955. Diplomate: Am. Bd. Neurology and Psychiatry, Pan. Am. Med. Assn. (hon.). Intern U. Mich. Hosp., 1955-56; clin. assoc. Nat. Inst. Neurol. Diseases and Blindness, 1956-59; clin. clk. Nat. Hosp., London, 1959-60; with Nat. Inst. Neurol. Diseases and Stroke, 1960-81, chief med. neurology, 1963-78, chief neuromuscular diseases, 1978-81; clin. prof. neurology George Washington U., 1969-81; prof. neurology and pathology, chief div. neuromuscular diseases, dept. neurology U. So. Calif. Sch. Medicine, Los Angeles, 1981—; dir. U. So. Calif. Neuromuscular Center, Hosp. of Good Samaritan, Los Angeles, 1981—; Mem. med. adv. bd. St. Jude's Children's Research Hosp., Memphis, 1970-76, Myasthenia Gravis Found., 1970—, Amyotrophic Lateral Sclerosis Nat. Found., 1971—, Amyotrophic Lateral Sclerosis Soc. Am., 1980—; vis. prof., invited lectr., advisor internat. congresses in, Europe, S.Am., Can., Far East; cons. Nat. Naval Med. Center. Former Mem. editorial bd.: Archives of Neurology; contbr. numerous papers to profl. lit., poems to mags. Past pres. Citizens Assn., Bethesda, Md., Longhouse chief YMCA Indian Guides, 1965-66; past chmn. troop com. Boy Scouts Am.; mem. edn. adv. bd. Phronesis, Spain. Recipient Meritorious Service medal USPHS, 1971, various awards from Italian med. socs. Fellow Am. Acad. Neurology (S. Weir Mitchell award 1962); mem. AMA, Histochem Soc., Am. Soc. Cell Biology, Am. Assn. Neuropathologists, World Commn. Neuromuscular Disease (exec. com.), Am. Neurol. Assn., Société Belge d'Electromyographie (assoc.), Asociación de Distrofía Muscular de la República Argentina (hon. pres.), Soc. for Neurosci., Société Francaise de Neurologie (hon.). Office: U So Calif Neuromuscular Ctr Hosp Good Samaritan 637 S Lucas Ave Los Angeles CA 90017

ENGELBART, ROGER WILLIAM, banker; b. Ft. Dodge, Iowa, Apr. 28, 1923; s. William Eberhard and Julia Kathryn (Faulstick) E.; m. Elizabeth Emma Affleck, Sept. 20, 1947; 1 son, Roger Warren. Ed., Kansas City (Mo.) Jr. Coll., 1942. Bookkeeper Woolf Bros. Clothing Store, Kansas City, Mo., 1942-43; with United Mo. Bank of Kansas City (N.A.), 1946—, cashier, 1971—. Mem. Friends Am. Field Service Internat. Scholarships, 1970—. Served with AUS, 1943-46. Mem. Greater Kansas City C. Of C., Mail Users Council Greater Kansas City, Bank Adminstrn. Inst., Am. Security Council (nat. adv. bd.). Republican. Lutheran. (chmn. bd. 1969-71, 73-78). Home: 5002 W 71st Terr Prairie Village KS 66208 Office: 928 Grand Ave Kansas City MO 64106

ENGELBERT, ARTHUR FERDINAND, univ. dean; b. St. Johnsburg, N.Y., Dec. 18, 1903; s. Ferdin and Anna (Fetzer) E.; m. Ruth B. Bunt, Aug. 14, 1930; 1 dau., Carol (Mrs. Ervin S. Palmer). Student, Concordia Coll., 1922-24, Concordia Theol. Sem., 1924-27; M.A., U. Pitts., 1929, Ph.D., 1935; postgrad., Duke, 1941, U. Chgo., 1949. Asst. pastorate Immanuel Lutheran Ch., Braddock, Pa., 1927-31; grad. asst. U. Pitts, 1929-30, instr. modern langs., 1930-31; prof., head dept. modern langs. Mt. Union Coll., Alliance, Ohio, 1931-59; dean Coll. Liberal Arts, Washburn U., Topeka, 1959—, acting pres., 1961, also v.p. for acad. affairs.; Coordinator liberal arts com. N. Central Assn. Colls. and Secondary Schs., 1951-56. Contbr. articles to edn. jours.; Editorial bd.: Soc. for Acad. Achievement. U.S. rep. of Danish Internat. Student Com.; Chmn. Alliance chpt. ARC, 1956-58; mem. planning council for Shawnee County Health Facilities Commn. Mem Am. Assn. Acad. Deans, Acad. Deans Kan. Colls. and Univs. (pres. 1968-69), Tau Delta Pi, Psi Kappa Omega. Clubs: Rotarian., Sagamore, Fortnightly. Home: 1166 Collins St Topeka KS 66604 *It is only when men find peace with God that there will also be peace among men of good will.*

ENGELBRECHT, RICHARD STEVENS, environmental engineering educator; b. Ft. Wayne, Ind., Mar. 11, 1926; s. William C. and Mary Elizabeth (Stevens) E.; m. Mary Condrey, Aug. 21, 1948; children: William, Timothy. A.B., Ind. U., 1948; M.S., M.I.T., 1952, Sc.D., 1954. Teaching asst. Ind. U. Sch. Medicine, Indpls., 1949-50; research asst. M.I.T., Cambridge, 1950-52, instr., 1952-54; asst. prof. U. Ill., Urbana-Champaign, 1954-57, assoc. prof., 1957-59, prof. environ. engring., 1959—; dir. Advanced Environ. Control Tech. Research Center, 1979—; cons. Ill. EPA, U.S. EPA, WHO; mem. Ohio River Valley Water Sanitation Commn., chmn., 1980-82. Named Ernest Victor Balsom Commemoration Lectr., 1978; recipient Eric H. Vick award Inst. Public Health Engrs., U.K., 1979. Mem. Internat. Assn. Water Pollution Research and Control (pres. 1980—), Am. Water Works Assn. (George W. Fuller award 1974, Publ. award 1975), Water Pollution Control Fedn. (Eddy medal 1966, Arthur Sidney Bedell award 1973, pres. 1978), Nat. Acad. Engring., AAAS, Am. Soc. Microbiology, N. Am. Benthological Soc., Ill. Soc. Microbiology., Abwasser-technische Vereini-gung (hon.). Home: 2012 Silver Ct W Urbana IL 61801 Office: 3230 Newmark Civil Engring Lab 208 N Romine St Urbana IL 61801

ENGELDER, THEODORE CARL, physicist; b. Detroit, Aug. 31, 1927; s. Conrad John and Ruth Laura (Linsenmann) E.; m. Rita Marie Gaffney, Sept. 28, 1952; children—Laura, James. B.S., U. Mich., 1949; M.S., Yale U., 1950, Ph.D., 1953. Nuclear physicist Dow Chem. Co., Midland, Mich., 1952-56; nuclear engr. Chrysler Corp., Ann Arbor, Mich., 1956; chief exptl. physics sect. Babcock & Wilcox Co., Lynchburg, Va., 1956-67; asst. dir. Nuclear Devel. Center, 1967-71; dir. Research Center, 1971—. Contbr. tech. articles to profl. jours. Mem. Am. Nuclear Soc., Am. Phys. Soc., Atomic Indsl. Forum, Phi Beta Kappa, Sigma Xi. Patentee in field. Home: 2236 Taylor Farm Rd Lynchburg VA 24503 Office: PO Box 239 Lynchburg VA 24505

ENGELHARDT, ALBERT GEORGE, physicist, research engr.; b. Toronto, Ont., Can., Mar. 17, 1933; came to U.S., 1957, naturalized, 1965; s. Samuel and Rose (Menkes) E.; m. Elzbieta Szajkowska, June 14, 1960; children—Frederick, Leonard, Michael. B.A., U. Toronto, 1958; M.S., U. Ill., 1959, Ph.D. (grad. fellow), 1961. Research asst. elec. engring. U. Ill., Urbana, 1958-61; staff research and devel. center engr. Westinghouse Electric Co., Pitts., 1961-70, mgr., 1966-69, fellow scientist, 1969-70; sr. research scientist, group leader Hydro-Que. Research Inst., Varennes, Can., 1970-74; mem. staff Los Alamos Sci. Lab., 1974—; adj. prof. elec. engring. Tex. Tech. U., Lubbock, 1976—; vis. prof. U. Que., 1970-77. Contbr. articles to profl. jours. Group leader Boy Scouts Can., 1972-74. Mem. IEEE Nuclear and Plasma Scis. Soc., Am. Phys. Soc. Home: 549 Bryce St Los Alamos NM 87544 Office: Los Alamos Sci Lab MS554 PO Box 1663 Los Alamos NM 87545 *Since 1959 my basic research interest has been plasma physics and concomitantly nuclear fusion. The importance of the latter is that it shows great promise for providing us with renewable energy resources with acceptably small environmental and ecological perturbation.*

ENGELHARDT, HUGO TRISTRAM, JR., physician, educator; b. New Orleans, Apr. 27, 1941; s. Hugo Tristram and Beulah (Karbach) E.; m. Susan Gay Malloy, Nov. 25, 1965; children: Susan Elisabeth, Christina Tristram, Dorothea. B.A., U. Tex., Austin, 1963, Ph.D., 1969; M.D. with honors, Tulane U., 1972. Asst. prof. U. Tex. Med. Br., 1972-75, asso. prof., 1975-77; mem. Inst. Med. Humanities, 1973-77; Rosemary Kennedy prof. philosophy of medicine Georgetown U., 1977-82; sr. research scholar Kennedy Inst. Center for Bioethics, Washington, 1977-82; prof. depts. internal medicine and community medicine Baylor Coll. Medicine, Houston, 1983—, mem. Ctr. for Ethics, Medicine and Pub. Issues, 1983—. Author: Mind Body: A Categorial Relation, 1973; asso. editor: Ency. of Bioethics, 1973-78, Jour. Medicine and Philosophy, 1974—; mem. editorial adv. bd.: Social Sci. and Medicine, 1976—, Theoretical Medicine/Bioethics Reporter, 1983—; editor: (with others) Philosophy and Medicine series, 1974—, Evaluation and Explanation in the Biomedical Sciences, 1975, Philosophical Dimensions of the Neuro-Medical Sciences, 1976, Philosophical Medical Ethics, 1977, Mental Health, 1978, Clinical Judgment, 1979, Mental Illness: Law and Public Policy, 1980, Law-Medicine Relation, 1981, Concepts of Health and Disease, 1981, The Roots of Ethics: Science, Religion, and Values, 1981, New Knowledge in the Biomedical Sciences, 1982, Abortion and the Status of the Fetus, 1983. Mem. bioethics com. Nat. Found. March of Dimes, 1975—; dirs. adv. bd. Masters and Johnson Inst. Fulbright fellow, 1969-70. Fellow Inst. Soc., Ethics and the Life Scis.; mem. Am. Philos. Assn. Home: 2402 Bellefontaine Houston TX 77030 Star Route 3 Box 1 New Braunfels TX 78130 Office: Center for Ethics Medicine and Pub Issues Baylor Coll Medicine Houston TX 77030 *Success in the academic world is properly a function of faith in ideas—that they function and move the world, that they are, at least in part, the real world, that they are worthy of selfless love.*

ENGELHARDT, LEROY A., paper co. exec.; b. Saginaw, Mich., Mar. 15, 1924; s. Herman J. and Alma (Engelhard) E.; m. Arlene L. Papineau, July 12, 1947; children—Richard C., Kay C., Douglas R. B.B.A., U. Mich., 1949, M.B.A., 1950. Plant, div. or subsidiary controller Chrysler Corp., 1950-60; mgmt. controls cons. Diehl K.G., Nuremberg, Germany, 1960-63; sec. Genesee Brewing Co., Rochester, N.Y., 1963-67; v.p. fin. Consol. Papers, Inc., Wisconsin Rapids, Wis., 1967—, also dir.; dir. Consol. Water Power Co., Consoweld Corp., Mead Realty Corp. Bd. dirs. Consol. Civic Found. Served with AUS, 1943-46. Home: 444 2 Mile Ave Wisconsin Rapids WI 54494 Office: PO Box 50 Wisconsin Rapids WI 54494

ENGELHARDT, SARA LAWRENCE, found. exec.; b. Phila., Aug. 23, 1943; d. Ruddick Carpenter and Barbara (Dole) Lawrence; m. Dean Lee Engelhardt, June 20, 1970; children—Barbara Elizabeth, Margaret Ann. B.A., Wellesley Coll., 1965; M.A., Tchrs. Coll., Columbia U., 1970. Staff asst. Carnegie Corp., N.Y.C., 1966-70, asst. sec., 1972-74, asso. sec., 1974-75, sec., 1975—. Free-lance editor and writer, Storrs, Conn., 1970-72. Home: 173 Riverside Dr New York NY 10024 Office: Carnegie Corp 437 Madison Ave New York NY 10022

ENGELHARDT, THOMAS ALEXANDER, editorial cartoonist; b. St. Louis, Dec. 29, 1930; s. Alexander Frederick and Gertrude Dolores (Derby) E.; m. Katherine Agnes McCue, June 25, 1960; children—Marybeth, Carol Marie, Christine Leigh, Mark Thomas. Student, Denver U., 1950-51, Ruskin Sch. Fine Arts, Oxford (Eng.) U., 1954-56, Sch. Visual Arts, N.Y.C., 1957. Free-lance cartoonist, comml. artist, N.Y.C., 1957-60, Cleve., 1961-62; asst. editorial cartoonist, Newspaper Enterprise Assn., Cleve., 1960-61; editorial cartoonist: St. Louis Post-Dispatch, 1962—, one-man exhbns. of cartoons at, Fontbonne Coll. Art Gallery, St. Louis, 1972, Old Courthouse (Jefferson Nat. Meml.), St. Louis, 1981. Served with USAF, 1951-53. Office: 900 N 12th Blvd St Louis MO 63101

ENGELKE, GEORGE L., JR., banker; b. Englewood, N.J., Nov. 17, 1938; s. George L. and Marienne B. E.; married; children: Jennifer, Courtenay. B.S. in Bus. Adminstrn., Lehigh U., 1960. With Peat, Marwick, Mitchell & Co., N.Y.C., 1960-71, audit mgr., 1971; with Astoria Fed. Savs. and Loan Assn., Long Island City, N.Y., 1971—, exec. v.p., treas., 1974—, dir., 1983—. Mem. Am. Inst. C.P.A.s, N.Y. State Soc. C.P.A.s. Office: 37-16 30th Ave Long Island City NY 11103

ENGELMAN, DONALD MAX, molecular biophysics and biochemistry educator; b. Los Angeles, Jan. 25, 1941; s. Francis Leopold and Mildred Lillian (Bordsen) E.; m. Pamela Alice Rackliff, Dec. 14, 1963; children: Ian Kenton, Bevin Page. B.A., Reed Coll., Portland, Oreg., 1962; M.S., Yale U., 1964, Ph.D., 1967. Postdoctoral fellow U. Calif., San Francisco, 1967-68, Kings Coll., London, 1968-70; asst. prof. Yale U., 1970-74, assoc. prof., 1974-78, prof. molecular biophysics and biochemistry, 1978—; editor-in-chief Ann. Rev. Biophysics, 1982—; vis. prof. Cambridge U., Eng., 1978-79; guest biophysicist Brookhaven Nat. Lab., Upton, N.Y., 1974—; series cons. U.S. News Books, Washington, 1980-82. Editor: Biophysics Jour., Jours. Membrane Biology, Biosci. Report; contbr. numerous articles to internat. jours., sci. jours. Guffenheim fellow, 1978-79; NSF, NIH research grantee, 1970—. Mem. Orgn. Biophys. Soc., Am. Chem. Soc., AAAS. Home: 231 Park St New Haven CT 06511

ENGELMAN, IRWIN, food corporation executive; b. N.Y.C., May 9, 1934; s. Max and Julia (Shaoul) E.; m. Rosalyn Ackerman, Nov. 24, 1956; children: Madeleine F., Marianne L. B.B.A., CCNY, 1955; J.D., Bklyn. Law Sch., 1961. Bar: N.Y. 1962; C.P.A., N.J. Sr. acct. Pub. Acctg., N.Y.C., 1959-62; controller Razdow Labs., Inc., Newark, 1962-65; bus. mgr. Becker & Becker Asso., Inc., N.Y.C., 1965-66; with Xerox Corp., Rochester, N.Y., 1966-78, corp. v.p., 1975-78; v.p., chief fin. officer Singer Co., Stamford, Conn., 1978-81; exec. v.p., chief fin. officer Gen. Foods Corp., White Plains, N.Y., 1981—; assoc. prof. Monroe Community Coll., 1967-68. Bd. dirs. Citizens Tax League, 1971—, Long Wharf Theatre. Served with U.S. Army, 1957-58. Fellow Am. Bar Assn., Am. Inst. C.P.A.s.; mem. Acctg. Research Found., Fin. Execs. Inst., N.J. Soc. C.P.A.s. Clubs: Econ. of N.Y., University. Home: 12 Old Hill Rd Westport CT 06880 Office: Gen Foods Corp 250 North St White Plains NY 10625

ENGELMAN, KARL, physician; b. N.Y.C., June 23, 1933; s. Samuel and Lillian (Wachs) E.; m. Elaine Kaufman, June 10, 1956; children—Harold Kent, Ross Mitchell, Jeffrey Steven. B.S., Men's Coll. Arts and Scis., Rutgers U., 1955; M.D., Harvard U., 1959; M.A. (hon.), U. Pa., 1971. Diplomate: Am. Bd. Internal Medicine. Intern, asst. resident, resident in medicine Mass. Gen. Hosp., Boston, 1959-64; clin. asso., sr. investigator, attending physician Nat. Heart Inst., NIH, Bethesda, Md., 1961-70; asso. prof. medicine and pharmacology Sch. Medicine U. Pa., Phila., 1971—, chief hypertension sect., dir. clin. research center; cons. physician Phila. VA Hosp., Children's Hosp., Phila. Served with USPHS, 1961-63. Mem. Am. Coll. Clin. Pharmacology, A.C.P., Internat. Soc. of Hypertension (sci. council on hypertension), U.S. Pharmacopeia and Nat. Formullary (adv. council), Council for High Blood Pressure Research (adv. bd.), Am. Heart Assn. Jewish. Clubs: Phila., Doctors Golf Assn., Sea Pines. Patentee. Home: 65 Harrowgate Dr Cherry Hill NJ 08003 Office: Hosp of U Pa 3600 Spruce St Philadelphia PA 19104

ENGELMAN, MELVIN ALKON, dentist, business executive; b. Waterbury, Conn., July 27, 1921; s. Herman B. and Marion (Halpern) E.; m. Muriel Phillips, Aug. 27, 1949; children: Curtis Land, Suzanne Ruth. A.B., Ohio U., 1942; D.D.S., Western Res. U., 1944. Diplomate: Am. Bd. Oral Electrosurgery. Practice dentistry, Wappingers Falls, N.Y., 1949—; attending dentist, chmn. oral diagnosis and oral pathology sect., dir. oral diagnostic center St. Francis Hosp., Poughkeepsie, N.Y., 1963-77, dir. dept. dentistry, 1967, 71-74, 78; pres. Di-Equi Dental Products Distbn. Corp., 1980—, Dentifax Internat.; observer Meml. Hosp. Cancer and Allied Diseases, N.Y.C., 1962-66; mem. adv. bd. Dutchess Community Coll., 1963-69, lectr. dental assts., 1960-63; dir. 1st regional sci. fair, Dutchess County, N.Y., 1960-61; project dir. USPHS community cancer demonstration project, 1963-66; asst. chief med. officer Dutchess County N.Y. CD, 1963-68; cons. Nat. Cancer Inst., mem. clin. cancer tng. com., 1968-71, Profl. edn. com. for cancer control, 1972-73; attending dentist Central Dutchess Nursing Home, 1970—; cons. VA Hosp., Castle Point, N.Y., 1976-77, Lactona Corp., div. Warner Lambert, 1976-80. Co-author: Oral Cancer Examination Procedure, 16th edit, 1983; contbr. articles to profl. jours. Chmn. Wappinger Red Cross Fund Drive, 1956; committeeman Troop 6, Boy Scouts Am., Chelsea, N.Y., 1963-67; pres. Dutchess County unit Am. Cancer Soc., 1969-71. Served from ensign to lt. comdr. USNR, 1942-46; lt. comdr. Res. (ret.). Fellow Royal Soc. Health (Eng.), Am. Pub. Health Assn., AAAS (life mem.), Acad. Gen. Dentistry; mem. Am. Assn. Hosp. Dentists, ADA, Internat. Assn. Dental Research, Am. Prosthodontic Soc., Am. Public Health Assn., Assn. Mil. Surgeons, 9th Dist. Dental Soc., Dutchess County Dental Soc. (pres. 1965), Am. Acad. Dental Electrosurgery (pres. 1983), Wappinger Conservation Assn. (v.p. 1970-71), Wappingers Falls C. of C. (pres. 1952-54), Alpha Omega. Clubs: Masons (32 deg.), Shriners, B'nai B'rith (pres. So. Duchess lodge 1963-64). Clin. research, publs. and lectures in fixed prosthodontics, premedication, oral cancer, metallurgy. Home: Nutmeg Hill Wappingers Falls NY 12590 Office: 1 E Academy St Wappingers Falls NY 12590

ENGELMAN, ROBERT S., merchandising executive; b. Rahway, N.J., Sept. 25, 1912; s. Bernard and Lena (Pachman) E.; m. Mary Straus, Jan. 6, 1938; children: Tilden S., Robert S., John S. and Stephen B. (twins), Mary Margaret. A.B., Dartmouth, 1934. Re-buyer Spiegel, Inc., 1934-37, buyer, 1937-40, div. mdse. mgr., 1940-51, v.p., 1949-54, gen. mdse. mgr., 1951-54, pres., gen. mgr., 1954-60, exec. v.p., 1960-69, pres., 1970—, dir., 1951—; partner R.S. Engelman Assos., Bus. Cons., 1971—; pres. E.I.C. Inc., also; MRE Inc., 1971—; dir.

Acorn Fund, 1972—. Past pres., bd. dirs. Chgo. chpt. Anti-Defamation League; bd. dirs. Comprehensive Community Services Met. Chgo.; chmn. commerce div. Crusade of Mercy, Chgo., 1955, 56, 63, 70, 71; former treas., bd. dirs. Jewish Fedn. Met. Chgo., Community Fund Met. Chgo. Clubs: Mill Creek Hunt, Lake Shore Country, Tavern. Home: 61 Hazel St Highland Park IL 60035 Office: 2 N Riverside Plaza Chicago IL 60606

ENGELMANN, HUGO OTTO, educator; b. Vienna, Austria, Sept. 11, 1917; came to U.S., 1939, naturalized, 1944; s. Otto Hugo and Karolina (Skrceny) E.; m. Ruth Marie Gould, Oct. 4, 1941; 1 son, John Hugh. Student, U. Vienna Law Sch., 1935-38; B.A. in Polit. Sci, U. Wis., 1941; Ph.D. in Sociology, U. Wis., 1953. Instr. social sci. Mich. State U., 1945-48; from instr. to prof. sociology U. Wis.-Milw., 1948-69, chmn. dept., 1964-67; prof. sociology No. Ill. U., DeKalb, 1969—; Founder, 1965; since editor Clearinghouse for Sociol. Lit. Author: Essays in Social Theory and Social Organization, 1966, Theoretical Sociology-Its Bases and Place in Modern Science, 1966, Sociology-A Guided Study Text, 1969, also articles, book revs.; Asso. editor: Sociol. Quar, 1963-66, Internat. Rev. Sociology, 1971—, Internat. Jour. Contemporary Sociology, 1971—, Jour. Polit. and Mil. Sociology, 1973—; editor: Wis. Sociologist, 1960-69. Fellow AAAS, Am. Anthrop. Assn.; mem. Am., Wis. (pres. 1962-63) sociol. assns). Home: 421 W Hillcrest Dr DeKalb IL 60115

ENGELMANN, LOTHAR KLAUS, photographic science educator; b. Rudolstadt, Germany, Jan. 30, 1926; came to U.S., 1957, naturalized, 1969; s. Karl and Frida (Zange) E.; m. Gudrun Drewello, Jan. 10, 1948; children: Bettina, Randolph. Dr. phil. nat., J.W. Goethe U., Frankfurt, Germany, 1955. Mgr. photo-paper dept. Adox Fotowerke, Frankfurt, 1952-57; sr. photog. chemist Polaroid Corp., Cambridge, Mass., 1959-60; supr. silver halide research 3M Co., St. Paul, 1962-65, mgr. prodn. tech. dept., Rochester, N.Y., 1966-69; prof. photog. sci. and tech. Rochester Inst. Tech., 1969—, dean, 1969-81; dir. RIT Research Corp., 1981-82. Recipient Elmer G. Voight award, 1976, Friedman medal, 1978. Mem. Soc. Photog. Scientists and Engrs., Am. Chem. Soc., Royal Photog. Soc. Gt. Brit., Ges. Deutscher Chemiker, Tech. Assn. Graphic Arts, Deutsche Gesellschaft für Photographie (corr.), Phi Kappa Phi. Patentee tanning chemistry and photo sci. Home: 128 Thatcher Rd Rochester NY 14617

ENGELMANN, RUDOLF JACOB, oceanographer; b. Ward County, N.D, Mar. 11, 1930; s. Emil B. and Hazel Ella (Schwartz) E.; m. Virginia D. Fletcher, Dec. 27, 1952; children: Richard, Eric, Kurt, Peter, Aleta, Karsten. B.A., Augsburg Coll., 1950; postgrad., N.Y. U., 1952; Ph.D., U. Wash., 1964. Meteorologist Gen. Elec. Co., Hanford, Wash., 1958-66; chief fallout studies AEC, 1967-73; dep. mgr. environ. programs ERDA, 1973-75; dir. outer continental shelf environ. assessment program Nat. Oceanic and Atmospheric Adminstrn., Boulder, Colo., 1975—; dep. dir. Div. Environ. Assessment, UN Environment Program, Nairobi, Kenya, 1980-82; sr. oceanographer NOAA, Washington, 1983—. Served to 1st lt. USAF, 1950-57. Named Distinguished Alumnus Augsburg Coll., 1976. Mem. Am. Meteorol. Soc., Sigma Chi. Club: Elks. Home: 7137 Petursdale Ct Boulder CO 80301 Office: OAR NOAA Rockville MD 20852

ENGELS, LAWRENCE ARTHUR, metals company executive; b. Darlington, Wis., Sept. 26, 1933; s. Henry Morris and Nell Ellen (O'Connor) E.; m. Marilyn Rae Stellick, Sept. 6, 1958; children: Laurie, Michael, Thomas, Stephen. B.B.A., U. Wis., 1959; M.B.A., Northwestern U., 1970. Dist. credit mgr. U.S. Steel Corp., Chgo., 1959-69; asst. treas. Nat. Can Corp., Chgo., 1969-77; corp. treas. Comml. Metals Co., Dallas, 1977—, chief fin. officer and treas., 1979—, v.p., treas., chief fin. officer, Dallas, 1981—. Served with USN, 1952-55. Fellow Nat. Inst. Credit; mem. Cash Mgmt. Practitioners Assn. (Chgo. sec. 1975), Chgo. Midwest Credit Mgmt. Assn. (dir. 1973-75), Chgo. Midwest Credit Service Corp. (dir. 1975), Fin. Execs. Inst., Nat. Assn. Corp. Treas. Office: Commercial Metals Co 7800 Stemmons Freeway Dallas TX 75247

ENGEN, DONALD DAVENPORT, government official, retired naval officer; b. Pomona, Calif., May 28, 1924; s. Sydney Morris and Dorothy (Davenport) E.; m. Mary Ann Baker, Sept. 23, 1943; children: Donald T., Candace L., Christopher W., Charles T. B.S., George Washington U., 1968; grad., Naval War Coll., 1966. Commd. ensign U.S. Navy, 1943, advanced through grades to vice adm., 1976; comdg. officer U.S.S. Mt. Katmai, 1964, U.S.S. America, 1966-67; comdr. Carrier Div. 4, 1971-73; dep. comdr. in chief U.S. Naval Forces, Europe, 1973-76, Atlantic and U.S. Atlantic Fleet, 1976-78; ret., 1978; gen. mgr. Lakeland div. Piper Aircraft Corp., Fla., 1978-80; sr. assoc. Ketron, Inc., 1980-82; presdl. appointee Nat. Transp. Safety Bd., 1982-84; administrator Fed. Aviation Adminstrn., Washington, D.C., 1984—; past pres. Assn. for Rescue at Sea, N.Y.C. Contbr. articles to mil. mags. Decorated Navy Cross, D.S.M. (2), Def. D.S.M., Legion of Merit (2), D.F.C., Air medal (3). Mem. Soc. Exptl. Test Pilots. Clubs: Ends of Earth, European-Atlantic Group (London). Home: 809 Duke St Alexandria VA 22314 Office: Federal Aviation Adminstrn 800 Independence Ave SW Washington DC 20591

ENGEN, RICHARD BRUCE, librarian; b. Aberdeen, Wash., Nov. 23, 1927; s. Laurie Hammond and Esther (Howenstine) E.; m. Rebecca Lee Bartels, July 13, 1975; children—Kristen, Paul, Kyle, Tobin. B.S., Northwestern U., 1952; M.L.S., U. Wash., 1953. With Seattle Pub. Library, 1953-60; dir. Columbia River Regional Library Demonstration, Wenatchee, Wash., 1960; ref. asst. Evanston (Ill.) Pub. Library, 1960-61; county librarian Inyo-Mono counties, Calif., 1962-63; head field services Oreg. State Library, 1963-67; dir. Div. State Libraries and Museums, Alaska, 1967—; Mem. exec. bd. Pacific Northwest Bibliographic Center, 1972—. Served with AUS, 1946-48. Mem. Pacific N.W. (sec. 1967-69), Oreg. (pres. 1966), Alaska library assns., ALA (councilor 1970-74), Western Council of State Library Agys. (pres. 1981-82). Home: PO Box 1782 Juneau AK 99802 Office: Pouch G Juneau AK 99811

ENGER, WALTER MELVIN, cons. engr., former navy officer; b. Urbana, Ill., May 11, 1914; s. Melvin Lorenius and Mary (Crawford) E.; m. Charlotte Hope Tuttle, Dec. 25, 1935; children—Susan Hope (Mrs. K. Randall Myers), Thomas Arthur. B.S. in Civil Engring, U. Ill., 1935. Registered profl. engr., D.C. Jr. engr., asst. engr. Bur. Reclamation, Denver, Parker Dam, also Shasta Dam, Calif., 1935-41; commd. lt. (j.g.) Civil Engrs. Corps, USN, 1941, advanced through grades to rear adm., 1965; officer charge constrn. civil works contracts on West Coast, 1941-44; exec. officer 59th, 72d Naval Constrn. Bns., Guam and Japan, 1944-45; officer charge 72d, 31st Naval Constrn. Bns., Japan, 1945-46; dep. dist. pub. works officer 8th Naval Dist., New Orleans, 1946-48; instr. marine engring. U.S. Naval Acad., 1948-51; pub. works officers Marine Corps Base, Camp Pendleton and; Twenty-nine Palms, Calif., 1951-53; detail officer Civil Engr. Corps, Bur. Naval Personnel, 1953-56; dep. chief staff Naval Constrn. Forces Pacific, Pearl Harbor, 1956-59; pub. works officer Naval Air Sta., Point Mugu, Cal., 1959-61; asst. chief mil. readiness Bur. Yards and Docks, 1961-64; dir. Chesapeake Div. Bur. Yards and Docks, 1964-65; vice comdr. Naval Facilities Engring. Command, Washington, 1965-69, comdr.; chief of civil engrs. of Navy, 1969-73; ret., 1973; v.p. DeLeuw, Cather & Co. (Engrs.), Washington, 1973-76; engring. cons., 1976—; Chmn. Engrs. Joint Council Commn. on Engring. Information, 1973-76. Decorated Navy Commendation medal, D.S.M., Legion of Merit. Fellow ASCE, Soc. Am. Mil. Engrs.; mem. Am. Pub. Works Assn. (hon.), Kappa Sigma. Home and Office: 8360 Greensboro Dr Apt 618 McLean VA 22102

ENGERMAN, STANLEY LEWIS, economist, educator; b. Bklyn., Mar. 14, 1936; s. Irving and Edith (Kaplan) E.; m. Judith Rader, June 21, 1963; children—David, Mark, Jeffrey. B.S. cum laude, N.Y. U., 1956, M.B.A., 1958; Ph.D., Johns Hopkins, 1962. Asst. prof. econs. Yale, 1962-63; asst. prof., then asso. prof. U. Rochester, N.Y., 1963-71, prof. econs. and history, 1971—. Co-author: Time on the Cross: The Economics of American Negro Slavery, 1974; Co-editor: The Reinterpretation of American Economic History, 1971, Race and Slavery in the Western Hemisphere: Quantitative Studies, 1975. Mem. Econ. History Assn., Am. Econ. Assn., Am. Hist. Assn. Home: 181 Warrington Dr Rochester NY 14618

ENGGAS, CARL E., lawyer; b. Kansas City, Mo., June 3, 1900; s. Main C. and Eva M. (Killip) E.; m. Jane M. Greene, Feb. 4, 1925; 1 dau., Marion Jane (Mrs. John H. Kreamer). A.B., U. Mich., 1923, J.D., 1925. Bar: Mo. bar 1925. Since practiced in, Kansas City; asso. Ingham Hook, 1925-31, Watson, Gage, Ess, Groner & Barnett, 1931-36; mem. firm Watson, Ess, Marshall & Enggas (and predecessors), 1936—. Mem., sec. Kansas City Bd. Election Commrs., 1961-65; mem. Jackson County Charter Commn., 1957-58. Served with U.S. Army, World War I. Fellow Am. Coll. Trial Lawyers; mem. Am. Bar Assn., Mo. Bar, Lawyers Assn. Kansas City, Lawyers Club Ann Arbor (Mich.), Am. Judicature Soc., C. of C., Order of Coif, Alpha Tau Omega. Clubs: River; University (Kansas City) (past pres.). Home: 1200 W 60th Terr Kansas City MO 64113 Office: Home Savings Bldg Kansas City MO 64106

ENGGASS, ROBERT, art historian; b. Detroit, Dec. 20, 1921; s. Clarence H. and Helen (Strasburger) E.; m. Catherine Ann Cavanaugh, June 27, 1949. B.A., Harvard U., 1946; M.A., U. Mich., 1950, Ph.D. (Rackham fellow), 1955. Instr. Bryn Mawr Coll., Haverford Coll., 1955-56; asst. prof. Williams Coll., 1956-57, U. Buffalo, 1957-58; asso. prof. Pa. State U., 1958-65, acting head art history dept., 1963, chmn. grad. program, 1960-65; prof. art history, chmn. dept. La. State U., 1965-66; prof. art history Pa. State U., 1966-71, U. Kans., Lawrence, 1971-78, grad. adv., 1973-76; Callaway prof. art U. Ga., Athens, 1979—. Author: Baciccio, 1966, (with J. Brown) Italy and Spain 1600-1750 - Sources and Documents in Art History, 1970, Early 18th Century Sculpture in Rome, 1976 (Borghese prize 1977), (with Catherine Enggass) Vatican Library edit. Pio's Vite di Pittori, 1977, Malvasia's Reni, 1980, Ridulfi's Tintoretto, 1984; Contbr. numerous articles to profl. jours. Served with USAAF, 1942. Am. Council Learned Socs. grantee-in-aid, 1958, 70, 76; Fulbright research scholar U. Rome, 1963-64; Kress Found. grantee, 1966, 67, 69, 70; U. Kans. grantee, 1971-77. Mem. Coll. Art Assn., AAUP, Inst. di Studi Romani, Royal Soc. Arts, Am. Soc. Eighteenth Century Studies (editorial bd. quar. jour. 1979—), Southeastern Soc. 18th Century Studies (dir. 1984—). Democrat. Club: Accademia degli Ippopotami. Home: 340 W Lake Dr Athens GA 30606 Office: Art Dept U Ga Athens GA 30602

ENGLAND, ANTHONY W., astronaut, geophysicist; b. Indpls., May 15, 1942; s. Herman U. and Betty (Steel) E.; m. Kathleen Ann Kreutz, Aug. 31, 1962. S.B. S.M., M.I.T., 1965, Ph.D., 1970. With Texaco Co., 1962; field geology Ind. U., 1963; NSF grantee, 1965-67; scientist-astronaut NASA, 1967-72, 79—; with U.S. Geol. Survey, 1972-79. Asso. editor: Jour. Geophys. Mem. Am. Geophys. Union, Am. Geol. Inst., Internat. Glaciological Soc., Soc. Exploration Geophysicists, Sigma Xi. Research, 1976-79. Home: 15802 Craighurst Dr Houston TX 77059 Office: NASA Johnson Space Center Houston TX 77058

ENGLAND, ARTHUR JAY, JR., lawyer, former state justice; b. Dayton, Ohio, Dec. 23, 1932; s. Arthur Jay and Elsbeth (Weiskopf) E.; m. Morley Tenenbom, June 24, 1959 (div.); children: Andrea, Pamela, Ellen, Karen.; m. Deborah J. Miller, Mar. 31, 1984. B.S., U. Pa., 1955, LL.B., 1961; LL.M. in Taxation, U. Miami (Fla.), 1971. Bar: N.Y. 1961, Fla. 1961. Assoc. Dewey, Ballantine, Bushby, Palmer & Wood, N.Y.C., 1961-64; ptnr. Culverhouse, Tomlinson, Taylor & DeCarion, Miami, 1964-69, Scott, McCarthy, Steel, Hector & Davis, 1969-70; spl. tax counsel Fla. Ho. Reps., 1971-72; consumer adviser, spl. counsel to gov. Fla., 1972-73; ptnr. Paul & Thomson, Miami, 1973-74; justice Supreme Ct. Fla., 1975-81, chief justice, 1978-80; ptnr. Steel, Hector & Davis, Miami, 1981-84, Fine Jacobson Block England, 1984—; dep. chmn. Conf. of Chief Justices, 1978-80; chmn. Council of State Ct. Reps., Nat. Center for State Cts., 1979-80; chmn. adv. bd. Nat. IOLTA Clearinghouse, 1983—; pres. Fla. Bar Found., 1983-84; adj. prof. Fla. State U. Coll. Law. Contbr. articles to legal jours. Served with AUS, 1955-57. Mem. ABA, Fla. Bar, Am. Law Inst., Order of Coif, Beta Gamma Sigma. Jewish. Home: 6829 Veronese St Coral Gables FL 33146 Office: 2401 Douglas Rd Coral Gables FL 33134

ENGLAND, JAMES WALTON, college dean and official, mathematics educator; b. Newton, Kans, July 20, 1938; s. John L. and Ruth (Frazier) E.; m. Mary Margaret Ramsay, Aug. 11, 1961; children: Ruth, Ann. A.B., Kans. State Tchrs. Coll., 1960; M.A., U. Mo., 1962, Ph.D., 1964. Asst. prof. U. Va., Charlottesville, 1964-69; mem. Inst. for Advanced Studies, Princeton, N.J., 1967-68; assoc. prof. Swarthmore Coll. (Pa.), 1969-73, prof. math., 1973-81, chmn. dept. math., 1976-81; dean faculty, v.p. acad. affairs Occidental Coll., Los Angeles, 1982—; mem. evaluating team Middle State Assn. Colls., 1976-79; reviewer Math. Revs., 1978—. Author: Mathematical Theory of Entropy, 1981. Bd. dirs. Better Chance Program, Swarthmore, 1976-80; gen. mem. council Presbytery of Phila., 1978-79; mem. sch. bd. Wallingford-Swarthmore Sch. Dist., 1978-82. NSF postdoctoral fellow, 1967-68. Mem. Am. Math. Soc., Math. Assn. Am. Democrat. Presbyterian. Home: 1882 Campus Rd Los Angeles CA 90041 Office: Occidental College 1600 Campus Rd Los Angeles CA 90041

ENGLAND, JOSEPH WALKER, heavy equipment manufacturing company executive; b. Moline, Ill., June 21, 1940; s. Stanley B. and Mary (Walker) E.; m. Mary Jo Richter, Oct. 26, 1963; children: Kathleen, Amy, Sarah. B.S., U. Ill., 1962. With Deere & Co., Moline, Ill., 1963—, sr. v.p. acctg. control, 1981—. Bd. dirs. United Way, 1978—, pres., 1980,81. Served with AUS, 1963. Mem. Nat. Assn. Accountants, Ill. Soc. C.P.A.s, Am. Inst. C.P.A.s, Fin. Execs. Inst., U. Ill. Alumni Assn. (dir. 1977). Club: Short Hills Country. Home: 1105 24th Ave Moline IL 61265 Office: Deere & Co John Deere Rd Moline IL 61265

ENGLANDER, HAROLD ROBERT, dental researcher, educator; b. N.Y.C., Dec. 11, 1923; s. Samuel Harold and Elsie (Kimless) E.; m. Harriet Beecher, May 8, 1949; 1 son, Mark R. B.S., CCNY, 1945; student, Washington U., St. Louis, 1944; D.D.S., Columbia U., 1948, M.P.H., 1951. Diplomate: Am. Bd. Dental Pub. Health. Commd. lt. (j.g.) U.S. Navy, 1948, advanced through grades to lt. comdr., 1959; assigned U.S.S. Piedmont and U.S.S. Kearsarge, Korea, 1952-53; dir. naval dental research Inst. U.S. Naval Tng. Center, Gt. Lakes, Ill., 1953-58; sr. dental officer U.S.S. Pocono, 1959; resigned USNR, 1962; prof. dentistry U. Ill. Dental Sch., 1959-62; commd. officer USPHS, 1962; dental dir., chief clin. and field trials Nat. Inst. Dental Research, 1962-70, caries prevention and research br., 1970-75, ret., 1975; prof. dental public health Sch. Public Health, U. Tex., San Antonio, 1975—; vis. prof. Howard U., Johns Hopkins, U. Md.; adj. scientist SW Found. Research and Edn., 1977; cons. to govt., pvt. orgns. Served with AUS, 1942-44. Recipient Research Honor award Am. Dental Assn., 1975. Fellow Am. Coll. Dentists, Am. Pub. Health Assn., AAAS, Fedn. Dentaire Internat., Am. Assn. Pub. Health Dentists, Internat. Assn. Dental Research (sec., pres. Chgo. sect. 1958), Commd. Officers Assn., USPHS (del. 1967-68), Omicron Kappa Upsilon, Sigma Xi. Research, publs. oral research and epidemiology dental caries and periodontal diseases; effect of fluoride on exptl. dental caries, plaque and microbes in hamsters. Showed that fluoridated water may enhance health of gums and effective in lowering dental caries in adults; pioneered use of mouthpieces for topical fluorides and other drug application to teeth; field testing for possible anticaries antiplaque and antibacterial agts. Home: 11502 Whisper Bluff San Antonio TX 78230 Office: U Tex Health Sci Center 7703 Floyd Curl Dr San Antonio TX 78284

ENGLANDER, ROGER, producer, director; b. Cleve., Nov. 23, 1926; s. Will Cedric and Frieda (Osteryoung) E. Ph.B., U. Chgo., 1946, postgrad., 1947-49; postgrad., Chgo. Mus. Coll., 1948, Goodman Theater, Art Inst. Chgo., 1948. Stager entertainments for state Dinners at the White House for President's Kennedy and Johnson; vis. prof. Parsons Coll., Fairfield, Iowa, summers 1963-66, U. S.C., 1969, State U. N.Y. at Brockport, 1970, Conn. Coll., 1973-74, Fairfield U., 1980—; guest lectr. schs. including N.Y. U., Ind. U., Ohio State U., U. Chgo.; cons. N.Y. State Council on Arts, Pub. Relations Bd., Chgo. Asst., Cain Park Theatre, Cleve., 1945, Berkshire Music Center, Tanglewood, Mass., 1946; asst. to gen. mgr., Chgo. Opera Co., 1946-47; asst. to, Gian Carlo Menotti, producing 1st network TV operas, 1947-49; producer, NBC-TV, 1949-50; asso. dir., ABC-TV, 1950-53; producer, dir., CBS-TV, 1953-58; free-lance producer, dir., N.Y.C., 1958—; prod. Children's Concerts, Little Orch. Soc. N.Y., 1957-60; producer, dir., N.Y. Philharmonic Young People's Concerts with Leonard Berstein and Michael Tilson Thomas, 1958—; producer: Promenade Concerts, 1963-65; also program series: Camera Three, CBS, 1975—; sr. producer CBS Cable TV, 1980—; stage dir., N.Y. City Opera Co., 1959-63; also, Am. Opera Co.; instr., Sch. Arts, N.Y. U., 1966-73; master tchr. dept. mus. theatre, 1981—; instr., Inst. Film and TV, 1970-73; producer, co-founder, Am. Dance Theater, 1964; pres. bd. trustees; chmn. adv. panel public media and co-chmn. adv. panel on dance, Nat. Endowment Arts; dir.: The Performing Arts; Author: (with Mary Rodgers) works for narrator and orch. Three to Make Music, 1960, Mark Twain, 1964; Opera: What's all the Screaming About?, 1983; also ballet scenarios, TV scripts, articles. Trustee Mannes Coll. Music, N.Y.C.; bd. dirs. Profl. Children's Sch., N.Y.C., Dance Notation Bur., N.Y.C., Nat. Choral Council, N.Y.C., In Concerts for Peace, Washington. Recipient Emmy award Nat. Acad. TV Art and Scis., 1960, 61, 62, 65, 78, Producer's awards Ohio State U., 1960, 61, Saturday Rev., 1960, 62, 63, 64; Edison award, 1966; Broadcast Preceptor San Francisco State Coll., 1968; Prix Jeunesse, Munich, 1968; Christopher award, 1970; Peabody award, 1979; U. Chgo. Profl. Achievement award, 1980. Mem. Acad. TV Arts and Scis. (gov. N.Y. chpt. 1959-71, nat. trustee 1961-69, internat. dir. 1964-69, Dirs. Guild Am., Outstanding Achievement award 1974), Am. Guild Mus. Artists, Writers Guild Am., ANTA, Internationales Institut für Musik, Tanz und Theater in den Audio-visuellen Media (Vienna), Conseil International de la Musique (Paris), Renaissance Soc. U. Chgo. Club: Univ. (Chgo.) (mem. cabinet). Home: 15 St Lukes Pl New York NY 10014

ENGLE, DONALD EDWARD, railway executive, lawyer; b. St. Paul, Mar. 5, 1927; s. Merlin Edward and Edna May (Berger) E.; m. Nancy Ruth Frank, Mar. 18, 1950; children: David Edward, Daniel Thomas, Nancy Ann. B.A., Macalester Coll., St. Paul, 1948; J.D., U. Minn., 1952, B.S.L., 1950. Bar: Minn. bar 1952, Mo. bar 1972. Law clk., spl. atty. Atty. Gen.'s Office Minn., 1951-52; atty., asst. gen. solicitor, asst. gen. counsel G.N. Ry., St. Paul, 1953-70; asso. gen. counsel Burlington No., Inc., 1970-72; v.p., gen. counsel S.L.-S.F. Ry., St. Louis, 1972-79, v.p. law, sec., 1979-80; v.p. corp. law Burlington No., Inc., St. Paul, 1980-81, Burlington No. Ry., 1981-83, sr. v.p. law and govt. affairs, sec., 1983—, also dir.; dir. BN RR Properties, Inc., Clarkland, Inc., Clarkland Royalty, Inc., 906 Olive Corp., St. Paul Union Depot Co., Western Fruit Express Co.; continuing edn. lectr. U. Minn. Bd. dirs. YMCA, St. Paul, 1981—; bd. dirs. ARC, 1981-84. Served with USNR, 1945-46. Mem. Am., Mo., Minn., Ramsey County, St. Louis bar assns., Phi Delta Phi. Republican. Lutheran. Clubs: St. Paul, Athletic, Minnesota; Bellerive Country (St. Louis); North Oaks Golf. Office: 176 E 5th St Saint Paul MN 55101

ENGLE, HAROLD MARTIN, med. adminstr.; b. Chgo., Nov. 29, 1914; s. Nathan Hale and Sarah (Wolson) E.; m. Marilyn Roe Detweiler, Aug. 22, 1942; children—Maurine Sara Engle Francis, Paige Renee Engle Laun. Student, Northwestern U., 1931-32, Central Coll., 1932-35; B.S., U. Ill., 1937, M.D., 1939. Intern Michael Reese Hosp., Chgo., 1939-40; resident, 1940-42; med. officer Ft. Harrison VA Hosp., Helena, Mont., 1946-47; asst. chief med. service VA Hosp., Portland, Oreg., 1947-48, chief profl. service, Vancouver, Wash., 1948-50, chief med. service, Spokane, 1950-52, chief profl. service, Seattle, 1952-53; also asso. instr. med. U. Wash. Med. Sch.; dir. VA hosps., Salt Lake City, 1953-55, Denver, 1955-60; clin. asst. prof. medicine U. Colo. Med. Sch., Denver, 1953-55, clin. asso. medicine, 1955-60; dep. chief med. dir. VA Central Office, Washington, 1960-64; chief med. dir. VA, 1966-70; clin. prof. med. UCLA Med. Sch., 1964-66; vice-chancellor for health services U. Ill. Med. Sch., Chgo., 1970-76; spl. asst. to dean U. Calif. at San Diego Sch. Medicine, 1977-80; mem. nat. adv. health council Office of Surgeon Gen., USPHS, 1966-70, Pres.'s Nat. Adv. Commn. Health Manpower, 1966-70, Fed. Task Force Health, 1966-70. Bd. regents Nat. Library Medicine. Served to maj. M.C. AUS, 1942-46. Recipient Distinguished Service award Fed. Hosp. Inst. Alumni Assn., 1969. Fellow A.C.P.; mem. AMA (ho. dels. 1960-64, 66-70), Assn. Mil. Surgeons (exec. council 1966-70). Home: 1435 Sun Valley Rd Solana Beach CA 92075

ENGLE, JAMES BRUCE, ambassador; b. Billings, Mont., Apr. 16, 1919; s. Bruce Wilmot and Verbeaudah Margaret (Morgan) E.; m. Priscilla Joyce Wright, June 10, 1950; children—Stephen, Judith, Philip, Susan, John, Peter. Diploma, Burlington (Iowa) Jr. Coll., 1938; B.A., U. Chgo., 1940, postgrad., 1940-41, 46; diploma, Grad. Sch. Bus. Adminstrn., Harvard, 1945; Honours B.A. (Rhodes scholar), Exeter Coll., Oxford (Eng.) U., 1950, Honours M.A., 1954, U. per Stranieri, Perugia, Italy, 1949, Istituto Italiano Studi Storici, Naples, 1950-53; postgrad., Am. U., Washington, 1956-58; diploma, Goethe Institut, Germany, 1958; postgrad., King's Coll., Cambridge (Eng.) U., 1958-59. Dept. State liaison officer with Bd. Econ. Warfare, Washington, 1941-42; vice consul, Quito, Ecuador, 1942-44, Rio de Janeiro, Brazil, 1946-47, Naples, 1951-53; 2d sec. Am. embassy, Rome, 1953-54; Italian desk officer Dept. State, Washington, 1955-58; 1st sec. Am. embassy, London, 1958-59; consul, Frankfurt, Germany, 1959, Duesseldorf, Germany, 1959-60; labor attache Am. embassy, Bonn, Germany, 1960-61, 1st sec., Accra, Ghana, 1961-62, acting dep. chief mission, 1962-63, charge d'affaires, 1963; dep. chief mission, counselor embassy, Managua, Nicaragua, 1963-67, charge d'affaires, 1967; mem. sr. seminar in fgn. policy Dept. State, Washington, 1967-68; dep. chief reports and analysis div. CORDS, Mil. Assistance Command, Saigon, Vietnam, 1968; province sr. advisor, Phu Yen mil. region II, Tuy Hoa, Vietnam, 1969-70; dir. Vietnam working group, sec. com. on Vietnam, Nat. Security Council, Dept. State, Washington, 1970-71, spl. advisor to ambassador-at-large, 1971-72; spl. asst. to U.S. ambassador to

North Atlantic Council, Brussels, Belgium, 1972; exec. sec. spl. interdepartmental task force on Indochina Dept. State, Washington, 1972-73; consul gen., Nha Trang, Vietnam, 1973, dep. chief mission, counselor of embassy, Phnom Penh, Cambodia, 1973-74, charge d'affaires, 1974; ambassador to People's Republic of Bénin (Dahomey), Cotonou, 1974-76; polit. advisor with rank of ambassador to U.S. Comdr.-in-Chief Atlantic and Supreme Allied Comdr. Atlantic, 1976-78; sr. fgn. service insp. Dept. State, Washington, 1978—. Served to lt. (j.g.) USN, 1944-46. Recipient Rockefeller Pub. Service award to Cambridge (Eng.) U., 1958-59. Mem. Phi Beta Kappa. Episcopalian. Leader U.S. Andean expdns. in Ecuador, 1942-43. Home: RFD 2 Groton VT 05046 Office: Office Insp Gen Dept State Washington DC 20520

ENGLE, MARY ALLEN ENGLISH, physician; b. Madill, Okla., Jan. 26, 1922; d. Russell C. and Vera (Apperson) English; m. Ralph Landis Engle, Jr., June 7, 1945; children: Ralph Landis III, Marilyn Elizabeth. A.B. cum laude, Baylor U., 1942; M.D., Johns Hopkins, 1945. Diplomate: in pediatric cardiology Am. Bd. Pediatrics. Intern pediatrics Johns Hopkins Hosp., 1945-46, asst. dir. pediatrics outpatient dept., 1946-47, fellow pediatric cardiology, 1947-48; asst. resident Sydenham Hosp. Contagious Diseases, Balt., 1946, N.Y. Hosp., 1948-49, asst. attending pediatrician, 1952-60, asso. attending pediatrician, 1960-62, attending pediatrician, 1962—; instr. pediatrics Johns Hopkins, 1946-48; fellow pediatrics Cornell U., 1949-50, faculty pediatrics, 1950—, prof., 1969—, Stavros S. Niarchos prof. pediatric cardiology, 1979—; med. dir. Insts. in Care Premature Infant, 1952-55, dir. pediatric cardiology, 1963—; Mem. Pres.'s Adv. Panel on Heart Disease, 1972. Mem. editorial bd.: Am. Heart Jour. Hypertension; assoc. editor: Jour. Am. Coll. Cardiology. Recipient Spence-Chapin award for contbns. to pediatrics, 1958; award of merit Philoptochos Soc. N. and S. Am., 1978; Woman of Conscience award Nat. Council Women, 1979; citation Nat. Bd. Med. Coll. Pa., 1979; Disting. Achievement award, Baylor U., 1981. Mem. Am. Acad. Pediatrics (charter mem. sect. cardiology, founder's award cardiology sect. 1983), Am. Heart Assn. (Award of Merit 1975, Helen B. Taussig award 1976, dir. 1976-78), N.Y. Heart Assn. (dir. 1980—), N.Y. Acad. Medicine, Harvey Soc., Soc. Pediatric Research, Am. Coll. Chest Physicians, Assn. European Pediatric Cardiologists (corr.), Am. Coll. Cardiology (master tchr. 1969, 73, 76, trustee 1974-79, Theodore and Susan Cummings Humanitarian award, 1973, 76), Am. Pediatric Soc., Pediatric Cardiology Soc. Greater N.Y., N.Y. Cardiology Soc. (dir.), Explorers' Club, Phi Beta Kappa, Alpha Omega Alpha. Presbyn. Clubs: Pelham Country, Internat. Garden. Home: 1 Country Club Ln Pelham Manor NY 10803 Office: NY Hosp Cornell Med Coll 525 E 68th St New York NY 10021

ENGLE, MERLE L., manufacturing executive; b. Arcadia, Kans., Feb. 4, 1940; s. Ernest J. and Helen Engle. B.S. in Mech. Engring, U. Kans., 1962. With Electronics and Space div. Emerson Electric Co., St. Louis, 1968—, sr. v.p., 1978-80, pres., gen. mgr., 1980; group v.p. electronics and Space div. Emerson Electric Co., 1982. Chmn. Jack Beirne Pro-Am Golf Tournament, 1979-80; pres. Warson Woods Sch. PTA, 1974-75; pres. patrons assn. St. Joseph Inst. for Deaf, 1975-76. Served with U.S. Army N.G., 1959. Mem. Am. Def. Preparedness Assn., Am. Security Council, Navy League, Nat. Security Indsl. Assn., Assn. U.S. Army. Clubs: St. Louis, Bellerive. Office: Emerson Electric Co E&S Div Sta 3153 8100 W Florissant Ave Saint Louis MO 63136

ENGLE, PAUL HAMILTON, writer, English educator; b. Cedar Rapids, Iowa, Oct. 12, 1908; s. Hamilton Allen and Evelyn (Reinheimer) E.; m. Mary Nomine Nissen, July 3, 1936; children: Mary, Sara; m. Hualing Nieh, May 14, 1971. A.B., Coe Coll., 1931; A.M., State U. Iowa, 1932; postgrad., Columbia U., 1932-33; A.B., Merton Coll., Oxford (Eng.) U., A.M., 1939; Litt.D., Coe Coll., Monmouth Coll., Iowa Wesleyan U.; L.H.D. (hon.), U. Dubuque, 1981, U. Colo., 1981. Writer, prof. English, dir. program in creative writing U. Iowa, Iowa City, 1966-77; cons., co-founder Internat. Writing Program, 1967—. Librettist opera: produced TV Golden Child, 1960; (Recipient award for West of Midnight, Friends Am. Writers, Chgo. 1941), (with Hualing Nieh Engle) (Iowa award for disting. service to arts. Found. for Advancement Edn. fellow 1952-53); Author: books poetry including American Child, 1945, The Word of Love, 1951, Poems in Praise, 1959, A Prairie Christmas, 1960, Embrace; poems, 1969, Images of China, 1981; also, A Woman Unashamed, Golden Child; opera libretto, 1960, Golden Child; prose fiction, 1962, Women in the American Revolution, 1976; Images of China, Poems, 1982; Editor: anthology Midland, 1961, (with Joseph Langland) Poet's Choice; Past editor: On Creative Writing, 1964, An Old Fashioned Christmas, 1964, Portrait of Iowa, 1974; co-editor: Reading Modern Poetry; Translator: (with Hualing Nich Engle) Poems of Mao Tse-Tung, 1972; Contbr. to popular mags.: N.Y. Times. Pub. lectr. lit. at colls., Town Hall, N.Y.C., CBS-TV, others; participant Christmas Heritage Program, PBS, 1978; Mem. adv. com. John F. Kennedy Cultural Center, Washington; mem. nat. council on arts White House; judge Nat. Book Award, 1955, 70. Lamont award Acad. Am. Poets, 1958-61; Guggenheim Found. fellow, 1953-54. Mem. Phi Kappa Phi, Phi Gamma Delta. Home: 1104 N Dubuque St Iowa City IA 52240 *"A grindstone does its job by a perpetual turning in one place, wearing itself down slower than the steel."*

ENGLE, RALPH LANDIS, JR., physician, educator; b. Phila., June 11, 1920; s. Ralph Landis and Ruth (Enck) E.; m. Mary Allen English, June 7, 1945; children: Ralph Landis III (dec.), Marilyn Elizabeth Varela. B.S., U. Fla., 1942; M.D., Johns Hopkins U., 1945. Intern pathology N.Y. Hosp., 1945-46, intern medicine, 1948-49, asst. resident medicine, 1949-51, asst. attending physician, 1952-57, asso. attending physician, 1957-69, attending physician, 1969—; Am. Cancer Soc. research fellow anatomy Washington U. Med. Sch., St. Louis, 1951-52; practice medicine, specializing in internal medicine, N.Y.C., 1952—; chief div. med. systems and computer sci., dept. medicine N.Y. Hosp.-Cornell U. Med. Center, 1967-74; asst. prof. medicine Cornell U. Med. Coll., 1952-57, asso. prof., 1957-69, prof., 1969—, prof. pub. health, 1973—, asso. dir. Office Research and Sponsored Programs, 1975—; mem. com. on sci. and tech. communications Nat. Acad. Scis.-Nat. Acad. Engring., 1967-70; chmn. Ad Hoc Task Group on Toxicol. Info., 1969-70; mem. toxicol. info. program com., div. med. scis., 1969-72, 76-78; mem. cancer clin. investigation rev. com. Nat. Cancer Inst., 1968-72, chmn. cancer control supportive services rev. com., 1974-76, chmn. cancer control community activities rev. com., 1975, chmn. cancer control prevention, detection and pretreatment evaluation rev. com., 1976-78. Author: (with L.A. Wallis) Immunoglobulins, Immune Deficiency Syndromes, Multiple Myeloma and Related Disorders, 1969; also numerous articles. Served from 1st lt. to capt., M.C. AUS, 1946-48. Markle scholar in med. sci., 1952-57. Fellow ACP, N.Y. Acad. Medicine; mem. Internat., Am. socs. hematology, N.Y. Soc. for Study Blood (past pres.), Am. Fedn. Clin. Research, Soc. Exptl. Biology and Medicine, AAAS, Harvey Soc. (past sec.), Am. Clin. and Climatol. Assn., AMA, Am. Public Health Assn., Sigma Xi, Chi Phi, Nu Sigma Nu. Presbyn. Club: Pelham Country. Home: 1 Country Club Ln Pelham Manor NY 10803 Office: 525 E 68th St New York NY 10021 *Faith in God, trust in man, commitment to the responsibilities of life in the face of risk, and love of ones fellowmen are the keys to a successful and happy life.*

ENGLEHAUPT, WILLIAM MYLES, association executive; b. Bradford, Pa., Feb. 18, 1918; s. William Myles and Pearl Anne (Weir) E.; m. Dorothy Fuller, Mar. 9, 1947; children: William, Michael. B.A., South Mountain Coll., 1936. With Lever Bros. Co., 1941-50; with Helene Curtis Industries, Chgo., 1950-54, 68-70; v.p. mktg. Earle Ludgin Agy., Chgo., 1954-60; exec. v.p. Nat. Electronics Distbrs. Assn., Chgo., 1972-77; exec. dir. Foodservice Equipment Distbrs. Assn., Chgo., 1977—; editor, pub. News & Views mag., 1978—. Trustee Harris Sch., 1966-70. Mem. Am. Soc. Assn. Execs., Chgo. Soc. Assn. Execs., Sales and Mktg. Assn. Republican. Club: Ill. Athletic. Home: 3750 Lake Shore Dr Chicago IL 60613 Office: 332 S Michigan Ave Chicago IL 60604

ENGLEKIRK, JOHN EUGENE, educator; b. N.Y.C., Sept. 24, 1905; s. John and Lena (Didion) E.; m. Fern Carolyn Houp, Feb. 14, 1931; children—Robert E., June Carolyn (Mrs. Frederick T. Grade), John Allan. B.A., St. Stephen's Coll., Bard, N.Y., 1926; M.A. (teaching fellow), Northwestern U., 1928; diploma (travel fellow Instituto de las Españas), Columbia, also Residencia de Estudiantes, Madrid), Centro de Estudios Históricos, Madrid, Spain, 1930; Ph.D., Columbia, 1934; diploma (Chilean travel and study scholar Inst. Internat. Edn.), U. Chile, 1938. From instr. to asso. prof. Romance langs. U. N.Mex., 1928-39; asst., then instr. Spanish Columbia, 1931-33; asso. prof., prof., chmn. dept. Spanish and Portuguese Tulane U., 1939-58; prof. Spanish and Portuguese U. Calif. at Los Angeles, 1958—, chmn. dept., 1959-62; vis. prof. various univs.; dir. European office Inst. Internat Edn., Paris, 1950-51. Author: Poe in Hispanic Literature, 1934, 72, Bibliografía de obras norteamericanas en traducción española, 1944, A literatura norteamericana no Brasil, 1952, (with Gerald E. Wade) La novela colombiana, 1952, El epistolario Pombo-Longfellow, 1956, El teatro folklórico hispanoamericano, 1957, De lo nuestro y lo ajeno, 1966, (with M.M. Ramos) La narrativa uruguaya, 1967; editor, co-author: An Outline History of Spanish American Literature, 1965, 79, An Anthology of Spanish American Literature, 1968, also texts, numerous articles.; Co-editor: Revista Iberoamericana, 1940-53, 57-59; editor, 1959-61; co-editor: Hispanofila, 1958—. Tulane U. research grantee, Mexico, 1940, Venezuela and Colombia, 1947, Caribbean, 1954; Am. Council Learned Socs. grantee, Mexico, 1942, Uruguay and Brazil, 1959; Middle Am. Research Inst. grantee, Mexico, C.Am., Venezuela, 1957; Smith-Mundt fellow, lectr., Spain and Portugal, 1955-56; U. Calif. at Los Angeles research grantee, Uruguay and Brazil, 1959-60; Del Amo Found. fellow, Spain, 1962, 70, 75; Fulbright-Hays award for study in Latin Am., 1965; Am. Philos. Soc. grantee, Latin Am., 1966; Fulbright grantee, Spain, 1967. Mem. Instituto Internacional de Literatura Ibero-americana (founder mem., pres. 1940-42, v.p. 1961-63), Am. Assn. Tchrs. Spanish and Portuguese (pres. 1949), Modern Lang. Assn. (pres. S. Central sect. 1952), La. Fgn. Lang. Tchrs. Assn. (pres. 1953-55), Modern Lang. Assn. So. Calif. (pres. 1961-62), AAUP, Internat. Comparative Lit. Assn., Ateneo Americano de Washington (corr. mem.), Academia Norteamericana de la Lengua Española (founder 1973), Phi Kappa Phi, Theta Alpha Phi, Sigma Alpha Epsilon, Phi Sigma Iota, Sigma Delta Pi. Home: 11164 Ophir Dr Los Angeles CA 90024

ENGLEMAN, EPHRAIM PHILIP, physician; b. San Jose, Calif., Mar. 24, 1911; s. Maurice and Tillie (Rosenberg) E.; m. Jean Sinton, Mar. 2, 1941; children—Ephraim Philip, Edgar George, Jill. B.A., Stanford U., 1933; M.D., Columbia U., 1937. Intern Mt. Zion Hosp., San Francisco; resident U. Calif., San Francisco, Jos. Pratt Diagnostic Hosp., Boston; research fellow Gen. Hosp., Boston, 1937-42; practice medicine specializing in rheumatology, San Francisco, 1948—; mem. faculty U. Calif. Med. Center, San Francisco, 1949—, clin. prof. medicine, 1965—; dir. Rosalind Russell Arthritis Center, 1979—; mem. staff U. Calif., Wills Meml., Peninsula hosps.; Chmn. Nat. Commn. Arthritis and Related Diseases, 1975-76. Author: The Book on Arthritis: A Guide for Patients and Their Families, 1979; also articles, chpts. in books. Served to maj. M.C. USMCR, 1942-47. Recipient citation Arthritis Found., 1973; grantee Nat. Inst. Arthritis. Fellow ACP; Mem. Internat. League Against Rheumatism (pres. 1981—), Am. Rheumatism Assn. (pres. 1962-63), Nat. Soc. Clin. Rheumatologists, AMA, Am. Fedn. Clin. Research; hon. mrm. Japanese Rheumatism Soc., Spanish Rheumatism Soc., Uruguay Rheumatism Soc. Republican. Jewish. Club: Family (San Francisco). Office: 400 Parnassus St San Francisco CA 93537

ENGLER, JOHN GEORGE, II, business executive; b. Palmerton, Pa., Oct. 29, 1941; s. William Joseph and Mary Rita (King) E.; m. Rita Dever, June 24, 1965; children: John George, III, Brian Joseph, Craig King, Catherine Ann. B.A., U. Tex., 1963; M.B.A., U. Pa., 1970. Asst. to pres. Ronson Corp., Bridgewater, N.J., 1970-75, v.p. finance, treas., 1975-82; pres., chief exec. officer The Inteleplex Corp., Pleasantville, N.J., 1983—. Bd. dirs. Sport Billy Found., 1983—. Served with USN, 1963-69. Mem. Fin. Execs. Inst., Am. Finance Assn., Am. Mgmt. Assn., Naval Res. Assn. Roman Catholic. Home: 2 Pletcher Pl Morristown NJ 07960 Office: 1101 Black Horse Pike Pleasantville NJ 08232

ENGLER, MARTIN RUSSELL, JR., natural gas pipeline company executive; b. San Diego, July 30, 1924; s. Martin Russell and Lura (Griffin) E.; m. Mary Russell Belford, June 7, 1948; children: William Erickson, Mary Elizabeth, Kathryn Louise. B.S.M.E., Calif. State Poly. U., San Luis Obispo, 1950. Registered profl. engr., Calif., Tex., Ariz., N. Mex. Engr. gas div. San Diego Gas & Electric Co., 1950-65, v.p. gas div., 1965-73, exec. v.p., 1973-75; sr. v.p. El Paso LNG Co., Houston, 1976-79; exec. v.p. El Paso Marine Co., Houston, 1979-81; exec. v.p., dir. El Paso Natural Gas Co., 1981—; mem. Am. Bur. Shipping, 1979-81. Inventor portable LNG demonstrator, 1965; designer LNG powered Automobile, 1968. Pres. Internat. Aerospace Hall of Fame, San Diego, 1972, Reuben H. Fleet Space Theater, San Diego, 1975; bd. dirs. San Diego Mus. of Art, 1975. Served to capt. USAAF, 1943-45. Named Disting. Alumni Calif. State Poly. U., 1974. Fellow ASME (sect. pres. 1958-59); mem. Pacific Coast Gas Assn. (49er award with star 1978, Basford Trophy award 1966, bd. dirs. 1970-76), So. Gas Assn. (bd. dirs. 1982—), Soaring Soc. Republican. Presbyterian. Lodge: Rotary. Home: 804 Wingfoote El Paso TX 79912 Office: El Paso Natural Gas Co PO Box 1492 El Paso TX 79978

ENGLER, ROBERT, educator, author; b. N.Y.C., July 12, 1922; s. Isidore and Esther (Haber) E.; m. Rosalind Elowitz, May 16, 1946 (div. June 1960); children: Richard J., Elise P.; m. Inea Bushnaq, Sept. 5, 1968; 1 dau., Nadya Kate. B.S.S., CCNY, 1942; M.A., U. Wis., 1946, Ph.D., 1947. Mem. faculty U. Wis., 1946-47; mem. Syracuse U., 1947-50, Columbia U., 1959-63; prof. polit. sci. Queens Coll., CUNY, 1964-69, Bklyn. Coll. and Grad. Sch., CUNY, 1969—, Sarah Lawrence Coll., 1951-71; mem. faculty New Sch. Social Research, 1961-64; vis. prof. U. P.R., 1961, U. Sask., 1973; disting. vis. prof. Am. U., Cairo, 1978. Author: The Politics of Private Power and Democratic Directions, 1961, The Brotherhood of Oil: Energy Policy and the Public Interest, 1977; also articles, reviews; contbg. author: The Dissenting Academy, 1968; editor: America's Energy: 100 Years of Struggle for the Democratic Control of Our Resources, 1980. Asst. to pres. Nat. Farmers Union, Washington, 1950-51; dir. Encampment for Citizenship, N.Y.C., 1961, 64. Served with AUS, 1943-46; ETO. Recipient Sidney Hillman Found. prize award polit. writing, 1955. Mem. AAAS, ACLU. Home: 233 W 11th St New York NY 10014 Office: Graduate Center CUNY 33 W 42d St New York NY 10036

ENGLERT, ROY THEODORE, lawyer; b. Nashville, Sept. 11, 1922; s. Roy T. and Ruth Rowe (Tindall) E.; m. Helen Frances Wiggs, Sept. 25, 1948; children—Lee Ann, Roy Theodore. B.A., Vanderbilt U., 1943; LL.B., Columbia, 1951; LL.M., George Washington U., 1953. Bar: Tenn. 1951, D.C. 1952, Supreme Ct. 1955. Asst. supr. Nat. Life & Accident Ins. Co., Nashville; asst. counsel Office Comptroller of Currency, U.S. Treasury Dept., 1951-58, chief counsel, 1958-62, asst. gen. counsel of dept., 1962-66, dep. gen. counsel, 1966-73; sr. asso., sec. Charls E. Walker Assos., Inc., Washington, 1973—; pvt. practice, Washington, 1973—; mem. Sr. Seminar in Fgn. Policy, Dept. State, 1963-73, U.S. Assay Commn., 1975; lectr., writer on banking law. Served from apprentice seaman to lt. USNR, 1943-46. Recipient Treasury Exceptional Service and; Gen. Counsel awards. Mem. Fed., Am., D.C., Tenn. bar assns. Presbyn. Club: National Lawyers (Washington). Home: 6720 Bellamy Ave Springfield VA 22152 Office: 1730 Pennsylvania Ave Washington DC 20006

ENGLESMITH, TEJAS, curator; b. London, Nov. 28, 1941; s. lGeorge and Lydia Julia (Johnson-Briet) E. Student, U. St. Thomas, Houston, 1959-63. Asst. dir. Whitechapel Gallery, London, 1963-69; curator Contemporary Art Jewish Mus., N.Y.C., 1969-70; dir. Leo Castelli Gallery, N.Y.C., 1970-74, Max Hutchinson Gallery, Houston, 1977-78; arts program KPFT-FM, 1977—; art cons. various corps. and instns.; mem. adv. panel visual arts CACH, Houston, 1977—; judge art shows. Narrator: (film) Pas de Deux: A Dance of Two Countries: China and America, 1980; art cons. and interviewer: Curtain!, KUHT-TV, 1980-81; asst. dir. devel.: KUHT-TV, 1980—; writer mus. catalogues. Mem. N.Y. Drawing Soc. (selection com. 1970). Home: 406 Westmoreland Houston TX 77006 Office: KUHT 4513 Cullen Blvd Houston TX 77004

ENGLEY, DONALD BROWN, university librarian; b. Stafford Springs, Conn., July 19, 1917; s. Frank Ballantine and Annie (Brown) E.; m. Hope I. Lummis, Oct. 31, 1942. B.A., Amherst Coll., 1939, M.A. (hon.), 1959; B.S. in L.S, Columbia U., 1941; M.A., U. Chgo., 1947. Library asst. Amherst Coll., 1936-40, Columbia, 1940-41, N.Y. Pub. Library, 1941; librarian Am. Army U., Biarritz, France, 1945, Norwich U., Northfield, Vt., 1947-49; asso. librarian Trinity Coll., Hartford, Conn., 1949-51, librarian, 1951-72; asso. univ. librarian Yale U., 1972-82, supr. Lewis Walpole Library, 1982—; Sec. Trinity Coll. Library Assos., 1951-72; adv. com. Mark Twain Meml. and Library Commn., Hartford, 1954—; chmn. Conn. Gov.'s Com. Libraries, 1961-63; mem. Conn. State Library Com., 1964-73; mem. univ. council library com. Yale, 1966-70. Trustee Watkinson Library, Hartford, Stowe-Day Found. Served to capt. AUS, 1941-46. Decorated Bronze Star. Mem. Conn. Library Assn. (past pres.), Conn. Hist. Soc. (trustee), Amherst Assn. Conn., Bibliog. Soc. Am. Congregationalist. Clubs: Grolier (N.Y.C.); Acorn of Conn., Columbiad. Home: 30 Glenwood Rd West Hartford CT 06107

ENGLEY, FRANK B., JR., microbiologist, educator; b. Wallingford, Conn., Oct. 26, 1919; s. Frank B. and Anne (Brown) E.; m. Beatrice Winslow Doak, June 26, 1948; children: Karen Winslow, Elizabeth Anne, Heather Cooke, Frank B. III. B.S., U. Conn., 1941; M.S., U. Pa., 1944, Ph.D., 1949; postgrad., Johns Hopkins, 1946-47. Diplomate: Am. Bd. Microbiology. Research technician Atwater Animal Disease Labs., Storrs, Conn., 1938-41; asst. instr. microbiology U. Pa. Sch. Medicine, 1941-44; research microbiologist U.S. Govt., 1946-50; asso. prof. bacteriology and parasitology, cons. microbiologist Univ. Hosps., U. Tex. Med. Br., 1950-55; prof. microbiology, chmn. dept. U. Mo. Sch. Medicine, 1955-77, asst. dean, 1956-60, prof., acting chmn. dept. public health and preventive medicine, 1960-61; vis. prof., Lagos, Nigeria, 1972, Tripoli, Libya, 1979; cons. in field, 1954—; mem. Am. Inst. Biol. Scis. adv. com. to NASA on spacecraft sterilization, 1966-68, FDA com. on OTC antimicrobials, 1972-80; mem. council NIH, 1983—; cons. Armed Forces Epidemiol. Bd., 1983—. Author: Advanced and Elementary Laboratory Manuals for Medical Microbiology, 1955, 65, Pocket Reference Guide to Medical Microbiology, 1963, Persistence of Microorganisms, 1963, also numerous articles.; Editorial bd.: Cytobios and Microbios, Eng., Medizin und Hygiene, Germany. Served with AUS, 1944-46. Decorated Army Commendation ribbon; recipient Civil Service award, 1948; Osteon Faculty award U. Tex. Med. Br., 1954; Commonwealth Fund research and travel award, Switzerland, 1965-66; SAMA Faculty Teaching award, 1970. Fellow AAAS, Am. Pub. Health Assn. (pres. Mo. br. 1964), Am. Acad. Microbiology; mem. Am. Soc. Microbiology (pres. Mo. br. 1959), Research Soc. Am., AMA (affiliate), Royal Soc. Health, Am. Inst. Biol. Scis., AAUP, Soc. Exptl. Biology and Medicine, N.Y. Acad. Scis., Am. Assn. Med. Colls., Inst. Environ. Scis., Soc. Indsl. Microbiology, Conf. State and Provincial Lab. Dirs., Am. Sci. Film Assn., Am. Assn. Med. Instrumentation, Assn. Practitioners of Infection Control, Sigma Xi. Home: 609 Westmount Ave Columbia MO 65201

ENGLISH, ALEXANDER, professional basketball player; b. Columbia, S.C., Jan. 5, 1954. Ed., U. S.C. Forward Milw. Bucks, NBA, 1976-78, Indiana Pacers, NBA, 1978-80, Denver Nuggets, NBA, 1980—; player NBA All-Star Game, 1982, 83. Address: care Denver Muggets PO Box 4286 Denver CO 80204 *

ENGLISH, CHARLES BRAND, lawyer; b. Urbana, Ohio, June 10, 1924; s. Edwin L. and Margaret (Br) E.; m. Constance Coulter, 1946 (dec. 1953); 1 son, Thomas C.; m. Eva Uber, Oct. 3, 1954; children—Gwendolyn, Carolyn (dec.). Student, Dartmouth, 1941-42, Denison U., 1942-43; A.B., U. Mich., 1944, LL.B., 1947; L.H.D. (hon.), Urbana U., 1978. Bar: Ohio bar 1947. Since practiced privately in, Urbana., Farm mgr., 1950-60; Bd. dirs. Milk Producers Union, Cin., 1957-62, Nat. Milk Producers Fedn., 1966-69; v.p. Cin. Milk Sales Assn., 1966-72, dir., 1962-72. Contbr. articles to jours. Mem. bd. edn. Triad Sch. Dist., 1951-59, Glen Helen Adv. Bd., 1959-76; open space legal adviser Com. for Country Common, 1963-76; mem. Ohio Land Use Rev. Adv. Council, 1976-77; trustee Urbana Coll., 1966-77, vice chmn., 1969-73, sec., 1973-76; bd. dirs. Assn. Ind. Colls. and Univs. Ohio, 1969-77, Ohio Citizens' Council for Health and Welfare, 1973-77; mem. Champaign County Bd. Mental Retardation, 1967-75. Named One of Hon. 100 alumni Ohio State U. Sch. Natural Resources, 1970. Mem. ABA, Ohio Bar Assn., Champaign County Bar Assn. (pres. 1958), Ohio Conservation Found. (trustee 1969—, sec.-treas. 1969-73), Am. Humanist Assn. (dir. 1957-66, sec. 1959-66), Fellowship of Religious Humanists (sec. 1967-72), Community Water Resources Com. Champaign County (co-chmn. 1970-71), SW Ohio Water Devel. Study (adv. bd. 1969-72). Unitarian. Home: Rural Route Cable OH 43009 Office: 648 Bodey Circle PO Box 271 Urbana OH 43078

ENGLISH, DAN COUCH, surgeon, educator; b. Lubbock, Tex., May 5, 1931; s. Otis W. and Roxie (Couch) E.; m. Mary Lucille Dansby, June 20, 1953; children: Dana Leigh, Eric Otis, Mary Elaine. Student, Baylor U., 1948-51, M.D., 1955. Diplomate: Am. Bd. Surgery. Intern Jefferson Davis Hosp., 1955-56; resident George Washington U., 1956-57, 59-60, U. Pitts. VA Hosp., 1960-61, Phila. Gen. Hosp., 1961-63; gen. practice surgery, Lubbock, 1963-68, Tyler, Tex., 1968-70; mem. faculty Coll. Human Medicine, Mich. State U., East Lansing, 1971—, prof. surgery, chmn. dept., 1975-81; Robert Wood Johnson health policy fellow, Washington, 1980-81. Served with AUS, 1957-59. Fellow A.C.S.

ENGLISH, DAVID ANTHONY, book editor; b. Macclesfield, Cheshire, Eng., Jan. 9, 1942; came to U.S., 1946; s. Raymond and Mary (Jones) E.; m. Deirdre May Mills, Aug. 15, 1964; children:

Katherine Louise, Duncan Clive. B.A., Cambridge U., Eng., 1963. Sales rep. Harper & Row, Ann Arbor, Mich., 1964-69; English editor Macmillan Pub. Co., N.Y.C., 1969-74, English and econs. editor, 1974-79, exec. editor, 1979-82, editor-in-chief, 1982—, v.p. Coll. div. Episcopalian. Office: Macmillan Publishing Company 866 Third Ave New York NY 10022

ENGLISH, FLOYD LEROY, telecommunications company executive; b. Nicholas, Calif., June 10, 1934; s. Elvan L. and Louise (Corliss) E.; m. Wanda Parton, Sept. 8, 1955 (div. 1980); children: Roxane, Darryl; m. Elaine Ewell, July 3, 1981. A.B. in Physics, Calif. State U.-Chico, 1959, M.S., Ariz. State U., 1962, Ph.D., 1965. Div. supr. Sanida Labs., Albuquerque, 1965-73; gen. mgr. Rockwell Internat.-Collins, Newport Beach, Calif., 1973-75; pres. Darcom, Albuquerque, 1975-79; cons in energy mgmt. and acquisitions, Albuquerque, 1970-80; v.p. U.S. ops. Andrew Corp., Orland Park, Ill., 1980-82, pres., 1982—, dir., 1982—. Contbr. articles to profl. jours. Served to 1st lt. U.S. Army, 1954-57; served to capt. USAR, until 1969. Mem. IEEE. Republican. Presbyterian. Office: Andrew Corp 1055 W 153d St Orland Park IL 60462

ENGLISH, GLENN, Congressman; b. Cordell, Okla., Nov. 30, 1940; m. Jan Pangle, 1970. Grad., Southwestern State Coll., Weatherford, Okla., 1964. Mem. 94th-98th Congresses from 6th Okla. Dist.; Exec. dir. Okla. State Democratic Com. Served with U.S. Army Res., 1965-71. Office: 2235 Rayburn House Office Bldg Washington DC 20515 *

ENGLISH, JAMES FAIRFIELD, JR., college president; b. Putnam, Conn., Feb. 15, 1927; s. James Fairfield and Alice Bradford (Welles) E.; m. Isabelle Spotswood Cox, July 9, 1955; children: Alice, James Fairfield, Margaret, William. Grad., Loomis Sch., 1944; B.A., Yale U., 1949; M.A., Cambridge (Eng.) U., 1951; LL.B., U. Conn., 1956. With Conn. Bank & Trust Co., Hartford, 1951—, sr. v.p., 1961-63, exec. v.p., 1963-66, pres., 1966-70, chmn. bd., 1970-80; also dir.; v.p. fin. and planning Trinity Coll., Hartford, 1977-81, pres., 1981—; dir. Cigna Corp., Emhart Corp., Conn. Natural Gas Co. Bd. dirs. Inst. of Living. Served with AUS, 1944-46. Mem. United Ch. of Christ. Home: 31 Potter Ct Noank CT 06340 Office: Trinity Coll Hartford CT 06106

ENGLISH, JOSEPH T., physician, medical administrator; b. Phila., May 21, 1933; m. Ann Carr Sanger, Dec. 20, 1969; 3 children. A.B., St. Joseph's Coll., 1954; M.D., Jefferson Med. Coll., 1958. Intern Jefferson Med. Coll. Hosp., Phila., 1958-59; resident in psychiatry Inst. of Pa. Hosp., Phila., 1959-61, NIMH, Bethesda, Md., 1961-62; practice psychiatry, 1962—; psychiatrist Office of Dir., NIMH, 1964-65, asst. chief policy and program co-ordination, 1965-66, dept. chief office interagy. liaison, 1966; chief psychiatrist med. program div. Peace Corps, Washington, 1962-66; dep. asst. dir. health affairs OEO, Washington, 1966, acting asst. dir., 1966-68, asst. dir., 1969; adminstr. Health Services and Mental Health Adminstrn., HEW, 1969-70; pres. N.Y.C. Health and Hosps. Corp., from 1970; dir. dept. psychiatry St. Vincent's Hosp. and Med. Center, N.Y.C., 1973—; also dean; prof. psychiatry N.Y. Med. Coll., 1979—; adj. prof. psychiatry Cornell U.; Chmn. interagy. task force emergency food and med. program for U.S. OEO-HEW, U.S. Dept. Agr., 1968-69; chmn. Alaska Subcom. Fed. Health Programs Pres.'s Rev. Commn. Alaska, 1969—; chmn. adv. com. on accessible environments for disabled Bldg. Research Adv. Bd., Washington, 1974—; chmn. exec. com. of com. on mental health services Greater N.Y. Hosp. Assn., 1974—; exec. coordinator panels on mental health services delivery Pres.'s Commn. on Mental Health, 1977; mem. Health Adv. Council Gov. State N.Y., 1981. Author spl. reports on Peace Corps, other govtl. programs.; Contbr. articles to profl. jours. Served to capt. USAF Res., 1958-63; sr. surgeon USPHS, 1963-66. Named One of Outstanding Young Men of Year U.S. Jr. C. of C., 1964; recipient John XXIII medal Coll. New Rochelle, N.Y., 1966; Meritorious award for exemplary achievement pub. adminstrn. William A. Jump Meml. Found., 1966; Flemming award, also personal commendation Pres. of U.S., 1968. Fellow Am. Psychiat. Assn. (chmn. council financing psychiat. sers. 1981), N.Y. Acad. Medicine, Am. Coll. Psychiatrists, Inst. Medicine of Nat. Acad. Scis.; mem. AMA (chmn. mental health services to poor 1965-66), Insts. Religion and Health (profl. adv. bd. 1966—), Am. Public Health Assn., Group Advancement Psychiatry, Pa. Med. Soc., Soc. of Jefferson for Research (charter), Am. Coll. Mental Health Adminstrs., Am. Hosp. Assn. (chmn. bd. govs. Center Mental Health and Psychiatry), Arnold Air Soc., Alpha Omega Alpha, Kappa Beta Phi, Alpha Sigma Nu. Office: St Vincent's Hosp and Med Center 203 W 12th St New York NY 10011 *

ENGLISH, LOWELL EDWARD, former marine corps officer, mgmt. cons., mus. dir.; b. Fairbury, Nebr., July 8, 1915; s. George William and Hazel (Browning) E.; m. Eleanor R. McCallum, Feb. 24, 1941; children—Loellen Kay, Bruce Browning, Becky Lynne. B.A., U. Nebr., 1938. Commd. 2d lt. USMC, 1938, advanced through grades to maj. gen., 1967; various assignments, prior to World War II; mem. 3d Marine Div., World War II; mem. acad. staff U.S. Naval Acad., 1946-49; instr. mil. psychology and leadership U.S. Mil. Acad., 1949-52; comdg. officer 3d Bn.; regtl. exec. officer 1st Marines, Korea; mem. staff U.S. 8th Army, 1953; chief staff Recruit Tng. Command, San Diego, 1954; comdr. tng. and test regt., 1957; also Basic Sch., Marine Corps Schs., Quantico, Va., 1958-60; grad. Army War Coll., 1961; assigned Office Asst. Sec. Def., 1961-63; chief staff for comdr. in chief U.S. Naval Forces, Eastern Atlantic and Mediterranean, 1963-64; dep. chief plans directorate J-5, U.S. Strike Command, MacDill AFB, Fla., 1964-65; asst. div. comdr. 3d Marine Div., Vietnam, 1965-67; comdr. Marine Corps Recruit Depot, San Diego, 1967-69; mgmt. cons., 1969-72; dir. Mus. of Man, 1972—. Vice chmn. San Diego chpt. ARC; bd. dirs. San Diego 200th Anniversary, San Diego United Community Services, Childrens' Health Center, San Diego U.S.O. Decorated D.S.M. (2), Legion of Merit (2), Bronze Star (2), Purple Heart. Mem. Navy League (dir. San Diego council). Clubs: Kiwanian, Rotarian. Home: 5865 Madra San Diego CA 92120 *To achieve true greatness, one must have respect for himself. This respect comes from those values of all cultures, which he observes in his relationship with others. A man without respect for himself is incapable of respecting others.*

ENGLISH, NICHOLAS CONOVER, lawyer; b. Elizabeth, N.J., Apr. 12, 1912; s. Conover and Sara Elizabeth (Jones) E.; m. Agnes N. Perry, Mar. 18, 1939 (div. 1947); children—Henry H. P., Anne Whitall (Mrs. Edward J. Wardwell); m. Eleanor Morss, May 1, 1948; children—Priscilla (Mrs. Jonathan S. Vincent), Sara (dec.), Sherman, Eleanor. Grad., Pingry Sch., 1929; A.B., Princeton, 1934; LL.B., Harvard, 1937. Bar: N.J. bar 1937. Since practiced in, Newark; partner firm McCarter & English, 1947-77, counsel, 1978—. Bd. dirs. Summit (N.J.) YMCA, 1950-57, Newark YMWCA; chmn. exec. com. Central Atlantic Area YMCA, 1957-63; mem. nat. council YMCA, 1954, 58—, v.p., 1959-60, mem. nat. bd., 1960-71, 73-81, vice chmn., 1969-71, treas., 1977-81; trustee Kent Place Sch., 1959—, pres., 1961-72; bd. dirs. Nat. Legal Aid Assn., 1953-56. Served to lt. USNR, 1943-46. Mem. ABA (ho. of dels. 1957-58), N.J. Bar Assn., Essex County Bar Assn., Am. Bible Soc. (bd. mgrs. 1964—), Am. Law Inst. Republican. Conglist. Clubs: Essex (Newark); Princeton (N.Y.C.). Home: 12 Harrison Ct Summit NJ 07901 Office: 550 Broad St Newark NJ 07102

ENGLISH, O. SPURGEON, physician; b. Presque Isle, Maine, Sept. 27, 1901; s. G. Wesley and Annie L. (Hemphill) E.; m. Ellen Mary Brown, Feb. 28, 1933; children—Wesley, O. Spurgeon (dec.), Carroll, Cheryl Ann. Student, U. Maine, 1918-20; M.D., Jefferson Med. Coll., 1924, Berlin Psychoanalytic Inst., 1931-33. Intern Jefferson Med. Coll. Hosp., 1924-27, Boston Psychol. Hosp., 1927-28; resident physician Montefiore Hosp., N.Y.C., 1928-29; Commonwealth fellow in psychiatry, 1929-32; clin. prof. psychiatry Temple U. Med. Sch., 1933-38, prof. psychiatry, 1938—, head dept. psychiatry, 1938-64; pvt. practice psychiatry and psychoanalysis, Phila., 1938—. Author: (with G.H.J. Pearson) numerous books including The Emotional Problems of Living, 1945, Psychosomatic Medicine, (with Edward Weiss) Fathers are Parents, Too, (with Constance Foster), 1951, Introduction to Psychiatry, (with Stuart H. Finch), 1954, Direct Analysis and Schizophrenia, (with others), 1961. Fellow A.C.P., Am. Psychiat. Assn., AMA; mem. Am. Psychoanalytical Assn., Phila. Psychiat. Soc. (past pres.), Phila. Psychoanalytic Soc. (past pres.). Home and office: 449 Righters Mill Rd Narberth PA 19072

ENGLISH, PAUL WARD, geographer; b. Worcester, Mass., Feb. 20, 1936; s. James and Mary T. E.; married; children—Paul, Peter. B.A. (scholar), Clark U., 1957; fellow, Johns Hopkins U., 1957-58; M.A., U. Wis., 1959, Ph.D., 1965. Fellow U. Wis., 1960-61, Nat. Acad. Scis.-NRC fgn. area field research grantee, Madison, 1961-63; asst. prof. U. Tex., Austin, 1963-65; assoc. prof., asst. dir. Center for Middle Eastern Studies Mich. State U., 1966-69, prof. geography, dir. Center for Middle Eastern Studies, 1973-79; prof. geography U. Tex., Austin, 1979—, chair dept. geography, 1982—; vis. prof. dept. geography U. Calif., Berkeley, summer 1969; NSF summer fellow, 1959, vis. scientist, 1971-72. Author: City and Village in Iran, 1966 (Herfurth award in social scis.), (with R.C. Mayfield) Man, Space and Environment - Concepts in Contemporary Cultural Geography, 1972, World Regional Geography - A Question of Place, 1977; editorial bd.: Contemporary Arab World, Geography, Jour. Middle East Studies Assn. Univ. Research Inst. grantee, 1965, 67, 70, 80, 82, 83; grad. seminar devel. grantee, 1972; Fulbright faculty research fellow, Afghanistan, 1967; Joint Research grantee, 1971; Devel. grantee, 1971, 72, summer 1976; Earhart Found. grantee, summer 1975; Social Sci. research grantee, Isfahan, Iran, summer 1975; recipient medal Iranian Geog. Assn., 1977; named an Outstanding Coll. Tchr. Change Mag. Press, 1978. Mem. AAAS, Am. Inst. Iranian Studies, Assn. Am. Geographers, Council Soc. for Iranian Studies, Middle East Inst., Middle East Studies Assn. N.Am. (dir. 1977—), Nat. Council Geog. Edn., NSF Commn. on Coll. Geography. Office: U Tex GRG 334 Austin TX 78712

ENGLISH, ROBERT JOSEPH, electronic corporation executive; b. Jersey City, Dec. 5, 1932; s. John Joseph and Mary (Budrawiz) E.; m. Robyn Adele Allan, Dec. 27, 1958; children: Robert Joseph, Mark Allan, John Frederick. B.S., St. Peters Coll., 1954; LL.B., Georgetown U., 1958; M.B.A., NYU, 1963. Bar: D.C. 1958, N.J. 1959. Subcontract adminstr. ITT Fed. Labs. div., Nutley, N.J., 1959-60; with Fed. Electric Corp., Paramus, N.J., 1960—, sec., gen. counsel, 1964-66, dir. legal contracts, 1967-70; gen. counsel ITT Govt. and Comml. Services Group, 1970-72; v.p., sec., gen. counsel ITT Def. Communications and ITT Avionics divs., Nutley, 1972—; sec., gen. counsel Internat. Electric Corp., 1972—; dir. ITT Fed. Support Services Inc., ITT Tech. Services Inc., Intelex Systems Inc., Providence, Base Services Inc., Paramus, Internat. Standard Engring. Inc., Paramus. Contr. articles to profl. jours. Trustee Mahwah (N.J.) Hist. Soc., 1978—. Served to 1st lt., Chem. Corps U.S. Army, 1954-56. Mem. Am., Bergen, N.J., D.C. bar assns., Phi Delta Phi. Home: 36 Sunnyside Rd Mahwah NJ 07430 Office: 492 River Rd Nutley NJ 07110

ENGLISH, WOODRUFF JONES, lawyer; b. Elizabeth, N.J., Apr. 28, 1909; s. Conover and Sara Elizabeth (Jones) E.; m. Carolyn Barton, Dec. 19, 1942; children: Woodruff Jones II, Virginia English Sprenkle, Barton Conover, Elizabeth Cooper, Carolyn Whitaker. A.B., Princeton U., 1931; LL.B., Harvard U., 1934. Bar: N.J. 1935. Since practiced in Newark; partner McCarter & English, 1947-72, of counsel, 1972—; lectr. trusts and estates; dir. Jersey Mortgage Co. Pres. Summit (N.J.) United Appeal, 1947-48; mem. Summit Environ. Commn., 1971-76; trustee Presbyn. Hosp., Newark, 1947-58, United Hosps. Newark, 1959-70; chmn. bd. United Hosps. Newark, 1967-70; trustee Overlook Hosp., Summit, 1949-55, pres., 1953-55; trustee United Community Fund Newark, 1957-71, pres., 1961-65; trustee Frost Valley YMCA, 1959—, pres., 1967—; trustee Overseas Ministries Study Center, 1958—, sec., 1958-70, pres., 1970—; bd. dirs. Summit YMCA, 1935-39, Newark YM-YWCA, 1951—; pres. Newark YM-YWCA, 1957-61; mem. internat. com. nat. bd. YMCA, 1953-72, exec. com., 1953-72, sec. exec. com., 1960-64, vice chmn. student work com., nat. bd., 1952-62, mem. nat. council, 1973—, exec. com. internat. div. nat. bd., 1972-81; chmn. student work com. Central Atlantic Area, 1955-60; trustee N.J. region NCCJ, 1961-72; trustee Colonial Symphony Soc., 1951-61, v.p., 1959-61; trustee, mem. exec. com. Drew U., 1972—; pres. Summit Council Chs., 1948-50. Served to lt. comdr. USNR, 1941-45. Hon. award, 1973. Fellow Am. Coll. Probate Counsel; mem. Am. Law Inst., Am. Judicature Soc., Am., N.J., Essex County bar assns., Assn. Bar City N.Y., N.J. Soc. Hosp. Attys. (v.p. 1972). Republican. Presbyterian (ruling elder 1951—). Clubs: Essex (Newark); Nassau (Princeton, N.J.); Princeton (N.Y.C.). Home: 90 Whittredge Rd Summit NJ 07901 Office: 550 Broad St Newark NJ 07102

ENGLUND, JOHN ARTHUR, research co. exec.; b. Omaha, June 4, 1926; s. Arthur D. and Marguerite E. (Welsh) E.; m. Marilyn Ann Miller, Aug. 9, 1952; children—John Arthur, Ann E., George A., James M., Edward M. B.S., Creighton U., Omaha, 1949; S.M., M.I.T., 1951. Teaching fellow M.I.T., 1949-51; asst. prof. Creighton U., 1951-56; ops. analyst SAC, Omaha, 1956-62; mil. systems analyst U.S. Arms Control and Disarmament Agy., Washington, 1962-63; successively mathematician, br. chief, div. mgr. Analytic Services, Inc., Falls Church, Va., 1963-76, exec. v.p., 1976-81, pres., 1981—. Served with USAAF, 1944-46. Mem. Mil. Ops. Research Soc. (pres. 1979-80). Address: 400 Army-Navy Dr Arlington VA 22202

ENGLUND, PAUL THEODORE, biochemist, educator; b. Worcester, Mass., Mar. 25, 1938; s. Theodore John and Mildred Elizabeth (Anderson) E.; m. Jean Elizabeth Nelson, Aug. 12, 1961; children—Suzanne Elizabeth, Marcia Jean. B.A., Hamilton Coll., 1960; Ph.D., Rockefeller U., 1966. Postdoctoral fellow Stanford U., 1966-68; asst. prof. Johns Hopkins Sch. Medicine, Balt., 1968-74, asso. prof., 1974-80, prof., 1980—. Editorial bd.: Jour. Biol. Chemistry, Molecular and Biochem. Parasitology, 1982—; contbr. articles to profl. jours. Faculty research grantee Am. Cancer Soc., 1969-74; Fogarty Sr. Internat. fellow, 1980; grantee NIH, WHO.; Burroughs-Wellcome scholar in molecular parasitology, 1982—. Mem. Am. Chem. Soc., Am. Soc. Biol. Chemists, AAAS. Home: 1208 Roundill Rd Baltimore MD 21218 Office: 725 N Wolfe St Baltimore MD 21205

ENGLUND, RALPH CALDWELL, constrn. co. exec.; b. Gaffrey, S.C., Mar. 29, 1925; s. Carl G. and Anna (Hall) E.; m. Sallie Bozier Allen, Nov. 26, 1949; children—John, Susan, Virginia. B.S. in Civil Engring, Ga. Inst. Tech., 1945. Estimator, project mgr. Daniel Internat. Corp., Birmingham, Ala., 1946-54, asst. div. mgr., 1954-58, div. mgr., 1958-62, v.p., 1962—, Daniel Realty Corp., Birmingham, 1970-75, pres., 1975—. Served with USN, 1943-46. Methodist. Club: Kiwanis. Home: 2901 Warrington Rd Birmingham AL 35223 Office: 1900 Daniel Bldg Birmingham AL 35233

ENGMAN, LEWIS AUGUST, pharmaceutical association executive, lawyer, former government official; b. Grand Rapids, Mich., Jan. 6, 1936; s. H. Sigurd and Florence C. (Lewis) E.; m. Patricia Lynne Hanahan, Dec. 2, 1978; children: Geoffrey Ponton, Jonathan Lewis, Richard Ransford. A.B., U. Mich., 1957; postgrad., Univ. Coll. and London Sch. Econs., 1957-58; LL.B., Harvard U., 1961. Asso., then partner law firm Warner Norcross & Judd, Grand Rapids, 1961-70, Washington, 1976-79; pres. Pharm. Mfrs. Assn., Washington, 1979—; mem. council Internat. Fedn. Pharm. Mfrs. Assns., 1979—; pres. Nat. Drug Trade Conf., 1980; dir. legis. affairs Pres.'s Com. Consumer Interests, Washington, 1970; gen. counsel White House Office Consumer Affairs, Washington, 1970-71; asst. dir. Domestic Council, The White House, Washington, 1971-73; chmn. FTC, Washington, 1973-75; Mem. Council Adminstrv. Conf. of U.S., 1974-75; mem. 6th Circuit Jud. Conf. U.S.; Bd. advisors Columbia U. Center for Law and Econ. Studies, 1975-79, Mich. Franchise Adv. Com., 1977-79; mem. Western Mich. Areawide Comprehensive Health Planning Unit, 1969-70; chmn. Kent County (Mich.) Health Planning unit, 1969-70. Mem. Friends of Art adv. bd. Grand Valley State Coll., 1969-70; Mem. Kent County Republican Finance Com., 1965-70; Bd. dirs. Opera Assn. Western Mich., 1967-69; bd. dirs. Grand Rapids Symphony Soc., 1964-70, pres., 1968-70; trustee Blodgett Meml. Hosp., 1968-70, sec., 1969-70; bd. dirs. Dyer-Ives Found., 1964—, sec., 1961-70. Mem. ABA (mem. council sect. anti-trust law 1973-75), Fed. Bar Assn., D.C. Bar Assn., Mich. Bar Assn., Am. Soc. Internat. Law, Phi Beta Kappa, Delta Sigma Rho, Phi Kappa Phi, Phi Eta Sigma. Presbyterian. Clubs: Kent Country, University (Grand Rapids); George Town, Metropolitan (Washington). Home: McLean VA Office: 1100 15th St NW Washington DC 20005

ENIX, AGNES LUCILLE, editorial consultant; b. Drummond, Okla., Jan. 17, 1933; d. James Robert and Alma Frances (Hodges) E. B.S., Okla. State U., 1955; M.S., Northwestern U., 1966. Dietetic intern VA Hosp., Los Angeles, 1955-56; staff dietition, 1956-57; nutritionist Dairy Council Greater Kansas City, Mo., 1957-61; asso. dir. materials devel. Nat. Dairy Council, Chgo., 1961-65; reporter, feature writer Chgo. Tribune, 1966-67; copywriter Rogers & Smith Advt. Agy., Dallas, 1967-68; editor Dallas Mag., Dallas C. of C., 1968-75, Dallas Morning News, 1976-79; rep. Wilson Engraving Co., Inc., Dallas, 1979-80, Vision mag., Public Communications Found. for North Tex., 1980-81; editorial cons., 1981—; mag. cons. Am. Dietetic Assn., 1970-71; Mem. Wednesday Noon Forum YMCA, 1971-72; adv. bd. journalism dept. N. Tex. State U. Recipient award S.W. Journalism Forum, 1970, Journalism award Tex. Med. Assn., 1971, Matrix award Women in Communication, 1971, Katy award Dallas Press Club, 1982, Creative award Art Dirs. Mag., 1982. Mem. Omicron Nu, Phi Upsilon Omicron, Alpha Delta Pi. Home: 6932 Allview Dallas TX 75227

ENLOE, CORTEZ FERDINAND, JR., magazine publisher, physician; b. Jefferson City, Mo., June 1, 1910; m. Mary Josephine Greenlee, May 4, 1963; children: Margaret Mary Greenlee, David Goodridge, Cynthia Holden. B.A., U. Mo., Columbia, 1932; postgrad., Ruperto Carola U. Heidelberg, Ger., Ludwig Maximillians U. Munich, Ger.; M.D. cum laude, U. Berlin, 1937; grad., Sch. Aviation Medicine, 1942, Command and Gen. Staff Coll., 1943. Diplomate: Am. Bd. Preventive Medicine. Research intern Charity Clinic, Berlin, 1936-37; intern St. Anthony Hosp., St. Louis, 1937-38; practice medicine, specializing in internal medicine; asst. med. dir. Winthrop Chem. Co., N.Y.C.; exec. v.p., gen. mgr. G.F. Harvey Co., Saratoga Springs, N.Y.; dir. profl. services and clin. research William R. Warner, Inc., N.Y.C.; v.p. Murray Breese Assos., N.Y.C.; chmn. bd., pres. Cortez F. Enloe, Inc., N.Y.C.; pres. Mediphone, Inc., Washington; sr. partner Enloe, Stalvey & Assocs., Washington; chmn. bd., pres. Nutrition Today, Inc., Annapolis, Md., 1964—; editor, pub. Nutrition Today mag., 1964—; mem. med. adv. bd. Nat. Assn. Human Devel., Washington, 1980—; hon. Militare Samfunn lectr., Oslo, 1980; dir. Antarctic Nutrition Survey, 1968—; chmn. sci. adv. com. Am./Norwegian Trans Polar Expdn., 1968-69; ofcl. observer NATO High Arctic Exercises, 1980; Central European corr. Kansas City Star, 1933-37; cons. fed. adminstr. CD and dir. Office of Emergency Planning; adminstr. N.Y. State CD; cons. mem. Council Nat. Def., AMA; cons. Surgeon Gen. USAF; mem. N.Y. Gov's Adv. Com. Emergency Health Resources. Editor: The Flight Surgeon's Manual, 1954; contbr. articles to sci. jours. and yachting mags. Trustee Geriatrics Research Found. Served to maj. USAAF, 1946; CBI, PTO, ETO; med. advisor to Admiral Lord Louis Mountbatten, comdr.; CBI. Decorated Legion of Merit, Air medal, Bronze Star, Antarctic medal, numerous others; recipient Faculty-Alumni Gold medal U. Mo., 1973; citation Jefferson City Public Schs.; Nat. Air Power award Air Force Assn., 1955; Nat. Leica Photographers medal, 1939. Fellow N.Y. Acad. Medicine, Royal Soc. Medicine (London), Royal Geog. Soc. (London), Aerospace Med. Assn., Am. Coll. Angiology, Am. Geriatrics Soc., Explorers Club; mem. AMA, N.Y. State Med. Soc. (chmn. space medicine sect.), County N.Y. Med. Soc., Am. Coll. Preventive Medicine, Am. Chem. Soc., AAAS, Assn. Mil. Surgeons, Endocrine Soc. (emeritus), Space Med. Soc., World Med. Assn., Hollywood (Calif.) Acad. Medicine (hon. life), Hakluyt Soc. (London), Air Force Assn. (life, past dir.), Soc. Med. Friends of Wine (hon. life). Clubs: N.Y. Yacht (Atalantis trophy 1964, D.S.M. 1967), Manhasset Bay Yacht, Out Island Squadron, Bermuda Ocean Racing; Tuna (Atlantic City); Army and Navy (Washington); Wings, Overseas Press (N.Y.C.); Nat. Press. Office: PO Box 1829 Annapolis MD 21404

ENLOE, CYNTHIA HOLDEN, political science educator, writer; b. N.Y.C., July 16, 1938; d. Cortez F. and Harriet (Goodridge) E. B.A., Conn. Coll., 1960; M.A., U. Calif.-Berkeley, 1963, Ph.D., 1967. Acting asst. prof. polit. sci. U. Calif.-Berkeley, 1966-67; asst. prof. sci. Miami U., Oxford, Ohio, 1967-72; assoc. prof. govt. Clark U., Worcester, Mass., 1972-78, prof., 1978—, chmn. dept., 1980-82, coordinator women's studies, 1982—; Fulbright lectr. U. Guyana, Georgetown, 1971-72; chmn. com. on ethnicity Social Sci. Research Council, 1978-82. Author: Ethnic Conflict and Political Development, 1973, Comparative Politics of Pollution, 1975, Ethnic Soldiers, 1980, Does Khaki Become You? The Militarization of Women's Lives. Recipient Disting. Teaching Clark U., 1981; fellow Council Fgn. Affairs, 1975-76; recipient Outstanding Teaching Miami U., 1972; Internat. Conflict fellow Ford Found., 1972. Mem. Am. Polit. Sci. Assn., Caucus Women in Polit. Sci., Assn. Asian Studies. Office: Dept of Government Clark University Worcester MA 01610

ENLOE, JOSEPH R., JR., oil company executive, petroleum engineer; b. Seymour, Tex., Sept. 9, 1924; s. Joseph R. and Bessie (Taylor) E.; m. Jessie Christopher, Jan. 11, 1948; children: Holly Ann, Bary Layne. B.S., Tex. Tech. U., 1949. Registered profl. engr., N.D. Vice-pres. Amerada Hess Corp., Tulsa, 1950—. 1st lt. USAAF, 1943-46; PTO. Mem. Soc. Petroleum Engrs. of AIME (sect. chmn. 1957-58). Home: 6447 S Hudson St Tulsa OK 74136 Office: Amerada Hess Corp 218 W 6th St Tulsa OK 74102

ENLOW, DONALD HUGH, anatomist; b. Mosquero, N.Mex., Jan. 22, 1927; s. Donald Carter and Martie Blairene (Albertson) E.; m. Martha Ruth McKnight, Sept. 3, 1945; 1 dau., Sharon Lynn. B.S., U. Houston, 1949, M.S., 1951; Ph.D., Tex. A&M U., 1955. Instr. biology U. Houston, 1949-51; asst. prof. biology West Tex. State U., 1955-56; instr. anatomy Med. Coll. S.C., 1956-57; asst. prof. U. Mich. Med. Sch., Ann Arbor, 1957-62, assoc. prof., 1962-67, prof. anatomy, 1969-

72; dir. phys. growth program Center for Human Growth and Devel., 1966-72; prof., chmn. dept. anatomy W.Va. U. Sch. Medicine, Morgantown, 1972-77; Thomas Hill Disting. prof., chmn. dept. orthodontics Case Western Res. Sch. Dentistry, Cleve., 1977—, asst. dean for research and grad. studies, 1977—, acting dean, 1983; guest lectr. 19 fgn. countries, 1963—. Author: Principles of Bone Remodeling, 1963, The Human Face, 1968, Handbook of Facial Growth, 1975; Contbr. chpts. to 18 books, numerous articles to profl. jours. Served with USCGR, 1945-46. Recipient Outstanding Research award Tex. Acad. Sci., 1952. Fellow Royal Soc. Medicine, Am. Assn. Anatomists, Internat. Assn. Dental Research; hon. mem. Am. Assn. Orthodontists (Mershon Meml. lectr. 1968, Spl. Merit award 1969), Gt. Lakes Orthodontic Soc., Cleve. Dental Soc., Cleve. Orthodontic Soc., Omicron Kappa Upsilon. Republican. Methodist. Home: 1402 Cleveland Heights Blvd Cleveland Heights OH 44106 Office: Dept Orthodontics Sch Dentistry Case Western Res U Abington Rd Cleveland OH 44106

ENLOW, FRED CLARK, banker; b. Lewistown, Mont., Apr. 15, 1940; s. Guy Rucks and Jewell E.; m. Catherine F. Cantrell, Aug. 28, 1965; children: Brett D., Alyssa M. B.A., Eastern Wash. U., 1964; M.B.A., Ohio State U., 1965. Instr. mktg. Eastern Wash. U., 1965-67; with Continental Pipeline Co., 1967-68, Seattle First Nat. Bank, from 1968, sr. v.p., dir. mktg., from 1976; sr. v.p., mgr. personal banking SeaFirst Corp.; now sr. v.p., mgr. retail product devel. mktg. Bank of Am. Bd. dirs. Pacific N.W. Ballet, 1981-83; chmn. bd. trustees Eastern Wash. U., 1981-83. Served with USAR, 1959-62. Methodist. Office: 180 Montgomery Suite 3692 San Francisco CA 94104

ENNEY, JAMES CROWE, former air force officer, business executive; b. Youngstown, Ohio, Oct. 1, 1930; s. Edgar Earl and Mildred (Crowe) E.; m. Margaret Ann Reeve, Oct. 31, 1975. B.G.E., U. Nebr., Omaha, 1963; grad., Indsl. Coll. Armed Forces, 1971. Commd. 2d. lt. USAF, 1953, advanced through grades to maj. gen., 1980; chief Target Intelligence Center, 7th Air Force, Republic of Vietnam, 1965-66, Targets; spl. asst. to asst. chief staff Intelligence, Hdqrs. USAF, Washington, 1966-70; chief plans div. U.S. European Command, Stuttgart, Germany, 1971-74; chief Soviet/Warsaw Pact div. Def. Intelligence Agy., Washington, 1974-75, dep. dir. for info. systems, 1975-76; dep. dir. Nat. Strategic Target List, Joint Strategic Target Planning Staff, Offutt AFB, Nebr., 1976-79; dep. chief staff Intelligence SAC, 1979-82; v.p. Sci. Applications, Inc., McLean, Va., 1982—. Decorated Def. Superior Service medal, D.S.M., Legion of Merit with two oak leaf clusters, Joint Service Commendation medal, Air Force Commendation medal with one oak leaf cluster. Mem. Air Force Assn. Episcopalian. Home: 1815 Saint Boniface St Vienna VA 22180 Office: Sci Applications Inc 1710 Goodridge Dr McLean VA 22102

ENNIS, BILLY MACK, food co. exec.; b. Shoffner, Ark., Apr. 10, 1938; s. Rex Dale and Geraldine N. (McCoy) E.; m. Paula Joy Morgan, Nov. 27, 1960; children—Sherry, William Morgan. B.S., Ark. State U., 1965. Accountant Touche, Ross & Co., Memphis, 1965-68; v.p., dir. United Foods, Inc., Bells, Tenn., 1968—. Mem. Am. Inst. C.P.A.'s, Tenn. Soc. C.P.A.'s. Home: 85 Pine Tree Dr Jackson TN 38301 Office: 100 Dawson Ave Bells TN 38006

ENNIS, THOMAS ALLEN, lawyer; b. N.Y.C., Aug. 21, 1920; s. Thomas Lel and Madeleine Clark (Smith) E.; m. Alfreda Learoyd Wallace, Sept. 13, 1947 (div. Dec. 1974); children: Madeleine Elizabeth, Thomas Wallace; m. Mary S. Davlin, Oct. 23, 1975. Grad., St. Mark's Sch., 1938; B.A., Yale U., 1942; LL.B., Columbia U., 1949. Bar: N.Y. 1949. Assoc. Shearman & Sterling, N.Y.C., 1949-54; counsel Combustion Engring., Inc., 1954-57, sec. counsel, 1957-60, v.p., sec., counsel, 1960-63, v.p. adminstrn., counsel, 1963-73, v.p. adminstrn., 1973—, also dir.; dir. Combustion Engring.-Superheater Ltd., Montreal, Can., Lummus Group Inc., N.J., Munich Am. Reins. Co., N.Y.C. Served to 1st lt. USAAF, 1943-46. Mem. ABA, Assn. Bar City N.Y., Chi Psi. Episcopalian. Clubs: Links, Yale; Jupiter Hills (Fla.); Island (Hobe Sound, Fla.). Home: 1077 Oenoke Ridge Rd New Canaan CT 06840 Office: 900 Long Ridge Rd Stamford CT 06902

ENNIS, THOMAS ELMER, JR., educator; b. Salisbury, N.C., Jan. 1, 1930; s. Thomas Elmer and Annie (Williams) E.; m. Loraine May Van Dam, Aug. 21, 1959. B.S. in Bus. Adminstrn, U. N.C., 1952, M.B.A., 1955; Ph.D., U. Mich., 1964. Mem. faculty Washington and Lee U., 1955—, instr., 1955-57, asst. prof. accounting, 1957-64, assoc. prof., 1964-68, prof., 1968—. Served with AUS, 1952-54. Mem. Am. Accounting Assn., Nat. Assn. Accountants, Phi Beta Kappa, Beta Gamma Sigma, Omicron Delta Epsilon. Home: Maury Heights Route 5 Box 116 Lexington VA 24450 Office: 311 Commerce Bldg Washington and Lee U Lexington VA 24450

ENNIS, THOMAS MICHAEL, community mental health adminstr.; b. Morgantown, W.Va., Mar. 7, 1931; s. Thomas Edson and Violet Ruth (Nugent) E.; m. Julia Marie Dorety, June 30, 1956; children—Thomas John, Robert Griswold (dec.). Student, W.Va. U., 1949-52; A.B., George Washington U., 1954; J.D., Georgetown U; 1960. Subrogation-arbitration examiner Govt. Employees Ins. Co., Washington, 1956-59; asst., legis. analyst to v.p. pub. affairs Air Transport Assn. Am., Washington, 1959-60; dir. ann. support program George Washington U., 1960-63; nat. dir. devel. Project HOPE, People to People Health Found., Inc., Washington, 1963-66; nat. exec. dir. Epilepsy Found. Am., Washington, 1966-74; exec. dir. Clinton, Eaton, Ingham Community Mental Health Bd., 1974—; clin. instr. dept. community medicine and internat. health Georgetown U. Sch. Medicine, 1967-74; adj. asso. prof. dept. psychiatry Coll. Medicine Mich. State U., 1975—, lectr. Univ. Ctr. for Internat. Rehab., 1977—; cons. health and med. founds., related orgns.; cons. Am. Health Found., 1967-69, Reston, Va.-Georgetown U. Health Planning Project, 1967-69. Contbr. articles on devel. disabilities, mental health and health care to profl. jours. Mem. adv. bd. Nat. Center for Law and Handicapped; advisor Nat. Reye's Syndrome Found.; mem. Pres.'s Com. on Employment Handicapped, Internat. Bur. Epilepsy, Nat. Com. for Research in Neurol. Disorders; mem. nat. adv. bd. Developmental Disabilities/Tech. Assistance System, U. N.C.; Nat. del. trustee, v.p. Nat. Capitol Area chpt., bd. dirs., exec. com. Nat. Kidney Found., 1969—, Nat. trustee, 1970-74, pres., 1972—; bd. dirs. Nat. Assn. Pvt. Residential Facilities for Mentally Retarded; bd. dirs., mem. exec. com. Epilepsy Found. Am., Epilepsy Center Mich.; nat. bd. dirs. Western Inst. on Epilepsy, 1969-72; bd. dirs., pres. Mich. Mid-South Health Systems Agy. World Rehab. Fund fellow, Norway, 1980. Mem. Nat. Rehab. Assn., Am. Pub. Health Assn., Nat. Epilepsy League (bd. dirs.), Mich. Assn. Community Mental Health Bd. Dirs. (pres.), AAAS, Phi Alpha Theta, Phi Kappa Psi. Home: 4361 Wausau Okemos MI 48864 Office: 300 Washington Sq Lansing MI 48933

ENNS, MARK KYNASTON, electrical engineer; b. Hutchinson, Kans., Oct. 13, 1931; s. Harry and Bernice (Griffith) E.; m. Patricia Shupe, Dec. 23, 1956; children: Neil, Paul, Carol. B.S. in Elec. Engring, Kans. State U., 1953, M.S., U. Pitts., 1960, Ph.D., 1967. Elec. utility engr. Westinghouse Elec. Corp., East Pittsburgh, Pa., 1956-64, research labs., Pitts., 1964-67; asst. prof. elec. engring. Carnegie-Mellon U., Pitts., 1967-69; asso. prof. U. Mich., Ann Arbor, 1969-72, prof., 1972-78; dir. Power Systems Lab., 1969-78, Harris SAI, Inc., Ann Arbor, 1978-81; pres., chmn. bd. Electrocon Internat., Inc., Ann Arbor, 1981—. Editor: spl. issue Procs. of IEEE, 1974. Served with USAF, 1953-55. Fellow IEEE; mem. Sigma Xi, Eta Kappa Nu. Patentee in field. Home: 1010 Lincoln Ave Ann Arbor MI 48104 Office: Electrocon Internat Inc 611 Church St Ann Arbor MI 48104

ENO, BRIAN (BRIAN PETER GEORGE ST. JOHN DE LA SALLE ENO), composer, musician, producer; b. Woodbridge, Suffolk, Eng., 1948. Attended, Ipswich Art Sch.; F.A., Winchester Sch. Art, 1969. Early musical career with composer, LaMonte Young, and avant-garde band, Portsmouth Sinfonia; co-founder rock group, Roxy Music, 1971-73; solo musician, 1973—; worked as producer, composer, musician with other artists including, Robert Fripp, John Cale, Phil Manzanera, Robert Wyatt, David Bowie, Talking Heads, Harold Budd, Jon Hassell, Television, Devo, Ultravox, Edikanfo; founder label, Obscure Records, 1975; (with Robert Fripp) albums include Evening Star, (with David Byrne) My Life in the Bush of Ghosts, Here Come the Warm Jets, 1973, Taking Tiger Mountain (By Strategy), 1974, Another Green World, 1975, Before & After Science, 1977, Music for Airports. Office: care Island Records 444 Madison Ave New York NY 10022 *

ENO, CHARLES FRANKLIN, soil science educator; b. Atwater, Ohio, May 21, 1920; s. Clarence and Alice (Rhoads) E.; m. Fern A. Imler, Sept. 8, 1948; children: Charles Franklin, Mark Imler. B.S., Ohio State U., 1942, M.S., 1948; Ph.D., Purdue U., 1951. Asst. prof., assoc. prof., prof. soil microbiology U. Fla., Gainesville, 1950-65, prof., chmn. soil sci. dept., 1965-82, asst. dir. internat. programs, 1982—. Served to lt. col. AUS, 1942-46, 51-52. Decorated Bronze Star. Fellow Am. Soc. Agronomy (pres. 1983), Soil Sci. Soc. Am. (pres. 1975); mem. Council for Agrl. Sci. and Tech., Fla. Hort. Soc., Soil and Crop Sci. Soc. Fla. (pres. 1965), Sigma Xi, Gamma Sigma Delta. Republican. Methodist. Club: Gainesville Golf and Country. Home: 2607 NW 18th Way Gainesville FL 32605

ENOCH, JAY MARTIN, visual scientist, educator; b. N.Y.C., Apr. 20, 1929; s. Jerome Dee and Stella Sarah (Nathan) E.; m. Rebekah Ann Feiss, June 24, 1951; children—Harold Owen, Barbara Diane, Ann Allison. B.S. in Optics and Optometry, Columbia U., 1950; postgrad., Inst. Optics U. Rochester, 1953; Ph.D. in Physiol. Optics, Ohio State U., 1956. Asst. prof. physiol. optics Ohio State U., Columbus, 1956-58, assoc. supr. of, 1957-58; fellow Nat. Phys. Lab., Teddington, Eng., 1959-60; research instr. dept. ophthalmology Washington U. Sch. Medicine, St. Louis, 1958-59, research asst. prof., 1959-64, research asso. prof., 1965-70, research prof., 1970-74; fellow Barnes Hosp., St. Louis, 1960-64, cons. ophthalmology, 1964-74; research prof. dept. psychology Washington U., St. Louis, 1970-74; grad. research prof. ophthalmology and psychology U. Fla. Coll. Medicine, Gainesville, 1974-80, grad. research prof. physics, 1979-80; dir. Center for Sensory Studies, 1976-80; dean Sch. Optometry, prof. physiol. optics and optometry U. Calif., Berkeley, 1980—, prof. physiol. optics in ophthalmology, San Francisco, 1980—; chmn. subcom. contact lens Standards Am. Nat. Standards Inst., 1970-77; mem. nat. advisory eye council Nat. Eye Inst., NIH, 1975-77, 80—; exec. com., com. on vision NAS-NRC, 1973-76; mem. U.S. Nat. Com. Internat. Commn. Optics, 1976-79. Author numerous chpts. and articles on visual sci., receptor optics, perimetry, contact lenses and infant vision to sci. jours.; contbr. chpts. in field to med. books; hon. editorial bd.: Vision Research, 1974-80; editorial bd.: Internat. Ophthalmology, 1977—; asso. editor: Investigative Ophthalmology, 1965-75, Sight-Saving Rev, 1974—, Sensory Processes, 1974—; editorial bd. optical scis.: Springer-Verlag, Heidelberg, 1978—. Mem. nat. sci. advisory bd. Retinitis Pigmentosa Found., 1977—; U.S. rep. Internat. Perimetric Soc., 1974—; also exec. com., chmn. Research Group Standards.; Bd. dirs. Friends of Eye Research, 1977—; trustee Illuminating Engring. Research Inst., 1977-81. Served to 2d lt. U.S. Army, 1951-52. Recipient Career Devel. award NIH, 1963-73. Fellow AAAS, Am. Acad. Optometry (Glenn A. Fry award 1972, Charles F. Prentice medal award 1974), Optical Soc. Am. (chmn. vision tech. sect. 1974-76), Am. Acad. Ophthalmology Otolaryngology (asso.); mem. Assn. for Research in Vision and Ophthalmology (trustee 1967-73, pres. 1972-73, Francis I. Proctor medal 1977), Internat. Strabismological Assn., Internat. Soc. for Clin. Electro-retinography, Biophys. Soc., Psychonomic Soc., Am. Soc. for Photobiology, AAUP, Am. Psychol. Assn. (sect. 3), Contact Lens Soc. of U.K., Sigma Xi. Home: 54 Shuey Dr Moraga CA 94556 Office: Sch Optometry U Calif Berkeley CA 94720

ENOCHS, RODNEY LEE, insurance company executive; b. Midway, Ohio, Feb. 8, 1926; s. Edgar Ernest and Mary (Halliday) E.; m. Elizabeth M. Gunderson, Feb. 11, 1961; children: Karen Elizabeth, Ross Alexander. B.S. in Bus, Miami U., Oxford, Ohio, 1949; J.D., Fordham U., 1958. Bar: N.Y. bar 1959. With Equitable Life Assurance Soc. U.S., 1950—, sec., 1966-74, v.p., sec., 1974—; sec. Equitable Life Holding Corp., 1971-78, 80-83, Equitable Variable Life Ins. Co., 1972-78. Served with USAAF, World War II. Mem. Am. Soc. Corporate Secs., Am. Bar Assn., Pi Kappa Alpha, Delta Sigma Pi. Club: Ardsley Country. Home: 41 Carla Ln Irvington-on-Hudson NY 10533 Office: 1285 Ave of Americas New York NY 10019

ENOS, CHRIS, photographer; b. Burbank, Calif., Aug. 21, 1944; d. George Von and Wanda Ingred (Thorsen) Schlatter. A.A., Foothill Coll., Los Altos, Calif., 1965; B.A., San Francisco State U., 1969; M.F.A., San Francisco Art Inst., 1971. Instr. art Crystal Springs Sch., Hillsborough, Calif., 1968-69, Hamlin Sch., San Francisco, 1969-71; co-owner, instr. photography Let A Dark Photo Lab., San Rafael, Calif., 1971-73; instr. photography U. Calif., San Francisco, San Francisco Acad. Art, 1972-73, Windham Coll., Putney, Vt., 1974, Harvard U., summer 1980; asst. prof. photography Hampshire (Mass.) Coll., 1974-75, Boston U., summer 1975; instr., gallery dir. New Eng. Sch. Photography, 1977-78; artist in residence Light Work Syracuse, N.Y., 1978, U. Colo., Boulder, 1980, Internat. Center for Photography, N.Y.C., 1980; lectr. Md. Art Inst., Balt., 1979, Internat. Center Photography, N.Y.C., 1979, Colo. Mountain Coll., Breckinridge, 1979, Brown U./R.I. Sch. Design, Providence, 1979, Inst. Contemporary Art, Boston, 1983, others.; vis. artist Smith Coll., Northampton, Mass., 1982-83; vis. lectr. UCLA, 1983-84; artist in residence Light Work Internat. Center for Photography, N.Y.C., 1980. One-woman exhbns. include, Photography and Film Center West, Berkeley, Calif., 1972, M.I.T., 1974, Portland (Maine) Sch. Art, Hampshire Coll., Amherst, Mass., Gallery 115, Santa Cruz, Calif., 1975, Carl Siembab Gallery, Boston, Bibliothèque Nationale, Paris, Pine Manor Coll., Chestnut Hill, Mass., 1976, U. Calif., San Francisco, U. Rochester, N.Y., 1977; one-woman exhbns. include, Camerawork Gallery, San Francisco; One-woman exhbns. include, Wingspread Gallery, Northeast Harbor, Maine, 1978, U. Colo., Boulder, 1982, Thomas Segal Gallery, Boston; group exhbns. include, Boston Visual Artists Union Gallery, 1975, Fashion Inst., N.Y.C., Mus. Fine Arts, Boston, 1976, Womanspace Gallery, Boulder, Colo., 1977, Portland Mus. Art, M.I.T., 1973, 80, San Francisco Art Inst., Fogg Mus., 1974, 80, Photo Gallery, U. R.I., 1978, Anyart Gallery, Providence, Venezia 79, Venice, Italy, Santa Barbara Art Mus., 1979, Light Gallery, N.Y.C., 1980, Fogg Mus., Clarence Kennedy Gallery, Cambridge; represented in permanent collections, Wellesley Coll., Mus. Fine Arts Boston, Fogg Mus. Art, Portland Mus. Art, George Eastman House, Rochester, N.Y., Seagram Collection, N.Y., Polaroid Corp., Amsterdam, Shaklee Corp., Calif., San Francisco Mus. Art, Bibliothèque Nationale, Paris; Photographs pub. in various mags. Mass. Arts and Humanities Found. fellow, 1975; Cutler de long West Found. grantee, 1977; Artists Found. Inc. fellow, 1975, 80; Nat. Endowment for Arts grantee, 1980; project completion grant Artists' Found., Boston, 1982; other grants. Mem. Soc. Photog. Edn. (dir.), Visual Studies Workshop, Boston Inst. Contemporary Art. Office: UCLA Art Dept 405 Hilgard Ave Los Angeles CA 90024

ENOUEN, WILLIAM ALBERT, paper corporation executive; b. Columbus, Ohio, Nov. 7, 1928; s. John J. and Bertha (Thiry) E.; m. Joan Claire Batsche, June 20, 1953; children: William A., Robert, Kathryn, James, Patricia. B.S., U. Dayton, 1952; student advanced mgmt. program, Harvard, 1975. Various accounting positions Touche, Ross & Co., Dayton, Ohio, 1952-59; asst. to controller, asst. to group v.p. and fin. cons. affiliated cos. Mead Corp., Dayton, 1959-68, controller, 1969-72, v.p., controller, 1972-81, v.p. fin. resources and control, 1981—; v.p. Brunswick Pulp & Paper Co., 1968-69; dir. Northwood Forest Industries, Ltd., Brunswick Pulp & Paper Co., Mead Re Inc., Westbury Ins. Co., B.C. Forest Products Ltd., Morris Bean. Served with AUS, 1946-47. Mem. Ohio Soc. C.P.A.s (v.p. Dayton chpt. 1959-60). Home: 4617 Ackerman Blvd Dayton OH 45429 Office: Mead World Hdqrs Courthouse Plaza NE Dayton OH 45463

ENQUIST, IRVING FRIDTJOF, surgeon; b. Superior, Wis., June 25, 1920; s. Fridtjof Gunnar and Anna Margaret (Peterson) E.; m. Bertha Mildred Miller, June 2, 1944; children—Kristine Enquist Fach, Erik, Rolf. B.S., U. Minn., 1942, M.D., 1944; M.S. in Surgery, 1952. Diplomate: Am. Bd. Surgery. Intern St. Mary's Hosp., Mpls., 1944; resident in surgery Univ. Hosp., Mpls., 1947-52; asst. prof. surgery State U. N.Y., Bklyn., 1952-55, asso. prof., 1955-60, prof., 1960—; dir. surgery Methodist Hosp., Bklyn., 1965—; vis. surgeon Kings Hosp., Bklyn., 1956—; cons. VA Hosp., Bklyn., 1958—. Contbr. articles to profl. jours. Served to capt., M.C. U.S. Army, 1944-46. Fellow A.C.S., Am. Surg. Assn.; mem. Internat. Surg. Soc., Soc. Surg. Alimentary Tract, Sigma Xi, Alpha Omega Alpha. Congregationalist. Home: 168 Dogwood Ln Manhasset NY 11030 Office: 506 6th St Brooklyn NY 11215

ENRIGHT, WILLIAM BENNER, judge; b. N.Y.C., July 12, 1925; s. Arthur Joseph and Anna Beatrice (Plante) E.; m. Bette Lou Card, Apr. 13, 1951; children—Kevin A., Kimberly A., Kerry K. A.B., Dartmouth, 1947; LL.B., Loyola U. at Los Angeles, 1950. Bar: Calif. bar 1951, diplomate: Am. Bd. Trial Advs. Dep. dist. atty., San Diego County, 1951-54; partner Enright, Levitt, Knutson & Tobin, San Diego, 1954-72; judge U.S. Dist. Ct. So. Dist. Calif., San Diego, 1972—; Mem. adv. bd. Joint Legis. Com. for Revision Penal Code, 1970-72, Calif. Bd. Legal Specialization, 1970-72; mem. Jud. Council, 1972; Bd. dirs. Defenders, 1965-72, pres., 1972. Served as ensign USNR, 1943-46. Recipient Honor award San Diego County Bar, 1970; Extraordinary Service to Legal Professions award Mcpl. Ct. San Diego Jud. Dist., 1971. Fellow Am. Coll. Trial Lawyers, Am. Bar Found.; mem. ABA, San Diego County Bar Assn. (dir. 1963-65, pres. 1965), State Bar Calif. (gov. 1967-70, v.p. 1970, exec. com. law in a free soc. 1970—), Dartmouth Club San Diego, Am. Judicature Soc., Alpha Sigma Nu, Phi Delta Phi. Club: Rotarian. Office: Courtroom 3 US Courthouse 940 Front St San Diego CA 92189 *

ENRIGHT, WILLIAM FAIRLEIGH, JR., multi-bank holding company executive; b. St. Joseph, Mo., Feb. 21, 1920; s. William Fairleigh E. and Lucy Graham (Howell) Lucas; m. Patricia Anne Quinn, Nov. 12, 1947; children: Katherine A., Mary Jane, Sheila F., William Fairleigh III, Patricia I., Laura Q. B.S. in Econs., U. Pa., 1941; LL.D. (hon.), Mo. Western State Coll., St. Joseph, 1977. Cert. comm. lender Am. Bankers Assn., 1975. Vice pres. Empire Trust Co., St. Joseph, 1946-60; sr. v.p. Tootle-Enright Nat. Bank, St. Joseph, 1960-63; exec. v.p. to chmn. bd. Am. Nat. Bank, St. Joseph, 1963-78, dir., 1963—; chmn. Ameribanc, Inc., St. Joseph, 1978—; sec. Mo. state Banking Bd., Jefferson City, 1975-83; dir. Am. Bank, Plattsburg, Mo. Pres. St. Joseph Ecumenical Help Care, Inc., 1982—; bd. dirs. St. Joseph Area C. of C., 1978-81; pres. bd. regents Mo. Western State Coll., 1965-76. Served to maj. USAAF, 1940-46; served with USAF, 1951-52; ETO. Mem. Ind. Bankers Assn. (bd. dirs. Mo. 1966-72). Democrat. Roman Catholic. Clubs: St. Joseph Country (pres.) (1967-68); Benton (St. Joseph)). Lodges: Elks; K.C. Home: 630 N 8th St Saint Joseph MO 64501 Office: Ameribanc Inc 5th and Francis Sts Saint Joseph MO 64502

ENRIQUEZ SAVIGNAC, ANTONIO, public administrator; b. Mexico City, Aug. 17, 1931; s. Manuel and Cecilia (Savignac) Enriquez; m. Margarita Cabot, Sept. 28, 1957; children: Juan, Antonio. B.A., U. Ottawa-Ont., 1955; M.B.A., Harvard U., 1957. Mng. dir., chief exec. officer Fonatur, Mexico City, 1969-76; undersec. of tourism Tourism Secretariat, Mexico City, 1976-77; dir. indsl. promotion Banco Nacional de Mexico, Mexico City, 1977-81; dir. fin. Petroleos Mexicanos, Mexico City, 1981-82; undersec. Treasury Secretariat, Mexico City, 1982; sec. tourism Tourism Secretariat, Mexico City, 1982—; pres. Nat. Council Tourism, Mexico City, 1983—; lectr. in field. Recipient Gentlemen's Honor League award French Govt., 1977. Office: Secretaria de Turismo Presidente Masaryk 172 Mexico City DF Mexico 11587

ENROTH-CUGELL, CHRISTINA, neurophysiologist, educator; b. Helsingfors, Finland, Aug. 27, 1919; came to U.S., 1956, naturalized, 1962; d. Emil and Maja (Syren) Enroth; m. David W. Cugell, Sept. 5, 1955. M.D., Karolinska Inst., 1948, Ph.D., 1952. Resident Karolinska Sjukhuset, 1949-52; intern Passavant Meml. Hosp., 1956-57; with Northwestern U., Evanston, Ill., 1959—, prof. dept. neurobiology and physiology dept. engring. scis., 1974—; mem. vision research program com. Nat. Eye Inst., 1974-78, mem. nat. adv. eye council, 1980-84. Contbr. articles to profl. jours. Recipient Ludwig von Sallman award Internat. Assn. Research in Vision and Ophthalmology, 1982. Mem. Am. Assn. Research in Vision and Ophthalmology (co-recipient Friedenwald award 1983), Soc. Neuroscis., Am. Physiol. Soc. (asso.); mem. Am. Acad. Arts and Scis.; Mem. Physiol. Soc. (U.K.). Office: 2145 Sheridan Rd Evanston IL 60201

ENSIGN, CHESTER OSCAR, JR., geologist, exec.; b. Statesville, N.C., Oct. 23, 1924; s. Chester Oscar and Ruth (Dillon) E.; m. Elizabeth Dunlop, Mar. 18, 1950; children—Stephen Willard, Chester Oscar. B.S. in Bus. Adminstrn, U. N.C., 1948, 1950, M.S. in Econ. Geology, 1951; D.Bus. Adminstrn. (hon.), Colo. State Coll., D.Eng., Mich. Technol. U. Instr. geology U. N.C., 1949-51; supr. exploration, mines planning engr. Davison Chem. Corp., Bartow, Fla., 1951-55; sr. exploration geologist Am. Metal Climax, Inc., 1955-61; chief geologist Copper Range Co., N.Y.C., 1961-68, v.p. exploration, 1968-69, exec. v.p., chief operating officer, 1969-70, pres., chief exec. officer, 1970-77; v.p., group exec. for base metals AMAX, Inc., Greenwich, Conn., 1977-81, exec. v.p., 1981—. Contbr. articles to profl. jours. Served with USNR, 1943-46. Mem. Am. Inst. Mining, Metall. and Petroleum Engrs., Geol. Soc. Am., Soc. Econ. Geologists, Am. Inst. Profl. Geologists, Mining and Metall. Soc., Canadian Inst. Mining and Metallurgy, Soc. Exploration Geophysicists. Methodist. Clubs: Rotarian., Saugatuck Harbor Yacht (Westport); Westchester Country (Rye N.Y.). Home: 284 Mulberry Hill Rd Fairfield CT 06430 Office: Amax Center Greenwich CT 06830

ENSIGN, RICHARD PAPWORTH, Business executive; b. Salt Lake City, Jan. 20, 1919; s. Louis Osborne and Florence May (Papworth) E.; m. Margaret Anne Hinckley, Sept. 5, 1942; children: Judith Ensign

Lantz, Mary Jane Ensign Hofmeister, Richard L., James R., Margaret Ensign Aronson. B.S., U. Utah, 1941. With Western Air Lines, 1941-70, v.p. in-flight service, 1963-70, v.p. passenger service, 1970, Pan Am. World Airways, 1971, sr. v.p. field mgmt., 1973-74, sr. v.p. mktg., 1974; exec. v.p. Western Airlines, 1980-82; pres. R.P. Ensign & Assocs., 1982—; Mem. U. Utah Nat. Adv. Council; dir. Pacific Area Travel Assos. Nat. fund raising chmn. U. Utah, 1982-83, 83-84. Recipient Disting. Service award Fla. Internat. U., 1973; named Disting. Alumnus U. Utah, 1976. Mem. Am. Soc. Travel Agts., U.S.-Mex. C. of C., Nat. Aeros. Assn. Republican. Mormon. Club: Lochnvar. Patentee in field. Home: 3848 Malibu Country Dr Malibu CA 90265 Office: P.O. Box Malibu CA 90265

ENSIGN, WILLIAM JAMES, political science educator; b. Cleve., June 21, 1924; s. Harmon Oliver and Isabelle T. (McKay) E.; m. Joan Marie Kennedy, Nov. 18, 1950; children: Maria Therese, Kimberly Anne, Christopher William, Joel Francis, Madonna Maureen, Thomas Shannon. Student, Eastern Ill. State Coll., 1946-48; A.B., U. Notre Dame, 1950, A.M., 1951. Purchasing agt. Brodhead-Garrett Co., Cleve., 1941-42; caseworker, juvenile parole officer, South Bend, Ind., 1950-51; probation officer Lucas County, Ohio, 1951-60; exec. sec. Ohio Pardon and Parole Commn., 1960-63; welfare dir. Lucas County, 1963-67; mayor of Toledo, 1967-71; dir. Ohio Youth Commn., 1971-74, Ohio State Office Vol. Coordination, 1974-75; prof. polit. sci., dir. criminal justice program Ohio Dominican Coll., Columbus, 1975—; adj. prof. Xavier U., Cin., 1974—; part time instr. sociology Mary Manse Coll., 1953-60, 63-67; dir. Criminal Justice Assocs. Served with USMCR, 1942-46; PTO. Mem. U.S. Conf. Mayors, Nat. Leagues Cities, Am. Legion, DAV, Old Newsboys Goodfellow Assn., Sigma Tau Gamma. Democrat. Roman Catholic. Address: 1900 Northam Rd Columbus OH 43221

ENSIGN, WILLIAM LLOYD, architect; b. Trinidad, W.I., Dec. 14, 1928; s. Lloyd Gordon and Evelyn Barbara (Hobson) E.; m. June G. Pollinger, July 10, 1954; children: David Gordon, Evan Alexander. B.S.A.E., B.S.C.E., U. Colo., 1950; M. Arch., Columbia U., 1952. Mem. firm McLeod & Ferrara (Architects), Washington, 1955-65; partner McLeod Ferrara & Ensign, 1965-72; pres. McLeod Farrara Ensign, 1972-80; asst. architect of the Capitol, Washington, 1980—. Author: others. Educational Facilities. Served with C.E. USNR, 1952-55. Fellow AIA (dir., past pres. Washington chpt., chmn. various coms.); mem. Nat. Trust Historic Preservation, Council Ednl. Facility Planners Internat., Washington Bldg. Congress, Nat. Capitol Hist. Soc., Soc. Coll. and Univ. Planning. Episcopalian. Office: US Capitol Washington DC 20515

ENSLEN, RICHARD ALAN, judge; b. Kalamazoo, May 28, 1931; s. Ehrman Thrasher and Pauline Mabel (Dragoo) E.; m. Joan Arelne Dille, Sept. 8, 1951; children—David, Susan, Sandra, Thomas, Janet, Joseph. Student, Kalamazoo Coll., 1949-51, Western Mich. U., 1955; LL.B., Wayne State U., 1958. Bar: Mich. bar 1958, Western Dist. Mich 1960, Ct. Appeals for 6th Circuit 1971, 4th Circuit 1975, U.S. Supreme Ct 1975. Mem. firm Stratton, Wise, Early & Starbuck, Kalamazoo, 1958-60, Bauckham & Enslen, 1960-64, Howard & Howard, 1970-76, Enslen & Schma, 1977-79; dir. Peace Corps., Costa Rica, 1965-67; judge Mich. Dist. Ct., 1968-70; U.S. dist. judge, Kalamazoo, 1979—; mem. faculty Western Mich. U., 1961-62, Nazareth Coll., 1974-75; adj. prof. polit. sci. Western Mich. U., 1982—. Bd. dirs. Big Bros., St. Agnes Foundling Home, 1958-65; chmn. Negro Coll. Fund, Kalamazoo Alcoholism and Addiction Council, 1970-75. Served with USAF, 1951-54. Recipient Disting. Alumni award Wayne State Law Sch., 1980, Western Mich. U., 1982; Jewel Corp. scholar, 1956-57; Lampson McElhorne scholar, 1957. Mem. ABA, Am. Judicature Soc. (bd. dirs. 1983—), Mich. Bar Assn., Kalamazoo County Bar Assn. Office: 410 W Michigan Ave Kalamazoo MI 49005

ENSLIN, THEODORE VERNON, poet; b. Chester, Pa., Mar. 25, 1925; s. Morton Scott and Ruth May (Tuttle); m. Mildred Marie Stout, Aug. 1, 1945 (div.); children—Deirdre, Jonathan Morton; m. Alison Jane Jose, Sept. 14. 1969; 1 son, Jacob Hezekiah. Studied mus. composition with Nadia Boulanger, Cambridge, Mass., 1943-44. Author: New Sharon's Prospect, 1965, To Come To Have Become, 1966, Forms (5 vols.), 1970-74, The Country of Our Consciousness, 1971, The Median Flow, 1975, Synthesis, 1975, Carmina, 1976, Ranger, 2 vols., 1978-80, Readings and seminars various colls. and univs. Recipient Niemann award for weekly newspaper column The Cape Codder, 1955, Hart Crane Meml. award, 1969. Mem. Am. Found. for Homoeopathy. Address: RFD Box 289 Kansas Rd Milbridge ME 04658

ENSLOW, RIDLEY MADISON, JR., book publisher; b. Orange, N.J., Mar. 13, 1926; s. Ridley Madison and Virginia E.; m. Florence M. Fraser, Oct. 24, 1953; children—Ridley Madison III, Gregory F., Brian D. A.B., Colgate U., 1947. With Macmillan Co., 1949-52, McGraw Hill Book Co., 1952-54; v.p. Macrae Smith Co., Phila., 1954-56, Lothrop Lee & Shepard Co., N.Y.C., 1956-58; exec. v.p., sec. William Morrow & Co., N.Y.C., 1958-76; also dir.; pres. Enslow Publishers, Hillside, N.J., 1976—. Served with USMCR, 1944-46. Club: Racquets (Short Hills). Home: 60 Crescent Pl PO Box 301 Short Hills NJ 07078 Office: Bloy St and Ramsey Ave PO Box 777 Hillside NJ 07205

ENSMINGER, LUTHER GLENN, chemist; b. Mt. Perry, Ohio, Oct. 17, 1919; s. Charles Henry and Mary Elfa (Koehler) E.; m. Emma Jean Couch, May 12, 1951; children—Luther, Douglas, Phillip, Deborah. B.Sc., Ohio State U., 1942, 1948. Chemist FDA, Cin., 1948-56, chemist, lab. supr., Los Angeles, 1956-59, sci. adminstr., Washington, 1959-79; sci. cons., Arlington, Va., 1979—. Contbr. articles to profl. jours. Sec. Lee-Ballston Citizens Assn., 1965-75. Served with U.S. Army, 1942-45. Fellow Assn. Ofcl. Analytical Chemists (exec. sec. 1967-79, mem. exec. com. 1960-79), Beta Gamma Sigma. Republican. Presbyterian. Club: Capitol Dance. Address: 2310 N 10th St 303 Arlington VA 22201

ENSMINGER, MARION EUGENE, animal science educator, author; b. Stover, Mo., May 28, 1908; s. Jacob and Ella (Belt) E.; m. Audrey Helen Watts, June 11, 1941; children: John Jacob, Janet Aileen (dec.). B.S., U. Mo., 1931, M.S., 1932; Ph.D., U. Minn., 1941. Field agt. U. Mo., summers 1929-30; instr. Mo. State U., Marysville, summers 1931-32; asst. to supt. U.S. Soil Erosion Sta., Bethany, Mo., 1933; soil erosion specialist U.S. Dept. Interior, U.S. Dept. Agr., Ill., 1934; mgr. Dixon Springs (Ill.) project U.S. Dept. Agr., 1934-37; asst. prof. U. Mass., 1937-40; teaching asst. U. Minn., 1940-41; prof., chmn. dept. animal sci. Wash. State U., 1941-62; owner, pres. Consultants-Agriservices, Clovis, Calif., 1962—; Distinguished prof. U. Wis.-River Falls, 1963—; collaborator U.S. Dept. Agr., 1965—; adj. prof. Calif. State U., Fresno, 1973—, U. Ariz., Tucson, 1977; cons. nucleonics dept. Gen. Electric Co., AEC, 1947-66; Mem. nat. bd. field advisers SBA, 1959-60. Author: books including Animal Science, Beef Cattle Science, Sheep and Goat Science, Sevine Science, Dairy Cattle Science, The Complete Encyclopedia of Horses, Feeds and Nutrition, Food and Animals—A Global Perspective, The Complete Book of Dogs; (with others) China-The Impossible Dream, Foods and Nutriton Ency.; syndicated columnist: The Stockman's Guide, 1956—, Horses, Horses, Horses, 1962—, works transl. into fgn. langs., also books on record for blind. Mem. adv. bd. People-to-People Found.; pres. Agriservices Found., Pegus Co., Inc. Dept. agrl. scis. Hall of Fame Wash. State U., 1958; hon. mem. Indian Council for Farmers, New Delhi.; Named Hon. State Farmer Future Farmers Am.; recipient Wisdom Honor award, 1969, Faculty-Alumni Gold medal, citation of merit U. Mo., 1975. Fellow AAAS, Am. Soc. Animal Sci. (sec.-treas., v.p., pres. Western sect., Disting. Tchr. award, mem., plaque), Am. Genetic Assn., Soil Conservation Soc. Am., Am. Soc. Range Mgmt., Am. Dairy Sci. Assn., Am. Soc. Agrl. Consultants (1st pres.), Agrl. Inst. Can., CATEC France (hon. v.p.), Assn. Spanish Purebred Horse Breeders Guatemala (hon.), Sigma Xi, Alpha Zeta, Lambda Gamma Delta. Clubs: Boots and Spurs (hon. life) (Calif. State U. San Luis Obispo) 1973); Dairy (Calif. State U. Fresno) (hon. 1973). Address: 648 W Sierra Ave Clovis CA 93612

ENTEMAN, WILLARD FINLEY, college provost; b. Glen Ridge, N.J., Oct. 21, 1936; s. Verling Clair and Elizabeth Vance Rutherford (Dailey) E.; m. Kathleen Ffolliott, June 18, 1960; children: Sally Holyoke, David Finley. B.A., Williams Coll., 1959, LL.D. (hon.), 1978; M.B.A., Harvard U., 1961; M.A., Boston U., 1962, Ph.D., 1965; LL.D. (hon.), Colby Coll., 1980. Instr. in philosophy Wheaton Coll., 1963-65, asst. prof., 1965-69, assoc. prof., 1969-70; assoc. prof., chmn. dept. philosophy Union Coll., Schenectady, 1970-72, provost and assoc. prof., 1972-78; pres., prof. Bowdoin Coll., 1978-81; provost, v.p. acad. affairs R.I. Coll., 1982—; mem. New Eng. Bd. Higher Edn., 1978—; 2d v.p., trustee Colby-Bates-Bowdoin Ednl. Telecasting Corp., 1978—. Contbr. articles to profl. publs.; editor: The Problem of Free Will, 1967. Trustee Regional Meml. Hosp., Brunswick, Maine, 1978—, Hotchkiss Sch., 1980—; mem. long range planning com. Portland (Maine) Sch. Art, 1979—. Named 1 of 100 Top Young Leaders in Higher Edn. Change Mag., 1978. Mem. Nat. Assn. Ind. Colls. and Univs. (dir.), Brunswick C. of C. (trustee 1978—). Office: RI Coll 600 Mount Pleasant Ave Providence RI 02908

ENTHOVEN, ALAIN CHARLES, economist, educator; b. Seattle, Sept. 10, 1930; s. Richard Frederick and Jacqueline (Camerlynck) E.; m. Rosemary Fenech, July 28, 1956; children: Eleanor, Richard, Andrew, Martha, Nicholas, Daniel. B.A. in Econs, Stanford U., 1952; B.Phil. (Rhodes scholar), Oxford (Eng.) U., 1954; Ph.D. in Econs, MIT, 1956. Instr. econs. MIT, Cambridge, 1955-56; economist The RAND Corp., Santa Monica, Calif., 1956-60; ops. research analyst Office of Dir. Def. Research and Engring., Dept. Def., Washington, 1960, dep. comptroller, dep. asst. sec., 1961-65, asst. sec. for systems analysis, 1965-69; v.p. for econ. planning Litton Industries, Beverly Hills, Calif., 1969-71; pres. Litton Med. Products, Beverly Hills, 1971-73; Marriner S. Eccles prof. pub. and pvt. mgmt. Stanford (Calif.) U. Grad. Sch. Bus., 1973—; prof. health care econs. dept. family, community and preventive medicine Stanford U. Sch. Medicine, 1973—; cons. The Brookings Instn., 1956-60; vis. asso. prof. econs. U. Wash., 1958; mem. Stanford Computer Sci. Adv. Com., 1968-73; cons. The RAND Corp., 1969—; mem. vis. com. in econs. Mass. Inst. Tech., 1971-78; mem. vis. com. on environ. quality lab. Calif. Inst. Tech., 1972-77; mem. council Inst. Medicine, Nat. Acad. Scis., 1975-77; mem. vis. com. Harvard U. Sch. Pub. Health, 1974-80; cons. Kaiser Found. Health Plan, Inc., 1973—. Contbr. numerous articles on def. spending and on econs. and pub. policy in health care to profl. jours.; author: (with K. Wayne Smith) How Much is Enough? Shaping the Defense Program 1961-69, 1971, Health Plan: The Only Practical Solution to the Soaring Cost of Medical Care, 1980; editor: (with A. Myrick Freeman III) Pollution, Resources and the Environment, 1973. Bd. dirs. Georgetown U., Washington, 1968-73, Inter Study, Excelsior, Minn., 1984—; bd. regents St. John's Hosp., Santa Monica, 1971-73. Recipient Pres.'s award for Distinguished Fed. Civilian Service, 1963; Dept. Def. medal for Distinguished Pub. Service, 1969. Mem. Am. Econ. Assn., Council on Fgn. Relations, Am. Assn. Rhodes Scholars, Phi Beta Kappa. Home: 1 McCormick Ln Atherton CA 94025 Office: Grad Sch Business Stanford Univ Stanford CA 94305

ENTMACHER, PAUL SIDNEY, physician, medical services administrator; b. N.Y.C., Oct. 15, 1924; s. Charles and Fannie (Bleecker) E.; m. Viola Feldman, June 9, 1946; 1 dau., Susan DeWitt Entmacher. B.S. (war cert.), Harvard, 1945; M.D., N.Y. Med. Coll., 1947. Diplomate: Am. Bd. Internal Medicine, Bd. Life Ins. Medicine. Intern Jewish Hosp., Bklyn., 1947-48; resident Montefiore Hosp., Bronx, N.Y., 1949-50, Cushing VA Hosp., Framingham, Mass., 1950; practice medicine specializing in internal medicine, Great Neck, N.Y., 1953-55; asst. med. dir. Met. Life Ins. Co., N.Y.C., 1958-62, asso. med. dir., 1963-64, med. dir., 1965-73, v.p., chief med. dir., 1974—; cons. medicine North Shore U. Hosp., Manhassett, N.Y., 1966—; mem. Internat. Com. for Life Ins. Medicine, 1976—, Nat. Diabetes Data Group, Nat. Inst. Arthritis, Diabetes and Kidney Diseases, 1977—. Contbr. articles on diabetes and ins. to profl. publs. Mem. med. adv. com. President's Com. for Employment of Handicapped, 1970-80, chmn., 1981—; bd. dirs. Am. Blood Commn., 1976-77, Nat. Center for Health Edn., 1975—; vice chmn. Nat. Center for Health Edn., 1978-80; vice chmn. bd. dirs. Med. Care Group of St. Louis, 1979-81, chmn., 1981—; bd. dirs. Nat. Health Council, 1978-81; adv. council environ. health Johns Hopkins U., 1981—. Served with U.S. Army, 1943-46, 51-53. Fellow A.C.P., Am. Coll. Preventive Medicine, N.Y. Acad. Medicine (mem. com. on medicine in soc. 1975—), Council of Epidemiology of Am. Heart Assn.; mem. Am. Public Health Assn., Am. Soc. Internal Medicine, Health Ins. Assn. Am. (mem. med. relations com. 1974—), N.Y. Diabetes Assn. (mem. com. on employment and ins. 1963-64, chmn. 1966-67, pres. 1972-73, bd. dirs. 1967—), Assn. of Life Ins. Med. Dirs. Am. (exec. council 1972—, editor of transactions 1973-77, pres. 1980), Am. Diabetes Assn. (com. on employment and ins. 1961-65, chmn. 1970-75, bd. dirs. 1980-83), AMA, Am. Heart Assn., N.Y. Heart Assn., N.Y. C. of C. and Industry (chmn. com. public health and welfare 1974-80), N.Y. Acad. Scis. Club: Harvard of N.Y. Home: 84 Park View Dr Searingtown NY 11507 Office: 1 Madison Ave Metropolitan Life Insurance Co New York NY 10010

ENTORF, RICHARD CARL, cement company executive; b. Gettysburg, S.D., Feb. 11, 1929; s. Carl Luke and Violet (Carr) E.; m. Dorothy Ann Alexander, Nov. 23, 1951; children: Mark, Kimberly. B.S., U. Calif. at Berkeley, 1952. Methods engr. Boeing Aircraft Corp., 1952; successively prodn. mgr., dir. mfg., v.p. ops., v.p., gen. mgr., pres. Riverside Cement Co. div. Amcord, Inc., Los Angeles, 1957-75; successively v.p., gen. mgr. Fla. div., sr. v.p. Gen. Portland Inc., Dallas, 1975-81; sr. v.p. Fla. Crushed Stone Co., Leesburg, Fla., 1982—. Served with USAF, 1953-57. Home: 1648 Loves Point Drive Leesburg FL 32748 Office: PO Box 300 Leesburg FL 32748

ENTREMONT, PHILIPPE, conductor, pianist; b. Rheims, France, June 7, 1934; s. Jean and Renée (Monchamps) E.; m. Andree Ragot, Dec. 21, 1955; children: Félicia, Alexandre. Student, Conservatoire National Superieur de Musique, Paris, Jean Doyen. Profl. debut at 17, in Barcelona, Spain, Am. debut at 19, at Nat. Gallery, Washington, 1953, performs throughout world; pianist-condr. debut at, Mostly Mozart Festival, Lincoln Center, N.Y.C., 1971; rec. artist, Epic, Concert Hall and Columbia records; music guest condr., Royal Philharmonic, Orch. Nat. de France, Montreal Symphony, San Francisco Symphony, Vienna Chamber Orch., numerous others; music dir., prin. condr., New Orleans Philharmonic Symphony Orch., 1981—. Decorated Chevalier de l'Ordre National du Merite.; A finalist Queen Elizabeth of Belgium Internat. Concours, 1952; Grand Prix Marguerite Long-Jacques Thibaud Competition, 1953; Harriet Cohen Piano medal, 1953; 1st prize Jeunesses Musicales; Grand Prix du Disque, 1967, 68, 69, 70; Edison award, 1968; Nominee Grammy award, 1972. Former mem. Academie Internationale de Musique Maurice Ravel (pres. 1975-80). Office: New Orleans Philharm Symphony Maritime Bldg Suite 903 203 Carondelet St New Orleans LA 70130 *

ENTWISLE, DORIS ROBERTS, educator; b. Wilbraham, Mass., Sept. 28, 1924; d. Charles Edwin and Helen (MacMenigall) Roberts; m. George Entwisle, Aug. 31, 1946; children: Barbara, Beverly, George H. B.S., U. Mass., 1945; M.S., Brown U., 1946; Ph.D., Johns Hopkins U., 1960. Postdoctoral fellow Social Sci. Research Council Johns Hopkins U., Balt., 1960-61, research assoc. edn. and elec. engring., 1961-64, part-time asst. prof., 1964-67, assoc. prof., 1967-71, prof. social relations and engring. sci., 1971—. Author: (with S.G. Doering) The First Birth, 1981, (with L.A. Hayduk) Early Schooling, 1982; editor: Scoiology of Education, 1975-78; assoc. editor: Am. Sociol. Rev., 1972-75. Guggenheim fellow, 1976-77. Fellow Am. Psychol. Assn., Am. Sociol. Assn.; mem. Am. Ednl. Research Assn., Soc. Research in Child Devel. Office: Johns Hopkins U 304 Barton Hall Baltimore MD 21218

ENTWISLE, GEORGE, physician; b. Bolton, Eng., May 27, 1922; came to U.S., 1923, naturalized, 1936; s. Nathan and Edith (Wilkinson) E.; m. Doris Helen Roberts, Aug. 31, 1946; children—Barbara, Beverly, George. B.S., U. Mass., 1944; M.D., Boston U., 1948. Diplomate: Nat. Bd. Med. Examiners, Am. Bd. Internal Medicine. Intern Evans Meml. Hosp., 1948-49, fellow physiology, 1949-51, asst. resident medicine, 1951-52, resident medicine, 1952; lectr. physiology, then instr. medicine Boston U. Sch. Medicine, 1952-56; faculty U. Md. Sch. Medicine, 1956—, prof. preventive medicine, 1958—, chmn. dept., 1958-71. Served with AUS, 1943-44, 52-54. Fellow A.C.P., Am. Coll. Preventive Medicine, Am. Pub. Health Assn., Council on Epidemiology of Am. Heart Assn.; mem. Md. Rehab. Assn. (pres. 1963-64), Assn. Tchrs. Preventive Medicine (pres. 1967-68, Distinguished Service award 1977, editor newsletter 1971-78), Mass., Balt. med. socs., Med and Chirurg. Faculty Md., Am. Fedn. Clin. Research, Sigma Xi. Home: 905 East Wind Rd Baltimore MD 21204

ENTWISTLE, JOHN, musician; b. London, Sept. 10, 1944. Bassist with musical group, The Who, 1965—; solo recs. include Mad Dog; appeared in: films Woodstock, 1970, The Kids are Alright, 1979. Office: care Premier Talent Agency 3 E 54th St New York NY 10022 *

ENTZEROTH, ROBERT ELLEARD, architect; b. St. Louis, Jan. 24, 1926; s. Elleard Colburn and Erma (Braun) E.; m. Barbara Elizabeth Ingold, Aug. 18, 1950; children—Lee Catherine, Lyn Suzanne, Julie Ann. B.Arch., Washington U., St. Louis, 1951. Architect Harris Armstrong (Architect), St. Louis, 1949-51, Murphy & Mackey, 1951-52, 53-54; partner in charge design Smith-Entzeroth, St. Louis, 1955—; vis. prof. archtl. design Washington U. Sch. Architecture; mem. Mo. Bd. Architects, Profl. Engrs. and Land Surveyors. Prin. works include Pierre Laclede Center, Clayton, Mo., Coll. Center of Principia Coll, University City Pub. Library, Washington U. Chemistry and Engring. Labs, Safeco Ins. Co. Offices, St. Louis, Nashville, Chgo., Mo. State Office Bldg, St. Louis, Alumni House Principia Coll, AAA Hdqrs. Bldg, St. Louis County. Served with USNR, 1944-46. Recipient numerous archtl. design awards including Archtl. Forum, 1961, Am. Fedn. Arts, 1968, 40 under 40 Exhbn. of Architects' Works, 1968; LeBrun Traveling scholar, 1952. Fellow AIA. Mem. United Ch. Christ. Club: St. Louis. Home: 106 Mason Ave Saint Louis MO 63119 Office: 7701 Forsyth Blvd Saint Louis MO 63105

ENYEDY, GUSTAV, JR., chemical engineer; b. Cleve., Aug. 23, 1924; s. Gustav and Mary (Silay) E.; m. Zoe Agnes Zachlin, Aug. 25, 1956; children: Louise Elaine, Roseann Marie, Arthur Gustav, Lillian Alice, Edward Anthony. B.S. in Chem. Engring., Case Inst. Tech., 1950, M.S., 1955. Registered profl. engr., Ohio. Engr., Rayon Tech. div. E.I. duPont, Richmond, Va., 1950-51; project engr. Grasselli Chem. Div., Cleve., 1951-54; devel. engr. Diamond Alkali (Soda Products), Painesville, Ohio, 1954-60; process engr. Central Engring., Cleve., 1960-61, staff engr. research dept., Painesville, 1961-65, supr. computer services, 1965-68; mgr. Diamond Shamrock Corp., Painesville, 1968-73; engring. cons., 1973—; pres. PDQS, Inc., 1975—; lectr. chem. engring. Fenn Coll., Cleve., 1957-61, Cleve. State U., 1975-76. Contbr. articles to tech. jours., textbooks. Treas., cubmaster, chmn. Gates Mills Cub Scout Pack, 1970-71, 75-78. Served with AUS, 1943-46. Decorated Bronze Star medal, Combat Inf. badge. Fellow Am. Assn. Cost Engrs. (tech. v.p. 1966-68, pres. 1969-70, speakers' bur. program 1971—), Am. Inst. Chem. Engrs.; mem. Tau Beta Pi, Pi Delta Epsilon. Home: Sugarbush Ln Gates Mills OH 44040 Office: Route 1 Box 64 Gates Mills OH 44040 *Do each job with complete integrity. Do not gain favor by giving in to outside pressure to slant results.*

ENZLER, ELLEN ROCHELLE, investment consultant; b. Bklyn., Jan. 13, 1943; d. Milton Harold and Lillian Bernice (Arbeit) E. B.A., NYU, 1963; postgrad., CCNY Grad. Sch. Bus., 1963-64, UCLA, 1970. Research analyst Bache & Co., N.Y.C., 1965-68; cons. investments, Los Angeles, 1968-69; v.p. research H. Hentz & Co., Los Angeles, 1970-72, E.F. Hutton & Co., Inc., 1972-79; regional editor Pvt. Wire, 1976-79; asst. v.p. research Paine, Webber, Jackson & Curtis, Los Angeles, 1979-80; investment cons., 1980—; founder Trophy Room Books and Trophy Room Pub., 1980. Mem. Los Angeles Soc. Technol. Analysts (pres. 1975-76), Los Angeles Soc. Fin. Analysts, Los Angeles Analysts Soc., Fin. Analysts Fedn., Nat. Rifle Assn., Antiquarian Booksellers Assn. Am., Nat. Wildlife Fedn., Internat. League Antiquarian Booksellers. Clubs: Ducks Unltd., Safari Internat. Home: 4858 Dempsey Ave Encino CA 91436

EPEL, DAVID, biologist; b. Detroit, Mar. 26, 1937; s. Jacob A. and Anna K. (Karse) E.; m. Lois S. Ambush, Dec. 18, 1960; children: Andrea, Sharon, Elissa. A.B., Wayne State U., 1958; Ph.D., U. Calif., Berkeley, 1963. Postdoctoral fellow Johnson Research Found., U. Pa., 1963-65; asst. prof. Hopkins Marine Sta., 1965-70; asso. prof., then prof. Scripps Instn. Oceanography, 1970-77; prof. biol. scis. Hopkins Marine Sta., dept. biol. scis. Stanford U., Pacific Grove, Calif., 1977—; co-dir. embryology course Marine Biol. Lab., Woods Hole; mem. adv. panel on devel. and cell biology NSF. Mem. editorial bd.: Devel. Biology, Cell Differentiation, Gamete Research. Guggenheim fellow, 1976-77; Overseas fellow Churchill; Coll., Cambridge, Eng., 1976-77. Fellow AAAS (mem.-at-large, sect. G 1979—); mem. Am. Soc. Cell Biology (mem. council 1978-80), Soc. Devel. Biology, Internat. Soc. Devel. Biology, Soc. Gen. Physiologist, Am. Soc. Zoologists. Home: 25847 Carmel Knolls Dr Carmel CA 93923 Office: Hopkins Marine Station Pacific Grove CA 93950

EPHRAIM, CHARLES, lawyer; b. Chgo., Sept. 18, 1924; s. Max H. and Margaret Mary (O'Neill) E.; m. Marguerite Marie Lamont, Dec. 23, 1944; children—Linda Patrice, Charles Lamont. Ph.B., U. Chgo., 1948, J.D., 1951. Bar: D.C. bar 1951. Since practiced in, Washington; partner firm Ephraim and Flint, 1979—; sec., dir. Herner Co. Mng. editor: U. Chgo. Law Rev, 1950-51; Contbr. to profl. publs. Bd. dirs. Christ Ch. Child Center, Bethesda, Md., 1961-68, chmn., 1961-62; v.p., bd. dirs. Bethesda Fellowship House, 1976-78. Served to 1st lt. USAF, 1943-47. Mem. Am., D.C. bar assns., Motor Carrier Lawyers Assn. (pres. 1978-79), Phi Beta Kappa, Order of Coif. Home: 5604 Western

Ave Chevy Chase MD 20815 Office: 918 16th St NW Suite 406 Washington DC 20006

EPHRAIM, MAX, JR., mechanical engineer; b. Chgo., Oct. 15, 1918; s. Max and Margaret (O'Neill) E.; m. Audrey Charlotte Nelson, Nov. 22, 1941; children: Janet, Philip, Alice, Daniel, Gary, Paul, Stephen, Lois, James. B.S.M.E. with high honors, Ill. Inst. Tech., 1939. Registered profl. engr., Ill. With Electro-Motive div. Gen. Motors Corp., La Grange, Ill., 1939—, locomotive sect. engr., 1955-59, asst. chief engr., 1959-73, chief engr., 1973-83; mem. U.S. electrification del. USSR, 1975; co. rep. to USSR Govt. tech. discussions, Soviet Union, 1974; mem. task force Coll. Engring., Ill. Inst. Tech., 1975-76. Vice chmn. bd. Channel 38 TV, Chgo., 1974—; regional v.p. adv. council Evangel Coll., Springfield, Mo., 1960—. Served to lt. USNR, 1943-46. Recipient Order Golden Shield, 1978; Recipient Profl. Achievement award Ill. Inst. Tech., 1981. Fellow ASME (award for paper 1969); Mem. Locomotive Maintenance Officers Assn., Assn. Am. R.R.s (track train dynamics steering com.). Mem. Assembly of God. Author, patentee heavy-duty diesel engine design, maj. locomotive components. Home: 10001 Central Park Evergreen Park IL 60642 Office: 9301 E 55th St La Grange IL 60525 *Christ has guided my life and put my priorities in the right order—God first, my family next, and then my job. With the peace of God in my life, a wonderful wife and family to love and support me, I am well prepared to lead and manage an outstanding engineering department while making worthwhile contributions to my company and to the railroad industry.*

EPHRON, NORA, author; b. N.Y.C., May 19, 1941; d. Henry and Phoebe (Wolkind) E.; m. Carl Bernstein, Apr. 14, 1976; Jacob, Max. B.A., Wellesley Coll., 1962; L.H.D., Briarcliffe (N.Y.) Coll., 1975. Reporter N.Y. Post, 1963-68; free-lance writer, 1968—; contbg. editor, columnist Esquire mag., 1972-73, sr. editor, columnist, 1974-78; contbg. editor N.Y. mag., 1973-74. Author: Wallflower at the Orgy, 1970, Crazy Salad, 1975, Scribble Scribble, 1978, Heartburn, 1983; Screenwriter: (with Alice Arlen) Silkwood, 1983. Mem. Writers Guild Am., AFTRA, Authors Guild. Address: care Lynn Nesbit ICM 40 W 57th St New York NY 10019 *

EPLEY, LEWIS EVERETT, JR., lawyer; b. Ft. Smith, Ark., Apr. 28, 1936; s. Lewis Everett and Evelyn (Wood) E.; m. Donna Louise Swopes, Feb. 24, 1962. B.S., J.D., U. Ark., 1961. Bar: Ark. 1961. Since practiced in Eureka Springs, city atty., 1969-71; dir. Bank of Eureka Springs.; del. Ark. Constl. Conv., 1969-70. Mem. Ark. Bldg. Services Council, 1975-80, chmn., 1976-78; mem. Carroll County Central Democratic Com., 1964-68; bd. dirs. Eureka Springs Ozark Folk Festival, 1964-69; chmn. adv. bd. Eureka Springs Mcpl. Hosp., 1963-71; mem. Beaver Lake Adv. Com., 1982—. Mem. ABA, Ark. Bar Assn. (del. 1975-78), Carroll County Bar Assn. (past pres.), Eureka Springs C. of C. (dir., past pres.), Phi Alpha Delta, Kappa Kappa Psi. Baptist. Home: Pivot Rock Rd Eureka Springs AR 72632 Office: PO Box 470 104 Spring St Eureka Springs AR 72632

EPLEY, MARION JAY, JR., oil company executive; b. Hattiesburg, Miss., June 17, 1907; s. Marion Jay and Eva (Quin) E.; m. Dorris Glenn Ervin, Feb. 12, 1934; children: Marion Jay III, Sara Perry (Mrs. Richard H. Davis). LL.B., Tulane U., 1930. Bar: La. 1930. Practiced in, New Orleans, 1930-42, 45-47; gen. atty. Texaco, Inc., New Orleans, N.Y.C., 1948-58, v.p., asst. to chmn. bd., N.Y.C., 1958-60, sr. v.p., 1960-61, exec. v.p., 1961-64, pres., 1964-70, chmn. bd., 1970-71; also dir.; pres., dir. Mardor Fin. Corp., 1971—. Served as lt. USNR, 1942-45. Decorated officer Ordre de la Couronne, Belgium). Mem. Am., La. bar assns. Clubs: Boston (New Orleans); Everglades, Bath and Tennis, Seminole Golf (Palm Beach, Fla.); Roaring Gap (N.C.); Royal Norwegian Yacht (Norway). Address: 350 Cocoanut Row Palm Beach FL 33480

EPNER, STEVEN ARTHUR, computer consultant; b. Buffalo, July 23, 948; s. Robert and Rosann (Krohn) E.; m. Louise Berke, June 20, 1970; children: Aaron J., Brian D. B.S., Purdue U., 1970. Computer operator/programmer Union Carbide, Chgo. and London, 1966-68; system analyst process design III, Chgo., 1969; analyst, sr. systems analyst Monsanto Co., St. Louis, 1970-74; lead analyst Citicorp., St. Louis, 1974-76; cons., pres. The User Group, Inc., St. Louis, 1976—; lectr. U. Mo., St. Louis Bus. Program, 1981-83; mem. Commn. on Software Issues in the 80s, 1982—, SBA Task Force on Small Bus. Editor: The Independent, 1977-84; contbr. articles to profl. jours. Mem. Ind. Computer Cons. Assn. (dir., pres. chpt., nat. pres.). Office: 443 N New Ballas St Saint Louis MO 63141 *I am often asked about starting businesses. My normal reply is, "If it were easy and guaranteed, then it would already be done." Therefore, building a successful organization takes time, effort, and risk.*

EPP, ELDON JAY, religion educator; b. Mountain Lake, Minn., Nov. 1, 1930; s. Jacob Jay and Louise (Kintzi) E.; m. ElDoris Balzer, June 13, 1951; children: Gregory Thomas, Jennifer Elizabeth. A.B. magna cum laude, Wheaton Coll., 1952, B.D., Fuller Theol Sem., 1955; S.T.M., Harvard U., 1956, Ph.D., 1961. Spl. research asst. Princeton Theol. Sem., 1961-62; vis. instr. Drew U. Theol. Sch., 1962; asst. prof. religion U. So. Calif. Grad. Sch. Religion, 1962-65, asso. prof., 1965-67, asso. prof. classics, 1966-68; asso. prof. religion Case Western Res. U., Cleve., 1968-71, prof. religion, Harkness prof. bibl. lit., 1971—, dean humanities and social scis., 1977—; Mem. Am. exec. com. Internat. Greek New Testament Project, 1968—. Author: The Theological Tendency of Codex Bezae Cantabrigiensis in Acts, 1966; co-editor: New Testament Textual Criticism: Its Significance for Exegesis, 1981; Asso. editor: Jour. Bibl. Lit, 1971—; Mem. editorial bd.: Soc. Bibl. Lit. Monograph Series, 1969-72, Soc. Bibl. Lit. Centennial Publs, 1975—, Studies and Documents, 1971—; exec. sec.: Hermeneia: A Critical and Historical Commentary on the Bible, 1962—; mem. editorial bd., 1966—; Contbr. articles, reviews to publs. Active Boy Scouts Am., 1975-78; Bd. mgrs. St. Paul's Episcopal Cathedral, Los Angeles, 1964-68, clk., 1967-68. Recipient Harvard Div. Sch. fellowship, 1956-58, Harvard Faculty Arts and Scis. fellow, 1958-59, Rockefeller doctoral fellow in religion, 1959-60; postdoctoral fellow Claremont Grad. Sch., 1966-68; Guggenheim fellow, 1974-75. Mem. Am. Acad. Religion (sect. pres. 1965-66), Soc. Bibl. Lit. (chmn. textual criticism seminar 1966, 71—, mem. permanent Centennial com. 1975-80, mem. council 1980-82, del. Council on Study of Religion 1980-82), Studiorum Novi Testamenti Societas, Cath. Bibl. Assn., New Testament Colloquium (chmn. 1974), Soc. Mithraic Studies, Am. Assn. U. Profs. (chpt. exec. com. 1970-72), Inst. Antiquity and Christianity, Phi Beta Kappa. Home: 22399 Shelburne Rd Shaker Heights OH 44122 Office: Office of the Dean 7080 Crawford Cleveland OH 44106 *Personal integrity is the essential foundation for life in all its aspects. From integrity flow those qualities that will preserve, enrich, and ennoble human existence. Integrity is formative and substantive in every meaningful human relationship; in its absence, both the meaning and the relationship itself eventually disintegrate.*

EPPELSHEIMER, DANIEL SNELL, educator; b. Chgo., Mar. 17, 1909; s. Daniel and Florence Irvina (Snell) E.; m. Marion Elizabeth Vaughn, Apr. 11, 1936; children—Daniel Snell, David Vaughn. B.S. cum laude in Mining and Metallurgy, Harvard, 1932, D.Sc. in Phys. Metallurgy, 1935. Research asst., Harvard, 1929-35; research metallurgist Union Carbide & Carbon Research Lab., Niagara Falls, N.Y., 1935-38; prof., head engr. Exptl. Sta. U. N.H., 1938-45; chief. physics metallurgist, sales mgr. Metal Hydrides, Inc., Beverly, Mass., 1945-46; prof. nuclear and metall. engring. U. Mo. at Rolla, 1947—, chmn. dept. metallurgy, 1957-58, 63-64; cons. in field. Mem. Mo. AEC, 1959—; Mo. rep. So. Interstate Nuclear Bd., Atlanta, 1965—, chmn., 1970—; sci. adviser Gov. Mo., 1970—. Contbr. articles to profl. jours. Mem. Am. Inst. Mining, Metall. and Petroleum Engrs., Am. Soc. Metals, Am. Chem. Soc., Am. Crystallographic Assn., Am. Foundrymens Soc., Am. Soc. Engring. Edn., Brit. Inst. Physics, Brit. Inst. Metals, Brit. Iron and Steel Inst., Verein Deutscher Eisenhutten Leute, Franklin Inst., Sigma Xi, Pi Kappa Alpha. Clubs: Rotarian., Harvard (Boston); Missouri Athletic (St. Louis). Home: PO Box 299 Rolla MO 65401 Office: Metallurgy Dept U Mo Rolla MO 65401

EPPEN, GARY DEAN, educator; b. Austin, Minn., Apr. 28, 1936; s. Marldene Fredrick and Elsie Alma (Wendorf) E.; m. Ann Marie Sathre, June 14, 1958; children: Gregory, Peter, Paul, Amy. A.A., Austin Jr. Coll., 1956; B.S., U. Minn., 1958, M.S.I.E., 1960; Ph.D., Cornell U., 1964. Prof. mgmt. European Inst. Advanced Studies, Brussels, 1972-73; asso. dean Grad. Sch. Bus., U. Chgo., 1969-75, prof. indsl. adminstrn., 1970—, asso. dean Ph.D. studies, 1978—, dir. Life Officers Investment Seminar, 1975—, dir. Fin. Analysts Seminar, 1982—; Francqui prof. Cath. U. Leuven, Belgium, 1979; external examiner U. West Indies, 1979-82. Author: (with F.J. Gould) Quantitative Concepts for Management, 1979, (with Metcalfe and Walters) The MBA Degree, 1979, (with F.J. Gould) Introductory Management Science, 1984; contbr. articles to profl. jours. Mem. Ops. Research Soc. Am. (asso. editor jour.), Inst. Mgmt. Sci. Lutheran. Home: 801 Bruce St Flossmoor IL 60422 Office: Grad Sch Bus U Chgo 1101 E 58th St Chicago IL 60637

EPPENBERGER, FRED ARNOLD, lawyer; b. Chgo., Oct. 30, 1906; s. Arnold A. and Laura (Doerr) E.; m. Emily V. Hurd, Nov. 26, 1937; children—Katherine C., Frederick H. Student, St. Louis U., 1923; LL.B., Washington U., 1928. Bar: Mo. bar 1928. Asso. firm Husch, Eppenberger, Donohue, Elson & Cornfeld (and predecessors), St. Louis, 1928—, mem. firm, 1936—; Active drafting of adoption law, juvenile court code. Chmn. St. Louis County Commn. on Human Relations, 1964-70; vice chmn. joint adminstrv. com. St. Louis Constrn. Manpower Corp. (St. Louis Plan), 1968-74; vice chmn. St. Louis County Civil Service Commn., 1974, chmn., 1975-76; Bd. dirs. Mid-County YMCA, St. Louis; bd. dirs. Family and Children's Service of Greater St. Louis, v.p., 1955-58; mem. citizens adv. bd. Juvenile Ct. of St. Louis, chmn., 1963; adv. bd. St. Louis County Children's Treatment Center. Recipient Alumni citation Washington U., 1962; Disting. Alumni award Washington U. Law Sch., 1981. Fellow Am. Bar Found., Am. Coll. Probate Counsel; mem. Am. Bar Assn. (ho. dels. 1961-68), Am. Judicature Soc. (dir. 1962-65), Bar Assn. St. Louis (chmn. juvenile laws com.; exec. com. 1944-50), Mo. Bar (chmn. juvenile laws com., bd. govs. 1955—, pres. 1960, pres. Found. 1962-65), Nat. Assn. Coll. and Univ. Attys., Order of Coif, Phi Delta Phi. Conglist. Club: Missouri Athletic (St. Louis). Home: 7141 Washington St University City MO 63130 Office: 100 N Broadway Saint Louis MO 63102

EPPERLY, WILLIAM ROBERT, energy company executive; b. Christiansburg, Va., Mar. 17, 1935; s. William Rangeley and Myrtle Claire (Vest) E.; m. Sarah Ann Owen, June 9, 1957; children: William Robert, Jennifer Ann, Thomas. B.S., Va. Poly. Inst., 1956, M.S., 1958. With Exxon Research & Engring. Co., and parent co., 1957—; mgr. Baytown (Tex.) reseach research and devel. div., 1973-76, mgr. project devel. and planning, Florham Park, N.J., 1976-77, gen. mgr. liquefaction, 1977-79, gen. mgr. synthetic fuels dept., 1980-83, sr. program mgr., 1983—; mem. air pollution research adv. com. Coordinating Research Council, 1969-71; mem. fossil energy program adv. com. Oak Ridge Nat. Lab., 1978-81; mem. com. synthetic fuels safety NRC, 1982, mem. com. on coop. govt. industry research, 1983. Author. Mem. Am. Inst. Chem. Engrs. (award for chem. engring. practice 1983), Am. Petroleum Inst., AAAS. Methodist. Patentee in synthetic fuels, automotive emissions/gasoline composition, iron ore reduction, fuel cells, others. Home: 18 Gloucester Rd Summit NJ 07901 Office: Exon Research & Engring Co Clinton Twp Route 22E Annandale NJ 08801

EPPERSON, DAVID ERNEST, educator, dean; b. Pitts., Mar. 14, 1935; s. Robert N. and Bessie Lee (Tibbs) E.; m. Cecelia Trower, July 11, 1964; children: Sharon, Lia. B.A., U. Pitts., 1960, M.S.W., 1964, M.A. in Polit. Sci, 1971, Ph.D., 1975. World service worker YMCA, Hong Kong, 1961-62; coordinator equal opportunities program U. Pitts., 1964-65; dep. dir. Pitts. program OEO, 1965-67, exec. dir., 1967-69; univ. fellow in urban affairs U. Pitts., 1969-72; prof., dean Sch. Social Work, U. Pitts., 1972—; cons. specialist in social welfare, pub. policy and urban affairs. Pres. Urban League of Pitts.; vice chmn. Urban Redevel. Authority of Pitts., YMCA. Served with USAF, 1954-58. Mem. Council Social Work Edn., Nat. Assn. Social Workers, UN Assn., Nat. Conf. Social Welfare. Democrat. Office: Sch Social Work Univ of Pitts Cathedral of Learning Pittsburgh PA 15260 *

EPPINK, NORMAN ROLAND, artist; b. Cleve., July 29, 1906; s. Herman and Catherine (Koch) E.; m. Helen Louise Brenan, June 15, 1931; 1 dau., Karen Eppink Remington. B.E.A., Cleve. Art Inst., 1928; M.A., Western Res. U., 1936. Instr. art Lakewood (Ohio) public schs., 1928-30; med. illustrator Cleve. Clinic Found., 1930-33; lectr. Cleve. Mus. Art, 1935-36; tchr. art Cleve. public schs., 1936-37; instr. art Emporia (Kans.) State U., 1937-47, prof. art, head dept., 1947-75, prof. emeritus, 1975—; Bd. dirs. Kans. Fed. Art, 1946-49, Kans. Cultural Arts Commn., 1965-67. Author: 101 Prints, 1971; one man shows include, Wichita Art Mus., 1944, Nat. Gallery of Art, 1968-70, Cleve. Public Library, 1967, Denver U. Library, 1968, Topeka Public Library, 1969, Paine Art Center, Oshkosh, Wis.; represented in permanent collections at, Brit. Mus., Chgo. Art Inst., Cleve. Mus. Art, Los Angeles County Mus. Art, Met. Mus. Art.; (with wife) two-man show, Topeka Pub. Library Gallery, 1977. Club: Rotary. Address: 2101 Canterbury Rd Emporia KS 66801

EPPLER, JEROME CANNON, investment executive; b. Englewood, N.J., Mar. 16, 1924; s. William E. and Aileen (Vaughan) E.; children: Stephen Vaughan, William Durand, Margaret Nye, Elizabeth Scott, Edward Curtis. B.S. in Mech. Engring., Tex. A&M U., 1946; M.B.A., U. Pa., 1949. With Gen. Electric Supply Corp., Newark, 1949-50; investment banker Equitable Securities Corp., Nashville, mgr. Houston office, 1950-53; gen. partner Cyrus J. Lawrence & Sons, N.Y.C., 1953-61; (mem. N.Y. Stock Exchange), Eppler & Co., Inc., 1961-82; ltd. partner Alex, Brown & Sons, Balt., 1983—; dir. Esmark, Inc., Chgo., Pure Cycle Corp., Boulder, Colo., Castle Pines Land Co., Denver, Telecredit, Inc., Los Angeles, Gifford-Hill & Co. Inc., Dallas.; mem. indsl. adv. com. U. Calif., San Diego. Trustee Scripps Clinic and Research Found., La Jolla. Served to lt. (j.g.) USNR, 1942-46. Mem. N.Y. Soc. Security Analysts. Presbyterian. Clubs: Wharton Grad. Bus. Sch. (N.Y.) (dir.); Castle Pines Golf (Denver)). Office: 135 E Baltimore St Baltimore MD 21202

EPPLEY, ROLAND RAYMOND, financial services executive; b. Balt., Apr. 1, 1932; s. Roland and Verna (Garrettson) E.; m. LeVerne Pittman, June 20, 1953; children: Kimberly, Kent, Todd. B.A., Johns Hopkins U., 1952, M.A., 1953. Pres., chief exec. officr Comm. Credit Computer, Balt., 1962-68; pres., chief exec. officer CIPC, Balt., 1968-77; vice chmn. Eastern Staes Monetary, Lake Success, N.Y., 1982—; pres., chief exec. officer, dir. Affiliated Financial, Wilmington, Del., 1983—, Eastern States Bankcard, Lake Success, N.Y., 1971—; dir. Eastern States Monetary. Chmn. bd. trustees Calgary Bapt. Ch., Balt., 1969-71; chmn. investment com. Community Ch., Manhasset, N.Y., 1983—. Laucheimer grantee, 1952-53. Mem. Am. Bankers Assn., Data Processing Mgmt. Assn., Am. Mgmt. Assn. Pres. Assn., Electronic Funds Transfer Assn., Mensa, Phi Beta kappa, Omicron Delta Epsilon, Beta Gamma Sigma. Republican. Mem. Reformed Ch. Am. Clubs: Madison Square Garden, Meadowbrook, Plandome Country (dir. 1977—), Hillendale). Home: 77 Westgate Blvd Plandome NY 11030 Office: 4 Ohio Dr Lake Success NY 11042

EPPS, AUGUSTUS CHARLES, lawyer; b. Richmond, Va., Feb. 2, 1916; s. John Lindsey and Lily Madeline (Becker) E.; m. Rosalie Suzanne Garrett, Aug. 17, 1946; children: Augustus Charles, George Garrett, John Daniel. B.S., U. Va., 1936, LL.B., 1938. Bar: Va. 1937, U.S. Supreme Ct. 1950. Practice in, Richmond, 1938-42, 46—; assoc. atty. Christian, Barton & Parker, 1938-42; ptnr. Christian, Barton, Epps, Brent & Chappell, 1946—; dir., gen. counsel Richmond Life Ins. Co., 1952-69; dir. Truxmore Industries, Truxmore Internat. Inc., Va. Suppliers Inc., Wainwright Investment Co., Va. Legal Services Corp., Newbridge Mgrs. Inc., Garrett Groves, Inc. Editorial bd., bd. mng. editors: Va. Law Rev, 1936-38; contbr. articles to profl. jours. Mem. Richmond Sch. Bd., 1963-70; past pres. Met. Richmond Legal Aid Project; past pres., bd. dirs. Crippled Children's Hosp., Friends Richmond Pub. Library; past vice chmn., bd. dirs. Richmond YMCA; bd. dirs., exec. com. Legal Aid Soc. Met. Richmond, 1967-76, Richmond Symphony; bd. dirs. Va. Soc. for Performing Arts; mem. Richmond Public Library Bd.; past bd. dirs. Richmond Offender Aid and Restoration, 1969-75; trustee Roslyn Diocesan Center, Episcopal Diocese Va.; v.p., bd. dirs. V.O.I.C.E. Served to maj. AUS, 1942-46. Fellow Am. Bar Found., Am. Coll. Trial Lawyers; mem. ABA (past mem. com. on specialization, past mem. grievance com., past chmn. state com. legal edn., admission to bar, commn. on law and the economy), Va. Bar Assn. (pres. 1966-67, chmn. com. on specialization, past chmn. joint com. legis., law reform, past mem. exec. com., com. specialization), Richmond Bar Assn. (past chmn. legal aid com., past pres.), City of N.Y. Bar Assn., Am. Judicature Soc., Assn. Life Ins. Counsel, Fed. Jud. Conf., U. Va. Law Sch. Assn. (council, chmn. Law Day 1972, 73, past chmn. com. scholarships, pres. 1977-79), Phi Beta Kappa, Order of Coif, Phi Delta Phi, Alpha Tau Omega. Episcopalian. Home: 6323 Ridgeway Rd Richmond VA 23226 Office: Mutual Bldg Richmond VA 23219

EPPS, EDGAR GUSTAVUS, sociology educator; b. Little Rock, Aug. 30, 1929; s. Clifford and Odelle (Hil) E.; m. Marilyn Harryette Miller, Dec. 18, 1958; children: Carolyn, Raymond. A.B., Talladega Coll., 1951; M.A., Atlanta U., 1955; Ph.D., Wash. State U., 1959. Mem. faculty Tenn. State Coll., 1958-61; prof. Fla. A&M U., 1961-64; asso. prof., research asso. Inst. Social Research U. Mich., 1964-67; dir. Behavioral Sci. Research Tuskegee Inst., 1967-70; Marshall Field IV prof. urban edn. U. Chgo., 1970—. Author: (with Patricia Gurin) Black Consciousness, Identity, and Achievement, 1975; editor: Black Students in White Schools, 1972; Editor: Race Relations; Current Perspectives, 1973, Cultural Pluralism, 1974; contbr. articles to profl. jours. Mem. Bd. Edn. City of Chgo., 1974-80; bd. dirs. So. Edn. Found., 1976—. Served with AUS, 1951-53. Mem. Am. Sociol. Assn., Soc. Psychol. Study Social Issues, Am. Ednl. Research Assn., Phi Delta Kappa. Home: 5825 S Dorchester Ave Chicago IL 60637

EPREMIAN, EDWARD, government official; b. Schenectady, Sept. 3, 1921; s. Krikor and Rose (Momjian) E.; m. Mary Lou Feller, Nov. 29, 1948; children: Barbara Ellen, Jeffrey Louis. B.S., M.I.T., 1943; M.S., Rensselaer Poly. Inst., 1947; Sc.D. (Timken fellow 1949-51), Carnegie Inst. Tech., 1951. Research assoc. Gen. Electric Co. Research Lab., Schenectady, 1943-47; dep. sci. dir. U.S. Office Naval Research, London, 1951-54; chief metallurgy and materials br. AEC Div. Research, Washington, 1954-57; sr. metallurgist Research Lab., Union Carbide Metals Co., Niagara Falls, N.Y., 1957-59, tech. coordinator tech. dept., N.Y.C., 1960-61, mgr. new product mktg., 1961-63; asst. dir. research Carbon Products div. Union Carbide Corp., Cleve., 1964-65; gen. mgr. High Temperature Materials Co., Inc. subs., N.Y.C., 1965-67, gen. mgr. advanced materials dept., 1965-70, mgr. tantalum products Metals div., 1970-71, mgr. splty. products, 1971-72, dir. new ventures, 1973-76; exec. dir. Commn. Sociotech. Systems, NRC, Nat. Acad. Scis., Washington, 1976-82; spl. asst. to exec. dir. UN Indsl. Devel. Orgn., Vienna, 1983—; Mem. adv. com. U. Pa. Sch. Metallurgy and Materials Scis., 1969-73; mem. adv. council Coll. Engring., U. Md., College Park, 1978-83; bd. dirs. Acta Metallurgica, 1971-73. Editor: (with F. Sisco) Columbium and Tantalum, 1963. Trustee Webb Inst. Naval Architecture and Marine Engring., 1976-83. Rensselaer Poly. Inst. fellow grantee, 1948. Fellow AAAS, Am. Soc. for Metals; mem. AIME, Sigma Xi, Phi Kappa Phi. Patentee in field. Home: Taubstummengasse 2/12 1040 Vienna Austria Office: UNIDO PO Box 300 A-1400 Vienna Austria

EPSTEEN, CASPER MORLEY, physician, educator; b. East Chicago, Ind., May 6, 1902; s. Hyman and Sarah Ida (Goodman) E.; m. Aline Gertrude Grossman, Sept. 26, 1934; children: Lynn, Robert. B.Sc., U. Ill., 1923, M.D., 1925; D.D.S., Loyola U. Chgo., 1930. Diplomate: Internat. Bd. Surgery. Intern Michael Reese Hosp. and Med. Center, Chgo., 1925-26; now sr. attending surgeon; preceptorship with Dr. Truman W. Brophy, 1926-29; practice medicine specializing maxillofacial and plastic surgery, Chgo., 1926—; cons. Weiss Meml. Hosp., Jackson Park Community Hosp. and Med. Center, Central Community Hosp.; clin. prof. maxillofacial and plastic surgery Chgo. Med. Sch., 1960-84, clin. prof. emeritus, 1984—. Author: Tice's Practice of Medicine, 1948; Guest editor: Am. Jour. Surgery, Dec. 1952; editorial asso.: Internat. Jour. Surgery. Served to lt. col. AUS, 1942-46. Guest of honor 1st Internat. Congress Maxillofacial Surgeons, Venice, Italy, 1971; recipient hon. mention for research salivary glands Am. Soc. Plastic and Reconstructive Surgeons, 1953; Honor award Michael Reese Hosp. and Med. Center, 1955, Louis A. Weiss Meml. Hosp., 1960. Fellow Ill. Soc. for Med. Research, Ednl. and Sci. Found. Ill. Med. Soc.; mem. Am. Soc. Maxillofacial Surgeons (founder mem.; pres. 1960, Leadership award 1960, Distinguished award 1966, Presdl. Achievement award 1982), Chgo. Med. Soc. (pres. 1962-63, award merit 1963, founder ann. clin. conf., Testimonial of Appreciation 1978, Biog. Roll of Honor award 1983), Ill. Med. Soc. (1st v.p. 1968), AMA, Am., Internat. colls. surgeons, World Med. Assn., Internat. Assn. Burn Injuries, Chgo. Natural History Mus. (life), Am. Burn Assn., Art Inst. Chgo. Clubs: Quadrangle, Executive (Chgo.). Home: 5750 S Kenwood Ave Chicago IL 60637 *To alleviate pain—to heal the sick—to sustain and maintain life—to teach young people the principles of the above and also the tried and successful methods of so doing. To help my colleagues with sick people. To understand the psychological impact of congenital and traumatic deformities and to help the afflicted with understanding. To speak over and over the values of humanism and human understanding and thus to make the world a better place for all people.*

EPSTEIN, ALVIN, actor, director; b. Bronx, N.Y., May 14, 1925; s. Harry and Goldie (Rudnick) E. Student, Queens Coll., 1942-43, Martha Graham Sch. Dance, N.Y.C., 1946-47, Ecole de Mime Etienne Decroux, Paris, 1947-51, Sanford Meisner Profl. Class, N.Y.C., 1951-52. Tchr. Chamber Theatre, Israel, Neighborhood Playhouse, N.Y.C., Circle in Sq. Theatre Sch.; acting artistic dir. Yale Repertory Theatre, 1972-73, assoc. dir., 1973-77; acting tchr. Yale Drama Sch., 1968-77;

artistic dir. Guthrie Theatre, Mpls., 1978-79; mem. faculty Salzburg Am. Seminar, 1972. Actor, Theatre de Mime Etienne Decroux, Paris, 1947-51, Habima Theatre, Israel, 1952-55; made Am. profl. debut with Marcel Marceau, Phoenix Theatre, N.Y.C., 1955; has appeared in: many Broadway, off-Broadway touring and regional prodns., including The Fool in King Lear, N.Y.C., 1956; Lucky in original Broadway prodn. Waiting for Godot, 1956; Puck in A Midsummer Night's Dream, Empire State Music Festival, N.Y., 1956; O'Killigain in Purple Dust, N.Y.C.; Clov in Endgame, N.Y.C.; Luc Delbert in No Strings, N.Y.C.; title role in Enrico IV, Milw., Chgo.; Beranger in The Pedestrian in the Air, Chgo.; Theseus and Oberon in A Midsummer's Night Dream, N.Y.C.; Octave in Clerambard, N.Y.C.; various roles in Postmark Zero, N.Y.C.; Landau in The Latent Heterosexual, Los Angeles; Sgt. in Dynamite Tonite, N.Y.C.; appeared in: Whores, Wars and Tin Pan Alley, Chgo., New Haven, N.Y.C., Easthampton, A Place Without Doors, Long Wharf Theatre, New Haven, Staircase Theatre, N.Y.C., Goodman Theatre, Chgo., on U.S. tour, Los Angeles, Washington; mem., Yale Repertory Theatre, New Haven, 1968—; playing leading parts: Dynamite Tonite, God Bless, Story Theatre, The Bacchae, Greatshot, Crimes and Crimes, Olympian Games, Gimple the Fool, Woyzeck, Don Juan, Macbett (Ionesco), The Tempest, Happy End, the Possessed, Bingo, Ivanov, Goodman Theatre, on U.S. tour, Los Angeles, Washington; dir.: The Rivals, Caligula, Seven Deadly Sins, Bourgeois Gentleman, Rise and Fall of the City of Mahagonny, The Tempest, A Midsummer Night's Dream, Troilus and Cressida, Julius Caesar, others; appeared in many TV shows on all networks; dir.: The Pretenders, Beggars Opera, The Rivals; appeared in: Marriage, A Kurt Weill Cabaret, Monsieur de Moliere for, Guthrie Theatre; co-founder, actor, Berkshire Theatre Festival, Stockbridge, Mass., 1966; playing: Antrobus in Skin of Our Teeth, Berkshire Theatre Festivals, Stockbridge, Mass.; Skylock in Merchant of Venice, Berkshire Theatre Festival, Stockbridge, Mass.; dir.: Colette, Berkshire Theatre Festival, Stockbridge, Mass., 1974. Bd. dirs. Theatre Communications Group, N.Y.C., 1975-77. Served with AUS, 1943-46; ETO. Recipient Obie award for Dynamic Tonite, 1968, Creative Arts award in theatre Brandeis U., 1966; Ford Found. grantee, 1959-60; fellow Trumbull Coll., Yale U. Address: 344 W 84th St New York NY 10024 *

EPSTEIN, ARTHUR WILLIAM, physician, educator; b. N.Y.C., May 15, 1923; s. Jacob E. and Anne (Bass) E.; m. Leona Cruce, Mar. 2, 1955; children: David Byron, Nona Kathryn, Emily Vera, James Jacob. A.B., Columbia U., 1944, M.D., 1947. Intern Mt. Sinai Hosp., N.Y.C., 1947-48, resident, 1949-50; clin. asst. Norristown (Pa.) State Hosp., 1948-49; faculty Tulane U., New Orleans, 1954—, asso. prof. psychiatry and neurology, 1959-64, prof., 1964—; pvt. practice medicine, specializing in neuropsychiatry, New Orleans, 1954—; vis. physician Charity Hosp., New Orleans, 1951—; cons. U.S. Army Hosp., New Orleans, 1958-64, VA Hosp., 1969—; mem. med. staff Tulane Med. Center Hosp., 1976—. Author: An Anatomist's Dream of Love, 1966, The Dissecting Room, 1978, The Lady and the Serpent, 1981; contbr. articles to profl. jours. Med. adviser Social Security Adminstrn., 1968—; Bd. dirs. Ednl. Research and Treatment Center, New Orleans. Served with M.C. USNR, 1956-58. Fellow Am. Psychiat. Assn. (leisure time and its uses com.), Am. Acad. Psychoanalysis, Am. Acad. Neurology, AAAS, mem. Soc. Biol. Psychiatry (asst. sec. 1973-76, sec.-treas. 1976-79), Soc. Biol. Psychiatry (v.p. 1979-80, pres. elect 1980-81, pres. 1981-82), Soc. for Neurosci., Am. Epilepsy Soc., Alpha Omega Alpha. Home: 1664 Robert St New Orleans LA 70115 Office: 1430 Tulane Ave New Orleans LA 70112 *Amid the hurly-burly, keep awe and wonder. Pursue the ideal.*

EPSTEIN, BARBARA, editor; b. Boston, Aug. 30, 1929; d. H.W. and Helen (Diamond) Zimmerman; children: Jacob, Helen. B.A., Radcliffe Coll., 1949. Editor N.Y. Review of Books, N.Y.C., 1963—. Home: 33 W 67th St New York NY 10023 Office: NY Review of Books 250 W 57th St New York NY 10019

EPSTEIN, BARRY R., public relations counselor; b. N.Y.C., Mar. 22, 1942; s. Irving Henry and Libby Frieda (Ertel) E.; children: Larry Marc, Lori Ann. B.A., Kent State U., 1964. Promotion mgr. White Plains (N.Y.) C. of C., 1964-66; asst. mgr. Ypsilanti (Mich.) C. of C., 1966-67; exec. v.p. Warren County (Pa.) C. of C., 1967-71, Greater Hollywood (Fla.) C. of C., 1971-78, pres., chief exec. officer, 1974-78; exec. v.p. Orlando (Fla.) C. of C., 1978-79; pres. Barry R. Epstein Assos., Inc., Hollywood, Fla., 1979—; adj. prof. Broward Community Coll. Mem. Ypsilanti Youth Commn., 1966, Citizens Adv. Com., 1968, Pleasant Twp. Planning Commn., 1969, NW Pa. Regional Planning and Devel. Commn., 1970; mem. citizens adv. com. Broward County Area Planning Bd., 1973; mem. Hollywood Planning and Zoning Bd.; pres. Hollywood Hills Elementary PTA, 1976; sec.-treas. S. Broward Community Found., 1976—; mem. Com. of 100, 1975—. Recipient 1st prize Pa. Better Community Contest, Jaycee Spoke award, 1970; named Outstanding Young Man of Am.; Ky. col. Mem. Am. C. of C. Execs., Pa. C. of C. Execs. (dir. 1969-71), Fla. C. of C. Execs. (dir. 1974—, pres. 1977), Broward County C. of C. Execs. (chmn. 1976—). Home: 1747 Van Buren St Hollywood FL 33020 *Take time to "listen" to people. Don't just "hear" what they say. The Golden Rule still can't be improved upon for standards of conduct.*

EPSTEIN, CHARLES JOSEPH, physician, medical geneticist, pediatrics and biochemistry educator; b. Phila., Sept. 3, 1933; s. Jacob C. and Frieda (Savransky) E.; m. Lois Barth, June 10, 1956; children: David Alexander, Jonathan Akiba, Paul Michael, Joanna Marguerite. A.B., Harvard U., 1955, M.D., 1959. Diplomate: Am. Bd. Medical Genetics. Intern in medicine Peter Bent Brigham Hosp., Boston, 1959-60, asst. resident in medicine, 1960-61; research asso., med. officer and sect. chief Nat. Heart Inst. and Nat. Inst. Arthritis and Metabolic Diseases, NIH, Bethesda, Md., 1961-67; research fellow in med. genetics U. Wash., 1963-64; asso. prof. pediatrics and biochemistry U. Calif., San Francisco, 1967-72, prof., 1972—; investigator Howard Hughes Med. Inst., 1976-81; mem. human embryology and devel. study sect. NIH, 1971-75; mem. mental retardation research com. Nat. Inst. Child Health and Devel., 1979-83, chmn., 1981-83; mem. com. for study inborn errors of metabolism NRC, 1972-75; mem. sci. adv. bd. Nat. Down Syndrome Soc., 1981—. Asso. editor: Rudolph's Textbook of Pediatrics, 17th edit, 1982; editorial bd.: Biology of Reproduction, 1974-78, Cytogenetics and Cell Genetics, 1975-80, Am. Jour. Med. Genetics, 1977—, Human Genetics, 1981—, Devel. Genetics, 1983—, Jour. Embryology and Exptl. Morphology, 1983—. Served with USPHS, 1961-63. Recipient Henry A. Christian award Harvard Med. Sch., 1959, Research Career Devel. award NIH, 1967-72; John S. Guggenheim Meml. Found. fellow, 1973-74; Inst. Advanced Studies in Behavioral Scis. fellow. Mem. Am. Fedn. Clin. Research, Am. Soc. Human Genetics (dir. 1972-75), Am. Soc. Biol. Chemists, Soc. Pediatric Research (council 1972-75), Western Soc. Pediatric Research, Western Soc. Clin. Research, Am. Soc. Clin. Investigation, Am. Soc. Cell Biology, Soc. Devel. Biology, Am. Pediatric Soc., Western Assn. Physicians, Assn. Am. Physicians, Soc. Inherited Metabolic Disorders, Phi Beta Kappa, Alpha Omega Alpha. Jewish. Research, numerous publs. on human and med. genetics, devel. genetics and biochemistry. Home: 19 Noche Vista Ln Tiburon CA 94920 Office: Dept Pediatrics U Calif San Francisco CA 94143

EPSTEIN, CYNTHIA FUCHS, sociology educator. B.A. in Polit. Sci., Antioch Coll., 1955; postgrad., U. Chgo. Law Sch., 1955-56; M.A. in Sociology, New Sch. Social Research, 1960; Ph.D., Columbia U., 1968. Instr. anthropology Finch Coll., 1961-62; assoc. in sociology Columbia U., 1964-65, instr. Barnard Coll., 1965; instr. sociology Queens Coll., N.Y.C., 1966-67, asst. prof., 1968-70, assoc. prof., 1971-74, prof., 1974—, co-dir. NIMH tng. grant on sociology and econs. of women and work Grad. Ctr.; resident scholar Russell Sage Found., N.Y.C., 1982—; vis. prof. Health Sci. Ctr., SUNY-Stony Brook, 1975; cons., lectr. and speaker in field. Author: Woman's Place: Options and Limits in Professional Careers, 1970, Women in Law, 1981; editor: (with William J. Goode) The Other Half: Roads to Women's Equality, 1971; (with Rose Laub Cose) Access to Power: Cross-National Studies of Women and Elites, 1981; mem. editorial bds.: Signs, Women's Studies, Internat. Jour. Work and Occupations, Sociol. Focus, Women 1974, Dissent; contbr. chpts. to books, articles to profl. jours. Grantee Inst. Life Ins., 1974, Ford Found., 1975-77, Research Found. City N.Y., 1974-76, Guggenheim Meml. Found., 1976-77, Ctr. Advanced Study in Behavioral Scis., 1977-78; fellow NIH, 1963-66, MacDowell Colony, 1973, 74, 77, 80, Guggenheim, 1976-77, Ctr. Advanced Study in Behavioral Sci., 1977-78. Mem. Eastern Sociol. Soc. (v.p. 1977-79, exec. council 1973-74, pres. 1983-84, I. Peter Gellman award 1976), Am. Sociol. Assn. (council 1974-77, chmn. sect. on sociology of sex roles 1973-74), Social. Research Assn., AAAS, Internat. Sci. Commn. on Family. Office: Russell Sage Found 112 E 64th St New York NY 10025

EPSTEIN, DANIEL MARK, poet, dramatist; b. Washington, Oct. 25, 1948; s. Donald David and Louise Marietta (Tillman) E.; m. Wendy Roberts, May 29, 1976; 1 dau., Johanna Ruth. A.B. magna cum laude with highest honors in English, Kenyon Coll., 1970; postgrad., U. Va., 1970-71. Asst. mgr. Automatic Enterprises, Washington, 1967-70; cons. lit. div. Nat. Endowment for Arts, Washington, 1973; lectr. USIS tour German univs., 1977, tour, Africa, 1978; asst. prof. Johns Hopkins U.; Bd. dirs. Balt. Theatre Project; co-founder Balt. Poet's Theatre. Poet-in-residence, NDEA grantee, Garrett County, Md., 1972; master poet, Md. Arts Council Artists-in-the-Schs. program, 1974-77; appeared in numerous poetry readings; books of poetry include Appearances, 1969, No Vacancies in Hell, 1973, The Follies, 1977, Young Men's Gold, 1978, The Book of Fortune, 1982; plays include Young Men's Gold, 1974; appeared in: Jenny and the Phoenix, 1977, The Gayety Burlesque, 1978, The Midnight Visitor, 1981. Recipient Robert Frost prize, 1969; Prix de Rome AAAL, 1977; Danforth Found. grantee, 1971; Nat. Endowment for Arts fellow, 1974. Fellow Am. Acad. in Rome; mem. Phi Beta Kappa. Address: Overlook/Viking Press 625 Madison Ave New York NY 10022

EPSTEIN, DAVID GUSTAV, educator, lawyer; b. Alexandria, La., Dec. 7, 1943; s. Isaac and Alice (Fried) E.; m. Diane Floca, Feb. 16, 1969; 1 son, Daniel Stewart. LL.B., U. Tex., 1966; LL.M., Harvard U., 1969. Bar: Tex. bar 1966, Ariz. bar 1967, Ark. bar 1979. Asst. prof. N.C. Sch. Law, 1970-74; prof. law U. Tex., 1974-79, Fulbright and Jaworski prof. law, 1982—; dean Sch. Law, U. Ark., 1979-82; of counsel Sheinfeld, Maley & Kay, Houston, 1983—. Author: Basic Uniform Commercial Code Teaching Materials, 1977, Cases and Materials on Debtors and Creditors, 1973, rev. 2d edit., 1978, Debtor Creditor Law in a Nutshell, 1973, 2d rev. edit., 1979. Mem. Nat. Bankruptcy Conf., ABA, Am. Law Inst., Ark. Bar Assn., Order of Coif. Democrat. Jewish. Office: Sch Law U Tex Austin TX 78705

EPSTEIN, DAVID MAYER, composer, conductor; b. N.Y.C., Oct. 3, 1930; s. Joshua S. and Elizabeth (Mayer) E.; m. Anne Louise Merrick, June 21, 1953; children: Eve Miriam, Beth Sara. A.B., Antioch Coll., 1952; M.Mus., New Eng. Conservatory Music, 1953; M.F.A., Brandeis U., 1954, Princeton U., 1956, Ph.D., 1968. Asst. editor, music critic Musical America, N.Y.C., 1956-57; asst. prof. music Antioch Coll., 1957-61, asso. prof., 1962; musical dir. Ednl. Broadcasting Corp., N.Y.C., 1962-64; assoc. prof. music MIT, Cambridge, 1965-69, prof., 1970—; vis. fellow Max-Planck Inst., Seewiesen, West Ger., 1980-81; vis. prof. U. Munich, 1980-81, U. Lisbon, 1980; guest condr. Hourel Orch. Philharm. de Paris, 1982, 84, Haifa Symphony Orch., 1979, 81. Guest condr., Berlin (Germany) Radio Orch., 1967, Czech Radio Orch., Pilsen, Czechslovakia, 1966, Cleve. Orch., 1961, N.Y.C. Center, 1966, N.J. Symphony, 1961, Bavarian Radio Symphony, 1973, Vienna Tonkuenstlerorchester, Israel Broadcasting Orch., 1971, Royal Philharmonic Orch., 1974, Am. Symphony Orch., 1978, Bamberg Symphony Orch., Orchestre de la Suisse Romande, 1981, Jerusalem Orch., 1982, others, also Antioch Shakespeare Festival, 1957; music dir., Harrisburg Symphony Orch., 1974-78; composer mus. scores for documentary films produced by UN, Nat. Ednl. TV, 1964-65; Dir., Youth Symphony Orch. N.Y., 1963-66; music dir., Worcester Orch., Worcester Festival, 1976-80; Author: Beyond Orpheus: Studies in Musical Structure, 1979; also articles in profl. jours. Bd. dirs. New Eng. Lyric Theatre, Adirondack Found. of Arts, Young Audiences Boston. Recipient Louisville Orch. award, Fromm Found. award, BMI award N.Y. State Council for Arts commn., 1973; Boston Symphony Orch. Young People's Commn., 1972; Rockefeller Fedn. grantee, 1971; Ford Found. rec. grantee, 1971, 76; ASCAP awardee, 1964—, Mass. Arts and Humanities Found., 1977; Kulas Found. fellow. Mem. ASCAP, Am. Soc. Univ. Composers (exec. com. 1967-69), Am. Symphony Orch. League (chmn. univ. orch. sect. 1960-62), Am. Fedn. Musicians, Am. Music Center, Internat. Soc. for Study of Time (exec. bd.). Office: Music Dept Mass Inst Tech Cambridge MA 02139 *Communication with colleagues, with audiences, and with the brilliant creative minds that have given us our repertoire makes music an immensely satisfying profession. It is a profession that also demands self-discipline and continual striving for the highest standards.*

EPSTEIN, DENA JULIA, librarian; b. Milw., Nov. 30, 1916; d. William Samson and Hilda Rita (Satt) Polacheck; m. Morton Batlan Epstein, Oct. 24, 1942; children—William Eliot, Suzanne Louise. B.A., U. Chgo., 1937; B.S. in L.S, U. Ill., 1939, M.A., 1943. Cataloger art and music U. Ill., Champaign, 1939-43; sr. music librarian Newark Pub. Library, 1943-45; music cataloger, reviser copyright cataloging div. Library of Congress, 1946-48; asst. music librarian U. Chgo., 1964—. Author: Music Publishing in Chicago Before 1871: The Firm of Root and Cady, 1858-1871, 1969, Sinful Tunes and Spirituals: Black Folk Music to the Civil War, 1977. Grantee Am. Council Learned Socs., 1970, Ill. Arts Council, 1970, Nat. Endowment Humanities, 1971, 73; recipient Chgo. Folklore prize, 1978, Francis Butler Simkins prize So. Hist. Assn., 1979. Mem. Am. Library Assn., Music Library Assn. (pres. 1977-78), Am. Musicol. Soc., Internat. Folk Music Council, Internat. Assn. Music Libraries, AAUW. Home: 5039 S Ellis Ave Chicago IL 60615 Office: Room 361 Library Univ Chicago Chicago IL 60637

EPSTEIN, EDWARD S., meteorologist; b. N.Y.C., Apr. 29, 1931; s. Herman and Julia E.; m. Alice Katzenstein, June 6, 1954; children: Debra, Harry, Nancy, William. A.B., Harvard U., 1951; M.B.A., Columbia U., 1953; M.S., Pa. State U., 1954, Ph.D., 1960. Lectr. U. Mich., 1959-61, asst. prof., 1961-63, asso. prof., 1964-68, prof., 1969-73, chmn. dept. atmospheric and oceanic sci., 1971-73; asso. adminstr. for environ. monitoring and predictions NOAA, 1973-77, acting asst. adminstr. for research and devel., 1977-78, dir. Nat Climate Program Office, Rockville, Md., 1978-81, chief Climate and Earth Scis. Lab., 1981—, acting dir. research and applications Nat. Environ. Satellite, Data and Info. Services, 1982—; bd. dirs. Univ. Corp. for Atmospheric Research, 1969-73. Editor: Jour. Applied Meteorology, 1971-73; contbr. articles to profl. jours. Served with USAF, 1953-57. Fellow Am. Meteorol. Soc. (councillor 1974-77), AAAS (chmn. sect. hydrospheric scis. 1980); mem. Am. Geophys. Union. Jewish. Home: 8216 Inverness Hollow Terr Potomac MD 20854 Office: Fed Office Bldg 4 Suitland MD 20233

EPSTEIN, ELENI SAKES (MRS. SIDNEY EPSTEIN), editor; b. Washington, May 17, 1925; d. Constantine and Aspasia (Economon) Sakes; m. Sidney Epstein, Mar. 30, 1957. Student, George Washington U., 1943-45, Columbia U., 1947. Copygirl, women's staff writer Washington Star, 1945-46, fashion editor, 1946-81. Recipient J.C. Penney Fashion Writing award U. Mo., 1961; citation Nat. Women's party, 1966; N.Y. Fashion Reporters award, 1972; Frany award, 1973; Woman of Year award Am. Legion post Washington; Silver Cross Royal Order Benevolence Royal Greek embassy, 1973; decorated Order Al Merito, Italy). Mem. Washington Fashion Group, Washington Press Club (sec. 1949-50), Am. Newspaper Women's Club (v.p. 1952-54). Greek Orthodox. Home: 2807 Cathedral Ave NW Washington DC 20008

EPSTEIN, EMANUEL, plant physiologist; b. Duisburg, Germany, Nov. 5, 1916; came to U.S., 1938, naturalized, 1946; s. Harry and Bertha (Lowe) E.; m. Hazel M. Leask, Nov. 26, 1943; children: Jared H. (dec.), Jonathan H. B.S., U. Calif.-Davis, 1940, M.S., 1941; Ph.D., U. Calif.-Berkeley, 1950. Plant physiologist Dept. Agr., Beltsville, Md., 1950-58; lectr., assoc. plant physiologist U. Calif., Davis, 1958-65, prof. plant nutrition, plant physiologist, 1965—, prof. botany, 1974—; cons. to govt. and pvt. agys. Author: Mineral Nutrition of Plants: Principles and Perspectives, 1972; editorial bd.: Plant Physiology, 1962-71, 76—, CRC Handbook Series in Nutrition and Food, 1975—, The Biosaline Concept: An Approach to the Utilization of Underexploited Resources, 1978, Plant Sci. Letters, 1981—, Advances in Plant Nutrition, 1981—. Served with U.S. Army, 1943-46. Recipient Gold medal Pisa (Italy) U., 1962; Guggenheim fellow, 1958; Fulbright sr. research scholar, 1965-66, 74-75. Fellow AAAS; mem. Nat. Acad. Scis., Am. Soc. Plant Physiologists, Scandinavian Soc. Plant Physiology, Australian Soc. Plant Physiologists, Am. Inst. Biol. Scis., Crop Sci. Soc. Am., Am. Soc. Agronomy, Common Cause, Save-the-Redwoods League, Sierra Club, Sigma Xi. Club: U. Calif. at Davis Faculty. Research, publs. on ion transport in plants, mineral nutrition and salt relations of plants, salt tolerant crops. Office: Land Air and Water Resources U Calif Davis CA 95616

EPSTEIN, FRANKLIN HAROLD, educator, physician; b. Bklyn., May 5, 1924; s. Max and Florence (Geduld) E.; m. Sherrie Spivack, Aug. 12, 1951; children: Mark, Ann, Sara, Jonathan. B.A., Bklyn. Coll., 1944; M.D., Yale U., 1947. Diplomate: Am. Bd. Internal Medicine (chmn. subsplty. bd. in nephrology 1969-72). Asst. prof. medicine Yale U., 1954-59, assoc. prof., 1959-66, prof. medicine, 1966-72, chief, div. metabolism, 1965-72; prof. medicine Harvard U., 1972—, H.L. Blumgart prof. medicine, W. Applebaum prof. medicine; dir. Thorndike Meml. Lab., Boston City Hosp., 1972; physician-in-chief Beth Israel Hosp., 1973-80, dir. renal div., 1980—; Macy Found. fellow and vis. scientist Oxford (Eng.) U., 1980-81; Cons. U.S. Army Surgeon Gen., 1964—; mem. USPHS (metabolism study sect.), 1962-66, research career award, 1964; v.p. Mt. Desert Island Biol. Lab., 1981—. Assoc. editor: Jour. Clin. Investigation, 1957-62; Contbr. papers, book chpts. on renal physiology, disease of kidneys. Served to capt. M.C. AUS, 1950-53. Mem. Am. Soc. Clin. Investigation (v.p. 1970), Assn. Am. Physicians, Interurban Clin. Club, Sigma Xi, Alpha Omega Alpha. Jewish. Home: 294 Buckminster Rd Brookline MA 02146 Office: 330 Brookline Ave Boston MA 02215

EPSTEIN, GARY MARVIN, lawyer; b. Bklyn., Nov. 28, 1946; s. Arthur and Juliett (Winick) E.; m. Jeralyn Needel, June 29, 1969; children: Daniel, Deborah. B.S.E.E., Lehigh U., 1968; J.D., Harvard U., 1971. Engr. Gordon Engring. Co., Wakefield, Mass., 1967-70; assoc. firm. Arent, Fox, Kinter, Plotkin & Kahn, Washington, 1971-79, ptnr., 1979-81; chief Common Carrier Bur. FCC, Washington, 1981-83; ptnr. Latham, Watkins & Hills, Washington, 1983—. Mem. ABA, Fed. Bar Assn., D.C. Bar Assn., Eta Kappa Nu, Tau Beta Pi. Home: 5706 Ogden Rd Bethesda MD 20816 Office: FCC 1919 M St Washington DC 20554

EPSTEIN, HENRY DAVID, electronics company executive; b. Frankfurt, Germany, Apr. 5, 1927; came to U.S., 1940, naturalized, 1945; s. Julius S. and Lola C. (Heilbronner) E.; m. Henny Wenkart, Sept. 6, 1952; children: Jonathan, Heitzi, Ari. Sc.B. Engring., Brown U., 1948; S.M. (Baker scholar), Harvard U., 1950. Mgr. devel. engring. Metal & Controls Corp., Attleboro, Mass., 1952-59; mgr. precision controls dept. Tex. Instruments, Attleboro, 1959-67; mgr. div. control products, 1967-77, asst. v.p., 1969-77; sr. group v.p. Loral Corp., N.Y.C., 1977—; dir. N.E. Paper Converting Corp., Am. Beryllium Co., Corvus Corp. Served with Signal Corps U.S. Army, 1945-46. Fellow IEEE; mem. Friends of Harvard Hillel (treas.), Sigma Xi, Tau Beta Pi. Patentee elec. controls, automotive safety, pollution control. Home: 4 Shady Hill Sq Cambridge MA 02138 Office: 600 3d Ave New York NY 10016

EPSTEIN, HOWARD MICHAEL, pub. co. exec.; b. N.Y.C., Apr. 27, 1927; s. Samuel and Florence Leah (Gilbert) E.; m. Cynthia Paula Fuchs, July 3, 1954; 1 son, Alexander Maxim. B.A., Queens Coll.; certificate, Inst. d'Etudes Politiques, U. Paris, 1952; postgrad., U. Chgo., 1955-56. Wire news editor Xenia (Ohio) Gazette, 1952-54; Ohio corr. AP, UP, INS, 1952-54; fgn. news editor Facts on File Publs., N.Y.C., 1958-68, mng. editor, 1963-68, exec. v.p., 1968-75, pres., 1975—. Author: Revolt in the Congo, 1964. Active N.Y. Democratic Clubs, 1966-68. Served with USN, 1945-46. Office: 460 Park Ave S New York NY 10016

EPSTEIN, JASON, publishing co. exec.; b. Cambridge, Mass., Aug. 25, 1928; s. Robert and Gladys (Shapiro) E.; children—Jacob, Helen. B.A., Columbia, 1949, M.A., 1950. Editor Doubleday & Co., 1951-58; v.p., editorial dir. Random House, Inc., N.Y.C., 1958—; dir. N.Y. Rev. Books, Inc.; cons. Children's TV Workshop. Author: The Great Conspiracy Trial, 1970; co-author: Easthampton, a history and guide, 1975. Bd. dirs. Central Park Conservancy; dir., treas. Lit. Classics U.S. Mem. Phi Beta Kappa. Home: Box 1143 Sag Harbor NY 11963 Office: 201 E 50th St New York NY 10022

EPSTEIN, JEREMIAH FAIN, anthropologist, educator; b. N.Y.C., Feb. 14, 1924; s. Joseph and Carol (Fain) E.; (div.)children—Anne, Louise, Suzanne. B.S. in Agr, U. Ill., 1949, M.A. in Anthropology, 1951; Ph.D., U. Pa., 1957. Lectr. Hunter Coll., N.Y.C., 1954-58; research scientist anthropology U. Tex., Austin, 1958-60, mem. faculty, 1958—, prof. anthropology, 1970—; fieldwork in, Mex., Belize, Honduras, France, U.S. Contbr. articles to profl. jours. Served with AUS, 1942-45. Decorated Purple Heart; grantee NSF, 1963, 64, Wenner Gren Found., 1961, U. Tex. Inst. Latin Am. Studies, 1963, 75; Fulbright-Hays fellow, 1964. Mem. Am. Anthrop. Assn., Soc. Am. Archaeology, AAAS, Soc. Mexicana Anthropologia. Office: Dept Anthropology U Tex Austin TX 78712 *

EPSTEIN, JOHN HOWARD, dermatologist; b. San Francisco, Dec. 29, 1926; s. Norman Neman and Gertrude (Hirsch) E.; m. Alice Thompson, Nov. 1953; children: Norman H., Janice A., Beverly A. B.A., U. Calif., Berkeley, 1949, M.D., 1942; M.S., U. Minn., 1956. Diplomate: Am. Bd. Dermatology (dir. 1974—, pres. 1981—). Intern Stanford U. Med. Center, 1952-53; resident in dermatology Mayo

Clinic, Rochester, Minn., 1953-56; practice medicine specializing in dermatology, San Francisco, 1956—; chief dermatology Mt. Zion Hosp., 1970-80; clin. prof. U. Calif. Med. Sch., San Francisco, 1972—; cons. Letterman Army Med. Center, U.S. Naval Hosp., San Diego. Author articles in field.; Chief editor: Archives of Dermatology, 1973-78; asst. editor: Jour. Am. Acad. Dermatology, 1978—. Served with USNR, 1944-46. Fellow A.C.P.; mem. Am. Acad. Dermatology (pres. 1981-82, Silver award for exhibit 1962, Gold award 1969), Soc. Investigative Dermatology (v.p. 1979-80), Am. Dermatol. Assn. (bd. dirs. 1983—), Pacific Dermatol. Assn., San Francisco Dermatol. Soc. (pres. 1963-64), Am. Soc. Photobiology (councilor 1983—). Office: 450 Sutter St Suite 1306 San Francisco CA 94108

EPSTEIN, JOSEPH, publishing company executive; b. Chgo., Jan. 9, 1937; s. Maurice and Belle (Abrams) E.; m. Barbara Maher, Feb. 27, 1976; children: Mark, Burton. A.B., U. Chgo., 1959. Editor Am. Scholar, Washington, 1975—; vis. lectr. Northwestern U., Evanston, Ill., 1974—. Author: Divorced in America, 1975, Familiar Territory, 1980, Ambition, 1981, The Middle of My Tether, 1983, Plausible Prejudices, 1985; editor: Masters, 1981. Served with U.S. Army, 1958-60. Jewish. Office: American Scholar 1811 Q St NW Washington DC 20009

EPSTEIN, JOSEPH, educator; b. N.Y.C., Jan. 19, 1917; s. Isador and Ida (Snofsky) E.; m. Lucille Goldberger, June 22, 1940; children—Joshua Morris, Samuel David. B.S., Coll. City N.Y., 1939; Ph.D., Columbia, 1951; M.A. (hon.), Amherst Coll., 1961. Physicist research and devel. U.S. Army Signal Corps. Labs., 1942-44, Fed. Telephone & Radio Corp., Newark, 1944-46; from lectr. to asst. prof. Columbia, 1946-51; faculty Amherst (Mass.) Coll., 1952-71, prof. philosophy, 1961-71, Crosby prof. philosophy, 1976; vis. prof. philosophy Yale, 1966-67; mem. consulente aggregato Centro Superiore di Logica e Scienze Comparate, Bologna, Italy, 1972—. Editor: Alexandrian Editions, 1960, Rene Descartes: A Discourse on Method and Other Works, 1965, (with Gail Kennedy) The Process of Philosophy, 1967; Contbr. articles to profl. jours. Rockefeller Found. grantee, 1958; Ford Humanities grantee, 1972. Mem. Am. Philos. Assn., Symbolic Logic Assn., Am. Assn. Physics Tchrs., AAAS, AAUP, Mind Assn., Sigma Xi. Patentee in field. Home: 148 Lincoln Ave Amherst MA 01002

EPSTEIN, LAURA, social work educator, consultant; b. Chgo., Oct. 31, 1914; d. Ellik and Rose (Kwatnez) E. A.M., U. Chgo., 1936. Cert. Acad. Cert. Social Workers. Field instr. social work U. Chgo., 1967-70, asst. prof., 1970-72, assoc. prof., 1972-76, prof., 1976—; vis. prof. Wilfred Laurier U., Waterloo, Ont., Can., 1980-82; cons. W. Va. Dept. Social Welfare, Charleston, 1982, Villemarie Community Service, Montreal, Que., Can., 1982. Author: Helping People: The Task Centered Approach, 1980, (with William J. Reid) Task Centered Casework, 1972; editor: Task Centered Practice, 1977. Mem. Council on Social Work Edn. (del. 1980-83), Nat. Assn. Social Workers. Jewish. Home: 5530 S Shore Dr Chicago IL 60637 Office: U Chgo 969 E 60th St Chicago IL 60637

EPSTEIN, LEON DAVID, educator; b. Milw., May 29, 1919; s. Harry Aaron and Anna (LeKachman) E.; m. Shirley Galewitz, Jan. 12, 1947. B.A., U. Wis., 1940, M.A., 1941; Ph.D., U. Chgo., 1948; D.Litt. (hon.), U. Warwick, Eng., 1980. Jr., also asst. economist Nat. Resources Planning Bd., 1941-42; asst. prof. polit. sci. U. Oreg., 1947-48; faculty U. Wis., Madison, 1948—, prof. polit. sci., 1954—, Bascom prof., 1973-80, Hilldale prof., 1980—; chmn. dept., 1960-63; dean Coll. Letters and Sci., 1965-69; fellow Center for Advanced Study in Behavioral Scis., 1970-71. Author: Britain-Uneasy Ally, 1954, Politics in Wisconsin, 1958, British Politics in the Suez Crisis, 1964, Political Parties in Western Democracies, 1967, 2d edit., 1980, Governing the University, 1974; also articles. Served to capt. AUS, 1942-46. Fellow Am. Acad. Arts and Scis.; mem. Am. Polit. Sci. Assn. (pres. 1978-79), AAUP, Midwest Polit. Sci. Assn. (pres. 1971-72). Home: 2806 Ridge Rd Madison WI 53705

EPSTEIN, LEON JOSEPH, psychiatrist; b. Jersey City, June 7, 1917; s. Irving and Sara (Pomerantz) E.; children: Lisa, David. A.B., Vanderbilt U., 1937, M.A., 1938; Ph.D., Peabody Coll., 1941; M.D., U. Tenn., 1949. Intern Wesley Meml. Hosp., Chgo., 1950; resident in psychiatry St. Elizabeths Hosp., Washington, 1951-54, staff psychiatrist, 1954-56; dep. dir. Calif. Dept. Mental Hygiene, Sacramento, 1956-61; prof. psychiatry, asso. dir. Langley Porter Inst. U. Calif. Sch. Medicine, San Francisco, 1961—. Author books and articles in psychogerontology and psychopharmacology. Mem. San Francisco Crime Commn., 1969-71. Served to lt. comdr. USN, 1941-46. Recipient Sullivan award Peabody Coll., 1941; William A. White award St. Elizabeths Hosp., 1952, 53; J. Elliott Royer award U. Calif., 1976. Mem. Am. Coll. Psychiatry, Am. Coll. Neuropsychopharmacology, Am. Psychiat. Assn., Am. Psychopath. Assn., Gerontol. Soc. Jewish. Home: 2251 Steiner St San Francisco CA 94115 Office: 401 Parnassus Ave San Francisco CA 94143

EPSTEIN, LIONEL CHARLES, lawyer; b. N.Y.C., Apr. 7, 1924; s. David and Carrie (Roth) E.; m. Sarah Louise Gamble, June 10, 1951 (div. Apr. 12, 1983); children: David Bradley, James Roth, Richard Aldis, Miles Owen, Sarah Carianne. B.A., NYU, 1947; LL.B., Harvard U., 1950. With office gen. counsel U.S. Navy Dept., 1950-52; tax div. U.S. Justice Dept., 1952-57; mem. firms Ginsburg & Leventhal, 1957-67, Epstein, Friedman, Duncan & Medalie, Washington, 1967-74, Jones, Day, Reavis & Pogue, 1975—; spl. asst. to R. Sargent Shriver Peace Corps, 1962; Bd. dirs. Expt. in Internat. Living, Mus. Modern Art (N.Y.C.) Com. on Illustrated Books and Prints, Washington Print Club. Author art exhbn. catalogs. Served with inf. AUS, 1942-45. Decorated Purple Heart, knight's cross 1st class Order St. Olav, Norway). Mem. Am. Bar Assn. Clubs: Lawyers (founding mem.), Internat., 1925 F St., Harvard. Home: 700 New Hampshire Ave NW Washington DC 20037 Office: 1735 Eye St NW Washington DC 20036

EPSTEIN, LOUISE RALPH, food company executive; b. Sharon, Pa., Jan. 28, 1926; s. Samuel W. and Bess (Rosenblu) E.; m. Marlene Lurie, Aug. 13, 1950; children: Richard, Susan, Georgia. B.A., U. Rochester, 1949. Pres. Golden Dawn Foods, Inc., Sharon, until 1983; gen. mgr. wholesale div. P.J. Schmitt Co., Sharon, 1983—; dir. McDowell Nat. Bank, Sharon, Mercer County br. Pa. Economy League, 1983; dir., pres. Harry M. Pollock Co., Kittanning, Pa., 1979—. Trustee Buhl Trustees, Sharon, 1983; dir. Mercer County United Way, Sharon, 1983, past. pres.; mem. Pa. State Adv. Bd., Sharon, 1983. Served with Signal Corps. U.S. Army, 1943-46. Club: Sharon Country (dir.). Office: Peter J Schmitt Food Distbn Center 385 Shenango Ave Sharon PA 16146

EPSTEIN, MAX, electrical engineering educator; b. Lodz, Poland, Feb. 5, 1925; came to U.S., 1952, naturalized, 1958; s. Israel and Dola (Grad) E.; m. Judith R. Slotnikoff, Sept. 10, 1963; children—Michael, David, Deborah. B.S., Israel Inst. Tech., 1952; M.S., Ill. Inst. Tech., 1955, Ph.D., 1963. Elec. engr. Admiral Corp., Chgo., 1953-54; instr., asso. research engr. Ill. Inst. Tech., Chgo., 1954-58; research engr., then sr. research engr. Research Inst., 1958-67; prof. elec. engring., computer sci. and biomed. engring. Northwestern U., Evanston, Ill., 1967—. Sr. mem. IEEE; mem. Am. Phys. Soc., Optical Soc. Am., AAUP. Jewish. Office: Tech Inst Northwestern U Evanston IL 60201

EPSTEIN, NORMAN, chem. engr.; b. Montreal, Que., Can., Dec. 6, 1923; s. Louis and Leah E.; m. Marilyn Golub, Dec. 26, 1947; children—Michael, Rachel, Eric. B.Engring., McGill U., 1945, M.Engring., 1946; D.Engring. Sci., N.Y. U., 1953. Instr. chem. engring. dept. McGill U., Montreal, 1946-48; mem. faculty dept. chem. engring. U. B.C., Vancouver, 1951—, prof. chem. engring., 1965—; Mem. Com. of 100, Cambridge, Eng., 1961-62; bd. dirs. New Sch., Vancouver, 1963, 65. Author: (with Kishan B. Mathur) Spouted Beds, 1974. Killam sr. fellow, 1975-76. Fellow Chem. Inst. Can., Am. Inst. Chem. Engrs.; mem. Canadian Soc. Chem. Engring. (pres. 1979-80), Assn. Profl. Engrs. Province B.C., Canadian Sci. Pollution and Environ. Control Soc., Canadian Coalition Nuclear Responsibility, B.C. Civil Liberties Assn., Amnesty Internat. Home: 901-2233 Allison Rd Vancouver BC V6T 1T7 Canada Office: Dept Chem Engring U BC Vancouver BC V6T 1W5 Canada

EPSTEIN, RAYMOND, engring. and archtl. exec.; b. Chgo., Jan. 12, 1918; s. Abraham and Janet (Rabinowitz) E.; m. Betty Jadwin, Apr. 7, 1940; children: Gail, David, Norman, Harriet. Student, Mass. Inst. Tech., 1934-36; B.S., U. Ill., 1938. Registered architect; registered profl. engr. With A. Epstein & Sons Internat., Inc., Chgo., 1938—, chmn. bd., 1961-83, chmn. exec. com., 1983—; dir. Ampal-Am. Israel Corp., ARA Services, Inc. Past pres. Young Men's Jewish Council, Jewish Welfare Fund Met. Chgo.; dir. United Israel Appeal; mem. housing com. Mayor's Commn. Sr. Citizens; past pres. Nat. Council Jewish Fedn. and Welfare Funds, Inc.; past chmn. bd. dirs. Jewish United Fund; mem. exec. com. Am. Jewish Joint Distbn. Com.; bd. govs. Jewish Agy.; Trustee Chgo. Med. Sch.; mem. citizens bd. Loyola U.; life dir. Mt. Sinai Med. Research Found.; v.p., nat. bd. Jewish Telegraphic Agy.; bd. dirs. United Jewish Appeal; exec. com. Meml. for Jewish Culture; past chmn. public affairs com., past chmn. bd. gen. campaign Jewish United Fund of Met. Chgo.; past sec.-treas. Nat. Jewish Community Relations Adv. Council; mem. exec. com. Am. Israel Public Affairs Com.; past treas., bd. dirs. Welfare Council Met. Chgo.; bd. dirs. Chgo. Bldg. Congress; past sec., bd. dirs. Jewish Fedn. Met. Chgo. Decorated comdr. Legion of Honor, Ivory Coast; recipient Julius Rosenwald Meml. award J.F.C., Disting. Alumnus award U. Ill. Mem. Nat. Soc. Profl. Engrs., Soc. Civil Engrs. France, ASCE, Soc. Am. Registered Architects, Am. Concrete Inst., Western Soc. Engrs., Assn. Engrs. and Architects in Israel, French Engrs. in the U.S., Inc., Pi Lambda Phi. Clubs: Standard (past bd. trustee), Illini, M.I.T., Caxton (Chgo.). Home: 4950 S Chicago Beach Dr Chicago IL 60615 Office: 600 W Fulton St Chicago IL 60606

EPSTEIN, RICHARD LEWIS, lawyer, association executive; b. N.Y.C., Apr. 26, 1930; s. Harry Browdy and Sarah (Bussell) E.; children: Elizabeth Bussell, Sarah Denonn. B.A. cum laude, Amherst Coll., 1951; LL.B., Yale U., 1954. Bar: U.S. Supreme Ct. 1961, Ill. 1973, N.Y 1973. Assoc. firm Harris, Beach & Wilcox, Rochester, N.Y., 1954-63, partner, 1963-72; partner firm Sonnenschein Carlin Nath and Rosenthal, Chgo., 1973-77; group v.p. law Am. Hosp. Assn., Chgo., 1977-80, sr. v.p., gen. counsel, 1981—; mem. Fed. Services Impasses Panel, 1970-78; cons. labor relations Dept. State, 1972-78; mgmt. rep. Health Industry Wage Adv. Panel Cost of Living Council, 1973-75. Contbr. articles on health law and labor law to profl. jours.; mem. editorial bd.: Employee Relations Law Jour, 1975—. Mem. Ill. Gov.'s Employee Relations Council, 1974—; mem. nat. panel on edn. Am. Arbitration Assn., 1974—; Bd. advisors Rochester St. Mary's Hosp., 1967-72; pres. Planned Parenthood of Rochester and Monroe County, 1971. Recipient Leroy Snyder Meml. award Rochester Jaycees, 1965; named to Outstanding Young Men in Am. U.S. Jaycees, 1965. Mem. Am. Bar Assn., Am. Acad. Hosp. Attys. (pres. 1975-76), Rochester C. of C. (trustee 1969-73). Clubs: Metropolitan, Carlton (Chgo.); Genesee Valley, Rochester Yacht, Tennis of Rochester (Rochester). Home: 155 Harbor Dr Chicago IL 60601 Office: Am Hosp Assn 840 N Lake Shore Dr Chicago IL 60611

EPSTEIN, ROBERT MARVIN, anesthesiologist, educator; b. N.Y.C., Mar. 10, 1928; s. Nathan Batlan and Rebecca (Dickes) E.; m. Lillian Ray Cohen, Dec. 31, 1950; children: Judith Susan, Neal Myron, Charles Benjamin. B.S. with distinction, U. Mich., 1947, M.D. cum laude, 1951. Diplomate: Am. Bd. Anesthesiology (dir. 1972—, pres. 1979-80). Intern U. Mich. Hosp., 1951-52; resident in anesthesiology Presbyterian Hosp., N.Y.C., 1952-53, 55-56; instr. in anesthesiology and fellow in medicine Columbia U., 1956-57; asso., 1957-59, asst. prof., anesthesiology, 1959-65, asso. prof., 1965-70, prof., 1970-72; Alumni prof., chmn. anesthesiology U. Va., 1972—; mem. anesthesiology tng. com. Nat. Inst. Gen. Med. Scis., NIH, 1966-69; mem. com. on anesthesia NRC, 1970-71; mem. Nat. Bd. Med. Examiners, 1982—. Contbr. numerous articles to profl. jours.; editor: Anesthesiology, 1974-79. Bd. dirs., sec. U. Va. Health Services Found., 1980—. Served with M.C. U.S. Army, 1953-55. Guggenheim fellow Oxford (Eng.) U., 1966-67; N.Y. Heart Assn. fellow, 1956-57. Fellow Faculty of Anesthetists, Royal Coll. Surgeons (Eng.); mem. AAAS, Am. Physiol. Soc., Am. Soc. Anesthesiologists, Am. Soc. Pharmacology and Exptl. Therapeutics, Anaesthetic Research Soc. (U.K.), Assn. Univ. Anesthetists (pres. 1974-75), Phi Beta Kappa, Sigma Xi, Alpha Omega Alpha. Office: U Va Med Center Charlottesville VA 22908

EPSTEIN, SAMUEL STANLEY, physician, pathologist, toxicologist, environmentalist, educator; b. Middlesborough, Eng., Apr. 13, 1926; s. Isidore and Gertrude (Joseph) E.; m. Catherine Epstein; children: Mark, Julian, Emily. B.Sc., London (Eng.) U., 1947, M.B.B.S., 1950, diploma in Tropical Medicine and Hygiene, 1952, diploma in Pathology, 1954, M.D., 1958. Diplomate: Am. Bd. Microbiology. Demonstrator morbid anatomy Guys Hosp., London, 1950; house physician St. Johns Hosp., London, 1951; lectr. pathology and bacteriology Inst. Laryngology and Otology, U. London, 1955-58; Brit. Empire Cancer Campaign research fellow with Chester Beatty Cancer Research Inst.; also tumor pathologist Hosp. Sick Children, London, 1958-60; cons. pathology Meml. Hosp., Peterborough, Eng., 1960; research assoc. Children's Hosp. Med. Center and Children's Cancer Research Found., Inc., Boston, 1961-71; chief labs. carcinogenesis and environ. toxicology, applied microbiology and histology Children's Cancer Research Found., Inc., 1961-71, sr. research assoc. pathology, 1962-71, Harvard Med. Sch., Boston, 1962-71; Swetland prof. environ. health and human ecology Case Western Res. U. Sch. Medicine, Cleve., 1971-76; prof. occupational and environ. medicine Sch. Pub. Health, Abraham Lincoln Sch. Medicine, U. Ill. Med. Center, Chgo., 1976—; dir. Environ. Health Resource Center of State of Ill., 1978—; cons. com. on pub. works U.S. Senate, 1970-74, Center for Studies Narcotic and Drug Abuse, Nat. Inst. Mental Health, 1970; panel on polycyclic organic matter Nat. Acad. Scis.-NRC, 1970, Pesticide Bd. Mass., 1970, U.S. Senate sub-com. on exec. reorgn. and govt. research, com. on govt. ops., 1971, U.S. Ho. of Reps. com. on pub. works, 1973; adviser Environ. Def. Fund, Environ. Health Programs, Inc., Washington, 1970. Author: (with M. Legator) Mutagenicity of Pesticides, 1971, Chronic Non-Psychiatric Hazards Drugs of Abuse, 1971, (with D. Grundy) The Legislation of Product Safety: Consumer Health and Product Hazards, 2 vols, 1974, The Politics of Cancer, 1979, Hazardous Waste in America, 1982; also 250 sci. articles. Chairperson Commn. for Advancement Pub. Interest Orgn., Washington, 1974; pres. Rachel Carson Trust, Washington, 1974; mem. nat. air quality adv. com. EPA, 1971-75, mem. environ. health adv. com., 1975. Served with M.C. Royal Army, 1952-55. Recipient Montefiore Gold medal in tropical medicine, 1953, Ronald Martin prize in mil. surgery, 1953, Achievement award Soc. Toxicology, 1969. Fellow Royal Soc. Health, N.Y. Acad. Scis.; mem. Soc. Clin. Pathologists, Soc. Pathology and Bacteriology, Soc. Gen. Microbiology, Soc. Protozoologists, Air Pollution Control Assn. (com. chmn.), Am. Assn. Pathologists and Bacteriologists, Am. Soc. Exptl. Pathology, Am. Assn. Cancer Research, Soc. Toxicology, Environ. Mutagen Soc. (exec. sec. 1970-73), Soc. for Occupational and Environ. Health (pres.). Home: 860 N Lake Shore Dr Apt 25M Chicago IL 60611

EPSTEIN, SEYMOUR, author; b. N.Y.C., Dec. 2, 1917; s. Joseph and Jenny (Pomerantz) E.; m. Miriam Kligman, May 5, 1956; children—Alan, Paul. Student, Coll. City N.Y., 1937-38, N.Y. U., 1938-39. Worked at various jobs, to 1960; tchr. creative writing New Sch. Social Research, N.Y.C., 1963—; now prof. U. Denver. Author: Pillar of Salt, 1960, The Successor, 1961, Best Short Stories of 1962, Leah, 1964, Short Story 1, Caught in That Music, 1967, The Dream Museum, 1971, Looking for Fred Schmidt, 1973, Love Affair, 1979; contbr. short stories to popular mags. Served with USAAF, 1942-45; ETO. Recipient Edward Lewis Wallant Meml. Book award for Leah, 1964; Guggenheim fellow, 1965. Home: 3205 S Saint Paul St Denver CO 80210

EPSTEIN, SIDNEY, engineer, architect; b. Chgo., 1923; children: Donna Epstein Barrows, Laurie E. Lawton; stepchildren: Mary Rosenberg Kaltman, Ann Rosenberg Rakoff. B.S. in Civil Engring. with high honors, U. Ill., 1943. Chmn. bd., dir. A. Epstein & Sons Internat., Inc., Chgo.; dir. Amal. Trust & Savs. Bank, C. Trustee Northwestern Mut. Life Ins. Co.; Chmn. Chgo. Youth Centers; chmn. bd. trustees Michael Reese Hosp. and Med. Center; former mem. vis. com. U. Chgo.; bd. dirs. Lyric Opera Chgo.; trustee Orchestral Assn. Chgo. Mem. Polish-U.S. Econ. Council, Romanian-U.S. Econ. Council, Sigma Xi, Tau Beta Pi, Sigma Tau, Phi Kappa Phi, Phi Eta Sigma. Club: Standard (Chgo.) (past pres.). Office: 600 W Fulton St Chicago IL 60606

EPSTEIN, SIDNEY, editor; b. Wilmington, Del., Oct. 11, 1920; s. Abraham and Ida (Kelrick) E.; m. Eleni Sakes, Mar. 30, 1957; 1 dau., Diane. Student, George Washington U., 1937-41. With Washington Herald, 1937-54; city editor Washington Times-Herald, 1952-54, Washington Star, 1958-68, asst. mng. editor, 1968-74, mng. editor, 1974-78, exec. editor, 1978-81, assoc. pub. and editor, 1981—, also dir. Served to capt. USMCR, 1942-46. Home: 2807 Cathedral Ave NW Washington DC 20008

EPSTEIN, WILAM GELLER, advertising agency executive; b. b., N.Y.C., Jan. 6, 1946; d. Jack R. and Dorothy (Brill) Geller; m. Jeffrey L. Epstein, Oct. 27, 1968; 1 dau., Jill. Student, Bernard Baruch Sch. Bus., 1963-64, New Sch. for Social Research, 1964-65. Asst. planner Batten, Barton, Durstine & Osborne, N.Y.C., 1965-66; planner West Weir & Bartel, N.Y.C., 1966-68, Ogilvy & Mather, 1968-76, asst. media dir., 1976-79, v.p., 1976-79, sr. v.p., assoc. media dir., 1979—; dir. Bus. Pub.s Assn., N.Y.C., 1982—. Bd. dirs. Jewish Guild for Blind, N.Y.C., 1974-79. Office: Ogilvy and Mather 2 E 48th St New York NY 10028

EPSTEIN, WILLIAM, experimental psychologist; b. N.Y.C., Nov. 23, 1931; s. Jacob and Sarah (Kaplan) E.; m. Arlene Rita Cohen, Mar. 25, 1956; children: Sarah Ann, Edith Lynn. B.A., NYU, 1955; M.A., New Sch. Social Research, 1957, Ph.D., 1959. Asst. prof. psychology U. Kans., 1959-68, asso. prof., 1962-65, prof., 1965-68; prof. psychology U. Wis.-Madison, 1968—, chmn. dept., 1975-79; vis. prof. Cambridge (Eng.) U., 1972-73; Fulbright research fellow and vis. prof. Delhi (India) U., 1981-82. Author: Varieties of Perceptual Learning, 1967, (with F.C. Shontz) Psychology in Progress, 1971, Stability and Constancy in Visual Perception, 1977; Cons. editor: Perception and Psychophysics, 1971-82; editor: Jour. Exptl. Psychology: Human Perception and Performance, 1982—. NSF sr. postdoctoral fellow U. Uppsala, Sweden, 1966-67; NIMH grantee, 1959—. Mem. Am. Psychol. Assn., AAAS, Psychonomic Soc., Sigma Xi. Office: Psychology Bldg Univ of Wis Madison WI 53706

EPSTEIN, WILLIAM LOUIS, educator, physician; b. Cleve., Sept. 6, 1925; s. Norman N. and Gertrude (Hirsch) E.; m. Joan Goldman, Jan. 29, 1954; children—Wendy, Steven. A.B., U. Calif., Berkeley, 1949, M.D., 1952. Mem. faculty U. Calif., San Francisco, 1957—, asso. prof. div. dermatology, 1963-69, dir. dermatol. research, 1957-70, acting chmn. div. dermatology, 1966-69, chmn. dept. dermatology, 1970—; cons. dermatology Outpatient Dept.; cons. various hosps. Calif. Dept. Public Health; cons. Food and Drug Adminstrn., Washington, 1972—; dir. div. research Nat. Program Dermatology, 1970-73; Dohi lectr., Tokyo, 1982. Mem. AAAS, AMA, Am. Acad. Dermatology and Syph., Pacific Dermatologic Assn., Am. Fedn. Clin. Research, Soc. Investigative Dermatology (bd. dirs.), Am. Dermatol. Assn., Assn. Profs. Dermatology, Phi Beta Kappa, Sigma Xi. Home: 498 Sea Cliff San Francisco CA 94121

EPSTEIN, WOLFGANG, biochemist, educator; b. Breslau, Germany, May 7, 1931; came to U.S., 1936, naturalized, 1943; s. Stephan and Elsbeth (Lauinger) E.; m. Edna Selan, June 12, 1961; children: Matthew, Ezra, Tanya. B.A. with high honors, Swarthmore Coll., 1951; M.D., U. Minn., 1955. Postdoctoral fellow in physiology U. Minn., Mpls., 1959-60; postdoctoral fellow Pasteur Inst., Paris., 1963-65; postdoctoral fellow in biophysics Harvard Med. Sch., 1961-63, research asso., then asso. in biophysics, 1965-67; asst. prof. biochemistry U. Chgo., 1967-73, asso. prof., 1973-79, prof., 1979—, chmn. com. on genetics, 1976—. Served with M.C. U.S. Army, 1957-59. Mem. Am. Soc. Biol. Chemists, Am. Soc. for Microbiology, Biophys. Soc., AAAS. Home: 1120 E 50th St Chicago IL 60615 Office: 920 E 58th St Chicago IL 60637

EPTON, BERNARD EDWARD, lawyer; b. Chgo., Aug. 25, 1921; s. Arthur I. and Rose (Goldstein) E.; m. Audrey Issett, June 8, 1945; children: Teri Lynn, Jeffrey David, Mark Richard, Dale Susan. Student, U. Chgo., 1938-39, Northwestern U., 1939-40; student, DePaul U., 1947. Bar: Ill. bar 1947. Since practiced in, Chgo.; partner firm A.I. Epton & Sons, 1941-47, Epton, Mullin, Segal & Druth, Ltd., 1947—; mem. Ill. Gen. Assembly from 24th Dist., 1969-82; chmn. ins. com.; dir. Pemcor, Inc. Mem. South Shore O'Keefe Conservation Community Council, 1960-66; mem. Jewish Bd. Edn., 1965-70; past pres. Nat. Conf. Ins. Legislators; chmn. Ill. Ins. Study Commn., 1972-82; mem. Lloyds of London; bd. dirs., v.p. Jane Dent Home Aged Negros, 1961—; bd. dirs. Jewish Community Centers Chgo.; trustee Coll. Jewish Studies; mem. pres.'s council St. Xavier Coll.; mem. estate planning council DePaul U.; Republican candidate for mayor, Chgo., 1983. Served to capt. USAAF, 1942-45; ETO. Decorated D.F.C. with oak leaf cluster, Air medal with three oak leaf clusters. Mem. Ill., Chgo. bar assns., Decalogue Soc. Lawyers (bd. dirs. 1949, pres. 1961-62), Fedn. Ins. Counsel, Trial Lawyers Club, Am. Legion, Air Force Assn. (bd. dirs. 1947-50), South Shore C. of C. (dir., counsel 1953—, pres. 1959-61), Mil. Order World Wars (vice comdr.), Chgo. Hist. Soc. (life), U. Chgo. Alumni Assn. (life). Clubs: Standard (Chgo.); Idlewild Country (Flossmoor, Ill.) (dir. 1964-67). Home: 1110 N Lake Shore Dr Chicago IL 60611 Office: 140 S Dearborn St Chicago IL 60603 *Integrity has never been an abstract word or thought; it has been a way of life.*

EPTON, SAUL ARTHUR, lawyer, retired judge; b. Chgo., July 17, 1910; s. Arthur I. and Rose (Goldstein) E.; m. Ena Bollaert, June 2, 1935; 1 dau., Nancy Ann. Student, U. Mich., 1930; LL.B., John Marshall Law Sch., 1932. Bar: Ill. 1932. Since practiced in, Chgo.; now sr. partner firm Epton, Mullin, Segal & Druth, Ltd.; judge Circuit Court Cook County, 1959-77; dir. Uptown Fed. Savs. and Loan Assn.; Special asst. atty. gen. ins. matters, Ill., 1942-46. Mem. Ill. Civil Service Commn., 1953-59; Trustee Mt. Sinai Hosp., Chgo., Morgan Park (Ill.) Mil. Acad.; v.p. Chgo. Police Bd.; chmn. Coordinating Council on Arson for Profit, State of Ill. Arson Award Com.; sec. Greater Chgo. Boys Club. Mem. Am., Ill., Chgo. bar assns., Fedn. Ins. Council (past v.p.), Ill. State Judges Assn. Clubs: Standard, Tavern (Chgo.). Home: 100 E Walton St Chicago IL 60611 Office: Epton Mullin Segal & Druth Ltd 140 S Dearborn St Chicago IL 60603

ERASMUS, CHARLES JOHN, anthropologist, educator; b. Pitts., Sept. 23, 1921; s. Percy Thomas and Alice E.; m. Helen Marjorie O'Brien, Feb. 18, 1943; children: Thomas Glen, Gwendolyn. B.A., UCLA, 1942; M.A., U. Calif., Berkeley, 1950, Ph.D., 1955. Field ethnologist in Colombia Smithsonian Instn., 1950-52; applied anthropologist for AID, Western S.Am., 1952-54; research asso. culture exchange project U. Ill., 1955-59; vis. prof. anthropology Yale U., 1959-60; asso. prof. anthropology U. N.C., Chapel Hill, 1960-62, U. Calif., Santa Barbara, 1962-64, prof., 1964—, chmn. dept., 1964-68. Author: Man Takes Control: Cultural Development and American Aid, 1961, In Search of the Common Good: Utopian Experiments Past and Future, 1977, Contemporary Change in Traditional Communities of Mexico and Peru, 1978. Served with USN, 1942-45. Home: 6190 Barrington Dr Goleta CA 93017 Office: Dept Anthropology U Calif Santa Barbara CA 93106

ERAZMUS, ROBERT F., business executive; b. Chgo., May 12, 1942; s. Frank and Bernice (Wydra) E.; m. Margaret M. Meyer, July 16, 1966; children: Marilou, Elizabeth, Susan. B.A., St. Mary's Coll., Winona, Minn., 1964; M.B.A., DePaul U., 1966. Instr. acctg. St. Mary's Coll., Winona, 1966-68; with Arthur Andersen & Co., Mpls., Chgo., 1965-73, audit sr. mgr., 1968-73; controller Heizer Corp., Chgo., 1973-75; v.p. fin., treas. Internat. Jensen, Inc., Westchester, Ill., 1975-80; pres. Internat. Jensen Inc., 1980—. Mem. Am. Inst. C.P.A.s, Ill. C.P.A. Soc. Clubs: Economic (Chgo.); Presidents. Office: 4136 N United Pkwy Schiller Park IL 60176

ERB, DONALD, composer; b. Youngstown, Ohio, Jan. 17, 1927; s. Tod and Janet (Griffith) E.; m. Lucille Hyman, June 10, 1950; children: Christine, Matthew, Stephanie, Janet. B.S., Kent State U., 1950; Mus.M., Cleve. Inst. Music, 1953; Mus.D., Ind. U., 1964. Tchr. Cleve. Inst. Music, 1953-61, composer-in-residence, 1966-81; Meadows prof. composition So. Meth. U., 1981-84; grad. asst. Ind. U., 1961-62, 63-64; asst. prof. composition Bowling Green State U., 1964-65; vis. asst. prof. research electronic music Case Inst. Tech., 1965-67; composer-in-residence Dallas Symphony, 1968-69; vis. prof. Ind. U., 1975-76, Calif. State U., Los Angeles, 1977; prof. composition Ind. U., 1984—. Featured composer, lectr. condrs. festivals at, U. Minn., Ashland Coll., Albany State Coll., Tex. Technol. Coll., Oberlin Coll., U. Hartford, Wis. State U., Augustana Coll., Whitman Coll., Kent State U., U. Tex., others; co-dir.: contemporary music series Portfolio, Cleve., 1966-72; staff composer, Bennington Composers Conf., 1969-73; composer-librettist panelist, Nat. Endowment for Arts, 1973-79; chmn., 1977-79; performed at, Warsaw Autumn Festival, 1971-73; Composer: Dialogue for Violin and Piano, 1958, Correlations for Piano, 1959, Music for Violin and Piano, 1959, String Quartet No. 1, 1960, Music for Brass Choir, 1960, Sonata for Harpsichord and String Quartet, 1962, Chamber Concerto, 1961, Sonneries for Brass Choir, 1961, Four for Percussion, 1962, Bakersfield Pieces, 1962, Compendium, 1962, Dance Pieces, 1963, Cumming's Cycle, 1963, Hexagon, 1963, Concertant for Harpsichord and Strings, 1963, Antipodes, 1963, Symphony of Overtures, 1964, VII Misc, 1964, Fallout?, 1964, N, 1965, Reticulation, 1965, Phantasma, 1965, Concert Piece 1, 1966, Diversion for Two, 1966, Stargazing, 1966, Concerto for Solo Percussion and Orchestra, 1966, Andante for Piccolo, Flute and Alto Flute, 1966, String Trio, 1966, Summermusic, 1966, Kyrie, 1967, Reconnaissance, 1967, In No Strange Land, 1968, the Seventh Trumpet, 1969, Basspiece, 1969, Klangfarbenfunk I, 1970, God Love You Now, 1971, Fanfare, 1971, The Purple-Roofed Ethical Suicide Parlor, 1972, Harold's Trip to the Sky, 1972, Concerto for Trombone and Orchestra, 1976, Music for a Festive Occasion, 1976, Concerto for Violoncello and Orchestra, 1976, others. Served with USNR, 1945-46. Ford Found. composer-in-residence, Bakersfield, Calif., 1962-63; Rockefeller Found. grantee for performance Symphony of Overtures, 1965; Guggenheim fellow, 1965-66; grantee Nat. Council on Art, 1967-68; recipient Cleve. Arts prize; Distinguished Alumnus award Ind. U. Sch. Music; Naumberg Rec. award, 1974; Disting. Alumnus award Kent State U., 1982; Ohioana citation, 1978; fellow Bellagio Study and Conf. Center, 1979. Mem. Am. Music Center (pres. 1982-85), Broadcast Music, Cleve. Composers Guild, Am. Composers Alliance. Home: 2310 Queens Way Bloomington IN 47401

ERB, RICHARD DAVID, international agency executive; b. N. Bellmore, N.Y., Apr. 15, 1941; s. David and Margaret Harriet (Becker) E.; m. Joanna Reed Shelton, Mar. 22, 1980. B.A., SUNY-Buffalo, 1963; Ph.D., Stanford U., 1968. Asst. to gov. Fed. Res. Bd., Washington, 1967-69; with Arthur D. Little, N.Y.C., 1969-71; staff asst. to Pres. Nixon, 1971-74; fellow Council Fgn. Relations, 1974-76; dep. asst. sec. treasury, 1976-77; resident fellow Am. Enterprise Inst., 1977-81; U.S. exec. dir. IMF, 1981—; faculty Johns Hopkins Sch. Advanced Internat. Studies. Contbr. articles to profl. jours. Woodrow Wilson fellow. Mem. Am. Econs. Assn., Council Fgn. Relations, Middle East Inst., Phi Beta Kappa. Office: IMF 700 19th St NW Washington DC 20431

ERB, ROBERT ALLAN, phys. scientist; b. Ridley Park, Pa., Jan. 30, 1932; s. John Walter and Roma (Chapman) E.; m. Doretta Louise Barker, June 27, 1953; children—Sylvia Ann, Susan Doretta, Carolyn Joy. B.S. in Chemistry, U. Pa., 1953; M.S., Drexel Inst. Tech., 1959; Ph.D., Temple U., 1965. Chemist Gates Engring. Co., Wilmington, Del., 1953-54; with Franklin Research Center, Franklin Inst., Phila., 1954—, sr. staff chemist, 1965-68, prin. scientist, 1968-81, Inst. fellow, 1981—. Mem. Am. Chem. Soc., AAAS, Soc. Rheology, Soc. Plastics Engrs., Internat. Solar Energy Soc., Sigma Xi. Presbyterian. Inventor contraceptive systems, solar collectors, permanent systems for dropwise condensation. Home: Jug Hollow Rd PO Box 86 Valley Forge PA 19481 Office: Franklin Inst 20th and Parkway Philadelphia PA 19103

ERBER, THOMAS, physics educator; b. Vienna, Austria, Dec. 6, 1930; m. Audrey Burns. B.Sc., Mass. Inst. Tech., 1951; M.S., U. Chgo., 1953, Ph.D. in Physics, 1957. Asst. prof. physics Ill. Inst. Tech., Chgo., 1957-62, assoc. prof., 1962-69, prof., 1969—; Research fellow, Brussels, Belgium, 1963-64; vis. scientist Stanford Linear Accelerator Center, 1970; prof. physics U. Graz, 1971, 82, hon. life prof. physics, 1971—; prof. physics UCLA, 1978-79, U. Grenoble, 1982; adv. bd. Research Corp. Editorial bd.: Acta Physica Austriaca. Fellow Am. Phys. Soc., Am. Math. Soc.; mem. IEEE (sr.), European Phys. Soc., Oesterreichische Physikalische Gesellschaft, Am. Radio Relay League, Sigma Xi. Office: Dept Physics Ill Inst Tech Chicago IL 60616

ERBSEN, CLAUDE ERNEST, journalist; b. Trieste, Italy, Mar. 10, 1938; came to U.S., 1951, naturalized, 1956; s. Henry M. and Laura Elena (Treves) E.; m. Jill J. Prosky, July 16, 1959; 1 dau., Diana Lisa; m. Hedy Miriam Cohn, Apr. 7, 1970; children—Allan Henry, Michael David. B.A. cum laude, Amherst Coll., 1959; Inter-Am. Press Assn. scholar, U. Andes, Bogota, Colombia, 1960. Reporter-printer Amherst Jour.-Record, 1955-57; staff reporter El Tiempo, Bogota, 1960; with AP, 1960-1965, newsman in, N.Y.C., Miami, Fla.; and Washington, to chief of bur., Brazil, 1965-69, exec. rep. for, Latin Am., 1969-70; bus. mgr., adminstrv. dir. AP-Dow Jones Econ. Report, London, 1970-75, dep. dir. world services, N.Y.C., 1975-80; v.p., dir. AP-Dow Jones News Services, 1980—. Served to lt. USNR, 1961-65. Mem. Internat. Press Inst., Council Fgn. Relations. Club: Town (Scarsdale). Home: 27 Stratton Rd Scarsdale NY 10583 Office: AP 50 Rockefeller Plaza New York NY 10020

ERBURU, ROBERT F., newspaper publishing company executive; b. Ventura, Calif., 1930. Grad., U. So. Calif., 1952, Harvard U. Law Sch., 1955. Pres., chief exec. officer, dir. Times Mirror Co., Los Angeles; dir. Tejon Ranch Co.; mem. Bus. Roundtable, 1983—, Bus. Council, 1984—. Trustee Huntington Library, Art Gallery and Bot. Gardens, 1981—, Flora and William Hewlett Found., 1980—, Brookings Instn., 1983—. Mem. Am. Newspaper Pubs. Assn. (dir. 1980—), Council on Fgn. Relations (dir.). Home: 1518 Blue Jay Way Los Angeles CA 90069 Office: Times Mirror Sq Los Angeles CA 90053

ERDELY, STEPHEN LAJOS, music educator; b. Szeged, Hungary, May 6, 1921; came to U.S., 1949, naturalized, 1954; s. Jeno and Vilma (Lengyel) E.; m. Beatrice Eppinelle, Sept. 28, 1952. Absolutorium, Nat. Franz Liszt Music Acad., 1939-44, Franz Josef U., 1944; Ph.D., Case Western Res. U., 1962. Faculty Ohio State U., Toledo, 1966-73; prof. music M.I.T., Cambridge, Mass., 1973—, dir. music, 1976—. Soloist, Munich (Ger.) Chamber Music Dept., 1946-49, Cleve. Orch., 1951-66; concert artist with, The Erdely Duo, 1951—; Author: Methods and Principles of Hungarian Ethnomusicology, 1965; contbr. articles to profl. jours. Am. Philos. Soc. grantee, 1962; Am. Council Learned Socs. grantee, 1964; Nat. Endowment for Arts grantee, 1974-77. Mem. o2Am. Musicol. Soc. Soc. for Ethnomusicology (councilor 1970-73), Internat. Folk Music Council, Ohio Folklore Soc. (pres. 1967-69), Internat. Musicology Soc., Coll. Music Soc. Office: Dept Humanities MIT Cambridge MA 02139 *

ERDMAN, CARL L. N., ret. banker; b. Reading, Pa., Aug. 3, 1915; s. Lee Marcus and Ella (Nolde) E.; m. Carolyn M. Wilson, Sept. 10, 1938; children—Lee W., Christine N. (Mrs. Robert D. Keeler). B.A., Dartmouth, 1937. With Am. Bank and Trust Co. Pa., Reading, 1953-81, exec. v.p., 1966-81, ret., 1981. Mem. borough council, Wyomissing, Pa., 1964—; Bd. regents Mercersburg Acad., 1966—. Served with USNR, 1943-46, 50-52. Recipient Silver Beaver award Boy Scouts Am., 1961. Mem. Beta Theta Pi. Club: Rotarian. Home: 1415 Parkside Dr N Wyomissing PA 19610 Office: 35 N 6th St Reading PA 19603

ERDMAN, HOWARD LOYD, political science educator; b. Boston, Aug. 29, 1935; s. Simon and Eva (Freedman) E.; children: Karen, Deborah. B.A., Harvard U., 1958, M.A., 1960, Ph.D., 1964. From asst. prof. to prof. govt. Dartmouth Coll, Hanover, N.H., 1964—; vis. prof. various instns., U.S. And India; cons. Peace Corps, World Bank, Dept. State; mem. Dept. Edn. Contbr. articles to profl. jours. Sheldon travelling fellow Harvard U., 1962; Fulbright fellow; Am. Inst. Indian Studies fellow; Am. Philos Soc. fellow; Am. Council Learned Socs. fellow; recipient Deturs award Harvard Coll., 1956. Mem. Nat. Assn. Asian Studies. Democrat. Jewish. Club: Demolay. Home: 28 E Wheelock St Hanover NH 03755 Office: Dept Govt Darmouth Coll Hanover NH 03755

ERDMAN, PAUL EMIL, author; b. Stratford, Ont., Can., May 19, 1932; s. Horace Herman and Helen E.; m. Helly Elizabeth Boeglin, Sept. 11, 1954; children: Constance Anne Catherine, Jennifer Michele. Student, Concordia Coll., Ft. Wayne, Ind., 1950-51, Concordia Sem., St. Louis, 1952-53; B.A., Concordia Coll., St. Louis, 1954; B.Sc., Sch. Fgn. Service, Georgetown U., 1955; M.A., U. Basel, Switzerland, 1956, Ph.D., 1958. Econ. cons. European Coal and Steel Community, Luxembourg, Luxembourg, 1958; internat. economist Stanford Research Inst., Menlo Park, Calif., 1958-61; exec. v.p. Electronics Internat. Capital Ltd., Hamilton, Bermuda, 1962-64; vice chmn. United California Bank in Basel A.G., 1965-70; Cons. RAI Corp., TV corp., Italy.; host Moneytalk Sta. KGO, ABC, San Francisco, 1983—. Author, 1971—; Author: Swiss-American Economic Relations, 1959, Die Europaeische Wirtschaftsgemeinschaft und die Drittlaender, 1960, The Billion Dollar Sure Thing, 1973, The Silver Bears, 1974, The Crash of '79, 1976, The Last Days of America, 1981, Paul Erdman's Money Book: An Investor's Guide to Economics and Finance, 1984; Contbr. articles, revs. to popular mags. Mem. bd. advisors program in internat. bus. diplomacy Sch. fgn. Service, Georgetown U., Washington, 1980—. Recipient Champion Media award for econ. understanding Amos Tuck Sch. Bus. Adminstrn., Dartmouth Coll., 1984. Mem. Authors Guild, Mystery Writers Am. (Edgar award 1974). Lutheran. Address: 1817 Lytton Springs Rd Healdsburg CA 95448

ERDMAN, ROBERT LEE, ednl. adminstr., educator; b. Milw., Jan. 9, 1927; s. Henry H. and Nettie J. (Leister) E.; m. Mildred Weppler, June 11, 1949; children—Alan M., Steven H., Laura L. B.S., U. Wis., Milw., 1947; M.S., U. Ill., 1948, Ed.D., 1957. Tchr. spl. edn., public schs., Champaign, Ill., 1948-50; asso. prof. exceptional edn. U. Wis., Milw., 1952-58, prof., chmn. dept. exceptional edn., 1958-66; prof. spl. edn., chmn. dept. spl. edn. U. Utah, 1966-76, dean, prof., 1976—. Contbr. numerous articles to profl. publs. Fellow Am. Assn. on Mental Deficiency (Disting. Service award 1980); mem. Council Exceptional Children, Am. Ednl. Research Assn., Am. Assn. Tchr. Educators, Kappa Delta Pi, Phi Delta Kappa. Lutheran. Home: 854 Edgehill Rd Salt Lake City UT 84103 Office: 225MBH U Utah Salt Lake City UT 84112

ERDREICH, BEN, congressman; b. Birmingham, Ala., Dec. 9, 1938; s. Stanley and Corinne E.; m. Ellen Cooper, 1965; children: Jeremy C., Anna B. B.A., Yale U., 1960; J.D. with honors, U. Ala., 1963. Bar: Ala. 1963. Pvt. practice, Birmingham, 8 yrs.; mem. 98th Congress from 6th Dist. Ala. Mem. Ala. Ho. of Reps., 1970-74, Jefferson County Commn., 1974-80. Served to 1st lt. U.S. Army, 1963-65. Mem. Ala. Bar Assn., Birmingham Bar Assn., ABA. Democrat. Jewish. Office: 512 Cannon House Office Bldg Washington DC 20515 *

ERHARDT, WARREN RICHARD, publisher; b. West Allis, Wis., Nov. 14, 1924; s. George and Clara Katherine (Klafka) E.; m. Selma Gerber, Apr. 13, 1957; children—Amy, Eliza, Drew. Ph.B. in Journalism, Marquette U., 1950. Asso. media dir. Fuller & Smith & Ross Advt., N.Y.C., 1953-60; dir. corporate planning, asso. pub. McCall's Pub. Co., N.Y.C., 1960-71; asst. to pres. Downe Communications, N.Y.C., 1972; pub. Family Health mag., N.Y.C., 1973; pres., pub. Am. Home mag., N.Y.C., 1974-75; pub. Saturday Rev., 1975-77, Boys' Life, Boy Scouts Am., 1977-80; v.p., pub. Intermed Communications Inc., 1980—. Trustee Villagers Theatre, Middlebush, N.J. Served with USNR, 1943-46. Home: 455 Wakefield Dr Metuchen NJ 08840 Office: 1111 Bethlehem Pike Springhouse PA 19477

ERICH, JOHN BERNHARDT, plastic surgeon; b. Chgo., Jan. 14, 1907; s. John F. and Alma (Dow) E.; m. Edith Gebhardt, Mar. 26, 1932. B.S., U. Ill., 1929, M.D., 1932, D.D.S., 1933, M.S., 1935. Diplomate: Am. Bd. Plastic Surgery (mem. 1956-64), Am. Bd. Otolaryngology. Fellow plastic surgery Mayo Clinic, 1933-36, cons. plastic surgery, 1937—; head sect. plastic surgery, 1955-67, sr. cons. plastic surgery, 1967-76; prof. plastic surgery Mayo Med. Sch., 1949-76, prof. emeritus, 1976—. Served as lt. M.C. USNR, 1942-48. Fellow A.C.S., Am. Acad. Ophthalmology and Otolaryngology; mem. Am. Laryngol. Assn., Triological Soc., Am. Soc. Head and Neck Surgeons, AMA, Am. Assn. Plastic Surgeons, Am. Soc. Plastic and Reconstructive Surgeons, Am. Soc. Maxillofacial Surgeons (past pres.), Am. Fracture Soc. (v.p.), Minn. Acad. Ophthalmology and Otolaryngology, Minn. Med. Soc., So. Minn. Med. Assn., Sigma Xi. Home: 716 10th St SW Rochester MN 55901 Office: Mayo Clinic: Rochester MN 55901

ERICKSEN, EPHRAIM GORDON, sociologist, educator; b. Salt Lake City, Sept. 7, 1917; s. Ephraim Edward and Edna (Clark) E.; m. Darlene Anderson, Apr. 24, 1944; children—Craig, Heidi, Dana. B.S., U. Utah, 1938, M.S., 1939; Ph.D., U. Chgo., 1947. Mem. faculty U. Ind., 1946-47, U. Calif. at Los Angeles, 1947-49, U. Kans., 1949-65, U. Tenn., 1965-68; faculty Va. Poly. Inst. and State U., 1968—, prof. sociology, 1968-73, chmn. dept., 1968-72; cons. in field. Author: Urban Behavior, 1954, The West Indies Population Problem, 1962, The Territorial Experience: Human Ecology as Symbolic Interaction, 1980; contbr. articles to profl. jours. Fellow Am. Sociol. Assn.; mem. Midwest Sociol. Soc., Phi Delta Kappa, Pi Kappa Alpha.

ERICKSEN, GREGG EDWARD, manufacturing company executive; b. Fargo, N.D., Jan. 17, 1933; s. Arthur B. and Mignon I. (Schiede) E.; m. Lila Maxine Jorgenssen, Sept. 10, 1960; children: Bradley, Scott, Lori, Gail. B.B.S., U. Minn., 1955. Controller def electronics div. Honeywell, Seattle, 1974-80, controller avionics div., Mpls., 1980-81, v.p., controller control systems div., 1981-82, v.p., controller, 1983—. Served to lt. USN, 1966-69. Home: 14910 Woodruff Rd Wayzata MN 55391 Office: Honeywell Honeywell Plaza Minneapolis MN 55408

ERICKSEN, JERALD LAVERNE, educator, physicist; b. Portland, Oreg., Dec. 20, 1924; s. Adolph and Ethel Rebecca (Correy) E.; m. Marion Ella Pook, Feb. 24, 1946; children: Lynn Christine, Randolph Peder. B.S., U. Wash., 1947; M.A., Oreg. State Coll., 1949; Ph.D., Ind. U., 1951. Mathematician, solid state physicist U.S. Naval Research Lab., 1951-57; faculty Johns Hopkins U., 1957-83, prof. theoretical mechanics, 1960-83, U. Minn., Mpls., 1983—. Editorial adv. bd.: Internat. Jour. Solids and Structures; editorial bd.: Jour. Elasticity. Served with USNR, 1943-46. Recipient Bingham medal, 1968, Timoshenko medal, 1979. Mem. Soc. Rheology, Soc. Natural Philosophy, Soc. Interaction Mechanics and Math. Home: 10 Poplar Ln North Oaks MN 55110 Office: Mechanics Dept U Minn Minneapolis MN 55455

ERICKSON, CARL RUSSELL, retail company executive; b. Kansas City, Mo., Sept. 11, 1921; s. Charles John and Lotten (Seger) E.; m. Janet Rollins, June 11, 1949 (div. 1980); children: Kurt, Kim, Jan. B.S., U. Notre Dame, 1947; M.B.A., Harvard U., 1948. With Dayton's, Mpls., 1949-78, pres., 1968-76, chmn. bd., 1976-78; sr. v.p. Godchaux's, New Orleans, 1979-80, Joseph Magnin, San Francisco, 1980-82; exec. v.p. Liberty House, Honolulu and San Francisco, 1982—. Served to lt. USN, 1942-46. Office: Liberty House PO Box 2690 Honolulu HI 96845

ERICKSON, CHARLES BURTON, savs. bank exec.; b. Monett, Mo., Oct. 17, 1932; s. Albion Burton and Ruth Elizabeth (Harris) E.; m. Dolores Imbrowicz, June 16, 1977; children—Catherine, Charles. Student, U. Mo., 1950-52, A.B., 1958, LL.B., 1960. Bar: Ill. bar 1960. Atty. First Nat. Bank of Chgo., 1960-63, United Airlines, 1963-64; v.p. Jewel Companies, Inc., Chgo., 1964-75; sr. v.p. ops., sec., gen. counsel First Fed. of Chgo., 1975—; instr. De Paul U. Law Sch. Dir. Chgo. USO. Served with USMC, 1952-55. Mem. Chgo. Econ. Club, Chgo. Bar Assn. Republican. Methodist. Club: Union League. Home: 6525 Main Unit 304 Downers Grove IL 60516 Office: 7 S Dearborn Chicago IL 60603

ERICKSON, DENNIS DUANE, bank holding company executive; b. Duluth, Minn., July 16, 1938; s. David and Catherine Mary (Dennis) E.; m. Mary Louise Erickson, Dec. 26, 1964; children: Dana Catherina, Nissa Lynn. B.A. in Bus. Adminstrn., U. Minn.-Duluth, 1960; cert, Coll. William and Mary, 1971; cert. with honors, U. Wis. Sch. Bank Adminstrn., 1976. C.P.A., Colo. Corp. acctg. mgr. United Banks of Colo., Inc., Denver, 1971-74, controller, 1974-80, v.p., controller, 1980-82, v.p., treas., 1979-82, sr. v.p. fin., treas, 1982—; treas., asst. sec. Fidelity Ins. Co. and Lincoln Agy., Inc., Denver, 1978-82; dir. United Bank of Arvada, Colo., 1978-82, United Banks Arapahoe, Durango, Colo., 1981-82, Durango & Ignacio United Bank of Cherry Creek, Denver, 1982-83. Republican. Roman Catholic. Office: United Banks of Colorado Inc 1700 Lincoln Suite 3200 Denver CO 80274

ERICKSON, DON, editor; b. Kansas City, Kans., Mar. 25, 1932; s. Iver and Mildred (Gocke) E. B.A., Yale, 1953, Oxford (Eng.) U., 1955, M.A., 1960. Editor Am. Cyanamid Co., N.Y.C., 1959-64; with Esquire mag., N.Y.C., 1964—, exec. editor, 1972-73, editor, 1973-75, editor-in-chief, 1975-77, editorial dir., 1977—; with public TV, 1980; editor Dial Mag. Rhodes scholar, 1953-55. Mem. Am. Soc. Mag. Editors, Phi Beta Kappa. Office: 304 W 58th St New York NY 10019

ERICKSON, FLORENCE HENRIETTA, nurse, educator; b. McKeesport, Pa., Feb. 22, 1914; d. Harry and Esther (Johnson) E. Grad., McKeesport Hosp. Sch. Nursing, 1935; B.S. in Nursing Edn, U. Pitts., 1947, Ph.D., 1957; M.S., Yale, 1954. Orthopedic staff nursing N.Y. Orthopedic Hosp., N.Y.C., 1935-36; indsl. nursing Jones & Laughlin Steel Co., McKeesport Tin Plate, 1936-44; instr. pediatric nursing, asst. prof., then prof., chmn. dept. U. Pitts., 1945-77, prof. nursing care of children, 1977-80, prof. emeritus, 1980—; Chmn. interdivisional council maternal and child health nursing Pa. League for Nursing, 1953; mem. nursing research study sect. NIH, 1965-67, project dir. nurse scientist tng. grant, 1970-76. Author monograph.; Co-editor: Maternal-Child Nursing Jour, 1972-80. Mem. Am. Nurses Assn., Nat. League for Nursing (steering com. inter-div. council on maternal and child health 1957-61, vice chmn. and chmn. elect 1963-67), Alpha Tau Delta (past nat. treas., nat. pres. 1947). Presbyterian. Home: RD 1 Harrisville PA 16038

ERICKSON, FRANK WILLIAM, composer; b. Spokane, Wash., Sept. 1, 1923; s. Frank O. and Myrtle L. (Leck) E.; m. Mary A. Smith, Aug. 15, 1981; children by previous marriage—William, Richard, Christian. Mus.B., U. So. Calif., 1950, Mus.M., 1951. Rep. Bourne Co. (music pubs.), 1952-58; lectr. U. Calif., Los Angeles, 1958; prof. music San Jose (Calif.) State U., 1959-61. Composer, arranger, 1961—; works include 1st Symphony for Band, 1954, 2d Symphony for Band, 1959, Toccata for Band, 1957, Air for Band, 1956, Balladair, 1956, Double Concerto for Trumpet, Trombone and Band, 1951, Fantasy for Band, 1955, Concerto for Alto Saxophone and Band, 1961, Sonatina for Band, 1962, Rhythm of the Winds, 1964, Citadel, 1964, Blue Ridge Overture, 1976, Overture Jubiloso, 1978, Overture Pastorale, 1981.

Served with USAAF, 1942-46. Mem. ASCAP, Phi Mu Alpha Sinfonia, Pi Kappa Lambda, Phi Beta Mu.

ERICKSON, HOMER THEODORE, educator; b. Pulaski, Wis., Mar. 8, 1925; s. Elmer and Luella (Thorson) E.; m. Carolyn J. Cochran, Sept. 10, 1955; children—Ann, Jean, Charles, Neal. B.S., U. Wis., 1951, M.S., 1953, Ph.D., 1954; Prof. Honorus Causa, Fed. U., Vicosa, Minas Gerais, Brazil, 1963. Asst. prof. U. Maine, 1954-56; mem. faculty Purdue U., 1956, prof. horticulture, 1964—, head dept., 1967-75; research center coordinator with Spanish govt., Zaragoza, 1975-76; Cons. in horticulture, Ghana, 1972. Served with AUS, 946-47. Mem. Am. Genetics Assn., Am. Soc. Hort. Sci., Nat. Audubon Soc., Delta Theta Sigma; founder, hon. mem. Brazilian Hort. Soc. Lutheran. Club: Optimist Internat. Home: 1409 N Salisbury St West Lafayette IN 47906

ERICKSON, JAMES HARRISON MILLER, college president; b. Mankato, Minn., Oct. 25, 1923; s. Arvid S. and Johanna (Miller) E.; m. Mittie M. Berry, June 3, 1956; children: Karen, Mark. B.S. cum laude, U. Minn., 1949; M.Ed. U. Colo, 1949; Ed.D., U. Wyo., 1954. English tchr. pub. schs., to 1954; asst. prof. English Ball State U., 1954-55; asst. prof. edn., chmn. secondary edn. dept. Ariz. State U., 1955-58; prof. edn. U. Wis., La Crosse, 1958-73, dean Grad. Coll., 1963-73; dean Sch. Profl. Studies Central Wash. U., Ellensburg, 1974-78; pres. No. Mont. Coll., Havre, 1978—; dir. First Bank Havre. Served with AUS, 1943-46, 51-52. Mem. Havre C. of C. (dir.), Kappa Delta Pi, Phi Delta Kappa, Phi Kappa Phi. Presbyn. (elder). Home: 11 Park Rd Havre MT 59501 Office: No Mont Coll Office of Pres Havre MT 59501

ERICKSON, JAMES HUSTON, physician; b. Omaha, Sept. 7, 1931; s. Paul Ferdin and Naomi Marie (Berglund) E.; m. Shirley Arlene Nordling, Dec. 26, 1959; children: Jonathan, Ingrid, Sonja. A.A., N. Park Coll., 1950; A.B., Stanford U., 1952; M.D., U. Colo., 1959; M.P.H., U. Minn., 1975; M.S. (hon.), Loyola U. of Md., 1982. Diplomate Am. Bd. Preventive Medicine. Intern Swedish Covenant Hosp., Chgo., 1959-60, med. resident; and VA Hosp., Hines, Ill., 1963-65; dir. med. edn. Swedish Covenant Hosp., Chgo., 1965-69; dir. health service N. Park Coll., Chgo., 1965-69; flight surgeon United Airlines, Chgo., 1969; commd. comdr. USPHS, 1970, advanced through grades to rear adm., 1976—; asst. surgeon gen., dir. Bur. Med. Services, Hyattsville, Md., 1976-81; dir. health services, prof. allied health scis. No. Ill. U., DeKalb, 1981—; vis. fellow in preventive medicine Christian Med. Coll., Ludhana, India, 1965; instr. medicine Northwestern U., Evanston, Ill., 1967-68; asst. prof. preventive medicine U. Ill., Chgo., 1968-70; asso. prof. family medicine and health services U. Wash., Seattle, 1975-76; adj. prof. Uniformed Services Univ. Health Scis., 1977-81. Troop chaplain Boy Scouts Am., 1976-81; mem. Civil Air Patrol, 1971—. Served with USN, 1960-63, 69-70. Decorated Bronze Star Medal; recipient Rear Admiral Richard L. Fowler award Naval Reserve Assn., 1968; cert. of merit Republic of Vietnam, 1970; Physicians Recognition award AMA, 1970, 73, 76, 79; Meritorious Service medal USPHS, 1981. Fellow Am. Coll. Preventive Medicine, Royal Soc. Health; mem. Aerospace Med. Assn., Am. Heart Assn., Am. Soc. Law and Medicine, Assn. for Hosp. Med. Edn., Assn. of Mil. Surgeons of U.S., Christian Med. Soc., Soc. for Health and Human Values, USPHS Commd. Officers Assn. Mem. Evangel. Covenant Ch. Office: Univ Health Service No Ill U DeKalb IL 60115

ERICKSON, JAMES RICHARD, psychologist, educator; b. Mpls., June 21, 1934; s. Clarence Gustave and Lillie Mae (Evenson) E.; m. Shirley Faye Warren, Dec. 21, 1957 (div. 1978); children: Kenton Richard, Marcus Richard, Stuart Richard; m. Mary Lina Berndt, July 8, 1978 (div. 1982). B.S., U. Minn., 1958, Ph.D. (NIH fellow 1961-62), 1963. From asst. prof. to prof. psychology Ohio State U., Columbus, 1962-75; vis. asso. prof. U. Colo., Boulder, 1968-69; prof. psychology, chmn. dept. U. Tex., Arlington, 1975—. Author articles on exptl. psychology; cons. editor: Jour. Exptl. Psychology, 1972-80. Grantee NIMH, 1966-72; NSF, 1976-81. Fellow Am. Psychol. Assn.; mem. Midwest Psychol. Assn., AAAS, Psychonomic Soc., Psychometric Soc., Southwestern Psychol. Assn. Office: Dept Psychology Univ Tex Arlington TX 76019

ERICKSON, JOHN DUFF, mining engineering educator; b. Crawford, Nebr., Apr. 1, 1933; s. Harold Edward and Ruth Isabel (Duff) E.; m. Janet Eileen Lind, Dec. 28, 1955; children: Gregory Duff, Sheryl Ann. B.S. in Mining Engring., S.D. Sch. Mines and Tech., 1955; M.S. in Indsl. Mgmt., MIT, 1965. Mine planning engr. Kennecott Copper Corp., Salt Lake City, 1965-67, truck ops. supt., 1968-69; mine mgr. Bougainville Copper Ltd., North Solomons Papua, New Guinea, 1970-72, exec. mgr. tech. services, 1973-75, asst. gen. mgr., 1976-77; head dept. mining engring. S.D. Sch. Mines and Tech., Rapid City, S.D., 1978—; mining cons. Bechtel Civil and Minerals, San Francisco, 1979—, Fluor Engrs., Redwood City, Calif., 1983—; dir. So. Hills Mining Co., Rapid City, S.D., 1982—. Served to capt. AUS, 1961-62. Sloan Fellow awardee, 1964-65. Mem. AIME (chmn. Black Hills sect. 1983—), Black Hills Mining Assn. Republican. Clubs: Arrowhead Country, Elks. Home: 2958 Tomahawk Dr Rapid City SD 57702 Office: SD Sch Mines and Tech 500 E St Joseph St Rapid City SD 57701

ERICKSON, KIRBY JOHN, hospital administrator; b. Dodgeville, Wis., Mar. 30, 1940; s. Ralph Chester and Alice Juliet (Ege) E.; divorced; children: Christopher, Jacqueline, Kimberly. B.S., N.D. State U., 1962; M.S., U. Minn., 1965. Pharmacist St. Luke's Hosp., Duluth, Minn., 1962-63; resident in adminstrn. Franklin County Pub. Hosp., Greenfield, Mass., 1964-65; adminstrv. asst. Fairview Hosp, Mpls., 1965-67; asst. adminstr. Fairview-Southdale Hosp., Edina, Minn., 1967-74, assoc. adminstr., 1974-76, adminstr., 1976-83, v.p., 1983—; mem. Met. Health Bd. Mpls., 1981—. Recipient Mac Eachern award citations Am. Soc. Hosp. Pub. Relations, 1970, 71. Mem. Am. Coll. Hosp. Adminstrs., Am. Hosp. Assn., Greater Edina C. C. Republican. Episcopalian. Home: 6670 Vernon Ave S Edina MN 55436 Office: Fairview-Southdale Hosp 6401 France Ave S Edina MN 55435

ERICKSON, LAWRENCE WILHELM, educator; b. Huron, S.D., Aug. 5, 1915; s. Hilding M. and Hildur (M. (Johnson) E.; children: Michael, Jeffrey Sellwood. B.S., UCLA, 1942; M.S., 1945; Ed.D., 1955. With Wohl Shoe Co., Huron, 1931-32, Armour & Co. (various cities), 1932-35, Chgo. & Northwestern Ry., 1935-38; tchr. Beverly Hills (Calif.) High Sch., 1943-44; mem. faculty U. San Francisco, 1949-50, Columbia U., 1952-58, UCLA, 1945—, prof. edn., 1967—, asst. dean, 1967-82; cons. to bus., industry, ednl. instns. Author: The Secretary's Book, 1955, 20th Century Typewriting, 6th to 9th edits, 1952-67, Typing Our Language, 1970, Clerical Office Typing, 1972, Century 21 Typewriting, 1972, 77, 82, Typewriting—Learning and Instruction, 1979, Microcomputer Keyboarding/Formatting Applications, 1983, Alphabetic Keyboarding and Numeric Keypad Operations, 1983; coordinating editor: Nat. Assn. Bus. Tchrs. Edn. Rev, 1973—. Mem. Nat. Assn. Bus. Tchrs. Edn. (pres. 1971-73), Western, Calif. bus. edn. assns. Home: 16954 Strawberry Dr Encino CA 91436 Office: 405 Hilgard Ave Los Angeles CA 90024

ERICKSON, LEROY ALEXANDER, electronics executive; b. Valley City, N.D., June 22, 1921; s. Henry Oscar and Myrtle Eleanor (Jacobson) E.; m. Mary Dixon, Dec. 22, 1946; children: Carol, David. B.S., U. Oreg., 1947. Pres., Luminator, Inc., 1962-70; chmn., pres., chief exec. officer, dir. Varo, Inc., Garland, Tex., 1971-74, Ozite Corp., 1976—; dir. Met. Savs. & Loan, Altec Corp., Anaheim, Calif., Wing Industries Inc., Universal Resources Inc., Dallas. Mem. Phi Delta Theta. Clubs: Preston Trail Golf (Dallas); De Caza y Pesca Las Cruces (Baja, Calif.); Waverley Country (Portland, Oreg.). Home: 11956 Tavel Circle Dallas TX 75230 Office: 12200 Park Central Dr Dallas TX 75251

ERICKSON, LUTHER EUGENE, educator, chemist; b. Pulaski, Wis., June 30, 1933; s. Elmer and Luella (Thorson) E.; m. Jenny Sue Payne, June 22, 1957; children—Louise Elizabeth, Hans Luther. B.A., St. Olaf Coll., 1955; Ph.D., U. Wis., 1959. Asst. prof. chemistry Dickinson Coll., Carlisle, Pa., 1959-62; mem. faculty Grinnell (Iowa) Coll., 1962—, prof. chemistry, 1968—, Dodge prof., 1974—. Contbr. articles to profl. jours. NSF sci. faculty fellow, 1968-69; recipient Catalyst award Chem. Mfrs. Assn., 1983. Mem. Am. Chem. Soc., Iowa Acad. Scis., AAAS. Home: 1415 Summer St Grinnell IA 50112

ERICKSON, RALPH ERNEST, lawyer; b. Jamestown, N.Y., Oct. 3, 1928; s. Lawrence Harold and Myrtle (Jespersen) E.; m. Janet Cass, June 6, 1953; children: Sandra Lynne, John Cass. B.S., Cornell U., 1952; J.D., Harvard U., 1955. Bar: Calif. 1956, U.S. Supreme Ct. 1968, D.C. 1973. Assoc. firm Musick, Peeler & Garrett, Los Angeles, 1952-62, ptnr., 1962-71, 73-76; asst. atty. gen. U.S. Dept. Justice, Washington, 1971-72, dep. atty. gen., 1972-73; ptnr. Erickson, Zerfas & Adams, Los Angeles, 1976-79, Jones, Day, Reavis & Rouge, 1979—; spl rep. of U.S. for Am. Indian Movement Wounded Knee negotiations, 1973. Founding mem., trustee Victor Gruen Found. Environ Planning; chmn. legal adv. com. San Marino Sch. Dist., Calif., 1979-81; mem. Investment Commn., 1979—, Los Angeles Citizens Olympics Commn. Mem. Calif. State Bar, ABA (ho. of del. 1972-73). Republican. Episcopalian. Clubs: Calif. (Los Angeles); Met. (Washington); Springs (Rancho Mirage, Calif.); Annandale Golf (Pasadena, Calif.); Town Hall (Los Angeles) (life mem.). Office: 2029 Century Park E Suite 3600 Los Angeles CA 90067

ERICKSON, RAYMOND LEROY, university dean, psychologist; b. Jamestown, N.Y., Feb. 11, 1925; s. Raymond J. E. and Grace (Erickson) Myers; m. Barbara Joan Golden, Apr. 29, 1956; children: Leslie Ann, Laurel Meredeth, Douglas Alan. B.A. magna cum laude, State U. N.Y. at Buffalo, 1951; M.A., UCLA, 1954, Ph.D., 1962. Psychol. intern Calif. Dept. Corrections, 1954; lectr. U. Md. Overseas Program, 1956-58; instr., then asst. prof. Whittier Coll., 1958-63; mem. faculty U. N.H., 1963—, prof. psychology, 1967—, chmn. dept., 1965-71, dean Grad. Sch., 1974—, assoc. v.p. acad. affairs, 1981—. Served with AUS, 1943-46. Mem. Am. Psychol. Assn., N.H. Psychol. Assn. (pres. 1967-68), Phi Beta Kappa. Home: 4 Lantern Ln Exeter NH 03833

ERICKSON, RICHARD AMES, physicist, emeritus educator; b. Bryant, S.D., Sept. 12, 1923; s. Ray and Mabel Gabriella (Arneson) E.; m. Frances Irene Boyd, June 13, 1943; children—Donna Mae (Mrs. Don Smith), Jeanne Marie, David Ray, Kristine Ann (Mrs. Scott Stewart). B.Sc., S.D. Sch. Mines and Tech., 1944; Ph.D., Tex. A. and M. U., 1952. Predoctoral fellow Oak Ridge Inst. Nuclear Studies, 1949-51; asst. prof. physics U. Tenn., 1951-54; asst. prof. Ohio State U., 1954-61, asso. prof., 1961-74, prof., 1974-79, prof. emeritus, 1979—, sec. faculty, 1975-77; cons. Lockheed Research Lab., Palo Alto, Calif., 1964, AID, India, 1965; Mem. Univ. Area Commn., Columbus, Ohio, 1973-74. Contbg. author: Methods of Experimental Physics, vol. 3, 1961; Contbr. articles to profl. jours. Served with USNR, 1944-46. Mem. Am. Phys. Soc., AAAS, AAUP, Univ. Community Assn., Sigma Xi. Lutheran. Club: Ohio State U. Faculty. Home: 1981 Indianola Ave Columbus OH 43201 Office: 174 W 18th Ave Columbus OH 43210

ERICKSON, RICHARD CARL, psychologist, educator; b. Seattle, Oct. 28, 1937; s. Richard Carl and Winona Elizabeth (Dinges) E.; m. Joyce Quiring, Sept. 12, 1958; children: Diana Laureen, David Mark, Jonathan Park Dong Myung. Student, Seattle Pacific Coll., 1955-56; B.S., U. Wash., 1959, Ph.D., 1969; M.Div., Fuller Theol. Sem., 1962. Intern Olympic Center for Mental Health and Mental Retardation, Bremerton, Wash., 1968-69; psychologist mental hygiene clinic Seattle VA Hosp., 1969-70, psychologist day hosp. unit, 1970-74, psychologist rehab. medicine service, 1974-78; inpatient psychiatrist Portland (Oreg.) VA Center, 1979—; instr. dept. psychiatry and behavioral scis. U. Wash. Med. Sch., Seattle, 1971-73, asst. prof., 1973-77, asso. prof., 1977-78; asso. prof. dept. med. psychology U. Oreg. Health Scis. Center, 1979—; ordained minister United Presbyn. Ch. in U.S.A., 1967. Contbr. articles to profl. jours. Mem. Am., Western psychol. assns., Assn. for Advancement Psychology. Office: 3710 SW US Veterans Hospital Rd Portland OR 97201

ERICKSON, RICHARD THEODORE, retail company executive; b. St. Paul, Feb. 8, 1932; s. Louis Amil and Leona Ruth (Bergeron) E.; m. Pearl Margaret Desimone, June 12, 1954; children: Patricia, Michael, Richard, Shari. B.A. in Bus., U. Wash., 1954. With J.C. Penney Co., Inc., 1956—, from mgmt. trainee to regional personnel mgr., Buena Park, Calif., successively dist. mgr., Buena Park, stores personnel mgr., N.Y.C., personnel mgr., v.p. personnel, 1981-82, sr. v.p. personnel, 1982—; dir. Unemployment Benefits Advisors, Washington, 1983—. Served to lt. (j.g.) USN, 1954-56; PTO. Mem. N.Y.C. C. of C. and Industry (chmn. social ins. com. 1983). Home: 26 Hermit Ln Westport CT 06880 Office: J C Penney Co Inc 1301 Ave of the Americas New York NY 10019

ERICKSON, ROBERT ARLEN, engr.; b. Brainerd, Minn., Jan. 12, 1932; s. Benjamin Bernhart and Ruth Amelia (Linn) E.; m. Naomi Marie Hepburn, May 18, 1956; children—Catherine, John, Benjamin. Student, Brainerd Jr. Coll.; B.A. in Physics, U. Minn., 1958. Physicist Sperry Univac Def. Systems div., St. Paul, Minn., 1958-62, sr. physicist, 1962-64, supr. engr., 1964-65, mgr., 1965-66, group mgr., 1966-70, dir. research and devel., 1970-74, dir. engring., 1974-78, v.p. product engring., 1978-80, v.p., gen. mgr. Semicondr. div., 1980—. Contbr. articles to profl. jours. Served with USAF, 1951-55. Mem. Am. Legion, various mgmt. and tech. groups, several conservation orgns. Republican. Patentee in field. Home: 2182 Garnet Point St Paul MN 55122 Office: 333 Pilot Knob Rd St Paul MN 55165

ERICKSON, ROBERT PORTER, educator; b. South Bend, Ind., Feb. 13, 1930; s. Carl Gustav and Elinor (Porter) E.; children: Lars, Nils, David. Ph.D., Brown U., 1958. Prof. psychology Duke U., Durham, N.C., 1961—. Served to lt. (j.g.) USN, 1951-54. Mem. Am. Physiol. Soc., Soc. Neuroscis., Am. Chemoreception Soc. Home: 564 Rockwood Rd Route 1 Hillsborough NC 27278 Office: Duke U Durham NC 27706

ERICKSON, ROLAND AXEL, financial and management consultant; b. Worcester, Mass., Sept. 8, 1913; s. Axel and Anna (Erickson) E.; m. Roxie Erickson, Apr. 6, 1940; children: Brent, Lorna (Mrs. E. Long). A.B. summa cum laude, Clark U., 1935; A.M., Tufts U., 1937; LL.B., Susquehanna U., 1970. Instr. econs. Tufts U., 1935-37; economist Norton Co., 1937-41; v.p. Guaranty Bank & Trust Co., 1941-45, v.p., treas., dir., 1945-47, pres., 1947-64, hon. dir.; sr. v.p., dir. Gen. Foods Corp., 1964-66, exec. v.p., dir., 1966-70; fin. mgmt. cons., 1970—; vice chmn. Bofors Am., Inc.; dir. Norton Co., State Mut. Life Assurance Co.; dir., chmn. bd. Am., Marine Savs. and Loan of Fla.; Wain-Roy Co., Inc. Contbr. articles on corporate fin., money and banking, fiscal policy to profl. publs. Trustee emeritus Clark U.; past pres. Swedish Council Am., Worcester (Mass.) United Way. Decorated knight Royal Order Vasa 1st class, knight comdr. Royal Order North Star, Sweden). Mem. Newcomen Soc., Nat. Assn. Bus. Economists, Am. Econ. Assn., Am. Acad. Polit. and Social Sci., Phi Beta Kappa. Conglist. Clubs: Mason (32 deg.), Worcester, University (N.Y.C.); Worcester Country (Odin); Royal Poinciana (Naples, Fla.). Home: The Laurentians Apt 8C 1285 Gulf Shore Blvd N Naples FL 33940 Home: Hi-Acres Hubbardston MA 01452 Office: 1140 Mechanics Tower Worcester MA 01608

ERICKSON, ROY BERNHARDT, lawyer; b. Portland, Oreg., Dec. 6, 1921; s. Roy Bernhardt and Anna Emeline (Lindstrom) E.; m. Kimi Hatano, Aug. 26, 1951; Marcia Emeline, Meredity Marie, Millicent Jean. A.B., Harvard U., 1943, postgrad. in econs., 1951, J.D. cum laude, 1952; cert., Indsl. Coll. Armed Forces, 1962. Bar: Oreg. 1952, U.S. Supreme Ct. Civilian adminstr. U.S. Occupation Forces, Japan, 1946-49; lawyer Bonneville Power Adminstrn., 1952-54; atty. adviser Corps of Engrs., 1955-56; atty. Japan Plocurement Agy, Yokohama, 1956-62; lawyer AEC, Richland, Wash., 1962-66, asst. chief counsel, 1966-75, ERDA, 1975-77, Dept. Energy, 1978—; lectr. law U. Md. Far East Div., 1957-60. Contbr. articles to profl. jours. U.S. observer Asian Conf. World Peace Through Law, 1961; mem. Richland Human Rights Commn., 1966-68; spl. legal adviser Commn. Govt. Contracts, 1970-72; bd. dirs. Benton-Franklin Community Action Com., Richland, 1971-73. Capt. inf. AUS, 1943-46. Recipient award for superior performance Dept. Army, 1962, for significant contbn. AEC, 1967, Mgrs. award Dept. Energy, 1980. Mem. Ben Franklin Legal Aid Assn. (dir., vice chmn. 1969-76, chmn. 1977-79), ACLE (dir., chpt. chmn. 1969-73), ABA, Oreg. Bar Assn., Benton Franklin County Bar Assn., Fed. Bar Assn., Nat. Legal Aid and Defender Assn. Home: 3120 Hamilton Ave Richland WA 99352 Office: Federal Bldg Richland WA 99352

ERICKSON, ROY FREDERICK, JR., hospital administrator; b. Chgo., Aug. 16, 1928; s. Roy Frederick and Irene Elsa (Jacobson) E.; m. Julia Ellen Raffington, Oct. 18, 1958; children: Elizabeth, Peter, Stephen. B.S., Northwestern U., 1950, M.S., 1956. Asst. adminstr. Decatur (Ill.) Meml. Hosp., 1956-60; adminstr. Passavant Meml. Area Hosp., Jacksonville, Ill., 1960-64, Blessing Hosp., Quincy, Ill., 1964-72; pres. Ball Meml. Hosp., Muncie, Ind., 1972—; adj. prof. physiology and health sci. Ball State U., Muncie, 1979—; bd. dirs. Bi-State Regional Med. Program, 1969-72; mem. assoc. faculty Muncie Center for Med. Edn.; mem. adv. council Health Systems Agy., Area II. Bd. dirs. Cancer Soc.; div. chmn. United Fund; mem. Citizens Adv. Council for Vocat. Edn. Served with USAF, 1950-54. Mem. Am. Hosp. Assn., Ill. Hosp. Assn. (trustee 1968-70), Ind. Hosp. Assn. (dir. 1976-82), Am. Mgmt. Assn., Am. Coll. Hosp. Adminstrs. Methodist. Club: Rotary. Home: 4201 University Ave Muncie IN 47304 Office: 2401 University Ave Muncie IN 47303

ERICKSON, ROY LYDEEN, agribusiness exec.; b. Kelliher, Minn., Apr. 20, 1923; s. Albert E. and Victoria (Lydeen) E.; m. Beverly E. Hurrle, July 12, 1957. B.B.A., U. Minn., 1948; J.D., Wm. Mitchell Coll. Law, 1961. Bar: Minn. bar 1961. With treas. dept. financial and computer areas Archer-Daniels-Midland Co., Decatur, Ill., 1948-60, atty., asst. sec., 1961-68, sec., gen. counsel, 1969—, v.p., 1970—; practice law, Mpls., 1961-69, Decatur, Ill., 1969—; Chmn. Planning and Zoning Com., Columbia Heights, Minn., 1962; spl. Municipal Ct. judge, Columbia Heights, 1964-68. Served with USNR, 1940-45. Mem. Am., Minn., Hennepin County bar assns. Home: 494 Shoreline Dr Decatur IL 62521 Office: 4666 Faries Pkwy Decatur IL 62525

ERICKSON, W(ALTER) BRUCE, business and economics educator; b. Chgo., Mar. 4, 1938; s. Clifford E. and Mildred B. (Brinkmeier) E. A.B., Mich. State U., 1959, M.A., 1960, Ph.D. in Econs., 1965. Research asso. Subcom. on Antitrust and Monopoly, U.S. Senate, 1960-61; asst. prof. econs. Bowling Green (Ohio) U., 1964-66; asst. prof. bus. and govt. Coll. Bus. Adminstrn., U. Minn., Mpls., 1966-70, asso. prof., 1971-75, prof., 1975—, chmn. dept. mgmt., 1977-80; cons. rock salt antitrust cases for atty. gens., Mich., cons. rock salt antitrust cases for atty. gens. of, Calif., Ill., Wis., Minn.; cons. U.S. Justice Dept. Author: An Introduction to Contemporary Business, 3d edit., 1981, Government and Business, 1980; contbr. articles to profl. jours. Mem. Am. Econ. Assn., Royal Econs. Soc. Office: 869 Mgmt and Econs Bldg Minneapolis MN 55455

ERICKSON, WILLIAM HURT, chief justice state supreme court; b. Denver, May 11, 1924; s. Arthur Xavier and Virginia (Hurt) E.; m. Doris Rogers, Dec. 24, 1953; children: Barbara Ann, Virginia Lee, Stephen Arthur, William Taylor. Petroleum Engr., Colo. Sch. Mines., 1947; postgrad., U. Mich., 1949; LL.B., U. Va., 1950. Bar: Colo. 1951. Practiced law, Denver; now chief justice Colo. Supreme Ct.; faculty N.Y. U. Appellate Judges Sch.; mem. exec. com. Commn. on Accreditation of Law Enforcement Agys. Served with USAAF, 1943. Recipient award of merit Colo. Com. Continuing Legal Edn., 1968. Fellow Internat. Acad. Trial Lawyers (former sec.), Am. Coll. Trial Lawyers, Am. Bar Found., Internat. Soc. Barristers (past pres.); mem. Am. Law Inst. (council), Practising Law Inst. (nat. adv. council), Colo. (bd. govs.), Denver Bar Assn., past pres., trustee), Am. Bar Assn. (bd. govs., past chmn. spl. com. on standards criminal justice, former chmn. council criminal law sect., chmn. com. to implement standards criminal justice, mem. long-range planning com., action com. to reduce ct. costs and delay), Order of Coif, Scribes (pres. 1978). Home: 10 Martin Ln Englewood CO 80110 Office: State Judicial Bldg 2 E 14th Ave Denver CO 80203

ERICKSTAD, RALPH JOHN, state supreme ct. justice; b. Starkweather, N.D., Aug. 15, 1922; s. John T. and Anna Louisa (Myklebust) E.; m. Lois Katherine Jacobson, July 30, 1949; children—John Albert, Mark Anders. Student, U. N.D., 1940-43; B.Sc. in Law, U. Minn., 1947, LL.B., 1949. Bar: N.D. bar 1949. Practiced in, Devils Lake, 1949-62, State's atty., Ramsey County, 1953-57; mem. N.D. Senate from, Ramsey County, 1957-62, asst. majority floor leader, 1959, 61; asso. justice Supreme Ct. N.D., 1963-73, chief justice, 1973—; Treas. N.D. States Attys. Assn., 1955, v.p., 1956; mem. N.D. Legislative Research Com., 1957-59, N.D. Budget Bd., 1961-63, Gov. N.D. Spl. Com. Labor, 1960. Past mem. exec. com. Mo. Valley council Boy Scouts Am.; chmn. bd. trustees Mo. Valley Family YMCA, 1966-77. Served with USAAF, 1943-45; ETO. Recipient Silver Beaver award Boy Scouts Am., 1967; Sioux award U. N.D., 1973; 1st Disting. Service award Missouri Valley Family YMCA, 1978. Mem. Am., N.D., Burleigh County bar assns., Nat. Conf. Chief Justices (exec. council), Am. Judicature Soc., Am. Law Inst. Lutheran (del. 1st biennial conv., mem. nominating com.). Clubs: Am. Legion, VFW., Kiwanian. Office: Supreme Ct North Dakota State Capitol Bismarck ND 58505

ERICSON, JAMES DONALD, lawyer; b. Hawarden, Iowa, Oct. 12, 1935; s. Elmer H. and Martha (Sydness) E.; children: Linda Jean, James Robert. B.A. in History, State U. Iowa, 1958, J.D., 1962. Bar: Wis. 1965. Asso. firm Fitzgerald, Brown, Leahy, McGill & Strom, Omaha, 1962-65; with Northwestern Mut. Life Ins. Co., Milw., 1965—, asst. to pres., 1972-75, dir. policy benefits, 1975-76, v.p., gen. counsel, sec., 1976-80, sr. v.p., 980; pres. Grand Ave. Corp.; dir. Allen & O'Hara, Inc., Memphis, Krueger Holdings, Inc. Past chmn. bd. dirs.

Wis. Conservatory of Music; bd. dirs. United Performing Arts Center, Florentine Opera Co., Milw. Repertory Theater, Wis. chpt. Nat. Multiple Sclerosis Soc. Mem. Am., Wis. bar assns., Assn. Life Ins. Counsel, Phi Beta Kappa. Republican. Presbyterian. Office: 720 E Wisconsin Ave Milwaukee WI 53202

ERICSON, RICHARD FERDINAND, management educator; b. Chgo., June 12, 1919; s. Ferdin and Irene (Purdon) E.; m. Davida Gloria Kerr, Aug. 23, 1941; children: Kurt Ferdinand, Dana Morse. A.B., U. Chgo., 1943, M.B.A. with honors, 1948; Ph.D., Ind. U., 1952. Instr. fin. Ind. U., 1949-52; prof., chmn. dept. econs. Stetson U., 1952-56; asso. prof. mgmt. and hosp. adminstrn. U. Iowa, 1956-59; prof. mgmt. George Washington U., 1960—; also dir. program in mgmt. systems and organizational cybernetics; cons. Ohio Depts. Fin. and Hwys., 1959-62; mgmt. devel. and tng. cons. numerous pvt. firms, also fed. agys.; Mem. environ. liaison bd., chmn. Working Group G, Internat. Assembly Nongovtl. Orgns. Concerned with the Environment.; Bd. dirs., sec. Gen. Systems Sci. Inst., Santa Barbara, Calif. Fellow AAAS, World Orgn. Cybernetics and Gen. Systems (hon.); mem. Soc. Gen. Systems Research (v.p., mng. dir. 1968-77, pres. 1978-79), Acad. Mgmt., Inst. Mgmt. Sci., Soc. Gen. Systems Research, Phi Beta Kappa, Beta Gamma Sigma. Home: 12613 Bunting Ln Bowie MD 20715 Office: Lisner Hall 2023 G St George Washington U Washington DC 20052

ERICSON, ROGER D(ELWING), paper company executive; b. Moline, Ill, Dec. 21, 1934; s. Carl D. and Linnea E. (Challman) E.; m. Norma F. Brown, Aug. 1, 1957; children: Catherine Lynn, David. A.B., Stetson U., DeLand, Fla., 1958, J.D., 1958; M.B.A., U. Chgo., 1971. Bar: Fla. 1958, Ill. 1959, Ind. 1974. Atty. Brunswick Corp., Skokie, Ill., 1959-62; asst. sec., asst. gen. counsel Chemetron Corp., Chgo., 1962-73; asst. v.p. Inland Container Corp., Indpls., 1973-75, v.p., gen. counsel, sec., 1975—; v.p., sec., dir. Ga. Kraft Co.; pres., dir. Kraft Land Services, Inc.; vice chmn. bd., pres., dir. G.K. Investments, Inc.; dir. Anderson Box Co., Fastex Packaging Inc., El Morro Corrugated Box Corp., INDISC, Inc., Inland Paper Co., Inc., Inland Real Estate Investments, Inc. Trustee Chgo. Homes for Children, 1971-74; mem. alumni council U. Chgo., 1972-76; mem. Palatine Twp. Youth Commn., 1969-72; sect. chmn. Chgo. Heart Assn., 1972, 73; alumni bd. dirs. Stetson U. Mem. ABA, Chgo. Bar Assn., Ill. State Bar Assn., Ind. Bar Assn., Fla. Bar Assn., Indpls. Bar Assn. (chmn. corp. counsel sect., mem. profl. responsibility com. 1982), Am. Soc. Corp. Secs., Am. Paper Inst. (past mem. govt. affairs com.), Indpls. C. of C. (mem. govt. affairs com.), Omicron Delta Kappa, Phi Delta Phi. Clubs: Plum Grove (Chgo.) (pres. 1969); Crooked Stick Golf (Carmel, Ind.)). Home: 11191 Crooked Stick Ln Carmel IN 46032 Office: Inland Container Corp 151 N Delaware St PO Box 925 Indianapolis IN 46206

ERICSON, WILLIAM ARNOLD, educator; b. Larchmont, N.Y., Jan. 9, 1934; s. Leonard William and Martha (Cassell) E.; m. Peggy R. Lapsley, June 6, 1959; children—Marta Elisabeth, William Leonard. B.S., U. Pa., 1955, M.A., 1958; Ph.D., Harvard, 1963. Asst. prof. math. U. Mich., 1962-67, asso. prof. math. and statistics, 1967-70, prof., 1970—, chmn. dept. statistics, 1969-77; dir. Statis. Research Lab., 1970—; Cons. U.S. Census Bur., 1965-67; Del. to County and State Democratic convs., 1968. Asso. editor: Jour. Am. Statis. Assn, 1967-75; Contbr. articles to sci. jours. Fellow Am. Statis. Assn.; mem. Biometric Soc., Inst. Math. Statistics, AAUP, Beta Gamma Sigma. Home: 3231 Charing Cross Ann Arbor MI 48104

ERIKSEN, CHARLES WALTER, psychologist, educator; b. Omaha, Feb. 4, 1923; s. Charles Hans and Luella (Carlson) E.; m. Garnita Tharp, July 22, 1945 (div. Jan. 1971); children—Michael John, Kathy Ann; m. Barbara Becker, Apr. 1971. B.A., U. Omaha, 1943; Ph.D., Stanford, 1950. Asst. prof. Johns Hopkins, 1949-53, research scientist, 1954-55; lectr. Harvard, 1953-54; faculty U. Ill., Urbana, 1956—, prof., 1959—; Prop. farm; research cons. VA, 1960-80; mem. psychobiology panel NSF, 1963; mem. expt. psychology study sect. NIH, 1958-62, 66-70. Author: Behavior and Awareness, 1962; Editor: Am. Jour. Psychology, 1968; prin. editor: Perception and Psycho Physics, 1971—; cons. editor: Jour. Exptl. Psychology, 1965-71, Jour. Gerontology, 1980—; Contbr. articles to profl. jours. Recipient Stratton award Am. Psychopath. Assn., 1964, NIMH Research Career award, 1964. Mem. Psychonomic Soc., Soc. Exptl. Psychologists, Midwestern Psychol. Assn., AAAS, Sigma Xi. Home: Rural Route I Oakland IL 61943 Office: Psychol Bldg Champaign IL 61820

ERIKSEN, JOHN GEORGE, political science educator; b. Mpls., Aug. 14, 1918; s. N. Henry and Caroline (Hagen) E.; m. Anne Laurette Duenbostle, May 1, 1948; 1 son, Mark John. B.S., U. Minn., 1942, M.A., 1950, Ph.D., 1957; certificate, U. Iowa, 1944, U. Marburg, Germany, 1948. Teaching asst., then instr. polit. sci. U. Minn., 1947-48, 49-50, 50-51; mem. faculty U. Okla., 1951-68, prof. polit. sci., 1965-68, asso. dean Coll. Arts and Sci., 1954-66, dir. honors, 1963-64; dir. U. Munich (Germany) Center, 1963-68, dir. internat. programs, 1967-68; dean Coll. Arts and Scis. Bowling Green (Ohio) State U., 1968-81, dean emeritus, 1983—, prof. polit. sci., 1968-81, provost, 1981-83, Trustee prof. polit. sci., 1983—. Author articles.; Editor: The Development of Soviet Society: Plan and Performance. Served with AUS, 1943-46. Mem. Am. Polit. Sci. Assn., Am. Assn. Advancement Slavic Studies. Home: 427 N Prospect Ave Bowling Green OH 43402

ERIKSEN, OTTO LOUIS, manufacturing company executive; b. Pitts., Jan. 28, 1930; s. Gabriel Soma and Catherine Lilian (Veatch) E.; m. Carmen Licano, July 4, 1981; children by previous marriage: Victor Soma, Catherine Ethel, Gregory Louis. Certificate in indsl. engring., Internat. Corr. Schs., 1965; student law, LaSalle U., 1966-68. Product line mgr. ITT Marlow Co., Midland Park, N.J., 1964-69; gen. mgr. ITT Jabsco, Costa Mesa, Calif., 1969-71; pres. ITT Marine & Recreation Components, Costa Mesa, 1971-83, ITT Jabsco-Worldwide, 1983—. Republican. Episcopalian. Clubs: Balboa Bay (Newport Beach, Calif.); Alta Vista Country (Placentia, Calif.). Home: 4495 Mimosa Dr Yorba Linda CA 92686 Office: 1485 Dale Way Costa Mesa CA 92626

ERIKSEN, PETER BENDTSEN, investment co. exec.; b. Chgo., Oct. 19, 1918; s. Peter A.S. and Ruth M. (Bendtsen) E.; m. Mary Alice Hill, Aug. 20, 1941 (dec. 1968); children—Judith Lynne Eriksen Buren, Kristen Mary; m. Mary Skiles, June 27, 1969. B.S. in Commerce, Northwestern U., 1939. Retail auditor Hart, Schaffner & Marx, Chgo., 1939-42; controller Baskin Clothing Co., Chgo., 1947-52; with Baker, Fentress & Co., Chgo., 1952—; now sr. v.p., sec., treas.; with Medford Corp., Chgo., 1953-81, sec. until, 1981. Served to capt. U.S. Army, 1942-46. Episcopalian. Club: Mid-Day. Home: 207 S Kaspar Ave Arlington Heights IL 60005 Office: Suite 2200 208 S LaSalle St Chicago IL 60604

ERIKSON, ERIK HOMBURGER, psychoanalyst; b. Frankfurt-am-Main, Germany, June 15, 1902; came to U.S., 1933, naturalized, 1939; (parents Danish citizens); m. Joan Mowat Serson, Apr. 1, 1930; children: Kai T., Jon M., Sue Erikson Bloland. Grad., Vienna Psychoanalytic Inst., 1933; M.A. (hon.), Harvard, 1960, L.L.D., 1978; LL.D., U. Calif., 1968, Brown U., 1972; D.Sc. (hon.), Loyola U. at Chgo., 1969, D. Social Sci., Yale, 1971, U. Lund, 1980. Psychoanalyst, 1933—, tng. psychoanalyst, 1942—; teaching, research Harvard Med. Sch., 1934-35, Yale Sch. Medicine, 1936-39, U. Calif. at Berkeley and San Francisco, 1939-51; sr. staff mem. Austen Riggs Center, Stockbridge, Mass., 1951-60; vis. prof. U. Pitts. Sch. Medicine, 1951-60; prof. human devel., lectr. psychiatry Harvard, 1960-70, prof. emeritus, 1970—; sr. cons. in psychiatry Mt. Zion Hosp., San Francisco, 1972—. Author: Childhood and Society, 1950, 2d edit., 1963, Young Man Luther, 1958, Insight and Responsibility, 1964, Identity; Youth and Crisis, 1968, Gandhi's Truth, 1969 (Nat. Book award 1970, Pulitzer prize 1970, Melcher award 1970), Dimensions of a New Identity, 1973, Jefferson Lectures, 1974, Life History and the Historical Moment, 1975, Toys and Reasons: Stages in the Ritualization of Experience, 1977, Identity and the Life Cycle, 1980, The Life Cycle Completed, 1982; Editor: Youth: Change and Challenge, 1963, Adulthood, 1978. Recipient Foneme prize, Milan, 1969, Aldrich award Am. Acad. Pediatrics, 1971, Montessori medal Am. Montessori Soc., 1973, McAlpin Research award Nat. Assn. for Mental Health, 1974. Fellow Am. Acad. Arts and Scis.; mem. Nat. Acad. Edn. (emeritus), Am. Psychoanalytic Assn. (life), Cambridge Sci. Club, Signet Soc., Phi Beta Kappa (hon.). Home: 1705 Centro W Tiburon CA 94920

ERIKSON, KAI, educator, sociologist; b. Vienna, Austria, Feb. 12, 1931; came to U.S., 1933, naturalized, 1937; s. Erik H. and Joan (Serson) E.; m. Joanna M. Slivka, Jan. 27, 1961; children: Keith S., Christopher J. B.A., Reed Coll., 1953; M.A., U. Chgo., 1955, Ph.D., 1963. Instr. psychiatry U. Pitts., 1959-63; assoc. prof. psychiatry Emory U., 1963-66; prof. sociology Yale U., 1966—, master Trumbull Coll., 1969-73. Author: Wayward Puritans: A Study in the Sociology of Deviance, 1976—, Everything in Its Path, 1977; Editor: Yale Rev., 1979—. Served with AUS, 1955-57. Fellow Am. Sociol. Assn. (MacIver award 1967, Sorokin award 1977, pres. 1984-85); mem. Soc. Study Social Problems (pres. 1970-71), Eastern Sociol. Soc. (pres. 1980-81). Home: 115 Blake Rd Hamden CT 06517

ERIKSON, RAYMOND LEO, biology educator; b. Eagle, Wis., Jan. 24, 1936; married, 1958. B.S., U. Wis., 1958, M.S., 1961, Ph.D. in Molecular Bilogy, 1963. From asst. prof. to assoc. prof. U. Colo., Denver, 1965-72, prof. pathology, 1972-82; prof. cellular and devel. biology Harvard U., 1982—. USPHS fellow, 1963-65. Mem. Am. Soc. Biol. Chemists, Am. Soc. Microbiology. Office: Dept Biology Harvard Univ Cambridge MA 02138 *

ERIM, KENAN TEVFIK, classics educator; b. Istanbul, Turkey, Feb. 13, 1929; came to U.S., 1947; s. Kerim Tevfik and Fahime (Osan) E. Student, Coll. de Geneve, 1941-46; B.A., NYU, 1953; M.A., Princeton U., 1955, Ph.D., 1958; Vis. instr., Ind. U., 1957-58. Asst. prof. NYU, N.Y.C., 1958-62, assoc. prof. classics, 1962-71, prof., 1971—; field dir. research project, 1961, now dir. excavation archeol. discovery Aphrodisias in Turkey. Recipient Franklin L. Burr prize Nat. Geog. Soc., 1973; Guggenheim fellow, 1961-62. Mem. Archaeol. Inst. Am. Royal Numis. Soc., Explorers Club, Turk Tarih Kurumu (corr.), Phi Beta Kappa. Research in field. Home: 48 Nassau St Princeton NJ 08542

ERLANDSON, RAY SANFORD, former business educator; b. Wausau, Wis., May 3, 1893; s. Paul and Torgine (Olson) E.; m. Margery McKillop, Aug. 22, 1919; children: Paul McKillop, Ray Sanford, William. A.B., U. Wis., 1918; M.A., George Washington U., 1921. Sch. adminstr., Chippewa Falls, Wis., 1913-16; asst. sec., bus. mgr. NEA, 1919-24; bus. mgr. Internat. Council Religious Edn., 1924-27; sales exec. John Rudin & Co., 1927-29, Grigsby Grunow Co., 1929-32, Zenith Radio Corp., 1932-35; v.p. Rudolph Wurlizer Co., 1935-45, San Antonio Music Co., 1945-50, pres., 1950-53, Bledsoe Furniture Co., 1950-53; dir. 1st Fed. Savs. & Loan Assn., San Antonio; chmn. dept. bus. adminstrn. Trinity U., 1953-64, prof. emeritus, 1980—. Author: (with others) Principle of Retailing, 1955, Marketing, 1958, Principles of Advertising. Pres., chief exec. officer Children's Fund, San Antonio, 1964-70; pres. Am. Inst. Character Edn., 1970-74, chmn. bd., 1970—; bd. dirs. SW Research Center, 1954—; founder Am. Sch. of Air, 1929; pres. Am. Music War Council, 1942-44; chmn. nat. trade practice code com., music industry, 1944-53; Nat. vice chmn. ARC, 1959-60; past bd. dirs. San Antonio chpt., San Antonio Symphony Soc., Taxpayers League, Community Welfare Council; bd. dirs., exec. com. S.W. Research Inst., chmn. bd. of control, 1961-64. Served as lt. F.A. U.S. Army, World War I; cons. joint Army-Navy com. on welfare, recreation, World War II. Named Father of Year, San Antonio, 1951; Distinguished Alumnus award Wis. State U., 1969. Mem. NEA (life), San Antonio Chamber Music Soc. (pres. 1950-56), Research and Planning Council (pres. 1957), San Antonio Council Presidents (pres. 1951), Nat. Assn. Music Mchts. (pres. 1950-52, hon. life). Republican. Presbyterian. Clubs: Masons, Rotary (gov. dist. 584 internat. 1958-59), Rotary (hon. life mem.), Rotary (pres. 1954), Knife and Fork (pres. 1954), Breakfast (pres. 1953), San Antonio.). Home: 401 Shook Ave San Antonio TX 78212 Office: 342 W Woodlawn Ave San Antonio TX 78212

ERLANGER, BERNARD FERDINAND, biochemist, educator; b. N.Y.C., July 13, 1923; s. Leo and Frieda (David) E.; m. Rachel Fenichel, June 23, 1946; children—Laura, Louis, Leon. B.S., Coll. City N.Y., 1943; M.A., N.Y.U., 1949; Ph.D., Columbia, 1951. Chemist U.S. Indsl. Chems. Co., Inc., Newark, 1943-44; tech. adviser Manhattan Project, U.S. Army, Los Alamos, 1944-46; prodn. mgr. Hexagon Labs., Inc., N.Y.C., 1946-48; faculty Columbia, 1951—, prof. microbiology, 1966—; Vis. scientist Instituto Superiore di Sanita, Rome, Italy, 1961-62, Inst. Cell Biology, Shanghai, Peoples Republic China, 1978; cons. to industry; mem. Fulbright-Hays Award Com., 1966-72. Fulbright scholar, U. Republic Uruguay, 1967; Guggenheim fellow Inst. Biologie Physico-Chimique, Paris, 1969; Am. Cancer Soc. scholar, 1979. Mem. Am. Chem. Soc., Am. Soc. Biol. Chemists, Biochem. Soc., Harvey Soc., Am. Soc. Immunologists, Am. Soc. Photobiology. Research on mode of action of antibiotics; investigation of mechanisms of enzyme catalysis, immunochemistry of macromolecules concerned with genetics, photoregulation, biol. receptors. Home: 163-16 15th Dr Beechhurst NY 11357 Office: Columbia U 701 W 168th St New York NY 10032 *The scientist, like the artist, contributes most when he allows his work to be an extension of his individuality. The risks to his ego and security are great, but success brings with it the satisfaction of making a personal imprint on the future of society.*

ERLENBORN, JOHN NEAL, congressman; b. Chgo., Feb. 8, 1927; s. John H. and Veronica M. (Moran) E.; m. Dorothy C. Fisher, May 10, 1952; children: Debra Lynn, Paul Nelson, David John. Student, U. Notre Dame, 1944, U. Ill., 1945-46; J.D., Loyola U., Chgo., 1949. Bar: Ill. bar 1949. With law office Joseph S. Perry, Wheaton, 1949-50; partner firm Erlenborn & Bauer, Elmhurst, 1952-63, Erlenborn, Bauer and Hotte, 1963-71; mem. 89th-98th congresses from 13th Dist., Ill.; Asst. states atty. DuPage County, Ill., 1950-52; mem. Ill. Ho. of Reps. from DuPage County, 1956-64. Served with USNR, 1944-46. Home: Glen Ellyn IL 60137 Office: House Office Bldg Washington DC 20515

ERLICH, VICTOR, educator; b. Petrograd, Russia, Nov. 22, 1914; came to U.S., 1942, naturalized, 1943; s. Henryk and Sophie (Dubnov) E.; m. Iza Sznejerson, Feb. 27, 1940; children: Henry Anthony, Mark Leo. M.A., Free Polish U., Warsaw, 1937; Ph.D., Columbia U., 1951; M.A. (hon.), Yale U., 1963. Asst. lit. editor New Life mag., Warsaw, 1937-39; research writer Yiddish Ency., 1942-43; from asst. prof. to prof. Slavic lit. and langs. U. Wash., 1949-63; Bensinger prof. Russian lit. Yale, 1963—, chmn. dept. Slavic langs., 1963-68, 78-81; Del. congress Fedn. Modern Lang. and Lit., 1957, Internat. Congress Slavists, Sofia, 1963, Warsaw, 1973, Congress Internat. Comparative Lit. Assn., Belgrade, 1967. Author: Russian Formalism: History, Doctrine, 1955, The Double Image: Concepts of the Poet in Slavic Literatures, 1964, Gogol, 1969; Editor: Twentieth Century Russian Criticism, 1975, Pasternak: Twentieth-Century Views, 1977. Served with AUS, 1943-45; ETO. Decorated Purple Heart.; Ford Fellow, 1953-54; Fulbright lectr. U. Leyden, 1957-58; Guggenheim fellow, 1958, 64, 76-77; Nat. Endowment for Humanities fellow, 1968-69. Mem. Am. Assn. Advancement Slavic Studies (v.p.), MLA (exec. council), Internat. Assn. Slavic Langs. and Lits. (exec. council 1957-62), AAUP, Am. Comparative Lit. Assn., Am. Soc. Aesthetics. Home: 25 Glen Pkwy Hamden CT 06517 Office: Yale Univ New Haven CT 06520

ERLICHT, LEWIS HOWARD, broadcasting company executive; b. N.Y.C., Aug. 6, 1939; s. Harry and Estelle (Silk) E.; m. Wilma Binder, June 10, 1961; children: Paul Jon, Jamie Blake. B.A. in Psychology, L.I. U., 1962. With ABC-TV, 1962—, account exec., 1965-70; sales mgr. Sta. WABC-TV, 1970-73, gen. sales mgr., 1973-74; gen. mgr. Sta. WLS-TV, Chgo., 1974-77, v.p. programming, N.Y.C., 1977-79; v.p., asst. to pres. ABC Entertainment, Los Angeles, 1979-80, sr. v.p., asst. to pres., 1980-81, sr. v.p. prime time programming, 1981-83, pres., 1983—. Served with USAF, 1956-60. Mem. Hollywood Radio and TV Soc. (dir.). Office: 2040 Ave of the Stars Los Angeles CA 90067

ERLICK, EVERETT HOWARD, broadcasting company executive; b. Birmingham, Ala., Sept. 12, 1921; s. Julian H. and Bertha Lorraine (Engel) E.; m. Nancy Ruth Jacobs, July 11, 1953; children—James M., Lorre Bert. A.B., Vanderbilt U., 1942; LL.B., Yale, 1948. Bar: N.Y. 1948. Assoc. atty. Engel, Judge & Miller, N.Y. C., 1948-51; asst. gen. counsel Young & Rubicam, N.Y.C., 1951-55, v.p; asso. dir. media relations dept., 1955-58, v.p. radio-TV dept., 1959-61; v.p., gen. counsel Am. Broadcasting-Paramount Theatres, Inc. (now Am. Broadcasting Cos., Inc.), 1961-68, dir., 1962—, group v.p., gen. counsel, 1968-72, sr. v.p., gen. counsel, 1972—; dir. AB-PT, Inc., WLS, Inc.; Mem. Pres.'s Bus. Adv. Com. on Desegregation, 1963, Pres.'s Nat. Citizens Com. for Community Relations, 1964, Nat. Com. for Immigration Reform, 1965. Mem. campaign Am. Cancer Soc., 1965—; nat. chmn. parents com. Duke U., 1974-76, pres.'s assoc., 1976—; trustee Everglades Protection Assn., 1980—. Mem. Phi Beta Kappa. Home: 22 Chester Dr Rye NY 10580 Office: 1330 Ave Americas New York City NY 10019

ERMAN, JOHN, film and TV director; b. Chgo., Aug. 3, 1935; s. Milton G. and Lucile Arlie (Straus) E. B.A. in Applied Arts, UCLA, 1957. Founder The Faculty, Acting Sch., Los Angeles. Free lance actor, 1954-59; casting dir., 20th Century Fox, 1959-63; head TV casting, 20th Century Fox, 1960-61; dir. films including: Making It, 1970, Ace Eli and Rodger of the Skies, 1972; dir. TV films including: Roots, 1977, Just Me and You, 1978, Child of Glass, 1978, Alexander, The Other Side of Dawn, 1977, Roots, The Next Generation, 1979, My Old Man, 1979, Moviola, 1980, The Letter, 1981, Eleanor, First Lady of the World, 1982, Who Will Love My Children, 1983, A Streetcar Named Desire, 1983, Atlanta Child Murders, 1984. Mem. Dirs. Guild Am. Office: Suite 900 10900 Wilshire Blvd Los Angeles CA 90024 *I always try to find a positive statement in the material I'm directing and then endeavor to decide how I can best express that statement and help my fellow creators to do the same.*

ERMENC, JOSEPH JOHN, mechanical engineering educator; b. Milw., Nov. 11, 1912; s. John and Mary (Jeray) E.; m. Mary Wilkinson Steele, June 30, 1952; children: Christine, Elsie, Joseph Steele. B.S., U. Wis., 1934; M.S., U. Mich., 1940; M.A. (hon.), Dartmouth Coll., 1945. Instr. Purdue U., 1936-37, Rensselaer Poly. Inst., 1937-42; asst. prof. mech. engring. Thayer Sch. Engring., Dartmouth, 1942-45, prof., 1945—; Hon. research assoc. U. Coll., London, Eng., 1962-63; Mem. N.H. SSS adv. com. on sci., engring. specialized personnel; mem. com. on power sources for developing countries Nat. Acad. Scis., 1973-74; sci. adv. N.H. Legislature, 1982. Contbr. articles on history of tech. to profl. jours. NSF Sci. Faculty fellow, 1962-63. Mem. ASME (history and heritage com. 1971-82, chmn. 1978-82), N.H. Legis. Acad. Sci. and Tech. (pres. 1982). Home: 77 E Wheelock St Hanover NH 03755

ERMOLAEV, HERMAN SERGEI, educator; b. Tomsk, Russia, Nov. 14, 1924; came to U.S., 1949, naturalized, 1956; s. Sergei and Vera (Kozminykh) E.; m. Tatiana Kuzubova, June 8, 1975; children: Michael, Natalia, Katherine. Student, U. Graz, Austria, 1949; B.A., Stanford U., 1951; M.A., U. Calif.-Berkeley, 1954, Ph.D., 1959. Mem. faculty Princeton U., 1959—, prof. Slavic langs. and lits., 1970—. Author: Soviet Literary Theories, 1917-1934, The Genesis of Socialist Realism, 1963, 77, Mikhail Sholokhov and His Art, 1981, Soviet Literature, 1982; articles; translator: (Gorky): Untimely Thoughts, 1968. McCosh fellow, 1967-68. Mem. Am. Assn. Advancement Slavic Studies, Am. Assn. Tchrs. Slavic and E. European Langs. (pres. 1971-72). Home: 30 N Stanworth Dr Princeton NJ 08540

ERNEST, ALBERT DEVERY, JR., banker; b. Mobile, Ala., June 7, 1930; s. Albert Devery and Dorothy (Griffith) E.; m. Donna Barnett Sims, Nov. 20, 1954; children: Albert Devery III, Lise Sims. B.A., U. Va., 1954; postgrad., Harvard U., 1974. Mgmt. trainee St. Regis Paper Co., N.Y.C., 1954, asst. to v.p., timberlands div., 1958-61; founder, pres. Albert Ernest Enterprises, investment and mgmt. cons., Jacksonville, Fla., 1961-76, Allied Timber Co., Jacksonville, 1968-76; pres., chief exec. officer Barnett Bank of Jacksonville, 1977-82, now dir.; sr. exec. v.p. met. banking Barnett Bank of Fla., Inc., 1982—; vice chmn., dir. Barnett Banks of Fla., Inc., 1984—; pres., chief exec. officer Barnett Bank of South Fla., 1982—, dir., chmn., 1984—; dir. Barnett Bank of Tampa, Barnett Bank of Central Fla., Barnett Banks Trust Co. Bd. dirs. Arts Assembly, Jacksonville, 1978-80, Channel 7, 1978; bd. dirs. Cummer Gallery Art, 1979—, pres., 1981; bd. dirs. World Bus. Council, Inc., 1980, Jacksonville Community Council, Inc., 1978-80, Jacksonville Symphony Assn., 1979—; trustee Jacksonville U., 1975—; pres. Leadership Jacksonville, 1977-78, bd. dirs., 1977-81; trustee Southside Country Day Sch., 1971-78, pres., 1974-76; mem. exec. com. United Way, Jacksonville, 1978—, campaign chmn., 1981-82, pres., 1983. Mem. Am. Bankers Assn., Assn. Res. City Bankers, Forest Farmers Assn. (dir. 1960-76), Mgmt. Policy Council, Fla. Bankers Assn., Fla. Forestry Assn. (dir. 1961-76), Fla. C. of C. (dir. 1980), Jacksonville C. of C. (pres. 1982). Democrat. Episcopalian. Clubs: Deerwood, Farmington Country; Harvard (N.Y.C.); River (dir. 1978—), Timuquana Country). Office: 100 Laura St Jacksonville FL 32202

ERNEST, ROBERT C., consumer products executive; b. 1924. Ed., U. Wis., MIT. With Kimberly-Clark Corp., 1952—, v.p. paper products, 1971, group v.p. fine paper and spltys. group, 1971, dir., 1971, exec. v.p., 1972, pres., 1978—. Office: Kimberly Clark Corp 2100 Winchester Rd Neenah WI 54956

ERNST, CALVIN BRADLEY, vascular surgeon, surgery educator; b. Detroit, May 12, 1934; s. Edward William and Irene Marie (Doelker) E.; m. Elizabeth Abbott, Dec. 21, 1957; children: Lisa Anne, Matthew Abbott, David William, Susan Elizabeth. M.D., U. Mich., 1959. Intern Ohio State U. Med. Ctr., Columbus, 1959-60; resident U. Mich. Med. Ctr., Ann Arbor, 1960-65; instr. surgery U. Mich., 1968-69, asst. prof., 1969-72, assoc. prof., 1972, U. Ky., Lexington, 1972-74, prof., 1974-79; prof. surgery Johns Hopkins U., 1979—, surgeon hosp., 1979—; chmn.

surg. scis. Balt. City Hosps., 1979—; cons. surgeon Loch Raven VAHosp., Balt., 1979—. Contbr. chpts. to books. Served to capt. U.S. Army, 1962-65. Fellow ACS; mem. Soc. Vascular Surgery, Internat. Cardiovascular Soc. (recorder 1977-82), So. Assn. Vascular Surgery (sec. treas. 1976-81, pres. 1980-81), Alpha Omega Alpha. Home: 7915 Ellenham Ave Baltimore MD 21224 Office: Baltimore City Hospitals 4940 Eastern Ave Baltimore MD 21224

ERNST, JIMMY, artist; b. Cologne, Germany, June 24, 1920; naturalized, 1951; s. Max and Louise Amalia (Straus) E. Student, Lindenthal Real-Gymnasium, Cologne, 1932-36, Sch. Arts and Crafts, Altona, Germany, 1938. Prof. dept. art Bklyn. Coll., 1951—; Am. specialist Dept. State's Cultural Exchange Program to, Russia and Poland, 1961; vis. artist Norton Galleries, Palm Beach, Fla. One-man shows, Milw. Art Center, Grace Borgenicht Gallery, N.Y.C., Venice Biennial, Brussels World Fair, Kunstverein Cologne (Germany) Mus., 1963, other nat. and internat. shows, work represented permanent collections, Mus. Modern Art, Met. Mus. Art, Corcoran Gallery, Washington, Guggenheim Mus., Chgo. Art Inst., Albright Art Gallery, Buffalo, others, mural commns. include, exec. dining room Gen. Motors Tech. Center, Am. President Lines, S.S. Adams, Continental Nat. Bank, Lincoln, Nebr.; lectr., various museums in U.S.; exhbns. in, Cologne, Germany, Bielefeld Mus., Germany, 1963-64, Am. House, Berlin. (Recipient Brandeis creative arts award 1957), Am. House, Berlin. (Guggenheim grant for creative painting 1961). Home: Lee Ave East Hampton NY 11937 also 3860 Casey Key Rd Nokomis FL 33555 Office: One Armstrong Gallery 50 W 57th St New York NY 10019 *

ERNST, LOIS GERACI, advertising agency executive; b. Utica, N.Y., Aug. 16, 1933; d. Frank and Mary (Geraci); m. John L. Ernst, June 12, 1971. B.A. summa cum laude, Elmira Coll., 1955; M.A. in English, Duke U., 1957. Successively dir. Interpublic's New Product Devel. Co.; sr. v.p., creative dir. Marshalk Agy., N.Y.C.; sr. v.p., dir., creative dir. Foote, Cone & Belding, N.Y.C.; founder, pres., creative dir., dir. Advt. to Women, Inc., N.Y.C., 1975—. Composer: Imprevu, 1965, You're Not Getting Older, You're Getting Better. Bd. dirs. Elmira Coll., Kidney Found. N.Y. Recipient Triple Threat creative award Internat. Film Festival; recipient 1st Women in Business Entrepreneurial award, 1981; many Effie and creative advt. awards for film prodn. and composition. Mem. Am. Assn. Advt. Agys., Advt. Women N.Y., ASCAP, Phi Beta Kappa. Home: River House 435 E 52d St New York NY 10022 Office: 777 3d Ave New York NY 10017

ERNST, RICHARD JAMES, community college president; b. Niagara, Wis., Feb. 3, 1933; s. Seymour and Rose Marie (Berger) E.; m. Elizabeth Lyle McGeachy, Dec. 23, 1959; children: Marie Elizabeth, Theresa Ann, Richard James. B.S. with high honors, U. Fla., 1956, M.Ed. (univ. fellow), 1959; Ed.D., Fla. State U., 1965. Tchr. Pinellas and Hillsborough County pub. schs., Fla., 1958-62; adminstrv. intern Pinellas County Pub. Schs., 1962-63; instr., asst. dean instrn. St. Petersburg (Fla.) Jr. Coll., 1963-65, dean acad. affairs, 1965-68; pres. No. Va. Community Coll., Annandale, 1968—; Bd. dirs. Consortium for Continuing Higher Edn. in No. Va., 1972—, chmn. bd., 1978; mem. extension and pub. service adv. com. Va. Council Higher Edn., 1972-73, mem. gen. profl. adv. council, 1978—; mem. nat. commn. on acad. affairs Am. Council on Edn., 1972-74, mem. commn. on mil.-higher edn. relations, 1978—; mem. adv. com. nat. orgns. Corp. for Pub. Broadcasting, 1972-74; mem. Va. Adv. Council Vocat. Edn., 1976—, Va. adv. com. Nat. Identification Program for Advancement of Women in Higher Edn. Adminstn., 1977—, Va. Forum on Edn., 1978—; chmn. fin. com., chmn. personnel com., mem. exec. com., adv. council pres.'s, mem. research and edn. com. Va. Community Coll. System; adv. bd. Jr. Service League, No. Va., 1969-71. V.p. bd. trustees Fairfax Hosp., 1972—; also mem. exec. com., chmn. planning and program devel. com., chmn. joint conf. com.; mem. fin. com., mem. adv. panel on hosp.-physician contracts Fairfax Hosp. Assn., 1978—; bd. dirs. Interfaith Center on Corp. Responsibility, 1975—, Coop. for Advancement Community-Based Community Coll. Edn., 1975—; trustee, chmn. acad. affairs com. Mary Baldwin Coll., 1976—, also mem. exec. com. bd. trustees; mem. trustees assembly United Way of Nat. Capitol Area; appointee Gov.'s Task Force on Sci. and Tech.; mem. gen. assembly mission bd. Presbyterian Ch. in U.S., 1974—, chmn. investment com., 1974—, chmn. long-range planning task force, vice chmn. div. central support services, chmn. fiscal and data sub-div. Served with AUS, 1956-58. Fla. Ho. of Reps. scholar, 1952-56. Mem. No. Va. Ednl. TV Assn., So. Assn. Colls. and Schs. (com. on standards and reports, chmn. commn. on colls., chmn. accrediting coms.), Am. Assn. Jr. Colls. (nat. commn. on instrn.), Phi Eta Sigma, Phi Kappa Phi, Kappa Delta Pi, Phi Delta Kappa. Presbyn. (deacon, elder). Home: 8524 Pappas Way Annandale VA 22003

ERNST, ROGER, consultant on development; b. N.Y.C., June 2, 1924; s. Morris L. and Marguerite (Samuels) E.; m. Jean O'Mara, Mar. 15, 1952; children: Deborah, David. B.A. cum laude, Williams Coll., 1948; fgn. area and lang. study, U. Md., 1944; grad., Nat. War Coll., 1956. Joined U.S. Fgn. Service, 1948; Austria desk officer Marshall Plan State Dept., 1948-50; asst. dir NATO, Dept. Def., 1950-55; asst. dir. planning Dept. Def., 1956-59; mem. staff President's Com. Study Fgn. Aid Program, 1958-59; asst. dir. AID mission to India, 1959-62; rep. Peace Corps in India, 1961-62; dep. dir. AID mission to China, 1962-64, AID mission to Korea, 1964-68; dir., econ. minister AID mission to Ethiopia, 1968-73; dir.-minister AID mission to Thailand, Bangkok, 1973-76; spl. cons. to adminstr. tech. applications Tech. Assistance Bur., AID, Washington, 1976-77; coordinator So. African devel. analysis Bur. for Africa, 1977-78; coordinator internat. devel. programs U. Hawaii Coll. Tropical Agr., Honolulu, 1978-80; cons. on devel., 1980—; pres. Devel. Consultancy Internat., Inc. Served with AUS, 1943-47. Decorated Bronze Star; Civil Merit medal, Republic of Korea; recipient William Jump award for exemplary pub. service. Mem. Nantucket Hist. Assn. Lodge: Rotary. Home: 5400 Duvall Dr Bethesda MD 20816 Nantucket MA 02554 *Success comes from: good preparation; "no indecision, no regret" when taking action; "catching the tide;" Having "fun" while doing; Being experimental and able to correlate the unrelated elements in a situation. Management succeeds when managers focus on directing peoples energies, not money or physical resources which are finite.*

ERNST, ROGER CHARLES, natural resource cons., assn. exec.; b. Denver, May 9, 1914; s. Alexander Frederick and Elizabeth Jackson (Rogers) E.; m. Mary Louise Young, Apr. 4, 1942; children—Michael, Judith, Jeanne. B.S. in Commerce, U. Denver, 1937. Investment counselor, 1937-39; tech. report writer R.J. Tipton, Denver, 1940-42; exec. sec. Frying-Pan-Ark. Project, Pueblo, Colo., 1947-50; asst. to gen. mgr. Salt River Project, Phoenix, 1950-52; mgr. Wellton-Mohawk Irrigation Dist, Wellton, Ariz., 1952-53; land commr. Ariz., Phoenix, 1953-57, asst. sec. interior, Washington, 1957-60; cons. Ariz. Pub. Service Co., Phoenix, 1961—; mem. Alaska Rail and Hwy. Commn., 1957-60, Nat. Water Commn., 1969-73; mem. bd. Central Ariz. Water Conservation Dist., 1971—, pres., 1971-77. Served with AUS, 1943-46. Mem. Sigma Alpha Epsilon. Republican. Episcopalian. Home: 4047 E Rancho Dr Phoenix AZ 85018 Office: PO Box 21666 Phoenix AZ 85036

ERNST, WALLACE GARY, geology educator; b. St. Louis, Dec. 14, 1931; s. Fredrick A. and Helen Grace (Mahaffey) E.; m. Charlotte Elsa Pfau, Sept. 7, 1956; children: Susan, Warren, Alan, Kevin. B.A., Carleton Coll., 1953; M.S., U. Minn., 1955; Ph.D., Johns Hopkins U., 1959. Geologist U.S. Geol. Survey, Washington, 1955-56; fellow (Geophys. Lab.), Washington, 1956-59; mem. faculty UCLA, 1960—, prof. geology and geophysics, 1968—, chmn. geology dept. (now earth and space scis. dept.), 1970-74, 78-82. Author: Amphiboles, 1968, Earth Materials, 1969, Metamorphism and Plate Tectonic Regimes, 1975, Subduction Zone Metamorphism, 1975, Petrologic Phase Equilibria, 1976, The Geotectonic Development of California, 1981, The Environment of the Deep Sea, 1982. Mem. Nat. Acad. Sci. (chmn. geology sect. 1979-82), AAAS, Am. Geophys. Union, Am. Geol. Inst., Geol. Soc. Am., Geochem. Soc., Mineral. Soc. Am. (recipient award 1969, pres. 1979-80), Mineral. Soc. London. Home: 16939 Livorno Dr Pacific Palisades CA 90272 Office: Dept Earth and Space Scis U Calif Los Angeles CA 90024

ERNST, WILLIAM THEODORE, rubber co. exec.; b. Canton, Ohio, Apr. 24, 1920; s. William Addison and Helen (Kauffman) E.; m. Carolyn Leahy, Apr. 24, 1943 (div.); 1 son, William Theodore. A.B., Harvard U., 1941; postgrad., Bus. Sch., 1941-42. With Mohawk Rubber Co., 1946—, sec.-treas., Akron, Ohio, 1956-65, v.p. fin., 1965-74, exec. v.p., Hudson, Ohio, 1974-79, pres., 1979—, dir., 1960—. Served to lt. USNR, 1942-46. Mem. New Eng. Soc. of N.Y., Phi Beta Kappa. Clubs: Clevelander, Univ. of Cleve. Home: 18200 Shaker Blvd Shaker Heights OH 44120 Office: 50 Executive Pkwy Hudson OH 44236

ERNSTROM, CARL ANTHON, food science educator; b. Draper, Utah, Mar. 28, 1922; s. Carl Ludvig and Jennie Charlotte (Nielsen) E.; m. Maurine A. Lawrence, Aug. 24, 1949; children—Brian, Carl R., Jean, Maren. Student, U. Colo., 1943-44; B.S., Utah State U., 1949, M.S., 1951; Ph.D., U. Wis., 1956. With Wis. Extension Service, 1953-54; researcher Hansen Lab., Milw., j71955-56; asst., then asso. prof. dept. dairy and food industries U. Wis., 1956-65; prof., head dept. food sci. and industries Utah State U., Logan, 1967-71, head dept. nutrition and food sci., 1971—; Cons. to industry. Assoc. editor: Jour. Dairy Sci., 1974—. Served with USMCR, 1943-46, 51-52. Fellow Inst. Food Technologists; mem. Am. Dairy Sci. Assn. (Pfizer award 1968), Sigma Xi, Phi Kappa Phi. Home: 730 Mountain View Dr Logan UT 84321

EROLA, JUDITH ANNABEL, Canadian government official; b. Sudbury, Ont., Can., Jan. 16, 1934; s. Niilo M. and Laura (Rauhala) Jacobsen) E.; m. Voltto Erola, Aug. 27, 1955; children: Laura Elizabeth, Kelly Ann. Interviewer, commentator, performer CKSO and CKNC-TV, 1950—; account exec. Radio Sta. CHNO, 1976-80; co-owner, operator Marina & Tourist Outfitting Bus.; mem. House of Commons Nickel Belt, Ont., Can., 1980—, minister of state for mines, 1980—; minister for status of women, 1981—, minister consumer and corporate affairs; Sec.-treas. Nickel Belt Riding Assn.; past bd. dirs. Meml. Hosp., Sudbury; mem. Sudbury Folk Art Council; founding mem. Sudbury Little Theatre. Mem. Sudbury Dist. C. of C. (mem. advt. com.). Liberal. Lutheran. Home: Rural Route 1 Whitefish ON P0M 3E0 Canada Office: 707 Confederation Bldg Ottawa ON K1A 0X2 Canada

EROS, PETER, symphony orchestra conductor; b. Budapest, Hungary, Sept. 22, 1932; came to U.S., 1972; s. Egon and Agnes (Rozgonyi) E.; m. Georgy Weiser, Dec. 4, 1956; children: George Otto, Andrew Robert. Grad. piano, composition, conducting, Franz Liszt Music Acad., Budapest, 1956. Mem. faculty Amsterdam Mus. Conservatory, 1960-65. Asst. condr., Holland and Salzburg Festivals, 1958-61; asso. condr., Amsterdam Concertgebouw Orch., 1960-65; internat. guest condr., 1963—; chief condr., Malmo (Sweden) Symphony, 1966-68; prin. guest condr., Melbourne (Australia) Symphony, 1969-70; music dir., San Diego Symphony Orch., 1972-80; condr. laureate, 1980-81; resident condr., Peabody Symphony, Johns Hopkins U., 1982—. Clubs: Melbourne Savage; Cuyamaca, Kona Kai (San Diego). Home: 7019 Bobhird Dr San Diego CA 92119

ERSEK, ROBERT ALLEN, plastic surgeon, inventor; b. Ridley Twp., Pa., June 19, 1938; s. Joseph Martin and Theda Louise (Kromes) E.; m. Gerry Avenelle Mullins, Mar. 28, 1958; children: Stephanie Louise, Cynthia Leigh. B.S., Morris Harvey Coll., 1961; M.D., Hahnemann Med. Coll., 1966. Diplomate Nat. Bd. Med. Examiners. Intern surgery U. Minn. Hosps., Mpls., 1966-67; research fellow U. Pa., 1962, Hahnemann Med. Coll., Phila., 1963-65; med. fellow dept. surgery U. Minn., 1967-73; resident dept. plastic and reconstructive surgery Tulane U., New Orleans, 1975-77; fellow in plastic surgery U. Miss., Jackson, 1978; clin. instr. plastic surgery U. Tex. Health Sci. Center, San Antonio, 1979; chmn. bd., med. dir. Med. Gen. Inc., 1969—; dir., med. dir. Genetic Labs., 1970—; chmn. bd. Remedco, 1980—; gen. partner Ersek & Beisang; med. dir., dir. Emerald Airlines, Inc. Author: Pain Control, 1981; Co-editor: Organ Perfusion and Preservation, 1969; contbr. articles to med. jours. Bd. dirs. Austin Civic Ballet. Served to maj. USAF, 1973-75. Recipient Alan Edelsohn prize Hahnemann Med. Coll., 1966; Grand award for exhibit Student Am. Med. Assn. Squibb Nat. Contest, 1967; award of excellence in med. writing Minn. Medicine, 1970. Mem. A.C.S. (candidate group), Am. Coll. Emergency Physicians, AMA, La. Med. Soc., Soc. for Cryosurgery, Am. Soc. Plastic and Reconstructive Surgeons, Am. Soc. Artificial Internal Organs, Nat. Acad. Sci., Am. Med. Writers Assn., Smithsonian Inst., Nat. Assn., Flying Physicians, AAUP, Am. Trauma Soc., Tex. Med. Assn., Travis County Med. Soc., Am. Burn Assn., Serpent Soc., Aesculpulation Soc., Austin Knights of Symphony, Phi Kappa Delta. Patentee numerous surg. devices. Home: 2300 Cypress Point W Austin TX 78746 Office: 309 Park St Davids 800 E 30th St Austin TX 78705

ERSKINE, ROBERT BRUCE, hotel company executive; b. Hackensack, N.J., Oct. 31, 1982; s. Kenneth W. and Elise (Kraimer) E.; m. Jeanette Harbison, June 5, 1954; children: Ronald, Laura, Catherine, Jennifer. B.M.E., Villanova U., 1955. Vice pres. A.I. Kearney, Inc., Chgo., 1966-74; with I.U. Distbn. Service, Phila., 1974-77; sr. v.p. Holiday Inns, Inc., Memphis, 1977-82; v.p. support services Harrah's Hotel Casino, Atlantic City, 1982—. Served to lt. (jg.) USN, 1955-58. Home: Six Mill Ln Linwood NJ 08221 Office: Harrah's Marina Hotel Casino 1752 Brigantine Blvd Atlantic City NJ 08401

ERTEGUN, AHMET MUNIR, record co. exec., profl. soccer club exec.; b. Istanbul, Turkey, July 31; s. M. Munir and Hayrunisa Rustem (Temel) E.; m. Ioana Maria Banu, Apr. 6, 1961. B.A., St. John's Coll., Annapolis, Md., 1944; postgrad., Georgetown U., 1944-46. Co-founder Atlantic Records, N.Y.C., 1947, chmn. bd., chief exec. officer, 1947—; co-founder Cosmos Soccer Club, N.Y.C., 1971, pres., 1971—; Chmn. bd. Am. Turkish Soc.; bd. govs., bd. visitors St. John's Coll.; mem. adv. council dept. Near Eastern Studies. Producer various Grammy-Award-winning records; writer various award-winning songs. Princeton U. Recipient Humanitarian award Conf. Personal Mgrs., 1977; Humanitarian of Yr. award T.J. Martell Found. Leukemia Research, 1978; named Man of Yr. United Jewish Appeal, 1970. Mem. Rec. Industry Assn. Am. (dir.), Black Music Assn. (dir.), Nat. Assn. Record Merchandisers (Presdl. award 1977), Nat. Acad. Rec. Arts and Scis., ASCAP, Broadcast Music Industry, N. Am. Soccer League. Office: 75 Rockefeller Plaza New York NY 10019

ERTEL, ALLEN EDWARD, congressman; b. Williamsport, Pa., Nov. 7, 1936; s. Clarence and Helen (Froehner) E.; m. Catharine Bieber Klepper, June 20, 1959; children—Taylor John, Edward Barnhardt, Amy Sara. B.A., Dartmouth Coll., 1958; M.S. in Bus. Adminstrn, Amos Tuck Sch. Bus. Adminstrn., Thayer Sch. Engring., 1959; LL.B., Yale U., 1965. Bar: Pa., Del., U.S. Supreme Ct. bars. Law clk. U.S. Dist. Ct. of Del., 1965-66; asso. firm Candor, Youngman, Gibson & Gault, Williamsport, 1967-72, Ertel & Kieser, 1972-76; dist. atty., Lycoming County, Pa., 1967-76; mem. 95th-97th Congresses from 17th Pa. Dist.; Del. Democratic. Nat. Conv., 1972. Served with USN, 1959-62. Mem. Pa., Del. bar assns., Dartmouth Soc. Engrs. Lutheran. Club: Lions. *

ERTEL, INTA J(ANNERS), pediatrics educator, pediatrician; b. Riga, Latvia, Jan. 5, 1932; came to U.S., 1950; d. Nikolajs B. and Alma (Steikmehis) Janners; m. Paul Y. Ertel, Aug. 20, 1955; children: Dace, Lynne. A.A., Lycoming Coll., 1952; B.S., Mary Washington Coll., 1955; M.D., U.Va., 1959. Diplomate: Am. Bd. Pediatrics. Rotating intern Cleve. Met. Gen. Hosp., 1959-60; resident in pediatrics U. Mich., Ann Arbor, 1960-62, instr. pediatrics, pediatric hematology-oncology, 1962-66, asst. prof., assoc. prof., 1966-77, prof., 1977—. Mem. Am. Acad. Pediatrics, Am. Soc. Clin. Oncology, Ambulatory Pediatric Assn., Cancer Research Assn., Am. Med. Women's Assn. Democrat. Lutheran. Home: 13453 Piker Rd Chelsea MI 48118 Office: Pediatrics OPD Annex Univ Mich Ann Arbor MI 48118

ERTESZEK, JAN JAKUB, apparel manufacturing company executive; b. Krakow, Poland, Dec. 26, 1913; s. Mer and Rosalia (Latner) E.; m. Olga Bertram, Dec. 6, 1939; children: Victoria, Mary, Christina. LL.D., U. Krakow, 1938, Whittier Coll., 1978. Legal asst., Krakow, 1936-38; founder, chmn. bd. The Olga Co., Van Nuys, Calif., 1942—. Recipient Gold medal Am. Freedom Found., 1950, Am. Patriot award Americanism Ednl. League, 1983. Mem. Beta Gamma Sigma. Republican. Presbyterian. Office: 7900 Haskell Ave Van Nuys CA 91409

ERVANIAN, ARMEN, manufacturing company executive; b. Chgo., Sept. 25, 1937; s. Arthur and Annie (Tatoian) E.; m. Joan Strelecky, Aug. 21, 1960; children: Renee Ruth, James Armen. A.A. in Psychology and Engleis, Wilson Jr. Coll., 1958; student, Roosevelt U., 1958-60, John Marshall Law Sch., 1960-61; Ins. Cert., Ins. Inst. Am., 1964; B.Law, LaSalle Extension U., 1969; cert. of Completion, Wharton Sch. Bus., 1979. Claims adjuster Continental Ins. Co., Chgo., 1961-62; claims supr. Security Ins. Group, Chgo., 1962-66; real estate mgr. Armour & Co., Chgo., 1967-71; dir. real estate The Greyhound Corp., Phoenix, 1971-73, v.p. real estate, 1973—; pres., chief exec. officer Greyhound Realty Corp., Phoenix, 1981—. Treas. Madison Meadows Elem. Sch., 1975; pres. bd. dirs. Recreation Assn. Brophy Dads Club, Phoenix, 1973-76; bd. dirs. Brophy Coll. Prep Sch., 1978-79. Recipient Leadership and Achievement award Nat. Assn. Corp. Real Estate Execs., 1982. Mem. Nat. Assn. Rev. Appraisers, Nat. Assn. Corp. Real Estate Execs. (group v.p. 1980), Am. Planning Assn., Ariz. Planning Assn., Phoenix C. of C. (dir.). Clubs: Ariz., Watering Hole Racquet. Office: Greyhound Greyhound Tower Phoenix AZ 85077

ERVIN, JOHN, JR., publisher; b. Mt. Vernon, N.Y., Jan. 8, 1927; s. John and Edith Gertrude (Atkinson) E.; m. Jean Adams, June 17, 1950; children: Keith, Andrew, Bruce, Alec, John A. B.S. with honors, Yale U., 1949. Editorial staff Princeton U. Press, 1952-57; dir. U. Minn. Press, 1957—; mem. governing bd. for nat. enquiry into prodn. and dissemination of scholarly knowledge Am. Council Learned Socs.; cons. Nat. Hist. Publs. and Records Commn., 1974-75, Nat. Endowment for Humanities, 1977-78, 83. Author: (with Jean Ervin) The Twin Cities Explored; Contbr. articles to profl. jours. Served with USNR, 1945-46. Mem. Assn. Am. Univ. Presses (dir. 1964-65, v.p. 1970-71, dir. 1979-81), Am. Univ. Press Services (dir. 1964-65, v.p. 1970-71), Minn. Book Pubs. Roundtable (pres. 1978-79), Phi Beta Kappa, Phi Kappa Phi. Club: Campus. Home: 59 Seymour Ave SE Minneapolis MN 55414 Office: U Minn Press 2037 University Ave SE Minneapolis MN 55455

ERVIN, ROBERT MARVIN, lawyer; b. nr. Ocala, Fla., Jan. 19, 1917; s. Richard William and Carrie (Phillips) E.; m. Frances Anne Cushing, Dec. 25, 1941; children: Anne Cushing (Mrs. Henry Lamar Rowe), Robert Marvin. B.S. in Bus. Adminstrn, U. Fla., 1941, LL.B., 1947. Bar: Fla. 1947. Practice in, Tallahassee, 1947—; partner firm Ervin, Varn, Jacobs, Odom & Kitchen (and predecessor firms), 1947—; U.S. referee in bankruptcy No. Dist. Fla., part time, 1952-72. Mem. Fla. Constn. Revision Commn., 1966-68; Trustee U. Fla. Law Center Assn.; mem. bd. visitors Fla. State U. Coll. Law. Served with USMCR, 1941-45; PTO; col. Res.ret. Recipient Distinguished Service award for legal edn. John B. Stetson U., 1966, Armed Forces League, 1966. Fellow Fla. Bar Found., Am. Bar Found., Nat. Coll. Criminal Def. Lawyers, Internat. Acad. Trial Lawyers, Am. Coll. Trial Lawyers; mem. Fla. Bar (pres. 1965-66, Disting. Service award 1966), Am. Bar Retirement Assn. (pres. 1980-82), ABA (ho. of dels., bd. govs., chmn. sect. criminal justice 1975-76), Am. Coll. Trial Lawyers (regent), Nat. Conf. Referees in Bankruptcy (pres. 1963-64), Res. Officers Assn., Marine Corps Res. Officers Assn., Fla. Blue Key, Phi Alpha Delta, Alpha Kappa Psi. Democrat. Baptist. Club: Elk. Home: 1434 Crestview Ave Tallahassee FL 32303 Office: 305 S Gadsden St PO Box 1170 Tallahassee FL 32302

ERVIN, SAMUEL JAMES, III, federal judge; b. Morganton, N.C., Mar. 2, 1926; s. Sam E. B.S., Davidson Coll., 1948; LL.B., Harvard U., 1951. Bar: N.C. Pvt. practice law, Morganton, 1952-57; mem. firm Patton, Ervin & Starnes (and predecessors), Morganton, 1957-67; judge Superior Ct. 25th Jud. Dist. N.C.; now judge U.S. Ct. Appeals (4th cir.), Morganton; solicitor Burke County (N.C.) criminal Ct., 1954-56. Pres. Davidson Coll. Nat. Alumni Assn., 1973-74; trustee Davidson Coll., 1982-86. Named Young Man of Yr. Morganton Jaycees, 1954. Mem. Borke County C. of C. (pres. 1962). Office: PO Drawer 2146 Morganton NC 28655 *

ERVIN, SAMUEL JAMES, JR., former U.S. senator; b. Morganton, N. C., Sept. 27, 1896; s. Samuel J. and Laura Theresa (Powe) E.; m. Margaret Bruce Bell, June 18, 1924; children: Samuel James III, Margaret Leslie (Mrs. Gerald Hansler), Laura Powe (Mrs. William E. Smith). A.B., U. N.C., 1917, LL.D., 1951; LL.B., Harvard, 1922; LL.D., Western Carolina Coll., 1955, Wake Forest U., 1971, George Washington U., Davidson Coll., St. Andrews Presbyn. Coll., 1972, Boston U., 1973, U. N.C. at Charlotte, 1974, Drexel U., 1974, Colgate U., 1974, U. Cin., 1974, Belmont Abbey Coll., 1975, Warner Pacific Coll., 1975, Anderson Coll., 1976, U. N.C.-Greensboro, 1983; Dr. Pub. Adminstrn., Suffolk U., Boston, 1957; L.H.D., Wilkes Coll., 1973, Chgo. State U., 1977; Litt.D., Catawba Coll., 1974; D.Con.L., Appalachian U., 1974; J.D., New Eng. Sch. Law, 1975; D. Pub. Service, U. West Fla., 1983. Bar: N.C. 1919. Engaged in gen. practice, Morganton, 1922—; rep. from Burke County N.C. Gen. Assembly, 1923, 25, 31; judge Burke County Criminal Ct., 1935-37, N.C. Superior Ct., 1937-43; resigned to resume practice law; rep. in Congress from 10th N.C. Dist., 1946-47; asso. justice N.C. Supreme Ct., 1948-54; U.S. senator from N.C., 1954-74; mem. Senate armed services com., judiciary com., chmn. separation of powers subcom., govt. operations com., Presdl. campaign activities select com.; Mem. N.C. Bd. Law Examiners, 1944-46, N.C. Democratic Exec. Com., 1930-37. Author: The Watergate Conspiracy, Humor of a Country Lawyer. Trustee Morganton Graded Schs., 1927-30, U. N.C., 1932-35, 1945-46, Davidson Coll., 1948—. Served with Co. I, 28th Inf., 1st div. U.S.

Army, World War I; French front. Decorated French Fourragere, Purple Heart with oak leaf cluster, Silver Star, D.S.C.; U.D.C. cross mil. service. Mem. ABA, N.C. Bar Assn., N.C. State Bar, Jr. Am. Legion, V.F.W., D.A.V., Soc. 1st Div., Army and Navy Legion Valor, Morganton C. of C., Am. Judicature Soc., N.C. Lit. and Hist. Assn., So. Hist. Assn., Soc. Mayflower Descs. N.C. (gov. 1950-52), Gen. Alumni Assn. U.N.C. (pres. 1947-48), Soc. Cincinnati, S.A.R., Sigma Upsilon, Phi Delta Phi. Democrat. Presbyn. Clubs: Mason (33 deg., K.T.), Moose, Kiwanian, Kip. Home: PO Box 69 Morganton NC 28655

ERVIN, THEODORE ROBERT, public health administrator, health consultant; b. Lansing, Mich., May 12, 1928; s. Grant D. and Queen L. (Munger) E.; m. Yarda D. Anderson, Sept. 11, 1948; children: Christine K., Timothy P. B.A. in Communications, Mich. State U., 1960, M.A. in Sociology and Anthropology, 1962. Info. officer Mich. Assn. TB., Lansing, 1947-55; asst. to dir. Mich. Dept. Pub. Health, Lansing, 1955-63, assoc. dir., 1964-74, dep. dir., 1974—; health cons. Citrin Corp., Romulus, Mich., 1981—; chmn. bd. Astho Pub. Health Found., McLean, Va., 1982-83; chmn. mgmt. com. Assn. State and Territorial Health Ofcl., Washington, 1965-70; cons. Mich. State Univ. Coll. Human Medicine Devel., E. Lansing, 1975—. Author: Crosscurrents of Influence, 1964; editor: Annual Proceedings Health Policy Guide, 1963-83. Recipient Dist. Service award Mich. Health Officers Assn., Lansing, 1973, Leadership award Mich. Acad. Family Practice, Lansing, 1978. Fellow Am. Pub. Health Assn.; mem. Mich. Pub. Health Assn. Office: Mich Dept Pub Health 3500 N Logan Lansing MI 48909

ERVING, JULIUS WINFIELD, basketball player; b. Roosevelt, N.Y., Feb. 22, 1950; s. Callie Erving Lindsey. Student, U. Mass. With Virginia Squires, Am. Basketball Assn., 1971-73, N.Y. Nets, Am. Basketball Assn., 1973-76, Phila. 76ers, Nat. Basketball Assn., 1976—; mem. Nat. Basketball Assn. Championship team, 1983; player Nat. Basketball Assn. All-Star Game, 1976-84. Appeared in: film The Fish That Saved Pittsburgh, 1979. Named Rookie of Year, 1972. Office: care Phila 76ers Veterans Stadium PO Box 25040 PA 19147

ERWIN, ALBERT RICH, educator, physicist; b. Charlotte, N.C., May 1, 1931; s. Albert Rich and Lois (Lee) E.; m. Mary Jane Murray, June 12, 1954; 1 dau., Christy Lee. B.S., Duke, 1953; Ph.D., Harvard, 1958. Research asso. Brookhaven Nat. Lab., 1956-58; faculty U. Wis., 1959—, prof. physics, 1965—. Spl. research on high energy particles physics. Home: 1150 University Ave Madison WI 53706

ERWIN, DAVID WILLIAMS, insurance company executive; b. Clarksville, Tex., Jan. 21, 1923; s. Roy M. and Mamie Catherine (Williams) E.; m. Mary Jane Dinwiddie, Sept. 29, 1945; children: Andrew, Matthew, John, Mary Catherine. Student, U. Tex., 1940-46. With Travelers Ins. Co., 1948-61; agency mgr. Tenn. Life Ins. Co., Houston, 1961, v.p., dir. agencies, 1961-66, sr. v.p., dir. agencies, 1966-68, pres., 1968-72, Phila. Life Ins. Co., 1972-73, chmn. bd., chief exec. officer, 1973—, Phila. Am. Life Ins. Co.; dir. Fidelity Corp. Pa. Served with USAAF, 1943-46. Mem. Gen. Agts. and Mgrs. Assn., Nat., Phila. assns. life underwriters. Methodist. Clubs: Union League (Phila); Pine Valley (N.J.) Golf; Merion Golf (Ardmore, Pa.). Home: 1309 Partridge Ln Villanova PA 19085 Office: One Independence Mall Philadelphia PA 19106

ERWIN, ELMER LOUIS, cement company executive; b. Visalia, Calif., Oct. 6, 1926; s. Louis Nelson and Myra Erla (Hector) E.; m. Jeanne Prothero, Feb. 27, 1954; children: Catherine Lynn, Christopher Lawrence. B.S., U. Calif.-Berkeley, 1950. Registered profl. engr., Calif. With Kaiser Cement Corp., Oakland, Calif., 1957-80, v.p. mfg. and distbn., 1980—. Office: Kaiser Cement Corp 300 Lakeside Dr Oakland CA 94612

ERWIN, FRANK WILLIAM, mgmt. cons., pub. co. exec.; b. Elizabeth, N.J., Nov. 22, 1931; s. Frank J. and Jessie (Rugero) E.; m. Bridget E. Taddeo, June 26, 1965. B.A. cum laude, N.Y. U., 1957. With MBS, 1957-62, asst. to pres., asst. sec. to bd. dirs., 1960-62; dep. dir. div. selection, dir. recruiting ops. Peace Corps, 1962-65; exec. asst. to sec. labor, 1965-68; pres. Richardson, Bellows, Henry & Co., Inc., 1968—. Served with AUS, 1949-52. Mem. Am. Mgmt. Assn., Am. Psychol. Assn., Am. Soc. Personnel Adminstrn., Am. Numis. Assn. Home: 1400 S Joyce St Arlington VA 22202 Office: 1140 Connecticut Ave NW Washington DC 20036

ERWIN, JAMES OTIS, clergyman, educator, religious organization executive; b. Marion, N.C., Apr. 28, 1922; s. John Adam and Idella (Cannon) E.; m. Adeline Comer, Aug. 13, 1947; children: JoNina Marie Erwin Abron, Janet Ann Erwin Hall, Judith Kathryn. B.A., Johnson C. Smith U., 1943; M.Div., Garrett Theol. Sem., 1946; M.R.E., Iliff Sch. Theology, 1953, S.T.M., 1979; LL.D., Rust Coll., 1971, W.Va. Wesleyan U., 1972; postgrad., U. Iowa, 1966-67. Ordained to ministry United Meth. Ch., 1946; chaplain, instr. Morristown (Tenn.) Coll., 1946-48, pres., 1970-72; chaplain, chmn. dept. religion, philosophy Wiley Coll., Marshall, Tex., 1948-53; asst. prof. philosophy Lincoln U., Jefferson City, Mo., 1953-66; founder Wesley Found., 1953, minister, dir., 1953-66; assoc. minister Wesley Found., U. Iowa, 1966-67; pastor Wesley United Meth. Ch., 1968-70; dean students, chaplain Philander Smith Coll., Little Rock, 1967-70; pres. Morristown (Tenn.) Coll., 1970-72; pastor St. James United Meth. Ch., Chgo., 1972-76; dist. supt., Western dist. conf. United Meth. Ch., 1976—; pastor South Shore United Meth. Ch., 1982—; adminstr. Child Care Ctr. St. James United Meth. Ch., Chgo.; Exec. dir. Found. for Preservation St. James, Inc., 1974-76. Contbr. articles to profl. jours. Mem. citizens participation com. Douglas-Cherokee Office Econ. Opportunity, 1970-72; active Cherokee Guidance Center, Morristown, 1970-72; vice chmn. Boy Scouts Am., Little Rock, 1968-70; mem. adv. bd. No. Ill. U. Center for Inner City Studies, 1976—; rec. sec. Council Presidents United Meth. Colls., 1971-72; bd. dirs., rec. sec. Ch. Fedn. Greater Chgo.; bd. dirs. Meth. Youth Services; mem. nat. com. Meth. Fedn. for Social Action, 1974—; mem. exec. com. Interdenoml. Ministers Alliance, Chgo., 1976—; treas. Ministerial Assn. of South Shore; mem. South Shore Council of Chs., 1982—; mem., co-chmn. higher edn. com. No. Ill. United Meth. Conf.; Bd. dirs. United Meth. Found. No. Ill., 1974—; Trustee Rust Coll., 1979—. Mem. Assn. Pvt. Minority Jr. Colls. (co-founder 1970, nat. pres. 1970—), Insts. Religion and Health, Phi Beta Sigma, Alpha Phi Omega. Home: 7659 S Cregier Ave Chicago IL 60649 Office: 7350 S Jeffrey Blvd Chicago IL 60649

ERWIN, J(OHN) D(AVID), service merchandise executive; b. Harrison, Ark., Oct. 26, 1935; s. Jethro Tom and Donna Clayton (Owens) E.; m. Judith Ann Merriweather, June 18, 1954; children: Linda, John. Br. mgr. Pepsi-Cola Bottling Co., Springdale, Ark., 1951-56; salesman, supr. Sav-A-Stop, Springfield, Mo., 1956-61; asst. dir. sales Mass Merchandisers, Inc., Harrison, 1961-63, v.p., dir. sales, 1963-75, exec. v.p. sales, 1975-80, exec. v.p. trade relations, 1980-81, pres. service sales, 1981-82, pres., 1983—. Mem. Nat. Assn. Service Merchandisers (dir.), Harrison C. of C. (dir.). Methodist. Home: Route 1 PO Box 152 Harrison AR 72601 Office: Mass Merchandisers Inc PO Box 790 Harrison AR 72601

ERWIN, RICHARD C., federal judge; b. McDowell County, N.C., Aug. 23, 1923; s. John Adam and Flora (Cannon) E.; m. Demerice Whitley, Aug. 25, 1946; children—Richard Cannon, Jr., Aurelia Whitley. B.A., Johnson C. Smith U., 1947; LL.B., Howard U., 1951; LL.D., Pfeiffer Coll., 1980, Johnson C. Smith U., 1981. Bar: N.C., U.S. Supreme Ct. Practice law, Winston-Salem, N.C., 1951-77; judge N.C. Ct. Appeals, 1978, U.S. Dist. Ct. Middle Dist., N.C., 1980—; rep. N.C. Gen. Assembly, chmn. hwy. safety com. Trustee Forsyth County Legal Aid Soc., Amos Cottage, Inc.; chmn. bd. trustees Bennett Coll.; bd. dirs. N.C. 4-H Devel. Fund, Inc.; bd. visitors Div. Sch., Duke U.; trustee Children's Home, Winston-Salem; mem. steering com. Winston-Salem Found.; bd. dirs. United Fund; bd. dirs., pres. Citizens Coalition Forsyth County and Anderson High Sch., PTA.; mem. N.C. Bd. Edn., 1971-77, N.C. State Library Bd. Trustees, 1968-69; mem., chmn. personnel com. Winston-Salem/Forsyth County Sch. Bd.; chmn. bd. trustees St. Paul United Methodist Ch. Mem. N.C. Assn. Black Lawyers, Forsyth County Bar Assn. (pres.), N.C. State Bar. Office: PO Box 89 Greensboro NC 27402

ERWITT, ELLIOTT ROMANO, photographer, cinematographer; b. Paris, July 26, 1928; U.S., 1939; s. Boris and Jeanette (Trepel) E.; m. Lucienne Van Kan, 1953 (div. 1962); children: Ellen, Misha, David, Jennifer; m. Susan Lynn Ringo, Dec. 21, 1976; children: Alexandra, Amelia. A.A., Los Angeles City Coll., 1947. Freelance photographer, N.Y.C., 1945—; photographer Magnum Photos, N.Y.C., 1953—, pres., 1966-70; cinematographer Elliott Erwitt Enterprises, Inc., N.Y.C., 1968—. Author: Photographs and Anti Photographer, 1972, Son of Bitch, 1974, Recent Developments; photographer Observations on American Architecture, 1972. Served with U.S. Army, 1951-53; ETO. Am. Film Inst. grantee, 1973. Mem. Am. Soc. Mag. Photographers, Soc. Motion Picture Technicians and Engrs. Office: Magnum Photos 251 Park Ave S New York NY 10010

ESAKI, LEO, physicist; b. Osaka, Japan, Mar. 12, 1925; came to U.S., 1960; s. Soichiro and Niyoko (Ito) E.; m. Masako Araki, Nov. 21, 1959; children: Nina Yvonne, Anna Eileen, Eugene Leo. B.S., U. Tokyo, 1947, Ph.D., 1959. With Sony Corp., Japan, 1956-60; with Thomas J. Watson Research Center, IBM, Yorktown Heights, N.Y., 1960—, IBM fellow, 1967—, mgr. device research, 1965—; dir. IBM-Japan. Recipient Morris N. Liebmann Meml. prize I.E.E.E., 1961; Stuart Ballantine medal Franklin Inst., 1961; Japan Acad. award, 1965; Nobel Prize in physics, 1973; decorated Order of Culture Govt. of Japan, 1974. Fellow Am. Phys. Soc. (councillor-at-large 1971-74), IEEE, Japan Phys. Soc., Am. Vacuum Soc. (dir. 1973-74); mem. Am. Acad. Arts and Scis., Nat. Acad. Scis. (fgn. asso.), Nat. Acad. Engring. (fgn. asso.), Academia Nacional de Ingenieria Mex. (corr.), Japan Acad. Inventor tunnel diode, 1957. Home: 16 Shady Ln Chappaqua NY 10514 Office: Watson Research Center IBM PO Box 218 Yorktown Heights NY 10598 *

ESBENSEN, ERIC THORVALD, lawyer; b. Eagle River, Wis., Mar. 22, 1939; s. Duane Herbert and Janet Helen (Adams) E.; m. Noreen J. Lemal, Aug. 20, 1976. B.A., Fla. Atlantic U., 1966; J.D., U. Fla., 1969. Bar: Fla. 1969, D.C. 1969. Ptnr. Pittman, Lovett, Ford & Hennessey, Washington, 1969-77; sr. ptnr. Esbensen & Powell, Washington, Phila. and Gainesville, Fla., 1982—; pres., mng. ptnr. Sunshine Wireless Co., Fort Lauderdale, Fla., 1978—; pres., dir. N.Am. Media Assos., 1981—, N.Am. Cable Radio Corp., 1982—; sec., gen. counsel Am. Communications and TV, Inc., Gainesville, 1983—. Mem. Fla. Bar Assn., Nat. Assn. Broadcasters, So. Fla. Radio Broadcasters Assn., ABA, Fort Lauderdale C. of C., Boca Raton C. of C. Republican. Club: Boca Raton Hotel and Club. Home: 1632 NW 19th Circle Gainesville FL 32605 Office: 4801 Massachusetts Ave NW Suite 400 Washington DC 20016

ESBJORNSON, ROBERT GLENDON, educator; b. Duluth, Minn., Apr. 6, 1918; s. Per Hjalmer and Victoria (Swenson) E.; m. Ruth Bernice Bostrom, May 6, 1945; children—Ruth Louise, Carl Daniel. Student, Duluth Jr. Coll., 1937-39; A.B., Gustavus Adolphus Coll., 1941; grad., Augustana Theol. Sem., 1945; S.T.M., Yale, 1954. Ordained to ministry Luth. Ch., 1945; pastor Holy Trinity Luth. Ch., Newington, Conn., 1945-50; tchr. religion Gustavus Adolphus Coll., St. Peter, Minn., 1950—; pastor Bethany Luth. Ch., Judson, Minn., 1960-72; fellow Center for Ecumenical and Cultural Studies, Collegeville, Minn., 1973. Author: Luther W. Youngdahl: A Christian in Politics, 1955. Pres. bd. dirs. Riverbend Assn., St. Peter, 1968-74; bd. dirs. Northwestern Theol. Sem., St. Paul, 1967-76. Mem. Am. Acad. Religion, Soc. Sci. Study Religion, World Future Soc. Democrat. Home: 748 Valley View Rd St Peter MN 56082

ESCH, MARVIN L., cons.; b. Flinton, Pa., Aug. 4, 1927; m. Olga Jurich; children: Emily, Leo, Thomas. A.B. in Polit. Sci, U. Mich., 1950, M.A., 1951, Ph.D., 1957. Prof. Wayne State U.; also cons. U. Mich.-Wayne State U. Inst. Labor and Indsl. Relations, 1951-64; mem. Mich. Ho. of Reps., 1965-66, 90th to 94th Congresses from 2d Dist. Mich.; dir. pub. affairs U.S. Steel Corp., Washington, 1977-80; vis. fellow Am. Enterprise Inst., 1977, dir. programs and seminars, 1981—; pres. Esch Assos., Chen and Esch Internat. Ltd., 1980—. Served with U.S. Army, U.S. Maritime Service, World War II. Home: Washington DC Office: 1133 15th St NW Suite 620 Washington DC 20005

ESCH, ROBIN ERNEST, educator, mathematician; b. Chevy Chase, Md., Feb. 25, 1930; s. Fred Henry and Harriette (Fish) E.; m. Joan L. Brockway, June 25, 1965; children: Elizabeth Francesca, David Nathaniel, Thomas Benjamin. B.A., Harvard, 1951, M.A., 1953, Ph.D., 1957. Asst. prof. Harvard, 1957-62; head applied mechanics dept. Sperry Rand Research Center, Sudbury, Mass., 1962-66; prof. math. Boston U., 1966—, chmn. dept., 1968—; co-chmn. Boston Numerical Math. Seminar, 1967-72. Mem. Am. Math. Soc., Math. Assn. Am., Soc. Indsl. and Applied Math., Amateur Chamber Music Soc. Home: 371 Plainfield Rd Concord MA 01742 Office: 111 Cummington St Boston MA 02215

ESCHBACH, JESSE ERNEST, judge; b. Warsaw, Ind., Oct. 26, 1920; S. Jesse Ernest and Mary W. (Stout) E.; m. Sara Ann Walker, Mar. 15, 1947; children: Jesse Ernest III, Virginia. B.S., Ind. U., 1943, J.D. with distinction, 1949. Bar: Ind. bar 1949. Partner firm Graham, Rasor, Eschbach & Harris, Warsaw, 1949-62; city atty., Warsaw, 1952-53; dep. pros. atty. 54th Jud. Circuit Ct. Ind., 1952-1954; judge U.S. Dist. Ct. Ind., 1962-81, chief judge, 1974-81; judge U.S. Ct. Appeals (7th cir.), 1981—; Pres. Endicott Church Furniture, Inc., 1960-62; sec., gen. counsel Dalton Foundries, Inc., 1957-62. Editorial staff: Ind. Law Jour, 1947-49. Trustee Ind. U., 1965-70. Served with USNR, 1943-46. Hastings scholar, 1949; Recipient U.S. Law Week award, 1949. Mem. U.S. C. of C. (labor relations com. 1960-62), Warsaw C. of C. (pres. 1955-56), Nat. Assn. Furniture Mfrs. (dir. 1962), Ind. Mfrs. Assn. (dir. 1962), ABA, Ind. Bar Assn. (bd. mgrs. 1953-54, ho. dels. 1950-60), Fed. Bar Assn., Am. Judicature Soc., Order of Coif. Presbyn. Club: Rotarian (pres. Warsaw 1956-57). Home: 2000 N Bay Dr Warsaw IN 46580 Office: US Courthouse Room 243 1300 S Harrison St Fort Wayne IN 46802

ESCHENBACH, CHRISTOPH, pianist; b. Breslau, Silesia, Germany, Feb. 20, 1940. Attended, Hamburg (W. Ger.) Conservatory, State Conservatory Music, Cologne, W. Ger. Performed with leading orchs., including, Concertgebouw, Amsterdam, Netherlands, Lamoureux Orch., Paris, London Symphony, Berlin Philharm., Cleve. Orch.; soloist with Cleve. Orch. during European Festival Tour, 1967; N.Am. debut, Expo '67, Montreal, Que., Can., 1967; soloist with, Cleve. Orch., 1969, Carnegie Hall debut with Cleve. Orch.; toured, Europe, North and South Am., USSR, South Africa, Israel, Japan; appeared at festivals, including, Salzburg, Austria, Lucerne, Switzerland, Bonn, W. Ger., Aix-en-Provence, France; appeared as condr. in, Europe, N.Am.; rec. artist, Deutsche Grammophon. Winner, Munich (W. Ger.) Internat. Competition, 1962, Clara Haskil Concours, Lucerne, 1965. Office: care Columbia Artists Mgmt Inc 165 W 57th St New York NY 10019 *

ESCHENBERG, KATHREYN (MARCELLA), bilogical science educator; b. St. Louis, Dec. 12, 1923. B.A., Miami U., 1946; M.A., U. Colo., 1950; Ph.D., U. Wash., 1957. Ast. biologist, vertebrate physicologist U. Colo., 1948-49, inst., 1949-51; asst. zoology, embryology, cell physiology U. Wash., 1951-56; Nat. Cancer Inst. research fellow Princeton U., 1957; asst. prof. zoology cell biology, embryology Mt. Holyoke Coll., South Hadley, Mass., 1958-64, assoc. prof. biol. scis., 1964-70, prof. biol. sci., chmn. dept., 1970-80, Ida and Marion Van Natta prof. biol. sci., 1980—. Mem. AAAS, Am. Inst. Biol. Sci., Am. Soc. Zoology, Soc. Devel. Biology. Office: Dept Biol Scis Mt Holyoke Coll South Hadley MA 01075 *

ESCHMEYER, WILLIAM NEIL, marine scientist; b. Knoxville, Tenn., Feb. 11, 1939; s. Reuben William and Ruth Elizabeth (Willey) E.; m. Lydia R. Berardelli, Sept. 9, 1967 (div. 1981); children: Lisa Ruth, David Paul, Lanea Cathleen. B.S., U. Mich., 1961; M.S., U. Miami, Fla., 1964, Ph.D., 1967. Asst. curator, then asso. curator Calif. Acad. Scis., San Francisco, 1967-73, curator, 1973—, dir. research, 1977-83, sr. curator, 1983—. Author books, research papers, articles in field. Grantee NSF. Mem. Am. Soc. Ichthyologists and Herpetologists, other biol. socs., Zeta Psi. Address: Calif Acad Scis Golden Gate Park San Francisco CA 94118

ESHBACH, WILLIAM WALLACE, architect; b. Allentown, Pa., Mar. 12, 1917; s. William W. and Jennie (Krum) E.; m. Hilda Kern Campbell, Nov. 5, 1943; 1 son, William Wallace. B.Arch., U. Pa., 1941. With DuPont Co., Wilmington, 1941-43, George Daub (architect), Phila., 1946-47; asso. and project mgr. Vincent G. Kling, Phila., 1947-52; ptnr. William W. Eshbach (architect and assos.), Phila., 1952-54, Eshbach, Pullinger, Stevens & Bruder (architects and engrs.), 1954-72, Eshbach Glass Kale and Assos. (architects, engrs. and planners), 1972-79; chmn. bd. TEI Cons. Engrs., Inc., 1970-72, pres., 1972-81; ptnr. Eshbach-Kale & Assos., 1979—; chmn. bd., pub. interest dir. Fed. Home Loan Bank Pitts., 1973-75; mem. panel Am. Arbitration Assn., 1958—; mem. pub. adv. panel on archtl. services GSA, 1969-73; mem. adv. panel on new sch. arch. Temple U., Phila., 1970-74. Prin. archtl. projects include State Office Bldg., Harrisburg, Arts and Humanities Bldg., Pa. State U., housing complex, U. Pa., Kent & Queen Anne's Hosp., Chestertown, Md., Class and Adminstrn. Bldg., Rutgers U., Camden, N.J., Law School and Social Sci., Temple U., Mus. at Valley Forge Nat. Park; prin. engring. projects include: regional mass transp. study for Buffalo area, extension to subway system Phila. N.E. Freeway, Phila. Served from ensign to lt. USNR, 1943-46; PTO. Fellow AIA (v.p. 1964-65, mem. vis. nat. archtl. accreditation teams, chmn. various coms. regional dir. nat. bd. 1961-63, Edward C. Kemper award 1966), Pa. Soc. Architects (dir. 1956-57, sec. 1957-58, pres. 1959-60, dir. 1956-60, chmn. com. Pa. interprofl.-govt. relations com. 1967-71). Club: Union League (Phila.). Home: 1023 West Ave Springfield PA 19064 Office: 225 S 15th St Philadelphia PA 19102

ESHELMAN, RAYMOND HARRY, telephone directory advertising executive; b. Dayton, Ohio, July 10, 1925; s. Harry and Winifred Ann (LeJeune) E.; m. Alice Joyce McMullen, Sept. 20, 1952; children: Peter, Julie, Timothy. Student, U. Nebr., 1945-46. Account exec. Pat Patrick Advt. Agy., Glendale, Calif., 1946; with L.M. Berry and Co., Dayton, 1947—, gen. sales mgr., 1963, v.p. sales, 1965, exec. v.p. ops., 1973-80, pres., chief operating officer, 1980—, dir.; pres., dir. L.M. Berry and Co.-NYPS, 1977, L.M. Berry Services Inc., 1980—, L.M. Berry and Co.-Cellular, Inc., 1982—; dir. ITT World Directories, ITT World Directories (U.K.), Intermedia, Inc. Trustee Loren M. Berry Found., 1979—, Wright State Found., Dayton Performing Arts Fund, 1982—; trustee Dayton Opera Assn., 1982—; bd. dirs. Dayton Philharm. Orch. Assn., 1983—, Jr. Achievement. Served with USNR, 1943-46. Mem. Nat. Yellow Pages Services Assn. (pres. 1976-77, exec. com. 1976—), Dayton C. of C. Republican. Roman Catholic. Clubs: Moraine Country (dir.), Racquet, Bicycle, The Hundred (Dayton); Wilderness Country (Naples, Fla.); Seaview Country (Absecon, N.J.). Home: 4557 Troon Trail Dayton OH 45429 Office: PO Box 6000 3170 Kettering Blvd Dayton OH 45401

ESHELMAN, WILLIAM ROBERT, librarian, editor; b. Oklahoma City, Aug. 1921; s. Cyrus Lenhert and Fern (Reed) E.; m. Mimi Blau, July 3, 1952 (div. Aug. 1956); m. Eve Kendall, June 21, 1957 (div. Apr. 1975); children: Ann, Benjamin, Zachary; m. Pat Rom, Dec. 29, 1977. A.B., Chapman Coll., Los Angeles, 1943; M.A. (Shirle Robbins Poetry prize 1949), U. Calif. at Los Angeles, 1950; B.L.S., U. Calif. at Berkeley, 1951. Conscripted in civilian pub. service, Waldport, Oreg., 1943-46, asst. dir., 1944-45; teaching asst. UCLA, 1949-50, library asst., 1950; faculty Los Angeles State Coll., 1951-65, asst. librarian, 1954-59, librarian, 1959-65; librarian, prof. bibliography Bucknell U., 1965-68; editor Wilson library Bull., 1968-78; pres. Scarecrow Press, Metuchen, N.J., 1979—; editor Calif. Librarian, 1960-63; partner Untide Press, Pasadena, 1946-65; dir. Grolier Edn. Corp.; Mem. adv. council edn. for librarianship, U. Calif., 1961-64; mem. acad. senate Calif. State Colls., 1964-65. Editorial bd.: Choice, 1966-71. Mem. Am. Assn. U. Profs. (v.p. Los Angeles State Coll. 1958-59, pres. 1964-65), ALA (1 Library Periodicals Award 1960, editorial com. 1964-66, mem. council 1972-76, com. accreditation 1977-79), Calif. Library Assn. (chmn. intellectual freedom com., pres. So. dist. 1965), Assn. Coll. and Research Libraries (publs. com.), Assn. Calif. State Coll. Profs., Am. Civil Liberties Union, Friends Com. Legislation, N.J. Library Assn. Clubs: Book of Calif.; Rounce and Coffin (Los Angeles) (sec.-treas 1953-56); Typophiles (N.Y.C.)). Home: 74 7th St Edison NJ 08837 Office: 52 Liberty St Metuchen NJ 08840

ESHLEMAN, CLAYTON, poet, translator, editor, educator; b. Indpls., June 1, 1935; s. Ira Clayton and Gladys Maine (Spencer) E.; m. Caryl Reiter, May 21, 1969; 1 son by previous marriage, Matthew. B.A. in Philosophy, Ind. U., 1958, M.A.T. in English Lit, 1961. Instr. in English U. Md. Far Eastern Div., Taiwan, Korea and Japan, 1961-62; tchr. English lang. program Matsushita Electric Corp., Osaka, Japan, 1962-64; instr. Am. Lang. Inst., N.Y. U., 1966-68, Sch. Critical Studies, Calif. Inst. Arts, 1970-72; tchr. 20th century world poetry and creative writing pvt. workshop, Sherman Oaks, Calif., 1973; instr. contemporary Am. poetry Am. Coll. in Paris, 1974; lectr. advanced poetry workshop extension UCLA, 1975—; Dreyfuss lectr. in creative writing Calif. Inst. Tech., Pasadena, 1979-83; participant poetry in the schs. program, N.Y.C., 1967, Los Angeles, 1974-75; cons., bd. dirs. Coordinating Council Lit. Mags., 1968-71; co-organizer N.Am. Poetry Circuit, 1969. Recorded poetry, transls., Sta. KBCA, N.Y.C., 1964, Sta. KPFK, Los Angeles and San Francisco, 1968; Author numerous books, the most recent being, Bearings, 1971, Altars, 1971, The Sanjo Bridge, 1972, Coils, 1973, Human Wedding, 1973, Aux Morts, 1974, Realignment, 1974, Portrait of Francis Bacon, 1975, The Gull Wall, 1975, The Woman Who Saw Through Paradise, 1976, Grotesca, 1977, The Name Encanyoned River, 1977, Core Meander, 1977, What She Means, 1978, Nights We Put The Rock Together, 1980, The Lich Gate,

1980, Our Lady of the Three-pronged Devil, 1981, Hades In Manganese, 1981, Fracture, 1983; contbg. author: Erotic Poetry, 1963, Contemporary Latin American Literature, 1970, The Voice that is Great within Us, 1970, Doors and Mirrors, 1972, Messages, 1973, Open Poetry, 1973, America A Prophecy, 1973, Giant Talk, 1975; translator: Residence on Earth (Pablo Neruda), 1962, (with Denis Kelly) (Aimé Césaire), 1966, Human Poems (César Vallejo), 1968, Artaud The Mômo (Antonin Artaud), 1972, Letter to André Breton (Antonin Artaud), 1974, (with José Rubia Barcia) Take This Cup From Me (César Vallejo), 1974, (with Norman Glass) To Have Done with the Judgment of God (Antonin Artaud), 1975, (with José Rubia Barcia) César Vallejo: The Complete Posthumous Poetry, 1978; translater: (with Annette Smith) Aime Cesaire: The Collected Poetry, 1983; editor: Folio, 1959-60; editor, pub.: Caterpillar mag, 1966-73; Caterpillar Books series, including At Bottom (Cid Corman), 1967, Sing Song (Paul Blackburn), 1967, Crystals (Frank Samperi), 1967, Definitions (David Antin), 1967, Terms of Articulation (D. Alexander), 1967, The Counted (Robert Vas Dias), 1967, August Light Poems (Jackson MacLow), 1968; editor, contbg. author: A Caterpillar Anthology, 1971. Recipient award for translating Vallejo Nat. Transl. Ctr., 1967, Fels award for non-fiction prose Coordinating Council Lit. Mags., 1975, P.E.N. Transl. award, 1976, Nat. Book award for Cesar Vallejo: The Complete Posthumous Poetry, 1979; Nat. Transl. Center grantee, 1967, 68; Center Inter-Am. Relations grantee, 1968; Coordinating Council Lit. Mags. grantee, 1968, 70, 73; Guggenheim fellow in poetry, 1978; Nat. Endowment for Humanities grantee, Summer 1980, 1981. Address: care Black Sparrow Press Box 3993 Santa Barbara CA 93105 *I increasingly seek to develop a poetry that includes imaginative presentations of all the political, mythical and intimate cross-currents that preoccupy me on a daily basis, against a background of deepening otherness that seems to be no less than early Homo Sapiens consciousness, or Paleolithic imagination and the Construction of the Underworld; thus I work a time-frame that includes American policy in El Salvador, the presence of my wife and cave paintings done around 15,000 BC.*

ESHLEMAN, EDWIN D., former congressman, educator; b. Lancaster County, Pa., Dec. 4, 1920; s. Reeder L. and Mary (Barbara) E.; m. Kathryn E. Dambach, Dec. 26, 1942; children: E. Bruce, R. Lee. B.S. in Polit. Sci., Franklin and Marshall Coll., 1942; postgrad., Temple U., 1948. Tchr. pub. schs., 1946-49; mem. Pa. Ho. of Reps. from Lancaster County, 1954-66; majority and minority whip; mem. 90th-94th congresses 16th Dist. Pa.; circuit prof. Franklin and Marshall Coll.; dir. Lancaster 1st Fed. Savs. & Loan Assn.; Vice chmn. Pa. Higher Assistance Agy., 1963-67. Author: Congress, The Pennyslvania Dutch Seat. Served with USCGR, 1942-45. Recipient Disting. Service award Pa. Jr. C. of C., 1956; Disting. Alumni award Franklin and Marshall Coll., 1974; Nat. Silver medal of Merit, VFW, 1975; named to Pa. Young Rep. Hall of Fame, 1966. Mem. Am. Legion (Outstanding Citizen award 1976), VFW, Amvets. Home: 2173 West Ridge Dr Lancaster PA 17603

ESHMAN, AARON RICHARD, investment executive; b. Los Angeles, Apr. 21, 1927; s. Louis Aaron and Leah (Fink) E.; m. Sari Vogel, July 1, 1951; children: Lisa Ann, Mark L., Robert A. Student, UCLA, 1946-48; B.A., U. Calif. at Berkeley, 1950. With Drexel Burnham Lambert, Inc.; mems. N.Y. Stock Exchange, Los Angeles, 1950—, partner, 1959-65, sr. v.p., dir., 1965-70; pres., chief exec. officer Stern, Frank, Meyer & Fox, Inc., 1970-77, sr. v.p., dir., regional mgr. for So. Calif., 1977-83; bd. govs. Am. Stock Exchange, 1972-75, Pacific Stock Exchange, 1980-81; mem. Nat. Market Adv. Bd., 1975-77. Mem. Los Angeles Community Relations Com., 1959-65; exec. com. Anti-Defamation League, 1958-75; pres. Spring St. Forum, 1966-67; bd. dirs. Vista Del Mar Child Care Center, Cedars-Sinai Med. Center, 1978—; mem. exec. bd. Am. Jewish Com., 1978—. Served with USNR, 1945-46. Recipient Outstanding Leadership award Jewish Fedn. Council, Los Angeles, 1958. Mem. Securities Industry Assn. (chmn. Calif. group 1972, nat. dir., treas. 1975, bd. govs. 1971-76), Zeta Beta Tau. Jewish. Clubs: Hillcrest Country, Stock Exchange (Los Angeles); Stock Exchange Luncheon, Wall Street (N.Y.C.). Office: 1901 Ave of Stars Los Angeles CA 90067

ESKANDARIAN, EDWARD, advt. agy. exec.; b. Telford, Pa., Nov. 20, 1936; s. Michael and Katherine (Arslanian) E.; m. Nancy Rose Boujicanian, June 20, 1965; children—Wendy, Kristin, Jill. B.S., Villanova U., 1958; M.B.A., Harvard, 1965. Engr. Pitman Dunn Labs., Phila., 1958-60; project engr. Gen. Electric Corp., Phila., 1961-63; v.p., account supr. Compton Advt., Inc., N.Y.C., 1965-71; pres., dir. Humphrey, Browning, MacDougall, Inc., Boston, 1971—. Served with USAF, 1959-60. Mem. Advt. Club Boston (pres. dir), Harvard Bus. Sch. Assn. Boston (dir.). Clubs: Harvard, Algonquin, Weston Golf. Home: 21 Decatur Ln Wayland MA 01778 Office: 1 Beacon St Boston MA 02108

ESKEW, RHEA TALIAFERRO, newspaper publisher; b. Lebanon, Tenn., Nov. 16, 1923; s. Robert Edward and Sammie (Taylor) E.; m. Nancy Portlock Hall, June 13, 1953; children: Rhea Taliaferro, Elizabeth Vaughan Landers, Tucker Alexander, Hall Edward. Student, U. Tenn., 1941-42; B.A., Emory U., 1948. With UPI, 1948-55, bus. rep., N.C., S.C., Va., 1951-55; dept. pub. relations So. Bell Telephone Co., 1955-56; with UPI, 1956-73, gen. mgr. communications, N.Y.C., 1963-64, So. div. mgr., Atlanta, 1964-73; v.p., gen. mgr. Greenville (S.C.) News-Piedmont, 1973-77, pub., 1978—; v.p., dir. Multimedia, Inc.; pres. Multimedia Newspaper Co., 1978—; cons. on communications. Served with AUS, 1942-45; ETO. Mem. S.C. Press Assn. (pres. 1981), So. Newspaper Pubs. Assn. (pres. 1982-83), Sigma Delta Chi (former regional dir.). Methodist. Clubs: Greenville Country, Poinsett, Atlanta Commerce. Home: Route 2 Huntington Rd Greenville SC 29607 Office: 305 S Main St Greenville SC 29601

ESLER, ANTHONY JAMES, historian, novelist; b. New London, Conn., Feb. 20, 1934; s. James Arthur and Helen Wilhelmina (Kreamer) E.; m. Carol Eaton Clemeau, June 17, 1961; children: Kenneth Campbell, David Douglas. B.A., U. Ariz., 1956; M.A., Duke U., 1958, Ph.D., 1961. Mem. faculty Coll. William and Mary, 1962—, prof. history, 1972—; vis. prof. Northwestern U., 1968-69. Author: The Aspiring Mind of the Elizabeth Younger Generation, 1966, Bombs, Beards and Barricades: 150 Years of Youth in Revolt, 1971, The Youth Revolution: The Conflict of Generations in Modern History, 1974, Castlemayne, 1974, Hellbane, 1975, Lord Libertine, 1976, Forbidden City, 1977, The Freebooters, 1979, Babylon, 1980, Bastion, 1980, Generations in History: An Introduction to the Concept, 1982, The Generation Gap in Society and History: A Select Bibliography, 1984. Fulbright fellow, U. London, 1961-62; research fellow Am. Council Learned Socs., 1969-70; Fulbright travel grantee, Ivory Coast and Tanzania, 1983. Mem. Am. Hist. Assn., Authors Guild, Amnesty Internat. Home: 1523 Jamestown Rd Williamsburg VA 23185 Office: History Dept Coll William and Mary Williamsburg VA 23185

ESLER, JOHN KENNETH, artist; b. Pilot Mound, Man., Can., Jan. 11, 1933; s. William John and Jennie Mae (Thompson) E.; m. Annemarie Schmid, June 26, 1964; children—William Sean, John Derek. B.F.A., U. Man., B.Ed., 1962. Mem. faculty dept. art Alta. Coll. Art, 1964-68; mem. faculty U. Calgary, Alta., Can., 1968-80; chmn. Print and Drawing Council Can., 1976-78. One man exhbn., Gallery Moos, Toronto, Ont., 1978; represented in permanent collections, Victoria and Albert Mus., London, Eng., Albright Knox Gallery, Buffalo, N.Y., Mus. Modern Art, N.Y.C., Nat. Gallery Can., Ottawa, Ont. Mem. United Ch. of Can. Address: Box 2 Site 7 SS 1 Calgary AB T2M 4N3 Canada

ESLICK, LEONARD JAMES, educator, philosopher; b. Denver, Nov. 8, 1914; s. Theodore Parker and Leila (Van Natta) E.; m. Florence Elizabeth Weber, May 3, 1935. A.B., U. Chgo., 1934; M.A., Tulane U., 1936; Ph.D., U. Va., 1939. Instr. philosophy Drake U., Des Moines, 1939-42; tutor St. John's Coll., Annapolis, Md., 1943-48; asso. prof. St. Louis U., 1948-57, prof., 1957—; vis. prof. U. Va. at Charlottesville, 1961, U. Ill. at Urbana, 1965, U. Notre Dame, 1968. Asso. editor: Modern Schoolman, 1950—; editorial Bd.: Process Studies, 1970—; Contbr. articles on metaphysics, Plato, A.N. Whitehead to philos. jours., books. Served with AUS, 1942. Mem. Am. Philos. Assn., Mo. Philos. Assn. (pres. 1958-59), Metaphys. Soc. Am., Cath. Commn. Intellectual and Cultural Affairs. Home: 4253 Flora Pl St Louis MO 63110

ESLINGER, FRANK ROBERT, real estate executive; b. Washington, Ind., Feb. 4, 1923; s. Frank J. and Marie Rosine (Simmick) E.; m. Barbara Louise Denny, May 18, 1946; children: Barbara Patricia, Robert Denny. B.S., U. N.Mex., 1946; J.D., George Washington U., 1951. Bar: D.C. 1951, Supreme Ct. 1951. With Equitable Life Ins. Co., McLean, Va., 1940-82, treas., 1958-65, sr. v.p., 1965-73, exec. v.p., 1973-82, also dir.; pres. First Oxford Corp., Washington, 1983—; mem. adv. bd. trustees Columbia Real Estate Title Co. Served with USNR, 1941-46. Fellow Life Mgmt. Inst.; Mem. Sigma Chi. Republican. Roman Catholic. Clubs: Congressional Country, Downtown Washington. Lodge: Kiwanis (past chmn. vocat. guidance com., program com.). Home: 8513 Timber Hill Ln Potomac MD 20854 Office: 3524 K St NW Washington DC 20007

ESMAN, MILTON JACOB, educator; b. Pitts., Sept. 15, 1918; s. Mayer and Hermoine (Bernstein) E.; m. Janice Newman, Oct. 23, 1949; children—Michael, Oliver, Judith. B.A., Cornell U., 1939; Ph.D., Princeton, 1942. Program planning officer CSC, 1947-51; intelligence research officer Dept. State, 1951-54; fgn. aid adminstr., Washington and Saigon, Vietnam, 1954-59; prof., head dept. econ. and social devel. Grad. Sch. Pub. and Internat. Affairs, U. Pitts., 1959-66, research dir., 1963-66; sr. adviser devel. adminstrn. Prime Minister's Dept., Govt. Malaysia, 1966-68; dir. Center for Internat. Studies; John S. Knight prof. Cornell U., 1969—. Served with AUS, 1942-46. Home: 903 Triphammer Rd Ithaca NY 14850

ESMAY, MERLE LINDEN, agricultural engineer; b. Greene County, Iowa, Dec. 27, 1920; s. Earl Stephen and Ruth Marie E.; m. Katherine Ann Paskin, July 25, 1942; children: Katherine Linda, Merle Dennis. B.S. in Agrl. Engring, S.D. State U., 1942; M.S., Iowa State U., 1947, Ph.D., 1951. Registered profl. engr., Iowa, Mich. Extension agrl. engr. S.D. State U., 1946; asst. prof. agrl. engring. Iowa State U., 1947-51; asso. prof. U. Mo., Columbia, 1951-55; mem. faculty Mich. State U., E. Lansing, 1955—, prof. agrl. engring., 1957—, chief party on ednl. tech. assistance program for Taiwan, 1962-64; adviser numerous postgrad. students; cons. in field; participant numerous internat. confs. leader U.S. delegation agrl. engrs. to China, 1979, mem. sci. exchange team to China, 1981. Author: Principles of Animal Environment, 1969, Agricultural Mechanization in Developing Countries, 1973, Rice Postproduction Technology in the Tropics, 1979, also numerous papers, bulls. Served to capt. C.E. AUS, 1942-46. Recipient Disting. Alumnus award S.D. State U., 1980, Disting. Engr. award S.D. State U., 1983. Fellow Am. Soc. Agrl. Engrs. (dir. internat. dept. 1979-80, engr. of Year award Mich. sect. 1966, nat. Structures and Environment award 1966, Internat. Kishida award 1982); mem. Am. Soc. Engring. Edn., Am. Poultry Sci. Assn., Sigma Xi, Alpha Zeta, Phi Kappa Phi, Tau Beta Pi, Gamma Sigma Delta. Home: 1272 Scott Dr East Lansing MI 48823 Office: Agrl Engring Dept Mich State U East Lansing MI 48824

ESOGBUE, AUGUSTINE ONWUYALIM, indsl. engr., educator; b. Kaduna, Nigeria, Dec. 25, 1940; came to U.S., 1961; s. Nwanze and Helen (Nwakuso) E. Student, U. Calif., Berkeley, 1962; B.S. in Elec. Engring, UCLA, 1964; M.S. in Indsl. Engring, Columbia U., 1965; Ph.D. in Systems Engring. and Ops. Research, U. So. Calif., 1968; postgrad., M.I.T., 1975. Research asso. Schs. Engring. and Medicine, U. So. Calif., Los Angeles, 1965-68; devel. engr. Water Resources Center, Sch. Engring. and Applied Sci., UCLA, 1966-67; asst. prof. dept. ops. research Case-Western Res. U., Cleve., 1968-72; asso. prof. Sch. Indsl. and Systems Engring., Ga. Inst. Tech., Atlanta, 1972-77, prof., 1977—; asso. faculty Univ. Seminar on Water Resources and Pollution, Columbia U., N.Y.C., 1970—; adj. prof. dept. community medicine Morehouse Sch. Medicine, Morehouse Coll., Atlanta, 1979—; dept. math. scis. Atlanta U., 1980; mem. Water Resources Task Force, Atlanta Regional Commn.; faculty adv. Ga. Tech. Soc. Black Engrs., 1975; founder, pres. AESO Systems, Inc., 1980; v.p. Atlantic Systems, Inc., 1972-78; cons. to govt. agys. and public orgns., 1969—; N. Am. sci. del. to 6th Pan African Congress, Dar Es Salaam, Tanzania, 1974; mem. various sci. panels NRC, 1973, Nat. Acad. Scis., 1973; Vice pres. adv. bd. Council on Internat. Programs, 1977. Author: Mathematical Aspects of Scheduling and Applications; Adv. editor: Internat. Jour. Fuzzy Sets and Systems, 1976—; asso. editor: Jour. Math. Analysis and Applications, 1978—, Jour. Computer Sci. and Its Applications, 1980—; contbr. articles on theory and application of ops. research to profl. jours. Recipient Disting. Service award internat. affairs com. UCLA, 1964, Disting. Faculty Adv. award Nat. Soc. Black Engrs., 1979, Profl. Engr. and Acad. Excellence award Atlanta Council Black Profl. Engrs., 1979. Fellow AAAS; mem. Ops. Research Soc. Am. (nat. chmn. vis. lectr. program 1979), Am. Inst. Indsl. Engrs. (Speaker award 1970), IEEE, Inst. Mgmt. Scis., Sigma Xi, NAACP. Office: Sch of Indsl and Systems Engring Ga Inst Tech Atlanta GA 30332

ESPENSHADE, EDWARD BOWMAN, JR., geographer, educator; b. Chgo., Oct. 23, 1910; s. Edward B. and Mary E. (Jones) E.; m. Dorothy Elizabeth Barrows, June 17, 1939; children—Jean Ellen, Nancy Elizabeth. B.S., U. Chgo., 1931; Ph.D., 1944. Asso. prof. geography Northwestern U., 1948-55, prof., 1958-78, prof. emeritus, 1979—, chmn. dept., 1958-76; geog. cons., geog. editor Rand McNally & Co.; Chmn. div. earth scis. Nat. Acad. Sci.-NRC, 1960-62; mem. exec. bd. N. Central Assn. Commn. Higher Edn., 1972-77. Editor: Goode's World Atlas, 1947—. Mem. Assn. Am. Geographers (pres. 1964-65, chmn. commn. on coll. geography 1967-69), Geog. Soc. Chgo. (past sec., pres. 1969-71). Home: 2811 Garrison Ave Evanston IL 60201

ESPING, EDWARD D., wholesale food distribution company executive. Pres. Cardinal Foods Inc., Columbus, Ohio. Office: 315 Phillipi Rd Columbus OH 43228

ESPINOSA, GUSTAVO ADOLFO, radiologist, educator; b. Colombia, June 8, 1944; U.S., 1969, naturalized, 1976; s. Hector Octavius and Olga I. (Milanes) E.; m. Cecilia Troncoso, June 4, 1968; children: Gustavo Aldolfo, David A., Susan M. B.S., St. Joseph Coll., Colombia, 1960; M.D. magna cum laude, U. Xaveriana, Colombo, 1968. Diplomate: Am. Bd. Radiology. Intern Providence Hosp., Washington, 1969-70; resident in radiology Cook County Hosp., Chgo., 1971-75, attending radiologist, 1976—, West Side VA Hosp., Chgo., 1977—, chmn. dept., 1977—; attending U. Ill. Hosp., 1977—; assoc. prof. U. Ill. Med. Sch.; med. dir. Sch. X-ray Tech. Malcolm X Coll., Chgo. Mem. Radiol. Soc. N.Am., AMA, Am. Coll. Radiology, Am. Inst. Ultrasound in Medicine, Ill. Med. Soc., Ill. Radiol. Soc., Chgo. Med. Soc., Chgo. Roentgen Soc., Chgo. Ultrasound Soc. Office: 820 S Damen Ave Chicago IL 60680

ESPOSITO, ALBERT CHARLES, ophthalmologist; b. Pitts., Nov. 9, 1912; s. Charles Micali and Elizabeth (Cuda) E.; m. V. Elizabeth Dodson, July 17, 1940; children—Bettina (Mrs. Peter F. Kelly), Mary Alice (Mrs. Andrew Tartler), Gregory C. B.S., U. Pitts., 1933; M.D. cum laude, Loyola U., 1938; D.Sc. (hon.), Marshall U., 1976. Diplomate: Am. Bd. Ophthalmology. Intern St. Francis Hosp., Pitts., 1938-39; resident Ohio State U. Med. Coll. Hosp., 1940-43; practice medicine specializing in ophthalmology, Huntington, W.Va., 1946—; instr. ophthalmology Ohio State U. Med. Coll., 1943-45, asso. prof., 1945-47; chmn. dept. ophthalmology St. Mary's Hosp., Huntington, 1950—, pres. staff, 1966-67; cons. VA Hosp., C. & O. Ry.; attending ophthalmologist Cabell Huntington, Huntington and Morris Meml. hosps.; clin. prof., chmn. dept. ophthalmology Sch. Medicine, Marshall U., 1976—; Pres. S. W.Va. Blue Shield; dir. First City Bank, Huntington; mem. W.Va. Ho. of Reps., 1974—; minority whip, minority chmn. health, welfare, edn., banking and ins. coms.; alt. del. Rep. Nat. Conv., Detroit, 1980; chmn. med. sch. com., bd. dirs., mem. faculty Marshall U. Found. Contbr. articles to profl. jours. Trustee Doctors Meml. Hosp., C. & O. R.R. Employes' Hosp. Assn.; sec.-treas. Norval Carter Trust Fund. Served to maj. M.C. AUS, World War II. Recipient Outstanding Ophthalmologist in South award, 1970, Marshall U. Distinguished Service award, 1973; Appreciation award City of Huntington, 1974; Stritch medal, 1974; Distinguished W. Virginian award, 1976. Fellow Internat. Coll. Surgeons (regent W.Va. chpt.), A.C.S., Oxford (Eng.) Congress Ophthalmology, Am. Acad. Ophthalmology (teaching staff 1967—, Honor award 1977), Am. Assn. Ophthalmology (pres.); mem. AMA, So. Med. Assn. (past pres., trustee, chmn. sect. ophthalmology), W.Va. Med. Assn. (past pres.), Assn. Univ. Profs., Ophthalmology, Société Française d'Opthalmologie (France), Greater Huntington C. of C. (dir.), W.Va. Acad. Ophthalmology (pres.), Alpha Omega Alpha. Clubs: Elk., Guyan Golf and Country, Huntington Gun, Serena Yacht. Home: 171 Woodland Dr Huntington WV 25705 Office: 420-422 11th St Huntington WV 25701 *Throughout my life I have been sustained by a love of God and a burning desire to do what I could to help my fellowman. Any success that I have achieved in life, I feel is a direct result of constantly keeping this objective in mind. Hard work and a consistent desire to achieve the goals set forth have made so many of them possible. As I look back, there have been times of stress, illness, deep troubles, and almost hopeless situations which faith and the objectives I adhered to have enabled me to rise above.*

ESPOSITO, ALFRED LEWIS, consultant, former air force officer; b. Newark, Sept. 26, 1923; s. Thomas Matthew and Romelia Mari (Moressi) E.; m. Theresa Marie Harlow, Nov. 18, 1972; children: Sharon Marie, Carolyn Gwen Esposito Stephens, Carol Ann Dross. B.S. in Aero. Engring, Air Force Inst. Tech., 1957; M.B.A., U. Conn., 1963. Commd. 2d lt. USAAF, 1944; advanced through grades to brig. gen. USAF, 1968; dir. procurement policy Office Sec. Def., 1972-73; ret., 1973; gen. mgr. Fairchild Burns Co. div. Fairchild Industries, Inc., Winston-Salem, N.C., 1973-75; mgmt. cons., Winston-Salem, 1975-78; pres. Merrell Furniture Co., Inc., Mocksville, N.C., 1977-80; cons. to govt. and industry, 1980—. Decorated Legion of Merit with 2 oak leaf clusters, Joint Service Commendation medal, Air Force Commendation medal, Army Commendation medal. Home: 207 Stanaford Rd Winston-Salem NC 27104

ESPOSITO, MICHAEL PATRICK, JR., banker; b. Hackensack, N.J., Oct. 6, 1939; s. Michael Peter and Maria Carmela E.; m. Ellen Lyons, Sept. 2, 1962; children: Michael, John, James. B.B.A., Notre Dame U., 1961; M.B.A., N.Y.U., 1967. Supr. Chase Manhattan Bank, N.Y.C., 1965-66, acctg. officer, 1967-68, 2d v.p., 1968-70, v.p., 1970-74, sr. v.p., 1975-83, exec. v.p., 1983—. Served with USMCR, 1961-63. Mem. Bank Adminstrn. Inst. (chmn. acctg. and fin. commn. 1981-83), Nat. Assn. Accts., Fin. exec. Inst. Republican. Roman Catholic. Office: Chase Manhattan Bank NA 1 Chase Manhattan Plaza New York NY 10081

ESPY, WILLARD R., author; b. Olympia, Wash., Dec. 11, 1910; s. Harry Albert and Helen Medora (Richardson) E.; m. Hilda S. Cole, 1940; m. Louise J. Manheim, 1962. B.A., U. Redlands, 1930; student, U. Paris, Sorbonne, 1930-31. Reporter Tulare (Calif.) Times, 1932, Brawley (Calif.) News, 1932; asst. editor World Tomorrow, N.Y.C., 1933-35; copy editor L'Agence Havas, 1937-40; mgr. promotion and pub. relations Reader's Digest, 1941-57; producer, interviewer radio program Personalities in Print, 1957-58; creative advt. dir. Famous Artists Schs., 1958-63; publisher Charter Books, 1963-66; pub. relations cons., N.Y.C., 1963-75; panelist Harper Dict. Contemporary Usage, 1976, 83. Contbg. editor: Harvard Mag, 1978—; author: Bold New Program, 1951, The Game of Words, 1972, An Almanac of Words at Play, 1975, Oysterville: Roads to Grandpa's Village, 1977, The Life and Works of Mr. Anonymous, 1977, O Thou Improper, Thou Uncommon Noun, 1978, Say It My Way, 1980, Another Almanac of Words at Play, 1980, Have a Word on Me, 1981, Espygrams, 1982, A Children's Almanac of Words at Play, 1982, Word Puzzles, 1983, The Garden of Eloquence, 1983; Contbr.: articles to periodicals. Recipient Gov.'s award for contbn. to cultural life of Wash., 1973, 76; Capt. Robert Gray medal Wash. State Hist. Soc., 1979. Mem. New Eng. Soc. in City of N.Y., PEN, Nat. Book Critics' Circle, Authors Guild. Clubs: Century Assn., Dutch Treat, Coffee House (N.Y.C.). Home: 529 W 42nd St New York NY 10036 also Oysterville WA 98641

ESREY, WILLIAM TODD, telecommunications company executive; b. Phila., Jan. 17, 1940; s. Alexander J. and Dorothy (B.) E.; m. Julie L. Campbell, June 13, 1964; children: William Todd, John Campbell. B.A., Denison U., Granville, Ohio, 1961; M.B.A., Harvard U., 1964. With Am. Tel & Tel. Co., also N.Y. Telephone Co., 1964-69; pres. Empire City Subway Ltd., N.Y.C., 1969-70; mng. dir. Dillon, Read & Co. Inc., N.Y.C., 1970-80; exec. v.p. United Telecommunications, Inc., Westwood, Kans., 1980-82, pres., 1982—; dir. United Mo. Bank, Kansas City, Mo. Bd. dirs. U. Kansas City; bd. dirs., treas. Kansas City Philharm.; trustee Pembroke Country Day Sch. Mem. Phi Beta Kappa. Clubs: Mission Hills Country, River, Links. Office: 2330 Johnson Dr Westwood KS 66205

ESS, HENRY NEWTON, III, lawyer; b. Kansas City, Mo., Aug. 17, 1921; s. Henry Newton and Mildred (McBaine) E. A.B., Princeton U., 1942; LL.B., Harvard U., 1944. Bar: N.Y. 1945, U.S. Supreme Ct. 1961. Assoc. Sullivan & Cromwell, N.Y.C., 1944-53, ptnr., 1953—. Trustee William Nelson Cromwell Found., 1961—, Princeton Library, N.Y.C., 1970—, Vincent Astor Found., 1973—. Mem. ABA, N.Y. State Bar Assn., N.Y. County Lawyers Assn. (pres. 1973-75), Am. Bar Found., Assn. Bar City N.Y., Am. Judicature Soc., Am. Coll. Probate Counsel. Home: 80 Park Ave New York NY 10016 Office: Sullivan & Cromwell 125 Broad St New York NY 10004

ESSELMAN, WALTER HENRY, research institute administrator; b. Hoboken, N.J., Mar. 19, 1917; s. Gustav and Stephanie (Winter) E.; m. Margaret Esselman, June 19, 1943; children—Walter J., Thomas

C., Marie J., Peter C. B.S.E.E., Newark Coll. Engring., 1938; M.S.E.E., Stevens Inst. Tech., 1944; D.E.E., Poly. Inst. Bklyn., 1953. With Westinghouse Electric Corp., 1938-75; dir. Hanford Engring. Devel. Lab., 1970-72; pres. Westinghouse Hanford (Wash.), 1970-72; dir. strategic planning Electric Power Research Inst., Palo Alto, Calif., 1975-81, tech. dir. engring. assessment and analysis, 1981—. Recipient E. Weston award Newark Coll. Engring., 1962, A.J. Cullimore award, 1968. Fellow IEEE, Am. Nuclear Soc. (past dir.); mem. AIAA, AAAS, Inst. Energy Economists. Roman Catholic. Home: 1141 Buckingham Dr Los Altos CA 94020 Office: 3412 Hillview Ave Palo Alto CA 94303

ESSELSTYN, CALDWELL BLAKEMAN, JR., physician; b. N.Y.C., Dec. 12, 1933. A.B., Yale U., 1956; M.D., Western Res. U., 1961. Am. Bd. Surgery, Nat. Bd. Med. Examiners. Intern Cleve. Clinic Hosp., 1961-62, resident in gen. surgery, 1962-66; sr. registrar St George's Hosp., London, 1965; mem. staff Cleve. Clinic, 1969—; chmn. med. staff Cleve. Clinic Found., 1977, trustee, gov., 1979—; asst. prof. surgery Case Western Res. U., 1974—, sr. clin. instr. community health, 1974—. Contbr. numerous articles to profl. jours. Bd. dirs. Caldwell B. Esselstyn Found. Served to capt. M.C. U.S. Army, 1966-68. Recipient gold medal for 8 oared rowing Olympics, 1956. Mem. Med. Alumni Assn. Case Western Res. U. (trustee), ACS, AMA, Cleve. Surg. Soc., Central Surg. Assn., Cleve. Acad. Medicine, Collegium Internationale Chirurgiae Digestivae, Eastern Surg. Soc., Internat. Assn. Endocrine Surgeons, Ohio Med. Assn., Pan Pacific Surg. Assn., Rupert Turnbull Surg. Soc., Internat. Surg. Soc., Am. Assn. Endocrine Surgeons, Am. Soc. Bone and Mineral Research, Am. Surg. Assn., Nu Sigma Nu. Office: Cleveland Clinic 9500 Euclid Ave Cleveland OH 44106

ESSENBURG, FRANKLIN, mechanician, educator; b. Holland, Mich., Aug. 2, 1924; s. Frank and Katherine (Bakker) E.; m. Doloris May Gerhardt, Sept. 18, 1946; children—Sally Kay, Sandra Karen. B.S. in Mech. Engring, U. Mich., 1945, J.D., 1948, M.S. in Physics, 1949, 1950, Ph.D., 1956. Bar: Mich. bar 1948. Patent atty. Bell Telephone Labs., Murray Hill, N.J., 1950-51; engaged in pvt. constrn. bus., Holland, Mich., 1951-53; instr., then asst. prof. mechanics U. Mich., 1953-58; asso. prof., then prof. mechanics Ill. Inst. Tech., 1958-62; prof. mechanics, 1962—, 80—; chmn. dept. mech. engring. U. Colo., Boulder, 1962-70, chmn. dept. aerospace engring. scis., 1976-79; dean engring. Mich. Technol. U., Houghton, 1979-80. Served with USNR, 1943-45. Fellow ASME; mem. Mich. Bar. Assn., Sigma Xi, Pi Tau Sigma, Phi Kappa Phi, Tau Beta Pi. Office: Dept Mech Engring U Colo Boulder CO 80309

ESSER, CARL ERIC, lawyer; b. Montclair, N.J., Feb. 12, 1942; s. Josef and Elly (Graber) E.; m. Barbara A. B. Stelzer, Oct. 12, 1968; children: Jennifer, Alison, Eric, Brian. A.B., Princeton U., 1964; J.D., U. Mich., 1967. Bar: Pa. 1967. Assoc. firm Reed Smith Shaw & McClay, Phila, 1967-72; ptnr. Reed Smith & McClay, Phila, 1973—. Served with USMCR, 1965. Mem. ABA, Pa. BarAssn., Phila. Bar Assn. Republican. Clubs: Racquet (Phila.); Pennllyn (Pa.). Home: 10 Haddon Pl Fort Washington PA 19034 Office: 1600 Ave of the Arts Bldg Philadelphia PA 19107

ESSEX, HARRY, writer; b. N.Y.C., Nov. 29, 1915; s. Wolfe Wilhelm and Sarah (Bratter) E.; m. Lee Berman, June 22, 1945; 1 son, David. B.B.A., St. Johns U., 1936. Writer Columbia Studio, 1945-48, RKO, 1949-51, Universal, 1951-56, MGM, 1960-62, United Artists, 1962-68; script writer, story editor Warner Bros. Writer, NBC Movie of Week, 1974—; scenarist: films The Lonely Man, 1956, Man and Boy, 1973, The Amigos, 1974, Sons of Katie Elder, 1964, He Walked by Night, 1948, It Came from Outer Space, 1953; playwright: Broadway prodns. Something For Nothing, 1954, Neighborhood Affair, 1960, One for the Dame, 1961, Twilight, 1980; owner, head writer: Target the Corruptors, 1961-62; author: novels I Put My Right Foot In, 1954, Man and Boy, 1971, Marina, 1981; writer: series TV Untouchables, Playhouse 90. Served with AUS, 1942-44. Recipient Theatre Guild award for playwriting, 1940, Vencie Festival award for motion picture He Walked by Night, 1949. Mem. Dramatists League, Writers Guild Am., West Acad. Motion Picture Arts and Scis. Home: 9303 Readcrest Dr Beverly Hills CA 90210

ESSEX, MARTIN WALKER, educational administrator; b. Ray, Ohio, Mar. 25, 1908; s. John S. and Cora (McCormick) E.; m. Blanche Davis, Aug. 12, 1933. B.S., Ohio State U., 1930, M.A., 1934; D.Pd. (hon.), Baldwin-Wallace Coll., 1950; LL.D., U. Akron, 1958, Ohio U., 1970; D.Pub.Service, Miami U., 1975; H.H.D., Capital U., 1976. Tchr., Middleport, Ohio, 1930-32, high sch. prin., 1932-35, supt. schs., 1935-41, prin., East Liverpool, Ohio, 1941-43, supt. schs., 1943-45, prin., Ferndale, Mich., 1945-46, supt. schs., 1946-47, Lakewood, Ohio, 1947-55, Akron, 1955-66; supt. pub. instruction State of Ohio, 1966-77; exec. dir. Ohio Adv. Council Vocat. Edn., 1977—; guest lectr. Cornell U., Harvard, U. Mo., Northwestern U., U. Oreg., Tex. A&M U., U. Toledo, U. Wis., 1958, others; mem. exec. com. Joint Council on Econ. Edn.; chmn. adv. council on vocat. edn. HEW, 1966-67; nat. chmn. sch. savs. program; U.S. Treasury Dept., 1966-68; chmn. adv. council Nat. Merit Scholarship Corp.; pres. Council Chief State Sch. Officers, 1974; cons. to Am. schs. in Europe, U.S. Dept. State, 1970; chmn. Nat. Adv. Council for Community Edn., HEW, 1974-77; Treas. Nat. PTA, 1974-76; study tour, Russia, 1959, 64, 74, China, 1980. Editorial bd.: The Nation's Schs. and Colls. Named Man of Year Am. Vocat. Assn., 1968; Distinguished Service award Buckeye Assn. Sch. Adminstrs., Ohio Youth in Govt.; Am. Educators medal Freedoms Found., 1969; Martin W. Esse Sch. for Gifted dedicated Ohio State U., 1981; named to McGuffey Hall of Fame, 1981. Mem. NEA (Service award), Am. Assn. Sch. Adminstrs. (pres. 1959-60, Disting. Service award 1978), Vocat. Edn. Profl. Soc., Omicron Tau Theta (hon.), Phi Alpha Theta, Phi Delta Kappa. Lodge: Rotary. Home: 3117 Carisbrook Rd Columbus OH 43221 Office: 750 Brooksedge Blvd Suite 105 Westerville OH 43081

ESSLIN, MARTIN JULIUS, author, critic, drama educator; b. Budapest, Hungary, June 8, 1918; s. Paul and Charlotte (Schiffer) Pereszlenyi; m. Renate Gerstenberg, Sept. 13, 1947; 1 dau., Monica. Diploma, Reinhardt Seminar of Dramatic Art, Vienna, 1938; D. Litt. (hon.), Kenyon Coll., 1978. Scriptwriter, dir. BBC, London, 1940-55, asst. head European prodns. dept., 1955-60, asst. head radio drama, 1960-63, head drama, radio, 1963-77; prof. drama Stanford U., Calif., 1977—; lit. adv. Royal Shakespeare Co., London, 1963-72, chmn. drama panel, 1976; dramaturg Magic Theatre, San Francisco, 1977. Author: Brecht-A Choice of Evils, 1959, The Theatre of the Absurd, 1961, Pinter, the Playwright, 1970, Meditations, 1981, The Age of Television, 1982. Decorated Order Brit. Empire. Club: Garrick (London). Home: 1766 Willow Rd Apt 403 Palo Alto CA 94304 Office: Drama Dept Stanford U Stanford CA 94305

ESSON, JAMES DOUGLAS, meat packing company executive; b. Peterborough, Ont., Can., Nov. 13, 1940; s. James Edgar and Augustine (Laird) E.; children: James Andrew, Matthew Lingle. A.B. in Econs, Princeton U., 1963. Mgmt. trainee and prodn. supr. Shulton Inc., Clifton, N.J., 1963-65; beef lugger DaFran Meats, Bronx, N.Y., 1965; with Seitz Foods, Inc., St. Joseph, Mo., 1965—, v.p. beef ops., 1971-74, pres., 1974-76, pres., chief exec. officer, chmn. bd., 1976—; dir. Am. Nat. Bank; adv. Stanford Bus. Exec. Program for Small Cos. Bd. dirs. Jr. Achievement, 1977-80, Albrecht Art Mus., 1967-69; bd. dirs., 1st v.p. St. Joseph C. of C., 1969-72; mem. St. Joseph Sch. Dist. Adv. Bd., 1977-79. Mem. Am. Meat Inst. (dir.). Office: Seitz Foods Inc PO Box 247 Saint Joseph MO 64502

ESTABROOK, REED, artist, educator; b. Boston, May 31, 1944; s. F. Reed and Nancy (Vogel) E.; 1 son, August. B.F.A., R.I. Sch. Design, Providence, 1969; M.F.A., Art Inst. Chgo., 1971. Instr. U. Ill., 1971-74; asst. prof. U. No. Iowa, Cedar Falls, 1974-78, assoc. prof., 1978-83, head dept. photog. program, 1974-83; advisor visual arts Iowa Arts Council, Des Moines, 1977-78, mem. art purchase com., 1977-78; chmn. photog. dept. Kansas City Art Inst., Mo., 1983—. Exhibited one-man shows, Sioux City Art Ctr., Iowa, 1981, Klein Gallery, Chgo., 1982, James Madison U., Harrisonburg, Va., 1983, Orange Coast Coll., Costa Mesa, Calif., Portland State U., Oreg., others, group shows, U. Colo., Boulder, 1977, 82, Mus. Modern Art, N.Y.C., 1978, Santa Barbara Mus. Art, Calif., 1979, San Francisco Mus. Modern Art, 1982, others; represented permanent collections, Mus. Modern Art, N.Y.C., Mpls. Inst. Arts, Hallmark Collection, Kansas City, Mo., Boise Gallery Art, Idaho, Walker Art Ctr., Mpls., R.I. Sch. Design, U. Colo., Fogg Mus. Art, Harvard U., Spencer Mus. Art, U. Kans., Lawrence, Internat. Mus. Photography, Rochester, N.Y., Art Inst. Chgo., Humbolt State U., Arcata, Calif., Cedar Arts Forum Black Hawk County, Iowa, Smithsonian Instn., Washington. W.R. French fellow Art Inst. Chgo., 1971; Nat. Endowment for Arts fellow, 1976. Mem. Soc. for Photog. Edn., Fedn. Digestive Diseases Socs. (council 1978-80), Am. Assn. Study of Liver Disease, Cuy ahoga County Acad. Medicine, Interstate Postgrad. Med. Assn. (pres. 1984), Sigma Xi, Alpha Omega Alpha. Home: 1717 Wyandotte Kansas City MO 64108 Office: Kansas City Art Inst 4415 Warwick Blvd Kansas City MO 64111

ESTABROOK, ROBERT HARLEY, editor, publisher; b. Dayton, Ohio, Oct. 16, 1918; s. Charles and Christianne M. (Harley) E.; m. Mary Lou Stewart, Dec. 22, 1942; children: John Stewart, James Ross, David Morse, Margaret Harley. A.B., Northwestern U., 1939; postgrad., Am. Press Inst., Columbia, 1947; L.H.D., Colby Coll., 1972. City editor Emmet County Graphic, Harbor Springs, Mich., 1936; editor Daily Northwestern, Northwestern U., 1938-39; reporter Cedar Rapids (Iowa) Gazette, 1939-40, editorial writer, 1940-42, Washington Post, 1946-53, editor, 1953-61, London corr., 1961-62, chief fgn. corr., London, 1962-65; UN and Can. corr., 1966-71; editor, pub. Lakeville (Conn.) Jour., 1971—; lectr. journalism U. Md., 1948-49. Asso. editor, 1965-66. Served from pvt. to capt. AUS, 1942-46; in charge Army newspaper and radio sta., 1945; Brazil. Recipient John Peter Zenger award U. Ariz., 1979, Eugene Cervi award, 1980, Horace Greeley award, 1980. Mem. Nat. Conf. Editorial Writers (founder, life mem. pres. 1951), Council Fgn. Relations, Conn. Editorial Assn. (pres. 1975-76), Conn. Council on Freedom of Info. (chmn. 1981-82), New Eng. Press Assn. (pres. 1983), Phi Beta Kappa, Sigma Delta Chi (award for best editorial 1954), Deadline Club (award for UN corr. 1969, Golden Quill award for best editorial 1973, 78, Herbert Brucker award 1977), Delta Tau Delta. Unitarian. Home: Reservoir Rd Lakeville CT 06039 Office: Lakeville Jour Lakeville CT 06039

ESTABROOK, RONALD WINFIELD, chemistry educator; b. Albany, N.Y., Jan. 3, 1926; s. George Arthur and Lillian Florence (Childs) E.; m. June Elizabeth Templeton, Aug. 23, 1947; children: Linda Estabrook Gilbert, Laura Estabrook Verinder, Jill Estabrook, David Estabrook. B.S., Rensselaer Poly. Inst., 1950; Ph.D., U. Rochester, 1954, D.Sc. (hon.), 1980, M.D., Karolinska Inst., Stockholm, 1981. Johnson Research Found. fellow U. Pa. Sch. Medicine, 1955-58; research asso., 1958-59, asst. prof. phys. biochemistry, 1959-62, asso. prof., 1961-65, prof., 1965-68; prof. biochemistry U. Tex. Health Sci. Center, Dallas, 1968-82, dean, 1973-76; chmn. basic sci. rev. com. VA, 1972-74; cons. in field. Bd. sci. advisers St. Judes Hosp., Memphis, 1978-81; chmn. bd. toxicology and environ. health Nat. Acad. Sci., 1980—; mem. Atlantic Richfield Sci. Adv. Council, 1981—. Exec. editor: Archives of Biochemistry and Biophysics, 1966-73, Cancer Research, 1980—; editor: Jour. Pharmacology and Exptl. Therapeutics, 1969-74, Xenobiotica, 1970—, Life Scis, 1973—; Contbr. articles to profl. jours. Served with USNR, 1943-46. Recipient Disting. Scientist award Fedn. Am. Socs. Exptl. Biologist, 1977; Claude Bernard medal U. Montreal, 1969. Mem. Inst. Medicine, Nat. Acad. Scis., Pan Am. Assn., Biochem. Socs. (sec.-gen. 1972-75), Am. Assn. Med. Schs. (adminstrv. bd. council acad. socs.; task force cost med. edn. 1971-72, liaison com. med. edn. 1975-80), Am. Soc. Biol. Chemists, Am. Soc. Pharmacology and Exptl. Therapeutics, Sigma Xi. Home: 5208 Preston Haven Dallas TX 75229 Office: U Tex Health Sci Center 5323 Harry Hines Blvd Dallas TX 75235

ESTCOURT, VIVIAN FITZGEORGE, consulting electrical and mechanical engineer; b. London, May 31, 1897; U.S., 1912, naturalized, 1921; s. Rowland Metzner and Constance A. (Swain) E.; m. Helen Grant, June 21, 1929 (dec. Dec. 1977). A.B., Stanford U., 1922. Lic. profl. elec. and mech. engr., Calif. Mech. draftsman Consol. Copper Co., 1922-23; efficiency engr. Pacific Gas and Electric Co., San Francisco, 1923-36, asst. supt. steam dept., 1936-39, asst engr. ops., 1939-45, engr. steam and gas, San Francisco, 1945-50, gen. supt. steam generation dept., 1950-60, mgr. steam generation dept., 1960-62, cons. engr., 1962-64, Bechtel Power Corp., 1963—; mem. accreditation of engring. colls. com. Engrs.' Council for Profl. Devel., N.Y.C., 1958-64; mem. com. on furnace safeguards Nat. Fire Protection Assn., Boston, 1958—; mem. tech. adv. com. on sea water conversion U. Calif.-Berkeley, 1960-64; chmn. joint steering com. on stack plume opacity Edison Electric Inst. and USPHS, Washington, 1960-64. Contbr. articles, sect. to profl. publs., 1953—. Recipient Newcomen Soc. Gold medal in steam Franklin Inst., Phila., 1966. Fellow ASME (chmn. San Francisco sect. 1940-41, Prime Movers Com. award 1958, hon. mem. 1963, Centennial medal 1980), Power Engring. Soc. of IEEE (hon. mem. generation com. 1983), IEEE (sr. mem.); mem. ASTM, Nat. Acad. Engring. Clubs: Commonwealth of No. Calif., Engrs.' of San Francisco (San Francisco). Lodge: Masons. Home: 40 Kittredge Terr San Francisco CA 94118 Office: Bechtel Power Corp PO Box 3965 Sa Francisco CA 94119

ESTEE, CHARLES REMINGTON, chemistry educator; b. Hecla, S.D., Oct. 7, 1921; s. Charles William and Vera Alice (Hines) E.; m. Doris Evelyn Erickson, Aug. 1, 1943 (dec. Oct. 1974); children: Barbara Ellen Estee Schmelz, Elizabeth Ann Estee Mollet, Charles Steven. B.S., Jamestown Coll., 1942; M.S., U. Iowa, 1944, Ph.D., 1947. Chemist Tenn. Eastman Corp., Oak Ridge, 1944-45; duPont fellow, grad. asst. instr. U. Iowa, 1945-47; mem. faculty U. S.D., Vermillion, 1947—, prof., chmn. chemistry dept., 1952—; Sci. faculty fellow U. Minn., 1957-58; Harrington lectr. U. S.D., 1969. Contbg. editor: Jour. Coll. Sci. Teaching, 1971—; contbr. articles to sci. jours. Fellow Iowa Acad. Sci., AAAS; mem. Am. Chem. Soc. (past chmn. Sioux Valley sect.), S.D. Acad. Sci. (past pres.), Nat. Sci. Tchrs. Assn., Soc. Coll. Sci. Tchrs. (pres. 1982-83), Sigma Xi, Phi Lambda Upsilon. Republican. Methodist. Lodges: Masons; Lions. Home: 110 S Yale Vermillion SD 57069

ESTENSON, NOEL KEITH, agricultural exchange executive; b. Climax, Minn., Dec. 26, 1938; s. Ordean Parnell and Helen Marie (Charis) E.; m. Ethel Hanson, June 3, 1960; children: Keith, Craig, Kim, Dennis. Student, N.D. State U., 1957-61, U. Minn. With Farmers Union Central Exchange, Inc., St. Paul, 1963—, mgr. gen. credit, 1967-74, v.p. fin. services, 1974-81, sr. v.p. petroleum and fin., 1981—. Mem. Inver Grove Heights Planning Commn. Served to 2d lt. AUS, 1961-63. Mem. South St. Paul/Inver, Grove Heights C. of C. (pres. 1980-81), Fin. Execs. Inst. Democrat. Clubs: St Paul Athletic, Lilydale Tennis. Office: PO Box 64089 St Paul MN 55164

ESTERHAI, JOHN LOUIS, lawyer; b. Phoenixville, Pa., Jan. 26, 1920; s. Louis and Mary (Wolarik) E.; m. I. Louise Moyer, Nov. 13, 1943; children: John Louis Jr., Louise Clayton (Mrs. William A. Ratcliffe). B.S.C., Temple U., 1940; LL.B., U. Pa., 1946. Bar: Pa. 1947. Law clk. to Hon. Herbert F. Goodrich, 1946-47; assoc. legal dept. Philco Corp., Phila., 1947-58; v.p., sec., dir. Philco Finance Corp., 1958-62; asst. counsel Penn Mut. Life Ins. Co., 1962-65, assoc. counsel, 1965-69, asso. gen. counsel, 1970-83, sec., 1971-77, dir. govt. relations, 1977-83. Author: (with others) Trademark Management, 1955. Bd. mgrs. Meml. Hosp., Roxborough, chmn., 1969-77, hon. chmn., 1977—; mem. ho. of dels. Am. Hosp. Assn., 1974-79; bd. dirs. Med. Tech. Fund, Inc., PRO Fund, Inc., PRO Income Fund, Inc. Served to lt. USNR, 1942-45. Recipient Disting. Service award Hosp. Assn. Pa., 1979. Mem. Am., Pa., Phila. bar assns., U.S. Trade Mark Assn. (pres. 1958-60), Internat. Assn. Protection Indsl. Property (treas. 1954-58), Assn. Life Ins. Counsel. Republican. Baptist. Clubs: Mason., Union League (Phila.). Home: 8423 Pembrook Rd Philadelphia PA 19128

ESTERLY, JOHN ROOSEVELT, pathologist, educator; b. Friedensburg, Pa., Mar. 13, 1933; s. John E. and Della (Nein) E.; m. Nancy Burton, June 15, 1957; children: Sarah, Anne, John, Henry. B.S., Yale U., 1955; M.D., Johns Hopkins U., 1959. Intern Johns Hopkins Hosp., Balt., 1959-60, resident, 1960-63; asst. prof. dept pathology U. Chgo., 1968-72, assoc. prof., 1972-75, prof., 1975—. Contbr. articles to profl. jours. Served with U.S. Army, 1966-68. Mem. Internat. Acad. Pathology, Am. Assn. Pathologists, Histochem. Soc., Teratology Soc., Pediatric Path. Club, Am. Thoracic Soc. Office: Dept Pathology U Chgo Chicago IL 60637

ESTERLY, NANCY BURTON, physician; b. N.Y.C., Apr. 14, 1935; d. Paul R. and Tanya 21E. (Pasahow) Burton; m. John R. Esterly, June 16, 1957; children—Sarah Burton, Anne Beidler, John Snyder, II, Henry Clark, II. A.B., Smith Coll., 1956; M.D., Johns Hopkins U., 1960. Intern, then resident in pediatrics Johns Hopkins Hosp., 1960-63, fellow in dermatology, 1964-67; instr. pediatrics Johns Hopkins U. Med. Sch., 1967-68; instr., trainee La Rabida U. Chgo. Inst.; also dept. pediatrics U. Chgo. Med. Sch., 1968-69; asst. prof. Pritzker Sch. Medicine, U. Chgo., 1969-70, asso. prof., 1973-78; asst. prof. dermatology Abraham Lincoln Sch. Medicine, U. Ill., 1970-72, asso. prof. dermatology and pediatrics, 1972-73; dir. div. dermatology, dept. pediatrics Michael Reese Hosp. and Med. Center, Chgo., 1973-78; prof. pediatrics and dermatology Northwestern U. Med. Sch., 1978; head div. dermatology, dept. pediatrics Children's Meml. Hosp., Chgo., 1978—. Contbr. numberous articles to profl. jours. Mem. Internat. Soc. Pediatric Dermatology, Am. Acad. Dermatology, Soc. Investigative Deramtology, Soc. Pediatric Research, Soc. Pediatric Dermatology, Soc. Dermatol. Genetics, Chgo. Dermatol., Soc., Chgo. Pediatric Soc., Sigma Xi. Office: Children's Meml Hosp 2300 Children's Plaza Chicago IL 60614

ESTEROW, MILTON, magazine editor, publisher; b. Bklyn., July 28, 1928; s. Bernard and Yetta (Barash) E.; m. Jacqueline Levine, Jan. 6, 1951; children: Judith, Deborah. Student, Bklyn. Coll., 1946-49. Reporter, N.Y. Times, N.Y.C., 1948-63, asst. to cultural news dir., 1963-68; asso. dir. Kennedy Galleries, N.Y.C., 1968-72; editor, pub. ARTnews, N.Y.C., 1972—, The ART newsletter, 1975—; chmn. ARTnews Books, 1980—, Corp. ARTnews, 1984—; lectr. numerous colls., univs., museums. Author: The Art Stealers, 1966. Office: 5 W 37th St New York NY 10018

ESTES, CARL L., II, lawyer; b. Fort Worth, Tex., Feb. 9, 1936; s. Joe E. and Carroll E.; m. Gay Gooch, Aug. 29, 1959; children: Adrienne Virginia, Margaret Ellen. B.S., U. Tex., 1957, LL.B., 1960. Bar: Tex. 1960. Law clk. U.S. Supreme Ct., 1960-61; assoc. firm Vinson & Elkins, Houston, 1961-69, ptnr., 1970—. Bd. dirs. St. Lukes Meth. Ch., Houston, 1978—. Fellow Am Bar Found., Tex. Bar Found.; Mem. Am. Law Inst., Am. Coll. Probate Counsel, ABA; mem. Internat. Bar Assn.; Mem. Tex. Bar Assn., Internat. Fiscal Assn., Internat. Acad. Estate and Trust Law. Clubs: Houston, Ramada, Houston Country, Allegro. Home: 101 Broad Oaks Circle Houston TX 77056 Office: 3400 First City Nat Bank Tower Houston TX 77002

ESTES, CARROLL LYNN, sociologist, educator; b. Ft. Worth, May 30, 1938; d. Joe Ewing and Carroll (Cox) E.; m. Philip R. Lee; 1 dau., Duskie Lynn Gelfand. A.B., Stanford U., 1959; M.A., So. Meth. U., 1961; Ph.D., U. Calif.-San Diego, 1972. Research asst. and assoc. Brandeis U. Social Welfare Research Center, 1962-67; research dir. Simmons Coll., 1963-64; asst. prof. social work San Diego State Coll., 1967-72; asst. prof. dept. psychiatry U. Calif., San Francisco, 1972-75, coordinator human devel. tng. program, 1974-75, asso. prof. dept. social and behavioral scis., 1975-79, prof., 1979—, chair dept. social and behavioral scis., 1981—; dir. Aging Health Policy Research Center, 1979—; Mem. Calif. Commn. on Aging, 1974-77; cons. U.S. Senate Spl. Com. on Aging, 1976—, U.S. Congress Office of Tech. Assessment, 1982—. Author: The Decision-Makers: The Power Structure of Dallas, 1963; author: The Aging Enterprise, 1979, Austerity and Aging, 1983; contbr. articles to profl. jours. Trustee, The Villers Found., 1982—. Recipient Matrix award Theta Sigma Phi, 1964; award for contbns. to lives of older Californians, Calif. Commn. on Aging, 1977; NIMH spl. fellow for research, 1970-72. Mem. ACLU, Am. Sociol. Assn., Inst. Medicine of Nat. Acad. Scis., Assn. Gerontology in Higher Edn. (pres. 1980-81), Western Gerontol. Soc. (pres. 1982—), Soc. Study of Social Problems (sect. chair 1979), Pi Beta Phi. Democrat. Home: 485 Dewey Blvd San Francisco CA 94116

ESTES, DONALD WAYNE, trucking company executive; b. Allen, Kans., Sept. 15, 1930; s. Frank Lester and Florence M. (Lewis) E.; m. Arlene Joyce Hahn, Aug. 10, 1957; children: Gayla Dawn, Julie Ann. B.B.A., Washburn U., 1958. Account mgr. Ryder Truck Rental, Inc., 1964-65, dist. mgr., Little Rock, 1965-70, regional mgr., Milw., 1970-74, area v.p., Miami, Fla., 1974-79, sr. v.p., 1979-81, exec. v.p., 1981-82, exec. v.p. ops., 1982-83, pres., 1983—; pres. Catrala Assocs., 1969-71, others. Served with USN, 1950-54. Mem. Ark. Bus and Truck Assn. (v.p., dir. 1965-71), Truck Rental and Leasing Assn, (dir. 1983—). Democrat. Methodist. Home: 7195 SW 101st St Miami FL 33156 Office: 3600 NW 82d Ave Miami FL 33166

ESTES, EDWARD HARVEY, JR., medical educator; b. Gay, Ga., May 1, 1925; s. Edward Harvey and Veola (Jarrell) E.; m. Jean Anderson, Oct. 15, 1948; children: Sara Estes Brown, Susan Estes Jones III, Rebecca Estes Dunn, John, Elizabeth Estes Smith. B.S., Emory U., 1944, M.D., 1947. House officer, research fellow Grady Meml. Hosp., Atlanta, 1947-50; mem. faculty dept. medicine Duke U., 1952—, prof. chmn. dept. community and family medicine, 1966—. Author: (with R.P. Grant) Spatial Vector Electrocardiography, 1950. Mem. Inst. Medicine, Am. Soc. Internal Medicine (named Distinguished Internist of Year 1975), AMA, ACP, N.C. Med. Soc. (pres. 1977-78). Home: 3542 Hamstead Ct Durham NC 27707

ESTES, ELAINE ROSE GRAHAM, librarian; b. Springfield, Mo., Nov. 24, 1931; d. James McKinley and Zelma Mae (Smith) Graham; m. John Melvin Estes, Dec. 29, 1953. B.S. in Bus. Adminstrn, Drake

U., 1953, teaching cert., 1956; M.S. in L.S, U. Ill., 1960. With Public Library, Des Moines, 1956—, coordinator extension services, 1977-78, dir., 1978—; lectr. antiques, hist. architecture, libraries; mem. conservation planning com. for disaster preparedness for libraries, Iowanet adv. com. Iowa Library Commn. Author bibliographies of books on antiques; contbr. articles to profl. jours. Mem. Des Moines Mayor's Sister City Commn., 1970-80; chmn. Des Moines Mayor's Hist. Dist. Commn.; bd. dirs. Des Moines Art Center, 1972—; mem. nominations rev. com. Iowa State Nat. Hist. Register. Recipient recognition for outstanding working women—leadership in econ. and civic life of Greater Des Moines YWCA, 1975, Disting. Alumni award Drake U., 1979. Mem. ALA, Iowa Library Assn. (pres. 1978-79), Iowa Urban Public Library Assn., Library Assn. Greater Des Moines Metro Area (pres.), Iowa Soc. Preservation Hist. Landmarks. Clubs: Links, Quester's, Inc. (pres. 1982). Office: 100 Locust St Des Moines IA 50308

ESTES, ELEANOR, author; b. West Haven, Conn., May 9, 1906; d. Louis and Caroline (Gewecke) Rosenfeld; m. Rice Estes, Dec. 8, 1932; 1 dau., Helena. Grad., Pratt Inst. Sch. Library Sci., (Caroline M. Hewins scholar), 1932. Children's librarian Free Pub. Library, New Haven, 1924-31, N.Y. Pub. Library, 1932-40. Author: The Moffats, 1941, The Middle Moffat, 1942, The Sun and the Wind and Mr. Todd, 1943, Rufus M, 1943, The Hundred Dresses, 1944, The Echoing Green, 1947, The Sleeping Giant, 1948, Ginger Pye, 1951 (winner Herald Tribune Spring Book Festival award), A Little Oven, 1955, Pinky Pye, 1958, The Witch Family, 1960, The Alley, 1964, Miranda The Great, 1967, The Lollipop Princess, 1967, The Tunnel of Hugsy Goode, 1972, The Coat-Hanger Christmas Tree, 1973, The Lost Umbrella of Kim Chu, 1978, The Moffat Museum, 1983. Recipient Newbery medal for distinguished contbn. to Am. lit. for children, 1951; ann. Alumni award Pratt Inst., 1967; N.Y. State assn. Supervision and Curriculum Devel. award for outstanding contbn. to childrens lit., 1961. Mem. P.E.N. Episcopalian. Home: New Haven CT 06511

ESTES, ELLIOTT M., automobile executive; b. Mendon, Mich., Jan. 7, 1916. Student, Gen. Motors Inst., 1932-36; M.S. in Mech. Engring., U. Cin., 1940; D.Sc. (hon.), U. Cin., 1971; LL.D. (hon.), Kalamazoo Coll., 1975, No. Mich. U., 1976. Chief engr. Pontiac Motor div. Gen. Motors Corp., 1956-61, gen mgr., corp. v.p., 1961-65, v.p., gen. mgr. Chevrolet Motor div., 1965-69, group exec. car and truck group, 1969-70, group v.p. overseas ops., 1970-72, exec. v.p. ops. staff, dir., 1972-74, pres., chief operating officer, dir., Detroit, 1974-81; dir. Owens-Ill. Inc., Kellogg Co., McDonnell Douglass Corp., COMSAT. Mem. Sigma Chi. Address: 4441 Clarke Dr Saint Clair MI 48079

ESTES, EMORY DOLPHOUS, English educator; b. Marshal, Tex., July 1, 1925; s. Emory Dolphous and Thelma (Pyle) E.; m. Dorothy Louise Southerland, Aug. 30, 1947; children: Emory Dolphous, Shannon Gayle. B.A., East Tex. Bapt. Coll., Marshall, 1969; M.A., North Tex. State U., Denton, 1956; Ph.D., Tex. Christian U., 1970. Prof. English U. Tex., Arlington, 1956—, chmn. dept., 1971—. Served with U.S. Army, 1943-46. Mem. MLA, Coll. English Assn. (Tex. pres. 1966-67). Episcopalian. Office: Dept of English Univ of Texas Arlington TX 76019

ESTES, GERALD WALTER, newspaper executive; b. Memphis, Apr. 21, 1928; s. Edward Leon and Grace Virginia (Knight) E.; m. Mary Charlene Owen, Nov. 7, 1953 (div. July 1975); children: Patricia Estes Tischler, Charles, Susan, Jacqueline; m. Bernice Pendleton O'Mery, Mar. 20, 1976. Student, Memphis State U., 1949-50. Research asst. Washington Star, 1954-56, asst. prodn. mgr., 1956-68; prodn. mgr. Richmond (Va.) Newspapers, 1968-69; v.p., gen. mgr. SE Media, Inc., Richmond, 1969-73; v.p. newspaper div. Media Gen., Inc., Richmond, 1974-77, sr. v.p., 1977—; dir. Computer Software Co. Served with USAF, 1946-49. Mem. Am. Newspaper Pubs. Assn., So. Newspaper Pubs. Assn., So. Prodn. Program (dir.), Va. Cable TV Assn. (dir.), Central Richmond Assn., Richmond C. of C. Republican. Methodist. Clubs: Bull and Bear, Willow Oaks Country. Home: 6505 River Rd Richmond VA 23229 Office: Media Gen Inc 333 E Grace St Richmond VA 23229

ESTES, HOWELL MARION, JR., former air force officer, airline exec.; b. Ft. Oglethorpe, Ga., Sept. 18, 1914; s. Col. Howell Marion and Juanita (Dickson) E.; m. Annah Verbeck, Mar. 8, 1941; children—Howell Marion III, Michael Summer, Charles Dickson. B.S., U.S. Mil. Acad., 1936; grad., Flying Schs., 1940, Air War Coll., 1949. Commd. 2d lt. Cav. U.S. Army, 1936, USAAF, 1940-69; advanced through grades to gen. USAF, 1964; assigned (7th Cav.), Ft. Bliss, Tex., 1936-37, acting a.d.c. to comdr., 1937-39, flight instr., Brooks Field, 1940; comdt. cadets Advanced Flying Sch., 1940-42, dir. flying, 1942-43, dir. tng., 1943-44; comdg. officer, Lackland Air Base, Waco, Tex., 1944, comdr., Lubbock Army Air Field, 1944-45; chief plan and policy br., operations div. USAAF Europe, Wiesbaden, Germany, 1946, chief staff for operations, 1946-47, asst. chief staff for plans, 1947; assigned (22d Bomb Wing), March Air Base, Calif., 1949, comdr., 1949, with, U.K., 1949-5O, dep. comdr., chief staff, 195O-51, comdr., March Air Base, 1951, vice comdr., 1951, comdr., March Air Base, 1951-52, 1952-53, 1952-54; dir. weapon systems operations Wright Air Devel. Center, Air Research and Devel. Command, Wright-Patterson AFB, Ohio, 1954-55; asst. dep. comdr. for weapon systems, comdr. detachment no. 1 Hdqrs. Air Research and Devel. Command, dir. systems mgmt., 1955-57; asst. chief staff for air def. systems Hdqrs. USAF, Washington, 1957-58, asst. dep. chief of staff, operations, 1958-61; dep. comdr. aerospace systems (Air Force Systems Command), Los Angeles, 1961-62, vice comdr., Andrews AFB, 1962-64, comdr., 1964-69, ret., 1969; sr. v.p. World Airways, Inc., Oakland, Calif., 1969-71, exec. v.p., 1971, pres., 1971-74, also dir.; chmn. bd., chief exec. officer, dir. Fed. Express Corp., Memphis, 1974-75; chmn. bd. Vanguard Internat. Aircargo Inc., 1975—. Decorated Legion of Merit with two clusters, D.F.C., Air Medal with 2 clusters, D.S.M. Army, D.S.M. with oak leaf cluster USAF; War Cross, Czechoslovakia).; Recipient Gen. H. H. Arnold trophy. Mem. Nat. Def. Transp. Assn. (def. adv. council). Address: 7603 Shadywood Rd Bethesda MD 20817

ESTES, JAMES MILTON, reinsurance company executive; b. Polo, Mo., June 2, 1927; s. James Floyd and Lela (Fowler) E.; m. Shirley Jeanne Mallen, Sept. 25, 1954; 1 son, James Todd. Student, U. Mo., 1948-50, Kansas City U., 1956-58. C.P.C.U. Casualty auditor Kemper Ins. Corp., Chgo., 1954-56; underwriter casualty reins. Employers Rein. Corp., Overland Park, Kans., 1956-80, exec., 1980—; dir. Bates-Turner Inc., Overland Park, Kans. Served as cpl. USAF, 1946-47. Mem. C.P.C.U. Soc. Office: Employers Reinsurance Corp 5200 Metcalf PO Box 2991 Overland Park KS 66201

ESTES, JOE EWING, judge; b. Commerce, Tex., Oct. 24, 1903; s. Joe Guinn and Della Marshall (Loy) E.; m. Carroll Virginia Cox, Dec. 1, 1931; children: Carl Lewis, Carroll. Student, E. Tex. State Tchrs. Coll., 1923-24; LL.B., U. Tex., 1927; LL.D., E. Tex. State U., 1974. Bar: Tex. 1927. Partner Crosby & Estes, Commerce, 1928-30, Phillips, Trammell, Estes, Edwards & Orn, Ft. Worth, 1930-45, Sanford, King, Estes & Cantwell, Dallas, 1946-52, Estes & Cantwell, 1952-55; U.S. dist. judge, Dallas, 1955-60; chief judge U.S. Dist. Ct. No. Dist. Tex., Dallas, 1959-79, sr. judge, 1979—; also judge Temp. Emergency Ct. Appeals U.S., 1972—; mem. adv. com. on rules evidence U.S. Supreme Ct. Contbr. articles to profl. jours.; also to: Handbook of Recommended Procedures for the Trial of Protracted Cases; co-author: Handbook for Newly Appointed U.S. District Judges; editorial bd.: Manual for Complex Litigation. Trustee, mem. exec. com. S.W. Legal Found.; Research fellow, mem. med.-legal com., chmn. Oil and Gas Inst. of S.W. Legal Found.; chmn. exec. com. bd. trustees St. Mark's Sch. of Tex., Dallas, 1951-55. Served as lt. comdr. USNR, 1942-45; mem. Res. Recipient Hatton W. Sumners award S.W. Legal Found., 1972. Fellow Am. Bar Found.; mem. Nat. Conf. Commrs. on Uniform State Laws, Am. Law Inst., Inter-Am., Fed., ABA (chmn. sect. jud. administrn. 1961-62, mem. ho. dels.), Dallas Bar Assn. (past v.p.), Fort Worth Bar Assn. (past dir.), State Bar Tex., Am. Judicature Soc., Jud. Conf. U.S. (chmn. com. on trial practice and technique, mem. exec. com. 1969-71, dist. judge rep.), Nat. Lawyers Club, Inst. Jud. Adminstrn., Philos. Soc. Tex., Newcomen Soc., Am. Legion, Chancellors, Phi Delta Phi, Kappa Sigma, Order of Coif. Methodist. Clubs: Masons (33 deg.), Shriners (hon. insp. gen.), Shriners (Jester). Home: 5846 Desco Dr Dallas TX 75225 Office: US Court House Dallas TX 75242 *What characterizes my life is faith, hard work, and determination.*

ESTES, RICE, librarian; b. Spartanburg, S.C., Apr. 27, 1907; s. Elliott and Sadie Jane (Smith) E.; m. Eleanor Rosenfeldt, Dec. 8, 1932; 1 dau., Helena Estes Haeseler. A.B., U. S.C., 1928; B.L.S., Pratt Inst., 1932; A.M., U. So. Calif., 1941; postgrad., Columbia, 1943-45. Librarian U. S.C. Sch. Edn., 1931, Housing Study Guild, 1933; library asst. Bklyn. Coll., 1933-35, reference librarian, 1938-43; library asst. Stuyvesant High Sch., N.Y., 1936-38; alumni sec. Pratt Inst., 1944, sec., 1956-71, asst. prof. library sci., 1944-48, acting dean, 1955-56, librarian, 1955-72, librarian emeritus, 1972—, asso. prof., 1955-59, prof. bibliography, 1959; asst. librarian U. So. Calif., 1948-52; librarian Fairfield (Conn.) Pub. Library, 1952-53; chief asst. librarian George Washington U., 1953-55; asso. librarian Albertus Magnus Coll., New Haven, 1972—; Dir. Bklyn. coll. libraries research project Council for Higher Ednl. Instns., N.Y., 1962-63. Author: A Study of Seven College Libraries and Their Cooperative Potential; Contbr. articles to profl. jours.; Book reviewer. Mem. Eastern Coll. Librarians Conf. (chmn. 1965), A.L.A. (chmn. Grolier award com. 1965-66, chmn. Clarence Day award com. 1968-69), N.Y. Library Assn., Conn. (sec. 1953), Spl. Libraries Assn., Assn. Colls. and Research Libraries, Acad. Libraries of Bklyn. (pres. 1969-7O), Bibliog. Soc. Am., Am. Assn. U. Profs., Met. Coll. Inter-Library Assn. (pres. 1962-63), Phi Beta Kappa, Beta Phi Mu (hon. mem., exec. council 1968-71). Episcopalian. Clubs: Archons of Colophon, New York Library (pres. 1961-62). Home: 324 Willow St New Haven CT 06511

ESTES, RICHARD, painter; b. Evanston, Ill., 1936. Student, Chgo. Art Inst., 1952-56. Works rep., Whitney Mus. Am. Art, N.Y.C., Rockhill Nelson Mus., Kansas City, Mo., Toledo Mus., Chgo. Art Inst., Des Moines Art Center, numerous exhbns. including, Documenta V, Kassel, W. Ger., 1972, Venice Biennale, Whitney Mus. Ann., Va. Mus. Fine Arts, 1974, Boston Mus. Fine Arts, 1975, 78. Address: 300 central park west New York NY 10024

ESTES, WALTER EUGENE, civil engineer; b. Quincy, Ill., Aug. 27, 1923; s. Walter and Vena Davis (Jones) E.; m. June Elizabeth Weiss, Oct. 16, 1943; Children: Steven Alan, Joan Elizabeth, Sally Ann. B.S. in Civil Engring., U. Ill., 1944, M.S., 1947. Registered profl. engr., Calif., Hawaii, Guam, Del., Ont., N.B. Project mgr. Standard Oil Co. Calif., San Francisco, 1947-62; head gen. engring. dept. Iranian Oil Exploration and Producing Co., Iran, 1958-60; v.p., gen. mgr. Irvings Cos., Can., 1962-66; partner Dames & Moore, Los Angeles, 1966—; dir. engring. and constrn. cos. Mem. N.B. Research and Productivity Council, 1963-67. Co-author: What Every Engineer Should Know About Project Management, 1981. Served with AUS, 1943-46. Fellow ASCE; mem. Project Mgmt. Inst., Soc. Mil. Engrs. Club: Los Angeles Rotary. Home: 1797 Brooksfall Ct Westlake Village CA 91361 Office: 445 S Figueroa St Suite 3500 Los Angeles CA 90071

ESTES, WILLIAM KAYE, psychologist, educator; b. Mpls., June 17, 1919; s. George D. and Mona; m. Katherine Walker, Sept. 26, 1942; children: George E., Gregory W. Mem. faculty Ind. U., 1946-62, prof. psychology, 1955-60, research prof. psychology, 1960-62; faculty research fellow Social Sci. Research Council, 1952-55; lectr. psychology U. Wis., summer 1949; vis. prof. Northwestern U., spring 1959; fellow Center Advanced Study Behavioral Scis., 1955-56; spl. univ. lectr. U. London, Eng., 1961; prof. psychology, mem. Inst. Math. Studies Social Scis., Stanford, 1962-68; prof. Rockefeller U., 1968-79, Harvard U., 1979—. Author: An Experimental Study of Punishment, 1944, Learning Theory and Mental Development, 1970; co-author: Modern Learning Theory, 1954, Models of Learning, Memory, and Choice, 1982; also numerous articles.; Editor: Handbook of Learning and Cognitive Processes, 1975, Jour. Comparative and Physiol. Psychology, 1962-68, Psychol. Rev., 1977-82; asso. editor: Jour. Exptl. Psychology, 1958-62. Served with AUS, 1944-46. Fellow Am. Psychol. Assn. (pres. div. exptl. psychology 1958-59, Distinguished Sci. Contbn. award 1962), AAAS, Am. Acad. Arts and Scis.; mem. Nat. Acad. Scis., N.Y. Acad. Sci. (hon. life), Soc. Exptl. Psychologists (Warren medal 1963), Psychometric Soc., Midwestern Psychol. Assn. (pres. 1956-57). Home: 95 Irving St Cambridge MA 02138 Office: 620 W James Hall 33 Kirkland Cambridge MA 02138

ESTEVES, VERNON RAFAEL, educator; b. Mayaguez, P.R., Oct. 24, 1920; s. Luis Raul and Lupe (Navarro) E.; m. Isabel Loyd, June 4, 1948; children—Vernon Xavier, Maria Cristina, Maria Isabel. B.A., U. P.R., 1942; M.Econ., Harvard, 1945, Ph.D., 1948. Mem. faculty U. P.R., Río Piedras, 1947, 65-69, 71—, dean, 1965-69, 78—, prof. fin., 1971—, acad. dean, 1979—; sr. economist IMF, Washington, 1948; econ. adviser to Gov. P.R., 1949-51; exec. sec. Finance Council, 1958-65; fgn. payments specialist ECA U.S. (Marshall Plan), Paris, 1951-53; pvt. practice econ. cons., Miami, Fla., 1953-58; v.p. Govt. Devel. Bank P.R., 1958-65; exec. dir. Gov.'s Adv. Council for Devel. Govt. Programs, 1969-71; mem. adv. bd. Ins. Commr. P.R., 1966-69; dir. Housing Bank P.R.; Bd. dirs. Commonwealth Job Devel. Center, Phillips P.R. Core, Inc. Contbr. articles to profl. jours. Mem. Am. Econ. Assn., Soc. Internat. Devel., Assn. Puertorriquena de Economía y Estadisticas. Home: Laguna Terr 12A 6 Joffre St Condado PR 00907 Office: Box AU U PR Station Rio Piedras PR 00931

ESTEVEZ, LUIS DE GALVEZ, designer, mfr.; b. Havana, Cuba; came to U.S., 1944, naturalized, 1960; s. Luis Estevez y Navarro and Gloria Cortinas de Galvez y Benitez de Lugo; m. Betty Dew Menzies. Student, U. Havana, 1948-49, Traphagen Sch. Fashion, 1951-51. Display at Lord & Taylor, N.Y.C., 1950, Jean Patou, Paris, 1951-52; prin. Grenelle-Estevez, N.Y.C., 1955-58; prin., partner Estevez, N.Y.C., 1959-65; owner, operator Estevez/Gabor-Estevez/Estevez Resort Sports Wear, 1973-76; partner with Neal Diamond Estevez Dress Firm, Los Angeles, 1977—. Designer, Pat Hartley, N.Y.C., 1953-54, Neal of Calif., Los Angeles, 1968-72, films and TV, Universal Studios, 1969-70; Betty Ford's wardrobe, 1975-77; designer home furnishings for Dan River also houses and real estate devel.; presented: fashion openings Broadway shows Hair, 1969, Hello Dolly, 1974; Contbr.: articles on fashion to Phila. Inquirer, 1956-66. Recipient Fla. Sunshine award, 1955, Coty Am. Critics award, 1956, Chgo. Gold Coast awards, 1959, 60, 62, Denver Symphony award, Goldwaters Phynix award, Bambergers Fashion award, 1962, Silk award, Traphagen Fashion award, 1975, Am. Schiffli Embroidery award, 1963. Mem. Costume Designers Guild Los Angeles, Acad. Motion Pictures Arts and Scis., Council Fashion Designers Am. Roman Catholic. Office: 122 E 7th St Los Angeles CA 90014 *I believe that you should only wear what is flattering regardless what fashion dictates.* *

ESTEY, GEORGE FISHER, rhetoric educator; b. Cody's, N.B., Can., Jan. 21, 1924; s. Clarence A. and Eileen (Fisher) E.; m. Barbara Alice Brown, Aug. 25, 1951; children: Roger Scott, Gregory Alan. B.A. magna cum laude, Tufts Coll., 1952; M.A., U. Conn., 1954; Ph.D., U. Ill., Urbana, 1960. Instr. U. Conn., Storrs, 1952-54, U. Ill., Urbana, 1954-59; mem. faculty Boston U., 1959—, asso. prof., 1964-68, prof. rhetoric, 1968—. Author: (with Harry H. Crosby) College Writing, 1968, 2d edit., 1975, Just Rhetoric, 1972; editor: (with Doris Hunter) Non-Violence, 1971, Violence, 1971, Interdisciplinary Perspectives, 1976-82. Served with USAAF, 1942-47. Mem. Nat. Council Tchrs. English, Conf. Coll. Composition and Communication, Assn. for Gen. and Liberal Studies, Phi Beta Kappa. Home: 54 Colony Rd Lexington MA 02173 Office: Boston U 871 Commonwealth Ave Boston MA 02215

ESTEY, RALPH HOWARD, plant pathologist; b. Millville, N.B., Can., Dec. 9, 1916; s. Walter Clay and Hazel May (Howard) E.; m. Dorean Elizabeth Pridham, June 22, 1944; children: Ronald Harry, Frank Pridham. B.Sc. in Agr, McGill U., Montreal, Que., Can., 1951, Ph.D., 1956; M.S., U. Maine, 1954; B.Ed., U. N.B., 1960; D.I.C., Imperial Coll., London, 1965. Tchr. Que. High Sch., Quebec City, 1945-50; instr. vocat. agr. Carleton County (N.B.) Vocat. Sch., Woodstock, 1951-53; lectr. botany U. Conn., Storrs, 1956-57; asst. prof. plant pathology Macdonald Coll., McGill U., Ste. Anne de Bellevue, Que., 1957-61, assoc. prof., 1961-72, prof., 1972-82, emeritus prof., 1982—, chmn. dept. plant pathology, 1970-76. Served with Can. Army, 1942-45. Fellow Linnean Soc. London; mem. La Corporation Professionnelle des Agronomes du Que., Soc. Nematologists, Can. Phytopathol. Soc., Agrl. History Soc., Mycol. Soc. Am., Can. Assn. Univ. Tchrs., Agrl. Inst. Can. Home: 91 Devon Rd Baie d'Urfe PQ Canada H9X 2X3 Office: Macdonald Coll McGill U Ste Anne de Bellevue PQ Canada H9X 1C0

ESTEY, WILLARD ZEBEDEE, judge; b. Saskatoon, Sask., Can., Oct. 10, 1919; s. James Wilfred and Muriel (Baldwin) E.; m. Marian Ruth McKinnon, June 14, 1946; children—Wilfred McKinnon, John Willard, Eleanor Ruth, Paul Norman. B.A., U. Sask., 1940, LL.B., 1942; LL.M., Harvard U., 1946; LL.D. (hon.), Wilfrid Laurier U., 1977, U. Toronto, 1979, U. Western Ont., 1980, Law Soc. Upper Canada, 1981. Bar: Called to bar Sask 1942, Ont 1947, apptd. Q.C 1960. Prof. Coll. Law, U. Sask., 1946-47; lectr. Osgoode Hall Law Sch., 1947-51; individual practice law, Toronto, Ont., 1947-72; judge Ct. of Appeal, Supreme Ct., Ont., 1973-75; chief justice High Ct., 1975-76; chief justice of Ont., 1976-77; puisne judge Supreme Ct. of Can., Ottawa, Ont., 1977—; commr. steel profits inquiry Royal Commn. of Inquiry, 1974, commr. Air Can. inquiry, 1975. Past chmn. bd., past pres. Can. Cablesystems, Ltd.; Chmn. bd. dirs. Hockey Can.; hon. life mem., bd. govs. York-Finch Gen. Hosp. Served with Can. Army and RCAF, World War II. Mem. Can. Bar Assn. (past pres. Ont.), Law Soc. Upper Can. (past bencher), Can. Inst. for Advanced Legal Studies (v.p.), Can. Judges Conf. (hon. chmn.). Office: Supreme Ct of Can Ottawa ON K1A 0J1 Canada

ESTIN, HANS HOWARD, investment exec.; b. Prague, Czechoslovakia, Sept. 8, 1928; came to U.S., 1941, naturalized, 1946; m. Gay Parker Semler, Mar. 1957; children: Hilary Parker, Alexandra Howard. A.B., Harvard U., 1949; LL.D., Merrimac Coll., 1972, Boston U., 1977. Vice chmn., pres., chmn. bd. Harbor Nat. Bank, Boston, 1964-67; vice chmn. N.Am. Mgmt. Corp., Boston, 1974—; dir. Boston Safe Deposit & Trust Co., Boston Co., Inc., Putnam Vista Fund, Putnam Voyager Fund, Yellowknife Bear Resources Inc., Toronto, Can.; trustee Putnam Daily Dividend Trust, Putnam Convertible Fund, Putnam High Yield Trust, Putnam Equities Fund, Putnam Option Income Trust, Putnam Income Fund, Putnam Tax Exempt Income Fund, George Putnam Fund of Boston, Putnam Info. Scis. Trust, Depositors Investment Trust, Putnam Growth Fund., Putnam Calif. Tax Exempt Income Fund. Trustee French Library in, Boston, New Eng. Aquarium, Proctor Acad.; chmn. bd. trustees Boston U., 1969-76; mem. corp. Mass. Gen. Hosp.; trustee Tabor Acad.; bd. overseers Boys and Girls Clubs of Boston, Inc.; mem. vis. com., com. on resources Harvard U. Served as 1st lt. USAF, 1951-55. Decorated Knight Order of Crown, Belgium; Recipient Distinguished Service citation Boston U. Sch. Medicine, 1967; named hon. consul of Belgium at, Boston, 1970. Clubs: Somerset, Essex County (Manchester, Mass.). Home: Summer St Manchester MA 01944 Office: 28 State St Boston MA 02109

ESTLOW, EDWARD WALKER, newspaper executive; b. Snyder, Colo., Mar. 20, 1920; s. Edward G. W. and Mary Rachel (McConnel) E.; m. Charlotte Ann Schroder, Mar. 27, 1943; children: Susan Lyday, Nancy Hawes, Sally Baier, Mary Erculiani. A.B., U. Denver, 1942, postgrad. law sch., 1946-49. Gen. mgr. Lovington (N.Mex.) Press, 1949-52; account exec. Rocky Mountain News, Denver, 1952-55, personnel mgr., 1955-64; v.p., bus. mgr. Denver Pub. Co., 1964-70; asst. gen. bus. mgr. Scripps-Howard Newspapers, N.Y.C., 1970-72, v.p., gen. bus. mgr., 1972-76; pres., dir., mem. exec. com. E.W. Scripps Co., 1976—, N.Mex. State Tribune, Birmingham Post Co., Herald-Post Pub. Co., El Paso, Fullerton (Calif.) Pub. Co., Denver Pub. Co.; pres., dir. Grant County News, Ky., Leader, Inc.; v.p., dir., mem. exec. com. Evansville Press Co., Ind., San Juan Star Co., P.R., Scripps-Howard Supply Co.; pres., pub., dir. Cary Publs. Inc., Fla.; v.p., dir. Albuquerque Pub. Co.; dir., mem. exec. com. Sun Tattler Co., Hollywood, Fla., Knoxville News-Sentinel Co., Tenn., Memphis Pub. Co., Pitts., Press Co., Stuart News Co., Fla., Newspaper Enterprise Assn., Inc., United Features Syndicate, Inc., United Press Internat., Inc.; dir. Scripps-Howard Broadcasting Co., Newspaper Printing Corp., El Paso, Tex., United Media Enterprises, Inc., Berkley-Small, Inc., Dataway, Inc. Pres. Mile High Red Cross, Denver, 1965-66; bd. dirs. Denver Jr. Achievement, 1964-70, Denver Better Bus. Bur., 1968-70; trustee U. Denver, 1976—; v.p. Newspaper Advt. Bur., 1976—. Served to capt. USAAF, 1942-45. Mem. U. Denver Alumni Assn. (pres. 69-71). Office: E W Scripps Co 1100 Central Trust Tower Cincinnati OH 45202 *

ESTRADA, ERIK (BORN ENRIQUE ESTRADA), actor; b. N.Y.C., Mar. 16, 1949. Attended, Am. Musical Dramatic Acad., N.Y.C. Appeared in: films Midway; appeared in: TV films Fire!; star of: TV series CHIPs, 1977—; other TV appearances include Medical Center. Office: care Azevedo Internat 1875 Century Park E 6th Floor Los Angeles CA 90067

ESTRADA, RODNEY JOSEPH, utility co. exec.; b. New Orleans, Aug. 22, 1937; s. Louis Orlando and Loretta Patricia (Taillon) E.; m. Roxanne Gatipon, June 3, 1961; children—Rochelle, Ronel, Ronda, Roquel. B.S., La. State U., 1959. Sr. staff acct. Deloitte, Haskins & Sells, 1959-65; staff acct. Middle South Services, 1965-67, sr. acct., 1967-68, asst. treas., asst. sec., 1968-70, controller, 1970-79; asst. treas. Middle South Utilities, New Orleans, 1978-79, treas., 1979—. Mem. Am. Inst. C.P.A.'s, Edison Electric Inst. (chmn. application acctg. principles com. 1979-80). Roman Catholic. Home: 4929 Wade Dr Metairie LA 70003 Office: Middle South Utilities 225 Baronne St New Orleans LA 70112

ESTRIDGE, RONALD B., paper company executive; b. 1937. B.S. in Chem. Engring., N.C. State U.; M.S. in Chemistry and Engring., Inst. Paper Chemistry, Ph.D. Prodn. mgr. bleached kraft pulpmill Mean Corp., 1974; with James River Corp. Va., Richmond, 1974—; v.p. corp. devel., exec. v.p. James River-Mass Inc., 1974-78; v.p. James River Corp., Va., 1978-79, exec. v.p., 1979—. Office: James River Corp Va Tredegar St Box 2218 Richmond VA 23221 *

ESTRIN, HERBERT ALVIN, entertainment co. exec.; b. Jamaica, N.Y., May 4, 1925; s. Joseph and Minnie (Haskell) E.; m. Phyllis Glassman, Jan. 28, 1951; children—Myrna Hope, Richard Lawrence. B.S. in Acctg, N.Y. U., 1949. With Columbia Pictures Industries, Inc., N.Y.C., 1953-73, v.p., 1971-73; v.p., treas., chief fin. officer Prudential Bldg. Maintenance Corp., N.Y.C., 1973-79; v.p., treas. Bolt Corp., South Laguna, Calif., 1979; sr. v.p. fin. and adminstrn. Warner Home Video Inc. (subs. Warner Communications), 1981—. Served with U.S. Army, 1943-46. Office: 3 E 54th St New York NY 10022

ESTRIN, HERMAN ALBERT, educator; b. North Plainfield, N.J., June 2, 1915; s. Morris I. and Ida Ruth (Bender) E.; m. Pearl Simon, June 26, 1949; children: Robert Keith, Karen Ruth. A.B., Drew U., 1937; M.A., Columbia U., 1942, Ed.D., 1954. Instr. social sci., South Plainfield, N.J., 1938-42; mem. faculty N.J. Inst. Tech., Newark, 1946—, prof. English, 1958-81; lectr. U. Paris, 1978, 79, 80, 81; lectr.; cons. Author: (with Paul Obler) The New Scientist: Essays on the Methods and Values of Science, 1963, Technical and Professional Writing: A Practical Anthology, 1963, (with Delmer Good) College and University Teaching, 1966, (with Arthur Sanderson) Freedom and Censorship of the College Press, 1966, (with Esther Lloyd-Jones) The American Student and His College, 1967, How Many Roads?, The 70's, 1970, (with Donald Mehus) The American Language in the 70's, 1974; editor: (with Donald Cunningham) The Teaching of Technical Writing, 1975, The Best Student Poetry in New Jersey, 1978, 79, 80, 81, 82, 83, 84, Poetic Engineers, 1983; author brochures and articles. Adv. bd. Donor Estrin scholarships, 1971-81. Served to capt. U.S. Army, 1942-46. Recipient Alumni Achievement award in arts Drew U., 1958; Gold Key award Columbia Scholastic Press Assn., 1962; Robert Van Houton award N.J. Inst. Tech. Alumni Assn., 1970; Nat. Disting. Newspaper Adviser award Nat. Council Coll. Publs. Advisers, 1970; Western Electric Fund award, 1971; Outstanding Tchr. Tech. Writing award Assn. Tech. Writing Tchrs., 1975; plaque Soc. Collegiate Journalists, 1981; named Outstanding Faculty Mem. N.J. Inst. Tech., 1979-80; also recipient citation Div. Continuing Edn., 1981, also James Robbins award, 1979. Mem. Nat. Council Tchrs. English (past dir., Disting. Service Award 1980), N.J. Council Tchrs. English (past pres., Disting. Tchrs. Award 1973), N.J. Coll. Press Assn. (founder), Nat. Council Publs. Advisers (past pres.), Coll. English Assn. (past regional pres.), N.J. Writers Conf. (dir. 1966—), N.J. Authors Luncheons (dir. 1959—), AAUP, Am. Soc. Engring. Edn., Phi Beta Kappa, Omicron Delta Kappa (award for service 1981), Alpha Pi Omega, Phi Delta Kappa (award for service 1980), Kappa Delta Pi, Phi Eta Sigma, Pi Delta Epsilon (past pres.). Home: 315 Henry St Scotch Plains NJ 07076 Office: Student Center NJ Inst Tech Newark NJ 07102

ESTRIN, RICHARD WILLIAM, editor; b. N.Y.C., Apr. 16, 1932; s. Max and Ruth (Lillienthal) E.; m. Alison Kiendl Stewart, Mar. 13, 1971. B.A., CCNY, 1953. Reporter Park Row News Service, N.Y.C., 1953-55; with Newsday, Inc., Long Island, N.Y., 1955—, sucessively sunday news editor, Part II editor, sr. editor news, until 1983, exec. news editor N.Y.C. Newsday, 1983—. Recipient First Place Lifestyle Journalism awards U.C. Penney-U. M., 1974, 75. Mem. Phi Beta Kappa. Office: Newsday Inc Long Island NY 11747

ESTRUP, PEDER JAN ZWERGIUS, educator; b. Copenhagen, July 15, 1931; U.S., 1956; s. Lauritz A. and Alice (Horneman) E.; m. Faiza Fawaz, Sept. 15, 1960. M.Sc., Poly. Inst. Denmark, Copenhagen, 1954; Ph.D. (Fulbright fellow, Sheffield Sci. fellow), Yale, 1959; Postdoctoral fellow, European Center Nuclear Research, Geneva, 1959-61. Mem. tech. staff Bell Telephone Labs., Murray Hill, N.J., 1961-64; research scientist Bartol Research Found., Swarthmore, Pa., 1964-67; prof. physics, chemistry Brown U., Providence, 1967—. Editor: Surface Phenomena, 1970; Contbr. articles to profl. jours. Served to lt. Danish Army, 1954-56. Fellow Am. Phys. Soc.; mem. Am. Chem. Soc., Am. Vacuum Soc. (exec. com. surface sci. div.). Research in physics and chemistry of surfaces. Home: 15 Adelphi Ave Providence RI 02906

ESTY, DAVID CAMERON, communications executive; b. Mt. Kisco, N.Y., May 26, 1932; s. John Cushing and Virginia (Place) E.; Elizabeth Gunn; children: John Philip, Mary Virginia, David Cameron, Cynthia Elizabeth. B.A., Amherst Coll., 1954. Vice-pres. J. Walter Thompson, N.Y.C., 1964-70; pres. T.D.I., N.Y.C., 1970-74, Douglas Leigh, Inc., 1975-76, Catalyst Corp., 1976-78, BIS Communications Corp., N.Y.C., 1979-82, Airnetwork Corp., 1982—. Author: Somebody Close to You is on Drugs, 1971. Mem. Nat. Ski Patrol; emergency med. technician; chmn. class officers com. Amherst Coll., pres. Class of '54. Served to capt. USAF, 1954-57. Mem. The Advt. Council (dir., mem. exec. com.), Young Pres. Orgn. Club: N.Y. Athletic (N.Y.C.). Office: 310 E 46th St New York NY 10017

ESTY, JOHN CUSHING, JR., education association executive; b. White Plains, N.Y., Aug. 9, 1928; s. John Cushing and Virginia e6(Place) E.; m. Katharine Woolsey Cole, Dec. 21, 1955; children: Daniel Cushing, Paul Cameron, Benjamin Cole, Joshua Dwight. B.A., Amherst Coll., 1950, L.H.D., 1970; M.A., Yale U., 1951; postgrad., U. Calif., Berkeley, 1959-60. Asst. dean, asst. dir. admissions Amherst Coll., 1953-58, asso. dean, 1958-63, lectr. math., 1958-63; headmaster Taft Sch., Watertown, Conn., 1963-72; research asso. in edn. Harvard U., 1972-73; scholar-in-residence U. Mass. Sch. Edn., 1972-73; sr. staff asso. Edn. Devel. Center, Newton, Mass., 1973-74; staff asso. Rockefeller Bros. Fund, N.Y.C., 1973-78; pres. Nat. Assn. Ind. Schs., 1978—; adj. lectr. U. Mass., 1978—. Author: Choosing Private School, 1974. Trustee Robert Coll. of Istanbul. Served to 1st lt. USAF, 1951-53; capt. Res. Mem. Phi Beta Kappa, Sigma Xi, Psi Upsilon. Clubs: Univ., Century Assn. (N.Y.C.). Address: 25 Everett St Concord MA 01742

ETCHELECU, ALBERT DOMINIC, energy company executive; b. Santa Barbara, Calif., Sept. 30, 1937; s. John and Etiennette E.; m. Judith Ann Matthews, June 7, 1975; children: Steven, Scott, Cheri, Michael, David. Student, U. Calif., Santa Barbara, 1957; student program for mgmt. devel., Harvard U. Bus. Sch., 1972. Prodn. mgr. East Tex. Sun Co., 1972-79; v.p., gen. mgr. Sun Info. Services, Phila., 1979-80; pres., chmn. bd. Sperry-Sun, Inc., Houston, 1980; pres., chief exec. officer Minnegasco, Inc., Mpls., 1980—, also dir.; dir. Lane Mgmt. Co. State chmn. Am. Cancer Soc., 1981-82. Mem. Am. Gas Assn. Club: Minneapolis. Office: Minnegasco, Inc 201 S 7th St Minneapolis MN 55402 *

ETCHESON, WARREN WADE, educator; b. Bainbridge, Ind., May 15, 1920; s. Raymond W. and Rosetta (Evans) E.; m. Marianne Newgent, May 30, 1947; children: Denise Elene, Crayton Wade. B.S., Ind. U., 1942; M.B.A., U. Iowa, 1951, Ph.D., 1954. Adminstrv. sec., exec. sec., nat. sec. Delta Chi Nat. Fraternity, 1946-56; lectr. Santo Tomas U., Manila, 1946, U. Iowa, 1951-54; asst. prof. U. Wash., 1954-56, asso. prof., 1956-60, prof. Sch. Bus. Adminstrn., 1960—; asso. dean Bus. Adminstrn., 1974—, Fulbright prof., Istanbul, Turkey, 1963-64. Author: Consumerism, 1972. Trustee Seattle-King County Mcpl. League. Served to lt. U.S. Army, 1942-46. Mem. Am. Mktg. Assn., Alpha Kappa Psi, Phi Eta Sigma, Beta Gamma Sigma, Delta Chi. Club: Rainier. Home: 6625 NE 132d St Kirkland WA 98033 Office: Univ of Wash Seattle WA 98195

ETHEREDGE, FOREST DEROYCE, state senator, former community college president; b. Dallas, Oct. 21, 1929; s. Gilbert Wybert and Theta Erlene (Tate) E.; m. Joan Mary Horan, Apr. 30, 1955; children: Forest William, John Bede, Mary Faith, Brian Thomas, Regina Ann. B.S., Va. Poly. Inst. and State U., 1951; M.S., U. Ill., 1953; postgrad., Northwestern U., 1953-55; Ph.D., Loyola U., Chgo., 1968. Mem. faculty City Colls. Chgo., 1955-65, chmn. phys. sci. dept., 1963-65; dean instrn. Rock Valley Coll., 1965-67, v.p., 1966-67; pres. McHenry County Coll., 1967-70, Waubonsee Community Coll., 1970-81; senator from 21st Legis. Dist. Ill. Senate, minority spokesman senate revenue com., transp. and higher edn. coms., vice chmn. legis. info. system, intergovtl. cooperation commn. Bd. dirs. Mercy Center for Health Care Services, Aurora, Ill.; mem. citizens' adv. council Dangerous Drugs Commn.; mem. Sci. Adv. Council. Mem. Ill. Council Public Community Coll. Presidents (chmn. 1971-72), Chgo. Met. Higher Edn. Council (dir.), No. Ill. Public TV Consortium (dir.), Suburban Community Coll. TV Consortium (dir.). Republican. Roman Catholic. Club: Rotary (Aurora) (pres. club 1978-79). Home: 68 S LeGrande Blvd Aurora IL 60506 Office: 52 W Downer St Aurora IL 60506 Stratton Office Bldg Rm 1012 Springfield IL

ETHEREDGE, ROBERT FOSTER, lawyer, state legislator; b. Birmingham, Ala., July 14, 1920; s. Joel H. and Nell (Cain) E.; m. Joanna Carson, Aug. 28, 1948; children: Robert Foster, Carson, Nancy. A.B., U. Ala., 1946, LL.B., 1949. Bar: Ala. 1949. Since practiced in, Birmingham; partner firm Spain, Gillon, Riley, Tate & Etheredge (and predecessors), 1949—. Mem. Ala. Ho. of Reps. from Jefferson County, 1963—; mem. adv. com. Family Ct.; Pres. Ala. Soc. for Crippled Children and Adults, 1972-73; bd. dirs. Jefferson County Soc. Crippled Children and Adults, No. Ala. Rehab. Facility. Served to 1st lt. AUS, 1943-46. Recipient citation for meritorious service Rotary Found. Mem. Am., Birmingham bar assns., Ala. State Bar, Internat. Assn. Ins. Counsel, Ala. Law Inst., Ala. Def. Lawyers Assn., Farrah Law Soc., Newcomen Soc. N.Am., Am. Legion, VFW, Omicron Delta Kappa, Pi Kappa Alpha. Democrat. Methodist. Clubs: Elks, Eagles, Rotary (pres. 1981-82), Birmingham Country, Relay House (Birmingham). Home: 3748 Locksley Dr Birmingham AL 35223 Office: John Hand Bldg Birmingham AL 35203

ETHERIDGE, JACK PAUL, judge; b. Atlanta, Mar. 16, 1927; s. Anton Lee and Jessie Shephard (Brown) E.; m. Ursula Schlatter, Feb. 2, 1952; children: Jack Paul, Margaret Ann, Mary Elizabeth. Grad., Darlington Sch., Rome, Ga., 1945; B.S., Davidson Coll., 1949; J.D., Emory U., 1955. Bar: Ga. bar 1955. Since practiced in, Atlanta; mem. firm Huie, Etheridge & Harland, 1959-66; mem. Ga. Gen. Assembly from Fulton County, 1963-66; judge Fulton Superior Ct., 1966-76, sr. judge, 1977—; faculty Nat. Jud. Coll., Coll. Criminal Justice, Law Sch., U. S.C., 1977-80; assoc. dean Emory U. Law Sch., Atlanta, 1981—; mem. Ga. Crime Commn., 1971-73; sr. assoc. Inst. Social Change, Emory U.; Bd. dirs. Atlanta Legal Aid Soc., 1960-70. Trustee Davidson Coll., 1966-75, Arts Festival of Atlanta, 1971-74, Atlanta U., 1977—; chmn. bd. dirs. Atlanta Neighborhood Justice, Inc., Wolfcreek Wilderness Schs., Inc.; Fellow Harvard Law Sch., 1980. Served with USNR, 1945-46; Served with with AUS, 1949-52. Named Young Man of Year in Professions Atlanta Jr. C. of C., 1962. Fellow Internat. Acad. Trial Judges; mem. Atlanta Bar Assn. (pres. 1962-63), Nat. Conf. State Trial Judges (chmn. 1978-79), Atlanta Hist. Soc. (trustee 1969-75), Nat. Acad. Public Adminstrn., Beta Theta Pi, Omicron Delta Kappa, Phi Alpha Theta. Presbyterian. Home: 4715 Harris Trail NW Atlanta GA 30327 Office: Courthouse Atlanta GA 30303 also Emory U Law Sch Atlanta GA 30322

ETHERIDGE, RICHARD EMMET, educator, zoologist; b. Houston, Sept. 16, 1929; s. Jerry Haller and Ethel (Hans) E. B.S., Tulane U., 1951; M.S., U. Mich., 1952, Ph.D., 1959. NSF fellow U. So. Calif., 1959-60, lectr., 1960-61; mem. faculty zoology San Diego State U., 1961—, prof., 1968—, chmn. dept., 1969-72; Research asso. Los Angeles County Mus., 1961—, Ohio State U., 1961-62; curator herpetology San Diego Natural History Mus., 1962-73; interim curator herpetology U. Fla., 1963-64. Editorial bd.: Herpetologica, 1966-77; Contbr. articles profl. jours. Served with USNR, 1952-56. Mem. Am. Soc. Ichthyologists and Herpetologists (gov. 1967-69), So. Calif. Acad. Scis. (dir. 1967-70), Herpetologists League (exec. council 1967-70). Home: 4865 Lucille Pl San Diego CA 92115

ETHERINGTON, EDWIN DEACON, lawyer, business executive, educator; b. Bayonne, N.J., Dec. 25, 1924; s. Charles K. and Ethel (Bennett) E.; m. Katherine Colean, Sept. 11, 1953; children: Edwin Deacon, Kenneth C., Marion (dec.), Robert. B.A. with honors and distinction, Wesleyan U., 1948; J.D., Yale U., 1952. Bar: D.C 1953, N.Y. 1955. Asst. dean, instr. English, Wesleyan U., 1948-49; asst. instr. Yale Law Sch., 1951-52; law clk. to judge Ct. Appeals, Washington, 1952-53; asso. Wilmer & Broun, Washington, 1953-54, Milbank, Tweed, Hope & Hadley, N.Y.C., 1954-56; sec. N.Y. Stock Exchange, 1956-58, v.p., 1958-61; partner Pershing & Co., 1961-62; pres. Am. Stock Exchange, 1962-66, Wesleyan U., Middletown, Conn., 1966-70, now pres. emeritus; pres. Nat. Center for Voluntary Action, Washington, 1971, chmn., 1972; dir. Am. Express Co., N.Y.C., Am. Can Co., Greenwich, Conn., Am. Express Internat. Banking Corp., U.S. Trust Co. of N.Y., Automatic Data Processing Corp., Saudi-U.S. Trust Co., Tech. Transitions Inc.; chmn. Nat. Advt. Rev. Bd., 1973-74, Conn. Gov.'s Commn. on Services and Expenditures, 1971-72. Mem. Commn. on Pvt. Philanthropy and Pub. Needs; mem. nat. adv. council Ariz. Heart Inst.; incorporator Nat. Housing Partnership; vice chmn. bd. visitors U.S. Naval Acad., 1966-68; mem. bd. visitors U.S. Mil. Acad., 1969-71; hon. trustee Hammonasset Sch., North Madison, Conn.; trustee Alfred P. Sloan Found., 1969-76; hon. trustee The Schumann Found. Served with AUS, 1943-44. Mem. Phi Beta Kappa Assos., Kappa Beta Phi, Phi Delta Phi, Order of Coif. Congregationalist. Clubs: Down Town Assn. (N.Y.C.); Black Hall Golf, Old Lyme (Conn.) Country, Old Lyme Beach; Jupiter Island (Fla.); Hobe Sound (Fla.) Yacht; Seminole Golf, North Palm Beach (Fla.). Home: 102 Bassett Creek Trail Hobe Sound FL 33455

ETHERINGTON, ROGER BENNETT, banker; b. Bayonne, N.J., Nov. 18, 1923; s. Charles K. and Ethel (Bennett) E.; m. Barbara H. Dean, Nov. 22, 1946; children—Sandra, Kim Anne, Caryn, R. Barrie. Student, Conn. Wesleyan U., Middletown, 1941-43, 47-48; A.B., Columbia U., 1950. With Am. Nat. Bank & Trust N.J., Morristown, N.J., 1950—, pres., 1969-76, chmn. bd., chmn. exec. com., 1976—; chmn. Horizon Bancorp., N.J.; dir., chmn. Horizon Trust Co. N.A., 1981—; dir. Horizon Creditcorp., Marine Nat. Bank, Wildwood, N.J., Care Dwellings, Inc. Trustee Montclair Ambulance Assn., Fairleigh Dickinson U., Waterloo Found. for Arts, Mt. Hebron Cemetery Assn.; v.p. Montclair YMCA; bd. dirs., chmn. bd. Greer-Woodycrest Children's Services; mem. bus. adv. bd. Community Coll. Morris. Served as officer AUS, 1943-46, 51-52; PTO. Recipient Peace medal, 1981. Mem. Morris County C. of C. (dir., past pres.), Nat. Alliance Bus. (bus. adv. bd.), Morgan Horse Club, N.J. Morgan Horse Assn. (pres. 1967). Congregationalist (trustee, treas. 1964-67). Clubs: Montclair Golf, Sky Top, Morristown; Nassau (Princeton, N.J.); Green Boundary (Aiken, S.C.). Home: 465 Park St Upper Monclair NJ 07043 Office: 334 Madison Ave Morristown NJ 07960

ETHINGTON, RAYMOND LINDSAY, geology educator, researcher; b. State Center, Iowa, Aug. 28, 1929; s. Lindsay E. and Hilda Ruby (Weuve) E.; m. Leslie Ann Nielsen, June 15, 1955; children: Elaine Marie, Mary Frances. B.S., Iowa State U., 1951, M.S., 1955; Ph.D., U. Iowa, 1958. Asst. prof. geology Ariz. State U., Tempe, 1958-62; asst. prof. U. Mo., Columbia, 1962-65, assoc. prof., 1965-68, prof., 1968—. Served with U.S. Army, 1951-53. NSF grantee, 1966. Fellow Geol. Soc. Am.; mem. Soc. Econ. Paleontologists and Mineralogists (editor Jour. Paleontology 1969-74, spl. publs. editor 1980-83, chmn. publs. com. 1974-76), Am. Assn. Petroleum Geologists, Palaeontol. Assn. Gt. Brit., Paleontol. Soc. Mormon. Home: 1012 Pheasant Run Columbia MO 65201 Office: Dept Geology U Mo Columbia MO 65211

ETHRIDGE, JAMES MERRITT, publishing company executive; b. Atlanta, May 21, 1921; s. Eugene Wright and Addie Lee (Echols) E.; m. Elaine Bierfield Baer, 1950 (div.); children: Steven Bruce, Nancy Lee; m. Suzanne Lovett Fleisher, 1980. Ph.B., U. Chgo., 1947, M.A., 1953. Mem. editorial staff A.N. Marquis Co. (later Marquis Who's Who, Inc.), Chgo., 1949-53, research dir., 1953-59, v.p. research and pub. relations, 1959-62; editorial dir., sr. v.p., exec. v.p., dir. Gale Research Co., Detroit, 1962—; editor Contemporary Authors, 1962-65; propr. Info. Enterprises, Detroit, 1976—; editor Directory Info. Service and Directory of Directories, 1976—. Served with AUS, 1942-45. Home: 16784 Westbrook St Detroit MI 48219 Office: Gale Research Co Penobscot Bldg Detroit MI 48226

ETHRIDGE, SAMUEL BROUGHTON, educational association executive; b. Brewton, Ala., Dec. 22, 1923; s. Frank and Lillie (Foster) E.; m. Cordia Elizabeth Baylor, Nov. 11, 1946; children: Samuel David, Sherman George, Camille LaVerne, Steven Edsel. Student, Stillman Jr. Coll., 1940-42; A.B., Howard U., 1948; M.Ed., U. Cin., 1957. Tchr., Central High Sch., Mobile, Ala., 1948-54; prin. Chickasaw Terrace Sch., Mobile County, 1954-56; supr. secondary schs., Mobile, 1956-58; asst. dir. intergroup relations Nat. Found.-March of Dimes, N.Y.C., 1958-60; free lance fund raising, pub. relations, N.Y.C., 1960-62; dir. So. region United Negro Coll. Fund, Atlanta, 1962-64; asst. sec. Commn. on Profl. Rights and Responsibilities, NEA, Washington, 1964-65, asso. sec., 1965-67; dir. Center for Human Relations, 1967—, dir. tchr. rights, 1969—, asst. to exec. dir., 1975—; asso. Nat. Tng. Labs. Camping chmn., Mobile Area, Boy Scouts Am., 1951-58; chmn. alumni fund dr. Stillman Coll., 1966-68, trustee, 1972; mem. exec. com. Nat. Reading is Fundamental, 1972-76; asst. to exec. dir. NEA, 1976—; bd. dirs. Nat. Com. Against Discrimination in Housing, Martin Luther King Jr. Found. Served with USAAF, 1943-46. Mem. Am. Bridge Assn. (pub. relations dir. 1965-67). Home: 1602 Allison St NW Washington DC 20011 Office: 1201 16th St NW Washington DC 20036

ETKES, RAPHAEL, film co. exec.; b. Paris, May 6, 1930. Student, U. So. Calif. Joined MCA, 1961; v.p. Universal Pictures, 1973, sr. v.p., 1979; v.p. MCA, Inc., 1978; pres., chief exec. officer Am. Internat. Pictures, Inc., 1980—. Address: Filmways Pictures Inc 9033 Wilshire Blvd Beverly Hills CA 90211 *

ETLING, JOHN CHARLES, reinsurance company executive; b. Bklyn., Nov. 14, 1935; s. John and Josephine (Weisman) E.; m. Marilyn Gloria Silvestri, Apr. 6, 1958; 1 dau., Jacquelyn Carla. B.A., Manhattan Coll., 1957. Property underwriter Atlantic Cos., N.Y.C., 1957-61, Gen. Reinsurance Corp., Greenwich, Conn., 1961-70, v.p., 1970-76, sr. v.p., 1976-82, exec. v.p., 1982—, dir.; chmn. Herbert Clough Inc., 1981—; dir. Gen. Reassurance Corp., Gen. Re Services, North Star Mgmt. Corp. Republican. Roman Catholic. Clubs: Paterson (Fairfield, Conn.); Landmark (Stamford, Conn.); Fairfield Fish and Game, Ducks Unlimited, Safari.

ETNIER, STEPHEN MORGAN, artist; b. York, Pa., Sept. 11, 1903; s. Carey and Susan Ellen (Smith) E.; m. Mathilde Gray, June 1926 (div. 1932); m. Elizabeth Jay, June 1933 (div. 1948); m. Jane Pearce, Sept. 1948 (dec. June 1949); m. Samuella Rose, Apr. 5, 1950; children—Suzanne Etnier Collins, Penelope Etnier Dinsmore, Stephanie Etnier Doane, Victoria Etnier Villamil, John, David. Student, Yale, 1926, Haverford Coll., 1928, Pa. Acad. Fine Arts, 1925-29; A.F.D., Bates Coll., 1969, Bowdoin Coll., 1969. Paintings represented permanent collections, Met. Mus., N.Y.C., Boston Mus., Avery Meml., Hartford, Conn., Toledo Mus., New Britain Mus., Phillips Meml. Mus., Washington, Farnsworth Mus., Rockland, Maine, Vassar Coll., Pa. Acad. Fine Arts, Bowdoin Coll., Brunswick, Maine, Fairleigh Dickinson Coll., Rutherford, N.J., Buck Hill Art Assn., Buck Hill Falls, Pa., IBM, Dallas, Los Angeles, Springfield (Mass.) museums, Marine Mus., Searsport, Maine, Brooks Meml. Mus., Memphis, Parrish Art Mus., Southampton, L.I., others, murals, Everett (Mass.), Spring Valley (N.Y.) post offices. Served as lt. USNRF, World War II. Recipient Hon. mention Chgo. Art Inst., 1932; Saltus gold medal N.A.D., 1955; 2d Altman prize, 1956; Samuel F.B. Morse medal, 1964; purchase prize Butler Art Inst., Youngstown, Ohio. Academician N.A.D. Home: Old Cove South Harpswell ME 04079 Address: Midtown Galleries 11 E 57th St New York NY 10022 also Frost Gully Gallery 25 Forest Ave Portland ME

ETRIS, SAMUEL FRANKLIN, assn. exec.; b. Port Huron, Mich., Dec. 3, 1922; s. Samuel and Mildred Susan (Davis) E.; m. Mary Jane Lytle, June 29, 1957; children—Andrew Brooke, Edward Lytle. A.B., Temple U., 1947; M.S., Rutgers U., 1951. With Foote Mineral Research Labs., Phila., 1947-49, spl. asst. to mng. dir. for nat. affairs, editor, 1967-80; editor Am. Soc. for Testing and Materials, Phila., 1953—; v.p. Klein of Sacs, Inc.; mgrs. Silver Inst., Gold Inst.; mem. numerical data adv. bd. NRC. Contbr. articles and editorials to profl. publs. Tchr. measurement course Phila. Pkwy. Sch.; Scoutmaster Boy Scouts Am., 1954-57, troop com. chmn., 1957-61. Served to 1st lt. USAAF, 1944-46; Served to 1st lt. USAF, 1951-52; CBI. Recipient Scoutmaster's Key award, 1957. Mem. Nat. Inst. Ceramic Engrs., Am. Ceramic Soc. Home: 115 Runnymede Ave Wayne PA 19087 Office: 1001 Connecticut Ave Washington DC 20036

ETTER, BETTY, editor; b. Sigourney, Iowa, Aug. 3, 1911; d. William Luther and Flora Alice (Cotton) E. Student, Wilson Coll., 1927-29; B.J., U. Mo., 1931. Reporter Ponca City (Okla.) Daily News, 1931-32; society editor Cedar Rapids (Iowa) Gazette, 1932-34; asso. editor Bankers mag., 1935-37, Am. Home, 1938-40; editor Ideal Pub. Co., 1941-51, Lady's Circle, N.Y.C., 1967-74, contbg. editor, 1974—; tchr. mag. editing Coll. City N.Y. Club: Overseas Press of (N.Y.C.). Home: 500 The Esplanade 506 Venice FL 33595

ETTER, DAVID PEARSON, poet, editor; b. Huntington Park, Calif., Mar. 18, 1928; s. Harold Pearson and Judith (Goodenow) E.; m. Margaret Ann Cochran, Aug. 8, 1959; children: Emily Louise, George Goodenow. B.A., U. Iowa, 1953. Editor Northwestern U. Press, Evanston, Ill., 1961-63; asst. editor Ency. Brit., Chgo., 1964-66, staff writer, 1966-69; staff editor Compton's Ency., Chgo., 1969-73; manuscript editor No. Ill. U. Press, DeKalb, 1974-80; free-lance writer, editor, 1980—. Author: poems Go Read the River, 1966, The Last Train to Prophetstown, 1968, Strawberries, 1970, Voyages to the Inland Sea, 1971, Crabtree's Woman, 1972, Bright Mississippi, 1975, Well You Needn't, 1975, Central Standard Time: New and Selected

Poems, 1978, Alliance, Illinois, 1978, Open to the Wind, 1978, Riding the Rock Island through Kansas, 1979, Cornfields, 1980, West of Chicago, 1981, Boondocks, Alliance, Illinois; contbr. poems to lit. mags., anthologies, textbooks. Served with AUS, 1953-55. Home: 414 Gates St Elburn IL 60119

ETTING, EMLEN, artist; b. Phila., Aug. 24, 1905; s. Emlen Pope and Florence (Lucas) E.; m. Gloria Braggiotti, June 20, 1938. Student, Ecole Nouvelle, Lausanne, Switzerland, 1914-17; B.S., Harvard U., 1928, Academie Andre Lhote, Paris, 1929-32. Instr. drawing, paintings Tyler Sch. Fine Arts, 1949-52, Fla. So. Coll., 1952-54, Phila. Mus. and Sch. Art, 1953—. One-man shows, Paris, Phila., N.Y.C., Cleve., Boston, Phoenix Mus., Fla. So. Coll., Allentown Mus., retrospective exhbns., Melvin Gallery, Fla. So. Coll., Lakeland, 1974, Allentown Mus., murals include, Market St. Nat. Bank, Italian Consulate, Phila, works represented in, Whitney Mus., Addison Gallery, Pa. Acad. Fine Arts, Phila. Mus. Art, also pvt. collections; translator, illustrator: (Paul (Valéry) The Graveyard by the Sea; illustrator: Drawing the Ballet, 1945, Ecclesiastes, Amerika, (Franz Kafka) Born in a Crowd; designer sculpture monument to Mayor Richardson Dilworth of Phila., 1982. Served as assimilated capt. French radio div. OWI, 1944-45. Decorated Italian Star of Solidarity; chevalier Legion d'Honneur, France). Mem. Phila. Art Alliance, Artists Equity Assn. (hon. pres.), Alliance Française (hon. pres.), Soc. of Cincinnati, Nat. Soc. Mural Painters. Club: Century Assn. Office: care Midtown Galleries 11 E 57th St New York NY 10022 *

ETTINGER, AUSTEN ARNOLD, advertising executive; b. N.Y.C., Feb. 23, 1923; s. Bertr and Lucy E. (Costabile) E.; m. Shirley Riche, June 5, 1944; 1 son, John R. With McCall Corp., N.Y.C., 1956-62, advt. promotion mgr., 1956-58; asst. pub. Redbook mag., 1958-62; with Crowell-Collier Pub. Co., 1962-63; asst. gen. mgr. Collier Books, N.Y.C.; pres. Jameson Advt., Inc., N.Y.C., 1963—, chmn., 1984—. Home: 345 E 56th St New York NY 10022 Office: 750 3d Ave New York NY 10017

ETTINGER, CECIL RAY, church executive; b. Taylorville, Ill., July 26, 1922; s. Cecil Ray and Minnie Elizabeth (Sloan) E.; m. Betty Jean Russell, Aug. 1, 1946; children: Cecil Ray, Stephanie Lynn Ettinger Kelley, David Alexander. A.A., Graceland Coll., 1942; B.A., U. Iowa, 1948; Th.M., Am. Div. Sch., 1955, Th.D., 1957. With Reorganized Ch. of Jesus Christ of Latter-day Saints, 1947—, radio minister, 1958-60; mem. Council of Twelve Apostles, 1960-74, in charge of European mission, 1962-66; minister to Africa 1963, 67, exec. asst. to 1st presidency, 1974—; prison counselor, tchr. Leavenworth Fed. Penitentiary, also Lansing (Kans.) State Prison, 1958—. Served with USAAF, 1942-45; ETO. Decorated D.F.C., Air medal with 9 clusters. Lodges: Lions (pres. 1973-74,, zone chmn. 1974-75,, dep. dist. gov. 1975-76,, dist. gov. 1976-77,, internat. dir. 1983-85). Home: 2413 S Whitney Ave Independence MO 64057 Office: PO Box 1059 Independence MO 64051

ETTINGER, GEORGE HAROLD, physiologist; b. Kingston, Ont., Can., May 9, 1896; s. John George and Elizabeth Jane (Watts) E.; m. Pearl Elizabeth Blyth, Dec. 21, 1920 (dec. 1958); 1 dau., Barbara Joan Ettinger Hinton; m. Margaret Elizabeth Mackay Sawyer, Apr. 19, 1969. B.A. Queen's U, Kingston, 1916; M.D., C.M., Kingston, 1920; LL.D. (hon.), Kingston, 1967; postgrad., U. Chgo., 1923, U. Edinburgh, Scotland, 1928-29; D.Sc. (hon.), U. Western Ont., London, 1958, M.D., U. Ottawa, Ont., 1963. Lectr. in physiology Queen's U., 1920-29, asst. prof. physiology, 1929-33, asso. prof., 1933-35, prof., 1935-62, dean medicine, 1949-62; dir. med. planning Addiction Research Found., Toronto, Ont., 1962-70; ret. 1970; research asso. U. Toronto, 1931-35; hon. sec. Asso. Com. on Med. Research, Nat. Research Council Can., Ottawa, 1939-46, asst. dir. div. med. research, 1946-58. Author: History of the Associate Committee on Medical Research of NRC, 1946, History of the Canadian Physiological Society, 1970. Served with Royal Canadian Army M.C., 1918-19. Decorated mem. Order Brit. Empire; Queen's Jubilee medal Can. Govt. Fellow Royal Soc. Can.; mem. Am. Physiol. Soc., Physiol. Soc. Gt. Brit., Am. Assn. Anatomists, Can. Physiol. Soc., Can. Med. Assn. (sr.). Mem. United Ch. of Canada. Research, numerous publs. on physiology. Home: Cartwright Point Kingston ON K7K 5E2 Canada

ETTINGER, RICHARD PRENTICE, publishing company executive; b. N.Y.C., Sept. 27, 1922; s. Richard Prentice and Elsie (Davis) E.; m. Sharon Whitaker, May 1, 1971; children: Deborah, Pamela, Heidi, Barbara, Wendy, Richard Prentice, Ronene, Jean, James, Christian, Leland, Matthew. A.B., Dartmouth Coll., 1944; Litt.D., Whittier Coll., 1973. Field rep. coll. div. Prentice-Hall, Inc., 1947-50, Western div. mgr., 1951-54, asst. to pres., 1955, dir., 1951-58, 82—; pres. Wadsworth Pub. Co., Belmont, Calif., 1957-64, chmn., 1964-77, Dickenson Pub. Co., Los Angeles, 1968-77, Allyn & Bacon, Inc., Boston, 1980-81; Chmn. bd. trustees Ednl. Found. Am., Westport, Conn. Mem. bd. visitors U. Calif. at Los Angeles Grad. Sch. Bus.; trustee Whittier (Calif.) Coll., 1970-76; bd. overseers Dartmouth Med. Sch., 1976-79. Mem. Belmont C. of C. (pres. 1969-70), U.S. Yacht Racing Assn., Stanford Sailing Assn. (trustee 1977-81), SAR. Republican. Episcopalian. Clubs: St. Francis Yacht, Transpacific Yacht, Windjammers, Indian Harbor Yacht, Newport Harbor Yacht. Home: 350 Buena Vista Balboa CA 92661

ETTINGTON, RICHARD MARTIN, pump company executive; b. Tulsa, July 2, 1925; m. Elizabeth K. Kirkpatrick, Dec. 22, 1951; children: Martin, Kathryn. B.S.M.E., Rennesslaer Poly Inst., 1947. Dir. corp. labor relations Ingersoll Rand, 1947-67, gen. mgr. compressor and engine mfg. and engring. ops., 1947-67; div. pres. Alco div. Stud-Worthington, 1967-73; group v.p. Worthington Pump Group Stud-Worthington, 1967-73; exec. v.p., chief ops. Internat. Basic Economy Corp., 1973-75; pres. Baltech Corp., 1979-81, Pacific Pumps div. Dresser Industries, Huntington Park, Calif., 1981—. Served to lt.(j.g.) USNR, 1943-46; PTO. Mem. Hydraulic Inst. Republican. Clubs: Jonathan (Los Angeles); Rolling Hills Golf (Palos Verdes, Calif.); Baltusrol Golf (Springfield, N.J.). Home: 4211 Cartesian Circle Palos Verdes Peninsula CA 90274 Office: Dresser Industries Pacific Pump Div 5715 Bickett St Huntington Park CA 90255

ETTRE, LESLIE STEPHEN, chemist; b. Szombathely, Hungary, Sept. 16, 1922; came to U.S., 1958, naturalized, 1965; s. Stephen and Mary Therese (Dunay) E.; m. Kitty Polonyi, May 16, 1953; 1 dau., Julie Suzanne. Diploma Chem. Engring, U. Tech. Scis., Hungary, 1945, D.Tech. Scis. Chemist G. Richter Pharm. Works, Budapest, Hungary, 1946-49; research chemist Research Inst. for Heavy Chem. Industries, Veszprem, Hungary, 1949-51, head tech. office, 1951-53; sr. lectr. chemistry U. Veszprem, 1951-53; head indsl. dept. Research Inst. for Plastics Industry, Budapest, 1953-56; chemist Lurgi Cos., Frankfurt, W. Ger., 1957-58; applications chemist Perkin-Elmer Corp., Norwalk, Conn., 1958-60, product specialist, 1960-62, chief applications chemist, 1962-68, sr. staff scientist, 1972—; exec. editor Ency. Indsl. Chem. Analysis John Wiley & Sons, N.Y.C., 1968-72; research asso. dept. engring. and applied scis. Yale U., New Haven, 1977-78; adj. prof. U. Houston, 1978—; chmn. Anniversary Symposium on Chromatography Am. Chem. Soc., N.Y.C., 1972, Symposium on Selective Chromatography Detectors, San Francisco, 1976, Symposium on Standard Materials in Chromatography, Atlanta, 1981; co-chmn. Summer Symposium on Analytical Chemistry Miami U., Oxford, Ohio, 1973; lectr. in, U.S., Can., Europe, Asia, Africa; participant lecture tours of Chromatography Council of Acad. Scis., USSR, 1976, 78, 79, 80, 81, Estonian Acad. Scis., 1979, 81, Chinese Acad. Scis., 1980, Georgian Acad. Sci., 1981. Author: Open Tubular Columns in Gas Chromatography, 1965, (with A. Zlatkis) The Practice of Gas Chromatography, 1967, (with W.H. McFadden) Ancillary Techniques of Gas Chromatography, 1968 (transl. into Russian, 1972), Practical Gas Chromatography, 1972, Introduction to Open Tubular Columns, 1974 (transl. into German, 1976, Spanish, 1978), (with A. Zlatkis) 75 Years of Chromatography-A Historical Dialogue, 1979, Basic Relationships of Gas Chromatography, 1977, (with R.W. Yost and R.D. Conlon) Practical Liquid Chromatography, 1980; (translated into Spanish and French, 1981), (with J.L. DiCesare, M.N. Dong) Introduction to High-Speed Liquid Chromatography, 1981 (translated into Spanish 1982); mem. editorial bd.: Jour. Chromatographic Sci, 1963—; editor: (with R.W. Yost and R.D. Conlon) Chromatographia, 1971—; contbr. numerous articles to profl. jours. Recipient Commemorative Chromatography medal Acad. Scis., USSR, 1978, Internat. Chromatography award, 1978, L.S. Palmer award Minn. Chromatography Forum, 1980, A.J.P. Martin award Brit. Chromatography Discussion Group, 1982. Fellow Am. Inst. Chemists; mem. ASTM (chmn. subcom. research of com. E-19 1966-70, subcom. on nomenclature of com. E-19 1970-73), Am. Chem. Soc., Chromatography Discussion Group Eng., N.Y. Acad. Scis., Internat. Union Pure and Applied Chemistry (nomenclature com. 1981—). Home: 157 Grumman Ave Norwalk CT 06851 Office: Perkin-Elmer Corp Main Ave Norwalk CT 06856

ETZEL, JAMES EDWARD, environmental engineering educator; b. Reading, Pa., Nov. 9, 1929; s. Edward John and Ruth Anna (Getrost) E.; m. Barbara Dawn Shoup, Sept. 3, 1950; children: Pamela Dawn, Gregory John, Mark Raymond, Scott Edward, Christopher James. B.S. in San. Engring, Pa. State U., 1951; M.S. in Civil Engring, Purdue U., 1955, Ph.D., 1957. Registered profl. engr., Ind. Engr. Capitol Engring. Co., Dillsburg, Pa., 1951, du Pont Co., Wilmington, Del., 1957-58; engr., dir. research Roy F. Weston, engrs., Newtown Sq., Pa., 1958-59; mem. faculty Purdue U., 1959—, prof. environ. engring., 1964—, Water Refining Co. prof., 1978—; head environ. engring. area Sch. Civil Engring., 1971—; chmn. Tippecanoe County (Ind.) Solid Wastes Com., 1971—; mem. W. Lafayette Environ. Commn., 1968-76; cons. to industry, 1960. Served with C.E., 1951-53; AUS. Named Outstanding Prof. in Civil Engring. Purdue U., 1979. Mem. Water Pollution Control Fedn. Ind. Water Pollution Control Assn. (past pres.). Lutheran. Patentee in field. Home: 710 Cardinal Dr Lafayette IN 47905 Office: Sch Civil Engring Purdue U West Lafayette IN 47907

ETZIONI, AMITAI WERNER, educator, sociologist; b. Cologne, Germany, Jan. 4, 1929; s. Willi Falk and Gertrude Hannauer (Falk) E.; m. Minerva Morales, Sept. 14, 1965; children: Ethan, Oren, Michael, David, Benjamin. B.A., Hebrew U., Jerusalem, 1954, M.A., 1956; Ph.D. in Sociology, U. Calif.-Berkeley, 1958. Mem. faculty Columbia U., 1958-80; research assoc. Inst. War and Peace Studies, 1961—, prof. sociology, 1967—, chmn. dept., 1969—; dir. Center for Policy Research, 1968—; guest scholar Brookings Instn., 1978-79; sr. advisor White House, 1979-80; Univ. prof. George Washington U., Washington, 1980—; mem. Econ. Forum The Conf. Bd., 1983. Author: A Comparative Analysis of Complex Organizations, 1961, Modern Organizations, 1964, Political Unification; A Comparative Study of Leaders and Forces, 1965, Studies in Social Change, 1966, The Active Society, 1968, Genetic Fix, 1973, Social Problems, 1976, An Immodest Agenda, 1982, Capital Corruption, 1984; Contbr. numerous articles to profl. jours.; Editorial bd.: Science, 1969-71. Mem. governing council Am. Jewish Congress, 1973—. Social Sci. Research Council faculty fellow, 1960-61, 67-68; fellow Center for Advanced Study in Behavioral Scis., 1965-66; Guggenheim fellow, 1968. Fellow AAAS; mem. Am. Sociol. Assn. Developed organizational analysis, a typology based on means used to control participants in orgns., how orgns. change, survive and are integrated into larger social units. Home: 7110 Arran Pl Bethesda MD 20817

ETZKORN, K. PETER, university administrator, sociologist, author; b. Karlsruhe, Germany, Apr. 18, 1932; came to U.S., 1952, naturalized, 1958; s. Johannes and Luise (Schlick) E.; m. Hildegard Elizabeth Garve, Sept. 3, 1953; children: Kyle Peter, Lars Peter. A.B., Ohio State U., 1955; student, Ind. U., 1955-56; A.M., Princeton, 1958, Ph.D., 1959. Asst. prof. U. Calif., Santa Barbara, 1959-63; asso. prof. Am. U. Beirut, Lebanon, 1963-64; dir. Office Instl. Research; chmn. dept. sociology and anthropology U. Nev., 1964-67; prof., chmn. faculty sociology and anthropology U. W. Fla., 1967-68; prof. sociology San Fernando Valley State Coll., 1968-69, U. Mo.-St. Louis, 1969—; asso. dean Grad. Sch., 1978—; dir. Office of Research, 1979—; vis. prof. U. Münster, Germany, 1975-76; cons. in field. Author: The Conflict in Modern Culture, 1968, Music and Society, 1973; Contbr. articles to profl. jours. Mem. Gov. Nev. Com. on Dept. Correction, 1966; Mo. Gov. liaison German-Am. Tricentennial Task Force, 1983; mem. Mo. Adv. Com. on Humanities; chmn. Univ. Symposia Com. Bicentennial Horizons Am. Music; mem. St. Louis-Stuttgart Sister City Com.; Mo. state rep. Sister Cities Internat., 1976—; cons. Nat. Endowment Arts, NSF.; pres. St. Louis New Music Circle; bd. dirs. Am. Kantorei; v.p. Internat. Inst. Met. St. Louis, 1982—; gov. of Mo. liaison German-Am. Tricentennial Task Force, Washington, 1983—. Fellow Am. Sociol. Assn., Am. Anthrop. Assn.; mem. Soc. Ethnomusicology (council 1963-71, 76-79, editor spl. publs.), Inst. Internat. Sociologie (mem. bur.), Interam. Orgn. Higher Edn. (dep. council 1980—), Town Affiliation Assn. U.S. (dir. 1981—), St. Louis Council Sister Cities (chmn. 1981—). Home: 21 Ladue Ridge Saint Louis MO 63124

ETZWILER, DONNELL DENCIL, pediatrician; b. Mansfield, Ohio, Mar. 29, 1927; s. Donnell Seymour and Berniece Jean (Meek) E.; m. Marion Frances Grassby, June 28, 1952; children—Nancy, Lisa, Diane, David. B.A. cum laude, Ind. U., 1950; M.D., Yale U., 1953. Intern dept. pediatrics Yale U. Sch. Medicine, New Haven, 1953-54; resident dept. pediatrics N.Y. Hosp.-Cornell U. Sch. Medicine, N.Y.C., 1954-55, Nat. Inst. Arthritis and Metabolic Diseases fellow, 1956-57; instr. pediatrics Cornell U. Med. Sch., 1956-57; mem. faculty U. Minn. Med. Sch., Mpls., 1957—, clin. asso. prof. pediatrics, 974—; practice medicine specializing in pediatrics, 1957—; pediatrician St. Louis Park Med. Center, 1957—; instr. Project Hope, Trujillo, Peru, 1962; founder, bd. dirs. Diabetes Edn. Center, Mpls., 1967—; bd. dirs., pres. St. Louis Park Med. Center Research Found., 1969-71; mem. Nat. Commn. on Diabetes, 1975-77; pres. Health Edn. for Living program, 1973—; mem. Internat. Study Group Diabetes in Children and Adolescents, Inst. of Medicine, Nat. Acad. Sci., 1981. Author: Education and Management of the Patient with Diabetes Mellitus, 1973, also articles, reports. Served with USNR, World War II. Recipient Good Neighbor award Sta. WCCO, 1976. Fellow All India Inst. Diabetes; mem. Am. Diabetes Assn. (dir. 1971-78, pres. 1976-77, chmn. profl. subsect. juvenile diabetes 1977—, cert. of award 1977, Disting. Service to Youth award 1976, Banting medal 1977, Becton-Dickinson award 1978, Upjohn award), Twin Cities Diabetes Assn. (dir. 1959-73), Am. Diabetes Assn. Minn. (dir. 1975—), Mpls. Soc. Blind (dir. 1977—), Internat. Diabetes Fedn. (exec. com., dir., bd. mgmt., chmn. internat. com. juvenile diabetes 1978—, v.p. 1979), Soc. Public Health Educators, Am. Group Practice Assn., Am. Hosp. Assn., Am. Dietetic Assn. (hon.), AMA, Minn. Med. Assn., European Assn. for Study of Diabetes. Presbyterian. Office: 5000 W 39th St Minneapolis MN 55416

EU, MARCH KONG FONG, state ofcl.; b. Oakdale, Calif., Mar. 29, 1927; d. Yuen and Shiu (Shee) Kong; children by previous marriage—Matthew Kipling Fong, Marchesa Suyin Fong You; m. Henry Eu, July 30, 1973; stepchildren—Henry, Adeline, Yvonne, Conroy, Alaric. Student, Salinas Jr. Coll.; B.S., U. Calif. at Berkeley; M.Ed., Mills Coll., 1951; Ed.D., Stanford, 1956; postgrad., Columbia, Calif. State Coll. at Hayward. Chmn. div. dental hygiene U. Calif. Med. Center, San Francisco; dental hygienist Oakland (Calif.) Pub. Schs.; supr. dental health edn. Alameda County (Calif.) Schs.; lectr. health edn. Mills Coll., Oakland; mem. Calif. Legislature, 1966-74, chmn. select com. on agr., foods and nutrition, 1973-74; mem. com. natural resources and conservation, com. commerce and pub. utilities, select com. med. malpractice; sec. state State of Calif., 1975—, chief of protocol, 1975—; spl. cons. Bur. Intergroup Relations, Calif. Dept. Edn.; ednl., legis. cons. Sausalito (Calif.) Pub. Schs., Santa Clara County Office Edn., Jefferson Elementary Union Sch. Dist., Santa Clara High Sch. Dist., Santa Clara Elementary Sch. Dist., Live Oak Union High Sch. Dist.; mem. Alameda County Bd. Edn., 1956-66, pres., 1961-62, legis. adv., 1963. Mem. budget panel Bay Area United Fund Crusade; mem. Oakland Econ. Devel. Council; mem. tourism devel. com. Calif. Econ. Devel. Commn.; mem. citizens com. on housing Council Social Planning; mem. Calif. Interagy. Council Family Planning; edn. chmn., mem. council social planning, dir. Oakland Area Baymont Dist. Community Council; charter pres., hon. life mem. Howard Elementary Sch. PTA; charter pres. Chinese Young Ladies Soc., Oakland; mem., vice chmn. adv. com. Youth Study Centers and Ford Found. Interagy. Project, 1962-63; chmn. Alameda County Mothers' March, 1971-72; bd. councillors U. So. Calif. Sch. Dentistry, 1976; mem. exec. com. Calif. Democratic Central Com., mem. central com., 1963-70; asst. sec.; del. Dem. Nat. Conv., 1968; dir. 8th Congl. Dist. Dem. Council, 1963; v.p. Dems. of 8th Congl. Dist., 1963; dir. Key Women for Kennedy, 1963; women's vice chmn. No. Calif. Johnson for Pres., 1964; bd. dirs. Oakland YWCA, 1965. Recipient ann. award for outstanding achievement Eastbay Intercultural Fellowship, 1959; Phoebe Apperson Hearst Disting. Bay Area Woman of Yr. award; Woman of Yr. award Calif. Retail Liquor Dealers Inst., 1969; Merit citation Calif. Assn. Adult Edn. Adminstrs., 1970; Art Edn. award; Outstanding Woman award Nat. Women's Polit. Caucus, 1980. Mem. Am. Dental Hygienists Assn. (pres. 1956-57), No. Calif. Dental Hygienists Assn., Oakland LWV, AAUW (area rep. in edn. Oakland br.), Calif. Tchrs. Assn., Calif. Sch. Bd. Assn., Alameda County Sch. Bd. Assn. (pres. 1965), Alameda County Mental Health Assn., So. Calif. Dental Assn. (hon.), Bus. and Profl. Women's Club, Chinese Retail Food Markets Assn. (hon.), Delta Kappa Gamma. Office: 1230 J St Sacramento CA 95814

EUBANK, J. THOMAS, lawyer; b. Port Arthur, Tex., Mar. 17, 1930; s. J.T. and Ada (White) E.; m. Nancy Moore, Feb.10, 1956; children: John, Marshall, Stephen, Laura. B.A., Rice U., 1951; J.D., U. Tex., 1954. Bar: Tex. 1954, U.S. Supreme Ct. 1960. Assoc. Barker & Botts, Houston, 1954-66; ptnr. Baker & Botts, Houston, 1966—, sr. ptnr., 1979—. Mem. joint editorial bd.: Uniform Probate code, 1972—. Mem. ABA (chmn. sect. real property, probate and trust law 1378-79), Am. Coll. Probate Counsel (pres.-elect 1983-84), State Bar Tex. (chmn. sect. real estate, probate and trust law 1972-73), Am. Bar Found., Tex. Bar Found., Houston Philos. Soc., Rice U. Alumni Assn. (pres. 1979-80), Am. Law Inst., Internat. Acad. Estate and Trust Law. Home: 26 Liberty Bell Circle Houston TX 77024 Office: Baker & Botts 1 Shell Plaza Houston TX 77002

EUBANKS, LUTHER BOYD, judge; b. Caprock, N.Mex., July 31, 1917; s. J.P. and Evelyn (Downs) E.; m. Lois Stevens, Sept. 5, 1942; children: Nancy Eubanks McClaran, Carolyn Eubanks Bryan, Stephen. B.A., U. Okla., 1940. Bar: Okla. bar 1944. County atty., Cotton County, Okla., 1946-49; mem. Okla. House Reps. from, Cotton County, 1949-53; district judge, Lawton, Okla., 1956-65; U.S. dist. judge Western Dist. Okla., after 1965, now chief judge. Served with AUS, World War II; ETO. Club: Rotarian. Address: 3301 Fed Courthouse Bldg 200 NW 4th St Oklahoma City OK 73102

EUBANKS, ROBERT ALONZO, civil engineer, educator, consultant; b. Chgo., June 3, 1926; s. Gilbert and Pollie Cundiff; m. Helaine L. Eubanks, Apr. 5, 1969. B.S., Ill. Inst. Tech., 1950, M.S., 1951, Ph.D., 1953. Registered profl. engr., Ill. Asst. prof. mechanics Ill. Inst. Tech., Chgo., 1950-54; sci. adviser Research Inst., Ill. Inst. Tech., 1960-65; sr. research engr. Bulova R&D Lab., Flushing, N.Y., 1954-55; research engr. mechanics research dept. Am. Machine and Foundry Co., Chgo., 1955-56; scientist Research Ctr., Borg-Warner Corp., Des. Plaines, Ill., 1956-60; George A. Miller vis. prof. civil engring. U. Ill., Urbana, 1964-65, prof. civil engring. theoretical and applied mechanics, 1965—; vis. disting. prof. civil engring., mech. and aerospace engring. and math. U. Del., Newark, 1973-74; mem. Bldg. Code Bd. Appeals City Urbana. Editorial bd.: Jour. Elasticity; contbr. articles to profl. jours. Bd. dirs., mem. exec. com., v.p. Nat. Consortium for Grad. Degrees for Minorities in Engring., Inc.; bd. dirs. Champaign County Urban League, Ill. Served with U.S. Army, 1942-46. Fellow Am. Acad. Mechanics; mem. ASME, AAUP, Soc. Indsl. and Applied Maths., Am. math. Soc., Acoustical Soc. Am., ASCE, Am. Soc. Engring. Edn., Sigma Xi, Sigma Pi Sigma, Chi Epsilon. Office: 3129 NCEL U Ill 208 N Romine St Urbana IL 61801 *

EUELL, JULIAN THOMAS, museum director; b. N.Y.C., May 23, 1929; s. Thomas Bass and Helen Lillian (Adams) E.; m. Dolores Lolita Brown (div.); children: Julian, Juliette, Dana, Denise, Simeon; m. Barbara Jean Tiggs, Mar. 5, 1967 (div. 1966); 1 son, Miles. B.S., NYU; postgrad., Columbia U., Julliard Sch. Music, George Washington U. Profl. musician, 1959-62; dir. arts and culture HARYOU-ACT, Inc., N.Y.C., 1962-66; dir. arts program Einstein Coll. Medicine, Bronx, N.Y., 1967-70; asst. sec. pub. service Smithsonian Instn., Washington, 1968-82; dir. Oakland Mus., Calif., 1982—; mem. jazz panel Nat. Endowment of the Arts. Mem. NCAAP legal Def. and Edn. Fund., Urban League, Washington, Reading is Fundamental, Washington. Served with U.S. Army, 1946-47. Recipient Martin Luther King award NYU, 1968, Pub. Service award Smithsonian Instn., 1974. Mem. Am. Assn. Mus., Nat. Hist. Soc., Nat. Trust Hist. Preservation, Am. Mus. Nat. History, Nat. Soc. Lit. and the Arts. Democrat. Club: Rotary (Oakland, Calif.). Home: 6301 Wood Dr Oakland CA 94611 Office: Oakland Mus 1000 Oak St Oakland CA 94607

EULAU, HEINZ, educator, polit. scientist; b. Offenbach, Germany, Oct. 14, 1915; s. Arthur and Martha (Spier) E.; m. Cleo Mishkin, June 8, 1946; children—Lauren, Peter. A.B., U. Calif. at Berkeley, 1937, M.A., 1938, Ph.D., 1941. Research asso. Library of Congress, 1941-42; sr. analyst Spl. War Policies Unit, Dept. Justice, 1942-44; asst. editor New Republic, 1944-47; from asst. prof. to prof. Antioch Coll., 1947-57; prof. polit. sci. Stanford, 1958—, William Bennett Munro prof., 1973—; vis. legis. research prof. U. Calif. at Berkeley, 1961-62; vis. prof. Inst. Advanced Studies, Vienna, Austria, 1964-65; mem. behavioral sci. div. NRC, 1969-73; bd. overseers, chmn. Nat. Election Studies, 1977—; asso. dir. Inter-Univ. Consortium for Polit. and Social Research, 1978—. Author: Class and Party in the Eisenhower Years, 1962, The Legislative System, 1962, Journeys in Politics, 1963, The Behavioral Persuasion in Politics, 1963, Micro-Macro Political Analysis, 1969, Labyrinths of Democracy, 1973, Technology and Civility, 1977, The Politics of Representation, 1978. Fund Advancement Edn. fellow, 1951-52; Center Advanced Study Behavioral Scis. fellow, 1957-58; Guggenheim Found. fellow, 1979-80.

Fellow AAAS, Am. Acad. Arts and Scis.; mem. Am. Polit. Sci. Assn. (pres. 1971-72). Home: 753 Frenchmans Rd Stanford CA 94305

EUMONT, JACK VOCTIR, oil company executive; b. New Orleans, Dec. 6, 1928; s. Clarence Yves and Lena Theresa (Scariano) E.; m. Joyce Marie Raphael, Mar. 3, 1951; children: Jannelle, Jack Victor, Judy, Jill, Jeffrey, Jerry. B.B.A., Loyola U., New Orleans, 1949. C.P.A., La. Chief acct. Nat. Tax and Record Service, New Orleans, 1949-51; sr. acct. Peat, Marwick, Mitchell & Co., New Orleans, 1953-57; acct., treas., v.p. La. Land & Exploration Co., New Orleans, 1957-74, sr. v.p., 1974—. Mem. Mid-Continent Oil and Gas Assn., La. Soc. C.P.A.s, Petroleum Club New Orleans (bd. dirs.). Democrat. Roman Catholic. Home: 733 Fairfield Ave Gretna LA 70053 Office: La Land & Exploration Co 225 Baronne St Suite 1200 New Orleans LA 70112

EURE, THAD, state official; b. Gates County, N.C., Nov. 15, 1899; s. Tazewell A. and Armecia (Langstun) E.; m. Minta Banks, Nov. 15, 1924; children: Armecia (Mrs. J. Norman Black, Jr.), Thad. Student, U. N.C., 1917-19, Law Sch., 1921-22; LL.D., Elon Coll., 1958. Lawyer; mayor, City of Winton, N.C., 1923-28, atty., Hertford County, N.C., 1923-31; prin. clk. N.C. Ho. of Reps., 1931, 33, 35, 36; sec. state State of N.C., Raleigh, 1936—; Mem. N.C. Ho. of Reps., 1929; keynote speaker N.C. Democratic Conv., 1950, permanent chmn., 1962. Chmn. bd. trustees Elon Coll. Mem. Nat. Assn. Secs. of State (pres. 1942, dean 1961), Am. Legion, 40 and 8, Theta Chi. Mem. United Ch. of Christ. Club: Elk. Office: Office of Sec of State State Capitol Bldg Capitol Sq Raleigh NC 27611

EURICH, ALVIN CHRISTIAN, educator; b. Bay City, Mich., June 14, 1902; s. Christian H. and Hulda (Steinke) E.; m. Nell P. Hutchinson, Mar. 15, 1953; children: Juliet Ann, Donald Alan. B.A., N. Central Coll., 1924, Litt.D., 1949; M.A.; 4U. Maine, 1926; LL.D., 1965; Ph.D., U. Minn., 1929; LL.D., Hamline U., 1944; Alfred U., Clark U., 1950, Miami U., 1951, Yeshiva U., 1954, Redlands U., 1960; Litt.D., New Sch. Social Research; L.H.D., U. Fla., 1953, U. Miami, Fla., 1968, Albion Coll., 1965, Fairfield U., 1971; Sc.D., Akron U., 1960. Instr. U. Maine, 1924-26; served from asst. in ednl. psychology to prof., also asst. to pres. U. Minn., 1926-37; prof. edn. Northwestern U., 1937-38, Stanford, 1938-48, v.p., 1944-48, acting pres., 1948; chmn. Stanford Research Inst.; 1st chancellor State U. N.Y., 1949-51; v.p. Ford Fund Advancement Edn., 1951-64, mem. bd. dirs., 1952-67; exec. dir. edn. div. Ford Found, 1958-64; pres. Aspen Inst. Humanistic Studies, 1963-67; founder, pres. Acad. Ednl. Devel., 1961—; pres. Phonemic Spelling Council; trustee Internat. Council for Ednl. Devel., Center for Public Resources; cons. U.S. govt. agys. during and following war years; supr. various ednl. surveys; served as mem. or cons. various commns. including Hoover Commn., Pres. Truman's Commn. Higher Edn., Pres. Kennedy's Task Force Edn.; chmn. Surgeon Gen.'s Commn. Nurses; cons. NASA, AID, Peace Corps; chmn. U.S. nat. commn. UNESCO, chmn. U.S. del. to gen. conf., Paris, 1968; chmn. adv. com. Haile Selassie U.; planning adviser U. Patras, Greece; ednl. adviser, Libya; mem. Nat. Commn. Libraries; vis. prof. various univs.; vis. fellow Clare Coll., U. Cambridge, Eng., 1967; mem. U.S. Council for World Communications Yr., 1983. Author or co-author books and studies in education; also psychol. and achievement tests, including Time Mag.'s Current Affairs Tests; contbr. articles to profl. jours.; author: Reforming American Education, 1969; co-author: Educational Psychology, 1935; editor: Campus, 1980, 1968, High School, 1980, 1970, Major Transitions in the Human Life Cycle, 1981. Bd. dirs. Lovelace Found. Served from lt. comdr. to comdr. USNR, 1942-44; dir. standards and curriculum div. Naval Personnel. Recipient Outstanding Achievement award U. Minn., 1951; Times Sq. Club's 4th Ann. award, 1953; Ann. award N.Y. Acad. Pub. Edn., 1963. Fellow AAAS (council 1941-45), Am. Psychol. Assn., Aspen Inst.; mem. Sigma Xi, Phi Delta Kappa. Clubs: Univ., Century, Coffee House (N.Y.C.); Cosmos (Washington); Athenaeum (London). Home: 24 W 55th St New York NY 10019 Office: 680 Fifth Ave New York NY 10019 *Throughout a long life, I've been exceptionally fortunate both personally and professionally. I seem to have been at the right place at the right time. This has given me the opportunity to have close associations with outstanding educational, governmental, and business leaders of our time and to be creative in my profession throughout my career.*

EURICH, NELL, former educator, association executive; b. Norwood, Ohio, July 28, 1919; d. Clayton W. and Adah (Palmer) Plopper; m. Alvin C. Eurich, Mar. 15, 1953; children: Juliet Ann, Donald Alan. A.A., Stephens Coll., 1939; B.A., Stanford U., 1941, M.A., 1943; Ph.D., Columbia U., 1959. Dir. student union U. Tex., 1942-43; resident counselor Barnard Coll., 1944-46; asst. to pres. Woman's Found., 1947-49; officer charge pub. relations State U. N.Y., 1949- 52; acting pres. Stephens Coll., 1953-54; asst. prof. English N.Y. U., 1959-64; academic dean New Coll., Sarasota, Fla., 1965; dir. project to reorganize curriculum Aspen (Colo.) Pub. High Sch., 1966; dean faculty, prof. English Vassar Coll., 1967-70; provost, dean faculty, prof. English, v.p. acad. affairs Manhattanville Coll., Purchase, N.Y., 1971-75; sr. cons. Internat. Council for Ednl. Devel., 1975-82, Acad. for Ednl. Devel., 1982—; mem. nat. selection com., chmn. Rocky Mountain regional com. Nat. Endowment Humanities, 1966-67, cons., 1970-71; mem. Middle States commn. Marshall Scholarships, 1967-68; chmn. Northeastern region, 1969-71; mem. U.S. Commn. on Ednl. Tech., HEW, 1968-69; mem. overseer's com. on summer sch. and univ. extension vis. com. Harvard, 1969-75; mem. panel of judge's Fed. Woman's award, 1969; cons. Acad. for Ednl. Devel., 1970-71; mem. career minister rev. bd. U.S. Dept. State, 1972; participant Ditchley Conf. V, 1973; mem. Rhodes Scholarship Selection Com., 1976; moderator exec. seminar Aspen Inst. for Humanistic Studies, 1977, 79, 80. Author: Science in Utopia, 1967, Higher Education in Twelve Countries: A Comparative View, 1981, (with B. Schwenkmeyer) Great Britain's Open University, 1971; contbg. author: (Alvin Toffler) Learning for Tomorrow, 1974, From Parnassus: Essays for Jacques Barzun, 1976; Contbr.: articles to profl. jours. Past trustee Bank St. Coll., Salisbury Sch., Hudson Guild Neighborhood House, Colo. Rocky Mountain Sch.; trustee New Coll. Found., Bennington Coll., Carnegie Found. for Advancement Teaching, 17-24 Corp., Soc. for Right to Die; mem. Carnegie Council on Policy Studies in Higher Edn. Mem. Modern Lang. Assn., Am. Assn. Colls. (spl. com. on liberal studies 1966-70), World Soc. Ekistics, Nat. Council Women (hon.). Home: 24 W 55th St New York NY 10019 also Hubbell Mountain Rd Sherman CT 06784

EURY, LYNN WADE, utility executive; b. Polkton, N.C., Jan. 18, 1937; s. James L. and Zula Mae (Whitley) E.; m. Alice Faye Young, Sept. 27, 1959; children: Beth, Leigh, Faith. B.S. in E.E., N.C. State U., 1959. Registered profl. engr., N.C., S.C. With Carolina Power & Light Co., Raleigh, N.C., 1959—, v.p. systems planning and coordiantion, 1979-80, v.p. power supply, 1980, sr. v.p. power supply, 1980—; mem. EEI Nuclear Power Exec. Adv. Com., Washington, 1982—; bd. dirs. N.C. Engring. Found., Inc., Raleigh, 1981—; v.p. Carolina Va. Nuclear Power Assn., Inc., Columbia, 1982—. Chmn. fin. com. Hayes Barton Meth. Ch., 1983. Served with U.S. Army, 1960. Mem. IEEE, Profl. Engrs. N.C., N.C. Soc. Engrs., Am. Nuclear Soc., Eastern Carolinas sect. Am. Nuclear Soc., Health Physics Soc. Republican. Methodist. Club: Glen Forest Swim (pres. 1983).

EUSDEN, JOHN DYKSTRA, theology educator, clergyman; b. Holland, Mich., July 20, 1922; s. Ray Anderson and Marie (Dykstra) E.; m. Joanne Reiman, June 14, 1950; children: Andrea Bonner, Alan Tolles, John Dykstra, Sarah Jewell. A.B., Harvard U., 1943, postgrad in law, 1946; B.D. cum laude, Yale U., 1949; Ph.D. in Religion, Yale U., 1954. Ordained to ministry United Ch. of Christ, 1949. Instr. in religion Yale U., 1953-55, asst. prof., 1955-60; asst. prof. religion, chaplain Williams Coll., Williamstown, Mass., 1960-65, prof. chaplain, 1965—, Nathan Jackson prof. Christian theology, 1970—; theologian-in-residence Am. Ch. in Paris, 1972; lectr. Doshisha U., Kyoto, Japan, 1976, 82; dir. Associated Kyoto Program, Japan, 1981-82. Author: Puritans, Lawyers and Politics in Early 17th Century England, 1958, Zent and Christian: The Journey Between, 1981, (with John W. Westerhoff III) The Spiritual Life: Learning East and West, 1982; contbr. (articles to profl. jours.); translator, editor, author introduction: The Marrow of Theology (William Ames), 1968; author introduction, editor: New Covenant and Saints Qualification (John Preston), 1980. Mem. adv. council, campus ministry program Danforth Found., 1966-70; bd. dirs. Wellesley Coll. Parents Assn., 1972-75, pres., 1974-75; trustee Lingnan U., N.Y.C., 1964—, Buxton Sch., Williamstown, Mass., 1970—; leader trips, People's Republic of China, 1978,81. Served to 1st lt. USMCR, 1943-45. Scholar, Harvard U.; faculty fellow Am. Assn. Theol. Schs., 1958-59; fellow Folger Shakespeare Library, 958-59, 71-72; Lilly postdoctoral grantee, 1963-64; Danforth campus ministry grantee, 1963-64; research fellow Kyoto U., Japan, 1963-64; fellow Am. Council Learned Socs., 1967-68; Fulbright research travel grantee, 1967-68; research fellow U. Utrecht, Netherlands, 1968; research grantee Williams Coll., 1976. Mem. Am. Acad. Religion, AAUP, Am. Soc. Ch. History, Am. Soc. Christian Ethics, Nat. Assn. Coll. and Univ. Chaplains, Soc. Values in Higher Edn. Clubs: Appalachian Mountain, Randolph Mountain (pres. 1973-75). Home: 75 Forest Rd Williamstown MA 01267 Office: Stetson Hall Williams Coll Williamstown MA 01267

EUSTER, JOANNE REED, librarian; b. Grants Pass, Oreg., Apr. 7, 1936; d. Robert Lewis and Mabel Louise (Jones) Reed; m. Stephen L. Gerhardt, May 14, 1977; children: Sharon L., Carol L., Lisa J. Student, Lewis and Clark Coll., 1953-56; B.A., Portland State Coll., 1965; M.Librarianship, U. Wash., 1968, M.B.A., 1977; postgrad., U. Calif.-Berkeley, 1981—. Asst. librarian Edmonds Community Coll., Lynnwood, Wash., 1968-73, dir. library-media center, 1973-77; univ. librarian Loyola U. of New Orleans, 1977-80; library dir. J. Paul Leonard Library, San Francisco State U., 1980—; cons. Union Ejidal, La Penita, Nayarit, Mexico, 1973; co-cons. Office of Mgmt. Studies Assn. of Research Libraries, 1979—. Author: Changing Patterns of Internal Communication in Large Academic Libraries, 1981; contbr. articles to profl. jours. Mem. ALA, Am. Soc. Info. Sci., AAUP, Calif. Library Assn., Coll. and Research Libraries, Library Adminstrn. and Mgmt. Assn. Unitarian. Office: J Paul Leonard Library San Francisco State U 1630 Holloway Ave San Francisco CA 94132

EUSTIS, ALBERT ANTHONY, lawyer, diversified industry corporate executive; b. Mahanoy City, Pa., Nov. 8, 1921; s. Anthony and Anna E.; m. Mary Hampton Stewart, Apr. 25, 1959; children: Thomas Stewart, David Anthony. B.S., Columbia U., 1948; LL.B., Harvard U., 1951. Bar: N.Y. 1952, U.S. Dist. Ct. (So. dist.) N.Y 1955. Atty. firm Kelley, Drye & Warren, N.Y.C., 1951-61; atty. W.R. Grace & Co., N.Y.C., 1961-66, asst. gen. counsel, 1966-76, v.p., gen. counsel, sec., 1976-78, sr. v.p., gen. counsel, sec., 1978-82, exec. v.p., gen. counsel, sec., 1982—; chmn. bd. trustees President's Pvt. Sector Survey on Cost Control; adj. prof. law Fordham Law Sch. Served with AUS, 1942-46. Mem. ABA, Am. Soc. Corp. Secs., Am. Arbitration Assn. (comml. arbitration panel). Clubs: Harvard, Am. Yacht. Home: 2 Northwest Way Bronxville NY 10708 Office: W R Grace & Co 1114 Ave of the Americas New York NY 10036

EUSTIS, ROBERT HENRY, mech. engr.; b. Mpls., Apr. 18, 1920; s. Ralph Warren and Florence Louise E.; m. Katherine Vik Johnson, Mar. 20, 1943; children—Jeffrey Nelson, Karen V. B.M.E., U. Minn., 1942, M.S., 1944; Sc.D., M.I.T., 1953. Instr. U. Minn., 1942-44; research scientist NASA, 1944-47; asst. prof. M.I.T., 1947-51; chief engr. Thermal Research and Engring. Corp., 1951-53; mgr. heat and mech. sect. S.R.I. Internat., 1953-55; mem. faculty dept. mech. engring. Stanford U., 1955—; prof. 1962, dir. high temperature gasdynamics lab, 1961-80; chmn. tech. adv. council Emerson Electric Corp. Contbr. articles to profl. jours. Recipient medal Soviet Sci. Acad., 1973. Fellow AIAA; mem. ASME, Am. Soc. Engring. Edn., Combustion Inst. Home: 862 Lathrop Dr Stanford CA 94305 Office: Mech Engring Dept Stanford Univ Stanford CA 94305

EUSTIS, WARREN PENHALL, lawyer, educator; b. Fairmont, Minn., Nov. 30, 1927; s. Irving Nelson and Florence (Penhall) E.; m. Doris Anne Grieser, Mar. 1951 (div. Nov. 1968); children: Lillian, Paul; m. Nancy N. Anderson, Jan. 15, 1971; 1 son, Soren. B.A., Carleton Coll., 1950; J.D., U. Chgo., 1953; M.A., U. Ark., 1956. Bar: Minn. 1953. Since practiced in Rochester and Mpls.; mem. firm Van Eps & Gilmore; prof. law U. Minn., 1974—; pres. Granville, Inc.; counsel Upper Midwest Research and Devel. Council; dir. Twin Cities Health Project, 1972—; orgnl. cons. in health and ednl. delivery systems. Mem. Rochester Charter Commn., 1960-70, Minn. Higher Edn. Commn., 1965-67; pres. Rochester Council Chs., 1966, Minn. Chem. Dependency Assn.; chmn. 1st Congl. Dist. Minn. Democratic-Farmer Labor Party, 1959-66; state fin. chmn. 1962-67. Served with Sci. and Profl. Corps, AUS, 1954-56. Mem. Minn. Trial Lawyers Assn. (gov.), Olmsted County Bar Assn. (past pres.), Delta Upsilon, Phi Alpha Theta. Home: 58 Groveland Terr Minneapolis MN 55403 Office: 140 Sheland Plaza N Minneapolis MN 55426

EVANOFF, GEORGE C., database publishing executive; b. W. Deer, Pa., June 5, 1931; s. Christ and Luba (Georgieff) E.; m. Mary E. Yelavich, Nov. 21, 1964; 1 son, Michael. B.S. cum laude, U. Detroit, 1952, M.B.A., 1956. Engr. Gen. Motors Corp., Detroit, 1953-57; supervisory, mgmt. and exec. positions in sales, marketing, and product devel. Ford Motor Co., Dearborn, Mich., 1957-68; staff v.p. mktg., v.p. corporate planning, v.p. corporate devel. group RCA Corp., N.Y.C., 1968-76; with Norton Simon, Inc., Los Angeles and New York, 1977-82; v.p. corp. planning, interim pres. Max Factor & Co., 1977-78; pres. Max Factor Internat., 1979-82; pres., chief exec. officer Cordura Publs., Inc., San Diego, 1984—; dir. Nat. CSS, Wilton, Conn., 1974-79. Served with USAF, 1952-53. Roman Catholic. Home: Box 8043 Fairbanks Ranch Rancho Santa Fe CA 92067

EVANS, ALFRED SPRING, physician, educator; b. Buffalo, Aug. 21, 1917; s. John H. and Ellen (Spring) E.; m. Brigitte Kluge, July 26, 1952; children: John Kluge, Barbara Spring, Christopher Paul. A.B., U. Mich., 1939, M.P.H., 1960; M.D., U. Buffalo, 1943; M.A. (hon.), Yale U., 1966. Diplomate: col. Res. ret. Diplomate Am. Bd. Internal Medicine. Intern U. Pitts. Hosps., 1943-44; resident Goldwater Hosp., N.Y.C., 1944; USPHS postdoctoral research fellow Yale Med. Sch., 1947-48, from instr. to asst. prof. medicine, 1949-50, prof. epidemiology, dir. WHO serum reference bank, dept. epidemiology and pub. health, 1966—, John Rodman Paul prof. epidemiology, dir. div. infectious disease, 1982—; resident Buffalo Gen. Hosp., 1948-49; assoc. prof. preventive medicine and med. microbiology U. Wis. Sch. Medicine, 1952-59; prof., chmn. dept. preventive medicine, also dir. Wis. State Lab. Hygiene, 1959-66; mem. microbiology fellowship panel NIH, 1960-64; mem. microbiol. panel space flight NRC/NASA; cons. Philippine Health Dept., WHO, 1962, 1964, cons. tropical diseases, 1977—; cons. epidemiology Surgeon Gen. U.S. Army, 1969—, USN Bur. Medicine, 1973-76. Editor: Yale Jour. Biology and Medicine, 1971-73; editor-in-chief, 1973-76; editor: Viral Infections of Humans, 1976, (with H.A. Foldman) Bacterial Infection of Humans, 1982; contbr. articles on med. history, infectious diseases and epidemiology to profl. jours. Served to capt. M.C. AUS, 1944-46, 50-52. Fellow Am. Pub. Health Assn., Am. Coll. Epidemiology (bd. dirs.); mem. Am. Soc. Tropical Medicine, Soc. Epidemiol. Research, Am. Epidemiol. Soc. (sec.-treas. 1968-73, pres. 1973-74), Infectious Disease Soc. Am., Internat. Epidemiol. Assn., Am. Assn. History of Medicine, Central Soc. Clin. Research, Soc. Med. Consultants to Armed Forces (chmn. preventive medicine 1973-76, council 1976—, v.p. 1979-80, pres. 1980—), Delta Omega, Beaumont Med. Club (pres. 1973-74). Home: 38 Dogwood Circle Woodbridge CT 06525 Office: 333 Cedar St New Haven CT 06510

EVANS, ANTHONY HOWARD, college president; b. Clay County, Ark., Sept. 24, 1936; s. William Raymond and Thelma Fay (Crews) Romine; m. Lois Fay Kirkham, Aug. 29, 1959. B.A., East Tex. Bapt. Coll., Marshall, 1959; M.A., U. Hawaii, 1961; Ph.D., U. Calif.-Berkeley, 1968. Program dir. Peace Corps., Seoul, Korea, 1970-75; dir. planning Peace Corps, Washington, 1972-75; exec. v.p. Eastern Mich. U., Ypsilanti, 1975-78, acting pres., 1978-79, v.p.acad. affairs, 1979-82; pres. Calif. State Coll.- San Bernardino, 1982—. Mem. Orgn. Am. Historians, Phi Kappa Phi. Home: 855 Vista Dr. San Bernardino CA 92405 Office: Calif State College 5500 State College Pkwy San Bernardino CA 92407

EVANS, AUDREY ELIZABETH, physician, educator; b. York, Eng., Mar. 6, 1925; came to U.S., 1957, naturalized, 1962; d. Llewellyn and Phyllis Mary (Miller) E. Licentiate Sch. Medicine, Royal Coll. Surgeons, Edinburgh, 1950. Intern Royal Infirmary, Edinburgh, 1950-52; physician tumor therapy Children's Hosp., Boston, 1957-65; instr. pediatrics Harvard U. Med. Sch., 1961-65; asst. prof. pediatric hematologist U. Chgo., 1965-69; prof. pediatrics U. Pa., 1969—; dir. oncology Children's Hosp., Phila., 1969—. Home: 2010 Spruce St Philadelphia PA 19103 Office: Children's Hosp 3400 Civic Center Blvd Philadelphia PA 19104

EVANS, AUSTIN JAMES, hosp. adminstr.; b. Mt. Pleasant, Iowa, Feb. 26, 1920; s. William Henry and Estelle (Lamb) E.; m. Wilma Mildred Stephens, Mar. 26, 1944; children—Mary Beth, Susan Louise. B.S., Iowa Wesleyan Coll., 1941, D.Sc., 1976; M.S., Yale, 1950. Adminstrv. resident State U. Iowa Hosps., 1949-51; bus. adminstr. Mental Health Inst., Independence, Iowa, 1951-54; adminstr. Hadley Meml. Hosp. and Rehab. Center, Hays, Kans., 1954-63; dir. Cleve. Met. Gen. Hosp., 1963-65; adminstr. Lake View Meml. Hosp., Danville, Ill., 1965-75; field rep. Joint Commn. on Accreditation of Hosps., Chgo., 1975—; hosp. cons. Methodist Bd. Hosps. and Homes, Evanston, Ill., 1965—. Contbr. articles to profl. jours. Chmn. Independence chpt. ARC fund drive, 1951-53; Hays service unit Salvation Army, 1954-63; pres. Cerebral Palsy Vermilion County; chmn. Citizens' Referendum Com., Danville; bd. dirs. Danville United Fund, YMCA; trustee Danville Jr. Coll. Served to lt. USNR, 1942-46. Named Man of Year in Independence, 1953. Fellow Am. Coll. Hosp. Adminstrs.; mem. Am. Hosp. Assn. (life), Danville C. of C. (dir.), Kans. Hosp. Assn. (pres. 1958), Danville Musical Cycle (pres.). Methodist. Club: Rotary (pres. Danville). Home: 1128 Walnut St Danville IL 61832 Office: 875 N Michigan Ave Chicago IL 60611

EVANS, BENJAMIN HAMPTON, architectural educator, consultant; b. Premont, Tex., Oct. 27, 1926; s. Clyde Allen and Grace Ruth (Pierce) E.; m. Gwendolyn Jones, July 29, 1950; children: Ann Elizabeth, Sara Lynn, Gail Leigh. B.Arch., Tex A&M U., 1952; M.Arch., Tex. A&M U., 1962. Research architect Tex. Engring. Expt. Sta., 1952-63; assoc. prof. Tex. A & M U., 1955-63; dir. research and edn. AIA, Washington, 1963-69; asst. dir. Nat. Acad. Scis., Washington, 1959-75; prof. architecture Va. Tech. U., Blacksburg, 1975—; prin. Daylight-Energy Design Assocs., Blacksburg, Va., 1975—. Author: Emerging Techniques, 1969, Daylight in Architecture, 1981. Served with AUS, 1944-46. Fellow AIA (pres. Brazos chpt. 1960-61), Illuminating Engring. Soc. (chmn. daylighting com.). Republican. Mem., Disciples of Christ Ch. Club: Lions.

EVANS, BERNARD WILLIAM, geologist, educator; b. London, July 16, 1934; U.S., 1961, naturalized, 1977; s. Albert Edward and Marjorie (Jordan) E.; m. Sheila Campbell Nolan, Nov. 19, 1962. B.Sc., U. London, 1955; D.Phil., Oxford U., 1959. Asst. U. Glasgow, Scotland, 1958-59; departmental demonstrator U. Oxford, 1959-61; asst. research prof. U. Calif., Berkeley, 1961-65, asst. prof., 1965-66, asso. prof., 1966-69; prof. geology U. Wash., Seattle, 1969—, chmn. dept. geol. scis., 1974-79. Contbr. articles to profl. jours. Mem. Geol. Soc. Am., Mineral. Soc. Am. (award 1970), Geochem. Soc., Geol. Soc. London, Mineral. Soc. Gt. Britain, Swiss Mineral. Soc., AAAS. Home: 8001 Sandpoint Way NE Apt C55 Seattle WA 98115 Office: Dept Geol Scis Univ of Wash Seattle WA 98195

EVANS, BILL (JAMES WILLIAM EVANS), dancer, choreographer, educator, arts adminstr.; b. Lehi, Utah, Apr. 11, 1940; s. William Ferdin and Lila (Snape) E.;, Aug. 27, 1962 (div. 1965); 1 dau., Thais. B.A. in English, U. Utah, 1963, M.F.A., 1970; dance student various pvt. dance schs. and studios. Profl. ballet dancer, Salt Lake City, N.Y.C., Chgo., 1965-67; mem., choreographer, artistic coordinator Utah Repertory Dance Theatre, U. Utah, 1967-75; founder, artistic dir. Bill Evans Dance Co., Salt Lake City, 1975-76, Seattle, 1976—; founder, tchr., artistic dir. Bill Evans Dance/Seattle Sch., 1977—; founder Seattle Summer Inst. and Festival of Dance, 1977—; dance/movement specialist Artist-in-Schs. program Nat. Endowment for Arts; guest prof. dance U. Wash., 1979-81. Free-lance dancer, 1969—, including, Berlin Ballet, 1969, Jacob's Pillow Dance Festival, Lee, Mass., 1973, Harvard U., 1973, 74; choreographer numerous works for various ballet and modern dance cos., 1967—; Creator Evans technique for tng. body. Am. Arts Alliance rep. before House and Senate appropriations coms., 1979. Served as officer U.S. Army, 1963-65. Recipient various choreographic awards, including from Nat. Endowment for Arts, 1972-75, 77, 78, Western States Arts Found., 1975, Utah Bicentennial Com., 1976; Guggenheim fellow, 1976-77; recipient Teaching Plaudit award Nat. Dance Assn., 1981. Mem. Dancers, Inc. (adv. bd.). Home: 1221 Minor Ave 1010 Seattle WA 98101 Office: 704 19th Ave E Seattle WA 98112

EVANS, BILLY LEE, Congressman; b. Tifton, Ga., Nov. 10, 1941; children—Christopher, William Corry, Autumn Lee. A.B., U. Ga., 1963, LL.B., 1964. Bar: Ga. bar 1965. Individual practice law, Macon, Ga., 1965-76; mem. Ga. Ho. of Reps., 1969-76, 95th-96th Congresses from 8th Ga. Dist., Pub. Works and Transp. Com., House Judiciary Com. Mem. Ga., Macon bar assns., Ga. Farm Bur. Democrat. Clubs: Elks, Moose, Eagles, Masons, Shriners.

EVANS, BLACKWELL BUGG, pediatric urologist; b. Forksville, Va., Nov. 5, 1927; s. Clarence Meredith and Saluda Ann Rebecca (Bugg) E.; m. June Helen Banks, Oct. 8, 1949; 1 son, Blackwell Bugg. B.A., U. Va., 1955; M.D., Med. Coll. Va., 1959. Diplomate: Am. Bd. Urology. Intern, resident in surgery Johnston-Willis Hosp., Richmond, Va., 1959-61; resident in urology, research fellow in urology Tulane U. Med. Center, 1961-65; clin. asst. urology Med. Coll. S.C., 1965-67; mem. faculty Tulane U. Med. Center, 1967—, prof. pediatrics, 1975—, prof. urology, 1974-82; Sobin prof. pediatric urology, 1982—; chief sect. pediatric urology Tulane U. Med. Center, 1978-82, chmn. dept. urology, 1982—; dir. urologic edn. Children's Hosp., New Orleans, 1978—, pres. med. staff, 1981-83; med. adv. bd. La. Kidney Found., 1973-74; med. adv. com. La. Handicapped Children's Service Program, 1976—; cons. in field. Served as officer USAF, 1951-53. Fellow A.C.S., Am. Acad. Pediatrics, Internat. Coll. Pediatrics; mem. Am. Urol. Assn. (dir., chmn. fin. com. Southeastern sect. 1979-83), Soc. Pediatric Urology, Soc. Univ. Urologists, Royal Soc. Medicine, Internat. Soc. Nephrology, AMA, Pan-Am. Med. Assn., So. Med. Assn., Am. Assn. Med. Colls., N.Y. Acad. Scis., So. Soc. Pediatric Research, La. Urol. Assn. (pres. 1977-78), United Ostomy Assn. (profl. adv. bd. 1974-79), Greater New Orleans Ostomy Assn. (med. adv. bd. 1980—), Sigma Xi. Address: Tulane U Med Sch 1430 Tulane Ave New Orleans LA 70112

EVANS, BOB OVERTON, electronics executive; b. Grand Island, Nebr., Aug. 19, 1927; s. Walter Bernard and Lillian (Overton) E.; m. Maria Bowman, Nov. 19, 1949; children: Cathleen L., Robert W., David D., Douglas B. B.E.E., Iowa State U., 1949. Electric operating engr. No. Ind. Pub. Service Co., Hammond, 1949-51; with IBM, 1951-82; v.p. devel. Data Systems div., 1962-64; pres. Fed. Systems div., 1965-69, Systems Devel. div., 1970-74, Systems Communication div., 1975-77; v.p. IBM engring., programming and tech., 1977-84; ptnr. Hambrecht and Quist, 1984—; mem. Stark Draper Labs., Inc.; cons. govt. agys.; area bd. mem. Md. Nat. Bank; mem. Def. Sci. Bd. Mem. exec. bd. Nat. Capital Area council Boy Scouts Am.; trustee Rensselaer Poly. Inst., N.Y. Pub. library; mem. elec. engring. vis. com. MIT. Served with USNR, 1945-46. Recipient Disting. Pub. Service award NASA; Disting. Alumni citation Iowa State U. Fellow IEEE (chmn. computer group conf. 1970, Armstrong award 1984); mem. Nat. Acad. Engring., Profl. Group Electronic Computers, Nat. Security Indsl. Assn. (trustee), Armed Forces Communications and Electronics Assn. (trustee), Aerospace Industries Assn. (exec. bd.). Presbyterian. (elder). Designed and developed large digital electric computers. Home: Ivanhoe Ln Greenwich CT 06830 Office: 325 Montgomery St San Francisco CA 94015

EVANS, BRUCE DWIGHT, lawyer; b. Mt. Hope, W.Va., May 27, 1934; s. M. Albert and Eleanor E. (Fowler) E.; m. Sallie Lee Hazen, Aug. 24, 1957 (div. Jan. 1974); children: Scott C., Leigh F., Randolph D.; m. Doris N. Stritzinger Webster, Sept. 2, 1978. A.B., Princeton U., 1956; LL.B., Harvard U., 1959. Bar: N.Y. 1960, Pa. 1970. Assoc. Debevoise, Plimpton, Lyons & Gates, N.Y.C., 1959-68; ptnr. Reed Smith Shaw & McClay, Pitts., 1969—. Trustee Ellis Sch., Pitts., 1972-78. Mem. ABA, Allegheny County Bar Assn., Phi Beta Kappa. Republican. Episcopalian. Clubs: Harvard-Yale-Princeton; Rivers (Pitts.). Office: Reed Smith et al 747 Union Trust Bldg Pittsburgh PA 15219

EVANS, BRUCE HASELTON, art museum director; b. Rome, N.Y., Nov. 13, 1939; s. E. Arnold and Joan Sawyer (Haselton) E.; m. Margo Elizabeth Frey, July 14, 1962; children: Barton Haselton, Christopher Andrew. B.A., Amherst Coll., 1961; M.A., NYU, 1964. Asst. curator Dayton (Ohio) Art Inst., 1965-66, curator, 1967-68, chief curator, 1969-72, asst. dir., 1973-74, dir., 1975—; mem. adv. panels Nat. Endowment for Arts and Humanities, 1973—; v.p. Midwest Museums Conf. Council; Active Dayton River Corridor Design Rev. Com., Historic Architecture Com. Author: Fifty Treasures of the Dayton Art Institute, 1969, The Paintings of Jean-Leon Gerome, 1972, The Paintings of Edward Edmondson, 1972. Mem. Assn. Art Mus. Dirs., Ohio Mus. Assn. (pres.), Intermus. Conservation Assn. (trustee), Am. Assn. Museums, Internat. Council Museums. Home: 334 Marathon Ave Dayton OH 45406 Office: PO Box 941 Dayton OH 45401

EVANS, CARLETON CANNON, physician; b. Salt Lake City, July 20, 1934; s. David Wooley and Beatrice (Cannon) E.; 1 son, Jonathan Urquhart. A.B. in History, U. Calif., Berkeley, 1958; M.D., U. Minn., 1966. Intern San Francisco Gen. Hosp., 1966-67; resident U. Calif., San Francisco, San Francisco VA Hosp., 1967-70; chief ambulatory care sect. VA Med. Center, San Francisco, 1970, asso. chief staff, 1970-71, asso. chief staff ambulatory care, 1971-72; dir. health services research and devel. service VA, Washington, 1972-79; scholar-in-residence, dir. div. health care Nat. Acad. Scis.-Inst. Medicine, Washington, 1979-81; dir. allocation devel. service VA, Washington, 1981—; instr. medicine U. Calif., San Francisco, 1970-72; guest lectr. Harvard Sch. Public Health, Ga. Inst. Tech., U. Calif., Berkeley, Yale Center for Health Services; project officer Nat. Acad. Scis. Study of VA Health Care. Mem. health services devel. grants study sect. HEW; mem. com. on sci., engring. and tech. resources and research disciplines NSF; mem. steering com. VA-M.I.T. Center for Health Care Mgmt., Boston. Served with U.S. Army, 1956-58. Ford Found. fellow, 1951-54. Mem. Am. Public Health Assn., Beta Theta Pi. Home: 3912 N Vacation Ln Arlington VA 22207 Office: 2101 Constitution Ave NW Washington DC 20418

EVANS, CLIFFORD JESSIE, manufacturing executive; b. Sayre, Okla., May 3, 1923; s. Roy and Maggie May (Blackburn) E.; m. Lillian Jerry Furlong, Jan. 11, 1942; children: Garry Lee, Charlotte Ann Evans Kretzmeier, William Joe, Elena Kay, Pandora Leigh (dec.), Stephen Kelley. Ed. high sch. Newspaper distbr., 1934-42, home and apt. builder, 1946-49; inventor, mfr., pres. Jetco Alhambra, trenching equipment, 1948—; pres. Dallas-Jetco, 1960—, Tulsa-Jetco, 1964—, Dallas-Jetco, Grand Prairie, 1971—, Flying E Inc., Valley Mills, Tex., 1975—, Highland Park Water Supply Corp.; pres., owner Highland Park Apts., Ft. Worth, 1973—; pres. Highland Park Estates, China Springs, Tex. Served with AUS, 1943-46. Decorated Bronze Star, Purple Heart; named to Pipeliners Hall of Fame, 1970, Salesman of Year, U.S. and Can., Salesmen Internat., 1960-70. Home: Flying E Ranch: Route 2 Valley Mills TX 76689 Office: Waco Hwy 2490 Route 2 Valley Mills TX 76689

EVANS, COOPER, congressman; b. Cedar Rapids, Iowa, May 26, 1924; s. Thomas and Ora E.; m. Jean Marie Ruppelt, June 20, 1948; children: Jim, Charles. B.S., Iowa State U., 1949, M.S., 1955. Registered profl. engr., Iowa. With C.E. U.S. Army, 1949-65; dir. advanced manned lunar missions NASA, Washington, 1963-65; farmer, mng. ptnr., nr. Grundy Center, Iowa, 1965—; mem. Iowa Ho. of Reps., Des Moines, 1974-79, 98th Congress from 3d Iowa Dist. Served to lt. col., inf. U.S. Army, 1943-46. Decorated Army Commendation medal. Mem. Am. Legion. Republican. Methodist. Lodge: Rotary. Office: US Ho of Reps 127 Cannon House Office Bldg Washington Dc 20515

EVANS, DANIEL FRALEY, college administr., banker, business consultant; b. Crawfordsville, Ind., Feb. 24, 1922; s. Benjamin C. and Ruth (Fraley) E.; m. Julia Delo Sloan, Oct. 15, 1945; children: Daniel Fraley, David Sloan, Julia Anne. A.B., Wabash Coll., 1944, LL.D., 1976; M.B.A., Harvard U., 1948; LL.D., Ind. Central U., 1969. With L.S. Ayres Co., Indpls., 1948-76, treas., 1958-64, exec. v.p., 1964-65, pres., 1965-74, chmn., 1974-76; treas. Wabash Coll., Crawfordsville, Ind., 1975—; dir. Midwest Nat. Corp., vice chmn., 1981—, Meridian Mut. Ins. Co., Ball Stores, Inc., Flanner & Buchanan, Inc., Stokely-Van Camp, Inc.; Chmn. Ind. Tax and Financing Policy Commn., 1967-69. Author: It's All Relative, Part I, 1978, It's All Relative, Part II, 1982, Changing from a What to a Who, 1977. Mem. Ind. Ann. Conf. Meth. Ch., also mem. commn. on structure; chmn. Indpls. Community Devel. Task Force, 1976, 77; bd. dirs. Ayres Found., Meth. Hosp. Found.; trustee Meth. Hosp. Ind., pres., 1965-68; trustee Wabash Coll., Wesley Med. Care Corp., Oak Hill Cemetery Co. Served as lt. (j.g.) USNR, World War II; PTO. Decorated Bronze Star with 4 clusters; recipient medal of honor U. Evansville, 1970, Alumni award merit Wabash Coll., 1968; Sagamore of Wabash, 1962, 76, 81. Mem. Ind. Retail Council (pres. 1961-64), NAACP (life), Indiana Academy, Phi Beta Kappa (asso.). Clubs: University, Columbia, Traders Point, Meridian Hills. Home: 6463 N Illinois St Indianapolis IN 46260 Office: Wabash Coll Crawfordsville IN 47933

EVANS, DANIEL JACKSON, U.S. senator; b. Seattle, Oct. 16, 1925; s. Daniel Lester and Irma (Ide) E.; m. Nancy Ann Bell, June 6, 1959; children: Daniel Jackson, Mark L., Bruce M. B.S. in Civil Engring, U. Wash., 1948, M.S., 1949. Registered profl. engr., Wash. Asst. mgr. (Mountain-Pacific chpt.); Asso. Gen. Contractors, Seattle, 1953-59; cons. civil engr., Seattle, 1949-51; partner Gray & Evans, structural and civil engrs., Seattle, 1959-65; mem. Wash. Ho. of Reps. from, King County, 1956-65, Republican floor leader, 1961-65; gov., State of Wash., 1964-77; pres. Evergreen State Coll., Olympia, 1977-83; mem. U.S. Senate from Wash. State, 1983—; mem. Adv. Council on Intergovernmental Relations, 1972-77, Fed. Adv. Commn. Project Independence, 1974, Nat. Commn. on Productivity and Work Quality, 1975, President's Vietnamese Refugee Adv. Com., 1975; chmn. Pacific NW Electric Power and Conservation Planning Council, 1981-83. Keynote speaker Rep. Nat. Conv., 1968; mem. Nat. Gov.'s Conf., chmn., 1973-74; chmn. Western Gov.'s Conf., 1968-69; trustee Carnegie Found. for Advancement of Teaching, Nature Conservancy, 20th Century Fund. Served to lt. USNR, 1943-46, 51-53. Recipient Human Rights award Pacific N.W. chpt. Nat. Assn. Intergroup Relations Ofcls., 1967; Service to the Profession award Cons. Engrs. Council, 1969; Scales of Justice award Nat. Council Crime and Delinquency, 1968; Pub. Ofcl. of Year award Wash. Environmental Council, 1970; Distinguished Eagle, Silver Beaver, Silver Antelope awards Boy Scouts Am.; Distinguished Citizen award Nat. Municipal League, 1977. Congregationalist. Address: US Senate Washington DC 20510

EVANS, DAVID C., computer company executive; b. Salt Lake City, Feb. 24, 1924; s. David W. and Beatrice (Cannon) E.; m. Joy Frewin, Mar. 21, 1947; children: Gayle Evans Scheidel, Susan Evans Foote, David F., Ann Evans Brown, Peter F., Douglas F., Katherine E. B.S., U. Utah, 1949, Ph.D. in Physics, 1953. Dir. engring. computer div. Bendix Corp., Los Angles, 1953-62; prof. elec. engring. and computer sci. U. Calif.-Berkeley, 1962-66; prof. elec. engring. and computer sci., chmn. dept. U. Utah, Salt Lake City, 1965-73; chmn. bd., pres. Evans & Sutherland Computer Corp., Salt Lake City, 1968—. Served in U.S. Army, 1942-45. Recipient Silver Beaver award Boy Scouts Am.; named to Computer Hall of Fame. Fellow IEEE; mem. Nat. Acad. Engring. Republican. Mem. Ch. of Jesus Christ of Latter-day Saints. Home: 1393 E South Temple Salt Lake City UT 84102 Office: PO Box 8700 Salt Lake City UT 84108

EVANS, DAVID STANLEY, astronomy educator; b. Cardiff, Wales, U.K., Jan. 28, 1916; came to U.S., 1968; s. Arthur C. and Kate (Priest) E.; m. Betty Hall Hart, Mar. 8, 1949; children: Jonathan Gareth Weston, Barnaby Huw Weston. B.A., Cambridge U., Eng., 1937, M.A., 1941, Ph.D., 1941, Sc.D., 1971. Research asst. Obs. U. Oxford, Eng., 1938-46; 2d asst. Radcliffe Obs., Pretoria, South Africa, 1946-51; chief asst. Royal Obs., Cape Town, South Afria, 1951-68; assoc. dir. research McDonald Obs. U. Tex., Austin, 1968-81, prof. astronomy, 1968—; vis. prof., researcher various univs. Author: Frontiers of Astronomy, 1946, Teach Yourself Astronomy, 1952, Observation in Modern Astronomy, 1968; editor (with others) Herschel at the Cape, 1969; The Shadow of The Telecope, 1970, External Galaxies and Quasistellar Objects, 1972, Photometry, Kenematics and Dynamics of Galaxies, 1979; contbr. articles to profl. jours. Rcipient Tyson medal Cambridge U., 1937; recipient Raleigh prize Tyson medal, 1938, Macintyre award Astron. Soc. South Africa, 1972; Nat. Sci. Sr. vis. scientist fellow, 1965-66. Fellow Royal Astron. Soc. London, Brit. Inst. Physics; mem. Internat. Astron. Union, Astron. Soc. South Africa, Am. Astron. Soc. Clubs: Owl, Western Province Sports (Cape Town); Town and Gown (Austin). Address: Dept Astronomy Univ Tex Austin TX 78712

EVANS, DENNIS EDWARD, banker; b. N.Y.C., Aug. 3, 1938; s. Robert Thomas and Ellen (Martin) E.; m. Mary Jayne Boeger; children: Thomas, James, Robert, David. B.S., Ind. U., 1960, M.B.A., 1961. Vice pres. Glore Forgan William R. Staats Co., investment bankers, N.Y.C., 1969-72; v.p., dir. research, then exec. v.p. resources mgmt. and planning group First Nat. Bank Mpls., 1972-80, former pres., now chmn., chief exec. officer, 1980—, also dir. Bd. dirs. Mpls. Jr. Achievement. Mem. Fin. Analysts Fedn., Twin Cities Soc. Cert. Fin. Analysts. Clubs: Minneapolis, Wayzata Country. Office: 120 S 6th St Minneapolis MN 55402 *

EVANS, DENNIS HYDE, chemist, educator; b. Grinnell, Iowa, Mar. 28, 1939; s. Leonard Hyde and Clara Ethel (Parmley) E.; m. Ruth Elizabeth Turnbull, June 28, 1958; children: Susan Katherine, John Hyde, Andrew Turnbull. B.S., Ottawa U., 1960; A.M., Harvard U., 1961, Ph.D., 1964. Instr. chemistry Harvard U., Cambridge, 1964-66; asst. prof. chemistry U. Wis., Madison, 1966-70, asso. prof., 1970-75, prof., 1975—, chmn. dept., 1977-80, assoc. dean Coll. of Letters and Sci., 1983—. Contbr. articles to profl. jours. Danforth fellow, 1960-64; NIH fellow, 1961-64; NSF grantee, 1968—. Mem. Am. Chem. Soc., Internat. Soc. Electrochemistry. Baptist. Home: 2209 Hollister Ave Madison WI 53705 Office: 1101 University Ave Madison WI 53706

EVANS, DEREK THOMAS, manufacturing company executive; b. Lampeter, Cardigan, Wales, Dec. 3, 1940; emigrated to Can., 1971; s. Thomas and Sarah Anne (Thomas) E.; m. Marlene Hill, Apr. 8, 1963; children: Mark Damion, Simon Timothy. B.Engr., Sheffield U., Sheffield, Eng., 1963. Registered profl. engr., Ont. Plant supt. Can. Packers, Toronto, Ont., Can., 1971-72; mfg. control mgr. ITT Can., Guelph, Ont., 1972-74; mfg. mgr. Kockums Industries, Guelph, Ont., 1974-77, N.Am. mfg. mgr., Malmo, Sweden, 1977-79, gen. mgr., Fredericton, N.B., 1979-80; pres., gen. mgr. Koehring Can., Brantford, Ont., 1980—; bd. dirs. Ont. Ctr. Resource Machinery, Sudbury, 1982—. Mem. Profl. Engrs. Ont. Club: Golf & Country (Brantford). Lodge: Rotary. Home: 72 Golfdale Rd Brantford ON Canada N3T 5H9 Office: Koehring Canada Market St Brantford ON Canada N3T 5P6

EVANS, DONALD DWIGHT, educator; b. Thunder Bay, Ont., Can., Sept. 21, 1927; s. Ira Dwight and Jessie (Milliken) E.; m. Sybil Ruth Blenkinsop, June 28, 1952 (div. Feb. 1983); children: Stephen, Gregory, Luke, Nicholas.; m. Frances Ann Smith, May 21, 1983. B.A., U. Toronto, Ont., Can., 1950; B.Phil., Oxford (Eng.) U., 1953, D.Phil., 1962; B.D., McGill U., 1955. Ordained to ministry United Ch. Canada, 1955; pastor, Grand Forks, B.C., Can., 1955-58; asst. prof. divinity McGill U., Montreal, Que., Can., 1960-64; asso. prof. philosophy U. Toronto, 1964-68, prof., 1968—. Author: The Logic of Self-Involvment, 1963, Communist Faith and Christian Faith, 1964, Struggle and Fulfilment, 1980, Faith, Authenticity and Morality, 1980; editor: Peace, Power and Protest, 1967. Home: 395 Markham St Toronto ON Canada

EVANS, DONALD JOHN, lawyer; b. Springfield, Mass., Jan. 29, 1926; s. Daniel G. and Marcia M. (Shaughnessy) E.; m. Sheila Sweeney, Apr. 24, 1954; children—Daniel Shields, Elizabeth Hendrick, Martha Cunningham. A.B., Dartmouth Coll., 1947; J.D., Harvard U., 1952. Bar: Mass. 1952. Asso. firm Goodwin, Procter & Hoar, Boston, 1952-59, partner, 1960—; dir., sec., mem. exec. and nominating com. Barry Wright Corp.; dir. BIW Cable Systems, Inc.; sec., clk., dir. DesignPak Inc.; exec. com., trustee, corporator Home Savs. Bank; dir., sec. Interstate Uniform Services Corp.; mem. exec. com., sec., dir. Mass. Bus. Devel. Corp.; sec., clk. Mass. High Tech. Council, Inc., Savs. Mgmt. Computer Corp., Mass. Cert. Devel. Corp.; clk. Allison Acoustics Inc.; asst. sec. Barry Realty Corp. Corporator Big Brother Assn. Boston; trustee, exec. com., chmn. nominating com. Boston Ballet Co.; bd. dirs. Boston Opera Assn., World Affairs Council; corporator New Eng. Bapt. Hosp.; mem. adminstrn. and fin. adv. com. Cardinal and Archbishop of Boston.; sec., trustee Pinellas Found. Fellow Am. Bar Found.; mem. ABA (past chmn. corp., banking and bus. Law sect., chmn. com. on long range issues affecting bus. law practice, mem. counsel responsibility and liability comm., audit inquiry, bus. mgmt. liability ins., com. on coms., corp. laws, fed. regulation of securities com., mem. various other coms., chmn. adv. Bus. Lawyer), Am. Law Inst., Boston Bar Assn., Mass. Bar Assn., Am. Coll. Investment Counsel. Clubs: Bay, Cohasset Golf, Cohasset Tennis and Squash, Cohasset Yacht Club (past commodore, exec. com.); Union Club (Boston) (pres. 1980-82). Home: 72 Main St Cohasset MA 02025 Office: 28 State St Boston MA 02109

EVANS, DONALD LEE, well drilling company executive; b. Jacksonville, Ill., Dec. 23, 1931; s. Paul Edward and Eleanor (Barthlow) E.; m. Donna Jean Potter, June 28, 1958; children: Sandra Lynn, Brian Keith. B.S. in Chem. Engring., Mo. Sch. Mines and Metallurgy, 1961, M.S., 1964; C.E., U. Mo., 1981. Registered profl. engr., Ill.; registered land surveyor, Mo. Instr. Mo. Sch. Mines and Metallurgy, Rolla, 1961-64; sales engr. Layne-Western Co., Aurora, Ill., 1964-72, dist. mgr., Columbus, Ohio, 1972-74, exec. v.p., Mission, Kans., 1974-77, pres., 1977—. Mem. Am. Water Works Assn., Nat. Water Works Assn., Mo. Assn. Registered Land Surveyors. Republican. Methodist. Office: Layne-Western Co Inc 5800 Foxridge Dr Mission KS 66202

EVANS, DOUGLAS MCCULLOUGH, surgeon, educator; b. Vandergrift, Pa., July 31, 1925; s. Archibald Davis and Helen Irene (McCullough) E.; m. Thelmajean Volkers, Aug. 1, 1959; children: Matthew Kirk, Daniel Scott. Student, Ohio State U., 1943, 46-48; M.D., Western Res. U., 1952; postgrad., U. Mich., 1956-58. Diplomate: Am. Bd. Surgery. Resident in surgery Henry Ford Hosp., 1952-57, chief resident in surgery, 1957-58, mem. surgery staff, 1959-60, Akron (Ohio) Gen. Hosp., 1960-70; chmn. dept. surgery Akron Gen. Med. Center, 1971—; prof., chmn. surgery Northeastern Ohio U. Coll. Medicine. Served with AUS, 1943-46. Fellow A.C.S.; mem. Midwest Surg. Soc., AMA, Ohio Med. Assn., Soc. Surg. Chmn. Republican. Presbyterian. Clubs: Akron City, Cascade. Office: 400 Wabash Ave Akron OH 44307 *

EVANS, EARL ALISON, JR., biochemist; b. Balt., Mar. 11, 1910; s. Earl Alison and Florence (Lewis) E. Student, Balt. Poly. Inst., 1924-28; B.Sc., Johns Hopkins, 1931; Ph.D., Columbia, 1936. Research asst. pharmacology Johns Hopkins Med. Sch., 1931-32, asst. lab. endocrine research, 1932-34; univ. fellow biochemistry Columbia, 1934-36; instr. biochemistry U. Chgo., 1937-39, asst. prof., 1939-41, asso. prof. biochemistry, acting chmn. dept., 1941-42; on leave, 1947-48, prof., 1942—; chmn. dept. biochemistry 1942-72; fellow Rockefeller Found. U. Sheffield, Eng., 1939-40; chief sci. officer Am. embassy, London, 1947-48; cons. to sec. state, 1951-53; mem. bd. sci. counselors Nat. Inst. Arthritis and Metabolic Diseases, NIH, 1960-63; mem. div. med. scis. NRC, 1962-65; chmn. postdoctoral fellowships Nat. Acad. Sci.-NRC, 1963-65; mem. divisional com. biol. and med. scis. NSF, 1963-66. Author: Biochemistry of Bacterial Viruses, 1952, (with others) Biological Symposia V, 1941, Symposium on Respiratory Enzymes, 1942; Editor: Biological Action of the Vitamins, 1942; Contbr. articles to sci. jours. Adv. bd. Am. Found. Continuing Edn. Fellow All Souls Coll., Oxford U., 1969, Pierpont Morgan Library; Soc. Scholars Johns Hopkins U.; Recipient Gold Key U. Chgo. Sch. Medicine Alumni Assn. Fellow AAAS; mem. Am. Chem. Soc. (Eli Lilly prize in biol. chemistry 1942), Am. Soc. Biol. Chemists, Biochem. Soc. (Britain), Am. Soc. Bacteriologists, Asociacion Quimica Argentina, Sigma Xi, Tau Beta Pi. Episcopalian. Clubs: Cosmos (Washington); Quadrangle, Univ., Racquet (Chgo.); R.A.C., Travellers (London). Home: 1120 N Lake Shore Dr Chicago IL 60611

EVANS, EDWARD PARKER, publishing and information services company executive; b. Pitts., Jan. 31, 1942; s. Thomas Mellon and Elizabeth Parker (Kase) E. B.A., Yale U., 1964; M.B.A., Harvard U., 1967. Vice pres. Evans & Co., Inc., N.Y.C., 1975-82; chmn. bd. H.K. Porter Co., Inc., Pitts., 1976-82, Mo. Portland Cement Co., 1975-82, Fansteel, Inc., 1977-82, Evans Broadcasting Corp., Mo., 1977-82, Macmillan, Inc., N.Y.C., 1980—. Served with Air N.G., 1965-71. Clubs: Duquesne (Pitts.); River, Harvard Bus. Sch. (N.Y.C.); Round Hill (Greenwich, Conn.); Rolling Rock (Ligonier, Pa.); Blind Brook (Purchase, N.Y.); Lyford Cay (Nassau, Bahamas). Office: Macmillan Inc 866 3d Ave New York NY 10022

EVANS, EDWIN CHARLES, consultant,, former manufacturing executive; b. Waterford, N.Y., May 23, 1910; s. Edwin Bernard and Sarah (Slavin) E.; m. Renette Wendell, July 22, 1944. Student, Rensselaer Poly. Inst., 1930-31, Siena Coll., 1939-40, Harvard Grad. Sch. Bus. Adminstrn., 1949. Civil engr. N.Y. State Engring. Dept., 1928-34; with Behr-Manning div. (now Abrasive and Tape divs.) Norton Co.), Troy, N.Y., 1934-68, beginning as mem. sales analysis dept., successively staff purchasing dept., asst. purchasing agt., purchasing agt., asst. to v.p. charge engring. and mfg. asst. gen. mgr., 1955-59, gen. mgr., 1959-68, pres., 1961-68; cons. N.Y. State Dept. Commerce, 1970—, asst. dep. commr., 1972-75; v.p. Norton Co., Worcester, Mass., 1961-68. Bd. dirs. Samaritan Hosp.; trustee Russell Sage Coll., Albany Med. Coll. of Union U. Mem. Harvard Bus. Sch. Assn. Clubs: Troy, Troy Country. Home: East Acres Troy NY 12180

EVANS, EDWIN CURTIS, physician; b. Milledgeville, Ga., June 30, 1917; s. Watt Collier and Bertha Chambers E.; m. Marjorie Claire Wood, Nov. 27, 1945; children: Nancy, Edwin, Marjorie, Jane and Jill (twins), Carol. B.S., U. Ga., 1936; M.D., Johns Hopkins U., 1940. Diplomate: Am. Bd. Internal Medicine, also recertified. Intern Hartford (Conn.) Hosp., 1940-42; resident in medicine Balt. City Hosp., 1946-47; fellow in pathology Hosp. of U. Pa., Phila., 1947-48; practice medicine specializing in internal medicine, Atlanta, 1948—; clin. asso. prof. medicine Emory U. Sch. Medicine, 1972—; adj. prof. medicine Sch. Pharmacy, Mercer U., 1980—; chief of staff Ga. Baptist Med. Center, Atlanta, 1973-79; pres. Atlanta Blue Shield, 1968-70. Contbr. articles to profl. jours. Served to maj. M.C. AUS, 1942-46. Fellow A.C.P. (gov. Ga. 1972-76), Am. Coll. Chest Physicians; mem. Diabetes Assn. Atlanta (pres. 1958), Ga. Diabetes Assn. (pres. 1965), Med. Assn. Atlanta (Pres. 1973), Ga. Soc. Internal Medicine (pres. 1963), Am. Soc. Internal Medicine (pres. 1972-73), So. Med. Assn. (pres. 1981-82), Med. Assn. GA., AMA, Am. Heart Assn., Inst. Medicine Nat. Acad. Scis. Republican. Methodist. Club: Cherokee Town and Country. Home: 500 Westover Dr NW Atlanta GA 30305 Office: 340 Boulevard NE Atlanta GA 30312

EVANS, ELLIS DALE, educator, psychologist; b. Topeka, Nov. 6, 1934; s. Ellis Meredith and Ruth Alice (Burchinal) E.; m. Cynthia Ann McClure, Dec. 23, 1961; children—Jennifer Ann, Alicia Ruth. B.Music Edn., U. Kans., 1956; M.S. in Edn, Ind. U., 1962, Ed.D., 1964. Tchr. Shawnee Mission, Kans., 1957; field rep. Delta Upsilon, 1960-61; research asst., teaching asso. Ind. U., 1961-64; mem. faculty U. Wash., 1964—, prof. ednl. psychology, 1971—; spl. instr. Shoreline Community Coll., Seattle, 1973-75; cons. in field. Author: Development and Classroom Learning, 1973, Children and Youth; Psychosocial Development, 1973, rev. edit., 1978, Contemporary Influences in Early Childhood Education, 1975, The Transition to Teaching, 1976; cons. editor: Charles E. Merrill Pubs.; Author also articles. Active local music orgns. Shoreline Schs. Served to capt. USAF, 1957-60. Fellow U.S. Office Edn., 1970-71.; Mem. Am. Psychol. Assn., Am. Ednl. Research Assn., Nat. Assn. Edn. Young Children, Nat. Soc. Study of Edn., Soc. for Research in Child Devel., Phi Delta Kappa, Omicron Delta Kappa, Delta Upsilon. Home: 19045 46th St NE Seattle WA 98155

EVANS, ELLSWORTH E., lawyer; b. Cedar Rapids, Iowa, 1903; 2 children. LL.B., John Marshall Law Sch., 1928. Bar: S.D. bar 1928. Mem. firm Davenport, Evans, Hurwitz & Smith; former state's atty. and asst. atty. gen. Fellow Internat. Acad. Trial Lawyers; mem. Am., Minnehaha County bar assns., State Bar S.D. (pres. 1958-59), Am. Coll. Trial Lawyers. Address: Nat Res Bldg Sioux Falls SD 57102

EVANS, EMORY GIBBONS, educator, historian; b. Richmond, Va., Jan. 21, 1928; s. Wallace R. and Margaret (Strickl) E.; m. Winifred Burton, Dec. 19, 1953; children—Jeffrey, Christopher, Philip. B.A., Randolph-Macon Coll., 1950; M.A., U. Va., 1954; Ph.D., 1957. Instr. Darlington Sch., Rome, Ga., 1950-52, U. Pitts., 1958-60, asst. prof., 1960-64; instr. U. Md., College Park, 1956-58, prof., chmn. dept. history, 1976—; asso. prof. No. Ill. U., DeKalb, 1964-68, prof., 1968—, chmn. history dept., 1964-74, acting v.p. and provost, 1975-76; vis. prof. U. Va., Charlottesville, 1969-70. Author: Thomas Nelson of Yorktown: Revolutionary Virginian, 1975, also essays in books, periodicals, mags. Served with AUS, 1946. Recipient grants-in-aid, summers; Am. Philos. Soc., 1959, 64; Colonial Williamsburg, Inc., 1959, 60, 61, 62, 64. Mem. Am. Hist. Soc., AAUP, Orgn. Am. Historians, So. Hist. Assn., Va., Md. hist socs. Home: 12910 Forest View Dr Beltsville MD 20705

EVANS, ERSEL ARTHUR, manufacturing company executive; b. Trenton, Nebr., July 17, 1922; s. Arthur E. and Mattie Agnes (Perkins) E.; m. Patricia A. Powers, Oct. 11, 1945; children: Debra Lynn (dec.), Paul Arthur. B.A., Reed Coll., Portland, Oreg., 1947; Ph.D., Oreg. State U., 1950. Registered profl. engr., Calif. With Gen. Electric Co., 1951-67, supr. ceramics research and devel., Hanford, Wash., 1961-64; mgr. plutonium devel. Vallecitos Lab., Pleasanton, Calif., 1964-67; mgr. fuels and materials dept. Battelle Meml. Inst., Richland, Wash., 1967-70; with Westinghouse Electric Corp., 1970—; v.p. Westinghouse Hanford Co., Richland, 1972—; tech. dir. Hanford Engrng. Devel. Lab., 1976—; mem. vis. com. Coll. Engrng., U. Wash., Seattle, 1974—. Author. Bd. dirs. Mid-Columbia Mental Health Center, Richland, 1975—. Served with USNR, 1943-45. DuPont fellow, 1950-51; grantee Research Corp. Am., 1949-50; recipient Westinghouse Order of Merit. Fellow Am. Nuclear Soc. (Spl. Merit award 1964, Performance award 1980), Am. Inst. Chemists, Am. Soc. Metals, Am. Ceramic Soc.; mem. Nat. Acad. Engrng., Phi Kappa Phi. Patentee in field. Home: 2033 Weiskopf Ct Richland WA 99352 Office: PO Box 1970 Richland WA 99352 *Inspiration and guidance for my career have often been provided by Justice Oliver Wendell Holmes, "... certainty generally is illusion, and repose is not the destiny of man." (Harvard Law Review 1897)*

EVANS, FRANCIS COPE, ecologist; b. Phila., Dec. 2, 1914; s. Edward Wyatt and Jacqueline Pascal (Morris) E.; m. Rachel Worthington Brooks, June 12, 1942; children—Kenneth Richardson, Katharine Cope, Edward Wyatt II, Rachel Howe. B.S., Haverford Coll., 1936; D.Phil. (Rhodes scholar), Oxford U., 1939; Claypole fellow, U. Calif., Berkeley, 1939-40. Research asst. Hooper Found., San Francisco, 1939-41; jr. zoologist U. Calif., Davis, 1941-43; instr., asst. prof. Haverford (Pa.) Coll., 1943-48, acting dean, 1944; asst. prof., assoc. prof. U. Mich., Ann Arbor, 1948-59; prof., assoc. dir. E.S. George Res., 1959-82; prof. emeritus, 1982—. Editor publs.: Mus. Zoology, Ann Arbor, 1968-78; Contbr. sci. articles to profl. jours. Recipient Painton award Cooper Ornithol. Soc., 1963; Guggenheim fellow, 1962-63; Erskine fellow U. Canterbury, Christchurch, N.Z., 1976-77. Fellow AAAS; mem. Ecol. Soc. Am. (pres. 1983), Brit. Ecol. Soc., Am. Soc. Naturalists, Soc. for Study Evolution. Quaker. Home: 2019 Day St Ann Arbor MI 48104 Office: 4129 Natural Sci Bldg U Mich Ann Arbor MI 48109

EVANS, FRANKLIN BACHELDER, emeritus advertising educator; b. Chgo., Feb. 9, 1922; s. Franklin B. and Arline (Brown) E.; m. Barbara V. Both, Sept. 16, 1943; children: Mary A., Amy B., Geoffrey B., Christopher G. A.A., U. Chgo., 1941, A.B., 1943, M.B.A., 1954, Ph.D., 1959. Asst. prof. mktg. U. Chgo., 1957-64; prof. mktg. U. Hawaii, 1964-69; prof. advt. Northwestern U., 1969-80, prof. emeritus, 1981—; cons. to bus. and industry. Contbr. articles to profl. jours. Served with AUS, 1943-45; CBI. Decorated Bronze Star. Mem. Am. Statis. Assn., Am. Sociol. Assn., Am. Mktg. Assn., Am. Acad. Advt., AAAS, AAUP, Psi Upsilon. Research on consumer motivation. Home: Box 32 Macatawa MI 49434

EVANS, FREDERICK HARRIS, otolaryngologist; b. Terre Haute, Ind., Feb. 1, 1916; s. Frederick H. and Grace (Wilson) E.; m. Shirley Richardson, Jan. 10, 1939; children: Frederick Harris III, Noel G. B.A., Fisk U., 1941; M.D., Meharry Med. Coll., 1944; postgrad., Columbia U., Harvard U. Diplomate: Am. Bd. Ophthalmology and Otolaryngology. Intern Freedmens Hosp., Washington, 1944-46; gen. practice, Indpls., 1946-52; resident otolaryngology Ind. U. Med. Center, Marion County Gen. Hosp., 1955-58; practice medicine specializing in otolaryngology, Indpls., 1958—; chmn. otolaryngology sect. Methodist Hosp., 1966-70, mem. staff, 1970—, St. Vincent Hosp.; asso. otalaryngolgy dept. Ind. U. Med. Center, 1958—; mem. exec. bd. Ind. State Bd. Health. Mem. Indpls. Mus. Art; guarantor Clowes Hall; bd. dirs. Our Lady of Fatima Retreat House, St. Mary's Child Center; trustee Vincennes U. Served as capt. AUS, 1952-54. Decorated Bronze Star; recipient Wisdom award of Honor, Wisdom Hall Fame; Brotherhood award NCCJ, 1974. Fellow Am. Acad. Otolaryngology-Head and Neck Surgery; mem. Nat. Med. Assn., Hoosier State Med. Soc. (pres. 1965-66), Ind., Marion County, Aesculapian med. socs., Ind. Acad. Ophthalmology and Otolaryngology, Pan Pacific Surg. Assn., N.Y. Acad. Scis., Pan-Am. Assn. Oto-Rhino-Laryngology and Broncho-Esophagology, Am. Bridge Assn., Am. Contract Bridge League, NAACP (life), Nat. Urban League, Nat. Council Cath. Men, Sigma Pi Psi, Kappa Alpha Psi. Roman Catholic. Clubs: Serra Internat. (dir.), Rotary.). Home: 1705 Kessler Blvd W Dr Indianapolis IN 46208 Office: 3901 N Meridian St Indianapolis IN 46208

EVANS, FREDERICK JOHN, psychologist; b. Wollongong, Australia, Nov. 17, 1937; came to U.S., 1963; s. Frederick John and Phyllis Lurline (Wiffen) E.; m. Barbara Joan Marcelo, June 8, 1968; children: Christopher Arthur, David Troy, Mark Fredrick, Diana Joy. B.A. Honors Class I, U. Sydney, Australia, 1959, Ph.D., 1965. Teaching fellow U. Sydney, 1959-63; research psychologist Mass. Mental Health Center, 1963-64; from instr. psychology in psychiatry U. Pa. Sch. Medicine, Phila., 1965-66, to asso. prof. psychiatry, 1972-81, asso. prof. psychology, 1974-79; sr. research psychologist Unit for Exptl. Psychiatry Inst. of Pa. Hosp., Phila., 1964-79; vis. fellow psychology Yale U., 1970-71; trustee Inst. Exptl. Psychiatry, Boston, 1970-79; adj. prof. U. Medicine and Dentistry N.J.-Rutgers Med. Sch., 1979—; dir. research div. Carrier Found., Belle Mead, N.J. Adv. editor: Internat. Jour. Clin. and Exptl. Hypnosis, 1968-69; assoc. editor, 1969—; cons. editor: Jour. Abnormal Psychology, 1979-85; co-editor: Functional Disorders of Memory, 1979, Springer Series in Behavior Modification and Behavioral Medicine; contbr. chpts. to textbooks, articles to profl. jours. Served to capt. Australian Army, 1961-63. Fulbright grantee, 1963-66. Fellow AAAS, Am. Psychol. Assn. (div. 30 program chmn. 1972, chmn. ethics and standards com. 1972-75, sec.-treas. 1973-75, pres. 1978-79), Am. Soc. Clin. Hypnosis (chmn. liaison com. 1975—), N.J. Psychol. Soc., Pa. Psychol. Soc., Soc. Clin. and Exptl. Hypnosis (co-chmn. scientific program 1970, chmn. research workshop 1971, 76, 79, 80, sec. 1973-75, co-chmn. publs. com. 1975-77, v.p. 1979-81, pres. 1981-83); mem. Assn. Psychophysiol. Study of Sleep, Am. Pain Soc. (dir. 1977-80), Australian Psychol. Assn., Internat. Assn. Study of Pain, Internat. Soc. Hypnosis (sec.-treas. 1973-79, co-chmn. 7th Internat. Congress Hypnosis 1976, vice chmn. bd. dirs. 10th Internat. Congress 1985), Soc. Exptl. Social Psychologists. Home: 36 Knickerbocker Belle Mead NJ 08502 Office: Carrier Found Belle Mead NJ 08502

EVANS, GEORGE R., bishop; b. Denver, Sept. 22, 1922. Student, Notre Dame U., St. Thomas Sem., Colo., Apollinare Univ., Rome. Ordained priest Roman Catholic Ch., 1947. Ordained titular bishop Tubyza and aux. bishop, Denver, 1969—. Office: St Rose of Lima Ch 1320 W Nevada Pl Denver CO 80223 *

EVANS, GEORGE ROBERT, JR., graphic arts executive; b. San Antonio, June 24, 1931; s. George Robert and Maude Ellen (Davis) E.; m. Alma Emma Behling, Feb. 23, 1952 (dec.); children: Sandra, Robert, Teri, John, James, Patrick, Michelle.; m. Charlotte P. Mortimer, Sept. 4, 1982. B.S., Wagner Coll., 1953; postgrad., U. Pa., 1963-64, UCLA, 1967-69. Works mgr., dir. mktg., v.p., gen. mgr. U.S. Gypsum Co., 1953-69; pres. U.S. Gypsum Export Co., 1966-68; pres., chief exec. officer, dir. Kingsport Press, Inc., Tenn., 1969-71; group v.p. Arcata Nat. Corp., N.Y.C., 1971—; pres., chief exec. officer Arcata Graphics Corp., N.Y.C., 1971-73; dir., exec. v.p., chief operating officer Arcata Corp., Menlo Park, Calif., 1973-82, pres., chief exec. officer, 1982—; dir. Shaklee Corp.; mem. adv. com. Rochester Inst. Tech.; dir. Environ. Conservation Bd. of Graphic Industries. Trustee Wagner Coll.; mem. Nat. UN Com., 1971—; chmn. U. Tenn. Devel. Council. Mem. Book Mfg. Inst. (dir.), Printing Industries Am., Conf. Bd., Graphic Arts Tech. Found. (dir.), Newcomen Soc. N.Am. Lutheran. Clubs: Commonwealth of Calif., San Francisco Stock Exchange, Rotary. Home: 47 Ralston Rd Atherton CA 94025 Office: 700 Kings Mountain Rd Woodside CA 94062

EVANS, GEORGE RUSSELL, financial company executive; b. Hubbard, Ohio, Apr. 25, 1910; s. Evan E. and Ellen L. (Thomas) E.; m. Arabelle Chute, Sept. 5, 1936; children: Jill Evans Farris, Jane Evans Hill. B.S. in Bus. Adminstrn, Ohio U., 1933. Case work supr. Trumble County (Ohio) Relief Commn., 1933-35; with, Beneficial Corp, Wilmington, Del., 1935—, mem. exec. com., 1975—, vice chmn., pres., dir., 1977—; sr. v.p. Beneficial Mgmt. Corp., Morristown, N.J., 1970-73, exec. v.p., 1973-74, pres., 1974-78, chmn. bd., 1978-79; also dir.; pres. Beneficial Finance Co. of Can., 1974-76, chmn. bd., 1976—, also dir.; chmn. chief exec. officer, chmn. exec. com. Western Auto Supply Co., 1979—; dir. First Tex. Fin. Corp., Spiegel Co., Midland Internat. Corp., Peoples Bank & Trust Co., Beneficial Finance Internat. Corp.; Trustee Hodson Trust. Mem. Nat. Consumer Finance Assn., Nat. Second Mortgage Assn., Assn. Canadian Financial Corps., Phi Delta Theta. Republican. Presbyterian. Clubs: Masons, Shriners, Baltusrol Golf (bd. govs.). Home: 83 Tanglewood Dr Summit NJ 07901 Office: Beneficial Center Peapack NJ 07960

EVANS, GERAINT LLEWELLYN, opera singer; b. Wales, Feb. 16, 1922; s. William John and Gladys May (Thomas) E.; m. Branda Evans Davies, Mar. 27, 1948; children: Alun Grant, Huw Grant. Student, Guildhall Sch. Music; Mus.D. (hon.), U. Wales, 1963, U. Leicester, 1969, Council Nat. Acad. Awards, 1980, U. London, 1982. Prin. baritone, Royal Opera House, appearances include, Covent Garden, London, 1948—, Glyndebourne Festival Opera, 1950—, also, Vienna State Opera, La Scala, Milan, Italy, Met. Opera, N.Y.C., San Francisco Opera, Lyric Opera, Chgo., Salzburg (Germany) Opera, Edinburgh Festival Opera, Paris Opera, Teatro Colon, Buenos Aires, Mexico, City Opera, Welsh Nat. Opera, Scottish Opera, Berlin Opera, Teatr Wielki, Warsaw, Poland. Decorated comdr. Brit. Empire, 1959, knight bachelor, 1969; Fellow Guildhall Sch. Music, 1960; recipient Sir Charles Santley Meml. award Worshipful Co. of Musicians, 1963, Harriet Cohen Internat. Music award, 1967; fellow Royal No. Coll. Music Univ. Coll., Cardiff, 1976, 1978, Jesus Coll., Oxford, 1979, Royal Coll. Music, 1981. Hon. mem. Royal Acad. Music. Home: 17 Highcliffe 32 Albemarle Rd Beckenham Kent England

EVANS, GIL, musician, composer; b. Toronto, Ont., Can., May 13, 1912. Formerly mus. arranger for bands lead by, Claude Thornhill, Miles Davis; now pianist and leader of own band: (with M. Davis) compositions include Sketches of Spain (Grammy award 1960). Winner Down Beat Readers Poll as Best Arranger, 1966, 74-77 *

EVANS, GREGORY THOMAS, justice Supreme Ct. Ont.; b. McAdam, N.B., Can., June 13, 1913; s. Thomas Vincent and Mary Ellen E.; m. Zita Callon, Oct. 1, 1941; children: Thomas, John, Gregory, Rory, Mary, Kerry, Brendan, Catherine, Erin. B.A., St. Joseph's U., 1934; postgrad., Osgoode Hall Law Sch., Toronto, 1939; LL.D., St. Thomas U., Fredericton, N.B., 1963; Ph.D., U. Moncton, 1964. Bar: Called to bar; created queen's counsel 1953. Sr. partner firm Evans, Evans, Bragagnolo, Perras & Sullivan, Timmons, Ont., Can., 1939-63; apptd. to Supreme Ct. Ont., 1963, Ct. Appeal, Ont., 1965; apptd. chief justice High Ct., Supreme Ct., Ont., Toronto, 1976—; vice chmn. Can. Jud. Council, 1981. Pres. Ont. English Catholic Edn. Assn., 1961. Decorated knight comdr. Order St. Gregory the Great. Mem. Canadian Inst. Advanced Legal Studies (v.p.). Roman Catholic. Club: Univ. (Toronto). Office: Osgoode Hall 130 Queen St W Toronto ON M5H 2N5 Canada

EVANS, GROSE, educator, former curator; b. Columbus, Ohio, Dec. 15, 1916; s. Marshall Blakemore and Elizabeth Theodora (Grose) E.; m. Grace Elizabeth Orvis, Jan. 4, 1946; 1 dau., Grace Elizabeth Grose. B.F.A., Ohio State U., 1938, A.M., 1940; Ph.D., John Hopkins U., 1953. Lectr. Nat. Gallery of Art, Washington, 1946-54, asst. curator ednl. work, 1954-58, asso. curator, 1958-60; curator decorative arts Index Am. Design and Extension Service, 1960-70, curator exhbns. and loans, 1970-73, curator decorative arts, 1973, ret., 1973; adj. prof. art history George Washington U., 1973—, lectr. modern art, 1953-56, professorial lectr. theories of art, 1956-61; guest lectr. baroque and modern art Cath. U. Am., 1948-49; guest lectr. modern art Am. U., 1952-53; curriculum dir. Research in Tchr. Tng. Program U.S. Office Edn., 1966, Arts and Humanities Inst., 1967. Author: Subtle Satire of Magnasco, Gazette des Beaux Arts, 1948, Benjamin West and the Taste of His Times, 1959, Van Gogh, 1968. Home: 2308 Glasgow Rd Hollin Hills Alexandria VA 22307 Office: Art Dept George Washington U Washington DC 20052

EVANS, GWYNNE BLAKEMORE, educator; b. Columbus, Ohio, Mar. 31, 1912; s. Marshall Blakemore and Theodora (Grose) E.; m. Florence Elizabeth Richey, June 1, 1943; children—Michael Blakemore, Pamela Grose. A.B., Ohio State U., 1934; M.A., U. Cin., 1936; Ph.D., Harvard, 1940. Asst. tutor Bklyn. Coll., 1940-41; instr. U. Wis., 1941-42, 45-46, asst. prof., 1946-47, U. Ill., 1947-51, asso. prof., 1951-56, prof., 1956-67; prof. English and lit. Harvard, Cambridge, Mass., 1967-75, Cabot prof. English lit., 1975—. Author: Plays and Poems of William Cartwright, 1951, Supplement Vol. to Variorum I Henry IV, 1957, Shakespearean Prompt-Books of the 17th Century, 6 vols, 1960-80, Complete Works of Shakespeare (textual edit.), 1974; Editor: Jour. of English and Germanic Philology, 1955-62; editorial bd.: Publs. of Modern Lang. Assn, 1963-69. Served with Signal Corps Intelligence AUS, 1942-45. Dexter Traveling fellow, 1940; Guggenheim fellow, 1948-49. Mem. Renaissance English Text Soc., Acad. Lit. Studies. Home: 985 Memorial Dr 201 Cambridge MA 02138 Office: Warren House Harvard Cambridge MA 02138

EVANS, HAROLD J., plant physiologist, biochemist, educator; b. Franklin, Ky., Feb. 19, 1921; s. James H. and Allie (Uhls) E.; m. Elizabeth Dunn, Dec. 14, 1946; children: Heather Mary, Pamela. B.S., U. Ky., 1946, M.S., 1948; Ph.D. (Cook-Vorhees fellow), Rutgers U., 1950. Asst. prof. botany N.C. State U., 1952-54, asso. prof., 1954-57, prof., 1957-61; postdoctoral fellow Johns Hopkins U., Balt., 1952; prof. plant physiology Oreg. State U., Corvallis, 1961—; dir. Lab. for Nitrogen Fixation, 1978—; vis. prof. U. Sussex, Eng., 1967; George A. Miller vis. prof. U. Ill., Urbana, 1973; mem. panel for metabolic biology NSF, 1964-68; mem. U.S.-Japan Coop. Sci. Program, 1976. Contbr. articles to profl. jours. Recipient Hoblitzelle Nat. award Tex. Research Found., 1964; Basic Research award Oreg. State U., 1965; N.W. Sci. award Gov. Oreg., 1967; named Disting. Alumnus U. Ky., 1975; recipient George G. Ferguson Disting. Prof. award and Milton Harris research award Oreg. State U., 1983. Mem. Am. Soc. Plant Physiologists (pres. 1971, trustee 1977—), Biochem. Soc. (U.K.), Am. Soc. Biol. Chemists, U.S. Nat. Acad. Scis., Sigma Xi (award 1968), Phi Kappa Phi. Democrat. Home: 2939 Mulkey St Corvallis OR 97330 Office: Lab for Nitrogen Fixation Research Oreg State U Corvallis OR 97331

EVANS, HARRISON SILAS, psychiatrist, ednl. adminstr.; b. Monroe, Iowa, Aug. 4, 1911; s. Clifton and Coral Aletha (Oldham) E.; m. Ruth Harding, Feb. 15, 1934; children: Judith Ann, Richard Fuller. Student, Union Coll., 1929-31; M.D., Loma Linda U., 1935. Diplomate: Am. Bd. Psychiatry and Neurology. Intern Los Angeles County Hosp., 1935-36; resident in psychiatry Harding Hosp., Worthington, Ohio, 1936-39, co-dir. hosp., 1942; pvt. practice psychiatry, Worthington, 1936-62; asso. prof. neurology and psychiatry Ohio State U., Columbus, 1946-62; prof., chmn. dept. psychiatry Loma Linda (Calif.) U., 1962—; dean Sch. Medicine, 1975-77, v.p. med. affairs, 1976-79, 82—. Contbr. articles to profl. jours. Bd. dirs. Harding Hosp., Worthington, 1974—. Served to lt. col. AUS, 1942-46. Life fellow Am. Psychiat. Assn.; mem. Am., Calif. med. assns., Am. Acad. Psychoanalysis, Central Neuropsychiat. Hosp. Assn. (past pres.), Nat. Assn. Pvt. Psychiat. Hosps. (past pres.), Alpha Omega Alpha. Republican. Seventh-day Adventist. Home: 11553 Hillcrest Ct Loma Linda CA 92354 Office: Loma Linda U Loma Linda CA 92354

EVANS, HOWARD ENSIGN, educator, entomologist; b. East Hartford, Conn., Feb. 23, 1919; s. Archie J. and Adella (Ensign) E.; m. Mary Alice Dietrich, June 6, 1954; children: Barbara, Dorothy, Timothy. B.A., U. Conn., 1940; M.S., Cornell U., 1941, Ph.D., 1949. Asst. prof. Kans. State Coll., Manhattan, 1949-52; asst. prof. entomology Cornell U., 1954-59; asso. curator Mus. Comparative Zoology, Harvard U., 1959-63, curator, 1963-69, Alexander Agassiz prof. zoology, 1969-73; prof. entomology Colo. State U., Fort Collins, 1973—. Author: Song I Sing, 1950, Studies on the Comparative Ethology of Digger Wasps of the Genus Bembix, 1957, Wasp Farm, 1963 (nominated for Nat. Book award 1964), The Comparative Ethology and Evolution of the Sand Wasps, 1966, Life on a Little Known Planet, 1968, (with M.J.W. Eberhard) The Wasps, 1970, (with M.A. Evans) William Morton Wheeler, Biologist, 1970, Australia A Natural History, 1983, Insect Biology, 1984; Contbr. (with M.A. Evans) articles to profl. jours. Served to 2d lt. AUS, 1942-45. Mem. Soc. Study Evolution, Nat. Acad. Scis. Home: 304 Off Shore Rd Fort Collins CO 80524

EVANS, HOWARD MOUZON, retail co. exec.; b. Galax, Va., Oct. 31, 1922; s. Robert Lee and Blanche (Bradley) E.; m. Carole Jeanne Pugh, Jan. 3, 1944; children—Larry H., H. Stephen, Suzanne. Student, U. Tenn., 1941-42, Niagara U., 1943. Mgmt. trainee J.C. Penney Co., Knoxville, Tenn., 1946-52, mgr., Norfolk, Va., Audubon, N.J., Wheeling, W.Va., also; Denver, 1952-68, v.p., N.Y.C., 1969-80, sr. v.p., 1981—. Bd. dirs. Nat. Goodwill Industries Am., Council Better Bus. Burs. Served with C.E. U.S. Army, 1943-46. Mem. Am. Mktg. Assn., Assn. Nat. Advertisers Inc. Club: Rotary. Home: 77 Colt Rd Summit NJ 07901 Office: 1301 Ave of Americas New York NY 10019

EVANS, HOWARD VERNON, educator; b. Red Granite, Wis., Sept. 29, 1922; s. Robert L. and Ethel (Newbold) E.; m. Charlotte Buff, July 4, 1947; children—Robert Thomas, Janice Elizabeth. Ph.B., U. Wis., 1948, M.S., 1950, Ph.D., 1955. Asst. dir. edn. U.S. Armed Forces Inst., 1952-56; prof. history, dean of coll. Muskingum Coll., 1956-67, v.p. acad. affairs, dean of coll., 1967-69; asso. prof. history Central Mich. U., 1969-71; prof. history 1972, chmn. dept. history, 1974-76. Author: Nootka Sound Controversy in Anglo-French Diplomacy, 1790, Women Artists in Eighteenth Century France. Served to lt. col., inf. AUS, 1942-46. Mem. Mich. Acad. Sci., Arts and Letters, Am. Soc. Eighteenth-Century Studies, Soc. French Hist. Studies, Am. Hist. Assn., Phi Eta Sigma, Phi Alpha Theta. Presbyterian. Club: Rotary. Home: 30 Cedar Dr Mount Pleasant MI 48858

EVANS, HUGH E., pediatrician; b. N.Y.C., July 6, 1934; s. David and Geraldine (Krebs) E.; m. Ruth L. Orloff, June 5, 1960; children: Margo Lynn, Marc Douglas. A.B. cum laude, Columbia U., 1954; M.D., State U. N.Y., Downstate Med. Center, 1958. Intern Johns Hopkins Hosp., Balt., 1958-59, asst. resident, 1959-60; sr. asst. resident NIH, Bethesda, Md., 1960-62, chief resident outpatient dept., 1962-63; practice medicine, Bellaire, Ohio, 1963-66; asso. dir. pediatrics Harlem Hosp. Center, N.Y.C., 1966-73; dir. dept. pediatrics Jewish Hosp. and Med. Center, Bklyn., 1973—; asso. clin. prof. pediatrics Columbia U., 1968-73; prof. pediatrics State U. N.Y., Downstate Med. Center, Bklyn., 1973—; cons. Catholic Med. Center, St. Johns Episcopal Hosp., Englewood (N.J.) Hosp., Hackensack (N.J.) Hosp.; trustee Bergen-Passiac County Lung Assn., 1973—. Author: (with Leonard Glass) Perinatal Medicine, 1976, Lung Diseases of Children, 1979; contbr. articles to profl. jours. Served to sr. asst. surgeon USPHS, 1960-62. Mem. Soc. Pediatric Research, Harvey Soc., Am. Soc. Microbiology, Am. Acad. Pediatrics, Am. Thoracic Soc., Am. Pediatric Soc., Soc. Exptl. Biology and Medicine, N.Y. Pediatric Soc. (pres. 1982-83), Bklyn. Acad. Pediatrics (v.p. 1976, pres. 1977), Infectious Diseases Soc., Alpha Omega Alpha. Home: 165 Serpentine Rd Tenafly NJ 07670 Office: 555 Prospect Pl Brooklyn NY 11238

EVANS, JACK W., supermarkets and drug stores company executive; b. Dallas, 1922. Student, So. Meth. U., Birmingham So. Coll., Harvard Bus. Sch. With Kroger Co., Dallas, 1955-66; exec. v.p. Tom Thumb Stores Inc. subs., Dallas, 1966-67, pres., 1967—; pres., dir. Cullum Cos. Inc., Dallas; pres. Page Drug Stores, Dallas; dir. White Rock Bank, Dallas-Fort Worth Airport. Mayor City of Dallas, until 1983; pres. Dallas United Way; vice chmn., treas., bd. dirs. Children's Med. Ctr. Served with USAAF, 1942-45. Office: Cullum Cos Inc 14303 Inwood Rd Dallas TX 75234 *

EVANS, JAMES HURLBURT, corporate executive; b. Lansing, Mich., June 26, 1920; s. James L. and Marie (Hurlburt) E.; m. Mary Johnston Head, 1984; children by previous marriage: Eric Bertram, Carol Ruth, Joan McLeod. A.B., Centre Coll., 1943; J.D., U. Chgo., 1948; LL.D. (hon.), Millikin U., 1978. Bar: Ill. 1949. Atty., loan officer Harris Trust & Savs. Bank, Chgo., 1948-56; sec.-treas. Reuben H. Donnelley Corp., Chgo., 1956-57, v.p., N.Y.C., 1957-62, also dir., 1961, financial v.p., 1962-65, dir., 1962-77; pres. Seamen's Bank for Savs., N.Y.C., 1965-68, chmn. bd., 1968, trustee, 1965-78; pres. Union Pacific Corp., 1969-77, chmn., chief exec. officer, 1977-83, chmn., 1977—, dir., 1969—; dir. U.P. R.R., 1965—, vice chmn. bd., 1969-77, 83—, chmn. bd., 1977-83; vice chmn. bd., dir. Mo. Pacific R.R. Co., 1983—; dir. AT&T, Citicorp, Citibank N.A., Gen. Motors Corp., Met. Life Ins. Co. Bd. govs. N.Y. Hosp.; trustee Union Pacific Found., Rockefeller Bros. Fund, U. Chgo., George C. Marshall Research Found.; chmn. bd. trustees Centre Coll. Ky.; trustee Nat. Recreation Found., pres., 1971-75; bd. dirs. Council Fin. Aid to Edn.; founding chmn., life trustee Nat. Recreation and Park Assn.; founding mem. Citizens Adv. Com. on Environ. Quality, 1966-70; bd. govs. Am. Nat. Red Cross, 1970-76, nat. fund chmn., 1974-76; bd. dirs. Catalyst United Way Tri-State; bd. mgrs. N.Y. Bot. Garden. Served to lt. USNR, 1943-46. Mem. Am., Chgo. bar assns., Am. Petroleum Inst. (past mem. exec. com.), Nat. Petroleum Council, Bus. Roundtable (past co-chmn.), Bus. Council (exec. com.), Fgn. Policy Assn. (gov.), Pilgrims of U.S., Phi Beta Kappa, Omicron Delta Kappa, Delta Kappa Epsilon. Presbyterian. Clubs: Down Town Assn., River, Racquet and Tennis, Links, Knickerbocker (N.Y.C.); Metropolitan (Washington). Office: 345 Park Ave New York NY 10154

EVANS, JERRY NORMAN, director; b. Santa Monica, Calif.; s. William and Jeanne (Davidson) E.; m. Meta Baron, Oct. 3, 1971; children: Allison, Katlin. B.A. in English Lit., U. Calif., Berkeley, 1958; M.F.A., Yale U., 1962. Asst. prof. theatre and speech Fairleigh Dickinson U., 1963-68; dir. artistic involvement Upward Bound, 1967-70; Playwrights Conf. TV dir. O'Neill Theatre Center, Waterford, Conn., 1976. Staff asst. dir., stage mgr.: Somerset and Another World, NBC-TV, N.Y.C., 1968-72; asst. producer and dir.: Secret Storm and Love of Life, CBS-TV, N.Y.C., 1972-75; dir.: Ryan's Hope, Labine-Mayer Prodns., ABC-TV, N.Y.C., 1976—. Recipient Emmy awards for outstanding direction, 1979, 80. Mem. Dirs. Guild Am., Nat. Acad. TV Arts, Scis. Jewish. Home: 1 Sunset Dr Summit NJ 07901 Office: ABC Studio 16-433 W 53d St New York NY 10019

EVANS, JOHN, artist; b. Sioux Falls, S.D., Aug. 24, 1932; s. William Voil and Alice Loretta (Sauers) E.; m. Margaret McConnell, Dec. 3, 1976; children—India Alexandra and Honor Flavia (twins). B.F.A., Art Inst. Chgo., 1961, M.F.A., 1963. Author collection of 38 collage books, 1966-75; Exhbns. include, Phila Acad. Fine Art, 1964, Sonraed Gallery, N.Y.C., 1971, Rubin-Magnusson Galeri, Copenhagen, Blue Parrot Gallery, N.Y.C., 1972, Newport Harbor Art Mus., Newport Beach, Calif., 1974, Buecker & Harpsichords, N.Y.C., 1976, Davidson (N.C.) Nat. Drawing Competition, Kornblee Gallery, N.Y.C., U. Calif., La Jolla, 1977, Gruenebaum Gallery, N.Y.C., Franklin Furnace, N.Y.C., 1978, Dayton (Ohio) Art Inst., 1978-79, Key Gallery, N.Y.C., 1979, Cordier & Ekstrom Gallery, N.Y.C., 1980, 81, Alex Rosenberg Gallery, N.Y.C., 1980, Summit (N.J.) Art Center, Eastern Mont. State U., Billings, Arts Club, Chgo., 1982, Gracie Mansion Gallery, N.Y.C., numerous mail-art exhbns., U.S. and abroad. Served with U.S. Army, 1953-55. Home: 199 E 3d St New York NY 10009 Office: Box 1004 New York NY 10009

EVANS, J(OHN) HARVEY, naval architect; b. Rochester, N.Y., May 1, 1914; s. John and Mabel (Harvey) E.; m. Edith Miriam Price, July 3, 1943; children: Harvey David, Gail Edith. B.Engring., U. Liverpool, Eng., 1937. Engr. and supr. Bethlehem Steel Co., 1937-47; mem. faculty Mass. Inst. Tech., 1947—, prof. naval architecture, 1961-78, emeritus prof., 1978—; cons. to industry, 1947—; mem. maritime transp. research bd. Nat. Acad. Sci., 1965-68, 75-78. Editor; major author: Ship Structural Design Concepts, Ship Structural Design Concepts, 2d cycle, 1983; Contbr. articles to profl. jours. Del. Internat. Ship Structures Congress, 1961—; chmn. 6th congress, 1976. Fellow Royal Instn. Naval Architects, Soc. Naval Architects and Marine Engrs. (hon. mem., Davidson medal 1976, council 1966-69, 73—, exec. com. 1969-70, v.p. 1977-80, hon. v.p. 1980—); mem. ASME, Soc. Naval Architects Japan, Sigma Xi, Tau Beta Pi. Home: 8 Doran Farm Ln Lexington MA 02173 Office: Mass Inst Tech Cambridge MA 02139

EVANS, JOHN JAMES, management consultant; b. N.Y.C., Aug. 12, 1923; s. James J. and Mary (Galan) E. Student, U. Nebr., 1943; B.B.A. cum laude, CCNY, 1948, M.B.A., 1950; postgrad., NYU, 1951. Certified mgmt. cons. Mgr. Roman Silversmiths, 1946-49; systems Addressograph-Multigraph Corp., 1949-53; mgmt. cons., v.p. Fairbanks Assos., Greenwich, Conn., Fairbanks Assocs., N.Y.C. and Washington, 1953-59; pres., 1959—. Contbr. articles to profl. jours. Served with AUS, 1943-46; ETO. Mem. Inst. Mgmt. Consultants, Am. Soc. Assn. Execs., Am. Mgmt. Assn., Beta Gamma Sigma. Office: PO Box 1009 Alamo CA 94507

EVANS, JOHN JOSEPH, III, banker; b. Lancaster, Pa., Oct. 10, 1928; s. John Joseph and Lucille Johnson (Dye) E.; m. Noreen Blakeley, June 16, 1951; children: Anne, John J. IV, Elizabeth. B.A., Wesleyan U., 1950. Vice pres. Mfrs. Hanover Trust Co., N.Y.C., 1963-70, sr. v.p., 1970-73, exec. v.p., 1973—, also dir. Mem. gen. adminstrv. bd. Jr. warden St. John's Episcopal Ch., Cold Spring Harbor, N.Y., 1976; treas. St. Paul's and St. Mary's Schs. Com., L.I. Cathedral Chpt., Garden City, N.Y. Served with USAF, 1951-52. Mem. Bank Adminstrn. Inst., Am. Bankers Assn. (vice chmn. exec. com. ops. div.). Republican. Clubs: Racquet and Tennis (N.Y.C.); Cold Spring Harbor Beach. Office: 350 Park Ave New York NY 10022 *

EVANS, JOHN LESLIE, member Canadian Parliament, economist; b. Seattle, July 12, 1941; emigrated to Can., 1970; s. Leslie Nathaniel and Edith Alice (Williams) E.; m. Ann Elizabeth Powell, Dec. 10, 1966 (div. 1974); children: Julie Ann, Susan Elizabeth; m. Suzanne Duval, Oct. 18, 1975. B.A., Central Wash. U., 1964; M.B.A., U. Wash., 1966, Ph.D., 1968. Prof. U. N.C., Chapel Hill, 1968-70, U. B.C., Vancouver, 1970-75; dir. Govt. of Can., Ottawa, 1975-79; mem. Can. Parliament, 1979—, parliamentary sec., 1980-82. Mem. Can. Econ. Assn., Am. Econ. Assn. Mem. Liberal Party. Roman Catholic. Clubs: Royal Vancouver Yacht; Carlton Golf and Yacht (Manotick, Ont.). Home: 17 Impala Crescent Ottawa ON Canada K1B 9V7 Office: House of Commons Ottawa ON Canada K1A 0A6

EVANS, JOHN MARTIN, educator; b. Cardiff, Wales, Feb. 2, 1935; s. Evan Arthur and Edith Kathleen (Loveluck) E.; m. Mariella LaFranchi, Aug. 5, 1963; children: Jessica Rachel, Joanna Rebecca. B.A., Jesus Coll., Oxford (Eng.) U., 1958, postgrad., 1958-61; M.A., D.Phil., Merton Coll., 1963. Asst. prof. English Stanford U., 1963-68, assoc. prof., 1968-75, prof., 1975—, assoc. dean humanities and scis., 1977-81. Author: Paradise Lost and the Genesis Tradition, 1968, America: The View From Europe, 1976, The Road From Horton, 1983. Served with RAF, 1953-55. Nat. Endowment for Humanities fellow; Am. Council Learned Socs. grantee. Office: English Dept Stanford U Stanford CA 94305

EVANS, JOHN MARTIN, lawyer; b. Boulder, Colo., Apr. 18, 1911; s. Herbert Silas and Daisy Edith (Hiltner) E.; m. Elizabeth Dulaney Cassidy, Dec. 31, 1936; children: John Martin, Carol Elizabeth (Mrs. William V. Markowitz, Jr.). B.S. in Elec. Engring, U. Colo., 1933; postgrad., George Washington U., 1934-35; LL.B., Yale U., 1937. Bar: Calif. bar 1938, Colo. bar 1942. With Gen. Electric Co., Schenectady, 1933-34, Washington, 1934-35; asso. firm Pillsbury, Madison & Sutro, San Francisco, 1937-42; asst. atty. gen., Colo., 1946-48, 51-60, individual practice law, Denver, 1948-55; partner firm Fuller & Evans, Denver, 1955-80, of counsel, 1980—; instr. U. Denver Law Sch., 1946-47. Sr. warden St. Aidans Episcopal Ch.; dist. chmn. Boy Scouts Am., 1950's; mem. bd. Colo. Chautauqua Assn., 1977-79, pres., 1977-78; Denver chmn. Young Republicans, 1946-48, Colo. chmn., 1948-50, nat. gen. counsel, 1948-50; bd. dirs. Boulder Philharmonic Soc., 1960-66, pres., 1963-66; mem. Engring. Devel. Bd., U. Colo. Served with USN, 1942-45. Mem. Am., Calif., Colo., Denver bar assns., Denver Law Club, Tau Beta Pi, Sigma Tau, Sigma Pi Sigma, Eta Kappa Nu, Phi Kappa Psi. Clubs: University (Denver); Univ. (Boulder); Boulder Country, Cactus, Torch, Town and Gown. Home: 500 13th St Boulder CO 80302 Office: 900 Equitable Bldg Denver CO 80202

EVANS, JOHN REESE, government official; b. Bisbee, Ariz., June 1, 1932; s. Marius Oman and Mary Helena (Huish) E.; m. Gale Gagon, Dec. 18, 1964; children: John, Michael, Richard, Marianne, Carolyn. B.S. in Econs, U. Utah, 1957, M.S., 1959. Research asst. Bur. of Econ. and Bus. Research, U. Utah, 1960-61, research analyst, 1961-63, instr. econs., 1962; econs. asst. Sen. Wallace Bennett, Washington, 1963-64; minority staff dir. Com. on Banking, Housing and Urban Affairs, U.S. Senate, 1964-71, profl. staff mem., 1971-73; commr. SEC, Washington, 1973—. Republican. Mormon. Home: 9208 Seven Locks Rd Bethesda MD 20817 Office: 450 5th St NW Washington DC 20549

EVANS, JOHN ROBERT, former university president, physician; b. Toronto, Ont., Can., Oct. 1, 1929; s. William Watson and Mary Evelyn Lucille (Thompson) E.; m. Jean Gay Glassco, 1954; children: Derek, Mark and Michael (twins), Gillian, Timothy, Willa. M.D., U. Toronto, 1952; D.Phil. (Rhodes scholar), Oxford U., 1955; LL.D., Dalhousie U., McMaster U., McGill U., 1972, Queen's U., 1974, Wilfred Laurier U., 1975, York U., 1977, U. Toronto, 1980, U. Western Ont., 1982, Yale U., 1978; D.Sc., Meml. U., 1973, U. Montreal, 1977; D.H.L., Johns Hopkins U., 1978; D.U., U. Ottawa, 1978. Intern Toronto Gen. Hosp., 1952-53, chief resident physician, 1958-59; practice medicine specializing in cardiology, Toronto, 1961—; assoc. dept. medicine U. Toronto Med. Sch., 1961-65, prof., 1972—, pres. univ., 1972-78; dir. population, health and nutrition dept. World Bank, Washington, 1979-83; chmn., chief exec. officer Allelix Inc., Mississauga, Ont., 1983—; physician Toronto Gen. Hosp., 1961-65; dean Faculty Medicine McMaster U., Hamilton, Ont., 1965-72, v.p. health scis., 1967-72.; Dir. Defasco, Inc., Hamilton, Ont., Crown Life Ins. Co., Toronto, Ont., Data Crown Inc. Trustee Rockefeller Found, N.Y.C., 1982—. Decorated companion Order of Can.; Markle scholar, 1960-65. Fellow A.C.P., Royal Coll. Physicians. Home: 58 Highland Ave Toronto ON M4W 2A3 Canada Office: 6850 Goreway Dr Mississauga ON Canada L4V 1P1

EVANS, JOHN VAUGHAN, physicist; b. Manchester, Eng., July 5, 1933; s. Gyril John and Gertrude Veronica (Bayliss) E.; m. Maureen Vervain Patrick, Oct. 19, 1958; children: Carol, David, Lesley. B.Sc. in Physics with honors, Manchester U., 1954, Ph.D., 1957. Leverhulme research fellow Jodrell Bank Exptl. Sta., U. Manchester, 1957-60; mem. staff Lincoln Lab. MIT, Lexington, 1960-66, 67-70; G.A. Miller vis. prof. U. Ill.-Urbana, 1966-67; assoc. group leader surveillance techniques group Lincoln Lab. MIT, 1970-72, group leader, 1972-74, assoc. div. head aerospace div., 1974-77, asst. dir. lab., 1977-83; dir. Haystack Obs., MIT, 1980-83; also prof. meteorology; dir. research COMSAT Labs., Gaithersburg, Md., 1983—. Editor: (with T. Hagfors) Radar Astronomy, 1968; contbr. numerous articles to sci. jours. Served with Royal Brit. Army, 1951-57. Recipient Appleton prize Royal Soc., London, 1954. Fellow IEEE; mem. Am. Geophys. Union, AAAS, Internat. Astron. Union, Internat. Union Radio Scis., Sigma Xi. Unitarian. Club: Cosmos (Washington). Office: COMSAT Labs Gaithersburg MD 20877

EVANS, JOHN VICTOR, governor of Idaho; b. Malad City, Idaho, Jan. 18, 1925; s. David Lloyd and Margaret (Thomas) E.; m. Lola Daniels, 1945; children: David L., John Victor, Martha Anne, Susan Dee, Thomas Daniels. B.A. in Bus. and Econs, Stanford U., 1951. Mem. Idaho Senate, 1953-74, majority leader, 1957-59, minority leader, 1969-74; mayor, Malad, 1960-66, former farmer, rancher, businessman; lt. gov., Idaho, 1975-76, gov., 1977—; past v.p., dir. J.N. Ireland Bank, Malad; past v.p. Bear River Water Users; past pres. Deep Creek Irrigation Co., Oneida R.C. & D. Served with inf. AUS, 1944-46; PTO. Recipient Distinguished Service award for meritorious service during legis. career Assn. Idaho Cities, 1974; Idaho Conservationist of Yr. award, 1978. Mem. Nat. Govs. Assn. (chmn. subcom. on nuclear energy 1979), Western Govs. Assn. (chmn. 1978-79), Am. Legion, VFW, Farm Bur. Democrat. Mem. Ch. of Jesus Christ of Latter-day Saints. Clubs: Masons, Kiwanis, Eagles. Office: Statehouse Boise ID 83720 *

EVANS, JOHN WAINWRIGHT, JR., astrophysicist, geophysicist; b. N.Y.C., May 14, 1909; s. John Wainwright and Edith (Claggett) E.; m. Elizabeth F. Harlan, Aug. 23, 1932; children: Wainwright, Nancy Jane, Jeanne Harlan. A.B., Swarthmore Coll., 1932, Sc.D., 1970; student, U. Pa., 1932-34; A.M., Harvard, 1936, Ph.D., 1938; D.Sc., U. N.Mex., 1967. Tchr. astronomy U. Minn., 1937-38, Mills Coll., 1938-42; research, devel. optical instruments Inst. Optics, U. Rochester, 1942-46; research solar activity and terrestrial effects, devel. telescopes, coronagraphs, spectroprgraphs High Altitude Obs., Boulder, Colo., 1946-52; dir. Sacramento Peak Obs., Sunspot, N.Mex., 1952-75, sr. scientist, 1975-79, Cons., 1979—; leader obs. Eclipse Expdn. to, Sudan, 1952, to Puka Puka, Cook Islands, 1958. Recipient Newcomb Cleveland prize AAAS (with Schwarzschild and Rogerson), 1957; Distinguished Civilian Service award Dept. Def., 1965; Rockefeller Pub. Service award, 1969. Fellow Am. Acad. Arts and Scis., AAAS (past v.p. for astronomy), Optical Soc. Am. (emeritus mem.); mem. Internat. Astron. Union, Am. Astron. Soc. (past rep. NRC, mem. council 1967-70, Geory Ellery Hale prize 1982). Constructed and developed optical theory of birefringent filters, 1940. Home: Box 124 High Rolls NM 88325 Office: Sacramento Peak Observatory: Sunspot NM 88349

EVANS, JOSEPH PATRICK, neurological surgeon, educator; b. La Crosse, Wis., Nov. 29, 1904; s. Edward and Sarah (Thompson) E.; m. Hermene Eisenman, June 24, 1929; children: Mary Frances Bapst, Edward, Frederick Nicholas, Caroline de Villa, Anne W. Lanctot, Hermene Wolfe, John Fisher, Thomas More. Student, U. Notre Dame, 1921-23; A.B., Harvard U., 1925, M.D. cum laude, 1929; M.Sc., McGill U., 1930, Ph.D., 1937; postgrad., U. Chgo., U. Minn., Yale U., Cambridge U., London U., Nat. Hosp., Queen Sq., London, Breslau; D.Sc. (hon.), Loyola U., Chgo., 1964. Diplomate: Am. Bd. Neurol. Surgery (mem. 1944-50), Am. Bd. Psychiatry and Neurology. Asso. prof. surgery charge neurol. surgery U. Cin., 1937-54; prof. emeritus neurol. surgery U. Chgo., 1970; dir. div. neurol. surgery U. Chgo. Clinics, 1954-67; fellow Adlai Stevenson Inst. Internat. Affairs, 1967-69, hon. fellow, 1969; Rockefeller fellow, 1935-36; research asso. physiology Yale U., 1948; med. mission, Austria, 1947; Latin Am. liaison rep. ACS, 1971-76, asst. dir., 1974-79; dir. Internat. Office, 1979-82; cons. Pan Am. Fedn. Assns. Med. Schs., 1971-76; dir. N.Am. Liturgical Conf., 1960-66; mem. investigating commn. Dissent and Disorder, 1968-69. Contbr. articles to med. jours. Washington area rep. Internat. Physicians for Prevention of Nuclear War, 1982—. Recipient Condecoracion de Salud y Merito Asistencial Republic of Colombia. Fellow ACS (Disting. Service award 1981), Academia Medicina, Instituto Chile (hon.); mem. Am. Acad. Neurol. Surgery (pres. 1940-41), AMA, Assn. Research Nervous and Mental Diseases, Am. Assn. Neurol. Surgeons (v.p. 1961-62), Soc. Neurol. Surgeons (v.p. 1963-64, Disting. Service award 1980), Am. Neurol. Assn. (v.p. 1966-67), Sigma Xi, Alpha Omega Alpha, mem. hon. fgn. socs. Roman Catholic. Club: Quadrangle (Chgo.). Home: 10203 Frederick Ave Kensington MD 20895 Office: PO Box 274 Kensington MD 20895

EVANS, LANE, congressman; b. Rock Island, Ill., Aug. 4, 1951; s. Lee Herbert and Joycelene (Saylor) E. B.A., Augustana Coll., 1974; J.D., Georgetown U., 1978. Bar: Ill. 1978. Mng. atty. Western Ill. Legal Assistance Found., Rock Island, 1978-79; mem. nat. staff Kennedy for Pres., Washington, 1978-80; atty., ptnr. Community Legal Clinic, Rock Island, Ill., 1981-82; mem. 96th Congress from 17th Ill. Dist., 1983—. Served with USMC, 1969-71. Mem. AmVets, Am. Legion, Marine Corps League, Vietnam Vets Ill. Democrat. Roman Catholic. Home: 1516 37th St Rock Island IL 61201 Office: US Ho of Reps 1427 Longworth House Office Bldg Washington DC 20515

EVANS, LARRY MELVYN, journalist, chess expert; b. N.Y.C., Mar. 22, 1932; s. Harry and Bella (Shotl) E.; m. Ingrid Carla Hamann, Sept. 15, 1968; children—Karin Louise, Michael Charles, Gary Dean. B.A. with honors, Coll. City N.Y., 1954. Columnist Chgo. Tribune, 1972, Denver Post, 1971—, Washington Post, 1975—; commentator World Chess Tournament ABC-TV, 1972; mem. U.S. Olympic chess team, 1950, 1968, 1970, 76; European chess tour for U.S. State Dept., 1956. Author: Trophy Chess, 1956, New Ideas in Chess, 1958, Modern Chess Openings, 1965, Chess: Beginner to Expert, 1967, Modern Chess Brilliancies, 1970, Chess Catechism, 1970, What's the Best Move?, 1973, Evans on Chess, 1974, World Championship: Fischer v. Spassky, 1972, The Chess Opening for You, 1975; Contbg. editor: Chess Life and Rev, 1950—, Chess Digest, 1970—, Americana Ann, 1972—, Games, 1979. Recipient Internat. Chess Grandmaster award, 1957. Mem. U.S. Chess Fedn. N.Y. chess champion, 1948, U.S. chess champion, 1951, 62, 68, 80, U.S. Open chess champion, 1951, 52, 54, 71, Canadian Open chess champion 1956, 68. Office: Box 1182 Reno NV 89504

EVANS, LAWRENCE BOYD, chemical engineering educator; b. Fort Sumner, N.Mex., Oct. 27, 1934; s. Marval Darrow and Ruby Lee (Lyon) E.; m. Beverley Ann Broughton, Aug. 24, 1963; children: Stephen Alan, Michael Patrick. Student, Central Okla. State U., 1952-54; B.S., U. Okla., 1956; M.S.E., U. Mich., 1957, Ph.D., 1962. Asst. prof. chem. engring. Mass. Inst. Tech., Cambridge, 1962-68, asso. prof., 1968-73, prof., 1973—, exec. officer dept. chem. engring., 1972-74; founder, treas. Cache Corp., Cambridge, 1974-80; pres. Aspen Tech. Inc., 1981—; Donald L. Katz lectr. U. Mich., 1980; cons. to industry, 1962—. Contbr. articles to profl. jours. Mem. Am. Inst. Chem. Engrs. (dir. 1981—, Computing and systems tech. div. award 1982), Am. Chem. Soc., Assn. for Computing Machinery, Nat. Acad. Engring. Mexico (corr.), ASME, Sigma Xi, Tau Beta Pi, Sigma Tau, Phi Kappa Psi. Home: 29 Coolidge Hill Rd Cambridge MA 02138 Office: Dept Chem Engring Mass Inst Tech Cambridge MA 02139

EVANS, LLOYD ROBERTS, physician; b. Columbus, Ohio, Nov. 22, 1911; s. William Lloyd and Cora (Roberts) E.; m. Myrtle Elizabeth Tierney, June 8, 1940; children: Thomas David, Mary Jane. B.A., Ohio State U., 1933; M.D., Harvard U., 1940. Diplomate: Am. Bd. Internal Medicine. Intern Peter Bent Brigham Hosp., Boston, 1941-42; resident in internal medicine Ohio State U. Hosp., Columbus, 1945-47; USPHS fellow Mass. Gen. Hosp., Boston, 1947-48; practice medicine, specializing in internal medicine, Laramie, Wyo., 1948-63, 71—; asso. prof. medicine Ohio State U., Columbus, 1963-65, prof., 1965-71, asst. dean, 1963-69, asso. dean, 1969, univ. vice provost for curriculum, 1969-71; lectr. nursing U. Wyo., 1952-62, clin. prof. medicine, 1977—; mem. Wyo. Bd. Health, 1953-63, Western Interstate Commn. for Higher Edn., 1959-63, zu2Ohio State Med. Bd, Ohio Gov.'s Citizens Com. on Mental Health, 1964-65, Rhodes Scholarship Selection Com. for Wyo., 1963, Nat. Bd. Med. Examiners, 1969-77, mem. exec. com., 1974-77; cons. Ohio Police and Firemen Retirement System, 1968-71; mem. exam. com. Fedn. State Bds. Med. Examiners, 1968—; chmn. FLEX Bd., 1977—. Mem. editorial bd.: Hosp. Med. Staff, 1978-80. Served to maj. U.S. Army, 1942-45. Recipient A.H. Robins Community Service Award Wys. Med. Soc., 1982. Fellow A.C.P.; mem. AMA (task force on future directions for med. edn. 1980—), Am. Hosp. Assn. (council on physicians 1977-80), Sigma Xi, Alpha Omega Alpha, Beta Theta Pi. Congregationalist. Club: Westerners. Lodges: Masons; Rotary. Home: 1059 Alta Vista Dr Laramie WY 82070 Office: Laramie WY 82070

EVANS, LOREN KENNETH, manufacturing company executive; b. Aurora, Ind., May 8, 1928; s. Fred W. and Wilma (Walser) E.; m. Margaret A. Ingels, June 18, 1950; children: Michael, Elaine, Scott. B.S., Ind. U., 1950. Ops. mgr. Arvinyl, Arvin Industries, Columbus, Ind., 1964-68, gen. mgr., 1968-73, pres., 1973-75, Arvin Auto, 1975—, group v.p., 1977—. Served to 1st lt. U.S. Army, 1951-53. Office: 1531 13th St Columbus IN 47201

EVANS, LYNNE SMITH, hospital administrator; b. Montgomery, Ala., July 28, 1947; d. Braxton Wilson and Katie Elizabeth (Reynolds) Smith; m. William H. Evans, Jr., Apr. 7, 1973; 1 son, William Hunter. B.A., U. Ala., 1969; M.P.A., U. Tenn., 1975. Research assoc. Mid-Cumberland Health Planning Council, Nashville, 1970-73; adminstrv. asst. Dede Wallace Mental Health Ctr., Nashville, 1973-74; adminstr. asst. dir. Tenn. Health Facilities Commn., Nashville, 1974-76; assoc. exec. dir. U. Tenn. Hosp., Memphis, 1976-79; adminstr. U. Tenn. William F. Bowld Hosp., Memphis, 1979-83; asst. dir. U. Tenn. Med. Ctr., Memphis, 1983—; mem. project rev. com. Mid-South Med. Ctr. Council, Memphis, 1979-82; adj. prof., clin. preceptor Memphis State U., 1980—; chmn. adv. com., respiratory therapy program N.W. Miss. Jr. Coll., Senatobia, 1982—. Bd. dirs. Lifeblood-Mid-South Regional Blood Ctr., Memphis, 1982—, Memphis chpt. March of Dimes, 1983—; mem. hosp. relations com. Memphis-Shelby Country Med. Soc., 1983—. Mem. Am. Coll. Hosp. Adminstrs., Memphis Young Adminstrs. Forum (sec. 1978, pres. 1979), Memphis Hosp. Council (treas. 1979-80, sec. 1980-81, v.p. 1981-82, pres. 1982-83), Tenn. Hosp. Assn., Am. Acad. Health Adminstrn. (nat. sec. 1977-78), Tenn. Alpha Delta Pi Alumnae Assn. (state pres. 1974-76). Clubs: Zonta Internat. (dir. 1981-83); U. Tenn. Faculty Women's (Memphis)). Office: U Tenn Med Ctr 951 Court Ave Memphis TN 38103

EVANS, MARI, author; b. Toledo. Student, U. Toledo; L.H.D. (hon.), Marian Coll., 1975. Instr. black lit., writer-in-residence Ind. U.-Purdue U. at Indpls., 1969-70; asst. prof. black lit., writer-in-residence Ind. U., Bloomington, 1970-78; asst. prof. Purdue U., 1978-80; vis. asst. prof. Washington U., St. Louis, 1980, Cornell U., 1981-84, Northwestern U., 1972-73; cons. Discovery Grant Program, Nat. Endowment for Arts, 1969-70; cons. ethnic studies Bobbs-Merrill Co., 1970-73. Producer, dir., writer: TV program The Black Experience, WTTV, Indpls., 1968-73; Author: poems Where Is All the Music, 1968, I Am A Black Woman, 1970, Nightstar, 1980; juveniles J.D, 1973, I Look at Me, 1974, Singing Black, 1976, Jim Flying High, 1979; playwright, dir.: River of My Song, 1977; playwright: stage musical Eyes, 1982; editor: (non-fiction) Black Women Writers 1950-80: A Critical Evaluation, 1984; Contbr. poetry to textbooks, anthologies, periodicals. Chmn. lit. adv. panel Ind. Arts Commn., 1976-77; chmn. Statewide Com. for Penal Reform; mem. bd. mgmt. Fall Creek Pkwy. YMCA; bd. dirs. 1st World Found.; mem. Ind. Corrections Code Commn. Woodrow Wilson Found. grantee, 1968; recipient Ind. U. Writers Conf. award, 1970, 1st Ann. Poetry award Black Acad. Arts and Letters, 1971; John Hay Whitney fellow, 1965-66; MacDowell fellow, 1975; Copeland fellow Amherst Coll., 1980; Nat. Endowment Arts grantee, 1981-82. Mem. Authors Guild, Authors League Am., African Heritage Studies Assn. Home: PO Box 483 Indianapolis IN 46206

EVANS, MARK LEWIS, lawyer; b. Bklyn., Dec. 2, 1942; s. Harry and Gloria (Orans) E.; m. Janet Rogers, Dec. 11, 1967; children: Matthew, Daniel. A.B., Hamilton Coll., 1964; J.D., Cornell U., 1968. Bar: N.Y. State 1968, D.C. 1969, U.S. Supreme Ct. 1971. Law clk. U.S. Ct. Appeals, Washington, 1968-69; mem. firm Shea & Gardner, Washington, 1969-72; asst. to solicitor gen. Dept. Justice, 1972-76; gen. counsel ICC, Washington, 1976-79; ptnr. Miller & Chevalier, Washington, 1979—. Mem. ABA, Order of Coif, Phi Kappa Phi. Office: 655 15th St NW Washington DC 20005

EVANS, MARY JOHNSTON, business executive, corporate director; b. Shawnee, Okla., Feb. 28, 1930; d. Paul Xenophon and Helen Elizabeth (Alford) Johnston; children by previous marriage: Marcia Lee Head, Paul Johnston Head, Eric Talbott Head. Student, Wellesley Coll., 1947-48, U. Okla., 1949. Dir. Amtrak, 1974-80, vice chmn., 1975-79; dir. Household Internat., Inc., CertainTeed Corp., Am. Hosp. Supply Corp., The Sun Co., Inc., Butler Mfg. Co., Delta Air Lines. Pres. Jr. League Oklahoma City, 1968-69; trustee Nat. Council Crime and Delinquency, 1971-75, Presbyn. Med. Center, Oklahoma City, 1969-75; bd. dirs. St. Anthony Hosp., Oklahoma City, 1973-75; bd. visitors U. Pitts. Grad. Sch. Bus., 1978—; trustee Mary Baldwin Coll., Staunton, Va., 1976-83. Recipient Law Day award-Liberty Bell award Oklahoma Bar Assn., 1971, Disting. Service award U. Okla., 1981; named one of Top 100 Corporate Women Bus. Week mag., 1976; named to Okla. Hall of Fame, 1978. Mem. Conf. Bd. (Sr.), Pi Beta Phi. Presbyn. (elder). Club: Colony. Address: 200 E 66th St New York NY 10021

EVANS, MEDFORD STANTON, newspaper editor; b. Kingsville, Tex., July 20, 1934; s. Medford Bryan and Alice Josephine (Stanton) E.; m. Sue Ellen Moore, Apr. 14, 1962. B.A., Yale, 1955; postgrad., N.Y. U., 1955. Asst. editor Freeman, 1955; editorial staff Nat. Rev., 1955-56, asso. editor, 1960-68; mng. editor Human Events, 1956-59, contbg. editor, 1968—; publs. dir. Intercollegiate Soc. Individualists, 1956-59, trustee, 1960; chief editorial writer Indpls. News, 1959-60, editor, 1960. Broadcaster: Spectrum series, CBS Radio, from 1971; Author: Revolt on the Campus, 1961, The Fringe on Top, 1962, The Liberal Establishment, 1965, The Politics of Surrenders, 1966, The Lawbreakers, 1968, The Future of Conservatism, 1968, Assassination of Joe McCarthy, 1970. Recipient Freedoms Found. awards for editorial writing, 1959, 60, 65, 66; award for outstanding editorial pages Nat. Headliners Club, 1960. Mem. Am. Soc. Newspaper Editors, Nat. Headliners Club, Am. Conservative Union (chmn.), Indpls. C. of C., Phi Beta Kappa, Sigma Delta Chi. Republican. Methodist. Clubs: Capitol Hill (Washington); Elizabethan (Yale); Indpls. Press, Indpls. Athletic, Yale of Ind. Office: care Human Events 422 1st St SE Washington DC 20003 *

EVANS, MELVIN HERBERT, ambassador, physician; b. Christiansted, St. Croix, V.I., Aug. 7, 1917; s. Charles Herbert and Maude Eloise (Rogiers) E.; m. Mary Phyllis Anderson, Aug. 26, 1945; children: Melvin Herbert, Robert Rogiers, William Charles, Cornelius Duncan. S.B., Howard U., 1940, M.D., 1944, LL.D. hon., 1972; M.P.H., U. Calif.-Berkeley, 1967; L.H.D. hon., Morgan State U., Balt., 1971. Physician in charge Frederiksted Mcpl. Hosp., St. Croix, 1945-48; chief mcpl. physician V.I. Govt., St. Croix, 1951-56, 57-59, commr. of health, 1959-67; gov. U.S. V.I., 1969-75; mem. 96th Congress from V.I., 1979-80; ambassador to Trinidad and Tobago, 1981—; fellow in cardiology Johns Hopkins Hosp., Balt., 1956-57; chmn. V.I. Bd. Med. Examiners, 1959-67. Chmn. bd. trustees Coll. of V.I., 1962-69; chmn. So. Govs. Assn., 1973-74; mem. Republican Nat. Com. from V.I., 1976—. Sr. asst. surgeon USPHS, 1948-50. Recipient Disting. Alumni award Howard U., 1970, Trustee Merit award Fairleigh Dickinson U., 1970. Fellow ACP; mem. Am. Assn. Pub. Health Physicians (charter), V.I. Med. Soc. (past pres.), Pan Am. Med. Assn., St. Croix C. of C. (pres. 1977-78). Mem. Wesleyan Ch. Lodges: St. Croix Rotary; Masons. Home: Box E Christiansted St Croix VI 00820 Office: Am Embassy PO Box 752 Port of Spain Trinidad

EVANS, MICHAEL JONAS, actor, writer; b. Salibury, N.C., Nov. 3, 1949; s. Theodore and Anna Sue (Murdock) E. Ed., Los Angeles City Coll.; grad. in prodn., Am. Film Inst., 1983. Played role of Lionel in TV show: All in the Family, 1970-75, The Jeffersons, 1975, 79-81; co-author TV show: Good Times. Mem. Big Bros. Am., Acad. TV Arts and Scis. Address: PO Box 581 Van Nuys CA 91408

EVANS, NOLLY SEYMOUR, lawyer; b. Augusta, Ga., Sept. 16, 1927; s. Nolly Seymour and Laura (Taylor) E.; m. Judith Anne Leach, Feb. 18, 1965; children—Samantha, Meredydd, Clelia, Nolly. B.F.A. in Music, U. Ga., 1948, M.A. in English Lit, 1950; LL.B., Yale U., 1956. Bar: N.Y. bar 1956. Asso. firm Milbank, Tweed, Hadley & McCloy, N.Y.C., 1956-64; fin. counsel Amax, Inc., N.Y.C., 1964-70; gen. counsel Gilman Paper Co., N.Y.C., 1970-74; gen. counsel, sec. Crouse-Hinds Co., Syracuse, N.Y., 1976-82; counsel Hancock & Estabrook, Syracuse, N.Y., 1982—. Served with U.S. Army, 1947-48. Mem. Am., N.Y. bar assns. Clubs: Century (Syracuse); Confrerie des Chevaliers du Tastevin, Commanderie de Bordeaux. Home: 26 Lyndon Rd Fayetteville NY 13066 Office: Hancock & Estabrook One Mony Plaza Syracuse NY 13202

EVANS, NORMAN ALLEN, scientist; b. Spearfish, S.D., Dec. 3, 1922; s. Allen C. and Claire (Doscher) E.; m. Jean Cole, Dec. 26, 1943; children—Douglas Robert, Elizabeth Ann, Garth William, Mathew. B.S., S.D. State U., 1944; M.S., Utah State U., 1947; Ph.D., Colo. State U., 1963. Registered profl. engr., Colo. Asst. prof. N.D. State U., 1947-51; from asst. prof. to prof. civil engring. Colo. State U., Ft. Collins, 1951-59, prof., head dept. agrl. engring., 1956-69; dir. Environ. Resources Center, 1966-78; asso. dir. U. Expt. Sta., 1970-71; dir. Office Gen. U. Research, 1970-72; dir. Water Resources Research Inst., 1966—; cons. in field; dir. Engrs. Council for Profl. Devel., 1970-76; mem. Colo. Water Pollution Control Commn., 1966-80, vice chmn., 1970-72; mem. Ft. Collins City Water Bd., 1963—, chmn., 1966-68, vice chmn., 1968—. Served to 1st lt. AUS, 1944-46. Fellow AAAS; mem. ASCE, Am. Soc. Agrl. Engrs. (v.p. 1968-70), Sigma Xi, Phi Kappa Phi, Chi Epsilon, Alpha Epsilon, Gamma Sigma Delta. Home: 1847 Michael Ln Fort Collins CO 80521

EVANS, ORINDA D., federal judge; b. Savannah, Ga., Apr. 23, 1943; d. Thomas and Virginia Elizabeth (Grieco) E.; m. Roberts O. Bennett, Apr. 12, 1975; 1 son, Wells Cooper. B.A., Duke U., 1965; J.D. with distinction, Emory U., 1968. Bar: Ga. 1968. Ptnr. Alston, Miller & Gaines, Atlanta, 1974-79; U.S. dist. judge No. Dist. Ga., Atlanta, 1979—; adj. prof. Emory U. Law Sch., 1974-77; counsel Atlanta Crime Commn., 1970-71. Bd. dirs. Ansley Park Civic Assn., 1975-76. Mem. State Bar Ga., Atlanta Bar Assn. (dir. 1979). Democrat. Episcopalian. Home: 200 The Prado NE Atlanta GA 30309 Office: 1988 US Courthouse 75 Spring St SW Atlanta GA 30303

EVANS, ORMOND KEISTER, JR., association executive; b. Ringgold, Va., May 10, 1939; s. Ormond Keister and Catherine (Booth) E.; m. Judith May Carson, Nov. 21, 1962; children: Emily Catherine, Ellen Carson. B.Sc., Va. Poly. Inst., 1961, M.S., 1968. Cert. assn. exec. Asst. agrl. extension agt., Virginia Beach, Va., 1961-62, agrl. extension agt., Newport News, Va., 1963-64; exec. sec., editor Am. Rose Soc., Columbus, Ohio, 1964-69; sec. Am. Rose Found., 1964-69, Columbus Rose Commn., 1964-69; registrar Internat. Rose Registration Authority, 1964-69; exec. dir. Am. Hort. Soc., 1970-76; exec. v.p. Internat. Hardwood Products Assn., 1976—. Mem. Am. Soc. Assn. Execs., Washington Soc. Assn. Execs., Nat. Assn. Execs. Home: 7601 Ridgecrest Dr Alexandria VA 22308 Office: Internat Hardwood Products Assn 417 N Lee St Alexandria VA 22314

EVANS, ORRIN BRYAN, educator; b. Baraboo, Wis., Oct. 6, 1910; s. Evan Alfred and Mary (Rountree) E.; m. Margaret Louise Searle, Feb. 18, 1933; children—Margaret Aspinwall, Evan George, David Rountree. A.B., U. Wis., 1931, LL.B., 1935; J.S.D., Yale, 1940. Asst. prof. law U. Idaho, 1937-38; from asst. prof. to prof. U. Mo., 1938-47, atty. for univ., 1940-47; prof. U. So. Calif., 1947-52, Henry W. Bruce law prof., 1952-79, George Phleger prof. law, 1979—; asso. dean Law Sch., 1952-63, dean, 1963-67, dean and Phleger prof. emeritus, 1980—; vis. prof. law Yale, U. Wis., Northwestern U., U. Calif., others. Commr. Los Angeles CSC, 1961-65; state inheritance tax referee, 1967-73; public trustee Food and Drug Law Inst. Mem. Am., Mo., Wis., Los Angeles County bar assns., Assn. Am. Law Schs. (exec. com. 1955), Order of Coif, Selden Soc., Phi Kappa Sigma, Phi Alpha Delta, Phi Kappa Phi. Episcopalian. Home: 3371-2A Punta Alta Laguna Hills CA 92653

EVANS, PHILIP MORGAN, newspaper editor; b. N.Y.C., Nov. 21, 1933; s. Cowden and Margaret (Morgan) E.; m. Carol Ness, June 26, 1977; 1 dau., Leslie. Reporter Salisbury (Md.) Times, 1953-56; newsman AP, 1956-59; reporter Balt. Evening Sun, 1959-65, city editor, 1965-68, asst. mng. editor, 1968-69; exec. editor Annapolis (Md.) Evening Capital, 1969-71; city editor Phila. Evening and Sunday Bull., 1971-73, mng. editor, 1973-75; sr. asst. mng. editor Washington Star, 1975-78, mng. editor, 1978-79; dep. mng. editor Washington Times, 1982—. Served with AUS, 1954-56. Mem. Soc. Profl. Journalists, Sigma Delta Chi. Home: 129 North Carolina Ave SE Washington DC 20003 Office: Washington Star 225 Virginia Ave SE Washington DC 20003

EVANS, R. O., construction materials company executive; b. 1922; married. Student, Jackson Sch. Bus.-U. Chgo. Purchasing agt. J.A. Jones Constrn. Co., 1949-52; v.p. Concrete Materials Inc., 1953-57; pres. Concrete Supply Inc., 1957-67; v.p. southeastern region constrn. materials div Gifford-Hill & Co. Inc., Dallas, 1968-69; v.p. constrn. materials div. Gifford-Hill & Co. Inc., Dallas, 1969-72, exec. v.p., 1972—, dir. Served with AUS, 1943-46. Office: Gifford-Hill & Co Inc 8435 Stemmons Freeway Box 47127 Dallas TX 75247 *

EVANS, RICHARD BATES, banker; b. Indpls., Nov. 8, 1934; s. Percy Griffith and Anna (Jones) E.; m. Carolyn Ruth Robinson, June 12, 1956; children: Deborah Lynn, Michael Robert, Barbara Bates. B.A., DePauw U., 1956; J.D., Ind. U., 1965. Bar: Ind. 1965. Salesman Coll. Life Ins. Co., Indpls., 1956; v.p., trust officer Am. Fletcher Nat. Bank & Trust Co., Indpls., 1957-69; pres. Indpls. Office Supply Co., 1970; exec. v.p., sr. trust officer Commonwealth Nat. Bank, Harrisburg, Pa., 1970—; dir. WITF-FM/TV. Past asst. chmn. spl. gifts div. Tri-County United Way; past pres. bd. dirs. Seidle Meml. Hosp., Mechanicsburg, Pa.; past bd. dirs. Central Pa. YMCA. Served with AUS, 1957-59. Mem. Am., Ind., Indpls. bar assns., Harrisburg C. of C. Home: 130 Townhouse Briarcrest Hershey PA 17033 Office: PO Box 1010 10 S Market Sq Harrisburg PA 17108

EVANS, RICHARD VIRDIN, educator; b. Balt., Mar. 29, 1930; s. George Heberton and Elinor (Virdin) E.; m. Elizabeth Morgan Eaton, June 28, 1958; children—Dorothy Eaton, Sally Morgan, Margaret Canby, Richard Virdin. A.B., Princeton, 1951; D.Eng., Johns Hopkins, 1959. Instr. U. Mich., 1958-59, asst. prof., 1959-62, U. Calif., Los Angeles, 1962-65; asso. prof. Case Western Res. U., 1965-69; prof. bus. adminstrn. U. Ill., Urbana, 1969—, acting head dept., 1969-70. Contbr. articles to profl. jours. Served to 2d lt. AUS, 1951-54. Lord Baltimore Press fellow, 1956-58. Mem. Ops. Research Soc. Am. (asso. editor jour. 1965-74), Inst. Mgmt. Sci., Inst. Math. Statistics, Royal Statis. Soc., Assn. Computing Machinery, Soc. Indsl and Applied Math. Home: 2507 Melrose Dr Champaign IL 61820 Office: Commerce West U Ill Urbana IL 61801

EVANS, ROBERT, motion picture producer; b. N.Y.C., June 29, 1930; m. Ali MacGraw (div.); 1 son, Joshua; m. Phyllis George, 1977 (div. 1978). Grad. high sch. Child actor on radio programs; actor: motion pictures including The Man of a Thousand Faces, 1957, The Sun Also Rises, 1957, The Fiend Who Walked the West, 1958, The Best of Everything, 1959; ind. producer, 20th Century Fox; successively v.p. prodn., Paramount Pictures Corp.; v.p. world-wide prodn., 1969-71; exec. v.p., 1971-75; now ind. producer; producer: films Chinatown, 1974, Marathon Man, 1976, Black Sunday, 1977, Players, 1979, Popeye, 1980, Urban Cowboy, 1980, Cotton Club, 1984. Office: Paramount Pictures Corp 5555 Melrose Ave Los Angeles CA 90038

EVANS, ROBERT, JR., university dean, economics educator; b. Sterling, Colo., Mar. 20, 1930; s. Robert and Mary Louise (Paradise) E.; m. Lois Ellen Herr, Nov. 6, 1955; children: Karen E., Robert, Janet K., Thomas W., L. Midori, Laura E., Katherine Joan. S.B., MIT, 1954; Ph.D. (Hillman fellow), U. Chgo., 1959. Asst. prof. indsl. relations MIT, 1959-65; assoc. prof. Brandeis U., 1965-71, chmn. dept. econs., 1970-72, 73-75, prof., 1971—, dean Coll. Arts and Scis., 1975-81, Atran prof. labor econs., 1975—; vis. prof. Keio U., Tokyo, 1966-67, 72-73, 82-83; research dir. study on prison industries Can. Corrections Assn., 1968-69. Author: Public Policy Toward Labor, 1965, The Labor Economics of Japan and the United States, 1971, Developing Policies for Public Security and Criminal Justice, 1973. Mem. Acton (Mass.) and Acton Boxborough Regional Sch. Com., 1971-72, 74-82, regional chmn., 1972, 79-80, town chmn., 1975-77; trustee Tech. Devel. Corp. Served with AUS, 1955-57. Mem. Am. Econ. Assn., Indsl. Relations Assn., Assn. Asian Studies. Home: 43 High St Acton MA 01720 Office: Dept Econs Brandeis U Waltham MA 02254

EVANS, ROBERT JAMES, architect; b. Alameda, Calif., Apr. 15, 1914; s. Edwin Florence and Idella Mary (Cranna) E.; m. Carol Ann Benton, Sept. 11, 1937; children: Joan Carlson, Ann Lockey, Marcia Mothorn. A.B., U. Calif., Berkeley, 1935. Registered architect, Calif. Draftsman Wm. C. Hays Architect, San Francisco, 1935-37, U. Calif., 1937-41, architect, 1941-45, univ. architect, 1945-72, asst. v.p., 1971-72; cons. architect, Marshall, Calif., 1973—; asst. to chancellor U. Mich.-Flint, 1972-73; supervising architect U. Calif., Davis, 1942-45, Berkeley, 1948-55; cons. architect campus plan U. Ryukuas, Okinwa, 1969; cons. architect campus paln U. N.C., Greensboro, 1979-82; cons. architect campus plan Kabul U., Afghanistan, 1955, U. Hawaii, 1960-62, U. Rykus, Okinwa, 1969, U. N.C., Greensboro, 1979-82. Founder Tomales Bay Assn., Marshall Calif., 1964. Fellow AIA; mem. Assn. Univ. Architects (pres. 1955-57). Clubs: Richmond Yacht (treas.) (1961); Inverness Yacht). Address: 18545 Hwy 1 Marshall CA 94940

EVANS, ROBERT L., restaurant executive; b. Sugar Ridge, Ohio, May 30, 1918; s. Stan and Elizabeth E.; m. Jewell Waters, 1940; children: Stanley, Robin, Gwen, Debbie, Steve, Bobbie. Grad., Ohio State U. Engaged in restaurant bus., 1944—; now pres. Bob Evans Farms, Inc., Columbus, Ohio.; mem. Vet. Medicine Adv. Com. Ohio, Dept. Agr. Meat Adv. Bd.; dir. council Food Industries Ctr. Fund raising chmn. Ohio Soc. Prevention Blindness, 1977; hon. chmn. Heart Fund Drive, 1979; state chmn. Easter Seal Campaign; mem. exec. bd. Rio Grande Coll.; sponsor Ohio 4-H Conservation Camp; trustee Ohio Forestry Assn. Served with AUS, 1944-45. Named Ohio Soil Conservationist of Year, 1969, Ohio Wildlife Habitat Conservationist of Year, 1972, 80; named Ohio Ambassador Natural Resources, 1981; named to Hall of Fame Ohio State Fair, 1976, Ohio 4-H, 1982; recipient Bus. Tourism award, 1973, Gov. Ohio award, 1978, Meritorious Service award Ohio State U. Coll. Agr., 1978, Ohio Conservation Achievement award, 1978, Wildlife Council Service award, 1978, 79, Meritorius Service award Ohio State U. Coll. Agr. Alumni, 1983, Hon. award Furture Farmers Am., Disting. Service award Gallia County Soil and Water Conservation Dist., Nat. Charolais Congress Breeders award. Mem. Am. Charolais Assn. (past dir.), 4-H Club (adv. bd. Ohio), Ohio Charolais Assn. (dir.), Ohio Wildlife Council, Ohio C. of C. (dir.); mem. Spanish-Barb Mustang Breeders Assn. (founding mem.). Home: Route 2 Mt Zion Rd Bidwell OH 45614 Office: Route 25 Box 154 Rio Grande OH 45674

EVANS, ROBERT VAN ORMAN, lawyer; b. Cleve., Jan. 15, 1920; s. Miles Erland and Edna (Koncana) E.; m. Virginia Michael, June 15, 1945; children: Amanda, Miles, David, Alison. B.A., Dartmouth Coll., 1941; LL.B., U. Mich., 1948. With CBS, 1950—, gen. counsel, v.p., 1968-76. Served with USNR, 1942-45. Fellow Am. Bar Found.; mem. Am. Bar Assn., Assn. Bar City N.Y. Republican. Home: Box 4068 Milford CT 06460 also Les Marmottes 1961 Arolla Switzerland

EVANS, ROBLEY DUNGLISON, physicist; b. University Place, Nebr., May 18, 1907; s. Manley Jefferson and Alice (Turner) E.; m. Gwendolyn Elizabeth Aldrich, Mar. 10, 1928; children: Richard Owen, Nadia Ann, Ronald Aldrich. B.S., Calif. Inst. Tech., 1924-28, M.S., 1929, Ph.D., 1932. With research lab. C.F. Braun & Co., Alhambra, Calif., 1929-31; instr. Poly. Sch., Pasadena, Calif., 1931-32; nat. research fellow U. Calif. at Berkeley, 1932-34; asst. prof. Mass. Inst. Tech., Cambridge, 1934-38, asso. prof., 1938-45, prof., 1945-72, prof. emeritus, 1972—; dir. Radioactivity Center, 1935-72, cons., 1972-81; vis. prof. Ariz. State U., 1966-67; staff cons. Peter Bent Brigham Hosp., Boston, 1945-72; cons. surgeon gen. Dept. Army, 1962-69, USN Radiol. Def. Lab., 1952-69; cons. div. biology and medicine AEC, 1950-75; spl. project asso. Mayo Clinic, 1973—; cons. div. biol. and environ. research ERDA, Dept. Energy, 1975—; cons. physics Mass. Gen. Hosp., 1948-73, USPHS, 1961-71, Fed. Radiation Council, 1965-69, Roger Williams Hosp., Providence, 1965—; Chmn. Internat. Conf. Applied Nuclear Physics, Cambridge, 1940; vice chmn. com. on nuclear sci. NRC, 1946-72; mem. Nat. Acad. Scis.-NRC panel 231 adv. to NBS on radiation physics, 1963-66, chmn., 1964; chmn. standing com. for radiation biology aspects of supersonic transport FAA, 1967; mem. com. on radioactive waste mgmt. Nat. Acad. Scis., 1968-70; adviser U. Chgo., 1964-68; sci. adv. bd. New Eng. Deaconess Hosp., 1963-69; sr. U.S. del. Internat. Assn. Radiation Research, Cortina, 1966; mem. organizing com. U.S. Nat. Com. Med. Physics, 1966-69; vis. com. med. dept. Brookhaven Nat. Lab., 1965-68; cons. Blood Research Inst., 1967-74; vice chmn. adv. com. to U.S. Transuranium Registry, 1968—; mem. tech. adv. com. Ariz. Atomic Energy Commn., 1971-72; spl. project asso. Mayo Clinic, 1973—. Author: The Atomic Nucleus, 1955; Editorial bd.: Internat. Jour. Applied Radiation and Isotopes, 1955-69; hon. mem. editorial bd., 1976—; editorial bd.: Mt. Washington Obs. Bull, 1962—, Health Physics, 1962-70, Physics in Medicine and Biology, 1963-66; editor physics: Radiation Research, 1959-62; Contbr. sci. research papers to various publs. Vice pres. Found. for Study and Aid of Emotionally Unstable, 1948—. Recipient Theobald Smith medal in Med. Scis., 1937; Presdl. certificate of Merit, 1948; Hull award and Gold medal AMA, 1963; Silvanus Thompson medal Brit. Inst. Radiology, 1966. Fellow AAAS, Am. Phys. Soc., Am. Acad. Arts and Scis., N.Y. Acad. Scis.; mem. Am. Assn. Physicists in Biology and Medicine, Radiation Research Soc. (v.p., pres. 1965-67), Am. Roentgen Ray Soc. (asso.), Am. Indsl. Hygiene Assn., Am. Assn. Physics Tchrs., Am. Nuclear Soc., Health Physics Soc. (pres. 1972-73, Disting. Achievement award 1981), Nat. Com. Radiation Protection and Measurements (council 1965-71, hon. mem. 1975—), Soc. Nuclear Medicine (hon. mem.), Royal Sci. and Lit. Soc. (hon.), Kungliga Vetenshapoch Vitterhets-Samhallet (Goteborg, Sweden), Sigma Xi, Kappa Gamma, Tau Beta Pi, Pi Kappa Delta. Republican. Home: 4621 E Crystal Ln Scottsdale AZ 85253 Office: Mass Inst Tech Cambridge MA 02139

EVANS, ROWLAND, JR., newspaper columnist; b. White Marsh, Pa., Apr. 28, 1921; s. Rowl and Elizabeth Wharton (Downs) E.; m. Katherine Winton, June 18, 1949; children: Rowland Winton, Sarah Warren. Grad., Kent Sch., 1939; student, Yale, 1940-41; A.A., George Washington U., 1950. With A.P., 1945-55; mem. staff N.Y. Herald Tribune, 1955-63, syndicated columnist, 1963—. Roving editor: Readers Digest mag.; TV panelist and commentator.; Author: (with Robert Novak) Lyndon B. Johnson: The Exercise of Power, 1967, Nixon in The White House: The Frustration of Power, 1971, The Reagan Revolution, 1981. Served with USMCR, 1941-44. Home: 3125 O St NW Washington DC 20007 Office: 1750 Pennsylvania Ave Washington DC 20006

EVANS, RUPERT NELSON, vocational education educator; b. Terre Haute, Ind., Apr. 6, 1921; s. Loran Nelson and Hazel Mae (Rupert) E.; m. Barbara Jean Barbre, June 29, 1941; children: Ellen Anne (Mrs. Roger Collins), Catherine Nell (Mrs. Ronald Westman), Nancy Jean (Mrs. Paul McNabb). Student, Butler U., 1938-39; B.S., Ind. State Tchrs. Coll., 1946; M.S., Purdue U., 1949, Ph.D., 1950, D. Vocat. Edn. (hon.), 1970, D.Edn., Eastern Mich. U., 1980, Eastern Ky. U., 1982. Foreman Allison div. Gen. Motors Co., 1940-44; instr. Elkhart (Ind.) High Sch., 1946-48; grad. asst. Purdue U., 1948-50; mem. faculty U. Ill., 1950—, prof. vocat. and tech. edn., 1956—, dean, 1964-69; Fulbright lectr., Japan, 1957-58; mem. Edn. Professions Devel. Council, 1968-72. Mem. sch. bd., Champaign, Ill., 1960-64. Mem. Am. Vocat. Assn., Am. Indsl. Arts Assn., Mississippi Valley Indsl. Tchr. Edn. Conf. (chmn. 1970-80), Ill. Vocat. Edn. Adv. Council (past chmn.), Nat. Assn. Indsl. Tchr. Educators (past pres.), Am. Ednl.

Research Assn., Ill. Vocat. Edn. Assn., Ill. Indsl. Edn. Assn. (past pres.), Nat. Council Employment Policy, Sigma Xi, Phi Delta Kappa, Kappa Delta Pi, Iota Lambda Sigma, Epsilon Pi Tau. Home: 1842 Maynard Dr Champaign IL 61820 Office: Education Bldg U Ill Urbana IL 61801

EVANS, SAMUEL LONDON, impresario; b. Leon County, Fla., Nov. 11, 1902; s. Reuben L. and Penny U. (Underwood) E.; m. Edna H. Hoye, Nov. 20, 1928; 1 dau., Retha Evans Kelly. Student, Columbia U., 1948, N.Y. U., 1951-53; Mus.D. (hon.), Combs Coll. Music, 1968. Pres., nat. chmn., chief exec. officer AFNA Plan: New Access Routes to Profl. Careers, Phila., 1968—; founder, pres., chmn. Am. Found. for Negro Affairs, 1968—; impresario, performing classical arts producer; producer Phila. Chamber Orch. Soc., 1961-71; exec. v.p., 1976; Bicentennial Corp., 1971—; designer, founder African Am. Hall of Fame Garden. Author: Nothing to Fear, An Incident About the Scientist, J. Robert Oppenheimer and the McCarthy Era, Second Phase of Democracy, An American Manifesto, National Preventive Med. Plam and Crime Control Design. Sec. Pa. Athletic Commn., 1941-45; coordinator U.S. Div. Phys. Fitness, 1941-45; chmn. Phila. Anti-Poverty Action Commn., 1965-71; mem. Mayor's Com. on Municipal Services, 1969-70; bd. dirs. Am. Trauma Soc., Phila. Gen. Hosp.; bd. dirs., prodn. gen. mgr. Phila. Coffee Concerts Com.; mem. Nat. Trust Historic Preservation, Am. Pub. Health Assn. Recipient Black Expn. 72' Service award 3d World '76, Inc., 1972, Achievement award Phila. Cotillion Soc., 1972, Community Service award Phila. Opportunities Industrialization Centers, 1972, Achievement award NAACP Region II, 1972; commendation Educator's Roundtable, 1978; cert. of achievement Commonwealth of Pa., 1978; Charles R. Drew, M.D. award, 1978; life-size bronze bust Phila. Acad. Sci., 1981; shield award; others. Mem. Internat. Assn. Impresarios and Concert and Festival Mgrs. Office: IVB Bldg 1700 Market St Suite 2020 Philadelphia PA 19103 *Throughout my life I have been impelled with an innermost desire to achieve two basic philosophies: "That it is better to give than to receive:"... because it is difficult for the receiver in many ways to be equal with the giver... This is a Herculean task. Yet, the reward is sufficient. It leaves my conscience clear and my spirit satisfied. The first is second only to my commitment to life and the human species - - that all may feel safe in my presence.*

EVANS, TERENCE THOMAS, judge; b. Milw., Mar. 25, 1940; s. Robert Hansen and Jeanett (Walters) E.; m. Joan Marie Witte, July 24, 1965; children: Kelly Elizabeth, Christine Marie, David Rourke. B.A., Marquette U., Milw., 1962, J.D., 1967. Bar: Wis. 1967. Law clk. to justice Wis. Supreme Ct., 1967-68; dist. atty., Milw. County, 1968-70, pvt. practice, 1970-74, circuit judge, State of Wis., 1974-80; judge U.S. Dist. Ct. Eastern Dist. Wis., Milw., 1980—. Mem. ABA, State Bar Wis., Milw. Bar Assn. Roman Catholic. Office: 517 E Wisconsin St Room 376 Milwaukee WI 53202 *

EVANS, THOMAS BEVERLEY, JR., former congressman, lawyer; b. Nashville, Nov. 5, 1931; s. Thomas Beverley and Hannah (Hundley) E.; m. Mary Page Hilliard, Sept. 23, 1961; children: Thomas Beverley, III, Robert S., Page. B.A., U. Va., 1953, LL.B., 1956. Bar: Va. 1956. Dir. Delaware Devel. Dept., 1969-70; co-chmn. Republican Nat. Com., 1971-73; mem.-at-large 95th-97th Congresses from Del.; ptnr. O'Connor & Hannan; dir. Chronar Corp.; mem. exec. bd. Environ. Study Conf.; del. UN Law of Sea Conf., 1977, African Am. Conf., 1978; Rep. nat. commiteeman for, Del., 1970-77; dep. chmn., exec. com. Rep. Nat. Finance Com., 1969-70; exec. com. Rep. Nat. Com., 1971-77; del. Rep. Nat. Conv., 1972, 76, 80; vice chmn. nat. bd. advisors Reagan-Bush '84 Campaign. Mem. Delmarva Regional council Boy Scouts Am.; bd. dirs., exec. com. Wesley Coll., Dover, Del.; Delaware chmn. Radio Free Europe, 1966-67; chmn. United Negro Coll. Fund, 1968-69; bd. advisers Lewes U. Spl. Services Center, Chgo.; bd. dirs. Ford's Theatre, Washington.; trustee Woodberry Forest Sch., 1973-76; vice chmn. Environ. and Energy Study Inst. Served with Del. N.G., 1956-60. Mem. Am. Legion (Employment of Handicapped award 1970), Delta Phi, Phi Alpha Delta. Clubs: Wilmington Country, Wilmington, Pine Valley Golf. Home: 1111 Brandon Ln Wilmington DE 19807 Office: O'Connor and Hannan 1919 Pennsylvania Ave NW Washington DC 20006

EVANS, THOMAS MELLON, manufacturing company executive; b. Pitts., Sept. 8, 1910; s. Thomas M. and Martha S. Jarnagin; m. Elizabeth Parker, June 26, 1935 (div.); children: Thomas M., Edward Parker, Robert Sheldon; m. Josephine Schlotman Mitchell, Aug. 7, 1953 (dec. May 1977); m. Betty Barton Loomis, Nov. 4, 1977. B.A., Yale U., 1931. Chmn. exec. com. H.K. Porter Co., Inc., Pitts., 1939—; chmn. Crane Co., N.Y.C., 1959—; pres. Evans & Co., Inc., N.Y.C., 1956—. Bd. dirs. Children's Village, Dobbs Berry, N.Y.; trustee Hirshhorn Mus., Washington, Historic Deerfield, Mass. Republican. Presbyterian. Office: 300 Park Ave New York NY 100022

EVANS, TREVOR HEISER, advt. exec.; b. Grafton, Nebr., Dec. 10, 1909; s. George Augustus and Lydia Rebecca (Heiser) E.; m. Elsie Brooke, Feb. 12, 1938; children—Brooke, Gwyneth Evans Lindbo. B.A. in English, U. Wash., 1934. With Sta. KOMO-KJR, Seattle, 1935-39; radio dir. Erwin-Wasey, 1939-41, Wash. Def. Council, 1941-43; with Pacific Nat. Advt., Seattle, 1944—, account exec., 1946—, pres., 1954—; chmn. bd. Evans/Pacific Inc.; guest lectr. U. Wash., 1959-66, City Coll. Seattle, 1977—; mem. radio history com. Wash. State U. Actor, free lance writer, 1934-35. Chmn. pub. relations com. United Good Neighbors, 1960-66; trustee Cystic Fibrosis Found., 1968; dir. pub. relations, sec. N.W. Kidney Center. Named Seattle Advt. Man of Year, 1956. Mem. Am. Assn. Advt. Agys. (chmn. bd. govs. western region 1955-56), Advt. Assn. West (dir. 1953-56), Am. Fedn. Advt. (nat. edn. com. 1965), Seattle Advt. Rev. Bd. (pres. 1972-74), Acad. TV Arts and Scis. (treas. Seattle chpt. 1966, Gov.'s award 1976), Seattle Advt. Fedn., Seattle C. of C., Seattle Better Bus. Bur. (chmn. bd.), U. Wash. Alumni Assn., Phi Kappa Sigma, Alpha Delta Sigma. Clubs: Seattle Advt. (pres. 1955-56), Wash. Athletic, Blue Ridge (past dir., treas.), Advt. Golfers Assn. (dir.), Harbor.). Home: 1472 NW Woodbine Way Seattle WA 98177 Office: 300 Elliott Ave W Seattle WA 98119

EVANS, VAN MICHAEL, advertising agency executive, consultant; b. N.Y.C., July 18, 1916; s. Michael James and Catherine (Conte) Livadas; m. Mary Bota, Nov. 8, 1942; children: Stephen, Barbara. B.A., NYU, 1938. Sales and editorial positions Social Spectator mag., N.Y.C., 1938-39; account exec. Deutsch & Shea Advt. Agy., N.Y.C., 1940-46, v.p., exec. v.p., 1946-68, pres., 1969-80, chmn. exec. bd., 1981-83; cons. Foote Cone & Belding div. Deutsch & Shea Advt. Agy., N.Y.C., 1983—; cons. Morality and Media Inc., N.Y.C., 1970-78; bd. dirs. Pension and Profit Sharing Fund Am. Assn. Advt. Agys., 1971-73. Editorial cons.: The Coming Revolution in Human Resources, 1978; editor: The Complete Job Book, 1980; contbr. artilces to publs. Nat. chmn. United Greek Charities, Inc., N.Y.C., 1973-74; adviser Greek Orthodox Youth Council, Inc., 1973-76. Served with Signal Corps U.S. Army, 1942-46. Greek Orthodox. Clubs: Solon Culture Soc. (pres. chpt. 1972-74), Ahepa (chaplain Delphi chpt. 1948-52). Office: Deutsch Shea & Evans Inc 49 E 53d St New York NY 10022 *My Credo for leadership is to foment change. . ..the application of imagination wedded to a quality of restlessness.*

EVANS, WALTER J., business executive; b. Toronto, Ont., Can., Feb. 3, 1916; s. Walter E. and Emma (Richey) E.; m. Mary Dorothy Squire, Aug. 3, 1940; children—Barry M., Paul H., Joan C. R.I.A., De LaSalle Coll., Toronto. Vice pres., asst. gen. mgr. G. H. Wood & Co., Ltd.; pres., gen. mgr. S.F. Lawrason Chems. Ltd., Lawrason Holdings Ltd., 1955-72; dir. S.F. Lawrason & Co. Ltd., Multi-Tek Inc., Adrian, Mich. Dir. Can. Nat. Inst. Blind, Western Fair Bd., St. Joseph's Hosp.; past pres. Plaza East Assn. Fla.; mem. adv. bd. Huron Coll. Found.; chmn. bd. St. Mary's Hosp., London; dir. U. Western Ont.; trustee YM-YWCA, London, Ont. Mem. London C. of C. (pres. 1963-64). Club: London Hunt and Country. Office: 4300 N Ocean Blvd Apt 7L Fort Lauderdale FL 33308

EVANS, WILLIAM BUELL, mathematician; b. Monticello, Miss., June 5, 1918; s. Walter Price and Lillian G. (Hancock) E.; m. Margaret Polk Peters, Oct. 12, 1945; children: Patricia Irene, Margaret Faye, David Buell. B.S. with highest honors in Math. and Chemistry, U. So. Miss., 1939; M.S. in Math. and Physics, La. State U., 1941, M.I.T., 1944; Ph.D. in Math, U. Ill., 1950. Instr. in math. A&M Coll. Tex., College Station, 1941-42; asst. prof. math. U. Ill., Urbana, 1948-50; asso. prof. math. Ga. Inst. Tech., Atlanta, 1950-60; vis. asso. prof. engring. math. UCLA, 1960-64; prof. math. Emory U., Atlanta, 1965—, prof. biometry, 1965—, acting chmn. dept. biometry, 1969-71, dir. Computing Ctr., 1965-81. Contbr. articles on applied math. and meteorology to sci. publs. Served with USAAF, 1942-46, 51-53. Mem. Math. Assn. Am., Biometry Soc., Am. Math. Soc., Soc. Indsl. and Applied Math., Assn. Computing Machinery, Sigma Xi, Phi Kappa Phi. Baptist. Office: Uppergate House Emory U Atlanta GA 30322 *Superior ability is an asset in striving for high goals, but persistence and integrity form the team on which one must depend if worthwhile objectives in life are to be attained.*

EVANS, WILLIAM LEE, cytologist, biologist; b. Calvert, Tex., Aug. 28, 1924; s. James Herman and Lilly Australia (O'Neal) E.; m. Lillian Mary Madden, July 30, 1948; children—Kathy A., David C., Susan. B.A. with honors, U. Tex., Austin, 1949; M.A., U. Tex.-Austin, 1950, Ph.D., 1955. Mem. faculty U. Ark., Fayetteville, 1955—, prof. zoology, 1968—, chmn. dept. biology, 1967-70. Author articles, lab. manuals. Served with AUS, 1942-46; Served with USAF, 1951-52. Decorated Air medal with oak leaf cluster; recipient award for classroom teaching Omicron Delta Kappa, 1959; grantee NSF, 1959-62, NIH, 1960-63; grantee U. Ark. Found., 1979, Fulbright Coll. Arts and Sci., 1982. Mem. Am. Genetic Assn., AAAS, Ark. Acad. Sci. (treas. 1972-82, pres.-elect 1983—), Audubon Soc., Am. Philatelic Soc., Phi Beta Kappa, Sigma Xi. Baptist. Home: 111 Nolan Ave Fayetteville AR 72701 Office: Dept Zoology SE 632 U Ark Fayetteville AR 72701

EVANS, WILLIAM SPEARING, architect and engineer; b. Shreveport, La., Feb. 24, 1913; s. James Parham and Edith (Fuqua) E.; m. Catherine McDowell Murphey, Mar. 15, 1940; children: William Spearing, Judith Evans Reilly, Jonathan M. B.A., Yale U., 1937, M.F.A., 1939, M.Arch., 1940, M.Engring. (univ. scholar), 1942. With archtl. firms in, N.Y.C. and Shreveport, 1940-41, 42, pvt. practice, Shreveport, 1945-70; with project planning div. TVA, 1942-43; with Manhattan Project, Tenn. Eastman, 1943-45; partner firm Evans & Evans, Shreveport, 1970—; Vice chmn. Shreveport City Bldg. Code Commn., 1951-54; mem. Shreveport City Planning Comm., 1954-56; vice chmn. Shreveport Met. Planning Commn., 1962-63, Shreveport Met. Bd. Appeals, 1972-73, sec., 1971-72; pres. Downtown Shreveport Unlimited, 1973-75; chmn. Shreveport Downtown Devel. Authority, 1978-79. Prin. works include St. Paul's Episcopal Ch, Shreveport, 1951-62, United Gas Bldg, Jackson, Miss., 1956, Sport Yacht Club, 1973, Student Activity Center, NW State Sch., Bossier, La., 1978, others. Bd. dirs. Shreveport Jr. Achievement, 1968-70; chmn. environ. health com. N.W. La. Areawide Health Planning Council, 1974-75. Fellow AIA (Gulf States regional award 1956), ASCE; life mem. ASHRAE; mem. La. Assn. Architects (award of merit 1976), Constrn. Specifications Inst., Illuminating Engring. Soc., ASCE, Engring. and Sci. Council Shreveport, La. Land Surveyors Assn., Nat. Soc. Profl. Engrs., Profl. Engrs. in Pvt. Practice. Republican. Episcopalian. Clubs: Shreveport, Shreveport Yacht, Jeems Bayou Fishing and Hunting. Office: 320 Texas St Shreveport LA 71101

EVANSON, ROBERT VERNE, pharmacy educator; b. Hammond, Ind., Nov. 3, 1920; s. Evan and Dorothy (Gordon) E.; m. Helen Louise Wolber, June 29, 1947; children: Yvonne Louise Evanson Nash, Karen Denice Evanson Yaeger. B.S. in Pharmacy, Purdue U., 1947, M.S. in Indsl. Pharmacy, 1949, Ph.D. in Pharmacy Adminstrn., 1953. Apprentice pharmacist Physician's Supply Co., Hammond, 1946; grad. asst. pharmacy Sch. Pharmacy, Purdue U., 1947-48, mem. faculty, 1948—, prof. pharm. adminstrn., 1963—, head dept., 1966-72; cons. in field. Contbr. articles to profl. jours.; contbg. author: Central Pharm. Jour., 1964-72. Served with AUS, 1943-46. Recipient Lederle Faculty award, 1964. Fellow Am. Found. Pharm. Edn., Am. Pharm. Assn.; mem. Ind. Pharm. Assn., Am. Assn. Coll. Pharmacy (dir., Disting. Educator award 1982), Am. Assn. Coll. Pharmacy Council Faculties, Acad. Pharm. Scis., Acad. Pharmacy Practice, Soc. Preservation and Encouragement Barbershop Quartet Singing in Am., Sigma Xi. Mem. Fed. Ch. W. Lafayette. Home: 400 Lindberg Ave West Lafayette IN 47906

EVARTS, CHARLES MCCOLLISTER, orthopaedic surgeon; b. Dunkirk, N.Y., Aug. 16, 1931; s. Charles Melville and Laura (McCollister) E.; m. Nancy Joan Lyons, July 2, 1955; children: Cynthia Ann, Charles Mark, Robert Alan. A.B. cum laude, Colgate U., 1953; M.D., U. Rochester, 1957. Diplomate: Am. Bd. Orthopaedic Surgery (mem. bd., vice chmn. residency rev. com.). Intern Strong Meml. Hosp., 1957-58, resident in orthopaedic surgery, 1961-64; with Cleve. Clinic Found., 1964-74, chmn. dept. orthopaedic surgery, 1970-74; prof., chmn. dept. orthopaedics U. Rochester, 1974—, Dorris H. Carlson prof., 1975—. Editor: Orthopaedic Clinics of North America, Vol. 12, 1971, Vol. 15, 1973, Clinical Orthopaedics and Related Research, Vol. 107, 1975, Proc. of the Hip Society, 1976, Reconstructive Surgery of the Knee, 1977, Instructional Course Lectures, 1983, Surgery of the Musculoskeletal System, 4 vols., 1983; contbr. articles to profl. jours. Served with USNR, 1959-61. Nat. Found. fellow, 1964. Fellow A.C.S. (gov., chmn. adv. council for orthopedics); mem. Am. Acad. Orthopaedic Surgeons, Orthopaedic Research Soc., Internat. Knee Soc., Scoliosis Research Soc., Am. Orthopaedic Assn., Assn. Orthopedic Chmn. (pres. 1982-83), AMA, Am. Rheumatism Assn., Société Internationale de Chirurgie Orthopedique et de Traumatologie, Continental, 20th Century, Interurban orthopaedic socs., Alpha Omega Alpha. Club: Fortnightly. Home: 150 Pelham Rd Rochester NY 14610 Office: 601 Elmwood Ave Rochester NY 14642

EVARTS, HARRY FRANKLIN, association executive; b. Troy, N.Y., July 20, 1928; s. Leslie Herbert and Lenora Marie (Chapman) E.; m. Drusilla Ann Riley, Sept. 9, 1951 (div. Aug. 1969); children: Dale Irene, Leslie Alan, Valerie Dru, Jill Ann. Student, Sampson (N.Y.) Coll., 1948-49; B.S.C., Ohio U., 1951, M.S., 1952; D.B.A., Harvard U., 1959. Work standards and methods engr. Gen. Motors Corp., 1952-55; indsl. engr. Gardner Bd. & Carton Co., 1955-57; asst. prof. prodn. mgmt. Northwestern U., 1958-63; asso. prof. Ohio U., 1963-65, prof. bus. adminstrn., dean Coll. Bus. Adminstrn., 1965-70; pres. Bryant Coll., Smithfield, R.I., 1970-76, also trustee; dir. ednl. services Am. Mgmt. Assns., 1976-80, v.p. ednl. services, 1980-82, group v.p. R&D, 1982—; Cons. ICA and Japan Productivity Center, 1960; dir. Internat. Data Sci., Inc. Author: (with others) Operations Management, 1961, Introduction to PERT, 1964; also articles, chpts. in books. Trustee Nichols Coll., 1978; bd. dirs. Ohio Council Econ. Edn., 1966-70, R.I. Council Econ. Edn., 1971-76, Internat. Mgmt. Devel-Inst., Kenya, 1970, Internat. Mgmt. Devel-Inst., Zambia, 1971, 73. Served with AUS, 1946-48; PTO. Ford Found. fellow, 1956-58. Mem. Acad. Mgmt., Beta Gamma Sigma. Unitarian. Club: University. Home: 159 W 53d St New York NY 10019

EVELEIGH, VIRGIL WILLIAM, educator; b. Dexter, N.Y., Aug. 20, 1931; s. Malcolm N. and Doris M. (Gilmore) E.; m. Eleanor L. Langenmayr, June 9, 1956 (div. 1980); m. 2d Barbara A. Beaman, May 11, 1980. B.S.E.E., Purdue U., 1957, M.S.E.E., 1958, Ph.D., 1961. Technician Gen. Electric, Syracuse, N.Y., 1953-54, engr., 1961-64; prof. elec. and computer engring. Syracuse U., 1964—; v.p. engring. JDR Systems Corp., Syracuse, 1978—; pres., treas. Data Functions Corp., Syracuse, 1974—. Contbr. articles to profl. jours.; author: Adaptive Control and Optimization Techniques, 1967. Served with USAF, 1949-52. RCA scholar, 1956-57; RCA teaching fellow, 1957-61. Mem. IEEE, AAUP, Sigma Xi, Tau Beta Pi, Eta Kappa Nu. Republican. Presbyterian. Home: 753 James St 223 Syracuse NY 13203 Office: Syracuse Univ 111 Link Hall Syracuse NY 13210

EVELYN, DOUGLAS EVERETT, museum executive; b. Ossining, N.Y., Sept. 19, 1941; s. Everett Edward and Marie Georgette (Davis) E.; m. Martha Ellen Hutchins MacCornack, Aug. 14, 1965; children: Sarah Ellen, Elizabeth Jane. B.A. cum laude, Wesleyan U., Middletown, Conn., 1963; grad. student, Howard U., 1966-69. Staff asst., then adminstrv. asst. to dir. Am. Assn. Museums, 1963-67; adminstrv. asst. Democratic Nat. Com., 1968; asso. cons. Monroe Bush & Assos. (mgmt. cons.), Washington, 1969; asst. to dir. Nat. Portrait Gallery, Washington, 1969-71, asst. dir., 1973, dep. dir., 1978—, Nat. Mus. Am. History, Smithsonian Instn., Washington, 1979—. Bd. dirs. Cultural Alliance of Greater Washington. Mem. Am. Assn. Museums (treas.). Home: 2318 King Pl NW Washington DC 20007 Office: Nat Mus Am History Smithsonian Instn Washington DC 20560

EVEN, FRANCIS ALPHONSE, lawyer; b. Chgo., Sept. 8, 1920; s. George Martin and Cecilia (Neuman) E.; m. Margaret Hope Herrick, Oct. 16, 1945; children: Janet Beth, Dorothy Elizabeth. B.S. in Mech. Engring, U. Ill., 1942; J.D., George Washington U., 1949. Bar: D.C. bar 1949, Ill. bar 1950. Engr. Gen. Electric Co., 1945-49; partner firm Fitch, Even, Tabin & Flannery (patent and trademark law), Chgo., 1952—. Mem. bd. edn., River Forest, Ill., 1963-69; trustee West Suburban Hosp., Oak Park, Ill., 1974-77. Served with combat engrs. AUS, 1942-45. Fellow Am. Coll. Trial Lawyers; mem. Am. Patent Law Assn. (bd. mgrs. 1963-66), Am., Ill., Chgo. bar assns., Patent Law Assn. Chgo. (bd. mgrs. 1972-73). Republican. Clubs: Union League (Chgo.); Oak Park (Ill.) Country, River Forest Tennis. Home: 1018 Park Ave River Forest IL 60305 Office: 135 S LaSalle St Chicago IL 60603

EVEN, ROBERT LAWRENCE, artist; b. Breckenridge, Minn., June 7, 1932; s. William A. and Carrie M. (Nelson) E.; m. Christa Jo Altier, Dec. 30, 1967. B.S., Valley City State Coll., 1951; M.A., U. Minn., 1952, Ph.D., 1963. Artist Brown & Biglow Corp., St. Paul, 1954; instr. U. Minn., 1955-57, 63; tchr. art Alexander Ramsey High Sch., 1958-62; mem. faculty dept. art No. Ill. U., DeKalb, 1964—, prof., 1968—, chmn. dept., 1974—. Served with U.S. Army, 1952-54. Mem. Coll. Art Assn. Am., Nat. Assn. Schs. Art, Nat. Art Adminstrs. Council, Nat. Art Edn. Assn. Office: Art Dept Northern Illinois University DeKalb IL 60115

EVENS, RONALD GENE, physician, educator; b. St. Louis, Sept. 24, 1939; s. Robert and Dorothy (Lupkey) E.; m. Hanna Blunk, Sept. 3, 1960; children: Ronald Gene, Christine, Amanda. B.A. in Econs., Washington U., St. Louis, 1960, M.D., 1964, postgrad. in bus. and edn., 1970-71. Intern Barnes Hosp., St. Louis, 1964-65; resident Mallinckrodt Inst. Radiology, 1965-66, 68-70; research asso. Nat. Heart Inst., 1966-68; asst. prof. radiology, v.p. Washington U. Med. Sch., 1970-71; prof., head dept. radiology, dir. Mallinckrodt Inst. Radiology, 1971-72; Elizabeth Mallinckrodt prof., head radiology dept., dir. Mallinckrodt Inst., 1972—; radiologist in chief Barnes and Children's Hosp., St. Louis, 1971—; chmn. bd. Med. Care Group, St. Louis, 1980—; mem. bd. Washington U. Med. Center, 1980—; mem. adv. com. on splty. and geog. distbn. of physicians Inst. Medicine, Nat. Acad. Scis., 1974-76; dir. Charter Bank St. Louis.; Hickey lectr., Detroit, 1975, Carmen lectr., St. Louis, 1983, Hampton lectr., Boston, 1984. Contbr. over 120 articles to profl. jours. Lodge adviser Order Arrow, Boy Scouts Am., 1975—; elder Glendale and Kirkwood Presbyn. Ch., 1971-74; bd. dirs. St. Louis Comprehensive Neighborhood Health Center, OEO, 1970-74. Served with USPHS, 1966-68. James Picker Found. advanced acad. fellow, 1970; recipient Disting. Service award St. Louis C. of C., 1972, Disting. Eagle Scout award Nat. Council Boy Scouts Am., 1984. Fellow Am. Coll. Radiology; mem. Mo. Radiol. Soc. (pres. 1977-78), Soc. Nuclear Medicine (trustee 1971-75), AMA, St. Louis Med. Soc., Mo. Med. Assn., Soc. Chairmen Acad. Radiology Depts. (pres. 1979), Radiol. Soc. N.Am., Assn. Univ. Radiologists, Am. Roentgen Ray Soc. (v.p. 1982, treas. 1983—), Phi Beta Kappa, Alpha Omega Alpha (Sheard-Sanford award). Office: 510 S Kingshighway Saint Louis MO 63110

EVENSON, MERLE ARMIN, chemist, educator; b. LaCrosse, Wis., July 27, 1934; s. Ansel Bernard and Gladys Mabel (Nelson) E.; m. Peggy L. Kovats, Oct. 5, 1957; children—David A., Donna L. B.S., U. Wis., LaCrosse, 1956; M.S. in Guidance, Madison, 1960, Madison, 1960; Ph.D. in Analytical Chemistry, Madison, 1966. Diplomate: Am. Bd. Clin. Chemistry (v.p. 1978-81). Tchr. math. and physics St. Croix Falls (Wis.) High Sch., 1956-57; tchr. chemistry Central High Sch., LaCrosse, 1957-59; instr. dept. medicine U. Wis., Madison, 1965-66, asst. prof., 1966-69, asso. prof., 1971-75, prof., 1975—, prof. dept. pathology, 1979—; asst. dir. clin. lab. Univ. Hosps., 1965-66, dir. clin. chemistry lab., 1966-69, dir. toxicology lab., 1971—; chmn. Gordon Research Conf. on Analytical Chemistry, 1978; vis. lectr. Harvard Med. Sch., 1969-71; mem. staff Peter Bent Brigham Hosp., Boston, 1969-71; cons. in field to AEC, FDA, NIH, Nat. Bur. Standards. Bd. editors: Chemical Instrumentation, 1973—, Analytical Chemistry, 1974-77, Jour. Analytical Toxicology, 1976-79, Selected Methods in Clin. Chemistry, 1977-81; editor: Contemporary Topics in Analytical and Clincal Chemistry, 1974—; contbr. numerous chpts. to books, articles to profl. jours. NIH fellow, 1970-71; recipient Maurice O. Graff Disting. Alumni award U. Wis., LaCrosse, 1981. Mem. Acad. Clin. Lab. Physicians and Scientists, AAAS, Am. Assn. Clin. Chemists (bd. editors Clin. Chemistry 1970-80), Am. Chem. Soc., Sigma Xi, Kappa Delta Pi. Patentee continuous oil hemoperfusion unit. Office: 600 Highland Ave Madison WI 53792 *As a teacher, the fostering of the development of creativity in people who then make contributions to our society is an exciting process. The most significant professional reward I receive is the observation of the successes of others with whom I have interacted and taught.*

EVENSON, PATTEE EDWARD, orch. condr., educator; b. Spokane, Wash., June 2, 1910; s. Edward Winter and Rowena (Pattee) E.; m. Flavis Richards, Mar. 23, 1951. Pre-law student, U. Chgo., 1930; B.Sc., U. Minn., 1931; Mus.M., U. Mich., 1935; D.Mus. Arts, U. So. Calif., 1960; postgrad., Eastman Sch. Music, U. Rochester, N.Y., 1942-49. Chmn. music dept. San Diego State Coll., 1949-57; dir. grad. studies in music Mt. St. Marys Coll., Los Angeles, 1957-64; guest condr., lectr., clinic dir., adjudicator state and nat. music festivals. Curriculum cons., mem. coll. accreditation com. Calif. Bd. Edn. First chair trumpet, Mpls. Symphony Orch., 1929-34, Rochester Philharmonic and Civic orchs., 1935-49, Boston Pops Orch., summer 1945; condr., dept. head, Eastman Sch. Music, Rochester, 1935-49; condr., Inglewood (Calif.) Symphony Orch., Am. Symphony of Los Angeles, Burbank (Calif.) Symphony, others, 1964—; Mem. editorial adv. bd.: Music Jour, 1968—; Contbr. articles to profl. jours. Bd. dirs. Los Angeles chpt. Young Audiences of Am. Mem. Am. Fedn. Musicians, Opera Guild So. Calif. (charter mem. San Diego chpt.), Music Educators Nat. Conf. (chmn. com. music in higher edn.), Phi Mu Alpha Sinfonia, Pi Kappa Lambda. Address: 3622 Terra Granada Dr 1A Walnut Creek CA 94595

EVERBACH, OTTO GEORGE, lawyer; b. New Albany, Ind., Aug. 27, 1938; s. Otto G. and Zelda Marie (Hilt) E.; m. Nancy Lee Stern, June 3, 1961; children: Tracy Ellen, Stephen George. B.S., U.S. Mil. Acad., 1960; LL.B., U. Va., 1966. Bar: Va. 1967, Ind. 1967, Calif. 1975, Mass. 1978. Counsel CIA, Langley, Va., 1966-67; corp. counsel Bristol-Meyers Co., Evansville, Ind., 1967-74, Alza Corp., Palo Alto, Calif., 1974-75; sec., gen. counsel Am. Optical Corp., Southbridge, Mass., 1976-81; assoc. gen. counsel Warner-Lambert Co., Morris Plains, N.J., 1981-83; v.p., gen. counsel Kimberly-Clark Corp., Neenah, Wis., 1984—. Sec. So. Ind. Higher Edn., Inc., 1972-74. Served with U.S. Army, 1960-63. Mem. Am., Va., Ind., Calif. bar assns. Office: Kimberly-Clark Corp 400 N Lake St Neenah WI 54956

EVERETT, C. CURTIS, lawyer; b. Omaha, Aug. 9, 1930; s. Charles Edgar and Rosalie (Cook) E.; m. Joan Rose Bader, Sept. 7, 1951; children: Jeffrey, Ellen, Amy, Jennifer. B.A. cum laude, Beloit Coll., 1952; J.D., U. Chgo., 1957. Bar: Ill. 1957. Since practiced in, Chgo.; partner firm Bell, Boyd, Lloyd, Haddad & Burns, 1965-81; partner successor firm Bell, Boyd & Lloyd, 1981—; Vice pres., sec., dir. H. Bader, Cons., Inc., Clearwater, Fla. Editorial bd.: U. Chgo. Law Rev, 1956-57. Chmn., So. suburban area Beloit Coll. Ford Found. challange program, 1964-65; pres. The Players, Flossmoor, 1970-71. Served with AUS, 1952-54. Mem. Am., Ill., Chgo. bar assns., U. Chgo. Law Sch. Alumni Assn. (dir. 1973-76, pres. Chgo. chpt. 1979-80), Order of Coif, Order Demolay (past master counselor Rock River chpt.), Sigma Chi, Phi Alpha Delta. Mem. Community Ch. (deacon). Clubs: Legal, Law, Monroe (bd. govs. 1976—), Univ. (Chgo.)). Home: 2302 MacDonald Ln Flossmoor IL 60422 Office: 3 First Nat Plaza 70 W Madison St Chicago IL 60602

EVERETT, DONALD EDWARD, educator; b. Auburn, Ala., Dec. 10, 1920; s. Edward and Mary Rebecca (Hopkins) E.; m. Mary Lou Melancon, Sept. 4, 1949; children—John Lauchlin, Mary Melancon. B.A., U. Fla., 1941; M.A., Tulane U., 1950, Ph.D. (Ford Found. fellow), 1952. Instr. history Tulane U.; also editorial asst. Mississippi Valley Hist. Rev., 1952-53; faculty Trinity U., San Antonio, 1953—, prof. history, 1964—, chmn. dept., 1967-81; Piper prof., 1970. Editor: Chaplain Davis and Hood's Texas Brigade, 1962; Author: Trinity University: A Record of One Hundred Years, 1968, San Antonio: The Flavor of Its Past, 1845-1898, 1975; compiler: San Antonio Legacy, 1979; contbr. articles to hist. jours. Mem. Bexar County Hist. Survey Com., 1961—. Served with USAAF, 1942-45. Mem. Orgn. Am. Historians, So. Hist. Assn., Tex.Hist. Assn., San Antonio Hist. Assn. (pres. 1962), Yanaguana Soc., Phi Alpha Theta, Pi Sigma Alpha. Presbyterian (elder). Home: 142 Laurel Heights Pl San Antonio TX 78212

EVERETT, DURWARD R., JR., banker; b. Robersonville, N.C., Feb. 20, 1925; s. Durward R. and Fannie M. (Smith) E.; m. Iris Taylor, June 21, 1947; children—Amy, Janet, Patricia. Student, Davidson Coll., 1941-42; B.S. in Commerce, U. N.C., 1947; postgrad., Stonier Grad. Sch. Banking, 1956. Mgmt. trainee Wachovia Bank & Trust Co., Raleigh, N.C., 1947-51, asst. v.p., 1951-58, v.p., 1958-69, sr. v.p., 1969—, city exec., Durham, N.C., 1970-74, western region exec., Asheville, 1974—; dir. Gen. Telephone Co. of S.E.; trustee U.N.C.-Asheville. Trustee Meml. Mission Hosp.; sec.-treas. Asheville Regional Airport Authority. Served to lt. (j.g.) USNR, 1943-46. Mem. Asheville Area C. of C. (dir., pres. 1980). Clubs: Biltmore, Forest Country, Asheville Downtown City. Home: 11 Stuyvescent Crescent Biltmore Forest NC 28803 Office: PO Box 2510 Asheville NC 28802

EVERETT, EUGENE FRANCIS, JR., banker; b. Springfield, Mo., Aug. 29, 1925; s. Eugene F. and Helen L. (Jacobi) E.; m. Juliana E. Johnson, June 11, 1949; children—Constance Everett White, Susan Everett Provance, Thomas, Diane, John. B.A. in Econs, Drury Coll., 1948; cert., Sch. Fin. Public Relations, Northwestern U., 1955. Exec. trainee Mississippi Valley Trust Co., St. Louis, 1948-51; with Union Nat. Bank, Springfield, Mo., 1952—, v.p., 1959-69, exec. v.p., 1969-75, pres., 1975-78, chmn. bd., 1978—, chief exec. officer, 1978—; dir. Boatmen's Bancshares Inc., St. Louis; instr. adult edn. dept. Drury Coll., Springfield, 1962-68, Basic Sch. Banking, Omaha, 1969-76, Intermediate Sch. Banking, from 1969; dir. Boatmen's Bank of Pulaski County, Richland, Mo., Boatmen's Bank of Taney County, Forsyth, Mo., Boatmen's Springfield Nat. Bank; chmn. bd. Heer-Andres Investment Co., Springfield, 1976—; pres. Finance Investment Co., Springfield, 1977—, Better Bus. Bur. S.W. Mo., Inc., 1971—. Pres. Easter Seal Soc. S.W. Mo., 1975-76, Ozark Regional Heart Assn., 1973-74, Mo. Public Expenditure Survey, Jefferson City, Mo., 1976-79; mem. adv. bd. St. John's Hosp., Springfield, 1978—; bd. dirs. United Way of Springfield and Greene County, Mo., 1977—, ARC, Greene County chpt., 1972-75, Springfield Greene County Hist. Mus., 1978-79, Community Orgn. for Drug Abuse Control, 1973-74, Cath. Found. of Diocese of Springfield-Cape Girardeau, Mo., 1977—, Springfield Art Mus.; chmn. Springfield Art Mus., 1969; trustee Drury Coll., 1976—, chmn., 1981-83. Served to 1st lt. USAAF, 1943-45, 51-52. Recipient Disting. Alumni award Drury Coll., 1970. Mem. Am. Inst. Banking, Mo. Bankers Assn. (chmn. 1968-69), Bank Adminstrn. Inst. (pres. S.W. Mo. chpt. 1959-60), Springfield C. of C. (dir. 1976-79). Republican. Roman Catholic. Clubs: Hickory Hills Country., Ironwood Country. Home: 2333 Fritts Ln Springfield MO 65804 Office: PO Box 1157 SSS Springfield MO 65805

EVERETT, JAMES LEGRAND, III, utility executive; b. Charlotte, N.C., July 24, 1926; s. James LeGr and Charlotte (Keesler) E.; m. Marjorie Miriam Scherf, Sept. 3, 1947; children: James LeGrand IV, Christopher Glenn, John Keesler. B.S. in Mech. Engring, Pa. State U., 1948, M.S., 1949; M.S. in Indsl. Mgmt, MIT, 1959. Registered profl. engr., Pa. Instr. mech. engring. Pa. State U., 1948-50; instr. civil and mech. engring. Drexel Evening Coll., 1950-52; head fuel sect. Atomic Power Devel. Assos., 1953-55; with Phila. Electric Co., 1950—, exec. v.p., 1968-71, pres., 1971-82, chmn., chief exec. officer, 1982—, also dir., mem. exec. com. parent co., dir. subsidiaries; chmn., dir. Radiation Mgmt. Corp., 1971—; dir. Phila. Nat. Bank, Fidelity Mut. Life Ins. Co., Tasty Baking Co., Martin Marietta Corp. Mem. sci. and arts com. Franklin Inst. Served to ensign USNR, 1944-46. Sloan fellow, 1958-59; Recipient Outstanding Young Man of Year award Phila. Jr. C. of C., 1961; Ann. Engring. Tech. award Temple U., 1963; Distinguished Alumnus award Pa. State U., 1971; George Washington medal, 1974; Humanitarian award Am. Jewish Com., 1976; PAL award Police Athletic League, 1978; Exemplar award for interracial cooperation Phila. NAACP, 1981; named Engr. of Year, Delaware Valley, Pa., 1972; Delaware Valley Council Citizen of Yr., 1972; YMCA Outstanding Layman of Yr., 1975. Fellow ASME; mem. Am. Nuclear Soc., Franklin Inst., IEEE, Soc. Am. Mil. Engrs., Nat. Acad. Engring., Engrs. Club Phila., Nat., Pa. socs. profl. engrs., Tau Beta Pi, Pi Tau Sigma, Pi Mu Epsilon. Office: Phila Electric Co 2301 Market St Philadelphia PA 19101 *

EVERETT, LUCIUS THEODORE, utility exec.; b. Paterson, N.J., Jan. 14, 1920; s. Lucius Theodore and Louise Harriet (Puster) E.; m. Marian Florence Greenwood, May 11, 1946; children—Louise Harriet, Ruth Anne, Marjorie Carol, Virginia Sue. A.B., Clark U., Worcester, Mass., 1941; postgrad., Bklyn. Poly. Inst. With Public Service Electric & Gas Co., Newark, 1941-59, sr. rate asst., 1956-59; with N.Y. State Electric & Gas Corp., Ithaca, 1959—, asst. to pres., then v.p., 1969-74, sr. v.p., 1974—. Chmn. budget com. Tompkins County (N.Y.) United Fund, 1965-66. Served to 1st lt. C.E. AUS, 1943-46. Republican. Club: Masons. Home: 1114 Hanshaw Rd Ithaca NY 14850 Office: PO Box 287 Ithaca NY 14850

EVERETT, MARK ALLEN, dermatologist, educator; b. Oklahoma City, May 30, 1928; s. Mark Ruben and Alice (Allen) E.; 1 son, Howard Dean. B.A. in Polit. Sci, U. Okla., 1947, M.D., 1951. Intern in pediatrics U. Mich. Med. Sch., 1951, resident in dermatology, 1954-57, instr. dermatology, 1956-57; intern in public health Tulane Med. Sch., 1951; mem. faculty U. Okla. Med. Sch., 1959—, chmn. dept. dermatology, 1964—, prof. dermatology, head dept., 1967—, adj. prof. pathology and anatomy, 1975—, prof., interim head dept. pathology, 1979—, Regents prof., 1982—, chmn. faculty bd., 1974—; chief staff Okla. Meml. Hosp., 1980—; vice chmn. bd. Bone and Joint Hosp., Oklahoma City, 1976—; chmn. Internat. Com. for Dermatopathology, 1980—. Author 200 articles in field, chpts. in books. Pres. Okla. Ballet Soc., 1973, 77-80, Oklahoma City Chamber Orch., 1979-81; pres. trustees Allen Everett Found., 1961—; adv. bd. World Lit. Today, 1970—, Bizzell Library Soc., 1982—. Served with USAF, 1952-54. Recipient Bronze medal U. Okla. Fedn.; grantee Am. Cancer Soc., NIH. Mem. Am. Acad. Dermatology (chmn. long-range planning council 1975-80, dir. 1978—), Assn. Profs. Dermatology (pres. 1976-78), Am. Soc. Dermatopathology (pres. 1980), AMA, Am. Assn. Cancer Research, Internat. Acad. Pathology, Am. Dermatol. Assn., Am. Soc. Clin. Investigation, Soc. Investigative Dermatology, Radiation Research Soc., Okla. Med. Soc., Coll. Physicians Phila., N.Y. Acad. Scis., N.Mex. Dermatol. Soc., Pacific Dermatol. Assn., S. Central Dermatol. Soc., Austrian Dermatology Soc., Gourgerot Soc., Phi Beta Kappa. Democrat. Roman Catholic. Club: Lotos (N.Y.C.). Office: 619 NE 13th St Oklahoma City OK 73104

EVERETT, ROBERT GEORGE, food company executive; b. Binghamton, N.Y., Mar. 15, 1931; s. Robert L. and Madeline E.; m. Betty J. Whitten, Sept. 9, 1950; children: Elizabeth, Karen, Robert, Thomas. B.S. in Accounting, Harpur Coll., 1953; M.B.A., Cornell U., 1955. Various financial positions up to div. controller, corporate dir. financial planning IBM, 1955-69; exec. v.p. Great Western United Corp., Denver, 1969-72, pres., 1972-75; exec. v.p. Fisher Foods, Inc., Beford Heights, Ohio, 1977-79, vice chmn. bd., chief fin. officer, 1979—, pres., 1981—. Served with USNR, 1949-54. Mem. Fin. Execs. Inst. Clubs: Larchmont Shore, Larchmont Yacht. Home: 30 Larchmont Ave Larchmont NY 10538 Office: 5300 Richmond Rd Bedford Heights OH 44146

EVERETT, ROBERT RIVERS, manufacturing company executive; b. Yonkers, N.Y., June 26, 1921; s. Chester McKenzie and Ruth (Melius) E.; m. Helen Burns, Oct. 21, 1944 (div. 1972); children—Robert F., Bruce M., Douglas F., Theodore J., Michael B.; m. Jean M. McGrath, Nov. 4, 1972 (dec. Nov. 1980); m. Ann T. Russell, Mar. 26, 1982. B.S., Duke, 1942; M.S., Mass. Inst. Tech., 1943. With Servomechanisms Lab. of Mass. Inst. Tech., 1942-51, asso. dir., 1951; asso. div. head Lincoln Lab., 1951-56, div. head, 1956-58; tech. dir. The Mitre Corp., Bedford, Mass., 1958-59, v.p. tech. operations, 1959-69, exec. v.p., 1969, pres., 1969—; mem. sci. adv. bd. USAF; mem. sci. adv. group Def. Communications Agy.; trustee No. Energy Corp.; cons. Def. Sci. Bd.; cons. div. adv. group Electronic Systems div. Air Force Systems Command.; Mem. sci. adv. bd. U.S. Air Force. Contbr. articles to tech. jours. Fellow IEEE; mem. Assn. Computing Machinery, AAAS, Nat. Acad. Engring., Phi Beta Kappa, Sigma Xi, Tau Beta Pi. Club: Cosmos (Washington). Patentee digital computers. Home: 80 Rollingwood Ln Concord MA 01742 Office: PO Box 208 Bedford MA 01730

EVERETT, WARREN SYLVESTER, government official; b. Wichita, Kans., Oct. 19, 1910; s. Carl S. and Effie (Barton) E.; m. Ruthmary Francis, June 13, 1935; children: Mary Margaret (Mrs. R.L. Graham), Judith Ann (Mrs. D.L. McKee), Warren Douglas. B.A., U. Wichita, 1932; B.S., U.S. Mil. Acad., 1935; M.S., Cornell, 1939; student, Army Engr. Sch., 1939-40, Army Command and Gen. Staff Coll., 1942, Princeton, 1945, Armed Forces Staff Coll., 1949, Army War Coll., 1956-57. Registered profl. engr., Wash. Commd. 2d lt. U.S. Army, 1935, advanced through grades to col., 1951; dir. U.S. Army Constrn. Agy., France, 1959-61; dist. engr., Vicksburg, Miss., 1961-63, ret., 1963; chief pub. works div. USOM to Vietnam, 1963-65; chief engr. U.S. AID mission to Nigeria, 1965-66, Vietnam Bur., AID, 1966-67; dir. excess property program AID, 1967-68; cons. Office Emergency Preparedness, Exec. Office Pres., 1968-69; exec. archtl.-engring. firm, Saigon, Vietnam, 1969-71; dep. dir. U.S. Property Disposal Agy., Vietnam, 1971-74; dep. dir. Office Planning and Mgmt., chief commodity mgmt. and merchandising divs. Def. Property Disposal Service, Battle Creek, 1974—. Contbr. articles to profl. jours. Organizer nat. fallout shelter survey and marking program, 1961; Pres. P.T.A., Am. Sch., Tokyo, 1953-54. Decorated Legion of Merit with oak leaf cluster; Ulchi medal with silver star (Korean Distinguished Service medal); Presdl. citation, Korea; Chuong-My Outstanding Service medal, Vietnam). Fellow Am. Soc. C.E., Soc. Am. Mil. Engrs. (past pres. Vicksburg and Saigon); mem. Nat. Soc. Profl. Engrs., Am. Security Council (nat. adv. bd.). Home: 340 Watkins Ln Battle Creek MI 49015 Office: Def Property Disposal Service (DPDS-MM Federal Center). Battle Creek MI 49016

EVERETT, WOODROW WILSON, electrical engineer, educator; b. Newton, Miss., Oct. 11, 1937; s. Woodrow Wilson and Katherine (Thrash) E.; m. Cherry Donna Sarff, Aug. 23, 1958; children: Woodrow W., Cherry Leanne Everett. B.E.E., George Washington U., 1959; M.S., Cornell U., 1965, Ph.D., 1968. Project engr. Scott Paper Co., 1959; Ihaca Research Labs., Atlantic Research Corp., Ithaca, N.Y., 1962-64; postdoctoral program dir. Rome (N.Y.) Air Devel. Center, 1964-75; chmn. bd. Southeastern Center for Elec. Engring. and N.E. Consortium for Engring. Edn., St. Cloud, Fla., 1975—; dir. Device Assos. Corp. N.Y., Masonwood, Inc., Sunoric Corp., Groton Community Devel. Corp. Author works in field. Democratic committeeman, Madison County, N.Y., 1976-79; pres. Village of Groton (N.Y.) Appeals Bd., 1966-69; chmn. Groton Planning Bd., 1968-69. Served with USAF, 1959-62. Fellow IEEE; mem. Instrument Soc. Am., N.Y. Acad. Sci. Club: Rotary. Home: Cherwood-Alligator Lake Rt 5 Box 919 St Cloud FL 32769 Office: 1101 Massachusetts Ave St Cloud FL 32769

EVERHART, DAVID LESLIE, hospital administrator; b. Granville, Ohio, May 24, 1928; s. William Alfred and Mary Elder (Lough) E.; m. Margaret Weber, June 23, 1951; children: John David, Barbara Weber, Margaret Leslie. B.A., Denison U., 1950; M.S. in Hosp. Adminstrn., Columbia U., 1953. Adminstrv. intern Ohio State U. Hosp., Columbus, 1950-51; adminstrv. resident Henry Ford Hosp., Detroit, 1952-53, adminstrv. asst., 1953-55, asst. dir., 1955-61, assoc. dir., 1961-63; adminstr., adminstrv. v.p. John Hopkins Hosp., Balt., 1963-70; exec. dir. New Eng. Med. Ctr. Hosp., Boston, 1970-75; pres. Northwestern Meml. Hosp., Chgo., 1976—. Mem. Am. Hosp. Assn., Am. Coll. Hosp. Adminstrs., Assn. Am. Med. Colls., Soc. Health Service Adminstrs., Am. Pub. Health Assn., Ill. Hosp. Assn. (trustee 1976-82), Inst. Medicine, Phi Gamma Delta, Blue Key. Presbyterian. Office: Northwestern Meml Hosp Superior St and Fairbanks Ct Chicago IL 60611

EVERHART, EDGAR, astronomer; b. Akron, Ohio, June 20, 1920; s. Edgar and Eleanor Pauline (Schmidt) E.; m. Elizabeth Saward Merry, June 7, 1943; children—Stanley David, Kathleen. A.B., Oberlin Coll., 1942; Ph.D. in Physics, Mass. Inst. Tech., 1948. Instr. Dartmouth Coll., 1948-50; mem. faculty U. Conn., 1950-69, prof., 1960-69; prof. physics and astronomy U. Denver, 1969—. Contbr. articles in atomic collisions, comets, celestial mechanics, and astronom. photographs. Fellow Am. Phys. Soc.; mem. Am. Astron. Soc., Internat. Astron. Union. Discovered 2 comets. Home: 985 Dick Mountain Dr Bailey CO 80421 Office: Physics Dept U Denver Denver CO 80208

EVERHART, REX, actor, director, photographer; b. Watseka, Ill., June 13, 1920; s. Arthur Mark and Jeanette (Dodson) E.; m. Jill Reardon, Feb. 11, 1944 (div. 1957); m. Claire Violet Richard, Dec. 22, 1962; 1 dau., Degan Jeanette. Student, U. Mo., 1938-40; B.T.A., Pasadena Playhouse, 1942; B.S., NYU, M.A., 1949. Actor films, TV, radio, 23 Broadway or pre-Broadway state prodns., TV commls., regional theatres, repertory theatres including 7 seasons Am. Shakespeare Theatre, touring cos., London prodn. of the Odd Couple, 1966-67. Served to 1st lt. USN, 1942-46. Nominated Antoinette Perry (Tony) award, 1978. Mem. Actors' Equity Assn. (councillor 1968-75), Screen Actors' Guild, AFTRA. Democrat. Club: Players (N.Y.C.).

EVERHART, THOMAS EUGENE, physicist, electrical engineer, educator; b. Kansas City, Mo., Feb. 15, 1932; s. William Elliott and Elizabeth Ann (West) E.; m. Doris Arleen Wentz, June 21, 1953; children—Janet Sue, Nancy Jean, David William, John Thomas. A.B. in Physics magna cum laude, Harvard, 1953; M.Sc., U. Calif. at Los Angeles, 1955; Ph.D. in Engring, Cambridge (Eng.) U., 1958. Mem. tech. staff Hughes Research Labs., Culver City, Calif., 1953-55; mem. faculty U. Calif. at Berkeley, 1958-78, prof. elec. engring. and computer scis., 1967-78, Miller research prof., 1969-70, chmn. dept., 1972-77; prof. elec. engring., Joseph Silbert dean engring. Cornell U., Ithaca, N.Y., 1979—; fellow scientist Westinghouse Research Labs., Pitts., 1962-63; guest prof. Inst. für Angewandte Physik, U. Tuebingen, W. Germany, 1966-67, Waseda U., Tokyo, also Osaka (Japan) U., fall 1974; vis. fellow Clare Hall, Cambridge U., 1975; chmn. Electron, Ion and Photon Beam Symposium, 1977; cons. to industry; mem. sci. and ednl. adv. com. Lawrence Berkeley Lab., 1978—, chmn., 1980—; mem. sci. adv. com. Gen. Motors Corp., 1980—; mem. tech. adv. com. R.R. Donnelley & Sons, 1981—. NSF sr. postdoctoral fellow, 1966-67; Guggenheim fellow, 1974-75. Fellow IEEE; mem. AASS, Nat. Acad. Engring., Electron Microscopy Soc. Am. (council 1970-72, pres. 1977), Microbeam Analysis Soc. Am., Deutsche Gesellschaft für Elektronenmikroskopie, Assn. Marshall Scholars and Alumni (pres. 1965-68), Sigma Xi, Eta Kappa Nu. Club: Faculty (Cornell U.). Home: 102 Willard Way Ithaca NY 14850 Office: Coll Engring Cornell U Ithaca NY 14853

EVERILL, CHARLES HENRY, consumer direct marketing executive, communications-media company executive; b. Beloit, Wis., Mar. 25, 1943; s. Royal B. and Alice M. (Grenawalt) E.; m. Martha Ann Brownell, June 26, 1965; children: Charles Henry, Sara Elaine. B.A. cum laude, Harvard Coll., 1965, M.B.A. with highest distinction, 1972. Corp. dir. mktg. Harte-Hanks Communications, Inc., San Antonio, 1972-74, pres. nat. newspaper group, 1976-80, sr. v.p. mktg., 1980—; acting pres. Harte-Hanks Cable, 1981-82; pres. consumer direct mktg. Hart-Hanks Communications, Inc., 1982—; pub. The Jour. News, Hamilton, Ohio, 1974-80. Founding mem. Hamilton Devel. Corp. Served to lt. USN, 1965-70. Baker scholar Harvard Grad. Sch. Bus. Adminstrn., 1972; named Outstanding Young Ohioan Ohio Jaycees, 1976, Outstanding Young Man Hamilton Jaycees, 1976. Mem. Am. Newspaper Pubs. Assn., Inland Daily Press Assn., Am. Soc. Newspaper Editors, San Antonio C. of c. (chmn. mktg.-communications com. 1981-83). Republican. Congregationalist. Home: 3726 Mary Mont San Antonio TX 78217 Office: Harte-Hanks Communications Inc 40 NE Loop 410 San Antonio TX 78216

EVERINGHAM, LYLE J., grocery chain executive; b. Flint, Mich., May 5, 1926; s. Kenneth L. and Christine (Everingham) E.; m. Rlene Lajiness, Mar. 31, 1929; children: Nancy, Mark, Christine. Student, U. Toledo, 1956-63. With Kroger Co., 1946—, v.p., Ohio, 1963-64, v.p. produce merchandising, Cin., 1964-65, successively v.p., from 1966; sr. v.p., pres., now chmn., chief exec. officer; pres. Wesco Foods. Active Mt. Lookout Civic Club; Mem. Cin. Bus. Com.; mem. adv. bd. Cin. Salvation Army. Served with cav. AUS, 1943-46. Roman Catholic. Clubs: Cin. Country, Queen City, Comml. (Cin.). Office: Kroger Co 1014 Vine St Cincinnati OH 45201

EVERITT, GEORGE BAIN, banker; b. Forest Hills, L.I., N.Y., Apr. 21, 1914; s. George B. and Lois E. (Richter) E.; m. Barbara Taylor, Mar. 25, 1944; children: Lois V., (Mrs. Paul R. Anderson), Margaret M. (Mrs. Manfred Gerling), Emily A., Elizabeth S. Caldwell. B.A., Duke, 1936. With Sears, Roebuck & Co., 1936; with Merchandise Nat. Bank of Chgo., 1936—, asst. v.p., 1941-49, dir., 1946—, v.p., 1949-60, pres., 1960-65, chmn. bd., 1965—. Sec. Hadley Sch. for Blind, Winnetka, Ill., 1950-64, v.p., 1964—. Served with USNR, 1942-46. Mem. North Side Bankers Assn. (past pres.). Office: Merchandise Nat Bank of Chicago Merchandise Mart Chicago IL 60654

EVEROTE, WARREN PETER, film and pub. co. exec.; b. Farmington, Minn., Oct. 12, 1913; s. Peter William and Gladys (Ritter) E.; m. June Meriam, Mar. 18, 1940; children—Jan Deneige, Linda Ann. B.A., U. Calif. at Los Angeles, 1935, M.A., 1936; Ph.D., Columbia, 1943. Instr. pub. schs., Los Angeles, 1938-42; research asso. Bur. Ednl. Research in Sci., Columbia, 1942-43; instr. sci. Lincoln Sch., N.Y.C., 1942-43; with Ency. Brit. Films, 1945-66, v.p. research and prodn., 1955-62, pres., 1962-64, dir., 1962-66; pres. Ency. Brit. Press, 1964-65, Ency. Brit., Ltd., 1965—, Ency. Brit. Devel. Corp., 1966-67, Ency. Brit. Edn. Corp., 1967-70, v.p., 1970—; dir. Ency. Brit., 1962-70; Mem. phys. sci. study sect. Nat. Studies Ednl. Improvement, 1957-58, chemistry study sect., 1960-62. Author: Agricultural Science to Serve Youth, 1943, also articles on film prodn. Served to lt. comdr. USNR, World War II. Recipient Scholastic Tchr. mag. award, 1949, 54, Inter-Agrl. Congress award, 1953. Fellow A.A.A.S., Ill. Acad. Sci.; mem. Nat. Assn. Research Sci., Teaching, N.Y. Acad. Sci., L'Ordre des Anysetiers du Roy (Paris), Phi Delta Kappa. Episcopalian. Home: 4265 Cresta Ave Santa Barbara CA 93110

EVERS, WALTER, mgmt. cons.; b. Englewood, N.J., May 9, 1914; s. Fritz Otto and Liesel Clara (Micho) E.; m. Emlen Davies Grosjean, Sept. 19, 1970; children by previous marriage—Alison Evers Everett, Jr., Ridgely Clyde. A.B., St. John's Coll., 1935; grad. student, Georgetown U. Sch. Fgn. Service, also Maxwell Sch. of Syracuse U. Pres. Walter Evers & Co., mgmt. cons., Cleve., 1960—, Walter Evers,

Inc., 1962—; dir. Medusa Corp., Cleve.; Dir. exec. recruitment WPB, 1941-42; exec. sec. def. mgmt. com. Office Sec. Def., 1949-50. Mem., past chmn. bd. visitors and govs. St. John's Coll., Annapolis, Md., Santa Fe, N.Mex., 1958—. Served to lt. USNR, 1942-47. Republican. Episcopalian. Clubs: University (N.Y.C.); Chagrin Valley Hunt (Gates Mills, Ohio). Home: PO Box 99 Newbury OH 44065 Office: 54 Lyman Circle Shaker Heights OH 44122

EVERS, WILLIAM DOHRMANN, lawyer; b. San Francisco, May, 6, 1927; s. Albert John and Sepha (Pischel) E.; m. Edwina Bigelow Benington, Aug. 26, 1950 (div. May 1978); children: Elliot B., Anne B., Albert John II, William Dohrmann; m. Britte-Marie Emblad, May 27, 1978. B.A., Yale U., 1949; LL.B., J.D., U. Calif. at Berkeley, 1952. Bar: Calif. bar 1952. Asso. firm Chickering & Gregory, San Francisco, 1953-56; legal asst. to commr. SEC, 1956-57; asso. atty. Allen, Miller, Groezinger, Keesling & Martin, San Francisco, 1957-60; partner Pettit, Evers & Martin, San Francisco, 1960-78; chmn. On-Line Bus. System, Inc., 1980—; chmn., chief exec. officer Precision Techs., 1982—; dir. Comml. Bank San Francisco, Boreal Ridge Corp. Pres. Econ. Devel. Council City and County of San Francisco, 1978-80; Chmn. San Francisco Bay Conservation and Devel. Commn., 1972-75; pres. Calif. Roadside Council, 1959-60, SPUR, San Francisco, 1975-78; chmn. assistance and adv. council Calif. Gov.'s Office Planning and Research, 1977-78; founder, pres. Planning and Conservation League, 1965-68; mem. air quality adv. bd. EPA, 1970-73; Vice chmn. San Francisco Republican County Central Com., 1959-63; Trustee Marin County Day Sch., 1967-70, 79—, Katherine Branson Sch., 1976-78; bd. dirs. Yosemite Inst., 1979—, Wilderness Soc., 1983—. Served with USNR, 1944-45. Mem. ABA, San Francisco Bar Assn., State Bar Calif. Clubs: Bohemian, Pacific Union (San Francisco). Home: 704 Greenfield Rd St Helena CA 94574 *Intelligence, industry, integrity and humor are the essential elements for business or professional success and, of these, integrity is the most important.*

EVERS, WILLIAM LOUIS, found. exec.; b. Pitts., Aug. 13, 1906; s. Louis and Anna (Trbovic) E.; m. Mary Alice Rice, Aug. 28, 1963; 1 dau., Danica Evers Ridgway. B.S., U. Akron, 1928; M.S., Northwestern U., 1929; Ph.D., Pa. State U., 1932. Research chemist Mobil Oil Co., 1932-36; research mgr. Rohm & Haas Co., Bridesburg, Pa., 1936-52; mgr. exploratory research Celanese Corp., N.Y.C., 1952-68; exec. dir. Camille and Henry Dreyfus Found., N.Y.C., 1968—; cons. in field. Mem. vis. com. in phys. scis. U. Chgo., 1978—; mem. vis. com. in chemistry Harvard U., 1981—. Mem. Assn. Research Dirs., Am. Chem. Soc., Sigma Xi. Republican. Presbyterian. Club: Univ. (N.Y.C.). Patentee in field. Home: 104 Essex Rd Summit NJ 07901 Office: 445 Park Ave New York NY 10022

EVERSLEY, FREDERICK JOHN, sculptor, engr.; b. Bklyn., Aug. 28, 1941; s. Frederick William and Beatrice Agnes (Syphax) E. B.S.E.E., Carnegie-Mellon U., 1963. Aerospace engring. exec. Wyle Labs., El Segundo, Calif., 1963-67. One man shows include, Whitney Mus. Am. Art, N.Y.C., 1970, Nat. Acad. Sci., Washington, 1976, 81; Los Angeles Inst. Contemporary Art, 1976, Santa Barbara Mus., Newport Harbor Art Mus., Oakland Mus. Art, 1977, Palm Springs Desert Mus., 1978, AIA, 1981, Va. Mus.; represented in permanent collections, Smithsonian Instn., Washington, Calif. State Coll. at Los Angeles, Oakland (Calif.) Art Mus., Milw. Art Center, Whitney Mus. Am. Art, N.Y.C., John Marin Meml. Collection, N.Y.C., U., Kans. Art Gallery, Lawrence, Long Beach (Calif.) Mus. Art, Currier Gallery Art, Manchester, N.H., Taft Mus. Art, Cin., Cranbrook Art Gallery, Bloomfield Hills, Mich., Nat. Acad. Sci., Washington, Nat. Collection Fine Arts, Washington, M.I.T., Cambridge, Neuberger Mus. Art, Purchase, N.Y., Newport Harbor Art Mus., Newport Beach, Calif., Guggenheim Mus., N.Y.C., Smith Coll. Mus. Art, Northhampton, Mass., Nat. Air and Space Mus.; artist in residence, Nat. Air and Space Mus., Washington, 1977-80. Nat. Endowment Arts grantee, 1972. Mem. Los Angeles Inst. Contemporary Art, Artworkers Coalition. Address: 1110 W Washington Blvd Venice CA 90291 also 29 Mercer St New York NY 10013

EVERSON, LEONARD CHARLES, container manufacturing company executive, lawyer; b. Schenectady, July 7, 1923; m. Marjory Whitty; children: Mark, Charles W. Student, Duke U.; J.D., Harvard U., 1948. Staff atty. Ford Motor Co., Detroit, 1950-57; v.p., gen. counsel Internat. Basic Economy Corp., N.Y.C., 1957-72, Nat. Bulk Carriers, 1972-75; v.p., chief legal officer Nat. Can Corp., Chgo., 1975—. Served with U.S. Army, 1943-45. Mem. Am. Bar Assn. Home: 74 Woodland Rd Lake Forest IL 60045 Office: Nat Can Corp 8101 W Higgins Rd Chicago IL 60631

EVERSON, WILLIAM OLIVER, poet; b. Sacramento, Sept. 10, 1912; s. Louis Waldemar and Francelia Marie (Herber) E.; m. Edwa Poulson, 1938 (div. 1948); m. Mary Fabilli, 1948 (div. 1960); m. Susanna Rickson, Dec. 13, 1969; 1 stepson, Jude. Student, Fresno State Coll., 1931, 34-35. With Civilian Conservation Corps, 1933-34; with Civilian Public Service, 1943-46; dir. Fine Arts Group, Waldport, Oreg., 1944-46; with U. Calif. Press, 1947-49, Catholic Worker Movement, 1950-51, Dominican Order, Province of West, 1951-69; poet-in-residence Kresge Coll., U. Calif., Santa Cruz, 1971-81; master printer Lime Kiln Press, U. Calif., Santa Cruz, 1971-81. Author: verse The Residual Years, Poems, 1934-48, 1968, Man-Fate, 1974, The Veritable Years, Poems, 1949-1966, 1978, The Masks of Drought, 1980; prose Robinson Jeffers Fragments of an Older Fury, 1967, Archetype West, 1976, Earth Poetry: Selected Essays and Interviews, 1980, Birth of a Poet: The Santa Cruz Meditations, 1982. Recipient Silver medal Commonwealth Club, 1967; Shelley Meml. award, 1978; Book of Yr. award Conf. on Christianity and Lit., 1978; Guggenheim fellow, 1949; Nat. Endowment Arts grantee, 1981. Home: 312 Swanton Rd Davenport CA 95017

EVERT, RAY FRANKLIN, botany educator; b. Mt. Carmel, Pa., Feb. 20, 1931; s. Milner Ray and Elsie (Hoffa) E.; m. Mary Margaret Maloney, Jan 2, 1960; children: Patricia Ann, Paul Franklin. B.S., Pa. State U., 1952, M.S., 1954; Ph.D., U. Calif. at Davis, 1958. Mem. faculty Mont. State U., 1958-60; mem. faculty U. Wis.-Madison, 1960—, prof. botany, 1966-77, prof. botany and plant pathology, 1977—, chmn. dept., 1973-74, 77-79; vis. prof. U. Natal, Pietermaritzburg, S. Africa, winter, spring 1971, U. Göttingen, W.Ger., summer 1971, 74-75; Mem. gen. biology and genetics fellowship rev. panel NIH, 1964-68. Co-author: Biology of Plants; contbr. articles on food conducting tissue in higher plants and leaf structure-function relationships. Recipient Alexander von Humboldt award, 1974-75, Emil H. Steiger award for excellence in teaching, 1981; Guggenheim fellow, 1965-66. Mem. Bot. Soc. Am. (Merit award 1982), Am. Inst. Biol. Scis., AAAS, Wis. Acad. Scis., Sigma Xi, Phi Kappa Phi, Phi Sigma, Phi Epsilon Phi., Pi Alpha Xi. Home: 810 Woodward Dr Madison WI 53704

EVERT-LLOYD, CHRISTINE MARIE (CHRIS EVERT), profl. tennis player; b. Ft. Lauderdale, Fla., Dec. 21, 1954; d. James and Colette Evert; m. John Lloyd, Apr. 17, 1979. Amateur tennis player, until Dec. 1972, U.S. jr. champion, 1970-71; now profl. player, mem. Women's Pro Tennis Tour; Mem. Wightmen Cup team, 1971, 72, 73, 75, 76, Bell Cup team, 1972, 73. Recipient Most Valuable Player trophy Wightman Cup Championship, 1971; Lebair Sportsmanship trophy, 1971; named Female Athlete of Yr. AP, 1974, 75; Athlete of Yr. Sports Illustrated, 1976; ranked Number 1 Woman Player World Tennis and Tennis mags., 1974-78. Mem. U.S. Lawn Tennis Assn. (named Top Women's Singles Player 1974), Nat. Honor Soc. Singles titlist U.S. Clay Ct. Championship, 1972, 73, 74, 75, 80, South African Open, 1973, Wimbledon, 1974, 76, 81, Italian Open, 1974, 75, 80, French Open, 1974, 75, 80, Canadian Open, 1974, 80, Family Circle Mag. Cup tournament, 1974, 75, 77, 78, U.S. Open, 1975, 76, 77, 78, 80, Va. Slims Championship, 1975, 77, U.S. Indoor Championship, 1978, Tokyo Invitational, 1978, numerous others *

EVERTS, CONNOR, artist; b. Bellingham, Wash., Jan. 24, 1926; s. William Edward and Sophia (Mehan) E.; m. Chizuko Sugita, Mar. 15, 1953; children—Anon Connor, Meigan Mariko, Geoffrey, Tamura. A.A., El Camino Coll., 1950; B.A., U. Wash., 1952. Mem. faculty dept. art Calif. State U., Northridge, 1960-62, Calif. Inst. Arts, 1962-65, Calif. State U., Long Beach, 1965, San Francisco Art Inst., 1966, U. So. Calif., 1967-69, U. Calif.-, Riverside, 1972-76; graphics chmn. Cranbrook Acad. Art, Bloomfield Hills, Mich., 1976-81; exchange prof. Prahran Coll. Advanced Studies, Melbourne, Australia; artist in residence Calif. Inst. Tech., 1970-71. One man exhbns. include, Pasadena Art Mus., 1960, Michael Walls Gallery, San Francisco, 1967-69, Los Angeles Mcpl. Gallery, 1971, Meckler Gallery, Los Angeles, 1979, World Print Council, 1982, retrospective exhibit, Los Angeles Mus., 1983; group exhbns. include Tokyo Biann. Painting Exhbn, 1967, Homage to Lithography, Mus. Modern Art, N.Y.C., 1969, Printmaking, Oskokunst Forening, Oslo, Norway, 1974; represented in permanent collections, Chgo. Art Inst., Long Beach Mus. Art, Los Angeles County Mus. Art, Milw. Art Center, Mus. Modern Art, N.Y.C., Pasadena Art Mus., San Francisco Mus. Modern Art, Washington Gallery Modern Art, others. Pres. adv. bd. Los Angeles Mcpl. Gallery, 1968. Served with USCG, 1946. Mem. AAUP, Los Angeles Printmaking Soc., Mich. Assn. Printmakers, Artists Equity. Studio: 2351 Sonoma St Torrance CA 90501 *Circumstances, time and place of birth, sex, race, religion, economic status, and the resultant formulative years, determine the rough shape of our lives. But we, above all, are the largest factors in determining the kinds of persons we become. Let it be by conscious choice. If we will be shaped, let it be by ideas and challenge.*

EVERY, RUSSEL B., business exec.; b. Bridgewater, Mich., Oct. 13, 1924; s. William Ward and Ola M. (Bennet) E.; m. Marion J. Olson, May 12, 1945; children—Gloria, David, William. Student, Cleary Coll. With Midland-Ross Corp., 1969-76, v.p., gen. mgr. frame div., group v.p. automotive, until 1976; an organizer Midland Steel Products Co., Cleve., 1976; with Midsco, Inc. (merged into Lamson & Sessions Co.), Lakewood, Ohio, chmn., pres., 1979—; pres., chief operating officer, dir. Lamsom & Sessions Co., 1980—. Served with USN. Mem. Am. Mgmt. Assn., Ohio Mfrs. Assn., Ohio C. of C., Greater Cleveland Growth Assn., Presidents Assn., Soc. Automotive Engrs. Clubs: Lakewood Country, Detroit Athletic, Mid-Day, Clevelander, Union, Pepper Pike (Ohio) Country. Office: 2000 Bond Ct 1300 E 9th St Cleveland OH 44114

EVINRUDE, RALPH, outboard motors mfg. exec.; b. Milw., Sept. 27, 1907; s. Ole and Bessie (Cary) E.; m. Marion Armitage, Jan. 3, 1931 (dec.); m. Frances Langford, Oct. 6, 1955. Ed., U. Wis. Testing mgr. Elto Outboard Motor Co., 1927-30; export sales mgr. Outboard Motor Corp., 1930-32, prodn. mgr., 1932-34, pres., 1934-36; chmn. bd., chmn. exec. com. Outboard Marine Corp. (formerly Outboard Marine & Mfg. Co.), 1936—. Mem. Phi Gamma Delta. Clubs: University, Yacht, Milw. Athletic (Milw.); Eldorado Country; Crown Colony (Bahamas). Home: PO Box 96 Jensen Beach FL 33457

EVIRS, HOWARD WESLEY, JR., utility exec.; b. Boston, Oct. 3, 1925; s. Howard Wesley and Inez (Harriman) E.; m. Helen G. Keefe, Mar. 12, 1949; children—Howard Wesley, Diane E., Patricia A. B.S. in Elec. Engring. with honors, Northeastern U., Boston, 1951, M.B.A., 1970. Registered profl. engr., Mass. Asst. elec. engr. Exeter & Hampton Electric Co., N.H., 1951-52; asst. exec. engr. Brockton Taunton Gas Co. (Mass.), Concord Electric Co. (N.H.), Fitchburg Gas and Electric Co. (Mass.), Orange and Rockland Utilities, Inc. (Mass.), Springfield Gas Light Co. (Mass.), 1952-63; with Fitchburg Gas and Electric Light Co., 1963—, exec. v.p., 1969-70, pres., dir., 1970—; dir. Fitchburg Fed. Savs. & Loan Assn.; adv. dir. Worcester County Nat. Bank; instr., chmn. elec. theory Lincoln Coll., Boston, 1952-64. Mem. exec. com. New Eng. Power Pool; pres. Fitchburg Energy Devel. Corp., Fitchburg Area Econ. Devel. Corp.; Bd. dirs. Jr. Achievement Montachusett Area; bd. dirs. United Fund Greater Fitchburg, v.p., 1969-71; mem. pres.'s circle Fitchburg State Coll. Served with USNR, 1943-46. Mem. IEEE (past chmn. Boston), Nat. Soc. Profl. Engrs., Edison Electric Inst., Am., Gas Assn., New Eng. Gas Assn. (dir.), Electric Council New Eng. (dir.), Fitchburg C. of C. (past chmn., past pres.), Eta Kappa Nu (past pres.), Tau Beta Pi. Clubs: Masons, Rotary (past dir. Fitchburg), Fay (pres.); Braintree (Mass.); Yacht (past commodore); Commodores of Am. (Mass.); Down East Yacht (Maine). Home: 10 Hemlock Dr Lunenberg MA 01462 Office: 655 Main St Fitchburg MA 01420 *

EVITT, WILLIAM ROBERT, geology educator; b. Balt., Dec. 9, 1923; s. Raymond W. and Elsa (Schwarz) E.; m. Gisela Cloos, July 29, 1950; children: Eric R., Steven D., Glenn M. A.B., Johns Hopkins, 1942; Ph.D., 1950. Instr. U. Rochester, 1948- 51, asst. prof. geology, 1951-55, asso. prof., 1955-56, acting chmn. dept. geology, 1955-56; sr. research geologist Jersey Prodn. Research Co., Tulsa, 1956-59, research asso., 1959-62; vis. prof. Stanford, 1961, prof. geology, 1962—; vis. sr. research scientist Continental Shelf Inst., Oslo, 1976. Served to capt. USAF, 1943-46. Decorated Bronze Star. Fellow Calif. Acad. Scis., Geol. Soc. Am.; mem. Am. Assn. Stratigraphic Palynologists (Sci. Excellence award 1982), Paleontol. Soc. (editor 1953-56, v.p. 1957), Internat. Assn. Plant Taxonomists. Home: 882 Cedro Way Stanford CA 94305 Office: Dept Geology Stanford U Stanford CA 94305

EVONS, HARRY, research co. exec.; b. N.Y.C., Dec. 25, 1914; s. Saul and Augusta (White) E.; m. Laura Marie Anderson, July 16, 1937; children—Richard Harry, Thomas Henry. Student, N.Y. U., 1934. Mgr. Photo Reflex Studios, Boston, Kansas City, Mo. and Rochester, N.Y., 1936-40; U.S. regional and nat. dir. Arthur Murray Studios, 1940-56; pres., dir. Forsyth Oil Co., San Antonio, 1959-63; v.p., dir., chmn. exec. com. Signal Pictures Corp., San Antonio, 1959-64; pres., dir., treas. Arthur Murray, Inc., N.Y.C., 1964-67; chmn. bd., pres., dir. Kargl Instruments, Inc., San Antonio, 1961-64; v.p., dir., exec. com. Fed. Mart Corp., San Diego, 1957-67; chmn. bd. Fed. Mart World Tours, Inc., San Diego, 1967-69; pres., dir. Nat. Fiberglass Co., San Antonio, 1957-62, Evons Travel Enterprises, San Diego, 1969-72, Markham Research Services, Ltd., London, 1976—; pres. Markham Co. Research Services, Inc., N.Y.C., 1974—. Pres. San Antonio Safety Council, 1950-51; treas. Bexar County chpt. Am. Cancer Soc., 1953-54; commr. Nat. Milk Bowl, 1955-64; v.p., dir. Boys Homes Am., 1955; bd. dirs. Philanthropic Inst., Dallas, 1960; mem. vol. bd. Tex. Hosps., 1950-61. Served with USNR, 1942-45. Recipient George Washington Honor medal Freedoms Found. at Valley Forge, 1957. Mem. Stock Transfer Assn., Corp. Transfer Agts. Assn., AIM (pres.'s council). Clubs: Friars, Masons, Lions (pres. 1958). Office: 39 Broadway New York NY 10006

EVOY, JOHN JOSEPH, psychology educator; b. Seattle, Apr. 14, 1911; s. Martin and May (Harpur) E. A.B., Gonzaga U., Spokane, 1936, M.A., 1937; S.T.L., St. Louis U., 1944; Ph.D., Loyola U., Chgo., 1953. Joined Soc. of Jesus, 1930; ordained priest Roman Cath. Ch., 1943; mem. faculty Gonzaga U., 1951-76, prof. psychology, 1957-76, prof. emeritus, author-in-residence, 1976—, chmn. dept. psychology, 1971-75; asso. editor America mag., 1966-67; counselor, lectr. in field. Co-author: 4 books, including The Rejected, 1981. Mem. Am. Psychol. Assn., Brit. Psychol. Soc. Home: Gonzaga Univ Spokane WA 99202 *I joyously view life as opportunity to care about and benefit others, within a picture of reality that is meaningful and worth-while.*

EWALD, EARL, utility exec.; b. St. Paul, July 2, 1908; s. Martin P. and Minna L. (Neumann) E.; m. Marian Borglum, June 9, 1930; children—Carol Ewald Johnson, Clark, Paula Wagner. B.S., U. Minn., 1930, postgrad., 1938-40. With No. States Power Co., Mpls., 1930-75, v.p. charge ops., 1954-62, exec. v.p., 1962-64, pres., 1964-65, 1965-68, chmn. bd., 1968-72, chief exec. officer, 1965-71, dir., 1972-75, now ret. Mem. IEEE, Nat. Soc. Profl. Engrs., Triangle. Club: Masons. Home: 7108 Cedarwood Circle Boulder CO 80301

EWALT, GEORGE W., electrical contracting company executive; b. Balt., May 25, 1935; s. George W. E. and Lilly (Harrison) Floyd Ewalt; m. Patricia C. Ewalt, Sept. 30, 1961; children: Gretchen Walther, Paige Noel. B.S., U. Md.; postgrad., George Washington U. Contract adminstr., program coordinator Melpar, Inc., Washington, 1969-71; v.p. facilities mgmt. Dynalectron Corp., McLean, Va., 1971-73, group v.p., 1973-77, sr. v.p., 1977—. Mem. Am. Mgmt. Assn., Nat. Elec. Contractors Assn., Nat. Joint Apprenticeship and Tng. Com. for Elec. Industry. Home: Route 4 Box 518 Leesburg VA 22075 Office: Dynalectron Corp 1313 Dolley Madison Blvd McLean VA 22101

EWAN, GEORGE THOMSON, educator; b. Edinburgh, Scotland, May 6, 1927; s. Alexander Farmer and Jeannie Young (Taylor) E.; m. Maureen Louise Howard, Aug. 7, 1952; children—Elizabeth Louise, Robert Alexander. B.S., Edinburgh U., 1948, Ph.D., 1952. Asst. lectr. Edinburgh U., 1950-52; research asso. McGill U., 1952-53, NRC Can. fellow, 1953-55; asst. research officer Atomic Energy Can. Ltd., Chalk River, Ont., Can., 1955-58, asso. research officer, 1958-62, sr. research officer, 1962-70; prof. physics Queen's U., Kingston, Ont., 1970—, head dept. physics, 1974-77; Vis. scientist Lawrence Radiation Lab., Berkeley, 1966, CERN, Geneva, Switzerland, 1977-78. Contbr. articles to profl. jours. Recipient Radiation Industry award Am. Nuclear Soc., 1967; Ford Found. fellow Niels Bohr Inst., Copenhagen, Denmark, 1961-62. Fellow Am. Phys. Soc., Royal Soc. Can.; mem. Canadian Assn. Physicists. Home: 66 Fairway Hill Crescent Kingston ON Canada

EWART, DONALD LINSLEY, coal company executive; b. Pitts., Dec. 7, 1929; s. John A. and Grace (McConnell) E.; m. Martha J. McMichael, June 7, 1952; children: Ann, Donald Linsley, Ellen. A.B., U. Pitts., 1951, J.D., 1956. Bar: Pa. 1957. Practice in, Pitts., 1956-62; assoc., then ptnr. Rose, Houston, Cooper & Schmidt, 1956-62; asst. sec. Consol. Coal Co., Pitts., 1963-65, asst. v.p., 1965-66, gen. counsel, sec., 1966-70, v.p., 1968-71, pres. Midwestern div., 1971-72, v.p. ops. Midwestern div., 1972-74, sr. v.p. Midwestern div., 1974-76; pres. Gilbert Fuel Co., Inc., 1976-80, Minerals Mgmt. Assos., 1977—; mem. firm Corcoran, Hardesty, Ewart, Whyte & Polito, 1981—. Served with USAF, 1951-53. Mem. ABA, Pa. Bar Assn., Allegheny County Bar Assn., Order of Coif, Omicron Delta Kappa, Sigma Alpha Epsilon. Club: Duquesne (Pitts.). Home: 217 Trotwood West Dr Pittsburgh PA 15241 Office: Two Chatham Center Suite 210 Pittsburgh PA 15219

EWELL, ALBERT HUNTER, JR., psychologist; b. Phila., Nov. 30, 1925; s. Albert Hunter and Emma (Kind) E. B.A., Haverford Coll., 1946; postgrad., Princeton U., 1946-49; Ph.D., N.Y. U., 1954. Instr. Middlebury (Vt.) Coll., 1952-55, asst. prof., 1955-61, chmn. dept. psychology, 1956-75, asso. prof., 1961-67, prof. psychology, 1967—; cons. Vt. Rehab. Center, Burlington, 1959-67; research analyst Vt. Div. Vocat. Rehab. Spl. Project, 1964-66. Mem. Optical Soc. Am., Acoustical Soc. Am., France and Colonies Philatelic Soc., Collectors Club N.Y., Phi Beta Kappa. Home: 28 Weybridge St Middlebury VT 05753

EWEN, DAVID, musician, author; b. Lemberg, Austria, Nov. 26, 1907; s. Isaac and Helen (Kramer) E.; m. Hannah Weinstein, Sept. 10, 1936; 1 son, Robert. Student, Coll. City N.Y., 3 years; mus. edn. with pvt. tutors; also spl. courses, Columbia; Mus.D. (hon.), U. Miami, 1975. Dir. Allen, Towne & Heath, Inc., 1946-49; adj. prof. music U. Miami, Fla., 1965-72. Music editor, Cue, 1937-38; serious music record critic, Stage, 1938-39; editor, Mus. Facts, 1940-41; Author many books on music and musicians, 1933-46; Haydn: A Good Life, 1946, Songs of America, 1947, American Composers Today, 1949, The Story of Irving Berlin, 1950, The Story of Arturo Toscanini, 1951, The Complete Book of Twentieth Century Composers, 1952, The Story of Jerome Kern, 1953, European Composers Today, 1953; (with Milton Cross) including The Milton Cross Encyclopedia of Great Composers, rev. edit, 1969; The Home Book of Musical Knowledge, 1954, Encyclopedia of the Opera, completely rewritten, 1969, A Journey to Greatness: The Life and Music of George Gershwin, completely rewritten, 1970, Panorama of American Popular Music, 1957, Richard Rodgers, 1957, The Complete Book of the American Musical Theatre, 1958, Ency. of Concert Music, 1959, The World of Jerome Kern, 1960, Leonard Bernstein: A Biography for Young People, 1960, The Story of the American Musical Theater, 1961, David Ewen Introduces Modern Music, 1962, The Book of European Light Opera, 1962, With A Song in His Heart (a young people's biography of Richard Rodgers), 1963, The Life and Death of Tin Pan Alley, 1964, The Complete Book of Classical Music, 1965, The Cole Porter Story, 1965, Great Composers: 1300-1900, 1966, American Popular Songs: From The Revolutionary War to the Present, 1966, Famous Modern Conductors, 1967, The World of Twentieth Century Music, 1968, Composers for the American Musical Theatre, 1968, Composers Since 1900, 1969, 1st supplement, 1981, Great Men of American Popular Song, 1970, New Complete Book of the American Musical Theater, 1970, Composers of Tomorrow's Music, 1971, Opera, 1972, Orchestral Music, 1973, Solo Instrumental and Chamber Music, 1974, Vocal Music, 1975, All the Years of American Popular Music, 1977, Musicians Since 1900: Performers in Opera and Concert, 1978, American Composers: A Biographical Dictionary, 1982; Contbr. articles to periodicals, encys. Mem. bd. Greater Miami Philharmonic Orch., Fla. Philharmonic, Community Concerts Miami. Served with AUS, 1944-45; authorized to write history Am. paratroopers. Hon. life mem. Miami Beach Music and Arts League. Address: Century Village Preston A-18 Boca Raton FL 33434

EWEN, HAROLD IRVING, physicist; b. Chicopee, Mass., Mar. 5, 1922; s. Arthur and Ruth Francis (Fay) E.; m. Mary Ann Whitney, Feb. 10, 1956; children—Donald, Jim, Bruce, Mark, David, Deborah, Daniel, Rebecca. B.A., Amherst Coll., 1943; M.A., Harvard U., 1948, Ph.D., 1951. Mem. faculty Amherst Coll., 1943; co-dir. Harvard Radio Astronomy Program, 1952-58, research asso. astronomy dept., 1958-65, asso., 1965-80; pres. Ewen Knight Corp., Weston, Mass., 1952—, Ewen Dae Corp., 1958—; sci. advisor to Cin. Electronics Corp. for USAF Air Weather Service; mem. Global Solar Radio Telescope Network, 1977—. Contbg. author: Advances in Microwaves, vol. 5, 1970, Electromagnetic Sensing of the Earth from Satellites, 1967, Geoscience Instrumentation, 1974, also articles. Served to lt. USNR, 1943-46. NRC fellow, 1946-49; recipient service award Harvard Coll., 1977. Fellow Am. Acad. Arts and Scis., IEEE (Morris E. Leeds award

1970), AAAS, Phi Beta Kappa, Sigma Xi. Co-discoverer 21 cm interstellar hydrogen line, 1951; remote sensing of atmospheric ozone distribution (resonant line at 102 GHz), 1966; patentee in field of intermediate frequency interferometry.

EWERS, JOHN CANFIELD, museum administrator; b. Cleve., July 21, 1909; s. John Ray and Mary Alice (Canfield) E.; m. Margaret Elizabeth Dumville, Sept. 6, 1934; children: Jane (Mrs. Robinson), Diane (Mrs. Peterson). A.B., Dartmouth Coll., 1931, D.Sc., 1968; M.A., Yale U., 1934; LL.D., U. Mont., 1966. Field curator Nat. Park Service, Washington, Morristown, N.J., Berkeley, Calif., Macon, Ga., 1935-40; curator Mus. Plains Indian, Browning, Mont., 1941-44; asso. curator ethnology U.S. Nat. Mus., Smithsonian Instn., Washington, 1946-56, planning officer, 1956-59, asst. dir. Mus. History and Tech., 1959-64, dir., 1964-65, sr. scientist, 1965-79, now ethnologist emeritus; research assoc., hon. trustee Mus. Am. Indian Heye Found., N.Y.C., 1979—; mus. planning cons. Bur. Indian Affairs, 1948-49, Mont. Hist. Soc., 1950-54; cons. Am. Heritage, 1959. Author: Plains Indian Painting, 1940, The Horse in Blackfoot Indian Culture, 1955, The Blackfoot: Raiders on the Northwestern Plains, 1958, Artists of the Old West, 1965, Indian Life on Upper Missouri, 1968, Murals in the Round: Painted Tipis of the Kiowa and Kiowa-Apache Indians, 1978; Editor: Adventures of Zenas Leonard, Fur Trader, 1959, Crow Indian Medicine Bundles, 1960, Five Indian Tribes of the Upper Missouri, 1961, O-Kee-pa, A Religious Ceremony and Other Customs of the Mandans, (George Catlin), 1967, Jean Louis Berlandier's Indians of Texas in 1830, 1969, Jose Francisco Ruíz, Report on the Indian Tribes of Texas in 1828, 1972, Indian Art in Pipestone, George Catlin's Portfolio in the British Museum, 1979, Jour. Washington Acad. Scis, 1955-56; Mem. editorial bd.: The American West, 1965—, Gt. Plains Quar, 1979—; contbr. articles to profl. publs. Served with USNR, 1944-46. Recipient 1st Exceptional Service medal Smithsonian Instn., 1965, Oscar O. Winther Meml. award Western History Assn., 1976. Fellow Am. Anthrop. Assn., Rochester Mus. Arts and Scis.; mem. Western History Assn. (hon. life), Am. Indian Ethnohist. Conf. (pres. 1960-61), Anthrop. Soc. Washington. Clubs: Cosmos, Explorers (N.Y.C.). Home: 4432 26th Rd N Arlington VA 22207 Office: Smithsonian Instn Washington DC 20560

EWICK, CHARLES RAY, librarian; b. Shelbyville, Ind., Sept. 13, 1937; s. Laurel R. and Loraine Pearl (Tufts) E.; m. Joann Hotchkiss, June 14, 1958; children—David Lee, Jeffrey Allen. B.A., Wabash Coll., 1962; M.A., Ind. U., 1966. Cons. Ind. State Library, Indpls., 1966-68, asst. dir., 1968-72, dir., 1978—; dir. Rolling Prairie Libraries, Decatur, Ill., 1972-78. Mem. ALA, Ind. Library Assn., Phi Beta Mu. Presbyterian. Office: Ind State Library 140 N Senate Ave Indianapolis IN 46204

EWIGLEBEN, ROBERT LEON, coll. pres.; b. Lansing, Mich., Apr. 6, 1928; s. Albert H. and Freda M. (Ruger) E.; m. Esther Sayer, Dec. 4, 1948; children—Lynne (Mrs. J. Seymour Case), Lezley (Mrs. Thomas Buford), Robert, Jan, Thomas. B.S., Mich. State U., 1952, M.A., 1956; Ed.D., 1959; Dr. Pub. Service, Central Mich. U., 1971. Tchr. Croswell (Mich.) High Sch., 1952, Montrose (Mich.) High Sch., 1953-55; prin. Stoner (Mich.) Sch., 1955; supt. schs., Crystal, Mich., 1956-58; dean, prof. Purdue U., Ft. Wayne Campus, 1959-65; v.p. adminstrn. Humboldt State Coll., Calif., 1965-68; pres. Coll. of San Mateo, Calif., 1968-71, Ferris State Coll., Big Rapids, Mich., 1971—; chmn. bd. Mich. No. Railroad Inc., 1977—; dir. Mich. Nat. Bank, 1980—. Cons. Asia Found.; examiner N. Central Accrediting Assn.; bd. dirs. Council on Post Secondary Accreditation, 1978—, Mich. C. of C., 1979—. Served with; AUS, 1946-48. Ford Found. fellow, 1959. Office: Office of Pres Ferris State Coll Big Rapids MI 49307

EWING, BAYARD, lawyer; b. Sorrento, Maine, Aug. 19, 1916; s. Thomas and Anna (Cochran) E.; m. Harriet M. Kelley, Sept. 2, 1939; children: Linda L. (Mrs. C. Hamlin), Gillian Ewing Ehrich, Bayard C., Gifford P., Harriet K. (Mrs. R. Hannan). Grad., St. Paul's Sch., Concord, N.H., 1934; A.B., Yale, 1938; LL.B., Harvard, 1941. Bar: R.I. 1941. Partner firm Tillinghast, Collins & Graham, Providence, 1949—; Dir. Old Stone Trust Co., Watering Inc., Hilliard Oil & Gas, Inc. Mem. Commn. on Pvt. Philanthropy and Pub. Needs, 1972-76; Del. Republican Nat. Conv., 1948, 52, 56, 60, 64, 68; rep. R.I. Gen. Assembly, 1950-52; candidate U.S. Senate from R.I., 1952, 58; mem. R.I. Public Expenditures Council, Rep. Nat. Com., 1955-68; Trustee Sch. Design, 1957; chmn., United Way Am., 1969-72; vice chmn. United Way Am., 1972-76; trustee Am. Fedn. Arts, 1977—, pres., 1977-80; trustee Nat. Info. Bur., 1976—, Ind. Sector Inc., 1980—; chmn. Coalition of Nat. Vol. Orgns., 1977-80. Mem. Am., R.I. bar assns. Episcopalian. Club: Mason (32 deg.). Home: 41 Waterman St Providence RI 02906 Office: 2000 Hospital Trust Tower Providence RI 02903

EWING, BENJAMIN BAUGH, engineering educator; b. Donna, Tex., Apr. 4, 1924; s. Joshua Fulkerson and Bula Betty (Baugh) E.; m. Elizabeth Malone, Apr. 3, 1947; children: Melissa, Douglas Malone, Frederick Joshua. B.S., U. Tex., Austin, 1944, M.S., 1949; Ph.D., U. Calif. at Berkeley, 1959. Diplomate: Am. Acad. Environ. Engrs. Instr., asst. prof. U. Tex., Austin, 1947-55; asso. in civil engrng., asst. research engr. U. Calif. at Berkeley, 1955-58; asso. prof., prof. U. Ill., Urbana, 1958—, dir., 1966-73, 1972—; Cons. engr., 1959—. Trustee Urbana and Champaign San. Dist., 1974-80; public mem. Ill. Water Resources Commn., 1975—. Served to lt. (j.g.) CEC. USNR, 1943-46. Recipient Epstein award dept. civil engrng. U. Ill., 1961, Harrison Prescott Eddy award for noteworthy research, 1968. Fellow ASCE; mem. Am. Water Works Assn. (life), Am. Geophys. Union, Water Pollution Control Fedn., AAAS, Assn. Environ. Engrng. Profs. Club: Rotarian. Home: 2212 Cottage Grove Urbana IL 61801 Office: 408 S Goodwin St Urbana IL 61801

EWING, DAVID WALKLEY, magazine editor; b. Grand Rapids, Mich., May 19, 1923; s. Walkley Bailey and Harriet Elissa (Edwards) E.; m. Elizabeth Weld Bennett, Sept. 11, 1948; children—Elizabeth (Mrs. Phillip A. Cook), Bennett, Sarah, Rebecca. Student, Amherst Coll., 1941-43, Williams Coll., 1943-44; J.D., Harvard U., 1949. Asst. editor Harvard Bus. Rev., Boston, 1949-63, assoc. editor, 1963-68; sr. assoc. editor, 1968-72, exec. editor, planning, 1972-81, mng. editor, 1981—; tchr. Harvard U. Bus. Sch., 1966-68. Author: The Managerial Mind, 1964, The Practice of Planning, 1968, The Human Side of Planning, 1969, Freedom Inside the Organization, 1977, Writing for Results: In Business, Government, Science, and the Professions, 1978, Do It My Way or You're Fired, 1983; editor: Mgmt. Thinking, 1961-68, Technological Change and Management, 1970, Long-Range Planning for Management, 1972, Science Policy and Business, 1973, others; Contbr.: articles to others. Chmn. Winchester (Mass.) Unitarian Soc., 1973-74. Served with USNR, 1944-46. Mem. ACLU, AAAS, Alpha Delta Phi. Club: Monday (Winchester). Home: 195 Cambridge St Winchester MA 01890 Office: Harvard Business Review Teele Hall Boston MA 02163

EWING, EDGAR LOUIS, artist, educator; b. Hartington, Nebr., Jan. 17, 1913; s. David E. and Laura (Buckendorf) E.; m. Suzanna Peter Giovan, Feb. 12, 1941. Grad., Art Inst. Chgo., 1935; studied, in France, Eng., Italy, 1935-37. Mem. faculty Art Inst. Chgo., 1937-43, U. Mich., Ann Arbor, 1946; asst. prof. fine arts U. So. Calif., 1946-54, assoc. prof., 1954-59, prof., 1959-78, prof. emeritus, 1978—; Mellon prof. Carnegie-Mellon U., Pitts., 1968-69. Exhibitor: one-man shows M.H. Young Meml. Mus., San Francisco, 1948, San Francisco, Long Beach Mus. Art, 1955, Dalzell Hatfield Galleries, Los Angeles, 1954, 56, 58, 61, 63, 65, Hewlett Gallery-Carnegie Mellon U., Pitts., 1969, Nat. Gallery, Athens, Greece, 1973, Los Angeles Mcpl. Art Gallery, 1974, Palm Springs (Calif.) Desert Mus., 1976-77; group exhbns. Cin Art Mus., Corcoran Gallery Art, Washington, Denver Art Mus., Dallas Mus. Fine Arts, Fort Worth Art Ctr., Met. Mus., N.Y.C.; represented: San Francisco Mus. Art, Dallas Mus. Fine Arts, Ft. Worth Art Ctr., Met. Mus., N.Y.C., Sao Paulo (Brazil) Mus. Art, Wichita Art Mus. Served with C.E. U.S. Army, 1943-46; PTO. Recipient Aberle Floresheim Meml. Prize for Oil Painting Art Inst. Chgo., 1943, Purchase award for oil painting Los Angeles County Mus. Art, 1952, Samuel Goldwyn award, 1957, Ahmanson Purchase award City of Los Angeles Exhbn., 1962; Louis Comfort Tiffany grantee, 1948-49; grantee Jose Drudis Found., Greece, 1967. Mem. AAUP, Nat. Watercolor Soc. (v.p. 1952, pres. 1953). Democrat. Home: 4226 Sea View Ln Los Angeles CA 90065 Home: Odos Piraeus 6 Athens Greece 104-31

EWING, FRANK MARION, lumber company executive, industrial land developer; b. Albany, Ga., Apr. 24, 1915; s. Frank Marion and Alpharetta (Tucker) E.; m. Hanna Anderson, June 15, 1935; children: Grace Marit (Mrs. Paul Atherton), Linda Tucker (Mrs. Richard R. Mace), Frances Marion (Mrs. Brian Tennery); m. Jo Anne Bacon Hilley, Mar. 12, 1964; children: Andrew L., (adopted) Kathleen Melinda, Wayne Edgar; m. Marilyn Hassett Petrie. B.A. (Sereno Gaylord scholar), Yale, 1936. Pres., chmn. bd. Frank M. Ewing Co., Inc., Washington, 1937—, Lumber Distbn. Co., Petersburg, Va., 1942-57, Ewing Lumber & Millwork Corp., Beltsville, Md., 1958-71; chmn. bd. Kettler Bros. Inc., Gaithersburg, Md., 1965—; developer Beltsville Indsl. Center, 1950—; dir. Martin Marietta Corp., Washington Mut. Investors Fund.; Mem. industry adv. com. WPB, 1942-46; industry adv. com. to sec. commerce, 1947-50, dept. asst. sec. def., 1955-56; mem. bd. Met. Washington Bd. Trade, 1957-61. Gen. campaign chmn. Prince Georges Community Chest, 1955; Bd. dirs. Childrens Hosp., Washington. Mem. Prince Georges C. of C. (pres. 1956-57). Clubs: Kiwanian (bd. dirs. Prince Georges 1948-52), Mason., Chevy Chase, Metropolitan, Burning Tree (Washington); St. Andrew's Royal and Ancient Golf (Scotland). Home: 5304 Woodlawn Chevy Chase MD 20015 Office: 9624 Stewartown Rd Gaithersburg MD 20760

EWING, GEORGE EDWARD, chemist; b. Charlotte, N.C., Nov. 28, 1933; s. Allen Conover and Margaret (Morse) E.; m. Louise Stuart, Aug. 11, 1972; children: Alice, Christina, Tamara, James, Ross, Sondra. B.S., Yale U., 1956; Ph.D., U. Calif., Berkeley, 1960. Sr. scientist Jet Propulsion Lab., Pasadena, Calif., 1960-63; instr. chemistry Ind. U., 1963-64, asst. prof., 1964-68, asso. prof., 1968-71, prof., 1971—; vis. scientist Nat. Center Atmospheric Research, Boulder, Colo., summer 1968; mem. staff Bell Telephone Labs., Murray Hill, N.J., 1969-70; directeur des researches Ecole Polytechnique, Paliseau, France, 1976-77; Isaac Taylor vis. prof. Technion-Israel Inst. Tech., Haifa, spring 1981; Guggenheim fellow Oxford U., 1983-84. Office: Dept Chemistry Ind U Bloomington IN 47401

EWING, GEORGE H., pipeline company executive; b. San Antonio, June 11, 1925; s. H.L. and Miriam (Galloway) E.; m. Doris Ann Cannan, May 31, 1947; children: Susan, Beverly, Mary, Bryan. B.C.E., Tex. A & M, 1948. Registered profl. engr., La. With Tex. Eastern Transmission Corp., Houston, 1948—, chief plans and research div., 1956-58, supervising engr., 1958-64, v.p., chief engr., 1965-71, v.p. engrng. and supplemental fuels, 1971-76, sr. v.p. gas supply, 1976; pres., chief exec. officer Tex. Eastern Gas Pipeline Co., 1979—, Transwestern Pipeline Co., 1979—. Served with USNR, 1943-46. Mem. ASME, Am. Gas Assn., Ind. Natural Gas Assn. Houston. Presbyterian. Club: Petroleum (Houston). Home: 502 W Forest St Houston TX 77079 Office: PO Box 2521 Houston TX 77252

EWING, JOHN ALEXANDER, psychiatrist; b. Fife, Scotland, Mar. 17, 1923; came to U.S., 1951, naturalized, 1959; s. James Anderson and Esther Stratton (Turner) E.; m. Janet S.G. Combe, Oct. 31, 1946; children: Christine, Ian James. M.B., Ch.B., U. Edinburgh, 1946, M.D., 1954; D.P.M., U. London, 1950. Intern, Royal Infirmary, Preston and Gogarburn Hosp., Edinburgh, 1946-47; resident in psychiatry U. Durham (Eng.) Hosp., 1947-50; sr. registrar Cherry Knowle Hosp., Sunderland, Eng., 1950-51; psychiatrist Alcoholic Rehab. Center, Butner, N.C., 1951-54; mem. faculty U. N.C. Med. Sch., Chapel Hill, 1954—, prof. psychiatry, 1963—, chmn. dept., 1965-70, dir. Center Alcohol Studies, 1970—; cons., vis. lectr. in field. Author: Drinking to your Health, 1981; Co-editor: Drinking, 1978; Contbr. articles to profl. jours. Fellow Royal., Am. colls. psychiatrists, Am. Psychiat. Assn., Am. Acad. Psychoanalysis; mem. Am., Brit. med. assns., Am. Med. Soc. on Alcoholism, N.C. Med. Soc., N.C. Neuropsychiat. Assn. Home: 9 Bluff Trail Chapel Hill NC 27514 Office: Dept Psychiatry Sch Medicine Univ NC Chapel Hill NC 27514

EWING, JOHN ARTHUR, research administrator; b. Euchee, Tenn., June 24, 1912; s. James Anderson and Harriette Mahala (Moulton) E.; m. Frances Mowry Burleson, Dec. 26, 1936; children: John Arthur, Ward Burleson, Jack Dunn. B.S.A., U. Tenn., 1933, M.S., 1946; D.P.A., Harvard U., 1956. Vocat. agr. tchr., Erwin, Tenn., 1934-35, asst. county agt., Carter County, Tenn., 1935-44; asst. supt. Middle Tenn. Expt. Sta., Columbia, 1944-46, supt., 1946-49; asst. dir. Agrl. Expt. Sta., U. Tenn., Knoxville, 1949-55, vice dir., 1955-59, dir., then dean, 1957-76, dean emeritus, 1976—, sr. vice dean Coll. Agr. and Home Econs., sr. vice dir. Agrl. Extension Service, 1955-57; project leader AEC Agrl. Lab., U. Tenn., 1955—; Bd. dirs. Tenn. Research Corp., Knoxville; adminstrv. adviser So. region for grain marketing research, soybean research, water resources; mem. Nat. Cotton Seed policy com.; mem. nat. tobacco adv. com. sec. agr.; dir.'s rep. So. Land Econ. Research Com.; mem. Tenn. Air Pollution Control Bd., Cotton Breeding Policy Com. Named Man of Yr. in Tenn. Agr., 1974. Mem. Expt. Sta. Dirs. in South (dir., chmn.), Agronomy Soc., So. Agrl. Workers Assn. (pres.), Am. Assn. Land Grant Colls. (chmn. expt. sta. sect.), Sigma Xi, Omicron Delta Kappa, Epsilon Sigma Phi, Phi Kappa Phi, Pi Kappa Alpha, Alpha Zeta, Delta Sigma Phi, Gamma Sigma Delta. Episcopalian (vestry). Club: Block and Bridle (Knoxville). Lodges: Rotary; Masons. Home: Route 1 Euchee Rd Ten Miles TN 37880

EWING, JOHN ISAAC, geophysicist; b. Lockney, Tex., July 5, 1924; s. Floyd Ford and Hope Ethyl (Hamilton) E.; m. Ellen Elizabeth Thomas, June 26, 1948; children: Valerie Margaret, Martha Ann, John Thomas. B.S. in Physics, Harvard U., 1950. Research scientist Lamont-Doherty Geol. Obs., Columbia U., N.Y.C., 1950-61, sr. research asso., 1961-76, asso. dir. for research, 1972-76; adj. prof., 1974—; sr. scientist, chmn. dept. geology and geophysics Woods Hole Oceanographic Instn., 1976—. Contbr. numerous articles to books and profl. jours. Served with USAAF, 1943-46. Recipient Shepard medal Soc. Econ. Paleontologists and Mineralogists, 1976, Maurice Ewing medal Am. Geophys. Union/USN, 1982. Fellow Am. Geophys. Union.; Mem. AAAS, Soc. Exploration Geophysicists. Home: 288 Elm Rd Falmouth MA 02540 Office: Woods Hole Oceanographic Instn Woods Hole MA 02543

EWING, KY PEPPER, JR., lawyer; b. Victoria, Tex., Jan. 7, 1935; s. Ky Pepper and Sallie (Dixon) E.; m. Almuth Rott, Apr. 6, 1963; children: Kenneth Patrick, Kevin Andrew, Kathryn Diana. B.A. cum laude, Baylor U., 1956, LL.B., Harvard U., 1959. Bar: D.C. 1959, U.S. Supreme Ct 1963. Assoc. firm Covington & Burling, Washington, 1959-64; partner firm Prather, Seeger, Doolittle, Farmer & Ewing, Washington, 1964-77; dep. asst. atty. gen. antitrust div. Dept. Justice, Washington, 1978-80; partner firm Vinson & Elkins, Washington, 1980—; dir., sec. Washington Inst. Fgn. Affairs. Pres. Potomac Valley League, 1977, Carderock Springs Citizens Assn., 1975-78. Mem. ABA, D.C. Bar Assn., Fed. Bar Assn., Am. Soc. Internat. Law. Democrat. Episcopalian. Clubs: Metropolitan, 1925 F Street (Washington). Home: 8317 Comanche Ct Bethesda MD 20817 Office: 1101 Connecticut Ave NW Washington DC 20036

EWING, LYNN MOORE, JR., lawyer; b. Nevada, Mo., Nov. 14, 1930; s. Lynn Moore and Margaret Ray (Blair) E.; m. Peggy Patton Adams, July 10, 1954; children: Margaret Grace, Melissa Lee, Lynn Moore. A.B., U. Mo., Columbia, 1952, J.D., 1954. Bar: Mo. 1954. Former partner Ewing, Carter, McBeth, Smith, Gosnell, Vickers & Hoberock, Nevada, Mo.; pres. Farm & Home Savs. Assn., Nevada; dir. Citizens State Bank, Nevada; trustee Mo. Law Sch. Found., 1974—, pres., 1981—. Mem. Mo. Ho. of Reps., 1959-64; mem. Nevada City Council, 1967-73, mayor, 1979-70, 72-73; mem. Nevada Charter Commn., 1978-79, Mo. Land Reclamation Commn., 1971-75; bd. dirs. Nevada Hosp., 1974—; vestryman All Saints Episcopal Ch. Served to 1st lt. USAF, 1954-56. Recipient Legis. award St. Louis Globe-Democrat, 1960, 62; named Citizen of Year, Nevada Rotary Club, 1975. Mem. Internat. Bar Assn., ABA, Am. Coll. Probate Counsel, Am. Coll. Mortgage Attys., Am. Judicature Soc., U.S. League Savs. Assn. (chmn. attys. com. 1977-79), Mo. Bar (adv. com. 1975—, bd. govs. 1974-78), Mo. League Savs. Assns., Vernon County Bar Assn. Democrat. Episcopalian. Clubs: Nevada Rotary (pres. 1969-70), Nevada Country; University (Kansas City, Mo.); Elks. Home: 146 Country Club Dr Nevada MO 64772 Office: 221 W Cherry St Nevada MO 64772

EWING, MARIA, mezzo-soprano; b. Detroit; m. Peter Hall, Feb. 1982. Recital Raviania Festival performances with, Chgo. Symphony, 1973; then appeared, Lyric Opera Chgo., Washington Opera, San Francisco Spring Opera, Opera Co. Boston, Santa Fe Opera, Houston Grand Opera, Cologne Opera, Los Angeles Philharmonic, Phila. Orch., Pitts. Symphony, Cin. Symphony; Met. Opera debut as Cherubino in: Le Nozze de Figaro, 1976; La Scala debut in: Pelleas et Melisande; N.Y. Philharmonic debut in its, Mahler Festival; title role Cenerentola, Geneva Opera, 1981, Paris recital debut, 1981; summer festival appearances, Ravinia, London's South Bank Festival, Glyndebourne Festival; appeared with, Concertgebouw Orch., Amsterdam and Toronto (Ont., Can.) Symphony; other roles include: Blanche in The Dialogues of the Carmelites, Met. Opera, 1981, Rosina, Composer, Perichole, Dorabella, Elvila. Address: care Columbia Artists Mgmt Inc 165 W 57th St New York NY 10019

EWING, RAYMOND CHARLES, foreign service officer; b. Cleve., Sept. 7, 1936; s. Thomas D. and Marion (Andrews) E.; m. Jerelyn Patten, Jan. 19, 1962; children: Gregory, Edward Thomas, Joyce. B.A., Occidental Coll., 1957; M.P.A., Harvard U., 1970. Commd. fgn. service officer Dept. State, 1957, assignments in Tokyo, Vienna, Pakistan, 1957-69, econ. officer Am. Embassy, Rome, 1970-73, counselor econ. affairs Am. Embassy, Bern, Switzerland, 1973-75, dir. Office of So. European Affairs, Washington, 1977-79, dep. asst. sec. European Affairs, 1980-81, U.S. ambasador to Cyprus, Nicosia, 1981—. Recipient meritorious honor award Dept. State, 1968. Mem. Am. Fgn. Service Assn. Presbyterian. Home: Am Embassy Dositheos and Therissou Sts Nicosia Cyprus Office: Am Embassy PO Box 4536 Nicosia Cyprus

EWING, RICHARD TUCKER, diplomat, educator, publisher; b. Albany, Ga., Sept. 25, 1918; s. Francis Marion and Alpharetta (Tucker) E.; m. Jacquelyn Randolph Knapp, Apr. 26, 1947; children—Maitland Marshall, Sara Almand, Richard Tucker, Elizabeth Harrison, Alpharetta Tucker, John Randolph. B.A., Yale U., 1940, M.A., 1942, postgrad., 1946-47, 49-51. With Fgn. Service Dept. State, 1946-70; attache U.S. Legation, Bern, Switzerland, 1947-49; 2d sec. Am. embassy, Taipei, Taiwan, China, 1951-56, 1st sec., Rangoon, 1959-62; dept. dir. div. research and analysis for Asia Dept. State, 1963-65; dept. dir. Office S.E. Asian Affairs, 1965-66, country dirs., Burma and Cambodia, 1966-67; faculty Nat. War Coll., Washington, 1967-70; dir. dept. internat. relations and area studies; sr. v.p., editorial dir. Congl. Info. Service, Inc., Bethesda, Md., 1970-80. Pres. local sch. chpt. P.T.A., Rockville, Md., 1967-68, Trustee, 1968-69. Served to capt. AUS, 1942-46. Decorated Bronze Star medal, Order Yun Huei. Mem. Kingsley Trust Assn., Fgn. Service Assn., Phi Beta Kappa. Home: Red Hall Box 26 Dunkirk MD 20754

EWING, ROBERT, lawyer; b. Little Rock, July 18, 1922; s. Esmond and Frances (Howell) E.; m. Elizabeth Smith, May 24, 1947; 1 dau., Elizabeth Milbrey. B.A., Washington and Lee U., 1943; LL.B., Yale U., 1945. Bar: Conn. 1945. Assoc. Shipman & Goodwin, Hartford, Conn., 1945-50, partner, 1950—; asst. pros. atty., West Hartford, Conn., 1953-55; dir. Poly Choke Co., Inc. Incorporator Hartford Hosp., Mt. Sinai Hosp.; bd. dirs. Travelers Aid Soc. of Hartford, 1951-57, treas., 1954-57; bd. dirs. Family Service Soc., 1961-65, Hartford Hosp. Assn.; bd. dirs., chmn. Greater Hartford chpt. ARC, 1977-79. Mem. Am., Conn., Hartford County bar assns., Am. Law Inst., Conn. Hist. Soc. (dir., v.p. 1983—, v.p. 1982—), Newcomen Soc. N.Am. Congregationalist. (sr. deacon 1972-75). Clubs: Twentieth Century (pres. 1975-76), Hartford (counsel), Mory's Assn., Dauntless, Rotary (pres. Hartford 1966-67). Home: 28 Birch Rd West Hartford CT 06119 Office: 799 Main St Hartford CT 06103

EWING, ROBERT EDWARD, publishing company executive; b. Glen Ridge, N.J., Nov. 29, 1921; s. Edward Graham and Edith (Powell) E.; m. Virginia Ann Harwood, Jan. 6, 1942; children: Robert Edward, John Harwood, William Michael, Andrew Graham, Jean Ann, Edward Clinton. B.A., St. Lawrence U., 1943. Copywriter Schwab & Beatty, Advt., N.Y.C., 1946-47; gen. mgr. McGraw Hill Book Co., N.Y.C., 1948-68, v.p., 1968-70; pres. Van Nostrand Reinhold Co., N.Y.C., 1970-82, chmn. bd., chief exec. officer, 1983—. Served with AUS, 1943-46. Mem. St. Lawrence U. Alumni Council, Alpha Tau Omega. Home: 4 Acre View Dr Northport NY 11768 Office: 135 W 50th St New York NY 10020

EWING, ROBERT PAUL, insurance company executive; b. Kirksville, Mo., Feb. 8, 1925; s. Leo M. and Eva (Dodson) E.; children: Robert I., Michael J., Patricia; m. Nancy Best, 1972. B.S., N.E. Mo. State Coll., 1948. With Bankers Life & Casualty Co., Chgo., 1948—, exec. v.p., 1965-74, pres., 1974—, chmn. bd., 1978—; chmn. Bankers Life and Casualty Co. of N.Y., 1978—; dir. Bankers Multiple Line Ins. Co., Des Moines, 1970—, Constn. Life Ins. Co., Chgo., Union Bankers Ins. Co., Dallas., Citizens Bank and Trust Co., Park Ridge, Ill. Bd. dirs. Evanston (Ill.) Hosp. Corp., John D. and Catherine T. Mac Arthur Found.; trustee Retirement Research Found., Park Ridge. Served with USAAF, 1943-45. Mem. Internat. Assn. Health Underwriters, Nat. Assn. Life Underwriters, Health Ins. Assn. Am. Club: Glen View Country. Office: 4444 Lawrence Ave Chicago IL 60630

EWING, SAMUEL DANIEL, JR., financial executive; b. Topeka, Aug. 9, 1938; s. Samuel Daniel and Jane Elizabeth (Smith) E. B.E.E., U. Cin., 1961; M.S., U. Conn., 1963-64; M.B.A., Harvard U., 1968. Asso. devel. engr. Norden Labs. div. United Aircraft Corp., Norwalk, Conn., 1961-62; engr. Bendix Research Lab. div. Bendix Corp., Southfield, Mass., 1962-63; staff mem., cons. Lincoln Labs., MIT, Lexington, 1964-67; security analyst, registered rep. Gruss & Co., N.Y.C., 1968-69; sr. asso. corp. fin. Salomon Bros., N.Y.C., 1969-75; v.p., dir. pvt. placement Bankers Trust Co., N.Y.C., 1975-78; dir. Fed. Savs. and Loan Ins. Corp., Fed. Home Loan Bank Bd., Washington, 1978-80; pres. and chief exec. officer Broadcast Capital Fund, Inc., Washington, 1980-81; pres. Ewing Capital, Inc., Washington, 1981—; Bd. dirs. D.C. Housing and Fin. Agy., 1980—. Author: (with C.H.W. Maloney) Minority Capital Resource Handbook, 1978; contbr. sci., bus. articles to profl. jours. Dayton Bd. Edn. scholar, 1956; Nat. Assn. Elec. Distbrs. scholar, 1956. Fellow Fin. Analysts Assn.; mem. N.Y. Soc. Security Analysts (sr.), 100 Black Men N.Y.C. (dir.), Afro Am. Alumni Assn., Harvard Bus. Sch. (chmn. vis. com. 1978, chmn. bd. dirs. 1978-79), Urban League (Black Execs. Exchange Program), Kappa Alpha Psi. Clubs: Harvard of Washington, Harvard Bus. Sch. of Washington. Office: Ewing Capital Inc 1016 16th St NW Suite 650 Washington DC 20036

EWING, SIDNEY ALTON, veterinarian, parasitologist; b. Emory U., Ga., Dec. 1, 1934; s. Aubrey Coleman and Grace Eliza (Prickett) E.; m. Margaret Jane Steffens, Aug. 16, 1963; children—Holly Annette, Ann Krull, Leah Grace. B.S.A., D.V.M., U. Ga., 1958; M.S., U. Wis., 1960; Ph.D., Okla. State U., 1964. Instr. U. Wis., 1960; mem. faculty Okla. State U. at Stillwater, 1960-65, 68-72, prof., head dept. vet. parasitology, microbiology and public health, 1968-72, 79—; asso. prof. Kans. State U., 1965-67; prof., head dept. Miss. State U., 1967-68; dean Coll. Vet. Medicine, U. Minn., St. Paul, 1973-78; mem. adv. bd. Morris Animal Found., Denver, 1967-69, cons., 1969—; Mem. animal health com. NRC, 1971—. Recipient Outstanding Tchr. of Year award Okla. State U. Coll. Veterinary Medicine, 1970. Mem. N.Y. Acad. Scis., Am., Minn., Okla. vet. med. assns., Am. Assn. Vet. Parasitologists, World Assn. Advancement Veterinary Parasitology, Am. Soc. Parasitologists, Conf. Research Workers in Animal Diseases (council 1980—), Sigma Xi, Phi Kappa Phi, Phi Zeta, Alpha Zeta, Alpha Psi (past nat. pres.), Gamma Sigma Delta, Aghon, Omicron Delta Kappa. Office: Dept Vet Parasitology Microbiology and Public Health Oklahoma State U Stillwater OK 74078

EWING, WAYNE TURNER, coal company executive; b. Beech Creek, Ky., Dec. 1, 1933; s. O.E. and Elizabeth E.; m. Jane Gray, June 3, 1960; children—Allyson, Sally. B.A., Georgetown Coll.; M.A., Western Ky. U. With Peabody Coal Co., 1963—, pres., St. Louis, 1983—; dir. First Nat. Bank of Belleville, Ill., 1981-83. Trustee McKendree Coll., Lebanon, Ill., 1980-82; mem. bd. assos. Georgetown Coll., 1980-82. Served with U.S. Army, 1955-57. Mem. Nat. Coal Assn., Ill. Coal Assn. Methodist. Clubs: Mason, St. Clair Country. Office: Peabody Coal Co 301 N MEMORIAL DRIVE Saint Louis MO 63102

EWING, WILLIAM HICKMAN, JR., U.S. attorney; b. Memphis, June 11, 1942; s. William Hickman and Addie Carolyn (Young) E.; m. Mary Clair Deyling, May 13, 1972; children: Jessica, Adam, Abigail. B.A., Vanderbilt U., 1964; J.D., Memphis State U., 1972. Bar: Tenn. 1972, U.S. Supreme Ct. 1978, U.S. Ct. Appeals, 5th cir. 1974. Asst. U.S. atty. Dept. Justice, Memphis, 1972-77, 1st asst. U.S. atty., 1977-81, U.S. atty., 1981—; chmn. law enforcement coordinating com. Western Dist. Tenn., 1981—. Served with USN, 1964-69. Mem. Memphis and Shelby County Bar Assn. (dir. young lawyers sect. 1974-75), Tenn. Bar Assn., ABA, Fed. Bar Assn. Office: US Attys Office 1026 Federal Bldg Memphis TN 38103

EXLEY, CHARLES ERROL, JR., manufacturing company executive; b. Detroit, Dec. 14, 1929; s. Charles Errol and Helen Margaret (Greenizen) E.; m. Sara Elizabeth Yates, Feb. 1, 1952; children: Sarah Helen, Evelyn Victoria, Thomas Yates. B.A., Wesleyan U., Middletown, Conn., 1952; M.B.A., Columbia U., 1954. With Burroughs Corp., Detroit, 1954-76, controller, 1960-63, corp. controller, 1963-66, v.p., group exec. office products group, 1966-71, v.p. fin., 1971-73, exec. v.p. fin., 1973-76; also dir.; pres. NCR Corp., Dayton, Ohio, 1976—, chief exec. officer, 1983—, also dir., mem. exec. com. Trustee Wesleyan U. Mem. Fin. Execs. Inst. Clubs: Grosse Pointe (Grosse Pointe Farms, Mich.); Moraine Country (Dayton); Dayton Racquet. Home: 5 Volusia Ave Oakwood OH 45409 Office: NCR Corp 1700 S Patterson Blvd Dayton OH 45479

EXLINE, RALPH VALENTINE, psychologist, educator; b. Cleve., Dec. 23, 1922; s. Ralph Valentine and Violet V. (Knaus) E.; m. Frances M. Howard, June 11, 1944; children—Ann, Elizabeth. A.B., Ohio U., 1947, M.A., 1949; Ph.D., U. Ill., 1954. Asst. prof. ednl. psychology Butler U., 1954-55; asst. prof. to asso. prof. dept. psychology and Center for Research on Social Behavior U. Del., 1955-69, prof., 1969—, chmn. dept. psychology, 1973—; vis. fellow Wolfson Coll., Oxford U., 1980; cons. AID, VA, Del. Div. Mental Health; research prof. psychiatry Thomas Jefferson U. Mem. editorial bd.: Jour. Personality, 1975, Jour. Nonverbal Behavior, 1979. Served with AUS, 1943-46. Office Naval Research grantee; NIMH Tng. grantee; NIMH Research grantee. Fellow Am. Psychol. Assn.; mem. Soc. Exptl. Social Psychology, Phi Beta Kappa, Psi Chi, Phi Delta Theta. Democrat. Mem. United Ch. of Christ. Research on nonverbal communication, small group behavior and personality. Home: 108 Cheltenham Rd Newark DE 19711 Office: Dept Psychology U Del Newark DE 19711

EXON, JOHN JAMES, senator; b. Geddes, S.D., Aug. 9, 1921; s. John James and Luella (Johns) E.; m. Patricia Ann Pros, Sept. 18, 1943; children: Stephen James, Pamela Ann, Candace Lee. Student, U. Omaha, 1939-41. Mgr. Universal Finance Corp., Nebr., 1946-53; pres. Exon's, Inc., Lincoln, Nebr., 1954-71; gov., Nebr., 1971-79; mem. U.S. Senate from Nebr., 1979—. Active state, local, nat. Democratic coms., 1952—; del. Dem. Nat. Conv., 1964-74; Dem. nat. committeeman, 1968—. Served with Signal Corps AUS, 1942-45. Mem. Am. Legion, VFW. Clubs: Masons (32 deg.), Shriners, Elks, Eagles, Optimist Internat. Office: 340 Dirksen Senate Office Bldg Washington DC 20510 *

EXUM, GLENN, musician, mountaineer; b. Topaz, Idaho, June 24, 1911; s. Oliver Kinch and Allie Vaughn (Tolman) E.; m. Beth Pauline Noben, Nov. 28, 1939; children: Edward Sherman, Glenda Lynne. B.S. in Edn, U. Idaho, 1934; mus. tng., St. Georges Boys Choir, Windsor Castle, Eng., 1935, 38. Mountaineer in Grand Teton Nat. Park, Jenny Lake, Wyo., 1930—; operator Exum Sch. Am. Mountaineering and Guide Service, Grand Teton Nat. Park, 1946-78; supr. music Sch. Dist. 391, Kellogg, Idaho, 1934-71; Adjudicator, dir. Massed Bands and Choruses in, Alaska and Idaho; judge solo, ensemble music festivals in, Wash., Alaska, Ida. Pres. Shoshone County Community Concerts Assn., 1942-57; chmn. Kellogg Planning Commn., 1957-58; bd. dirs. Jackass Ski Bowl, 1965-67, pres., 1967; participant Am. Celebraties Against Cancer, Altanta, 1983. Named Man of Year Jr. C. of C., 1940; recipient Outstanding Citizenship award C. of C., 1959; Certificate of Recognition Gov. State of Idaho, 1971; Exum Glacier in Antarctic named in his honor; also Exum Cup given at Jackass Ski Bowl Races. Mem. Gyro Internat., Nat. Ski Patrol (charter mem.), Am. Alpine Club, Sigma Nu. Clubs: Kellogg Country (chmn. 1970), Jackson Hole Country, Bloomington (Utah) Country. Pioneered Exum Route on Grand Teton, 1931; first Am. to make solo ascent of Swiss Matterhorn, 1935; featured in films on 50th anniversary of Exum Ridge climb. Home: XM Chalet 95 Ranch Moose WY 83012

EXUM, JAMES GOODEN, JR., state justice; b. Snow Hill, N.C., Sept. 14, 1935; s. James Gooden and Mary Wall (Bost) E.; m. Judith McNeill Jamison, June 29, 1963; children—James Gooden, Steven Jamison, Mary March Williams. B.A., U. N.C., (1957), Chapel Hill; LL.B., N.Y. U., 1960. Bar: N.C. bar 1960. Law clk. to Justice Emery Denny, N.C. Supreme Ct., 1960-61; asso. firm Smith, Moore, Smith, Schell & Hunter, Greensboro, N.C., 1961-67; resident judge Superior Ct., 1967-74; assoc. justice N.C. Supreme Ct., Raleigh, 1975—; mem. adj. faculty Law Sch. U. N.C., 1977, 81. Rep. N.C. Gen. Assembly, 1967; vice chmn. central selection com. Morehead Scholarships; parliamentarian Episcopal Diocese N.C. Served to capt. USAR, 1963-67. Recipient Disting. Service award Greensboro Jaycees, 1969, Psi Disting. Achievement and Service award Psi chpt. Sigma Nu, 1974. Mem. ABA (council criminal justice sect.), N.C. Bar Assn. (mem. com. on civil practice, appellate rules), Wake County Bar Assn., U.S. Power Squadron. Democrat. Clubs: Raleigh Racquet, Capital City., Milburie Fishing. Home: 2240 Wheeler Rd Raleigh NC 27607 Office: PO Box 1841 Raleigh NC 27602

EYDE, RICHARD HUSTED, curator, botanist; b. Lancaster, Pa., Dec. 23, 1928; s. Richard Husted and Thelma (Somers) E.; m. Lorriane Sylvia Dittrich, June 8, 1957; children: Douglas Alan, Dana Everest. B.S. in Biology, Franklin and Marshall Coll., 1956; M.S. in Botany, Ohio State U., 1957; Ph.D. in Biology, Harvard U., 1962. Research asst., then assoc. curator botany Smithsonian Instn., Washington, 1961-69, curator, 1969—. Fulbright scholar, India, 1960-61. Mem. AAAS, Am. Inst. Biol. Scis., Am Soc. Plant Taxonomists, Bot. Soc. Am., Goethe Gesellschaft, Goethe Soc. N.Am., Internat. Assn. Angiosprem Paleobotany, Internat. Assn. Plant Taxonomy, Internat. Soc. Plant Morphologists, Internat. Orgn. Palaeobotany, Soc. Systematic Zoology, Torrey Bot. Club. Office: Dept. Botany Smithsonian Instn Washington DC 20560

EYE, GLEN GORDON, teacher educator; b. Miltonvale, Kans., Oct. 19, 1904; s. Christopher J. and Dillie G. (Park) E.; m. Lucile Terry, June 21, 1927 (dec. 1978); children—Miriam Gale Eye Blum, Kathryn Elaine Eye Bading; m. Lanore A. Netzer, 1979. B.A., Kans. Wesleyan U., 1925, L.H.D., 1957; Ph.M., U. Wis., 1930, Ph.D., 1942. Tchr. math. Sweetgrass County High Sch., Big Timber, Mont., 1925-27; prin. pub. schs., Park City, Mont., 1927-28; asst. prin. Custer County High Sch., Miles City, Mont., 1928-29; supt. schs., Miles City, 1929-37; asst. prin. Sr. High Sch., Ogden, Utah, 1937-39, prin., 1939-41, Wis. High Sch.; asst. prof., then asso. prof. U. Wis.-Madison, 1941-48, dir. student teaching, asso. prof., then prof., 1948-56, acting dean, Milw., 1956-57, prof. edn., Madison, 1957-59, prof., chmn. dept. edn., 1959-62, chmn. dept. ednl. adminstrn., 1962-65, prof. ednl. adminstrn., 1962-72, A.S. Barr Distinguished prof., 1972-75; research dir. U.S. Office Edn. project, 1963-66; vis. prof. U. Oreg., summer 1951. Author: (with Milton O. Pella) Elementary Arithmetic Workbook, 1946, Basic Arithmetic Book I, 1947, Basic Arithmetic Book II, 1947, (with Kurt R. Schoenoff) Objectives of Education, 1951, (with W. R. Lane) The New Teacher Comes to School, 1956, (with L. A. Netzer) Supervision of Instruction: A Phase of Administration, 1965, School Administrators and Instruction, 1969, (with others) Interdisciplinary Foundations of Supervision, 1969, Education, Administration and Change, 1970, Instructional Technology and the School Adminstrator, 1970, (with L. A. Netzer and R.D. Krey) Supervision of Instruction, 1971, As Far As Eye Can See, 1976, (with others) Strategies for Instructional Management, 1979; also articles. Mem. Wis. Joint Com. Edn., 1944; mem. U. Wis. Athletic Bd., 1951-56; Chmn. Wis. Post War Planning Com., 1943; chmn. Wis. Surplus Commodity Com., 1945. Recipient Your Madisonian award Wis. State Jour., 1970; Meritorious Service citation State of Wis., 1974; Wis. Outstanding Educator award Wis. Assn. Tchr. Educators, 1974; certificate of appreciation Wis. Dept. Pub. Instrn., 1974; award of distinction Wis. Elementary Sch. Prins. Assn., 1975; William H. Kiekhofer Distinguished Teaching award U. Wis.-Madison, 1975; certificate of commendation Wis. State Legislature, 1975; Distinguished Service award U. Wis. Alumni Assn., 1975; Distinguished Achievement award Kans. Wesleyan U., 1974; also named to Hall of Fame, 1981. Mem. Wis. Edn. Assn. (commn. chmn., editor handbook), Wis. Secondary Sch. Prins. Assn. (past pres.), Am. Assn. Sch. Adminstrs., Wis. Assn. Sch. Bds. (hon. mem.), Wis. Assn. Sch. Dist. Adminstrs. (Outstanding Educator of Year 1969), Nat. Assn. Supervision and Curriculum Devel. (dir.), Wis. Assn. Supervision and Curriculum Devel. (hon. mem., Distinguished Scholar of Supervision award 1975), Wis. Edn. Research Assn. (hon.), Phi Delta Kappa. Home: 110 S Henry St Madison WI 53703 *My moments of greatest satisfaction have been those in which I helped others achieve and have those persons feel that they did it on their own power.*

EYE, JOHN DAVID, educator; b. Franklin, W.Va., June 22, 1923; s. Benjamin Claude and Jane (McQuain) E.; m. Margaret Marie Mullenax, Jan. 31, 1946; children—Nancy Eye Gant, Sarah Eye Cobb, Linda Eye Lotton, Patricia. B.S. in Civil Engring, Va. Poly. Inst., 1948, M.S., 1949; Sc.D. in Occupational Health, U. Cin., 1966. Faculty U. So. Calif., Los Angeles, 1949-51, Va. Poly. Inst., 1951-56; prof. environmental engring. U. Cin., 1956—; Cons. on environmental engring., water pollution control. Contbr. articles to profl. jours. Served with AUS, 1943-45. Mem. ASCE, Am. Water Works Assn., Am. Soc. Engring. Edn., Water Pollution Control Fedn., Sigma Xi, Chi Epsilon, Tau Beta Pi, Phi Kappa Phi. Home: 2899 Mt Airy Ave Cincinnati OH 45239

EYEN, TOM, playwright, dir.; b. Cambridge, Ohio, Aug. 14, 1941; s. Abraham L. and Julia (Farhad) E.; m. Liza Giradeux, Aug. 10, 1963; children: Jacque, Christopher, David. M.A. in English, Ohio State U., 1960. Dir. repetory company in residence, La Mama E.T.C., Theatre of the Eye, N.Y.C., 1965—; Author: Frustrata, The Dirty Little Girl with the Red Paper Rose Stuck in Her Head, Is Demented!, 1963, White Whore and The Bit Player, 1964, Miss Nefertiti Regrets, 1965, Dirtiest Show in Town, 1970, 2008 1/2 (A Spaced Oddity), 1974, (with Gary William Friedman) Why Hanna's Skirt Won't Stay Down, 1964, Paris, 1974, Women Behind Bars, 1974, London, 1976; TV writer: Mary Hartman, Mary Hartman, 1976-77, Millken Show, 1977, 78, Bette Midler TV Spl., 1977, Neon Woman, 1978, Melody of the Glittering Parrot, 1980; writer, dir.: (for Showtime TV) The Dirtiest Show in Town, 1980; musical Dreamgirls, 1981; dir., writer: repertory co. Theatre of Big Dreams, 1982-83. Rockefeller fellow, 1967; Guggenheim fellow, 1970. Address: care Bridget Aschenberg ICM 40 W 57th St New York NY 10011

EYERLY, JEANNETTE HYDE, author; b. Topeka, June 7, 1908; d. Robert and Mabel (Young) Hyde; m. Frank Eyerly, Dec. 6, 1932; children—Jane (Mrs. Lawrence Kozuszek), Susan (Mrs. Joseph A. Pichler). B.A., State U. Iowa, 1930. Tchr. creative writing Des Moines adult edn. classes, 1955-57; lectr. A.P. Mng. Editors Assn., Seattle, 1959, Clarke Coll., 1953, State U. Iowa, 1963, Am. Soc. Newspaper Editors Conv., Washington, 1963, State U. Iowa, 1966. Contbr. to mags.: McCalls, 1941-57; book reviewer: Des Moines Sunday Register; author: (with Valeria Winkler Griffith) Dearest Kate, 1961, More Than a Summer Love, 1962, Drop-Out, 1963, The World of Ellen March, 1964, Gretchen's Hill, 1965 (Susan Glaspell award 1965), A Girl Like Me, 1966, The Girl Inside, 1968, Escape from Nowhere, 1969 (Christopher award 1970), Radigan Cares, 1970, The Phaedra Complex, 1971, Bonnie Jo, Go Home, 1972, Goodbye to Budapest, 1974, The Leonardo Touch, 1976, He's My Baby, Now, 1977, See Dave Run, 1978, If I Loved You Wednesday, 1980, The Seeing Summer, 1981, Seth and Me and Rebel Makes Three, 1983. Pres. Polk County Mental Health Center; dir. Des Moines Child Guidance Center, 1949-54, St. Joseph Acad. Guild, 1954-57; mem. acquisition com. Des Moines Art Center, 1960-63; mem. Iowa Commn. for Blind, 1977-80. Mem. Authors League Am., Nat. Audubon Soc. Roman Catholic. Home: 231 42d St Des Moines IA 50312

EYERMAN, THOMAS JUDE, architect; b. Columbus, Ohio, June 11, 1939; s. Raymond Jacob and Lucille (Garno) E.; m. Mary Kay Evans, Nov. 3, 1962; children: Matthew, David, Nicole. B.Arch., Ohio State U., 1963; M.B.A., Harvard U., 1965. With Skidmore, Owings & Merrill, Chgo., 1966—, asso. partner, 1971-73, gen. partner, 1973—. Author: Financial Management Concepts and Techniques for the Architect, 1973. Trustee, mem. research and policy com. Com. for Econ. Devel.; mem. research and policy bd. Chgo. Orch. Assn.; bd. dirs. Harvard U. Bus. Sch. Club Chgo., 1980-81, mem. dean's fund, 1980-81; mem. com. for tomorrow Ohio State U., 1981; mem. governing bd. Art Inst. Chgo., 1981; mem. Ill. Indsl. Revenues Bond Authority. Recipient Texnikoi Outstanding Alumnus award Ohio State U. Coll. Engring., 1974. Mem. AIA (treas. Chgo. chpt. 1972, chmn. offices practices com. 1974, pres. Chgo. chpt. 1984), Harvard U. Bus. Sch. Assn., Phi Delta Theta. Clubs: Harvard, Arts, Metropolitan, Monroe, Chicago (Chgo.); Presidents (U. Chgo.). Home: 1046 N Grove Ave Oak Park IL 60302 Office: 33 W Monroe St Chicago IL 60603

EYES, RAYMOND, magazine publisher; b. New Bedford, Mass.; s. Joseph Chester and Florence (Morgan) E.; m. Anne Coleman, Dec. 27, 1947; children—Peter, Virginia, David, Edward. B.A., U. Conn. Engaged advt. sales N.Y. News, 1950-53, Advt. Agy. mag., 1953-54; with McCall Corp., 1954—, now pres., pub.; pub. Working Mother mag., Redbook mag., 1966-69; dir. Select Mags., N.Y.C.; sec., bd. dirs. Pubs. Info. Bur., Inc. Bd. dirs. Madison Square Boys' Club. Served with AUS, 1944-46. Mem. Mag. Pubs. Assn. (dir., treas.). Clubs: Cedar Point Yacht (Westport); Conn. Golf (Easton, Conn.). Office: 230 Park Ave New York NY 10169

EYLER, WILLIAM ROSS, physician; b. Van Wert, Ohio, Apr. 13, 1918; s. William H. and Florence (Ross) E.; m. Freda Warner, June 13, 1942; children: Lee, Ross, Steven, James, Ann. A.B., Harvard U., 1939, M.D., 1943. Successively intern, resident physician, staff radiologist Mass. Gen. Hosp., Boston, 1943-52; asst. clin. prof. radiology U. Ill. Med. Sch., 1952-53; radiologist Henry Ford Hosp., Detroit, 1953-83, chmn. dept., 1955—; clin. prof. radiology U. Mich. Editor: Radiology, 1966—. Served to capt., M.C. AUS, 1944-46; ETO. Fellow Am. Coll. Radiology; mem. Detroit Roentgen Ray Soc. (pres. 1961-62), Am. Roentgen Ray Soc., Radiol. Soc. N. Am., AMA. Office: 2799 W Grand Blvd Detroit MI 48202

EYMAN, RICHARD KENNETH, psychologist, educator; b. Joliet, Ill., Nov. 26, 1931; s. Robert Kennedy and Helen E. (Reick) E.; m. Vivian Kolodziej, Jan. 31, 1959. B.S., U. Ill., Urbana, 1954, M.A., 1955; Ph.D., U. So. Calif., 1966. Diplomate: Am. Bd. Profl. Psychology. Personnel research specialist Gen. Motors, South Gate, Calif., 1955-56; asst. research psychologist U.S. Army Def. Human Research Unit, Ft. Bliss, Tex., 1956-58; with Pacific State Hosp., Pomona, Calif., 1958-73, research specialist III, 1967-68; research specialist VA, 1968-73; chief research Pacific State Hosp., 1972-73; asso. research psychologist Pacific State Hosp. research group Neuropsychiat. Inst., UCLA, 1973-75, adj. asso. prof. III, 1975-76, adj. prof., 1976-80, prof.-in-residence, 1980—; research educationist UCLA, 1981; lectr. statistics and edn. U. Calif., Riverside, 1974-81, prof. edn., 1981—; cons. in field. Editorial cons.: CHOICE, Assn. Coll. and Research Libraries div. ALA, 1968—, Am. Jour. Mental Deficiency, 1969—, Mental Retardation, 1971—, Hosp. and Community Psychiatry, 1974—, Sci, 1975—, Nature, 1975—; contbr. articles to profl. jours. Mem. subcom. on population and geography Mental Retardation Program Bd., Area 10, Los Angeles County, 1972—; mem. adv. panel on vocat. rehab. reporting system State U. N.Y., Stony Brook, 1973—. Served with U.S. Army, 1956-57. Calif. Dept. Mental Hygiene grantee, 1962-64; NIMH grantee, 1964-71; Nat. Inst. Child Health and Human Devel. grantee, 1976-81; Div. Developmental Disabilities Rehab. Services Adminstrn. grantee, 1972-75; Office Econ. Opportunity grantee, 1974-75. Fellow Am. Assn. Mental Deficiency, Am. Psychol. Assn.; mem. Am. Acad. Mental Retardation (pres. 1974-75, research adv. bd. 1974—), Am. Ednl. Research Assn., Am. Statis. Assn., Psychometric Soc., Western Psychol. Assn., Sigma Xi. Home: 20286 Lorencita Dr Covina CA 91724 Office: Sch Edn U Calif Riverside CA 92521

EYRE, IVAN, artist, educator; b. Tullymet, Sask., Can., Apr. 15, 1935; s. Thomas and Kay E.; m. Brenda Fenske, June 14, 1957; children: Keven, Tyrone. Mem. faculty U. N.D., 1958-59; mem. faculty U. Man., Can., Winnipeg, 1959—, prof. drawing and painting, 1975—, head drawing dept., 1974-78. One-man shows include, Montreal Mus. Fine Arts, 1964, Winnipeg Art Gallery, 1964, 66, 74, Fleet Galleries, Winnipeg, 1965, 69, 71, Albert White Galleries, Toronto, 1965, Atelier Vincitore Gallery, Brighton, Eng., 1967, Yellow Door Gallery, Winnipeg, 1966, Jerrold Morris Gallery, Toronto, 1969, 71, 73, Frankfurter Kunst Kabinett, Frankfurt, Ger., 1973, Burnaby Art Gallery, Siemens Werk, Erlangen, Germany, 1974, N.B. Mus., St. John, 1976, Mira Godard Gallery, Toronto, 1978, Equinox Gallery, Vancouver, 1978, 81, Robert McLaughlin Gallery, Oshawa, 1980, Mira Godard Gallery, Toronto, Rodman Hall Arts Centre, St. Catherines, Ont., Art Gallery Windsor, Ont., 1981, Beaverbrook Art Gallery, Fredericton, N.B., London (Ont.) Regional Art Gallery, Sir George Williams Galleries, Montreal, MacDonald Stewart Art Centre, Guelph, Ont., Burlington (Ont.) Art Centre, 1982, Winnipeg Art Gallery, Can. Cultural Centre, Paris, Can. House Gallery, London, Eng., Talbot Rice Gallery, Edinburgh, Scotland, group shows include, London Art Gallery, 1963, Agnes Lefort Gallery, Montreal, 1964, Nat. Gallery, Ottawa, 1965, 67, 74, Yellow Door Gallery, Winnipeg, 1965, Toronto Gallery, 1968, Montreal Mus. Fine Arts, 1970, 76, Art Gallery Ont., Winnipeg Art Gallery, 1976, Glenbow-Alta. Inst., Calgary, Vancouver Art Gallery, 1977, London (Ont.) Art Gallery, Saskatoon Art Gallery, 1977, 82, Harbourfront Art Gallery, Toronto, 1977, Edmonton (Alta., Can.) Art Gallery, 1981; represented in permanent collections, Winnipeg Art Gallery, Nat. Gallery, Ottawa, Vancouver Art Gallery, Montreal Mus. Fine Arts, Art Gallery Ont., Toronto. Decorated Queen's Silver Jubilee medal; recipient Silver Commemorative medal Montreal Mus. Fine Arts, 1979; Acad. of Italy with gold medal, 1980; Can. Council sr. fellow, 1966. Mem. Royal Acad. Arts. Subject of book Ivan Eyre (Woodcock), 1981. Home: 1098 Trappistes Saint Norbert MB R3V 1B8 Canada Office: Dept Art U Manitoba Winnipeg MB Canada *To live a civil existence we compromise our behavior and actions so that others may have a portion of freedom and privacy. But in artistic matters there must be no compromises in feeling or thought. My work projects towards that which is "essential" in me and in you, towards our unconditional and* *unpersuaded selves. It concerns itself with the passage of time and time's inversion in memory and contemplation.*

EYRING, EDWARD MARCUS, chemical educator; b. Oakland, Calif., Jan. 7, 1931; s. Henry and Mildred (Bennion) E.; m. Marilyn Murphy, Dec. 28, 1954; children—Steven C., Valerie, David W., Sharon K. B.A., U. Utah, 1955, M.S., 1956, Ph.D., 1960. Asst. prof. chemistry U. Utah, 1961-65, asso. prof., 1965-68, prof., 1968—, chmn. dept., 1973-76. Author: (with H. Eyring) Modern Chemical Kinetics, 1963, (with others) Statistical Mechanics and Dynamics, 1964; Contbr. numerous articles to sci. jours. Served to lt. USAF, 1955-57. NSF Postdoctoral fellow to U. Goettingen, 1960-61; NATO sr. sci. fellow, 1976; J.S. Guggenheim Found. fellow, 1982-83. Mem. Am. Chem. Soc., AAAS, Phi Beta Kappa, Sigma Xi, Phi Kappa Phi. Mem. Ch. Jesus Christ of Latter-day Saints (Bishop, 1966-69). Home: 4570 Sycamore Dr Salt Lake City UT 84117

EYRING, LEROY, chemist, educator; b. Pima, Ariz., Dec. 26, 1919; s. Edward Christian and Emma (Romney) E.; m. Ruth LaReal Patton, July 21, 1941; children—Michelle, Patricia, Cynthia, Gregory. B.S., U. Ariz., 1943; Ph.D., U. Calif. at Berkeley, 1949. Asst. prof., then asso. prof. State U. Iowa, 1949-61; prof. chemistry Ariz. State U., 1961—, chmn. dept., 1961-69, dir. Center for Solid State Sci., 1969-72, 74-76. Editor: Progress in the Science and Technology of the Rare Earths, vol. I, 1964, vol. II, 1966, vol. III, 1967, Advances in High Temperature Chemistry, vol. I, 1967, vol. II, 1969, vol. III, 1971, vol. IV, 1971, Rare Earth Research III, 1965, The Chemistry of Extended Defects In Non-Metallic Solids, (with M. O'Keeffe), 1970, (with K. Gschneidner) Handbook on the Physics and Chemistry of Rare Earths, Vol. 1, 1978, vols. 2, 3 and 4, 1979, vol. 5, 1982; Mem. editorial adv. bds.: Jour High Temperature Sci; Contbr. articles sci. publs. Served with USNR, 1944-46. Spl. postdoctoral fellow U. Gottingen, Imperial Coll., and U. Stockholm, 1958-59; Guggenheim fellow, also Fulbright Hays Program awardee U. Melbourne, Australia, 1959-60. Mem. Am. Chem. Soc. (chmn. solid state chemistry subdiv. 1979), AAAS, Ariz. Acad. Sci., Phi Beta Kappa, Sigma Xi, Phi Kappa Phi, Phi Lambda Upsilon, Pi Mu Epsilon. Mem. Ch. Jesus Christ of Latter Day Saints (missionary 1939-41). Home: 6995 E Jackrabbit Rd Scottsdale AZ 85253

EYSENBACH, MARY LOCKE, coll. dean, economist; b. Hartford, Conn., Dec. 19, 1932; s. Ernest and Margaret (Perkins) E. B.A., Reed Coll., 1954, Oxford U., 1956, M.A., 1960; Ph.D., Stanford U., 1970. Commd. fgn. service officer Dept. State, 1957; positions in, Frankfurt am Main, Germany, 1958-60, Athens, 1960-61, 62-63, Thessaloniki, Greece, 1961-62; asst. prof. econs. U. Wash., Seattle, 1966-73, U. Utah, 1973-74; dean curriculum Grinnell Iowa Coll., 1974-77; provost U. Redlands, Calif., 1977-78; dean coll., prof. econs. Knox Coll., Galesburg, Ill., 1978—. Author: American Manufactures Exports: 1879-1914, 1976; contbr. articles to profl. jours. Fulbright fellow, 1954-56. Mem. Am. Econ. Assn., Western Econ. Assn., Assn. Acad. Deans, Sierra Club. Office: Knox Coll Galesburg IL 61401

EYSTER, FRANKLIN SPANGLER, II, lawyer, business executive; b. York, Pa., July 3, 1941; s. Franklin S. and Mary Virginia (Watson) E.; children: Kendra E., Franklin S. III. B.A., Williams Coll., 1963; LL.B, U. Pa., 1966. Bar: Del. 1967. Assoc. Richards, Layton & Finger, Wilmington, Del., 1966-73; sr. v.p., gen. counsel Atlantic Aviation Corp., Wilmington, Del., 1973—. Mem. ABA, Del. Bar. Assn. Home: 6 Bedford Ct Wilmington DE 19805 Office: Atlantic Aviation Corp PO Box 15000 Wilmington DE 19850

EYSTER, MARY ELAINE, hematologist, educator; b. York, Pa., Mar. 21, 1935; d. Charles Gable and March Viola (Schriver) E.; m. Robert E. Dye, Jan. 2, 1965; children: Robert E., Charles. A.B., Duke U., 1956, M.D., 1960. Intern. N.Y. Hosp.-Cornell Med. Coll., N.Y.C., 1960-61, resident in medicine, 1961-63, fellow in hematology, 1963-66, instr. medicine, 1966-67, asst. prof. medicine, 1967-70, Milton S. Hershey Med. Ctr., Pa. State U., Hershey, 1970-73, assoc. prof., 1973-82, prof., 1982—; chief hematology div., dept. medicine Pa. State U. Coll. Medicine, 1973—; dir. Hemophilia Ctr. of Central Pa., 1973—; faculty research assoc. Am. Cancer Soc., 1966-71; mem. State Hemophilia Adv. Com., 1973—, chmn., 1977-79; mem. policy bd. Coop. F VII inhibitor study Nat. Heart, Lung and Blood Inst., 1975-79; mem. med. and sci. adv. council Nat. Hemophilia Found., 1976-77, chmn. med. adv. com. Delaware Valley chpt., 1979—; co-investigator, mem. multi-agy. task force on AIDS, established by HHS, 1982—. USPHS grantee, 1976—. Fellow ACP; mem. Pa. Med. Soc., Am. Fedn. Clin. Research, World Fedn. Hemophilia, Am. Soc. Hematology, Am. Assn. Blood Banks, Internat. Soc. Thrombosis and Haemostasis, Internat. Soc. Hematology, Pa. Soc. Hematology, Oncology (bd. dirs. 1982—), Am. Heart Assn. Council on Thrombosis, Phi Beta Kappa, Alpha Omega Alpha. Office: Milton S Hershey Med Ctr Hershey PA 17033

EYSTER, WILLIAM BIBB, lawyer; b. Decatur, Ala., June 21, 1921; s. Charles Harris and Katharine C. (Bibb) E.; m. Ann J. Kimbrough, May 29, 1948; children—Katharine Ann, William B. B.A. with honors, U. South, 1941; postgrad., Law Sch., U. Va., 1941-42; LL.B., U. Ala., 1947. Bar: Ala. bar. Sr. partner firm Eyster, Eyster, Key & Tubb (and predecessors), Decatur, 1947—; dir., chmn. bd. 1st Nat. Bank Decatur, Ala. Bancorp. Past v.p. Decatur C. of C. Served with USNR, 1942-46. Fellow Am. Coll. Trial Lawyers; mem. Ala., Am., Morgan County bar assns. Episcopalian. Home: 2010 Country Club Rd SE Decatur AL 35601 Office: 402 E Moulton St Decatur AL 35602

EYTAN, RACHEL, novelist, educator; b. Israel, May 4, 1932; came to U.S., 1967, naturalized, 1979; d. Yaacov Litai and Sara (Zweig); m. Jerry H. Fishman, Oct. 1967; children: Omry, Hamutal, Yonatan. B.A., Hakibutzim Tchrs. Coll., Israel, 1950, NYU, 1973, M.A., 1975, doctoral student, 1976-79. Tchr. Israeli Kibbutz, Tel Aviv, 1950-53; prof. Israeli lit. Gratz Coll., Phila., 1967-68; prof. Israeli, Hebrew and Yiddish lit. Hofstra U., 1968—; lectr. Am., European and Israeli univs., TV and radio. Novelist: book The Fifth Heaven, 1963; Shida Veshidot, 1973; contbr. short stories and articles to Am. lit. mags.; editor, contbr. to Israel and Am. Lit. mags. and newspapers. Active Israeli-Arab Peace Movement, NOW, Coalition of Am.-Israel Civil Liberties, Women Ink W Writers, Union of Concerned Scientists. Recipient Brenner prize for Lit., Israel, 1966, Founders Day award NYU, 1973. Mem. MLA, AAUP, Israeli PEN Club, Israeli Writers Assn. Home: 227 Central Park W New York NY 10024 Office: Hofstra U Hempstead NY 11550 *The new engage, involved literature must not become a new didacticism—but rather the creation of new idiom. We must create, each in her/his own fashion, a psychological climate of healing. A climate for easing the fears and hatreds, for dispelling the suspicions, and the political machismo. We must break the tribal mold of egocentricity, and put all the national and racial stereotypes back where they belong—in Madame Tussaud's Wax Museum. We must wake up a world that is apathetically waiting for the final blow, give the lie to the fallacy that Humanism is dangerous to humanity, and give ourselves, once again, the dynamic of time flowing into the future and the megalomania of art.*

EYTON, JOHN TREVOR, lawyer, business executive; b. Quebec, Que., Can., July 12, 1934; s. John and Dorothy Isabel E.; m. Barbara Jane Montgomery, Feb. 13, 1955; children: Adam Tudor, Christopher Montgomery, Deborah Jane, Susannah Margaret, Sarah Elizabeth. B.A., Victoria Coll., 1957; LL.B., U. Toronto, 1960. Bar: Ont. 1962, created queen's counsel. Read law Tory, Tory, DesLauriers & Binnington, Toronto, Ont., 1960-62, assoc., 1962-67, ptnr., Toronto, 1967—; pres., chief exec. officer Brascan Ltd., Toronto, 1979—; pres., dir. Nat. Hees Enterprises Ltd.; dir. Astral Bellevue Pathe Ltd., Brasca de Resource Ltd., Carena-Bancorp, Inc., CFGM Broadcasting Ltd., Edper Equities Ltd., Edper Investments Ltd., Great Lakes Power Corp. Ltd., Westmin Resources Ltd., Hume Pub. Ltd., London Life Ins. Co., Noranda Mines Ltd., John Labatt Ltd., Royal Trustco Ltd., Scott Paper Co., Trilon Fin. Corp., Union Gas Ltd., Radio IWC Ltd., Trizec Corp. Ltd. Mem. Upper Can. Law Sch., Can. Bar Assn. Progressive Conservative. Mem. United Ch. of Can. Clubs: Toronto Bd. Trade, Univ., Can., Toronto, Chingaucousy Golf and Country, Royal Can. Yacht, Empire, Caledon Ski, Caledon Riding and Hunt; Coral Beach and Tennis (Bermuda). Home: RR 2 Caledon ON Canada L0N 1C0 Home: 15 Elm Ave Toronto ON Canada M4W 1M9 Office: Brascan Ltd Commerce Ct W PO Box 48 Toronto ON Canada M5L 1B7

EYZAGUIRRE, CARLOS EDWARDS, educator, neurophysiologist; b. Santiago, Chile, Apr. 28, 1923; came to U.S., 1957; s. Carlos Gormaz and Ines (Edwards) E.; m. Elena Fontaine, Aug. 31, 1947; children—Carlos A., Elena M., Rodrigo J. B.A., U. Chile, 1940, M.D., 1947; D.Sc. (hon.), Cath. U. Chile, 1972; Dr. h.c., Universidad Complutense de Madrid, 1975. Mem. faculty Cath. U. Chile, Santiago, 1942-47, 50-52, asso. prof. neurophysiology, 1952-57; lectr. physiology Tchrs.'s Coll., U. Chile, 1951-53; asst. research prof. physiology U. Utah Coll. Medicine, Salt Lake City, 1957-59, asso. prof., 1959-62, prof., 1962—, chmn. dept., 1965—; fellow Johns Hopkins, 1947-48, Emanuel Libman fellow, 1948-50; fellow Wilmer Inst., John S. Guggenheim Meml. Found. fellow, 1953-55; Vis. prof. U. Montevideo, 1957; vis. praelector U. St. Andrews, 1965; spl. cons. USPHS neurol. scis. research tng. com., 1966-69, 1970-74, chmn., 1973-74, 1977—. Recipient USPHS Research Career Devel. award, 1964; Distinguished Research award U. Utah, 1974; USPHS Sr. Research fellow, 1959-64. Mem. Am. Physiol. Soc., Biol. Soc. Santiago, Biol. Soc. Montevideo (hon.), Soc. for Neurosci. Research, publs. in physiology of nervous system, physiology receptors and chemoreceptors, initiation of impulses in these areas. Home: 2217 Laird Way Salt Lake City UT 84108

EZEKIEL, WALTER NAPHTALI, plant pathologist, mycologist, research microbiologist; b. Richmond, Va., Apr. 26, 1901; s. Jacob Levy and Rachel (Brill) E.; m. Sarah Ritzen, Feb. 15, 1926 (dec. Feb. 1972); children: Herbert M. (dec.), David H., Joseph L., Raphael S., Miriam (Mrs. Joseph E. Bernhardt); m. Denise Levy Tourover, Sept. 27, 1972 (dec. Jan. 1980). B.S., U. Md., 1920, M.S., 1921, Ph.D., 1924; postgrad, U.S. Dept. Agr. Grad. Sch., 1922-24; NRC fellow, U. Minn., 1925-27. Asst. plant pathologist Md. Agrl. Expt. Sta., 1920-25; agt. Bur. Plant Industry, 1927-28; plant pathologist Tex. Agrl. Expt. Sta.; mem. grad. faculty Tex. A. and M. U., 1928-44; prin. mycologist Naval Ordnance Lab., Silver Spring, Md., 1944-46; head mycologist in charge fungus and moisture proofing program Bur. Ordnance, Navy Dept., 1946-53, Bur. Yards and Docks, 1953-54; tech. reports officer Bur. Mines, 1955-56, technologist (microbiology), 1956-64; microbiologist Bur. Mines Research Center, College Park, Md., 1964-69, research microbiologist health div., coal mine health and safety, 1969-71; dir. research Bioteknika Internat., Inc., 1973-78, v.p. research and devel., 1978—. Editor: Coal Chronicle, 1962-64. Mem. Va. Capital Bicentennial Commn., 1938; Trustee United Jewish Appeal of Greater Washington, chmn., Brazos County, Tex., 1940-44; vice chmn. Navy Dept., 1946-54; chmn. Interior Dept., 1957-64, exec. com. bd. dirs., vice chmn. govt. div., 1968—. Recipient Meritorious Civilian Service award with citation Bur. Ordnance, 1946. Fellow AAAS, Tex. Acad. Sci.; mem. Am. Technion Soc. (chmn. Washington chpt. 1947-49), Zionist Orgn. Am., Friends Hebrew U., Am. Phytopath. Soc., Mycol. Soc.·Am., Am. Soc. Microbiology, Am. Inst. Biol. Scis., Soc. Indsl. Microbiology (organizer 1949, dir. 1952-54, hon. 1963—), Sigma Xi, Phi Sigma Delta. Jewish. Research and publs. on fruit-rotting Sclerotinias, root rot of plants, alleviation of pollution by petroleum and other organic compounds, also other areas. Address: 4545 Connecticut Ave NW Apt 926 Washington DC 20008

EZELL, BOYCE FOWLER, III, lawyer; b. Miami, Fla., Apr. 8, 1942; s. Boyce Fowler and Sara E.; m. Katherine Ann Warthen; children: Boyce Fowler IV, William D. Student, Fla. State U., 1963; J.D., Stetson Coll., 1968. Bar: Fla. 1968. Assoc. firm Turner, Hendrich, Fascell, Guilford, Goldstein & McDonald, Miami, 1968-71, George Jahn, 1971-72; ptnr. Gautier & Ezell, 1972-80, Holland & Knight, Miami, 1980—. Served with USAF, 1963-69. Mem. ABA, Fla. Bar Assn. (gov. 1977-83), Dade County Bar Assn., Am. Bar Found., Dade County Trial Lawyers Assn., Acad. Fla. Trial Lawyers, Assn. Trial Lawyers Am. Democrat. Methodist. Clubs: University, Tiger Bay. Office: Holland & Knight PO Box 015441 Miami FL 33101

EZELL, JOHN SAMUEL, historian; b. Louisville, Mar. 9, 1917; s. Samuel Jones and Grace (Hicks) E.; m. Martha Jean McLean, Feb. 17, 1945; children—John McLean, Margaret Jean. B.A., Wake Forest Coll., 1938; M.A., Harvard, 1941, Ph.D., 1947. Faculty Carnegie Inst. Tech., 1947-48; mem. faculty U. Okla., 1948—, prof. history, 1959-65, chmn. dept., 1962-65, David Ross Boyd prof. history, 1965—, dean, 1965-73; curator Western history collections, 1974—; Summer sch. tchr. Howard Coll., 1947, Wake Forest Coll., 1961; cons. Pan Am. Petroleum Co., Service Pipe Line Co. Co-editor: Readings in American History, 2 vols., 4th edit, 1976, Fortune's Merry Wheel: The Lottery in America, 1960, The South Since 1865, 2d edit, 1975, Innovations in Energy: The Story of Kerr-McGee, 1979; Editor: The New Democracy in America: Travels of Francisco de Miranda in the United States, 1783-84, 1963; Contbr.: articles to hist. jours. Dictionary Am. Biography. Mem. U. adv. council for Inst. Life Ins., 1967-78. Mem. Am., So. hist. assns., Orgn. Am. Historians, Phi Beta Kappa, Omicron Delta Kappa. Home: 801 Hoover St Norman OK 73069

EZELL, KERRY MOORE, utility company executive; b. Sharon, Tenn., Aug. 17, 1935; s. Will Allen and Robbie (Moore) E.; m. Dorothy Laird, June 21, 1957; children: Krista, Darren. Student, U. Tenn., Martin, 1953-55; B.B.A., U. Miss., 1957. Accountant Ford Motor Co., Memphis, 1957; pvt. practice acctg., Sharon, Tenn., 1958-59; accountant Greenetone Record Distbg. Co., Nashville, 1959-60; v.p., treas. Miss. Power Co., Gulfport, 1960-83, v.p. fin., 1983—. Mem. Miss. Econ. Council. Served with U.S. Army, 1957-58. Mem. Am. Inst. C.P.A.s, Miss. Soc. C.P.A.s, Southeastern Electric Exchange, Edison Electric Inst., Southeastern Assn. Tax Reps. (chmn. 1976), Miss. Mfrs. Assn. Baptist. Club: Gulfport Yacht. Office: 2992 W Beach Blvd Gulfport MS 39501

EZELLE, ROBERT EUGENE, foreign service officer; b. Mattoon, Ill., Dec. 5, 1927; s. Zonner Robert and Nina Leora (Smith) E.; m. Lesly Marion Hopkins, Apr. 30, 1955; children: Robert, Lesley, John, Paul. Student, U. So. Calif., 1947-49, U. Bonn, 1954-56, U. Munich, 1956-57; Ph.D., U. Vienna, 1960; M.S. (Sloan fellow), Stanford Grad. Sch. Bus., 1977; Dr.h.c., Nat. U., 1981. Instr. Bonn, Munich and Vienna, 1954-60; dir. lang. sch., San Mateo, Calif., 1960-61; joined U.S. Fgn. Service, 1961; internat. relations officer State Dept., Washington, 1961-62; staff asst. Fgn. Service Inst., 1962-63; assigned, Hong Kong, 1963-65, Bern, Switzerland, 1965-69, Naples, Italy, 1969-72; chief consular affairs sect. Am. Embassy, Bonn, 1972-75; internat. relations officer State Dept., Washington, 1975-76; dep. consul gen. Am. Embassy, London, 1977-80; consul gen. State Dept., Tijuana, Mex., 1980—. Served with USAF, 1949-53. Home: PO Box 1358 San Ysidro CA 92073

EZEQUELLE, RICHARD MARTIN, publisher; b. Norwalk, Conn., Apr. 12, 1936; s. Robert E. and Sylvia B. (Martin) E.; m. Marcia K. O'Connell, June 7, 1958; children—Lauren B., Robert M., Andrew M. B.A., U. Vt., 1960. Sales rep. Fisher Sci. Co., Pitts., 1960-66; regional mgr. Scherago Assos., N.Y.C., 1966-72; founder, 1972; since pres., publisher, chmn. bd. Clin. Lab. Products, Amherst, N.H. Mem. Medfield (Mass.) Planning Bd., 1967-72, Caldwell (N.J.) Republican Town Com., 1962-66, Medfield Rep. Town Com., 1968-72. Mem. Assn. Indsl. Advertisers, Bus. and Profl. Advt. Assn., Midwest Pharm. Advt. Club, Biomed. Mktg. Assn. Club: Boggestow Ski (founder). Home: Cricket Corner Rd Amherst NH 03031 Office: Route 101A Amherst NH 03031

EZER, MITCHEL JULIAN, lawyer; b. Chgo., Jan. 3, 1935; s. Meyer Wolf and Celia (Goldstein) E.; m. Frances Suhd, Oct. 30, 1971; children—Renee, David. B.S., Northwestern U., 1956; J.D., Yale, 1959. Bar: Calif. bar 1960; C.P.A., Ill. Teaching asso. UCLA Sch. Law, 1959-60; asso. Hastings & Lasker, Beverly Hills, 1960-63; staff counsel Universal Studios, Universal City, Calif., 1963-64; pvt. practice law, Beverly Hills and Los Angeles, 1964; partner Rich & Ezer, Los Angeles, 1964—; Lectr. law Loyola U. Sch. Law, 1963-67; vol. atty. ACLU, 1961—. Author: Uniform Commercial Code Bibliography, 1972; Contbr. articles to legal periodicals. Mem. Beverly Hills Bar Assn., Am. Arbitration Assn. (nat. panel arbitrators 1961—), Yale Law Sch. Assn., Order of Coif, Phi Alpha Delta, Beta Gamma Sigma. Home: 1153 Lachman Ln Pacific Palisades CA 90272 Office: 1888 Century Park E Los Angeles CA 90067

FAAS, ANDREW STANLEY, newspaper executive; b. Seattle, Sept. 9, 1936; s. Frank William and Annie Marie (Grant) F.; m. Judith Diane Anderson, Aug. 15, 1965. B.A. in Bus. with honors, U. Wash., Seattle, 1962. C.P.A., Wash. From jr. auditor to audit mgr. Price Waterhouse & Co., Seattle and Caracas, Venezuela, 1963-69; J1with; Seattle Times Co., 1969—, controller, 1973-76, treas., 1974-76, v.p. fin., 1976-79, v.p. fin. and adminstrn., 1979-81, v.p. ops., 1981—. Bd. dirs. Chief Seattle council Boy Scouts Am., 1978—; chmn. acctg. adv. panel U. Wash., 1982-83. Recipient cert. of service U. Wash. Acctg. Dept., 1976. Mem. Am. Inst. C.P.A.s, Wash. Soc. C.P.A.s, Fin. Execs. Inst. (pres. elect. Seattle chpt. 1979-80, dir. 1980-81, western area v.p. 1981-82). Clubs: Wash. Athletic, Rainier, Meydenbauer Bay Yacht, Glendale Golf. Address: PO Box 70 Seattle WA 98111

FAAS, LARRY ANDREW, educator; b. Iowa City, Sept. 25, 1936; s. Merlin Andrew and Verla Lavonne (Cheney) F.; m. Patricia Middleton, Dec. 18, 1962; children—Anna Rachel, Eric Andrew, Audra Beth. B.S., Iowa State U., 1959; M.A., U. No. Colo., 1961; Ed.D., Utah State U., 1967. Instr. vocat. agr. English Valley Community Schs., North English, Iowa, 1959-60; sch. psychologist Tri-County Spl. Edn., Decorah, Iowa, 1961-63, dir. spl. edn., 1963-65; asst. prof., dir. spl. edn. U. Nev., 1966-67; asst. prof. edn. Ariz. State U., Tempe, 1967-70, asso. prof., 1970-75, prof. edn., 1975—. Author: The Emotionally Disturbed Child, 1970, Learning Disabilities, 1972, Learning Disabilities: A Competency Based Approach, 1976, 2d edit., 1981, Children with Learning Problems: A Handbook for Teachers, 1980. Mem. Council Exceptional Children, Phi Delta Kappa. Home: 519 E Del Rio Dr Tempe AZ 85282 *My goals in life are to work with my wife in raising our children to be honest, sensitive, responsible, productive, self-sufficient adults, and to function personally and professionally in a manner which will make it possible for me to assist others in their personal and professional growth.*

FABBRI, BRIAN JOHN, economist; b. Union City, N.J., July 15, 1944; s. Mario and Eugenia (Soracco) F.; m. Andrea Frances Koryal; 1 dau., Briana Jean. B.S. in Econs., NYU, 1966, M.B.A. in Econs. with distinction, 1968, doctoral candidate, 1972. Economist, monetary aggregates unit, fed capital markets unit Fed. Res. Bank of N.Y., N.Y.C., 1973-74; sr. economist, v.p. bond market research Salomon Bros., Inc., N.Y.C., 1974—; econs. and fin. cons. Contbr. articles to profl. publs.; editor: Comments on Credit. Served with U.S. Army, 1968-70. Marcus Nadler fellow, 1970-72. Mem. Nat. Assn. Bus. Economists, Am. Econ. Assn., N.Y. Assn. Bus. Economists, NYU Money Marketeers. Roman Catholic. Clubs: Meadowlands Racquet, Tiger Racquet. Office: Salomon Bros Inc 1 New York Plaza New York NY 10004

FABER, ADELE, author, educator; b. N.Y.C., Jan. 12, 1928; d. Morris and Betty (Kamay) Meyrowitz; m. Leslie Faber, Aug. 27, 1950; children—Carl, Joanna, Abram. B.A. in Theatre and Drama, Queens Coll., 1949; M.A. in Edn, N.Y. U., 1950; student, Dr. Haim Ginott, 1964-74. Speech tchr. N.Y. Sch. Printing, N.Y.C., 1950-51, Girls High Sch., 1952-58; Keynote speaker, condr. workshops on communication skills for parents and tchrs. at confs., throughout U.S., 1974—, lectr., cons. in field, 1972—; mem. faculty C.W. Post Coll., L.I. U., 1975—, New Sch. Social Research, 1976; co-dir. Liberating Relationships, Inc. Author: (with Elaine Mazlish) book Liberated Parents/Liberated Children, 1974 (Book-of-Month Club selection, 1974, Christopher award 1975), How To Talk So Kids Will Listen and Listen So Kids Will Talk, 1980 (Literary Guild selection); also How To Talk So Kids Will Listen Group Workshop Kit, 1980; booklet Breaking Barriers: Communication Skills for Teenagers, 1976; TV scripts The Princess, ABC, 1975, Mr. Sad-Sack, 1975, You Can Live With Your Family series, CBS, 1976; appeared numerous times on local, nat. radio, TV, 1974—. Home and Office: 351 I U Willets Rd Roslyn Heights NY 11577

FABER, DAVID ALAN, United States attorney; b. Charleston, W.Va., Oct. 21, 1942; s. John Smith and Wilda Elaine (Melton) F.; m. Deborah Ellayne Anderson, Aug. 24, 1968; 1 dau., Katherine Peyton. B.A., W.Va. U., 1964; J.D., Yale U., 1967. Bar: W.Va. 1967, U.S. Ct. Mil. Appeals 1970, U.S. Supreme Ct. 1974. Assoc. Dayton, Campbell & Love, Charleston, W.Va., 1967-68, Campbell, Love, Woodroe, 1972-74; ptnr. Campbell, Love, Woodroe & Kizer, Charleston, 1974-77, Love, Wise, Robinson & Woodroe, 1977-81; U.S. atty. U.S. Dept. Justice, Charleston, 1982—; counsel to ethics commn. W.Va. State Bar, Charleston, 1974-76. Served to capt. USAF, 1968-72. Nat. law scholar Yale Law Sch., New Haven, 1964-65. Mem. ABA, W.Va. State Bar, W.Va. Bar Assn., Phi Beta Kappa. Republican. Episcopalian. Home: 1417 Longridge Rd Charleston WV 25314 Office: US Atty W Va 500 Quarrier St Charleston WV 25301

FABER, JOHN HENRY, photographer; b. N.Y.C., Feb. 13, 1918; s. John Martin and Jennie (Wacker) F.; m. Gertrud Margot, Oct. 26, 1964; children: John, Karin Faber Clothier, Marlene Faber Pang, Donald, Dorian Faber Jenssen, Dana, Erich. Student, U. Ala. With Eastman Kodak Co., N.Y.C., 1950-83, indsl. photography tech. specialist, 1970-83; chief photographer Ala. Ordnance Works, 1941-43; with Bechtel-McCone-Parsons Corp., Birmingham, Ala., 1943-46; dir. photography Birmingham News, 1946-50; lectr. in field. Author: Industrial Photography, 1948, Great Moments in News Photography, 1960, Humor in News Photography, 1961, Travel Photography, 1971, Great News Photos and the Stories Behind Them, 1978; columnist: On the Record, Nat. Press Photographer mag., 1956-68, 79—; photography editor: The Explorer's Jour.; contbr. articles to mags., newspapers. Recipient Pres.'s medal (3) Nat. Press Photographers Assn., 1961, Kenneth P. McLaughlin award, 1958, hon. fellowship award, 1971, Joseph A. Sprague Meml. highest honor award, 1974, Joseph Costa award, 1979; disting. service award N.Y. Press Photographers Assn., 1973; George Eastman award Eastman Kodak Co., 1975. Fellow Am. Photog. Hist. Soc.; mem. N.Y. Press Photographers Assn., Explorer's Club, Royal Photographic Soc. Gt. Britain, Nat. Press Photographers Assn. (past regional v.p., nat. sec. 1948-50, historian 1956—), European Soc. History of Photography, Soc. Am. Historians, Am. Mus. Photography (past bd. trustees). Home: 23 Fernwood Pl Mountain Lakes NJ 07046

FABER, SANDRA MOORE, astronomer, educator; b. Boston, Dec. 28, 1944; d. Donald Edwin and Elizabeth Mackenzie (Borwick) Moore; m. Andrew L. Faber, June 9, 1967; children: Robin, Holly. B.A., Swarthmore Coll., 1966; Ph.D., Harvard U., 1972. Asst. prof., astronomer Lick Obs., U. Calif.-Santa Cruz, 1972-77, assoc. prof., astronomer, 1977-79, prof., astronomer, 1979—; mem. NSF astronomy adv. panel; vis. prof. Princeton U., 1978, U. Hawaii, 1983; Phillips visitor Haverford Coll., 1982; mem. Nat. Acad. Astronomy Survey Panel, 1979-81; chmn. vis. com. Space Telescope Sci. Inst., 1983—. Assoc. editor: Astrophys. Jour. Letters 1982—; editorial bd.: Ann. Revs. Astronomy and Astrophysics 1982—; contbr. articles to profl. jours. Recipient Bart J. Bok prize Harvard U., 1978; NSF fellow, 1966-71; Woodrow Wilson fellow, 1966-71; Alfred P. Sloan fellow, 1977-81. Mem. Am. Astron. Soc. (councilor 1982-84), Internat. Astron. Union, Phi Beta Kappa, Sigma Xi. Office: Lick Obs U Calif Santa Cruz CA 95060

FABIAN, FRANCIS GORDON, JR., corp. exec.; b. Evanston, Ill., Jan. 25, 1915; s. Francis G. and Dorothy (Gardner) F.; m. Gretchen Hauschild, Oct. 1, 1938; children—Richard G., Jennifer C. Grad. cum laude, Choate Sch., 1933; B.S. in Indsl. Engring, Yale, 1937. Asst. to v.p. engring. and mfg., chief design engr. Lindsay Corp., Chgo., 1946-48, v.p., 1949-50; asso. and bus. planning mgr. Booz Allen Hamilton, 1950-53; asst. to gen. mgr. Dresser Mfg. div. Dresser Industries, 1953-55, gen. mgr., 1955-58, pres., 1958-60, exec. v.p. parent co., Dallas, 1960-62, pres., dir., mem. exec. com., 1962-65; pres., dir. finance com. Hunt Food Industries, Inc., Fullerton, Calif., 1965-68; chmn., pres. For Better Living Inc., Laguna Niquel, 1969—. Home: 43 Monarch Bay South Laguna CA 92677 Office: 27665 Forbes Rd Laguna Niguel CA 92677

FABIAN, GEORGE STEPHEN, advertising agency executive; b. Budapest, Hungary, May 7, 1930; s. Alexander S. and Edith (Kern) F.; m. Norma A. MacInnes, Nov. 20, 1964; children: Jennifer S., Alexander K. B.A., Columbia U., 1950; M.B.A., U. Chgo., 1954. Dir. advt., media research Young & Rubicam, N.Y.C., 1956-66; mgr. mktg. research Johnson & Johnson Domestic Operating Cos., New Brunswick, N.J., 1966-68; dir. mktg. devel. and research Chesebrough-Pond's, Greenwich, Conn., 1968-77; dir. mktg. Campbell Soup Co., Camden, N.J., 1977-80; exec. v.p. SSC&B, Inc., N.Y.C., 1980—; lectr. CCNY Grad. Bus. Sch., 1962-64. Mem. exec. com. VITAM, 1974-77. Mem. Advt. Research Found. (dir. 1974—, exec. com.), Am. Mktg. Assn. (dir. 1977-80), Market Research Council (dir. 1974-76). Clubs: Aronomink Golf, Merion Cricket. Home: 843 Muirfield Rd Bryn Mawr PA 19010 Office: One Dag Hammarskjold Plaza New York NY 10017

FABIAN, JOHN M., astronaut; b. Goosecreek, Tex.; m. Donna Kay Buboltz; 2 children. B.S., Wash. State U., 1962; Ph.D., U. Wash., 1974. Astronaut NASA, Houston, 1978—, mission specialist Challenger Flight #2. Served with USAF; Vietnam. Decorated Vietnam Cross of Gallantry. Office: Lyndon B Johnson Space Center NASA Houston TX 77058 *

FABIAN, LARRY LOUIS, foundation executive; b. Aurora, Ill., May 25, 1940; s. Louis and Emma (Mayer) F.; m. Terese Sulikowski, Dec. 1, 1978; 1 son, Christopher Klement. B.A., Cath. U. Am., 1961, M.A., 1963; Ph.D., Columbia U., 1971. Staff mem. Bur. Intelligence and Research, Dept. State, Washington, 1962; staff mem. Carnegie Endowment for Internat. Peace, N.Y.C., 1964; research staff fgn. policy studies program Brookings Instn., Washington, 1965-71, research asso., co-dir. program on tech. and Am. fgn. policy, 1971-73; sr. assoc., dir. Middle East program Carnegie Endowment for Internat. Peace, Washington, 1974-77, sec., N.Y.C., 1977—; cons. Hudson Inst., N.Y.C., Rockefeller Found. Author: Soldiers without Enemies, 1971, (with others) Regimes for the Ocean, Outer Space and Weather, 1973; co-editor: Israelis Speak: About Themselves and the Palestinians, 1976. Mem. Council Fgn. Relations, Am. Soc. Internat. Law, Am. Polit. Sci. Assn., Internat. Inst. Strategic Studies, Middle East Inst., Antiquarian Horological Soc. Democrat. Roman Catholic. Club: Century (N.Y.C.). Office: 11 Dupont Circle NW Washington DC 20036 *

FABIAN, MICHAEL ROBERT, advertising executive; b. Budapest, Hungary, Dec. 7, 1932; came to U.S., 1941; s. Tibor and Elisabeth (Partos) F.; m. Betty B. Borjeson, July 28, 1956; children: David, John, Jennifer. B.A., Wesleyan U., 1954. Asst. account exec. Grey Advt., N.Y.C., 1956-58; asst. advt. mgr. Hudson Pulp & Paper, N.Y.C., 1958-60; mktg. dir. W.B. Doner Co., Phila., 1960-62; pres., chief exec. officer March Direct Mktg., N.Y.C., 1962—; pres. Barry Blau & Ptnrs., Westport, Conn., 1984—. Served with U.S. Army, 1954-56. Mem. Direct Mktg. Assn. (chmn. pres.'s club 1972-74, Silver Mailbox award 1978), Direct mktg. Creative Guild (pres. 1976-78, 82—), Direct Mktg. Idea Exchange. Clubs: Hundred Million, Weston Field. Home: 59 Lords Hwy Weston CT 06883 Office: March Direct Mktg 485 Lexington Ave New York NY 10017

FABIAN, ROBERT HART, lawyer; b. St. Paul, Dec. 27, 1914; s. Arthur Vincent and Maria (Hart) F.; m. Virginia Ritt, Oct. 1, 1940; children—Patrick, Ellen (Mrs. Christopher Braithwaite), Ann, Mark, Jane. B.A., Coll. St. Thomas, 1936; J.D., U. Minn., 1938. Bar: Minn. bar 1938, Calif. bar 1948, also U.S. Supreme Ct 1948. Atty. Dept. Justice, 1938-41; dep. zone adminstr. War Assets Adminstns., 1946-48; trial atty. Bank Am., N.T. & S.A., Los Angeles, 1948-67, sr. v.p. gen. counsel, San Francisco, 1967-73, exec. v.p., gen. counsel, 1973-75; partner firm Sullivan Roche and Johnson, 1975—; Mem. exec. com. Nat. Legal Aid and Defender Assn.; co-chmn. San Francisco Lawyers Com. for Urban Affairs, 1968-70. Note editor: Minn. Law Rev, 1937-38. Served to lt. col. C.E. AUS, 1942-46. Decorated Legion of Merit; recipient Distinguished Service award St. Thomas More Soc., 1970. Mem. ABA, Internat. Bar Assn. (vice chmn. comml. banking com.), Bar Assn. San Francisco (pres. 1974), Am. Bankers Assn., Calif. Bankers Assn. (chmn. govtl. affairs group), Phi Delta Phi. Home: 215 Cherry St San Francisco CA 94118 Office: 220 Bush St San Francisco CA 94104

FABIANI, DANTE CARL, industrialist; b. Waterbury, Conn., Aug. 13, 1917; s. Rosato Francis and Barbara (Poscente) F.; m. Virginia Parnham, July 15, 1944; children: Barbara Camille Fabiani Henriques, James Parnham, Kathryn Louise Fabiani Bartholomew. B.S., Tri-State Coll., 1938; postgrad., Purdue U., 1942. Employed with Auburn Rubber Corp., Ind., 1938-42, Gen. Electric Co., Ft. Wayne, Ind., 1942-45, Continental Can Co., Van Wert, Ohio, 1945-47; controller, asst. mgr. Standard Products Co., Toledo, 1948-51; dir., sec.-treas. Townsend Co., New Brighton, Pa., 1951-59; v.p. finance H. K. Porter Co., Inc., Pitts., 1959-60; dir., v.p. finance McDonnell Aircraft Corp., St. Louis, 1960; exec. v.p. Crane Co., 1960-61, pres., 1961-80, dir., 1961—; ret., 1980; dir. C.F.I. Steel Corp. subs. Crane Co., Pueblo, Colo., 1970—, Medusa Corp. subs. Crane Co., Cleve., Huttig Sash & Door Co. subs. Crane Co., St. Louis, Kearney Nat., Inc., N.Y.C., Graniteville Co. (S. C.), Grossman's, Brookline, Mass., Textron, Inc., Southeastern Pub. Service Co., Evans Products Co., Varlen Corp.; chmn., dir. Pirelli Cable Corp., 1983—. Republican. Clubs: Patterson (Westport, Conn.); Garden of the Gods (Colorado Springs, Colo.). Home: 15 North Ave Westport CT 06880 Office: 277 Park Ave New York NY 10022

FABRAY, NANETTE, actress; b. San Diego, Oct. 27; d. Racul Bernard and Lillian (McGovern) Fabares; m. David Tebet, Oct. 26, 1947 (div. July 1951); m. Ranald MacDougall, 1957 (dec. Dec. 1973); 1 son, Jamie. Student, Los Angeles City Coll.; D.H.L. (hon.), Gallaudet Coll., 1970, D.F.A., Md. Coll., 1972. Appeared as actress in: Broadway shows Let's Face It, 1941, Meet the People, 1940, By Jupiter, 1943, Bloomer Girl, 1944, High Button Shoes, 1947, Arms and the Girls, 1950, Love Life, 1948, Make A Wish, 1951, Mr. President, 1962, Jackpot, 1973, No Hard Feelings, 1973, Applause, 1973-74, Plaza Suite, 1973-74, The Secret Affairs of Mildred Wild, 1977; co-star: (with Sid Caesar on) Caesar's Hour, CBS-TV, 1954-56; star: TV series Yes, Yes Nanette, 1961-62; spls. Happy Birthday & Goodby, 1974, George M!, 1970; motion pictures include Private Lives of Elizabeth and Essex, 1939; The Bandwagon, 1952, The Happy Ending, 1969, A Child is Born, 1940, Cockeyed Cowboys of Calico County, 1970, That's Entertainment, Part 2, 1976, Harper Valley PTA; TV appearances include: One Day at a Time, CBS-TV; (Recipient two Donaldson awards for High Button Shoes 1947). Trustee Eugene O'Neill Meml. Found., Nat. Theatre of Deaf; bd. dirs., v.p. Nat. Assn. Hearing and Speech Agys.; bd. dirs. Pres.'s Nat. Adv. Com. on Edn. Deaf, Pres.'s Com. on Employment Handicapped, Muses of Calif. Mus. Found.; mem. Nat. Council on Handicapped, 1982—. Recipient two Donaldson awards for High Button Shoes, 1947, Tony award for Love Life, 1949, Emmy award as best comedienne, 1955, 56, best supporting performer Caesar's Hour, 1955, Eleanor Roosevelt Humanitarian award, 1964, Human Relations award Anti-Defamation League, 1969, 1st ann. Cogswell award Gallaudet Coll., 1970, Pres.'s Distinguished Service award, 1970; named Woman of Year Radio and TV Editors, 1963, Jewish War Vets. Am., 1969. *

FABRICAND, BURTON PAUL, educator, physicist; b. N.Y.C., Nov. 22, 1923; s. Irving Kermit and Frances (Sobler) F.; m. Heather C. North, Dec. 15, 1972; children (from previous marriage): Nicole Diane, Lorraine Stewart. A.B., Columbia U., 1947, A.M., 1949, Ph.D., 1953. Project engr. Philco Corp., Phila., 1952-54; lectr., research asso. U. Pa., 1954-56; sr. research scientist Columbia Hudson Labs., Dobbs Ferry, N.Y., 1957-69; prof. physics Pratt Inst., Bklyn., 1969—; mng. ptnr. Fabricand Assocs., 1970—; cons. Moore Sch. Elec. Engring., U. Pa., 1954-60, Indsl. Electronic Hardware Corp., N.Y.C., 1960-64. Author: Horse Sense: A New and Rigorous Application of Mathematical Methods to Successful Betting at the Track, 1965, Beating the Street, 1969, Horse Sense: Updated and Expanded Edition, 1976, The Science of Winning: A Random Walk on the Road to Riches, 1979. Mem. Am. Phys. Soc., Sigma Xi. Home: 47 Plaza St Brooklyn NY 11217 Office: 215 Ryerson St Brooklyn NY 11205

FABRICANT, ARTHUR E., lawyer, corporate executive; b. N.Y.C., Aug. 8, 1935; s. Henry and Rita (Wilson) F.; m. Inger Olsson, Nov. 1, 1975; children: Jill, Mary, John, James, Ann. A.B., U. St. Andrews, Scotland, 1954, Union Coll., 1956; J.D., Harvard U., 1959. Bar: N.Y. Atty. spl. group organized crime Office U.S. Atty. Gen., 1959-60; mem. firm Abeles & Clark, N.Y.C., 1960-61; v.p. Seligman & Latz Inc., N.Y.C., 1962-67, pres. internat. div., London, 1967—; dir. New Eng. Ice Cream Co., U.K., New Eng. Food Co. Fellow Inst. Dirs. Clubs: Lansdowne (London); Royal Wimbledon Golf. Home: Old Warren Farm Wimbledon Common England Office: 6 Curzon Pl London W1 England

FABRICK, HOWARD DAVID, lawyer; b. Milw., July 30, 1938; s. Seymour C. and Ruthe (Levine) F.; m. Myrna Taylor, June 29, 1958; children: Kenneth, Douglas, Tracy. A.B., Stanford U., 1960, J.D., 1962. Bar: Calif. 1963, U.S. Dist. Ct. (cen. dist.) Calif. 1963, U.S. Dist. Ct. (no. dist.) Calif. 1980. Atty. NLRB, Washington, 1962-64; sole practice, Beverly Hills, Calif., 1966-70; v.p. Burbank Studios, Calif., 1971-72, Assn. Motion Picture and TV Producers, Los Angeles, 1973-74; ptnr. firm Loeb & Loeb, Los Angeles, 1975-81, firm Proskauer, Rose, Goetz & Mendelsohn, 1981—; vis. instr. U. So. Calif., UCLA Extension. Pres., bd. dirs. Found for Junior Blind. Mem. Calif. Bar Assn., Phi Alpha Sigma. Office: 2049 Century Park E Suite 2290 Los Angeles CA 90067

FABRIKANT, BENJAMIN, educator; b. N.Y.C., Jan. 4, 1924; s. Samuel and Marcia (Fabryk) F.; m. Laurine Merriam Zucker, Aug. 28, 1949; children—Craig S., Gary K., Gail L. Student, Va. Mil. Inst., 1944-45, Shriveham Am. U., 1945; B.A., Bklyn. Coll., 1948; M.A., Temple U., 1950; Ph.D., U. Buffalo, 1953; postdoctoral, Am. U., 1958, L.I.U., 1962. Diplomate: Am. Bd. Profl. Psychology, Am. Bd. Profl. Hypnosis, Am. Bd. Family Practice. Psychologist Topeka State Hosp., 1952-53; psychologist, asst. chief, chief psychol. research VA Hosp., Buffalo, 1953-59; chief psychologist Psychol. Service Center, Teaneck, N.J., 1959-62; mem. faculty Fairleigh Dickinson U., Teaneck, 1962—, prof., dir. clin. programs, 1971—; lectr. Grad. Sch. Orthodontics, 1964—; cons. in field. Author: (with J. Barron, J. Krasner) Psychotherapy, 1971, (with M. Protell and J. Krasner) Psychodynamics of Dental Practice, (with J. Barrow and J. Krasner) To Live is to Enjoy: A Primer of Psychotherapy; Asso. editor: Psychotherapy Bull, 1976-80; editor, 1980—; cons. editor: New Jersey Psychologist, Jour. Psychotherapy; editor: The Relationship jour, 1979-81; contbr. articles to profl. jours. Bd. trustees North Bergen County YMHA, 1969-70; pres. Fabrikant Family Found. Served with AUS, 1942-45. Fellow Soc. Personality Projective Assessment, Am. Psychol. Assn. (adminstrv. coordinator div. psychotherapy 1980—, chmn. subcom. on profl. edn. and tng. bd. profl. affairs 1980-81); mem. Bergen County Psychol. Assn. (past pres.), N.J. Psychol. Assn., N.J. Group Psychotherapy Assn. (past pres.), Am. Acad. Psychotherapists, Soc. Clin. Exptl. Hypnosis, Sigma Xi. Home: 18 Chimney Ridge Ct Westwood NJ 07675 *There is no measure of success in any area of life unless and until a person is completely honest with himself. The praise and or criticism of those around you are simply guidelines, to be evaluated in the light of your ability to see yourself completely honestly.*

FABRYCKY, WOLTER JOSEPH, industrial and systems engineer; b. Queens County, N.Y., Dec. 6, 1932; s. Louis Ludwig and Stephanie (Wadis) F.; m. Luba Swerbilow, Sept. 4, 1954; children: David Jon, Kathryn Marie. B.S., Wichita State U., 1957; M.S., U. Ark., 1958; Ph.D. (Ethyl Corp. fellow), Okla. State U., 1962. Instr. indsl. engring. U. Ark., 1957-60; assoc. prof. indsl. engring. and mgmt. Okla. State U., 1962-65; prof. indsl. engring. and ops. research Va. Poly. Inst. and State U., 1965—, assoc. dean engring., 1970-76, dean research, 1976-81; mem. Engring. Edn. Del. to People's Republic of China, 1978. Author: Economic Decision Analysis, 2d edit., 1980, (with G.J. Thuesen) Engineering Economy, 6th edit., 1984, (with P.M. Ghare and P.E. Torgersen) Applied Operations Research and Management Science, 1984, (with B.S. Blanchard) Systems Engineering and Analyses, 1981; Editor: (with J.H. Mize) Prentice-Hall International Series in Industrial and Systems Engineering, 1972—. Fellow AAAS, Inst. Indsl. Engrs. (exec. v.p. 1982-84, Book of Year award 1973); mem. Am. Soc. Engring. Edn. (v.p. 1977-78), Ops. Research. Soc. Am., Sigma Xi, Alpha Pi Mu, Sigma Tau. Home: 1200 Lakewood Drive Blacksburg VA 24060 Office: 360 Whittemore Hall Va Poly Inst and State U Blacksburg VA 24061

FABRYCY, MARK ZDZISLAW, economist; b. Sosnoviec, Poland, Nov. 18, 1922; came to U.S., 1959, naturalized, 1964; s. Ludomir Adam and Alicia Barbara (Bielska) F.; m. Marie Barbara Fabierkiewicz, Jan. 25, 1949. B. Commerce with honors, U. London, 1950; M.A., City U.N.Y., 1962, Ph.D., 1967. Overseas contracts engr. Crompton Parkinson, Ltd. (elec. mfrs.), London, 1950-53; pres. Mark Z. Fabrycy & Assos. (econ. research cons.), Montreal, N.Y.C. and Dayton, Ohio, 1953—; asst. prof. econs. N.Y. U., 1965-67, asso. prof., 1967-72; prof. econs. Wright State U., Dayton, 1972—, chmn. dept., 1978—; prin. Urban Research Assos., N.Y.C., 1966-69, Tech-Mark Research Assos., 1967—. Contbr. articles to profl. jours. Served with Brit. Army, 1942-45. Decorated Mil. Cross, Army Cross. Mem. Econometric Soc., Am. Econ. Assn., Royal Econ. Soc. Club: Racquet. Home: 6710 Carinthia Dr Dayton OH 45459 Office: Dept of Economics Wright State University Dayton OH 45431

FACCINTO, VICTOR PAUL, artist, gallery administrator; b. Albany, Calif., Oct. 30, 1945; s. Victor A. and Betty Jean (Smith) Pearson; 1 dau., Denise Michelle. B.A. in Psychology, Calif. State U.-Sacramento, 1969, M.A. in Art, 1972. Instr. art Calif. State U., 1972-74; asst. to dir. Nancy Hoffman Gallery, N.Y.C., 1974-78; dir. art gallery Wake Forest U., Winston Salem, 1978—, dir. Rockefeller vis. artist program, 1978—. Exhibited one man shows, Mus. Modern Art, N.Y.C., 1975, Collective for Living Cinema, N.Y.C., 1976, Phyllis Kind Gallery, N.Y.C., 1980, 82, group shows include, Whitney Mus. Am. Art, 1972, 73, 74, Mus. Modern Art, N.Y.C., 1978, Barbara Gladstone Gallery, N.Y.C., 1983, Monique Knowlton Gallery, N.Y.C.; represented in permanent collections, Mus. Modern Art, N.Y.C., Philip Morris, Inc.; maker: animated film Shameless, 1974. N.Y. CAPS fellow, 1977; N.C. Arts Council fellow, 1982; recipient 1st prize NYU Small Works Competition, 1983. Baptist. Home: 155 Harmon Ave Winston Salem NC 27106 Office: Wake Forest U PO Box 7232 Winston Salem NC 27109

FACHES, WILLIAM GEORGE, lawyer; b. Cedar Rapids, Iowa, Feb. 15, 1928; s. George Vlasios and Androniki (Panagopoulos) F.; m. Mary Matzanias, Dec. 6, 1959; children: Andrea Lynn, Allison Lynn. Student, Coe Coll., 1947-48; B.A., U. Iowa, 1951, J.D., 1955. Bar: Iowa bar 1955, U.S. Supreme Ct 1971. Mem. firm Reilly & Faches, Cedar Rapids, 1955-67; 1st asst. county atty., Linn County, 1965-67, county atty., 1967-74; sr. mem. firm Faches, Gloe and Quint, and predecessors, Cedar Rapids, 1967—. Mem. Mayor's Ad Hoc Com. on Alcholism, 1967-68, Linn County Crime Commn., 1971-73, Linn County Bd. Suprs., 1978; pres. Young Democrats, 1960; mem. central com. Linn County Dem. Com., 1956-58, 60-68; bd. dirs. Linn County Assn. Mentally Retarded, 1968-72, Cedar Rapids Teen Club, 1968-74; chmn., mem. bd. 6th Jud. Dist. Iowa Dept. Correctional Services, 1978—; inheritance tax appraiser 6th Jud. Dist., 1980—; pres. St. John's Hellenic Orthodox Ch., 1981—. Served with Air Corps AUS, 1946-47. Recipient Civil Libertarian award Iowa Civil Liberties Union, 1974. Mem. Iowa, Linn County bar assns., Am. Trial Lawyers Assn., Iowa County Attys. Assn., Nat. Dist. Attys. Assn., Am. Judicature Soc., Criminal Law Assn. Linn County (pres. 1976), Iowa Correctional Services Assn. (Citizen of Yr. award 1980), Am. Legion (trustee Hanford Post 5 1982—), Phi Alpha Delta. Home: 1901 5th Ave SE Cedar Rapids IA 52403 Office: 318 Paramount Bldg Cedar Rapids IA 52401

FACKENHEIM, EMIL LUDWIG, educator; b. Halle, Germany, June 22, 1916; emigrated to Can., 1940; s. Julius and Meta (Schlesinger) F.; m. Rose Komlodi, Dec. 28, 1957; children—Michael Alexander, Susan Sheila, David Emmanuel, Joseph Jonatan. Student, U. Halle, 1937-38, U. Aberdeen, Scotland, 1939-40; Ph.D. in Philosophy, U. Toronto, Can., 1945; LL.D., Laurentian U., Sudbury, Ont., 1969, Sir George Williams U., Montreal, Que., 1971; D.D., St. Andrew's Coll., Saskatoon, Sask., 1972; D.H.L., Hebrew Union Coll., Cin., 1974; D.L., Barry U., Miami, Fla. Rabbi, 1939; rabbi Congregation Anshe Sholom, Hamilton, Ont., Can., 1943-48; from lectr. to prof. dept. philosophy U. Toronto, 1948—, Univ. prof., 1979; vis. prof. Hebrew U., 1982—. Author: Metaphysics and Historicity, 1960, Paths to Jewish Belief, 1961, The Religious Dimension in Hegel's Thought, 1968, 70, Quest for Past and Future, 1968, 70, God's Presence in History, 1970, 73, Encounters Between Judaism and Modern Philosophy, 1973, 80, The Jewish Return Into History, 1978, 80, To Mend the World, 1982. Recipient Pres.'s medal U. Western Ont., London, 1954; Guggenheim fellow, 1957-58; Killam fellow, 1977-78. Fellow Royal Soc. Can.; mem. Canadian Philos. Assn., Can. Zionist Fedn. Home: 563 Briar Hill Ave Toronto M5N 1N1 ON Canada *Ever since 1933, or shortly thereafter, I have been trying to respond, through philosophical understanding and Jewish religious thought, to what gradually emerged as being a catastrophe without precedent, the Nazi assault on God and Man, on the human family in general and, in particular, on the Jewish people, the most radically singled out victim. And, after fifty years, I believe that the bulk of the task still lies ahead.*

FACKLER, BENJAMIN LLOYD, utility executive; b. Meansville, Ga., Oct. 20, 1926; s. Ferris L. and Sallie (Storey) F.; m. Patricia Cheney, Oct. 20, 1951; children: Gena Fackler Conrad, Carole Fackler Cooper. Student, N. Ga. Coll. at Dahlonega, 1942-44; B.B.A. in Acctg., U. Ga., 1947. With Atlanta Gas Light Co., Ga., 1947—, asst. treas., asst. sec., 1967-68, treas., 1968-77, sr. v.p. fin., 1977—, dir., 1978—. Served with USNR, 1944-46. Mem. Fin. Execs. Inst. (dir.), Am. Gas Assn. (mng. com., fin. com.), Ga. Freight Bur. (dir.), Phi Kappa Phi. Republican. Baptist (chmn. bd. deacons; Sunday sch. supt., fin. com.). Club: Kiwanis. Home: 2381 Sagamore Hills Dr Decatur GA 30033 Office: PO Box 4569 235 Peachtree St NE Atlanta GA 30302

FACKLER, JOHN PAUL, JR., university dean, chemistry educator; b. Toledo, July 31, 1934; s. John P. and Ruth (Moehring) F.; m. Naomi Paula Steege, Sept. 2, 1956; children: Katherine G., Cheryl R., Karla S., John M., Dorothy L. Student, MIT, 1952; B.A., Valpraiso U., 1956; Ph.D., MIT, 1960. Jr. chemist Sun Oil Co., 1953-56; teaching asst. MIT, 1956-59, research assoc., 1960; asst. prof. U. Calif., 1960-62, Case Inst. Tech., 1962-64; asso. prof. chemistry Case Western Res. U., 1964-69, prof., 1970-82, chmn. dept., 1972-77; dean Coll. Sci., prof. chemistry Tex. A&M U., 1983—, 1983—; vis. prof. U. Calif. at Santa Barbara, 1969; Fulbright lectr. Colombia, 1969; cons. in chemistry Central State U., 1967-69. Author: Symmetry in Coordination Chemistry, 1971; Editor: Symmetry in Chemical Theory, 1973, Inorganic Syntheses, Vol. 21, 1982; Contbr. articles to profl. jours. Bd. dirs. Luth. Met. Ministry, 1969-72; bd. dirs. Luth. High Sch. Assn., 1974-80, chmn., 1979. J.S. Guggenheim fellow, 1976; Recipient Tech. Achievement award Cleve. Tech. Soc., 1971. Mem. Am. Chem. Soc. (councilor 1972-73, chmn. elect 1974, chmn. Cleve. sect. 1975, chmn. elect 1978, chmn. inorganic div. 1979), Gordon Research Conf. (council 1979-82, trustee 1982—), Chem. Soc. London, AAAS, Am. Crystal. Assn., Sigma Xi, Phi Lambda Upsilon, Phi Delta Theta.

Lutheran. Home: Route 3 Box 303 College Station TX 77840 Office: Tex A&M U College Station TX 77843

FACKLER, WALTER DAVID, economist, educator; b. Aitkin, Minn., Aug. 27, 1921; s. Leonard D. and Ruth (Wanous) F.; m. Hazel Shepardson, May 24, 1951; children—Mark Duval, Neil Evan, Paul Leonard. A.B. with distinction and spl. honors, George Washington U., 1950; postgrad., Johns Hopkins, 1951-54. Accountant Pub. Service Co. of Ind., 1939-42; asst. prof. econs. George Washington U., Washington, 1950-56, asst. to dean faculties, 1953-56, dir. fgn. service rev. program, 1950-54; instr. polit. economy Johns Hopkins, 1952-54; asst. dir. econ. research dept. U.S. C. of C., Washington, 1956-59; sr. economist Cabinet Com. on Price Stability for Econ. Growth, Washington, 1959-60; asso. prof. bus. econs. U. Chgo. Grad. Sch. Bus., 1960-62, prof., 1962—, asso. dean, 1962-69, acting dean, 1968-69, dir. mgmt. programs, 1970—; Bus. and govt. cons., 1950—, lectr., 1950—; mem. Ill. State Bd. Banks and Trust Cos., 1979—. Contbr. articles to profl. publs. Served to capt. AUS, 1942-46. Decorated Bronze Star. Mem. Am. Econ. Assn., Am. Statis. Assn., Phi Beta Kappa. Clubs: Economic, University (Chgo.). Home: 5811 S Dorchester Ave Chicago IL 60637

FACKLER, WILLIAM MARION, banker; b. Canton, Ga., June 24, 1938; s. Newman Eidson and Mary Edna (Williams) F.; m. Judith Virginia Tomme, June 27, 1965; children: William Marcus, Michael Tomme. B.A., Emory U., 1960; M.B.A., Ga. State U., 1967; diploma, Stonier Grad. Sch. Banking, 1970. Vice pres. mktg. research, planning and product devel. First Nat. Bank Atlanta, 1975—; sr. v.p., dir. mktg. First Nat. Bank Birmingham, Ala., 1983; also AmSouth Bancorp.; now exec. v.p. Barnett Banks of Fla., Inc.; mem. faculty Ga. Banking Sch., Stonier Grad. Sch. Banking. Editorial rev. bd.: Jour. Retail Banking. Served with USAF, 1961. Mem. Am. Mktg. Assn. (Mktg. Person of Year, Birmingham chpt. 1980), Bank Mktg. Assn. (dir., exec. com.), Am. Inst. Banking, Sales and Mktg. Execs. Methodist. Home: 3809 Timuquara Rd Jacksonville FL 32210 Office: 100 Laura St Jacksonville FL 32210

FACTOR, ALAN JAY, film producer; b. Chgo.; s. John Jacob and Rella (Cohen) F.; m. Phyllis Ezrach, Feb. 25, 1961; children: Mitchell, Daniel, Robert, Angela Steven. B.F.A., Northwestern U.; student, Art Inst. Chgo., Goodman Theatre. Vice pres. Calumet Agy., 1953-60; story editor Karzmar Prodns., 1961-62; prodn. exec. Fox Prodns., 1962-63, Screen Gems, 1963-64; pres. Bedford Prodns., Hollywood, Calif., 1965-76, Factor-Newland PLrodns., Hollywood, 1975—; mem. spl. adv. com. TV Acad. Awards, 1974. Dir.: TV programs Bewitched, The Next Step Beyond, People Need People, El Rosario Story, Spl. Olympics; commls., others; producer: Something Evil, Siege, Terror on the Beach, A Sensitive, Passionate City, The Five of Me, others. Pres. Beverly Hills Charitable Found., 1964; v.p. Eddie Cantor Charitable Found., 1970; dir., v.p. ANTA. Served with Armed Forces Radio Service, 1950-52. Recipinet Masada award State of Israel, 1973. Mem. Producers Guild Am., Dirs. Guild Am., Screen Actors Guild, Actors Equity Assn., Hollywood Radio and TV Soc. (dir., v.p.), Tau Delta Phi. Club: B'nai B'rith (past pres.). Home: 817 N Roxbury Dr Beverly Hills CA 90210 Office: 1438 N Gower St Hollywood CA 90028

FACTOR, TED H., advertising executive; b. St. Louis, June 15, 1914; s. Nathan and Rose (Heiman) F.; m. Margot Kadel, Oct. 19, 1946; m. Barbara Currey Wood, July 11, 1965. Student, U. Calif., 1931-33, U. So. Calif., 1933-34. Internat. publicity dir. Max Factor & Co., 1934-36; pres. Ted. H. Factor Agy., named changed to Factor-Breyer, Inc., 1951, merged with Doyle Dane Bernbach, Inc., 1954, 1936-54; sr. v.p. charge West Coast ops. Doyle Dane Bernbach, Inc., 1954, exec. v.p. West Coast ops., 1969-74; now vice chmn. Doyle Dane Bernbach Internat., also dir., past mem. exec. com.; past dir. Econ. Resources Corp., Milici/Valenti Advt. Agy., Honolulu, Doyle Dane Bernbach Hong Kong Ltd. Mem. exec. bd. Art Center Coll. Design; adv. com. on Communications Los Angeles County Mus. Art; founding mem. Center Study Democratic Instns. Named Man of Yr. Western States Advt. Agys., 1970. Mem. Am. Assn. Advt. Agys., Tau Delta Phi. Clubs: Beverly Hills Tennis (past v.p.); Palm Springs Racquet, World Trade. Home: 1374 Laurel Way Beverly Hills CA 90210 Office: 5900 Wilshire Blvd Los Angeles CA 90036

FADELEY, EDWARD N., lawyer, state legislator; b. Williamsville, Mo., Dec. 13, 1929. A.B., U. Mo., 1951; J.D., U. Oreg., 1957. Bar: Oreg. 1957. Practice law, Eugene, Oreg., 1957—; mem. Oreg. Ho. of Reps., 1961-63, Oreg. Senate, 1963—, pres., 1983—. Chmn. Oreg. Dem. Party, 1966-68; chmn. law and justice com. Nat. conf. Legislators, 1977-78. Lt. USNR, 1951-54. Recipient Pioneer award U. Oreg., 1980. Mem. ABA, Oreg. State Bar Assn. (chmn. uniform laws com. 1962-64), Order of Coif, Alpha Pi Zeta, Phi Alpha Delta. Office: Fadeley & Fadeley 350 Forum Bldg 777 High St Eugene OR 97401 *

FADELEY, HERBERT JOHN, JR., banker, lawyer; b. Ambler, Pa., Feb. 14, 1922; s. Herbert John and Jennie Miller (Lewis) F.; m. Eleanor A. Battafarano, Feb. 8, 1947; children: Herbert John, Brett Duane, Theresa Jane, Scott Lewis. B.S. in Commerce, Drexel U., 1946; J.D., Temple U., 1953; postgrad., Stonier Sch. Banking, Rutgers U., 1957. Bar: U.S. Supreme Ct. bar 1957. Asst. cashier First Nat. Bank, Media, Pa., 1951; v.p. Boardwalk Nat. Bank, Atlantic City, N.J., 1957-60, Indsl. Trust Co., Phila., 1960-62; v.p., trust officer County Trust Co., White Plains, N.Y., 1963-68; pres. Troy Savs. Bank, N.Y., 1969—, chmn. bd., chief exec. officer, 1982—, also trustee.; pres., dir. 32 second St. Inc.; dir. Realty Umbrella Ltd.; Lectr. banking and law Drexel U., 1962, Rockland Community Coll., Suffern, N.Y., 1964-68, Westchester County chpt. Am. Inst. Banking, 1965-68, Hudson Valley Community Coll., Troy, 1970. Chmn. Rensselaer County Am. Cancer Fund Crusade, 1970-73; also v.p., dir. Cancer Soc., 1970-73, pres., 1975-76; bd. dirs. Troy Downtown Devel. Found.; mem. Troy Downtown Devel. Council, Tri-county Fifty Group.; Bd. dirs. Russell Sage Coll., chmn. fin. com., past treas., gen. chmn. 1972 fund drive; bd. dirs. United Community Services, Soc. Friendly Sons St. Patrick; pres. Soc. Friendly Sons St. Patrick, 1976-77; bd. dirs. Mary Warren Free Inst., also v.p.; bd. dirs., v.p. Uncle Sam Mall, Inc., 1971-73. Served to lt. (j.g.) USNR, 1942-43, 48-59; maj. Old Guard; City of Phila. Named Outstanding Alumnus Drexel U., 1961; recipient trust div. sch. awards N.Y. State Banker's Assn., 1967, 68. Mem. Am. Bar Assn., Am. Inst. Mgmt. (mem. pres.'s council), Am. Judicature Soc., Assn. U.S. Army, Lambda Chi Alpha, Phi Alpha Delta (named outstanding alumnus 1957, chief justice Dr. Elden S. Magaw Alumni chpt. 1955-56), Greater Troy C. of C. (dir. 1969-75, pres. 1973-74). Episcopalian. Clubs: Mason, Shriner, Jester., Troy (Troy). Home: 37 Brunswick Rd Troy NY 12180 Office: 32 2d St Troy NY 12180

FADEN, CHARLES A., corporate executive; b. Troy, N.Y., Dec. 14, 1930; s. Charles A. and Helen M. (Lang) F.; m. L. Dolores Faden, Feb. 21, 1959; children: Leigh, Kerry, Lynne. B.Sc., Siena Coll., 1952; M.B.A., U. Mich., 1958. With Parke-Davis & Co., 1958-62, dir. sales research and devel., 1960-62; with Squibb Corp., 1962-78; pres. E.R. Squibb & Sons, Inc., 1974-78, Warner-Lambert Europe, Morris Plains, N.J., 1978-79, Warner-Lambert, Pan Am.-Asia, 1980-83; v.p. health care div. Monsanto Co., St. Louis, 1983—; dir. Squibb Corp., 1975-78. Served as lt. USNR, 1952-56. Clubs: Metropolitan (N.Y.); Bedens Brook (Princeton, N.J.); Hurlingham (London). Office: Monsanto Co 800 Lindbergh Blvd Saint Louis MO 63166

FADER, DANIEL NELSON, English educator; b. Balt., Jan. 4, 1930; s. Maurice Abraham and Ida Eunice (Browne) F.; m. Martha Alice Agnew, Oct. 8, 1955 (div. 1982); children: Paul Frederick, Lisa Jeanine. B.A., Cornell U., 1952, M.A., 1954; Ph.D., Stanford U., 1963. Research scholar Christ's Coll., Cambridge (Eng.) U., 1955-57; acting instr. Stanford (Calif.) U., 1957-61; instr. U. Mich., Ann Arbor, 1961-63, asst. prof., 1963-68, asso. prof., 1968-73, prof. English lang. and lit., 1973-76, prof. English, chmn. English composition bd., 1976—; lectr., cons. in field. Author: books including Hooked on Books, 1966, The Naked Children, 1971, Paul and I Discover America, 1975, (with others) New Hooked on Books, 1976; contbr. articles to profl. jours. Served with U.S. Army, 1954-55. Mem. AAUP, MLA, Nat. Council Tchrs. of English. Home: 2222 Fuller St Ann Arbor MI 48105 Office: Angell Hall U Mich Ann Arbor MI 48109

FADER, SHIRLEY SLOAN (MRS. SEYMOUR J. FADER), writer; b. Paterson, N.J., Feb. 24; d. Samuel Louis and Miriam (Marcus) Sloan; m. Seymour J. Fader, June 26, 1951; children: Susan Deborah, Steven Micah Kimchi. B.S., M.S., U. Pa. Writer, journalist, author, Paramus, N.J., 1956—; chmn., coordinator ann. writers seminar Bergen Community Coll., 1973-76. Writer of: Jobmanship and People and You columns, Family Weekly, 1971-81; contbg. writer, 1977-82; contbg. editor: Glamour mag, 1978-81; writer: column How to Get More from Your Job; contbr. articles to nat. mags., 1956—; writer: Start Here column, Working Woman mag., 1980—; contbg. editor, Working Woman Mag., 1980—; writer: Women Getting Ahead column, Ladies' Home Jour., 1981—; author: The Princess Who Grew Down, 1968, From Kitchen to Career, 1977, Jobmanship, 1978, Successfully Ever After, 1982. Mem. Authors Guild, Am. Soc. Journalists and Authors (nat. v.p. 1976-77, mem.-at-large nat. exec. council 1976-78, 83-85), Nat. Press Club. Address: 377 McKinley Blvd Paramus NJ 07652

FADIMAN, CLIFTON, writer, editor, radio and TV entertainer; m. Pauline Rush (div.); m. Annalee Whitmore Fadiman; children: Jonathan, Kim, Anne. A.B., Columbia U., 1925. Editor Simon and Schuster (book pubs.), 1929-35; book editor The New Yorker, 1933-43; mem. selecting com. Book-of-the-Month Club, 1944—; lectr.; cons. Ency. Brit. Ednl. Corp., 1963-70; Regents lectr. U. Calif. at Los Angeles, 1967; Children's book juror Nat. Book Awards, 1973. Contbr. to numerous magazines, 1924—; master of ceremonies on: radio program Information Please, 1938-48, Conversation, 1954-57; TV program This is Show Business; formerly regular essayist, Holiday Mag.; bd. editors, Ency. Brit., 1959—; Author: Party of One, 1955, Any Number Can Play, 1957, The Lifetime Reading Plan, 1959, rev. edit., 1977, Enter Conversing, 1962, Wally the Wordworm, 1964; co-author: The Joys of Wine, 1975, Wine-Buyer's Guide, 1977, Empty Pages, 1979; editor: Reading I've Liked, 1941, The American Treasury, 1955, Fantasia Mathematica, 1958, The Mathematical Magpie, 1962, Dionysus, 1962, Fifty Years, 1965, World Treasury of Children's Literature, vols. 1 and 2, 1984; bd. advisors: Cricket, 1972-79; assoc. editor: Gateway to the Great Books; editorial adv. bd.: Réalités, 1980; columnist, 1981; book reviewer: Signature, 1981-84; commentator: First Edition (TV show), 1983-84. Bd. dirs. Council Basic Edn. Address: 3222 Campanil Dr Santa Barbara CA 93109

FADUM, RALPH EIGIL, university dean; b. Pitts., July 19, 1912; s. Torgeir Bleken and Mimi (Knudsen) F.; m. Nancy Isabelle Fields, July 19, 1939; 1 dau., Jane Fields. B.S. in Civil Engring, U. Ill., 1935; M.S., Harvard, 1937, S.D., 1941; D.Eng., Purdue U., 1963. Registered profl. engr., N.C. Parttime asst. civil engring. Harvard, 1935-37, instr., 1937-41, faculty instr., 1941- 43; asst. prof. soil mechanics Purdue U., 1943-45, asso. prof., 1945-47, prof., 1947-49; head of civil engring. dept. and prof. of civil engring. N.C. State U., Raleigh, 1949-62, dean of engring., 1962-78; cons. Dept. Def., U.S. Corps Engrs.; Mem. Army Sci. Bd. Dept. Army, 1959-81; mem. research adv. com. Fed. Hwy. Adminstrn., 1963-70; adv. bd. Ford Found., 1963-69; vice chmn. Army Sci. Adv. Panel, Dept. Army, 1966-70; chmn. adv. group to comdr. gen. Tank Automotive Command, 1967-70. Contbr. articles to profl. jours. Chmn. N.C. Water Control Adv. Council; bd. dirs. Nat. Driving Center, 1973-77; commr. Raleigh Housing Authority, 1962-72; pres. Atlantic Coast Conf., 1966-67, 71-72; v.p. Nat. Collegiate Athletic Assn., 1972-76; Chmn. bd. dirs. N.C. Water Resources Research Inst., U. N.C. Recipient Patriotic Civilian Service award Dept. Army, 1967, Meritorious Civilian Service medal, 1967, Outstanding Civilian Service medal, 1973, 77; Distinguished Civil Engring. Alumnus award U. Ill., 1969. Mem. ASCE (hon. mem., Outstanding Civil Engr. N.C. award 1971); mem. Nat. Acad. Engring., U.S. Nat. Council Soil Mechanics and Found. Engring., Nat. Soc. Profl. Engrs., N.C. Soc. Engrs. (Outstanding Engring. Achievement award 1971), Raleigh Engrs. Club (Outstanding Engr. award), Am. Soc. Engring. Edn. (hon. mem.; v.p., mem. exec. com. 1973-74, dir.), Sigma Xi, Tau Beta Pi, Chi Epsilon (nat. honor mem.), Phi Kappa Phi, Delta Upsilon. Clubs: Rotary (Raleigh); Carolina Country. Address: 408 Mann Hall NC State U Raleigh NC 27695

FAFIAN, JOSEPH, JR., diversified financial services company executive; b. N.Y.C., Apr., 17, 1939; s. Joseph M. and Mary (Alonso) F.; m. Nathalie Coluccio, Oct. 5, 1963; children—John Joseph, Michael Francis. B.A., Bklyn. Coll., 1959. Asso. actuary U.S. Life Ins. Co., N.Y.C., 1967; 2d v.p. USLIFE Corp., 1967-69, v.p., 1969-72, sr. v.p. ops., 1972-76, exec. v.p. life ins., 1976-77, sr. exec. v.p. life ins., 1977-78; pres., chief exec. officer, dir. U.S. Life, 1978-80; pres., dir. Beneficial Nat. Life Ins. Co., N.Y.C., 1980-82, chmn. bd., chief exec. officer, 1982—; dir. Assoc. Madison., pres., chief operating officer, 1982—. Trustee, treas. S.I. Acad.; Trustee S.I. Hosp. Served with N.G., 1962-67. Fellow Soc. Actuaries; mem. Acad. Actuaries. Home: 74 Mason St Staten Island NY 10304 Office: 125 Maiden Ln New York NY 10038 *Guide my actions by three principles: Always be proud of what I am doing; Always seek to improve what I am doing; Always learn more about what I am doing.*

FAGALY, WILLIAM ARTHUR, curator; b. Lawrenceburg, Ind., Mar. 1, 1938; s. William James and Dorothy Rae (Wheeler) F. B.A., Ind. U., 1962, M.A., 1967. Asst. registrar Art Mus., Ind. U., Bloomington, 1965-66; with New Orleans Mus. Art, 1966—, curator collections, 1967-73, chief curator, 1973-80, asst. dir for art, 1980—; guest curator La. Folk Painting exhibit, Mus. Am. Folk Art, N.Y.C., 1973; mem. adv. panel visual arts and crafts, div. arts La. Arts Council, 1978—; panelist Nat. Endowment Arts GSA Art in Architecture Commn., 1974, 76, 78; guest lectr., cons. Contbr. articles to profl. jours. Mem. Am. Assn. Mus. Methodist. Home: 915 Saint Philip St New Orleans LA 70116 Office: PO Box 19123 New Orleans LA 70179

FAGAN, GEORGE VINCENT, librarian-historian; b. Phila., Oct. 4, 1917; s. William J. and Mary A. (Carrigan) F.; m. Ernestine M. Hudak, Nov. 21, 1942; children: George Vincent, William J., John E., Ernestine A.T., Terence P. B.S., Temple U., 1940, M.A., 1941; M.A. in L.S, U. Denver, 1957; Ph.D., U. Pa., 1954. Instr. history Temple U., 1940-41, 46-51; instr. U.S. Naval Acad., 1951-54; asso. editor Air U. Press, 1954-55; asso. prof. USAF Acad., 1955-56, prof. history and dir. library, 1956-69; lectr. Regis Coll., Denver, 1957-59, U. Denver, 1960-63, U. Colo., 1960-68; prof. library sci., head librarian Tutt Library, Colo. Coll., 1969-83; library cons., 1983—; exec. dir. Colo. Com. for Nat. Library Week, 1959-63. Author: Alexander Dallas Bache, Educator, 1941, Study Guide for American History, 1948-57, Self-Evaluation, United States Air Force Academy, 1958, (with W.W. Jeffries) Geography and National Power, 1953, Pikes Peak Region and USAF Academy, 1962; Contbr. articles to periodicals. Trustee Colorado Springs Fine Arts Center, 1961-66. Commd. 2d lt. AUS, 1942; advanced through grades to col. USAF, 1963. Mem. Am. Hist. Assn., Orgn. Am. Historians, ALA. Home: 1408 N Cascade Ave Colorado Springs CO 80907

FAGAN, JOHN PAUL, financial executive; b. Yonkers, N.Y., Apr. 28, 1930; s. John J. and Winifred R. (Murray) F.; m. Theresa A. Kivlon, Aug. 20, 1955; children—Robert, Nancy, Thomas. B.B.A., Pace Coll., 1962; grad. Advanced Mgmt. Program, Harvard, 1973. Sr. asst. treas. N.Y.C. R.R., N.Y.C., 1953-68; asst. v.p. I.C. R.R., Chgo., 1968-69; treas. IC Industries, Chgo., 1969—, v.p., 1972—, v.p. finance, treas., 1975-81, sr. v.p. fin., 1981-82, exec. v.p. fin., 1982—; dir. Philipsborn Equities, Inc., Chgo., IC Leasing Co., Chgo. Bank of Commerce, Mut. Marine Fire & Inland Ins. Co., Phila., Evanston Ins. Co., Ill. Mem. adv. bd. Cath. Charities, Chgo.; Bd. dirs. Better Bus. Bur., Chgo.; trustee Chgo. Pops Orch. Assn., Ill. Inst. Tech.; also bd. govs. Research Inst. Served with USMCR, 1951-53. Mem. Newcomen Soc. N.Am. Clubs: Chicago, Economics; North Shore Country (Glenview, Ill.). Home: 1319 Southwind Dr Northbrook IL 60062 Office: 111 E Wacker Dr Chicago IL 60601

FAGAN, JOSEPH FRANCIS, III, psychologist, educator; b. Hartford, Conn., Sept. 7, 1941; s. Joseph F. F. B.A., U. Hartford, 1963; M.A., U. Conn., 1965, Ph.D., 1967. Grad. research asst. U. Conn., 1966-67; research assoc. Case Western Res. U., Cleve., 1967-68, asst. prof., 1968-71, assoc. prof., 1971-78, prof., 1978—. Recipient career devel. award NIH, 1972-77; predoctoral fellow Nat. Inst. Child Health and Human Devel., 1967

FAGEN, DONALD, musician; b. N.J. Mem.: musical group Steely Dan, 1972—; recordings include Can't Buy a Thrill, Countdown to Ecstasy, Pretzel Logic, Katy Lied, The Royal Scam, Aja, Gaucho. Winner Down Beat mag. Readers polls for rock-blues group, 1978, 79. Office: care Front Line Mgmt 8380 Melrose Ave Los Angeles CA 90069 *

FAGEN, RICHARD REES, educator, author; b. Chgo., Mar. 1, 1933; s. Abel E. and Mildred (Rees) F.; children: Sharon, Ruth, Elizabeth, Michael. B.A. in English, Yale U., 1954; M.A. in Journalism, Stanford U., 1959; Ph.D. in Polit. Sci., Stanford U., 1962. Asst. prof. Stanford U., 1962-66, assoc. prof., 1966-70, prof. polit. sci., 1970—, Gildred prof. Latin Am. studies, 1981—; cons. Ford Found., Santiago, Chile, 1972-73; prof. Latin Am. Sch. Social Sci., Santiago, 1972-73; cons. Rockefeller Found., 1977-80; chmn.com. on Latin Am. studies Social Sci. Research Council, N.Y.C., 1981-83. Author Politics and Communication, 1966; co-author: (with David Finley and Ole Holsti) Enemies in Politics, 1967; co-aurthor: (with Richard Brody and Thomas O'Leary) Cubans in Exile: Disaffaction and the Revolution, 1968; author: The Transformation of Political Culture in Cuba, 1969; co-author: (with William Tuohy) Politics and Privilege in a Mexican City, 1972, (with Albert Fishlow, Carlos Diaz Alejandro. Roger Hansen) Rich and Poor Nations in the World Economy, 1978; author: The Nicaraguan Revolution, 1981; editor, translator: Cubs: The Political Content of Adult Education, 1964; editor. author: (with Wayne Cornelius) Political Power in Lation America, 1969; editor, author: (with Julio Cotler) Latin America and The United States, 1974; editor: Capitalism and the State in U.S.-Latin American Relations, 1979, (with Olga Pellicer) The Future of Central America: Policy Choices for the U.S. and Mexico, 1983. Mem. internat. adv. bd. Amnesty Internat., 1976—. Served with U.S. Army, 1954-56. Fellow Social Sci. Research Council, 1960-61, Social Sci. Research Council, 1964, Am. Council Learned Socs., 1964, Ford Found., 1965-67, Fgn. Area Fellowship Program, 1965-67; grantee Ford Found., 1969, 79-80, 81; fellow NSF, 1970-71, 82—, Rockefeller Found., 1977; grantee Rockefeller Found., 1978-80, Com. on Scholarly Exchange with the People's Republic of China, 1983. Office: Dept Polit Sci Stanford U Stanford CA 94305

FAGG, GEORGE GARDNER, judge; b. Eldora, Iowa, Apr. 30, 1934; s. Ned and Arleene (Gardner) F.; m. Jane E. Wood, Aug. 19, 1956; children: Martha, Thomas, Ned, Susan, George, Sarah. B.S. in Bus. Adminstrn., Drake U., 1965, J.D., 1958. Bar: Iowa 1958. Ptnr. Cartwright, Druker, Ryden & Fagg, Marshalltown, Iowa, 1958-72; judge Iowa Dist. Ct., 1972-82, U.S. Ct. Appeals (8th cir.), 1982—; chmn. Iowa Dist. Ct., 1980-82; adv. com. rules of civil procedure Iowa Supreme Ct., 1981-82; mem. faculty Nat. Jud. Coll., 1979. Bd. dirs. Marshalltown United Campaign, Marshalltown YMCA. Mem. Am. Judicature Soc., ABA, Iowa Bar Assn., Order of Coif. Office: US Courthouse E 1st and Walnut Sts Des Moines IA 50309

FAGG, JOHN EDWIN, history educator; b. San Saba, Tex., Nov. 21, 1916; s. Edwin Earl and Bessie (Sanderson) F. B.A., U. Tex., 1938; M.A., U. Chgo., 1939, Ph.D., 1942. Mem. faculty NYU, 1946—, prof. history, 1962-80, prof. emeritus, 1982—, chmn. dept. Washington Sq. Coll., 1961-69, dir. Portuguese-Brazilian Center, 1961-65, dir. Center for Latin Am. Studies, 1977-79; expert cons. USAF, 1946-51, 56-57; vis. prof. U. Va., 1976-77. Author: essays Rafael Altamira, 1942, Sir Charles Webster, 1961, Latin America: A General History, rev. edit., 1977, Cuba, Haiti, The Dominican Republic, 1965; Panamericanism, 1982; also sects. ofcl. history, USAF. Served with USAAF, 1942-46. Mem. Am. Hist. Assn., Phi Beta Kappa (hon.), Kappa Sigma. Episcopalian. Home: 1107 W Commerce San Saba TX 76877 Office: New York Univ New York NY 10003

FAGGIN, FEDERICO, electronics executive; b. Vicenza, Italy, Dec. 1, 1941; U.S., 1968, naturalized, 1978; s. Giuseppe and Emma (Munari) F.; m. Elvia Sardei, Sept. 2, 1967; children: Marzia, Marc, Eric. Grad., Perito Industriale Instituto A. Rossi, Vicenza, 1960; D.Physics, U. Padua, Italy, 1965. Sect. head Fairchild Camera & Instrument Co., Palo Alto, Calif., 1968-70; dept. mgr. Intel Corp., Santa Clara, Calif., 1970-74; founder, pres. Zilog Inc., Cupertino, Calif., 1974-80; v.p. computer systems group Exxon Enterprises, N.Y.C., 1981; co-founder, pres. Cygnet Technologies, Inc., Sunnyvale, Calif., 1982—. Developed silicon gate tech. for MOS fabrication, first microprocessor. Office: 1296 Lawrence Station Rd Sunnyvale CA 94089

FAGIN, CLAIRE MINTZER, educational administrator; b. N.Y.C., Nov. 25, 1926; d. Harry and Mae (Slatin) Mintzer; m. Samuel Fagin, Feb. 17, 1952; children: Joshua, Charles. B.S., Wagner Coll., 1948; M.A., Tchrs. Coll. Columbia, 1951; Ph.D., N.Y. U., 1964; D.Sc. (hon.), Lycoming Coll., 1983. Staff nurse Sea View Hosp., Staten I., N.Y., 1947, clin. instr., 1947-48, Bellevue Hosp., N.Y.C., 1948-50; psychiat. nurse cons. Nat. League for Nursing, N.Y.C., 1951-52; asst. chief psychiat. nursing service clin. center NIH, 1953-54, supr., 1955; research project coordinator Children's Hosp. Dept. Psychiatry, Washington, 1956; instr. psychiat.-mental health nursing N.Y. U., N.Y.C., 1956-58, asst. prof., 1964-67, dir. grad. programs in psychiat. mental health nursing, 1965-69, asso. prof., 1967-69; chmn. nursing dept., prof. Herbert H. Lehman Coll., CUNY, N.Y.C., 1969-77; dir. Health Professions Inst., Montefiore Hosp. and Med. Center, 1975-77; dean sch. of nursing U. Pa., Phila., 1977—; mem. task force Joint Commn. Mental Health of Children, 1966-69; gov.'s com. on children N.Y. State, 1971-75; pres. Council on Deans of Nursing, Sr. Colls. and Univs. N.Y. State, 1974-76; cons. to many pub. and private univs. and health care agys.; cons. Pan Am. Health Nursing, Washington, 1972-

74, WHO, Geneva, Switzerland, 1974—, NIMH, HEW, 1974-76, NIMH, 1979, 83; mem. expert adv. panel on nursing WHO, 1974—; mem.-at-large Nat. Bd. Med. Examiners, 1980—; Bd. dirs. Provident Mut. Ins. Co., 1977—, audit com., 1978—. Editorial bds.: Cancer Nursing: An International Jour. of Cancer Care, 1977—, Jour. of Pub. Health Policy, Am. Jour. Nursing; Chmn. editorial bd.: Jour. for Nursing Leadership, 1978-81; speaker profl. convs.; contbr. articles to profl. publs.; speaker radio and TV. Recipient achievement award Wagner Coll., 1956, Wagner Coll. Sch. Nursing, 1973, Tchrs. Coll., 1975, disting. alumna award N.Y. U., 1979, Founders award Sigma Theta Tau, 1981; NIMH fellow, 1950-51, 60-64. Mem. Inst. of Medicine, Nat. Acad. Scis. (governing council 1981-83), Am. Acad. Nursing (governing council 1976-78), Am. Orthopsychiat. Assn. (bd. dirs. 1972-75, exec. com. of bd. 1973-75), Am. Assn. Colls. Nursing (data bank task force). Office: Nursing Education Bldg Univ Pennsylvania Philadelphia PA 19104

FAGIN, DAVID KYLE, natural resource company executive; b. Dallas, Apr. 9, 1938; s. Kyle Marshall and Frances Margaret (Gaston) F.; m. Margaret Anne Hazlett, Jan. 22, 1959; children—David Kyle, Scott Edward. B.S. in Petroleum Engring, U. Okla., 1960; postgrad., Am. Inst. Banking, So. Meth. U. Grad. Sch. Bus. Adminstrn. Registered profl. engr., La., Okla., Tex. Trainee Magnolia Petroleum Co., 1955-56; jr. engr., engr., then partner W.C. Bednar (petroleum cons.), Dallas, 1958-65; petroleum engr. First Nat. Bank, Dallas, 1965-68; v.p. Rosario Resources Corp., N.Y.C., 1968-75, exec. v.p., 1975-77, dir., 1977-80, pres., 1977-82; v.p. AMAX Inc. (merged with Rosario Resources Corp. 1980), N.Y.C., 1980-82; chmn., dir., pres., chief exec. officer Fagin Resources Corp., Denver, 1982—; dir. Compania Fresnillo, S.A., Savance Corp., San Francisco, AMAX Petroleum Can. Ltd., Bruneau Mining Co. Chmn. council ministries New Canaan United Methodist Ch. Mem. Soc. Petroleum Engrs., AIME (chmn. investment fund 1979-82), Dallas Geol. Soc. Clubs: Conn.-R.I. Lightning Assn., Denver Petroleum; Mining (N.Y.C.). Office: Suite 4380 City Center 4 1801 California St Denver CO 80202

FAGIN, HENRY, educator; b. N.Y.C., Apr. 9, 1913; s. Philip A. and Ester (Brody) F.; m. Eleanor Fine, Aug. 3, 1940; children: David Henry, Mara Eleanor. B.Arch., Columbia, 1937, M.S. in Planning, 1938. Registered profl. architect, N.Y. Editor Fed. Writers Project, N.Y.C., 1938; architect, draftsman Mayer & Whittlesey, N.Y.C., 1939-42; planning dir. Churchill-Fulmer Assos., N.Y.C., 1946-49, North Westchester (N.Y.) Joint Planning Program, 1949-51, Regional Plan Assn., N.Y.C., 1952-58, exec. dir., 1959; research prof. U. Calif. at Berkeley, 1958; exec. dir. Pa.-Jersey Transp. Study, Phila., 1959-62; prof. planning U. Wis. at Madison, 1962-67; prof. adminstrn. Grad. Sch. Mgmt., U. Calif., Irvine, 1967-80, research dir. pub. policy research orgn., 1967-74; prof. seminar Am. studies Salzburg, 1965, cons., 1950—; Chmn. panel I, spl. com. urban transp. research Hwy. Research Bd., Nat. Acad. Sci., 1961-62. Author: (with R. C. Weinberg) Planning and Community Appearance, 1958, The Policies Plan; Instrumentality for a Community Dialogue, 1965, (with Leo F. Schnore) Urban Research and Policy Planning, 1967; Bd. contbrs.: Archtl. Forum, 1965—; contbr.: Colliers Ency. Mem. Mayor Madison Civic Adv. Com., 1963-67, chmn., 1967. Served with USNR, 1944-46. Mem. Wis. Civil Liberties Union (v.p. 1965-67), Regional Sci. Assn. (v.p. 1963-64), Am. Inst. Planners (pres. N.Y.-Pa. chpt. 1954-55), Am. Soc. Pub. Adminstrn. (pres. Wis. Capitol chpt. 1967). Home and Office: 1649 Sunset Ridge Dr Laguna Beach CA 92651

FAGIN, RICHARD, retail exec.; b. St. Louis, Aug. 10, 1935; s. Harry and Sylvia (Weiss) F.; m. Margaret Strauss, June 19, 1960; children—David Robert, Steven Todd, Daniel Roger. B.S. in Retailing, Washington U., St. Louis, 1957. Dept. mgr. Famous-Barr Co., St. Louis, 1958-62; with promotion devel. dept. Procter & Gamble Co., Cin., 1962-66; with bus. devel. dept. Federated Dept. Stores, Inc., Cin., 1966-69; v.p., asso. dir. corp. devel. div. U.S. Shoe Corp., Cin., 1969-72; operating v.p. long range planning Federated Dept. Stores, 1972—. Vice pres. Jewish Vocat. Service, Cin., 1978-80; chmn. allocations com. Community Chest Cin., 1977-79, mem. planning bd., 1981—. Served with USAR, 1957. Office: 7 W 7th St Cincinnati OH 45202

FAGOT, JOSEPH BURDELL, corp. exec.; b. Forest River, N.D., Apr. 23, 1917; s. Peter J. and Minnie (Eldredge) F.; m. Joyce Bodell Cawley, Aug. 31, 1940; children—JoAnn, Joel, Don, Larry, Lynne. B.B.A. with distinction, U. Minn., 1940. Sales corr. Montgomery Ward & Co., St. Paul, 1940-41; exec. trainee, asst. dept. mgr. Sears-Roebuck & Co., Mpls., 1941-43; profl., adminstrv. and exec. placement Walker Employement Service, Mpls., 1943-44; placement mgr. Marathon Corp., Menasha, Wis., 1944-52; v.p. personnel and indsl. relations Omar, Inc., Omaha, 1952-58; v.p. orgn. and personnel Fibreboard Corp., 1958-62; v.p. ops. Gold Bond Stamp Co., Mpls., 1962-66; pres., dir. Fed. Mart Stores, Inc., San Diego, 1966-69; pres., owner J B Mgmt., Inc., San Diego, 1969—. Author articles in field. Republican. Roman Catholic. Address: 804 La Jolla Rancho Rd La Jolla CA 92037

FAHEY, JOHN ALOYSIUS, musician, composer; b. Takoma Park, Md., Feb. 28, 1939; s. Aloysius John and Jane (Cooper) F.; m. Melody Brennan. B.A., Am. U., Washington, 1962; M.A. in Folklore and Mythology, UCLA, 1967. Founder Takoma Records, Los Angeles. Composer, performer Am. guitar music; albums include Voice of the Turtle; Author: biography Charley Patton. Office: Rounder Records 1 Camp St Cambridge MA 02140

FAHEY, JOSEPH FRANCIS, JR., banker; b. Stamford, Conn., Dec. 19, 1925; s. Joseph Francis and Margaret (Hoffkins) F.; m. June Alice Gleason, July 8, 1950; children—Janice, Jill, Christopher, Colleen, Moira, Kevin, Brian. B.A., U. Notre Dame, 1949; postgrad. real estate law, U. Conn., 1951; credit mgmt., Bridgeport U., 1952, Sch. Mortgage Banking, Stanford, 1958, Sch. Mortgage Banking, Northwestern U., 1960, Grad. Sch. Bank Mgmt., Columbia, 1965. With Greenwich Trust Co., Conn., 1947-58, asst. treas., 1954-58; asst. v.p. mortgage dept. Nat. Bank & Trust Co., Stamford, 1958-59, v.p. mortgage adminstrn., 1959-62; sr. v.p. mortgage dept. State Nat. Bank Conn., Bridgeport, 1962-65, sr. v.p. in charge loan portfolio, chmn. loan com., 1965-74, pres., 1973-82, chmn. bd., 1974-82, Conn. Bank, 1982—; pres. CBT Corp., 1982—; 1st chmn. Southwestern Regional Planning Agy., 1963-64; mem. faculty Am. Inst. Banking, 1964-69; pres. Stamford Devel. Corp., 1967—. Chmn. gen. unit United Fund, 1962, chmn. comml.-fin. div. advance gifts, 1963, campaign chmn., Stamford, 1965, bd. dirs., 1965-68; mem. citizen's adv. com. Ferguson Library, 1964-74; treas. Community Council study com., 1965-68, 4th Congl. Dist. Voter Edn. Com., 1965-69, Stamford March Dimes, 1965; mem. adv. council New Haven U. New Products and Concepts Lab., 1973; Bd. dirs. Citizens Action Council, Stamford, 1965-70, mem. exec. com., 1966-71; regent, treas. St. Mary's Coll., Notre Dame, Ind., 1977—, Bapt. Econ. Devel. Council, 1976-78; bd. dirs. Stamford Hosp., 1965—, treas., 1967-70, v.p., 1970-72, pres., 1972—; trustee Hartman Theatre, Stamford, 1976-78; bd. dirs. Aspetuck Land Trust, Inc., 1967-71, treas., 1967-71; bd. dirs. Rehab. Center So. Fairfield County, Inc., 1966-70, treas., 1966-70; trustee Fairfield U., 1974-82, mem. adv. council, 1972-74; dir., sec. Bridgeport Econ. Devel. Council, 1976-78; chmn. Samford Econ. Assistance Corp., 1978—. Served with AC USNR, 1943-46. Named Young Man of Year Stamford Jr. C. of C., 1961. Mem. Mortgage Bankers Assn. Am., Conn. Bankers Assn. (pres. 1973-74), Conn. C. of C., Am. Bankers Assn. (nat. conf. commrs. on uniform state laws), Conf. Bd., Southwestern Area Commerce and Industry Assn. (dir. 1970-71, 75—). Clubs: Roasters (treas., founding mem.), Stamford Yacht (Stamford) (dir., mem. exec. com. 1969-73); Landmark (gov. 1973-83); Woodway Country (Darien, Conn.)). Home: CBT CORP 1 CONSTITUTION PLAZA HARTFORD CT 06115 Office: One Atlantic St Stamford CT 06901

FAHEY, WALTER JOHN, elec. engr., educator; b. Winnipeg, Man., Can., Apr. 10, 1927; came to U.S., 1928, naturalized, 1956; s. Gordon Joseph and Agnes (Larsen) F. B.S., Case Inst. Tech., 1957, M.S., 1959, Ph.D., 1963. Instr. elec. engring. Case Inst. Tech., 1959-62; asst. prof. Ohio U., 1963-65, asso. prof., chmn. dept. elec. engring., 1965-67, prof., dean, 1967-68; prof. elec. engring. U. Ariz., Tucson, 1969—; dean Coll. Engring., 1969-77; Mem. Ohio Crime Commn., 1967-68; mem. Ariz. Bd. Tech. Registration, 1969-71; mem. tech. adv. com. Ariz. AEC, 1971-74; chmn. Tucson Master Tech. Com., 1971-74; mem. adv. com. USAF Inst. Tech., 1974-78; mem. product adv. com. Internat. Tape Assn., 1974-77. Bd. dirs. Aviation Research and Edn. Found., pres., 1973-74; bd. dirs. Devel. Authority Tucson Economy, 1971-75, pres., 1973-74. Served with USN, 1945-48, 1950-52. Recipient Outstanding Grad. award Case Inst. Tech., 1957; Internat. Achievement award Internat. Tape Assn.; named Engr. of Year Ariz. Council Engring. and Sci. Assns., 1972; Am. Council on Edn. fellow, 1967-68. Mem. IEEE (sr.), Am. Soc. Engring. Edn., Tucson C. of C. (dir. 1971-75), Sigma Xi, Tau Beta Pi, Eta Kappa Nu, Tau Kappa Alpha, Theta Tau, Phi Kappa Phi, Blue Key. Office: Dept Elec Engring U Ariz Bldg 20 Tucson AZ 85721

FAHIEN, LEONARD AUGUST, physician; b. St. Louis, July 26, 1934; s. John Henry and Alice Katherine (Schubkegel) F.; m. Rose Marian Burmeister, June 21, 1958; children—Catherine, Lisa, James. A.B., Washington U., 1956, M.D., 1960. Intern U. Wis., Madison, 1960-61; surgeon NIH, Bethesda, Md., 1964-66; asst. prof. dept. pharmacology U. Wis. Med. Sch., Madison, 1966-69, asso. prof., 1969-74, prof., 1974—, asso. dean, 1979—. Contbr. chpts. to books; contbr. articles to profl. jours. Served with USPHS, 1964-66. Numerous NIH grants, 1966—. Mem. Phi Beta Kappa, Sigma Xi. Lutheran. Home: 3212 Topping Rd Madison WI 53705 Office: 426 N Charter Madison WI 53706

FAHLGREN, HERBERT SMOOT, advertising agency executive; b. Parkerburg, W.Va., Aug. 17, 1930; s. C. Herbert and Julia (Smoot) F.; m. Judith Anne Henniger, Dec. 7, 1952; children: Steven, Becky, John. Student, Marietta Coll., 1948, 52; B.S. in Bus. Adminstrn., U. Va., 1952. Founder, pres. Fahlgren & Ferriss, Parkersburg, W.Va., 1962—. Elder 1st Presbyn. Ch., Parkersburg. Mem Am. Assn. Advt. Agys (treas. 1978-79, dir. 1981—). Home: Route 9 PO Box 218 Parkersburg WV 26101 Office: Fahlgren & Ferriss PO Box 1628 Parkersburg WV 26101

FAHRENKOPF, FRANK JOSEPH, JR., lawyer; b. Bklyn., Aug. 28, 1939; s. Frank J. and Rose (Freeman) F.; m. Mary Ethel Bandoni, Aug. 25, 1962; children: Allison Marie, Leslie Ann, Amy Michelle. B.A., U. Nev., 1962; J.D., U. Calif., Berkeley, 1965. Bar: Nev. 1965, D.C. bar 1983. Assoc. atty. Breen & Young, Reno, Nev., 1965-67; partner, atty. Sanford, Sanford, Fahrenkopf & Mousel, Reno, 1967-75, Fahrenkopf, Mortimer, Sourwine, Mousel & Sloane, 1976—; Instr. criminal law U. Nev., 1967-82; panelist reporter Citizens Conf. on Nev. Cts., 1968; mem. Nev. Bd. Bar Examiners, 1971—; judge pro tem Reno Municipal Ct., 1972—; Mem. faculty Nat. Jud. Coll., Reno, 1974—. Chmn. lawyers div. United Fund, 1969-70; chmn. Rep. Nat. Com., 1983—, Nev. Republican Com., 1975-83; gen. counsel Nev. Republican Com., 1972-75; No. Nev. co-chmn. Com. for Re-election of Pres., 1972; mem. exec. bd. Nev. Rep. Central Com., 1972—, Washoe County Rep. Central Com., 1969—; nat. committeeman Nev. Young Reps., 1969-73; mem. Rep. Nat. Com., 1975—; del. Rep. Nat. Conv., 1972, 76, 80; chmn. Western States Rep. Chairmen's Assn., 1978-83; nat. chmn. Rep. State Chairman's Assn., 1981-83; chmn. Rep. Nat. Com., 1983—; bd. dirs. Nev. Cancer Soc., chmn., 1978—; bd. dirs. Washoe County Legal Aid Soc., Babe Ruth Baseball League, Nev. Opera Guild, Reno YWCA, Sierra Sage council Camp Fire Girls, 1974-76, Nat. Endowment Democracy, 1983—, Am. Polit. Found., 1983—, Am. Council Young Polit. Leaders, 1983—; trustee U.S. Presdl. Yacht, 1983—. Served with AUS, 1957. Recipient Disting. Service award U.S. Jaycees, 1973, Humanitarian award NCCJ, 1981. Mem. Am. Judicature Soc., Comml. Law League Am., Am., Bar Assn., Am. Trial Lawyers Assn., No. Nev. Trial Lawyers Assn. (v.p. 1969), State Bar Nev., Washoe County Bar Assn. (pres. 1973-74), Execs. Assn. Reno (dir. 1973-74), Nat. Assn. Gaming Attys. (v.p. 1981, pres. 1982-83), Barristers Club Nev. (v.p. 1969-73), Alpha Tau Omega. Home: 1040 LaRue Ave Reno NV 89509 Office: PO Box 460 Reno NV 89504 310 1st St SE Washington DC 20013 *I believe each of us as a citizen of this country has an obligation to serve the community, state and nation. The rights of citizens and benefits of citizenship must be balanced by a duty to serve others.*

FAHRINGER, CATHERINE HEWSON, savings and loan association executive; b. Phila., Aug. 1, 1922; d. George Francis and Catherine Gertrude (Magee) Hewson; m. Edward F. Fahringer, July 8, 1961; 1 son by previous marriage, Francis George Beckett. Grad. diploma, Inst. Fin. Edn., 1965. With Dade Savs. and Loan Assn. (formerly Dade Fed. Savs. and Loan Assn. of Miami), Miami, Fla., 1958—, v.p., 1967-74, sr. v.p., 1974—, sec., 1975-79, head savs. personnel and mktg. div., 1979-82, exec. v.p., dir., 1982—. Contbr. articles to profl. jours. Trustee, co-chmn. audit com. United Way of Dade County, Fla.; trustee Public Health Trust, Dade County, 1974, sec., 1976, vice chmn., 1977-78, chmn. bd., 1979-81, chmn. Joint Conf. Com., 1982; hon. bd. govs. U. Miami, Soc. for Research in Med. Edn.; trustee So. Fla. Blood Services, Miami, 1979—, vice chmn., 1980, chmn., 1982-84; trustee Dade County Vocat. Found., 1977-81, Fla. Internat. U. Found., 1976—; v.p. bd. Fla. Internat. U. Found., 1978-81, pres., 1982-84. Named Woman of Yr. in fin. Zonta Internat., 1975, ambassador Air Def. Arty., U.S. Army Air Def. Command, 1970, Community Headliner Women in Communication, 1983; recipient Trail Blazer award Women's Council of 100, 1977. Mem. U.S. League of Savs. Assn., Nat. League Savs. and Loan Assn., Fla. Savs. and Loan League, Am. Soc. Personnel Adminstrs., Fla. Women's Network (dir. 1983), Dade Bus. and Profl. Women's Club (past pres., Woman of Yr. 1974), Bus. and Profl. Women, Inst. Fin. Edn. (life; nat. dir., past pres. Local Greater Miami chpt.), Savs. and Loan Mktg. Soc. South Fla. (past pres.), Savs. and Loan Personnel Soc. South Fla. Democrat. Congregationalist. Clubs: Coral Gables Country, Bankers. Office: 101 E Flagler St Miami FL 33131

FAHRNEY, DELMER STATER, ret. naval officer, aero. engr.; b. Grove, Okla., Oct. 23, 1898; s. Albert Franklin and Lillian (Pugh) F.; m. Agnes Whiting Kelly, June 2, 1925 (dec. Nov. 1969); children: Dawn Fahrney Knotts, Delmer Stater (dec.), Carol, Paula Fahrney Yon (dec.); m. Helen Sheehan Arthur, Nov. 27, 1970. B.S., U.S. Naval Acad., 1919; M.S., Mass. Inst. Tech., 1930. Commd. ensign USN, 1919, advanced through grades to rear adm., 1950; served on following ships and stas. (U.S.S. Utah, U.S.S. Wadsworth, U.S.S. Stewart, U.S.S. Wright, U.S.S. W.Va., U.S.S. Lexington, Naval Air Station), Pensacola, Fla., also, Pearl Harbor; insp. naval aircraft Wright Aeroplane Corp., Naval Aircraft Factory, Phila.; also Bur. of Aeros.; served as first comdr. of Naval Air Missile Test Center, Point Mugu, Calif., 1948-50; cons. guided missiles since, 1936; pioneered radio controlled aircraft, and guided missiles; cons. Eastern rep. Coleman Engring. Co., Culver City, Calif., 1951-52; naval historian on guided missiles Bur. Aero., Navy Dept., 1954-58; sec. to com. on sci. and arts Franklin Inst., 1957-73. Decorated Legion of Merit; awarded commendation for work on guided missiles Bur. Aero.; commendation for radio control achievements USN, 1938, 41; Gold star in lieu 2d Legion of Merit, 1957; for devel. of assault drone guided missile. Asso. fellow AIAA; mem. Franklin Inst., SAR, Mil. Order World Wars, Sigma Xi. Holder patents on aircraft, guided missile developments. Home: 10245 Vivera Dr La Mesa CA 92041

FAIGIN, LARRY BERNARD, real estate executive, lawyer; b. Cleve., Nov. 10, 1942; s. Leonard A. and Ethyl (Wax) F.; m. Pamela Heishman, Oct. 7, 1979. A.B., Western Res. U., 1965, J.D., 1968. Bar: Ohio 1968, N.Y. 1969, Ga. bar 1972, Calif. bar 1977. With firm Willkie Farr & Gallagher, N.Y.C., 1968-72, Alston, Miller & Gaines, Atlanta, 1972-75; v.p., gen. counsel Shapell Industries, Inc., Beverly Hills, Calif., 1976-80, sr. v.p., gen. counsel, 1980-83, sr. v.p., 1983—, dir., 1980—, vice chmn., 1983—; dir. Shapell Industries, Inc.; of counsel firm Hurt, Richardson, Garner, Todd & Cadenhead, Atlanta, 1979-81; lectr. Yale U. Law Sch., spring 1973, fall 1974. Bd. dirs. Friends of Beta Falasha Community in Ethiopia, 1970-73; mem. vis. com. Case Western Res. U. Law Sch., 1979-81; mem. Los Angeles Olympic Citizens Commn., 1980—; alt. mem. Gov.'s Commn. on Affordable Housing, 1980—, also author interim report. Dewit scholar, 1966; Alumni scholar, 1967. Mem. ABA (mem. com. civil and criminal procedure anti-trust sect.), N.Y. State Bar Assn., Ga. Bar Assn., Atlanta Bar Assn., Calif. Bar Assn., Los Angeles County Bar Assn., Beverly Hills Bar Assn., Assn. Bar City N.Y., Alpha Epsilon Pi, Phi Alpha Delta. Club: Ansley Golf (Atlanta). Home: 228 S McCadden Pl Los Angeles CA 90004 Office: 8383 Wilshire Blvd Suite 700 Beverly Hills CA 90211

FAILEY, GEORGE LEO, JR., public utility executive; b. Binghamton, N.Y., Aug. 7, 1928; s. George Leo and Marion (Corliss) F. B.S., Notre Dame U., 1952. Accountant Arthur Andersen & Co. (C.P.A.s), 1952-59; with North Penn Gas. Co., Port Allegany, Pa., 1960—, exec. v.p., 1964-72, pres., 1972—, also dir.; v.p., dir. Penn Fuel System, Inc., 1976—; exec. v.p., dir. Penn Fuel Gas, Inc.; dir. 1st Nat. Bank, Port Allegany, Pa. & So. Gas. Co. Served with AUS, 1946-48. Mem. Pa. Soc., Am. Gas Assn., Pa. Gas Assn. (pres. 1970-71, dir. 1970—). Club: Rotarian. Home: PO Box 27 Port Allegany PA 16743 Office: 76-80 Mill St Port Allegany PA 16743

FAILING, GEORGE EDGAR, editor, clergyman, educator; b. Kingston, Ont., Can., Nov. 25, 1912; s. Roy Augustus and Nellie (Richardson) F.; m. Phyllis Ogden, Apr. 12, 1939; children: Bunnie Jean, Alice Joy, Lynn Odgen. B.A. magna cum laude, Houghton Coll., 1940, Litt.D., 1960; M.A., Duke U., 1947. Ordained to ministry Wesleyan Meth. Ch., 1938; pastor in, Fillmore, N.Y., 1935-41, Louisville, 1941-44, Marion, Ind., 1953-56; prof. Central S.C. Wesleyan Coll., 1944-47, Houghton (N.Y.) Coll., 1947-53, dir. pub. relations, 1947-53; editor Sunday Sch. Lit. Wesleyan Meth. Ch., Marion, Ind., 1956-59, Wesleyan Methodist, 1959-68; chancellor Satellite Christian Inst., San Diego, 1968-73; prof. Greek and N.T. United Wesleyan Coll., Allentown, Pa., 1973; gen. editor Wesleyan Advocate, Marion, 1973-84. Author: 1 Corinthians, 1963, Presence, 1977, Secure and Rejoicing, 1980, Did Christ Die for All?, 1980; contbg. author: Ency. World Methodism, 1974; contbg. author, editor: And They Shall Prophesy, 1978, With Open Face, 1983, Way of Wonder, 1983. Mem. gen. bd. trustees Wesleyan Meth. Ch. Am., 1959-68, 74—. Mem. Soc. Bibl. Lit. and Exegesis, Evang. Press Assn. (pres. 1965-67), Am. Schs. Oriental Research. Home: PO Box 669466 Charlotte NC 28266 Office: 2300 Alleghany St Charlotte NC 28208

FAIMAN, CHARLES, endocrinologist; b. Winnipeg, Man., Can., Dec. 6, 1939; s. Max and Bessie (Freedman) F.; m. Carol Lee Fien, June 16, 1963; children—Barton Shale, Gregg Howard, Matthew Randall. B.Sc. in Medicine; Harry Silverberg, Isbister, Lederle scholar, U. Man., 1962, M.D., 1962, M.Sc., 1966. Intern Winnipeg Gen. Hosp., 1962-63, resident, 1963-64, Med. Research Council Can. fellow, 1964-65, U. Ill. Coll. Medicine, 1965-67, Mayo Clinic, Rochester, Minn., 1967-68; asst. prof. physiology and medicine U. Man., 1968-71, assoc. prof., 1971-75, prof., 1975—; dir. clin. investigation unit Winnipeg Gen. Hosp., 1971-74; head sect. endocrinology and metabolism dept. medicine U. Man. and Health Scis. Centre, Winnipeg, 1977—. Bd. dirs. Winnipeg Hebrew Sch., 1969-76, 77—, Pres., 1982-83. Med. Research Council Can. scholar, 1968-73; recipient Prowse prize for research, 1966. Fellow Royal Coll. Physicians Can.; mem. Endocrine Soc., Am. Soc. Clin. Investigation, Am. Fedn. Clin. Research, Soc. Exptl. Biology and Medicine, Canadian Soc. Clin. Investigation, Canadian Soc. Endocrinology and Metabolism (pres. 1979-80), N.Y. Acad. Scis., AAAS, Canadian Fertility Soc., Sigma Xi. Home: 1430 Mathers Bay E Winnipeg MB Canada Office: Health Scis Center 700 William Ave Winnipeg MB Canada

FAIMAN, ROBERT NEIL, academic administrator; b. Excelsior, Minn., June 25, 1923; s. Clarence C. and Henrietta (Baker) F.; m. Eunice A. Kessler, Mar. 12, 1944; children: Robert Neil Jr., John Charles. B.S. in Elec. Engring, N.D. State Coll., 1947, M.S., U. Wash., 1948; Ph.D., Purdue U., 1956. Registered profl. engr., Ohio. Asso. elec. engring. U. Wash., 1947-48; from asst. prof. to prof. N.D. State Coll., 1948-58, chmn. dept., 1951-58; engr., engring. scis. program NSF, 1957-59; dean Coll. Tech., dir. Engring. Expt. Sta. U. N.H., 1959-67, v.p. research, 1967-74; acad. dir. Air Force Inst. Tech., Wright-Patterson AFB, Ohio, 1974—. Mem. N.H. Bd. Registration for Profl. Engrs., 1971-74. Served with USAAF, 1943-46; maj. Res. Recipient Alumni Achievement award N.D. State U., 1966. Mem. IEEE (sr.), Am. Soc. Engring. Edn., Ohio, Soc. Profl. Engrs., AAAS, Soc. Am. Mil. Engrs., Air Force Assn., Sigma Xi, Tau Beta Pi, Eta Kappa Nu, Phi Kappa Phi. Club: Rotarian. Home: 3246 Maplewood Dr Xenia OH 45385

FAIN, HASKELL, philosophy educator; b. N.Y.C., July 1, 1926; s. Max and Ethel (Frankenstein) F.; m. Elaine Folk, Sept. 14, 1949 (dec. May 1980); children—Jonathan Simon, Madeline Alessandra. B.S., U. Ill., 1948; M.A., U. Calif. at Berkeley, 1951, Ph.D., 1956. Mem. faculty U. Wis., Madison, 1956—, prof. philosophy, 1966—, chmn. dept., 1968-70, 72-73; sr. Fulbright prof. U. Bergen, Norway, 1961-62; vis. asso. prof. U. B.C., 1963-64; vis. fellow Linacre Coll., Oxford U., 1966-67; lectr. Oxford U., 1967; vis. prof. Fla. State U., 1970-71, U. Mich., 1974; cons. World Book Ency., 1961-65, Empire State Coll. State U. N.Y., 1972-73, Nat. Endowment for Humanities, 1975—. Author: Between Philosophy and History, 1970. Served with AUS, 1944-46. Mem. Am. Philos. Assn. Home: 2306 Van Hise Ave Madison WI 53705

FAIN, RICHARD DAVID, shipping company executive; b. Boston, Oct. 9, 1947; s. Morton Edgar and Libby Miriam (Winer) F.; m. Colleen Jo Ferris, July 27, 1969; children: Julie Merideth, Sara Elizabeth, Benjamin Alfred. B.S., U. Calif., Berkeley, 1969; M.B.A., U. Pa., 1972. Mgr. internat. fin. IU Internat. Corp., Phila., 1972-75; sr. v.p. fin. Gotaas Larsen Shipping Corp., N.Y.C., 1975—. Club: Univ. Home: 36 Marryat Rd Wimbledon London England

FAIN, SAMMY, composer, singer, pianist; b. N.Y.C., June 17, 1902. Began career as mem. staff, Music pub. co.; composer: songs for films include Majorie Morningstar, Weekend at the Waldorf, Sweet Music,

Anchors Aweigh; film scores include Just You and Me Kid, Alice in Wonderland, Peter Pan, Calamity Jane, Mardi Gras, Jazz Singer, Three Sailors and a Girl, April Love; Broadway stage scores include Something More; Broadway stage scorces include Hezapoppin; Broadway stage scores include George White's Scandals, Flahooley, Around the World in Eighty Days, Ankles Aweigh, Christine; songs include Secret Love (Acad. award 1953), Love is a Many-Splendored Thing (Acad. award 1955), Let a Smile Be Your Umbrella, Wedding Bells Are Breaking Up That Old Gang of Mine, When I Take My Sugar To Tea, You Brought a New Kind of Love To Me, Was That the Human Thing to Do?, I Can Dream, Can't I?, Are You Havin' Any Fun?, I'm Late, Dickey Bird Song, Something I Dreamed Last Night, That Old Feeling, I'll Be Seeing You, Dear Hearts and Gentle People, A Very Precious Love, Tender Is the Night, A Certain Smile, By a Waterfall, April Love, Strange are the Ways of Love (Acad. award nomination), A World That Never Was (Acad. award nomination), If Every Day Were Valentine's Day, Someone's Waiting for You (Acad. award nomination), Katie. Recipient 10 Acad. award nominations, Nashville Country Music award, Diploma di Benemerenza Hall of Artists, Nice, France; Augusto Messinese Gold award, Italy; 2 Laurel awards; named to Songwriters Hall of Fame.

FAINI, MARIA LUISA TERESA, concert pianist, educator; b. Rome; U.S., 1950. Piano diploma, Santa Cecilia Conservatory, Rome; artist diploma, Santa Cecilia Acad., Rome. Piano chmn. Hartford Conservatory, Conn., 1954-59; artist faculty mem. Eastman Sch. Music, Rochester, N.Y., 1966—. Recipient Eisenhart award, Eastman Sch. Music, 1979. Mem. Sigma Alpha Iota. Home: 30 Thayer St Rochester NY 14607

FAINTER, JOHN WELLS, JR., state official; b. Pecos, Tex., Apr. 20, 1939; s. J. Wells and Ruth (Alexander) F.; m. Frances Barclay; 1 son, John III. B.A., U. Tex., 1962, LL.B., 1963. Bar: Tex. Investigator Tex. Securities Bd., Austin, 1963-64; asst. atty. gen. Tex., Austin, 1964-69, 1st atty. gen., 1979-83, sec. state, 1983—; v.p. Underwood, Neuhaus & Co. Inc., Houston, 1969-79; chmn. Tex. Bar study election laws; adv. com. asset mgmt. Tex. Treasury; joint select com.fiscal policy; mem. coordinator bd. Tex. Coll. and Univ. System, 1975-78. Bd. advisors Leadership Austin, 1983-84; Hobby-Clayton commr., 1975-76; adv. council Coll. Bus. Adminstrn. Found., U. Tex.-Austin; pub. affairs com. U. Tex.-Austin Ex-Student Assn.; bd. dirs. Law Sch. Assn. Mem. Nat. Assn. Secs. State (com. campaign finance). Democrat. Episcopalian. Clubs: Headliners, Austin Country (Austin). Office: Secretary State Room 127 Capitol Bldg 11th St at Congress Ave Austin TX 78711

FAIR, HAROLD LLOYD, publishing executive; b. Tyronza, Ariz., Aug. 2, 1924; s. James Asberry and Clara (Williamson) F.; m. Agnes H. Fair, Apr. 2, 1976; children by previous marriage: Kathryn, Robert. B.A., U. Miss., Oxford, 1952; B.D., Vanderbilt U., 1954, M.A., 1968, Ph.D., 1971. Assoc. editor United Meth. Pub. House, Nashville, 1957-72, mng. editor, 1972-81; gen. mgr. Abingdon Press, Nashville, 1981—. Author: Class Devotions, 1975—. Served with U.S. Army, 1944-46. Mem. Soc. Am. Historians, Am Soc. Ch. History, Am. Hist. Assn. Democrat. Methodist. Home: 853 General Patton Rd Nashville TN 37221 Office: Abingdon Press 201 8th Ave S Nashville TN 37202

FAIR, JAMES MILTON, agricultural cooperative company executive; b. Lloydminster, Alta., Can., Apr. 14, 1934; s. James and Evelyn (Warren) F.; m. Joyce Dennis, Aug. 4, 1956; children: Dennis, Donna Fair Frentz. Student, Harvard U., 1981. Chartered acct. With audit dept. govt. of Alta., Edmonton, 1951-59; with computer devel. div. Govt. of Alta., Edmonton, 1959, sr. systems analyst, 1959-65; systems mgr. Sask. Wheat Pool, Regina, 1965-66, asst. treas., 1966-70, corp. treas., 1970-76, dir. adminstrn., dep. gen. mgr., 1976-79, gen. mgr. ops., 1979-81, chief exec. officer, 1981—; dir. Pacific Elevators Ltd., Vancouver, B.C., Western Pool Terminals Ltd., CSP Foods Ltd., Saskatoon, Sask., Can., XCAN Grain Ltd., Winnipeg, Man., Can., Prince Rupert Grain Ltd., Vancouver, Western Co-op Fertilizers Co., Calgary, Alta. Mem. Sask. Inst. Chartered Accts., Alta. Inst. Charteed Accts. Am. Baptist. Lodge: Rotary. Home: 2650 Thornicroft Bay Regina SK Canada S4V 0T8 Office: Saskatchewan Wheat Pool 2625 Victoria Ave Regina SK Canada S4T 7T9

FAIR, JAMES RUTHERFORD, JR., chemical engineering educator, consultant; b. Charleston, Mo., Oct. 14, 1920; s. James Rutherford and Georgia Irene (Case) F.; m. Merle Innis, Jan. 14, 1950; children: James Rutherford III, Elizabeth, Richard Innis. Student, The Citadel, 1938-40; B.S., Ga. Inst. Tech., 1942; M.S., U. Mich., 1949; Ph.D., U. Tex., 1955; D.Sc. (hon.), Wash. U., 1977. Research engr. Shell Devel. Co., Emeryville, Calif., 1954-56; with Monsanto Co., 1942-52, 56-79, engring. dir. corp. engring. dept., St. Louis, 1969-79; Cockrell prof. chem. engring. U. Tex., Austin, 1979—; dir., v.p. Fractionation Research, Inc., Bartlesville, Okla., 1969-79. Author: North Arkansas Line, 1969, Distillation, 1971; Contbr. numerous articles to profl. publs. Bd. dirs. Nat. Mus. Transport. Recipient profl. achievement award Chemical Engineering mag., 1968. Fellow Am. Inst. Chem. Engrs. (bd. dirs. 1965-67, Walker award 1973, Practice award 1975, Founders award 1977, Inst. lectr. 1979); mem. Am. Chem. Soc., Nat. Acad. Engring., Am. Soc. Engring. Edn., Nat. Soc. Profl. Engrs., Sigma Nu. Republican. Presbyterian (elder). Clubs: Faculty (U. Tex.); Headliners (Austin). Home: 2804 Northwood Rd Austin TX 78703 Office: Dept Chem Engring U Tex Austin TX 78712

FAIR, JEAN EVERHARD, emeritus teacher educator; b. Evanston, Ill., July 21, 1917; d. Drury Hampton and Bess Marion (Everhard) F. B.A., U. Ill., 1938; M.A., U. Chgo., 1939, Ph.D., 1953. Tchr. Evanston (Ill.) Twp. High Sch., 1940-48, 1954-58; tchr. U. Minn. High Sch., 1948-49, U. Ill. High Sch., 1951-53; prof. edn. Wayne State U., Detroit, 1958-82, now prof. emeritus. Contbr. articles to profl. jours. Mem. Nat. Council for Social Studies (pres. 1972, dir. 1958-61, 73-75), Assn. for Supervision and Curriculum Devel., AAUP, LWV, Phi Beta Kappa. Mem. United Ch. Christ. Home: 10 Clinton Ln Dearborn MI 48120

FAIR, WILLIAM ROBERT, physician; b. Norristown, Pa., Mar. 29, 1935; m. Mary Ann Collins, Sept. 9, 1961; 1 son, William. B.S., Phila. Coll. Pharmacy, 1956; M.D., Jefferson Med. Coll., Phila., 1960. Diplomate: Am. Bd. Urology. Intern Womack Army Hosp., Ft. Bragg, N.C., 1960-61; resident in gen. surgery Martin Army Hosp., Ft. Benning, Ga., 1963-64; resident in urology Stanford U. Med. Center, 1964-68, asst. prof., then asso. prof., 1968-75; prof. surgery, chmn. div. urology Washington U. Med. Sch., St. Louis, 1975—, acting head dept. surgery, 1978-81. Asst. editor: Jour. Urology, 1974—; internat. editorial bd.: Jour. Internat. Med. Research, 1972—; editorial bd.: Urology Digest, 1971, Investigative Urology, 1973-79; contbr. articles med. jours. Served as officer M.C. USAR, 1960-64. Mem. Internat. Soc. Nephrology, Nat. Kidney Found. (trustee), Nat. Urol. Forum, AAAS, Am. Soc. Nephrology, A.C.S., Am. Urol. Assn., Am. Fedn. Clin. Research, Soc. Univ. Surgeons, Assn. Acad. Surgery, Pan Pacific Surg. Assn., Soc. Univ. Urologists, Am. Assn. Genitourinary Surgeons, Alpha Omega Alpha. Home: 13253 Takara Dr St Louis MO 63131 Office: Washington Univ Med Sch 660 S Euclid St St Louis MO 63110 *Despite the imperfections in our society, we still maintain an environment wherein individuals from any background can achieve recognition and where the principles of hard work, discipline and pursuit of excellence are encouraged and rewarded.* *

FAIRAND, BARRY PHILIP, physicist; b. Watertown, N.Y., May 20, 1934; s. Charles Francis and Dorothy Marie (Piche) F.; m. Jeanine Fontana, June 13, 1959; children: Mary, Joan, John, Amy, Ann. B.S., LeMoyne Coll., 1955; M.S., Detroit U., 1957; Ph.D., Ohio State U., 1969. Sr. scientist Battelle Meml. Inst., Columbus Labs., 1957-80; pres. Laser Tech. Inc., Columbus, 1980—. Contbr. articles to profl. jours.; patentee laser generated x-rays, applying radiation. Mem. Am. Phys. Soc., Photo-optical Instrumentation Engrs., Soc. N.Y. Acad. Scis., Sigma Xi, Sigma Pi Sigma. Home: 1169 Regency Dr Columbus OH 43220 Office: Laser Tech Inc 368 W Park Ave Columbus OH 43223

FAIRBANK, JOHN KING, historian, educator; b. Huron, S.D., May 24, 1907; s. Arthur Boyce and Lorena C. V. (King) F.; m. Wilma Cannon, June 29, 1932; children: Laura, Holly. A.B. summa cum laude, Harvard U., 1929; Ph.D., Oxford U., Eng., 1936; LL.D., Korea U., 1964, U. Toronto, 1967, Swarthmore Coll., 1968, Harvard, 1970, Oberlin Coll., 1971, U. Cin., 1973; L.H.D., U. Wis., 1969, U. Mass., 1974, Middlebury Coll., 1975, Northwestern U., 1978, Brandeis U., 1979, Clark U., 1979, U. S.D., 1981, U. Mich., 1982, Johns Hopkins U., 1983. Mem. faculty dept. history Harvard U., 1936—, Higginson prof. history, dir., 1959-77; chmn. (Council East Asian Studies), 1973-77; with co-ordinator of info. and O.S.S., Washington, 1941-42; spl. asst. to Am. ambassador in, Chungking, China, 1942-43; with OWI, Washington, 1944-45; dir. USIS, in China, 1945-46. Author: several books including The United States and China, 1948, 4th rev. edit., 1979, enlarged edit., 1983, A Documentary History of Chinese Communism, 1921-50, (with Conrad Brandt and Benjamin Schwartz), 1951, Trade and Diplomacy on the China Coast, 1954, China's Response to the West, (with S. Y. Teng), 1954, East Asia; The Great Tradition, (with E. O. Reischauer), 1960, East Asia; The Modern Transformation, 1965, East Asia: Tradition and Transformation, 1972, China Perceived, 1974, Chinabound, 1982; Contbr. articles to nat. periodicals. Mem. Far Eastern Assn. (v.p. 1950-51), Am. Inst. Pacific Relations (trustee 1947-51), Council on Fgn. Relations, Am. Hist. Assn. (pres. 1968), Assn. for Asian Studies (pres. 1959), Nat. Com. U.S.-China Relations, Am. Acad. Arts and Scis., Am. Philos. Soc., Mass. Hist. Soc., Am. Council of Learned Socs. (Far Eastern studies com.). Home: 41 Winthrop St Cambridge MA 02138 Office: 1737 Cambridge St Cambridge MA 02138

FAIRBANK, WILLIAM MARTIN, physicist, educator; b. Mpls., Feb. 24, 1917; s. Samuel Ballantine and Helen Leslie (Martin) F.; m. Jane Davenport, Aug. 16, 1941; children: William Martin, Robert Harold, Richard Dana. A.B., Whitman Coll., Walla Walla, Wash., 1939, D.Sc. (hon.), 1965; postgrad. fellow, U. Wash., 1940-42; M.S., Yale, 1947, Ph.D. (Sheffield fellow), 1948; D.Sc., Duke U., 1969, Amherst Coll., 1972. Mem. staff radiation lab. Mass. Inst. Tech., 1942-45; asst. prof. physics Amherst Coll., 1947-52; asso. prof. Duke, 1952-58, prof., 1958-59; prof. physics Stanford, 1959—. Bd. overseers Whitman Coll. Named Calif. Scientist of Year Calif. Museum Sci. and Industry, 1961; recipient Fritz London award, 1968; Wilbur Lucius Cross medal Yale U., 1968; Guggenheim fellow, 1976-77. Fellow Am. Phys. Soc. (Oliver E. Buckley Solid State Physics prize 1963, Research Corp. award 1965); mem. AAAS (chmn. physics sect. 1980-81), Nat. Acad. Scis., Am. Acad. Arts and Scis., Am. Philos. Soc. Spl. research microwave radar systems, microwave propagation, cryogenics, quantized flux in superconductors, properties liquid helium II, He3, liquid helium bubble chambers, superconducting electron accelerators, quarks, exptl. gravitations. Home: 141 E Floresta Way Menlo Park CA 94025 Office: Physics Dept Stanford Univ Stanford CA 94305

FAIRBANKS, CHARLES HERRON, educator, anthropologist; b. Bainbridge, N.Y., June 3, 1913; s. Louis Byron and Henrietta Fox (Herron) F.; m. Evelyn Adams Timmerman, Feb. 8, 1941; children: Charles Herron, Marie Timmerman. Student, Swarthmore Coll., 1931-32; A.B., U. Chgo., 1939; M.A., U. Mich., 1949, Ph.D., 1954. Archeologist, U. Tenn.-TVA, 1937-38; Archeologist Ocmulgee Nat. Monument; Nat. Park Service, Macon, Ga., 1938-43; supt. Fort Frederica Nat. Monument, St. Simons Island, Ga., 1946-48; with Nat. Park Service, 1950-54; mem. faculty Fla. State U., 1954-63; prof. anthropology U. Fla., 1963-76, disting. service prof., 1976-83, emeritus, 1983—, chmn. dept., 1963-70; Collaborator Indian claims div. Dept. Justice, 1958-65. Author numerous articles, revs., monographs in field; asst. editor: Am. Antiquity, 1958-60. Chmn. Fla. Marine Salvage Com., 1964-65; mem. hwy. salvage com. Fla. Road Dept., 1958-66; Mem. Fla. Rev. Bd. Nat. Register Historic Sites; mem. Fla. Rev. Council, 1973-78. Served with AUS, 1943-46. Mem. Soc. Am. Archaeology, Fla. Anthrop. Soc. (sec. 1955, pres. 1956, editor 1957-59, 61-66), Assn. Current Anthropology, N.C. Archaeol. Soc., Soc. Hist. Archaeology (dir. 1968, pres. 1971), Soc. Profl. Archeologists, Sigma Xi. Home: 717 Northeast Blvd Gainesville FL 32601

FAIRBANKS, CHARLES HERRON, JR., government official, Soviet specialist; b. Macon, Ga., Nov. 17, 1944; s. Charles Herron and Evelyn (Timmerman) F.; m. Joan Helen Roth, Feb. 20, 1983; 1 dau., Eve Rebecca. B.A., Cornell U., 1966; Ph.D., U. Chgo., 1975. Lectr. dept. polit. economy U. Toronto, 1971-73; staff mem. The Rand Corp., Santa Monica, Calif., 1973, cons., 1972-79; asst. prof. polit. sci. Yale U., 1974-81, assoc. prof., 1981-83; mem. policy planning staff U.S. Dept. State, Washington, 1981-82, dep. asst. sec. of state Bur. Human Rights and Humanitarian Affairs, 1982—; cons. Ambassador Moynihan U.S. Mission to UN, N.Y.C., 1975; cons. Office Sec. of Def., Washington, 1978-80; vis. fellow Am. Enterprise Inst., Washington, 1980; fgn. policy advisor Reagan Campaign for the Presidency, 1980. Author: The Soviet Bureaucratic Process, 1979; contbr. chpts. to books. Grantee Twentieth Century Fund, 1976-81, NEH, 1980—. Mem. Am. Polit. Sci. Assn., Am. Assn. Advancement of Slavic Studies, Phi Beta Kappa. Republican. Home: 2853 Ontario Rd NW Washington DC 20009 Office: Bur Human Rights and Humanitarian Affairs US Dept State 2201 C St NW Washington DC 20520

FAIRBANKS, CHARLES LEO, football coach; b. Detroit, June 10, 1933; s. Ronald John and Grace Mary (Qubesh) F.; m. Virgeleen Thomson; children—Charles, Gwenn, Melissa, Tyler, Tobin. B.A., Mich. State U., 1955. Student asst. coach Mich. State U., 1955; head coach Ishpeming (Mich.) High Sch., 1955-57; asst. coach Ariz. State U., 1958-61, U. Houston, 1961-65, U. Okla., 1966, head coach, 1967-73; gen. mgr., head coach New Eng. Patriots Football Club, Inc., Foxboro, Mass., 1973-79; head football coach U. Colo., Boulder, after 1979; pres., head coach N.J. Gens., U.S. Football League; dir. Am. Exchange Bank, Norman, Okla., Foxboro Savs. Bank. Chmn. Mass. Easter Seal campaign, 1975; panel judge Boston Jaycees Ten Outstanding Young Leaders, 1976; hon. Christmas seal chmn. Norfolk County-Newton Lung Assn., 1978. Named Man of Year Football News, 1976; Nat. Football League Coach of Year, 1976; Am. Football Conf. Coach of Year, 1976; named to Okla. U. Hall of Fame, 1976. Mem. Am. Football Coaches Assn. Baptist. Address: care NJ Gens 3 Empire Blvd South Hackensack NJ 07606

FAIRBANKS, DOUGLAS ELTON, JR., actor, producer, writer, corp. dir.; b. N.Y.C., Dec. 9, 1909; s. Douglas Elton and Anna Beth (Sully) F.; m. Mary Lee Epling, Apr. 22, 1939; children:— Daphne Fairbanks Kay, Victoria, Melissa Fairbanks Morant. Ed., Bovee and Collegiate Schs., N.Y.; attended, Knickerbocker Greys, N.Y., Pasadena Poly., Harvard Mil. Sch., Los Angeles; D.F.A. (hon.), Westminster Coll., 1966, Sr. Churchill fellow; vis. fellow, St. Cross Coll., Oxford U.; M.A., Oxford U., 1971; LL.D. (hon.), Denver U., 1974; fellow, Boston U. Libraries, 1978. Chmn. Dougfair Corp. and subsidiaries, The Fairbanks Co., Calif., 1946, Fairtel Corp., N.Y., 1969, Douglas Fairbanks Ltd., U.K.; (and asso. cos.), 1952-58; past pres. Boltons Trading Co., Inc.; also past dir. or cons. several internat. bus. corps., U.S., Europe, Asia; gov. Am. Mus. in Britain; trustee Edwina Mountbatten Trust; mem. exec. com., bd. govs. Royal Shakespeare Theatre, Stratford on Avon, U.K.; bd. govs. Ditchley Found.; mem. adv. com. Denver Center for Performing Arts; chmn. Internat. Cultural Center for Youth, Jerusalem.; lectr. attached Joint Chiefs Staff, 1971—. Author of screen plays, articles, polit. essays, short stories.; Exhibitor paintings and sculpture.; Began film career, 1923, stage career, 1927; acted in more than 75 films including 3 in French (produced or co-produced 15 in U.S. and U.K.), and 20 plays both U.S. and U.K.; produced 160 1-act TV plays, 1953-58; films include Stella Dallas, Woman of Affairs, The Barker, Chances, Union Depot, Little Caesar, Dawn Patrol, Catherine the Great, The Little Accident, The Amateur Gentleman, Outward Bound, Morning Glory, The Narrow Corner, The Young in Heart, Having Wonderful Time, The Joy of Living, Prisoner of Zenda, Gunga Din, Rage of Paris, Corsican Brothers, Angels Over Broadway, Lady in Ermine, Sinbad the Sailor, The Exile, The Fighting O'Flynn, State Secret, Ghost Story, others; plays include The Dummy, Toward the Light, Romeo and Juliet, Young Woodley, The Jest, Man in Possession, Saturday's Children, Moonlight is Silver, My Fair Lady, The Pleasure of His Company, The Secretary Bird, Present Laughter, Out on a Limb; numerous TV and radio plays for, CBS, NBC, ABC, BBC, TV narrations for symphony orchs. throughout, U.S., various song recordings for, Columbia, Caedman, others; organized own prodn. co., Criterion Films Corp., U.K., 1934. Nat. vice-chmn. Com. Defend America by Aiding Allies, 1940-41, Franco-British War Relief Assn., 1939-41; Presdl. envoy for spl. S.Am. mission, 1941; spl. advisor to comdr. 6th Fleet, NATO, 1969-70; U.S. naval del. SEATO Conf., London, 1971; Nat. v.p. Am. Assn. For UN, 1966-63; nat. chmn. Com. for CARE, 1946-50; chmn. Am. Relief for Korea, 1950-53. Commd. lt. (j.g.) USNR, 1941; advanced through grades to capt., 1952. Decorated Silver Star, Combat Legion of Merit with valor attachment, U.S.; knight comdr. Order Brit. Empire; knight Order St. John of Jerusalem; D.S.C., U.K.; officer Legion of Honor (mil. and civil); Croix de Guerre with palm, France; knight comdr. Order George I, Greece; comdr. Order Orange-Nassau, Netherlands; War Cross for Mil. Valor; comdr. Order of Merit; Star of Italian Solidarity, Italy; knight comdr. Order of Merit, Chile; officer Order So. Cross, Brazil; officer Order of the Crown, Belgium; Nat. medal of Korea; Hon. Citizen of Korea; others; recipient Gold Medal of Honor VFW, 1966; Armed Forces award, 1972; Am. Image award, 1976; award for contbn. to arts U. Notre Dame, 1971; award for contbn. to world understanding and peace World Affairs Council, Phila., 1978; Spl. award for internat. artistic achievements New Sch. for Social Research, 1978; Nat. Humanitarian award NCCJ, 1979; Nat. Brotherhood award Salvation Army, 1980; Ann. Nat. Vet.'s Day award, 1981; Apptd. spl. post-war missions State Dept. Mem. Council Fgn. Relations (councilor), Brit-Am. Alumni Assn. (pres. 1950), Am. Friends Order St. John Jerusalem (gov. 1970—), Groupe Navale d'Assaut (hon.), Battalion de Choc (hon.), Assn. des Anciens Combatants (France). Episcopalian. Clubs: Racquet (Chgo.); Brook, Century, Knickerbocker (N.Y.C.); Myopia Hunt (Hamilton, Mass.) (hon.); Metropolitan (Washington); Newport (R.I.) Reading Room; White's, Buck's, Beefstake, Garrick, Naval and Military, R.A.C. (London); Traveller's (Paris); Puffin's (Edinburgh). Office: Inverness Corp 380 Madison Ave New York NY 10022 Office: Farnesworth Co Ltd 21 Cavendish Pl London England

FAIRBANKS, HAROLD VINCENT, metall. engr., educator; b. Des Plaines, Ill., Dec. 7, 1915; s. Oscar William and Muriel (Hulet) F.; m. Marilyn Elizabeth Markussen, July 20, 1951; children—Elizabeth Muriel, William Martin. B.S. in Chem. Engring, Mich. State U., 1937, M.S. in Phys. Chemistry, 1939; postgrad., M.I.T., 1939-40. Registered profl. engr., Ind., W.Va. Instr. in chem. engring. U. Louisville, 1940-42; asst. prof. dept. chem. engring. Rose Poly. Inst., 1942-46, W.Va. U., Morgantown, 1946-49, asso. prof. metall. engring., 1949-55, metall. engr., 1949—, prof. metall. engring., 1955—, asso. chmn. dept. chem. engring., 1973—; adviser for mining and metall. engring. dept. Taiwan Provincial Cheng Kung U., Republic of Free China, 1957-59; cons. to various mfg. firms, govt. agys. and utility cos., 1939—. Contbr. numerous articles on corrosion and metall. engring. to profl. jours. Tau Beta Pi scholar, 1933-34. Fellow AAAS; mem. Am. Inst. Metall. Engrs., Am. Inst. Chem. Engrs., ASTM, Nat. Soc. Profl. Engrs. (pres. Morgantown chpt. 1962-64), IEEE, Internat. Metallographic Soc., Instrument Soc. Am., Profl. Engrs. in Edn. (W.Va. state chmn. 1966-69), Nat. Assn. Corrosion Engrs., Am. Ordnance Assn., Am. Powder Metallurgy Inst., W.Va. Acad. Sci. (chmn. engring. sci. sect. 1969), Acoustical Soc. Am., W.Va. Soc. Profl. Engring., Am. Soc. Metals, Chinese Inst. Engrs., Sigma Xi, Tau Beta Pi, Phi Mu Alpha, Phi Kappa Phi. Home: 909 Riverview Dr Morgantown WV 26505 Office: Dept Chemical Engineering WVa U Morgantown WV 26506 *Always try to leave a place a little brighter than before entering. Help others to progress. Give support only when needed. A question asked is worth listening to-before answering. Never let an opinion stop experimentation for the facts.*

FAIRBANKS, JONATHAN LEO, museum curator; b. Ann Arbor, Mich., Feb. 19, 1933; s. Avard T. and Beatrice Maude (Fox) F.; m. Louise Ann Eckenbrecht, Feb. 12, 1954; children: Theresa Louise, Hilary Ann. B.F.A., U. Utah, 1953; student, Pa. Acad. Fine Arts, 1956-57; M.F.A., U. Pa., 1957; M.A., U. Del., 1961. Curatorial asst. to assoc. curator Winterthur Museum, Del., 1961-71; co-founder Am. Prints Confs., 1970—; curator Am. decorative arts Museum of Fine Arts, Boston, 1971—; adj. lectr. U. Del.; extension teaching U. Utah, Brigham Young U., W.Va.; adj. prof. Am. New Eng. Studies program Boston U.; trustee Tex. Pioneer Arts Found.; trustee, incorporator Dublin Seminar for Early New Eng. Folklife. Curator: exhbns. and catalogues Paul Revere's Boston-1735-1818; also others. Overseer Strawbery Banke, Inc.; bd. dirs. Revere House, Boston. Served with USNR, 1953-55. Winterthur fellow, 1959-61; recipient Disting. Service award Antiques Monthly, 1983, Robert H. Lord award for excellence in hist. studies. Emmanuel Coll., 1983. Fellow Pilgrim Soc., Am. Inst. Conservation; mem. Victorian Soc. Am. (past v.p.), Internat. Inst. Conservation, Am. Assn. Museums, Soc. Archtl. Historians, Nat. Trust for Historic Preservation, Colonial Soc. Mass., Decorative Arts Soc. (v.p. 1978-79), Dunlap Soc. (dir.), Westwood Hist. Soc. (pres. 1978-81), Am. Soc. Interior Designers (hon.). Mural executed Hall of Earth History, Acad. Natural Scis., Phila., 1957. Office: Museum of Fine Arts Boston MA 02115

FAIRBANKS, RICHARD MONROE, broadcasting company executive; b. Indpls., Mar. 27, 1912; s. Richard Monroe and Louise (Hibben) F.; m. Virginia Nicholson Brown, Oct. 26, 1968; children by previous marriage: Anthony Caperton, Richard Monroe, III, Scott Andrew, Charles Hibben (dec.). Grad., Yale U., 1934. Reporter, asst. mng. editor Indpls. News, 1934-42; pres. Sta. WIBC, Indpls., 1947-83, Sta. WNAP, 1968-83, Sta. WKOX, Framingham, Mass., 1970—, Sta. WVBF, Framingham and Boston, 1971—, Fairbanks Broadcasting Co. Inc., Indpls., 1968—, WRMF, Inc. and stas. WJNO, West Palm Beach, WRMF, Palm Beach, Fla., 1979—, Fairwest Studios, Inc., Dallas, 1979-84, Fairbanks Cable of Ind., Dearborn County, 1981—, Fairbanks Cable of Fla., Delray Beach, 1981—, Fair Hill Realty, Indpls., 1981, Fairwind and Traffic-copters; dir. FairWind, Inc., Traffic-copters, Inc., Fairbanks Broadcasting Co. of Kansas City (Mo.), Profl. Helicopter Services, Inc. Bd. dirs. Trinity Episcopal Ch. Meml. Fund, Indpls.; bd. dirs. Cornelia Cole Fairbanks Found., 1958—, pres., 1968—; bd. corporators Crown Hill Cemetery, Indpls., 1965—; trustee Butler U., 1966—. Served to lt. comdr. USNR, World War II. Clubs: Dramatic, Woodstock (Indpls.); Ocean Reef, Card Sound Golf, Card Sound Sailing, Racquet, Key Largo Anglers (Key Largo, Fla.); Governors (West Palm Beach, Fla.). Home: Snapper Point Dr Ocean Reef Key Largo FL 33037 Office: Servico Ctr 1601 W Belvedere Dr West Palm Beach FL 33406

FAIRBANKS, RICHARD MONROE, III, government official; b. Indpls., Feb. 10, 1941; s. Richard Monroe, Jr. and Mary Evans (Caperton) F.; m. Ann Shannon O'Connor, June 13, 1962; children: Woods Alexander, Jonathan Barcroft. A.B., Yale U., 1962; J.D. magna cum laude, Columbia U., 1969. Bar: D.C. Assoc. Arnold & Porter, 1969-71; spl. asst. to adminstr. EPA, 1971; staff asst. Domestic Council, Exec. Office of Pres., White House, 1971-72, asso. dir. energy, environ. and natural resources, 1972-74; founding partner firm Beveridge, Fairbanks & Diamond, Washington, 1974-81; asst. sec. congressional relations Dept. State, 1981-82, ambassador, spl. negotiator for Middle East peace process, ambassador-at-large, 1984—; adj. prof. law Georgetown U. Law Sch., 1971-72; dir. Fairbanks Broadcasting Co., 1974-81. Founder, 1st pres. Washington chpt. Am. Refugee Com., 1978, mem. nat. bd. dirs., 1977—; trustee Meridian House Internat., 1978—; mem. com. natural resources Republican Nat. Com., 1977-80; mem. Pres.'s Citizens Adv. Com. Environ. Quality, 1974-77. Served as officer USNR, 1962-66. Mem. ABA, D.C. Bar Assn. Clubs: Burning Tree, Metropolitan of Washington; Yale (N.Y.C.). Office: Dept State Washington DC 20520 *

FAIRBANKS, RUSSELL NORMAN, univ. adminstr.; b. N.Y.C., Oct. 4, 1919; s. Carleton Forrest and Norna (Johnson) F.; m. Rachel France Fain, Apr. 28, 1942; children—Russell Norman, Jonathan, Norna. A.B., Harvard, 1941; LL.B., Columbia, 1952. Bar: D.C. bar 1953, N.J. bar 1975. Commd. 2d lt. U.S. Army, 1941, advanced through grades to lt. col., 1962; chief legal officer U.S.-Japan Procurement Agy., 1955-57; dir. acad. dept. Judge Adv. Gen.'s Sch., Charlottesville, Va., 1960-62; ret., 1962; asso. dean Columbia Law Sch., 1964-67; prof. law, dean Sch. Law, Rutgers U., 1967—, provost, Camden, N.J.; Cons. Congl. Commn. on Govt. Procurement. Mem. policy com., legal services unit Moblzn. for Youth; mem. nat. adv. com. Am. Vets. Com.; Trustee Camden County Legal Services, Inc., N.J. Inst. for Continuing Legal Edn. Decorated Bronze Star. Mem. Am., Camden County bar assns., Assn. Bar City N.Y. Democrat. Clubs: Harvard (Boston); Englewood Field, Riverton Country, Camden City. Home: 729 Signal Light Rd Moorestown NJ 08057 Office: 5th and Penn Sts Camden NJ 08102

FAIRBANKS, VIRGIL FOX, hematologist; b. Ann Arbor, Mich., June 7, 1930; s. Avard Tennyson and Beatrice Maude (Fox) F.; m. Sheary Jill Eggertsen, Nov. 25, 1955; children: Eric, Julie, Caroline. B.A., U. Utah, 1951; M.D., U. Mich., 1954. Intern Bellevue Hosp., N.Y.C., 1954-55; resident in internal medicine Salt Lake County Hosp., VA Hosp., Salt Lake City, 1957-59; fellow Scripps Clinic, LaJolla, Calif., 1959-60; hematologist City of Hope Med. Center, Duarte, Calif., 1960-63, Los Angeles County Hosp., 1960-63, Permanente Med. Group, Portland, Oreg., 1964-65; cons. in hematology and lab. medicine Mayo Clinic and Found., Rochester, Minn., 1965—; prof. lab. medicine Mayo Med. Sch., 1974—; mem. faculty U. Calif. Coll. Medicine, Los Angeles, 1963-64, U. Oreg. Med. Sch., 1964-65. Author: (with E. Beutler and J.L. Fahey) Clinical Disorders of Iron Metabolism, 1963, 1971, Hemoglobinopathies and Thalassemias, 1980, Current Hematology, Vols. I-III, 1981, 82, 83; contbr. articles to med. jours. and textbooks. Served with USN, 1955-57. Fellow Internat. Soc. Hematology; mem. Am. Fedn. Clin. Research, AMA, Am. Soc. Hematology, A.C.P., Academic Clin. Lab. Physics and Scientists, Central Soc. Clin. Research, Zumbro Valley Med. Soc., Minn. Med. Soc. Democrat. Home: 620 Colombia Ct NE Rochester MN 55901 Office: Mayo Clinic 200 1st St SW Rochester MN 55901

FAIRBURN, DAVID H., corporation executive; b. 1937; married. A.B., Harvard U., 1959. With Keyes Fibre Co., Stamford, Conn., 1961—, sales rep., 1961-63, product mgr., 1963-64, asst. mgr. and dir. European ops., 1964-68, regional sales mgr. U.S.A., 1968-70, mgr. European ops., 1970-74, v.p. corp. ops., 1974-76, exec. v.p., 1976—. Served with USAR. Office: Keyes Fibre Co 3003 Summer St Stamford CT 06905 *

FAIRBURN, ROBERT GORDON, business executive; b. Cleve., July 2, 1911; s. William Armstrong and Louise (Ramsay) F.; m. Mary Whitwell, July 15, 1933; children: Anne, Louise Fairburn Lumley; m. Margaret Taylor Watson, July 2, 1951; 1 son, Robert Gardner; m. Eileen Baker Rickard, Aug. 12, 1972. A.B., Princeton U., 1932. With Berst-Forster-Dixfield Co., N.Y.C., 1932-47, pres., gen. mgr., 1942-47; dir. Diamond Match Co., 1941-57, pres., 1947-57; (Diamond Match Co. merged with Gardner Board & Carton Co. to become Diamond Gardner Corp. 1957; Diamond Gardner Corp. merged with U.S. Printing & Lithograph Corp. to become Diamond Nat. Corp. 1959); chmn. bd., dir. Diamond Nat. Corp., to 1961, Keyes Fibre Co., N.Y.C., 1961-78; dir. Arcata Co., 1978-83; trustee Ataca Liquidating Corp., 1983—; pres. William Gordon Corp.; co-owner, treas. H.R. Dunham Co., Waterville, Maine. Chmn. bd., trustee Thomas Coll., Waterville; trustee Marine Research Soc. of Bath, Maine. Mem. Masters of Fox Hounds Assn. Am. Presbyterian. Clubs: Princeton Quadrangle; Spring Valley Hounds (New Vernon, N.J.); Cumberland (Portland, Maine); Carmel Valley (Calif.) Golf and Country. Home: RFD 1 Fairfield ME 04937 Office: 64 Main St Waterville ME 04901

FAIRCHILD, CLEM WILLIAM, lawyer; b. Valley Falls, Kans., Oct. 11, 1919; s. Charles Clement and Ada (Baker) F.; m. Winifred A. Kipp, Apr. 20, 1945; children—Roberta A., Judith W., Kipp C., Charles W. B.S. in Bus. Adminstrn, U. Kans., 1939; LL.B., U. Mo. at Kansas City, 1947. Bar: Mo. bar 1947. Since practiced in, Kansas City; partner firm Linde, Thomson, Fairchild, Langworthy & Kohn (and predecessors), 1946—; instr. U. Mo. Law Sch. at, Kansas City, 1948; dir. Stuart Hall Co., Inc. Mem. 16th Jud. Commn., 1963-70; Chmn. Kansas City Citizens Assn., 1955-58; co-chmn. Jackson County (Mo.) Charter Commn., 1970. Served with USMCR, 1941-45, 51-52. Mem. Mo. Bar Assn., Kansas City Bar Assn. (pres. 1965), Mil. Order World Wars, Sigma Nu. Republican. Congregationalist. Club: Carriage (Kansas City, Mo.) (pres. 1969-70). Home: 3204 W 84th Pl Leawood KS 66206 Office: City Center Sq 27th Floor 12th and Ballmore Kansas City MO 64196

FAIRCHILD, JAMES DELANO, assn. exec.; b. Buffalo, Mar. 26, 1942; s. George C. and Harriett L. (Kepley) F.; m. Pamella Ann Tutton, July 22, 1962; children—Patricia, Tamara, Thomas James. Student, State U. N.Y., 1962. News reporter radio and TV, 1966-69; govtl. affairs mgr. C. of C. of Greenville, S.C., 1969-73; legis. and polit. program mgr. S.W. div. C. of C. of U.S., Dallas, 1973-75; exec. v.p. Norfolk C. of C., 1975-81, Providence C. of C., 1981—. Mem. Greenville Tax Appeals Bd., 1971-73; chmn. Young Life; bd. regents Inst. Orgn. Mgmt. Mem. So. Assn. C. of C. Execs., New Eng. Assn. C. of C. Execs., Am. C. of C. Execs. Presbyterian. Home: 15 Langlais Dr Hope RI 02831 Office: 10 Dorrance St Providence RI 02903

FAIRCHILD, JOHN BURR, publisher; b. Newark, Mar. 6, 1927; s. Louis W. and Margaret (Day) F.; m. Jill Lipsky, June 8, 1950; children: John Longin, James Burr, Jill and Stephen (twins). B.A., Princeton, 1950. Mem. research dept. J.L. Hudson Co., Detroit, 1950-51; with Fairchild Publs., Inc., N.Y.C., 1951—; pub. Women's Wear Daily, Daily News Record, 1960—, editor-in-chief corp. publs., 1964-65, pub. dir., 1965-66, pres., 1966-70, chmn. bd., chief exec. officer corp. publs., 1970—; exec. v.p., dir. Capital Cities Broadcasting Corp.; exec. v.p. Capital Cities Communications, Inc. Author: The Moonflower Couple, The Fashionable Savages. Served with AUS, 1947-48. Decorated chevalier de L'Ordre National de Merite, France). Clubs: Travellers, Tir aux Pigeons (Paris, France); Century (N.Y.C.). Office: 7 E 12th St New York NY 10003

FAIRCHILD, MAHLON LOWELL, educator, entomologist; b. Spencer, Iowa, Oct. 13, 1930; s. Herbert Elmer and Faye (Eaton) F.; m. Shirley Jean Natvig, Aug. 16, 1954; children: Bruce Charles, Jeanette Marie, Julie Ann. B.S., Iowa State U., 1952, M.S., 1953, Ph.D., 1959. Grad. research asst. Iowa State U., 1952-53, 55-56; entomologist European Corn Borer Lab., Ankeny, Iowa, 1957-59; mem. faculty U. Mo. at Columbia, 1959—, prof. entomology, 1967—, chmn. dept., 1969-80, coordinator integrated pest mgmt., 1980—. Author articles in field. Served with AUS, 1953-55. Mem. Entomol. Soc. Am. (pres. N. Central br. 1974-75, exec. com. N. Central br. 1966-69, chmn. plant protection div. 1968-69), Cosmopolitan Internat. (gov. Mo.-Kans. fedn. 1968-69, mem. internat. gov. bd. 1969-71, 3d internat. v.p. 1971-72, 2d internat. v.p. 1972-73, internat. pres. 1974-75), Sigma Xi, Gamma Sigma Delta (pres. Mo. chpt. 1968-69, award of merit 1965). Home: 1209 Sunset Dr Columbia MO 65201

FAIRCHILD, THOMAS E., U.S. judge; b. Milw., Dec. 25, 1912; s. Edward Thomas and Helen (Edwards) F.; m. Eleanor E. Dahl, July 24, 1937; children: Edward, Susan, Jennifer, Andrew. Student, Princeton, 1931-33; A.B., Cornell U., 1934; LL.B., U. Wis., 1938. Bar: Wis. 1938. Practiced, Portage, Wis., 1938-41, Milw., 1945-48, 53-56; atty. OPA, Chgo., Milw., 1941-45; hearing commr. Chgo. Region, 1945; atty. gen., Wis., 1948-51; U.S. atty. for Western Dist. Wis., 1951-52; justice Supreme Ct. Wis., 1957-66, U.S. Ct. Appeals for 7th circuit, 1966—. Dem. candidate Senator from Wis., 1950, 52. Mem. Am., Wis., Fed., Milw. bar assns., Am. Judicature Soc., Am. Law Inst., Phi Delta Phi. Democrat. Presbyterian. Club: K.P. Office: Ct Appeals 219 S Dearborn Chicago IL 60604 *

FAIRHURST, CHARLES, civil engineering educator; b. Widnes, Lancashire, Eng., Aug. 5, 1929; came to U.S., 1956, naturalized, 1967; s. Richard Lowe and Josephine (Starkey) F.; m. Margaret Ann Lloyd, Sept. 7, 1957; children: Anne Elizabeth, David Lloyd, Charles Edward, Catherine Mary, Hugh Richard, John Peter, Margaret Mary. B.Eng., U. Sheffield, Eng., 1952, Ph.D., 1955. Mining engr. trainee Nat. Coal Bd., St. Helens, Eng., 1949-56; research assoc. U. Minn., Mpls., 1956-67, prof., 1967-70, head Sch. Mineral and Metall. Engring., 1969—, prof. dept. civil and mineral engring., 1970—, head dept., 1972—, E.P. Pfleider prof. mining engring. and rock mechanics, 1983; cons. U.S. Army C.E., Petrobras, Brazil.; Chmn. U.S. nat. commn. rock mechanics Nat. Acad. Scis., 1971-74. Mem. AIME, S. African Inst. Mining and Metallurgy, ASCE (chmn. rock mechanics com. 1978-80), Internat. Soc. Rock Mechanics (past dir.), Am. Underground Space Assn. (pres. 1976-77), Royal Swedish Acad. Engring. Scis. (fgn.), Sigma Xi. Roman Catholic. Home: 417 5th Ave N South Saint Paul MN 55075 Office: Dept Civil and Mineral Engring U Minn Minneapolis MN 55455

FAIRLEY, FRANCIS HILLIARD, lawyer; b. Monroe, N.C., Oct. 3, 1915; s. Frank Hilliard and Janie (Phifer) F.; m. Ella Doris McGuinn, Aug. 24, 1951; children—Mary Jane, Ella Frances. B.A. with honors, U. N.C., 1935; student and teaching-fellow, Grad. Sch., 1935-36, LL.B., 1939, Columbia U. Sch. Law, 1936-38. Bar: N.C. bar 1939, also U.S. Supreme Ct., Ct. Claims, ICC, FCC, Tax Ct., Treasury Dept., U.S. Ct. Internat. Trade 1939. Law clk. to chief judge U.S. Ct. Appeals, 4th Circuit, 1939-40; sr. partner firm Fairley, Hamrick, Monteith & Cobb, Charlotte, N.C., 1939—; pros. atty. City of Charlotte, 1941; sr. asst. U.S. atty. Western Dist. N.C., 1948-53; Dir., vice chmn. So. Nat. Bank; dir., chmn. bd. Ruth's Salads Corps. of N.C. and S.C.; dir., sec. Catawba Loan & Finance Co.; dir. Daniels Constrn. Co., Lawyers Service Corp., Lenoir Finance Co., J.V. Griffith Co., Eastover Assn.; instr. negotiable instruments and comml. law Am. Inst. Banking, 1946-49, 51-52; Mem. Charlotte Estate Planning Council; chmn. Nat. Conf. Lawyers and Life Ins. Cos., 1976—, vice chmn., 1974-76. Contbr. articles to profl. jours. Mem. N.C. Democratic Exec. Com., 1960—; Bd. dirs. N.C. Law Found. Served to lt. comdr., naval aviator USNR, 1941-45; ETO, PTO. Fellow Am. Bar Found., Am. Coll. Probate Counsel, Comml. Law Found. (dir. 1968—); mem. Am. Acad. Polit. and Social Scis., Acad. Polit. Sci., Am. Law Inst. (life), Am. Judicature Soc., Assn. Bar City N.Y., Internat. Bar Assn., N.C. Bar Assn. (past v.p.), Inter-Am. Bar Assn., Fed. Bar Assn., ABA (life; ho. dels. 1962—, vice chmn. life ins. law com., banking law com.), Mecklenburg County Bar Assn. (exec. com. 1950-54, past chmn. programs com. 1949-55), N.C. State Bar (pres. 1962-63, past v.p., chmn. exec. com., mem. council), Am. Legion (life; post comdr.), 40 and 8, Comml. Law League Am. (bd. govs. 1963-69, v.p. 1966-67, pres. 1967-68), S.A.R. (life; v.p. 1979-80, pres. 1980-81), S.C.V., Fedn. Ins. Counsel, Nat. Assn. Probate and Bank Attys., Def. Research Inst., Nat. Conf. Bar Presidents, U. N.C. Law Alumni Assn. (dir. 1953-64, pres. 1959-60), V.F.W., N.C. Law Found., N.C. Ednl. Found., Robert Burns Soc., U. N.C. Gen. Alumni Assn. (life; dir. 1948-51, class agt. ann. alumni giving), Columbia U. Law Sch. Alumni Assn. (Harlan Fiske Stone fellow; ann. fund dir.), Charlotte Opera Assn., Mint Mus. Art, Charlotte Symphony Soc., Charlotte Regional Ballet, Order of Grail, Order of Golden Fleece, Charlotte C. of C., Scribes, Phi Beta Kappa Assos., Phi Delta Phi (province pres. 1947-64, internat. pres. 1967-69, chief justice 1969—). Episcopalian (sr. warden, lay leader). Clubs: Carmel Country (pres. 1957), City, Execs., Cotillion; Charlotte Country, Univ., Rams, Towne (Charlotte). Home: Fairley Hall 424 Eastover Rd Charlotte NC 28207 Office: Suite 1014 Law Bldg 830 East Trade St Charlotte NC 28202

FAIRLEY, HENRY BARRIE, anesthesiologist; b. London, Apr. 24, 1927; Can., 1955, naturalized, 1965; s. Robert Fleming and Helen Ramsay (Barrie) F.; m. Dorothy Jean Orr, Feb. 11, 1950; children—Pamela Gay, David Barrie, Jennifer Anne. Student, King's Coll., U. London, 1943-46; M.B., B.S., Westminster Med. Sch., 1949. Intern Westminster Hosp., London, 1948-49, resident, 1949-51, Brompton Hosp., London, 1954-55; mem. anesthesia staff Toronto (Ont.) Gen. Hosp., 1955-69; clin. tchr. U. Toronto, 1955-59, asso., 1959-62, asso. prof., 1962-67, prof., 1967-69, U. Calif., San Francisco, 1969—; also asso. dean Sch. Medicine; chief anesthesia San Francisco Gen. Hosp., 1973—. Contbr. numerous articles to profl. publs.; asso. editor: Survey of Anesthesiology, 1968—. Served with RAF, 1951-54. Can. Med. Research Council grantee, 1962-69; NIH grantee, 1970—. Fellow Royal Coll. Physicians and Surgeons (Can.), Faculty Anaesthetists, Royal Coll. Surgeons, mem. (diploma), Royal Coll. Physicians (Eng.) (lic.), Med. Council Can. (lic.), Assn. Univ. Anesthetists, Calif. Soc. Anesthesiology, Am. Soc. Anesthesiology, Am. Thoracic Soc., Can. Soc. Anaesthesia, Soc. Critical Care Medicine (charter); hon. mem. New Eng. Soc. Anesthesia, Australian Soc. Anesthesia., N.Z. Soc. Anesthesia. Research in respiratory physiology as applied to anesthesia and intensive care. Office: Dept Anesthesia U Calif San Francisco CA 94143

FAIRMAN, JOEL MARTIN, investment banking executive; b. N.Y.C., Mar. 12, 1929; s. Philip A. and Isabelle (Glackman) Feinberg; m. Claire Martin, Oct. 1, 1959; children: Elizabeth, David, Helen. B.A., Amherst Coll., 1952; J.D., Yale U., 1955. Assoc. Patterson Belknap & Webb, N.Y.C., 1956-61; asst. to pres., v.p. Gianis & Co., Inc., N.Y.C., 1961-65; sr. assoc., asst. v.p., v.p., 1st v.p., sr. v.p. and dir. corp. fin. communications group Prudential-Bache Securities and predecessor firms, N.Y.C., 1965—. Clubs: Bond Club of N.Y.; The Recess, Madison Sq. Garden (N.Y.C.); Piping Rock (Locust Valley, N.Y.); Beaver Dam (Locust Valley) (gov. 1978—). Home: Bayville Rd Locust Valley NY 11560 Office: Prudential-Bache Securities Inc 100 Gold St New York NY 10292

FAIRMAN, ROBERT L., government official; b. London, 1931; m. Jane F. Fairman; children: Scott, Colin. B.Indsl. Engring., U. Fla.; M.S. in Mgmt., Fla. State U., D.Bus. Adminstrn. Chief indsl. engring. br. Warner Robins AFB, Ga., 1959-63; various positions NASA Kennedy Space Ctr., 1963-73; dir. mgmt. planning div. Dept. Transp., 1973-78, dep. asst. sec. for adminstrn., 1978-81, asst. sec. for adminstrn., 1981—. Mem. Am. Inst. Indsl. Engrs., Acad. Mgmt., Sigma Iota Epsilon. Office: Office Adminstrn Dept Transportation 400 7th St SW Washington DC 20590 *

FAIRWEATHER, OWEN, lawyer; b. Chgo., Aug. 18, 1913; s. George O. and Nellie (Dieter) F.; m. Sally Hallberg, May 4, 1940; children—Ellen Vail, Peter Gustav. A.B., Dartmouth, 1935; J.D., U. Chgo., 1938. Bar: Ill. bar 1938. Since practiced in, Chgo.; partner firm Seyfarth, Shaw, Fairweather & Geraldson, 1945—. Author: also internat. comparative labor law texts. Practice and Procedure in Labor Arbitration; Contbr. to legal jours. Mem. ABA (council sect. labor and employment law), Ill. Bar Assn., Chgo. Bar Assn. Home: 59 Hawthorne Rd Barrington IL 60010 Office: 55 E Monroe St Chicago IL 60603

FAIRWEATHER, ROBERT GORDON LEE, lawyer; b. Rothesay, N.B., Can., Mar. 27, 1923; s. Jack H.A.L. and Agnes Charlotte (Mackeen) F.; m. Nancy E. Broughall, June 1, 1946; children—Michael, Wendy, Hugh. B.C.L., U. N.B., 1949, LL.D. (hon.), 1973, St. Thomas U., 1977, Queens U., 1978, St. Francis Xavier U., 1980. Bar: Called to bar N.B 1949, created Queen's Counsel 1958. Partner firm McKelvey, MacAulay, Machum & Fairweather, St. John, 1957-77; atty. gen., N.B., 1958-60; chief Can. Human Rights Commn., Ottawa, Ont., 1977—. Mem. Legis. Assembly N.B., 1952-62; M.P., 1962-77. Served with Royal Can. Navy, 1941-45. Decorated officer Order of Can. Mem. Can. Bar Assn., N.B. Barristers Soc. Home: 71 Somerset St W 1802 Ottawa ON K2P 2G2 Canada Office: 257 Slater St Ottawe ON K1A 1E1 Canada

FAISON, EDMUND WINSTON JORDAN, business educator; b. Rocky Mount, N.C., Oct. 13, 1926; s. Nathan Marcus and Margery Lucille (Jordan) F.; m. Lois Harper Parker; children: Charles, Dorothy Anne, Barbara Jeane. A.B. in Psychology, George Washington U., 1948, M.A., 1950, Ph.D., 1956. Research asst. NRC, Washington, 1948-49; mgr. exptl. lab. Needham, Louis and Brorby, Chgo., 1955-56; account exec. Leo Burnett Co., 1957-58; v.p. Market Facts, Inc., Chgo., 1959; pres. Visual Research Internat., Zurich, Switzerland, 1960-61; adviser AID, Dept. State. Latin Am., 1963-68; prof. bus. adminstrn. U. Hawaii, Honolulu, 1968—, chmn. mktg. dept., 1975—; chmn. bd. East-West Research and Design, Inc.; vis. prof. London Grad. Sch. Bus. Studies, 1974-75. Author: Advertising: A Behavioral Approach for Managers, 1980; editorial bd.: Jour. of Mktg, 1958-63; contbr. articles to profl. jours. Served with USN, 1944-46; Served with USAF, 1950-54. Mem. Am. Psychol. Assn., Soc. Consumer Behavior, Am. Mktg. Assn. (pres. Honolulu chpt. 1973-74), Acad. Mktg. Sci., Acad. Mgmt., Am. Acad. Advt., Am. Assn. Public Opinion, Sales and Mktg. Execs. Internat., Advt. Research Found., Honolulu Advt. Fedn., Market Research Soc. (U.K.), C. of C. of Hawaii, Small Bus. Assn. Hawaii, Honolulu Acad. Arts, All-Industry Packaging Assn. (chmn. 1961), European Packaging Fedn. (U.S. rep. 1961), Sigma Xi, Pi Sigma Epsilon. Clubs: Pacific, Oahu Country, Kaneohe Yacht, Rotary. Home: Box 1207 Kailua HI 96734 Office: East West Research Inst 146-103 Hekili St Kailua HI 96734 U Hawaii Honolulu HI 96822 *My entire career has been devoted to helping domestic and international businesses successfully compete within the private enterprise system. The more experience I gain, the more I appreciate the benefits such a system offers for all segments of society.*

FAISON, SETH SHEPARD, insurance broker; b. N.Y.C., Jan. 18, 1924; s. John Williams and Caroline Goree (Shepard) F.; m. Susan Tyler, Apr. 14, 1956 (dec. 1978); children: Katharine Tyler, Seth Shepard, Sarah, Ann Badger; m. Sara Williams Rose Chew, Mar. 29, 1980; stepchildren: Sara Holten Chew, Katherine Rose Chew, Arthur Duncan Chew. B.A. with honors, Wesleyan U., 1947. Personnel mgr. NBC, N.Y.C., 1948-53; div. mgr. Am. Mgmt. Assn., N.Y.C., 1953-58; asst. v.p. Johnson & Higgins, Inc., N.Y.C., 1958-68, v.p., 1968—; trustee Kings Hwy. Savs. Bank, Bklyn., 1969-71. Chmn. Bklyn. Acad. Music, 1966-72, hon. chmn., 1979—; trustee Bklyn. Inst. Arts and Scis., 1963—, v.p., 1965-71, exec. v.p., 1971-74, vice chmn., 1974-79, chmn., 1979-81; vice chmn. Bklyn. Mus., 1981—; trustee Bklyn. Hosp., 1963—, v.p., 1968—, vice chmn., 1982; trustee Poly Prep., 1962-77; bd. dirs. Police Athletic League N.Y., 1957-73, Chelsea Theater Center, 1969-77; regent St. Francis Coll., Bklyn., 1961-70; mem. N.Y.C. Commn. for Cultural Affairs., 1981—. Served to lt. (j.g.) USNR, 1943-46. Recipient N.Y. State award for Acad. Music (rehab. of 1 of state's most venerable theaters), 1969. Mem. Citizens Union, Ins. Brokers Assn. State N.Y., Huguenot Soc. Am. Unitarian (deacon). Clubs: Down Town Assn. (N.Y.C.); Heights Casino, Rembrandt (Bklyn.); Bellport Bay Yacht (Bellport, N.Y.). Home: 1 Pierrepont St Brooklyn NY 11201 Office: 95 Wall St New York NY 10005

FAITH, CARL CLIFTON, mathematics educator; b. Covington, Ky., Apr. 28, 1927; s. Herbert Spencer and Vila Belle (Foster) F.; m. Betty Frances Compton, Aug. 11, 1951 (div. Apr. 28, 1981); children: Heidi, Cindy. Student, U. Cin., 1947; Algernon Sidney Sullivan fellow, U. Ky., 1949-51, B.S. cum laude with honors in Math., 1951; M.A. in Math., Purdue U., 1953, Ph.D., 1955. Asst. prof. math. Mich. State U., 1955-57; asst., asso. prof. Pa. State U., 1957-62; prof. math. Rutgers U., 1962—; vis. prof. U. Heidelberg, Germany, 1959-60; vis. mem. Inst. Advanced Study, Princeton, N.J., 1960-62, 73-74, 77-78, assoc. mem., 1983—; vis. prof. Israel Inst. Tech. (Technion), Haifa, 1976; vis. scholar U. Calif.-Berkeley, 1965-66; vis. Ford scholar Tulane U., 1970; cons. AID, NSF, India, 1968; screening com. Sr. Fulbright Awards, 1970-73. Author: Lectures on Injective Modules and Quotient Rings, 1967, Algebra: Rings, Modules and Categories, 1973, rev. edit., 1981, Russian transl., 1978, (with J.H. Cozzens) Simple Noetherian Rings, 1975, Algebra II: Ring Theory, 1976, Russian transl., 1979, (with S. Wiegand) Module Theory, 1979, Injective Modules and Injective Quotient Rings, 1982, (with S.S. Page) FPF Ring Theory: Faithful Modules and Generators of Mod-R, 1983; also articles. Block capt. Princeton Assn. Human Rights, 1963—; mem. Movement for a New Congress, Princeton, 1970. Served with USNR, 1945-46. NSF grantee; NATO postdoctoral fellow, Heidelberg, 1959-60; NSF postdoctoral fellow, 1960-61; Rutgers faculty fellow, 1965-66, 69-70; acad. sabbatical, 1973-74, 81-82. Mem. Am. Math. Soc. Home: 199 Longview Dr Princeton NJ 08540

FAJANS, JACK, tech. inst. dean; b. N.Y., Nov. 17, 1922; s. Harry and Fanny Fajans; m. Eleanor Belfert, Mar. 5, 1944; children—Anita, Joel. B.Chem.Engring., CCNY, 1944; Ph.D., M.I.T., 1950. Engr. Western Electric Co., Kearny, N.J., 1944; group mgr. Sylvania Electric Co., Bayside, N.Y., 1950-53; mem. faculty Stevens Inst. Tech., Hoboken, N.J., 1953—, prof. physics, 1953—, dean, 1974—; exchange prof. Kabul (Afghanistan) U., 1963-65, 67-69; cons. in field, 1956—. Author. Served with AUS, 1944-46. Mem. Am. Phys. Soc., M.I.T. Alumni Assn., CCNY Alumni Assn., Sigma Xi. Patentee in field. Home: 1133 Magnolia Rd Teaneck NJ 07666 Office: Stevens Inst Tech Hoboken NJ 07030

FAJANS, STEFAN STANISLAUS, physician; b. Munich, Ger., Mar. 15, 1918; came to U.S., 1936, naturalized, 1942; s. Kasimir M. and Salomea (Kaplan) F.; m. Ruth Stine, Sept. 6, 1947; children: Peter S., John S. B.S., U. Mich., Ann Arbor, 1938, M.D., 1942. Intern Mount Sinai Hosp., N.Y.C., 1942-43; resident U. Mich., 1947-49, research fellow, 1946-47, 49-51; mem. faculty U. Mich. Med. Sch., 1950—, prof. internal medicine, 1961—, head div. endocrinology and metabolism, also dir. metabolism research unit, 1973—; dir. Mich. Diabetes Research and Tng. Center, 1977—; mem. endocrinology study sect. NIH, 1958-62, mem. diabetes and metabolism tng. grants com., 1966-70; chmn. Am. zone internat. sci. adv. com. Congresses Internat. Diabetes Fedn., 1977-79; Banting meml. lectr., 1978. Contbr. articles med. publns. Served as officer M.C. AUS, 1943-46. Research fellow in medicine A.C.P., 1949-50; fellow Life Ins. Med. Inst., 1950-51. Mem. Am. Diabetes Assn. (pres. 1971-72, Banting medal 1972, Banting Meml. award 1978), Endocrine Soc. (council 1967-71, 78-81), ACP (master), Endocrine Soc. (v.p. 1970-71), Am. Fedn. Clin. Research, Am. Soc. Clin. Investigation, Assn. Am. Physicians, Central Soc. Clin. Research, Sigma Xi, Alpha Omega Alpha. Home: 2485 Devonshire Rd Ann Arbor MI 48104 Office: Univ Mich Hosp Ann Arbor MI 48109

FAJEN, STEPHEN RANDOLPH, advertising executive; b. N.Y.C., Sept. 24, 1940; s. Randolph B. and Lee (DeCunzo) F.; m. Diane Sue Fajen Miller, Sept. 24, 1967; children: Kimberly N., Brett Randolph. B.A. in Math, NYU, 1962. Group account dir. A.C. Nielsen, N.Y.C., 1962-67; v.p. media and research J. Walter Thompson, N.Y.C., 1967-75; media dir. McCaffrey & McCall, N.Y.C., 1975-77; sr. v.p., gen. mgr. and media dir. Needham Harper & Steers, N.Y.C., 1977-81; pres., chief operating officer David Deutsch Assocs., N.Y.C., 1981-82; sr. v.p., exec. media dir. Compton Advt., N.Y.C., 1982—; cons. Advt. Age, N.Y.C., 1982—. Contbr. articles to profl. jours. Commr., mgr. Youth Soccer League, Larchmont, N.Y., 1978—. Served with U.S. Army, 1962-68. Mem. Internat. Radio and TV Soc., Nat. Acad. Arts and Scis., 4 A's Media Research Council.

FALAHEE, JAMES BURNS, power company executive; b. Jackson, Mich., May 31, 1924. A.B., U. Mich., 1948, J.D., 1950. Bar: Mich. 1950. Atty. Consumers Power Co., Jackson, 1950-58, gen.atty., 1958-76, v.p., gen. counsel, 1976-77, sr. v.p., 1977—; also vice chmn. Pres. St. Joseph Home for Boys, Jackson, 1971; bd. dirs. Foote Hosp., Jackson, 1976—. Mem. Jackson County Bar Assn., Mich. Bar Assn., ABA. Office: 212 W Michigan Ave Jackson MI 49201

FALB, PETER LAWRENCE, mathematician, investment company executive; b. N.Y.C., July 26, 1936; s. Harry and Bertha (Kirschner) F.; m. Karen Forslund, Oct. 9, 1971. A.B., Harvard U., 1956, M.A., 1957, Ph.D., 1961. Mem. staff Mass. Inst. Tech. Lincoln Lab., Cambridge, 1960-66; asso. prof. applied math. U. Mich., Ann Arbor, 1966; prof. Brown U., Providence, 1967—; prin. Dane, Falb, Stone & Co., Inc., Boston, 1977—; chmn. Barberry Corp., 1968—; also dir.; dir. FES Computing Co.; vis. prof. Lund (Sweden) Inst. Tech., summers 1971, 72, 74, 76, 78; cons. NASA, Bolt, Beranek & Newman Co. Author: (with M. Athans) Optimal Control: An Introduction to the Theory and its Applications, 1966, (with R. Kalman and M. Arbib) Topics in Mathematical System Theory, 1969, (with J. deJong) Some Successive Approximation Methods in Control and Oscillation Theory, 1969. Home: 245 Brattle St Cambridge MA 02138 Office: Dept Applied Mathematics Brown Univ Providence RI 02912 also Dane Falb Stone & Co 10 Liberty Sq Boston MA 02109

FALCK, R. H., chain department store executive; b. 1926; married. With K Mart Corp., Troy, Mich., 1948—, asst. store mgr., 1950-56, store mgr., 1956-59, dist. mgr., 1959-61, asst. sales dir., 1961-64, asst. sales mgr., promotion mgr., 1964-65, assoc. buyer men's wear, 1965-68, sr. buyer hardware and bldg. materials, 1968-70, v.p. sales, gen. mdse. mgr., 1970-72, sr. v.p. sales, gen. mdse. mgr., 1972-77, sr. v.p., treas., 1977-81, sr. v.p. distbn., transp. and mdse. systems, 1981-82, exec. v.p. merchandising, 1982—. Served with USAF, 1944-45. Office: K Mart Corp 3100 W Big Beaver Troy MI 48084 *

FALCO, LOUIS, dancer, choreographer, dance co. dir.; b. N.Y.C., Aug. 2, 1942. Studied with, Jose Limon, Charles Weidman, Martha Graham, Am. Ballet Theatre Sch. Participant Nat. Endowment Dance Touring Program; artist-in-residence numerous colls. and univs. throughout U.S. Prin. dancer, Jose Limon Dance Co., 1960-70; toured, South and Central Am., N.Am., Europe and Far East; formed, The Louis Falco Dance Co. Inc., 1967; since toured with co., throughout U.S., Can., Mexico and Europe, 10th tour, 1975; presents ann. seasons, N.Y.C.; works include Argot, 1967, Huescape, 1968, Timewright, 1969, Caviar, 1970, Ibid, 1970, Sleepers, 1971, Soap Opera, 1972, Avenue, 1973, Twopenny Portrait, 1973, Storeroom, 1974, Eclipse, 1974, Caterpillar, 1975, Pulp, 1975, Champagne, 1976, Hero, 1977, Tiger Rag, 1977, Escargot, 1978, Saltibocca, 1979, Early Sunday Morning, 1979, Kate's Rag, 1980, Service Compris, 1980; revived with: Rudolph Nureyev Moor's Pavane, 1974, filmed for Dutch and German TV, choreographed works for, La Scala Opera Ballet, Alvin Ailey Dance Theatre, Boston Ballet, Washington Opera Soc., Caramoor Festival, Australian Ballet, Les Ballets Jazz de Montreal, Ballet Rambert and the, Netherlands Dance Theatre; choreographer: film (F)AME, 1979; choreographer, performer 6 episodes of TV series for, RAI-TV of Italy, 1981; The Louis Falco Dance Co. Inc. is a non-profit corp. supported in part by, Nat. Endowment for Arts, N.Y. State Council on Arts, many works are collaborations with prominent artists, including, Robert Indiana, Stanley Landsman, William Katz, Marisol; incorporates spoken dialogue in works. Recipient Harkness award, 1979. Address: 131 W 24th St New York NY 10011

FALCO, MARIA JOSEPHINE, polit. scientist; b. Wildwood, N.J., July 7, 1932; d. John J. and Mafalda M. (Barbieri) F. A.B., Immaculata (Pa.) Coll., 1954; Fulbright scholar, U. Florence, Italy, 1954-55; M.A., Fordham U., 1958; Ph.D., Bryn Mawr (Pa.) Coll., 1963; postdoctoral research fellow, Yale, 1965-66; NSF grantee, U. Mich., summer 1968. Instr., asst. prof. history and polit. sci. Immaculata Coll., Pa., 1957-63; asst. prof. polit. sci. Washington Coll., Chestertown, Md., 1963-64; research asst. Genevieve Blatt, candidate for U.S. Senator from, Pa., 1964-65; asst. prof., asso. prof. polit. sci. Le Moyne Coll., Syracuse, N.Y., 1966-73, chmn. polit. sci. dept., 1967-73; prof. polit. sci. Stockton State Coll., Pomona, N.J., 1973-76; chmn. social and behavioral scis. faculty U. Tulsa, 1976-79; dean Coll. Arts and Scis., Loyola U., New Orleans, 1979—. Author: Truth and Meaning in Political Science: An Introduction to Political Inquiry, 1973, Through the Looking-Glass: Epistemology and the Conduct of Political Inquiry: An Anthology, 1979, Bigotry!: Ethnic, Machine and Sexual Politics in a Senatorial Election, 1980, also articles.; Cons. editor: Political Parties and the Civic Action Groups. Pres. Syracuse chpt. New Democratic Coalition, 1970-71. Named Outstanding Educator in U.S., 1975; Faculty fellow in state and local politics Nat. Center for Edn. in Politics, 1964. Mem. Womens Caucus Polit. Sci. (pres. 1976), Am. Polit. Sci. Assn. (mem. Benjamin Evans Lippincott award com. 1976, chmn. sect. program com. 1975, mem. com. acad. freedom and profl. ethics), Midwestern Polit. Sci. Assn. (mem. com. status of women), Northeastern Polit. Sci. Assn., SW Polit. Sci. Assn. (outstanding conv. paper com.), AAUP (v.p. LeMoyne chpt. 1971-72), Founds. Polit. Theory Group, Common Cause. Roman Catholic. Home: 4817 Belle Dr Metairie LA 70002 Office: Coll Arts and Scis Loyola U New Orleans LA 70118 *Despite the fact that it's different being a woman in a man's world, I would rather be a woman.*

FALCONE, ANTOINETTE D., business executive; b. Phila., Mar. 10, 1939; d. Joseph and Maria G. F. Ed., St. Joseph's U., 1968. With N.W. Ayer & Son, Inc., N.Y.C., 1956-81; adminstrv. asst. N.W. Ayer ABH Internat., 1960, asst. corp. sec., 1977, corp. sec., 1978-79, stock transfer agt., 1969-79, info. specialist, 1979-81; exec. v.p. Help Bus. Services, Inc., Swarthmore, Pa., 1980—. Office: Help Business Services Inc 417 Dartmouth Ave Swarthmore PA 19081

FALCONER, DONALD PEARSON, sugar company executive; b. Oakland, Calif., May 21, 1920; s. Eric A. and Janet (Pearson) F.; m. Lavina Kelly, Jan. 3, 1945; children: John, Ethan, Julia. A.B., U. Calif. at Berkeley, 1940, LL.B., 1947. Bar: Calif. bar 1947. With Calif. and Hawaiian Sugar Co., 1947—, v.p., gen. counsel, sec., 1964—, sr. v.p., 1977—; exec. com. U.S. Cane Sugar Refiners Assn., 1964—. Served to capt. AUS, 1942-46. Mem. Am., Calif., San Francisco bar assns., Order of Coif. Club: Banker's. Home: 1226 King Dr El Cerrito CA 94530 Office: One California St San Francisco CA 94106

FALES, HALIBURTON, II, lawyer; b. N.Y.C., Aug. 7, 1919; s. DeCoursey and Dorothy Mildred (Mitchell) F.; m. Katharine Ladd, Dec. 27, 1941; children: Nancy, Haliburton, Priscilla, Lucy, William E. Ladd. Student, Harvard U., 1938-41; LL.B., Columbia U., 1947. Bar: N.Y. 1948, U.S. Supreme Ct. 1957, D.C. 1974. Assoc. firm White & Case, N.Y.C., 1947-58, ptnr. firm, 1959—; counsel Frick Collection. Contbr. articles to profl. jours. Trustee, sec., pres. Pierpont Morgan Library; vice chmn. St. Barnabas Hosp.; trustee Victoria Found.; sr. warden St. Luke's Ch. Served to lt. comdr. USNR, 1941-45. Fellow Am. Bar Found., N.Y. Bar Found. (dir.), Inst. Judicial Adminstrn., Am. Coll. Trial Lawyers; mem. Albert Gallatin Assos., Am. Bar Assn., Am. Judicature Soc., Am. Law Inst., Am. Soc. Internat. Law, Assn. Bar City N.Y., Internat. Bar Assn. (patron), Internat. Law Assn., Internat. Legal Aid and Defender Assn., N.Y. County Lawyers Assn., N.Y. State Bar Assn. (pres. 1983-84). Home: Pottersville Rd Gladstone NJ 07934 Office: 1155 Ave of Americas New York NY 10036

FALETTI, RICHARD JOSEPH, lawyer; b. Spring Valley, Ill., Nov. 15, 1922; s. Michael Joseph and Alfonsa M. (Delo) F.; m. Barbara Louise Shaft, Aug. 11, 1947; children: Martha DeWitt, Joan Delo, Carol Louise, Michael John, Margaret Mary. B.S., U. Ill., 1947, J.D., 1948. Bar: Ill. 1949. Assoc. Arrington & Healy, Chgo., 1948-50; asst. prof. law U. Ill., Urbana, 1950-55; assoc. Winston & Strawn, Chgo., 1955-58, ptnr., 1958—; chmn. exec. com., dir. Bank of Clarendon Hills, Ill., 1976—, chmn. bd., 1984—; dir. Bank of Wheaton, Ill.; sec. Carus Corp., LaSalle, Ill., 1956. Governing life mem. Art Inst. Chgo., 1975—; chmn. fin. com., village trustee Village of Clarendon Hills, 1960-64. Served to 1st lt. USAAF, 1944-46. Decorated Air medal with 3 oak leaf clusters. Mem. ABA, Ill. State Bar Assn., Chgo. Bar Assn., Am. Judicature Soc., Order of Coif. Republican. Roman Catholic. Clubs: Mid-Day (Chgo.); Hinsdale Golf. Home: 1 Hamill Ln Clarendon Hills IL 60514 Office: Winston & Strawn 1 First Nat Plaza Chicago IL 60603

FALICOV, LEOPOLDO MAXIMO, physicist; b. Buenos Aires, Argentina, June 24, 1933; came to U.S., 1960, naturalized, 1967; s. Isaias Felix and Dora (Samoilovich) F.; m. Marta Alicia Puebla, Aug. 13, 1959; children: Alexis, Ian. Licenciado in chemistry, Buenos Aires U., 1957; Ph.D. in Physics, Cuyo U. Instituto J. A. Balseiro, Argentina, 1958, Cambridge U., 1960, Sc.D., 1977. Research asso. dept. physics Inst. Study Metals, U. Chgo., 1960-61, instr. physics, 1961-62, asst. prof. physics, 1962-65, asso. prof., 1965- 68, prof., 1968-69; prof. physics U. Calif., Berkeley, 1969—, Miller research prof., 1979-80, chmn. dept. physics, 1981—; cons. in field. Author: Group Theory and Its Physical Applications, 1966, La Estructura Electronica de los Solidos, 1967; contbr. articles to profl. jours. Alfred P. Sloan Found. fellow, 1964-68; vis. fellow Fitzwilliam Coll., Cambridge, Eng.; Fulbright fellow, 1969; OAS vis. prof., Argentina, 1970; Nordita vis. prof. U. Copenhagen, 1971-72; Fulbright lectr., Spain, 1972; Guggenheim fellow, 1976-77; vis. fellow Clare Hall, Cambridge, Eng., 1976-77; exchange prof. U. Paris, 1977. Mem. Nat. Acad. Sci. Home: 90 Avenida Dr Berkeley CA 94708 Office: Dept Physics U Calif Berkeley CA 94720

FALISE, ROBERT ALPHONSE, lawyer; b. N.Y.C., Oct. 28, 1932; s. Alphonse and Anne K. (Tiedemann) F.; m. Katharine Keith Stephenson, Apr. 21, 1967; children: Katherine Prentice, Elizabeth Stephenson Gill, William McIntyre Gill, Christina Sumner. A.B., Columbia U., 1954, J.D., 1956. Bar: N.Y. State 1957. Assoc. firm Donovan, Leisure, Newton & Irvine, N.Y.C., 1956-61; dep. asst. dir. U.S. Commn. on Civil Rights, Washington, 1960-61; assoc. firm Olwine, Connelly, Chase, O'Donnell & Weyher, N.Y.C., 1961-66; v.p., sec., gen. counsel Dictaphone Corp., N.Y.C., 1966-80; staff v.p., gen. atty.-corp. affairs RCA, N.Y.C., 1980—. U.S. del. Internat. Civil Aviation Orgn., 1958. Served to maj. JAGC USAR, 1957-60. Mem. ABA, N.Y. State Bar Assn. (chmn. corp. counsel sect.), Assn. Bar City N.Y., Fed. Bar Assn., Westchester/Fairfield Corporate Counsel Assn. (founder, past pres.). Episcopalian. Clubs: Am. Yacht (Rye, N.Y.); Metropolitan, Doubles (N.Y.C.); Westchester Country. Home: Quarry" Poundridge Rd Bedford NY 10506 Office: RCA 30 Rockefeller Plaza New York NY 10020

FALK, BERNARD HENRY, trade assn. exec.; b. N.Y.C., Sept. 10, 1926; s. Max and Sadie (Orwin) F.; m. Iris G. Tannenbaum, June 13, 1954; children—Cindy, Amy, David. B.E.E., Coll. City N.Y., 1950; grad. student, Columbia Sch. Bus., 1954. Field engr. RCA, 1950-52; sales engr. Gen. Precision Corp., 1953-56; exec. sec. Nat. Elec. Mfrs. Assn., 1956-65, v.p. govt. relations, 1966-71, pres., 1972—; Chmn. adv. com. elec. goods Dept. Commerce, 1974—; mem. exec. adv. com. nat. power survey FPC, 1972—; mem. Bus. Adv. Council on Fed. Reports. Served with USNR, 1944-46. Mem. Am. Nat. Standards Inst. (dir.), Am. Soc. Assn. Execs. (v.p. 1978, dir.), N.Y. State Soc. Assn. Execs. (pres. 1975). Home: Watergate South Washington DC 20037 Office: 2101 L St Washington DC 20037

FALK, CARL ANTON, investment banker; b. Omaha, Dec. 12, 1907; s. Charles E. and Amanda C. (Quarnstrom) F.; m. Gladys M. Gustafson, June 30, 1928; children—Carolyn (Mrs. Scott), Robert, Virginia (Mrs. Olson), Suzanne (Mrs. Ahlstrand). Student pub. schs. and bus. coll., Omaha; L.H.D., Midland Coll. Former chmn. bd. Kirkpatrick, Pettis, Smith, Polian, Inc. (investment bankers), Omaha. Mem. Nebr. Investment Bankers Assn. (past pres.), Omaha C. of C., Omaha Council Chs. (past pres.), Aksarben. Clubs: Rotarian, Masons (33 deg.), Shriners., Omaha, Omaha Country, Noon Day (past pres.), Plaza (Omaha); De Anza Desert Country (Borrego Springs, Calif.); Garden of Gods (Colorado Springs, Colo.). Home: 9966 Fieldcrest Dr Omaha NE 68114 Office: 9110 Dodge St Embassy Bldg Omaha NE 68114

FALK, EDGAR ALAN, pub. relations exec.; b. Bklyn., Nov. 4, 1932; s. Ralph P. and Lillian (Freud) F. A.B., N.Y. U., 1954, postgrad., 1957-59. Pub. relations asst. Western Electric Co., N.Y.C., 1957-59; dir. pub. relations Ritter, Sanford, Price & Chalek, N.Y.C., 1959-60; account supr. pub. relations Batten, Barton, Durstine & Osborn, N.Y.C., 1960-67; group dir. pub. relations N.W. Ayer & Son, N.Y.C., 1967-73; v.p., dir. pub. relations div. Cunningham & Walsh, Inc., N.Y.C., 1973-79; dir. communications NBA, 1979—. Mem. Kings County Republican County Com., 1958-61. Served to 1st lt. U.S. Army, 1954-56; lt. col. Res. ret. Recipient Freedoms Found. award, 1971. Mem. Public Relations Soc. Am. (Silver Anvil award 1970, 71, 73), Assn. U.S. Army, Res. Officers Assn. Home: 301 E 78th St New York NY 10021 Office: 645 Fifth Ave New York NY 10022 *Know what you want out of life... and seek those "wants." If you want them badly enough, you will get them. And avoid being an if "onlyer." Don't look back at past decisions and say "if only."*

FALK, EUGENE HANNES, educator; b. Czechoslovakia, Aug. 10, 1913; U.S., 1946, naturalized, 1953; s. Herman and Helen (Kircova) F.; m. Ellen Wien, 1938 (div.); children—Ingrid Helen, Ronald Jonathan. Ph.D. in French, Victoria U., Manchester, Eng., 1942; M.A. (hon.), Dartmouth, 1966. Asst., then asst. lectr. German U. Manchester, Eng., 1939-42; master French Alcester (Eng.) Sch., 1943-46; mem. faculty U. Bridgeport, Conn., 1946-53, prof. fgn. langs., 1948-53, chmn. dept. fgn. langs., 1947-53; vis. prof. French U. Minn., 1953-54, mem. faculty, 1954-63, prof. French, 1957-63, chmn. dept. comparative lit., 1956-63, chmn. dept., 1960-63; mem. faculty Dartmouth, 1963-67, chmn. dept., 1964-67, Edward Tuck prof. French, 1964-67; prof. French and comparative lit. U. N.C., 1967—, chmn. comparative lit., 1972-80, Marcel Bataillon prof. comparative lit., 1973—; Fulbright prof., Brazil, 1981. Author: Renunciation as a Tragic Focus, 1954, Types of Thematic Structure, 1967, The Poetics of Roman Ingarden, 1980. Fellow Fund Advancement Edn., 1952-53, Nat. Humanities Center, 1982; decorated Ordre des Palmes Académiques, France). Mem. MLA, Am. Assn. Tchrs. French, AAUP, Assn. Internat. d'Etudes Francaises, Am. Assn. Comparative Lit. Home: 348 Wesley Dr Chapel Hill NC 27514

FALK, FERDIE ARNOLD, distilling and importing co. exec.; b. New Orleans, Nov. 3, 1928; s. Ferdinand N. and Beatrice (Roseman) F.; m. Ursula Blum, May 8, 1971; children by previous marriage: Lori Rose, Christopher. Student, La. State U., 1946-48. With Seagram and Sons, 1955-71; exec. v.p. Gen. Wine and Spirits Co., 1969-71, Schenley Affiliated Brands Corp., 1971-74; pres., dir. Fleischmann Distilling Corp., 1974-76, New Eng. Distillers, Inc.; sr. v.p., group exec. Nabisco Products, Inc., N.Y.C., 1978—; chmn., chief exec. officer Julius Wile Sons and Co., Inc., 1978-82; chmn., chief exec. officer, prin. shareholder Ancient Age Distillery Co. Inc., Frankfort, Ky., 1983—; dir. L.J. McGuiness Co., Ltd., Can. and All Brand Importers, Inc., Mark Bouwer, Ltd.; chmn. com. on econ. devel. Spirits Industry. Bd. dirs. Am. Cancer Soc., Fund for Higher Edn.; chmn. N.Y. council drive Boy Scouts Am., 1983; pres. Sky Ranch for Boys.; chmn. United Negro Coll. Fund Drive, 1983. Recipient Louis Berger Meml. award Am. Cancer Soc., N.Y.C., 1979; Sword of Haganah award State of Israel, 1979. Mem. Nat. Assn. Alcoholic Beverage Importers (past dir.), Brit. Export Mktg. Adv. Com., Brit. Am. C. of C. (past v.p., dir.), French-Am. C. of C. in U.S. (councillor). Clubs: Shelter Rock, Sands Point., Deepdale Golf. Office: 36 Main St Roslyn NY 11570

FALK, ISIDORE SYDNEY, bacteriologist, pub. health med. economist, social security expert; b. Bklyn., Sept. 30, 1899; s. Samsin and Rose (Stolzberg) F.; m. Ruth Hill, Mar. 18, 1925 (dec. July 17, 1982); children: Sydney Westervelt, Stephen Ackley. Spl. student, Sheffield Sci. Sch. Yale U., 1915-17, Ph.B., 1920, Ph.D., 1923. Asst. dept. pub. health Yale U., 1915-20, instr., 1920-23, prof. pub. health, 1961-68, prof. emeritus, adj. lectr., 1968—; asst. prof. bacteriology U. Chgo., 1923-26, asso. prof., 1926-29, prof., 1929; asst. dir. Bur. Child Welfare, Chgo. Dept. Health, 1926-27; asso. dir. Com. on Costs of Med. Care, 1929-33; research asso. Milbank Meml. Fund, 1933-36; staff mem. U.S. Com. on Econ. Security, 1934-35; with Div. Research and Statistics, Social Security Adminstrn., Washington, 1936-54, dir., 1940-54; cons. on health services United Steelworkers of Am., 1958-80; pvt. cons. on pub. health and social security. Author numerous books, since 1923, primarily in field med. care.; Conducted several health surveys and; compiled reports thereon.; Contbr. numerous tech. papers to jours.; mem. editorial bds. various profl. jours. Vice chmn. bd. dirs., exec. dir. Community Health Care Center Plan, New Haven, 1967-79. Served with AUS, 1918; Mem. govt. adv. coms., World War II. Decorated Congl. Selective Service medal; officer Ordre de Honneur et Merite, Haiti, 1953; cabalero Orden de Vasco Nunez de Balboa, Panama, 1956; recipient various profl. awards and hon. memberships. Fellow Am. Public Health Assn. (Sedgwick Meml. Gold medal 1973), AAAS; mem. and officer several profl. assns. Research in eugenics of infant welfare, theory of microbic virulence, microbic cause of influenza, econs. of med. care and pub. health, social ins., nat. health ins. group practice prepayment plans and health maintenance orgns., quality of med. care. Home: 472 Whitney Ave New Haven CT 06511

FALK, JAMES H., lawyer; b. Tucson, Aug. 17, 1938; s. George W. and Elsie L. (Higgins) F.; m. Bobbie Jo Vest, July 8, 1960; children—James H., John Mansfield, Kathryn Colleen. B.S., B.A., U. Ariz., 1960, LL.B., 1965. Bar: Ariz. bar, D.C. bar, U.S. Supreme Ct. bar. Counsel El Paso Natural Gas Co., Tex., 1965-66, The Anaconda Co., Tucson, 1967-68; partner Waterfall Economidas, Falk & Caldwell, Tucson, 1968-71; staff asst. Exec. Office of the Pres., Washington, 1971-73; asso. dir. Domestic Council, Washington, 1973-76; mem. firm Touche Ross & Co., Washington, 1976-78; partner Coffey, McGovern, Noel & Novogroski, Washington, 1978-81, Larkin, McCarthy, Noel & Falk, 1981—; rep. of U.S. Pres. to state and local govts., D.C., U.S. territories, 1974-75, Asst. city prosecutor, city atty., Tucson, 1966-67. Pres., chmn. bd. Tucson Transit Authority Inc., 1970-71. Mem. Am. Arbitrators Assn. (mem. nat. panel arbitrators), Nat. Conf. Commrs. on Uniform State Laws. Home: 9430 Cornwell Farm Rd Great Falls VA 22066 Office: 1301 Pennsylvania Ave NW Washington DC 20004

FALK, KARL L., savings and loan executive; b. Berkeley, Calif., Sept. 12, 1911; s. Henry and Helen S. (Ruecker) F.; m. Doris Finger, June 21, 1936. A.B., Stanford U., 1932; Ph.D., U. Berlin, 1936. Mem. faculty dept. fgn. lang. Fresno State Coll. (now Calif. State U. at Fresno), 1938-42, faculty div. soc. sci., 1946-68, head div. social sci., 1950-63, prof. econs., prof. econs. emeritus, 1968—, acting pres. coll., 1969-70; chem. economist Dept. Commerce, Washington, 1942; dean Sierra Summer Sch., 1948; Fulbright lectr. Technische Hochschule Stuttgart, Germany, 1954-55; pres. First Savs. & Loan Assn., 1957-75, chmn. bd., 1957-81; dir. Calif. State Internat. Programs, Germany and Sweden, 1963-64; dir. internat. affairs Calif. State Colls., 1965-66; lectr. U.S. Dept. State in, Germany, Austria, 1955, 56, 60, 64. Author articles on chem. developments, European problems, housing and urban renewal problems, others. Mem. U.S. Nat. Commn., UNESCO, 1957-59; Chmn. Fresno City Housing Authority, 1951-69; vice chmn.

Fresno County Housing Authority, 1981—; pres. Nat. Assn. Housing and Redevel. Ofcls., 1960-61; mem. Calif. Commn. for Housing and Community Devel., 1966-67; Bd. dirs., vice chmn. Found. for Coop. Housing, 1965-80, chmn., 1981—. Served with AUS, 1943-46. Mem. Am. Econ. Assn., Phi Beta Kappa, Pi Gamma Mu, Beta Gamma Sigma. Office: 1515 E Shaw Fresno CA 93710

FALK, LEE HARRISON, author, director, producer; b. St. Louis; s. Benjamin and Eleanor (Allina) F.; m. Elizabeth Moxley, Dec. 31, 1976; children: Valerie, Diane, Conley. B.A., U. Ill. Pres. Provincetown (Mass.) Acad. of Arts, 1964-72, Truro (Mass.) Center for Arts at Castle Hill, 1979-82. Creator: comic strips Mandrake The Magician, 1934—, The Phantom, 1936—; producer, dir. summer theatres, 1940-60; Winkelberg, 1960; Author: plays Passionate Congressman, 1945, Eris, 1965, Home at Six, 1965, (with Alan Cranston) The Big Story, 1940; musicals Mandrake, 1974, (with John LaTouche) Happy Dollar, 1950. Served with AUS, 1944-45. Mem. Nat. Cartoonist Soc., Features Council, Dramatists Guild. Club: Players (N.Y.C.). Address: PO Box Z Truro MA 02666

FALK, MARSHALL ALLEN, physician, univ. dean and ofcl.; b. Chgo., May 23, 1929; s. Ben and Frances (Kamins) F.; m. Marilyn Joyce Levoff, June 15, 1952; children: Gayle Debra, Ben Scott. B.S., Bradley U., 1950; M.S., U. Ill., 1952; M.D., Chgo. Med. Sch., 1956. Diplomate: Am. Bd. Psychiatry. Intern Cook County Hosp., Chgo., 1956-57; resident Mt. Sinai Hosp., Chgo., 1964-67; gen. practice medicine, Chgo., 1959-64; resident in psychiatry, faculty dept. psychiatry Chgo. Med. Sch., 1964-67, prof., acting chmn. dept. psychiatry, 1973-74, dean, 1974—, v.p. med. affairs, 1981-82, exec. v.p., 1982—; med. dir. London Meml. Hosp., 1964-74; mem. cons. com. commr. health, City of Chgo., 1979—; mem. Gov.'s Commn. to Revise Mental Health Code Ill., 1973-77, Chgo. Northside Commn. on Health Planning, 1970-74, Ill. Hosp. Licensing Bd., 1981—. Contbr. articles to profl. jours. Served to capt. AUS, 1957-59. Recipient Bd. Trustees award for research Chgo. Med. Sch., 1963; Distinguished Alumni award Chgo. Med. Sch., 1976. Fellow Am. Psychiat. Assn., Am. Coll. Psychiatrists, Ill. Council Deans (pres. 1981—), Sigma Xi, Alpha Omega Alpha. Home: 3860 Mission Hills Rd Northbrook IL 60062 Office: 3333 Greenbay Rd North Chicago IL 60064 *Consistent effort, with an attempt to make decisions based on situations as they occur—with as little prejudgment as possible.*

FALK, PETER, actor; b. N.Y.C., Sept. 16, 1927; s. Michael and Madeline (Hauser) F.; m. Alyce Mayo, Apr. 17, 1960 (div. 1976); children: Jackie, Catherine; m. Shera Danese, Dec. 1977. B.A., New Sch. Social Research, 1951; M.P.A., Maxwell Sch., Syracuse U., 1953; pupil of, Eva Le Gallienne, 1955, Sanford Meisner, 1957. Theatrical appearances include Don Juan, 1956, The Changeling, 1956, The Iceman Cometh, 1956, St. Joan, 1956, Diary of a Scoundrel, 1956, The Lady's Not for Burning, 1957, Purple Dust, 1957, Bonds of Interest, 1956, Comic Strip, 1958, The Passion of Josef D, 1964, The Prisoner of Second Avenue; motion picture appearances include Murder, Inc, 1960, Pocketful of Miracles, 1961, The Balcony, 1962, It's a Mad, Mad, Mad, Mad World, 1963, Italiano Bravo-Gente, 1963, Robin and the 7 Hoods, 1964, The Great Race, 1965, Luv, 1967, Anzio, 1968, Castle Keep, 1969, Machine Gun McCann, 1970, Husbands, 1970, A Woman Under the Influence, 1976, Murder by Death, 1976, Mikey and Nicky, The Brink's Job, 1978, The Cheap Detective, 1978, The In-Laws, 1979; numerous TV appearances, 1960—; including Columbo in, NBC Mystery Theater, 1971-78, Phoenix and Griffin. Recipient Emmy award for TV prodn. The Price of Tomatoes, for best performance in Columbo, 1972. Address: care Creative Artists Agy 1888 Century Park E Los Angeles CA 90067

FALK, RICHARD SANDS, JR., brokerage firm executive; b. Milw., Aug. 26, 1941; s. Richard Sands and Dorothy Jane (Herman) F.; m. Dorothy Ann Johnson, Sept. 7, 1975; children: Burton, Brooke. B.A., Stanford U., 1963, postgrad., 1964-65; postgrad., Milw. Sch. Engring., 1966. Product mktg. mgr. Falk Corp., Milw., 1966-69; v.p. sales Mitchell Hutchins Co., N.Y.C., 1969-75; first v.p., nat. sales mgr. Paine Webber Mitchell, Hutchins, Inc., N.Y.C., 1976-78, sr. v.p., 1979—, also dir., mem. exec. com.; bd. counselors S.E. Asset Mgmt., Memphis; nat. adv. bd. AMR Internat., N.Y.C. Mem. Securities Industries Assn., Delta Sigma. Republican. Congregationalist. Club: DAC. Office: 140 Broadway New York NY 10005 *The single most important ingredient for success is determination.*

FALKER, JOHN RICHARD, food company executive; b. Detroit, July 15, 1940; s. John J. and Helen K. (Loeffler) F.; m. Mary Eileen Jacobsen, Nov. 7, 1964; children: Mary anne, John, Peter. B.A. in English, U. Mich., 1962; M.B.A. in Fin., U. Detroit, 1980. With Chrysler Corp., Detroit, 1964-77; v.p., treas. Chrysler Fin. Corp., 1974-77; treas. Internat. Multifoods Corp., Mpls., 1977—. Served to lt. (j.g.) USNR, 1962-64. Mem. Am. Radio Relay League (life). Republican. Roman Catholic. Clubs: Interlachen Country, Mpls. Athletic. Office: PO Box 2942 Minneapolis MN 55402

FALKNER, FRANK TARDREW, educator, physician; b. Hale, Eng., Oct. 27, 1918; came to U.S., 1956, naturalized, 1963; s. Ernest and Ethel (Letten) F.; m. June Dixon, Jan. 1948; 2 children. M.D., Cambridge U., 1945. Diplomate: Am. Bd. Clin. Nutrition. Intern London Hosp., 1945; resident Guys Hosp., London, 1947-48, Children's Hosp., Cin., 1948-50; practice medicine specializing in pediatrics, U.K. and, Paris, 1948-56, Louisville, 1956-70, Yellow Springs, Ohio, 1971—; chmn. dept. pediatrics U. Louisville, 1963-70; dir. Fels Research Inst., Yellow Springs, 1971-79; Fels prof. pediatrics, prof. obstetrics and gynecology U. Cin. Coll. Medicine, 1971-79; prof. child and family health U. Mich., 1979-81; prof. and chmn. maternal and child health U. Calif., Berkeley, 1981—. Contbr. articles to profl. jours.; syndicated columnist on children's and young people's health. Fellow Am. Acad. Pediatrics, Royal Coll. Physicians; mem. Am. Pediatric Soc., Soc. Pediatric Research. Home: 145 Forest Ln Berkeley CA 94708 Office: Maternal and Child Health Sch Public Health U Calif Berkeley CA 94720

FALKOW, STANLEY, microbiologist, educator; b. Albany, N.Y., Jan. 24, 1934; s. Jacob and Mollie (Gingold) F.; m. Rhoda Mae Falkow, Jan. 18, 1958; children: Lynn Beth, Jill Stuart.; m. Lucy Stuart Thompkins, Dec. 3, 1983. B.S. in Bacteriology cum laude, U. Maine, 1955, D.Sc. (hon.), 1979; M.S. in Biology, Brown U., 1960, Ph.D., 1961. Asst. chief dept. bacterial immunity Walter Reed Army Inst. Research, Washington, 1963-66; prof. microbiology Med. Sch. Georgetown U., 1966-72; prof. microbiology and medicine U. Wash., Seattle, 1972-80; prof., chmn. dept. med. microbiology Stanford (Calif.) U., 1981—; Karl H. Beyer vis. prof. U. Wis., 1978-79; Sommer lectr. U. Oreg. Sch. Medicine, 1979; Kinyoun lectr. NIH, 1980; Rubbro orator Australian Soc. Microbiology, 1981; Stanhope Bayne-Jones lectr. Johns Hopkins U., 1982; Mem. Recombinant DNA Molecule Com.; mem. task force on antibiotics in animal feeds FDA; mem. microbiology test com. Nat. Bd. Med. Examiners. Author: Infectious Multiple Drug Resistance, 1975; Editor: Jour. Bacteriology, Jour. Infection and Immunity, Jour. Infectious Diseases. Recipient Ehrlich prize, 1981. Fellow Am. Acad. Microbiology; mem. Infectious Disease Soc. Am. (Squibb award 1979), Am. Soc. Microbiology, Genetics Soc. Am., AAAS, Sigma Xi. Home: 87 Peter Coutts Circle Stanford CA 94305 Office: Dept Microbiology Stanford U Stanford CA 94305

FALLACI, ORIANA, author, journalist; b. Florence, Italy, June 29, 1930; d. Edoardo and Tosca (Cantini) F. Grad., Liceo Classico Galileo Galilei, Italy; student, U. Florence Faculty Medicine, 1946-48; Litt.D. (hon.), Columbia Coll., Chgo., 1977. Editor and spl. corr. Europeo Mag., Milan, Italy, 1958-77; collaborator with major publs. throughout world, including Look mag., Life mag., The Washington Post, N.Y. Times, London Times; dir. Rizzoli Pubs. Corp. Author: (essay) The Useless Sex, 1964; The Egotists, 1965; (novel) Penelope at War, 1966; (non-fiction) If the Sun Dies, 1967, Nothing and So Be It, 1972 (Bancarella award); Interview with History, 1976; (novel) Letter to a Child Never Born, 1977, A Man, 1979 (Viareggio prize award). Recipient St. Vincent award for Journalism, 1971, 73. Office: 712 Fifth Ave New York NY 10019

FALLDING, HAROLD JOSEPH, Sociology educator; b. Cessnock, New South Wales, Australia, May 3, 1923; s. Frederick and Alice Bessie (Chopping) F.; m. Margaret Hurlstone Hardy, Dec. 18, 1954; children: Marion, Ruth, Helen. Cert., Library Sch., Public Library of New South Wales, 1941; B.Sc., U. Sydney, Australia, 1950, B.A., 1951, diploma of edn., 1952, M.A. with honors, 1955; Ph.D., Australian Nat. U., 1957. Tchr. high sch. English and history New South Wales Dept. Edn., 1952-53; sr. research fellow in sociology, dept. agrl. econs. U. Sydney, 1956-58; sr. lectr. sociology U. New South Wales, 1959-62; vis. asso. prof. sociology Grad. Sch., Rutgers U., N.J., 1963-65; prof. sociology U. Waterloo, Ont., Can., 1965—. Author: The Sociological Task, 1968, The Sociology of Religion: An Explanation of the Unity and Diversity in Religion, 1974, Drinking, Community and Civilization. The Account of a New Jersey Interview Study, 1974; poems Word of the Tangling Fire, 1969. Mem. Clare Hall, U. Cambridge, 1971-72. Served in Australian Army, 1942-46. Fellow Royal Soc. Can.; mem. Am. Sociol. Assn., Can. Soc. Sociology and Anthropology, Internat. Sociol. Assn., Soc. Sci. Study of Religion, Assn. Sociology of Religion, Internat. Conf. Sociology of Religion, Can. Sci. and Christian Affiliation, Social Sci. Fedn. Can. (dir.). Mem. United Ch. Can. Club: Kitchener-Waterloo Torch. Office: U Waterloo Waterloo ON N2L 3G1 Canada *My life has seemed like a series of arrivals at the same crossroads, compelling me to confirm a decision on priorities made very early, that loyalty to truth comes before achievement. Any achievements have consequently seemed surprises - like spin-offs from giving effect to that loyalty.* *

FALLER, DONALD ELMER, marketing executive; b. Jersey City, Mar. 1, 1927; s. Louis John and Gertrude Louise (Hupfield) F.; m. Dolores Adeline Smith, Aug. 28, 1948; children: Mark William, Kyle Lindsay Fernandez, Kimberly Willard, Donald Mark, Krystn Judith, Kelly Bridget Christina. B.S., Mich. State U., 1948. Prodn. mgr. Sealtest Foods Kraft, Detroit, 1958-60, dist. mgr., 1960-67, div. mktg. mgr., Cleve., 1967-70; v.p. mktg. Citrus Central Inc., Orlando, Fla., 1970-78, exec. v.p. mktg. and adminstrn., 1978-83; gen. sales mgr. Sunkist Growers Inc., Ontario, Calif., 1984—; dir. Combank Apopka Freedom Savs. & Loan Assn., Winter Park, Fla. Bd. dirs. Pace Sch., Alamonte Springs, Fla., 1976-82. Mem. Blue Key, Alpha Zeta (pres. 1947-48). Republican. Roman Catholic. Clubs: Orlando Country; Sweetwater Country (Longwood, Fla.). Office: Sunkist Growers Sunkist Ave Ontario CA

FALLER, JAMES ELLIOT, physicist, educator; b. Mishawaka, Ind., Jan. 17, 1934; s. Elmer Edward and Leona Maxine (Forstbauer) F.; m. Elisabeth Andrea Jost, June 6, 1959; children: William Edward, Peter James. A.B. summa cum laude, Ind. U., 1955; M.A., Princeton U., 1957, Ph.D., 1963; M.A. (hon.), Wesleyan U., Middletown, Conn., 1972. Instr. Princeton U., 1959-62; mem. Joint Inst. Lab. Astrophysics, Boulder, Colo., 1963-66, fellow, 1972—; asst. prof. physics Wesleyan U., 1966-68, asso. prof. physics, 1968-71, prof., 1971—. Nat. Acad. Sci./NRC postdoctoral fellow, 1963-64; Sloan fellow, 1972-73; recipient Precision Measurement award Nat. Bur. Standards, 1970, Arnold O. Beckman award Instrument Soc. Am., 1970, Exceptional Sci. Achievement medal NASA, 1973. Mem. Am. Phys. Soc., AAAS, Am. Geophysical Union, Phi Beta Kappa, Sigma Xi. Home: 303 Hollyberry Ln Boulder CO 80303 Office: Joint Inst Lab Astrophysics Univ Colorado Boulder CO 80309

FALLETTA, JOHN MATTHEW, pediatrician; b. Arma, Kans., Sept. 3, 1940; s. Matthew John and Norma (Luke) F.; m. Carolyn Ontjes, June 22, 1963; children—Elizabeth, Matthew. A.B., U. Kans., 1962, M.D., 1966. Diplomate: Am. Bd. Pediatrics, with subsply. hematology-oncology. Resident in pediatrics Baylor Coll. Medicine; then hematology-oncology fellow; asso. prof. pediatrics Duke, no chief div. hematology-oncology, dir., 1976—. Served with USPHS, 1967-67. Mem. Am. Assn. Cancer Research, So. Soc. Pediatric Research (pres. 1981-82), Phi Beta Kappa, Alpha Omega Alpha. Office: PO Box 2916 Duke U Med Center Durham NC 27705

FALLOWS, JAMES MACKENZIE, editor; b. Phila., Aug. 2, 1949; s. James Albert and Jean (Mackenzie) F.; m. Deborah Jean Zerad, June 22, 1971; children: Thomas Mackenzie, Tad Andrew. B.A. magna cum laude, Harvard U., 1970; diploma in econ. devel. (Rhodes scholar), Oxford U., 1972. Staff editor Washington Monthly, 1972-74; freelance mag. writer, 1972-76; assoc. editor Tex. Monthly, 1974-76; chief speech-writer Pres. U.S., Washington, 1977-79; Washington editor Atlantic Monthly, 1979—. Author: National Defense, 1981; contbr. articles to numerous mags. and jours. Home: 4780 Dexter St Washington DC 20007 Office: Atlantic Monthly 8 Arlington St Boston MA 02116

FALLS, EDWARD JOSEPH, educator, business exec., lawyer; b. N.Y.C., Feb. 24, 1920; s. Edward A. and Anne (Sincher) F.; m. Marie A. Andreas, Aug. 23, 1942; children: Rita, Christina Falls Hutchison, Sharon Falls Cantello, Loretta Falls Greer. B.S., St. John's U., 1940, J.D., 1946; postgrad., Sch. Bus., Stanford U., 1959. Bar: N.Y. State 1947, Ill. 1955, Calif. 1979; Lic. real estate broker, Calif. Atty., asst. counsel Prudential Ins. Co., 1947-57; adminstrv. v.p. Pacific Fidelity Life Ins. Co., Los Angeles, 1957-60; v.p., gen. counsel, sec. Beneficial Standard Corp., Los Angeles, 1960-74; v.p., gen. counsel Beneficial Nat. Life Ins. Co., N.Y.C., 1974-77; exec. v.p., gen. counsel, sec., dir. Pelorus Group, Inc., N.Y.C., 1977-78; pres. Total Corporate Planning, Los Angeles, 1977-80; regional dir. legal and govt. relations Am. Internat. Group, 1977—; cons. Taxpayer Alert Com.; prof. Calif. State U., Long Beach, 1979—. Served with AUS, 1942-46; ETO. Mem. Am. Bar Assn., Calif. Bar Assn., Stanford Bus. Sch. Assn., Am. Soc. Corp. Secs., Assn. Life Ins. Counsel, Mensa, Phi Delta Phi. Office: 695 Town Center Dr Costa Mesa CA 92626

FALLS, JOSEPH FRANCIS, sports writer and editor; b. N.Y.C., May 2, 1928; s. Edward and Anna (Zincak) F.; m. Mary Jane Erdei, Oct. 10, 1975; children by previous marriage: Robert, Kathleen, Susan, Janet, Michael. Grad. high sch. Reporter AP, N.Y.C., 1946-56; sports writer Detroit Times, 1956-60; sports editor, sports writer Detroit Free Press, 1960-78; sports writer Detroit News, 1978—, sports editor, 1980—; columnist Sporting News, St. Louis, 1965—, Hockey News, Toronto, 1981; sports commentator WWJ Radio, Detroit, 1980. Author: Man in Motion, 1973, The Detroit Tigers, 1975, The Boston Marathon, 1977. Mem. Baseball Writers Assn. Am., Football Writers Assn. Am., Hockey Writers Assn., Pro Basketball Writers Assn., Golf Writers Assn. Home: 8115 Deerwood Rd Clarkston MI 48016 Office: Detroit News Detroit MI 48231

FALLS, RAYMOND LEONARD, JR, lawyer; b. Youngstown, Ohio, Feb. 24, 1929; s. Raymond Leonard and Vernita Belle (Bowden) F.; m. Alice Van Fleet, June 22, 1952; children: Janette Rae, Nancy Margaret, Raymond Taylor, Thomas Alan, Lawrence David. B.A., Coll. of Wooster, 1950; LL.B., Harvard U., 1953. Bar: N.Y. 1957, U.S. Supreme Ct. 1961. Law clk. to judge U.S. Ct. Appeals 2d Cir., 1955-56; assoc. Cahill, Gordon & Reindel, N.Y.C., 1956-63, ptnr., 1963—; assoc. adj. prof. NYU Law Sch., 1967-73. Mem. Mayor's Task Forces on Reorgn. Govt., N.Y.C, 1965-66. MEM. Am. Coll. Trial Lawyers; mem. ABA, Assn. Bar City N.Y. Office: Cahill Gordon & Reindel 80 Pine St New York NY 10005

FALLS, ROBERT, NATO official. Chmn. mil. com. NATO, Brussels. Office: Mil Com NATO Brussels Belgium 1110

FALLS, ROBERT GLENN, educator; b. Lubbock, Tex., Dec. 9, 1921; s. Cecil O. and Mamie Lou (Glenn) F.; m. Ruth A. Wagner, Apr. 5, 1942; children—Carolyn Ruth, Barbara Ann. A.B., Anderson Coll., 1948; M.B.A., Ind. U., 1950, D.B.A., 1954. C.P.A., Ind. Instr. Ind. U., Bloomington, 1948-52; instr. Anderson (Ind.) Coll., 1952-53, asst. prof., 1953-58, asso. prof., 1958-62, prof., 1962—; chmn. bd. Pay Less Supermarkets, Inc., Anderson, 1966—, Laymen Life Ins. Co., 1970—; dir. Anderson Banking Co., Conren, Duo, Action, other cos. Active Madison County United Way, 1965—. Served to 1st lt. U.S. Army, 1942-46. Recipient Alumni Disting. Service award Anderson Coll., 1981. Mem. Am. Inst. C.P.A.'s, Ind. Assn. C.P.A.'s, Am. Mgmt. Assn. Mem. Ch. of God. Club: Rotary (dir., treas. 1976-80). Home: 610 Maplewood Ave Anderson IN 46012 Office: E Fifth and College Sts Anderson IN 46012 *As much as possible I make life decisions on the basis of my Christian commitments and my understanding of my reason for being which springs from, or led to that commitment.*

FALOON, WILLIAM WASSELL, physician, educator; b. Pitts., July 6, 1920; s. Joseph Coulter and Martha Louise (Wassell) F.; m. Roberta Jane Emery, Sept. 11, 1948; children—Karen L., William Wassell, Nancy. B.A., Allegheny Coll., 1941; M.D., Harvard U., 1944. Diplomate: Am. Bd. Internal Medicine. Intern Pa. Hosp., Phila., 1944-45; asst. resident in medicine Albany (N.Y.) Hosp., 1945-46, resident in medicine, 1946-47; research fellow in medicine Harvard Med. Sch., Thorndike Meml. Lab., Boston City Hosp., 1947-48; asst. prof. oncology, instr. medicine Albany Med. Coll., 1948-50; instr. medicine State U. N.Y. Coll. Medicine, Syracuse, 1950-51, asst. prof., 1951-56, asso. prof., 1956-64, prof. medicine, 1964-68; program dir. Adult Clin. Research Center, Syracuse, 1965-68; physician-in-chief, dir. clin. research and edn. Santa Barbara (Calif.) Gen.-Cottage Hosps., 1968-69; prof. medicine U. Rochester (N.Y.) Sch. Medicine, 1969—; mem. Univ. Senate, 1971-74; mem. staff Strong Meml. Hosp., Rochester, Highland Hosp., 1969—, chief medicine, 1970-80, dir. gastroenterology and nutrition, 1970—. Mem. editorial bd.: Am. Jour. Clin. Nutrition, 1970-76; contbr. articles to profl. jours. Bd. mgrs. Camp Dudley YMCA, 1962-67, 69-74, chmn. bd., 1966-67, 71-73; bd. dirs. Onondaga County Met. Health Council, Syracuse, 1959-61; mem. adv. com. Onondaga County Health Dept., 1966-68. Fellow A.C.P., Rochester Acad. Medicine (dir. 1979—); mem. Am. Fedn. Clin. Research (councillor 1956-59), AAAS, Onondaga County Med. Soc. (exec. com. 1964-66), Am. Assn. for Study Liver Disease, Am. Inst. Nutrition, Am. Soc. Clin. Nutrition, Endocrine Soc., Am. Gastroent. Assn., Western Soc. for Clin. Research, Med. Soc. Monroe County, Internat. Assn. for Study Liver, Assn. Program Dirs. Internal Medicine (councillor 1978-80), Sigma Xi, Phi Delta Theta. Presbyterian (deacon 1958-61, elder 1963-65). Clubs: Gt. Lakes Interurban (sec. 1977—), Eastern Gut; Oak Hill Country (Rochester). Home: 4 Whitecliff Dr Pittsford NY 14534 Office: Highland Hosp South Ave Rochester NY 14620

FALSGRAF, WILLIAM WENDELL, lawyer; b. Cleve., Nov. 10, 1933; s. Wendell A. and Catherine J. F.; children: Carl Douglas, Jeffrey Price, Catherine Louise. A.B. cum laude, Amherst Coll., 1955; J.D., Case Western Res. U., 1958. Bar: Ohio 1958, U.S. Supreme Ct. 1972. Partner firm Baker & Hostetler, Cleve., 1971—; Chmn. vis. com. Case Western Res. U. Law Sch., 1973-76. Trustee Case Western Res., 1976—, chmn. bd. overseers, 1977-78; trustee Cleve. Health Mus. Recipient Disting. Service award; named Outstanding Young Man of Year Cleve. Jr. C. of C., 1962. Fellow Am. Coll. Probate Counsel, Am. Bar Found., Ohio Bar Found.; mem. ABA (chmn. young lawyers sect. 1966-67, mem. ho. of dels. 1967-68, 70—, bd. govs. 1971-74, asst. treas. 1972-73, pres.-elect 1984—, bd. dirs., v.p., treas. Am. Bar Endowment 1974—, chmn. standing com. on scope and correlation of work 1978-79), Ohio Bar Assn. (mem. council of dels. 1968-70), Cleve. Bar Assn. (trustee 1979—), Amherst Alumni Assn. (pres. N.E. Ohio 1964). Clubs: Union, Canterbury Golf. Home: 616 North St Chagrin Falls OH 44022 Office: 3200 National City Center Cleveland OH 44114

FALSONE, ANNE MARIE MCMAHON, state ofcl.; b. N.Y.C., May 20, 1937; d. Thomas Henry and Betty May (Stansel) McMahon; m. James H. Kennedy. B.S., Memphis State U., 1956, M.A., 1968; M.L.S., George Peabody Coll., Vanderbilt U., 1969. Head librarian White Station Jr./Sr. High Sch., Memphis, 1966-71; asst. head history dept. Memphis Public Library, 1971-72; cons. sch. libraries Colo. State Library, 1972-75; supr. state sch. library programs Colo. Dept. Edn., Denver, 1975-76; asst. commr. Office Library Services, 1976—; trustee Bibliog. Center Research, Nat. Rehab. Info. Center; mem. Western Council of State Libraries, Colo. Gov.'s Commn. on Public Telecommunications. Mem. ALA, Colo. Library Assn., Colo. Ednl. Media Assn., Chief Officers of State Library Agys., Colo. Assn. Scn. Execs., Phi Alpha Theta, Beta Phi Mu, Alpha Lambda Delta, Alpha Delta Pi. Home: 2835 S Monaco Pkwy Apt 2-108 Denver CO 80222 Office: 1362 Lincoln St Denver CO 80203 *Since I am the first woman to hold the rank of assistant commissioner, I am often asked what factors contributed to this. Sometimes I make the flippant response that any woman who is willing to work 70 hours a week can achieve the same position. Seriously, the answer is not that far off target. Somehow we must convince young women that there is a vast difference between a job and a career. Many women spend years of their lives working at a job when they might have chosen to have a career if they had realized the amount of their lifespan that would be spent in a work situation. To me the difference between a job and a career is directly realted to the commitment that exists and the goals which have been established. A job can just happen; a career takes careful planning.*

FALSTEIN, EUGENE I., psychoanalyst, psychiatrist; b. Chgo., Oct. 29, 1908; s. Samuel and Pearl (Levin) F.; m. Charlotte Rosenfield, Dec. 25, 1932. B.S., U. Ill., 1928, M.D., 1930; Rockefeller fellow psychoanalytic tng., Chgo. Inst. Psychoanalysis, 1936-42. Diplomate: Am. Bd. Psychiatry and Neurology. Intern psychiatry Elgin State Hosp., 1930-31, psychiatrist, 1933-37; intern Michael Reese Hosp. and Med. Center, Chgo., 1931-33, psychiat. clinic staff, 1933-40; now senior attending psychiatrist dept. of psychiatry, chief adolescent care Inst. Psychosomatic and Psychiat. Research and Tng.; faculty Northwestern U. Med. Sch., 1933-37; child psychiatrist Inst. Juvenile Research, 1937-42; asst. prof. dept. criminology U. Ill., 1937-51; attending psychiatrist children's div. Ill. Neuropsychiat. Inst., 1940-51; now clin. prof. emeritus in psychiatry Chgo. Med. Sch.; pvt. practice psychoanalysis and psychiatry, 1946—; psychiat. cons., adv. bd. Jewish Children's Bur.; hon. cons. Nicholas Pritzker Children's Center. Author sci. articles, chpts. in books. Bd. dirs. Am. Friends of Hebrew U., founder med. sch.; bd. dirs. Jewish Fedn. Met. Chgo., Am. Jewish

Physicians Com. Served as lt. comdr. USNR, 1942-46. Recipient Israel Scroll, 1957, Torch of Learning award Hebrew U., Jerusalem, 1976. Fellow Am. Psychiat. Assn. (life), Am. Orthopsychiat. Assn. (life), Am. Acad. Psychoanalysis (life), Am. Acad. Child Psychiatry (life), AMA; mem. Ill. Med. Soc. (life mem.; mem. 50 Yr. Club), Chgo. Psychoanalytic Soc. (life), Chgo. Neurol. Soc. (life), Am. Psychoanalytic Assn., Internat. Psychoanalytic Assn., AAAS, Pan Am. Med. Assn. (life), Chgo. Council Child Psychiatry (life mem., past pres.), Ill. Psychiat. Soc. (past sec., life mem.), Alpha Omega Alpha, Phi Delta Epsilon. Club: Ravisloe Country. Home: 1300 N Lake Shore Dr Chicago IL 60610 Office: 25 E Washington St Chicago IL 60602

FALSTEIN, LOUIS, author; b. Ukraine, May 1, 1909; U.S., 1925, naturalized, 1936; s. Joseph and Bessie (Kammerman) F.; m. Shirley Gesser, Apr. 9, 1949; children—Jessica, Joshua. Student, Lewis Inst., Chgo., 1930- 32, N.Y.U., 1946-48. Tchr. novel workshops N.Y.U., 1949-50; tchr. short story writing Coll. City N.Y., 1956. Author: Face of A Hero, 1950, Slaughter Street, 1953, Sole Survivor, 1954, Spring of Desire, 1958, Laughter On A Weekday, 1965, The Man Who Loved Laughter: The Story of Sholom Aleichem; biography, 1968; Editor: The Martyrdom of Polish-Jewish Physicians, 1963. Served with USAAF, 1943-45. Decorated Purple Heart, Air medal with three clusters. Mem. Authors League Am. Address: 2571 Hubbard St Brooklyn NY 11235

FALTER, VINCENT EUGENE, army officer; b. Akron, Ohio, Dec. 20, 1932; s Alois S. and Prunella (Scharf) F.; m Anna Marta Stephen, Sept. 6, 1958; children: Vincent Eugene, Laura Dianne. B.E., U. Nebr.-Omaha, 1963; grad., Command and Gen. Staff Coll., 1968, U.S. War Coll., 1973; M.P.A., Shippensburg State Coll., 1972. Served as enlisted U.S. Army, 1953, commd. 2d lt., 1954, advanced through grades to maj. gen., 1981, served with 750th F.A. Bn., Germany, 1954-57, served with Mortar Battery 2d BG 60th Inf., 1958-59, served with hdqrs. 1st Cav. Div., Korea, 1959-60, instr. F.A. Sch., 1960-63, battery comdg. officer 17th F.A. Bd., 1963-64, asst. G-1, 7th Army, Germany, 1964-66, exec. officer 2d Bn., 13th F.A. Bn., Vietnam, 1966-67; staff officer Dept. Army Office Dept. Chief of Staff for Ops., Washington, 1968-70; comdg. officer 2d Bn. 19th F.A. U.S. Army, Vietnam, 1970-71, exec. officer F.A. Br., Washington, 1971-72, sec. F.A. Sch., 1973-74, comdg. officer 75th F.A Group, 1974-76; dir. nuclear and chem. ops. Dept. Army, Office Dep. Chief of Staff for Ops., Washington, 1977-79; comdg. gen. VII Corps Arty. U.S. Army, Germany, 1979-81, dep. insp. gen., Washington, 1981-82, with Office Chief of Staff, 1982-83; comdg. gen. Mil Personnel Ctr., 1983—. Decorated Legion of Merit with 2 oak leaf clusters, Bronze Star with 3 oak leaf clusters, Air Medal with 15 oak leaf clusters. Mem. F.A. Assn. Roman Catholic. Club: Rotary Internat. Home: 7914 Colorado Springs Dr Springfield VA 22113 Office: Mil Personnel Ctr Alexandria VA 22332

FALWELL, JERRY L., clergyman; b. Lynchburg, Va., Aug. 11, 1933; s. Cary H. and Helen V. (Beasley) F.; m. Macel Pate, Apr. 12, 1958; children: Jerry L., Jeannie, Jonathan. B.A., Baptist Bible Coll., Springfield, Mo., 1956; D.D. (hon.), Tenn. Temple U., LL.D., Calif. Grad. Sch. Theology, Central U., Seoul, Korea. Ordained to ministry Bapt. Ch.; founder, 1956; since sr. pastor Thomas Rd. Bapt. Ch., Lynchburg; founder, 1979; since pres. Moral Majority Inc. Author: Listen, America!, 1980, The Fundamentalist Phenomenon, 1981, Finding Inner Peace and Strength, 1982, When It Hurts Too Much to Cry, 1984, Wisdom for Living, 1984, Stepping Out on Faith, 1984; co-author: Church Aflame, 1971, Capturing a Town for Christ, 1973. Recipient Clergyman of Year award Religious Heritage Am., 1979, Jabotinsky Centennial medal, 1980; named Christian Humanitarian of Year Food for the Hungry Internat., One of 20 Most Influential People in Am. U.S. News & World Report, 1982. Mem. Nat. Assn. Religious Broadcasters (dir.). Conservative. Address: Thomas Rd Bapt Ch Lynchburg VA 24514

FAMBROUGH, DON PRESTON, former football coach, government official; b. Longview, Tex., Oct. 19, 1922; s. Ivan Holt and Willie Albertine (Whittington) F.; m. Delfred Few, Oct. 4, 1941; children: James Preston, Robert Raymond. Student, U. Tex., 1941-42; B.S., U. Kans., 1948; postgrad., E. Tex. State U., 1952-53. Asst. football coach U. Kans., Lawrence, 1948-52, 58-69, head football coach, 1970-74, dir. pub. relations athletic dept., Lawrence, 1975-78, head football coach, 1978-82; now legis. rep. for Sen. Robert Dole; asst. football coach East Tex. State Coll., Commerce, 1952-56, Wichita (Kans.) U., 1956-57. Served with USAAF, 1943-46. Mem. Nat. Collegiate Athletic Assn. Club: Elks. Home: 1118 W Hills Pkwy Lawrence KS 66044

FAN, KY, educator, mathematician; b. Hangchow, China, Sept. 19, 1914; came to U.S., 1945, naturalized, 1954; s. Chi-Han and Wu-Shien (Fang) F.; m. Yu-Fen Yen, Apr. 26, 1936. B.S., Nat. Peking U., 1936; D.Sc. in Math., U. Paris, 1941. French Nat. Sci. fellow, charge de recherches Centre Nat. de la Recherche Scientifique, 1942-45; mem. Inst. for Advanced Study, 1945-47; faculty math. U. Notre Dame, 1947-60, prof., 1952-60; prof. math. Wayne State U., Detroit, 1960-61, Northwestern U., 1961-65; vis. prof. math. U. Tex., Austin, spring 1965; prof. math. U. Calif., Santa Barbara, 1965—, chmn. dept. math., 1968-69; vis. prof. math. U. Hamburg, Germany, summer 1972, U. Paris IX, Dauphine, fall 1981. Contbr. articles to math. jours. Mem. Academia Sinica, Am. Math. Soc., Math. Assn. Am. Home: 1402 Santa Teresita Dr Santa Barbara CA 93105

FANCHER, GEORGE HOMER, petroleum engr., cons.; b. San Francisco, Sept. 3, 1901; s. William Woodruff and Gertrude (Frisbie) F.; m. Mattie Stanfield, Sept. 10, 1931; children—Charles Cornell, George Homer, Carol Sue. B.S., U. So. Calif., 1923; Chem. Engr., U. Md., 1926, U. Mich., 1928; D.Sc., Colo. Sch. Mines, 1930. Chem. engr. Universal Oil Products Co., 1923-24; gas engr. C.C.M. Oil Co., 1924-25; instr. U. Md., 1925-26; research fellow U. Mich., 1926-28; instr. Colo. Sch. Mines, 1928-29, asst. prof., 1920-30, asso. prof., 1930-31; asst. prof. Pa. State U., 1931-34; petroleum engr. York State Oil Co., 1934-35; prof. petroleum engring. U. Tex. at Austin, 1935-39, grad. prof. petroleum engring., 1939-60, chmn. dept., 1956-60, George Homer Fancher prof. petroleum engring., 1981—; v.p. gen. mgr., dir. Sinclair Research, Inc., Tulsa, 1960-65; v. p., dir. Sinclair Oil & Gas Co., 1965-66; petroleum cons., Austin, 1966—; Cons. Ministry Mines and Petroleum, Alta., Can., 1948-49, Nat. Petroleum Council, Colombia, 1948-49, Ministry Mines and Petroleum, Venezuela, 1952-53, Empressa Colombiana de Petroleus, 1954-59, to pres. U. Americas, Mexico, 1969, 70, 71; Mem. Internat. Exec. Service Corps, 1966—; dir. Tex. Petroleum Research Com., 1949-60; adviser land commr., Tex.; mem. gov.'s com. Interstate Oil Compact Commn.; adviser formulation nat. policy of conservation, Colombia.; Adv. bd. Internat. Oil and Gas Center, S.W. Legal Found. U. Tex. at Dallas; bd. dirs. Colo. Sch. of Mines Research Found.; adv. bd. to trustees Colo. Sch. of Mines; dir. Internat. Petroleum Expn., 1963—. Author: Secondary Recovery of Petroleum in Arkansas, 1946, Oil Resources of Texas, 1954, Calculation of Flowing and Static Bottom Hole Pressures of Natural Gas Wells, 1959; Contbr. articles to various publs. Recipient Citation Venezuelan Govt., Distinguished Achievement medal Colo. Sch. Mines, 1963. Fellow Am. Inst. Chemists, Inst. Petroleum, Tex. Acad. Sci.; mem. Am. Inst. Mining Engrs. (John Franklin Carll award Soc. Petroleum Engrs. 1968), Am. Petroleum Inst., Am. Arbitration Assn. (nat. bd. arbitrators), Am. Chem. Soc. (emeritus mem.), A.I.M., S.A.R. (pres. Patrick Henry chapter Tex. 1969, registrar 1975—), Tex. Soc. Mayflower Descs. (surgeon 1981-82, gov. San Antonio colony 1981—), Huguenot Soc. Tex. (pres. chpt. 1979—), Sigma Xi (emeritus mem.), Tau Beta Pi, Phi Lambda Upsilon, Sigma Gamma Epsilon, Alpha Chi Sigma, Sigma Nu (past pres. home assn., chpt. advisor, Legion of Honor 1956), Pi Epsilon Tau (hon.). Episcopalian (vestry). Clubs: Headliners, Rotary, The Citadel, University (Austin, Tex.); American Club (Mexico City, Mexico). Home: 600 E 32d St Austin TX 78705

FANCHER, MICHAEL REILLY, newspaper editor; b. Long Beach, Calif., July 13, 1946; s. Eugene Arthur and Ruth Leone (Dickson) F.; m. Nancy Helen Edens, Nov. 3, 1967 (div. 1982); children: Jason Michael, Patrick Reilly; m. 2d Carolyn Elaine Bowers, Mar. 25, 1983. B.A., U. Oreg., 1968; M.S., Kans. State U., 1971. Reporter, asst. city editor Kansas City Star, Mo., 1970-76, city editor, 1976-78; reporter Seattle Times, 1978-79, night city editor, 1979-80, asst. mng. editor, 1980-81, mng. editor, 1981—. Ruhl fellow U. Oreg., 1983. Mem. Associated Press Mng. Editors, Soc. Profl. Journalists. Office: Seattle Times PO Box 70 Seattle WA 98111

FANESTIL, DARRELL DEAN, physician, educator; b. Great Bend, Kans., Oct. 31, 1933; s. Carl Leonard and Esther (Fail) F.; m. Dorthy Ann Smith, Aug. 14, 1955; children—Bradley, John, Jane, Katherine. B.A., U. Kans., 1955, M.D., 1958. Intern Los Angeles Gen. Hosp., 1958; fellow Lahey Clinic, Boston, 1959, Scripps Clinic and Research Found., La Jolla, Calif., 1960-62, U. Calif., San Francisco, 1964-66; asst. prof. Kans. U. Med. Sch., 1966-68, asso. prof., 1968-70, U. Calif., San Diego, 1970-72, prof., 1972—; mem. staff Univ. Hosp. San Diego; established investigator Am. Heart Assn., 1966-71. Served with USPHS, 1962-64. Markle scholar in acad. medicine, 1966-71. Mem. Am. Soc. Nephrology, Am. Physiol. Soc., Am. Fedn. Clin. Research, Am. Soc. Clin. Investigation. Home: 8491 Cliffridge Ln La Jolla CA 92037 Office: U Calif San Diego La Jolla CA 92093

FANG, BERTRAND TIEN-CHUEH, research co. exec.; b. Nanking, China, Feb. 2, 1932; came to U.S., 1955, naturalized, 1972; s. Thome H. and Lillian (Kao) F.; m. Bernice B. Feng, June 25, 1960; children—Elaine, Daniel, Harry, Roger, Constance. B.S., Nat. Taiwan U., 1952; M.S., Ia. State U., 1957; Ph.D., U. Minn., 1962. Research fellow U. Minn., 1957-61; mech. engr. Advanced Tech. Lab., Gen. Electric Co., 1962-63; asst. prof. The Catholic U. Am., 1963-65, asso. prof., 1965-69, prof., 1969-74; sr. sci. specialist EG & G Wolf Research & Devel. Corp., Riverside, Md., 1974-77, prin. scientist, 1977-79; sr. prin. engr. Computer Scis. Corp., Silver Spring, Md., 1979—. Home: 15005 Argyle Club Rd Silver Spring MD 20906 Office: 8728 Colesville Rd Silver Spring MD 20910

FANG, CHING SENG, civil engr., marine scientist, educator; b. Chung-Ching, China, Nov. 23, 1938; came to U.S., 1962, naturalized, 1972; s. Tien and Funchuen I. F.; m. Carol Sang, June 18, 1966; children—Edward, James. B.S., Nat. Taiwan U., 1961; M.S., N.C. State U., 1964, Ph.D., 1969. Research asst. dept. agrl. engring. N.C. State U., 1962-64, teaching asst., 1964-65, research asst. dept. civil engring., 1965-67, research asso. and teaching asst. dept. engring. mechanics and civil engring., 1967-68; research engr. Camp Dresser & McKee Co., Boston, 1968-69; asst. prof., marine scientist Va. Inst. Marine Sci., U. Va. and Coll. William and Mary, Gloucester Point, 1969-70, head dept. phys. oceanography and hydraulics, 1970—; asso. prof. marine sci. U. Va. and Coll. William and Mary, 1974-78, prof., 1979—; gen. mgr. Coastal Environ. Assos., Gloucester Point, 1971—; cons. environ. engring. UN, 1976. Contbr. numerous articles on hydrodynamics, environ. engring., marine sci. to profl. jours. Mem. ASCE, Am. Geophys. Union. Office: Va Inst Marine Sci Gloucester Point VA 23062

FANG, JOONG, philosophy educator; b. Piongyang, Korea, Mar. 30, 1923; came to U.S., 1948, naturalized, 1962; s. Gabiong and Igab (Kim) F.; children: Eva Maria, Guido Andreas. Student, Chuo U., Tokyo, 1939-41; B.S., Coll. Tech. Seoul, Korea, 1944; M.A., Yale U., 1950; Dr.Phil., U. Mainz, Germany, 1957. Asst. prof. math. Jinhae Coll., also U. Pusan, Korea, 1945-48, Valparaiso (Ind.) U., 1958-59, St. John's U., 1959-61, U. Alaska, 1961-62; assoc. prof. No. Ill. U., 1963-67; prof. math. and philosophy Memphis State U., 1967-73; prof. philosophy Old Dominion U., Norfolk, Va., 1974—; vis. prof. U. Münster, Germany, 1971. Author: Das Antinomienproblem, 1957, Abstract Algebra, 1963, Kant-Interpretationen, I, 1967, Towards a Philosophy of Modern Mathematics, I, 1970, II, 1970, Mathematicians from Antiquity to Today, I, 1972, Sociology of Mathematics and Mathematicians, 1975, The Illusory Infinite: A Theology of Mathematics, 1976, Logic Today, Basics and Beyond, 1979; editor: Philosophia Mathematica, 1964—. Mem. Am. Math. Soc., Am. Philos. Assn., Math. Assn. Am. Address: 251 Portview Norfolk VA 23503

FANGER, DONALD LEE, educator; b. Cleve., Dec. 6, 1929; s. Max Leon and Rae (Bercu) F.; m. Margot Taylor, June 18, 1955; children: Steffen, Ross, Katharine. B.A., U. Calif.-Berkeley, 1951, M.A., 1954; Ph.D., Harvard U., 1962. Mem. faculty Brown U., 1960-66, asso. prof. Slavic langs. and lit., 1964-66; asso. prof. Slavic, dir. div. Stanford U., 1966-68; prof. Slavic and comparative lit. Harvard U., 1968—, chmn. dept. Slavic langs. and lits., 1973-82; mem. bd. syndics Harvard U. Press, 1968-73. Author: Dostoevsky and Romantic Realism, 1965, The Creation of Nikolai Gogol, 1979; editor: Brown U. Slavic Reprint Series, 1962-66. Mem. program com. Internat. Research and Exchanges Bd., 1968-69, 70-73. Served with AUS, 1953-55. Guggenheim Found. fellow, 1975-76. Mem. MLA, Am. Acad. Arts and Scis., Acad. Lit. Studies, Internat. Comparative Lit. Assn. Home: 74 Putnam St West Newton MA 02165 Office: Boylston Hall Harvard Univ Cambridge MA 02138

FANNIN, WILLIAM WARNER, JR., curator; b. San Antonio, Tex., June 15, 1946. B.A., U. Tex., Austin, 1974, postgrad., 1974-76. Curator exhibits San Jacinto Mus. History, Deer Park, Tex., 1975-76; asst. dir. The Spindletop Mus., Beaumont, Tex., 1976-78; curator Jefferson Landing State Historic Site, Mo. State Mus., Jefferson City, 1979—. Served with USN, 1968-71. Mem. Am. Assn. State and Local History, Mo. Museums Assos., Mo. Civil War Re-enactors Assn., Tex. Assn. Museums, Co. Mil. Historians. Office: PO Box 176 Jefferson City MO 65102

FANNING, BARRY HEDGES, lawyer; b. Olney, Tex., Dec. 5, 1950; s. Robert Allen and Carolyn (Parker) F.; m. Rebecca Sue Cobbs, May 24, 1975. B.B.A., Baylor U., 1972, LL.B., 1973. Bar: Tex. 1973, Fla. 1974. Mem. firm Fanning, Harper, Wilson, Martinson & Fanning, Dallas, 1974—. Social v.p. Dallas Symphony Orch. Guild, 1975-77; mem. Dallas Metro Young Life Bd., 1977—, fund raising chmn., 1982-84. Mem. Am. Bar Assn. (vice-chmn. young lawyers com. 1980, public relations com. torts sect.), Baylor U. Student Found. (steering com. 1971-72), Baylor Alumni Assn. (dir. 1978-82), Tryon Coterie (pres. 1971), Phi Eta Sigma, Omicron Kappa Delta. Baptist. Clubs: Dervish, Calyx, Dallas Baylor (dir. 1976—), Dallas Baylor (pres. 1981-82), Christian Men's (Dallas)). Home: 3319 Milton Dallas TX 75205 Office: 4303 N Central Expressway Dallas TX 75205

FANNING, KATHERINE WOODRUFF, editor; b. Chgo., Oct. 18, 1927; d. Frederick William and Katherine Bower (Miller) Woodruff; m. Marshall Field, Jr., May 12, 1950 (div. 1963); children: Frederick Woodruff, Katherine Woodruff, Barbara Woodruff; m. Lawrence S. Fanning, 1966 (div. 1971); m. Amos Mathews, Jan. 6, 1984. B.A., Smith Coll., 1949; LL.D. (hon.), Colby Coll., 1979; Litt. D. (hon.), Pine Manor Jr. Coll., 1984; L.H.D. (hon.), Northeastern U., 1984. With Anchorage Daily News, 1965—, editor, pub., 1972-83; editor The Christian Science Monitor, 1983—. Mem. Anchorage Urban Beautification Commn., 1968-71, Alaska Ednl. Broadcasting Commn., 1971-75; dir. Alaska Repertory Theater, 1975-81; pres. Greater Anchorage Community Chest, 1973-74. Recipient Elijah Parish Lovejoy award Colby Coll., 1979; Smith Coll. medal, 1980; Mo. medal of Honor, U. Mo. Journalism award, 1980. Mem. Am. Soc. Newspaper Editors (dir., treas. 1984), Sigma Delta Chi. Office: One Norway St Boston MA 02115

FANNING, LOUIS ALBERT, historian, educator; b. Berwyn, Ill., Jan. 31, 1927; s. Louis Albert and Alice Winifred (Moysey) F.; m. Helen Marie Hoffsommer, July 14, 1952; children: Jeanne, Kurt. B.A., U. Ill., 1951; M.A., C.W. Post Coll., L.I. U., 1966; Ph.D., St. John's U., Jamaica, N.Y., 1975. Personnel dir., various cos. in pvt. industry, 1953-63; instr. SUNY, Farmingdale, 1963-66, asst. prof. history, 1966-68, asso. prof., 1968-75, prof., 1975—; spl. cons. on student affairs to pres. U. Hartford, Conn., 1968; adv. to Senate Fgn. Relations Com., 1967; vis. lectr. Vietnamese studies U.S. Army Spl. Warfare Center, Ft. Bragg, N.C., 1967. Author: Betrayal in Vietnam, 1975. Served to maj. U.S. Army, 1951-53; Japan. Mem. Conservative Historians' Forum, Irish-Am. Soc. (dir. 1974-75), SAR. Republican. Research on Versailles Treaty. Office: SUNY Melville Rd Farmingdale NY 11735
Determination in the face of adversity, perseverance in the attainment of goals, and loyalty to my family and friends have been the guiding principles of my life. Whatever success I have enjoyed in this world has been due, in part, to the following of these principles, the inspiration of some great teachers, a helpful family and a few strong friends.

FANNING, WILLIAM JAMES, baseball club official; b. Chgo., Sept. 14, 1927; s. Frank and Gladys Leona (Lighter) F. B.A. in phys. edn., Buena Vista Coll, 1951; M.Phys. Edn., U. Ill., 1961. Profl. baseball player Chgo. Cubs, 1954, 56, 57; player, mgr. Tulsa Oilers, Tex. League, 1958, Dallas Rangers, Am. Assn., 1959-60, Venezuela, Eau Claire Braves, Wis., 1961-62; spl. assignment scout Milw. Braves, 1963-64, asst. gen. mgr., 1964-66; asst. gen. mgr., farm and scouting dir. Atlanta Braves, 1966-67; 1st dir. Major League Scouting Bur., 1967-68; gen. mgr. Montreal Expos., 1968-73, v.p., gen. mgr., 1973-77, v.p. player devel., 1977-81, field mgr., 1981-82, v.p. player devel. and scouting, 1982—; mem. numerous Major League coms. Service with U.S. Army, 1945-47. Methodist. Office: PO Box 500 Station M Montreal Canada PQ H1V 3P2

FANO, ROBERT MARIO, educator; b. Torino, Italy, Nov. 11, 1917; came to U.S., 1939, naturalized, 1947; s. Gino and Rosetta (Cassin) F.; m. Jacqueline M. Crandall, Mar. 26, 1949; children—Paola C., Linda, Carl. B.S. in Elec. Engring, Mass. Inst. Tech., 1941, Sc.D., 1947. Teaching asst. elec. engring. dept. Mass. Inst. Tech., 1941-43, instr., 1943-44, staff mem., 1944-46, research asso. elec. engring. dept. and research lab. electronics, 1946-47, asst. prof. elec. engring dept., 1947-51, group leader, 1950-53, asso. prof. elec. engring. dept., 1951-56, prof., 1956-62, Ford prof., 1962—; dir. Project MAC, 1963-68, asso. head for computer sci. and engring. elec. engring. dept., 1971-74; cons. to indsl. labs. Author: (with R. B. Adler and L. J. Chu) Electromagnetic Fields, Energy and Forces; Electromagnetic Energy Transmission and Radiation, 1960, Transmission of Information, 1961. Fellow IEEE (Ednl. medal 1977), Nat. Acad. Scis., Nat. Acad. Engring., Am. Acad. Arts and Scis.; mem. Assn. Computing Machinery, Sigma Xi, Eta Kappa Nu. Home: 9 Edmonds Rd Concord MA 01742 Office: Mass Inst Tech Cambridge MA 02139

FANO, UGO, physicist, educator; b. Turin, Italy, July 28, 1912; came to U.S., 1939, naturalized, 1945; s. Gino and Rosa (Cassin) F.; m. Camilla V. Lattes, Feb. 8, 1939; children: Mary, Virginia. Sc.D., U. Turin, 1934; D.Sc. (hon.), Queen's U., Belfast, No. Ireland, 1978, U. Pierre and Marie Curie, Paris, 1979. Lectr., U. Rome, 1937-38; fellow, resident investigator Carnegie Instn., Washington, 1940-46; cons. ballistition U.S. Army Ordnance, 1944-45; physicist X-ray sect. Nat. Bur. Standards, Washington, 1946-49, chief radiation theory sect., 1949-60, sr. research fellow, 1960-66; prof. physics James Franck Inst., U. Chgo., 1966-82, prof. emeritus, 1982—, chmn. dept., 1972-74; lectr. George Washington U., 1946-47; vis. prof. U. Calif., Berkeley, summer 1958, 68, Cath. U., Washington, 1963-64. Author: (with G. Racah) Irreducible Tensorial Sets, 1959, (with L. Fano) Basic Physics of Atoms and Molecules, 1959, Physics of Atoms and Molecules, 1972; also articles. Recipient Rockefeller Pub. Service award, 1956, Exceptional Service award Dept. Commerce, 1957; Stratton award Nat. Bur. Standards, 1963; Davisson-Germer prize Am. Phys. Soc., 1976. Mem. Nat. Acad. Scis., Am. Acad. Arts and Scis., Am. Phys. Soc., Radiation Research Soc. Home: 5801 S Dorchester Ave Chicago IL 60637

FANSHEL, DAVID, social worker; b. N.Y.C., July 29, 1923; s. Hyman and Clara (Kratchman) F.; m. Florence Greenberg, Apr. 10, 1949; children—Ethan Jules, Merrie Lee. B.S.S., CCNY, 1947; M.S., N.Y. Sch. Social Work, 1947; D.S.W. (fellow Russell Sage Found. 1957-59), Columbia U., 1960. Research dir. Family and Children's Service, Pitts., 1955-58; dir. research Child Welfare League Am., 1958-63; mem. faculty Columbia U. Sch. Social Work, 1962—, prof. social work, 1965—. Co-author: Therapeutic Discourse, 1977, Children in Foster Care, 1978. Served with USAAF, 1942-45. Decorated D.F.C., Air medal. Mem. AAUP, Am. Sociol. Assn., Nat. Assn. Social Workers. Home: 537 Cumberland Ave Teaneck NJ 07666 Office: 622 W 113th St New York NY 10025

FANT, EUGENE ROBERT, steel co. exec.; b. Cleve., Jan. 17, 1919; m. Fay F., Nov. 17, 1959; children—Glenda, Nancy, Robert, Richard, Gina. With U.S. Steel Corp., 1939-41; with New Process Steel Corp., Houston, 1945—, now pres., chief exec. officer. Served with USAAF, 1941-45. Republican. Methodist. Office: New Process Steel Corp 5800 Westview Dr Houston TX 77055 *

FANTA, PAUL EDWARD, educator, chemist; b. Chgo., July 24, 1921; s. Joseph and Marie (Zitnik) F.; m. LaVergne Danek, Sept. 3, 1949; children—David, John. B.S., U. Ill., 1942; Ph.D., U. Rochester, 1946. Postdoctoral research fellow U. Rochester, 1946-47; instr. Harvard, 1947-48; mem. faculty Ill. Inst. Tech., 1948—, prof. chemistry, 1961—; exchange scholar Czechoslovak Acad. Sci., Prague, 1963-64, Soviet Acad. Sci., Moscow, 1970-71. Contbr. articles to profl. jours. NSF fellow Imperial Coll., London, Eng., 1956-57. Mem. Am. Chem. Soc., AAAS, ACLU, Sigma Xi, Phi Lambda Upsilon. Home: 947 S Clinton Ave Oak Park IL 60304 Office: Ill Inst Tech Tech Center Chicago IL 60616

FANTON, JONATHAN FOSTER, university president; b. Mobile, Ala., Apr. 29, 1943; s. Dwight F. F. and Marion (Foster) Fantan Bemer. B.A., Yale U., 1965, M.Phil., Ph.D., 1978. Carnegie teaching fellow in history Yale U., 1965-66, lectr. history, 1966-78, coordinator spl. ednl. programs, 1968-70, spl. asst. to pres., 1970-73, exec. dir. Summer Plans, 1973-76, assoc. provost, 1976-78; v.p. acad. resources and instn. planning U. Chgo., 1978-82; pres. New Sch. Social Research, N.Y.C., 1982—. Editor: John Brown. Trustee Bank St. Coll., N.Y.C., 1983—. Mem. Am. Hist. Assn. Clubs: Quadrangle (Chgo.); Yale (N.Y.C.); Lawn (New Haven). Home: 21 W 11th St New York

NY 10011 Office: New Sch for Social Research 66 W 12th St New York NY 10011

FANUCCI, JEROME BENEDICT, educator; b. Glen Lyon, Pa., Oct. 7, 1924; s. Benjamin and Celia (Lanuti) F.; m. Janice C. Bavitz, Jan. 26, 1952; children—Jerome Paul, Karen Marie. B.S. in Aero. Engring, Pa. State U., 1944, M.S., 1952, Ph.D., 1956. Aero. engr. Eastern Aircraft Corp., Trenton, N.J., 1944-45, Republic Aviation Corp., Farmingdale, N.Y., 1947-49; asst. prof. aerospace engring. Pa. State U., 1956-57; research engr. Gen. Electric Aerospace Sci. Lab., Phila., 1957-59; sr. research scientist Plasma and Space Applied Physics Lab., RCA, Princeton, N.J., 1959-64; prof. aerospace engring. W.Va. U., Morgantown, 1964—, chmn. dept., 1964-81; indsl. cons. Contbr. articles profl. jours. Served with USAAF, 1946-47. Fellow Am. Inst. Aeros. and Astronautics (asso.); mem. Am. Radio Relay League, Am. Soc. for Engring. Edn., Sigma Xi, Sigma Gamma Tau, Pi Tau Sigma. Co-designer first STOL aircraft using circulation control wing. Home: 1313 Anderson Ave Morgantown WV 26505

FANWICK, ERNEST, lawyer, business executive; b. N.Y.C., Feb. 28, 1926; s. Jacob and Jeanette (Lossof) F.; m. Lee Nathan, Sept. 1, 1951; children: Lewis Leslie, Eric. B.E.E., Pa. State U., 1948; J.D., Columbia U., 1951. Bar: N.Y. 1952, U.S. Patent Office 1952, U.S. Ct. Appeals (2d cir.) 1952, U.S. Ct. Appeals (fed. cir.) 1982, U.S. Supreme Ct. 1958. Sr. patent atty. ITT Fed. Telephone Labs., Nutley, N.J., 1951-55; div. counsel Avion div. ACF, Paramus, N.J., 1955-57; patent counsel Burndy Corp., Norwalk, Conn., 1957-65, dir. legal dept., 1965-75, gen. counsel, 1975-82, v.p., counsel, sec., 1982—; mem. faculty Practising Law Inst., N.Y.C., 1964—; lectr. Conf. Legal Execs., Pa., 1970, 72. Bd. dirs. Aid to Retarded, Stamford, Conn., pres., Stamford, Conn., 1982; arbirtator Am. Arbitration Assn. Mem. ABA, Am. Patent Law Assn., Am. Soc. Corp. Secs., Conn. Patent Law Assn. (pres. 1966), N.Y. Patent Law Assn., Westchester-Fairfield Corp. Counsel Assn. Club: Masons. Home: 1403 Newfield Ave Stamford CT 06905 Office: Burndy Corp Richards Ave Norwalk CT 06856

FARABOW, FORD FRANKLIN, JR., lawyer; b. Charlotte, N.C., Jan. 6, 1938; s. Ford Franklin and Louise (Botts) F.; children—Ford Franklin, III, Amy Kathryn, Andrew Leighton. B.S. in Chem. Engring, Clemson U., 1959; J.D. with honors, George Washington U., 1963. Bar: D.C. bar 1965, S.C. bar 1963. With law dept. Swift & Co., Washington, 1959-62; asso. firm Nexsen & Pruet, Columbia, S.C., 1962-64; with patent dept. Hercules, Inc., Wilmington, Del., 1964-65; partner firm Finnegan, Henderson, Farabow, Garrett & Dunner, Washington, 1965—; lectr. to Am. Bar Assn., Am. Patent Law Assn., also others. Contbr. articles to profl. publs. Mem. Am., S.C. bar assns., Am. Judicature Soc., Bar Assn. D.C., Am. Patent Law Assn., U.S. Trademark Assn. (chmn. internat. adv. group), Am. Chem. Soc., Clemson U. Alumni Assn., Tiger Brotherhood, Order of Coif, Phi Eta Sigma, Delta Theta Phi. Clubs: Bethesda (Md.) Country; Touchdown, Nat. Lawyers (Washington); Clemson IPTAY. Home: 5511 Greystone Chevy Chase MD 20815 Office: 1775 K St NW Washington DC 20006

FARAGE, DONALD J., lawyer. A.B., U. Pa., 1930, LL.B. with 1st honors, 1933; LL.D. hon., Dickinson Sch. Law, 1966. Bar: Pa. 1933. Asst. to prof. Francis H. Bohlen, reporter for Restatement of Torts, 1933-36; prof. law Dickinson Sch. Law, 1934-46, 50—, George Washington U. Law Sch., 1948-50; former sr. ptnr. firm Farage & Colleran, Phila.; now sr. ptnr. firm Farage & McBride, Phila.; vis. prof. med. jurisprudence Jefferson Med. Coll., Phila., 1948-76. Author: Pennsylvania Annotations to Restatement of Restitution, 1940, Pennsylvania Annotations to Restatement Judgements, 1957; co-editor: Hazards of Medication, 1971, 2d edit., 1978. Fellow Law Sci. Acad.; fellow Internat. Soc. Barristers (dir. 1971-74), Am. Coll. Trial Lawyers, Internat. Acad. Law and Sci., Southwestern Legal Found., Internat. Acad. Trial Lawyers (pres. 1970-71); mem. ABA (council, chmn. com. on rules and procedure, sect. ins., negligence and compensation law 1971-73, mem. council sect. torts and ins. practice law 1977-81, chmn. class actions com. 1981-83, chmn. motions and resolutions com. 1983—), Pa. Bar Assn. (ho. of dels. 1966-73, 75-78, 82—), Phila. Bar Assn., Assn. Trial Lawyers Am. (v.p. Pa. chpt. 1956-58). Club: Lawyers (Phila.). Office: 836 Suburban Sta Bldg 1617 John F Kennedy Blvd Philadelphia PA 19103

FARAH, CAESAR ELIE, Middle Eastern and Islamic studies educator; b. Portland, Oreg., Mar. 13, 1929; s. Sam Khalil and Lawrice F.; m. Marsha B. McDonald, June 5, 1977; children by previous marriage: Ronald, Christopher, Ramsey, Laurence, Raymond, Alexandra. Student, Internat. Coll. Beirut, 1941-45; B.A., Stanford U., 1952; M.A., Princeton U., 1955, Ph.D., 1957. Pub. affairs asst., cultural affairs officer ednl. exchanges USIS, New Delhi, 1957-58, Karachi, Pakistan, 1958; asst. to chief Bur. Cultural Affairs, Washington, 1959; asst. prof. history and Semitic langs. Portland State U., 1959-63; asst. prof. history Calif. State U.-Los Angeles, 1963-64; assoc. prof. Near Eastern studies Ind. U., Bloomington, 1964-69; prof. Middle Eastern and Islamic studies U. Minn., Mpls., 1969—; cons. U.S. Army, 1962-63; vis. prof. Harvard U., summers 1964-65; guest lectr. Fgn. Ministry, Spain, Iraq, Lebanon, Ministry Higher Edn., Saudi Arabia, Syrian Acad. Scis.; resource person on Middle East, media and service group Minn., 1977—. Author: The Addendum in Medieval Arabic Historiography, 1968, Islam: Beliefs and Observances, 2d edit., 1981, Eternal Message of Muhammad, 1964, 3d edit., 1981, (3 vols.) Ta'rikh Baghdad li-Ibn-al-Najjar, 1980-83; contbr. articles to profl. jours. Mem. Oreg. Republican Com., 1960-64. Recipient cert. of merit Syrian Ministry Higher Edn.; Fulbright Hayes scholar, 1966-68; fellow Am. Philos. Soc., 1970-71; grantee others. Mem. Stanford U. Alumni Assn. (leadership recognition award), Stanford Club Minn. (dir., pres. 1979), Am. Oriental Soc., Royal Asiatic Soc. Gt. Britain, Am. Hist. Assn., Middle East Studies Assn. N.Am., Am. Assn. Tchrs. Arabic (exec. bd.), Pi Sigma Alpha. Greek Orthodox. Club: Princeton. Home: 3847 York Ave S Minneapolis MN 55410 Office: Univ Minn 160 Klaeber Ct Minneapolis MN 55455

FARAH, JOSEPH FRANCIS, newspaper editor, writer; b. Paterson, N.J., July 6, 1954; s. John Joseph and Loretta Gertrude (Comeau) F.; m. Judith Gale Smagula, Apr. 16, 1983. B.A., William Paterson Coll., 1977. Reporter, editor Pascack Publs., Park Ridge, N.J., 1977-78; reporter Paterson News, 1978, news editor, 1978; asst. news editor Herald Examiner, Los Angeles, 1979-80, news editor, 1980-82, exec. news editor, Los Angeles, Los Angeles, 1979-80; instr. UCLA, 1982. Mem. Religion Newswriter Assn., Soc. Profl. Journalists. Baptist. Office: Los Angeles Herald Examiner 1111 S Broadway Los Angeles CA 90015

FARARO, THOMAS JOHN, sociologist, educator; b. N.Y.C., Feb. 11, 1933; s. Joseph and Anna (Marcello) F.; m. Irene Johanna Famasch, Dec. 30, 1955; children: Ramona, Raymond D. B.A., CCNY, 1959; Ph.D., Syracuse U., 1963. Asst. prof. sociology Syracuse U., 1963-64; vis. scholar Stanford U., 1964-67; prof. sociology U. Pitts., 1967—, chmn. dept. sociology, 1980—. Author: Mathematical Sociology, 1973, Mathematical Sociology, Japanese translation, 1980; assoc. editor: Jour. of Math. Sociology, 1978—; mem. editorial bd. (Am. Jour. Sociology), 1977-79, Am. Sociol. Rev., 1980-82. Served with USAF, 1952-56. Grantee Social Sci. Research Council, 1968, NSF, 1969-72. Mem. Am. Sociol. Assn., Soc. Gen. Systems Research, Internat. Network for Social Network Analysis. Office: Department of Sociology Univ Pitts 230 Boquet St Pittsburgh PA 15260 *I have devoted my intellectual life to the advancement of theoretical sociology by the use of mathematical methods in presenting theories, clarifying and formalizing concepts, representing social processes and social structures, and explaining social phenomena.*

FARBER, BERNARD, educator, sociologist; b. Chgo., Feb. 11, 1922; s. Benjamin and Esther (Axelrod) F.; m. Annette Ruth Shugan, Dec. 21, 1947 (div. 1970); children—Daniel, Michael, Lisa, Jacqueline; m. Rosanna Bodanis, June 10, 1971; 1 dau., Tanya. A.B., Roosevelt U., Chgo., 1943; A.M., U. Chgo., 1949, Ph.D., 1953. Research asso. U. Chgo., 1951-53; asst. prof. Henderson State Tchr. Coll., Arkadelphia, Ark., 1953-54; mem. faculty U. I., 1954-71, prof. sociology, 1964-71; asso. dir. Inst. Research Exceptional Children, 1967-69; prof. Ariz. State U., 1971—, chmn. dept. sociology, 1971-75; cons. in field, 1957—. Author: Family: Organization and Interaction, 1964, Mental Retardation: Its Social Context and Social Consequences, 1968, Kinship and Class, 1971, Guardians of Virtue, 1972, Family and Kinship in Modern Society, 1973, Conceptions of Kinship, 1981. Mem. mental retardation research com. Nat. Inst. Child Health and Human Devel., 1971-75. Served with AUS, 1943-46. Recipient E.W. Burgess award Nat. Council on Family Relations, 1975; Disting. Research award Ariz. State U., 1980. Mem. Am. Sociol. Assn. (council mem. family sect. 1966-69), Ill. Sociol. Assn. (founding pres. 1965-66), Am. Anthrop. Assn. Jewish. Home: 739 E Loyola Tempe AZ 85282 Office: Dept Sociology Ariz State U Tempe AZ 85287

FARBER, EMMANUEL, pathologist, biochemist, educator; b. Toronto, Ont., Can., Oct. 19, 1918; emigrated to U.S., 1946, naturalized, 1956; s. Morris and Mary (Madorsky) F.; m. Ruth Wilma Diamond, Apr. 16, 1942; 1 dau., Naomi Beth. M.D., U. Toronto, 1942; Ph.D. in Biochemistry (Am. Cancer Soc. fellow 1947-49), U. Calif., Berkeley, 1949. Diplomate: Am. Bd. Pathology. Intern, resident pathology Hamilton (Can.) Gen. Hosp., 1942-43, 44-46; Am. Cancer Soc. fellow Hektoen Inst. Med. Research, Cook County Hosp., Chgo., 1949-50; instr., asst. prof. pathology and biochemistry Tulane U. Sch. Medicine, 1950-55, asso. prof., 1955-59, Am. Cancer Soc. research prof., 1959-61; prof., chmn. pathology U. Pitts., 1961-70; Am. Cancer Soc. research prof. pathology and biochemistry Fels Research Inst., Temple U., Phila., 1970-74; prof. pathology and biochemistry, dir. Fels Research Inst., 1974-75; prof., chmn. dept. pathology U. Toronto, 1975—; Mem. Surgeon Gen.'s Adv. Com. Smoking and Health, 1962-64; chmn. pathology B study sect. NIH, 1966-70; mem. Nat. Adv. Cancer Council, 1966-70; mem. sci. adv. bd. cons. Armed Forces Inst. Pathology, 1966-70; sci. adv. bd. Nat. Central Toxicol. Research, 1972-74; chmn. biochem. carcinogen rev. panel Am. Cancer Soc., 1972-75; cons. Carcinogenic Prog. Etiology area, 1972—; mem. Lung Cancer Task Force, 1971—; mem. cancer research tng. grants com. Nat. Cancer Inst., 1971-72; mem. grants rev. panels Nat. Cancer Inst. Can., 1975-79. Editorial bd.: Chemico-Biol. Interactions; contbr. articles to sci. jours. Served from lt. to capt., M.C. Royal Canadian Army, 1943-46. Recipient Am. Cancer Soc. scholarship, 1951-55, Parke-Davis award exptl. pathology, 1958, Bertha Goldblatt Teplitz Meml. award, 1961; Samuel R. Noble Found. award, 1976. Fellow Royal Soc. Can., AAAS, Royal Coll. Physicians; mem. Am. Assn. Pathologists and Bacteriologists (council 1974—), Am. Soc. Exptl. Pathology (council; v.p. 1972-73, pres. 1973-74), Am. Chem. Soc., Am. Soc. Biol. Chemists, Am. Assn. Cancer Research (dir. 1964-67, 70-73, v.p. 1971-72, pres. 1972-73), N.Y. Acad. Scis., Biochem. Soc., Histochem. Soc. (pres. 1966-67), Internat. Acad. Pathology, Am. Soc. Cell Biologists, Soc. Exptl. Biology and Medicine, N.Y. Acad. Scis., Sigma Xi. Home: 23 Tranby Ave Toronto ON M5R 1N4 Canada Office: Dept Pathology U Toronto 100 College St Toronto ON M5G 1L5 Canada

FARBER, EVAN IRA, librarian; b. N.Y.C., June 30, 1922; s. Meyer M. and Estelle H. (Shapiro) F.; m. Hope Wells Nagle, June 13, 1966; children—Cynthia, Amy, Jo Anna, May Beth; stepchildren—David, Jeffrey and Lisa Nagle. A.B., U. N.C., 1944, M.A., 1953, B.S. in L.S, 1953; D.H.L., St. Lawrence U., 1980. Instr. polit. sci. U. Mass., Amherst, 1948-49; asst. documents dept. U. N.C. Library, 1951-53; librarian State Tchrs. Coll., Livingston, Ala., 1953-55; chief serials and binding div. Emory U. Library, Ga., 1955-62; head librarian Earlham Coll., Richmond, Ind., 1962—; dir. seminar on non-Western studies for coll. librarians Columbia U. Sch. Library Ser., summers, 1966, 68, 69; cons. Austin Coll., Asbury Theol. Sem., Malone Coll., Nazareth Coll., Maryville Coll., Knox Coll., Ill. Coll., Messiah Coll., Hiram Coll., Convenant Theol. Sem., Colby Coll., Ga. State U., Ripon Coll., Hampshire Coll., Rockhurst Coll., Nat. Endowment for Humanities. Asso. editor: Southeastern Librarian, 1959-62; asst. editor: Explorations in Entrepreneurial History, 1964-66; co-editor: Earlham Rev, 1965-72; columnist: Choice Mag, 1974—; Author: (with Andreano and Reynolds) Student Economists Handbook, 1967, Classified List of Periodicals for the College Library, 5th edit, 1972; editor: (with Ruth Walling) Essays in Honor of Guy R. Lyle; Editor: Combined Retrospective Index to Book Revs. in Scholarly Jours., 1886-1974, 1979-83, Combined Retrospective Index to Revs. in Humanities Jours., 1802-1974, 1983—. Recipient Librarian of Yr. award, 1980. Mem. Assn. Coll. and Research Libraries (pres. 1978-79), ALA (council 1969-71, 79—). Home: 331 College Ave Richmond IN 47374 Office: Lilly Library Earlham College Richmond IN 47374

FARBER, HAROLD D., life ins. co. exec.; b. Buffalo, June 3, 1907; s. Simon and Matilda (Goldstein) F.; m. Grace Weber, 1929; 1 dau., Lois Carol (Mrs. Leonard A. Dopkins); m. Lillian Robertson, 1947 (dec. Aug. 1979); children—Eric A., Michael H., Paul C. Student, U. Buffalo, 1924-27. Engaged in ins. bus., 1927—; 1st pres., chmn. bd. Internat. Life Ins. Co. N.Y., Buffalo, 1960—; pres. chmn. bd. Internat. Life Holding Corp.; dir. Protective Closures Co., Inc., Buffalo, Standard Electronics, Inc.; founder, dir. Lake Ledge Park, Inc., Williamsville. Mem. Million Dollar Round Table (life) *

FARBER, ISADORE E., psychologist, educator; b. St. Joseph, Mo., May 21, 1917; s. Jacob and Rose (Malkin) F.; m. Billie Frances Gulko, May 5, 1942; children: Ronna Ellen, Deborah. Student, St. Joseph Jr. Coll., 1934-36; B.A., U. Mo., 1939, M.A., 1940; Ph.D., U. Iowa, 1946. Instr. psychology U. Rochester, 1946-47; asst. prof. to prof. psychology U. Iowa, 1947-64; vis. prof. U. Wis., 1955, Stanford, 1960; research cons. Med. Sch., U. of Okla., 1956-57; prof. psychology U. Ill., Chgo., 1964—, head dept. psychology, 1964-68, 76-81; vis. prof. Hebrew U., Jerusalem, 1971-72. Founding editor: Jour. Exptl. Research in Personality, 1965-71; editor: Psychology series, Dodd, Mead & Co., 1965-73; Cons. editor: Jour. Abnormal and Social Psychology, 1955-61, Jour. of Personality, 1955-61, Jour. Abnormal Psychology, 1973-79; Contbr. articles to profl. jours. Served with Q.M.C. AUS, 1941-42; to 2d lt. USAAF, 1942-45. Fulbright fellow, 1971-72. Mem. Am. Psychol. Assn., Midwestern Psychol. Assn. (past pres.), Psychonomic Soc., AAUP, Am. Profs. for Peace in the Middle East, Phi Beta Kappa, Sigma Xi. Jewish. Home: 7912 Church St Morton Grove IL 60053 Office: Dept Psychology U Ill Chgo Circle Harrison and Morgan Sts Chicago IL 60680

FARBER, JACKIE, editor; b. Jersey City, Apr. 16, 1927; d. Herman B. and Pauline (Birnbaum) Levine; m. Samuel Farber, June 25, 1960 (div. 1981); children: Thomas Adam, John David; m. 2d Jay Topkis, Sept. 27, 1981. B.A., Smith Coll., 1949. Editor Bernard Gris Assocs., N.Y.C., 1963-72; sr. editor Delacorte Press, N.Y.C., 1972-74, exec. editor, 1980-81, editor-in-chief, 1981—; sr. editor William Morrow, N.Y.C., 1974-78, Random House, 1978-80. Democrat. Jewish. Club: Provincetown Tennis (Mass.). Home: 155 E 72d St New York NY 10021 Office: Delacorte Press 1 Dag Hammarskjold Plaza New York NY 10017

FARBER, JAY JOEL, educator; b. Phila., Nov. 6, 1932; s. Albert and Sarah (Efter) F.; m. Ada Sachs, Apr. 5, 1952; children—Jonathan, Jeremy. B.A., U. Chgo., 1952, M.A., 1954; Ph.D. (Kellogg fellow), Yale, 1959. Instr. classics U. Chgo., 1957-60; asst. prof. classics Rutgers U., 1960-63; asso. prof. classics, chmn. dept. Franklin and Marshall Coll., Lancaster, Pa., 1963-70, John W. Wetzel prof. classics, 1970—; Vis. research asso. Center for Internat. Studies, Princeton, 1962-63; mem. com. examiners Coll. Entrance Exam. Bd., 1971-74. Mem. Am. Philol. Assn., Classical Assn. Atlantic States, Pa. Classical Assn. (pres. 1968-70, editor Bull. 1971-78). Home: 1415 Hillcrest Rd Lancaster PA 17603

FARBER, JOHN, chemical company executive; b. Timisoara, Rumania, Aug. 23, 1925; s. Eugene and Magda (Reiter) F.; m. Maya Kleyman, June 28, 1953; children: Sandra, Deborah, Michael, Claudia. M.S., U. Cluj, Timisoara, 1948; Ph.D., Poly. Inst. Bklyn., 1956. Research chemist Sun Chem. Co., N.Y.C., 1951-52; cons. Soc. des Peintures et Vernis Bouvet, Tournus, France, Verneba A.G. Neuallschwill, Basel, Switzerland, Foster Grant Co., Inc., Leominster, Mass., Chemische Fabrik Kalk GmbH, Koln, Kalk, Germany, Asahi Chem. Industry Co., Ltd., Tokyo, 1953-56; pres., chief exec. officer ICC Industries, Ind., N.Y.C.; chmn. bd. Zenith Labs., Inc., Northvale, N.J.; pres. Primex Plastics Corp., Oakland, N.J., Dover Chem. Corp., Ohio; dir. Electrochem. Industries (Frutarom) Ltd., Haifa, Israel, UMB Bank & Trust Co., N.Y.C. Mem. Am. Chem. Soc., Soc. Plastics Industry, Soc. Plastics Engrs., Nat. Petroleum Refiners Assn., Chem. Mfrs. Assn. Office: 720 Fifth Ave New York NY 10019 *

FARBER, NORMA, musician, poet; b. Boston, Aug. 6, 1909; d. G. Augustus and Augusta (Schon) Holzman; m. Sidney Farber, July 3, 1928; children: Ellen, Stephen, Thomas, Miriam. A.B., Wellesley Coll., 1931; M.A., Radcliffe Coll., 1932. Singer, soprano, solo recitals, appearances with small ensemble groups and orchs., 1940—; author: poetry The Hatch, 1955, Look to the Rose, 1958, A Desperate Thing, 1973, Household Poems, 1975, Something Further, 1979; juvenile Did You Know It was the Narwhale, 1967, I Found Them in the Yellow Pages, 1973; juvenile books Where's Gomer?, 1974; juvenile This Is the Ambulance Leaving the Zoo, 1975, As I Was Crossing Boston Common, 1975 (nominated for Nat. Book award), Six Impossible Things Before Breakfast, 1977, A Ship in a Storm on the Way to Tarshish, 1978, Three Wanderers from Wapping, 1978, How the Left-Behind Beasts Built Ararat, 1978, There Once Was a Woman Who Married a Man, 1978, Never Say Ugh! to a Bug, 1979, Small Wonders, 1979, There Goes Feathertop!, 1979, How Does It Feel to be Old?, 1979, Up the Down Elevator, 1979, How the Hibernators Came to Bethlehem, 1980, A Night on Gars Mountain, 1981; novel Mercy Short, 1982; co-translator: To Live in Pronouns, 1974. Recipient premier prix in singing Jury Central des Etudes Musicales, Belgium, 1936, prizes Poetry Soc. Am., Borestone award, 1957, 73, 75, 76, Golden Rose award N.E. Poetry Club. Mem. Phi Beta Kappa. Address: 1010 Memorial Dr Cambridge MA 02138

FARBER, PAUL ALAN, educator; b. Bklyn., Sept. 13, 1938; s. Joseph and Dorothy (Trager) F.; m. Judith Goldblatt, Aug. 14, 1960; children—Leslie, Donna Lynn. A.B., U. Mich., 1960, D.D.S., 1962; Ph.D., U. Rochester, 1967. USPHS grad. research fellow U. Rochester, N.Y., 1962-67; asst. prof. microbiology Temple U. Sch. Dentistry, 1967-70; NIH spl. fellow, guest worker Nat. Inst. Dental Research, NIH, Bethesda, Md., 1970-71; guest worker Albert Einstein Med. Center, 1975-76; asso. prof. pathology Temple U. Sch. Dentistry, Phila., 1972-78, prof. pathology, 1978—; clin. prof. N.Y. U. Coll. Dentistry, 1980—. Served as maj. Dental Corps U.S. Army, 1966. NIH research grantee, 1972. Mem. AAAS, Am. Soc. Microbiology, Am. Assn. Pathologists, Res. Officers Assn., Assn. Mil. Surgeons U.S., NIH Alumni Assn. Home: 21 Glenn Circle Erdenheim PA 19118 Office: Temple U Sch Dentistry 3223 N Broad St Philadelphia PA 19140

FARBER, ROBERT HOLTON, emeritus dean; b. Geneseo, Ill., Jan. 12, 1914; s. Charles William and Hulda E. (Ogden) F.; m. Edna Earle Klutts, Jan. 6, 1946; children: Betty Jean, Charles Robert. A.B., DePauw U., 1935; M.A., U. Chgo., 1940; Ed.D., Ind. U., 1951. Field rep. DePauw U., 1935-36, sec. admissions, 1937-41, asst. dean students, dir. Edward Rector Scholarship Found., 1946-1952, dean of univ. Edward Rector Scholarship Found., from 1952, now dean emeritus; v.p. Edward Rector Scholarship Found., 1974—, acting pres., 1976-77, chief adminstrv. officer, 1962-63; tchr. speech Bloomington (Ind.) High Sch., 1936-37; Chmn. Stillwater Nat. Deans Conf., 1972; mem. nat. coordinating commn. Nat. Council Accreditation for Colls. for Tchr. Edn.; task force mem. Ind. Commn. on Higher Edn.; dir. Study Tour, Europe and Russia, People to People Orgn., 1970, Japan, 1972. Del. White House Conf. on Aging, 1981. Served as maj. AUS, 1941-46. Decorated Bronze Star, Meritorious Service plaque. Mem. Am. Assn. Colls. for Tchr. Edn., North Central Assn. Acad. Deans (pres.), Nat. Assn. Acad. Deans., Ind. Assn. Acad. Deans (past chmn.), Ind. Assn. Ind. and Ch.-Related Colls., Am. Assn. Ret. Persons (pres. Putnam County, chmn. state legis. commn.), Putnam County Health Careers Assn. (chmn.), Blue Key, Phi Delta Kappa. Republican. Methodist. Clubs: Masons (32 deg.), Kiwanis). Home: 712 Highridge Ave Greencastle IN 46135 *The function of education in bringing out the best in terms of personality and character, as well as scholarship, is to me a fundamental process. All of our educational institutions must be directed toward that end in order to give all persons, regardless of status, a fair chance to make the most of their abilities.*

FARBER, SEYMOUR MORGAN, physician, university administrator; b. Buffalo, June 3, 1912; s. Simon and Matilda (Goldstein) F.; children: Burt, Margaret, Roy. B.A., U. Buffalo, 1931; M.D., Harvard, 1939; D.H.L. (hon.), St. Mary's Coll., Moraga, 1964, LL.D., Pepperdine U., 1977. Individual practice medicine, specializing in chest diseases, San Francisco, 1946—; instr. dept. medicine U. Calif. at San Francisco, 1942-47, asst. prof., 1947-53, asso. prof., 1953-61, prof. clin. medicine, 1961—, asst. dean for continuing edn. medicine and health scis., 1956-63, dir. instrn. in extension, 1960-61, dir. continuing edn. medicine and health scis., 1963-70, dean ednl. services, 1963-70, dean continuing edn. in health scis., 1970-73, vice-chancellor pub. programs and continuing edn., 1973—; lectr. U. Calif. Sch. Pub. Health, Berkeley, 1948—; chief U. Calif. Tb and chest service San Francisco Gen. Hosp., 1945-65, sr. cons., 1965—; exec. dir. Howard Florey Inst. Am.; fellow Howard Florey Inst. Melbourne, Australia; spl. cons. Nat. Cancer Inst., 1958-60; nat. cons. continuing edn. and chest diseases to surg. gen. USAF, 1962. Author: Cytological Diagnosis of Lung Cancer, 1950, Lung Cancer, 1954; Editor: The Air We Breathe, 1961, Control of the Mind, 1961, Man and Civilization: Conflict and Creativity, 1963, The Potential of Woman, 1963, Man Under Stress, 1964, The Challenge to Women, 1966, Food and Civilization, 1966, Teen-Age Marriage and Divorce, 1967, Sex Education and the Teen-Ager, 1967; Editorial board: Diseases of Chest, 1948-61, General Practice, 1958- 61; bd. cons.: Pre-Med. Jour, 1965—; Contbr. to profl. publs. Mem. Pres.'s Commn. on Status of Women, 1962-63; mem. Council Med. TV, Bay Area Council on Alcoholism; commr. Asian Art Commn. San Francisco, 1977—, Calif. Postsecondary Edn. Commn.; vice chmn. Calif. Postsecondary Edn.

Commn., 1978-81, chmn., 1983—; mem. Air Quality Adv. Com. San Francisco Bay Area, 1979—; mem. nat. planning com., nat. adv. bd. John Muir Med. Film Festival, 1980—; chmn. com. on health maintenance White House Conf. on Aging, 1981—. Fellow Am. Coll. Chest Physicians (past pres.), Am. Coll Cardiology; mem. AMA (chmn. chest diseases sect. 1959-60), Calif. Med. Assn., San Francisco County Med. Soc., Calif. Soc. Internal Medicine, Am. Fedn. Clin. Research, N.Y. Acad. Scis., Am. Trudeau Soc., Internat. Acad. Pathology, AAAS, Pan Am. Med. Assn. (pres. sect. chest diseases), Assn. Am. Med. Colls., Am. Geriatrics Soc. Office: U Calif San Francisco CA 94143

FARBER, VIOLA ANNA, dancer, choreographer; b. Heidelberg, Germany, Feb. 25, 1931; emigrated to U.S., 1938, naturalized, 1944; d. Eduard and Dora (Schmidt) F.; m. Jeffrey Clarke Slayton, June 14, 1971. Student, Am. U., 1949-51, Black Mountain Coll., 1951-52. Dance tchr. Merce Cunningham Studio, N.Y.C., 1961-69; dancer Merce Cunningham Dance Co., N.Y.C., 1952-65; instr. dance Adelphia U., N.Y.C., 1959-67, Bennington (Vt.) Coll., 1967-68, N.Y. U., 1971-73; dir., tchr. Viola Farber Dance Studio, N.Y.C., 1969—; also artistic dir., choreographer, dancer Viola Farber Dance Co., N.Y.C., 1969—; artistic dir. Centre National de Danse Contemporaine, Angers, France, 1981-83; guest tchr. The Place, London, 1983-84; dir. Found. Contemporary Performance Arts, TAG Found., Ltd., Dance Ring. Choreographer, Viola Farber Dance Co., Théâtre Contemporain d'Angers, France, Ballet Théâtre Français, Repertory Dance Theatre Utah, Manhattan Festival Ballet, Nancy Hauser Dance Co., Dance depts. Adelphi, N.Y. U., Ohio State U. and U. Utah, Janet Gillespie and Present Co.; commd. by, Heinz Found.; collaborated with, Robert Rauschenberg and David Tudor on; video tape Brazos River, 1976; choreographed: Jeux Chorégraphique for, Ballet Théâtre Français de Nancy; performed at, Centre Pompidou, Paris, 1979. Recipient Gold medal Paris Dance Festival, 1971; NEA choreography grantee, 1975, 79; NEA prodn. grantee, 1976; NEA grantee, 1981; N.Y. State Council on Arts grantee, 1974-79; CAPS grantee, 1974, 78; N.Y. Dept. Cultural Affairs grantee, 1977; Guggenheim fellow, 1982-83. Mem. Assn. Am. Dance Cos. Studio: 30 E 31st St New York NY 10016

FARBERMAN, HAROLD, conductor, composer; b. N.Y.C., Nov. 2, 1930; s. Louis and Lena (Kramer) F.; m. Corinne Curry, June 22, 1958; children—Thea, Lewis. Diploma (scholarship 1947-51), Juilliard Sch. Music, 1951; B.S., New Eng. Conservatory Music, 1956, M.S., 1957. Percussionist, Boston Symphony Orch., 1951-63; condr., New Arts Orch., Boston, 1955-63; guest condr., Royal Philharmonic Orch., London, Eng., Denver Symphony Orch., BBC Symphony, Victoria (Can.) Philharmonic, Miami (Fla.) Philharmonic, N.Y. Philharmonic, New Philharmonia Orch., London, Eng.; condr., Colorado Springs (Colo.) Philharmonic, 1967-68; music dir., condr., Oakland Symphony Orch., 1971-79; rec. artist (condr. or composer) for, Columbia, Capitol, Mercury, Vanguard, Cambridge, Serenus, Boston records; rep. U.S. in, Paris (France) Internat. Composition Competition, 1959; Composer symphonies, string quartet, chamber music, operas, jazz.; Pioneered recorded works of, Charles E. Ives.; Author in field. Mem. ASCAP, Nat. Assn. Composers and Conductors. Address: 271 Central Park W New York NY 10024

FARBMAN, AARON ABRAHAM, surgeon; b. Odessa, Russia, Apr. 24, 1902; came to U.S., 1904; s. Samuel and Bertha (Rubin) F.; m. Marie Arlene Prager, July 23, 1944; children—Leslie, Robin. A.B., Columbia, 1923, M.A., 1924, M.D., 1928. Diplomate: Am. Bd. Abdominal Surgery. Began practice of surgery, 1930; research with Drs. David J. Sandweiss, Harry C. Saltzstein on relationship of sex hormones to peptic ulcer, 1936; company surgeon Continental Motors Corp., 1941-47; attending surgeon in gen. surgery North End Clinic, 1931-55; attending surgeon Cottage Hosp., Grosse Pointe, Mich.; Grosse Pointe asso. emeritus in surg. Sinai Hosp., Detroit; sr. attending surgeon Detroit Meml. Hosp.; asso. fellow postgrad. med. edn. U. Mich., 1951—. Contbr. articles on endocrine and surg. to med. jours. Pres., founder Chamber Music Players of Grosse Pointe, 1962; Trustee Detroit Music Settlement Sch., 1962-76. Recipient certificate of merit, for class I Sci. Exhibit by A.M.A., 1938. Fellow A.C.S., Internat. Coll. Surgeons, Am. Geriatric Soc., A.M.A., Amateur Chamber Music Players (nat. exec. com.), Phi Delta Epsilon. Jewish religion. Clubs: Columbia University of Mich. (trustee), Economic, Clef. Home: 809 Berkshire Rd Grosse Pointe Park MI 48230 Office: 20261 Kelly Rd Detroit MI 48225 *I have always followed the principle "Do unto others as thou wouldst have others do unto you." I have never decided on any treatment for a patient without questioning myself as to whether I would accept that same treatment for myself or any member of my family under similar circumstances.*

FARELLA, FRANK EUGENE, lawyer; b. Seattle, Aug. 14, 1929; s. Frank and Vere D. (LaRue) F.; children: Elizabeth, Ann, Thomas, William. B.A., San Francisco State U., 1951; J.D., Stanford U., 1954; student, Oreg. State U., 1947-49. Bar: Calif. 1954. Assoc. firm Bronson, Bronson & McKinnson, 1957-62; partner, founder Farella, Braun & Martel, San Francisco, 1962—; propr. Farella/Mt. George Vineyards, Napa, Calif. Mem. exec. com. bd. visitors Stanford U. Served with U.S. Army, 1955-57. Mem. Bar Assn. of San Francisco (pres. 1978), State Bar Calif., Am. Bar Assn., San Francisco Stanford Law Alumni No. Calif. and Nev. (pres. 1963), Can. Am. Soc., San Francisco Mus. Modern Art. Clubs: Marin Tennis, Calif. Tennis, Bankers. Home: Sausalito CA Office: 235 Montgomery St San Francisco CA 94104

FARENTHOLD, FRANCES TARLTON, lawyer, former coll. pres.; b. Corpus Christi, Tex., Oct. 2, 1926; d. Benjamin Dudley and Catherine R. (Bluntzer) Tarlton; m. George E. Farenthold, Oct. 6, 1950; children—Tarlton, George E., Emilie, James. A.B., Vassar Coll., 1946; J.D., U. Tex., 1949. Bar: Tex. bar 1949. Pvt. practice, 1949-65, 67-76, 80—; dir. Nueces County Legal Aid Soc., 1965-67; pres. Wells Coll., Aurora, N.Y., 1976-80. Mem. Tex. Ho. of Reps. from 404th Dist., 1968-73. Democrat. Address: 2100 Travis St Suite 1203 Houston TX 77002

FARENTINO, JAMES, actor; b. Bklyn., Feb. 24, 1938; s. Anthony and Helen (Enrico) F.; m. Michele Lee Dusick, Feb. 20, 1966; 1 son, David Michael. Ed., Am. Acad. Dramatic Arts. Broadway appearance in Night of the Iguana, 1961; also appeared in: Days and Nights of BeeBee Fenstermaker, 1963, In the Summer House, 1964, One Flew Over the Cuckoo's Nest, 1973, Streetcar Named Desire, 1973; film appearances include The War Lord, 1964, The Pad (And How to Use It), 1966, Rosie, 1966, Me Natalie, 1968, Story of A Woman, 1968, Banning, 1965, Ride to Hangman's Tree, 1965, The Final Countdown, 1980, Dead and Buried, 1982; starring: TV appearances in Death of a Salesman, 1966, Vanished, 1971; series The Bold Ones, 1970-72, John Dos Passos: U.S.A, 1971, Cool Million, 1972, Dynasty, 1982-83, Blue Thunder, 1984—; TV movie The Elevator, 1974, Police Story, 1974, 75, Crossfire, 1975; spl. Emily, Emily, 1977, Jesus of Nazareth, 1977, Eva Peron, 1981; movie The Possessed, 1978 (Recipient Golden Globe award for most promising newcomer 1966, award for best actor in Chicago 1973, Theater World award 1973, Charles MacArthur award Chgo. Drama League 1974). Named hon. chmn. Ill. Assn. Retarded Citizens. Office: care William Morris Agy Inc 151 El Camino Blvd Beverly Hills CA 90212 *

FARER, TOM J., legal educator, writer; b. N.Y.C., July 28, 1935; s. Louis and Lola (Garfinkel) F.; m. Mika V. Ignatieff, Dec. 26, 1964; children: Paola E., Thomas V. A.B, Princeton U., 1957; postgrad., Glasgow (Scotland) U., 1957-58; LL.B., Harvard U., 1961. Bar: N.Y. Program officer AID, Washington, 1962; spl. asst. Dept. Def., Washington, 1962-63; advisor Somaili Police Force, Mogadishu, Somalia, 1963-64; assoc. Davis, Polk & Wardwell, N.Y.C., 1965-66; asst. prof., then assoc. prof. Columbia U., 1966-71; disting. prof. law Rutgers U., Camden, 1971—. Author: Warclouds on the Horn of Africa, 1975; author, editor: Toward A Humanitarian Diplomacy, 1980, Future of Inter-American System, 1979. Mem. Inter-Am. Commn. Human Rights, 1976-83, pres., 1980-82; spl. asst. Dept. State, 1975. Sr. fellow Carnegie Endowment, 1974; sr. research fellow Council Fgn. Relations, 1975; Fulbright scholar, U.K., 1957-58; Woodrow Wilson fellow, 1983. Mem. Am. Soc. Internat. Law. Clubs: Cosmos (Washington); Princeton (N.Y.C.). Office: Rutgers U Law Sch 5th and Penn Sts Camden NJ 08102

FARGIS, PAUL MCKENNA, publisher, editor; b. N.Y.C., Mar. 19, 1939; s. George Bertrand and Elizabeth Harlin (McKenna) F.; m. Elizabeth Hackett, Aug. 22, 1964; children: John Hackett, Alison Kathryn; m. Dawn Sangrey, Apr. 23, 1977; 1 son, Christopher Sangrey. Student, Cath. U. Am., 1958; B.Social Sci., Fairfield U., 1961; M.A. (Publs. Tuition scholar), N.Y. U., 1962. Editorial asst. Prentice-Hall, Inc., Englewood Cliffs, N.J., 1961-62; editor Hawthorn Books, Inc., N.Y.C., 1963-67, v.p., editorial dir., 1967-71; v.p., editor-in-chief Thomas Y. Crowell Co. and Funk & Wagnalls divs. Dun-Donnelley Pub. Corp., N.Y.C., 1971-77; editor-in-chief Apollo Books, N.Y.C., 1972-77; managing dir. Thomas Y. Crowell div. Harper and Row, N.Y.C., 1977-78; pub., editor-in-chief The Stonesong Press div. Grosset & Dunlap, Inc., N.Y.C., 1978-80; founder, pres. and pub. The Stonesong Press, Inc., 1980—; pub. cons., 1980—; founder, owner The Biblioswitch, Bedford Hills, N.Y., 1973—; mem. advisory bd. Grad. Sch. Corp. and Polit. Communication Fairfield U., 1969—; pub. arbitrator Am. Arbitration Assn., 1982—. Author: The Consumer's Handbook, 1966, rev. edit., 1974, Company's Coming, 1965; Am. editor: Twentieth Century Ency. Catholicism, 1963-67. Exec. dir. Harrison (N.Y.) Town Recreation Commn., 1970-72; dir. Harrison Town Forum, 1969-73; former bd. dirs. U.S. Cath. Hist. Soc.; trustee Unitarian Fellowship of No. Westchester. Mem. Assn. Am. Pubs., Am. Book Producers Assn. (dir.). Office: 319 E 52d St New York NY 10022

FARGO, DONNA, singer, songwriter; b. Mt. Airy, N.C., Nov. 10, 1945. Grad. coll. Formerly tchr. English, Calif., now singer, songwriter. Numerous appearances TV and stage; recs. include Funny Face (Named Top Female Vocalist, Acad. Country Music 1972-73, recipient Grammy award, Female Country Performance of Year 1973, Best Selling Female Country Artist award Nat. Assn. Record Merchandisers 1972, 73, Country and Western Record of Yr. on Jukeboxes award for Funny Face, Music Operators Am. 1973, Robert J. Burton award for most performed country song 1972-73, Single Record of Yr. award Country Music 1972, Country Music award as best new female artist Billboard mag. 1972, best female artist 1973, best female singles artist 1974, U.S., Australian gold single records for Happiest Girl in U.S.A., Funny Face, Can. gold single record for Funny Face, U.S., Can. gold albums for Happiest Girl in the U.S.A., also U.S. platinum album). Recipient numerous awards, 1972—. Song. U.S. of A. adopted as So. Nev. Bicentennial Theme Song. Address: PO Box 150527 Nashville TN 37215

FARHI, LEON ELIE, physiology educator, researcher; b. Cairo, Oct. 9, 1923; U.S., 1958; s. Elie Salomon and Victoria (Anzarut) F.; m. Haya Youlus, July 12, 1948; children: Nitza Ellis, Eli Ralph. B.Sc., Am. U., Beirut, 1939; M.D., U. St. Joseph, Beirut, 1947. Asst. prof. physiology, 1958-62; assoc. prof. SUNY, Buffalo, 1962-66, prof., 1966—, chmn., 1982—; cons. in field. Contbr. to books, sci. jours. and reviews. NSF fellow, 1965-66. Mem. Am. Physiol. Soc., Am. Thoracic Soc., Am. Heart Assn., Undersea Biomed. Soc., Biomed. Engring. Soc. Jewish. Home: 158 North Dr Eggertsville NY 14226 Office: SUNY Buffalo NY 14214

FARICY, RICHARD THOMAS, architect; b. St. Paul, Minn., June 1, 1928; s. Roland J. and Clare (Sullivan) F.; m. Carole Murphy, Juen 24, 1961; children: Althea, Bridget. Architect, Minn., Wis., N.D., Colo., N.Mex., Fla., Tex., Ind., Okla. V.p. The Cerny Assocs., Mpls., 1961-71; exec. v.p. Winson/Faricy Architects, Inc., St. Paul, 1971—. Pres. Merrick Community Ctr., St. Paul, 1969, Ramsey County Hist. Soc., St. Paul, 1981-82; chmn. Blue Cross Blue Shield Minn., St. Paul, 1974-77, HMO Minn., St. Paul, 1974-76. Served to 1st lt. USAR, 1952-57. Fellow AIA; mem. Minn. Soc. Architects (dir. 1973-77), St. Paul AIA (pres. 1974). Clubs: St. Paul Athletic (pres. 1980); Minnesota (St. Paul)). Home: 2211 St Clair Ave Saint Paul MN 55105 Office: Winsor/Faricy Architects Inc 28 W 5th St Saint Paul MN 55102

FARIES, BELMONT, editor; b. Wilmington, Del., June 3, 1913; s. Clarence D. and Elva (Eddingfield) F.; m. Bette Jane Bonine, Sept. 5, 1945; children: Jain, Nancy, Jennifer. B.A., U. Pa., 1935. Reporter Jour. Every Evening, Wilmington, Del., 1935-38; copy editor Evening Star, Washington, 1938-56, news editor, 1956-75, stamp editor, 1955-81; Editor Soc. Philatelic Ams. Jour., 1962—, Minkus Stamp and Coin Jour., 1966—, U.S. specialist, 1981—; Mem. Postmaster Gen.'s Stamp Adv. Com., 1967-69, 71-75, chmn., 1975—. Served to 2d lt. AUS, 1942-46. Mem. Phi Beta Kappa. Home: 11713 Chapel Rd Clifton VA 22024

FARIES, CHARLES EDWARD, JR., pulp and paper company executive; b. Belzonia, Miss., Apr. 8, 1933; s. Charles Edward and Velma (Berry) F.; m. Charlotte Mayers, Mar. 19, 1954; children: Charles Edward, Daniel, Cary. B.S., Miss. State U., 1957. Project engr. Internat. Paper Co., 1957-62; supr. engring. and planning Am. Can. Co., Naheola, Ala., 1962-64; project mgr. Boise Cascade Corp., Wallula, Wash., 1964-70, St. Helens, Oreg., 1964-70, DeRidder, La., 1964-70, resident mgr., v.p. mfg., 1970-77, v.p. mgr. mfg., Portland, 1977-80; v.p., gen. mgr. Boise Cascade-Paper Group, Portland, 1980—. Served with USN, 1951-53. Mem. Am. Paper Inst. (pulp producers exec. bd. 1980—). Republican. Club: Waverly. Home: 12535 SW Iron Mountain Blvd Portland OR 97219 Office: 1600 SW 4th Ave Portland OR 97201

FARINELLA, PAUL JAMES, educational institution executive; b. Trenton, Sept. 28, 1926; s. Nicholas E. and Grace (Cubberly) F.; m. Margaret Pippitt, May 29, 1948; children: Dianne, Deborah. B.S. in Commerce and Bus. Adminstrn., Rider Coll., 1953. C.P.A., N.J. Pub. acct. Peat, Marwick, Mitchell & Co., Newark, 1953-61; assoc. comptroller U. Rochester, N.Y., 1961-67; v.p. bus. and fin. sec.-treas. Ithaca Coll., 1967-76; pres., trustee Munson-Williams-Proctor Inst., Utica, N.Y., 1977—. Served with USAAF, 1945-47. Office: 310 Genesee St Utica NY 13502

FARINHOLT, LARKIN HUNDLEY, found. exec.; b. Balt., Sept. 24, 1905; s. Leroy Whiting and Elizabeth (Gwin) F.; m. Mary Kathryn Snyder, Dec. 26, 1947; children-Larkin, Kathryn, Mary Victoria. B.S. in Chemistry, Johns Hopkins, 1927, grad. study, 1927-28; D. Phil. (Rhodes scholar), Oxford U., 1931; D.Sc. (hon.), Clarkson Coll. of Tech., 1967. Asst. prof. chemistry Washington and Lee U., 1933-37, asso. prof., 1937-41; asso. prof. chemistry Columbia, 1947-54, prof., 1954-60; dir. Chem. Labs., 1953-60; adminstr. program for basic research in phys. scis. Alfred P. Sloan Found., N.Y.C., 1960-73, v.p., 1962-70, trustee, 1962-69, cons., 1971-73; dept. sci. adviser State Dept., 1958-60; sci. attaché Am. Embassy, London, 1951-52; Exec. officer Explosives Research Lab., NDRC, OSRD, 1941-45; spl. asst. to chmn. NDRC, 1945-46; mem. Com. Internat. Exchange of Persons, 1953-56. Recipient Presdl. Certificate of Merit. Mem. Am. Chem. Soc., AAAS, Phi Gamma Delta, Omicron Delta Kappa, Tau Beta Pi. Club: Cosmos (Washington). Home: 10201 Grosvenor Pl Rockville MD 20852

FARIS, ESRON MCGRUDER, lawyer, educator; b. Norfolk, Va., May 24, 1925; s. Esron McGruder and Highland Louise (Stevens) F.; m. Helen Marie Davis, Feb. 18, 1950; children: Anne Martin, Douglas McGruder. B.S., Washington and Lee U., 1949, J.D., 1951; LL.M., Duke U., 1954. Bar: Va. bar 1952, N.C. bar 1960. Asst. prof. law Washington and Lee U., 1951-57; mem. faculty Sch. of Law Wake Forest U., Winston-Salem, N.C., 1957-65, 67-78; practice law, Williamsburg, Va., 1965-67; founder, dir. Overseas Program for Am. Law Students, Exeter U., Eng., 1967; vis. prof. law U. S.C., 1972-73, U. N.C., 1976-77; prof. law Stetson U., St. Petersburg, Fla., 1978—. Author: Accounting for Lawyers, 1964, 4th edit., 1982, Accounting and Law, 1984. Republican nominee for N.C. Senate, 1978. Served with USAAF, 1943-46. Presbyterian (elder). Clubs: Kiwanis, Masons. Home: 1401 61st St S Saint Petersburg FL 33707 Office: Stetson Law School Saint Petersburg FL 33707

FARISH, C(HARLES) WEBB, specialty chemicals company executive; b. Noxapater, Miss., Feb. 28, 1929; s. Earl J. and Willie Lenora (Webb) F.; m. Annie Lou McRae, July 13, 1951; children: Tony, Ronnie, Terri. B.S., U. So. Miss., 1952, M.A., 1953. Exec. v.p. ops. Petrolit Corp., St. Louis, 1982—. Home: 14718 Greenleaf Valley Dr Saint Louis MO 63017 Office: Petrolite Corp 369 Marshall Ave Saint Louis MO 63119

FARISON, JAMES BLAIR, electrical engineer, educator; b. McClure, Ohio, May 26, 1938; s. Blair Albert and Marie Lucille (Ballard) F.; m. Gail Donahue, Mar. 30, 1961; children: Jeffrey James, Mark Donahue. B.S. summa cum laude in Elec. Engring, U. Toledo, 1960; M.S., Stanford U., 1961, Ph.D., 1964. Registered profl. engr., Ohio. Asst. prof. elec. engring. U. Toledo, 1964-67, asso. prof., 1967-74, prof., 1974—, asst. dean engring., 1969-71, dean engring., 1971-80. Contbr. tech. articles to profl. jours. Recipient Outstanding Young Man of 1971 award Toledo Jr. C. of C., 1972, Boss of Year award Limestone chpt. Am. Bus. Women's Assn., 1973. Fellow Ohio Acad. Sci.; mem. Nat. Soc. Profl. Engrs, Ohio Soc. Profl. Engrs. (Young Engr. of Year award 1973), Toledo Soc. Profl. Engrs. (Young Engr. of Year award 1973, citation award 1983), IEEE (Toledo Elec. Engr. of Year awards 1972, 74, 76), Instrument Soc. Am., Am. Soc. Engring. Edn., Tech. Soc. Toledo, Blue Key, Sigma Xi, Tau Beta Pi, Pi Mu Epsilon, Phi Kappa Phi, Eta Kappa Nu (Outstanding Young Elec. Engr. award 1971). Home: 2314 Secor Rd Toledo OH 43606 Office: U Toledo 2801 W Bancroft St Toledo OH 43606

FARKAS, PHILIP FRANCIS, musician; b. Chgo., Mar. 5, 1914; s. Emil Nelson and Anna (Cassady) F.; m. Margaret Groves, May 11, 1939; children—Carol, Lynn, Jean Ann, Margaret. Studied with, Louis Dufrasne, Chgo. Civic Orch.; Mus.D. (hon.), Eastern Mich. U., 1978. Disting. prof. music Ind. U., 1960—. Solo hornist, Kansas City Philharmonic, 1934-36, Chgo. Symphony Orch., 1936-41, 47- 60, Cleve. Orch., 1941-45, 46-47, Boston Symphony Orch., 1945-46; French horn player symphony orch., radio, other orchestras.; Author: The Art of French Horn Playing, 1956, The Art of Brass Playing, 1962, A Photographic Study of 40 Virtuoso Horn Players' Embouchures, 1970, The Art of Musicianship, 1976; Editor of: French Horn Excerpts from the Modern French Repertoire. Home: 5994 E State Rd 46 Bloomington IN 47401

FARKAS, ROBIN LEWIS, retail company executive; b. N.Y.C., Oct. 13, 1933; s. George and Ruth (Lewis) F.; m. Suzanne Ellen Gold, July 5, 1959 (dec. Aug. 1971); children: Andrew Lawrence, Bradford Lewis; m. Carol S. Garner, Oct. 17, 1972; adopted children: Judi Beth, Andrea Lee, Charles Hugh. B.A., Harvard U., 1954, M.B.A., 1961. From jr. exec. trainee to asst. store mgr. Alexander's Dept. Stores, N.Y.C., 1955-59; staff cons. Arthur D. Little Inc., Cambridge, Mass., 1961-63; pres. Alexander's Rent-A-Car, 1963-69; sr. v.p., dir., treas. Alexander's Dept. Stores, 1963-81, chmn. exec. com., 1976-81, chmn. bd., 1981—; dir. Refac Tech. Corp., Electronics Research Assos. Mem. vis. com. on adminstrn. Harvard U., 1974-77, mem. vis. com. on Harvard Coll., 1983—; mem. Assn. for Better N.Y.; v.p. Met. Mchts. Assn. N.Y.C., 1970-82, pres., 1983—; mem. Nat. Democratic Fin. Com., 1974-77. Served with AUS, 1955-57. Recipient award service to youth Westchester-Bronx YMCA, 1966; Distinguished and Exceptional Service award City N.Y., 1972. Mem. Aircraft Owners and Pilots Assn. Clubs: Harvard (Boston and N.Y.C.); Harvard Business School (N.Y.C.); University, Beach Point Yacht. Home: 730 Park Ave New York NY 10021 Office: 500 7th Ave New York NY 10018

FARKAS, RUTH LEWIS (MRS. GEORGE FARKAS), personnel and community relations consultant, former ambassador; b. N.Y.C., Dec. 20, 1906; d. Samuel and Jennie (Bach) Lewis; m. George Farkas, June 17, 1928; children: Alexander Spencer, Robin Lewis, Bruce Russell, Jonathan Dale. B.A., N.Y. U., 1928, Ed.D. (Founder's Day scholar), 1957; M.A., Columbia U., 1932. Psychol. tutor Fedn. Jewish Charities, N.Y.C., 1941-45; instr. N.Y. U. Sch. Edn., 1949-55; personnel cons., community relations dir. Alexander's, Inc., N.Y.C., 1955-72; also dir., mem. exec. com. Alexander's Dept. Stores, Inc.; pres. Dolma Realty Corp., Ft. Lauderdale, Fla., 1955-70; U.S. ambassador to Luxembourg, 1973-76, personnel and community relations cons., 1977—; Andrew Wellington Cordier II fellow Columbia U. Sch. Internat. Affairs, 1976. Chmn. pres.'s adv. council N.Y. U. Grad. Sch. Social Work, 1966-73, hon. chmn., 1974—; nat. chmn. Albert Einstein Med. Coll. Women's Div., 1965-68; mem. Women's Council N.Y. State, 1964-71, Pres.'s Com. for Handicapped, 1964-70; founder, mem. Gov.'s Scholastic Program, 1964-71; mem. U.S. Commn. to UNESCO, 1964-71; mem. exec. com. Behavioral Sci. commn., 1968-71; part time sociol. cons. U.S. State Dept., 1963, 65, 68; v.p. Maferr Found., 1965—; pres. Role Found., 1967—, Bethabraham Hosp., 1963-73; vice chmn. Center for Study Presidency, 1978-79, chmn., 1980—; patron Met. Opera Assn.; Bd. dirs. Montifiore Hosp., Nat. Council Social Work; trustee N.Y. U., Town Hall Found. Recipient honor Pres.'s Com. on Handicapped, 1966; Am. Med. Center Humanitarian award, 1969; Alumnae Achievement award N.Y. U., 1970; Alumnae Achievement award Columbia U. Tchrs. Coll., 1982; Achievement award women's div. Albert Einstein Med. Coll., 1973; Founders' Day scholar N.Y. U., 1957; Gallatin fellow N.Y. U., 1983; Mental Health Assn. award N.Y. and Bronx Counties, 1978; Women's Achievement award N.Y. U. Alumni Assn., 1980; decorated Grand Croix Ordre de Merite, Luxembourg). Mem. Met. Mus. Art, Am. Fgn. Service Assn. (vice chmn. public mems. 1977-79), Alumnae Council Tchrs. Coll. Columbia (dir.), Alpha Kappa Delta. Clubs: Lotos, Harmonie, New York University (founder, gov. 1955-58), Palm Beach (Fla.) Country; Capitol Hill (Washington). Patentee roller muff. Home: 110 E 57th St New York NY 10022 also 172 S Ocean Blvd Palm Beach FL 33480

FARLEY, ANDREW NEWELL, lawyer; b. Brownsville, Pa., Oct. 31, 1934; s. Andrew Polycarp and Sarah Theresa (Landymore) F.; m. Marta Olha Pisetska, May 5, 1963; children—Andrew Daniel, Mark Landymore. A.B., Washington and Jefferson Coll., 1956; M.P.A., U. Pitts., 1961, J.D., 1961; diploma, U.S. Army Command and Gen. Staff

Coll., 1972, Indsl. Coll. Armed Forces, 1967; grad., U.S. Army War Coll., 1976. Bar: Pa. Supreme Ct. bar 1962, U.S. Supreme Ct. bar 1965. Asso. firm Reed Smith Shaw & McClay, Pitts., 1961—, partner, 1966—; lectr. in fed. jurisprudence and adminstrv. law U. Pitts; adminstrv. asst. Pa. Atty. Gen., 1959; counsel to Pa. Constl. Conv., 1968; mem. Pa. Atty. Gen.'s Task Force on Adminstrn., 1970. Asso. editor: Pitts. Legal Jour, 1963—; contbr. articles to law jours. Mem. Luth. Council Region III; chmn. Pitts. Area Consortium Ind. Schs.; bd. dirs. Ind. Schs. Chmn. Assn., World Affairs Council, Pitts. Served with U.S. Army; col. Res. Decorated Meritorious Service medal, Army Commendation medal; recipient Gubernatorial citation Commonwealth of Pa., 1978; Omicron Delta Kappa award, 1960; Nat. Def. Transp. Assn. fellow, 1956. Mem. Pa. Bar Assn. (ho. of dels., chmn. sect. internat. law), Am. Law Inst., Am. Bar Assn. (vice chmn. sect. adminstr. law com. on ombudsman), Assn. U.S. Army (pres. Ft. Pitt chpt.). Clubs: Pitts. Athletic Assn., Duquesne (Pitts.); Masons, Pa. State Grange. Office: 747 Union Trust Bldg Pittsburgh PA 15230

FARLEY, CAROLE, soprano; b. Le Mars, Iowa, Nov. 29, 1946; d. Melvin and Irene (Reid) F.; m. Jose Serebrier, Mar. 29, 1969; 1 dau., Lara Adriana Francesca. Mus.B., Ind. U., 1968. Fulbright scholar Hochschule für Musik, Munich, 1968-69. (Musician of Month, Musical Am./Hi Fidelity 1977), Am. debut at, Town Hall, N.Y.C., 1969, Paris debut, Nat. Orch., 1975, London debut, Royal Philharmonic Soc., 1975, S.Am. debut, Teatro Colon, Philharmonic Orch., Buenos Aires, 1975; soloist with, major Am. and European symphony orchs., 1970—; soloist, Welsh Nat. Opera, 1971, 72, Cologne Opera, 1972-75, Phila. Lyric Opera, 1974, Brussels Opera, 1972, Lyon Opera, 1976, 77, Strasbourg Opera, 1975, Linz Opera, 1969, N.Y.C. Opera, 1976, New Orleans Opera, 1977, Cin. Opera, Met. Opera Co., N.Y.C., 1977—, Zurich Opera, 1979, Chgo. Lyric Opera, 1981, Can. Opera Co., 1980, Düsseldorf Opera, 1980, 81, 84, Palm Beach Opera, 1982, Theatre Mcpl. Paris, 1983, Theatre Regale de la Monnaie Brussels, Teatro Regio, Turin, Italy, Nice Opera (France), 1984; TV film for ABC Australia La Voix Humaine; recorded for, Deutsche Gramophone, CBS, BBC records. Named Alumni of Year Ind. U., 1976. Mem. Am. Guild Mus. Artists. Home: 270 Riverside Dr New York City NY 10025 *A young opera singer today has a much greater responsibility than his predecessors 50 years ago. The age of the 200-pound soprano expiring of consumption at the end of "La Traviata" is a thing of the past. Now we must "look" the part, and be able to act as well as sing.*

FARLEY, EDWARD MILTON, III, lawyer; b. Hampton, Va., Oct. 26, 1927; s. Edward Milton, Jr. and Anna (Latham) F.; m. Joan D. Midkiff, Oct. 11, 1952; children: Mary Joan, Edward Milton, IV, Anna Bernardine, Peter, Matthew. Student, Mt. St. Mary's Coll., Emmitsburg, Md., 1945-46, 47-49; J.D. cum laude, U. Notre Dame, 1952. Bar: Va. 1952, D.C. 1981. Practiced law, Richmond, Va., 1952-81; partner Hunton & Williams (and predecessors), Richmond, 1959-81, Washington, 1981—; past dir., gen. counsel Va. Transit Co.; permament mem. U.S. 4th Circuit Jud. Conf., 1975—, mem. adv. com. appellate rules, 1973—. Past bd. dirs. Benedictine High Sch., Richmond; past trustee United Givers Fund of Richmond, Henrico and Chesterfield; past sec. Richmond Commn. on Community Relations. Served with AUS, 1946-47. Fellow Am. Coll. Trial Lawyers; Mem. ABA, D.C. Bar Assn., Va. Bar Assn., Richmond Bar Assn. (past pres.), U. Notre Dame Law Sch. Alumni Assn. (past dir.), Mil. Order Malta. Democrat. Roman Catholic. Clubs: Country of Va., KC (Richmond) (past chancellor). Office: 2000 Pennsylvania Ave NW Washington DC 20036

FARLEY, EDWARD RAYMOND, JR., mining and mfg. co. exec.; b. S.I., N.Y., Sept. 30, 1918; s. Edward Raymond and Ruth Veronica (Joyce) F.; m. Irene Daly, Feb. 19, 1948; children—Thomas Joyce, Nancy Seaver, Jane Campbell, Edward Raymond III. A.B., Princeton, 1940; J.D., Harvard, 1943. Bar: N.Y. bar 1944. With firm Simpson, Thacher & Bartlett, N.Y.C., 1944-55; v.p. Atlas Corp., N.Y.C., 1956-64, chmn. bd. dirs., 1964—, pres., 1966—; trustee, chmn. exec. com. Lincoln Savs. Bank, Bklyn., 1973—; dir. Am. Nuclear Energy Council, 1979—. Active local United Fund; trustee, pres. bd. Lawrenceville Sch., 1970—; trustee, chmn. bd. Princeton Med. Center, 1976—. Mem. Atomic Indsl. Forum, Dial Lodge (trustee). Clubs: Beden's Brook, Pretty Brook Tennis, Nassau (Princeton). Home: 188 Parkside Dr Princeton NJ 08540 Office: 353 Nassau St Princeton NJ 08540

FARLEY, JAMES DUNCAN, banker; b. Chgo., June 24, 1926; s. Donald Stephen and Alice (Duncan) F.; m. Mary Kay Tracy, Feb. 27, 1960; children—Frances, James Duncan, Kathryn, Andrew. B.S., Georgetown U., 1949. Trainee, mgr. First Nat. City Bank, Buenos Aires, Argentina, 1950-64, v.p. overseas div., N.Y.C., 1964-67; exec. v.p., gen. mgr. Merc. Bank of Can., 1967-68; sr. v.p. personal banking group First Nat. City Bank (now Citibank N.A.), N.Y.C., 1968, exec. v.p., 1969—, exec. v.p. mcht. banking group, 1975; exec. v.p. Caribbean (C. Am. and S. Am. banking group), 1980—; dir. Moore Corp., Pvt. Export Funding Corp., Chesebrough-Pond's, Inc. Trustee Georgetown U., Manhattan Coll., John Hartford Found. Served to ensign USNR, 1945-46; lt., 1951-52. Clubs: Skating, Round Hill (Greenwich, Conn.); Wequetonsing (Mich.) Golf; Lyford Cay (Nassau, Bahamas); Sky, Univ. (N.Y.C.); Blind Brook (Purchase, N.Y.). Home: 1 Pheasant Ln Greenwich CT 06830 Office: 399 Park Ave New York NY 10043

FARLEY, JAMES PARKER, retired advertising executive; b. Newark, Sept. 16, 1924; s. James Joseph and Margaret (Parker) F.; m. Irene Florence Reinert, July 1, 1950; children: James Bernard, Catherine Elizabeth, Robert Craig, Margaret Patricia. B.A. in Bus. Adminstrn, Rutgers U., 1949. Asst. advt. mgr. Gen. Electric Co., Syracuse, N.Y., 1949-51, merchandising mgr., Bridgeport, Conn., 1951-56; account dir. McCann-Erickson, Inc., N.Y.C., 1956-62; dir., pres. McCann Erickson-Hakuhodo, Tokyo, 1962-78, chmn., chief exec. officer, 1978-79, chmn., 1979-82; exec. v.p., regional mgr. Pacific, McCann-Erickson Internat., N.Y.C., 1972-82; dir. McCann-Erickson Internat., N.Y.C., 1974-82, Hakuhodo, Inc., Tokyo. Served with USNR, 1943-46. Mem. Internat. Advt. Assn., Am. C. of C. Japan, Am.-Japan Soc., Fgn. Corr. Club Japan, Young Pres. Orgn., Zeta Psi. Club: Tokyo Am. (past pres.). Home: 62 Rivergate Dr Wilton CT 06897

FARLEY, JAMES THOMAS, hosp. exec.; b. Chgo., Apr. 12, 1925; s. Thomas Walter and Nona F. (Kelly) F.; m. Mary Jean Powers, Oct. 4, 1947; children—James Thomas, Mary Margaret, Michael, Thomas, Patricia, Donal Joseph (dec.). B.S.A., Loyola U., Chgo., 1950; M.S. in Hosp. Adminstrn, Northwestern U., 1956. Vice pres. Meml. Sloan-Kettering Cancer Center, N.Y., 1964-68; pres. St. John Hosp., Detroit, 1968—; Cons. NIH, 1969-70. Contbr. articles to profl. jours. Trustee St. Vincents Hosp., N.Y.C., 1967-68. Served with USAAF, 1943-46. Fellow Coll. Hosp. Adminstrs.; mem. Am., Mich. hosp. assns., Soc. Hosp. Adminstrv. Assos., Knights Malta. Clubs: Grosse Pointe, Detroit Athletic, Grosse Pointe Hunt. Home: 3 Foxbriar Hilton Head SC 29928 Office: 22101 Moross Rd Detroit MI 48236

FARLEY, JOHN JOSEPH, univ. dean; b. N.Y.C., Mar. 19, 1920; s. John Anthony and Margaret (Green) F.; m. Rita Johnston, Feb. 26, 1944; children—Janet, Eugene, Marian, Joseph, Veronica. B.A., Cath. U., 1940; M.A., Columbia, 1950, M.S., 1953; Ph.D., N.Y. U., 1964. Tchr., N.Y.C. schs., 1940-50, high sch. librarian, Cranford, N.J., 1952-53, W. Hempstead, N.Y., 1953-58; curriculum dir. Sewanhaka Central High Sch. Dist., N.Y., 1958-60; successively asst. prof., asso. prof., chmn. dept. library scis. Queens Coll. of City U.N.Y., 1960-67; vis. prof. library sci. San Jose (Calif.) State Coll., 1967; prof. library sci. SUNY at Albany, 1967—, dean, 1967-77; cons. in field, 1958—. Author: Introduction to Library Science, 1969, also articles. Served with USAAF, 1943- 46. Recipient Founders Day award N.Y. U., 1964; Pius X medal for distinguished service to confraternity Christian doctrine, 1966. Mem. ALA, AAUP, Nat. Council Tchrs. English, Am. Soc. Information Sci. Democrat. Roman Catholic. Home: 12 Granada Dr Clifton Park NY 12065 Office: State U N Y at Albany Albany NY 12222

FARLEY, JOHN MICHAEL, steel company executive; b. Bklyn., July 10, 1930; s. John F. and Lucile J. F.; m. Dorothy O. Stacy, Nov. 29, 1959; children: Anne L., Joan E., John O. B.C.E. magna cum laude, Syracuse U., 1952; M.S., U. Ill., 1954. Registered prof. engr., Ohio, Pa. Project mgr. Cleve. works Jones & Laughlin Steel Corp., 1957-64, mem. engring. staff, Aliquippa, Pa., 1964-67, with gen. office, Pitts., 1967-71, gen. mgr. planning, engring. and constrn., 1972-73, v.p. research and engring., 1974-75, v.p. raw materials, 1975-77, pres. raw materials div., 1977-82, v.p. raw materials, purchasing, traffic, 1982—. Served with USNR, 1954-57. Mem. Am. Iron Ore Assn., Am. Iron and Steel Inst., AIME, Iron and Steel Soc., Assn. Iron and Steel Engrs., Engrs. Soc. Western Pa., Tau Beta Pi. Clubs: Duquesne, Longue Vue Country (Pitts.). Office: Jones & Laughlin Steel Corp 3 Gateway Center Pittsburgh PA 15263

FARLEY, JOSEPH MCCONNELL, electric utility executive; b. Birmingham, Ala., Oct. 6, 1927; s. John G. and Lynne (McConnell) F.; m. Sheila Shirley, Oct. 1, 1958 (dec. July 1978); children: Joseph McConnell, Thomas Gager, Mary Lynne. Student, Birmingham-So. Coll., 1944-45; B.S. in Mech. Engring., Princeton U., 1948, Grad. Sch. Commerce and Bus. Adminstrn., U. Ala., 1948-49; LL.B., Harvard, 1952; L.H.D., Judson Coll., 1974; LL.D. (hon.), U. Ala.-Birmingham, 1983. Bar: Ala. 1952. Assoc. firm Martin, Turner, Blakey & Bouldin, Birmingham, 1952-57; partner successor firm Martin, Balch, Bingham & Hawthorne, 1957-65; exec. v.p., dir. Ala. Power Co., 1965-69, pres., dir., 1969—; v.p. So. Electric Generating Co., 1970-74, pres., 1974—, also dir.; pres., dir. Ala. Property Co., Columbia Fuels, Inc.; dir. AmSouth Bank, N.A., Am South Bancorp., The So. Co., So. Co. Services, Inc., Torchmark Corp., Assoc. Industries Ala. Mem. adv. bd. Salvation Army; vice chmn., trustee Gorgas Scholarship Found.; mem. exec. bd. Southeastern Electric Reliability Council, chmn., 1974-76; Mem. Jefferson County Republican Exec. Com., 1953-65; counsel, mem. Ala. Rep. Com., 1962-65; permanent chmn. Ala. Rep. Conv., 1962; alternate del. Rep. Nat. Conv., 1956; Bd. dirs. Edison Electric Inst., 1976-79, Southeastern Electric Exchange; pres. Southeastern Electric Exchange, 1984; Bd. dirs. Ala. Safety Council, Inc., Kidney Found. Ala., Inst. Nuclear Power Ops., Ala. Bus. Hall of Fame, Coll. Football Hall of Fame Bowl, Birmingham Area YMCA, Operation New Birmingham, Warrior-Tombigbee Devel. Assn., Jefferson County Community Chest; chmn. bd. trustees So. Research Inst.; trustee Thomas Alva Edison Found., Tuskegee Inst., Ala. Symphony Assn.; trustee, pres. bd. trustees Children's Hosp. Birmingham; mem. pres.'s council U. Ala.-Birmingham, U. Ala.-Tuscaloosa; bd. visitors U. Ala. Sch. Commerce; mem. bus. adv. council Sch. Bus., U. Ala., Birmingham. Mem. Naval Res., 1948; now lt. ret. Mem. Ala., Birmingham bar assns., Ala. Assn. Ind. Colls. (bd. govs.), Ala. C. of C. (dir., pres. 1984), Birmingham Area C. of C. (dir., pres. 1974), Newcomen Soc. N.Am., Phi Beta Kappa, Kappa Alpha, Tau Beta Pi, Beta Gamma Sigma (hon.). Episcopalian. Clubs: Rotarian., Birmingham Country, Relay House, Downtown (gov.), Princeton of New York, Mountain Brook (gov.), The Club, Inc.). Home: 3333 Dell Rd Birmingham AL 35223 Office: 600 N 18th St Birmingham AL 35291

FARLEY, PHILIP JUDSON, government official; b. Berkeley, Calif., Aug. 6, 1916; s. Guy E. and Ernestine (Kennedy) F.; m. Mildred Bowling, 1938; children: Paul, Katherine, Kenneth. B.A., U. Calif.-Berkeley, 1937, M.A., 1938, Ph.D., 1941. Teaching fellow U. Calif., 1938-41; faculty Corpus Christi Jr. Coll., 1941-42; staff AEC, 1947-54; with Dept. State, 1954-73, spl. asst. sec. state for disarmament and atomic energy, 1957-61; spl. asst. sec. of state for atomic energy and outer space, 1961-62; chief polit. sect. U.S. Mission to NATO, Paris, 1962; dep. U.S. rep. to NATO, 1965-67; dep. asst. sec. state for polit.-mil. affairs, 1967-69; dep. dir. ACDA, also alt. U.S. rep. for U.S.-Soviet strategic arms talks, with personal rank of ambassador, 1969-73; sr. fellow Brookings Instn., Washington, 1973—; guest scholar Stanford, 1976—. Home: 18190 Saratoga-Los Gatos Rd Monte Sereno CA 95030 Office: Stanford U Palo Alto CA

FARLEY, RICHARD CHARLES, mfg. co. exec.; b. Harrisburg, Pa., Feb. 14, 1926; s. Thomas and Helen Margaret F.; m. Greta Margaret Galvin, June 14, 1975; children—Steven, David, Douglas, Lisa. B.S.B.A., Elizabethtown (Pa.) Coll., 1952. Dir. European ops. AMP Inc., Harrisburg, Pa., 1951-65; v.p. Premier Industries, Cleve., 1965-66; group v.p. bus. equipment Bell & Howell, Chgo., 1966-70; corp. v.p. Burndy Corp., Norwalk, Conn., 1970-71, exec. v.p., 1971-72, pres., 1972—, also dir.; dir. Burndy Corp., Mchts. Bank Norwalk, Sybron Corp., Rochester, N.Y. Trustee Elizabethtown Coll., YMCA Norwalk. Served with USN, 1944-46. Club: Shorehaven Country. Office: Burndy Corp Richards Ave Norwalk CT 06850

FARLEY, ROBERT DONALD, lawyer, business executive; b. Oneida, N.Y., Aug. 14, 1941; s. Donald William and Marian Elizabeth (Sawner) F.; m. Jennifer Lynn McCord, Dec. 1, 1967; 1 son, Jonathan Brett. B.S., Fordham U., 1962; J.D., Georgetown U., 1965. Bar: D.C. 1966, N.Y. 1971. Asso. firm Dewey, Ballantine, Bushby, Palmer & Wood, N.Y.C., 1965-66, 69-75; sec., corp. counsel Esterline Corp., Darien, Conn., 1975-77, sec., gen. counsel, 1977-79, v.p., gen. counsel, sec., 1979—. Bd. editors: Georgetown Law Jour, 1964-65. Served with JAGC USNR, 1966-69. Mem. Am. Bar Assn., N.Y. State Bar Assn., Westchester-Fairfield Corp. Counsel Assn. Clubs: Country of Darien.; Wilson Cove Yacht (Rowayton, Conn.). Office: 1120 Post Rd Darien CT 06820

FARLEY, TERRENCE MICHAEL, banker; b. N.Y.C., Mar. 6, 1930; s. Terrence M. and Mary A. (Dundon) F.; m. Audrey E. Churchill, June 8, 1952; children: Elizabeth Farley Coots, Peter, Matthew. B.B.A., Coll. City N.Y., 1955. With Brown Brothers Harriman & Co., N.Y.C., 1951—, partner, 1972—. Clubs: University, Broad Street (N.Y.C.); Echo Lake Country (Westfield, N.J.); Wianno (Osterville, Mass.). Home: 867 Bradford Ave Westfield NJ 07090 Office: Brown Bros Harriman & Co 59 Wall St New York NY 10005

FARLEY, WALTER LORIMER, author; b. N.Y.C., June 26, 1922; s. Walter Patrick and Isabelle (Vermilyea) F.; m. Rosemary Lutz, May 26, 1945; children: Pamela, Alice, Walter Steven, Timothy. Grad., Mercersburg (Pa.) Acad., 1936; also ed. at, Columbia U., 1941. Author: The Black Stallion, 1941, Black Stallion and Flame, 1960, Black Stallion and Satan, 1949, Black Stallion Challenged, 1964, Black Stallion Mystery, 1957, Black Stallion Returns, 1945, Black Stallion Revolts, 1953, Black Stallion's Courage, 1956, Black Stallion's Filly, 1952, Black Stallion's Sulky Colt, 1954, Blood Bay Colt, 1950, Great Dane Thor, 1968, Horse Tamer, 1958, Horse that Swam Away, 1965, Island Stallion, 1948, Island Stallion Races, 1955, Island Stallion's Fury, 1951, Little Black, a Pony; Little Black Goes to the Circus, 1963, Little Black Pony Races, 1968, Man O'War, 1962, Son of the Black Stallion, 1947, Big Black Horse, 1953, Black Stallion's Ghost, 1969, Black Stallion and the Girl, 1971, The Black Stallion Picture Book, 1979, The Black Stallion Returns Picture Book, 1983, The Black Stallion Comic Book, 1983, The Black Stallion Legend, 1983. Served with AUS, 1941-46. Address: care of Random House 201 E 50th St New York NY 10022

FARLEY, WILLIAM F., corporation executive; b. Pawtucket, R.I., Oct. 10, 1942; m. Jackie Merrill, Sept. 30, 1978; children: Natalie, Ned. A.B., Bowdoin Coll., 1964; J.D., Boston Coll., 1969; postgrad., NYU Grad. Sch. Bus., 1969-72. Bar: Mass. 1969. Sales mgr. Crowell Collier and MacMillan, 1966; dir. mergers and acquisitions NL Industries, N.Y.C.; head corp. fin. dept. Chgo. office Lehman Bros., Inc., 1973-78; chmn., owner Farley Industries, Chgo., 1977—; owner Anaheim Citrus Products Co., Doehler Jarris Products, So. Screw Co., Magnus metal Co. Tool & Engring. Co.; chmn. Baumfolder Corp., Health Foods, Inc. Corp.; co-owner, dir. Chgo. White Sox Baseball Club. Bd. dirs. Goodman Theatre; trustees Bowdoin Coll. Mem. Mass. Bar Assn., Am. Bar Assn., Young Pres.'s Orgn. Clubs: Saddle and Cycle, Chicago.

FARLOW, CARL PEARSON, JR., iron and steel manufacturing executive; b. Albertville, Ala., May 21, 1921; s. Carl Pearson and Margaret (Hood) F.; m. Mary Ann Nance, Sept. 2, 1943; children: Sam, Margaret Farlow Lee. B.S.M.E., U. Ala., 1943; B.A., U. Minn., 1960, B.Arch., 1960. Registered profl. engr., Ala. Engr. Am. Cast Iron Pipe Co. (Acipco), Birmingham, Ala., 1939-43, 46-47, sales engr., 1948-51, N.Y.C., 1952, design engr., Birmingham, Ala., 1953-55, chief engr., 1956-63, v.p. engring., 1963-76, exec. v.p., 1976-78, pres., 1978—, dir. various subs.; dir. First Ala. Bank of Birmingham. Bd. govs. Brookwood Med. Ctr., Birmingham; bd. visitors Berry Coll., Birmingham; mem. pres.'s council U. Ala., Birmingham; bd. dirs. Community Chest, Jr. Achievement, Warrior-Tombigbee Devel. Assn., Birmingham Area Alliance of Bus., Met. Devel. Bd. Birmingham, Operation New Birmingham, ARC; mem. adv. bd. Salvation Army. Served with USN, 1943-46. Mem. ASME (past dir.), Assn. Iron and Steel Engrs. (dir., past dist. chmn.), Nat. Mgmt. Assn. Methodist. Clubs: Birmingham, The Club, Downtown, Shoal Creek, Kiwanis. Home: 3617 Springhill Rd Birmingham AL 35223 Office: PO Box 2727 Birmingham AL 35202

FARLOW, TALMAGE HOLT, musician; b. Greensboro, N.C., June 7, 1921; s. Clarence E. and Annice B. (Holt) F.; m. Tina Zwirlein, Feb. 14, 1973. Jazz guitarist with musical groups, Red Norvo, Buddy De Franco, Artie Shaw; formed jazz trio, 1956—; toured, U.S., Europe; recorded over 25 albums; guest jazz guitarist with numerous jazz artists. Address: 16 Peninsula Ave Sea Bright NJ 07760

FARMAKIDES, JOHN BASIL, lawyer; b. Symi Island (Dodecanese), Italy; s. Basil John and Anna Maria (Zouroudis) F.; m. Maria T. Kambanis, July 12, 1964; children: Basil J., George S. B.S., Case Western Res. U., 1950; J.D. with honors, George Washington U., 1956; LL.M., Georgetown U., 1958. Bar: D.C. 1957, U.S. Supreme Ct. 1958. Research analyst Patent Trademark Found., George Washington U., 1954-55; patent examiner U.S. Patent Office, 1955-59; atty. U.S. Air Force, 1960-62; atty., supervising atty. NASA, 1962-70, mem. bd. contract appeals, 1968-70; asst. gen. counsel NSF, 1970-72; chmn. atomic safety bds. AEC (NRC), mem. NRC appeals bd., 1972-75; chmn. bd. contract appeal, contract adjustment bd., patent compensation bd. invention licensing appeals bd., fin. assistance appeals, bd., adminstrv. appeals bd. ERDA, Dept. Energy, 1975—; professorial lectr. in law Am. U. Law Sch.; U.S. del. Internat. Conf. on Govt. Computer Experts, Geneva, 1972; chmn. FCST Subcom. on Legal Aspects of Info. Systems, 1969-72; mem. OMB/OFPP task group on 1978 Contract Disputes Act; cons. HEW, NSF; chmn. Nat. Conf. on Legal Aspects of Computerized Info. Systems-FCST, 1969-72; dir. Joint Army, Navy, Air Force Spl. Analyn Div., U.S. Army Res., 1972-74; mem. U.S. Chinese Workshop on Computerized Info. Systems, Nat. Acad. Sci. Contbr. articles to profl. jours. Served to 1st lt. U.S. Army, 1951-53; to col. Res., 1974. Recipient letters of appreciation U.S. Army, HEW, NASA, NSF; Exceptional Service medal Dept. Energy. Mem. Am. Judicature Soc., Am. Bar Assn., Fed. Bar Assn., IEEE, Am. Soc. Public Adminstrn., Am. Hellenic Ednl. Progressive Assn., Phi Delta Phi, Lambda Chi Alpha. Clubs: Cosmos, Washington Golf, Nat. Lawyers. Office: Dept of Energy Washington DC 20545

FARMER, CROFTON BERNARD, atmospheric physicist; b. Cardiff, Wales, May 30, 1931; came to U.S., 1967; s. Francis Herbert and Cicely (Arnott) F.; m. Roberta Josephine Stewart, June 20, 1956; children—Louise Josephine, Joanna Cicely, Philippa Bernice. B.S., U. London, 1952, Ph.D., 1968. Research physicist EMI Electronics, Ltd., Eng., 1952-60, head infrared research dept., 1960-62; led sci. expdns. to Bolivian Andes, 1962, 64; mem. tech. staff Jet Propulsion Lab., Calif. Inst. Tech., Pasadena, 1967-72, mgr. planetary atmospheres, 1972-75; prin. investigator NASA Viking Mars, 1975-77, Shuttle Spacelab, 1977—; mem. subcoms. on planetary atmospheres and stratospheric research NASA; cons., lectr. remote sensing of atmospheres. Contbr. articles on solar-terrestrial spectroscopy and composition of planets' atmospheres to sci. jours. Recipient Exceptional Sci. Achievement medal NASA, 1975, 77. Home: 2525 Hollister Terr Glendale CA 91206 Office: 4800 Oak Grove Dr Pasadena CA 91103

FARMER, DONALD EDWIN, television anchorman; b. St. Louis, Sept. 27, 1938; s. William S. and Doris K. (Stephenson) F.; m. Chris Curle, Feb. 27, 1972; children: Laurie Lynn, Justin James. B.J., U. Mo., 1960. Polit. reporter WRCV-TV, Phila., 1963-65; with ABC News, N.Y.C., 1965-66, Chgo., 1966-68, bur. chief, Atlanta, 1968-71, London corr., 1971-73, bur. chief, Bonn, W. Ger., 1973-75, congressional corr., Washington, 1975-78, nat. corr., 1978-80. Anchor-host: Take Two, Cable News Network, 1980—; anchor: Evening Edition, Cable News Network. Recipient Headliners Club award, 1963, Overseas Press Club team award for Cyprus coverage, 1974. Mem. Radio and Television Corrs. Assn. (exec. bd. U.S. Capitol). Office: Cable News Network Techwood Dr Atlanta GA 30318

FARMER, GUY, lawyer; b. Foster Falls, Va., Sept. 13, 1912; s. Harbert and Kate (Bell) F.; m. Helen Joura (dec.); children: Mary, Mark, Jane. B.A., W.Va. U., 1934, LL.B., 1936; Rhodes scholar, Oxford (Eng.) U., 1936-37. Bar: W.Va., D.C., U.S. Supreme Ct. Asso. gen. counsel NLRB, 1943-45, atty., 1945, chmn., 1953-55; asso. Steptoe & Johnson, 1945-49, partner, 1949-60; sr. partner Farmer, Wells, McGuinn, Flood & Sibal, 1960-83; of counsel Vedder, Price, Kaufman & Kamholtz, 1983—; lectr. labor law W.Va. U., 1948-49, Georgetown U., 1957-59; dir. Bartlett Tree Co., Stamford, Conn. Author articles labor topics. Mem. Am., D.C., W.Va. bar assns., Order of Coif, Phi Beta Kappa, Phi Alpha Delta. Club: Cosmos. Home: 3600 Macomb St Washington DC 20016 Office: 1000 Potomac St NW Suite 402 Washington DC 20007

FARMER, JAMES, civil rights leader and former trade union official; b. Marshall, Tex., Jan. 12, 1920; s. James Leonard and Pearl Marion (Houston) F.; m. Lula A. Peterson, May 21, 1949 (dec. May 1977); children: Tami, Abbey. B.S., Wiley Coll., Marshall, 1938; B.D., Howard U., 1941; H.H.D., Morgan State Coll., Balt., 1964. Founder

Congress of Racial Equality (CORE), 1942, nat. chmn., 1942-44, 50, nat. dir., 1961-66; race relations sec. Fellowship of Reconciliation, 1941-45; organizer Upholsterer's Internat. Union N.Am., 1945-47; lectr. race and labor problems, 1948-50; student field sec. League Indsl. Democracy, 1950-54; internat. rep. State, County and Municipal Employees Union, 1954-59; program dir. NAACP, 1959-61; leader CORE Freedom Ride, 1961; pres. Center for Community Action Edn., 1965—; asst. sec. for adminstrn. HEW, 1969-70; pres. Council on Minority Planning and Strategy, 1973-76; exec. dir. Coalition of Am. Pub. Employees, 1977-82; adj. prof. N.Y. U., 1968; prof. social welfare Lincoln (Pa.) U., 1966-67; vis. prof. Antioch U., 1983-84; Nat. exec. bd. Am. Com. on Africa, 1959-64; chmn. Council United Civil Rights Leadership, 1963—; sponsor Am. Negro Leadership Conf. on Africa, 1962—. Author: Freedom When?, 1965; also author essay, also numerous articles. Vice chmn. Liberal Party N.Y. County, 1954-61; Bd. dirs. League Indsl. Democracy, Friends of Earth, Nat. Citizens Com. Broadcasting, Black World Found., ACLU, Americans Dem. Action. Recipient Am. Vets. Com. award, 1962, John Dewey award League Indsl. Democracy, 1962, Distinguished Postgrad. Achievement Alumni award Howard U., 1964, Omega Psi Phi award, 1961, 63. *

FARMER, JOE SAM, petroleum co. exec.; b. Hot Springs, Ark., Mar. 2, 1931; s. Walter L. and T. Naomi F.; m. Elizabeth Jean Keener, Dec. 27, 1952; children: J. Christopher, David E., Kathryn L. Student, Ohio State U., 1950-51; B.Sc., Tex. A & M U., 1955. Cert. petroleum geologist. Geologist Lion Oil Co., Shreveport, La., 1955; geologist, then asst. chief geologist Placid Oil Co., New Orleans, Shreveport and Dallas, 1958-68; exploration mgr. N.Am. div. Union Carbide Petroleum Corp., Houston, 1968-71; v.p. domestic exploration and prodn. Ashland Exploration Inc., Houston, 1971-73, exec. v.p., 1973-77, adminstrv. v.p., Ashland, Ky., 1977-79; v.p. Mesa Petroleum Co., Houston, 1979-80; pres. chief operating officer Union Tex. Petroleum Corp., Houston, 1980—; dir. Bank of the S.W., Houston. Served with USAF, 1955-57. Mem. Am. Assn. Petroleum Geologists, Assn. Profl. Geol. Scientists, Am. Petroleum Inst., Mid-Continent Oil and Gas Assn., Ind. Producers Assn. Am., Houston Geol. Soc. Clubs: Petroleum (Houston); April Sound Country (Conroe, Tex.). Office: PO Box 2120 Houston TX 77252

FARMER, JOHN DAVID, museum administrator; b. Washington, Ga., Jan. 25, 1939; s. John Lloyd and Frances Heard (Woolley) F.; m. Patricia Phelps Dow, Aug. 21, 1965; children: Emily Dow, Rachel Aldrich. B.A., Columbia U., 1960; M.A., U. N.C., 1963; M.F.A., Princeton U., 1965, Ph.D., 1981. Curatorial asst. Worcester (Mass.) Art Mus., 1967-69; curator Busch-Reisinger Mus. Germanic Art, Harvard, 1969-72; curator earlier painting Art Inst. Chgo., 1972-75; dir. Birmingham (Ala.) Mus. Art, 1975-78; lectr. fine arts Clark U., Worcester, 1968-69; lectr. art Harvard U., 1970; lectr. U. Ala., Birmingham, 1976-78; exec. dir. Commn. for Ednl. Exchange between U.S.A., Belgium and Luxembourg, Brussels, 1979-80; dir. U. Calif.-Santa Barbara Art Mus., 1981—; adj. prof. art history U. Calif.-Santa Barbara, 1981—. Author: The Virtuoso Craftsman: Northern European Design in the 16th Century, 1969, Concepts of the Bauhaus, 1971, German Master Drawings of the 19th Century, 1972, James Ensor, 1976, also articles. Bd. dirs. Boston Musica Viva, 1971-72. Albert M. Friend fellow, 1963-64, 65-66; Fulbright-Hayes fellow, Belgium, 1966-67. Mem. Coll. Art Assn., Assn. Am. Museums, Nat. Assn. Amateur Oarsmen, Assn. Art Mus. Dirs., U.S. Rowing Assn. Club: Odd Volumes (Boston). Office: Art Museum U Calif Santa Barbara CA 93106

FARMER, PHILIP JOSÉ, author; b. North Terre Haute, Ind., Jan. 26, 1918; s. George and Lucile Theodora (Jackson) F.; m. Elizabeth Andre, May 10, 1941; children: Philip Laird, Kristen. B.A., Bradley U., 1950. Laborer, steel mill, Peoria, 1941-52, tech. writer, various cos., 1956-69. Author: 60 books including Strange Relations, 1960, The Lovers, 1961, The Alley God, 1962, Riverworld Series: To Your Scattered Bodies Go, 1971, The Fabulous Riverboat, 1971, The Dark Design, 1977, The Magic Labyrinth, 1980, Riverworld and other Stories, 1979, Tarzan Alive, 1972, Venus on the Half-Shell (as Kilgore Trout), 1975; Author: The Adventure of the Peerless Peer by John H. Watso, M.D., 1974, The Cache, 1981, A Barnstormer in Oz, 1982; short stories Riverworld, 1980. Recipient Hugo award, 1953, 68, 72. Address: 5617 N Fairmont Dr Peoria IL 61614 *Most of my works are science-fiction. These spring from imaginative speculations-extrapolations on science, technology, psychology, sociology, linguistics, philosophy, and theology. The main emphasis, however, is on the human beings trapped in a bewildering cosmos but fighting to understand it. One of my premises is that if the Creator has not given us physical immortality, then we will make our own. This may be one of the goals of homo sapiens evolution.*

FARMER, RICHARD GILBERT, physician, foundation adminstrator; b. Kokomo, Ind., Sept. 29, 1931; s. Oscar Irvin and ElizabethJane (Gilbert) F.; m. Janice Mae Schrank, Nov. 29, 1958; children: Amy Lynn, David Richard. Student, Ind. U., 1949-52; M.D., U. Md., 1956; M.S. in Medicine, U. Minn., 1960. Diplomate: Am. Bd. Internal Medicine. Fellow in internal medicine Mayo Clinic, Rochester, Minn., 1957-60; mem. staff Cleve. Clinic Found., 1962—, chmn. dept. gastroenterology, 1972-82, chmn. div. medicine, 1975—, mem. med. ops. group, 1975—, bd. govs., 1974-79, mem. exec. com. bd. trustees, 1975-77; mem. adv. com. Cleve. Clinic Internat. Ctr. Splty. Studies, 1977—; assoc. clin. prof. medicine Case Western Res. U. Sch. Medicine, Cleve., 1980—; mem. nat. adv. bd. Nat. Commn. Digestive Diseases, 1977-79; mem. nat. sci. adv. bd. Nat. Found. Ileitis and Colitis, 1973—; chmn. grants rev. com. Nat. Found. Ileitisand Colitis, 1981—. Editor 2 books; contbr. articles to sci. jours., chpts. to books. Served as lt. comdr. USNR, 1960-62. Fellow ACP (gov. Ohio 1980—, health and pub. policy com. 1982—), Am. coll. Gastroenterology (pres. 1978-79), Am. Coll. Gastroenterology (trustee, exec. com. 1975-80); mem. Assn. Program Dirs. in Internal Medicine (founding, pres. 1977-79, chmn. steering com. new orgn. 1977), Council Subsplty. Socs. in Internal Medicine (council 1978—), Inst. Medicine of Nat. Acad. Scis., Am. Soc. Internal Medicine (chpt. trustee 1980—), Am. Gastroent. Assn. (commn. on future 1973-74, tng. and edn. com. 1975-78, chmn. subcom. grad. edn. 1975-78). Democrat. Presbyterian. Home: 150 Hunting Trail Chagrin Falls OH 44022 Office: Cleve Clinic Found 9500 Euclid Ave Cleveland OH 44106

FARMER, RICHARD NEIL, educator; b. Alameda, Calif., Aug. 19, 1928; s. George Albert and Alice (Mellin) F.; m. Barbara Jean Flaherty, Sept. 18, 1951; children-Christine, Geoffrey, Sarah, Daniel. B.A., U. Calif. at Berkeley, 1950, M.A., 1951, Ph.D., 1957. Asst. prof. Am. U. Beirut, 1957-59; gen. mgr. Gen. Contracting Co., Al Khobar, Saudi Arabia, 1959-61; lectr. U. Calif., Davis, 1961-62, asst. prof., Los Angeles, 1962-64; prof. bus. Ind. U., Bloomington, 1964—; also adviser Black Entrepreneurial Program. Author: (with B. Richman) Comparative Management and Economic Progress, 1964, International Business, 1965, Management in the Future, 1967, International Management, 1968, New Directions in Management Information Transfer, 1968, Benevolent Aggression, 1972, (with W.D. Hogue) Corporate Social Responsibility, 1973, The Real World of 1984, 1974, (with B. Richman) Leadership, Goals and Power in Higher Education, 1975, Management and Organizations, 1975, Why Nothing Seems to Work Any More, 1977. Served with AUS, 1951-53. Fellow Acad. Mgmt., Acad. Internat. Bus. (pres. 1977-78); mem. Soc. Internat. Devel. Home: 1115 E Wylie St Bloomington IN 47401

FARMER, ROBERT LINDSAY, lawyer; b. Portland, Oreg., Sept. 29, 1922; s. Paul C. and Irma (Lindsay) F.; m. Carmen E. Engebretson, Sept. 8, 1943; children—Cort W., Scott L., Eric C. B.S., U. Calif. at Los Angeles, 1946; LL.B., U. So. Calif., 1949. Bar: Calif. bar 1949. Since practiced in, Los Angeles; mem. firm Forster, Gemmill & Farmer, Los Angeles, 1949—. Trustee Edward James Found., West Dean Estate, Chichester, Eng. Served with AUS, 1943-46. Mem. Am., Los Angeles County bar assns., Order of Coif, Beta Gamma Sigma, Kappa Sigma, Phi Delta Phi. Clubs: Annadale Golf (Pasadena, Calif.); California (Los Angeles). Home: 251 S Orange Grove Blvd Apt 1 Pasadena CA 91105 Office: 900 Wilshire Blvd Los Angeles CA 90017

FARMER, SUSAN LAWSON, secretary of state Rhode Island; b. Boston, May 29, 1942; d. Ralph and Margaret (Tyng) Lawson; m. Malcolm Farmer, III, Apr. 6, 1968; children: Heidi Benson, Stephanie Lawson. Student, Garland Jr. Coll., 1960-61, Brown U., 1961-62. Mem. Providence Home Rule Charter Commn., 1979-80; sec. of state State of R.I., Providence, 1983—; spl. advocate R.I. Family Ct., 1978—. Bd. dirs. Justice Resources Corp., Marathon House, Inc.; mem. Mayor's Task Force on Child Abuse; v.p. Miriam Hosp. Found. Mem. R.I. Women's Polit. Caucus (Woman of Yr. award 1980), LWV, Common Cause, Save the Bay, Women for a Non-nuclear Future, Providence Preservation Soc. Republican. Home: 147 Lloyd Ave Providence RI 02906 Office: State House Providence RI 12903

FARMER, THOMAS ALBERT, JR., physician, university chancellor; b. Smithfield, N.C., Jan. 28, 1932; s. Thomas Albert and Oma Martha (Adams) F.; m. Nancy Josephine Nussear, Aug. 25, 1956; children: Thomas Albert III, David Crown, Steven Adams, Kelly Elizabeth. Student, Davidson Coll., 1950-51; B.S., U. N.C., 1954, M.D., 1957. Diplomate: Am. Bd. Internal Medicine. Asst. prof. medicine, asst. dean curriculum matters U. Ala. Med. Center, Birmingham, 1965-67, asso. dean, dir. student affairs and curriculum, 1967-68, asso. prof. medicine, 1967-69, exec. asso. dean, dir. undergrad. med. edn., 1968-72, prof. medicine, 1969-72; dean Sch. Medicine, U. Tenn., Memphis, 1972-75; chancellor U. Tenn. Center for Health Scis., 1975-80; now chancellor U. Md., Balt., 1981—. Contbr. articles to profl. publs. Served to capt. AUS, 1961-63. Fellow A.C.P. Home: 3112 Old Court Rd Pikesville MD 21208

FARMER, THOMAS LAURENCE, lawyer; b. Berlin, Germany, July 26, 1923; s. Laurence and Else (Dienemann) F.; m. Elizabeth Fairchild Becker, Sept. 1951 (div. Aug. 1970); children-Daniel Fairchild, Sarah Bennett, Elizabeth Lanham. A.B., Harvard, 1943, LL.B., 1950; B.A., Brasenose Coll., Oxford (Eng.) U., 1948, M.A., 1953. Bar: D.C. bar 1951, N.Y. bar 1956. Law clk. to Judge M.O. Hudson; mem. Internat. Law Commn. of UN, Geneva, Switzerland, 1950; asso. firm Simpson, Thacher & Bartlett, N.Y.C., 1954-57, Washington, 1958-64; gen. counsel AID, Washington, 1964-68; partner Kominers, Fort, Schlefer, Farmer & Boyer, Washington, 1968-70, Prather, Seeger, Doolittle & Farmer, 1970—. Chmn. bd. Nat. Capital Transp. Agy., 1961-64; mem., chmn. Pres.'s Intelligence Oversight Bd., 1977-81; Mem. vis. com. Harvard, 1959-65; trustee Lincoln U., 1959-77; dir. Overseas Devel. Council, Washington. Served with AUS, 1943-46. Mem. Am., Fed. bar assns., Am. Soc. Internat. Law, Grey's Inn Soc. Democrat. Clubs: Federal City, Metropolitan (Washington). Home: 3456 Macomb St NW Washington DC 20016 Office: 1101 16th St NW Washington DC 20036

FARMER, THOMAS WOHLSEN, neurologist, educator; b. Lancaster, Pa., Sept. 18, 1914; s. Clarence R. and Laura (Wohlsen) F.; m. Phyllis McCormick, July 19, 1941; children: Pamela Farmer Henderson, Thomas Wohlsen. A.B., Harvard U., 1935, M.D., 1941; M.A., Duke U., 1937; postgrad., U. Copenhagen, 1957-58, U. Calif., San Diego, 1971-72. Diplomate: Am. Bd. Psychiatry and Neurology (dir. 1969—, pres. 1977). Intern Pa. Hosp., Phila., 1941-42; resident Boston City Hosp., 1942-43, Johns Hopkins Hosp., 1943-44, 46-47; mem. staff N.C. Meml. Hosp., Chapel Hill, 1952-79; instr. medicine Johns Hopkins U., 1947-48; asst. prof. neurology Southwestern Med. Sch., U. Tex., Dallas, 1948-49, asso. prof., 1949-50, prof., 1950-52, prof. medicine, acting chmn. dept. medicine, 1951-52; prof. neurol. medicine, head div. neurology U. N.C., Chapel Hill, 1952—, Sarah Graham Kenan prof. medicine, 1975—. Author: Pediatric Neurology, 1964, 3d edit., 1983, Neurologia Pediatrica, 1972. Served with USNR, 1944-46. Mem. Am. Acad. Neurology (nat. sec. 1955-57), Am. Neurol. Assn., Am. Acad. Neurology, ACP, AMA, Assn. Research Nervous and Mental Diseases, Child Neurology Soc. Home: 1304 Mason Farm Rd Chapel Hill NC 27514 Office: U NC Sch Medicine Clin Scis Bldg Chapel Hill NC 27514

FARMER, WELFORD STUART, banker, lawyer; b. Richmond, Va., Oct. 19, 1925; s. Joseph L. and Cora (Chamberlain) F.; m. Ellen Azalee Harpe, Sept. 10, 1949 (dec. Aug. 1977); children: Welford Stuart, Joseph A., Neil P., Alison H.; m. Bonnie Hyler Fowlkes, Jan. 16, 1982. B.S.B., U. Richmond, 1948, J.D., 1950. Bar: Va. 1951. With Fed. Res. Bank Richmond, 1950—, gen. counsel, 1961-63, v.p., gen. counsel, 1964-68, sr. v.p., gen. counsel, 1969-71, sr. v.p., spl. legal adviser, 1971—. Served with USNR, 1944-46. Mem. Va., Richmond bar assns., Sigma Alpha Epsilon, Phi Alpha Delta. Methodist. Clubs: Country of Va., Westwood Racquet (Richmond). Office: Fed Res Bank 701 E Byrd St Richmond VA 23261

FARMER, WILLIAM CARTER, lawyer; b. Gentry, Ark., Oct. 20, 1915; s. Hon Carter and Jennie (Brockman) F.; m. Clarice Loxley, Feb. 10, 1972; children—Barry Joe, Shelley Suzanne. A.B., U. Kans., 1939, J.D., 1941. Bar: Kans. bar 1941, U.S. Supreme Ct. bar 1955. Spl. agt. FBI, 1941-48; individual practice law, Wichita, Kans., 1948-50, 58—, chief dep. county atty., Wichita, 1950-53; U.S. atty. Dist. Kans., Topeka, 1953-58; chmn. Kans. Supreme Ct. Nominating Com., 1980—. Mem. Kans. State Senate, 1961-65; vice-chmn. Gov's Econ. Devel. Com., 1963-66; bd. trustee Wichita State U., 1973—, pres., 1978-80; mem. Ark. River Valley Devel. Council, 1970—; trustee Osteo. Hosp. Wichita, 1965—. Recipient Recognition award Wichita State U., 1974. Fellow Am. Bar Found., Am. Coll. Trial Attys.; mem. Am. Bar Assn. (Kans. del. 1979—, coms.), Kans. Bar Assn. (pres. 1978-79, exec. council 1973—), Wichita Bar Assn. (pres. 1971-72), Am. Bd. Trial Advocates, Kans. Trial Attys. Assn., Am. Judicature Soc., Wichita C. of C. (dir. 1966-68), Phi Alpha Delta. Republican. Presbyterian. Clubs: Crestview Country, Wichita, Masons, Scottish Rite, Moose, Hi-12. Home: 823 Brookfield Wichita KS 67206 Office: Suite 830 200 W Douglas Wichita KS 67202

FARNAN, JOSEPH JAMES, JR., lawyer; b. Phila., June 15, 1945; s. Joseph James and Philomena (DeLaurentis) F.; m. Patricia Candice Winner, June 28, 1969; children: Joseph James III, Brian, Kelly, Tracie, Michael. B.A., King's Coll., (Pa.), 1967; J.D., U. Toledo Coll. Law, 1970. Bar: N.J. 1970, Del. 1972. Dir. crime justice program Wilmington Coll., New Castle, Del., 1970-73; sole practice law, Wilmington, 1973-76; asst. pub. defender State Del., Wilmington, 1973-75; county atty. New Castle County, Wilmington, 1976-79; chief dep. atty. gen. Del. Dept. Justice, Wilmington, 1979-81; U.S. atty. U.S. Dept. Justice, Wilmington, 1981—. Mem. ABA, Del. State Bar Assn., N.J. State Bar Assn., Am. Trail Lawyers Assn., Fed. Bar Assn. Republican. Roman Catholic. Home: 7 Crenshaw Dr Wilmington DE 19810 Office: US Attys Office 844 King St Wilmington DE 19801

FARNER, DONALD SANKEY, biologist; b. Waumandee, Wis., May 2, 1915; s. John and Lillian O. (Sankey) F.; m. Dorothy S. Copps, Dec. 21, 1940; children: Carla M., Donald C. B.S., Hamline U., 1937, D.Sc. (hon.), 1962; M.A., U. Wis., 1939, Ph.D., 1941. Instr. zoology U. Wis., 1941-43; asst. prof. zoology U. Kans., 1946-47; faculty Wash. State U., 1947-65, prof. zoophysiology, 1952-65, dean, 1960-64; prof. zoophysiology U. Wash., Seattle, 1965—, chmn. dept. zoology, 1966-81; Fulbright research scholar, hon. lectr. zoology U. Otago, N.Z., 1953-54; Guggenheim fellow U. Western Australia, 1958-59; chmn. div. biology and agr. Nat. Acad. Sci.-NRC, 1969-73; sr. U.S. scientist Alexander von Humboldt Stiftung, 1978; pres. XVII Internat. Ornithol. Congress, 1978. Served to lt. USNR, 1943-46; capt. Res. ret. Fellow AAAS (council 1964-80), Am. Ornithologists Union (Brewster award 1960, pres. 1973-75); mem. Am. Physiol. Soc., Am. Soc. Zoologists (pres. 1984), Am. Inst. Biol. Scis., Am. Chem. Soc., Internat. Union Biol. Scis. (pres. 1967-73, chmn. div. zoology 1973-82), Soc. Systematic Zoology, Cooper Ornithol. Soc. (hon. mem.; bd. govs. 1965-71), Deutsche Ornithologen-Gesell. (hon.), Ornitologiska Foreningen: Finland (hon.), Soc. for Endocrinology, Soc. for Study Reproduction, Phi Beta Kappa, Sigma Xi, Phi Kappa Phi, Phi Sigma (hon. pres. 1973-80), Gamma Alpha, Omicron Delta Kappa. Methodist. Club: Cosmos (Washington). Research and publs. in avian biology and physiology. Home: 4533 W Laurel Dr Seattle WA 98105 Office: Dept Zoology U Washington Seattle WA 98195

FARNHAM, ANTHONY EDWARD, English educator; b. Oakland, Calif., July 2, 1930; s. Willard Edward and Frances Fern (Hicks) F.; m. Frances Anne Larkey, Dec. 28, 1957; children: Allen Nicholas, Timothy John. A.B., U. Calif.-Berkeley, 1951; M.A., Harvard U., 1957, Ph.D., 1964. Instr. English Mt. Holyoke Coll., South Hadley, Mass., 1961-64, asst. prof., 1964-69, assoc. prof., 1969-72, prof., 1972—, dept. chmn., 1979—. Editor: A Sourcebook in the History of English, 1969. Served with M.I. U.S. Army, 1953-56. Mem. MLA, Modern Humanities Research Assn., Medieval Acad. Am., Phi Beta Kappa. Roman Catholic. Home: 23 Atwood Rd South Hadley MA 01075 Office: Dept English Mt Holyoke Coll South Hadley MA 01075

FARNHAM, GEORGE RAILTON, lawyer; b. Ft. Wayne, Ind., Feb. 1, 1914; s. George Ross and Mae R. (Railton) F.; m. Constance Amberg, June 6, 1942; children: Carolyn F., Pamela F., Marjorie F., Laurie J., George L. A.B. cum laude, Harvard U., 1936, J.D., 1939. Bar: N.Y. 1939. Job locator N.Y.C. Lawyers Placement Com. Assn. or Bar N.Y.C., 1946; atty. War Assets Adminstrn., N.Y.C., 1946, Finch & Schaefler, 1946-48; assoc. Coudert Bros., N.Y.C., 1948-59, ptnr., 1960—. Mem. Bd. Edn. Union Free Sch. , Eastchester, N.Y., 1955-59; trustee, chmn. Prescott Coll., Ariz., 1965-75; trustee Embry Riddle Aero. U., Daytona Beach, Fla., 1978—; bd. govs. Children's Health Service, N.Y. County, 1970-76; dir., v.p., pres. Mental Health Assn., Westchester County, N.Y., 1973—; bd. dirs. Legal Aid Soc., N.Y.C., 1980—. Served to maj. U.S. Army, 1941-46. Mem. ABA, N.Y. Bar Assn., Assn. Bar City N.Y., Am. Judicature Soc. Club: Harvard. Home: 41 Drake Rd Scarsdale NY 10583 Office: Coudert Bros 200 Park Ave New York NY 10166

FARNHAM, WALLACE DEAN, historian; b. Sibley, Iowa, Apr. 2, 1928; s. Harley W. and Vera I. (Cates) F.; m. Marilynn Pfeiffer, Aug. 26, 1950 (div. 1977); children—Anne, Leonard. B.A., Cornell Coll., Iowa, 1949; M.A., Columbia U., 1951; Ph.D., U. Oreg., 1955. Asst. prof. history U. No. Iowa, 1955-56; asst. prof. U. Alta., Edmonton, Can., 1956-60, asso. prof., 1960-64; asso. prof. history U. Wyo., 1964-65, prof., 1965-67; prof. history U. Ill., Urbana, 1967—; vis. prof. Warsaw (Poland) U., 1971-73, 75-77, 80; asso. dir. Am. Studies Center, Warsaw U., 1975-77. Gen. editor: American Scene, 1966-72; contbr. articles to profl. jours. Served with U.S. Army, 1953-55. Fulbright fellow, 1971-73. Mem. Am. Hist. Assn., Orgn. Am. Historians, Phi Beta Kappa. Episcopalian. Home: 502 W Main 202 Urbana IL 61801 Office: History Dept Univ of Ill Urbana IL 61801

FARNHAM-DIGGORY, SYLVIA, educator, psychologist; b. Lynchburg, Va., Aug. 16, 1927; d. Albert Ayrton and Lola Marshall Farnham; children—Matthew, Jonathan. Ph.B., U. Chgo., 1946; Ph.D. in Psychology, U. Pa., 1961. Asst. prof. psychology Carnegie-Mellon U., Pitts., 1966-70, asso. prof., 1970-75; prof. U. Tex., Dallas, 1975-76, head programs in psychology and human devel., 1975-76; H. Rodney Sharp prof. ednl. studies U. Del., Newark, 1976—. Author: Cognitive Processes in Education, 1972, Learning Disabilities, 1978; contbr. articles to profl. jours. Fellow Nat. Inst. Edn., 1976. Mem. Soc. Research in Child Devel., Cognitive Sci. Soc., Soc. of Friends. Democrat. Office: Willard Hall Univ Del Newark DE 19711

FARNSLEY, CHARLES ROWLAND PEASLEE, publisher; b. Mar. 28, 1907; s. Burrel Hobson and Anna May (Peaslee) F.; m. Nancy Hall Carter, Feb. 27, 1937; children: Sally (Mrs. Robert S. Bird, Jr.), Ann, Alexander, Burrel Charles Peaslee, Douglass Charles Ellerbe. LL.B., U. Louisville, 1930, A.B., 1942, LL.D., 1950; postgrad., U. Ky., 1943-44; LL.D., Wesleyan U., Middletown, Conn., 1959. Practiced law, 1930-48, 54-64; mem. Ky. Ho. of Reps., 1936-40; mayor, Louisville, 1948-54; mem. 89th Congress, 3d dist. of Ky.; pres. Lost Cause Press, Charley Farnsley Distilling Co. Trustee U. Louisville, 1946-48, sec., 1947-48, mem. bd. overseers, 1948-64; curator Transylvania U., Lexington, Ky., 1947-58; trustee Louisville Free Pub. Library, 1945-48; bd. dirs. Louisville Philharmonic Soc., 1947-48, 54—, Louisville Orch., 1954—. Mem. Soc. Colonial Wars, Delta Upsilon, Omicron Delta Kappa. Democrat. Episcopalian. Clubs: River Valley, Pendennis, Wynn Stay, Filson (Louisville) (pres. 1979-80); Century, Grolier (N.Y.C.). Lodge: Masons (Louisville). Home: Glenview KY 40025 Office: Starks Bldg Louisville KY 40202

FARNSWORTH, ALAN COYLE, construction company executive; b. New Orleans, June 4, 1926; s. Richard A. and Dorothy (Coyle) F.; m. Mary Osborn, Oct. 19, 1951; children: Alan Kent, Randal Lee. Student, Tulane U., 1943, Va. Poly. Inst., 1944; B.S., U. Tex., Austin, 1948. Vice pres. Farnsworth & Chambers Co., Inc., Houston, 1949-57; dir. H.A. Lott, Inc., Houston, 1957—, pres., 1959-80, chmn., 1980—. Served with AUS, 1944-46. Mem. Phi Delta Theta, Tau Beta Pi, Chi Epsilon. Republican. Presbyn. Club: Forest. Home: 10 Bayou Shadows Houston TX 77024 Office: 6315 Gulfton St Houston TX 77036

FARNSWORTH, EDWARD ALLAN, lawyer, educator; b. Providence, June 30, 1928; s. Harrison Edward and Gertrude (Romig) F.; m. Patricia Ann Nordstrom, May 30, 1952; children—Jeanne Scott, Karen Ladd, Edward Allan, Pamela Ann. B.S., U. Mich., 1948; M.A., Yale, 1949; LL.B. (Ordronaux prize 1952), Columbia, 1952. Bar: D.C 1952, N.Y. bar 1956. Mem. faculty Columbia, 1954—, prof. law, 1959—, Alfred McCormack prof. law, 1970—; vis. prof. U. Instanbul, 1960, U. Dakar, 1964, U. Paris, 1974-75, Harvard Law Sch., 1970-71; mem. faculty Salzburg Seminar Am. Law, 1963, Columbia-Leyden-Amsterdam program Am. law, 1964, 69, 73; dir. orientation program Am. law Assn. Am. Law Schs., 1965-68; U.S. rep. UN Commn. Internat. Trade Law, 1970—; reporter Restatement of Contracts 2d, 1971-80; cons. N.Y. State Law Revision Commn., 1956, 58, 59, 61; mem. coms. validity and agy. internat. sales contracts Internat. Inst. Unification Pvt. Law, Rome, 1966-72, mem. governing council, 1978—; spl. counsel city reorgn. N.Y.C. Council, 1966-68; U.S. del. Vienna Conf. on Internat. Sales Law, 1980, Bucharest Conf. on Internat. Agy., 1979. Author: An Introduction to the Legal System of the United States, 1963, 2d edit., 1983, (with J. Honnold) Cases and Materials on Commercial Law, 3d edit, 1976, (with W.F. Young) Cases and Materials on Contracts, 3d edit, 1980, Cases and Materials on Commercial Paper, 2d edit, 1976, (with J. Honnold) Cases and Contracts, 1982. Served to capt. USAAF, 1952-54. Mem. Am. Bar Assn., Am. Law Inst., Assn. Bar City N.Y. (chmn. com. fgn. and comparative law 1967-70), Phi Beta Kappa, Phi Delta Phi. Unitarian. Home: 201 Lincoln St Englewood NJ 07631 Office: 435 W 116th St New York NY 10027

FARNSWORTH, FRANK ALBERT, economics educator; s. Frank Adelbert and Lancing Claudine (Miller) F.; m. Elizabeth Hoyt, Dec. 6, 1971; children: Frank A., Ruth Farnsworth McDowell, John C., Elizabeth Martire Cutter, Amy Martire, John Martire. A.B. in Econs. with honors, Colgate U., 1939; A.M., Harvard U., 1946, Ph.D., 1952. With dept. econs. Colgate U., 1941—, prof., 1957—; dept. chmn., vis. research assoc. Harvard U. Grad. Bus. Sch., 1947-48; Fulbright prof. Norwegian Sch. Econs., Bergen, 1954-55; vis. prof. small bus. Wake Forest U., 1975; vis. fellow Massey Coll.-U. Toronto, 1968; pres. Madison Bus. Devel. Corp.; treas. Madison County Indsl. Devel. Agy.; dir. Victory Markets Inc., N.Y.; cons. in econs.; dir. Susquehan and Western R.R. Mem. AAUP, N.Y. State Econ. Devel. Council, Alpha Chi Epsilon. Republican. Am. Baptist. Lodge: Masons. Home: 17 E Kendrick Ave Hamilton NY 13346 Office: Colgate U 412 Alumni Hall Hamilton NY 13346

FARNSWORTH, JACK LEE, educational publisher; b. Detroit, Feb. 18, 1946; s. Lee J. Farnworth and Mary E. (Smith) F.; m. Nancy R. Young, Jan. 30, 1963 (div.); children: Lori, Kristine. B.A., U. Iowa, 1968. Sales rep. McGraw-Hill-Coll. div., Iowa, 1969-71, editor math. and physics, N.Y.C., 1971-73, mktg. mgr. arts and sci., 1973-76, editor-in-chief, 1976-77; editorial dir. McGraw-Hill-Coll. dir., N.Y.C., 1977-81; mktg. dir. McGraw-Hill-Coll. div., N.Y.C., 1981-82, gen. mgr. McGraw-Hill-Webster div., 1982—2; lectr. CUNY, U. Pa., Denver; v.p., treas. Jamie Laughridge Creative Services, N.Y.C., 1976—. Mem. Assn. Am. Pubs. Democrat. Home: 44 W 62d St New York NY 10023 Office: McGraw-Hill Book Co 1221 Ave of the Americas New York NY 10021

FARON, LOUIS CHARLES, educator; b. Bklyn., July 16, 1923; s. Louis C. and Erna (Rost) F.; m. Sally Rogers, Dec. 18, 1974; children by previous marriage—Amy, Kenneth. A.B., Columbia, 1949, Ph.D., 1954. Research asso. dept. anthropology U. Ill., Champaign-Urbana, 1955- 59; asst. prof. dept. anthropology Calif. State Coll. at Los Angeles, 1959- 62; asso. prof. dept. anthropology U. Pitts., 1962-64; prof. State U. N.Y., Stony Brook, 1964—, chmn. dept. anthropology, 1964-71; engaged in field work, Chile, 1952-54, Peru, 1957-59, Panama, 1960, Mexico, 1963. Served with AUS, 1943-46. Guggenheim Found. fellow, 1970—. Fellow Am. Anthrop. Assn.; mem. Internat. Congress of Americanists. Home: Main St Stony Brook NY 11790

FARQUHAR, GORDON NESBITT, insurance company executive; b. Olney, Md., Nov. 13, 1923; s. Arthur Douglas and Helen Thomas (Nesbitt) F.; m. Virginia Fischer, 1951; children: Jean, Ellen Brooke. B.A., Yale U., 1948; LL.B., U. Conn., 1954; postgrad., Harvard U. Bus. Sch., 1972. With Aetna Life & Casualty Co., Hartford, Conn., 1948-73, v.p., 1969-73; pres. Excelsior Life Ins. Co., Toronto, 1973—, Aetna Casualty Co. Can. Bd. dirs. Toronto Symphony. Served to capt. AUS, 1943-46; served to capt. U.S. Army, 1951-52. Home: Apt 204 350 Lonsdale Rd Toronto ON Canada M5P 1R6 Office: 20 Toronto St Toronto ON Canada M5C 2C4

FARQUHAR, JOHN WILLIAM, physician, educator; b. Winnipeg, Man., Can., June 12, 1927; came to U.S., 1934, naturalized, 1950; s. John Giles and Marjorie Victoria (Roberts) F.; m. Christine Louise Johnson, July 14, 1968; children: Margaret F., John C.M.; children by previous marriage: Bruce E., Douglas G. A.B., U. Calif., Berkeley, 1949, M.D., 1952. Intern U. Calif. Hosp., San Francisco, 1952-53; resident, 1953-54, 57-58, postdoctoral fellow, 1955-57; resident U. Minn., Mpls., 1954-55; research asso. Rockefeller U., N.Y.C., 1958-62; asst. prof. medicine Stanford (Calif.) U., 1962-66, asso. prof., 1966-73, prof., 1973—; dir. Stanford Heart Disease Prevention Program, 1973—; mem. staff Stanford U. Hosp.; adviser, cons. Inst. of Medicine of Nat. Acad. Scis. Author: The American Way of Life Need Not Be Hazardous to Your Health, 1978; contbr. articles to profl. jours. Served with U.S. Army, 1945-46. Recipient James D. Bruce award ACP, 1983. Mem. Am. Soc. Clin. Investigation, Acad. Behavioral Medicine, Harvey Soc., Gold Headed Cane Soc., Sigma Xi, Alpha Omega Alpha. Episcopalian. Office: Sch Medicine Stanford U Stanford CA 94305

FARQUHAR, MARILYN GIST, biologist; b. Tulare, Calif., July 11, 1928; d. Brooks DeWitt and Alta Gertrude (Green) Gist; m. George E. Palade, June 7, 1970; children—Bruce, Douglas. A.B., U. Calif., Berkeley, 1949, M.A., 1953, Ph.D., 1955. Asso. to prof. pathology U. Calif. Sch. Medicine, San Francisco, 1962-69; prof. Rockefeller U., N.Y.C., 1970-73; prof. cell biology Yale U. Sch. Medicine, New Haven, 1973—; fellow Branford Coll. Yale U., 1977—. Mem. editorial bd.: Jour. Cell Biology, 1966-70, Endocrinology, 1974-79, Kidney Internat. Jour, 1974—, Jour. Exptl. Medicine, 1976—, Jour. Histochemistry Cytochemistry, 1970-77; contbr. articles on cell biology, exptl. pathology and endocrinology to profl. jours. Nat. Inst. Arthritis Metabolism and Digestive Diseases research grantee, 1962—; Nat. Inst. Gen. Med. Scis. career awardee, 1965-73. Mem. Am. Soc. Cell Biology (pres. 1981-82), Am. Assn. Pathologists, Am. Assn. Anatomists, Endocrine Soc., Electron Microscope Soc. Am., Histochemical Soc., Internat. Acad. Pathology. Home: 22 Coachmans Ln Woodbridge CT 06525 Office: 333 Cedar St New Haven CT 06510

FARQUHAR, NORMAN, securities company executive; b. Olney, Md., May 10, 1921; s. Arthur Douglas and Helen (Thomas Nesbitt) F.; m. Ann Randolph Jennings, Oct. 4, 1947 (dec.); children: Katherine, Douglas Brooke, Edward Pleasants, William Thomas Nesbitt, Witt Jennings; m. Elinor Kenney Brown, Jan. 3, 1981; stepchildren: Elizabeth M. Brown, Sarah K. Brown, Marcia B. Brown. B.A., U. Va., 1943; LL.B., Nat. U., 1954. Bar: D.C. 1954. Asst. sec. Savs. Instn. Sandy Spring, Md., 1946; rep. Alex Brown & Sons, Washington, 1948-58, gen. partner, 1958—; dir. Cin. New Orleans Tex. Pacific Ry., Washington, Montgomery Mut. Ins. Co., Sandy Spring. Served to capt. C.E., AUS, 1942-45. Mem. Securities Industry Assn. (past chmn. Mid-Atlantic div.), Delta Psi. Clubs: Princess Anne Country, Metropolitan, Chevy Chase. Home: 2425 Kalorama Rd NW Washington DC 20008 Office: Alex Brown & Sons 730 15th St NW Washington DC 20005

FARQUHAR, ROBIN HUGH, university president; b. Victoria, B.C., Can., Dec. 1, 1938; s. Hugh Ernest and Jean (MacIntosh) F.; m. Frances Harriet Caswell, July 6, 1963; children: Francine Jean, Katherine Lynn, Susan Ann. B.A. with honors, U. B.C., 1960, M.A., 1964; Ph.D., U. Chgo., 1967. Tchr., counsellor, coach Edward Milne Secondary Sch., Sooke, B.C., 1962-64; assoc. dir., then dep. dir. Univ. Council Ednl. Adminstrn., Columbus, Ohio, 1966-71; chmn. ednl. adminstrn. dept., asst. dir. Ont. Inst. Studies in Edn., Toronto, 1971-76; prof., dean Coll. Edn., U. Sask., Saskatoon, 1976-81; pres. U. Winnipeg, 1981—. Author: The Humanities in Preparing Educational Administrators, 1970, Preparing Educational Leaders: A Review of Recent Literature, 1972, Social Science Content for Preparing Educational Leaders, 1973, Educational Administration in Australia and Abroad: Analyses and Challenges, 1975, Canadian and Comparative Educational Administration, 1980; editorial bd.: Jour. Edn. Adminstrn., 1973—; Editorial bd.: Internat. Jour. Ednl. Adminstrn., 1984—. Served with Can. Navy Res., 1956-64. Recipient Edward L. Bernays Found. prize, 1968. Fellow Commonwealth Council Ednl. Adminstrn. (pres.); Mem. Can. Soc. Study Edn. (past pres.), Can. Edn. Assn. (dir.), InterAm. Soc. for Ednl. Adminstrn. (dir.). Mem. United Ch. Can. Clubs: Man., Rotary (Winnipeg). Home: 49 Oak St Winnipeg MB R3M 3P6 Canada

FARQUHARSON, GORDON MACKAY, lawyer; b. Charlottetown, P.E.I., Can., July 12, 1928; s. Percy Alfred and Rachael Lillian (MacKay) F.; m. Judy Lynne Bridges, Oct. 10, 1980; 1 son, Trevor; children by previous marriage: Douglas, Tanyss, Robbie, Karen. B.A., U. Toronto, 1950; LL.B., Osgoode Hall Law Sch., 1954. Bar: Called to Ont. bar 1954. Since practiced in, Toronto; partner Lang, Michener, Cranston, Farquharson & Wright, 1964—; instr. bar admission course Osgoode Hall Law Sch., 1959-66; dir. GSW Ltd., Cameo Inc., Valleydene Corp. Ltd., Showerlux Can. Ltd., Mony Life Ins. Co. Can., Shaw Industries Ltd., Doverhold Investments Ltd. Conv. chmn. for Mitchell Sharp in Fed. Leadership campaign, 1968. Mem. Can. Bar Assn., German-Can. Bus. and Profl. Assn., Phi Gamma Delta (pres. 1954). Club: Univ. (Toronto). Home: 245 Borden St Toronto ON Canada Office: PO Box 10 First Canadian Pl Toronto ON M5X 1A2 Canada

FARR, CHARLES SIMS, lawyer; b. Hewlett, N.Y., June 29, 1920; s. John and Hazel Zealy (Sims) F.; m. Mary Randolph Rue, Dec. 21, 1946 (dec. Dec. 1980); children: Charles Sims, Virginia Farr Ramsey, Randolph Rue, John, II. Student, Princeton U., 1938-40; LL.B., Columbia U., 1948. Bar: N.Y. State 1949. Assoc. firm White & Case, N.Y.C., 1948-58, partner, 1959—; mem. bd. visitors Columbia U. Sch. Law. Contbr. articles to profl. publs. Chmn. Commonwealth Fund, N.Y.C.; trustee St. Luke's-Roosevelt Hosp. Center, N.Y.C., Gen. Theol. Sem., N.Y.C., 1968-77, N.Y. Zool. Soc.; mem. bd. fgn. parishes Protestant Episc. Ch., 1954—, pres., 1977; chancellor to pres. bishop Protestant Episc. Ch. in U.S.A., 1977—; mem. vestry St. James' Ch., N.Y.C., 1966-76, sr. warden, 1973-76, 77—; mem. council Rockefeller U.; Sec. Am. Hosp. in Paris Found. Served to lt. comdr. USN, 1941-45; PTO. Decorated Sec. Navy Commendation Ribbon; recipient Alumni Assn. medal Columbia U., 1977. Fellow Am. Coll. Probate Counsel, Am. Bar Found.; mem. Am. Law Inst., ABA, N.Y. State Bar Assn. Republican. Clubs: Century, Links, Racquet and Tennis, Pilgrims. Home: 139 E 79th St New York NY 10021 Office: 1155 Ave of the Americas New York NY 10036

FARR, HENRY BARTOW, JR., lawyer; b. N.Y.C., June 16, 1921; s. H. Bartow and Mildred (Blair) F.; m. Mary Elizabeth Roberts, Jan. 22, 1972; children: H. Bartow, Preston Putnam, Christopher Blair. B.A. magna cum laude, Princeton U., 1943; LL.B. (Stone scholar), Columbia U., 1948. Bar: U.S. Ct. Appeals (2d Cir.) 1950, U.S. Dist. Ct. 1950. Asso. Sullivan & Cromwell, 1948-53; asst. atty. gen. N.Y. State Crime Commn., 1951-53; asso. Wilkie, Farr & Gallagher, N.Y.C., 1953-58; mng. atty. IBM, N.Y.C., 1959-64, Armonk, N.Y., 1964-65, group counsel data processing group, Harrison, N.Y., 1965-68; v.p., gen. counsel World Trade Corp., N.Y.C., 1968-72, v.p., gen. counsel, sec., 1972-74, World Trade Europe, Paris, 1974-77; v.p., gen. counsel Singer Co., N.Y.C., 1977-80; dep. gen. counsel R.J. Reynolds Industries, Inc., Winston-Salem, N.C., 1980—. Served with USNR, 1943-46. Mem. ABA. Episcopalian. Clubs: Racquet & Tennis, Travellers Old Town. Home: 1020 Kent Rd W Winston-Salem NC 27104 Office: RJ Reynolds Industries Winston-Salem NC 27102

FARR, JAMIE, actor; b. Toledo, July 1; s. Samuel N. and Jamelia M. (Abodeely) Farah; m. Joy Ann Richards, Feb. 16, 1963; children—Jonas Samuel James, Yvonne Elizabeth Rose. B.A. in Film, Columbia Coll., Los Angeles; student, Pasadena Playhouse Theatre Arts. Appeared in: stage prodns. including Chapter Two; appeared in: numerous films including Canonball Run, CBS-TV, The Rebels Return; appears in TV series MASH as Corporal Klinger; appeared in: other TV series including Chicago Teddy Bears; nightclub comedy entertainer, 1975—. Served with U.S. Army, 1957-59. Mem. Writers Guild Am., Screen Actors Guild, AFTRA, Actors Equity. Eastern Orthodox. Office: care Internat Creative Mgmt 8899 Beverly Blvd Los Angeles CA 90048 *I just wouldn't give up—failures for me were merely stepping stones to eventual success. I refused to give up a business I loved—I didn't treat it as an affair, but a lasting romance.* *

FARR, RICHARD CLABORN, manufacturing company executive; b. Wynne, Ark., Nov. 2, 1928; s. Jesse William and Francis Adele (Hooper) F.; m. Marcille Mullikin, Dec. 25, 1950; children: Denise Farr Isaac, Richardson Lloyd, David Randall. B.A. in Philosophy, Hendrix Coll., Conway, Ark., 1952; postgrad., Stanford U., So. Methodist U. With Procter & Gamble Co., 1952-65; v.p. Continental Grain Co., N.Y.C. and Paris, 1965-70; mng. dir. Lehman Bros., Inc., N.Y.C., 1970-71; corp. v.p. Heublein, Inc., Farmington, Conn., 1971-79; sr. v.p. Crown Zellerbach Corp., San Francisco, 1979—; chmn., chief exec. officer Farr Investment Co., 1980—; dir. United Vintners, Inc., Air Sunshine, Inc., Seal, Inc., Bouton Corp., Lincoln Logs Ltd., Hunter Environ. Services, Inc.; chmn. bd. Bituminous Coal Corp., Inc. Bd. dirs. United Way San Francisco. Served with AUS, 1946-48. Fulbright scholar, 1952; Mgmt. Devel. fellow, 1965. Mem. Personnel Round Table (dir.), Consumer Fin. Inst. (chmn. exec. com.), Conf. Board (dir. com. mgmt.), Am. Platform Tennis Assn. (dir.). Clubs: Univ. (N.Y.C.); Hartford Golf, Hartford Tennis; University (Hartford); Oyster Harbors (Osterville, Mass.). Home: 40 Colony Rd West Hartford CT 06117 3555 Jackson St San Francisco CA 94118 Office: 1 Bush St San Francisco CA 94104 also PO Box 7-367 West Hartford CT 06107 *Self-confidence is a prerequisite to great undertakings.*

FARR, RICHARD STUDLEY, physician; b. Detroit, Oct. 30, 1922; s. Hiram Grant and Gretchen (Wyman) F.; m. Janet Elizabeth Rothrock, June 17, 1944; children: Peter Rothrock, Andrew Grant. Student, Hamilton Coll., 1940-43; M.D., U. Chgo., 1946. Intern U.S. Naval Hosp., Annapolis, Md., 1946-47; postdoctoral fellow, research fellow M.C. USN, 1947-54; sr. research fellow Calif. Inst. Tech., 1953-54; resident U. Chgo. Sch. Medicine, 1954-55; instr. dept. medicine U. Chgo., 1954-55, asst. prof., 1955-56; asso. research prof. anatomy U. Pitts., 1956-57, asst. prof., head sect. clin. immunology, 1957-60, asso. prof. medicine, head clin. immunology sect., 1960-62; head div. allergy, immunology and rheumatology Scripps Clinic and Research Found., La Jolla, Calif., 1962-69; head dept. allergy-clin. immunology Nat. Jewish Hosp. and Research Center, Denver, 1969-72, chmn. dept. medicine, 1972-77; also prof. medicine (clin. immunology) U. Colo. Med. Center, 1972—; Mem. tng. grant com. USPHS, 1963-66, immunobiology study sect., 1968-72; chmn. rev. panel for bacterial vaccines and antigens FDA, 1973-78. Contbr. profl. jours. Served with M.C. USNR, 1946-54. Recipient Distinguished Service award U. Chgo., 1975. Fellow Am. Acad. Allergy (pres. 1969-70), AAAS, Am. Coll. Allergists (hon.), Can. Soc. Allergy and Clin. Immunology (hon.); mem. AMA (chmn. 1966-67), Am. Soc. Clin. Investigation, Am. Assn. Immunologists. Developed ammonium sulfate and other primary tests to detect antibodies. Office: Nat Jewish Hosp and Research Ctr Nat Asthma Ctr Denver CO 80206 *On Human Experimentation: An experiment should not be done on a human if the investigator would not do the same experiment on each of the following: his/her mother, father, sister, brother, wife/husband, son and daughter. One can have hidden hostilities toward a mate or relative but I've yet to meet anyone without a strong affection for at least one of the persons listed above. The investigator is excluded from this list because we sometimes do foolish things to ourselves.*

FARR, WALTER GREENE, JR., lawyer; b. Wenonah, N.J., Feb. 24, 1925; s. Walter Greene and Florence (Miner) F.; m. Louise Evans, June 24, 1950; children: Judith Evans, Catherine Austin, Elizabeth Lawton, Stephen Nicholas. B.S., Yale U., 1948, LL.B., 1951. Bar: N.Y. 1951. Asso. firm Paul, Weiss, Rifkind, Wharton & Garrison, N.Y.C., 1951-54, Gumbart, Corbin, Tyler & Cooper, New Haven, 1955-58, partner, 1958-62; with AID, 1962-67; dep. regional adminstr. Bur. Near East and S. Asian Affairs, 1964-67; dir. model cities adminstrn. HUD, 1967-69; prof. law NYU Law Sch., 1969-77; chief counsel Econ. Devel. Adminstrn., Dept. Commerce, Washington, 1977-78; dep. asst. sec. community planning and devel. HUD, 1978-81; exec. dir. Calif. Housing Fin. Agy., 1981-83; sr. v.p. Wells Fargo Mktg. Co., 1983—; vis. lectr. Yale Law Sch., 1958-62. Served with AUS, 1943-45. Home: 460 Cragmont Ave Berkeley CA 94708

FARRALL, ARTHUR W., author, educator, engineer, inventor; b. Harvard, Nebr., Feb. 23, 1899; s. John W. and Olive A. (Frazell) F.; m. E. Luella Buck, June 20, 1923; children: Margaret Longnecker, Robert Arthur. B.S., U. Nebr., 1921, M.S., 1922, D.Eng. (hon.), 1955; post grad., U. Calif., 1926. Tchr., U. Calif., 1922-29; research dir. Douthitt Engrng. Co., Chgo., 1929-33; research engr., dir. research Creamery Package Mfg. Co., 1933-45; prof. agrl. engrng., chmn. dept. Mich. State U., 1945-64, prof., 1965-68, prof., chmn. emeritus, 1968—, chmn. food tech., 1959-60; U.S. del. Internat. Dairy Congress, Stockholm, 1949; cons. U.S. Dept. Agr., 1964-65, Ford Found., Punjab Agr. U., India, 1968-69; cons. to industry in dairy and agrl. engrng.; cons. food engrng., Brazil, 1970; mem. research adv. com. Food Industry Research Center, Nat. Restaurant Assn., 1958-61; gen. chmn. Centennial Farm Mechanization, 1955. Author: Dairy Engineering, 1942, Engineering for Dairy and Food Products, 1963, History of the Farrall and Frazell Families, 1970; also bulls., tech. papers; co-author: Ency. Food Engineering, 1971; editor: dairy engrng. sect. Am. Jour. Dairy Sci., 1945-52; asso. editor, co-author: Dairy Handbook and Dictionary, 1958; editor-in-chief, co-author: Agriculture Engineering-A Dictionary and Handbook, 1965; contbr.: Refrigeration Handbook, 1937; author: Food Engineering Systems 1, Operations, 1975; contbr.: Food Engineering Systems 2, Utilities, 1979; editor: Hall of Fame, Food Engineering, 1978, Dictionary of Agricultural and Food Engineering, 2d edit., 1979. Sponsor Arthur and Luella Farrall fellowship Mich. State U., 1979—, A.W. Farrall Engrng. Faculty award, 1979—; pres. East Lansing Sr. Citizens, 1980-81; gen. chmn. Mich. State U. Retirees Service Corps. Recipient Gold Medal award Dairy and Food Equipment Assn.-Am. Soc. Agrl. Engrs., 1972. Fellow Am. Soc. Agrl. Engrng. (pres. 1962-63, chmn. food engrng. com. 1965-66, editor Food Engrng. newsletter 1966-68, Massey Ferguson Ednl. Gold Medal award 1971, sponsor ann. award to young educator 1972—); mem. Am. Soc. Engrng. Edn. (chmn. agr. engrng. div. 1949, 60), AAUP, Am. Dairy Sci. Assn., Inst. Food Tech., AAAS, Mid-Mich. Geneal. Soc. (pres. 1971-73), Am. Legion, Phi Kappa Phi (exec. sec. Mich. State U. chpt. 1968—), Sigma Xi, Alpha Gamma Rho, Alpha Zeta, Tau Beta Pi, Pi Tau Sigma, Alpha Epsilon. Congregationalist. Club: Mich. State Univ. Patentee inertial propulsion system; frost prevention, machine, freezer controller, continuous ice cream freezer, fruit feeder, continuous butter machine, electric battery powered automobile. Home: 1858 Cahill Dr East Lansing MI 48823 *Service to others is a sound basis for continuing satisfaction in life.*

FARRAR, DONALD KEITH, financial executive; b. Indio, Calif., May 18, 1938; s. Keith and Sarah S. (Turner) F.; m. Jo Ann Puttler, Dec. 16, 1961; children: Daniel K., Donald S., Douglas S., Kimberly. B.S. in Bus. Adminstrn, U. So. Calif., 1960, M.B.A., Harvard U., 1965. With planning div. Paul Revere Life Ins. Co., Worcester, Mass., 1965, budget supr., 1966, asst. to pres., 1967, asst. sec., 1968-73, v.p. investment, 1969-73; v.p. planning Avco Corp., Greenwich, Conn., 1973-74, sr. v.p., chief acct. officer, 1975-77, exec. v.p., 1978-81, pres., dir., 1981—. Mem. fin. com. Hahnemann Hosp., Worcester, 1969-73. Served with USNR, 1960-63. Home: 115 Lower Cross Rd Greenwich CT 06830 Office: 1275 King St Greenwich CT 06830

FARRAR, EDWARD, geologist, educator; b. London, Sept. 7, 1937; s. Harry and Betty (Crickmay) F.; m. Mary Patricia Thomas, June 11, 1966; children: Scott, Ross, Jean, Andrew. B.A. in Physics, U. Toronto, 1959, M.A., 1960, Ph.D., 1966. Meterologist Can. Dept. Transport, Goose Bay, Labrador, 1960-63; prof. geol. sci. Queens U., Kingston, Ont., Can., 1966—, head dept. geol. scis., 1981—. Contbr. articles to profl. publs. Mem. Am. Geophys. Union. Home: RR 1 Inverary ON Canada K0H 1X0 Office: Queen's U Dept Geol Scis Kingston ON Canada K7L 3N6 *I hope that when my time comes I will have left more than I have taken away.*

FARRAR, FREDERICK M., banker; b. Ft. Collins, Colo., Sept. 10, 1912; s. Fred and Mary H. (McMenemy) F.; m. Katherine E. Thatcher, June 20, 1941; children: Katherine Farrar Spahn, Logan, Elizabeth, Janet Farrar Timmerman. Student, Colo. Sch. Mines, 1931-33; B.S. in Bus., U. Colo., 1936; LL.B., U. Denver, 1941. Bar: Colo. bar 1945. Practice in, Denver, 1945-58; mem. firm Farrar and Martin; chmn. bd. First Nat. Bank, Pueblo, Colo., 1963-74, Colo. Comml. Bank, Colorado Springs, 1967-72, Exchange Nat. Bank, 1970-74; founder, chmn. Mountain Banks, Ltd., Colorado Springs, 1971-74; chmn. Citadel Bank, Colorado Springs, 1975-80, Garden of the Gods Bank, 1977—. Mem. bd. edn. Air Acad. Sch. Dist., 1963-69; chmn. Western Mus. Mining and Industry, 1971—; trustee Colo. Coll. Served with USAAF, 1942-45. Episcopalian. Clubs: Cheyenne Mountain, El Paso (Colorado Springs); Cactus (Denver). Office: 4520 Northpark Dr Colorado Springs CO 80907

FARRAR, MARTIN WILBUR, chemical company executive; b. Hazlehurst, Miss., Dec. 25, 1922; s. Thomas Martin and Hettie (Ashley) F.; m. Lorraine Williams, Feb. 11, 1944; children—James Martin, Michael David. B.S. in Chemistry, Miss. Coll., 1943; Ph.D., U. Pitts., 1950. Sr. research chemist Monsanto Chem. Co., St. Louis, 1950-54; project leader Ethyl Corp., Baton Rouge, 1954-55; with Monsanto Co., 1955—, mgr. research and devel., 1965-74, dir. research and devel., 1974—. Bd. dirs. Mo. Baptist Found., 1969-74. Served with USNR, 1943-46. Recipient Barnhill Meml. award chemistry Miss. Coll., 1943; AEC fellow, 1948-50. Mem. Mo. Acad. Sci. (councilor 1974-77), Soc. Plastics Engrs., Sigma Xi, Phi Lambda Upsilon. Author, patentee organic chemistry. Home: 858 Briarfarm Ln Kirkwood MO 63122 Office: 800 N Lindbergh Blvd Saint Louis MO 63167

FARREHI, CYRUS, cardiologist, educator; b. Malayer, Iran, Jan. 26, 1935; s. Mansoor and Nikzad (Agah) F.; m. Z. Jane Christensen, June 6, 1964; children: Peter M., Paul C., Lisa N., Mary M. M.D., U. Tehran, 1958. Diplomate: Am. Bd. Internal Medicine, Am. Bd. Cardiovascular Diseases. Intern Wayne County Gen. Hosp., Eloise, Mich., 1959-60, resident, 1960-62; fellow in cardiology U. Oreg. Med. Sch., 1962-64; teaching fellow dept. medicine U. Alta., 1964-66; asst. prof. medicine U. Oreg.; also dir. cardiac catherization lab. VA Hosp., Portland, Oreg., 1966-69; chmn. dept. medicine McLaren Gen. Hosp.,

Flint, Mich., 1971-73, dir. cardiovascular diagnostic service, 1973—; clin. assoc. prof. medicine Mich. State U., 1973-78, clin. prof., 1978—; cons. cardiovascular diseases, Flint, 1969—; bd. dirs. Ind. Practice Assocs., 1979—, sec., 1979-83; adj. prof. health care and human services U. Mich., Flint, 1981—. Contbr. articles med. jours. Fellow A.C.P., Royal Coll. Physicians and Surgeons of Can., Am. Coll. Cardiology, Clin. Council Am. Heart Assn., Genesee County Med. Soc. (dir. 1980—); mem. Detroit Heart Club. Roman Catholic. Home: 8398 Old Plank Rd Grand Blanc MI 48439 Office: 1071 N Ballenger Hwy Flint MI 48504

FARREL, GEORGE T., bank holding co. exec.; b. 1931; (married). B.S., U. Notre Dame, 1953. With Mellon Bank (N.A.), 1955—, asst. v.p. credit dept., 1962-64, asst. v.p. internat. dept., 1964, v.p. internat. dept., 1966-74, sr. v.p. internat. dept., 1974, exec. v.p., 1978-80, vice chmn., 1980-81, pres., 1981—, also dir.; dir. Banco Bozano, Network Fin. Ltd., First Boston (Europe) Ltd.; v.p. Mellon Nat. Corp. Served with U.S. Army. Mem. Bankers Assn. Fgn. Trade (dir.). Office: Mellon Bank Mellon Sq Pittsburgh PA 15230

FARRELL, AUSTIN JAMES, lawyer; b. Rockville Centre, N.Y., June 10, 1932; s. James Hyslop and Grace (Moseley) F.; m. Margaret Root Auch, Sept. 8, 1955; children: Emily, Benjamin. B.A., Haverford Coll., 1954; J.D., Columbia U., 1957. Bar: N.Y. 1959, Wash. 1973. Asso. firm Thacher, Proffitt, Prizer, Crawley & Wood, 1957-65; with Crowell Collier and Macmillan, Inc., 1965-72, sr. counsel, sec., 1967-72, v.p., sec., 1971; asst. gen. counsel PACCAR Inc., Bellevue, Wash., 1972-73; gen. counsel Rocket Research, Corp., Redmond, Wash., 1973—, sec.-treas., 1974-76; v.p. adminstrn., counsel Flow Industries, Inc., Kent, Wash., 1976-77; partner firm Holman & Farrell, Seattle, 1977-78; sr. partner firm Farrell & Cool (and predecessor), Bellevue, Wash., 1979—; arbitrator Am. Arbitration Assn.; mem. Wash. State Bar Examiners. Mem. Am., N.Y. State, Wash., Seattle-King County bar assns., Assn. Bar City N.Y. Clubs: College (Seattle); Bellevue Athletic, Mercer Island Beach. Home: 8230 84th Ave SE Mercer Island WA 98040 Office: 301 116th SE Suite 100 Bellevue WA 98004

FARRELL, DAVID COAKLEY, department store executive; b. Chgo., June 14, 1933; s. Daniel A. and Anne D. (O'Malley) F.; m. Betty J. Ross, July 9, 1955; children: Mark, Lisa, David. B.A., Antioch Coll., Yellow Springs, Ohio, 1956. Asst. buyer, buyer, br. store gen. mgr., mdse. mgr. Kaufmann's, Pitts., 1956-66, v.p., gen. mdse. mgr., 1966-69, pres., 1969-74; v.p. May Dept. Stores Co., St. Louis, 1969-75, dir., 1974—, pres., chief operating officer, 1975-79, pres., chief exec. officer, 1979—; dir. 1st Nat. Bank, St. Louis. Bd. dirs. St. Louis Symphony Soc., St. Louis Area council Boy Scouts Am., Arts and Edn. Fund Greater St. Louis; trustee Com. for Econ. Devel., St. Louis Children's Hosp., Washington U., St. Louis; active Salvation Army; mem. Bus. Com. for Arts, Civic Progress. Mem. Nat. Retail Mchts. Assn. (dir.). Roman Catholic. Clubs: University (N.Y.C.); Duquesne (Pitts.); Bogey, Mo. Athletic, Noonday, St. Louis, St. Louis Country (St. Louis). Office: 611 Olive St Saint Louis MO 63101 *

FARRELL, EDMUND JAMES, author, English language educator; b. Butte, Mont., May 17, 1927; s. Bartholomew J. and Lavinia H. (Collins) F.; m. Jo Ann Hayes, Dec. 19, 1964; children—David, Kevin, Sean. A.B., Stanford U., 1950, M.A., 1951; Ph.D., U. Calif., Berkeley, 1969. Chmn. English dept. James Lick High Sch., San Jose, Calif., 1954-59; supr. secondary English U. Calif., Berkeley, 1959-70; adj. prof. English U. Ill., Urbana, 1973-78; prof. English edn. U. Tex., Austin, 1978—; pres. Farrell Ednl. Services, Inc., 1981—; participant revision lit. objectives Nat. Assessment of Ednl. Progress, Denver, 1972-73, 78; mem. adv. com. Center for the Book, Library of Congress, 1980—; chmn. adv. com. on English Coll. Bd., N.Y.C., 1974-79, mem. council acad. affairs, 1978-79; guest lectr. local, state and nat. confs. of English tchrs., 1954—; reader compositions for advanced placement program Rider Coll., Princeton, N.J., 1969, 72-77. Author: (with others) Exploring Life Through Literature, 1964, Counterpoint in Literature, 1967, Projection in Literature, 1967, Outlooks in Literature, 1973, Fantasy: Forms of Things Unknown, 1974, Science Fact/Fiction, 1974, Comment, 1976, Myth, Mind and Moment, 1976, I/You, We/They, 1976, Traits and Topics, 1976, Up Stage/Down Stage, 1976, To Be, 1976, Conflict in Reality, 1976, Arrangement in Literature, 1979, Purpose in Literature, 1979, Album U.S.A., 1983. Served with USN, 1945-46. Mem. Nat. Council Tchrs. English (field rep. 1970-71, asst. exec. sec. 1971-73, asso. exec. dir. 1973-78, chmn. commn. lit. 1979—, trustee research found. 1979—, Disting. Service award 1982), Coll. English Assn., Phi Delta Kappa, Pi Lambda Theta. Unitarian. Home: 6500 Sumac St Austin TX 78731 Office: Dept Curriculum and Instruction Univ Texas Austin TX 78712

FARRELL, EDWARD JOSEPH, educator; b. San Francisco, Mar. 28, 1917; s. Christopher Patrick and Ethel Ann (Chesterman) F.; m. Pearl Philomena Rongone, Aug. 21, 1954; children: Paul, Paula. B.Sc., U. San Francisco, 1939; M.A., Stanford U., 1942. Faculty U. San Francisco, 1941—, prof. math., 1968-82, prof. emeritus, 1982—; Guest lectr. regional and nat. meetings Nat. Council Tchrs. Math., 1966, 67, 69; cons. math. text pubs. Mem. adv. panels NSF, 1966—, dir. summer and in-service insts., 1960—, dir. confs. geometry, 1967, 68, 70-75; mem. rev. panel Sci. Books. Author math. reports; editor studies teaching contemporary geometry. Served with AUS, 1944-46. NSF faculty fellow, 1956-57. Mem. AAAS, Am. Assn. Physics Tchrs., Nat. Council Tchrs. Math., Sch. Sci. and Math. Assn. Republican. Roman Catholic. Home: 2526 Gough St San Francisco CA 94123

FARRELL, EILEEN, singer, soprano; b. Williamantic, Conn., Feb. 13, 1920; d. Michael John and Catherine (Kennedy) F.; m. Robert V. Reagan, Apr. 4, 1946; children: Robert V., Kathleen. Degrees hon., U. R.I., Loyola U., U. Hartford, Notre Dame Coll., N.H., Wagner Coll., Cin. Conservatory. Vis. prof. Hartford U. Made debut as singer, Columbia Broadcasting Co., 1941; singer own program, CBS, 6 yrs; made opera debut in: Il Trovatore with, San Francisco Opera; singer with major symphony orchs. in, U.S.; toured throughout, U.S. and in S.Am.; performer pops, blues and jazz with symphony orchs.; rec. artist, ABC Dunhill, Columbia, RCA, London, Angel records. (Recipient Grammy award.). Address: ICM Artists Ltd 40 W 57th St New York NY 10019

FARRELL, JAMES PATRICK, lawyer, foundation executive; b. Montclair, N.J., Jan. 22, 1903; s. Patrick J. and Martha (Farrell) F.; m. Kathryn Fischer, Oct. 24, 1929; children: James P., Mary Patricia Farrell Russell, Kathryn Anne Farrell Noumair, Hazel Claire Farrell Murray, Jr. LL.B., Fordham U., 1926, LL.D., 1976; LL.D., U. R.I., 1973, Trinity Coll., 1982. Bar: N.Y. 1932. Mem. firm Frueauff, Farrell, Sullivan & Bryan, N.Y.C., 1926-74, partner, 1936-80; former dir. Wigton-Abbott Corp., Cities Service Co., Tiffany & Co.; sec./treas. W. Alton Jones Found., Inc., 1944-71, pres., 1971—; v.p. Charles A. Frueauff Found., Inc. Trustee Trinity Coll., Washington, Madison Sq. Boys Club, N.Y.C. Decorated Assn. Master Knights Sovereign Mil. Order Malta U.S.A., 1958, Knights and Ladies Equestrian Order Holy Sepulchre Jerusalem, 1962. Mem. Assn. Bar City N.Y., N.Y. County Lawyers Assn., N.Y., Am. Bar Assn., Gamma Eta Gamma. Home: 132 S Mountain Ave Montclair NJ 07042

FARRELL, JOHN JOSEPH, surgeon, educator; b. Seneca, Wis., Sept. 6, 1917; s. Thomas Emmett and Caroline Mae (Nugent) F.; children: Mary Eileen, John Joseph, Patricia Ann. A.B., Loras Coll., 1938; M.D., Harvard U., 1942. Diplomate: Am. Bd. Surgery. Intern St. Joseph's Hosp., Lexington, Ky., 1942-43; resident surgery Albany (N.Y.) Hosp. and Albany Med. Coll., 1946-50; instr., then asst. prof. surgery Albany Med. Coll., 1950-54; prof. surgery, chmn. dept. U. Miami (Fla.) Sch. Medicine, 1954-61, clin. prof. surgery, 1962-65; surgeon-in-chief Jackson Meml. Hosp., Miami, 1954- 61; dir. surgery Coral Gables (Fla.) VA Hosp., 1956-61, Kendall Hosp., Miami, 1958-63; Bd. dirs. John Elliott Blood Bank, Dade County, 1956-65, Dade County chpt. Am. Cancer Soc., 1958-65, Palm Beach County chpt. Am. Cancer Soc., 1966-83. Served to capt., M.C. AUS, 1943-46; ETO. Fellow exptl. surgery Dazian Found., 1948-49. Fellow A.C.S. (bd. govs. 1960-63); mem. Pan Am. Med. Assn., AMA, Southeastern Surg. Congress, Soc. Surgery Alimentary Tract, AAAS, N.Y. Acad. Scis, Fla. Assn. Gen. Surgeons (pres. 1972-74), Alpha Omega Alpha. Home: 2354 Waterside Dr Lake Worth FL 33461 Office: 3003 S Congress Suite 1D Palm Springs FL 33461

FARRELL, JOHN L., JR., lawyer, business executive; b. N.Y.C., Jan. 24, 1929; s. John Lawrence and Edna (Ziegler) F.; m. Kathleen Lynch, Oct. 5, 1973; children: John Lawrence, III, Maureen, Jayne, Dianne, Michael. B.A., St. Peters Coll., N.J., 1950; LL.B., St. John's U., 1955; M.B.A., NYU, 1960. Bar: N.Y. bar 1956. Asst. counsel ACF Industries, Inc., N.Y.C., 1955-61; counsel, sec., asst. to chmn. Knox Glass, Inc., N.Y.C., 1961-68; adminstrv. liaison Williams Cos., Tulsa, 1968-69; cons. on mergers and acquisitions, 1969-71; sr. v.p. law and adminstrn., sec. U.S. Filter Corp., N.Y.C., 1971-82; pres., chief operating officer FRACORP, Tulsa, 1983—; mem. adv. bd. Internat. Comparative Law Center, Dallas. Mem. Ardsley (N.Y.) Sch. Bd., 1965-68. Served to 1st lt. U.S. Army, 1951-53. Mem. Am. Soc. Corp. Secs., Am., N.Y. State bar assns., Am. Soc. Internat. Law, Phi Delta Phi. Republican. Roman Catholic. Home: 4635 S Wheeling Tulsa OK 74105 Office: 1717 S Boulder Tulsa OK 74119

FARRELL, JOHN TIMOTHY, hospital administrator; b. St. Louis, Feb. 22, 1947; s. Michael James and Jane Frances (Lautenschlager) F.; m. Martha Anne Paynter, June 4, 1971; children: Kathleen Marie, Margaret Mary, Anne Elizabeth, John Timothy. B.A. in Philosophy, Cardinal Glennon Coll., 1969; postgrad., U. Mo., 1969-71; M.H.A., St. Louis U., 1973. Adminstrv. resident St. John's Mercy Med. Center, St. Louis, 1970-72, 73, exec. v.p., 1979—; asst. exec. dir. St. Mary's Hosp., Richmond, Va., 1973-74, asso. exec. dir., 1974-76; adminstr. St. Francis Mercy Hosp., Washington, Mo., 1976-78, exec. v.p., 1978—; mem. health adv. bd. Sisters of Mercy of the Union, Province St. Louis, 1976-79, mem. personnel com., 1978-79; mem. Catholic health care facilities com. Mo. Cath. Conf., Jefferson City, 1976-82, chmn., 1979-82, mem. health affairs task force, 1977-82; mem. adv. com. med. records technician program St. Mary's Coll., O'Fallon, Mo., 1978-79; mem. subcom. on services pediatric tech. adv. group Health Systems Agy., 1978—; mem. mental health task force St. Louis-Jefferson-Franklin Counties, Devel. Mental Health Facilities, 1977-79; mem. steering subcom. Health Systems Agy. Local Impact Com., 1979. Mem. mgmt. adv. com. Washington (Mo.) Sch. Dist., 1976-79; bd. dirs. St. Francis Mercy Hosp., 1979-82, Mercy Health Conf., 1982—, Family Planning Council St. Louis, 1979-81; mem. personnel com. Family Planning Council St. Louis, 1979-81, budget com., 1980; bd. dirs. Tri County Hosp., Mansfield, Mo., 1983. Mem. Am. Coll. Hosp. Adminstrs., Mo. Hosp. Assn. (vice chmn. budget com. 1979—), Hosp. Assn. Met. St. Louis (council on fin. 1979—, chmn. environ. services com. 1981, mem. council mgmt. services). Home: 537 Meadow Creek Ln Saint Louis MO 63122 Office: 615 S New Ballas Rd Saint Louis MO 63141

FARRELL, JOSEPH, research co. exec., writer, sculptor; b. N.Y.C., Sept. 11, 1935; s. John Joseph and Mildred Veronica (Dwyer) F. A.B. summa cum laude, St. John's Coll., 1958; A.M., U. Notre Dame, 1959; J.D., Harvard U., 1965. Bar: N.Y. bar 1965. With firm Milbank, Tweed, Hadley & McCloy, N.Y.C., 1964-65; exec. asso. Carnegie Corp. N.Y., 1965-66; dir. spl. projects, then exec. v.p., chief operating officer Am. Council of Arts, 1966-71; pres. Nat. Research Center of Arts, N.Y.C., 1971-76; exec. v.p. Louis Harris & Assos. (Harris Poll), N.Y.C., 1974-76, vice chmn., 1977; pres., chief exec. officer Nat. Research Group, Inc., Los Angeles, 1977—; movie mktg. analyst and cons., 1978—. Author, editor: Americans and the Arts, 1973, 75, Museums: USA, 1973, The Cultural Consumer, 1973, The U.S. Arts and Cultural Trend Data System, 1977; sculptor, 1958—. Mem. Gov. N.Y. Task Force on Arts, 1975; founder, bd. dirs. Vol. Lawyers for Arts, 1968-76; bd. dirs. Arts and Bus. Council N.Y., 1973-76, Aman Folk Ensemble, 1979—. Woodrow Wilson fellow, 1958.

FARRELL, MIKE, actor; b. St. Paul, Feb. 6; m. Judy Hayden, 1963; children: Josh, Erin. Ed., Los Angeles City Coll., Orange Coast Coll., U. Calif. at Los Angeles, Jeff Corey Workshop, Hollywood. Profl. debut in little theatre prodn. Rain, 1961; motion pictures include Captain Newman, M.D, 1964, The Americanization of Emily, 1964, The Graduate, 1967, Targets, 1968, September 30, 1955, 77; numerous TV appearances include Harry O; regular on: TV series Days of Our Lives, NBC-TV, The Interns, CBS-TV, 1970-71, The Man and the City, ABC-TV, 1971-72, M*A*S*H, CBS-TV, 1975-83; TV spls. include Ladies of the Corridor, PBS, 1975, Child Sexual Abuse, PBS, 1984; TV movie The Questor Tapes, The Longest Night, Battered, Sex and the Single Parent, Rank, Damien... The Leper Priest. Involved in polit. and social causes. Office: care Bauman Hiller & Assocs 9220 Sunset Blvd Los Angeles CA 90069 *

FARRELL, NEAL JOSEPH, banker; b. Bklyn., Aug. 31, 1932; s. Joseph D. and Gertrude B. (Behan) F.; m. Joan Pendergast, Aug. 13, 1955; children—Michael J., Daniel S., Patrick J., Nancy E. B.A., Dartmouth Coll., 1954; grad. Advanced Mgmt. Program, Harvard U., 1970. With Chase Manhattan Bank, N.Y.C., 1956-78, sr. v.p., 1971-78; pres., dir. Mercantile Trust Co. (N.A.), St. Louis, 1978—; vice chmn., dir. Mercantile Bancorp. Inc. Bd. dirs. United Way St. Louis, Laclede's Landing Redevel. Corp., Arts and Edn. Fund Greater St. Louis, St. Louis Regional Commerce and Growth Assn.; trustee St. Louis Art Mus., St. Louis U., St. Louis Children's Hosp. Served to lt. (j.g.) USNR, 1954-56. Mem. Am. Bankers Assn., Assn. Rev. City Bankers. Clubs: Old Warson Country, St. Louis (St. Louis); Log Cabin. Office: Mercantile Trust Co NA Mercantile Tower St Louis MO 63166

FARRELL, PAUL EDWARD, naval officer; b. Upper Darby, Pa., Nov. 15, 1926; s. James Patrick and Marie Edythe (Kerk) F.; m. Romayne A. Farrell, Aug. 23, 1952; children: Anne Marie, Paul Edward. D.D.S., U. Pa., 1951. Commd. lt. (j.g.) Dental Corps, U.S. Navy, 1951, advanced through grades to rear adm., 1976; head naval reserve br. Bur. Medicine and Surgery, 1970-73, exec. officer, dir. clin. services Naval Regional Dental Center, Norfolk, Va., 1973-76, insp. gen. dental Bur. Medicine and Surgery, Navy Dept., 1976-77, chief Navy Dental Corps, asst. chief for dentistry, chief dental div. BUr. Medicine and Surgery, 1977-80; prof., chmn. dept. operative dentistry Temple U., Phila., 1980—. Bd. overseers Sch. Dental Medicine, U. Pa., 1979—. Decorated Legion of Merit, Navy Commendation medal. Fellow Am. Coll. Dentists, Internat. Coll. Dentists; mem. ADA, Am. Assn. Dental Schs., Acad. Operative Dentistry, Am. Acad. Gold Foil Operators, Omicron Kappa Epsilon, Delta Sigma Delta. Republican. Roman Catholic. Home: 442 Timber Ln Devon PA 19333

FARRELL, PAUL HARRY, lawyer, business executive; b. Cambridge, Mass., Sept. 14, 1927; s. Harrry Gordon and Frances Rose (Fay) F.; m. Blanche Ada Church, Oct. 24, 1948; children: James, John, Joan, Peter, William. A.B., U. Pitts., 1950; J.D., Harvard U., 1954. Bar: Mass. 1954, Ohio 1974, Calif. 1981. Assoc. firm Goodwin, Procter & Hoar, Boston, 1954-63; asst. gen. counsel United Fruit-United Brands, Boston, N.Y.C., The Hauge, Paris, 1963-73; sr. v.p., gen. counsel Buckeye Internat., Inc., Columbus, Ohio, 1973-79; v.p., gen. counsel, sec. Clorox Co., Oakland, Calif., 1979—; mem. adminstrn. and legal processes com. Mills Coll., Oakland, 1980—. Served with USN, 1945-48. Mem. ABA, San Francisco Bar Assn. Republican. Clubs: Harvard (N.Y.C.); Bankers (San Francisco). Home: 56 Iron Ship Plaza San Francisco CA 94111 Office: Clorox Co 1221 Broadway Oakland CA 94612

FARRELL, ROBERT WILLIAM, investment banker; b. Bklyn., Jan. 4, 1927; s. John Arthur and Ann V. (Hayes) F.; children: Kathleen, Michael, James. A.B., Cornell U., 1947, M.B.A., 1949. Jr. analyst Affiliated Fund, N.Y.C., 1949-52; investment supr. N.Y. Life Ins. Co., N.Y.C., 1952-58; sr. analyst Laurence M. Marks & Co., N.Y.C., 1958-59; partner Faulkner, Dawkins & Sullivan, N.Y.C., 1959-67; v.p., dir. research E.F. Hutton Co., N.Y.C., 1967-71; sr. exec. v.p. Bache Halsey Stuart Shields Inc., N.Y.C., 1971-82; pres. Farrell Assocs., Inc., N.Y.C., 1983—. Served with USNR, 1944-46. Mem. Inst. Chartered Fin. Analysts, N.Y. Soc. Security Analysts, Phi Kappa Psi. Republican. Roman Catholic. Clubs: City Midday, Bond (N.Y.C.). Office: 420 Lexington Ave New York NY 10017

FARRELL, RODGER EDWARD, mfg. and distbn. co. exec.; b. N.Y.C., Aug. 1, 1932; s. Edward Thomas and Anna Marie (Pace) F.; m. Rutty Delgado, Dec. 24, 1960; children—Linda, Edward, Diana, Marisa, John. A.B. in Econs, Brown U., 1953. With Gen. Elec. Co., N.Y.C., 1955-59; financial, marketing and adminstrv. positions Gen. Elec. de Colombia, 1959-73, pres., gen. mgr., 1973-76, Gen. Elec. de Venezuela, 1976-81; v.p. Gen. Elec. Co. and; gen. mgr. Andean Countries Bus. Div., Coral Gables, Fla., 1981—. Pres. bd. dirs. Camp Alegre Sch.; bd. dirs. N.Am. Assn. Served with USN, 1953-55. Mem. Venezuelan Am. C. of C. (pres.), Caracas C. of C. (dir.). Republican. Club: Caracas Country. Office: Gen Elec Co 2801 Ponce de Leon Blvd Coral Gables FL 33134

FARRELL, ROGER HAMLIN, educator; b. Greensboro, N.C., July 23, 1929; s. Charles A. and Anne (McKaughan) F.; m. LeMoyne Goodman, Dec. 29, 1967. Ph.B., U. Chgo., 1947, M.S., 1951; Ph.D., U. Ill., 1959. Faculty Cornell U., Ithaca, N.Y., 1959—, now prof. math. Contbr. articles to profl. jours. Served with U.S. Army, 1954-56. Mem. Am. Math. Soc., Inst. Math. Statistics, Am. Statis. Assn. Home: 120 Eastwood Terr Ithaca NY 14850

FARRELL, SHARON, actress; b. Sioux City, Iowa, Dec. 24, 1949; d. D.L. and H.R. F.; m. Dale Trevillion, Feb. 14, 1975; 1 son, Chance Boyer. Actress: movies include Out of the Blue (Named Best Actress, 7th Festival Internat. de Paris du Film Fantastique et de Science-Fiction for The Premonition 1976); (movies include) The Reivers, Marlowe, The Love Machine, It's Alive, Last Ride of the Dalton Gang, Stuntman, Sweet Sixteen, Lonewolf McQuade. Mem. Women in Film, Equity, Acad. Arts and Scis., AFTRA, Screen Actors Guild.

FARRELL, SUZANNE, ballerina; b. Cin.; m. Paul Mejia, Feb. 1969. Studied ballet, Cin. Conservatory Music with Marian LaCour; Ford Found. scholar, Sch. Am. Ballet, 1960; hon. doctorate, Georgetown U., 1984. Hon. lectr. dance U. Cin.; mem. faculty Sch. Am. Ballet.; guest artist, artistic adv. Chgo. City Ballet. With, N.Y. City Ballet, 1961-69, 75—; became featured dancer, 1962; prin. dancer, 1965-69; roles include: film version Midsummer Night' Dream; with, Bejart Ballet of 20th Century, Brussels, Belgium, 1971-75; created role in: other ballets include Ah, Vous Dirais Je, Maman?; Juliet in: Romeo and Juliet; created: The Young Girl in Rose in Nijinsky... Clown of God, 1971, Bolero, The Rite of Spring; Laura in: I Trionfi; created roles with, N.Y.C. Ballet in New Ravel Festival, Tzigane, In G Major, 1976; featured in TV show: Balanchine Dance in Am., Parts I-IV. Recipient Spl. award of merit in creative and performing arts U. Cin., 1965; Merit award Mademoiselle mag., 1965; Dance Mag. award, 1976; Creative Arts award in dance Brandeis U., 1980; award of honor for arts and culture, N.Y.C., 1980. Address: care New York City Ballet Lincoln Center Plaza New York NY 10023

FARRER, WILLIAM CAMERON, lawyer; b. Cleve., Apr. 27, 1922; s. William M. and Jean (Cameron) F.; m. Constance Webb, July 25, 1953; children: William W., Cameron W., Jonathan S., Webb M. A.B., UCLA, 1943; J.D., Duke U., 1949. Bar: Calif. 1950. Practiced in, Los Angeles, 1950—; atty. Hill, Farrer & Burrill, 1950—, partner, 1958—; del. Calif. Bar Conf., 1952-71; dir. First Fed. Savs. & Loan Assn. San Gabriel Valley. Mem. Calif. Coordinating Council on Higher Edn., 1970; Bd. dirs. Greater Los Angeles Zoo Assn., 1968-71; regent U. Calif., 1970-71; adv. bd. Orthopaedic Hosp., 1974—; trustee U. Calif. at Los Angeles Found., 1970-74; bd. counsellors U. So. Calif. Law Center, 1972-77; bd. dirs. Dunn Sch., 1977-80. Served to capt., inf. AUS, 1943-46. Decorated Bronze Star medal. Fellow Am. Bar Found. (life); mem. Am. Bar Assn. (ho. of dels. 1957-80, mem. council sect. internat. law 1964-72, bd. govs. 1973-76), UCLA Alumni Assn. (pres. 1969-71), Am. Law Inst., Am. Judicature Soc. (dir. 1972-75), Duke Law Alumni Council, Newcomen Soc. N.Am., Bel Air Assn (dir. 1981), Phi Gamma Delta, Phi Alpha Delta. Clubs: California, Beach (dir. 1972-73), Lincoln, Chancery (pres. 1973-74), Chevaliers du Tastevin.). Home: 1047 Moraga Dr Los Angeles CA 90049 Office: 445 S Figueroa St 34th Floor Los Angeles CA 90071

FARRINGTON, JERRY S., utility holding company executive; b. Burkburnett, Tex. B.B.A., North Tex. State U., 1955, M.B.A., 1958. With Tex. Electric Service Co., 1957-60; v.p. Tex. Utilities Co. (parent co.), 1970-76, pres., Dallas, 1983—, Dallas Power & Light Co., chief exec. officer, 1976-83; chmn. Tex. Electric Co. Office: Tex Utilities Co 2001 Bryan Tower Dallas TX 75201 *

FARRIOR, JOSEPH BROWN, otologist; b. Tuscaloosa, Ala., Dec. 22, 1911; married; 2 children. B.S., U. Fla., 1932; M.D., Tulane U., 1936; M.S. in Otolaryngology, U. Mich., 1942. Diplomate: Am. Bd. Otolaryngology. Intern Tampa (Fla.) Gen. Hosp., 1936-37; resident in otolaryngology Roosevelt Hosp., N.Y.C., 1937-38; resident and instr. U. Mich. Med. Sch., 1938-42; cons. otology New Orleans Ear, Nose and Throat Hosp., 1945-48; asst. prof. Tulane U. Med. Sch., 1946-48; vis. surgeon Charity Hosp., New Orleans, 1947-48; practice medicine specializing in ear surgery, Tampa, Fla., 1948—; mem. staff St. Joseph's, Tampa Gen. hosps.; clin. prof. otolaryngology U. South Fla. Med. Sch., 1972-77, founding chmn. and clin. prof. otolaryngology emeritus, 1977—, chief dept., 1972-75; Wherry Meml. lectr., 1976; Disting. Alumnus lectr. Tulane U. Med. Sch., 1976; Francis E. LeJeune Meml. lectr., 1978. Author papers in field. Served as officer M.C. AUS, 1942-45. Fellow Am. Acad. Ophthalmology and Otolaryngology (Gold medal 1973, Presdl. citation 1982), A.C.S., Am. Laryngol., Rhinol. and Otol. Soc., Otosclerosis Study Group (pres. 1965-66); mem. Am. Otol. Soc. (award of Merit 1981, Guest of Honor 1984, pres. 1981-82), Triological Soc. (v.p. So. sect. 1975), AMA (Billings Gold medal 1959, 69), So. Med. Assn., Fla. Med. Assn., Centurian Club (pres. 1966, life), Fla. Soc. Ophthalmology and Otolaryngology, corr. mem. various fgn. med. assns. Clubs: Palma Ceia Golf and Country, Tampa Yacht and Country, Tampa Rotary. Office: 509 Bay St Tampa FL 33606

FARRIS, CHARLES LOWELL, city official; b. Washington, Ind., Dec. 18, 1910; s. Bain and Pauline Frances (Love) F.; m. Ruby Alberta Buzan, July 2, 1935; children: Charles M., William P., John T. A.B., U. Notre Dame, 1933; student, Army Indsl. Coll., Washington, 1944. Govt. ofcl., Washington and Dallas, 1935-49; chief field ops. div. slum clearance and urban redevel. Housing and Home Finance Agy., 1949-51, dep. dir., 1951-53; exec. dir. Land Clearance for Redevel. Authority, St. Louis, 1953-66, St. Louis Housing Authority, 1955-66; pres. Urban Programming Corp., 1966-69; exec. dir. St. Louis Land Clearance for Redevel. Authority, 1969—. Past chmn. City Plan Commn.; bd. dirs. Urban Programming Corp., 1969-72, 77—; commr. Community Devel. Agy. Served as lt. USNR, 1943-45. Recipient Levee Stone award Downtown St. Louis, 1976, award Real Estate Bd. Met. St. Louis, 1983, Disting. Service award Mo. chpt. Am. Planning Assn., 1984; named Man of Yr. Bldg. and Constrn. Trades Council, 1983. Mem. Nat. Assn. Housing and Redevel. Ofcls. (pres. 1959-60, M. Justin Herman Meml. award 1978, Disting. Service award Southwest regional chpt. 1983), Nat. Housing Conf., Inc. Democrat. Roman Catholic. Clubs: K.C., Notre Dame (St. Louis). Home: 6515 Nottingham Ave Saint Louis MO 63109 Office: 1300 Convention Plaza Dr Saint Louis MO 63103

FARRIS, FRED JOSEPH, insurance company executive; b. Gary, Ind., Sept. 24, 1939; s. James George and Julia (Rehal) F.; m. Diane Barbara Novosel, Apr. 19, 1964; children: Martin, Fred, Timothy, David. B.S., Ariz. State U., 1961. Actuarial trainee Continental Assurance Co., Chgo., 1963; asst. sec. First United Life Co., Gary, Ind., 1963-67, N. Am. Co. For Life, Chgo., 1967-71; sr. v.p. Capitol Life Ins. Co., Denver, 1972. Pres. Bon Aire Civic Assn., Merrillville, Ind., 1969; precinct committeeman Rep. Party, Arapahoe County, Colo., 1974. Served with U.S. Army, 1962. Republican. Roman Catholic. Club: Valley Country (Aurora, Colo.). Lodge:. Home: 6587 S Helena St Aurora CO 80016 Office: Capitol Life Ins Co PO Box 1200 Denver CO 80201

FARRIS, HANSFORD WHITE, electrical engineer, educator, consultant; b. Blackford, Ky., Oct. 7, 1919; s. Jacob Duncan and Georgia Zola (White) F.; m. Vera June Maybury, June 2, 1942; children: Frances Diane, Lawrence White. B.S., Eastern Ky. U., 1941, M.A., 1942; M.E.E., U. Ill., 1948, postgrad., 1951-53; Ph.D., U. Mich., 1958. Asst. prof. elec. engring. U. Ky., 1948-51; asst. prof., dir. electronics lab. U. Mich., 1958-60, asso. prof., 1960-62, prof., 1962—, chmn. elec. engring. dept., 1965-68, asso. dean engring. for dept. adminstrn., 1968-73, acting dean engring., 1980-81; asso. dir. Inst. Sci. and Tech. responsible for univ.-industry relations, 1963-65. Author, host: TV series Future Without Shock. Served with AUS, 1942-46. Recipient Amoco Outstanding Teaching award U. Mich., 1976, Outstanding Alumnus award East Ky. U., 1981. Mem. IEEE (sr., dir. 1971-73), Nat. Electronics Conf. Inc. (pres. 1966, dir., chmn. 1969-71), Eta Kappa Nu, Tau Beta Pi, Sigma Xi. Presbyn. (elder 1957—). Club: Rotarian. Home: 2 Caisson Crossing Savannah GA 31411

FARRIS, JEFFERSON DAVIS, univ. adminstr.; b. Springdale, Ark., Sept. 30, 1927; s. Jeff D. and Loretta J. (Grunder) F.; m. Patricia Ann Camp, July 31, 1948; children—Rebecca, Elizabeth, Jefferson Davis III. B.S. in Engring, U. Central Ark., 1949; M.A., Peabody Coll., 1950; M.P.H. (USPHS fellow), U. Mich., 1957; Ed.D., U. Ark., 1963. Tchr. public high sch., Pine Bluff, Ark., 1950-57; dir. public health edn. Ark. Dept. Health, Little Rock, 1957-61; prof. health edn. U. Central Ark., Conway, 1961—, chmn. dept. health and phys. edn., 1961-68, dean, 1968-75, univ. pres., 1975—; mem. adv. com. Nat. Endowment Humanities. Editor: A Guide for School Health Education, 1956, Handbook for Elementary Physical Education, 1964. Mem. Ark. Gov.'s Council on Youth Fitness.; Bd. dirs. Conway (Ark.) Meml. Hosp., 1971—; civilian aide for Ark. to sec. of army, 1979-81. Served with USN, 1946-48. Named Layman of Yr. Ark. Assn. Dentistry for Children, 1970. Mem. Ark. Assn. Deans (pres. 1968-75). Methodist. Club: Rotary (pres. local). Home: 140 Donaghey St Conway AR 72032 Office: Office Pres U Central Ark Conway AR 72032

FARRIS, JEROME, judge; b. Birmingham, Ala., Mar. 4, 1930; s. William J. and Elizabeth (White) F.; m. Jean Shy, June 27, 1957; children—Juli Elizabeth, Janelle Marie. B.S., Morehouse Coll., 1951, LL.D. (hon.), 1978; M.S.W., Atlanta U., 1955; J.D., U. Wash., 1958. Bar: Wash. State bar 1958. Mem. firm Weyer, Roderick, Schroeter and Sterne, Seattle, 1958-63, Schroeter, Farris, Bangs and Horowitz, 1963-65, Farris, Bangs and Horowitz, 1965-69; judge Wash. State Ct. of Appeals, Seattle, 1969-79, U.S. Ct. of Appeals for 9th circuit, 1979—; lectr. U. Wash. Law Sch. and Sch. of Social Work, 1976—; mem. faculty Nat. Coll. State Judiciary, U. Nev., 1973; adv. bd. Nat. Center for State Cts. Appellate Justice Project, 1978—; founder First Union Nat. Bank, Seattle, 1965, dir., 1965-69. Del. White House Conf. on Children and Youth, 1970; mem. King County (Wash.) Youth Commn., 1969-70, U. Wash. Law Sch. Found., 1978—; vis. com. U. Wash. Sch. Social Work, 1977—; mem. King County Mental Health-Mental Retardation Bd., 1967-69; trustee Pacific N.W. Ballet, 1978—; past bd. dirs. Seattle United Way. Served with Signal Corps U.S. Army, 1952-53. Recipient Disting. Service award Seattle Jaycees, 1965, Clayton Frost award, 1966. Mem. ABA (exec. com. appellate judges conf. 1978—, chmn. conf. 1982-83), Washington Council on Crime and Delinquency (chmn. 1970-72), State-Fed. Jud. Council of State of Wash. (vice chmn. 1977—). Home: 1908 34th Ave S Seattle WA 98144 Office: 912 US Courthouse Seattle WA 98104

FARRIS, PAUL LEONARD, agricultural economist; b. Vincennes, Ind., Nov. 10, 1919; s. James David and Fairy Julia (Kahre) F.; m. Rachel Joyce Rutherford, Aug. 16, 1953; children: Nancy, Paul, John, Carl. B.S., Purdue U., 1949; M.S., U. Ill., 1950; Ph.D., Harvard U., 1954. Asst. prof. agrl. econs. Purdue U., West Lafayette, Ind., 1952-56, asso. prof., 1956-59, prof., 1959—, head dept. agrl. econs., 1973-82; agrl. economist Dept. Agr., Washington, 1962; project leader for meat and poultry Nat. Commn. Food Mktg., Washington, 1965-66. Editor: Market Structure Research, 1964, Future Frontiers in Agricultural Marketing Research, 1983; contbr. articles to profl. jours. Served with AUS and USAAF, 1941-46. Mem. Am. Agrl. Econs. Assn., Am. Econ. Assn. Home: 1510 Woodland Ave West Lafayette IN 47906 Office: Dept Agrl Econs Purdue U West Lafayette IN 47907

FARRIS, VERA KING, college president. Pres. Stockton State Coll., Pomona, N.J., 1983—. Office: Office of Pres Stockton State Coll Pomona NJ 08240§

FARROW, MIA VILLIERS, actress; b. Los Angeles, Feb. 9, 1945; d. John Villiers and Maureen Paula (O'Sullivan) F.; m. Andre Previn, Sept. 10, 1970 (div. Feb. 1979); children: Matthew Phineas and Sascha Villiers (twins), Lark Song, Fletcher Farrow, Summer Song, Gigi Soon Mi, Misha. Student pub., pvt. schs. Actress appearing in TV and films. Debut: The Importance of Being Earnest, N.Y.C., 1964; starred in: TV series Peyton Place; films include Hurricane, Rosemary's Baby, The Great Gatsby, Peter Pan, The Wedding, Death on the Nile, A Midsummer Night's Sex Comedy, Zelig, Broadway Danny Rose; appeared in: stage plays Romantic Comedy, Mary Rose, The Three Sisters, The House of Bernarda Alba, Ivanov; joined, Royal Shakespeare Co., London, 1974. Recipient Golden Globe award, 1967; Recipient best actress award French Acad., 1969, Rio de Janero Film Festival award, 1969, Italian Acad. award, 1970. Address: care Lionel Larner Ltd 850 7th Ave New York NY 10019 *

FARSON, RICHARD EVANS, psychologist; b. Chgo., Nov. 16, 1926; s. Duke Mendenhall and Mary Gladys (Clark) F.; m. Elizabeth Lee Grimes, May 21, 1954 (div. 1962); children: Lisa Page, Clark Douglas; m. 2d Dawn Jackson Cooper, Jan. 4, 1964; children: Joel Andrew, Ashley Dawn, Jeremy Richard. B.A., Occidental Coll., 1947, M.A., 1951; postgrad., UCLA, 1948-50; Ph.D., U. Chgo., 1955. Dean Sch. Design Calif. Inst. Arts, Valencia, 1969-73; pres. Esalen Inst., Big Sur and San Francisco, 1973-75; faculty Saybrook Inst., San Francisco, 1975-79; pres. Western Behavioral Scis. Inst., LaJolla, Calif., 1959-68; chmn. bd. Western Behavior Scis. Inst., LaJolla, Calif., 1968-79, pres., 1979—; dir. Internat. Design Conf. in Aspen, Colo., 1971—, pres., 1976-80. Editor: Science and Human Affairs, 1967; author: Birthrights, 1974, (with others) The Future of the Family, 1969. Served to lt. j.g. USNR, 1955-57. Ford Found. fellow, 1953-54. Mem. Am. Psychol. Assn., Sigma Xi, Psi Chi. Democrat. Home: 636 Prospect St LaJolla CA 92037 Office: 1150 Silverado St LaJolla CA 92037

FARST, DON DAVID, zoo director, veterinarian; b. Wadsworth, Ohio, Feb. 25, 1941; s. Walter K. and Ada (Stetler) F.; m. Jan Rae Harber, June 17, 1980; children: Julie K., Jenny Lynn. D.V.M., Ohio State U., 1965. Veterinarian, mammals curator Columbus Zoo, Ohio, 1969-70; assoc. dir. Gladys Porter Zoo, Brownsville, Tex., 1970-74, dir., 1974—. Editor: Jour. Zoo Animal Medicine, 1973-77. Mem. Am. Assn. Zool. Parks and Aquariums (pres. 1979-80, chmn. animal health), Am. Assn. Zoo Veterinarians. Home: Rt 5 Box 640 San Benito TX 78586 Office: Gladys Porter Zoo 500 Ringgold St Brownsville TX 78520

FARWELL, ALBERT EDMOND, government official; b. Providence, June 7, 1915; s. Albert Potter and Elizabeth (Shelmerdine) F.; m. Elizabeth Fuller Thurlow, May 18, 1940 (dec. Apr. 21, 1975); children: Bruce Albert, Christopher James; m. Gertrude Cochran Ridgely, Sept. 9, 1978. A.B., Brown U., 1935; M.A., U. Ariz., 1937. Various non govtl. positions, 1939-45; exec. dir. Fgn. Trade Found., 1945-46; sr. editor Bur. Nat. Affairs, Washington, 1946-48; chief procedures and publ. br. Dept. Commerce, 1948-49; econ. analyst ECA, Greece, 1949-51; dep. dir. strategic controls div. Dept. Commerce, 1951-52; program analyst MSA, FOA, 1952-54; chief Near East div. FOA, ICA, 1955; chief program officer Near East and So. Asia ICA, 1956-59; spl. asst. to undersec. mut. security Dept. State, 1959-60; dep. dir. AID, Nepal, 1960-65, dir., Costa Rica, 1965-67, dep. dir., Laos, 1967, dir., 1968, asso. dir., Vietnam, 1969-73, dir. labor relations, 1973-74, cons. econ. devel. planning and adminstrn., 1974—; pres. Alphi Assos., 1979. Recipient Meritorious Service award ICA, 1953, 55, Dept. State, 1960; Pub. Safety award Govt. of Costa Rica, 1967; Vietnam Service award AID, 1970; Superior Honor award, 1974; Presdl. Order of Merit; Def. Honor medal; numerous others. Mem. Am. Acad. Polit. and Social Sci., Soc. Labor Relations Profls., Am. Fgn. Service Assn. Address: 10417 Hunters Valley Rd Vienna VA 22180

FARWELL, BYRON EDGAR, writer; b. Manchester, Iowa, June 20, 1921; m. Ruth Saxby; children: Joyce, Byron John, Lesley. Student, Ohio State U., 1939-40; M.S., U. Chgo., 1968. Dir. adminstrn. Chrysler Internat., Geneva, 1959-70; archeologist. Author: The Man Who Presumed, 1953, 57, Burton: A Biography of Sir Richard Francis Burton, 1963, 75, Prisoners of the Mahdi, 1967, 71, Queen Victoria's Little Wars, 1972, The Great Anglo-Boer War, 1976, For Queen and Country, 1981, The Gurkhas, 1984; lectr. in field; contbr. numerous articles to newspapers, revs., mags.; editorial bd.: Small Towns Inst. Mayor Hillsboro, Va. Fellow Royal Soc. Lit. (U.K.). Address: PO Box 81 Hillsboro VA 22132

FARWELL, ELWIN D., former college president, consultant; b. Branch County, Mich., May 1, 1919; s. Don J. and Dessa (Clingan) F.; m. Helen Irene Hill, Aug. 23, 1942; children: Don Lucian, Helen Kay, James Lyman, Judith Anne. B.S., Mich. State U, 1943; M.S., Mich. State U., 1947; Ed.D., U. Calif. at Berkeley, 1959; B.D., Pacific Lutheran Theol. Sem., Berkeley, 1959; LL.D., Loras Coll., Valparaiso U.; L.H.D., St. John's U., St. Olaf Coll. Instr. animal husbandry Mich. State U., 1947-49, asst. prof., 1949-55; cons. point 4 program State Dept. U. Nacional, Colombia, 1952; adminstrv. asst. to chmn. Center Study Higher Edn., U. Calif. at Berkeley, 1956-59; ordained to ministry Luth. Ch., 1958; pastor in, Andrew, Iowa, 1959-61; academic dean Calif. Luth. Coll., Thousand Oaks, Calif., 1961- 63; pres. Luther Coll., Decorah, Iowa, 1963-82; vis. scholar U. Calif.-Berkeley, 1982; profl. cons., 1983—. Author: Livestock Development and Selection, 1951, (with others) Stability of Change, 1964; contbr. articles to profl. jours., encys. Mem. Iowa Gov.'s Com. Conservation Natural Resources, 1964-68, Iowa Gov.'s Commn. Coop. State and Local Govt., 1964-66; mem. Iowa Coordinating Council Higher Edn., 1967-70, pres., 1968-69; chmn. Com. Intergovtl. Coop. and Communication, 1964-65, Gov.'s Com. on Govt. Reorgn., 1966, State Adv. Com. on Community and Jr. Coll., 1965-69; mem. exec. com. Iowa Assn. Pvt. Colls. and Univs., 1964-73, 76-78, chmn., 1971-72; chmn. Council Coll. Pres.'s, Am. Luth. Ch., 1976-77; Mem. Decorah Human Relations Council, 1968-72; mem. exec. com. Norwegian-Am. Mus. Assn., 1965-71; chmn. World Brotherhood Found., 1962-77, Iowa Coll. Found., 1968-69; mem. Iowa Campaign Fin. Disclosure Commn., 1977—, chmn., 1980-81; mem. Iowa Mental Health Adv. Council, 1978-81, Am. Scandinavian Found.; bd. govs. Calif. Luth. Ednl. Found., 1957-59; bd. dirs. Inst. European Studies, 1977-81; bd. Nat. Luth. Campus Ministry, 1966-69; pres. Luth. Ednl. Conf. N.Am., 1973-74, mem. legis. policy com., 1978-81; counselor Luth. Council U.S.A., 1975-79; bd. dirs. Gundersen Med. Found., La Crosse, Wis., 1976—. Served to capt. AUS, 1943-46; PTO. Decorated Knight's Cross 1st class Order St. Olav, 1975, Knight's Cross 1st class Order No. Star, 1977; Sweden). Mem. Symra Soc., World League Norsemen, Central States Coll. Assn. (dir. 1964-76, chmn. 1967), Nat. Assn. Ind. Colls. and Univs. (dir. 1977-78), Norwegian-Am. Hist. Assn., Phi Delta Kappa, Alpha Gamma Rho, Alpha Zeta. Club: Rotarian. Home: 308 Leif Erickson Dr Decorah IA 52101

FARWELL, F. EVANS, land and mineral company executive; b. New Orleans, 1906. Grad., U. Va., 1929. Pres. Milliken & Farwell, Inc., New Orleans, also dir.; pres., dir. Westover Planting Co., Ltd.; v.p., dir. Avoca, Inc.; dir. Internat. Trade Mart; pres. S.C. Minerals, Inc. Mem. New Orleans Pub. Belt R.R. Commn.; mem. exec. com. Am. Sugar Cane League. Home: 5824 St Charles Ave New Orleans LA 70115 Office: Whitney Bldg New Orleans LA 70130

FARWELL, FRANK LESTER, ins. co. exec.; b. Worcester, Mass., May 28, 1914; s. Frank Lester and Flora Louise (Arrington) F.; m. Mary Lincoln Chambers, Sept. 24, 1938; children—Louise A. (Mrs. Charles W. Domina), Linda (Mrs. William Lange). B.B.A., Boston U., 1937; Advanced Mgmt. Program, Harvard, 1957; L.H.D., Boston U., 1969. With Liberty Mut. Ins. Co., Boston, 1934—, successively clk., asst. treas., treas., 1934-58, v.p., 1959-61, exec. v.p., 1961-62, pres., 1962—, chmn., 1974-81, hon. chmn., 1981—, dir.; hon. chmn. Liberty Mut. Fire Ins. Co.; dir. Liberty Life Assurance Co., First Nat. Bank Boston, First Nat. Boston Corp., Boston Edison Co., Dennison Mfg. Corp. Trustee Northeastern U. Served as officer USNR, World War II. Clubs: Wellesley Country, Algonquin, Comml. Office: 175 Berkeley St Boston MA 02117

FARWELL, LYNDON JAMES, priest, theological school president; b. Los Gatos, Calif., Oct. 29, 1940; s. Lyndon James and Louise Catherine (Bacigalupi) F. B.A., Gonzaga U., 1964; M.A. in History, UCLA, 1968; S.T.M. in Theology, Jesuit Sch. of Theology, Berkeley, 1972; Ph.D. in Religion, Claremont Grad. Sch., 1976. Joined Soc. of Jesus, 1958; ordained priest, 1971; asst. prof. theology U. San Francisco, 1976-78; exec. asst. to provincial Calif. Province of Soc. of Jesus, Los Gatos, 1978-81; pres. Jesuit Sch. of Theology, Berkeley, Calif., 1981—. Trustee U. Santa Clara, 1977—, U. San Francisco, 1981—, Grad. Theol. Union, 1981—. Mem. Am. Acad. Religion, Am. Hist. Assn., Internat. Assn. History of Religions, N.Am. Acad. Liturgy, Soc. Calif. Pioneers. Democrat. Roman Catholic. Home: 2535 Le Conte Ave Berkeley CA 94709 Office: Jesuit Sch of Theology 1735 Le Roy Ave Berkeley CA 94709

FASANO, CLARA, sculptor; b. Castellaneta, Italy, Dec. 14, 1900; emigrated to U.S., 1907, naturalized, 1939; d. Pasquale and Julia (de Feudis) F.; m. Jean de Marco, July 8, 1936. Student, Cooper Union Art Inst., Art Students League, N.Y.C., 1917-21, Julien Academie and Colarossi Academie, Paris, 1924-26; scholar, Rome, Italy, 1922-24. Tchr. sculpture adult edn. Bd. Edn., N.Y., 1948-58; tchr. Manhattanville Coll. Exhibited at, Salon d'Automne, Paris, 1925; worked in own studio, exhibited in, Rome, 1926-32; exhibited in numerous shows, including, Worlds Fair, N.Y.C., 1939, Whitney Museum, NAD, Pa. Acad., Art Inst. Chgo., Met. Mus. Art, Am.-Brit. Center, N.Y.C., Ferragil, Buckholz galleries; works represented in permanent collections at, Met. Mus. Art, N.Y.C., Manhattanville Coll. Sacred Heart, Purchase, N.Y., Norfolk Mus. Arts and Scis., Smithsonian Instn., Washington, Syracuse U., also pvt. collections, U.S., abroad; important works include series of twelve portraits in bronze, the last being of His Excellency Giuseppe Cataldi, pres. Corte dei Conti of Italy. Grantee, recipient citation Nat. Inst. Arts and Letters, 1952; recipient medal of Honor with citation Am. Artists Mag., Audubon Annual Exhbn., 1956, hon. mention Archtl. League N.Y., Gold Medals Exhbn., 1956, Daniel Chester French medal NAD, 1965, Peter Caesar Alberti award Italian Execs. Am. Inc., 1967, Dessie Greer award for sculpture NAD, 1968, 2d pl. sculpture competitions for entrance Supreme Ct. of Bklyn., for fountain sculpture for lobby 100 Church St. bldg., N.Y.C., sculpture commn. for relief Middleport (Ohio) Post Office U.S. Treasury Dept. competition for Apex Bldg. in Washington. Academician NAD.; Fellow Nat. Sculpture Soc. (hon. mention 1956); mem. Audubon Artists (M. Grumbacher prize 1954), Sculptors Guild, Nat. Assn. Women Artists (Anonymous prize 1945, Marcia Brady Tucker prize 1950, medal of Honor for sculpture 63d ann. exhbn. 1955). Subject of articles, works reproduced in Am. Artist mag., Nat. Sculpture Rev., also books Sculpture in Modern America, Contemporary American Sculpture, The Materials and Methods of Sculpture. Home: Cervaro-Prov Frosinone Italy Office: 1083 Fifth Ave New York NY 10028

FASCELL, DANTE B., congressman; b. Bridgehampton, N.Y., Mar. 9, 1917; s. Charles A. and Mary (Gullotti) F.; m. Jeanne-Marie Pelot (div. Sept. 19, 1941); children: Sandra J., Toni F. J.D., U. Miami, Coral Gables, Fla., 1938. Bar: Fla. 1938. Practiced in, Miami, 1938-41, 46—, legal attaché state legislative delegation, Dade County, Fla., 1947-50; mem. Fla. Legislature, 1950-54, 84th-98th Congresses from 19th Dist. Fla.; chmn. house fgn. affairs com.; Am. rep. 24th Gen. Assembly UN, 1969; chmn. Commn. Security and Cooperation in Europe; U.S. del U.S.-Canadian Interparliamentary Group, 1977—; chmn. house del. North Atlantic Assembly. Pres. Dade County Young Democratic Club, 1947-48. Served as officer AUS, 1942-46. Named one of ten outstanding legislators Fla. Legislature, 1951, 53; one of five outstanding men in Fla. Fla. Jr. C. of C., 1951. Mem. Miami Jr. C. of C. (pres. 1947-48), Am., Fed., Dade County, D.C. bar assns., Fla. Bar, Am. Legion, Kappa Sigma, Omicron Delta Kappa. Democrat. Club: Italian-American (pres. 1947-48). Lodges: Lions; Moose. Home: 6300 SW 99th Terr Miami FL 33156 Office: 7855 SW 104th St Suite 220 Miami FL 33156 also 2222 Ponce de Leon Blvd Coral Gables FL 33134 House Office Bldg Washington DC 20515

FASCIA, REMO MARIO, aviation consultant, airplane manufacturing company executive; b. Villa Ballester, Buenos Aires, Argentina, Oct. 5, 1922; came to U.S., 1956; s. Remo Raul and Maria Juana (Dematteis) F.; m. Olive G. Parsons, July 24, 1960 (dec. Feb. 15, 1983). B.S. in Elec. Engring., Otto Krause Indsl. Sch., Buenos Aires, 1941; M.S. in Aero. Engring., U. La Plata, 1948. Quality control engr. Def. Dept., Argentina, 1942-48; flight test engr. Argentine Air Force, 1949-54; faculty mem. aerodynamics and aircraft structures Air Force Inst., Buenos Aires, 1950-53; chief procurement testing engr. Techint-Dalmine, Argentina, 1955-56; sr. design engr. Convair Corp., San Diego, 1956-60; asst. project engr. Ford Motor Co., Buenos Aires, 1960; structural engr. Lockheed Aircraft Corp., Burbank, Calif., 1960; sr. structural engr. Norair Aircraft div. Northrop Corp., Hawthorne, Calif., 1961-62, sec. chief engr., 1966-70; sr. design engr. N.Am. Aviation Corp., Downey, Calif., 1962-63; scientist specialist Douglas Aircraft Corp., Long Beach, Calif., 1963-66; dir. Fascia Aviation cons., St. Louis, 1965—; configuration synthesis engr. specialist McDonnel Douglas Co., St. Louis, 1970—; mgr. S.Am. Mktg. Cons., St. Louis, 1970—; ptnr. Profl. Profile, Leadership and Creativity Evaluation Services, St. Louis, 1975—; guest lectr. profl. creativity vs. graphoanalysis, 1975—. Hon. rep. City of St. Louis mayor-St. Louis Ambassadors, 1975—; treas. McCarthy for Pres. campaign, mo., 1976; state advisor U.S. Congl. Adv. Bd., Washington, 1982—; arbitrator St. Louis Better Bus. Bur., 1983. Mem. AIAA, Internat. Graphoanalysis Soc., Soc. Aero. Weight Engrs., Internat. Platform Assn., St. Louis Council World Affairs. Roman Catholic. Clubs: Marriot Swim and Tennis (St. Louis); Gaslight (Chgo.). Office: Fascia Aviation Consultants 1 Alden Ln Saint Louis MO 63141

FASCIANA, SALVATORE, untility company executive; b. N.Y.C., July 2, 1925; s. Angelo S. and Valeria M. (Billi) F.; m. Margaret Mary Lusk, Jan. 20, 1951; children: Barbara, Robert, Elizabeth. B.C.E., Poly. Inst. Bklyn., 1948, M.C.E., 1950. Registered profl. engr., N.Y. Instr. civil engring. Poly. Inst. Bklyn., 1948-51; cons. engring., N.Y.C., 1951-54; constrn. engr. Western Electric Co., N.Y.C., 1954-57; structural engr. Ebasco Services, N.Y.C., 1957-65; project mgr. M.W. Kellogg Co., N.Y.C., 1965-70; v.p. constrn. Consol. Edison Co. of N.Y., Inc., N.Y.C., 1970—. Mem. Chi Epsilon, Sigma Chi. Home: 76 Oneck Rd PO Box 364 Westhampton Beach NY 11978 Office: Consol Edison of NY Inc 4 Irving Pl New York NY 10003

FASMAN, GERALD DAVID, educator; b. Drumheller, Alta., Can., May 28, 1925; came to U.S., 1955, naturalized, 1964; s. Morris and Sarah (Stauffer) F.; m. Jean Schalit, Dec. 27, 1953; children—Michael, Daniel, Jonathan. B.S., U. Alta., 1948; Ph.D., Calif. Inst. Tech., 1952; postgrad., Cambridge (Eng.) U., 1951-53, Eidg. Technische Hochschule, Zurich, Switzerland, 1953-54, Weizmann Inst. Sci., Rehovoth, Israel, 1954-55. Research asst. Children's Cancer Research Found., Children's Med. Center, Boston, 1955-56; research asso. pathology Children's Med. Center and Children's Cancer Research Found., Boston, 1957-61; asst. in pathology Harvard Med. Sch., 1957-58, research asso. pathology, 1958-60, research asso. biol. chemistry, 1960-61; lectr. protein chemistry Boston U., 1958-59; asst. head biophys. chemistry lab. Children's Cancer Research Found., Boston, 1959-61; tutor in biochem. sci. Harvard, 1960-62; established investigator Am. Heart Assn., 1961-66; asst. prof. biochemistry Brandeis U., Waltham, Mass., 1961-63, assoc. prof., 1963-67, prof., 1967—, Rosenfield prof. biochemistry, 1971—; Cons. African Primary Sci. Program, Ednl. Services, Inc., Dar es Salaam, Tanzania, 1966, mem. program steering com., Accra, Ghana, 1967, mem. adv. group, 1968-

69; mem. sci. adv. com. Am. Cancer Soc., 1979-83; mem. molecular biology adv. panel NSF, 1980—. Editor: Biophys. Jour, 1976-79; adv. bd.: Biopolymers, 1975—; editorial bd.: Internat. Jour. Peptide and Protein Research, 1976-82. NSF sr. postdoctoral fellow Protein Inst., Osaka (Japan) U. and; Weizmann Inst. Sci., 1967-68; Guggenheim fellow, 1974-75; research fellow Japan Soc. for Promotion of Sci., 1979. Fellow AAAS, Am. Inst. Chemists; mem. Am. Chem. Soc., Biophys. Soc., Am. Soc. Biol. Chemists, Chem. Soc. (London), N.Y. Acad. Sci., Sigma Xi. Home: 69 Kingswood Rd Newton MA 02166 Office: Brandeis U Waltham MA 02154

FASS, PETER JOSEF, chemical company executive; b. Vienna, Austria, May 15, 1937; came to U.S., 1939, naturalized, 1945; s. Bennett and Gertrude (Ehrenfeld) F.; m. Elizabeth Anne Steere, Mar. 23, 1959; children: David Jessica, Joshua, Rachel. B.A. summa cum laude, Mich. State U., 1959; postgrad., U. Calif., Berkeley, 1960. With Reichhold Chems., Inc., White Plains, N.Y., 1963—, v.p. purchasing, 1968-72, exec. v.p., 1972-75, pres., 1975—; dir. Reichhold Internat., Inc., Reichhold Chems. Ltd., Reichhold Energy Corp., Sterling Varnish Co., Ltd., Doverstrand Ltd., Eng., Reichhold Quimica, Mexico, Japan Reichhold Chems., Inc. Bd. dirs. Goodwill Industries. Served to 1st lt. USAF, 1960-63. Mem. Mfg. Chemists Assn., Soc. Plastics Industry, Nat. Paint and Coatings Assn. (dir.), Soc. Chem. Industry (adv. bd.), Psi Kappa Psi. Home: 2 Fountain Ln Scarsdale NY 10583 Office: 525 N Broadway White Plains NY 10603

FASS, PETER MICHAEL, lawyer; b. Bklyn., Apr. 11, 1937; s. Irving and Bess (Fordin) F.; m. Alice Joan Williams, Dec. 21, 1961; children: Brian Samuel, Lyle Williams. B.S. in Econs. with honors, U. Pa., 1958; J.D. cum laude, Harvard U., 1961; LL.M., N.Y. U., 1964. Bar: N.Y. 1965; C.P.A. Since practiced in, N.Y.C.; mem. firm Carro, Spanbock, Fass, Geller, Kaster & Cuiffo, N.Y.C., 1968—; adj. asst. prof. real estate N.Y. U.; lectr. for Practising Law Inst., N.Y. Law Jour., Instl. Investor mag., Ill. Inst. for Continuing Legal Edn.; spl. cons. Calif. Commr. of Corps. Real Estate Adv. Com.; mem. ad hoc com. Real Estate Securities and Syndication Inst., chmn. regulatory legis. and taxation com., 1975-76; adviser Nat. Center for Paralegal Tng., Adelphi U. Co-author: Tax Sheltered Investments-Securities and Taxation, 1977-80, Tax Sheltered Investment Handbook, 1980-83; contbr. articles to profl. jours. Recipient Haskins award for outstanding achievement in N.Y. State C.P.A.'s exam., 1964. N.Y. Mem. Am. Bar Assn. (chmn. real estate investment com., real property, probate and trust sect.), N.Y. State Bar Assn., Am. Inst. C.P.A.'s, N.Y. State Soc. C.P.A.'s, Pi Lambda Phi, Beta Gamma Sigma, Beta Alpha Psi. Home: 45 E 89th St New York NY 10028 Office: 1345 Ave of Americas New York NY 10105

FASSEL, VELMER ARTHUR, educator, science administrator, physical chemist; b. Frohna, Mo., Apr. 26, 1919; s. Arthur Edward and Alma (Poppitz) F.; m. Mary Alice Katschke, July 25, 1943. B.A., S.E. Mo. State U., 1941; Ph.D., Iowa State U., 1947. Chemist, Manhattan Project, Iowa State U., Ames, 1942-47, mem. faculty, 1947—, prof. chemistry, sr. scientist, 1956—, disting. prof. sci. and humanities, 1976—; sect. chief Ames Lab., U.S. Dept. Energy, 1966-69; dep. dir. Ames Lab., Energy and Mineral Resources Research Inst., 1969—; Titular mem., sec., chmn. Commn. Spectrochem.; Methods of Analysis, Internat. Union Pure and Applied Chemistry. Recipient Disting. Alumni award S.E. Mo. State U., 1965, award Spectroscopy Soc. Pitts., 1969, Maurice F. Hasler award, 1971, Anachem award, 1971. Fellow AAAS, Optical Soc. Am.; mem. Soc. for Applied Spectroscopy (Ann. medal 1964), Am. Chem. Soc. (Chem. Instrumentation award 1983, Fisher award 1979, Iowa award 1983), Japan Soc. Analytical Chemistry (hon. mem., medal 1981), Assn. Ofcl. Analytical Chemists (Harvey Wiley award), Am. Inst. Physics, Sigma Xi. Research, publs. on analytical atomic emission and absorption spectroscopy, spectroscopic instrumentation, analytical chemistry. Home: 2307 Timberland Rd Ames IA 50010

FASSER, PAUL JAMES, JR., labor arbitrator; b. Gary, Ind., June 15, 1926; s. Paul James and Julia (Thomas) F.; m. Mae Ann Carino, July 31, 1954; children: Paula, Michael, Thomas. B.S., Cornell U., 1951; student, Grove City Coll., 1946-48, U. Pitts., 1948-49. Nat. staff rep. United Steelworkers of Am., 1951-70; dep. asst. sec. Manpower and Manpower Adminstrn., U.S. Dept. Labor, Washington, 1970-73, asst. sec. labor mgmt. relations, 1973-76; labor arbitrator, asso. impartial chmn. Postal Service and Postal Workers Unions; mem., panelist Am. Arbitration Assn.; panelist UMWA/BCOA dist. 5, 17, 28 and 30, Nat. Mediation Bd.; arbitrator Republic Steel, Armstrong Rubber Co., Jones & Laughlin Steel Corp., Youngstown Sheet & Tube, Allegheny Ludlum, Dept. Labor, Social Security Administrn., Armstrong Rubber Co., Jones & Laughlin Steel Corp., Youngstown Sheet & Tube, Allegheny Ludlum, Bituminous Coal Operators Assn., United Mine Workers Am.; panelist Pa. Mediation Service, Pa. Gov.'s Office, Fed. Mediation Conciliation Service. Served with AUS, World War II. Recipient Judge William B. Groat Alumni award; Pres.'s award for Employment of Handicapped. Mem. Nat. Acad. Arbitrators. Home: 2309 Concert Ct Vienna VA 22180 Office: PO Box 909 Vienna VA 22180

FASSETT, DAVID WALTER, toxicologist, physician; b. Broadalbin, N.Y., Nov. 13, 1908; s. Herbert A. and Clara (Smith) F.; m. Charlotte Cloudman, Dec. 22, 1934; children—Matthew, Myra, Clara. A.B., Columbia, 1933; M.D., N.Y. U., 1940. Diplomate: Am. Bd. Preventive Medicine. Intern Bellevue Hosp., N.Y.C., 1940-41; research fellow dept. medicine, asst. dept. therapeutics N.Y. U., 1942-45; acting chief dept. pharmacology FDA, 1943-45; practice medicine specializing in cardiology and anticoagulant research, Miami, Fla., 1945-48; dir. health and safety lab. Eastman Kodak Co., Rochester, N.Y., 1948-73; cons. toxicology Nat. Acad. Scis., 1973—; clin. asso. prof. preventive medicine and community health U. Rochester Sch. Medicine and Dentistry; vis. lectr. Sch. Pub. Health, Harvard, 1965—. Asso. editor: Patty-Industrial Hygiene and Toxicology; Contbr. articles to profl. jours. Cons. Nat. Inst. Occupational Safety and Health, 1972—; mem. subcom. on toxicology, food protection com. NRC-Nat. Acad. Scis., 1950-72; mem. com. naturally occuring toxicants Nat. Acad. Scis., also mem. toxicology com., com. on non-nutritive sweetners, com. on food irradiation, adv. bd. on mil. supplies; mem. tech. adv. com. N.Y. State Air Pollution Control Bd., 1963; chmn. N.Y. State Action for Clean Air Com., 1970-71. Fellow Soc. Toxicology (disting. fellow, Merit award 1979); mem. Am. Soc. Pharmacology and Extpl. Therapeutics, Soc. Exptl. Biology and Medicine, AAAS (council 1969-73), Am. Indsl. Hygiene Assn. (pres. 1969-70, Cummings award 1978), Sigma Xi, Alpha Omega Alpha. Home: 13 Summer St Box 739 Kennebunk ME 04043

FAST, HOWARD, author; b. N.Y.C., Nov. 11, 1914; s. Barney and Ida (Miller) F.; m. Betty Cohen, June 6, 1937; children: Rachel Ann, Jonathan. Ed., George Washington High Sch., N.Y.C., N.A.D. Began writing, 1932; European corr. for Esquire and Coronet mags., 1945; mem. overseas staff OWI, 1942-43; Army film project, 1944. (Emmy award for The Ambassador, Benjamin Franklin 1974); Author: novels Two Valleys, 1932, Strange Yesterday, 1933, The Children, 1936, Place in the City, 1937, Conceived in Liberty, 1939; biography Haym Salomon, 1941; novel The Last Frontier, 1941; biography Baden Powell, 1941; novel Tail Hunter, 1942, The Unvanquished, 1942; biography Goethals and the Panama Canal, 1942; novel Citizen Tom Paine, 1943, Freedom Road, 1944; Peekskill, U.S.A, 1951; novel Spartacus, 1952; The Naked God, 1957; novel Moses, Prince of Egypt, 1958, Tony and the Wonderful Door, 1968, The Crossing, 1971; General Zapped an Angel, 1971, Last Frontier, 1971; novel The Hessian, 1972; My Glorious Brothers, 1972, A Touch of Infinity, 1973, (under name E.V. Cunningham) Sylvia, 1960, Phyllis, 1962, Alice, 1963, Helen, 1966, Margie, 1966, Sally, 1967, Samantha, 1967, Cynthia, 1968, Millie, 1973; Editor: Selected Works of Paine, 1945, Collection of Short Stories: Patrick Henry and the Frigate's Keel, 1945, The American (biography of Peter Altgeld, former gov. of Ill.), 1946, Carkton, 1947, My Glorious Brothers, 1948, Departure, 1949, Literature and Reality, 1949, The Proud and the Free, 1950, The Passion of Sacco and Vanzetti, 1953, 1972, Silas Timberman, 1954, The Story of Lola Gregg: The Winston Affair, 1959, April Morning, 1961, Power, 1962, The Crossing; play, 1962, Agrippa's Daughter, 1964, The Hill; drama, 1963, Torquemada, 1966, The Hunter and the Trap, 1967, The Jews, 1968, The Hessians, 1970, The Immigrants, 1977, Second Generation, 1978, The Establishment, 1979, The Legacy, 1981, Max, 1982. Mem. World Peace Council, 1950-55; Am. Labor Party Congl. candidate 23d Dist., N.Y., 1952. Jewish. Office: care Houghton Mifflin Co 2 Park St Boston MA 02107

FAST, JULIUS, author, editor; b. N.Y.C., Apr. 17, 1919; s. Barnett Arthur and Ida (Miller) F.; m. Barbara Hewitt Sher, June 8, 1946; children: Jennifer, Melissa, Timothy Hewitt. B.A., NYU, 1941. Sr. writer Smith, Kline & French Pharms., Phila., 1955-57; chief dept. med. communications Purdue Fredericks, N.Y.C., 1957-62; feature editor Med. News, 1962-63; sr. editor Med. World News, 1963-64; editor Ob-Gyn Observer, N.Y.C., 1965-75. Author: mystery novels Watchful at Night, 1945, Bright Face of Danger, 1946, Walk in Shadow, 1948, Model for Murder, 1956, Street of Fear, 1959; sci.-fiction League of Grey-Eyed Women, 1970; non-fiction Blueprint for Life, 1963; Beatles, 1968, What You Should Know About Sexual Response, 1966, Body Language, 1970, Incompatibility of Men and Women, 1971, You and Your Feet, 1971, The New Sexual Fulfillment, 1972, Bisexual Living, 1974, The Pleasure Book, 1975, Creative Coping, 1976, The Body Language of Sex Power and Aggression, 1977, Psyching Up, 1978, Weather Language, 1979, Talking Between the Lines, 1979, Body Politics, 1980, The Body Book, 1981, Sexual Chemistry, 1983, Ladies Man, 1983. Served with AUS, 1942-46. Recipient Mystery Writers Am. award, 1944. Home: Peter Rd Southbury CT 06488

FATE, MARTIN EUGENE, JR., utility company executive; b. Tulsa, Jan. 9, 1933; s. Martin Eugene and Frances Mae (Harp) F.; m. Ruth Ann Johnson, Aug. 28, 1954; children: Gary Martin, Steven Lewis, Mary Ann. B.E.E., Okla. State U., 1955; grad. Advanced Mgmt. Program, Harvard U., 1981. With Public Service Co. of Okla., Tulsa, 1955—, v.p. power, 1973-76, exec. v.p., 1976-82, pres., chief exec. officer, 1982—; dir. Central & S.W. Corp., First Bancorp., Tulsa; Ash Creek Mining Co. Bd. dirs. Okla. Osteo. Hosp.; trustee Phillips U., Enid, Okla. Served to capt. USAF, 1955-57. Mem. Phi Kappa Phi, Eta Kappa Nu, Sigma Tau, Kappa Sigma. Mem. Christian Ch. Club: Tulsa Summit. Office: PO Box 201 Tulsa OK 74102

FATELEY, WILLIAM GENE, scientist, educator, adminstr.; b. Franklin, Ind., May 17, 1929; s. Nolan William and Georgia (Scott) F.; m. Wanda Lee Glover, Sept. 1, 1953; children—Leslie Kaye, W. Scott, Kevin L., Jonathan H., Robin L. A.B., Franklin Coll., 1951, D.Sc. (hon.), 1965; postgrad., Northwestern U., 1951-53, U. Minn., 1956-57; Ph.D., Kans. State U., 1956. Head phys. measurement Dow Chem. Co., Williamsburg, Va., 1958-60; fellow Mellon Inst., Pitts., 1960-62, head sci. relations, 1962-64, asst. to pres., 1964-67, sr. fellow in ind. research, 1965-72; asst. to v.p. for research, 1967-72; prof. chemistry Carnegie-Mellon U., 1970-72; prof., head dept. chemistry Kans. State U., 1972-79; vis. prof. chem. dept. U. Tokyo, 1973, 81; pres. D.O.M. Assos., Internat., 1979—; dir. Pitts. Conf. on Analytical Chemistry and Applied Spectroscopy, 1964-65, pres., 1970-71; editor Jour. Applied Spectroscopy, Raman Newsletter, also finance chmn., steering com. for interferometry. Author: Infrared and Raman Selection Rules, 1973, Characteristic Raman Frequencies, 1974, also numerous sci. papers.; Contbr. articles to profl. jours. Recipient Coblentz award for outstanding contbn. to molecular spectroscopy, 1965; Spectroscopy award Pitts. Conf. Analytical Chemistry and Applied Spectroscopy, 1976; named 1st outstanding grad. chemistry Kans. State U., 1964; H.H. King award, 1979. Fellow Optical Soc. Am.; mem. Am. Chem. Soc. (pres. phys.-inorganic sect. Pitts. 1969-70), Phi Beta Kappa (hon.), Sigma Xi, Sigma Alpha Epsilon, Phi Lambda Epsilon, Pi Mu Epsilon. Home: 1928 Leavenworth Manhattan KS 66502 *Be nice to young people on their way up. Students are our greatest natural resources.*

FATEMI, NASROLLAH SAIFPOUR, social sciences educator; b. Nain, Iran, June 15, 1910; came to U.S., 1946, naturalized, 1960; s. Saifulolma and Tuba (Tabe Tabai) F.; m. Shayesteh Ostowar, May 10, 1932; children—Faramarz, Fariborz, Farivar. B.A. with honors, Stuart Meml. Coll., Isfahan, Iran, 1932; M.A., Columbia, 1949; Ph.D., New Sch. Social Research, 1954; LL.D., Kyung Hee U., Korea, 1973. Mem., v.p. legislative council, Province Isfahan, Iran, 1936-39, mayor, Shiraz, Iran, 1939-41, gov.-gen., Province Fars, Iran, 1941-43; mem. Iranian Parliament, 1943-47; rep. Iran UNESCO Conf., 1948, Internat. Congress Americanists, 1949; del. Iran to UN, 1952-53; mem. Iranian Mission presenting case of Iran to UN Security Council, 1951; econ., polit. adviser Permanent Delegation Iran to UN, 1952-53; lectr. Asia Inst., 1949; tchr. Oriental culture and civilization Princeton, 1950-55; prof. social scis. Fairleigh Dickinson U., 1955—, chmn. dept., 1960—, Distinguished prof-internat. affairs, 1971—, dean, 1965-71, dir., 1971—; chmn. exec. com. Inter-Univ. Centre Post-Grad. Studies, Dubrovnik, Yugoslavia, 1972—; dir. Midland Bank, N.J. Author: Diplomatic History of Persia, 1951, Oil Diplomacy, 1954, The Dollar Crisis, 1964, While the United States Slept, 1981; also 5 books in Persian.; Co-author: Humanities in the Age of Science, 1967; Editor: Problems of Balance of Payment and Trade, 1974, Multinational Corporations, 1975, Love, Beauty, and Harmony in Sufism, 1978. Mem. environmental com. Borough of Saddle River.; Bd. dirs. United Fund of Bergen County, Health and Welfare Council of Bergen County; trustee North Jersey Cultural Council., Jersey State Coll. Fellow Royal Acad. Arts and Scis.; mem. Internat. Assn. Univ. Pres. (mem.-at-large governing bd.), Acad. Polit. Sci., Inst. Mediterranean Affairs (vice chmn.). Home: 47 Chestnut Ridge Rd Saddle River NJ 07458 Office: 1000 River Rd Teaneck NJ 07666

FATES, JOSEPH GILBERT, TV producer; b. Newark, Sept. 29, 1914; s. Joseph and Dora (Racicot) Faatz; m. Faye Appleberry Smith, Sept. 29, 1946; children—Decia, Amy, Dailey Gilbert. B.S., U. Va., 1937. Actor, stage mgr. Broadway legitimate theatre, 1937-40; writer, producer, performer CBS-TV, 1941-50; free-lance TV producer, 1950-53; exec. producer Goodson-Todman Prodns.; v.p. Goodson-Todman Enterprises, Ltd., 1953—; TV program cons. CTV, Can., BBC, ATV, London Weekend TV and Scottish TV, Gt. Britain, RAI, Italy. Exec. producer: I've Got a Secret; Author: "What's My Line?"-TV's Most Famous Panel Show, 1978. Served to lt. USCGR, 1942-46. Mem. Sigma Nu. Home: Boulder Brook Rd Greenwich CT 06830 Office: 375 Park Ave New York City NY 10022

FATHAUER, GEORGE HARRY, educator; b. Cleve., Apr. 15, 1918; s. Otto Fred and Emma Cecelia (Fuerhoff) F.; m. Johanne Wilma Wainwright, June 6, 1942. A.B., Miami U., Oxford, Ohio, 1940; M.A., U. Chgo., 1942, Ph.D., 1950. Mem. faculty Hobart Coll., Geneva, N.Y., 1947-48; faculty Miami U., 1948—, prof. anthropology and sociology, 1960—; Mem. staff seminars in communications Mich. State U.-AID, 1961—. Served with Signal Corps AUS, 1942-46. Social Sci. Research Council fellow, 1946-47; Walgreen fellow, 1941-42; Am. Philos. Soc. fellow, 1956-57. Fellow Am. Anthrop. Assn., Am. Sociol. Assn., Soc. Applied Anthropology; mem. Central States Anthrop. Soc. (pres. 1966-67, editor Bull. 1966-71), Sigma Xi, Phi Beta Kappa, Alpha Kappa Delta, Psi Chi, Phi Eta Sigma. Home: 205 Springwood Dr Oxford OH 45056

FAUBER, BERNARD M., retail exec.; b. 1922; (married). With K Mart Corp., 1942—, sr. exec. v.p., chief adminstrv. officer, 1977-80, chmn. bd., chief exec. officer, 1980—; also dir.; dir. K Mart Can. Ltd., K Mart Apparel Corp. Served with USNR, 1941-45. Office: K Mart Corp 3100 W Big Beaver Troy MI 48084

FAUBER, JOSEPH EVERETTE, JR., architect, historian; b. Charlottesville, Va., Aug. 15, 1908; s. Joseph Everette and Alma (Carter) F.; m. Ella Whitmore Williams, Sept. 5, 1936; children—Joseph Everette III, Rodger Williams, Stuart Carter. B.S. in Architecture, U. Va., 1929. Archtl. draftsman Perry, Shaw & Hepburn, Boston, 1930-32; partner Fauber & Poston, Lynchburg, Va., 1933-41; chief architect Wiley & Wilson, Camp Ritchie, Md., 1941-43; prin. J. Everette Fauber, Jr. (F.A.I.A.), Lynchburg, 1945-80; instr. U. Va., 1929-30; Mem., chmn. Va. Bd. Examiners Architects, Engrs. and Land Surveyors, 1949-59; Commonwealth of Va. Preservation Coordinator, 1968-73, 74-81; mem. adv. bd. Historic Lexington, Inc., 1969—. Restoration architect for: Library of Congress, Washington, John Marshall House, Richmond, Old Greek Revival Courthouse (Lynchburg), 1855, Christ Ch, Savannah, Ga., St. Patrick's Ch, Newcastle, Maine, Carlyle House, Bank of Alexandria, Gadsby's Tavern, Mount Vernon, Alexandria. Pres. Citizens Com. Greater Lynchburg, 1968; mem. Lynchburg Planning Commn., 1950-52; trustee Patrick Henry Shrine, Red Hill, Va., 1976-80; mem. Edenton Hist. Commn., 1977—. Recipient William C. Noland award Va. chpt. AIA, 1967. Fellow AIA (nat. com. on historic resources 1974-77); mem. Soc. Archtl. Historians, Assn. for Preservation Tech., Nat. Trust for Historic Preservation, Smithsonian Assn., Assn. for Preservation Va. Antiquities (life). Home: 501 Ves Rd Ct 13 Westminster Centre Lynchburg VA 24503 Office: Box 162 Forest Village Sq Forest VA 24551

FAUCETT, PHILIP MATSON, JR., business executive; b. Chgo., Mar. 28, 1917; s. Philip Matson and Beulah Woodward (Bach) F.; m. Elizabeth Pusey Lohmann, Sept. 7, 1946; children: Philip Matson III, Melissa Jane, Carolyn Woodward. B.S., U. Ill., 1940, postgrad. in Econs, 1947-50; M.B.A., Harvard, 1942, U. Chgo., 1950-52. Economist Fed. Res. Bank of Chgo., 1950-52; lectr. Grad. Sch. Bus. Adminstrn., Northwestern U., 1952-58; sr. economist, dir. research Wolf Mgmt. Engring. Co., Chgo., 1958-63; with AID, State Dept., 1963-75; banking adviser, Bolivia, 1963-65, capital assistance officer, 1965-66; asst. dir. operations Regional Office, Guatemala, 1966-67, dep. mission dir., Bolivia, 1967-69; asst. dir. industry, Vietnam, 1969, asst. dir. commodity mgmt. and indsl. devel., 1970, dep. asso. dir. comml. and capital assistance, 1970-71, dep. dir. mission, Ecuador, 1971-73; dir. Office of Argentine, Paraguay and Uruguay Affairs, U.S. Dept. State, Washington, 1973-75; pres. Youth Concerts Found., Bethesda, Md., 1975—; exec. v.p., treas. Nat. Acad. Arts, Champaign, Ill., 1976-78, bd. dirs., 1976—; pres. Faucett Communications, 1981—; adviser to Agrl. Bank of Bolivia, Mining Bank of Bolivia, Indsl. Devel. Bank of Bolivia, Central Am. Bank for Econ. Integration, Bolivia Ministry Economy, Artisan's Bank, Israel, Israel Productivity Center, Indsl. Devel. Center, Vietnam. Chmn. bd. Am. Embassy Commissary, Bolivia; bd. dirs. Coop. Sch., La Paz, Bolivia, 1968-69; pres. Champaign County Arts and Humanities Council, 1979-80. Served with USAAF, 1943-44. Mem. Order of Artus, Beta Theta Pi, Beta Gamma Sigma. Clubs: University (Chgo.); Kenwood Country (Bethesda, Md.); Champaign County Country, Rotary (Champaign). Home: 69 Greencroft Rd Champaign IL 61820 Office: 505 S Mattis Ave Champaign IL 61820

FAUCETT, THOMAS RICHARD, educator, mech. engr.; b. Hatton, Mo., Aug. 22, 1920; s. Thomas A. and Nora (Craghead) F.; m. Ruth G. Phelps, May 23, 1942; children—Thomas W., John P., Lucia A., Dennis R. B.S. in Mech. Engring, U. Mo., 1942; M.S., Purdue U., 1949, Ph.D., 1952. Design analyst Cleve. diesel engine div. Gen. Motors Corp., 1942-46; instr. mech. engring. Purdue U., 1946- 52; asso. prof. U. Rochester, 1952-60; prof. Mo. Sch. Mines and Metallurgy, 1960-62; prof. mech. engring., head dept. State U. Iowa, 1962-65; prof., chmn. mech. and aero. engring. dept. U. Mo. Rolla, 1965-78, prof. mech. engring., 1978—; cons. mech. engr., 1946—; dir. KDI Inc., Rochester, N.Y., 1958-60. Author articles design analysis, vibrations stress analysis. Mem. ASME, Am. Soc. Engring. Edn., Sigma Xi, Tau Beta Pi, Pi Tau Sigma. Presbyterian. (elder, trustee). Home: 25 McFarland Dr Rolla MO 65401

FAUCHER, ALBERT, economic historian; b. Beauce, Que., Can., July 20, 1915; s. Joseph and Tardif Corinne F.; m. Louisette Couture, Aug. 10, 1946; children—Louis, Adele Faucher Mainguy, Antoine, Francois. B.A., U. Montreal, (1938); licentiate social sci., Laval U., 1941; M.A., U. Toronto, 1945. Prof. econ. history U. Laval, 1945—; vis. prof. McGill U., 1970-71. Author: Histoire economique et Unite Canadienne, 1970, Quebec en Amerique au XiXe Siecle, 1973. Nuffield fellow Eng., 1953-54; Can. Council fellow, 1969-70; Recipient Can. Gov. gen.'s Lit. award, 1973. Mem. Royal Soc. Can., Societe Canadienne d'Economique, Can. Econ. Assn., Can. Hist. Assn. Social Democrat. Roman Catholic. Home: 1246 Ave Forget Sillery PQ G1S 3Y7 Canada Office: Laval U Quebec PQ G1K 7P4 Canada

FAUGHT, HAROLD FRANKLIN, elec. equipment mfg. co. exec.; b. Washington, Oct. 16, 1924; s. Robert A.N. and Bessie I. (Towns) F.; m. Kathleen M. Quinn, June 21, 1947; 1 son, Richard H. B.M.E., Cornell U., 1945; M.M.E., U. Pa., 1951; grad. Advanced Mgmt. Program, Harvard U., 1961. Registered profl. engr., Pa. Div. gen. mgr. Westinghouse Electric Corp., 1946-69; sr. asst. postmaster gen. U.S. Postal Service, 1969-73; group v.p. Emerson Electric Co., St. Louis, 1973—. Served with USNR, 1943-46. Mem. AIAA. Club: Old Warson Country (St. Louis). Home: 1527 Candish Ln St Louis MO 63017 Office: 8000 W Florrisant Ave St Louis MO 63136

FAUGHT, THOMAS FLYNN, JR., corporate executive; b. Salem, Oreg., Oct. 1, 1929; s. Thomas Flynn F. and Jessie Viola (Miller) Shinn; m. Leta Jean Evans, June 26, 1949; children: Kellee Shannon, Kimberlee Jo, Michael Flynn, Mitchell Thomas. B.S. in indsl. Mgmt., Oreg. State U., 1951; M.B.A., Harvard U., 1953; postgrad., MIT, 1952-53. With Ford Motor Co., Detroit, 1953-57, Booz Allen & Hamilton, N.Y.C., Washington, Europe, 1957-68, Gould, Inc., Chgo., 1968-71, F. & M. Schaffer Corp., N.Y.C., 1971-74; sr. v.p. fin., chief fin. officer, dir. Dravo Corp., Pitts., 1974-77, exec. v.p., 1977-81, pres., chief operating officer, 1981-83, pres., chief exec. officer, 1983—, dir., 1977—; regional advisor Liberty Mut. Ins. Co., Boston, 1978—. Co-chmn. Pitts. United Way Planning and Allocations Com., 1979—; trustee Duquesne U., 1978—. Served to 1st lt. USMC, 1946-48. Mem. Newcomen Soc. Clubs: Links; Harvard (N.Y.C.); Rolling Rock; Laurel Valley Golf (Ligonier, Pa.); Duquesne (dir.), Fox Chapel Golf,

Pitts. Athletic Assn. Home: 5525 Dunmoyle St Pittsburgh PA 15217 Office: Dravo Corp One Oliver Plaza Pittsburgh PA 15222

FAUL, GEORGE JOHNSON, former college president; b. Santa Ana, Calif., Oct. 11, 1918; s. George William and Esther Francis (Johnson) F.; m. June Patricia Lynch, Dec. 22, 1949; children: Robert M., Alison. Student, Santa Ana Jr. Coll., 1936-38; A.B., Stanford U., 1941, M.A., 1947, Ed.D., 1954; H.H.D. (hon.), Monterey Inst. Internat. Studies, 1980. Counselor Visalia Coll., 1947, Stanford U., 1947-48; dir. guidance Coll. of the Sequoias, 1948-50; dean student personnel Contra Costa Coll., 1950-58, pres., 1958-64; pres., supt. Monterey (Calif.) Peninsula Coll., 1964-80, pres. emeritus, 1980—; lectr. U. Calif., Stanford U.; mem. ednl. adv. bd. Sci. Research Assos. Mem. exec. com., chmn. Richmond Park and Recreation Commn., 1958-64; pres. Community Welfare Council, West Contra Costa County, 1960-62; bd. dirs. Monterey Peninsula Community Chest, Community Theater of Carmel, Bach Festival Monterey Jazz Festival, Alcoholism Council of Monterey Peninsula, USO; pres. Monterey Peninsula Mus. Art; exec. sec. Carmel Tomorrow Found.; bd. govs. Monterey Peninsula Found. Served with USNR, 1942-47. Mem. Assn. Calif. Community Coll. Adminstrs., Western Coll. Assn. Clubs: Old Capital, Pacific Biol. Lab. Home: PO Box 4365 Carmel CA 93921

FAULCONER, ROBERT JAMIESON, pathologist; b. Sedlescombe, Sussex, Eng., July 11, 1923; came to U.S., 1925, naturalized, 1932; s. Robert Hoffman and Gladys Alice (Jamieson) F.; m. Virginia Myrl Davis, Aug. 11, 1945; children: Anne, Elizabeth, Mary Waite, John. B.S., Coll. William and Mary, 1943; M.D., Johns Hopkins U., 1947. Intern Johns Hopkins U., 1948, fellow, 1948-49; resident Presbyn.-U. Pa. Med. Center, Phila., 1949-52; pathologist DePaul Hosp., Norfolk, Va., 1954-78, pathologist, dir. labs., 1965-78; clin. prof. pathology Med. Coll. Va., 1972-79; prof. pathology Eastern Va. Med. Sch., 1974—, chmn., 1978—; cons. pathologist U.S. Naval Hosp., Portsmouth, Va., VA Hosp., Hampton, Va., Children's Hosp., Norfolk.; Bd. visitors Coll. William and Mary. Nat. bd. dirs., mem. exec. com. Am. Cancer Soc. Served with USNR, 1943-46; M.C. U.S. Army, 1952-54. Recipient J. Shelton Horsley award merit Va. div. Am. Cancer Soc., 1966. Fellow AAAS; mem. Internat. Acad. Pathology, Am. Soc. Clin. Pathologists, Coll. Am. Pathologists, Am. Assn. Anatomists, AMA, Am. Soc. Clin. Oncology, Am. Assn. Phys. Anthropologists, Va. Soc. Pathology (past pres.), Am. Assn. History of Medicine, Sigma Xi. Episcopalian. Clubs: Commonwealth (Richmond); Yacht and Country, Harbor (Norfolk). Home: 1507 Buckingham Ave Norfolk VA 23508 Office: Eastern Va Med Sch 700 W Olney Rd Norfolk VA 23507

FAULHABER, ROBERT WILLIAM, economist, educator; b. Cleve., July 28, 1920; s. Frank F. and Agnes J. (Youkel) F.; m. Martha L. Finke, June, 17, 1950; children: Roberta, Peter, Christina. Elizabeth. Cert., Am. Inst. Banking, 1942; A.B., Cath. U. Am., 1948; M.A., U. Chgo., 1950; Doctorate, U. Paris, 1952. Messenger-teller Cleve. Trust Co., 1939-42; instr. econs. Loyola U., Chgo., 1949-50; mem. faculty DePaul U., Chgo., 1952—, prof. econs., 1964—, chmn. dept. econs., 1972-77; vis. tutor Grad. Inst., St. John's Coll., Santa Fe, N.Mex., summers 1973-74. Asso. editor: Rev. Social Economy. Mem. long-range planning com. Cath. Interracial Council Chgo., 1959; treas. Greater Ill. Faculty Com. on Vietnam, 1965-74; Chmn. legis. com. Ind. Voters Ill., 1954; mem. steering com. Com. Nuclear Overkill Moratorium, 1976—. Served with USAAF, 1942-45; PTO. Mem. Am. Econs. Assn., Assn. for Social Econs. (1st v.p. 1978-79, pres. 1980, exec. council 1981—), AAUP, Phi Beta Kappa, Pi Gamma Mu. Roman Catholic. Home: 5653 S Harper Ave Chicago IL 60637

FAULISO, JOSEPH J., state official; b. Stonington, Conn., Feb. 23, 1916; s. Anthony and Rose M. (Grills) F.; m. Ann Marie Derrico; 1 son, Richard J. Student, Providence Coll.; LL.B., Boston U., 1939. Bar: Conn. Former assoc. firm Bailey & Wechsler; partner firm Fauliso, Katz & Hansen, Hartford, Conn.; lt. gov. of, Conn., 1981—; Mem. Conn. Senate, former pres. pro-tem, 1981—; formerly judge City and Police Ct. of Hartford, Conn. Circuit Ct. Mem. Am., Conn., Hartford County bar assns. Democrat. Roman Catholic. Office: State Capitol Hartford CT 06115 *

FAULK, WILLIAM GILBERT, JR., newspaper executive; b. Monroe, La., Aug. 1, 1943; s. William Gilbert and Jean Carrington (Hartsook) F.; m. Patricia Carroll Rooney, June 22, 1963; children: William Gilbert, Page Carrington. B.A., Hampden-Sydney (Va.) Coll., 1965; LL.B. cum laude, Washington and Lee U., 1968. Bar: Va. 1968. With Dow Jones & Co., Inc., N.Y.C., 1968—, dir. labor relations, house counsel, 1972-77, v.p. legal and govtl. affairs, 1977—; pres. Dow Jones Realty Co.; dir. Nat. Delivery Service, Inc.; speaker in field. Contbr. articles to law revs. Recipient Am. Jurisprudence award constl. law, labor law. Mem. Am. Bar Assn., Fed. Bar Assn., Va. Bar Assn. Episcopalian. Club: Trenton (N.J.) Country. Home: 2005 Makefield Rd Yardley PA 19067 Office: 22 Cortlandt St New York NY 10007

FAULKNER, ADELE LLOYD, interior designer, color consultant; b. Los Angeles, Dec. 26, 1913; d. Lloyd Lawrence and Coralynn (DeVoe) Lloyd; m. William Carl Quinn, Dec. 22, 1963; 1 son by previous marriage, Lloyd Nelson Faulkner. Grad., Woodbury Coll., 1932. Pres. Adele Faulkner & Assos., Inc.; syndicated columnist Copley News; dir. Los Angeles Community Design Center, 1972-76; tchr. U. Calif. at Los Angeles extension, U. Calif. at Irvine; mem. adv. council, bd. visitors Fiden Nat. Accrediting Body for Univs. Teaching Interior Design. Recipient award of Merit Women in Design, 1980, nat. design awards Acad. Interior Design, 1968-69. Fellow Am. Soc. Interior Designers (twice past chpt. pres., v.p. nat. bd. govs., nat. sec. 1972-73, regional v.p. 1973-75), Home Fashions League; mem. Profl. Women for So. Calif. Symphony. Office: Box 112 North Hollywood CA 91603

FAULKNER, CLAUDE WINSTON, educator; b. Barbourville, Ky., Apr. 24, 1916; s. James Edward and Eulah (Swearingen) F.; m. Nancy Isabel McCallum, Dec. 9, 1944; children—Linda Jo, Keith Edward, Sally Ann, Charles Douglas. A.B., Union Coll., Ky., 1936, Litt.D., 1962; M.A., U. Ky., 1938; Ph.D., U. Ill., 1947. Instr. English U. Ill., 1947; faculty U. Ark., 1947—, prof. English, 1953—, chmn. dept., 1953-74. Author: Writing Good Sentences, 1950, rev. edit., 1981; Co-author: Writing Good Prose, 1961, 4th edit., 1977. Served to capt. USAAF, 1942-46; lt. col. Res. Named Distinguished Alumnus Union Coll., 1954. Mem. Modern Lang. Assn., Phi Beta Kappa, Phi Kappa Phi. Home: 306 W Prospect St Fayetteville AR 72701 *Do your work as well as you can. Savor small pleasures. Don't take yourself too seriously.*

FAULKNER, EDWIN JEROME, insurance company executive; b. Lincoln, Nebr., July 5, 1911; s. Edwin Jerome and Leah (Meyer) F.; m. Jean Rathburn, Sept. 27, 1933. B.A., U. Nebr., 1932; M.B.A., U. Pa., 1934. With Woodmen Accident & Life Co., Lincoln, 1934—, successively claim auditor, v.p., 1934-38, pres., dir., 1938-77, chmn. bd., chief exec. officer, 1977—; pres., dir. Comml. Mut. Surety Co., 1938—; dir. Lincoln Tel. & Tel. Co., Universal Surety Co., Inland Ins. Co.; Chmn. Health Ins. Council, 1959-60; mem. adv. council on social security HEW, 1974-75. Author: Accident and Health Insurance, 1940, Health Insurance, 1960; Editor: Man's Quest for Security, 1966. Chmn. Lincoln-Lancaster County Plan Commn., 1948-67; mem. medicare adv. com. Dept. Def., 1957-70; Neb. Republican State Finance chmn., 1968-73; Chmn., trustee Bryan Meml. Hosp.; trustee Doane Coll., 1961-70, Lincoln Found., Am. Coll. Life Underwriters, Cooper Found., Newcomen Soc. N.Am.; chmn. bd. trustees U. Nebr. Found.; bd. dirs. Nebraskans for Pub. TV., Bus. Industry Polit. Action Com., Washington. Served from 2d lt. to lt. col. USAAF, 1942-45. Decorated Legion of Merit; recipient Disting. Service award U. Nebr., 1957; Harold R. Gordon Meml. award Internat. Assn. Health Ins. Underwriters, 1955, Ins. Man of Year award Ins. Field, 1958; Exec. of Yr. award Am. Coll. Hosp. Adminstrs., 1971; Nebr. Builders award, 1979; Disting. Service award Lincoln Kiwanis Club, 1980. Mem. Health Ins. Assn. Am. (1st pres. 1956), Am. Legion, Am. Life Conv. (exec. com. 1961-70, pres. 1966-67), Ins. Econs. Soc. (chmn. 1971-73), Nebr. Hist. Soc. (pres. 1982—), Ins. Fedn. Nebr. (pres.), Phi Beta Kappa, Phi Kappa Psi, Alpha Kappa Psi (hon.). Republican. Presbyn. Clubs: Mason, Elk. Home: 4100 South St Lincoln NE 68506 Office: 1526 K St Lincoln NE 68508

FAULKNER, ELIZABETH COONLEY, civic worker; b. Chgo., Dec. 3, 1902; d. Avery and Queene (Ferry) Coonley; m. Waldron Faulkner, Nov. 18, 1926; children: Avery Coonley, Winthrop Waldron, Celia Ferry (Mrs. Raymond C. Cleveger III). Grad., Madeira Sch., Greenway, Va., 1920; A.B., Vassar Coll., 1924. Bd. dirs. Madeira Sch. Alumnae Assn., 1943-68; trustee Vassar Coll., 1958-66, Potomac Sch., 1948-51; pres. bd. D.C. YWCA, 1951-53; chmn. women's activities, centennial conv. AIA, 1957; mem. vestry St. Margaret's Episcopal Ch., 1953-55; dirs. bd. Episcopal Center Children, 1962-68. Clubs: Cosmopolitan (N.Y.C.); Sulgrave, City Tavern (Washington). Address: 3415 36th St NW Washington DC 20016

FAULKNER, FRANCIS MARION, artist; b. Sumter, S.C., July 27, 1946; s. Francis Marion and Mary Kate (Austin) F. B.F.A., U. N.C., 1968, M.F.A., 1972. One-man exhbns. include, Monique Knowlton Gallery, N.Y.C., 1976, 77, 79, 80, 81, 83, Galeri Alexandra Monett, Brussels, Belgium, 1978, Arts Club, Chgo., 1980, Schneebeck Gallery, Cin., 1981, Roy Boyd Gallery, Los Angeles, 1983, Davis McLean Gallery, Houston, group exhbns. include, Phoenix Mus., 1979, Whitney Mus., Lerner Hellon Gallery, N.Y.C., 1981, Neuberger Mus., 1982, Davos, Switzerland, 1983, Va. Mus., spl. project, Fabric Workshop, 1981, N.Y. Subway Project, Burrough Hall, 1983; represented in permanent collections, Hirshhorn Mus. and Sculpture Garden, Washington, Nat. Collections Fine Arts, Washington, Ludwig Mus., Cologne, Ger., Albright Knox Mus., Springfield Mus.; commn., Orlando Internat. Airport, 1981. Nat. Endowment Arts grantee, 1975. Address: 150 W 26 St New York NY 10001 *Painting should be, a visual experience. I believe that all art is, first of all, formalist, and should be accessible to everybody, at least on a sensual level. The best art has the most meaning to the most people on the most levels.*

FAULKNER, FRANK M., artist; b. Sumter, S.C., July 27, 1946; s. Francis M. and Mary Kate (Austin) F. B.F.A., U. N.C., 1968, M.F.A., 1972. One-man shows include, Monique Knowlton Gallery, N.Y.C., 1976, 77, 78, 79, 80, 81, 82, 83, 84, Chgo. Arts Club, 1981, Roy Boyd Gallery, Chgo., 1981, Los Angeles, 1983; One-man shows include, Davis McClain Gallery, Houston, 1983; exhibited in group show, Whitney Biennial, 1975, SECCA, Winston-Salem, N.C., 1983; represented in permanent collections, Hirschhorn Mus., Albright-Knox Mus., Smith Coll. Mus., N.C. Mus., Nat. Collection Fine Arts, Ludwig Mus., Aachen, W.Ger. Mem. Phi Beta Kappa. Address: 150 W 26th St New York NY 10001

FAULKNER, JAMES HARDIN, state justice; b. Louisville, Miss., Mar. 17, 1921; m. Eleanor Jane Wyatt; children: Kate Faulkner Hubbard, Christopher. Ed., San Diego State Coll.; J.D., U. Ala.; LL.M., U. Va.; postgrad., U. Calif., Boalt Hall; attended, N.Y. U. Sch. Law Seminar for Appellate Judges, Am. Acad. Jud. Edn., U. Colo., (Appellate Judges Seminars), La. State U. Sch. Law. Bar: Ala. bar 1949. Practiced law, Birmingham, Ala., 1949-51, Birmingham and Montevallo, 1958-72; with Dept. Treasury, 1951-55; asso. justice Ala. Supreme Ct., Montgomery, 1972—; former city atty., City of Montevallo; former judge Recorder Ct.; trust officer Birmingham Trust Nat. Bank, 1955-58; instr. Am. Inst. Banking. Mem. Ala. State Bar, Birmingham Bar Assn., Shelby County Bar Assn. Club: Masons. Office: Judicial Bldg PO Box 218 Montgomery AL 36104

FAULKNER, JAMES HUGH, aluminum company executive; b. Montreal, Mar. 9, 1933; s. George V. F. and Cecil E. (Baird) MacLaren; m. Jane E. Meintjies, Dec. 21, 1973; children: Julian, Adrian, Antonia. B.A., McGill U., 1956; Diploma, Internat Mgmt. Inst., Geneva, 1958. Mem. Parliament, House of Commons, Ottawa, Ont., Can., 1965-79, dep. speaker, 1968-70; cabinet minister Govt. of Can., Ottawa, 1972-79; v.p. Alcan Aluminum Ltd., Montreal, 1981-83; mng. dir. Indian Aluminum Co., Calcutta, 1983—. Chmn. Can. Inst. Internat. Affairs, Montreal, 1982-83; conseil D' adminstrn. World Film Festival, Montreal, 1980-82, Nat. Theatre Sch., Montreal, 1982-83. Liberal. Clubs: University (Montreal); Delhi Gymkhanna (Delhi, India); Tullygunmgh (Calcutta). Home: White House Gardens 17 Alipore Rd Calcutta India Office: Indian Aluminum Co Ltd 1 Middleton Rd Calcutta India

FAULKNER, JOHN ARTHUR, physiologist, educator; b. Kingston, Ont., Can., Dec. 12, 1923; s. Jack and Winifred (Esdaile) F.; m. Margaret Isabel Rowntree, Apr. 9, 1955; children: Laura Megan, Melanie Anne. B.A., Queen's U., 1949, B.P.H.E., 1950; M.S., U. Mich., 1956, Ph.D., 1962. Tchr. sci. Glebe Collegiate Inst., Ottawa, Ont., Can., 1952-56; asst. prof. phys. edn. U. Western Ont., 1956-60; asst. prof. edn. U. Mich., 1962-65, asso. prof. edn., 1965-67, asso. prof. physiology, 1966-70, prof. physiology, 1970—. Contbr. articles on altitude acclimatization, cardiovascular response to swimming and running, skeletal muscle adaptation, and transplantation and regeneration of skeletal muscles to profl. jours. Served with RCAF, 1942-45. Burke Aaron Hinsdale scholar, 1962. Fellow AAAS.; Mem. Am. Coll. Sports Medicine (pres. 1971-72, Citation award 1978), Am. Physiol. Soc. Home: 2200 Navarre Circle Ann Arbor MI 48104 Office: Dept Physiology U Mich Med Sch Box 024 Ann Arbor MI 48109

FAULKNER, LARRY RAY, chemistry educator; b. Shreveport, La., Nov. 26, 1944; s. James Clifford and Doris Louise (Koch) F.; m. Mary Ann Jordan, Aug. 14, 1965; children: Brian Jordan, Susan Louise. B.S., So. Meth. U., 1966; Ph.D., U. Tex., Austin, 1969. Asst. prof. chemistry Harvard U., 1969-73; asst. prof. chemistry U. Ill., Urbana-Champaign, 1973-75, assoc. prof., 1975-79, prof., 1979—; mem. Materials Research Lab., 1978—; corp. dir. Anderson Physics Labs., Inc., Urbana. Author: (with A. J. Bard) Electrochemical Methods, 1980; div. editor: Jour. Electrochem. Soc, 1975-80; U.S. regional editor: Jour. Electroanalytical Chemistry, 1980—. NSF grad. fellow, 1966-69. Mem. Electrochem. Soc. (Edward Weston fellow 1969, Young Authors prize 1976), Am. Chem. Soc., Phi Beta Kappa (Grad. Research award Tex. Gamma chpt. 1969-70), Phi Kappa Phi. Home: 19 Montclair Rd Urbana IL 61801 Office: Dept Chemistry U Ill 1209 W California St Urbana IL 61801

FAULKNER, WALTER THOMAS, lawyer; b. New Haven, Sept. 17, 1928; s. Walter Thomas and Alice Marion (McGushin) F.; m. Joan Lee Hills, Mar. 17, 1956; children: John, Andrew, George, Susan. A.B., Providence Coll., 1952; LL.B., Columbia U., 1955. Bar: N.Y. State 1956. Since practiced in, N.Y.C.; asso. firm Rogers, Hoge & Hills, 1959-69, partner, 1969-79, sr. partner, 1979—; sec. Sterling Drug Inc., 1973-78; sec., dir. Bacardi Corp.; dir. Raymond Holdings Inc. Served with AUS, 1946-48. Mem. Assn. Bar City N.Y., ABA, N.Y. State Bar Assn. Clubs: Larchmont Yacht (trustee 1967—); Union League (N.Y.C.)). Home: 64 Woodbine Ave Larchmont NY 10538 Office: 90 Park Ave New York NY 10016

FAULKNER, WINTHROP WALDRON, architect; b. Bronxville, N.Y., Feb. 26, 1931; s. Waldron and Elizabeth (Coonley) F.; m. Jeanne Hawes, July 9, 1955; children: Edith G., David M., Andrew W., Elizabeth W., Celia A. B.A., Trinity Coll., 1953; M.Arch., Yale U., 1959. Registered architect, D.C. Md., Va. Architect Metcalf & Assocs., Washington, 1959-61, Keyes, Lethbridge & Condon, 1961-65; ptnr. Wilkes Faulkner Jenkins & Bass and predecessor firm, Washington, 1965-80, sr. ptnr., 1980—; designer archtl. master plan U.S. Embassy, Jakarta, Indonesia, 1979, Singapore, 1980. Trustee Trinity Coll., 1971-77; mem. Coonley Found., 1965—, Kingsbury Ctr., Washington, 1978—. Mem. AIA (Coll. of Fellows, recipient design 1982). Clubs: Cosmos (art com. 1976-80, house com. 1981—. Office: Wilkes Faulkner Jenkins & Bass 1147 20th St NW Washington DC 20036

FAULSTICH, ALBERT JOSEPH, banking consultant; b. New Orleans, May 28, 1910; s. Albert and Mary (Balser) F.; m. Anna Emily Collignon, June 30, 1940; children: Albert Joseph, Richard Charles. B.S. in Accounting and Econs, Columbus U., Washington, 1938, M.S. in Accounting and Finance, 1948. With Treasury Dept., 1939-64; dir. Office Security, 1961; spl. asst. Office Sec., 1961-64, asst. to comptroller currency, 1962-64, coordinator of banking, 1964-65; dir. FDIC, 1965-66, dep. adminstr. nat. banks, 1965-74, mem. bd. rev., spl. com., com. liquidations, loans and purchases assets, 1966-74; cons. Financial Gen. Bankshares, Inc., 1974-76; cons. for banks and govt., 1976—; dir. Am. Nat. Bank of Md., 1975-77. Chmn. comptroller currency orgn. for nation-wide campaign for Kennedy Library Fund, 1964. Served to lt. USNR, 1943-46. Recipient Naval Commendation medal; commendation Treasury Dept., 1962; 3 citations, 1972; meritorious service award, 1973; Albert Gallatin award; Am. Flag award; Equal Opportunity award, 1974. Democrat. Roman Catholic. Home and Office: 505 Elderwood Rd Silver Spring MD 20904

FAUNCE, SARAH CUSHING, museum curator; b. Tulsa, Aug. 19, 1929; d. George Jr. and Helen Pauline (Colwell) F. B.A., Wellesley Coll., 1951; M.A., Washington U., St. Louis, 1959; postgrad., Columbia U., 1960-63. Tchr. history Hartridge Sch., Plainfield, N.J., 1954-56; tchr. art Mary C. Wheeler Sch., Providence, 1958-59; instr. art history Barnard Coll., N.Y.C., 1962-64; sec. adv. council art history Columbia U., 1963-70, registrar, curator, 1965-70; curator paintings and sculpture Bklyn. Mus., 1970—; exhbn. cons. Jewish Mus., N.Y.C., 1968-70; adv. bd. Skowhegan Sch. Painting and Sculpture, N.Y.C., 1978—; adv. council art history dept. Columbia U., 1970—. Exhbn. catalog author: Anne Ryan Collages, 1974, Carl Larsson, 1982; author, editor: Belgian Art 1880-1914, 1980; editor: Northern Light: Realism and Symbolism in Scandinavian Painting 1880-1910, 1982. Travel grantee Columbia U., 1963. Mem. Coll. Art Assn., Victorian Soc., Am. Assn. Mus., Phi Beta Kappa. Democrat. Episcopalian. Home: 28 E 92d St New York NY 10028 Office: The Bklyn Mus Eastern Pkwy New York NY 11238

FAUNTROY, WALTER E., congressman; b. Washington, Feb. 6, 1933; s. William T. and Ethel (Vine) F.; m. Dorothy Simms, Aug. 3, 1957; 1 son, Marvin Keith. B.A. cum laude, Va. Union U., 1955; B.D., Yale U. Divinity Sch., 1958, Muskingum Coll., 1971, Va. Union U., 1968, Yale U., 1969, Georgetown U. Law Center, 1979. Ordained to ministry Baptist Ch., 1958; pastor New Bethel Baptist Ch., Washington, 1958—; founder, former dir. Model Inner City Community Orgn. Inc., Washington; mem. 92d-98th Congresses; chmn. Congl. Black Caucus, from 1981; Dir. Washington bur. So. Christian Leadership Conf., 1960-71; now chmn. bd. dirs.; coordinator March on Washington for Jobs and Freedom, 1963; chmn. D.C. Coalition of Conscience, 1965; coor. Selma to Montgomery March, 1965; vice chmn. White House Conf. to Fulfill these Rights, 1966; nat. coordinator Poor People's Campaign, 1969; mem. Leadership Conf. on Civil Rights, Yale U. Council, 1969-74; Vice-chmn. D.C. City Council, 1967-69. Vice pres. bd. dirs. Martin Luther King Jr. Center for Social Change, from 1969. Office: 2135 Rayburn House Office Bldg Washington DC 20515 *

FAUPEL, LEONARD, advt. agy. exec.; b. Irvington, N.J., June 24, 1920; s. Brigham Bishop and Dorothy A. (Beet) F.; m. Jacqueline C. Kuett, May 31, 1947; children—Caroline Faupel Keating, Mark, John. Grad. high sch., Irvington. Advt. mgr. P. Ballantine & Sons, 1956-65; sr. v.p. William Esty Co., N.Y.C., 1966—. Formerly chmn. adv. com. Maplewood (N.J.) Recreation Dept. Served with USAAF, 1942-45. Decorated Bronze Star. Home: 2 Pinewood Ct Short Hills NJ 07078 Office: 100 E 42d St New York NY 10017

FAURE, GUNTER, geology educator; b. Tallinn, Estonia, May 11, 1934; s. Arnulf and Stella (von Harpe) F.; m. Barbara L.L. Goodell, Sept. 5, 1959; children: Mary Jennifer, John Eric, Pamela Anne, David Christopher. B.Sc., U. Western Ont., 1957; Ph.D., MIT, 1961; fellow, Sch. Advanced Studies, 1961-62. Asst. prof. geology Ohio State U., 1962-65, asso. prof., 1965-68, prof., 1968—; field work, Antarctica. Author: (with J.L. Powell) Strontium Isotope Geology, 1972, Principles of Isotope Geology, 1977; editor-in-chief: Jour. Isotope Geosci.; contbr. articles to profl. jours. Recipient univ. gold medal in honours geology U. Western Ont., 1957, disting. teaching award Ohio State U., 1970, 83; Antarctic Service medal, 1976. Fellow Geol. Soc. Am., Ohio Acad. Scis.; mem. Geochem. Soc., AAAS, Planetary Soc., Sigma Xi. Home: 2047 Fairfax Rd Columbus OH 43221

FAURE, HUBERT RENE JOSEPH, machinery manufacturing company executive; b. Brueil-en-Vexin, France, Sept. 5, 1919; came to U.S., 1975; s. Frederic and Jacqueline (de Vendegies) F.; m. Christine Genevieve Polonceau, June 22, 1973. Ed., Ecole Libre Sciences Politiques, 1939-45. Attache French embassy, Bogota, Colombia, 1947; mgr. Ateliers Metallurgiques St. Urbain, 1949; pres. Ascinter-Otis, 1961-72, Otis Europe, Paris, 1969—; pres., chief operating officer Otis Elevator Co., N.Y.C., 1975-77, pres., chief exec. officer, 1977-79, chmn. bd., pres., chief exec. officer, 1979-81, chmn. bd., chief exec. officer, 1981—; sr. exec. v.p. bldg. systems sector United Technologies Corp.; dir. Société Imetal, Grands Magasins Jones, United Technologies Corp. Decorated Chevalier, French Legion of Honor. Mem. Am. C. of C., Assn. Elevator Lift Mfrs. France (pres. 1970-72). Clubs: Nouveau Cercle; Racquet and Tennis, Brook (N.Y.C.). Home: 960 5th Ave New York NY 10021 Office: care Otis Elevator Co 750 3d Ave New York NY 10017

FAURER, LOUIS, photographer; b. Phila., Aug. 28, 1916; s. Morris and Sarah F.; 1 son by previous marriage, Mark. Student public schs., Phila. Caricature artist, Atlantic City, 1934-37; poster letterer Warner Bros. Theatres, Phila., 1937-42; comml. photographer, 1947-70; affiliated with Light Gallery (exclusive agt.); lectr. photography seminar Parsons Sch. Design, N.Y.C., 1975-77, New Sch. Social Research, 1977, SUNY, Purchase, 1978, Stockton (N.J.) State Coll., 1980, Internat. Center Photography, N.Y.C., 1981, Golden Photography Collections and Workshop, 1981, U. Md. Art Gallery, College Park, 1981. Contbr. to, Harpers Bazaar, Vogue, Life, Time, Fortune, and, Look mags., Flair Cowles Publs., Glamour, Madamoiselle, Seventee, Elle, Paris, Jardin des Modes (Paris) mags., one man shows include, Marlborough Gallery, N.Y.C., 1977, U. Md. Art Gallery, College Park, 1981, Limelight Gallery, N.Y.C., 1960, group exhbns. include, Los Angeles County Mus. Art, 1950, Mus. Modern Art, N.Y.C., 1954-78, Marlborough Gallery, 1977, Whitney Mus. Am. Art, N.Y.C., 1978, Light Gallery, N.Y.C., Fed. Plaza, N.Y.C., 1979, N.Y.C. City Hall, Westbeth Gallery, N.Y.C., 1980, Am. Children, Mus. Modern Art, N.Y.C., 1981, 19th and 20th Century Photography, Lunn Gallery, Washington, 1980, Quality of Presence, 1978; represented in: permanent collections including Quality of Presence, Mus. Modern Art, Seagrams Collections, N.Y.C., Harry Lunn Jr. Graphics Internat. Ltd., Washington, New Orleans Mus. Art; Contbr.: photographs to Local Color (Trumen Capote), 1950, Family of Man, 1965, 100 Years of the American Female, 1967, Aperture, 1978, American Children, Collection Mus. Modern Art, 1981, Contact Theory, 1980, Fall 1980 Photography Courses, New Sch., N.Y.C., 1980. Creative Artists Public Service fellow, 1977-78; Nat. Endowment Arts fellow, 1978; John Simon Guggenheim Meml. Found. fellow, 1979-80. Office: Westbeth Group 463 West St New York NY 10014 *Truth transforms adversity and evil into victories of love and hope.*

FAUS, WARREN WILSON, educator, artist; b. Ismay, Mont., Feb. 12, 1919; s. Walter Josiah and Anna (Steen) F.; m. Frances Mist Korb, July 24, 1956; stepchildren—Marion Mist Kennedy, Frances Louise Collins. Student, Mpls. Sch. Art, 1938-39; B.A., Mont. State Coll., 1942; M.A., Stanford, 1954. Mem. art faculty San Jose (Calif.) State U., 1946-74, prof., 1961—, chmn. dept., 1960-67, dean, 1972-74; watercolorist and Asian art historian. Served to maj. AUS, 1942-46. Decorated Bronze Star. Mem. Western Assn. Art Museums (pres. 1960-61), Soc. Asian Art (dir. 1968-81), Phi Kappa Phi, Delta Phi Delta. Home: 2 Pelican Point Belvedere CA 94920

FAUSETT, WILLIAM DEAN, artist; b. Price, Utah, July 4, 1913; s. George and Helen J. (Bryner) F. Student, Brigham Young U., 1930, Art Students League, N.Y.C., 1930-35, Beaux Arts Sch. Design, N.Y.C., 1935-37. Portraitist, landscapist, muralist, sculptor; instr. Henry Street Settlement, N.Y.C., 1936-38; artist cons. USAF, Washington, 1952-60; pres. So. Vt. Art Ctr., Manchester, 1958-61, Found. Preservation of Traditional Values in Fine Arts, N.Y.C., 1975—. One-man shows Kraughaar Gallery, N.Y.C., 1944, 46, 52, Vose Gallery, Boston, 1947, So. Vt. Art Ctr., Manchester, Vt., 1953, 57, 66, 73, 74, 82, Ariz. State U., Tempe, 1970, Palm Springs Desert Mus., Calif., 1970, 71; group shows Art Inst., Chgo., 1933, Whitney Mus. Am. Art, 1939-47, Carnegie Inst., 1940, 41, 42, 43, 44, 46, 47, Mus. Modern Art, 1940, 44-45, Wildenstien Gallery, N.Y.C., 1960; represented: permanent collections Met. Mus. Art, Whitney Mus. Am. Art, Mus. Modern Art, Whitney Gallery Western Art, Buffalo Bill Hist. Ctr., Cody, Wyo., Worchester Mus., Art Inst. Chgo., Canajorharie Mus., Bennington Mus., New Britain Mus., Springville Art Gallery, Los Angeles County Mus., So. Vt. Art Ctr., Witte Mus., San Antonio, Ft. Ligonier Mus., Ligonier, Pa., Mus. Fine Arts, Smith Coll., San Diego Mus. Fine Arts, Colorado Springs Fine Arts Ctr., Cornwall Art Ctr., Palm Springs Desert Mus., Eccles Fine Arts Ctr., Yuma Fine Arts Ctr., Augusta Mus. Art, Herbert Inst. Art, Mus. Art, Salt Lake City, Univs. Iowa, Nebr., Vt., Ariz., Utah, Princeton U., Brigham Young U., Ind. State U., Montclair State Coll., Williams Coll., Union Coll., Andover Coll., Ariz. State U., No. Ariz. State U., Utah State U., Weber Coll., Coll. Eastern Utah, Casper State Coll., Snow Coll., Norwich U., U. St. Andrews, Scotland. Recipient Carnegie prize, Pitts., 1940, 47, Salamagundie prize Salamagundie Club, N.Y.C., 1952, Franklin S. Harris award Brigham Young U., 1969; Tiffany fellow, 1932, 33, 34; Guggenheim fellow, 1941, 43. Fellow Art Students League N.Y.; mem. Nat. Soc. Mural painters (hon., pres. 1979—). Mormon. Home: 1 W 67th St New York NY 10023

FAUSOLD, MARTIN LUTHER, history educator; b. Irwin, Pa., Nov. 11, 1921; s. Samuel and and Edna (Breegle) F.; m. Daryl Ethel Clement, June 18, 1949; children: Sharon Ann, Cynthia Lynn, Marti Clement, Martin Samuel. B.A., Gettysburg Coll., 1945; Ph.D., Syracuse U., 1953. Partner Fausold Dairy Co., Blairsville, Pa., 1946-49; from asst. prof. to prof. history and govt. State U. N.Y., Cortland, 1952-58; prof. history and govt., chmn. social sci. div. SUNY, Geneseo, 1959-69, prof. Am. history, 1969—; Mem. univ. awards com. SUNY, chmn., 1970-78, joint awards council, 1970—. Author: Gifford Pinchot: Bull Moore Progressive, 1961, James W. Wadsworth: The Gentleman from New York, 1975, also articles, book revs. profl. jours.; Editor: The Hoover Presidency: A Reappraisal, 1974; Cons. editor, Kennikut Press, 1969-74. Chmn. Cortland Bd. Pub. Works, 1956; mem. Cortland County Civil Service Commn., 1956; trustee Wadsworth Library, 1976—. Served to lt. (j.g.) USNR, 1942-46. Research grantee SUNY Research Found., Nat. Endowment for Humanities, Herbert Hoover Presdl. Library Assn.; SUNY Faculty Exchange Scholar, 1978. Mem. Faculty Assn. State U. N.Y. (pres. 1964- 67), Orgn. Am. Historians, Am. Hist. Assn. Democrat. Presbyn. (elder 1968-70). Home: 29 Oak St Geneseo NY 14454

FAUST, A. DONOVAN, communications executive; b. Indpls., May 31, 1919; s. Glenn L. and Lela Vivien (Smith) F.; m. Barbara Lou Wilson, Aug. 4, 1951; 1 son, Thomas. Student, Taylor U., 1936-37, Purdue U., 1937-39. Broadcasting performer, producer, exec., 1939-54; gen. mgr. Sta. WJRT-TV, Flint, Mich., 1954-65; with Gen. Electric Broadcasting Co., 1966-82; gen. mgr. Sta. WNGE-TV, Nashville, 1966-70, Sta. KOA-TV, Denver, 1970-71, v.p. sta. ops., 1971-73, pres., Schenectady, 1979-82; v.p., gen. mgr. Gen. Electric Cablevision Corp., Schenectady, 1974-78, pres., 1979-82; chmn. Evansville Cable TV, Ind.; dir. Tau Epsilon Music, Inc., N.Y.C., Tomorrow Program Syndication, Inc. Bd. dirs. Com. of Sponsors, Flint Coll. and Cultural Devel., 1958-65, United Way Middle Tenn., 1968-70, 78-84, YMCA, Flint, Mich., 1958-64, YMCA, Nashville, 1967-70, YMCA, Denver, 1971-73, Nashville Better Bus. Bur., 1968-70, 78-80, Service Corps of Ret. Execs.; mem. Mich. Gov's. Council on Traffic Safety, 1962-64, Colo. Gov's. Task Force on Jobs for Vets., 1972-73. Named Newsmaker of Tomorrow Time Mag.-Pitts. C. of C., 1953. Mem. Nat. Assn. Broadcasters (mem. radio code bd. 1967-70), UHF TV Assn. (v.p., dir. 1953-54), ABC-TV Network Affiliates Assn. (bd. govs. 1966-70), Soc. TV Pioneers. Home: 501 Lynnwood Blvd Nashville TN 37205

FAUST, IRVIN, author, educator; b. N.Y.C., June 11, 1924; s. Morris and Pauline (Henschel) F.; m. Jean S. Faust, Aug. 29, 1959. B.S., CCNY, 1949; M.A., Columbia U. Tchrs. Coll., 1952, Ed.D., 1960. Tchr. jr. high sch. N.Y.C. public schs., 1949-53, 55, high sch. guidance counselor, 1956-60, dir. guidance, 1960—; lectr. fiction and creative writing U. Rochester, New Sch. for Social Research, Swarthmore Coll., CCNY. Author: non-fiction Entering Angel's World, 1963; fiction Roar Lion Roar And Other Stories, 1965; novels The Steagle, 1966 (made into film 1971), The File on Stanley Patton Buchta, 1970, Willy Remembers, 1971, Foreign Devils, 1973, A Star in the Family, 1975, Newsreel, 1980; contbr.: stories to Paris Rev., Sewanee Rev., Esquire mag., Atlantic Monthly, Northwest Rev., Carleton Miscellany, San Francisco Rev., Saturday Evening Post, Transatlantic Rev.; author: various anthologiesincluding Prize Stories, O. Henry Awards, 1983; contbr. to: Voice of Am. series: American Writing Today. Served with U.S. Army, 1943-46; ETO; Served with U.S. Army; Philippines. Mem. PEN, Nat. Assn. Coll. Admissions Counselors. Office: care Gloria Loomis A Watkins Inc 77 Park Ave New York NY 10016

FAUST, JOHN WILLIAM, JR., engineering educator; b. Pitts., July 25, 1922; s. John William and Helen (Crowther) F.; m. Mary Claire Barton, June 7, 1947; children: Mary Faust Baumert, Elizabeth Wickham Kemp, John William III, Charles Barton, Ann Louise Faust Spires, Susan Bosley, Helen Crowther, Thomas McCullough. B.S. in Chem. Engring., Purdue U., 1943; M.A., U. Mo., 1949, Ph.D., 1951. Research scientist Westinghouse Research Labs., Pitts., 1951-63, mgr. materials characterization lab., 1963-65, project mgr. crystal growth, 1965-67; prof. materials sci. Pa. State U., State College, 1967-69; prof. engring. U. S.C., Columbia, 1969—; research physicist Naval Research Labs., 1980-81; cons. Wright Patterson Air Force Research Center, 1957, Corning Glass Research Labs., 1968-70, Dow Corning Semiconductor Div., 1967-69, Gen. Tel. & Tel. Labs., 1968, cons. Sylvania materials div., 1968-70; cons. Langley Air Force Research Labs., 1970, Air Force Materials Lab., Wright Patterson AFB, 1977, Borg-Warner Corp., 1982—, Silaq Corp., 1979-80, Morgan Semicondr. Corp., 1982—; co-chmn. Internat. Com. on Silicon Carbide, 1969-75; chmn. tech. adv. panel solar energy S.C. State Legislature, 1979—. Editor: The Surface Chemistry of Metals and Semiconductors, 1960, Silicon Carbide, 1973; cons. editor, Marcel Dekker, Inc., 1967-71; div. editor, Jour. Electrochem. Soc., 1971—; contbr. articles to profl. jours. Served with USNR, 1943-46. Fellow Am. Inst. Chemists; mem. Electrochem. Soc. (editorial com. 1971—), AIME, AAAS (councillor 1967-69), Am. Phys. Soc., Am. Soc. Metals, Am. Chem. Soc., Sigma Xi, Eta Kappa Nu, Tau Beta Pi. Patentee in field. Home: 2455 Robincrest Dr W Columbia SC 29169 *I have always had an insatiable curiosity to find out why things were as they were. In addition, my thirst for knowledge has kept me a student all my life, and an open mind has allowed me to learn from people in all walks of life and all ages. I have always attempted to work at my maximum efficiency. This has meant making use of every moment and, perhaps most important, not taking the time to worry about whether my co-workers might be more highly paid or doing less work than I.*

FAUST, RICHARD EDWARD, pharmaceutical chemist; b. Greenfield, Mass., Oct. 26, 1927; s. Gotthold E. and Marjorie (Bonk) F.; m. Joan Louise Allen, June 6, 1953; children: Mark, Timothy, Gretchen. B.S., Mass. Coll. Pharmacy, 1951; M.S., Purdue U., 1953, Ph.D., 1955; M.B.A., Columbia U., 1968. Asst. prof. pharmacy Ferris State Coll., Big Rapids, Mich., 1955-57; dir. research Cuticura Labs., Malden, Mass., 1957-61; mgr. new products creation Merck & Co., Rahway, N.J., 1961-63; dir. product devel. Johnson & Johnson, New Brunswick, N.J., 1963-68; dir. research planning and devel. Hoffmann-La Roche Inc., Nutley, N.J., 1968—; adj. prof. Fairleigh Dickinson U.; exec. asso. Denver Research Inst. Author papers in field, chpts. in books. Served with AUS, 1946-48. Mem. AAAS, Am. Chem. Soc., Am. Pharm. Assn., N.Am. Soc. Corp. Planning, Acad. Pharm. Scis., Drug Info. Assn., Project Mgmt. Inst., Lic. Execs. Soc., Soc. Research Adminstrs., Assn. Research Dirs. Home: 80 Bayberry Ln Watchung NJ 07060 Office: 340 Kingsland St Nutley NJ 07110

FAUVER, JOHN WILLIAM, business executive; b. Detroit, Dec. 11, 1921; s. John Newton and Margaret Burns (Schofield) F.; m. Margaret M. Miller, Dec.7, 1943; children: John, Johanna, Jeffrey. B.S.M.E., U. Mich., 1943. With J.N. Fauver Co., Madison Heights, Mich., 1946—, now chmn., chief exec. officer. Trustee Cranbrook Schs., 1970-80; pres. Boys Clubs Met. Detroit, 1972; mayor City of Bloomfield Hills, Mich., 1976-77, 81—, city commr., 1972—. Served to capt. AUS, 1942-46. Mem. Nat. Indsl. Distbrs. Assn. (pres. 1979-80), Fluid Power Ednl. Found. (trustee). Republican. Presbyterian. Clubs: Lost Tree, Bloomfield Hills Country, Orchard Lake Country, Jupiter Hills, Torch Lake Yacht, Belvidere Country, Detroit Rotary (past pres.), Masons.). Home: 11080 Turtle Beach Rd North Palm Beach FL 33408 Office: 1500 Avis Madison Heights MI 48071

FAVORITE, FELIX, oceanographer; b. Quincy, Mass., Mar. 18, 1925; s. Felix Christian and Irene Vibert (Doyle) F.; m. Betty Lou Donnelly, Nov. 2, 1951; children: Lee H., Kim C., Kit C., Felix Scott. B.S., Mass. Maritime Acad., 1950; postgrad., Boston U., 1949-50; B.S., U. Wash., 1956, M.S., 1966; Ph.D., Oreg. State U., 1968. Research oceanographer U. Wash., 1957; dir. oceanographic research Bur. Comml. Fisheries Biol. Lab., Seattle, 1957-70; program mgr. oceanography Nat. Maritime Fisheries Service, Seattle, 1971-75, resource ecology studies coordinator, 1977—; prin. investigator Outer Continental Shelf Environ. Assessment Program, 1976-78; expert in oceanography Internat. No. Pacific Fisheries Commn., 1959-72. Served to lt. comdr. USNR, 1947-48, 50-53. Recipient Silver medal Dept. Commerce, 1973. Mem. Oceanography Soc. Japan, N.Y. Acad. Scis., Sigma Xi. Club: Sheridan Beach Community of Seattle (trustee 1960-61). Home: 16103 41st St NE Seattle WA 98155 Office: 2725 Montlake Blvd E Seattle WA 98112

FAVORS, MALACHI, jazz musician, bassist; b. Chgo., Aug. 22, 1937., (With Andrew Hill) Rec., 1958; played in (with Roscoe Mitchell) group, 1961; with, Muhal Richard Abrams' Exptl. Band, 1960's, Assn. Advancement of Creative Musicians, 1965, Joseph Jarman, Roscoe Mitchell and later Lester Bowie and Don Moye, now known as Art Ensemble of Chgo.; performed in, France, 1969-71; recs. include Certain Blacks and Others, Reese and the Smooth Ones, Message to Our folks, People in Sorrow, Tutankhamun, Fanfare for the Warriors, Nice Guys; appeared at, Ann Arbor Blues and Jazz Festival, 1972, Chgo. Jazz Festival, 1980, others. Office: care Rasa Artists 144 W 27th St New York NY 10001 *

FAVREAU, DONALD FRANCIS, consultant; b. Cohoes, N.Y., Sept. 7, 1919; s. Alphonse Emille and Millie Loretta (Smith) F.; m. Helen Patricia Rafferty, June 2, 1945; 1 dau., Susan Debra. B.A., Knox Coll., 1949; M.A., SUNY, 1954. Prof. mil. sci. LaSalle Inst., Troy, N.Y., 1949-54; mgr. tng. Ford Motor Co., Cleve., 1954-57, Am. Bosch Arma Corp., Garden City, N.Y., 1957-59; asst. to v.p. Royal Metal Corp., N.Y.C., 1959-60; mgr. personnel devel. N.Y. Stock Exchange, N.Y.C., 1960-62; manpower coordinator N.Y. State Dept. Labor, 1962-65; asso. dir. Center for Exec. Devel. SUNY-Albany, 1965-69, dir. Center for Exec. Devel. and Pub. Safety Mgmt., 1969-83, prof. emeritus, 1983—; pres. Don Favreau Assocs., 1983—; adj. instr. Western Res. U., 1952-54; adj. prof. C.W. Post Coll., 1975—; cons. in field. Author: Introduction to Fire Protection, 1972, Criminal Victimization of the Elderly, 1977, Modern Police Administration, 1978. Mem. Saratoga Performing Arts Center; met. bd. dirs. Nat. Alliance Bus., 1979—; vice chmn. Pvt. Industry Council, 1980—; v.p. Northeast Alliance of Bus., 1982—; bd. dirs. Vis. Nurse Assn. of Albany, 1984—. Served with U.S. Army, 1943-46. Named hon. citizen Ville de Lafayette; recipient commendation Pres. Carter, 1978, Pres. Reagan, 1982, cert. of merit State of N.Y., 1983; named hon. fire chief City and County of Denver, 1983. Mem. Internat. Fire Adminstrn. Inst. (exec. dir. 1965-73), Am. Mgmt. Assn., Nat. Fire Protection Assn., Internat. Assn. Chiefs of Police, N.Y. State Assn. Fire Chiefs, AAUP, NEA, Soc. Advancement of Mgmt., Am. Soc. Tng. Dirs., Nat. Assn. 10th Mountain Div. Assn., Friendly Sons St. Patrick (dir. 1984—), Sigma Nu. Club: Elks. Home: 32 Hemlock Dr Clifton Park NY 12065

FAVRET, LOUIS MARTIN, management consultant; b. Columbus, Ohio, June 5, 1928; s. Louis E. and Marie A. (Smyth) F.; m. Patricia L. Fitzburgh, June 28, 1952; children: Michele, Gerald, Diane, Richard, Paul, John. B.S.M.E., Ohio State U., 1951, M.S.M.E., 1951. Mgr. market research Babcock & Wilcox, Barberton, Ohio, 1961-65, proposal mgr. nuclear power plants, 1965-69, mgr. planning and comml. ops., 1969-70, gen. mgr. nuclear equipment div., 1970-71, v.p. nuclear equipment div., 1971-73, v.p. nuclear divs., 1973-78, exec. v.p. power generation group, 1979, exec. v.p. bus. integration group, New Orleans, 1980-82; mgmt. cons., New Orleans, 1982—; mem. mech. engring. adv. com. Ohio State U., 1973-81. Recipient Disting. Alumnus award Ohio State U., 1974. Mem. Atomic Indsl. Forum (vice chmn.), ASME. Roman Catholic. Home: 5735 Durham Dr New Orleans LA 70114 Office: 5735 Durham Dr New Orleans LA 70114

FAW, CHARLES DENNIS, retail food store chain executive; b. Wilkes County, N.C., Oct. 31, 1937; s. Roby Charles and Sue Lee F.; m. Patricia Ann Shumaker, June 30, 1957; children: Gregory Charles, Stephanie Ann, Leslie Denise. Student, Appalachian State U., 1957. With Lowe's Food Stores, Inc., Wilkesboro, N.C., 1954—, v.p. store ops., 1965-69, exec. v.p., gen. mgr., 1969-84, pres., 1984—, dir., 1965—; dir. Piedmont Fed. Savs. and Loan. Mem. adv. bd. Wilkes Community Coll., 1976-79, chmn., 1979-80. Mem. Wilkes County C. of C. (pres. 1979—), Food Market Inst., N.C. Mchts. Assn., N.C. Food Dealers Assn. (v.p.), Am. Mgmt. Assn., Western Carolina Industries, Va. Food Dealers Assn. Baptist. Clubs: Oakwoods Country, Elks. Office: PO Box 700 Wilkesboro NC 28697

FAW, DUANE LESLIE, lawyer, educator; b. Loraine, Tex., July 7, 1920; s. Alfred Leslie and Noma Leigh (Elliott) F.; m. Lucile Elizabeth Craps, Feb. 20, 1943; children: Cheryl Leigh, Bruce Duane, Debra Leoma, Melanie Loraine. Student, N. Tex. State Coll., 1937-41; J.D., Columbia U., 1947. Bar: Tex. 1948, D.C. 1969, U.S. Supreme Ct. 1969. Individual practice law Denton and Van Horn, Tex., 1948-52; with USMC, 1942-45, 52-71, commd. 2d lt., 1942, advanced through grades to brig. gen., 1969; aviator, 1942-45, atty., Calif., 1952-53, Korea/Japan, 1954, Parris Island, S.C., 1955-58; with Amphibious Warfare Sr. Sch., 1958-59; bn. comdr., 1959-61, staff judge adv. marine div., 1961-62; policy analyst Marine Hdqrs., 1964-67; dep. chief of staff III Marine Amphibious Force, 1967-68; judge Navy Ct. Mil. Rev., 1968-69; dir. Judge Adv. Div. Marine Hdqrs., Washington, 1969-71; prof. law Pepperdine U. Sch. Law, Malibu, Calif., 1971—, U. London, 1983. Co-author: The Military in American Society, 1978. Decorated Air medal with gold star, Navy Commendation medal, Legion of Merit with combat V; UN Cross of Gallantry with gold star; VN Honor medal 1st class. Mem. ABA (adv. com. mil. justice 1969-71, adv. com. lawyers in Armed Forces 1969-71), Fed. Bar Assn. (council), Judge Advs. Assn. Club: Masons. One of original 12 judges Navy Ct. Mil. Rev.; 1st gen. officer head Marine Corps Judge Advs. Address: 24311 Baxter Dr Malibu CA 90265 *People are placed upon this planet for a purpose greater than self-maintenance and self-indulgence. True success and happiness require a personal discovery of, and commitment to, a system of values which furthers the implementation of the Divine plan.*

FAWCETT, DON WAYNE, anatomist; b. Springdale, Iowa, Mar. 14, 1917; s. Carlos J. and Mabel (Kennedy) F.; m. Dorothy Marie Secrest, 1941; children: Robert S., Mary Elaine, Donna, Joseph. A.B. cum laude, Harvard, 1938, M.D., 1942; D.Sc. (hon.), U. Siena, Italy, 1974, N.Y. Med. Coll., 1975, U. Chgo., 1977, U. Cordoba, Argentina, 1978, M.D., U. Heidelberg, Germany, 1977, D.V.M., Justus Liebig U., Giessen-Lahn, Germany, 1977. Intern surgery Mass. Gen Hosp., Boston, 1942-43; instr. anatomy Harvard Med. Sch., 1946-48, asso. anatomy, 1948-51, asst. prof. anatomy, 1951-55, Hersey prof. anatomy, 1958—, James Stillman prof. comparative anatomy, 1962—, sr. asso. dean preclin. affairs, 1975-77; prof. anatomy Cornell Med. Coll., 1955-58; scientist Internat. Lab. Research on Animal Diseases, Nairobi, Kenya, 1980—. Author: The Cell, 1966, 2d edit., 1981, Textbook of Histology, 1968, 10th edit., 1975. Served as capt. M.C. AUS, 1943-46; bn. surgeon A.A. John and Mary Markle scholar med. sci., 1949-54; recipient Lederle Med. Faculty award, 1954. Fellow Am. Acad. Arts and Sci., Nat. Acad. Sci., Royal Microscopical Soc. (hon.); mem. AAAS, N.Y. Acad. Sci., Am. Assn. Anatomists (pres. 1964- 65, Henry Gray award 1983), N.Y. Soc. Electron Microscopists (pres. 1957-58), Histochem. Soc., Tissue Culture Assn. (v.p. 1954-55), Soc. Exptl. Biology and Medicine, Assn. Anatomy Chairmen (pres. 1973-74), Am. Soc. Zoologists, Am. Soc. Mammalogists, Electron Microscope Soc. Am., Soc. Study Devel. and Growth, Harvey Soc., Am. Soc. Cell Biology (pres. 1961-62), Argentine Nat. Acad. Sci., Anat. Soc. So. Africa (hon.), Japanese Anat. Soc. (hon.), Anat. Soc. Australia and N.Z. (hon.), Japanese Electron Microscope Soc., Internat. Fedn. Soc. Electron Microscopy (pres. 1976-78), Am. Soc. Andrology (pres. 1977-78), Soc. Study Reprodn., Mexican (hon.), Canadian (hon.) assns. anatomists. Office: Internat Lab Research in Animal Diseases PO Box 30709 Nairobi Kenya

FAWCETT, FARRAH LENI, actress, model; b. Corpus Christi, Tex., Feb. 2, 1947; d. James William and Pauline Alice (Evans) F.; m. Lee Majors, July 28, 1973 (div. 1982). Student, U. Tex. at Austin. Works as model. Movie debut in Myra Breckenridge, 1970; other film appearances Love is a Funny Thing, 1970, Logan's Run, 1976, Somebody Killed Her Husband, 1978, Sunburn, 1979, Strictly Business, 1979, The Helper, 1979, Saturn 3, 1980, Cannonball Run, 1981; TV movies The Girl Who Came Gift-Wrapped, 1974, Murder on Flight 502, 1975, Charlie's Angels, 1976, Murder in Texas, 1981, The Red Light Sting, 1984; regular TV series Charlie's Angels, 1976-77; other TV appearances include Harry O; N.Y.C. Stage debut (off-Broadway) Extremities, 1983. Mem. Delta Delta Delta. With Lee Majors formed prodn. co. Fawcett-Majors Prodns. Office: care William Morris Agy 151 El Camino Beverly Hills CA 90212 *

FAWCETT, HENRY MITCHELL, rubber co. exec.; b. Canton, Ohio, Nov. 30, 1919; s. John Andrew and Pauline (Heingartner) F.; m. Mary Ellen Bloch, Mar. 27, 1943; children—Mary Ellen Fawcett Tobin, Jane M. Fawcett Comunale, Julie Ann Fawcett Deane. B.A., Colgate U., 1941, Harvard, 1943. Various sales positions Mohawk Rubber Co., Akron, Ohio, 1946-51, asst. pres., 1951-56, pres., chief exec. officer, 1956-81, chmn., chief exec. officer, Hudson, Ohio, 1981—, also dir.; dir. Twin Coach Co., Buffalo, 1st Nat. Bank Akron, Pfleuger Corp., Akron. Trustee Boy Scouts Am., YMCA, Salvation Army, Children's Hosp. Akron, Akron City Hosp.; bd. dirs. Assos. Harvard Bus. Sch.; bd. govs. Mass. Gen. Hosp., Boston. Served as lt. USNR, 1942-45. Mem. Akron C. of C. (trustee), Harvard Bus. Sch. Alumni Assn., Newcomen Soc., Sigma Nu. Club: Portage Country. Home: 470 Delaware Ave Akron OH 44303 Office: 50 Executive Pkwy Hudson OH 44236

FAWCETT, JAN, psychiatrist; b. Jamestown, N.Y., Mar. 31, 1934; s. James Earl and Gretchen (Benney) F.; (married); 5 children. B.S., U. Rochester, N.Y., 1956; M.D., Yale U., 1960. Diplomate: Am. Bd. Psychiatry and Neurology. Intern USPHS Hosp., San Francisco, 1960-61; resident in psychiatry Langley Porter Neuropsychiat. Inst., San Francisco, 1961-63, U. Rochester Med. Center, 1963-64; clin. asso. NIMH, Bethesda, Md., 1964-65; chief research unit, then asso. dir. research Ill. State Psychiat. Inst., Chgo., 1966-72; prof. psychiatry, chmn. dept. Rush-Presbyn. St. Lukes Med. Center, Chgo., 1972—; prin. investigator NIMH grants, 1970—. Author papers in field.; Cons. editor: Life Threatening Behavior, 1970; mem. editorial bds. profl. jours. Served with USN, 1952-54. Recipient Anna-Monika award, Basel, Switzerland, 1973. Mem. Am. Psychiat. Assn., Am. Psychosomatic Soc., Am. Soc. Adolescent Psychiatry, Am. Assn. Suicidology, Psychiat. Research Soc., Central Neuropsychiat. Soc., Am. Coll. Neuropsychopharmacology, Central Found. Med. Care, Am. Psychopathol. Assn., Ill. Psychiat. Soc. (pres. 1974-75), Chgo. Med. Soc. Address: 1720 W Polk St Chicago IL 60612

FAWCETT, JOHN WILLIAM, III, lawyer; b. Oil City, Pa., May 4, 1920; s. John William and Mary (Chambers) F.; m. Margaret B. Hoyer, May 30, 1957; children—John William, Jennifer Wales, Erik Hoyer. B.A., Yale U., 1942; LL.B., Temple U., 1950. Bar: Pa. bar 1950. Partner firm Montgomery, McCracken, Walker & Rhoads, Phila.; consul of France for Phila. Trustee La Napoule Found., Alpes-Maritimes, France. Served to lt. USNR, 1942-46. Named chevalier l'Ordre du Merite. Mem. Internat. Law Assn., Internat. Fiscal Assn., Am., Phila. bar assns. Clubs: Yale (Phila. and N.Y.); Union League, Corinthian Yacht (Phila.); Rittenhouse. Home: 126 Montrose Ave Rosemont PA 19010 Office: 3 Parkway Philadelphia PA 19102

FAWCETT, SHERWOOD LUTHER, research laboratory executive; b. Youngstown, Ohio, Dec. 25, 1919; s. Luther T. and Clara (Sherwood) F.; m. Martha L. Simcox, Feb. 28, 1953; children: Paul, Judith, Tom. B.S., Ohio State U., 1941; M.S., Case Inst. Tech., 1948, Ph.D., 1950; hon. degrees, Ohio State U., Gonzaga U., Whitman Coll., Otterbein Coll., Detroit Inst. Tech. Registered profl. engr., Ohio. Mem. staff Columbus Labs. Battelle Meml. Inst., 1950-64, mgr. physics dept., 1959-64; dir. Pacific Northwest Labs., Richland, Wash., 1964-67; exec. v.p. Battelle Meml. Inst., Columbus, Ohio, 1967- 68, pres., 1968-80, chmn., chief exec. officer, 1981—. Served with the USNR, 1941-46. Decorated Bronze Star. Mem. Am. Phys. Soc., Am. Nuclear Soc., Nat. Soc. Profl. Engrs., Am. Inst. Metall. Engrs., Sigma Xi, Delta Chi, Sigma Pi Sigma, Tau Beta Pi. Home: 2820 Margate Rd Columbus OH 43221 Office: 505 King Ave Columbus OH 43201

FAWLEY, JOHN JONES, banker; b. Phila., Oct. 1, 1921; s. James L. and Edna (Jones) F.; m. Ann Kemp, Jan. 8, 1944; children: Jo Ann (Mrs. Richard High), Christine, James K. B.S. in Econs, Wharton Sch., U. Pa., 1948; grad., Rutgers U. Grad. Sch. Banking, 1957. With First Pa. Bank, Phila., 1948-69, sr. v.p., 1968- 69; pres., dir. United Va. Bank/First & Citizens Nat. Bank, Alexandria, Va., 1969-72; exec. v.p. Indsl. Valley Bank, Phila., 1973-83, Dauphin Deposit Bank, Harrisburg, Pa., 1983—; lectr. Comml. Lending Sch., U. Okla., 1969. Trustee Hahnemann U. Served with AUS, 1942-45. Mem. Robert Morris Assocs. (nat. pres. 1972-73). Presbyterian (past trustee). Lodge: Masons. Home: 5 Hound Rum Whitpainfarm BlueBell PA Office: 213 Market St Harrisburg PA 17105

FAX, ELTON CLAY, author, artist; b. Balt., Oct. 9, 1909; s. Mark Oakl and Willie Estelle (Smith) F.; m. Grace Elizabeth Turner, Mar. 12, 1929 (dec.); children: Betty Louise (Mrs. James Evans), Virginia Mae (dec.), Leon. B.F.A., U. Syracuse, 1931. Tchr. Claflin Coll., Orangeburg, S.C., 1934-36; artist-tchr. WPA, N.Y.C., 1936-40; free lance artist-writer, 1940—; Lectr.-cons. prep. schs., colls., New Eng., N.Y., Midwest, Calif., 1960—; participant Union Bulgarian Writers Conf., Sofia, 1977. Author: Contemporary Black Leaders, 1970, Seventeen Black Artists, 1971, Garvey, 1972, Through Black Eyes, 1974, Black Artists of the New Generation, 1977, Hashar, 1980, El-Chun, 1984. MacDowell Colony fellow, 1967; State Dept. travel grantee to S.Am., 1955, W.Africa, 1963, E.Africa, Egypt, 1964; invited by Soviet writers USSR, 1970, 73; recipient Louis E. Seley NACAL Gold medal for oil painting for USN, 1971, Coretta Scott King Authors award, 1972. Mem. Authors Guild Am., P.E.N. Am. Home: 51-28 30th Ave Woodside NY 11377 Office: PO Box 2188 Long Island City NY 11102 *To be true to my craft and fair to my fellowman at all times and under all circumstances no matter what the cost, is what being an artist means to me.*

FAY, ALBERT HILL, bldg. materials co. exec.; b. Bklyn., Aug. 19, 1911; s. Albert Hill and Clara (Constable) F.; m. Leona May Anderson, Sept. 4, 1934. B.Arch., Columbia, 1934, M.S., 1935. Product mgr., then prodn. mgr. Flintkote Corp., 1936-50; advt. mgr. Asbestone Corp., New Orleans, 1950-53; dir. product mgmt. Nat. Gypsum Co., Buffalo, 1953-65, v.p. mktg., 1965-69, v.p. research and mktg., 1969-76; pres. Constrn. Mktg. Services, 1977—; mem. bldg. research adv. bd. Nat. Acad. Sci., 1974—. Past trustee Niagara Frontier Housing Devel. Corp.; Trustee Nat. Council of Housing Industry, 1969-75, vice chmn., 1970-72; Bd. dirs. Brand Names Found., Better Bus. Bur. Western N.Y., 1978—. Served to lt. USNR, 1944-46. Consultative mem. Nat. Inst. Bldg. Scis.; mem. Nat. Home Improvement Council (pres. 1971-73, dir.), Asbestos Cement Products Assn. (pres. 1962-74), Asbestos Information Assn. N.Am. (pres. 1972-73). Home: 63 Jordan Rd Williamsville NY 14221

FAY, FREDERIC ALBERT, former government official; b. Oneonta, N.Y., July 4, 1911; s. Earl Donovan and Madoline (Lewis) F.; m. Wray Hass, Feb. 9, 1936 (dec. 1956); 1 dau., Anne Madoline; m. Virginia Easton Ford, Feb. 11, 1961. B.S., Syracuse U., 1933; postgrad., Harvard U., 1934, U. Va., 1942. Asst. landscape architect Central N.Y. State Parks Commn., Syracuse, 1933-34; asst. landscape architect Nat. Parks Service, Gatlinburg, Tenn., Richmond, Va., 1934-41; tech. dir., asst. exec. dir. Portsmouth (Va.) Redevel. and Housing Authority, 1941-49; architect-engr. George T. McLean Co., Inc., Portsmouth, 1949-50; exec. dir. Richmond Redevel. and Housing Authority, 1950-80; mem. Va. Housing Devel. Authority, chmn., 1972-80; mem. slum clearance adv. com. U.S. HHFA; mem. Va. Adv. Legis. Council, 1957, 78—, Va. Emergency Resources Planning Com., 1965; mem. jury PHA Honor Awards for Design Excellence Program, 1964. Contbr. articles to profl. jours. Bd. dirs. Richmond Symphony, Hist. Richmond Found., March of Dimes, Va. Center for Performing Arts, St. Joseph's Villa Housing Corp.; chmn. Richmond Chaplaincy Service, 1982—; trustee Old Dominion Symphony Council, treas., 1974-78, pres., 1978—; vestryman St. Stephen's Ch., Richmond, St. John's Ch., Portsmouth. Named Honorary Citizen Nashville, 1955, New Orleans, 1967, Grant's Pass, Oreg., 1967, Portland, Oreg., 1967. Fellow Am. Soc. Landscape Architects; hon. mem. AIA; mem. Am. Soc. Planning Ofcls., Am. Inst. Planners, Nat. Assn. Housing and Redevel. Ofcls. (pres. 1965-67, gov. 1957-73), General Research Inst. Va. (dir.), Sigma Chi. Democrat. Episcopalian. Clubs: Commonwealth, Rotary (Richmond). Home: 801 St Christophers Rd Richmond VA 23226

FAY, JAMES ALAN, engineering educator; b. Southold, N.Y., Nov. 1, 1923; s. William Joseph, Jr. and Margaret (Keenan) F.; m. Agatha Marie Kelly, Jan. 12, 1946; children: David Anthony, Mark Bernard, Colin Michael, Jamie Martin, Peter Robert, Michele Marie. B.S., Webb Inst. Naval Architecture, 1944; M.S., MIT, 1947; Ph.D., Cornell U., 1951. Research engr. Lima-Hamilton Corp., 1947-49; asst. prof. engring. mechanics Cornell U., 1951-55; mem. faculty Mass. Inst. Tech., 1955, prof. mech. engring., 1960—; dir. SCA Services, Inc.; cons. to govt. and industry; mem. NRC Environ. Studies Bd., 1973-78, 80—,. Author: Molecular Thermodynamics, 1965; also articles. Chmn. Boston Air Pollution Commn., 1969-72, Mass. Port Authority, 1972-77; bd. dirs. Union Concerned Scientists, 1978—. Served with USNR, 1942-46. Fellow Am. Acad. Arts and Scis., Am. Phys. Soc. (exec. com. div. fluid dynamics 1964-67), AAAS, AIAA (chmn. plasmadynamics com. 1966-68); mem. ASME, Air Pollution Control Assn., AAUP, Mass. Audubon Soc. (dir. 1978-82), Sigma Xi. Home: 36 Spruce Hill Rd Weston MA 02193 Office: Mass Inst Tech Cambridge MA 02139

FAY, PETER THORP, judge; b. Rochester, N.Y., Jan. 18, 1929; s. Lester Thorp and Jane (Baumler) F.; m. Claudia Pat Zimmerman, Oct. 1, 1958; children: Michael Thorp, William, Darcy. B.A., Rollins Coll., 1951, LL.D., 1971; J.D., U. Fla., 1956; LL.D., Biscayne Coll., 1975. Bar: Fla. 1956, U.S. Supreme Ct. 1961. Partner firm Nichols, Gaither Green, Frates & Beckham, Miami, Fla., 1956-61, Frates, Fay, Floyd & Pearson (and predecessors), Miami, 1961-70; judge U.S. Dist. Ct. for So. Fla., Miami, 1970-76, U.S. Ct. Appeals (5th cir.), 1976-81, U.S. Ct. Appeals (11th cir.), 1981—; prof. Fla. Jr. Bar Practical Legal Inst., 1959-65; lectr. Fla. Bar Legal Inst., 1959—; faculty Fed. Jud. Center, Washington, 1974—; Mem. Jud. Conf. Com. for Implementation Criminal Justice Act, 1974-82, Adv. Com. on Codes of Conduct, 1980—. Mem. Orange Bowl Com., 1974—; dist. collector United Fund, 1957-70; mem. adminstrv. bd. Biscayne Coll., 1970—. Served with USAF, 1951-53. Mem. Law Sci. Acad., Fla. Acad. Trial Attys., Am., Fla., Dade County, John Marshall (past pres.) bar assns., Fla. Council of 100, U. Fla. Alumni Assn. (dir.), Miami C. of C., Medico Legal Inst., Order of Coif, Phi Delta Phi (past pres.), Omicron Delta Kappa (past pres.), Pi Gamma Mu (past pres.), Phi Kappa Phi, Phi Delta Theta (past sec.). Republican. Roman Catholic. Clubs: Wildcat Cliffs (N.C.); Snapper Creek Lakes, Coral Oaks (Miami). Home: 11000 Snapper Creek Rd Miami FL 33156 Office: US Courthouse Miami FL 33101

FAY, PETER WARD, history educator; b. Paris, France, Dec. 3, 1924; s. Willis Ward and Joan (Peters) F.; m. Phyllis Ford, 1950 (div. 1955); 1 dau., Jennifer; m. Mariette Robertson, Dec. 21, 1957; children: Todor, Lisa, Jonathan, Benjamin. B.A., Harvard U., 1947, Ph.D., 1954; B.A., Oxford U., 1949. Instr. Williams Coll., 1951-55; asst. prof. history Calif. Inst. Tech., 1955-60, assoc. prof., 1960-70, prof. history, Pasadena, Calif., 1970—. Author: The Opium War 1840-42, 1975. Served with AUS, 1943-46. Rhodes scholar, 1947. Mem. Am. Hist. Assn., Assn. for Asian Studies. Democrat. Club: Signet Soc. Home: 590 Auburn St Sierra Madre CA 91024 Office: 228-77 Calif Inst Tech Pasadena CA 91125

FAY, ROBERT CLINTON, chemist, educator; b. Kenosha, Wis., Mar. 14, 1936; s. Clinton Edward and Selma (Lenz) F.; m. Carol Lee Baker, Aug. 25, 1960. A.B., Oberlin Coll., 1957; postgrad., Wheaton Coll., 1957-58; M.S., U. Ill., 1960, Ph.D., 1962. Teaching fellow Wheaton (Ill.) Coll., 1957-58; teaching asst. U. Ill., Urbana, 1958-59; inorganic chemist Nat. Bur. Standards, Washington, summers 1957-60; asst. prof. chemistry Cornell U., Ithaca, N.Y., 1962-68, asso. prof., 1968-75, prof., 1975—. Contbr. articles to profl. jours. NSF fellow, 1960-62; NSF faculty fellow U. East Anglia, U. Sussex, Eng., 1969-70; Sci. and Engring. Research Council vis. fellow and NATO/Heineman sr. fellow Oxford (Eng.) U., 1982-83; NSF grantee, 1964-80; recipient Clark Disting. Teaching award Cornell U., 1980. Mem. Am. Chem. Soc., Chem. Soc. (London), Am. Crystallographic Assn., Sigma Xi, Phi Kappa Phi, Phi Beta Kappa, Phi Lambda Upsilon, Pi Mu Epsilon. Home: 318 Eastwood Ave Ithaca NY 14850 Office: Dept Chemistry Cornell Univ Ithaca NY 14853

FAY, ROBERT JESSE, lawyer; b. Cleve., Apr. 9, 1920; s. Horace Byron and Florence (Keating) F.; m. Ann Regan, Sept. 24, 1948 (div.); children—Regan, Laura, Karen, Michael, Molly, Ford, Genny. B.S., Mass. Inst. Tech., 1942; J.D., Case Western Res. U., 1948. Bar: Ohio bar 1948, D.C. bar 1964. Patent examiner U.S. Patent Office, Washington, 1948-49; since practiced in, Cleve.; partner firm Fay and Sharpe; pres. Gridiron Steel Co.; adj. prof. law Case Western Res. Sch. Law, 1960-75. Mem. Lakewood (Ohio) Planning Commn., 1961-70. Served with U.S. Army, 1942-46. Mem. Am. Patent Law Assn., IEEE, AAAS, Am., Ohio, Cleve., Cleveland County bar assns., Am. Chem. Soc. Clubs: Rotary, Cleve. Athletic. Office: 1113 E Ohio Bldg Cleveland OH 44114

FAY, THOMAS A., philosophy educator; b. Utica, N.Y., July 18, 1927; s. Thomas A. and Theresa A. (Miller) F. B.A., Cath. U. Am., 1952; M.A., U. Laval, Quebec, 1963; Ph.D., Fordham U., 1970. Asst. prof. philosophy St. Bernard Coll., 1963-64; mem. faculty St. John's U., Jamaica, N.Y., 1967—, prof. philosophy, 1977—; chmn. dept. philosophy St John's U., Jamaica, N.Y.; vis. prof. Drew U., 1969. Author: Heidegger: The Critique of Logic, 1977, And Smoking Flax Shall He Not Quench: Reflections on New Testament Themes, 1979; contbr. articles to profl. jours.; first violinist, Forest Hills Symphony Orch. Served with U.S. Army, 1945-46. Mem. Am. Cath. Philos. Assn. (pres. Met. chpt.), Internat. Thomistic Soc. (v.p.), Internat. Soc. Metaphysics, Am. Philos. Assn., Medieval Acad. Am. Home: 43-44 Kissena Blvd Flushing NY 11355 Office: Philosophy Dept St Johns U. Jamaica NY 11439

FAY, WILLIAM MICHAEL, judge; b. Pittston, Pa.; s. William Morris and Carolyn (Runner) F.; m. Jean Burke, 1945; 1 son, W. Michael. Student, Georgetown U., 1939; LL.B., Cath. U. Am., 1942. Bar: D.C. 1942. Asst. counsel atomic energy com. U.S. Senate, 1946; exec. sec. U.S. Senator McMahon, 1946-48; with Chief Counsel's Office, IRS, 1948-61, asst. regional counsel, 1957-61; judge U.S. Tax Ct., 1961—. Served with USNR, 1942-45. Mem. Am. Bar Assn., Bar Assn. D.C. Office: US Tax Ct Washington DC 20217 *

FAYERWEATHER, JOHN, management and international business specialist, educator; b. Pittsfield, Mass., Mar. 17, 1922; s. Charles S. and Margaret Doane (Gardiner) F.; m. Ruth Elizabeth Selina, Aug. 2, 1947; children: John Charles, James George. B.S. in Geol. Engring., Princeton U., 1943; M.B.A., Harvard U., 1948, D.C.S., 1954. Research asst. Grad. Sch. Bus. Adminstrn., Harvard U., 1948-49, instr., 1949-51, asst. prof., 1952-58; founder, mng. editor The Internat. Exec., 1959—; asso. prof. Grad. Sch. Bus., Columbia U., N.Y.C., 1958-60, dir. 1st mgmt. program in internat. ops., 1959-60; adj. asso. prof. Grad. Sch. Bus. Adminstrn., NYU, N.Y.C., 1961, prof. mgmt. and internat. bus., 1962-82, prof. emeritus, 1982—, dir. workshops for profs. of internat. bus., 1964-72, coordinator internat. bus. programs, 1962-73; cons. and lectr. U.S. Govt. Aid program overseas, 1960-61, co. exec. programs, 1961—; mem. faculty Salzburg (Austria) seminar in Am. studies, 1977; mem. adv. com. on bus. and internat. edn. U.S. Nat. Commn. for UNESCO, 1971-73; mem. task force on bus. and internat. edn. Am. Council on Edn., 1976-78. Author: The Executive Overseas, 1959, Management of International Operations, 1960, Facts and Fallacies of International Business, 1962, International Marketing, 1964, (with Boddewyn and Engberg) International Business Education, Curriculum Planning, 1966, International Business Management, A Conceptual Framework, 1969, Foreign Investment in Canada: Prospects for National Policy, 1973, The Mercantile Bank Affair, 1974, (with Ashok Kapoor) Strategy and Negotiation for the International Corporation, 1976, International Business Strategy and Administration, 1978, Host National Attitudes Toward Multinational Corporations, 1982; contbr. articles to profl. publs.; editor: International Business-Government Affairs, 1973, International Business Policy and Administration, 1976. Served from pvt. to 1st lt. C.E., U.S. Army, 1943-46, 51-52; ETO and Korea. Fellow Acad. Internat. Bus., Internat. Acad. Mgmt., Acad. Mgmt.; mem. U.S. C. of C. (mem. fgn. commerce com. 1955-62), Acad. Internat. Bus. (1st pres. 1961-62). Home: PO Box 860 White River Junction VT 05001

FAZIO, JOHN, supermarket executive; b. Cleve., Jan. 23, 1920; s. Charles and Josephine (Russo) F.; children—Charles Walter, John, Janice Jo Janis. Student, U. Tulsa, 1944. Engaged in food bus., 1941—; pres., chief exec. officer Fazio's Supermarkets, Cleve., 1957—; pres. Fisher Foods Inc., Cleve., 1965-79, dir., cons., 1979—; pres. J.F. Enterprises, Chagrin Falls, Ohio, 1978—, Jote's Inc., Willowick, Ohio, 1982—. Served with AUS, 1943-46. Mem. Supermarket Inst., Asso. Retail Bakers. Baptist. Office: 29700 Lake Shore Blvd Willowick OH 44094

FAZIO, VIC, congressman; b. Winchester, Mass., Oct. 11, 1942; m. Judy Kern; children: Dana, Anne. B.A., Union Coll., Schenectady, 1965; postgrad., Calif. State U., Sacramento. Congressional and legis. cons., 1966-75; mem. Calif. State Assembly, 1975-78, 96th-98th Congresses from Calif. 4th Dist., mem. appropriations, budgets and standards of ofcl. conduct coms., chmn. legis. br. appropriations com., majority whip-at-large, mem. exec. com. Democratic Study Group, also vice-chmn. Fed. Govt. Services Task Force; Former mem. Sacramento County Charter and Planning Commns. Founder: Calif. Jour. Coro Found. fellow.; Named Environmentalist of Yr., Calif. Planning and Conservation League. Mem. Air Force Assn., Navy League, UNICO. Democrat. Office: Room 1421 Longworth House Office Bldg Washington DC 20515

FEAGLES, ROBERT WEST, insurance company executive; b. Ft. Wayne, Ind., July 23, 1920; s. Ralph L. and Mary Anna (West) F.; m. Anita Marie MacRae, Sept. 15, 1951; children: Wendy Lee, Cuyler MacRae, Priscilla Jane, Patrick Emerson. B.S., Ga. Inst. Tech., 1943, Am. Grad. Sch. of Internat. Mgmt., 1951; cert. of banking, Rutgers U. Grad. Sch. Banking, 1958. Sr. v.p. Citibank, N.Y.C., 1951-76, Travelers Ins. Co., Hartford, Conn., 1976—; chmn., chief exec. officer Travelers Asset Mgmt. Internat. Corp., N.Y.C., 1979—. Bd. fellows Am. Grad. Sch. Internat. Mgmt., Glendale, Ariz., 1973—; mem. council bd. Internat. Exec. Service Corps. Council, N.Y.C., 1970—; chmn. Hartford Area Manpower Planning Council, 1978-79, Hartford Area Pvt. Industry Council, 1979—, State job Tng. Coordinating Council, Hartford, 1983—. Served to capt. U.S. Army, 1943-47. Recipient Jonas Mayer award Am. Grad. Sch. Internat. Mgmt., 1978. Mem. Bus. Roundtable (employee relations com.), Labor Policy Assn. (bd. dirs.), Personnel Round Table, Greater Hartford C. of C. Republican. Presbyterian. Clubs: University (N.Y.C.); Royal Automobile (London); Hartford Golf (West Hartford, Conn.); Fishers Island (N.Y.). Home: 182 Fern St West Hartford CT 06119 Office: Travelers Ins Co One Tower Sq Hartford CT 06115

FEAHENY, THOMAS JOSEPH, automobile company executive; b. Detroit, Aug. 15, 1931; s. Thomas J. and Marie Teresa (May) F.; m. Dorothy Ellen Crowley, Aug. 15, 1959; children: Thomas, Maura, Laura, Ellen, James, Daniel. B.M.E., U. Detroit, 1953, M.B.A., 1959. With hydraulic div. Gen. Motors, 1953-57; custom car planning mgr. product planning Ford Motor Co., Dearborn, Mich., 1957-65, cat engring., 1965-70, engine mfg., 1971-77, v.p. car engring., 1977—. Chmn. pres's cabinet U. Detroit. Mem. Soc. Automotive Engrs., Engring. Soc. Detroit. Republican. Roman Catholic. Club: Detroit Athletic. Home: 1585 Lone Pine Rd Bloomfield Hills MI 48013 Office: Ford Motor Co. 20000 Rotunda Dr Dearborn MI 48121

FEAKER, DARRELL L., natural resources company executive; b. Topeka, Oct. 27, 1936; s. Frederick Jackson and Nellie Eleanor (Wells) F.; m. Carolyn Kay Berg., Dec. 28, 1958 (dec.); children: Deborah Denise, Tamara Leigh; m. Lucille Ann. Sanders, June 10, 1979. B.S., Kans. State U., 1958; postgrad., Harvard U., 1975, Northwestern U., 1981. Salesman Procter & Gamble, Wichita, Kans., 1962-66; internat. fin. mgr. Internat. Minerals and Chem. Corp., Skokie, Ill., 1966-67, treas., Northbrook, Ill., 1974-78, v.p., 1978—; dir. Mill-Tech. Products, Barrington, Ill., 1980—. Dir. United Way, Lake County, Ill., 1983—; active Jr. Achievement No. div., Chgo. chpt., 1983. Served to 1st lt. USAF, 1958-61. Mem. Fin. Execs. Inst., Econ. Club Chgo. Presbyterian. Club: Meadow (Rolling Meadows, Ill.). Home: 744 Oak Rd Barrington IL 60010 Office: Internat Minerals and Chem Corp. 2315 Sanders Rd Northbrook IL 60062

FEAMAN, PAUL ARMSTRONG, retail chain store cons.; b. Browning, Ill., May 5, 1920; s. Ralph Lee and Bertha Matilda F.; m. Joan Patricia Rolfe, Sept. 10, 1978. B.S., U. Ill., 1941; M.B.A., U. Chgo., 1951. Indsl. engr. U.S. Steel Corp., 1941-43; ops. mgr. Marshall Field & Co., Chgo., 1946-52; partner Robert Heller Assos., Cleve., 1952-62; dir. distbn. Colgate Palmolive Co., 1963-68; v.p., dir. distbn. J.C. Penney Co., N.Y.C., 1968-80; pres. Armstrong Assos., N.Y.C., 1980—. Served to lt. USNR, 1943-45. Mem. Nat. Council Distbn. Mgmt., N.Y. Council Distbn. Mgmt. (pres. 1972-74). Home: 133 Sandstone Circle Venice FL 33595 Office: Pan Am Bldg 200 Park Ave 303 E New York NY 10166

FEARN-BANKS, KATHLEEN, publicist; b. Chattanooga, Nov. 21, 1941; d. James E. and Kayte (Marsh) Fearn. B.A., Wayne State U., 1964; M.S. Will Rogers scholar, UCLA, 1965, postgrad. in theatre arts, 1965-69; postgrad. in instrnl. tech., U. So. Calif., 1978-80. Instr. journalism and English Los Angeles Valley Coll., 1966-67; feature writer Los Angeles Times, 1967; news writer, producer, reporter CBS affiliate KNXT-TV, 1967-69; publicist NBC-TV, Burbank, Calif., 1969—; instr. journalism and creative writing Los Angeles Community Colls., 1965-78. Author: (with David Burleigh) The Story of Western Man, 1969, 4 vols; Contbr. articles to profl. jours. Recipient Calif. Sun mag. writing award U. Calif., Los Angeles, 1964. Mem. Writers Guild of Am., Publicists Guild (sec.), Nat. Acad. TV Arts and Scis., Delta Sigma Theta (cons. Operation Head Start), Theta Sigma Phi. Office: NBC Press Dept 3000 W Alameda Burbank CA 91505

FEARON, ROBERT HENRY, banker; b. Oneida, N.Y., Aug. 7, 1900; s. Henry D. and Mary A. (Fuller) F.; m. Ruby J. Kilts, Aug. 27, 1926; children—Robert Henry, Patricia A. (Mrs. Richard H. Howarth). B.S., Syracuse U., 1922. With Blair & Co., 1922-24; with Oneida Valley Nat. Bank, 1924—, pres., 1942-71, chmn., 1971—; pres. Sylvan Spring Water Co., Sylvan Beach, N.Y., 1948—; also dir.; dir., treas. Marcellus Lumber Co., Oneida, 1942-70. Trustee N.Y. State Bankers Retirement System, 1939-67; Treas. Madison County council Boy Scouts Am., 1930-58; Treas., bd. dirs. bd. dirs. Oneida Library, Oneida Area Industries. Served with USNR, 1918. Recipient Silver Beaver award Boy Scouts Am., 1935, 80. Mem. N.Y. State (past chmn. group IV, past treas. assn.), Madison County (past pres.), bankers assns., Delta Kappa Epsilon. Republican. Methodist (past trustee, trustee Central N.Y. Conf. 1960-72). Clubs: Elk, Rotarian (Oneida) (past pres.). Home: 501 Broad St Oneida NY 13421 Office: Oneida Valley Nat Bank: Oneida NY 13421

FEARS, JOHN RIDER, hosp. exec.; b. Oklahoma City, July 19, 1941; s. Joe B. and Ethel Mae (Rider) F.; m. Marcia McMurray, Feb. 17, 1967; children—Jeffrey, Scott, Robin, Jonathan. B.S., U. S.C., 1963; J.D., U. Okla., 1966. Asst. dir. VARO, Indpls., 1973-74; asst. dir. VA Med. Center, San Juan, P.R., 1974-75, dir., 1975-78, VA Hosp., Hines, Ill., 1978—. Served with U.S. Army, 1965-66. Mem. Fed. Bar Assn., Am. Colls. Hosp. Adminstrs., Am. Legion, DAV. Club: Lions. Office: Veterans Administration Hospital Hines IL 60141 *

FEASTER, GEORGE ERWIN, agricultural company executive; b. Indpls., Aug. 30, 1941; s. Ned and Maxine Myrtle (McCallian) F.; m. Becky Jane Evans, June 23, 1962; children—Tamera Deann, Raymond Clark, Stephanie Suzanne, Bradley Curtis. A.A., Cerritos Jr. Coll., 1961; B.S., Calif. State Poly. Coll., 1963. Br. mgr. United Calif. Bank, Brawley, Calif., 1963-70; v.p., gen. mgr. Western Beef, Inc., Amarillo, Tex., 1970-71, pres., 1971—; v.p., dir. Cal-Tex Feed Yard, Inc., Clifton Cattle Co., Inc., Western Beef Cattle Fund, Inc.; pres. CNT Fin. Corp. Mem. Am. Soc. Animal Sci., Tex. Cattle Feeders Assn. (dir. 1972—),

Alpha Zeta. Home: 4206 Southpark Dr Amarillo TX 79104 Office: PO Box 2638 Amarillo TX 79189

FEATHER, LEONARD GEOFFREY, composer, music critic, lecturer, author; b. London, Sept. 13, 1914; U.S., 1935, naturalized, 1948; s. Nathan and Felicia (Zelinski) F.; m. Jane Larrabee, May 18, 1945; 1 dau., Lorraine. Student, Univ. Coll. Sch., London, 1920-26, St. Paul's Sch., London, 1926-31. Writer, London Melody Maker, 1933—, Esquire mag., 1943-56, Down Beat, 1951—, Playboy, 1956-62, Internat. Musician, 1961—, Show Mag., 1962-66, Rolling Stone, 1975-77, Contemporary Keyboard, 1976—; also for mags., in London, Paris, Stockholm, Berlin; arranger, Count Basie, other orchs.; composer lyrics and music, various popular singers; emcee radio shows; condr.: jazz programs Voice of Am, 1950-52; weekly program, 1967—; also broadcasts for, BBC, London, 1969; producer: Jazz Show, KNBC, Los Angeles, 1970-71, KUSC, Los Angeles, 1977; host: TV series L.A. Jazz, KUSC, 1982; producer: music quiz Platterbrains, ABC Radio Network, 1953—; toured Europe: with own prodn. Jazz Club U.S.A, 1954; composer: music The Weary Blues for record album of Langston Hughes poems, 1958; cons.: Ednl. TV series The Subject is Jazz, NBC, 1958; adv. bd.: Newport (R.I.) Jazz Festival; script writer: TV series Jazz Scene U.S.A, 1962-63; commentator at jazz concerts; lectures. Regents lectr. history of jazz, U. Calif., Riverside, 1973, 74, Loyola-Marymount U., 1972-74, Calif. State U., Northridge, 1977; Author: Inside Jazz, 1949, Encyclopedia of Jazz, 1955, Book of Jazz, 1957, New Yearbook of Jazz, 1958, New Encyclopedia of Jazz, 1960, Laughter From the Hip, 1964, The Encyclopedia of Jazz in the '60s, 1966, From Satchmo to Miles, 1972, The Pleasures of Jazz, 1976, The Encyclopedia of Jazz in the '70s, 1977, The Passion for Jazz, 1981; contbr. to, World Book Ency. and yearbooks, 1955-81. Mem. Acad. Rec. Arts and Scis. (bd. govs. 1968-69), ASCAP, Am. Fedn. Musicians, NAACP. Home: 13833 Riverside Dr Sherman Oaks CA 91423

FEATHER, MILTON SHORB, biochemistry educator; b. Canton, Ohio, Mar. 14, 1936; s. Ralph Raymond and Armintha (Shorb) F.; m. Betty Lou Werner, Aug. 17, 1957; children: Peter Milton, Erik James. B.S., Heidelberg Coll., 1958; M.S., Purdue U., 1960, Ph.D., 1962. Chemist Forest Service U.S. Dept. Agr., Madison, Wis., 1962-67; asst. prof. U. Mo., Columbia, 1967-69, assoc. prof., 1970-72, prof., 1972—, chmn. dept. biochemistry, 1981—; research fellow Swedish Wood Research Ctr., Stockholm, 1964-65; cons. Travenol Labs., Morton Grove, Ill. Contbr. chpts. to books, articles to profl. jours. Mem. Am. Soc. Biol. Chemists, Am. Chem. Soc., AAAS. Home: 904 Colgate Columbia MO 65201 Office: Dept Biochemistry 322 Chemistry Bldg U Mo Columbia MO 65201

FEATHER, RICHARD KELTZ, newspaper executive; b. Latrobe, Pa., Nov. 21, 1927; s. Isaac Kelley and Sylverine (Keltz) F.; m. Doris Evelyn Foy, May 21, 1949; children: Karen, Richard, Kirk, Jeffrey. Student, Bryant and Stratton bus. Coll., Buffalo, 1947-49. Paymaster Buffalo Evening News, 1957-77, personnel mgr., 1962-77, v.p., indsl. relations, 1977-83, sr. v.p., dir. indsl. relations, 1983—; dir. Blue Cross of Western N.Y., 1982. Bd. dirs. Crippled Children's Camp, Buffalo, 1980—. Served with U.S. Army, 1946-47. Mem. Newpaper Personnel Relations Assn., Indsl. Relations Research Assn. Republican. Home: 457 Woodstock Ave Tonawanda NY 14150 Office: Buffalo Evening News Inc 1 News Plaza Buffalo NY 14240

FEATHERSTON, C. MOXLEY, federal judge; b. Jayton, Tex., June 6, 1914; s. William Matthew and Fannie Eva (Roberts) F.; m. Rose Darlington Ross, Dec. 29, 1938; children: Ross Moxley, Neal Roberts, Rose Anne. A.B., Hardin-Simmons U., 1935; J.D., George Washington U., 1939. Bar: D.C. 1939, Tex. 1940. Pvt. practice, Hereford, Tex., 1940; atty. Dept. Agr., 1940-42, War Relocation Authority, 1942-45; asst. gen. counsel Inst. Inter-Am. Affairs, 1949-51; atty. Dept. Justice, 1945-49, 51-67; judge U.S. Tax Ct., 1967-77, chief judge, 1977-81. Mem. Order of Coif, Alpha Chi. Office: US Tax Ct 400 2d St NW Washington DC 20217 *

FEAVER, DOUGLAS DAVID, classics educator; b. Toronto, Ont., Can., May 14, 1921; came to U.S., 1948; s. Charles John and Margaret Adeline (Brett) F.; m. Margaret Ruth Seaman, June 10, 1950; children: David, John, Paul, Ruth, Peter. B.A., U. Toronto, 1948; M.A., Johns Hopkins U., 1949, Ph.D., 1951; postgrad., Am. Sch. Classical Studies, 1951-52. Instr. Yale U., New Haven, 1952-56; mem. faculty Lehigh U., Bethlehem, Pa., 1956—, prof. classics, 1966—; jr. fellow Ctr. Hellenic Studies, 1967-68; ann. research prof. Am. Sch. Classical Studies, 1976-77; dir. Humanties Perspectives on Tech., 1972-75; cons. in field. Author: El mundo en que vivio Jesus, 1972; contbr. articles to profl. jours. Served with RCAF, 1940-45. NEH scholar, 1971-84; cons. NEH, 1975—. Mem. Am. Philol. Assn., Archaeol. Inst. Am., Classical Assn. Atlantic States. Presbyterian. Home: 1227 Lorain Ave Bethlehem PA 18018 Office: 249 Maginnes 9 Lehigh U Bethlehem PA 18015

FEAVER, JOHN CLAYTON, educator, philosopher; b. Fowler, Calif., June 24, 1911; s. Ernest Albion and Agnes Katherine (Hansen) F.; m. Margaret Storsand, June 21, 1936; children: John Hansen, Katherine Elaine, Margaret Ellen. A.B., Fresno State Coll., 1933; student, San Francisco Theol. Sem., 1934; B.D., Pacific Sch. Religion, 1936; Ph.D., Yale U., 1949. Asst., then asso. prof. philosophy Berea Coll., 1941-51; Kingfisher Coll. prof. philosophy religion and ethics U. Okla., 1951-81, emeritus, 1981—, David Ross Boyd prof. philosophy, 1959-81, emeritus, 1981—; chmn. exec. com. Coll. Liberal Studies U. Okla., 1961-73; chmn. exec. com. S.W. Center Human Relations Studies, 1971-81. Co-editor: Religion in Philosophical and Cultural Perspective, 1967. Recipient Disting. Service citation U. Okla., 1979. Mem. Am. Philos. Assn., Southwestern Philos. Soc. (pres. 1960), Soc. Philosophy Religion, Am. Acad. Religion, AAUP, Phi Beta Kappa, Omicron Delta Kappa. Home: 900 E Boyd St Norman OK 73071

FECK, LUKE MATTHEW, newspaper editor; b. Cin., Aug. 15, 1935; s. John Franz and Mercedes Caroline (Rielag) F.; m. Gail Ann Schutte, Aug. 12, 1961; children: Lisa, Mara, Paul. B.A., U. Cin., 1957. Copyboy Cin. Enquirer, 1956, reporter, TV editor, columnist, 1957-64, asst. features editor, 1969-70, mag. editor, 1970, news editor, 1971-73, mng. editor, 1974-75, exec. editor, 1975, editor, 1976-80, Columbus Dispatch, 1980; pres. Ackerman and Feck Press, Inc., 1964-69, Feicke Web, Inc., 1974-75. Served to 1st lt. AUS, 1957-59. Mem. Am. Newspaper Pubs. Assn., Am. Soc. Newspaper Editors, AP Mng. Editors Assn. (dir.), AP Soc. Ohio, Sigma Delta Chi (pres. chpt.), Phi Kappa Theta. Clubs: Literary of Cin., Kit Kat, Columbus Athletic, Muirfield Village Country. Home: 2494 Sheringham Columbus OH 43220 Office: 34 S 3d St Columbus OH 43216

FEDDER, JOEL DAVID, lawyer, accountant; b. Balt., Nov. 15, 1931; s. Morris and Bess (Cohen) F.; m. Ellen Francine Sachs, Aug. 14, 1956; children—Michael, Alan, Amy Sue. A.B., Goddard Coll., 1954; LL.B., U. Md., 1958. Bar: Fed. bar 1961; certificate accounting John Hopkins, 1964. Partner firm Fedder & Garten, Balt., 1961—; instr. taxation Eastern Coll. Commerce and Law; pres. Balt. Estate Planning Council, 1979-80. Contbr. articles to profl. jours. Bd. dirs. Asso. Jewish Charities, Balt., 1963-64, chmn. young leadership council, 1963-64; bd. dirs. Jewish Welfare Fund, Balt., 1962-63, Lexindale Hebrew Home and Infirmary; chmn. bd. dirs. Central Md. chpt. Am. Heart Assn., 1977-79, Md. affiliate, 1980-82. Served with AUS, 1954-56. Recipient Outstanding Service award Nu Beta Epsilon, 1958, 59; Young Leadership award Asso. Jewish Charities, 1964. Mem. Fed. Bar Assn. (sec. 1961, 2d v.p. 1964-65, chmn. Balt. chpt. nat. young lawyers com. 1963), ABA, Md. Bar Assn. (tax council), Balt. Bar Assn. (orphan's ct. com.), Law League Am., Nu Beta Epsilon. Jewish. Mem. B'nai B'rith. Home: 5 Garrison Farms Ct Baltimore MD 21208 Office: 2300 Charles Center S Baltimore MD 21201

FEDDERS, JOHN MICHAEL, lawyer; b. Covington, Ky., Oct. 21, 1941; s. Aloysius Henry and Mary Margaret (Schmidt) F.; m. Charlotte Louise O'Donnell, Aug. 13, 1966; children: Luke D., Mark A., Matthew C., John Michael (dec.), Andrew M., Peter J. B.A. in Journalism, Marquette U., 1963; LL.B., Cath. U. Am., 1966. Bar: N.Y. 1967, D.C. 1967. Assoc. firm Cadwalader, Wickersham & Taft, N.Y.C., 1966-71; exec. v.p. Gulf Life Holding Co. (now Gulf United Corp.), Dallas, 1971-73; with firm Arnold & Porter, Washington, 1973-81; partner, 1975-81; dir. Div. of Enforcement, SEC, 1981—; lectr. corp. securities and fin. Contbr. articles to legal jours. Recipient Service award Marquette U., 1977, Achievement award Cath. U. Am. Alumni Assn., 1982, Chmn.'s award for excellence SEC, 1982. Mem. ABA, Assn. Bar City N.Y., D.C. Bar, Sigma Delta Chi, Phi Alpha Delta. Republican. Roman Catholic. Club: Congressional Country. Office: 500 N Capitol St Washington DC 20549

FEDER, AARON, physician, educator; b. N.Y.C., May 1, 1915; s. Herman and Fannie (Trenner) F.; m. Beatrice Wallance, Dec. 25, 1941; children: Carol (Mrs. Philip Glatsein), Jane Louise (Mrs. Harlan M. Dellsy). Student, N.Y.U., 1931-34; Exchange scholar, Harvard Med. Sch., 1937; M.D. with honors, U. Md., 1938. Intern Hosp. Joint Diseases, N.Y.C., 1938-40, resident, 1940; practice medicine specializing in internal medicine, Jackson Heights, N.Y., 1940-83; mem. faculty Cornell U. Med. Sch., 1940—, clin. prof. medicine, 1965—, 1st Irene and I. Roy Psaty Disting. prof. in clin. medicine, 1984—; vis. prof. LaGuardia Hosp., 1974; attending physician N.Y. Hosp., L.I. Jewish Hillside Med. Center; vis. physician Bellevue Hosp., 1953-68; mem. med. malpractice panel N.Y. State Supreme Ct.; cons. physician Booth Meml. Hosp., North Shore U. Hosp., Long Beach Meml. Hosp.; cons. NIH, 1976-79; mem. med. adv. bd. Hebrew U.-Hadassah; del. internat. Congresses in field. Contbr. articles to profl. jours.; Asso. editor: N.Y. State Jour. Medicine. Co-chmn. physicians div. United Jewish Appeal Greater N.Y., 1963—, past chmn., Queens div.; mem. exec. com. Fedn. Jewish Philanthropies, 1950—; gov. YMHA-YWHA of Central Queens. Served from 1st lt. to maj., M.C. AUS, 1942-45; PTO. Recipient Myrtle Wreath award for disting. service Hadassah; U. Md. Med. Alumni Assn. award for outstanding contbns. to medicine and disting. service to mankind, 1980. Fellow A.C.P. (founding pres. chpt., council), Am. Coll. Cardiology, N.Y. Acad. Medicine, N.Y. Acad. Scis., N.Y. Cardiol. Soc. (past dir.), Royal soc. Health Gt. Britain, Royal Soc. Medicine, Cornell U. Med. Coll. Alumni (hon.), U. Md. Med. Alumni (v.p. 1978-79, 82-84); mem. Med. Soc. State N.Y. (past del., past sect. chmn., com. on prizes and awards), Harvey Soc., Am. Fedn. Clin. Research, Am. Soc. Tropical Medicine, Am. Heart Assn., Assn. Am. Med. Colls., Assn. Mil. Surgeons, AAAS, Sigma Xi, Alpha Omega Alpha (hon.). Home: 28 Meadow Woods Rd Great Neck NY 11020 Office: 40-42 75th St Jackson Heights NY 11373 NY Hosp Cornell Med Ctr 525 E 68th St New York NY 10021

FEDER, ALLAN APPEL, management consultant; b. Chgo., Aug. 6, 1931; s. Tobias M. and Belle (Appel) F.; m. Joan Feldman, Nov. 19, 1961; children: Steven, Michael, Lisa, Valerie. B.S., Syracuse U., 1952; M.B.A., U. Pa., 1953. With Topps Chewing Gum, Inc., Duryea, Pa., 1965-70; gen. ops. mgr., also dir.; v.p. mfg. Life Savers subs. Squibb Corp., N.Y.C., 1970-72, exec. v.p. Dobbs Life Savers subs., 1972-73, pres., Memphis, 1973-76; pres. mfg. group Gt. Atlantic & Pacific Tea Co. Inc., Montvale, N.J., 1976-82, also corp. sr. exec. v.p. and dir.; mgmt. cons., 1982—; dir. Edward Don & Co., Topps Chewing Gum, Inc. Mem. Nat. Food Processors Assn. (past dir.).

FEDER, ARTHUR A., lawyer; b. N.Y.C., Mar. 23, 1927; s. Leo and Bertha (Franklin) F.; m. Ruth Musicant, Sept. 4, 1949; children—Gwen Lisabeth, Leslie Margaret, Andrew Michael. B.A., Columbia Coll., 1949; LL.B., Columbia U., 1951. Bar: N.Y. 1951. Assoc. firm Fulton Walter & Halley, 1951-53; research asst. Am. Law Inst. Fed. Income, Estate and Gift Tax Project, 1953-54; asso., partner firm Roberts & Holland, N.Y.C., 1954-66; partner firm Willkie, Farr & Gallagher, N.Y.C., 1966-69, Fried, Frank, Harris, Shriver & Jacobson, 1970—; lectr. in law Columbia U., 1961-63; lectr. Am. Law Inst., N.Y. U. Inst. on Fed. Taxation, Practicing Law Inst., various profl. groups. Contbr. articles on fed. income tax to various publs. Served with USN, 1945-46. Mem. Am. Bar Assn. (sect. of taxation, chmn. com. on real property tax problems 1964-66, com. on legis. drafting 1968—), Assn. of Bar of N.Y.C. (various coms.), N.Y. State Bar Assn. (exec. com. sect. of taxation), Internat. Fiscal Assn. (council U.S.A. Br.), Am. Law Inst., Phi Beta Kappa. Democrat. Club: University. Home: 25 W 81st St New York NY 10024 Office: 1 New York Plaza New York NY 10004

FEDER, HAROLD A., lawyer; b. Denver, Aug. 22, 1932; s. Harry A. and Surriee A. (Aarons) F.; m. Flora Sue Dunn, June 6, 1954; children: Harlan M., Sharon J., Janet B. B.A., U. Colo., 1954, LL.B., 1959, J.D., 1968. Bar: Colo. 1959, Circuit Ct. Appeals 1969, U.S. Supreme Ct. 1971. Stockholder, pres. firm Feder, Morris & Tamblyn (P.C.), Denver, 1959—; spl. asst. atty. gen. State of Colo., 1961-69; dir. Reichart-Silversmith, Inc.; adj. prof. law U. Denver, 1963; arbitrator Am. Arbitration Assn.; also lectr. Contbr. articles to profl. jours. Mem. Gov.'s Planning Commn. Mental Retardation, 1965; bd. dirs. George Washington Home Owners Assn., Jewish Community Center of Denver, 1972-77; trustee BMH Synagogue, Denver, 1960-62. Served with USNR, 1954-56. Mem. Fed. Bar Assn., ABA (mem. council econs. of law practice sect.), Colo. Bar Assn. (bd. govs. 1972-74), Denver Bar Assn., First Jud. Dist. Assn., Trial Lawyers Am. (state committeeman), Colo. Trial Lawyers Assn. (pres. 1971-72, bd. dirs. 1968—), Internat. Soc. Barristers, Am. Judicature Soc., Sons of Italy, Phi Delta Phi, Sigma Nu. Home: 460 S Marion Pkwy 1556 Denver CO 80209 Office: 1441 18th St Suite 400 Denver CO 80202

FEDER, MORRIS LOUIS, ship chartering company executive; b. Handlova, Czechoslovakia, Mar. 28, 1917; came to U.S., 1947, naturalized, 1953; s. Simon and Hermine (Gassner) F.; m. Lucy Kraus, June 22, 1950; children: Harry Simon, Karen Hermine. Student, Comml. Acad., Zlin, Czechoslovakia. Mem. export dept. Bata Shoe Co., Zlin, Czechoslovakia, 1933-38; mgr. Far East export dept., 1939-41; police officer Shanghai Mcpl. Police, 1942-45; dir. immigration dept. UN Relief and Rehab. Assn., Am. Jewish Joint Distbn. Com., Shanghai, China, 1945-47; traffic mgr. Am. Israeli Shipping Co., 1948-52; exec. v.p. Maritime Overseas Corp., 1953-75; sr. v.p. Overseas Shipholding Group, Inc., N.Y.C., 1975—. Mem. Assn. Shipbrokers and Agts. Democrat. Jewish. Clubs: Fgn. Commerce, Am.-Israel Cultural Found. (N.Y.C.). Office: 1114 Ave of Americas New York NY 10036

FEDERER, HERBERT, educator, mathematician; b. Vienna, Austria, July 23, 1920; came to U.S., 1938, naturalized, 1944; s. Josef and Louise (Schlesinger) F.; m. Leila Raines, June 30, 1949; children—Andrew, Wayne, Leslie. B.A. in Math. and Physics, U. Cal. at Berkeley, 1942, Ph.D., 1944. Mem. faculty Brown U., 1945—, asst. prof., 1946-48, asso. prof., 1948-51, prof. math., 1951—, Florence Pirce Grant U. prof., 1966—; Mem. NRC, 1966-69. Contbr. articles to profl. jours. Served with AUS, 1944-45. Alfred P. Sloan research fellow, 1957-60; NSF sr. postdoctoral fellow, 1964-65; John Simon Guggenheim fellow, 1975-76. Fellow Am. Acad. Arts and Scis.; mem. Am. Math. Soc. (asso. sec. 1967-68, colloquium lectr. 1977), Nat. Acad. Scis. Spl. research geometric measure theory. Home: PO Box 456 North Scituate RI 02857

FEDERICI, WILLIAM R., justice N.Mex. Supreme Court; b. Cimarron, N.Mex., July 15, 1917; m. Elsie, Mar. 20, 1945; children: Linda Federici Stevens, Richard, Larry, Gina. B.A., U. N.Mex., 1939; J.D., U. Colo., 1941. Bar: N.Mex. 1941. Began practice law, Santa Fe, 1941; with Atty. Gen.'s Office, 1942, 46-48; justice N.Mex. Supreme Ct., 1977—. Served with aircraft arty. U.S. Army, 1942-46. Mem. State Bar N.Mex., First Jud. Dist. Bar Assn., Am. Bar Assn., vets. orgns. Democrat. Roman Catholic. Club: Elks. Office: Supreme Ct Bldg Santa Fe NM 87503 *

FEDERICI, WILLIAM VITO, newspaper reporter; b. Bklyn., June 22, 1931; s. Theodore and Margaret (DeMaio) F.; m. Arlene Ann McAuliffe, Oct. 1, 1955; children—William Theodore, Robert Gerard. Student, Hofstra Coll., 1949-50, St. John's U., 1954-56. With N.Y. Daily News, 1950—, nat. corr., until 1965, spl. reporter, 1965-72, asst. city editor in charge investigations, 1975-79, Bklyn. editor, 1979—; Dir. spl. projects Office Spl. State Prosecutor, N.Y.C., 1972-75. Author series on child abuse which initiated N.Y. laws to protect children, 1969. Served with USN, 1950-54; Korea. Recipient several journalism awards, including George Polk award Long Island U., 1970, Sigma Delta Chi award for met. reporting, 1975. Office: 220 E 42d St New York NY 10017

FEDERMAN, DANIEL DAVID, medical educator, educational administrator, endocrinologist; b. N.Y.C., Apr. 16, 1928; m. Elizabeth Buckley; children: Lise, Caroline. B.A., Harvard U., 1949, M.D., 1953. Am. Bd. Internal Medicine. Instr. to prof. Harvard Med. Sch., Boston, 1961-72, prof. medicine and dean for students and alumni, 1977—; chmn. medicine Stanford Med. Sch., Palo Alto, Calif., 1973-77. Author: med. textbook Abnormal Sexual Development, 1967; editor: Scientific American Medicine. Mem. ACP (pres. Phila. 1982-83). Home: 1 Evergreen Way Belmont MA 02178 Office: Harvard Med Sch 25 Shattuck Boston MA 02115

FEDERMAN, IRWIN, semiconductor company executive; b. N.Y.C., Aug. 9, 1935; s. Alfred B. and Rose F.; m. Sheila Schwartzbard, June 9, 1956; children—Jaime Robin, Eric Stuart, Alex David, Carolyn. B.S. in Econs, Bklyn. Coll., 1956. C.P.A., Calif. Successively C.P.A. S.D. Leidesdorf & Co.; treas. Optics Tech., Inc.; v.p. fin. Data Recognition Corp.; now chief exec. officer Monolithic Memories, Inc., Sunnyvale, Calif., also dir.; dir. Corvus Systems, Inc. Bd. dirs. NCCJ, Greater San Jose Jewish Fedn. Served with U.S. Army, 1961-62. Mem. Am. Inst. C.P.A.'s. Office: Monolithic Memories Inc 2175 Mission College Blvd Santa Clara CA 95050

FEDOR, GEORGE EDWARD, lawyer; b. Slovakia, Mar. 28, 1909; U.S., 1913, naturalized, 1921; s. George and Mary (Talas) F.; m. Helen R. Evansick, Apr. 24, 1934; children: Bruce G., Dennis G., Donna Fedor Wimbiscus, Thomas J., Mark Q., Louise Fedor Ortiz, Renee Fedor Bauchmoyer, Christopher A. B.A., Western Res. U., 1931; LL.B. magna cum laude, Cleve. Law Sch., 1939. Bar: Ohio 1940. Since practiced in, Cleve.; chmn. bd., dir. Home Fed. Savs. and Loan Assn., Lakewood, Ohio; law dir. City of Lakewood, 1956-59; Mem. Ohio Ho. of Reps. from Cuyahoga County Dist., 1949-52, Lakewood Planning Commn., 1953-55; chmn. speaker's bur. Cuyahoga County Democratic Com., 1947-48. Trustee Cleve. Citizens League, 1955-61, Cleve. Diocese Catholic Charities Corp.; former trustee St. Augustine Manor, Cleve. Former Mem. Am., Ohio, Greater Cleve., Cuyahoga County bar assns.; Mem. Am. Judicature Soc. Roman Catholic. Home: 18603 W Valley Ln Fairview Park OH 44126 Office: 600 Terminal Tower Cleveland OH 44113

FEEHAN, THOMAS JOSEPH, engineering and construction company executive; b. New Orleans, Feb. 12, 1924; s. Hugh Alphonse and Rena Martha (Hill) F.; m. Virginia Waters Arnold, Sept. 3, 1949; children: Anne, Mary, Catherine. B.Engring., Tulane U., 1944. Prodn. supr. Flintkote Co., 1946-47; with Brown & Root, Inc., Houston, 1947—, corp. pres., 1977—, chmn. bd., 1983—; also dir. Brown & Root Co.; dir. Halliburton Co., 1st City Bank Corp. Houston. Served with USMC, 1944-46. Mem. Am. Inst. Chem. Engrs., Houston Engrng. Soc., Tex. Research League., Nat. Ocean Industries Assn. (dir.), Tex. Assn. Taxpayers (dir.). Roman Catholic. Clubs: Petroleum of Houston, Ramada (Houston); Sky (N.Y.C.); River Oaks Country. Office: PO Box 3 Houston TX 77001

FEELEY, HENRY JOSEPH, JR., advertising agency executive; b. Cambridge, Mass., July 9, 1940; s. Henry Joseph and Florence Patricia (O'Connor) F.; m. Mary Diane Dudenhoefer, May 14, 1966; children: Kathleen Anne, Mary Patricia, Henry Joseph III, James Brian. B.A., Coll. Holy Cross, 1963; grad., Inst. Advanced Advt. Studies, Northwestern U., 1966; P.M.D., Harvard Bus. Sch., 1976. With Leo Burnett Co., Inc.,, Chgo., 1965—, v.p., 1973-76, sr. v.p., 1976-82, exec. v.p., 1982—. Bd. dirs. Mary Bartelme Homes, Chgo., 1982—; pres. Sacred Heart Bd. Edn., Winnetka, Ill., 1982-83; mem. Irish Fellowship Chgo., 1982—. Served to lt. USN, 1963-65. Republican. Roman Catholic. Club: Plaza (Chgo.). Home: 1080 Pelham Rd Winnetka IL 60093 Office: Leo Burnett Co Inc Prudential Plaza Chicago IL 60601

FEELEY, JOHN PAUL, paper co. exec.; b. Akron, Ohio, July 17, 1918; s. John Joseph and Pauline (Wallace) F.; m. Patricia; children—Joanne, Suzanne. B.S. in Bus. Adminstrn, U. Akron, 1941. Civilian with Dept. of Navy, 1946-56; chief Navy Mgmt. Office, 1955-56; sec.-treas. Am. Colortype Corp., 1956-57; treas. Rapid Am. Corp., 1958-59; asst. controller Remington Rand Co., 1960-62; v.p., dir. APS Paper Corp., 1963-64, Allied Paper Inc., Kalamazoo, 1964-72, sr. v.p., 1972—. Served to lt. comdr. USNR, World War II. Home: 6091 Breed Rd Gobles MI 49055 Office: 2030 Portage St Kalamazoo MI 49001

FEELY, ROBERT MORIARTY, lawyer; b. N.Y.C., Apr. 29, 1928; s. Robert Moriarty and Marie Adele (O'Connell) F.; m. Audrey Robinson, June 15, 1954 (dec. 1966); children: Robert (dec.), Erin Robinson; m. Margot Hirsh, June 11, 1972; stepchildren: Thomas Biow, Douglas Biow. B.A., Williams Coll., 1950; LL.B., Harvard U., 1955. Bar: N.Y. 1956. Assoc. Shearman & Sterling, N.Y.C., 1955-62, ptnr., 1962—; dir. West World Holding Corp., 1982—. Served to lt. (j.g.) USNR, 1951-53. Home: 1220 Park Ave New York NY 10128 Office: Shearman & Sterling 153 E 53d St New York NY 10022

FEENEY, CHARLES STONEHAM, baseball executive; b. Orange, N.J., Aug. 31, 1921; s. Thaddeus and Mary Alice (Stoneham) F.; m. Margaret Ann Hoppock, July 10, 1948; children: Katharine Willard, Charles Stoneham, John Hoppock, William McDonald, Mary Patrick. B.A., Dartmouth Coll., 1943; LL.B., Fordham U., 1949. Vice pres. San Francisco Giants, 1946-69; pres. Nat. League Profl. Baseball Clubs, San Francisco, 1970-77, N.Y.C., 1977—. Served to lt. USNR, 1943-46. Mem. Casque and Gauntlet, Phi Kappa Psi. Clubs: Pacific Union, Burlingame (Calif.) Country. Home: 405 E 63d St New York NY 10022 Office: 350 Park Ave New York NY 10022

FEENEY, FLOYD FULTON, legal educator; b. Franklin, Ind., Sept. 26, 1933; s. Burla L. and Ona Marie (McMillian) F.; m. Peggy Ann Ballard, June 15, 1956; children: Elizabeth, Linda. B.S. in History with honors, Davidson Coll., 1955; LL.B., NYU, 1960. Bar: N.C. 1960, D.C. 1961. Law clk. U.S. Supreme Ct., 1961-62; spl. asst. to solicitor of labor Dept. Labor, 1962-63; dep. spl. counsel Pres.'s Com. on Equal Employment Opportunity, 1963; asst. dir. Pres.'s Crime Commn., 1966-67; spl. asst. to adminstr. AID, 1963-68; prof. law U. Calif.-Davis, 1968—; mem. adv. com. Calif. Bur. Criminal Stats., 1980—; mem. Calif. Bail Reform Evaluation Com., 1980—; cons. Nat. Ctr. for State Cts., 1973, 76-80. Author: The Police and Pretrial Release, 1982, (with Roger Baron) Juvenile Diversion Through Family Counseling—An Exemplary Project, 1976. Served to 1st lt. U.S. Army, 1956-58. Recipient Pepperdine award, 1978. Mem. ABA, Am. Assn. Law Schs., Am. Law Inst., D.C. Bar Assn., N.C. Bar Assn., Assn. for Criminal Justice Research Calif. (bd. dirs.). Home: 1228 Colby Dr Davis CA 95166 Office: U Calif Sch Law Davis CA 95616

FEER, MARK CECIL ISELIN, investment banker; b. N.Y.C., July 31, 1928; s. H. Ernest and Cecile (Iselin) F.; m. Helene de Lone, May 31, 1952 (dec. Nov. 1973); children—Camilla H., Barbara S., M. Peter de L.; m. Susan Hecht Cramer, June 21, 1975; stepchildren—Cathy A., Robert S., Wendy S. A.B., Dartmouth Coll., 1949; postgrad., U. Geneva, 1949-50, Sorbonne, 1950; M.A., Fletcher Sch. Law and Diplomacy, 1951, Ph.D., 1954. Econ. cons. Arthur D. Little, Inc., Cambridge, Mass., 1954-55; with First Boston Corp., 1957-65, asst. v.p., 1961-64, v.p., 1964-65; dep. asst. sect. for fin. policy U.S. Dept. Commerce, Washington, 1965-68; asso. Kuhn, Loeb & Co., N.Y.C., 1968, gen. partner, 1969-77; mng. dir. Lehman Bros., Kuhn, Loeb, Inc., N.Y.C., 1977-79, advt. dir., 1979—; dir. W.R. Grace & Co., N.Y.C., Share Australia Mgmt. Co. Ltd., Sydney; vice chmn. Pvt. Investment Co. for Asia, 1973-74, dir., 1969-74; adj. prof. internat. econs. Fletcher Sch. Law and Diplomacy, Tufts U., Medford, Mass., 1980—, Grad. Sch. Internat. Affairs, Columbia U., 1980—; mem. Pvt. Investment Mission to Korea, 1967. Pres. Westchester chpt. Assn. for Retarded Children, 1958-60; bd. dirs. Am.-Swiss Assn., Inc., 1970-78, U.S.-Korea Econ. Council, Population Council, N.Y.C., 1980—; mem. bd. visitors Fletcher Sch. Law and Diplomacy, Tufts U., 1980—. Served with AUS, 1955-57. Fulbright grantee India, 1952-53. Mem. Council Fgn. Relations, Asia Soc., Japan Soc., Phi Beta Kappa (treas. United chpts. 1975—), Theta Delta Chi. Clubs: India House (N.Y.C.); Sunningdale Country; Fox Meadows Tennis (Scarsdale, N.Y.). Home: 133 E 64th St New York NY 10021 Office: Lehman Bros Kuhn Loeb Inc 55 Water St New York NY 10041

FEERICK, JOHN DAVID, college dean, lawyer; b. N.Y.C., July 12, 1936; s. John J. and Mary J. F.; m. Emalie Platt, Aug. 25, 1962; children: Maureen, Margaret, Jean, Rosemary, John, William. B.S., Fordham U., 1958, LL.B., 1961. Bar: N.Y. 1961. Assoc. firm Skadden, Arps, Slate, Meagher & Flom, N.Y.C., 1961-68, partner, 1968-82; dean Fordham U. Sch. Law, 1982—; mem. labor law adv. com. Practising Law Inst. Author: From Failing Hands: The Story of Presidential Succession, 1965, The 25th Amendment, 1976; co-author: The Vice Presidents of the United States, 1967, NLRB Representation Elections-Law, Practice and Procedure, 1980; also articles.; Editor-in-chief: Fordham Law Rev., 1960-61; bd. editors: Nat. Law Jour. Trustee Fordham U.; chmn. trustees Center Info. on Am. Recipient Eugene J. Keefe award Fordham U. Law Sch., 1975, spl. award Fordham U. Law Rev. Assn., 1977. Fellow Am. Bar Found.; mem. Am. Bar Assn. (chmn. spl. com. election law and voter participation 1976-79, spl. award 1966), N.Y. State Bar Assn. (chmn. com. fed. constn. 1979—), Assn. Bar City N.Y., Am. Arbitration Assn., Fordham U. Law Sch. Alumni Assn. (dir. 1972—, medal of achievement 1980), Phi Beta Kappa.

FEFERMAN, SOLOMON, mathematics and philosophy educator, researcher; b. N.Y.C., Dec. 13, 1928; s. Leon and Helen (Grand) F.; m. Anita Burdman, Dec. 9, 1948; children: Rachel, Julie. B.S., Calif. Inst. Tech., 1948; Ph.D., U. Calif.-Berkeley, 1957. Instr. math. and philosophy Stanford U., Calif., 1956-58, asst. prof., 1958-62, assoc. prof., 1962-68, prof., 1968—; cons. Stanford Research Inst., Menlo Park, Calif., 1958-63; editor Springer Pub. Co., N.Y.C. and Berlin, 1979—. Author: The Number Systems, 1964; co-author monograph, 1981. Served with U.S. Army, 1953-55. Postdoctoral fellow NSF Inst. Advanced Study, Princeton U., sr. postdoctoral fellow, Paris and Amsterdam, 1959-60; Guggenheim fellow, Oxford and Paris, 1972-73; vis. fellow All Souls Coll. Oxford U., 1979-80. Mem. Am. Math. Soc. (editor 1976-69), Assn. Symbolic Logic (exec. com. 1964-67, pres. 1980-83), Math. Assn. Am. Office: Dept Math Stanford U Stanford CA 94305

FEFFER, GERALD ALAN, lawyer; b. Washington, Apr. 24, 1942; s. Louis Charles and Elsie (Glick) F.; 1 son, Andrew. B.A. with honors, Lehigh U., 1967; J.D., U. Va., 1967. Bar: N.Y. 1968, D.C. 1980. Assoc. Mudge, Rose, Guthrie & Alexander, N.Y.C., 1967-71; asst. U.S. atty. So. Dist. N.Y., 1971-76, asst. chief criminal div., 1975-76; ptnr. Kostelanetz & Ritholz, N.Y.C., 1976-79; dep. asst. atty. gen. tax div. Dept. Justice, Washington, 1979-81; ptnr. Steptoe & Johnson, Washington, 1981—. Contbr. articles to profl. jours. Mem. ABA (civil and criminal tax penalties com., chmn. subcom. on constl. and atty.-client privileges, chmn. task force on underground economy, white collar crime com., complex crimes com.). Home: 407-A 4th St SE Washington DC 20003 Office: 1250 Connecticut Ave NW Washington DC 20036

FEFFERMAN, CHARLES LOUIS, educator, mathematician; b. Washington, Apr. 18, 1949; s. Arthur Stanely and Liselott Ruth (Stern) F.; m. Julie Anne Albert, Feb. 1975; children: Nina Heidi, Elaine Marie. B.S., U. Md., 1966; hon. doctorate, 1979; Ph.D., Princeton U., 1969; hon. doctorate, Knox Coll., 1981. Instr. math. Princeton U., 1969-70, prof. math., 1974—; mem. faculty U. Chgo., 1970-74, prof. math., 1971-74. Author research papers. Recipient Salem prize for outstanding work in fourier analysis by young mathematician, Alan T. Waterman award, 1976, Fields medal Internat. Congress Mathematicians, 1978. Mem. Nat. Acad. Scis., Am. Math. Soc., Am. Acad. Arts and Scis. Home: 234 Clover Ln Princeton NJ 08540 Office: Fine Hall Princeton Univ Princeton NJ 08540

FEGLEY, KENNETH ALLEN, educator; b. Mont Clare, Pa., Feb. 14, 1923; s. Henry Stanley and Bertha (Malone) F.; m. Virginia Ruth Weaver, Sept. 1, 1951; children—Alan Donald, John David, Paul Andrew. B.S., U. Pa., 1947, M.S., 1950, Ph.D., 1955. Instr. elec. engring. U. Pa., 1947-53, asso., 1953-55, asst. prof., 1955-58, asso. prof., 1958-66, prof., 1966—, chmn. dept. systems engring., 1973-75; cons. to industry. Contbr. articles to profl. jours. Dir. Pa. Assn. Retarded Children, 1968-70. Served with USNR, 1946-48. Fellow AAAS, IEEE; mem. Am. Soc. Engring. Edn. (chmn. Middle Atlantic sect. 1967). Presbyterian. Home: 115 Park Ave Paoli PA 19301 Office: U Pa Philadelphia PA 19104

FEGLEY, ROBERT LEROY, JR., former public relations executive; b. Allentown, Pa., Dec. 2, 1919; s. Robert LeRoy and Mollie Minerva (Wei) F.; m. Alice Blaine Longfellow, Aug. 30, 1941; children: Molly Fegley Rayner, Susan Fegley Osmond. A.B., Columbia U., 1941. With Gen. Electric Co., N.Y.C., 1941-81, beginning in indsl. advt., successively mgr. visual edn., mgr. instl. advt., mgr. public issues analysis, mgr. exec. communications, mgr. public relations planning, 1941-73, staff exec., chief exec. officer communications, Fairfield, Conn., 1973-81. Author: (with R. J. Cordiner) New Frontiers for Professional Managers, 1956; pub.: GE Forum Mag, 1960-66. Bd. dirs. Silvermine Artists Guild, 1958-60, New Canaan (Conn.) United Fund, 1967-68, New Canaan YMCA, 1969-74. Recipient Woodberry poetry prize Columbia U., 1941; named PR Profl. of Year PR News, 1979, U. Tex., 1981, among 10 Top Corporate PR Profls. in U.S. Bus. Week mag., 1979. Mem. Public Relations Seminar (chmn. 1978), Nat. Elec. Mfrs. Assn. (chmn. public relations council 1963-66), NAM (public relations council 1966-75), Bus. Roundtable (chmn. public info. com. 1975-80), Public Relations Soc. Am. (accredited), Found. Public Relations Edn. and Research (dir. 1969-73), Wiseman Soc., Public Relations Soc. N.Y., New Canaan Hist. Soc., N.Y. Gen. and Biog. Soc., Stamford Geneal. Soc., John Jay Assn. Republican. Methodist. Home: 36 Comstock Hill Rd New Canaan CT 06840

FEHLBERG, ROBERT ERICK, architect; b. Kalispell, Mont., Apr. 28, 1926; s. Otto Albert Erick and Mary Grace F.; m. LaDonna Karen Rognlie, May 31, 1953; children: Kolby J., Kenje A., Kurt E., Klee J. B.S. in Architecture, Mont. State U., 1951. Architect in tng. with Gehres D. Weed Architect, Kalispell, 1952-55; partner Weed & Fehlberg Architects, Kalispell, 1955-57; pvt. practice, Kalispell, 1957-58; with Cushing Terrell Assos., Billings, Mont., 1958-72, partner, 1960-72; v.p. CTA Architects Engrs., Inc., Billings, 1973—. Bd. dirs. Yellowstone Art Center Found., 1965—, 1st pres., 1965; bd. dirs. Mont. Inst. Arts Found., 1976—, pres., 1976-80, treas., 1980—. Served with AUS, 1944-46. Recipient (with wife) Gov.'s award for arts, 1983. Fellow AIA (pres. Mont. 1965, nat. dir. 1971-74), Mont. Inst. Arts (pres. 1963-64); mem. Prodn. Systems for Architects and Engrs. (dir. 1971-74, chmn. 1974). Home: 2050 Rimrock Rd Billings MT 59102 Office: 1500 Poly Dr PO Box 1439 Billings MT 59103 Office: Boise ID Office: Anchorage AK

FEHNEL, EDWARD ADAM, chemist, educator; b. Bethlehem, Pa., Apr. 22, 1922; s. Edward Franklin and Marguerite (Paull) F.; m. Dorothy Gary Lynn, Oct. 21, 1944; children—Lynn Susan, Gary Edward. B.S., Lehigh U., 1943, M.S., 1944, Ph.D., 1946. Instr. chemistry Moravian Prep. Sch., Bethlehem, 1943-44; chemist Central Research Lab. Allied Chem. & Dye Corp., Morristown, N.J., 1944-45; research fellow, lectr. U. Pa., 1946-48; asst. prof. chemistry Swarthmore (Pa.) Coll., 1948-57, asso. prof., 1957-66, prof., 1966—, Edmund Allen prof. chemistry, 1972—. Mem. editorial bd.: Organic Electronic Spectral Data, 1957-60; Contbr. profl. jours. NSF Sci. Faculty fellow U. Cambridge, Eng., 1962; vis. prof. chemistry Ind. U., summer 1968. Mem. Am. Chem. Soc., Phi Beta Kappa, Sigma Xi, Tau Beta Pi. Home: 120 Paxon Hollow Rd Rose Tree Media PA 19063

FEHR, KENNETH MANBECK, capital equipment co. exec.; b. Schuylkill Haven, Pa., Feb. 21, 1928; s. Theodore E. and Eva (Manbeck) F.; m. Jean Alice Greenawalt, June 28, 1952; children—K. Craig, Karen Jean, K. Todd. B.S., Pa. State U., 1951; M.B.A., U. Pitts., 1953. With U.S. Steel Corp., 1951-62, div. controller, 1962; controller Interlake Steel Corp., Chgo., 1962-68; v.p. fin. Hallicrafters Co., 1968-71, E.W. Bliss Co., Salem, Ohio, 1971-74; treas. Alliance Machine Co., Ohio, 1974—; Night sch. tchr. U. Pitts., 1956-57. With USNR, 1945-46. Mem. Fin. Execs. Inst., Nat. Assn. Accountants. Club: Mason. Home: 725 S Lincoln Rd Salem OH 44460 Office: 1149 S Mahoning Ave Alliance OH 44601

FEHR, WALTER RONALD, agronomist, researcher, educator; b. East Grand Forks, Minn., Dec. 4, 1939; s. Eilert Peter and Clara (Luithle) F.; m. Elinor Lee Otis, July 1, 1961; children: Susan, Steven, Kevin. B.S., U. Minn.-St. Paul, 1961, M.S., 1962; Ph.D., Iowa State U., 1967. Cert. agronomist. Grad. asst. U. Minn., St. Paul, 1961-62; instr. Congo Poly Inst., Zaire, 1962-64; research assoc. Iowa State U., Ames, 1964-67, prof. dept. agronomy, 1967—. Author: Applied Plant Breeding, 1982; editor: Hybridization of Crop Plants, 1980; contbr. writings to book chpts. and profl. articles. Sunday Sch. supt. First Bapitst Ch., Ames, 1983; leader Broken Arrow council Boy Scouts Am., Ames, 1979; coach Little League Baseball, Ames, 1980; pres. Friends of Ames Swimming, 1983. Grantee Nat Crop Ins. Assn., 1968—, Iowa Soybean Promotion Bd., 1972—, U.S. Dept. Agr., 1982-84. Fellow Am. Soc. Agronomy (Crops and Soils Mag. award 1969); mem. Crop Sci. Soc. Am. (div. chmn. 1982-83, assoc. editor), Am. Soybean Assn. (Meritorious Research award 1981, grantee 1981—). Office: Iowa State Univ Dept Agronomy Amex IA 50011

FEHRENBACHER, DON EDWARD, history educator; b. Sterling, Ill., Aug. 21, 1920; s. Joseph H. and Mary (Barton) F.; m. Virginia Ellen Swaney, Feb. 9, 1944; children: Ruth Ellen Fehrenbacher Gleason, Susan Jean Fehrenbacher Koprince, David Charles. B.A., Cornell Coll., 1946; M.A., U. Chgo., 1948, Ph.D., 1951; M.A., Oxford U., 1967; D.H.L., Cornell Coll., 1970. Asst. prof. history Coe Coll., Cedar Rapids, Iowa, 1949-53; asst. prof. history Stanford U., 1953-57, asso. prof., 1957-62, prof., 1962-66, William R. Coe prof. Am. history, 1966—; Harmsworth prof. Am. history Oxford U., 1967-68; Harrison prof. history Coll. William and Mary, 1973-74; tchr. Rutgers U., summer 1959, Northwestern U., 1964, Harvard U., 1967, U. B.C., 1970; Commonwealth Fund lectr. U. London, 1978; Walter Lynwood Fleming lectr. La. State U., 1978; Seagram lectr. U. Toronto, 1981. Author: Chicago Giant: A Biography of Long John Wentworth, 1957, Prelude to Greatness: Lincoln in the 1850s, 1962, The Era of Expansion, 1969, The Dred Scott Case: Its Significance in American Law and Politics, 1978 (Pulitzer prize in history 1979), The South and Three Sectional Crises, 1980, Slavery, Law and Politics, 1981; editor: History and American Society: Essays of David M. Potter, 1973, The Impending Crisis (David M. Potter), 1976, Freedom and Its Limitations in American Life (David M. Potter), 1976; contbr. articles to profl. jours. Served to 1st lt. USAAF, 1943-45. Decorated D.F.C., Air medal with 3 oak leaf clusters.; Guggenheim fellow, 1959-60; NEH fellow, 1975-76. Mem. Am. Acad. Arts and Scis., Am. Hist. Assn. (pres. br. 1983-84), So. Hist. Assn., Am. Soc. Legal History, Soc. Historians of Early Am. Republic, Soc. Am. Historians, Orgn. Am. Historians (mem. editorial bd. 1965-68), Am. Antiquarian Soc. Home: 625 Salvatierra St Stanford CA 94305

FEIBLEMAN, JAMES KERN, emeritus philosophy educator, author; b. New Orleans, July 13, 1904; s. Leopold and Nora (Kern) F.; m. Dorothy Steinam, 1928 (div.); 1 son, Peter Steinam; m. Shirley Ann Grau, Aug. 4, 1955; children: Ian, Nora, William, Katherine. Student, U. Va., 1924; pvt. study Europe; D.Litt., Rider Coll., 1973; L.H.D., U. Louisville, 1976; LL.D., Tulane U., 1977. Asst. mgr. dept. store, 1924-29; v.p., gen. mgr. James K. Feibleman Realty Co., Inc., 1930-54; partner of Leopold Investment Co., 1954-71; acting asst. prof. English Coll. Arts and Scis., Tulane U., 1943-44, acting asst. prof. philosophy, 1945-46, grad. prof., since 1946, head dept. philosophy, 1951-56, chmn., 1956-69, W.R. Irby prof. of philosophy, 1969-74, Andrew W. Mellon prof. humanities, 1974-75, prof. philosophy emeritus, 1975—; lectr., univs., assns., founds. Author: numerous books, most recent being The Dark Bifocals, 1952, The Institutions of Society, 1956, The Pious Scientist, 1958, Inside the Great Mirror, 1958, Religious Platonism, 1959, The Foundations of Empiricism, 1962, Biosocial Factors in Mental Illness, 1962, Mankind Behaving: Human Needs and Material Culture, 1963, The Two-Story World, 1966, Moral Strategy, 1967, The Reach of Politics, 1969, The Way of A Man, 1970, The New Materialism, 1970, In Praise of Comedy, 1970, Great April, 1971, Scientific Method, 1972, The Quiet Rebellion, 1972, Understanding Philosophy, 1973, Collected Poems, 1975, Understanding Civilizations: The Shape of History, 1975, The Stages of Human Life, A Biography of Entire Man, 1975, Understanding Oriental Philosophy: A Popular Account for the Western World, 1976, Adaptive Knowing, 1977, Understanding Human Nature: A Popular Guide to the Effects of Technology on Man and His Behavior, 1978, New Proverbs for Our Day, 1978, Assumptions of Grand Logics, 1979, Ironies of History, 1980; Contbr. chpts. to books and numerous book reviews and articles. Fellow Charles S. Pierce Soc. (pres. 1948-49); mem. AAUP, Am. Philos. Assn. (eastern, pacific and western divs.), Am. Soc. Aesthetics, Art Assn. New Orleans, Assn. for Symbolic Logic, Inst. Applied Logic, Metaphys. Soc. Am., Mind Assn., Modern Lang. Assn. Am., New Orleans Acad. Sci. (pres. 1958-59), Royal Inst. Philosophy, South Central Moderan Lang. Assn., So. Soc. Philosophy and Psychology, Southwestern Philos. Soc. (v.p., program chmn. 1979-80, pres. 1980-81), Phi Beta Kappa, Phi Sigma Tau (v.p. 1956-57). Home: 12 Nassau Drive Metairie LA 70005 Office: 1424 First Nat Bank Commerce Bldg New Orleans LA 70112 *I have not allowed external events to interfere with the peaceful pursuit of my chosen goal of trying to discover some useful truths and so leave the world when I have to a slightly better place than I found it.*

FEICHTEL, CARL JOSEPH, banker; b. Allentown, Pa., Oct. 1, 1931; s. Charles J. and Laura E. (Eby) F.; m. Julia Ann Green, Jan. 29, 1955; children: Denise, Carl Joseph, Joseph, Jean. Cert. achievement, Pa. State U., 1955, Bucknell U., 1960, Sch. Consumer Banking, U. Va., 1964, Nat. Comml. Lending Sch., U. Okla., 1971, Grad. Sch. Bus., Columbia U. Cert. comml. lender. With Mchts. Nat. Bank, Allentown, 1949—, sr. v.p., 1973, exec. v.p. loan div., 1973-74, pres., 1974—, chief exec. officer, 1976—, also dir.; past instr. Am. Inst. Banking. Past bd. dirs. Lehigh County Indsl. Devel. Corp., Sacred Heart Hosp.; past bd. dirs., v.p. Asso. Credit Bur. Services, Inc.; trustee Allentown Coll. of St. Francis De Sales; mem. Lehigh County Authority. Served with AUS, 1952-54. Mem. Pa. Bankers Assn. (agy. relations com.; exec. com. group III, also 2d vice-chmn.), Robert Morris Assos., Allentown-Lehigh County C. of C. (dir., treas.). Republican. Roman Catholic. Clubs: Rotary, Lehigh Country. Home: 560 Sand Spring Rd Schnecksville PA 18078 Office: Merchants Nat Bank 702 Hamilton Mall Allentown PA 18101

FEICK, WILLIAM, JR., corp. exec.; b. Bklyn., Dec. 12, 1924; s. William and Clara (Nichols) F.; m. Joan Meeske, Sept. 1, 1950; children—William Kurt, Matthew Fritz, Alexander Nichols. B.A., Amherst Coll., 1947. Asst. v.p. Crocker First Nat. Bank of San Francisco, 1948-56; treas. Flintkote Co., N.Y.C., 1956-59, v.p., 1959-62, MacKay-Shields Fin. Corp., N.Y.C., 1963-66, pres., 1966-72, exec. dir., 1973—; Felmont Oil Corp. Served as lt. (j.g.) USNR, 1944-46. Mem. Phi Delta Theta. Republican. Episcopalian. Clubs: Bohemian (San Francisco); University, Country (New Canaan). Home: Lambert Rd New Canaan CT 06840 also Stratton VT 05155 Office: 551 Fifth Ave New York NY 10017

FEICKERT, CARL WILLIAM, lawyer; b. Belleville, Ill., Sept. 24, 1906; s. Christian Arthur and Elizabeth (Brosius) F.; m. Emma Joanne Heinl, Apr. 12, 1941; children: Carl A., Elissa Ann, John C. LL.B., U. Ill., 1931. Bar: Ill. 1931, Mo. 1931. Practice law, East St. Louis and Belleville, 1932-61; atty. regional office HOLC, Chgo., 1934-35; asst. U.S. atty., East St. Louis, 1937-40; U.S. atty. Eastern Dist. Ill., East St. Louis, 1961-69; asst. St. Clair County states atty., 1969-74; mem. firm Jones, Ottesen, Feickert & Derango, Belleville, 1974—. Mem. Belleville Twp. High Sch. and Jr. Coll. Bd. Edn., 1957-63, pres., 1960; Pres. United Fund, Belleville, 1959. Served to maj. Judge Adv. Gen.'s Dept. USAAF, 1942-46. Mem. Am., Ill., St. Clair County bar assns., Am. Legion, Belleville Philharmonic Soc., St. Clair County Hist. Soc. (dir. 1979-84), Nat. Assn. Former U.S. Attys., U.S. (dir. 1938-40), Internat. Jr. C. of C., Ill. Jr. C. of C. (pres. 1939-40), Belleville C. of C., U. Ill. Alumni Assn., Demolay Legion Honor, Theta Xi, Phi Delta Phi. Democrat. Clubs: Illini, Downtown Optimist, Elks (Belleville). Home: 44 N Pennsylvania Ave Belleville IL 62221 Office: 3d Floor First Nat Bank Bldg Belleville IL 62220

FEIFFER, JULES, cartoonist-writer; b. N.Y.C., Jan. 26, 1929; s. David and Rhoda (Davis) F.; m. Judith Sheftel, Sept. 17, 1961 (div. 1983); 1 dau., Kate.; m. Jennifer Allen, Sept.11, 1983. Student, Art Students League, N.Y.C., 1946, Pratt Inst., N.Y.C., 1947-48, 49-51. Asst. to syndicated cartoonist Will Eisner, 1946-51; co-chmn. maj. funds com. Yaddo Corp. Cartoonist, author: syndicated Sunday page Clifford; engaged in various art jobs, 1953-56; contbg. cartoonist: Village Voice, N.Y.C., 1956—; cartoons pub. weekly in London (Eng.) Observer, 1958-66, 72-82; regularly in Playboy mag, 1959—; cartoons nationally syndicated U.S., 1959—; (Recipient Acad. award for animated cartoon, Munro 1961, spl. George Polk Meml. award 1962, Outer Circle Drama Critics award 1969, 70); Author: books Sick, Sick, Sick, 1959, Passionella and other stories, 1960, The Explainers, 1961, Boy, Girl, Boy, Girl, 1962, Hold Me, 1962; mus. revue The Explainers, 1961; one act play Crawling Arnold, 1961; novel Harry, The Rat with Women, 1963; Feiffer's Album, 1963, The Unexpurgated Memoirs of Bernard Mergendeiler, 1965, The Great Comic Book Heroes, 1965, Feiffer's Marriage Manual, 1967; play Little Murders (voted best fgn. play of yr. by London critics, Obie award), 1967 (Outer Circle Drama Critics award), Feiffer on Civil Rights, 1967, God Bless, 1968, The White House Murder Case, 1970; screenplays Little Murders, 1971, Carnal Knowledge, 1971; books Pictures at a Prosecution, 1971, Feiffer on Nixon: The Cartoon Presidency, 1974; play Knock-Knock, 1976; revue Hold Me!, 1977; novel Ackroyd, 1977; cartoon novel Tantrum, 1979; screenplay Popeye, 1980; play Grownups, 1981, A Think Piece, 1982; book Jules Feiffer's America: From Eisenhower to Reagan, 1982. Served with AUS, 1951-53. Mem. Authors Guild, Dramatists Guild (council, pres. found. 1982-83), P.E.N. Office: care Universal Press Syndicate 4400 Johnson Dr Fairway KS 66205

FEIGELSON, PHILIP, scientist, biochemist, educator; b. N.Y.C., Apr. 20, 1925; s. David and Rose (Venitsky) F.; m. Muriel Horowitz, Mar. 30, 1947; children—Janet Lauren, Eric Dennis. B.S., Queens Coll., 1947; M.S., Syracuse U., 1948; Ph.D., U. Wis., 1951. Asst. prof. biochemistry Antioch Coll., Yellow Springs, Ohio, 1951-54; research asso. Fels Research Inst., 1951-54; mem. faculty Coll. Phys. and Surg. Columbia U., N.Y.C., 1954—, assoc. prof. biochemistry, 1961-70, prof. biochemistry, 1970—; Mem. study sect. pharmacology USPHS, 1966-70. Mem. editorial bd.: Cancer Research, 1973-76, Jour. Biol. Chemistry, 1977-82. Fellow AAAS, N.Y. Acad. Scis. (bd. govs. 1970—, chmn. div. biochemistry 1967-69, pres. 1975), World Acad. Arts and Scis.; mem. Am. Soc. Biol. Chemists, Am. Chem. Soc., Am. Assn. Cancer Research, Harvey Soc. Home: 265 Tenafly Rd Tenafly NJ 07670 Office: Inst Cancer Research Dept Biochemistry Columbia U New York NY 10032

FEIGEN, RICHARD L., art dealer; b. Chgo., Aug. 8, 1930; s. Arthur P. and Shirley (Bierman) F.; m. Sandra Elizabeth Canning Walker, Feb. 23, 1966 (dec. div. 1978); children: Philippa Canning, Richard Wood Bliss. B.A., Yale U., 1952; M.B.A., Harvard U., 1954. Asst. treas. Beneficial Standard Life Ins. Co., Los Angeles, 1955-56; mem. N.Y. Stock Exchange, 1956-57; pres., dir. Richard L. Feigen & Co., Inc., N.Y.C. and Chgo., 1957—; chmn. bd., treas. Castelli Feigen Corcoran Gallery, Inc.; mem. com. works fine art N.Y. State Office Bldg., Harlem; lectr. in field. Contbr. articles to art publs. Candidate, del. Democratic Nat. Conv., 1972; trustee John Jay Homestead Assn.,

Katonah, N.Y., 1976—. Fellow Mpls. Soc. Fine Arts, Met. Mus. Art, Art Inst. Chgo.; mem. Art Dealers Assn. Am. (dir. 1972-76), Harvard Bus. Sch. Assn., Phi Gamma Delta. Clubs: Arts, Tavern (Chgo.). Home: 953 Fifth Ave New York NY 10021 also Cantitoe House Cantitoe St Katonah NY 10536 Office: 113 E 79th St New York NY 10021

FEIGENBAUM, ARMAND VALLIN, systems engineer, systems equipment executive; b. N.Y.C., Apr. 6, 1920; s. S. Frederick and Hilda (Vallin) F. B.S., Union Coll., 1942; M.S., Mass. Inst. Tech., 1948, Ph.D., 1951. Engr. test program Gen. Electric Co., Schenectady, 1942-45, factory tng. course, 1945-47, sales engr., 1947-48, supr. tng. mfg. personnel, Lynn, Mass., 1948-50, asst. to gen. mgr. aircraft gas turbine div., Cin., 1950-52, mgr. aircraft nuclear propulsion dept., N.Y.C., 1952, co. mgr. quality control, 1956, company-wide mgr. mfg. operations and quality control, 1958-68; pres., chief exec. officer Gen. Systems Co., Inc., Pittsfield, Mass., 1968—; pres. Internat. Acad. for Quality, 1966-79, chmn. bd. dirs., 1979—; trustee, mem. bd. investment Berkshire County Savs. Bank.; Adv. group U.S. Army, 1966—; lectr. Mass. Inst. Tech., U. Cin., Union Coll., U. Pa. Author: Quality Control-Principles and Practice, 1951, Total Quality Control-Engineering and Management, 1961, Management Programming, 1980, The Organization Process, 1980, Total Quality Control, 3d edit., 1983; Contbr. articles to profl. jours. Chmn. inst. adminstrn., mgmt. council Union Coll., 1963—. Recipient Founders medal, 1977. Fellow Am. Soc. Quality control (pres. 1961-63, chmn. bd. 1963-64, Edwards medal 1966, Lancaster medal 1982), AAAS; mem. Nat. Security Indsl. Assn. (nat. award merit 1965), ASME, Nat. Soc. Profl. Engrs., IEEE, Inst. Math. Statistics, Acad. Polit. and Social Scis., Am. Econ. Assn., Soc. for Advancement Mgmt., Indsl. Relations Research Soc., Council for Internat. Progress in Mgmt. (chmn. bd. 1968-70). Home: 123 Ann Dr Pittsfield MA 01201 Office: Berkshire Common South St Pittsfield MA 01201

FEIGENBAUM, EDWARD ALBERT, computer science educator; b. Weehawken, N.J., Jan. 20, 1936; s. Fred J. and Sara Rachman; m. H. Penny Nii, 1975; children: Janet Denise, Carol Leonora, Sheri Bryant, Karin Bryant. B.S. in Elec. Engring., Carnegie Inst. Tech., 1956, Ph.D. in Indsl. Adminstrn., 1960. Asst., then assoc. prof. bus. adminstrn. U. Calif. at Berkeley, 1960-64; assoc. prof. computer sci., then prof. Stanford U., 1965—; prin. investigator heuristic programming project, 1965—; dir. Computation Center Stanford U., 1965-68, chmn. dept. computer sci., 1976-81; pres. Intelli Genetics Inc., 1980-81, mem. tech. adv. bd., 1983—; cons. to industry, 1957—; dir. Sperry Corp.; Mem. computer and biomath. scis. study sect. NIH, 1968-72, mem. adv. com. on artificial intelligence in medicine, 1974—; mem. adv. com. Health Care Tech. Center, U. Mo., Columbia; mem. Math. Social Sci. Bd., 1975-78; computer sci. adv. com. NSF, 1977-80; mem. Internat. Joint Council on Artificial Intelligence, 1973—. Author: (with others) Information Processing Language V Manual, 1961, (with P. McCorduck) The Fifth Generation; author: (with R. Lindsay, B. Buchanan, J. Lederberg) Applications of Artificial Intelligence to Organic Chemistry: the Dendral Program; Editor: (with J. Feldman) Computers and Thought, 1963, (with A. Barr and P. Cohen) Handbook of Artificial Intelligence, 1981, 82; Mem. editorial bd.: Jour. Artificial Intelligence, 1969—. Fulbright scholar Gt. Britain, 1959-60. Fellow AAAS; Mem. Assn. Computing Machinery (nat. council 1966-68, chmn. spl. interest group on biol. applications 1973-76), Am. Assn. Artificial Intelligence (pres. 1980-81), Cognitive Sci. Soc. (council 1979-81), Am. Psychol. Assn., AAAS, Sigma Xi, Tau Beta Pi, Eta Kappa Nu, Pi Delta Epsilon. Home: 1017 Cathcart Way Stanford CA 94305 Office: Computer Sci Dept Stanford U Stanford CA 94305

FEIGENBAUM, HARVEY, cardiologist, educator; b. East Chicago, Ind., Nov. 20, 1933; s. Julius and Tillie (Sol) F.; m. Phyllis M. Cohn, Oct. 20, 1957; children—Steven, Thomas, Lyle. A.B., Ind. U., 1955, M.D., 1958. Diplomate: Am. Bd. Internal Medicine. Intern Phila. Gen. Hosp., 1958-59; resident Ind. U. Med. Center, Indpls., 1959-61, cardiology fellow, 1961-62; instr. Ind. U. Sch. Medicine, Indpls., 1962-64, asst. prof., 1964-67, assoc. prof., 1967-71, prof., 1971-80, Disting. prof., 1980—; research assoc. Krannert Inst. Cardiology, Indpls., 1962-73, sr. research assoc., 1973—. Author: Echocardiography, 3d edit, 1981; contbr. articles to profl. jours.; mem. editorial bd.: Am. Jour. Medicine, Circulation, Cardiology, Jour. of Am. Coll. Cardiology, Am. Heart Jour. Bd. dirs. Regenstrief Found. for Delivery of Health Care. Fellow A.C.P., Am. Coll. Cardiology; mem. Central Soc. for Clin. Research, Am. Soc. for Clin. Investigation, Assn. Am. Physicians, Am. Soc. Echocardiography (pres. 1975-78), Am. Heart Assn. (council on clin. cardiology), Am. Inst. Ultrasound in Medicine (dir. 1969-72), Phi Beta Kappa, Alpha Omega Alpha. Jewish. Office: 926 Michigan St Indianapolis IN 46223

FEIGENBAUM, MITCHELL JAY, physics educator; b. Phila., Dec. 19, 1944; s. Abraham Joseph and Mildred (Sugar) F. B.E.E., CCNY, 1964; Ph.D., MIT, 1970. Research assoc., instr. physics dept. Cornell U., Ithaca, N.Y., 1970-72, prof. physics, 1982—; research assoc. physics dept. Va. Poly. Inst., Blacksburg, 1972-74; staff mem. theory div. Los Alamos Nat. Lab., 1974-81, lab. fellow, 1981-82; vis. mem. Inst. Advanced Study, Princeton, N.J., 1978, Institute des Hautes Recherches Scientifiques, Bueres-sur-Yvette, France, 1980—. Editorial bd.: Jour. Statis. Physics, 1982—. Recipient Disting. Performance award Los Alamos Nat. Lab., 1980; recipeint Ernest O. Lawrence award U.S. Dept. Energy, 1983. Mem. N.Y. Acad. Scis., Am. Phys. Soc., Sigma Xi. Discovered theory period doubling route to turbulence, 1976-79. Home: 100 Fairview Sq 5E Ithaca NY 14850 Office: Physics Dept Cornell Univ 538 Clark Hall Ithaca NY 14853

FEIGHAN, EDWARD FARRELL, Congressman, lawyer; b. Lakewood, Ohio, Oct. 22, 1947; s. Francis X. and Rosemary (Ling) F.; m. Nadine Hopwood, Apr. 24, 1976; children: Lauren, David. B.A., Loyola U., New Orleans, 1969; J.D., Cleve.-Marshall Coll. Law, 1978. Bar: Ohio 1978. Tchr., Cleve., 1969-72; mem. Ohio Ho. of Reps., 1973-78; county commr. Cuyahoga County, Cleve., 1979-82; mem. firm Carney, Rains & Feighan, Cleve., 1982—; mem. 97th-98th Congresses from 19th Ohio Dist. Author of anthology, 1983. Mem. Ohio Bar Assn., Cleve. Bar Assn., LWV, Citizen League, City Club. Democrat. Roman Catholic. Home: Old River Rd Gates Mills OH 44040 Office: Room 1223 Longworth House Office Bldg Washington DC 20515

FEIGIN, BARBARA SOMMER, advertising executive; b. Berlin, Germany, Nov. 16, 1937; came to U.S., 1940, naturalized, 1949; d. Eric Daniel and Charlotte Martha (Denmer) Sommer; m. James Feigin, Sept. 17, 1961; children: Michael, Peter, Daniel. B.A., Whitman Coll., Walla Walla, Wash., 1959; cert., Harvard-Radcliffe Program Bus. Adminstrn., 1960. Mktg. research asst. Richardson-Merrell Co., 1960-61; market research analyst SCM Corp., 1961-62; group research supr. Benton & Bowles, Inc., N.Y.C., 1962-68; assoc. research dir. Marplan Research Co., N.Y.C., 1968-69; exec. v.p., dir. mktg. and research Grey Advt. Inc., N.Y.C., 1969—. Author articles in field. Bd. overseers Whitman Coll. Mem. Advt. Research Found., Am. Mktg. Assn. (dir. N.Y. chpt.), Copy Research Council, Market Research Council, Agy. Research Dirs. Council. Home: 535 E 86th St New York NY 10028 Office: 777 3d Ave New York NY 10017

FEIGIN, RALPH DAVID, pediatrician; b. N.Y.C., Apr. 3, 1938; s. Jack Bernard and Dorothy Phyllis (Strauss) F.; m. Judith Sue Zobel, June 26, 1960; children: Susan M., Michael E., Debra F. A.B., Columbia U., 1958; M.D., Boston U., 1962. Diplomate: Am. Bd. Pediatrics. Pediatric intern Boston City Hosp., 1962-63; pediatric resident Boston City Hosp. and Mass. Gen. Hosp., 1963-65; teaching fellow pediatrics Harvard U. Med. Sch., 1964-65; from asst. prof. to prof. pediatrics Washington U. Med. Sch., St. Louis, 1968-77, dir. div. infectious diseases, dept. pediatrics, 1973-77; prof. pediatrics, chmn. dept. Baylor Coll. Medicine, Houston, 1977—; physician-in-chief Tex. Children's Hosp., 1977—; pediatric service Harris County Hosp. Dist., 1977—; pediatrician-in-chief Methodist Hosp., 1980—; adv. ad hoc study group spl. infectious disease problems U.S. Army Med. Research and Devel. Command, 1974—; vis. prof., cons. in field; pres. Pediatric Research Found., 1982—. Co-editor: Nutrition and the Developing Nervous System, 1975, Textbook of Pediatric Infectious Diseases, 1981; editorial bd.: Pediatrics, 1978—, Jour. Pediatric Infectious Diseases; assoc. editor: Jour. Infectious Diseases, 1984—; contbr. articles to med. jours., chpts. to books. Served with M.C., USAR, 1965-67. Recipient Research Career Devel. award USPHS, 1970, Founders Day award Washington U. Med. Sch., 1977, Sr. Class Outstanding Tchr. award Baylor Coll. Medicine, 1979, 80, 81, 82, 83, Minnie Stevens Piper Professorial award, 1984; Alumni Teaching scholar Washington U. Med. Sch., 1975. Mem. Am. Pediatric Soc., Soc. Pediatric Research (pres. 1982-83), Am. Acad. Pediatrics, Infectious Disease Soc. Am., Am. Soc. Microbiology, N.Y. Acad. Scis., AMA, Assn. Med. Sch., Pediatric Dept. Chmn., AAAS, Tex. Med. Assn., Tex. Pediatric Soc., Harris County Med. Soc., Houston Pediatric Soc. Office: Baylor Coll Medicine Dept Pediatrics 1200 Moursund Ave Houston TX 77030

FEIGL, DOROTHY MARIE, chemistry educator; b. Evanston, Ill., Feb. 25, 1938; d. Francis Philip and Marie Agnes (Jacques) F. B.S., Loyola U., Chgo., 1961; Ph.D., Stanford U., 1966; postdoctoral fellow, N.C. State U., 1965-66. Asst. prof. chemistry St. Mary's Coll., Notre Dame, Ind., 1966-69, asso. prof., 1969-75, prof., 1975—, chmn. dept. chemistry and physics, 1977—, bd. regents, 1976-82. Author: (with John Hill) Chemistry and Life, 1983, Foundations of Life, 1983; contbr. articles to chem. jours., (with John Hill) chpts. to texts. Recipient Spes Unica award St. Mary's Coll., 1973, Maria Pieta award, 1977. Mem. Am. Chem. Soc., Royal Soc. Chemistry, Midwestern Assn. Chemistry Tchrs. at Liberal Arts Colls., Sigma Xi, Iota Sigma Pi. Democrat. Roman Catholic. Office: Dept of Chemistry Saint Marys College Notre Dame IN 46556

FEIKENS, JOHN, judge; b. Clifton, N.J., Dec. 3, 1917; s. Sipke and Corine (Wisse) F.; m. Henriette Dorothy Schulthouse, Nov. 4, 1939; children: Jon, Susan Corine, Barbara Edith, Julie Anne, Robert H. A.B., Calvin Coll., Grand Rapids, Mich., 1939; J.D., U. Mich., 1941; LL.D., U. Detroit, 1979, Detroit Coll. Law, 1981. Bar: Mich. 1942. Gen. practice law, Detroit; dist. judge Eastern Dist. Mich., 1960-61, 70-79, chief judge, 1979—; past co-chmn. Mich. Civil Rights Commn.; past chmn. Rep. State Central Com.; past mem. Rep. Nat. Com. Past bd. trustees Calvin Coll. Fellow Am. Coll. Trial Lawyers; mem. ABA, Detroit Bar Assn. (dir. 1962, past pres.), State Bar Mich. (commr. 1965-71). Club: University of Michigan. Home: 10750 Koebbe Rd Manchester MI 48158 Office: Fed Bldg Detroit MI 48226

FEIN, A. EDWIN, mgmt. co. exec.; b. N.Y.C., Apr. 9, 1898; s. Samuel and Anne (Fein) F. Student, N.Y. U., 1919-1925, Columbia, 1925-26. Marketing-tech. cons. Walter Kidde & Co., Bloomfield, N.J., 1934-35; dir. sales DCA Food Industries, N.Y.C., 1936-38; chmn. Research Co. Am., N.Y.C., 1939-73; v.p., sec. United Indsl. Corp., N.Y.C., 1959—, also dir.; sec., dir. Affiliated Hosp. Products, Inc.; dir. Detroit Stoker Co., Neo Products Co. Author: This Is My Life; also ann. edits.: Brewing Industry Survey (Ann. Advt. award), Basic Marketing Chart of U.S; Contbr. articles to profl. jours. Served with U.S. Army, 1918-1919. Fellow Soc. Advancement Mgmt.; mem. Four Freedoms Found., Internat. Platform Assn., Assn. Corporate Growth, Am. Soc. Corporate Secs., N.Y. Zool. Soc. (chmn. industry com.), N.Y. C. of C., Am. Legion (comdr. 1931). Clubs: City, Explorers (N.Y.C.). Home: 303 E 57th St Apt 22H New York City NY 10022 Office: 18 E 48th St New York NY 10017

FEIN, BERNARD, investments exec.; b. N.Y.C., Jan. 15, 1908; s. Samuel and Anna (Fine) F.; m. Elaine Schneir, Dec. 26, 1948; children—Kathy Joyce, Lawrence Seth, Susan, Adam, David. LL.B., St. Lawrence U., 1929. Bar: N.Y. bar 1931. Practice of law, N.Y.C., 1931-41; pres., chmn. bd. United Indsl. Corp., N.Y.C; pres., chmn. Affiliated Hosp. Products, Inc, St. Louis; chmn. bd. Neo Products Corp., Chgo.; pres. Affiliated Med. Products Ltd., Toronto, Ont.; chmn. exec. com. Internat. Controls Corp., Thomaston, Conn.; dir. Aircraft Armaments, Inc., Balt. Home: 80 Garden Rd Scarsdale NY 10583 Office: 18 E 48th St New York NY 10017

FEIN, BRUCE E., government official; b. Cambridge, Mass., Mar. 12, 1947; married; 3 children. Student, Swarthmore Coll., 1965-67; B.A., U. Calif.-Berkeley, 1969; J.D. cum laude, Harvard U., 1972. Bar: Calif. 1973, U.S. Supreme Ct. 1977. Law clk. to judge U.S. Dist. Ct. Md., 1972-73; atty., advisor Office Legal Counsel Dept. Justice, Washington, 1973-74, asst. dir. Office Policy and Planning, 1974-75, spl. asst. to asst. atty. gen Antitrust div., 1975-77, sr. trial atty. appellate sect., 1977-81, assoc. dep. atty. gen., 1981-82; gen. counsel FCC, Washington, 1982—. Contbr. articles to profl. jours. Mem. ABA, Phi Beta Kappa. Office: FCC 1919 M St NW Washington DC 20554 *

FEIN, IRVING ASHLEY, television and motion picture executive; b. Bklyn., June 21, 1911; s. Harry and Fannie (Milstein) F.; m. Florence Kohn, Dec. 25, 1941 (dec.); children: Michael Anthony, Patricia Ann; m. Marion Sheppard Schechter, June 21, 1969. Student, U. Balt., 1928-29, U. Wis., 1930-32; LL.B., St. Lawrence U., 1936. Publicity and advt. dept. Warner Bros., N.Y.C., 1933-36; dir. exploitation and radio West Coast studios, 1936; asst. publicity dir. Samuel Goldwyn, 1941; dir. exploitation and radio Columbia Pictures, Hollywood, 1946; publicity, advt. dir. Amusement Enterprises, Inc., 1947; with CBS, Inc., 1948-56, dir. exploitation, Hollywood, 1950; dir. publicity and exploitation CBS Radio, Hollywood, 1951-53, dir. pub. relations, 1953-55, v.p. sales promotion, advt. and press info., N.Y.C., 1955-56; pres. J & M Prodns., Inc., Beverly Hills, Calif., 1956-65; exec. v.p. JAC Prodns., 1965-75, J.B. Prodns.; pres. TV Prodn. Co. Producer George Burns TV spls., 1975-84; producer film: Just You and Me Kid, Oh God! You Devil; Author: Jack Benny—An Intimate Biography, 1976. Home: 1100 N Alta Loma Rd Los Angeles CA 90069

FEIN, JOHN MORTON, educator; b. Chgo., Dec. 23, 1922; s. Louis Julius and Lola (Dubin) F.; m. Lucille Blumenthal, Sept. 11, 1946; children: David, Judith, Joanna, Laura. B.A., M.A., Harvard U., 1944, Ph.D., 1950. Teaching fellow, tutor Harvard U., 1944-49, instr., 1949-50; mem. faculty Duke U., 1950—, prof. Romance langs., 1963—, chmn. dept., 1964-73, 79-81, vice provost undergrad. edn., 1974-79; dean Trinity Coll., 1974-79; vis. prof. U. Chile, U. Catolica, Chile, 1957-58, Ind. U., 1964, Stanford U., summer 1965, U. Wyo., summer 1967, Dartmouth Coll., summer 1971, U. N.Mex., 1982. Author: Modernismo in Chilean Literature: The Second Period, 1965. Mem. Modern Lang. Assn., Am. Assn. Tchrs. Spanish and Portuguese (exec. com.). Home: 2726 Montgomery St Durham NC 27705

FEIN, LEONARD J., educator, author; b. Bklyn., July 1, 1934; s. Isaac M. and Clara (Wertheim) F.; m. Zelda Kleiman, 1955 (div.); children: Rachel, Naomi, Jessica. A.B., U. Chgo., 1953, B.A., 1955, M.A., 1957; Ph.D., Mich. State U., 1962. Asst. prof. MIT, 1962-66, asso. prof., 1966-70; dep. dir., dir. research MIT-Harvard Joint Center for Urban Studies, 1968-70; prof. polit. and social policy Brandeis U., 1970-73, Klutznick prof. contemporary Jewish studies, 1973-80; cons. Upward Bound, Grad. Sch. Edn., Harvard U., Sch. Edn., NYU, Union Am. Hebrew Congregations, Inst. Jewish Life. Author: Politics in Israel, 1967, Israel: Politics and People, 1968, The Ecology of the Public Schools: An Inquiry Into Community Control, 1971; editor: American Democracy: Essays on Image and Realities, 1965; editor-in-chief: Moment Mag., 1974—. Chmn. research adv. council Mass. Commn. Against Discrimination, 1963-66; chmn. commn. on urban affairs Am. Jewish Congress, 1968-70; mem. exec. com. Am.-Israel Pub. Affairs Com., 1969-74; Trustee, mem. exec. com. Combined Jewish Philanthropies, Boston, 1969-75, life trustee, 1982—; trustee Am. Zionist Youth Found. Social Sci. Research Council fellow, 1961-63, 66; recipient Smolar award, 1979, 83. Jewish. Home: 189 Marlborough St Boston MA 02116 Office: 462 Boylston St Boston MA 02116

FEIN, RASHI, educator; b. N.Y.C., Feb. 6, 1926; s. Isaac M. and Clara (Wertheim) F.; m. Ruth Judith Breslau, June 19, 1949; children—Alan, Michael, Karen, Bena. Student, Bridgeport Jr. Coll., 1942-43; B.A., Johns Hopkins, 1948, Ph.D., 1956. Mem. staff Pres.'s Commn. on Health Needs, 1952; from lectr. to asso. prof. U. N.C., 1952-61; statistician Bur. of Census, 1958-59; sr. staff Pres.'s Council Econ. Advisers, 1961-63; sr. fellow Brookings Inst., 1963-68; prof. Harvard, 1968—; sr. fellow Brookdale Inst., Jerusalem, 1978—; Heath Clark lectr. London Sch. Hygiene & Tropical Medicine, 1980; Chmn. med. assistance adv. council to sec. HEW, 1967-69; mem. adv. com. research and devel. Social Security Adminstrn., 1968-71; mem. Nat. Manpower Policy Task Force, 1967-79; mem. acad. adv. council Nat. Inst. for Research in Behavioral Scis., Israel; mem. tech. bd. Milbank Meml. Fund, 1975-78; mem. Office Tech. Assessment, Health Adv. Panel. Author: Economics of Mental Illness, 1958, The Doctor Shortage; An Economic Diagnosis, 1967, (with Gerald Weber) Financing Medical Education; An Analysis of Alternative Policies and Mechanisms, 1971, (with Charles Lewis and David Mechanic) A Right to Health; The Problem of Access to Primary Medical Care, 1976; Editorial bd.: Milbank Meml. Fund Quar; advisory editorial bd.: Jour. Human Resources. Trustee Beth Israel Hosp., Boston, Hebrew Rehab. Home for Aged; bd. dirs. Harvard Community Health Plan Found., 1980—. Served with USNR, 1944-46. Recipient John M. Russell award for advancement knowledge in medicine, 1971; Fellow Inst. History Medicine Johns Hopkins, 1951-52; traveling fellow WHO, 1971. Mem. Inst. Medicine of Nat. Acad. Scis., Am. Econ. Assn., Am. Assn. U. Profs., Am. Pub. Health Assn. Jewish. Home: 205 Commonwealth Ave Boston MA 02116 Office: 25 Shattuck St Boston MA 02115

FEINBERG, GERALD, educator, physicist; b. N.Y.C., May 27, 1933; s. Leon and Florence (Weingarten) F.; m. Barbara J. Silberdick, Aug. 9, 1968; children—Jeremy Russell, Douglas Loren. B.A., Columbia U., 1953, M.A., 1954, Ph.D., 1957. Mem. Inst. Advanced Study, Princeton, N.J., 1956-57; research assoc. Brookhaven Nat. Lab., Upton, N.Y., 1957-59, cons., 1960-74; prof. physics dept. Columbia U., N.Y.C., 1959—, chmn., 1980-82. Author: The Prometheus Project, 1969, What is the World Made Of?, 1977, Consequences of Growth, 1977, Life Beyond Earth, 1980, The Future of Science, 1984; div. assoc. editor: Phys. Rev. Letter, 1983—; Contbr. articles to profl. jours. Sloan Found. fellow, 1960-64; Overseas fellow Churchill Coll., Cambridge, Eng., 1963-64; Guggenheim fellow, 1973-74. Fellow Am. Phys. Soc.; mem. Sigma Xi. Home: 535 E 86th St New York NY 10028

FEINBERG, IRWIN L., manufacturing company executive; b. Bklyn., Mar. 4, 1916; s. Philip F. and Rose (Meyers) F.; m. Helen Kadison, Dec. 3, 1944; children: Marjorie, Phyllis. B.S., NYU, 1936. Sr. ptnr. Feinberg & Kadison, N.Y.C., 1947—; exec. v.p., dir. Mallory Randall Corp., N.Y.C., 1971-76, pres., chief exec. officer, dir., 1976—; chmn. bd. Savoy Industries, Inc., 1982. Mem. Am. Inst. C.P.A.s, N.Y. State Soc. C.P.A.s, NYU Alumni Assn. Clubs: NYU, B'nai B'rith. Home: 3 Jaegger Dr Old Brookville NY 11545 Office: 122 E 42d St New York NY 10168

FEINBERG, JOEL, educator; b. Detroit, Oct. 19, 1926; s. Abraham J. and Marion (Tahl) F.; m. Betty Grey Sowers, May 29, 1955; children—Melissa, Benjamin. Student, U. Ill., 1944-45; B.A., U. Mich., 1949, M.A., 1951, Ph.D., 1957. Instr. philosophy Brown U., 1955-57, asst. prof., 1957-62, Princeton U., 1962-64, asso. prof., 1964-66; prof. U. Calif. at Los Angeles, 1966-67; prof. philosophy Rockefeller U., N.Y.C., 1967-77, U. Ariz., 1977—. Author: Doing and Deserving, 1970, Social Philosophy, 1973, Rights, Justice and the Bounds of Liberty, 1980; contbg. author: Philosophy in America, 1965, Educational Judgments, 1973, Philosophy and Environmental Crisis, 1974; editor: Reason and Responsibility, 1965, Moral Concepts, 1969, The Problem of Abortion, 1973, Philosophy of Law, 1975. Served with AUS, 1944-46. Fellow Center for Advanced Study in Behavioral Scis., 1960-61; liberal arts fellow in law and philosophy Harvard Law Sch., 1963-64; Guggenheim Found. fellow, 1974-75. Fellow Am. Acad. Arts and Scis., Am. Philos. Assn. (v.p. Pacific div. 1980-81, pres. 1981-82); mem. Am. Soc. Polit. and Legal Philosophy (program chmn. 1963, sec.-treas. 1971-72), Soc. Health and Human Values, Council Philos. Studies. Home: 5322 N Via Entrada Tucson AZ 85718

FEINBERG, LAWRENCE BERNARD, psychologist, university dean; b. Bklyn., June 2, 1940; s. Robert Erwin and Geraldine F.; children: Ronald, Nancy. B.A., U. Buffalo, 1961; M.S., SUNY, Buffalo, 1963, Ph.D., 1966. Lic. psychologist, Calif.; cert. rehab. counselor. Lectr. dept. counselor edn. SUNY, Buffalo, 1965-66; prof. spl. edn. and rehab. Syracuse U., 1966-67, dir. rehab. edn., 1967-77; prof. counselor edn. San Diego State U., 1977—, adj. prof. public health, 1981—, assoc. dean grad. div. and research, 1977—; cons. psychologist VA Hosp., Syracuse, 1970-77; cons. Rehab. Services Adminstrn., HEW, Washington, 1976-77, Nat. Inst. Handicapped Research, U.S. Dept. Edn., 1982; chmn. Nat. Commn. Accreditation of Rehab. Edn., 1974-76; bd. dirs. Nat. Commn. Rehab. Counselor Cert., 1973-77. Author: (with others) Rehabilitation and Poverty: Bridging the Gap, 1969, Rehabilitation in the Inner City, 1970, Education for the Rehabilitation Services, 1974; cons. editor 6 profl. jours.; contbr. articles to profl. jours. Recipient 20 fed. grants, 4 nat. profl. service awards. Fellow Am. Psychol. Assn. (treas. div. rehab. psychology 1980-83, pres. div. rehab. psychology 1984-85); mem. Am. Rehab. Counseling Assn. (pres. 1973, dir. 1980—), Am. Personnel and Guidance Assn. (dir. 1974), N.Y. State Rehab. Counseling Assn. (pres. 1970), Council Rehab. Counselor Educators (regional dir. 1969-71). Home: 1428 Beryl St San Diego CA 92109 Office: Grad Div and Research San Diego State U San Diego CA 92182

FEINBERG, LEONARD, English educator; b. Vitebsk, Russia, Aug. 26, 1914; came to U.S., 1923, naturalized, 1933; s. Samuel and Belle (Feinberg) Aleshker; m. Lilian Okner, Nov. 26, 1938; children: Thomas (dec.), Ellen. B.S., U. Ill., 1937, M.A., 1938, Ph.D., 1946. Instr. U. Ill., Urbana, 1946; asst. prof. English Iowa State U., Ames, 1946-50, asso. prof., 1950-57, prof., 1957-82, Distinguished prof. sci. and humanities, 1973-82, ret., 1982; Fulbright lectr. U. Ceylon, 1957-58; vis. lectr., India, Japan, Hong Kong, Hungary, Poland, Yugoslavia. Author: Man and Laughter, 1955, Satirist, 1963, Introduction to

Satire, 1967, Asian Laughter, 1971, Secret of Humor, 1978. Served with USN, 1943-45. Home: 111 Lynn St Ames IA 50010

FEINBERG, MORTIMER ROBERT, psychologist; b. N.Y.C., Aug. 26, 1922; s. Max and Frieda (Siegel) F.; m. Gloria Granditer, June 22, 1947; children—Stuart Andrew, E. Todd. B.S., Coll. City N.Y., 1944; M.S., Ind. U., 1945; Ph.D., N.Y. U., 1950. Diplomate Am. Bd. Examiners in Indsl. Psychology. Instr. psychology N.Y. U., 1945-50; chief psychologist Research Inst. Am., 1953-58; prof. psychology Bernard M. Baruch Coll., City U., 1958—, acting chmn. dept. psychology, 1969-70, dir. advanced mgmt., asst. dean, 1974—; pres. BFS Psychol. Assos., 1960-74, chmn., 1974—; prin. lectr. Am. Mgmt. Assn.; lectr. Young Pres.'s Orgn.; indsl. psychology cons. psychiatry div. Mt. Sinai Hosp.; Research adviser City of N.Y. Exec. Tng. Program, 1959—. Publisher: Interaction; Author: (with D. Fryer) Developing People in Industry, 1956, Effective Psychology for Managers, 1965, New Psychology for Managing People, (with G. Feinberg and J. Tarrant) Leavetaking, 1978, (with R. Dempewolff) Corporate Bigamy; Contrbr.: Wall St. Jour. Fellow Am. Psychol. Assn., AAAS. Clubs: Yale, N.Y. Sales Execs. (dir. 1974-76). Home: 34 Brook Ln Peekskill NY 10566 Office: 666 Fifth Ave New York NY 10103

FEINBERG, RICHARD EDWARD, economist; b. N.Y.C., Jan. 10, 1947; s. I. Robert and Lucille (Greenberg) F.; m. Diane Bette Gotkin, Dec. 24, 1977; 1 dau., Sonya. B.A., Brown U., 1969; Ph.D., Stanford U., 1978. Vol. Peace Corps, Chile, 1969-71; economist U.S. Dept. Treasury, Washington, 1975-77; mem. policy planning staff U.S. Dept. State, Washington, 1977-80; sr. economist banking com. Ho. of Reps., Washington, 1982; v.p. Overseas Devel. Council, Washington, 1983—; research fellow Brookings Instn., 1974-75; adj. prof. Georgetown U., 1980—. Author: The Intemperate Zone: The Third World Challenge to U.S. Foreign Policy, 1983, Subsidizing Success: The Export-Import Bank in the U.S. Economy, 1982; editor: Central America: International Dimensions of the Crisis, 1982. Woodrow Wilson fellow, 1980-81; Council of Fgn. Relations fellow, 1981-82. Address: 1717 Massachusetts Ave NW Washington DC 20036

FEINBERG, WALTER, educator; b. Boston, Aug. 22, 1937; s. Nathan and Adeline (Weisberger) F.; m. Eleanor Kemler, June 21, 1964; children—Deborah Lee, Jill Suzanne. A.B., Boston U., 1960, Ph.D., 1966. Asst. prof. edn. Oakland U., 1965-67; asst. prof. philosophy edn. U. Ill., Urbana, 1967-70, asso. prof. ednl. policy studies, 1970-75, prof. ednl. policy studies, 1975—, prof. Bur. Ednl. Research, 1977-80, dir. Medicine and Society Faculty Program, 1981—. Author: Reason and Rhetoric, 1975 (One of Outstanding Books in Edn., Choice mag. 1975), Understanding Education, 1983; Co-editor: Work, Technology and Education, 1975, Knowledge and Values in Social and Educational Research, 1982; asso. editor: Ednl. Theory, 1969—; corr. editor: Theory and Society, 1977; editor: Equality and Social Policy, 1978. U. Ill. faculty fellow, 1969; Nat. Inst. Edn. grantee, 1976. Mem. Philosophy Edn. Soc., Am. Ednl. Studies Assn. (pres. 1979), Am. Philosophy Assn. Jewish. Home: 1704 Henry St Champaign IL 61820 Office: 188 Education Bldg U Ill Urbana IL 61801

FEINBERG, WILFRED, fed. judge; b. N.Y.C., June 22, 1920; s. Jac and Eva (Wolin) F.; m. Shirley Marcus, June 23, 1946; children—Susan, Jack, Jessica. B.A., Columbia, 1940, LL.B., 1946. Bar: N.Y. bar 1947. Law clk. U.S. dist. judge, 1947-49; asso. firm Kaye, Scholer, Fierman & Hays, N.Y.C., 1949-53; mem. firm McGoldrick, Dannett, Horowitz & Golub, N.Y.C., 1953-61; dep. supt. N.Y. State Banking Dept., 1958; U.S. judge So. Dist. N.Y., 1961-66, Ct. Appeals 2d Circuit, 1966-80, chief judge, 1980—. Editor-in-chief: Columbia Law Rev, 1946. Served with AUS, 1942-45. Mem. Assn. Bar City N.Y., Am. Bar Assn., N.Y. County Lawyers Assn., Am. Judicature Soc., Phi Beta Kappa. Home: 15 Pasadena Pl Mount Vernon NY 10552 Office: US Courthouse Foley Sq New York NY 10007

FEINDEL, WILLIAM HOWARD, neurosurgeon, educator; b. Bridgewater, N.S., Can., July 12, 1918; s. Robert Ronald and Annie (Swansburg) F.; m. Faith Lyman, July 28, 1945; children: Christopher, Alexander, Patricia, Janet, Michael, Anna. B.A., Acadia U., 1939, D.Sc. (hon.), 1963; Rhodes scholar, Nova Scotia and Merton Coll., Oxford (Eng.) U., 1939; M.Sc. in Physiology, Dalhousie U., 1942; M.D., C.M., McGill U., 1945; D.Phil. in Neuroanatomy, Oxford (Eng.) U., 1949. Diplomate: Am. Bd. Neurol. Surgery. Demonstrator biology Acadia U., 1937-39; demonstrator physiology Dalhousie U., 1940-42, Banting Found. research grantee, 1941; fellow neuropathology Montreal Neurol. Inst., 1943-44; research asst., demonstrator anatomy Oxford U., 1946-49; demonstrator neurosurgery, then lectr. McGill U. Sch. Medicine, 1951-55, chmn. dept. neurology and neurosurgery, 1972-77; research fellow neurophysiology Montreal Neurol. Inst., 1951-52, Reford postgrad. fellow, 1953-55; prof. surgery U. Sask. Med. Sch., also Univ. Hosp., 1955-59; 1st William Cone prof. neurosurgery McGill U. Med. Sch., 1959—; neurosurgeon-in-chief Montreal Neurol. Hosp., 1963-72, dir. gen., 1972—, v.p. bd. corp., 1972; founder, dir. Cone Lab. Neurosurg. Research, 1959—; dir. Montreal Neurol. Inst., 1972—; attending neurosurgeon Catherine Booth Hosp., 1950-73; neurologist and neurosurgeon-in-chief Royal Victoria Hosp., 1972—; cons. neurosurgeon Sherbrooke Gen. Hosp.; Sigma Xi lectr., 1969; guest lectr. U. Calif. at Los Angeles and San Francisco, U. Sask., Yale, Columbia, U. Oreg., U. Vt., Dalhousie U., U. Toronto, U. Giessen, Queen's U., N.Y. U., U. Padua, U. Milan, U. Tokyo, U. Hakkaido; dir. 4th Can. Congress of Neurol. Scis.; mem. Conseil de la politique scientifique Govt. Que., 1974-77; cons. neuroscis. WHO, 1974—. Editor: (with A. Dawson) Prospect and Retrospect in Neurology, 1944, Medical Aspects of Traffic Accidents, 1955, Memory, Learning and Language: The Physical Basis of Mind, 1960, Thomas Willis: The Anatomy of the Brain and Nerves, 1965; Editorial bd. jour.: Stroke, 1972-75, Jour. History of Medicine. Bd. curators Osler Library, McGill U., 1965—; bd. dirs. McGill Hosps. Joint Inst. Decorated Order of Can.; NRC grad. fellow, 1949-50. Fellow Royal Soc. Can., Royal Coll. Physicians and Surgeons Can. (com. on neurosurgery 1970—), A.C.S. (adv. com. neurosurgery 1970); mem. Inst. Nat. Neurol. Mexico (hon.), Am. Assn. Neurol. Surgeons, Soc. Neurol. Surgeons, Am. Acad. Neurol. Surgery (pres. 1975), Am. Acad. Neurology, A.A.A.S., Am. Neurol. Assn. (v.p. 1975), Am. Assn. History of Medicine, Royal Soc. Medicine, Montreal Medico-Chir. Soc. (pres. 1975), Anat. Soc. Gt. Britain and Ireland, Montreal Neurol. Soc., Canadian Neurosurg. Soc. (v.p. 1966, pres. 1968-69), Vancouver Med. Assn. (hon.), Alpha Omega Alpha. Home: 4021 Avenue de Vendôme Montreal PQ H4A 3N2 Canada Office: 3801 University St Montreal PQ H3A 2B4 Canada

FEINGOLD, DAVID SIDNEY, microbiology educator; b. Chelsea, Mass., Nov. 15, 1922; s. Louis Edward and Miriam (Young) F.; m. Batia Babette Haber, Nov. 15, 1949; children: Oded, Anat, Michele. B.S., MIT, 1944; Ph.D., Hebrew U., Jerusalem, Israel, 1956. Chemist Lucidol Corp., Buffalo, 1944; jr. research biochemist U. Calif. at Berkeley, 1957-60; asst. prof. biology U. Pitts., 1960-62, asso. prof., 1962-65, prof., 1965—; prof. microbiology Sch. Medicine, 1966—. Contbr. articles to profl. jours. Served with USNR, 1944-46. Recipient State of Israel prize in natural sci., 1957, Career Devel. award NIH, 1965-75. Mem. Am. Chem. Soc., Am. Soc. Biol. Chemists, Am. Soc. Microbiology, Infectious Disease Soc. Am. Home: 6420 Bartlett St Pittsburgh PA 15217

FEINGOLD, HENRY LEO, history educator; b. Mannheim, Germany, Feb. 6, 1931; s. Marcus and Frieda (Singer) F.; m. Vera Schiff, Feb. 7, 1954; children: Margo Rachel, Judith Eva. B.A., Bklyn. Coll., 1953, M.A., 1954; Ph.D., N.Y.U., 1966. Asst. prof. CUNY, 1967-68; prof. history Baruch Coll., 1978—, chmn. Faculty Seminar on Holocaust; lectr. in field. Author: The Politics of Rescue: The Roosevelt Administration and the Holocaust 1938-45, 1970 (Leon Jolson award, Commentary Book Club selection), Zion in America: The Jewish Experience from Colonial Times to the Present, 1971 (Commentary Book Club selection), A Midrash on American Jewish History, 1982; contbr. articles to profl. jours.; editor: Am. Jewish History; mem. editorial bd.: YIVO Ann., Shoah, Reconstructionist. Served with U.S. Army, 1954-57, 61. Mem. Am. Jewish History Soc. (acad. council), Jewish History Soc. N.Y. (exec. com.), Assn. Jewish Studies (exec. com.). Jewish. Home: 280 9th Ave New York NY 10001 Office: 17 Lexington Ave New York NY 10010

FEINGOLD, MICHAEL, critic translator, stage director; b. Chgo., May 5, 1945; s. Bernard C. and Elsie F. B.A., Columbia U., 1966; M.F.A., Yale U., 1970. Drama critic Columbia Daily Spectator, N.Y.C., 1963-66; founding editor Yale-Theatre, 1968; editor Winter House Ltd., 1969-72; lit. mgr. Yale Repertory, 1972-76; artistic dir. Theatre-at-Noon, N.Y.C., 1975-76; lit. dir. Guthrie Theatre, Mpls., 1977-79; drama critic Village Voice, N.Y.C., 1971—. Translator: Brecht's Rise and Fall of the City of Mahagonny, 1974, Happy End, 1972, Ibsen's When We Dead Awaken, 1971, Moliere's The Bourgeois Gentleman, 1974, Diderot's Rameau's Nephew, 1976, Thomas Berhard Force of Habit, 1976; others; operas Offenbach, Donizetti; dir. Off-Broadway plays, Yale Theatre, Guthrie Theatre; Two-Part Inventions, Circle Repertory Theater, 1976, Goodman Theatre, Chgo., 1979, Speakeasy, Am. Place Theatre, 1983; contbr. articles: New Republic, N.Y. Sunday Times, Saturday Rev. Lit. Guggenheim fellow, 1978. Office: care Village Voice 842 Broadway New York NY 10003

FEINGOLD, S. NORMAN, psychologist; b. Worcester, Mass., Feb. 2, 1914; s. William and Aida (Salit) F.; m. Marie Goodman, Mar. 24, 1947; children: Elizabeth Anne, Margaret Ellen, Deborah Carol, Marilyn Nancy. A.B., Ind. U., 1937; M.A., Clark U., 1940; Ed.D., Boston U., 1948; LL.D., Edward Waters Coll., Saints Coll. Dir. vocat. service, also ednl. and vocat. dir. Hecht. Neighborhood House, Boston, 1940-43; exec. dir. Boston Jewish Vocat. Service and Work Adjustment Center, 1946-58; nat. dir. B'nai B'rith Career and Counseling Services, Washington, 1958-80, pres. Nat. Career Counseling Services, 1980—; pvt. practice, 1980—; faculty Internat. Coll.; exec. adviser Rehab. Services, Boston, 1953-58; dir. ednl. and vocat. workshop United Cerebral Palsy of Greater Boston, Inc., 1957-58; cons. to Scholarships, Fellowships and Loans News Service, Social Security Adminstrn., 1962—; instr., spl. lectr. Boston U., 1951-58; profl. lectr. Am. U. Rehab. Counseling Adv. Panel, 1963-65; mem. Am. Bd. Counseling Services, 1962-65, 70—. Author: It Pays to Advertise, 1975, Occupations and Careers, 1969, The Vocational Expert in the Social Security Disability Program, 1969, A Counselor's Handbook, 1972; past editor: Counselors Information Service; author: Counseling for Careers in the 80's, 1979, Whither Counseling, 1981, Making It on Your Own. A Guide to Financial Success, 1981, Emerging Careers: New Occupations for the Year Two Thousand and Beyond, 1983, The Professional and Trade Association Job Finder, 1983, Getting Ahead: A Woman's Guide to Career Sources, 1983. Chmn. Gov.'s Council on Aging, 1956-58, Washington Bus.-Industry Group, 1963-64; mem. Pres.'s Com. on Employment Handicapped, 1950—; mem. adv. com. Nat. Health Council; mem. Nat. Home Study Accrediting Commn.; chmn. human relations com. Dept. Agr. Grad. Sch.; mem. profl. adv. bd. Epilepsy Found. Served from pvt. to 1st lt. AUS, 1943-46; ETO and PTO. Recipient Community Service award B'nai B'rith, 1957, Brotherhood and Americanization award, 1958, Eminent Career award Nat. Capital Personnel and Guidance Assn. Fellow Am. Psychol. Assn.; mem. Greater Boston Personnel and Guidance Assn. (pres. 1952-53), Am. Personnel and Guidance Assn. (pres. 1974-75), Mass., Eastern psychol. assns., Nat. Vocat. Guidance Assn. (pres. 1968-69), Am. Assn. Adult Edn., AAAS, Am. Gerontol. Assn., Am. Assn. Marriage and Family Counselors (clin.), Internat. Council Psychologists, Nat. Rehab. Assn., Phi Delta Kappa. Clubs: Torch, New Century (dir. 1957-58). Home: 9707 Singleton Dr Bethesda MD 20034 Office: 1522 K St NW Suite 336 Washington DC 20005 *Any success I may have attained is because of conscientiousness, a love of life, a high energy level, a supportive family, close friends, and being an optimist by temperament and conviction. I believe in people and the tremendous potential of all people. To me, everyone is a Very Important Person, who can make a contribution. My premise is that our most precious resource is people, and everything we do individually or collectively now or in the future depends on that conviction and acting accordingly.*

FEININGER, ANDREAS BERNHARD LYONEL, photographer; b. Paris, France, Dec. 27, 1906; s. Lyonel and Julia (Lilienfeld) F.; m. Gertrud Wysse Hägg, Aug. 30, 1933; 1 son, Tomas G.A. Ed. schs., in Germany; studied under, Walther Gropius at the Bauhaus, Weimar, Germany, 1922-25; student architecture, Staatliche Bauschule, in Zerbst, Germany, passed summa cum laude, 1928; learned trade of a cabinet maker at the Bauhaus, 1922-25; passed journeyman examination, 1925. Practiced architecture, Dessau and Hamburg, Germany, 1928-31; worked with LeCorbusier, Paris, 1932-33. Profl. photographer specializing in archtl. and indsl. photography, Stockholm, Sweden, 1933-39; freelance photographer, Black Star Photo Agy., N.Y.C., 1940; under own name, 1941-43; staff photographer specializing in "on location" assignments, Life mag., 1943-62, One-man exhbn. of photographs, Smithsonian Instn., 1963, one-man comprehensive retrospective exhbn., Internat. Center of Photography, 1976; Author of 38 books. Charter mem. Am. Soc. Mag. Photographers; mem. Explorers Club. Research work in telephotography and graphic control processes. Exptl. photography in connection with lenses of very long and very short focal lengths. Home: 18 Elizabeth Ln New Milford CT 06776

FEININGER, THEODORE LUX, artist; b. Berlin, Germany, June 11, 1910; s. Charles Lyonel and Julia (Lilienfeld) F.; m. Patricia Randall, Dec. 17, 1954; children: Lucas, Conrad, Charles. Grad., Bauhaus, Dessau, Germany, 1929. Instr. Sarah Lawrence Coll., 1950-52; lectr. drawing and painting Harvard U., 1953-62; instr. drawing and painting Boston Fine Arts Mus. Sch., 1962-75. Author: Lyonel Feininger: City at the Edge of the World, 1965, Photographs of the 20s and 30s (illustrated catalogue), 1980; Exhibitions include Am. Realists and Magic Realists, Mus. Modern Art, N.Y.C., 1943, Revolution and Tradition in Modern Am. Art, Bklyn. Mus., 1951, Whitney Mus. Am. Art Annual, N.Y.C., Am. Painters, M.I.T., 1954, Retrospective, Busch-Reisinger Mus., 1962, Wheaton Coll., 1973, Wamsutta Club, New Bedford, Mass., 1974, Prakapas Gallery, N.Y.C., 1980; represented in permanent collections at, Mus. Modern Art, N.Y.C., Busch-Reisinger Mus. and Fogg Art Mus., Harvard U., Altonaer Mus., Hamburg, W.Ger., Schleswig-Holstein Landes Mus., Mus. Folkwang, Essen, W.Ger. Served with U.S. Army, 1942-45. Mem. Westport Art Group. Democrat. Address: 22 Arlington St Cambridge MA 02140 *The practice and teaching of art has shown me that I must seek progress on the basis of understanding and assimilating tradition; that every individual incorporates both revolutionary and conservative tendencies; and that the task of the individual lies in assessing and acting upon his findings, his own proportionate share of these two conflicting trends. I am Society, and Society cannot do without me.*

FEINSTEIN, ALLEN LEWIS, lawyer; b. N.Y.C., Apr. 18, 1929; s. Jacob and Kate (Goldberg) F.; m. Charlesa Joan Wolfe, Dec. 14, 1957. A.B., CCNY, 1949; LL.B., Columbia U., 1952. Bar: N.Y. 1952, Ariz. 1960, U.S. Supreme Ct. 1960. Practice in, N.Y.C., 1953-59, Phoenix, 1960—; law clk. Surrogate Frankenthaler, 1953-55; asso. Proskauer Rose Goetz & Mendelsohn, 1955-59; law clk. Supreme Ct. Justice Charles C. Bernstein, Phoenix, 1959-61; 1st adminstrv. dir. Supreme Ct. Ariz., 1961-64; individual practice law, 1964—; partner firm Daughton Feinstein & Wilson, Phoenix, 1972—; Mem. Phoenix Housing Code Com., 1968; vice chmn. adv. com. State Legislative com. on Medicaid; mem. Phoenix Charter Review Com., 1969; mem. exec. com. Phoenix Sister City Commn., 1973-75. Bd. dirs. Meml. Hosp. Phoenix, chmn., 1973-76; also chmn. Meml. Hosp. Found.; bd. dirs. Community Council, 1970-76; bd. dirs., chmn. council trustees, mem. exec. com. Ariz. Hosp. Assn., 1981—; Ariz. del. to nat. conf. governing bds. Served with USAF, 1952-53. Mem. Am. Arbitration Assn., Am., Ariz., Maricopa County bar assns., Am. Judicature Soc., State Bar Ariz. (chmn. com. civil practice and procedure 1971-74, mem. ethics com., chmn. long range com. 1980), Phi Beta Kappa, Phi Delta Phi. Democrat. Jewish religion. Club: University of Phoenix (pres. 1971-72). Home: 2110 Encanto Dr SW Phoenix AZ 85007 Office: 100 W Washington St Phoenix AZ 85003

FEINSTEIN, ALVAN RICHARD, physician; b. Phila., Dec. 4, 1925; s. Joel B. and Bella (Ukasz) F.; m. Linda Louise Marean, Oct. 20, 1968; children: Miriam Anne, Daniel Joel Bennett. B.S., U. Chgo., 1947, M.S. in Math, 1948, M.D., 1952; M.A. (hon.), Yale U., 1969. Intern, then resident Yale-New Haven Hosp., 1952-54; research fellow Rockefeller Inst., 1954-55; resident Columbia-Presbyn. Med. Center, N.Y.C., 1955-56; clin. dir. Irvington House, N.Y.C., 1956-62; instr., then asst. prof. N.Y. U. Sch. Medicine, 1956-62; chief clin. pharmacology VA Hosp., West Haven, Conn., 1962-64, chief clin. biostatistics, 1964-74; mem. faculty Sch. Medicine, Yale U., 1962—, prof. medicine and epidemiology, 1969—, dir. clin. scholar program, 1974—; chief Eastern Research Support Center, VA, 1967-74; Pres. New Haven area chpt. Assn. Computing Machinery, 1968-69. Author: Clinical Judgment, 1967, Clinical Biostatistics, 1977; editor: Jour. Chronic Diseases; also articles. Served with AUS, 1944-46. Recipient Francis G. Blake award for outstanding teaching Yale Med. Sch., 1969. Mem. Assn. Am. Physicians, Am. Soc. Clin. Investigation, Am. Epidemiol. Soc., A.C.P., Inst. Medicine, Am. Fedn. Clin. Research, Am. Soc. Clin. Pharmacology Therapeutics, Am. Statis. Assn., Assn. Computing Machinery, Biometric Soc., Am. Heart Assn., Am. Assn. History Medicine, Alpha Omega Alpha. Home: 45 Edgehill Rd New Haven CT 06511 Office: 333 Cedar St New Haven CT 06510

FEINSTEIN, DIANNE, mayor San Francisco; b. San Francisco, June 22, 1933; d. Leon and Betty (Rosenburg) Goldman; m. Bertram Feinstein, Nov. 11, 1962; 1 dau., Katherine Anne. B.S., Stanford U., 1955. Intern in pub. affairs Coro Found., San Francisco, 1955-56; asst. to Calif. Indsl. Welfare Commn., Los Angeles, also San Francisco, 1956-57; mem., vice-chmn. Calif. Women's Bd. Terms and Parole, Los Angeles, also San Francisco, 1962-66; chmn. San Francisco City and County Adv. Com. for Adult Detention, San Francisco, 1967-69; supr. City and County of San Francisco, 1970-78; mayor of San Francisco, 1978—; pres. San Francisco City and County Bd. Suprs., 1970-72, 74-76, 78; mem. Mayor's Com. on Crime, 1967-69; chmn. Environ. Mgmt. Task Force, Assn. Bay Govts., 1976-78, exec. com., del. gen. assembly, 1970—; bd. govs. Bay Area Council, 1972—; mem. Bay Conservation and Devel. Commn., 1973-78. Chmn. bd. regents Lone Mountain Coll., 1972-75. Recipient Women of Achievement award Bus. and Profl. Women's Clubs of San Francisco, 1970, Disting. Woman award San Francisco Examiner, 1970. Mem. Multi-Culture Inst. (dir.), Calif. Tomorrow, Bay Area Urban League, Planning and Conservation League, Friends of Earth, Chinese Culture Found., N. Central Coast Regional Commn. Clubs: Sierra, Propeller, Commonwealth. Office: Office of the Mayor City Hall San Francisco CA 94102

FEINSTEIN, IRWIN KEITH, mathematics educator; b. Chgo., Aug. 29, 1914; s. Mike and Rose (Katz) F.; m. Lena S. Zimmerman, July 9, 1954; children: Kate Ann, Ronald Sam. B.S., Ill. Inst. Tech., 1936; M.A., Northwestern U., 1946, Ph.D., 1952. Mem. faculty U. Ill. at Chgo., 1946—; prof. math. U. Ill. at Chgo. Circle, 1962—; Vis. prof. R.I. Coll., 1960, Northwestern U., 1962, Nat. Coll. Edn., 1956-62; cons. in field. Author: Analytic Geometry, 1949, College Algebra, 1957, rev. edit., 1981, Accountants Handbook, 1963, rev. edit., 1973, Spanish edit., 1976, New Math I, New Math II, New Math III, 1968-69; Contbr. articles to profl. jours. Served to lt. USCGR, 1942-46. Mem. AAUP, Math. Assn. Am., Nat. Council Tchrs. Math., Ill. Council Tchrs. Math. (Max Beberman award for contbns. to math. edn. 1983), Sch. Sci. and Math. Assn. Clubs: Men's Mathematics (Chgo.); Mem. B'nai B'rith (dir. Educator's Lodge 1968-71, 74-77, pres. Educator's Lodge 1972, 73. Home: 735 Lamon Ave Wilmette IL 60091 Office: Univ of Ill at Chicago Chicago IL 60607

FEINSTEIN, JOSEPH, electronics engineer, educator; b. N.Y.C., July 8, 1925; s. David and Edith (Morgenstern) F.; m. Elaine Cantor, Mar. 2, 1952; children: Susan, David, Jonathan. B.E.E., Cooper Union, 1944; M.A. in Physics, Columbia U., 1947, Ph.D., NYU, 1951. Mem. staff Nat. Bur. Standards, Washington, 1949-54; mem. tech. staff, dept. head Bell Telephone Labs., Murray Hill, N.J., 1954-59; dir. research S-F-D Labs., Union, N.J., 1959-64, exec. v.p., 1960-64; v.p. research Varian Assocs., Palo Alto, Calif., 1964-79; dir. electronics and phys. scis. Dept. Def., 1980-83; vis. prof., cons. in electronics Stanford U. (Calif.), 1983—. Editor, contbg. author: Crossed Field Microwave Devices, 1968, Electronics Engineers Handbook, 1975, 81. Fellow IEEE; mem. Nat. Acad. Engring. Patentee in communications, microwaves, electron tubes. Home: 2398 Branner Dr Menlo Park CA 94025 Office: Stanford U Dept Elec Engring Stanford CA

FEINSTEIN, SELWYN, reporter; b. N.Y.C., Nov. 5, 1931; s. Jacob and Kate (Goldberg) F.; m. Eve Gellerman, June 27, 1954; children—Jeffrey Eliot, Robert Michael. B.A., Queens Coll., N.Y.C., 1952; M.S. in Journalism, Columbia, 1953. Reporter United Press, Pitts., 1955-58; asso. editor Tide mag., 1958-59; sr. editor Printers' Ink mag., 1959-61; reporter Wall St. Jour., N.Y.C., 1962-66, in Hong Kong, 1966-67, in Chgo., 1967, N.Y.C., 1968—, asst. fgn. editor, 1977—. Contbg. editor: Ency. Americana, 1958-61. Served with AUS, 1953-55. Address: 73 Tompkins Ave Hastings-on-Hudson NY 10706

FEIR, DOROTHY JEAN, entomologist, physiologist, educator; b. St. Louis, Jan. 29, 1929; d. Alex R. and Lillian (Smith) F. B.S., U. Mich., 1950; M.S., U. Wyo., 1956; Ph.D., U. Wis., 1960. Instr. biology U. Baffalo, 1960-61; mem. faculty St. Louis U., 1961—, prof. biology, 1967—; mem. tropical medicine and parasitology study sect. NIH, 1980—. Editor: Environ. Entomology, 1977—. Mem. Entomol. Soc. Am., AAAS, Am. Physiol. Soc., N.Y. Acad. Sci., Mo. Acad. Sci., Sigma Xi, Soc. Devel. and Comparative Immunology. Office: Biology Dept St Louis U St Louis MO 63103

FEIRER, JOHN LOUIS, industrial education educator; b. Menomonie, Wis., Mar. 14, 1915; s. John and Elizabeth (Berger) F. B.S. in Vocat. Edn, Stout State Coll., 1936, postgrad., 1937; M.A., U. Minn., 1939; Ed.D., U. Okla., 1946. Tchr. indsl. arts Roosevelt Jr.

High Sch., Appleton, Wis., 1936-37, pub. schs., Mpls., 1938-40; asso. prof. indsl. edn. Western Mich. U., Kalamazoo, 1940-43, prof., head dept., 1946—; prof. U. Mich., 1941-42; founder, dir. Center of Metric Edn., Kalamazoo, 1972—; vis. prof. Stout State Coll., summers 1939, 40, 53, San Jose State Coll., summer 1950, U. Hawaii, summers 1955, 58, 60, Oreg. State U., summer 1956, U. P.R., summer 1967, Colo. State U., summer 1975; vis. prof., state tchr. trainer U. Hawaii, 1959-60; cons. vocat. edn. Chgo. Pub. Schs., 1963; cons. indsl. edn. Los Angeles Area Pub. Schs., 1963; cons. metro-rural visitor project State of Hawaii, 1965; cons. film div. Ency. Brit., 1965-69; cons. NASA, 1965-72; chmn. com. for space resources for high sch./indsl. arts resource units; mem. Com. on Nat. Tchr. Exams. for Indsl. Arts, 1948; mem. Mich. State Adv. Com. on Indsl. Edn., 1948-65; mem. conf. on indsl. edn. U.S. Office of Edn., 1950; mem. yearbook planning com. Am. Council on Indsl. Arts Tchr. Edn., 1963—; mem. workshop adv. com. Mid-Pacific Conf., Honolulu, 1971. Author: Industrial Arts Woodworking, 1977, SI Metric Handbook, General Metals, 1979, Spanish edit., 1970, Advanced Woodworking and Furniture Making, 1954, 4th edit., 1982, Woodworking for Industry, 1979, Metalwork, 1975, Cabinetmaking and Millwork, 1982; co-author: Basic Electricity, 1943, General Industrial Education, 1979, Machine Tool Metalworking, 1976, Carpentry and Building Construction, 1981, Furniture and Cabinet Making, 1983, Guide to Residential Carpentry, 1983; editor: Indsl. Edn. mag, 1959—. Phase officer Aviation Metalsmith Sch. Naval Air. Tech. Tng. Center, 1943-46; Norman, Okla. Named Man of Year in Indsl. Edn. Am. Council Indsl. Arts Tchr. Edn., 1963; recipient Apollo Achievement award NASA, 1969; Disting. Achievement award Ednl. Press Am., 1975; Disting. Faculty Scholar. Mem. Assn. Indsl. Tchr. Trainers (research com.), Am. Vocat. Assn. (editorial com. bull.), Mich. Indsl. Arts Assn., Mich. Ednl. Assn., Indsl. Arts Conf. Miss. Valley, Phi Delta Kappa, Epsilon Pi Tau (trustee, hon. citation 1967), Alpha Pi Omega. Home: 2433 Alta Vista Kalamazoo MI 49008

FEIRSTEIN, FREDERICK, poet, playwright, psychotherapist; b. N.Y.C., Jan. 2, 1940; s. Arnold and Nettie (Schechter) F.; m. Linda Bergton, June 9, 1963; 1 son, David Ben. B.A., U. Buffalo, 1960; M.A., N.Y. U., 1961. Author: poetry Survivors, 1974 (Outstanding Book award Choice), Manhattan Carnival, 1981; plays The Family Circle, 1973, Carnival, 1981, Fathering, 1982. Guggenheim fellow in poetry, 1979-80; recipient award in playwriting OADR, 1976, award in poetry CAPS, 1977, John Masefield award Poetry Soc. Am., 1977. Mem. P.E.N., Dramatists Guild, Writers Guild East, Poetry Soc. Am. Jewish. Address: 355 E 86th St New York NY 10028

FEISEL, LYLE DEAN, electrical engineering educator, university dean; b. Tama, Iowa, Oct. 16, 1935; s. Clyde Edward and Clara Maria (Ehlers) F.; m. Dorothy Evelyn Stadsvold, June 15, 1957; children: Patricia, Margaret, Kenneth. B.S. in E.E., Iowa State U., 1961, M.S., 1963, Ph.D., 1964. Registered profl. engr., S.D. Engr. Honeywell, Mpls., 1961-62; staff engr. IBM Corp., Poughkeepsie, N.Y., 1963, Burlington, Vt., 1967; mem. faculty of elec. engring. S.D. Sch. of Mines, Rapid City, 1964-83, head elec. engring. dept., 1975-83; dean Watson Sch., SUNY-Binghamton, 1983—; vis. prof. Cheng Kung U., Tainan, Taiwan, 1969-70; research engr. Northrop Corp., Los Angeles, 1974. Nat. Def fellow, 1961-64; recipient Ben Dasher award IEEE, 1983. Mem. IEEE Edn. Soc. (pres. 1978-79, Meritorious Service award 1981), Am. Soc. Engring. Edn. (dir. 1982-83), S.D. Renewable Energy Assn. (pres. 1979-81). Democrat. Lutheran. Office: University Center Binghamton State University New York Binghamton NY 13901

FEIST, GENE, theatre director; b. N.Y.C., Jan. 16, 1930; s. Henry and Hattie (Fishbein) F.; m. Elizabeth Owens, Feb. 10, 1957; children: Nicole, Gena. B.F.A., Carnegie Mellon U., 1951; M.A., N.Y. U., 1952. Lectr., cons. Debut as dir., Nashville, 1958, N.Y.C., 1962; founder, Fourth St. Theatre, N.Y.C.; producer, dir., Roundabout Theater Co., Inc., 1965—; also staged prodns., Cherry Lane Theatre, East End Theatre, Actors' Studio; Author: plays James Joyce's Dublin, 1975, Jocasta and Oedipus, 1970, also others; adapted: plays for stage including Ibsen's The Master Builder, Chekhov's Uncle Vanya, Pirandello's Naked, also others. Mem. Soc. Stage Dirs. and Choreographers, League N.Y. Theaters and Producers, League Resident Theatres. Club: Players (N.Y.C.). Office: 333 W 23d St New York NY 10011 *

FEIST, LEONARD, assn. exec.; b. Pelham, N.Y., Dec. 12, 1910; s. Leo and Bessie (Meyer) F.; m. Mary Regensburg, Dec. 6, 1937; children—Linda S. (Mrs. Montgomery), Betsy. Grad., Worcester Acad., 1928; B.A., Yale, 1932; postgrad., Columbia, 1933-34; Mus. Doc. (h.c.), Peabody Inst. Conservatory Music, 1976. Sec. Leo Feist, Inc., 1932-35; pres. Century Music Pub. Co.-Mercury Music Corp., 1936-56, Asso. Music Pubs., Inc., 1956-64; exec. v.p. Nat. Music Pubs. Assn., N.Y.C., 1965-76, pres., 1976—; Pres. Seaview (N.Y.) Assn., 1954-56. Contbr. articles to mags. Served with AUS, 1944-46. Mem. Nat. Music Council (dir. 1963-66, treas. 1966-71, pres. 1971-76, chmn. bd. 1976-79), Music Pubs. Assn. U.S. (pres. 1952-54), Nat. Acad. Popular Music (v.p.), Copyright Soc. U.S. (v.p. 1974-78), Am. Music Conf. (dir. 1978—), Phi Mu Alpha (hon. life), Sigma Alpha Iota (nat. arts associated mem.). Clubs: Internat. (Washington); Century Assn. (N.Y.C.). Home: 49 E 86th St New York NY 10028 Office: 110 E 59th St New York NY 10022

FEITLER, ROBERT, shoe company executive; b. Chgo., Nov. 19, 1930; s. Irwin and Bernice (Gombrig) F.; m. Joan Elden, May 30, 1957; children: Pamela, Robert, Richard, Dana. B.S., U. Pa., 1951; LL.B., Harvard U., 1954. Vice pres., gen. mgr. Scott Publs. div. Esquire, Inc., N.Y.C., 1958-64; pres., treas. Weyenberg Shoe Mfg. Co., Milw., 1964-72, pres., 1972—; chmn. Hynite Corp., 1975—; dir. Bank of Commerce., Parts Rebuilders, Inc. Trustee Smart Family Found. Served with U.S. Army, 1954-56. Jewish. Clubs: University, Milwaukee Athletic (Milw.); Harvard (N.Y.C.). Home: 1712 E Cumberland Blvd Whitefish Bay WI 53211 Office: 234 E Resevoir St Milwaukee WI 53201

FEIWEL, JEAN LESLIE, editorial director; b. N.Y.C., Feb. 5, 1953; d. Henry and Maria (Weschler) F. B.A., Sarah Lawrence Coll., 1976. Asst. to mng. editor Avon Books, N.Y.C., 1976-77, asst. to children's book editor, 1977, sr. editor, children's books, 1977-81, editorial dir. books for young readers, 1981-83; editorial dir., div. v.p. Secondary Book Group, Scholastic, Inc., N.Y.C., 1983—. Mem. Children's Book Council (dir. 1982—), Am. Assn. Pubs. (dir. intellectual freedom com. 1983—). Office: Scholastic Inc 730 Broadway New York NY 10003

FEJER, ANDREW AKOS, mechanical engineer, educator; b. Budapest, Hungary, June 4, 1913; came to U.S., 1938, naturalized, 1948; s. Eugene and Ilona (Haas) F; m. Edith Behal, June 12, 1938; children: Theodore William, Mark Eugene, Ilona Anne. M.E., Czech Tech. U., 1936; M.S., Calif. Inst. Tech., 1939, Ph.D., 1945. Mech. engr. Skoda Works, Prague, Czechoslovakia, 1936- 38; research fellow Hydraulics Machinery Lab., Calif. Inst. Tech., 1939- 41, instr. mech. and aero. engring., 1941-45; research engr. aircraft engine div. Packard Motor Car Co., 1945-48; prof., chmn. depts. aero. and mech. engring. U. Toledo, 1948-58; prof., dir. mech. engring. dept. Ill. Inst. Tech., 1958-64, chmn. mech. and aerospace engring. dept., 1964-71, prof. emeritus, 1978—; sr. advisor gas turbine research Inst. Gas Tech., 1978—; lectr. aeros. U. Mich., 1950-51; vis. prof. Inst. Engring Scis., U. Nancy, France, 1967, Nat. Inst. Applied Scis., Lyon, France, 1968; vis. lectr. U.S. Dept. State ednl. and cultural exchange prof., Equatorial Africa, 1969; U.S. del. to 1st Internat. Symposium on Air-breathing Engines, Marseille, France, 1972; engring. cons. Chevalier dan l'ordre des Palmes Academiques (France). Fellow ASME (internat. div.); asso. fellow AIAA (adv. group aerospace research and devel. NATO 1972); mem. Am. Assn. Engring. Edn., N.Y. Acad. Scis., AAAS, Sigma Xi, Phi Kappa Phi, Tau Beta Pi, Pi Tau Sigma. Home: 122 LeMoyne Pkwy Oak Park IL 60302 Office: 3110 S State St Chicago IL 60616

FELCH, WILLIAM CAMPBELL, internist, editor; b. Lakewood, Ohio, Nov. 14, 1920; s. Don Harold Willison and Beth (Campbell) F.; m. Nancy Cook Dean, Aug. 4, 1945; children: Patricia Felch Monokoski, William Campbell, Robert Dean. B.A., Princeton U., 1942; M.D., Columbia U., 1945. Diplomate: Nat. Bd. Med. Examiners, Am. Bd. Internal Medicine. Intern St. Luke's Hosp., N.Y.C., 1945-46, resident in internal medicine, 1948-51; practice medicine specializing in internal medicine, Rye, N.Y., 1951—; chief staff United Hosp., Port Chester, N.Y., 1975-77; med. dir. Osborn Home, Rye, N.Y., 1979—. Author: Aspiration and Achievement, 1981; editor: The Internist, 1975—, Acme Almanac, 1978—. Trustee N.Y. Med. Coll., Valhalla, 1971-73. Served to capt. U.S. Army, 1946-48. Recipient award of merit N.Y. State Soc. Internal Medicine, 1976; named Internist of Distinction Internal Medicine Soc. N.Y. County, 1973. Mem. ACP, Alliance for Continuing Med. Edn. (exec. v.p.), Am. Soc. Internatl Medicine (pres. 1973-74), Inst. of Medicine of Nat. Acad. Scis., AMA (chmn. council on legislation 1977-79). Republican. Club: Am. Yacht (Rye, N.Y.). Home: 105 Grandview Ave Rye NY 10580 Office: 265 Purchase St Rye NY 10580

FELCHLIN, JAMES ALOIS, investment banker; b. Los Angeles, Dec. 29, 1919; s. Alois H. and Clay (Dare) F.; m. Diane Gordon Oliver, Oct. 3, 1975; children—James Christopher, John Timothy, Clay Monica, Dare Valerie. A.B., U. Calif., Berkeley, 1941; postgrad., Wharton Sch., U. Pa., U. Calif. grad. bus. extension. Account exec. Dean Witter & Co., San Francisco, 1946-53; partner F.S. Smithers Co., San Francisco and N.Y.C., 1953-65; with Dean Witter Reynolds Inc. and predecessor, 1966—, mng. dir., San Francisco, also dir.; dir. Tejon Agrl. Corp. Mem. exec. bd. Bay Area council Boy Scouts Am.; bd. dirs. Comprehensive Health Services, San Francisco.; trustee, mem. exec. com. World Affairs Council of No. Calif. Served to maj. USAAF, 1941-45. Decorated Air medal. Mem. Sigma Chi. Republican. Episcopalian. Clubs: San Francisco Golf, Villa Taverna, Pacific Union (San Francisco); Racquet and Tennis (N.Y.C.). Home: Armsby Circle Ross CA 94957 Office: 101 California St San Francisco CA 94111

FELD, ALAN DAVID, lawyer; b. Dallas, Nov. 13, 1936; s. Henry R. and Rose (Scissors) F.; m. Anne Sanger, June 1, 1957; children: Alan David, Elizabeth S., John L. B.A., So. Methodist U., 1957, LL.B., 1960. Bar: Tex. bar 1960. Since practiced in Dallas; partner Akin, Gump, Strauss, Hauer & Feld, 1966—; lectr. Southwestern U. Med. Sch.; dir. Knoll Internat. Inc., Collin Creek Bank. Contbr. articles to legal jours. Bd. dirs. Dallas Day Nursery Assn., Timberlawn Found. Mem. Am., Tex., D.C., Dallas bar assns., Salesmanship Club, Phi Delta Phi. Clubs: Dallas, Royal Oaks Country. Home: 4235 Bordeaux St Dallas TX 75205 Office: 2800 Republic Bank Bldg Dallas TX 75201

FELD, ALAN L., lawyer, educator; b. N.Y.C., Feb. 5, 1940; s. Max and Rachel F.; m. Marcia Marker, Dec. 30, 1962; children: William, Harold, Samuel. A.B., Columbia U., 1960; LL.B., Harvard U., 1963. Bar: N.Y. 1963, Mass. 1974. Practiced law, N.Y.C., 1964-71; asso. prof. law Boston U., 1971-74, prof., 1974—; vis. prof. U. Pa., 1977-78. Author: Tax Policy and Corporate Concentration, 1982. Mem. ABA, Am. Law Inst. Home: 5 Hamlin Rd Newton MA 02159 Office: 765 Commonwealth Ave Boston MA 02215

FELD, ELIOT, dancer, choreographer; b. Bklyn., July 5, 1942; s. Benjamin Noah and Alice (Posner) F. Student, High Sch. Performing Arts, N.Y.C., 1954-58. Debut as child prince in: The Nutcracker, N.Y.C. Ballet, 1954; mem. cast: West Side Story, 1958; with co.: I Can Get It for You Wholesale, 1962; began dancing with, Am. Ballet Theatre, 1963; later resident choreographer, Am. Ballet Theatre; solo dance appearances in: Les Noces, Wind in the Mountains, Dark Elegies, Fancy Free, Billy the Kid, Helen of Troy, Giselle; founder, Am. Ballet Co., 1968; subsequently prin. dancer, mgr., chief choreographer, Am. Ballet Co., 1969-71; with, Bklyn. Acad. Music, two seasons; guest choreographer, N. Am. and Europe, 1971-73; founder, artistic dir., chief choreographer: The Feld Ballet, N.Y.C., 1973; founder, New Ballet Sch, 1978; Choreographed: Harbinger, 1967, At Midnight, 1967, Meadowlark, 1968, Intermezzo, 1969, Cortege Burlesque, 1969, Pagan Spring, 1969, Early Songs, 1970, Cortege Parisien, 1970, The Consort, 1970, A Poem Forgotten, 1970, Romance, 1971, Theatre, 1971, The Gods Amused, 1971, A Soldier's Tale, 1971, Eccentrique, 1971, Winters Court, 1972, Jive, 1973, Sephardic Song, 1974, Tzaddik, 1974, The Real McCoy, 1974, Mazurka, 1975, Excursions, 1975, Impromptu, 1976, Variations on America, 1977, A Footstep of Air, 1977, Santa Fe Saga, 1978, La Vida, 1978, Danzon Cubano, 1978, Half-Time, 1978, Papillon, 1979, Circa, 1980, Anatomic Balm, 1980, Scenes for the Theater, 1980, Scenes, 1980, Play Bach, 1981, Over the Pavement, 1982, Straw Hearts, 1982, Summer's Lease, 1983, Three Dances, 1983, Adieu, 1984, The Jig Is Up, 1984. Address: Feld Ballet 890 Broadway New York NY 10003

FELD, FRITZ, actor, writer, dir.; b. Berlin, Germany, Oct. 15, 1900; came to U.S., 1923, naturalized, 1930; s. Heinrich and Martha (Guttman) F.; m. Virginia Christine, Nov. 10, 1940; children—Steven, Danny. Ed., Gymnasium, Germany, 1907-17. Chmn. So. Calif. chpt. Am. Nat. Theatre ANTA, 1968—. Performer in: The Miracle, Prof. Max Reinhardt Theaters, Berlin, 1917-23, Century Theatre, N.Y.C., 1923-27; actor, writer, dir., Hollywood motion picture studios, 1923—; actor, dir.: Grand Hotel, Nat. Theatre, 1930—, Berlin, George M. Cohan Theatre, N.Y.C., 1931—. Recipient award for 60 years in movies, 1977, Nat. Film Soc.; named KNX Radio Citizen of Week, hon. mayor of Brentwood Calif. Brentwood C. of C., 1979. Mem. Screen Actors Guild (dir. 1970—, chmn. Hollywood Mus. project com. 1976—), Acad. Motion Picture Arts and Scis. Community theater named in his honor. Address: 12348 Rochedale Ln Los Angeles CA 90049

FELD, IRVIN, circus producer; b. Hagerstown, Md., May 9, 1918; s. Isaac and Jennie (Mansh) F.; m. Adele Schwartz, Mar. 5, 1946 (dec.); children—Karen, Kenneth. Grad. high sch.; hon. degree, Lehigh U., 1976. Pres. Super Music City, 1940-56; pres., producer Super Attractions, Inc., Washington, 1954-67; producer Carter Barron Amphitheatre Summer Series for Dept. Interior, Washington, 1954-74; personal mgr. Paul Anka, 1957-64; pres., producer, chief exec. officer Ringling Bros.-Barnum & Bailey Combined Shows, Inc., Washington, 1968-82; chmn., chief exec. officer Ice Follies & Holiday on Ice, Inc., 1979-82; owner, chmn., chief exec. officer, producer Ringling Bros.-Barnum & Bailey Combined Shows, Inc and Ice Follies & Holiday on Ice, Inc., 1982—; producer Walt Disney's Ice Shows, 1981—, Siegfried & Roy, Superstars of Magic, Frontier Hotel, Las Vegas, Nev., 1981—, Broadway play Barnum, 1980; hon. dir. Barnett Bank of Winter Haven N.A.; mem. Met. Washington Bd. Trade.; Pres. Amity Club of Washington, 1951; Founder Ringling Brothers and Barnum & Bailey Clown Coll., 1968. Contbr. to: The Language of Show Biz, 1973, Variety newspaper. Mem. endowment com. Circus World Mus.; adv. council Wilmer Opthalmol. Inst., Johns Hopkins U. Sch. Medicine. Recipient Champion of Liberty award Anti-Defamation League of B'nai B'rith, 1984. Clubs: Nat. Press Club, Variety, Friars, Circus Saints and Sinners., Woodmont Country. Office: 3201 New Mexico Ave NW Washington DC 20016 *I have found that if you give the public more than their money's worth while maintaining a high standard of quality they will respond fully with their support. I have always insisted on giving the paying public more than they expect.*

FELD, LIPMAN GOLDMAN, credit agency executive; b. Kansas City, Mo., Jan. 16, 1914; s. Emel and Celia (Goldman) F.; m. Anne Brozman, Apr. 30, 1942; children: Robert David, Celia Ann (Mrs. Terry Harms). B.S. cum laude, Harvard, 1935; J.D., U. Mo., 1935-38. Bar: Mo. 1938. Asso. firm Butler Disman, Kansas City, 1938-41; v.p., counsel Century Acceptance Corp., Kansas City, 1946-79, sr. v.p., 1973-79; v.p. CenCor Inc., Kansas City, 1968-79; counsellor to ofcl. child learning facilities, income tax offices, colls. of med. and dental assts., profl. practice mgmt. services, temporary labor centers, consumer finance offices. Author: Harrassment and Other Collection Taboos, 1976, Bad Checks and Fraudulent Identity, 1978; contbr. numerous articles profl. jours. Served to capt. AUS, 1941-46. Mem. Mo. Bar Assn., Am. Jewish Com., Am. Jewish Hist. Soc. Jewish (hon. trustee congregation B'nai Jehudah). Clubs: 40 Year Ago, Harvard of Kansas City. Home: 1233 W 69th St Kansas City MO 64113 *Shyness means oblivion; it does not hurt to ask.*

FELD, MICHAEL STEPHEN, educator; b. N.Y.C., Nov. 11, 1940; s. Albert and Lillian R. Norwalk; m. Frances Aschheim, Mar. 2, 1980; children—David A., Jonathan R. S.B. in Humanities and Sci, M.I.T., 1963, S.M. in Physics, 1963, Ph.D., 1967. Postdoctoral fellow M.I.T., Cambridge, 1967-68, asst. prof., 1968-73, asso. prof., 1973-79, prof. physics, 1979—, dir. spectroscopy lab., 1976—, dir. regional laser center, 1979—. Editorial bd.: Laser Focus Mag; co-editor: Fundamental and Applied Laser Physics, 1973, Coherent Nonlinear Optics, 1980. Alfred P. Sloan research fellow, 1973; recipient Disting. Service award M.I.T. Minority Community, 1980. Fellow Am. Optical Soc., Sigma Xi; mem. Am. Phys. Soc. Condr. research laser saturation spectroscopy. First exptl. demonstration of superradiance. Home: 56 Hinckley Rd Waban MA 02168 Office: 77 Massachusetts Ave Cambridge MA 02139

FELD, NICHOLAS, foreign service officer; b. Vicksburg, Miss., Dec. 5, 1915; s. Nicholas and Mabel (Phillips) F.; m. Cora Helene Hochstein, Dec. 27, 1949; 1 dau., Evelyn Dana. A.B., Harvard U., 1936, postgrad., 1937-38. Apptd. fgn. service officer, unclassified, vice consul career, sec. Diplomatic Service, pres., 1981-83; assigned vice consul Diplomatic Service, Zurich, Switzerland, 1939, Basel, 1939; with Fgn. Service Officers Tng. Sch., Dept. State, Washington, 1940; vice consul, Madras, India, 1940, 3d sec., Pretoria, Union South Africa, 1944, 2d sec., 1945, commd. consul, 1948, consul, Dar-es-Salaam, Tanganyika Ty., East Africa (now Tanzania), 1948, Geneva, 1950; officer in charge West, Central and East African affairs Office African Affairs, Dept. State, 1951; consul, Singapore, 1954-56; officer in charge trusteeship affairs Office Dependent Area Affairs, Dept. State, 1956-60; counselor, Budapest, Hungary, 1960-62; chief, jr. officer personnel Dept. State, Washington, 1963-65; acting dir. Office West African Affairs, 1965; dep. dir. Office Inter-African Affairs, Bur. African Affairs, Dept. State, 1965, country dir., Kenya, Tanzania, Seychelles and Uganda, 1967; U.S. adviser Entente Guaranty Fund, Abidjan, Ivory Coast, 1969. Clubs: Harvard of Cape Cod.(v.p. 1980-81, pres. 1981-83. Home: PO Box 62 North Chatham MA 02650

FELD, STUART P., art gallery director; b. Passaic, N.J., Aug. 10, 1935; s. Samuel B. and Maude (Breitner) F.; m. Sue Kessler, May 29, 1970; children: Elizabeth, Peter. A.B., Princeton U., 1957; A.M., Harvard U., 1958. Curatorial asst., assoc. curator in charge dept. Am. paintings and sculpture Met. Mus., N.Y.C., 1961-67; pres., dir. Hirschl and Adler Galleries, N.Y.C., 1967—. Author: (with Albert TenEyck Gardner) American Paintings in the Collection of the Metropolitan Museum, 1965; contbr. articles on Am. fine arts and decorative arts to profl. jours. Office: Hirschl and Adler Galleries 21 E 70th St New York NY 10021

FELD, WERNER JOACHIM, political scientist, educator; b. Duesseldorf, Ger., Apr. 10, 1910; came to U.S., 1938, naturalized, 1944; s. Bruno and Irma (Loebl) F.; m. Elizabeth Lloyd Tandy, Oct. 1, 1957. Student law, U. Berlin, 1930-33; Ph.D. in Polit. Sci., Tulane U., 1962. Dist. mgr. sales E. Edelmann & Co., Chgo., 1938-43, 46; pres. Dixie Specialty Co., Inc., Mobile, 1947-50, 52-61; prof., chmn. dept. polit. sci. and econ. Moorhead (Minn.) State Coll., 1962-65; prof., chmn. dept. polit. sci. U. New Orleans, 1965—; vis. prof. Bologna Center, Johns Hopkins U., 1969, Free U. Berlin, 1977, U. Innsbruck, 1984; adviser to asst. sec. for European affairs State Dept., 1966-68, cons., 1965-70. Author: Reunification and West German-Soviet Relations, 1963, The Court of the European Communities: New Dimension in International Adjudication, 1964, The European Common Market and the World, 1967, The Enduring Questions of Politics, 1969, Transnational Business Collaboration Among Common Market Countries, 1970, Nongovernmental Forces and World Politics, 1972, The European Community in World Affairs, 1976, Domestic Political Realities and European Unification, 1977, the Foreign Policies of West European Socialist Parties, 1978, International Relations: A Transnational Approach, 1979, Multinational Corporations and U.N. Politics, 1980, West Germany and the European Community, 1981, American Foreign Policy: Aspirations and Reality, 1984; co-author, co-editor: Comparative Regional Systems, 1980, NATO and the Atlantic Defense, 1982, International Organizations: A Comparative Approach, 1983. Dir. Civil Def., Mobile, 1955-57. Served with AUS, 1943-46, 50-52. Decorated Army Commendation medal; Fulbright scholar Coll. Europe, Bruges, Belgium, 1968-69. Mem. Am. Polit. Sci. Assn., So. Polit. Sci. Assn. (sec. 1967-68), Internat. Studies Assn. (pres. S. dist.), UN Assn. (pres.). Home: 2362 Killdeer St New Orleans LA 70122 *Aggressiveness, adaption to changing conditions, and strict adherence to ethical principles.*

FELDBERG, CHESTER BEN, banker, lawyer; b. N.Y.C., Dec. 16, 1939; s. William and Janet (Mesh) F.; m. Lynn Lea Uebelhack, Sept. 17, 1963; children: Gregory Howard, Suzanne. A.B., Union Coll., Schenectady, 1960; LL.B., Harvard, 1963. Bar: N.Y. bar 1963. Atty. Fed. Res. Bank of N.Y., N.Y.C., 1964-68, asst. counsel, 1968-73, sec., 1969-73, v.p., 1975-83, sr. v.p., 1984—; sec. bd. govs. Fed. Res. System, 1973-74. Office: Federal Reserve Bank NY 33 Liberty St New York NY 10045

FELDBERG, MEYER, univ. dean; b. Johannesburg, South Africa, Mar. 17, 1942; s. Leon and Sarah (Kretzmer) F.; m. Barbara Erlick, Aug. 9, 1965; children—Lewis Robert, Ilana. B.A., Witwatersrand U., Johannesburg, 1962; M.B.A., Columbia U., 1965; Ph.D., Cape Town (South Africa) U., 1969. Product mgr. B.F. Goodrich Co., Akron, Ohio, 1965-67; dean Grad. Sch. Bus., U. Cape Town, 1968-79; asso. dean J.L. Kellogg Sch. Mgmt., Northwestern U., Evanston, Ill., 1979-81; prof., dean Sch. Bus., Tulane U., New Orleans, 1981—; dir. ICL, South Africa; vis. prof. M.I.T., 1974, Cranfield Inst. Tech., 1970-76; cons. in field. Author: Organizational Behaviour: Text and Cases, 1975, American Universities, Divestment of Stock in South Africa, 1978, also articles. Named Jaycee Young Man of Yr., 1972. Office: Tulane U Sch Bus New Orleans LA 70118 *

FELDBERG, SUMNER LEE, retail company executive; b. Boston, June 19, 1924; s. Morris and Anna (Marnoy) F.; married; children—Michael S., Ellen R.; stepchildren: Mollye S., Beth, James. B.A., Harvard, 1947, M.B.A., 1949. With New Eng. Trading Corp., 1949-56; treas. Zayre Corp., 1956-73, sr. v.p., 1965-68, exec. v.p., 1969-73, chmn. bd., 1973—; dir. Mass. Mut. Income Investors, Mass. Mut. Corporate Investors, Zayre Corp. Trustee Beth Israel Hosp., Combined Jewish Philanthropies of Greater Boston. Served to 1st lt. USAAF, 1943-46. Address: PO Box 910 Framingham MA 01701

FELDBRILL, VICTOR, conductor; b. Toronto, Ont., Can., Apr. 4, 1924; s. Nathan and Helen (Lederman) F.; m. Zelda Mann, Dec. 30, 1945; children: Debbi (Mrs. Ted Ross), Aviva. Artist's diploma, U. Toronto, 1949. Music dir., condr. Winnipeg Symphony, 1958-68; condr.-in-residence U. Toronto, 1969—; resident condr. Toronto Symphony, from 1970; condr. Canadian Opera Co., from 1967; regular appearances in, Japan, 1979—; Ann. conducting for BBC, in Eng.; regular guest condr. throughout Can. with Nat. Youth Orch. of Can., 1960—; founder, condr. Toronto Symphony Youth Orch. Served with Canadian Navy, 1942-45. Recipient Canadian Music citation, Can. Centennial medal, Sr. Arts award Can. Council., City of Tokyo medal, 1978 *

FELDER, RODNEY OTTO, college president; b. Redwood, N.Y., May 25, 1927; s. Otto and Pearl Maybelle (Lambert) F. B.S. SUNY-Albany, 1949; M.A., Columbia U., 1953, Ed.D., 1957. Tchr. public schs., Worcester, N.Y., 1949-50, Morristown, N.Y., 1950-52; instr. Santa Barbara City Coll., 1953-55; chmn. bus. and econs. Finch Coll., 1955-59, asst. dean, 1959-60, dean, 1960-69, v.p., 1969-70, pres., 1970-77, Finch Coll. Mus. Art, 1969-77, Upsala Coll., 1977—; vis. prof. econs. UCLA, 1962; mem. N.J. Dept. Higher Edn. Master Planning Com. Contbr. numerous bus. and econ. articles to profl. jours., 1952-62. Bd. dirs. Ind. Coll. Fund N.J.; numerous radio, TV appearances on pvt. colls.; Past pres. Council Lutheran Ch. in Am. Colls. Served with U.S. Army, 1945-47. Mem. Assn. Ind. Colls. and Univs. N.J. (exec. com.). Office: Upsala Coll East Orange NJ 07019

FELDHUSEN, JOHN FREDERICK, educational psychology educator; b. Waukesha, Wis., May 5, 1926; s. John C. and Luella Elsie (Gruetzmacher) F.; m. Hazel J. Artz, Dec. 20, 1954; children: Jeanne, Anne. B.A., U. Wis., 1949, M.S., 1955, Ph.D., 1958. Counselor Wis. Sch. for Boys, 1949-51; tchr. Northwestern Acad., Lake Geneva, Wis., 1951-54; instr. Madison Bus. Coll., 1955-58, U. Wis., Eau Claire, 1958-59, asst. prof., 1959-61, assoc. prof., 1961-62; assoc. prof. ednl. psychology Purdue U., West Lafayette, Ind., 1962-65, prof., 1965—; dir. Gifted Edn. Resource Inst., 1979—. Author: (with W. Krypsin) Writing Behavioral Objectives: A Guide for Planning Instruction, 1974, Analyzing Classroom Dialogue, 1974, Developing Classroom Tests, 1974, (with S.J. Moore, D.J. Treffinger) Global and Componential Evaluation of Creativity Instructional Materials, 1970, (with D.J. Treffinger, P. Pine and others) Teaching Children How to Think, 1975, (with D.J. Treffinger) Creativity and Problem Solving in Gifted Education, 1980; contbr. numerous articles on ednl. psychology and teaching methods to profl. jours.; editorial bd.: Gifted Child Quar, 1976—; editor: The Ednl. Psychologist, 1966-69, Ednl. Psychology Series, 1976—; cons. editor: Burgess Pub. Co, 1967-76. Pres. West Lafayette P.T.A., 1969. Served with AUS, 1944-45. U.S. Office edn. grantee, 1967-71. Fellow Am. Psychol. Assn.; mem. Am. Ednl. Research Assn., Nat. Assn. Gifted Children (pres.-elect 1981), Council Exceptional Children, Phi Delta Kappa. Home: 2187 Tecumseh Park Ln West Lafayette IN 47906 Office: Educational Psychology Purdue University West Lafayette IN 47906

FELDMAN, A. DANIEL, lawyer; b. South Bend, Ind., May 18, 1932; s. Benjamin H. and Fannie F.; m. Jessica Ann Tenofsky, July 3, 1955; children: Stephanie, Susan, Laurence, Valerie. B.A., U. Chgo., 1952, J.D., 1955. Bar: Calif. 1956, Ill. 1958. Law clk. U.S. Ct. Appeals for 9th Circuit, San Francisco, 1955-56; asso. firm Isham, Lincoln & Beale, Chgo., 1958-64, partner, 1965—. Pres. United Community Services of Evanston, 1968-70; bd. dirs. Consumer Health Group, Evanston, Ill., 1974-81; mem. Chgo. exec. com. Anti-Defamation League, 1976—; mem. Bd. Ethics, Evanston, 1981—. Served with U.S. Army, 1956-58. Mem. ABA, Chgo. Bar Assn., Am. Law Inst. Jewish. Clubs: Mid Day, Legal (Chgo.). Home: 808 Sheridan Rd Evanston IL 60202 Office: 3 First National Bank Plaza Chicago IL 60202

FELDMAN, ALVIN LINDBERGH, airline exec.; b. N.Y.C., Dec. 14, 1927; s. Harry and Rose (Lefkowitz) F.; m. Rosemily Petrison, Feb. 15, 1952 (dec. July 1980); children—David, John, Susan. B.S. in Mech. Engring, Cornell U., 1949; S.E.P., Stanford U. Grad. Sch. Bus., 1966. With Cornell Aeros. Lab., 1949-52; engr. Convair div. Gen. Dynamics Corp., San Diego, 1952-54; asst. gen. mgr. Liquid Rocket Co.; pres. Aerojet Nuclear Systems Co., Aerojet-Gen. Corp., Sacramento, 1954-71; pres., chief exec. officer Frontier Airlines, Inc., Denver, 1971-80, Continental Airlines, Inc., Los Angeles, 1980—; chmn. bd., dir. Denver br. Fed. Res. Bank of Kansas City, 1977-79; dir. Pub. Service Co. Colo.; pub. mem. Nat. Transp. Policy Study Commn., 1976—. Asso. fellow AIAA, Air Transport Assn. (dir.), Denver C. of C. (dir. 1975-76). Clubs: LaJolla Country, Hiwan Golf, Aero of Washington.

FELDMAN, ARTHUR MITCHELL, museum dir.; b. Phila., Dec. 22, 1942; s. Joseph and Cecilia (Levin) F.; m. Laurel Hollis Bucky, June 22, 1969. B.S., Villanova (Pa.) U., 1964; M.A. in Art History and Archaeology, U. Mo., Columbia, 1970. Vis. curator Nelson Gallery, Atkins Mus., Kansas City, Mo., 1969-70, Victoria and Albert Mus., London, 1970-71; asso. curator Renwick Gallery, Smithsonian Instn., Washington, 1971-72; dir. Spertus Mus. of Judaica, Chgo., 1972—; profl. appraiser, 1974—. Author museum catalogues, 1973—. NDEA fellow, 1965-70. Mem. Am. Assn. Museums, Council Am. Jewish Museums (pres. 1976, 80, 81). Address: 618 S Michigan Ave Chicago IL 60605

FELDMAN, BURTON GORDON, advertising executive; b. Chgo., Dec. 19, 1915; s. Maurice J. and Goldye (Gordon) F.; m. Dorothy Straus, Dec. 28, 1942 (dec. d. 1969); children: Roger, Susan; m. Judith Levinson Miller, 1970. B.S., Northwestern U., 1933. Group copy chief Foote, Cone & Belding, Chgo., 1942-46; v.p. charge Chgo. office Buchanan & Co., 1946-48; exec. v.p. Gordon Best/Post, Keyes, 1948-59; pres. Burton G. Feldman, Inc., 1959-68; chmn. bd. Feldman & Assocs. Advt., Inc., Chgo., 1968-74; pres. Instant Printing Corp., Chgo., 1972—; pres. Phoenix Electric Co., Chgo., 1963-68, chmn. bd., 1968—, dir., 1963—; v.p. mktg., dir. Cummins Tool Corp., 1977—. Pres. James Gordon Grant for Gov., 1962—; v.p. bd. fellows Brandeis U., 1981—; v.p., bd. dirs. Chgo. Chamber Orch. Assn., 1982—. Mem. Pi Lambda Phi, Sigma Delta Chi. Clubs: Columbia Yacht, Arts of Chgo., Brandeis U. of Chgo. (pres. 1980—). Home: 175 E Delaware Chicago IL 60611 Office: 228 N LaSalle St Chicago IL 60601

FELDMAN, CLARICE ROCHELLE, lawyer; b. Milw., Dec. 2, 1941; d. Harry and Beatrice (Hiken) Wagan; m. Howard J. Feldman, July 11, 1965; 1 son, David Lewis. B.S., U. Wis., 1963, LL.B., 1965. Bar: Wis. 1965. Appellate atty. NLRB, Washington, 1965-69; co-counsel to Joseph A. Yablonski, Washington, 1969; atty. Washington research project Clark Coll., 1970-72; asso. gen. counsel United Mine Workers Am., Washington, 1972-74; partner Becker, Channell, Becker & Feldman, Washington, 1974-76, Becker & Feldman, 1976-77; gen. counsel Ams. for Energy Independence, Washington, 1978-80; atty. Office of Spl. Investigations, Dept. Justice, 1980-84; sole practice, Washington, 1984—. Advisor Assn. Union Democracy. Mem. Wis., D.C. bar assns. Democrat. Jewish. Home: 4455 29th St NW Washington DC 20008 Office: 2001 S St NW Suite 400 Washington DC 20009

FELDMAN, DAVID, real estate companies executive; b. London, June 27, 1946; emigrated to Can., 1969; s. Barnet and Dinah F. Diploma of Bldg., Hertfordshire Coll. Bldg., 1966; grad. student, Georgre Wimpey & Co. Ltd., London, 1966-69. Project mgr. Cadillac Fairview Corp., Toronto, 1969-76; gen. mgr. Tower Glen Devels. Ltd., Toronto, 1976—; pres. Camrost Group of Cos., Toronto, 1980—; mem. Urban Land Inst. U.S., Urban Devel. Inst., Toronto. Bd. dirs. Mt. Sinai Hosp., Toronto, 1983. Recipient Gold Standard award Duke of Edinburgh, 1966, award of honor Jewish Lad's Brigade, London, 1967. Mem. Can. Inst. Quantity Surveyors, Bd. of Trade Met. Toronto. Club: Cambridge (Toronto).

FELDMAN, EDMUND BURKE, art critic; b. Bayonne, N.J., May 6, 1924; s. Lucian Theodore and Bertha (Seldin) F.; m. Lailah G. Link, Mar. 15, 1953; children—Eva Jeanne, Jessica Marion. B.F.A., Syracuse U., 1949; M.A., U. Calif., Los Angeles, 1951; Ed.D., Columbia U., 1953. Curator painting and sculpture Newark Mus., 1953; asso. prof. art Livingston (Ala.) State U., 1953-56, Carnegie Inst. Tech., 1956-60; head art div. State U. Coll., New Paltz, N.Y., 1960-66; vis. prof. art Ohio State U., 1966; prof. art U. Ga., Athens, 1966—, Alumni Found. distinguished prof. art, 1973—; vis. prof. aesthetic edn. U. Calif., Berkeley, 1974; bd. govs. Pitts. Plan for Art, 1964-66; mem. U.S. Office Edn., Art Television Project, Whitney Mus., 1967, Ednl. Testing Service, N.Y.C., 1969-70, Coll. Entrance Exam. Bd., Princeton, N.J., 1969-70, Nat. Instructional Television Center, Bloomington, Ind., 1969-71; editorial cons. art Prentice-Hall, Inc. (arts and humanities Canfield Press subs. Harper & Row); adviser Ga. Council for Arts, 1973-74; cons. J. Paul Getty Trust, 1981—. Author: Art as Image and Idea, 1967, Varieties of Visual Experience, 1971, 2d edit., 1981, The Artist, 1982; Editor: Art Bull, Eastern Arts Assn., 1957-60, Art in American Higher Institutions, 1970; Mem. editorial bd.: Rev. of Research in Visual Arts Education, 1975-77; mem. editorial adv. bd.: Jour. of Aesthetic Education, 1976—; chmn. editorial bd.: Georgia Rev, 1977. Served with USAAF, 1942-46. Recipient Roswell Hill prize in painting Syracuse U., 1948. Mem. Nat. Art Edn. Assn. (pres. 1981-83), Coll. Art Assn., U.S. Soc. for Edn. Through Art, Tau Sigma Delta, Kappa Delta Pi, Kappa Pi, Phi Kappa Phi. Jewish. Home: 140 Chinquapin Pl Athens GA 30605 Office: U Ga Art Dept Athens GA 30602

FELDMAN, EGAL, historian, educator; b. N.Y.C., Apr. 9, 1925; s. Morris and Chaya F.; m. Mary Kalman, June 28, 1959; children: Tyla, Auora, Naomi. B.A., Bklyn. Coll., 1950; M.A., N.Y. U., 1954; Ph.D., U. Pa., 1959. Asst. prof. history U. Tex. at Arlington, 1960-66; asso. prof. history U. Wis.-Superior, 1966-68, prof., 1968—, chmn. dept. history and philosophy, 1973—, dean, 1977-82. Author: Fit for Men: History of New York's Clothing Trade, 1960, The Dreyfus Affair and the American Conscience, 1895-1906, 1981; Contbg. author books; contbr. articles to profl. publs. Named Tchr. of Year U. Wis., 1969; recipient Inst. Jewish Research award, 1954, Max Levine award, 1975. Jewish. Home: 2019 Weeks Ave Superior WI 54880 Office: 230 Sundquist Hall Superior WI 54881

FELDMAN, FRANKLIN, lawyer; b. N.Y.C., Nov. 12, 1927; s. Reuben and Anne (Schulman) F.; m. Naomi Goldstein, June 3, 1956; children: Sarah, Eve, Jacob. B.A., NYU, 1948; LL.B., Columbia U., 1951. Bar: N.Y. 1952. Mem. office Gen Counsel U.S. Air Force, Dept. Def., Washington, 1951-53; atty. office gen. counsel to gov. State of N.Y., 1954; assoc. firm Stroock & Stroock & Lavan, N.Y.C., 1955-64, ptnr., 1965—; cons. Temp. N.Y. Commn. on Constl. Conv., 1967. Editor-in-chief: Columbia U. Law Rev., 1950-51; author: (with Stephen E. Weil) Art Works-Law, Policy and Practice, 1974; contbr. articles to profl. jours. Mem. ABA, N.Y. State Bar Assn., Assn. Bar City N.Y., N.Y. County Lawyers Assn., Internat. Found. for Art Research (pres. 1971-76). Home: 15 W 81st New York NY 10024 Office: Stroock & Stroock & Lavan 7 Hanover Sq New York NY 10004 *Don't take yourself too seriously; don't underestimate others; don't overestimate your own judgement or wisdom; and don't try to keep score.*

FELDMAN, GORDON, educator; b. Windsor, Ont., Can., Dec. 6, 1928; s. Henry and Veta F.; m. Janet Mary Robson, Mar. 23, 1968; children—Leonard Carl, Joanna, Matthew. B.A., U. Toronto, Ont., 1950, M.A., 1951; Ph.D., U. Birmingham, Eng., 1953. Research asso. U. Birmingham, 1953-55; mem. Inst. Advanced Study, Princeton, N.J., 1955-56; research asso. U. Wis., Madison, 1956-57; asst. prof. to asso. prof. physics Johns Hopkins U., Balt., 1957-64, prof., 1964—; vis. prof. Imperial Coll., London, 1968-69, 73-75. Contbr. numerous articles to profl. jours. Raymond Priestly fellow; Guggenheim fellow, 1962-63. Home: 4832 Keswick Rd Baltimore MD 21210 Office: Johns Hopkins U Baltimore MD 21218

FELDMAN, IRVING, poet; b. Bklyn., Sept. 22, 1928; m. Carmen Alvarez del Olmo, 1955; 1 son, Fernando R. Ed., CCNY, Columbia U. Formerly prof. English U. P.R., Rio Piedras, Kenyon Coll., Gambier, O.; prof. English State U. N.Y., Buffalo, 1964—. Author: Works and Days, 1961, The Pripet Marshes, 1965, Magic Papers, 1970, Lost Originals, 1972, Leaping Clear, 1976, New and Selected Poems, 1979, Teach Me, Dear Sister, 1983; Contbr. to periodicals. Recipient Poetry prize Jewish Book Council Am., 1962; Ingram Merrill Found. grantee, 1963; Nat. Inst. and Am. Acad. Arts and Letters award, 1973; Guggenheim fellow, 1973; N.Y. State CAPS grantee, 1980. Home: 349 Berryman Dr Buffalo NY 14226 Office: Dept English State U NY Buffalo NY 14260

FELDMAN, JAY N., film and TV production company executive, lawyer; b. N.Y.C., Nov. 11, 1936; s. Morris Kenneth and Della (Newman) F.; m. Nancy Tobias, Dec. 7, 1963; children—Nina Cheryl, Karen Elise. A.B. magna cum laude, Colgate U., 1958; J.D., Harvard U., 1961. Bar: N.Y. 1962. Asso. firm Jacobs Persinger and Parker, 1961-68; sec., treas., gen. counsel Lynch Corp., 1968-69; counsel Allied Artists Industries, Inc., N.Y.C., 1970-80, sec., 1970-76, v.p., 1975-76, v.p. adminstrn., 1976-77, group v.p., 1977-80, dir., 1973-80; sec. Allied Artists Pictures Corp., 1973-74, dir., 1974-80; sec., counsel, dir. PSP, Inc., 1970-76; sec., dir. D. Kaltman & Co., Inc., 1970-79, v.p., 1977-79; sec., dir. Vitabath, Inc., 1970-72, Apollo Motor Homes, Inc., 1970-80, v.p., 1977-80; sec., dir. Westwood Import Co., Inc., 1972-79, v.p., 1977-79; sec., dir. Paul-Marshall Products Inc., 1972-75, Adstat Co., 1972-74; v.p., sec., dir. Allied Artists Video Corp., 1978-80; v.p., dir. Palmland Fashions, Inc., 1971-78; resident counsel Lorimar Prodns., Inc., 1980-83; corp. atty. NYNEX, 1983—; Mem. com. on criminal cts. Legal Aid Soc., 1969-72. Mem. Am. Bar Assn., N.Y. State Bar Assn., Phi Beta Kappa. Home: 61 Roger Dr Port Washington NY 11050 Office: 1095 Ave of the Americas New York NY 10036 *Dare to be different—the path to success is the road least travelled*

FELDMAN, JEROME ARTHUR, computer scientist; b. Pitts., Dec. 5, 1938; s. Rudolph Abraham and Deborah Ruth (Appleman) F.; m. Janice Sharla Auerbach, Nov. 16, 1961; children—Michael Alan, Benjamin Noah. B.A. with distinction, U. Rochester, N.Y., 1960; M.A., U. Pitts., 1961; Ph.D. in Math. and System Sci, Carnegie-Mellon U., 1964. Engr. Westinghouse Electric Corp., 1960-61; asst. research scientist Carnegie-Mellon U., 1963-64; mem. staff Lincoln Lab., MIT, 1964-66; mem. faculty Stanford U., 1966-74, assoc. prof. computer sci., 1969-74, assoc. dir. artificial intelligence lab., 1972-74, vis. prof., 1979; vis. prof. math. Hebrew U., Jerusalem, 1970-71; prof. computer sci. U. Rochester, 1974—, chmn. dept., 1974-81, John H. Dessauer prof., 1982—, vice provost computing, 1977-79; chmn. ad-hoc com. exptl. computer sci. NSF, 1979; cons. in field. Author papers in field. Fulbright grantee, 1970-71. Fellow AAAS; Mem. Assn. Computing Machinery, Cognitive Sci. Soc., Artificial Intelligence Soc. (gov.), Scientists and Engrs. Social and Polit. Action. Home: 386 Oakdale Dr Rochester NY 14618 Office: Computer Sci Dept U Rochester Rochester NY 14627

FELDMAN, JEROME IRA, lawyer, patent development executive; b. N.Y.C., July 17, 1928; s. George and Tanya (Rubenstein) F.; m. Terry Jean Harmon, Oct. 23, 1964; children: Rebecca Page, Michael Dana, Kyra Joelle, Sarah Allison. B.A., Ind. U., 1949; LL.B., N.Y. U., 1951, J.D., 1951. Bar: N.Y. 1951. Partner firm Feldman & Pollak, N.Y.C., 1953-60; pres. Nat. Patent Devel. Corp., N.Y.C., 1960—, also dir.; dir. Interferon Scis. Inc., Internat. Hydron Corp., Wombat Prodns. Inc. Trustee Bard Coll. Mem. N.Y. Bar Assn. Jewish. Office: 375 Park Ave New York NY 10152

FELDMAN, JEROME MYRON, physician; b. Chgo., July 27, 1935; s. Louis and Marian (Swichkow) F.; m. Gaye Arleen Friedman, Sept. 4, 1960; children: Karen Joy, Ellen Deborah, Mark Steven. B.S., Northwestern U., 1957, M.D. with distinction, 1961. Diplomate: Am. Bd. Internal Medicine. Mem. faculty Duke U. Med. Sch., 1968—, assoc. prof. medicine, 1972—, dir. diabetes clinic, 1970-73; assoc. dir. diabetes sect. Regional Med. Program N.C., 1967-70; clin. investigator Durham VA Hosp., 1971-74, chief endocrinology service, 1971—. Editor Jour. Clin. Endocrinology and Metabolism, 1983—; Contbr. articles to med. jours., chpts. to books. Served as officer M.C. USAR, 1965-67. Fellow A.C.P.; mem. Am. Diabetes Assn., Endocrine Soc., Am. Fedn. Clin. Research, So. Sugar Club, N.C. Diabetes Assn. (pres. 1973-74), Phi Beta Kappa, Sigma Xi, Alpha Omega Alpha. Jewish. Home: 2744 Sevier St Durham NC 27705 Office: Box 2963 Duke Univ Med Center Durham NC 27710

FELDMAN, JOEL STEVEN, life insurance company executive; b. Charleston, S.C., Dec. 18, 1940; s. Morris Aaron and Rita (Karesh) F.; m. Marilyn M. Musgrove, Nov. 18, 1976; children: Ryan, Dana. B.A., The Citadel, 1963; J.D., Tulane U., 1969. Bar: Conn. 1970, Colo. 1983. Atty. Conn. Mut. Life Ins. Co., Hartford, 1969-71; v.p., gen. counsel Horace Mann Ins. Group, Springfield, Ill., 1971-77; sr. v.p., sec., gen. counsel Capitol Life Ins. Co., Denver, 1977—, dir., 1982—; dir. Am. Pacific Life Ins. Co., San Rafael, Calif.; officer Providence Ins. Co., Wilmington, Del., 1982—, Providence Capitol Corp., 1982—, Providence Capitol Ltd., Hamilton, Bermuda, 1982—. Served to capt. U.S. Army, 1963-66. Mem. ABA, Colo. Bar Assn., Am. Corp. Counsel Assn. Home: 6040 E Geddes Circle Englewood CO 80112 Office: Capitol Life Ins Co 1600 Sherman St Denver CO 80203

FELDMAN, LOUIS HARRY, educator; b. Hartford, Conn., Oct. 29, 1926; s. Sam and Sarah (Vine) F.; m. Miriam Blum, Mar. 8, 1966; children—Moshe Yaakov, Sarah Rivkah, Leah Chanah. B.A., Trinity Coll., 1946, M.A., 1947; Ph.D., Harvard, 1951. Ford found. teaching fellow in classics Trinity Coll., Hartford, Conn., 1951-52, instr., 1952-53; instr. classics Hobart and William Smith Coll., 1953-55; instr. humanities and history Yeshiva and Stern Coll., N.Y.C., 1955-56; asst. prof. classics Yeshiva Coll., 1956-61, asso. prof., 1961-66, prof., 1966—. Author: Scholarship on Philo and Josephus, 1963, Josephus, Jewish Antiquities, Books XVIII-XX, 1965, Prolegomenon, The Biblical Antiquities of Philo, 1971; Asso. editor: Classical Weekly, 1955-57; mng. editor: Classical World, 1957-59; deptl. editor: Hellenistic lit. Ency. Judaica, 1967-71; Contbr.: classical and religious jours. Ency. Brit. Guggenheim fellow, 1963-64; Am. Council Learned Socs. sr. fellow, 1971-72; Am. Philos. Soc. fellow, 1972-73, 79-80; Littauer Found. fellow, 1973-74; Wurzweiler Found. fellow, 1974-75; grantee Am. Acad. Jewish Research, 1976-77, Meml. Found. for Jewish Culture, 1969-70, 80-81. Mem. Am. Philol. Assn., Phi Beta Kappa. Jewish religion. Home: 69-11 Harrow St Forest Hills NY 11375

FELDMAN, MARK B., lawyer; b. Rochester, N.Y., Oct. 3, 1935; s. Edward P. and Grace (Relin) F.; m. Marcia Smith, Nov. 23, 1963; children: Ilana, Rachel. A.B., Wesleyan U., 1957; LL.B., Harvard U. 1960. Bar: N.Y. 1961, D.C. 1974. Assoc. Kaye, Schuler, Fierman, Hap & Handley, N.Y.C., 1960-65; with Office Legal Advisor, Dept. State, 1965-81, dep. legal advisor, 1974-81; of counsel Donovan, Leisure, Newton & Irvine, Washington, 1981—; adj. prof. law Gerogetown U. Mem. Council Fgn. Relations, Am. Law Inst., Am. Soc. Internat. Law, ABA, Internat. Law Assn. Address: 4010 48th St NW Washington DC 20016

FELDMAN, MARTIN L. C., federal judge; b. St. Louis, Jan. 28, 1934; s. Joseph and Zelma (Bosse) F.; m. Melanie Pulitzer, Nov. 26, 1958; children: Jennifer Pulitzer, Martin L.C. B.A., Tulane U., 1955, J.D., 1957. Bar: La., Mo. 1957. Law clk. to Hon. J.M. Wisdom, U.S. Ct. Appeals, 1958-59; asso. firm Bronfin, Heller, Feldman & Steinberg, New Orleans, 1959-60, partner firm, 1960-83; U.S. dist. judge, New Orleans, 1984—; trustee, former chmn. Sta. WYES-TV. Contbr. articles to profl. jours. Former nat. sec. Anti-Defamation League; former pres. bd. mgrs. Touro Infirmary; bd. dirs. Public Broadcasting Service. Mem. ABA, La. Bar Assn. (chmn. law reform com. 1981), Mo. Bar Assn., Am. Law Inst., Order of Coif. Republican. Jewish. Home: 12 Rosa Park New Orleans LA 70115 Office: 500 Camp St New Orleans LA 70130

FELDMAN, MARVIN, college president; b. Rochester, N.Y., May 24, 1927; s. Max and Blanche F.; m. Dorothy Owens, July 29, 1954; children—Brian, Michael. Student, U.S. Mil. Acad., 1948-51; A.B., San Francisco State U., 1953; Ph.D. in Edn, Northeastern U., 1973. Tchr. math. public schs., San Francisco, 1952-57; v.p. Cogswell Coll., 1958-64; program officer Ford Found., N.Y.C., 1964-69; asst. to spl. com. office edn. HEW, Washington, 1969-71; asst. dir. OEO, 1969-71; pres. Fashion Inst. Tech., 1971—; dir. Gerber Garmet Tech. Corp.; mem. Pres.'s Nat. Adv. Council on Vocat. Edn., 1968-79. Contbr. articles to profl. jours. Bd. dirs. 34th St. Midtown Assn., N.Y.C., DeVry Inst., Shankar Coll. Served with USN, 1944-46. Served with U.S. Army, 1948-53; PTO. Recipient Meritorious award Nat. Adv. Council on Vocat. Edn., 1972, 75, 78. Mem. Orgn. Rehab. through Tng., Pres.'s Assn., West Point Soc. Home: 41 S Mountain Ave Montclair NJ 07042 Office: 227 W 27th St New York NY 10001

FELDMAN, MELVIN J., metallurgist; b. South Bend, Ind., Jan. 6, 1926; s. Benjamin and Fannie (Glaser) F.; m. Nancy Ann McCarty, June 11, 1945; children—David, Cynthia, Martha, Benjamin, Matthew. B.S. in Metall. Enging, Purdue U., 1950; M.S., U. Tenn., 1956. Supr. hot cells, solid state div. Oak Ridge Nat. Lab., 1950-56; supr. metallurgy and hot cells Westinghouse Electric Corp., 1956-60; mgr. EBR-11 fuel cycle facility Argonne Nat. Lab., Idaho Falls, Idaho, 1960-72; asso. dir. Argonne-West div., 1973-75; mgr. engring. systems Consol. fuel reprocessing program Oak Ridge Nat. Lab., 1975—; adj. asso. prof. metallurgy U. Utah, thesis adviser. Author papers in field. Served with USNR, 1944-46. Fellow Am. Nuclear Soc. (pres. 1975-76); mem. Am. Soc. Metals, Sigma Xi. Democrat. Unitarian. Club: Oak

Ridge Country. Home: 224 Connors Circle Oak Ridge TN 37830 Office: PO Box X Oak Ridge TN 37830

FELDMAN, MILTON, publisher; b. N.Y.C., June 28, 1920; s. Abraham and Sarah (Bader) F.; m. Pearl Bell, Dec. 8, 1946; children: Stuart, Nancy. B.S., NYU, 1942. Public acct. Anchin, Block & Anchin, N.Y.C., 1941-46; with Grune & Stratton Inc. (med. pub.), N.Y.C., 1947—, v.p., 1965-77, pres., chief operating officer, 1978—, chmn., pub., 1982—; treas., adv. Intercontinental Med. Book Corp., N.Y.C., Henry M. & Lillian Stratton Found. for Med. Research. Pub., adv.: Am. Soc. Hematology. Recipient Recognition award Internat. Soc. Transplantation, 1976. Mem. Am. Mgmt. Assn. Club: Free Sons of Israel. Office: Grune & Stratton Inc 111 Fifth Ave New York NY 10003

FELDMAN, MYER, lawyer; b. Phila., June, 1917; s. Israel and Bella (Kurland) F.; m. Adrienne Arsht, Sept. 28, 1980; children by previous marriage: Jane Margaret, James Alan. Student, Girard Coll., Phila., 1922-31; B.S. in Econs., U. Pa., 1935; LL.B. (fellow 1938-39), U. Pa., 1938. Bar: Pa. 1938, D.C. 1965, U.S. Supreme Ct. 1965. Pvt. practice, Phila. and D.C., 1939-42, 65—; spl. counsel, exec. asst. to chmn. SEC, 1946-54; counsel banking and currency commn. U.S. Senate, 1955-57; legis. asst. to Senator John F. Kennedy, 1958-61; dep. spl. counsel to Presidents Kennedy and Johnson, 1961-64; counsel to Pres. Johnson, 1964-65; partner Ginsburg Feldman & Bress, Washington, 1965—; lectr. law U. Pa., 1941-42; prof. law Am. U., 1955-56; pres. Radio Assos., Inc., 1959-81; partner Key Stas., 1960-79; chmn. bd. Speer Publs., 1972-77, Capital Gazette Press, Inc., 1972-77, Bay Publs., 1972-77; dir. Flying Tiger Line, Inc., 1966-82, Nat. Savs. & Trust Co., Flame Hope, Inc., Media and Art Services, Inc., WSSH, Inc., Internat. Fusion Energy Systems Co., Inc., WLLH Broadcasters, WLAM Broadcasters, Lazare Kaplan, Inc. Author: Standard Pennsylvania Practice, 4 vols., 1958; also articles. Pres. N.Y. Art Festival, Inc., 1972-80; del. Democratic Nat. Conv., 1968; pres. McGovern for Pres. Com., 1971-72; vice chmn. Congl. Leadership for Future, 1970; finance chmn. Bayh for Pres. Com., 1975-76; bd. dirs. Weitzman Inst., 1963-84, Spl. Olympics, Inc.; trustee Eleanor Roosevelt Meml. Found., 1963—; bd. dirs. Henry M. Jackson Found., 1984—; trustee Declaration of Independence, House and Library, 1965-75; bd. dirs. John F. Kennedy Library, 1983—; trustee Jewish Publ. Soc., 1966-78; bd. overseers V.I. U., 1962—. Served with USAAF, 1942-46. Mem. U. Pa. Law Alumni Assn. Washington (pres. 1952-58), Tau Epsilon Rho (pres. 1938). Home: 2801 New Mexico Ave NW Washington DC 20007 Office: 1700 Pennsylvania Ave NW Washington DC 20006

FELDMAN, RAYMOND, psychiatrist; b. Chgo., Oct. 27, 1909; s. Phillip and Jennie (Cohen) F.; m. Anne M. Reganis, July 13, 1941; 1 dau., Marie Anne Feldman Mactavish. B.A., Northwestern U., 1930, M.B., 1932, M.D., 1933. Diplomate: Am. Bd. Psychiatry and Neurology, Am. Bd. Family Practice (dir. 1969-76). Intern Cook County Hosp., Chgo., 1933-34; asso. physician, resident in psychiatry VA hosps., Little Rock, 1936, Chillicothe, Ohio, 1937, Bedford, Mass., 1939-41; camp and dist. surgeon Civilian Conservation Corps, Camp Custer Dist., Mich., 1934-36; med. officer USPHS, Cristobal, C.Z., 1937-39; with VA regional office, Denver, 1946-52, dept. medicine and surgery, Washington, 1952-57; with NIH, Bethesda, Md., 1957-66; chief tng. br. NIMH, 1959-63, asso. dir. extramural programs, 1963-65, dep. dir. inst., 1965-66; dir. gen. practitioner edn. program Am. Psychiat. Assn., 1965-66; former dir. mental health programs Western Interstate Commn. Higher Edn., Boulder, Colo., 1967-75; clin. prof. dept. psychiatry U. Colo. Med. Sch.; Mem. Adv. Health Com. Montgomery County, Md., 1962-66. Bd. dirs. Joint Commn. Correctional Manpower and Tng., 1969-74. Served with AUS, 1941-46. Fellow, founder Am. Coll. Psychiatrists; mem. AMA, Group for Advancement Psychiatry, Am. Psychiat. Assn. (council med. edn. and career devel. 1968-77), Am. Orthopsychiat. Assn., Colo. Med. Assn., Colo. Psychiat. Soc. Home: 205 Devon Pl Boulder CO 80302

FELDMAN, ROBERT GEORGE, med. educator; b. Cin., Apr. 27, 1933; s. Jacob and Katie (Green) F.; m. Gail Poliner, Dec. 25, 1960; children—John, Elise. B.A., U. Cin., 1954, M.D., 1958. Diplomate: Am. Bd. Psychiatry and Neurology (asst. examiner 1972), Am. Bd. Electroencephalography. Research asst. pharmacology U. Cin., 1949-54; jr. pharmacologist William S. Merrell Co., Reading, Ohio, 1951-56; fellow Nat. Assn. Mental Health, U. Calif. at Los Angeles, 1957; intern Los Angeles County Hosp., 1958-59; resident neurology Yale-New Haven Med. Center, 1959-63, W. Haven VA Hosp., 1961; fellow metabolic diseases Yale Med. Sch., 1961-62; USPHS spl. fellow, 1962-63, practice medicine, specializing in neurology, Boston, 1963—; neurologist-in-chief Univ. Hosp., 1969—; mem. staff Boston City Hosp., Carney Hosp., Quincy City Hosp., 1963; vis. fellow Montreal (Can.) Neurol. Inst., 1962, Mayo Clinic and Found., Rochester, Minn., 1962; asso. electroencephalographer Yale-New Haven Med. Center, 1962-63; mem. faculty Harvard Med. Sch., 1963—, lectr., 1968—, Sch. Public Health, 1978—; mem. faculty Boston U. Sch. Medicine, 1963—, prof. neurology, 1970—, chmn. dept., 1969—, prof. pharmacology, 1977—; lectr. Tufts U. Sch. Medicine, 1977—; chief neurology services Boston VA hosps., 1966—; Mem. nat field adv. group Neurology VA, 1972—; mem. sci. council Com. to Combat Huntington's Disease, 1972-75; chmn. Zone 1 Profl. Standards Rev. Orgn., 1973-78; mem. profl. advisory bd. Epilepsy Found., 1976. Editor-in-chief: Jour. Club Neurology; contbg. editor: Am. Jour. Indsl. Medicine, 1980—. Bd. dirs. Postgrad. Med. Inst., 1973; bd. dirs. Norfolk County Med. Soc.; v.p. Mass. Med. Soc., 1973. Fellow Am. Acad. Neurology (councillor 1979—); mem. Am. Epilepsy Soc., Am. Assn. Electromygraphy and Electrodiagnosis, Am. Assn. Profs. Neurology, Boston Soc. Psychiatry and Neurology (pres. 1972-73), Am. Acad. Clin. Toxicology, Am. Neurol. Assn., Eastern EEG Soc., Am. Med. EEG Assn., Am. Heart Assn. (fellow stroke council), AMA, Mass. Med. Soc., Am. Pub. Health Assn. Home: 74 Rita Rd Braintree MA 02184 Office: 80 E Concord St Boston MA 02118

FELDMAN, ROGER DAVID, lawyer; b. N.Y.C., Apr. 7, 1943; s. Louis and Dora (Goldsmith) F.; m. Gail Steg, May 31, 1969; children: Rebecca, Seth. A.B., Brown U., 1962; LL.B., Yale U.; M.B.A., Harvard U. Bar: N.Y. 1966, D.C. 1977. Ops. research analyst Office Asst. Sec. Def., Washington, 1967-68; staff asst. Office of Pres. U. S., Washington, 1968-69; assoc. de Boeuf Lamb Leiby & MacRae, 1969-75; ptnr. de Boeuf Lamb Lieby & MacRae, 1977—; dep. asst. adminstr. Fed. Energy Adminstrn., Washington, 1975-77; dir. Pan Atlantic Group Inc., R.J. Rudden & Assocs. Inc.; mem. bd. advisors Energy Bur. Inc. Mem. bd. editors: Law Jour., Yale Law Sch., 1965. Mem. ABA (chmn. energy law com. 1980—, chmn. alt. energy sources com. 1981—, spl. com. on energy law 1981—), Fed. Energy Bar Assn. (chmn. cogeneration com.), Phi Beta Kappa. Office: 1333 New Hamphire Ave NW Suite 1100 Washington DC 20036

FELDMAN, RUTH SPERO, association administrator; b. N.Y.C., Oct. 18, 1932; d. and Eva Zarrow; m. Robert D. Spero, Dec. 21, 1964 (dec.); children—Ilene, Karen, Janice Berger.; m. Seymour Feldman, Oct. 31, 1982. B.A., Tufts U., 1953; postgrad., U. Miami, 1961-63. Music therapist So. Fla. State Hosp., 1958-60; in field human relations and inter-group relations, 1960-63; dir. cultural arts and vol. services Jewish Center Buffalo, 1965-68; dir. creative arts therapist Children's Rehab. Center, Buffalo, 1968-70; dir. creative arts therapies research exceptional edn. div. Niagara Falls (N.Y.) Schs., 1970-71; exec. dir. Day Care Council Erie County (N.Y.), 1971-73; head div. social rehab. and creative arts therapies dept. Buffalo Psychiat. Center, N.Y. State Div. Mental Hygiene, 1973-76; dir. devel. Buffalo Philharmonic Orch., 1976-77, mgr., 1977-80, exec. dir., 1980-82; nat. exec. dir. B'nai B'rith Women, 1983—; mem. faculty SUNY, Buffalo, 1974-76; mem. U.S. Pres.'s Commn. on Employment Handicapped, 1975—. Author: Opening Ears to the Performing Arts—A Guide to Serving the Hearing Impaired, 1981; contbr. articles to profl. publs. Pres. Action for Rehab. Bd., Buffalo, 1975-76; mem. adv. bd. Erie County Manpower, 1976-81, Daimon Coll., Erie Community Coll., Medaille Coll. Recipient Woman of Yr. award SUNY, Buffalo, 1980; SUNY, Buffalo fellow, 1976—. Mem. Am. Symphony Orch. League, Nat. Rehab. Assn., Nat. Assn. Music Therapy (registered music therapist), Am. Assn. Music Therapy (cert. music therapist), Am. Art Therapy Assn., Am. Dance Therapy Assn., N.Y. State Assn. Edn. Young Child. Democrat. Jewish. Club: Zonta (Buffalo). Office: 1640 Rhode Island Ave NW Washington DC 20036

FELDMAN, SAMUEL MITCHELL, psychologist, educator; b. Phila., Sept. 26, 1933; s. Boris and Fannie B. (Shrager) F.; children—Lee Stephen, David Saul. B.A., U. Pa., 1954; M.A., Northwestern U., 1955; Ph.D., McGill U., 1959. Fellow in physiology U. Wash., Seattle, 1958-60; from instr. to asso. prof. physiology Albert Einstein Coll. Medicine, 1960-71; prof. psychology N.Y. U., 1971—, head dept., 1972-76; mem. psychol. sci. study sect. NIMH, 1968-72, chmn., 1970-72, mem. biol. sci. tng. grant rev. com., 1977—; cons. in field. Contbr. articles to profl. jours. Fellow USPHS, 1958-60; recipient Career award, 1969-71, research grantee, 1963—. Mem. Eastern Psychol. Assn., Am. Physiol. Soc., Soc. Neurosci., Sigma Xi. Home: 37 Washington Sq W New York NY 10011 Office: Dept Psychology New York Univ New York NY 10003

FELDMAN, STANLEY GEORGE, judge; b. N.Y.C., Mar. 9, 1933; s. Meyer and Esther Betty (Golden) F.; m. Norma Arambula; 1 dau., Elizabeth L. Student, U. Calif., Los Angeles, 1950-51; LL.B., U. Ariz., 1956. Bar: Ariz. 1956. Practiced in, Tucson, 1956—; partner firm Miller, Pitt & Feldman, 1968—; justice Ariz. Supreme Ct., 1982—; lectr. Coll. Law, U. Ariz., 1965-76, adj. prof., 1976—. Bd. dirs. Tucson Jewish Community Council. Mem. Am. Bd. Trial Advocates (past pres. So. Ariz. chpt.), ABA, Ariz. Bar Assn. (pres. 1974-75, bd. govs. 1967-76), Pima County Bar Assn. (past pres.), Am. Trial Lawyers Assn. (dir. chpt. 1967-76). Democrat. Jewish. Home: 3490 Via Guadalupe Tucson AZ 85717 Office: ARIZONA SUPREME CT STATE CAPITAL BLDG PHOENIX AZ 85007

FELDMAN, STEPHEN, university president; b. N.Y.C., Sept. 11, 1944; s. Harry and Mae (Morris) F.; m. Constance M. Lerudis, June 1, 1969; 1 dau., Jennifer Dawn. B.B.A., CCNY, 1966, M.B.A., 1968, Ph.D. (fellow), 1971. Chmn. dept. banking, fin. and investments Hofstra U., Hempstead, N.Y., 1969-77, asso. prof., 1974-77; dean Sch. Bus. and Public Adminstrn., Western Conn. State U., Danbury, 1977-83, univ. pres., 1981—; dir. Macrolease Internat. Corp., Consol. Lithography Corp., Ednl. Reading Aids Corp.; cons. IBM, Revlon, N.Y. Telephone Co. Editor: Credit Unions, 1974, Handbook of Wealth Management, 1977; contbr. articles to profl. publs. Trustee, Danbury Hosp., United Way. Mem. Am. Assn. State Colls. and Univs. (vice-chmn. com. external relations). Home: Little River Ln RD 4 Redding CT 06896 Office: Western Conn State U Danbury CT 06810 *As well as using creativity, reliability, honest and hard work as vehicles for success, one should attempt to remember to enjoy the contest and not only the victory.*

FELDMAN, WALTER SIDNEY, artist; b. Lynn, Mass., Mar. 23, 1925; s. Hyman and Fradel (Gordon) F.; m. Barbara Rose, June 4, 1950; children—Steven, Mark. B.F.A., Yale U., 1950, M.F.A., 1951; studied with, Willem de Kooning, 1950-51; M.A. (hon.), Brown U., 1953. Instr. painting Yale U., 1951-53; mem. faculty dept. art Brown U., 1953—, prof., 1961—, chmn. studio div., 1973—; vis. prof. Harvard U., 1968, U. Calif., Riverside; artist-in-residence Dartmouth Coll., 1978; cons. Providence Lithography Co. One-man shows, Kruaushaar Galleries, N.Y.C., 1958, 61, 63, Obelisk Gallery, Boston, 1965-66, 67, Inst. Contemporary Arts, London, 1967-68, Bristol Mus., 1975, Hopkins Center, Dartmouth Coll., 1978, group shows include, Mus. Modern Art, 1954, 55, Bklyn. Mus., 1957-58, Corcoran Gallery, Washington, 1959, Bklyn. Mus., 1960, Butler Inst. Am. Art, Youngstown, Ohio, Harvard U. Carpenter Center for Visual Arts, 1963, Lowe Are Center, Syracuse, 1964, Inst. Contemporary Art, Boston, 1961, 66; represented in permanent collections, Brown U., Fogg Mus., Los Angeles County Mus., Met. Mus. Art, Mus. Modern Art, Phoenix Art Mus., Princeton U., Yale U. Art Gallery, Lehigh U. Art Collection, U. Mass., Mexican-Am. Inst., others. Served with U.S. Army, 1943-46. Decorated Purple Heart.; Fulbright fellow, 1956-57; Eliza Howard fellow Mex., 1961; recipient Gov.'s award for arts, 1980. Mem. Color Print Soc. Am. Home: 107 Benevolent St Providence RI 02906 Office: 64 College St Brown Univ Providence RI 02912

FELDMANN, EDWARD GEORGE, pharmaceutical chemist; b. Chgo., Oct. 13, 1930; s. Edward Louis and Vera (Arneson) F.;; foster mother and Helen Whitney; m. Mary J. Evans, Aug. 30, 1952; children: Ann Marie, Edward William, Robert George, Karen Lynn. B.S. in Chemistry, Loyola U., Chgo., 1952; M.S. in Pharmacy (research fellow Am. Found. Pharm. Edn. 1953-55), U. Wis., 1954; Ph.D. in Pharm. Chemistry-Biochemistry, U. Wis., 1955; postgrad., Northwestern U., 1956, U. Chgo., 1958. Teaching asst. Loyola U., Chgo., 1951-52; research asst. U. Wis., 1952-53; sr. chemist Am. Dental Assn., 1955-58, dir. div. chemistry, 1958-59; asso. dir. sci. div. Am. Pharm. Assn., 1959-60, dir., 1960—, asso. exec. dir. for sci. affairs, 1970-83, v.p. sci. affairs, 1983—, asso. editor sci. edit. assn. jour., 1959-60; exec. sec. Acad. Pharm. Scis., 1983—; editor Am. Pharm. Assn., 1960; asso. dir. revision Nat. Fomulary, 1959-60, dir. revision, 1960-70; Mem. adv. panel dental drugs Nat. Formulary, 1955-60; reviewer Internat. Pharmacopeia, WHO, 1958; spl. lectr. drug standards George Washington U., 1960-64; del. conf. on fellowships Nat. Health Council, 1960; mem. coordinating com. Nat. Conf. Antimicrobial Agts., Soc. Indsl. Microbiology, 1960-63; mem. adv. panel pharm. nomenclature A.M.A.-Am. Pharm. Assn.-U.S. Pharmacopeia, 1961-66, mem. nomenclature com., 1962-66; sec. U.S. Com. Internat. Drug Standards, 1964-65; adv. panel food chems. codex Nat. Acad. Scis.-NRC, 1961-71, liaison rep. to drug research bd., 1968-76; spl. liaison rep. to Commn. of Life Scis., Nat. Acad. Scis.-NRC, 1973—; mem. lab. com. Am. Pharm. Assn. Found., 1961-75; mem. com. Ebert prize, 1961-75; judge Lunsford-Richardson Pharmacy Awards, 1962-69; cons. Council on Drugs, A.M.A., 1962; vis. scientist Am. Assn. Colls. of Pharmacy, NSF, 1963-66; mem. expert adv. panel on internat. pharmacopeia and pharm. preparation World Health Orgn., 1963-75; drug cons. Office Sec., U.S. Dept. Health, Edn. and Welfare, 1967-70; nomenclature cons. to Commr., U.S. Food and Drug Adminstrn., 1968-71; mem. expert working group Indsl. Devel. Orgn., UN, 1969; mem. organizing com. 31st Internat. Congress Pharm. Scis., 1970-71; mem. NRC, 1971—; del. U.S. Pharmacopeia, 1970—; mem. Nat. Council on Drugs, 1976-83; expert witness congressional drug legis. hearings; lectr. in field. Asso. editor (1959-60) Drug Standards; editor (1960); chmn. (1960-70) Nat. Formulary Bd.; editor Jour. Pharm. Scis., 1961-75; cons. editor, 1975—; editor APS Acad. Reporter, 1983—; Author articles in field.; Editorial adv. bd.: Index Chemicus, 1968-71. Mem. membership com. Ravenwood Park Citizens Assn., Falls Church, Va., 1962, mem. nominating com., 1971-72; mem. Lake Barcroft Community Assn., 1975—. Recipient Man of Yr. award Nat. Assn. Pharm. Mfrs., 1970; Distinguished citation U. Wis., 1971; G.A. Bergy Lectr. award U. W.Va., 1975. Acad. Fellow Acad. Pharm. Scis.; life mem. Am. Pharm. Assn.; mem. Am. Chem. Soc., N.Y. Acad. Scis., Nat. Soc. Med. Research (council 1961-69), Am. Testing Materials, Council Biology Editors, A.M.A. (affiliate), Fedn. Internat. Pharm., U.S. Tennis Assn., Sigma Xi, Rho Chi, Lambda Chi Sigma. Roman Catholic. Clubs: K.C., Sleepy Hollow Bath and Racquet (Falls Church, Va.); Arlington Tennis and Squash. Home: 6306 Crosswoods Circle Falls Church VA 22044 Office: 2215 Constitution Ave NW Washington DC 20037

FELDMANN, SHIRLEY CLARK, psychology educator; b. Niagara Falls, N.Y.; d. Franklin T. and Mildred L. (Payne) Clark; m. Robert Feldmann, June, 1952 (dec.); m. Horace S. Bush. B.A., Barnard Coll., 1951; M.A., Columbia U., 1952, Ph.D., 1961. Asst. prof. edn. SUNY-Fredonia, 1958-60; asst. research prof. psychiatry N.Y. Med. Coll., N.Y.C., 1960-63; prof. sch. edn. City Coll., CUNY, N.Y.C., 1963—, prof., exec. officer Ph.D. program in ednl. psychology Grad. Sch., 1976—. Contbr. articles to prof. jours. Mem. Am. Psychol. Assn., Internat. Reading Assn., Am. Ednl. Research Assn., Soc. for Research in Child Devel. Home: 600 W End Ave New York NY 10024 Office: Grad Sch CUNY 33 W 42d St New York NY 10036

FELDSHUH, TOVAH S., actress; b. N.Y.C., Dec. 27, 1952; d. Sidney and Lillian (Kaplan) F.; m. Andrew Harris-Levy, Mar. 20, 1977. B.A., Sarah Lawrence Coll., Bronxville, N.Y.; McKnight fellow, Guthrie Theatre-U. Minn. Broadway debut in: Cyrano de Bergerac, 1973; starring role in: Yentl, N.Y.C., 1974, Yentl Goes to Broadway, 1975; leading lady, Am. Shakespeare Festival, Stratford, Conn., 1976; TV appearances in The Amazing Howard Hughes, 1976, Holocaust, 1977, Beggarman-Thief, 1980, The Women's Room, 1980; CBS pilot Murder Inc, 1981; off-Broadway appearance in Three Sisters, 1977; nat. tour in Peter Pan, 1978; starring role in: Broadway musical Sarava, 1978; films include The Idolmaker, 1980, Cheaper to Keep Her, 1980, Daniel, 1983; leading lady, Nat. Shakespeare Festival, 1980, 81; one-woman show, Guthrie Theater, 1980, 81. Recipient Theatre World award, Outer Critics Circle award, Drama Desk award, Israeli Govt. Friendship award. Address: care Internat Creative Mgmt 40 W 57th St New York NY 10019

FELDSTEIN, ALBERT B., editor; b. Bklyn., Oct. 24, 1925; s. Max and Beatrice (Segal) F.; m. Claire Szép, Sept. 2, 1944 (div. Jan. 13, 1967); m. Natalie (Lee) Sigler, Jan. 27, 1967; children—Leslie, Susan (dec.), Jamie, Alan Weiss, Mark. Student, Bklyn. Coll., 1942-43; League scholar, Art Students League, 1942-43. Free-lance artist-writer comic book industry, N.Y.C., 1945-47; freelance artist-writer, editor, E. C. Publs. Inc., N.Y.C., 1947-55; editor, MAD Mag., 1955—; supr.: MAD TV Spl, 1974; Author TV scripts; illustrator children's record album covers. Served with USAAF, 1943-45. Home: 400 E 56th St New York NY 10022 Office: 485 Madison Ave New York NY 10022

FELDSTEIN, JOEL ROBERT, public relations executive; b. Boston, May 20, 1942; s. David and Gertrude (Wexler) F.; married; 1 son, David Reid. B.A., Ohio Wesleyan U., 1963; M.S., Northwestern U., 1964. Mem. pub. relations staff Internat. Minerals & Chems. Corp., Libertyville, Ill., 1964-66; asst. mgr. communications programs Quaker Oats Co., Chgo., 1966-69; pres. Corp. Communications Inc., Chgo., 1969-71; v.p. Aaron D. Cushman & Assos., Inc., Chgo., 1971-74, N.W. Ayer Internat., 1974—; mem. adv. council SBA, 1971. Recipient Medallion award Publicity Club Chgo., 1972. Home: 720 Gordon Terr Chicago IL 60613 Office: 111 E Wacker Dr Chicago IL 60601

FELDSTEIN, JOSEPH, corporate executive, lawyer; b. N.Y.C., Apr. 20, 1933; s. Oscar and Minna (Buchweitz) F.; m. Joyce I. Rogol, June 10, 1962; children: Marc Stuart, Eliot Paul, Jessica Claire. A.B. magna cum laude, Harvard U., 1954, J.D., 1959. Bar: N.Y. bar 1959. Asso. firm Friedman, Lowenstein & Myers, N.Y.C., 1959-61, Jacobs Persinger & Parker, 1961-64; asst. mgr. legal dept. Inmont Corp., N.Y.C., 1964-71; v.p., gen. counsel DPF Inc., Hartsdale, N.Y., 1971-72, Engelhard Industries div. Engelhard Minerals & Chems. Corp., Murray Hill, N.J., 1972-76, sr. v.p., gen. counsel, 1976-81, exec. v.p. adminstrn., 1981—. Mem. Gov.'s Task Force on Future of Tri-State Regional Planning Commn., 1978—. Served with U.S. Army, 1954-56. Mem. N.Y. State Bar Assn., Harvard U. Alumni Assn. Club: Harvard of N.J. (schs. com. 1975—). Home: 46 Charles Rd Bernardsville NJ 07924 Office: 70 Wood Ave S Iselin NJ 08830

FELDSTEIN, MARTIN STUART, economist; b. N.Y.C., Nov. 25, 1939; s. Meyer and Esther (Gevarter) F.; m. Kathleen Foley, June 19, 1965; children—Margaret, Janet. A.B. summa cum laude, Harvard U., 1961; M.A., Oxford U., 1964, D.Phil., 1967. Research fellow Nuffield Coll., Oxford U., 1964-65, ofcl. fellow, 1965-67, lectr. pub. fin., 1965-67; asst. prof. econs. Harvard U., 1967-68, assoc. prof., 1968-69, prof., 1969—; pres. Nat. Bur. Econ. Research, 1977-82; chmn. Council Econ. Advisers, 1982—. Fellow Am. Acad. Arts and Scis., Econometric Soc. (council 1977-82), Nat. Assn. Bus. Economists; mem. Am. Econ. Assn. (John Bates Clark medal 1977, mem. exec. com. 1980-82), Inst. Medicine Nat. Acad. Scis., Council on Fgn. Relations, Phi Beta Kappa. Home: 147 Clifton St Belmont MA 02178 Office: The White House Washington DC 02138

FELDT, ROBERT HEWITT, pediatric cardiologist, educator; b. Chgo., Aug. 3, 1934; s. Robert Hewitt and Frances (Swanson) F.; m. Barbara Ann Fritz, Aug. 17, 1957; children: Christine, Susan, Kathryn. B.S., U. Wis., 1956; M.D., Marquette U., 1960; M.S., U. Minn., 1965. Diplomate: Am. Bd. Pediatrics, Am. Bd. Pediatric Cardiology. Intern Miller Hosp., St. Paul, 1960-61; resident in pediatrics cardiology Mayo Found., Rochester, Minn., 1961-65; cons. pediatrics Mayo Clinic, Rochester, Minn., 1966—, chmn. dept. pediatrics, 1980—, prof. pediatrics; examiner Am. Bd. Pediatrics; chmn. sci. council Am. Heart Assn. Author numerous sci. articles, book chpts., monographs. Fellow Am. Acad. Pediatrics, Am. Cardiology Coll.; mem. Minn. Heart Assn. (pres. 1982), Midwest Soc. Pediatric Research, Am. Pediatric Soc. Presbyterian. Home: 1804 Walden Ln SW Rochester MN 55901 Office: Mayo Clinic Dept Pediatrics 200 1st St SW Rochester MN 55901

FELICIANO, JOSE, entertainer; b. Larez, P.R., Sept. 10, 1945; s. Jose and Hortencia (Garcia) F. Pres. Feliciano Enterprises. Folk singer in, Greenwich Village, N.Y.C., 1962; rec. artist for, Motown Records; TV appearances Feliciano:-Very Special, 1969, Monsanto Night Presents Jose Feliciano, 1972, Soul Train, 1974, over 100 others; has performed with major symphonies worldwide.; composer some of own material, including: Affirmation, Rain, Chico and the Man, Romance in the Night; composer: guitar concerto Concerto de Paulinho; (Recipient Grammy award (2) 1969, Best Folk Guitarist award Guitar Player Mag. 1973, Best Pop Guitarist award 1973-77). 30 Gold Albums. Address: care Internat Creative Mgmt 8899 Beverly Blvd Los Angels CA 90048 *The greatest tragedy for many so-called handicapped people is that they let others convince them that there are limits to what they can accomplish. It's just not so.*

FELICIOTTI, ENIO, food company executive; b. Southbridge, Mass., Oct. 9, 1926; s. Olimpio and Ida (Cesolini) F.; m. Mary Ann Patti, May 28, 1960; children: Sandra, Michele, Delia; m. 2d Carol Hagerty, May 23, 1974; children: Gregory, Charles. B.A., Boston U., 1949, M.A., 1954; Ph.D., U. Mass., 1956. Food technologist Hazel-Atlas

Glass Co., Wheeling, W.Va., 1956-57; mgr. customer service Continental Can Co., Chgo., 1957-60; asst. dir. research Thomas J. Lipton, Inc., Englewood Cliffs, N.J., 1960-65, dir. research, 1965-67, v.p. research, 1967-78, sr. v.p. sci. and tech., 1978—, dir., 1978—. Pres. Haworth Bd. Edn., N.J., 1971-72, Alpine Community Chest, N.J., 1980-83. Served with USN, 1944-46. Recipient presdl. citation Rutgers U., 1983. Fellow Inst. Food Technologists; mem. Am. Chem. Soc., Sigma Xi, Phi Tau Sigma. Roman Catholic. Home: Closter Dock Rd Box 708 Alpine NJ 07620 Office: Thomas J Lipton Inc 800 Sylvan Ave Englewood Cliffs NJ 07632

FELIG, PHILIP, physician, medical researcher, educator, pharmaceutical executive; b. N.Y.C., Dec. 18, 1936; s. Elias M. and Rose (Horn) F.; m. Florence Lee Farber, June 22, 1958; children: Clifford, David, Elliot. A.B. magna cum laude, Princeton U., 1957; M.D. cum laude, Yale U., 1961, Karolinska Inst., 1978. Diplomate: Am. Bd. Internal Medicine. (mem. subsplty. bd. endocrinology 1983-84). Intern Yale-New Haven (Conn.) Hosp., 1961-62, resident, 1962-63, 1965-67; practice medicine specializing in internal medicine, New Haven, 1969-84; asst. prof. medicine Yale U. Sch. Medicine, New Haven, 1969-72, assoc. prof., 1972-75, prof. medicine, 1975-84, C.N.H. Long prof. medicine, 1978-80, vice chmn. dept. internal medicine, 1975-80, chief sect. endocrinology, 1975-80, dir. Clin. Research Center, 1971-80, clin. prof. medicine, 1984—; dir. med. service Presbyn. Hosp., N.Y.C., 1980; Samuel Bard prof. dept. medicine Columbia U., Coll. Physicians and Surgeons, summer, 1980; pres. Sandoz Research Inst., Sandoz Inc., East Hanover, N.J., 1984—; cons. to FDA, 1977, Center for Disease Control, 1978, 82, Nat. Acad. Scis., 1980; com. on small bus. U.S. Senate, 1974; mem. metabolism study sect. NIH, 1974-75, 76-80; chmn. test com. on medicine Nat. Bd. Med. Examiners, 1982-84. Contbr. articles on research in metabolism, endocrinology and diabetes to profl. jours.; editorial bd.: Diabetes, 1974-77, Annals of Internal Medicine, 1977-79, Archives Internal Medicine, 1976—, Am. Jour. Physiology, 1976-82; assoc. editor: Clinical Research, 1971-74, Clin. Physiology, 1980—; editor-in-chief: Endocrinology and Metabolism, 1981. Mem. Mayor's Com. for Commemoration of the Holocaust, New Haven, 1977-79; chmn. groundbreaking and dedication New Haven Holocaust Meml., 1978; bd. dirs. New Haven Jewish Fedn., 1977-80. Served to capt. USAF, 1963-65. Recipient Teaching and Research scholar award Am. Coll. Physicians, 1969-72, Research Career Devel. award NIH, 1972-77, Alvarenga prize award Swedish Med. Soc., 1975, Mary Jane Kugel award Juvenile Diabetes Found., 1977, Louis D. Brandeis award Zionist Orgn. Am., 1979, John Claude Kellion lectr. Australian Diabetes Assn., 1977. Fellow A.C.P.; mem. Endocrine Soc., Am. Diabetes Assn. (vice chmn. nat. program com. 1975-76, Lilly award 1976, established investigator award 1977-82, bd. dirs. 1979-81, 81-84), Conn. Diabetes Assn. (pres. 1974-76, Jonathan May award 1979, Sci. Achievement award 1981), Soc. for Exptl. Biology and Medicine, Am. Fedn. Clin. Research (nat. council 1972-74), Am. Soc. Clin. Nutrition, Am. Physiol. Soc., Assn. Am. Physicians, Am. Soc. Clin. Investigation (nat. council 1977-80), Interurban Clin. Club, N.Y. Acad. Scis., Sigma Xi, Alpha Omega Alpha (pres. Yale chpt. 1960-61). Jewish. Home: 15 Edgewood Way New Haven CT 06515 Office: Route 10 East Hanover NJ 07936

FELIX, ANTHONY G., JR., banker; b. Phila., May 8, 1909; s. Anthony G. and Anna Mabel (Young) F.;, June R. Spreter,; Oct. 28, 1939. B.S. in Econs, U. Pa., 1931, LL.B., 1934. Bar: Pa. bar 1935. Asso. firm Hepburn & Norris, Phila., 1935-42; partner firm Norris, Lex, Hart & Eldredge Esqs., Phila., 1942-56; v.p. First Pa. Banking & Trust Co., Phila., 1956-58, v.p., sec., 1958-63, sr. v.p., sec., 1963-68, exec. v.p., sec., 1968-72, vice chmn., 1972-74; also dir.; sec. First Pa. Corp., 1968-69, v.p., sec., 1969-72, vice chmn., 1972-74, chmn. exec. com., 1974-77; also dir.; sec. 1st Pa. Mortgage Trust, 1970-77, sec., treas., 1977-80; Mem. Banking Bd. Commonwealth Pa., 1964-80. Mem. Am., Pa., Phila. bar assns., Am. Law Inst. Clubs: Merion Golf; Philadelphia Country, Racquet (Phila.). Home: 1127 Wyndon Ave Rosemont PA 19010

FELIX, DAVID, economics educator; b. N.Y.C., June 10, 1918; s. Oscar and Jenny (Rosen) F.; m. Gretchen Louise Schafer, Aug. 20, 1945; children: Tonia, Gianna. B.A., U. Calif.-Berkeley, 1942, M.A., 1947, Ph.D. in Econs., 1955. Asst. prof. econs. U. Wash., Seattle, 1950-52; lectr. bus. adminstrn. U. Calif., Berkeley, 1952-54; from asst. prof. to prof. econs. Wayne State U., Detroit, 1954-63; prof. econs. Washington U., St. Louis, 1964—; vis. prof. econs. U. Calif., Berkeley, 1956, UCLA, 1980, Nat. U. Montevideo, 1967; research assoc. Ctr. Econ. Devel. U. Chgo., 1957-58, 59; research cons. devel. adv. service Harvard U., Argentina, 1964-66, research assoc. Ctr. Internat. Affaris, Cambridge, Mass., 1967-68; cons. UN Econ. Commn. for Latin Am., 1974, Central Bank of Ecuador, Quito, 1976, 78, U. Sao Paulo (Brazil), 1978; vis. fellow Inst. Devel. Studies U. Sussex (Eng.), 1973; state dept. ICA lectr., Holland, Germany, Romania, U.K., 1981. Contbg. editor: Latin Am. Handbook, 1962-65; editorial bd.: Latin Am. Research Rev., 1970-72, 82—, Jour. Econ. History, 1978—; contbr. articles to profl. jours. Mem. exec. com. Eastern Mo. chpt. Ams. Dem. Action, 1971—. Served to lt. USN, 1942-46; PTO. Rockefeller Found. postdoctoral fellow, 1957-58; faculty fellow Ford. Found., 1962-63; research fellow Social Sci. Research Council, 1972. Mem. Am. Econ. Assn., Econ. History Assn., Latin Am. Studies Assn., AAUP. Home: 712 Pennsylvania University City MO 63130 Office: Washington Univ Box 1208 Saint Louis MO 63130

FELKER, CLAY S., editor; b. St. Louis, Oct. 2, 1928; s. Carl T. and Cora F. B.A., Duke, 1951. Editor Duke Chronicle, 1950; reporter Life mag., 1951-57; features editor Esquire mag., 1957-62, pres., 1977; cons. editor Viking Press, 1963-66; editor Infinity, Am. Soc. Mag. Photographers mag., 1965-66, Sunday mag. of N.Y. Herald Tribune, 1963-67, Bookweek mag. and Sunday mag. N.Y. World Jour. Tribune, 1966-67; founder, editor, pub. New York Mag., 1967-77; editor-in-chief, pub. Village Voice, 1974-77, New West mag., 1976-77; pres. NYM Corp., 1967-77; dir., pres. N.Y. Mag. Co., Inc., 1969-77; editor Esquire mag., 1977-79; editor afternoon edit. Daily News, 1980-81. Mem. Phi Delta Theta, Sigma Delta Chi. Home: 322 E 57th St New York NY 10022

FELKER, JEAN HOWARD, electrical engineer; b. Centralia, Ill., Mar. 14, 1919; s. Henry Adam and Olga Fay (Snider) F.; m. Joan Woodman, Aug. 14, 1943 (div. 1981); children: Dittany R., Christopher H.; m. Elizabeth Byers Holtz, Apr. 4, 1981. B.E.E., Washington U., St. Louis, 1941. With Bell Telephone Labs., 1945-59; with AT&T, 1959-62, asst. chief engr., 1960-62; v.p. ops., dir. N.J. Bell Telephone Co., 1962-69; bus. cons., 1969-71; v.p. Bell Telephone Labs., 1971-81; dir., fin. com. Chubb-Life Ins. Co. Am. Fellow IEEE; mem. Nat. Acad. Engring. Home: Box 3 RD 1 Kintnersville PA 18930

FELKER, RICHARD REEVES, investment company executive; b. Monroe, Ga., Aug. 25, 1929; s. Paul M. and Anne (Reeves) F.; m. Rebecca White; children: Ric, Betty. A.B., Vanderbilt U., 1951. With Equitable Securities Corp., 1951-54; v.p. firm Robinson-Humphrey, Inc., Atlanta, 1955-58; chmn. bd. Fin. Service Corp. Am., Atlanta, 1958-72; pres. Richard Felker Co., Atlanta, 1973—; mem. Midwest Stock Exchange, Chgo., 1969-72, Phila.-Balt. Stock Exchange, 1966-72. Chmn. Fulton County chpt. Am. Cancer Soc., 1971—; mem. alumni bd. Vanderbilt U., 1961-62, Com. of 100, Emory U., 1967-74; bd. dirs. Atlanta Community Chest; commr. Atlanta Community Relations Commn. Mem. Atlanta C. of C. (dir. 1968-71, 77, pres. Downtown Council), Apt. Owners and Mgrs. Assn. (past pres., dir.). Clubs: Piedmont Driving, Atlanta City (dir. 1972—), Atlanta City (Atlanta) (chmn. bd. govs. 1977-81). Home: 800 Fairfield Rd NW Atlanta GA 30327 Office: 100 Peachtree St NE Atlanta GA 30303

FELKNOR, BRUCE LESTER, publishing company executive; b. Oak Park, Ill., Aug. 18, 1921; s. Audley Rhea and Harriet (Lester) F.; m. Joanne Sweeney, Feb. 8, 1942 (div. Jan. 1952); 1 dau., Susan Harriet Felknor Pickard; m. Edith G. Johnson, Mar. 1, 1952; children: Sarah Anne, Bruce Lester II. Student, U. Wis., 1939-41. Reporter Dunn County News, Menomonie, Wis., 1937-39; freight brakeman Pa. R.R., N.Y.C., 1941, asst. yardmaster, 1942; prodn. coordinator Hwy. Trailer Co., Edgerton, Wis., 1943; radio officer U.S. Maritime Service, 1944-45; flight radio officer Air Transport Command, 1945; mem. pub. relations dept. Am. Airlines, 1945; writer pub. relations dept. ITT, 1946; Southeast regional pub. relations dir. Ford Motor Co., Chester, Pa., 1946-48; free lance pub. relations, N.Y.C., 1948-49; pub. relations exec. Foote, Cone & Belding, Inc., N.Y.C., 1950-53; v.p. Market Relations Network, N.Y.C., 1954-55; exec. dir. Fair Campaign Practices Com., Inc., N.Y.C., 1956-66; asst. to William Benton (chmn. and pub. Ency. Brit.), 1966-70; dir. mktg. info. internat. div. (Ency. Brit.), 1970-73, dir. advt. and promotion, 1973, dir. pub. info., 1974-76, exec. editor, 1977-83; dir. yearbooks Ency. Brit., 1983—; vis. lectr. Hamilton Coll., 1966, 75, 82. Author: Fair Play in Politics, 1960, State-by-State Smear Study, 1956, You Are They, 1964, (with C.P. Taft) Prejudice & Politics, 1960, Dirty Politics, 1966, reprinted, 1975, (with Frank Jonas et al) Political Dynamiting, 1970; editor: The U.S. Government; How and Why it Works, 1978; also various newspaper, jour. and yearbook articles on politics. Chmn. Citizens Com. for Sch. Centralization in Armonk, N.Y., 1957-61; Mem. bd., exec. com. Fair Campaign Practices Com.; Mem. nat. adv. bd. Amigos de las Americas, 1982—, Am. U., Washington, 1982—; mem. Ill. Gov.'s Council Literacy Am. U., Washington, 1984—. Mem. Am. Polit. Sci. Assn., Authors League Am., Authors Guild. Democrat. Presbyn. (ruling elder, chmn. com. religion and race Presbytery Hudson River 1963-67, mem. nat. council on ch. and soc. 1966-72). Clubs: Arts, Tavern (Chgo.); Nat. Democratic (Washington); Dutch Treat (N.Y.C.). Home: 620 Smith Ave Lake Bluff IL 60044 Office: 310 S Michigan Ave Chicago IL 60604 *Man's greatest gifts are empathy and the ability to penetrate balderdash.*

FELL, FREDERICK VICTOR, publisher; b. Bklyn., May 21, 1910; s. Samuel and Victoria (Greenhut) F.; m. Selma Shampain, May 18, 1975; children: Linda Fell Firestein, Nancy. Student, NYU, 1928-31; LL.B., Bklyn. Law Sch., 1935. Pres. Frederick Fell Pubs., Inc., N.Y.C., 1943-81; prin. Frederick Fell & Assocs., Inc., Literary Agts., Hollywood, Fla., 1981—. Author: (pseudonym Vic Fredericks) Crackers in Bed, 1953, More For Doctors Only, 1953, Jest Married, 1958, For Golfers Only, 1964, Wit and Wisdom of Presidents, 1966, others. Trustee Long Beach (N.Y.) Library, 1948-50; councilman City of Long Beach, 1950-54, pres. city council, 1950-52; pres. Long Beach Hosp. Club, 1949, 59; chmn. book pubs. div. crusades N.Y.C. div. Am. Cancer Soc., 1977-81. Mem. Assn. Am. Pubs., Am. Booksellers Assn., Book Group South Fla. Democrat. Jewish. Clubs: Engrs. Country, Roslyn (L.I.); Hillcrest County, Hollywood (Fla.). Home: 3800 Hillcrest Dr Apt 1120 Hollywood FL 33021

FELL, JOHN LOUIS, film educator, author; b. Westfield, N.J., Sept. 19, 1927; s. Shelby G. and Frances (Hildebr) F.; m. Suzanne Shillington, Dec. 5, 1958; children: Justine Richmond, John Shillington, Eliza Marritt. A.B., Hamilton Coll., 1950; M.A., NYU, 1954, Ph.D., 1958. Dept. head Film and TV Center, State U. Mont., 1958-60; mem. faculty San Francisco State U., 1960-84, chmn. film dept., 1967-70, 75-76, prof. film dept., 1970—. Film writer, N.Y.C., 1952-58; musician, N.Y.C., 1950-58; Author: Film and the Narrative Tradition, 1974, Film: An Introduction, 1975, A History of Films, 1979, Film Before Griffith, 1983; also articles in field; assoc. editor: Cinema Jour.; editorial bd.: Film Quar. Served with USAAF, 1946-47. Mem. Writers Guild Am., Univ. Film Assn., Soc. Cinema Studies (pres. 1981-83), Am. Fedn. Musicians, Phi Beta Kappa, Kappa Delta Pi, Alpha Epsilon Rho. Home: 254 Limokiln Rd Dover Plains NY 12522

FELLENDORF, GEORGE WILLIAM, foundation executive; b. Glen Cove, N.Y., Sept. 11, 1925; s. Frederick and Sarah (Bouton) F.; m. Hazel Maisey, Nov. 30, 1946; children: Carol Elaine, Linda Jean, Joyce Ellen. B.S. in Elec. Engring, Union Coll., Schenectady, 1947,, M.S., Rensselaer Poly. Inst., 1949; Ed.D. in Edn, Columbia, 1974. Jr. engr. Western Electric Co., 1946-47; project adminstr. Hazeltine Electronics Corp., 1949-51; contracts adminstr. Airborne Instruments Lab., Hicksville, N.Y., 1951-52; v.p. Instruments for Industry, Inc., Mineola, N.Y., 1952-58; pres. Planetronics, Inc., Easton, Pa., 1958-62; exec. dir. Alexander Graham Bell Assn. for Deaf, Washington, 1962-78, Hearing Ednl. Aid and Research Found., Inc., 1978—; pres. Fellendorf Assocs., Inc., 1980—. Author: papers in field; Editor: Bibliography on Deafness, 1967, 77, Current Developments in Assistive Devices, 1982, Develop and Deliver!, 1984; also periodical Volta Rev, 1962-76. Mem. Nat. Adv. Council on Vocat. Edn., 1982—. Mem. Council Exceptional Children, Consumers Orgn. for Hearing Impaired, Am., Md., Fla. speech and hearing assns., Acad. Rehab. Audiology, Acad. Health Adminstrn., IEEE, AAAS, Rehab. International. Republican. Lutheran. Clubs: Kiwanis (pres. Georgetown, D.C. club 1975), Cosmos.). Home: 1300 Ruppert Rd Silver Spring MD 20903 Office: Box 32227 Washington DC 20007

FELLER, ROBERT LIVINGSTON, chemist, art conservator; b. Newark, Dec. 27, 1919; s. William Henry and Edna (Buckelew) F.; m. Ruth M. Johnston, Mar. 31, 1975. A.B., Dartmouth Coll., 1941; M.S., Rutgers U., 1943, Ph.D., 1950. Sr. fellow Nat. Gallery Art Research Project, Mellon Inst., Pitts., 1950-76; dir. Research Center on Materials of Artist and Conservator, Carnegie-Mellon Inst. Research, Pitts., 1976—; vis. scientist Conservation Center, Inst. Fine Arts, NYU, 1961; pres. Nat. Conservation Adv. Council, 1975-79. Co-author: On Picture Varnishes and their Solvents, 2d rev. edit., 1971. Served with USN, 1944-46. Fellow Internat. Inst. Conservation Hist. and Artistic Works, Am. Inst. Conservation Hist. and Artistic Works, Illuminating Engring. Soc.; mem. Am. Chem. Soc., Internat. Council Museums (pres. conservation com. 1969-78), AAAS, Fedn. Socs. Coatings Tech., Inter-Soc. Color Council, Am. Assn. Museums, Am. Inst. Conservation. Clubs: Cosmos (Washington); Univ. (Pitts.). Research on deterioration of varnishes, paper, pigments and dyes used by artists. Home: 220 N Dithridge St Pittsburgh PA 15213 Office: Mellon Inst Research Carnegie-Mellon U 4400 5th Ave Pittsburgh PA 15213

FELLERS, JAMES DAVISON, lawyer; b. Oklahoma City, Apr. 17, 1913; s. Morgan S. and Olive R. (Kennedy) F.; m. Margaret Ellen Randerson, Mar. 11, 1939; children: Kay Lynn Fellers Pellow, Lou Ann (Mrs. James B. Street), James Davison. A.B., U. Okla., 1936, J.D., 1936; LL.D. (hon.), Suffolk U., 1974, William Mitchell Coll. Law, 1976, San Fernando Valley U., 1976, D.H.L., Okla. Christian Coll., 1974. Bar: Okla. 1936. Since practiced in, Oklahoma City; sr. mem. Fellers, Snider, Blankenship, Bailey & Tippens; mem. U.S. Com. Selection of Fed. Jud. Officers, 1977-79; Mem. bd. Nat. Legal Aid and Defender Assn., 1973-76; bd. dirs. Am. Bar Endowment, 1977—; mem. adv. bd. Internat. and Comparative Law Center. Trustee Southwestern Legal Found.; hon. consul Belgium, for Okla., 1972—. Served to lt. col. USAF, 8 campaigns, 1941-45; ETO, MTO. Decorated Bronze Star; recipient Hatton W. Sumners award, 1975; Distinguished Service citation U. Okla., 1976; selected as outstanding young man Oklahoma City C. of C., 1948; named to Okla. Hall of Fame, 1982. Fellow Am. Coll. Trial Lawyers, Am. Bar Found., Okla. Bar Found., Nat. Jud. Coll. (dir. 1967-70); mem. Am. Bar Assn. (nat. chmn. jr. bar conf. 1946-47, gov. 1962-65, chmn. ho. of dels. 1966-68, pres. 1974-75), Barra Mexicana (hon. mem.), Can. Bar Assn. (hon. mem.), Internat. Bar Assn., Inter-Am. Bar Assn., Minn. Bar Assn. (hon. mem.), Okla. Bar Assn. (pres. 1964), W.Va. Bar Assn. (hon. mem.), Am. Judicature Soc., Am. Law Inst. (com. continuing legal edn. 1947-49), Inst. Jud. Adminstrn., Internat. Assn. Ins. Counsel (v.p. 1955-56), Nat. Conf. Bar Pres.'s, World Peace through Law Center, Fellows of Young Lawyers Am. Bar (hon. chmn. 1977-79), Oklahoma City C. of C. (dir. 1976), Phi Kappa Psi. Episcopalian. Clubs: Beacon, Petroleum. Home: 6208 Waterford Blvd Apt 92 Oklahoma City OK 73118 Office: 2400 First National Center Oklahoma City OK 73102

FELLEY, DONALD LOUIS, chemical company executive; b. Memphis, Feb. 7, 1921; s. Alfred and Helen Ruth (Meek) F.; m. June Pack, Oct. 1, 1949; children: James D., Douglas C., Richard B., David L., Mary L. B.S., Ark. State Coll., 1941; M.S., U. Ill., 1947, Ph.D., 1949. With Rohm and Haas Co., 1949—, v.p., gen. mgr. internat. div., 1970-76, v.p., regional dir. N.Am., 1976-78, pres., dir., Phila., 1978—; chmn. Greater Phila. 1st Corp., 1984—. Bd. dirs. Phila. World Affairs Council, 1976—, Greater Phila. C. of C., 1978—, Abington (Pa.) Meml. Hosp., 1978—. Served to capt. F.A. AUS, 1942-46. Mem. Am. Chem. Soc., Soc. Chem. Industry (bd.), Sigma Xi, Alpha Chi Sigma, Phi Lambda Upsilon. Office: Rohm and Haas Co Independence Mall W Philadelphia PA 19105

FELLIN, PHILLIP ALEXANDER, univ. dean; b. Marshfield, Mo., Aug. 26, 1931; s. Peo James and Anna (Sperandio) F.; m. Phyllis LaPee, June 29, 1959; children—Christopher, Annette, Cecilia, Campion, Mary. A.B., St. Benedict's Coll., 1953; M.S.W., St. Louis U., 1957; M.A., U. Mich., 1959, Ph.D., 1962; D.H.L., Benedictine Coll., 1972. Asst. prof. St. Louis U., 1961-64, asso. prof., 1964-65, U. Mich., 1965-68, prof., 1968—, asst. dean, 1970-71, dean, 1971; Mem. commn. accreditation Council on Social Work Edn., 1970—. Co-author, editor: The Assessment of Social Research, 1969, Exemplars of Social Research, 1969, Social Program Evaluation, 1972, Social Workers at Work, 1972. Dir. Family Service of Ann Arbor, 1967-70, Office Econ. Opportunity, 1968-70; bd. dirs. Washtenaw County Juvenile Ct., 1967—. Served with AUS, 1953-55. Russell Sage Found. scholar, 1959. Mem. Acad. Certified Social Workers, Council Social Work Edn., Nat. Assn. Social Workers. Home: 1543 Waltham St Ann Arbor MI 48103

FELLINI, FEDERICO, film director, writer; b. Rimini, Italy, Jan. 20, 1920; s. Urbano and Ida (Barbiani) F.; m. Giulietta Masina, Oct., 1943. Student, U. Rome. Journalist, 1937-39, writer radio dramas, 1939-42, screen writer, 1943—, dir., 1952—. Writer: films, including Open City (N.Y. Film Critics Circle award for best fgn. lang. film 1946), Paisan, (N.Y. Film Critics Circle award for best fgn. lang. film 1948), Ways of Love, 1950 (N.Y. Film Critics Circle award for best fgn. lang. film 1950), Senza Pieta, 1950; dir.: The White Sheik, 1952, I Vitelloni, 1953, La Strada, 1954 (Acad. award 1957), Il Bidone, 1955, Notti di Cabiria, 1957 (Acad. award for best fgn. film 1958), La Dolce Vita, 1959 (Cannes Festival Gold Palm award 1960, N.Y. Film Critics Circle award for best fgn. lang. film 1961), 8 1/2, 1963 (Acad. award for best fgn. film 1964, N.Y. Film Critics Circle award 1963), Juliet of the Spirits, 1965, Never Bet the Devil Your Head, 1968, Histoires Extraordinairies, 1968, Satyricon, 1969, The Clowns, 1970, Fellini's Roma, 1972, Amarcord, 1974 (Acad. award for best fgn. film 1975), Casanova, 1977, Orchestra Rehearsal, 1979, City of Women, 1981; Author: Amarcord, 1974, Quattro Film, 1975, Fellini on Fellini, 1977. Office: 110 Via Margutta Rome Italy *

FELLMAN, DAVID, political science educator; b. Omaha, Sept. 14, 1907; s. Jacob and Brandel (Gubermann) F.; m. Sara Ann Dinion, Aug. 6, 1933; children: Laura Ann, Michael Dinion. A.B., U. Neb., 1929, A.M., 1930, LL.D., 1966; Ph.D., Yale, 1934. Instr. U. Neb., 1934-39, asst. prof. polit. sci., 1939-43, asso. prof., 1943-47; prof. polit. sci. U. Wis. at Madison, 1947-79, Vilas prof. polit. sci., 1964-79, emeritus prof., 1979—; vis. instr. U. Mo., summer 1938; instr. G.I.U. of Florence, Italy, 1945; Brown and Haley lectr. Coll. Puget Sound, 1959; Gaspar G. Bacon lectr. Boston U., 1963-64; Sperry-Hutchinson lectr. U. S.C., 1965; C.H. Dillon lectr. U. S.D., 1969. Author: (with T.C. McCormick, ed.) Problems of the Postwar World, 1945, Twentieth Century Political Thought, (with J.S. Roucek, ed.), 1946; Editor: Post-War Governments of Europe, 1946, Readings in American National Government, 1947, 2d edit., 1950, The Defendants Rights, 1958, The Limits of Freedom, 1959, The Supreme Court and Education, 1960, 3d edit., 1976, State Constitutional Revision, 1960, (with W.B. Graves) The Constitutional Right of Association, 1963, Religion in American Public Law, 1965, The Defendant's Rights under English Law, 1966, (with Barbara N. McLennan) Crime in Urban Society, 1970, The Defendant's Rights Today, 1976; bd. editors: Am. Polit. Sci. Rev, 1947-49; editor: Midwest Jour. Polit. Sci, 1956-59; Contbr. articles to polit. sci., law jours., encys. Mem. Am. Polit. Sci. Assn. (mem. exec. council 1952-55, v.p. 1959-60), AAUP (pres. U. Wis. chpt. 1950-51, mem. nat. council 1958-61, 67-72, pres. 1964-66), ACLU, Midwest Conf. Polit. Scientists (pres. 1955-56), Sigma Alpha Mu (nat. scholarship chmn. 1943-48), Phi Beta Kappa, Phi Kappa Phi. Home: 3207 Stevens St 4 Madison WI 53705

FELLNER, MICHAEL JOSEF, dermatologist; b. N.Y.C., Sept. 15, 1936; s. Stephen and Selma (Ehrlich) F.; m. Fredda Ginsberg, Aug. 27, 1961; children: Jonathan, Melinda. A.B. in Chemistry, Cornell U., 1956; M.D., U. Md., 1960. Diplomate: Am. Bd. Dermatology. Intern Kings County Hosp., State U. N.Y., Bklyn., 1960-61; resident Mt. Sinai Hosp., N.Y.C., 1961-63; NIH tng. fellow N.Y. U. Med. Center, N.Y.C., 1963-64; NIH research tng. fellow in allergy and immunology, dept. dermatology N.Y. U., N.Y.C., 1964-66, Am. Allergy Found. fellow, 1966-67; practice medicine specializing in dermatology, N.Y.C., 1966—; dir. dermatology Bird S. Coler Hosp., N.Y.C., 1973-79, chief of dermatology, 1979—; mem. staff Met. Hosp., Gracie Sq. Hosp.; asst. prof. dermatology N.Y. U. Sch. Medicine, N.Y.C., 1966-70, asso. prof., 1970-72; prof. dermatology N.Y. Med. Coll., N.Y.C., 1973—; reviewer Archives of Dermatology. Author: Immunology of Skin Diseases, 1980; contbr. numerous articles on immunology, allergy and dermatology to med. jours.; corr. editor: Internat. Jour. Dermatology, 1976-81; mem. N.Am. editorial bd., 1981—. Recipient Fred Wise Meml. award N.Y. Acad. Medicine, 1963; Gold medal Am. Dermatol. Assn., 1967; award N.Y. State Med. Soc., 1973; NIH grantee, 1967-73; John A. Hartford Found. grantee, 1972-78. Mem. Am. Acad. Dermatology, Am. Acad. Allergy, Dermatologic Soc. Greater N.Y. (Henry Silver award 1964), Am. Fedn. Clin. Research, Soc. Investigative Dermatology, Am. Dermatologic Soc. for Allergy and Immunology (founding mem., sec.-treas. 1977-79, pres. 1979-80), N.Y. Acad. Scis., N.Y. State Dermatology Soc., N.Y. County Soc. Medicine, Internat. Soc. Tropical Dermatology, AAAS. Office: 30 E 60th St New York NY 10022

FELLOWES, FREDERICK GALE, JR., naval officer; b. Buffalo, Jan. 12, 1930; s. Frederick Gale and Adalaide Elisabeth (Evans) F.; m. Sarah Campbell Sharpe, Apr. 16, 1955; children—Ashley Elisabeth, Sarah Gale. Student, Dartmouth Coll., 1948-49; B.S., U.S. Naval

Acad., 1953. Commd. ensign U.S. Navy, 1953, advanced through grades to rear adm., 1977; personal aide to (Chief Naval Ops.), 1969-71, exec. officer, 1971-72, comdg. officer, 1972-74, 1974-76; chief of staff, comdr. Naval Air Force, U.S. Pacific, 1976-77; comdr. (Fighter Airborne Early Warning Wing, U.S. Pacific Fleet), 1977-79; with Office Chief Naval Ops., Pentagon, Washington, 1979—. Decorated Legion of Merit, D.F.C. (3), Navy Commendation medal, others. Home: 1503 Snughill Ct Vienna VA 22180 Office: Office Chief Naval Ops (Code 982 The Pentagon) Washington DC 20301

FELLOWS, GEORGE HARVEY, city manager; b. Ft. Dodge, Iowa, Sept. 22, 1920; s. William Harvey and Ellen (Saville) F.; m. Bertha Jean Abbe, July 4, 1944; children: Jonathon Allen, Thomas Lee, Georganne. B.C.E., Iowa State Coll., 1944. City engr., City of Spencer, Iowa, 1947-49, asst. city engr., City of Waterloo, Iowa, 1949-53; dir. pub. service City of Greeley, Colo., 1953-57; dir. pub. works City of Pueblo, Colo., 1957-59, city mgr., 1959-66, City of Colorado Springs, Colo., 1966—. Mem. exec. com. ARC, Pueblo, 1961-65, sec., 1965; bd. dirs. Goodwill, Pueblo, 1964-65, Pueblo YMCA; mem. citizens adv. council U. Colo., El Paso Community Coll. Served as ensign USNR, 1944-46. Mem. Internat. Assn. City Mgrs., Pueblo, Colorado Springs chambers commerce. Presbyterian. Clubs: Elks, Kiwanis, Masons. Home: 3134 San Luis Dr Colorado Springs CO 80909 Office: City Adminstrn Bldg Colorado Springs CO 80901

FELLOWS, HAYNES HAROLD, JR., communications company executive; b. N.Y.C., Apr. 10, 1919; s. Haynes Harold and Madeleine Masten (Day) F.; m. Joan J. Blackwell, Feb. 20, 1983; 7 children. A.B. cum laude, Wesleyan U., Middletown, Conn., 1940. With Met. Life Ins. Co., 1940-41; with New Eng. Tel. & Tel. Co., 1946-52, 55—, v.p., comptroller, 1963-65, v.p. for planning, 1965, v.p. ops., 1965-73, v.p. finance, 1973—, also dir.; with AT&T, 1953-54; dir., chmn. exec. com. State St. Bank & Trust Co., Boston, State St. Boston Corp.; dir., mem. exec. com., chmn. fin. com. Blue Cross of Mass.; dir. Commonwealth Energy System. Mem. corp. Boston Mus. Sci., Wentworth Inst.; chmn. bd. sponsors New Eng. Eye Bank; bd. dirs. N.E. region NCCJ; mem. exec. bd., chmn. fin. com. Norumbega council Boy Scouts Am.; trustee Mass. Eye and Ear Infirmary. Served to maj. Q.M.C. AUS, 1941-46. Mem. Fin. Execs. Inst., Newcomen Soc., Phi Beta Kappa, Delta Kappa Epsilon. Clubs: Downtown, Commercial (Boston); Lake Sunapee (N.H.); Yacht. Home: 301 Highland St Weston MA 02193 Office: 185 Franklin St Boston MA 02107

FELLOWS, ROBERT ELLIS, medical scientist, educator; b. Syracuse, N.Y., Aug. 4, 1933; s. Robert Ellis and Clara (Talmadge) F.; children—Kara, Lisa, Ari. A.B., Hamilton Coll., 1955; M.D., C.M., McGill U., 1959; Ph.D., Duke U., 1966. Intern N.Y. Hosp., N.Y.C., 1959-60, asst. resident, 1960-61, Royal Victoria Hosp., Montreal, Que., Can., 1961-62; asst. prof. dept. medicine Duke U., Durham, N.C., 1966-76, asst. prof. dept. physiology and pharmacology, 1966-70, assoc. prof. dept. physiology and pharmacology, asso. dir. med. scientist tng. program, 1972-76; prof., chmn. dept. physiology and biophysics U. Iowa Coll. Medicine, dir. med. sci. tng. program, 1976—; mem. Nat. Pituitary Agy. Adv. Bd.; cons. NIH. Mem. editorial bd.: Endocrinology. Mem. AAAS, Am. Chem. Soc., Am. Fedn. Clin. Research, Am. Physiol. Soc., Am. Soc. Biol. Chemists, Am. Soc. Cell Biology, Assn. Chairmen Depts. Physiology, Biochem. Soc., Biophys. Soc., Endocrine Soc., Internat. Soc. Neuroendocrinology, N.Y. Acad. Scis., Soc. for Neurosci., Tissue Culture Assn., Sigma Xi, Alpha Omega Alpha. Home: 15 Prospect Pl Iowa City IA 52240 Office: 5-660 Bowen Scis Bldg Iowa City IA 52242

FELLOWS, RUSSELL COLEMAN, retail chain executive; b. Rentz, Ga., Sept. 26, 1938; s. Rufus C. and Myrtice Lucille (Brown) F.; m. Patsy Patterson, June 26, 1960. Student pvt. schs., Macon, Ga. With Scott's Supermarket, Macon, 1946-60; asst. mgr.; mgr. Handy Andy Food Stores, Macon; also partner, gen. mgr.; gen. mgr. food stores Munford, Inc., Atlanta, then v.p., gen. mgr., sr. v.p., pres. food stores, 1974-76, sr. v.p. corporate devel., 1976-81, sr. v.p. petroleum mktg., 1978, sr. v.p. mktg., 1979-81, pres., 1981—, chief operating officer, 1982—, also dir. Mem. Nat. Assn. Convenience Stores (dir.), Ga Retail Food Dealers Assn. (past dir.). Baptist. Home: 649 Old Club Rd S Macon GA 31210 Office: 1860-74 Peachtree Rd NW Atlanta GA 30309

FELMER, ANDREW ROBERT, utility executive; b. Cleve., Mar. 10, 1924; s. Michael and Hermine (Fleger) F.; m. Joan Elaine White, Mar. 12, 1945; children: Diane, Janet. B.A., Baldwin-Wallace Coll., Berea, Ohio, 1947; student, Advanced Mgmt. Course, Case Western Res. U. With Cleve. Electric Illuminating Co., 1948—, asst. treas., 1957-74, sec., 1974—. Bd. dirs. Am. Cancer Soc. Served with USAAF, 1942-43; Served with USNR, 1943-45. Mem. Am. Soc. Corp. Secs. (treas. 1982), Edison Electric Inst., Greater Cleve. Growth Assn. Episcopalian. Clubs: Mid-Day, Kiwanis (past pres.), Masons.). Home: 5164 Park Ln North Olmsted OH 44070 Office: PO Box 5000 Cleveland OH 44101

FELS, RENDIGS, economist, educator; b. Cin., June 11, 1917; s. Clifford George and Estella Luella (Rendigs) F.; m. Beatrice Carmichael Baker, Dec. 27, 1941; children: Charles Wentworth Baker, Carmichael. A.B., Harvard, 1939, Ph.D., 1948; A.M., Columbia, 1940. Mem. faculty Vanderbilt U., 1948—, prof. econs., 1956—, dir. grad. program econ. devel., 1956- 57, chmn. dept. econs. and bus. adminstrn., 1962-65, 77-79; Chmn. Univs.-Nat. Bur. Com., 1962-67. Author: American Business Cycles, 1865-1897, 1959, Challenge to the American Economy, an Introduction to Economics, 1961, 2d edit, 1966, (with C. Elton Hinshaw) Forecasting and Recognizing Business Cycle Turning Points, 1968; Editor: (with Stephen Buckles) Casebook of Economic Problems and Policies, 5th edit, 1981. Served with USAAF, 1942-46. Mem. Am. Econ. Assn. (sec.-treas. 1970-75, treas. 1976—), Midwest Econ. Assn. (pres.-elect 1983-84), So. Econ. Assn. (pres. 1967-68). Home: 917 Westview Ave Nashville TN 37205

FELSEN, LEOPOLD B., engineer, educator; b. Munich, Germany, May 7, 1924; m. Sima Laks, May 10, 1944; children: Michael, Judy. B.E.E., Poly. Inst. Bklyn., 1948, M.E.E., 1949, D.E.E., 1952; D.Tecnices (hon.), tech. U. Denmark, 1979. Research asst. prof. Poly. Inst. N.Y., Bklyn., 1952-56, research asso. prof., 1956-61, prof. electrophysics, 1961-74, dean engring., 1974-78, inst. prof., 1978—. Contbr. articles to profl. jours. Served with U.S. Army, 1943-46. Recipient Balthasar Van der Pol gold medal Internat. Union Radio Sci., 1975; Humboldt Sr. Scientist award, 1980; Guggenheim fellow, 1973. Fellow IEEE, Optical Soc. Am.; mem. Internat. Union Radio Sci., Am. Soc. Engring. Edn., Nat. Acad. Engring. Home: 2 Bay Club Dr Bayside NY 11360 Office: Polytechnic Inst of NY Route 110 Farmingdale NY 11735

FELSENFELD, GARY, govt. ofcl.; b. N.Y.C., Nov. 18, 1929; (married), 1956; 3 children. A.B., Harvard, 1951; Ph.D. in Chemistry (NSF fellow), Calif. Inst. Tech., 1955; postgrad. (NSF fellow), Oxford (Eng.) U., 1954-55. Officer NIH, USPHS, HEW, 1955-58; chief phys. chemistry sect., lab. molecular biology Nat. Inst. Arthritis and Metabolic Diseases, 1961—; asst. prof. biophysics U. Pitts., 1958-61; cons. NIMH, 1958-61; vis. prof. Harvard, 1963; Merck disting. lectr. Rutgers U., 1977. Mem. editorial bd.: Jour. Biol. Chemistry, 1965-70, Jour. Molecular Biology, 1967-73, Biophys. Chemistry, 1973-76, Biopolymers, 1975-77, Ann. Rev. of Biochemistry, 1975-80, Quar. Rev. of Biophysics, 1975—, Cell, 1979—, Jour. Molecular and Cellular Biology, 1980—. Fellow AAAS; mem. Am. Chem. Soc., Am. Biophys. Soc., Am. Assn. Biol. Chemists, Nat. Acad. Scis., Am. Acad. Arts and Scis. Office: Lab Molecular Biology Nat Inst Arthritis Diabetes, Digestive, and Kidney Diseases Bethesda MD 20205

FELSON, BENJAMIN, physician, educator; b. Newport, Ky., Oct. 21, 1913; s. Solomon and Esther (Bussell) F.; m. Virginia Raphaelson, Mar. 18, 1936; children: Stephen, Nancy (Mrs. Paul Rubin), Marcus, Richard, Edward. B.S., U. Cin., 1933, M.D., 1935. Intern Cin. Gen. Hosp., 1935-36, resident pathology, 1936-37, resident radiology, 1937-40; fellow in cancer therapy Indpls. City Hosp., 1940-41; practice radiology, Tulsa, 1941-42; asst. prof. radiology U. Cin., 1945-48, asso. prof., 1948-51, prof. radiology, 1951—, dir. radiology, 1951-73; radiologist Cin. Gen. Hosp., 1945-48, asso. dir. radiology, 1948-51, dir., 1951-73; Cons. Wright-Patterson AFB Hosp., Dayton and Cin. VA hosps., USPHS, VA Central Office, U.S. Army M.C.; cons. U.S. Navy Med. Dept.; Cons. Walter Reed Hosp., Armed Forces Inst. Pathology. Author: Fundamentals of Chest Roentgenology, 1960, Index for Roentgen Diagnoses, 1961, (with A. Weinstein, H.B. Spitz) Principles of Chest Roentgenology, 1965 (Gold Book award), (with J.F. Wiot) Case of the Day, 1966, Chest Roentgenology, 1973, (with M.M. Reeder) Gamuts in Radiology, 1974; editor: Roentgen Techniques in the Laboratory Animal, 1968, Radiology of The Acute Abdomen, 1974, Gall Bladder and Biliary Tract, 1976, Fractures and Dislocations, 1978, Computerized Cranial Tomography, 1977, Tuberculosis, 1979, Lymphomas and Leukemias, 1980, Interventional Radiology, 1981; jour. Seminars in Roentgenology, 1966—; mem. editorial bd.: Chest, 1962-72, JAMA (Jour. AMA), 1974-79; Contbr. numerous articles to sci. jours. Nat. bd. dirs. Friends of Hebrew U., Israel, U. Negev, Israel. Served from capt. to maj. M.C. AUS, 1942-45; ETO. Fellow Am. Coll. Chest Physicians, Am. Coll. Radiology (chmn. commn. on edn. and chancellor 1966-69, Gold medal 1977), Royal Coll. Radiology (hon.) (Gt. Britain), Royal Coll. Radiology Australia (hon.), Royal Coll. Surgeons in Ireland (hon.); mem. Cin. Acad. Medicine, Am. Roentgen Ray Soc. (1st v.p. 1972, Cert. appreciation 1982), Roentgen Soc. Chgo. (Gold medal), Ohio Med. Assn., Radiol. Soc. N.Am. (1st v.p. 1959, Gold medal 1979), Ohio Radiol. Soc., Greater Cin. Radiol. Soc., Fleischner Chest Radiol. Soc. (pres. 1975), Alpha Omega Alpha, Pi Kappa Epsilon; hon. mem. Cuban, Brazilian, Colombian, Peruvian, Central Am., Costa Rican, Spanish, Japanese, South African, Canadian radiol. socs., Nat. Acad. Medicine Colombia, Venezuelan Thoracic Soc., Med. Soc. Okinawa. Home: 3994 Rose Hill Ave Cincinnati OH 45229

FELT, DONALD LINN, naval officer; b. San Diego, June 6, 1931; s. Harry Donald and Kathryn Cowley F.; m. Marguerite Denver Synon, July 6, 1957; children—Kathryn Linn, Mary Eleanor, Marguerite Elizabeth, George Andrew, Sara Denver. B.S., U.S. Naval Acad., 1953; Aero. Engr., U.S. Naval Postgrad. Sch., 1963. Commd. ensign U.S. Navy, 1953, advanced through grades to rear adm., 1980; comdg. officer (Attack Sqfuadron 27), Lemore, Calif., 1969-70, 1974-76,, comdr., after 1978, comdg. officer. Decorated Bronze Star, Air Medal, others. Mem. Sigma Xi. Office: Joint Chief Staff Washington DC 20301

FELT, IRVING MITCHELL, foundation executive, corporation executive; b. N.Y.C., Jan. 25, 1910; s. Abraham and Dora (Mandel) F. B.S., U. Pa., 1929. Pres. Felt Found., Inc., N.Y.C., 1941—; pres. Graham-Paige Corp., 1955—, now chmn.; hon. chmn. Felt Forum; chmn. bd. Madison Sq. Garden Corp.; dir., chmn. exec. com. Trafalger Industries, Inc.; Chmn. bd., mem. exec. com. Republic Corp.; dir. Triangle Industries, Inc. Hon. chmn., former pres. Fedn. Jewish Philanthropies; bd. dirs., mem. exec. com. Met. Opera Assn.; chmn. nat. exec. bd. NCCJ; hon. chmn., past pres. Jewish Child Care Assn.; bd. dirs. Joffrey Ballet. Mem. Navy League of U.S. (nat. v.p., dir.), N.Y. Conv. and Visitor's Bur. (dir.). Clubs: Met. Opera, Madison Sq. Garden, Harmonie (N.Y.C.); Racquet, Tamarisk Golf, Springs (Palm Springs, Calif.); Hillcrest Country (Los Angeles). Home: 800 Fifth Ave New York NY 10021 Office: 2 Pennsylvania Plaza New York NY 10001

FELTEN, JOHN CHARLES, transportation equipment manufacturing company executive; b. Chgo., Dec. 1, 1930; s. Frank N. and Mabel Rose (Hansch) F.; m. Sally Louise McDougall, Oct. 20, 1956; children: Leslie Margaret, John William. B.S., U. Ill., 1952. Sales rep. Shell Oil Co., 1956-58; v.p. mktg. MCM Industries, 1958-63; pres., gen. mgr. subs. Medalist Mfg. Co., 1963-67; with U.S. Ry. Mfg. Co. (now Evans Transp. Co.), Chgo., 1967-73, pres., 1970-73; exec. v.p., gen. mgr. transp. systems and indsl. group Evans Products Co., Chgo., 1973-74, pres., 1974—, exec. v.p., dir., Portland, Oreg., 1975—; dir. First Nat. Bank, Des Plaines, Ill. Bd. dirs. N.W. Suburban YMCA. Served to lt. USNR, 1952-55. Mem. Am. Ry. Car Inst. (dir. 1969), Ry. Supply Inst. (dir. 1972), Ry. Progress Inst. (gov. 1972), Nat. Freight Traffic Assn., Young Presidents Orgn., Alpha Sigma Phi. Republican. Lutheran. Home: 21446 N Andover Rd Kildeer IL 60047 Office: 2550 Golf Rd Rolling Meadows IL 60008

FELTENSTEIN, HARRY DAVID, JR., chemical executive; b. St. Joseph, Mo., Nov. 6, 1920; s. Harry David and Isabel (Rosenbaum) F.; m. Rosalie Goldstein, Jan. 18, 1945 (dec. Sept. 1977); children: Andrew, Martha; m. Carmen Arechabala Fernandez, Aug. 24, 1979; 1 son, Henry. B.S., Harvard U., 1942. Engaged in book pub., 1946-50; with Merrill Lynch, Pierce, Fenner & Smith, 1951-57, Lithium Corp., Am. Inc., N.Y.C., 1957-69, financial v.p., treas., 1957-58, exec. v.p., treas., 1958-60, pres., treas., 1960-69; pres., dir. Beryllium Metals & Chems. Corp., 1962-69, Gt. Salt Lake Minerals and Chems. Corp., 1967-69; exec. v.p., dir. Gulf Resources & Chem. Corp., 1967-69; pres. dir. Fuel Mgmt. Corp., Washington, 1970—, Internat. Wine Investors, Ltd., 1972—, Wildenstein & Co., 1972-74; European rep. C & K Coal Co. div. Gulf Resources & Chem. Corp., 1981-82. Served with USNR, 1942-46. Home: Fernandez de la Hoz 78 Madrid-3 Spain also Calle Marqués de Salvatierra 5 Ronda (Málaga) Spain

FELTHAM, IVAN REID, business executive; b. Brandon, Man., Can., May 13, 1930; s. Reginald F. and Ethel L. (Graham) F.; m. Kristine Strombeck, May 30, 1958; children: Derek Bruce, Andrea Lynn. B.A., U. B.C., 1951, LL.B., 1954; B.C.L., Oxford U., 1956. Bar: barrister and solicitor B.C. 1957, barrister and solicitor Ont. 1962, Queen's Counsel 1969. Asst. prof. U. B.C., Vancouver, 1957-61; prof., co-dir. Comml. Law Program Osgoode Hall Law Sch., Toronto, 1961-65; assoc. Baker & McKenzie, Chgo., 1965-67; prof., dir. bus. law program Osgood Hall Law Sch., Toronto, 1967-74; exec., gen. counsel Canadian Gen. Electric Co. Ltd., Toronto, 1974—. Rhodes scholar, 1954. Mem. Can. Bar Assn., Law Soc. Upper Can., Internat. Bar Assn., Internat. Law Assn., Am. Soc. Internat. Law. Club: Granite (Ont.). Office: Can Gen Electric Co Ltd PO Box 417 Commerce Ct N Toronto ON Canada M5L 1J2

FELTON, DEAN RUSSELL, engring. co. exec.; b. Kewanee, Ill., Feb. 28, 1926; s. George William and Hazel Louise (Hepner) F.; m. Shirley Jean Wilson; children—David, Michael, Mark, Julie. B.A. in Civil Engring, U. Ill., 1951. Registered profl. engr. and land surveyor, Mo., others. Asst. hwy. engr. Calif. Div. Hwys., 1951-55; project mgr. Warren & Van Praag, Inc. (Engrs.), St. Louis, 1955-57, sr. design engr., 1957-62, head St. Louis office, 1963, asso., 1965—, v.p., 1968-74, exec. v.p., 1974-76; pres. Dean R. Felton, Inc. (Cons. Engrs.), St. Louis, 1976—; dir. Cons. Engrs. Council Mo. Served with U.S. Army, 1944-46. Fellow ASCE, Am. Water Works Assn., Am. Cons. Engrs. Council; mem. Nat., Mo. socs. profl. engrs. Republican. Mem. United Ch. of Christ. Club: Masons. Home: 615 Hollywood Pl Webster Groves MO 63119 Office: 320 West Port Plaza Suite 202 Saint Louis MO 63141

FELTON, GORDON H., publishing exec.; b. New Virginia, Iowa, Nov. 20, 1925; s. Elmer Harold and Velda Ann (Frederick) F.; m. Elizabeth Lanza, July 22, 1961. B.A., Rollins Coll., Winter Park, Fla., 1946; M.A., U. Denver, 1951. Asst. to v.p. Look mag., N.Y.C., 1960-64; bus. mgr. Cowles Communications Books Co., N.Y.C., 1965-67; v.p. Cambridge Book Co., N.Y.C., 1968-70; gen. mgr. publs. NEA, Washington, 1971—. Served with AUS, 1950-52. Mem. NEA, Am. Soc. Curriculum Devel., Internat. Reading Assn., Modern Lang. Assn. Home: 2122 California St NW Washington DC 20008 Office: 1201 16th St NW Washington DC 20036

FELTON, JEAN SPENCER, physician; b. Oakland, Calif., Apr. 27, 1911; s. Herman and Tess (Davidson) F.; m. Janet E. Birnbaum, June 27, 1937; children: Gary, Keith, Robin. A.B., Stanford U., 1931, M.D., 1935. Diplomate: Am. Bd. Preventive Medicine, Am. Bd. Indsl. Hygiene. Intern Mt. Zion Hosp., San Francisco, 1934-35, resident in surgery, 1935-36, Dante Hosp., San Francisco, 1936-38; practice medicine, San Francisco, 1938-40; guest lectr. indsl. sociology U. Tenn. at Knoxville, 1946-53; med. dir. Oak Ridge Nat. Lab., 1946-53; cons. dept. medicine, prof. dept. preventive medicine, pub. health U. Okla. Med. Sch., 1953-58; cons. indsl. hygiene Okla. State Dept. Health, 1953-58; past cons. VA, St. Louis area; prof. occupational health U. Calif. Schs. Medicine and Pub. Health, Los Angeles, 1958-68; dir. occupational health service Dept. Personnel, County Los Angeles, 1968-74; med. dir. occupational health Naval Regional Med. Center, Long Beach, Calif., 1974-78; clin. prof. community medicine U. So. Calif., 1968-82, clin. prof. emeritus, 1982—; clin. prof. community and environ. medicine U. Calif., Irvine, 1975—; cons. occupational health NASA, USN, VA, AEC, USPHS, Social Security Adminstrn., 1955-62. Author: (with A. H. Katz) Health and Community; Man, Medicine, and Work; Bd. editors: Exerpta Medica, Sect. XXXV, The Netherlands.; Contbr. articles to med. jours. Past mem. Youth Service Com. Oak Ridge Welfare Council, 1946-53, Tenn. State Commn. on Children, Welfare Services Dept.; chmn., mem. adv. bd. Oak Ridge; past mem. Gov.'s Com. Utilization Physically Handicapped, Pres.'s Com. Employment Handicapped. Served to lt. col., M.C. AUS, 1940-46; transport surgeon on St. Mihiel and Pres. Pierce, 1941; between San Francisco and the Orient; indsl. med. officer; Philippines and Japan; indsl. med. officer Sixth Army, 1945. Decorated Army Commendation Ribbon, 1946; recipient Citation for Excellence in Med. Authorship by Am. Assn. Indsl. Physicians and Surgeons, 1948; Knudsen award Indsl. Med. Assn., 1968; Physician of Yr. award Calif. Gov.'s Com. on Employment of Handicapped, 1979, Pres.'s Com. on Employment of Handicapped, 1979. Fellow Am. Coll. Preventive Medicine (pres. 1966-67), Am. Acad. Occupational Medicine, Am. Occupational Med. Assn. (Meritorious Service award 1965, Health Achievement in Industry award 1983), Am. Pub. Health Assn.; mem. AMA (sec., vice chmn. sect. preventive and indsl. medicine and pub. health 1949-53, chmn. sect. 1953), Am. Indsl. Hygiene Assn., Nat. Rehab. Assn. So. Calif. (dir.), So. Calif. Ind. Hygiene Assn. (past pres.). Unitarian. Prepared standard operating procedure of U.S. Army indsl. med. program at San Francisco Port of Embarkation (adopted by the U.S. Army Chief of Transp. for use by all Ports of Embarkation). Home: 275 Bellino Dr Pacific Palisades CA 90272 Office: Dept Community and Environ Medicine U Calif Coll Med 19727 MacArthur Blvd Irvine CA 92717

FELTON, JOHN CHARLES, transportation equipment manufacturing company executive; b. Chgo., Dec. 1, 1930; s. Frank N. and Mabel Rose (Hansch) Felten; m. Sally Louise McDougall, Oct. 20, 1956; children: Leslie Margaret, John William. B.S., U. Ill., 1952. Sales rep. Shell Oil Co., 1956-58; v.p. mktg. MCM Industries, 1958-63; pres., gen. mgr. subs. Medalist Mfg. Co., 1963-67; with U.S. Ry. Mfg. Co. (now Evans Transp. Co.), Chgo., 1967-73, pres., 1970-73; exec. v.p., gen. mgr. transp. systems and indsl. group Evans Products Co., Chgo., 1973-74, pres., 1974—, exec. v.p., Portland, Oreg., 1975—, dir.; dir. First Nat. Bank, Des Plaines, Ill. Bd. dirs. N.W. Suburban YMCA, Palatine, Ill. Served to lt. USNR, 1952-55. Mem. Am. Ry. Car Inst. (bd. dirs. 1969), Ry. Supply Inst. (bd. dirs. 1972), Ry. Progress Inst. (gov. 1972), Nat. Freight Traffic Assn., Young Pres. Orgn., Alpha Sigma Phi. Republican. Lutheran. Office: Evans Products Co 1121 SW Salmont St Portland OR 97208

FELTON, LURTON EUGENE, food processing executive; b. Grand Tower, Ill., June 30, 1899; s. Samuel W. and Maude (Norton); m. Zola H. Dillavou, Sept. 8, 1923; children—James E., Carol Ann. B.S., U. Ill., 1923. C.P.A., Ill. Certified pub. accountant Albert T. Bacon & Co., Chgo., 1923-26; with Green Giant Co., LeSueur, Minn., 1926—, successively auditor, controller, treas., sec.-treas., 1926-52, v.p. finance and treas., 1952-58, exec. v.p., 1958-59, pres., treas., 1959-60, pres., 1960-64, chmn. bd., 1964-69, hon. chmn., 1969-79; dir. emeritus Valley Nat. Bank, LeSueur, Employers Mut. of Wausau. Mem. U. Ill. Found.; mem. Pres.'s Council U. Ill.; trustee Sarasota Meml. Hosp. Found. Mem. Fin. Execs. Inst., Beta Alpha Psi, Beta Gamma Sigma. Home: 435 S Gulfstream Ave Apt 604 Sarasota FL 33577

FELTON, NORMAN, motion picture producer; b. London, Eng., Apr. 29, 1913; came to U.S., 1929, naturalized, 1939; s. John Thomas and Gertrude Anne (Francis) F.; m. Aline Stotts, Sept. 15, 1940; children: Julie Anne, John Christopher, Aline Elizabeth. B.F.A., U. Iowa, 1939, M.A., 1940. Dir., St. Paul Civic Theatre, 1940-41, Saginaw (Mich.) Civic Theatre, 1941-42; producer, NBC Radio, Chgo., 1944-48; exec. producer central div., NBC TV, 1948-50; dir.: Robert Montgomery TV dramatic series, 1950-54; writer, dir. TV dramas, N.Y.C., 1950-56; producer: Studio One, CBS-TV, 1957-59; exec. producer, CBS West Coast, 1959-60; dir. TV programs, 1960-61, TV films, Metro-Goldwyn-Mayer, 1961—; pres., Arena Prodns., 1961—; developed TV series: The Psychiatrist; also produced: (features) To Trap a Spy, 1964; features The Spy With My Face, 1965, One Spy Too Many, 1966, The Spy in the Green Hat, 1966, The Karate Killers, 1967, The Helicopter Spies, 1967, How to Steal the World, 1968, God Bless the Children, 1970; exec. producer: TV series The Psychiatrist, 1971, Baffled, 1972; TV feature Hawkins on Murder, 1973; producer: TV film Babe, 1975, Executive Suite, 1976, And Your Name is Jonah, 1979. Recipient Emmy award for TV direction, 1953, Sylvania award for Disting. Achievement, 1952, 56, Christopher award, 1954, 56, TV Guide Gold medal, 1952, TV Guide award 1963, 64; others. Mem. Screen Producers Guild (past pres.), Caucus Producers, Writers and Dirs. Am. (co-chmn.). Address: Arena Prodns Inc 22146 Pacific Coast Hwy Malibu CA 90265

FELTON, WARREN LOCKER, II, surgeon; b. Bartlesville, Okla., Oct. 25, 1925; s. Warren Locker and Elizabeth (Keller) F.; m. Judith Ann Mead, July 25, 1969; children—Warren Locker, III, Susan Elizabeth Felton Skove, Richard John Conrad, Alecia Ann, Christina Jane. B.S., Washington U., St. Louis, 1949, M.D., 1949. Diplomate: Am. Bd. Surgery, Am. Bd. Thoracic Surgery. Intern, then resident in surgery and instr. Yale-New Haven Med. Center, 1949-56; practice medicine specializing in thoracic and vascular surgery, Oklahoma City, 1958—; mem. staff Mercy Health Center, St. Anthony Hosp., Baptist Med. Center; clin. prof. U. Okla. Med. Sch. Contbr. articles to med. jours. Bd. dirs. Travelers Aid Soc., Oklahoma City, 1961-64; mem. U.

Okla. Assos., 1980. Served with USN, 1943-45; M.C. U.S. Army, 1956-58. Mem. AMA, A.C.S., Am. Thoracic Soc., Am. Assn. Thoracic Surgery, Soc. Thoracic Surgeons, Southwestern Surg. Congress, Sigma Xi, Alpha Omega Alpha. Episcopalian. Club: Oklahoma City Golf and Country. Home: 1612 Dorchester Dr Oklahoma City OK 73120 Office: 5700 NW Grand Blvd Oklahoma City OK 73112

FELTS, JAMES MARTIN, physiologist, educator; b. Austin, Tex., Mar. 11, 1923; s. Amos Martin and Ilene (Lytton) F. A.B., U. Calif., Berkeley, 1948, Ph.D., 1955. Asst. prof. Tufts U. Med. Sch., Boston, 1955-59; asst. prof., then prof. physiology U. Calif., San Francisco, 1959-69, prof. physiology, 1972—; cons. dept. surgery, 1973-74; prof. med. research U. Toronto, 1969-71. Author articles, chpts. in books. Served with USAAF, 1943-44. Sr. research fellow NIH, 1957-59; recipient Career Devel. award, 1961-69; med. investigator VA, 1973-77. Mem. Am. Physiol. Soc., Western Soc. Clin. Research, Am. Diabetes Assn., Am. Heart Assn. Office: VA Hosp 151 L 4150 Clement St San Francisco CA 94121

FELTS, WILLIAM ROBERT, JR., physician; b. Judsonia, Ark., Apr. 24, 1923; s. Wylie Robert and Willie Etidorpha (Lewis) F.; m. Jeanne E. Kennedy, Feb. 17, 1954 (div. 1971); children: William R. III, Thomas Wylie, Samuel Clay, Melissa Jeanne. B.S., U. Ark., 1944, M.D., 1946. Intern Garfield Meml. Hosp., Washington, 1946-47; resident in medicine Gallinger Mcpl. Hosp., Washington, 1949-51, George Washington U. Hosp., 1951-53, trainee in rehab. (rheumatology), 1955-57; asst. chief arthritis research unit VA Hosp., Washington, 1953-54, adj. asst. chief, 1954-58, chief, 1958-62; cons. in rheumatology U.S. Naval Hosp., Bethesda, Md., 1957-70; mem. faculty dept. medicine George Washington U., 1962—, asso. prof., 1962-80, prof., 1980—, dir. div. rheumatology, 1970-79; mem. Nat. Commn. on Arthritis and Related Musculoskeletal Diseases, 1975-76, Nat. Arthritis Adv. Bd., 1977-80, 80-83; mem. nat. com. on health policy Project Hope, 1977; cons. health affairs and mem. profl. adv. bd. Control Data Corp., 1976—; mem. D.C. Health Planning Adv. Com., 1969-72; chmn. med. adv. com. D.C. chpt. Arthritis Found., 1963—, v.p., 1983; bd. dirs. Symposium on Computer Applications in Med. Care, 1980—, pres.-elect, 1982-83; mem. WHO Task Force on Rheumatology in Developing Countries, 1982. Author articles in field, especially med. socioecons.; Mem. editorial adv. bd., cons. internal medicine: Current Procedural Terminology, 3d edit, 1972-73; chmn. editorial cons. panel, CPT-TV, 1980—; editorial adv. bd.: Internal Medicine News, 1976—. Bd. dirs. Nat. Capital Med. Found., 1979—, pres., 1980-81. Served with AUS, 1943-46, 47-49. Mem. Am. Soc. Internal Medicine (dir. 1969-78, pres. 1976-77), AMA (council on legis. 1980—, chmn. editorial adv. panel CPT-4 1980—), Am. Fedn. Clin. Research, Am. Rheumatism Assn., Inst. Medicine of Nat. Acad. Scis., D.C. Med. Soc. (chmn. legis. com. 1972-76), D.C. Soc. Internal Medicine (exec. council 1975-78), N.Y. Acad. Scis., So. Med. Assn. (sec. sect. internal medicine 1978-79, vice-chmn. 1979-80, chmn. 1980-81, asso. councilor 1979-81), Rheumatism Soc. D.C. (pres. 1963-64), Internat. League against Rheumatism (chmn. subcom. on classification and nomenclature 1982—), Alpha Epsilon Delta, Phi Chi, Kappa Sigma. Republican. Baptist. Clubs: Masons, George Wever. Home: 4827 N 27th Pl Arlington VA 22207 Office: 2150 Pennsylvania Ave NW Washington DC 20037

FENDER, CLARENCE LEO, guitar manufacturing company executive; b. Anaheim, Calif., Aug. 10, 1909; s. Clarence Montraville and Harriet Elvina (Wood) F.; m. Esther Marie Klotzly, Aug. 1, 1934 (dec. Aug., 1979); m. Phyllis Marie Dalton, Sept. 20, 1980. Jr. Acct., Fullerton Jr. Coll. Acct. Calif. Hwy. Dept., San Luis Obispo, 1931-35; owner, pres. radio repair shop, Fullerton, Calif., 1935-44; owner, pres. Fender Instruments, Fullerton, Calif., 1944-65, C.L.F. Research, Inc., 1976-80, G & L Musical Products, Inc., 1980—; cons. CBS Musical Instruments, Fullerton, 1965-70. Patentee in field. Recipient Pres.'s award Country Music Assn., Nashville, 1965, Pioneer award Acad. Country Music, Hollywood, Calif., 1982. Republican. Club: Century (Fullerton). Office: G & L Musical Products Inc 2548 E Fender Ave C Fullerton CA 92631

FENDER, FREDDY (BALDEMAR HUERTA), singer; b. San Benito, Tex., June 4, 1937; s. Serapio and Margarita (Garza) Huerta; m. Evangalina Muniz, Aug. 10, 1957; children: Baldemar, Tammy, Daniel. Student, Del Mar Jr. Coll., Corpus Christi, Tex., 1973-74. Country music performer and rec. artist: records include Tex Mex, Enter My Heart; (Recipient Grammy, Billboard awards, Outstanding Mexican-Am. award 1977). Served with USMC, 1954-56; Korea. Mem. Country Music Assn., AFTRA, Am. Fedn. Musicians U.S. and Can., Broadcast Music Inc. Office: care William Morris Agy 2325 Crestmoor Rd Box 15245 Nashville TN 37215 *

FENDLER, JANOS HUGO, chemistry educator; b. Budapest, Hungary, Aug. 12, 1934; came to U.S., 1964; s. Janos and Vilma (Csiky) F.; m. Eleanor Johnson, June 15, 1965 (div. 1975); children: Michael, Lisa; m. Ann Fendler, Feb. 15, 1976; children: Peter, Monika. B.Sc., U. Leicester, Eng., 1960; Diploma in Radiochemistry, Leicester Coll. Tech., 1961; Ph.D., U. London, 1964, D.Sc., 1978. Postdoctorial fellow U. Calif.-Santa Barbara, 1965-66; fellow Mellon Inst., Pitts., 1966-70; assoc. prof. chemistry Tex. A&M U., College Station, 1970-75, prof., 1975-81, Clarkson Coll., Potsdam, N.Y., 1982—; indsl. cons., vis. prof., Japan, 1975, Switzerland, 1979, Sweden, 1981. Author: Catalysts in Micellar and Macromolecular Systems, 1975, Membrane Mimetic Chemistry, 1982; research, numerous publs. in field; contbr. revs. to chem. jours.; editorial bd.: Jour. Organic Chemistry, 1978-82, Jour. Colloid and Interface Sci., 1981—. Mem. Am. Chem. Soc. (Kendall award 1982), Royal Chem. Soc., Internat. Assn. Colloid and Interface Scientists. Home: 103 Leroy St Potsdam NY 13676 Office: Clarkson Coll Tech Potsdam NY 13676

FENDLER, OSCAR, lawyer; b. Blytheville, Ark., Mar. 22, 1909; s. Alfred and Rae (Sattler) F.; m. Patricia Shane, Oct. 26, 1946; children—Tilden P. Wright III (stepson), Frances Shane. B.A., U. Ark., 1930; LL.B., Harvard, 1933. Bar: Ark. bar 1933. Practice in, Blytheville, 1933-41, 46—; spl. justice Ark. Supreme Ct., 1965; Mem. Ark. Jud. Council, 1959- 60; pres. Conf. Local Bar Assn., 1958-60; pres. bd. dirs. Ark. Law Rev., 1961-67; mem. Ark. Bd. Pardons and Paroles, 1970-71. Mem. Miss. County Democratic Central Com., 1948—. Served with USNR, 1941-45. Fellow Am. Coll. Probate Counsel, Am. Bar Found.; mem. ABA (chmn. gen. practice sect. 1966-67, mem. council sect. gen. practice 1964—, ho. dels. 1968-80, mem. com. edn. about Communism 1966-70, com. legal aid and indigent defendants 1970-73, chmn. com. law lists 1973-76), Ark. Bar Assn. (chmn. exec. com. 1956-57, pres. 1962-63), Am. Judicature Soc. (dir. 1964-68), Scribes, Nat. Conf. Bar Presidents (exec. council 1963-65), Blytheville C. of C. (past v.p., dir.), Navy League, Am. Legion. Clubs: Blytheville Country, Blytheville Rotary (past pres.). Home: 1062 W Hearn St Blytheville AR 72315 Office: 104 N 6th St Blytheville AR 72315

FENDRICH, CHARLES WELLES, JR., environmental and energy company executive; b. Washington, Nov. 18, 1924; s. Charles Welles and Ellen Frances (Friel) F.; m. Roberta Knope, Sept. 8, 1948; children: Kathleen, Patricia, Charles, Anne. B.S., Dartmouth Coll., 1946; postgrad., Tuck Sch. Bus. Adminstrn., 1947-48, NYU, 1954-56. Sales engr. Link Belt Co., N.Y.C., 1948-54, Mech. Handling Systems Inc., Detroit, 1954-56; assoc. Stewart, Dougall & Assocs., N.Y.C., 1956-60; dir. mktg. research Walworth Co., N.Y.C., 1960-62; dir. mktg. services B.F. Goodrich co., Akron, OH, 1962-67; v.p. mktg. Ohio Rubber div. Eagle Picher Industries, 1967-69; mgr. mktg. projects ITT, N.Y.C., 1969-73, Brussels, 1969-73, worldwide product line mgr. pumps, compressors, indsl. products, 1973-75; sr. v.p., mem. exec. com. Research Cottrell Inc., Somerville, N.J., 1975—. Bd. dirs., vice chmn. N.J. Research and Devel. Council, Environ. Industry Council, Washington, 1975-80; mem. adv. bd. Stuart Country Day Sch., Princeton, N.J., 1976—; trustee N.J. Sci. and Tech. Ctr., 1980—. Served to lt. (j.g.) USNR, 1943-47. Mem. N. Am. Planning Assn. Republican. Roman Catholic. Home: 122 Gallup Rd Princeton NJ 08540 Office: Research Cottrell Inc PO Box 1500 Somerville NJ 08876

FENDRICK, ALAN BURTON, advertising executive; b. Bronx, N.Y., Mar. 22, 1933; s. Louis and Esther (Silberberg) F.; m. Beverly R. Schoenfeld, June 12, 1960; children—Sarah Lin, Lisa Augusta. A.B. with honors in Econs, Columbia, 1954; M.B.A., Harvard, 1958. Asst. sales mgr. splty. div. Hankins Container Co., 1958-60; mgr. bus. adminstrn., operations and engring. NBC, 1960-67; with Grey Advt. Inc., 1967—, exec. v.p., sec., treas., 1972—. Trustee Woodlands High Sch. Scholarship Fund, Greenburgh, N.Y., pres., 1977-78; mem. Greenville Community Theater. Served with AUS, 1954-56. Mem. Am. Assn. Advt. Agys. (chmn. com. on fiscal control 1979-81), Advt. Agy. Financial Mgmt. Group (chmn. exec. com. 1980-82, pres. 1982-84), Harvard Bus. Sch. Club N.Y., Fin. Execs. Inst. Jewish (trustee temple). Home: 30 Canterbury Rd White Plains NY 10607 Office: 777 3d Ave New York NY 10017

FENELLO, MICHAEL JOHN, government agency executive; b. Rochester, N.Y., Jan. 22, 1916; s. Frank and Mamie (Mazza) F.; m. Eileen Claire McPadden, Sept. 21, 1947; children: Carol Ann, Jean Marie, Lois Ann. B.S., SUNY-Buffalo, 1938; M.A., NYU, 1941. Tchr. high sch. Westchester County, N.Y.C., 1938-41; pilot Eastern Airlines, N.Y.C., 1946-68, v.p., Miami, 1968-81; dep. adminstr. FAA, Washington, 1981—. Bd. dirs. United Fund, Miami; mem. adv. bd. Air and Space Mus., Washington, 1981—. Served to lt. USN, 1938-41. Mem. Airline Pilots Assn. (exec. 1948-52). Republican. Roman Catholic. Clubs: Rotary, K.C. Office: Fed Aviation Adminstrn 800 Independence Ave SW Washington DC 20591

FENG, TSE-YUN, computer engineer, educator; b. Hangchow, China, Feb. 6, 1928; s. Shih-ching and Lin Shao; m. Elaine Hu, Jan. 28, 1965; children: Wu-chun, Wu-chi, Wu-che, Wu-chang. B.S., Nat. Taiwan U., 1950; M.S., Okla. State U., 1957; Ph.D., U. Mich., 1967. Asst. engr. Taiwan Power Co., 1950-56; sr. designer Ebasco Services, N.Y.C., 1957-60; teaching fellow U. Mich., 1962-65, research asst., 1965-66, asst. research engr., 1966, research asso., 1967; asst. prof. elec. and computer engring. Syracuse U., 1967-71, asso. prof., 1971-75; prof. elec. and computer engring. Wayne State U., Detroit, 1975-79; prof. computer sci. Wright State U., Dayton, Ohio, 1979-80, chmn. dept., 1979-80; prof. computer and info. sci. Ohio State U., 1980—; cons. Transidyne Gen., Syracuse U., Pattern Analysis and Recognition Corp., N.Y. State Bd. Edn.; chmn. Internat. Conf. on Parallel Processing, 1975—, Internat. Conf. on Computers and Applications, 1983—; dir. N.E. Consortium for Engring. Edn., 1976—; participant U.S. Technol. Policy Conf., 1978; cons. USAF. Contbr.: numerous articles to others. Fellow IEEE (chmn. computer soc. standards com. 1974-78, mem. numerous other coms., presiding officer computer soc. governing bd. 1979-80, computer soc. disting. visitor 1973-78, pres. 1979-80, chmn. nominations com. 1981—, jr. past pres. 1981—, Best Paper award 1975, Honor Roll award 1978, Spl. award 1981, mem. del. to Chinese Electronics Soc. 1978, leader del. 1980, del. to Popov Soc. Congress, USSR 1978, editor-in-chief Trans. on Computers 1982—); Mem. Am. Fedn. Info. Processing Socs. (dir. 1979-80, 82—, nominating com. 1979-80), Assn. Computing Machinery, Am. Nat. Standards Inst. (info. systems standards mgmt. bd. 1974-78), Sagamore Computer Conf. (chmn., editor proc. 1972-75), Hon. Order of Ky. Cols., Sigma Xi, Phi Kappa Phi, Tau Beta Pi, Eta Kappa Nu, Phi Tau Phi. Patentee in field. Home: 1604 Stormy Ct Xenia OH 45385 Office: Dept Computer and Info Sci Ohio State U Columbus OH 43210

FENG, YEN TSAI, librarian; b. Peking, China, Jan. 17, 1923; came to U.S., 1946, naturalized, 1961; d. C.C. and B.Y. (Hu) F.; m. Philip J. McNiff, Aug. 18, 1978. A.B., U. Shanghai, 1945; A.M., Colo. State Coll., 1947; Ph.D., U. Denver, 1953; M.S. in L.S, Columbia U., 1955; D.H.L., New Eng. Coll., 1975; D.Litt., Regis Coll., 1981, Smith Coll., 1982—. Library trainee N.Y. Pub. Library, 1953-55; from reference asst. to asst. librarian Harvard Coll. Library, 1955-67; asst. dir. research library services Boston Pub. Library, 1967-77; librarian of Wellesley Coll., 1977-80; librarian Harvard Coll., 1980—; Roy E. Larsen librarian librarian, 1982—. Mem. Depository Library Council to Pub. Printer, 1975-78; bd. dirs. New Eng. Library Info. Network, 1978-81, Polaroid Corp., 1981—; vis. lectr. Simmons Coll. Sch. Library and Info. Scis., Boston, 1972, 73, 76; mem. vis. com. libraries MIT, 1979—. Mem. Gov. Mass. Task Force Ethnic Heritage, 1974, Mass. Council Arts and Humanities, 1976-78; bd. dirs. Boston YWCA, 1976-79; visitor dept. pub. edn. Boston Mus. Fine Arts, 1973—; community adv. bd. WGBH Ednl. Found., 1979-81; mem. corp. Boston Mus. Sci., 1980—. Mem. ALA. Home: 101 Waban Hill Rd Chestnut Hill MA 02167 Office: Widener Library Harvard Univ Cambridge MA 02138

FENIGER, JEROME ROLAND, JR., broadcasting executive; b. Peoria, Ill., June 16, 1927; s. Jerome Rol and Marie Dorothy (Miller) F.; m. Marian Laura Schwartz, June 24, 1951; children: Robin Jean, Bruce David. B.A., U. Ia., 1948; postgrad., Columbia U., 1948, N.Y. U., 1949-50. Account exec. Biow Co. (advt.), N.Y.C., 1949-50; chief time buyer firm Cunningham & Walsh (advt.), N.Y.C., 1950-51, v.p., 1954-60; sales exec. CBS, N.Y.C., 1952-54; exec. Cowles Communications Co., N.Y.C., 1960-65; v.p. Grey Advt. Inc., N.Y.C., 1965-70; pres. Horizons Communications Corp., N.Y.C., 1970-83; mng. dir. Sta. Reps. Assn., Inc., N.Y.C., 1983—; Vice pres. Louise Wise Services. Trustee Columbia Grammar and Prep. Sch., 1965-77, treas., 1970-77. Served with USAAF, 1945-46. Mem. Internat. Radio and TV Soc. (pres. 1975-77). Democrat. Clubs: Friars, Dutch Treat (N.Y.C.). Home: 16 W 77th St New York NY 10024 Office: 230 Park Ave New York NY 10169

FENIMORE, GEORGE WILEY, mfg. co. exec.; b. Bertrand, Mo., 1921. B.S. in Fin. and Bus. Adminstrn, Northwestern U., 1941; LL.B., Harvard U., 1947; postgrad. exec. program, UCLA, 1954-55. Bar: Mich. bar 1948. Asst. to dir. planning Ford Motor Co., 1947-48; exec. to v.p. and gen. mgr. Hughes Aircraft Co., 1948-53; adminstrv. mgr. tech. products Packard Bell Electronics Co., 1954-55; with TRW, Inc., 1955-64; v.p., gen. mgr. TRW Internat., 1959-64; v.p. internat. ops. Bunker Ramo Corp., 1964-65; dir. public relations, then corp. sec. Litton Industries, Inc., Beverly Hills, Calif., 1965-73, v.p., corp. sec., 1973-81, sr. v.p., corp. sec., 1981—. Chmn. bd. dirs. Southwestern U.; bd. dirs., past pres. Beverly Hills YMCA. Served with USAAF, World War II. Named Citizen of Yr. Beverly Hills Lions Club, 1976. Mem. Am. Soc. Corp. Secs. (dir., past nat. dir., past pres. Los Angeles Group), Beverly Hills C. of C. (past pres., Citizen of Yr. award 1979), Mandeville Canyon Assn. (past pres.). Presbyterian. Clubs: Beverly Hills Rotary (past pres.; Paul Harris fellow Rotary Internat. 1972), Beverly Hills Men's, Shriners. Address: Litton Industries Inc 360 N Crescent Dr Beverly Hills CA 90210

FENINGER, CLAUDE, bus. exec.; b. Cairo, Jan. 15, 1926; U.S., 1960; s. Paul and Therese (DeRogatis) F.; m. Ruth Lee Rohlfs, July 10, 1965; children—Paul Gordon, Eric. Student, Lausanne (Switzerland) Sch. Hotel Mgmt., 1948, Am. U., Cairo, 1945, Lincoln Sch., Cairo, 1943, Lycee Francais, Cairo, 1935. With Hilton Internat., 1955-67; product line mgr. ITT, 1967-68; pres. Sheraton Internat., 1968-74; chmn. bd., chief exec. officer Omni Internat. Hotels, Inc., Atlanta, 1974-80; pres. ARA-Internat., Phila., 1980—; cons. in field, 1960—; dir. VS Services, Can., Traulsen Refrigeration Co., N.Y.C., Internat. Forum. Mem. Am. Mgmt. Assn., Am. Hotel Assn., New Eng. Internat. Center. Home: 302 Julip Run Saint Davids PA 19087 Office: ARA Services Inc Independence Sq W Philadelphia PA 19106

FENLON, THOMAS BOLGER, lawyer; b. Long Branch, N.J., Nov. 12, 1904; s. John T. and Elizabeth (Cole) F.; m. Juliet O. Ludford, June 30, 1930; children—Mary Ann (Mrs. William V. Knowles), Henry L., Thomas Bolger, Juliet (Mrs. Frederick L. Nagle, Jr.), Lois (Mrs. Michael W. Brinkman). A.B., Georgetown U., 1925; LL.B., Columbia, 1928. Bar: N.Y. bar 1928. Partner firm Emmet, Marvin & Martin, N.Y.C., 1942—; Village atty. North Pelham, N.Y., 1933-35; town supr., Pelham, 1942-43. Mem. Pelham Bd. Edn., 1945-58, pres., 1955-58; Bd. dirs., mem. exec. com. United Fund of Westchester, 1969—; trustee St. Catharine's Ch., Pelham. Named Man of Year in Pelham, 1967. Mem. ABA, N.Y. State Bar Assn. (chmn. com. state legislation 1944-46), Assn. Bar City N.Y. (chmn. com. state legislation 1944-46). Clubs: Pelham Mens (pres. 1952-53); Down Town Assn. (N.Y.C.); Huguenot Yacht (New Rochelle, N.Y.). Home: 72 Clifford Ave Pelham NY 10803 Office: 48 Wall St New York NY 10005

FENN, CHARLES VAN ORDEN, mgmt. exec.; b. Montclair, N.J., Aug. 14, 1908; s. George T. and Frances I. (Geary) F.; m. Isabelle Williams, July 2, 1932; children—June Marilyn, William Charles. M.E., Stevens Inst. Tech., 1929. With Carrier Corp., Syracuse, N.Y., 1929-72, successively student engr., mem. constrn. dept., mgr. spl. order shop, dist. mgr. charge sales engring., constrn. and service Southeastern states, mgr. direct dept. covering nat. sales engring., constrn. and service, v.p. and gen. sales mgr. machinery and systems div., 1953-57, gen. mgr. machinery and systems div., 1957-60, v.p. charge corporate staff group, 1960-62, asst. to pres., 1968, exec. v.p. charge all ops., 1968, pres., 1968-72, dir., 1960-79; pres. Elliot Co. div. Carrier Corp., 1962-68. Mem. Tau Beta Pi, Beta Theta Pi. Clubs: Onondaga Golf and Country (Syracuse); Bent Pine Golf, John's Island (Vero Beach). Home: 500 Beach Rd John's Island Vero Beach FL 32960

FENN, DAN HUNTINGTON, JR., library director, educator; b. Boston, Mar. 27, 1923; s. Dan Huntington and Anna (Yens) G.; m. Nancy Ring, Dec. 28, 1946 (div. 1965); children—Peter, Anne, David, Thomas O.; m. Lenore O. Sheppard, Oct. 10, 1969; children—W. Gregory, W. Marie, Christopher G. A.B. magna cum laude, Harvard, 1946; student, Grad. Sch. Arts and Scis., 1946-48, A.M., 1972; LL.D., Nasson U., 1972, New Eng. Coll., 1976; L.H.D., U. Mass.-Boston, 1983. Asst. dean freshmen Harvard, 1946-49; exec. dir. World Affairs Council, Boston, 1949-55; asst. editor Harvard Bus. Rev.; mem. faculty, also editor Harvard Bus. Sch. Bull., Harvard Bus. Sch., 1955-61; spl. asst. to Senator Smith, 1961; staff asst. to Pres. Kennedy, 1961-63; mem. U.S. Tariff Commn., 1963-67, vice chmn., 1964-65; pres. Center Bus.-Govt. Relations, Inc., Washington, 1969-71; dir. John F. Kennedy Library, Boston, 1971—; mem. faculty, lectr. Harvard Grad. Sch. Bus. Adminstrn., 1976-80, Kennedy Sch. Govt., 1980—; also sr. asso. Mass. Inst. Tech-Harvard Joint Center on Urban Studies, 1969-72; dir. Home Owners Fed. Savs. and Loan, Boston. Author: Citizens Guide to International Relations, 1953; Editor: Management Guide to Overseas Operations, 1957, Management in a Rapidly Changing Economy, 1958, Management's Mission in a New Society, 1959, Business Responsibility in Action, 1960, Managing America's Economic Explosion, 1961; co-author: Cases in Business and Government, 1966, The Social Audit, 1972; Co-editor: Planning the Future Strategy of your Business, 1956, Incentives for Executives, 1962, Management of Materials Research, 1962. Mem. pres.'s Delegation to Algerian Independence Day, 1963; Sec. Lexington (Mass.) Sch. Com., 1957-61; mem. Lexington Town Meeting, 1953-61, 71-78; Del. Mass. Democratic Conv., 1954, 56, 58, 60; Dem. nominee for Mass. Legislature, 1952; alternate del.-at-large Dem. Nat. Conv., 1960; Trustee Browne and Nichols Sch., 1959-61. Served with USAAF, 1943-45; ETO. Decorated by Govt. Morocco, 1952. Mem. Phi Beta Kappa. Unitarian. Home: 130 Worthen Rd Lexington MA 02173 Office: John F Kennedy Library Boston MA 02125 also Kennedy Sch Govt Harvard U Cambridge MA

FENN, JOHN BENNETT, chemist educator; b. N.Y.C., June 15, 1917; s. Herbert Bennett and Jeanette Clyde (Dingman) F.; m. Margaret Elizabeth Wilson, June 6, 1939; children: Margaret Marianne, Barbara Leigh, John Bennett. A.B., Berea Coll., 1937; Ph.D., Yale U., 1940. Research chemist (Monsanto Chem. Co.), Anniston, Ala., 1940-43, Sharples Chems., Inc., Wyandotte, Mich., 1943-45; v.p. Experiment, Inc., Richmond, Va., 1945-52; dir. Project SQUID, Princeton, 1952-62, prof. mech. engring., 1959-63, prof. aerospace scis., 1963-66; prof. applied sci. and chemistry Yale U., 1967—; pres. Relay Devel. Corp., 1975—; vis. scientist N.Am. Aviation Sci. Center, 1965-66; vis. prof. U. Trento, Italy, 1976, U. Tokyo, 1979; dir. Thermal Research & Engring. Corp., 1952-59; sci. liaison officer Office Naval Research, London, 1955; dir. Aero Chem. Research Labs., 1956-60. Author: with W.H. Freeman Engines, Energy and Entropy, 1982; Editor: (with A.B. Cambel) Transport Properties in Gases, 1958, Dynamics of Conducting Gases, 1960. Mem. Am. Chem. Soc., AAAS, Am. Inst. Chem. Engrs., Sigma Xi. Home: 226 Pleasant Point Rd Branford CT 06405

FENN, RAYMOND WOLCOTT, JR., metallurgical engineer; b. Torrington, Conn., Feb. 4, 1922; s. Raymond W. and Josephine (Mueller) F.; m. Beatrice Myra Christian, Jan. 19, 1946; children—Carol Louise, Ralph Christian. B.Metall. Engring., Rensselaer Poly. Inst., 1943; M.Engring., Yale, 1947, D.Engring., 1949. Registered profl. engr., Calif. Metall. engr. Gen. Electric Co., West Lynn, Mass., 1943-44; supr. testing lab., chief testing and instrumentation sect. Metall. Lab., Dow Chem. Co., Midland, Mich., 1949-61; cons. scientist, sr. mem. research lab., mgr. materials and prodn. systems engring., mgr. mfg. research, also mgr. material and process labs. Lockheed Missiles & Space Co., Sunnyvale, Calif., 1961—. Contbr. articles to profl. jours. Served with USNR, 1944-46. Fellow Am. Soc. Metals (trustee 1969-71, chmn., mem. exec. com. Santa Clara Valley chpt. 1966-69); mem. Am. Soc. Testing Materials (dir. 1966-69, R.E. Templin award 1961), Am. Inst. Mining and Metall. Engrs., Research Soc. Am., Am. Welding Soc., Soc. Mfg. Engrs., Soc. for Advancement of Material and Process Engring. (chmn. No. Calif. chpt. 1973-74, dir. 1974-76, 2d v.p. 1976-77, 1st v.p. 1977-78, pres. 1978-79), Nat. Mgmt. Assn., Sigma Xi. Home: 13428 Carillo Ln Los Altos Hills CA 94022 Office: 1111 Lockheed Way Sunnyvale CA 94086

FENNEMA, OWEN RICHARD, food chemistry educator; b. Hinsdale, Ill., Jan. 23, 1929; s. Nick and Fern Alma (First) F.; m. Ann Elizabeth Hammer, Aug. 22, 1948; children: Linda Gail, Karen Elizabeth, Peter Scott. B.S., Kans. State U., 1950; M.S., U. Wis., 1951, Ph.D., 1960. Project leader for research and devel Pillsbury Co., Mpls., 1953-57; asst. prof. food sci. dept. U. Wis., Madison, 1960-64, assoc. prof., 1964-69, prof., 1969—, chmn. dept., 1977-81; cons. Pillsbury

Co., Mpls., 1979-82; mem. sci. adv. com. Nutrition Found., N.Y.C., 1980-83. Author: Low Temperature Preservation of Foods, 1973; editor: (with others) Principles of Food Science, 2 vols., 1976, Proteins at Low Temperatures, 1979; mem. editorial bd.: Cryobiology, 1966-82, Jour. Food Sci., 1975-77. Served to 2d lt. U.S. Army, 1951-53. Recipient Excellence in Teaching award U. Wis., Madison, 1977. Fellow Inst. Food Technologists (pres. 1982-83, Excellence in Teaching award 1978); mem. Am. Chem. Soc., Am. Inst. Nutrition, Soc. Cryobiology, Am. Dairy Sci. Assn. Home: 5010 Lake Mendota Dr Madison WI 53705 Office: U Wis 1605 Linden Dr Madison WI 53706

FENNER, GEORGE GLEASON, finance company executive; b. Newark, Mar. 24, 1934; s. John David and Janice G. (Gleason) F.; m. Janice N. Netland, Aug. 30, 1955; children—Richard P., John T. A.B., Dartmouth Coll., 1956; M.B.A., Columbia U., 1958. With Gen. Motors Acceptance Corp., N.Y.C., 1958—, regional fin. mgr., 1967-70, gen. asst. exec. office, 1970-73, asst. mgr. plans dept., 1973-75, dir. lease financing, 1975-76, dir. spl. financing, 1976-78, v.p. fin., 1981—; exec. v.p. Motors Ins. Corp., 1978-81. Pres. Chatham (N.J.) Recreation Bd., 1964. Mem. Fin. Execs. Inst. Republican. Clubs: Minisink, Westhampton Yacht Squadron., Birmingham Athletic. Home: 411 Linden Rd Birmingham MI 48011 Office: 3044 W Grand Blvd Detroit MI 48202

FENNER, MILDRED SANDISON (MRS. ERNEST G. REID), circus executive; b. Huntsville, Mo., July 9, 1910; d. John Forte and Minnielee (Holliday) Sandison; m. H. Wolcott Fenner, Feb. 1, 1940 (dec. Oct. 1972); m. E.G. Reid, Aug. 30, 1975. B.S., N.W. Mo. State Tchrs. Coll., 1931; M.A., George Washington U., 1938, Ed.D., 1942; Litt.D., Glassboro State Coll., 1962. With NEA Jour. (now Today's Education), 1931-75, beginning as mem. staff, successively asst. editor, mng. editor, 1931-54, editor, 1954-75; dir. dept. ednl. services Ringling Bros.-Barnum & Bailey Combined Shows, 1975—. Author: (with Eleanor Fishburn) Pioneer American Educators, 1944, NEA History, 1945, (with H.W. Fenner) The Circus: Lure and Legend, 1970; also articles in field. Mem. Woman's Nat. Democratic Club. Mem. Am. Assn. U. Women, Edn. Press Assn. Am. (sec.-treas. 1951-60, rep. Internat. Ednl. Editors' Workshop, Manila summer 1956, Amsterdam 1961), Horace Mann League (1st woman mem., pres. 1971-72), Common Cause, Smithsonian Assos., Pi Lambda Theta, Sigma Sigma Sigma. Methodist. Home: 530 N St SW Washington DC 20024 Office: Ringling Bros Circus 3201 New Mexico Ave NW Washington DC 20016

FENNESSEY, JOHN JOSEPH, JR., manufacturing company executive; b. Morristown, N.J., Sept. 3, 1941; s. John Joseph and Kathryn Myrtle (Miller) F.; m. Deborah Ann Bremer, June 17, 1961 (div. Dec. 1982); children: Scott John, Lisa Hay. B.A., Cornell U., 1963; M.B.A., Columbia U., 1969. Vice pres. Bankers Trust Co., N.Y.C., 1963-71; asst. treas. N.Am. Philips Co., N.Y.C., 1971-75; treas. Midland Ross Corp., Cleve., 1975—, v.p., 1977-80, sr. v.p., 1980-82, exec. v.p., 1982—. Mem. Fin. Execs. Inst., Cleve. Treasurers Club, Beta Gamma Sigma. Republican. Clubs: Shaker Heights (Ohio) Country, Cleve. Racquet, Seabrook Island; Board Room (N.Y.C.). Home: 3237 Fox Hollow Dr Pepper Pike OH 44124 Office: 20600 Chagrin Blvd Shaker Heights OH 44122

FENNINGER, LEONARD DAVIS, medical educator, association executive; b. Hampton, Va., Oct. 3, 1917; s. Laurence and Natalie Ayers (Bourne) F.; m. Jane Thomas, Mar. 20, 1943; children: David McClure, Anne Randolph. A.B., Princeton U., 1938; M.D., U. Rochester, 1943. Diplomate: Am. Bd. Internal Medicine. Asso. dean, prof. health services, chmn. dept., prof. medicine U. Rochester; also physician, med. dir. Strong Meml. Hosp., 1961-67; dir. Bur. Health Manpower, USPHS, 1967-69; asso. dir. health manpower NIH, 1969-73; dir. dept. grad. med. edn. AMA, Chgo., 1973-76, group v.p. med. edn., 1976-80, v.p. med. edn. and sci. policy, 1981—. Home: 847 Valley Rd Glencoe IL 60022 Office: AMA 535 N Dearborn St Chicago IL 60610

FENNO, RICHARD FRANCIS, JR., political science educator; b. Winchester, Mass., Dec. 12, 1926; s. Richard Francis and Mary Brooks (Tredennick) F.; m. Nancy Davidson, Sept. 10, 1948; children: Mark Richard, Craig Pierce. Student, Williams Coll., 1944-46; A.B., Amherst Coll., 1948; Ph.D., Harvard U., 1956. Instr. govt. Wheaton (Mass.) Coll., 1951-53; instr. polit. sci. Amherst Coll., 1953-56, asst. prof., 1956-57; mem. faculty U. Rochester, N.Y., 1957—, prof., 1964—, Don Alonzo Watson prof. polit. sci., 1971-78, William R. Kenan prof. polit. sci., 1978—. Author: The President's Cabinet, 1959, The Power of the Purse, 1966, Congressmen in Committees, 1973, Home Style: U.S. House Members In Their Districts, 1978 (Woodrow Wilson Found. award 1979, D.B. Hardeman prize 1980), (with F. Munger) National Politics and Federal Aid to Education, 1962; Editor: The Yalta Conf, 1956, 73; book rev. editor: Am. Polit. Sci. Rev., 1969-71. Served with USNR, 1944-46. Social Sci. Research Council fellow, 1960-61; Rockefeller Found. fellow, 1963-64; Ford fellow, 1971-72; Guggenheim fellow, 1976-77; Russell Sage Found. grantee, 1978—. Mem. Am. Polit. Sci. Assn. (council 1971-73, v.p. 1975-76, pres. 1984), Nat. Acad. Scis., Social Sci. Research Council (dir. 1973-75), Am. Acad. Arts and Scis., Phi Beta Kappa. Home: 108 Farm Brook Dr Rochester NY 14625

FENSELAU, CATHERINE CLARKE, pharmacology educator; b. York, Nebr., Apr. 15, 1939; d. Lee Keckley and Muriel (Thomas) Clarke; m. Allan Herman Fenselau, Dec. 27, 1962 (div. 1980); children: Andrew Clarke, Thomas Stewart. A.B., Bryn Mawr Coll., 1961; Ph.D., Stanford U., 1965. Research scientist U. Calif.-Berkeley, 1965-67; instr. to assoc. prof. Johns Hopkins U., Balt., 1967-82, prof. pharmacology; cons. NIH, NSF, U.S. Dept. Agr., U.S. Army; mem. FDA; cons. others. Contbr. articles to profl. jours.; editor: Biomed. Mass Spectrometry, 1973—. Mem. Am. Soc. Mass Spectrometry (pres.), Am. Chem. Soc., AAAS, Am. Soc. Pharmacology and Exptl. Therapeutics. Office: Johns Hopkins Univ Sch Medicine 725 N Wolfe St Baltimore MD 21205

FENSTER, SAUL, institute technology president; b. N.Y.C., Mar. 22, 1933; s. Samuel and Rose (Glass) F.; m. Roberta Schamis, Jan. 11, 1959; children: Deborah, Lisa, Jonathan. Student, Bklyn. Coll., 1949-51; B.Mech. Engring., City U. N.Y., 1953; M.S., Columbia, 1955, N.Y. U., 1955-56; Ph.D. (Shell fellow 1957-58), U. Mich., 1958. Lectr. mech. engring. City U. N.Y., 1953-56; teaching fellow engring. mechanics U. Mich., 1956-57; with univ. Research Inst., 1957-58; research engr. Sperry-Rand Corp., 1959- 62; prof. engring. Fairleigh Dickinson U., Teaneck, N.J., 1962-78, chmn. dept. physics, 1962-63, chmn. dept. mech. engring., 1963-70, grad. adminstrv. asst. to dean, 1965-70, asso. dean, 1970-71, exec. asst. to pres., 1971—, provost, 1972-78; pres. N.J. Inst. Tech., Newark, 1978—, 1978—; dir. Howard Savs. Bank N.J., Prudential Series Fund, Inc., Pruco Life Series Fund, Inc.; cons., 1962—. Author: (with Wallace Arthur) Mechanics, 1969, (with A. Cahit Ugural) Advanced Strength and Applied Elasticity, 1975; Contbr. chpts. in books, tech. papers. Mem. Hudson River Waterfront Study and Planning Commn., 1979-80; bd. dirs. N.J. Assn. Colls. and Univs., 1980—; trustee Newark Boys Chorus Sch., 1980—; mem., vice chmn. N.J. Water Supply Authority, 1981—; mem. Gov.'s Commn. on Sci. and Tech., 1982—; bd. dirs. N.J. Alliance for Action, 1982—. Mem. AAAS ASME, Am. Soc. Engring. Edn., Assn. Ind. Colls. and Univs. N.J. (vice chmn. bd. 1975-78, chmn. bd. 1978-80, dir. 1980—), N.Y. Acad. Scis., Greater Newark C. of C. (dir. 1980—), Newcomen Soc., Sigma Xi, Tau Beta Pi, Omicron Delta Kappa, Pi Tau Sigma. Home: 524 Bernita Dr River Vale NJ 07675 Office: NJ Inst Tech Newark NJ 07102

FENSTERBUSCH, JACK ALVIN, insurance company executive; b. Rock Island, Ill., June 28, 1916; s. Alvin B. and Matilda (Klingebiel) F.; m. Jeanette Henchon, Aug. 10, 1940; children: Alan Kent, Susan Kay Fensterbusch Thomas. Student higher accountancy, LaSalle Extension U., 1935-38. With Bituminous Casualty Corp., Rock Island, 1935—, pres., 1967-71, chmn. bd., chief exec. officer, 1971-81, chmn. bd., 1981—, also dir.; chmn. bd., chief exec. officer, dir. Bituminous Fire and Marine Ins. Co., 1973-81, chmn. bd., 1981—; chmn. bd., chief exec. officer, dir. Bitco Corp. Pres. Rock Island County United Way, 1971-72; chmn. bd. United Appeal Rock Island County, 1969; co-chmn. Rock Island Family Y Bldg. Fund, 1974. Served with AUS, World War II. Mem. Adminstrv. Mgmt. Soc. (past chpt. pres.), Rock Island C. of C. (past pres.). Lutheran. Clubs: Rock Island Arsenal Golf, Union League, Masons. Home: 3510 15th St Rock Island IL 61201 Office: 320 18th St Rock Island IL 61201

FENTER, FELIX WEST, aerospace company executive; b. Paris, Tex., Sept. 16, 1926; s. Felix Franklin and Haidee (West) F.; m. Duanne Raye Moore, Jan. 28, 1951; 1 dau., Susan Elaine Fenter Barner. B.S., U. Tex., 1953, M.S., 1954, Ph.D. in Aerospace Engring. 1960. With aeromech. div. Def. Research Lab., U. Tex., 1952-58; research engr. Chance Vought Aircraft, Inc. (now Vought Corp.), Grand Prairie, Tex., 1958-60, sr. scientist, 1960-61; supr. aerophysics group LTV Research Center div. LTV, Grand Prairie, 1961-62, asst. dir., 1962-66, asso. dir., 1966-71; v.p. Vought Advanced Tech. Center, Inc., Grand Prairie, 1971-73, pres., chmn. bd., 1973—; v.p. research and advanced tech. Vought Corp., 1977-83, v.p. advanced programs and tech., 1983—; mem. NSF Indsl. Panel on Sci. and Tech. Councilor, Tex. A. and M. U. Research Found.; mem. vis. com. dept. aerospace engring. and engring. mechanics U. Tex. at Austin. Mem. tech. adv. council So. Meth. U.; mem. adv. com. Coll. Engring., U. Tex-Arlington. Served with USN, 1945-49. Named Disting. Grad. U. Tex. Coll. Engring.; named to Engring. Hall Achievement U. Tex.-Arlington. Asso. fellow Am. Inst. Aeros. and Astronautics (marine systems com.); mem. Sigma Xi, Tau Beta Pi. Home: 4114 Wingren St Irving TX 75062 Office: PO Box 225907 Dallas TX 75265

FENTON, ALAN, artist; b. Cleve., July 29, 1927; s. Morris and Ethel (Beal) F.; m. Naomi J. Feigenbaum, July 31, 1955; children: Danielle D., David Efrem. B.F.A., Pratt Inst., 1959; student, Art Students League, N.Y.C., 1956-57. Prof. Pratt Inst., N.Y.C., Housatonic State Coll., Stratford, Conn.; tchr. Cleve. Inst. Art, 1977—; lectr. museums. Exhibited group shows, Art U.S.A., N.Y.C., 1958, City Center, N.Y.C., 1959 (hon. mention), Am. Inst., Mexico City, 1965, Cleve. Sch. Art., 1950, New Sch., N.Y.C., 1958, N.Y. U., Cleve. Mus. Art, 1959-61 (1st prize 1960, 61), San Francisco Mus. Art, 1963, Fed. Pavillion, N.Y. World's Fair, 1964, Larry Aldrich Mus., 1968, Light Show, Conn., Corcoran Gallery Art, Washington, 1970, Corcoran worldwide touring exhibit, 1971—, Tokyo, 1983, Munich, W.Ger.; exhibited one-man shows, Pace Gallery, N.Y.C., 1964, Bridgeport (Conn.) Mus. Art, 1973, N.Y. Cultural Mus., N.Y.C., 1974, Washington Post Exec. Offices, 1975, Iseton Gallery Art, Tokyo, 1975—, Iowa Mus. Art, Iowa City, 1976, Phillips Collection, Washington, 1977, Houston, N.C., Ft. Wayne (Ind.) museums art, Barbara Fiedler Gallery, Washington, 1982; travelling exhbn., Barbara Fiedler Gallery, Washington, 1980. Served with U.S. Mcht. Marine, World War II. Studio: 333 Park Ave S New York NY 10010 *I have during the last 10 years considered myself not a Minimalist but a "Nothingness", a blank painter. It is a doctrine that social conditions are so bad that destruction of the system is preferable to the present state. I rejoice in making do with nothing even as I claim attention to the daily depredations of existence on our decreasing physical and mental potencies. I allow my pictures to be less and less, but my drama becomes more and more energetic, more authoritative and more dominating. No compromise is possible.*

FENTON, EDWARD A., metallurgical engineer; b. N.Y.C., Nov. 17, 1925; s. Philip and Rose (Poppick) F.; m. Elaine B. Schlam, June 27, 1953; children: Ellen, Eliot. B.Mech. Engring., CCNY, 1947; M.Metall. Engring., Poly. Inst. Bklyn., 1951. Various positions in metall. field in shipbldg., r.r., oil refinery, chem. plant, aircraft industry, 1947-54; mem. staff Am. Welding Soc., Inc., N.Y.C. and Fla., 1954-75, tech. dir., 1957-69, exec. dir., sec., 1969-75; cons. engr. industry and govt., 1959—; lectr. in field; head U.S. del. to fgn. meetings Internat. Inst. Welding, Internat. Orgn. for Standardization, also Internat. Electrotech. Commn. Author: Marks Handbook for Mechanical Engineers, 1978, Index of Standards From 23 Nations, 1968, The AWS Bibliographies, 1968; also articles; contbr. to: Merit Students Ency., Book of Knowledge, Ency. Brit. Jr., others; author, editor over 200 articles and books on welding, metallurgy and engring., works transl. into French, German, Russian, Arabic, Italian, Norwegian, Portuguese, Turkish, others. Home and office: 7190 SW 99th St Miami FL 33156

FENTON, LEWIS LOWRY, lawyer; b. Palo Alto, Calif., Aug. 20, 1925; s. Norman and Jessie (Chase) F.; m. Gloria J. Palmieri, Aug. 21, 1978; children: Lewis Lowry, Juanita Chase, Daniel Norman. B.A., Stanford U., 1948, LL.B., 1950. Bar: Calif. 1950. Atty. Calif. Dept. Pub. Works, 1950-52; pres. Hoge, Fenton, Jones & Appel, Inc., Monterey, San Luis Obispo and San Jose, 1952—. Mem. bldg. com. Community Hosp. Monterey Peninsula, Carmel, 1961-62; found. dir. Monterey Jazz Festival, 1958; Trustee Monterey Peninsula Coll. (pres. 1971-72), Monterey Inst. Fgn. Studies; pres. trustees York Sch., Monterey, Calif., 1960-74. Served to 2d lt. USAAF, 1942-46. Fellow Am. Coll. Trial Lawyers; mem. Assn. Def. Counsel (pres. 1969), Nat. Bd. Trial Advocacy, Monterey Bar Assn. (pres. 1963), Stanford U. Alumni Assn. (pres. 1966-67). Episcopalian (vestryman, sr. warden 1956-58). Clubs: Cypress Point, Old Capital, Pacheco., Pacific Union. Home: PO Box 791 Monterey CA 93940 Office: PO Box 791 Monterey CA 93940

FENTON, NOEL JOHN, computer systems manufacturing company executive; b. New Haven, May 24, 1938; s. Arnold Alexander and Carla (Mathiasen) F.; m. Sarah Jane Hamilton, Aug. 14, 1965; children: Wendy, Devon, Peter, Lance. B.S., Cornell U., 1959; M.B.A., Stanford U., 1963. Research asst. Stanford (Calif.) U., 1963-64; v.p. Mail Systems Corp., Redwood City, Calif., 1964-66; v.p., gen. mgr. products div. Acurex Corp., Mountain View, Calif., 1966-72, pres., chief exec. officer, dir., 1972-83, Covalent Systems Corp., Santa Clara, Calif., 1983—; dir. Elpac Electronics, Inc., Micro Mask Inc., RPC Industries. Chmn. adv. council Resource Center for Women; mem. San Jose Econ. Devel. Task Force, 1983, Pres. Reagan's Bus. Adv. Panel. Served to lt. (j.g.) USN, 1959-61. Mem. Am. Electronics Assn. (chmn. 1978-79, dir. 1976-80), Young Pres.'s Orgn., Santa Clara County Mfrs. Group (dir.), Stanford Bus. Sch. Alumni Assn. (pres. 1976-77, dir. 1971-76). Republican. Episcopalian. Home: 60 Hayfields Rd Portola Valley CA 94025 Office: Coualent Systems Corp 585 Maude Court Sunnyvale CA 94086

FENTON, ROBERT LEONARD, lawyer; b. Detroit, Sept. 14, 1929; s. Ben B. and Stella Frances (Saffir) F.; children: Robert L., Cynthia R. A.B., Syracuse U., 1952; LL.B., U. Mich., 1955. Bar: Mich. 1955. Asso. Marks, Levi, Thill & Wiseman, Detroit, 1955-60; partner Fenton, Nederlander & Dodge, Detroit, 1960—; Lectr. Flint and Lansing Real Estate Bds., 1966-68; spl. counsel Detroit Fire Dept., 1975—, Mich. Motion Picture and TV Commn., 1979. Treas. Oakland County Democratic Com., 1960-64; mem. Dem. State Finance Com., 1966-69, Nat. Finance Com., 1962-74, Dem. Pres.'s Club, 1962-74; financial adviser to Mayor Roman S. Gribbs, 1969-73, Mayor Coleman A. Young, 1974—; chmn. State of Mich. Film and TV Commn.; Bd. dirs. Detroit Bi-Centennial Commn., Rivers and Harbour Congress of U.S.; mem. adv. bd. NAACP, U. Mich. Pres.'s Club. Served with USAF, 1950-52, Recipient Distinguished Pub. Service medal City of Detroit, 1973; named Man of the 60's City of Detroit, 1964; decorated Order of St. Johns of Jerusalem, 1980. Mem. Am., Mich., Detroit bar assns., Econs. Club, Acad. Magical Arts, Soc. Preservation Variety Arts. Jewish. Clubs: Mason (Shriner), Franklin Hills Country, Town and Country, Standard, Recess (Detroit); Les Ambassadors (Eng.); Racquet, Jockey (Miami Beach, Fla.). Home: Gateway III Ltd 27265 S Gateway Dr Bldg 12 Apt 206 Farmington Hills MI 48018 Office: 1930 Buhl Bldg Detroit MI 48226

FENTON, TERRY LYNN, art gallery director; b. Regina, Sask., Can., July 1, 1940; s. John Albert and Gertrude (Hirons) F.; m. Sheila Ann Cowie, Dec. 1, 1962; 1 son, Mark. B.A. in English Lit., U. Sask., 1962. Social worker Province of Alta., Edmonton, 1962-65; asst. to dir. Mackenzie Gallery, Regina, 1965-71; dir. Edmonton Art Gallery, 1972—. Co-author: Modern Painting in Canada, 1978; author books and catalogues on contemporary art; painter landscapes. Mem. Can. Mus. Assn., Can. Art Mus. Dirs. Assn., Council Assoc. Mus. Dirs. Home: 15713 89A Edmonton AB Canada T5R 4T1 Office: Edmonton Art Gallery 2 Churchill Sq Edmonton AB Canada T5J 2C1

FENTON, THOMAS TRAIL, journalist; b. Balt., Apr. 8, 1930; s. Matthew Clark and Beatrice (Trail) F.; m. Simone France Marie Lopes-Curval, Jan. 10, 1959; children: Ariane France, Thomas Trail. A.B., Dartmouth Coll., 1952. Mem. staff Balt. Sun, 1961-70, chief Rome bur., 1966-68, chief Paris bur., 1968-70; reporter-producer Rome bur. CBS News, 1970-73, corr. Tel Aviv bur., 1973-77, corr. Paris bur., 1977-79, sr. European corr., London, 1979—. Served with USN, 1952-61. Recipient citation for articles from Paris Overseas Press Club Am., 1968, award for coverage Indo-Pakistan War, 1971, for coverage Middle East War, 1973, Sadat visit to Jerusalem, 1977, for Mountbatten funeral, 1980, hunger in Africa, 1981, award for report on Africa, Nat. Acad. TV Arts and Scis., 1981. Mem. Soc. of Cincinnati, Assn. Am. Corrs., Internat. Inst. Strategic Studies (Royal United Services Inst. Def. Studies), Reform Club, Delta Upsilon. Office: CBS News Bowater House 68 Knightsbridge London SW1 England

FENTON, WILLIAM NELSON, anthropologist, emeritus educator; b. New Rochelle, N.Y., 1908; s. John William and Anna Belle (Nourse) F.; m. Olive Louise Ortwine, 1936; children: Elizabeth Fenton Snyder, John W., Douglas Bruce, Harry (dec.). A.B., Dartmouth Coll., 1931; Ph.D., Yale U., 1937; LL.D., Hartwick Coll., 1968. Community worker U.S. Indian Service (N.Y. Agency, in charge Tonawanda and Tuscarora Reservations), 1935-37; instr. sociology and anthropology St. Lawrence U., 1937-38, asst. prof., 1938-39; instr. (summers) Allegany Sch. Natural History, U. Buffalo, 1938, St. Lawrence U., 1938; vis. prof. Northwestern U., 1947, U. Mich., 1951, U. Ariz., 1963; lectr. Johns Hopkins U., 1949-50, Cath. U. Am., 1950-51; asso. anthropologist Bur. Am. Ethnology, Smithsonian Instn., 1939-43, sr. ethnologist, 1943-51, mem. and sec., war com., 1942-44; research asso. Ethnogeographic Bd., 1943-45; exec. sec. div. anthropology and psychology NRC, 1952-54; dir., asst. commr. N.Y. State Mus. and Sci. Service, 1954-68; research prof. anthropology State U. N.Y., Albany, 1968-74, disting. prof., 1974-79, emeritus disting. prof., 1979—; U.S. del. IV Internat. Congress Anthrop. and Ethnol. Sci., Vienna, 1952; mem. Am. del. VII Internat. Congress on Anthropology and Ethnology, Moscow, 1964; ethnol. field trips to Iroquois Indian Reservations; Nat. Endowment Humanities fellow Huntington Library, 1978-79; mem. Iroquois Documentary History Project, Newberry Library, 1979-81. Author: Area Studies in American Universities, 1947, Iroquois Eagle Dance, 1953, Indian and White Relations to 1830, 1957, Parker on the Iroquois, 1968; co-editor, transl.: Customs of the American Indians (J.F. Lafitau) 2 vols, 1974, 76; contbr. numerous articles to profl. jours. Mem. com. on Lang. and Areal Implications, Commn. on Implication of Armed Service Ednl. Programs, Am. Council Edn., 1946; trustee Mus. Am. Indian-Heye Found., 1976-80, 82—. Recipient Cornplanter medal for Iroquois Research, 1965, Citizen Laureate award SUNY Found., 1978; Dartmouth Coll. Class of 1930 award, 1979; named Dean in Perpetuum of Iroquoian Studies 30th Conf. on Iroquois Research, 1979; Fulbright-Hays research fellow to N.Z., 1975; NEH sr. fellow, 1982-83. Fellow AAAS, Royal Anthrop. Inst., Am. Folklore Soc. (pres. 1959-60), Am. Anthrop. Assn. (exec. bd. 1963-65), Am. Ethnol. Soc. (pres. 1959), Am. Soc. Ethnohistory (pres. 1962), Anthrop. Soc. Washington (former sec., v.p., pres.), Keene Valley Library Assn. (trustee 1970-73), Sigma Xi. Episcopalian. Club: Trout Unltd. (pres. Clearwater chpt. 1979-81). Home: 7 N Helderberg Pkwy Slingerlands NY 12159 (summer) Keene Valley NY 12943

FENVES, STEVEN JOSEPH, civil engr.; b. Subotica, Yugoslavia, June 6, 1931; came to U.S., 1950, naturalized, 1953; s. Louis and Clara (Gereb) F.; m. Norma Jean Horwitz, July 3, 1955; children—Gregory L., Carol E., Peter D., Laura R. B.C.E., U. Ill., 1957, M.S., 1958, Ph.D., 1961. Prof. U. Ill., 1957-71; prof., head dept. civil engring. Carnegie-Mellon U., Pitts., 1972-75, Univ. prof., 1975—; vis. prof. M.I.T., 1962-63, Nat. U. Mex., 1965, 70, Cornell U., 1970-71; cons. to pvt. corps., govt. agys. Author: Stress Programming System, 1964, Computer Methods in Civil Engineering, 1967; contbr. numerous articles to tech. jours. Served with U.S. Army, 1952-53. Mem. Nat. Acad. Engring., ASCE (Research prize 1965), Assn. Computing Machinery, Sigma Xi, Tau Beta Pi, Chi Epsilon. Home: 1125 Folkstone Dr Pittsburgh PA 15243

FENWICK, MILLICENT HAMMOND, diplomat, former congresswoman; b. N.Y.C., Feb. 25, 1910; d. Ogden Haggerty and Mary Picton (Stevens) Hammond; children: Mary Fenwick Reckford, Hugh. Student, Columbia Extension Sch., New Sch. for Social Research. Assoc. editor Conde Nast Publs., N.Y.C., 1938-50; mem. N.J. Gen. Assembly, 1970-73; dir. div. consumer affairs N.J. Dept. Law and Pub. Safety, 1973-74; mem. 94th-97th Congresses from N.J. 5th Dist.; U.S. del. UN Food and Agr. Orgn., 1983—. Author: Vogue's Book of Etiquette, 1948, Speaking Up, 1982. Vice chmn. N.J. advisory com. to U.S. Commn. on Civil Rights, 1958-72; mem. Bernardsville (N.J.) Bd. Edn., 1938-41; mem Bernardsville Borough Council, 1958-64. Republican. Office: Food and Agriculture Organization Via delle Terme di Caracalla Rome Italy 00100

FENYVESI, CHARLES, journalist, editor; b. Debrecen, Hungary, Nov. 23, 1937; came to U.S., 1956, naturalized, 1963; s. Aladar and Anna (Schwarcz) F.; m. Elisabeth Kelemen, Dec. 21, 1965; children: Shamu, Daniel, Malka. B.A. cum laude, Harvard U., 1960; M.A., Madras U., 1962. Washington corr. Jerusalem Post, 1966-69, Ha'aretz, Tel Aviv, 1969-74, Israel Radio, 1970-81; editor Nat. Jewish Monthly, Washington, 1972-81; staff writer Washington Post, 1981-83; editor Washington Jewish Week, 1983—; garden columnist Washington Post,

1983—. Author: Splendor in Exile, The Ex-Majesties of Europe, 1979. Office: Nat Press Bldg Washington DC 20045

FENZA, WILLIAM JOSEPH, JR., financial co. exec.; b. Ridley Park, Pa., May 21, 1929; s. William Joseph and Leona (Lane) F.; m. Myra Ann Wolf, Dec. 14, 1968; children—David, Christine, Jennifer, Richard. A.B., Johns Hopkins U., 1951; LL.B., U. Pa., 1956. Bar: Pa. bar. Law clk. firm Joseph E. Pappano, Chester, Pa., 1956-57; claims office mgr. State Farm Ins. Co., Dover, Del., 1957-59; partner firm Bernstein, Corcoran, Mueller & Fenza, Upper Darby, Pa., 1960-62; with Finance Am. Corp., Allentown, Pa., 1962—, sr. v.p., gen. counsel. Served with AUS, 1951-53. Mem. Am., Pa., Lehigh County bar assns. Home: 2830 Old S Pike Ave Allentown PA 18103 Office: 1105 Hamilton St Allentown PA 18101

FERBEL, THOMAS, physics educator, physicist; b. Radom, Poland, Dec. 12, 1937; came to U.S., 1949, naturalized, 1955; s. Joseph and Natalie (Gotfryd) F.; m. Barbara G. Goolnick, Apr. 20, 1963; children: Natalie, Peter Jordan. B.S., Queens Coll., 1959; M.S., Yale U., 1960, Ph.D., 1963. Research staff physicist Yale U., New Haven, 1963-65; research assoc. U. Rochester, N.Y., 1965, asst. prof. physics, 1965-69, assoc. prof., 1969-73, prof., 1973—; sci. assoc. CERN, Geneva, 1980-81; mem. program adv. com. Stanford Linear Accelerator Ctr., Calif., 1974-76, Brookhaven Lab., Upton, N.Y., 1981-84. Editor: Techniques and Concepts of High Energy Physics, 1981, Silicon Detectors in High Energy Physics, 1982; mem. editorial bd.: Phys. Rev., 1978-80, Zeitschrift fur Physik, 1981-84. Alfred P. Sloan fellow, 1970; John S. Guggenheim fellow, 1971. Mem. Am. Phys. Soc. (sec.-treas. div. particles and fields 1983—). Office: Dept. Physics U Rochester Rochester NY 14627

FERBER, HERBERT, artist; b. N.Y.C., Apr. 30, 1906; s. Louis and Hattie (Lebowitz) Silvers; m. Edith Popiel, Feb. 1967. Student, CCNY, 1927, Columbia U., 1930. Free-lance painter and sculptor, 1930—; one-man shows include, Andre Emmerich Gallery, N.Y.C., 1960-77, Kootz Gallery, N.Y.C., 1955, 57, Betty Parsons Gallery, 1947, 56, 57, Walker Art Center, Mpls., 1962, Whitney Mus. Am. Art, 1961, Knoedler & Co., 1978-80, Houston Mus. Fine Arts, 1981, group shows include, Mus. Modern Art, N.Y.C., 1952, 68, Antwerp (Belgium) Biennale, 1971, Nat. Coll. Fine Arts, Washington, 1976, represented permanent collections mus. throughout U.S. and Europe including, Nat. Gallery Fine Arts, Washington, Mus. Modern Art, N.Y.C., Met. Mus. Art, N.Y.C., Whitney Mus. Am. Art, N.Y.C., Houston Mus. Fine Arts, Norton Simon Mus., Pasadena, Calif., Princeton Art Gallery, N.J., Centre Georges Pompidou, Paris; subject of book by Eugene Goossen. Address: 44 MacDougal St New York NY 10012

FERBER, SAMUEL, advertising executive; b. N.Y.C., June 6, 1920; s. Isidor and Sadie (Irgang) F.; m. Beatrice Ruth Ziman, June 18, 1944; children: Bruce Joseph, Joel David. B.B.A., CCNY, 1941; postgrad., Columbia U., 1946-48. Promotion dir. Nat. Advt. Service, Inc., N.Y.C., 1946-50, Boys' Life mag., 1950-52; promotion dir. Esquire mag., N.Y.C., 1952-58, advt. mgr., 1959-65, sr. v.p., assoc. pub., 1965-70, advt. dir., 1970-74, pub., 1974-76, co-dir., 1966-74, dir., 1972-75; sr. v.p., prin. Altman, Stoller, Weiss Advt., 1976-80, exec. v.p., 1980—; mem. faculty econs. and advt. Latin Am. Inst., N.Y.C., 1946-49; lectr. on mag. pub. at various colls. and univs. Mem. arts adv. bd. N.Y. Bd. Trade, 1969-73; Leader Gt. Books Discussion Group. Served with Adj. Gen.'s Dept. AUS, 1942-46. Home: 17 Solar Ln Searingtown NY 11507 Office: 1350 Ave of Americas New York NY 10019 *I have always subscribed to the philosophy of my colleague, Arnold Gingrich, that one should "never leave well enough alone". When things are progressing smoothly is the precise moment to plan the evolutionary change that insures progress and vitality. In my time, I have seen pillars of industry and publishing fall by the wayside because their emphasis has been on self-preservation rather than innovation.*

FERDERBER, JOSEPH, electronics consultant; b. Cleve., Oct. 23, 1919; s. Andrew and Anna (Yurkovich) F.; m. Georgia Lucille Pesek, Sept. 26, 1942 (div. Jan. 1970); children: Lawrence Joseph, Julie Ann, Michael James; m. Anna Ruth Spasser, May 1979. B.S. in Elec. Engring., Case Inst. Tech., 1942; postgrad., Syracuse U., 1945-46; grad. exec. program, UCLA, 1958. Test engr. Gen. Electric Co., Syracuse, N.Y., 1943-44, head test, 1944-46, asst. gen. head test, 1946-48, asst. gen. head inspection, 1948-49; chief prodn. test Hughes Aircraft Co., Culver City, Calif., 1949-50, supt. assembly, 1950-52, mgr., El Segundo, Calif., 1956-66, v.p. mfg., 1966-83, mem. policy bd., 1956-83, v.p., 1962-83; cons., 1983—. Mem. Aerospace Industries Assn. (mfg. com.), Machinery and Allied Products Inst. (mfg. council), Am. Def. Preparedness Assn., Sigma Xi, Eta Kappa Nu, Tau Beta Pi. Unitarian (dir., treas.). Home and Office: 27553 Sunnyridge Rd Palos Verdes Peninsula CA 90274

FEREBEE, STEPHEN SCOTT, JR., architect; b. Detroit, July 30, 1921; s. Stephen Scott and Caroline (Cheatham) F.; m. Mary Elizabeth Cooper, July 7, 1945; children: Scott III, John, Caroline. B.Archtl. Engring., N.C. State U., 1948. Job capt. A.G. Odell, Jr. & Assocs. (Architects), Charlotte, N.C., 1948-53; partner Higgins & Ferebee (Architects), Charlotte, 1953-59, Ferebee & Walters (Architects), 1959-64; pres. Ferebee, Walters & Assos. (Architects/Planners), Charlotte, 1964—; dir. Prodn. Systems for Architects and Engrs., Inc., Washington, 1969-71, 77-78, Republic Bank & Trust Co., Charlotte, John Crosland Co., Charlotte. Projects have included East Bay Trading Co. Restaurant, Charleston, S.C., 1980, Hickory Ridge Mall, Memphis, Tenn., 1981, Tech. Center for Union Carbide Agrl. Products Co., Inc, Research Triangle Park, N.C., 1982, Sch. Vet. Medicine, N.C. State U., Raleigh, 1983. Pres. N.C. Design Found., 1966-68, 78-79. Served to capt., 101st Airborne Div. AUS, 1942-46; maj. gen. Res.; ret.). Decorated D.S.M., Bronze Star, Purple Heart; Croix de Guerre, France and Belgium). Fellow AIA (pres. N.C. 1964, chmn. commn. profl. practice 1971, nat. pres. 1973, Sec. Coll. of Fellows 1984—); mem. Internat. Union Architects (council 1975-81), Charlotte C. of C. (v.p. 1975-76), N.C. State U. Alumni Assn. (pres. 1980-81), Phi Kappa Phi. Methodist (past chmn. ofcl. bd.). Club: Rotarian. Home: 2329 Rock Creek Dr Charlotte NC 28226 Office: 8008 Corporate Center Drive PO Box 2029 Charlotte NC 28211

FERETIC, EILEEN SUSAN, editor; b. N.Y.C., Aug. 31, 1949; d. Joseph Anthony and Eileen Helen (Sohl) F. B.A., Fordham U., 1971. Editor Manpower Edn. Inst., N.Y.C., 1970-72, UTP div. Hearst Bus. Communications, L.I., N.Y., 1972—, Corporate Systems mag., 1975-80, Office Products News, 1972-82, Today's Office, 1982—; editorial dir., 1978—; also editorial dir. Office Group, 1978—; industry rep. U.S. Dept. Commerce, 1980, 83; mem. Pres.' Pvt. Sector Survey on Cost Control/Office Automation Task Force, 1982. Editor, Manpower Edn. Inst., N.Y.C., 1970-72, UTP div. Hearst Bus. Communications, L.I., N.Y., 1972—, Corporate Systems mag, 1975-80; editor: Office Products News, 1972—; editorial dir., 1978—; also editorial dir.: Office Group, 1978—; Co-author textbook on adminstrv. procedures in electronics office, 1979. Recipient N.Y. Daily News award journalism, 1970. Mem. Am. Bus. Press Editors Assn. Home: 115 Rita Dr East Meadow NY 11554 Office: 645 Stewart Ave Garden City NY 11530

FERGER, LAWRENCE A., gas distribution utility executive; b. Des Moines, May 3, 1934; s. Cleon A. and Helen K. (Jacobs) F.; m. LaVon Stark, Oct. 20, 1957; children: Kirsten A., Jane S. B.S. in Bus. Adminstrn., Simpson Coll., Indianola, Iowa, 1956. Auditor Arthur Andersen & Co., Chgo., 1956-64; dir. data processing Ind. Gas Co., Inc., Indpls., 1964-74, v.p. planning, 1974-79, v.p., treas., 1979-80, sr. v.p. fin., 1980-81, exec. v.p., 1981-84, pres., 1984—. Served with U.S. Army, 1957-59. Mem. Ind. Gas Assn. (treas. 1966-80, sec. 1966-70, dir. 1980—). Office: Indiana Gas Co Inc 1630 N Meridian St Indianapolis IN 46202

FERGUSON, ALLEN RICHMOND, economist; b. Pawtucket, R.I., Sept. 27, 1919; s. Duncan Hector Campbell and Margaret Esther (Allen) F.; m. Audrey Irene Mitscher, Jan. 12, 1944; children: Allen Richmond, Rondell Audrey, William Duncan, Duncan Campbell. A.B., Brown U., 1941, M.A., 1943; Ph.D., Harvard, 1949. Asst. prof. econs. U. Va., 1949-51; economist OPS, 1951, CIA, 1952; dep. head logistics dept. Rand Corp., 1953-58; dir. research Transp. Center, Northwestern U., 1958-60; sr. economist Rand Corp., 1960-63; coordinator internat. aviation State Dept., 1963-65; dep. mgr. systems econs. div., dir. policy research Planning Research Corp., 1965-71; ind. economist, 1971-72; founder, pres. Pub. Interest Econs. Center and Found., 1972—; chmn. Nat. Inst. Econs. and Law; adviser Office Sec. Def., 1958-59; coordinator research Nat. Com. for Effective Congress, 1970; cons. Ho. Com. on Banking and Currency, 1971, Internat. Bank for Reconstrn. and Devel. Govt. Man., Can., 1972, Commodities Futures Trading Commn., 1976. Author: The Economic Value of the United States Merchant Marine, 1960; also articles.; Editor: Measuring Benefits of Health and Safety Regulation; Agenda for Regulatory Research for the, 1980's. Served as 1st lt., pilot USAAF, 1943-45. Decorated D.F.C., Air medal with 2 oak leaf clusters. Mem. Am. Econ. Assn., Phi Beta Kappa. Home: 4440 Sedgwick St NW Washington DC 20016 Office: 1525 New Hampshire Ave NW Washington DC 20036

FERGUSON, ANDREW BOYD, JR., TV producer and director; b. Indpls., Oct. 6, 1936; s. Andrew Boyd and Alberta (Clemons) F.; m. Claudette Buchanan, Sept. 6, 1970; children: Sybil, Gregory, Cynthia, Heather, Davin. B.A., U. Rochester, 1958; postgrad., Nat. Acad. TV and film engr. Sta. WGBH-TV, Boston, 1961-68; assoc. producer, audio engr., tech. producer dir. pub. affairs programming, 1968-69; asso. producer Sta. WABC-TV, N.Y.C., 1969-70; lectr. mass media arts and scis. Hampton Inst., 1970-71; producer Electric Company, Public Broadcasting System, 1972-79; pres. A.B. Ferguson Prodns. Corp., 1979—; ptnr. Am. Video Network; cons. in field.; instr. N.Y. U.; Mem. exec. bd. ACLU, also; chmn. publicity com., 1970. (Silver Hugo award, Chgo. Film Festival 1974, Emmy award Nat. Acad. TV Arts and Scis 1977, Achievement award Action for Childrens TV 1976); prodns. include IBM Spl. with Petulia Clark Mus. Spl. Served with USN, 1958-60. Recipient numerous awards including awards Ohio State U., 1973, Japan Prize, 1973. Mem. Dirs. Guild Am., Nat. Assn. Ednl. Broadcasters, Acad. TV Arts and Scis. Home: 555 Main St Roosevelt Island New York NY 10044 *I've lived my years in the heat of blood and have drunk the dreamer's wine, so let my soul house built of mud not topple to the dust a vacant shrine. Let me be like the tuned swept fiddler's string that feels the master's melody and snaps*

FERGUSON, CHARLES ALBERT, Linguist, consultant on language problems; b. Phila., July 6, 1921; s. Albert T. and Mary B. (Kohler) F.; m. Joanna Eichmuller, Sept. 16, 1944 (div. 1962); children: Lisa J., Christina M.; m. Shirley Brice Heath, Mar. 25, 1979; children: Brice W. Heath, Shannon K. Heath. B.A., U. Pa., 1942, M.A., 1943, Ph.D., 1945. Sci. linguist Fgn. Service Inst.-U.S. Dept. State, Washington, 1946-55; lectr. linguistics Harvard U., Cambridge, Mass., 1955-59; dir. pres. Ctr. for Applied Linguistics, Washington, 1959-66; prof. linguistics Stanford (Calif.) U., 1967—; trustee Ctr. for Applied Linguistics, 1967-82; mem., chmn. Social Sci. Research Council Com. on Sociolinguistics, 1963-79; dir. Lang. Survey of Ethiopia, 1968-69. Mem. editorial bd.: Language in Society, Jour. Child Language, 1974—; author: Language Structure and Language Use, 1972; co-author, editor: Language Problems of Developing Nations, 1968, Talking to Children, 1977, Language in the USA, 1981. Fellow Ctr. For Advanced Study in Behavioral Scis., 1970-71, Sch. Oriental and African Studies-London, 1975; Guggenheim fellow India, Australia, 1980. Fellow Am. Acad. Arts and Scis.; mem. Linguistic Soc. Am. (pres. 1970), Internat. Assn. for Study of Child Lang. (pres. 1973-75), Am. Assn. for Applied Linguistics (exec. com. 1971-83). Lutheran. Home: 711 Ensign Way Palo Alto CA 94303 Office: Stanford U. Stanford CA 94305

FERGUSON, CHARLES AUSTIN, newspaper editor; b. New Orleans, Mar. 16, 1937; s. Austin and Josephine Hayes (Gessner) F.; m. Jane Pugh, Dec. 21, 1961; children: Elizabeth Hayes, Caroline Pugh. B.A., Tulane U., 1958, LL.B., 1961. Bar: La. bar 1961. From reporter to editor States-Item, New Orleans, 1961-80; editor Times-Picayune/States-Item, New Orleans, 1980—; anchorman TV program City Desk, New Orleans, 1971-78. Trustee Dillard U., New Orleans, 1972—, chmn. exec. com., 1978—; trustee Inst. Politics, Loyola U., New Orleans, 1968-75, pres., 1971-75; co-chmn. Louis Armstrong Meml. Park Com., New Orleans, 1971-79. Recipient Torch of Liberty award Anti-Defamation League of B'nai B'rith, 1981; Nieman fellow, 1965-66. Mem. Am. Soc. Newspaper Editors, La. Bar Assn. Club: New Orleans Lawn Tennis. Home: 1448 Joseph St New Orleans LA 70115 Office: 3800 Howard Ave New Orleans LA 70140

FERGUSON, CHARLES RAY, management consultant; b. Duncanville, Tex., Jan. 15, 1925; s. John Herbert and Thelma Inez (Brandenburg) F.; m. Billie Lucille Benson, Nov. 11, 1945; children: John Benson, Rebecca, Rachel. B.S., So. Meth. U., 1945, M.S., 1953. Engr. U.S. Steel Co., Dallas, 1945-47, adminstrv. asst., Oil City, Pa., 1948-49, asst. to gen. mgr. mfg., Dallas, 1950-54; instr. indsl. engring. So. Meth. U., 1955-56; founding mem., mng. prin. LWFW, Inc., Dallas, 1955—, now chmn. bd., chief exec. officer; dir. Fibergrate Corp. Author: Measuring Corporate Strategy, 1974. Bd. dirs. Dallas County Mental Health, Mental Retardation Center, 1975-76; pres., bd. dirs. Spl. Care Sch., Dallas, 1975-76; chmn. bd. govs. Dallas Symphony Orch.; mem. Dallas Citizens Council, 1962—; pres. bus. adv. council U. Tex. at Arlington. Served with USNR, 1943-45. Mem. Inst. Mgmt. Consultants (a founder), Assn. Cons. Mgmt. Engrs. (dir. 1972, 75). Club: City (Dallas). Home: 5511 Park Ln Dallas TX Office: 12700 Park Central Pl Dallas TX 75251

FERGUSON, CHARLES WINSTON, retired insurance company executive; b. Bryan, Tex, Dec. 7, 1913; s. John M. and Nell Elizabeth (Jones) F.; m. Julia Locke McCall, Mar. 8, 1935; children—Judith Olivia, Patricia Nell. Grad., Tex. A&M U., 1935. With Texas Co., 1935-40; with Houston Gen. Ins. Co. (and predecessor), 1940-58, sr. v.p., 1954-58; pres. Balboa Ins. Co., Newport Beach, Calif., 1958-76; chmn. Assos. Ins. Group, Dallas, 1976—, Cumberland Life Ins. Co., Emmco Ins. Co., Hallmark Life Ins. Co., Sydney, N.S.W., Australia, 1966-76, Hallmark Gen. Ins. Co., Sydney, 1968-76; pres. Atlantic Gen., Hamilton, Bermuda, 1968-76. Bd. dirs. Dallas Boys Clubs, Boys Club of Palm Springs; exec. com., bd. dirs. Dallas Symphony; mem. fin. com. Calif. Democratic party. Mem. Lloyds of London. Presbyterian. Clubs: Mill Creek Golf (Salad., Tex.); Seven Lakes, Desert Island (Palm Springs); Masons. Home: 4506 Stagecoach Trail Temple TX 76502 401 Desert Lakes Palm Springs CA 92264

FERGUSON, DONALD JOHN, surgeon, educator; b. Mpls., Nov. 19, 1916; s. Donald Nivison and Arline (Folsom) F.; m. Lillian Elizabeth Mack, June 26, 1943; children—Anne Elizabeth, Donald John, Merrill James. B.S., Yale, 1939; M.D., U. Minn., 1943, M.S. in Physiology, 1951, Ph. D. in Surgery, 1951. Intern, then resident U. Minn. Hosp., 1947-52; asst. prof. surgery U. Minn., 1952-54; asso. prof., 1954-56, prof., 1956-60; prof. surgery U. Chgo., 1960—. Contbr. articles in field. Served to capt. M.C. AUS, 1943-46. Mem. ACS, Am. Surg. Assn., Soc. U. Surgeons. Home: 5629 Blackstone Ave Chicago IL 60637

FERGUSON, EDWARD CLIFTON, III, ophthalmology educator, physician; b. Beaumont, Tex., Mar. 11, 1926; s. Edward Clifton and Marie Louise (Meador) F. B.S., Northwestern U., 1946; B.M., Northernwestern U., 1949; M.D., NorthwesternU., 1950. Diplomate: Am. Bd. Ophthalmology; lic. physician, Iowa, Wash., Colo., Ill., Tex. Rotating intern Evanston Hosp. Assn., Ill., 1950; intern Cook County Hosp., Chgo., 1950-51; resident in ophthalmology Ill. Eye and Ear Infirmary, U. Ill.-Chgo., 1954-56; fellow in Neuro-ophthalmology Howe Lab., Boston, 1956-57; Head fellow in strabismus Columbia U. Coll. Physicians and Surgeons Eye Inst., N.Y.C., U. Iowa City, 1957; asst. prof. ophthalmology U. Iowa, 1957-63; assoc. prof. ophthalomology U. Tex. Med. Br., Galveston, 1964-69, prof. ophthalmology, 1969—, chmn. dept., 1964-81; head retina service U. Iowa, 1958-63; mem. staff USAF Gen. Hosp., Lackland AFB, 1951-53, Brook Gen. Hosp., San Antonio, 1952, U. Iowa Hosps., 1957-63, U. Tex. Med. Br. Hosp., 1964—; cons. St. Mary's Hosp., Galveston. Contbr. articles to profl. jours. Served to capt. M.C. USAFR, 1951-53. Recipient Career Devel. award Nat. Inst. Neurol. Disease and Blindness, 1957, deptl. devel. award Nat. Inst. Neurol Disease and Blindness, 1964. Fellow ACS; mem. Am. Acad. Ophthalmology, Tex. Ophthal. Assn. (councilor 1968-70), Tex. Soc. Ophthalmology and Otolaryngology, Houston Ophthal. Assn., AMA, Galveston Med. Soc., Pan Am. Ophthal. Assn., Assn. Research in Vision and Ophthalmology, Am. Intraocular Implant Soc., Internat. Glaucoma Congress, Am. Soc. Contemporary Ophthalmology; mem. Assn. Univ. Profs. of Ophthalmology, Contact Lens Assn. Ophthalmology, Ill. Eye and Ear Alumni (pres. 1964-65), So. Med. Assn. (chmn. sect. ophthalmology 1971), Sigma Xi, Alpha Omega Alpha. Episcopalian. Club: Arty (Galveston). Office: Dept of Ophthalmology U of Texas Medical Branch Galveston TX 77550

FERGUSON, ELDON EARL, physicist; b. Rawlins, Wyo., Apr. 23, 1926; s. George Earl and Bess (Pierce) F. B.S., Okla. U., 1949, M.S., 1950, Ph.D., 1953. Physicist U.S. Naval Research Lab., Washington, 1954-57; prof. physics U. Tex., Austin, 1957-62; dir. aeronomy lab. NOAA, Dept. Commerce, Boulder, Colo., 1962—. Served with U.S. Army, 1944-45. Guggenheim Found. fellow, 1960; Humboldt fellow, 1979-80. Mem. Am. Phys. Soc., Am. Chem. Soc., Am. Geophys. Union. Office: 325 Broadway Boulder CO 80302

FERGUSON, ELI HALL, insurance company consultant; b. Philip, S.D., Oct. 27, 1909; s. Messer A. and Susie Anne (Hall) F.; m. Hazel Mae Bell, Dec. 26, 1934; 1 dau., Faye Jean Cartmell. B.S., S.D. State U., 1932, D.Sc. (hon.), 1963. Cattle rancher, 1926-33; fieldman First Nat. Bank, Philip, S.D., 1933-34; various positions U.S. Dept. Agr., Lincoln, Neb., 1934-36; with Equitable Life Assurance Soc. U.S., N.Y.C., 1936-74, 2d v.p., 1953-59, charge farm mortgages, 1956-60, v.p., 1959—, v.p. corporate planning on staff of chief exec. officer, 1960-71, sr. v.p. corporate planning, 1971-74; chmn. bd., chief exec. officer Student Life Funding, Inc., 1971-74; dir. Equitable Environ. Health, Houston Gen. Ins. Co., Traders & Gen. Ins. Co., Insurers Indemnity & Ins. Co., Traders Indemnity Co., Asso. Employers Gen. Agy., Inc., 1974-78. Mem. N.J. Natural Resources Council, 1972-77; Bd. dirs., treas. Nat. Soc. to Prevent Blindness; bd. dirs., sec. N.J. Soc. to Prevent Blindness. Mem. Am., Western farm econ. assns., N.Am. Soc. Corp. Planning, Am. Risk and Ins. Assn. Clubs: Mason., Economic (N.Y.C). Home: 680 Wellington Rd Ridgewood NJ 07450

FERGUSON, FRANCIS EUGENE, insurance company executive; b. Batavia, N.Y., Feb. 4, 1921; s. Harold M. and Florence (Munger) F.; m. Patricia J. Reddy, Aug. 11, 1945; children: Susan Lee, Patricia Ann. Student, Cornell U., 1938-39; B.S., Mich. State U., 1947. Asst. sec.-treas. Fed. Land Bank Assn., Lansing, Mich., 1947-48; appraiser Fed. Land Bank, St. Paul, 1948-50; specialist agrl. econs. Mich. State U. Extension, 1951; with Northwestern Mut. Life Ins. Co., Milw., 1951—, specialist, 1951-52, asst. mgr. farm loans, 1952-56, mgr. farm loans, 1956-62, gen. mgr. mortgage loans, 1962-63, v.p. mortgage loans, 1963-67, pres., 1967-80, chmn., chief exec. officer, 1980-83, chmn. bd., 1983—; dir. Allen-Bradley Co., Milw., Djinnii Industries, Dayton, Kaneb Services, Houston, Singer Co., Stamford, Conn., Ralson Purina Co., St. Louis, Green Bay Packaging Inc., Wis., WICOR, Wis. Gas Co., Rexnord, Inc., Milw. Gen. campaign chmn. United Fund, 1965; corp. mem. Milw. Children's Hosp.; bd. dirs. Com. Econ. Devel., Greater Milw. Com., Columbia Hosp. Served to capt. USAAF, 1942-45. Decorated Purple Heart. Mem. Milw. Assn. Commerce (dir.). Republican. Methodist. Clubs: Milwaukee, Milwaukee Country, University. Home: 817 W Autumn Path Ln Milwaukee WI 53217 Office: 720 E Wisconsin Ave Milwaukee WI 53202

FERGUSON, FRANK CAHAN, marketing association executive; b. Hamilton, Ont., Can., Nov. 26, 1923; s. Cecil George and Ethel Elizabeth (Dyer) F.; m. Verna Louise Stephenson, July 11, 1947 (div. May 1975); children: Diane, Frederick, John; m. 2d Nola Anne Moody, Nov. 14, 1975. Student, McMaster U., 1946-48, U. Toronto, 1958-61. Salesman Archtl. Aluminum, Hamilton, 1949-58; sales mgr. Reynolds Extrusion Co., Toronto, Ont., 1958-65; dir. research G.L. Sutin & Assoc., Cons. Engrs., Hamilton, 1965-74; exec. dir. Reinforcing Steel Inst., Toronto, 1974-77; pres. Can. Direct Mktg. Assn., Toronto, 1977—. Editor: Ad Mail Canada, 1980. Bd. dirs. Canadian Advt. Found., Toronto, 1977—. Served with RCAF, 1943-46. Mem. Inst. Indsl. Engr. (chpt. pres. 1973), Can. Soc. Indsl. Engrs., Can. Inst. Mgmt. Clubs: Donaldo (Toronto); Royal Hamilton Military Institute. Home: 15 Highfield Crescent Box 5 RR 1 Keswick ON Canada L4P 3C8 Office: Canadian Direct Marketing Association 405-150 Consumers Rd Willowdale ON Canada M2J 1P9

FERGUSON, FREDERICK PALMER, physiologist, government official; b. Middletown, Conn., Mar. 19, 1916; s. Frederick Burns and Frances Van Norstrand (Palmer) F.; m. Dorothy Helen Delano, June 14, 1941; children: Ruth, Kathleen, Barbara, James, Thomas. B.A. with honors, Wesleyan U., 1938, M.A., 1939; Ph.D. (C.P. Sigerfoos fellow), U. Minn., 1943. Asst. biology Wesleyan U., Middletown, Conn., 1938-39, asst. prof., 1947-49; asst. zoology U. Minn., Mpls., 1939-43; instr. physiology La. State U., New Orleans, 1943-45; research assoc. Rutgers U., New Brunswick, N.J., 1945-46, asst. prof. physiology, 1946-47, U. Md., Balt., 1949-51, assoc. prof., 1951-55, prof., 1955-60; with NIH, Bethesda, Md., 1960—; program coordinator biophysics and physiol. scis. program Nat. Inst. Gen. Med. Scis., 1984—; mem. adv. com. Life Scis. Research Office, Fedn. Am. Socs. Exptl. Biology, 1972-79. Contbr. articles to profl. jours. Recipient Sustained High Quality Performance award NIH, 1970, Dir.'s award, 1978. Fellow AAAS, N.Y. Acad. Scis.; mem. Am. Physiol. Soc., Am. Soc. Zoologists, Biomed. Engring. Soc. (dir. 1980-82), Soc. for Exptl. Biology and Medicine, Sigma Xi, Phi Beta Kappa. Research on physiology of heart and kidney, protein metabolism, responses to hypoxia. Home: 10228 Hatherleigh Dr Bethesda MD 20814 Office: Nat Inst Gen Med Scis NIH Bethesda MD 20205

FERGUSON, GARY WARREN, public relations executive; b. Stockton, Kans., May 5, 1925; s. Richard and Nelle (McBee) F.; m. Doris Drisler, Oct. 2, 1948; children: Arthur Richard, Frances, Robert Warren, Scott William. A.B., Yale U., 1946; M.S. in Journalism, Columbia U., 1948. Reporter Providence Jour. Bull., 1948-49, Richmond (Va.) News Leader, 1949-52; reporter St. Louis Post-Dispatch, 1954-55, spl. writer, 1955-60; counselor Fleishman-Hillard, Inc., St. Louis, 1961-62, sr. partner, 1962-71; pres. Gary Ferguson, Inc. (pub. relations), 1971—; First v.p. St. Louis Newspaper Guild, 1959-60. Mem. founding bd. Greater St. Louis Council Alcoholism, 1965, pres., 1966-69; pres. Mental Health Assn. of St. Louis, 1980-81; bd. dirs. Repertory Theatre of St. Louis. Served with USNR, 1946-47, 52-53. Recipient Bishop's award Episcopal Diocese Mo., 1965. Mem. Pub. Relations Soc. Am. (accredited) (dir. St. Louis chpt.), Soc. Profl. Journalists, Sigma Delta Chi. Club: Noonday (St. Louis). Home: 130 Plant Ave Webster Groves MO 63119 Office: 555 Shell Bldg Saint Louis MO 63103

FERGUSON, GEORGE WAGONER, JR., lawyer, utility company executive; b. Charlotte, N.C., Jan. 19, 1933; s. George Wagoner and Edna Louise (McCorkle) F.; m. Elizabeth Eugenia Allen, Nov. 23, 1957; children: Traci Lynne, George Wagoner. B.A., U. N.C., 1954, LL.B., 1956. Bar: N.C. bar 1956. Individual practice law, Charlotte, 1960-62; asst. gen. counsel Duke Power Co., Charlotte, N.C., 1962-71, asso. gen. counsel, 1971-75, sec., asso. gen. counsel, 1975, sec., dep. gen. counsel, 1976-80, v.p. govtl. affairs, 1980-82, v.p., dep. gen. counsel, 1982—. Served with USN, 1956-60. Mem. Am. Bar Assn. (public utility sect.), Twenty-Sixth Jud. Dist. Bar Assn., N.C. State Bar, N.C. Bar Assn., Phi Beta Kappa, Phi Alpha Delta, Pi Kappa Alpha. Democrat. Methodist. Clubs: Masons, Charlotte Lodge of Perfection. Home: 2301 Whilden Ct Charlotte NC 28211 Office: PO Box 33189 422 S Church St Charlotte NC 28242

FERGUSON, GLENN WALKER, consultant; b. Syracuse, N.Y., Jan. 28, 1929; s. Forrest Erwin and Mabel Gertrude (Walker) F.; m. Patricia Lou Head, June 22, 1950; children: Bruce Walker, Sherry Lynn, Scott Sherwood. B.A., Cornell U., 1950, M.B.A., 1951; student, U. Santo Tomas, Manila, 1952-53, U. Chgo. Law Sch., 1955-56; J.D., U. Pitts., 1957; D.S. (hon.), Worcester Poly. Inst., 1973, LL.D., Sacred Heart U., 1974. Staff asso. Govtl. Affairs Inst., Washington, 1954-55; asst. editor, asst. sec.-treas. Am. Judicature Soc., Chgo., 1955-56; asst. to chancellor and asst. dean Grad. Sch. Pub. Affairs, U. Pitts., 1956-60; with McKinsey & Co. (mgmt. cons.), Washington, 1960-61, Peace Corps, 1961-64, dir. Thailand, 1961-63, asso. dir., Washington, 1963-64; dir. Vols. in Service to Am., Washington, 1964-66; U.S. ambassador to Kenya, 1966-69; pres. Clark U., 1970-73, U. Conn., 1973-78, Radio Free Europe/Radio Liberty, Munich, Ger., 1978-82, Lincoln Ctr. Performing Arts, N.Y.C., 1983-84; cons. govt. agys., 1959-64, TV moderator fgn. affairs, Pitts., 1957-60; dir. Pvt. Export Funding Co., 1972-81, Equator Bank Ltd., 1977-79. Contbr. articles to profl. jours. Human rights commr. City of Worcester, 1971-72; trustee Cornell U., 1972-76. Served to 1st lt. USAF, 1951-53; Korea. Recipient Arthur S. Flemming award, 1968; Asso. fellow Timothy Dwight Coll., Yale U. Mem. Fed. Bar Assn., ABA, Am. Judicature Soc., Council Fgn. Relations, Fgn. Policy Assn. (dir. 1974-83), Phi Beta Kappa, Psi Upsilon, Phi Delta Phi. Clubs: Nat. Press, Internat. (Washington); Century (N.Y.C.).

FERGUSON, HARRY, engring. scientist; b. Dayton, Ohio, May 1, 1914; s. Robert and Isabella (Gamble) F.; m. Helen B. Baker, July 7, 1941. B.S., Boston U., 1939; A.M., Harvard U., 1949; Ph.D., U. Pitts., 1958. Mem. Faculty Ohio U., Northeastern U., Tufts U., 1939-50; applied mathematician, Wright-Patterson AFB, 1950-56, aero. research engr., 1956-59; asso. prof. math. U. Cin., 1959-66, prof. engring. scis., 1966—; v.p., owner Ferguson Sales, Inc., Alpha, Ohio. Mem. Am. Math. Soc., Math. Assn. Am., Soc. Indsl. and Applied Math., Soc. Natural Philosophy, Am. Soc. Engring. Edn., Alpha Tau Omega. Methodist. Clubs: Harvard (Dayton); Masons, Shriners. Home: 5105 Weston Circle Dayton OH 45429 Office: Dept Engring Sci U Cin Cincinnati OH 45221

FERGUSON, HENRY, history educator; b. Schenectady, May 31, 1927; s. Charles Vaughan and Harriet Esther (Rankin) F.; m. Joan Alice Metzger, July 18, 1953; children: Jean Rankin Gerbini, Cynthia Harriet, Henry Closson, Margaret Susan. A.B., Union Coll., 1950; A.M., Harvard U., 1954, Ph.D., 1958. With Conn. Gen. Life Ins. Co., Hartford, 1950-53; lectr., asst. prof., asso. prof. history, chmn. Non-Western studies com. Union Coll., Schenectady, 1957-69; N.Y. State Edn. Dept. dir. Ednl. Resources Center, New Delhi, India, 1967-69; spl. lectr. Trinity Coll., Hartford, 1969-72; pres., dir. InterCulture Assos., Inc., Thompson, Conn., 1969-79; dir. Center for Internat. Programs, N.Y. State Dept. Edn., Albany, 1979—. Author: (with Joan M. Ferguson) Village Life Study Kit Guide and Village Life Study Kit, 1970, Changing Africa, a Guide, 1973, Manual for Multicultural and Ethnic Studies, 1977, (with N. Abramowitz) Opportunities for Interprofessional Collaboration, 1980; editor: Handbook on Human Rights and Citizenship, 1981, Community Resource Manual on Human Rights and Citizenship, 1981, Ferguson Fortnightly, 1979, Cross Cultural Currents, 1980—. Trustee Rectory Sch., Pomfret, Conn., Freedom Forum, Schenectady, 1963-66; citizen del. White House Conf. on Library and Info. Services, 1979; pres. Internat. Center of Capital Region, 1981-82. Served with USN, 1945-46. Sr. fellow Oriental studies Columbia U., 1960-61; N.Y. State Bd. Regents sr. fellow in Non-Western studies, 1965-66; Fulbright research grantee Osmania U., India, 1961; Fulbright sr. research grantee, 1966-67. Mem. Soc. Intercultural Edn., Tng. and Research, Nat. Council Social Studies, Conn. Book Pubs. Assn. (pres. 1978-79). Episcopalian. Clubs: Fishers Island (N.Y.); Yacht; Fort Orange (Albany). Lodge: Rotary. Home: Chestnut Hill N Albany NY 12211 Office: NY State Dept Edn Albany NY 12230

FERGUSON, JAMES A., surgeon; b. Grand Rapids, Mich., Aug. 22, 1915; s. Ward Smith and Ethel Ann (Gray) F.; m. Margaret Alice Bevan, June 25, 1940; children—Bevany Ann Ferguson Farmer, Margaret Ferguson Booras, James A II. A.S., Grand Rapids Jr. Coll., 1934; M.D., U. Mich., 1939. Diplomate: Am. Bd. Surgery, Am. Bd. Colon and Rectal Surgery (pres. 1974-75). Intern St. Joseph's Hosp., Lexington, Ky., 1939-40; resident in surgery Multnomah County Hosp., U. Oreg., Portland, 1940-41, U. Mich. Hosps., Ann Arbor, 1945-48; practice medicine specializing in colon and rectal diseases, Grand Rapids, 1948-79; sr. surgeon, chmn. bd. dirs. Ferguson-Droste-Ferguson Hosp.; staff physician VA Outpatient Clinic, Ft. Meyers, Fla., 1980—. Contbr. profl. jours. Served with M.C. AUS and USAAF, 1942-45. Fellow A.C.S.; mem. AMA, Frederick Collier Surg. Soc., Am. Soc. Colon and Rectal Surgeons (pres. 1970), Mich. Med. Soc., Kent County Med. Soc. (pres. 1968), Royal Soc. Medicine (hon.). Club: Cypress Lake Country (Fort Myers, Fla.). Home: 9844 Madera Rd Fort Myers Beach FL 33931

FERGUSON, JAMES JOSEPH, JR., medical school dean, researcher, educator; b. Glen Cove, N.Y., Feb. 1, 1926; s. James Joseph and Elizabeth Marie (Madine) F.; m. Martha Randolph Saunders, Nov. 29, 1952; children: James Joseph III, William L., Nancy G., Katherine E. B.A., U. Rochester, 1946, M.D., 1950. Intern, resident medicine Mass. Gen. Hosp., Boston, 1950-55; research fellow Case Western Res. U., Cleve., 1956-59; faculty U. Pa., Phila., 1959—, assoc. dean Sch. Medicine, 1975—. Served with USNR, 1943-45, 52-55. Markle fellow, 1960-65; recipient NIH research career devel. award, 1965, grantee, 1963-75. Mem. A.C.P., Soc. Clin. Investigation, Endocrine Soc., Phila. Doctors Symphony Assn. (pres. 1982—). Club: Merion Cricket. Home: 831 Amies Ln Bryn Mawr PA 19010 Office: Dean's Office Sch Medicine U Pa Philadelphia PA 19104

FERGUSON, JAMES LARNARD, food co. exec.; b. Evanston, Ill., Mar. 16, 1926; s. J. Larnard and Justine (Dickson) F.; m. Elizabeth Rich, June 17, 1950; children—Deborah, John Dickson, Douglas. A.B., Hamilton Coll., 1949; M.B.A., Harvard, 1951. Asso. advt. mgr. Procter & Gamble, Cin., 1951-62; sr. v.p., account supr. Lennon & Newell Advt., N.Y.C., 1962-63; asst. to mktg. mgr. Birds Eye div. Gen. Foods Corp., White Plains, N.Y., 1963, mktg. product devel. positions, 1963-67, gen. mgr., 1967-68, corp. v.p., 1968-70, corp. group v.p., 1970-72, exec. v.p., 1972, pres., 1972-77, chief exec. officer, 1973—, chief operating officer, 1972, chmn., 1974—, dir., 1972—; dir. Union Carbide Corp.; dir., mem. exec. com. and compensation com. Chase Manhattan Bank (N.A.); dir. Sawyer-Ferguson-Walker Co. Mem. audit com. Council Fin. Aid to Edn.; trustee Hamilton Coll.; mem. Outward Bound, Bus. Com. for Arts; bd. dirs. Assos. Harvard Bus. Sch. Served with C.E. U.S. Army, 1944-46. Mem. Grocery Mfrs. Am. (dir., chmn., exec. com.), Bus. Roundtable (exec. com., policy com.), SRI Internat. Council, Econ. Club, Conf. Bd., Confrerie des Chevaliers du Tastevin. Episcopalian (sr. warden 1971—). Clubs: Wilton Riding, Blind Brook, Clove Valley Rod and Gun; Silver Spring Country (Ridgefield, Conn.); Links, Woodway Gun. Home: 77 Middlebrook Farm Rd Wilton CT 06897 Office: 250 North St White Plains NY 10625

FERGUSON, JAMES SHARBROUGH, history educator; b. Anguilla, Miss., Dec. 31, 1916; s. James Elbert Jenkins and Delle Prudence (Clark) F.; m. Frances Hardy Cottrell, June 3, 1939 (dec. Nov. 1978); children: Frances Cottrell, Elizabeth Lynn; m. Sarah Thompson Shepherd, Oct. 18, 1980. A.B., Millsaps Coll., 1937, LL.D., 1974; A.M., La. State U., 1940; Ford scholar, Yale U., 1952-53; Ph.D., U. N.C., 1953. Instr. math. Amory (Miss.) High Sch., 1937-39; teaching fellow La. State U., 1939-42; Gen. Edn. Bd. fellow U. N.C., 1942-43, instr. history, 1943-44; asst. prof. history Millsaps Coll., 1944-46, asso. prof., 1946, prof., 1947-62, acad. dean, 1954-62; prof. history U. N.C. at Greensboro, 1962—, dean grad. sch., 1962-64, acting chancellor, 1964-65, 66-67, vice chancellor, 1966, chancellor, 1967-79, Univ. Disting. prof., 1979—; vis. asso. prof. summer session Tulane U., 1947. Contbr. articles hist. jours. Dir. Christian Citizenship Seminar, Miss. Meth. Youth Fellowship, 1954; trustee St. Andrew's Presbyn. Coll. Mem. AAUP, Orgn. Am. Historians, So., Miss. hist. assns., N.C. Lit. and Hist. Assn., Phi Beta Kappa (hon.), Pi Kappa Alpha, Alpha Epsilon Delta, Eta Sigma Phi, Phi Kappa Phi, Pi Kappa Delta, Omicron Delta Kappa. Methodist. Club: Civitan (Greensboro). Home: 4 Greenbrook Ct Greensboro NC 27408

FERGUSON, JO MCCOWN, lawyer; b. Central City, Ky., Apr. 5, 1915; s. Jo Marvin and Willie Mae (Cain) F.; m. Margarita Hauser, July 12, 1947; children—Rita, Diane, Jo Frances. A.B., U. Ky., 1937, LL.B., 1939. Bar: Ky. bar 1939. Practiced in, Central City, 1939-42, asst. atty. gen., Ky., 1948-56, atty. gen., 1956-60, commr. econ. security, 1960-61; partner firm Harper, Ferguson & Davis. Chmn. Gov.'s Com. on Constl. Revision, 1961-62; chmn. Gov.'s Task Force on Fin., 1976-77. Served as capt. AUS, 1944-47; ETO; chief Property Control br. Mil. Govt., 1946-47; Bavaria. Mem. Am., Ky. bar assns., VFW, So. Attys. Gen. (chmn. 1957-58). Democrat. Episcopalian. Home: 403 Duff Ln Louisville KY 40207 Office: 310 W Liberty St Louisville KY 40202

FERGUSON, JOHN BOWIE, professional hockey team executive; b. Vancouver, B.C., Can., Sept. 5, 1938; m. Joan Ferguson; children: Christine, Cathy, John, Joanne. Player Montreal Canadiens, NHL, 1963-72; asst. coach Team Can., 1972; coach, gen. mgr. N.Y. Rangers, NHL, 1976-78; v.p., gen. mgr. Winnipeg Jets, NHL (formerly with World Hockey Assn.), 1978—. Mem. B.C. Sports HALL Of Fame. Mem. Stanley Cup Championship Team, 1965, 66, 68, 69, 71; player NHL All-Star Game, 1965, 67. Office: Winnipeg Jets 15-1430 Maroons Rd Winnipeg MB Canada R3G 0L5 *

FERGUSON, JOHN HENRY, retired political science educator; b. Lexington, Nebr., Aug. 22, 1907; s. Leonard Calvin and Dicie Shirley (Sipes) F.; m. Ruth Arvilla Benton, June 10, 1930 (dec. Oct. 28, 1976); children: Milton O., Richard B., David J., Rachel A. (Mrs. Rider); m. Eleanor Ely Mackey, June 26 1977. A.B., Nebr. Central Coll., 1929; M.A., U. Pa., 1932, Ph.D., 1937. Prin., tchr. Monroe (Nebr.) High Sch., 1929-30; dir. boys work Friends Neighborhood Guild, Phila., 1930-34; instr. polit. sci. Pa. State U., 1934-37, asst. prof., 1937-41, assoc. prof., 1941-47, prof., 1947—, head dept., 1947-48; dir. Social Sci. Research Center, 1953-55, Inst. Pub. Adminstrn., 1959-65, head dept. polit. sci., 1963-65; dean sch. politics New Sch. Social Research, 1948-49; vis. prof. U. Nebr., summer 1948; dir. program evaluation Office Gov. of Pa., 1955-56, sec. of adminstrn., 1956-59, budget sec., 1957-59; vis. lectr. U. Pa., 1966-77. Author: American Diplomacy and the Boer War, 1939, (with Dr. Dean E. McHenry) The American System of Government, 14th edit, 1981, The American Federal Government, 14th edit, 1981, Elements of American Government, 9th edit, 1971, (with Dr. Charles F. LeeDecker) Municipally Owned Waterworks in Pennsylvania, 1948, Municipally Owned Electric Plants in Pennsylvania, 1950, (with Drs. Dean E. McHenry and E. B. Fincher) American Government Today, 1951, (with David L. Cowell) The Minor Courts of Pennsylvania, 1962. Co-dir. research Pa. Constl. Conv., 1967-68; pres. Better Govt. Assos., Inc., 1967-77; sr. asso. Berger Assos., 1976-81; exec. dir. Commonwealth Compensation Commn., 1976-80; Mem. bd. Pub. Service Inst., Commonwealth Pa.; chmn. Commonwealth Pa., 1963-73; bd. dirs. Lincoln U., 1960-72; Dir. Civilian Public Service Camp, Gatlinburg, Tenn., 1943-44; adminstrv. asst. Am. Friends Service Com., 1944-45, exec. bd., 1950-56, 57-60. Recipient Hall of Fame award William Penn Coll., 1980. Mem. Am. Polit. Sci. Assn. (exec. council 1951-53), Northeastern Polit. Sci. Assn., Pa. Polit. Sci. Assn. (pres. 1958-60), Am. Soc. Pub. Adminstrn. (award for disting. achievement 1958), AAUP. Quaker. Home: 555 W Ridge Ave State College PA 16801

FERGUSON, JOHN MARSHALL, lawyer; b. Marion, Ill., Oct. 14, 1921; s. John Marshall and Vessie (Widdows) F.; m. Jeanne Harmon, Sept. 23, 1950; children: Marcia Ann Ferguson Velde, Mark Harmon, John Scott, Mary Sue. Student, So. Ill. U., 1939-41, S.E. Mo. Tchrs. Coll., 1941; LL.B., J.D., Washington U., St. Louis, 1948. Bar: Ill. 1949, U.S. Ct. Appeals (7th cir.) 1956, U.S. Supreme Ct 1960. Asst. mgr. I.W. Rogers Theaters, Inc., Anna, Ill., 1934-42; atty. U.S. Fidelity & Guaranty Co., St. Louis, 1948-51; assoc. Baker, Kagy & Wagner, East St. Louis, Ill., 1951-56, ptnr., 1956-59, Wagner, Ferguson, Bertrand & Baker, East St. Louis and Belleville, Ill., 1959-72; pres. bd. Arch Aircraft, Inc., 1966-68; disciplinary commr. Ill. Supreme Ct., 1957—, mem. joint com. on revision disciplinary rules, 1972-74; mem. hearing bd. Ill. Registration and Disciplinary Commn., 1974—; pres. 1st Dist. Fedn. Bar Assns. Precinct committeeman Stookey Twp., St. Clair County (Ill.) Republican Com., 1958-62; bd. dirs., v.p. East St. Louis chpt. ARC. Served to capt. AUS, 1941-45. Mem. ABA, Ill. Bar Assn. (gen. chmn. 1971-74, profl. ethics com. 1975—, sec. 1977—), St. Clair County Bar Assn., 7th Fed. Circuit Bar Assn. (bd. govs.), Delta Theta Phi. Clubs: East St. Louis City (pres. 1960-61); Illinois (gov., pres. 1966-67), St. Clair Country (St. Louis) (pres. 1972-73). Lodges: Masons; Elks. Home: 12 Oak Knoll Belleville IL 62223 Office: 65 S 65th St Belleville IL 62223

FERGUSON, JOHN ROBERT, JR., former steel co. exec.; b. Berkeley, Calif., Dec. 25, 1915; s. John Robert and Jane (Gray) F.; m. Dorothy Berry, Dec. 29, 1939; children—Darryl, John Robert III. S.B., Mass. Inst. Tech., 1937; M.B.A., U. Chgo., 1950. Registered profl. engr., Ill. and Pa. With Carnegie Ill. Steel Corp., 1940-50; asst. chief engr. Orinoco Mining Co., 1950-54; chief engr. project devel. U.S. Steel Corp., 1954-55, asst. v.p. engring., 1956-63, v.p. design and constrn., 1963-66, v.p. for appropriations, 1966-69, exec. v.p. engring. and research, 1974-79, sr. v.p., asst. to pres., 1979-80; v.p. engring. services USS Engrs. and Consultants, Inc., 1969-73, pres., 1973-74. Vice pres. Action Housing, Inc., 1967-68, pres., 1968-71, mem. bd., 1967—, chmn. bd., 1975—; chmn. bd., chmn. exec. com. Allegheny Housing Rehab. Corp., 1968-70, mem. bd. exec. com., 1970-74; Trustee Sewickley Valley Hosp., 1973—; pres. Valley Care Assn., 1980—. Mem. Am. Inst. Mining, Metall. and Petroleum Engrs., Engrs. Soc. Western Pa., Am. Iron and Steel Inst., Assn. Iron and Steel Engrs. Clubs: Allegheny Country, Duquesne, Edgeworth. Home: 335 Grant St Sewickley PA 15143

FERGUSON, JOSEPH GANTT, chemical engineer; b. Charleston, W.Va., May 26, 1921; s. Ernest Pendleton and Evelyn Harvey (Gantt) F.; m. Margaret Whaley, Oct. 23, 1948; 1 son, Joseph Gantt; m. Nell C. Kennamer, Dec. 29, 1979. B.S. in Chem. Engring., Clemson U., 1942. Lab. asst. Taylor-Colquitt Co., Spartanburg, S.C., 1942; with Internat. Paper Co., 1947-83, Georgetown, S.C. and Mobile, Ala. mills, 1947-55, Erling Riis Research Lab., 1955-82, chief paper research, 1961-63, 1st asst. dir., then dir. research So. Kraft div., 1963-76, mgr. mfg. research, 1976-77, mgr., Mobile, 1977, mgr. tech. and adminstrv. services, 1977-82. Served as officer USN, 1942-46; lt. comdr. Res. ret. Decorated Navy Commendation medal. Mem. TAPPI, Mobile C. of C., Alpha Chi Sigma, Phi Kappa Phi. Episcopalian. Clubs: Fairhope Yacht, Internat. Trade. Home: 4104 Ursuline Dr Mobile AL 36608

FERGUSON, LEONARD WILTON, psychologist; b. Turlock, Calif., Mar. 2, 1912; s. William Ward and Sara Minium (Kaufman) F.; m. Edith Beverly Phemister, July 1, 1939; children: Barbara Ferguson Needham, Margaret Ferguson Gibson, Kathryn Ferguson McCarthy. A.B., Stanford U., 1933, M.A., 1935, Ph.D., 1942. Diplomate: in indsl. psychology Am. Bd. Examiners in Profl. Psychology. Instr. to asst. prof. psychology U. Conn., Storrs, 1939-43; asst. staff supr. Met. Life Ins. Co., 1943-51; research asst. Aetna Life Affiliated Cos., 1951-53; research asso. Life Ins. Agy. Mgmt. Assn., Hartford, Conn., 1953-55, program dir., 1955-63; prof. psychology Ohio U., Athens, 1966-77; sec. com. on tests Life Office Mgmt. Assn., 1940-47, sec. clerical salary study com., 1943-44, chmn., 1944-49; lectr. NYU, summer 1949, U. Conn. extension div., 1953-54, 54-55; treas. Joint Council Psychologists for Legis. in N.Y. State, 1951; mem. adv. com. on job evaluation Nat. Mgmt. Council, 1950. Editor: The Journal Press, Provincetown, Mass., 1964-65; Author: Personality Measurement, 1952, The Heritage of Industrial Psychology (series), Cape Cod Collection, a series; numerous articles in profl. jours.; Editor: Clerical Salary Administration, 1947. Selectman Town of Provincetown, Mass., 1980-81. Home: 450 East 100 South, #29 Salt Lake City UT 84111

FERGUSON, LLOYD NOEL, chemist; b. Oakland, Calif., Feb. 9, 1918; s. Noel Swithin and Gwendolyn Louise (Johnson) F.; m. Charlotte Olivia Welch, Jan. 2, 1944; children—Lloyd Noel, Stephen Bruce, Lisa Annette. B.S., U. Calif. at Berkeley, 1940, Ph.D., 1943; D.Sc., Howard U., 1970, Coe Coll., 1979. Research asst. Nat. Def. Project, U. Calif. at Berkeley, 1941-44; asst. prof. Agr. and Tech. Coll., Greensboro, N.C., 1944-45; faculty Howard U., 1945-65, prof. chemistry, 1955-65, chmn. dept., 1958-65; prof. chemistry Calif. State U., Los Angeles, 1965—, chmn. chemistry dept., 1968-71; vis. prof. U. Oreg., summers 1958, 60, 63, U. Nairobi, Kenya, 1971-72; govt. chemist Nat. Bur. Standards, Naval Ordnance Lab. and Dept. Agr., summers 1950, 51, 67; vis. scientist, div. chem. edn. Am. Chem. Soc., 1959—; touring lectr. N.Y. State, 1956, Okla., 1974; series lectr., Copenhagen, Denmark, and Lund, Sweden, 1954; cons. Coll. Chemistry Cons.'s Service. Author: Electron Structures of Organic Molecules, 1952, Textbook of Organic Chemistry, 1958, The Modern Structural Theory of Organic Chemistry, 1963, Organic Chemistry: A Science and an Art, 1972, Highlights of Alicyclic Chemistry, Vol. 1, 1973, Vol. 2, 1977, Organic Molecular Structure, 1974; also, numerous articles. Recipient Mfg. Chemists award, 1974; Outstanding Prof. award Calif. State U., Los Angeles, 1974; Oakland Mus. Assn. award, 1973; Distinguished medallion Am. Found. Negro Affairs, 1976; Outstanding Teaching award Nat. Orgn. Black Chemists, 1979; Outstanding Prof. award Calif. State U. and Colls., 1981; Guggenheim fellow Carlsberg Lab., Copenhagen, 1953-54; NSF faculty fellow Swiss Fed. Inst. Tech., Zurich, 1961-62. Fellow Chem. Soc. London, AAAS, Am. Inst. Chemists; mem. Am. Chem. Soc. (award Chem. Edn. 1978, chmn. chem. edn. div. 1980), AAUP, Nat. Inst. Sci., Sigma Xi. Home: 4221 S Cloverdale Ave Los Angeles CA 90008

FERGUSON, MARY ANNE HEYWARD, educator; b. Charleston, S.C., July 25, 1918; d. William and Annie (Sinkler) Walker Heyward; m. Alfred Riggs Ferguson, May, 1948; children: Margaret W., Jean Ferguson Carr, Lucy Ferguson Allen. A.B., Duke U., 1938, M.A., 1940; Ph.D., Ohio State U., 1965. Teaching asst. Duke U., 1938-40; instr. English U. N.C., 1945-46, U. Conn., 1946, Queens Coll., Flushing, N.Y., 1947, Ohio Wesleyan U., 1949-62, Ohio U., 1965-66; instr. Ohio State U., 1962-64, Elizabeth Howald postdoctoral fellow, 1969-70; asst. prof. English U. Mass., Boston, 1966-69, 70-72, prof., 1973—, chmn. dept., 1979—, fellow Carnegie Project Women in Higher Edn., 1974—; project dir. Women's Studies, U. Mass., Nat. Endowment for Humanities, 1973-75. Author: Bibliography of English Translations from Medieval Sources, 1974, Images of Women in Literature, 1973, 77, 81; contbr. to: Eudora Welty: Critical Essays, 1979; contbr. articles to profl. jours. Wellesley Mellon fellow, 1979. Mem. Modern Lang. Assn. Am. (Commn. on Status of Women 1970-73, del. assembly 1973-76), Nat. Women's Studies Assn., Phi Beta Kappa. Democrat. Episcopalian. Home: 57 Berwick St Belmont MA 02178 Office: English Dept University of Massachusetts at Boston Harbor Campus Boston MA 02125 *Though mixing family and career has cost me some success by quantitative measures, I feel that the quality of my professional work has been enriched by my experience as wife and mother, and vice versa. I wouldn't have missed any of it.*

FERGUSON, MAYNARD, trumpet player; b. Montreal, Que., Can., May 4, 1928; came to U.S., 1949. Trumpet player, Stan Kenton Orch., 1950-53; free-lance musician, Los Angeles, 3 years; formed own touring 13-piece orch., 1957-65; formed sextet, 1965; lived in, Eng. and India, 1967-71; Records for, Columbia Records. Recipient Gold record Conquistador, 1978. Address: care New Vintage Mgmt PO Box 716 Ojai CA 93023 *You don't have to suffer to gain musical "soul"—just enjoy what you're playing. My instrument is a thing of pleasure, and I play it only because I enjoy it. The most important thing is doing what feels right for me. If I were to play as I did 10, 20, 30 years ago, I'd have to think the same as I did then, but of course I've grown and that brings change and therefore my music has changed.*

FERGUSON, MILTON CARR, JR., lawyer; b. Washington, Feb. 10, 1931; s. Milton Carr and Gladys (Emery) F.; m. Marian Evelyn Nelson, Aug. 21, 1954; children: Laura, Sharon, Marcia, Sandra. B.A.,

Cornell U., 1952; LL.B., 1954; LL.M., N.Y. U., 1960. Bar: N.Y. State 1954. Trial atty. tax div. Dept. Justice, Washington, 1954-60, asst. atty. gen., 1977-81; asst. prof. law U. Iowa, 1960-62; asso. prof. N.Y. U., 1962-65, prof., 1965-77; vis. prof. law Stanford (Calif.) U., 1972-73; of counsel Wachtell, Lipton, Rosen & Katz, N.Y.C., 1969-76; partner firm Davis Polk & Wardwell, N.Y.C., 1981—; spl. cons. to Treasury Dept., Commonwealth P.R., 1974. Author: (with others) Federal Income Taxation Legislation in Perspective, 1965, Federal Income Taxation of Estates and Beneficiaries, 1970. Mem. Am., N.Y. State bar assns., Soc. Illustrators. Home: 32 Washington Sq W New York NY 10011 Office: Davis Polk & Wardwell One Chase Manhattan Plaza New York NY 10005

FERGUSON, NEIL TAYLOR, savings and loan executive; b. Alameda, Calif., Mar. 15, 1922; s. Hector Donald and Erna (Taylor) F. B.A., San Jose State Coll., 1944. Mgr. Fields Store, Campbell, Calif., 1946-48; partner Paul C. Rudolph & Co., San Jose, Calif., 1948-51; pres., dir. Mut. Fund Assos., Inc., San Rafael, Calif., 1951-71; chmn., dir. Putnam Fin. Services, Inc., 1972-74, Western Travelers Life Ins. Co., Inc., 1972-74; pres., dir. Funded Investors, Inc., 1971-74; chmn. bd. Centennial Savs. and Loan Assn., 1976—; pres. Union R.R. Oreg., 1978—; partner Jamestown Hotel (R.R. Consultants); chmn. Sierra Western Rail Corp., 1980—; dir. Forestville Park Devel. Inc. Mem. Forestville Citizens Adv. Com.; v.p. Forestville Sch. Facilities Corp.; bd. dirs. Big Bros. and Sisters of Sonoma County, Clear Water Ranch Childrens House, Inc., Russian River Region Inc., Sonoma State U. Pres.'s Assos.; adv. Prime Timers, Forestville, 1978—; adv. bd. Ret. Sr. Vol. Program, Santa Rosa, Calif., 1979—, Pres.'s Assos., 1978-80; mem. adv. bd. Sonoma State U.; bd. dirs. Community Found. Sonoma County. Served to lt. USNR, 1942-46. Mem. Marin County C. of C. (dir. 1971-74), Forestville C. of C. (v.p., dir.), Nat. Assn. Securities Dealers (vice chmn. dist. bus. conduct com. 1972-75), Am. Assn. Pvt. Railroad Car Owners (v.p. 1980), UN Orgn., Native Sons Golden West, Forestville Grange. Clubs: Optimist., Commonwealth (San Francisco). Home: 10650 Woodside Dr Forestville CA 95436

FERGUSON, OLIVER WATKINS, educator; b. Nashville, June 7, 1924; s. John Lambuth and Olive Andrews (Watkins) F.; m. Joanne O'Kelly, Aug. 18, 1949; children—John Andrews, Charles Edward. B.A., Vanderbilt U., 1947, M.A., 1948; Ph.D., U. Ill., 1954. Instr. German U. Miss., summer 1947; instr. English U. Ark., 1948-50; instr., then asst. prof. English Ohio State U., 1954-57; mem. faculty Duke U., 1957—, prof. English, 1967—, chmn. dept., 1967-73. Author: Jonathan Swift and Ireland, 1962; also articles.; Asso. editor: S. Atlantic Quar, 1961-72; editor, 1972—. Served with inf. AUS, 1943-45; ETO. Rotary Internat. Found. fellow, 1952-53; Guggenheim fellow, 1963-64. Mem. Modern Lang. Assn., Am. Soc. 18th Century Studies, Southeastern Am. Soc. 18th Century Studies, South Atlantic Modern Lang. Assn. Home: 1212 Arnette Ave Durham NC 27707

FERGUSON, PHIL MOSS, engr.; b. Bartlett, Tex., Nov. 10, 1899; s. William Simpson and Annie Leonora (Moss) F.; m. Marion Hicks, Feb. 23, 1939 (div. 1940); 1 son, Yale Hicks. B.S. in Civil Engring, U. Tex., 1922, C.E., 1923; M.S., U. Wis., 1924. Registered profl. engr., Tex. Tutor in physics U. Tex. at Austin, 1922-23, asso. prof. civil engring., 1928-39, prof., 1939-76, prof. emeritus, 1976—, chmn. dept. civil engring., 1943-57, Dean T.U. Taylor prof. civil engring., 1968-72; structural engr. Dwight P. Robinson & Co., N.Y.C., 1924-28, summer 1930; field insp., designer R.O. Jameson, Dallas, summer 1929; designer bridge div. Tex. Hwy. Dept., summers 1931, 32, 35, 39; designer on Buchanan Dam, S.W. Engring. Co., Austin, Tex., summer 1936. Author: Plate Girder Theory, rev, 1935, Reinforced Concrete Fundamentals, 1958, 4th edit., 1979, also numerous papers on reinforced concrete and frame analysis. Chmn. bd. U. Coop. Soc., 1952-54. Recipient research award ASCE, 1961; Distinguished Service citation U. Wis., 1970; named Distinguished Engring. Grad. U. Tex. at Austin, 1972; Honor award Concrete Reinforcing Steel Inst., 1977; Balcones Structural Lab. renamed Phil M. Ferguson Structures Research Lab. in his honor, 1979. Mem. Nat. Acad. Engring., Am. Concrete Inst. (Wason medal for research 1954, 58, 68, pres. 1959, hon. mem. 1968, Lindau award 1972, Raymond C. Reese research medal 1973, Turner medal 1976, Kelly award 1977, Charles S. Whitney award 1979), ASCE (pres. Tex. sect. 1967, hon. mem. 1971), Reinforced Concrete Research Council, Comité Européen du Béton, Internat. Assn. Bridge and Structural Engring. (U.S. alt. dir. 1966-70), Nat. Soc. Profl. Engrs. (dir. 1966-70, S.W. regional vice chmn. Profl. Engrs. in Edn. 1968-71), Tex. Soc. Profl. Engrs. (pres. 1962), Sigma Xi, Tau Beta Pi, Phi Kappa Phi, Chi Epsilon. Methodist. Home: 3102 Beverly Rd Austin TX 78703

FERGUSON, ROBERT BURY, mineralogy educator; b. Cambridge, Ont., Can., Feb. 5, 1920; s. Alexander Galt and Harriet Henrietta (Bury) F.; m. Margaret Irene Warren, Dec. 29, 1948; children: Evelyn Bury, Robert Warren, Marion Galt. B.A., U. Toronto, 1942, M.A., 1943, Ph.D., 1948. Asst. prof. mineralogy U. Man. (Can.), Winnipeg, 1947-50; assoc. prof. U. Man, Winnipeg, Can., 1951-59; prof. U. Man.(Can.), Winnipeg, 1959—, disting. prof., 1983. Fellow Royal Soc. Can., Mineral Soc. Am.; mem. Mineral Soc. Great Britain, Mineral Assn. Can. (Hawley award 1981), Am. Crystallographic Assn. New Democratic Party. Unitarian. Home: 184 Wildwood Park Winnipeg MB Canada R3T 0E2 Office: Dept Earth Scis U Man Winnipeg MB Canada R3T 2N2

FERGUSON, ROBERT DOYLE, lawyer; b. New Castle, Pa., Dec. 17, 1905; s. James M. and Floy (Robertson) F.; m. Phyllis S. Marschall, July 20, 1939; children—Phyllis M., James M. A.B., Westminster Coll., 1927; LL.B., Harvard, 1931. Bar: Pa. 1931. Partner Patterson, Crawford, Arensberg & Dunn, 1931-43; v.p. trusts Pitts. Nat. Bank, 1943-70, exec. v.p., 1960-68, chmn. trust com., 1968-70; partner firm Tucker, Arensburg, Very & Ferguson, 1971-80. Bd. dirs. Magee-Womens Hosp.; trustee Westminster Coll., Bd. Family and Childrens Service. Mem. Am., Pa. bar assns., Am. Bankers Assn. (past pres. trust div.). Republican. Presbyn. Clubs: Duquesne, Longue Vue Country. Home: 19 Churchill Rd Pittsburgh PA 15235 Office: 1110 Pittsburgh Nat Bank Bldg Pittsburgh PA 15222

FERGUSON, ROBERT LOUIS, corporate executive; b. Dover, Idaho, Oct. 26, 1932; s. James and Lydia (Sindelar) F.; m. Catherine Crosby, June 2, 1956; children: Catherine Maureen, Colleen Marie. B.S. in Physics, Gonzaga U., 1954; postgrad., Wash. State U., 1957-58, Oak Ridge Sch. Reactor Tech., 1962, Fed. Exec. Inst., 1977. Dep. asst. mgr. Chgo. ops. office AEC, 1961-70, dir. contract adminstrn. div. Richland (Wash.) ops. office, 1971, asst. mgr. for programs, 1972-73; dir. Fast Flux Test Facility Project office Dept. Energy, Richland, 1973-78, program dir. for nuclear energy, Washington, 1978-79, dep. asst. sec. for nuclear reactor programs, 1979-80; chief exec. officer Wash. Public Power Supply System, Richland, 1980-83; chmn. UNC Nuclear Industries, Inc., 1983—; pres. Tri-Cities Nuclear Indsl. Council; dir. Pacific Nuclear Systems, Inc., Frontier Fed. Savs. and Loan Assn. Bd. regents Gonzaga U. Served with Ordinance Corps, U.S. Army, 1954-57. Recipient Meritorious Achievement award ERDA, 1976; Presdl. Meritorious Exec. award. Roman Catholic.

FERGUSON, ROBERT R., JR., bank holding company executive; b. Savannah, Ga., Dec. 31, 1923; s. Robert R. and Frances (McDonald) F.; m. Betty Jane King, Nov. 26, 1949; children: Robert R. III, James P. B.A., Lehigh U., 1947; M.B.A., U. Pa., 1949; LL.D., Seton Hall U., 1981; L.H.D. hon., Caldwell Coll., 1983. Trainee Fed. Res. Bank, Phila., 1947-49; v.p. Fed. Trust Co., Newark, 1949-58; pres., chief exec. officer First Nat. State Bank, Newark, 1958—, First Nat. State Bancorp., 1969—; dir. Pub. Service Electric & Gas Co., 1980—. Episcopalian. Office: First Nat State Bancorp 550 Broad St Newark NJ 07101

FERGUSON, ROBERT WILLI, broadcasting exec.; b. Barberton, Ohio, June 18, 1913; s. Guy Henry and Abbiegaie (Dauchy) F.; m. Dorothy Denison, Oct. 28, 1939 (dec. Apr. 1976); 1 dau., Ann; m. Eloise Morris, Sept. 22, 1979. B.S. in Journalism, Ohio State U., 1939. With Scripps-Howard Bur., Columbus, 1938-39; mem. staff Eagle-Star, Marientte, Wis., 1939-40; advt. mgr. Wooster (Ohio) Daily Record, 1940-41, Times-Leader, Martins Ferry, Ohio, 1941-43, bus. mgr., 1946-47; v.p., gen. mgr. radio sta. WTRF, Bellaire, Ohio, 1947-53; pres. sta. WTRF-TV, Wheeling, W.Va., 1953-79; sr. v.p. corp. projects Forward Communications Corp., 1979—; dir. Half Dollar Trust & Savs. Bank, Wheeling; vis. prof. journalism W.Va. U., 1972, 76—; lectr. Wheeling Coll.; Mem. W.Va. Ednl. Broadcasting Authority, 1967—, W.Va. Legis. Compensation Commn., 1968—. Contbr. articles to profl. jours. Pres. Belmont County chpt. ARC, 1949; chmn. Wheeling Area Conf. Community Devel., 1959-61; Bd. fellows Bethany (W.Va.) Coll.; trustee Ohio Valley Med. Center; mem. president's council Wheeling Coll.; bd. dirs. Oglebay Park Zoo. Served to lt. USNR, 1943-45. Mem. W.Va. Broadcasters Assn. (past pres., Distinguished Service award 1975), NBC-TV Affiliates (chmn. bd. dels. 1971-75), Nat. Assn. Broadcasters (chmn. TV dirs. 1967-70, chmn. TV code bd. 1964-66), Broadcast Pioneers (pres. 1969, pres. found. 1975-80), Wheeling C. of C. (dir. 1970-74), Phi Gamma Delta (pres. 1938-39), Kappa Tau Alpha, Alpha Kappa Psi. Republican. Presbyn. Clubs: Overseas Press (N.Y.C.); Nat. Press (Washington); La Quinta (Calif.) Country, Wheeling Country; Belmont Hills Country (St. Clairsville, Ohio). Home: 44 Forest Hills Wheeling WV 26003 Office: 1324 Chapline St Fort Henry Wheeling WV 26003

FERGUSON, ROGER NEPHI, franchise bus. exec.; b. Ocean Park, Calif.; s. Robert Byron and Fawn Berncie (Christensen) F.; m. Sybil Rae Clarke, 1952; children—Debra Kay, Michael David, Wade Clarke, Lois Christine, Julie Xarissa. Student, Brigham Young U., 1952. Pres. Diet Center, Inc., Rexburg, Idaho, U.S., Can., 1972; owner, chmn. bd., dir. Dietology Sch., Diet Center Inn, Ferguson's Pharms. Labs., Audio-Visual Studio, Diet Center Shipping and Receiving Co., Diet Center Print Shop; dir. Internat. Livestock Inc., Sybils, Inc., Ferguson & Assos.; co-owner Ferguson Farms; also Big Grassy potato ranch; regional mgr. Bio-Chem. Farm Products Co.; pres. Local Insulators in Indsl. Trade, 1960-62. Recipient award Rick's Coll. Boosters Club, 1977-81. Mem. U.S. C. of C., Rexburg C. of C. Mormon. Club: Rexburg Golf Assn. (dir. 1981).

FERGUSON, RONALD EUGENE, reinsurance company executive; b. Chgo., Jan. 16, 1942; s. William Eugene and Elizabeth (Hahanneman) F.; m. Carol Jean Chapp, Dec. 27, 1964; children: Brian, Kristin. B.A., Blackburn Coll., 1963; M.A., U. Mich., 1965. Statistician Lumbermans Mut. Casualty Co., Long Grove, Ill., 1965-59; actuary Gen. Reins. Corp., Greenwich, Conn., 1969-72, asst. v.p, 1972-74, v.p., 1974-77, sr. v.p., 1977-82, exec. v.p., 1982—, dir., 1983, pres., 1983—; v.p., group exec. Gen. Re Corp., Greenwich, Conn., 1981—; chmn., pres., dir. Gen. Re Services Corp., Greenwich, Conn., 1981—; dir. Trident Ins. Cos., London, Nat. Guardian Corp. Contbr. articles to profl. jours. Served with USPHS, 1966-68. Fellow Casualty Actuarial Soc. (dir. 1978-81); mem. Am. Acad. Actuaries (dir. 1981—). Congregationalist. Clubs: Patterson (Fairfield, Conn.); Landmark (Stamford, Conn.). Office: General Reinsurance Corp 600 Steamboat Rd Greenwich CT 06830

FERGUSON, SYBIL RAE, franchise business executive; b. Barnwell, Alta., Can., Feb. 7, 1934; came to U.S., 1938, naturalized, 1975; d. Alva John and Xanssia (Merkley) Clarke; m. Roger N. Ferguson, July 10, 1952; children: Debra Kay, Michael David, Wade Clarke, Lois Christine, Julie Xarissa. Student public schs. Founder, owner Diet Center, Inc., Rexburg, Idaho, 1970—; dir. Dietology Sch., Diet Center Inn, Ferguson's Pharm. Labs., Diet Center Shipping and Receiving Co., Diet Center Print Shop, Audio Visual Studio, Sybils, Inc., Ferguson & Assos.; Charter mem. women's aux. Madison Meml. Hosp., Rexburg. Author: The Diet Center Program; Lose Weight Fast and Keep It Off Forever, 1983. Recipient Bus. Leader of Yr. award Ricks Coll., 1980. Mem. Rexburg C. of C. (program dir. 1976). Mormon. Clubs: Rexburg Civic, Soroptimists (v.p. Rexburg 1975), Soroptimists (award 1979). Office: Diet Center Inc 220 W 2d St S Rexburg ID 83440

FERGUSON, THOMAS BRUCE, cardiothoracic surgeon; b. Oklahoma City, May 6, 1923; s. Walter Scott and Lucia Caroline (Loomis) F.; m. Doris Elizabeth Shanley, Jan. 31, 1948; children—Linda Anne Ferguson Benoist, Thomas Bruce, Scott Shanley. B.S., Duke U., 1947, M.D., 1947. Diplomate: Am. Bd. Surgery, Am. Bd. Thoracic Surgery (chmn. 1977-79). Intern in surgery Duke U. Hosp., 1947-48, asst. resident, 1949-50; USPHS fellow in physiology Harvard U. Med. Sch., 1948-49; asst. resident in surgery, then fellow in thoracic surgery Barnes Hosp., St. Louis, 1953-56, mem. staff, 1956—; instr. Duke U. Hosp., 1950; mem. faculty Washington U. Med. Sch., St. Louis, 1956—, prof. clin. surgery, 1973—; pres. Chest Service, Inc., 1975—; mem. staff Barnes, Deaconess, Robert Koch, St. Louis City, St. Louis Children's, St. Luke's hosps; vis. prof./lectr., panelist, cons. in field. Editorial bd.: Chest, 1977-82, Annals of Thoracic Surgery, 1973-83; editor, 1984—; Contbr. numerous articles med. jours. Served as officer M.C. U.S. Army, 1951-52. Recipient Disting. Alumnus award Duke U. Med. Sch., 1979. Mem. Am. Assn. Thoracic Surgery (v.p. 1980-81, pres. 1981-82), Am. Cancer Soc., Am. Coll. Chest Physicians, Am. Bd. Med. Specialties (v.p. 1980-81, pres. 1982-84), A.C.S., Am. Soc. Extra-corporeal Tech. (med. adv. bd. 1974-78), AMA (Physicians Recognition award 1977-80), Council Med. Specialty Socs. (pres. 1978-80), Am. Heart Assn. (Disting. Service medal Hillsborough County (Fla.) chpt. 1963), Samson Thoracic Surg. Soc. (hon.), Soc. Thoracic Surgeons (pres. 1976-77), St. Louis Heart Assn. (pres. 1970-72, Arthur E. Strauss award 1977), St. Louis Met. Med. Soc. (award of merit 1980), Am. Surg. Assn., Central Surg. Assn., Deryl Hart Soc., Internat. Assn. Study Lung Cancer, Internat. Cardiovascular Soc., St. Louis Surg. Soc. (council 1973—), Williams Greeleaf Eliot Soc., Phi Beta Kappa, Alpha Omega Alpha. Episcopalian. Club: Bellerive Country. Home: 14 Hacienda St Louis MO 63124

FERGUSON, THOMAS H., newspaper executive. Pres. Washington Post Newspaper. Office: Office to the President Washington Post 1150 15th St NW Washington DC 20071

FERGUSON, TRACY HEIMAN, lawyer, educational administrator; b. Syracuse, N.Y., Sept. 2, 1910; s. George Joshua and Fannie (Heiman) F.; m. Babbette R. Oberdorfer, Dec. 22, 1938; children: Babbette Tracy, Earl Mark. A.B., Syracuse U., 1931; LL.B., Harvard, 1934. Bar: N.Y. 1934, U.S. Supreme Ct 1944, other U.S. cts 1934. Practice in, Syracuse, 1934—; partner firm Bond, Schoeneck & King, 1947—; mem. faculty Syracuse U. Coll. Law, 1946-48; adj. prof. labor law U. Miami, 1977-78, Nova U., 1978. 79; adj. prof. Maxwell Sch. Citizenship, Syracuse U., 1981—. Contbr. articles legal jours. Industry mem. N.Y.-N.J. Regional Wage Stblzn. Bd., 1951-52; v.p. Citizens Found. Syracuse, 1949-50; nat. vice chmn. jr. div. Am. Jewish Joint Distbn., 1937; chmn. Syracuse Jewish Welfare Fedn., 1950-51, 62, pres., 1951; chmn. Onondaga County chpt. March of Dimes, 1956; mem. labor mgmt. adv. panel N.Y. State Mediation Bd., 1969-78; mem. nat. adv. com. N.Y. U. Inst. Labor Relations, 1968—; Pres. Republican Citizens Com. Onondaga County, 1962-63; Regent LeMoyne Coll., Syracuse, 1967-72; bd. dirs., sec. Community-Gen. Hosp. Greater Syracuse, 1967-74, hon. dir., 1976—; former bd. dirs. Midtown Hosp., Syracuse, United Community Chest and Council; trustee Onondaga County Community Coll., 1961-66, Cazenovia Coll., 1965-66, Syracuse Pub. Library, 1965-69, Union of Am. Hebrew Congregations, 1969-83; bd. dirs. N.Am. Bd., World Union for Progressive Judaism, 1981-83. Served as officer USNR, 1943-46. Recipient Letterman of Distinction award Syracuse U., 1976, Alumni award Syracuse U., 1983. Fellow Am. Bar Found.; mem. ABA (chmn. labor relations law sect. 1963-64, mem. council 1957-66, hon. mem. council 1973—, sect. del. 1965-66), Fed. Bar Assn. (pres. N.Y. upstate chpt. 1973-74, mem. nat. council), N.Y. Bar Assn. (chmn. labor law com. 1964-66), Onondaga County Bar Assn., Am. Arbitration Assn. (mem. exec. com. 1977-79, former chmn. N.Y. State adv. council), Indsl. Relations Research Assn. Central N.Y. (co-pres. 1979-80). Jewish (trustee temple, pres. 1966-71). Clubs: Century, University (Syracuse); Nat. Press, Nat. Lawyers (Washington). Home: 15 Pebble Hill Rd S Syracuse (Dewitt) NY 13214 also 9003 Cocoplum Circle Plantation FL 33324 Office: 1 Lincoln Center Syracuse NY 13202

FERGUSON, WARREN JOHN, federal judge; b. Eureka, Nev., Oct. 31, 1920; s. Ralph and Marian (Damele) F.; m. Laura Keyes, June 5, 1948; children: Faye F., Warren John, Teresa M., Peter J. B.A., U. Nev., 1942; LL.B., U. So. Calif., 1949; LL.D. (hon.), Western State U., San Fernando Valley Coll. Law. Bar: Calif. bar 1950. Mem. firm Ferguson & Judge, Fullerton, Calif., 1950-59; city atty. for cities of, Buena Park, Placentia, La Puente, Baldwin Park, Santa Fe Springs, Walnut and Rosemead, Calif., 1953-59, municipal ct. judge, Anaheim, Calif., 1959-60; judge Superior Ct., Santa Ana, Calif., 1961-66, Juvenile Ct., 1963-64, Appellate Dept., 1965-66; U.S. dist. judge, Los Angeles, 1966-79; judge U.S. Circuit Ct. 9th Circuit, Los Angeles, 1979—; faculty Jud. Center, Practising Law Inst., U. Iowa Coll. Law, N.Y. Law Jour.; asso. prof. psychiatry (law) Sch. Medicine, U. So. Calif.; asso. prof. Loyola Law Sch. Served with AUS, 1942-46. Decorated Bronze Star. Mem. Phi Kappa Phi, Theta Chi. Democrat. Roman Catholic. Office: 34 Civic Ctr Plaza Santa Ana CA 92701 *Having been born and raised in Nevada, I have adopted an old prospector's philosophy: "Live today; look every man in the eye; and tell the rest of the world to go to hell."*

FERGUSON, WILLIAM CHARLES, telecommunications executive; b. Detroit, Oct. 26, 1930; s. William and Bessie F. (Barr) F.; m. Joyce G. Soby, June 14, 1952; children: Laura, Ellen, Joanne. B.A., Albion Coll., 1952. With Mich. Bell Telephone Co., 1952-77, 78—, dist. mgr., 1961-63, div. mgr., 1963-68, gen. traffic mgr., 1968-72, v.p. ops. staff and engring., 1972-73, v.p. metro, 1973-76, v.p. personnel, 1976-77, exec. v.p., chief operating officer, 1978-82; pres. N.Y. Telephone Co., 1983—; v.p. N.Y.C. region N.Y. Telephone Co., 1977; dir. Marine Midland Bank. Bd. dirs. Detroit Symphony, 1979-82; mem. adv. bd. United Found., 1979-82; co-chmn. corp. drive Artrain, 1979-80; trustee Albion Coll., 1980; bd. dirs. N.Y. State Bus. Council, N.Y.C. Partnership. Served with U.S. Army, 1952-54. Mem. Engring. Soc. Detroit. Home: 5 Dogwood Dr Armonk NY 10504 Office: 1095 Ave of the Americas New York NY

FERGUSON, WILLIAM EMMETT, retired securities broker; b. Quincy, Mass., Dec. 21, 1902; s. Patrick J. and Margaret (O'Brien) F.; m. Loretta Mahon, July 6, 1935. Ed. high sch. With Thomson, McKinnon Securities Inc. (formerly Thomson & McKinnon, Inc.), N.Y.C., 1919—, gen. partner, 1948; former pres., chmn. bd., chief exec. officer, dir., now hon. chmn. bd. Formerly mem. bd. govs., vice chmn. exec. com. Midwest Stock Exchange, Chgo. Mem. Chgo., Kansas City bds. trade. Clubs: Beverly Country, Union League (Chgo.); N.Y. Athletic (N.Y.C.). Office: One New York Plaza New York NY 10004

FERGUSON, WILLIAM MCDONALD, banker, former state ofcl.; b. Wellington, Kans., Dec. 2, 1917; s. William McDonald and May (Deems) F.; m. Harriet Shelden, Sept. 12, 1939; children—Joan, William McDonald III. A.B., U. Kans., 1938; LL.B., Harvard, 1941. Bar: Kans. bar 1946. City atty., Wellington, 1948-57, gen. practice law, 1948-73, atty. gen., Kans., 1961-65; Pres. Security State Bank, Wellington, 1959-71, chmn. bd., 1972—. Author: (with John Q. Royce) Maya Ruins of Mexico in Color, 1977. Mem. Kans. Ho. of Reps. 69th Dist., 1949-57. Served to lt. (s.g.) USNR, 1942-46. Mem. ABA (ho. dels. 1961-62), Kans. Bar Assn. (exec. council 1952-61, v.p. 1961, pres. 1963), Am. Legion, Sigma Alpha Epsilon. Republican. Club: Elk. Home: 1023 S Washington St Wellington KS 67152

FERGUSSON, FRANCIS, lit. critic; b. Alburquerque, N.Mex., Feb. 21, 1904; s. Harvey Butler and Clara Mary (Huning) F.; m. Marion Crowne, Jan. 16, 1931 (dec. 1959); children—Harvey, Honora; m. Peggy Kaiser, July 26, 1962. Student, Harvard, 1921-23; B.A. (Rhodes scholar), Oxford U., 1926. Asso. dir. Am. Lab. Theatre, N.Y., 1926-30; drama critic The Bookman mag., N.Y., 1930-32; lectr., exec. sec. New Sch. for Social Research, N.Y.C., 1932-34; prof. humanities and drama Bennington (Vt.) Coll., 1934-47; mem. Inst. for Advanced Study, Princeton, N.J., 1948-49; dir. Princeton Seminars in lit. criticism, 1949-52, adv. bd. humanities program, Princeton, 1952-58; vis. prof. English Ind. U., 1952-53; prof. comparative lit. Rutgers U., 1953-68, Princeton, 1973—. Author: books including The Idea of a Theatre, 1949, Plays of Moliere, Critical Introduction, 1950, Dante's Drama of the Mind (Christian Gauss award 1953), Aristotle's Poetics, Critical Introduction, 1961, Poems, 1962, Dante, 1966, Shakespeare: The Pattern in His Carpet, 1970, Literary Landmarks, 1976; also contbr.: poems to Critical Essays; The Human Image, 1957; Gen. editor: Laurel Shakespeare, 1957—; mem. editorial bd.: Comparative Lit, 1952-60. Recipient award for lit. Nat. Inst. Arts and Letters, 1953. Mem. Nat. Inst. Arts and Letters. Home: Box 143 Kingston NJ 08528

FERGUSSON, ROBERT GEORGE, retired army officer; b. Chgo., May 20, 1911; s. Archibald Campbell and Anne (Sheehan) F.; m. Charlotte Lawrence, Nov. 18, 1937; 1 son, Robert Lawrence (dec.). Student, Beloit Coll., 1929-32; B.S., U.S. Mil. Acad., 1936; M.A. in Internat. Relations, Boston U., 1959. Commd. 2d lt. U.S. Army, 1936, advanced through grades to maj. gen., 1962; comdg. officer 14th Inf. Regt., Hawaii, 1955-57; chief army adv. group Naval War Coll., Newport, R.I., 1957-61; asst. div. comdr. 24th Inf. Div., Augsburg, Ger., 1961-62; chief staff Hdqrs. Central Army Group (NATO), Heidelberg, Ger., 1962-65; comdg. gen. U.S. Army Tng. Center, Inf., Ft. Ord, 1965-67; comdr. U.S. Forces, Berlin, 1967-70; ret., 1970; corp. group v.p. manpower planning Dart Industries, Inc., Los Angeles, 1970-78; cons., 1978-82, ret., 1982. Decorated D.S.M., Legion of Merit with oak leaf cluster, Bronze Star with 3 oak leaf clusters, Purple Heart (U.S.); knight comdr. Cross with badge and star Order of Merit (W.Ger.); officer Legion of Honor (France). Mem. Clan Fergusson Soc. (Scotland), Beta Theta Pi. Clubs: Cypress Point (Pebble Beach); Old Capitol (Monterey, Calif.). Home: Box 1515 Pebble Beach CA 93953

FERKISS, VICTOR CHRISTOPHER, political science educator; b. Richmond Hill, N.Y., Aug. 2, 1925; s. Joseph and Pauline (Kiss) F.; m. Barbara Ellen Jouvenal, Oct. 16, 1948 (dec. 1981); children: Michael,

Deborah, Ethan. A.B., U. Calif.-Berkeley, 1948, A.M., 1949; M.A., Yale U., 1950; Ph.D., U. Chgo., 1954. Asst. prof. polit. sci. U. Mont., 1954-55; asst. to asso. prof. polit. sci. St. Mary's Coll. Calif., 1955-59, 60-62; asso. prof. govt. Georgetown U., Washington, 1962-66, prof., 1966—; Field dir. ICA Tng. for Africa Program, Boston U., 1959-60; cons. Peace Corps, 1961. Author: Technological Man, 1969, Africa's Search for Identity, 1966, Communism Today, 1962, The Future of Technological Civilization, 1974, Futurology, 1977. Sec. Cath. Commn. on Intellectual and Cultural Affairs, 1978-81. Served with AUS, 1943-46; to 1st lt., 1951-52. Decorated Combat Inf. badge, Bronze Star; Rockefeller Found. fellow, 1958-59; Fulbright prof. U. West Indies, Trinidad, 1968-69; Eli Lilly prof. sci., theology and human values Purdue U., spring 1976. Mem. Am. Polit. Sci. Assn., Am. Soc. Pub. Adminstrn., AAAS, Fedn. Am. Scientists. Roman Catholic. Home: 4114 Edgevale Ct Chevy Chase MD 20815

FERLAND, E. JAMES, electric utility executive; b. Boston, Mar. 19, 1942; s. Ernest James and Muriel (Cassell) F.; m. Eileen Kay Patridge, Mar. 9, 1964; children: E. James, Elizabeth Denise. B.S., U. Maine, 1964; M.B.A., U. New Haven, 1979; postgrad. in program mgmt. devel., Harvard U. Grad. Sch. Bus. Adminstrn. Electric utility engr. HELCO, New London, Conn., 1964-67; supt. nuclear ops. NNECO, Waterford, Conn., 1967-78; dir. rate regulation N.E. Utilities, Berlin, Conn., 1978-80, pres., chief operating officer, 1983—, dir. subs., Conn., Mass.; exec. v.p., chief fin. officer NUSCO, Berlin, 1980-83; dir. Conn. Yankee Co., Vt. Yankee Co., Maine Yankee Co., Yankee Atomic Co. Mem. Am. Mgmt. Assn., Am. Nuclear Soc. Office: Northeast Utilities 107 Selden St Berlin CT 06037

FERLIN, FRANK, JR., labor orgn. exec.; b. Olphant Furnace, Pa., Nov. 24, 1935; s. Frank J. and Ann D. (Bandzuch) F.; m. Margaret T. Patchan, Feb. 13, 1960; children—Mark E., Marilyn A. Student, California (Pa.) State Tchrs. Coll., 1959, John Carroll U., 1960. With Pa. Dept. Hwys., 1957; structural engr. to resident engr. Nickel Plate R.R., Cleve., 1957-70; v.p. and vice gen. chmn. Nickel Plate Lodge 563-5, Am. Ry. and Airway Suprs. Assn., 1964-68, pres. and gen. chmn., 1968-70; v.p., field rep., mem. bd. Grand Lodge, 1970-72, fin. sec.-treas., 1972-74; gradn pres. and chmn. bd. Am. Ry. and Airway Suprs. Assn., 1974—. Editor: Supr.'s Jour, 1974—. Labor mem. Nat. R.R. Adjustment Bd., 1974—; mem. edn. com. AFL-CIO, 1974—. Served in USMC, 1954-57. Mem. Ry. Labor Execs. Assn. (exec. bd.), Am. R.R. Editors. Democrat. Roman Catholic. Club: K.C. *

FERLINGHETTI, LAWRENCE, poet; b. Yonkers, N.Y., 1920; s. Charles and Clemence (Mendes-Monsanto) F.; 1951; children—Julie, Lorenzo. A.B., U. N.C.; M.A., Columbia, Doctorat De L'Université, Sorbonne, 1950. Founder (with Peter D. Martin), first all paperbound bookstore in U.S., City Lights Books, San Francisco, firm also publishes works of modern poets and writers; widely traveled poetry reader, also painter.; Participant (with Allen Ginsberg), Pan Am. cultural conf., U. Concepcion, Chile, 1960; participant, One World Poetry Festival, Amsterdam, 1981; Author: poetry Pictures of the Gone World, 1955, A Coney Island of the Mind, 1958, Starting from San Francisco, 1961, After the Cries of the Birds, The Secret Meaning of Things, Open Eye, Open Heart, 1973, Who Are We Now?, 1976, Landscapes of Living and Dying, 1979, Endless Life: Selected Poems, 1981; novel Her, 1960, Routines; plays Back Roads to Far Places; poetry and prose jour. Northwest Ecolog, 1978, (with Nancy J. Peters) Literary San Francisco: A Pictorial History, 1980; Editor: City Lights Books, Anarchist Resistance Press. Served with USNR, World War II. Address: City Lights Bookstore 261 Columbus Ave San Francisco CA 94133

FERM, DEANE WILLIAM, clergyman; b. Lebanon, Pa., May 22, 1927; s. Vergilius T.A. and Nellie (Nelson) F.; m. Paulie Swan, June 26, 1949 (div. 1976); children: William, Linnea, Robert, Laurie; m. Debra Campbell, Dec. 21, 1976. B.A., Coll. Wooster, 1949; B.D., Yale U., 1952, M.A., 1953, Ph.D., 1954. Ordained to ministry Presbyterian Ch., 1952; minister Fishers Island Union Chapel, N.Y., 1952-54; dir. Sch. Religion, Mont. State U., 1954-59; asst. dir. Danforth Found., 1958; dean Coll. Chapel, Mt. Holyoke Coll., South Hadley, Mass., 1959-81; lectr. Smith Coll., 1960-63; vis. prof. St. Mary's Coll., St. Andrew's U., Scotland, 1980. Author: Responsible Sexuality Now, 1971, Contemporary American Theologies: A Critical Survey, 1981, Contemporary American Theologies II: A Book of Readings, 1982, Alternative Life Styles Confront the Church, 1983; contbr. articles to profl. jours. Served with USNR, 1945-46. Danforth Campus Ministry grantee, 1965-66; Poulson fellow Am. Scandinavian Found., 1965-66. Mem. Nat. Assn. Coll. and Univ. Chaplains. Home: 867 Biglerville Rd Gettysburg PA 17325

FERM, VERGIL HARKNESS, embryologist; b. West Haven, Conn., Sept. 13, 1924; s. Vergilius T.A. and Nellie (Nelson) F.; m. Ruth Eleanor Rowe, June 5, 1948; children—Daniel W., David V., Judith N., Susan C. A.B., Coll. Wooster, 1946; M.D., Western Res. U., 1948; M.S., U. Wis., 1950, Ph.D., 1955; M.A. (hon.), Dartmouth, 1967. Asst. prof. Ind. U., 1955-57; asso. prof. U. Fla., 1957-61; asso. prof. pathology Dartmouth Med. Sch., Hanover, N.H., 1961-66, prof. anatomy and embryology, 1966—, also chmn. dept. anatomy. Mem. Am. Assn. Anatomists, Am. Soc. Human Genetics, Teratology Soc. Exptl. Pathology, Phi Beta Kappa, Sigma Xi. Research, publs. on environ. and genetic factors causing birth defects. Home: Dogford Rd Etna NH 03750

FERMAN, IRVING, lawyer, educator; b. N.Y.C., July 4, 1919; s. Joseph and Sadie (Stein) F.; m. Bertha Paglin, June 12, 1946; children—James Paglin, Susan Paglin. B.S., N.Y.U., 1941; J.D., Harvard, 1948. Bar: La. bar 1948, D.C. bar 1974. Partner Provensal, Faris & Ferman, New Orleans, 1948-52; dir. Washington office Am. Civil Liberties Union, 1952-59, Am. Civil Liberties Clearing House, 1952-54; exec. vice chmn. Pres.'s Com. Govt. Contracts, 1959-60; v.p. Internat. Latex Corp., 1960-66; pres. Piedmont Theaters Corp., 1966-69; adj. asso. prof. mgmt. N.Y.U. Grad. Sch. Bus., 1964-68; adj. prof. law Howard U., 1968-69, prof. law, 1969—; dir. Project for Legal Policy, 1976—; vis. prof. law Am. U., 1971-72; Mem. Am. Com. Cultural Freedom, 1954—; mem. Com. of Arts and Scis. for Eisenhower, 1956; mem. citizens adv. com. U.S. Commn. on Govt. Security, 1957; chmn. Police Complaint Review Bd., 1965-73; mem. Dept. HEW Reviewing Authority, 1969-79. Contbr. to books and revs. Mem. bd. dirs. New Orleans Acad. Art, 1948-51. Served from cadet to 1st lt. USAAF, 1942-46. Mem. Am., La., D.C., New Orleans bar assns. Jewish. Clubs: Capitol Hill, International (Washington); Army-Navy Country (Arlington, Va.); Harvard, Caterpillar (N.Y.C.). Home: 3818 Huntington St Washington DC 20015 also Route 1 Sullivan Harbor ME 04689 Office: 2935 Upton St NW Washington DC 20015

FERN, ALAN MAXWELL, art historian, museum director; b. Detroit, Oct. 19, 1930; s. Martin and Rose (Coral) F.; m. Lois Ann Karbel, Mar. 17, 1957. A.B., U. Chgo., 1950, M.A., 1954, Ph.D., 1960; Fulbright scholar, Courtauld Inst., U. London, 1954-55. Asst., instr., asst. prof. humanities The Coll., U. Chgo., 1952-61; asst. curator prints and photographs div. Library of Congress, Washington, 1961, curator fine prints, 1962-64, asst. chief, 1964-73, chief, 1973-76, dir. research dept., 1976-78, dir. spl. collections, 1978-82; dir. Nat. Portrait Gallery, 1982—. Author: A Note on the Eragny Press, 1957, (with others) Art Nouveau, 1960, (with M. Constantine) Word and Image, 1968, Leonard Baskin, 1970, (with Constantine) Revolutionary Soviet Film Posters, 1974; introductory essay Lasansky: Printmaker, 1975, Eichenberg, The Wood and the Graver, 1977; contbr. articles to profl. jours. Decorated chevalier Ordre de la Couronne (Belgium). Mem. Print Council Am. (past pres., dir.), Coll. Art Assn. Am., Am. Antiquarian Soc., AIA (hon.), Double Crown Club (hon.). Clubs: Cosmos (Washington); Grolier (N.Y.C.); Balt. Bibliophiles. Home: 3605 Raymond St Chevy Chase MD 20815 Office: NATIONAL PORTRAIT GALLERY F STREET AT 8TH NW Washington DC 20560

FERNALD, CHARLES EDWARD, transportation company executive; b. Dowmington, Pa., Sept. 28, 1902; s. Josiah Pennell and Sophia (Weltner) F.; m. Getrude Marie Connell, Oct. 17, 1936; 1 son, Charles Edward. Student mech. engring., Drexel Inst. Tech., 1921-24, Wharton Sch. U. Pa., 1926-30. C.P.A., Pa., N.J., N.Y., Ill. With credit dept. Notaseme Hosiery Co., 1919-22; purchasing agt. Haslett Chute & Conveyor Co., Oaks, Pa., 1922-24; sr. partner Fernald & Co., Phila., 1924-63; now sec., dir., chmn. finance com. Chem. Leaman Corp., Lionville, Pa. Active Republican Party.; Past pres. Credit Research Found., Inc. Served as lt. (j.g.) spl. assignments USN, USCGR, World War II. Mem. Am. Inst. C.P.A.s, Pa., N.J., N.Y., Ill. socs. C.P.A.s, Nat. Assn. Credit Mgmt. (past nat. pres.). Clubs: Union League (Phila.) (life); (Chgo.) (life); JDM Country (Palm Beach Gardens, Fla.)). Home: 2600 N Flagler Dr West Palm Beach FL 33407 Mailing address: PO Box 179 Downington PA 19335 *Ideals and goals which were impressed upon me during my home and school life were: love of country; respect of parents; morality in business dealings; and always be able to walk the streets with dignity. These ideals have remained with me to this day and I feel that more ideals of this nature should be included in our educational system.*

FERNALD, DAVID GORDON, foundation executive; b. Glen Ridge, N.J., Aug. 16, 1923; s. Charles Barker and Olga Elleda (Hoff) F.; m. Julia Ida Gregg, May 19, 1957; children: David Gordon, Julia Dana, John Gregg. A.B., Brown U., 1944; M.B.A., Harvard U., 1947; J.D., N.Y. U., 1956. Bar: N.Y. 1957; C.P.A., N.Y., N.J. Staff accountant Loomis, Suffern & Fernald (C.P.A's), N.Y.C., 1947-57; staff accountant, partner Lybrand, Ross Bros. & Montgomery (C.P.A.'s), N.Y.C., 1957-67; mgr. accounting and taxes Rockefeller Family & Assos., N.Y.C., 1967—; treas. Rockefeller Bros. Fund, also; Rockefeller Family Fund, JDR 3d Fund, Martha Baird Rockefeller Fund for Music, Rockefeller & Co., all N.Y.C., 1967—; trustee Montclair Savs. Bank, N.J. Trustee emeritus Brown U.; trustee Mt. Hebron Cemetery Assn., Montclair, First Montclair Housing Corp.; treas. Passaic County (N.J.) chpt. Full Gospel Bus. Men's Fellowship Internat. Served to lt. (j.g.) USNR, 1943-46. Mem. Am. Inst. CP.A.'s, N.Y. State Soc. C.P.A.'s, Tax Execs. Inst., Soc. Mining Engrs., Tax Mgmt. (adv. bd.), Phi Beta Kappa, Sigma Xi. Republican. Methodist. Clubs: Union League (past gov.), Mining, Rockefeller Center Luncheon (N.Y.C.); Montclair Golf (past treas.), Montclair Republican (past pres.), Cosmopolitan (Montclair) (past pres.). Home: 102 Lorraine Ave Upper Montclair NJ 07043 Office: Room 5600 30 Rockefeller Plaza New York NY 10112 *Honesty, integrity, due consideration for others, and hardwork are essential elements of a responsible position in civilized society. We must find a way to preserve Judeo-Christian principles and beliefs as a basis for our society if we are to continue both free and democratic.*

FERNALD, HAROLD ALLEN, publishing executive; b. Haverhill, Mass., June 1, 1932; s. Harold Allen and Leona Swan (Horton) F.; m. Sally Camilla Carroll, June 23, 1956; children: Robert Arthur, Melissa Anne, Thomas Allen. B.A. in Psychology, U. Maine, 1954; M.B.A., NYU, 1964. Trainee Nat. Shawmut Bank, Boston, 1954-55; sales Carter's Ink Co., Cambridge, Mass., 1955-56; sect. chief Western Electric Co., Andover, Mass., 1956-60, buyer, N.Y.C., 1960-64; corp. devel. Holt Rinehart & Winston, N.Y.C., 1964-66, personnel dir., 1966-68, mgr. adminstrn., 1968-70, v.p. adminstrn., 1970-77, v.p., gen. mgr. coll. pub. div., 1971-77; pub. Down East mag., Rod and Reel mag., Fly Tackle Dealer Mag.; pres. Down East Enterprise, Inc., Camden, Maine, 1977—, Twin City Printery, Inc., Lewiston, Maine, 1978-80, Fernald-Spahn Enterprise, Inc., Rockport, Maine, 1978-80; pres., treas. Hanson Energy Products, Inc., Newcastle, Maine, 1981—; dir. John Wiley & Sons, Inc., N.Y.C. Vice chmn. Maine Gov.'s Council Vacation Travel, 1979—; bd. dirs. N.E. Health Found., 1982—, U. Maine-Orono Devel. Found., 1982—, Bay Chamber Concerts, Inc., 1981—. Mem. Assn. Am. Pubs., Regional Mag. Pubs. Assn. (dir.), Camden-Rockport C. of C. (dir. 1977—), Alpha Tau Omega, Sigma Mu Sigma. Clubs: Masons, Camden Outing (dir. 1979). Home: 1 Beauchamp St Rockport ME 04856 Office: Commercial St Rockport ME 04856

FERNALD, PETER J., pub. co. exec.; b. N.Y.C., Dec. 12, 1928; s. Paul R. and Kathryn (Miley) F. B.A., Wesleyan U., 1950; M.A., Harvard, 1956, M.B.A., 1959. Profl. staff Arthur D. Little, Inc., Cambridge, Mass., 1956-67; asst. to pres. for corp. devel. Times Mirror, Los Angeles, 1967, corp. dir. planning, 1968, v.p. planning devel., 1969—. Served with USAF, 1951-55. Club: University (Los Angeles). Home: 1338 Glen Oaks Blvd Pasadena CA 91105 Office: Times Mirror Sq Los Angeles CA 90053

FERNANDES, JOSEPH EDWARD, business executive; b. Madeira Island, Portugal, Mar. 12, 1923; came to U.S., 1924, naturalized, 1946; s. Jose and Rosa (Teixeira) F.; m. Annabelle Watson, Apr. 24, 1954; children: Joseph, Marcia, Donna Maria. B.S. in Bus. Adminstrn, Boston U., 1947; D.Comml. Sci. (hon.), Stonehill Coll., 1964. With Fernandes Super Markets, Inc., Norton, Mass., 1948—, pres., treas., 1952—; chmn. bd., to, 1979; pres. treas. Fernandes Realty Corp., Brockton East Shopping Plaza, Inc., Fernandes Twin-City Realty Corp.; pres. Portuguese Times, Inc., 1976—, C & F Communications, Sta. WICE, Providence, 1982—, Portuguese Cable TV Network, 1980—; dir. Mass. Blue Shield, Fall River Line Pier (Mass.). Pres., Annawon council Boy Scouts Am., 1974-75; area dir. N.E. Boy Scouts Am., 1971—; former chmn., 1st pres. Portuguese Am. Fedn. U.S. and Can.; cons. Alliance for Progress, Uruguay, 1962; bd. dirs. U.S.S. Massachusetts Meml. Com.; v.p. Assn. for Devel. Cath. U. Portugal, 1976—; bd. dirs., mem. exec. com. R.I. Philharm. Orch., 1980; pres. Bristol County Devel. Council, 1980; chmn. Portuguese Cultural Found., 1980. Served with AUS, 1943-45. Decorated knight St. Gregory the Great; Order Prince Henry the Navigator, Portugal; recipient Man of Year award NCCJ; Peter Francisco award Portuguese Continental Union, 1966. Mem. Internat. Assn. Chain Stores (pres. 1968-71). Home: Fernandes Circle Norton MA 02766 Office: 378 S Worcester St Norton MA 02766

FERNANDEZ, EUSTASIO, JR., educator; b. Tampa, Fla., Dec. 11, 1919; s. Eustasio and Carmen (Aguera) F.; m. Athena Lozos, Dec. 3, 1950; children—Christopher Tasio, Alexandra Athena. B.S., U. Fla., 1941; M.A., U. Md., 1947, Middlebury Coll., 1950; Doctor en Letras, Nat. U. Mexico, 1960. Instr. Spanish U. Tampa, 1951-52, asst. prof., 1952-60, asso. prof., 1960-64, prof. modern langs., 1964—, acting chmn. modern lang. dept., 1958-60, chmn., 1960—; Spanish lang. cons. legal and engring. firms, pub. ofcls. Fla. edn. rep. Fla.-Colombia Alliance, 1965—; chmn. Tampa-Barranquilla (Colombia) Sister City Com., 1970—. Author: La Proyeccion Social en las Novelas de Gregorio Lopez y Fuentes, 1960, The Ybor City Story, 1976. Served with M.I. AUS, 1942-45. Recipient certificate of merit AID, 1970; Inst. Internat. Edn. (N.Y.) fellow U. Havana, 1947; Father Felix Varela fellow U. Havana, 1949. Mem. Am. Assn. Tchrs. Spanish and Portuguese, Modern Lang. Assn., South Atlantic Modern Lang. Assn., AAUP, Tampa World Trade Council (dir.), Theta Chi, Phi Delta Kappa. Democrat. Presbyn. Clubs: Sertoma Internat. (Tampa) (v.p. 1957, pres. 1970), Centro Espanol de Tampa, University Spanish. Home: 104 S Lincoln Tampa FL 33609

FERNANDEZ, LOUIS, chemical company executive; b. Cleve., May 13, 1924; m. Katherine Ritz; 5 children. B.S., Case Western U., Ph.D. in Chemistry. With Monsanto Co., 1949—, dir. devel. inorganic chems. div., St. Louis, 1961-64, dir. mktg., 1964-67, group mgr. new enterprise div., 1967-68, gen. mgr. inorganic div., 1968-69, corp. v.p., gen. mgr. textiles div., 1969-73, group v.p., 1973-76, exec. v.p., 1976-80, vice chmn., 1980-83, chmn., 1983—, dir., 1971—, chmn. corp. adminstrv. com.; dir. Boatmen's Bancshares, Inc., Trane Co., Petrolite Corp. Trustee St. Louis U.; mem. exec. bd. St. Louis Area Council Boy Scouts Am. Mem. Soc. Chem. Industry (exec. com.), Chem. Mfrs. Assn. (chmn. 1983-84). Office: Monsanto Co 800 N Lindbergh Blvd Saint Louis MO 63167

FERNANDEZ, MARIANO HUGO, banker; b. Havana, Cuba, Apr. 29, 1939; came to U.S., 1944, naturalized, 1959; s. Jesus M. and America (Sire) F.; m. Mary Patricia Demeritt, Aug. 27, 1960; children: Mariano Hugo II, Theresa Marie. Grad. with honors, Miami Dade Community Coll.; standard certificate, Am. Inst. Banking, 1965; grad., Fla. Trust Sch., 1974, Stonier Grad. Sch. Banking, Rutgers U., 1979. Chartered bank auditor; certified internal auditor. With First Nat. Bank Miami, Fla., 1957—, auditor, 1967-68, S.E. Banking Corp., Miami, 1968—. Served with USCGR, 1959-67. Mem. Bank Adminstrn. Inst. (bd. dirs. S. Fla. chpt. 1968-71), Inst. Internal Auditors (sec. Miami chpt. 1971-73, 1st v.p. 1974-75, pres. 1975-76, dist. v.p. 1978-79), Am. Bankers Assn. (task force on bank internal auditing 1982-83). Home: 7441 SW 174th St Miami FL 33157 Office: PO Box 014057 Miami FL 33101 also 100 S Biscayne Blvd Miami FL 33131

FERNANDEZ ARTEAGA, JOSÉ, bishop; b. Santa Inés, Mex., Sept. 12, 1933. Ordained priest Roman Cath. Ch., 1957; elevated to bishop of, Apatzingán, Mex., 1974, consecrated, 1974, named bishop of, Colima, Mex., 1980. Address: Palacio Episcopal Hidalgo 135 Apartado 1 Colima Mexico

FERNANDEZ-MORAN, HUMBERTO, biophysicist; b. b, Maracaibo, Venezuela, Feb. 18, 1924; s. Luis and Elena (Villalobos) Fernandez-M.; m. Anna Browallius, Dec. 30, 1953; children—Brigida Elena, Veronica. M.D., U. Munich, Germany, 1944, U. Caracas, Venezuela, 1945; M.S., U. Stockholm, Sweden, 1951, Ph.D., 1952. Fellow neurology, neuropath. George Washington U., 1945-46; intern George Washington U. Hosp., 1945-46; resident Serafimerlasarettet, Stockholm, 1946-58; fgn. asst. Neurosurg. Clinic, Stockholm, 1946-48; research fellow Nobel Inst. Physics, Stockholm, 1947-49, Inst. Cell Research & Genetics, Karolinska Institutet, 1948-51, asst. prof., 1952; prof., chmn. dept. biophysics U. Caracas, 1951-58; dir. Venezuelan Inst. Neurology and Brain Research, Caracas, 1954-58; asso. biophysicist neurosurg. service Mass. Gen. Hosp., Boston, 1958-62; vis. lectr. dept. biology Mass. Inst. Tech., 1958-62; research asso. neuropath. Harvard, 1958-62; prof. biophysics U. Chgo., 1962—, now A.N.; Pritzker prof. biophysics. Sci. and cultural attaché to Venezuelan legations, Sweden, Norway, Denmark, 1947-54; head Venezuelan commn. Atomic Energy Conf., Geneva, 1955; chmn. Venezuelan commn. 1st Inter-Am.-Symposium on Nuclear Energy, Brookhaven, N.Y., 1957; minister of edn., Venezuela, 1958; mem. Orgn. Am. States adv. commn. on sci. devel. in Latin Am., Nat. Acad. Scis., 1958; mem. U.S. Nat. Com. UNESCO, 1957. Author: The Submicroscopic Organization of Vertebrate Nerve Fibres, 1952, The Submicroscopic Organization of the Internode Portion of Vertebrate Myelinated Nerve Fibers, 1953, Cryoelectronmicroscopy; Superconductivity; Diamond Knife Ultramicrotomy, 1955-76; author series publs. in fields molecular biology, nerve ultrastructure, electron and cryo-electron microscopy, electron and x-ray diffraction, cell ultrastructure, neurobiology, superconducting lenses, superconductivity, others.; Editorial bd., Jour. of Cell Biology, 1961. Decorated Knight of Polar Star, Sweden; Claude Bernard medal, Canada; Medalla Andres Bello, Venezuela, 1973; Recipient Gold medal City Maracaibo, 1968, John Scott award for invention of diamond knife, 1967; medal Bolivarian Soc. U.S., 1973. Fellow Am. Acad. Arts and Sci.; mem. Venezuelan Acad. Medicine (hon.), Academia Ciencias Fisicas y Matematicas (Caracas), Am. Acad. Neurology (corr. mem.), Internat. Soc. Cell Biology, Buenos Aires, Santiago, Lima, socs. Neurology, Buenos Aires, Santiago, Lima, Porto Alegre societies surgery, Electron Microscopy Soc. Am. (spl. citation), Am. Nuclear Soc., Pan Am. Med. Assn., Sociedad Bolivárianade Arquitectos (Venezuela) (hon.), Pan Am. Assn. of Anatomy (hon.). Home: Apartado 362 Maracaibo Venezuela Office: Research Insts U Chgo 5640 S Ellis Ave Chicago IL 60637

FERNBACH, ROBERT DENNIS, lawyer; b. Cheektowaga, N.Y., May 27, 1917; s. Louis P. and Katherine (Kinsella) F.; m. Beth M. Hager, July 18, 1947; children—Robert Dennis, John P. Grad. cum laude, U. Notre Dame, 1938; LL.B. with distinction, Cornell U., 1941. Bar: N.Y. bar 1941. With Moot, Sprague, Marcy, Landy & Fernbach (now Moot & Sprague), Buffalo, 1941—; now mem. firm Moot, Sprague, Marcy, Landy & Fernbach; dir. Monroe Abstract & Title Corp.; lectr. U. Buffalo Sch. Bus. Adminstrn., 1947-50, Law Sch., 1950-54. Bd. dirs., mem. exec. com., now chmn. Greater Buffalo Devel. Found.; chmn. legal div. United Way of Buffalo.; Pres., bd. dirs. Downtown Buffalo Mgmt. Corp.; Bd. dirs. Western N.Y. Tech. Devel. Center, Devel. Downtown Inc.; Mem. exec. com. Erie County Indsl. Devel. Agy.; Bd. dirs. Buffalo Waterfront Devel. Corp.; Mem. Main-Genesee Urban Design Task Group. Served with USAAF, 1942-45. Decorated Bronze Star medal. Mem. Am., N.Y. State, Erie County bar assns., Trial Lawyers Assn., Ry. Trial Counsel Assn. Republican. Roman Catholic. Home: 117 Hyledge Dr Eggertsville NY 14226 Office: 2300 Main Place Tower Buffalo NY 14202

FERNEA, ROBERT ALAN, anthropology and Middle Eastern studies educator, consultant; b. Vancouver, Wash., Jan. 25, 1932; s. George Jacob and Alta Lorraine (Carter) F.; m. Elizabeth Warnock, June 8, 1956; children: Laura Ann, David Karim, Laila Catherine. B.A., Reed Coll., 1954; M.A., U. Chgo., 1955, Ph.D., 1959. From asst. prof. to assoc. prof. anthropology and Middle Eastern studies Am. U., Cairo, 1959-65; prof. U. Tex., Austin, 1966—, dir. Ctr. for Middle Eastern Studies, 1966-73; vis. prof. UCLA, 1968, U. Wash., 1970; cons. in field. Author: Shaykh and Effendi, 1970, Nubians in Egypt (recipient Tex. Writer of Yr. award). Mem. exec. com., bd. govs. Am. Reserch Ctr. in Egypt, Inc., 1981—. French Govt. scholar French Ministry of Culture, 1976; NEH fellow, 1980-81; Fulbright-Hays fellow, 1971. Fellow Am. Anthrop. Assn., Middle East Studies Assn. (founder). Home: 3003 Bowman Ave Austin TX 78703 Office: Dept Anthropology Univ Tex Austin TX 78712

FERNIE, JOHN DONALD, astronomer, educator; b. Pretoria, South Africa, Nov. 13, 1933; emigrated to Can., 1961, naturalized, 1967; s. John Fernie and Nell (Beattie) F.; m. Yvonne Anne Chaney, Dec. 23, 1955; children—Kimberly Jan, Robyn Andrea. B.Sc., U. Cape Town, 1953, 1954, M.Sc., 1955; Ph.D., Ind. U., 1958. Lectr. physics, astronomy U. Cape Town, 1958-61; asst. prof. astronomy U. Toronto, 1961-64, asso. prof., 1964-67, prof., 1967—, chmn. dept., 1978—; dir. David Dunlap Obs., 1978—. Author: Variable Stars in Globular

Clusters and Related Systems, 1973, The Whisper and the Vision, 1976; Contbr. articles to profl. jours. Fellow Royal Soc. Can.; mem. Royal Astron. Soc. Can. (past pres.), Internat. Astron. Union, Am. Astron. Soc., Astron. Soc. Pacific, Can. Astron. Soc. Office: Dunlap Observatory Box 360 Richmond Hill ON L4C 4Y6 Canada

FERNLEY, ROBERT CLUTE, trade association executive; b. Phila., Dec. 21, 1922; s. George Adamson and Mildred (Bougher) F.; children: Thomas James III (dec.), George Adamson Taylor, John Randolph, Robert Clute, David, Charles Jared. B.S., U. Pa., 1943. Chmn. bd. Fernley & Fernley, Inc.; mng. dir. Nat. Welding Supply Assn., 1947—, Am. Brush Manufacturers Assn., 1947—, Nat. Indsl. Distbrs. Assn., 1951—. Mem. S.R. Republican. Episcopalian. Clubs: Racquet, St. Anthony. Home: 660 Penllyn Pike Blue Bell PA 19422 Office: 1900 Arch St Philadelphia PA 19103

FERNSLER, JOHN PAUL, lawyer; b. Lebanon, Pa., Dec. 24, 1940; s. K. Paul and Elizabeth Mary (Snyder) F.; m. Christine Joan Chester, July 31, 1965; children: Euan, Scott. A.B., Dickinson Coll., 1962; J.D., U. Mich., 1965. Bar: Pa. 1965. Assoc. Balmer, Mogel, Speidel & Roland, Reading, Pa., 1965-66; dep. atty. gen. Commonwealth of Pa., Harrisburg, 1968-70; area counsel HUD, Pitts., 1970-81; ptnr. Reed Smith Shaw & McClay, Pitts., 1981—. Contbr. articles to profl. jours. Mem. Mt. Lebanon Zoning Hearing Bd., 1979—, sec., 1979-82; bd. dirs., counsel Council for Luth. Campus Ministry in Greater Pitts., 1979—. Served to capt. U.S. Army, 1966-67. Decorated Commendation medal. Mem. ABA, Pa. Bar Assn., Allegheny County Bar Assn., Fed. Bar Assn., Am. Judicature Soc. Republican. Lutheran. Home: 852 Meadowcroft Ave Pittsburgh PA 15216 Office: Reed Smith Shaw & McClay Union Trust Bldg PO Box 2009 Pittsburgh PA 15230

FERNSTROM, MEREDITH MITCHUM, financial services company executive, public responsibility professional; b. Rutherfordton, N.C., July 26, 1946; d. Lee Wallace and Ellie (Saine) Mitchum; m. John Richard Fernstrom, Dec. 28, 1968. B.S., U. N.C.-Greensboro, 1968; M.S., U. Md., 1972. Tchr. home econs. Prince Georges County pub. schs., Md., 1968-72; assoc. dir. market research H.J. Kaufman Advt., Washington, 1972-74; dir. consumer edn. Washington Consumer Affairs Office, 1974-76; dir. consumer affairs U.S. Dept. Commerce, Washington, 1976-80; v.p. consumer affairs Am. Express Co., N.Y.C., 1980-82, sr. v.p.-pub. responsibility, 1982—; mem. consumer adv. council Fed. Res. System, Washington, 1982—; bd. dirs. Nat. Consumers League, Washington, 1982—, N.Y. Met. Better Bus. Bur., N.Y.C., 1983—, Internat. Consumer Credit Assn., 1984—. Contbr. articles to profl. jours. Mem. Va. Citizen's Consumer Council, 1980. Recipient Consumer Edn. award Nat. Found. Consumer Credit, 1981. Mem. Soc. Consumer Affairs Profls. (1st v.p. 1983—, pres.-elect 1984). Office: Am Express Co 125 Broad St New York NY 10004

FERON, JAMES MARTIN, newspaperman; b. Woodside, N.Y., June 23, 1928; s. James J. and Flora (Trostler) F.; m. Jeanne Margaret Clare, Feb. 28, 1953; children—Robert, Michael, Andrew, Margaret. B.A., Marietta Coll., 1950; M.S., Columbia, 1955. With N.Y. Times, 1952—; beginning as copy boy, successively news clk., radio news writer, gen. assignment N.Y. area corr. UN, 1959-61, London, 1961-65, Israel, 1965-70, Warsaw, 1970-73, N.Y., 1973—. Contbr. to: Ency. Year Book, 1963-66. Served with Signal Corps AUS, 1948-50. Pulitzer travelling fellow, 1955. Address: care New York Times 229 W 43d St New York City NY 10036

FERRAND, JEAN CLAUDE, oil co. exec.; b. Lyon, France, Feb. 10, 1930; s. Jean A. and Andree (Desire) F.; m. Bayote Odette, Feb. 20, 1960; children—Jean Pascal, Isabelle, Patrick. Engr.'s degree, Ecole de L'Air France, 1952; research asst., Calif. Inst. Tech., 1958-59, advanced mgmt. program Harvard Bus. Sch., 1970-71. Geophysicist in France and Africa for Compagnie Generale de Geophysique, 1955-58; mgr. Compagnie Reynolds de Geophysique, Algeria, 1959-61; adviser to Australian Govt. with French Inst. Petroleum, 1961-63; geophysicist, Australia; then chief geophysicist, asst. to exploration mgr. New Zealand for local subsidiaries Societe Nationale des Petroles d'Aquitaine, 1963-65; exec. v.p., dir. Aquitaine Oil Corp., 1965-73; v.p., dir. First Bus. Computing Corp., 1969-73; gen. mgr. internat. ops. Tex. Eastern Transmission Corp., Houston, 1973-74; pres. J.C. Ferrand & Assos., Houston, 1974—, Kemerton Energy Cy., Inc., 1976—; v.p., dir. Compagnie des Petroles Transcontinental (S.A.), France, 1974-76. Served as officer French Army, 1951-55. Mem. European Assn. Exploration Geophysicists, Soc. Exploration Geophysicists, Am. Assn. Petroleum Geologists, Ind. Petroleum Assn. Am., Harvard Alumni Assn. Home: 13630 Barryknoll St Houston TX 77079 Office: One Allen Center Houston TX 77002 13046 Trail Hollow Houston TX 77079

FERRANTE, JOAN MARGUERITE, English and comparative literature educator; b. N.Y.C., Nov. 11, 1936; d. Nicholas Henry and Josephine (Pisacane) F. Student, Brearley Sch., 1950-54, Radcliffe Coll., 1954-55; B.A., Barnard Coll., 1958; M.A., Columbia U., 1959, Ph.D., 1963. Asst. prof. English and comparative lit. Columbia U., N.Y.C., 1966-70, assoc. prof., 1970-74, prof. English and comparative lit., 1974—; lectr. modern langs. Swarthmore (Pa.) Coll., 1968; lectr. medieval studies Fordham U., N.Y.C., 1976; Andrew Mellon prof. humanities Tulane U., 1984. Author: The Conflict of Love and Honor, 1973, Guillaume d'Orange, Four Twelfth Century Epics, 1974, Woman as Image in Medieval Literature from the Twelfth Century to Dante, 1975, (with Robert Hanning) The Lais of Marie de France, 1978, The Political Vision of the Divine Comedy, 1984; editor: (with George Economou) In Pursuit of Perfection, Courtly Love in Medieval Literature, 1975; mem. adv. bd.: Speculum, 1975-78; cons. editor: Records of Civilization, Columbia U. Press, 1975—; dir.: Center for Italian Studies, Columbia U., 1977-80. Am. Council Learned Socs. fellow, 1969-70; Nat. Endowment Humanities fellow, 1980-81. Fellow Medieval Acad. Am. (councillor); Mem. Dante Soc. Am. (councillor, v.p. 1978-83), MLA, Internat. Arthurian Soc., Renaissance Soc. Am., Comparative Lit. Assn., Phi Beta Kappa (senator 1979—). Office: 616 Philosophy Hall Columbia U New York NY 10027

FERRANTE, VICTOR RALPH, television executive; b. Chgo., Sept. 21, 1937; s. Ralph and Josephine (Discepolo) F.; m. Margaret Mary Ryan, Oct. 29, 1966; children: Lisa, Michelle. B.S., U. Ill., 1961. Sales rep. R.H. Donnelley, Chgo., 1961-63, Branham Co., 1963-65; sr. v.p. Katz Communications, N.Y.C., 1965—, dir. Served with USNR, 1955-57. Mem. Television Bur. of Advt. (dir.), Station Reps. Assn. (sec., dir.). Club: Darien Country. Office: Katz Communications Inc 1 Dag Hammarskjold Pl New York NY 10017

FERRARA, ARTHUR VINCENT, insurance company executive; b. N.Y.C., Aug. 12, 1930; s. Thomas Joseph and Camille Virginia (Crescenzi) F.; m. Isabel D. Flynn, Dec. 26, 1953; children: Thomas G., Margaret Mary, James X. B.S., Holy Cross Coll., 1952. Group sales rep. Conn. Gen. Life Ins. Co., N.Y.C., 1955-56, Guardian Life Ins. Co. of Am., 1957-60; agy. v.p. Guardian Life Ins. Co. of Am., N.Y.C., 1972-77, sr. v.p., 1977-80, exec. v.p., 1981—; v.p. sales Guardian Ins. & Annuity Co., N.Y.C., 1972-78, dir., 1972—, Guardian Investor Services Corp., 1981. Served to 1st lt. U.S Army, 1952-55. Mem. Am. Soc. C.L.U.s, Nat. Life Underwriters Assn., N.Y. Life Suprs. Assn., N.Y. Life Underwriters Assn., Golden Key Soc. of C.L.U.s. Home: 43 Brendon Hill Rd Scarsdale NY 10583 Office: Guardian Life Ins Co Am 201 Park Ave S New York NY 10003

FERRARA, PETER JOSEPH, lawyer, author, government official; b. N.Y.C., Apr. 26, 1955; s. Joseph B. and Betty (San Filippo) F.; m. Consuelo M. Suarez, July 17, 1982. B.A., Harvard U., 1976, J.D., 1979. Bar: N.Y. 1980. Assoc. firm Cravath, Swaine & Moore, N.Y.C., 1979-81; spl. asst. to asst. sec. for policy devel. and research HUD, Washington, 1981-82; mem. sr. staff White House Office Policy Devel., Washington, 1982—; adj. scholar CATO Inst., Washington, 1979—. Author: Social Security: The Inherent Contradiction, 1980, (with others) Enterprise Zones Sourcebook, 1981, Social Security: The Family Security Plan, 1982, Social Security: Averting the Crisis, 1982. Mem. ABA. Republican. Club: Harvard (N.Y.C.). Office: White House Office Policy Devel Old Executive Office Bldg Washington DC 20500

FERRARA, V(ERNON) PETER, editor, publisher; b. Providence, Jan. 23, 1912; s. Peter and Grace (Cracknell) F.; m. Lyna Lambooy, May 7, 1932; children: Stephen, Kathleen Ferrara Kusta. B.A., Kalamazoo Coll., 1934; B.S., Northwestern U., 1938, M.S., 1941; M.A., Roosevelt U., 1960; postgrad., U. Chgo., 1961-62. Publisher-editor Nelson-Hall Book Pub. Co., Chgo., 1937—; pres. Adams Advt. Agys., Inc., Chgo., 1946—, Perfect Voice Inst., 1947—; pub. Practical Knowledge Pub. Co., N.Y.C., 1948—; dir. Madison-Chgo. Corp. Author: How to Get Along in This World, 1948, Effective Employment Practices, 1950, Personality Development, 1952, Psychology of Success, 1956; editor: Practical Knowledge Monthly, 1961—. Bd. dirs. Chgo. Boys Clubs, Chgo. council Boy Scouts Am., Art Inst. Chgo., Chgo. Council Fgn. Relations. Mem. World Assn. Document Examiners (dir.), Internat. Graphoanalysis Soc. (pres. 1970-75), Am. Psychol. Assn. Conglist. (trustee). Clubs: Masons, Executives (officer), Metropolitan (charter), Union League (Chgo.) (officer). Home: 400 Utley Rd Elmhurst IL 60126 Office: 111 N Canal St Chicago IL 60606

FERRARI, MICHAEL RICHARD, JR., university administrator; b. Monongahela, Pa., May 12, 1940; s. Michael Richard and Lillian Ann (Cristina) F.; m. Janice Bjurstrom, Sept. 5, 1964; children: Elizabeth Anne, Michael, III. B.A., Mich. State U., 1962, M.A., 1963, D.B.A. (Ford Found. fellow), 1968. Asst. to dean men U. Cin., 1965-66; asst. to dir. residence life, resident hall head advisor Mich. State U., 1966-68; acting chmn. dept. adminstrv. scis. Kent (Ohio) State U., 1970-71; mem. adminstrv. staff Bowling Green (Ohio) State U., 1971—, v.p. resource planning, 1973-78, provost, exec. v.p., 1978-81, interim pres., 1981-82; vis. scholar U. Mich., 1982-83; prof. mgmt., provost Wright State U., Dayton, 1983—; dir. Mid-Am. Nat. Bank and Trust Co., Bowling Green; bd. dirs. J. Preston Levis Regional Computer Center; mgmt. cons., 1968—. Author: Profiles of American Presidents, 1970, Measuring the Quality of Universities, 1970, National Study of Student Personnel Manpower Planning, 1972. Trustee Maumee Valley Country Day Sch., 1979-80, Consortium Health Edn. Northwestern Ohio, 1978—. Research fellow Am. Coll. Testing Program, 1970. Mem. Acad. Mgmt., Soc. Coll. and U. Planning, Inter-Univ. Council Ohio Provosts (chmn. 1980-81), Omicron Delta Kappa, Phi Kappa Phi, Beta Gamma Sigma, Pi Gamma Mu. Episcopalian. Home: 1746 W Rahn Rd Dayton OH 45459 Office: Wright State Univ Colonel Glenn Hwy Dayton OH 45435

FERRARI, ROBERT JOSEPH, educator, former banker; b. Bklyn., Dec. 3, 1936; m. Patricia A. Cantalupo, Sept. 6, 1958; children—Robert Joseph, James G., Judith A., Thomas A. B.S. in Econs, Villanova U., 1958; M.B.A., N.Y. U., 1962; grad. certificate, Brown U., 1969, Henry George Sch. Social Sci., 1961; D.Sc., London Inst., 1973. With arbitrace dept. Goodbody & Co., 1957; analyst Pinkerton's Inc., N.Y.C., 1958-60, Old Town Corp., 1960; bank auditor Fed. Res. Bank, N.Y.C., 1960-65; v.p. Franklin Savs. Bank (formerly Kings Hwy. Savs. Bank), N.Y.C., 1965-81; asst. prof., chmn. dept. econs. and bus. Marymount Coll., Tarrytown, N.Y., 1981—; Cons. LaCorte Agy., Inc., 1963-65; adj. lectr. C.W. Post Coll., 1963-65; adj. lectr. econs. N.Y. U., 1968-81; adj. prof. Mercy Coll., 1976—, N.Y. Inst. Tech., 1976—. Vice pres. Better Bklyn. Com.; v.p., bd. dirs. Kensington Flatbush Preservation Assn.; treas. Boy Scouts Am. Mem. Flatbush/ Flatlands Republican Assn., Am. Econ. Assn., Am. Finance Assn., Am. Statis. Assn., Nat. Assn. Bus. Economists, Nat. Economists Club, N.Y. State, Met. econ. assns., Am. Acad. Polit. and Social Sci. Club: University (N.Y.C.). Home: 114 Parkville Ave Brooklyn NY 11230 Office: Box 1301 Marymount Coll Tarrytown NY 10591

FERRARIO, JOSEPH ANTHONY, bishop; b. Scranton, Pa., Mar. 3, 1926; s. Angelo and Angelina (Mangione) F. B.A., St. Mary Sem./U. Balt., 1947; S.T.L., Catholic U. Am., 1951; M.S., U. Scranton, 1956. Ordained priest Roman Catholic Ch., 1951; sem. prof. St. Joseph's Coll., Mountain View, Calif., 1951-57, St. Stephen's Sem., Kaneohe, Hawaii, 1957-66; aide to Bishop Scanlan Diocese Honolulu, 1966-73, pastor parish, 1973-78, aux. bishop, 1978-82, ordinary bishop, 1982—. Bd. regents Chaminade U., Honolulu, 1979-82; mem. exec. bd. Aloha council Boy Scouts Am.; bd. dirs. Aloha United Way, Honolulu. Office: Roman Catholic Diocese Honolulu 1184 Bishop St Honolulu HI 96813

FERRARO, EDWARD JAMES, city mgr.; b. McKees Rocks, Pa., Sept. 12, 1928; s. Frederick and Catherine (Hughmanic) F.; m. Karen Virginia Isaac, Apr. 12, 1973; children—Vincent, Michael. B.A. In Polit. Sci, UCLA, 1956, M.A. in Public Adminstrn, 1958. Adminstrv. trainee, then adminstrv. analyst Chief Adminstr.'s Office, Los Angeles County, 1957-59; city adminstr., Lawndale, Calif., 1960-62, asst. city mgr., Torrance, j5Calif., 1962-64, city mgr., 1964—; asst. prof. Center Public Policy and Adminstrn., Calif. State U., g Beach; st lectr in field. Author articles, reports. Served with AUS, 1941-53. Mem. Internat. City Mgmt. Assn., Am. Soc. Public Adminstrn. (chmn. policy com. Los Angeles, Clarence A. Dykstra award Los Angeles chpt. 1980), Am. Acad. Polit. and Social Sci. (dir.), Calif. Assn. Public Adminstrn. Edn., South Bay City Mgrs. Assn. (pres.), League Calif. Cities (program com. city mgr.'s dept., public safety com. Los Angeles County div.). Home: Box 3576 Torrance CA 90510 Office: 3031 Torrance Blvd Torrance CA 90503

FERRARO, GERALDINE ANNE, congresswoman; b. Newburgh, N.Y., Aug. 26, 1935; d. Dominick and Antonetta L. (Corrieri) F.; m. John Zaccaro, 1960; children: Donna, John, Laura. B.A., Marymount Coll., 1956; J.D., Fordham U., 1960; postgrad., N.Y. U. Law Sch., 1978. Bar: N.Y. 1961, U.S. Supreme Ct. 1978. Individual practice law, N.Y.C., 1961-74, asst. dist. atty., Queens County, N.Y., 1974-78, chief spl. victims bur., 1974-78; mem. 96th-98th Congresses from 9th N.Y. Dist.; sec. House Democratic Caucus. Chmn. Dem. Platform Com., 1984. Mem. Queens County Bar Assn., Queens County Women's Bar Assn. (past pres.). Roman Catholic. First woman vice-presidential nominee. Office: 312 Cannon House Office Bldg Washington DC 20515 108-18 Queens Blvd Forest Hills NY

FERRARO, JOHN RALPH, chemist; b. Chgo., Jan. 27, 1918; s. Charles and Jennie (Carlotta) F.; m. Mary J. Leo, June 21, 1947; children: Lawrence, Janice, Victoria. B.S., Ill. Inst. Tech., 1941, Ph.D., 1954; M.S., Northwestern U., 1948. Chemist Kankakee (Ill.) Arsenal, 1941-42; with Argonne Nat. Lab., 1948-80, sr. chemist, 1968-80; spectroscopy adv. bd. Chem. Rubber Co., Cleve., 1971—; vis. prof. U. Rome, Italy, 1966-67, U. Ariz., 1973-74, adj. prof. planetary scis., 1974—; Searle prof. chemistry Loyola U., Chgo., 1980—. Author: (with J.S. Ziomek) Introductory Group Theory and Its Application to Molecular Structure, 1969, 2d edit., 1976, Low Frequency Vibrations of Inorganic and Coordination Compounds, 1971, (with L.J. Basile) Fourier Transform Infrared Spectroscopy—Applications to Chemical Systems, Vol. 1, 1978, Vol. 2, 1979, Vol. 3, 1982; editor: The Sadtler Infrared Spectra Handbook of Minerals and Clays, 1982; asst. editor: Applied Spectroscopy, 1967-68; editor, 1968-74. Served with USAAF, 1942-46. Recipient Outstanding Achievements in Spectroscopy award N.Y. sect. Soc. for Applied Spectroscopy, 1970, Distinguished Scientist award Argonne Univs. Assn., 1973, Meggers award, 1975; NATO sr. scientist fellow, 1978. Mem. Am. Chem. Soc., Research Soc. Am., Coblentz Soc. (bd. mgrs. 1969-73), Soc. for Applied Spectroscopy (pres. 1965, hon. mem., Profl. Achievement in Spectroscopy award Chgo. sect. 1975), Am. Inst. Chemists, N.Y., Ill. acads. sci., Sigma Xi, Sigma Pi Sigma. Home: 568 Saylor Ave Elmhurst IL 60126 Office: 6525 N Sheridan Rd Chicago IL 60626

FERRARO, MICHAEL DENNIS, baseball team manager; b. Kingston, N.Y., Aug. 18, 1944; s. Peter and Yolanda (Sisco) F.; m. Pam Houghtaling, Apr. 5, 1965 (div. 1973); children: Michele, Michael; m. Mary Catherine McLeod, May 16, 1979; 1 dau., Tracy. Coach N.Y. Yankees, Bronx, 1979-82; mgr. Cleve. Indians, 1983—. Home: 6195-B Laurel Ln Tamarac FL 33319 Office: Cleveland Indians Boudreau Blvd Cleveland OH 44114

FERRARO, NIEL PATRICK, naval officer; b. Bronx, N.Y., Oct. 13, 1931; s. Michael Angelo and Vincenza Rose (Rossi) F.; m. Rita Jane, June 12, 1954; children: Patrick Michael, Michelle Marie. Student, Cath. U. Am. Sch. Architecture, 1949; B.S., U.S. Naval Acad., 1954; M.S. with honors in Indsl. Mgmt, Purdue U., 1961; disting. grad., Indl. Coll. Armed Forecs, 1972-73. Commd. ensign U.S. Navy, 1954, advanced through grades to rear adm., 1980; supply officer U.S.S. Zellars, 1956-57, U.S.S. Albany, 1965-67; aide/spl. asst. to asst. sec. of navy, Washington, 1967-70; dir. aircraft procurement div. Naval Air Systems Command, Washington, 1973-75, asst. comdr. for contracts, 1975-78; vice comdr. Naval Supply Systems Command, Washington, 1982-83; dep. chief staff for logistics, comdr.-in-chief Atlantic Fleet, Norfolk, Va., 1983—; dir. Joint Logistics over the Shore; chmn. Icelandic Def. Coordination Group; lectr. U. Hawaii. Author several weapons acquisition studies related to organizational, procedural, budgetary aspects. Decorated Legion of Merit with gold star, Meritorious Service medal, Navy Commendation medal. Mem. Nat. Contract Mgmt. Assn. Roman Catholic. Home: 4218 Sleepy Hollow Rd Annandale VA 22003 Office: Dep Chief Staff Logistics CINCLANT Fleet Norfolk VA 22003

FERRATER, JOSE MARIA, humanities educator; b. Barcelona, Spain, Oct. 30, 1912; came to U.S., 1947, naturalized, 1960; s. Maximiliano and Carmen (Mora) F. B.A., Institute Maragall, Barcelona, 1932; Licenciado en Filosofia, U. Barcelona, 1936; Ph.D. (hon.), 1979. Prof. philosophy U. Chile, 1942-47; lectr. philosophy Bryn Mawr Coll., 1949-51, asso. prof., 1951-56, prof., 1956—, Fairbank prof. humanities, 1975—, chmn., 1971; vis. prof. Princeton, 1951-52, Johns Hopkins, 1955-56, Temple U., 1970-71. Cons. editor: Abraxas; Author: Unamuno: A Philosophy of Tragedy, 1962, Man at the Crossroads, 1957, Ortega y Gasset; An Outline of His Philosophy, 1956, Philosophy Today, 1960, Being and Death, 1967, Diccionario de Filosofía, 6th edit., 4 vols, 1979, El Ser y El Sentido, 1967, Indagaciones sobre el lenguaje, 1970, Las palabras y los hombres, 1972, El hombre y su medio, 1972, Cambio de marcha en filosofía, 1974, De la materia a la razón, 1979, Etica aplicada, 1981, Claudia, mi Claudia, El mundo del Escritor, 1983, Fundamentos de Filosofía, 1984. Guggenheim fellow, 1947-49; Am. Council Learned Socs. fellow, 1963-64. Mem. Institut Internat. de Philosophie (Paris), Am. Philos. Assn., Assn. for Symbolic Logic, Hispanic Soc. Am. (hon.). Home: 1518 Willowbrook Ln Villanova PA 19010 Office: Bryn Mawr Coll Bryn Mawr PA 19010

FERRE, ANTONIO LUIS, cement company executive; b. Ponce, P.R., Feb. 6, 1934; s. Louis A. and Lorenza (Ramirez de Arellano) F.; m. Luisa Rangel, Feb. 23, 1963; children: Maria Luisa, Antonio Luis, Luis Alberto, Maria Eugenia, Maria Lorenza. A.B. magna cum laude, Amherst Coll., 1955; M.B.A., Harvard U., 1957, Inst. for Sr. Mgmt. and Govt. Execs., Dartmouth Coll., 1978. Asst. plant mgr. Ponce Cement Co., Inc., 1957-59; pres. Puerto Rican Cement Co., Inc., San Juan, 1960—, co-chmn. bd., 1976; dir. Banco de Ponce, Am. Airlines; chmn., pub. El Nuevo Dia. Pres. P.R. Council on Higher Edn., 1966-68, Gov.'s Adv. Council, 1968-72; mem. Gov.'s Labor Adv. Council, 1975; bd. dirs. Colegio Puertorriqueño de Niñas. Served with U.S. Army, 1958. Recipient Presdl. citation, 1976. Mem. P.R. Mfrs. Assn. (pres. 1965-66), Am. Mgmt. Assn., Inc. (pres.'s assn. 1963—), P.R. C. of C., Phi Beta Kappa. Democrat. Roman Catholic. Clubs: Dorado Beach and Golf, Caribe Hilton Swimming and Tennis, Bankers of P.R., Ponce Yacht, Deportivo de Ponce. Home: Guaynabo PR 00657 Office: Chase Manhattan Bank Bldg 12th Floor Hato Rey PR 00918

FERRÉ, FREDERICK POND, philosophy and religion educator; b. Boston, Mar. 23, 1933; s. Nels F.S. and Katharine Louise (Pond) F.; m. Marie Booth, June 8, 1954 (div. July 18, 1980); 1 dau., Katharine Marie.; m. Barbara Meister, June 12, 1982. Student, Oberlin Coll., 1950-51; A.B. summa cum laude (Prof. Augustus Howe Buck fellow), Boston U., 1954; M.A., Vanderbilt U., 1955; Ph.D. (Fulbright fellow, Kent fellow), U. St. Andrews, Scotland, 1959. Comml. pilot; certified flight instr. Vis. asst. prof. philosophy Vanderbilt U., 1958-59; asst. prof. religion Mt. Holyoke Coll., 1959-62; asso. prof. philosophy Dickinson Coll., Carlisle, Pa., 1962-67, prof. philosophy, 1967-80, Charles A. Dana prof., 1970-80; prof. philosophy, head dept. philosophy and religion U. Ga., Athens, 1980—; vis. prof. So. Meth. U., 1964-65, Bucknell U., 1965-66, Pitts. Theol. Sem., 1968-69, Princeton Theol. Sem., 1970-71, Vancouver Sch. Theology, 1978, Iliff Sch. Theology, 1983; Eli Lilly vis. prof. sci., theology and human values Purdue U., 1974-75; vis. prof. philosophy and tech. and pub. policy Vanderbilt U., 1977-78. Author: Language, Logic and God, 1961, Exploring the Logic of Faith, 1962, Paley's Natural Theology, 1963, Basic Modern Philosophy of Religion, 1967, Comte's Introduction to Positive Philosophy, 1970, Shaping the Future, 1976; editorial bd.: Am. Jour. Theology and Philosophy, Am. Philos. Quar., Environ. Ethics, Philos. Forum, Proteus; chmn. editorial bd.: Ga. Rev. Nat. Endowment Humanities fellow, 1969-70, Nat. Humanities Inst., U. Chgo., 1978-79. Mem. Am. Assn. U. Profs. (nat. council 1973-76), Am. Philos. Assn. (program com. 1973-74, nominating com. 1980-82), Philosophy Sci. Assn., Metaphys. Soc. Am. (program chmn. 1971-72, councillor 1975-79), Am. Theol. Soc. (exec. com. 1970-73, treas. 1972-73, v.p. 1975-76, pres. 1976-77), Nat. Humanities Faculty, Am. Council Learned Socs. (del. 1982—), Phi Beta Kappa (pres. chpt. 1971-74). Home: 513 Milledge Circle Athens GA 30606

FERRE, JOSE ANTONIO, corp. ofcl.; b. Ponce, P.R., Sept. 13, 1902; s. Antonio and Mary Aguayo (Casals) F.; m. Florence Salichs, Dec. 31, 1933; children—Maurice, Mary Ann; m. Joanne Singleterry, Oct. 31, 1961; children—Jo, Noel, Tony; m. Patricia Christensen, March 29, 1967; children—Emile Antonio, Christina. B.B.A., Boston U., 1924; M.B.A., U. Miami, 1955. Pres. Pan Am. Investment, Inc., Miami Caribe Investments, Caribe Panama Investments. Trustee Boston U., U. Miami. Mem. Navy League. Clubs: Elk, Rotarian., N.Y. Athletic,

Advertising (N.Y.C.); Yacht, Bankers (San Juan). Home: 7 Aleazar St Ponce PR 00732

FERRE, MAURICE ANTONIO, mayor, corporate consultant; b. Ponce, P.R., June 23, 1935; s. Jose Antonio and Florence (Salichs) F.; m. Maria Mercedes Malaussena, Aug. 25, 1955; children: Mary Isabel, Jose Luis, Carlos Maurice, Maurice Raimundo, Francisco Antonio, Florence. Grad., Lawrenceville (N.J.) Sch., 1953; B.S. in Archtl. Engring, U. Miami (Fla.), 1957. Mem. Fla. Ho. of Reps., 1967—; mayor of, Miami, 1973—; Mem. City of Miami Commn., 1968-70. Trustee U. Miami. Office: Office of Mayor 3500 Pan American Dr Miami FL 33133 *

FERREIRA, ARMANDO THOMAS, sculptor, educator; b. Charleston, W.Va., Jan. 8, 1932; s. Maximiliano and Placeres (Sanchez) F.; children—Lisa, Teresa. Student, Chouinard Art Inst., 1949-50, Long Beach City Coll., 1950-53; B.A., UCLA, 1954, M.A., 1956. Asst. prof. art Mt. St. Mary's Coll., 1956-57; mem. faculty dept. art Calif. State U., Long Beach, 1957—, prof., 1967—, chmn. dept. art, 1971-77; lectr., cons. One man shows include, Pasadena Mus., 1959, Long Beach Mus., 1959, 69, Eccles Mus., 1967, Clay and Fiber Gallery, Taos, 1972, group shows include, Los Angeles County Art Mus., 1948, 66, Wichita Art Mus., 1959, Everson Mus., 1960, 66, San Diego Mus. Fine Arts, 1969, 73, Fairtree Gallery, N.Y.C., 1971, 74; vis. artist, U. N.D., 1974; exhibited widely abroad including, Poland, Portugal, Morocco, Spain, France. Fulbright lectr., Brazil, 1981. Mem. Nat. Assn. Schs. Art (dir.), Internat. Video Network (dir.), Assn. Calif. State Univ. Profs. Office: Calif State U Long Beach CA 90840 *I suppose much of my own life has been shaped by my experience as a first generation American. What modest success I may have had in my work is considerably due to that sense of ambition with which immigrant parents imbue their children. My vision as an artist is also shaped by the strong sense of Spanish culture that was part of my upbringing.*

FERRELL, CONCHATA GALEN, actress; b. Charleston, W.Va., Mar. 28, 1943; d. Luther Martin and Mescal Loraine (George) F.; 1 dau., Samantha Ferrell Anderson. Student, W.Va. U., 1961-64, Marshall U., 1967-68. N.Y. theater appearances The Hot L Baltimore, 1973, The Sea Horse, 1973-74 (OBIE award and Drama Desk award 1974), Battle of Angels, 1975; appeared in: Los Angeles plays Getting Out, 1978; appeared in TV series: The Hot L Baltimore, 1975, B.J. and the Bear, 1979, McClain's Law, 1981, E.R., 1984; appeared in movies: Network, 1975, Heartland, 1981; appeared in TV movies: A Girl Called Hatter Fox, 1977, A Death in Canaan, 1977, The Orchard Children, 1978, Before and After, 1979, Bliss, 1979, Reunion, 1980, The Rideout Case, 1980, The Great Gilley Hopkins, 1981. Wrangler award Nat. Cowboy Hall of Fame, 1981; Most Promising Newcomer award Threatre World, 1974. Mem. Circle Repetory Theatre, Actors Equity Assn., Screen Actors Guild, AFTRA, ACLU, NOW. Democrat. Office: care Jack Fields and Co 9255 Sunset Blvd Los Angeles CA 90069 *Do the best you can with what you have to work with. And if there is a choice between laughter and tears, always go for the laughter. Where there is laughter, there is life.*

FERRELL, DAVID LEE, public relations agency executive; b. Canton, Ohio, Feb. 13, 1937; s. Arthur Glen and Evelyn Theresa (Bortz) F.; m. Beverly Jean Zarick, May 13, 1961; children: David Lee, Amy Elizabeth. B.S. in Journalism, Ohio U., Athens, 1960. Bur. editor Wooster (Ohio) Daily Record, 1957-60; editor employee publs. Firestone Tire & Rubber Co., Akron, Ohio, 1960-62, Air Line Pilot mag., Chgo., 1962-65; account exec. Carl Byoir & Assocs., N.Y.C., 1965-72; exec. v.p. Gray & Rogers, Inc., Phila., 1972-82; pres., chief exec. officer Ferrell-Cleary, Inc., Phila., 1983—; also dir. Gray & Rogers, Inc. Mem. Public Relations Soc. Am., Nat. Investor Relations Inst., Aviation and Space Writers Assn., Sigma Delta Chi, Tau Kappa Epsilon. Republican. Roman Catholic. Club: Waynesborough Country. Home: 1565 Stanford Ln Paoli PA 19301 Office: 602 Ave of Arts Bldg. Broad and Chestnut Sts Philadelphia PA 19107

FERRELL, JAMES EDWIN, energy company executive; b. Atchison, Kans., Oct. 17, 1939; s. Alfred C. and Mabel A. (Samson) F.; m. Elizabeth J. Gillespie, May 10, 1959; children: Kathryn E., Sarah A. B.S. in Bus. Adminstrn., U. Kans., 1963. Pres. Ferrell Cos., Inc., Liberty, Mo., 1965—; chmn., chief exec. officer Gas Service Co., Kansas City, Mo., 1983—; dir. United Mo. Bancshares, Kansas City, Gas Service Co., Ferrell Cos., Inc. Served to 1st lt. U.S. Army, 1963-65. Republican. Lutheran. Address: Ferrell Cos Inc 1 Liberty Plaza Liberty MO 64068

FERRELL, JAMES K., chemical engineering educator; b. Maryville, Mo., Jan. 18, 1923; s. Harry K. and Susie (Bruce) F.; m. Dorothy I. Dobransky, Mar. 19, 1943; children: Janet Marion, John K. BS., U. Mo., 1948, M.S., 1949; Ph.D., N.C. State U., 1954. Asst. prof. chem. engring. N.C. State U., Raleigh, 1954-56, Alcoa prof., 1961—, head dept. chem. engring., 1961-80, dir. energy and environ. programs, 1980—; group leader nuclear div. Martin Co., Balt., 1956-58; sect. chief atomic energy div. Babcox & Wilcox Co., Lynchburg, Va., 1958-61; dir. Hydra Computer Co., Raleigh, N.C. Oil Recycling Demonstration Program. Contbr. articles to profl. jours. Bd. dirs. N.C. Ednl. Computing Service, Research Triangle, N.C. Served to 1st lt., F.A. AUS, 1943-46. Mem. Am. Inst. Chem. Engrs. (various offices), Am. Chem. Soc., Sigma Xi. Home: 4205 Rowan St Raleigh NC 27609

FERRELL, RAY EDWARD, JR., geology educator, consultant; b. New Orleans, Jan. 29, 1941; s. Ray Edward and Viola Olive (Naffe) F.; m. Suzanne Mary Haulard, Dec. 22, 1962; children: Ray Eric, Nancy Suzanne, Andrew Edward, Benjamin Thomas. B.S., U. Southwestern La., 1962; M.S., U. Ill., 1965, Ph.D., 1966. Asst. prof. La. State U., Baton Rouge, 1966-71, assoc. prof., 1971-77, prof. geology, 1977—, chmn., 1978-82; corp. officer Materials Evaluation Lab., Baton Rouge, 1972-76. Mem. Clay Minerals Soc. (councilor 1982-84), Am. Assn. Petroleum Geologists. Home: 595 Maxine Dr Baton Rouge LA 70808 Office: La State U Dept Geology Baton Rouge LA 70803

FERRELL, ROBERT HUGH, historian, educator; b. Cleve., May 8, 1921; s. Ernest Henry and Edna Lulu (Rentsch) F.; m. Lila Esther Sprout, Sept. 8, 1956; 1 dau., Carolyn Irene. B.S. in Edn., Bowling Green State U., 1946, B.A., 1947, LL.D. (hon.), 1971; M.A., Yale U., 1948, Ph.D., 1951. Intelligence analyst U.S. Air Force, 1951-52; lectr. in history Mich. State U., 1952-53; asst. prof. history Ind. U., 1953-58, asso. prof., 1958-61, prof., 1961-74, Disting. prof., 1974—; vis. prof. Yale U., 1955-56, Am. U. at Cairo, 1958-59, U. Conn., 1964-65, Cath. U. Louvain, Belgium, 1969-70, Naval War Coll., 1974-75. Author: Peace in Their Time, 1952, American Diplomacy in the Great Depression, 1957, American Diplomacy: A History, 1959, 2d rev. edit., 1969, 3d edit., 1975, Frank B. Kellogg and Henry L. Stimson, 1963, (with M.G. Baxter and J.E. Wiltz) Teaching of American History in High Schools, 1964, George C. Marshall, 1966, (with R.B. Morris and W. Greenleaf) America: A History of the People, 1971, (with others) Unfinished Century, 1973, Harry S. Truman and the Modern American Presidency, 1983, Truman: A Centenary Remembrance, 1984; editor: Off the Record: The Private Papers of Harry S. Truman, 1980, The Autobiography of Harry S. Truman, 1980, The Eisenhower Diaries, 1981, Dear Bess: The Letters from Harry to Bess Truman, 1984, (with Samuel Flagg Bemis) American Secretaries of State and Their Diplomacy, 9 vols., 1963-80. Served with USAAF, 1942-45. Mem. Am. Hist. Assn., Orgn. Am. Historians, Soc. Historians Am. Fgn. Relations. Home: 512 S Hawthorne St Bloomington IN 47401 Office: Dept History Ind U Bloomington IN 47405

FERRELL, WILLIAM WILSON, pipeline company executive; b. Danville, W.Va., Mar. 9, 1924; s. Robert F. and Isabel (Childress) F.; m. B. Annette Robinson, Dec. 27, 1947; children: Barbara Ann, William Wilson, Robert R. Student, Georgetown Coll., 1941-42; B.S. in Mining Engring, W.Va. U., 1949. Registered profl. engr., W.Va. Jr. engr. United Fuel Gas Co., 1949-56, asst. production supt., 1956-59, production and storage supt., 1959-62, v.p. ops., 1962-67; v.p. Charleston Group Cos.—Columbia Gas System, 1967-68, pres., 1968-72, pres., chief exec. officer, 1972-73; pres. Columbia Gas Transmission Corp., Charleston, W.Va., 1973-74, pres., chief exec. officer, 1974-76, chmn. bd., chief exec. officer, 1976-83, chmn. bd./pres., chief exec. officer, 1983—, dir., 1962—; pres., dir. Big Marsh Oil Co.; dir. Columbia Gas System Service Corp. Mem. vis. com. Coll. Mineral and Energy Resources, W.Va. U. Served with Q.M.C. USNR, 1943-46. Mem. W.Va. C. of C. (dir.). Clubs: Rotary (Charleston); Edgewood Country, Berry Hills Country. Office: PO Box 1273 Charleston WV 25325

FERREN, JOHN MAXWELL, appellate judge; b. Kansas City, Mo., July 21, 1937; s. Jack Maxwell and Elizabeth Anne (Hansen) F.; m. Ann Elizabeth Speidel, Sept. 4, 1961; children—Andrew John, Peter Maxwell. A.B. magna cum laude, Harvard U., 1959, LL.B., 1962. Bar: Ill. bar 1962, Mass. bar 1967, D.C. bar 1970. Asso. firm Kirkland, Ellis, Hodson, Chaffetz & Masters, Chgo., 1962-66; dir. Neighborhood Law Office Program, Harvard Law Sch., 1966-68, teaching fellow, dir., 1968-69, lectr. law, dir., 1969-70; partner firm Hogan & Hartson, Washington, 1970-77; asso. judge D.C. Ct. Appeals, Washington, 1977—, mem. disciplinary bd., 1972-76; mem. exec. com., bd. dirs. Council on Legal Edn. for Profl. Responsibility, 1970-82; exec. com. Washington Lawyers Com. for Civil Rights Under Law, 1970-77. Contbr. articles to profl. jours. Treas., bd. dirs. Firman Neighborhood House, Chgo., 1964-66; legis. subcom. on consumer credit Chgo. Commn. on Human Relations Com. on New Residents, 1964-66; originator, chmn. Neighborhood Legal Advice Clinics, Ch. Fedn. Greater Chgo., 1964-66; bd. dirs. Peoples Devel. Corp., Washington, 1970-74; exec. com. of legal adv. com. Nat. Com. Against Discrimination in Housing, 1974-77; steering com. Nat. Prison Project of ACLU Found., 1975-77; bd. dirs. George A. Wiley Meml. Fund, 1974—, Nat. Resource Center for Consumers of Legal Services, 1973-77. Fellow Am. Bar Found.; mem. ABA (Commn. on Nat. Inst. Justice 1972-80, mem. Consortium on Legal Services and Public 1972-73, 76-79, chmn. 1979-82, chmn. spl. com. on public interest practice 1976-78), Am. Law Inst., Nat. Legal Aid and Defender Assn., Phi Beta Kappa. Presbyterian. Home: 3404 Legation St NW Washington DC 20015 Office: DC Court Appeals 500 Indiana Ave NW Washington DC 20001

FERRER, ALBERTO, legal educator, lawyer; b. San Juan, P.R., Dec. 13, 1919; s. Miguel and Floria (Rincon) F.; m. Nellie Gonzalez, Jan. 17, 1944; children: Alberto, Gloria, Teresa. A.B., Cornell U., 1940, J.D., 1943. Bar: U.S. Dist. Ct. P.R. 1943, P.R. 1943, U.S. Ct. Appeals (1st cir.) 1959, U.S. Supreme Ct. 1977, D.C. 1978. Law clk. Supreme Ct., P.R., 1943-44; gen. counsel Land Authority, San Juan, P.R., 1944-58; dir. office legis. services P.R. Legislature, 1958-67; sr. ptnr. Canales & Ferrer, San Juan, 1967-76; sole practice, San Juan, 1976-78; dean Inter Am. U. Sch. Law, Santruce, P.R., 1978-82; Disting. prof. law Inter. Am. U. Sch. Law, Santurce, P.R., 1982—; of counsel Doval, Munoz, Acevedo, Otero & Trias, San Juan, 1982—; mem. Nat. Conf. Commrs. Uniform State Laws, 1975—, P.R. Jud. Conf., 1978—; dir., sec. Caribbean Fed. Savs. and Loan Assn., P.R. Author: Law of Condominium, 2 vols., 1967; bd. editors: P.R. Bar Assn. Law Rev., 1961-65. Recipient Gold medal III Internat. Congress on Registry Law, San Juan, 1979. Mem. P.R. Bar Assn. (dir. Found. 1973—, Disting. Membership award 1968), Fed. Bar Assn., Am. Judicature Soc., Phi Alpha Delta. Democrat. Roman Catholic. Clubs: Association Fraternal de Amigos (San Juan); Riomar Country (Rio Grande, P.R.). Office: Inter Am U Sch Law Fernandez Juncos Sta PO Box 8897 Santruce PR 00910

FERRER, JOSÉ VICENTE, actor, producer, director; b. Santurce, P.R., Jan. 8, 1912; s. Rafael and Maria Providencia (Cintrón) F.; m. Uta Hagen, Dec. 8, 1938 (div. 1948); 1 dau., Leticia Thyra; m. Phyllis Hill, June 19, 1948 (div. 1953); m. Rosemary Clooney, July 13, 1953 (div. 1967); m. Stella Daphne Magee; children: Miguel, Maria, Gabriel, Monsita, Rafael. A.B., Princeton U., 1933, M.A. (hon.), 1947; H.H.D. (hon), U. P.R., 1949. Asst. stage mgr., Suffern N.Y., 1935; appeared in: Let's Face It; as Iago to: Paul Robeson's Othello, 1943; producer, dir.: Strange Fruit, 1945, Stalag 17, 1952, Anything Can Happen; motion picture, 1951, The Fourposter, 1952, The Chase, 1952; producer and actor: Cyrano de Bergerac, 1946; played Dauphin to: Ingrid Bergman's Joan of Arc, 1948 (motion picture); played: The Silver Whistle, 1948, 4 Chekov 1-act plays; produced and acted in: The Insect Comedy of, N.Y. City Theatre Co., Twentieth Century, 1950, The Shrike, 1952 (Pulitzer prize play), Richard III, Charley's Aunt, all 1953-54; dir.: My Three Angels, 1953, The Dazzling Hour, 1953, Return to Peyton Place, 1961; gen. dir., N.Y. Theatre Co.; acted in: Whirlpool, 1949, Crisis, 1950, Cyrano de Bergerac, 1950; motion pictures Moulin Rouge, 1952, Miss Sadie Thompson, 1953, The Caine Mutiny, 1953, Deep in My Heart, 1954, The Shrike, 1954, The Cockleshell Heroes, 1955, The Great Man, 1956, I Accuse, 1957, The High Cost of Living, 1957, Nine Hours to Rama, 1963; star: Lawrence of Arabia, 1962, Ship of Fools, 1965, The Greatest Story Ever Told, 1965; producer, dir. star: theatre Edwin Booth, 1959; dir., co-author: Oh Captain, 1958; dir.: The Andersonville Trial, 1960; star: play The Girl Who Came to Supper, 1963-64, The Man of La Mancha, Broadway, 1966-67; appeared in: films Enter Laughing, 1967, Cervantes, 1966, The Marcus-Nelson Murders, 1973, Crash, 1977, Forever Young, Forever Free, 1977, The Sentinel, 1977, The Swarm, 1978, Fedora, 1979, The 5th Musketeer, 1979, Natural Enemies, 1979, The Big Brawl, 1980, Midsummer Night's Sex Comedy, 1981, And They're Off, 1982, To Be Or Not To Be, 1983, The Evil that Men Do, 1983, Dune, 1983; did 2 complete live TV prodns. What Makes Sammy Run, A Case of Libel; mini-series The French Atlantic Affair, 1979; documentaries and numerous guest appearances; appeared in: TV movies The Missing Are Deadly, 1975, The Art of Crime, 1975, Exo-Man, 1977; TV dramatic spl. Truman at Potsdam, 1976; TV ltd. series The Rhinemann Exchange, 1977; TV show Gideon's Trumpet, 1979; TV series Quincy, 1982, This Girl for Hire, George Washington, Samson and Delilah, 1983. Recipient Tony awards as best dramatic actor, 1947, 52, Motion Picture Acad. Arts and Scis. Oscar award as best actor of, 1950. Address: PO Box 616 Coconut Grove FL 33133

FERRER, MARIE IRENE, physician; b. Elberon, N.J., July 30, 1915; d. Jose Maria and Irene (O'Donohue) F.; 1 adopted dau., Marianne Ferrer Killian. B.A., Bryn Mawr Coll., 1937; M.D., Columbia U., 1941. Intern Bellevue Hosp., N.Y.C., 1941-43, resident, 1943-44; prof. clin. medicine Coll. Phys. and Surg. Columbia, 1972—; dir. electrocardiographic labs. Columbia. Presbyn. Med. Center, 1956—, Doctors Hosp., 1953—. Bd. dirs. N.Y. Heart Assn. Recipient Salute to Women award Republican Women in Industry and Professions, 1966. Mem. Am. Heart Assn., N.Y. Acad. Med., Am. Soc. Clin. Investigation, Am. Fed. Clin. Research (emeritus), Am. Med. Women's Assn. (editor jour.). Club: Cosmopolitan (N.Y.C.). Cardiopulmonary research with Dr. A. Cournand and Dr. D. W. Richards (Nobel prize winners 1956). Office: 962 Park Ave New York NY 10028

FERRERA, ARTHUR RODNEY, food distribution company executive; b. Boston, Feb. 1, 1916; s. James F. and Mary (Mangini) F.; m. Mildred Grace Rugg, Sept. 9, 1944; children: Kenneth Grant, James Howard. A.B., Harvard U., 1938. Co-founder James Ferrera & Sons, Inc., 1945—, pres., 1945-57, chmn. bd., 1957—; dir. Commonwealth Bank of Boston, 1966-70; past dir. Romi Foods, Toronto.; Chmn. food div. CD, Mass., 1966. Served with AUS, 1942-46. Mem. New Eng. Wholesale Food Distbrs. Assn. (dir., past pres.), Nazareth Food Assn. (dir.), DAV (life). Republican. Roman Catholic. Clubs: Winchester Swim and Tennis (Mass.); Officers (Bedford, Mass.). Home: 5 Longfellow Rd Winchester MA 01890 Office: 135 Will Dr Canton MA 02021

FERRERA, KENNETH GRANT, food distbn. co. exec.; b. Mass., Dec. 1, 1945; s. Arthur R. and Mildred G. (Rugg) F.; m. Donna Marie LaMura, June 30, 1977; children—Kristian Garett, Danielle Marie. B.A., Am. Internat. Coll., Springfield, Mass., 1969. With James Ferrera & Sons, Inc., Canton, Mass., 1970—, v.p., 1974-77, exec. v.p., 1977—. Mem. Frozen Food Assn. New Eng. (pres. 1977-78), New Eng. Wholesale Food Distbrs. Assn. (v.p. 1976—). Office: 135 Will Dr Canton MA 02021

FERRETTI, OLGA, found. exec.; b. Raritan, N.J., Oct. 17, 1922; d. John Nathan and Victoria (Conti) F. R.N., St. Elizabeth's Hosp. Sch. Nursing, 1956. Sec. Ortho Research Corp., Raritan, 1947-53; sec.-nurse Johnson & Johnson, New Brunswick, N.J., 1958-68; corp. asst. sec. Robert Wood Johnson Found., Princeton, N.J., 1968—. Bd. mgrs. Am. Cancer Soc. Somerset County, Somerville, N.J. Home: 109 Stockton Blvd Sea Girt NJ 08750 Office: PO Box 2316 Princeton NJ 08540

FERREY, EDGAR EUGENE, association executive; b. Columbia City, Ind., May 22, 1920; s. Ralph Roy and Sarah Delilah (Dowell) F.; m. Claudis Sue Leininger, Jan. 29, 1944; 1 son, Steven Edgar. A.B., Ind. U., 1942. Mem. editorial staff Ft. Wayne News-Sentinel, Ind., 1942-43; news dir. Sta. WHAS, Louisville, 1943-46; pub. relations dir. Farnsworth TV, Ft. Wayne, 1946-48; editor news bur. Ind. U., Bloomington, 1948-52; pub. relations dir. Lenkurt Electric Co., San Carlos, Calif., 1952-60; pres. and chief exec. officer Am. Electronics Assn.(formerly Western Electronic Mfrs. Assn.), Palo Alto, Calif., 1960—. Dir. San Mateo County Devel. Assn., 1953-54, Golden Gate chpt. ARC, 1959-60; v.p. Sequoia Dir., 1958-60; v.p., dir. Sequoia YMCA, 1953-60; dir., pres. San Carlos C. of C., 1956. Mem. Am. Soc. Assn. Execs. (dir. 1982—, chartered assn. exec.), Pub. Relations Soc. Am., Armed Forces Communications and Electronics Assn., Am. Mgmt. Assn., Ind. U. Alumni Assn., Sigma Delta Chi, Sigma Alpha Epsilon. Republican. Presbyterian. Home: 26350 Espenanza Dr Los Altos Hills CA 94022 Office: Am Electronics Assn 2670 Hanover St Palo Alto CA 94303

FERRIER, ILAY CHARLES, textile company executive; b. Aug. 1927; m. Elizabeth Jean O'Brien; 6 children. B.Comm., McGill U., Montreal, 1948. Chartered accountant, Que., 1951; With Canron Ltd., Montreal, 1953-75, v.p., gen. mgr. elec. div., 1971-75; v.p. fin. services, then v.p. fin. Dominion Textile Inc., Montreal, 1975-77, sr. v.p. fin., 1977—. Bd. dirs. Sacred Heart Sch. Montreal; former bd. dirs. Can. Arthritis Soc., Montreal Symphony Orch. Mem. Fin. Execs. Inst. Can. (nat. chmn., dir., past pres. Montreal chpt.), Fin. Execs. Inst. U.S. (dir., area v.p.). Clubs: Univ., Badminton and Squash (Montreal). Office: PO Box 6250 Montreal PQ Canada H3C 3L1

FERRIES, JOHN CHARLES, advt. agy. exec.; b. Boston, Dec. 7, 1937; s. Harry Smith and Elizabeth (McGaffin) F.; m. Donna Jean Steele, Feb. 3, 1968. A.B., Dartmouth, 1959; M.B.A., Amos Tuck Sch. Bus. Adminstrn., 1960. Sales rep. Am. Hosp. Supply Corp., Evanston, Ill., 1960-63; account exec. Benton & Bowles Inc., 1965-67, v.p., account supr., 1967-70, mgmt. supr., 1970, sr. v.p., 1970-80, mng. dir., Europe, 1980—, also dir. Served with AUS, 1960-61. Mem. Kappa Sigma. Home: Ave Leo Errera 68 1180 Brussels Belgium Office: Rue du Commerce 23 1040 Brussels Belgium

FERRIL, THOMAS HORNSBY, poet, editor; b. Denver, Feb. 25, 1896; s. Will C. and Alice Lawton (MacHarg) F.; m. Helen Drury Ray, Oct. 5, 1921; 1 dau., Anne Milroy. A.B., Colo. Coll., 1918; hon. M.L., U. Colo., 1934, Litt.D., 1960; LL.D., U. Denver, Colo. Coll. Reporter and dramatic editor Denver Times, The Rocky Mountain News, 1919-21; engaged in motion picture advt., Denver, 1921-26; editor Through the Leaves and The Sugar Press (mags. of Great Western Sugar Co.), 1926-68; asso. and contbg. editor Rocky Mountain Herald, since 1918; Lectr. and mem. Regional Authors' Council of Writers Conf. in The Rocky Mountains, U. of Colo.; lectr. on poetry and Western culture, various univs. Author: New and Selected Poems, 1952, Words for Denver and Other Poems, 1966, April of Roses, 1983, (with Mrs. Ferril) The Rocky Mountain Herald Reader, 1966; also poetry, prose and book revs. in many newspapers and mags.; writer 9 verse texts used in connection with Boettcher murals, Colo. State Capitol; author: (poems) Trial by Time, 1944; Author: (prose) I Hate Thursday, 1946; contbr.: Harper's Mag.; author: (drama) And Perhaps Happiness, 1957 (1,000 award 1958); Author: (dramatization of poems) Feril, Etc (produced PBS-TV 1975). Commd. 2d lt. Aviation sect. Signal Corps, 1918. Recipient prize Acad. Am. Poets, 1939; Ridgely Torrence Poetry prize Soc. Am., 1953; prize Denver Post, and Perhaps Happiness, 1958; Service to Mankind award, Sertoma, 1958; Robert Frost poetry award Poetry Soc. Am. Contest, 1960; named Centennial-Bicentennial Poet for Colo., 1975; apptd. Poet Laureate of Colo., 1979; award Western Am. Lit. Assn., 1982; named to Cowboy Hall of Fame, 1983; award Denver Press Club, 1983. Mem. Am. Hist. Trails Assn. (hon.), The Westerners, Phi Beta Kappa, Phi Delta Theta, Sigma Delta Chi. Clubs: Cactus, Mile High, Denver Press (Denver). One of 31 poets commd. by Steuben Glass Co. to participate in Poetry in Crystal exhbn., N.Y.C., 1963. Home: 2123 Downing St Denver CO 80205

FERRIN, ALLAN WHEELER, association executive; b. Mt. Vernon, N.Y., Aug. 10, 1921; s. Dana Holman and Eleanor (Wheeler) F.; m. Barbara Hogate, Sept. 18, 1943; children: Barbara Ann Ferrin Lane, Allan Hogate. A.B., Princeton U., 1943. Salesman, advt. mgr. F.S. Crofts & Co. (book pubs.), N.Y.C., 1946-48; with Appleton-Century-Crofts, Inc., N.Y.C., 1949-62, adminstrv. asst. to chmn. bd., 1956-58, v.p., 1958-60, pres., dir., 1960-62; gen. mgr. ednl. div. Meredith Corp., N.Y.C., 1961-73, v.p., 1968-73, also dir.; pres. AMACOM div. Am. Mgmt. Assns., N.Y.C., 1973-78, corp. v.p., 1978-79, sr. v.p., 1979-81; pres. Am. Mgmt. Assns./Internat., 1981-83, sr. v.p., chief fin. officer, 1983—. Served to 1st lt. F.A. AUS, 1943-46. Mem. Phi Beta Kappa (pres. Scarsdale 1959-60), Phi Beta Kappa Assos. (dir. 1972-81, pres. 1975-79, hon. dir. 1981—). Clubs: Scarsdale Golf (Hartsdale, N.Y.); Quaker Hill Country (Pawling, N.Y.). Home: 50 Popham Rd Scarsdale NY 10583 Office: 135 W 50th St New York NY 10020

FERRIN, CHARITON ARNOLD, JR., univ. athletic dir.; b. Salt Lake City, July 29, 1925; s. Chariton Arnold and Ellen (Copening) F.; m. RoLayne Rasmussen, June 22, 1948; children—Chariton Arnold III, Richard Bard, Louanne, Shawn Christian. B.S., U. Utah, 1948. Profl. basketball player Mpls. Lakers, 1949-51; sales exec. in western, U.S., 1951-71; dir. regional programs U. Utah Alumni Assn., 1971-72; gen.

mgr. Utah Star Profl. Basketball Team, 1972-76; dir. athletics U. Utah, Salt Lake City, 1976—; pres Rocky Mountain Enterprises; sec. Wagon Wheel Trailer Ct.; dir. R.C. Wiley, Inc., Copper State Thrift & Loan Co. Served with AUS, 1945. Named to Helms Basketball Hall of Fame; Utah Hall of Fame. Mormon. All-Am. basketball player, 4 yrs. Home: 2698 E Sherwood Dr Salt Lake City UT Office: U Utah Dept Athletics Spl Events Center Salt Lake City UT 84112 *Two of my favorite verses are: "that which you inherit from your father you must earn in order to possess". (by Stanley Marcus-Goethe). "Let your friend's dignity be as dear to you as your own". (by Gerson D. Cohen-Talmud).*

FERRIS, BARTON PURDY, JR., investment banking executive; b. N.Y.C., June 5, 1940; s. Barton Purdy and Evelyn (Van Dyk) F.; m. Susan Sheldon Moore, Apr. 17, 1965; children: Juliana, Jeffrey, Nathaniel. B.A., Princeton U., 1962; M.B.A., Columbia U., 1966. Actuarial trainee Equitable Life Assurance, N.Y.C., 1963-64; spl. asst. to dir. Office Fgn. Direct Investments, U.S. Dept. Commerce, Washington, 1970; v.p. Morgan Stanley & Co. Inc., N.Y.C., 1966-77; mng. dir. Morgan Stanley Can. Ltd., Montreal, Que., 1975-77; sr. v.p. E.F. Hutton & Co. Inc., N.Y.C., 1977-83, James D. Wolfensohn Inc., 1983—; mng. dir. investment banking Advest, Inc., Hartford, Conn., 1983—; dir. Moore Investment Co., St. Clair, Mich. Treas., bd. dirs. 610 West End Corp., N.Y.C., 1979-82; mem. Twilight Park Assn., Haines Falls, N.Y. Served with U.S. Army, 1963-64. Mem. Sigma Xi. Clubs: Princeton, Union (N.Y.C.); University (Hartford). Home: 149 Main St Farmington CT 10024 Office: Advest Inc 6 Central Row New York NY

FERRIS, BENJAMIN GREELEY, JR., physician, environ. researcher; b. Watertown, Mass., Jan. 24, 1919; s. Benjamin Greeley and Margaret (Wright) F.; m. Sarah Brooks Upham, Dec. 20, 1942 (dec. Oct. 13, 1979); children—Pamela Ferris Barneby, Margaret Upham Zimmerman, Kathrine Ferris Goddard, Patience Brooks Sandrof, Sarah Elizabeth; m. Stefana Puleo, Dec. 7, 1980. A.B., Harvard U., 1940, M.D., 1943. Diplomate: Am. Bd. Pediatrics, Am. Bd. Preventive Medicine. Research fellow Harvard U., Boston, 1948-50, asso. in physiology, 1950-53, asst. prof., 1953-58, asso. prof. environ., health and safety, 1958—, prof., 1971—; dir. environ. health and safety Univ. Health Service, 1958—; cons. medicine Mass. Gen. Hosp.; cons. environ. health Children's Med. Center; sr. cons. internal medicine Lemuel Shattuck Hosp., Boston, 1955-56; vis. prof. U. B.C., Can., 1974-78; lectr. medicine Tufts U., Boston, 1965—. Editor emeritus: Safety Report, Am. Alpine Club; Contbr. articles to profl. jours. Served with M.C. U.S. Army, 1945-47. Fellow Am. Pub. Health Assn.; mem. AAAS, Am. Physiol. Soc., Am. Epidemiol. Soc., Royal Soc. Medicine (affiliate), Sigma Xi. Clubs: Am. Alpine, Appalachian Mountain, Harvard, St. Boloph. Home: Box 305 Town House Rd Weston MA 02193 Office: 665 Huntington Ave Boston MA 02115

FERRIS, CHARLES BIRDSALL, civil engineer; b. N.Y.C., Mar. 5, 1904; s. Charles and Florence (Birdsall) F.; m. Laura Soper, Apr. 6, 1929 (div.); m. Geraldine Beyerly, July 18, 1949 (dec. March 1957); m. Laura Soper, Apr. 1958. B.S., N.Y.U., 1926, C.E., 1927; certificate Fine Arts, N.Y. U. Sch. Architecture, 1939. Registered profl. engr., N.Y., N.J., Mass., Pa., Conn., Wis., Fla; registered architect-engr., Geneva, Switzerland. Engr. Thompson-Starrett Co., 1927-31, Cross & Brown Co., 1931-34; engr. real estate dept. Guaranty Trust Co., 1934-37; in charge archtl. dept. Mut. Life Ins. Co., N.Y.C., 1937-40; v.p. Gramatan Nat. Bank & Trust Co., also Gramatan Co., Bronxville, N.Y., 1946-48; pres. Ferris Constrn. Co., N.Y.C., 1948-78, White Plains, N.Y., Charles B. Ferris Inc., N.Y.C., 1951—; sec.-treas. Flagsim Co., Inc., White Plains, 1951-58; propr. Charles B. Ferris Asso. Architects & Engrs., N.Y.C., 1979—, C.B. Ferris Asso., Geneva, Switzerland, Paris, N.Y.C., 1951—, pres., 1960—; partner Ferris-Heck Inc., 1979—; Cons. and dir. operations housing and redevel. bd. charge urban renewal and slum clearance, N.Y.C., 1960-62. Works include Barnert Meml. Hosp, Paterson, N.J., 1966-68; 3 hosps. in, France, med. depot, signal depot command support center, France; various coll. campus bldgs., mil. bases, libraries, schs. World Affairs Center, N.Y.C., Met. Ednl. TV Sta. Served from pvt. to maj. 102d Engrs., 27th Div. N.Y. N.G., 1925-41; col. C.E. and G.S.C., 1942-46; brig. gen., 1947; comdg. gen. 410th Engr. Brigade U.S. Army Res.; comdg. all engr. troops in res. in; N.Y. State; ret., 1961. Decorated Legion of Merit with Cluster, Bronze Star with cluster, Purple Heart, commendation medal. Fellow ASCE, Soc. Licensed Profl. Engrs., Res. Officers Assn. (past pres. N.Y. chpt.), SAR, Am. Legion, Mil. Order World Wars, N.Y. Soc. Mil. Order Fgn. Wars, Sojurners, Am. C. of C. in Paris, Assn. U.S. Army (v.p. N.Y. chpt.), Explorers Club, Kappa Sigma. Episcopalian (warden). Clubs: Columbia U., Princeton U., Army and Navy, Masons. Office: 320 E 54th St New York NY 10022

FERRIS, CHARLES DANIEL, lawyer, former government official; b. Boston, Apr. 9, 1933; s. Henry Joseph and Mildred Mary (MacDonald) F.; m. Patricia Catherine Brennan; children: Caroline, Sabrina. A.B., Boston Coll., 1954, J.D., 1961, LL.D. (hon.), 1978; grad. advanced mgmt. program, Harvard U., 1971. Bar: Mass. Supreme Jud. Ct. bar 1961, D.C. bar 1969. Jr. physicist Sperry Gyroscope Co., Gt. Neck, N.Y.C., 1954-55; asst. prof. naval sci. Harvard U., 1958-60; trial atty. Dept. Justice, Washington, 1961-63; gen. counsel U.S. Senate Democratic Policy Com., U.S. Senate Majority Counselor; also chief counsel to U.S. Senate Majority Leader Mansfield, 1963-76; gen. counsel U.S. Ho. of Reps. Speaker Thomas P. O'Neil, 1977; chmn. FCC, Washington, 1977-81; ptnr. firm Mintz, Levin, Cohn, Ferris, Glovsky & Popeo, Washington and Boston, 1981—. Served with USN, 1955-60. Mem. Mass. Bar Assn., D.C. Bar Assn. Democrat. Roman Catholic. Office: 1825 Eye St Washington DC 20006

FERRIS, DAKIN BENNETT, JR., financial services firm executive; b. Mineola, N.Y., Mar. 17, 1926; s. Dakin Bennett and Antoinette Respress (Smith) F.; m. Joyce Loveridge Egan, Apr. 6, 1950; children: Virginia Antoinette, Caroline Atwater. Student, Ga. Tech., 1946-50, Columbia Mil. Acad., 1943-44. With Merrill Lynch, Pierce, Fenner & Smith, Inc., 1947—, group v.p., 1970-74, exec. com., 1971—, exec. v.p., 1974-76; dir. Merrill Lynch & Co., 1968—, exec. v.p., 1976—; chmn. Merrill Lynch Realty Inc., 1982—; dir. Family Life Ins. Co., AMIC Co.; Vice chmn. Securities Industry Assn., 1978. Chmn. bd. Greater Atlanta United Fund, 1967; trustee Episcopal Radio and TV Found., 1965—, Ga. Tech. Found., 1969—. Served with A.C. AUS, 1944-45. Mem. Phi Delta Theta. Republican. Episcopalian (vestryman 1973-78). Clubs: Apawamis, Am. Yacht, Blind Brook (Purchase, N.Y.); Piedmont Driving, Peachtree Golf (Atlanta); Bond (N.Y.) (gov. 1978). Home: 973 Forest Ave Rye NY 10580 Office: 165 Broadway New York NY 10080

FERRIS, ERNEST JOSEPH, radiology educator; b. Adams, Mass., Nov. 17, 1932; m. Alice Manchester, May 28, 1960; children: Susan, Paul, Kathryn, Donald. B.S. cum laude, Coll. of Holy Cross, 1954; M.D., Tufts U., 1958. Diplomate: Am. Bd. Radiology. Intern Boston City Hosp., 1958-59, resident in radiology, 1961-64; resident in medicine Boston VA Hosp., 1959-60; prof. radiology Boston U. Sch. Medicine, 1968-76; assoc. prof. radiology Tufts U. Sch. Medicine, Boston, 1967-68, lectr., 1970; clin. instr. radiology Harvard U., Boston, 1970; prof. chmn. dept. radiology U. Ark. Med. Sci., Little Rock, 1977—; trustee U. Ark. Med. Sci., Little Rock, 1982-83. Author: Venography of the Inferior Vena Cava, 1969, Urinary Tract and Adrenal Glands, 1980; contbr. articles to radiol jours. Fellow Am. Coll. Radiology (program chmn. Ark. chpt. 1980-83), Am. Coll. Chest Physicians; mem. Am. Roentgen Ray Soc. (lectr., com. participant 1981-83), Radiol. Soc. N.Am. (com. participant), Soc. Chmn. Acad. Radiology Depts. (exec. com. 1983—), Soc. Nuclear Magnetic Resonance. Club: Little Rock. Home: 13241 Rivercrest Dr Little Rock AR 72212 Office: Dept Radiology U Ark Med Scis 4301 W Markham St Little Rock AR 72205

FERRIS, GEORGE MALLETTE, investment banker; b. Newtown, Conn., Sept. 25, 1894; s. George B. and Bertha E. (Clark) F.; m. Charlotte Hamilton, Apr. 14, 1920; children: Gene, George M. A.B., Trinity Coll., 1916; LL.D.; LL.D., Gallaudet Coll. Engaged in investment banking, 1920—; sr. partner Ferris Co., Washington, 1946—; pres. Ferris & Co., Inc., Washington, 1933-71, chmn. bd., 1971—; dir. Perpetual Am. Fed. Savs. & Loan Assn. Former chmn. bd. govs. Chevy Chase Village.; Mem. N.Y. Stock Exchange.; Mem. bd. Sibley Hosp.; trustee, treas. emeritus Gallaudet Coll.; trustee emeritus Trinity Coll. Mem. Washington Bd. Trade, Alpha Chi Rho. Clubs: Mason., Rotary, Chevy Chase, Columbia; Metropolitan (Washington); Burning Tree. Home: 5810 Cedar Pkwy Chevy Chase MD 20015 Office: 1720 I St NW Washington DC 20006

FERRIS, GEORGE MALLETTE, JR., investment banker; b. Washington, Mar. 11, 1927; s. George Mallette and Charlotte (Hamilton) F.; m. Nancy Strouce, Jan. 25, 1964; children: George Mallette III, Bradley, Kimberly Anne, David Hamilton. B.S. in Engring. summa cum laude, Princeton U., 1948; M.B.A., Harvard U., 1950. Chief exec. officer Ferris & Co., Inc., Washington, 1971—; dir. Entron, Inc., Internat. Exec. Service Corps, MSG Investment Co., Armstrong Cement & Supply Corp.; cons. in field; past bd. govs. N.Y. Stock Exchange. Gen. chmn. United Givers Fund campaign, 1966, Nat. Symphony Orch. sustaining fund drive, 1959, 60; trustee Mt. Vernon Coll., St. Albans Sch.; mem. Pres.'s Task Force Internat. Pvt. Enterprise; chmn. loan rev. bd. AID. Recipient Princeton in Nation's Service award, 1968, Washingtonian award Jaycees, 1959, Order Red Triangle award YMCA Greater Washington, 1966, Silver Beaver award Boy Scouts Am., 1967. Mem. Securities Industry Assn., Washington Soc. Investment Analysts (past pres.), Washington Execs. Assn., Phi Beta Kappa, Tau Beta Phi. Clubs: Harvard Business School (past pres., dir.), Metropolitan (Washington); Chevy Chase, Burning Tree (Md.). Home: 5601 Kirkside Dr Chevy Chase MD 20015 Office: 1720 I St NW Washington DC 20006

FERRIS, MELTON, writer, consultant; b. Modesto, Calif., June 25, 1916; s. Leslie Allen and Georgia (Melton) F.; m. Mary Jane Kirby, Oct. 9, 1947; children: Kirby, Leslie Allen II, Roxana Winifred Lee. A.A., Riverside Coll., 1935; student, U. Calif. at Berkeley, 1935-37, Calif. Sch. Fine Arts, 1951-52. Cert. assn. exec. Newspaper reporter, photographer San Jose (Calif.) Mercury Herald, 1937-40, Hilo (Hawaii) Tribune Herald, 1940-41; polit. reporter Internat. News Service, Sacramento, 1941-42; account exec. Gardner Advt. Co., St. Louis, 1948-50; photography editor San Francisco Chronicle, 1951-53; exec. v.p. Calif. council AIA, San Francisco, 1954-78; partner M. & M. Ferris, Corte Madera, Calif. Author articles on photography, sailing, knife making. Chmn. Marin Parks and Recreation Commn., 1963-69; dir. Calif. Roadside Council, 1967-68, Bolinas Community Inc., 1965-69. Served to maj. C.E. USAAF, 1942-48. Mem. AIA (hon.), Design Profls. Safety Assn. (dir. 1976—), Knife Makers' Guild, Nat. Knife Collectors Assn., Calif. Knife Makers Assn., Oreg. Knife Collectors Assn., Am. Soc. Assn. Execs. Clubs: Sausalito Yacht; Sutter (Sacramento). Home: Mill Valley CA 94941 Office: Corte Madera CA 94925

FERRIS, RAYMOND WEST, toy company executive; b. Boston, May 12, 1941; s. Raymond West and Phyllis (Vernon) F.; m. Janice Elaine Rudeen, June 24, 1966; children: Raymond West, Koren Alexandra, Adam James, Colin Matthew. B.A., Denison U., 1963; LL.B., UCLA, 1966. Bar: Calif. 1967. Atty. Dept. Corps., State Calif., Los Angeles, 1966-68, Republic Corp., 1968-72, sec., 1971-72; asst. gen. counsel, sec. Mattel, Inc., Hawthorne, Calif., 1972-73, sec., 1973—, v.p., gen. counsel, 1973-78, sr. v.p., gen. counsel, 1978-79, sr. v.p. corp. devel.; sec., 1979-83; sr. v.p. bus. devel. Mattel Electronics, 1983—. Office: 5150 Rosecrans Ave Hawthorne CA 90250

FERRIS, RICHARD J., airline executive; b. Sacramento, 1932. B.S., Cornell U., 1962; postgrad. in Bus., U. Wash. Staff analyst, restaurant mgr. Olympic Hotel; with Anchorage Westward Hotel; gen. mgr. Continental Plaza Hotel, Carlton Hotel; project officer-new constrn. Western Internat. Hotels; pres. carrier's food service div., then sr. v.p.-mktg. United Air Lines, Inc., 1971-75, pres., 1975-77, chmn., 1982—, chief exec. officer, 1976—; also dir.; dir. Western Internat. Hotels, Westin Hotel Co., Standard Oil Co., Ind. Office: United Air Lines PO Box 66100 Chicago IL 60666 *

FERRIS, ROBERT ALBERT, corporate executive, lawyer; b. N.Y.C., May 11, 1942; s. Albert Gerard and Helen Elizabeth (Jones) F. A.B., Boston Coll., 1963; J.D., Fordham U., 1966; grad. Advanced Mgmt. Program, Harvard Bus. Sch., 1974. Bar: N.Y. 1967, Calif. 1973. Asso. firm Carter Ledyard & Milburn, N.Y.C., 1966-71; v.p., sec., gen. counsel Arcata Corp., Menlo Park, Calif., 1972-82. Bd. dirs. Herbert Hoover Meml. Boys' Club Am., 1973-74, Girls' Club Mid-Peninsula, 1977-79, Legal Aid Soc. Served with AUS, 1966-67. Mem. Am. Judicature Soc., ABA. Club: Commonwealth of Calif. Home: 87 Fair Oaks Ln Atherton CA 94025 Office: 3000 Sand Hill Rd Bldg II Suite 140 Menlo Park CA 94025

FERRIS, ROBERT EDMUND, lawyer; b. Chgo., May 22, 1918; s. Edmund H. and Rose M. (Collins) F.; m. Jane H. Conybear, June 7, 1941; children: Robert E., John F., Kathy. A.B., U. Ill., 1939, J.D., 1941. Bar: Ill. 1941, Fla. 1946. Mem. firm McCune, Hiaasen, Crum, Ferris & Gardner (and predecessors), Fort Lauderdale, Fla., 1947—. Author: Cooperative Apartments Florida Real Property Practice II. Mem. Bd. Pub. Instrn. Broward County, 1955-58, chmn., 1958; founding bd. trustees Nova U.; chmn. Planning and Zoning Bd. Plantation, Fla., 1953-68; chmn. bd. trustees Broward Community Coll., 1959-71. Served with AUS, 1941-46; lt. col. Res. (ret.). Mem. Am., Fla., Broward County bar assns., Kappa Delta Rho. Presbyterian. Clubs: Lauderdale Yacht, Fort Lauderdale Country. Home: 120 N Bel Air Dr Plantation FL 33317 Office: 25 S Andrews Ave Fort Lauderdale FL 33302

FERRIS, RONALD CURRY, bishop; b. Toronto, Ont., Can., July 2, 1945; s. Harold Bland and Marjorie May (Curry) F.; m. Janet Agnes Walker, Aug. 14, 1965; children: Elisa, Jill, Matthew, Jenny, Rani, Jonathon. Grad., Toronto Tchrs. Coll., 1965; B.A., U. Western Ont., London, 1970; M.Div., Huron Coll., London, 1973, D.D. hon., 1982. Ordained to ministry Anglican Ch., 1970. Tchr. Pape Ave. Sch., Toronto, 1965-66; prin. Carcross Elem. Sch., Y.T., 1966-68; incumbent St. Luke's Ch., Old Crow, Y.T., 1970-72; rector St. Stephen's Ch., London, Ont., 1973-81; bishop Diocese of Yukon, Whitehorse, 1981—. Home: 41 Firth Rd Whitehorse YT Canada Y1A 4R5 Office: Diocese of Yukon PO Box 4247 Whitehorse YT Canada Y1A 3T3

FERRIS, THOMAS FRANCIS, physician; b. Boston, Dec. 27, 1930; s. Henry J. and Mildred M. (MacDonald) F.; m. Carol A. Connor, June 15, 1957; children—Richard C., Deirdre D., Thomas M., Claudia C. A.B., Georgetown U., 1952; M.D., Yale U., 1956. Intern Johns Hopkins Hosp., 1956-57; resident Yale—New Haven Hosp., 1951-53, fellow in renal diseases, 1961-63; fellow Linacre Coll., Oxford U., 1966-67; asst. prof. medicine Yale U. Med. Sch., 1964-67; prof. Ohio State U. Med. Sch., 1967-78; prof. medicine, chmn. dept. U. Minn. Med. Sch., Mpls., 1978—. Author articles on hypertension, renal disease. Served as officer M.C. AUS, 1957-59. Home: 1535 Hunter Dr Wayzata MN 55391 Office: 420 Delaware St Minneapolis MN 55455

FERRIS, VIRGINIA ROGERS, nematologist, educator; b. Abilene, Kans.; d. Ames P. and Virginia (Lucas) Rogers; m. John M. Ferris, June 20, 1953; children: Jeffrey Ames, Susan Virginia. Student, U. Kans., 1945-46; B.A. (Durant scholar), Wellesley Coll., 1949; M.S., Cornell U., 1952; Ph.D. (NSF fellow, Horton-Hallowell fellow), Cornell U., 1954. Teaching asst. plant pathology Cornell U., 1949-52, asst. prof. (1st woman prof. in dept.), 1954-55; cons. nematology, West Lafayette, Ind., 1956-65; asst. prof. nematology, entomology Purdue U., 1965-70, asso. prof., 1970-74, prof., 1974—, asst. dean Grad. Sch., 1971-75, asst. provost, 1976-79; cons. NSF, 1979-82. Asso. editor: Nematology News Letter, 1963-66, Jour. Nematology, 1974-76; contbr. articles to sci. jours. Recipient H.B. Schleman Gold medallion, 1973, Outstanding Faculty award Asso. Women Students. Mem. Am. Phytopath. Soc., N.Y. Acad. Sci., Helminthological Soc. Washington, Soc. Systematic Zoology (council 1978-81), Hennig Soc. (council 1981—), Entomol. Soc. Am., Soc. Nematologists (sec. 1965-68, v.p. 1968-69, pres. 1969-70), European Soc. Nematologists, Assn. Systematics Collections (dir. 1975-76, 78-81), AAAS, Am. Inst. Biol. Sci., Phi Beta Kappa (senator United chpts. 1979—), Phi Beta Kappa Assocs., Sigma Xi, Mortar Bd. (hon.), Phi Kappa Phi, Kappa Kappa Gamma, Sigma Delta Epsilon, Gamma Sigma Delta (hon.); fellow Ind. Acad. Sci. Home: 2237 Delaware Dr West Lafayette IN 47906 Office: Dept Entomology Purdue U West Lafayette IN 47907

FERRISS, DAVID PLATT, advertising executive; b. St. Louis, Jan. 27, 1919; s. Henry Theodore and Edith (Platt) F.; m. Marion Harris Ford, July 9, 1942 (div. July 1951); children: Carol (dec. 1967), Marion Wilson; m. Elizabeth Lashly States, May 17, 1952 (div. July 1963); m. Jean O. Browne, Jan. 18, 1964 (div. Mar. 1976); m. Ruth Knight Schneider, Sept. 2, 1976. B.A., Yale U., 1940. Reporter, St. Louis Star-Times, 1940-41; v.p. Gardner Advt. Co., St. Louis, also N.Y.C., 1946-70; pres. Ralph Jones Advt., Inc., Cin., 1970-75; chmn. Fahlgren & Ferriss Advt., 1975-78; pub. Cin. Mag., 1979-80; v.p. The Angus Group, exec. search firm, 1980—; Former asso. lectr. English, Washington U., 1947-51, George Washington U., 1951-52; lectr. bus. communications U. Cin. Served to capt. CIC, AUS, 1941-45; capt. CIA, 1951-52. Mem. Advt. Club Cin. (pres. 1979), Am. Mktg. Assn. (chpt. pres. 1982-83). Republican. Episcopalian. Clubs: St. Louis Country; Cincinnati Country, Queen City (Cin.); Yale (N.Y.C.). Home: 3649 Traskwood Circle Cincinnati OH 45208

FERRO, WALTER, artist; b. N.Y.C., Oct. 6, 1925; s. Joseph Salvador and Mary Elizabeth (Potezna) F.; m. Lore Gausmann, Sept. 20, 1966; children—Elizabeth, Paula. Certificate, Bklyn. Mus. Art Sch., 1952. Art cons. Mobil Corp. One-man exhbns. include, Wakefield Gallery, N.Y.C., 1960, Dominican Coll., Racine, Wis., 1962, Kings Coll., Briarcliff, N.Y., 1967, group exhbns. include, Bklyn. Mus., 1953, U. Okla., 1959, Jersey City Mus., 1966, Phila. Mus.; represented in permanent collections, Met. Mus. Art. Served with USNR, 1942-44. Recipient Kenneth Hayes Miller Meml. award Audubon Artists, 1953; Kate W. Arms Meml. award Soc. Am. Graphic Artists, 1959; Guggenheim fellow, 1972. Address: Rural Route 2 Hoyt Rd Pound Ridge NY 10576

FERRY, ANDREW PETER, ophthalmic surgeon, medical educator; b. N.Y.C., June 15, 1929; s. John Francis and Ingrid (Hammer) F.; m. Mercedes Kobasa, Mar. 7, 1964. B.S., Manhattan Coll., 1950; M.D., Georgetown U., 1954. Intern Duke U. Hosp., 1954-55; resident in medicine U. Mich. Hosp., Ann Arbor, 1957-58; resident in ophthalmology N.Y. Hosp.-Cornell Med. Center, N.Y.C., 1958-61; spl. fellow Armed Forces Inst. Pathology, Washington, 1961-63; dir. corneal surgery service Eye Bank Jordan, Jerusalem, 1964; prof. ophthalmology, dir. ophthalmic pathology lab. Mount Sinai Sch. Medicine, City U. N.Y., 1965-77; prof. and chmn. dept. ophthalmology Med. Coll. Va. Va. Commonwealth U., 1978—; dir. ophthalmology Med. Coll. Va. Hosps., 1978—, prof. pathology, 1980—; practice medicine specializing in ophthalmic surgery and pathology; cons. Richmond VA Hosp., 1978—, Beth Israel Med. Center, 1967—; W. Yerby Jones lectr. State U. N.Y. Med. Sch., Buffalo, 1970; McLean lectr. N.Y. Acad. Medicine, 1973. Author: Ocular and Adnexal Tumors, 1972; co-author: Pathology and Systemic Disease, 1977; contbr. articles to med. publs. Served to capt. USAF, 1955-57. Recipient Kober medal Georgetown U., 1954, Billings medal AMA, 1965; decorated Knight Grand Priory British Realm Order of Hosp. St. John of Jerusalem; guest of honor European Ophthalmic Pathology Soc., 1978. Fellow Am. Acad. Ophthalmology (Merit award), A.C.S., N.Y. Acad. Medicine; mem. Am., N.Y. ophthalmol. socs., Assn. Research Vision and Ophthalmology, N.Y. Soc. Clin. Ophthalmology (sec. 1970-75, v.p. 1976, pres. 1977), Verhoeff Soc. (pres. 1979), Armed Forces Inst Pathology Alumni Assn. (pres. 1981), Am. Assn. Ophthalmic Pathologists, Assn. Univ. Profs. Ophthalmology, Alpha Omega Alpha. Clubs: Commonwealth (Richmond); N.Y. Athletic (N.Y.C.). Office: Medical Coll Va Va Commonwealth Univ Dept Ophthalmology Richmond VA 23298

FERRY, BRYAN, singer, songwriter; b. Eng., Sept. 26, 1945. Founder rock group, Roxy Music, 1970, reformed group, 1979; appeared in concert tours as solo musician and with group in, Europe, U.S.; albums with Roxy Music include Roxy Music, For Your Pleasure, Stranded, Country Life, Siren, Manifesto, Flesh and Blood, Avalon; solo albums include These Foolish Things, Another Time, Another Place, Let's Stick Together, The Bride Stripped Bare. Office: care EG Mgmt Inc 161 W 54th St New York NY 10019 *

FERRY, MILES YEOMAN (CAP), state senator; b. Brigham City, Utah, Sept. 22, 1932; s. John Yeoman and Alta (Cheney) F.; m. Suzanne Call, May 19, 1952; children: John, Jane Ferry Stewart, Ben, Helen, Sue. D.S.J., Utah State U., 1954. Rancher, Corinne, Utah, 1952; gen. mgr. J.Y. Ferry & Son, Inc.; mem. Utah Ho. of Reps., 1965-66, Utah Senate, 1967—, minority whip, 1975-76, minority leader, 1977-78, pres. senate, 1979—; mem. governing bd. Council State Govts., 1983-84. Pres. Brigham Jr. C. of C., 1956-61; v.p. Utah Jr. C. of C., 1960-61; nat. dir. Utah Jaycees, 1961-62; pres. Farm Bur. Box Elder County, 1958-59; commr., bd. dirs., mem. council com. Lake Bonneville council Boy Scouts Am. Named outsatnding young man of yr. Brigham City Jr. C. of C., 1957, outstanding nat. dir. U.S. Jaycees, 1962, outstanding young man in Utah Utah Jr. C. of C., 1961, outstanding young farmer, 1958, one of 3 outstanding young men of Utah, 1962; recipient award of merit Boy Scouts Am., 1976, alumni of yr. award Utah State U., 1981, award of merit Utah Vocat. Assn., 1981. Mem. Sons Utah Pioneers (dir. Box Elder chpt.), Phi Kappa Phi, Phi Kappa Alpha, Utah Cattlemen's Assn., Nat. Golden Spike Assn. (dir. 1958—). Republican. Office: Office of Pres Utah Senate State Capitol Salt Lake City UT 84114 Address: PO Box 70 Corinne UT 84307

FERRY, ROBERT DEAN, professional basketball team executive; b. St. Louis, May 31, 1937; s. Willard Francis and Elsie (Neuman) F.; m. Rita Brooks, June 25; children: Laura, Robert, Daniel. B.A., St. Louis U., 1959. Player Nat. Basketball Assn., 1959-70; asst. coach, scout

Washington (formerly Balt.) Bullets, 1968-73, gen. mgr., 1973—; mem. Md. Phys. Fitness Commn.; dir. Jefferson Bank & Trust. Active local Big Bros. Named NBA Gen. Mgr. of Yr. Sporting News, 1978-79, 81-82. Mem. Nat. Basketball Assn. Players Assn. Address: care Washington Bullets Capital Centre Landover MD 20785 *

FERRY, WILBUR HUGH, foundation consultant; b. Detroit, Dec. 17, 1910; s. Hugh Joseph and Fay (Rutson) F.; m. Jolyne Marie Gillier, Oct. 23, 1937 (div. 1972); children: Lucian (stepson), Denise, Fay Ferry Christiansen, Robin F. Cook; m. Carol Underwood Bernstein, 1973; stepchildren: Katherine, John. A.B., Dartmouth Coll., 1932; L.H.D., Starr King Sch., Berkeley, Calif., 1969. Instr. Choate Sch., 1932-33; newspaperman, 1933-35, 37-41; dir. publicity Eastern Air Lines, 1936; chief investigator in N.H. for OPA, 1942-44; cons. ILO, 1940-44; dir. pub. relations CIO-Polit. Action Com., 1944; partner Earl Newsom & Co., 1945-54; v.p. Center Study Democratic Instns., 1954-69, cons., 1969—. Author: The Corporation and The Economy, 1959, The Economy Under Law, 1961, Caught on the Horn of Plenty, 1962, What Price Peace, 1963, Masscomm as Educator, 1966, Farewell to Integration, 1967, Tonic and Toxic Technology, 1967, The Police State Is Here, 1969, The Zaca Manifesto, 1980; editor: Warming Up for Fifty Years, 1982, Letters from Tom, 1983. Address: PO Box 657 Scarsdale NY 10583

FERST, BARTON E., lawyer; b. Phila., Jan. 23, 1920; s. Abe and Helen (Kaufman) F. B.S. in Econs., U. Pa., 1940, LL.B., 1944; M.A. in Govt., La. State U., 1941. Bar: Pa. 1944. Assoc. Herman H. Krekstein, Phila., 1944-52, firm Blank & Rudenko, 1952-55; ptnr. Blank, Rome, Comisky & McCauley, Phila., 1955—; lectr. in field. Co-author: Basic Accounting for Lawyers, 1976. Vice pres. Fedn. Jewish Agys. of Greater Phila., 1973-76; bd. dirs. United Way, Phila., 1974-79; chmn. bd. overseers Gratz Coll., 1978-83. Mem. Pa., Phila. bar assns., Order of Coif. Office: Blank Rome et al 4 Penn Center Plaza 11th-13th Floors Philadelphia PA 19103

FERTEY, MAURICE C., automobile company executive. Pres. Am. Motors Can. Inc., Brampton, Ont. Office: Am Motors Can Inc 350 Kennedy Rd S Brampton ON Canada L6V 2M3§

FERTIG, HOWARD, publisher, editor; b. N.Y.C.; s. Benjamin and Rose (Mallman) F.; m. Ellen C. Bandler; children: Paul, Daniel. B.A., NYU. Book reviewer Village Voice, N.Y.C., 1956-57; editor Queens Post, N.Y.C., 1957-60; asst. editor Commentary mag., N.Y.C., 1960; editor Alfred A. Knopf, Inc., N.Y.C., 1961-62; chief editor Univ. Library Paperbacks, Grosset & Dunlap, Inc., N.Y.C., 1962-65; pres., editor-in-chief Howard Fertig, Inc., N.Y.C., 1966—. Mem. MLA, P.E.N., Am. Hist. Assn., Friends of Columbia Library. Home: 315 E 68th St New York NY 10021 Office: 80 E 11th St New York NY 10003

FERTIG, LAWRENCE, economist; b. N.Y.C., Mar. 19, 1898; m. Bertha Alexander, Aug. 1932. A.B., N.Y. U., 1919; A.M., Columbia, 1920. Founder Lawrence Fertig & Co., Inc., 1923, pres., 1923-60; syndicated econ. columnist, 1944—. Author: Prosperity Through Freedom, 1961. Trustee N.Y U., 1954—; pres. Alumni Fedn., 1950-52; chmn. bd. trustees Found. Econ. Edn. Mem. Mont Pelerin Soc., Phi Beta Kappa. Home: 2 Sutton Pl S New York NY 10022 Office: 50 E 42d St New York NY 10017

FERTIS, DEMETER GEORGE, civil engineering educator; b. Athens, Greece, July 25, 1926; s. George P. and Athanasia (Papazschari) F.; m. Vaslike J. Beltsos, July 26, 1953; children—Athanasia, Evaggelia. B.S., Mich. State U., 1952, M.S., 1955, D. Engring., 1964; diploma in engineering, Nat. Tech. U., Athens, 1962. Planner-in-charge Ohio, Army C.E., Greece, 1948-50; research engr. Mich. Hwy. Dept., Lansing, 1952-57; asst. prof. mechanics dept. Wayne State U., Detroit, 1957-63; vis. prof. Nat. tech. U., 1963-64; asso. prof. U. Iowa, 1964-66; prof. civil engring. U. Akron, Ohio, 1966—; cons. in field. Author: Tranverse Vibration Theory, 1961, Deflection and Vibration of Engineering Structures, 1964, Notes on Structural Dynamics, 1966, Dynamics of Structural Systems, Vol. 1, 1971, Vol. 2, 1972, Dynamics and Vibration of Structures, 1973; contbr. articles profl. publs. Mem. ASCE, Am. Soc. Engring. Edn., Ohio Planners-in-Charge, Am. Concrete Inst., Indsl. Math. Soc., N.Y. Acad. Scis., Contemporary Authors. Greek Orthodox. Home: 2961 Chamberlain Rd Akron OH 44313

FERY, JOHN BRUCE, manufacturing executive; b. Bellingham, Wash., Feb. 16, 1930; s. Carl Salvatore and Margaret Emily (Hauck) F.; m. Delores Lorraine Carlo, Aug. 22, 1953; children: John Brent, Bruce Todd, Michael Nicholas. B.A., U. Wash., 1953; M.B.A., Stanford U., 1955. Asst. to pres. Western Kraft Corp., 1955-56; prodn. mgr., 1956-57; with Boise Cascade Corp., Idaho, 1957—, pres., chief exec. officer, 1972-78, chmn. bd., chief exec. officer, 1978—; dir. Albertson, Inc., Idaho First Nat. Bank, Union Pacific Corp., Union Pacific R.R.; mem. adv. com. Chase Internat. Mem. adv. council Sch. Bus. Stanford U.; chmn. bd. trustees St. Alphonsus Hosp. Served with USN, 1950-51. Recipient Ernest Arbuckle award Sch. Bus. Stanford U., 1980; named Most Outstanding Chief Exec. Officer Fin. World, 1977, 78, 79, 80. Mem. Am. Paper Inst. (past chmn., mem. exec. com.). Clubs: Elks, Arid, Hillcrest Country, Link's, Arlington. Office: 1 Jefferson Sq Boise ID 83728 *

FESHBACH, HERMAN, physicist, educator; b. N.Y.C., Feb. 2, 1917; s. David and Ida (Lapiner) F.; m. Sylvia Harris, Jan. 28, 1940; children: Carolyn Barbara, Theodore Philip, Mark Frederick. B.S., CCNY, 1937; Ph.D., MIT, 1942; D.Sci., Lowell Tech. Inst., 1975. Tutor CCNY, 1937-38; instr. MIT, 1941-45, asst. prof., 1945-47, asso. prof., 1947-55, prof., 1955—, Cecil and Ida Green prof. physics, 1976-83, Inst. prof., 1983—, dir. Center for Theoretical Physics, 1967-73, head dept. physics, 1973-83; cons. AEC; chmn. nuclear sci. adv. com. of Dept. Energy and NSF, 1979-82. Author: (with P.M. Morse) Methods of Theoretical Physics, 1953, (with A. deShalit) Theoretical Nuclear Physics, 1974; also sci. articles tech. jours.; Editor: Annals of Physics. Recipient Harris medal Coll. City N.Y., 1977; John Simon Guggenheim Meml. Found. fellow, 1954-55; Ford fellow CERN, Geneva, Switzerland, 1962-63. Mem. Am. Phys. Soc. (chmn. div. nuclear physics 1970-71, divisional councillor 1974-78, exec. com. 1974-78, chmn. panel on pub. affairs 1976-78, v.p. 1979-80, pres. 1980-81, Bonner prize 1973), Nat. Acad. Scis., NRC, Am. Acad. Arts and Scis. (v.p. Class I 1973-76, pres. 1982-85). Home: 5 Sedgwick Rd Cambridge MA 02138

FESHBACH, SEYMOUR, psychology educator; b. N.Y.C., June 21, 1925; s. Joseph and Fannie (Katzman) F.; m. Norma Deitch, Aug. 16, 1947; children: Jonathan, Laura, Andrew. B.S., Coll. City N.Y., 1947; M.A., Yale U., 1948, Ph.D., 1951. Project dir. Army Attitude Assessment Br., 1951-52; from asst. prof. to asso. prof. U. Pa., Phila., 1952-63; prof. U. Colo., Boulder, 1963-64; prof. psychology U. Calif., Los Angeles, 1964—, chmn. dept., 1977—; dir. Fernald Sch., 1964-73; cons. CBS, Ednl. TV, 1972; vis. fellow Wolfson Coll., Oxford (Eng.) U., 1980-81. Author: Television and Aggression, 1970, Psychology, An Introduction, 1977; also others; co-author: Personality, 1982; editor: Aggression and Behavior Change: Biological and Social Processes, 1979; cons. editor: Jour. Abnormal Psychology, 1973—; Contbr. chpts. to books, articles to profl. jours. Served to 1st lt., inf. AUS, 1943-46; PTO. Recipient Ward medal Coll. City N.Y., 1947, Townsend Harris medal, Distinguished Alumnus award, 1972, Fellowship award Found. Fund Advancement of Psychiatry, 1980-81, Disting. Scientist award Calif. Psychol. Assn., 1983; NIMH grantee; NSF grantee. Fellow Am. Psychol. Assn.; mem. Western Psychol. Assn. (pres. 1976-77), AAAS, Soc. for Study of Social Issues, Soc. for Research in Child Devel., Internat. Soc. for Applied Psychology, Internat. Soc. for Study of Aggression, Internat. Soc. for Study of Behavior Devel., ACLU, Phi Beta Kappa. Democrat. Jewish. Home: 743 Hanley Ave Los Angeles CA 90049 Office: Dept Psychology U Calif 405 Hilgard Ave Los Angeles CA 90024

FESLER, DAVID RICHARD, banker; b. Mpls., Sept. 21, 1928; s. John K. and Elsie L. F.; m. Sherrill E.; children—Dael F. Norum, Nancy K., Janet C. B.B.A. with distinction, U. Minn., 1950. Pres. Lampert Yards, Inc., 1950-79, Liberty State Bank, St. Paul, 1950-82, chmn. bd., 1982—; treas. Mason City Builders Supply Co., Inc., 1975—, The Sussel Co., Inc., 1975-79; pres. Wim Co., St. Paul, 1952-79, Liberty Agency, Inc., 1952-75. Bd. dirs., mem. fin. com., exec. com. Shattuck Sch., Inver Grove Heights (Minn.) Planning Commn.; active Indianhead council Boy Scouts Am., St. Croix Valley council Girl Scouts U.S., YMCA, Salvation Army, Family Service, Edgcumbe Presbyn. Ch., Presbyn. Homes Minn. Mem. Ramsey County Hist. Soc., Beta Gamma Sigma, Phi Delta Theta. Club: St. Paul Athletic. Home: Route 2 Box 80 Hudson WI 54016 Office: 176 Snelling Ave N Saint Paul MN 55164

FESS, PHILIP EUGENE, accountant; b. Troy, Ohio, Nov. 25, 1931; s. Charles E. and Margaret (Furlong) F.; m. Suzanne E. Cuthbert, Sept. 17, 1955; children: Linda Marie, Virginia Sue, Martha Ann. B.S., Miami U., Oxford, Ohio, 1953; M.S., U. Ill., 1955, Ph.D., 1960. C.P.A., Ill. Asso. prof. accounting U. Ill. at Urbana, 1953-55, 57-68, prof. accountancy, 1968—, Arthur Andersen & Co. Alumni prof., 1975—, asso. dean, 1978-80. Author: (with C.R. Niswonger) Accounting Principles, 9th, 10th, 11th, 12th, 13th edits, 1966-81, (with C.R. Niswonger, J. Parker) Accounting Principles, Can. edit, 1975, 2d edit., 1980; contbr. articles to profl. jours. Treas. Champaign County (Ill.) Am. Cancer Soc., 1966-67; trustee Ill. C.P.A. Found., 1975-77. Served to 1st lt. USAF, 1955-57. Mem. Am. Inst. C.P.A.'s (auditing standards bd. 1980, 81), Ill. Soc. C.P.A.'s (dir. 1975-77), Am. Accounting Assn., U. Ill. Alumni Assn. (treas., dir. 1969—, acting chief exec. 1983), Phi Beta Kappa, Beta Alpha Psi, Delta Sigma Pi, Omicron Delta Kappa, Beta Gamma Sigma, Sigma Chi. Home: 2408 Melrose Dr Champaign IL 61820

FEST, THORREL BROOKS, educator, consultant; b. Audubon, Iowa, Aug. 23, 1910; s. Albert F. and Augusta (Boers) F.; m. C. Lucille Etzler, June 5, 1934; children—Stephen, Bruce. B.A., State Coll. Iowa, (now No. Iowa U.), 1932; M.Ph., U. Wis., 1938, Ph.D., 1952. Tchr. secondary schs. Griswold and Spencer, Iowa, 1932-39; asst. prof. U. N.D., 1939-40, Albion Coll., 1940-44; staff Manhattan Project, 1944-45; mem. extension faculty U. Tenn., 1945; asst. prof. U. Colo., 1945-53, asso. prof., 1953-58, prof., 1958-79, prof. emeritus, 1979—, acad. dean, 1979, chmn. dept. speech, 1960-68; vis. prof. Western State Coll., 1957, U. Hawaii, 1959, 63, Syracuse U., 1961; vis. lectr. U. New South Wales, Australia, spring 1970, summer 1975, Autonomous U. of Guadalajara, 1961-80; sr. vis. fellow Caulfield Inst. Tech., Melbourne, Australia, 1980-81; Cons. N.Am. Def. Command Hdqrs. Staff, 1956-71, U.S. C. of C., 1959-76, Colo. Div. Wildlife, B.C. Tchrs. Fedn., 1968-77, Colo. Tax Commn., 1965—; v.p. Nat. Center Communication Arts and Scis., 1965-78, program dir., 1966—; pres. Fest Farms, Inc., 1947-79. Author: (with Martin Cobin) Speech and Theater, 1964, Registry of Communications Research, 1970, (with R.V. Harnack and B.S. Jones) Group Discussion: Theory and Technique, 2d edit, 1977, (with J. Robbins) Cross Cultural Communications and the Trainer, 1976; also profl. articles. Bd. govs. Nat. Installment Bankers Inst., 1972-79; Mem. adv. com. Alexander Hamilton Bicentennial Commn., 1956-58; Chmn. bd. trustees Intercultural Sch. Rockies, 1968-71; mem. internat. founding com. Center for Audio Visual Instrn. via Satellite, 1968-79. Recipient Disting. Service award U. Colo., 1971, Disting. Alumni award No. Iowa U., 1978. Fellow Internat. Inst. Arts and Letters (hon.), Societè Internationale pour le Dėvelopment Des Organisations (hon.); mem. Nat. U. Extension Assn., Nat. Collegiate Players, Am. Forensic Assn. (1951-53), Adult Edn. Assn., Speech Communication Assn. (legislative council 1955-57, exec. council 1957-60, chmn. com. on curricula and certification 1963-66, legis. 1963-65, 67-69), Canadian Speech Assn., Colo.-Wyo. Acad. Sci., Am. Edn. Theatre Assn., AAUP (pres. chpt. 1960-62), Colo. (pres. state conf. 1962-64), Western (v.p.), Central, So. speech assns., Colo. Speech and Drama Assn. (Disting. Contbn. award 1981), Indsl. Communication Council, Indsl. Relations Research, Assn., Nat. Soc. Tng. and Devel., Internat. Communication Assn. (nat. council 1955-62, nat. pres. 1960-61), Internat. Soc. Gen. Semantics, Izaak Walton League, Delta Sigma Rho (editor Gavel 1949-53, nat. pres. 1953-57, distinguished award 1972), Lambda Delta Lambda, Kappa Delta Pi, Theta Alpha Phi. Home: 1546 Sunset Blvd Boulder CO 80302 *We must learn from the past although we cannot change it. The future is before us and everything we do affects it. As we aspire to goals that are both worthy and challenging, we must realize our interdependence with others and value their contributions and potentials.*

FETLER, ANDREW, author, educator; b. Riga, Latvia, July 24, 1925; came to U.S., 1939, naturalized, 1944; s. Basil Andreyevitch and Barbara (Kovalevski) Fetler-M.; m. Carol J. McMahon, Aug. 29, 1960; 1 son, Jonathan. Student, U. Chgo., 1946-48; B.A., Loyola U., Chgo., 1959; M.F.A., U. Iowa, 1964. Tchr. Master Fine Arts Program in English, U. Mass., Amherst, 1964—, now prof. English. Author: The Travelers, 1965, To Byzantium, 1976; contbr. fiction to lit. quars. Served with AUS, 1944-46. Recipient grants for fiction writing Iowa Industries, 1962-63; grantee Mass. Arts and Humanities Found., 1976, Nat. Endowment for Arts, 1976-77, 83-84, Guggenheim Found., 1978-79; recipient O. Henry awards, 1977, 84. Mem. Authors Guild, PEN Am. Center. Office: Dept English U Mass Amherst MA 01003

FETLER, PAUL, composer; b. Phila., Feb. 17, 1920; s. William Basil and Barbara (Kovalevsky) Fetler-M.; m. Ruth Regina Pahl, Aug. 13, 1947; children: Sylvia, Daniel, Beatrix. Mus.B., Northwestern U., 1943; Mus.M., Yale U., 1948; Ph.D., U. Minn., 1956. Instr. to prof. music theory and composition U. Minn., Mpls., 1948—; vis. composer, condr. and lectr. various colls. and univs. Composer Contrasts for Orchestra, 1958, Soundings, 1962, Jubilate Deo, 1963, Te Deum, 1963, Four Symphonies, 1948-67, Cantus Tristis, 1964; opera Sturge Maclean, 1965, A Contemporary Psalm, 1968, Cycles, 1970, The Words From the Cross, 1971, First Violin Concerto, 1971, Dialogue, 1973, Lamentations, 1974, Three Venetian Scenes, 1974, Six Pastoral Sketches, 1974, Dream of Shalom, 1975, Songs of the Night, 1976, Whitman Poems, 1975, Pastoral Suite, 1976, Celebration, 1976, Three Impressions, 1977, Five Piano Games, 1977, Sing Alleluia, 1978, Song of the Forest Bird, 1978, Six Songs of Autumn for guitar, 1979, Second Violin Concerto, 1980, Missa de Angelis, 1980, Serenade, 1981; Rhapsody for violin and piano, 1982; song cycle The Garden of Love, 1983; numerous sacred and secular choral compositions. Served with AUS, 1943-45. Recipient Guggenheim awards, 1953, 60, Soc. for Publ. Am. Music award, 1953, Yale U. Alumni Assn. certificate of merit, 1975, NEA award, 1975, 77; Ford Found. grantee, 1958. Mem. ASCAP (Ann. award 1962—). Home: 420 Mount Curve Blvd Saint Paul MN 55105 Office: 203 Scott Hall U Minn Minneapolis MN 55455 *Ultimately there is no way to explain a new work of art if it does not explain itself.*

FETNER, CHARLES ANTHONY, hospital administrator; b. Lineville, Ala., Feb. 12, 1951; s. Leon and Doris (Proctor) F.; m. Lynne Walker, Apr. 26, 1975; children: Matt, Molly. B.S., U. Ala.-Tuscaloosa, 1972; J.D., Jones Law Inst., Montgomery, Ala., 1976. Bar: Ala. 1977. Pub. auditor State Examiners, Montgomery, 1974-75; budget mgr. Ala. Dept. Mental Health, Montgomery, 1975-77; asst. dir. Bryce Hosp., Tuscaloosa, 1977-81, hosp. dir., 1981—. Bd. dirs. United Way, Tuscaloosa, 1983—. Mem. Ala. Bar Assn., ABA. Home: 93 Heritage Hills Tuscaloosa AL 35406 Office: Bryce State Hosp University Blvd Tuscaloosa AL 35403

FETNER, ROBERT HENRY, radiation biologist; b. Savannah, Ga., Feb. 22, 1922; s. William Westcott and Lucille Fedora (Goodrich) F.; m. Mary Carolyn Guiney, July 8, 1972; 1 dau., Amber. B.S., U. Miami, Fla., 1950, M.S., 1952; Ph.D., Emory U., 1955. Mem. faculty Ga. Inst. Tech., Atlanta, 1955—, prof. radiation biology, 1963—, dir., 1964-70; cons. in field. Contbr. articles in field to profl. jours. Served with AUS, 1942-45. Decorated Combat Inf. badge. Mem. Ga. Acad. Sci. (editor bull. 1960-64), Sigma Xi, Phi Kappa Phi. Presbyterian. Patentee computer digitizer. Address: 2219 Walker Dr Lawrenceville GA 30245 *My most rewarding career experience has been as a participant in the search for knowledge in science.*

FETRIDGE, CLARK WORTHINGTON, publisher; b. Chgo., Nov. 6, 1946; s. William Harrison and Bonnie-Jean (Clark) F.; m. Jean Hamilton Huebner, Apr. 19, 1980; 1 son, Clark Worthington. B.A., Lake Forest (Ill.) Coll., 1969; M.B.A., Boston Coll., 1971. Money market specialist Continental Ill. Nat. Bank, Chgo., 1971-73; with Dartnell Corp., Chgo., 1973—, sr. v.p., 1977-78, pres., 1978—. Author: Office Administration Handbook, 1975. Trustee Lake Forest Coll., Jacques Holinger Meml. Fund; mem. U.S. Found. Internat. Scouting; vice-chmn. Nat. Eagle Scout Assn.; mem. internat. com. Boy Scouts Am.; chmn. 1200 Club Ill.; bd. govs. United Republican Fund Ill.; Rep. candidate for Congress, 1972; del. Rep. Nat. Conv., 1976. Mem. Latin Sch. Chgo. Alumni Assn. (treas), Tau Kappa Epsilon. Republican. Episcopalian. Office: 4660 Ravenswood Ave Chicago IL 60640

FETRIDGE, WILLIAM HARRISON, corporate executive; b. Chgo., Aug. 2, 1906; s. Matthew and Clara (Hall) F.; m. Bonnie Jean Clark, June 27, 1941; children: Blakely (Mrs. Harvey H. Bundy III), Clark Worthington. B.S., Northwestern U., 1929; LL.D., Central Mich. U., 1954. Asst. to dean Northwestern U., 1929-30; editor Trade Periodical Co., 1930-31, Chgo. Tribune, 1931-34, H. W. Kastor & Son, 1934-35, Roche, Williams & Cleary, Inc., 1935-42; mng. editor Republican Mag., 1939-42; asst. to pres. Popular Mechanics mag., 1945-46, v.p., 1946, exec. v.p., 1953-59; v.p. Diamond T Motor Truck Co., Chgo., 1959-61; exec. v.p. Diamond T div. White Motor Co., 1961-65; pres. Dartnell Corp., Chgo., 1965-77, chmn. bd., 1977—; dir. Bank of Ravenswood, Chgo. Author: With Warm Regards, 1976; Editor: The Navy Reader, 1943, The Second Navy Reader, 1944, American Political Almanac, 1950, The Republican Precinct Workers Manual, 1968. Trustee Greater North Michigan Ave. Assn., 1949-58; Chmn. Ill. Tollway Dedication com., 1958; pres. United Republican Fund of Ill., 1968-73, 79-80; fin. chmn. Ill. Rep. Party, 1968-73; alt. del.-at-large Rep. Nat. Conv., 1956, del.-at-large, 1968, hon. del.-at-large, 1972; mem. Rep. Nat. Finance Com.; chmn. Midwest Vols. Nixon, 1960, Rep. Forum, 1958-60, Nixon Recount Com.; Trustee Jacques Holinger Meml. Assn., Am. Humanics Found.; mem. nat. exec. bd., nat. v.p. Boy Scouts Am., 1958-76, chmn. nat. adv. bd., 1976-77; vice chmn. World Scout Found., Geneva, 1977—; trustee Lake Forest Coll., 1969-77; pres. U.S. Found. for Internat. Scouting, 1971-79, hon. chmn., 1979—; past pres. trustees Latin Sch. Chgo.; chmn. bd. dirs. Johnston Scout Mus., North Brunswick, N.J.; mem. Am. com. Westminster Abbey Appeal. Served as lt. comdr. USNR, 1942-45. Decorated chevalier Grand Priory of Malta, Order St. John of Jerusalem; recipient Abraham Lincoln award United Republican Fund, 1980; Recipient Silver Antelope, Silver Beaver, Silver Buffalo Boy Scouts Am., 1956, Bronze Wolf award World Scout Conf., 1973, Distinguished Eagle award, 1976. Mem. Navy League U.S. (past regional pres.), Ill. C. of C., Ill. St. Andrew Soc. (Disting. Citizen award 1980), Newcomen Soc., Soc. Midland Authors, Beta Theta Pi. Clubs: The Casino, Chicago, Union League, Saddle and Cycle, Rotary (Chgo.); Capitol Hill (Washington); Chikaming Country (Lakeside, Mich.). Office: 4660 Ravenswood Ave Chicago IL 60640

FETT, EUGENE WERNER, banker; b. Austin, Minn., Mar. 18, 1932; s. Werner August and Isabelle Martha (Schumann) F.; m. Charlotte R. Fenske, May 1, 1966; 1 son, Michael Eugene. Grad. high sch. Teller Austin State Bank, Minn., 1950-53; operations analyst Northwest Bancorporation, Mpls., 1953-68, corp. sec., 1971-74; v.p. cash Third Northwestern Nat. Bank Mpls., 1974-80, sr. v.p., cashier, 1980—; v.p., controller Northwest Computer Services, Mpls., 1968-71. Lutheran (treas.). Home: 4805 Dunberry Ln Edina MN 55435 Office: 425 E Hennepin Av Minneapolis MN 55414

FETTER, ALEXANDER LEES, theoretical physicist; b. Phila., May 16, 1937; s. Ferdinand and Elizabeth Lean Fields (Head) F.; m. Jean Holmes, Aug. 4, 1962; children: Anne Lindsay, Andrew James. A.B., Williams Coll., 1958; B.A., Balliol Coll., Oxford U., 1960; Ph.D., Harvard U., 1963. Miller research fellow U. Calif., Berkeley, 1963-65; mem. faculty dept. physics Stanford U., 1965—, prof., 1974—, asso. dean undergrad. studies, 1976-79; vis. prof. Cambridge U., 1970-71; Nordita vis. prof. Tech. U., Helsinki, Finland, 1976. Author: (with J.D. Walecka) Quantum Theory of Many Particle Systems, 1971, Theoretical Mechanics of Particles and Continua, 1980. Alumni trustee Williams Coll., 1974-79. Rhodes scholar, 1958-60; NSF fellow, 1960-63; Sloan Found. fellow, 1968-72; Recipient W.J. Gores award for excellence in teaching Stanford U., 1974. Fellow Am. Phys. Soc., AAAS; mem. Sigma Xi. Home: 904 Mears Ct Stanford CA 94305 Office: Physics Dept Stanford Univ Stanford CA 94305

FETTER, RICHARD ELWOOD, industrial company executive; b. Lewisburg, Pa., Feb. 25, 1923; s. Elwood M. and Emily (Rogers) F.; m. Mary Virginia Gabriel, June 22, 1947; 1 dau., Molly Elizabeth. B.S. in Commerce and Finance, Bucknell U., 1947. With Gen. Electric Co., 1947-64, fin. mgr. indsl. heating dept., Shelbyville, Ind., 1954-64; controller F.W. Dodge Co. div. McGraw- Hill, Inc., 1964-65, v.p., 1965-67; financial v.p., treas. Standard & Poor's Corp., 1967-70; v.p. fin., adminstr. Research-Cottrell, Inc., Bedminster, 1970-75; v.p. fin., sec.-treas. Debron Corp., St. Ann, Mo., 1975-81; v.p. fin. Fasco Industries, Inc., Boca Raton, Fla., 1981—. Mem. fin. adv. com. Chatham Twp., 1971-74; Bd. dirs. Shelby County United Fund, 1963-64. Served with USAAF, 1945-47. Decorated Air medal. Mem. Financial Execs. Inst., Am. Soc. Corp. Secs., Phi Gamma Delta, Omicron Delta Kappa. Presbyn. (trustee 1960-63). Clubs: Rotarian (Shelbyville) (dir. 1960-61); Boca Raton Hotel and Club (Boca Raton, Fla.)). Home: 3512 Pine Haven Circle Boca Raton FL 33431 Office: Fasco Industries Inc 601 N Federal Hwy Boca Raton FL 33432

FETTER, ROBERT BARCLAY, administrative sciences educator; b. Berwyn, Ill., May 6, 1924; s. Russell M. and Dorothy (Dupuis) F.; m. Audrey Louise Lillard, Feb. 7, 1951; children: Sarah Anne, Robert Alan, Martha Sue. B.S., Va. Poly. Inst., 1947; M.B.A., Ind. U., 1949, D.B.A., 1952; M.A. (hon.), Yale U., 1963. Instr., asst. prof. Ind. U., 1949-53; asst. prof. Mass. Inst. Tech., 1953-58; asso. prof. Yale U., 1958-63, prof. adminstrv. scis., 1963—, chmn. adminstrv. scis., 1969-

72; dir. Health Systems Mgmt. Group, Sch. Orgn. and Mgmt., 1976—, Instn. Social and Policy Studies, 1976—; cons. Rand Corp., 1963-71, E.I. duPont de Nemours & Co., Inc., 1960-72, McKinsey & Co., Inc., 1960—; cons. editor R.D. Irwin, Inc., Homewood, Ill., 1960—, WHO, 1972-73; v.p. Puter Assos., Inc., 1971-77, chmn., 1977-82; v.p., dir. Health Systems Internat. Inc., 1982—; dir. Dead River Group of Cos., 1984—. Served with USNR, 1944-46. Ford Found. fellow, 1964. Fellow Acad. of Mgmt., Am. Inst. Decision Scis.; mem. Ops. Research Soc. Am., Inst. Mgmt. Scis. Home: 313 St Ronan St New Haven CT 06511 Office: 12 Prospect Pl New Haven CT 06520

FETTER, THEODORE HENRY, entertainment consultant; b. Ithaca, N.Y., June 10, 1906; s. Frank Albert and Martha (Whitson) F.; m. Suzanne Merandon Pleven, Apr. 26, 1946; children: Frank Albert II, (foster son) Patrick Alfred Pleven. Student, The George Sch.; A.B., Swarthmore Coll., 1928. V.p., nat. dir. programs ABC TV Network, 1956-68; curator theatre and music collection Mus. of City of N.Y., 1974-79, entertainment cons., 1979—. Actor: Abraham Lincoln, 1929, Garrick Gaieties, 1930, Jubilee, 1935, Many Mansions, 1936; lyric writer: The Little Show, 1930, The Show Is On, 1936, Naughty Naught, 1937, The Fireman's Flame, 1937, The Girl from Wyoming, 1938, Billy Rose's Aquacade, 1939, Cabin in the Sky, 1939; TV prodns. Your Hit Parade, 1950-53, Jack Paar Show, 1954-56, One Man Show, 1969-70, Secret Challenge, 1970-71; Published songs include Taking a Chance on Love. Mem. ASCAP, Nat. Acad. TV Arts and Scis., Am. Arbitration Assn., Soc. of Friends. Clubs: Seabright Lawn Tennis and Cricket, Seabright Beach, Coffee House. Co-producer of first live intercontinental TV program, U.S. to Europe via satellite, 1962. Home: 114 E 71st St New York NY 10021

FETTER, THEODORE SEARCH, management consultant; b. Phila., June 6, 1913; s. Theodore Search and Mabel Florence (Wicks) F.; m. Sarah Venable Walker, Oct. 7, 1944; children: Theodore W., Elizabeth A., John B. B.S. in Civil Enging, U. Pa., 1935; cert. elec. enging., Drexel U., 1937. With Phila. Electric Co., 1935-78, staff engr., mech. enging. div., 1953-56, exec. engr., enging. dept., 1956-60, asst. to pres., 1960-62, asst. to chmn. bd., 1962-75, corporate sec., 1975-78; mem. advisory com., civil and urban enging. dept. U. Pa., 1973—, chmn., 1973-80; mem. exec. com. Univ. City Sci. Center, 1972-79. Mem. distbn. com. Phila. Found., 1967-78, chmn. distbn. com., 1972-75; mem. steering com. Community Leadership Seminar, 1968-80; v.p. Crime Commn. of Phila., 1965-70. Served as lt. USNR, 1942-46. Fellow ASME. Republican. Presbyterian. Club: Merion Cricket (Haverford, Pa.). Home: 1606 Lark Lane Villanova PA 19085 Office: 2301 Market St Philadelphia PA 19101

FETTERMAN, JOHN HENRY, JR., naval officer; b. Ashland, Pa., Aug. 4, 1932; s. John Henry and Mary (Horvath) F. B.A., Albright Coll., 1954; grad., Naval War Coll., 1964-65; postgrad., Harvard U., 1981. Commd. ensign U.S. Navy, 1955, advanced through grades to rear adm., 1981; comdg. officer USS Roosevelt, Carrier Air Wing 8, USS Nimitz, 1975-76, USS LaSalle, 1977-78, Naval Base, Guantanamo Bay, Cuba, 1979-81, Tactical Wings Atlantic NAS Oceana, Va., 1981-83; comdr. tng. U.S. Atlantic Fleet, Norfolk, Va., 1983—. Decorated Legion of Merit (3), Meritorious Service medal. Lodge: Elk. Home: 1324 Carolyn Dr Virginia Beach VA 23451 Office: Comdr Tng US Atlantic Fleet Bldg N-30 Naval Sta Norfolk VA 23511

FETTEROLF, CHARLES FREDERICK, aluminum company executive; b. Franklin, Pa., July 18, 1928; s. Harry B. and Beryl (Linsey) F.; m. Frances Spang, Apr. 11, 1953; children: Regan J., Scott F. B.S. in Chemistry, Grove City Coll., 1952. Sales trainee Alcoa Aluminum Co., Pitts., 1952, chemist, gen. salesman, 1953, Louisville, 1959, San Francisco, 1961, industry asst. flexible packaging, 1965, div. sales mgr., 1965-69, asst. dist. sales mgr., Los Angeles, 1969; dist. sales mgr. Alcoa Aluminum, Phila., 1971; industry mgr. def. Alcoa Aluminum Co., Phila., 1974, gen. mgr. mktg., 1975, gen. mgr. ops., 1977, v.p., 1977, v.p. Alcoa smelting process project, 1979, v.p. ops., 1979, v.p. sci. and tech., 1981, exec. v.p. mill products, 1981, dir., pres., 1983—. Mem. vestry St. Stephen's Episcopal Ch., 1974—; bd. dirs. Grove City Coll.; trustee Shadyside Hosp.; mem. adv. bd. Coalition for Addictive Disease of S.W. Pa., 1982—. Served with USN, 1946-48. Recipient Alumni Achievementaward Grove City Coll., 1978. Clubs: Duquesne, Laurel Valley, Internat., Allegheny Country. Office: 1501 Alcos Bldg Pittsburgh PA 15219

FETTIG, LESTER ALAN, consultant, writer; b. Bklyn., May 28, 1947; s. Lester and Bertha (van der Heiden) F.; m. Ilka Astrid Krohn, Dec. 17, 1966; children: Leslee, Butch, Jake, Zara. B.S. (N.Y. State Regents scholar, Lockheed Nat. Enging. scholar), Calif. Inst. Tech., 1968; M.S. (Calif. Scholarship Commn. fellow), U. So. Calif., 1969; postgrad. (N.Y. State Regents fellow), Rensselaer Poly. Inst., 1970. Cons. Center for Naval Analysis, 1969-71; Rockefeller Younger scholar Brookings Inst., 1972; cons. U.S. Congressional Commn. on Govt. Procurement, Washington, 1971-73; mem. staff U.S. Senate Com. on Aero. and Space Scis., Washington, 1973; staff dir. subcom. on fed. spending practices Com. on Govt. Ops., 1973-74, staff dir. subcom. on fed. spending practices, efficiency and open govt., 1975-77; adminstr. for fed. procurement policy Office Mgmt. and Budget, Washington, 1977-79, internat. cons., writer, businessman, 1979—; hon. prof. Def. Systems Mgmt. Coll., 1979. Author: Federal Contracting, 1981; mem. editorial adv. bd., Govt. Exec. mag.; Washington editor: Mil. Electronics, 1981-82, Mil. Scis. and Tech., 1981-82. Pres. Saratoga Community Assn., 1980-81; chmn. Pohick Valley Fedn., 1981-82; v.p. governing bd. Mt. Vernon Center Mental Health.; bd. dirs. Residential Youth Services. Mem. Calif. Inst. Tech. Alumni Assn., Nat. Contract Mgmt. Assn., Nat. Security Indsl. Assn. (hon.). Home: 8016 West Point Dr Springfield VA 22153 *Cherish and use the personal freedom this country offers to grow and to be. Develop a strong sense of internal counsel and guiding principles to rely upon. Listen to wise people who will gladly share their learning, if only asked. Challenge yourself, take personal risks to keep your spirit and sense of adventure alive. Be always grateful to God for your special gifts and strengths, whatever they might be.*

FETZER, JOHN EARL, broadcasting executive, professional baseball team executive;; b. Decatur, Ind., Mar. 25, 1901; s. John Adam and Della Frances (Winger) F.; m. Rhea Maude Yeager, July 19, 1926. Student, Purdue U., 1921; A.B., Andrews U., 1927, U. Mich., 1929; LL.D., Western Mich. U., 1958, Kalamazoo Coll., 1972, Andrews U., 1980; Litt.D., Elizabethtown Coll., 1972; D.Eng. (hon.), Lawrence Inst., 1979. Owner, chmn. bd. Fetzer Broadcasting Co., 1930—, Fetzer TV Corp., Kalamazoo-Grand Rapids, Mich., 1970—, Cornhusker TV Corp., Lincoln, Nebr., 1953—; chmn. bd., owner Detroit Tigers Am. League Baseball Club, 1956—, Fetzer Music Corp., Fetzer TV, Inc., Cadillac, Mich., 1958-79, John E. Fetzer, Inc., 1968—; chmn. Wolverine Cablevision, Inc., 1967—; dir. emeritus Am. Nat. Bank & Trust Co., Kalamazoo.; Chmn. Maj. League TV Com., 1963-71; U.S. Censor of radio, 1944-45; reporting to Gen. Eisenhower (engaged in ETO radio studies in), Eng., France, Russia, Germany, Italy and other European countries, 1945; fgn. corr. radio-TV-newspaper mission, Europe and Middle East, 1952; mem. mission Radio Free Europe, Munich, Germany, and Austrian-Hungarian border, 1956; mem. Broadcasters Mission to Latin-Am., Dept. State, 1962; Detroit Tiger Baseball tour of Japan, Okinawa, Korea, under auspices Dept. State, 1962; mem. A.P. tour, Europe, 1966; Dept. State del. Japanese-U.S. TV Treaty, 1972; mem. adv. bd. N.Am. Service, Radio Diffusion Française, Paris, 1946-47. Author: One Man's Family, 1964, The Men from Wengen and America's Agony, 1972; Contbr.: Radio and Television Project, Columbia, 1953. Trustee Kalamazoo Coll., 1954—. Recipient Broadcast Pioneers award, 1968; Distinguished service award Nat. Assn. Broadcasters, 1969; Mich. Frontiersman award, 1969; Fourth Estate award Am. Legion, 1972; citation Mich. Legislature, 1972; Tiger 75th Anniv. award, 1976; Mich. Legis. citation, 1976; Nebr. Pub. TV citation, 1976; Abe Lincoln Railsplitter award, 1979. Fellow Royal Soc. Arts London; mem. Nat. Assn. Broadcasters (chmn. TV bd. 1952), C. of C. (past pres., Summit award 1977), Nat. Geneal. Soc., Acad. Polit. Sci., Am. Soc. Mil. Engrs., I.E.E.E. (life mem.), Internat. Radio and TV Execs. Soc., Broadcast Pioneers (19th Mike award 1981), Alpha Kappa Psi. Presbyn. Clubs: Mason (33 deg., Shriner), Elk., Park, Kalamazoo Country (Kalamazoo); Economic, Detroit Athletic, Press, Detroit (Detroit); Tucson Country. Office: Kalamazoo MI 49008 also Tiger Stadium Detroit MI 48216

FETZNER, RICHARD WALTER, oil company executive; b. St. Joseph, Mo., Mar. 22, 1929; s. Walter G. and Mildred (Conner) F.; m. Reva Spohr, Dec. 27, 1951; children: Charles Richard, Caron Ann, William Walter. B.A., Augustana Coll., Rock Island, Ill., 1951; M.S., U. Wis., 1956, Ph.D., 1958; M.B.A., Drexel U., Phila., 1970. Geologist, Standard Oil Co. Ohio, Oklahoma City, 1956; research mgr. Sun Oil Co., Dallas, 1958-68, mgr. orgn. analysis, St. Davids, Pa., 1968-70; v.p., gen. mgr. Peruvian Sun Oil Co., Lima, 1970-74; chief geologist Sun Oil Internat., Inc., Phila., 1974-75; pres. Sun Transp., Inc., Wayne, Pa., 1975-77, Sun Overseas Transp. Ltd., 1975-77, Sunoco Terminals, Inc., 1975-77, Sun Internat., Inc., 1977-79, Sun Exploration & Prodn. Co., Dallas, 1981—; group v.p. Sun Co., Inc., Radnor, Pa., 1979. Contbr. articles profl. jours. Served with USNR, 1951-55. Mem. Am. Assn. Petroleum Geologists, Am. Inst. Profl. Geologists, Am. Petroleum Inst., Tex. Mid Continent Oil and Gas Assn. Home: 7210 Elmridge Dr Dallas TX 75240 Office: 5420 LBJ Freeway Two Lincoln Ctr Dallas TX 75240

FEUCHT, DONALD LEE, research institute executive; b. Akron, Ohio, Aug. 25, 1933; s. Henry George and Dorothy Fern (Kroeger) F.; m. Janet Wingerd, Aug. 16, 1958; children: Lynn Janet, Paul Henry. B.S., Valparaiso U., 1955; M.S., Carnegie Inst. Tech., 1956, Ph.D., 1961. Electronics engr. Convair, San Diego, 1956; instr. elec. enging. Carnegie-Mellon U. (formerly Carnegie Inst. Tech.), Pitts., 1958-61, asst. prof., 1961-65, assoc. prof., 1965-69, prof., assoc. head dept., 1969-73, prof. elec. enging., assoc. dean, 1973-77; chief advanced materials research and devel. br. Dept. Energy, Washington, 1977-78; mgr. photovoltaic program office Solar Energy Research Inst., Golden, Colo., 1978-80, mgr. photovoltaics div., 1980-81, acting dir. for research and devel., 1981, dep. dir., 1981—; research scientist IBM Research Center, Yorktown Heights, N.Y., 1961; cons. Power Components Inc., Scottsdale, Pa., 1965-67, PPG Industries, Pitts., 1967-69, Essex Internat., 1967-74. Author: (with A.G. Milnes) Heterojunctions and Metal Semiconductor Junctions, 1972; Contbr. sci. publs. Recipient Alumni award Valparaiso U., 1979. Fellow IEEE (past treas., dir. Pitts.), Group Electron Devices (past chmn. Pitts.); mem. Am. Phys. Soc., Electrochem. Soc., Sigma Xi, Phi Kappa Phi, Tau Beta Pi, Theta Chi. Patentee method for making semicondrs. for solar cells. Home: 8102 W 22d Way Lakewood CO 80215

FEUCHTWANG, THOMAS EMANUEL, physics educator; b. Budapest, Hungary, May 21, 1930; came to U.S., 1950, naturalized, 1972; s. Benno Meir and Rose Rachel;; s. Benno Meir and Schwartz F.; m. Sheila Shulamit Winer, Sept. 1, 1953; children: Orna, Daphna, Jonathan, Ilani. B. in E.E., Ga. Tech. U., 1953; M.S. in E.E., Calif. Tech. U., 1954; Ph.D. in E.E., Stanford U., 1960. Research asst. Microwaves Lab., Stanford U., 1954-59; research asso., postdoctoral fellow dept. physics U. Ill., Urbana, 1960-62; asst. prof. physics U. Minn., Mpls., 1962-65; asso. prof. physics Pa. State U., University Park, 1965-70, prof., 1970—; vis. prof. U. Tel Aviv, 1971-72; vis. Lady Davis prof. Technion, Israel Inst. Tech., 1978-79; vis. prof. U. Hawaii, Manoa, 1980-81. Contbr. numerous articles to profl. jours. Served with Israeli Def. Force, 1948-50. Francis E. Cole fellow, 1953-54. Fellow Am. Phys. Soc., Sigma Xi; mem. Tau Beta Pi, Eta Kappa Nu, Phi Kappa Phi. Democrat. Jewish. Club: B'nai B'rith. Office: 104 Davey Laboratory Pennsylvania State University University Park PA 16802

FEUER, CY, theatrical and motion picture exec.; b. N.Y.C., Jan. 15, 1911; s. Herman and Ann (Abrams) F.; m. Posy Greenberg, Jan. 20, 1945; children—Robert, Jed. Student, Inst. Mus. Art Julliard Found., 1928-32. Head music dept. Republic Pictures, 1938-42, 45-47; partner Feuer and Martin Prodns., N.Y.C., 1947—. Theatrical prodns. include Where's Charley, 1948, Guys and Dolls, 1950, Can-Can, 1953, The Boy Friend, 1954, Silk Stockings, 1955, Whoop-Up, 1958, How To Succeed in Business Without Really Trying, 1961 (Pulitzer prize for drama), Little Me, 1962, Skyscraper, 1965, Walking Happy, 1966, The Goodbye People, 1968, The Act, 1977; producer: motion pictures Cabaret, 1972 (winner 8 Acad. awards), Piaf, 1975; mng. dir., Los Angeles-San Francisco Civic Light Opera Assn., 1975. Office: 505 Park Ave New York NY 10022

FEUER, HENRY, emeritus educator, chemist; b. Stanislau, Austria, Apr. 4, 1912; came to U.S., 1941, naturalized, 1946; s. Jacob and Julia (Tindel) F.; m. Paula Berger, Jan. 19, 1946. M.S., U. Vienna, Austria, 1934, Ph.D., 1936. Postdoctoral fellow U. Paris, France, 1939; with dept. chemistry Purdue U., Lafayette, Ind., 1943-79, prof. chemistry, 1961-79, prof. emeritus, 1979—; vis. prof. Hebrew U., Jerusalem, Israel, 1964, Indian Inst. Tech., Kanpur, India, 1971, Peking (China) Inst. Tech., 1979. Mng. editor: Organic Nitro Chemistry, 1982—. Fellow AAAS; mem. Am. Chem. Soc., Chem. Soc., Sigma Xi, Phi Lambda Upsilon. Research, publs. in organic nitrogen compounds; discovered new methods for syntheses nitro compounds, cyclic hydrazides; research on mechanism of these reactions. Home: 726 Princess Dr West Lafayette IN 47906 Office: Dept Chemistry Purdue U Lafayette IN 47907

FEUER, LEO JOSEPH, manufacturing company executive; b. Bad Aussee, Austria; came to U.S., 1937, naturalized, 1942; s. Leon and Margaret Rose (Pengg) F.; m. Marguerite Taylor Brink, June 15, 1946; children: Robert, Jonathan, Gretchen, Charles, Elisabeth. B.S., Mass. Inst. Tech., 1943. Engr. Atlantic Research Assn., Newton, Mass., 1943-46; dir. research and devel. William Carter Co., Needham Heights, Mass., 1946-67, exec. v.p., 1967-70, pres., 1970-73, chmn., 1973—; dir. Shawmut Needham Bank. Mem. ASTM, Am. Apparel Mfrs. Assn. (dir. 1971—, 1st vice chmn. 1981, chmn. 1982-83). Roman Catholic. Clubs: Brae Burn Country, Longwood Cricket. Home: 43 Fairmont Ave Newton MA 02158 Office: 963 Highland Ave Needham Heights MA 02194

FEUER, LEWIS S., sociologist, educator, philosopher; b. N.Y.C., Dec. 7, 1912; s. Joseph and Fannie (Weidner) F.; m. Kathryn Jean Beliveau, Oct. 13, 1946; 1 dau., Robin Kathryn (Mrs. Miller). B.S., Coll. City N.Y., 1931; A.M., Harvard U., 1932, Ph.D., 1935. Asst. in philosophy Harvard, 1935-37; instr. philosophy Coll. City N.Y., 1939-42; faculty Vassar Coll., 1946-51, U. Vt., 1951-57; prof. philosophy and social sci. U. Calif. at Berkeley, 1957-66; prof. sociology U. Toronto, 1966-76; Univ. prof. sociology and govt. U. Va., Charlottesville, 1976—; cons. Radio Liberty, Fgn. Service Inst., Internat. Communication Agy., 1970—. Author: Psychoanalysis and Ethics, 1955, Spinoza and the Rise of Liberalism, 1958, The Scientific Intellectual, 1963, The Conflict of Generations, 1969, Marx and the Intellectuals, 1969, Einstein and the Generations of Science, 1974, Ideology and the Ideologists, 1975; Editor: Marx and Engels, Basic Writings on Politics and Philosophy, 1959. Served with AUS, 1942-46. Ford fellow for Advancement of Edn., 1954-55; exchange scholar Inst. Philosophy, Soviet Acad. Sci., Moscow, USSR, 1963; recipient Bowdoin medal Harvard, 1935. Mem. Am. Sociol. Assn., Am. Philos. Assn., Am. Polit. Sci. Assn., Am. Jewish Hist. Soc. (Leo Wasserman award 1982), Assn. Sociol. Study of Jewry, Cambridge Union U. Tchrs. (sec. 1935-37), AAUP (pres. Vt. chpt. 1955-56), Authors Guild, Phi Beta Kappa. Research, numerous publs. Home: 1519 Dairy Rd Charlottesville VA 22903

FEUER, PAULA BERGER, physicist, educator; b. N.Y.C., Feb. 11 1922; d. Morris and Lottie (Greenwald) Berger; m. Henry Feuer, Jan. 19, 1946. B.A., Hunter Coll., 1941; M.S., Purdue U., 1946, Ph.D., 1951. Instr. physics Purdue U., 1946-55, asst. prof. enging. scis., 1955-57, asso. prof., 1957-65, prof. aeros., astronautics and enging. scis., 1965—; vis. prof. physics Hebrew U., Jerusalem, 1964. Contbr. articles to sci. jours. Active Vols. for Youth. Mem. League Women Voters, Soc. Enging. Sci. (founding dir., treas. 1964-69), Am. Phys. Soc., Sigma Xi. Pi Mu Epsilon, Sigma Pi Sigma. Club: Canadian Alpine. Home: 726 Princess Dr West Lafayette IN 47906

FEUERLEIN, WILLY JOHN ARTHUR, economist, educator; b. Zurich, Switzerland, May 8, 1911; came to U.S., 1933, naturalized, 1940; s. Gustave Otto and Kate Elizabeth (Dickes) F.; m. Margaret Elizabeth Gammons, Apr. 11, 1942; 1 dau., Elizabeth. A.B., George Washington U., 1935, M.A., 1935; Ph.D., Yale U., 1939; LL.D. hon., Fla. Atlantic U., 1983. Statistician Fed. Res. Bank of N.Y., 1940-42; economist Fgn. Econ. Adminstrn., Washington, 1942-44; fgn. trade specialist E. I. du Pont de Nemours & Co., Wilmington, Del., 1944-50; lectr. econs. and bus. adminstrn. Temple U., 1946-47, U. Del., 1947-49; mem. U.S. Econ. and Financial Mission to Peru, 1949-50; cons. UN and Internat. Monetary Fund, 1950-52; head UN Tech. Assistance Mission to El Salvador, 1952-56; vis. prof. econs. U. Fla., 1956-57; indsl.-economist ICA, U.S. Ops. Mission, Karachi, Pakistan, 1957-62; asst. dir. for devel. Office Brazil Affairs, AID State Dept., Washington, 1962-65; prof. econs. Fla. Atlantic U., Boca Raton, 1965-81, prof. emeritus, 1981—, chmn. dept., 1974-81, Rockefeller research fellow, 1938-39. Author: (with Hannan) Dollars in Latin America, 1940; also; UN publ., articles profl. jours. Mem. Am. Econ. Assn., Fla. Atlantic U. Found., English Speaking Union. Home: 6035 S Verde Trail Apt J-111 Boca Raton FL 33433 Office: Dept Econs Fla Atlantic U Boca Raton FL 33431

FEUERSTEIN, DONALD MARTIN, lawyer; b. Chgo., May 30, 1937; s. Morris Martin and Pauline Jean (Zagel) F.; m. Dorothy Rosalind Sokolsky, June 3, 1962 (dec. Mar. 1978); children: Eliza Carol, Anthony David. B.A. magna cum laude, Yale U., 1959, J.D., Harvard U., 1962. Bar: N.Y. 1962. Asso. firm Cleary, Gottlieb, Steen & Hamilton, N.Y.C., 1962-63; law clk. to U.S. dist. judge, N.Y.C., 1963-65; asso. firm Saxe, Bacon & Bolan, N.Y.C., 1965; asst. gen. counsel, chief counsel instl. investor study SEC, Washington, 1966-71; partner, counsel Salomon Bros., N.Y.C., 1971-81; mng. dir., sec. Salomon Bros. Inc., 1981—; sec. Salomon Bros. Found., Inc., 1971—; mem. adv. council U. Pa. Center for Study of Fin. Instns., 1973—; mem. adv. bd. U. Calif. Securities Regulations Instn., 1972-76. Mem. editorial adv. bd.: Securities Regulation Law Jour, 1973—; bd. editors: Nat. Law Jour, 1978—. Bd. dirs. 1st All Children's Theatre, 1976—, chmn., 1976-82; mem. vis. com. Northwestern U. Law Sch., 1980—; bd. dirs. Arts and Bus. Council, 1981—, Legal Aid Soc., 1983—; trustee Summer Camp Fund, 1982—, Dalton Sch., 1983—. Served with U.S. Army, 1962-63. Mem. Am., N.Y. State bar assns., Assn. Bar City N.Y., Phi Beta Kappa, Pi Sigma Alpha. Club: Harvard. Home: 778 Park Ave New York NY 10021 Office: 1 New York Plaza New York NY 10004

FEUERWERKER, ALBERT, history educator; b. Cleve., Nov. 6, 1927; s. Martin and Gizella (Feuerwerker) F.; m. Yi-tsi Mei, June 11, 1955; children: Alison, Paul. A.B., Harvard U., 1950, Ph.D., 1957. Lectr. history U. Toronto, Ont., Can., 1955-58; research fellow Harvard U., Cambridge, Mass., 1958-60; asso. prof. history U. Mich., Ann Arbor, Mich., 1960-63, prof., 1963—, chmn. dept., 1984—, dir. Center for Chinese Studies, 1961-67, 72-83; directeur d'études École des Hautes Etudes en Scis. Sociales, Paris, 1981; vis. scholar Acad. Social Scis., Shanghai, China, 1981; mem. joint com. on contemporary China, Social Sci. Research Council-Am. Council Learned Socs., 1966-78, 80-83, chmn., 1970-75; mem. com. on scholarly communication with the People's Republic of China, Nat. Acad. Scis.-Social Sci. Research Council-Am. Council Learned Socs., 1971-78, 81-83, vice chmn., 1975-78. Author: China's Early Industrialization, 1958, History in Communist China, 1968, The Chinese Economy 1870-1911, 1969, Rebellion in 19th Century China, 1975, The Foreign Establishment in China, 1976, Economic Trends in the Republic of China, 1977, Chinese Social and Economic History from the Song to 1900, 1982; bd. editors: Am. Hist. Review, 1970-75, The China Quar, 1967—, Comparative Studies in Soc. and History, 1964—. Served with AUS, 1946-47. Nat. Endowment for the Humanities fellow, 1971-72; Social Sci. Research Council-Am. Council of Learned Socs. fellow, 1962-63. Fellow AAAS; mem. Assn. for Asian Studies, Am. Hist. Assn., Nat. Com. on U.S.-China Relations. Home: 1224 Ardmoor Ave Ann Arbor MI 48103 Office: Center for Chinese Studies U of Mich Lane Hall Ann Arbor MI 48109

FEUERZEIG, HENRY LOUIS, territorial judge; b. Chgo., Dec. 12, 1938; s. Samuel Alexander and Esther Fleeger; m. Penny Zweigenhaft, Apr. 8, 1967; children: Paul Lawrence, Darcy Elizabeth. B.S. tchr.'s certificate (Evans scholar), U. Wis., 1962; J.D., George Washington U., 1970. Bar: D.C., V.I., Fla., Md. Reporter various newspapers, Dubuque, Iowa, Chgo., Madison, Wis., Cin. and Washington, 1962-64, 65-67; assoc. firm Sachs, Greenebaum, Frohlich & Tayler, Washington, 1970-72; asst. atty. gen. V.I. Dept. Law, St. Thomas, 1972-73, chief civil and adminstrv. law div., 1973-74, 1st asst. atty. gen., 1974; partner firm Feuerzeig & Zebedee, St. Thomas, 1974-76; judge Territorial Ct. V.I., St. Thomas, 1977—; del., chmn. jud. powers and functions com. 4th V.I. Constl. Conv., 1981; mem. supervisory bd. V.I. Law Enforcement Planning Commn., 1978—; mem. V.I. Juvenile Code Revision Task Force, 1978-83, V.I. Criminal Code Revision Task Force, 1978—. Mem. Montgomery County (Md.) Democratic State Central Com., 1970-72; mem. V.I. Indsl. Devel. Commn., 1976; bd. dirs. Environ. Studies Program, St. Thomas, 1977—; bd. reps. Hebrew Congregation of St. Thomas, 1983—. Sigma Delta Chi scholar, 1962; Congressional fellow Am. Polit. Sci. Assn., 1964-65. Mem. ABA, D.C. Bar Assn., Fla. Bar Assn., V.I. Bar Assn. (pres. 1976), Am. Judges Assn., Nat. Council Juvenile and Family Ct. Judges, Am. Law Inst., Am. Judicature Soc., Assn. Trial Lawyers Am., Sigma Delta Chi, Order of Coif, Phi Delta Phi. Jewish. Club: Rotary. PO Box 4823 Saint Thomas VI 00801 Office: Territorial Ct PO Box 70 Saint Thomas VI 00801

FEUILLE, RICHARD HARLAN, lawyer; b. Mexico City, Mexico, June 10, 1920; s. Frank and Margaret (Levy) F.; m. Louann Johnston Hoover, Oct. 20, 1948; children: Louann H., Richard H., Robert R., Joseph L. (dec.), James M., Patrick F. (dec.), Margaret J. B.A., U. Va., 1947, LL.B., 1948. Bar: Tex. 1948. Assoc. Jones, Hardie, Grambling & Howell, El Paso, Tex., 1948-53; ptnr. Hardie, Grambling, Sims &

Feuille, El Paso, 1953-57; sr. ptnr. Scott, Hulse, Marshall & Feuille, El Paso, 1957—; Dir. El Paso Nat. Bank, Northgate Nat. Bank El Paso. Active United Fund El Paso, 1963—, founder, v.p. trust fund, 1969—, pres., 1968, 75—, bd. dirs., 1966—; pres. El Paso Community Concert Assn., 1961-67; mem. adv. council U. Tex. at El Paso, 1968—, mem. exec. com., 1968-70; Bd. dirs. St. Clement's Episcopal Parish Sch., El Paso; trustee YWCA, El Paso.; bd. dirs. El Paso Community Found., 1980—, pres., 1983—. Served to maj. USAAF, 1941-46; PTO. Mem. ABA (estate and gift tax com.), El Paso County Bar Assn. (pres. 1972-73), Tex. Bar Assn., Greater El Paso Tennis Assn. (bd. dirs.), Order Coif, Phi Beta Kappa, Omicron Delta Kappa. Episcopalian (vestryman, sr. warden). Clubs: Coronado Country, El Paso Tennis (El Paso) (pres. 1973). Home: 1021 Broadmoor St El Paso TX 79912 Office: 11th Floor El Paso Nat Bank Bldg El Paso TX 79901

FEULNER, EDWIN JOHN, JR., research foundation executive; b. Chgo., Aug. 12, 1941; s. Edwin John and Helen J. (Franzen) F.; m. Linda C. Leventhal, Mar. 8, 1969; children: Edwin John III, Emily V. B.Sc., Regis Coll., Denver, 1963; M.B.A., U. Pa., 1964; PH.D., U. Edinburgh, 1981; hon. degree, Nichols Coll., Dudley, Mass., 1981, Universidad Francisco Marraquin, Guatemala City, 1982, Hanyang U., Seoul, Korea, 1982. Richard Weaver fellow London Sch. Econs., 1965; pub. affairs fellow Hoover Instn., 1965-67; Confidential asst. to sec. def. Melvin Laird, 1969-70; adminstrv. asst. to U.S. Congressman Philip M. Crane, 1970-74; exec. dir. Republican Study Com., Ho. of Reps., 1974-77; pres. Heritage Found., Washington, 1977—, Inst. Research on Econs. of Taxation, 1977—; chmn. Inst. European Strategic and Def. Studies, London, 1979—; chmn. adv. com. on pub. diplomacy USIA; mem. sci. commn. Ctr. Applied Econ. Research, Rome; adv. council Inst. Economique de Paris; nat. adv. bd. Ctr. for Edn. and Research in Free Enterprise, Tex. A&M U. Author: Congress and the New International Economic Order, 1976, Looking Back, 1981, Conservatives Stalk the House, 1983; contbr. articles to profl. jours., chpts. to books. Trustee Manhattan Inst. Policy Research, N.Y.C., Lehrman Inst., N.Y.C., Intercollegiate Studies Inst., Rockford Inst., Roe Found., Am. Council on Germany. Mem. Am. Econs. Assn., So. Econs. Assn., Am. Polit. Sci. Assn., Internat. Inst. Strategic Studies, U.S. Strategic Inst., Transp. Research Forum, Phila. Soc. (treas. 1964-79, pres. 1982-83), Nat. Economists Club, Mont Pelerin Soc. (treas.). Republican. Roman Catholic. Clubs: Union League (N.Y.C.); University (Washington); Reform (London). Office: 214 Massachusetts Ave NE Washington DC 20002

FEVANG, LEROY CONRAD, pharmacist, assn. exec.; b. High Prairie, Alta., Can., Sept. 22, 1936; s. Siguard David and Pearl (Wakefield) F.; m. Patricia Russell, Aug. 31, 1957; children—Monty, Sharon. B.Sc., U. B.C., 1958, M.B.A., 1968. Mgr. Glacier Drugs Ltd., 1958-66; mgr. corp. pharmacy Cunningham Drugs Ltd., 1968-71; registrar Coll. Pharmacists B.C., 1971-78; exec. dir. Can. Pharm. Assn., Ottawa, 1978—. Dir. Narcotics Addiction Found. B.C., Pharmacy Exam. Bd. Can. Mem. B.C. Coll. Pharmacists, Can. Pharm. Assn., Conf. Pharmacy Registrars Can., Inst. Assn. Execs., Am. Soc. Assn. Execs. Anglican. Club: Ottawa Athletic. Office: 1815 Alta Vista Dr Ottawa ON K1G 3Y6 Canada

FEWELL, TERRY GLENN, moving co. exec.; b. Greenwood, Ind., Jan. 11, 1940; s. Wilbur Glenn and Martha Jean (Petrakos) F.; m. Johanna Theresa Planker, July 15, 1962; children—John Bradley, Jason Glenn, Jeffrey Joseph, Johanna Theresa, II. A.B., Wabash (Ind.) Coll., 1962; J.D., Ind. U., 1965. Bar: Ind. bar 1965, Ill. bar 1979. Atty., then gen. atty. N. Am. Van Lines, Inc., Ft. Wayne, Ind., 1965-76; v.p., gen. counsel Allied Van Lines, Inc., Broadview, Ill., 1976—. Mem. Ill. Bar Assn., Ind. Bar Assn. Republican. Lutheran. Home: Route 2 West County Line Rd Barrington IL 60010 Office: Allied Van Lines Inc 25th Ave and Roosevelt Rd Broadview IL 60153

FEY, DOROTHY (MRS. GEORGE JAY FEY), former assn. exec.; b. Chgo., Aug. 5, 1917; d. Charles H. and Lottie (Brousseau) F.; m. George Jay Fey, Oct. 1, 1957. Student, Bryant and Stratton Bus. Coll., Chgo. Acad. Fine Arts; also trademark registration, N.Y. U. Account exec. Steve Hannagan Assos., 1943-44; asst. to pres. Don Spencer Co., Inc., 1944-46; sec., dir. pub. relations, media dir. Hiram Ashe Advt. Inc., N.Y.C., 1946-51; exec. sec. U.S. Trademark Assn., 1952-59, exec. dir., 1959-81. Home: 3147 Buchanan St Hollywood FL 33021

FEY, HAROLD EDWARD, editor, clergyman; b. Elwood, Ind., Oct. 10, 1898; s. Edward Henry and Eva (Gant) F.; m. Golda Esper Conwell, July 20, 1922; children: Russell C., Gordon Edward (dec.), Constance Fey Thullen. A.B., Cotner Coll., 1922; B.D., Yale U., 1927; D.D. (hon.), Chgo. Theol. Sem., 1948; Litt.D., Park Coll., 1960; H.H.D., Culver Stockton Coll., 1963. Ordained to ministry Christian Ch. (Disciples of Christ), 1923; minister 1st Christian Ch., Hastings, Nebr., 1927-29; prof. Union Theol. Sem., Manila, 1929-32; editor World Call mag., Indpls., 1932-35, Fellowship mag.; also nat. exec. Fellowship Reconciliation, N.Y., 1935-40; field editor, then mng. editor Christian Century, Chgo., 1940-56, editor, 1956-64, contbg. editor, 1964—; prof. social ethics Christian Theol. Sem., Indpls., 1964-68, emeritus, 1968—; editor World Council Chs. ecumenical history com., 1968—; pres. Christian Century Found., 1956-64, Associated Ch. Press, 1951-52; editor In Common, newsletter; also book rev. editor World Call, 1964—. Author: The Lord's Supper: Seven Meanings, 1948, Cooperation in Compassion, 1966, Life-New Style, 1968, With Solemn Reverence, 1974, How I Read the Riddle (autobiography), 1982; editor: (with D'Arcy McNickle) Indians and Other Americans, 1959, The Ecumenical Advance, vol. II, 1970, Kirby Page, Social Evangelist, 1975. Served with U.S. Army, 1918. Recipient Disting. Service award Nat. Congress Am. Indians, 1955, citation Ill. chpt. ACLU, 1964, Leadership in Christan Journalism award Christian Ch., 1969; Disciples Peace Fellowship award, 1981; Sutphin lectr. Ind. Central Coll., 1972; Oreon E. Scott lectr. Christian Theol. Sem., 1973. Mem. Council Christian Unity, Cons. on Ch. Union, Sigma Delta Chi. Home: 770 Alden Rd Claremont CA 91711 *On the greatest matters, we have to choose between contradictory possibilities without the benefit of scientific certainty. Before half our questions are answered, we have to act, to come down on one side or the other. We have to do it ourselves; we cannot delegate our destiny. So we act, in faith. In Faith we define our relationships with other people and with the universe. In faith we make the commitments by which our fate is determined. In faith we choose to walk humbly with God or to walk proudly into nihilism. I walk, often stumbling, toward the light I believe is God.*

FEY, JOHN THEODORE, insurance company executive; b. Hopewell, Va., Mar. 10, 1917; s. Raymond B. and Ruth (St. Fultz) F.; m. Jane K. Gerber, Apr. 5, 1947 (dec); 1 son, John Theodore; m. Mary Callimanopulos, Aug. 1, 1976. Student, Washington and Lee U., 1935-37, LL.D., 1978; LL.B., U. Md., 1940; M.B.A., Harvard U., 1942; J.S.D., Yale U., 1952; LL.D., Middlebury Coll., Alma Coll., 1961, U. Vt., 1967, St. Augustins Coll., 1981. Bar: Md. 1940, D.C. 1953, Vt. 1959, N.Y. 1977. County atty., Md., 1947-49; faculty Law Sch., George Washington U., 1949-53, dean, 1953-56, professorial lectr., 1956; clk. Supreme Ct. U.S., 1956-58; pres. U. Vt., 1958-64, U. Wyo., 1964-66, Nat. Life Ins. Co., 1966-74, also dir., 1966-74; chmn. bd. Equitable Life Assurance Soc. U.S., N.Y.C., 1974-82, Nat. Bank N.Am., Fidelity Union Life Ins. Co.; dir. Consol. Foods Co., Certain-Teed Co.; mem. Md. Legislature, 1946-50. Trustee Getty Mus., Malibu, Calif. Served to col. USMCR, 1942-46. Mem. Am. Coll. Life Underwriters (chmn. bd. trustees), Order of Coif. Home: Sugar House Hill Stowe VT 05672

FEY, THOMAS HOSSLER, soft drink co. exec.; b. Chgo., Sept. 17, 1939; s. Stanley Edgar-All and Mary (Hossler) F.; m. Carolyn Hurlbut Lenfestey, Dec. 30, 1973; children—Josephine B., Caroline H. B.S., Pa. State U., 1962; M.B.A., Northwestern U., 1967. Group product mgr. United Brands, Boston, 1971-73; pres. A & W Beverages Inc., N.Y.C., 1973—; dir. Am. Concrete Products, F. Hurlbut Co. Served with USAF, 1962-66. Mem. Am. Mgmt. Assn., Am. Mktg. Assn. Office: 1271 Avenue of the Americas New York NY 10020 *

FEYERABEND, PAUL KARL, philosopher, educator; b. Vienna, Austria, Jan. 13, 1924; came to U.S., 1959. Student, Vienna Mus. Acad.; Dr. Phil., U. Vienna, 1951; U. London, 1952-53; D.H.L. (hon.), Loyola U., Chgo., 1970. Lectr., Vienna Inst. Scis. and Fine Arts, 1951-56, Bristol (Eng.) U., 1955-59; fgn. cons. Library of Congress, Washington, 1952-53; assoc. prof. philosophy U. Calif., Berkeley, 1959-62, prof., 1962—, Humanities Research fellow, 1972-73, Humantities Research prof., 1975-76; chmn. dept. history and philosophy of sci. Univ. Coll., London, 1968-70, Free U. Berlin, 1968-70; prof. philosophy Yale U., New Haven, 1969-70; prof. philosophy of sci. Fed. Inst. Tech., Zurich, Switzerland, 1979—; spl. lectr. Am. Council of Learning, 1968-69; numerous vis. appointments in field and otherwise. Author: Against Method, 1975, Science in a Free Society, 1978, Erkenntnis für freie Menschen, 1979, Probleme des Empirismus, 1980, Philosophical Papers, 2 vols., 1980, Wissenschaft als Kunst, 1984; contbr. numerous articles in philosophy, theatre, physics, history of sci. and history of ideas to profl. and non-profl. jours. Served to lt. German Army, 1942-45. Decorated Iron Cross; recipient Austrian Pres. Scis. and Fine Arts award, 1952; fellow Minn. Center Philosophy of Sci., 1956, 62, 64, 70, 76; NSF grantee, 1962, 65, 68, 76. Mem. Busoni Soc. (exec. v.p.). Office: Dept Philosophy U Calif Berkeley CA 94720 *My life has been the result of accidents, not of goals and principles. My intellectual work forms only an insignificant part of it. Love and personal understanding are much more important for I believe, with I.B. Singer, that the story of creation is basically a love story. Leading intellectuals with their zeal for objectivity kill these personal elements. They are the criminals, not the liberators, of mankind.*

FEYNMAN, RICHARD PHILLIPS, physicist; b. N.Y.C., May 11, 1918; s. Melville Arthur and Lucille (Phillips) F. B.S., Mass. Inst. Tech., 1939; Ph.D., Princeton, 1942. Staff atomic bomb project Princeton, 1942-43, Los Alamos, 1943-45; asso. prof. theoretical physics Cornell U., 1945-50; prof. theoretical physics Calif. Inst. Tech., 1950—. Author Quantum Electrodynamics, Theory of Fundamental Processes, Character of Physical Law, Statistical Mechanics; contbr. theory of quantum electrodynamics, beta decay and liquid helium. Recipient Einstein award, 1954; Nobel prize in physics, 1965; Oersted medal, 1972; Niels Bohr Internat. Gold medal, 1973. Mem. Am. Phys. Soc., AAAS, Royal Soc. (fgn. mem.), Pi Lambda Phi. Address: Physics Dept California Institute of Technology Pasadena CA 91125 *

FIACCONE, HUBERT NOVELLINO, former drug/chemical company executive; b. Phila., Feb. 12, 1918; s. Novellino S. and Florence (Ahern) F.; m. Doris Katherine Brewster, June 13, 1943; children: Katherine Ann Fiaccone Daley, William Brewster. B.S., Syracuse U., 1941. Foreman Gen. Chem. Co., 1941-42; with Merck & Co., Inc., 1942-81, dir. ops., Rahway, N.J., 1964-65, v.p., gen. mgr., 1965-67, sr. v.p., 1967-70, pres. chem. div., corp. sr. v.p., 1970-81; dir. Summit Fed. Savs. and Loan Assn. Bd. dirs. Summit YMCA. Fellow Am. Inst. Chem. Engrs.; mem. Am. Chem. Soc. Home: 35 Dale Dr Summit NJ 07901

FIALKOV, HERMAN, investment banker; b. Bklyn., Mar. 23, 1922; s. Isidore and Pearl (Heinish) F.; m. Elaine Dampf, Nov. 25, 1942; children: Carol Fran, Jay Michael. Student, CCNY, 1938-41; B.Adminstrv. Engring., NYU, 1951. Engr. Emerson Radio Corp., 1941-47, MBS, 1947-49, Tele-Tone Radio Corp., 1949-51; chief engr. Radio Receptor Co., 1951-54; pres. Gen. Transistor Corp. (merged with Gen. Instrument Corp. 1960), 1954-60; v.p., dir. Gen. Instrument Corp., 1960-67, sr. v.p., 1967-68; partner Geiger & Fialkov, 1968-78, Venture Capital Investments, 1978—; dir. Wells-Benrus Corp., Ridgefield, Conn., Standard Microsystems Corp., Hauppauge, N.Y., EMS Devel. Corp., Radyne Corp., Control Transaction Corp. Panelist Am. Arbitration Assn.; trustee Adelphi U., Garden City, 1959-70, Poly. U. N.Y., Heinish Found. Served with AUS, 1943-46. Decorated Bronze Star with oak leaf cluster; Conspicuous Service Cross, N.Y. Mem. IEEE, Am. Technion Soc. (dir.), Tau Beta Pi, Alpha Pi Mu. Home: One Kensington Gate Great Neck NY 11021 Office: One Old Country Rd Carle Place NY 11514

FIALKOW, PHILIP JACK, medical educator; b. N.Y.C., Aug. 20, 1934; s. Aaron and Sarah (Ratner) F.; m. Helen C. Dimitrakis, June 14, 1960; children: Michael, Deborah. B.A., U. Pa., 1956; M.D., Tufts U., 1960. Diplomate: Am. Bd. Internal Medicine, Am. Bd. Med. Genetics. Instr. medicine U. Wash., Seattle, 1965-66, asst. prof., 1966-69, assoc. prof., 1969-73, prof. medicine, 1973—, chmn. dept. medicine, 1980—; chief med. service Seattle VA Ctr., 1974-81; physician-in-chief Univ. Hosp., Seattle, 1980—; attending physicians Harborview Med. Ctr., Seattle, 1965—; cons. Children's Orthopedic Hosp., Seattle, 1964—. Contbr. articles to profl. jours. Trustee Fred Hutchinson Cancer Research Ctr., Seattle, 1982—. NIH fellow, 1963-65; NIH grantee, 1965—. Fellow ACP; mem. Am. Soc. Clin. Investigation, Assn. Am. Physicians, Assn. Profs. Medicine, Am. Soc. Human Genetics (dir. 1974-77), Alpha Omega Alpha. Office: Dept Medicine RG 20 Seattle WA 98195

FIBICH, HOWARD RAYMOND, editor; b. Oak Park, Ill., Jan. 6, 1932; s. Raymond Clarence and Vivian (Barrie) F.; m. Carrol Jean Anderson, June 5, 1954; children: Linda, Steven, Barbara. B.S., Northwestern U., 1954, M.S., 1955; postgrad., Columbia U., 1966. Reporter Kokomo (Ind.) Tribune, 1955-56; copy editor Milw. Jour., 1956-64, telegraph editor, 1964, asst. news editor, 1964-67, news editor, 1967-84, asst. mng. editor, 1984—; free lance writer, 1959-63; Chmn. Mid-Am. Press Inst. Mem. AP Mng. Editors Assn. (new tech. com.), Milw. Press Club, Kappa Tau Alpha. Home: 2537 N Swan Blvd Wauwatosa WI 53226 Office: 333 W State St Milwaukee WI 53201

FIBIGER, JOHN ANDREW, life insurance company executive; b. Copenhagen, Apr. 27, 1932; U.S., 1934, naturalized, 1953; s. Borge Rottboll and Ruth Elizabeth (Wadmond) F.; m. Barbara Mae Stuart, June 22, 1956; children: Karen Ruth, Katherine Louise. B.A., U. Minn., 1953, M.A., 1954; postgrad., U. Wis. With Lincoln Nat. Life Ins. Co., Ft. Wayne, Ind., 1956-57; with Bankers Life Ins. Co. Nebr., Lincoln, 1959-73, sr. v.p. group, 1972-73; with New Eng. Mut. Life Ins. Co., Boston, 1973—, pres., chief adminstrv. officer, 1981—; dir. Texet Corp. Vice pres. United Way Mass. Bay, 1980-81, past mem. bd. dirs.; corporator Museum Sci., Boston, 1980-81; bd. govs. New Eng. Med. Center, Boston; mem. Mass. Taxpayers Pension Com., 1980-81, President's Council for Internat. Youth Exchange; v.p. Boston Classical Orch.; bd. overseers Boston Symphony Orch. Served with AUS, 1957-59. Fellow Soc. Actuaries; mem. Health Ins. Assn. Am. (chmn. adminstrv. com. 1979-81), Am. Acad. Actuaries (v.p.), Boston Actuaries Club. Club: Algonquin (Boston). Office: 501 Boylston St Boston MA 02117

FIBKINS, ROBERT JAMES, magazine publisher; b. Springfield, Mass., Feb. 17, 1936; s. William James and Jean (Helmar) F. A.B., Harvard U., 1960, M.B.A., 1964. With Time, Inc., N.Y.C., 1964-70, mktg. info. mgr., 1967, circulation dir., Can., 1969; gen. mgr., circulation dir. Sail mag., Boston, 1970-74; pub. Horticulture mag., Boston, 1974-78, Conservative Digest, Falls Church, Va., 1978-79; pres. Fibkins Publs., Inc. (pubs. gardening books), 1978—, FFG, Inc. (pubs. The Family Food Garden); lectr., cons. in field. Served with AUS, 1956-58. Recipient Nat. Mag. award Mag. Pubs. Assn.-Columbia Sch. Journalism, 1976. Mem. Mag. Pubs. Assn. Home: 7 Delawanda Rd Hull MA 02045 Office: FFG Inc 464 Commonwealth Ave Boston MA 02215

FICCA, DAVID R., lawyer; b. Atlas, Pa., June 30, 1931; s. Frank E. and Edith (Pizzoli) F. B.S., Fordham U., 1953; LL.B., Georgetown U., 1959; LL.M., George Washington U., 1960. Bar: D.C. bar 1960. Atty., adviser SEC, 1961-67; staff counsel Kidde, Inc., Saddlebrook, N.J., 1967-69, sec., 1969-71, v.p., 1971-77, sr. v.p., 1977-82, exec. v.p., 1982—, sec., 1971—, sr. legal officer, 1978—, dir., 1983—. Mem. Am. Bar Assn. Home: 296 Feather Ln Franklin Lakes NJ 07417 Office: Park 80 W Plaza II Saddlebrook NJ 07662

FICHENBERG, ROBERT GORDON, newspaper editor; b. Phila., Jan. 1, 1920; s. Samuel Harrison and Katherine (Gordon) F.; m. Ruth Pollard, Sept. 14, 1947; children: Ruth Ann, Kathryn Leigh. B.S., Syracuse U., 1940. City editor Adirondack Daily Enterprise, Saranac Lake, N.Y., 1940-42; reporter, copy editor, asst. city editor Binghamton (N.Y.) Press, 1942-57; mng. editor Knickerbocker News, Albany, N.Y., 1957-66, exec. editor, 1966-78; chief Washington bur. Newhouse Newspapers, editor Newhouse News Service, 1979—. Served to 1st lt. Signal Corps AUS, 1942-46; to capt. U.S. Army, 1951-52. Mem. Am. Soc. Newspaper Editors, N.Y. State Soc. Newspaper Editors (pres.), AP Mng. Editors Assn., White House Corr. Assn., N.Y. State AP Assn. (past pres.), Nat. Press Club, Sigma Delta Chi. Clubs: Fed. City, Internat., Gridiron, Washington Press (Washington). Office: Suite 1320 1750 Pennsylvania Ave Washington DC 20006

FICHTEL, RUDOLPH ROBERT, association executive; b. N.Y.C., Dec. 12, 1915; s. Paul Gotthard and Helen (Szapka) F.; m. Elsie E. Terebesy, Dec. 24, 1942; children: Nancy Lynn, Robert Paul, Richard John. B.B.A. cum laude, Coll. City N.Y., 1938; cert., Am. Inst. Banking, 1941; diploma fin. pub. relations, Northwestern U., 1950; M.B.A., NYU, 1951; diploma banking, Rutgers U. Stonier Grad. Sch. Banking, 1954. Tchr. N.Y.C. Pub. Schs., 1938-39; adminstr. East River Savs. Bank, 1939-42; dir. pub. relations, editor, asst. sec. Savs. Banks Assn. N.Y. State, 1945-53; dir. pub. relations council, savs. and mortgage div. Am. Inst. Banking of Am. Bankers Assn., N.Y.C., Washington, 1953-78; regional v.p. United Student Aid Funds, Inc., N.Y.C., 1978—; mem. lender relations com. Higher Edn. Loan Programs; mem. faculty Am. Inst. Banking, Stonier Grad. Sch. Banking; contbg. editor Am. Inst. Banking textbooks; speaker. Contbr. articles to profl. jours. Served to capt. AUS, 1942-45; ETO. Recipient highest award citation Internat. Council Indsl. Editors, 1948, Dr. Marcus Nadler award for excellence in finance; N.Y. U., 1951. Mem. Beta Gamma Sigma. Home: 65-19 170th St Flushing NY 11365 Office: 200 E 42d St New York City NY 10017 *Success in my life has been the result of hard work, continuing search for knowledge, constant effort to understand and relate to people, and total dedication to excellence in full partnership with a loving family.*

FICHTER, JOHN L., food company executive; b. Kobe, Japan, 1924; m. B.A., U. So. Calif., 1946, M.S. in Chem. Engring., 1949. With Anderson, Clayton & Co., Houston, 1949—, v.p. agrl. and indsl. ops., mem. exec. com., 1964-74, exec. v.p., mem. exec. com., dir., 1974—. Office: Anderson Clayton & Co Interfirst Plaza 1100 Louisiana Houston TX 77002

FICHTER, JOSEPH H., clergyman, educator; b. Union City, N.J., June 10, 1908; s. Charles J. and Victoria (Weiss) F. A.B., St. Louis U., 1935, M.A., 1939; Ph.D., Harvard U., 1947. Entered Soc. Jesus, 1930; ordained priest Roman Cath. Ch., 1942; instr. Spring Hill Coll., 1935-36, Loyola U., New Orleans, 1944-45, prof., chmn. dept. sociology, 1947-64, 72—; vis. prof. sociology Muenster U., Germany, 1953-54; vis. prof. sociology, dir. research Notre Dame U., 1956-57, U. Chile, Santiago, 1961-62; vis. prof. sociology U. Chgo., 1964-65; Stillman prof. Harvard U., 1965-70; vis. prof. State U. N.Y. at Albany, 1971-72; Favrot prof. Tulane U., 1974-75. Author: Roots of Change, 1939, Man of Spain, 1940, Christianity, 1947, Social Relations in the Urban Parish, 1954, Sociology, 1957, Soziologie der Pfarrgruppen, 1958, Parochial School, 1958, Religion as an Occupation, 1961, Cambios Sociales en Chile, 1962, Priest and People, 1965, America's Forgotten Priests, 1968, One-Man Research, 1973, Organization Man in the Church, 1974, Catholic Cult of the Paraclete, 1975, Ardent Spirits Subdued, 1981. Founder Southeastern. Region Coll. Students Interracial Commn., 1948; mem. New Orleans Commn. Human Rights, 1948, New Orleans Com. Race Relations. Mem. Nat. Urban League, Am. Sociol. Assn. (exec. council), So. Sociol. Soc. (past pres.), Soc. Study Social Problems, AAUP, Assn. for Sociology Religion, Soc. Sci. Study Religion (past pres.), Religious Research Assn. Address: Loyola U New Orleans LA 70118

FICKINGER, WAYNE JOSEPH, advertising executive; b. Belleville, Ill., June 23, 1926; s. Joseph and Grace (Belton) F.; m. Joan Mary Foley, June 16, 1951; children: Michael, Joan, Jan, Ellen, Steven. B.A., U. Ill., 1949; M.S., Northwestern U., 1950. Overnight editor U.P., Chgo., 1950-51; spl. project writer Sears-Roebuck & Co., Chgo., 1951-53; account exec. Calkins & Holden Advt. Agy., Chgo., 1953-56; account supr. Foote, Cone & Belding Advt. Agy., Chgo., N.Y.C., 1956-63; sr. v.p. J. Walter Thompson Co., Chgo., 1963-72, v.p., dir. U.S. Western div., 1972-75, exec. v.p., dir., 1975-78, pres., chief operating officer, N.Am. div., 1978-79, trustee retirement fund, dir., mem. exec. com., 1980-82; mng. dir. Spencer Stuart & Assocs., 1982-83; vice chmn., dir., mem. exec. com. Bozell & Jacobs Inc., Chgo., 1984—; pres., dir., mem. exec. com. JWT Group; dir. Monroe Communicats Corp., 1982—, EValucom, 1982—. Fund raising cons. Nat. Mental Health Assn., 1970; Communications counselor Cook County (Ill.) Republican Orgn., 1970; Trustee Salvation Army, 1973—; bd. dirs. Off-the-Street Club, Chgo., 1974-77. Served with USNR, 1943-46. Recipient Five-Year Meritorious Service award A.R.C., 1963, Service award Mental Health Assn., 1970. Mem. Am. Assn. Advt. Agys.; Mem. Council Fgn. Relations (Chgo. com.), Sigma Delta Chi, Alpha Delta Sigma. Clubs: Exmoor Country (Highland Park, Ill.); N.Y. Athletic; Mid-Am., Internat. (Chgo.). Office: 360 N Michigan Ave Chicago IL 60610

FICKINGER, WILLIAM JOSEPH, physicist, educator; b. N.Y.C., July 18, 1934; s. Robert Henry and Alice Virginia (Etchingham) F. B.S. in Physics, Manhattan Coll., 1955, Ph.D., Yale U., 1961. Asst. prof. physics U. Ky., 1961-62; research asst. physicist Brookhaven Nat. Lab., 1962-63, 65; physicist Centre D'Etudes Nucleaires de Saclay, France, 1963-64; asso. prof. physics Vanderbilt U., 1965-67, Case Western Res. U., Cleve., 1967-76, prof., 1976—. Contbr. articles to profl. jours. NSF grantee, 1972—. Mem. Am. Phys. Soc., AAUP. Office: Dept Physics Case Western Res U Cleveland OH 44106

FICKLING, WILLIAM ARTHUR, JR., health care company executive; b. Macon, Ga., July 23, 1932; s. William Arthur and Claudia Darden (Foster) F.; m. Neva Jane Langley, Dec. 30, 1954; children: William Arthur III, Jane Dru, Julia Claudia, Roy Hampton. B.S. cum laude, Auburn U., 1954. Exec. v.p. Fickling & Walker, Inc.,

Macon, Ga., 1954-74; chmn. bd., chief exec. officer Charter Med. Corp., Macon, Ga, 1969—; dir. Ga. Power Co., South Ga. Ry. Co., Riverside Ford, Southlake Ford; chmn., dir. Atlanta Fed. Res. Bank. Trustee Wesleyan Coll., Macon. Mem. Macon Bd. Realtors, Kappa Alpha, Delta Sigma Phi, Phi Kappa Phi. Methodist. Home: 4918 Wesleyan Woods Dr Macon GA 31210 Office: Charter Med Corp 577 Mulberry St Macon GA 31298

FIDDICK, PAUL WILLIAM, broadcasting company executive; b. St. Joseph, Mo., Nov. 20, 1949; s. Lowell Duane and Betty Jean (Manring) F.; m. Julie Hanna Lorms, July 31, 1983. B.J., U. Mo., 1967-71. Account exec. radio sta. KCMO-KFMU, Kansas City, Mo., 1971-72, WFXW, Milw., 1972-74, dir. sales mktg., 1974-76, v.p., gen. mgr., 1976-81; sr. v.p. Multimedia Radio, Milw., 1981-82, pres., Cin., 1982—; dir. Radio Advt. Bur., N.Y.C.; mem. faculty U. Wis.-Milw., 1978-82. Producer: indsl. film Marketing of Radio, 1975. Mem. Comprehensive Planning Task Force, Shorewood, Wis. Recipient Up and Coming Radio Exec. of Yr. award Radio Only mag., 1983. Club: Bankers (Cin.). Office: Multimedia Broadcasting Co 140 W 9th St Cincinnati OH 45202

FIDDLER, THOMAS ROBERT, retail executive; b. N.Y.C., Mar. 24, 1921; s. Earl Thomas and Margaret (Martsolf) F.; m. Jane Carol Sundlof, Sept. 12, 1942; children: Martha J., Thomas N. (dec.), Kathryn A. A.B., Princeton U., 1942. With Marshall Field & Co., Chgo., 1945-51, buyer, 1950-54; with Rich's Inc., Atlanta, 1954-60, gen. mgr., Tenn., 1955-60; with Frederick Atkins, N.Y.C., 1960-67, pres., 1963-67; with D.H. Holmes Co. Ltd., New Orleans, 1967—, pres., 1972—; dir. Hibernia Nat. Bank, Delchamps, Inc.; tchr. mktg. U. Ga., evenings 1952-54; bd. dirs. Internat. Trade Mart, 1983—; mem. council advisers Tulane U. Grad. Sch. Bus. Bd. dirs., exec. com. New Orleans Econ. Devel. Council, 1974—; chmn. maj. gifts United Way, 1974-75; sr. v.p. Council for a Better La., 1983; bd. dirs. New Orleans Met. Area Com., 1970—, New Orleans Symphony, 1974, 79, New Orleans Tourist Commn., 1969—; pres. New Orleans Tourist Commn., 1977-78, chmn., 1979; trustee King Sch., Stamford, Conn., 1962-66, Low Heywood Sch., Stamford, 1964-67, Xavier U., 1979; bd. dirs., exec. mgmt. com., v.p. La. World Expn., 1980—. Served to lt. comdr. USNR, 1942-45. Mem. Nat. Retail Mchts. Assn. (dir. 1974—), Am. Retail Fedn. (dir. 1981—), New Orleans Retail Mchts. Council (pres. 1972-73), New Orleans C. of C. (dir., exec. com.), Internat. House (dir., exec. com.). Republican. Episcopalian. Clubs: Univ. (N.Y.C.); New Orleans Country, Boston, Plimsoll (New Orleans); Pass Christian Golf, Pass Christian Yacht (Miss.); Diamondhead. Home: 5418 Dayna Ct New Orleans LA 70124 Office: DH Holmes Co Ltd 819 Canal St New Orleans LA 70160

FIDLER, RONALD HERBERT, company executive; b. Slough, Eng., July 26, 1933; s. Harry H. and Clen L. (Gorton) F.; m. Patricia Beard, Feb. 14, 1959; 1 dau., Giuliana. Student, Brit. schs. With Black & Decker Mfg. Co., 1955-83, gen. mgr. Italy, South Europe, then European gen. mgr., 1971-75, pres. European Internat. Group, Brussels, 1975-81, chief operating officer, exec. v.p., 1981-82, pres., 1982-83. Fellow Chartered Inst. Secs. and Adminstrs., Inst. Dirs.; mem. Brit. Inst. Mgmt. (companion). Mem. Ch. of Eng. Club: Villa d'Este (Como, Italy). Home: Stonehouse Grange Church Rd Penn Bucks MDEngland HP10 8NX

FIDO, FRANCO, language and literature educator; b. Venice, Italy, July 15, 1931; came to U.S., 1963; s. Spiridione Mario and Maria (Baseggio) F.; m. Marie-Josephe Rolin, July 31, 1958; children—Anne-Claire, Silvia C. D.Lett., U. Pisa, 1953; postgrad., Libera Docenza, Italy, 1969; M.A. ad eundem, Brown U., 1971. Lectr., Italian Faculte des Lettres, Dijon, 1954-58; instr. U. Calif., Berkeley, 1958-61; lectr. Italian Faculte des Lettres, Grenoble, 1961-63; asst. prof. to prof. Italian UCLA, 1963-69, chmn. dept., 1966-69; prof., dir. Italian studies Brown U., Providence, 1969-78, univ. prof. Italian, 1979—; R. Pierotti prof. Italian lit. Stanford U., 1978-79; vis. prof. McGill U., 1971, 76, Middlebury Coll., summers 1973-74, U. Venice, 1973, Queens Coll. and Grad. Center, CUNY, 1975, Yale U., 1975. Author: Machiavelli-Storia della Critica, 1965, Guida a Goldoni-Teatro e Societa nel Settecento, 1977, Le Metamorfosi del Centauro-Studi da Boccaccio a Pirandello, 1977. Recipient L. Russo prize, Italy, 1978; Krieble Delmas Found. fellow, 1977; Nat. Endowment Humanities fellow, 1979; Am. Council Learned Socs. grantee, 1978. Mem. MLA (H.R. Marraro prize 1978), Dante Soc. Am. Home: 34 Pratt St Providence RI 02906 Office: Box E Brown U Providence RI 02912

FIEBACH, H. ROBERT, lawyer; b. Paterson, N.J., June 7, 1939; s. Michael M. and Silvia Irene (Nadler) F.; m. Elizabeth D. Carlton, Mar. 17, 1984; children by previous marriage: Jonathan, Rachel. B.S., U. Pa., 1961, LL.B. cum laude, 1964. Bar: Pa. 1965, U.S. Supreme Ct. 1971. Law clk. to Chief Judge U.S. Ct. Appeals for 3d Cir., 1964-65; assoc. Wolf, Block, Schorr and Solis-Cohen, Phila., 1965-71, ptnr., 1971-79, sr. ptnr., 1979—; permanent mem. U.S. Jud. Conf. for 3d cir., 1967—; arbitrator Phila. Common Pleas Ct., U.S. Dist. Ct. (ea. dist.) Pa., Am. Arbitration Assn., 1966—. Research editor: U. Pa. Law Rev., 1964-65; contbr. articles to legal jours. Mem. Phila. adv. bd. Anti-Defamation League of B'nai B'rith, Greater Phila. Regional Commn. on Law and Social Action, Am. Jewish Congress; bd. dirs. Greater Phila. chpt. ACLU, past chmn. criminal justice and police practices com.; bd. dirs. Pa. chpt. ACLU, Welsh Valley Civic Assn.; past pres. Welsh Valley Civic Assn.; past bd. dirs., treas. A Better Chance in Lower Merion; founder, mem. bd. dirs. Penn Valley Jr. Sports Assn.; mem. legal com. Main Line Reform Temple, Phila. Mem. ABA (litigation sect. 3d cir. discovery com.), Pa. Bar Assn. (ho. of dels. 1983—, vice chmn. jud. selection com., chmn. jud. retention election com. 1980-83, spl. com. on profl. liability, chmn. polit. action com. for merit retention of judges 1980-83), Phila. Bar Assn. (chmn. fed. cts. com., past. sec., vice chmn. arbitration com., past mem. spl. com. to study appellate cts., chmn. spl. com. on instns. 1983—, mem. civil jud. precedures com., speaker various panels), Am. Judicature Soc., Assn. Trial Lawyers Am., Phila. Trial Lawyers Assn. (chmn. bus. litigation com.), Defender Assn. Phila. (bd. dirs.), Order of Coif (past dir. U. Pa. chpt.). Home: Independence Pl Philadelphia PA 19106 Office: 12th Floor Packard Bldg Philadelphia PA 19102

FIEDEROWICZ, WALTER MICHAEL, lawyer; b. Hartford, Conn., Aug. 23, 1946; s. Michael and Sylvia Christine (Ramunno) F.; m. Gerry Prattson, June 1, 1968; children: Michael, Catherine. B.A., Yale U., 1968; J.D. (DuPont fellow), U. Va., 1971. Bar: Conn. bar 1971, U.S. Supreme Ct. bar 1977. Mem. firm Cummings, & Lockwood, Stamford, Conn., 1971-76, ptnr. firm, 1979—; White House fellow, 1976-77; spl. asst. to Atty. Gen., Dept. Justice, Washington, 1976-77; assoc. dep. Atty. Gen., 1977-79. Mem. editorial bd.: Va. Law Review, 1969-71. Bd. dirs. Conn. Prison Assn., VITAM Found.; mem. grad. council Loomis-Chaffee Sch. Bd. Mem. Am. Bar Assn., Conn. Bar Assn., Order of the Coif. Roman Catholic. Home: 55 Cross Hwy Redding CT 06875 Office: City Place Hartford CT

FIEDLER, BOBBI, congresswoman; b. Santa Monica, Calif., Apr. 22, 1937; children—Lisa, Randy. Student, Santa Monica City Coll., Santa Monica Tech. Sch.; LL.D. (hon.), West Coast Coll. Law, 1979. Owner, mgr. 2 pharmacies; mem. Los Angeles Bd. Edn., 1977; co-founder BUSTOP antibusing orgn.; mem. 97th-98th congresses from 21st Dist. Calif. Bd. dirs. Com. Investigating Valley Ind. City/County; mem. sponsors bd. B'nai B'rith Youth Orgn. Mem. Bus. and Profl. Women's Assn. Republican. Office: 1607 Longworth House Office Bldg Washington DC 20515 *

FIEDLER, JOHN FRANCIS, rubber company executive; b. Akron, Ohio, May 22, 1938; s. Leon Francis and Elizabeth (Klaras) F.; m., July 16, 1960; children: Michael, Jill, Caroline. B.S., Kent State U.; postgrad. in bus. adminstrn., U. Del., Newark; S.M., MIT. Asst. to chmn. Goodyear Tire & Rubber Co., Akron, Ohio, 1979-80, v.p. gen. products research and devel., 1982—; mng. dir. Goodyear Malaysia, Kuala Lumpua, 1980-82. Sloan fellow. Home: 2390 Brunswick Ln Hudson OH 44236

FIEDLER, LESLIE AARON, actor, author; b. Newark, Mar. 8, 1917; s. Jacob J. and Lillian (Rosenstrauch) F.; m. Margaret Ann Shipley, Oct. 7, 1939 (div. 1972); children—Kurt, Eric, Michael, Deborah, Jenny, Miriam; m. Sally Andersen, 1973; stepchildren—Soren and Eric Charles Andersen. B.A., N.Y. U., 1938; M.A., U. Wis., 1939, Ph.D., 1941; postdoctoral student, Harvard, 1946-47. Mem. faculty U. Mont., 1941-64, instr. to asso. prof. English, 1941-53, prof., 1953-64, chmn. dept., 1954-56; prof. English State U. N.Y. at Buffalo, 1965—; vis. prof. U. Rome, 1951-52, U. Bologna and Ca Foscari U., 1952-53, Princeton, 1956-57, Athens, 1961-62, U. Sussex, 1967-68, U. Paris, 1970-71; jr. fellow Ind. U. Sch. Letters, 1951—; asso. fellow Calhoun Yale U., 1969—. Author: (with others) Leaves of Grass: 100 Years After, 1955, An End to Innocence, 1955, The Art of the Essay, 1959, rev. 1969, The Image of the Jew in American Fiction, 1959, Love and Death in the American Novel, 1960, rev. 1966, No. In Thunder, 1960, Pull Down Vanity (stories), 1962, The Second Stone (novel), 1963, (with J. Vinocur) The Continuing Debate, 1964, Waiting for the End, 1964, Back to China, 1965, (with others) The Girl in the Black Raincoat, 1966, The Last Jew in America, 1966, The Return of the Vanishing American, 1967, Nude Croquet and Other Stories, 1969, Being Busted, 1970, Collected Essays, 1971, The Stranger in Shakespeare, 1972, The Messengers Will Come No More, 1974, In Dreams Awake, 1975, Freaks, 1977, A Fiedler Reader, 1977, The Inadvertent Epic, 1979; Editor: Master of Ballantrae, 1951, Waiting for God (S. Weil), 1952, Poems of Whitman, 1959, (with Arthur Zeiger) O Brave New World, 1967; asso. editor: Ramparts, 1959-65; contbg. editor: Am. Judaism; lit. editor: Running Man, 1967-69; Contbr. short stories, poems, articles to jours. U.S. and abroad. Served from ensign to lt. (j.g.) USNR, 1942-46. Rockefeller fellow humanities, 1946-47; recipient Furioso prize for Poetry, 1951; Fulbright fellow, 1951-53; Kenyon rev. fellow in criticism, 1956-57; Christian Gauss lectr., 1956; award Nat. Inst. Arts and Letters, 1957; grant-in-aid Am. Council Learned Socs., 1960, 61; Guggenheim fellow, 1970-71. Mem. English Inst., Modern Lang. Assn., AAUP, Dante Soc. Am., P.E.N. Club, Phi Beta Kappa. Home: 154 Morris Ave Buffalo NY 14214

FIELD, ARTHUR NORMAN, lawyer; b. N.Y.C., Sept. 28, 1935; s. Harry and Rose (Lemberg) F.; m. Doris Helen Rabbiner, Sept. 1, 1957; children: Michael, Karen. B.B.A., CCNY, 1955; LL.B., Harvard U., 1958. Assoc. firm Shearman & Sterling, N.Y.C., 1959-68, ptnr., 1968—; dir. Bank of Montreal Trust Co., N.Y.C., N. Central Oil Corp., Houston, Sunset Realty Corp., Punta Groda, Fla., Trizec Stamford Inc.; chmn. bd. Western Maine Radio Inc., Rumford, 1981—. Bd. dirs. Wave Hill Inc., N.Y.C., 1968-80, Washington Sq. Legal Services, N.Y.C., 1979—; chmn., dir. Community Action for Legal Services, N.Y.C., 1972-77; trustee Brookdale Found., N.Y.C., 1983—. Fellow N.Y. Bar Found.; mem. N.Y. County Lawyers Assn. (dir.), N.Y. State Bar Assn. (mem. ho. of dels.), ABA, Assn. Bar City of N.Y. Club: Metropolitan.

FIELD, CYRUS ADAMS, lawyer; b. Fergus Falls, Minn., Oct. 27, 1902; s. Nicolai F. and Ida (Adams) F.; m. Mary Emily Kutz, Dec. 26, 1953. A.B., U. Minn., 1923; J.D., Harvard, 1926. Bar: Minn. bar 1926. Since practiced in, Fergus Falls; sr. partner Field, Arvesen, Donoho Lundeen & Hoff, 1952-76; dir. Western Minn. Savs. & Loan Assn.; mem. adv. com. on rules practice and procedure Supreme Ct. Minn., 1950-78. Past pres. Fergus Falls Community Chest.; Trustee Minn. Bar Found., 1968-76, Fergus Falls Salvation Army, Lake Region Hosp. Assn. Mem. ABA (ho. dels. 1963-65), Minn. Bar Assn. (pres. 1962-63, bd. govs. 1960-64), Fergus Falls C. of C. (past pres.), Harvard Law Sch. Assn., Delta Chi. Conglist. Clubs: Mason (Shriner), Rotarian (Fergus Falls) (past pres.); Elk., Harvard of Minn. Home: 324 S Lakeside Dr Fergus Falls MN 56537 Office: 125 S Mill St Fergus Falls MN 56537

FIELD, ELOIS RACHEL, nurse, educator; b. Farnum, Nebr., Apr. 19, 1921; d. Joseph Walter and Mary Jane (Johnston) F. A.A., Jr. Coll. S.E. Colo., 1940; R.N., Baylor U., 1943; B.A., Wheaton Coll., 1945; M. Nursing, U. Wash., 1949; Ph.D., U. Chgo., 1961. Supr. polio epidemic ARC, N.W. Tex. Hosp., Amarillo, 1943, pvt. duty nurse, 1943-44, supr. medicine, surgery, 1945, instr. sch. nursing, 1945-46, 50-51; instr. St. Luke's Hosp. Sch. Nursing, Denver, 1946, Baylor Sch. Nursing, Dallas, 1947-48, 54-57, asst. dean, 1951-53; lectr. U. Calif., 1959-60; dir. baccalaureate programs Emory U. Sch. Nursing, Atlanta, 1962-64; dean Sch. of Nursing, U. Ark. Med. Center, 1964-78; prof. U. Tex., Arlington, 1979—. Author articles profl. jours. Mem. Am. Nurses Assn., Nat. League Nursing, Am. Ednl. Research Assn., Sigma Theta Tau, Pi Lambda Theta. Baptist. Office: U Tex Arlington PO Box 19407 Arlington TX 76019

FIELD, GEORGE BROOKS, theoretical astrophysicist; b. Providence, Oct. 25, 1929; s. Winthrop Brooks and Pauline (Woodworth) F.; m. Sylvia Farrior Smith, June 23, 1956 (div. Oct. 1979); children: Christopher Lyman, Natasha Suzanne. B.S. in Physics, M.I.T., 1951; Ph.D. in Astronomy, Princeton U., 1955. Asst. prof., then asso. prof. astronomy Princeton U., 1957-65; vis. prof. Calif. Inst. Tech., 1964; prof. astronomy U. Calif., Berkeley, 1965-72, chmn. dept., 1970-71; Phillips visitor Haverford (Pa.) Coll., 1965, 71; vis. prof. Cambridge (Eng.) U., 1969; prof. astronomy Harvard U., 1972—; also dir. coll. obs.; dir. Smithsonian Astrophys. Obs., Center Astrophysics; lectr. Ecole d'Ete de Physique Theorique, Les Houches, France, 1974. Recipient Public Service medal NASA, 1977, cert. exceptional service Smithsonian Inst., 1977; Guggenheim fellow, 1960-61. Fellow Am. Phys. Soc.; mem. Am. Astron. Soc., AAAS, Astron. Soc. Pacific, Internat. Astron. Union, Sigma Xi. Office: 60 Garden St Cambridge MA 02138 *

FIELD, GEORGE REED, university chancellor; b. La Crosse, Wis., Feb. 23, 1929; married, 1952; 5 children. B.A., Carleton Coll., 1950; M.A., U. Colo., 1953; Ph.D., U. Wis., 1965. Asst. to pres. U. Wis., Madison, 158-61, exec. asst. to pres., 1961-65, v.p., 1967-68, chancellor, River Falls, 1968—. A.C. Nielsen fellow. Office: Office of the Chancellor U Wis River Falls WI 54022 *

FIELD, HAROLD DAVID, JR., lawyer; b. Mpls., Aug. 21, 1927; s. Harold David F. and Gladys (Jacobs) (Field); m. Joyce Fineman, Sept. 3, 1950; children: Stephen, Lawrence, Richard. S.B., MIT, 1948; LL.B., Yale U., 1951. Bar: Minn. 1951, N.Y. 1952, U.S. Dist. Ct. Minn. 1953, U.S. Ct. Appeals (8th cir.) 1956. Assoc. Paul, Weiss, Rifkind, Wharton & Garrison, N.Y.C., 1951-52, Leonard, Street and Deinard, Mpls., 1952-58, ptnr., 1959—. Mem. Minn. Pollution Control Agy. Bd., 1971-79, chmn., 1973-75. Mem. ABA, Minn. Bar Assn., Hennepin County Bar Assn. Club: Minneapolis. Office: Suite 1200 Nat City Bank Bldg Minneapolis MN 55402

FIELD, HENRY, anthropologist; b. Chgo., Dec. 15, 1902; m. Julia Rand Allen, Feb. 6, 1953; 1 dau., Juliana Lathrop; 1 dau. by previous marriage, Mariana Field Hoppin. Ed. in Eng.; student, Eton Coll., 1916-21, New Coll., Oxford, 1921-26; B.A., Oxford U., 1925; Diploma in Anthropology, Oxford U., 1926, M.A., 1929, D.Sc., 1937; research, U. Heidelberg, 1926, Peabody Mus., Harvard, 1936-37. Anthropologist Field Mus. Natural History, 1926-41, asst. curator phys. anthropology, 1926-36, curator, 1937-41; research for F.D. Roosevelt and H.S. Truman at Library of Congress, 1941-45; Mem. archaeol. expdn. in, Europe, Africa, Southwestern Asia, 1927-55, Mongolia, 1973; leader Marshall Field Archaeol. Expdns. to, Europe, N. Arabian Desert, Iraq, Jordan and Saudi Arabia; mem. other expdns. Research fellow phys. anthropology Harvard, 1950-69, hon. asso. in phys. anthropology, 1969—; adj. prof. U. Miami, 1966—; Forbes Hawkes lectr. U. Miami, Lowell Inst., Boston, 1952. Author: (with David Hooper) books on different geog. areas, including Useful Plants and Drugs of Iran and Iraq, 1937, The Anthropology of Iraq, 1939, 40, 48, 51, 52, Contributions to the Anthropology of the Caucasus, 1953, The Track of Man, 1953, Los Indios de Tepoztlan, Morelos, Mexico, 1954, Ancient and Modern Man in S.W. Asia, I, 1956, II, 1961, Bibliographies on S.W. Asia I-VII, 1953-61, Supplements I-VIII, 1963-73, Anthropological Reconnaissance in West Pakistan, 1959, North Arabian Desert Archaeological Survey, 1925-50, 1960, "M" Project for F.D.R.; Studies on Migration and Settlement, 1962, Physical Anthropology of India, 1970, Anthropology of Saudi Arabia, 1971, Arabian Desert Tales, 1976, Mongolia Tour, Mongolia Today, 1978, Trail Blazers, 1980; editor: Peabody Mus. Russian Translation Series, 1960-70, Field Research Projects, 1963—. U.S. del. to internat. congresses and sci. confs.; Mem. U.S. mission to Moscow and Leningrad for 220th anniversary of Acad. Scis. USSR, 1945, Internat. Congress, Moscow, 1964, Internat. Geog. Congress, London, 1964. Hon. mem. Glasgow Archaeol. Soc.; corr. mem. several fgn. sci. socs.; Mem. U.S. and fgn. profl. and scientific socs. and assns., anthropol., archaeol., and other spl. orgns.; Fellow AAAS, Royal Geog. Soc., Royal Central Asian Soc., Asiatic Soc. Bengal (Gold medal) Royal Anthrop. Inst., Zool. Soc., Prehistoric Soc., and others; mem. Acad. Arts and Scis. Ams. (pres. 1964-75). Club: Explorers (N.Y.) (pres. S. Fla. chpt.). Home: 3551 Main Highway Coconut Grove Miami FL 33133 Office: Peabody Museum Harvard Cambridge MA 02138

FIELD, HENRY AUGUSTUS, JR., lawyer; b. Wisconsin Dells, Wis., July 8, 1928; s. Henry A. and Georgia (Coakley) F.; m. Patricia Ann Young, Nov. 30, 1957 (dec. 1980); children: Mary Patricia, Thomas Gerard, Susan Therese. Student, Western Mich. Coll., 1946-47; Ph.B., Marquette U., 1950; LL.B., U. Wis., 1952. Bar: Wis. bar 1952. Asst. U.S. atty. Western Dist. of Wis., 1956-57; asso. Roberts, Boardman, Suhr, Bjork & Curry, 1957-62; jr. partner Roberts, Boardman, Suhr & Curry, 1962-70; partner Boardman, Suhr, Curry & Field, Madison, Wis., 1970—; mem. Wis. Jud. Council, 1974-79. Dir. Family Service Soc., 1969-75, treas., 1971-72, pres., 1973-74. Served with C.I.C. AUS, 1952-55. Fellow Am. Coll. Trial Lawyers (state chmn. 1982-83), Am. Bar Found.; mem. ABA (Wis. chmn. legis. com. 1975-76), 7th Fed. Circuit Bar Assn., Wis. Bar Assn. (chmn. negligence sect. 1971-72), Milw. and Dane County Bar Assn. (pres. 1971-72), Phi Delta Phi, Sigma Tau Delta, Order of Coif. Republican. Roman Catholic. Club: Madison. Home: 4410 Keating Terr Madison WI 53711 Office: 1 S Pinckney St Madison WI 53703

FIELD, HENRY FREDERICK, lawyer; b. Weston, Mass., June 3, 1941; s. E. Olsen and Harriet (Jacobs) F.; m. Martha Heineman, 1962; children—Thalia L., Jessica M.; m. Mary Jo Laflin, 1979. B.A., Harvard U., 1962; J.D. cum laude, U. Chgo., 1965. Bar: Ill. bar 1965, D.C. 1966, U.S. Supreme Ct. 1971. Law clk. to Justice Schaefer, Ill. Supreme Ct., 1965-66; asst. U.S. atty. Dept. Justice, Washington, 1966-67; spl. asst. to pres. U. Chgo., 1968-69; assoc. firm Mayer, Brown & Platt, Chgo., 1969-74, partner, 1975-79; partner firm Friedman & Koven, Chgo., 1979—; mem. character and fitness com. Ill. Supreme Ct. Contbr. articles to profl. jours.; editor: U. Chgo. Law Rev. Bd. dirs. Taylor Inst., Chgo., 1976—. Mem. Chgo. Council Lawyers (dir. 1969-75), Am. Law Inst., Am. Bar Assn., Chgo. Bar Assn., Order of Coif. Clubs: Mid Day, Saddle and Cycle. Home: 2344 Lincoln Park W Chicago IL 60614 Office: 208 S LaSalle St Chicago IL 60604

FIELD, HERMANN HAVILAND, educator, architect; b. Zurich, Switzerland, Apr. 13, 1910; s. Herbert Haviland and Nina (Eschwege) F.; m. Jean Clark, 1932 (div. 1940); m. Kate Thornycroft, June 14, 1940; children: Hugh, Alan, Alison. B.A., Harvard, 1933; student, Grad. Sch. Design, 1932-34; Diplom Architekt, Swiss Fed. Poly. Inst., Zurich, 1936. Resident architect Roche Products Ltd., Welwyn Garden City, Eng., 1936-38; field rep. in Poland and Eng. Czech Refugee Trust Fund, 1939-40; site planner Tuttle, Seelye, Place and Raymond, N.Y.C., 1941-45; research dir. Raymond and Rado (architects), N.Y.C., 1945-47; dir. bldg. plans Western Res. U., 1947-49; planning dir. Tufts-New Eng. Med. Center, Boston, 1961-72; dir. planning project for innovative Boston elementary sch., 1966-72; prof. environmental planning, dir. grad. program urban social and environmental policy Tufts U., 1972-78, prof. emeritus polit. sci., advisor grad. dept. urban and environ. policy, 1978—; v.p. Cambridge Interfaith Housing Corp., Mass., 1969-79. Author: (with Stanislaw Mierzenski) Angry Harvest, 1958 (German version selection Europaischer Buchklub, Stuttgart 1962; English, Polish, Swedish edits.), Duck Lane, 1961 (also Polish edit), (with others) Problems of Pediatric Hospital Design, 1965, Evaluation of Hospital Design, 1972, Environment and Cognition, 1973. Mem. Gov. Mass. Task Force Transp., 1969-70, Joint Regional Transp. Commn., 1973-79, Shirley (Mass.) Conservation Commn., 1969-83, Shirley Historic Dist. Commn., 1973—, Cambridge (Mass.) Conservation Commn., 1975-81; mem. working com. Boston Transp. Planning Rev., 1971-72; bd. dirs. Mass. Assn. Conservation Commns., 1976—, v.p., 1979—; bd. dirs. H.J. Coolidge Ctr. Environ. Leadership, 1983—, Global Tomorrow Coalition, 1982—, Nashua River Watershed Assn., 1981—; adv. bd. Health Facilities Research, Inc., 1972-74; non-govtl. observer UN Habitat Conf., 1976. Fellow AIA; mem. Am. Planning Assn., Boston Soc. Architects (sec., mem. bd. 1968-74), Boston Archtl. Center, Harvard Grad. Sch. Design Assn. (council 1968-70, 74-76), Am. Inst. Cert. Planners, Internat. Union for Conservation of Nature and Natural Resources (commn. on environ. planning 1980—), AAUP. Victim of kidnapping in Cold War incident, secretly held in Polish prison cellar, Miedzeszyn, 1949-54; preparation of prison novels, London, 1955, Boston, 1956-60. Home: Valley Farm Shirley MA 01464 Office: Tufts Univ Medford MA 02155

FIELD, JAMES ALFRED, JR., educator, historian; b. Chgo., Mar. 9, 1916; s. James Alfred and Amy Morehead (Walker) F.; m. Lila Ruth Breckinridge, Aug. 30, 1941; children—Charles Walker, Mary Breckinridge. Grad., Milton (Mass.) Acad., 1933; S.B., Harvard, 1937, A.M., 1939, Ph.D., 1947; student, Trinity Coll., Cambridge (Eng.) U., 1937-38. Exec. asst. Nat. Resources Com., 1939; teaching fellow Harvard, 1940-42, 47; mem. faculty Swarthmore Coll., 1947—, prof. history, 1958—, chmn. dept., 1963-68, 79-80; vis. prof. maritime history U.S. Naval War Coll., 1954-55, prof. strategy, 1975-76. Author: The Japanese at Leyte Gulf, 1947, History of U.S. Naval Operations, Korea, 1962, America and the Mediterranean World, 1969. Mem. hist. adv. com. Dept. of Army, 1964-68; mem. Sec. Navy's Adv. Com. on Naval History, 1976—. Served with USNR, 1942-46. Mem. Am. Hist.

Assn., Soc. Historians Am. Fgn. Relations, Orgn. Am. Historians. Home: 605 Hillborn Ave Swarthmore PA 19081

FIELD, JAMES BERNARD, internist, educator; b. Fort Wayne, Ind., May 28, 1926; s. Abraham and Clara (Ridner) F.; m. Dorothy Spivey, Sept. 25, 1954; children—Carolyn, Nancy, Douglas, Susan. Student, Harvard Coll., 1946-47; M.D. cum laude, Harvard Med. Sch., 1951. Diplomate: Am. Bd. Internal Medicine. Intern internal medicine Mass. Gen. Hosp., Boston, 1951-52, asst. resident internal medicine, 1952-53, resident internal medicine, 1953-54; practice medicine specializing in endocrinology, Pitts., 1962-78, Houston, 1978—; med. officer USPHS, Nat. Inst. Arthritis and Metabolic Diseases, Bethesda, Md., 1954, sr. asst. surgeon, 1954-58, sr. investigator, 1958-60, surgeon, 1958-60, sr. surgeon, 1960-61; asst. in medicine diabetic dept. Kings Coll. Hosp., London, 1957-58; head div. endocrinology and metabolism U. Pitts. Sch. Medicine, 1962-78, asso. prof. medicine, 1962-66, prof. medicine, 1966-78, dir. clin. research unit, 1962-78; Rutherford prof. medicine Baylor Coll. Medicine, Houston, 1978—, head div. endocrinology and metabolism, 1978—, also dir. Diabetes and Endocrinology Research Ctr.; med. adv. bd. Nat. Pituitary Agy., 1967-69; research collaborator Brookhaven Nat. Lab., 1972—; mem. nat. diabetes adv. bd. HEW, 1977—, chmn., 1982—; mem. endocrinology study sect. USPHS, 1965-69, chmn., 1968-69, endocrinology and metabolism tng. grant com., 1970-74, gen. clin. research center rev. com., 1976-79; mem. VA merit rev. com. on endocrinology and metabolism, 1982—. Contbr. numerous articles on research studies in endocrinology to profl. jours.; assoc. editor: Metabolism, 1959-69; editor-in-chief, 1969—; editor: Jour. Cylic Nucleotide Research, 1974-79; mem. editorial bd.: Clin. Research, 1965, Postaglandins, 1968-72. Bd. dirs. Gen. Clin. Research Centers, 1977-79. Served with U.S. Army, 1944-45. Decorated Purple Heart; recipient Van Meter prize award Am. Goiter Assn., 1961. Mem. Assn. Am. Physicians, Endocrine Soc. (mem. council 1972-75, internat. liaison com. 1972-75, mem. awards com. 1977-80, chmn. 1980, nominating com. 1982—, chmn. 1983), Am. Diabetes Assn. (dir. 1968-74, vice chmn. com. on research 1972-73, chmn. 1975-77, Eli Lilly award 1958), Am. Fedn. Clin. Research, Am. Clin. and Climatol. Assn., Am. Physiology Soc., Am. Soc. Clin. Investigation, Alpha Omega Alpha. Clubs: Briar, Univ. (Houston); Fox Chapel Racquet (Pitts.); Sea Pines Racquet (Hilton Head, S.C.). Home: 3020 Locke Ln Houston TX 77019 Office: 6720 Bertner St Houston TX 77025

FIELD, JOHN A., JR., U.S. circuit judge; b. Charleston, W.Va., Mar. 22, 1910; s. John A. and Mayme (Butler) F.; m. Elaine Cochran Goode, Apr. 1, 1933 (dec.); children: John A., William Claiborne; m. Colleen Conety Ball, Dec. 27, 1980. A.B., Hampden-Sydney Coll., 1932; LL.B., U. Va., 1935. Bar: W.Va. 1935. With firm Brown, Jackson & Knight, Charleston, 1935-43; individual practice, Charleston, 1946-57, tax commr., W.Va., 1957-59; U.S. judge for So. Dist. W.Va., 1959-71; U.S. circuit judge 4th Circuit Ct. Appeals, 1971—, sr. judge, 1976—. Mem. Charleston City Council, 1947-55, pres., 1951-55. Served to lt. (s.g.) USNR, 1944-46. Mem. Am., W.Va., Charleston bar assns., Am. Law Inst., Order of Coif, Chi Phi, Omicron Delta Kappa. Presbyterian. Home: 102 Wilderness Dr Apt 2116 Naples FL 33942 Office: Fed Ct House 500 Quarries St Charleston WV 25301

FIELD, JOHN HARDIN, chemical company executive; b. Lexington, Ky., Oct. 31, 1925; s. John Utterback and Ethel Constance (Fletcher) F.; m. Vivian Eileen Miller, June 2, 1962; children—Thomas Burnam, John Douglas, Jennifer Myung Ja. B.S. in Chem. Engring, Yale U., 1946. With Union Carbide Corp., 1946—; v.p., dir. Union Carbide Can. Ltd., 1971-75, corp. v.p. strategic planning, N.Y.C., 1975-82, exec. v.p., 1982—. Mem. Galveston County (Tex.) Mosquito Control Dist. Bd., 1964-68; bd. dirs. Salvation Army, Victoria, Tex., 1962-64, Munster (Ind.) Hosp., 1968-70. Served to lt. (j.g.) USNR, 1944-46. Mem. Am. Inst. Chem. Engrs. Republican. Home: 68 St John's Pl New Canaan CT 06840 Office: Old Ridgebury Rd Danbury CT 06817

FIELD, JOHN LOUIS, architect; b. Mpls., Jan. 18, 1930; s. Harold David and Gladys Ruth (Jacobs) F.; m. Carol Helen Hart, July 23, 1961; children: Matthew Hart, Alison Ellen. B.A., Yale, 1952; M. Arch., 1955. Individual practice architecture, San Francisco, 1959-68; v.p. firm Bull, Field, Volkmann, Stockwell (Architects), San Francisco, 1968-83; ptnr. Field/Gruzen (Architects), San Francisco, 1983—; Guest lectr. Stanford, 1970; Chmn. archtl. council San Francisco Mus. Art, 1969-71; mem. San Francisco Bay Conservation and Devel. Commn., Design Rev. Bd., 1980—; Founding chmn. San Francisco Bay Architects Review, 1977-80. Co-author, producer, dir.: film Cities for People (Broadcast Media award 1975, Golden Gate award San Francisco Internat. Film Festival 1975, Ohio State award 1976); documentary film maker: The Urban Preserve (Central Calif. AIA Commendation of excellence 1982); Co-author, producer, dir.: design for New Alaska Capitol City (winner design competition). Recipient Archtl. Record award, 1961, 1972; AIA, Sunset mag. awards, 1962, 64, 69; No Calif. AIA awards, 1967, 82; Central Calif. AIA award, 1982; certificate excellence Calif. Gov.'s Design awards, 1966; Homes for Better Living awards, 1962, 66, 69, 71, 77; Albert J. Evers award, 1974; Nat. Endowment for Humanities grantee, 1972; Nat. Endowment for Arts fellow, 1975. Fellow AIA (exec. com. chpt., mem. com. on design); mem. Nat. Council Archtl. Registration Bds. Club: Yale (San Francisco). Address: 2561 Washington St San Francisco CA 94115 Office: 251 Post St San Francisco CA 94108

FIELD, KENNETH EDWARD, real estate development company executive; b. Toronto, Ont., Can., Nov. 17, 1943; s. Lewis E. and Sue F.; children: Lisa, Howard, Peter. B.A., U. Toronto, 1965; LL.B., Osgoode Hall Law Sch., Toronto, 1969; cert. in bus. adminstrn., U. Waterloo, (Ont.), York U., (Ont.). Bar: Ont. 1970. Pres. Bramalea Ltd., Toronto, Ont., Can., 1979—, dir., 1979—; dir. Coseka Resources, Calgary, Alta., Can., Coho Resources; pres. Eros Holdings Ltd., Toronto, Ont., Can. Mem. Young Pres.' Assn. Office: Bramalea Ltd 1867 Yonge St 11th Floor Toronto ON Canada M4S 1Y5

FIELD, LAMAR, educator, chemist; b. Montgomery, Ala., July 19, 1922; s. Samuel Lamar and Nelle (Brock) F.; m. Betty Leyden, Jan. 1, 1948; children—Patricia Leyden, Brock Lamar. S.B., Mass. Inst. Tech., 1944, Ph.D., 1949. Jr. chemist Merck and Co., 1944-46; Socony-Vacuum fellow Mass. Inst. Tech., 1947-48; mem. faculty Vanderbilt U., 1949—, prof. chemistry, 1959—, chmn. dept., 1961-67; indsl. cons., 1955—; cons. NIH, 1965-69, N.Y. State Edn. Dept., 1974, So. Assn. Colls. and Schs., 1976, 83; Coulter lectr. U. Miss., 1968; vis. fellow dept. exptl. pathology John Curtin Sch. Med. Research, also; hon. fellow Research Sch. Chemistry, Australian Nat. U., 1974; external examiner grad. theses from, Australia, Can., Egypt and India. Editorial bd. Sulfer Reports, 1982; Editorial bd Sulfur Letters, 1982—; Contbr. numerous publs. in field chemistry. Recipient Boit prize Mass. Inst. Tech., 1941, 42, Roger's award, 1944; Thomas Jefferson award Vanderbilt U., 1974; E.A. Jones faculty award, 1982; S.A.A.C.S. awards for teaching, 1980, 83. Mem. Am. Chem. Soc. (chmn. Nashville sect. 1955, councilor 1960-68, mem. council com. on publs. 1963-68, mem. award canvassing com. 1978—, mem. award selection com. 1981—, vis. scientist 1966-73, vis. assoc. com. profl. tng. 1963-82, student-affiliate tour speaker 1971—), Royal Soc. Chemistry, Phi Beta Kappa (hon.), Sigma Xi (L.C. Glenn award Vanderbilt chpt. 1952), Alpha Chi Sigma, Delta Tau Delta. Office: Box 1507 Station B Vanderbilt U Nashville TN 37235

FIELD, LEOPOLD MCDONALD, cons. engr.; b. Georgetown, Guyana, S. Am., Aug. 3, 1930; s. Edward Nathaniel and Henrietta Amelia (Smith) F.; m. Gretna Dorita Gibbs, Aug. 30, 1952; children—Linda Joan, Lesley Sandra. B.S.E.E., Battersea Coll. Tech., 1961; M.Sc., U. Aston, Eng., 1968; postgrad., Poly. Inst. Bklyn., 1969-71. Registered profl. engr., N.Y. Technician engring. dept. Brit. Post Office, London, 1952, design draftsman, exec. asst. engr., to 1962; chmn. dept. elec. engring. Tech. Inst., Georgetown, Guyana, 1962-69; project engr. RCA Global Communications, N.Y.C., 1969-73; chmn. elec. trades George Washington Tech. and Vocat. Sch., Bklyn., 1973-75; founder, pres. Field Assos. (Cons. Engrs.), Freeport, N.Y., 1975—, now chmn. bd. Contbr. articles to profl. jours. Bd. dirs. Roosevelt Youth Center, 1974-76, Target Youth Center, Hempstead, 1974-78; mgr., trainer George Washington High Sch. Soccer Club. Mem. Inst. Elec. Engrs. U.K., IEEE, Inst. Radio and Electronic Engrs. (Eng.), N.Y. Soc. Profl. Engrs., Nassau County Profl. Engrs., Kings County Profl. Engrs., NAACP. Republican. Methodist. Clubs: Holiday Spa Health, Masons. Home: 87 W Clinton Ave Roosevelt NY 11575 Office: 113 W Sunrise Hwy Freeport NY 11520

FIELD, LYMAN, lawyer; b. Kansas City, Mo., Oct. 6, 1914; s. Russell and Gertrude (Brown) F.; 1 dau. by previous marriage, Kathleen; m. Jo Ann Straube, Apr. 10, 1965; 1 dau., Jennifer Ann. A.B., U. Kans., 1936; LL.B., Harvard U., 1939. Bar: Mo. 1939. Since practiced in Kansas City; partner Field, Gentry, Benjamin & Robertson; spl. commr. Supreme Ct. Mo., 1953-54. Founding bd. dirs. Greater Kansas City Mental Health Found., 1950-58; pres. Council Social Agys., Kansas City, Mo., 1951-55; gen. chmn. Citizens Regional Planning Council of Greater Kansas City, 1949-53, Mayor's Mcpl. Services Commn., 1951-53; pres. Bd. Police Commrs., Kansas City, Mo., 1957-61; mem. Mo. State Council on Arts, 1965-75, chmn., 1966-73; chmn. N.Am. Assembly State and Provincial Art Agencies, 1968-70; co-chmn. Midwest Regional Assembly on Future of Performing Arts, 1979; participant 46th Am. Assembly on Art Mus., Arden House, N.Y.; mem. and chmn. Thomas Hart Benton Homestead Meml. Adv. Commn. Mo., 1975—; trustee Thomas Hart Benton and Rita P. Benton testamentary trusts; trustee, v.p. Kansas City Philharm. Orch. Assn., 1961-71; trustee Samuel H. Kress Found., N.Y.C.; bd. dirs. Cross Found., Kansas City Soc. Western Art, Mid-Am. Arts Alliance, Mo. Inst. for Justice, Mo. Repertory Theater; trustee, bd. dirs. Kansas City Art Inst., 1969-74. Served from pvt. to maj. USMCR, 1942-46; PTO. Decorated Bronze Star medal. Fellow Am. Coll. Trial Lawyers; mem. Am., Mo., Kansas City bar assns., Am. Judicature Soc., Internat. Assn. Ins. Counsel, Lawyers Assn. Kansas City, Beta Theta Pi, Phi Delta Phi. Clubs: Kansas City Country, University, Carriage (Kansas City, Mo.); Century Assn. (N.Y.C.). Home: 5815 State Line Rd Kansas City MO 64113 Office: 600 E 11th St Kansas City MO 64106

FIELD, MARSHALL, business executive; b. Charlottesville, Va., May 13, 1941; s. Marshall IV and Joanne (Bass) F.; m. Joan Best Connelly, Sept. 5, 1964 (div. 1969); 1 son, Marshall; m. Jamee Beckwith Jacobs, Aug. 19, 1972; children: Jamee, Stephanie Caroline, Abigail Beckwith. B.A., Harvard U., 1963. With N.Y. Herald Tribune, 1964-65; pub. Chgo. Sun-Times, 1969-80, Chgo. Daily News, 1969-78; dir. Field Enterprises, Inc., Chgo., 1965-84, mem. exec. com., 1965-84, chmn. bd., 1972-84, Field Corp., 1984—, Cabot, Cabot & Forbes, 1984—; pub. World Book-Childcraft Internat. Inc., 1973-78, dir., 1965-80; dir. First Chgo. Corp., First Nat. Bank of Chgo. Mem. Chgo. com. Chgo. Council Fgn. Relations; adv. bd. Broader Urban Involvement and Leadership Devel., Inc., Chgo.; trustee, vice-chmn. Art Inst. Chgo.; trustee Field Mus. Natural History, Mus. Sci. and Industry, Rush-Presbyn.-St. Luke's Med. Center; bd. dirs. Field Found. of Ill., Smithsonian Instn., Internat. Atlantic Salmon Found., McGraw Wildlife Found., Restoration Atlantic Salmon In Am., Inc., Lincoln Park Zool. Soc., Chgo. Boys Clubs, Nat. Bldg. Mus.; hon. bd. dirs. Open Lands Project (CorLands); governing mem. Orchestral Assn., Chgo.; adv. bd. Chgo. area council Boy Scouts Am., Presdl. Classroom for Young Ams.; mem. com. to visit coll. and com. univ. resources Harvard Coll.; mem. adv. bd. Brookfield Zoo; dir. hon. bd. Nat. Commn. Prevention Child Abuse. Mem. Nature Conservancy, Chgo. Zool. Soc. Clubs: River (N.Y.C.); Chicago, Merchants and Manufacturers, Mid-Am., Tavern, Commercial, Harvard, Hundred of Cook County, Casino, Racquet (Chgo.); Onwentsia (Lake Forest, Ill.); Somerset (Boston); Jupiter Island (Hobe Sound, Fla.). Office: 333 N Wacker Dr Chicago IL 60606

FIELD, MARTHA AMANDA, law educator, lawyer; b. Boston, Aug. 20, 1943; d. Donald T. and Adelaide (Anderson) F.; children: Maria Adelaide, Gabriel Hartry, Lucas Anthony. B.A., Harvard U., 1965; J.D., U. Chgo., 1968. Bar: D.C. 1969. Law clk. to Justice Abe Fortas, U.S. Supreme Ct., 1968-69; from asst. prof. to prof. law U. Pa., 1969-78; prof. law Harvard U., 1978—. Contbr. numerous articles to law revs. Office: Harvard U Law Sch Langdell Hall 225 Cambridge MA 02138

FIELD, MICHAEL, retired research company executive, consultant; b. N.Y.C., Feb. 21, 1914; s. Max and Anna (Heller) F.; m. Ruth V. Clendening, Jan. 24, 1942; children: David, Janice. B.S. in Mech. Engring, Coll. City N.Y., 1937, M.S., Columbia U., 1938; Ph.D. in Physics, U. Cin., 1948; Sc.D. in Engring. (hon.), Chalmers U. Tech., Sweden, 1980. Research engr. Cin. Milling Machine Co., 1938-48; pres., gen. mgr. Metcut Research Assocs., Inc., Cin., 1948-78, chmn. bd., chief exec. officer, 1978-82, ret., 1982; cons., 1982—. Contbr. articles to profl. jours. Active U. Cin., Columbia corporate fund drives, Boy Scouts Am., United Appeal. Named Engr. of Year, Cin., 1966; recipient Gold Medal award Soc. Mfg. Engrs., 1968, Distinguished alumni award U. Cin., 1969, Joseph Whitworth prize Instn. Mech. Engrs., 1968; Am. Machinist award, 1978. Fellow Am. Soc. Metals (William H. Eisenman award 1971), Soc. Exptl. Stress Analysis (chmn. chpt. 1963-65), Soc. Automotive Engrs., Aircraft Industries Assn., Am. Inst. Aeros. and Astronautics, Am. Ordnance Assn., AAAS, Numerical Control Soc., Soc. Mfg. Engrs. (dir. 1972-76), Sigma Xi; mem. ASME (hon.), Nat. Acad. Engring. Home: 9060 Spooky Ridge Ln Cincinnati OH 45242

FIELD, ROBERT WARREN, chemistry educator; b. Wilmington, Del., June 13, 1944; s. Edmund Kay Huebsch (Field). A.B., Amherst Coll., 1965; M.A., Harvard U., 1971, Ph.D., 1972. Adj. asst. prof. chemistry U. Calif.-Santa Barbara, 1974; asst. prof. chemistry M.I.T., Cambridge, 1974-78, assoc. prof. phys. chemistry, 1978-82, prof., 1982—. Mem. editorial bd.: Jour. Molecular Spectroscopy, Jour. Phys. Chemistry; contbr. articles to profl. jours. Alfred P. Sloan fellow, 1975-77. Fellow Am. Phys. Soc. (H.P. Broida prize 1980); mem. Am. Chem. Soc. Office: Dept Chemistry Room 6-223 MIT Cambridge MA 02139

FIELD, RON, theatrical director, choreographer. Grad., High Sch. Performing Arts. Profl. debut at age 8 in: Lady in the Dark; appeared: Broadway plays The Boy Friend; mem., Jack Cole Dancers; choreographer: Zorba; dir., choreographer: On The Town, 1971; staged nightclub acts for, Liza Minnelli, Carol Lawrence, Chita Rivera, TV dances for, Fred Astaire and, Angela Lansbury; staged and choreographed: King of Hearts, 1978 (Recipient Tony award for choreography of Cabaret 1967, and for best dir.-choreographer of Applause 1970, Emmy award for choreography in America Salutes Richard Rodgers 1977). Office: 5 W 19th St New York NY 10011 *

FIELD, SALLY, actress; b. Pasadena, Calif., 1946; (div.)children: Peter, Eli. Student, Actor's Studio, 1973-75. Starred in: TV series Gidget, 1965, The Flying Nun, 1967-69, The Girl With Something Extra, 1973; theatrical film debut in The Way West, 1967; other films include Stay Hungry, 1976, Heroes, 1977, Smokey and the Bandit, 1977, Hooper, 1978, The End, 1978, Norma Rae, 1979 (Cannes Film Festival Best Actress award 1979, Acad. award 1980), Beyond the Poseidon Adventure, 1979, Smokey and the Bandit II, 1980, Back Roads, 1981, Absence of Malice, 1981, Kiss Me Goodbye, 1982; TV movies include Maybe I'll Come Home In the Spring, 1971, Marriage: Year One, 1971, Home for the Holidays, 1972, Bridges, 1976, Sybil, 1976 (Emmy award 1977) *

FIELD, THOMAS STEWART, coll. pres.; b. Chgo., June 2, 1915; s. Thomas Robertson and Ann (Stewart) F.; m. Virginia Margaret Leach, 20, 1939; ldren—Melinda (Mrs. Donald Ross Duncan), Rebecca (Mrs. James Edward Montgomery). B.S., Wheaton (Ill.) Coll., 1937, D.D., 1957; B.D., Eastern Baptist Theol. Sem., 1941. Ordained to ministry Baptist Ch., 1941; pastor First Bapt. Ch., Quitman, Ga., 1950-52, La Grange, Ga., 1952-57, Lake Charles, La., 1957-60, Springfield, Mo., 1960-70; pres. William Jewell Coll., Liberty, Mo., 1970-80, pres. emeritus, 1980—; Mem. exec. bd. Ga. Bapt. Conv., 1954-57, La. Bapt. Conv., 1958-60, Mo. Bapt. Conv., 1961-70, pres., 1967-69; mem. exec. com. So. Bapt. Conv., 1969-70, mem. found. bd., 1965-71, mem. relief annuity bd., 1957-60, mem. edn. commn. Chmn. ARC, La Grange, 1956; chmn. adv. bd. Salvation Army, Springfield, 1968-69; mem. exec. com. Community Chest, Lake Charles, 1957; pres. bd. dirs. Ozark Christian Counseling Service, Springfield; v.p. trustees Cox Med. Center, Springfield; bd. dirs. Mo. Council Econ. Devel.; trustee Northland Med. Found., Kansas City, Mo. Recipient Freedoms Found. award for address Let Freedom Ring, 1968. Mem. Am. Assn. U. Adminstrs., So. Bapt. Hist. Soc., C. of C. Liberty, Harry S. Truman Inst. for Nat. and Internat. Affairs, Am. Assn. Presidents Ind. Colls. and Univs., Assn. So. Bapt. Colls. and Schs., Newcomen Soc., Smithsonian Assos.

FIELD, THOMAS WALTER, JR., supermarket chain executive; b. Alhambra, Calif., Nov. 2, 1933; s. Thomas Walter and Pietje (Slagveld) F.; m. Ruth Inez Oxley, Apr. 10, 1959; children: Julie, Sherry, Cynthia, Thomas Walter, III, James. Student, Stanford U., 1951-53. Vice pres. retail ops. Alpha Beta Co., La Habra, Calif., 1972-73, sr. v.p., 1973-75, exec. v.p., 1975-76, pres., chief exec. officer, 1976-81; pres. Am. Stores Co., 1981—. Bd. dirs. La Habra Boys' Club. Mem. Calif. Retailers Assn. (dir.), Automobile Club So. Calif. (adv. bd.). Republican. Office: Am Stores Co PO Box 27447 Salt Lake City UT 84127 *

FIELD, WILLIAM NOÉ, clergyman, educator; b. Orange, N.J., Dec. 22, 1915; s. William Noé and Marie Natalie (O'Mara) F. A.B., Seton Hall, 1936; student, Immaculate Conception Sem., 1936-40; postgrad., Columbia, 1940-52, M.L.S., 1960. Ordained priest Roman Catholic Ch., 1940; mem. faculty Seton Hall U., South Orange, N.J., 1940—, prof. English, 1940—, dir. libraries, 1963—, dir. devel., 1959-61, now curator rare books and archival collections, univ. archivist; lectr. Adult Sch., Chatham, N.J., 1964-66, Montclair, N.J., 1973—; moderator various employee groups. Editorial bd.: Advocate, 1951—; Author: poetry Hear My Heart, 1950; also articles, book revs. Trustee Cath. Forum, Newark Mus., South Orange Hist. Commn.; trustee, mem. exec. bd. N.J. Cath. Hist. Records Commn.; sec. No. N.J. chpt. Am. Diabetes Assn. Mem. N.J. Library Assn. (pres.-elect coll. and univ. div. 1966—, mem. com. for disadvantaged 1973), Met. Cath. Library Assn. (pres.), Nat. Assn. Cath. Archivists (exec. bd.), Renascence Soc. (pres. 1971—, trustee, Serra of Orange moderator 1955—), Cath. Poetry Soc. Am., South Orange Hist. Soc. (pres.). Address: Seton Hall U South Orange NJ 07079

FIELDER, CHARLES ROBERT, business executive; b. Lubbock, Tex., Mar. 9, 1943; s. Clarence Daniel and Ola Marie (Sewell) F.; m. Mary Ruth Wills, May 31, 1964; 1 dau., Sara Elizabeth. B.B.A., Tex. Tech. U., 1965, M.S. in Acctg., 1972. C.P.A., Tex. Staff acct. Peat, Marwick, Mitchell & Co., Dallas, 1965-66, Arthur Andersen & Co., 1968-69; treasury acct. Halliburton Co., Dallas, 1969-71, treasury supr., 1971-72, asst. treas., 1972-78, treas., 1978—. Mem. Am. Inst. C.P.A.'s, Tex. Soc. C.P.A.'s, Phi Eta Sigma, Beta Alpha Psi, Beta Gamma Sigma, Phi Kappa Phi. Republican. Mem. Churches of Christ. Clubs: Chaparral; Plaza Athletic (Dallas). Office: Halliburton Co. 400 N Olive LB 263 Dallas TX 75201

FIELDER, JOHN THOMAS, retail consultant; b. Austin, Tex., July 13, 1919; s. Hammett Hardy and Emma (Monoghan) F.; m. Mary Elizabeth Holland, June 20, 1949; children: John Thomas, William Hammett, James Hardy, Elizabeth Holland. B.C.S., Benjamin Franklin U., 1940; student, George Washington U., 1940-41. Vice pres., dir. Julius Garfinckel & Co., Washington, 1953-59; pres. A. DePinna Co., N.Y.C., 1953-59; v.p., dir. Brooks Bros., N.Y.C., 1953-55; exec. v.p., dir. J.B. Ivey Co., Charlotte, N.C., 1960-75, pres., 1975-83; sr. v.p. Marshall Field & Co., 1980-82; cons. Batus Retail, 1983. Served to lt., aviator USNR, 1942-46. Office: 127 N Tyron St PO Box 30600 Charlotte NC 28230

FIELDER, PARKER CLINTON, legal educator; b. Chgo., Oct. 20, 1918; s. Harold Clinton and Adrienne (Parker) F.; m. Marguerite Sparks, June 16, 1943 (dec. 1976); children—Sydney (Mrs. Terry Seaver), Pamela (Mrs. Robert Wyatt); m. Bonnie Cummins, Feb. 12, 1977. B.S. in Commerce, Northwestern U., 1941; LL.B., U. Tex., 1948. Bar: Tex bar 1948, also U.S. Supreme Ct., other fed. cts 1948. Accounting-auditor Sears, Roebuck & Co., Chgo., 1941-42; prof. law U. Tex., 1948-53, William H. Francis, Jr. prof. law, 1961—; partner firm Turpin, Kerr, Smith & Dyer, Midland, Tex., 1953-61; vis. prof. U. Pa., 1964-65, So. Meth. U., summer 1968, U. Utah, 1976, Am. U., 1983; research asso. charge tax project Tex. Legis. Council, 1950; gen. counsel, dir. Permian Corp., 1959-61; spl. cons. Tex. Legis. Property Tax Com., 1974-75. Author articles in field.; Editor in chief: Tex. Law Rev, 1947-48. Served to capt. AUS, 1942-46; col. Res. Mem. Am. Bar Assn., State Bar Tex. (vice chmn. com. continuing legal edn. 1961-64), Am. Law Inst., Order of Coif, Phi Delta Phi, Chancellors. Mem. Christian Ch. (mem. bd., tchr.). Home: 906 Terrace Mountain Dr Austin TX 78746 Office: 727 E 26th St Austin TX 78705

FIELDING, ALLEN FRED, oral and maxillofacial surgeon, educator; b. Paterson, N.J., Jan. 22, 1943; s. Fred W. and Emily Claire (Boehm) F. B.S., Fairleigh Dickinson U., 1959, D.M.D., 1963; postgrad. in oral surgery, N.Y. U., 1965-66. Diplomate: Am. Bd. Oral Surgery. Intern in oral surgery Roosevelt Hosp., N.Y.C., 1966-67; resident in oral surgery Phila. Gen. Hosp., 1967-69; practice dentistry specializing in oral-maxillo facial surgery, Phila., 1969—; prof., chmn. dept. oral and maxillofacial surgery Temple U., Phila., 1969—, staff prof., chief dept. oral and maxillofacial surgery univ. hosp.; cons. VA Hosp., Wilmington, Del.; staff St. Christopher's Hosp. for Children, Phila.; cons. staff Quakertown (Pa.) Hosp., Lawndale Hosp., Phila.; cons. Gt. Lakes Naval Hosp., Ill.; lectr. in field. Contbr. articles to profl. jours. Served to capt. USAF, 1963-65. Fellow Am. Dental Soc. Anesthesiology, Royal Soc. Health; fellow Am. Soc. Oral Surgeons; mem. AAUP, Assn. Mil. Surgeons, Am. Assn. Dental Schs., Pa. Soc. Oral Surgeons, Delaware Valley Soc. Oral Surgeons (com. resident tng. 1973—, exec. com.), Am. Assn. Hosp. Dentists (sec.-treas. Delaware County chpt. 1972-74, v.p. 1974, pres. 1976), ADA, Pa., Phila. County dental socs., Internat. Assn. Maxillo-Facial-Surgery, Great Lakes, Mid-Atlantic socs. oral maxillofacial surgeons, Temple U. Oral Surgery Honor Soc. (advisor), Omicron Kappa Upsilon. Home: 1203 Rodman St Philadelphia PA 19147 Office: 3223 N Broad St Philadelphia PA 19140 also 3207 Kensington Ave Philadelphia PA 19134 *

FIELDING, ELIZABETH M(AY), public relations executive, editor; b. New London, Conn., May 16, 1917; d. Frederick James and Elizabeth (Martin) F. A.B., Conn. Coll. for Women, 1938; M.A., Am. U., 1944. Research writer Republican Nat. Com., Washington, 1940, acting dir. research, 1944, asst. dir. research, 1948-53; govt. statistician, personnel clk., economist, 1941-42, research writer, 1942-48, staff writer, spl. cons. to several U.S. congressmen, 1944-52; exec. sec., legis. asst. to Senator Alexander Wiley of Wis., 1953-54; asso. dir. research Rep. Nat. Com., 1954-57; researcher, speech writer, 1960-61; legis. analyst, newsletter editor Nat. Assn. Electric Cos., 1957-60; pub. relations dir. Nat. Fedn. Rep. Women, 1961-68; spl. asst. to asst. postmaster gen. U.S. Post Office Dept., 1969-71; pub. affairs dir. Pres.'s Council on Youth Opportunity, 1970-71; asst. adminstr. for pub. affairs Nat. Credit Union Adminstrn., 1971-75; pres. Profl. Enterprises, 1975—; editorial asst. U.S. Ho. of Reps., 1976—. Author: A History of the Republican Party, 1854-1944. Editor Rep. Clubwoman, 1961-68; dir. spl. activities women's div. United Citizens for Nixon-Agnew, 1968; fin. coordinator Inaugural Com., 1968-69; citizen mem. rev. panel Atty. Grievance Commn., State of Md., 1980—. Recipient medal of achievement for outstanding govt. service Conn. Coll., 1971; Distinguished Service award Nat. Fedn. Rep. Women, 1964, 67. Mem. Am. Polit. Sci. Assn., Am. Acad. Polit. and Social Sci., AAAS, Soc. for Scholarly Pub., Nat. Assn. Govt. Communicators, Nat. Assn. Women Bus. Owners, Pub. Relations Soc. Am., Exec. Link, Soc. for Tech. Communication, Internat. Biog. Assn., Am. Soc. Dowsers, Internat. Platform Assn., Rep. Women of Capitol Hill, Rep. Women's Fed. Forum, South Potomac Environ. Council, Nat. Soc. for Hist. Preservation, Senate Toastmasters, Nat. Fedn. Press Women, Phi Beta Kappa. Methodist. Clubs: Nat. Press, Washington Press, Am. News Women's, Capital Press Women, Capitol Hill, Congressional Flying, Capital Yacht, U.S. Senate Staff, U.S. Congl. Staff, Antique Auto of Am., Packards Internat. Home: 1312 Thornton Pkwy Fort Washington MD 20744 McFarland Shores New Harbor ME 04554 Office: PO Box 55513 Fort Washington MD 20744

FIELDING, FRED FISHER, lawyer; b. Phila., Mar. 21, 1939; s. Fred P. and Ruth Marie (Fisher) F.; m. J. Maria Dugger, Oct. 21, 1967; children: Adam Garrett, Alexandra Caroline. A.B., Gettysburg Coll., 1961; LL.B., J.D., U. Va., 1964. Bar: Pa., D.C. Asso. firm Morgan, Lewis & Bockius, Phila., 1964-65, 67-70; asso. counsel to Pres. of U.S., 1970-71, dep. counsel, 1971-74; partner firm Morgan, Lewis & Bockius, Washington, 1974-81; counsel to Pres. of U.S., 1981—; mem. Judicial Conf. D.C. Circuit, 1976—; conflict of interest counsel Office of Pres.-Elect., 1980. Mem. Commn. on White House Fellowships, 1981—, President's Commn. for German-Am. Tricentennial, 1982—. Served to capt. AUS, 1965-67. John McKee Found. fellow. Mem. ABA, Fed. Bar Assn., D.C. Bar Assn., Pa. Bar Assn., Am. Arbitration Assn. (nat. panel), Phi Gamma Delta, Omicron Delta Kappa, Pi Delta Epsilon, Pi Lambda Sigma, Phi Delta Phi. Republican. Lutheran. Clubs: Federal City, Washington Golf and Country, F Street. Office: The White House 1600 Pennsylvania Ave NW Washington DC 20500

FIELDING, GABRIEL (ALAN GABRIEL BARNSLEY), novelist, English language educator; b. Hexham, Northumberland, Eng., Mar. 25, 1916; s. George and Katherine Mary (Fielding-Smith) Barnsley; m. Edwina Eleanora Cook, Oct. 31, 1943; children: Michael Fielding, Jonathan Milne, Mario Simon George Gabriel, Felicity Ann, Mary Gabriel Elizabeth. B.A., Trinity Coll., Dublin, Ireland, 1940; mem., Royal Coll. Surgeons; licentiate, Royal Coll.Physicians, St. Georges Hosp., London, 1942; D.Litt. (hon.), Gonzaga U., 1967. Physician in gen. practice, Maidstone, Eng., 1948—; part-time med. officer Her Majesty's Tng. Establishment, Maidstone, 1952—; occasional broadcaster BBC, 1961—; author in residence Wash. State U., Pullman, 1966-67, prof. English, 1966—. Author: poetry The Frog Prince and Other Poems, 1952; novel Brotherly Love, 1954, In the Time of Greenbloom, 1956, Eight Days, 1959, Through Streets Broad and Narrow, 1961, XXVIII Poems, 1955, The Birthday King, 1963 (W. H. Smith prize 1963, St. Thomas More Soc. gold medal, Chgo.), Gentlemen in Their Season, 1966, New Queens for Old, 1972, Pretty Doll Houses, 1979; poems Songs without Music, 1979. Served to capt. Royal Army Med. Corps, 1943-46. Hon. librarian Univ. Philos. Soc., Trinity Coll., 1938; recipient Anatomy prize, 1937, Silver medal for oratory, 1938; Journalism award Cath. Press Assn., 1965. Roman Catholic. Home: NE 945 Monroe St Pullman WA 99163 also 19 High Barrow Rd Addiscombe Surrey England

FIELDING, IVOR RENE, chemist; b. Jefferson, Iowa, July 3, 1942; s. Leslie Wayne and Roberta (Oakes) F.; m. Anna Theresa Damasa, Aug. 10, 1968; children: Maria Ona, Krista Terese. B.A., Simpson Coll., 1964; postgrad., U. Colo., 1964, Kans. State U., 1964-66; M.S., Creighton U., 1970; Ph.D., U. Pitts., 1970; M.S., Midwest Coll. Engring., 1977. Teaching asst. Kans. State U., Manhattan, 1964-66, Creighton U., Omaha, 1966-68; teaching, research asst. U. Pitts., 1968-70; research chemist Amoco Chems. Corp. div. Standard Oil Ind., Naperville, Ill., 1970-77, sr. research chemist, Naperville, 1977—. Class agt. Simpson Coll. Alumni Ann. Fund, 1972-73, class coordinator, 1974-75. Grantee Simpson Coll., 1960-64, NSF, 1968-70. Mem. Am. Chem. Soc., Am. Inst. Chemists, Sigma Xi, Sigma Tau Delta, Phi Lambda Upsilon. Home: 115 N Brainard St Naperville IL 60540 Office: PO Box 400 Naperville IL 60566

FIELDING, J. WILLIAM, orthopaedic surgeon; b. Toronto, Ont., Can., Feb. 17, 1923; came to U.S., 1947, naturalized, 1952; s. Samuel and Elizabeth (Robertson) F.; m. Doris Alma Toogood, Jan. 20, 1950; children: Pamela Joan, Bruce Robertson, Deborah Elizabeth, Victoria Alma. M.D., U. Toronto, 1946. Diplomate: Am. Bd. Orthopaedic Surgery. Rotating intern Vancouver (B.C.) Gen. Hosp., 1946-47; resident in pathology St. Luke's Hosp., N.Y.C., 1947; sr. intern in pathology Montreal (Que.) Gen. Hosp., 1948; sr. rotating intern in gen. surgery Shaughnessy Hosp., Vancouver, 1948-49; asst. resident in orthopaedic surgery St. Luke's Hosp., 1949-50, resident, 1951-52; resident in orthopaedic surgery Seaview Hosp., Staten Island, 1950-51; postgrad. Columbia U. Coll. Physicians and Surgeons, 1951; practice medicine specializing in orthopaedic surgery, N.Y.C., 1952—; asst. attending Beekman-Downtown Hosp., 1961-71, Columbia-Presbyn. Med. Center, 1957-61; attending Bronx VA Hosp., 1965-68, Lenox Hill Hosp., 1972—, St. Luke's Hosp., 1952—, dir. dept. orthopaedic surgery, 1973—; dir. dept. Orthopaedics St. Vincent's Hosp., Staten Island, 1962-77, cons., 1977—; cons., vis. physician numerous area hosps.; clin. prof. Columbia U. Coll. Physicians and Surgeons, 1973—; asso. prof. N.Y. Med. Coll., 1971—. Mem. editorial bd. various profl. jours.; Contbr. numerous articles to med. jours. Served with M.C. Canadian Army, 1944-46; as flight lt. RCAF, 1948-49. Recipient Cine Eagle award for film, 1970. Fellow Royal Coll. Surgeons Can.; mem. Am. Acad. Cerebral Palsy, Am. Acad. Orthopaedic Surgeons (Gold medal 1952, Kappa Delta award 1963, 2d v.p. 1981-82, 1st v.p. 1982-83, pres. 1983-84), AMA (chmn. orthopaedic sect. council 1969-70, award of merit 1954), Assn. Bone and Joint Surgeons (chmn. membership com. 1965-66, Nicholas Andry award 1975), A.C.S., Am. Orthopaedic Assn. (traveling fellow 1957), Am. Orthopaedic Foot Soc. (pres. 1981-82), Assn. Orthopaedic Chairmen, Can. Orthopaedic Assn., Cervical Spine Research Soc. (pres. 1973, 74), Internat. Soc. Study Lumbar Spine (pres. 1975-76), Orthopaedic Research and Edn. Found. (regional chmn. 1971-76), N.Y. Acad. Medicine (chmn. orthopaedic sect. 1960-61), N.Y. Clin. Soc. (pres. 1975-76), Internat. Soc. Orthopaedics and Traumatology, AAAS, Am. Orthopaedic Soc. Sports Medicine, also numerous regional med. assns.; hon. mem. other med. socs. Episcopalian. Clubs: St. Andrew's Soc., Univ. Office: 105 E 65th St New York NY 10021

FIELDING, JONATHAN EVAN, public health administrator, educator; b. Nyack, N.Y., Oct. 4, 1942; s. Robert and Gertrude; m. Karin Barter, Sept. 19, 1976. B.A. magna cum laude, Williams Coll., 1964; postgrad., La Sorbonne, L'Ecole de science politique, l'Ecole du Louvre, Paris, 1962-63; M.A. (Josiah Macy fellow), Grad. Sch. Arts and Scis., Harvard U., 1969; M.D. cum laude, Grad. Sch. Arts and Scis., Harvard U., 1969; M.P.H. (USPHS fellow), Grad. Sch. Arts and Scis., Harvard U., 1971; M.B.A., U. Pa., 1977. Diplomate: Am. Bd. Pediatrics, Am. Bd. Preventive Medicine. Intern Children's Hosp. Med. Center, Boston, 1969-70, resident, 1970-71, Georgetown U., 1972-73; spl. asst. Office Adminstr. Health Services and Mental Health Adminstrn. HEW, and; prin. med. service officer Office Dir. Job Corps, Dept. Labor, Washington, 1971-73; spl. asst. to dir. Health Services and Mental Health Adminstrn., HEW and; prin. med. officer Officer Dir. Job Corps, Dept. Labor, 1973; dir. div. peer rev. Health Service Adminstrn., HEW, Washington, 1974-75; commr. pub. health Commonwealth of Mass., Boston, 1975-79; lectr. Harvard U. Sch. Pub. Health, Boston U., Mass. Inst. Tech., 1975-79; prof. pediatrics and public health UCLA, 1979—, co-dir., 1979—; vis. prof. U. Calif., Los Angeles, 1976-78; trustee U. Mass., 1975-79; commr. Mass. Group Ins. Commn., 1975-79; bd. dirs. Postgrad. Med. Inst. and Mass. Health Research Inst., Inc., 1975-79; mem. Mass. Spl. Commn. on Med. Profl. Liability Ins., 1977-79; mem. adv. bd. Industry Network for Social, Urban and Rural Efforts, N.Y.C.; mem. adv. council on edn. for health Clearinghouse on Corp. Social Responsibility, Washington; mem. Calif. Gov.'s Council on Wellness and Phys. Fitness; chmn. editorial adv. bd. HEALTHFAX, N.Y.C.; cons. HEW, 1976—. Editor: Problems in Comprehensive Ambulatory Health Care for High Risk Adolescents, 1973; asso. editor: Ann. Rev. of Pub. Health, Pub. Health and Preventive Medicine; editor column: New Eng. Jour. Medicine, 1975-79. Bd. dirs. Met. Cultural Alliance, Boston, 1976-79. Served with USPHS, 1971-75. Mem. Am. Acad. Pediatrics, Am. Pub. Health Assn., Soc. Adolescent Medicine, Ambulatory Pediatric Assn., Am. Coll. Preventive Medicine, Phi Beta Kappa. Office: UCLA Sch Pub Health 31-236 CHS Center for Health Enhancement and Research UCLA Los Angeles CA 90024

FIELDMAN, LEON, lawyer; b. Milw., Apr. 5, 1926; s. Nathan Lewis and Lena Rose (Horwitz) F.; m. Beverly L. Kaminsky, July 4, 1948 (dec.); children: Nancy, Susan, James, Jonathan; m. Mary D. Gatzert, Oct. 7, 1979. B.B.A., U. Wis., 1949, LL.B., 1951. Bar: Ill. 1951. Assoc. Jenner & Block, Chgo., 1951-60, ptnr., 1960—; sec. and dir. Chgo. Estate Planning Council, 1983—; dir. Chgo. Bar Found., 1977-81; lectr. Nat. Trust Sch., Evanston, Ill., 1968-80; inquiry bd. Atty. Registration and Disciplinary Commn. Supreme Ct. Ill., Chgo., 1980—. Contbg. author: Handling Business Interests in Estates, 1982, Closely Held Corporations, 1983, Illinois Estate Adminstration, 1983. Pres., dir. Pub. Interest Law Internship Inc., Chgo., 1982—; pres. Sch. Dist. 108, Highland Park, Ill., 1971-72. Served with U.S. Army, 1943-46. Fellow Am. Coll. Probate Counsel (chmn. probate practice com. 1967-68); mem. Chgo. Bar Assn., Ill. State Bar Assn. (chmn. probate, estate planning and trust law sect. 1973-74), ABA, Order of the Coif. Club: Law of City of Chgo. Home: 580 Hillside Dr Highland Park IL 60035 Office: Jenner & Block 1 IBM Plaza Chicago IL 60611

FIELDS, BERNARD NATHAN, microbiologist, physician; b. Bklyn., Mar. 24, 1938; s. Julius and Martha F.; m. Ruth Peedin, Sept. 10, 1966; children—John, Edward, Michael, Daniel, Joshua. A.B., Brandeis U., 1958; M.D., N.Y. U., 1962; A.M. (hon.), Harvard U., 1976. Intern Beth Israel Hosp., Boston, 1962-63, resident in medicine, 1963-64; officer USPHS, Nat. Communicable Disease Center, Atlanta, 1965-67; fellow Albert Einstein Coll. Medicine, N.Y.C., 1967-68, asst. prof. medicine and cell biology, 1968-71, asso. prof., 1971-75, chief infectious disease, 1971-75; prof. microbiology and molecular genetics Harvard Med. Sch., 1975—; chief infectious diseases Peter Bent Brigham Hosp., Boston, 1975—; mem. and chmn. exptl. virology study sect. NIH, 1977-81, spl. reviewer, 1973-75, cons. nat. vaccine adv. bd., 1973, mem. task force in virology, 1976; reviewer AEC carcinogenesis and somatic effects program Oak Ridge Nat. Lab., 1974; mem. Multiple Sclerosis Adv. Commn. on Fundamental Research, 1976. Contbr. articles to profl. jours. Recipient Faculty Research Asso. award Am. Cancer Soc., 1969-74, Irma T. Hirschel scholar, 1974-76; Career Scientist award Health Research Council N.Y., 1974—; 12th Ann. Redway medal N.Y. State Med. Soc., 1974; grantee Am. Cancer Soc., 1969-70, Multiple Sclerosis Soc., 1975—, NIH, 1969—. Mem. AAAS, Am. Soc. Microbiology, Am. Soc. Clin. Investigation, Harvey Soc., Am. Assn. Immunologists, Infectious Disease Soc. Am. Home: 281 Otis St West Newton MA 02165 Office: Dept Microbiology and Molecular Genetics Harvard Med Sch 25 Shattuck St Boston MA 02115

FIELDS, BERTRAM HARRIS, lawyer; b. Los Angeles, Mar. 31, 1929; s. H. Maxwell and Mildred Arlyn (Ruben) F.; m. Lydia Ellen Minevitch, Oct. 22, 1960; 1 son, James Eldar. B.A., UCLA, 1949; J.D. magna cum laude, Harvard U., 1952. Bar: Calif. 1953. Practiced in, Los Angeles, 1955—; assoc. firm Shearer, Fields, Rohner & Shearer (and predecessor firms), 1955-57, mem. firm, 1957-82; ptnr. Greenberg, Glusker, Fields, Claman & Machtinger, 1982—; Dir. Mark VII Ltd., other corps. Bd. editors: Harvard Law Rev, 1953-55; Subject of: descriptive report in Sheresky, On Trial-Masters of the Courtroom, 1977. Served as 1st. lt. USAF, 1953-55; Korea. Mem. Am., Los Angeles County bar assns., Assn. Comml. Trial Lawyers. Office: Greenberg Glusker Fields Claman & Machtinger 1900 Ave of the Stars Suite 2000 Los Angeles CA 90067

FIELDS, DOUGLAS PHILIP, building supply and home furnishings wholesale company executive; b. Jersey City, May 19, 1942; s. Douglas Philip and Priscilla (Wagner) F.; m. Paulette Susan Titko, Dec. 15, 1970; children: Douglas Philip, Priscilla Wagner. B.S. summa cum laude, Fordham U., 1964; M.B.A. with distinction, Harvard U., 1966. Investment analyst Lehman Bros., N.Y.C., 1966-67; asst. to pres. Talley Industries, Mesa, Ariz., 1967-69; pres. TDA Industries, Inc., N.Y.C., 1969—, chmn. bd., 1970—; founder Unimet Corp., N.Y.C., 1970-73; chmn. bd. Westco Corp., Boston, 1970-79, Cooper Distbrs. Inc., Miami, Fla., 1972—, Eagle Supply, Inc., Tampa, Fla., 1973—; pres., chmn. Westcalind Corp., R.I., 1971—; cons. U.S. Office Edn., 1973-74, Fed. Energy Adminstrn., 1974-75. Outside dir. NYU Grad. Sch. Bus., Mgmt. Decision Lab., 1973-78; mem. N.Y. State adv. com. U.S. Civil Rights Commn., 1974—; bd. dirs. YMHA-YWHA of Lower Westchester, Mt. Vernon, N.Y., 1981—. Mem. Young Pres.'s Orgn. Clubs: Harvard of N.Y.C., Harvard of Fairfield County (Conn.), Harvard Bus. Sch. of N.Y.C.; Midtown Tennis (N.Y.C.) (pres. 1969—). Office: 122 E 42d St New York NY 10168

FIELDS, EMMETT B., history educator; b. Ft. Smith, Ark., Nov. 19, 1923; s. Emmett B. and Rose Almeda (Black) F.; m. Mary Christine Arnold, Aug. 31, 1947; children: Ross Christopher, Laura Alison, Mary Leslie. B.A. magna cum laude, Ouachita Coll., Arkadelphia, Ark., 1948; M.A., Vanderbilt U., 1950, Ph.D. in Am. History, 1953. Asst., then fellow in history Vanderbilt U., 1950- 52; asso. prof. history Jacksonville (Ala.) State Coll., 1952-54, prof., chmn. dept., 1955-57; dir. summer sessions, assoc. dean Coll. Arts and Scis. Vanderbilt U., 1957-60, dean Coll. Arts and Scis., 1960-69, pres., 1977-82, prof. history, 1982—; dean of faculties U. Houston, 1969-75, v.p., 1969-71, exec. v.p., 1971-75; pres. State U. N.Y. at Albany, 1975-77. Mem. Tex. Com. for Humanities, 1972-75, Sea Grant Adv. Council for Tex., 1972-74; bd. dirs. Nashville Inst. for Arts, 1980—; mem. commn. colls. and univs. So. Assn. Colls. and Schs., 1961-65, chmn. commn., 1964-65, pres. assn., 1969-70, trustee, 1965-75; bd. dirs. S.W. Center for Urban Research, 1969-75, v.p., 1971; bd. dirs. Albany Symphony Orch., 1976-77; trustee Dudley Obs., 1975-77. Mem. So. Conf. Acad. Deans, Am., So. hist. assns., Orgn. Am. Historians, Tenn. Council Pvt. Colls. (treas. 1980—), Assn. Am. Colls. (dir. 1980—), Am. Conf. Acad. Deans (exec. council 1969), Nashville C. of C. (gov.). Presbyterian. Club: Rotary (Nashville). Office: History Dept Vanderbilt U Nashville TN 37240

FIELDS, JACK MILTON, congressman; b. Houston, Feb. 3, 1952; s. Jack Milton and Jessie Faye F.; m. Roni Sue Haddock, Mar. 10, 1979. B.A., Baylor U., 1974, J.D., 1977. Bar: Tex. Practiced in, Humble, Tex., 1977-79; v.p. Rosewood Meml. Park Cemetery, 1977-79; mem. 97th-98th congresses from 8th dist. Tex. Republican. Baptist. Lodge: Masons. Office: 4B Cannon House Office Bldg Washington DC 20515 *

FIELDS, JOHN EDWIN, univ. adminstr.; b. Bismarck, N.D., Jan. 20, 1915; s. Paris Ransom and Clara (Collins) F.; m. Jean Maxine Rogers, June 21, 1941; children—Christopher Clay, Julie Ransom. B.S., Northwestern U., 1936; student Japanese lang., history, econ. politics, militarism, 1937-43; M.B.A., UCLA, 1960. Free lance writer, Japan, China, 1937; alumni, pub. relations Northwestern U., 1938-43; acting chief Japan-Korea sect. Pacific bur. psychol. warfare (overseas shortwave broadcasting), O.W.I., San Francisco, 1943, chief, 1944-45, Japan sect. internat. broadcasting div. Dept. State, San Francisco, 1945-46; editor, pub. Far East Trader, 1946-49; pres. Farm Implement Co., 1947-48; v.p. U.S. Tractor & Engring. Co., 1947-48; dir. devel. U. So. Cal., 1948-52, v.p. charge devel., 1952-56; exec. v.p. Maple Investment, Inc., 1957-66; also partner Valley Vista Investment Co., Phoenix, 1960-68; pres. Apsco Products, Inc. div. Maple Industries, Inc., dir. parent co., 1958-71; v.p. Northwestern U., 1971—; dir. Computer Equipment Corp., Placer County Land Co., CETEC Corp. Trustee Hugh O'Brian Youth Fedn., Japan Found. Mem. Am. Alumni Council (v.p. 1941-42, dir. 1942-43), Am. Coll. Pub. Relations Assn. (v.p. 1953-56), Pub. Relations Soc. Am. (dir. 1952-56, western regional v.p. 1956). Presbyterian. Clubs: Tavern, Chicago (Chgo.); Westmoreland Country (Wilmette, Ill.). Home: 624 Noyes Evanston IL Office: 633 Clark Evanston IL 60201

FIELDS, LOUIS GLENN, JR., ambassador; b. Miami, Fla., May 21, 1929; s. Louis Glenn and Martha Emily (Holbrook) F.; m. Katherine Armistead Guerrant, Nov. 7, 1953; 1 dau., Frances Holbrook. B.A., U. Fla., 1950; J.D., U. Va., 1956. Bar: Va. 1956. Sole practice law, Richmond, Va., 1956-60; title atty. Lawyers Title Ins. Corp., Richmond, 1960-62; atty. A.H. Robins Co. Inc., Richmond, 1962-66; mem. staff Senator A. Willis Robertson, Washington, 1966-67; cons.-expert AID, Saigon, 1967-69, Washington, 1967-69; atty.-adviser Dept. State, Washington, 1969-70, asst. legal adviser, 1970-81; ambassador, U.S. rep. Com. on Disarmament, UN, 1982—; lectr. in forensic medicine Med. Coll. Va., 1957-66, U.S. Air Force Spl. Ops. Sch., 1969-81; participant confs. in internat. terroism; dir. Community Bank & Trust Co., Springfield, Va., First Comml. Bank, Arlington, Va. Contbr. textbook on forensic medicine. Mem. Bd. Fire Appeals, Richmond, 1965-70; bd. dirs. ARC, Richmond chpt., 1960-65, Gamble's Hill Community Ctr., Richmond, 1960-63. Served with AUS, 1952-54. Fellow Internat. Consular Acad.; mem. Fed. Bar. Assn., Va. State Bar Assn. (chmn. joint com. local bar orgn. 1963-64), Am. Mgmt. Assn. (co-chmn. seminar on mergers and acquisitions 1964). Clubs: Capitol Hill (Washington); country of Va. (Richmond). Office: US Mission to UN 799 United Nations Plaza New York NY 10017 *

FIELDS, PAUL ROBERT, research nuclear chemist, consultant; b. Chgo., Feb. 4, 1919; s. Alexander and Anna (Greene) F.; m. Bernice White, Jan. 3, 1943; children: Marlene Frances, Rita Norine, Donald Brian. B.S., U. Chgo., 1941. Chemist TVA, Wilson Dam, Ala., 1941-43, Metall. Lab. U. Chgo., 1943-45, Standard Oil Co., Whiting, Ind., 1945-46; with Argonne Nat. Lab., Ill., 1946—, dir. Chemistry Div., 1971-81, dir. Sci. Support Div., 1982—; cons. Simon & Schuster, Cleve., 1982—. Author, editor: Laboratory Experiments in Heavy Element Chemistry, 1955, Lanthanide-Actinide Chemistry, 1967, Cleaning our Environment, 1978; contbr. articles in field to profl. jours.; co-discoverer 3 new elements; patentee in field. Fellow AAAS, Am. Nuclear Soc.; mem. Am. Chem. Soc. (recipient Nuclear Applications in Chemistry award 1970), Am. Phys. Soc., Phi Beta Kappa. Home: 7308 N California Ave Chicago IL 60645 Office: Argonne Nat Lab 9700 S Cass Ave Argonne IL 60439

FIELDS, RALPH RAYMOND, educator; b. Prescott, Ariz., Apr. 29, 1907; s. Ralph Henson and Edna (Holmes) F.; m. Catherine Julia Tinker, Aug. 24, 1931; children: Ralph Rodney, Kay Louise. Student, Phoenix Jr. Coll., 1924-26; A.B., U. Ariz., 1929; A.M., Stanford, 1934, Ed.D., 1940. Instr. Phoenix Union High Sch., 1930-34, asst. dir. research and guidance, 1934-35; curriculum field sec. Stanford U. Santa Barbara Curriculum Project, 1936-38; asst. prof. edn. Stanford, 1938-41; curriculum dir. San Jose (Calif.) Unified Sch. Dist., 1941-42, asst. supt. schs., 1942-45, supt. schs., 1945-47; asso. supt., chief div. instrn. Calif. State Dept. Edn., 1947-48; exec. officer div. of instrn., prof. edn. Tchrs. Coll., Columbia, 1948-50, dir. div. instrn., prof. edn., 1950-59, asso. dean, 1959-61, prof. higher edn., 1961-74, prof. emeritus, 1974—; chief party Tchrs. Coll. ICA Mission, East Africa, 1961-62, AID sponsored project in, Peru, 1966-68; dir. Office Overseas Projects, 1969-71; chief party Tchrs. Coll. AID sponsored project in, Afghanistan, 1971-74; Mem. survey staff for P.R. pub. schs., 1948-49; mem. Calif. State Curriculum Commn., 1945-47; Dir. or cons. ednl. workshops and curriculum programs; dir. Community Coll. Study, Pa. Bd. Edn., 1964-65; liaison officer, cons. Asso. Colls. Mid-Hudson Area. Author: Kingsborough Community College: Final Report, The Community College Movement; Contbr. to: fifty-fifth year-book The Public Junior College, Nat. Soc. Study Edn., 1956, articles to profl. jours. Chmn. The Calif. Framework Com., 1947-48. Mem. NEA, AAUP, Am. Assn. Sch. Adminstrs., Am. Ednl. Research Assn., Am. Assn. Jr. Colls. (chmn. com. on curriculum and adult edn. 1952-53). Home: 234 Amesbury Circle Sun City Center FL 33570

FIELDS, ROBERT CHARLES, retired printing company executive; b. Tipton, Iowa, Aug. 18, 1920; s. Forrest Filson and Frieda (Werling) F.; m. Velma Mae Ohlsen, Oct. 26, 1941; children—Michael, David. B.S. in Mech. Engring, Iowa State U., 1949; grad., Advanced Mgmt. Program, Harvard U., 1961. With R.R. Donnelley & Sons Co., 1949-82, mfg. div., 1958-63, v.p., 1959-65, dir. sales div., 1963-68, sr. v.p., 1965-71, group dir., 1968-71, group v.p., 1971-75, exec. v.p., 1975-81, vice chmn., 1981-82, dir., 1972—. Bd. govs. Iowa State U. Found. Served to 2d lt. USAF, 1942-45. Mem. Newberry Library Assn., Art Inst., Field Mus. Clubs: Iowa State Univ., Harvard Business (Chgo.). Home: 5317 Turvey Ct Downers Grove IL 60515

FIELDS, VICTOR ALEXANDER, author, educator, vocal research specialist; b. Phila., Feb. 3, 1901; s. Solomon Alexander and Julia (Ross) F.; m. Mary Elizabeth Cameron, Jan. 27, 1943. Student singing, music and dramatics privately, Julliard Sch. Music, Teachers Coll., Columbia U., U.S.A. and Europe, 1919-30; B.S., Coll. City N.Y., 1926; M.A., Columbia U., 1930, Ph.D., 1946. Tchr. voice, dramatics and speech; prof. voice and diction City Coll. N.Y., 1926-68, emeritus prof. voice and diction, 1969—, dir. voice and speech clinic, 1932-57, deptl. supr., evening div., 1941-66; vis. prof. U. Oreg., summer, 1938. 40, Butler U., 1949. Began musical career in, 1919; sang in opera, oratorio, church and concert; Author: Training the Singing Voice, 1947, The Singer's Glossary, 1951, Foundations of the Singer's Art, 1977; Co-author: books including Taking the Stage, 1939, Voice and Diction, 1949. Asst. in speech rehab. of disabled war vets. VA, Army Hall speech Clinic, 1946-49; mem. N.Y. City Bd. Edn. com. surveying handicapped children in pub. schs., 1936-39. Mem. Music Educators Nat. Conf., Assn. for Higher Edn., Nat. Assn. Tchrs. Singing, Music Tchrs. Nat. Assn., Collegiate Chorale, NEA, Acoustical Soc. Am., Phi Mu Alpha, Phi Delta Kappa. Club: Mason. Home: 1514 Kennedy Plaza Utica NY 13502 *In every aspect of our existence, we live to grow. Ideals are implanted to provide incentives and to stimulate our growth. We should, therefore, cherish our ideals and seek to emulate those who exemplify them. We grow toward our ideals.*

FIELDS, WILLIAM ALBERT, lawyer; b. Parkersburg, W.Va., Mar. 30, 1939; s. Jack Lyons and Grace (Kelley) F.; m. Prudence Brandt Adams, June 26, 1964. B.S. magna cum laude, Ohio State U., 1961; postgrad., Harvard Law Sch., 1961-64. Bar: Ohio bar 1964. Since practiced in, Marietta, city prosecutor, 1964-65; acting Judge Marietta Municipal Ct.; dir. elections, Washington County, 1967-74, profl. bass-baritone soloist. Chmn. Washington County Heart Assn., 1965-67; county chmn. Am. Cancer Soc., 1967; mem. dist. exec. com. Boy Scouts Am., 1967-74; Treas. County Republican Exec. Com., 1966—; county chmn. Nixon for Pres., 1968, Saxbe for Senator, 1968; Trustee YMCA, Salvation Army; pres. bd. trustees Washington Tech. Coll., Marietta; exec. com., trustee Coll. Adminstrv. Scis., Ohio State U.; trustee Appalachian Bible Inst., Bradley, W.Va., 1974-77. Recipient Meritorious Service award Am. Heart Assn., 1968, Wall St. Jour. award, 1961; named Outstanding Young Man of Marietta, 1968. Mem. Ohio, Washington County bar assns., Marietta Area C. of C. (v.p., trustee), Am. Mensa., Sigma Chi, Beta Gamma Sigma. Clubs: Rotarian (pres. 1970-71), Marietta Country (trustee). Home: 129 Hillcrest Dr Marietta OH 45750 Office: 217 2d St Marietta OH 45750 *Without the light of Christ, all is darkness and vain machination.*

FIELEKE, NORMAN SIEGFRIED, economist; b. Kankakee, Ill., Aug. 22, 1932; s. Lessly and Catharine M. (Nicholson) F.; m. Carol A. Curtiss, June 16, 1962; children—Andrew, Eric, Michael. B.A. summa cum laude, Amherst Coll., 1954; A.M., Harvard U., 1955; Ph.D. (Littauer fellow, NSF fellow), 1969. Economist, budget examiner Office Mgmt. and Budget, Washington, 1959-64; industry economist Office U.S. Trade Rep., Exec. Office Pres., 1964-65; v.p., economist Fed. Res. Bank of Boston, 1967—; dir. econ. research U.S. Internat. Trade Commn., Washington, 1980; adj. prof. Boston U., 1975-76. Author: The Welfare Effects of Controls over Capital Exports from the United States, 1971; contbr. articles to profl. jours. Served to lt. USAF, 1955-57. Home: 5 Canterbury Rd Winchester MA 01890 Office: 600 Atlantic Ave Boston MA 02106

FIELSTRA, HELEN ADAMS (MRS. CLARENCE FIELSTRA), teacher educator; b. Elkhorn, W.Va., Feb. 26, 1921; d. Fred Russell and Clara Sue (Williams) Adams; m. Edmond T. Dooley, Jr., Nov. 15, 1941 (div. 1948); 1 dau., Dereth Dooley Pendleton; m. Clarence Fielstra, Jan. 1, 1956. A.B., UCLA, 1950; M.A., Stanford U., 1954, Ed.D., 1967. Tchr. Santa Monica (Calif.) Unified Sch. Dist., 1947-50; elem. coordinator San Diego County Schs., 1950-52; lectr. edn. Stanford U., 1953-54, UCLA, 1957-58; gen. elementary supr. Burbank (Calif.) Unified Sch. Dist., 1954-56, Beverly Hills (Calif.) Unified Sch. Dist., 1959-61; asst. prof. edn. Calif. State U., Northridge, 1961-67, asso. prof., 1967-70, prof., 1970—; sec.-treas., editor Fielstra Publs., Inc., Pacific Palisades, Calif.; sec.-treas. Hadco, Inc., Los Angeles.; Tng. coordinator Office Econ. Opportunity Tng. and Devel. Center, 1965-66; cons., speaker curriculum devel. and instructional supervision, 1952—; prin. investigator U.S. Office Edn. Project Tchr. Edn. for Disadvantaged, 1968-70; dir. interdisciplinary social sci. projects NSF, 1972-83; dir. Western Regional Center Edn. Devel. Center, 1974-76; chief cons. early childhood edn. Listener Corp. Author: (with L.G. Thomas, A. Coladarci, Lucien Kinney) Perspective on Teaching, 1961, (with Clarence Fielstra) Africa With Focus on Nigeria, 1963, Relationship Between Selected Factors and Pupil Success in Elementary School Foreign Languages Classes; also various monographs, curriculum guides, 2 ednl. films. Trustee, mem. exec. com. Calif. State U. Found., Northridge, 1970-72. Recipient Disting. Prof. award Calif. State Univ. and Coll. System, 1969, certificate of service Asso. Students Calif. State U., Northridge, 1970. Mem. Nat. Soc. for Study Edn., Am. Ednl. Research Assn., Nat. Council Social Studies (mem. publs. bd. 1970-72), Calif. Tchrs. Assn. (life), NEA (life), Congress of Faculty Assns. (founder), Assn. Supervision and Curriculum Devel., Stanford U. Alumni Assn., Calif. Assn. Supervision and Curriculum Devel. (chmn. state com. on supervision in structure public edn.), Calif. Council on Edn., AAUP, Calif. Higher Edn. Assn. (dir. 1970-74, pres. 1973-74), Calif. Coll. and U. Faculty Assn. (pres. chpt. 1969-70, state pres. 1972-73), Delta Zeta, Pi Lambda Theta, Delta Kappa Gamma (pres. Beta Eta chpt. 1960-62). Democrat. Clubs: Stanford (Los Angeles County); Palisadian Woman's. Home: 14177 Sunset Blvd Pacific Palisades CA 90272 Office: Calif State U Northridge CA 91330

FIENBERG, STEPHEN ELLIOTT, statistician; b. Toronto, Ont., Can., Nov. 27, 1942; came to U.S., 1964. B.S., U. Toronto, 1964; A.M., Harvard U., 1965, Ph.D., 1968. Asst. prof. dept. stats. and theoretical biology U. Chgo., 1968-72; asso. prof. dept. applied stats. U. Minn., St. Paul, 1972-76, prof., 1976-80, chmn. dept., 1972-78; prof. dept. stats. and social sci. Carnegie-Mellon U., Pitts., 1980—, head dept. stats., 1981—; chmn. com. on nat. stats. NRC, 1981—. Author: (with others) Discrete Multivariate Analysis: Theory and Practice, 1975, Analysis of Cross-classified Categorical Data, 1977, 2d edit., 1980, Beginning Statistics with Data Analysis, 1983; editor: (with A. Zellner) Studies in Bayesian Econometrics and Statistics, 1975, (with D.V. Hinkley) R.A. Fisher: An Appreciation, 1980, (with A.J. Reiss, Jr.) Indicators of Crime and Criminal Justice: Quantitative Studies, 1980. Fellow AAAS, Am. Statis. Assn., Inst. Statisticians, Inst. Math. Stats., Royal Statis. Soc.; mem. Biometric Soc., Internat. Statis. Inst., Psychometric Soc. Office: Dept Stats Carnegie-Mellon U Pittsburgh PA 15213

FIERING, NORMAN, historian, library adminstrator; b. N.Y.C., Jan. 8, 1935; s. Benjamin and Dora (Karp) F.; m. Renee Dashiell, May 29, 1958; children: Benjamin, Jason, Cassandre. B.A., Dartmouth Coll., 1956; Ph.D., Columbia U., 1969. Instr. Stanford U., Calif., 1964-69; postdoctoral fellow Inst. Early Am. History and Culture, Williamsburg, Va., 1969-72, editor publs., 1972-82, acting dir., 1982-83; dir., librarian John Carter Brown Library, Providence, 1983—. Author: Jonathan Edward's Moral Thought, 1981 (Orgn. Am. Historians Merle Curti award 1981); Moral Philosophy at 17th-Century Harvard, 1981. Fellow NEH, 1975-76, Nat. Humanities Ctr., Research Triangle Park, N.C., 1978-79. Mem. Am. Antiquarian Soc., Am. Hist. Assn. Home: 19 Lorraine Ave Providence RI 02906 Office: John Carter Brown Library PO Box 1894 Providence RI 02912

FIERY, BENJAMIN FRANKLIN, lawyer; b. Martinsburg, W.Va., Apr. 19, 1894; s. Samuel V. and Emily (Dukehart) F.; m. Virginia Biechele, Sept. 13, 1924; 1 dau., Anne (Mrs. Richard C. Bryan). A.B., Washington and Lee U., 1913; LL.B., Harvard, 1916. Bar: W.Va. bar 1916, Ohio bar 1917, U.S. Supreme Ct 1921. With firm Baker, Hostetler & Sidlo, Cleve., 1916-17; pvt. sec. to sec. of war Newton D. Baker, 1920-21; mem. firm Baker, Hostetler & Patterson, Cleve., from 1925; now mem. firm Baker Hostetler, Cleve. Trustee Law Library Assn. Served as 2d lt., air service U.S. Army, 1917-19. Mem. Am., Ohio, Cleve. bar assns., Am. Judicature Soc., Omicron Delta Kappa., Delta Tau Delta. Clubs: Union, Nisi Prius (Cleve.); Chagrin Valley Hunt. Home: 2676 Eaton Rd Cleveland OH 44118 Office: 3200 National City Center Cleveland OH 44115

FIESTER, CLARK GEORGE, communications company executive; b. Hazleton, Pa., Jan. 25, 1934; s. Benjamin Francis and Grethel (Tressler) F.; m. Thelma Christine Simpson, Mar. 16, 1957; children: Thomas Clark, Nancy Ann. B.S., Pa. State U., 1955; postgrad., Ohio State Grad. Ctr., Dayton, 1956-57; M.S., Stanford U., 1960. Mem. tech. staff Bell Telephone Labs., Murray Hill, N.J., 1955; research and devel. officer U.S. Air Force, Wright Patterson AFB, Ohio, 1955-57; v.p. and gen. mgr. GTE Communications Products Corp., Sylvania Group, Mountain View, Calif., 1957—; dir. Nat. Secutity Agr. adv. bd., Ft. George G. Meade, Md., 1983; chmn. Nat. Electronic Warfare Symposium Assn. of Old Crows, San Francisco, 1981. Chmn. Jr. Achievement Campaign, San Jose, Calif., 1980; bd. dirs. Santa Clara County Mfg. Group, San Jose, 1981—; chmn. United Way Campaign policy com., Santa Clara, 1981—, Santa Clara Bond Drive, 1978-79. Gen. Electric scholar, 1954. Office: GTE Communications Products Corp Sylvania Systems Group-WD PO Box 7188 Mountain View CA 94039

FIEVE, RONALD ROBERT, psychiatrist; b. Stevens Point, Wis., Mar. 5, 1930; s. Bjarne Elertson and Evelyn Anna (Knudson) F.; m. Katia Von Saxe, Dec. 12, 1963; children: Lara, Vanessa. B.S. in Engring, U. Wis., 1951; M.D., Harvard U., 1955. Intern Columbia U. Med. Service, Bellevue Hosp., N.Y.C., 1955-56; resident internal medicine and cardiology New York Hosp.-Cornell U., 1956-57; resident in psychiatry N.Y. State Psychiat. Inst., N.Y.C., 1957-60, research asst., 1960-63, dir. acute psychiat. service, 1962; chief psychiat. research Lithium Clinic, 1963—; attending physician Vanderbilt Clinic, Columbia Presbyn. Hosp.; med. dir. Found. for Depression and Manic-Depression, Inc., 1974—; prof. clin. psychiatry Coll. Phys. Surgs. Columbia U., 1973—; prin. investigator NIMH grant, 1967-70, 72, 79-81, N.Y. State Mental Hygiene grant, 1970-73, Columbia-Millhouser Depression grant, 1973—. Author: Moodswing: The Third Revolution in Psychiatry, 1975, A Physician's Guide to Depression, 1975; editor: (with D. Rosenthal and H.Brill) Genetic Research in Psychiatry, 1975; contbr. articles to sci. publs. Recipient Richard H. Hutchings award, 1971, N.Y. State Mental Hygiene Distinguished Service citation, 1972. Fellow Am. Psychiat. Assn., Am. Coll. Neuropsycho-Pharmacology; mem. Am. Psychopathological Assn., Psychiat. Research Soc., Harvey Soc., Coll. Internat. Neuro-Psycho-pharmacology, Soc. Practitioners of Columbia Presbyn. Med. Center. Lutheran. Clubs: Harvard, Southampton. Office: 722 W 168th St New York NY 10032

FIFE, AUSTIN EDWIN, former educator, author; b. Lincoln, Idaho, Dec. 18, 1909; s. Robert H. and Mary Elizabeth (Stocks) F.; m. Alta Stevens, Mar. 27, 1934; children: Carolyn (Mrs. David S. Langdon), Marian (Mrs. Burton Baldwin). B.A., Stanford U., 1934, Ph.D., 1939; M.A., Harvard U., 1937. Prof. French Occidental Coll., Los Angeles, 1946-58; specialist for langs. U.S. Office Edn., 1959-60; prof. French, head dept. langs. Utah State U., Logan, 1960-75. Author: (with Mrs. Fife) Saints of Sage and Saddle, 1956, 81, Borzoi Book of French Folk Tales, 1956, Songs of the Cowboys, 1966, Cowboy and Western Songs, 1968, Ballads of the Great West, 1970, Forms upon the Frontier, 1969, Heaven on Horseback, 1970; Contbr. articles to profl. jours. Served to lt. col. USAF, 1942-45, 51-53. Recipient Distinguished Service award Utah State U., 1976; Fulbright exchange prof. French Nat. Museums, 1950-51; Guggenheim fellow, 1958-59; Sr. fellow NEH, 1971-72. Fellow Am. Folklore Soc., Utah Hist. Soc., Utah Heritage Found., Utah Acad. Sci., Arts and Letters; mem. MLA, Rocky Mountain Modern Lang. Assn. Home: 686 E 10th North Logan UT 84321

FIFE, EUGENE V(AWTER), investment banking executive; b. Hinton, W.Va., Sept. 23, 1940; s. Clark E. and Margaret Ellen (Morton) F.; children: David E., Amy S. B.S., Va. Poly. Inst., 1962; M.B.A., U. So. Calif., 1968. With Northrop Corp., Los Angeles, 1965-66; assoc. corp. fin. Blyth & Co., Inc., N.Y.C., 1968-70; assoc. investment banking Goldman, Sachs & Co., San Francisco, 1970-80, v.p., 1976-80, ptnr. investment banking, 1980—; dir. Medfrord Corp., (Oreg.). Bd. dirs. San Francisco Opera, 1982, Met. YMCA, San Francisco, 1982. Served to 2d lt USAF, 1962-65. Clubs: Union (N.Y.C.); Bankers, Commonwealth (San Francisco). Office: Goldman Sachs & Co 555 California St San Francisco CA 94104

FIFE, JONATHAN DONALD, educator; b. Washington, Nov. 9, 1941; s. G. Donald and Marie D. (Wall) F.; m. Janice McKenna, Aug. 10, 1968 (div. May 1980); children: Patrick McKenna, Timothy Kingston, Brendan Martin; m. Lynn Barnett, June 6, 1980; stepchildren: Brian Stonner Haupt, Alison Lynn Haupt. B.B.A., U. Mass., 1965; postgrad., U. Cin., 1965-67; M.S., SUNY-Albany, 1970; Ed.D., Pa. State U., 1975. Mem. staff Student Union, U. Cin., 1965-67; asst. dir. student activities SUNY-Buffalo, 1967-69; research asst. Ctr. for Study Higher Edn., Pa. State U. (State Coll.), 1970-72; assoc. dir. ERIC Clearinghouse on Higher Edn., George Washington U., Washington, 1972-77, dir., 1977—; adj. asst. prof. George Washington U. ERIC Clearinghouse on Higher Edn., George Wahington U., 1977-79; assoc. prof. ERIC Clearinghouse on Higher Edn., George Washington U., Washington, 1979-84, prof., 1984—; bd. dirs. Nat. Ctr. for Higher Edn. Mgmt. Systems, Boulder, Colo., 1980-82. Editor: monograph series ERIC Higher Education Research Reports, 1972—; mng. editor: Rev. Higher Edn., 1980—; cons. editor: Change, 1981—; contbr. articles to profl. jours. Pres. Wheaton Sq. East Condominium, 1973-78. Mem. Assn. Study Higher Edn. (exec. sec.-treas. 1978—), Am. Ednl. Research Assn., Higher Edn. Group Washington (sec. 1979-81), Assn. Instnl. Research, Spl. Interst Group in Higher Edn. (sec. 1976-81), Phi Kappa Phi, Omicron Delta Kappa. Home: 8912 Flower Ave Silver Spring MD 20901 Office: George Washington U 1 Dupont Circle Suite 630 Washington DC 20036

FIFE, WILLIAM FRANKLIN, drug company executive; b. Buffalo, W.Va., Nov. 6, 1921; s. Alfred Charles and Grace (Pitchford) F.; children—Scott Franklin, Susan Elizabeth, Cindy Francine. A.B., Berea Coll., 1949; M.S., U. Wis., 1950. Operating mgr. McKesson & Robbins, Chgo. and Kansas City, Mo., 1950-56; Cleve. Wholesale Drug Co., 1956-58; with Owens, Minor & Bodeker, Inc., 1958—; sr. v.p. Owens, Minor & Bodeker, Inc. (now Owens & Minor, Inc.), Richmond, Va., 1981—; also dir. Owens, Minor & Bodeker, Inc. Served with C.E. U.S. Army, 1942-46. Mem. Nat. Wholesale Drug Assn. Democrat. Club: Rotary. Home: 8711 Gayton Rd Richmond VA 23229 Office: Owens Minor & Bodeker Inc 2727 Enterprise Pkwy Richmond VA 23229

FIFE, WILMER KRAFFT, chemistry educator; b. Wellsville, Ohio, Oct. 19, 1933; s. Wilmer George and Lourene Elizabeth (Krafft) F.; m. Betsy Louise Jones, Dec. 26, 1959; children: Kimberly, Julia, Steven. B.Sc. in Chemistry, Case Inst. Tech., 1955; Ph.D. in Organic Chemistry, Ohio State U., 1960. Applications chemist Monsanto Chem. Co., Dayton, Ohio, summers 1955, 57; instr. Muskingum (Ohio) Coll., 1959-60, asst. prof., 1960-64, asso. prof., 1964-70, prof., 1970-71, chmn. dept. chemistry, 1966-71; prof. chemistry Ind. U.-Purdue U. at Indpls., 1971—, chmn. dept., 1971-80. NIH postdoctoral fellow Harvard U., 1965-66, Columbia U., 1968-69; NSF fellow, 1955-56; Sinclair Oil Co. fellow, 1958-59; DuPont fellow, 1960; Danforth asso., 1969—; others. Mem. Am. Chem. Soc., AAAS, Sigma Xi, Tau Beta Pi, Phi Lambda Upsilon. Home: 7102 Dean Rd Indianapolis IN 46240

FIFER, CHARLES NORMAN, English educator; b. Evanston, Ill., Aug. 29, 1922; s. Warren Taylor and Margaret (McMillen) F.; m. Norma Crow, Aug. 20, 1955. B.A., Northwestern U., 1947, M.A., 1949; Ph.D., Yale U., 1954. Instr. in English Iowa State Coll., Ames, 1949, Lawrence Coll., Appleton, Wis., 1949-51, U. Ill., 1954-56; asst. prof. English Stanford U., 1956-61, assoc. prof., 1961-69, prof., 1969—, assoc. exec. head, dir. grad. studies dept. English, 1964-69. Editor: The Correspondence of James Bowell with Certain Members of the Club, 1976, George Farquhar's The Beaux Strategem, 1977; co-editor: (with others) English Literature: 1600-1800: A Bibliography of Modern Studies, vols. 5 and 6, 1972. Served with AUS, 1943-46. Mem. MLA, Soc. for 18th Century Studies, Johnson Soc. of Lichfield, AAUP. Democrat. Office: Dept English Stanford U Stanford CA 94305

FIFIELD, GARY MORTON, opera producer; b. Los Angeles, May 1, 1939; s. Howard C. and Esther S. F. Student, Jr. Coll. Kansas City, Mo., 1957-59; student in English lit., U. Mo., 1960-61. Bus. mgr. Kansas City Lyric Theater, 1962-65; asst. to gen. dir. San Francisco Opera Assn., 1965-69; exec. dir. Opportunity Resources for Arts, 1971-76; mng. dir. Washington Opera, 1976—; guest lectr. in arts mgmt. Wharton Sch. U. Pa., SUNY, Bklyn. Coll., George Washington U. Mem. Opera Am. (dir.), Cultural Alliance Greater Washington (dir.). Office: Washington Opera John F Kennedy Center Washington DC 20566 *

FIFIELD, RUSSELL HUNT, political science educator; b. Readfield, Maine, Feb. 21, 1914; s. Charlie Belle and Emma (Hunt) F. A.B., Bates Coll., 1935, LL.D., 1963; M.A., Clark U., 1940, Ph.D., 1942. Specialist hist. research State Dept., 1944-45; Am. Fgn. service officer, China and Formosa, 1945-47; mem. faculty U. Mich., 1947—, prof. polit. sci., 1954—; Fulbright research prof. U. Philippines, 1953-54; prof. fgn. affairs Nat. War Coll., 1958-59, participant nat. security seminars, 1979, 80; asso. research E. Asian Research Center, Harvard U., 1967-68; sr. research asso. S.E. Asia program Cornell, Spring 1972; vis. fellow Inst. SE Asian Studies, Singapore, fall 1978; Mem. adv. panel E. Asia and Pacific, State Dept., 1966-69; cons. Bur. Intelligence and Research, State Dept., 1953-54, 67-70; sec. gen. XXVII Internat. Congress Orientalists, 1964-67; exec. com. XXVIII and XXIX Congress, 1970, 73. Author: Woodrow Wilson and the Far East, 1952, Diplomacy of Southeast Asia, 1945-58, 1958, Southeast Asia in U.S. Policy, 1963, Americans in Southeast Asia, 1973, Nat. and Regional Interests in ASEAN, 1979; Contbr.: Asian Wall St. Jour, 1980—. Guggenheim fellow, 1958-59; Council Fgn. Relations fellow, 1959-60; research fellow St. Antony's Coll., Oxford (Eng.) U., 1963-64, Twentieth Century Fund, 1967-69; Earhart Found. fellow, 1971-72, fall 1978. Mem. Assn. Asian Studies (sec. 1961-63, sec.-treas. 1983—), Am. Hist. Assn. (George Louis Beer prize 1953), Detroit Com. Fgn. Relations (chmn. 1970-71), Council Fgn. Relations N.Y., Phi Beta Kappa, Phi Kappa Phi. Club: Cosmos. Home: 400 Maynard St Ann Arbor MI 48104

FIFIELD, WILLARD MERWIN, ret. assn. exec.; b. Schenectady, Jan. 17, 1908; s. Stephen H. and Letty (Gates) F.; m. Hazel Hook, July 22, 1935 (dec. Apr. 21, 1976). B.S.A., U. Fla., 1930, M.S., 1932; post-grad., Cornell U. With U. Fla., 1930-62, beginning as grad. asst., successively asst. horticulturist, horticulturist charge, asst. dir. sta. system, dir., 1950-55, provost for agr., 1955-62; sec., mgr. Fla. Agrl. Research Inst., 1962-75, ret., 1975; Past chmn. agrl. div. Fla. C. of C. Contbr. articles profl. publs. Served to lt. col. USAAF, 1942-46. Recipient Distinguished Service award Fla. Seedmen's Assn., 61953; named Man of Year in Fla. Agr. Progressive Farmer mag., 1955; Ann. Distinguished Service award Fla. Fruit and Vegetable Assn., 1959. Fellow A.A.A.S.; mem. Assn. So. Agrl. Workers (past pres.), Assn. So. Agrl. Expt. Sta. Dir. (past chmn.), Com. of Nine (past chmn.), Fla. Hort. Soc. (pres. 1964), Soil Sci. Soc. Fla., Sigma Xi, Delta Tau Delta, Gamma Sigma Delta, Alpha Zeta, Phi Sigma, Gamma Sigma Epsilon, Fla. Blue Key, Scabbard and Blade. Presbyn. Club: Rotarian. Home: 1823 NW 7th Ave Gainesville FL 32603

FIFIELSKI, EDWIN PETER, lawyer; b. Chgo., Oct. 4, 1916; s. Walter A. and Bessie (Dombrowski) F.; m. Jewel Weglarz, June 18, 1944. LL.B., John Marshall Law Sch., 1940, J.D., 1950. Bar: Ill. bar 1940. Since practiced in, Chgo.; Chmn. bd. Jefferson State Bank; pres. Spring Realty & Mortgage Co., Emancipator Ins. Agy., Inc. Alderman 45th ward, Chgo., 1963-79; Mem. com. Chgo. council Boy Scouts Am., 1958—. Served from pvt. to capt. AUS, 1940-46. Mem. AMVETS (state comdr. 1959-61, nat. comdr. 1961-62), Jefferson Park C. of C. (pres. 1959-61), Ill. Bar Assn., Am. Judicature Soc., Nat. Advocates Soc., Am. Legion, V.F.W., Chgo. Soc. (pres. 1971). Clubs: K.C., Jefferson Park Lions (pres. 1966-67). Office: 4758 N Milwaukee Ave Chicago IL 60630

FIFLIS, TED J., lawyer, educator; b. Chgo., Feb. 20, 1933; s. James P. and Christine (Karakitsos) F.; m. Vasilike Pantelakos, July 3, 1955; children: Christina, Antonia, Andreanna. B.S., Northwestern U., 1954; LL.B., Harvard U., 1957. Bar: Ill. 1957, Colo. 1975. Individual practice law, Chgo., 1957-65; mem. faculty U. Colo. Law Sch., Boulder, 1965—, prof., 1968—; vis. prof. N.Y. U., 1968, U. Calif., Davis, 1973, U. Chgo., 1976, U. Va., 1979, Duke U., 1980, Georgetown U., 1982, Am. U., 1983; cons. Rice U. Author: (with Homer Kripke) Accounting for Business Lawyers, 1970, 3d edit., 1984; Editor-in-chief: Corp. Law Review, 1977—; Contbr. articles to profl. jours. Mem. Am. Assn. Law Schs. (past chmn. bus. law sect.), Colo. Bar Assn. (council mem. sect. of corp., banking and bus. law 1974-75), Am. Law Inst., ABA. Greek Orthodox. Home: 1636 Columbine Boulder CO 80302 Office: Univ of Colo Law Sch Boulder CO 80309

FIGG, ROBERT MCCORMICK, JR., lawyer; b. Radford, Va., Oct. 22, 1901; s. Robert McCormick and Helen Josephine (Cecil) F.; m. Sallie Alexander Tobias, May 10, 1927; children: Robert McCormick, Emily Figg Dalla Mura, Jefferson Tobias. A.B., Coll. of Charleston, 1920, Litt.D., 1970; law student, Columbia U., 1920-22; LL.D., U. S.C., 1959. Bar: S.C. 1922. Practiced, in Charleston, 1922-59; gen. counsel S.C. State Ports Authority, 1942-72; circuit solicitor 9th Jud. Circuit of S.C., 1935-47; spl. circuit judge, 1957, 75, 76; dean Law Sch., U. S.C., 1959-70; sr. counsel Robinson, McFadden, Moore, Pope, Williams, Taylor & Brailsford, Columbia, 1970—; dir. Home Fed. Savs. & Loan Assn., Charleston. Co-author: Civil Trial Manual (joint com. Am. Coll. Trial Lawyers-Am. Law Inst.-Am. Bar Assn.), 1974. Mem. S.C. Reorgn. Commn., 1948—, chmn., 1951-55, 71-75; elector Hall Fame for Gt. Americans, 1976; mem. S.C. Ho. of Reps., 1933-35; past pres., now hon. life chmn. Coll. of Charleston Found.; trustee

Saul Alexander Found., Columbia Mus. Art. Recipient DuRant award for disting. pub. service S.C. Bar Found., 1982. Fellow Am. Coll. Trial Lawyers; mem. Am. Soc. Internat. Law, Am. Acad. Polit. Sci., Am. Law Inst. (life), Am. Judicature Soc., Inst. Jud. Adminstrn., World Assn. Lawyers, Inter-Am. Bar Assn., Charleston County Bar Assn. (pres. 1953), ABA (ho. of dels. 1971-72, com. fair trial-free press 1965-69, com. spl. study legal edn. 1974—), S.C. Bar Assn., S.C. State Bar (pres. 1971), Phi Beta Kappa (hon.), Phi Delta Phi (hon.), Blue Key (hon.). Clubs: Forum, Forest Lake, U. S.C. Faculty. Lodges: Masons (33°, grand master S.C. 1972-74). Home: 1522 Deans Ln Columbia SC 29205 Office: Jefferson Bldg Columbia SC 29201

FIGGE, FREDERICK H., JR., publishing executive; b. Chgo., Apr. 8, 1934; s. Frederick H. and Theodora M. (Hosto) F.; m. Beverly J. Menz, June 20, 1956; children: Dora, Ann, Jane, Fred C. B.S., U. Ill., 1956. C.P.A., Ill. With Arthur Young & Co. (C.P.A.s), Chgo., 1958-64; controller Ency. Brit., Inc., Chgo., 1964-74, v.p., treas., 1974—. Bd. dirs. Coll. Commerce, U. Ill.; mem. LaGrange (Ill.) Citizens Council. Served with USNR, 1956-58. Mem. Beta Theta Pi, Beta Gamma Sigma. Democrat. Congregationalist. Club: LaGrange Country. Home: 633 S Stone St LaGrange IL 60525 Office: 310 S Michigan Ave Chicago IL 60604

FIGGIE, HARRY E., JR., corp. exec.; b. 1923; (married); 3 children. B.S., Case Inst. Tech., 1947, M.S. in Indsl. Engring, 1951; M.B.A., Harvard U., 1949; LL.B., Cleve. Marshall Law Sch., 1953. Formerly with Western Automatic Screw Machine Co., Parker-Hannifin Corp. and; Booz, Allen & Hamiliton; group v.p. indsl. products A. O. Smith Corp., 1962-64; with Figgie Internat. (formerly A-T-O Inc.), 1964—, chmn. bd., chief exec. officer, 1960—; also dir.; chmn. Clark Reliance Corp.; dir. Western Union. Mem. World Bus. Council. Address: 4420 Sherwin Rd Willoughby OH 44094

FIGGINS, DAVID FORRESTER, construction company executive; b. Belfast, No. Ireland, Mar. 21, 1929; came to U.S., 1957, naturalized, 1966; s. David Peter and Irene Evelyn (Boomer) F.; m. Margaret McConnell, July 28, 1954; children: Margaret Lynne, David Peter, Michael Robert, Barbara Ann. B.S.C. in Civil Engring, Queen's U., Belfast, 1953. Field supt. Farrans Ltd., Belfast, 1952-54; gen. field supt. T.O. Lazarides & Assos., Toronto, Ont., Can., 1954-56, partner, 1956-57; with Mellon-Stuart Co., Pitts., 1957—, v.p., 1963-72, exec. v.p., 1972-78, sr. exec. v.p., 1978-80, pres., 1981—; dir. Bell Fed. Savs. & Loan Assn. Vice pres. Enterprise and Edn. Found., Pitts., 1977—; chmn. adv. bd. Salvation Army, Pitts., 1978-80, mem. nat. adv. council, 1980—; trustee Sewickley Acad., Sewickley, Pa., 1978-82; bd. dirs. Pitts. Symphony Soc., 1982—; trustee Civic Light Opera Assn., 1983—. Mem. Ont. Soc. Profl. Engrs., Nat. Soc. Profl. Engrs., Pa. Soc. Profl. Engrs., Pa. C. of C. (bd. dirs.). Republican. Episcopalian. Clubs: Duquesne, Oakmont Country, Fellows, Queen's U. Belfast Number 533, Rotary (dist. gov. 1979-80). Office: 1 North Shore Ctr Pittsburgh PA 15212

FIGLEY, MELVIN MORGAN, physician, educator; b. Toledo, Dec. 5, 1920; s. Karl Dean and Margaret (Morgan) F.; m. Margaret Jane Harris, Mar. 16, 1946; children: Karl Porter, Joseph Dean, Mark Thompson. Student, Dartmouth, 1938-41; M.D. magna cum laude (John Harvard fellow), Harvard, 1944. Diplomate: Am. Bd. Radiology (trustee 1967-72). Intern, resident internal medicine Western Res. U., 1944-46; resident radiology U. Mich., 1948-51, instr., asst. prof., asso. prof. radiology, 1950-58; practice medicine, specializing in radiology, Seattle, 1958—; prof. radiology, chmn. dept. U. Wash., 1958-78, prof. radiology and medicine, 1979—; mem. radiation study sect. NIH, 1963-67; mem. com. on radiology Nat. Acad. Scis.-NRC, 1964-69, chmn., 1968-69. Editor: Am. Jour. Roentgenology, 1976—; Contbr. articles profl. jours. Bd. dirs. James Picker Found., 1970—. Served to capt. M.C. AUS, 1946-48. John and Mary R. Markle scholar, 1952-57. Fellow Am. Coll. Radiology; hon. fellow Royal Coll. Radiologists (London), Royal Australian Coll. Radiologists; hon. mem. Royal Soc. Medicine; mem. Assn. Univ. Radiologists (pres. 1966, Gold medal 1983), Am. Roentgen Ray Soc. (exec. council 1970—, pres. 1983-84), N. Am. Soc. Cardiac Radiology (pres. 1974), Fleischer Soc., Radiol. Soc. N.Am., AMA, Boylston Med. Soc., Wash. Heart Assn. (past trustee), Soc. Chmn. Acad. Radiology Depts. (exec. council 1969-71), Phi Beta Kappa, Sigma Xi, Alpha Omega Alpha, Sigma Alpha Epsilon. Episcopalian. Home: 7010 51st Ave NE Seattle WA 98115 Office: Univ Hosp Dept Radiology Seattle WA 98105

FIGUEIREDO, GUSTAVO JOSE, health care company executive; b. Shanghai, China, Mar. 7, 1921; came to U.S., 1945; s. Henrique Alves and Emilia Angelina (Garcia) F.; m. Doris Vivian Nyland, Sept. 18, 1948; children: Richard Steven, Lucille Ann, Steven John. B.S. in B.A., NYU, 1951. Controller Warner-Lambert Co., Rio de Janeiro, Brazil, 1960-62, gen. mgr., 1962-63, Manila, 1963-71; regional dir. Asia Warner-Lambert, Hong Kong, 971-73; v.p. fin. Asian Mgmt. Ctr. Warner-Lambert Co., Hong Kong, 1973-76, v.p. fin. Europe, Morris Plains, N.J., 1976-79, internat. controller, 1979-80, v.p. fin. and adminstrn. internat., 1980-81, pres. Asia/Australia, 1981—. Served with U.S. Army, 1946-47. Mem. Pharm. Mfrs. Assn. (mem. Asia com.). Republican. Roman Catholic. Club: Hong Kong Jockey. Home: 5 Copperfield Way Convent Station NJ 17961 Office: 201 Tabor Rd Morris Plains NJ 07950

FIKE, CLAUDE EDWIN, educator; b. Delmar, Md., Mar. 31, 1920; s. Claude Edwin and Rosa (PEgram) F.; m. Helen Frances Duke, Nov. 21, 1951; 1 son, Claude Edwin IV. B.A., Duke, 1941; M.A., Columbia, 1947; Ph.D., U. Ill., 1950. Instr. dept. history Carnegie Inst. Tech., 1950-52; asst. prof. then asso. prof. Coll. Charleston, 1952-57; asso. prof. U. So. Miss., 1957-59, prof. history, 1959—, dean, 1961-76, univ. archivist, dir. grad. library, 1976—. Contbr. articles profl. jours. Served to lt. comdr. USNR, 1941-46. Fellow Royal Soc. Arts; mem. Inst. Am. Strategy (planning and devel. com.), Soc. Miss. Archivists (pres. 1978-79), S.A.R., Miss. Hist. Soc. (dir.), SCV, Scabbard and Blade, Pi Gamma Mu, Phi Alpha Theta, Omicron Delta Kappa, Kappa Kappa Psi, Sigma Delta Xi, Pi Delta Phi, Theta Xi, Phi Kappa Phi. Home: 102 Beverly Ln Hattiesburg MS 39401

FIKE, EDWARD LAKE, newspaper editor; b. Delmar, Md., Mar. 31, 1920; s. Claudius Edwin and Rosa Lake (Pegram) F.; m. s. Rosa Amanda Drake, Apr. 1, 1952; children—Rosa, Evelyn, Amy, Melinda. B.A., Duke U., 1941; postgrad., U. Cin., 1941-42. Editor, co-pub. Nelsonville (Ohio) Tribune, 1945-48; dir. bur. public info. Duke U., 1948-52; mem. U.S. del. N. Atlantic Council, Paris, 1952-53; asso. editor Rocky Mount (N.C.) Evening Telegram, 1953-57; editor, pub. Fike Newspapers, Lewistown and Glendive, Mont., also; Wilmington and Tujunja, Calif., 1957-68; asso. editor Richmond (Va.) News Leader, 1968-70; dir. news and editorial analysis Copley Newspapers, 1970-77; editor editorial pages San Diego Union, 1977—; lectr. journalism San Diego State U., San Diego Evening Coll. Bd. dirs. San Diego Salvation Army, San Diego United Way, El Cajon (Calif.) Boys Club. Served to lt. USNR, 1942-45. Recipient George Washington award Freedoms Found., 1969, 70, 71, 73, 78; Editorial Writing awards N.C. Press Assn., 1954, 55, Va. Press Assn., 1969, Calif. Newspaper Pubs. Assn., 1969, 80. Republican. Methodist. Home: 12244 Fuerte Dr El Cajon CA 92020 Office: 350 Camino de la Reina San Diego CA 92108

FILAS, FRANCIS LAD, priest, theology educator; b. Cicero, Ill., June 4, 1915; s. Thomas Martin and Emily (Seery) F. A.B., Loyola U. Chgo., 1937, M.A., 1943; S.T.D., W. Baden (Ind.) Pontifical U., 1952. Joined Soc. of Jesus, 1932; ordained priest Roman Catholic Ch., 1945; tchr. theology U. Detroit, 1946-48; prof. theology Loyola U., Chgo., 1950—, chmn. dept., 1959-67; writer, lectr. Cana Conf., also; family counselling; spl. research theology St. Joseph; lectr. radio, TV. Vice pres. Documentation and Research Center, North Am. Soc. of Josephology, St. Joseph's Oratory, Montreal, Can., 1952-62. Author: The Man Nearest to Christ, 1944, The Family for Families, 1947, Joseph and Jesus, 1952, His Heart in Our Work, 1952, Joseph Most Just, 1956, The Parables of Jesus, 1959, St. Joseph and Daily Christian Living, 1959, Joseph: The Man Closest to Jesus, 1962, Sex Education in the Family, 1966, St. Joseph After Vatican II, 1968, How to Read Your Bible, 1978; Recorded albums and tapes on family life, mental depression and philosophy of religion, 1964—; filmstrips on Bibl. history and geography of Israel Documentaries on Shroud of Turin. Mem. Am. Mariological Soc., Cath. Bibl. Assn., Holy Shroud Guild (v.p.). Spl. research on Pontius Pilate coins' imprints on Shroud of Turin. Address: 6525 N Sheridan Rd Chicago IL 60626 *The moment anyone of us makes himself or herself an idolatrous god by basking complacently in our supposed success, we have abdicated our commitment to human values. With an outlook such as that, "success" becomes the ultimate goal, howsoever "success" be defined, and the human beings in the way of that goal appear as so many obstacles, no matter what their rights may be. Instead, I believe we should have a deep concept of personal self-value because of goodness placed in us by the Creator, which we are to cherish and appreciate and extend to others as far as we can. Only if we are deeply convinced of our ultimate and lasting value can we live according to it.*

FILBY, PERCY WILLIAM, consultant; b. Cambridge, Eng., Dec. 10, 1911; came to U.S., 1957, naturalized, 1960; s. William Lusher and Florence Ada (Stanton) F.; m. Nancie Elizabeth Giddens (div. 1957); children: Ann Veronica Filby Chesworth, Jane Vanessa Filby Maisey, Roderick, Guy; m. Vera Ruth Weakliem, 1957. Student, Cambridge U. Librarian Cambridge U., 1930-37, dir. sci. library, 1937-40; sec. to Sir James Frazer, 1934-39; sr. researcher, archivist Brit. Fgn. Office, 1946-57; asst. dir. Peabody Inst., Balt., 1957-65; librarian, asst. dir. Md. Hist. Soc., Balt., 1965-72, dir., 1972-78, ret., 1978; 1978—; also; library cons.; cons. on rare books, calligraphy; appraiser rare books and manuscripts. Author: Cambridge Papers, 1936, Calligraphy and Handwriting in America, 1710-1962, 1963, (with others) Two Thousand Years of Calligraphy, 1965, American and British Genealogy and Heraldry, 1970, 3d edit., 1983, (with others) Star Spangled Books, 1972, Passenger Lists Bibliography, 1538-1900, 1981, (with others) Passenger and Immigration Lists Index, 3 vols, 1981, 1982 supplement, 1983, Philadelphia Naturalizations, 1982. Served to capt. Intelligence Corps. Brit. Army, 1940-46. Fellow Evergreen House, La Casa del Libro; mem. St. George's Soc., ALA, Spl. Libraries Assn. (pres. Balt. chpt. 1961-62), Soc. Scribes (v.p.), Soc. for Italic Handwriting, Soc. Am. Archivists, Manuscript Soc. (pres. 1976-78), Typophiles, Balt. Bibliophiles (pres. 1963-65), Am. Antiquarian Soc., Bibliog. Soc. Am. (council 1978-82). Club: Grolier (N.Y.C.) (mem. library com.). Home: 8944 Madison St Savage MD 20763 Office: 201 W Monument Baltimore MD 21201

FILDERMAN, ROBERT JAY, investment company executive; b. Phila., Dec. 1, 1937; m. Marilyn; children: Jay Robert, Robin. B.A., Dartmouth Coll., 1959. Account exec. E.F. Hutton & Co., New Orleans, 1966-69, mgr., Mobile, Ala., 1969-72, regional sales mgr., v.p., Houston, 1972-82, sr. v.p., nat. mktg. dir., La Jolla, Calif., 1982—. Served to 1st lt. U.S. Army, 1959-61. Mem. Internat. Assn. Fin. Planners, Inst. Cert. Fin. Planners. Republican. Jewish. Home: 4277 Cosoy Way San Diego CA 92103 Office: EF Hutton & Co Inc 11011 Torrey Pines Rd La Jolla CA 92038

FILEP, ROBERT THOMAS, communications company executive; b. New Brunswick, N.J., Dec. 2, 1931; s. John Kossuth and Irma Antonio (Matyus) F.; m. Francis Tudor Moxley, Aug. 8, 1964; children: Felicia Allison, Ian Robert. B.S., Rutgers U., 1953; M.A., Columbia U., 1957; Ph.D., U. So. Calif., 1966. Tchr. sci., coach Teaneck (N.J.) High Sch., 1953-56; asst. dir. admissions Rensselaer Polytechnic Inst., Troy, N.Y., 1957-59; dir. admissions and aid Mills Coll. of Edn., N.Y.C., 1959-61; sec. corp., dir. info. and tng. div. Center for Programed Instrn., Inst. Ednl. Tech., Columbia U., 1961-63; asso. investigator cinema research U. So. Calif., 1963-65; human factors scientist System Devel. Corp., Santa Monica, Calif., 1965-67; v.p., dir. studies Inst. Ednl. Devel., El Segundo, Calif., 1967-72; asso. commr., dir. Nat. Center for Ednl. Tech., U.S. Office of Edn., HEW, 1972-73; dir. Univ.-Wide Learning Systems Center; prof. communications and edn. U. So. Calif., Los Angeles, 1974-79; pres. Communications 21 Corp., 1979—. Editor: Prospectives in Programming, 1963; Contbg. editor: Ednl. Communications Tech. Jour, 1964—; contbr. chpts. to books, articles to profl. jours, 1968—. Mem. Commn. on NASA's Space Research and Tech. Programs Nat. Acad. Sci. and Engring.; mem. Mayor's Commn. on Cable TV.; pub. mem. Fgn. Service Selection Bur., Dept. State, 1982-83. Served with USAF, 1953-55. Fulbright-Hays lectr., India, 1975. Mem. Nat. Soc. Performance and Instrn. (past pres.), Ednl. Media Council (past pres.), Am. Psychol. Assn., English-Speaking Union (bd. dirs. Los Angeles 1980—), Am. Inst. Aeros. and Astronautics, AAAS, Chi Phi. Home: 3104 Palos Verdes Dr N Palos Verdes Estates CA 90274 Office: 1611 S Pacific Coast Hwy Suite 206 Redondo Beach CA 90277

FILER, JOHN HORACE, insurance company executive; b. New Haven, Sept. 3, 1924; s. Harry Lambert and Ehrma (Green) F.; m. Marlene A. Klick, Feb. 2, 1977; children—Susan, Cynthia, Kathryn, Ann. B.A., Depauw U., 1947, LL.D., 1970; LL.B., Yale U., 1950. Bar: Conn. bar 1950. Practice in, New Haven, 1950-58; law clk. to U.S. dist. judge, 1950-51; asso., partner Gumbart, Corbin, Tyler & Cooper, 1951-58; gen. counsel Aetna Life & Casualty Co., Hartford, Conn., 1958-68, exec. v.p., 1968-72, chmn. bd., chief exec. officer, 1972—, also dir.; dir. U.S. Steel Corp., Twentieth Century-Fox Film Corp. Chmn. Bd. Edn. Farmington, 1963-67; mem. Conn. Commn. to Study Met. Govt., 1966-67, Conn. Senate, 1957-58; trustee Mt. Holyoke Coll., 1971-77. Served to ensign USNR, 1943-46. Mem. Am., Conn., Hartford County bar assns., Assn. Life Ins. Counsel, Sigma Chi. Episcopalian. Home: West Hartford CT 06107 Office: 151 Farmington Ave Hartford CT 06115

FILER, LLOYD JACKSON, JR., medical educator, clinical investigator; b. Grove City, Pa., Sept. 30, 1919; s. Lloyd Jackson and Frances Elsie (Hosack) F.; m. Evalyn Mae Rink, May 29, 1942; children: Lloyd Jackson, Margaret Ann, Thomas Ewing. B.S. in Chemistry, U. Pitts., 1941, Ph.D. in Biochemistry, 1944; M.D., U. Rochester, 1952. Med. research fellow U. Pitts., 1944-45; instr. physiology U. Rochester, (N.Y.), 1945-47, research fellow in anatomy, 1945-52; med. dir., v.p. Ross Labs., Columbus, Ohio, 1952-65; instr., asst. clin. prof. Ohio State U., Columbus, 1952-65; prof. pediatrics U. Iowa, Iowa City, 1965—; chmn. food and nutrition bd. Nat. Acad. Sci., Washington, 1972-75; chmn. com. to evaluate generally regarded as safe substances, 1971—; trustee, bd. dirs. Nutrition Found., Washington, 1982—; bd. dirs. Am. Bd. Nutrition. Editor: Glutamic Acid, 1979, Parental Nutrition, 1983; jour. supplement Current Perspectives Hypertension, 1982. Served to capt. USAF, 1956-58. Recipient Joseph Goldberger award AMA, 1978, Outstanding Achievement award Am. Coll. Nutrition, 1979, Inst. Food Technologists, 1981. Fellow Am. Acad. Pediatrics (chmn. nutrition com. Evanston 1972-75); mem. Soc. Pediatric Research, Am. Pediatric Soc. Republican. Presbyterian. Club: Cosmos (Washington). Home: 216 Monroe St Iowa City IA 52240 Office: U Iowa Iowa City IA 52242

FILERMAN, GARY LEWIS, health association executive; b. Mpls., Nov. 16, 1936; s. Joseph H. and Bonnie (Kobrin) F.; m. Jane Harding, Sept. 15, 1962; children: Amy Beth, Joseph Harding, Suzanne Louise. B.A., U. Minn., 1959, M.Health Adminstrn. (Phillips Found. fellow 1959-60), 1961, M.A. (W.K. Kellogg fellow 1961-64), 1963, Ph.D. (Milbank travel grantee 1964, Orgn. Am. States fellow 1964), 1970. Adminstrv. resident Johns Hopkins Hosp., 1961-62; acting dir. Minn. Hosp. Assn., 1965; pres. Assn. Univ. Programs in Health Adminstrn., Washington, 1965—; exec. sec. Accrediting Commn. Edn. Health Services Adminstrn., 1968-80; mem. faculty Washington U. Med. Sch., St. Louis, George Washington U. Sch. Bus., Washington; guest scholar Brookings Instn., 1962; cons. in field. Editor: Jour. Health Adminstrn. Edn., 1982—; Author articles in field.; Mem. editorial bds. profl. jours. Mem. nat. health professions adv. council HHS, 1983—; Bd. dirs. Am. Refugee Commn., 1984—. Recipient Silver medal Leuven (Belgium) U., 1972, Disting. Contbn. award Assn. U. Programs Health Adminstrn., 1979, Outstanding Achievement award Regents of U. Minn., 1982. Fellow Am. Public Health Assn.; mem. Royal Soc. Health, Assn. Am. Med. Colls., Am. Assn. Can. Studies, Am. Health Planning Assn. (bd. dirs. 1982—), Nat. Audubon Soc., Wilderness Soc. Clubs: Cosmos (Washington); Banquo. Home: 1322 Banquo Ct McLean VA 22102 Office: 1911 Ft Myer Dr Suite 503 Arlington VA 22209

FILERMAN, MICHAEL HERMAN, TV producer; b. Chgo., May 4, 1938; s. Arthur Joseph and Anne Leah (Greenfield) F. B.S. in Communications, U. Ill., 1960. Gen. program dir. Sta. WGN-TV, Chgo., 1962-67; gen. program dir., dir. daytime programs CBS TV Network, N.Y.C., 1967-72; dir. series devel. Paramount TV, 1972-74; v.p. series devel. Lorimar Prodns., Culver City, Calif., 1976-83; with 20th Century Fox, 1983—; co-exec. producer Knots Landing, Falcon Crest, Emerald Point, N.A.S. Devel. exec.: Big Shamus, Little Shamus; exec. producer: Kings Crossing. Office: Box 900 Beverly Hills CA 90213

FILES, WILMER ROBERT, manufacturing company executive; b. Phila., Oct. 7, 1931; s. Wilmer Robert and Mary (Ryan) F.; m. Patricia Alice Culhane, Apr. 24, 1953; children: Christine, Bryan. B.S. in Econs., U. Pa., 1953. Various positions Gen. Electric Co., Schenectady, 1953-60, Phila., 1960-61, Cin., 1961-65; chief fin. officer Nat. Homes Corp., Lafayette, Ind., 1965—. Mem. Fin. Execs. Inst. Roman Catholic. Club: Lafayette Country (pres. 1980-81). Home: 3513 Cedar Ln Lafayette IN 47904 Office: Nat Homes Corp PO Box 7680 Lafayette IN 47902

FILIATRAULT, ALFRED CHARLES, JR., association executive; b. Duluth, Minn., Jan. 2, 1921; s. Alfred Charles and Alice (Shebetsky) F.; m. Mary Jane Smith, Sept. 13, 1952. B.S., U.S. Naval Acad., 1943. Commd. ensign U.S. Navy, 1943, advanced through grades to comdr., 1958; served in destroyers, S.W. Pacific, World War II, exec. officer, then comdg. officer destroyer escort, Pacific, 1946-48, comdg. officer mine location ship, Fla., 1948-49, aide to comdr. 7th Fleet, Korea, 1950-51; instr. NROTC, U. Minn., 1951-52; comdg. officer, then div. comdr. minesweep ships, Pacific, 1953-56, mil. asst. adv. group, Germany, 1957-59, comdg. officer two destroyers, Pacific, 1959-61; assigned Navy staff, The Pentagon, 1961-65; ret., 1965; exec. sec. Propeller Club U.S., 1965—. Trustee United Seaman's Service, 1965—, Nat. River Acad., 1972—. Decorated Bronze Star. Mem. Council Am. Master Mariners, Navy League, U.S. Naval Acad. Alumni Assn. Club: Mason. Home: 6512 Engel Dr McLean VA 22101 Office: 1730 M St NW Washington DC 20036

FILION, LOUIS JACQUES, management consultant, educator; b. Trois Rivieres, Que., Can., Aug. 9, 1945; s. Lionel and Estelle (Allary) F.; m. Maria Gagnon, May 27, 1972; 1 son, Charles Andre. B.A., U. Montreal, 1966, M.B.A., H.E.C., 1976; M.A., U. Ottawa, 1974. With Reynolds Metals Co., Baie Comeau, Que., 1968-72; cons. Govt. of Que., Quebec, 1972-73, Woods, Gordon, Montreal, Que., 1974; mktg. mgr. Quebec Trust, Montreal, Que., 1976-77; pub. Quinze Domino, C.E.J., Sogides, Montreal, 1977-80; prof. mgmt. sci. U. Montreal, 1981—; mgmt. cons. Fillon & Assocs., 1979—; prof. mgmt. sci. U. Trois-Rivieres, 1981—. Roman Catholic. Home: CP 612 Trois-Rivieres Quebec Canada G9A 5J3 *Management is the art of making other people happy to achieve your own dreams.*

FILION, MAURICE, professional sports team executive. Gen. mgr. Quebec Nordiques, Nat. Hockey League, Que., Can. Office: care Que Nordiques 2205 Ave du Colisee Quebec PQ Canada G1L 4W7§

FILIPPI, FRANK JOSEPH, lawyer; b. San Francisco, Dec. 18, 1907; s. Antonio and Rina (Linqua) F.; m. Olivia Cotta, Apr. 30, 1933. A.B., Lincoln U., 1928; LL.B., U. San Francisco, 1932. Bar: Calif. 1932, U.S. Supreme Ct. 1932. Sr. atty. Calif. Compensation Ins. Fund, 1934-44; supt. compensation ins. claims, Calif., 1944-49; now sr. partner Mullen & Filippi (with law offices in), San Francisco, San Jose, Sacramento, Fresno, Santa Rosa, Bakersfield; lectr. on ins. law. Mem. Calif. Rep. Central Com., 1946-56; bd. regents St. Mary's Coll. of Calif. Served with ARC, 1942-46. Mem. State Bar Calif., Internat. Bar Assn., Inter-Am. Bar Assn., ABA (mem. ho. of dels. 1967-77, vice chmn. workmen's compensation com.), San Francisco Bar Assn., Lawyers Club San Francisco (pres. 1959-60, bd. dirs. 1960-70), Am. Bd. Trial Advocates, Am. Trial Lawyers Assn., Am. Judicature Soc., Nat. Conf. Bar Presidents, Def. Research Inst., Def. Seminar Assn. San Francisco, Probate Attys. Assn. No. Calif., San Francisco C. of C., Bayview Mchts. Assn. (past pres.), Bay View Civic Club (past pres.), Central Council of Civic Clubs (dir.), Native Sons Calif. Clubs: San Francisco Athletic, Commonwealth of Calif. (San Francisco); Olympic City, Olympic Country. Home: 59 Iris Ave San Francisco CA 94118 Office: 115 Sansome St San Francisco CA 94104

FILIPPINE, EDWARD L., fed. judge; b. 1930. A.B., J.D., St. Louis U. Bar: bar 1957. Now judge U.S. Dist. Ct., Dist. Eastern Mo. Mem. Am. Bar Assn., Mo. Bar Assn., Bar Assn. Met. St. Louis, St. Louis County Bar Assn. Office: US Dist Ct Room 324 US Ct and Custom House 1114 Market St Saint Louis MO 63101

FILKINS, JAMES PAUL, physiology educator, researcher; b. Milw., Apr. 10, 1936; s. Lowell Stephen and Mildred Harriet (Pavalat) F.; m. Anneliese Margaret Cegler, Aug. 22, 1959; children: Mary Elizabeth, James Carl, Andrew Stephen, Patricia Anne, Joseph William, Margaret Ellen. B.S., Marquette U., 1957, M.S., 1959, Ph.D., 1964. Postdoctoral fellow in physiology Marquette U., Milw., 1964-65; asst. prof. physiology and biophysics U. Tenn. Med. Units, Memphis, 1965-70, assoc. prof., 1970-71; assoc. prof. physiology Loyola U. of Chgo., Maywood, Ill., 1971-75, prof. chmn. dept., 1971-75. Assoc. editor: Jour. Circulatory Shock; mem. editorial bd.: Jour. Leukocyte Biology; contbr. articles to profl. jours. Mem. Am. Physiol. Soc., Shock Soc. (pres. 1979-80), Assn. Chmn. Depts. Physiology, Chgo. Heart Assn. (research council 1981-84). Roman Catholic. Home: 734 S Vine Park Ridge IL 60068 Office: Loyola U Chgo 2160 S 1st Ave Maywood IL 60153

FILLER, BERNARD M., investment banker, lawyer; b. Cairo, Ill., Oct. 16, 1935; s. Leon and Jeanette (Sanofsky) F.; m. Judith Ann Sperling, June 16, 1957; children—Deborah Lynn, Mark Alan, Lisa Beth. B.S., U. Ill., 1957; L.L.B., Stanford, 1962. Bar: N.Y. bar 1963, Ill. bar 1970, Calif. bar 1975. Asso. firm Paul, Weiss, Rifkind Wharton & Garrison, N.Y.C., 1962-69; v.p. legal affairs Darborn-Storm Corp., Chgo., 1969-74; partner firm Holleb, Gerstein & Glass, Chgo., 1974-76; pres. Capital B Corp., Chgo., 1977—; lectr. bus. planning DePaul U. Law Sch., 1972-74, Loyola U. Law Sch., Chgo., 1972-73. Trustee Am. Jewish Com., Chgo., 1971—. Served as ensign USNR, 1957-59. Mem. Am., Ill., Chgo. bar assns., State Bar Calif., Order of Coif. Jewish (trustee temple). Club: Standard (Chgo.). Home: 1960 Partridge Ln Highland Park IL 60035 Office: 303 E Wacker Dr Chicago IL 60601

FILLER, ROBERT, educator, chemist, university dean; b. Bklyn., Feb. 2, 1923; s. Alfred Louis and Ethel (Schwab) F.; m. Lael Carol Rosenbloom, Oct. 7, 1945 (dec. 1954); children: Susan, Rebecca, Debby Vetter; m. Miriam G. Holland, Sept. 20, 1959; children: Michael, Daniel. B.S., CCNY, 1943; M.S., U. Iowa, 1947, Ph.D., 1949. Asst. prof. Union U., 1949-50; postdoctoral research fellow Purdue U., 1950-51; research chemist Wright Air Devel. Center, Dayton, Ohio, 1951-53; instr., asst. prof. Ohio Wesleyan U., 1953-55; asst. prof. Ill. Inst. Tech., Chgo., 1955-61, asso. prof., 1961-66, prof., 1966—, acting chmn. chem. dept., 1966-68, chmn., 1968-76, dean Lewis Coll. Scis. and Letters, 1976—; Research asso. Ben May Lab. for Cancer Research, U. Chgo., 1956-57; cons. U. Ill. Coll. Medicine, 1958-59, Ill. Inst. Tech. Research Inst., 1964-66; vis. scientist Weizmann Inst. Sci., Israel, 1974. Contbr. articles profl. jours.; editor 2 books on chemistry; mem. editorial bd.: Fluorine Chem. Revs. Served with AUS, 1944-46. Recipient NIH spl. postdoctoral fellow U. Cambridge, Eng., 1962-63. Mem. Am. Chem. Soc. (sec.-treas. div. fluorine chemistry 1972-74, chmn. 1976), Royal Soc. Chemistry (London), N.Y. Acad. Scis., AAAS, AAUP, Sigma Xi, Phi Lambda Upsilon. Home: 8453 Linder Ct Skokie IL 60077 *Be true to yourself, maintain your integrity, think positively, work hard, and keep your sense of humor.*

FILLIOS, LOUIS CHARLES, biochemistry educator; b. Boston, July 1, 1923; s. Charles Louis and Pagona (Kefalas) F.; m. Iphigenia Loomis, June 15, 1947; children: Despena, Diana, Hilary. A.B., Harvard, 1948, M.S., 1953, Sc.D., 1956. Research asso., then asso. Harvard, 1956-60; asst. prof. physiol. chemistry Mass. Inst. Tech., 1961-64, asso. prof., 1964-66; asso. research prof. biochemistry and pathology Boston U. Sch. Medicine, 1966-68, prof. biochemistry, 1970—, dir. div. basic sci., 1970-75, chmn. dept. nutritional scis., 1973—; cons. NIH, Am. Pub. Health Assn.; Chmn. Mass. Task Force Nutrition and Aging, 1970-71; cons. Mass. Office of Elder Affairs, 1971-73; co-chmn. nutrition sect. White House Conf. Aging, 1971-72; Cons. VA, Bedford, Mass., 1982—; Mem. pres.'s adv. council Hellenic Coll., 1968-73. Author numerous research articles fields biochemistry, pathology and nutrition; contbr. sci. and profl. jours. Vice chmn. Citizens Aviation Policy Assn., 1973-76. Served with USAAF, 1943-45. Decorated DFC; established investigator Am. Heart Assn., 1961-66; recipient Outstanding Educator of Am. award, 1972. Fellow Am. Heart Assn., AAAS; mem. Am. Inst. Nutrition (chmn. fellows award com. 1978-81), Biochem. Soc. London, AAUP, Sigma Xi, Omicron Kappa Upsilon. Home: 19 Eliot Rd Lexington MA 02173 Office: 100 E Newton St Boston MA 02118

FILLIPPS, FRANK PETER, insurance company executive; b. N.Y.C., June 29, 1947; s. John G. and Angela (Fusco) Filipps; m. Patricia Maria DeVito, Apr. 8, 1967; children: Todd Peter, Mark Peter. B.A., Rutgers U., 1969; M.B.A., NYU, 1971. Asst. treas. Chase Manhattan, N.Y.C., 1969-73, 2d v.p., 1974-75; v.p. investments Am. Life Ins. Co., N.Y.C., 1975-77, Am. Internat. Underwriters, 1978-81; treas. Am. Internat. Group Inc., N.Y.C., 1981—; dir. Latonia Investment Co., Geneva, Switzerland. Office: Am Internat Group Inc 70 Pine St New York NY 10270

FILLIUS, MILTON FRANKLIN, JR., food products company executive; b. N.Y., Nov. 17, 1922; s. Milton Franklin and Georgiana (Bergh) F.; m. Betty Williams, June 4, 1983; children—Julie, Karen, Anthony, Donald. B.A., Hamilton Coll., 1946; LL.B., U. Mich., 1949. Bar: Calif. bar 1950, also U.S. Supreme Ct 1950. Adminstrv. asst. to banker in, San Diego, 1949-51; treas., gen. mgr. Nat. Steel and Shipbldg. Co., San Diego, 1951-56, exec. v.p., gen. mgr., 1956-62; exec. v.p. Westgate-Calif. Corp., 1962-65; pres. Vita-Pakt Citrus Products Co., 1966—; dir. Fever, Dorland & Assos. Bd. dirs. San Diego YMCA, 1957—, San Diego council Boy Scouts Am., 1957—, San Diego County Heart Assn., 1959—, Childrens Home Soc., San Diego, 1959—, Mercy Hosp., San Diego, 1959—, Joseph Dean Found.; trustee Western Behavioral Scis. Inst., Hamilton Coll. Served with USNR, 1943-46. Mem. State Bar Calif., San Diego County Bar Assn., San Diego C. of C. (pres. 1962-64), Theta Delta Chi, Phi Alpha Delta. Home: 642 S Forestdale West Covina CA 91791 Office: 707 N Barranca St Covina CA 91722

FILLMORE, PETER ARTHUR, mathematician, educator; b. Moncton, N.B., Can., Oct. 28, 1936; s. Henry Arthur and Jeanne Margaret (Archibald) F.; m. Anne Ellen Garvock, Aug. 6, 1960; children: Jennifer Anne, Julia Margaret, Peter Alexander. B.Sc., Dalhousie U., 1957; M.A., U. Minn., 1960, Ph.D., 1962. Instr. U. Chgo., 1962-64; asst. prof. math. Ind. U., 1964-67, asso. prof., 1967-71, prof., 1971-72; vis. asso. prof. U. Toronto, 1970-71; Killam research fellow, prof. math. Dalhousie U., Halifax, N.S., Can., 1972-76, prof., 1976—; sr. vis. fellow U. Edinburgh, 1977—. Author: Notes on Operator Theory, 1970; editorial bd.: Jour. Integral Equations and Operator Theory; contbr. articles to profl. jours. Fellow Royal Soc. Can.; mem. Can. Math. Soc. (council 1973-75, 77-79, v.p. 1975-77), Am. Math. Soc. (council 1982-84). Home: 1384 Robie St Halifax NS B3H 3E2 Canada Office: Math Dept Dalhousie Univ Halifax NS B3H 4H8 Canada

FILOSA, GARY FAIRMONT RANDOLPH DE MARCO, II, financier; b. Wilder, Vt., Feb. 22, 1931; s. Gary F.R. de M. and Rosaline M. (Falzarano) F.; m. Edith Wilson du Motier Schoenberg (div.); children: Marc Christian Bazire de V., III, Gary Fairmont Randolph de Marco, III. Grad., Mt. Hermon Sch., 1950; Ph.B., U. Chgo., 1954; B.A., U. Americas, 1967; M.A., Calif. Western U., 1968; Ph.D., U.S. Internat. U., 1970. Sports reporter Claremont Daily Eagle, Rutland Herald, Vt. Informer, 1947-52; pub. The Chicagoan, 1952-54; account exec., editor house publs. Robertson, Buckley & Gotsch, Inc., Chgo., 1953-54; account exec. Fuller, Smith & Ross, Inc., N.Y.C., 1955; editor Apparel Arts mag. (now Gentlemen's Quar.), Esquire, Inc., N.Y.C., 1955-56; pres., chmn. bd. Teenarama Records, Inc., N.Y.C., 1956-62, Filosa Publs., 1956-61, Los Angeles, 1974-83; pres. Montclair Sch., 1958-60, Pacific Registry, Inc., Los Angeles, 1959-61, Banana Chip Corp. Am., N.Y.C., 1964-67; exec. asst. to exec. producer Desilu Studios, Inc., Hollywood, 1960-61; exec. asst. to Benjamin A. Javits, 1961-62; dean adminstrn. Postgrad. Center for Mental Health, N.Y.C., 1962-64; chmn. bd., pres. Producciones Mexicanes Internationales (S.A.), Mexico City, 1957-68, Filosa Films Internat., Hollywood, 1962-74, pres., Newport Beach, Calif., 1975-83, Palm Beach, Fla., 1984—; chmn. bd., pres. Cinematografica Americana Internationale (S.A.), Mexico City, 1964-74; v.p. acad. affairs World Acad., San Francisco, 1967-68; asst. headmaster, instr. Latin San Miguel Sch., San Diego, 1968-69; asst. to provost Calif. Western U., San Diego, 1968-69; assoc. prof. philosophy Art Coll., San Francisco, 1969-70; v.p. acad. affairs, dean of faculty Internat. Inst., Phoenix, 1968-73; chmn. bd., pres. Universite Universelle, 1970-73; bd. dirs., v.p. acad. affairs, dean Summer Sch., Internat. Community Coll., Los Angeles, 1970-72; chmn. bd., pres. Social Directory Calif., 1967-75, Am. Assn. Social Directories, Los Angeles, 1970-76; pres. Social Directory U.S., N.Y.C., 1974-76; chmn. bd. Internat. Assn. Social Directories, Paris, 1974—; surfing coach U. Calif. at Irvine, 1975-77; instr. history Coastline Community Coll., Fountain Valley, Calif., 1976-77; v.p. Xerox-Systemic, 1979-80. Pub.: Rustic Rhythm mags., Teenage, Teen Life, Rock & Roll Roundup, Stardust, Personalities, N.Y.C., 1956-61; editor: Sci. Digest, 1961-62; Author: Technology Enters 21st Century, 1966; (with Peter Duchin) musical Feather Light, 1966; No Public Funds for Nonpublic Schools, 1968, Creative Function of the College President, 1969, The Surfers Almanac, 1977; Contbr.: numerous articles to mags., and profl. jours. and encys. including Sci. Digest, World Book Ency. Candidate for Los Angeles City Council, 1959; chmn. Publishers for John F. Kennedy, 1960, Educators for Reelection of Ivy Baker Priest, 1970; mem. exec. and fin. com. Brown for Gov. Calif., 1974; patron Monterey Peninsula Mus. Art, 1978; mem. So. Calif. Com. for Olympic Games, 1977. Served with AUS, 1954-55. Recipient D.A.R. Citizenship award, 1959; Silver Conquistador award Am. Assn. Social Directories, 1970; Ambassador's Cup U. Ams., 1967; resolution Calif. Legislature, 1977; gold pendant Japan Surfing Assn., 1978. Mem. U.S. Surfing Found. (pres. 1974-76), Internat. Profl. Surfing Fedn. (pres. 1974-77, 83—), Am. Surfing Assn. (founder, pres. 1960-78, chmn. exec. com. 1974-78, pres. 1980—), Internat. Amateur Surfing Fedn. (chmn. bd., pres. 1960-77, 83—), Internat. Council of Assns. of Surfing (founder, pres. 1960—), Am. Assn. UN, Authors League, Authors Guild, Alumni Assn. U. Americas (pres. 1967-70), United Shareowners Am., Sierra Club, San Diego Zool. Soc., San Diego Opera Guild, NCAA (bd. dels. 1977-82), AAU (gov. 1978-82), NEA, NAACP, San Diego Hist. Soc., World Affairs Council San Francisco, Am. Acad. Polit. Sci., Mt. Herman Sch. Alumni Assn., Western Speech Assn., U. Chgo. Alumni Assn., Omicron Lambda. Democrat. Episcopalian. Clubs: Chapultepec, Jockey (Mexico City); Kona Kai (San Diego); Commonwealth (San Francisco); Embajadores (U. of Americas, Puebla, Mex.); Los Angeles Athletic, Town Hall (Los Angeles); Mt. Kenya Safari (Nairobi); Quarterback (Honolulu). Home: PO Box 2174 Palm Beach FL 33480 Office: PO Box 1315 Beverly Hills CA 92663 *My view of life is based on a blending of two ancient concepts: the Hellenic ideal of excellence and the full actualization of human potentialities, and the Hebraic ideal of duty and responsibility. The first implies a life of aspiration and freedom; the second a life of discipline and self-control.*

FIMRITE, RONALD DWAINE, journalism; b. Healdsburg, Calif., Jan. 6, 1931; s. Lester Thomas and Mildred Gladys (Ransom) F.; m. Joan Von Briesen, May 4, 1957 (div. 1970); children: Deborah, Peter; m. Mary Blake Green, Aug. 22, 1970 (div. 1977). B.A., U. Calif.-Berkeley, 1952. In pub. relations So. Pacific Co., 1954; reporter, columnist Berkeley Gazette, Calif., 1955-59, San Francisco Chronicle, 1959-71; sr. writer Sports Illustrated, N.Y.C., 1971—. Home: 3561 Jackson St San Francisco CA 94118 Office: Sports Illustrated Mag Time and Life Bldg New York NY 10020

FINA, THOMAS WITMER, business executive; b. Allentown, Pa., Mar. 25, 1924; s. Charles Carmen and Hazel Margaret (Witmer) F.; m. Eleanor Louise Stone, Sept. 14, 1946; children: Nancy Louise, Thomas Delmar, Robert Witmer. Student, Northeastern U., 1942-43; A.B. magna cum laude, Harvard U., 1948, M.A., 1950; postgrad., Middlebury Scuola Italiana, 1948, U. Florence, 1950, Bologna (Italy) Center Johns Hopkins, 1960-61, Nat. War Coll., 1968-69. Intelligence research Italian Desk, State Dept., Washington, 1950-55, 1956-57; asst. to dep. dir. Intelligence Coordination, 1957-58; economist mission OEEC, Paris, 1958-60; econ. officer Mission to European Communities, Luxembourg, 1961-63, polit. officer, Brussels, 1963-65; officer-in-charge European integration affairs State Dept., 1965-68; staff dir. gen. adv. com. ACDA, 1969-71; council internat. econ. policy White House, 1971; coordinator programs and planning Office Congl. Relations, State Dept., 1971-73; consul gen. Am. consulate gen., Milan, Italy, 1973-79; with Bur. Public Affairs, State Dept., 1979-80; gen. mgr. Weight Watchers Italiana, 1980—. Bd. dirs. Hollin Hills Civic Assn., 1970, 71. Served with USAAF, 1943-46. Harvard travelling fellow, 1949; Fulbright scholar, 1950; Recipient commendable service award State Dept., 1962, superior honor award, 1965, honor of commendatore (Italy), 1983. Office: Weight Watchers Italiana Viale Certosa 49 Milan Italy 20149

FINBERG, ALAN ROBERT, lawyer, communications company executive; b. Bklyn., July 2, 1927; s. Chester F. and Anne B. (Gorfinkle) F.; m. Barbara J. Denning, June 21, 1953. B.A., Yale U., 1950; J.D., Harvard U., 1953. Bar: N.Y. 1954, D.C. 1974, U.S. Supreme Ct. 1974. Assoc. firm Cravath, Swaine & Moore, N.Y.C., 1953-61; partner firm Stein, Kripke & Rosen, N.Y.C., 1961-64; asst. gen. counsel Gen. Dynamics Corp., N.Y.C., 1964-71; v.p., sec., gen. counsel Washington Post Co., Washington and N.Y.C., 1971—; dir. Newsweek, Inc., Daily Herald Co. Trustee Bard Coll. Served with USNR, 1945-46. Mem. Am. Bar Assn., Assn. Bar City N.Y., Am. Arbitration Assn. (arbitration panel), Am. Soc. Corporate Secs., Phi Beta Kappa. Democrat. Clubs: Board Room, Coffee House (N.Y.C.). Home: 165 E 72d St New York NY 10021 Office: Washington Post Co 444 Madison Ave New York NY 10022

FINBERG, BARBARA DENNING, foundation executive; b. Pueblo, Colo., Feb. 26, 1929; d. Rufus Raymond and Velma Aileen (Hopper) Denning; m. Alan R. Finberg, June 21, 1953. B.A., Stanford U., 1949; M.A., Am. U. of Beirut, Lebanon, 1951. Intern, then fgn. affairs officer Tech. Coop. Adminstrn., U.S. Dept. State, Washington, 1949-53; program specialist, area chief Inst. Internat. Edn., N.Y.C., 1953-59; editorial assoc., program officer Carnegie Corp. N.Y., N.Y.C., 1959-80, v.p. program, 1980—. Mem. adv. council N.C. Central U. Sch. Library Sci., Durham, 1973—; trustee Stanford U., 1976—, v.p. bd. dirs., 1982—; trustee N.Y. Found., 1979—, vice chmn. bd. dirs., 1983—. Rotary Found. fellow, 1950-51. Mem. Am. Ednl. Research Assn., Soc. for Research in Child Devel., Council on Fgn. Relations. Club: Cosmopolitan of N.Y. Home: 165 E 72d St Apt 19L New York NY 10021 Office: Carnegie Corp NY 437 Madison Ave New York NY 10022

FINBERG, DONALD RICHARD, government official; b. Balt., Nov. 23, 1931; s. Chester F. and Anne B. (Gorfinkle) F.; m. Hela Baumgardt, Oct. 19, 1958; children: Karen Anne, Dana. B.A., Amherst Coll., 1953; M.Pub. Affairs, Princeton U., 1955. With Office Sec. Def., Washington, 1955-59; asst. rep. Ford Found., Argentina and Chile, 1964-66; with AID, State Dept., 1960-62, Brazil, 1962-64, Peru, 1966-68, dep. dir., Paraguay, 1968-71, dep. dir. Regional Office for C.Am. and Panama, 1971-73, dir., Peru, 1973-77, dir. Ops. Appraisal Staff, 1977-79, AID rep. to, Portugal, 1979—. Served with AUS, 1957-58. Princeton fellow in pub. affairs, 1970-71. Mem. Phi Beta Kappa, Phi Alpha Psi.

FINBERG, LAURENCE, pediatrician; b. Chgo., May 20, 1923; s. Joseph and Anne (Malkow) F.; m. Harriet Levinson, June 17, 1945; children: Robert, Jeanne, James. B.S.; U. Chgo., 1944; M.D., 1946. Diplomate: Am. Bd. Pediatrics (examiner 1969—, bd. dirs. 1974-79, 82—, pres. 1978). Intern U. Chgo. Clinics, 1946-47; asst. resident pediatrics Balt. City Hosps., 1949-50, resident in pediatrics, 1950-51; practice medicine specializing in pediatrics, Balt., 1951-63, N.Y.C., 1963—; asst. chief pediatrician Balt. City Hosps., 1951-61, dir. pediatric out-patient dept., 1951-63, dir. premature nursery, 1951-59, asso. chief pediatrics, 1961-63; pediatrician Harriet Lane Home, 1951-63; chmn. dept. pediatrics Montefiore Hosp. and Med. Center, Bronx, N.Y., 1963-80, SUNY Downstate Med. Ctr., Bklyn., 1982—, prof. pediatrics, 1983—; instr. pediatrics Johns Hopkins U., 1951-56, asst. prof., 1956-63; prof. pediatrics Albert Einstein Coll. Medicine, Yeshiva U., Bronx, 1963—, chmn., 1968-80; cons. in field; mem. pediatric adv. com. N.Y.C. Dept. Health, 1970—. Mem. editorial bd.: Jour. Pediatrics, 1973—. Served with USPHS, 1947-49. Mem. Am. Pediatric Soc., Soc. Pediatric Research, Am. Acad. Pediatrics (com. on environ. hazards 1968—, chmn. 1979-83), Am. Coll. Nutrition, Am. Inst. Nutrition, Assn. Pediatric Ambulatory Services, Am. Soc. Clin. Nutrition, Am. Fedn. Clin. Research, AAAS, AMA, Sociedad Peruana de Pediatria, Sociedad Dominica De Peditria, Harvey Soc., N.Y. Acad. Medicine (past chmn. pediatric sec.), Phi Beta Kappa, Sigma Xi, Alpha Omega Alpha. Research in electrolyte physiology. Home: 57 Walden Rd Tarrytown NY 10591 Office: 450 Clarkson Ave Box 49 Brooklyn NY 11203

FINCH, CALEB ELLICOTT, neurobiology researcher, educator; b. London, July 4, 1939; U.S., 1939; s. Benjamin F. and Faith (Stratton) Campbell; m. Doris Nossamen, Oct. 11, 1975. B.S., Yale U., 1961; Ph.D., Rockefeller U., 1969. Guest investigator Rockefeller U., N.Y.C., 1969-70; asst. prof. Cornell U. Med. Coll., N.Y.C., 1970-72; asst. prof. biology, gerontology U. So. Calif., Los Angeles, 1972-75, assoc. prof., 1975-78, prof., 1978—; mem. cell biology study sect. NIH, Bethesda, Md., 1975-78. Editor: Handbook of Biology of Aging, 1977; editorial bd.: Jour. Gerontology, 1979—; contbr. numerous articles to sci. jours. Cons. Office of Tech. Assessment, U.S. Congress, Washington, 1982—. NIH research grantee, 1972—; postdoctoral fellow, 1969-71. Fellow Gerontol. Soc.; mem. Endocrine Soc., Neurosci. Soc., Psychoneuroendocrine Soc., Soc. Study Reprodn., Social Sci. Research Council. Home: 2144 Crescent Dr Altadena CA 91001 Office: U So Calif University Park Los Angeles CA 90007

FINCH, CHARLES BAKER, utilities exec.; b. N.Y.C., Mar. 1, 1920; s. Henry LeRoy and Mary (Baker) F.; m. Angela Cobb Sessions, Oct. 22, 1943; children—Charles Baker, William P. A.B., Yale U., 1941, LL.B., 1943. Bar: N.Y. bar 1943. With Milbank, Tweed & Hope (and successor firms), N.Y.C., 1943-54; v.p. Allegheny Power System, Inc., N.Y.C., 1954-72, pres., chief exec. officer, 1972—, chmn., 1981—; chmn. chief exec. officer West Penn Power Co., Monongahela Power Co., Potomac Edison Co. Bd. dirs. Josiah Macy, Jr. Found.; trustee Cooper Union. Mem. Municipal Art Soc., St. Nicholas Soc. City N.Y., Assn. Bar City N.Y., Phi Beta Kappa, Phi Delta Phi, Delta Kappa Epsilon. Clubs: Union, Church. Office: 320 Park Ave New York NY 10022

FINCH, CLEMENT A., physician; b. Broadalbin, N.Y., July 4, 1915; s. Percy Henry and Marion Elizabeth F.; m. Eugenia C. English, 1966; children—Clifton A., Carin A., Lisa, Derel. B.A., Union Coll., Schenectady, 1936; M.D., U. Rochester, 1941. Diplomate: Am. Bd. Internal Medicine. Fellow in pathology U. Rochester, 1938-39; med. intern Peter Bent Brigham Hosp., Boston, 1941-42, asst. resident in medicine, 1942-43, resident in medicine, 1944-46, jr. asso. in medicine, 1946-48; fellow in hematology Boston U., 1943-44; instr. medicine Harvard U., Boston, 1946-48, asso. in medicine, 1948-49; asso. prof. medicine U. Wash., 1949-55, prof., 1955—, head div. hematology, 1949—; attending physician Univ. Hosp., Seattle; cons. in field; mem. coms. Nat. Acad. Scis., NRC.; mem. adv. com. Nat. ARC; mem. adv. com. for biology and medicine AEC; mem. study sect. and council USPHS; chmn. blood diseases and resources adv. com. NIH. Contbr. numerous articles to profl. jours.; editorial positions: Haematologia. Recipient Goldberger award AMA, 1973, Wahle award in hematology SUNY, Buffalo, 1973. Mem. A.C.P., Am. Fedn. Clin. Research, Am. Soc. Clin. Investigation (pres. 1961), Am. Soc. Clin. Nutrition, Am. Physiol. Soc., Am. Soc. Hematology (pres. 1966, adv. com.), Assn. Am. Physicians, Internat. Soc. Hematology, King County Med. Soc., Nat. Acad. Arts and Scis., Nat. Acad. Scis., Soc. Exptl. Biology and Medicine, Societas Haematologica Helvetica (hon.), Wash. State Med. Assn., Western Assn. Physicians (pres. 1960-61), Western Soc. Clin. Research (Mayo Soley award 1972), Sigma Xi, Alpha Omega Alpha. Office: U Wash Med Sch Seattle WA 98105

FINCH, EDWARD RIDLEY, JR., lawyer, diplomat; b. Westhampton Beach, N.Y., Aug. 31, 1919. A.B. with honors, Princeton U., 1941; J.D., NYU, 1947; LL.D. hon., Mo. Valley Coll., 1963. Bar: N.Y. 1948, U.S. Supreme Ct. 1953, D.C. 1978, Fla. 1980. Ptnr. Finch & Schaeffer, N.Y.C., 1950—; commr. City of N.Y., N.Y., 1955-58; U.S. del. 4th UN Congress, Geneva, 1970, 5th UN Congress, Japan, 1975; U.S. spl. ambassador to, Panama, 1972; legal advisor U.S. Del. Unispace, Vienna, 1982; lectr. in field. Contbr. articles to legal jours. Mem. faculty adv. com. dept. politics Princeton U.; pres. N.Y. Inst. for Edn. of Blind, 1969-71; treas. Jessie Ridley Found., N.Y.C.; pres. Crippled Children's Friendly Aid Assn. Inc., Finch Trusts, Adams Meml. Fund Inc. Decorated Legion of Merit with oak leaf cluster, Order of Brit. Empire, Eng., Legion of Honor, France. Mem. ABA (ho. of dels. 1971-72, chmn. com. aerospace law of sect. internat. law 1973-79), Fed. Bar Assn., Inter-Am. Bar Assn., Internat. Bar Assn., Judge Advs. Assn. U.S. (past pres.), Am. Law Inst., Am. Judicature Soc., AIAA, Internat. Astronautical Acad. Am., Am. Arbitration Assn. (panelist), N.Y. State Bar Assn. Clubs: University, Union League, Union, Princeton. Home: 860 Park Ave New York NY 10021 Office: 36 W 44th St New York NY 10036

FINCH, HAROLD BERTRAM, JR., wholesale grocery company executive; b. Grand Forks, N.D., Oct. 13, 1927; s. Harold Bertram and Ruth M. F.; m. Catherine E. Cole, Sept. 6, 1950; children: Mark, James, Sarah, Martha, David. B.B.A., U. Minn., 1952, B.Chem. Engring., 1952. Div. mgr. Archer-Daniels-Midland Co., Mpls., 1960-66; dir. long-range planning, then v.p. sales and ops. Nash Finch Co., Mpls., 1966-78, pres., 1978—, chief exec. officer, 1982—. Bd. dirs. Jr. Achievement Mpls., 1977—, Mpls. YMCA, 1965-80. Served with U.S. Maritime Service, 1945-47. Mem. Nat. Assn. Wholesale Grocers Am. (bd. govs.), Food Mktg. Inst. Presbyterian. Office: 3381 Gorham Ave Minneapolis MN 55426

FINCH, H(AROLD) CURTIS, architect; b. Boise, Idaho, Oct. 22, 1926; s. Harold Clough and Clare May (Curtis) F.; children by previous marriage: Lisa M., Martin C., Timothy W., James A. B.Arch., U. Oreg., 1952. Ptnr. Dropping, Kelley & Finch (Architects), Boise, 1954-63, Fletcher/Finch/Farr Ptnrs. (and predecessor), Portland, Oreg., 1964—; pres. Oreg. Council Architects, 1977. Mem. council Portland Community Coll., 1968; mem. Lake Oswego (Oreg.) City Council, 1972-76. Served with USNR, 1944-45; Served with USAFR, 1951-53. Fellow AIA (pres. Idaho chpt. 1961, pres. Portland chpt. 1966). Republican. Presbyterian. Home: 2711 Lakeview Blvd Lake Oswego OR 97034 Office: 208 SW 1st Ave Portland OR 97204

FINCH, HENRY LEROY, JR., educator; b. Monmouth Beach, N.J., Aug. 8, 1918; s. Henry L. and Mary (Baker) F.; m. Margaret Rockwell, June 12, 1948; children—Margaret Julie, Martha Willard Kozlosky, Mary Dabney Baker, Annie Ridley Crane, Henry LeRoy III. Student,

Buckley Sch., Phillips Acad., Andover, Mass.; B.A., Yale U., 1940; M.A., Columbia U., 1950, Ph.D., 1952. Mem. faculty Sarah Lawrence Coll., Bronxville, N.Y., 1953-73; prof. philosophy Hunter Coll., N.Y.C., 1973—. Author: Wittgenstein-The Early Philosophy, 1970, Wittgenstein-The Later Philosophy, 1976; Editor: Conversations with Einstein, 1970, Talks with Tolstoi, 1969. Address: 106 Liberty Ave New Rochelle NY 10805 Office: Dept Philosophy Hunter Coll New York NY 10021

FINCH, HERMAN MANUEL, university trustee, former management consultant; b. Russia, July 7, 1914; came to U.S., 1921, naturalized, 1936; s. Nathan and Rose (Stark) F.; m. Frances G. Gutlow, Dec. 28, 1949; children: David S., Robert J., Mark J., Maurine. Student, Hebrew Theol. Coll., Chgo., 1929-32, U. Nebr., Omaha, 1932-36; Sc.D. (hon.), U. Health Scis., Chgo. Med. Sch., 1969. Head Herman M. Finch & Assocs. (mgmt. cons. in indsl. relations), Chgo., 1943-78; dir. Wilson Jones Co., 1954-59, Swingline, Inc., 1959-63, Nat. Bellas-Hess, Inc., 1971-76; Chmn. bd. trustees U. Health Scis., Chgo. Med. Sch., 1966—, chief exec. officer bd. trustees, 1980—; trustee Hebrew Theol. Coll., 1955-63; bd. dirs. Mt. Sinai Hosp. Med. Center, Chgo., 1960-65; Citizen fellow Inst. Medicine, Chgo. Jewish (v.p. ritual synagogue 1959-60, pres. Moriah congregation 1977-78). Clubs: Mid-America, Standard (Chgo.). Home: 415 Lambert Tree Rd Highland Park IL 60035 Office: 200 E Randolph Dr Chicago IL 60601 *The constant awareness that I arrived as a child to a land of freedom from a land without liberty and opportunity has evoked within me both ambition and humbleness. The ambition to strive for all that is possible in this land is tempered by humbleness and gratitude—thus the desire to give thanks in the form of service to others.*

FINCH, JAMES AUSTIN, JR., judge; b. St. Louis, Nov. 13, 1907; s. James Austin and Carrie (Lehman) F.; m. Helen E. Carroll, Aug. 28, 1937; children: Gail Carroll, James Austin III, John David. Student, S.E. Mo. State Coll., 1925-27; A.B., U. Mo., 1930, J.D., 1932, LL.D., 1966. Bar: Mo. bar 1931. Asst. atty. gen., Mo., 1932; mem. firm Finch, Finch & Knehans (formerly Finch & Finch), Cape Girardeau, 1933-65; judge Supreme Ct. Mo., 1965-78, chief justice, 1971-73; pros. atty., Cape Girardeau County, 1941-42; Bd. dirs. Nat. Center for State Cts., 1971-78, pres., 1975-77; mem. exec. council Appellate Judges Conf., 1972-77, sec., 1974-77; pres. Mo. Press-Bar Commn., 1979-80; chmn. Mo. Supreme Ct. Com. on Rules, 1980—; Mem. Mo. Citizens Adv. Com. on Higher Edn., 1956-57; govs. com. Edn. Beyond High Sch., 1958-60; chmn. Gov's Council Higher Edn., 1959-63, Adv. Council Mo. Commn. Higher Edn., 1963-64. Mem. bd. curators U. Mo., 1951-65, pres. bd., 1954-64; bd. dirs. Mo. Law Sch. Found., 1952-64, pres., 1958-59. Served as maj. USAAF, 1942-45. Recipient award for contbn. to Mo. edn. Phi Delta Kappa, 1964; Alumni Disting. Service award U. Mo., 1965; President's Disting. Service award U. Mo., 1982; Ann. Law Day award Law Sch., U. Mo. at Kansas City, 1968; Alumni Merit citation Sch. Law, U. Mo. at Columbia, 1970; Award of Merit Am. Judges Assn., 1976; Mo. Bar Found. Spurgeon Smithson award for service to justice in soc., 1977. Fellow Am. Bar Found.; mem. Am. Law Inst., Am. Judicature Soc. (dir. 1970-74), Am., Mo., Cole County, St. Louis bar assns., Mo. Hist. Soc., Am. Legion, Order of Coif, Inst. Jud. Adminstrn., Acad. Mo. Squires, Phi Beta Kappa Assos., Phi Delta Phi, Omicron Delta Kappa, Delta Sigma Rho, Phi Gamma Delta. Republican. Methodist. Clubs: Jefferson City (Mo.); Country, Rotary. Home: 404 Crystal View Terr Jefferson City MO 65101 Office: Supreme Ct Bldg Jefferson City MO 65101

FINCH, JAMES HARRISON, architect; b. Atlanta, Dec. 5, 1913; s. Harrison and Anne Cohutta (Gryder) F.; m. LewEllyn Grace Lundeen, Jan. 4, 1952; children: LewEllyn, Anne. B.S. in Arch, Ga. Inst. Tech., 1936; postgrad., Princeton, 1937-38. Draftsman Hentz, Adler & Shutze, 1938-41; designer Burge & Stevens, 1946-48; partner Finch, Barnes & Paschal, 1948-52, 54-58; pres. Finch Alexander Barnes Rothschild & Paschal, Atlanta, 1958—; v.p. Asso. Space Design, Atlanta, 1965—; pres. Fabrap, Inc., 1971—; asso. prof. arch. Ga. Inst. Tech., 1946-68; Mem. Ga. Commn. Arts, 1964—, chmn., 1966-67; mem. Atlanta Civic Design Commn., 1969—. Prin. works include Coca-Cola Co. Bldg, 1969, Atlanta Stadium, 1964, Ga. Power Co. Bldg, 1961, First Nat. Bank Bldg, 1969, all Atlanta, Riverfront Stadium, Cin., 1971, Scottish Rite Hosp, 1976, So. Bell Hdqrs, 1977, Coca-Cola Hdqrs, 1977, Ga. Inst. Tech. Student Athletic Complex, 1976. Trustee Ga. Conservancy. Served with USMC, 1941-46, 52-54; col. Res. Recipient Ivan Allen award N. Ga. chpt. AIA, 1968. Fellow AIA. Presbyn. Clubs: Commerce, Piedmont Driving, City (Atlanta). Home: 37 Inman Circle NE Atlanta GA 30309 Office: Finch Alexander Barnes Rothschild & Paschal 100 Peachtree St NW Atlanta GA 30303

FINCH, JEREMIAH STANTON, English language educator; b. Albany, N.Y., Apr. 27, 1910; s. Jeremiah Calvin and Nina (Tree) F.; m. Mathilde Effler, July 21, 1937 (div. 1960); children: Jeremiah (dec.), Anne Judith, Abigail Kathryn; m. Nancy Goheen Wallis, June 28, 1961. A.B., Cornell U., 1931, M.A., 1933, Ph.D., 1936; L.H.D. (hon.), St. Lawrence U., 1972, Litt.D., Ripon Coll., 1980. Instr. English Cornell U., 1934-36; successively instr. English, asst. prof. pub. speaking, asst. to dean of faculty, asst. dean of coll., lectr. English, assoc. dean of coll. Princeton U., 1936-55, dean, 1955-61, prof. English, 1956-75, prof. emeritus, 1975—; sec. univ. Princeton, 1966-74; study tchr. edn. with James B. Conant, 1961-62; exec. sec. Princeton Program for Servicemen, 1944-48. Author: Sir Thomas Browne: a Doctor's Life of Science and Faith, 1950; co-author: The Princeton Graduate School: A History, 1978, The Princeton Campus in World War II, 1978; contbr. articles to profl. jours. Trustee Danforth Found., 1964-71, Ripon Coll., 1971—. Mem. Charles Lamb Soc., AAUP (council 1946-48), Middle States Assn. (pres. 1970, mem. commn. on higher edn. 1958-64), Phi Kappa Phi. Club: Century Assn. (N.Y.C.). Home: 99 McCosh Circle Princeton NJ 08540

FINCH, RAYMOND LAWRENCE, judge; b. Christiansted, St. Croix, V.I., Oct. 4, 1940; s. Wilfred Christopher and Beryl Elaine (Bough) F.; m. Lenore Luana Hendricks, June 8, 1963; children—Allison, Mark, Jennifer. A.B., Howard U., 1962, J.D., 1965. Bar: V.I. bar 1971, Third Circuit Ct. of Appeals bar 1976. Law clk. Judge's Municipal Ct. of V.I., 1965-66; partner firm Hodge, Sheen, Finch & Ross, Christiansted, 1970-75; judge Territorial Ct. of V.I., Charlotte Amalie, 1975—; instr. Am. Inst. Banking, 1976—. Bd. dirs. Boy Scouts Am., Boys Club Am. Served to capt. U.S. Army, 1966-69. Decorated Army Commendation medal, Bronze Star medal. Mem. Am. Judges Assn., Am., Nat. bar assns., Internat. Assn. Chiefs of Police. Democrat. Lutheran. Home: 81 Tan Tan Terr Christiansted Saint Croix VI 00820 Office: PO Box 929 Christiansted Saint Croix VI 00820

FINCH, ROGERS BURTON, association executive; b. Broadalbin, N.Y., Apr. 16, 1920; s. Cecil Clement and Olga Ulrika (Lofgren) F.; m. Barbara Ellen Hine, Jan. 3, 1942; children: David Rogers, John Richard, Steven Alan, Kathryn Ann, Elizabeth Gale. B.S., Mass. Inst. Tech., 1941, M.S., 1947, Sc.D., 1950. Prof. Mass. Inst. Tech., 1946-53; dir. U.S. Fgn. Aid Mission, Rangoon, Burma, 1953-54; dir. research Rensselaer Poly. Inst., Troy, N.Y., 1954-61, v.p. planning, 1963-72; dir. univ. relations Peace Corps, Washington, 1961-63; exec. dir. ASME, N.Y.C., 1972-81; cons., 1981—; exec. v.p. Illuminating Engineering Soc. N.Am., 1982—. Contbr. articles profl. jours. Served to maj. AUS, 1941-46; to brig. gen. U.S. Army Res.; ret., 1975. Decorated Army Commendation medal, Legion of Merit. Fellow ASME (life), AAAS; mem. AIAA, Am. Soc. Assn. Execs., Am. Soc. Engring. Edn., Council Engring. and Sci. Soc. Execs. (past pres.), Illuminating Engring. Soc. N.Am., Sigma Xi, Tau Beta Pi. Home: 12 Sherwood Rd Little Silver NJ 07739

FINCH, RONALD M., JR., savings and loan executive; b. Mpls., Jan. 21, 1932; s. Ronald M. and Lynda (Stapel) F.; m. Arline Anne Atkins, Sept. 17, 1961. B.S., U. Fla., 1954; certificate of recognition, Ind. U., 1965. With First Fed. Savs. & Loan Assn., Lake Worth, Fla., 1958—, dir., 1969—, pres., 1970—. Sec., bd. dirs. United Community Fund Lake Worth; bd. dirs. Lake Worth Utilities Authority, 1969-73; trustee Employees Retirement System City Lake Worth, 1965-69; bd. dirs. Lake Worth Pub. Library, 1967-78, Palm Glades council Girl Scouts U.S.A., 1978-80, United Way Palm Beach County, 1978—, Council of 100, Palm Beach County, Inc., 1978—, Better Bus. Bur. Palm Beach County, 1973—. Served as 1st lt. USAF, 1955-58. Mem. Lake Worth C. of C. (past pres. dir.), Am. Savs. and Loan Inst. (past pres. Palm Beach County chpt.), Fla. Savs. and Loan League (dir. Orlando 1976-77), Alpha Tau Omega. Conglist (trustee 1967, moderator 1981, 82). Club: Kiwanis (past pres., dir.). Home: 413 Muirfield Dr Atlantis FL 33462 Office: 2601 10th Ave N Lake Worth FL 33460

FINCH, STUART MCINTYRE, child psychiatrist; b. Salt Lake City, Aug. 16, 1919; s. Elmer E. and Ann (McIntyre) F.; m. Dorothy Ellen Standish, Sept. 2, 1941; children: Craig Standish, Ellen Stuart. Premed. student, U. Utah, 1936-39; M.D., U. Colo., 1944. Diplomate: Am. Bd. Psychiat. and Neurology (mem. com. on certification in child psychiatry 1968). Intern Alameda County Hosp., Oakland, Calif., 1943-44; resident psychiatry Temple U. Hosp. and Sch. Medicine, 1946-49, Phila. Psychoanalytic Inst., 1947-53; instr. psychiatry Temple U. Sch. Medicine, 1949, asso. prof., 1954; attending psychiatrist St. Christopher's Hosp. Children, Phila., 1953-56; mem. faculty U. Mich. Med. Sch., 1956-73, prof. psychiatry, chief children's psychiat. service, 1960-73; lectr. U. Ariz. Sch. Medicine, 1973-83; practice medicine, specializing in child psychiatry, Tucson, 1973-83; prof. dept. psychiatry Med. Coll. Ga., Augusta, 1983—; Mem. adv. council Mich. Dept. Mental Health, 1968-73; Bd. dirs. Washtenaw County Community Mental Health Center, 1965—. Author: (with O.S. English) Introduction to psychiatry, 3d edit, 1964, Fundamentals of Child Psychiatry, 1960, (with J.F. McDermott) Psychiatry for Pediatricians, 1970. Mem. Am. Psychiat. Assn. (chmn. com. psychiatry childhood and adolescence 1964-70), Group Advancement Psychiatry, Am. Orthopsychiat. Assn., AMA, Am. Acad. Child Psychiatry, Am. Psychoanalytic Assn. Home: 3528 W Lake Dr Augusta GA 30907

FINCH, THOMAS AUSTIN, JR., furniture manufacturing company executive; b. Thomasville, N.C., Aug. 12, 1922; s. Thomas Austin and Ernestine (Lambeth) F.; m. Meredith Clark Slane, June 4, 1949; children: Thomas Austin III, John Lambeth, David Slane, Sumner Slane, Meredith Kempton. Grad., Woodberry Forest Sch., 1940; B.S. in Engring, Princeton U., 1943. With Thomasville Furniture Industries, Inc., 1946—, chmn. bd., 1979—; group v.p. parent co. Armstrong Cork Co., Lancaster, Pa., 1979—, also dir.; dir. Wachovia Bank and Trust Co., Winston-Salem, N.C., Norfolk So. R.R., Washington. Trustee Duke U., 1963-81, Woodberry Forest Sch., 1967-72, Community Gen. Hosp., Thomasville, 1964-71, 74-80, Davidson County Pub. Library System, 1974—, Madeira Sch., 1981—. Served to lt. (j.g.) USNR; World War II. Named Furniture Man of Yr. Am. Furniture Mart Corp., 1963, Industrialist of Yr. Thomasville Family YMCA, 1975. Mem. Furniture Factories Mktg. Assn., Phi Beta Kappa. Methodist (ofcl. bd.). Club: Rotarian (pres. Thomasville 1958). Office: Thomasville Furniture Industries Inc 401 E Main St Thomasville NC 27360 *

FINCH, WILLIAM GEORGE HAROLD, radio engineer; b. Birmingham, Eng., June 28, 1897; came to U.S., 1906; s. William Joseph and Amelia (Skelding) F.; m. Elsie Grace George, Nov. 29, 1916 (dec. May 1967); 1 dau., Eloise Grace Finch Tholen; m. Helen Stork Ambler, Feb. 1, 1969. Grad., Woodward High Sch., Cin.; elec. engring. course with, Allis-Chalmers, Norwood, Ohio; radio communication course, Marconi Inst., N.Y.C., 1917; completed spl. course radio engring. and patent law, Columbia U., 1923; D.Sc. (hon.), Fla. Inst. Tech., 1983. Registered profl. engr., N.Y.; patent atty. Asst. engr. Cleve. Electric Illuminating Co., 1916-17; inspecting engr. Nat. Dist. Telegraph Co., N.Y.C., N.Y. Compensating Rating Bd., 1917-19; elec. engr. Royal Indemnity Co., 1919-21; radio engr. and editor Internat. News Service, 1921—; chief engr. Hearst Radio, 1928-34; asst. chief engr. and chief telephone engring. div. FCC and chief engr. fed. investigation telephone cos., 1934-35; pres. Finch Telecommunications, Inc., N.Y.C., 1935-41, Conn. Indsl. Research Corp., Newtown, 1956—; founder, owner Sta. WGHF-FM, N.Y.C., 1946-49; v.p. Sta. WCAE, Pitts.; dir. communications Rowley Newspapers of Ohio, Ashtabula; dir. Telecommunication Cons. Internat. Inc., Washington; patent atty., U.S. and Can.; cons. profl. engr., electronic, facsimile communications and patent engring. Mem. Internat. Radio Consultive Com.; mem. tech. com. on radio and cable communication Am. Newspaper Pubs. Assn., 1924—; mem. com. allocation of frequency Fourth Nat. Radio Conf.; del. Internat. Telegraphic and Radio Telegraphic Conf., Madrid, 1932, N.Am. Radio Conf., Mexico City, 1933. Contbr. numerous articles to profl. jours. Mem. 1st F.A., N.Y. N.G., 1917-18; lt. (s.g.) USNR; exec. officer U.S. Navy Communication Res., 3d Naval Dist., 1929—; N.Y.C.; also detailed communication officer U.S.S. Wheeling; comdr. USN, 1943-45; asst. chief Office Naval Research; capt., 1944-57; ret. Recipient Presdl. award; decorated Legion of Merit; Wisdom award, 1971. Fellow IEEE (award 1956), Radio Club Am. (dir. emeritus, Amstrong medal 1976, Dr. Lee DeForest award 1984); mem. N.Y. Acad. Scis., Armed Forces Communications and Electronics Assn., Mil. Order World Wars, Am. Legion, AAAS, Am. Phys. Soc., Franklin Inst. Episcopalian (vestryman). Clubs: Mason., Bankers, Army and Navy (N.Y.); Masons (Buffalo); Army and Navy (Washington); Crown Point Country, N.Y. Yacht, N.Y. Athletic; Saint and Sinners Yacht (Port St. Lucie, Fla.) (sec. 1965—, commodore 1978-79); St. Lucie (Stuart, Fla.) (rear commodore); Anchor Line Yacht (Jensen Beach, Fla.)). Established 1st radiotypewriter press circuit between N.Y.C. and Chgo., 1932, 1st internat. radiotypewriter circuit between N.Y.C. and Havana, 1933. Owner of the schooner Night Hawk and Yacht Helena II. Home: 3025 Morningside Blvd Port St Lucie FL 33452 also 1913 Stuart Ave Richmond VA 23220 *Do right and fear no one.*

FINCHER, CAMERON LANE, educator; b. Douglas County, Ga., Nov. 4, 1926; s. Andrew Jackson and Ada (Swafford) F.; m. Mary Frances Cutts, June 15, 1957; children: Marcel, Matt, Mandy, Melissa. B.C.S., Ga. State U., 1950; M.A., U. Minn., 1951; Ph.D., Ohio State U., 1956. Dir. testing and counseling Ga. State Coll., Atlanta, 1956-65; asso. dir. Inst. Higher Edn., U. Ga., Athens, 1965-69, dir. Inst., 1969—, prof. higher edn. and psychology, 1965—, Regents prof. higher edn. and psychology, 1981—; cons. various indsl. and comml. cos., also colls. and univs. Mem. Gov.'s Com. on Postsecondary Edn., 1978-83; mem. research panel So. Edn. Found., 1978—. Author: A Preface to Psychology, 1972; contbg. columnist: Athens Banner-Herald, 1970—; contbg. editor: Research in Higher Edn, 1978—; contbr. articles to profl. jours. Served with USNR, 1944-46. Recipient Disting. Achievement in Public Service medallion U. Ga., 1980, Ben W. Gibson award So. Regional Council, Coll. Bd., 1982. Mem. Am. Psychol. Assn., Am. Ednl. Research Assn., Assn. Study of Higher Edn., Am. Assn. Higher Edn., Assn. Instnl. Research (Disting. Mem. 1983, Outstanding Service award 1980), Nat. Council Measurement in Edn., Alpha Kappa Psi, Phi Delta Kappa, Golden Key. Office: Inst Higher Edn Candler Hall U Ga Athens GA 30602

FINCHER, JOHN ALBERT, college official, consultant; b. Union, S.C., Sept. 8, 1911; s. Robert C. and Addie (Murphy) F.; m. Ruby C. Broom, Aug. 19, 1939; children: Judith Ellen, Janice Manette, John Albert. B.S., U. S.C., 1933, M.S., 1935; Ph.D., U. N.C., 1939. Prin. Pineview Sch., 1933-34; instr. U. S.C., 1934-35; grad. asst. U. N.C., 1935-39; instr. biology Cumberland Coll., 1939-40; asst., asso. prof. Millsaps Coll., 1940-46; prof., head dept. Samford U., Birmingham, Ala., 1946-57, asst. to pres., 1955-57, dean, 1957-68; pres. Carson-Newman Coll., Jefferson City, Tenn., 1968-77, pres. emeritus, 1977—; v.p. for acad. affairs Bapt. Coll. at Charleston (S.C.), 1983—; pres. Mid-Appalachia Coll. Council, 1969-72; Chmn. edn. commn. So. Bapt. Conv., 1962-66. Contbr. sci. articles to profl. jours. Trustee Gorgas Scholarship Found., 1947-68; bd. dirs. East End Meml. Hosp., 1958-68, v.p. bd., 1966-68; bd. dirs. Douglas-Cherokee Authority, 1968-77. Fellow AAAS; mem. Ala. Acad. Sci. (pres. 1952-53), Am. Soc. Zoology, Jefferson City C. of C. (dir., pres. 1972), Am. Assn. for Higher Edn., Tenn. Council Pvt. Colls. (vice chmn. 1969-72, chmn. 1972-74), Assn. So. Baptist Colls. and Schs. (pres. 1975-76), Tenn. Coll. Assn. (pres. 1975-76), Phi Beta Kappa, Sigma Xi, Alpha Epsilon Delta (nat. councilor 1954-60, nat. v.p. 1960-62), Omicron Delta Kappa (province dep. 1968), Pi Kappa Alpha, Beta Beta Beta, Phi Sigma Tau, Kappa Delta Pi, Blue Key. Democrat. Baptist. Club: Rotarian. Home: 4 Sabina Ct Hanahan SC 29405

FINCHER, JOSEPH, zoological park-entertainment center executive. Gen. mgr. Busch Gardens (The Dark Continent), Tampa, Fla. Office: Busch Gardens (The Dark Continent) PO Box 9158 Tampa FL 33674§

FINCHER, JULIAN HAYES, college dean; b. Union, S.C., July 22, 1935; s. Robert Charles and Addie (Murphy) F.; m. Betty Jane Jarrell Smith, June 2, 1966; 1 son, Timothy Kyle. B.S., U. S.C., 1958; M.S., U. Ga., 1962; Ph.D., U. Conn., 1964. Pharmacist Smith's Drug Store, Union, 1958, S.C. State Hosp. Pharmacy, 1959; instr. U. S.C., 1958-59, U. Ga., 1959-61; asst. prof. U. Miss., 1964-67, asso. prof., 1967-70, chmn. pharmaceutics, asso. prof., 1970-72; prof. pharmacy U. S.C., 1972—, dean, 1972—; research participant med. div. Oak Ridge Inst. Nuclear Studies, summer 1965; cons. H.A. Salzman & Co., Rock Island, Ill., 1967-73. Contbg. author: Experiments in Physical and Technical Pharmacy, 1968; co. author: The History of Pharmaceutical Education at the University of South Carolina, 1865-1978, 1982; Contbr.: chpts. to Solutions of Electrolytes; articles sci. jours. Recipient AEC grant, 1966, 68; Salzman Research Project grants, 1969, 70, 71; USPHS Capitation grantee, 1972-80. Fellow Am. Found. Pharm. Edn.; mem. Am. Pharm. Assn., Acad. Pharm. Scis., Am. Chem. Soc., Am. Assn. Colls. Pharmacy (chmn. Council of Deans 1981-82), S.C. Pharm. Assn., Sigma Xi, Phi Delta Chi, Rho Chi, Phi Lambda Upsilon, Omicron Delta Kappa. Democrat. Baptist. Club: Rotary. Home: 161 Morgan Dr Lexington SC 29072 Office: Coll Pharmacy U SC Columbia SC 29208 *Personal experiences are excellent teachers if they are viewed in the proper perspectives and the lessons heeded. These must always be tempered with the wise counsel and advice of personal associates in all areas of life. The ultimate source of strength and wisdom to cope with life's problems and make the right decisions comes from a constant personal relationship and prayerful requests with and of the God of our universe.*

FINCK, FURMAN JOSEPH, artist, educator; b. Chester, Pa., Oct. 10, 1900; s. Harry August and Caroline Emma (Smith) F.; m. Mildred Price Smith, June 18, 1938; 1 son, Nicolas. Student, Pa. Acad. Fine Arts, Phila., 1921-24, Ecole des Beaux Arts, Academie Julian, Paris, 1924; studied abroad, 1930, 32, 54, 66, 68, 69, 70, 71, 72, 83; A.F.D. (hon.), Muhlenburg Coll., 1954. Emeritus prof. drawing, painting Tyler Coll. Fine Arts, Temple U., Phila; tchr. Blai Coll., Ocean County Coll.; faculty Cheltenham Art Center, Phila. Mus. Art, Sch. of Nat. Acad. of N.Y.; dean du Cret Sch. Art; lectr. Phila. Art Inst. Portrait and landscape artist; Exhibited widely in ann., biennial, nat. and internat. group shows, 50-yr. retrospective, Woodmere Gallery, Phila.; represented in collections, Lyman Allyn Mus., New London, Conn., Nat. Theater, Nat. Portrait Gallery, Washington, Toledo Mus., State Capitol, Montpelier, Vt., State House, Hartford, Conn., Harvard, Pa., Princeton, Temple, Vt., Weidner, Yale, L.I., N.C., Ga., Iowa, Utah, Wash., Md., Rutgers, Loyola, Mich., Conn. univs., Muhlenburg, Muskingum, Western Md., Ann Arundel, Fla. So. colls., Akron, Drexel insts., Nat. Dem. Club N.Y.C., Union League Club, Am. Cancer Soc., various hosps. and med. centers, Wyeth Labs., Phila. Coll. Pharmacy, Farragut Med. Bldg., Washington, Berliz Collection, Zurich, John Weinberger, Geneva, Dartmouth House, London, Babcock Clinic, others; works include composition 34 med. portraits, Burnett Clinic, composition 8 med. portraits, Churchill Clinic, Chamberlain Clinic, composition 7 med. portraits, portraits of govt. ofcls. including two Presidents of U.S.; author: The Meaning of Art in Education, 1938, Complete Guide to Portrait Painting, 1970, 2d edit., 1974, (with others) The Artist as Teacher, 1950; Author: film lecture series The Art of Ancient Egypt; Contbr.: articles on art edn. to profl. publs. NBC TV U. of Air; (also subject of film). Recipient Cresson Travelling European scholarship Pa. Acad., 1924; Carnegie award Nat. Acad., N.Y.C., 1943; Popular award Worcester Mus., 1945; Krindler prize Salmagundi Club, N.Y.C., 1954; 1st Altman prize Nat. Acad., 1955, Am. Acad. Rome, 1966. Mem. Artists Equity, Artists Fellowship, Inc. (pres. 1973-77), English-Speaking Union, St. George Soc. Clubs: Dutch Treat, Players, Salmagundi (N.Y.C.); 25 Year (Temple U.). Studio: 285 Central Park W New York NY 10024

FINCK, WILLIAM ALBERT, chemical company executive; b. Balt., Feb. 1, 1924; s. William John and Elaine Vivian (deMott) F.; m. Bonnie Gutbub, Aug. 20, 1949; children: Karen Susanne Finck Grimm, Kevin William. B.S. in Chemistry, Western Md. Coll., 1948. Chemist Lever Bros. Co., 1948-51; successively foreman, shift supt., plant supt. Los Angeles Soap Co., 1951-60; with Purex Industries, 1960—, gen. mgr. mfg., 1965-68, v.p. mfg., 1968-70, group v.p., gen. mgr. indsl., instl. and comml. divs., 1970-79, exec. v.p., Lakewood, Calif., 1979—, also dir.; chmn. bd. Air Work Corp., Pacific Airmotive Corp.; dir. Brillo Corp., Brillo Eng., Ellio Pizza, T.P. Indsl. Served with USNR, 1942-46. Mem. Soap and Detergent Assn. (dir.). Republican. Methodist. Club: Hacienda Golf. Lodge: Masons. Office: 5101 Clark Ave Lakewood CA 90712

FINDER, THEODORE ROOSEVELT, lawyer; b. N.Y.C., Oct. 28, 1914; s. Henry H. and Wilhelmina (Kirschner) F. A.B., Columbia U., 1936, J.D., 1938. Bar: N.Y. 1938. Assoc. Fearey, Allen, Johnston & Smyth (and successor firms), 1938-42; assoc. firm Beekman & Bogue, N.Y.C., 1945-49, partner, 1950-81; partner firm Gaston Snow Beekman & Bogue, N.Y.C., 1981—, Boston, 1981—, Coral Gables, Fla., 1981—, Palo Alto, Calif., 1981—, San Francisco, 1981—; v.p., asst. sec., dir. B. Fischer & Co., Inc., N.Y.C., 1951-54, asst. sec., dir., 1957-64; pres., dir. Asher Am., Inc., Calgary, Alta., Can., 1952-53, asst. sec., 1953-58; dir. Redwater Am., Inc., Calgary, 1952-55, pres., 1953, asst. sec., 1953-55; v.p., dir. Gen. Fertilizer Corp., Walla Walla, Wash., 1958-64; asst. sec., dir. Calvan Am., Inc., Calgary, 1951-61, asst. treas., 1952-61; asst. sec., dir. Cola Beverage Corp., Jacksonville, Fla., 1958-64; dir. Studebaker Packard Corp., South Bend, Ind., 1958-60, fin. com., 1958-59, personnel com., 1958-60, exec. com., 1959-60. Served with USAAF, 1942-45; disch. as capt. Decorated D.F.C. (2), Air medal with clusters, Bronze Star medal; Presdl. Unit citation with cluster. Mem. Am., N.Y. State, N.Y. County, N.Y.C. bar assns., Delta Upsilon. Episcopalian. Clubs: Broad St. (N.Y.C.); Knickerbocker Country (Tenafly, N.J.); Desert Forest Golf (Carefree, Ariz.). Home: 136 E 76th St New York NY 10021 Home: 4620 N 68th St Scottsdale AZ 85251 Office: 14 Wall St New York NY 10005

FINDLAY, ERIC FRASER, dairy executive; b. Toronto, Ont., Can., July 16, 1926; s. Hugh Fraser and Etta (MacPherson) F.; children: Judith Ann, Craig Fraser, Scott Fraser. B.Commerce, U. Toronto, 1948. With Findlay Dairy Ltd. (later Findlay Kemp Dairies Ltd.), London, Ont., Can., 1948-66, v.p., 1954-65, pres., 1965-66; asst. to mng. dir. Silverwood Dairies Ltd., London, Ont., 1966-68, v.p., gen. mgr., 1968-70; exec. v.p. Silverwood Industries Ltd., 1970-71, chmn. bd., chief exec. officer, 1971—, pres., 1972—; pres. Execsil Corp.; dir. T.I. Industries Ltd., Can. Trust Co. Trustee, McMichael Canadian Collection. Mem. Milk Industry Found. (dir.). Clubs: London, London Hunt; Granite (Toronto). Home: 65 Harbour Sq Apt PH1 Toronto ON Canada Office: 6205 Airport Rd Mississauga Ontario Canada L4V 1E1

FINDLAY, JOHN WILSON, physicist; b. Kineton, Eng., Oct. 22, 1915; came to U.S., 1956, naturalized, 1963; s. Alexander Wilson and Beatrice Margaret (Thornton) F.; m. Jean Melvin, Dec. 14, 1953; children—Stuart E.G., Richard A.J. B.A., Cambridge U., 1937, M.A., 1940, Ph.D., 1950. With British Air Ministry, 1939-40; fellow, lectr. in physics Queens' Coll., Cambridge, Eng., 1945-52; asst. dir. for electronics research Ministry of Supply, London, 1952-56; with Nat. Radio Astronomy Obs., Charlottesville, Va., 1956—, dep. dir., 1961-65; dir. Arecibo Obs., 1965-66, sr. scientist, 1978—; mem. space sci. bd. Nat. Acad. Scis., 1961-71; chmn. lunar and planetary missions bd. NASA, 1967-71; chmn. space sci. bd. study Scientific Uses of the Space Shuttle, 1973. Contbr. articles to profl. jours. Served with RAF, 1940-45. Decorated Order of Brit. Empire. Fellow IEEE, AAAS; mem. Internat. Sci. Radio Union, Internat. Astron. Union. Clubs: Cosmos, Farmington. Home: Millbank Greenwood VA 22943 Office: Nat Radio Astronomy Observatory Edgemont Rd Charlottesville VA 22901

FINDLAY, RONALD EDSEL, economist; b. Rangoon, Burma, Apr. 12, 1935; came to U.S., 1969, naturalized, 1976; s. George and Hilda Beryl (Noble) F.; m. Tin Tin Aye, Dec. 16, 1961; 1 dau., Vanessa. B.A., Rangoon U., 1954; Ph.D. (Ford Found. fellow), M.I.T., 1960. Tutor in econs. Rangoon U., 1954-57, lectr. in econs., 1960-65, prof. econs., 1965-69; Ragnar Nurkse prof. econs. Columbia U., 1969—; Ford research prof., 1972-73. Author: Trade and Specialization, 1970, International Trade and Development Theory, 1973. Mem. Am. Econ. Assn. Home: 29 Claremont Ave New York NY 10027 Office: Columbia U New York NY 10027

FINDLAY, THEODORE BERNARD, management consultant; b. Grand Rapids, Mich., Jan. 23, 1939; s. Theodore Francis and Marie M. (Miltgen) F.; m. Ellen M. Tervo, June 27, 1964; children: Patrick John, Victoria Marie. A.B., Aquinas Coll., Grand Rapids, 1960. Reporter-desk man Grand Rapids Herald, 1955-59, Grand Rapids Press, 1959-60; metro editor Today, Cocoa, Fla., 1968-71; mng. editor Rockford (Ill.) Register-Star, 1971-74, Port Huron (Mich.) Times Herald, 1974-75; editor Racine (Wis.) Jour.-Times, 1975-77; exec. editor Quincy (Ill.) Herlad Whig, 1977-79; public relations Ford Motor Co., 1960-62; bur. chief, asst. city editor Miami (Fla.) Herald, 1964-69; metro editor Today, Cocoa, Fla., 1969-71; mng. editor Rockford (Ill.) Register-Star, 1971-74, Port Huron (Mich.) Times Herald, 1974-75; editor Racine (Wis.) Jour.-Times, 1975-77; exec. editor Quincy (Ill.) Herald Whig, 1977-79; dir. promotion, communications Universal Press Syndicate, Fairway, Kans., 1979-83; part-owner Equi-Plus, Inc., Overland Park, KS, 1983—; instr. communications, mgmt. Northwestern U., 1975-78, Culver-Stockton Coll., Canton, Mo., 1978-79; discussion leader Am. Press Inst., 1972—; newspaper, mgmt. cons., 1976—. Author: Above the Thunder, 1982. Served with AUS, 1962-64. Named to Northwestern Faculty Honor Roll, 1975-76; recipient AP Mng. Editors Leadership award, 1974, 76, 77. Roman Catholic. Club: Kiwanis. Home: 10566 Noland Rd Overland Park KS 66215 Office: Equi-Plus Inc Suite 100 10550 Barkley Overland Park KS 66212

FINDLAY, WALSTEIN C., JR., art gallery director; b. Kansas City, Mo., 1903. Student, U. Mo., 1925. Pres., dir. Wally Findlay Galleries, Inc., Chgo., Palm Beach, Fla., N.Y.C. and; Beverly Hills, Calif., Wally Findlay Galleries Internat., Inc., Chgo., Wally Findlay Galleries Internat., SARL, Paris. Decorated croix de chevalier Ordre Nat. du Mérite, France). Life mem. Art Inst. Chgo. Clubs: Univ. (Kansas City); Metropolitan, Raffles (N.Y.C.). Office: 814 N Michigan Ave Chicago IL 60611

FINDLEY, CHARLES H., manufacturing company executive; b. Saegertown, Pa., Jan. 14, 1924; s. Homer L. and Marian L. (Luce) F.; m. Helen Fyler, June 17, 1949; children: Robin, Susan, Alison. A.B., Baldwin-Wallace Coll., 1947; LL.B., Cleveland-Marshall Law Sch., 1952. With Gen. Electric Co., Ill. and Tenn., 1957-61, supt., employee relations mgr., 1961-63, plant mgr., 1964-69; gen. mgr. Clyde and St. Paul divs. Whirlpool Corp., 1971-78; pres., chief exec. officer Heil-Quaker Corp., Nashville, 1978—; dir. Clyde Savs. Bank, Northwestern Bank. Bd. dirs. Fremont Hosp., 1971-76, Better Bus. Bur., Mpls./St. Paul, 1976-78; mem. Sch. Bd. Murfreesboro, Tenn., 1968-71, Water Bd., 1967-71. Served with USNR, 1943-46. Mem. C. of C., Gas Appliance Mfrs. Assn., Air Conditioning and Refrigeration Inst. Republican. Methodist. Clubs: Kiwanis, Rotary. Office: Heil-Quaker Corp 635 Thompson Ln Nashville TN 37204 *

FINDLEY, PAUL, congressman; b. Jacksonville, Ill., June 23, 1921; s. Joseph S. and Florence Mary (Nichols) F.; m. Lucille Gemme, Jan. 8, 1946; children—Craig Jon, Diane Lillian. A.B., Ill. Coll., 1943, LL.D., 1972; L.H.D. (hon.), Lindenwood Coll., 1969. Pres., pub. Pike Press. Inc., Pittsfield, Ill., 1947—; mem. 87th-97th congresses 20th Ill. Dist., mem. Fgn. Affairs com., mem. Agr. com.; chmn. factfinding mission to Paris, 1965; chmn. Republican NATO Task Force, 1965-68; chmn. com. to investigate internat. problems caused by agrl. support policies Ditchley (Eng.) Conf., 1973; del. N. Atlantic Assembly, 1965-70, 72-79, Munich Conf. German Relations, 1969-71; Ditchley Conf. Atlantic Trade, 1967, European Parliament, 1974-76; mem. 7th Congl. Del. to People's Republic China, 1975; chmn. Ill. Trade Mission to, USSR, 1972; chmn. Ill. Trade Mission to, People's Republic of China, 1978; Dir. Federal Union, Inc. Author: Abraham Lincoln: The Crucible of Congress, The Federal Farm Fable; contbr. numerous articles on fgn. policy and agr. to periodicals. Trustee Ill. Coll.; bd. dirs. Abraham Lincoln Assn. Served to lt. (j.g.) USNR, World War II. Named laureate Lincoln Acad., 1980; decorated Grand Cross Order of Merit Fed. Republic of Ger.; inducted into Golden Age Hall of Fame Nat. Alliance Sr. Citizens; recipient Outstanding Service to Agr. citation So. Ill. U.; Hon. Am. Farmer degree Future Farmers Am.; also outstanding achievement award Alumni Assn.; citation Nat. Assn. State Univs. and Land-Grant Colls. Mem. Ill. Press Assn. (past dir.), Am. Legion, V.F.W., Navy League, Amvets, Phi Beta Kappa. Republican. Conglist. Lodges: Lions; Rotary. Home: 115 W Jefferson St Pittsfield IL 62363 Office: Suite 913 1730 Rhode Island Ave NW Washington DC 20036

FINDLEY, TIMOTHY IRVING, writer; b. Toronto, Ont., Canada, Oct. 30, 1930; s. Allan Gilmour and Margaret Maude (Bull) F. Student of acting, Toronto, London, 1950-53. Actor Stratford Shakespearean Festival, 1953; contract player H.M. Tennet, London, 1953-56; actor theatres, London; actor theaters Edinburgh Festival; tours, Moscow, radio, TV stage roles, Can., 1959-62, writer, 1962—; writer-in-residence Nat. Arts Centre, Ottawa, Ont., 1974-75, U. Toronto, 1979-80. Author novels including: The Last of the Crazy People, 1967; author: The Butterfly Plague, 1969, The Wars (transl. into 8 langs., film based on book), 1981, Famous Last Words, 1981; author play: Can You See Me Yet?, 1977. Recipient Armstrong, 1971; recipient with William Whitehead ACTRA award for best documentary, 1975, Anik, 1980, City of Toronto Book award, 1977, Gov. Gen.'saward, 1977; Can. Council jr. arts grantee, 1968; Can. Council sr. arts grantee, 1978, 83. Mem. Actors' Equity, ACTRA, Writers' Union Can. (chmn. 1977-78). Office: care Nancy Colbert & Assocs 303 Davenport Rd Toronto ON Canada M5R 1K5

FINDLEY, WILLIAM NICHOLS, mechanical engineering educator; b. Mankato, Minn., Feb. 12, 1914; s. Joseph Stillwell and Florence Mary (Nichols) F.; m. Ruth Woolsey, Aug. 31, 1939; 1 dau., Elizabeth Jo. A.B., Ill. Coll., 1936, D.Sc., 1970; B.S.E. in Math. and Mech. Engring, U. Mich., 1937; M.S. (McMullen scholar), Cornell U., 1939. Instr. engring. George Washington U., 1938-39; instr. engring. U. Ill., 1939-42, asso., 1942-43, asst. prof., 1943-47, asso. prof., 1947-54; prof. engring. Brown U., 1954—; dir. Central Facility for Mech. Testing, 1965-68; mem. sci. adv. council Picatinny Arsenal, Dover, N.J., 1951-62; cons. Lawrence Livermore Lab., 1962-78; lectr. Colloquium on Fatigue, Stockholm, Sweden, 1955; Mem. organizing com. Joint Internat. Conf. on Creep, 1963; mem. panels on rapid deformation and on European creep practice. Author: (with J. Lai, K. Onaran) Nonlinear Creep and Relaxation of Viscoelastic Materials, 1976; Cons. editor: Bull. Mech. Engring. Edn; Contbr. articles to tech. jours., chpts. in books. Recipient Charles B. Dudley medal ASTM, 1945; prize for paper Soc. Plastics Engrs., 1949, 50; Richard L. Templin award ASTM, 1953, 64; Office Naval Research-AIAA research scholar in naval structural mechanics, 1978. Fellow ASME; mem. Am. Soc. Engring. Edn., ASTM, Soc. Exptl. Stress Analysis, Soc. Rheology, Atlantic Union Com., Sigma Xi, Phi Kappa Phi, Tau Beta Pi. Home: 35 Mayfair Dr Rumford RI 02916 Office: Barus & Holley Physics and Engring Bldg Providence RI 02912

FINDLY, SARAH ELIZABETH, librarian; b. Winfield, Kans., Apr. 2, 1908; d. Guy H. and Vera Irene (Kindig) F. A.B., Drake U., 1929; B.S.L.S., U. Ill., 1934; A.M. in L.S., U. Mich., 1945. Tchr., jr. and sr. high sch., Geneva, Iowa, 1929-33; asst. circulation dept. U. Iowa Library, summer 1934; sr. asst. reference dept. Library U. Oreg., 1934-35, sr. asst. circulation dept., 1935-37, reference dept., 1937-47, head reference librarian, 1947-50, head gen. reference and documents div., 1950-66, head reference librarian, 1966-68, prof. Sch. Librarianship, 1968-77, dean, 1973-74; vis. prof. Melbourne (Australia) State Coll., 1978. Contbr. profl. jours. Sec. Wesley Found. at U. Oreg., 1938-61, chmn. exec. bd., 1975-78, sec., 1978-80; coordinator Christian edn. 1st United Meth. Ch., Eugene, Oreg., 1978-79; chmn. exec. bd. Campus Interfaith Ministry, 1978-79. Mem. ALA (mem. council 1965-69), Pacific N.W. Library Assn. (2d v.p. 1967-69, chmn. library edn. div. 1970-73), Oreg. Library Assn. (past pres.), Assn. Am. Library Schs., AAUP, Assn. Coll. and Reference Libraries (past sect. chmn.), Pacific N.W. Bibliographic Center (past chmn. bd. mgrs.), Phi Beta Kappa. Methodist. Club: Altrusa. Home: 860E 39th Ave Eugene OR 97405 Office: Trailer D Room 27 U Oreg Eugene OR 97403

FINDORFF, ROBERT LEWIS, air filtration equipment mfg. co. exec.; b. Mpls., Apr. 15, 1929; s. Hugo Clarence and Elfriede Louise (Schade) F.; m. Jocelyn J. Curtis, June 20, 1953; children—Robert H., Jean, Paul, Laura, Mary, Karl, John. B.B.A., U. Minn., 1952, M.B.A., 1956; J.D. magna cum laude, William Mitchell Coll. Law, 1962. Bar: Minn. bar 1962. Trust accounting mgr. No. Trust Co., Chgo., 1953-54; personnel mgr. purchasing dir. Donaldson Co., Inc., Mpls., 1955-62, plant mgr., v.p. mfg., v.p., gen. mgr., 1965—; asso. firm Oppenheimer, Hodgeson, Brown, Wolf & Leach, St. Paul, 1962-64; dir. Donaldson Micro Pore S.A. de C.V., TCOIC; instr. property law William Mitchell Coll. Law, 1964-65. Trustee William Mitchell Coll. Law, 1981—. Served with AUS, 1947-48; Served with USAF, 1962-68. Recipient Minn. State Bar Scholarship award, 1962. Roman Catholic. Home: 6812 Paiute Dr Edina MN 55435 Office: 1400 W 94th St Minneapolis MN 55431

FINE, DAVID HYMAN, chemist; b. Johannesburg, S. Africa, Sept. 17, 1942; came to U.S., 1969, naturalized, 1975; s. Morris and Esther (Schloshberg) F.; m. Celia Shull, Jan. 12, 1964; children—Karen Ruth, Michael Jonathan. Postdoctoral student chemistry, Leeds (Eng.) U., 1967-68, U. Man., Winnipeg, Can., 1968-69. Registered profl. engr., Mass. Research asso. Mass. Inst. Tech., 1969-72; sr. research scientist, mgr. cancer research dept. Thermo Electron Research Center, Waltham, Mass., 1972-78, dir. research, 1980—, New Eng. Inst. Life Scis., Waltham, 1978—; Mem. U.S. Acad. Sci. com. on amines, 1979-80, com. on nitrates and nitrites, 1981-82. Author numerous articles environ. distbn. N-nitroso compounds, worker exposure to nitrosamines, analytical chemistry, chem. carcinogenesis, air pollution chemistry, combustion, combustion control, explosions. Mem. Am. Chem. Soc., Chem. Soc. London, Combustion Inst., Canadian Chem. Inst., Soc. Occupational and Environ. Health. Patentee chem. instrumentation for nitrosamines, hydrazines and organic nitrogen compounds. Home: Whispering Pine Sudbury MA 01776 Office: New Eng Inst Life Scis 125 2d Ave Waltham MA 02154

FINE, DONALD IRVING, editor, publisher; b. Ann Arbor, Mich., Apr. 19, 1922; s. Morris Seide and Kathleen (Perlis) F.; 1 son, Stephen Morris. A.B., Harvard, 1944; grad. student, Columbia, 1947. Mng. editor Western Printing & Lithographing Co., 1951-58; editor in chief Popular Library, Inc., 1958-60; v.p., editor in chief Dell Pub. Co., 1960-68; exec. v.p., editor in chief Coward-McCann, Inc., 1968-69; founder, pres., pub. Arbor House Pub. Co., N.Y.C., 1969-83; founder, pres. Donald I. Fine, Inc., N.Y.C., 1983—. Contbr. to: The American Reading Public. Active Nassau County Stevenson for Pres., 1952. Served with AUS, 1943-46; PTO. Decorated Presdl. citation with 2 oak leaf clusters. Mem. P.E.N. Clubs: Harvard, Players (N.Y.C.). Home: 128 E 36th St New York NY 10016 Office: 128 E 36th St New York NY 10016

FINE, JERRY, lawyer; b. Los Angeles, Feb. 8, 1923; s. Nathan and Augusta (Kaufman) F.; m. Gwen Nicolson, Dec. 25, 1956; children: Carolyn, Rex, Gary, Gregory. Student, Stanford U., 1941-43; B.A., UCLA, 1947; J.D., Loyola U. at Los Angeles, 1950. Bar: Calif. 1951. Since practiced in, Los Angeles; ptnr. Fine, Perzik & Friedman, 1956—; adj. instr. Loyola U. Law Sch., Los Angeles; lectr., cons. in field; dir. World Team Tennis, 1973-74; Pres. Los Angeles Strings Tennis Team, 1974. Contbg. author: New Dimensions in School Board Leadership, 1969, The Integration of American Schools, 1975, Representing Professional Athletes and Teams, 1981; Contbr. articles to legal jours. Mem. nat. council YMCA, 1956-58; mem. bd. edn. Inglewood Unified Sch. Dist., 1963-71, pres., 1965-66, 69-71; chmn. bd. dirs. Westchester YMCA, 1955-58; bd. govs. Nat. Athletic Health Inst., 1972—; mem. Calif. Commn. for Econ. Devel., 1972-77. Served with AUS, 1943-46. Decorated Purple Heart. Fellow Am. Coll. Mortgage Attys.; mem. Inglewood Dist. Bar Assn. (pres. 1955), Los Angeles Bar Assn., Calif. Bar Assn. (chmn. governing com., continuing edn. of bar 1980-82), ABA, Calif. Sch. Bd. Assn. (dir. 1967-71). Office: Suite 1900 10960 Wilshire Blvd Los Angeles CA 90024

FINE, JULES, advt. exec.; b. Pa., Jan. 25, 1931; s. Morris and Lena F. B.B.A., City Coll. N.Y., 1952. With Blow Advt. Agency, N.Y.C., 1952-56; with Ogilvy & Mather, N.Y.C., 1956—, dir. media, 1966—, sr. v.p., 1969-76, exec. v.p., 1976—, dir. mktg. services, 1970—, also dir.; Vice chmn. bd. Audit Bur. Circulations. Named Media Man of Yr. Medicisions Mag., 1980. Mem. Am. Assn. Advt. Agys. (chmn. media policy com. 1978), Media Dirs. Council (pres. 1970—), Radio TV Research Council (pres. 1970—). Home: 415 E 52d St New York NY 10022 Office: 2 E 48th St New York NY 10017

FINE, MICHAEL JOSEPH, publishing and communications company executive; b. N.Y.C., Jan. 30, 1937; s. William and Rosa F.; m. Marlene Rosen, Apr. 4, 1959; children: Antony Adeus, Kaethe Elizabeth. Student, U. Fla., 1953-54; B.A., Bklyn. Coll., 1957; postgrad., State U. Iowa, 1959-60. Propr. The Paper Place Bookstore, Iowa City, 1960-63; v.p. Paperback Affiliates, Inc., N.Y.C., 1963-74; mgr., co-owner The Paperback Forum Bookstore, N.Y.C.; co-owner The Manhattanville Bookforum, Manhattanville Coll., Purchase, N.Y.; asst. to pres. Simon & Schuster, Inc., N.Y.C., 1964-65, assoc. dir. Washington Square Press, 1964-69, v.p., Assoc. Ednl. Services, 1965; founder, pub. Clarion Books (Simon & Schuster's trade paperback line); v.p. Associated Ednl. Services, 1966-67; co-founder Bookthrift, Inc., 1972, pres., 1978-81; sr. v.p. Ingram Book Co., Nashville, 1981-83; pres., chief exec. officer Ingram Ventures, Inc., N.Y.C., 1981-83; mem. editorial bd. Simon & Schuster. Contbr. to profl. jours. Chmn. bd. dirs. St. Michaels Montessori Sch., N.Y.C., 1973-75; Bd. dirs. Morningside Area Alliance, Inc., N.Y.C., 1974-83; active United Jewish Appeal. Mem. N.Y. Acad. Sci. (publs. com.).

FINE, MORRIS EUGENE, materials engineer, educator; b. Jamestown, N.D., Apr. 12, 1918; s. Louis and Sophie (Berrington) F.; m. Mildred Eleanor Glazer, Aug. 13, 1950; children: Susan Elaine, Amy Lynn. B.Metall. Engring. with distinction, U. Minn., 1940, M.S., 1942, Ph.D., 1943. Instr. U. Minn., 1942-46; mem. tech. staff Bell Telephone Labs., Murray Hill, N.J., 1946-54; prof., chmn. dept. metallurgy Tech. Inst., Northwestern U., Evanston, Ill., 1955-57, chmn. dept. materials sci., 1958-60, prof. and chmn. materials research center, 1960-64, Walter P. Murphy prof. materials sci., 1963—, asso. dean grad. studies and research, 1973—; vis. prof. dept. materials sci. Stanford U., 1967-68; JSPS vis. scholar, Japan, 1979; asso. engr. Manhattan Project, U. Chgo., also, Los Alamos, World War II; mem. materials adv. bd. Nat. Acad. Sci., 1963-68; mem. com. geol. and materials scis. NRC, 1979-82; co-chmn. Engring. Socs. Conf. on Fatigue Crack Initiation, 1980; chmn. adv. bd., program on modular methods for teaching materials Pa. State U., 1973-77; chmn. vis. com. metallurgy and materials Sci. and Materials Research Center, Lehigh U., 1965-75; vis. com. Lawrence Berkeley Lab., 1978-81, chmn., 1981, vis. com. Ames Dept. Energy Lab., 1976-80. Author numerous tech. and sci. articles on mech. properties of metals and ceramics, fatigue of metals, phase transformations and other subjects.; author: Introduction to Phase Transformation in Condensed Systems. Named Chicagoan of Year in Sci., 1961. Fellow Am. Phys. Soc., AAAS, Am. Soc. Metals (chpt. chmn. 1963, Campbell lectr. 1979), Metall. Soc. of AIME (chmn. inst. metals div. 1966-68, dir. 1968-71, dir. inst. 1972-75, Mathewson gold medal for research 1981, James Douglas Gold medal), Am. Ceramic Soc. (keynote lectr. electronic materials div. 1972); mem. Nat. Acad. Engring. (mem. astronautics space engring. bd. 1973-77, membership com. 1974-79, chmn. 1977-78), Am. Assn. Engring Edn., ASTM, AAUP, Fedn. Am. Scientists, Engring. Com. for Profl. Devel. (accreditation panel for metallurgy and materials), Sigma Xi, Tau Beta Pi, Alpha Sigma Mu, Sigma Alpha Sigma. Home: 1101 Manor Dr Wilmette IL 60091 Office: Northwestern U Evanston IL 60201

FINE, MORTON SAMUEL, consulting engineer; b. Worcester, Mass., June 3, 1916; s. Jacob and Mary (Savatsky) F.; m. Frances D. Kaufman, 1940; children: Philip J., Paula J. B.S. with high distinction, Worcester Poly. Inst., 1937. Draftsman Riley Stoker Corp., Worcester, 1937-38; bridge designer Cleverdon, Varney and Pike, Boston, 1938; office engr. U.S. Engr.'s Office, 1939-43; tool designer Marc A. Porter Co., Hartford, Conn., 1943-46; asst. dir., supr. instrn. Porter Sch. Tool and Machine Design, Hartford, 1946-48; partner, dir., instr. Home Contractor's Inst., Sch. Home Bldg., Hartford, 1948-49; instr. dept. engring. Trinity Coll., Hartford, 1950-52; cons. civil engr., landscape architect, planner, land surveyor, prin. Morton S. Fine & Assos., Inc., Hartford, 1950-75; exec. dir. Nat. Council Engring. Examiners, Clemson, S.C., 1976-82; program dir. Mfg. Engring. Applications Center Worcester Poly. Inst., (Mass.), 1982-83; cons. engr., Hartford, Conn., 1983—; pres. Nat. Council Engring. Examiners, 1974-75; Mem. Town Planning and Zoning Comm., West Hartford, Conn., 1958-63, chmn, 1960; mem. engring. adv. com. U. Hartford, 1971-76. Chmn. bd. trustees Hartford Conservatory Music, 1966-76; bd. dirs. Musical Theatre Guild, Hartford, 1974-76; trustee Congregation Beth Israel, West Hartford, 1960-72; mem. Conn. Fedn. Planning and Zoning Agys., 1958-63. Fellow ASCE; mem. Nat. Soc. Profl. Engrs. (nat. chmn. pvt. practice div. 1970-71), Am. Congress on Surveying and Mapping, Am. Soc. Engring. Edn., Am. Cons. Engrs. Council, Sigma Xi, Tau Beta Pi.

FINE, PERLE, artist; b. Boston, May 1, 1908; d. Simon and Sarah (Fine) F.; m. Maurice Berezov. Studied with, Hans Hofmann, Atelier 17. Assoc. prof. fine art Hofstra U.; vis. prof. art Cornell U., 1961; tchr., lectr. Provincetown Art Assn., pvt. groups. Contbr. articles on art.; One-man shows, Marian Willard, 1945, DeYoung Mus., 1947, Nierendorf, 1946, 47, Tanager, 1955, Betty Parsons galleries, 1949, 51, 52, 53, Graham Gallery, N.Y.C., 1961, 63, 64, 67, Bykert Gallery, Springs, N.Y., Andre Zarre Gallery, 1976, 77, Ingber Gallery, N.Y.C., 1982-84, Benson Gallery, Bridgehampton, N.Y.; also exhibited nat. group annuals, U.S. and abroad, retrospective exhbn., Guild Hall, works in permanent collections, Whitney Mus., Smith Coll. Mus., Rutgers U., Los Angeles County Mus., Parrish Mus., Brandeis U., Bklyn. Mus., Mus. Non-Objective Art, Munson-Williams-Proctor Inst., N.Y. U., U. Calif. at Berkeley, Hofstra U., Mus. Modern Art, Guild Hall, Easthampton, Ind. U., pvt. collections. Recipient Guggenheim scholarship; purchase award for color woodcut Bklyn. Mus., 1956; 1st prize for oil paintings Silvermine Art Guild, 1961; 1st prize, collage, 1963; award for wood collage, 1967; 1st prize for wood collage Guild Hall, Easthampton, 1970; Nat. Endowment for Arts grantee, 1979; Am. Acad. Arts and Letters grantee, 1974. Mem. Am. Abstract Artists, Fedn. Modern Painters and Sculptors, Guild Hall. Address: 538C Old Stone Hwy The Springs NY 11937

FINE, RALPH IRWIN, lawyer; b. Boston, Dec. 7, 1939; s. Joseph and Ann (Rosenblum) F. A.B. cum laude, U. Pa., 1961; LL.B. cum laude (Harlan Fiske Stone scholar), Columbia U., 1964. Bar: N.Y. 1965, Mass. 1967. Assoc. Gilbert, Segal & Young, N.Y.C., 1964-66, Fine & Ambrogne, Boston, 1966-75, ptnr., 1975—; dir. South Shore Pub. Co., 1969—; chmn. bd. Real Paper Inc., 1975-81, pub., 1977-79. Chmn. Fin. Commn. Boston, 1972-75; pres. bd. League Sch. Boston, 1972-76. Mem. Boston Bar Assn., Assn. Bar City N.Y. Office: 133 Federal St Boston MA 02110

FINE, RICHARD ISAAC, lawyer; b. Milw., Jan. 22, 1940; s. Jack and Frieda F.; m. Maryellen Olman, Nov. 25, 1982. B.S., U. Wis., 1961; J.D., U. Chgo., 1964; Ph.D. in Internat. Law, U. London, 1967; cert., Hague (Netherlands) Acad. Internat. Law, 1965, 66; cert. comparative law, Internat. U. Comparative Sci., Luxembourg, 1966; diplome superiere, Faculte Internat. pour l'Enseignment du Droit Compare, Strasbourg, France, 1967. Bar: Ill. 1964, D.C. 1972, Calif. 1973. Trial atty. fgn. comml. sect. Dept. Justice, 1968-72; chief antitrust div. Los Angeles City Atty.'s Office, also spl. counsel gov. efficiency com., 1973-74; prof. internat., comparative and EEC antitrust law U. Syracuse (N.Y.) Law Sch. (overseas program), summers 1970-72; individual practice, Los Angeles, 1974; mem. antitrust adv. bd. Bur. Nat. Affairs, 1981—. Contbr. articles to legal publs. Mem. Am. Bar Assn. (chmn. subcom. internat. antitrust and trade regulations, internat. law sect. 1972-77, co-chmn. com. internat. econ. orgn. 1977-79), Am. Soc. Internat. Law (co-chmn. com. corp. membership 1978-83, mem. exec. council 1984—), Am. Fgn. Law Assn., Internat. Law Assn., Brit. Inst. Internat. and Comparative Law, World Peace Through Law Center, State Bar Calif. (chmn. antitrust and trade regulation law sect. 1981—), Los Angeles County Bar Assn. (chmn. antitrust sect. 1977-78), Ill. Bar Assn., Phi Delta Phi. Address: Suite 250 10100 Santa Monica Blvd Los Angeles CA 90067

FINE, SEYMOUR HOWARD, marketing educator; b. N.Y.C., Apr. 21, 1925; s. Max and Sylvia (Topol) F.; m. Adell Gross, Jan. 24, 1948; children: Michael David, Paul Robert. M.S. magna cum laude in Math., Fairleigh Dickinson U., 1968; Ph.D., Columbia U., 1978. Pres. Fine Mktg. Assocs. Inc., N.Y.C., 1948—; prof. mktg. Rutgers U., Newark, 1977—. Author: The Marketing of Ideas and Social Issues, 1981. Recipient Consumer Research award, 1979. Mem. Assn. Consumer Research, Am. Acad. Advt., Am. Mktg. Assn., Am. Inst. Decision Scis., Pvt. Industry Council Passaic County. Address: 138 Gaynor Pl Glen Rock NJ 07452

FINE, SIDNEY, educator, historian; b. Cleve., Oct. 11, 1920; s. Morris Louis and Gussie (Redalia) F.; m. Jean Schechter, Dec. 5, 1942; children—Gail Judith, Deborah Ann. B.A. summa cum laude, Western Res. U., 1942; M.A., U. Mich., 1944, Ph.D., 1948. Mem. faculty U. Mich., 1948—, prof. history, 1959—, Andrew Dickson White prof. history, 1974—, chmn. dept., 1969-71; mem. faculty Salzburg Seminar Am. Studies, 1959; Mem. Nat. Archives Adv. Council, 1968-71. Author: Laissez Faire and the General Welfare State, 1956, The Automobile Under the Blue Eagle, 1963 (U. Mich. Press Book award 1965), (with G.S. Brown) The American Past, 2 vols, 1961, Recent America, 1962, Sit-Down: The General Motors Strike of 1936-1937, 1969 (U. Mich. Press Book award 1971), Frank Murphy: The Detroit Years, 1975, Frank Murphy: The New Deal Years, 1979; also articles.; Bd editors: Jour. Am. History, 1964-67, Revs. in American History, 1973-80; bd. editors: Labor History, 1963—; chmn. editorial bd., 1976—. Rackham predoctoral fellow U. Mich., 1946-48; Guggenheim fellow, 1957-58; Recipient Distinguished Faculty Achievement award U. Mich., 1969. Mem. Am. Hist. Assn., Orgn. Am. Historians, Labor Historians (pres. 1969-71), U. Mich. Research Club (pres. 1983-84), U. Mich. Sci. Club, Phi Beta Kappa (chpt. pres. 1975-76), Phi Kappa Phi. Home: 825 Russett Rd Ann Arbor MI 48103

FINE, STANLEY SIDNEY, business executive, former naval officer; b. N.Y.C., Sept. 26, 1927; s. Morris and Sophie (Brajer) F.; m. Eleanore D. Baker, July 21, 1955 (dec.); children: Lauren Allison, Stephen Sidney. Student, NYU, 1944-45; B.S., U.S. Naval Acad., 1949; postgrad., Coll. William and Mary, 1955-56, U. Va., 1956-57, Am. U., 1957-59, Harvard U., 1963-65. Commd. ensign U.S. Navy, 1949, advanced through grades to rear adm., 1972; comdg. officer U.S.S. Hawk, 1954-56, Polaris Program, 1956-59, U.S.S. Lowe, 1961-63; comdr. Escort Div. 33, 1963; comdg. officer U.S.S. Ingraham, 1965-67; br. head Navy Material Command, Washington, 1967-68; exec. asst., naval aide to asst. sec. Navy, 1968-70; study dir. Center for Naval Analysis Navy Dept., Washington, 1970; dep. dir. Navy Program Info. Center, 1970-71; br. head OPNAV, 1971; spl. asst. to dir. Navy Program Planning, Washington, 1971-72; dep. chief Programs and Fin. Mgmt.; comptroller Naval Ship Systems Command, Washington, 1972-73; dir. fiscal mgmt. div. Office Chief Naval Ops., Washington, 1973-78; dir. budget and reports Navy Dept., 1975-78; sec.-treas., dir. First United Corp., Jackson, Miss.; v.p., dir. United-Guardian, Inc., L.I., N.Y.; dir. Redhead Corp., Shreve., Ohio, Nat. Equipment Leasing Corp., McLean, Va., Globus Resources Ltd., Hong Kong; cons. Arthur Andersen & Co., Harbridge House, GSA, GAO, Dept. Commerce. Contbr. articles to profl. jours. Mem. Presdl. Transition Team, 1980-81. Decorated D.S.M., Legion of Merit with gold star; recipient Outstanding Mgmt. Analyst award Am. Soc. Mil. Comptrollers, 1971. Mem. Naval Inst., Am. Assn. Budget and Program Analysis. Harvard Bus. Sch. Alumni Assn. Home: 5133 Westbard Ave Bethesda MD 20816

FINE, TERRENCE LEON, electrical engineering and statistics educator; b. N.Y.C., Mar. 9, 1939; s. Abraham and Lola (Breidberg) F.; m. Susan Woodward, June 12, 1964 (div. Mar. 1981); children: David M., Jennifer E.; m. Silence Michelet, Oct. 11, 1982. B.E.E., CCNY, 1958; S.M., Harvard U., 1959, Ph.D., 1963. Research assoc., lectr. Harvard U., 1963-64; Miller Inst. fellow U. Calif.-Berkeley, 1964-66; prof. elec. engring. and stats. Cornell U., Ithaca, N.Y., 1966—; vis. prof. elec. engring. Stanford U., 1979-80; cons. in field. Author: Theories of Probability, 1973; patentee statis. delta modulation. Fellow IEEE; mem. Inst. Math. Stats. Democrat. Home: 201 Elmwood Ave Ithaca NY 14850 Office: Sch Elec Engring Cornell U. Ithaca NY 14853

FINE, TIMOTHY HERBERT, lawyer; b. Washington, Oct. 11, 1937; s. Nathan and Emily Newhall (Brown) F.; m. Mary Ellen Fox, June 16, 1960; children: Margaret Carol, Susan Emily, Rachel Winslow. B.E.E., U. Va., 1959; M.S. in E.E., U. So. Calif., 1962; LL.B., U. Calif.-Berkeley, 1965. Bar: Calif. 1966, U.S. Dist. Ct. (no., ea. and cen. dists.) Calif. 1966, U.S. Ct. Appeals (9th cir.) 1966, U.S. Supreme Ct. 1971. Law clk. to Hon. William T. Sweigert, U.S. Dist. Judge, San Francisco, 1965-67; asso. G. Joseph Bertain, Jr., San Francisco, 1967-77; prin. Law Offices of Timothy H. Fine, San Francisco, 1977—; del. White House Conf. Small Bus., 1980, Calif. State Confs. Small Bus., 1980, 82, 84; chmn. San Francisco Bay Area Small Bus. Caucus, 1984; author, lectr., cons., trial atty. on antitrust, franchise and small bus. legal matters.; Mem. nat. adv. council U.S. Senate Small Bus. Com., 1983—; mem. adv. bd. Calif. Senate Select Com. Small Bus., 1983—; mem. Calif Bd. Registration Profl. Engrs., 1982—. Served to lt. USAF, 1959-62. Mem. ABA (mem. governing bd., forum com. on franchising), Fed. Bar Assn., State Bar of Calif., The Bar Assn. San Francisco, Lawyers Club of San Francisco. Home: 747 San Diego Rd Berkeley CA 94707 Office: 25 Kearny St Suite 300 San Francisco CA 94108 *I have spent the past 16 years of my life representing small business and seeking to preserve and strengthen it in the face of galloping trends toward economic concentration, cartels monopolies in the United States.*

FINE, VIVIAN, composer; b. Chgo., Sept. 28, 1913; d. David and Rose (Fincer) F.; m. Benjamin Karp, Apr. 5, 1935; children: Margaret, Nina. Student composition with, Ruth C. Seeger, Roger Sessions; piano with, Djane Lavoie-Herz, Abby Whiteside. Mem. faculty Bennington (Vt.) Coll.; Vice pres. Am. Composers Alliance, 1961-65. Composer: Race of Life, 1937, Suite for Piano, 1940, Four Elizabethan Songs, 1943, The Great Wall of China, 1947, A Guide to the Life Expectancy of a Rose, 1956, String Quartet, 1957, Concertante for Piano and Orchestra, 1944, Sonata for Violin and Piano, 1952, Alcestis, 1960, Sinfonia and Fugato for Piano, 1963, Quintet for Trumpet, Harp and String Trio, 1967, Paean for brass ensemble and female chorus, 1969, Concerto for Piano Strings and Percussion, 1972, Missa Brevis for 4 cellos and taped voice, 1972; chamber opera The Women in the Garden, 1977; Quartet for Brass, 1978, Drama for Orch., 1982; Works rec. for CRI by, Imperial Philharmonic Tokyo, Japanese Philharmonic. Recipient Dollard award, 1966, comms. B. de Rothschild Found., 1956, Wykeham Rise, 1967, Woolley, 1972; Am. Acad./Inst. Arts and Letters award, 1979; Ford Found. grantee, 1969; Nat. Endowment for Arts grantee, 1974; Guggenheim fellow, 1980. Mem. ASCAP (awards 1967-79), Am. Acad. and Inst. Arts and Letters. Address: RFD 2 Box 630 Hoosick Falls NY 12090

FINE, WILLIAM CLYDE, management consultant, retired paint and chemical company executive; b. Aledo, Okla., Nov. 29, 1917; s. Henry Nathan Floyd and Deva Dolores (Campbell) F.; m. Helen Margaret Goodin, Dec. 31, 1938; 1 son, Robert Hayden. B.S. in Bus. Adminstrn, U. Wichita, 1938. With Firestone Tire & Rubber Co., 1938-41; with Sherwin-Williams Co., Cleve., 1941-80, sec., 1962—, asst. treas., 1966-67, asst. v.p. fin., 1967-68, v.p. fin. ops., 1968-70, v.p. fin., 1970-71, sr. v.p. fin. and adminstrn., 1971-73, exec. v.p., 1973-75, pres., chief operating officer, 1975—, chmn. bd., 1979-80, also dir., until 1980; mgmt. cons.; dir. Society Corp., Clark Consol. Industries, Inc.; Pioneer Standard Electronics, Inc. Trustee Fairview Gen. Hosp., 1971—, chmn., 1976-79; trustee Dyke Coll. Served to lt. (s.g.) USNR, 1943-46. Decorated Commendation medal. Mem. Greater Cleve. Growth Assn., Am. Mgmt. Assn., Pres.'s Assn., Sigma Phi Epsilon. Clubs: Masons, 50 of Cleve., Bluecoats, Inc., Westwood Country, Pepper Pike, Union of Cleve. Home: 3769 E Surrey Ct Rocky River OH 44116 Office: 20525 Detroit Rd Rocky River OH 44116

FINE, WILLIAM MICHAEL, textile corporation executive; b. N.Y.C., July 1, 1926; s. J. George and Susan (Morse) F.; m. Patricia Purdy, Aug. 22, 1948 (div. Apr. 1967); children: Brewster, Douglas, Timothy; m. Rosaleen Garvey, June 15, 1980; 1 son, Alexander Garvey. B.A., Kenyon Coll., 1950. Pub. dir. Harpers Bazaar and Town & Country, N.Y.C., 1960-67, Hearst Mags., 1967-69; pres., chief exec. officer Bonwit Teller, N.Y.C., 1969-74; pres., chier exec. officer Wamsutta Mills, N.Y.C., 1974-77; chmn., chief exec. officer Frances Denney Corp., Inc., Phila., 1977-82; pres. Dan River Mills, Inc., Danville, Va., 1982—, N.Y.C., 1982—; dir. Warnaco, Bridgeport, Conn., 1967—, Debenhams, Inc., N.Y.C., London, 1976—, Galway Crystal Co., (Ireland), 1982—, Towle Co., Boston, 1983—; cons., dir. Hermes, Paris, 1982—. Author: That Day with God, 1964; contbr. articles to various mags. Mem. Adv. Council of the Arts-Presdl. Commn., Washington, 1982—; bd. dirs. Fifth Ave. Assn., U.S.-Ireland Council; trustee Georgian Soc., Ireland. Served with inf. AUS, 1944-46; ETO. Decorated Bronze Star. Republican. Clubs: Wee Burn Country (Darien, Conn.); Union League (N.Y.C.). Home: 42 Dan's Hwy New Canaan CT 06840 Office: Dan River Inc 111 W 40th St New York NY 10018

FINEBERG, HARVEY VERNON, physician, educator; b. Pitts., Sept. 15, 1945; s. Saul and Miriam (Pearl) F.; m. Mary Elizabeth Wilson, May 16, 1975; children: Todd Peter, Mark Peter. A.B., Harvard U., 1967, M.D., 1972, M.P.P., 1972, Ph.D., 1980. Intern Beth Israel Hosp., Boston, 1972-73; asst. prof. Harvard Sch. Pub. Health, Boston, 1973-78, assoc. prof., 1978-81, prof., 1981—; physician Harvard Street Health Ctr., Boston, 1976—, East Boston Health Ctr., 1974-76. Co-author: Clinical Decision Analysis, 1980, The Epidemic That Never Was, 1983. Trustee Newton Wellesley Hosp., (Mass.), 1981—; study sect. chmn. Nat. Ctr. Health Services Research, Rockville, Md., 1982—; active Pub. Health Council, Mass., 1976-79. Jr. fellow Harvard U., 1974-75; Mellon fellow, 1976. Mem. Inst. Medicine, Nat. Acad. Scis., Soc. Med. Decision Making (pres. 1980-81). Jewish. Home: 125 Shornecliffe Rd Newton MA 02158 Office: Harvard Sch Pub Health 677 HuntingtonAve Boston MA 02158

FINEBERG, HERBERT, chemist; b. Portland, Maine, Jan. 16, 1915; s. Abraham Eliyahu and Esther Naomi (Tiferes) F.; m. Geraldine Shirley Morris, Dec. 25, 1941; children: Joan Susan, Sharon Rachael. B.S., Trinity Coll., 1935; Ph.D., U. Ill., 1941. Research chemist Eastman Kodak Co., 1935-38; research mgr. Conn. Hard Rubber Co., 1941-45; pres. Gen. Chem. Co., 1945-48; v.p. research Glyco Chem., 1948-62; research mgr. Archer-Daniels-Midland Co., 1962-67, Tech. Info. Center Ashland Chem. Co., Ky., 1967—. Contbr. article to profl. jour. Mem. Am. Oil Chem. Assn., Am. Chem. Soc., Chem. Mktg. Research Assn., Am. Inst. Chem. Engrs. Club: Slaty Hollow Trout. Home: 2848 Maryland Ave Columbus OH 43209 Office: 5200 Blazer Pkwy Dublin OH 43017

FINEBERG, S(OLOMON) ANDHIL, human relations cons.; b. Pitts., Nov. 29, 1896; s. Nathan and Libbie (Landau) F.; m. Hilda Cohen, 1925. A.B., U. Cin., 1917; Rabbi, Hebrew Union Coll., 1920, D.D., 1958; Ph.D., Columbia U., 1932. Rabbi, Niagara Falls, N.Y., 1920-24, Pitts., 1924-25, Mt. Vernon, N.Y., 1929-37; nat. community relations cons. Am. Jewish Com., 1939-64; cons. NCCJ, 1965-80; coordinator N.Y. Interracial Colloquoy, 1966-78; specialist in human relations U.S. State Dept. Internat. Exchange Program in Germany, 1954. Author: Overcoming Anti-Semitism; Punishment Without Crime, 1949 (Anisfield Wolf Lit. award), The Rosenberg Case, Report on Germany, Deflating the Professional Bigot, Religion Behind the Iron Curtain, Plight of Soviet Jews. Served with USMC, 1917-19. Recipient Am. Heritage Freedom award, 1959; Interreligious Leadership award NCCJ, 1978. Mem. Central Conf. Am. Rabbis, Nat. Assn. Inter-group Relations Ofcls. (dir. 1954-56), Jewish Community Relations Workers Assn. (pres. 1950-54), U.S. Jewish War Vets. (nat. chaplain 1932-36). Home: 19 William St Mount Vernon NY 10552

FINEG, JERRY, veterinarian, educator; b. Buffalo, Jan. 7, 1928; s. Bert D. and Rose K. F.; m. Joan Erb, Apr. 23, 1955; children—David V., Mary K., Steven T., Susan L. B.S., Tex. A&M U., 1949, D.V.M., 1953; M.S., U. So. Calif., 1964. Practice vet. medicine, Phoenix, 1953-54; commd. 2d lt. U.S. Air Force, 1954, advanced through grades to col., 1968; chief vet. sci. br., chief biodynamics br. Aeromed. Research Lab., Holloman AFB, N.Mex., 1964-67; dep. chief vet. scis. div. USAF Sch. Aerospace Medicine, Brooks AFB, Tex., 1969-70, chief vet. scis. div., 1970-73; ret., 1973; prof. physiology, pharmacology U. Tex., Austin, 1973—; dir. Animal Resources Center, 1973—; pres. U. Tex. System-Wide Animal Care Facilities Com., 1978—. Contbr. articles to profl. jours.; editorial bd.: Jour. Med. Primatology, 1981—. Decorated Legion of Merit.; NSF grantee, 1973-75. Mem. Am. Assn. Lab. Animal Sci. (pres. Tex. br. 1979, mem. exec. com. 1980-81, dist. trustee 1981-82), Bexar County Vet. Med. Assn. (v.p. 1971-72), AVMA, Internat. Primatological Soc., Internat. Zoo Veterinarians Assn., Am. Soc. Lab. Animal Practitioners. Office: 2701 Speedway Univ of Tex Austin TX 78712

FINEGAN, PAUL GREVILLE, banker; b. Bryn Mawr, Pa., July 11, 1933; s. Edmund Randolph and Marjorie Greville (Stanford) F.; m. Joanne McDowell, Oct. 7, 1961; children: Paul Stanford, Caryn, John Leland. B.A., Dartmouth Coll., 1955; postgrad., Wharton Sch. Fin., U. Pa., 1959-60. Security analyst Phila. Nat. Bank, 1959-61, v.p., head investment research, 1969-76, v.p., head investment mgmt. div., 1976-78, sr. v.p., head trust and investment mgmt. divs., 1978—; security analyst Ins. Co. N.Am., Phila., 1962-63; trust and comml. officer First Pa. Bank, 1964-68. Served to capt. USAF, 1955-58. Mem. Fin. Analysts Phila. Republican. Episcopalian. Office: Broad and Chestnut Sts Philadelphia PA 19101 *

FINEGAN, THOMAS ALDRICH, economist; b. Long Beach, Calif., Sept. 1, 1929; s. Edward and Hazel Irene (Aldrich) F. B.A. summa cum laude, Claremont Men's Coll., 1951; M.A. In Econs. (Harry A. Millis fellow 1951-52, Univ. fellow 1952-53), U. Chgo., 1953; Ph.D. in Econs. (Ford Found. fellow), U. Chgo., 1960. Asst. prof. econs. Princeton U., 1960-64, research asso. indsl. relations sect., 1962-64, vis. research economist, 1967, vis. sr. research economist, spring 1971; asst. prof. Vanderbilt U., 1964-65, asso. prof., 1965-70, prof., 1970—, chmn. econs. dept., 1974-77; vis. research asso. Princeton U. Woodrow Wilson Sch., spring, 1966; cons. Nat. Commn. on Employment and Unemployment Statistics, 1977-78. Author: (with William G. Bowen) The Economics of Labor Force Participation, 1969; contbr. articles to profl. jours. Served with USNR, 1954-57. Recipient Lawrence R. Klein award Monthly Labor Rev., 1972, Ellen Gregg Ingalls award Vanderbilt U., 1975; grantee Dept. Labor, 1967, NSF, 1971-73, NIMH, 1980-82. Mem. Am. Econ. Assn. (nominating com. 1983), So. Econ. Assn. (edit. bd. So. Econ. Jour. 1968-70, exec. bd. 1972-74, v.p. 1978), Indsl. Relations Research Assn., AAUP. Home: 1043 Davidson Rd Nashville TN 37205 Office: Box 1526 Sta B Nashville TN 37235

FINEGOLD, SYDNEY MARTIN, physician; b. N.Y.C., Aug. 12, 1921; s. Samuel Joseph and Jennie (Stein) F.; m. Mary Louise Saunders, Feb. 8, 1947; children: Joseph, Patricia, Michael. A.B., UCLA, 1943; M.D., U. Tex., 1949. Diplomate: Am. Bd. Med. Microbiology (mem. bd. 1978-85), Am. Bd. Internal Medicine. Intern USPHS, Galveston, Tex., 1949-50; fellow in medicine U. Minn. Med. Sch., 1950-52, research fellow, 1951-52; resident medicine Wadsworth Hosp., VA Center, Los Angeles, 1953-54; instr. medicine U. Calif. Med. Center, Los Angeles, 1955-57, asst. clin. prof., 1957-59, asst. prof., 1959-62, asso. prof., 1962-68, prof., 1968—; chief chest and infectious disease sect. Wadsworth Hosp., 1957-61, chief infectious disease sect., 1961—; Mem. pulmonary disease research program com. VA, 1961-62, infectious disease research program com., 1961-65, merit rev. bd. (infectious diseases), 1972-74, med. research program specialist, 1974-76, adv. com. on infectious disease, 1974—; mem. NRC-Nat. Acad. Sci. Drug Efficacy Study Group, 1966-69; mem. subcom. on gram-negative anaerobic bacilli Internat. Com. on Nomenclature Bacteria, 1966—, chmn., 1972-78; mem. adv. panel U.S. Pharmacopoeia, 1970-75. Editorial bd.: Calif. Medicine, 1966-73, Western Jour. Medicine, 1974-77, Applied Microbiology, 1973-74, Jour. Clin. Microbiology, 1975-85, Am. Rev. Respiratory Disease, 1974-76, Current Prescribing, 1974-80, Infection, 1976—, Antimicrobial Agts Chemotherapy, 1980-85, Jour. Infectious Disease, 1979-82, Asian Jour. Infectious Disease, 1979—, Diagnostic Microbiology and Infectious Diseases, 1982—; sect. editor: infectious disease vols. Clinical Medicine, 1978-82. Served with USMCR; Served with USNR, 1943-46; to 1st. lt. AUS, 1952-53. Fellow ACP, Am. Pub. Health Assn., Am. Acad. Microbiology, AAAS, Infectious Disease Soc. Am. (councilor 1976-79, pres.-elect 1980-81, pres. 1981-82, exec. com. 1980-83); mem. Am. Soc. Microbiology (chmn. subcom. on taxonomy of Bacteroidaceae 1971-74), Am. Thoracic Soc., Western Soc. Clin. Research, Western Assn. Physicians, Wadsworth Med. Alumni Assn. (past pres.), Soc. Intestinal Microbiology Ecology and Disease (interim pres. 1982—), Am. Fedn. Clin. Research, Sigma Xi, Alpha Omega Alpha. Democrat. Jewish. Home: 421 23d St Santa Monica CA 90402 Office: Wadsworth Hosp VA Center Los Angeles CA 90073

FINELL, MARVIN, bank exec.; b. Chattanooga, July 30, 1924; s. Morris and Rose (Baras) Finkelstein; m. Karen Kraus, Sept. 9, 1961; children—Steven, Stephanie. A.B., Harvard U., 1947, LL.B., 1950. Bar: Calif. bar 1951. Practiced in, Beverly Hills; mem. firm Wyman, Bautzer, Finell, Rothman & Kuchel, 1952-71; exec. v.p. ins. ops. and fin. services Nat. Gen. Corp., 1971-73, also dir.; chmn. bd. Republic Ind. Co., Gt. Am. Ins. Co., Am. Nat. Ins. Co., Constellation Reins. Co., Gt. Am. Life Ins. Co.; chmn. bd., pres. Plaza Fin. Corp.; chmn. loan com., dir. 1st Los Angeles Bank; chmn. bd. Energy Scis. Inc.; dir. First Ins. Co. Hawaii, Energy Conservation Systems, Inc.; cons. Gt. Am. Ins. Co., Am. Fin. Corp. Editor: Harvard Law Rev, 1949-50. Bd. dirs. Calif. Coll. Podiatric Medicine, 1965-68; trustee Marianne Frostig Center Ednl. Therapy. Served as navigator USAAF, World War II. Mem. Am., Calif., Los Angeles, D.C., Beverly Hills bar assns., Calif. Podiatry Assn. (hon.), Phi Beta Kappa. Home: 1020 Ridgedale Dr Beverly Hills CA 90210 Office: 2 Century Plaza 2049 Century Park E Los Angeles CA 90067

FINERTY, JOHN CHARLES, univ. adminstr.; b. Chgo., Oct. 20, 1914; s. John Lawrence and Hulda (Schulte) F.; m. Mildred King, Dec. 28, 1940; children—Olivia Lou (Mrs. John L. Moore), Donna Elizabeth (Mrs. James D. Gatewood). A.B., Kalamazoo Coll., 1937; M.S., Kan. State Coll., 1939; Ph.D., U. Wis., 1942. Rackham Found. postdoctoral fellow U. Mich., 1942-43, instr. anatomy, 1943-46; asst. prof. anatomy Washington U., St. Louis, 1946-49; asso. prof., then prof. anatomy U. Tex. at Galveston, 1949-56, asst. dean, 1954-56; prof. anatomy, chmn. dept. U. Miami (Fla.) Sch. Medicine, 1956-66; also asso. dean.; prof. anatomy, dean La. State U. Sch. of Medicine, New Orleans, 1966-71; vice chancellor La. State Med. Center, 1971—, also dean Sch. Grad. Studies, 1974—; Mem. com. pathogenesis cancer Am. Cancer Soc., 1960-63, chmn. exec. com., 1977-79; bd. dirs. La. Regional Med. Program, Bur. Govtl. Research, New Orleans, 1976-79, Greater New Orleans Health Planning Council, treas., 1971, pres., 1973; anatomy test com. Nat. Bd. Med. Examiners, 1964-68, mem. rev. com. on med. sch. constrn., 1968-70. Fellow AAAS; mem. Am. Assn. Anatomists (program sec. 1966-74, pres. 1975), Am. Physiol. Soc., Endocrine Soc., Radiation Research Soc., Soc. Exptl. Biology and Medicine, Tex. Acad. Sci. (pres. 1955-56), Sigma Xi (pres. U. Tex. med. chpt. 1955-56), Phi Kappa Phi, Omicron Delta Kappa. Clubs: Audubon Golf, Nicolet Country, Rotary. Home: 5561 Jacquelyn Ct New Orleans LA 70124

FINESHRIBER, WILLIAM H., JR., motion picture and broadcasting executive; b. Davenport, Iowa, Nov. 4, 1909; s. William H. and Mae (Wallerstein) F.; m. Clotilde Heller, Apr. 12, 1933 (dec.); children: Joy, William H. III (dec.); m. Ruth Moskin, Aug. 9, 1959. B.A. summa cum laude, Princeton, 1931; student, Sorbonne U., 1931. Pub. relations exec. CBS, 1931-34, dir. music, 1937-40, dir. shortwave programs, 1940-43, asst. dir. broadcasts, 1943-46, gen. mgr. program dept., 1946-49; mgr. Carnegie Hall, 1934-37; v.p. in charge programs MBS, 1949-51, exec. v.p., 1951-53, dir., 1952-53; v.p., gen. mgr., radio and TV networks NBC, 1953, v.p. in charge radio networks, 1954-56; v.p. Television Programs of Am., Inc., 1956-57; dir. internat. operations Screen Gems, Inc., until 1959; v.p. Motion Picture Assn. Am., Motion Picture Export Assn. Am., 1960-84; Dir., mem. exec. com. Broadcast Advt. Bur.; chmn. radio and TV com. Am. Jewish Tercentenary. Author: Stendhal, the Romantic Rationalist, 1932. Mem. Pres.'s Citizen Food Com., 1947; co-chmn. nat. radio div. Nat. Found. Infantile Paralysis, 1951-55. Mem. Nat. Assn. Broadcasters (program exec. bd.), Radio Diffusion Francaise (adv. com. 1946-48), NCCJ (commn. mass communications 1951-55), Acad. TV Arts and Scis., Radio and TV Execs. Club, Phi Beta Kappa. Clubs: Radio Pioneers (v.p.), Rockefeller Luncheon, Princeton (N.Y.C.). Home: 15 E 91st St New York NY 10028

FINESILVER, SHERMAN GLENN, judge; b. Denver, Oct. 1, 1927; s. Harry M. and Rebecca M. (Balaban) F.; m. Annette Warren, July 23, 1954; children—Jay Mark, Steven Brad, Susan Lynn. B.A., U. Colo., 1949; LL.B., U. Denver, 1952; certificate, Northwestern U. Traffic Inst., 1956; LL.D. (hon.), Gallaudet Coll., Washington, 1970. Bar: Colo. bar 1952, also U.S. Supreme Ct 1952, U.S. Ct. of Appeals 1952, 10th Circuit, U.S. Dist. Ct., Colo 1952. Legal asst. Denver City Atty.'s Office, 1949-52; asst. Denver city atty., 1952-55; judge Denver County Ct., 1955-62, Denver Dist. Ct., 2d Jud. Dist., 1962-71, presiding judge domestic relations div., 1963, 67, 68; judge U.S. Dist. Ct., Denver, 1971—; Faculty Denver Opportunity Sch., 1949-54, U. Denver Coll. Law and Arts and Sci. Sch., 1955—, Westminster Law Sch., 1955-61, Nat. Coll. Judiciary, Reno, 1967—, Atty. Gen.'s Advocacy Inst., Washington, 1974—, seminars for new fed. judges, 1974—; cons. HEW, 1958-62. Author: Model Law for Interpreters in Court Proceedings, 1968, Protect Your Life-Wise Words for Women, 1969, Timely Tips When Disaster Strikes-No Second Chance, 1970; Contbr.: chpt. to Epilepsy Rehabilitation, 1974; Editor: Proceedings Nat. Symposium on the Deaf, Driving and Employability, 1964; Contbg. editor: Lawyers Coop. Pub. Co, Rochester, N.Y., 1958-60, Teaching Driver and Traffic Safety Education, 1965; Contbr. articles to profl. jours. Founder Denver Driver Improvement Sch., 1959, dir., 1959-71; chmn. Denver Citizenship Day, 1967; organizer Denver Youth Council, 1968; dir. leadership conf. Neighborhood Youth Corps, 1969; mem. Pres.'s Task Force on Hwy. Safety, 1969-71; mem. advisory com. Nat. Hwy. Traffic Safety Adminstrn., Dept. Transp., 1969-72; mem. task force White House Conf. on Aging, 1972; chmn. Gov.'s Adv. Com. on Hwy. Safety, 1960-71; commr. Gov.'s Commn. on Aging, 1967-71; mem. nat. youth commn. B'nai B'rith, 1970-74; Pres. Jewish Family and Childrens Service of Colo., 1962-64; bd. dirs. Nat. Council Orgns. Serving Deaf, Washington, 1968-71; trustee Am. Med. Center, Denver, 1960-72. Decorated Knight Comdr. Ct. of Honor K.C., Rocky Mountain Consistory, 1967; recipient numerous awards including citation Nat. Safety Council, 1958, Paul Gray Hoffman award Automotive Safety Found., 1960, spl. award N.Am. Judges Assn., merit award Colo. Assn. Deaf and Nat. Soc. Deaf, 1966, Service to Mankind award Denver Sertoma Club, 1969, Freedoms Found. award, 1969, medallion for outstanding service by a non-handicapped person to physically disabled Nat. Paraplegia Found., 1972, certificate of commendation Sec. Transp., 1974, numerous others. Mem. ABA (nat. chmn. Am. citizenship com. 1968, award of merit Law Day 1968), Colo. Bar Assn. (chmn. Law Day 1964, chmn. Am. citizenship com. 1963), Denver Bar Assn. (chmn. Law Day 1964), Am. Judicature Soc., Hebrew Ednl. Alliance, Allied Jewish Community Council, Phi Sigma Delta (trustee 1960-66); mem. B'nai B'rith. Clubs: Mason (Shriner), Am. Amateur Radio.). Office: Room C-236 US Courthouse 1929 Stout St Denver CO 80294 *

FINESTONE, ARNOLD BARON, chemical executive; b. N.Y.C., Dec. 19, 1929; s. Irving and Jean (Rosenhaus) F.; m. Susan Frohlich, Aug. 15, 1954; children: Jeanne Lee, Jacqueline Mary, Jessica Carla. B.A., NYU, 1951; Ph.D. in Polymer Chemistry (fellow), Poly. Inst. Bklyn., 1955. Research chemist Westinghouse Research Lab., Westinghouse Electric Corp., Pitts., 1955-56, group leader, 1956-57; group leader long range research Foster Grant Co., Inc., Leominster, Mass., 1957-59, mgr. styrene polymer research, 1959-62, co-dir. research and devel., 1962-64, dir. research and devel. and market devel., 1964-65, v.p., dir. research and devel. and market devel., 1965-68, v.p., dir. planning and devel., 1968-70; exec. v.p. Dart & Kraft Inc., Paramus, N.J., 1970-82, pres. Dartco Mfg. Inc. subs., 1982—. Contbr. articles profl. jours. First v.p. Leominster United Fund, 1970-71, Leominster YMCA, 1969-71; pres. Leominster Cancer Found., 1966; mem. adv. council Bergen County (N.J.) United Fund, 1971-74; trustee Leominster Library, Plastics Inst. Am.; mem. Poly. Adv. Council for Chemistry. Poly. Inst. N.Y. fellow, 1977. Mem. Am., Brit. chem. socs., Soc. Plastic Engrs., Soc. Plastic Industries, Mfg. Chemists Assn., Soc. Plastic Industries (chmn. pigment task force), N.Y. Chemist Club, Sigma Xi. Jewish. Clubs: Edgewood Country (Rivervale, N.J.); President's Country (West Palm Beach, Fla.). Patentee in field. Home: 51 Indian Dr Woodcliff Lake NJ 07675 Office: W 115 Century Rd Paramus NJ 07652

FINETTE, FLORENCE, nurse educator; b. Aurora, Ill., July 4, 1906; d. Frank Monroe and Anna (Madden) Durham; m. Carl G. Finette, Aug. 2, 1938. Student, St. Charles Sch. Nursing, Aurora, 1923-26; B.S., DePaul U., 1941; M.S., U. Chgo., 1947, also postgrad. work. Instr. St. Charles Sch. Nursing, Aurora, 1927-29; dir., edn. dir. St. Mary Sch. Nursing, Kakakee, Ill., 1929-34; edn. dir., acting dir. Garfield Park Sch. Nursing, Chgo., 1934-39; edn. dir. St. Joseph Mercy Sch. Nursing, Aurora, 1939-44; instr. Loyola U., Chgo., 1944-47; chmn., prof. nursing DePaul U., 1947-72; Mem. health edn. commn. Ill. Bd. Higher Edn. Mem. Nat. League Nursing, Am. Nurses Assn. (past mem. exec. com. of educators, adminstrs. sect.), Ill. League Nursing (pres. 1955-59, dir.), Chgo. League Nursing (pres. 1941-45), Ill. Hosp. Assn. (hon.), AAUP, Am. Adult Edn. Assn. Home: 450 W Downer Pl Aurora IL 60506 *Before any ideas can be engendered which would lead to conclusion, actions to be taken, etc., there must be acceptance of the individual with whom you are concerned.*

FINFIELD, JAMES G., food company executive; b. St. Louis, 1942. B.B.A., So. Methodist U.; M.B.A., Methodist U. Mkg. asst. Gen. Mills. Inc., 1965-71, market dir. shaped snacks, chips, potatoes and new ventures, Mpls., 1971-73, corp. v.p., mgr. Golden Valley div., 1973-76, corp. v.p., gen. mgr. new bus. div., 1976-78, corp. group v.p., Mpls., 1978-81, exec. v.p. toy group, 1981—. Office: General Mills Inc 9200 Wazata Blvd Minneapolis MN 55440 General Mills Inc 41 Madison Ave New York NY 10010 *

FINGARETTE, HERBERT, philosopher, educator; b. Bklyn., Jan. 20, 1921; m. Leslie J. Swabacker, Jan. 23, 1945; 1 dau., Ann Hasse. B.A., UCLA, 1947, Ph.D., 1949. Mem. faculty U. Calif.-Santa Barbara, 1948—, Phi Beta Kappa Romanell prof. philosophy, 1983—; William James lectr. religion Harvard U., 1971; W.T. Jones lectr. philosophy Pomona Coll., 1974; Evans-Wentz lectr. Oriental religions Stanford U., 1977; Gramlich lectr. human nature Dartmouth Coll., 1978; cons. NEH; mem. Calif. Council for Humanities. Author: The Self in Transformation, 1963, On Responsibility, 1967, Self Deception, 1969, Confucius: The Secular as Sacred, 1972, The Meaning of Criminal Insanity, 1972, Mental Disabilities and Criminals Responsibility, 1979. Washington and Lee U. Lewis law scholar, 1980; fellow NEH, NIMH, Walter Meyer Law Research Inst., Battelle Research Ctr., Addition Research Inst., Royal Coll. Psychiatry. Mem. Am. Philos. Assn. (pres. Pacific div. 1977-78). Home: 1507 APS Santa Barbara CA 93103 Office: Philosophy Dept U Calif Santa Barbara CA 93106

FINGER, FRANK WHITNEY, psychology educator; b. Naples, N.Y., Apr. 16, 1915; s. Jacob and Elizabeth Ethel (Lewis) F.; m. Eleanor Ford Varn, June 14, 1958; children: Elizabeth, William, Eleanor, Louise. B.A., Syracuse U., 1936, M.A., 1937; Ph.D., Brown U., 1940. Instr. psychology Brown U., 1940-42; asst. prof. U. Va., 1942-48, asso. prof., 1948-55, prof., 1955-76, alumni prof., 1976—; vis. prof. U. Wis., 1952, Yale U., 1953-54, Sussex (Eng.) U., 1975-76, U. Canterbury, N.Z., 1981. Contbr. numerous articles in field. Mem. Am. Psychol. Assn., Eastern Psychol. Assn., Southeastern Psychol. Assn., Va. Psychol. Assn., AAAS, Phi Beta Kappa, Sigma Xi. Episcopalian. Office: Gilmer Hall University of Virginia Charlottesville VA 22901

FINGER, HAROLD B., energy systems analyst, space scientist, urbanologist; b. N.Y.C., Feb. 18, 1924; s. Beny and Anna (Perlmutter) F.; m. Arlene Karsch, June 11, 1949; children: Barbara Lynn, Elyse Sue, Sandra Ruth. B.M.E., CCNY, 1944; M.S. in Aero Engring, Case Inst. Tech., 1950. With NASA (and predecessor), 1944-69; mgr. joint AEC-NASA Space Nuclear Propulsion Office, 1960-67; dir. space nuclear systems div. AEC, 1965-67; dir. nuclear systems NASA, 1961-64, dir. nuclear systems and space power, 1964-67, asso. adminstr. for orgn. and mgmt., 1967-69; asst. sec. for research and tech. HUD, 1969-72; gen. mgr. Center for Energy Systems, Gen. Electric Co., Washington, 1972-80; staff exec. Power Systems, Strategic Planning and Devel., Fairfield, Conn., 1980-83; pres., chief exec. officer U.S. Com. for Energy Awareness, Washington, 1983—. Bd. dirs. Nat. Housing Conf., AIA Research Corp. Co-recipient Manley Meml. award Soc. Automotive Engrs., 1957; recipient Outstanding Leadership medal NASA, 1966; James H. Wyld propulsion award Am. Inst. Aeros. and Astronautics, 1968. Mem. Am. Inst. Aeros. and Astronautics, Am. Soc. Pub. Adminstrn., AIA (hon.), Nat. Acad. Pub. Adminstrn. Home: 6908 Millwood Rd Bethesda MD 20817 Office: 1735 I St NW Suite 500 Washington DC 20006

FINGER, JOHN HOLDEN, lawyer; b. Oakland, Calif., June 29, 1913; s. Clyde P. and Jennie (Miller) F.; m. Dorothy C. Riley, Dec. 30, 1950; children: Catherine, John Jr., David, Carol. A.B., U. Calif., 1933. Bar: Calif. 1937. Pvt. practice of law, San Francisco, 1937-42; chief mil. commn. sect. Far East Hdqrs. War Dept., Tokyo, 1946-47; mem. firm Hoberg Finger Brown Cox & Molligan, San Francisco, 1947—; adv. bd. Central Savs. & Loan Assn.; Trustee Pacific Sch. Religion, bd. chmn., 1969-78; bd. dirs. Calif. Maritime Acad., San Francisco Legal Aid Soc., 1955-70; bd. visitors Judge Adv. Gen. Sch., Charlottesville, Va., 1964-76, Stanford U. Law Sch., 1969-71. Pres. Laymen's Fellowship, No. Calif. Conf. Congl. Chs., 1951-53, moderator, 1954-55. Served to maj. JAGC AUS, 1942-46; col. Res. ret.; comdg. officer 5th Judge Adv. Gen. Detachment, 1962-64; U.S. Army Judiciary, 1967-68. Decorated Legion of Merit. Fellow Am. Bar Found., Am. Coll. Trial Lawyers; mem. Am. Judicature Soc., Am. Bar Assn. (ho. of dels. 1970-78, council jud. adminstrn. div. 1972-77, standing com. assn. communications), Bar Assn. San Francisco (dir. 1960-62, recipient John A. Sutro award for legal excellence 1980), Judge Adv. Assn. (dir. 1957—, pres. 1964-65), Lawyers Club San Francisco (pres. 1953, dir. 1950—), State Bar Calif. (bd. govs. 1965-68, pres. 1967-68), Sierra Club (exec. com. legal def. fund), Phi Alpha Delta, Sigma Phi Epsilon, Alpha Kappa Phi. Home: 12675 Skyline Blvd Oakland CA 94619 Office: 703 Market St San Francisco CA 94103

FINGER, KENNETH FRANKLIN, scientist; b. Antigo, Wis., Jan. 2, 1929; s. Otto Edward and Elsie (Kuehn) F.; m. Lois Eleanor Hoppe, Nov. 16, 1951; 1 son, William Lee. B.S., U. Wis., 1951, M.S., 1953, Ph.D., 1955. Sr. investigator Chas. Pfizer & Co. Bklyn., 1955-57, 1959-60, research supr., 1960-61, research mgr., 1961-63; asso. prof. Sch. Pharmacy, U. Wis., Madison, 1963-67, prof., 1967-68; dean Coll. Pharmacy, U. Fla., 1968-74, asso. v.p. health affairs, 1974—; guest worker Nat. Heart Inst., 1957-59; mem. HEW Nat. Adv. Council on Alcoholism and Alcohol Abuse. Author publs. on adrenergic drugs. Recipient Teaching award Sch. Pharmacy, U. Wis., 1967, citation of Merit award, 1977. Mem. Am. Soc. Pharmacology and Exptl. Therapeutics., Am. Pharm. Assn., Wis. Acad. Sci., Arts and Letters, Am. Assn. Colls. Pharmacy, Acad. Pharm. Scis., Sigma Xi, Rho Chi. Home: 1615 NW 31st Terr Gainesville FL 32605

FINGER, SEYMOUR MAXWELL, political science educator, former ambassador; b. N.Y.C., Apr. 30, 1915; s. Samuel and Bella (Spiegel) F.; m. Helen Kotcher, Apr. 5, 1956; 1 son, Mark. B.S., Ohio U., 1935; postgrad., U. Cin., 1942, Littauer Sch. Pub. Affairs, Harvard U., 1953-54. Branch mgr. Photo Reflex Studios, Inc., 1935-37, 1938-40, regional supr., 1940-43, asst. to v.p., 1945-46; tchr. O'Keefe Jr. High Sch., 1937-38; vice consul Am. consulate, Stuttgart, Germany, 1946-49; 2d sec. Am. embassy, Paris, France, 1949-51; 2d sec., econ. officer Am. legation, Budapest, Hungary, 1951-53; econ. def. officer Am. embassy, Rome, 1954-55, 1st sec., Vientane, Loas, 1955-56; sr. econ. adv. U.S. Mission to UN, 1956-65; counselor of mission to UN, 1965-67; ambassador, sr. adviser to permanent rep. U.S. Mission to UN, 1967-71; prof. govt. and internat. orgn. City U. N.Y., Coll. of S.I., 1971—; prof. polit. sci. Grad. Sch., City U. N.Y., 1973—; dir. Ralph Bunche Inst. on UN, 1973—; sr. adviser policy studies UN Assn. of U.S.A., N.Y.C., 1971-73; mem. U.S. del. to UN Gen. Assembly, 11th-25th sessions, chmn. security council com. on sanctions in, Rhodesia; mem. UN com. on contbrs.; spl. cons. to Brookings Instn., 1964; mem. Task Force for Nuclear Test Ban. Author: People, Politics and Bureaucracy in the Making of Foreign Policy, 1980; editor: others The New World Balance and Peace in the Middle East, 1975; Terrorism: Interdisciplinary Perspectives, 1978, U.S. Policy in International Institutions, 1978; contbr. articles to nat. newspapers, mags. and jours. Bd. dirs. Travel Program for Fgn. Diplomats, South Nassau Communities Hosp., 1973-74. Served as staff sgt. AUS, 1943-45. Mem. Council on Fgn. Relations, Inst. for Mediterranean Affairs (pres. 1971—), Am. Soc. Internat. Law, Acad. Polit. Sci., Soc. Internat. Devel. (pres. N.Y. chpt.), Commn. for Study Orgn. Peace, Phi Beta Kappa, Kappa Delta Pi. Club: American (Paris, Rome). Home: 476 Morris Ave Rockville Centre NY 11570 Office: 33 W 42d St New York NY 10036

FINGERHUT, MARTIN WILLIAM, railroad company executive; b. Bklyn., Sept. 17, 1934; s. Jack and Gussie (Teitelbaum) F.; m. Phyllis Matthew, Aug. 19, 1958; children: Glenn, Laura, Jill. B.A., Yeshiva U., N.Y.C., 1956; LL.B., Bklyn. Coll., 1961; postgrad. exec. program, Stanford U., 1978. Legal asst. NLRB, Washington, 1962-65; assoc. Schoene and Kramer, Washington, 1965-68; sr. v.p. human resources Ill. Central R.R., Chgo., 1969—, dir. Mem. ABA, Fed. Bar Assn., R.R. Personnel Assn. Office: Ill Central Gulf Railroad 233 N Michigan Ave Chicago IL 60601

FINGERS, ROLAND GLEN (ROLLIE FINGERS), profl. baseball player; b. Steubenville, O., Aug. 25, 1946; s. George Michael and Edna Pearl (Stafford) F.; 1 dau., Laurel Lynn. Student, Chaffey Jr. Coll., 1964-65. With Kansas City Athletics (various farm teams), 1964-68; relief pitcher Oakland A's, Oakland, Calif., 1968-76, San Diego Padres, 1977-81. Named World Series hero for Houston Sportswriters Assn., 1972; Man of Year Chgo. Sportswriters Assn., 1972, Upper Ohio Valley Dapper Dans Assn., 1972; Most Valuable Player 1974 World Series; named Fireman of Yr. Sporting News, 1977, 78, 80. Mem. Am. League All Star Team, 1973-76, Nat. League All-Star Team, 1978, 80. Office: care Milw Brewers Baseball Team Milwaukee County Stadium Milwaukee WI 53214 *

FINI, FRANK CAESAR, business executive; b. Leominster, Mass., Oct. 3, 1930; s. John and Sarah (Cappasso) F.; m. Valery Coles, Nov. 19, 1983; children: Lili Fini Zanuck, John N. Grad. high sch. Enlisted to USAF, 1947, advanced through ranks to chief master sgt., 1968; served with NATO in, Greece, Italy, Turkey and; Germany, ret., 1970; exec. dir. Air Force Sergeants Assn., Marlow Heights, Md., 1970-81; v.p. Assn. Growth Enterprises Inc., Washington, 1981—. Decorated Meritorious Service medal, Joint Services Commendation medal, Air Force Commendation medal with 4 oak leaf clusters, Army Commendation medal. Mem. Am. Soc. Assn. Execs., Am. Security Council, Am. Mgmt. Assn., Am. Legion, VFW. Home: Watergate at Landmark Apt 1016 Bldg 4 309 Yoakum Pkwy Alexandria VA 22304 Office: 4305 St Barnabas Rd Suite 400 Temple Hills MD 20748

FINK, ARTHUR EMIL, social worker; b. Phila., Jan. 20, 1903; s. Johann Christian and Phillipa (Schaefer) F.; m. Kathleen Boles, June 13, 1931; children—Susan Boles, Gretchen Boles, Christopher Boles. Student (elementary and high sch.), Girard Coll., 1912-20; A.B., U. Pa., 1924, A.M., 1930, Ph.D., 1936, M.S.W., 1937. Instr. sociology U. Pa., 1930-33, 1935-38; headworker Univ. Settlement House, Phila., 1933-34; asst. dir. Inter-Agy. Council for Youth, 1934-38; prof. social work, dir. social work tng. U. Ga., 1938-41; asso. dir., social protection div. Fed. Security Agy., Washington, 1941-45; prof. social work U. N.C., 1945-73, dean, 1945-65; Fulbright lectr. U. Birmingham, Eng., 1951-52. Author: Causes of Crime, 1938, The Field of Social Work, 1942, 7th rev. edit., 1978. Mem. Nat. Assn. Social Workers (chmn. Ga. 1939-41, mem. nat. bd. 1943-46), Nat. Conf. Social Work (chmn. social action sect. 1945-46), Nat. Probation and Parole Assn., AAUP, Am. Pub. Welfare Assn., Am. Assn. Schs. Social Work (dir. 1945-48), So. Sociol. Soc. (v.p. 1941-42), N.C. Conf. Social Service (dir. 1946-49), AAAS. Democrat. Presbyterian. Home: Laurel Ln Box 208 Little Switzerland NC 28749

FINK, CHESTER WALTER, pediatric rheumatologist, educator; b. N.Y.C., May 6, 1928; s. Murray and Estelle (Halbfinger) F.; m. Dorothy Crate, Dec. 3, 1955; children: Ellen L., Curtis M., Murray G. B.A., Duke U., 1947, M.D., 1951. Intern Kings County Hosp., Bklyn., 1951-52; resident in pediatrics Upstate Med. Center, Syracuse, N.Y., 1952-53, Babies and Children's Hosp., Cleve., 1953-54, chief resident, 1956-57; mem. faculty U. Tex. Southwestern Med. Sch., Dallas, 1957—, prof. pediatrics, 1971—, vice chmn. dept., 1977-82; mem. arthritis adv. com. FDA. Contbr. articles med. jours. Served as officer M.C. AUS, 1954-56. Mem. Soc. Pediatric Research, Am. Pediatric Soc., Am. Rheumatism Assn., So. Soc. Pediatric Research. Home: 4432 Hockaday Dr Dallas TX 75229 Office: 5323 Harry Hines Blvd Dallas TX 75235

FINK, CONRAD CHARLES, communications consultant, educator; b. Marquette, Mich., Sept. 16, 1932; s. Donald Ellsworth and Mary Ruth (Fox) F.; m. Sue Carol Henry, Sept. 4, 1954; children: Karen Sue, Conrad Stephan. B.S., U. Wis., 1954. Reporter Bloomington (Ill.) Daily Pantagraph, 1956-57; various positions to night city editor AP, Chgo., 1957-60, writer fgn. desk, 1961, fgn. corr. Tokyo Bur., 1961-64, bur. chief South Asia, New Delhi, India, 1964-67; dir. AP-Dow Jones Econ. Report, London, 1967-70; asst. to pres. AP, N.Y.C., 1970, v.p., 1971-77, sec., 1974-77; 1st v.p., dir. Wide World Photos, Inc.; v.p. Press Assn., Inc.; v.p., dir. AP (Can.), Ltd.; sec., dir. N.Y.C. News Assn., Inc.; exec. v.p. adminstrn. Park Broadcasting, Inc., Ithaca, N.Y., 1977-81, Park Newspapers, Inc., 1977-81; Disting. lectr. U. Ga., 1982; prof. newspaper mgmt. Sch. Journalism, U. Ga., 1983—; dir. Park Broadcasting. Served to 1st lt. USMCR, 1954-56. Recipient Disting. Service award U. Wis., 1969. Mem. Dutch Ref. Ch. Home: Alta Vista Farm Cherry Valley NY 13320 Office: Sch Journalism U Ga Athens GA 30606

FINK, DANIEL JULIEN, management consultant; b. Jersey City, Dec. 13, 1926; s. Joseph and Dorothy (Weisberger) F.; m. Tobie E. Weiss, June 24, 1951; children: Kenneth Wayne, Betsy Ilene, Karen Patrice. B.S., M.I.T., 1948, M.S., 1949. Registered profl. engr., Mass. Chief aircraft dynamics Bell Aircraft Corp., Buffalo, 1948; aeromechanics engr. Cornell Aero. Lab., Buffalo, 1949-52; with Allied Research Assos., Inc., Concord, Mass., 1952-63, v.p., 1959-63; spl. aerospace research, devel., mfg. dir. Hyperion Industries, Inc., 1961-63; asst. dir. def. research and engring. (def. systems) Dept. Def., 1963-65, dep. dir. def. research and engring. (strategic and space systems), 1965-67; with Gen. Electric Co., 1967-82, v.p., gen. mgr. space div., 1969-77, v.p., group exec. aerospace group, Phila., 1977-79, sr. v.p. corp. planning and devel., Fairfield, Conn., 1979-82; pres. D.J. Fink Assocs., Inc., 1982—; mem. def. sci. bd. Dept. Def., 1968-72, sr. cons., 1979—; nat. indsl. adv. council Opportunities Industrialization Centers, 1977-79; Mem. sci. adv. panel Dept. Army, 1971-74; mem. adv. council NASA, 1978-81, chmn. adv. council, 1982—; mem. corp. vis. dept. aeros. and astronautics MIT, 1972-82, Sloan Sch., 1982—; chmn. dept. adv. bd., dept. mech. engring. Rensselaer Poly. Inst., 1981—. Recipient Disting. Public Service award Dept. Def., 1967, Collier trophy, 1974. Hon. fellow AIAA (pres. 1974-75); Fellow AAAS; mem. Armed Forces Communications and Electronics Assn. (dir.), Am. Def. Preparedness Assn., Nat. Acad. Engring. (chmn. space applications bd. 1976-81, chmn. telecommunications and computer applications bd.). Clubs: Cosmos, Nat. Space (Washington) (dir.). Patentee vibration isolation, weapon systems mgmt., aerospace mgmt. and corp. planning. Home: 126 Merrimac Dr Trumbull CT 06611 Office: DJ Fink Assocs Suite 1120 1901 N Ft Myer Dr Arlington VA 22209

FINK, DAVID REAM, JR., ednl. adminstr.; b. Red Lion, Pa., Aug. 31, 1928; s. David Ream and Rachel (Heindel) F.; m. Barbara Lee Pickens, July 15, 1950; children—David Ream III, Julianne. B.A., Dartmouth, 1950; M.S., U. Pa., 1953, Ph.D., 1957. Tchr. Fenn Sch., Concord, Mass., 1950-52; mem. faculty U. Maine, 1957-76, prof. ednl. measurement Coll. Edn., 1957-65, dean Portland campus, 1965-68, provost, 1968-70, planner office of chancellor, 1970-71; pres., chmn. bd. Research Inst., Gulf, Maine, 1968-74; asso. dir. Inst. for Health Sci. Edn., U. Maine, 1974-76; dir. edn. York (Pa.) Hosp., 1976—. Mem. Phi Kappa Phi. Home: 1450 Bee Tree Rd York PA 17403 Office: York Hosp York PA 17405

FINK, DIANE JOANNE, physician; b. Chgo., July 27, 1936; d. Roman John and Mary Frances (Obrzut) Paluszek; (widow); children—Laura, Janice. B.S., Stanford U., 1957, M.D., 1960. Rotating intern, then resident in internal medicine Kaiser Found. Hosp., San Francisco, 1960-63; resident in internal medicine, then research asso. immunohematology VA Hosp., San Francisco, 1963-66, chief oncology sect., 1969-71, staff physician charge cancer chemotherapy sect., 1966-69, chmn. tumor bd., 1967-71; exec. sec., prin. investigator cancer chemotherapy group Pacific VA, 1966-71; program dir. chemotherapy, div. cancer research resources and centers Nat. Inst. Cancer, NIH, HEW, 1971-73, chief treatment br., then asso. dir. cancer control, cancer control program, 1973-74; dir. div. cancer control and rehab., 1974-79; asso. dir. Nat. Cancer Inst., 1979-81; v.p. Am. Cancer Soc., 1981—; mem. faculty U. Calif. Med. Center, San Francisco, 1967-71, asst. clin. prof. medicine, 1969-71; chmn. U.S. del. U.S.-USSR Exchange Cancer Control/Cancer Centers; mem. expert adv. panel on cancer WHO, 1977—; chmn. DES task force HEW, 1978; chmn. asbestos edn. task force HEW, 1978. Contbr. to med. jours. Recipient Gerard B. Lambert award Lambert Found., 1975; Superior Service Honor award NIH, 1975. Mem. Am. Assn. Cancer Research, Am. Assn. Cancer Edn., AMA, Am. Med. Women's Assn., Am. Pub. Health Assn., Am. Soc. Clin. Oncology, Am. Soc. Hematology, Exec. Women in Govt., Soc. Occupational and Environ. Health. Office: Am Cancer Soc 777 3d Ave New York NY

FINK, DONALD GLEN, engineer, editor; b. Englewood, N.J., Nov. 8, 1911; s. Harold Gardner and Margaret (Glen) F.; m. Alice Marjorie Berry, Apr. 10, 1948; children: Kathleen Marion, Stephen Donald, Susan Carol (Mrs. Daniel J. Ehrlich). B.S., MIT, 1933; M.S., Columbia U., 1942. Research asst. MIT, 1933-34; staff radiation lab. Mass. Inst. Tech., 1941-43, head Loran div., 1943; bd. dirs. McGraw-Hill Book

Co., Inc., 1947-52; cons. editor TV Series, 1949—; vice chmn. Nat. TV System Com., 1950-52, panel chmn., 1950-53; chmn. prep. com. TV Dept. State, 1951-55; with Philco Corp., 1952-62, dir. research, 1952-58, dir., gen. mgr. research div., 1959-62, v.p.-research, 1961; exec. dir., gen. mgr. IEEE, N.Y.C., 1962-74, exec. cons., 1975-76, dir. emeritus, 1974—; ops. dir. Assn. Coop. Engring., 1975-76; cons., Belgium, 1952; mem. bd. for internat. orgns. and programs Nat. Acad. Scis.; chmn. com. on internat. sci. and tech. info. NRC, 1975-78; chmn. com. UNESCO sci. programs NRC, 1976-81; mem. exec. com. World Fedn. Engring. Orgns., 1973-77; mem. U.S. Commn. for UNESCO, 1976-81; trustee Met. Reference and Research Library Agy., 1974-83; chmn. Study Group High Definition TV Soc. Motion Picture and TV Engis., 1977-83; expert cons. on radar and electronic nav. Office Sec. War, 1943-45; cons. to comdr. atom bomb tests, Bikini, 1946; mem. Army Sci. Adv. Panel, 1957-69; mem. com. nav. research and devel. bd. Dept. Def., 1948-51. Editorial staff: Electronics, 1934-52; editor in chief, 1946-52; Author: Engineering Electronics, 1938, Principles of TV Engineering, 1940, Microwave Radar, 1942, Radar Engineering, 1947, TV Engineering, 1952, Color Television Standards, 1955, Television Engineering Handbook, 1957, Physics of Television, 1960, Computers and the Human Mind, 1966, Standard Handbook for Electrical Engineers, 1978, Electronics Engineers' Handbook, 1981. Recipient Medal of Freedom, 1946; Presdl. Certificate Merit for wartime service, 1948; plaque for contbns. to TV IRE, 1951; Am. Technologists award N.Y. Inst. Tech., 1958; Outstanding Civilian Service medal U.S. Army, 1969; Citation for Outstanding Service to TV Internat. TV Symposium, Montreux, 1971. Fellow IEEE (pres. IRE 1958, Founders medal 1978, Consumer Electronics award 1978), Soc. Motion Picture and TV Engrs. (jour. award 1956, Progress medal 1979); mem. Nat. Acad. Engring., Radio Club Am. (Sarnoff citation 1979), Sigma Xi, Tau Beta Pi, Eta Kappa Nu (eminent mem.), Phi Mu Delta. Clubs: Cosmos (Washington); Heritage Hills (N.Y.) Country. Home: 103-B Heritage Hills Somers NY 10589 Office: 345 E 47th St New York NY 10017

FINK, GERALD RALPH, genetics educator; b. Bklyn., July 1, 1940; s. Benjamin and Rebecca F.; m. Rosalie P. Lewis, June 15, 1961; children: Julia, Jennifer. B.A., Amherst Coll., 1962; M.S., Yale U., 1964, Ph.D., 1965; D.Sc. (hon.), Amherst Coll., 1982. Asst. prof. genetics Cornell U., Ithaca, N.Y., 1967-71, asso. prof., 1971-76, prof., 1976-79, prof. biochemistry, 1979-82, Am. Cancer Soc. Life prof., 1981; prof. genetics Whitehead Inst. MIT, Cambridge, 1982—. Asso. editor: Genetics, 1970-74, Jour. Bacteriology, 1973-78, Molecular and Gen. Genetics, 1980—; editor: Gene, 1978—. Chmn. Am. Cancer Soc., 1976-77. Recipient U.S. Steel award in molecular biology Nat. Acad. Scis., 1981; Guggenheim Found. fellow, 1974-75. Mem. Genetics Soc. Am. (award 1982), Am. Soc. Microbiologists. Office: Dept Biology MIT Cambridge MA 02139

FINK, JOHN, newspaperman; b. Farmington, Ill., Mar. 15, 1926; s. Walter Phillip and Alta Blanche (Payton) F.; m. Eloise Darlene Bradley, Aug. 8, 1949; children—Sara, Joel, Alison. B.A., Millikin U., 1949; M.A., U. Ill., 1950; postgrad., U. Wis., 1950-51. Reporter City News Bur. Chgo., 1952-53; mem. staff Chgo. Tribune, 1953—, asst. Sunday editor, 1961-67. Editor: Tribune mag, 1963—; Editor: WGN, a Pictorial History, 1961. Served USNR, 1944-46. Mem. Chgo. Press Club, Chgo. Headline Club, Sigma Delta Chi. Home: 547 Hawthorn Ln Winnetka IL 60093 Office: Chicago Tribune Tribune Tower IL 60611

FINK, JOHN FRANCIS, publishing company executive; b. Ft. Wayne, Ind., Dec. 17, 1931; s. Francis Anthony and Helen Elizabeth (Hartman) F.; m. Marie Therese Waldron, May 31, 1955; children: Regina Marie, Barbara Ann, Robert Paul, Stephen Lawrence, Therese Rose, David Francis, John Noll. B.A., U. Notre Dame, 1953. Assoc. editor Our Sunday Visitor, Religious Pub. Co., Huntington, Ind., 1956-68; editor Family Digest, 1956-67, mktg. mgr., 1967-72, exec. v.p., 1972-76, pres., 1976-82, pub., 1982—; chmn. Noll Printing Co., 1978—; dir., mem. exec. com. First Nat. Bank, Huntington; vice chmn. Religious Communications Congress, 1980; bd. dirs. Center for Applied Research in the Apostolate, 1978—, Internat. Cath. Orgns. Center, 1979—; mem. Cath. Com. for White House Conf. on Families, 1980; mem. communications com. U.S. Cath. Conf., 1981-84. Chmn. United Fund Drive, 1963; pres. United Way of Huntington County, 1973-74, bd. dirs., 1971-74; bd. dirs. YMCA, Huntington, 1966-78, Cath. Journalism Scholarship Fund, Founds. and Donors Interested in Cath. Activities, 1977—; trustee Huntington Coll., 1978-81; bd. dirs. Huntington Coll. Found., 1977—, pres. bd., 1978-81; bd. dirs. Huntington Med. Meml. Found., 1978—. Served as 1st lt. USAF, 1954-56. Recipient Disting. Service award Huntington Jaycees, 1960; named Chief of Flint Springs Tribe, 1971; decorated knight of Malta, knight of Holy Sepulchre; recipient St. Francis de Sales award Cath. Press Assn., 1981. Mem. Internat. Fedn. Cath. Press Assns. (v.p. 1974-80, pres. 1980—), Internat. Cath. Union of the Press (council, mem. bur. 1974—), Cath. Press Assn. (pres. 1973-75, dir. 1965-75), Mag. Pubs. Assn., Printing Industries Am. Republican. Roman Catholic. Clubs: Cosmopolitan, Rotary, K.C. Office: Noll Plaza Huntington IN 46750

FINK, LARRY B., photographer, educator; b. BKlyn., Mar. 11, 1941; s. Bernard and Sylvia (Caplan) F.; m. Joan Snyder, 1969 (div. 1968); 1 dau., Molly Felicia Snyder. Asst. prof. Parson Sch. Design, N.Y.C., 1969-74, Lehigh U., Bethlehem, Pa., 1977-78; prof. Yale U., New Haven, 1978-79; prof. photography Cooper Union, N.Y.C., 1979—. One-man shows, Mus. Modern Art, N.Y.C., 1979, numerous others; group shows, Mus. Modern Art, 1979, San Francisco Mus. Modern Art, 1982. John Simon Guggenheim fellow, 1976, 79; Nat. Endowment for Arts fellow, 1978. Club: Black Panthers. Home: PO Box 295 Martins Creek PA 18062

FINK, LAWRENCE ALFRED, educator; b. N.Y.C., Jan. 20, 1930; s. Merwin Jesse and Claudia (Lowenthal) F.; m. Barbara Louise Gross, Aug. 30, 1959; children—Laura Alison, James Merwin, Hilary Lynn. A.B., Stanford U., 1951; M.A., Columbia, 1958, Ed.D., 1964. Tchr. history New Rochelle (N.Y.) High Sch., 1957-60; instr. Tchrs. Coll. of Columbia, 1960-62; asst. prof. edn. Smith Coll., 1963-66, asso. prof., chmn. dept. edn. and child study, 1966-70, prof., chmn. dept., 1970—, dir. grad. study, 1978—, athletic dir., 1981—; Sr. asso. Edn. Assos.; cons. Pres.'s Com. Mental Retardation, 1969-70; cons. editor Random House. Author: Honors Teaching in American History, 1969, Crisis in Urban Education, 1971. Trustee Northampton Instn. Savs.; Bd. dirs. Hampshire United Fund, Northampton, Mass., 1968—; trustee Northampton Sch. for Girls, Williston Acad. Served with C.I.C. AUS, 1953-55. Mem. Am. Hist. Assn., Nat. Council Social Studies, Orgn. Am. Historians, Am. Ednl. Research Assn., Am. Ednl. Studies Assn. Home: 96 Maynard Rd Northampton MA 01060

FINK, LYMAN ROGER, engr.; b. Elk Point, S.D., Nov. 14, 1912; s. Willis James and Helen (Black) F.; m. Frances Louise Kelly, Dec. 17, 1937; children—William R., Patricia H., James W. B.S., U. Calif. at Berkeley, 1933, M.S., 1934, Ph.D., 1937. Mgr. electronics lab. Gen. Electric Co., 1947-49, mgr. engr. radio and TV dept., 1949-55, mgr. research application dept., 1955-57, gen. mgr. X-ray dept., 1957-59, gen. mgr. atomic products div., 1959-63, v.p., 1962-63, Otis Elevator Co., 1963-66; v.p., chief tech. officer The Singer Co., 1966-68, group v.p., 1968-70; exec. v.p., dir. Church's Fried Chicken, Inc., 1970-73; pres. Diversitek Co., 1973—; Dir., v.p. Atomic Indsl. Forum, 1961-63; trustee S.W. Research Inst., 1976—. Recipient Charles A. Coffin award Gen. Electric Co., 1948. Fellow IEEE; mem. N.Y. Acad. Scis., AAAS, Sigma Xi, Phi Beta Kappa, Tau Beta Pi, Kappa Delta Rho. Club: Oak Hills Country (San Antonio). Home: 4309 Muirfield Dr San Antonio TX 78229 Office: 4438 Centerview San Antonio TX 78228

FINK, PETER R., corporation executive; b. Detroit, 1933. Student, U. Pa., U. Mich. With R.P. Scherer Corp., Troy, Mich., 1966—, Pres., chief exec. officer, dir., 1979—. Office: R P Scherer Corp 2075 W Big Beaver Rd Troy MI 48084 *

FINK, RICHARD DAVID, chemistry educator; b. N.Y.C., July 14, 1936; s. Merwin Jesse and Claudia (Lowenthal) F.; m. Alice Christine Hovenden, Sept. 8, 1961; children: Rebecca Elisabeth, Johanna Hovenden. A.B., Harvard U., 1958; Ph.D., M.I.T., 1962; M.A. (hon.), Amherst Coll., 1971. NSF fellow in chemistry Yale U., 1962-63; NIH fellow, 1963-64; asst. prof. chemistry Amherst (Mass.) Coll., 1964-67, assoc. prof., 1967-71, prof., 1971—, Mellon prof., 1977—, chmn. dept., 1970—, dean of faculty, 1983-85; NSF fellow King's Coll., U. London, 1968-69, vis. prof., 1972-73, 76-77, 80-81, U. Kans., 1980-81; sr. cons. Edn. Assos., Inc. Contbr. articles to profl. jours. Sloan Found. fellow, 1970-74; Dreyfus Found. tchr.-scholar prize, 1971; NSF Profl. Devel. award, 1979. Mem. Am. Phys. Soc., Am. Chem. Soc., AAAS, Sigma Xi. Home: 30 Orchard St Amherst MA 01002 Office: Amherst Coll Amherst MA 01002

FINK, RICHARD WALTER, educator, nuclear physicist, chemist; b. Detroit, Jan. 13, 1928; s. Bernard and Ann (Walter) F.; m. Gunilla Gustafsson, Oct. 4, 1960; children: Kerry Leif, Roger Gunnar. B.S. in Chemistry, U. Mich., 1948; M.S., U. Calif. at Berkeley, 1949; Ph.D., U. Rochester, 1953. Asso. prof. U. Ark., Fayetteville, 1953-61; prof. dept. physics Marquette U., Milw., 1961-65; vis. prof. Werner Inst. for Nuclear Chemistry, U. Uppsala, Sweden, 1959-60, Inst. for Exptl. Physics, U. Hamburg, Germany, 1963-64; prof. Sch. Chemistry, Ga. Inst. Tech., Atlanta, 1965—; research nuclear chemist Knolls Atomic Power Lab., Schenectady, 1949-50; Cons. Lawrence Radiation Lab., U. Calif., 1961-69, Phillips Petroleum Co., Bartlesville, Okla., 1957-65; cons. on natural radiocarbon counting Coca-Cola Co., Atlanta, 1972-73; chmn. Internat. Conf. on Inner Shell Ionization Phenomena, Atlanta, 1972; Fulbright Travel grantee, 1963-64, Fulbright lectr., Europe, 1964, Nat. Acad. Sci. exchange lectr., Yugoslavia, 1971, Poland, 1977; Internat. Atomic Energy Agy. cons. to Greek Atomic Energy Commn., Nuclear Research Center, Demokritos, Athens, 1975-76. Contbr. articles to profl. jours. Fellow Am. Phys. Soc.; mem. Sigma Xi (Research prize 1971, 77, 79, 83). Office: Sch Chemistry Ga Inst Tech Atlanta GA 30332

FINK, ROBERT MORGAN, educator; b. Greenville, Ill., Sept. 22, 1915; s. William Harvey and Pearl (Smith) F.; m. Kathryn L. Ferguson, Jan. 6, 1941; children—Patricia Kay, Suzanne Joyce. Student, Kans. State Coll., 1933-35; A.B., U. Ill., 1937; postgrad., Lehigh U., 1937-38; Ph.D., U. Rochester, 1942. Mem. faculty U. Calif. at Los Angeles, 1947—, prof. biol. chemistry, 1963-78, prof. emeritus, 1978—; research biochemist VA, 1947-54; Mem. subcom. on internal dose, nat. com. radiation protection Nat. Bur. Standards, 1947-49. Author: Biological Studies with Polonium, Radium and Plutonium, 1950. Mem. Am. Soc. Biol. Chemists. Research and publs. on chromatographic and radioactive tracer techniques for thyroid hormone prodn., photosynthesis and nucleic acid metabolism. Home: 1340 Avenida de Cortez Pacific Palisades CA 90272

FINK, ROBERT RUSSELL, university dean, music theorist; b. Belding, Mich., Jan. 31, 1933; s. Russell Foster and Frances (Thornton) F.; m. Ruth Joan Bauerle, June 19, 1955; children: Denise Lyn, Daniel Robert. B.Mus., Mich. State U., 1955, M.Mus., 1956, Ph.D., 1965. Instr. music SUNY, Fredonia, 1956-57; instr. Western Mich. U., Kalamazoo, 1957-62, asst. prof., 1962-66, assoc. prof., 1966-71, prof., 1971—, chmn. dept. music, 1972-78; dean Coll. Music U. Colo., Boulder, 1978—; prin. horn Kalamazoo Symphony Orch., 1957-67; accreditation examiner Nat. Assn. Schs. Music, Reston, Va., 1973—, grad. commr., 1981—. Author: Directory of Michigan Composers, 1972, The Language of 20th Century Music, 1975; composer: Modal Suite, 1959, Four Modes for Winds, 1967, Songs for High School Chorus, 1967; contbr. articles to profl. jours. Bd. dirs. Kalamazoo Symphony Orch., 1974-78, Boulder Bach Festival, 1983—. Mem. Coll. Music Soc., Mich. Music Tchrs. Assn. (dir.), Mich. Orch. Assn. (pres.), Phi Mu Alpha Sinfonia (province gov.), Pi Kappa Lambda. Home: 643 Furnam Way Boulder CO 80303 Office: U Colo Boulder CO 80309

FINK, STUART SIMON, educator; b. N.Y.C., Apr. 16, 1934; s. Theodore and Sara F. B.S., CCNY, 1956, M.B.A., 1959; Ph.D., Union Grad. Sch., 1980. Securities analyst Bache & Co., N.Y.C., 1958-60; adv. analyst IBM, N.Y.C., 1960-64; v.p., dir. data processing Mai Corp., 1964-69; mem. faculty N.Y. U., N.Y.C., 1969—, prof. mgmt., 1972—; dir. Sch. Continuing Edn., 1969—. Author: Business Data Processing, 1974. Mem. Data Processing Mgmt. Assn., Assn. Systems Mgmt., Assn. for Computing Machinery. Office: New York University 50 W 4th St Room 327 New York NY 10003 *As a scientist/educator I hope to provide direction in the adoption of the new technologies in order to better our way of life while retaining our fundamental values and principles.*

FINKBEINER, OTTO KARL, church official; b. Phila., Jan. 6, 1923; s. Otto and Helen (Betcher) F.; m. Eileen Ramsay, June 10, 1944; children: Eric, Judith L., Janet L.; m. Joyce Barnes, Apr. 25, 1982. B.S., Temple U., 1947. With Westminster Press, 1947-52; with dept. adminstrn. Gen. Assembly United Presbyn. Ch. in U.S.A., 1953, mgr., 1954-67, asst. stated clk., 1967-74, asso. stated clk., treas., 1974—. Served as pilot USAAF, World War II. Mem. Adminstrv. Mgmt. Soc., Assn. Statisticians Am. Religious Bodies (pres. 1960-62, sec.-treas. 1980—), Religious Conv. Mgrs. Assn. (pres. 1980-83), Am. Soc. Assn. Execs. Republican. Office: 475 Riverside Dr Room 1201 New York NY 10115

FINKEL, DONALD, poet; b. N.Y.C., Oct. 21, 1929; s. Saul A. and Meta (Rosenthal) F.; m. Constance Urdang, Aug. 14, 1956; children: Elizabeth Antonia, Thomas Noah, Amy Maria. B.S., Columbia U., 1952, M.A., 1953. Poet-in-residence Washington U., St. Louis, 1965—; cons. prosody Random House Dictionary. Author: The Clothing's New Emperor, 1959, Simeon, 1964, A Joyful Noise, 1966, Answer Back, 1968, The Garbage Wars, 1970, Adequate Earth, 1972, A Mote in Heaven's Eye, 1975, Endurance and Going Under, 1978, What Manner of Beast, 1981. Recipient Theodore Roethke Meml. award, 1974; Morton Dauwen Zabel award, 1980; Guggenheim fellow, 1966; grantee Ingram Merrill Found., 1972, Nat. Endowment for Arts, 1973. Mem. Antarctican Soc., Cave Research Found., Phi Beta Kappa. Address: 6943 Columbia Pl Saint Louis MO 63130

FINKEL, E. JAY, lawyer; b. Phila., June 21, 1931. B.A., Swarthmore Coll.; M.A., J.D., George Washington U. Bar: U.S. Supreme Ct., Ct. Internat. Trade, U.S. Dist. Ct. D.C. Various positions Dept. Treasury, 1952-74, dep. dir. Office Internat. Fin. Policy Coordination and Ops., 1963-67, dir. Office Latin Am., 1967-70, dir. Multilateral Instns. Program Office, 1970-74; dir. Developing Nations Fin., 1974-75; asst. exec. sec. World Bank-IMF Devel. Com., 1975-77; alt. U.S. exec. dir. Inter-Am. Devel. Bank, Washington, 1977-81; of counsel Porter Wright Morris & Arthur, Washington, 1981—. Ret. lt. comdr. USNR. Mem. D.C. Bar. Address: Porter Wright et al 1133 15th St NW Suite 1200 Washington DC 20005

FINKEL, GERALD MICHAEL, lawyer; b. N.Y.C., July 29, 1941; s. Abraham B. and Elizabeth B. (Michales) F.; m. Beverly Lynne Jaffee, Aug. 26, 1962; children: Bruce David, Judith Michelle. B.A., NYU, 1962; J.D., U.S.C., 1970. Bar: S.C. 1970, U.S. Dist. Ct. S.C. 1970, U.S. Ct. Appeals (4thcir.) 1973, U.S. Supreme Ct. 1973, D.C. 1973. Prin. Finkel, Georgaklis, Goldberg, Sheftman and Korn, P.A., Columbia, S.C., 1970—; adj. prof. trial advocacy U.S.C.; mem. faculty fed. trial practice AM. Law Inst., ABA; lectr. S.C. Bar, S.C. Trial Lawyers Assn., Richland County Bar and Profl. Insts.; spl. judge Richland County Family Ct., 1974-78, Ct. Gen. Sessions 5th Jud. Cir., 1976. Author: (with Ralph C. McCullough II) A Guide to South Carolina Torts, 1981. Heating officer S.C. Dept. Health and Environ. Control, 1979—; mem. S.C. Appelate Def. Commn., 1982-83, Gov.'s Sentencing Guidelines Commn., 1982-83. Served to capt. U.S. Army, 1962-67. Recipient Outstanding Alumni cert. Phi Alpha Delta, 1972. Mem. ABA, Richland County Bar Assn., Am. Judicature Soc., Assn. Trial Lawyers Am., Am. Law Inst., S.C. Trial Lawyers Assn. (conv. chmn. 1978, treas. 1978-80, exec. bd. 1978-81, v.p. 1980-81, pres. 1982-83), Phi Alpha Delta (dist. justice 1976-78). Democrat. Jewish. Office: Finkel Georgaklis et al PO Box 1799 Columbia SC 29202

FINKEL, MARION JUDITH, physician, federal agency adminstr.; b. N.Y.C., Nov. 2, 1929; d. Israel and Bella (Stillman) F.; m. Simon V. Manson, Sept. 12, 1954. Pre-med. student, L.I. U., 1945-48; M.D. (Howard Sloan Meml. scholar), Chgo. Med. Sch., 1952. Intern Jersey City Med. Center, 1952-53; resident in internal medicine Bellevue Hosp., N.Y.C., 1953-56; med. editor Merck and Co., 1957-61; practice medicine specializing in internal medicine, N.Y.C., 1956-57, 1961-63, N.J., 1956-57, 1961-63; with FDA, 1963—, dir. div. metabolic and endocrine drugs, 1966-70, dep. dir. Bur. Drugs, Rockville, Md., 1970-71, 72-74, dir. office new drug evaluation, 1971-72, 74, assoc. dir. for new drug evaluation, 1974-82, dir. Office of Orphan Products Devel., 1982—. Contbr. chpts., numerous articles to profl. publs. Recipient award of merit FDA, 1974; Superior Service award USPHS, 1976; Fed. Woman's award Fed. Govt., 1976; Meritorious Exec. award, 1980; named Disting. Alumnus Chgo. Med. Sch., 1977, L.I. U., 1980. Mem. Am. Soc. Clin. Pharmacology and Therapeutics, Soc. Clin. Trials. Office: 5600 Fishers Ln Rockville MD 20857

FINKELSTEIN, BERNARD, lawyer; b. N.Y.C., Jan. 21, 1930; s. Irving and Sadie (Katz) F.; m. Adele S. Levine, June 29, 1952; children: Sharon Ann, Marcia Lyn. B.A., NYU, 1951; LL.B., Yale U., 1954. Bar: N.Y. 1954, D.C. 1970. Assoc. Paul, Weiss, Rifkind, Wharton & Garrison, N.Y.C., 1956-64, ptnr., 1965—; mem. wills and trusts adv. com. Practicing Law Inst. Fellow Am. Coll. Probate Counsel; mem. ABA, N.Y. State Bar Assn., Assn. Bar City N.Y. (chmn. gift and tax com.- tax sect. 1978-80), Am. Judicature Soc., N.Y. Bar Found., Yale Law Sch. Assn. (exec. com.), Phi Beta Kappa, Phi Alpha Delta, Order of Coif. Club: Elmwood Country (White Plains, N.Y.). Home: 1 Tory Ln Scarsdale NY 10583 Office: Paul Weiss Rifkind Wharton & Garrison 345 Park Ave New York NY 10154

FINKELSTEIN, DAVID, physicist, educator; b. N.Y.C., July 19, 1929; s. Isidore and Esther (Rubinstein) F.; m. Helene Cooper, 1948 (div.); children: Daniel, Beth, Eve; m. Shlomit Ritz, 1981; 1 dau., Aria. B.S., CCNY, 1949; Ph.D., MIT, 1953. Asst., then asso. prof. physics Stevens Inst. Tech., 1954-60; asso. prof. Yeshiva U., then prof., chmn., dean, 1960-79; prof. physics Ga. Inst. Tech., 1979—; vis. prof. Tougaloo Coll., 1965, Hebrew U. Jerusalem, 1974. Editor: Internat. Jour. Theoretical Physics. Ford Found. fellow, 1958; NSF grantee, 1954—; est grantee, 1977. Mem. Am. Phys. Soc., AAAS. Jewish. Research in topological physics, gravity, quantum logic. Office: GA Inst Tech School of Physics Atlanta GA 30332

FINKELSTEIN, EDWARD S., department store executive; b. New Rochelle, N.Y., Mar. 30, 1925; s. Maurice and Eva (Levine) F.; m. Myra Schuss, Aug. 13, 1950; children: Mitchell, Daniel, Robert. B.A., Harvard U., 1946, M.B.A., 1948. Successively trainee, buyer fabrics, mdse. adminstr. Macy's, N.Y.C., 1948-62; sr. v.p., dir. merchandising Bambergers, 1962-67, exec. v.p., merchandising and sales promotion, 1967-69; pres. Macy's, Calif., 1969-74, pres., chief exec. officer, New York, 1974-78, chmn. bd., chief exec. officer, 1978-80; chmn., chief exec. officer R.H. Macy & Co. Inc., 1980—; dir. R.H. Macy, Inc., 1971—; dir. Chase Manhatten Bank., Chase Manhattan Corp. Mem. nat. adv. council Cystic Fibrosis, 1975-80; trustee Cystic Fibrosis Found., 1977-80, hon. trustee, 1980—; mem. adv. bd. Yale U., 1983—; bd. dirs. adv. bd. Harvard Bus. Sch., 1983—. Served with USN, 1943-46. Jewish. Clubs: Harvard Bus. Sch. of Greater N.Y. (dir.), Economic (N.Y.C.)). Office: 151 W 34th St New York NY 10001

FINKELSTEIN, LOUIS, sem. adminstr.; b. Cin., June 14, 1895; s. Rabbi Simon J. and Hannah (Brager) F.; m. Carmel Bentwich, Mar. 5, 1922; children—Hadassah, Ezra, Faith. A.B., Coll. City of N.Y., 1915; Ph.D., Columbia, 1918; Rabbi, Jewish Theol. Sem. Am., 1919; S.T.D., Columbia, 1944; Litt.D., Boston U., 1950; D.H.L., Dropsie Coll., 1961, Woodstock Coll., 1972, Brandeis U., 1972; LL.D., Temple U., 1963, Manhattan Coll., 1965, Fordham U., 1966; L.H.D., S.E. Mass. Inst. Tech., 1966; S.T.D., N.Y.U., 1967; D.D., Yale, 1967. Rabbi Congregation Kehilath Israel, N.Y. C., 1919-31; instr. Talmud Jewish Theol. Sem., 1920-24, Solomon Schechter lectr. in theology, 1924-30, asso. prof. theology, 1930, Solomon Schechter prof. theology, 1931—, asst. to pres., 1934-37, provost, 1937-40, pres., 1940, chancellor, 1951-72, chancellor emeritus, 1972—; pres. Inst. Religious and Social Studies; Ingersoll lectr. Harvard Div. Sch., 1944; Active in ednl. publs. and ednl. coms. and commns. for various gen. and spl. purposes. Ambassador of Pres. Kennedy to Papal Coronation, 1963; hon. chmn. bd. edn. for recruiting young people for preprofl. jobs in war on poverty, 1964; dir. Am. Friends of Hebrew U.; adv. bd. Inst. for Advancement of Cultural and Spiritual Values. Author or co-author several books, 1924—; latest being Abot of Rabbi Nathan, 1950, The Pharisees: The Sociological Background of Their Faith, 1962, New Light on the Prophets, 1969, Pharisaism in the Making, 1972; Editor commentaries, biographies; co-editor numerous symposia; contbr. review and jours.; Vice pres. and mem. editorial bd.: Universal Jewish Ency. Phi Epsilon Pi Fraternity Nat. Service award, 1952; Townsend Harris medal, 1940; 125th Anniversary medal Coll. City N.Y., 1972. Fellow Am. Acad. of Arts and Scis., Acad. of Jewish Research, Jewish Acad. Arts and Scis.; past pres. Conf. Sci. Philosophy and Religion., Mem. several assns. and orgns. Home: 340 Riverside Dr New York City NY 10025 Office: 3080 Broadway: New York City NY 10027

FINKELSTEIN, RICHARD ALAN, microbiologist; b. N.Y.C., Mar. 5, 1930; s. Frank and Sylvia (Lemkin) F.; m. Helen Rosenberg, Nov. 30, 1952; children: Sheri, Mark, Laurie; m. Mary Boesman, June 20, 1976; 1 dau., Sarina Nicole. B.S., U. Okla., 1950; M.A., U. Tex., Austin, 1952, Ph.D., 1955. Teaching fellow, research scientist U. Tex., Austin, 1950-55; fellow, instr. U. Tex. Southwestern Med. Sch., Dallas, 1955-58; chief bioassay sect. Walter Reed Army Inst. Research, Washington, 1958-64; dep. chief, chief dept. bacteriology and mycology U.S. Army Med. Component, SEATO Med. Research Lab., Bangkok, Thailand, 1964-67; asso. prof. dept. microbiology U. Tex. Southwestern Med. Sch., Dallas, 1967-73, prof., 1973-79; prof., chmn. dept. microbiology Sch. Medicine U. Mo.-Columbia, 1979—; mem.

Nat. Com. for Coordination of Cholera Research, Ministry of Public Health, Bangkok, 1965-67; cons. WHO, 1970—; cons. to comdg. gen. U.S. Army Med. Research and Devel. Command, 1975-79; cons. Schwarz-Mann Labs., 1974-79; vis. asso. prof. U. Med. Scis., Bangkok, 1965-67; vis. prof. U. Chgo. Med. Sch., 1977; vis. scientist Japanese Sci. Council, 1976; Ciba-Geigy lectr. Waksman Inst., Rutgers U., 1975. Contbr. articles on cholera, enterotoxins, gonorrhea, role of iron in host parasite interactions to profl. jours. Recipient Robert Koch prize, Bonn, W. Ger., 1976. Fellow Am. Acad. Microbiology, Infectious Diseases Soc. Am.; mem. Am. Soc. Microbiology (div. councilor, chmn. program com. 1979-82, pres. Tex. br. 1974-75), Am. Assn. Immunologists, Soc. Gen. Microbiology, Pathol. Soc. Gt. Britain and Ireland. Home: 3207 Honeysuckle Dr Columbia MO 65201 Office: Dept Microbiology Sch Medicine Univ of Mo-Columbia Columbia MO 65212

FINKLEA, JOHN FURMAN, physician, public health educator; b. s. Florence, S.C., Aug. 27, 1933; s. Orion T. and Ruth F. (Townsend) F.; m. Florence Elizabeth Gregory, June 26, 1958; children: Elizabeth Gregory, John Townsend. B.S., Davidson Coll., 1954; M.D., Med. Coll. of S.C., 1958; M.P.H., U. Mich., 1964, D.P.H., 1967; grad., Fed. Exec. Inst., 1974. Diplomate: Am. Bd. Preventive Medicine. Intern Univ. Hosp., Ann Arbor, Mich., 1958-59, resident, 1959-61; teaching asst. in epidemiology Sch. Pub. Health, U. Mich., Ann Arbor, 1965; asso. in medicine Northwestern U. Med. Sch., Chgo., 1966; asso. prof. preventive medicine and pediatrics Med. Coll. of S.C., Charleston, 1968-69; chief ecol. research br. div. of health effects research Nat. Air Pollution Control Adminstrn., Durham, N.C., 1969-71; dir. div. health effects research Nat. Environ. Research Center, EPA, Research Triangle Park, N.C., 1971-72, dir., 1972, Nat. Inst. for Occupational Safety and Health, Rockville, Md., 1975-78; prof. pub. health U. Ala., Birmingham, 1978—; adj. asso. prof. epidemiology U. N.C., Chapel Hill, 1969-75; asst. clin. prof. community health Duke Med. Sch., Durham, 1969-75; cons. Northwestern U., Chgo., 1966-71, WHO, 1973-80, sci. adviser on environ. health criteria, 1973; mem. advisory panel Nat. Center for Health Statistics, 1971—; Bd. dirs. Internat. Reference Center of Air Pollution Control. Editorial bd.: Jour. Environ. Pathology and Toxicology, 1976—, Am. Jour. Indsl. Medicine, 1980—; Contbr. numerous articles on preventive medicine to med. jours. Served with USNR, 1959-61. Mem. Am. Pub. Health Assn., Am. Acad. Pediatrics, Am. Assn. Tchrs. Preventive Medicine, Am. Coll. Preventive Medicine, Am. Coll. Toxicology, Nat. Acad. Scis. (com. hearing bioacoustics 1972-75), AMA, Am. Occupational Med. Assn., Delta Omega, Alpha Omega Alpha. Home: 3912 Royal Oak Dr Birmingham AL 35243 Office: Medical Towers Bldg 7th Floor U Ala Birmingham AL 35294

FINKS, JAMES EDWARD, professional baseball club executive; b. St. Louis, Aug. 31, 1927; s. William T. and Margaret (Hays) F.; m. Maxine Anne Stemmons, Sept. 24, 1951; children: James Edward, Danny, David, Tommy. B.A., Tulsa U., 1949. Quarterback Pitts. Steelers Profl. Football Club, 1949-55; asst. coach U. Notre Dame, 1956-57; gen. mgr. Calgary (Can.) Canadian Football League, 1957-64, Minn. Vikings Profl. Football Club, 1964-74, v.p., 1969-73, exec. v.p., 1973-74; v.p., gen. mgr., chief operations officer Chgo. Bears Profl. Football Club, 1974-83; pres., chief exec. officer Chgo. Cubs Baseball Club, 1983—. Office: Wrigley Field Chicago IL

FINKS, ROBERT MELVIN, paleontologist, educator; b. Portland, Maine, May 12, 1927; s. Abraham Joseph and Sarah (Bendette) F. B.S. magna cum laude, Queens Coll., 1947; M.A., Columbia U., 1954, Ph.D., 1959. Lectr. Bklyn. Coll., 1955-58, instr., 1959-61; lectr. Queens Coll., 1961-62, asst. prof., 1962-65, acting chmn., 1963-64, asso. prof. geology, 1966-70, prof., 1971—; geologist U.S. Geol. Survey, 1952-54, 63—; research asso. Am. Mus. Natural History, 1961-77, Smithsonian Instn., 1968—; cons. in field. Author: Late Paleozoic Sponge Faunas of the Texas Region, 1960; Editor: Guidebook to Field Excursions, 1968; Contbr. articles profl. jours. Fellow AAAS, Geol. Soc. Am., Explorers Club; mem. Paleontol. Soc. (vice chmn. Northeastern sect. 1977-78, chmn. 1978-79), Paleontol. Assn. Britain, Soc. Systematic Zoology, Internat. Palaeontol. Assn., Geol. Soc. Vt. (charter mem.), Planetary Soc. (charter), Phi Beta Kappa, Sigma Xi. (exec. sec. Queens Coll. chpt. 1982—). *Be humble in studying nature.*

FINLAND, MAXWELL, physician; b. Russia, Mar. 15, 1902; came to U.S., 1906, naturalized, 1925; s. Frank and Rebecca (Povza) F. Ed., Wendell Phillips Sch., Boston, English High Sch.; B.S., Harvard U., 1922, M.D., 1926, D.Sc. (hon.), 1982, Western Res. U., 1964, D.H.L., Thomas Jefferson U., 1978. Asst. resident Boston Sanatorium, 1926-27; med. house officer Boston City Hosp., 1927-28, resident physician for pneumonia and med. service, 1928-29, became jr. vis. physician, 1938; chief IV Harvard) Med. Service, 1939-62, dir. II and IV, 1963-68, head dept. medicine, 1963-68, hon. physician, 1972—; asst. resident Thorndike Meml. Lab., 1929-32, asst. physician, 1932-41, asso. physician, 1941-50, asso. dir. lab., 1950-63, dir., 1963-68; epidemiologist Boston City Hosp., 1968-72; vis. physician Pondville Hosp., 1933-69; successively Charles Follen Folson teaching fellow in hygiene Harvard Med. Sch., 1928-29, asst., 1929-32, Francis Weld Peabody fellow, 1932-37, instr., 1935-37, asso., 1937-40; asst. prof. 1940-46, asso. prof., 1946-62, prof. medicine, 1962-63, George Richards Minot prof. medicine, 1963-68, George Richards Minot Prof. emeritus, 1968—; mem. subcom. infectious diseases NRC, 1946-54, chmn., 1955-59; mem. advisory com. on influenza research USPHS, 1959-63; mem. bacteriol. and mycol. study sect. NIH, 1958-63; asso. mem. commn. acute respiratory diseases Armed Forces Epidemiological Bd., 1950-67, mem., 1967-72; mem. drug research bd. Nat. Acad. Scis.-NRC, 1964-71; cons. VA, 1945-73, mem. clin. investigators com. dept. medicine and surgery, 1955-69, chmn., 1964-69, distinguished physician, 1973—; chmn. Com. for Lederle Med. Faculty awards, 1952-68. Contbr. articles, editorials and revs. to sci. jours. and med. text books.; Editor, co-editor numerous monographs on infectious diseases.; Mem. editorial bd.: N.E. Jour. Medicine, 1945-68, Applied Microbiology, 1964-74, Antimicrobiol. Agents and Chemotherapy, 1960-71, Jour. Infectious Diseases, 1969-72, Jour. AMA, 1973—, Jour. Clin. Microbiology, 1974—. Recipient Charles V. Chapin award City of Providence, 1960; Bristol award Infectious Diseases Soc. Am., 1966; Modern Medicine award, 1969; John Phillips Meml. award ACP, 1971; Oscar B. Hunter Meml. award Am. Soc. Clin. Pharmacology and Therapeutics, 1971; Sheen award AMA, 1971; Outstanding contbns. award in field of antibiotic research Bristol Meyers Co., Internat. Div., 1981; named hon. citizen City of Panama, 1970. Master ACP; fellow AAAS; mem. Assn. Am. Physicians (emeritus, Kober medalist 1978), Mass. Med. Soc., Am. Med. Assn., Soc. Exptl. Biology and Medicine, Am. Soc. Clin. Investigation (councillor 1942-45, v.p. 1947-48), Am. Bd. Internal Medicine, Infectious Diseases Soc. Am. (pres. 1963-64), Am. Assn. Immunologists, Soc. Am. Bacteriologists, Am. Acad. Arts and Scis., N.Y. Acad. Scis., Am. Epidemiol. Soc. (councillor 1957-60, v.p. 1961-62), Nat. Acad. Scis., Harvard Med. Alumni Assn. (pres. 1971-72), Assn. Clin. Pathologists (London) (corr.), Sigma Xi, Alpha Omega Alpha. Address: Boston City Hospital Boston MA 02118

FINLAY, JAMES CAMPBELL, museum director; b. Russell, Man., Can., June 12, 1931; s. William Hugh and Grace Muriel F.; m. Audrey Joy Barton, June 18, 1955; children: Barton Brett, Warren Hugh, Rhonda Marie. B.Sc., Brandon U., 1952; M.Sc. in Zoology, U. Alta., 1968. Geophysicist Frontier Geophys. Ltd., Alta., 1952-53; geologist, then dist. geologist Shell Can., Ltd., 1954-64; chief park naturalist and biologist Elk Island (Can.) Nat. Park, 1965-67; dir. hist. devel. and archives, dir. hist. and sci. service, dir. Nature Center, City of Edmonton, Alta., 1967—; founder Fedn. Alta. Naturalists, 1969. Author: A Nature Guide to Alberta, Bird Finding Guide to Canada. Named to Edmonton Hist. Hall of Fame, 1976. Mem. Can. Mus. Assn. (pres. 1976-78), Alta. Mus. Assn. (founding mem., past pres.), Am. Mus. Assn. (past council), Assn. Canadian Interpreters Assn., Alta. Hist. Soc., Cooper Ornith. Union, Am. Ornithol. Union. Home: 61 East Whitecroft 52313 Rge Rd 232 Sherwood Park Alberta Canada T8B 1B7 Office: John Janzen Nature Centre Edmonton AB Canada *I will walk but once on this earth. In this short time I hope to help my fellow man come to a greater awareness, appreciation and understanding of the world environment of which we are very much a part. I am trying to ensure that our descendants have a fit planet on which to live.*

FINLAY, JAMES CHARLES, university president; b. Roscommon, Ireland, Aug. 29, 1922; s. James Charles and Kathleen (O'Connor) F. Student, Fordham Coll., 1940-42; B.A., Loyola U., 1945; M.A., Georgetown U., 1952; S.T.L., L'Immaculee Conception, 1955; Ph.D., Duke U., 1960. Mem. S.J.; ordained priest Roman Catholic Ch., 1954; instr. St. Peter's Prep. Sch., 1948-50; instr. polit. sci. Fordham U., 1960, asst. prof., 1961-63, chmn. dept., 1963-67, asso. prof., dean Grad. Sch., 1968-72, pres., 1972—; mem. Commr.'s adv. group on proposed postsecondary regulations. Mem. adminstrv. bd. Malcolm-King Harlem Coll. Extension; trustee Assn. Colls. and Univs. State N.Y.; chmn. bd., trustee Commn. Ind. Colls. and Univs.; dir. Assn. Jesuit Colls. and Univs.; mem. adv. com. Office of Fed. Regulatory Affairs, Am. Council on Edn.; trustee Inst. Internat. Edn.; mem. adv. com. pvt. sector initiatives Fed. Regional Council; mem. adv. council UN Assn. N.Y. Author: The Liberal Who Failed, 1968. Mem. N.Y.C. Partnership, N.Y.C. Charter Commn.; mem. met. council Coalition for N.Y.; Bd. mgrs. N.Y. Bot. Garden; mem. Hundred Yr. Assn. N.Y., Inc. Mem. Phi Beta Kappa, Pi Sigma Alpha. Club: Century Assn. Address: Fordham U Bronx NY 10458

FINLAY, JOHN WALTER, banker; b. Worcester, Mass., Oct. 26, 1923; s. William K. and Ruth (Montgomary) F.; m. Regina M. Bolander, Jan. 24, 1948; children: John Scott, Melanie Gail. D.B.S., Becker Coll., Worcester, 1948. With Marine Midland Bank Southeastern N.Y., Poughkeepsie, 1948—, pres., from 1971; also dir.; now pres., chief exec. officer, dir. Mchts. Nat. Bank & Trust Co., Syracuse, N.Y.; dir. Rogers Cablesystems of Syracuse. Bd. dirs. Met. Devel. Assn., Eye Defect and Vision Research Found., Crouse-Irving Meml. Found., United Way Central N.Y.; mem. Downtown Com. Syracuse, Inc.; trustee Onondaga Indsl. Devel. Corp.; bd. regents LeMoyne Coll. Served with AUS, 1943-46. Mem. Syracuse C. of C. (dir.), Am. Inst. Banking. Presbyterian. Clubs: Onondaga Golf and Country (dir.), Century). Home: 7619 Northfield Ln Manlius NY 13104 Office: 216-220 S Warren St Syracuse NY 13201

FINLAY, ROBERT DEREK, food company executive; b. U.K., May 16, 1932; s. William Templeton and Phyllis F.; m. Una Ann Grant, June 30, 1956; children: Fiona, Rory, James. B.A. with honors in Law and Econs, Cambridge (Eng.) U., 1955, M.A., 1959. With Mobil Oil Co. Ltd., U.K., 1955-61; dir. McKinsey & Co., Inc., 1971-79; mng. dir. H.J. Heinz Co. Ltd., U.K., 1979-81, sr. v.p. corp. devel. world hdqrs., Pitts., 1981—. Mem. London com. Scottish Council Devel. and Industry, 1979—. Served to Capt. Gordon Highlanders, 1950-61; Malaya. Mem. Inst. Mktg., Inst. Mgmt. Consultants. Clubs: Highland Brigade, Leander, Duquesne., Allegheny. Office: PO Box 57 Pittsburgh PA 15230 *

FINLEY, CARMEN JOYCE, psychologist, research instn. adminstr.; b. Santa Rosa, Calif., Mar. 9, 1926; d. Perry E. and Ardith (Bobst) F.; m. J. Hayes Hunter, Dec. 20, 1956 (div. 1968). A.B. in Speech and Math, U. Calif. at Berkeley, 1947; M.A., Tchrs. Coll., Columbia, 1952, Ph.D., 1962. Tchr. math. Porterville (Calif.) Union High Sch., 1948-51; sch. psychologist, cons. in adminstrv. research, dir. research and data processing Sonoma County Schs., Santa Rosa, 1952-67; asso. dir. Nat. Assessment Ednl. Progress, Ann Arbor, Mich., 1968-70, Denver, 1971; prin. research scientist Am. Insts. for Research, Palo Alto, Calif., 1972—; cons. in planning and evaluation San Mateo County Schs., 1974-75; Vis. asst. prof. statistics Sonoma State Coll., Rohnert Park, Calif., summer 1963, lectr. counseling dept., 1976—; vis. asso. prof. U. Rochester, N.Y., summer 1964; project asso. in ednl. psychology U. Wis., Madison, summer 1965; mem. com. on research and devel. Coll. Entrance Examination Bd., 1966-67; mem. European seminar on learning and ednl. process Skepparholmen, Hasseludden, Sweden, summer 1968; mem. Calif. Adv. Council on Ednl. Research, 1964-68, 72-73; cons. to Calif. State Dept. Edn., 1965, 75—, Maine State Dept. Edn., 1972-73, Mo. State Dept. Edn., 1973-74, Minn., Ill., Mich. depts. edn., 1973—, La., Ohio depts. edn., 1975, Santa Rosa, Sonoma County city schs., 1973; sub-regional rep. Far West Lab. Ednl. Research, 1966; dir. Johns Hopkins U. Nat. Symposium on Ednl. Research, 1979-80. Adv. editor: Jour. Ednl. Measurement, 1968-70; editorial bd.: Calif. Jour. Ednl. Research, 1964-69, 72-73; cons.: Am. Ednl. Research Jour, 1974; rev. editor: Measurement and Evaluation in Guidance, 1977—; Author monograph, tests.; Contbr. numerous articles on ednl. and psychol. measurement to profl. jours. Mem. Am. Ednl. Research Assn. (chmn. com. state and regional research assns. 1967-69, chmn. nominating com. div. D 1969, chmn. award com. 1975, reviewer ednl. evaluation and policy analysis), Calif. Ednl. Research Assn. (sec. treas. 1963-64, v.p. 1965-66, pres. 1966-67), Calif. Ednl. Data Processing Assn., Am. Personnel and Guidance Assn., Am. Psychol. Assn. (research com. 1966), Calif. Tchrs. Assn., Assn. Measurement and Evaluation in Guidance (publ. com. 1965), Nat. Council on Measurement in Edn. (newsletter reporter 1969—, program chmn. western region 1968, dir. 1970-71, chmn. publs. policy com. 1971, editor Measurement in Edn. 1972-75), Sonoma County Supts. Staff Assn. (pres. 1955-56), Sigma Xi, Kappa Delta Pi, Pi Lambda Theta. Home: 4820 Rockridge Ln Santa Rosa CA 95404 Office: PO Box 1113 1791 Arastradero Rd Palo Alto CA 94302

FINLEY, CHARLES OSCAR, ins. co. exec., former baseball exec.; b. Birmingham, Ala., Feb. 22, 1918; s. Oscar A. and Burmah E. (Fields) F.; m. Shirley McCartney, May 9, 1941 (div. 1979); children—Sharon, Charles O., Kathryn, Paul, Martin, Luke, David. From laborer to foreman U.S. Steel Corp. mills, Gary, 1936-41; with Kingsbury Ordnance Plant, 1941-45, div. supt., 1945; pres., owner Charles O. Finley & Co., Inc. (gen. ins. brokers), Chgo., 1945—; chmn. bd., pres., owner Oakland (Calif.) A's Baseball Club (American League), 1960-80; Asso. mem. So. Med. Assn. for devel. group ins. for doctors and families, 1960. Nat. chmn. Christmas Seal campaign Nat. Tb Assn., 1961. Recipient trophy World Series, 1972. Presbyn. Clubs: Mason (32 deg., Shriner), Chicago Athletic.) *

FINLEY, GLENNA, author; b. Puyallup, Wash., June 12, 1925; d. John Ford and Gladys De Ferris (Winters) F.; m. Donald MacLeod Witte, May 19, 1951; 1 son, Duncan MacLeod. B.A. cum laude, Stanford U., 1945. Producer internat. div. NBC, 1945-49; film librarian March of Time, 1949; with news bur. Life Mag., 1950; publicity and radio writer, Seattle, 1950-51, freelance writer, 1951-57; contract writer New Am. Library Inc., N.Y.C., 1970—. Author: numerous books, latest Master of Love, 1978, Beware My Heart, 1978, The Marriage Merger, 1978, Wildfire of Love, 1979, Timed for Love, 1979, Love's Temptation, 1979, Stateroom for Two, 1980, Affairs of Love, 1980; munerous books, latest Midnight Encounter, 1981; numerous books, latest Reunion Engagement, 1981, One Way to Love, 1982. Named Matrix Table Woman of Achievement, 1976. Mem. Free-lances, Mystery Writers Am., Romance Writers Am. Republican. Anglican. Club: Women's Univ. (Seattle). Home: 2645 34th Ave W Seattle WA 98199

FINLEY, HAROLD MARSHALL, investment banker; b. McConnelsville, Ohio, Feb. 24, 1916; s. Harry Marshall and Kate (Cotton) F.; m. Jean Rowley, Sept. 19, 1943; 1 son, Robert W. B.S. cum laude, Northwestern U., 1933, B.D., Chgo. Theol. Sem., 1944; postgrad., U. Chgo., 1949; LL.D., Lincoln Meml. U., 1975. Vice-pres. Chgo. Title and Trust Co., 1963-76; sr. v.p. Burton J. Vincent Chesley & Co., Chgo., 1976—; dir. Bank of Lockport, Ill. Author: Everybody's Guide to the Stock Market, 1956, 59, 65, 68, The Logical Approach to Successful Investing, 1971; columnist: Market Trends, Chgo. Today, 1961-74, Chgo. Tribune, 1974-81. Bd. dirs. Chgo. Boys Club; mem. Lockport Twp. High Sch. Bd. Edn., 1961-64; trustee Alice Lloyd Coll., Chgo. Theol. Sem., Kobe Coll., Spertus Coll. of Judaica, Lewis U., Lincoln Meml. U.; chmn. Lincoln Meml. U., 1981—. Mem. Investment Analysts Soc. Chgo., Chartered Fin. Analysts, Transp. Securities Club Chgo., Delta Sigma Pi. Congregationalist. Clubs: Univ., Rotary (Chgo.) (pres. 1978-79). Home: 630 E 12th St Lockport IL 60441 Office: 230 W Monroe St Chicago IL *I have had a wide range of experiences and have enjoyed them all. I find each day and each person interesting and am continually thankful for the health to enjoy them.*

FINLEY, JAMES EDWARD, ind. oil operator; b. Elsberry, Mo., Dec. 26, 1922; s. Cyrus G and Vincil (Watts) F.; children—Sheryl, David. Student, S.W. Mo. State Coll., 1940-43; B.S. in Geology, U. Mo., 1948; M.S. in Indsl. Mgmt, Mass. Inst. Tech., 1960. With Continental Oil Co. (various locations), 1948—, group v.p. exploration and prodn. N. Am. petroleum operations, Houston, 1965-69, exec. v.p. exploration and prodn. western hemisphere petroleum div., 1969-75, exec. v.p. minerals, 1975-76, ret., 1976; ind. oil operator, 1976—. Served with USNR, 1943-46. Sloan fellow, 1959. Mem. Am. Petroleum Inst. (chmn. exploration com. 1973-74), Ind. Petroleum Assn. Am. (bd. dirs.), Houston C. of C., Am. Assn. Petroleum Geologists, soc. Exploration Geophysicists, Tex. Mid-Continent Oil and Gas Assn., Houston Geol. Soc., Geophys. Soc. Houston, Am. Soc. Oceanography. Presbyn. Club: Petroleum (Houston). Home: 821 Our Lane Circle Houston TX 77024

FINLEY, JOANNE ELIZABETH, physician, educator; b. Brockport, N.Y., Dec. 28, 1922; d. Frank Robert and Margaret (Matthews) Otte; m. Joseph E. Finley, July 19, 1950; children: Scott M., Ethan C., Lucinda M., William N. B.A. with highest honors, Antioch Coll., Yellow Springs, Ohio, 1944, M.P.H., Yale U., 1951; certificate, Washington Sch. Psychiatry, 1955; M.D., Case-Western Res. U., 1962. Diplomate: Am. Bd. Preventive Medicine. Research economist Office Alien Property Custodian, 1944; adminstrv. asst. U.S. Ho. of Reps., 1945-48; field dir. Nat. Inst. Social Relations, Muncie, Ind., 1948-49; pub. affairs analyst, writer Nat. Com. Effective Congress, 1949-50; health edn. dir. Montgomery County (Md.) Tb and Heart Assn., 1952-55; also grad. student field tng. supr. sociology U. Md., 1952-55; exec. dir. Montgomery County Planned Parenthood League, 1955-56; founder, dir. Parent and Child, Inc., part-time, 1956-57; intern Med. Coll. Pa., 1971; research dir. Cleve. Health Goals Project, 1963-66; dep. commr. med., acting health commr. Cleve. Div. Pub. Health, 1966-68; dir. health planning Phila. Dept. Pub. Health, 1968-72; v.p. med. affairs Blue Cross Greater Phila., 1972-73; dir. pub. health New Haven Dept. Health; also lectr. health adminstrn. dept. epidemiology, pub. health. Yale U. Med. Sch., 1973-74; commr. health State of N.J., from 1974; asst. clin. prof. community and preventive medicine Med. Coll. Pa., 1969—; vis. lectr. N.J. Coll. Medicine and Dentistry, 1972—; Commr. Kellogg Found. Commn. Edn. for Health Adminstrn., 1972-74. Author numerous papers in field. Mem. Assn. State and Territorial Health Officers, Am. Pub. Health Assn. Office: 201 W Preston St Baltimore MD 21201

FINLEY, JOSEPH EDWIN, lawyer, author; b. Portageville, Mo., Aug. 7, 1919; s. William V. and Nell (Whitten) F.; m. Joanne E. Otte, July 8, 1950; children—Scott M., Ethan C., Lucinda M., William N. B.J., U. Mo., 1942; LL.B., Yale, 1951. Bar: D.C. bar 1951, Ohio bar 1957, Pa. bar 1971. Pvt. practice, Washington, 1951-61, Cleve., 1957—; atty. Woll, Glenn & Thatcher, 1951-54; gen. counsel AFL; partner Metzenbaum, Gaines, Finley & Stern, 1961-74; counsel firm Metzenbaum, Gaines & Stern Co., 1974—; gen. counsel Office and Profl. Employees Internat. Union AFL-CIO, Internat. Brotherhood Pottery and Allied Workers AFL-CIO; also labor arbitrator. Author: The Corrupt Kingdom, 1973, White Collar Union, 1975, Missouri Blue; novel, 1976; Contbr. articles to profl. jours. Served to capt. AUS, 1942-46. Mem. Am. Bar Assn. Home: 57 Brookstone Dr Princeton NJ 08540

FINLEY, KAY THOMAS, chemistry educator; b. Elmira, N.Y., Aug. 29, 1934; s. Thomas Wolf and Helen Grace (Kennedy) F.; m. Patricia Joan Siegel, July 10, 1978; children: John, Sarah, Moira. B.S., Rochester Inst. Tech., 1959; Ph.D., U. Rochester, 1963. Asst. prof. Rochester Inst. Tech., 1962-66, asso. prof., 1966; sr. research chemist Eastman Kodak Co., Rochester, N.Y., 1966-70; prof. State U. N.Y. at Brockport, 1970—; asso. lectr. U. Rochester, 1969-70. Author: Mental Dynamics, 1966, Fundamental Organic Chemistry, 1970, The Triazoles, 1980; Contbr. articles to profl. jours. Served with USN, 1952-55. NSF fellow, 1961-62; grantee Petroleum Research Fund, 1962-64, 66-68, 73-75, State U. Research Found., 1971, 72, 73. Office: Dept Chemistry State Univ College Brockport NY 14420

FINLEY, MURRAY HOWARD, labor union official; b. Syracuse, N.Y., Mar. 31, 1922; m. Elaine Auerbach, July 14, 1946; children: Sharon, Susan. B.A., U. Mich., 1946; J.D., Northwestern U., 1949. Asst. regional atty. Amalgamated Clothing Workers Am., Chgo., 1949-55, asst. mgr. Detroit joint bd., 1955-61, mgr. Chgo. joint bd., 1961-62, internat. v.p., 1962-72, gen. pres., 1962-76, pres., 1976—; dir. Amalgamated Bank N.Y.; v.p., mem. exec. council AFL-CIO.; Trustee Nat. Planning Assn., Asian-Am. Free Labor Inst.; mem. Adv. Com. Trade Negotiations; mem. adv. com. Am. Ditchley Found.; co-chmn. Nat. Com. Full Employment; mem. Com. for Nat. Health Ins.; hon. vice chmn. Am. Trade Union Council for Histadrut; bd. dirs. A. Philip Randolph Inst., African-Am. Labor Center, Am. Productivity Center. Served with U.S. Army, 1942-45. Recipient various labor awards. Office: 15 Union Sq New York NY 10003 *

FINLEY, SARA CREWS, medical geneticist, educator; b. Lineville, Ala., Feb. 26, 1930; m. Wayne H. Finley; children: Randall Wayne, Sara Jane. B.S. in Biology, U. Ala., 1951, M.D., 1955. Diplomate: Am. Bd. Med. Genetics. Intern Lloyd Noland Hosp., Fairfield, Ala., 1955-56; NIH fellow in pediatrics U. Ala. Med. Sch., Birmingham, 1956-60; NIH trainee in med. genetics Inst. Med. Genetics, U. Uppsala, Sweden, 1961-62; mem. faculty U. Ala. Med. Sch., 1960—, co-dir. lab. med. genetics, 1966—, asst. prof. physiology and biophysics, 1968—, asso. prof. pub. health and epidemiology, 1975—, prof. pediatrics, 1975—; mem. staff Univ., Children's hosps.; cons. staff Lloyd Noland Hosp.; mem. ad hoc com. genetic counseling Children's Bur., HEW, 1966, mem. ad hoc rev. panel for genetic disease and sickle cell testing and counseling programs, 1980. Author papers on clin. cytogenetics, human congenital malformations, human growth and devel. Mem. Ala. Council Vol. Family Planning, 1974-75; adv. com. Internat. Conf.

Human Engring. and Future of Man, 1974-75; mem. White House Conf. Health, 1965; mem. research manpower rev. com. Nat. Cancer Inst., 1977-81. Mem. Am. Soc. Human Genetics, Am. Fedn. Clin. Research, Soc. Exptl. Biology and Medicine, N.Y. Acad. Scis., So. Soc. Pediatric Research, Med. Assn. Ala., Ala. Assn. Retarded Children (Ann. Med. award 1969), Ala. Acad. Sci., Jefferson County Med. Soc., Jefferson County Pediatric Soc., Jefferson County Aid Retarded Children, Phi Beta Kappa, Sigma Xi, Alpha Epsilon Delta, Omicron Delta Kappa. Home: 3412 Brookwood Rd Birmingham AL 35223 Office: University Station Birmingham AL 35294

FINLEY, WAYNE HOUSE, medical educator; b. Goodwater, Ala., Apr. 7, 1927; s. Byron Bruce and Lucille (House) F.; m. Sara Will Crews, July 6, 1952; children: Randall Wayne, Sara Jane. B.S., Jacksonville State U., 1948; M.A., U. Ala., 1950, M.S., 1955, Ph.D., 1958, M.D., 1960; postgrad., U. Uppsala, Sweden, 1961-62. Sci. tchr. High Sch., Tuscaloosa, Ala., 1949-51; intern U. Ala. Hosps. and Clinics, 1960-61; asst. prof. pediatrics U. Ala. Sch. Medicine, 1962-66, assoc. prof., 1966-70, prof., 1970—, asst. prof. biochemistry, 1965-75, assoc. prof., 1975-77, prof., 1977—, asst. prof. physiology and biophysics, 1968-75, assoc. prof., 1975—, prof. epidemiology, pub. health and preventive medicine, 1975—, adjunct prof. biology, 1980, dir. Lab. Med. Genetics, 1966—; chmn. med. Student Research Day, 1965-75, chmn. faculty council Sch. Medicine, 1977-78; mem. nat. adv. research resources council NIH-HEW, 1977-80; sr. scientist Comprehensive Cancer Center., Cystic Fibrosis Research Center. Contbr. articles on human malformations and clin. cytogenetics to tech. jours. Served with AUS, 1945-46, 51-53; lt. col. Res.; ret. Recipient Med. award Ala. Assn. Retarded Children, 1969; Disting. Alumni award U. Ala. Med. Sch. Alumni Assn., 1978, Tarlington award, 1982, Disting. Faculty lectr. award U. Ala. Med. Center, 1983. Mem. AAAS, N.Y. Acad. Scis., Soc. Exptl. Biology and Medicine, Am. Inst. Chemists, Am. Fedn. Clin. Research, Am. Soc. Human Genetics, So. Med. Assn., So. Soc. Pediatric Research, Med. Assn. Ala., Jefferson County Med. Soc. (maternal and child health com. 1975-79, chmn. 1976-77, mem., pres. 1983); Mem. Jefferson County Pediatrics Soc., U. Ala. Sch. Medicine Alumni Assn. (pres. 1974-75), Sigma Xi (pres. U. Ala. in Birmingham chpt. 1972-73), Kappa Delta Pi, Phi Delta Kappa, Alpha Omega Alpha, Phi Beta Pi (McBurney cup 1960), Omicron Delta Kappa. Baptist. Clubs: Caduceus, U. Ala. Sch. Medicine (pres. 1984-86), Kiwanis (pres. Shades Valley 1973-74). Home: 3412 Brookwood Rd Birmingham AL 35223

FINLINSON, BURNS LYMAN, coll. pres.; b. Oak City, Utah, Nov. 24, 1904; s. Joseph Trimble and Edith Elzina (Lyman) F.; m. Lydia Jennings, Sept. 1, 1937; children—Edith Zoe, David Burns, Harriett Ann. B.S., Brigham Young U., 1927, M.S., 1929; postgrad., U. Calif. at Berkeley, 1933-34, 42-43, Columbia, 1937-38. Instr. social scis. Delta (Utah) High Sch., 1927-28; instr. Latter-Day Saints Sem., Kanab, Utah, 1929-33; instr. history Br. Agrl. Coll., Cedar City, Utah, 1934-46, dept. chmn., 1944-46, dean of men, 1945-46; dir. Vets.' Guidance Center, Bakersfield (Calif.) Coll., 1946-49, dean admissions and records, 1949-56, dean ednl. services, 1956-58, v.p., 1958-68, pres., 1968-72, pres. emeritus, 1972—. Councilman Cedar City, 1944-46. Mem. Kern County (Calif.) Mus. Assn. (pres. 1960-61), Phi Delta Kappa. Home: 309 Garnsey Ave Bakersfield CA 93309

FINMAN, TED, lawyer, educator; b. San Francisco, Feb. 10, 1931; s. Samuel and Dora (Weinberg) F.; m. Susan F. Heifetz, Jan. 2, 1950; children—Rona Irene, Terry Janette. B.A., U. Chgo., 1950; LL.B., Stanford U., 1954. Pvt. practice law, 1954-59; asst. prof. law U. N.Mex. Law Sch., 1959-62; vis. asso. prof. Rutgers U. Law Sch., 1962-63; mem. faculty U. Wis., Madison, 1963—, prof. law, 1966—. Co-author: The Lawyers in Modern Society, 2d edit, 1976; contbr. articles to legal jours. Research grantee U. Wis., Am. Bar Found. Mem. Calif. Bar Assn., Order of Coif. Democrat. Jewish. Office: Law Sch U Wis Madison WI 53706 *

FINN, DANIEL FRANCIS, educational association executive; b. Norwich, Conn., Aug. 15, 1922; s. Daniel Francis and Elizabeth Ann (Elliott) F.; m. Gabrielle LaFayette Beausoleil, Aug. 26, 1948; children: Daniel, Mark, Chad, Beth, Bart. A.B. cum laude in Econs., Brown U., 1943; M.E., U. Maine, 1944; postgrad., U. Nancy, (France), 1945, Purdue U., 1957. Asst. puchasing agt. Brown U., Providence, 1946-48, puchasing agt., 1948-55, Purdue U., West Lafayette, Ind., 1955-61, bus. mgr., asst. treas., 1961-69; exec. v.p. Nat. Assn. Coll. and Univ. Bus. Officers, Washington, Ind., 1969—; chmn. nat. adv. panel Nat. Ctr. Higher Edn. Mgmt. Systems, Boulder, Colo. Contbr. articles in field. Mem. exec. bd. Tippecanoe council Boy Scouts Am., 1963-69, Lafayette Symphony Orch., 1965-69. Served with U.S. Army, 1943-45. Decorated Croix de Guerre. Mem. Nat. Assn. Ednl. Buyers, Ind. Assn. Coll. and Univ. Bus. Officers, Assn. Phys. Plant Adminstrs., Phi Beta Kappa. Democrat. Roman Catholic. Lodge: Rotary. Home: 8517 Warde Terr Potomac MD 20854 Office: Nat Assn Coll and Univ Bus Officers One Dupont Circle Suite 510 Washington DC 20036

FINN, DAVID, public relations company executive, artist; b. N.Y.C., Aug. 30, 1921; s. Jonathan and Sadie (Borgenicht) F.; m. Laura Zeisler, Oct. 20, 1945; children: Kathy, Dena, Peter, Amy. B.S., CCNY, 1943. Co-founder Ruder & Finn, Inc. (now Ruder Finn & Rotman, Inc.), N.Y.C., 1948; pres. Ruder & Finn, Inc. (now Ruder Finn & Rotman, Inc., N.Y.C., 1956-68; chmn. bd., chief exec. officer Ruder & Finn, Inc. (now Ruder Finn & Rotman, Inc.), N.Y.C., 1968—; adj. assoc. prof. NYU. One-man shows, New Sch. for Social Research, N.Y.C.; exhibited in group shows, Nat. Acad., Washington, Met. Mus. Art, N.Y.C., Boston Mus. Art, L'Orangerie, Paris, Andrew Crispo Gallery, N.Y.C., Westchester County Ctr., others; author: Public Relations and Management, 1956, The Corporate Oligarch, 1969; Photographer: books Embrace of Life, 1969, As the Eye Moves, 1970, Donatello: Prophet of Modern Vision, 1973, Henry Moore Sculpture and Environment, 1976, Michelangelo's Three Pietas, 1975, Oceanic Images, 1978, The Florence Baptistry Doors, 1980, Sculpture at Strom King, 1980, Busch-Reisinger Museum, 1980; Contbr. articles, chpts. to profl. jours., art publs., 1980. Mem. adv. bd. Council for Study Mankind; mem. adv. council advanced mgmt. programs Internat. Bus. Inst., Baruch Coll., N.Y.C.; bd. visitors CCNY; bd. dirs. New Hope Found., Ctr. for Research in Bus. and Social Policy, Victor Gruen Ctr. for Environ. Planning, Inst. Advanced Studies in Humanities, MacDowell Colony, Inst. for Future, Artists for Environment Found., Internat. Ctr. Photography, Am. Coll. Switzerland, Jewish Theol. Sem. Am.; bd. overseers Parsons Sch. Design, N.Y.C. Served to 1st lt. A.C. AUS, 1944. Mem. Am. Fedn. Arts, Am. Inst. Graphic Arts (past dir.), Internat. Pub. Relations Assn., Kappa Tau Alpha (hon.). Office: 110 E 59th St New York NY 10022

FINN, HAROLD BOLTON, III, lawyer; b. Bronxville, N.Y., Nov. 7, 1938; s. Harold Bolton and Anita Genevieve (Blackburne) F.; m. Catherine Cecelia Young, Sept. 11, 1965; children: Denyse, Alison, Douglas, Katherine. B.A., Yale Coll, 1960; LL.B. magna cum laude, Columbia U., 1966. Bar: N.Y. State 1967, D.C. 1968, Conn. 1974. Law clk. to Assoc. Justice Stanley F. Reed and Chief Justice Earl Warren, U.S. Supreme Ct., 1966-67; assoc. Covington & Burling, Washington, 1967-69, Cravath, Swaine & Moore, N.Y.C., 1969-73, Cummings & Lockwood, Stamford, Conn., 1973-74, partner, 1975—. Mem. adv. com. Conn. Banking Commr.; mem. Atty. Gen.'s Blue Ribbon Commn., Conn. Served with USN, 1960-63. Mem. Am. Bar Assn. (banking law com. and fed. regulation of securities com. sect. corps.), Conn. Bar Assn. (exec. com. sect. corps., exec. com. banking law sect.), Am. Law Inst. Club: Field of Greenwich (Conn.). Office: 10 Stamford Forum Stamford CT 06904

FINN, JAMES FRANCIS, consulting engineer; b. Jersey City, July 11, 1924; s. James Aloysius and Helen Edna (Brown) F.; m. Evelyn Teresa Dobbins, Sept. 9, 1950; children: Deirdre, Robert, John, Kerry, James. Student, St. Peters Coll., 1942-43, Stevens Inst. Tech., 1946-49; B.S. in Civil Engring., Newark Coll. Engring., 1953. Asst. engr., sr. engr. N.J. Dept. Conservation, Newark, 1949-56; hwy. design engr. Howard Needles Tammen & Bergendoff, N.Y.C., 1956-64, engring. mgr., gen. partner, Fairfield, N.J., 1965—; v.p. Howard Needles Tammen & Bergendoff Internat., Inc., Fairfield, 1965—; ptnr., adminstr. Howard Needles Tammon & Bergendorf S.de R.L.; v.p. HNTB, Inc., HNTB, P.C. (N.Y. Oreg., and Washington), HNTB, A&E, P.C. (Va., Fla.), HNTB, Inc., P.S. (Wash.), HNTB, Inc. (Ala., Alaska). Served as officer C.E. U.S. Army, 1943-46; ETO. Fellow Am. Cons. Engrs. Council, ASCE; mem. Am. Rd. Builders Assn., Nat., N.J. socs. profl. engrs., N.J. Soc. Planners, Internat. Bridge, Tunnel and Turnpike Assn., Transp. Research Bd., The Moles, Chi Epsilon. Roman Catholic. Home: 48 Hampshire Rd Washington Twp Westwood NJ 07675 Office: 330 Passaic Ave Fairfield NJ 07006

FINN, PETER MICHAEL, advertising executive; b. Milton, Mass., Feb. 19, 1936; s. Matthew Charles and Mary Germaine (Ireland) F.; m. Judith Mary Barry, Sept. 7, 1957; children: Pamela Ann, Mary Kathryn, Matthew Ireland. A.B., Holy Cross Coll., 1956; M.B.A., George Washington U., 1962; A.M.P., Harvard U., 1980. Account exec. J. Walter Thompson Co., N.Y.C., 1962-64, account supr., 1966-67; account exec. Foote Cone & Belding, N.Y.C., 1964-66, v.p., account supr., 1967-68, Doyle Dane Bernbach, N.Y.C., 1968-70; sr. v.p., dir. F.W. Free, N.Y.C., 1970-74; pres. Henderson Advt., Greenville, S.C., 1974-80, Bozell & Jacobs, Dallas, 1980—, also dir. Mem. Greater Greenville Planning Council, 1976-79, Dallas Citizens Council. Served to lt. USNR, 1957-62. Mem. Am. Assn. Advt. Agencies (bd. govs.), Am. Advt. Fedn., Am. Mktg. Assn. Office: Bozell & Jacobs Box 61200 DFW Airport TX 75261

FINN, ROBERT, music critic; b. Boston, July 13, 1930; s. Edward Anthony and E. Caroline (Seifert) F.; m. Mary Pacana, Oct. 12, 1957; children: Laurence, Elaine. B.A., Boston U., 1952. Staff reporter, music-drama critic New Bedford (Mass.) Standard-Times, 1956-59, Akron (Ohio) Beacon Jour., 1959-64; music critic Cleve. Plain Dealer, 1964—; mem. guest faculty Rockefeller Found. project for tng. music critics, 1965, 66. Contbr. to: Opera News mag. Served with AUS, 1953-56. Co-recipient ASCAP-Deems Taylor award for, 1972, 74, 78, 80. Mem. Music Critics Assn (exec. bd. 1975—, v.p. 1983—). Roman Catholic. Home: 1211 Blanchester Rd Lyndhurst OH 44124 Office: 1801 Superior Ave Cleveland OH 44114

FINN, TIMOTHY JOHN, deputy attorney general U.S.; b. Mpls., Nov. 23, 1950; s. Michael Charles and Muriel Ann (Findell) F.; m. Jacquelyn Greiner. A.B., Harvard U., 1973, J.D., 1976. Assoc. Jones, Day, Reavis & Pogue, Washington, 1977-81; dep. asst. atty. gen. U.S. Dept. Justice, Washington, 1981-83, assoc. dep. atty. gen., 1983—. Republican. Office: US Dept Justice 10th St and Constitution Ave NW Washington DC 20530

FINN, WILLIAM GOEBEL, former govt. ofcl.; b. Burlington, Ky., Mar. 13, 1900; s. Charles A. and Laura I. (Smith) F.; m. Bernice P. Kirkham, June 9, 1927; children—Susan M. (Mrs. Donald E. Smith), Carole B. (Mrs. David A. Fisher, Jr.). B.S. in Agr. cum laude, U. Ky., 1923; M.S. in Agrl. Econs, Iowa State U., 1927; advanced econ. studies, Grad. Sch. U.S. Dept. Agr., 1931-33, George Washington U., 1934-36. Field agt. U.S. Dept. Agr., 1922-23; asst. prof. agrl. econs. U. Ky., 1924-31; spl. cons. Met. Life Ins. Co., 1930; economist div. statis. and hist. research U.S. Dept. Agr., 1931-35; asst. dir. div. tobacco, sugar, rice and peanuts A.A.A., 1935-38, dir., 1938-42, asst. chief, 1942-46, asst. to adminstr. Prodn. and Mktg. Adminstrn., 1946-49; chief tech. assistance br., food and agr. U.S. Del. to Regional Orgns., Paris, France, 1949-54, dep. dir. food and agr., 1954-57, dir., 1957-61; pvt. cons., 1962—; livestock farmer. Bd. dirs. U.S. Dept. Agr. Grad. Sch., 1945-49; mem. coms. Combined Food Bd., World War II; rep. U.S. Dept. Agr. on strategic materials com. U.S. Munitions Bd., 1942-49. Author state univ. bulls., also Dept. Agr. documents, pvt. publs., and; contbr. to profl. jours. Served with U.S. Army, 1918. Named to Hall of Distinguished Alumni U. Ky.; recipient Presdl. citation for distinguished service to agr. Mem. Am. Farm Econs. Assn., Sigma Nu, Alpha Zeta. Clubs: American (Paris); Kiwanis. Address: 14508 Fiske Dr Silver Spring MD 20906

FINNEBURGH, MORRIS LEWIS, electronic manufacturing executive; b. Ft. Worth, Sept. 3, 1900; s. Lewis Henry and Lillie (Lewis) F.; m. Frieda Fox, Oct. 17, 1920; 1 son, Morris L. Student pub. schs.; LL.D., Ariz. Valley Tech. Coll., 1975, U. Ariz. Partner, adminstrv. exec. Finney Co., Bedford, Ohio, 1952—; chmn. exec. com.; chmn. bd. Finney Mfg. Co., 1952—, Bedford Realty Corp., 1952—. Author: The Black Book; Contbr. articles to profl. jours. Trustee, mem. exec. com. Superior Ind. TV Service Fund; mem. Heritage Found., Washington; sustaining mem. G.O.P. Fund. Decorated knight Royal Order Rosarians; recipient Bernon Humanitarian award, 1969; Friends of Service awards (13); Community Improvement award City of Cleve., 1976; hon. Ky. col.; 25 Yr. Recognition award City of Toledo; Man of Year award in electronics industry, 1978; recipient (with wife) Second Wind Hall of Fame award for accomplishments in name of goodwill, humanity and charity; named to Electronic Hall of Fame, 1969; Silver Beaver award Boy Scouts Am.; 50 Yr. Masonic award. Hon. mem. Tex. Navy.; Mem. All-Industry Electronics Conf. (nat. chmn. speakers bur. 1961—), Electronics Industry Council (chmn.), Nat. Alliance Technicians and Electricians Assns., Nat. Electronics Distbrs. Assn., Technicians Service Assn., Electronic Technicians Guild, Nat. Alliance TV and Electronic Service Assns. (hon. life, chmn. nat. merger com. with Nat. Electronics Assn.), Ariz. Electronic Service Assn. (hon. life), Nat. Electronics Assn. (hon. life mem.), Calif. Electonics Assn. (hon. life mem.), Kans. Electronics Assn. (hon. life mem.), La. Electronics Assn. (hon. life mem.), Va. Electronics Assn. (hon. life mem.), Tex. Electronics Assn., Nat. Heritage Assn. Found., Electronics Industry Assn. (hon. life), Maine Electronics Technicians Assn. (hon. life mem.), Ky. Electronics Technicians Assn. (hon. life mem.), TV Reception Industry Program (nat. chmn.), Order of Turtle, State Electronic Service Assn. Ill. (hon. life mem.), State Electronic Service Assn. Ind. (hon. life mem.), State Electronic Service Assn. Wis. (hon. life mem.), State Electronic Service Assn. Miss. (hon. life mem.), State Electronic Service Assn. Ark. (hon. life mem.), State Electronic Service Assn. Wash. (hon. life mem.), State Electronic Service Assn. N.Y. (hon. life mem.), State Electronic Service Assn. Ga. (hon. life mem.), State Electronic Service Assn. Va. (hon. life mem.). Clubs: Masons, Lake Forest Country, Forest Hills, Rotary of P.R. (hon.). Home: 3111 Monticello Blvd Cleveland Heights OH 44118 Office: 34 W Interstate St Bedford OH 44014 *We can be indifferent and possibly just get by or we can work intelligently and be paid more and more—commensurate with our productivity. Definitely there is no restriction on enthusiasm, ability, and ingenuity. Our children can begin where we leave off—to do more and live better.*

FINNEGAN, CYRIL VINCENT, university dean, zoology educator; b. Dover, N.H., July 17, 1922; emigrated to Can., 1958; s. Cyril Vincent and Kilda C. (McClintock) F.; children: Maureen A., Patrick S., Cathaleen C., Kevin S., Eileen D., Gormlaith R., Michaeleen S., Maired B., Conal E. B.S., Bates Coll., Lewiston, Maine, 1946; M.S., U. Notre Dame, 1948, Ph.D., 1951. From instr. to asst. prof. St. Louis U., 1952-56; asst. prof. U. Notre Dame, South Bend, Ind., 1956-58; from asst. prof. to prof. zoology U. B.C., Vancouver, 1958—, assoc. dean sci., 1972-79, dean sci., 1979—. Contbr. articles to sci. jours. Served to sgt F.A. and C.E. AUS, 1942-45; Natousa, CBI. Postdoctoral research fellow NIH, 1952-53; Killum sr. fellow, 1968-69. Mem. Soc. Devel. Biology, Can. Soc. Cell Biology, Tissue Cultrue Assn., Internat. Soc. Develop. Biology, Sigma Xi. Roman Catholic. Office: Faculty of Science University of British Columbia Vancouver BCCanada V6T 1W5

FINNEGAN, GEORGE BERNARD, JR., lawyer; b. Nevada City, Calif., June 13, 1903; s. George B. and Margaret (Gillespie) F.; m. Elisabeth B. Morgan, Oct. 23, 1926; children—Marcus B., George Bernard III, Dana G.; m. Dorothy J. Conte, Dec. 9, 1978. B.S., U.S. Mil. Acad., 1924; postgrad., George Washington Law Sch., 1926-27; J.D., Fordham U., 1929. Bar: N.Y. bar 1930. Asst. examiner U.S. Patent Office, 1926-27; since practiced in, N.Y.C.; sr. partner Morgan, Finnegan, Pine, Foley & Lee, 1939—. Served with U.S. Army, 1924-26; from maj. to col. AUS, 1942-46. Decorated Legion of Merit; recipient Nat. Patent prize, 1978. Mem. Am. Bar Assn., Am. Judicature Soc., Am., N.Y., N.J. patent law assns., Am. Coll. Trial Lawyers, Assn. Grads. U.S. Mil. Acad., West Point Soc. N.Y., West Point Alumni Found. (bd. dirs.), Newcomen Soc. Clubs: Army-Navy (Washington); Anglers, Marco Polo (N.Y.C.); Bohemian (San Francisco). Co-inventor, licensor Aetna Drivo-Trainer. Home: Cove Pl Mountain Lakes NJ 07046 Office: 345 Park Ave New York NY 10022

FINNEGAN, NEAL FRANCIS, banker; b. Boston, Mar. 28, 1938; s. Neal Francis and Mary Theresa (McNeil) F.; m. Rosemarie A. Eldracher; children: Theresa, Lynn, Neal, Wayne. B.S., Northeastern U., 1961; M.B.A., Babson Coll., 1969. With Shawmut Bank of Boston, 1961-80, sr. v.p. OIC comml. banking, 1977-80; pres., chief exec. officer Worcester Bancorp Inc., Mass., 1980-82; chmn., chief exec. officer Worcester County Nat. Bank, Worcester, 1980-82; sr. exec. v.p. Shawmut Corp., Boston, 1982-83, vice-chmn., 1983—, dir., 1982—; exec. v.p. Shawmut Bank of Boston, N.A., 1983—; dir. Mass. Bus. Devel. Corp.; pres., dir. FSCC Corp. Trustee St. Vincent's Hosp., Worcester, 1980—. Mem. Am. Bankers Assn. Office: 1 Federal St Boston MA 02211

FINNEGAN, RICHARD ALLEN, chemist, educator; b. Mpls., Feb. 5, 1932; s. James Clair and Grace Margaret (Mullin) F.; m. Marchand M. Hall, Aug. 4, 1956 (div. Feb. 1970); children: Catherine Marie, Sarah Grace, Elizabeth Hope; m. Adria M. Rossman Campbell, Feb. 3, 1974 (div. June 1980). B.A., U. Minn., 1953; Ph.D., MIT, 1957; postdoctoral fellow, U. Chgo., 1957-58, Wayne State U., 1958-59. Asst. prof. chemistry Ohio State U., 1959-63; assoc. prof. medicinal chemistry SUNY, Buffalo, 1963-66, prof., 1966—. Contbr. articles to profl. jours. Del. Nat. Conv. Socialist Party U.S.A., 1966. Research grantee The Research Corp., Petroleum Research Fund, NIH, NSF. Fellow Am. Inst. Chemists; mem. Am. Chem. Soc., Chem. Soc. (London), AAAS, Organic Chemists Club Western N.Y. (chmn. 1964-65), Am. Pharm. Assn., Acad. Pharm. Scis., N.Y. Acad. Scis., AAUP, Am. Soc. Pharmacognosy, Sigma Xi, Phi Lambda Upsilon, Alpha Chi Sigma. Club: Bison City Yacht. Home: 89 Vernon Pl Buffalo NY 14214

FINNEGAN, RITA MADONNA, association executive; b. Jefferson, Iowa, Feb. 10, 1933; d. Roger James and Ella Modonna (Piepel) F. Ph.B., Northwestern U., 1963, M.A. in Edn., 1965. Registered records adminstr. Dir. med. records Mercy Hosp., Des Moines, 1956-58; asst. dir. med. records U. Ill. Hosp., Chgo., 1958-62, dir. med. records, 1962-72; dir. curriculum in med. records adminstrn. U. Ill., Chgo., 1965-82; exec. dir. Am. Med. Records Assn., Chgo., 1982—; cons. Riyadh Mil. Hosp., Saudi Arabia, 1980-81, Geisinger Med. Ctr., Danville, Pa., 1979, Northwestern U. Med. Assn., Chgo., 1979, St. Joseph Hosp., 1979. Author: Data Quality and DRGs, 1983; handbooks, 1979; editor: jours. Topics in Med. Record Adminstrn., 1979—. Mem. Am. Med. Record Assn. (dir. 1971-74, pres. 1975-76), Ill. Med. Record Assn. (disting. mem.; pres. 1967-68), Internat. Fedn. Health Record Orgns. (U.S. rep. 1976-80). Democrat. Roman Catholic. Home: 2970 N Lake Shore Dr Chicago IL 60657 Office: Am Med Record Assn 875 N Michigan Ave Chicago IL 60611

FINNEGAN, SARA ANNE, publisher; b. Balt., Aug. 1, 1939; d. Lawrence Winfield and Rosina Elva (Huber) F.; m. Isaac C. Lycett, Jr., Aug. 31, 1974. B.A., Sweet Briar Coll., 1961; M.L.A., Johns Hopkins U., 1965. Tchr., chmn. history dept. Hannah More Acad., Reisterstown, Md., 1961-65; redactor Williams & Wilkins Co., Balt., 1965-66, asst. head redactory, 1966-71, editor book div., 1971-75, assoc. editor-in-chief, 1975-77, v.p., editor-in-chief, 1977-81, pres. book div., 1981—; editor Kalends, 1973-78; exec. sponsor jour. Histochemistry and Cytochemistry, 1973-77. Trustee St. Timothy's Sch., Stevenson, Md., 1974-83, sec. bd., 1974-81; adv. bd. Balt. Ind. Schs. Scholarship Fund, 1977-81; adv. council grad. study Coll. Notre Dame of Md., 1983. Mem. Assn. Am. Pubs. Republican. Lutheran. Office: Williams & Wilkins Co 428 E Preston St Baltimore MD 21202

FINNEGAN, THOMAS JOSEPH, JR., lawyer, ins. exec.; b. Wilkes-Barre, Pa., Aug. 14, 1935; s. Thomas Joseph and Marianne Jerome (Elligette) F.; m. Gail A. Ryan, Sept. 23, 1961; children—Kathleen, Daniel, Susan, Mark, Martha, Paul. A.B., Fordham U., 1957; J.D., Columbia U., 1961. Bar: N.Y. bar 1961, Mass. bar 1967. Asso. firm Townsend & Lewis, N.Y.C., 1961-66; asst. counsel Mass. Mut. Life Ins. Co., Springfield, 1966-67, asso. counsel, 1967-71, counsel, 1971-72, sec., asst. gen. counsel, 1972-80, 2d v.p., sec., asso. gen. counsel, 1980—; sec. MML Investment Co., Inc., Springfield, 1971-76. Served with AUS, 1958. Mem. Am. Bar Assn. Roman Catholic. Home: 5 Wright Pl Wilbraham MA 01095 Office: 1295 State St Springfield MA 01111

FINNELL, MICHAEL HARTMAN, oil company executive; b. Los Angeles, Jan. 27, 1927; s. Jules Bertram and Maribel Hartman (Schumacher) F.; m. Grace Vogel, Sept. 11, 1954 (div. June 1964); children: Lesley Finnell Blanchard, Carter Hartman, Hunter Vogel. Student, Asheville (N.C.) Sch., 1939-44; B.A., U. Toronto, 1950; M.B.A., Harvard, 1952; H.H.D. (hon.), Capital U., Columbus, Ohio, 1980. Sec.-treas. Triad Oil Co. Ltd., 1952-62, v.p., dir., 1962-65; pres. Devon-Palmer Oils Ltd., 1963-65; v.p. Elwill Devel. Ltd., 1966-72; v.p., dir. Canadian Hydrocarbons, Ltd., 1967-71, pres., 1971-72, Tamarack Corp., 1973—. Regent Capital U., Columbus, Ohio; trustee Columbus Mus. Art. Served with U.S. Mcht. Marine, 1944-46. Mem. Delta Upsilon (v.p. 1949-50). Clubs: Calif. (Los Angeles); Ranchmen's, Calgary Petroleum, Calgary Golf and Country; Anandale Golf (Pasadena, Calif.); La Grulla Gun (Baja, Calif.); Nantucket Yacht (Mass.). Home: 787 S Orange Grove Blvd Pasadena CA 91105 Office: 696 E Colorado Blvd Suite 222 Pasadena CA 91101

FINNEMORE, DOUGLAS KIRBY, educator; b. Cuba, N.Y., Sept. 9, 1934; s. David Jerome and Mildred (Bosworth) F.; m. Faith Romaine Watson, June 16, 1956; children—Martha, Susan, Sara. B.S., Pa. State

U., 1956; M.S., U. Ill., 1958, Ph.D., 1962. Mem. faculty Iowa State U., Ames, 1962—, asso. prof. physics, 1965-68, prof., 1968—, program dir. solid state physics, 1978—; program dir. quantum solids and liquids program NSF, 1976-77. Fellow Am. Phys. Soc.; mem. Sigma Xi. Home: 3312 Oakland St Ames IA 50010

FINNERTY, FRANK AMBROSE, physician; b. Montclair, N.J., Nov. 3, 1923; s. Frank A. and Agnes (Fitzsimmons) F.; m. Frances Martin, July 26, 1975. A.B., Georgetown U., 1943, M.D., 1947. Diplomate: Am. Bd. Internal Medicine. Intern D.C. Gen. Hosp., Washington, 1947-48, Boston City Hosp., 1948-49; research fellow in medicine D.C. Gen. Hosp., 1950-51, chief resident in medicine, 1951-52; research fellow Am. Heart Assn., Washington, 1955-57; practice medicine specializing in internal medicine and cardiovascular disease, Washington, 1955—; established investigator Am. Heart Assn., 1957-62; asst. prof. medicine Georgetown U. Med. Center, Washington, 1958-63, asso. clin. prof. pharmacology, 1963-68, asso. clin. prof. medicine, 1963-68, clin. prof. obstetrics, 1969-72, clin. prof. medicine, 1969-72, 77—, prof. medicine, 1972-76; chief of medicine Columbia Hosp. for Women, 1963-74; clin. prof. medicine George Washington U. Med. Center, 1977—; adj. prof. medicine Catholic U. Grad. Sch. of Nursing, 1975—; dir. Hypertension Center of Washington, 1976—; med. cons. Dept. Corrections, D.C. Jail, 1965-77; mem. Medcom, Inc., Faculty of Medicine, 1974, Task Force of Therapeutics, Southeastern Regional Med. Hypertension Program, 1974-75. Contbr. numerous articles on cardiology and hypertension to med. jours. Bd. dirs. Nat. Kidney Found., Citizens Com. for Treatment of High Blood Pressure. Served with M.C. U.S. Army, 1953-55. Fellow A.C.P., Am. Coll. Cardiology (trustee 1975—), Am. Coll. Angiology; mem. Am. Fedn. Clin. Research, Am. Therapeutic Soc., Am. Coll. Clin. Pharmacology and Therapeutics, Am. Heart Assn., D.C. Heart Assn., D.C. Med. Soc., AMA, So. Med. Assn., Am. Soc. Contemporary Medicine and Surgery, Georgetown U. Alumni Assn. (gov. 1971-75). Office: 1328 G St SE Washington DC 20003

FINNERTY, JEAN CLARE, education educator; b. N.Y.C.; d. John Joseph and Rose Marie (Bonser) F. B.A., Manhattan Coll., 1941; M.A., St. John's U., 1946; Ph.D., Fordham U., 1959. Elem. tch. Cath. schs., Bklyn., 1935-41; secondary tchr. math., Bklyn., 1941-59; grad. adviser elem. and secondary schs., over-all supr. curriculum dir. Rockville Centre, N.Y., 1959-66; prin. St. Agnes Acad. High Sch., College Point, N.Y., 1966-68; asst. supt. Woodcliff Lake (N.J.) Pub. Shcs., 1968-71; adj. prof. Montclair State Coll., 1968-71, Seton Hall U., 1968-71; assoc. prof. Seton Hall U. Grad. Div. Adminstrn. and Supervision, South Orange, N.J., 1971-74, prof., 1974—, acting dept. chmn., 1979-80; cons. several maj. textbook cos. in math. and social studies, 1959-70; instr. math. Manhattan Coll. Extension, 1946-53; instr. and asst. prof. English St. Joseph Coll., 1942-54(summers); dir. in-service math. Molloy Coll., L.I., 1959-66; dir. workshops for adminstrs., 1975—. Co-author series geography lessons, Channel 13 TV, 1960-66; author: spelling books Spell Correctly, 1965, Evaluative Criteria for the Elementary Catholic Schools, 1965; Revolution in Geography, Too, 1963; contbr. articles to profl. jours. Mem. panel Gov.'s Conf. NCCJ, 1959-66; mem. Cath. Interracial Council, Nassau Ecumenical Council, Nassau Community Mental Health Assn., Bklyn. Supt. Schs. Adv. Council, 1959-67; ofcl. observer as rep. for U.S. Cath. schs. Internat. Ednl. Conf., Geneva, 1964. Recipient Woman in Research citation ALA, 1976, Bicentennial Com. citation, 1976. Mem. Nat. Cath. Edn. Assn. (sec. elem. exec. com. 1960-63, chmn. supr. sect. 1966-68, mem. adv. com. 1968—, co-chmn. middle states 1970, exec. com. 1959-65, middle state team 1968), NEA, N.J. Edn. Assn., AAUP (v.p. chpt. 1976-77), Assn. for Supervision and Curriculum Devel., Am. Assn. Sch. Adminstrs. (conv. panelist, speaker), N.J. Assn. Sch. Adminstrs., Internat. Platform Assn., Am. Assn. Ednl. Psychotherapists (assoc.), World Youth Vocat. Edn. Assn. (trustee), N.J. Profs. Ednl. Adminstrn. and Supervision (v.p. 1977-79), Alumni Assn. Seton Hall U. (faculty adv. 1978-80), Phi Delta Kappa (planning com. Montclair State chpt. 1981—), Kappa Delta Pi (exec. com. 1977-79). Office: Seton Hall U South Orange NJ 07079

FINNEY, JOAN MARIE MCINROY, state official; b. Topeka, Feb. 12, 1925; d. Leonard L. and Mary M. (Sands) McInroy; m. Spencer W. Finney, Jr., July 24, 1957; children: Sally, Dick, Mary. B.A., Washburn U., 1974. Sec. Washington and Topeka offices U.S. Senator Frank Carlson, 1953-69; commr. elections, Shawnee County, Kans., 1970-72, adminstrv. asst. to mayor of Topeka, 1973-74; treas. State of Kans., Topeka, 1974—; Candidate for U.S. Ho. of Reps., 1972. Pres. Girls Club of Topeka. Mem. Kans. Women's Polit. Caucus. Topeka Bus. and Profl. Women's Club, Nat. Assn. State Treas.'s (regional v.p.), Sigma Alpha Iota. Catholic. Office: Office of State Treasurer 535 Kansas Topeka KS 66603 *

FINNEY, JOSEPH CLAUDE JEANS, physician, educator, institute executive; b. Urbana, Ill., Mar. 18, 1927; s. Claude Lee and Margaret Ellen (Boillin) F.; m. Mary Littlefield, Jan. 21, 1955; children: Carol, Michael, John, Ellen. B.A., Vanderbilt U., 1946; postgrad., U. Notre Dame, 1947; M.D., Harvard U., 1949, U. Calif. at Berkeley, 1950-51, 52-53; Ph.D., Stanford U., 1959; LL.B., LaSalle U., 1972; postgrad. in law, U. Ky., 1972-75. Bar: U.S. Supreme Ct. 1978; ordained priest, 1969. Med. intern Johns Hopkins Hosp., Balt., 1949-50; resident physician U.S. VA Hosp., Palo Alto, Calif., 1953-56; dir. Champaign County Mental Health Center, 1956-60; chief research Hawaii State Mental Health System, 1960-63; asso. prof. psychiatry U. Ky., 1963-67, prof. ednl. psychology, 1967-77; dir. continuing edn. Am. Inst. Higher Studies, 1977—; pres. Finney Inst. for Study Human Behavior, 1977—; dir. research in psychiatry Loyola U. of Chgo., 1980-83; chief psychiatry U.S. Army Hosp., Ft. Ord, Calif., 1983—; cons. U.S. Dept. Justice, 1967-79, U.S. Social Security Adminstrn., 1967-80; vice chmn. Am. Bar Assn. Liaison Com. Law and Psychiatry, 1973-76, 80-81, chmn., 1976-80; nat. chaplain mems.-at-large Liberal Cath. Ch. in U.S., 1979—; del. Internat. Liberal Cath. Synod, 1976, 81. Author: Culture Change, Mental Health and Poverty, 1969; editorial bd.: Jour. Marriage and Family Counseling, 1974-80, Family Law Quar, 1977-78, Jour. Psychol. Anthropology, 1976—. Del. Libertarian Party Nat. Conv., 1977, 79; sec. Ky. Libertarian Party, 1979-80; nominee Electoral Coll., 1980. Served to lt. (j.g.) USPHS, 1951-53. Recipient research grants NIMH, 1966-68, U.S. Social and Rehab. Services, 1967-70. Fellow Am. Psychiat. Assn., Am. Psychol. Assn., Am. Coll. Legal Medicine, Am. Anthrop. Assn.; mem. Am. Bar Assn., Linguistic Soc. Am., Assn. Research in Nervous and Mental Disease, Soc. Crosscultural Research, Soc. Sci. Study Religion, Religious Research Assn., Polynesian Soc., Soc. Sci. Study of Sex, Am. Assn. Sex Educators, Counselors and Therapists (dir. 1981-83), VFW, Mensa, Phi Beta Kappa. Liberal Catholic. Club: Kiwanis. Inventor, developer computer systems for interpretation psychol. tests. Office: 5623 Lawn Drive Western Springs IL 60558 *I have learned that most of the harm done in the world is done not by obvious bad guys, but by well-meaning people who seek to impose on other people their views of what is right and good. The world would benefit from more tolerance of divergent ways of life, more encouragement of originality.*

FINNEY, PAUL BURNHAM, editor; b. Flushing, N.Y., Oct. 28, 1929; s. Frank Burnham and Eleanor (Axline) F.; m. Joanne Lyman Brown, Dec. 27, 1952 (div. Oct. 1975); children: Christopher L.B., Suzanne P.W.; m. Linda Washburne Menke, Oct. 14, 1978; 1 son, Durham W. Student, Columbia U., 1946; grad. cum laude, Harvard U., 1950. With Bus. Week, N.Y.C., 1950-77, London corr., 1960, asst. mng. editor, 1961-65, mng. editor, 1966-77; exec. editor Fortune, N.Y.C., 1977-80; editorial dir. Internat. Thomson Orgn. Ltd., Oradell, N.J., 1980-83; editor Mgmt. Tech., Internat. Thomson Tech. Thomson Tech. Info., N.Y.C., 1983—; nat. syndicated radio commentator and interviewer; hon. sec. gen. Am. del. Bilderberg Meetings. Author: The Businessman's Guide to Europe, 1965, The Business Week Diary and Travel Planner, 1976; Contbr.: N.Y. Herald Tribune, 1967, Esquire, 1966-68, Travel & Leisure, 1976—. Mem. Citizens Adv. Com. for Transp. Quality, 1968-72; Vice pres., trustee Collegiate Sch., 1966-73. Served as 2d lt. Ordnance Corps U.S. Army, 1951-53. Mem. Council Fgn. Relations, Overseas Press Club (bd. govs.). Clubs: Harvard (N.Y.C.); Sakonnet Golf (Little Compton, R.I.). Home: 139 E 94th St New York NY 10128 Office: 135 W 50th St New York NY 10020

FINNEY, REDMOND CONYNGHAM STEWART, educational administrator; b. Balt., Oct. 19, 1929; s. George G. and Josephine (Stewart) F.; m. Jeannette Sheldon Brown, June 12, 1956; children: Jeannette Sheldon, Redmond Conyngham Stewart, Edward Brown, Katharine Elizabeth Finney. B.A., Princeton U., 1951; M.Ed., Harvard U., 1959; postgrad., Johns Hopkins U., 1959—. With Gilman Sch., Balt., 1954—, faculty adviser discipline and honor, 1963-68, mem. admissions com., 1956-68; dir. Upward Bound, 1967, headmaster, 1968—. Alumni trustee Princeton U., 1969-73; trustee St. Mary's Coll., Md., Park Heights Street Acad.; pres. Md. Athletic Hall of Fame, 1980—; mem. regional adv. bd. NCCJ. Served with USNR, 1951-53; PTO. Named to All-Am. football and lacrosse teams, 1951; named Coach of Year Md. Scholastic Assn., 1966; named to Md. Athletic Hall of Fame, 1970; recipient Brotherhood award NCCJ, 1974. Mem. Nat. Assn. Ind. Schs. (minority affairs com.), Country Day Sch. Headmasters Assn., Headmasters Assn., Phi Delta Kappa. Presbyn. (mem. session). Home: 5407-A Roland Ave Baltimore MD 21210

FINNEY, ROBERT ARTHUR, ins. exec.; b. Princeton, Ind., July 16, 1906; s. Charles M. and Mary (Fuhrer) F.; m. Gertrude Leitzbach, Aug. 12, 1933; children—Ona, Mary, Paul. A.B., Butler U., 1928; postgrad., U. Chgo., 1929-31. Tchr. econs. Allegheny Coll., 1931-34; motor car dealer, Galion, Ohio, 1934-37, breeder Aberdeen-Angus cattle, 1937—; pres., sec., gen. mgr. Humboldt Brick & Tile Co., Kans., 1947-68; pres., dir. Farm & Ranch Life Ins., Wichita, 1968—; dir. Farm & Ranch Fin., Inc., City Nat. Bank, Humboldt Nat. Bank, Humboldt Shale Mining Co., Neosho Valley Oil & Gas Trust Co.; Dir. Structural Clay Products Inst. Mem. Kans. Ho. of Reps., 1961-66; Trustee Coll. of Emporia, 1953—; bd. dirs. Wichita Symphony Soc., 1968—, Wichita Crime Commn., 1973—; pres. Wichita Crime Commn., 1974; mem. Eastborough (Kans.) City Council, 1967—. Mem. U. S. C. of C. (dir., v.p.), Kans. C.of C. (pres.), Humboldt C. of.C (past pres.), Wichita C. of C. (v.p.), Kans. Assn. Pvt. Univs. and Colls. (trustee). Presbyn. Clubs: Rotary (past pres.), Kansas City (Mo.); Wichita Country. Home: 23 Huntington Rd Eastborough Wichita KS 67206

FINNEY, ROSS LEE, composer; b. Wells, Minn., Dec. 23, 1906; s. Ross Lee and Caroline (Mitchell) F.; m. Gretchen Ludke, Sept. 3, 1930; children—Ross Lee, Henry C. Student, U. Minn., 1924-25; B.A., Carleton Coll., 1927, L.H.D., 1957, Harvard U., 1929; student of, Nadia Boulanger, 1928, Alban Berg, 1932, Francesco Malipiero, 1937; Mus.D., New England Conservatory of Music. Prof. music Smith Coll., 1929-48, Mt. Holyoke Coll., 1940-44; chmn. dept. mus. theory Hartt Sch. Music, Hartford, 1941-42, Amherst Coll., 1946-47; dir. Northampton Chamber Orch. Composer in residence, U. Mich., 1948-74; emeritus, 1974—; composer in residence, Am. Acad. in Rome, 1960; Composer: Piano Sonata, 1933, First String Quartet, 1935, Second String Quartet, 1936, Piano Trio, 1938, Eight Poems by Archibald MacLeish, 1935-37, Sonata for Viola and Piano, 1937, Bleheris, 1937, Fantasy for Piano, 1939, Third String Quartet, 1940, Slow Piece, 1940, Pole Star for This Year, 1939, Symphony Communique, 1942, Third Piano Sonata, 1942, Hymn, Fuguing and Holiday, 1943, Duo for Violin and Piano, 1944, Pilgrim Psalms, 1945, Fourth Piano Sonata, 1945, Poor Richard, 1946, Nostalgic Waltzes, 1947, 4th String Quartet, 1947, Six Spherical Madrigals, 1947, Violin Concerto, 1933-47, Three Love Songs, 1948, Piano Quartet, 1948, Piano Concerto, 1948, 5th String Quartet, 1948, 2d Sonata for Cello and Piano, 1950, 6th String Quartet, 1950, Sonata for Violin and Piano, 1951, 36 Songs; chamber music, 1952, Immortal Autumn, 1952, Variation for Piano, 1952, Piano Quintet, 2d Sonata for Viola and Piano, 3d Sonata for Violin and Piano, 1953, The Express; song Piano Trio, 1954, 7th String Quartet, Inventions for Piano, Variations for Orchestra, Fantasy for Solo Cello, all 1957, Fantasy for solo violin, command Yehudi Menuhin, String Quintet, commd. by Coolidge Found., all 1958, 2d Symphony, commd. by Koussevitsky Found., Edge of Shadow, commd. by Grinnell Coll., 1959, 8th String Quartet, commd. by U. Ala., 3d Symphony, 1960, 2d Piano Quintet, commd. by U. S.C., 1961, Still are New Worlds, May Festival, Ann Arbor, 1962, Sonata quasi una fantasia, Quincy (Ill.) Art Festival, 1961, Three Pieces for Strings, Winds, Percusion and Tape Recorder, 1962, Divertimento, 1963, Divertissement, commd. by Bowdoin Coll., 1964, Three Studies in Fours, commd. by Poznon Ensemble, 1965, Concerto for Percussion and Orch, commd. by Carleton Coll., 1965, Nun's Priest's Tale, commd. by Dartmouth Coll., 1965, The Martyr's Elegy, commd. U. Mich. Sesquicentennial, 1966, Symphony Concertante, commd. by Kansas City Philharmonic, 1967, Organ Fantasies, 1967, 32 Piano Games, 1968, 2d Concerto for Piano and Orch, 1968, The Remorseless Rush of Time, for Chorus and 13 Instruments, commd. Wis. State U., 1969, Summer in Valley City, for Concert Band, commd. U. Mich. Band, 1969, 24 Inventions for Piano, 1970, 2 Acts for 3 Players; clarinet, percussion and piano, commd. G. LaBlanc Corp., 1970, Landscapes Remembered, 1971, Spaces; for large orch., commd. N.D. Council Arts, 1971, Symphony No. 4, commd. for Balt. Symphony Orch., 1972, 2d Concerto for Violin and Orch, 1973, 2 Ballades for Flutes and Piano, 1973, Variations on a Memory, 1975, 7 Easy Pieces for Percussion, 1975, Narrative for Cello and Orch, 1975, Concerto for String, 1976, Skating on the Sheyenne for Concert Band, commd. by Bklyn. Coll., 1977, Earthrise for Chorus, Soli and Orch, commd. by U. Mich. Sch. Music Centennial, 1978, others.; Author: The Game of Harmony, 1947; editor-in-chief: Smith Coll. Music Archives, 1935-48; edited, for same: XII Sonatas for Violin and Figures Bass, by Francesco Geminiani, 1935; Editor, Valley Music Press. Chief Paris office Interdeptl. com. OSS, 1944-45. Recipient Purple Heart, Certificate of Merit; Conn. Valley prize, 1935; Boston Symphony award, 1955; Rockefeller grant, 1956; Acad. Arts and Letters award, 1956; Brandeis Creative Arts award, 1967; Johnson Found. fellow, 1927; Pulitzer fellow; Guggenheim fellow, 1939, 47. Mem. Am. Musicol. Soc., Nat. Inst. Arts and Letters, Am. Acad. Arts and Scis., Phi Beta Kappa, Pi Kappa Lambda, Phi Mu Alpha. Home: 2015 Geddes Ann Arbor MI 48104 Office: Sch Music: U Mich Ann Arbor MI 48109

FINNIE, IAIN, mechanical engineer, educator; b. Hong Kong, July 18, 1928; s. John and Jessie Ferguson (Mackenzie) F.; m. Joan Elizabeth Roth, July 28, 1969; 1 dau., Shauna. B.S. with honors, U. Glasgow, 1949; M.S., MIT, 1951, M.E., 1952, Sc.D., 1954; D.Sc. (hon.), U. Glasgow, 1974. With Shell Devel. Co., 1954-61, engr., to 1961; mem. faculty dept. mech. engring. U. Calif., Berkeley, 1961—, prof., 1963—; vis. prof. Cath. U. Chile, 1965, Ecole Polytechnique, Lausanne, Switzerland, 1976. Author: Creep of Engineering Materials, 1959; contbr. articles to profl. jours. Guggenheim Found. fellow, 1967-68. Fellow Brit. Inst. Mech. Engrs.; mem. Nat. Acad. Engring., ASME (hon.; Nadai award 1982), Soc. Exptl. Stress Analysis. Home: 2901 Avalon Ave Berkeley CA 94705 Office: 6187 Etcheverry Univ Calif Berkeley CA 94720

FINNIGAN, JOSEPH TOWNSEND, public relations executive; b. Springfield, Ill., Aug. 26, 1944; s. Joseph;; s. Thomas and Mary Frances (McCarthy) F.; m. Kathleen Burke, July 2, 1966; children: Matthew, Brendan, Patrick. A.B., Marquette U., 1966. With Fleishman-Hillard, 1972—, v.p., 1975-77, partner, 1975—, exec. v.p., St. Louis, 1977—. Mem. Sigma Delta Chi. Roman Catholic. Clubs: Sunset Country, St. Louis Press. Home: 12415 Ballas Trails Dr Des Peres MO 63122 Office: 1 Memorial Dr Saint Louis MO 63102

FINNMAN, PAUL GORDON, hospital administrator, physician, educator; b. Chgo., Apr. 15, 1917; s. Emil I. and Martha C. (Nelson) F.; m. Esther Louise Anderson, Dec. 4, 1943; children: David, Daniel, Douglas, Diane. A.B., Augustana Coll., Rock Island, Ill., 1939. Bus. mgr., asst. treas. Immanuel Med. Center, Omaha, 1940-53; adminstr. North Platte (Nebr.) Meml. Hosp., 1953-63, Loveland (Colo.) Meml. Hosp., 1963—; faculty preventive medicine U. Colo., Boulder, 1971—; now dir. devel. and community relations McKee Med. Center, Loveland, Colo.; cons. Luth. Hosps. and Homes Soc., Fargo, ND. Composer: Augustana Coll. alma mater, 1938. Bd. dirs. Larimer County (Colo.) Community Health Assn., 1973—, Larimer County Comprehensive Health Planning Assn., 1973—; chmn. planning and devel. sect. Protestant Health and Welfare Assembly, Chgo., 1981-82. Served with U.S. Army, 1942-46. Fellow Am. Coll. Hosp. Adminstrs.; mem. Am. Hosp. Assn. (trustee 1971—), Colo. Hosp. Assn., Lutheran Hosp. Assn. (trustee 1972—), Am. Assn. Hosp. Planning, Luth. Hosps. and Homes Soc. Clubs: Elk, Kiwanis, Rotary. Home: 1017 Shortleaf Ct Loveland CO 80537 Office: Luth Hosps and Homes Soc Box 2087 Fargo ND 58102

FINTEL, NORMAN DALE, college president; b. Monrovia, Calif., Jan. 21, 1925; s. Ernest A.H. and Nora (Koester) F.; m. Jeanette Kosbau, June 30, 1953; children: Peggy, William, Barbara. B.A., Wartburg (Iowa) Coll., 1951; M.A., U. Wis., 1959; Ph.D., U. Minn., 1972. Dir. pub. relations Wartburg Coll., 1951-60; asst. dir., bd. coll. edn. Am. Luth. Ch., 1960-64, exec. dir., 1964-75; pres. Roanoke Coll., Salem, Va., 1975—; dir. First Fed. Savs. & Loan Assn.; Pres. Nat. Luth. Campus Ministry, 1966-75, CLCAC, 1980; ednl. cons., div. ednl. services Luth. Council in U.S., 1966-75. Editor: Evaluating Pub. Relations Results, 1958. Bd. dirs. Community Hosp. Roanoke., Roanoke Mus. Fine Arts, Roanoke Symphony Soc., 1976—, Roanoke YMCA, 1982—. Served with USAAF, 1944-45. Mem. Council Ind. Colls. Va. (pres. 1980). Republican. Lutheran. Address: Roanoke Coll Salem VA 24153

FINUCAN, J(OHN) THOMAS, clergyman, educator; b. Eau Claire, Wis., Feb. 23, 1930; s. Edwin T. and Isabelle Genevieve (McDonald) F. A.B. cum laude, Loras Coll., Dubuque, Iowa, 1952; S.T.B., N.Am. Coll., Rome, 1954, S.T.L., 1956; M.S., U. Wis., 1964, Ph.D. in Ednl. Adminstrn, 1970. Ordained priest Roman Catholic Ch., 1955; asst. pastor St. Mary's Ch., Richland Center, Wis., 1956-58; tchr. Assumption High Sch., Wisconsin Rapids, Wis., 1958-60, prin., 1965-70; tchr., asst. prin., guidance dir. Newman High Sch., Wausau, Wis., 1960-62; asst. to pastor St. Vincent de Paul Parish, Wisconsin Rapids, 1965-70; pres. Viterbo Coll., La Crosse, Wis., 1970-80; pastor, adminstr. St. Stanislaus Parish, Stevens Point, Wis., 1981—; coordinator Regional Sem. Project, Milw., 1980-81; chmn. Wis. State Arts Bd., Madison, 1981—; vis. prof. grad. sch. edn. Loras Coll., Dubuque, Iowa, 1969, 70; bd. dirs. Viterbo Coll., 1970—, St. Mary's Coll., Winona, Minn., Lakeland Coll., Sheboygan, Wis., 1980—; vis. lectr., faculty mem., cons., evaluator colls. and high schs. Bd. dirs.: Times Review Newspaper, 1979—; contbr.: articles to publs. including Wis. Adminstr. Bd. dirs. Bethany-St. Joseph Nursing Home, 1976-80; mem. Gov.'s Task Force Dept. Natural Resources, 1979-80, Gov.'s Commn. on Cable TV, 1972-73; dist. chmn. NCCJ, 1972-74, Wis. Heart Assn., 1972-73; bd. dirs. Community Concert Assn., Wausau, 1960-62 bd. dirs. Community Concert Assn., Wisconsin Rapids, 1958-60 bd. dirs. Community Concert Assn., La Crosse, 1970-78; dist. chmn. Muscular Dystrophy Assn., 1973; bd. dirs. Greater La Crosse C. of C., 1972-74. Recipient Mother Seton award Lourdes Acad., Oshkosh, 1977; pres.'s award for community service La Crosse C. of C., 1979. Mem. Nat. Assn. Ind. Colls. and Univs., Nat. Cath. Edn. Assn., Council for Advancement of Small Colls. (dir. 1976-79), Wis. Assn. Ind. Colls. and Univs. (pres. 1977-79), Wis. Found. Ind. Colls., Wis. Assn. Higher Edn. (pres. 1974-78), Blue Key (hon.), Phi Delta Kappa. Clubs: K.C., Rotary. Address: St Stanislaus Church 838 Fremont St Stavens Point WI 54481

FINZI, JOHN CHARLES, library exec.; b. Campiglia Marittima, Italy, Mar. 27, 1920; came to U.S., 1941, naturalized, 1948; s. Otello and Gina (Pirani) F. Student, U. Rome, 1937-38; B.A. with highest honors (Univ. fellow), UCLA, 1944; M.A. with highest honors in Brit. History (Univ. fellow), UCLA, 1945, postgrad., 1945-50; M.L.S., U. Calif., Berkeley, 1957. Teaching asst. in English history UCLA, 1947-50; bibliographer William Andrews Clark Meml. Library, 1951-57; with Library of Congress, Washington, 1957—; dir. Public Law 480 Programs for South Asia, New Delhi, 1962-64, coordinator for devel. and orgn. of collections, Washington, 1964-71, asst. dir. library resources, reference dept., 1971-78, dir. collections devel. office, 1978—; cons. Nat. Central Library, Florence, Italy, 1967. Author: Oscar Wilde and His Literary Circle: A Catalog of Manuscripts and Letters in the William Andrews Clark Memorial Library, 1957, Report of a Survey of the National Central Library, Florence, 1968; contbr. articles to profl. jours. Recipient Meritorious Service award Library of Congress, 1959, 1962, Superior Service award, 1979. Mem. Am. Anthrop. Assn., Assn. Asian Studies, Am. Hist. Assn., ALA, Indian Library Assn., Phi Beta Kappa, Pi Gamma Mu. Home: 2700 Virginia Ave NW Washington DC 20037 Office: Library Congress Washington DC 20540

FIORATO, HUGO, conductor; b. N.Y.C., Aug. 28, 1914; s. Noe and Anna (Kress) F.; m. Joelyn Littauer; children—James, Jan. Student, Profl. Children's Sch., McBurney Tchrs. Coll., Damroch Sch. Music, Nat. Orchl. Assn., Soc. Applied Music. Past mem. faculty conducting and chamber music Columbia U. Tchrs. Coll., Sarah Lawrence Coll. Founder, violinist, sta. WQXR, Quartet, 1945; condr., N.Y.C. Ballet, 1955—, Boston Ballet, 1968, Washington Nat. Ballet, 1963; condr., mus. dir., L.I. Symphony, 1980—. Clubs: Fairfield County Hunt, Pequot Yacht, Devon Yacht. Home: 459 Hulls Hwy Southport CT 06490 Office: NY State Theatre Lincoln Center New York NY 10023

FIORE, JOSEPH ALBERT, artist; b. Cleve., Feb. 3, 1925; s. Salvatore Emmanuel and Gemma Marie (Cominelli) F.; m. Mary Falconer Fitton, Oct. 10, 1952; children—Thomas, Susanna. Student, Black Mountain Coll., 1946-48, 49, San Francisco Sch. Art Inst., 1948-49. Instr. painting, drawing Black Mountain (N.C.) Coll., 1949-56, chmn. art dept., 1951-56; free lance designer, N.Y.C., 1958-61; instr. painting Phila. Coll. Art, 1962-70, Md. Inst. Coll. Art, Balt., 1970-75; instr. landscape painting Nat. Acad. Design, N.Y.C., 1979, Parson's Sch. Design Summer Program, Dordogne, France, 1980; vis. artist-critic Artists for Environment Found., Walpack Center, N.J., 1972—. Exhibited one-man shows, Staempfli Gallery, N.Y.C., 1960, Robert Schoelkopf Gallery, N.Y.C., 1965, 69, Green Mountain Gallery, N.Y.C., 1973, John Bernard Myers Gallery, N.Y.C., 1974, Fischbach

Gallery, N.Y.C., 1977, 81, group shows include, Stable Gallery, N.Y.C., 1954, 55, Whitney Mus. Am. Art, 1959, U. Ill., Urbana, 1961, Am. Fedn. Art, Am. Acad. Arts and Letters, N.Y.C., 1981, Jersey City Mus., 1982, Farnsworth Mus., Rockland, Maine, travelling exhbn., 1964, Corcoran Gallery, Washington, 1975, State Mus., Augusta, 1976, Cape Split Pl., Addison, Maine, 1977, Landmark Gallery, 1981, Artists Choice Mus., 1983; represented in permanent collections, Whitney Mus. Am. Art, N.Y.C., N.C. State Mus. Art, Raleigh, Corcoran Gallery Art, Washington, Colby Art Mus., Waterville, Maine, Weatherspoon Gallery, Greensboro, N.C., Chase Manhattan Collection, N.Y.C. Served with AUS, 1943-46. Recipient 1st prize Met. Young Artists 1st Ann. Nat. Arts Club, N.Y.C., 1958; Artists for Environment Found. residence grantee, 1976; Nettie Marie Jones Fellow Ctr. Music, Drama and Art, Lake Placid, N.Y., 1983. Mem. Artists Equity Assn. N.Y., Nat. Audubon Soc., Nature Conservancy, Maine Audubon Soc., Natural Resources Council Maine. Home: RFD 1 Jefferson ME 04348 *My only wish is to impart to the painting a life of its own, through the means of color (light) and form, nurtured by the vast panorama of previous art from the caves to the present moment, by the infinitude of natural phenomena, and by the ferment of the imagination. If the work of art succeeds, it survives the vicissitudes of fashion.*

FIORENZA, JOSEPH FRANCIS, financial exec.; b. Bklyn., Dec. 16, 1921; s. Dominic and Concetta (Chiusano) F.; m. Mary J. Girimonti, Nov. 22, 1958; children—Stephanie, Joseph Francis. B.B.A., Coll. City N.Y., 1947. Jr. accountant McArdle & McArdle, N.Y.C., 1947-48; overseas resident controller Raymond Internat., Inc., Venezuela, Guatemala, France, Thailand, Brazil and Liberia, 1948-58, accounting mgr., N.Y.C., 1958-62, tax mgr., 1962-64, asst. treas., controller, 1965-68, treas., Houston, 1969-74, v.p., 1974—. Served with AUS, 1942-45; ETO. Decorated Bronze Star, Purple Heart with oak leaf cluster. Mem. Houston Soc. Fin. Analysts, Nat. Investor Relations Inst., 773d Tank Destroyer Bn. Assn. Home: 10502 Jaycreek Dr Houston TX 77070 Office: 1225 Galleria Towers E Houston TX 77027

FIORI, PAMELA ANNE, editor; b. Newark, Feb. 26, 1944; d. Edward A. and Rita Marie (Rascati) F.; m. Colton Givner. B.A. cum laude, Jersey City State Coll., 1966. Tchr. English Gov. Livingston High Sch., Berkeley Heights, N.J., 1966-67; assoc. editor Holiday Mag., N.Y.C., 1968-71, Travel and Leisure Mag., 1971-74, sr. editor, 1974-75, editor-in-chief, 1975-80; editor-in-chief, exec. v.p. Am. Express Pub. Corp. (Travel and Leisure/Food and Wine), 1980—. Contbr. articles to periodicals; columnist: Window Seat, 1976—. Named an Outstanding Young Woman of Am., 1976. Mem. Am. Soc. Mag. Editors (exec. com.), N.Y. Travel Writers, Women's Forum. Home: 1725 York Ave New York NY 10028 Office: 1120 Ave of Americas New York NY 10036

FIPPINGER, GRACE J., telephone co. exec.; b. N.Y.C., Nov. 24, 1927; d. Fred Herman and Johanna Rose (Tesio) F. B.A., St. Lawrence U., 1948; LL.D. (hon.), Marymount Manhattan Coll., 1980. Dist. mgr. N.Y. Telephone Co., South Nassau, 1957-65, div. mgr., 1965-71, gen. comml. mgr., Queens, 1971—, Bklyn., 1973—, v.p., sec., treas., 1974—; mem. Manhattan East adv. bd. Mfrs. Hanover Trust Co.; dir. L.I. Trust Co., Conn. Mut. Life Ins., Gulf & Western Industries, Inc., Pfizer, Inc., Greater N.Y. Fund. Former mem. State Manpower Adv. Council; mem. Gov.'s Econ. Devel. Adv. Council; past bd. dirs. Consumer Credit Counseling Service Greater N.Y., 1972—; hon. bd. dirs. Am. Cancer Soc., 1974—, YMCA Greater N.Y., 1975—; former dir. A.R.C., L.I., Nassau County Health and Welfare Council; trustee Citizens Budget Commn., 1974—; former dir. exec. bd. Nassau County Fedn. Republican Women. Named Woman of Year Bus. and Profl. Women Nassau County, 1969; Woman of Achievement Flatbush Bus. and Profl. Women's Assn., 1974; Woman of Year; hon. mem. Soroptimist Club Central Nassau, 1974; recipient John Peter Zenger award Nassau County Press Assn., 1975; honoree Catalyst Inc., 1977, Marymount Coll., 1978, Women's Equity Action League, 1978. Mem. Am. Mgmt. Assn. (exec. com., trustee 1974—), Fin. Execs. Inst., Am. Soc. Corp. Secs., N.Y. Chamber Commerce and Industry (chmn. mems. council 1977-79), L.I. Assn. Clubs: St. Lawrence of L.I., Board Room (N.Y.C.). Home: 31 Meadow Ln Hicksville NY 11801 Office: 1095 Ave of Americas New York NY 10036

FIPPINGER, RONALD ALAN, trade association executive; b. Melrose Park, Ill., June 1, 1942; s. Arthur William and Helen Anna (Hohensee) F.; m. Carol Marie McElroy, June 23, 1962; children: Lisa Marie, Peter Brian. Student, Inst. for Mgmt., Ill. Benedictine Coll., 1972-76. Adminstrv. asst. Nat. Housewares Mfrs. Assn., Chgo., 1966-79, mng. dir., 1979—; v.p. Ill. Inst. Diving, Glen Ellyn, 1960-73. Pres. Lombard Hist. Soc., Ill., 1975-78; dir. Congress of Ill. State Hist. Socs. and Mus., Springfield Ill, 1976, Lombard Hist. Commn., Ill., 1978—. Mem. Profl. Assn. Diving Instrs. (master instr.), Am. Soc. Assn. Execs., Nat. Assn. Expn. Mgrs., Trade Show Bur., Union Des Foires Internationales (Paris). Clubs: Merchants and Mfrs. (dir. 1979—), Housewares (Chgo.); Housewares of N.Y. (N.Y.C.); Internat. Pot and Kettle. Home: 308 Loy St Lombard IL 60148 Office: Nat Housewares Mfrs Assn 1324 Merchandise Mart Chicago IL 60654

FIRCHOW, EVELYN SCHERABON, German educator, author; b. Vienna, Austria; came to U.S., 1951; d. Raimund and Hildegrad (Nicki) Scherabon; m. Peter E. Firchow, 1969; 2 children. B.A., U. Tex., 1956; M.A., U. Mann., 1957; postgrad., U. Munich, 1960-61; Ph.D., Harvard U., 1963. Instr. coll. math. Balmoral Hall Sch., Winnipeg, Man., Can., 1953-55; teaching fellow in German Harvard U., Cambridge, Mass., 1957-58, 61-62; lectr. German U. Md. in Munich, 1961; instr. dept. German U. Wis., Madison, 1962-63, asst. prof., 1963-65; assoc. prof. German U. minn., Mpls., 1965-69; prof. German and Germanic philology U. Minn., Mpls., 1969—; vis. prof. U. Fla., Gainesville, 1973; fellow Inst. for Advanced Studies-U. Edinburgh, 1973; Fulbright research prof., Iceland, 1980; vis. research prof. Nat. Cheng Kung U., Tainan, Taiwan, 1982-83; dir. Cuomputer Clearing-House Project for German and Medieval Scandinavian. Editor: (under name E.S. Coleman) Taylor Stark-Fest-schrift, 1964, (under anme E.S. Coleman) Stimen aus dem Stundenglas, 1968, (under name E.S. Coleman) Studies by Einar Haugen, 1972, Studies for Einar Haugen, 1972, WAs Deutsche Lesen, 1973, Deutung und Bedeutung, 1973; translator: Einhard:Vita Caroli Magni, Das Leben Karis des Grossen, 1968, Einhard: Vita Caroli Magni, The Life of Charlemagne, 1972, Icelandic Short Stories, 1974, (with P.E. Firchow) East German Short Stories, 1979; contbr. articles and book revs. to profl. jours. Fulbright scholar, Tex., 195-52; Alexander von Humboldt-Stiftung fellow, Munich, 1960-61, Tubingen, 1974; Alexander von Humboldt-Stiftung fellow, Marburg, 1981; Fulbright fellow Iceland, 1978; McMilan fellow, 1969, 77; fellow Austrian Govt., 1977, NEH, 1980-81. Mem. MLA (chmn. div. German lit. to 1700 1979-80, vice chmn. pedagogical seminar on Germanic philology 1979-82), Medieval Acad. Am., German-Am. Studies, Internat. Comparative Lit. Assn., Soc. for Advancement Scandinavian Studies (chmn. Germanic philology 1979, text editing 1980), Assn. for Lang. and Linguistic Computing (fopund mem.), Am. Comparative Lit. Assn., Midwest Modern Lang. Assn. (chmn. German I 1965-66, chmn. Scandinavian 1979), Internationale Vereinigung der Germanisten, Am. Assn. Tchrs. German, Modern Humanities Research Assn., AAUP, Internat. Courtly Lit. Soc. Office: Dept German U Minn Minneapolis MN 55455

FIRCHOW, PETER EDGERLY, educator, author; b. Needham, Mass., Dec. 16, 1937; s. Paul Karl August and Marta Loria (Montenegro) F.; m. Evelyn Maria Scherabon Coleman, Sept. 18, 1969; 1 dau., Pamina Maria Scherabon. B.A., Harvard Coll., 1959; postgrad., U. Vienna, Austria, 1959-60; M.A., Harvard U., 1961; Ph.D., U. Wis., 1965. Asst. prof. English U. Mich., 1965-67; asst. prof. English and comparative lit. U. Minn., Mpls., 1967-69, asso. prof., 1960-73, prof., 1973—, chmn. Comparative Lit. Program, 1972-78; fellow Inst. for Advanced Studies in Humanities, Edinburgh, 1977; Disting. vis. prof. Nat. Cheng Kung U., Taiwan, 1982-83. Author: Friedrich Schlegel's Lucinde and the Fragments, 1971, Aldous Huxley, Satirist and Novelist, 1972, The Writer's Place: Interviews on the Literary Situation in Contemporary Britain, 1974, (with E.S. Firchow) East German Short Stories: An Introductory Anthology, 1979; Contbr. articles on modern lit. subjects to profl. jours. Mem. MLA, Midwest Modern Lang. Assn. (v.p. 1977, pres. 1978), Am. Comparative Lit. Assn. Home: 135 Birnamwood Dr Burnsville MN 55337 Office: 210K Lind Hall Dept English U Minn 207 Church St SE Minneapolis MN 55455

FIREMAN, SUSAN, advertising executive; b. Flint, Mich., July 12, 1943; d. Leon and Arleen (Schulman) Shurman; m. Marvin Fireman, May 12, 1972. Student, Phila. Mus. Sch. Art, 1962-63, U. Colo., 1963-65. Prodn. mgr. Film Fair, Los Angeles, 1965-67; TV producer Doyle Dane Bernbach, N.Y.C., 1967-70; dir. TV dept. Smith Greenland, N.Y.C., 1970; sr. producer TV Marschalk Co., N.Y.C., 1970-72; sr. v.p., dir. broadcast-print prodn., mgr. creative dept. Benton & Bowles, N.Y.C., 1972—. Office: Benton & Bowles 909 3d Ave New York NY 10022

FIRESIDE, HARVEY FRANCIS, political scientist; b. Vienna, Austria, Dec. 28, 1929; came to U.S., 1940, naturalized, 1945; s. Norbert and Frances F.; m. Bryna Joan Levenberg, Dec. 12, 1959; children—Leela Ruth, Douglas Leonard, Daniel Ephraim. B.A. magna cum laude, Harvard U., 1952, M.A., 1955; Ph.D., New Sch. Social Research, 1968. Info. specialist AEC, 1957-58; editor Palmerton Publishing Co., N.Y.C., 1959-60, Am. Cyanamid Co., 1960-61, Fgn. Policy Assn., 1961-62; freelance editor, 1962-64; asst. prof. polit. sci. N.Y. Inst. Tech., 1964-68; Charles A. Dana prof. politics Ithaca (N.Y.) Coll., 1968—; cons. in field. Author: Icon and Swastika: The Russian Orthodox Church under Nazi and Soviet Control, 1971, Soviet Psychoprisons, 1979, also articles. Group leader Amnesty Internat., Ithaca, 1973—; co-chmn. Working Group Against Psychiat. Abuse, 1980—, Socialist Studies Com., Ithaca, 1977—; bd. dirs. Tompkins County chpt. ACLU, 1968-71. Served with AUS, 1955-57. Fellow Harvard U. Russian Research Center, summers 1975, 80, Harvard U. Ukrainian Research Inst., summer 1976; grantee N.Y. Dept. Edn., 1965; vis. scholar Russian Inst., Columbia U., 1966. Mem. Am. Polit. Sci. Assn., Am. Assn. Advancement Slavic Studies. Democrat. Jewish. Home: 105 Valentine Pl Ithaca NY 14850 Office: Ithaca Coll Ithaca NY 14850

FIRESTEIN, CHESTER, mgmt. and mktg. cons., banker; b. Los Angeles, July 31, 1930. B.S., U. Calif. at Los Angeles, 1952, M.B.A., 1953. C.P.A., 1954. With Max Factor & Co., Hollywood, Calif., 1955-75, exec. v.p., 1968-73, pres., 1973-75, CLF Assos., 1976—; chmn. bd. First Beverly Bank, 1980—; dir. Neutrogena Corp. Treas. Jewish Fedn.-Council Greater Los Angeles, 1972, v.p., 1973-75, 77-81; gen. campaign chmn. United Jewish Welfare Fund Greater Los Angeles, 1971, 72; asso. chmn. Central Los Angeles region United Crusade, 1975-76; adv. bd. Concern Found. Cancer Research; mem. pres.'s council Brandeis U.; bd. govs. Cedars-Sinai Med. Center; mem. Beverly Hills Traffic and Parking Commn., 1977—, chmn., 1979-80. Recipient Robert Greenberg leadership award, 1961. Mem. Am. Inst. C.P.A.'s, Calif. Soc. C.P.A.'s, Acad. Motion Picture Arts and Scis. (asso.), Zeta Beta Tau, Beta Gamma Sigma (Dir.'s table). Office: 9777 Wilshire Blvd Beverly Hills CA 90212

FIRESTONE, BERNARD, holding co. exec.; b. N.Y.C., May 1, 1918; s. Martin and Kate (Chariton) F.; m. Sylvia Zussin, Dec. 24, 1939 (dec.); children—Franklin Joseph, Frances Katherine, Bethann, Mellisa Jan, Wendy Elyse; m. Bettie Kaplan, Apr. 2, 1961. B.S., Purdue U., 1939; M.A., Loyola U., Chgo., 1948. With Chgo. & Northwestern R.R. Co., 1939-68, treas., 1962-68; v.p., treas. Northwest Industries, Inc., Chgo., 1968—. Served with USN, 1944-46. Club: Union League. Home: 1240 Park Ave Highland Park IL 60035 Office: Northwest Industries Inc 6300 Sears Tower Chicago IL 60606

FIRESTONE, GEORGE, state official; b. N.Y.C., May 13, 1931; m. Nola A. Nissenson, Aug. 10, 1980. Ins. broker, 1952-61; with Gray Security Service, Miami, Fla., 1961-72; sec.-treas. Investco, Inc., Miami, 1972—; mem. Fla. Ho. of Reps., 1966-72, chmn. com. house adminstrn. and conduct, 1971-73; mem. Fla. Senate, 1972-78; chmn. legis. auditing and legis. mgmt. coms., vice chmn. rules com.; co-chmn. Fla. Energy Com., 1973-74; chmn. Dade County Personnel Adv. Bd., 1962-64; sec. of state Fla., Miami, 1979—; past mem. Miami Econ. Adv. Bd. Served with AUS, 1948-52. Recipient Good Govt. award Miami Jaycees, 1972; Man of Yr. award Fla. Consular Corps, 1980; Conservationist of Yr. Fla. Audubon Soc., 1980. Mem. Nat. Conf. State Legislators (past pres. com. legis. tng.), Miami Jr. C. of C. (past pres.), N.W. Miami Property Owners Assn. (past pres.), Dade County Council Civic Orgns. (past pres.). Democrat. Club: Tiger Bay (Miami). Office: Office Sec State New Capitol Bldg Monroe St Tallahassee FL 32301

FIRESTONE, MORTON H., mgmt. and fin. cons.; b. Chgo., Feb. 4, 1935; s. William and Lillian (Kliot) F.; m. Roberta (Bobbie) Schwartz, Feb. 3, 1957; children—Jeffrey, Scott, Danny. B.S., U. Calif., Davis, 1957; M.B.A., U. So. Calif., 1971. Vice pres. Security Pacific Nat. Bank, Los Angeles, 1957-77; exec. v.p. fin. and adminstrn., corp. sec. Elixir Industries, Los Angeles, 1977—; pres. Over Nat. Land Co., Los Angeles, 1980—; dir. Robert Burns & Sons, Inc., Logic Evaluation Corp., Data Tech. Corp. Past chmn. Los Angeles-Eilat Sister City Com. Mem. Fin. Execs. Inst., Beta Gamma Sigma. Clubs: Hollywood Optimist (past pres.), West Hollywood Kiwanis (past pres.). Office: PO Box 64706 Los Angeles CA 90064

FIRESTONE, RAYMOND CHRISTY, former rubber company executive; b. Akron, Ohio, Sept. 6, 1908; s. Harvey S. and Idabelle (Smith) F.; m. Laura An Lisk, Aug. 25, 1934 (dec. July, 1960); m. Jane Allen Messler, Apr. 28, 1962; children—Christy An Firestone Gordon-Creed, Judith An Firestone Thiel. A.B., Princeton U., 1933; LL.D., U. Akron, 1957; H.H.D., U. Liberia, 1960. Joined sales dept. Firestone Tire & Rubber Co., 1933, 1934, dist. store supr., Los Angeles, 1934, asst. mgr. Southeastern sales zone, Akron, 1934-35, dist. mgr., Richmond, Va., 1935-36, staff Firestone plant at, Memphis, 1936, pres. subs., 1937-49, dir. parent co., 1942—, v.p. research and devel., 1949-54, exec. v.p., 1954-57, pres., 1957-63, pres., chief exec. officer, 1963-64, chief exec. officer, 1964-74, chmn. exec. com., 1964-76, chmn. bd., 1966-76, ret., 1976. Bd. dirs. 4-H Service Com., 1953-76, v.p., 1958-76; bd. dirs. Le Bonheur Children's Hosp., Inc., Memphis. Served as maj. USAF, 1942-44. Recipient Humanitarian Service award Eleanor Roosevelt Found., 1961, Ohio Gov.'s award, 1964; distinguished fellow Cleve. Clinic Found., 1971; decorated grand band Order Star of Africa, knight grand cross Order of Merit of Italy, 1971. Episcopalian. Clubs: Detroit Athletic (Detroit); Union, Chagrin Valley (Cleve.); Indpls. Athletic; Genesee Valley, Rochester Country (Rochester, N.Y.); Country of N.C., Pinehurst Country (Pinehurst); Portage Country (Akron). Home: Lauray Farms Bath OH 44210

FIRKUSNY, RUDOLF, pianist; b. Napajedla, Czechoslovakia, Feb. 11, 1912; s. Rudolf and Karla (Sindelárová) F.; m. Tatiana Nevolova; children: Véronique, Igor. Student coll., Conservatory of Music, Brno, Praha, 1922-1930. Mem. piano faculty Juilliard Sch., N.Y.C., 1965—. First appeared with, Czech. Philharmonic Orch., 1922; made concert tours, Europe, 1930-39; appeared with, symphony orchs., including N.Y. Philharmonic, Boston, Phila., Chgo., Nat. Detroit, Mpls., Cleve., San Francisco, Los Angeles, Toronto, Montreal; played in recitals in all sects., U.S., S.Am. tours, 1943—, annual tours in, Europe, 1950—, tours of, Australia and Far East, 1959, 67, Japan, 1978, 83; Composer piano concerto (performed in), Praha, Czechoslovakia, piano pieces, songs. Home: Staatsburg NY 12580 also New York NY

FIRLIT, CASIMER FRANCIS, urology educator, urologist; b. Chgo., Dec. 7, 1939; m. Sharon Chwierut; children: Matthew, Michelle. B.S. in Biology, Loyola U., Chgo., 1961, M.S., 1965, M.D., 1965, Ph.D., 1971. Diplomate: Am. Bd. Urology. Intern Mercy Hosp. Med. Center, Chgo.; resident in urology VA Hosp., Hines, Ill., 1970-73, research and edn. assoc., 1970-73, attending urologist, 1973—; attending pediatric urologist Children's Meml. Hosp., Chgo., 1973—; dir. organ preservation VA Hosp., Hines, 1974—, chmn. div. urology, Hines., 1980—, acting surgeon in chief, 1980-83; attending urologist Northwestern Meml. Hosp., Chgo., 1973—, prof. urology, 1980—. Recipient award, Loyola U., 1960, Royal E. Cabell award, 1964, Merk Manual award, 1965. Fellow A.C.S.; mem. Chgo. Urol. Soc., Am. Urol. Assn., Am. Soc. Transplant Surgeons, AMA, Soc. Pediatric Urology, Am. Fedn. Clin. Research. Office: Children's Meml Hosp 2300 Childrens Plaza Chicago IL 60614

FIRMAGE, EDWIN BROWN, lawyer; b. Provo, Utah, Oct. 1, 1935; s. Edwin Raddon and Mary Myrtice (Brown) F.; m. Gloria Paramore, Aug. 15, 1955; children—Edwin James, Miriam Anne, Rebecca (dec.), Sarah Elizabeth, Zina Gloria, Joseph Paramore, Jonathan, David. Student, Brigham Young U., 1954-55, B.S. with highest honors, 1960, M.S., 1962; J.D., U. Chgo., 1963, LL.M., S.J.D., 1964. Bar: Utah bar 1963, U.S. Supreme Ct. bar 1966. Asst. prof. law U. Mo., 1964-66; White House fellow, mem. staff Vice-pres. Hubert Humphrey, 1965-66; asst. prof. U. Utah, 1966-68, asso. prof., 1968-70, prof., 1970—; internat. affairs fellow Council on Fgn. Relations, Geneva, 1970-71; vis. scholar UN, 1970-71; fellow in law and humanities Harvard U. Sch. Law, 1974-75. Author: (with Francis Wormuth) The War Powers. Missionary Ch. of Jesus Christ of Latter-day Saints, U.K., 1956-57; participant Utah's Little Hoover Commn., 1966-70; pres. Utah Opera Co., Salt Lake City, 1976—; Democratic nominee Utah 2d Congl. Dist., 1978. Recipient Univ. research award U. Utah, 1970-71, 74-75, Univ. Disting. Teaching award, 1977; Alumni Disting. Achievement award Brigham Young U., 1978; Nat. Honors scholar U. Chgo., 1960-63; Edwin Hinckley scholar, 1959-60. Mem. Am. Bar Assn., Utah Bar Assn., Am. Soc. Internat. Law (Civil War panel 1959-60), Am. Judicature Soc., White House Fellows Assn., Order of Coif (pres. Utah chpt. 1959-60), Phi Kappa Phi (pres. Utah chpt. 1959-60), Phi Alpha Delta, Pi Sigma Alpha. Home: 2171 Arbor Ln Salt Lake City UT 84117 Office: Dept Law U Utah Salt Lake City UT 84112

FIRMIN, PETER ARTHUR, JR., business educator; b. Meeker, La., Feb. 24, 1924; s. Peter Arthur and Charlotte (Aucoin) F.; m. Jean Cameron Nash, Sept. 3, 1959; children: William C., Renee, Therese, Kathryn, David A., Peter N., Michael C., Sandra. B.S., La. State U., 1943; M.B.A., U. Calif.-Berkeley, 1948; Ph.D., U. Mich., 1957. Instr. St. Mary's Coll., Calif., 1947-49; asst. prof. acctg. Tulane U., New Orleans, 1949-57, asso. prof., 1957-63, prof., 1963-74, W.R. Irby prof. acctg., 1966-74, dean Grad. Sch. Bus. Adminstrn., 1968-74; dean Grad. Sch. Bus. and Pub. Mgmt., also Coll. Bus. Adminstrn., U. Denver, 1974-79, prof., 1979—; asso. prof. Inst. Adminstrn. of Enterprises, U. Aix-Marseille, Aix-en-Provence, France, 1980-81; mem. firm M & A, Denver, 1979—; Mem. Met. New Orleans Goals Found. Council, 1970-71, La. Gov.'s Council Econ. Advisers, 1972-74, Colo. Gov.'s Revenue Estimating Com., 1974-76. Author: (with Hector R. Anton and Hugh D. Grove) Contemporary Issues in Cost Accounting, 1965, 3d edit., 1978, (with others) University Cost Structures and Behavior, 1967. Bd. dirs. Met. Crime Commn., New Orleans, 1971-72, Interracial Council for Bus. Opportunity, 1971-74, Am. Assembly Collegiate Schs. Bus., 1972-75, Met. Area Com., 1973-74, Pub. Affairs Research Council, 1972-74. Ford Found. fellow for study math. for application to bus., 1959-60. Mem. Am. Acctg. Assn. (v.p. 1967-68), Am. Inst. C.P.A.s, Nat. Assn. Accts., Am. Arbitration Assn., Assn. Corp. Growth, Pres. Assn., Fin. Execs. Inst. Republican. Roman Catholic. Home: 5582 W Geddes Pl Littleton CO 80123

FIRMINGER, HARLAN IRWIN, pathologist, educator; b. Mpls., Dec. 31, 1918; s. Harry and Emily (Irwin) F.; m. Jane Ryder Hollings, Sept. 14, 1942; children: Ann Laura Firminger Howard, Carol Jean Firminger Feeney, Barbara Lynn. A.B., Washington U., St. Louis, 1939, M.D., 1943. Diplomate: Am. Bd. Pathology. Intern Barnes Hosp., St. Louis, 1943; resident pathology Mass. Gen. Hosp., Boston, 1946-47; pathologist Nat. Cancer Inst., Bethesda, Md., 1948-51; practice medicine specializing in pathology, Kansas City, Kans., 1951-57, Balt., 1957—; asst. prof., prof. pathology U. Kans., 1951-57; prof., chmn. dept. pathology U. Md., 1957-67, prof. pathology, 1967-75; dir. anatomic pathology Gen. Rose Meml. Hosp., Denver, 1975-76; prof. pathology U. Colo., 1975—; dir. Univs. Asso. for Research and Edn. in Pathology, 1964-71, scientist-asso., 1971-75; mem. sci. adv. bd. Armed Forces Inst. Pathology, 1965-70; mem. com. on pathology div. med. scis. Nat. Acad. Scis.-NRC, 1966-72. Editor: Atlas of Tumor Pathology, 1966-75; editorial adv. com., 1975-83; contbr. articles to profl. jours. Pres. Md. div. Am. Cancer Soc., 1967-68. Served to capt. M.C. AUS, 1943-46. Mem. Am. Assn. Pathologists, Internat. Acad. Pathology, Am. Assn. Cancer Research, Soc. Mayflower Descs. (gov. Md. chpt. 1967-70), Md. Soc. Pathologists (pres. 1969-71), Alpha Omega Alpha. Office: U Colo Med Center 4200 E 9th Ave Denver CO 80262

FIROR, JOHN WILLIAM, physicist, research center director; b. Athens, Ga., Oct. 18, 1927; s. John William and Mary Valentine (Moss) F.; m. Carolyn Merle Jenkins, Sept. 17, 1950 (dec. 1979); children: Daniel William, Katherine Eleanor, James Leonhard, Susan Elizabeth. B.S. with honors, Ga. Inst. Tech., 1949; Ph.D., U. Chgo., 1954. Mem. staff, dept. terrestrial magnetism Carnegie Instn., Washington, 1953-61; dir. high altitude obs. Nat. Center for Atmospheric Research, Boulder, Colo., 1961-68, dir. center, 1968-74, exec. dir. center, 1974-80, dir. advanced study program center, 1980—; vis. prof. astronomy Am. Astron. Soc., 1960-61; vis. prof. Calif. Inst. Tech., 1963; Barnaby lectr. Nat. Soaring Mus., 1982. Trustee Boulder YMCA, pres. bd., 1972-75; trustee Environ. Def. Fund, 1973—, chmn., 1976-80, vice-chmn., 1980—; trustee Internat. Fedn. of Insts. Advanced Study, 1981—; trustee, pres. Colo. Music Festival, 1981—; trustee, mem. exec. com. World Resources Inst., 1982—. Served with C.E. U.S. Army, 1946. Mem. Am. Geophys. Union, Am. Meteoral. Soc., Internat. Astron. Union, Internat. Sci. Radio Union, AAAS (v.p. 1968), Am. Astron. Soc. (chmn. solar physics div. 1970), Soaring Soc. Am. Home: 6138 Simmons Dr Boulder CO 80303 Office: Box 3000 Boulder CO 80307

FIRST, HARRY, legal educator; b. 1945. B.A., U. Pa., 1966, J.D., 1969. Bar: Pa. 1969, N.Y. 1979. Law clk. to justice Supreme Ct. Pa., 1969-70; atty. U.S. Dept. Justice, Washington, 1970-72; asst. prof. U. Toledo Coll. Law, 1972-76; vis. assoc. prof. NYU Law Sch., N.Y.C.,

1976-77, assoc. prof., 1977-79, prof., 1979—. Mem. editorial bd.: Pa. Law Rev. Mem. Pa. Law Rev., Order of Coif, Phi Beta Kappa. Office: NYU Law Sch 40 Washington Sq S New York NY 10012 *

FIRST, JOSEPH MICHAEL, legal and management consultant; b. Phila., Apr. 1, 1906; s. Louis and Sarah (Selig) F.; m. Helen Gross, Dec. 27, 1931; children: Elsa, Abigail First Farber, Jonathan. B.S. in Econs. cum laude, Wharton Sch., U. Pa., 1927, J.D. cum laude (case editor U. Pa. Law Rev. 1929-30), 1930, LL.M. (Gowen fellow 1930-32), 1932, LL.D. h.c., 1980. Bar: Pa. bar 1930. V.p., gen. counsel Triangle Publs., Inc., 1940-75; also dir.; v.p. Triangle Financial, Inc., 1970-75, also dir.; legal, mgmt. cons., 1975—; First pres., hon. chmn. bd. dirs. Albert Einstein Med. Center, 1951—; v.p., sec. Annenberg Sch. Communications, 1958-80, hon. trustee, 1980—; v.p., sec. M.L. Annenberg Found., 1944—; sec., treas. Annenberg Fund, Inc., 1951—. Bd. dirs. Merion Civic Assn., 1951-77, Fedn. Jewish Philanthropies Phila., 1950-80; hon. life trustee Phila. chpt. Am. Friends Hebrew U.; bd. dirs. Phila. chpt. Am. Friends Technion U.; trustee Temple U., 1966-80, hon. life trustee, also mem. exec. com., mem. ednl. policies com., 1968-80; trustee Dropsie Coll., 1950-53; asso. trustee U. Pa., 1968; hon. trustee Akiba Hebrew Acad. Recipient Outstanding Alumnus award McKean Law Club, U. Pa., 1959, alumni award of merit, 1958. Mem. Brandeis Lawyers Soc., ABA, Pa. Bar Assn. (editor quar. 1941-68, emeritus editor 1968—, chmn. publs. com. 1960-67, Distinguished Service award 1961, spl. citation 1968), Phila. Bar Assn., Soc. TV Pioneers, Jewish Publ. Soc. (pres. 1966-69, hon. life trustee), Order of Coif. Jewish (life trustee Temple Har Zion). Club: Scribes. Office: 230 Orchard Way Merion Station PA 19066

FIRST, WESLEY, publishing company executive; b. Erie, Pa., Feb. 18, 1920; s. Orson John and Pearle (Unger) F.; m. Margaret Elizabeth Whittlesey, Apr. 3, 1943 (div. June 1967); children: Karen Lee, Michael; m. Dianne Jones, Dec. 1975 (div. Sept. 1981); m. Suzanne Lavenas, Jan. 9, 1982. Student, U. Mich., 1937-40; B.S., Columbia U., 1958; M.A., New Sch. for Social Research, 1963. Reporter Erie Dispatch, 1943-47, asst. city editor, 1947-48, asst. to editor, 1948-50; with N.Y. World-Telegram and Sun, N.Y.C., 1950-63, successively copyreader, night news editor, 1950-57, asst. mng. editor, 1957-60, mng. editor, 1960-63; prof. journalism Ohio State U., 1963-65; dir. univ. relations Columbia, N.Y.C., 1965-67; asst. to pres. Sarah Lawrence Coll., 1967-68, Juilliard School, N.Y.C., 1968-69; editor Travel Weekly, 1969-76; editor-in-chief Psychology Today, 1976-77; Staff v.p. editorial Ziff-Davis Pub. Co., 1977-82, cons., 1982—; guest lectr. newspaper design and makeup Fordham U.; instr. journalism Finch Coll., N.Y.C.; Rep. to newspaper design and makeup seminar Am. Press Inst., 1957. Editor: Columbia Remembered, University on the Heights. Served with USAAF, 1944-46. Woodrow Wilson Fellow, 1959. Mem. U. Mich., Columbia U. alumni assns., Phi Beta Kappa, Kappa Tau Alpha, Sigma Delta Chi. Clubs: Overseas Press, Silurians. Home: 305 E 86th St Apt 20-R W New York NY 10028

FIRSTENBERG, PAUL BARRY, educational communications company executive; b. N.Y.C., Oct. 3, 1933; s. Murray A. and Lucille P. (Pollard) F.; children: Debra Ann, Douglas Mark; m. Barbara Jousan, Sept. 1, 1980; stepchildren: Juli, Jeff and Jamey Jousan. A.B., Princeton U., 1955; LL.B., Harvard U., 1958. Bar: N.Y. bar 1958. Law clk. to Hon. J.E. Lumbard, U.S. 2d Circuit Ct. Appeals, 1958-59; asso. firm Gilbert, Segall and Young, N.Y.C., 1959-62; with AID, Washington, 1962-66; asst. treas. Standard Oil, Ind., 1967, Atlantic Richfield Oil Co., 1968-70; officer-in-charge program related investments Ford Found., N.Y.C., 1970-72; fin. v.p. Princeton U., 1972-76; exec. v.p., trustee Children's TV Workshop, N.Y.C., 1976-82; pres. Children's Computer Workshop, N.Y.C., 1982—; dir. Vanguard Group Investment Cos.; vis. lectr., mem. bd. advisors Yale U. Sch. Mgmt. Author: (with Burton G. Malkiel) Managing Risk in an Uncertain Era: An Analysis for Endowed Institutions, 1976. Home: 337 Engle St Tenafly NJ 07670 Office: 1 Lincoln Plaza New York NY 10023

FIRTH, EVERETT JOSEPH, timpanist; b. Winchester, Mass., June 2, 1930; s. Everett Emanuel and Rosemary (Scandura) F.; m. Olga Kwasniak, June 22, 1960; children—Kelly Victoria, Tracy Kimberly. Mus.B. with distinction, 1952. Faculty head New Eng. Conservatory, 1950—; mem. faculty Berkshire Music Center, 1956—; pres. Vic Firth Inc. (mfr. custom line of timpani and drum sticks.). Solo timpanist, Boston Symphony Orch., 1952—, Boston Pops Orch.; with, Boston Symphony Chamber Players; Recs. with, RCA Victor, Mercury, Columbia, Cambridge, Deutsche Grammophon. Mem. Phi Kappa Lambda, Phi Mu Alpha Sinfonia. Home: 3 Pine Wood Rd Dover MA 02030 Office: Box 10 Dover MA 02030

FIRTH, ROBERT, judge; b. Harrison, N.J., May 12, 1918; s. Thomas E. and Emily (Thomas) F.; m. Royleen A. Clark, Jan. 20, 1942; children: Robert C., Michael G., Deirdre M. B.A., Ind. U., 1940; LL.B., Harvard U., 1948. Bar: Calif. Partner firm Nichols, Stead, Boileau & Lamb, Pomona, Calif., 1950-67; judge Superior Ct., State of Calif., Los Angeles County, 1967-74; U.S. dist. judge Central Dist. Calif., Los Angeles, 1974-79, sr. U.S. dist. judge, 1980—. Served to lt. comdr. USNR, 1941-45. Office: US Courthouse 312 N Spring St Los Angeles CA 90012 *

FIRTH, ROBERT DALE, office equipment company executive; b. Litchfield, Ill., June 2, 1931; s. Joseph William and Annabelle (Pierard) F.; m. Rosemarie Enrico, Aug. 5, 1954; children: Robert Joseph. B.S., U. Ill., 1953. Regional sales mgr. Xerox Corp., Dallas, 1969-72, pres. Xerox of Can., Ltd., Toronto, Ont., 1972-73, regional gen. mgr., Santa Ana, Calif., 1973-75, v.p. personnel, Stamford, Conn., 1975-78, pres. bus. systems, Rochester, N.Y., 1979-82, sr. v.p., Stamford, Conn., 1982—; dir. Fuji Xerox Co., Ltd., Tokyo. Bd. dirs. Am. Liver Found., Cedar Grove, N.J., 1979—. Served to 1st lt. U.S. Army, 1954-56. Office: 800 Long Ridge Rd Stamford CT 06904

FIRTH, RODERICK, educator; b. Orange, N.J., Jan. 30, 1917; s. Leo Earl and Ida (Lake) F.; m. Maria Lee Goodwin, June 10, 1943; 1 son, Roderick. B.S., Haverford Coll., 1938; M.A., Harvard, 1940, Ph.D., 1943. Instr. philosophy and psychology Coll. William and Mary, 1943-45; instr. to asso. prof. philosophy Swarthmore Coll., 1945-53; asso. prof. philosophy Harvard, 1953-58, prof., 1958—, Alford prof., 1962—, chmn. dept., 1957-63; lectr. Summer Inst. Epistemology, 1972, Am. philosophy, 1975; Cowling prof. Carleton Coll., 1974; Disting. Philosopher lectr. U. Ariz., 1978. Guggenheim fellow, 1952- 53; fellow Am. Council Learned Socs., 1959-60, Center for Advanced Studies Behavioral Scis., 1964-65, 67-68. Mem. Am. Philos. Assn. (pres. Eastern div. 1980), Am. Acad. Arts and Scis., Council for Philos. Studies, Phi Beta Kappa. Mem. Soc. of Friends. Home: 2 Patriots Dr Lexington MA 02173 Office: Harvard University Cambridge MA 02138

FISCH, CHARLES, physician; b. Zolkiew, Poland, May 11, 1921; s. Leon and Janette (Deutscher) F.; m. June Spiegal, May 23, 1943; children—Jonathan, Gary, Bruce. A.B., Ind. U., 1942, M.D., 1944. Diplomate: Am. Bd. Internal Medicine, Am. Bd. Cardiovascular Medicine (mem. 1977—). Intern St. Vincent's Hosp., Indpls., 1945; resident internal medicine VA Hosp., Indpls., 1948-50; fellow gastroenterology Marion County Gen. Hosp., Indpls., 1950-51, fellow cardiology, 1951-53; asst. prof. medicine Ind. U. Med. Sch., 1953-59, asso. prof., 1959-63, prof., 1963—, Distinguished prof., 1975, dir. cardiovascular div., 1963—, dir., 1960—; mem. cardio-renal adv. com. HEW-FDA, 1973-77, 79—; AHA Connor lectr., 1980. Co-editor: Digitalis, 1969; contbr. articles to med. jours.; mem. editorial bd.: Am. Heart Jour, 1967—, Am. Jour. Electrocardiology, 1967—, Coer et Medicine Interne, 1970—, Am. Jour. Medicine, 1973—, Circulation, 1977—, Am. Jour. Cardiology, 1967—; asso. editor, 1977—. Served to capt. M.C. AUS, 1946-48. Fellow ACP, Am. Coll. Cardiology (pres., dir.); mem. Am. Fedn. Clin. Research, Central Soc. Clin. Research, Am. Physiol. Soc., Assn. Univ. Cardiologists, Assn. Am. Physicians. Home: 7901 Morningside Dr Indianapolis IN 46240

FISCH, MAX HAROLD, educator; b. Elma, Wash., Dec. 21, 1900; s. William F. and Bessie J. (Himes) F.; m. Ruth A. Bales, June 12, 1927 (dec. July 1974); children: Emily J. Fisch Maverick, Margaret E. Fisch Karl, William B. A.B., Butler U., 1924; Ph.D., Cornell U., 1930. Instr. philosophy Cornell U., 1926-28; asst. prof. philosophy Western Res. U., 1928-43; curator rare books U.S. Army Med. Library, 1942-45, chief history of medicine div., 1946; prof. philosophy U. Ill. at Urbana, 1946-69, asso. Center Advanced Study, 1961, 62, 63, 67, prof. emeritus, 1969—; vis. prof. State U. N.Y. at Buffalo, 1969-70, U. Fla., 1970-71; vis. univ. prof. Tex. Tech U., 1973-75; prof. philosophy Ind. U.-Purdue U. at Indpls., 1975—; vis. prof. U. Chgo., winter 1955, Keio U., Tokyo, 1958-59; Fulbright research prof. U. Naples, Italy, 1950-51; Matchette lectr. Purdue U., 1956; George Santayana Fellow Harvard University, 1960, honorary research asso. in philosophy, 1966-67; Mem. adminstrv. bd. Internat. Assn. Univs., 1950-55. Mem. adv. bd.: Works of William James, 1973—; Bd. editors: Jour. History Medicine and Allied Scis, 1946-57; gen. editor: Writings of Charles S. Peirce, 1975-83; cons. editor, 1983—; author, editor, translator numerous books and articles. Pres. C.S. Peirce Bicentennial Internat. Congress, 1976, Charles S. Peirce Found., 1977—. Decorated knight Order of Merit Italian Republic, 1976. Mem. Am. Philos. Assn. (chmn. 1956-58, pres. Western div. 1955-56), History Sci. Soc. (council 1951-53, del. Am. Council Learned Socs. 1955-58), Charles S. Peirce Soc. (pres. 1960-61), Semiotic Soc. Am. (v.p. 1977-78, pres. 1978-79); fgn. mem. Nat. Soc. Scis., Letters and Arts, Naples, Italy. Home: 5245 Whisperwood Ln Indianapolis IN 46226

FISCH, ROBERT OTTO, medical educator; b. Budapest, Hungary, June 12, 1925; came to U.S., 1957-65; s. Zoltan and Irene (Manheim) F.; m. Joyce D.E. Gulasch, May 30, 1969; 1 dau., Rebecca A. Med. diploma, U. Budapest, 1951; study art, Acad. Fine Arts, Budapest, 1943, Walker Art Ctr., Mpls., 1968-69, U. Minn., 1969-70, Mpls. Coll. Arts and Design, 1970-76. Gen. practice medicine, Hungary, 1951-55, pub. health officer, 1955; pediatrician Hosp. for Premature Children, Budapest, 1956; intern Christ Hosp., Jersey City, 1957-58; intern pediatrics U. Minn. Hosps., 1958-59, researcher, 1959-60, research fellow, 1961; instr. U. Minn. Sch. Medicine, 1961-63, asst. prof., 1963-72, assoc. prof., 1972-79, prof., 1979—, dir. phonyiketonuria clinic, 1961—, dir. child care clinic, 1972—; Minn. dir. child devel. study, collaborative study of 14 med. univs. of U.S., 1963-75. Contbr. articles to profl. jours.; exhibited art works in various one-man and group shows. Mem. Am. Acad. Pediatrics, Assn. Ambulatory Pediatric Services. Home: 2298 Folwell St Saint Paul MN 55108 Office: Mayo Hosp Univ Minn PO Box 384 Minneapolis MN 55455

FISCH, WILLIAM BALES, lawyer; b. Cleve., May 11, 1936; s. Max Harold and Ruth Alice (Bales) F.; m. Janice Heston McPherson, Sept. 2, 1961; children: Katherine Emily, Stephen McPherson. A.B., Harvard Coll., 1957; LL.B., U. Ill., 1960; M.Comparative Law (univ. fgn. law fellow), U. Chgo., 1962; J.U.D., U. Freiburg, Germany, 1972. Bar: Ill. 1961, Mo. 1982. Asso. firm Kirkland & Ellis, Chgo., 1962-65; asst. prof. law U. N.D., 1965-68, asso. prof., 1968-70, U. Mo., Columbia, 1970-74, prof., 1974—, Isador Loeb prof. law, 1977—. Author: Die Vortailsausgleichung im amerikanischen und deutschen Recht, 1974; bd. editors: Am. Jour. Comparative Law; contbr. articles, revs. to law jours. Alexander von Humboldt-Stiftung research fellow, 1968-69; Fulbright-Hays research scholar, Hamburg, Germany, 1980-81. Mem. Am. Law Inst., Am. Bar Assn., Amintaphil, AAUP. Office: Sch Law U Mo Columbia MO 65211

FISCHBACH, ALLEN DANIEL, business executive; b. N.Y.C., July 26, 1917; s. Henry and Beatrice (Adelman) F.; m. Patricia Cute (div.); 5 children; m. Sheila Gilmore (div.); 1 child. Student, Rensselaer Polytechnic Inst. With Fischbach Corp., N.Y.C., 1939—, vice chmn., chief exec. officer, 1966-82, cons., 1982. Trustee Manhattan Coll. Served with USAAF, 1942-45. Decorated Air Medal. Clubs: Eastpointe Country (Palm Beach Gardens, Fla.); Tamarack Country. Home: 13266 Sand Grouse Ct Palm Beach Gardens FL 33410 Office: 40 Milton Ct Portchester NY 10573

FISCHBACH, EPHRAIM, physicist; b. Bklyn., Mar. 29, 1942; s. Julius L. and Rae L. F.; m. Janie Bernstein, Sept. 12, 1971; children—Jonathan, Jeremy, Michael. A.B., Columbia U., 1963; M.S., U. Pa., 1964, Ph.D., 1967. Research asso. Inst. Theoretical Physics, SUNY, Stony Brook, 1967-69; research asso. Niels Bohr Inst., Copenhagen, 1969-70; asst. prof. physics Purdue U., 1970-74, asso. prof., 1974-78, prof., 1979—; vis. asso. prof. Inst. Theoretical Physics, Stony Brook, 1978-79. Mem. Am. Phys. Soc. Home: 120 Pathway Ln West Lafayette IN 47906 Office: Dept Physics Purdue Univ West Lafayette IN 47907

FISCHEL, DANIEL NORMAN, publishing company executive; b. Bklyn., Apr. 13, 1922; s. Joseph Louis and Liza (Herman) F.; m. Maxine Friedman, May 9, 1943; children: Anne, Jonathan, Lisa. B.A., N.Y. U., 1943. Mng. editor Am. Water Works Assn., N.Y.C., 1946-55; editor Dodge Books, N.Y.C., 1955-61; with McGraw-Hill Book Co., N.Y.C., 1962-78, v.p., gen. mgr. profl. and reference books div., 1970-78; pres. Elsevier North-Holland, Inc., N.Y.C., 1978-81, Gordon & Breach Sci. Pubs., 1982—; pub. cons., 1981—; Mem. exec. com. tech., sci. and med. div. Am. Assn. Pubs., 1972-78, 79-81. Author: Writing and Publishing Your Technical Book, 1959. Served with AUS, 1943-45. Home: 467 Palmer Ave Teaneck NJ 07666 office: 50 W 23rd St New York NY 10010

FISCHEL, DAVID, astrophysicist; b. DuBois, Pa., Sept. 12, 1936; s. Leonard and Elizabeth Mae (Brown) F.; m. Constance Jean Newham, June 11, 1960; children: Valerie Dawn, Walter David, Brenda Jill. Sc.B. in Physics, Brown U., 1958; M.A., Ind. U., 1960, Ph.D. in Astrophysics, 1963. Astrophysicist NASA Ames Research Center, Moffett Field, Calif., 1963-65; astrophysicist Lab. for Astronomy and Solar Physics, NASA Goddard Space Flight Center, Greenbelt, Md., 1965-79, earth resources system scientist, 1979-84; project mgr. Systems and Applied Scis. Corp., 1984—; co-organizer Internat. Conf. in Stellar Pulsation, 1974, 78. Vol. Boy Scouts Am., 1964—, with Balt. Area council, 1975—; chmn. Columbia (Md.) Coop. Ministry Refugee Resettlement Com., 1975-82; elder First Presbyn. Ch. of Howard Country. Mem. Internat. Astron. Union, Assn. Computing Machinery, Soc. Photo-optical Instrumentation Engrs. Research and publs. in field. Office: 5809 Annapolis Rd Hyattsville MD 20784

FISCHEL, EDWARD ELLIOT, physician; b. N.Y.C., July 29, 1920; s. Joseph L. and Lisa (Herman) F.; m. Pauline Dunieff, Dec. 26, 1943; children—Robert, Janet. B.A., Columbia U., 1941, Sc.D. in Medicine, 1948, M.D., 1944. Diplomate: Am. Bd. Internal Medicine. Intern Presbyn. Hosp., N.Y.C., 1944-45, asst. resident medicine, 1945-46; asst. in medicine Columbia U. Coll. Physicians and Surgeons, N.Y.C., 1947-50, asso. medicine, 1950-55, asso. clin. prof. medicine, 1969-72, lectr. medicine, 1972—; practice medicine specializing in internal medicine and rheumatology; asst. physician Presbyn. Hosp., N.Y.C., 1947-55; asso. clin. prof. Albert Einstein Coll. Medicine, Yeshiva U., N.Y.C., 1957-69, prof. medicine, 1972-80, vis. prof., 1980-81; dir. dept. medicine Bronx-Lebanon Hosp. Center, Bronx, N.Y., 1954-80; chief dept. medicine Mt. Sinai Hosp., Hartford, Conn. and prof. medicine U. Conn., 1980-83; chief of staff VA Med. Ctr., Northport, N.Y., 1983—; assoc. prof. medicine SUNY-Stony Brook, 1983—; mem. exec. com. Health Research Council City N.Y., 1966-75, chmn. allergy and infectious disease panel, 1968-75. Fellow A.C.P., N.Y., Acad. Medicine (past v.p., trustee 1972-80), AAAS (past mem. council); mem. Am. Soc. Clin. Investigation, Am. Assn. Immunologists, Am. Rheumatism Assn. (past pres.), Assn. Am. Med. Colls., Infectious Diseases Soc., Harvey Soc., Soc. Exptl. Biology and Medicine, Am. Fedn. Clin. Research, AMA, Bronx County Med. Soc., Am. Heart Assn. (past mem. research com.), N.Y. Tb and Health Assn. (past dir.), Phi Beta Kappa, Alpha Omega Alpha. Office: VA Med Ctr Northport NY 11768

FISCHER, CARL, photographer, artist; b. N.Y.C., May 3, 1924; s. Joseph Albert and Irma (Schwerin) F.; m. Marilyn Wolf, Oct. 30, 1949; children:Kim Alison Fischer Lloyd George, Douglas James, Kenneth Lee. Student, Cooper Union Sch. Art, 1948, B.F.A., 1975, Central Sch. Arts, London, 1952. Designer Columbia Records, 1948, Look mag., 1949-51; asst. art dir. William H. Weintraub & Co., 1952-54; art dir. Sudler & Hennessey, 1954-56, Grey Advt., 1956-58; owner Carl Fischer Photography, Inc., N.Y.C., 1958—, Carl Fischer Prodns., Inc., 1965—; vis. instr. art Cooper Union; TV, film cons. Exhibited, Mus. Modern Art, 1965, Whitney Mus. Am. Art, 1974; represented in permanent collections, Met. Mus. Art, Rose Art Mus., Amherst, Mass.; contbg. editorial photographer: London Observer. Served with AUS, 1942-45; PTO. Fulbright grantee, 1951; Art Dirs. Club N.Y. Gold medal, 1960; Silver medal, 1975; Profl. Achievement citation Cooper Union, 1966; St. Gaudens medal, 1969; Mark Twain Jour. award, 1971. Mem. Dirs. Guild, Art Dirs. Club N.Y., AIGA. Office: 121 E 83d St New York NY 10028

FISCHER, CARL CASTLE, ret. pediatrician, educator; b. Phila., Oct. 13, 1902; s. John Adolph and Millie (Leupold) F.; m. Mae Adelaide Charles, Mar. 7, 1931; children—Elaine Lois (Mrs. Alexander Marshack), Charles Thomas, John William. B.S., Princeton, 1924; M.D., Hahnemann Med. Coll. and Hosp., Phila., 1928, M.A. (hon.), 1938. Intern Hahnemann Hosp., Phila., 1928-29, chief dept. pediatrics, 1945-67, asso. dir. med. affairs, 1967-69; pvt. practice pediatrics, Phila., 1930-58; cons. pediatrician St. Vincent's, Misercordia, St. Lukes and Children's hosps., Phila., Crozer Hosp., Chester, Pa., Meml. Hosp., Pottstown, Pa.; faculty Hahnemann Med. Coll., 1930—, prof. pediatrics, head dept., 1945-67, emeritus prof. pediatrics, 1967—; dir. health service Girard Coll., Phila., 1958-67. Author: The Role of the Physician in Environmental Pediatrics, 1960; editor: The Handicapped Child, 1958; cons. editor: Dorland's Med. Dictionary (Pediatrics), 1973. Vol. physician Project Hope, Natal, Brazil, 1972 vol. physician Project Hope, Ganado, N.Mex., 1973; Chmn. Gov. Pa. Com. Children and Youth, 1956-59; mem. Gov. Pa. Com. Handicapped, 1959-60. Fellow A.M.A., A.C.P.; mem. Am. Acad. Pediatrics (pres. 1961-62), Pa. Heart Assn., Heart Assn. of Southeastern Pa. (dir., past pres.), Phi Chi, Alpha Omega Alpha. Unitarian. Club: Kiwanis (Delray Beach, Fla.). Home: 3351 Spanish Trail Apt B214 Delray Beach FL 33444 *Looking back on my life from the vantage point of retirement, I find my greatest joy in watching the careers and accomplishments of those whom I have had the privilege to teach in the years gone by—medical students, interns, and residents, especially. As these young men and women show evidence of real progress in helping to improve the future for children everywhere, I feel my own efforts on their behalf have been more than repaid.*

FISCHER, CARL HAHN, educator, actuary; b. Newark, Aug. 22, 1903; s. Carl H.H. Fisher and Minnie (Hahn) F.; m. Kathleen Kirkpatrick, Sept. 25, 1925; children: Patrick Carl, Michael John. B.S., Washington U., St. Louis, 1923; M.S., U. Iowa, 1930, Ph.D., 1932. Spl. engr. Am. Steel Foundries, 1923-26; instr. math. Beloit (Wis.) Coll., 1926-29; asst. U. Iowa, 1929-32; instr. U. Minn., 1932-33; spl. research asst. Northwestern Nat. Life Ins. Co., 1933-34; mem. faculty Wayne U., 1934-41, U. Mich., 1941—, prof. ins. and actuarial math., 1950-74, prof. emeritus, 1974—; vis. prof. U. Calif., Berkeley, 1951; prof. U. Hawaii, 1955, Hebrew U., Jerusalem, 1965, 67, Netherlands Sch. Econs., Rotterdam, 1966; dir. summer actuarial program John Hancock Mut. Life Ins. Co., 1959-61, Travelers Ins. Co., 1963; cons., actuary, 1939—. Author: (with P.R. Rider) Mathematics of Investment, 1951, (with W.O. Menge) Mathematics of Life Insurance, 1965, Vesting and Termination Provisions in Private Pension Plans, 1970; contbr. articles to profl. jours. Trustee Ann Arbor Employee Retirement System, 1948-73; actuary Tchrs. Retirement Fund, N.D., 1939-77; cons. Philippine Govt. Service Ins. System, 1956, Social Security System, Philippine Govt., 1956-62, Nat. Social Security and Welfare Corp., Liberia, 1977; mem. Adv. Council Social Security Financing, 1957-58; chmn. study com. mil. retired pay U.S. Senate, 1960-61; mem. Ann Arbor Bd. Edn., 1957-60. Fellow Soc. Actuaries, Conf. Actuaries in Pub. Practice (v.p. 1970-75), Fraternal Actuarial Assn.; mem. Am. Acad. Actuaries, Am. Risk and Ins. Assn., Am. Statis Assn., Math. Assn. Am., Acacia, Sigma Xi, Beta Gamma Sigma. Club: Mason. Home: 1706 Morton Ave Ann Arbor MI 481041 Office: U Mich Grad Sch Bus Adminstrn Ann Arbor MI 48109

FISCHER, CARL ROBERT, health care facility executive; b. Rahway, N.J., Nov. 15, 1939; s. Robert Carlton and Elsie Marie (Wolfarth) F.; m. Lynn Eliane Ekstrand, Mar. 12, 1966; children: Kresten, Leslie, Meredith, Kelly. B.S. in Nursing, Wagner Coll., 1964; M.S., SUNY-Buffalo, 1966; M.P.H., Yale U., 1968. With Yale-New Haven Hosp., 1968-77, assoc. dir., 1975-77; exec. assoc. adminstr. U. Cin. Med. Ctr., 1977-80; exec. dir. clin. programs U. Ark. for Med. Scis., Little Rock, 1980—. Bd. dirs. Luth. Social Services Ark., Little Rock, 1982—; pres. Hillsborough Property Owners Assn., Little Rock, 1983—. Served with USNR, 1957-60. Mem. Am. Coll. Hosp. Adminstrs., Am. Assn. Med. Colls. (rep. to assembley 1981—), Consortium for Study U. Hosps. (sec. 1983), Am. Hosp. Assn., Ark. Hosp. Assn. (bd. dirs. 1982—, pres. Met. Dist. 1982). Republican. Lutheran. Home: 10 Fenchley Ct Little Rock AR 72205 OSffice: U Ark for Med Scis 4301 W Markham St Little Rock AR 72205

FISCHER, DALE ARNOLD, financial executive; b. Chgo., Aug. 26, 1932; s. Arnold W. and Viola G. F.; m. Ruth Floie Gregory, Apr. 11, 1953; children: Scott, Dale Arnold, Bruce, Kenneth, Brian. B.S. with honors, U. Ill., 1954; M.B.A., Northwestern U., 1957. C.P.A. Auditor Peat, Marwick, Mitchell & Co., Chgo., 1954-60; systems analyst IBM, Chgo., 1960-62; asst. controller Wurlitzer Co., Chgo., 1962-64; controller Ventura Savs. & Loan Assn., 1965-66; account mgr. Xerox Corp., 1966-67; chief fin. officer U.S. Filter Corp., Whittier, Calif., 1967-69; corp. controller Volt Tech. Corp., El Segundo, Calif., 1969-77; v.p., treas. Presley Co., Newport Beach, Calif., 1977-80; chief fin. officer Am. Ednl. TV Network, Irvine, Calif. and McLean, Va., 1980—; lectr., instr. Northwestern U., 1958-64. Alderman City of Rolling Meadows, Ill., 1961-63. Mem. Fin. Execs. Inst. (v.p., chmn. memberships Orange County chpt. 1979-80), Am. Inst. C.P.A.s, Calif. Soc. C.P.A.s, Planning Execs. Inst. Lutheran. Home: 24941 Nellie Gail Rd Laguna Hills CA 92653

FISCHER, DAVID CHARLES, government official; b. Sandusky, Ohio, Jan. 21, 1948; s. Edward Henry and Freda (Hansen) F.; m. Katherine Toolson, Jan. 5, 1978; children: Tiffany Ann, Lindsey Diane, Jennifer Lynn. A.A., Hartnell Coll., 1968; B.S. in Polit. Sci., Calif. State Poly. Coll., 1971; J.D., Brigham Young U., 1976. Exec. asst. to Gov. Reagan, mem. public relations firm Deaver & Hannaford, Los Angeles, 1977-80; exec. asst. to Gov. Reagan and dir. advance ops., Los Angeles, 1980; spl. asst. to Pres., White House, Washington, 1981—. Republican. Mormon. Office: West Wing The White House Washington DC 20500

FISCHER, DAVID HACKETT, historian, educator; b. Balt., Dec. 2, 1935; s. John Henry and Norma (Frederick) F.; m. Judith Hummel, Nov. 23, 1960; children: Susan, Anne. A.B., Princeton U., 1958; Ph.D., Johns Hopkins U., 1962. Mem. faculty Brandeis U., Waltham, Mass., 1962—, prof. history, 1970—, Earl Warren prof., 1971—, chmn., 1974-75, 78-81, founder, chmn., 1981-83; vis. lectr. Harvard U., 1964-65; vis. prof. U. Wash., Seattle, 1975; vis. scholar U. Cambridge, Eng., 1976, 78. Author: Revolution of American Conservatism, 1965, Historians Fallacies, 1970, Growing Old in America, 1977, (with Mary Dobson) The Dying Time, 1979, Chronic Inflation, 1981; contbr.: (with James McPherson) Times Atlas of World History, 1978, Studies in Social History of Concord, 1983. Bd. dirs. learning programs Boston Pub. Library, 1974-77; bd. advisors Rockefeller Program in Family History, 1973-78; co-chmn. United Campuses Against Nuclear War, 1982-83. Mem. Am. Hist. Assn., Inst. Early Am. History, Hakluyt Soc., Orgn. Am. Historians, Soc. Am. Historians, Am. Antiquarian Soc. Democrat. Lutheran. Club: Dial. Home: 36 Rich Valley Rd Wayland MA 01778 Office: 415 South St Waltham MA 02154

FISCHER, ERNST OTTO, chemist, educator; b. Munich, Germany, Nov. 10, 1918; s. Karl T. and Valentine (Danzer) F. Diplom, Munich Tech. U., 1949, Dr. rer. nat., 1952, Habilitation, 1954, Dr. rer. nat. h.c., 1972, D.Sc.h.c., 1975, Dr. rer. nat. h.c., 1977, Dr.h.c., 1983. Asso. prof. inorganic chemistry U. Munich, 1957, prof., 1959; prof., dir. inorganic chemistry inst. Munich Inst. Tech., 1964—. Author: (with H. Werner) Metall-pi-Komplexe mit di- und oligoolefischen Liganden, 1963; transl. Complexes with di- and oligo-olefinic Ligands, 1966; Contbr. numerous articles in field to profl. jours. Recipient ann. prize Göttingen Acad. Scis., 1957, Alfred Stock Meml. prize Soc. German Chemists, 1959, Nobel Prize in Chemistry, 1973; Am. Chem. Soc. Centennial fellow, 1976. Mem. Bavarian Acad. Scis., Soc. German Chemists, German Acad. Scis. Leopoldina, Austrian Acad. Scis. (corr.), Accademia Nazionale dei Lincei, Italy (fgn.), Acad. Scis. Göttingen (corr.), Am. Acad. Arts and Scis. (fgn., hon.), Chem. Soc. (hon.). Spl. research in organometallic chemistry: metal pi complexes of arenes, olefins, carbene and carbyne complexes with metals, ferrocene type sandwich compounds, metal carbonyls. Address: 16 Sohnckestrasse Munich Federal Republic of Germany

FISCHER, FLOYD BRAND, educational and management consultant; b. Susquehanna, Pa., May 13, 1916; s. Fred Martin and Laura (Br) F.; m. Naomi Pauline Anderson, July 17, 1937; 1 son, Richard Brand. B.S. in Agrl. and Biol. Chemistry, Pa. State U., 1937; LL.D. (hon.), Lycoming Coll., Williamsport, Pa., 1973. Tech. salesman Wilbur-Suchard Chocolate Co., Lititz, Pa., 1937-38, Am. Chicle Co., N.Y.C., 1938-41; mem. staff continuing edn. div. Pa. State U., 1941-79, dir. continuing edn., 1964-71, v.p. continuing edn., 1971-79; dir. C-Cor Electronics, Inc., 1956—, v.p., 1956-64; dir. Centre Video Corp., 1956-71, v.p., 1956-64; dir. Sci. Systems Inc., 1977—, United Fed. Savs. and Loan Assn., State College, Pa., 1977—; cons. to univs., 1977—; pres. Nat. U. Continuing Edn. Assn., 1971-72; chmn. council extension Nat. Assn. State Univs. and Land Grant Colls., 1978-79. Author articles in field. Treas. Pa. Public TV Commn., 1970-79; Chmn. Centre County (Pa.) Republican Com., 1977-84; mem. adminstrv. bd. St. Paul's United Methodist Ch., State College, 1964—. Recipient citation Pa. Senate and Ho. of Reps., 1979. Mem. Nat. Univ. Continuing Edn. Assn. (Julius M. Nolte award 1978), Nat. Assn. Accts., Pa. Assn. Adult Edn. (Disting. Service award 1973). Clubs: Town and Gown, Elks (State College). Home: 1201 William St State College PA 16801

FISCHER, FRANK ERNEST, utility executive; b. N.Y.C., Dec. 8, 1933; s. Frank Ernest and Marcelle Jeanne (Cailleux) F.; m. Evelyn M. Rynne, Nov. 26, 1966; children: Cathleen, Maureen, Donald. B.E.E., Manhattan Coll., 1955. Registered profl. engr., N.Y., N.J. Chief elec. engr. Consol. Edison Co. N.Y., 1973-78; v.p. engring. and prodn. Orange and Rockland Utilities Inc., Pearl River, N.Y., 1978—; v.p. Rockland Electric Co., Pike County Light & Power Co.; dir. Empire State Electric Energy Research Corp.; U.S. rep. working group metalclad substa. Conf. Internat. Grands Reseaux Electriques a haute tension; adv. com. elec. engring. Manhattan Coll. Author articles in field. Mem. Rockland County Solid Waste Mgmt. Com. Served to capt. USAF, 1955-57. Mem. Electric Power Research Inst., Assn. Edison Illuminating Cos., IEEE, Am. Nuclear Soc., Edison Electric Inst., Edison Engring. Soc. (past pres.), N.Y. Power Pool (planning and operating com.). Clubs: N.Y. Athletic, Westchester Country. Patentee elec. power cable apparatus. Office: 1 Blue Hill Plaza Pearl River NY 10965

FISCHER, GEORGE HERMAN, III, utilities co. exec.; b. Jacksonville, Fla., June 27, 1923; s. George H. and Lucille (Lawson) F.; m. Dorothy Virginia Flory, Dec. 23, 1947; children—George, Cindy Fischer Burwell, Karen Fischer Loignon, David, Susan. LL.B., U. S.C., 1949; LL.M., Duke U., 1950. Bar: S.C. bar 1949. Mem. editorial dept. Lawyers Coop. Pub. Co., Rochester, N.Y., 1950-53; mem. firm Nelson, Mullins & Grier (Attys.), Columbia, S.C., 1953-59; v.p., gen. counsel S.C. Elec. & Gas Co., Columbia, 1959—; dir. Bankers Trust S.C. Campaign chmn. United Community Services, 1968; pres. United Way, 1970. Served with USAAF, 1943-46. Decorated Air medal. Mem. Am., S.C., Richland County, Fed. Power bar assns., Edison Elec. Inst., Mil. Order World Wars, C. of C. (v.p. 1966), Delta Theta Phi. Presbyn. (deacon). Clubs: Kiwanian (pres. Columbia club 1971), Forest Lake Country, Carolina Yacht, Palmetto. Home: 4737 Lockewood Ln Columbia SC 29206 Office: PO Box 764 Columbia SC 29218

FISCHER, HADWIN KEITH, physician; b. Williamsport, Pa., June 6, 1916; s. M. Hadwin and Alice (Gortner) F.; m. Dorothy Steiger, Mar. 11, 1944; children: David H., Ann Fischer Markel, Nancy Fischer Thomason. A.B., Gettysburg Coll., 1939; M.D., Temple U., 1943, M.S., 1949. Diplomate: Am. Bd. Psychiatry, subcert. in psychoanalysis. Intern Williamsport (Pa.) Gen. Hosp., 1943; resident in psychiatry Temple U. Health Scis. Center, 1946-49, with dept. psychiatry, 1949—, asso. prof., 1957-66, clin. prof. psychiatry, 1966—; pvt. practice psychiatry, psychoanalysis, pschosomatic medicine, Phila., 1949—; attending in psychiatry Chestnut Hill Hosp., 1977—; chmn. adv. com. Pa. Mental Health Inc., 1964-72; mem. Pa. State Adv. Com. on Mental Health and Mental Retardation, 1966-79; trustee Eastern Pa. Psychiat. Inst., 1980—, chmn., 1981. Contbr. articles to profl. jours.; Asso. editor: Psychosomatics, 1972—. Mem. Pa. Bd. Pub. Welfare, 1968-80, sec., 1976; cons. Lutheran Home for Orphans and Aged, U.S. Naval Hosp., Phila., Ancora Hosp., Trenton Hosp.; chmn. Pa. Med. Polit. Action Com., 1977-83, Phila. Med. Polit. Action Com., 1978-83. Served to lt. M.C. USNR, 1944-46. Fellow Phila. Psychiat. Soc. (pres. 1965), Phila. Psychoanalytic Soc. (life), Internat. Coll. Psychosomatic Medicine; mem. Pa. Psychiat. Soc. (pres. 1975, chmn. ethics com. 1978—), Am. Coll. Psychoanalysts, Am. Acad. Psychoanalysis, Acad. Psychosomatic Medicine (pres. 1976), Psychoanalytic Soc. (treas. 1964-66), Drs. Golf Assn. Phila (pres. 1971), Am. Psychoanalytic Assn., Am. Acad. Family Physicians (active tchr. 1978—), Med. Club Phila. (pres. 1976), Philadelphia County Med. Soc. (sec. 1983), Am. Med. Golf Assn. (pres. 1971), Phi Gamma Delta, Phi Chi. Lutheran. Clubs: Sci. and Art Germatown, Phila. Cricket, Union League (Phila.); Seaview Country. Home: 3037 W Queen Ln Philadelphia PA 19129 Office: 5450 Wissahichon Ave Philadelphia PA 19144 *The key to achieving the human "vital balances", where mental, spiritual, physical and social health, and creative potentials are optimum, lies in developing mental mastery of one's inner personality functions resulting in the freedom to implement wise choices.*

FISCHER, HARRY W., radiologist, educator; b. St. Louis, 1921; s. Harry William and Amy Babette (Gieselman) F.; m. Kay Fischer, 1943; 5 children. B.S., U. Chgo., 1943, M.D., 1945. Diplomate: Am. Bd. Radiology. Asst. prof., then asso. prof. radiology U. Ia. Med. Sch., 1956-63, prof., head sect. diagnostic radiology, 1963-66; prof. radiology U. Mich. Med. Sch., 1966-71; dir. dept. radiology Wayne County Gen. Hosp., 1966-71; prof. radiology, chmn. dept. U. Rochester (N.Y.) Sch. Medicine and Dentistry, 1971—. Editorial bd.: Investigative Radiology, 1966—, Radiology, 1971—. Served to lt. (j.g.) M.C. USNR, 1946-48. Fellow Am. Coll. Radiology; mem. Radiol. Soc. N.Am., Assn. Univ. Radiologists (Gold medal), Am. Roetgen Ray Soc., Uroradiology Soc., U. Chgo. Med. Sch. Alumni Assn., Sigma Xi. Home: 3565 Elmwood Ave Rochester NY 14610 Office: 601 Elmwood Ave Rochester NY 14642

FISCHER, HENRY GEORGE, Egyptologist; b. Phila., May 10, 1923; s. Henry G. and Agnes Beatrice (Hurdman) F.; m. Eleanor Armstrong Teel, Dec. 15, 1951; 1 dau., Katherine Fraser. B.A., Princeton U., 1945; Ph.D., U. Pa., 1955. Instr. English Am. U. Beirut, 1945-48; asst. Egyptian sect. U. Pa. Mus., 1949-56; mem. univ. expdn. to, Mit Rahineh, Egypt, 1955, 56; asst. prof. Egyptology Yale Grad. Sch., 1956-58; asst. curator Egyptian art Met. Mus. Art, 1958-63, asso. curator, 1963-64, curator, 1964-70, Lila Acheson Wallace curator in Egyptology, 1970-79, research curator, 1979—; adj. asst. prof. fine arts Inst. Fine Arts, N.Y. U., 1962-64, adj. asso. prof., 1964-66, adj. prof., 1966-80; vis. lectr. art history and archaeology Columbia U., 1960-61; sec.-treas. Am. Com. to Preserve Abu Simbel, 1964-70. Author: Inscriptions from the Coptite Nome: Dynasties VI-XI, 1964, Ancient Egyptian Representations of Turtles, 1968, Dendera in the Third Millennium B.C, 1969, Egyptian Studies I: Varia, 1976, II: The Orientation of Hieroglyphs, Part 1: Reversals, 1977, Ancient Egyptian Calligraphy, 1979. Trustee Am. Research Center in Egypt, 1955-66; bd. dirs. Ams. for Middle East Understanding, 1967—, v.p., 1971—. Guggenheim fellow, 1956-57. Mem. Am. Inst. Archaeology, Egypt Exploration Soc. (London), Société Française d'Egyptologie; mem. German Archaeol. Inst.; Mem. Phi Beta Kappa. Address: Rural Route 1 Box 389 Sherman CT 06784

FISCHER, JAMES ADRIAN, clergyman; b. St. Louis, Oct. 15, 1916; s. John and Agnes (Henke) F. A.B., St. Mary's Sem., Perryville, Mo., 1941; S.T.L., Cath. U. Am., 1949; S.S.L., Pontifical Bib. Inst., Rome, Italy, 1951; LL.D. (hon.), Niagara U., 1968. Joined Congregation of Mission, 1936; ordained priest Roman Cath. Ch., 1943; prof. sacred scripture St. John's Sem., San Antonio, 1943-45, St. Mary's Sem., Houston, 1951-56, Perryville, 1958-62; provincial Western province Vincentian Fathers, 1962-71, De Andreis Sem., Lemont, Ill., 1971-81; pres. Kenrick Sem., St. Louis, 1981—. Author: The Psalms, 1974, God Created Woman, 1979, How to Read the Bible, 1981. Chmn. bd. trustees De Paul U., Chgo., 1962-71. Mem. Cath. Bibl. Assn. (pres. 1976-77). Address: Kenrick Sem 7800 Kenrick Rd Saint Louis MO 63119

FISCHER, JANET JORDAN, physician, educator, researcher; b. Pitts., Apr. 28, 1923; d. W. Edward and Jeannette (Kinnear) Jordan; m. Newton D. Fischer, Aug. 7, 1951; children: Amelia Fischer Drake, Jeannette Fischer Stein, Duncan, Helen, Anne. A.B., Vassar Coll., 1944; M.D., Johns Hopkins U., 1948.. Intern John Hopkins Hosp., Balt., 1948-49, fellow in infectious disease, 1950-52; resident Salt Lake Gen. Hosp., Salt Lake City, 1949-50; instr. medicine U. N.C. Meml. Hosp., Chapel Hill, 1953-54, assoc. prof., 1968-73, prof., 1973—, Sarah Graham Kehan prof., 1981—. Mem. Durham Orange County Med. Soc., N.C. Med. Soc., Phi Beta Kappa, Alpha Omega Alpha. Office: U. NC Sch Medicine Meml Hosp Chapel Hill NC 27514

FISCHER, JEROME MORTON, consulting engineer; b. N.Y.C., Mar. 15, 1924; s. Lester and Hilda (Schwartz) F.; m. Rhoda Barsha, Sept. 2, 1946; children: Steven, Karen, Michael, Marion. B.C.E., N.C. State U., 1948; postgrad., Tex. A&M U., 1942-43. Registered profl. engr., N.Y., Vt.; chartered engr., U.K. WIth Parsons, Brinckerhoff, Hall & MacDonald, N.Y.C., 1948-52, Tippets-Abbett-McCarthy-Stratton, 1952-60; v.p., then sr. v.p. Frederic R. Harris, Inc., The Hague, Netherlands, 1960-66, exec. v.p., N.Y.C., 1966-72, chmn. bd., 1972—; also dir.; v.p. Internat. Planning Research Corp., 1974—; dir. Planning Research Corp., 1974—, exec. v.p., 1977—; pres. PRC Engring., Inc., 1981—. Author numerous papers in field. Served with C.E. AUS, 1942-46. Decorated Order Crown, Belgium; Medal of Honor Spanish Ministry Pub. Works. Fellow ASCE, Inst. Civil Engrs. (Gt. Britain); mem. Am. Cons. Engrs. Council, Am. Inst. Cons. Engrs., Am. Concrete Inst., Internat. Rd. Fedn., Internat. Toll Rd., Tunnel and Turnpike Assn., Nat. Soc. Profl. Engrs., Permanent Internat. Congress Rds., Royal Netherlands Inst. Engrs., Soc. Flemish Engrs., Soc. Am. Mil. Engrs., U.S. C. of C. in Netherlands (past dir.). Clubs: Petroleum (London); Scarsdale (N.Y.) Golf. Home: 18 Hampton Rd Scarsdale NY 10583 Office: 300 E 42d St New York NY 10017

FISCHER, JOSEF E., surgeon, educator; b. N.Y.C., May 7, 1937; s. Max and Molly (Ochs) F.; m. Karen Jean Down, Oct. 24, 1965; children: Erich, Alexandra. A.B. summa cum laude, Yeshiva Coll., 1957; M.D. magna cum laude, Harvard U., 1961. Diplomate: Am. Bd. Surgery, Nat. Bd. Med. Examiners. Surg. intern Mass. Gen. Hosp., Boston, 1961-62, 3d asst. surg. resident, 1962-63, 2d asst. surg. resident, 1965-66, asst. resident surgery, 1966-68, chief resident, 1969-70, asst. in surgery, 1970-73, chief surg. physiology lab., 1970-78, chief hyperalimentation unit, 1972-78, asst. surgeon, 1973-76, asso. vis. surgeon, 1976-78; practice medicine, specializing in surgery, Boston, 1970-78, Cin., 1978—; commd. med. officer USPHS, 1963; research asso. lab. clin. sci. NIMH, 1963-65; teaching fellow in surgery Harvard U. Med. Sch., 1968-69, instr. surgery, 1970-72, asst. prof., 1972-75, asso. prof., 1975-78; Christian R. Holmes prof., chmn. dept. surgery U. Cin. Med. Center, 1978—; surgeon-in-chief U. Cin. Hosp., Children's Hosp. Med. Center, Cin.; bd. dirs. Weston Med. Labs., Inc., 1973. Editor: Total Parenteral Nutrition, 1976, Liver Assist Devices, Internat. Jour. Artificial Organs, 1977—; editorial bd.: Jour. Surg. Research, 1976, AMA Archive of Surgery, Am. Jour. Surgery, Jour. Enteral and Parenteral Nutrition, Current Surgery; Contbr. articles to med. jours. Co-chmn. steering com. Seminarians; dept. Am. Decorative arts Boston Mus. Fine Arts, 1976-77; bd. dirs. Beacon Hill Nursery Sch., 1970-75, Maimonides Sch., 1976—; chmn. bd. dirs. Cin. Chamber Orch., 1982-84. Recipient McCurdy-Rinkel award, 1971; James IV surg. fellow, 1974-75. Fellow A.C.S.; mem. AAAS, Am. Assn. for Study Liver Disease, Am. Gastroent. Assn., Am. Soc. Clin. Investigation, Assn. for Acad. Surgery (exec. com. 1975, recorder 1976), Internat. Soc. Parenteral Nutrition, Soc. for Parenteral Alimentation, Am. Surg. Assn., Central Surg. Assn., Ill. Surg. Soc. (hon.), Soc. Univ. Surgeons (chmn. com. social and legis. issues 1981—, exec. council 1981—), Soc. Surgery of Alimentary Tract, Halsted Soc., Boston Inter-Hosp. Liver Group, Mass. Med. Soc., Boston Surg. Soc., N.Y. Acad. Scis., Chgo. Surg. Soc. (hon.), Ky. Surg. Soc. (hon.), Colombia Soc. Surgery (hon.), Cin. Surg. Soc., Acad. of Medicine of Cin., Soc. Surg. Chairmen. Office: U Cin Med Center DtDept Surgery 231 Bethesda Ave Cincinnati OH 45267

FISCHER, LEROY HENRY, history educator; b. Hoffman, Ill., May 19, 1917; s. Andrew LeRoy and Effie (Risby) F.; m. Martha Gwendolyn Anderson, June 20, 1948; children: Barbara Ann, James LeRoy, John Andrew. B.A., U. Ill., 1939, M.A., 1940, Ph.D., 1943; postgrad., Columbia U., 1941. Grad. asst. history U. Ill., 1940-43; asst. prof. history Ithaca (N.Y.) Coll., 1946, Okla. State U. at Stillwater, 1946-49, asso. prof. history, 1949-60, prof. history, 1960-72, Oppenheim Regents prof. history, 1973-78, Oppenheim prof. history, 1978-84, Oppenheim prof. emeritus, 1984—; exec. sec. honors program, 1959-61. Author: Lincoln's Gadfly, Adam Gurowski, 1964, (with Muriel H. Wright) Civil War Sites in Oklahoma, 1967, The Civil War Era in Indian Territory, 1974, The Western States in the Civil War, 1975, Territorial Governors of Oklahoma, 1975, The Western Territories in the Civil War, 1977, Civil War Battles in the West, 1981, Oklahoma's Governors, 1907-1979, 3 vols., 1981-84; contbr. articles to profl jours. Vice chmn. Honey Springs Battlefield Park Commn., 1968—; chmn. adv. com. Okla. Historic Preservation Rev. Commn., 1969-78, mem., 1978—, vice-chmn., 1978-81, chmn., 1981-83; bd. dirs. Nat. Indian Hall of Fame, 1969—, YMCA, 1951-54, 83-85. Served with Signal Corps, AUS, 1943-45. Recipient Lit. award Loyal Legion U.S., 1963; named Tchr. of Year, Okla. State U.-Okla. Edn. Assn., 1969. Mem. Am., So. hist. assns., Western History Assn., Am. Assn. State and Local History, AAUP, Okla. (dir. 1966—), Ill. hist. socs., Orgn. Am. Historians, Omicron Delta Kappa, Pi Gamma Mu, Phi Alpha Theta, Alpha Kappa Lambda. Methodist (chmn. various coms. 1946—, adminstrv. bd. 1950-77, chmn. 1976-77, lay leader 1970-71). Home: 1010 W Cantwell Ave Stillwater OK 74075

FISCHER, LOUIS, food co. exec.; b. Pitts., 1930. Grad., Ohio State U., 1953. Chmn. bd., pres. Gino's, Inc., King of Prussia, Pa. Office: Gino's Inc 215 W Church Rd King of Prussia PA 19406 *

FISCHER, LOUIS THEODORE, coll. adminstr.; b. Des Plaines, Ill., Apr. 1, 1913; s. Theodore H. and Augusta (Klein) F.; m. Edith W. Hesemann, Sept. 1, 1945; children—James L., Stephen F. B.A. in commerce, Northwestern U., 1939. Mem. research staff Blackett Sample Hummert, Chgo., 1939-42; with Dancer Fitzgerald Sample, Inc., N.Y.C., 1945-77, asst. account exec., 1945-46, time buyer, 1946-49, media dir., 1949-55, v.p., 1955-66, sr. v.p. for media, 1966-77; dir. fin. and bus. Concordia Coll., Bronxville, N.Y., 1977—; instr. advt. N.Y. Advt. Club (media seminars for Advt. Age.). Bd. dirs. Taxpayers Orgn. N.E. Yonkers, Luth. TV, 1975—. Served to lt. AUS, 1941-45; PTO. Decorated Bronze Star; recipient Gold Key award Sta. Reps. Assn. Mem. Media Dirs. Council (pres. 1967). Lutheran (pres., trustee). Club: Wykagyl Country (New Rochelle, N.Y.). Home: 51 Harvard Ave Yonkers NY 10710

FISCHER, MARGARET THOMPSON, business consultant; b. N.Y.C., July 10, 1924; d. Edwin Wilson and Lisbeth (Hacker) Thompson; m. Arno Fischer, Aug. 10, 1963; 1 son, Arno Bryant. A.B. cum laude, Bucknell U., 1946. Editor, feature writer Bergen Evening Record, Hackensack, N.J., 1943-45; journalist Time, Inc., 1946-71; researcher Time, 1946-50; reporter Life, 1950-52, Sports Illustrated, 1953-55; head reporter Life, 1956-58, mem. new bldg. com., 1958-61, mgr. info. processing dept., 1961-71; dir. info. services Xerox Edn. Group, Xerox Corp., Stamford, Conn., 1972; mgr. data services div. R.R. Bowker Co., N.Y.C., 1972-75; bus. cons., Greenwich, Conn., 1975—; pres. Mgmt. Decisions, Greenwich; dir. Edwit Corp., Jersey City, 1952—, sec., 1977—, v.p., 1978—, pres., 1980—; dir. client services LINK Resources, Inc. Editor: Online Database Report, 1979—. Trustee Bucknell U., 1970—, Found. Center, 1978—. Mem. AAUW (pres. No. Valley N.J. chpt. 1959-61), Am. Soc. Info. Sci. (chmn. Met. N.Y. chpt. 1965-66, nat. councilor 1971-74, 75-78, pres. 1976-77). Congregationalist. Club: Burning Tree Country. Office: 44 Taconic Rd Greenwich CT 06830

FISCHER, MICHAEL JOHN, computer science educator; b. Ann Arbor, Mich., Apr. 20, 1942; s. Carl Hahn and Kathleen (Kirkpatrick) F.; m. Alice Edna Waltz, June 1, 1963; children: Edward Michael, Robert Patrick, David Frederick. B.S., U. Mich., 1963; M.A. (NSF fellow), Harvard U., 1965, Ph.D., 1968. Teaching fellow Harvard U., 1965-67; asst. prof. computer sci. Carnegie-Mellon U., 1968-69; asst. prof. math. M.I.T., 1969-73, asso. prof. elec. engring., 1973-75; prof. computer sci. U. Wash., 1975-81, dir. Computer Sci. Lab.,, 1976-79; prof. computer sci. Yale U., 1981—; program chmn. 17th IEEE Symposium on Founds. Computer Sci., 1976, 11th Assn. Computing Machinery Symposium on Theory Computing, 1979—, Assn. Computing Machinery Symposium on Principles of Distributed Computing, 1982; sr. vis. fellow U. Warwick, Coventry, Eng., summer 1972; vis. asso. prof. U. Toronto, spring, 1974; gastprofessor U. Frankfurt, Germany, summer 1974, ETH, Zurich, summer 1975; mem. adv. com. for math. and computer scis NSF, 1978-81; mem. com. on recommendations for U.S. Army Basic Sci. Research, 1978-81; cons. Xerox Palo Alto Research Ctr., 1982. Contbr. numerous articles to profl. jours.; editorial bd.: Computer Lang, 1973—, Transactions on Math. Software, 1976-77, Acta Informatica, 1976—, Jour. Algorithms, 1979—, Jour. Assn. Computing Machinery, 1979-82; editor-in-chief, 1982—. NSF grantee, 1974-77, 77-80, 80—; ONR contractor, 1979—. Mem. Assn. Computing Machinery (sec.-treas. spl. interest group on programming langs. 1971-73, local arrangements chmn. conf. 1973), Am. Math. Soc., Soc. Indsl. and Applied Math., European Assn. Theoretical Computer Sci., Phi Beta Kappa, Phi Kappa Phi. Home: 80 Killdeer Rd Hamden CT 06517 Office: Dept Computer Sci PO Box 2158 Yale Station New Haven CT 06520

FISCHER, PATRICK CARL, computer scientist, educator; b. St. Louis, Dec. 3, 1935; s. Carl Hahn and Kathleen (Kirkpatrick) F.; m. Linda Loomis, Dec. 22, 1956 (div. Jan 1967); 1 son, Carl; m. Charlotte Froese, Apr. 2, 1967; 1 dau., Carolyn. B.S., U. Mich., 1957; M.B.A., 1958; Ph.D. (Woodrow Wilson fellow, NSF fellow), Mass. Inst. Tech., 1962. Asst. prof. Harvard, 1962-65; asso. prof. Cornell U., Ithaca, N.Y., 1965-68; vis. asso. prof. U. B.C., 1967-68; prof. computer sci. U. Waterloo, Ont., Can., 1968-74, chmn. dept. applied analysis and computer sci., 1972-74; prof. dept. computer sci. Pa. State U., State College, 1974-79, head dept., 1974-78; prof. dept. computer sci. Vanderbilt U., Nashville, 1980—, chmn. dept., 1980—; Partner with Carl H. Fischer (actuaries cons.), Ann Arbor, Mich., 1962-75; Mem. computing and info. sci. grant selection com. Nat. Research Council Can., 1973-76. Editor in chief: spl. publs. Assn. Computing Machinery, 1971—; asso. editor: metatheory Jour. Computer and System Scis, 1968-74; editor, 1974—, SIAM Jour. on Computing, 1974—; mem. editorial bd.: Jour. Computer Lang, 1974—; contbr. profl. jours. Research grantee, 1964-66, 66-68, 79-81, 82-84; Nat. Research Council Can. grantee, 1968-75. Fellow Soc. Actuaries; mem. Assn. Computing Machinery (founder, chmn. spl. interest group automata and computability theory 1968-73), IEEE, IEEE Computer Soc., Am. Math. Soc., Sigma Xi, Phi Beta Kappa, Phi Kappa Phi, Beta Gamma Sigma. Home: 221 Burlington Pl Nashville TN 37215 Office: Box 6026 Station B Vanderbilt U Nashville TN 37235

FISCHER, RAYMOND P., business consultant, writer; b. Wheaton, Ill., Oct. 15, 1900; s. Herman A. and Julia (Blanchard) F.; m. Marita McMillan, June 18, 1932; 1 dau., Elizabeth Christine Fischer Lilly. A.B., Wheaton Coll., 1918-20, Pomona Coll., 1922; J.D., Harvard U., 1969. Bar: Ill. 1925. Practiced law in, Chgo., 1925-41; exec. v.p. Cuneo Press, 1941-67; pres., chmn. Combined Paper Mills, 1945-69; bus. cons., investment adviser; chmn. Associated Cons.; co-trustee several investment trusts. Mem. Nat. Assn. Bus. Economists. Episcopalian (warden, vestryman, diocesan council Chgo.). Clubs: Univ. (Chgo.); Chgo. Golf (Wheaton, Ill.); Crystal Downs Country (Frankfort, Mich.). Office: 213 W Wesley St Wheaton IL 60187

FISCHER, RICHARD SAMUEL, lawyer; b. Buffalo, July 31, 1937; s. Richard D. and Isabel B. (Van Dorn) F.; m. Malinda Berry, June 3, 1960; children: Richard B., Van D. A.B., Harvard U., 1959, J.D., 1963. Bar: N.Y. 1963. Law clk N.Y. Ct. Appeals, Albany, 1963-65; assoc. Nixon, Hargrave, Devans & Doyle, Rochester, N.Y., 1965-71, ptnr., 1972—. Sec., trustee Highland Hosp.; mem. Upstate Health Systems, Inc.; pres. Harley Sch. Mem. ABA, N.Y. State Bar Assn. (com. profl. ethics, co-chmn. com. on employee benefits, tax sect.), Monroe County Bar Assn., NYU Inst. Fed. Taxation (adv. com.). Club: Genesee Valley Country (Rochester, N.Y.). Office: 2200 Lincoln Tower Rochester NY 14603

FISCHER, ROBERT GEORGE, microbiology educator; b. St. Paul, Oct. 17, 1920; s. Fred F. and Agnes (Cooney) F.; m. Margaret Mary Roddy, June 28, 1947; children: Mary, John, James. B.A., U. Minn., 1942, M.S., 1947, Ph.D., 1948. Diplomate: Am. Bd. Microbiology. Research assoc. U. Minn., 1946-48; mem. faculty U. N.D. Med. Sch., 1948—, prof. microbiology, 1955—, chmn. dept., 1962-81. Served to capt., Med. Service Corps AUS, 1942-45; ETO. Fellow Am. Acad. Microbiology; mem. Am. Soc. Microbiology. Research on transmission of viruses by anthropod vectors; murine and avian leukemia virus transmission. Home: 447 Campbell Dr Grand Forks ND 58201

FISCHER, ROBERT WILLIAM, corporate executive; b. Mpls., Nov. 15, 1918; s. William Carl and Louise (Zabel) F.; m. Birdie Zumpf, Feb. 9, 1946; children: Judith Ann, Robert William, Kathleen Joan, Ann Louise. B.B.A., U. Minn., 1942; C.P.A., U. Ill., 1947. C.P.A., Ill., Minn. With Lybrand, Ross Brothers & Montgomery, Rockford, Ill., 1942-47; sr. v.p. First Nat. Bank, Mpls., 1947-67; chief exec. officer Dain, Kalman & Quail, Mpls., 1967-76; exec. v.p. Data 100 Corp., Mpls., 1976-79; also dir.; pres. Robert W. Fischer & Co., Inc., 1979—; dir. BMC Industries Inc., Domain Inc., CompuScan, Inc., Ringer Corp., Diversified Energies Inc. Bd. dirs. YMCA of Mpls., Mpls. Med. Center. Served with USNR, 1942-45. Mem. Am. Inst. C.P.A.s, Minn. Soc. C.P.A.s, Financial Execs. Inst., Mpls. C. of C. (dir.). Clubs: Minneapolis, Hazeltine Nat. Golf, Interlachen., Sky. Lodge: Rotary. Home: 5609 Woodcrest Dr Edina MN 55424 Office: 4900 IDS Tower Minneapolis MN 55402

FISCHER, STANLEY, economics educator; b. Lusaka, Zambia, Oct. 15, 1943; came to U.S., 1966, naturalized, 1976; s. Philip and Ann (Kopelowitz) F.; m. Rhoda Keet, Dec. 12, 1965; children: Michael Adam, David Benjamin, Jonathan Phillip. B.Sc., London Sch. Econs., 1965, M.Sc., 1966; Ph.D., MIT, 1969. Fellow U. Chgo., 1969-70, asst. prof. econs., 1970-73; asso. prof. MIT, 1973-77, prof., 1977—; vis. sr. lectr. Hebrew U., Jerusalem, 1972, fellow, 1976-77; vis. fellow Hoover Instn., Stanford U., 1981-82. Author: (with R. Dornbusch) Economics, 1983, Macroeconomics, 1984; editor: Rational Expectations and Economic Policy, 1980; contbr. articles to profl. jours. Fellow Econometric Soc.; mem. Am. Acad. Arts and Scis. Office: E52-214 MIT Cambridge MA 02139

FISCHER, THOMAS V., manufacturing company executive; b. 1929; married. A.B., DePauw U., 1951; LL.B., U. Mich., 1956. With firm Stevenson, Conaghan Hackbert, Rooks & Pitts., 1956-63; sec., counsel North Am. Car Corp., 1963-65; with A.E. Staley Mfg. Co., 1965—, v.p. law and admistrn., 1969-72, dir., mem. exec. com., 1970, v.p., 1972-78, exec. v.p., 1978—; dir. Millikin Nat. Bank of Decatur, Mut. Trust Life Ins. Co., Overmyer Corp. Bd. dirs. United Way of Decatur and Macon County, 1976-77. Address: A E Staley Mfg Co Eldorado at 22d St Decatur IL 62525

FISCHER, WILLIAM DONALD, food company executive; b. Tell City, Ind., Nov. 16, 1928; s. William Charles and Faith Odelia (Roehm) F.; m. Lois Anne Poindexter, Aug. 12, 1955; children: Dean William, Jennifer Louise, Nancy Anne, John Richard. B.S. in Acctg., Ind. U., 1952. Audit mgr. Price Waterhouse & Co., Chgo., 1952-60; controller Vapor Corp., Niles, Ill., 1960-63, sec., treas., 1963-67; treas. Am. Meter Co., Phila., 1967-69, Allied Tube & Conduit Corp., Harvey, Ill., 1969-71; v.p. fin., sec., treas. Dean Foods Co., Franklin Park, Ill., 1971—, dir., 1979—. Active DuPage County council Boy Scouts Am., 1969-76; trustee First Congl. Ch. of Elmhurst, Ill., 1972-76, 80-81, treas., 1969-72, moderator, 1976-78. Served with USN, 1946-48. Mem. Ind. Soc. C.P.A.s, Ill. C.P.A. Soc., Am. Inst. C.P.A.s. Office: 3600 N River Rd Franklin Park IL 60131

FISCHER-DIESKAU, DIETRICH, baritone; b. Berlin, Germany, May 28, 1925; s. Albert and Dora (Klingelhoffer) Fischer-D.; m. Irmgard Poppen, Feb. 10, 1949 (dec. Dec. 1963); children—Mathias, Martin, Manuel. Student high sch., Berlin; studied music with, Georg A. Walter, Herman Weissenborn; D.Mus. (hon.), Oxford U., 1978, Sorbonne, 1980. Sang lyrical and title role baritone, Municipal Opera, Berlin, 1948, extensive concert tours, Europe, U.S., appearance festivals, including, Edinburgh, Vienna, London, Paris, Netherlands, Munich, Berlin, Salzburg; mem., Vienna State Opera, 1957—; hon. mem., Deutsche Oper, Berlin, 1978; Author: Texte Deutscher Lieder, 1968, Aufden Spuren der Schubert-Lieder, 1971, Wagner und Nietzche-Der Mystagoge und sein Abtrünniger, 1974; Chief roles include Wolfram, Jochanaan, Alamavive, Marquis Posa, Don Giovanni, Dr. Faust, Falstaff, Sachs, others. Served with German Army, World War II. Recipient award Internat. Gramophone Record, 1955, 57, 58, 60, 61, 64, 65, 68, 71, 73, 76, 77; art award, Berlin, 1950; Golden Orpheus, Mantua, 1955; Federal medal for distinguished services, 1st class, 1958; Naras award, 1962; Mozart-Medaille Wien, 1963; Ehrenmitgliedschaft Konzerthausgesellschaft Wien, 1963; Byerischer Kammersänger, 1959; Berliner, 1963; Edison award, 1962, 64, 67, 71; Sonning award, 1975; Grosser Verdienstorden des Bundesverdienstkreuzes, 1974; Friedrich Rückert award Schweinfurt, 1979; Award Siemens-Stiftung, Germany, 1980; named Hon. Mem. Deutsche Oper Berlin, 1978. Mem. Acad. Arts, Internat. Mahler Soc. Vienna, Internat. Music Council (German sect.), Royal Acad. Music, London, Royal Acad. Music, Stockholm. Prisoner of war. Address: care Colbert Artists Mgmt Inc 111 W 57th St New York NY 10019 *

FISCHOFF, EPHRAIM, humanities educator, clergyman; b. N.Y.C., Oct. 2, 1904; s. Aaron and Betty (Gunsberg) F.; m. Marion Judson, Dec. 28, 1943; children: Aronel, Gabriel and Raphael (twins), Michael, Bettina, Daniel. A.B., CCNY, 1924; M.H.L., Jewish Inst. Religion, 1928; D. Social Sci., New Sch. Social Research, 1942; D.D., Hebrew Union Coll., (Jewish Inst. Religions), 1982. Ordained rabbi, 1928. Ministry, religious edn. group work, 1928-42; lectr. sociology Pa. State U., 1935-36; lectr. Jewish Tchrs. Sem., N.Y., 1937-42; editorial cons. World Jewish Congress, 1941-45; lectr. New Sch. Social Research, N.Y.C., 1942-51, Hunter Coll. (CCNY), 1942-46; asst. editor Jour. Legal and Polit. Sci., 1943-45; acting exec. dir. Conf. Jewish Relations, 1946; head dept. sociology Am. Internat. Coll., Springfield, Mass., 1946-54; lectr. Hartford Sem. Found., 1953-54; dir. B'nai B'rith Hillel Found. (U. Calif.-Berkeley), 1954, 1954-58; prof. humanities and social sci., dir. honors program Lynchburg Coll., Va., 1960-69; prof. sociology, anthropology and Am. Studies U. Wis.-Stevens Point, 1969-76; vis. prof. social welfare Sangamon State U., Springfield, Ill., 1976, prof. humanities, 1978-83; lectr. So. Ill. Sch. Medicine, 1979-81, lectr., sr. cons., vis. prof. in med. humanities, 1981; vis. prof. Hollings Coll. U. Va., 1965-67, Coll. William and Mary, 1969, Sir George Williams U., Montreal, 1970. Author: William Beaumont, Elizabeth Blackwell, Oliver Wendell Holmes, Sir William Osler, Pearson Mus. Monograph Series, 1981-82; trans., editor: (M. Herschfeld) Sexual History of the World War, (Max Weber) Sociology of Religion, 1963; contbr.: Great Thinkers of the Twentieth Century, 1963, Contemporary Jewish Thought, A Reader, 1963, Economy and Society, 1968; contbr., dept. editor: Encyclopaedia Judaica, 1972; editorial cons.: From War to Peace Series, Inst. Jewish Affairs, World Jewish Congress, 1944-48. Mem. exec. bd. ARC, Pres.'s Com. Physically Handicapped, NCCJ. Fellow Am. Sociol. Assn. Fellow Soc. for Applied Anthropology; mem. Nat. Assn. Social Workers (charter mem.), Cert. Social Workers, Am. Philos. Assn., Am. Studies Assn., Am. Acad. Polit. and Social Scis., Central Conf. Am. Rabbis, Soc. for Pschol. Study Social Issues, Am. Soc. for History of Medicine, Soc. Sci. Study Religion, Societe Europenne de Culture, Ill. State Hist. Soc., Nat. Humanities Faculty. Office: Dept Humanities Sangamon State U. Shepherd Rd Springfield IL 62708

FISCHTHAL, GLENN JAY, musician; b. Shell Lake, Wis., Feb. 22, 1948; s. Jacob Henry and Lois (Clinton) F.; m. Elizabeth Anne Gravelle, Dec. 23, 1973; child, Raphael. Student, U. Ghana, West Africa, 1965-66; B.Mus., Cleve. Inst. Music, 1970; postgrad., Calif. Inst. of the Arts, 1970-71. Mem. faculty San Francisco Conservatory of Music. Subs. trumpet, Cleve. Orch., 1970; 2d trumpet, San Antonio Symphony, 1971-72, Nat. Ballet of Can., 1972-73; prin. trumpet, Hong Kong Philharmonic, 1974; 2d trumpet, Kansas City Philharmonic, 1974-76; prin. trumpet, Israel Philharmonic Orch., 1976-79, San Diego Symphony, 1979-80, San Francisco Symphony, 1980—. Home: 166 Liberty St San Francisco CA 94110

FISCINA, CARMINE MICHAEL, former chemical company executive; b. Bklyn., July 23, 1924; s. Mario and Antoinette (Novellino) F.; m. Joan Virginia Martin, Aug. 27, 1957; children: Diane, Robert. B.B.A., St. John's U., 1949. With Reichold Chems. Inc., 1950-83, asst. treas., 1959-65, treas., 1965-83, also v.p., dir., 1972-83. Served with USNR, 1943-46. Home: Indialantic FL 32903

FISH, BARBARA, psychiatrist, educator; b. N.Y.C., July 30, 1920; d. Edward R. and Ida (Citrin) F.; m. Max Saltzman, Dec. 12, 1953; children: Mark, Ruth Saltzman Deutsch. B.A. summa cum laude, Barnard Coll., Columbia U., 1942; M.D., NYU, 1945. Diplomate: Am. Bd. Psychiatry and Neurology, subsplty bd. in child psychiatry. Intern Bellevue Hosp., N.Y.C., 1945-47, resident in pediatrics, 1947-49, resident in psychiatry, 1949-52; practice medicine specializing in child psychiatry, N.Y.C., 1952-65; instr. psychiatry Cornell U. Med. Coll., N.Y.C., 1955-60, instr. pediatrics, 1955-56, asst. prof. clin. pediatrics, 1956-60; child psychiatrist dept. pediatrics N.Y. Hosp.-Cornell Med. Center, 1955-60; mem. faculty William A. White Inst. Psychoanalysis, N.Y.C., 1957-66; assoc. prof. psychiatry N.Y. U. Sch. Medicine, N.Y.C., 1960-70, prof., 1970-72, adj. prof., 1972—; dir. child psychiatry N.Y. U. Med. Center, 1960-72; prof. U. Calif. Sch. Medicine, Los Angeles, 1972—; assoc. mem. Mental Retardation Research Center, U. Calif., 1976—; mem. advisory com. mental health services for children N.Y.C. Community Mental Health Bd., 1963-72; mem. profl. advisory com. on children N.Y. State Dept. Mental Hygiene, 1966-72; mem. com. cert. child psychiatry Am. Bd. Psychiatry and Neurology, 1969-77; mem. clin. program projects research rev. com. NIMH, 1976-78. Contbr. articles on the antecedents of schizophrenia and other severe mental disorders, and on the psychiat. diagnosis and treatment of children; mem. editorial bd.: Jour. Am. Acad. Child Psychiatry, 1966-71, Jour. Autism and Childhood Schizophrenia, 1971-74, Child Devel. Abstracts and Bibliography, 1974—, Archives Gen. Psychiatry, 1975—. Recipient Woman of Sci. award UCLA, 1978; NIMH grantee, 1961-72, 78—; Harriett A. Ames Charitable Trust grantee, 1961-66; William T. Grant Found. grantee, 1977—; Scottish Rite schizophrenia research grantee, 1979—. Fellow Am. Psychiat. Assn., Am. Acad. Child Psychiatry, Am. Coll. Neuropsychopharmacology (charter); mem. Am. Psychopath. Assn. (v.p. 1967-68), Assn. for Research in Nervous and Mental Diseases, Soc. Research in Child Devel., Psychiat. Research Soc. Home: 16428 Sloan Dr Los Angeles CA 90049 Office: Neuropsychiatric Inst Univ Calif Los Angeles 760 Westwood Plaza Los Angeles CA 90024

FISH, CHET, publishing executive; b. Worcester, Mass., June 30, 1925; s. Chester Boardman and Mary Elizabeth (Sheehan) F.; m. Claire Margaret Commo, Sept. 10, 1948; children: Craig Michael, Scott Kevin, Maribeth Ann, Andrea Dawn, Brian John. B.A., Syracuse U., 1950, M.A., 1952. Asst. editor Boys' Life mag., N.Y.C., 1951-53; assoc. editor Sports Afield mag., N.Y.C., 1953-55; copy chief Am. Home mag., N.Y.C., 1955-57; assoc. editor Outdoor Life mag., N.Y.C., 1957-63, article editor, 1963-67, mng. editor, 1967-73, editor-in-chief, 1973-76; sr. editor David McKay Co., Inc. (book pubs.), N.Y.C., 1976-80; editor Charles Scribner's Sons (pubs.), N.Y.C., 1980-81; pub. cons. The Competitive Edge, Greenlawn, N.Y., 1981-83; editorial dir. Stackpole Books, Harrisburg, Pa., 1983—. Served with USNR, 1943-46; PTO. Mem. Outdoor Writers Assn. Am. Republican. Roman Catholic. Home: 709 Sutton Dr Carlisle PA 17013 Office: Cameron and Kelker Sts Harrisburg PA 17105

FISH, EDWARD ANTHONY, construction company executive; b. Boston, June 13, 1933; s. Joseph Nicholas and Evelyn Irene (O'Mally) F.; m. Gretchen Fish; children: Karen, Edward Anthony, John, Kevin, Melissa, Matthew, Michael. B.A. magna cum laude in Econs, U. N.H., 1957. With Peabody Constrn. Co., Inc., Braintree, Mass., 1957—, v.p., 1962-65, pres., 1965—; owner Peabody Properties, Inc., Bancroft Corp. Bd. dirs. Cardinal Cushing Sch., 1978-80; life mem. bd. dirs. Family Counseling and Guidance Centers; hon. dir. Handi-Kids.; trustee Meadowbrook Sch. Served with AUS, 1952-54; Korea. Club: 100. Office: 536 Granite St Braintree MA 02184

FISH, HAMILTON, publisher; b. Washington, Sept. 5, 1951; s. Hamilton and Julia (Mackenzie) F. B.A., Harvard U., 1973. Co-producer: film Memory of Justice, 1975-76; pub.: Nation Mag, N.Y.C., 1978—. Vice-pres. Nat. Movement for Student Vote, 1971-72. Office: Nation Mag 72 Fifth Ave New York NY 10011

FISH, HAMILTON, JR., Congressman; b. Washington, June 3, 1926; s. Hamilton and Grace (Chapin) F.; m. Julia Mackenzie (dec. Mar. 1969); children: Hamilton III, Julia Alexandra, Nicholas S., Peter L.; m. Billy Laster Cline, Apr. 3, 1971. A.B., Harvard U., 1949; LL.B., NYU, 1957; postgrad., John F. Kennedy Sch. Pub. Adminstrn. Bar: N.Y. Vice consul to Ireland, 1951-53; with firm Alexander and Green, N.Y.C., 1957-64; practice law, Poughkeepsie and Millbrook, N.Y., 1964—; mem. 91st-98th Congresses from N.Y. State, ranking minority mem. Judiciary com. Mem. Franklin Delano Roosevelt Meml. Commn.; mem. exec. com. Dutchess County council Boy Scouts Am. Served with USNR, 1944-46. Mem. Improved Order Red Men. Republican. Clubs: Masons, Elks. Office: 2227 Rayburn House Office Bldg Washington DC 20515

FISH, HENRY EVERETT, hospital equipment manufacturing company executive; b. Erie, Pa., Aug. 26, 1925; s. Howard MacFarl and Dorothy (Hall) F.; m. Laurana Schultz, Sept. 9, 1950; children—Susan, Henry Earl II, Dorathea. Grad., Phillips Exeter Acad., 1944; B.A. in Econs. cum laude, Princeton U., 1948; M.S. in Indsl. Mgmt, Mass. Inst. Tech., 1961. Bus. tng. course Gen. Electric Co., Schenectady, 1948-49; field rep. Am. Sterilizer Co., Erie, 1949-50, dir. market research, 1951-55, field sales mgr., 1955-57, gen. sales mgr., 1958-59, v.p., 1960-67, sr. v.p., 1967-70, pres., 1971—; also dir.; dir. Lord Corp., Security Peoples Trust Co., 1972, Sta. WQLN-TV, 1979—. Bd. dirs. Erie Day Sch., 1963; bd. incorporators St. Vincent Hosp., Hamot Hosp. Served with USNR, 1944-45. Mem. Princeton NW Pa. Alumni Assn. (pres. 1969-71), Health Industry Mfg. Assn. (dir. 1974—, chmn. 1977—), Soc. Sloan Fellows. Baptist. Clubs: Aviation Country, Kahkwa (Erie); Princeton (N.Y.C.); Univ. (Washington). Home: 3535 Hershey Rd Erie PA 16506 Office: Am Sterilizer Co 2222 W Grandview Blvd Erie PA 16512

FISH, HOWARD MATH, business executive, former air force officer; b. Melrose, Minn., Aug. 1, 1923; s. Nathaniel Bragg and Louise Margurite (Gaetz) F.; m. Jamie Katherine Tom, May 15, 1948; 1 son, Howard Math. Student, Air Command and Staff Coll., 1954; M.B.A., U. Chgo., 1957, Armed Forces Staff Coll., 1960-61; M.A., George Washington U., 1964; disting. grad., Air War Coll., 1964. Commd. 2d lt. USAAF, 1944; advanced through grades to lt. gen. USAF, 1974; served in, ETO, 1944-45, Wiesbaden, Ger., 1946-49, 1948-49, stationed in, Korea, 1950-51, Dreux, France, Frankfurt, Ger., 1957-60; staff officer Hdqrs. USAF, Washington, 1964-69, 70-74, dir. budget, 1973-74; dir. Def. Security Assistance Agy.; dep. sec. def. (internat. security affairs) security assistance Def. Security Assistance Agy., 1974-78; asst. vice chief staff USAF, 1978-79; U.S. mil. rep. UN, 1978-79; v.p. internat. Vought Corp., Dallas, 1979—; served in, Vietnam, 1969-70; instr. personnel mgmt. U. Md., 1957-60, 69-70. Mem. nat. aviation explorer com. Boy Scouts Am., 1979—. Decorated Legion of Merit, D.F.C., Air medal, Purple Heart, Def. D.S.M., Air Force D.S.M. Mem. Am. Soc. Mil. Comptrollers (pres. 1971-72), Arnold Air Soc. (chmn. bd. trustees 1972—), Beta Gamma Sigma. Roman Catholic. Clubs: Army and Navy Country (Washington); Las Colinas Country (Irving, Tex.). Home: 3401 Hidalgo University Hills Irving TX 75062 Office: Vought Corp PO Box 225907 Dallas TX 75265

FISH, JANET ISOBEL, artist; b. Boston, May 18, 1938; d. Peter and Florence F. B.A., Smith Coll., 1960; postgrad., Skowhegan (Maine) Art Sch., summer 1961; B.F.A., M.F.A., Yale U., 1963. Represented in permanent collections, Whitney Mus. Am. Art, N.Y.C., Met. Mus. Art, N.Y.C., Cleve. Mus. Art, Dallas Mus. Fine Arts, Am. Airlines, Am. Fedn. Arts., Am. Acad. Inst. Arts and Letters, Art Inst. Chgo., Nat. Gallery. Bd. govs. Skowhegan Sch. Painting and Sculpture. Recipient Harris award, Chgo. Bienale award, 1974; MacDowell fellow; Yale scholar; Australian Council for Arts grantee, 1975.

FISH, MARY MARTHA, economist; b. Albert Lea, Minn., July 17, 1930; d. Charles H. and Olga (Stennes) Thomassen; m. Donald C. Fish, Oct. 1954; children—Jill S., Lynn M., Jason M. B.B.A., U. Minn., 1951; M.B.A. in Econs, Tex. Tech. Coll., 1957; Ph.D. (AAUW fellow 1960), U. Okla., 1963. Statis. asst. Iowa Bd. Control, 1951-53; public health analyst State of Calif., 1953-54; analytical statistician 46th Med. Gen. Lab., U.S. Army Forces, Tokyo, 1954-57; instr. econs. and bus. Odessa (Tex.) Coll., 1957-58; asst. prof., then asso. prof. W.Tex. State U., 1961-66; prof. econs. U. Ala., 1966—; Fulbright lectr. U. Liberia, 1974-75; cons. in field. Co-author: Convicts, Codes and Contraband, 1974; contbr. articles to profl. jours. Grantee U. Ala., 1967-68, Dept. Labor, 1978. Mem. Am. Econ. Assn., So. Econ. Assn., Southwestern Econ. Assn. Mem. Baha'i Ch. Home: 4 High Forest Tuscaloosa AL 35406 Office: Room 130 Bidgood Hall Box J Coll Commerce and Bus Adminstrn U Ala University AL 35486

FISH, PAUL W., lawyer; b. Ligonier, Pa., Apr. 12, 1933; s. Edmund R. and Catherine (McGuiggan) F.; m. Jacquelyn A. Shea, Sept. 19, 1959; children: Charles M., Edmund J., Catherine G., John H., Jacquelyn A. B.S. in Elec. Engring, Cath. U. Am., 1959, M.E.E., 1961; LL.B., George Washington U., 1965. Bar: Wis. bar, N.Y. bar, Mich. bar. Patent agt., atty. Xerox Corp., Rochester, N.Y., 1965-66; patent atty., asst. dir. patent div. Burroughs Corp., Detroit, 1966, dir. patents, to 1976; asst. gen. counsel Jos. Schlitz Brewing Co., Milw., 1976-79, gen. counsel., 1979-83, Comdisco, Inc., Rosemont, IL, 1983—. Sec. North Shore Republican Club. Served with USN, 1951-55. Mem. Am. Bar Assn., Am. Patent Law Assn., U.S. Trademark Assn., State Bar Wis. Roman Catholic. Home: 130 Pine Tree Ln Riverwoods IL 60015 Office: Comdisco Inc. 6400 Shafer Ct Rosemont IL 60018

FISH, STANLEY EUGENE, English language and literature educator; b. Providence, Apr. 19, 1938; s. Max and Ida Dorothy (Weinberg) F.; m. Adrienne A. Aaron, Aug. 23, 1959 (div. 1980); 1 dau., Susan.; m. Jane Parry Tompkins, Aug. 7, 1982. B.A., U. Pa., 1959; M.A., Yale U., 1960, Ph.D., 1962. Instr. U. Calif., Berkeley, 1962-63, asst. prof., 1962-67, assoc. prof., 1967-69, prof., 1969-74; Kenan prof. English Johns Hopkins U., Balt., 1974—. Author: John Skelton's Poetry, 1965, Supprised by Sin: The Reader in Paradise Lost, 1967, Seventeenth Century Prose: Modern Essays in Criticism, 1971, Self-Consuming Artifacts, 1972, The Living Temple: George Herbert and Catechizing, 1978, Is there a Text in This Class?, 1980; editorial bd.: Milton Studies, Milton Quar. Recipient 2d place, Explicator prize, 1967; Am. Council Learned Socs. fellow, 1966; Guggenheim fellow, 1969. Mem. Modern Lang. Assn., Milton Soc., Spenser Soc. Office: Dept English Johns Hopkins U Baltimore MD 21218

FISH, STEWART ALLISON, obstetrician-gynecologist; b. Benton, Ill., Nov. 4, 1925; s. Floyd Hamilton and Mary Vivian (Fish) F.; m. Patsy June Patterson, Apr. 24, 1957; children: Jayne, Jeffrey, Carolyn, Mary. Student, Va. Poly. Inst., 1943-44, U. Va., 1944-45; M.D., U. Pa., 1949. Intern Hosp. of U. Pa., 1949-50; resident obstetrics and gynecology Columbia-Presbyn. Med. Center, N.Y.C., 1950-53; chief resident gynecology Free Hosp. Women, Boston, 1953-54; asst. prof. obstetrics and gynecology Southwestern Med. Sch. of U. Tex., 1954-56; pvt. practice obstetrics and gynecology, Dallas, 1956; asst. prof. U. Ark. Med. Sch., 1962-66; prof., chmn. dept. obstetrics and gynecology U. Tenn. Med. Sch., 1966-75; obstetrician and gynecologist in chief City of Memphis Hosps.; mem. staff Bapt. Meml. Hosp.; cons. U.S. Naval Hosp., St. Joseph Hosp., Meth. Hosp. Contbr. to med. jours. Served to ensign USNR, 1943-46. Recipient Golden Apple award U. Ark., 1966, 75; Bicentennial Silver medal Columbia Coll. Phys. and Surg., 1968. Fellow A.C.S., Am. Coll. Obstetricians and Gynecologists; mem. Central Assn. Obstetricians and Gynecologists, Tenn. Obstet. and Gynecol. Soc. (pres. 1972-73), Tex. Assn. Obstetricians and Gynecologists (council), So. Med. Assn., Sigma Xi, Sigma Chi, Phi Chi. Episcopalian. Home: 2220 Logansport Rd Nacogdoches TX 75961

FISHBEIN, MARTIN, educator, psychologist; b. N.Y.C., Mar. 2, 1936; s. Sydney and Gloria (Nadelstein) F.; m. Deborah Louise Kaplan, Dec. 26, 1959. A.B., Reed Coll., Portland, Ore., 1957; Ph.D., U. Cal. at Los Angeles, 1961. Mem. faculty U. Ill., Urbana, 1961—, prof. psychology, 1970—, head social sci. div., 1979—, also research prof., 1970—, exec. com., 1964-72, asso. mem., 1974-75; vis. scholar London Sch. Econs. and Polit. Sci., 1967-68, 74-75. Author: (with Steiner) Current Studies in Social Psychology, 1965, Readings in Attitude Theory and Measurement, 1967, (with Ajzen) Belief, Attitude, Intention and Behavior: An Introduction to Theory and Research, 1975, Progress in Social Psychology, vol. 1, 1980, Understanding Attitudes and Predicting Social Behavior, 1980; Contbr. articles to profl. jours. Guggenheim fellow, 1967-68. Fellow Am. Psychol. Assn.; mem. Midwestern Psychol. Assn., Am. Sociol. Assn., Psychonomic Soc. Home: 811 W University Ave Champaign IL 61820

FISHBEIN, PETER MELVIN, lawyer; b. N.Y.C., June 20, 1934; s. Arthur L. and Lotta (Chary) Fishbein; m. Bette Klinghoffer, June 16, 1957; children: Stephen, Bruce, Gregory. B.A. magna cum laude, Dartmouth Coll., 1955; J.D., Harvard U., 1958. Bar: N.Y. 1959, U.S. Supreme Ct. 1973. Note editor Harvard Law Rev., Cambridge, Mass., 1956-58; law clk. to Justice William J. Brennan, Jr. U.S. Supreme Ct., Washington, 1958-59; dep. sec.gen. Internat. Peace Corps., Washington, 1962-64; ptnr. Kaye, Scholer, Fierman Hays & Handler, N.Y.C., 1967—; chief counsel N.Y. State Counstl. Conv., Albany, 1967; mem. Presdl. Commn. to Nominate Candidates for Fed. Ct. of Appeals, N.Y.C., 1980. Contbr. articles to profl. jours. Trustee Goddard Coll., 1967-75; mem. N.Y. State Gov.'s Bd. Pub. Disclosure, Albany, 1975-77; trustee Fedn. Jewish Philanthropies, N.Y.C., 1975-81; compaign mgr. Justice Arthur J. Goldberg's Campaign for gov., 1970. Fellow Am. Coll. Trail Lawyers; mem. N.Y.C. Bar Assn., ABA, Phi Beta Kappa. Club: Beach Point (bd. govs.). Home: 101 Woodlands Rd Harrison NY 10528 Office: 425 Park Ave New York NY 10022

FISHBERG, ARTHUR MAURICE, physician; b. N.Y.C., June 17, 1898; s. Maurice and Bertha (Cantor) F.; m. Irene Levin, June 16, 1933. A.B., Columbia U., 1919, M.D., 1921; D.Sc. (hon.), Mt. Sinai Sch. Medicine, 1979. Intern City Hosp., 1921-22; adj. and asso. physician Mt. Sinai Hosp., 1926-46; physician-in-chief Beth Israel Hosp., 1946—; cons. physician St. Joseph's Hosp., 1944—; cons. Army Med. Center, Washington, 1947—; clin. prof. med. N.Y. U., 1947—; cons. physician Mount Vernon Hosp., 1957—; clin. prof. medicine Mt. Sinai Sch. Medicine, 1966—; Pres. Dazian Found. for Med. Research, 1956. Author: Hypertension and Nephritis, 1930, Heart Failure, 1937; Contbr. numerous articles dealing with cardiovascular and renal disease. Mem. Am. Soc. for Clin. Investigation, AMA, Am. Heart Assn., N.Y. Acad. of Medicine; hon. mem. Buenos Aires Med. Soc., Brazilian Cardiological Soc. Jewish. Conducted extensive investigations on cardiovascular and renal disease. Address: 1136 Fifth Ave New York City NY 10028

FISHEL, JOSPEH J., museum curator; b. Clifton Springs, N.Y., May 15, 1940; s. Joseph J. and Venus E. (Zarr) Rishel; m. Anne d'Harnoncourt, June 19, 1971. B.A., Hobart Coll., 1962; M.A., U. Chgo., 1968. Instr. art history Wooster Coll., 1966-67; asst. curator earlier painting and sculpture Art. Inst., Chgo., 1968-71; curator European Painting Before 1900, curator John G. Johnson Collection, Phila. Mus. Art, 1971—. Office: Phila Mus Art PO Box 7646 Philadelphia PA 19101 *

FISHEL, LESLIE HENRY, JR., historic site administrator; b. N.Y.C., Nov. 14, 1921; s. Leslie Henry and Thelma R. (Minzie) F.; m. Barbara G. Richards, June 30, 1943; children: Ruth, Timothy, Lesley, Andrew, John. A.B., Oberlin Coll., 1943; A.M., Harvard, 1947, Ph.D., 1954; Litt.D., Lakeland Coll., 1969; L.H.D., Defiance Coll., 1980, Tiffin U., 1984. Mem. faculty Mass. Inst. Tech., 1948-55; lectr. history Oberlin Coll., 1956-59, exec. dir., 1955-59; dir. State Hist. Soc. Wis., 1959-69; pres. Heidelberg Coll., Tiffin, Ohio, 1969-80; dir. R.B. Hayes Presdl. Center, 1980—; adj. prof. Bowling Green (Ohio) State U., 1980—; research asso. Nat. Sci. Fedn. History Sci. Project, 1953-55; Cons. Bancroft Library, U. Calif. at Berkeley, 1967; adv. com. Library of Congress Nat. Union Catalogue of Manuscripts, 1967-70; chmn. sponsoring com. Madison Friends Urban League, 1961-67. Author: (with B. Quarles) The Black American: A Documentary History, 1967, 3d edit., 1975; Contbr. articles to profl. jours. Sec. Wis. Hist. Found., 1959-69; exec. v.p. Historic Sites Found. Wis., 1960-69; mem. Roadstead Found., 1961-70; mem. nat. council Nat. Endowment for the Humanities, 1970-76; mem. exec. com. United Ch. of Christ Council Higher Edn., 1975-80, Ohio Found. Ind. Colls., 1976-80; bd. dirs. Univ. YMCA, Madison, 1962-69, United Way, 1974-80, Webster Industries Found., 1975—, Birchard Pub. Library of Sandusky County. Served lt. (j.g.) USNR, 1943-46. Mem. Am. Assn. State and Local History (gov. council 1964-70), Tiffin Area C. of C. (dir. 1971-73), Sandusky County C. of C. (dir.), Oberlin-Shansi Meml. Assn. (past trustee), Ohio Coll. Assn. (exec. com. 1974—, pres. 1975-76), Orgn. Am. Historians, Ohio Hist. Soc. (trustee 1975-76, 78-80). Mem. United Ch. of Christ (past trustee, moderator). Home: 1500 Buckland Ave Fremont OH 43420

FISHEL, PETER LIVINGSTON, business executive; b. Chgo., Apr. 25, 1935; s. Philip W. and Dorothy B. (Livingston) F.; m. Donna Swift, Dec. 17, 1961; children: Pamela Leslie, Patricia Jane, Françoise Suzanne. B.S., Wharton Sch., U. Pa., 1959. C.P.A., Pa., Fla. Agt.-in-charge investigation and civil rights div. Commonwealth of Pa. Dept. Justice, 1961-62; controller Internat. Playtex Corp., 1962-70, BVD Knitwear, 1970-71; corp. controller BVD Co., Inc., N.Y.C., 1971-73, v.p. fin., 1973; chief fin. officer Colebrook Mills, div. Bobbie Brooks, Inc., Hialeah, Fla., 1973-77; owner Gen. Bus. Services, 1978—, regional dir. SE Fla., 1982—; mem. adv. com. Oceanmark Fed. Savs. & Loan, 1983—. Mem. citizens adv. com. Met. Dade Police, Miami, Fla., 1981—. Served with M.P., U.S. Army, 1954-56. Mem. Am., Pa., Fla. insts. C.P.A.s, Nat. Assn. Accts., Mensa, North Dade C. of C. (dir., v.p., Businessman of Yr. 1980). Home: 1041 NW 203d St Miami FL 33269 Office: 16211 NE 12th Ct North Miami Beach FL 33162

FISHEL, STANLEY IRVYNG, advertising executive; b. N.Y.C., Jan. 2, 1914; s. Max and Mollie (Schulman) F. B.S., Columbia, 1934. Exec. trainee United Artists Corp., N.Y.C., 1934-35; advt. mgr. Imperial Art Galleries, Ltd., N.Y.C., 1935-37; partner, v.p. Jasper, Lynch & Fishel, Inc., N.Y.C., 1937-49; pres. Wilson-Irving Co., 1955—; exec. v.p. Fairfax, Inc., N.Y.C., 1949-76, chmn. bd., 1976-83. Mem. exec. com. advt. div. United Jewish Appeal/Fedn. Jewish Philanthropies N.Y., 1949—; bd. dirs., sec. Henry Kaufmann Campgrounds, 1953-70; bd. dirs. The Troupe Theatre Workshop, N.Y.C., 1979-83. Served to lt. (s.g.) USCGR, 1942-46. Mem. Zeta Beta Tau (nat. pres. 1956-60, pres. found. 1968-80, chmn. bd. 1980-83). Home: 870 7th Ave New York NY 10019 Office: 635 Madison Ave New York NY 10022

FISHER, ALAN WASHBURN, historian, educator; b. Columbus, Ohio, Nov. 23, 1939; s. Sydney Nettleton and Elizabeth E. (Scipio) F.; m. Carol L. Garrett, Aug. 24, 1963; children: Elizabeth, Ann Christy, Garrett. B.A., DePauw U., 1961; M.A., Columbia U., 1964, Ph.D., 1967. Instr. history Mich. State U., East Lansing, 1966-67, asst. prof., 1967-70, asso. prof., 1970-78, prof. Russian and Turkish history, 1978—. Author: Russian Annexation of the Crimea, 1772-1783, 1970, The Crimean Tatars, 1978, Ottoman Studies Directory, I, 1979, II, 1981, III, 1983. Am. Research Inst. in Turkey fellow, 1969, 73, 76; Am. Council Learned Socs. grantee, 1976-77. Fellow Royal Hist. Soc.; Mem. Middle East Studies Assn., Turkish Studies Assn. (pres. 1982-83), Inst. Turkish Studies (dir.). Office: Dept History Mich State U East Lansing MI 48824

FISHER, ALFRED FOSTER, medical association executive; b. Durham, N.C., Mar. 7, 1934; s. Miles Mark III and Ada Virginia (Foster) F.; m. Janice LaVerne Jones, Apr. 20, 1957; children: Rhonda Gisele, Lisa Annette, Jeri Eileen, James Edward II. A.B., N.C. Central U., 1956; M.Ed., Pa. State U., 1965. Tchr., pub. schs., Durham, 1960-64; manpower devel. specialist Dept. Labor, 1965-66; asst. dir. program devel., rev. and tech. asst. Manpower and Career Devel. Agy., N.Y.C., 1966-67, dir. skills tng. div., 1968; asst. to pres. Central State U., Wilberforce, Ohio, 1967-68; dir. mgmt. and tng. systems Community Programs, Inc., Washington, 1968-69; asso. dir. field services Center Community Change, Inc., Washington, 1969-70; v.p. health Nat. Urban Coalition, 1970-72; exec. dir. Health Manpower Devel. Corp., Washington, 1972-74; spl. asst. to pres. N.Y.C. Health and Hosps. Corps., 1974-75; exec. v.p. adminstrv. affairs Nat. Med. Assn., Washington, 1975—. Served with USAF, 1956-60. Recipient various service awards. Mem. Nat. Assn. Minority Med. Educators, Nat. Assn. Health Services Execs., Am. Pub. Health Assn., Am. Assn. Med. Soc. Execs., Am. Soc. Assn. Execs., Phi Delta Kappa. Baptist. Home: 302 Colesville Manor Dr Silver Spring MD 20904 Office: 1012 10th St NW Washington DC 20001

FISHER, ALLAN CARROLL, JR., editor, writer; b. Cumberland, Md., Feb. 17, 1919; s. Allan C. and Ella (Rees) F.; m. Mary Alice Michael, Jan. 20, 1944; children: Suzanne de Cessna (Mrs. Grayson Mattingly), Martha Rees (Mrs. Gordon Sheridan). A.B., U. Md., 1941. Staff writer Washington Post, 1941, Balt. Sun, 1941-43; editorial staff N.Y. bur. A.P., 1943-47; N.Y. public relations rep. Kaiser-Frazer Corp., 1947-48; v.p. Booke & Fisher, Inc. (pub. relations), Houston, 1948-49; assoc. Hammond Assocs. (public relations), Balt., 1949-50; mem. staff Nat. Geog. Mag., 1950-81, asst. editor charge articles, 1963-65, sr. asst. editor charge articles, 1965-70, sr. asst. editor, 1971-78, asst. editor, 1978-81; v.p. Suzanne Fisher Interiors, Annandale, Va., 1979—. Author: America's Inland Waterway: Exploring the Atlantic Seaboard, 1973; contbg. author: this England, 1966; Contbr.: numerous articles to Nat. Geog. Mag. Recipient James J. Strebig Meml. award Aviation Writers Assn., 1956, 60. Mem. Aviation/Space Writers Assn., Nat. Assn. Sci. Writers, Nat. Aero. Assn., AAAS. Episcopalian. Clubs: Cosmos, Nat. Space (bd. govs. 1961-62), Aero (Washington); Marshwood (Savannah, Ga.); Pups (Melbourne, Australia). Home: 11 Mercer Rd The Landings Savannah GA 31411

FISHER, ALLAN HERBERT, JR., lawyer; b. Balt., July 5, 1922; s. Allan Herbert and Esther (Kahn) F. A.B., Johns Hopkins U., 1942; LL.B., U. Md., 1949. Bar: Md. 1948, D.C. 1960. Partner firm Fisher & Winner, Balt.; lectr. domestic relations and pleading Sch. Law U. Balt., 1954-67; former mem. Balt. Fin. Disclosure Adv. Bd.; participant legal seminars. Trustee numerous pvt. trusts, founds. Served to 1st lt. AUS, 1943-46. Fellow Am. Coll. Probate Counsel; mem. ABA, Md. State Bar Assn. (past chmn. sect. estate and trust law), D.C. Bar Assn., Balt. City Bar Assn. Republican. Jewish. Home: 28 Allegheny Ave Towson MD 21204 Office: 315 N Charles St Baltimore MD 21201

FISHER, ALTON KINDT, dentist, pathologist, educator; b. Abrams, Wis., Nov. 1, 1905; s. Fred Ward and Edith Bertha (Kindt) F.; m. Marcelia Coad Neff, Aug. 15, 1931. Student, U. Wis., 1925-32; D.D.S., Marquette U., 1935; B.S., Loyola U., 1948; grad. study, Tulane U., 1948-49. Asst. anthropology Milw. Pub. Mus., 1927-32, research asso., since 1937; intern Milw. Children's Hosp., 1935-36; pvt. dental practice, Milw., 1936-40; instr. histology Marquette U., 1937-40; attending dentist St. Joseph's Hosp., 1937-40; asst. prof. pathology Loyola U., New Orleans, 1945-47, prof., 1947-49; prof., head dept. oral pathology U. Iowa, 1949-73, prof., head dept. stomatology, 1958-65, asst. dean for research, 1973-74, prof. emeritus, 1974—, adj. prof. anthropology, 1976—; phys. anthropologist Office of State Archeologist of Iowa, 1976—; vis. dental surgeon Charity Hosp. La., New Orleans, 1946-49; cons. VA Hosp., Des Moines, 1951-54, Iowa City, 1954-74. Author articles on pathology. Served to comdr. USN, 1940-46; rear adm. Res. ret. Recipient Lapham medal Wis. Archeol. Soc., 1946. Fellow Am. Coll. Dentists, Internat. Assn. Dental Research, Am. Acad. Oral Pathology, Am. Anthrop. Assn., AAAS, Explorers Club; mem. Internat. Acad. Pathology, ADA, Fedn. Dentaire Internationale, Am. Soc. Clin. Pathologists, Wis. Archeol. Soc., Archaeol. Inst. Am., Arctic Inst. N.Am., Am. Polar Soc., Am. Assn. Phys. Anthropologists, Sigma Xi, Omicron Kappa Upsilon. Episcopalian. Club: Mason. Research normal and pathologic tissue respiration, phys. anthropology and paleopathology, 1951—; arctic animals Naval Arctic Research Lab., Point Barrow, 1958-59, 68, 69-71. Home: 701 Oaknoll Dr Iowa City IA 52240

FISHER, ANDREW, management consultant; b. Richmond, Va., Dec. 17, 1920; s. Marion Nimmo and Sarah Randolph (Talcott) F.; m. Cornelia Johnson, Oct. 10, 1942; children: Peter R., Carolyn, Andrew R. B.A., Amherst Coll., 1943; M.B.A., Harvard U., 1947; D.Sc. (h.c.), Albany Med. Coll. Dir. indsl. relations Internat. Braid Co., Providence, 1947; with N.Y. Times, 1947-71, v.p., 1963-70, exec. v.p., 1971, ret., 1971; chmn., pres., pub. News Jour. Co., 1976-78; mgmt. cons. Trustee emeritus Albany Med. Coll. Served to capt. AUS, 1943-46. Home: 1780 Cedar Ln Vero Beach FL 32963

FISHER, ARTHUR, editor; b. N.Y.C., Mar. 10, 1931; s. Abraham G. and Sadie (Gold) F.; m. Liliane E. Kowarsky, Aug. 18, 1951; 1 son, Anthony E. B.A., NYU, 1951. Sr. research aide NYU, 1954-56; mng. editor Dodge Books, 1957-62, Sci. World & Sr. Sci., 1962-68; group editor sci. and engring. Popular Sci., N.Y.C., 1969—. Author: (with Ernest V. Heyn) Century of Wonders, 1972, Fire of Genius, 1976, The Healthy Heart, 1981; contbr. articles to mags. Recipient citations for excellence in sci. writing Deadline Club, 1973, 74; Claude Bernard Sci. Journalism award Nat. Soc. Med. Research; Sci. Writing award Am. Heart Assn., 1981. Mem. Nat. Assn. Sci. Writers. Home: 120 Cabrini Blvd New York NY 10033 Office: 380 Madison Ave New York NY 10017

FISHER, ARTHUR JOHN, glass fiber manufacturing company executive; b. London, Eng., Sept. 13, 1913; s. John Edward and Elizabeth (Dickinson) F.; m. Dorothy Edith Hipkin, Dec. 27, 1937; children: Gillian, Peter, Hugh, Valerie. Student, Eltham Coll., Kent, Eng., 1922-29; cert. in elec. engring., North Staffordshire Tech. Coll., Eng., 1935; D.Engring. (hon.). Registered profl. engr., Ont. With Callenders Cable & Constrn. Co., Eng., 1932-36, Johnson & Phillips, Ltd., 1936-39, Atomic Research Establishment, Harwell, Eng., 1945-48; plant mgr. Fiberglas Can. Inc., Sarnia, Ont., 1948-51, gen. mgr., Toronto, Ont., 1951-55, v.p. mfg. and engring., 1955-67, pres., 1967-78, chmn. bd., 1976-83, hon. chmn. bd., 1983—; dir. Gt. West Steel Industries Ltd., Vancouver, B.C., Can., Standard Chartered Bank of Can. Hon. pres. Canadian Arthritis and Rheumatism Soc.; trustee S.W. Research Inst., Tex. Served as lt. col., arty. Brit. Army, 1939-45. Decorated U.S. Legion of Merit. Mem. Inst. Elec. Engrs. Eng., Engring. Inst. Can. (mem. Canadian-Am. com.). Home: 8 Maytree Rd Willowdale ON Canada M2P 1V8 Office: 3080 Yonge St Toronto ON Canada

FISHER, BENJAMIN CHATBURN, lawyer; b. Coos Bay, Oreg., Feb. 6, 1923; s. Benjamin S. and Catherine Selina (Chatburn) F.; m. Jean L. Whiting, June 30, 1951; children: John, Richard, Robert. A.B. with highest honors, U. Ill., 1948; J.D. magna cum laude, Harvard U., 1951. Bar: D.C. 1951. Law clk. to Judge Learned Hand, 2d circuit, N.Y.C., 1951-52; mem. firm Fisher, Wayland, Cooper & Leader, Washington, 1952—; mem. edn. appeal bd. U.S. Office Edn., 1973-83; mem. Adminstrv. Conf. U.S., 1970-76; chmn. bd. dirs. Center Adminstrv. Justice, Washington, 1972-77; gen. counsel Commn. Population Growth and Am. Future, 1970-72. Contbr. articles to law jours. Bd. dirs. D.C. chpt. ARC, 1977—. Mem. Am. Bar Assn. (chmn. sect. adminstrv. law 1968-69, mem. ho of dels. 1970-72, 73-75), Fed. Communications Bar Assn. (pres. 1967-68), D.C. Bar Assn., Am. Law Inst., Am. Bar Found. and Inst. Jud. Adminstrn., Phi Beta Kappa, Phi Kappa Phi. Clubs: Cosmos, Rotary (dir. 1980—), Rotary (Washington) (pres. 1983-84). Home: 5118 Cammack Dr Bethesda MO 20816 Office: 1100 Connecticut Ave NW Washington DC 20036

FISHER, BENJAMIN COLEMAN, minister, religion executive, educator; b. Webster, N.C., May 27, 1915; s. Ben Franklin and Amy (Long) F.; m. Sara Gehman, Dec. 27, 1940; children: David Lincoln, Hugh Robert. A.B., Wake Forest Coll., 1938, D.D., 1971; M.Div., Andover Newton Theol. Sch., 1942; postgrad., U. N.C., 1946; LL.D., Campbell Coll., 1968; D.Lit., Mercer U., 1980, Grand Canyon Coll., 1980. Ordained to ministry So. Baptist Conv., 1938; pastor Castalia-Peachtree Bapt. Ch., 1938-39, First Bapt. Ch., Nashville, N.C., 1942-45, Newton, N.C., 1945-47; tchr. Gardner-Webb Coll., 1947-48, asst. to pres., dir. pub. relations, 1948-52; assoc. sec. Edn. Commn. So. Baptist Conv., 1952-54, exec. sec. treas. edn. com., 1970, exec. dir., 1970-78; exec. sec.-treas. Am. Assn. Presidents of Ind. Colls. and Univs., 1981; adj. prof. religion Campbell U., 1978—; asst. to pres. Southeastern Sem., 1954-62; exec. sec. N.C. Edn. Com., 1962-70; chmn. bd. dirs. Bibl. Recorder, 1960-63; Advisor Chowan Coll. Author: A Public Relations Manual for Church-Related Colleges, 1954, An Orientation Manual for Trustees of Church Related Colleges, 4th edit, 1980; editor: New Pathways: A Dialogue in Christian Higher Education, 1980. Address: Campbell U Buies Creek NC 27506 Home: 607 Union St P O Box 607 Murfreesboro NC 27855

FISHER, BENJAMIN REEVES, retired manufacturing company executive; b. Pitts., Apr. 5, 1916; s. Chester G. and Margaret (Aiken) F.; m. Lilian C. Hall, Apr. 10, 1939; children: Margaret Aiken Fisher McKean, Coburn Hall, Benjamin Reeves, Christine Chase Fisher Allen. B.S., Yale U., 1938. With Fisher Sci. Co., Pitts., 1938-81, pres., chief exec. officer, 1965-75, chmn. bd., 1975-81. Trustee Children's Hosp. Pitts., Carnegie Hero Fund Commn., Pitts.; mem. exec. com. Allegheny Conf. Community Devel., Pitts. Mem. Sci. Apparatus Makers Am. (bd. dirs. 1957-64), Am. Chem. Soc., Sigma Xi (assoc.). Home: 5452 Northumberland St Pittsburgh PA 15217 Office: 711 Forbes Ave Pittsburgh PA 15219

FISHER, BERNARD, physician; b. Pitts., Aug. 23, 1918; s. Reuben and Amma (Miller) F.; m. Shirley Kruman, June 5, 1947; children: Beth, Joseph, Louisa. B.S., U. Pitts., 1940, M.D., 1943. Diplomate: Am. Bd. Surgery. Intern Mercy Hosp., Pitts., 1943-44, resident in surgery, 1944-48; fellow in surg. research, resident in gen. surgery Harrison dept. surg. research U. Pa., Phila., 1950-52; exchange appointment in surgery London Postgrad. Med. Sch., Hammersmith Hosp., 1955-56; teaching fellow in pathology U. Pitts., 1944-45, teaching fellow in surgery, 1945-47, asso. prof., 1956-59, prof., 1959—, research fellow in exptl. endocrinology, 1947-50, dir. oncology, 1974—, dir.,; mem. surg. staff Presbyn.-Univ. Hosp., Children's Hosp. of Pitts.; cons. staff Magee-Womens Hosp., VA Hosp., Pitts.; mem. Am. Council Learned Socs.-Nat. Acad. Scis.; Social Sci. Research Council Cancer del. to, China, 1977; hon. mem. faculty Instituto Nacional de Enfermedades Neoplasicas, Peru; cons. Nat. Cancer Inst., NIH, 1967—; mem. adv. com. for anti-neoplastic drugs FDA, 1977-79; chmn. Nat. Surg. Adjuvant Project for Breast and Bowel Cancers, 1967—; mem. com. sci. advisers Vincent T. Lombardi Cancer Research Center, 1974—; mem. program com. XI Internat. Cancer Congress, Florence, Italy, 1971-74; mem. Pres.'s Cancer Council, 1979—, Com. on therapeutics U.S.-Italian Agreement for Cooperation in Cancer, 1980—, Kettering Selection Com., Gen. Motors Cancer Research Fedn., 1980—. Mem. editorial bd.: Transplatation, 1966-71, Cancer, 1969-73, 75—, Year Book of Cancer, 1973—, Internat. Jour. Radiation Oncology Biology Physics, 1975—, Cancer Clin. Trials, 1977—; asso. editor: Cancer Research, 1976—; mem. editorial adv. bd.: Cancer Treatment Reports, 1976-79, 80-83; editorial bd.: Seminars in Oncology, 1979, Breast Cancer Research and Treatment, 1980—; Editorial bd.: Invasion and Metastasis, 1981—, Cancer Metastasis Revs., 1981, Jour. Clin. Oncology, 1982, Internat. Jour. Breast and Mammary Pathology, 1982; contbr. numerous articles to med. jours. Bd. dirs. Allegheny County unit Am. Cancer Soc. Recipient Man of Year award in medicine Pitts. Jr. C. of C., 1966; Philip Hench Distinguished Alumnus award U. Pitts. Sch. Medicine, 1976; McGraw medal Detroit Surg. Assn., 1978, Lucy Wortham James Clin. Research award, 1981, Health Meml. award, 1982, Joseph H. Morton Meml. award, 1983, Julia Hudson Freund Meml. award, 1983; Markle scholar in med. sci. John and Mary Markle Found., 1953-58. Mem. AAAS, Am. Assn. Cancer Edn., Am. Assn. Cancer Research, Am. Soc. Clin. Oncology (Karnofsky award 1980), AAUP, A.C.S. (patient care com. commn. on cancer 1970—), AMA, Am. Physiol. Soc., Assn. Am. Med. Colls., Cell Kinetic Soc., Am., Central, Pan-Pacific surg. assns., Internat. Cardiovascular Soc., Internat. Soc. Lymphology, Internat. Soc. Surgery, N.Y. Acad. Scis., Soc. for Surgery Alimentary Tract, Soc. Surg. Oncology (com. on govt. relations 1979-80), Soc. Univ. Surgeons, Soc. Vascular Surgeons, Surg. Biology Club II, Transplantation Soc., Fedn. Am. Socs. for Exptl. Biology, Pa. Med. Soc., Allegheny County Med. Soc. (cancer com. 1976) med. socs, Man of Year 1983), Pitts. Acad. Medicine, Pitts. Surg. Soc. (pres. 1979—), Peruvian Acad. Surgery (hon.), Italian Surg. Research Soc. (corr.), Associaxione Italiana per la Divulgaxione Scientifica della Cancerologia Clinica, Internat. Assn. Breast Cancer Research (sr. council 1980—), Am.-Italian Fedn. Cancer Research (dir. 1980—), Phi Beta Kappa. Office: Room 914 Scaife Hall U Pitts Sch Medicine 3550 Terrace St Pittsburgh PA 15261

FISHER, CALVIN DAVID, food mfg. co. exec.; b. Nerstrand, Minn., June 10, 1926; s. Edward and Sadie (Wolf) F.; m. Patricia Vivian Capriotti, July 28, 1950; children—Cynthia, Nancy Joann, Michael. B.S., U. Minn., 1950. Dairy specialist U.S. Dept. Agr., Mpls., 1950-54, chemist and dairy specialist, Omaha, 1954-58; with Roberts Dairy Co., Omaha, 1958-80, sr. v.p., chief operating officer, 1967-70, pres., chief exec. officer, 1970-80, owner, chief exec. officer, 1975-80, Fisher Foods Ltd. and Plasti-Cyc, Lincoln, Nebr., 1980—; pres., dir. Master Dairies, Indpls., 1968—; bd. dirs. Internat. Assn. Ice Cream Mfrs. Milk Industry Found., 1973—. Bd. dirs., v.p. Omaha Safety Council, 1981; bd. dirs. Arthritis Found., 1972-81; mem. adv. council SBA. Served with USN, 1944-47. Mem. Omaha C. of C. (pres.'s council 1976, 78), Internat. Food Scientists Assn., Inst. Food Tech., Nat. Ind. Dairies Assn. Republican. Methodist. Clubs: Rotary, Omaha Country, Omaha Press. Patentee spray-dried ice cream mix, pasteurized egg products. Home: 5040 S 81st St Ralston NE 68127 Office: 220 S 20th St Lincoln NE 68510

FISHER, CARL FREDERICK, real estate services company executive; b. Tiffin, Ohio, June 12, 1924; s. Lawrence F. and Margaret (LaFountain) F.; m. Kathleen Griffith Denman, Dec. 18, 1948; 1 son, Kurt Denman. B.S. in Bus. Adminstrn, Ohio State U., 1949. With Gen. Motors Corp., 1949-51, Ford Motor Co., 1951-54, Chrysler Corp., 1954-58, Chrysler de Venezuela, 1958-60; v.p., treas. Garrett Corp., Los Angeles, 1960-67; chmn. bd., pres. Signal Equities Co., 1967-70;

sr. v.p. Tracor, Inc., Austin, Tex., 1970-74; v.p., treas. Cordura Corp., Chgo., 1974-76; cons., 1976-80; exec. v.p. Creative Computer Services, Inc., Dallas, 1980-82; pres. Shalimar Corp., Dallas, 1976—. Served with USAAF, 1943-45. Home: 2900 Shalimar St Plano TX 75023

FISHER, CARRIE FRANCES, actress; b. Oct. 21, 1956; d. Eddie and Debbie Reynolds. Ed. high sch., Beverly Hills, Calif. Mem.: chorus in Broadway musical Irene, 1972; appeared: motion pictures Shampoo, 1975, Star Wars, 1977, Mr. Mike's Mondo Video, 1979, The Blues Brothers, 1980, The Empire Strikes Back, 1980, Under the Rainbow, 1981; TV movie Come Back, Little Sheba, 1977, Leave Yesterday Behind, 1978. *

FISHER, CHARLES HAROLD, research adminstr.; b. Hiawatha, W.Va., Nov. 20, 1906; s. Lawrence D. and Mary (Akers) F.; m. Elizabeth Dye, Nov. 4, 1933 (dec. 1967); m. Lois Carlin, July 1968. B.S., Roanoke Coll., 1928; M.S., U. Ill., 1929, Ph.D., 1932; D.Sc. (hon.), Tulane U., 1953, Sc.D., Roanoke Coll., 1963. Teaching asst. chemistry U. Ill., 1928-32; instr. Harvard, 1932-35; asso. organic chemist U.S. Bur. Mines, Pitts., 1935-40; head carbohydrate div. E. Regional Research Lab., U.S. Dept. Agr., 1946-50, dir., New Orleans, 1950-72; adj. research prof. Roanoke Coll., 1972—. Pres. New Orleans Sci. Fair, 1967-69. Recipient So. Chemists award, 1956, Herty medal, 1959; Chem. Pioneer award Am. Inst. Chemists, 1966. Mem. Am. Inst. Chemists (hon., pres. 1962-63, chmn. bd. dirs.), Sci. Research Soc. Am., Oil Chem. Soc., Am. Chem. Soc. (dir. region IV), Chemurgic Council (dir.), Am. Assn. Textile Chemists and Colorists, Sigma Xi, Alpha Chi Sigma, Gamma Alpha, Phi Lambda Upsilon. Club: Cosmos (Washington). Office: Chemistry Dept Roanoke College Salem VA 24153 *I have worked hard as a physical scientist and research administrator because research is fun and offers the best way of benefiting mankind.*

FISHER, CHARLES J., holding co. exec.; b. 1920; (married). B.S., M.I.T., 1946. Jr. engr Hamilton Paper Co., 1947-56; v.p., gen. mgr. Wyemissing Corp., 1956-64; v.p., gen. mgr. specialty chems. div. Reliance Universal Inc., Louisville, 1969-78, pres., 1978—, chief operating officer, 1979—. Office: Reliance Universal Inc 1930 Bishop Ln 1600 Watterson Tower Louisville KY 40218 *

FISHER, CHARLES PAGE, JR., consulting geotechnical engineer; b. Richmond, Va., Sept. 24, 1921; s. Charles Page and Annie Laura (Wright) F.; m. Joyce Mayo Isom, Dec. 23, 1972. B.S.C.E., U. Va., 1949; S.M., Harvard U., 1950; Ph.D., N.C. State U., 1962. Registered profl. engr., Md., Va., N.C., S.C., Tenn. Instr. to asso. prof. civil engrng. N.C. State U., Raleigh, 1955-69; pres. Geotech. Engrng. Co., Research Triangle Park, N.C., 1963-78; prin. C. Page Fisher Cons. Engr., Durham, N.C., 1978—; corporate sec. Troxler Electronics Labs., Research Triangle Park, N.C., 1961—. Bd. dirs. Ravenscroft Sch., Raleigh, N.C. Served with USN, 1941-45. Fellow Am. Cons. Engrs. Council, ASCE; mem. ASTM, Nat. Soc. Profl. Engrs., Transp. Research Bd., Am. Arbitration Assn., Internat. Soc. Soil Mechanics and Found. Engrng., Cons. Engrs. Council N.C., Am. Coll. Constrn. Arbitrators. Democrat. Episcopalian. Home: 1 Stoneridge Circle Durham NC 27705 Office: 2534 1/2 Chapel Hill Blvd Durham NC 27705

FISHER, CHARLES THOMAS, III, banker; b. Detroit, Nov. 22, 1929; s. Charles Thomas, Jr. and Elizabeth Jane (Briggs) F.; m. Margaret Elizabeth Keegin, June 18, 1952; children: Margaret Elizabeth (Mrs. F. Macy Jones), Charles Thomas IV, Curtis William, Lawrence Peter II, Mary Florence. A.B. in Econs, Georgetown U., 1951; M.B.A., Harvard U., 1953. C.P.A., Mich. With Touche, Ross, Bailey & Smart (C.P.A.'s), Detroit, 1953-58; asst. v.p. Nat. Bank Detroit, 1958-61, v.p., 1961-66, sr. v.p., 1966-69, exec. v.p., 1969-72, pres., chief adminstrv. officer, 1972—, also dir.; pres., dir. NBD Bancorp, Inc., 1973—, chmn., 1982—; dir. Internat. Bank of Detroit, Detroit Edison Co., Hiram Walker Resources, Ltd., Gen. Motors Corp., Am. Airlines. Civilian aide to sec. army for State of Mich., 1974-77; Chmn. Mackinac Bridge Authority.; Bd. dirs. Greater Detroit Area Hosp. Council. Named Detroit Young Man of Year Detroit Jr. Bd. Commerce, 1961. Mem. Assn. Res. City Bankers, Am. Inst. C.P.A.s, Mich. Assn. C.P.A.s. Clubs: Bloomfield Hills (Mich.) Country; Country of Detroit (Grosse Pointe); Detroit Athletic, Detroit, Yondotega (Detroit); Links (N.Y.C.). Home: Grosse Pointe Farms MI 48236 Office: National Bank Detroit Detroit MI 48232

FISHER, CHARLES WORLEY, editor; b. Phila., July 30, 1917; s. Charles Worley and Emily (Kohler) F.; m. Mary McCain Wilcox, Nov. 28, 1941; children: Linda Fisher Eveland, Mary Emily Fisher Vigna, Charles Worley, Anthony Hay, Lisa McCain. Grad., Mercersburg Acad., 1935; student, Haverford Coll., 1936-40. With Benton & Bowles, Inc., N.Y.C., 1946-65. Producer: TV shows As the World Turns, 1956-60, The Edge of Night, 1960-65, Another World, 1965, Hidden Faces, NBC-TV, N.Y.C., 1970; editor: Hagerstown (Md.) Town & Country Almanack, 1973—; co-author scenario, dir.: motion picture Washington Crossing the Delaware, 1967; freelance theatrical dir., audio-visual cons. TV cons. Trenton (N.J.) Bd. Edn., 1972-81; cons. Friends of Hildene; dir. Dorset Players. Served to capt. AUS, 1942-46. Home: River Rd Arlington VT 05250 Office: Gruber Almanack Co 17 E Washington St Hagerstown MD 21740

FISHER, CHESTER LEWIS, JR., retired lawyer; b. Maplewood, N.J., May 30, 1911; s. Chester Lewis and Katherine Barton (Riddle) F.; m. Grace Annette Tainsh, Nov. 23, 1943; children: Chester Lewis III, Jane Alison Swiggett. Grad., Mercersburg Acad., 1929; A.B., Princeton U., 1933; J.D., Cornell U., 1936. Bar: N.Y. 1937, P.I. 1945, N.J. 1947, U.S. Supreme Ct 1972. Instr. phys. edn. Cornell U., 1933-36; practiced law, N.Y.C., 1936-39; atty. Met. Life Ins. Co., 1939-57, asst. v.p., asst. to pres. and chmn., 1957-60, 3d v.p., 1960-63, 2d v.p., 1963-65, v.p., 1965-76. Village trustee Briarcliff Manor, 1969-71, mayor, 1971-77. Served from 1st lt. to col. USAAF, 1940-46. Decorated Legion of Merit. Mem. Assn. Life Ins. Counsel (past pres.), SAR. Episcopalian. Club: Sleepy Hollow Country. Home: 164 Pine Rd Briarcliff Manor NY 10510

FISHER, CLARKSON SHERMAN, judge; b. Long Branch, N.J., July 8, 1921; s. Albert Emmanuel and Katherine Morris (Sherman) F.; m. Mae Shannon Hoffmann, Dec. 26, 1949; children—Albert James, Clarkson Sherman, Scott Laurus, Daniel Russell. LL.B. cum laude, U. Notre Dame, 1950. Bar: N.J. bar 1951. Law clk., atty. Jacob Steinbach, Jr. (Atty. at Law), Long Branch, 1950, 51; atty. Edward F. Juska (Lawyer), Long Branch, 1951-58; partner Juska & Fisher (Counsellors at Law), Long Branch, 1958-64; Monmouth County (N.J.) Ct. judge, 1964-66; judge N.J. Superior Ct., 1966-70, U.S. Dist. Ct., Dist. of N.J., 1970-79, chief judge, 1979—. Trustee Central Jersey Bank & Trust Co.; Atty. Long Branch Planning Bd., Partrolmen's Benevolent Assn., Long Branch, Monmouth County, and Bayshore (N.J.); Mem. West Long Branch Fire Co. 2, 1955—, West Long Branch Bd. Adjustment, 1958; mem. Borough Council, West Long Branch, 1959-64; N.J. State assemblyman from Monmouth County, 1964; Trustee Monmouth Coll., West Long Branch, 1971-76. Served to staff sgt. Signal Corps, also Inf. AUS, 1942-45. Mem. ABA., N.J. Bar Assn., Monmouth County Bar Assn. (trustee 1962-64), Am. Legion, Holy Name Soc. (pres. chpt. 1960), VFW. Home: 11 Pinewood Ave West Long Branch NJ 07764 Office: Post Office and Courthouse Bldg Newark NJ 07101

FISHER, CRAIG BECKER, film and television executive; b. Manila, Philippines, Jan. 19, 1932; s. Dale Davis and Francis Mary (Major) F.; m. Helen Rossi Ashton, Sept. 5, 1970; children: Christopher Ashton, Wenda Francis; children by previous marriage: Cathleen Anne, Dean Barnett. B.A., U. Md., 1954. With sta. WRC-TV, Washington, 1950, WTOP-TV, 1952, WMAL-TV, 1954; successively unit mgr., asso. producer, film dir. CBS News, 1957-60; producer, dir., writer NBC News, 1960-70; pres. Osprey Prodns., Inc., N.Y.C., 1970—; adj. asso. prof. film dept. St. John's U., N.Y. U.; cons. Nat. Commn. Population Growth and the Am. Future; judge D.W. Griffith Film Festival; cons. TV, radio and film dept. U. Md.; Bd. dirs., treas. Am. Friends of Brit. Acad. Film and TV Arts; pres. Fund for Arts and Scis. Films, Inc., 1981—; mem. selection com. Nat. Endowment for Humanities. Mem. exec. com. Scott Newman Drug Abuse Prevention Award. Served to capt. USAF, 1955-57. Recipient Thomas Alva Edison award, George Foster Peabody award, Ohio State U. award; Freedoms Found. award; Wrangler award Western Heritage Center; Criss award; Golden Eagle award Council Internat. Nontheatrical Events; IFPA Cindy award.; recipient Best Documentary Script on Current Events award Writers Guild Am., Best Film award Nat. Press Photographers Assn., Emmy award, All Am. award Radio-TV Daily, Fame award TV Today and Motion Picture Daily, Blue Ribbon award Am. Film Festival, Silver Oscella La Biennale di Venezia, cert. Venice Film Festival, Adelaide/Auckland (Australia) Internat. Film Festival. Mem. Writers Guild Am. East (pres. 1977-79, exec. dir. Found.), Nat. Acad. TV Arts and Scis. (nat. trustee, chmn. awards), Soc. Tech. Writers and Pubs., Am. Sci. Film Assn., AAAS, Am. Polar Soc., Internat. Oceanographic Found., Info. Film Producers Am., East African Wildlife Soc., Air Force Assn., Sigma Delta Chi, Sigma Chi. Clubs: Overseas Press, Explorers (N.Y.C.) (fellow). Home: 233 E 52d St New York NY 10022

FISHER, DALE JOHN, medical instrumentation researcher; b. Omro, Wis., June 4, 1925; m. Ruth J. Laird, Apr. 27, 1957; 1 dau., Shelley Dale. B.S., U. Wis., Oshkosh, 1947; Ph.D. (Univ. fellow), Ind. U., 1951. Staff mem. Inst. Paper Chemistry, Appleton, Wis., 1945; chemist City of Oshkosh, Wis., summers 1946-48; chemist ionic analyses group Oak Ridge Nat. Lab., 1951-52, group leader analytical instrumentation group, 1952-72, mem. dir.'s staff, 1972-73; physicist (nuclear medicine) VA Hosp., Gainesville, Fla., 1973-74, tech. dir. nuclear medicine, 1974-76; physicist FDA, Silver Spring, Md., 1976—, physicist div. in vitro diagnostic device standards, 1976-83, physicist Office Sci. and Tech., 1983—. Mem. Am. Chem. Soc. (award chem. instrumentation), Sigma Xi, Phi Lambda Upsilon. Research with computer-based instrumentation to obtain better info. for patient care; instrumentation concerns of diagnostic med. device standards and research; sci. basis for med. instruments. Conceived and directed research programs for devel. of and selected and applied physiochem., mech., electronic and optical principles in design of instrumentation and for new or improved instrumental methods. Home: 6319 Golden Hook Columbia MD 21044 Office: Office Sci and Tech Nat Center for Devices and Radiol Health FDA Dept Health and Human Services 8757 Georgia Ave Silver Spring MD 20910

FISHER, DAVID FORD, pianist, musical director; b. Akron, Ohio, Dec. 22, 1946; s. Stanley Ford and Olive Jean (Parsons) F. B.S., U. Akron, 1969, J.D., 1973; postgrad., Stanford U., 1967-68, U. San Diego Law Sch., 1969-70; student, Juiliard Sch. Music, Am. U., Rome. Pianist Akron Symphony Orch.; mus. dir. Ohio Ballet, Akron; concert pianist, condr. Home: 181 Marvin Ave Akron OH 44302 Office: 354 E Market St Akron OH 44302

FISHER, DAVID WOODROW, editor, publisher; b. N.Y.C., Jan. 7, 1927; s. Jacob and Mollie Rose (Friedman) F.; m. Naomi Rubin, June 21, 1951; children: Paul, Robert. B.A., N.Y. U., 1947. With N.Y. Times, 1945-51, radio news writer, 1948-51; rewrite man Agence France-Presse, 1951-53; asst. dir. public info. Am. Heart Assn., 1953-56; with Med. News, N.Y.C., 1956-61, exec. editor, 1960-61; med. publs. editor Sci. and Medicine Pub. Co., 1961-64; editorial dir., exec. v.p. Blake Cabot Assos., Inc., 1964-66; editorial dir. Hosp. Practice, N.Y.C., 1966—; v.p. HP Pub. Co., Inc., 1966-74, pres., chmn. bd. dirs., 1974—. Author: You and Your Heart, 1963; editor: (with R.A. Good) Immunobiology, 1971, (with F.J. Dixon) The Biology of Immunologic Disease, 1983. Chmn. bd. dirs. Del., Nat. Democratic Conv., 1968; pres. Adlai Stevenson Reform Dem. Club, 1971-73. Mem. Nat. Assn. Sci. Writers, ACLU. Office: 575 Lexington Ave New York NY 10022

FISHER, DELBERT ARTHUR, physician, educator; b. Placerville, Calif., Aug. 12, 1928; s. Arthur Lloyd and Thelma (Johnson) F.; m. Beverly Carne Fisher, Jan. 28, 1951; children: David Arthur, Thomas Martin, Mary Kathryn. B.A., U. Calif., Berkeley, 1950, M.D., 1953. Diplomate: Am. Bd. Pediatrics (examiner 1971-80, mem. subsplty. com. pediatric endocrinology 1976-79). Intern, then resident in pediatrics U. Calif. Med. Center, San Francisco, 1953-55; resident in pediatrics U. Oreg. Hosp., Portland, 1957-58, Irwin Meml. fellow pediatric endocrinology, 1958-60; from asst. prof. to prof. pediatrics U. Ark. Med. Sch., Little Rock, 1960-68; prof. pediatrics UCLA Med. Sch., 1968-73; prof. pediatrics and medicine, 1973—; research prof. devel. and perinatal biology Harbor-UCLA Med. Center, 1975—; mem. com. maternal and child health research NRC, 1975-76; cons. genetic disease sect. Calif. Dept. Health Services, 1978—; mem. organizing com. Internat. Conf. Newborn Thyroid Screening, 1977-82. Co-editor: Perinatal Thyroid Physiology and Disease, 1975; editor-in-chief: Jour. Clin. Endocrinology and Metabolism, 1978-83; contbr. articles profl. jours., chpts. to books. Served to capt. M.C. USAF, 1955-57. Recipient Career Devel. award NIH, 1964-68. Mem. Am. Acad. Pediatrics (Borden award 1981), Soc. Pediatric Research, Am. Pediatric Soc., Endocrine Soc., Am. Thyroid Assn., Am. Soc. Clin. Investigation, Lawson Wilkins Pediatric Endocrine Soc., Phi Beta Kappa. Home: 4 Pear Tree Ln Rolling Hills Estates CA 90274 Office: Dept Pediatrics Harbor-UCLA Med Center 1000 W Carson St Torrance CA 90509

FISHER, DONALD G., casual apparel chain stores executive; b. 1928; married. B.S., U. Calif., 1950. With M. Fisher & Son, 1950-57; former ptnr. Fisher Property Investment Co.; co-founder, pres. The Gap Stores Inc., San Bruno, Calif., dir. Office: The Gap Stores Inc 900 Cherry Ave Box 60 San Bruno CA 94066 *

FISHER, DONALD GRANT, educator; b. Winnipeg, Man., Can., June 23, 1934; s. Donald James and Ruth Una (Beardsley) F.; m. Carlean June Ginsburg, May 5, 1956; children: Lynn Ellen, Douglas Grant. B.E., U. Sask., 1956, M.Sc., 1957; Ph.D., U. Mich., 1965; M.R.E., McMaster U., 1976. Registered profl. engr., Alta. Group leader Polyolefin design Union Carbide Can. Ltd., Montreal, Que., 1957-61; asst. prof. U. Alta., 1964-66, assoc. prof., 1966-70, prof., 1970-71; vis. prof. U. Manchester (Eng.) Inst. Sci. and Tech., 1971-72; prof., chmn. dept. chem. engrng. U. Alta., 1972-75, prof., 1976—; vis. prof. McMaster U., 1975-76; pres. Systemation Ltd., Edmonton, 1967—; chmn. asso. com. on automatic control NRC, 1978-83; ordained to ministry Bapt. Ch., 1977. Asso. editor: IEEE Transactions on Automatic Control; contbr. articles to tech. jours. NRC of Can. research grantee, 1965—. Mem. Canadian Soc. Chem. Engrng. (pres. Edmonton sect. 1967), Am. Inst. Chem. Engrs., Assn. Profl. Engrs. Alta., IEEE. Home: 8453 118th St Edmonton AB T6G 1T2 Canada

FISHER, DONALD WAYNE, assn. exec.; b. Pitts., Mar. 2, 1946; s. David H.W. and Jean K. (Crum) F.; children by previous marriage—Kimberly Elizabeth, Jeffrey Wayne. A.A., Hinds Jr. Coll., 1966; B.S. in Biology and Chemistry, Millsaps Coll., 1968; M.S. in Anatomy, U. Miss., 1970, Ph.D., 1973; postgrad. in assn. mgmt., U. Md., 1977-79. Cert. assn. exec. Instr. dept. chemistry and biology Hinds Jr. Coll., Raymond, Miss., 1968-74; instr. dept. anatomy U. Miss. Sch. Medicine, Jackson, 1973-74, co-dir. and exec. officer physician asst. program, 1972-74; asst. professorial lectr. George Washington U. Sch. Medicine, 1974—; exec. dir. Assn. Physician Asst. Programs, Arlington, Va., 1974-80, Am. Acad. Physician Assts., Arlington, 1974-80; exec. v.p., chief exec. officer Am. Group Practice Assn., Alexandria, Va., 1980—, treas. polit. action com., 1980—; mem. Nat. Commn. on Allied Health Edn., 1977-80; mem. adv. com. for tng., devel. and utilization of physician extenders Systems Scis., Inc., 1975-80; Pres. Am. Acad. Physician Assts. Ednl. and Research Found., 1977-80; sec., treas. Am. Group Practice Found., 1980—. Robert Wood Johnson Found. grantee, 1973-80. Mem. Am. Soc. Assn. Execs. (govt. relations com. 1980—), Assn. Am. Med. Colls., AAAS, Greater Washington Soc. Assn. Execs., Fairfax County Hosp. Assn., Arlington (Va.) C. of C. Home: 3814 Ivanhoe Ln Alexandria VA 22310 Office: 1422 Duke St Alexandria VA 22314

FISHER, DONALD WIENER, lawyer; b. Sandusky, Ohio, Jan. 27, 1923; s. Albert Livingston and Orpha (Wiener) F.; m. Jeanne Marie Bolan, Oct. 4, 1952; children—Sarah Jeanne Fisher Schmitt, Laura Laskey Fisher Pories, John Bolan, Andrew Donald, Martha Emily. B.S., Ohio State U., 1947, J.D., 1949. Bar: Ohio bar 1949, D.C. bar 1970. Practiced in, Toledo, 1949—; atty. NLRB, ICC; counsel Sheet Metal Workers Internat. Assn. Served with AUS, 1943-45; PTO. Mem. Am., D.C., Toledo bar assns. Club: Toledo. Home: 3803 Hillandale Rd Toledo OH 43606 Office: Nat Bank Bldg Toledo OH 43604

FISHER, EDWARD JOSEPH, optometrist, educator; b. Winnipeg, Man., Can., Nov. 25, 1913; s. Joseph Thomas and Margaret (Cobean) F.; m. Eleanor Jessie Holmes, Sept. 28, 1936; children: Margaret Eleanor (Mrs. Bruce Brillinger), Gordon Joseph, Barbara Marion. Diploma, Coll. Optometry of Ont. at Toronto, 1934; B.A., U. Toronto, 1946, M.A., 1948; D.Sc., Pa. Coll. Optometry, 1969. Practice optometry, Lindsay, Ont., Can., 1934-37, Toronto, 1937-45, 57-67; clinician Coll. Optometry of Ont., 1937, clinic dir., 1938-48, dean, 1948-67; dir. U. Waterloo (Ont.) Sch. Optometry, 1967-75, prof., 1969-82; vis. prof. U. Benin, Nigeria, 1976-81, City U. London, 1976; Lectr. orgns. in, Can., U.S., U.K., South Africa. Contbr. numerous articles to profl. jours. Recipient Order of Merit U. Montreal, Que., Can., 1958; Can. Centennial medal, 1967. Mem. Royal Canadian Coll. Organists, Am. Acad. Optometry (pres. 1968-70), Optometrical Assn. Ont., Canadian Assn. Optometrists (award 1971), Am. Optometric Assn., Optical Soc. Am. Clubs: University Waterloo Faculty, Masons. Research in low vision aids, contact lenses. Home: 519 Oxbow Rd Waterloo ON Canada

FISHER, EVERETT, lawyer; b. Greenwich, Conn., May 23, 1920; s. Henry Johnson and Alice Gifford (Agnew) F.; m. Catherine Gray Marshall, Aug. 21, 1943; children: Catherine (Mrs. Eliot Field), Emily Trenholm Griswold. Grad., Phillips Acad., 1937; B.A., Yale U., 1941, LL.B., 1948. Bar: Conn. 1948, N.Y. 1949. Assoc. Littlefield, Miller & Cleaves, N.Y.C., 1948-51; ptnr. Pullman, Comley, Marshall & Parker, Greenwich, 1951-58, Parker, Badger & Fisher, 1958-72, Badger, Fisher, Cohen & Barnett, 1972—; Dir., sec., mem. exec. com. Times Mirror Mags., Inc.; trust bd. dirs. Union Trust Co. Past chmn. Bd. Estimate and Taxation, Greenwich.; Bd. dirs., v.p. Greenwich Boys' Club; trustee Internat. Coll., Beirut, Lebanon. Mem. Internat., Am. bar assns., State Bar of Conn., Am. Coll. Probate Counsel, Phi Delta Phi. Republican. Clubs: Pine Valley Golf (Clementon, N.J.); Royal and Ancient Golf (St. Andrews, Scotland); Round Hill (dir., past pres), Field (Greenwich); Yale (N.Y.C.); Royal St. George's Golf (Sandwich, Eng.); Honourable Company of Edinburgh Golfers (Muirfield, Scotland); U.S. Seniors Golf Assn. (sec., gov.). Home: 53 Pecksland Rd Greenwich CT 06830 Office: 49 W Putnam Ave Greenwich CT 06836

FISHER, FRANKLIN GEORGE, cons. engrng. co. exec.; b. Sinking Spring, Pa., Dec. 24, 1916; s. Franklin Philemon and Vesta (Gotschall) F.; m. Mary E. Eben, June 24, 1939; children—Linda L. Fisher Farrell, Marjorie A. Fisher Spuhler. Student, Internat. Corr. Schs., 1934-35, Wyomissing Poly. Inst., 1936-39, McCann's Bus. Sch., 1938-39, Pa. State U. Extension, 1940-52. Registered profl. engr., Pa. With Reading Co. R.R., 1938-73, gen. mgr., Phila., 1967-69, operating v.p., 1970-73; v.p. STV Engrs., Inc., N.Y.C., 1973-78; sr. v.p. rail transp. STV/SSV & K Inc., Pottstown, 1978—. Fellow ASME; mem. Nat. Soc. Profl. Engrs., Am. Ry. Engrng. Assn. Democrat. Lutheran. Clubs: Lehigh Valley, Green Valley Country, Heidelberg Country, Masons. Patentee R.R. components, 1950-70. Home: 1942 Palm St Reading PA 19604 Office: 99 Park Ave New York NY 10016

FISHER, FRANKLIN MARVIN, economist; b. N.Y.C., Dec. 13, 1934; s. Mitchell Salem and Esther (Oshiver) F.; m. Ellen Jo Paradise, June 22, 1958; children—Abraham Samuel, Abigail Sarah, Naomi Leah. A.B. summa cum laude, Harvard U., 1956, M.A., 1957, Ph.D., 1960. Asst. prof. econs. U. Chgo., 1959-60; asst. prof. econs. Mass. Inst. Tech., 1960-62, asso. prof., 1962-65, prof., 1965—; cons. various law firms; dir., cons. Charles River Assos. Inc. Editor: Econometrica, 1968-77. Trustee Combined Jewish Philanthropies, Boston, 1975—, bd. mgrs., 1979—; trustee Beth Israel Hosp., Boston, 1979—; chmn. faculty adv. cabinet United Jewish Appeal, 1975-77; bd. govs. Tel Aviv U., 1976—. NSF fellow, 1962-63; Ford Found. Faculty Research fellow, 1966-67; Guggenheim fellow, 1981-82. Fellow Econometric Soc. (council, v.p. 1977-78, pres. 1979), Am. Acad. Arts and Scis.; mem. Am. Econ. Assn. (John Bates Clark medal 1973). Home: 197 Holden Wood Rd Concord MA 01742 Office: E52-359 50 Memorial Dr Mass Inst Tech Cambridge MA 02139

FISHER, FREDERICK G., JR., lawyer. A.B., Bowdoin Coll., 1942; LL.B., Harvard U., 1948. Bar: Mass. 1948. Mem. Hale and Dorr, Boston. Mem. Boston Bar Assn. (chmn. Conf. Personal Fin. Law 1980—), Mass. Bar Assn. (pres. 1975-76), ABA (chmn. gen. practice sect. 1974-75). Office: Hale and Dorr 60 State St Boston MA 02109 *

FISHER, GARY ALAN, publisher; b. Akron, Ohio, Apr. 4, 1951; s. Paul McCray and Betty Elaine F.; m. Lauren Victoria Muschio, Aug. 11, 1979. A.B. in History, Princeton U., 1973. Founder, pub. Courselector (univ. curriculum guides series), Princeton, N.J. and Boston, 1973-75; bus. mgr. CBS Spl. Interest Mags., N.Y.C., 1976-78, dir. bus. ops., 1979; pub. Am. Photographer Mag., N.Y.C., 1980—. Mem. Mag. Pub.'s Assn., Photog. Mktg. Assn. Office: 1515 Broadway New York NY 10036

FISHER, GENE JORDAN, chemical company executive; b. Quitman, Mass., Mar. 26, 1931; s. Ira R. and Gertrude (Jordan) F.; m. Christine Ann Hodges, May 28, 1954; 1 dau., Denise. B.S., U. Tex., 1953. Research chemist to sr. research chemist Celanese Chem. Co., Corpus Christi, Tex., 1952-59, group leader, 1959-67, research mgr., 1967-77, dir. research, 1977-83, tech. dir., 1983—. Contbr. articles to profl. jours. Fellow Am. Inst. Chemists; mem. Am. Chem. Soc., Corpus Christi C. of C. Baptist. Club: Rotary. Patentee in field. Office: PO Box 9077 Corpus Christi TX 78469

FISHER, GEORGE WESCOTT, university dean, geology educator; b. New Haven, May 16, 1937; s. Irving Norton and Virginia (Hays) F.; m. Frances Louisa Gilbert, Dec. 26, 1959; children: Catherine Anne, Lynn Ellen, Cynthia Lee. A.B., Dartmouth Coll., 1959; Ph.D. (Woodrow Wilson fellow, NSF fellow), Johns Hopkins U., 1963. Postdoctoral fellow Geophys. Lab., Carnegie Instn., Washington, 1964-66; asst. prof. geology Johns Hopkins U., Balt., 1966-71, asso. prof., 1971-74, prof., 1974—, chmn. dept. earth and planetary scis., 1978-83, dean Div. Arts and Scis., 1983—; geologist U.S. Geol. Survey, Beltsville, Md., 1967-72. Editor: Studies in Appalachian Geology: Central and Southern, 1970. Served with Signal Corps U.S. Army, 1962-64. NSF grantee, 1971—. Mem. Geol. Soc. Am., Mineral. Soc. Am. (treas. 1974-76), Geol. Soc. Washington, Geochem. Soc., AAAS, Phi Beta Kappa, Sigma Xi. Research in Appalachian geology and metamorphic petrology. Home: 936 Cromwell Bridge Rd Towson MD 21204 Office: Div Arts and Sciences Johns Hopkins U Baltimore MD 21218

FISHER, GERALD SAUL, lawyer, financial consultant, publisher; b. Bronx, N.Y., Mar. 24, 1931; s. Abraham Samuel and Rose (Richards) F.; m. Sue Louise Chidakel, Apr. 7, 1957; children—Steven Lawrence, A. Jody, David Scott. B.B.A., Clark U., 1952; J.D., Boston U., 1955. Bar: Mass. bar 1955, D.C. bar 1962, also U.S. Supreme Ct 1962. Atty.-adviser div. corp. finance SEC, 1956-58; with SBA, 1958-67, asst. dep. adminstr. investment, 1963-65, asst. dep. adminstr. procurement and mgmt. assistance, 1965-67; adminstrv. v.p. internat. foods div. Internat. Industries; pres. Copper Penny Family Restaurants (an Internat. Industries Co.), 1969-71; v.p. real estate Internat. Industries, 1971-72; pres. Triota Orgn., 1972—; pres., chmn. Sir Speedy, Inc., 1975-78; pub. Tile & Decorative Surfaces mag., Worldwide Meetings and Incentives mag., Contemporary Dialysis mag., Encino, Calif., 1978—; lectr. franchising and small bus. financing Practising Law Inst. Author articles in field.; Sr. editor: Boston U. Law Rev. Recipient awards for outstanding service to govt. Mem. Am., Fed. bar assns., Phi Theta Kappa. Home: 4450 Callada Pl Tarzana CA 91356 Office: 17901 Ventura Blvd Encino CA 91316

FISHER, GRANVILLE CHAPMAN, artist; b. Nashville, Apr. 11, 1906; s. Henry Gordon and Blanche (Dickens) F.; m. Ijourie Bernice Stocks, Oct. 7, 1941; children—Douglas, April. Ph.B., U. Chgo., 1944, A.M., 1946, Ph.D., 1949; B.D., Meadville Theol. Sch., 1945; F.D., Boswell Soc., Chgo. Archtl. draftsman Asmus & Clark, 1925-28; ordained to ministry Baptist Ch., 1928; pastor, 1928-34; art dir. Surf Club, Miami Beach, Fla., 1932-42; Unitarian minister, 1942—; psychologist Cook County Criminal Ct., Chgo., 1945-46; prof. psychology U. Miami, 1946-71, chmn. dept., 1948-60; Founder, owner Granville Galleries, Coral Gables. Cartoonist So. Bapt. Pub. Bd., Nashville, 1922-24; dir., actor profl. theatre, 1935-37; Contbr. articles to jours.; one-man show, Rudolph Galleries, Coral Gables, 1954, Bass Mus., Miami Beach, 1965. Chmn. Fine Arts Commn., City Miami. Recipient Outstanding Tchr. award U. Miami, 1968; First Poetry award Fla. Poetry Festival, 1968; also numerous awards in painting, local and nat. Fellow Gerontol. Soc.; mem. Am., Fla. psychol. assns., AAUP, Sigma Xi, Psi Chi. Home: 6770 SW 59th St Miami FL 33143

FISHER, HAROLD WALLACE, chemical engineer; b. Rutland, Vt., Oct. 27, 1904; s. Dean Wallace and Grace Minot (Cheney) F.; m. Hope Elisabeth Case, Sept. 29, 1930; 1 son, Dean Wallace. S.B. in Chem. Engring, Mass. Inst. Tech., 1927; D.Sc., Clarkson Coll. Tech., Potsdam, N.Y., 1960. With Exxon Corp. (and affiliates), 1927-69; joint mng. dir. Iraq Petroleum Co., 1957-59; dir. Exxon Corp., 1959-69, v.p., 1962-69; mem. adv. bd. energy lab. Mass. Inst. Tech., 1974-80, mem. corp. devel. commn., 1975—; mem. marine bd. Nat. Acad. Engring., 1969-74. Co-author: The Process of Technological Innovation, 1969; also articles. Chmn. exec. com. Community Blood Council Greater N.Y., 1969-71; trustee Sloan-Kettering Inst. Cancer Research, N.Y.C., 1964—, chmn., 1970-74. Recipient Chem. Industry medal Am. sect. Soc. Chem. Industry, 1968; Bronze Beaver award Mass. Inst. Tech. Alumni Assn., 1970. Fellow AAAS; mem. Nat. Acad. Engring., Am. Chem. Soc., Am. Inst. Chem. Engrs., Pilgrims of U.S., Kappa Sigma, Alpha Chi Sigma, Tau Beta Pi. Republican. Clubs: University (N.Y.C.); Duxbury Yacht (Mass.); Community Men's; American (London). Patentee petroleum processing, petrochem. mfr. Home: 68 Goose Point Ln PO Box 1792 Duxbury MA 02331

FISHER, HERBERT, retail executive; b. N.Y.C., Nov. 14, 1921; s. Arthur and May (Schnitzer) F.; m. Florence Temkin, Nov. 17, 1951; children: Meredith, Judith, Lesley. Student, CCNY, 1940-42. Part owner A. Fisher & Sons, N.Y.C., 1945-50; owner Franklyn Shops, 1950-59, Royal Factory Outlet, Pittsfield, Mass., 1959-60; with Jamesway Corp., Secaucus, N.J., 1960—, chmn. bd., 1962—; dir. Sonoma Vineyards, Healdsburg, Calif., 1976—. Exec. adv. Coll. Bus. Adminstrn., Fairleigh Dickinson U., Madison, N.J., 1982—; chmn. polit. action com. Nat. Mass Retailing Inst., 1980—. Served with USAAF, 1942-45. Home: 994 Wildwood Rd Oradell NJ 07649 Office: Jamesway Corp 40 Hartz Way Secaucus NJ 07094

FISHER, JACK CARRINGTON, educator; b. Cortland, N.Y., Aug. 30, 1932; s. William J. and Jeannette (Carrington) F.; m. Katherine A. Probasco, June 15, 1957; children—John C., Margaret Lynn. B.A., Syracuse U., 1956, M.A., 1958, Ph.D. (Ford Found. fellow), 1961. Asst. prof. city and regional planning Cornell U., Ithaca, N.Y., 1962-68; asso. prof., asso. dir. urban studies Wayne State U., Detroit, 1969-72; prof. geography and environ. engring. Johns Hopkins U., Balt., 1972—; dir. Center for Met. Planning and Research, 1972—. Author: Yugoslavia; A Multinational State; editor: City and Regional Planning in Poland; contbr. articles to profl. jours. Served with U.S. Army, 1952-55. Mem. Am. Assn. Planning Ofcls., Am. Inst. Planning, Am. Assn. Geographers, Regional Sci. Assn. Office: Center Met Planning and Research Johns Hopkins U Baltimore MD 21218

FISHER, JAMES AIKEN, industrial marketing executive; b. Pitts., Mar. 15, 1920; s. Chester G. and Margaret R. (Aiken) F.; m. Edith C. Hall, June 12, 1955; children: George S., Chester G. III, James Aiken. Grad., Phillips Exeter Acad., 1938; B.A., Yale, 1942. Engr. Alcoa Niagara Works, 1942-45; with Fisher Sci. Co., Pitts., 1945-79, mem. sales staff, 1945-50, advt. staff, 1950-60, sr. v.p., dir., 1963-79; chmn., pres. Kipling Corp. (mktg. cons.), 1979—; dir. Dollar Savs. Bank, Pitts., EFT Corp., Nat. Sci. Programs, Inc. Trustee, v.p. Carnegie Inst.; trustee Carnegie Mus. Art, Phillips Exeter Acad. Mem. Am. Chem. Soc., Sci. Apparatus Makers Assn. (past pres.), Am. Mktg. Assn. Clubs: Harvard-Yale-Princeton, Duquesne, Rolling Rock, Rivers (Pitts.); Yale (N.Y.C.). Home: 5414 Kipling Rd Pittsburgh PA 15217 Office: 1422 Oliver Bldg Pittsburgh PA 15222

FISHER, JAMES BURKE, publishing company executive; b. Cin., Aug. 22, 1932; s. Gustave A. and Marcella (McCormack) F.; m. Nathalie Towne, June 27, 1959. B.A., Dartmouth Coll., 1954; M.A., NYU, 1962. Gen. mgr. McCall's Book Co., N.Y.C., 1968-70; v.p. Hearst Publs., N.Y.C., 1970-78; pub. ITT Consumer Book Group, N.Y.C., 1978-80; sr. v.p. Grosset & Dunlap, N.Y.C., 1980-82; pres. Network Pub. Group, San Francisco, 1983—; lectr. NYU Grad. Pub. Inst., 1978-81. Author: Prelude to War: The Anglo-Transvaal Crisis, 1962. Served with U.S. Army, 1955-57. Home: 85 4th Ave New York NY 10003 Office: 2200 Jackson St San Francisco CA 91415

FISHER, JAMES LEE, assn. exec., writer; b. Decatur, Ill., June 2, 1931; s. Morris Lee and Vera (Brant) F.; children—Kerry Brant, Kathryn Sue, Curtis James, John Benson. B.S., Ill. State U., 1956, M.S., 1957; Ph.D., Northwestern U., 1963; student, U. Mich., summer 1964; LL.D., Millikin U., 1975; D.H.L., Towson State U., 1979. Grad. asst. Ill. State U., 1956-57, dir. student fin. aids, dir. admissions, 1960-63, asso. prof. psychology, 1963-69, asst. to pres., 1963-65, exec. asst. to pres., 1965-66, v.p., dean info. and research services, 1966-69; tchr., counselor, coach Rich Twp. High Sch., Park Forest, Ill., 1957-59; asst. dir. admissions Northwestern U., 1959-60; pres. emeritus, prof. psychology Towson (Md.) State U., 1969-78; pres. Council Advancement and Support Edn., Washington, 1978—; adj. prof. Johns Hopkins U., 1975-77; radio commentator WBAL, 1975-78; newspaper columnist, feature writer Jeffersonian and Balt. Sun, 1975—; cons. White House on campus tensions, 1970-71. Author numerous articles, essays, monographs, papers. Sec. treas. Ill. State U. Found., 1960-63. Served with USMC, 1951-54. Named Assn. Educator of Yr. Am. Soc. Assn. Execs., 1981. Mem. Am. Psychol. Assn., Pi Gamma Mu, Phi Eta Sigma, Phi Delta Kappa. Home: 1330 New Hampshire Ave NW Washington DC 20036 *The one truth of which I am most certain is that the goodness of your life will be measured by the extent to which you maintain fidelity and trust in the personal relationships of your life—with individuals, one at a time, rather than with organizations, institutions, or even causes.*

FISHER, JAMES WILLIAM, medical educator, pharmacologist; b. Startex, S.C., May 22, 1925; s. Ernest Amaziah and Mamie V. (Turner) F.; m. Carol Barbara Brodarick, June 5, 1947; children: Candis Loreen Fisher Smith, Patricia E., Richard W., William E., John C., Elaine M. B.S., U. S.C., 1947; Ph.D. in Pharmacology (USPHS fellow), U. Louisville, 1958. Pharmacologist Armour Pharm. Research Labs., Chgo., 1950-53, Lloyd Bros., Cin., 1954-56; instr. pharmacology U. Tenn., 1958-60, asst. prof., 1960-62, asso. prof., 1962-66, prof., 1966-68; prof., chmn. dept. pharmacology Med. Sch., Tulane U., 1968—; vis. scientist Christie Hosp. and Holt Radium Inst., Manchester, Eng., 1963-64; dir. Tulane-Universidad Nacional del Nordeste, Corrientes, Argentina, Pan Am. Health Orgn. Physiol. Scis. Tng. Program, 1972—; lectr. in field; mem. com. erythropoietin Nat. Heart, Lung and Blood Inst., 1971-74, mem. hematology tng. grants com., 1977; mem. Cooley's Anemia Nat. Research Com., 1974—; pres. So. Blood Club, 1975-77; mem. Wellcome Professorship Com., 1976. Author: Readings on the History of Pharmacology; editor: Kidney Hormones, Vol. I, 1971, Vol. II, 1977, Renal Pharmacology, 1971; co-editor: Erythropoiesis, 1975, Erythropoietin and Erythropoiesis, 1981; cons. editor: Erythropoletin, 1968; editorial bd.: Proc. Soc. Exptl. Biology and Medicine, 1971—; contbr. articles to profl. jours. Served to lt. (j.g.) USNR, 1943-46; PTO. Recipient Purkinje Medal Czech. Med. Soc., 1975; Golden Sovereign award, 1976. Mem. Am. Soc. Pharmacology and Exptl. Therapeutics (awards com.), Soc. Exptl. Biology and Medicine, Am. Soc. Nephrology, Am. Soc. Hematology (chmn. erythropoietin sub-com., mem. sci. affairs com.), Assn. Med. Sch. Pharmacology (chmn. nominating com. 1975, mem. exec. com. 1979-82), AAAS, AAUP, N.Y. Acad. Scis., Sigma Xi. Research on effects of drugs on kidney erythropoietin prodn., anemia and kidney disease, kidney transplantation. Patentee antirheumatic drug and RIA for erythropoietin. Home: 4025 Pin Oak Ave New Orleans LA 70114 *Creativity and brilliance are very important in science but in order to test one's ideas these qualities must be adequately supplemented by the necessary amount of work at the bench.*

FISHER, JEROME, psychologist; b. Bklyn., Sept. 10, 1916; s. Joseph and Esther (Winter) F.; m. Rosalyn Ann Ossakow, Mar. 4, 1941; children: Robert Lawrence, Kenneth Stephen. B.A., Bklyn. Coll., 1937, M.A., 1939; Ph.D., U. Calif., Berkeley, 1950. Diplomate: Am. Bd. Profl. Psychology. Chief psychologist VA Hosp., San Francisco, 1949-60; prof. med. psychology, dept. psychiatry U. Calif. at, San Francisco, 1960—, now prof. emeritus; chief psychologist Langley Porter Neuropsychiat. Inst., 1960-79; mem. psychology faculty San Francisco State U., part-time 1950-77. Contbr. articles to profl. jours. Bd. dirs. San Francisco Assn. Mental Health, 1963-65. Served to capt. U.S. Army, 1942-46. Mem. Calif. Conf. Chief Psychologists (chmn. 1963-64), Am. Psycol. Assn., Western Psychol. Assn., Calif. Psychol. Assn., Sigma Xi. Home: 151 Devonshire Way San Francisco CA 94131 Office: Langley Porter Psychiat Inst U Calif San Francisco CA 94143

FISHER, JIMMIE LOU, state official. Treas. State Ark., Little Rock. Office: State Treas 220 State Capitol Bldg Little Rock AR 72201§

FISHER, JOEL HILTON, lawyer; b. N.Y.C., Mar. 28, 1918; s. Samuel and Jeanette Florence (Almour) F.; children by previous marriage: Susan and John (twins); m. Helene B. Aaronson, Nov. 26, 1958. B.A. magna cum laude, Syracuse U., 1939, J.D., 1941. Atty. office gen. counsel U.S. Treasury Dept., 1941-42; asst. to solicitor U.S. Dept. Commerce, 1945-46; dep. dir. Intervotl. Com. on Refugees, 1946-47; gen. counsel, Am. Joint Distbn. Com, 1947-49; pres. Fisher & Sinick (P.C.), Washington, 1949—; dir. Seaboard World Airlines, 1972-80; Spl. asst. atty. gen. Wash. State, 1964—. Bd. dirs., gen. counsel Nat. Aeros. Assn., 1972-80. Served to lt. comdr. USCGR, 1942-45. Mem. Fed. Bar Assn., ABA, D.C. Bar Assn., Internat. Bar Assn. (patron), Inter-Am. Bar Assn., Am. Soc. Internat. Law, Assn. Trial Lawyers Am., Comml. Law League Am., Washington Fgn. Law Soc., Am. Fgn. Law Soc. (Am. br. internat. law), Aerospace Med. Assn., Nat. Aeros. Assn., Am. Judicature Soc. Unitarian. Clubs: Nat. Aviation, Internat., Wings. Home: 3313 Cleveland Ave NW Washington DC 20008 Office: 2020 K St NW Washington DC 20006

FISHER, JOEL MARSHALL, political scientist, legal recruiter; b. Chgo., June 24, 1935; s. Dan and Nell (Kolvin) F.; m. Linda Joyce Buss, 1970; children: Sara Melinda, Matthew Nicholas. A.B., U. So. Calif., 1955; LL.B., U. Calif.-Berkeley, M.A.; Ph.D. in Govt., Claremont Grad. Sch., 1968. Orgn. dir. Republican Citizens Com. of U.S., Washington, 1964-65; dir. arts and scis. state legis. divs. Rep. Nat. Com., Washington, 1968-69; asst. dep. counsel to pres. U.S. White House, 1969-70; dep. asst. sec. econ. and social affairs U.S. Dept. State, Washington, 1969-71; vis. prof. comparative and internat. law Loyola U. Sch. Law, Los Angeles, 1972-73; dir. World Bus. Inst., Ctr. Internat. Bus., Pepperdine U., Los Angeles, 1974-75; prof. constl. law Southwestern U. Sch. Law, Los Angeles, 1974-76; dir. World Trade Inst. So. Calif., 1976—; prof. internat. law, asst. dean Whitter Coll. Sch. Law, Los Angeles, 1977-80; prin. Ziskind, Greene and Assocs., Placement, 1980-84; pres. Wells Internat.; ofcl. visitor The European Communities, 1974, 76; mem. U.S. dels. UN confs., 1969-71; chmn. Strategy for Peace Conf. Panel on U.S. and UN, 1972—; coordinator Series on the Contemporary Am. Presidency, 1972-73; cons. Interconti, Inc., 1975-76, Robert Taft Inst., 1977—, World Trade Inst.N.Y., 1977-80, Woodstock Prodns., 1978-81, Curtis, Hoxter & co., N.Y.C., 1978—. Co-author two books; contbr. articles on polit. sci. and law to profl. publs. Mem. steering com. Calif. Com. for Reelection of Pres., 1972; nat. chmn. Community Leaders for Ford, 1976; trustee Rep. Assocs., 1978—; mem. vestry St. Michael and All Angeles Ch., Studio City, Calif., 1983—. Fellow Nobel Found., 1958; Falk fellow, 1961-62; State legis. fellow Am. Polit. Sci. Assn., 1970-73. Mem. Am. Soc. Internat. Law, Am. Polit. Sci. Assn., Fgn. Law Assn. So. Calif., Brit.-Am. C. of C., German-Am. C. of C. Home: 4963 Bluebell Ave North Hollywood CA 91607 Office: 2049 Century Park E Suite 1650 Los Angeles CA 90067 *I have always attempted to be positive in outlook; two steps ahead of others—colleagues and competition alike; and to pay attention to detail. In terms of general ideas, much of my life has been influenced by two masters: Benjamin Disraeli and Ray Bliss of Ohio.*

FISHER, JOHN CHARLES, JR., humanities educator; b. Mendon, N.Y., Nov. 27, 1927; s. John Charles and Helen Catherine (Laramie) F.; m. Joanne Marie Byrnes, Aug. 18, 1956; children—Gerard David, Elizabeth Ann. B.A., Champlain Coll., SUNY, Plattsburgh, 1953; A.M., U. Mich., 1954, Ed.D., 1962. Teaching fellow, vis. lectr. U. Mich., 1954-61; mem. faculty SUNY, Oswego, 1957—, now prof. English, coordinator linguistic studies, 1966-73, chmn. dept. English, 1972-74, chmn. faculty assembly, 1977-78, 80-83; Fulbright lectr. linguistics U. Rome, 1963-64; vis. prof. U. Hawaii, Hilo, 1970, Inter-Am. U., P.R., 1970. Author: Linguistics in Remedial English, 1966, Transformational Grammar, 1970; contbr. articles to profl. jours. Democratic committeeman, 1970—; mem. budget com. Diocese of Syracuse, 1976-80. Served with USN, 1945-47, 51-52. Recipient Innovative Curriculum award SUNY, 1972; N.Y. State English Council fellow, 1971; SUNY Faculty grantee, 1976. Mem. Keats/ Shelley Assn., N.E. Modern Lang. Assn., MLA, Nat. Council Tchrs. English, N.Y. State English Council (exec. sec. 1968-70, pres. 1974-75, Outstanding Tchr. in Coll. English award 1979). Roman Catholic. Club: Oswego Rotary (pres. 1981-82). Home: Perry Hill Oswego NY 13126 Office: SUNY Oswego NY 13126

FISHER, JOHN EDWIN, insurance company executive; b. Portsmouth, Ohio, Oct. 26, 1929; s. Charles Hall and Bess (Swearingin) F.; m. Eloise Lyon, Apr. 25, 1949. Student, U. Colo., 1947-48, Ohio U., 1948-49, Franklin U., Columbus, Ohio, 1950-51. With Nationwide Mut. Ins. Co., Columbus, 1951—, v.p., office gen. chmn., 1970-72, pres., gen. mgr., dir., 1972-81, gen. chmn., chief exec. officer, 1981—, also dir.; gen. chmn., chief exec. officer, dir. Nationwide Gen. Ins. Co., Nationwide Mut. Fire Ins. Co., Nationwide Property & Casualty Ins. Co., Nationwide Life Ins. Co., Nationwide Variable Life Ins. Co.; chmn. Neckura-Neckermann Versicherungs A.G., Oberursel, Germany, 1976—; trustee Battelle Commons Corp. Chmn. bd. Nationwide Found., 1981—; trustee Children's Hosp. Mem. Chartered Property and Casualty Underwriters Assn., Chartered Life Underwriters Soc., Assn. Ohio Life Ins. Cos. (past pres.), Ohio Ins. Inst. (pres. 1975-77), Nat. Assn. Ind. Insurers, Am. Risk and Ins. Assn., Griffith Ins. Found. (chmn. 1981), Property-Casualty Ins. Council (chmn. 1981-82), Columbus C. of C. (chmn. 1981-82). Office: One Nationwide Plaza Columbus OH 43216

FISHER, JOHN HURT, educator; b. Lexington, Ky., Oct. 26, 1919; s. Bascom and Franke (Sheddan) F.; m. Jane Elizabeth Law, Feb. 21, 1942; children: Janice Carol Fisher Lowe, John Craig, Judith Law. B.A., Maryville Coll., 1940; M.A., U. Pa., 1942, Ph.D., 1945; L.H.D., Loyola U., Chgo., 1970; Litt.D., Middlebury Coll., 1970. Instr., English U. Pa., 1942-45, Yale U., summer 1944; instr. English N.Y. U., 1945-48, asst. prof., 1948-55; lectr. U. So. Calif., summer 1955; instr. English U. Mich., summer 1956; assoc. prof. Duke U., 1955-58, prof., 1958-60; prof. English Ind. U., 1960-62, N.Y. U., 1962-72; John C. Hodges prof. English U. Tenn., 1972—, chmn., 1976-78. Author: Tretys of Love, 1951, John Gower: Moral Philosopher and Friend of Chaucer, 1964, The College Teaching of English, 1965, In Forme of Speche Is Chaunge, 1973, An Anthology of Chancery English, 1984; editor: The Medieval Literature of Western Europe, 1966, The Complete Poetry and Prose of Geoffrey Chaucer, 1977; contbr. articles on medieval lit., English linguistics, English edn. to profl. jours. Mem. U.S. Commn. to UNESCO, 1963-69; bd. dirs. Woodrow Wilson Nat. Fellowship Found., 1972-75, Maryville Coll., 1972-74. Nat. Endowment for Humanities sr. fellow, 1975-76. Fellow Medieval Acad. Am.; Mem. Modern Lang. Assn. Am. (exec. sec. 1963-71, editor PMLA 1963-71, pres. 1974), New Chaucer Soc. (bd. dirs. 1978—, exec. sec. 1981—, pres. 1982-84), Linguistic Soc. Am., Nat. Council Tchrs. English, Fédération Internationale des Langues et Littératures Modernes, UNESCO (Am. v.p. 1972-78), Phi Beta Kappa (senator-at-large 1978-82). Home: 505 Scenic Dr Knoxville TN 37919 Office: McClung Tower U Tenn Knoxville TN 37916

FISHER, JOHN MORRIS, association official, educator; b. Fairhaven, Ohio, Apr. 20, 1922; s. Marion Hays and Bessie (Morris) F.; m. Thelma Ison, Feb. 2, 1947; children: Steven Roger, Linda Lucille. A.B., Miami U., Oxford, O., 1947; postgrad., Bklyn Law Sch., 1950-51, Northwestern U., 1954-55; LL.D. (hon.), Nasson Coll., 1972. With Belden Mfg. Co., Richmond, Ind., 1941; spl. agt. FBI, 1947-53; exec. trainee Sears Roebuck & Co., Chgo., 1953, exec. staff asst. to v.p. personnel and employee relations, 1953-57, chmn. security com., 1957-61; operating dir. Am. Security Council, 1956-57, pres., chief exec. officer, 1957—; pres. Am. Research Found., 1961—; pres., chief exec. officer Am. Security Council Found., Boston, Va., 1962—; pres. Communications Corp. Am., 1972-80, chmn. bd., 1980—; organizer, pres. Fidelifax, Inc., 1956-57; chmn. merc. div. Nat. Safety Council, 1959-60, 1st vice chmn. trades and services sect., 1961—; Chmn. Chgo. Retail Safety Conf., 1959-60; spl. adviser Ill. Supt. Pub. Instrn., 1963-64; cons. to Gov. Fla.; cons. to chmn. com. cold war edn. Nat. Gov.'s Conf., 1962-65, Ill. Civil Def. Advisory Council, 1965-68; pres. Am. Council World Freedom, 1971-72; mem. exec. com. Nat. Captive Nations Com., 1968—; adminstrv. chmn. Coalition for Peace Through Strength, 1978—. Bd. visitors Freedoms Found., 1964-65; bd. dirs. Am. Fgn. Policy Inst., 1976—, Security and Intelligence Fund, 1976—, James Monroe Meml. Fedn., 1977—. Served to 1st lt. USAAF, 1943-45. Decorated Air medal with clusters; recipient 10th Anniversary medal and scroll Assembly Captive European Nations; Order Lafayette Freedom award, 1973; Disting. Service award Chaplain of 4 Chaplains, 1979. Mem. Am. Soc. Indsl. Security (dir. 1959-62), Phi Kappa Tau. Republican. Presbyterian. Clubs: Mason., Tower; Culpeper (Va.); Country; Army Navy, Nat. Democratic, Capitol Hill (Washington). Office: Am Security Council Found Boston VA 22713

FISHER, JOHN P., wood and paper products company executive. Chmn. Fraser Inc., Edmundston, N.B., Can. Officer: Fraser Inc 27 Rice St Edmundston NB Canada E3V 1S9§

FISHER, JOHN RICHARD, construction company executive; b. Columbus, Ohio, Dec. 28, 1924; s. Don Alfred and Katherine Buchanan (Galigher) F.; m. Kitson Overmyer, Oct. 2, 1946; children—Scott Owen, Lani Kitson. B.S., U.S. Naval Acad., 1946; B.Civil Engring., Rensselaer Poly. Inst., Troy, N.Y., 1950, M.Civil Engring., 1950; grad. Advanced Mgmt. Program, Harvard, 1971. Registered profl. engr., S.C. Commd. ensign U.S. Navy, 1946, advanced through grades to rear adm., 1972; service in, N.Africa, Cuba, Philippines and, Vietnam, dep. comdr. Naval Facilities Engring. Command, also comdr. Chesapeake div. constrn. facilities U.S. Naval Acad. and Omega Nav. System, 1969-73, comdr. Pacific div. Naval Facilities Engring. Command, 1973-77, ret., 1977; v.p. Raymond Internat., Inc., 1977-81, sr. group v.p., 1981-83, exec. v.p., 1983—. Pres. Community Hosp. Assn. Mid-Am., Columbus, Ohio. Decorated DSM, Legion of Merit with combat V (2). Fellow Soc. Am. Mil. Engrs., ASCE; mem. Navy League of U.S. (nat. dir.), Mil. Order Carabao, Sigma Xi, Tau Beta Pi. Clubs: Outrigger Canoe (Honolulu); Army-Navy Country (Arlington, Va.). Home: 1030 Ivy Wall Dr Houston TX 77079 Office: 2801 Post Oak Blvd Houston TX 77056

FISHER, JOHN WESLEY, manufacturing company executive; b. Walland, Tenn., July 15, 1915; s. Arthur Justin and Rachel (Malott) F.; m. Janice Kelsey Ball, Aug. 10, 1940; children: Joan Crosley,

Michael J., James A., Jeffrey E., Judith Fisher Musselman, John Wesley III, Jerrold M. B.S., U. Tenn., 1938; M.B.A., Harvard U., 1942; LL.D. hon., Ball State U., 1972, Butler U., 1977, DePauw U., 1981. Field sec. Delta Tau Delta Frat., Indpls., 1938-40; trainee, various mfg., sales and adminstrv. positions Ball Corp., Muncie, Ind., 1941-70, pres., chief exec. officer, 1970-78, chmn. bd., chief exec. officer, 1978-81, chmn. bd., 1981—, also dir.; dir. Ind. Bell Telephone Co., Ransburg Corp., Inland Steel Co., Chgo., Muncie Airport, Inc., Minnetrista Corp., Am. Nat. Bank & Trust Co., Muncie, Kindel Furniture Co., Grand Rapids, Mich.; partner Blackwood & Nichols Corp., Oklahoma City. State del. Republican Party, Ind., 1950-70; mem. Rep. State Finance Com., 1952—, del. nat. conv., 1952, 54, 64, 68; trustee De Pauw U.; bd. dirs. Ball Meml. Hosp., Ball Bros. Found. Mem. Glass Packaging Inst. (trustee 1962-68, pres. 1965-67), Ind. C. of C. (dir. 1959—, pres. 1966-68), Muncie C. of C. (past pres.), Conf. Bd., NAM (chmn. 1979-80, dir.), Delta Tau Delta. Republican. United Methodist. Clubs: Rotary (past pres.), Muncie, Delaware Country (Muncie); Indpls. Athletic, Columbia (Indpls.); Metropolitan (Chgo.). Home: PO Box 832 Muncie IN 47305 Office: Ball Corp 345 S High St Muncie IN 47302

FISHER, JOSEPH JEFFERSON, fed. judge; b. San Augustine County, Tex.; s. Guy B. and Lula (Bl) F.; m. Kathleen Clark; children—Leila (Mrs. Leila F. Thomas), Joseph Jefferson, John Clark, Guy Cade, Kathleen Anne (Mrs. Fred Thomas Winslow). Student, Stephen F. Austin Coll., 1929; LL.B., U. Tex., 1936. Bar: Tex. bar 1936. Served as county atty., San Augustine County, 1936-39; dist. atty. 1st Jud. Dist. Tex., 1939-46, dist. judge, 1956-59; partner firm Fisher, Tonahill & Reavley, Jasper, Tex., 1947-56; U.S. dist. judge Eastern Dist. Tex., 1959—, chief judge, 1967—. Mem. ABA (chmn. jud. sect. 1957), 1st Jud. Bar Assn. (pres. 1956), Tex. Bar Assn., State Bar Tex. (legis. and exec. coms. 1957-59), Am. Judicature Soc., Tex. Hist. Assn., Sons of the Republic of Tex., Ex-Student Assn. U. Tex. (life), Stephen F. Austin State U. Ex-Students Assn. (life), Delta Kappa Epsilon. Methodist. Clubs: Mason, Lion (dist. gov., internat. dir., mem. exec. com. 1952-54), Order San Jacinto.). Home: 130 Central Caldwood Dr Beaumont TX 77707 Office: Box 88: Beaumont TX 77704

FISHER, JOSEPH LYMAN, economist, former congressman, state official; b. Pawtucket, R.I., Jan 11, 1914; s. Howard Colburn and Caroline (Nash) F.; m. Margaret Saunders Winslow, June 21, 1942; children: H. Benjamin, Caroline, Robert W., William B., Elizabeth, James H., Barbara W. B.S., Bowdoin Coll., 1935, D.S.C., 1965; postgrad., London Sch. Econs., 1935-36; M.A., Harvard U., 1938, Ph.D. in Econs. (teaching fellow 1946-47), 1947; M.A. in Edn, George Washington U., 1951; LL.D., Allegheny Coll., 1966; L.H.D., Starr King Sch. Ministry, 1971. Instr. econs. Allegheny Coll., 1938-40; planning technician Nat. Resources Planning Bd., 1939-43; economist Dept. State, 1943; economist, exec. officer Council Econ. Advisers, Washington, 1947-53; assoc. dir. Resources for the Future, Inc., Washington, 1953-59, pres., 1959-74; mem. 94th-96th Congresses from 10th Dist. Va.; dir. policy analysis The Wilderness Soc., 1981—; sec. human resources Commonwealth of Va., 1982—; vis. fellow George Mason U., 1981—; vis. prof. U. Colo., 1957, U. Calif., 1971, 76, Va. Commonwealth U., 1984—; staff dir. Cabinet Com. Energy Supplies and Policies, 1955; cons. to govt. agys. Author: (with others) World Prospects for Natural Resources, Resources in America's Future; Contbr. chpts. to books, articles to profl. jours. Mem. Arlington County Bd., 1964-74, chmn., 1965, 71; Trustee Unitarian Universalist Assn., 1961-65, moderator, chmn. bd. trustees, 1965-77; trustee Tchrs. Ins. and Annuity Assn., 1966-74, United Planning Orgn., 1966-71; bd. dirs. Met. Washington Council of Govts., 1966-74, pres., 1969, chmn., 1970; bd. dirs. Washington Met. Area Transit Authority, 1972-74, chmn., 1972; bd. overseers Bowdoin Coll.; adv. council Electric Power Research Inst., 1973-79, chmn., 1973-75; bd. dirs. Population Reference Bur. Served with inf. AUS, 1943-46. Mem. Am. Forestry Assn. (dir. 1966-84), Wilderness Soc. (dir. 1983—), Am. Econ. Assn., Am. Soc. Pub. Adminstrn., AAAS, Nat. Acad. Pub. Adminstrn., Phi Beta Kappa, Phi Delta Kappa. Clubs: Century (N.Y.C.); Cosmos (Washington). Home: 2608 N 24th St Arlington VA 22207 Office: Sec Human Resources Commonwealth of Va PO Box 1475 Richmond VA 23212

FISHER, JULES EDWARD, producer, lighting designer, theatre consultant; b. Norristown, Pa., Nov. 12, 1937; s. Abraham and Ann (Davidson) F. B.F.A., Carnegie Inst. Tech., 1960. Pres. Jules Fisher Assocs. Inc. Theatre Cons., N.Y.C., 1963—, Jules Fisher & Paul Marantz Inc. Archtl. Lighting Design, 1971—, Jules Fisher Enterprises Inc. Lighting Design and Theatrical Prodn., 1973—. Lighting designer: Broadway prodns. Pippin, 1973 (Tony award), Ulysses in Nightown, 1974 (Tony award), Dancin', 1978 (Tony award), La Cage aux Folles, 1983; dir. (all prodns.), Beatlemania; producer: Frankenstein, 1981 (Drama Desk award), Lenny, 1971; prodn. supr.: various rock tours Tommy, 1973; designer lighting: Simon and Garfunkel Concert, Central Park, N.Y.C., 1981; lighting designer: film A Star is Born, 1976; 1977 Acad. Awards Presentation, 1977; producer: The Rink, 1983. Office: Jules Fisher Enterprises Inc 126 Fifth Ave New York NY 10011

FISHER, KENNETH ROBINSON, flour milling executive; b. Seattle, Dec. 12, 1906; s. William Peter and Estelle (Meeker) F.; m. Margarett Olivia Lewis, Oct. 29, 1930; children: Phelps Kenneth, Ann Estelle (Mrs. Peter Charles Hanson). B.A., U. Wash., 1928; M.B.A., Harvard U., 1930. With Fisher Mills Inc. (formerly Fisher Flouring Mills Co.), Seattle, 1930—, dir., 1949—, asst. gen. mgr., treas., 1952-60, v.p., gen. mgr., treas., 1960-65, pres., gen. mgr., 1965-71, pres., 1971-73, chmn. bd., 1973—; chmn., dir. Fisher Properties, Technovators, Inc.; v.p., dir. Magic Prodns., Inc.; dir. emeritus Western Internat. Hotels. Fin. chmn. Wash. State Citizens for Abortion Reform, 1968-70; mem. regional citizen's adv. com. Wash. Dept. Social and Health Services, 1971-75; mem. Wash. state adv. com. U.S. Commn. on Civil Rights, 1974—; chmn. bd. trustees Seattle Art Mus.; Bd. dirs. Planned Parenthood Center of Seattle, Camp Brotherhood, Inc.; mem. vis. com. Grad. Sch. Pub. Affairs; mem. emeritus adv. com. Grad. Sch. Bus. Adminstrn., U. Wash.; bd. visitors Sch. Law, former univ. trustee U. Puget Sound; mem. disciplinary bd. Wash. State Bar Assn. Recipient Gulick award Campfire Girls, 1956, Man of Year award Planned Parenthood Center, Seattle, 1969, Disting. Alumnus award Broadway High Sch. Alumni Assn., 1976, Brotherhood award NCCJ, 1977; Nat. Jewish Fund honoree, 1978. Mem. Poor Richard Investors, Beta Theta Pi. Congregationalist. Clubs: Rainier, Broadmoor Golf, Seattle Golf, Tennis, 49, Harvard Bus. Sch. (Seattle). Home: Madison Park Pl Suite 402 2000 43d Ave E Seattle WA 98112 Office: 1525 One Union Sq Seattle WA 98101 *One who has the capacity to get things done in the community and fails to use it is wasting his most valuable asset.*

FISHER, KENNETH WALTER, biology educator; b. Heston, Middlesex, U.K., Dec. 30, 1931; s. Walter and Matilda (Hunt) F.; m. Mettie Marie Barton, July 17, 1965; children—Sean Hayes, Galen Hunt. B.Sc., Queen Mary Coll., U. London, Eng., 1953, M.Sc., 1954; Ph.D., Royal Postgrad. Med. Sch., 1957. Asso. prof. biochem. genetics, dir. grad. genetics research tng. program Kans. State U., Manhattan, 1966-70; prof. biology Rutgers U., New Brunswick, N.J., 1970—, chmn. dept. biology, 1972-78, dir. grad. program microbiology, 1975-78; mem. comprehensive assistance to undergrad. sci. edn. grant rev. panel NSF, 1976-78; mem. microbial chemistry rev. panel for selection recipients post-doctoral fellowships NIH, 1977. Contbr. numerous articles to sci. jours. Recipient spl. award Med. Research Council, 1957-58; research fellow Pasteur Inst., 1957-58, Princeton U., 1962-63; Rockefeller traveling fellow, 1962-63; NSF grantee, 1966-69; NIH grantee, 1966-70; Eli Lilly Co. grantee, 1967-69. Fellow Royal Phys. Soc. Edinburgh; mem. N.Y. Acad. Scis., Am., U.K. genetics socs., Am. Soc. Microbiology, Biochem. Soc., Soc. for Gen. Microbiology, Eastern Apicultural Soc. (chmn. info. com. 1980-81). Home: 33 Stuart Close Princeton NJ 08540 Office: Dept Biology Douglass Coll Rutgers U New Brunswick NJ 08903

FISHER, LARRY M., management consultant; b. Elizabeth, N.J., May 30, 1926; s. Roy G. and Macey M. (Bilyeu) F.; m. Geraldine Jane Vorres, Mar. 17, 1946; children: Susan, Linda, Larry; m. Margaret Mary Ryan, Mar. 18, 1978. B.S. in Commerce, Rider Coll., Trenton, N.J., 1950. With Blue Cross-Blue Shield, Chgo., 1950-54, Marsh-McLennan, 1954-58, Hewitt Assos., 1958-63; with A.S. Hansen, Inc., 1963—, pres., Lake Bluff, Ill., 1963—; trustee Employee Benefit Research Inst., C.E.B.S.; bd. dirs. Internat. Found. Employee Benefit Plans; lectr. labor relations U. Chgo.; lectr. ins. Ind. U.; lectr. pensions and welfare Roosevelt U., Chgo. Served with USMC, 1944-46. Mem. Assn. Pvt. Pension and Welfare Plans, Assn. Cons. Mgmt. Engrs. Clubs: Bob O'Link Golf, Chgo., East Bank, Mid-Day. Home: 514 Hunter Rd Glenview IL 60025 Office: 1080 Green Bay Rd Lake Bluff IL 60044

FISHER, LEON HAROLD, physicist, emeritus educator; b. Montreal, Que., Can., July 11, 1918; came to U.S., 1920, naturalized, 1925; s. Jacob and Rachel (Haimowitz) F.; m. Phyllis Kahn, Dec. 21, 1941; children: Robert Alan, Lawrence Edgar, Carol Lee (Mrs. Lawrence P. Slotnick), David Bruce. B.S., U. Calif.-Berkeley, 1938, M.S., 1940, Ph.D., 1943. Instr. physics U. Calif.-Berkeley, 1943, vis. physics prof., summers 1949, 51, 55, 83; instr. physics U. N.Mex., 1944; physicist Los Alamos Sci. Lab., 1944-46; asst. prof. physics NYU, 1946-50, assoc. prof., 1950-57, prof. physics, 1957-61; vis. physics prof. U. So. Calif., summer 1948, U. Wash., summer 1979; mgr. plasma physics Lockheed Missiles and Space Co., 1961-62, sr. mem. electronic scis. lab., 1963-67, 69-70, asst. mgr. lab., 1967-69; head plasma physics Gen. Telephone Electric Labs., 1962-63; prof. elec. engring., head dept. info. engring. U. Ill. at Chgo. Circle, 1971; prof. physics Calif. State U., Hayward, 1971-83, prof. physics emeritus, 1983—, dean Sch. Sci., 1971-79; sr. liaison scientist Office Naval Research, Tokyo, 1979-82; cons. Edgerton, Germeshausen & Greer, 1954-55, Radiation Research, 1957-58, Harry Diamond Labs., Wash., 1958-61, Xerox Corp., Rochester, N.Y., 1958-61, Gen. Applied Sci. Lab., N.Y.C., 1960, Army Research Office, Durham, N.C., 1958-64, Re-Entry Physics Panel, Nat. Acad. Scis., 1965-66, Monsanto Enviro-Chem. Systems, Inc., 1971; chmn. Gaseous Electronics Conf., 1948, 67, 68. Asso. editor: Phys. Rev, 1955-58; Contbr. articles to profl. publs. Fellow Am. Phys. Soc., AAAS, Explorers Club; sr. mem. IEEE; mem. Am. Assn. Physics Tchrs., Phi Beta Kappa, Sigma Xi, Pi Mu Epsilon. Office: Calif State Univ Hayward CA 94542

FISHER, LESLIE ROBERT, state ofcl.; b. Madill, Okla., Jan. 17, 1922; s. Alfred Fidella and Emma Theodosia (Gullege) F.; m. Ernestine Jewell Gilstrap, Oct. 11, 1941; children—Linda Fisher Garrison, Susan Fisher Boyd, David. B.S., Southeastern State U., Durant, Okla., 1951; M.Ed., U. Okla., 1954, Ed.D., 1963. High sch. prin., Lone Grove, Okla., 1951-54; supt. schs. Mountain Home and Ringling, Okla., 1954-57, Moore, Okla., 1961-70; supt. pub. instrn. State of Okla., Oklahoma City, 1970—; mem. Okla. Bd. Edn., Okla. Bd. Vocat. and Tech. Edn., Sch. Land Commn., State Accrediting Agy., State Edn. TV Authority. Bd. regents Okla. Colls. Served with USNR, 1942-45. Mem. Am. Assn. Sch. Adminstrs., Okla. Assn. Sch. Adminstrs. (past pres.), NEA, Okla. Edn. Assn. (past pres. E. Central dist., past pres. Tri-County), Phi Delta Kappa. Home: 3216 Fairway Dr Moore OK 73160 Office: 2500 N Lincoln Oklahoma City OK 73105

FISHER, LESTER EMIL, zoo administrator; b. Chgo., Feb. 24, 1921; s. Louis and Elizabeth (Vodicka) F.; m. Wendy Fisher, Jan. 23, 1981; children: Jane Serrita, Katherine Clark. V.M.D., Iowa State U., 1943. Supr. animal care program Northwestern U. Med. Sch., 1946-47; attending veterinarian Lincoln Park Zoo, Chgo., 1947-62, dir. zoo, 1962—; owner, dir. Berwyn (Ill.) Animal Hosp., 1947-68; producer, moderator ednl. closed circuit TV for nat. vet. meetings, 1949-66; asso. prof.-dept. biology DePaul U., 1968—; adj. prof. zoology U. Ill., from 1972. Editor: Brit. Small Animal Jour. and Small Animal Clinician, 1958-72. Mem. citizens com. U. Ill.; chmn. zoo and wildlife div. Morris Animal Found. Served to maj., Vet. Corps AUS, 1943-46. Recipient Alumni Merit Award Ia. State Univ., 1968. Mem. Am. Animal Hosp. Assn. (regional dir., outstanding Service award 1969), Am. Vet. Med. Assn., Nat. Recreation and Park Assn., Internat. Union Dirs. Zool. Gardens (v.p. 1980-83, pres. 1983-86), Am. Assn. Zoo Veterinarians (pres. 1966-69), Am. Assn. Zool. Parks and Aquariums (pres. 1972-73), Theta Xi. Clubs: Adventures (pres. 1971-72), Execs. of Chgo. (bd. dirs. 1968-71), Arts. Assoc.). Home: 3180 N Lake Shore Dr Chicago IL 60657 Office: Lincoln Park Zool Garden Chicago IL 60614

FISHER, LLOYD EDISON, JR., lawyer; b. Medina, Ohio, Oct. 23, 1923; s. Lloyd Edison and Wanda (White) F.; m. Twylla Dawn Peterson, Sept. 11, 1949; children: Karen S., Kirk P. B.S., Ohio State U., 1947, J.D., 1949. Bar: Ohio 1950. Practice in, Columbus, 1962—; mem. gen. hearing bd. Ohio Dept. Taxation, 1950-53; trust officer Huntington Nat. Bank, Columbus, 1953-62; partner firm Alexander, Ebinger Fisher, McAlister & Lawrence, Columbus, 1962—; adj. prof. law Ohio State U., 1967-69. Bd. dirs. Wesley Glen Retirement Center, 1974-80. Served with AUS, 1943-45. Fellow Am. Coll. Probate Counsel; mem. ABA, Ohio Bar Assn., Columbus Bar Assn., Order of Coif. Methodist (trustee). Home: 611 Lummisford Ln N Columbus OH 43214 Office: 1 Riverside Plaza Columbus OH 43215

FISHER, LUCY JANE, film company executive; b. N.Y.C., Oct. 2, 1949; d. Arthur Bertram and Naomi (Kislak) F. B.A. cum laude, Harvard U., 1971. Exec. charge creative affairs MGM, Culver City, Calif., 1978; v.p. prodn. 20th Century Fox Corp., Los Angeles, 1978-80; v.p., head world-wide prodn. Zoetrope Studios, Los Angeles, 1980-81; sr. v.p. theatrical prodn. div. Warner Bros., Burbank, Calif., 1981—.

FISHER, MARJORIE, investment mgmt. co. exec.; b. Barcelona, Spain, Nov. 10, 1920; d. George H.B. and Marjorie A. (Wheeler) F. (parents Am. citizens). B.A., Mt. Holyoke Coll., 1942. Mem. editorial staff Dun's Rev., N.Y.C., 1943-45; asst. field dir. ARC, Philippines and Japan, 1945-47; with Babson's Reports, Wellesley Hills, Mass., 1948-50; security analyst Capital Research & Mgmt. Co., Los Angeles, 1951-58, v.p., 1958—; exec. v.p. Am. Mut. Fund, Inc., Los Angeles, 1968-80; pres., 1980—, dir., 1968—. Trustee Fellowships Endowment Fund, AAUW, 1965-75, Mt. Holyoke Coll., 1962-67. Mem. Fin. Analysts Fedn. (chartered fin. analyst, chmn. admissions com. 1963-64, regent Fin. Analysts Seminar 1969-72, bd. govs. 1970-72), Los Angeles Soc. Fin. Analysts (pres. 1961-62). Republican. Clubs: Univ. (Los Angeles); Mt. Holyoke of So. Calif. Home: 21 Maygreen Ct Glendale CA 91206 Office: 51st Floor 333 S Hope St Los Angeles CA 90071

FISHER, MARSHALL LEE, educator; b. Wyandotte, Mich., Feb. 19, 1944; s. Gary Hamilton and Bernice (Druckenbrod) F.; m. Geraldine Ann DeFusco, Nov. 18, 1967; children: Kara, Kimberly, Tobin. B.S. in E.E, M.I.T., 1965, M.S., 1969, Ph.D., 1970. Asst. prof. mgmt. sci. Grad. Sch. Bus., U. Chgo., 1970-75; vis. prof. (asst.) dept. ops. research Cornell U., Ithaca, N.Y., 1974-75; asso. prof. Wharton Sch., U. Pa., Phila., 1975-79, prof. decision scis., 1979—; cons. Dupont, NASA, Dept. Def., Air Products & Chems., Inc., USM Corp., others. Editor: Mgmt. Sci, 1979—, SIAM Jour. Algebraic and Discrete Methodis, 1980—; contbr. articles to profl. jours. Recipient Lanchester prize Ops. Research Soc. Am., 1977. Mem. Inst. Mgmt. Sci. (Mgmt. Sci. Practice prize 1983), Math. Programming Soc., Am. Product and Inventory Control Soc., Sigma Xi. Club: Phila. Masters Track. Office: Decision Sci Dept Wharton Sch U Pa Phila PA 19104

FISHER, MAX MARTIN, diversified co. exec.; b. Pitts., July 15, 1908; s. William and Mollie (Brody) F.; m. Marjorie Switow, July 1, 1953; children—Jane (Mrs. D. Larry Sherman), Mary, Phillip, Julie (Mrs. Peter Cummings), Marjorie. B.S., Ohio State U., 1930, LL.D., 1971; D.H.L., Bar-Ilan (Israel) U., 1967, Mich. State U., 1971; D.B.A., Albion Coll., 1968; Dr. Humanities, Detroit Inst. Tech., 1969; D.H.L., Gratz Coll., 1971, Eastern Mich. U., 1973, Hebrew Union Colls., Jewish Inst. Religion, 1975, Yeshiva U., 1976. Chmn. bd. Aurora Gasoline Co., Detroit, 1932-59, Fisher-New Center Co., 1964-73; former chmn. bd. United Brands Co.; now hon. chmn.; dir. Mfrs. Nat. Bank, Dayco Corp., Taubman Co. Chmn., United Jewish Appeal, 1965-67; chmn. New Detroit, Inc., 1968-70; pres. Council Jewish Fedns., 1969-72; chmn. bd. govs. Jewish Agy. for Israel, 1971—; spl. cons. President Nixon on Vol. Action, 1969-70. Hon. chmn. United Found. Detroit, 1969—; bd. dirs. Sinai Hosp. of Detroit; chmn. bd. dirs. Detroit Renaissance, 1970—. Mem. Am. Petroleum Inst. (dir. 1957-74). Republican. Jewish. Clubs: Recess, Harmonie (N.Y.C.); Franklin Hills Country; Standard, Economic (Detroit) (dir.); Palm Beach Country.). Office: 2210 Fisher Bldg Detroit MI 48202

FISHER, MICHAEL ELLIS, mathematical physicist, chemist; b. Trinidad, W.I., Sept. 3, 1931; s. Harold Wolf and Jeanne Marie (Halter) F.; m. Sorrel Castillejo, Dec. 12, 1954; children: Caricia J., Daniel S., Martin J., Matthew P.A. B.S. with 1st class honors in Physics, King's Coll., London, 1951, Ph.D., 1957. Lectr. math. RAF, 1952-53; lectr. theoretical physics King's Coll., 1958-62, reader physics, 1962-64; prof. physics U. London, 1965-66; prof. chemistry and math. Cornell U., 1966-73, Horace White prof. chemistry, physics and math., 1973—, chmn. dept. chemistry, 1975-78; guest investigator Rockefeller Inst., 1963-64; vis. prof. applied physics Stanford U., 1970-71; Buhl lectr. theoretical physics Carnegie-Mellon U., 1971; Richtmyer Meml. lectr. Am. Assn. Physics Tchrs., 1973; S.H. Klosk lectr. NYU, 1975; 17th F. London Meml. lectr. Duke U., 1975; Walker-Ames prof. U. Wash., Seattle, 1977; Loeb lectr. physics Harvard U., 1979; vis. prof. physics MIT, 1979; Welsh Found. lectr. in physics U. Toronto, Ont., Can., 1979; 21st Alpheas Smith lectr. Ohio State U., 1982. Author: (with D.M. MacKay) Analogue Computing at Ultra-High Speed, 1962, The Nature of Critical Points, 1964, The Theory of Equilibrium Critical Phenomena, 1967; assoc. editor: Jour. Math. Physics, 1963-68, 72-74; adv. bd.: Jour. Theoretical Biology, 1969-82, Chem. Physics, 1972—, Discrete Math., 1971-78, Jour. Statis. Physics, 1978-81; contbr. 300 articles to profl. jours. Recipient award in phys. and math. scis. N.Y. Acad. Scis., 1978; Guthrie medal and prize Inst. Physics, London, 1980; Wolf prize in physics, 1980; Michelson-Morely award Case Western Res. U., 1982; Boltzmann medal IUPAP, 1983; Guggenheim fellow, 1970-71, 78-79. Fellow Am. Acad. Arts and Scis., Royal Soc. (London) (Bakerian lectr. 1979), Phys. Soc. London, Am. Phys. Soc. (Langmuir prize chem. physics 1970), Kings Coll. London; mem. Am. Chem. Soc., Soc. Indsl. and Applied Math., Math. Assn. Am., Nat. Acad. Scis. (Fgn. assoc., James Murray Lack award 1983), N.Y. Acad. Scis. Office: Baker Lab Cornell U Ithaca NY 14853

FISHER, MILES MARK, IV, university official; b. Huntington, W.Va., Sept. 25, 1932; s. Miles Mark and Ada Virginia (Foster) F. B.A., Va. Union U., 1954, M.Div., 1959; M.A., N.C. Central U., 1968; D.Min., Howard U., 1978. Ordained to ministry Baptist Ch., 1961; tchr. pub. schs., Durham, N.C., 1959-67; asst. prof. edn., counselor Norfolk (Va.) State Coll., 1967-69; cons. Model Cities Area of Recreation, Norfolk, 1968-69; exec.-sec. Nat. Assn. Equal Opportunity in Higher Edn., Washington, 1969-78; spl. cons. Inst. for Services to Edn., Washington, 1969-70; vis. asst. prof. Sch. Religion, Howard U., 1978-80; staff dir., com. clk. Com. of Whole, Council of D.C., Washington, 1979-83; spl. asst. to v.p. acad. affairs U. D.C., Washington, 1983—; Mem. task force employment of minority populations Nat. Recreation and Park Assn., 1970-71; mem. task force on edn. and Vietnam Era vet. VA, 1971-72; mem. steering com. U.S. Office of Edn. Common Core Data for the 70's, 1971—, Congl. Black Caucus Nat. Policy Conf. on Black Edn., 1972; mem. Nat. task force on Student Financial Aid Problems, 1974-75. Bd. dirs. Cooperative Coll. Registry, 1973-75; mem. adv. bd. Four-Year Servicemen's Opportunity Coll., 1974-77; mem. adv. com. to bd. dirs. Nat. Student Ednl. Fund, 1974-78; bd. dirs. Reading is Fundamental Program, 1977-79, Vis. Nurse Assn., 1974-80, D.C. Citizens for Better Public Edn., 1977; pres. D.C. Citizens for Better Public Edn., 1981, 83; bd. dirs. Voice Informed Community Expression, pres., 1982—; trustee Va. Union U., 1983—, Shaw U. Div. Sch., 1982—. Mem. Am. Assn. Higher Edn., Am. Acad. Polit. and Social Scis., Am. Acad. Religion, Am. Personnel and Guidance Assn., Am. Soc. Ch. History, Assn. for Non-White Concerns., Internat. Alumni Assn. Va. Union U. (pres. 1983—). Home: 4444 Connecticut Ave NW Apt 402 Washington DC 20008 Office: PO Box 2340 Washington DC 20013

FISHER, MILTON LEONARD, lawyer; b. Pitts., Jan. 17, 1922; s. Jacob Morris and Sara (Weiner) F.; m. Jean Freiler, Apr. 30, 1950; children: Susan Yellen, Janet Sara, Joseph Freiler. A.B., Oberlin Coll., 1943; J.D., Northwestern U., 1949. Bar: Ill. 1949, Ohio 1949. Assoc. Suekoff & Frost, Chgo., 1949-50, Mayer, Brown & Platt, 1950-60, ptnr., 1960—. Mem. ednl. region service commn. Ill. State Bd. Edn., 1979; chmn. Highland Park Civil Service Commn., Ill., 1959-68; bd. dirs. Better Govt. Assn.; mem. vis. com. Northwestern U. Sch. Law; mem. Chgo. Bar Found. Mem. ABA, Ill. Bar Assn., Chgo. Bar Assn., Chgo. Council Lawyers, Law Club. Clubs: Lake Shore Country (Glencoe, Ill.); Cliff Dwellers (Chgo.). Home: 349 Woodland Rd Highland Park IL 60035 Office: Mayer Brown & Platt 231 S LaSalle St Chicago IL 60604

FISHER, MORTON STEPHEN, retail store executive; b. N.Y.C., Dec. 7, 1927; s. Benjamin and Kate F.; m. Ruth Kaufman, Dec. 29, 1950; 1 dau., Barbara Jo. B.A., N.Y. U., 1948. Div. mdse. mgr. S. Klein on the Square, N.Y.C., 1948-60; v.p., mdse. mgr. Allied Stores Corp., N.Y.C., 1960-68; pres. Town and Country div. Lane Bryant Stores, N.Y.C., 1968-74; exec. v.p. King's Dept. Stores, Inc., Newton, Mass., 1974—, also dir., mem. exec. com.; exec. v.p. Cato Corp., Charlotte, N.C., 1982—. Mem. Nat. Retail Mchts. Assn. Office: 150 California St Newton MA 02158

FISHER, NEAL FLOYD, clergyman; b. Washington, Ind., Apr. 4, 1936; s. Floyd Russell and Florence Alice (Williams) F.; m. Ila Alexander, Aug. 18, 1957; children—Edwin Kirk, Julia Bryn. A.B., DePauw U., 1957, L.H.D., 1982; M.Div., Boston U., 1960, Ph.D., 1966. Ordained to ministry United Meth. Ch., 1958; pastor 1st United

Meth. Ch., Revere, Mass., 1960-63, North Andover, Mass., 1963-68; planning asso. United Meth. Bd. Global Ministries, N.Y.C., 1968-73, dir. planning, 1973-77; asso. dean, asst. prof. theology and society Boston U. Sch. Theology, 1977-80; pres., prof. theology and society Garrett Evang. Theol. Sem., Evanston, Ill., 1980—; Mendenhall lectr. DePauw U., Greencastle, Ind., 1982; Willson lectr., Nashville, Tenn., 1983; Voigt lectr. McKendree Coll., 1984; chaplain and preacher, Chautauqua, 1984; mem. panel on future Gen. Council on Ministries, mem. univ. senate United Meth. Ch. Author: Parables of Jesus: Glimpses of the New Age, 1979, Context for Discovery, 1981. Jacob Sleeper fellow, 1960-61. Mem. Assn. United Meth. Theol. Scis. Home: 2426 Lincolnwood Dr Evanston IL 60201 Office: 2121 Sheridan Rd Evanston IL 60201

FISHER, PETER ROWE, lawyer; b. N.Y.C., May 24, 1933; s. Frank Cyril and Julia Anne (Potter) F.; m. Cary Randolph Fox, June 28, 1957; children: Diane R., Julian P., Elizabeth C. A.B. cum laude, Harvard U., 1954; LL.B., U. Va., 1960. Bar: N.Y. 1960. Assoc. atty. Sullivan & Cromwell, N.Y.C., 1960-66, Rogers & Wells, 1967-69, ptrn., 1969—; adj. prof. law N.Y. Law Sch., N.Y.C., 1980—; village justice Village of Oyster Bay Cove, N.Y., 1981—. Mem. Town of Oyster Bay Landmarks Commn., 1978; trustee, v.p., treas. Theodore Roosevelt Assn., Oyster Bay, 1975—; trustee Oyster Bay Hist. Soc., 1973—, pres., 1977-81, treas., 1981-83, chmn., 1983—; trustee Soc. for Preservation of L.I. Antiquities, Setauket, N.Y., 1977. Mem. ABA. Republican. Episcopalian. Clubs: Seawanhaka Corinthian Yacht (trustee); Harvard (N.Y.C.)). Home: 200 E Main St Oyster Bay NY 11771 Office: 200 Park Ave New York NY 10166

FISHER, PIETER ALRICKS, investment banker; b. Balt., Apr. 15, 1931; s. Louis Miller and Katharine Busteed (Streett) F.; m. Margaret Morgan, Jan. 2, 1971 (div. June 1979); m. M. Helen Anderson, Sept. 8, 1979; children: Pieter A., Ellen McCrea. B.A., Princeton U., 1953; M.B.A., U. Va., 1957. Research exec. Young & Rubicam, Inc., N.Y.C., 1957-59; v.p. Doherty, Clifford, Steers & Shenfield, Inc., N.Y.C., 1959-65, Goldman Sachs & Co., 1965-74, gen. ptnr., 1974—. Chmn. David K.E. Bruce Found., Princeton, N.J., 1979—; trustee Que. Labrador Found., Ipswich, Mass., 1964—, Atlantic Ctr. for Environment, 1980—; dir. Vol. Cons. Group, N.Y.C., 1975—. Served as 1st lt. U.S. Army, 1953-55. Mem. Council Fgn. Relations, Fgn. Policy Assn., The Pilgrims, Newcomen Soc., Met. Mus. Art. Republican. Episcopalian. Clubs: River, Recess (N.Y.C.); Ivy (Princeton, N.J.); Duquesne (Pitts.). Home: 985 Fifth Ave New York NY 10021 Office: Goldman Sachs & Co 85 Broad St New York NY 10004

FISHER, RAYMOND GEORGE, business consultant; b. Heber City, Utah, June 30, 1911; s. John David and Maude (Van Wagoner) F.; m. Ruth Bitner, July 27, 1935; 1 son, Stephen Bitner. B.S. with honors, U. Utah, 1934; postgrad., George Washington U., 1936-38, Am. U., 1938-39. Jr. economist Bur. Labor Statistics, 1934-35; asst. economist Central Statis. Bd., 1935-39; research adv. U.S. Housing Authority, 1939-40; asst. chief munitions br. WPB, 1940-42, asst. to prodn. vice chmn., 1942-43; dir. program control div. Combined Chiefs Staff, 1943-44; adv. mil. programs Office of War Moblzn. and Reconversion, 1944-45; dir. reports and statistics Office of Mil. Govt. for Germany, 1945-46; asst. to bd. dirs. RFC, 1946; economist Rockefeller Office, 1946-52; on leave as asst. prodn to dir. Def. Moblzn., 1951; dir. econ. research Continental Can Co., 1952-58, v.p. mktg., 1958-62, v.p., gen. mgr. flexible packaging, 1962-65, v.p., gen. mgr. central metal div., 1965-67, group v.p. diversified products group, 1967-71, exec. v.p., 1971-73, vice chmn., 1974-76, chmn. exec. com., 1976-77; bus. cons., 1977—; chmn. Europemballage Corp.; dir. Continental Can Co., Continental Can Co. Can., Tee-Pak, Inc.; Adv. formulation European Recovery Program, 1948, Point Four Program, 1949-50. Mem. nat. adv. council U. Utah.; Trustee Inst. for Future. Served as capt. AUS, 1944. Decorated Medal of Freedom. Mem. Am. Statis. Assn., Owl and Key, Pi Kappa Alpha. Clubs: Pinnacle (N.Y.C.); Indian Harbour, Greenwich Country. Home and Office: Deer Park Ct Greenwich CT 06830

FISHER, RICHARD YALE, food company executive; b. Milw., 1933. B.B.A., U. Wis., 1954, LL.B., 1956. Bar: Wis. 1956. Sole pratice, 1956-69; with Farm House Foods Corp., Milw., 1966—, now chmn. bd., chief exec. officer, sec.; dir. Scot Lad Foods, Inc. Office: Farm House Foods Corp 777 E Wisconsin Ave Milwaukee WI 53202 *

FISHER, ROBERT CHARLES, publishing company executive, editor; b. Burlington, Iowa, Mar. 3, 1930; s. Ray Erwin and Blanche Columbia (Brolin) F. B.A. cum laude, Harvard U., 1955; postgrad., Columbia U. Law Sch., 1955-56, Tokyo U., 1957-59. Analyst, adjutant gen's. office U.S. Army, Kansas City, Mo., 1949-50, Washington, 1950-51; adv. Prime Minister Takeo Miki of, Japan, 1957-64; Far Eastern rep. Fodor Travel Guides, Tokyo, 1959-64, exec. editor, N.Y.C., 1964-66, 75-77, exec. v.p., 1975-77, pres., 1977-80, exec. editor, London, 1966-74; v.p. David McKay Co., N.Y.C., 1976-80; pres. Fisher Travel Guides, 1980—; Founder, dir. Kansas City Open Forum, 1949-50; bd. dirs. Internat. Assn. Med. Assistance to Travelers, 1972—. Author: Picasso, 1967, Klee, 1967, Guide to Japan, 1981. Served with CIC U.S. Army, 1952-54; Korea. Balt. Scholarship Fund grantee for study in Japan, 1956-59. Mem. Japan Soc. (N.Y.), Internat. House of Japan, Soc. Am. Travel Writers (dir. 1978-80, v.p. 1981-83), N.Y. Travel Writers Assn. (pres. 1979-81). Clubs: Harvard of N.Y.C., Overseas Press, Am. of Japan. Office: Fisher Travel Guides 401 Broadway Suite 2300 New York NY 10013

FISHER, ROBERT GEORGE, neurological surgeon, educator; b. Bound Brook, N.J., Jan. 6, 1917; s. F. LeRoy and Anna (Young) F.; m. Constance M. Sheehan, May 23, 1942; children: David, Carol, Robert. B.S., Rutgers U., 1938; M.D., U. Pa., 1942; Ph.D., U. Minn., 1949. Diplomate: Am. Bd. Neurol. Surgery, v.p., 1974. Intern Hosp. of U. Pa., Phila., 1942-43; fellow in neurosurgery Mayo Clinic, Rochester, Minn., 1946-49; sr. resident, staff neurosurgeon Johns Hopkins Hosp., Balt., 1949-51; chief dept. neurosurgery Dartmouth Coll., Hanover, N.H., 1951-67, U. Okla., Oklahoma City, 1967-74, Rutgers U., New Brunswick, N.J., 1978—. Contbr. articles to profl. jours., chpts. to books. Cubmaster Boy Scouts am., Hanover, 1961. Served to capt. AUS, 1943-46; PTO. Fellow ACS; mem. Congress Neurosurgery (editor 1955-58, sr. mem.), Am. Acad. Neurosurgery (v.p. 1973), Am. Assn. Neurosurgery (exec. com. 1973), Soc. Neurosurgeons, AMA. Republican. Home: 1175 Johnston Dr Watchung NJ 07060 Office: Rutgers Med Sch PO Box 101 Piscataway NJ 08854

FISHER, ROBERT HENRY, yacht and ship broker and, builder; b. Boston, May 20, 1925; s. Milton and Mae (Gurson) F.; m. Peggy von Lindenmayer, Aug. 3, 1954. Student, M.I.T., 1948; B.S., Boston U., 1948. Vice pres., gen. mgr. Gloucester Marine Rys. Corp. (affiliate Rocky Neck Shipyards, Inc.), Mass., 1950-59; v.p. Breen-Fisher & Assos. (yacht brokers), Ft. Lauderdale, Fla., 1960-63; pres., chief exec. officer Northrop & Johnson, Inc. (yacht and ship brokers), Ft. Lauderdale, 1964—; marine cons. Bd. dirs., mem. marine adv. com. Fla. Atlantic U.; bd. dirs. Fla. Ocean Scis. Inst. Served with USMC, 1941-46. Mem. North Am. Yacht Racing Union, So. Yacht Brokers Assn. (pres. 1964-65, v.p. 1977-80). Clubs: Storm Trysail (fleet capt. So. sta.); Royal Norwegian Yacht (Oslo); Propellor, Gulfstream Sailing (Ft. Lauderdale); Boston Yacht (Marblehead, Mass.); Indian Harbor Yacht (Greenwich, Conn.). Home: 401 Idlewyld Dr Fort Lauderdale FL 33301 Office: 1300 SE 17th St Fort Lauderdale FL 33316

FISHER, ROGER DUMMER, lawyer, educator; b. Winnetka, Ill., May 28, 1922; s. Walter Taylor and Katharine (Dummer) F.; m. Caroline Speer, Sept. 18, 1948; children: Elliott Speer, Peter Ryerson. A.B., Harvard U., 1943, LL.B. magna cum laude, 1948. Bar: Mass. bar 1948, D.C. bar 1950. Asst. to gen. counsel, then asst. to dep. U.S. spl. rep. ECA, Paris, 1948-49; with firm Covington & Burling, Washington, 1950-56; asst. to solicitor gen. U.S., 1956-58; lectr. law Harvard Law Sch., 1958-60, prof. law, 1960-76, Samuel Williston prof. law, 1976—; dir. Harvard Negotiation Project, 1980—; vis. prof. internat. relations dept. London Sch. Econs., 1965-66; cons. pub. affairs editor WGBH-TV, Cambridge, 1969. Originator, 1st exec. editor: series on pub. TV The Advocates, 1969-70; moderator, 1970-71; co-originator, exec. editor: series on pub. TV Arabs and Israelis, 1975; Author: International Conflict for Beginners, 1969, Dear Israelis, Dear Arabs, 1972, International Mediation: A Working Guide, 1978, International Crisis and the Role of Law: Points of Choice, 1978, Improving Compliance with International Law, 1981; Co-author: Getting to Yes: Negotiating Agreement Without Giving In, 1981; co-author, editor: International Conflict and Behavioral Science-The Craigville Papers, 1964; contbr. articles on internat. relations, internat. law and TV. Mem. Mass. Gov.'s Commn. on Citizen Participation, 1973-74; Bd. dirs. Council for Livable World, Overseas Devel. Council, Pub. Interest Communications Services; trustee Hudson Inst. Served to 1st lt. USAAF, 1942-46. Guggenheim fellow, 1965-66. Fellow Am. Acad. Arts and Scis.; mem. Am. Soc. Internat. Law (exec. council 1961-64, 66-69, v.p. 1982-84), Am., Mass. bar assns., Commn. to Study Orgn. of Peace, Council Fgn. Relations. Clubs: Metropolitan (Washington); Harvard (N.Y.C.). Home: 16 Fayerweather St Cambridge MA 02138 Office: Harvard U Law Sch Cambridge MA 02138

FISHER, ROVILLE EARL, JR., lawyer, venture capital consultant; b. LaCrosse, Wis., Jan. 24, 1944; s. Orville Earl and Mary Elaine (Davy) F.; m. Alexandra Grace Fleming; children: Kelly, Stephanie, Andrew, Angela, Matthew. B.A., U. Minn., J.D. Bar: Minn. V.p. Nat. Car Rental System Inc., Mpls., 1970-75, Jostens Inc., 1975—; dir. DFW Rental and Leasing Inc., Dallas. Mem. Fed. Bar Assn., ABA, Minn. State Bar Assn., Hennepin County Bar Assn., Am. Assn. Corp. Counsel, Direct Selling Assn., Am. Soc. Corp. Secs. Republican. Roman Catholic. Home: 1991 Fagerness Pt Rd Wayzata MN 55391 Office: Jostens Inc 5501 Norman Ctr. Dr Minneapolis MN 55437

FISHER, ROY MAC, journalism educator; b. Stockton, Kans., Sept. 5, 1918; s. Carey A. and Alice (Bales) F.; m. Anne Fallon, June 12, 1948; children: Leslie Anne, Patricia Alice, Mary Margaret, Sarah Harkin. B.S., Kans. State U., 1940, Harvard, 1950-51. Reporter Hastings (Nebr.) Tribune, 1940, Pratt (Kans.) Tribune, 1940-41; reporter Chgo. Daily News, 1945-52, asst. city editor, 1952-56, features editor, 1956-58, editor, 1966-71; prof., dean Sch. Journalism, U. Mo. at Columbia, 1971-82, prof., dir. Washington Reporting Program, 1982—; mng. editor World Book Ency., Field Enterprises Ednl. Corp., 1958-64, exec. editor, v.p., 1964-66; lectr. Medill Sch. Journalism, 1950-55. Bd. cons. NSF, Nat. Endowment for Humanities, German Marshall Fund, Benton Fedn.; U.S. del. UNESCO Conf. on World Press, Paris, 1975. Served to lt. comdr. USNR, 1941- 45; PTO. Recipient Nat. Headline award, 1953, Page One award, 1952; Nat. Sigma Delta Chi award, 1949, 69. Mem. Am. Soc. Newspapers Editors, Assn. for Edn. in Journalism, Sigma Delta Chi. Methodist. Club: Nat. Press (Washington). Office: Sch Journalism Univ Missouri National Press Bldg Washington DC 20045

FISHER, SYDNEY NETTLETON, educator; b. Warsaw, N.Y., Aug. 8, 1906; s. Addison Washburn and Pearl Ellen (Nettleton) F.; m. Elizabeth Evelyn Scipio, Sept. 3, 1938; children—Alan Washburn, Robert Lynn, Margaret Ellen Fisher McCarthy. A.B., Oberlin Coll., 1928, M.A., 1932; Ph.D., U. Ill., 1935; postdoctoral work, Princeton, 1935, U. Brussels, 1938. Tutor math. Robert Coll., Istanbul, Turkey, 1928-31, tutor English, 1936-37; instr. history Denison U., 1935-36, Ohio State U., 1937-42, asst. prof., 1942-47, asso. prof., 1947-54, prof., 1954-72, prof. emeritus, 1972—; coordinator (Grad. Inst. World Affairs), 1961-65; asso. chief econ. analysis Bd. Econ. Warfare, 1943, Fgn. Econ. Adminstrn., 1943-44; country specialist comml. policy div. Dept. State, 1944-46; lectr. Chautauqua Inst., 1940-42; vis. prof. Stetson U., 1949, U. So. Calif., 1954, 61; Dir. publs. Middle East Inst., 1952-53. Author: The Foreign Relations of Turkey, 1481-1512, 1948, Evolution in the Middle East: Revolt, Reform and Change, 1953, Social Forces in the Middle East, 1955, 68, 77, The Middle East: A History, 1959, 69, rev. edition, 1979, The Military in the Middle East, 1962, France and European Community, 1965; New Horizons for the United States in World Affairs, 1966; Editor: Middle East Jour, 1952-53. Grantee Am. Council Learned Soc., 1935, 38, Social Sci. Research Council, 1958-59. Fellow Royal Hist. Soc. (London), Ordinario, Accademia del Mediterraneo (Rome, Italy); mem. Middle East Studies Assn., Ohio Acad. History, Phi Beta Kappa, Phi Alpha Theta, Phi Kappa Phi. Presbyn. Home: 221 St Antoine Worthington OH 43085

FISHER, THOMAS GEORGE, lawyer, media company executive; b. Debrecen, Hungary, Oct. 2, 1931; came to U.S., 1951; S. Eugene J. and Viola Elizabeth (Rittersporn) F.; m. Rita Knisley, Feb. 14, 1960; children: Thomas G., Katherine Elizabeth. B.S., Am. U., 1957, J.D., 1959; student, Harvard U., 1956. Bar: Iowa 1977. Atty and legal asst. FCC, Washington, 1959-61, 65-66; pvt. law practice, Washington, 1961-65, 66-69; asst. counsel Meredith Corp., N.Y.C., 1969-72, assoc. gen. counsel, Des Moines, 1972-76, gen. counsel, 1976-80, v.p. gen. counsel, 1980—. Contbr. articles to profl. jours. Bd. dirs. Des Moines Met. Opera Co., Indianola, 1979—, Civic Music Assn., Des Moines, 1982—; chmn. legis. com. Greater Des Moines C. of C., 1976-77. Served with U.S. Army, 1952-54. Mem. Iowa State Bar Assn. (chmn. corp. counsel subcom. 1979-82), ABA, Fed. Communications Bar Assn., Polk County Bar Assn., Des Moines Com. Fgn. Relations. Clubs: Wakonda Country; Embassy (Des Moines). Office: Meredith Corp 1716 Locust Des Moines IA 50336

FISHER, WALTER CARL, electronics company executive; b. Uniontown, Pa., Sept. 25, 1918; s. William Lee and Manila H. (Nehls) F.; m. Margaret Jane DuQuin, May 25, 1941; children: W. Paul, J. David, Laura L., Margaret Anne. Student, Northwestern U., Pa. State U. Buyer, Montgomery Ward & Co., Chgo., 1946-52; div. merchandising mgr. Asso. Merchandising Corp., N.Y.C., 1952-54; v.p. sales Norge div. Borg Warner Corp., Chgo., 1954-61; chmn., dir. Zenith Radio Corp., Glenview, Ill., 1961—; pres. Zenith Sales Co., Zenith Internat. Sales Corp.; dir. Wylain Corp., Internat. Ins. Corp., Internat. Surplus Lines Ins. Corp., L.W. Biegler Corp. Served with C.E., AUS, 1943-46. Mem. Electronics Industry Assn. (gov., dir., past chmn. bd. consumers electronics group). Republican. Lutheran. Club: Sunset Ridge Country. Home: 545 Somerset Ln Northfield IL 60093 Office: 1000 N Milwaukee Ave Glenview IL 60025

FISHER, WALTER DUMMER, economist, educator; b. Chgo., Sept. 17, 1916; s. Walter Taylor and Katharine (Dummer) F.; m. Marjorie Smith, Dec. 21, 1948; children: Andrew, Carol, Dorothy. A.B., Harvard U., 1937; Ph.D., U. Chgo., 1943. Asst. economist U.S. Surplus Mktg. Adminstrn., Washington, 1940-42; instr. econs. U. Calif. at Berkeley, 1946-48, asst. prof., 1948-51, Kans. State U., Manhattan, 1951-54, asso. prof., 1954-57, prof., 1957-67; prof. econs. Northwestern U., Evanston, Ill., 1967—; cons. Pullman Bank, Chgo., 1951-53, Rand Corp., Santa Monica, Calif., 1958-62; vis. prof. U. Louvain, Belgium, 1971-72; dir. Nat. Bur. Econ. Research, N.Y.C., 1967-83. Author: Clustering and Aggregation in Economics, 1969, Statistics Economized, 1981; Contbr. articles to profl. jours. Served to capt. USAAF, 1943-46. Faculty research fellow Social Sci. Research Council, 1954-57; Guggenheim fellow, 1960-61. Fellow Econometric Soc.; mem. Am. Statis. Assn. Home: 2763 Garrison Ave Evanston IL 60201

FISHER, WALTER TAYLOR, lawyer; b. Chgo., Feb. 20, 1892; s. Walter Lowrie and Mabel (Taylor) F.; m. Katharine Dummer, Aug. 21, 1915 (dec. 1961); children—Walter, Ethel, John, Roger, Francis, Gerard Henderson; m. Margaret W. Rieser, Jan. 25, 1962 (dec. 1978); m. Laura K. Pollak, Nov. 2, 1979. Grad., Chgo. Latin Sch., 1909; A.B., Harvard, 1913; student law, U. Chgo., 1914-15; LL.B., Harvard, 1917. Bar: Ill. bar 1918. Law clk. with Matz, Fisher & Boyden, Chgo., 1917; and practiced law in, Chgo.; counsel firm Bell, Boyd & Lloyd.; Chmn. Ill. Commerce Commn., 1949-53; Asst. gen. counsel War Finance Corp., Washington, 1921-22; pres. Amalgamated Trust & Savs. Bank, Chgo., 1926-29; Counsel for Chgo. agy. RFC, 1932-33; alt. pub. mem. Nat. Def. Mediation Bd., 1941; mem. Pres.'s Emergency Bds. in nat. nonoperating railway employees case, 1943, and other cases; also mediator, arbitrator or permanent umpire for various labor disputes. Author: What Every Lawyer Knows, 1974, also articles in jours. Trustee U. Ill., 1929-31; Pres. Chgo. Council Fgn. Relations, 1944-46; lectr. Northwestern U. Law Sch., 1962. Mem. ABA (chmn. com. on lawyer referral service 1956-57), Ill. State Bar Assn., Chgo. Bar Assn. (chmn. com. initiating lawyer reference plan for low-cost legal service 1939-43). Clubs: Law, Legal (pres. 1936-37), City (pres. 1925-27), University, Attic. Home: 760 Bronson Ln Highland Park IL 60035 Office: 70 W Madison St Chicago IL 60602

FISHER, WAYNE H., corporation executive; b. Los Angeles, Dec. 27, 1920; s. Wayne Holmes and Lucille (Bartlett) F.; m. Theo Frisbee, May 26, 1942; children: William Noble, Robert Gregory, Elizabeth Helen. B.A., Pomona Coll., 1942; J.A., Harvard U., 1943; M.B.A., Stanford U., 1946. With Owl Drug Co., Los Angeles, 1947—, pres., 1960-62; with Lucky Stores, Inc., 1962—, exec. v.p., 1968-71, pres., 1971-74, chmn., 1974—, dir., chief exec. officer until, 1980; dir. Transam. Corp., 1979—, Denny's Inc., Standard Brands Paint Co., 1980—; Mem. bd. govs. and exec. com. Food Employers Council of Calif., 1963-80; past pres., past mem. bd. dirs. and adv. com. Western Assn. Food Chains, Inc., 1965-69; bd. dirs., mem. exec. com. Food Mktg. Inst., 1974-80; mgmt. chmn. Joint Labor Mgmt. Com., 1978-80; exec. in residence Food Industry Mgmt. Sch. Bus., U. So. Calif., 1978-80. Bd. dirs. Bay Area Council, 1972-79; mem. adv. council Stanford Grad. Sch. Bus., 1973-79; bd. govs., mem. long-range planning com. San Francisco Symphony Assn., 1975-80; trustee Pomona Coll., 1978—. Address: 6300 Clark Ave Dublin CA 94568

FISHER, WILLIAM LAWRENCE, geologist, educator; b. Marion, Ill., Sept. 16, 1932; s. Henry Adam and Madge Lenora (Moore) F.; m. Marilee Booth, Dec. 18, 1954; children: Leah, Karl, Peter. B.S., So. Ill. U., 1954; M.S., U. Kans., 1958, Ph.D. (Shell fellow), 1961. Research scientist Tex. Bur. Econ. Geology, Austin, 1960-68, asso. dir., 1968-70, dir., 1970-75, 77—; asst. sec. for energy and minerals Dept. Interior, Washington, 1975-77; Morgan J. Davis prof. dept. geol. scis., prof. LBJ Sch. Public Affairs, U. Tex., Austin, 1969—; chmn. council on energy resources; geologist State of Tex.; Mem. geology assoc. bd. U. Kans., 1972-74. Author: Mineral Resources of East Texas, 1964, Depositional Systems in the Wilcox Group, 1969, Delta Systems in the Exploration for Oil and Gas, 1969, Environmental Geologic Atlas of Texas Coastal Zone, 1972, National Energy Policies, 1977, 78, 79, 80. Served with AUS, 1954-56. Recipient Haworth Grad. award U. Kans., 1956, Disting. Alumni award, 1978; Alumni Achievement award So. Ill. U., 1978. Fellow Geol. Soc. Am.; mem. Am. Inst. Profl. Geologists (pres. Tex. sect. 1979), Am. Assn. Petroleum Geologists (Disting. Service award), Am. Assn. State Geologists (pres. 1981), Austin Geol. Soc. (pres. 1973-74), Nat. Acad. Scis. (bd. mineral and energy resources). Home: 8705 Ridgehill Dr Austin TX 78759 Office: University Sta Box X Austin TX 78712

FISHER, WILLIAM ROY, JR., investment banking company executive; b. Wilson, Va., June 7, 1936; s. William Roy and Virginia Elizabeth (Lewis) F.; m. Lyle Marie Rea, Oct. 6, 1962; children: William, Richard, Carol. B.S.E.E., Va. Poly. Inst., 1957; M.B.A., U. Va., 1968. Project engr. Sperry Rand Corp., Charlottesville, Va., 1957-66; security analyst Donaldson, Lufkin & Jenrette, N.Y.C., 1968-70, v.p., 1970-78, sr. v.p., 1978-81, exec. v.p., 1981—. Trustee Central Presbyn. Ch., Summit, N.J., 1983. Samuel Forest Hyde scholar U. Pa., 1968. Presbyterian. Presbyterian. Clubs: India House (N.Y.C.); Noe Pond (Chatham, N.J.); Summit Tennis (N.J.). Home: 11 Portland Rd Summit NJ 07901 Office: Donaldson Lufkin & Jenrette 140 Broadway New York NY 10005

FISHER, WILLIAM THOMAS, business administration educator; b. Central Falls, R.I., Mar. 15 1918; s. William L. and Sarah (Foley) F.; m. Mary Rowena Donnelly, Dec. 26, 1949; 1 son, William Thomas. B.S. with high honors, Am. Internat. Coll., 1949; M.Ed., Boston U., 1951; Ph.D., U. Conn., 1956; postgrad., Clark U., 1954, Columbia U., 1957, St. Thomas Sem., Bloomfield, Conn., evenings 1970-73; grad., Life Ins. Agy. Mgmt. Schs. Prodn. planner Belding Heminway Corp., Putnam, Conn., 1938-42; prin. Templeton (Mass.) Sch., 1949-50, Tourtellotte High Sch., Thompson, Conn., 1950-57; instr. Becker Jr. Coll., Worcester, Mass., 1955-57; asso. prof. State U. N.Y. at, Albany, 1957; asst. dean Sch. Ins., U. Conn., 1957-76, asst. dean adminstrn., 1976-77; adminstrv. dir. (Hartford M.B.A. program), 1957-64; vis. prof. Ohio U., summer 1962; dir. (IBM Advanced Ins. Industry Sch.), 1960-70; ednl. cons. IBM Corp., 1960-80; adminstr., asst. dir. Center for Ins. Edn. and Research, Hartford, 1976-81; asso. prof., lectr. mgmt. and adminstrv. scis. dept. Sch. Bus. Adminstrn., U. Conn., Storrs, 1976-81, mgmt. and orgn. dept., 1981—; Ordained permanent deacon Roman Catholic Ch. for Archdiocese of Hartford, 1973; assigned St. Joseph Cathedral, Hartford, part-time 1973-83; real estate broker, 1973—; owner Prairie Acre Farm, East Thompson, Conn., 1965—; Mem. Conn. State Ins. Com. and Conn. State Ins. Purchasing Bd., 1963-73, 75—, chmn. bd., 1971-73; past pres., now dir. Conn. Assn. Mcpl. Devel. Commns.; mem. Conn. adv. council SBA, 1964-70, chmn., 1967; chmn. various coms. Greater Hartford Council Econ. Edn., 1958—; mem. Thompson Bd. Finance, 1963-75; chmn. Thompson Indsl. and Devel. Com., 1964-70, 71-80, 81—. Contbr. articles to profl. jours. Pres. Thompson Indsl. Found., 1965-66; co-chmn. Quinebaug Valley Indsl. Devel. Council, 1962-64; mem. Gov.'s Conf. on Human Rights and Opportunities, 1967, Thompson Community Devel. Action Program, 1968-69, Northeastern Conn. com. Conn. Inst. for Blind, Hartford.; Organizer Conn. small bus. div. Businessmen for V.P. Humphrey, 1968; Trustee Am. Internat. Coll., 1963-71, mem. corp., 1972—; chmn. adv. bd. govs. Conn. Library Service Center, Willimantic, 1964-68, mem. exec. com., 1968-70; bd. dirs., sec. Edn. and Research Found. Profl. Ins. Agts. for States N.Y., N.J. and Conn., Glenmont, N.Y., 1973-83; past trustee, past pres. Thompson Library; corporator Day Kimball Hosp., Putnam, Conn.; trustee, mem. exec. com., personnel com. Annhurst Coll., Woodstock, Conn., 1977-84; active Conn. Small Bus. Devel. Ctr., summer 1982, 83; bd. dirs. Norwich-Quinebaug unit Am. Cancer Soc. Served with AUS, 1942-45. Recipient award of Year Hartford Assn. Ins. Women, 1969;

Presdl. Certificate Appreciation Conn. Assn. Mcpl. Devel. Commns., 1968. Mem. NEA (life), Am. Risk and Ins. Assn. (fellowship 1960, 62), Risk and Ins. Mgmt. Soc., Am. Soc. Personnel Adminstrn., Ins. Co. Edn. Dirs. Soc., Am. Acad. Mgmt., Eastern Acad. Mgmt., Internat. Platform Assn., Northeastern Indsl. Developers Assn., Conn. Council Advancement Econ. Edn., Nat. Hist. Soc., Conn. Hist. Soc., Smithsonian Assos., Nat. Trust Historic Preservation, AAUP, Am. Legion, Phi Delta Kappa, Delta Pi Epsilon. Home: Chase Rd Thompson CT 06277 also 174 Valley View Rd Manchester CT 06040 Office: Mgmt and Orgn Dept U-41 Sch Bus Adminstrn U Conn Storrs CT

FISHMAN, AARON HARRY, plastics manufacturing executive; b. Phila., July 18, 1922; s. Morris and Anna (Sevitsky) F.; m. Gloria Smith, Apr. 9, 1949; children: Laurie, Michael J. Pres., co-founder APL Corp., Miami Beach, Fla., 1946—, also dir. Served with AUS, 1942-45. Club: Seawane. Office: 101-01 Ave D Brooklyn NY 11236

FISHMAN, ALAN H., banker; b. 1946; (married). B.A., Brown U., 1968; M.A. in Econs, Columbia U., 1968. With Chem. Bank, N.Y.C., 1969—, v.p., 1974-76, sr. v.p., 1976-79, sr. v.p. fin., 1979-81, exec. v.p. fin., 1981—; also exec. v.p., chief fin. officer Chem. N.Y. Corp., 1981—. Office: Chemical Bank 277 Park Ave New York NY 10172 *

FISHMAN, ALFRED PAUL, physician; b. N.Y.C., Sept. 24, 1918; s. Isaac and Anne (Tinter) F.; m. Florence Howitz, Aug. 23, 1948 (dec.); children: Mark, Jay. A.B., U. Mich., 1938, M.S., 1939; M.D., U. Louisville, 1943; M.A. (hon.), U. Pa., 1971. Diplomate: Nat. Bd. Examiners, Am. Bd. Internal Medicine. Intern Jewish Hosp., Bklyn., 1943-44; Dazian Found. fellow pathology Mount Sinai Hosp., N.Y.C., 1946-47, asst. resident, resident medicine, 1947-48; Dazian Found. fellow cardiovascular physiology Michael Reese Hosp., Chgo., 1948-49; Am. Heart Assn. research fellow Bellevue Hosp., N.Y.C., 1949-50, established investigator cardiopulmonary lab., 1951-55; Am. Heart Assn. research fellow physiology Harvard U., Boston, 1950-51; instr. physiology N.Y. U., 1951-53; assoc. in medicine Columbia Coll. Physicians and Surgeons, N.Y.C., 1953-55, asst. prof., 1955-58, assoc. prof., 1958-66; prof. medicine U. Chgo., 1966-69; dir. Cardiovascular Inst., Chgo., 1966-69; dir. div. cardiovascular disease Michael Reese Hosp., Chgo., 1966-69; prof. medicine U. Pa., 1969—, William Maul Measey prof., 1972—, asso. dean, 1969-75; dir. cardiovascular-pulmonary div., dir. Robinette Found., Clin. Cardiovascular Research Center, U. Pa. Med. Center, 1969—; dir. Specialized Center of Research (Lung), 1973-81; attending physician Hosp. U. Pa., 1969—; sr. attending physician Phila. Gen. Hosp., 1970-78; physician Mass. Gen. Hosp., 1979; cons. to chancellor U. Mo., Kansas City, 1973-78; vis. prof. Harvard U., 1970, Oxford (Eng.) U., 1972, Washington U., St. Louis, 1973, Johns Hopkins U., 1974, Ben Gurion U., 1975, Emory U., Atlanta, 1976, U. Porto Alegra, Brazilia, Brazil, 1976, U. Zurich, Switzerland, 1978, Fu Wai Hosp., Peking, China, 1980; cons. Exec. Office Pres., 1961-69, U. Athens, Greece, 1980; mem. WHO Expert Panel, Geneva, 1973—, Nat. Adv. Heart and Lung Council, NIH, 1968-71; chmn. Gov.'s Com. for Research on Respiratory Diseases in Coal Miners, 1974-79, Internat. Conf. on Lung, Titisee, Germany, Florence, Italy, 1976; mem. Inst. of Medicine, Nat. Acad. Sci., 1980—. Editor: (with D.W. Richards) Circulation of The Blood-Men and Ideas, 1964, (with H.H. Hecht) The Pulmonary Circulation and Interstitial Space, 1969, Handbooks of Respiratory Physiology, Am. Physiol. Soc., 1967-72, 79—, Physiology in Medicine, New Eng. Jour. Medicine, 1969-79, Jour. Applied Physiology, 1981—; editorial bd.: Merck Manual, 1972—, Ann. Rev. Physiology, 1977—, Heart Failure, 1979, (with E. M. Renkin) Pulmonary Edema, 1979, Pulmonary Diseases and Disorders, 1979; contbr. articles to profl. jours. Bd. dirs. Polachek Found., Phila. Zool. Soc. Served to capt. M.C. U.S. Army, 1944-46. Recipient Disting. Alumni award U. Louisville, 1984. Fellow Am. Coll. Chest Physicians (hon.), Royal Coll. Physicians, A.C.P.; mem. Am. Physiol. Soc. (chmn. publs. bd. 1974-81, pres. 1983), Am. Soc. Clin. Investigation, AAAS, Royal Soc. Medicine (London), Assn. Am. Physicians, Am. Heart Assn. (dir. 1973—, chmn. council on cardiopulmonary disease 1972-74, research council 1974—, Disting. Achievement award 1980), N.Y. Heart Assn. (pres. 1965-67), Internat Union Physiol. Scis. (U.S. nat. com. 1982—), Internat. Union Physiol. Scis. (adv. com. div. health sci. policy 1982—), Am. Coll. Cardiology (hon.), Interurban Clin. Club, N.Y. County Med. Soc., Phila. Coll. Physicians, Heart Assn. Southeastern Pa. (bd. dirs.), Alpha Omega Alpha. Home: 2401 Pennsylvania Ave Apt 20-A7 Philadelphia PA 19130 Office: Hospital U Pennsylvania 3400 Spruce St Philadelphia PA 19104

FISHMAN, BERNARD, mech. engr.; b. Bklyn., June 26, 1920; s. Max and Mollie (Greenberg) F.; m. Sara Fishman, July 3, 1947; 1 dau., Carol Beth. Student, Bklyn. Coll., 1937-39; B.M.E., CCNY, 1942; M.M.E., Bklyn. Poly. Inst., 1951. Instr. CCNY Sch. Tech., 1942-44; design and mfg. engr. Star Auto Radio, 1944-45; rocket propulsion engr. M.W. Kellogg Co., 1946-53; chief hydro-mech. engr. Simmonds Precision Products, 1953-65; engring. specialist Reaction Motors div. Thiokol Corp., 1965-67; dir. research ASME, N.Y.C., 1967—. Contbr. articles to profl. jours. Mem. Bd. Edn., Ft. Lee, N.J., 1968-72. Served with USAF, 1945-46. Fellow ASME; mem. Nat. Soc. Profl. Engrs., Tau Beta Pi, Pi Tau Sigma. Patentee in field. Office: 345 E 47th St New York NY 10017

FISHMAN, ERWIN, research scientist; b. Cleve., Nov. 7, 1927; s. Herman B. and Rosanna (Feingold) F.; m. Suzanne Mulhollen, July 24, 1976; children—Stephen, Sarah, Rebecca, Elizabeth, Ellen. A.B., Oberlin Coll., 1950; Ph.D., Brown U., 1954. Research asso. U. Ill., 1954-55; prof. chemistry Syracuse U., 1955-69, U. Bordeaux, France, 1960; prof., chmn. dept. chemistry Union Coll., Schenectady, 1969-71; founder, head corp. Silar Labs., Inc., 1971-74; mem. tech. staff TRW Systems Group, 1974—. Served with AUS, 1945-46. Mem. Am. Chem. Soc., AAAS. Home: 447 Herondo Apt 107 Hermosa Beach CA 90254

FISHMAN, FRED NORMAN, lawyer; b. N.Y.C., Aug. 21, 1925; s. Arthur Elihu and Frederica (Greenspan) F.; m. Claire S. Powsner, Sept. 19, 1948; children: Robert J., Nancy K. S.B. summa cum laude, Harvard U., 1946, LL.B. magna cum laude, 1948; postgrad., Yale U., 1945-46. Bar: N.Y. State 1950, U.S. Supreme Ct. 1954. Law clk. to Chief Judge Calvert Magruder, U.S. Ct. Appeals, 1st Circuit, Boston, 1948-49; to Asso. Justice Felix Frankfurter, Supreme Ct. U.S., 1949-50; asso. firm Dewey, Ballantine, Bushby, Palmer & Wood (and predecessors), N.Y.C., 1950-57; with Freeport Minerals Co., N.Y.C., 1957-61, asst. sec., 1958-59, asst. v.p., 1959-61; partner firm Kaye, Scholer, Fierman, Hays & Handler, N.Y.C., 1962—, chmn. exec. com., 1981—. Editor, officer: Harvard Law Rev. Chmn. Harvard Law Sch. Fund, 1977-79; mem. Harvard Bd. Overseers' Com. to Visit Harvard Law Sch., 1975-81; chmn. Com. for Harvard Law Sch. Class of 1948 Twenty-Fifth Anniversary Gift; mem. Harvard U. Bd. Overseers' Com. to Visit Grad. Sch. Edn., 1971-77, Harvard Coll. Class of 1946 Permanent Class Com.; trustee Public Edn. Assn., N.Y.C., 1956-73, chmn. bd., 1970-71; dir. Harvard Alumni Assn., 1981-83; trustee Hosp. for Joint Diseases and Med. Center, N.Y.C., 1971-73, Lawyers' Com. for Civil Rights under Law, 1979—. Mem. Assn. Bar City N.Y. (chmn. com. fed. legis. 1963-66, exec. com. 1966-70, chmn. com. on corp. law 1980-82), ABA, N.Y. State Bar Assn., New York County Lawyers Assn., Am. Law Inst. (adviser corp. governance project 1980—), Harvard Law Sch. Assn. (trustee N.Y.C. 1966-69, v.p. N.Y.C. 1974-75, nat. council 1978-82, nat. exec. com. 1980-82), Phi Beta Kappa. Club: Harvard of N.Y.C. Home: 650 Park Ave New York NY 10021 Office: 425 Park Ave New York NY 10022

FISHMAN, JACK, biochemistry educator; b. Cracow, Poland, Sept. 27, 1930; s. Naftali and Rachel F.; m. Barbara White, Nov. 29, 1963; children: Howard, Neil, Leslie, Daniel. B.A., Yeshiva U., 1950; M.A., Columbia U., 1952; Ph.D., Wayne U., Detroit, 1955. Research asso. Sloan Kettering Inst., N.Y.C., 1956-59, asst., 1959-60, asso., 1960-63; investigator Inst. Steroid Research, Montefiore Hosp., Bronx, N.Y., 1963-70, sr. investigator, 1970-74, dir., 1974-77; asso. prof. Albert Einstein Coll. Medicine, N.Y.C., 1967-70, prof., 1971-80; adj. prof. Rockefeller U., N.Y.C., 1977-80, prof. biochem. endocrinology, 1980—; cons. FDA, WHO, Nat. Inst. Aging, NSF, Contraceptive Devel. Br. NIH, Endocrinology Study Sect. NIH, NRC Can. Recipient John Scott medal for invention of naloxone, 1983; USPHS fellow Oxford U., 1955-56. Mem. Am. Chem. Soc., Endocrine Soc., Am. Soc. Biol. Chemists, AAAS, N.Y. Acad. Scis. Jewish. Office: 1230 York Ave New York NY 10021

FISHMAN, JOSHUA AARON, educator, sociologist; b. Phila., July 18, 1926; s. Aaron S. and Sonia (Horwitz) F.; m. Gella Jeanne Schweid, Dec. 23, 1951; children: M. Manuel, David Eliot, Avrom Aaron. B.S., M.S. (Mayor Phila. competitive scholar 1944-48), U. Pa., 1948; Ph.D., Columbia U., 1953; Ped.D. (hon.), Yeshiva U., 1968. Tchr. elem. and secondary Jewish secular schs., 1945-50; ednl. psychologist, sr. research asso. dept. research and experimentation Jewish Edn. Com. N.Y., 1951-54; from lectr. to vis. prof. psychology CCNY, 1955-58; research assoc. to dir. research Coll. Entrance Exam. Bd., 1955-58; assoc. prof. human relations and psychology U. Pa., 1958-60; prof. psychology and sociology, dean Grad. Sch. Edn., Yeshiva U., 1960-66; disting. univ. research prof. social scis. Ferkauf Grad. Sch. Psychology, 1966—; univ. v.p. acad. affairs Ferkauf Grad. Sch. Humanities and Social Scis., 1973-76; Cummings lectr. McGill U., 1979; Linguistics Soc. Am. prof. Linguistics Inst., 1980; Mem. com. on sociolinguistics Social Sci. Research Council; adviser, cons. Am. Jewish Congress, Nat. Scholarship Service and Fund for Negro Students, Coll. Entrance Exam. Bd., Am. Assn. Jewish Edn., Ministry of Finance, Republic of Ireland; cons. Center for Applied Linguistics, Internat. Research Center on Bilingualism. Author: Studies on Polish Jewry, 1974, Sociology of Bilingual Education, 1976, The Spread of English, 1977, Advances in the Creation and Revision of Writing Systems, 1977, Advances in the Study of Societal Multilingualism, 1978, Never Say Die: A Thousand Years of Yiddish in Jewish Life and Letters, 1981, Bilingual Education for Hispanic Students in the U.S., 1982, The Rise and Fall of the Ethnic Revival, 1984, Readings in the Sociology of Jewish Languages, 1984; also numerous profl. publs.; assoc. editor: Jour. Ednl. Sociology, 1963-65; Assoc. editor: Yivo Ann., 1970—, Yidishe Sprakh, 1970—; assoc. editor: Yivo Bleter, 1970-74; editor, 1974-77, Jour. Social Issues, 1964-69; contbr. to: Sociology of Lang., 1971—; gen. editor: Internat. Jour. Sociology of Lang., 1973—. Pres.'s scholar E.C. Morris fellow Columbia Tchrs. Coll., 1952-53; postdoctoral research tng. fellow Social Sci. Research Council, 1954-55; NSF European Conf. grantee, 1960; Office of Edn. grantee, 1960-63, 66-68, 72-74, 79-80; Social Sci. Research Council European Conf. grantee, 1961; fellow Center Advanced Study Behavioral Scis., 1963-64; NIMH grantee Latin Am., 1963, 66; NSF grantee, Europe, 1966, also 79-83; sr. specialist Inst. Advanced Projects, East-West Center, 1968-69; Ford Found. grantee, 1969-72, 75-76; Meml. Found. Jewish Edn. grantee, 1970-71, 78-79, 82-83; Inst. Advanced Study fellow, 1975-76; sr. assoc. Multicultural-Bilingual div. Nat. Inst. Edn., 1976-77; Nat. Inst. Edn. grantee, 1978-79, 79-81; fellow Netherlands Inst. Advanced Study, 1982-83, Israel Inst. Advanced Studies, 1983. Fellow Am. Psychol. Assn., Am. Sociol. Assn., AAAS, Am. Anthrop. Assn.; mem. Am. Ednl. Research Assn., Linguistic Soc. Am., Yivo Inst. Jewish Research, Nat. Assn. Bilingual Edn., TESOL, AAUP. Home: 3340 Bainbridge Ave New York NY 10467 Office: Ferkauf Grad Sch Yeshiva U 1165 Morris Park Ave Bronx NY 10461 *I have had the incredible good fortune to be exposed simultaneously to modern Western and Jewish classical thought, to secular and religious values, to theoretical and applied emphases, to the comforts of a language of wider communication (English) and a language of ethnic intimacy (Yiddish) to the infinite world of science, the eternal land of my ancestors and the new world of democracy, opportunity and pluralism to which my parents came as immigrants. I have tried to combine all of these forces within myself and to contribute to them. I consider both the tensions and the creativity resulting from these varied stimuli to be a unique heritage: an American-Jewish heritage to be treasured, cultivated, improved and handed on.*

FISHMAN, LIBBY G., lawyer; b. Merion Station, Pa., Aug. 14, 1940; d. Hyman A. and Mollie M. Guth; m. Alan L. Fishman, Aug. 2, 1964; children: Beth L., Charles E. B.A., Barnard Coll., 1962; M.S., Columbia U., 1963; J.D., Temple U., 1968. Mem. firm Goodis, Greenfield, Henry, Shaiman & Levin, Phila., 1968-76, partner, 1973-76; asso. corp. counsel Franklin Mint Corp., Franklin Center, Pa., 1976-78; sr. v.p., gen. counsel, sec. Girard Bank, Phila., 1978—; assoc. gen. counsel Mellon Nat. Corp., 1983—. Mem. Am. Bar Assn., Am. Soc. Corp. Secs., Support Center for Child Advs., Forum Exec. Women, Phila. Bar Assn., Phila. Citizens for Children and Youth. Jewish. Office: Girard Bank Girard Plaza Philadelphia PA 19101 *

FISHMAN, MARVIN ALLEN, physician; b. Chgo., Feb. 16, 1937; s. Joseph and Mary (Schneider) F.; m. Gloria Brenda Greenberg, Dec. 20, 1959; children: Bradley Steven, Patricia Ann. B.S., U. Ill., 1959, M.D., 1961. Diplomate: Am. Bd. Pediatrics, Am. Bd. Psychiatry and Neurology (child neurology). Intern, then resident in pediatrics Michael Reese Hosp. and Med. Center, Chgo., 1961-64; resident in neurology Mass. Gen. Hosp., Boston, 1966-67; fellow in pediatric neurology St. Louis Children's Hosp., 1969-70, dir. Birth Defects Ctr., 1971-79; prof. pediatrics, neurology and preventive medicine Washington U. Med. Sch., St. Louis, 1970-79, dir. Irene Walter Johnson Inst. Rehab., 1974-79; prof. pediatrics and neurology, dir. pediatric neurology tng. program Baylor Coll. Medicine, Houston, 1979—; chief neurology service Tex. Children's Hosp., Houston, 1979—. Author articles in field, chpts. in books; editorial bd.: Jour. Pediatrics, 1980—. Served with USAR, 1964-66. Grantee HEW, Grant Found., Ga. Warm Springs Found., Nat. Found.-March of Dimes. Mem. Am. Soc. Neurochemistry (councillor 1977-79), Child Neurology Soc. (exec. com., councillor 1980-82), Am. Acad. Pediatrics, Am. Acad. Neurology, Am. Neurol. Assn., Am. Pediatric Soc., Soc. Pediatric Research, Soc. Neuroscis. Home: 130 Plantation Houston TX 77024 Office: Baylor Coll Medicine 1200 Moursund Ave Houston TX 77030

FISHMAN, ROBERT ALLEN, educator, neurologist; b. N.Y.C., May 30, 1924; s. Samuel Benjamin and Miriam (Brinkin) F.; m. Margery Ann Satz, Jan. 29, 1956 (dec. May 29, 1980); children: Mary Beth, Alice Ellen, Elizabeth Ann.; m. Mary Craig Wilson, Jan. 7, 1983. A.B., Columbia U., 1944; M.D., U. Pa., 1947. Mem. faculty Columbia Coll. Phys. and Surg., 1954-66, asso. prof. neurology, 1962-66; asst. attending neurologist N.Y. State Psychiat. Inst., 1955-66, Neurol. Inst. Presbyn. Hosp., N.Y.C., 1955-61, asso., 1961-66; co-dir. Neurol. Clin. Research Center, Neurol. Inst., Columbia-Presbyn. Med. Center, 1961-66; prof. neurology, chmn. dept. U. Calif. Med. Center, San Francisco, 1966—; cons. neurologist San Francisco Gen. Hosp., San Francisco VA Hosp., Letterman Gen. Hosp.; dir. Am. Bd. Psychiatry and Neurology, 1981—. Author: Cerebrospinal Fluid in Diseases of the Nervous System, 1980; Contbr. articles to profl. jours. Nat. Multiple Sclerosis Soc. fellow, 1956-57; John and Mary R. Markle scholar in med. sci., 1960-65. Mem. Am. Neurol. Assn. (pres. 1983-84), Am. Fedn. for Clin. Research, Assn. for Research in Nervous and Mental Diseases, Am. Acad. Neurology (v.p. 1971-73, pres. 1975-77), Am. Soc. for Neurochemistry, Soc. for Neurosci., N.Y. Neurol. Soc., Am. Assn. Univ. Profs. Neurology (pres. 1972-73), AAAS, Am. Epilepsy Soc., N.Y. Acad. Scis., AMA (sec. sect. on nervous and mental diseases 1964-67, v.p. 1967-68, pres. 1968-69), Alpha Omega Alpha (hon. faculty mem.). Home: 61 Cloudview Rd Sausalito CA 94965 Office: U Calif Med Center 794 Herbert C Moffitt Hosp San Francisco CA 94122

FISHWICK, JOHN PALMER, retired railroad executive, lawyer; b. Roanoke, Va., Sept. 29, 1916; s. William and Nellie (Cross) F.; m. Blair Wiley, Jan. 4, 1941; children: Ellen Blair (Mrs. Guyman Martin III), Anne Palmer (Mrs. Wesley Posvar), John Palmer. A.B., Roanoke Coll., 1937; LL.B., Harvard U., 1940. Bar: Va. 1939. Asso. Cravath, Swaine & Moore, N.Y.C., 1940-42; asst. to gen. solicitor N. & W. Ry., Roanoke, Va., 1945-47, asst. gen. solicitor, 1947-51, asst. gen. counsel, 1951-54, gen. solicitor, 1954-56, gen. counsel, 1956-58, v.p., gen. counsel, 1958-59, v.p. law, 1959-63, sr. v.p., 1963-70, pres., chief exec. officer, 1970-80, chmn., chief exec. officer, 1980-81, also dir.; ptnr. Windels, Marx, Davies & Ives, N.Y.C.; chmn., chief exec. officer Erie Lackawanna Ry. Co., 1968-70; pres., chief exec. officer Del. and Hudson Ry. Co., 1968-70; pres., dir. Dereco, Inc., 1968-81; dir. Allied Corp., Shenandoah Life Ins. Co., Norfolk So. Corp., Piedmont Aviation Inc. Trustee Roanoke Coll., 1964-72; trustee Va. Theol. Sem. (former chancellor Diocese S.W. Va.); former trustee Va. Mus. Fine Arts, Richmond. Served as lt. comdr. USNR, 1942-45. Episcopalian. Clubs: City Tavern Assn. (Georgetown); Metropolitan (Washington); Hillsboro (Pompano Beach, Fla.). Office: 1701 Pennsylvania Ave NW Suite 940 Washington DC 20006

FISK, CARLTON ERNEST, baseball player; b. Bellows Falls, Vt., Dec. 26, 1947. Ed., U. N.H. With Boston Red Sox, 1971-80; with Chgo. White Sox, 1980—. Am. League player in All-Star Game, 1972, 73, 76, 77, 78. *

FISK, GEORGE WILLIAM, container corporation executive, lawyer; b. Bklyn, Aug. 24, 1919; s. Willaim Millard and Georgia Leona (Winans) F.; m. Dorothy Lee Bowles, May 8, 1943; children: Robert William, Virginia Lee Fisk Dunphy, Margaret Grace Fisk Genvert. A.B., Colgate U., 1940; LL.B., Columbia U., 1948. Bar: N.Y. 1948, Pa. 1956, Ill. 1979. Assoc. Hubbell and Davis, N.Y.C., 1948-50; atty. Allied Corp., N.Y.C., 1950-55; assoc. gen. counsel Mobil Oil Corp., Phila., N.Y.C., 1955-79; gen. counsel Container Corp. Am., Chgo., 1979—. Served to maj. AUS, 1941-46; ETO. Decorated Bronze Star. Mem. ABA. Republican. Congregationalist. Clubs: Union League (N.Y.C.); Burning Tree (Greenwich, Conn.); Mission Hills Country (Northbrook, Ill.). Home: 1670 E Mission Hills Rd Northbrook IL 60062 Office: Container Corp Am One First Nat Plaza Chicago IL 60603

FISKE, DONALD WINSLOW, psychology educator; b. Lincoln, N.H., Aug. 27, 1916; m. Barbara Page; children: Alan, Susan. A.B., Harvard U., 1937, A.M., 1939; Ph.D., U. Mich., 1948. Instr. Cambridge Jr. Coll., 1939-41; research assoc. Phillips Acad., 1940-42; instr. Wellesley Coll., 1941; from asst. project dir. to instr. U. Mich., 1946-48; mem. faculty U. Chgo., 1948—, prof. psychology, 1960—, assoc. chmn. dept., 1963-68, chmn. dept., 1982—; Mem. study panel in mental health NIMH. Author: (with others) Assessment of Men, 1948, (with E.L. Kelly) The Prediction of Performance in Clinical Psychology, 1951, (with S. Maddi) Functions of Varied Experience, 1961, Measuring the Concepts of Personality, 1971, (with S. Duncan Jr.) Face to Face Interactions: Research, Methods, and Theory, 1977, Strategies for Personality Research: The Observation versus Interpretation of Behavior, 1978; also articles.; Editor: Multivariate Behavioral Research, 1971-73. Served with USNR, 1942-43, 46; with OSS, 1944-45. Fellow AAAS; mem. Am. Psychol. Assn. (chmn. com. psychol. tests 1957-58, conv. com. 1964-65, pres. div. evaluation and measurement 1977-78), Midwestern Psychol. Assn. (sec.-treas. 1955-58, pres. 1962-63), AAUP, Soc. Multivariate Exptl. Psychology (pres. 1968-69). Home: 5711 Blackstone Ave Chicago IL 60637

FISKE, EDWARD BOGARDUS, journalist; b. Phila., June 4, 1937; s. Edward R., Jr. and Jean (Bogardus) F.; m. Dale Alden Woodruff, July 12, 1963; children: Julia Woodruff, Suzanna Rawson. B.A., Wesleyan U., Middletown, Conn., 1959; M.A., Princeton Theol. Sem., 1963, Columbia U., 1965; LL.D. (hon.), Beaver (Pa.) Coll., 1980. Ordained to ministry United Presbyn. Ch., 1963; asst. minister Ch. of the Master, N.Y.C., 1963-64; news clk., then religion reporter N.Y. Times, 1964-69, religion editor, 1969-74, edn. editor, 1974—. Editorial bd.: Theology Today, 1976—; contbr. articles nat. periodicals. Trustee Wesleyan U., 1968-72, New Canaan (Conn.) Country Sch., 1977—. Mem. Edn. Writers Assn., Phi Beta Kappa. Home: 45 S Turkey Hill Rd Green Farms CT 06436 Office: 229 W 43d St New York NY 10036

FISKE, MARJORIE, social psychologist; b. Attleboro, Mass.; d. Harold M. and Lena (Wells) F.; 1 dau., Carol Lissance. B.A., Mt. Holyoke Coll., D.Sc. (hon.), 1976; M.A., Columbia U. Dep. dir. evaluation staff Internat. Broadcasting Service, Dept. State, N.Y.C., 1949-53; exec. dir. nat. planning com. on media research Ford Found., N.Y.C., 1953-54; research dir. Bur. Applied Social Research, Columbia U., N.Y.C., 1953-55; lectr. dept. sociology U. Calif.-Berkeley, 1955-56, dir. book selection and censorship study, also lectr. social research Sch. Librarianship, 1956-58; lectr. dept. psychiatry U. Calif. Med. Sch. at San Francisco, 1958-65, prof. social psychology, 1966—; dir. human devel. research and tng. program U. Calif. at San Francisco, 1958—, also chmn., founder Ph.D. program in human devel. and aging.; Cons. on adult devel. and aging to nat., internat., state and regional orgns. Author: (with Robert K. Merton and Alberta Curtis) Mass Persuasion, 1946, (with Robert K. Merton and Patricia Kendall) The Focused Interview, 1948, Book Selection and Censorship, 1959, Lives in Distress, 1964, (with P. Berkman) Aging and Mental Disorder in San Francisco, 1967, (with A. Simon and L. Epstein) Crisis and Intervention, 1970, (with M. Thurnher and D. Chiriboga) Four Stages of Life: A Comparative Study of Women and Men Facing Transitions, 1975, Middle Age: The Prime of Life?, 1979; contbr. articles to profl. jours and books. Bd. dirs. Fromm Inst. Lifelong Learning, U. San Francisco; trustee Fielding Inst. Recipient Library Lit. award ALA-Internat. Library Assn., 1959. Fellow Am. Sociol. Assn., AAAS, Am. Psychol. Assn., Am. Gerontol. Soc. (Kleemeler award 1973). Home: 1100 Gough St San Francisco CA 94109 Office: Human Devel And Aging Program U Calif 745 Parnassus Ave San Francisco CA 94143

FISKE, RICHARD SEWELL, geologist; b. Balt., Sept. 5, 1932; s. Franklin Shaw and Evelyn Louise (Sewell) F.; m. Patricia Powell Leach, Nov. 28, 1959; children: Anne Powell, Peter Sewell. B.S. in Geol. Engring, Princeton U., 1954, M.S., 1955; Ph.D. in Geology, Johns Hopkins U., 1960. With U.S. Geol. Survey, 1964-76; chief Office Geochemistry and Geophysics, Reston, Va., 1972-76; geologist, curator dept. mineral scis. Smithsonian Instn., Washington, 1976-80; dir. Nat. Mus. Natural History, 1980—. Am. Chem. Soc. postdoctoral fellow U. Tokyo, 1960-61; recipient Meritorious Service award Dept. Interior, 1976. Fellow AAAS; mem. Geol. Soc. Am., Am. Geophys. Union, Geol. Soc. Washington. Club: Cosmos (Washington). Home:

5901 Wynnwood Rd Bethesda MD 20816 Office: Dept Mineral Scis NHB-119 Smithsonian Instn Washington DC 20560

FISKE, ROBERT BISHOP, JR., lawyer; b. N.Y.C., Dec. 28, 1930; s. Robert Bishop and Lenore (Seymour) F.; m. Janet Tinsley, Aug. 21, 1954; children: Linda Goucher, Robert Bishop, Susan Seymour. B.A., Yale U., 1952; J.D., U. Mich., 1955. Bar: Mich. 1955, N.Y. 1956, U.S. Supreme Ct. 1961. Assoc. firm Davis, Polk, Wardwell, Sunderland & Kiendl, 1955-57; asst. U.S. atty. So. Dist. N.Y., 1957-61; assoc. firm Davis, Polk & Wardwell, 1961-64, partner firm, 1964-76, 80—; U.S. atty. So. Dist. N.Y., N.Y.C., 1976-80. Fellow Am. Coll. Trial Lawyers; mem. Am. Bar Assn., Bar Assn. City N.Y., Fed. Bar Council (pres.), N.Y. State Bar Assn. Republican. Congregationalist. Club: Noroton Yacht. Home: 19 Juniper Rd Darien CT 06820 Office: 1 Chase Manhattan Plaza New York NY 10005

FISKEN, ALEXANDER MCEWAN, forest products co. exec.; b. Seattle, Dec. 31, 1922; s. Keith Gazzam and Marian (McEwan) F.; m. Elizabeth S. Reynolds, Nov. 25, 1944; children—Marian Fisken Byse, Alexander McEwan, Sarah Fisken Knudsen. B.Engring., Yale U., 1943. With Weyerhaeuser Co., 1945—, sr. v.p. facilities planning and tech., Tacoma, Wash., 1979—; dir. King Broadcasting Co., Seattle. Trustee Inst. Paper Chemistry, 1979—. Episcopalian. Office: Weyerhaeuser Co Tacoma WA 98477

FISSINGER, EDWIN RUSSELL, music educator; b. Chgo., June 15, 1920; s. Paul Clevel and Isabel (Sweney) F.; m. Cecile Patricia Monette, Feb. 27, 1943; children: Edwin Monette, Laura. B.Mus., Am. Conservatory of Music, Chgo., 1947, M.Mus., 1951; D.Mus.Arts, U. Ill., 1962. Instr. music Am. Conservatory of Music, Chgo., 1947-54; instr. music U. Ill., Urbana, 1954-57, chmn. dept., 1957-67; prof., chmn. dept. music N.D. State U., Fargo, 1967—, dir. concert choir, 1967—; cons. in field. Composer: To Everything There Is a Season, 1976, Lux Aeterna, 1983, Babylon, 1976, Something has Spoken to Me in the Night, 1979. Served with USAAF, 1942-44. Decorated Purple Heart; recipient Kimball award for composition, 1950. Mem. Am. Choral Dirs. Assn., Music Educators Nat. Conf. Home: 57 15th Ave N Fargo ND 58102 Office: Music Dept UND Fargo ND 58105

FITCH, BRIAN THOMAS, linguist; b. London, Nov. 19, 1935; emigrated to Can., 1965; s. Thomas Charles and Hilda F.; m. Josette Ramel, Aug. 29, 1959; children: Rafaella, Fabrice, Sebastien. B.A. with honors, King's Coll., U. Durham (Eng.), 1958; postgrad., Bordeaux (France) U., 1958-59; Doctorat d'Université, Strasbourg (France) U., 1962. Lectr. in English, Strasbourg U., 1960-62; asst. lectr. in French, Manchester (Eng.) U., 1962-65; vis. asso. prof. French, Trinity Coll., U. Toronto, Ont., Can., 1965-66, Gerald Larkin prof. French, 1966—, asso. chmn. grad. studies, 1977-81. Author: Narrateur et Narration dans L'Etranger, 1960, Le Sentiment d'etrangeté chez Malraux, Sartre, Camus et S. de Beauvoir, 1964, Dimensions et structures chez Bernanos, 1969, Un Texte, ses lecteurs, leurs Lectures, L'Etranger de Camus, 1972, Dimensions, structures et Textualite chez Beckett, 1977, The Narcissistic Test: a Reading of Camus' Fiction, 1982, Monde à l'envers/Texte réversible: la fiction de Bataille, 1982. Can. Council leave fellow, 1970-71, 76-77, 82-83. Fellow Royal Soc. Can.; mem. MLA, Soc. French Studies (U.K.), Can. Assn. Univ. Tchrs. Home: 236 Rose Park Dr Toronto ON M4T 1R5 Canada Office: Dept French Trinity Coll U Toronto Toronto ON M4T 1R5 Canada

FITCH, COY DEAN, physician, educator; b. Marthaville, La., Oct. 5, 1934; s. Raymond E. and Joey (Youngblood) F.; m. Rachel Farr, Mar. 31, 1956; children: Julia Anne, Jaquelyn Kay. B.S., U. Ark., 1956, M.S., 1958, M.D., 1958. Diplomate: in internal medicine and endocrinology Am. Bd. Internal Medicine. Intern U. Ark. Sch. Medicine, 1958-59, resident, 1959-62, instr. biochemistry, 1959-62, asst. prof. medicine and biochemistry, 1962-66, asso. prof., 1966-67, dir., 1965-67; asso. prof. internal medicine and biochemistry St. Louis U. Sch. Medicine, 1967-73, prof. internal medicine, 1973—, prof. biochemistry, 1976—, head sect. metabolism, 1969-76, dir. div. endocrinology and metabolism, 1977—; chief med. service St. Louis U. Hosps., 1976-77, vice-chmn. dept. internal medicine, 1983—; practice medicine, specializing in internal medicine, Little Rock, 1962-67, St. Louis, 1969—; dir. Diabetic Clinic, U. Ark. Med. Ctr., 1962-67, head sect. metabolism and endocrinology, 1966-67; mem. nutrition study sect. div. research grants NIH, 1967-71. Asso. editor: Nutrition Revs., 1964; contbr. articles to profl. jours. Served from capt. to lt. col., M.C. AUS, 1967-69. Recipient Lederle Med. Faculty award, 1966-67; Russell M. Wilder-Nat. Vitamin Found. fellow, 1959-62. Fellow ACP; mem. Am. Fedn. Clin. Research, Am. Inst. Nutrition, Am., So. socs. clin. investigation, Am. Soc. Biol. Chemists, Central Soc. Clin. Research, Phi Beta Kappa, Sigma Xi. Office: 1402 S Grand Blvd Saint Louis MO 63104

FITCH, DAVID ROBNETT, emeritus finance educator; b. Brookfield, Mo., Dec. 10, 1921; s. Donald Colt and Helen Morton (Robnett) F.; m. Doris Griffin Stephenson, Aug. 1, 1952; children: Cynthia, Robin, Susan. B.A. in Econs., Tex. A&M U., 1942, M.S., U. Wis., 1948; Ph.D., U. Okla., 1956. C.L.U., Tex. Assoc. prof. Tex. A&M U., College Station, 1949-56, prof., 1956-60; prof., chmn. dept. finance, ins. and real estate North Tex. State U., Denton, 1960-83, prof. emeritus, 1983—. Served to capt. F.A. AUS, 1942-47. Mem. Am. Finance Assn., Am. Econ. Assn., Am. Risk and Ins. Assn., Assn. C.L.U.s, Southwestern Finance Assn. (pres.), Phi Delta Theta, Delta Sigma Pi, Beta Gamma Sigma. Home: 2719 Crestwood Denton TX 76201

FITCH, FRANK WESLEY, pathologist, educator; b. Bushnell, Ill., May 30, 1929; s. Harold Wayne and Mary Gladys (Frank) F.; m. Shirley Dobbins, Dec. 23, 1951; children—Mary Margaret, Mark Howard. M.D., U. Chgo., 1953, S.M., 1957, Ph.D., 1960. USPHS postdoctoral research fellow, 1954-55, 57-58; faculty U. Chgo., 1957—, prof. pathology, 1967—, Albert D. Lasker prof. med. sci., 1976—, asso. dean med. and grad. edn., 1976—; vis. prof. Swiss Inst. Exptl. Cancer Research, Lausanne, Switzerland, 1974-75. Contbr. chpts. to books, articles profl. jours. Recipient Borden Undergrad. Research award, 1953, Lederle Med. Faculty award, 1958-61; Markle Found. scholar, 1961-66; Commonwealth Fund fellow U. Lausanne (Switzerland) Institut de Biochimie, 1965-66; Guggenheim fellow, 1974-75. Mem. Am. Assn. Immunologists, Am. Assn. Pathologists, Chgo. Path. Soc., Radiation Research Soc., Reticuloendothelial Soc., Sigma Xi, Alpha Omega Alpha. Home: 5449 Kenwood Ave Chicago IL 60615

FITCH, HOWARD MERCER, lawyer, labor arbitrator; b. Jeffersonville, Ind., Dec. 23, 1909; s. J. Howard and Kate Orvis (Girdler) F.; m. Jane Rogers McCaw, Dec. 25, 1930 (dec. 1983); children: Catherine Mercer Druitt, Jane Rogers Butterworth. B.M.E., U. Ky., 1930, M.S., 1936, M.E., 1939; J.D. magna cum laude, U. Louisville, 1942. Registered profl. engr., Ky., Ky. 1942, Ill. 1954, U.S. Patent Office 1943. Engr. Western Electric Co., Kearney, N.J., 1930-32; joined Am. Air Filter Co. Inc., 1936, served as sales engr., prodn. mgr., mgr. legal and patent dept., asst. to exec. v.p., 1936-53, mgr. Herman Nelson div., 1953, v.p., 1954-72, dir. ops., 1958-63; practice law, Louisville, 1942—; ptnr. Hunt & Fitch, 1945-58. Patentee in field. Mem. nat. com. Atlantic Union Com.; mem. Louisville Labor-Mgmt. Council; bd. dirs. Louisville Urban League, Louisville Better Bus. Bur., Consumers Adv. Council. Mem. ASME, ASHRAE, Am. Arbitration Assn. (panel arbitrators), Nat. Acad. Arbitrators, ABA, Ky. Bar Assn., Louisville Bar Assn., Hon. Order Ky. Cols., Louisville C. of C., Assoc. Industries Quad Cities (past pres.), Am. Soc. Personnel Adminstrn., Louisville Personnel Assn. Episcopalian. Clubs: Filson, Pendennis, Arts, Ky. Soc. Natural History, Louisville Photog. Soc. Home and Office: 1704 Spruce Ln Louisville KY 40207

FITCH, JAMES ALEXANDER, banker; b. Chgo., Jan. 28, 1931; s. Morgan Lewis and Marian Louise (Ringer) F.; m. Marilyn Quan, Feb. 12, 1955; children: James Alexander, Edward Lewis, Alice Louise. B.S., Beloit Coll., 1952. Pres. South Chgo. Savs. Bank, 1968—, chmn., 1984—. Chmn. South Chgo. YMCA; pres. Morgan Park Acad., Bowen High Sch. Council.; Vice pres. Washington and Jame Smith Home; Bd. dirs. South Chgo. Community Hosp. Served with AUS, 1952-54. Recipient Distinguished Service award Harborland Jaycees; named Man of Year South Chgo. C. of C. Mem. South Chgo. C. of C. (pres.), Harborland Jaycees (pres.), South Side Bankers Assn. (pres.), Ill. Bankers Assn. (State pres.; Chgo. dist. pres.), Acad. Humanitarians. Office: 2959 E 92d St Chicago IL 60617

FITCH, JAMES MARSTON, architectural preservationist, architectural historian, critic; b. Washington, May 8, 1909; s. James Marston and Ellen (Payne) F.; m. Cleo Rickman. Student, U. Ala., 1925-26, Tulane U., 1927-28, Columbia U., 1946-48; L.H.D. (hon.), Columbia U., 1980, D.A., Kans. State U., 1979. Housing analyst Fed. Housing Adminstrn., Washington, 1934-35; assoc. editor Archtl. Record, N.Y.C., 1936-42; tech. editor Archtl. Forum, N.Y.C., 1945-49; archtl. editor House Beautiful, N.Y.C., 1949-53; asst. prof. architecture Columbia U., N.Y.C., 1954-60, assoc. prof., 1960-64, prof., 1964-77, prof. emeritus, 1977—; mem. Landmarks Preservation Commn., N.Y.C., 1977-79; dir. hist. preservation Beyer Blinder Belle, Architects & Planners, N.Y.C., 1979—; preservator Central Park, N.Y.C., 1974-76; pres. Ctr. for Bldg. Conservation, N.Y.C., 1980—; vis. prof. U. Ill., Chgo., Ill., 1968, U. Sao Paulo, Brazil, 1978; Centennial vis. prof. Tex. A & M U., 1976; disting. vis. prof. U. Cin., 1979; adj. prof. Grad. Sch. Arts U. Pa., 1979-83. Author: Walter Gropius, 1960, Esthetics of Plenty, 1960, American Building, 2 vols., 2d edit., 1962, Historic Preservation, 1982. Bd. dirs. Mcpl. Arts Soc., N.Y.C., 1970-72. Served in USAAF, 1942-45. Fulbright scholar, Peru, 1975; recipient Outstanding Achievement award Nat. Trust Hist. Preservation, 1974, Conservation Service award U.S. Dept. Interior, 1976, Preservation award Victorian Soc. Am., 1977; Brunner scholar, 1974; fellow Guggenheim Found., 1977-78, Nat. Endowment Arts, 1980; Wm. Kinney Fellows fellow, Greece and Turkey, 1959; recipient cert. of Merit Mcpl. Art Soc. N.Y., 1977, George McAreny medal Am. Hist. Preservation Soc., 1982, Merit award N.Y. Soc. Architects, 1983. Mem. AIA (hon., medal 1976, N.Y. chpt. award of Merit 1979), N.Y. Soc. Architects (award of Merit 1981), Soc. Archtl. Historians (dir. 1973-74), Assn. Preservation Tech. (founding). Clubs: Century (N.Y.C.); Athenaeum (Phila.). Home: 115 Charles St New York NY 10014 Office: Beyer Blinder Belle Architects & Planners 80 Fifth Ave New York NY 10011

FITCH, JOHN CECIL, construction company executive; b. Hingham, Mass., May 21, 1921; s. Aubrey Wray and Gwyneth (Conger) F.; m. Barbara Stackhouse, Sept. 30, 1950; children: David D., William S. Student, Trinity Coll., Hartford, Conn., 1941-42. Trainee Stone & Webster, Inc., N.Y.C., 1946-48; from salesman to pres., dir. Rackle Co., Houston, 1949-64; v.p., dir. Houston Contracting Co., Houston, 1965-73, exec. v.p., dir., 1974-83; dir. Tideland Signal Corp., Mobile Gas Service Corp.; pres., dir. CEPO Ltd. Bd. dirs. Hester House, Houston, 1960-65, Planned Parenthood, 1981—; Republican precinct and area chmn., 1955-62. Served as officer USNR, 1942-46; PTO. Decorated Bronze Star, Letter of Commendation. Mem. Internat. Pipeline Contractors Assn. (dir. 1976-77). Episcopalian. Clubs: Bayou (Houston); Tejas, Breakfast Assn., Christmas Cove Assn. Office: 2807 Buffalo Speedway Houston TX 77098

FITCH, LYLE CRAIG, economist; b. Merriman, Nebr., May 22, 1913; s. Fred B. and Frances (Logsdon) F.; m. Violet Vaughn, Sept. 4, 1937; 1 dau., Linda Fitch Andrews. B.S., Chadron (Nebr.) State Coll., 1935; M.A., U. Nebr., 1938; Ph.D., Columbia U., 1946. Econ. depts. Bklyn. Coll., Columbia U., Wesleyan U., 1939-50; assoc. prof. econs. Columbia U., 1953-54; sr. mgmt. econs. Office of Mayor, City N.Y., 1954-56, 1st dep. city adminstr., 1957-60, city adminstr., 1960-61; economist U.S. Treasury Dept., 1942; spl. asst. to Gov. Conn., 1949-50; dir. fiscal research Inst. Pub. Adminstrn., 1956-57, pres., 1961—, chmn. bd. trustees, 1982; cons. govts. in, Africa, S.Am., fed., state and local govts. Author and editor: (with Horace Taylor) Planning for Jobs, 1946; author: Taxing Municipal Bond Income, 1950, (with Robert Haig, Carl Shoup) The Financial Problem of the City of New York, 1952, (with Carl Shoup, others) The Fiscal Systems of Venezuela, 1958, Urban Transportation and Public Policy, 1964, (with Annmarie Hauk Walsh) Agenda for a City, 1970, Financing Transit, 1980; other books, numerous articles and reviews. Mem. Am. Econs. Assn., Nat. Tax Assn., Am. Soc. Pub. Adminstrn., Am. Polit. Sci. Assn., Internat. Pub. Fin. Assn., Nat. Acad. Pub. Adminstrn. Clubs: Century, Cosmos. Home: 121 Red Hill Rd Princeton NJ 08540 Office: 55 W 44th St New York NY 10036

FITCH, MORGAN LEWIS, JR., patent lawyer; b. Chgo., Nov. 21, 1922; s. Morgan Lewis and Marian (Ringer) F.; m. Helen Shearer, June 9, 1945; children: Ruth F. White, Mary F. White, Morgan Lewis, Frederick Shearer. B.S. in Chem. Enging., Ill. Inst. Tech., 1943; student, Princeton U., 1943, MIT, 1943-44; J.D., U. Mich., 1948. Bar: Ill. 1948. Since practiced in Chgo.; partner Fitch, Even, Tabin, & Flannery, 1953—; dir. South Chgo. Savs. Bank. Chmn. nat. splty. exploring com. Boy Scouts Am.; pres. Robert Crown Navy Meml. Found., John Crerar Library Assos.; trustee emeritus Tri-State Coll., Angola, Ind.; bd. mgrs. YMCA, Chgo. Served to lt. (s.g.) USNR, 1943-46. Recipient Disting. Pub. Service award Sec. Navy, 1960, 65. Mem. Am., Ill., Chgo. bar assns., Chgo. Patent Law Assn., Navy League U.S. (pres. 1965- 67), U.S. Naval Sea Cadet Corps (pres. 1963-65), Naval Commandery, Naval Res. Assn., Soc. Mayflower Descs. Clubs: Union League, Legal, Executives (Chgo.). Home: 4640 Clausen St Western Springs IL 60558 Office: 135 S LaSalle St Chicago IL 60603

FITCH, STEVEN RALPH, fine arts educator, artist; b. Tucson, Aug. 16, 1949; s. Ralph Lynn and Virginia (Lien) F.; m. Anna Lynn Griemes, June 14, 1980. B.A., U. Calif.-Berkeley, 1971; M.A., U. N.Mex., 1978; postgrad., San Francisco Art Inst., 1977; student, U. Calif.-Davis, 1967-68. Instr. A.S.U.C. Studio, U. Calif.-Berkeley, 1971-77; grad. teaching asst. U. N.Mex., Albuquerque, 1978-79; instr., lectr. U. Calif. extension-San Francisco, 1978, U. Colo., Boulder, 1979—. Exhibited one-man shows, Darkroom Workshop Gallery, Berkeley, 1975, Univ. Art Mus., Berkeley, Shado Gallery, Oregon, Oreg., Sacramento State U., Orange Coast Coll., Sosta Mesa, Calif., 1976, Coll. of Marin, Kentfield, Calif., Santa Fe Gallery of Photography, N. Mex., 1977, Foto Gallery, N.Y.C., 1979;; exhibited group shows, San Francisco Art Inst., 1973, Light and Substance, U. N.Mex., Albuquerque, 1974, Young Am. Photographers, kalamazoo Inst. Arts, 1975, Radical Photography and Bay Area Innovators, Sacred Heart Sch., Menlo Park, Calif., 1977, 12 Calif. Photographers, toured Australia and N.Z., 1977, The Aesthetics of Graffiti, San Francisco Mus. Modern Art, 1978, Color Photgraphs: 5 Photographers, Friends of Photography, Carmel, Calif., 1978, Attitudes: Photography in the 70's, Santa Barbara Mus. of Art, Calif., 1979, 8 x 10, Susan spiritus Gallery, Newport Beach, Calif., 1979, Beyond Color, San Francisco Mus. Modern Art, 1980; represented permanent collections, Mus. Modern Art, N.Y.C., Mus. Modern Art, N.Y.C., Fogg Art Mus., Harvard U., Cambridge, Mass., R.I. Sch. Design, Providence, Mpls. Inst. Arts, Houston Mus. Fine Arts, U. N.Mex., Albuquerque, Center for Créative Photography, U. Ariz., Tucson, Oakland Art Mus., Calif., Grunwald Center for Graphic Arts, UCLA; author: Diesels and Dinosaurs, 1976. Fellow NEA, 1973, 75, grantee, 1981. Mem. Soc. for Photog. Edn. Democrat. Home: 801 LaFarge Louisville CO 80027 Office: Fine Arts Dept U Colo Boulder CO 80309

FITCH, VAL LOGSDON, physics educator; b. Merriman, Nebr., Mar. 10, 1923; s. Fred B. and Frances Marion (Logsdon) F.; m. Elise Cunningham, June 11, 1949 (dec. 1972); children: John Craig, Alan Peter; m. Daisy Harper Sharp, Aug. 14, 1976. B.Eng., McGill U., 1948; Ph.D., Columbia U., 1954. Instr. Columbia, 1953; instr. physics Princeton, 1954-56, asst. prof., 1956-59, 1959-60, prof., 1960—, Class 1909 prof. physics, 1968-76, Cyrus Fogg Bracket prof. physics, 1976—; Mem. Pres.'s Sci. Adv. Com., 1970-73. Trustee Asso. Univ., Inc., 1961-67. Served with AUS, 1943-46. Recipient Research Corp. award, 1967; E.O. Lawrence award, 1968; Wetherill medal Franklin Inst., 1976; Nobel prize in physics, 1980; Sloan fellow, 1960. Fellow Am. Phys. Soc., Am. Acad. Arts and Sci., A.A.A.S.; mem. Nat. Acad. Sci. Office: Dept Physics Princeton U Princeton NJ 08544 *

FITCH, WILLIAM C., professional basketball coach; b. Cedar Rapids, Iowa, May 19, 1934. Student, Coe Coll. Basketball coach Coe Coll., Cedar Rapids, 1958-62, U. N.D., Grand Forks, 1963-67, Bowling Green State U., 1967-68, U. Minn., Mpls., 1968-70; coach Cleve. Cavaliers, NBA, 1970-79, Boston Celtics, NBA, 1979-83, Houston Rockets, NBA, 1983—. Named NBA Coach of Yr., 1976, 80; coach NBA championship team,, 1981. Office: Houston Rockets The Summit Ten Greenway Plaza E Houston TX 77046 *

FITCH, WILLIAM CHESTER, consulting mechanical engineer, former educator; b. Billings, Mont., Nov. 12, 1916; s. Harry Davis and Grace E. (McCormick) F.; m. Manzella Lucille Groth, Feb. 23, 1946; 1 son, David Paul. B.S. in Indsl. Engring, Mont. State Coll., 1938; M.S. in Engring. Valuation, Iowa State U., 1939, Ph.D., 1950. Registered profl. engr., Iowa, Pa. Tchr. engring. Iowa State U., 1939-45; asst. prof. indsl. engring. Mont. State Coll., 1945-46; lectr. mech. engring. U. Calif. at Berkeley, 1946-47; assoc. prof. Iowa State U., 1947-52; asst. dir. valuation div. Gannett Fleming Corddry & Carpenter (cons. engrs.), Harrisburg, Pa., 1952-58, 59-64; prof., head mech. engring. dept. Utah State U., 1958-59, Mich. Tech. U., 1964-68; prof., chmn. engring. and tech. dept. Western Mich. U., 1968-72, assoc. dean Coll. Applied Scis., 1972-73, dean Coll. Engring. and Applied Scis., 1973-82; dir. Center for Depreciation Studies; pres. Depreciation Programs, Inc., Fitch, Cowles & Wolf, Inc.; cons. engr., 1952—. Mem. ASME, Am. Soc. Engring. Edn., Nat. Soc. Profl. Engrs., Am. Inst. Indsl. Engrs., Tau Beta Pi, Phi Kappa Phi, Pi Mu Epsilon, Pi Tau Sigma, Lambda Chi Alpha. Presbyn. (elder). Club: Rotarian (bd. dirs. Houghton, Mich. 1966-68). Home: 2408 Waite Ave Kalamazoo MI 49008

FITCH, WILLIAM HAROLD, marine corps officer; b. Chattanooga, Nov. 6, 1929; s. William Elmer and Leila Nina F.; m. Margaret Marie Williams, Aug. 7, 1955. B.S. in Agr. U. Fla., 1950; M.S. in Internat. Affairs, George Washington U., 1971; grad., Naval Test Pilot Sch., 1958, Nat. War Coll., 1971. Naval aviation cadet U.S. Navy, 1950, designated naval aviator, 1952; commd. 2d lt. USMC, 1952, advanced through grades to lt. gen., 1982, designated test pilot, 1958; combat missions in, Vietnam; dep. chief staff research and devel. Hdqrs. USMC, 1977-80; comdg. gen. 1st Marine Aircraft Wing, 1980-82; dep. chief of staff aviation Hdqrs. Marine Corps, 1982—. Decorated Silver Star, D.F.C., Naval Commendation medal (2), Legion of Merit, Air medal (29). Mem. Marine Corps Assn., Marine Corps Aviation Assn. Episcopalian. Patentee multiple carriage bomb rack. Home: 8th& I St SE Washington DC 20390 Office: Dep Chief Staff Avn HQ USMC Washington DC 20380

FITCHEN, ALLEN NELSON, publisher; b. Syracuse, Aug. 8, 1936; s. John Frederick and Mary (Nelson) F. III; m. Jane Cady, June 13, 1959; children—Anne Wheeler, Christopher Hardy, William Mills. B.A. in English cum laude, Amherst Coll., 1958, M.A., Cornell, 1960. Coll. traveler Macmillan Co., N.Y.C., 1960-62, editor, 1962-67; humanities editor U. Chgo. Press, 1968-82, sr. editor, 1971-82; dir. U. Wis. Press, 1982—. Mem. Psi Upsilon. Club: University (Madison). Home: 603 Eugenia Ave Madison WI 53705 Office: 114 N Murray St Madison WI 53715

FITCHEN, DOUGLAS BEACH, physicist, educator; b. N.Y.C., June 8, 1936; s. Paul R. and Eleanor B. F.; m. Janet Mathews; children: John, Katherine, Sylvia. A.B., Harvard U., 1957; Ph.D., U. Ill., 1962. Asst. prof. physics Cornell U., Ithaca, N.Y., 1962-65, assoc. prof., 1965-71, prof., 1971—, chmn. dept. physics, 1977-82; vis. prof. Oxford U., 1968, U. Paris, Orsay, 1975. Alfred P. Sloan fellow, 1964-68. Research in optical studies of solids, Raman spectroscopy. Office: 524 Clark Hall Cornell U Ithaca NY 14853

FITCHEN, FRANKLIN CHARLES, electrical engineering educator; b. New Rochelle, N.Y., June 15, 1928; s. Fred William and Frances (Hess) F.; m. Barbara Eloise Stinnett, Aug. 5, 1950; children: Roy, Sally, Jeanne. B.E.E., U. R.I., 1950; M.E.E., Northeastern U., 1957; D.Eng., Yale U., 1964. Design engr. Gen. Electric Co., Lynn, Mass., 1950-54; asso. prof. U. R.I., 1956-65; head elec. engring. dept. S.D. State U., 1965-72; dean engring. U. Bridgeport, 1972-80, prof. engring., 1981—. Author: Transistor Circuit Analysis and Design, 2d edit, 1966, Electronic Integrated Circuits and Systems, 1970, Low-Noise Electronic Design, 1973, World Directory of Engineering Schools, 1977, 2d edit., 1980. Dir. Brookings Municipal Utility Bd., 1971-72. Served with USA, 1954-56. Mem. IEEE, Am. Soc. Engring. Edn. Home: 4 Austin Dr Ext Easton CT 06612 Office: Coll Engring U Bridgeport Bridgeport CT 06601

FITE, ELWIN, coll. adminstr.; b. Willow Springs, Mo., Nov. 25, 1913; s. Austin Roe and Minnie (Hiest) F.; m. Mildred Mae McKee, Dec. 23, 1936; children—Barbara (Mrs. William Scearce), James Elwin. B.S. in Edn, S.W. Mo. State Coll., 1934; M.M., Northwestern U., 1941; Ed.D., George Peabody Coll. Tchrs., 1953. Asst. prof. edn. Austin Peay State Coll., Clarksville, Tenn., 1948, S.W. Mo. Coll., Springfield, 1948-50; supr. student teaching George Peabody Coll. Tchrs., Nashville, Tenn., 1950-52; chmn. music dept. Amarillo (Tex.) Coll., 1952-53; chmn. div. edn. and psychology Northeastern State Coll., Tahlequah, Okla., 1960-62, dean of coll., from 1962, acting pres., 1977-78, v.p., 1978-79. Author: (with V. Travis) Student Teaching Handbook, 1959. Served with USNR, 1944-46. Mem. C. of C. Tahlequah (past bd. dirs.). Baptist. Club: Kiwanian. Home: Route 3 Box 311 Tahlequah OK 74464 *An unselfish and considerate approach to working with others is the beginning of a solution to most local, state, national, and world problems.*

FITE, GEORGE LIDDLE, editor; b. Austin, Tex., Feb. 20, 1904; s. Warner and Esther (Sturges) F.; m. Carolyn Keiper Wrinkle, Nov. 17, 1962. A.B., Haverford Coll., 1924; M.D., Harvard U., 1928. Intern Fifth Av. Hosp., N.Y.C., 1928-29; asst. and instr. pathology Johns Hopkins Med. Sch., 1929-32, Rockefeller Inst., N.Y.C., 1932-34; resident Balt. City Hosps., 1935; instr. pathology Northwestern U.

Med. Sch., Chgo., 1936; research in leprosy, Tb. NIH, USPHS, 1937-58; chief lab. Carville Leprosy Hosp., 1958-64; ret., 1964. Sr. editor: Jour. AMA, 1965-74. Mem. Am. Assn. Pathologists, Pacific Dermatology Assn., Internat. Leprosy Assn. Address: 5511 Glenwood Rd Bethesda MD 20034

FITE, GILBERT COURTLAND, history educator, author; b. Santa Fe, Ohio, May 14, 1918; s. Clyde and Mary (McCardle) F.; m. Alberta June Goodwin, July 24, 1941; children: James Franklin, Jack Preston. Student, Wessington Springs (S.D.) Coll., 1935-37; B.A., M.A., U. S.D., 1941, Litt.D., 1975; Ph.D., U. Mo., 1945, D.H.L. (hon.), 1983; Litt.D., Seattle Pacific Coll., 1962. Dir. pub. relations Wessington Springs Coll., 1941-42; instr. history U. Mo., 1943-45; prof. history U. Okla., 1945-71, research prof., 1958-71, chmn. dept., 1955-58; pres. Eastern Ill. U., Charleston, 1971-76; Richard B. Russell prof. history U. Ga., 1976—; prof. Am. history Jadavpur U., Calcutta, India, 1962-63; dir. Am. Studies Research Centre, Hyderabad, India, 1969-70; summer vis. prof. U. Mo., 1950, 51, Vanderbilt U., 1955, U. Ill., 1959, U. Wis., 1965; cons. Nat. Park Service, 1950. Author: Peter Norbeck Prairie Statesman, 1948, Mount Rushmore, 1952, Readings in American History, (with others), 1952, George N. Peek and the Fight for Farm Parity, 1954, (with Ladd Haystead) The Agricultural Regions of the United States, 1955, (with H.C. Peterson) Opponents of War, 1917-18, 1957, (with Jim E. Reese) An Economic History of the United States, 3d edit, 1973, Farm to Factory: A History of the Consumers Cooperative Association, 1965, The Farmer's Frontier, 1865-1900, 1966, (with others) A History of the United States, 2 vols, 1970, (with J. Carrol Moody) The Credit Union Movement, 1971, Recent United States History, 1972, Beyond the Fence Rows: A History of Farmland Industries, Inc. 1929-1978, 1978, American Farmers: The New Minority, 1981, also articles. Trustee Phillips U., 1969-76, Lexington Theol. Sem., 1973-76. Ford fellow, 1954-55; Guggenheim fellow, 1964. Mem. Agrl. History Soc. (pres. 1960-61), Am. Assn. State and Local History (council), Orgn. Am. Historians (exec. com. 1958-61), Am. Hist. Assn., So. Hist. Assn. (exec. council 1967-70, pres. 1974), Econ. History Assn., Phi Beta Kappa (hon.), Phi Alpha Theta (internat. v.p. 1980-81, pres. 1981-83). Methodist. Address: History Dept U Ga Athens GA 30602

FITES, DONALD VESTER, tractor company executive; b. Goshen, Ind., Jan. 20, 1934; s. Rex E. and Mary Irene (Sackville) F.; m. Sylvia Dempsey, June 25, 1960; children: Linda Marie. B.S. in Civil Engring., Valparaiso U., 1956; M.S., M.I.T, 1971. With Caterpillar Overseas S.A., Peoria, Ill., 1956-66, dir. internat. customer div., Geneva, 1966-67; asst. mgr. market devel. Caterpillar Tractor Co., Peoria, 1967-70, dir. engine capacity expansion program, 1975-76, mgr. products control dept., 1976-79, v.p. products, 1981—; dir. Caterpillar Mitsubishi Ltd., Toyko, 1971-75; pres. Caterpillar Brasil S.A., 1979-81. Bd. dirs., treas. Peoria County Bd. for Care and Treatment of Mentally Deficient Persons, 1982—; chmn. fin. com. First United Meth. Ch., 1983—. Republican. Club: Mt. Halwey Country. Home: 7614 N Edgewild Dr Peoria IL 61614 Office: 100 NE Adams St Peoria IL 61629

FITHIAN, FLOYD, congressman; b. Vesta, Nebr., Nov. 3, 1938; s. James Creston and Eva May (Ballard) F.; m. Marjorie Heim, Nov. 1, 1952; children—Cindy, Judy, John. B.A., Peru (Nebr.) State Coll., 1951; M.A. in History, U. Nebr., 1955; Ph.D. in Am. History, U. Nebr., 1964. Former tchr. history and govt. high schs.; asso. prof. Am. history Purdue U., Lafayette, Ind.; mem. 94th-97th Congresses from 2d Ind. Dist.; Active Democratic campaigns, Tippecanoe County, Ind.; head Win-Dems vol. group. Contbr. articles to profl. jours. Served with USN, 1951-54. Mem. Am. Legion, Am. Hist. Assn., Ind. Cattlemen's Assn., Lafayette Farm Bur. Coop., Orgn. Am. Historians, Tippecanoe County Hist. Soc., Ind. State Council Social Studies (past pres.). Methodist. (tchr., lay speaker).

FITT, ALFRED BRADLEY, lawyer; b. Highland Park, Ill., Apr. 12, 1923; s. Frank and Harriett (Bradley) F.; m. Lois D. Rice, Jan. 7, 1978. B.A., Yale U., 1946; J.D., U. Mich., 1948. Bar: D.C., Mich. With firm Lewis and Watkins, Detroit, 1948-54, partner, 1952-54; legal adviser to gov. Mich., 1954-60; asso. counsel subcom. adminstrv. practice U.S. Senate Judiciary Com., 1960-61; chief counsel spl. com. FAA adminstrv. procedures, 1961; dep. under sec. manpower Dept. Army, 1961-63; dep. asst. sec. for civil rights Dept. Def., 1963-64; gen. counsel Dept. Army, 1964-67; asst. sec. for manpower Dept. Def., 1967-69; spl. adviser to the pres. Yale U., 1969-75; gen. counsel Congl. Budget Office U.S. Congress, Washington, 1975—. Served with AUS, 1943-46. Home: 2332 Massachusetts Ave NW Washington DC 20008

FITT, MICHAEL GEORGE, insurance holding company executive; b. Whitstable, Kent, Eng., May 16, 1931; came to U.S., 1976; s. Walter H. and Dorothy A. (Young) F.; m. Doreen Elizabeth Leitch, Oct. 1, 1955; children: Colin, Anne, Ian. Student, Brit. schs. Jr. clk. Can. Underwriters Assn., 1953; with Royal Exchange Assurance Ltd., 1953-69, br. mgr., Montreal, Que., Can.; with Employers Reins. Corp., 1969—, exec. v.p., Overland Park, Kans., 1977-79, vice chmn. bd., 1979-81, chmn. bd., 1981—, also dir., pres., chief exec. officer, 1983—; chmn. bd., dir. Nat. Fidelity Life Ins. Co.; chmn. bd. First Excess and Reins. Corp.; chmn. bd., dir. Centennial Life Ins. Co.; chmn., pres., dir. First Fidelity Equity Corp., all Overland Park; chmn., pres., chief exec. officer First Excess and Reins. Corp. (Bermuda); chmn., dir. First Cons. & Adminstrn. Co., Inc., Kansas City, Mo.; dir. First Nat. Bank Kansas City (Mo.), Charter Corp., Kansas City, Mo., Bates Turner, Overland Park, Kans.; pres. bd. mgmt. Fgn. Reins. Mgmt. Corp., Zurich, Switzerland. Served with Brit. Navy, 1948-53. Fellow Ins. Inst. Can. Episcopalian. Clubs: Kansas City, Brookridge Country, Mission Hills Country. Home: 9100 W 106th St Overland Park KS 66212 Office: 5200 Metcalf Ave Overland Park KS 66201

FITTERON, JOHN JOSEPH, chemical company executive; b. Norwalk, Conn., Sept. 25, 1941; s. Joseph A. and Olivia F.; m. Leola Kellogg, Sept. 9, 1967; children: Derek, Deanne. B.S., U. Conn., 1967. C.P.A., Conn. Mgr. Arthur Andersen & Co., N.Y.C., 1967-75; controller Beker Industries Corp., Greenwich, Conn., 1975-76, v.p., controller, 1976-78, sr. v.p. fin., 1978-79, sr. v.p. fin., treas., 1979—. Served with USAF, 1959-63. Mem. Am. Inst. C.P.A.'s, Conn. Soc. C.P.A.'s (Scholastic award 1967), Fin. Execs. Inst. Home: 146 Cedar Rd Wilton CT 06897 Office: 124 W Putnam Ave Greenwich CT 06830

FITTON, DAVID EDWARDS, III, retail company executive; b. Little Rock, Aug. 15, 1945; s. David Edwards and Ruth (Martin) F.; m. Judith Sharon Elliott, June 6, 1967 (div. 1979); m. Cynthia Gale Corley, May 12, 1979; stepchildren: Missy, Adrian. B.S. in Bus. Adminstrn. and Fin., U. Ark., 1967, postgrad., 1968. Health and manpower planner NWAEDD, Harrison, Ark., 1972-74; exec. v.p. Mass Merchandisers Inc., Harrison, 1974-83; v.p. Sav-A-Stop-Hanes D.S.D., Jacksonville, Fla., 1983—. Served to capt. USAF, 1968-72. Recipient Cost Reduction award U.S. Air Force, 1970; named Supply Officer of Yr U.S. Air Force, 1970. Home: 4377 Springmoor Dr W Jacksonville FL 32225 Office: Savastop Hanes DSD PO Box 19050 Jacksonville FL 32245

FITTS, DONALD DENNIS, chemist, educator; b. Concord, N.H., Sept. 3, 1932; s. Russell P. and Elisabeth (Reille) F.; m. Beverly Hoffman, July 11, 1964; children: Robert K., William R. A.B., Harvard U., 1954; Ph.D., Yale U., 1957. NSF postdoctoral fellow U. Amsterdam, Netherlands, 1957-58; research fellow Yale U., 1958-59; mem. faculty U. Pa., 1959—, asso. prof. chemistry, 1964-69, prof. chemistry, 1969—, asst. chmn. dept., 1965-72, asso. dean grad. studies faculty arts and scis., 1978-82, 83—, acting dean arts and scis., 1982-83; cons. Am. Cyanamid Co., 1959-63. Author: Nonequilibrium Thermodynamics, 1962, Vector Analysis in Chemistry, 1974; also articles. Mem. Am. Phys. Soc., Assn. Harvard Chemists, Royal Soc. Chemistry (London), Yale Chemists Assn. Research on theory of optical activity, statis.-mech. theory of transport processes, nonequilibrium thermodynamics, molecular quantum mechanics, theory of liquids, intermolecular forces, surface phenomena. Home: 634 Revere Rd Merion Station PA 19066 Office: Dept Chemistry U Pa Philadelphia PA 19104

FITTS, E. GRANT, business executive; b. Montevallo, Ala., 1916. LL.B., U. Cin., 1940; LL.M., Harvard U., 1946. Bar: Ala., Tex. Assoc. firm White, Bradley, Arant, All & Rose, 1946-51; partner firm Deramus, Fitts & Johnston, 1952-61; v.p., gen. counsel Am. Life Ins. Co., 1961-62; pres. Greatamerica Corp., 1962-68; chmn., pres. Gulf Life Holding Co., from 1968; with Gulf Life Ins. Co., Jacksonville, Fla., 1962—, chmn. bd., 1968—, pres., from 1970, also dir.; chmn., chief exec. officer, former pres. Gulf United Corp.; chmn. Am.-Amicable Life Ins. Co., Fin. Computer Services, Inc., Gulf Fire & Casualty Co., KYXO, Inc., WGHP-TV, Inc., WKAP, Inc., WTSP-TV, Inc., others; dir. numerous cos. Mem. Am. Bar Assn., State Bar Tex., Am. Judicature Soc. Office: Gulf United Corp Gulf Life Tower Jacksonville FL 32207 *

FITTS, JAMES WALTER, educator; b. Ft. Riley, Kans., July 17, 1913; s. Josiah Burt and Eva Rose (Freeman) F.; m. Mary M. Kocher, June 4, 1935; children—Jerry Burt, Dorothy Louise (Mrs. J. H. Johnson), Donald James. B.S., Nebr. State Tchrs. Coll., 1935; M.S., U. Nebr., 1937; Ph.D., Iowa State U., 1952. Asst. prof. soil sci. U. Nebr., 1937-48; asst. prof. soil sci. Iowa State U., 1948-52; prof. soil sci. N.C. State U., Raleigh, 1952—, head soil dept., 1956-65, dir. internat. soil fertilizer evaluation project, 1964-75; pres. Agro Services Internat., Inc., 1973—. Contbr. articles to profl. jours. Recipient Research award Soil Sci. Soc. N.C., 1966, Service award Chadron State Coll., 1977. Fellow Am. Soc. Agronomy, Soil Sci. Soc. Am. (pres. 1960); mem. Internat. Soil Sci. Soc. (div. vice-chmn. 1960-64), Sigma Xi, Gamma Sigma Delta. Home: 550 N Leavitt Ave Orange City FL 32763

FITWATER, MAX MARLIN, deputy assistant secretary U.S. Treasury Department; b. Salina, Kans., Nov. 24, 1942; s. Max Malcolm Fitzwater and Phyllis Ethel (Seaton) F.; children: Bradley Charles, Courtney Lynn. B.S., Kans. State U., 1965. Writer-editor Appalachian Regulatory Commn., Washington, 1966-68; sec., speechwriter Dept. Transp., Washington, 1970-72; with dept. press relations and pub. affairs EPA, Washington, 1972-74, dir. press office, 1974-81; dep. asst. sec. pub. affairs U.S Dept. Treasury, Washington, 1981—. Served with USAF, 1968-70. Recipient Presdl. Merit award, 1982. Home: 3032 S Abingdon St Arlington VA 22206 Office: US Treasury Dept 15th and Pennsylvania Ave NW Washington DC 20220

FITZ, ANNETTE ELAINE, physician, educator; b. Jasper County, Iowa, Mar. 13, 1933; d. Eugene Elmer and Hazel Matilda (Wehrman) F. Student, Iowa State U., Ames, 1950-52; B.A., U. Iowa, Iowa City, 1954, M.D., 1958. Registered med. practitioner, Iowa. Intern U. Utah Affiliated Hosps., Salt Lake City, 1958-59; resident in internal medicine VA Hosp., Iowa City, 1959-62; clin. investigator VA, 1964-67; research fellow in cardiovascular research labs., dept. medicine U. Iowa, 1962-64, asst. prof. internal medicine, 1968-72, asso. prof., 1972-76, prof., 1976—; staff physician VA Hosp., 1968—; spl. NIH research fellow St. Mary's Hosp., London, 1967-68; cons. cardio-renal adv. com. FDA, 1973-78. Contbr. articles to profl. jours. NIH grantee, 1969—. Mem. AMA, Iowa State Med. Soc., Iowa Soc. Internal Medicine, Am. Fedn. Clin. Research, Central Soc. Clin. Research, Council High Blood Pressure Research (med. adv. bd. 1973—), Interam. Soc. Hypertension, Midwest Salt and Water Club, Am. Heart Assn., Nat. Kidney Found., Am. Soc. Nephrology, Soc. Exptl. Biology and Medicine, Sigma Xi, Alpha Omega Alpha. Club: Altrusa. Home: 716 River St Iowa City IA 52240

FITZ, RAYMOND L., S.M., university president; b. Akron, Ohio, Aug. 12, 1941; s. Raymond L. and Mary Lou (Smith) F. B.S. in Elec. Engring., U. Dayton, Ohio, 1964; M.S., Poly. Inst. Bklyn., 1967, Ph.D., 1969. Joined Soc. of Mary, Roman Catholic Ch., 1960; mem. faculty U. Dayton, 1968—, prof. elec. engring. and engring. mgmt., 1975—, exec. dir. Center Christian Renewal, 1974-79, univ. pres., 1979—. Author numerous papers, reports in field. Bd. dirs. various civic organs. Recipient Disting. Alumnus award Poly. Inst. Bklyn., 1980. Address: Office of Pres U Dayton Dayton OH 45469

FITZGEORGE, HAROLD JAMES, oil and gas co. exec.; b. Trenton, N.J., June 15, 1924; s. George T. and Cecilia M. (Jansen) F.; m. Bette M. Weidel, June 23, 1945; children—Barbara Marsh, Virginia Fisher, Patricia Dunning, Elizabeth Brown. A.B., Princeton U., 1948; M.B.M., M.I.T., 1964. Geologist Magnolia Petroleum Co., Oklahoma City, 1948; numerous positions with petroleum cos., 1948-60; with Mobil U.S. Exploration, N.Y.C., 1960-63; v.p. Mobil Exploration Can., 1964-66; mgr. Mobil Fgn. Exploration, N.Y.C., 1966-68; pres. Mobil de Venezuela, 1968-73; gen. mgr. Western U.S. Exploration & Prodn., Mobil Oil, Denver, 1973-77; cons. in field, 1977-78; pres. Pennzoil Exploration and Prodn., Houston, 1978—, also dir. Served with USMC, 1943-46, 50-52. Sloan fellow, 1963-64. Mem. Am. Assn. Petroleum Geologists, Assn. Profl. Engrs. and Geologists of Alta., Am. Petroleum Inst. Republican. Roman Catholic. Clubs: Princeton (N.Y.); Denver Petroleum, Houston. Office: Pennzoil Place PO Box 2967 Houston TX 77001

FITZGERALD, CHARLES PATRICK, record industry executive; b. Kingston, N.Y., Aug. 13, 1930; s. Frank X. and Ann (Daly) F.; m. Mary Elizabeth Onions, July 1957; children: Elizabeth, Timothy, Pamela, Michael, Daniel, Scott. B.S., Babson Inst., 1956; M.B.A., Western Res. U., 1962. Asst. controller Glidden Co., Cleve., 1965-67; controller Capitol Industries-EMI, Inc., Hollywood, CA, 1967-69, treas., 1969-70, v.p., 1971—, dir., 1973—; dir. EMI Music Worldwide Mgmt. Bd., London. Served to 2d lt. U.S. Army, 1951-53. Republican. Roman Catholic. Home: 4520 Park Livorno Calabasas CA 91302 Office: Capitol Industries-EMI Inc 1750 N Vine St Hollywood CA 90028

FITZGERALD, EDMOND JAMES, artist; b. Seattle, Aug. 19, 1912; s. Maurice F. and Elizabeth (Norton) F.; m. Mary Louise Streets, Sept. 7, 1940 (dec. Feb. 1977); children—Desmond, Ryder O'Bannon; m. Margaret Boyer Trent, Oct. 26, 1978. Student, Eustace P. Ziegler, Mark Tobey. Lectr., tchr. (Recipient grand prize Art USA 1958, Am. Artists Profl. League prize 1955, anonymous watercolor prize 1959, gold medal of honor Hudson Valley Art Assn. 1952, 58, 60, also, Jane Peterson prize for oil painting 1962, Famous Artists' Sch. award 1969, Washington Sch. Art award 1970); Author: Painting and Drawing in Charcoal and Oil, 1959, Marine Painting in Watercolor, 1972; One-man shows include, Seattle Art Mus., 1941, Grand Central Gallery, 1946; murals include Trail to Oreg, Ontario, Oreg., 1937, Pathfinders, Colville, Wash., 1939, Battle of Bear River, Preston, Idaho, 1940, Normandy Invasion, Nat. Maritime Union's Curran Plaza Bldg., Man and the Land, Am. Mus. Nat. History, 1949, Pasteur, Kenilworth, N.J., murals for, Union First Nat. Bank, N.J., 1958, Cranford (N.J.) Jr. Coll., 1959, Jamaica (N.Y.) Savs. Bank, 1964, Chem. Constrn. Co., N.Y.C., 1961, Revlon, Inc., N.Y.C., 1976; represented in permanent collections, White House, George Washington U., Swope Mus., Terre Haute, Ind., New Britain (Conn.) Mus., Seattle Art Mus., Frye Mus., Seattle, Wash. State Coll., U.S. Naval War Coll., IBM, Nat. Cash Register Co. Served as officer USNR, 1942-46; comdr. Res.; ret. Ranger Fund purchase N.A.D., 1963; Club prize, 1961; Frank B. Williams prize, 1958, Salmagundi Club. Academician NAD; fellow Royal Soc. Art; mem. Allied Artists Am. (pres., Jane Peterson prize 1956, Robert S. Brush award 1959), Am. Watercolor Soc. (v.p., dir., hon. pres. 1970—, Herb Olsen prize 1961), Nat. Soc. Mural Painters (first prize 1946). Club: Salmagundi (N.Y.C.). Home: 6585 Lisa Ln Cincinnati OH 45243 Office and Studio: 4620 Spring Grove Ave Cincinnati OH 45214

FITZGERALD, EDMUND BACON, electronics industry executive; b. Milw., Feb.5, 1926; s. Edmund and Elizabeth (Bacon) F.; m. Elisabeth McKee Christensen, Sept. 6, 1947; children: Karen, Kathleen, Edmund Greer, Rogers Christensen. B.S. in Elec. Engring, U. Mich., 1946. With Cutler-Hammer, Inc., Milw., 1946-78, v.p. charge engring., 1959-61, adminstrv. v.p., 1961-63, pres., 1964-69, chmn. and chief exec. officer, 1969-78; also dir.; vice chmn. Eaton Corp., Cleve., 1978-79; mng. dir. Hampshire Assos., Milw., 1979-80; pres., dir. No. Telecom Inc., Nashville, 1980-82; pres. No. Telecom Ltd., Mississauga, Ont., Can., 1982—; chmn., dir. Milw. Brewers Baseball Club, Inc.; dir. No. Telecom, Ltd., Toronto, Cleve.-Cliffs Iron Co., Koppers Co., Pitts.; trustee Northwestern Mut. Life Ins. Co. Trustee, vice chmn. Com. for Econ. Devel. Served to capt. USMCR, 1943-46, 51-52. Named Man of Year Milw. Jr. C. of C., 1956. Mem. Nat. Elec. Mfrs. Assn. (pres. 1968). Office: No Telecom Ltd Nashville House One Vantage Way Nashville TN 37228

FITZGERALD, EDWARD EARL, publisher, author; b. N.Y.C., Sept. 10, 1919; s. Francis J. and Mary Leona (Morgan) F.; m. Libuse P. Ostruk, June 6, 1942; children—Eileen Frances, Kevin Paul. Reporter Westchester County Pubs., Inc., 1937-42; editor Macfadden Pubs., Inc., 1946-60; editor-in-chief Sport mag., 1951-60, editorial dir. men's group, 1952-60, asst. to pres., 1958-60; editor-in-chief Lit. Guild of Am., 1960-64; v.p. Doubleday & Co., Inc., gen. mgr. book club div., 1964-67, sr. v.p. in charge book club div., pub. div., book shop div., 1967-68; pres., chief exec. officer McCall Publishing Co., 1968-71; v.p. Book-of-the-Month Club, 1971-73, pres., 1973—, chief operating officer, 1973-78, chief exec. officer, 1979—, chmn., 1981—. Author: (with Lou Boudreau) Player-Manager, 1949, (with Althea Gibson), I Always Wanted to be Somebody, 1958, (with Genevieve Caulfield) The Kingdom Within, 1960, (with Yogi Berra) Yogi, 1961, (with Mel Allen) You Can't Beat the Hours, 1964, (with John Unitas) Pro Quarterback. Served with infantry AUS, 1942-46. Home: 26 Claudet Way Eastchester NY 10709 Office: 485 Lexington Ave New York NY 10017

FITZGERALD, EDWIN ROGER, educator, physicist; b. Oshkosh, Wis., July 14, 1923; s. James C. and Edwina (Brown) F.; m. Carolyn H. Johnson, Aug. 30, 1946; children: Lucia Edwina, Margaret Mary, William Maurice, Alice Ann, Roger Edwin, Douglas Brendan, Thomas Michael, Jane Carolyn. B.S., U. Wis., 1944, M.S. in Physics, 1950, Ph.D., 1951. Registered profl. engr., Md. Physicist Phys. Research Lab., B.F. Goodrich Co., 1944-46; Project asso. chemistry U. Wis., 1951-52; mem. faculty Pa. State U., 1953-61, prof. physics, 1959-61; prof. dept. mechanics Johns Hopkins U., 1961—. Author: Particle Waves and Deformation in Crystalline Solids, 1966; Contbr. numerous tech. articles to profl. jours., sects. in books. Fellow Am. Phys. Soc. (exec. com., chmn. high polymer Physics 1958-59); mem. Acoustical Soc. Am., Materials Research Soc., Phi Beta Kappa, Sigma Xi, Eta Kappa Nu, Tau Beta Pi. Spl. research on mech. and dielectric properties solids. Home: 2445 Tracey's Store Rd Parkton MD 21120

FITZGERALD, ELLA, singer; b. Newport News, Va., Apr. 25, 1918; m. Ray Brown (div. 1953); 1 son, Ray. Began singing with, Chick Webb Orch., 1934-39; tours throughout, U.S., Japan, Europe; with: Jazz at the Philharmonic troupe, 1948-57; rec. artist for, Decca, 1936-55, Verve, from 1956; now, Pablo Records; appeared in: motion picture Pete Kelly's Blues, 1955; nightclub appearances include, Sahara Hotel, Caesar's Palace, both Las Vegas, Fairmont Hotel, San Francisco, Ronnie Scott's Club, London; appeared on TV in spls. with Frank Sinatra; also on: All Star Swing Festival, 1972, concert with, Boston Pops, 1972; later with more than 40 Symphony orchs., throughout U.S.; Records include At Duke's Place, 1966, Best, 1967, Clap Hands, 1961, Cote d' Azur, (with Ellington), 1967, Ella, Ella Fitzgerald; In Hamburg, 1965, Mack the Knife, Ella in Berlin, 1960, Sunshine of Your Love, Things Ain't What They Used to Be, Tribute to Porter, 1965, Whisper Not, 1966, Watch What Happens, 1972, Take Love Easy, 1975, Ella in London, 1975, Montreux Ella, numerous others. Recipient 8 Grammy awards, numerous popularity awards from Down Beat mag., Metronome mag., Musicians Poll, JAY Award Poll; named number 1 female singer 16th Internat. Jazz Critics Poll, 1968, Am. Music award, 1978; recipient Kennedy Center honor, 1979, Grammy award as best female jazz vocalist, 1981, 84. Address: care Norman Granz 451 N Canon Dr Beverly Hills CA 90210 *

FITZGERALD, EUGENE FRANCIS, orchard exec.; b. Jersey City, Mar. 15, 1925; s. Arthur Gregory and Anna (O'Rourke) F.; m. Ellen M. O'Connor, Sept. 1, 1951; children—Timothy, Mary Ellen, Eugene Francis, Maura, John, Ann, Katherine. B.S. in Bus. Adminstrn, Georgetown U., 1949. Spl. agt. FBI, 1951-52; mgr. Prudential Ins. Co. Am., Newark, 1953-65; agy. v.p. K.C., New Haven, 1965-67; v.p. Minn. Mut. Life Ins. Co., St. Paul, 1967-70; pres., dir. North Star Equities Co., St. Paul, 1969-70; exec. v.p. Southland Life Ins. Co., Dallas, 1970-72; also dir.; exec. v.p. Equitable Life Ins. Co., Washington, 1972-73; also trustee; v.p. Liberty Life Ins. Co., Greenville, S.C., 1974-81; pres. Mountain View Orchard, Inc., 1981—; dir. Nathan Hale Life Ins. Co. Served with USMCR, 1943-45. Decorated Bronze Star. Mem. Nat. Assn. Life Underwriters, Sales and Mktg. Execs. Internat., Newcomen Soc. Roman Catholic. Club: Green Valley Country. Home: 305 Aberdare Ln Greenville SC 29607 Office: Route 2 Campobello SC 29322

FITZ-GERALD, F. GREGORY, financial services company executive; b. Wichita, Kans., June 8, 1941; s. John F. and Lexie (Beverlin) Fitz-G.; children: J. Keith, Kerry L., Lori G. B.S. in Econs., U. Pa., 1963. With Merrill Lynch & Co., Inc., N.Y.C., 1969—, exec. v.p., chief fin. officer, 1978; mem. Wharton adv. council fin. dept. U. Pa., Phila., 1980—. Episcopalian. Office: Merrill Lynch & Co Inc 165 Broadway Ave New York NY 10080

FITZGERALD, FRANCES, author; b. 1940; d. Desmond and Marietta Peabody FitzGerald Tree. Grad. magna cum laude, Radcliffe Coll., 1962; studied Chinese and Vietnamese history, religion and culture informally with, Paul Mus. Writer: series of profiles Herald Tribune mag; freelance writer, Vietnam, 1966; Author: Fire in the Lake: The Vietnamese and the Americans in Vietnam, 1972, America Revised, 1979; contbr. articles to mags. Recipient Overseas Press Club award for interpretative reporting, 1967; Nat. Inst. Arts and Letters award, 1973; Pulitzer prize, 1973; Nat. Book award, 1973; Sydney Hillman award, 1973; George Polk award, 1973; Bancroft award for history, 1973. Address: care Random House Inc 201 E 50th St New York NY 10022 *

FITZGERALD, FRANCIS JOHN, chemical company executive; b. Springfield, Ill, Oct. 25, 1927; s. Francis John and Mayme (MacGrangh) F.; m. Patricia Ann Sullivan, June 10, 1950; children: Micky, John, Terry, Tim, Moira, Kerry, Megan. B.S., U. Notre Dame, 1950. Sales rep. Gerity Mich. Corp., Adrian, 1950-51; with Monsanto Co., 1951—; group v.p., mng. dir. Monsanto Europe-Africa, Brussels, 1978—; exec v.p., mng. dir. internat. Monsanto, St. Louis. Bd. dirs. Jr. Achievement, 1975-79; active Boy Scouts Am. Mem. Soap and Detergent Assn. (bd. dirs. 1972-75). Roman Catholic. Club: Bellerive Country. Office: Monsanto Co 800 N Lindbergh Blvd St. Louis MO 63166

FITZGERALD, JAMES F., professional sports team executive. Chmn. bd., pres. Milw. Bucks Basketball Team. Office: Milw Bucks 901 N Fourth St Milwaukee WI 53203§

FITZGERALD, JAMES FRANCIS, cable TV executive; b. Janesville, Wis., Mar. 27, 1926; s. Michael Henry and Chloris Helen (Beiter) F.; m. Marilyn Field Cullen, Aug. 1, 1950; children: Michael Dennis, Brian Nicholas, Marcia O'Loughlin, James Francis, Carolyn Jane, Ellen Putnam. B.S., Notre Dame U., 1947. With Standard Oil Co. (Ind.), Milw., 1947-48; pres. F.-W. Oil Co., Janesville, 1950-73; v.p. Creston Park Corp., 1957—; pres. Sunnyside, Inc., 1958—, Total TV, Inc. (cable TV Systems), Wis., 1965—, Janesville Indsl. Devel. Corp., 1966—; dir. First Nat. Bank, Koss Corp.; chmn. bd., pres. Milw. Profl. Sports and Services (Milw. Bucks). Bd. govs., chmn. TV com. NBA. Served to lt. (j.g.) USNR, 1944-45, 51-52. Recipient Janesville Man of Year award Jr. C. of C., 1956. Mem. Janesville C. of C. (dir. 1955-58), Chief Execs. Forum, World Bus. Council, Wis. Petroleum Assn. (pres. 1961-62). Roman Catholic. Clubs: Janesville Country, Milw. Athletic.; Vintage (Indian Wells, Calif.). Home: PO Box 348 Janesville WI 53547 Office: 839 Harding St Janesville WI 53545

FITZGERALD, JAMES MARTIN, judge; b. Portland, Oreg., Oct. 7, 1920; s. Thomas and Florence (Linderman) F.; m. Karin Rose Benton, Jan. 19, 1950; children: Dennis James, Denise Lyn, Debra Jo, Kevin Thomas. B.A., Willamette U., 1950, LL.B., 1951; postgrad., U. Wash., 1952. Bar: Alaska bar 1953. Asst. U.S. atty., Ketchikan and Anchorage, Alaska, 1952-56; city atty. City of Anchorage, 1956-59; legal counsel to Gov. Alaska, Anchorage, 1959; commr. pub. safety State of Alaska, 1959; judge Alaska Superior Ct., 3d Jud. Dist., 1959-69, presiding judge, 1969-72; assoc. justice Alaska Supreme Ct., Anchorage, 1972-75; judge U.S. Dist. Ct. for Alaska, Anchorage, 1975—. Mem. advisory bd. Salvation Army, Anchorage, 1962—, chmn., 1965-66; mem. Anchorage Parks and Recreation Bd., 1965-77, chmn., 1966. Served with AUS, 1940-41; Served with USMCR, 1942-46. Office: US Courthouse 701 C St Anchorage AK 99513 *

FITZGERALD, JANET ANNE, college president; b. Woodside, N.Y., Sept. 4, 1935; d. Robert W. and Lillian H. (Shannon) F. B.A. magna cum laude, St. John's U., 1965, M.A., 1967, Ph.D., 1971. Joined Sisters of St. Dominic of Amityville, Roman Catholic Ch., 1953; tchr. St. Ignatius Sch., 1955-56, St. Thomas Apostle Sch., Woodhaven, N.Y., 1956-65, Bishop McDonnell High Sch., Bklyn., 1965-69; NSF postdoctoral fellow Cath. U. Am., summer 1971; prof. philosophy Molloy Coll., Rockville Centre, N.Y., 1969—, pres., 1972—; Chmn. L.I. Regional Adv. Council on Higher Edn.; trustee Commn. on Ind. Colls. and Univs.; mem. instl. rev. bd. St. John's U.; trustee Diocese of Rickville Centre. Author: Alfred North Whitehead's Early Philosophy of Space and Time, 1979. Mem. Am. Council on Edn., Am. Cath. Philos. Assn., Philos. Assn., Philosophy of Sci. Assn., Nat. Cath. Edn. Assn. Office: Molloy College Rockville Centre NY 11570

FITZGERALD, JOHN WARNER, legal educator; b. Grand Ledge, Mich., Nov. 14, 1924; s. Frank Dwight and Queena Maud (Warner) F.; m. Lorabeth Moore, June 6, 1953; children: Frank Moore, Eric Stiles, Adam Warner. B.S., Mich. State U., 1947; J.D., U. Mich., 1954. Bar: Mich. 1954. Practiced in, Grand Ledge, 1955-64; chief judge pro tem Mich. Ct. Appeals, 1965-73; justice Mich. Supreme Ct., 1974-83, dep. chief justice, 1975-82, chief justice, 1982; mem. faculty Thomas M. Cooley Law Sch., Lansing, Mich., 1982—; mem. Mich. Senate from 15th Dist., 1958-64. Served with AUS, 1943-44. Mem. ABA, State Bar Mich., Am. Judicature Soc. Office: Thomas M. Cooley Law Sch PO Box 13038 Lansing MI 48901

FITZGERALD, JOSEPH FARLEY, city ofcl.; b. Chgo., Feb. 9, 1928; s. Joseph Francis and Cecelia (Farley) F.; m. Jean Freeburn, May 16, 1953; children—Laura, Linda, Thomas. B.S. in Archtl. Engring, U. Ill., 1951. Structural and archtl. designer Swift & Co., Chgo., 1951-54; archtl. plan examiner dept. bldgs. City of Chgo., 1954-56, structural plan examiner, 1956-58, asst. chief inspection, 1958-60, asst. commr. bldgs., 1960-68, dep. commr. bldgs., 1968-69, commr. bldgs., 1969-80; chmn. Mayor's Adv. Com. on Bldg. Code Amendments, 1969—; chmn. codes and safety subcom. Chgo. High Rise Com., 1969-80; chmn. Chgo. Conf. High Rise Fire Safety, 1971; mem. Underwriter Labs. Fire Council. Author Movement of Air Through Smoke Towers in High Rise Buildings, 1972. Chmn. Chgo. High Rise Com., 1980—. Served with U.S. Army, 1946-47. Fellow AIA (chmn. legis. com. Chgo. chpt. 1968-71, mem. codes and standards com. 1973—); mem. Nat. Fire Protection Assn. (com. on systems concepts for fire protection in structures 1971-80), Assn. Major Cities Bldg. Ofcls. (chmn.), ASTM (com. fire tests), Nat. Inst. Bldg. Scis. (rehab. guidelines policy com., consultative council ad hoc planning com. 1977-80), Council Tall Bldgs. and Urban Habitat (vice chmn. com. on fire and blast). Home: 9844 S Oakley St Chicago IL 60643 Office: 33 W Monroe St Chicago IL 60603

FITZGERALD, LAURINE ELIZABETH, university dean; b. New London, Wis., Aug. 24, 1930; d. Thomas F. and Laurine (Branchflower) F. B.S., Northwestern U., 1952, M.A., 1953; Ph.D., Mich. State U., 1959. Instr. English dir. devel. reading lab., head resident-dir. Wis. State Coll., Whitewater, 1953-55; area dir. residence and counseling Ind. U., 1955-57; teaching grad. asst. guidance and counseling, then instr., counselor Mich. State U., East Lansing, 1957-59; asst. prof. psychology and edn., assoc. dean students U. Denver, 1959-62; asst. prof. counseling psychology, staff counselor for Carnegie Found. project U. Minn., 1962-63; asst. dean, asst prof. Mich. State U., 1963-70, assoc. dean students. prof. adminstrn. and higher edn., dir. div. edn. and research, 1970-74; dean Grad. Sch., prof. counselor edn., dir. N.E. Wis. Coop. Regional Grad. Ctr. (U. Wis.-Oshkosh), 1974—; vis. lectr. U. Okla., Norman, 1961; vis. prof. Oreg. State U., 1977; cons. in field. Author numerous articles in field; co-author monograms, texts. Recipient Higher Edn. Rocky Mountain council Girl Scouts U.S.A., 1961, Evelyn Hosmer U. Denver, 1962; Elin Wagner Found. fellow, 1963-64. Mem. Am. Psychol. Assn., Mich. Psychol. Assn., Am. Personnel and Guidance Assn., Am. Coll. Personnel Assn. (sec. 1965-67, exec. bd. 1968-70, chmn. women's task force 1970-71, editor jour. 1976—), Assn. Couselor Edn. and Supervision, Am. Assn. Higher Edn., Nat. Assn. Women Deans, Adminstrs. and Counselors (pres. 1980), AAUP (chpt. treas. 1955-56), NEA, Mich. Assn. Women Deans, Adminstrs. and Counselors (pres. 1967-69, Harriet Meyer 1977), Mich. Coll. Personnel Assn., Wis. Coll. Personnel Assn., Midwest Assn. Grad. Schs. (pres. 1980—), Intercollegiate Assn. Women Students (editorial bd., nat. adviser), AAUW, Women's Equity Action League (past pres. Mich., nat. sec.-treas. legal and edn. def. fund), Bus. and Profl. Women's Club (Lena Lake Forest fellow 1966-67, named Most Disting. Women in Edn., Mich. 1973), Mortar Bd., Beta Beta Beta, Psi Chi, Alpha Lambda Delta, Delta Kappa Gamma. Clubs: Zonta (pres. Lansing club, chmn. internat. status of women com. Home: 3715 Pau Ko Tuk Ln Oshkosh WI 54901 Office: Grad Sch U Wis-Oshkosh 800 Algoma Blvd Oshkosh WI 54901

FITZGERALD, MARK JAMES, educator; b. Olean, N.Y., May 28, 1906; s. Edward W. and Helen M. (York) F. A.B., U. Notre Dame, 1928; M.B.A., Harvard, 1931; Ph.D., U. Chgo., 1950; student, St. Bonaventure's Coll., 1925-26, Holy Cross Coll., 1936-40. Ordained priest Congregation Holy Cross, Roman Catholic Ch., 1940; mem. faculty econs. U. Notre Dame, 1940—, dir. indsl. relations sect., 1953-75, prof., 1956—, mem. grad. council, 1956-59, president's com. for acad. appointments, 1958-61; Pub. panel mem. 6th regional WLB, World War II; mem. arbitration panels Fed. Mediation and Conciliation Service, 1955-75; pres. Holy Cross Ednl. Conf., 1955. Author: Britain Views Our Industrial Relations, 1955, The Common Market's Labor Programs, 1966. Mem. Cath. Econ. Assn. (pres. 1957), Cath. Assn. Internat. Peace (v.p. 1958-61), Nat. Acad. Arbitrators (research and edn. com. 1961-65), Am. Arbitration Assn. (arbitration panel 1954-75). Address: Dept Economics Univ Notre Dame Notre Dame IN 46556

FITZGERALD, MICHAEL LEE, state official; b. Marshalltown, Iowa, Nov. 29, 1951; s. James Martin and Clara Francis (Dankbar) F.; m. Sharon Lynn Wildman, Dec. 15, 1979; children: Ryan William, Erin Elizabeth. B.B.A., U. Iowa, 1974. Campaign mgr. Fitzgerald for Treas., Colo., Iowa, 1974; market analyst Massey Ferguson, Inc., Des Moines, 1975-83; treas. State of Iowa, Des Moines, 1983—. Democrat. Roman Catholic. Home: 211 SW Caulder St Des Moines IA 50315 Office: Treasurer of State State Capitol Des Moines IA 50319

FITZGERALD, PAUL RAY, parasitologist; b. Elsinore, Utah, May 2, 1920; s. Oliver Preston and Christy Josephine (Jensen) F.; m. Naomi Brower, June 4, 1941; children: Nancy Fitzgerald Dahl, Merrily Fitzgerald Noble, Robin Fitzgerald Fuellenbach, Patrick Ray. Ed., Brigham Young U., 1938-42, U. Wis., 1943; B.S., Utah State U., 1949, M.S., 1950, Ph.D., 1961; postgrad., U. Ill., 1956-57, Oak Ridge Inst., 1964, La. State U., 1971. Instr. zoology Utah State U., Logan, 1949-53; naturalist U.S. Park Service, Grand Canyon, Ariz., 1949-50; parasitologist U.S. Dept. Agr., Logan, 1953-66; research asso. vet. pathology and hygiene U. Ill., Urbana, 1956-57, prof. vet. pathobiology, 1966—; cons. pharm. cos., state and fed. health agys. Author 2 books; contbr. articles to profl. jours. Served with AUS, 1944-46. Fulbright fellow, 1961. Mem. Am. Soc. Parasitologists, Soc. Protozoologists, Wildlife Disease Assn., Conf. Research Workers in Animal Diseases, Sigma Xi. Mem. Ch. Jesus Christ of Latter-Day Saints. Club: Kiwanis (pres. 1965-66). Home: 402 E Colorado Urbana IL 61801 Office: Coll Vet Medicine U Ill Urbana IL 61801

FITZGERALD, ROBERT (STUART FITZGERALD), writer; b. Geneva, N.Y., Oct. 12, 1910; s. Robert Emmet and Anne Montague (Stuart) F.; m. Sarah Morgan, Apr. 19, 1947 (div. div. 1982); children—Hugh Linane, Benedict Robert Campion, Maria Juliana, Peter Michael Augustine, Barnaby John Francis, Caterina Maria Teresa.; m. Penelope Laurans, May 16, 1982. Grad., Choate Sch., Wallingford, Conn., 1929; A.B., Harvard U., 1933; student, Trinity Coll., Cambridge (Eng.) U., 1931-32. Reporter N.Y. Herald Tribune, 1933-35; writer Time mag., 1936-49; instr. lit. Sarah Lawrence Coll., 1946-53, Princeton, 1950-51; fellow Sch. Letters, Ind. U., 1952—; vis. prof. U. Notre Dame, 1957, U. Wash., 1961, Mt. Holyoke Coll., 1964, Harvard U., 1964-65, Nicholas Boylston prof., 1965—, prof. emeritus, 1981. Author: Poems, 1935, A Wreath for the Sea, 1943, In the Rose of Time, 1956, Spring Shade, 1971; Translator: Oedipus at Colonus (Sophocles), 1941, Odyssey (Homer), 1961, Chronique, Birds (St. John Perse), 1961-66, Iliad (Homer), 1974, Aeneid (Virgil), 1983, (with Dudley Fitts) Alcestis (Euripides), 1935, Antigone (Sophocles), 1939, Oedipus Rex (Sophocles), 1949. Guggenheim fellow, 1953, 71; recipient Shelley award Poetry Soc. Am., 1955; grantee creative writing Ford Found., 1959, Bollingen prize for transl., 1961, Landon award for transl., 1976; Ingram Merrill Lit. award, 1978. Fellow Am. Inst. Arts and Letters (award 1957), Am. Acad. Arts and Scis., Acad. Am. Poets (chancellor 1968). Roman Catholic. Clubs: Harvard (N.Y.C.); Saturday (Boston). Address: Warren House Cambridge MA 02138

FITZGERALD, ROBERT SCHAEFER, physioloist, educator; b. Detroit, July 12, 1931; s. Edmond William and Edith Regina (Thompson) F. Litt.B., Xavier U., Cin., 1954; M.A., Spring Hill Coll., 1957; Ph.D., U. Chgo., 1963; S.T.B., Woodstock Coll., 1965, S.T.M., 1967. Tchr. St. Ignatius High Sch., Cleve., 1957-59; asst. prof. physiology Johns Hopkins U., Balt., 1967-70, assoc. prof., 1970-78, prof., 1978—, assoc. chmn. dept. environ. health sci., 1980; ad hoc cons. Nat. Heart, Lung and Blood Inst. NSF. Editor: Regulation of Respiration During Sleep and Anesthesia, 1978. Mem. Am. Physiol. Soc., Am. Thoracic Soc., N.Y. Acad. Scis., Alpha Omega Soc. Democrat. Roman Catholic. Home: 3944 Cloverhill Rd Baltimore MD 21218 Office: Johns Hopkins U 615 N Wolfe St Baltimore MD 21205

FITZGERALD, RUSSELL EDWARD, banker; b. Ardsley, Pa., Dec. 30, 1930; s. Russell E. and Kathryn B. (Rooney) F.; m. Frances Louise Cervasio, June 30, 1956; children: Russell, Stephen, Susan, Elizabeth, Joseph. Student, LaSalle Coll., Stonier Grad. Sch. Banking, 1963. With Broad Street Trust Co. Continental Bank, Phila., 1950-60; v.p. Continental Bank, Phila., 1960-67, sr. v.p., 1967-68, exec. v.p., 1968-71, pres., 1971—; state rep. BankPac, 1983—; vice chmn. Pa. Bankers Pub. Affairs Com., 1983—. Trustee Phila. Found., 1983—; treas. Jr. Baseball Fedn., 1983—; bd. dirs. March of Dimes, Phila., 1983—, Police Athletic League, 1983—; treas. Jewish Nat. Fund, 1983—. Served with U.S. Army, 1951-54. Named Bicentennial Man of Yr. Jewish Nat. Fund, 1976, Man of Yr. Delta Sigma Pi, 1976; recipient Humanitarian award Nat. Hemophilia Found., 1974, Spirit of Life award City of Hope, 1975. Club: Variety (Phila.) (pres. 1980-81). Lodge: K.C. Office: 1500 Market St Philadelphia PA 19102

FITZGERALD, THOMAS ROLLINS, university president; b. Washington, Feb. 23, 1922; s. Thomas Rollins and Bessie (Sheehy) F. B.A., Woodstock (Md.) Coll., 1945, M.A., 1948; S.T.L., Facultes St. Albert de Louvain, Belgium, 1953; Ph.D., U. Chgo., 1957. Joined Soc. of Jesus, 1939; ordained priest Roman Catholic Ch., 1952; instr. classics Novitiate St. Isaac Jogues, Wernersville, Pa., 1957-58, dean studies, asst. prof. classics, 1958-64; dean Coll. Arts and Scis., Georgetown U., 1964-66, acad. v.p., 1966-73; pres. Fairfield (Conn.) U., 1973-79, St. Louis U., 1979—. Pres. Conn. Conf. Ind. Colls., 1975-77; mem. New Eng. Bd. Higher Edn., 1977-79; trustee Gonzaga High Sch., Washington, 1969-74; chmn. bd. trustees St. Peter's Coll., Jersey City, 1969-75; trustee U. Scranton, Pa., 1974-77, Boston Coll. High Sch., 1976-79, Mo. Bot. Garden, 1981—, U. Detroit, 1982—; bd. dirs. Nat. Assn. Ind. Colls. and Univs., 1977-79, 82—. Democrat. Address: Saint Louis University Saint Louis MO 63103

FITZGERALD, WILLIAM FRANCIS, savings and loan association executive; b. Omaha, Jan. 20, 1908; s. James J. and Katherine (O'Rourke) F.; m. Mary Allingham, Sept. 29, 1934; children: Mary Frances (Mrs. J. Emmet Root), William A., Katherine A. (Mrs. A. R. Grandsaert, Jr.). Student, Creighton U., 1926-27, LL.D. (hon.), 1979; B.S. in Mech. Engring., Iowa State Coll., 1931. With Comml. Fed. Savs. & Loan Assn., Omaha, 1932—, sec., 1942-50, pres., 1950—, chmn. bd., 1975—, also dir.; dir. Hennen Realty Co., United Seed Co., Wynn Co., Hannon Co.; vice chmn., dir. Fed. Home Loan Bank, Topeka, 1960-64; Mem. Fed. Savs. and Loan Adv. Council, Washington, 1962-63. Chmn. Creighton U. Alumni Fund drive, 1960-61; Bd. dirs. United Community Fund, Omaha, 1958-61; bd. regents Creighton U., 1961-68; mem. pres.'s council 1968, mem. pres.'s research council, 1967—. Mem. U.S. Savs. and Loan League (dir. 1955-57), Omaha C. of C. (dir. 1958-61), Beta Gamma Sigma (hon.). Clubs: Omaha Country, Omaha, Omaha Press, Plaza (Omaha); Ak-Sar-Ben (king 1976-77), Kiwanis (charter, bd. dirs., past pres. South Omaha). Home: 685 N 57th St Omaha NE 68132 Office: 4501 Dodge St Omaha NE 68101

FITZ GERALD, WILLIAM HENRY GERALD, corporation executive; b. Boston, Dec. 23, 1909; s. William Joseph and Mary Ellen (Smith) Fitz) G.; m. Annelise Petschek, July 2, 1943; children: Desmond, Anne. B.S., U.S. Naval Acad., 1931; student, Harvard Law Sch., 1934-35; D.Sc. (hon.), Adelphi U., 1962. With Borden Co., N.Y.C., 1936-41; personal bus. interests, Mexico, 1946-47; organized Metall. Research & Devel. Co., Washington, 1947, v.p., treas., 1947-56, pres., 1956-58, 60—, chmn., 1960-82; chmn. bd. Nat. Metallizing Corp., Trenton, N.J., 1956-58, The Cottages, Ltd., Jamaica, B.W.I., 1960-70, Linden Corp., Washington, 1962-70, N.Am. Housing Corp., 1971—; chmn. Supramar, Ltd., Lucerne, Switzerland, 1963-69, dir., 1970-75; pres. Nat. Media Analysis, Inc., Washington, 1968-70, chmn., 1970-72; partner Hornblower & Weeks, Hemphill-Noyes, Inc., 1970-72, 1st. v.p., 1972-77; vice chmn., dir., exec. com. Fin. Gen. Bankshares, Inc., 1977-82; dir., mem. exec. com. First Am. Bank (N.A.), Washington, 1977-83, Avemco Corp.; dir. Cosmadent, Ltd., Zurich, Switzerland, 1964-75, Chase Fund of Boston, Chase Convertible Fund, Income & Capital Shares Inc., 1970-75, Pyrotector, Inc., Hingham, Mass., 1963-76; cons. to dir. ICA, Washington, 1957; dep. dir. for mgmt. ICA, Dept. State, 1958-60; U.S. conciliator Internat. Center for Investment Disputes, 1975-82; dir. Inst. Inter Am. Affairs, 1958-60; mem. President's Adv. Bd. on Internat. Investments, 1976-78; treas. Presdl. Inaugural Com., 1981; trustee Presdl. Inaugural Trust, 1981—; mem. Nat. Adv. Com. Internat. Edn., 1982—. Trustee Fed. City Council, 1962—, Wash. Inst. fgn. Affairs, 1966—; bd. dirs. Atlantic Council U.S., 1976—, treas., chmn. fin. com., 1979—; trustee Fgn. Student Service Council, 1963—, Oblate Coll. (Cath. U.), 1966—, Corcoran Gallery Art, 1977—; also mem. exec. com., chmn. devel. com. Corcoran Gallery Art; pres. Soc. for a More Beautiful Nat. Capital, Inc., 1974-77; bd. dirs., mem. exec. com., treas. Nat. Tennis Found. and Hall of Fame of Tennis, 1974—; trustee White House Preservation Fund, 1979—, chmn., 1982—; trustee, mem. nominating com. U.D.C., 1982—. Served as ensign USN, 1931-34; from lt. (j.g.) to comdr., 1941-46. Decorated Order Militar de Ayacucho, Peru, Knight Grand Cross Sovereign Mil. Order Malta; knight grand cross Equestrian Order Holy Sepulchre; Knight grand Cross Sacred Mil. Constantinian Order of St. George. Mem. Newcomen Soc. N.Am. So. Assn. in U.S.A., Sovereign Mil. Order of Malta (pres. 1975-79). Roman Catholic. Clubs: Army-Navy Country, University, Harvard, 1925 F St, International (Washington); River (N.Y.C.); Metropolitan (Washington); Essex County (Manchester, Mass.). Home: 2305 Bancroft Pl Washington DC 20008 Office: 1730 M St NW Washington DC 20036

FITZGERALD, WILLIAM THOMAS, tire company executive; b. Akron, Ohio, Sept. 1, 1926; s. John William and Mary Elizabeth (McAlonan) F.; m. Rita B. Gerraghty, Sept. 6, 1947; children: Thomas Joseph, Dennis Michael, John William, James Patrick. B.S. with distinction, U. Akron, 1950; postgrad. Advanced Mgmt. Program, Harvard U., 1969. Vice pres. mktg. Cooper Tire & Rubber Co., Findlay, Ohio, 1968-71, pres. Tire div., 1971—, exec v.p., 1982—, dir., 1970—; dir. Citizens Savs. & Loan, Tiffin, Ohio. Pres. Findlay council Boy Scouts Am., 1977-79. Served with USN, 1944-46. Mem. Am. Mgmt. Assn. Roman Catholic. Clubs: Country; Skeet (Findlay); Catawba Island (Port Clinton, Ohio). Office: Cooper Tire and Rubber Co Western and Lima Aves Findlay OH 45840

FITZGIBBON, JOHN FRANCIS, philosophy educator; b. Rock Island, Ill., Sept. 12, 1923; s. James Francis and Gertrude Marie (Schikan) F.; m. Elizabeth Jane Burke, Sept. 1, 1951; children: Elizabeth, John, Margaret, Mara, Timothy. A.B., St. Mary's of Barrens, 1946; A.M., St. Louis U., 1950; Ph.D., U. Notre Dame, 1956. Instr. U. Notre Dame, 1953-54; instr. Georgetown U., 1955-57, asst. prof., 1957-58, St. Ambrose Coll., Davenport, Iowa, 1958-60, asso. prof., 1960-66, prof., 1966—, chmn. dept. philosophy, 1967-74, 75-81, chmn. div. philosophy and theology, 1969-79; Participant Council on Religion and Internat. Affairs seminars, 1967, 68, Am. Maritain Assn. seminar, 1980. Author: Ethics: Fundamental Principles of Moral Philosophy, 1983. Pres. Rock Island chpt. Citizens for Ednl. Freedom, 1963-64; mem. Davenport (Iowa) Cath. Interracial Council, 1959-70, R.I. County Interracial Council, 1965-70. Mem. AAUP (chpt. pres. 1960-61, 62-63, 68-70), Am. Cath. Philos. Assn., Metaphys. Soc. Am., Iowa Philos. Assn. Home: 2728 26th Av Rock Island IL 61201

FITZ GIBBON, THOMAS PATRICK, savs. and loan exec.; b. St. Paul, Apr. 21, 1913; s. William Patrick and Helen Cecil (Davis) Fitz) G.; m. Jeanne F. Foley, Dec. 15, 1942 (dec. 1963); children—Thomas, Patricia Fitz Gibbon Curran, Michael, Kathleen Fitz Gibbon Moore, Mary Fitz Gibbon Kelly, Jeanne Fitz Gibbon Engel, James, Helen Fitz Gibbon Kegley; m. Mary H. Lambert, Jan. 28, 1967. With First Fed. Savs. & Loan Assn. of, St. Paul, 1946—, corporate sec., 1952-57, exec. v.p., dir., 1957-65, pres., dir., 1965—; sr. vp., dir. Midwest Fed. Savs. & Loan Assn., 1974—. Served with cav. AUS, 1942-45. Home: 660 Montcalm Pl Saint Paul MN 55116 Office: Cedar at 5th Saint Paul MN 55101

FITZGIBBONS, DAVID JOHN, drug co. exec.; b. Paterson, N.J., Jan. 18, 1906; s. David John and Elizabeth (Hynes) F.; m. Eleanor Corry Kelly, Feb. 22, 1941; children—Robert Anton, David James. Grad., Drake Bus. Coll., Paterson, 1925, Pace Inst., 1928. Office mgr., sec. Standard Plumbing & Heating, Inc., 1928-35; with Price, Waterhouse & Co. (C.P.A.'s), 1935-37; chief accountant Am. Ferment Co., 1937-39; v.p., treas. Sterling Products Internat., Inc., 1939—, Sydney Ross Co., 1939—, Winthrop Products, Inc., 1949—; v.p. Sterling Drug, Inc., 1960-61, exec v.p., 1961-63, pres., 1963-74, chmn. finance com., 1974—, also mem. exec. com., dir. Former bd. dirs. Nat. Fgn. Trade Council. Clubs: Essex Country (W. Orange, N.J.); Country of Fla., Delray Beach (Fla.). Home: 2000 S Ocean Blvd Delray Beach FL 33444 Office: 90 Park Ave New York City NY 10016

FITZHENRY, ROBERT IRVINE, publisher; b. N.Y.C., Apr. 10, 1918; s. Irvine and Margaret (Lane) F.; m. Hilda Anderson, Jan. 22, 1949; children—Sharon, Bridget, Hollister. B.A., U. Mich., 1939. Reporter, editor, night mgr. United Press Assn., Cleve. and Columbus, Ohio, 1939-41; from salesman, sales mgr. to dir. gen. sales Harper & Row Pubs., N.Y.C., 1946-66; co-founder, 1966; pres. Fitzhenry & Whiteside Ltd. (publishers), Markham, Ont., Can., 1966—, Beaverbooks Ltd., Markham, Ont., 1973—. Editor: Fitzhenry-Whiteside Book of Quotations, 1981, Barnes & Noble Book of Quotations, 1983. Chmn. Pound Ridge Democratic party, 1960-64. Served with USAAF, 1941-45. Mem. Am. Book Pubs. Council (chmn. book distbn. com. 1946-48, Canadian Book Pubs. Council, exec. com. 1972-73). Club: Canadian (N.Y.C.). Home: Box 508 62 Mill St

Uxbridge ON L0C 1K0 Canada 195 All State Pkwy Markham ON Canada L3R 4T8

FITZ-HUGH, GLASSELL SLAUGHTER, otolarynogologist, educator; b. Charlottesville, Va., May 1, 1907; s. Glassell and Orie (Slaughter) Fitz-H.; m. Dorothea Minor Meredith, Sept. 9, 1937; children: Glassell Slaughter, George Meredith, Elizabeth Morrison. Student, Augusta Mil. Acad., 1925-27; M.D., U. Va., 1933. Diplomate: Am. Bd. Otolaryngology. Intern, resident Charity Hosp., New Orleans, 1933-35, U. Va. Hosp., Charlottesville, 1935-37; faculty sch. medicine U. Va., 1937—, prof. otolaryngology, 1951-77, prof. emeritus, 1977—, chmn. dept., 1951-75, vice chmn. dept., 1975-77; Former mem. communicative disorder research tng. com. NIH. Served as capt. to lt. col. M.C. AUS, 1942-46. Fellow A.C.S. (past rep. to residency rev. com. for otolaryngology); mem. AMA, So. Med. Assn., Med. Soc. Va., Va. Soc. Ophthalmology and Otolaryngology, Am. Acad. Ophthalmology and Otolaryngology, Am. Laryngol. Rhinol. and Otological Soc. (pres. 1967), Am. Acad. Facial Plastic and Reconstructive Surgery, Am. Otological Soc., Am. Laryngol. Assn. (pres. 1974), AAUP, Thomas Jefferson Soc., U. Va. Gen. Alumni Assn. (bd. mgrs.), Am. Soc. Head and Neck Surgery, Soc. U. Otolaryngologists, Va. Acad. Scis., Va. Hearing Found., Am. Council Otolaryngology, Nat. Rehab. Assn., Alpha Omega Alpha. Presbyn. Home: 1415 Blue Ridge Rd Charlottesville VA 22903 Office: U Va Hosps Box 430 Charlottesville VA 22908

FITZHUGH, WILLIAM WYVILL, JR., business executive; b. Bklyn., June 27, 1914; s. William Wyvill and Portia (Starr) F.; m. Florence Hardy, Dec. 13, 1941; children: William, Priscilla, John, Portia. A.B., Dartmouth, 1935; B.A., Trinity Coll., Cambridge U., 1937, M.A., 1938; M.Phil., Columbia U., 1977; J.D., Pace U., 1980. Fellow Carnegie Endowment Internat. Peace, 1938-39; sec.-rapporteur Internat. Studies Conf., League of Nations, 1938-39; instr. govt., Columbia, 1939-42; pres. William W. Fitzhugh, Inc., N.Y.C., 1945—, New Haven Board & Carton Co., Inc., 1960-64; partner Dalsemer, Fitzhugh & Catzen, N.Y.C., 1964-66; pres. Newspaper Preprint Corp., N.Y.C., 1966-75. Past chmn. Chappaqua Orchestral Assn. Served to lt. USNR. Mem. Gravure Tech. Assn. (past pres.), Folding Paper Box Assn. Am. (past pres. met. N.Y. group), Label Mfrs. Assn. (past dir.), Bklyn. C. of C. (past dir.), Phi Beta Kappa, Sigma Chi. Republican. Episcopalian. Home and Office: Pine Tree Rd PO Box 356 Norwich VT 05055

FITZMORRIS, JAMES EDWARD, JR., former lt. gov. La.; b. New Orleans, Nov. 15, 1921; s. James Edward and Romolia E. (Hanning) F.; m. Gloria Lopez, Sept. 15, 1945; 1 dau., Lisa Marie. Student, Loyola U. of South, 1946. With Kansas City So. Lines, New Orleans, 1940-72, v.p., 1969-72; lt. gov. La., 1972-80; asst. for econ. devel. to Gov. of La., 1980—. Chmn. bd. La. Dept. Commerce; dir. La. State Bond and Bldg. Bank of New Orleans.; Mem. La. Energy Commn., La. Tourist Devel. Commn.; mem. La. Bd. Pub. Welfare, 1952-54; bd. govs. La. Civil Service League, 1953-55; coordinator internat. relations State of La.; chmn. energy and natural resources com. Nat. Conf. Lt. Govs.; Mem. bd. Total Community Action, 1965-67; regional v.p. Nat. Municipal League, 1966-71; mem. La., Miss. Export Expansion Council, 1966-69; dir. New Orleans Bd. Trade, 1967-69; mem. select port com. Port of New Orleans, 1970; pres. Miss. Valley World Trade Council, 1968, mem. exec. com., 1967-71; v.p. Greater New Orleans Homestead Assn., 1952-77; pres. Cultural Attractions Fund of Greater New Orleans, 1971; chmn. Brotherhood Week NCCJ, 1963, Nat. Transp. Week, 1967-69; sec. Met. New Orleans Safety Council, v.p., 1971-72; sustaining membership chmn. Girl Scouts Southeast La., 1973; mem. orgnl. bd. Chep Morrison Meml. Scholarship Fund, 1964-70; gen. chmn. U.S. Savs. Bond Share in Freedom, 1968; chmn. La. employees div. United Fund, 1973-77, trustee, 1965-70; mem. La. Stadium and Exposition Dist., 1974-76; Councilman, also councilman-at-large City New Orleans, 1954-66; Trustee nat. bd. Leukemia Soc.; bd. dirs. Internat. Trade Mart. Recipient ann. conf. award, 1976, Weiss Meml. award, 1976; Recipient Leukemia Soc. Leadership award, 1964; deLesseps S. Morrison Meml. award, 1965; Nat. Municipal League Distinguished Citizens award, 1968; Jesuit High Sch. award of Honor, 1969; named Jesuit Blue-Jay Outstanding Alumnus of the Year-The F. Edward Hebert award, 1972; recipient Ray Mock Meml. award, 1973, Service to Mankind award Sertoma Club, 1976; named One of 10 Outstanding Persons of Yr. Inst. Human Understanding, 1976. Mem. C. of C. Greater New Orleans, Internat. House (vice-chmn. 1970-71, dir. 1969-77, membership com. 1970-71), La. Outdoor Drama Assn. (adv. council 1972-73), Nat. Def. Transp. Assn. (nat. v.p. 1968-72). Clubs: Young Men's Business (pres. 1951), Commercial Athletic Assn. K.C. (grand knight 1951-52), Commercial Athletic Assn. K.C. (pres. Met. council 1952-53), Commercial Athletic Assn. K.C. (state speakers chmn. 1951-52), Commercial Athletic Assn. K.C. (4 deg.). Office: State Capitol PO Box 44243 Baton Rouge LA 70804 *

FITZPATRICK, EDWIN J., investor; b. N.Y.C., Ap. 15, 1910; s. James E. and Anna (Gallagher) F.; m. Betty C. Roney, July 5, 1940; children—Edwin J., Anne Roney. A.B., Cornell U., 1932. Asst. instr. econs. Cornell U., 1932-33; v.p. charge sales Clapp's Baby Foods, Inc., 1933-41; asst. chief food div. W.P.B., 1941-42; pres. Chef Boy-ar-dee Foods, Inc., Milton, Pa., 1946-49; also dir., v.p. Am. Home Foods, Inc., N.Y.C., 1946-49; pres. Permacel Tape Corp., New Brunswick, N.J., 1949-55; gen. partner Orvis Bros. & Co., N.Y.C., 1955-63; private investor, 1963—; Cons. bus. and def. service adminstrn. Dept. Commerce, 1954-55. Trustee Muhlenberg Hosp., Plainfield, N.J., Central N.J. Health Facilities Planning Council, Wardlaw Country Day Sch.; pres. Alumni Inter-frat. Council Cornell U. Served as maj. to col. Q.M.C.; ETO; Served as maj. to col. Q.M.C. U.S. Army, 1942-46. Decorated Legion of Merit, Bronze Star. Mem. Phi Beta Kappa, Chi Phi, Quill and Dagger. Clubs: Genesee Valley (Rochester, N.Y.); Plainfield (N.J.); Country; University (N.Y.C.); Bath, Indian Creek Country (Miami Beach). Home: 1734 Sleepy Hollow Ln Plainfield NJ 07060 Office: 120 Depot Park Plainfield NJ 07060

FITZPATRICK, F. W., diversified company executive. Chmn. Bralorne Resources Ltd., Calgary, Alta., Can. Office: Bralorne Resources Ltd 2900-205 5th Ave SW Calgary AB Canada T2P 2V7§

FITZPATRICK, GLADYS EVE, psychologist; b. Bklyn.; d. Frank A. and Bertha M. (Fehleisen) F.; m. Locke L. Mackenzie. B.A., Hunter Coll., 1953; M.A., CUNY, 1957; Ph.D., Fordham U., 1964. Adminstrv. dir. Astoria (N.Y.) Med. Group, 1949-60; research asst. Ittleson Center Child Research, Riverdale, N.Y., 1961-62; staff psychologist, devel. evaluation clinic Albert Einstein Coll. Medicine, Bronx, 1963-65; chief psychologist Bronx-Lebanon Hosp., Bronx, 1965—; dir. children's services Bronz-Lebanon Hosp., Bronz, 1969-74; sr. psychologist children's unit Creedmoor State Hosp., Queens, N.Y.; chmn. Boroughwide Com. Children's Services, 1980-82; chmn. profl. adv. bd. Crotona Park Community Mental Health Center., 1981—. Mem. Am. Psychol. Assn., Soc. Pediatric Psychology, Am. Orthpsychiat. Assn., Internat. Council Psychologists, Sigma Xi. Home: 61 E 77th St New York NY 10021 Office: 1285 Fulton Ave Bronx NY 10456

FITZPATRICK, JOSEPH EDWARD, temporary employment service company executive; b. Auburn, N.Y., Oct. 14, 1931; s. Joseph E. and Stella (Bannon) F.; m. Jean M. Cuddy, May 1, 1954; children: Michael, Kevin, Brian, Mary Jo. B.B.A., LeMoyne Coll., 1953. C.P.A., N.Y., Calif. Staff acct. Price Waterhouse & Co., N.Y.C., 1955-58, sr. acct., Rochester, N.Y., 1958-61, audit mgr., Bogota, Colombia, 1961-63, Phila., 1963-64; v.p. fin. group, treasury ops. Saga Corp., Menlo Park, Calif., 1964-79; controller, treas. Western Temporary Services, Inc., Walnut Creek, Calif., 1979—. Served to cpl. AUS, 1953-55. Mem. Am. Inst. C.P.A.s, N.Y. State Soc. C.P.A.s. Democrat. Roman Catholic. Home: 600 Guadalupe Dr Los Altos CA 94022 Office: Box 9280 230 N Wiget Ln Walnut Creek CA 94596

FITZPATRICK, KIRBY WARD, architect; b. Ada, Okla., Feb. 17, 1935; s. Leon Shannon and Mary Louvenia (Patterson) F. B.Arch., U. Pa., 1957. Designer Reid and Taries (AIA), San Francisco, 1964-69, Skidmore, Owings and Merrill, 1969; pvt. practice architecture, San Francisco, 1970-80; founder firm Fitzpatrick, Karren & Seals, San Francisco, 1980—; juror Homes for Better Living, 1977; vis. lectr. dept. architecture U. Calif., Berkeley, 1979. Works published in Arts and Architecture, 1963, Archtl. Record, 1976, Home Mag. Los Angeles Times, 1977, San Francisco Mag, 1977, Oakland Tribune Ann. Home Improvement Edit, Apr. 24, 1977, House Beautiful, Mar. 1978, Hudson Home Guide, Homes for Better Living, 1977. Bd. dirs. San Francisco Lung Assn., pres., 1983-84. Served to 1st lt. USAF, 1957-60. Recipient AIA-House and Home Homes for Better Living awards, 1973, 76, 79, AIA-Sunset award, 1975-76, Am. Plywood Assn. award, 1976; Red Cedar Shingle and Handsplit Shake Bur. award, 1975. Mem. AIA, Calif. Council AIA, No. Calif. AIA (chmn. house com.), U. Pa. Alumni Assn. (pres. No. Calif. chpt. 1970-74), San Francisco Symphony Found., San Francisco Ballet Assn., San Francisco Mus. Art, Oakland Art Mus., San Francisco Planning and Urban Renewal Assn. Home: 123 Liberty St San Francisco CA 94110 Office: 447 Sutter St San Francisco CA 94108

FITZPATRICK, MARTIN FRANCIS, JR., government official; b. Joliet, Ill., Dec. 24, 1952; s. Martin Francis and Jacqueline Marie (Bennie) F. B.A., Drake U., Des Moines. Residence hall dir. U. Mo., Columbia, 1975-76; staff asst. to George M. O'Brien U.S. Ho. of Reps., Washington, 1976-77; organizational dir. Republican Party of Va., Richmond, 1977-79; legis. dir., agr. advisor Sen. Roger Jepsen, Washington, 1979-81; dir. Office of Transp. Dept. of Agr., Washington, 1981—. Agr. advisor Reagan-Bush Com., 1980; staff asst. to platform com. Republican Nat. Conv., 1980. Mem. Transp. Research Forum, Smithsonian Soc., Sigma Alpha Epsilon. Roman Catholic. Home: 401 N Armistead St 209 Alexandria VA 22312 Office: Dept of Agr. 14th and Independence Ave SW Washington DC 20250

FITZPATRICK, MARY BLANCHE, economist, educator; b. Medford, Mass.; d. Joseph Leo and Elizabeth Dorothy (Bresnahan) F. A.B. summa cum laude, Tufts U., 1950; A.M., Stanford U., 1950; Ph.D., Harvard U., 1966. Labor relations analyst Raytheon, Boston, 1949; price economist Dept. Labor, Boston, 1949-53; dir. sales analysis Polaroid, Cambridge, Mass., 1953-58; faculty econs. Lesley Coll., 1958-64; asst. prof. Calif. State U., Fullerton, 1964-65, Boston U., 1965-66, assoc. prof., 1966-71, prof. econs., 1971—; chair econs Goucher Coll., 1980-82; lectr. Harvard U. Extension, 1971-77; mem. faculty adv. com. Md. Bd. Higher Edn., 1981-82; cons. in field. Author: Women's Inferior Education: An Economic Analysis, 1976. Mem. Mass. Gov.'s Commn. on Status of Women, 1971-74, Mass. Bd. Higher Edn., 1975-76; trustee U. Lowell, 1975-78. Mem. Am. Econ. Assn., Eastern Econ. Assn., Indsl. Relations and Research Assn., Chesapeake Assn. Econ. Educators, Phi Beta Kappa. Office: Boston U 270 Bay State Rd Boston MA 02215

FITZPATRICK, ROBERT JOHN, college president; b. Toronto, Ont., Can., May 18, 1940; came to U.S., 1952, naturalized, 1962; s. John and Maxine (Dunn) F.; m. Sylvie M. Blondet, Jan. 1966; children: Joel Denis, Michael Sean, Claire Valerie. B.A. magna cum laude, Spring Hill Coll., 1963, M.A., 1964; student (Woodrow Wilson fellow), Johns Hopkins U., 1964-65. Asst. prof. French U. Maine, 1965-68; mem. staff McCarthy Nat. Campaign Hdqrs., 1968; staff asst., campaign aide to Sen. Joseph D. Tydings, Washington, 1970; chmn. dept. modern langs. Gilman Sch., Balt., 1968-72; dean of students Johns Hopkins U., 1972-75; pres. Calif. Inst. of Arts, Valencia, 1975—. Mem. Balt. City Council, 1971-75; v.p. Mayor's Com. on Cultural Affairs, Los Angeles, 1976-79, Calif. Confedn. of Arts, 1977-79; dir. Olympic Arts Festival, Los Angeles, 1984; mem. Md. Democratic State Central Com., 1970-74; mem. adv. com. Next Wave Festival, Bklyn. Coll.; trustee Craft and Folk Art Mus., Los Angeles, Los Angeles Chamber Orch., 1977-81, Dunn Sch., Los Olivos, Calif., Bennington Coll., Vt.; mem. interdisciplinary panel Interarts program Nat. Endowment for Arts. Mem. Advocates for the Arts, Internat. Council Fine Arts Deans, Nat. Assn. Schs. Art, Assn. Ind. Calif. Colls. and Univs. (exec. com.). Democrat. Home: 16065 Royal Oak Rd Encino CA 91436 Office: 24700 McBean Pkwy Valencia CA 91355

FITZPATRICK, SHEILA MARY, historian, educator; b. Melbourne, Victoria, Australia, June 4, 1941; d. Brian F. and Dorothy Mary (Davies) Firtzpatrick. B.A. with honors, U. Melbourne, 1961; D.Phil., Oxford U., Eng., 1969. Researcher fellow Sch. Slavonic and Eastern European Studies, London, 1969-71; research fellow London Sch. Econs. and Polit. Sci., 1971-72; lectr. Slavic dept. U. Tex., Austin, 1972-73, prof. history, 1981—; assoc. prof. history St. John's U., Queens, N.Y., 1974-75; from asst. prof. to assoc. prof. history Columbia U., N.Y.C., 1975-80. Author: The Commissariat of Englightenment, 1970, Education and Social Mobility in the Soviet Union, 1921-1934 1979, The Russian Revolution, 1983; editor: Cultural REvolution in Russia, 1928-31 1978. Trustee Nat. council for Soviet and Eastern European Research, Washington, 1983—. Exchange scholar Moscow State U., Brit. Council, 1969-70; vis. scholar Australian Nat. U., 1979; Woodrow Wilson fellow, 1981-82. Mem. Am. Hist. Assn., Am. Assn. Advancement Slavic Studies. Office: History Dept Univ Tex Austin TX 78712

FITZPATRICK, WILLARD EDMUND, ins. co. exec.; b. Milw., Oct. 26, 1924; s. Christopher Edward and Catherine Alice (Mee) F.; m. Jeanne Keller, Feb. 5, 1955; children—Gerald, John, Michael. B.A., U. Wis., 1952, J.D., 1952. Bar: Wis. bar 1952. Claims atty. Am. Family Ins. Co., Madison, Wis., 1952-55; claims mgr. Bolivar Ins. Co., Bogotá, Colombia, 1955-57; exec. v.p. Universal Ins. Co., Bogotá, 1957-60; with Nationwide Ins. Cos., Columbus, Ohio, 1960—; asst. to pres. 1965-72, v.p. sec., asst. to gen. chmn., 1972—; mem. Internat. Ins. Devel. Bur. Served with AUS, 1943-46. Mem. Wis. Bar Assn., Soc. C.P.C.U.'s, Soc. C.L.U.'s, Am. Soc. Corp. Secs. Republican. Roman Catholic. Clubs: Univ., Brookside Country (Columbus). Home: 4169 Rowanne Rd Columbus OH 43214 Office: 1 Nationwide Plaza Columbus OH 43216

FITZROY, NANCY DELOYE, technology executive, engineer; b. Pittsfield, Mass., Oct. 5, 1927; d. Jules Emile and Mabel Winifred (Burr) deLoye; m. Roland Victor Fitzroy, Jr., Mar. 24, 1951. B. in Chem. Engring., Rensselaer Poly. Inst., Troy, 1949. Registered profl. engr., N.Y. Heat transfer engr. corp. research and devel. Gen. Electric Co., Schenectady, N.Y., 1950-71, mgr. heat transfer consulting, 1971-74, strategy planner, 1974-76, mgr. program devel., gas turbine div., 1976-82, mgr. energy and environ. program, 1982—; dir. West Hill Devel. Corp., Rotterdam, N.Y., 1955-61, 62-65; mem. adv. com. for research NSF, Washington, 1972-74; cons. in field. Author, editor: Heat Transfer and Fluid Flow, Data Books, 1955—; patentee in field. Recipient Demers medal Rensselaer Poly. Inst., 1975, Power Systems Engring. award Gen. Electric Co., 1979. Fellow ASME (gov. 1963—, sr. v.p. 1981-83); mem. Soc. Women Engrs. (Achievement award 1972), Am. Inst. Chem. Engrs., Nat. Acad. Engring. Republican. Episcopalian. Clubs: Ninety-Nines, Whirly-Girls. Home: 2125 Rosendale Rd Niskayuna NY 12309 Office: Gen Electric Co Gas Turbine Div 500-237 Schenectady NY 12345

FITZSIMMONS, JOHN ROBERT, landscape architect; b. Leadville, Colo., Aug. 22, 1896; s. Charles Andrew and Mary Lincoln (Irel) F.; m. Dorothy Proctor, Aug. 13, 1928; children—John Robert, Susan Jane Fitzsimmons Lessin. B.S., Colo. State U., 1921; M. Landscape Architecture (Scholar), Harvard U., 1924. State landscape architect Iowa Conservation Commn., Des Moines, 1924-36; mem. staff extension service Iowa State U., 1924-50, prof., head landscape architecture dept., Ames, 1950-62, part-time prof., 1962-79; free-lance landscape architect, Denver, 1979—; Landscape Architect Miss. River Planning Commn., 1950-52; mem. Iowa State Capitol Planning Commn., 1950-60. Precinct chmn. Republican Party, Denver, 1975—; mem. exec. com. Tall Corn council Boy Scouts Am. Served in 62d Inf. U.S. Army, 1917-18. Fellow Am. Soc. Landscape Architects; mem. Am. Inst. Planners, AAUP, Iowa Planning Assn. (hon.). Roman Catholic. Clubs: Rotary, Newman, Topiarian, K.C. Home: 1200 St Paul St Denver CO 80206

FITZSIMMONS, JOSEPH JOHN, publishing executive; b. Newark, Nov. 10, 1934; s. Joseph A. and Frances E. (Baume) F.; m. Nancy L. Lind, June 11, 1957; children: Joseph John, Michael, Patricia, Susan, Thomas. B.Chem. Engring., Cornell U., 1957. With Xerox Corp., Rochester, N.Y., 1957-65; v.p., gen. mgr. Xerox Univ. Microfilms, Ann Arbor, Mich., 1974-75; pres. Univ. Microfilms Internat., Ann Arbor, 1976—. Dir. Ann Arbor Bank & Trust Co.; Gen. campaign chmn. Washtenaw United Way, 1977-78; devel. com. St. Joseph's Hosp. Mem. Nat. Micrographics Assn., Internat. Micrographics Congress, ALA, Info. Industry Assn. Roman Catholic. Home: 2073 Chaucer Dr Ann Arbor MI 48103 Office: 300 N Zeeb Rd Ann Arbor MI 48106

FITZSIMMONS, RICHARD M., manufacturing executive, lawyer; b. New Haven, Apr. 4, 1924; s. Irving F. and Nina G. (Moore) FitzS.; m. Estelle M. Naughton, Nov. 27, 1954; children: Estelle J., Anne H. B.A., Hamilton Coll., 1947; J.D., Yale U., 1950. Bar: N.Y. 1950, U.S. Supreme Ct. 1954, Wis. 1958, Ill. 1964, Ky. 1966. Asso. Winthrop, Stimson, Putnam & Roberts, N.Y.C., 1950-51, Satterlee, Warfield & Stephens, 1951-54; counsel Gen. Electric Co., various locations, 1954-70, counsel Hotpoint div., Chgo., 1963-66, appliance and TV group, Louisville, 1966-70; gen. counsel, sr. v.p., sec. Allis-Chalmers Corp., Milw., 1970—; dir. Allis-Chalmers Gt. Britain Ltd., Allis-Chalmers Material Handling-Europe, Fiat-Allis, Inc., Fiat-Allis B.V., Allis-Chalmers Power Systems, Inc., Utility Power Corp., Marine Trust (N.A.); mem. adv. bd. Internat. and Comparative Law Center, Southwestern Legal Found., Dallas, 1970—. Editor Yale Law Jour., 1948-50; contbr. articles to profl. jours. Trustee Hamilton Coll., 1975-79. Served to capt. USAAF, 1943-46. Mem. Am., Wis., N.Y.C., Chgo., Ky. bar assns., Am. Arbitration Assn. (panel arbitrators), Corbey Ct., Yale Law Sch. Assn. (exec. com. 1978), Delta Kappa Epsilon, Phi Delta Phi. Clubs: Milwaukee Country, University of Milwaukee; Shenorock (Rye, N.Y.); Yale (N.Y.C.). Home: 4720 N Lake Dr Milwaukee WI 53211 Office: 1205 S 70th St West Allis WI 53214

FITZSIMONS, PATRICK S., police chief; b. N.Y.C., Apr. 16, 1930; s. Patrick Joseph and Mary (Brabazon) F.; m. Olga Parker, Aug. 18, 1959. B.S., Fordham U., 1954; J.D., 1972; J.D. fellow criminal justice, Harvard U. Law Sch., 1972-73. Bar: N.Y. bar. Adj. prof. John Jay Coll. Grad. Sch., N.Y.C.; mem. N.Y.C. Police Dept.; asst. chief programs and policies; now chief of police City of Seattle; mem. Gov. Wash. Council Criminal Justice, Wash.; Bd. Law Enforcement Tng. and Standards; mem. bd. Nat. Criminal Info. Center, Police Rxecs. Research Forum. Bd. dirs. Chief Seattle council Boy Scouts Am. Served to 1st lt. USMC, 1953-56. Recipient award criminal justice Am. Soc. Public Adminstrn. Mem. Fordham U. Law Sch. Alumni Assn., Harvard U. Law Sch. Alumni Assn. Clubs: Wash. Athletic, 101. Office: 610 3d Ave Seattle WA 98104

FITZSIMONS, RUTH MARIE, educator; b. Pawtucket, R.I.; d. Leo A. and Helena (Hollis) F. B.Ed., R.I. Coll., 1940; M.Ed., Boston U., 1949, D.Ed., 1955; postgrad., N.Y. U., 1956, Brandeis U., summer 1958. Tchr., prin. Warwick (R.I.) Sch. Dept., 1940-49, speech and hearing therapy coordinator, 1949-68; prof. speech and lang. pathology U. R.I., Kingston, 1969—; lectr. Boston U., 1956, 58, 59, U. Maine, summer 1966; cons. speech and hearing therapy R.I. Dept. Edn., Providence, 1968-69; cons. Meeting St. Sch. Childrens Rehab. Center, Providence, 1969; cons. editor T.J. Denison & Co., Mpls., 1966—. Author: Stuttering and Personality Dynamics, 1960, Christopher Listens, 1966, Make Believe with Mike, 1968; contbr. articles to profl. jours.; designer ednl. software. Mem. R.I. Speech and Hearing Assn. (pres. 1964-65), Am. Speech and Hearing Assn. (legislative councillor 1969-71), Am. Psychol. Assn., Am. Acad. Psychotherapists, Soc. for Research in Child Devel. Home: 38 Mystic Dr Warwick RI 02886 Office: Dept Speech U of Rhode Island Kingston RI 02881

FITZWATER, BONNIE, editor; b. Watonga, Okla., Nov. 16, 1923; d Clarence Eugene and Evelyn Ellen (Funk) F. B.A. magna cum laude, U. Okla., 1945; M.A., Northwestern U., 1947. Announcer, scriptwriter Radio Sta. WNAD, 1941-45; counselor dormitory Northwestern U., 1945-46, grad. asst. dept. psychology, 1945-47; asst. to dir. personnel indsl. relations dept. Atlantic Refining Co., Dallas, 1947-48; dir. social activities So. Meth. U., 1948-50, dir. student activities, 1950-57, dean women, 1957-61; asst. dean women Stanford U., 1961-62, asso. dean, 1962-65; pub.'s rep. Wadsworth Pub. Co., Belmont, Calif., 1966-67; spl. projects editor Brooks/Cole Pub. Co., Monterey, Calif., 1967-75, sociology/anthropology editor, 1975-78; freelance editor, 1978—. Mem. P.E.O., Nat., Tex., Calif. assns. women deans and counselors, Am. Sociol. Assn., Am. Anthrop. Assn., Phi Beta Kappa, Sigma Xi, Kappa Alpha Theta, Alpha Lambda Delta, Mortar Board. Presbyterian. Home: 721 N Noble St Watonga OK 73772 Office: Brooks/Cole Pub Co 555 Abrego St Monterey CA 93940

FIX, GEORGE JOSEPH, mathematics educator, consultant; b. Dallas, May 10, 1939; s. George Joseph and Francis (Barlett) F.; m. Linda Mitchell, June 30, 1962; children: Paige, Blake. B.S., Tex. A&M U., 1963; M.S., Rice U., 1965; Ph.D., Harvard U., 1968. Engr. Tex. Instruments, Dallas, 1963-64; assoc. prof. U. Md., 1972-73, U. Mich., 1973-75; prof., head dept. math. Carnegie-Mellon U., Pitts., 1975—; cons. Author 2 books, numerous articles. Served in USMC, 1958-62. NASA fellow, 1981-83; grantee Office Naval Research, Army Research Office, NSF. Mem. Am. Math. Soc., Soc. Indsl. and Applied Math., AAAS, Sigma Xi, Tau Beta Pi. Office: Carnegie-Mellon U Pittsburgh PA 15213

FIX, WILBUR JAMES, department store executive; b. Velva, N.D., Aug. 14, 1927; s. Jack J. and Beatrice D. (Wasson) F.; m. Beverly A. Corcoran, Sept. 20, 1953; children: Kathleen M., Michael B., Jenifer L. B.A., U. Wash., 1950. Credit mgr. Bon Marche, Yakima, Wash., 1951-54, controller, ops. mgr., Boise, Idaho, 1954-58, sr. v.p., Seattle, 1970-76, exec. v.p., 1976-77, pres., chief exec. officer, 1978—; chmn. Wash. Retail Council, 1983-84. Mem. pres.'s adv. com. Allied Stores Corp.,

N.Y., 1968-72; dir. Northgate Centers, Tacoma Mall Corp., Columbia Center Corp., Southcenter Corp.; Mem. citizens adv. com. Seattle Pub. Schs., 1970-71; v.p. Citizens Council Against Crime. Served with AUS, 1946-47. Mem. Nat. Retail Mchts. Assn., Controllers Congress, Seattle Retail Controllers Group (past pres.), Fin. Execs. Inst., Western States Regional Controllers Congress (past pres.), Seattle C. of C. (exec. com., bd. dirs.), Assn. Wash. Bus. (fin. adv.), Downtown Seattle Devel. Assn. (exec. com., trustee), Pi Kappa Alpha, Alpha Kappa Psi, Phi Theta Kappa. Episcopalian. Clubs: Wash. Athletic, Seattle Yacht, Elks. Home: 5403 W Mercer Way Mercer Island WA 98040 Office: 3d and Pine Sts Seattle WA 98181

FIXLER, DAVID ELLSWORTH, pediatric cardiologist; b. South Bend, Ind., Apr. 26, 1938; s. Harry and Evelyn F.; m. Susan J. Shaw, Sept. 1, 1962; children: Heidi Chris, Bradford Donovan, Rebekah Shaw. B.S., U. Notre Dame, 1960; M.D., U. Chgo., 1964; M.Sc. in Epidemiology, U. London, 1982. Diplomate: Am. Bd. Pediatrics, Am. Bd. Pediatric Cardiology. Intern, then resident in pediatrics and fellow in cardiology Children's Meml. Hosp., Chgo., 1964-67; NIH postdoctoral research fellow U. Calif. Med. Center, San Francisco, 1969-71; mem. faculty U. Tex. Health Scis. Center, Dallas, 1971—, prof. pediatrics, 1979—; dir. pediatric cardiology Children's Med. Center, Dallas, 1977—. Served as officer M.C., USAF, 1967-69. Grantee Tex. Heart Assn., 1971-79, Am. Heart Assn., 1974-79; Milbank Meml. Found. scholar, 1981-82; Grantee NIH, 1976-83; recipient Nat. Research Service award, 1981-82. Mem. Am. Acad. Pediatrics, Am. Coll. Cardiology, Soc. Pediatric Research, Am. Fedn. Clin. Research, Am. Heart Assn. (councils epidemiology, high blood pressure research, cardiovascular disease in young), Alpha Omega Alpha. Episcopalian. Home: 7123 La Sobrina St Dallas TX 75248 Office: Dept Pediatrics Univ Tex Health Scis Center 5323 Harry Hines Blvd Dallas TX 75235

FIXMAN, MARSHALL, educator, chemist; b. St. Louis, Sept. 21, 1930; s. Benjamin and Dorothy (Finkel) F.; m. Marian Ruth Beatman, July 5, 1959 (dec. Sept. 1969); children—Laura Beth, Susan Ilene, Andrew Richard; m. Branka Ladanyi, Dec. 7, 1974. A.B., Washington U., St. Louis, 1950; Ph.D., Mass. Inst. Tech., 1954. Jewett postdoctoral fellow chemistry Yale, 1953-54; instr. chemistry Harvard, 1956-59; sr. fellow Mellon Inst., Pitts., 1959-61; prof. chemistry, dir. Inst. Theoretical Sci., U. Oreg., 1961-64, prof. chemistry, research asso. inst., 1964-65; prof. chemistry Yale, New Haven, 1965-79; prof. chemistry and physics Colo. State U., Ft. Collins, 1979—. Asso. editor: Jour. Chem. Physics, 1962-64, Jour. Phys. Chemistry, 1970-74, Macromolecules, 1970-74. Served with AUS, 1954-56. Fellow Alfred P. Sloan Found., 1961-63; recipient Governor's award Oreg. Mus. Sci. and Industry, 1964. Mem. Nat. Acad. Scis., Am. Acad. Arts and Scis., Am. Chem. Soc. (award pure chemistry 1964), Am. Phys. Soc. (high polymer physics award 1980), Fedn. Am. Scientists. Address: Dept of Chemistry Colo State U Fort Collins CO 80523

FIXX, JAMES FULLER, editor, writer; b. N.Y.C., Apr. 23, 1932; s. Calvin Henry and Marlys (Fuller) F.; m. Mary J. Durling, June 11, 1957 (div. 1973); children: Paul, John, Elizabeth, Stephen. Student, Ind. U., 1950-52; B.A., Oberlin Coll., 1957. Reporter, Sarasota (Fla.) Jour., 1957-58; feature editor Saturday Rev., 1958-66; exec. editor McCall's, 1966-67, editor, 1967-69; sr. editor Life, 1969-71; articles editor Audience mag., 1971-72; mng. editor Horizon, 1974-76; cons. Pres.'s Council on Phys. Fitness and Sports, 1979—. Author: Games for the Superintelligent, 1972, More Games for the Superintelligent, 1976, The Complete Book of Running, 1977, Solve It!, 1978, Jim Fixx's Second Book of Running, 1979, Jackpot!, 1982. Mem. Conn. Gov.'s Com. on Fitness, 1980—. Home: 14 Knoll St Riverside CT 06878

FJELLMAN, ANEL GILBERT, bishop; b. Cedar Rapids, Iowa, Apr. 27, 1917; s. Anders Gustaf and Huldah C. (Johnson) F.; m. Lorine Cecilia Hoeger, Dec. 28, 1944; children: Ruth, Jonathan. B.A., Augustana Coll., Rock Island, Ill., 1942, M.Div., 1945; D.D. hon., Pacific Luth. U., Tacoma, 1963. Ordained to ministry Lutheran Ch. in Am., 1945; pastor St. Michael's Ch., Sun Valley, Calif., 1945-51, Good Sheperd Ch., Duluth, Minn., 1952-55; dir. Bd. Am. Missions, Los Angeles, 1955-62; bishop Pacific N.W. synod. Luth. Ch. in Am., Seattle, 1963-83; dir. Pacific Luth. Sem. and Univ., 1963-83. Mem. Wash. Asn. Chs. (pres. 1965-67), Luth. Student Assn. (pres. 1941-42). Democrat. Club: Swedish (Seattle). Home: 3217 30th Ave W Seattle WA 08199

FJELLMAN, CARL GUSTAF, organization executive; b. Cedar Rapids, Iowa, May 7, 1919; s. Anders Gustaf and Huldah Cornelia (Johnson) F.; m. Carolyn Elizabeth Schock, June 28, 1945; children: Susan Babette, Thomas Conrad. Student, State U. Iowa, 1937-38; B.A., Augustana Coll., Rock Island, Ill., 1941, L.H.D., 1967; B.D., Augustana Theol. Sem., 1945, U. Calif. at Berkeley, 1946; Ph.D., Drew U., 1955; Litt. D., Upsala Coll., 1976. Ordained to ministry Lutheran Ch., 1945; pastor, Alameda, Cal., 1945-47; mem. faculty Upsala Coll., East Orange, N.J., 1947—, v.p., dean coll., 1951-65, acting pres., 1965-66, pres., 1966-75, chancellor, 1975-76. Exec. dir. Turrell Fund, 1976—. Office: 33 Evergreen Pl East Orange NJ 07018

FJELSTAD, RALPH SYLVESTER, polit. scientist; b. Emmons, Minn., Nov. 12, 1915; s. Rudolf Malvin and Gena (Loken) F.; m. Margaret Dorothy Haugseth, Dec. 30, 1941; children—Mary, Carol, Paul. B.A., Concordia Coll., 1937; student, U. Minn., 1938-39; Ph.D., Northwestern U., 1948. Dir. personnel ordnance dept. Ill. Ordnance Plant, Carbondale, Ill., 1941-43; Edward C. Congdon Found., prof. govt. Carleton Coll., 1948—; Cons. Small Bus. Adminstrn., 1958; chmn. state Constl. Revision Com., 1962-63; cons. examiner Commn. on Instns. Higher Edn., N. Central Assn., 1967-77, mem. commn., 1970-74. Mem. Northfield Community Chest, 1954-57, pres., 1956-57; sec. Northfield City Charter Commn., 1958-61; mem. Northfield Sch. Bd., 1963-69. Classification specialist USAAF, 1943-46. Norman Walt Harris fellow polit. sci. Northwestern U., 1939-41; faculty fellow Fund for Advancement Edn., 1952-53; study Norwegian Parliament under travel grant Louis W. and Maude Hill Family Found., 1961. Mem. Am. Polit. Sci. Assn., Midwest Conf. Polit. Scientists. Republican. Home: 909 S Division St Northfield MN 55057

FLACCUS, EDWARD, biology educator; b. Lansdowne, Pa., Feb. 3, 1921; s. Louis William and Laura Lynne (Kimball) F.; m. Sarah Emlen, Mar. 15, 1947; children: Jennifer Ann, Chrisipher Edward, Lynnette Marie. B.S., Haverford Coll., 1942; M.S., U. N.H., 1952; Ph.D., Duke U., 1959. Relief worker Am. Friends Service Com., Germany(British Zone), 1946-47; tchr. High Mowing Sch., Wilton, N.H., 1948-50, Loomis Sch., Windsor, Conn., 1951-55; asst. assoc. prof. U. Minn.-Duluth, 1958-68; vis. scientist Brookhaven Nat. Lab., Upton, N.Y., 1968-69, SUNY-Stony Brook, 1968-69; prof. biology Bennington (Vt.) Coll., 1969—. Author: North Country Cabin, 1979. Recipient Student Faculty award U. Minn., 1961; NSF fellow, 1957-58. Fellow AAAS; mem. Ecol. Soc. Am., Bot. Soc. Am., N.Y. Acad. Sci., Sigma Xi. Quaker. Home: 110 Putnam St Bennington VT 05201 Office: Bennington Coll Bennington VT 05201

FLACH, VICTOR H., designer, educator; b. Portland, Oreg., May 31, 1929; s. Victor H. and Eva M. (Huget) F. Student of, Jack Wilkinson, W.R. Hovey; B.S., U. Oreg., 1952, M.F.A., 1957; postgrad., U. Pitts., 1959-65. Archtl., elec. engring. and cartographic draftsman with various cos. and U.S. govt. agy., 1948-62; teaching fellow, curator Henry Clay Frick Fine Arts Dept. and Gallery, U. Pitts., 1959-63; docent Frank Lloyd Wright's Fallingwater, Western Pa. Conservancy, 1963-64; prof. art, design, painting, theory and history U. Wyo., Laramie, 1965—; participant R. Buckminster Fuller Geodesic Prototype Projects, 1953, 59; interviewer Heritage series TV program Sta. PBS-TV, 1965; cons. Nat. Symposium on Role of Studio Arts in Higher Edn., U. Oreg., 1967. Participant: various TV programs including Arts in Practice series, 1971-77; designer multi-walled murals, U. Oreg., Eugene, 1952, Rainbow Club, 1954, Clear Lake Sch., Eugene, 1956, Sci. Center, U. Wyo., Laramie, 1967, one-man and group shows of paintings, photographs, exptl. films and drawings, 1949—; Author and editor: IJHTBIW20 Poems, 1949, 12 New Painters, 1953, IN/SERT Active Anthology for the Creative, 1955-62, Gloss of the Four Universal Forms, 1959, The Anatomy of the Canvas, 1961, The Eye's Mind, 1964, By These Presents, 1975, The Stage, 1978, Contra/verses Selected Poems, 1980, Contextualist Manifesto, 1982; contbr. poems, articles and photographs to lit. jours., 1949—. Served with U.S. Army, 1953-55. Office: Dept Art U Wyo Laramie WY 82071

FLACK, AUDREY, artist, educator; b. Bklyn., May 30, 1931; d. Morris and Jeannette (Flack) F.; m. H. Robert Marcus, June 7, 1970; children—Melissa, Hannah. Grad., Cooper Union U., 1951; B.F.A., Yale U., 1952. Instr. anatomy N.Y. U., 1964-70; instr. drawing and painting Pratt Inst., 1963-70; instr. drawing, painting Sch. of Visual Arts, 1969-72; prof. art U. Bridgeport, 1975—. One-woman shows include, Roko Gallery, 1959-63, French and Co., N.Y.C., 1972, Louis K. Meisel Gallery, N.Y.C., 1974, 76-78, Joseloff Gallery, U. Hartford, Conn., 1974, Carlson Gallery, U. Bridgeport, 1975, group exhibitions include, Riverside Mus., 1969, Whitney Mus., 1970, 78, Wadsworth Athaneum, Hartford, 1974, Nat. Gallery Australia, Canberra, 1977-78; represented in permanent collections including, Met. Mus. Art, N.Y.C., Mus. Modern Art, N.Y.C., Guggenheim Mus., N.Y.C., Whitney Mus. Am. Art, St. Louis Mus. Art, Allen Meml. Art Mus., Oberlin, Ohio, Nat. Gallery, Canberra, Australia, Melbourne (Australia) Mus.; represented by, Louis K. Meisel Gallery, N.Y.C. Address: care Louis K Meisel Gallery 141 Prince St New York City NY 10012 *A new vision is a threat to the established order of things. The truly original artist who is breaking the boundaries of art history will meet with great resistance. It is important to overcome this resistance and survive in one's life and work.*

FLACK, JAMES MONROE, former business executive; b. Baxterville, Miss., Aug. 29, 1913; s. Jesse James and Lenora (Lucas) F.; m. Hertha E. Eisenmenger, Aug. 30, 1941; children: James Monroe, Sonya Karen, Robert Frank, Suzanne Margaret. B.S., Delta State U., 1935; M.Div., Yale U., 1942; postgrad., Harvard U., 1952. Prin. Shaw (Miss.) High Sch., 1935-39; with employee relations dept. Standard Oil Co. of N.J., 1946; officer, dir. subs. Textron, Inc., 1946-53; v.p., dir. Indian Head, Inc., 1953—, vice chmn., 1972-74. Served as lt. comdr. USN, 1942-45. Clubs: N.Y. Athletic, Yale of N.Y.C., Red Fox Country, Tyron (N.C.) Country. Home: 165 Wilderness Rd Tryon NC 28782

FLACK, JOE FENLEY, county and municipal official, former insurance executive; b. Menard, Tex., Feb. 23, 1921; s. Frank H. and Evelyn (Fenley) F.; m. Ann Tarry, Jan. 21, 1945; children: Kate T., Joan E., Joe Fenley. B.B.A., U. Tex., 1943. C.P.A., Tex. Acct. Ernst & Ernst (C.P.A.s), Houston, 1946-47; with Am. Gen. Ins. Co., 1947-81, treas., 1951-81, sr. v.p., 1968-81, also dir.; chief fin. officer, auditor Harris County and Port of Houston, 1981—; partner John L. Wortham and Son, Houston, 1947-65; chmn. bd., pres., treas., dir. Knickerbocker Corp.; v.p., dir. Md. Casualty Co., Maine Bonding & Casualty Co., Robert Hampson & Son, Ltd.; v.p., treas., dir. Am. Gen. Fire & Casualty Co., Nat. Standard Ins. Co., Am. Gen. Leasing & Finance Corp., Atlas Realty Co., Am. Gen. Investment Corp., Am. Gen. Realty Co.; v.p. Assurance Co. Am., Marasco Co., Inc., No. Ins. Co. N.Y.; dir. Am. Gen. Capital Corp., Am. Gen. Life, Tex., Am. Gen. Life Del. Exec. bd. Boy Scouts Am.; mayor pro-tem Bunker Hill Village, Tex., 1959-61, mayor, 1961-65; trustee, v.p. sch. bd. Spring Branch Ind. Sch. Dist., 1967-75; bd. dirs. Kappa Sigma Found., U. Tex., Houston chpt. Salvation Army; bd. govs. Park Plaza Hosp., Houston; mem. exec. com. U. Tex. Health Sci. Center, Houston. Served to lt. USNR, 1943-45. Mem. U. Tex. Ex-Students Assn. (exec. council, regional v.p.). Methodist. Clubs: River Oaks Country, Petroleum (Houston). Home: 3623 Ella Lee Ln Houston TX 77027 Office: PO Box 13450 Houston TX 77219

FLACK, ROBERTA, singer; b. Black Mountain, N.C., Feb. 10, 1939; d. Laron and Irene F.; m. Stephen Novosel, 1966 (div. 1972). B.A. in Music Edn, 1958. Tchr. music and English lit. pub. schs., Farmville, N.C. and, Washington, 1959-67; rec. artist Atlantic Records, 1968—. Star: ABC TV spl. The First Time Ever, 1973; Composer: (with Jesse Jackson and Joel Dorn) Go Up, Moses. Recipient Gold Record for The First Time Ever I Saw Your Face, 1972, Grammy award for song and record of year, 1972; winner Downbeat's reader poll as best female vocalist, 1971-73; Grammy award best popular female vocal for Killing Me Softly with His Song, 1973; City of Washington celebrated Roberta Flack Human Kindness Day, 1972. Mem. Sigma Delta Chi. Address: care Atlantic Records 75 Rockefeller Plaza New York NY 10019 *

FLADELAND, BETTY, historian, educator; b. Grygla, Minn., Jan. 18, 1919; d. Arne O. and Bertha (Nygaard) F. B.S., Duluth State Coll., 1940; M.A., U. Minn., 1944; Ph.D. (Rackham fellow), U. Mich., 1952. Mem. faculty Wells Coll., Aurora, N.Y., 1952-55, Central Mich. U., 1956-59, Central Mo. State Coll., 1959-62; mem. faculty So. Ill. U., Carbondale, 1962—, prof. history, 1968—; vis. prof. U. Ill., summer 1966. Author: James Gillespie Birney: Slaveholder to Abolitionist, 1955, Men and Brothers: Anglo-American Antislavery Cooperation, 1972, also articles. Recipient Anisfield-Wolf award in race relations, 1972; grantee Am. Philos. Soc., 1963, 75, Lilly Found., 1962. Mem. Am. Hist. Assn., So. Hist. Assn. (exec. council), Orgn. Am. Historians (exec. bd.), Assn. Study Afro-Am. Life and History, Norwegian-Am. Hist. Soc., Soc. Historians Early Am. Republic (adv. bd., bd. editors, pres.-elect), ACLU, Phi Beta Kappa, Phi Kappa Phi. Home: Rt 2 Carbondale IL 62901 Office: Dept of History Southern Illinois University Carbondale IL 62901

FLAGELLO, EZIO DOMENICO, basso; b. N.Y.C., Jan. 28, 1932; s. Dionisio and Genoveffa (Casiello) F.; children: Genoveffa, Dante, Josine, Christine. Student, Manhattan Sch. Music, U. Perruggia, Italy. Pres. Opus Enterprises, Inc.; lectr. master classes numerous univs. Leading roles as basso at, Met. Opera, N.Y.C.; appeared major opera houses throughout world, including, La Scala, Milan, Italy, Vienna (Austria) State Opera, Berlin Opera; performed at opening night inaugural opera, Met. Opera, inaugural performance, Philharmonic Hall, Lincoln Center, N.Y.C.; rec. artist, RCA Victor, Columbia Deutschegrammaphon, Decca/London, Delhi, Scope, Internos, Musical Heritage Series. Served with U.S. Army, 1952-54. Recipient Grammy award Alumni award Evander Childs High Sch., N.Y.C., award Manhattan Sch. Music; Fulbright fellow. Roman Catholic. Home and Office: 2005 Samontee Rd Jacksonville FL 32211

FLAHERTY, DANIEL LEO, clergyman, editor; b. Chgo., July 29, 1929; s. Daniel Leo and Marguerite (Pauly) F. Student, Xavier U., 1950-51; A.B., Loyola U., Chgo., 1952, M.A., 1957; Ph.L., West Baden (Ind.) Coll., 1954, S.T.L., 1961; postgrad., Northwestern U., 1959-60. Joined Soc. of Jesus, 1947; ordained priest Roman Catholic Ch., 1960; book editor America, 1962-65, exec. editor, 1965-71; sec. America Press, Inc., 1965-71; mem. bd. Catholic Book Club, 1962-71; exec. dir. Loyola U. Press, Chgo., 1971-73, 79-80, dir., 1980—. Author: (with W.D. Ciszek) With God in Russia, 1964, He Leadeth Me, 1973; editor: National Jesuit News, 1972-73. Exec. sec. Chgo. Province Assembly, 1972-73; provincial Chgo. Province, S.J., 1973-79; Mem. selection bd. Campion award, 1962-71; Bd. dirs. John La Farge Inst., 1970-71; bd. dirs. Appeal of Conscience Found., 1967-72; trustee Loyola U., Chgo., 1970-73, 80—, vice-chmn., 1971-73, 80—; trustee U. Detroit, 1970-73, chmn. bd., 1972-73; trustee Loyola U., New Orleans, 1980—, Loyola Acad., Wilmette, Ill., 1980—. Address: 3441 N Ashland Ave Chicago IL 60657

FLAHERTY, JOHN P., state justice; b. Pitts., Nov. 19, 1931; s. John Paul and Mary G. (McLaughlin) F. B.A. in Philosophy, Duquesne U., Pitts., 1953; J.D., U. Pitts., 1958. Bar: Pa. 1958. Pvt. practice, Pitts., 1958-73; mem. faculty Carnegie-Mellon U., 1958-73; judge Ct. Common Pleas Allegheny County, 1973-79, pres. judge civil div., 1978-79; justice Supreme Ct. Pa., 1979—. Served as officer AUS, 1953-55. Named Man of Year in Law and Govt. Greater Pitts. Jaycees, 1978. Mem. Pa. Acad. Sci. (Disting. Alumnus 1977, chmn. hon. exec. bd. 1979—), Pa. Soc., Mil. History Soc. Ireland, Irish Soc. Pitts., Friendly Sons St. Patrick, Irish-Am. Cultural Inst., Gaelic Arts Soc., Knights Equity, Ancient Order Hibernians, Am. Legion. Home: 901 William Penn Ct Pittsburgh PA 15221 Office: 6 Gateway Center Pittsburgh PA 15222 *The law is the energy of the living world, and although developed and defined by the judiciary in our Anglo-American society, it is applied and is derived by and from the people. It exists only to protect one person from being hurt, physically or economically, by another. Serious problems face our age. In the final analysis, the judiciary must accomodate the various solutions which will be forthcoming. I hope that my brothers have the foresight and the stamina to accomodate what might be quite novel innovations in the law, which is the living energy, to make this world a place in which it's worth living, since that is the function of the law. Every case involves people. There is no such thing as a small case*

FLAHERTY, MICHAEL, lawyer, savings and loan executive; b. Fitchburg, Mass., Apr. 3, 1945; s. Paul J. and Loretta (Carroll) F.; m. Bonnie Darcy, July 26, 1969. B.A., Boston U., 1968; J.D., Cath. U. Am., 1971. Bar: D.C. 1972, U.S. Supreme Ct. 1976. Asst. librarian U.S. Ho. of Reps., Washington, 1969-72; counsel Subcom. on Domestic Fin., Com. on Banking, Currency and Housing, U.S. Ho. of Reps., 1972-75; gen. counsel House Com. on Banking, Fin. and Urban Affairs, 1975-82; chmn. bd. So. Calif. Savs.; v.p. Wright Patman Fed. Credit Union; pres. Nat. Trust Group Inc. Sec., bd. govs. Nat. Democratic Club. Mem. Am. Bar Assn., Fed. Bar Assn. (chmn. banking law sect.). Democrat. Roman Catholic. Home: 126 Kentucky Ave SE Washington DC 20003 Office: 9100 Wilshire Blvd Beverly Hills CA 90212

FLAHERTY, TINA SANTI, corporate communications executive; b. Memphis, May 18; d. Clement Alexander and Dale (Pendergrast) Santi; m. William Edward Flaherty, Feb. 22, 1975. B.A., Memphis State U., 1961; hon. Doctorate, St. John's U., 1979. Commentator guest interview program Sta. WMC-TV, Memphis, 1960-61; newscaster, commentator Sta. WHER, Memphis, 1961-62; community relations specialist Western Electric Co., N.Y.C., 1964-66; v.p. pub. relations div. Grey Advt., N.Y.C., 1966-72; dep. dir. corporate relations Colgate-Palmolive Co., N.Y.C., 1972-75, dir. corp. relations, 1975-76, corp. v.p., v.p. in charge of communications, 1976-83; v.p. pub. affairs GTE Corp., Stamford, Conn., 1984—. Gen. chmn. YWCA-N.Y.C., Salute to Women in Business, 1979; former chmn. Bus. Council; chmn. UN Decade for Women; bd. dirs. Nat. Jr. Achievement, 1978—, Nat. Girls Club, 1979—, Hugh O'Brian Youth Found.; v.p., bd. dirs. Women's Forum, 1979; mem. White House Pub. Affairs Advisors. Recipient Jr. Achievement Colgate Meml. award, 1984; Named One of 8 Outstanding Women in Bus. and Labor Women's Equity Action League, 1978; One of N.Y.C.'s Outstanding Women of Achievement NCCJ, 1978; One of 100 Top Corp. Women Bus. Week, 1976. Mem. Com. of 200. Home: 50 E 89th St New York NY 10028 Office: One Stamford Forum Stamford CT 06904 *Persistence alone is omnipotent.*

FLAHIFF, GEORGE BERNARD CARDINAL, former archbishop of Winnipeg; b. Paris, Ont., Can., Oct. 26, 1905; s. John James and Eleanor Rose (Fleming) F. B.A., St. Michael's Coll., U. Toronto, 1926; student, U. Strasbourg, France, 1930-31; Dipl. Archiviste-Paleographe, Ecole Nat. des Chartes, Paris, 1935, U. Seattle, 1965, U. Notre Dame, 1969, U. Man., 1969, U. Windsor, 1970, U. Winnipeg, 1972, U. Toronto, 1972, U. St. Francis Xavier, 1973, Laval U., 1974, St. Bonaventure U., 1975, U. St. Thomas, Houston, 1977. Ordained priest Roman Catholic Ch., 1930; prof. medieval history Pontifical Inst. Medieval Studies and U. Toronto, 1935-54, sec. inst., 1943-51; superior-gen. Basilian Fathers, 1954-61; archbishop of, Winnipeg, Can., 1961-82. Mem. Sacred Congregation for Religious. Named to Coll. Cardinals, 1969; Decorated companion Order of Can., 1974. Home: 39 Bishop's Lane Winnipeg MB R3R 0A8 Canada Office: 50 Stafford St Winnipeg MB R3M 2V7 Canada *

FLAMSON, RICHARD JOSEPH, III, banker; b. Los Anageles, Feb. 2, 1929; s. Richard J. and Mildred (Jones) F.; m. Arden Black, Oct. 5, 1951; children: Richard Joseph IV, Scott Arthur, Michael Jon, Leslie Arden. B.A., Claremont Men's Coll., 1951; cert. Pacific Coast Banking Sch., U. Wash., 1962. With Security Pacific Nat. Bank, Los Angeles, 1955—, v.p., 1962-69, sr. v.p., 1969-70, exec. v.p. corp. banking dept., 1970-73, vice-chmn., 1973-78, pres., chief exec. officer, 1978-81, chmn., chief exec. officer, 1981—, dir.; vice-chmn. Security Pacific Corp., 1973-78, pres., 1978-81, chief exec. officer, 1978—, chmn., 1981—; dir. Northrop Corp., Kaufman and Broad. Trustee Claremont Men's Coll. 1st lt. AUS, 1951-53. Mem. Res. City Bankers, Robert Morris Assocs., Town Hall, Stock Exchange Club. Clubs: Caif. Los Angeles Country; Balboa Bay, Balboa Yacht (Newport Beach, Calif.). Office: Security Pacific Corp 333 S Hope St Los Angeles CA 90071

FLANAGAN, ALVIN GEORGE, broadcasting executive; b. Oaji, Calif., Jan. 1, 1915; m. Effie Mims Davis. B.A., U. Fla., 1941. Pres. Nafi Broadcasting Co., Los Angeles, 1955-62, Mullins Broadcasting Co., Denver, 1962-69, Combined Communications, 1969-78, Gannett Broadcasting Co., 1978-83; chmn. Gannett Broadcasting Group, Atlanta, 1983—. Served to capt. USMC, 1942-45. Recipient Disting. Alumnus award U. Fla., 1981, Alvin G. Flanagan Broadcast News Center award U. Fla., 1982, Alvin G. Flanagan Endowment Fundaward U. Boulder, 1980. Home: 3355 Chatam Rd NW Atlanta GA 30305 Office: Gannett Broadcasting Group 1611 W Peachtree St NE Atlanta GA 30309

FLANAGAN, BARBARA, journalist; b. Des Moines; d. John Merrill and Marie (Barnes) F.; m. Earl S. Sanford, 1966. Student, Drake U., 1942-43. With promotion dept. Mpls. Times, 1945-47; reporter Mpls. Tribune, 1947-58; women's editor, spl. writer Mpls. Star and Tribune, 1958-65; columnist Mpls. Star, 1965—. Author: Ovation, Minneapolis. Mem., exec. com. Minn. Gov.'s Bicentennial Commn.; hon. mem. bd. Minn. Valley Historic Preservation Projects.; trustee Am. Swedish Inst. Mem. Mpls. Soc. Fine Arts (life), Mpls. Inst. Arts (founding mem. Minn. Arts Forum), Kappa Alpha Theta, Sigma Delta Chi.

Episcopalian. Home: 1510 Mt Curve Ave Minneapolis MN 55403 Office: Mpls Star 5th and Portland Sts Minneapolis MN 55415

FLANAGAN, CARROLL EDWARD, mathematics educator; b. nr. Clifford, Wis., Dec. 18, 1911; s. William Dennis and Elizabeth Bertha (Brueske) F.; m. Kathrine G. Snodgrass, June 3, 1939; children: Carolyn (Mrs. Warren Schroeder), Thomas B. Student, U. Wis., Madison, 1929-30, Ph.M., 1943, Ph.D., 1960, B.E., 1933. Prin. elementary sch., Waukau, Wis., 1933-36, tchr. math. jr. and sr. high sch., Merrill, Wis., 1936-42; instr. math Superior (Wis.) State Tchrs. Coll., 1942-45; welder Walter Butler Shipbuilders, Superior, Wis., 1945-46; tchr. edn. Milton (Wis.) Coll., 1946; prof. math. U. Wis.-Whitewater, 1946-82, part-time lectr., 1982—, chmn. dept., 1952-81; Tech. cons. math. Nigeria Tchr. Edn. Project U. Wis.-Ford Found., Ilorin, Nigeria, 1965-68. Editor: Wis. Tchr. Math, 1953-56. Pres. ARC, Whitewater, 1962-64; Trustee, treas. U. Wis.-Whitewater Found. Mem. Am. Math. Soc., Math. Assn. Am. (Wis. pres. 1948-49), Nat. Council Tchrs. Math., Wis. Math. Council, Math. Educators Wis., Assn. U. Wis. Faculty, Sigma Tau Gamma, Phi Delta Kappa. Roman Catholic. Clubs: K.C., Kiwanian (pres. 1969-70). Home: 281 N Park St Whitewater WI 53190 *To be of service to others has always been a guiding goal in my life.*

FLANAGAN, DENNIS, editor; b. N.Y.C., July 22, 1919; s. John Richard and Nan (Apotheker) F.; m. Geraldine A. Lux, Jan. 9, 1948; children: Cara Louise, John Gerard; m. Ellen Raskin; Oct. 17, 1966. A.B., Mich., 1941. Staff writer Life mag., 1941-47; mng. editor Scientific Am., 1947-50, editor, 1950—; Vis. fellow St. Cross Coll., Oxford, 1974—. Trustee Marine Biol. Lab., Woods Hole, Mass., 1975—. Recipient Outstanding Achievement award U. Mich., 1961, Kalinga prize UN Ednl., Sci. and Cultural Orgn., 1982. Fellow Am. Acad. Arts and Scis.; mem. Am. Soc. Mag. Editors (pres. 1977-79). Home: 12 Gay St New York NY 10014 Office: 415 Madison Ave New York NY 10017

FLANAGAN, EDWARD MICHAEL, JR., business executive, former army officer; b. Saugerties, N.Y., July 13, 1921; s. Edward Michael and Marie (Sinnott) F.; m. Marguerite Farrell, Dec. 26, 1945; children—Edward Michael III, Maureen Ann, Terrence Girard, Patricia Marie and Kathleen Mary (twins). B.S., U.S. Mil. Acad., 1943; grad., U.S. Army Command and Gen. Staff Coll., Ft. Leavenworth, Kans., 1946, Armed Forces Staff Coll., Norfolk, Va., 1955, U.S. Army War Coll., Carlisle Barracks, Pa., 1959; M.A., Boston U., 1960. Commd. 2d lt. U.S. Army, 1943, advanced through grades to lt. gen., 1972; comdg. gen. (U.S. Army John F. Kennedy Center for Mil. Assistance and), comdt., Ft. Bragg, N.C., 1968-71, comdg. gen., Ft. Riley, Kans., 1971-73; comptroller of Army, 1973; dep. comdg. gen. (8th U.S. Army), Korea, 1974-75, comdr., San Francisco, 1975-78, ret., 1978; bus. mgr. Dowling Law Firm, Beaufort, S.C., 1978—. Author: The Angels, A History of the 11th Airborne Division, 1948; Contbr. articles to profl. jours. Decorated D.S.M. with oak leaf cluster, Legion of Merit with oak leaf cluster, Bronze Star, Air medal with oak leaf cluster, Army Commendation medal; Vietnam Nat. Order of Merit (knight class); Vietnam Army Distinguished Service Order 1st class; Vietnam Gallantry Cross with gold star; Vietnam Medal of Honor; Korean Order of Nat. Security Merit. Roman Catholic. Home: Parade Rest 2 Oyster Catcher Rd Beaufort SC 29902 *Leadership: Be hard but fair with compassion.*

FLANAGAN, EDWIN WALLACE, financial and trust company executive; b. Sacramento, Dec. 18, 1923; s. Edwin J. and Alta Irene (Willard) F.; m. Nora McCabe, Sept. 3, 1951; children—Frank, Maureen, Peggy, Timothy. B.A., U. So. Calif., 1948; exec. devel. mgmt. program, Stanford U., 1961. With Pacific Finance Corp., 1948-66; pres. Trans Can. Credit Corp. Ltd., 1966-75, dir., 1966—; with Traders Group Ltd., Toronto, Can., 1966—, exec. v.p. finance group, 1974-76, pres., 1976—, also dir.; vice chmn. bd., dir. Guaranty Trust Co. Can. Served with USMCR, 1942-46. Clubs: Bayview Country, Canadian, Downtown Tennis. Home: 2993 Elbow Dr SW Calgary AB T2S 2J3 Canada Office: Gulf Canada Sq 401 9th Ave SW Calgary AB Canada

FLANAGAN, EUGENE JOHN THOMAS, tobacco company executive; b. N.Y.C., Mar. 27, 1923; s. Thomas F. and Louise V. (Verhoff) F.; m. Lucette A. Stumberg, Sept. 7, 1951; children: Claire (Mrs. David Duhaime), Janet (Mrs. Emory Morsberger), Anne, Thomas, Gail. B.S., Yale U., 1946; J.D., Harvard U., 1948; M.B.A., NYU, 1957, LL.M., 1960. Bar: N.Y. bar 1949. Asso., partner Bartels & Hartung (and predecessor firms), N.Y.C., 1949-56, Conboy, Hewitt, O'Brien & Boardman, 1958-71; asst. sec. The Best Foods, Inc., N.Y.C., 1956-58; asso. gen. counsel Philip Morris Inc., N.Y.C., 1970—, sec., 1971—, v.p., 1978—; adj. prof. law NYU Sch. Law, 1960—. Chmn. New Rochelle Youth Bur., 1966; mem. New Rochelle Bd. Appeals on Zoning, 1971-74; Bd. dirs. NYU Alumni Fedn. Served with AUS, 1943-46. Recipient NYU Alumni Meritorious Service award, 1973. Mem. Am. Soc. Corp. Secs. (chmn., chief exec. officer 1982-83), Am., N.Y. State bar assns., Assn. Bar City N.Y., NYU Grad. Bus. Sch. Alumni Assn. (pres. 1963-65), Am. Arbitration Assn. (nat. panel). Clubs: Westchester Country (Rye, N.Y.) (gov., mem. exec. com.); N.Y. Univ. (N.Y.C.) (pres. 1979-81). Home: 153 Dorchester Rd Scarsdale NY 10583 Office: 100 Park Ave New York NY 10017

FLANAGAN, FIONNULA MANON, actress, writer, producer; b. Dublin, Ireland, Dec. 10, 1941; came to U.S., 1968; d. Terence Niall and Rosanna (McGuirk) F.; m. Garrett O'Connor, Nov. 26, 1972. C.I.H.E., U. Fribourg, Switzerland, 1962; student, Abbey Theatre Sch., Dublin, 1964-66. Pres. The Rejoycing Co., 1978—; fellow Study Center for Orgn. and Leadership Authority, 1976—. Stage appearances include: Ulysses in Nighttown, N.Y.C., 1974, Lovers, 1968; author, actress one-woman shows: James Joyce's Women, 1977 (Los Angeles Drama Critics award, San Francisco Theatre Critics award, Drama-Logue award); films include: In The Region of Ice; films: Patman, 1980, James Joyce's Women, 1984; TV appearances include: Rich Man Poor Man, 1976 (Emmy award for most outstanding support role 1976), How The West Was Won, 1977-79 (Emmy nominee 1978). Mem. Actors' Equity, Screen Actors' Guild, AFTRA, Irish Actors Equity.

FLANAGAN, FRANCIS DENNIS, corporate executive; b. Dunkirk, N.Y., Mar. 6, 1912; s. Mark Francis and Margaret (Ready) F.; m. Margaret L. McNamara, Nov. 23, 1939; children—Sheila Flanagan Cones, Mark F., Martha Flanagan Casper, Catherine, Nora Flanagan Nutter, Moira Flanagan Cates, Dennis F., Molly, Patricia. Ph.B., Canisius Coll., Buffalo, 1933; LL.B., Georgetown U., 1938. Bar: D.C. bar 1937. Spl. agt. FBI, 1939-44; chief investigator war investigating com. U.S. Senate, 1944-46, asst. chief counsel, then chief counsel permanent subcom. investigations, 1946-54; asst. v.p. W.R. Grace & Co., 1954-67, v.p., mgr. Washington ops., 1967—. Mem. Soc. Former Agts. FBI, Friendly Sons St. Patrick, Washington Bar Assn. Clubs: Univ. (Washington); Congressional Country (Bethesda, Md.). Home: 2838 28th St NW Washington DC 20008 Office: WR Grace & Co 1511 K St NW Washington DC 20005

FLANAGAN, JAMES LOTON, electrical engineer. B.S. in Elec. Engring, Miss. State U., 1948, S.M., M.I.T., 1950, Sc.D., 1955. Mem. elec. engring. faculty Miss. State U., 1950-52; mem. tech. staff Bell Labs., Murray Hill, N.J., 1957-61, head dept. speech and auditory research, 1961-67, head dept. acoustics research, 1967—. Author: Speech Analysis, Synthesis and Perception, 1972; contbr. numerous articles to profl. jours. Mem. evaluation panel Nat. Bur. Standards/NRC, 1972-77; mem. adv. panel on White House tapes U.S. Dist. Ct. for D.C., 1973-74; bd. govs. Am. Inst. Physics, 1974-77; mem. sci. adv. bd. Callier Center, U. Tex., Dallas, 1974-76; mem. sci. adv. panel on voice communications Nat. Security Agy., 1975-77; mem. sci. adv. bd. div. communications research Inst. Def. Analyses, 1975-77. Recipient Disting. Service award in sci. Am. Speech and Hearing Assn., 1977. Fellow IEEE (mem. fellow selection com. 1979-81), Acoustical Soc. Am. (asso. editor Speech Communication 1959-62, exec. council 1970-73, v.p. 1976-77, pres. 1978-79); mem. Acoustics, Speech and Signal Processing Soc. (v.p. 1967-68, pres. 1969-70, Achievement award 1970, Soc. award 1976), Nat. Acad. Engring. of Nat. Acad. Scis. U.S. and fgn. patentee in field. Office: 600 Mountain Ave Murray Hill NJ 07974

FLANAGAN, JOHN CLEMANS, research institute executive; b. Armour, S.D., Jan. 7, 1906; s. Charles Gibbons and Gertrude (Clemans) F.; m. Katherine Ross, Jan. 18, 1930; children: John Ross, Scott Calhoun; m. Ruth Colonna; June 21, 1962. B.S., U. Wash., 1929; M.A., 1932; Ph.D., Harvard U., 1934. Diplomate: in personnel psychology Am. Bd. Examiners in Profl. Psychology. Tchr. sci. and math. Renton (Wash.) High Sch., 1929-30; tchr. math. Cleveland High Sch., Seattle, 1930-32; asst. in edn. Harvard U., 1934-35; lectr. Columbia Tchrs. Coll., 1936-41; assoc. dir. Coop. Test Service, N.Y.C., 1935-41; prof. psychology U. Pitts., 1946-72; chmn. bd. Am. Inst. Research, Pitts., 1946—. Served to col. USAAF, 1941-46; dir. aviation psychology program. Decorated Legion of Merit, 1946; recipient Raymond F. Longacre award Aero. Med. Assn., 1954, Edward Lee Thorndike award Am. Psychol. Assn., 1972, Profl. Practice award, 1982, Distinguished Contbn. award, 1976; Meritorious Contbn. award Phi Delta Kappa, 1977; Disting. Profl. Service award Ednl. Testing Service, 1978. Mem. AAAS (chmn. edn. sect.), Am. Ednl. Research Assn. (v.p. 1973), Am. Psychol. Assn. (pres. div. eval. and measurement 1956-57, pres. div. mil. psychology 1961-62, div. gen. psychology 1963-64, div. ednl. psychology 1969-70), Am. Statis. Assn., N.Y. Acad. Scis. (v.p. 1936), Psychometric Soc. (pres. 1952), Sigma Xi. Home: 1290 Sharon Park Dr Menlo Park CA 94025 Office: PO Box 1113 Palo Alto CA 94302

FLANAGAN, JOHN THEODORE, educator; b. St. Paul, Jan. 15, 1906; s. John Joseph and Emma (Hamm) F.; m. Virginia McGuigan, July 24, 1929; children: Sheila Virginia Flanagan Paulsen, Moira Ellen Flanagan Harris, Cathleen Coyla. B.A., U. Minn., 1927, M.A., 1928, Ph.D., 1935. Instr. English, U. N.D., 1928-29; instr., asst. prof. U. Minn., 1929-45; prof. English, So. Methodist U., 1945-46; asso. prof. English, U. Ill., Urbana, 1946-49, prof., 1949-72, prof. emeritus, 1972—; vis. prof. Ind. U., summer 1949, Kyoto U., summer 1952; Fulbright lectr. U. Bordeaux, 1952-53, univs. Liege, Ghent, Brussels, 1960-61; vis. lectr. U. Moscow, U. Leningrad, 1963. Author: James Hall, Literary Pioneer of the Ohio Valley, 1941, The American Way, 1953; editor: America Is West, 1945, (with Arthur Palmer Hudson) Folklore in American Literature, 1958, (with Clarence Brown) American Literature, A College Survey, 1961, Profile of Vachel Lindsay, 1970, Edgar Lee Masters: The Spoon River Poet and His Critics, 1974, Theodore C. Blegen, A. Memoir, 1977, (with Cathleen C. Flanagan) A Bibliography of American Folklore, 1950-74, 1977, (with R.B. Downs and H.W. Scott) Memorable Americans 1750-1950, 1983; editorial bd.: Am. Lit., 1968-71; contbr.: chpt. on folklore to Am. Lit. Scholarship, An Annual, 1965-74; articles and revs. to lit. and hist. jours. Recipient award for contbns. Soc. Study of Midwestern Lit., Mich. State U., 1977; Newberry Library fellow, 1943-44; Guggenheim fellow, 1943-44. Mem. Modern Lang. Assn., Minn. Hist. Soc., Ill. Hist. Soc., Soc. Midland Authors, Phi Beta Kappa. Republican. Clubs: Caxton (Chgo.); Dial (Urbana). Home: 705 W Michigan Ave Urbana IL 61801

FLANAGAN, JOSEPH PATRICK, JR., lawyer; b. Wilkes-Barre, Pa., Sept. 18, 1924; s. Joseph P. and Grace B. F.; m. Mary Elizabeth Mayock, Aug. 5, 1950; children: Maureen Elizabeth Flanagan Carrol, Joseph P. B.S., U.S. Naval Acad., 1947; J.D., U. Pa., 1952. Bar: Pa. 1953, U.S. Dist. Ct. (ea. dist.) Pa. 1953, U.S. Ct. Appeals (3d cir.) 1953. Assoc. Saul, Ewing, Remick & Saul, Phila., 1952-56; ptnr. Ballard, Spahn, Andrews & Ingersoll, Phila., 1956—. Editor: Practicing Law Inst., Health Facilities Financing, 1976; editor-in-chief: U. Pa. Law Rev., 1951-52; contbr. articles to profl. jours. Bd. dirs. Phila. Com. of 70, 1952-56. Served to lt. (j.g.) USN, 1946-49. Fellow Am. Bar Found.; mem. Phila. Bar Assn. (chmn. tax exempt fin. com., past chmn. profl. edn. com., client's security fund com., fee disputes com.), Pa. Bar Assn., ABA (mem. council urban state and local govt. sect.), Pa. Bar Inst. (pres. 1983, chmn. curriculum and course planning com. 1976-83), Am. Law Inst. Republican. Roman Catholic. Clubs: Racquet of Phila., Phila. Cricket, Urban of Phila., Army Navy Country of Va.; Princeton (N.Y.C.). Home: 401 E Mill Rd Flourtown PA 19031 Office: 30 S 17th St 20th Floor Philadelphia PA 19103

FLANAGAN, MARTHA LANG, corporate secretary; b. Cin., Mar. 23, 1942; d. Gordon Walter and Alma Marie (Strobl) Lang; m. John A. Flanagan, May 8, 1982. B.S. in Fine Arts, U. Cin., 1978. Various exec. secretarial positions, 1960-75; corp. sec., asst. to pres. Cin. Enquirer, 1973—. Mem. Cin. Police Chief Communications Adv. Com., 1976—, Cin. Music Hall Centennial Com., 1976-78; mem. Cin. chpt. Am. Heart Assn. Mem. Cin. Hist. Soc., Cin. Art Mus. Republican. Roman Catholic. Office: The Cincinnati Enquirer 617 Vine St Cincinnati OH 45202

FLANAGAN, MICHAEL KENDALL, professional baseball player; b. Manchester, N.H., Dec. 16, 1951. Student, U. Mass. Pitcher Balt. Orioles (Am. League), 1975—. Recipient Cy Young award, 1979. Mem. Am. League All-Star Team, 1978. Office: care Balt Orioles Meml Stadium Baltimore MD 21218 *

FLANAGAN, NEIL, lawyer; b. Chgo., Dec. 2, 1930; s. Norris Cornelius and Virginia (Riddell) F.; m. Mary Mead, Nov. 19, 1960; children: John Mead, Margot, Nancy, Jill. B.A., Yale U., 1953; J.D., U. Mich., 1956. Bar: Ill. 1956. Assoc. Leibman, Williams, Bennett, Baird & Minow, Chgo., 1960-66, ptnr., 1966-72, Sidley & Austin, 1972—. Bd. dirs. Dr. Scholl Found., Chgo., 1973—. Served to 1st lt. AUS, 1956-59. Fellow Am. Coll. Investment Counsel; mem. ABA, Chgo. Bar Assn. Clubs: University; Law (Chgo.); Indian Hill (Winnetka). Home: 1010 Mt Pleasant Winnetka IL 60093 Office: Sidley & Austin One First Nat Plaza Chicago IL 60603

FLANAGAN, ROBERT MATTHEW, securities company executive; b. N.Y.C., Sept. 13, 1928; s. Matthew and Viola M. (Van Derveer) F.; m. Joyce F. Carlstrom, June 25, 1950; children: Robert, Stephen, Kevin. Student, CCNY, 1949-52; M.B.A., Pace U. Exec. v.p. Dean Witter & Co. Inc. (now Dean Witter Reynolds Inc.), N.Y.C., 1953—. Served with AUS, 1950-51. Home: 15 Silver Brook Rd Shewsbury NJ 07701 Office: Dean Witter Reynolds Inc 5 World Trade Ctr New York NY 10048

FLANAGAN, ROBERT MICHAEL, communications company executive; b. Springfield, Mass., Apr. 18, 1930; s. Charles Patrick and Catherine Theresa (Perry) F.; m. Mary Bossell Laird, June 9, 1956; children: Christopher, Katherine, Sarah, Martha. A.B., St. Michael's Coll., 1951; M.B.A., Harvard U., 1956. With Raytheon Co., Boston, 1956-64, ITT, 1964-71; treas. Chgo. Pneumatic Tool Co., N.Y.C., 1971-73; v.p., comptroller Western Union Telegraph Co., Upper Saddle River, N.J., 1973-79, chmn. bd., chief exec. officer, 1979—; exec. v.p. Western Union Corp., 1978-79, chmn. bd., chief exec. officer, 1979—. Served to 2d lt. AUS, 1951-54. Democrat. Clubs: Nantucket Yacht; Union League (N.Y.C.). Office: Western Union Telegraph 1 Lake St Upper Saddle River NJ 07458 *

FLANDERS, DWIGHT PRESCOTT, economist; b. Rockford, Ill., Mar. 14, 1909; s. Daniel Bailey and Lulu Iona (Nichol) F.; m. Mildred Margaret Hutchison, Aug. 27, 1939 (dec. Dec. 1978); children—James Prescott, Thomas Addison. B.A., U. Ill., Urbana, 1931, M.A., 1937; teaching certificate, Beloit (Wis.) Coll., 1934; Ph.D. in Econs, Yale U., 1939. With McLeish, Baxter & Flanders (realtors), Rockford, 1931-33; instr. U.S. history and sci. in secondary schs., Rockford, 1934-36; asst. prof. econs. Coll. Liberal Arts and Scis.; also statistics Maxwell Grad. Sch., Syracuse (N.Y.) U., 1939-42; acad. staff econs. dept. social sci. U.S. Mil. Acad., West Point, N.Y., 1942-46; mem. faculty U. Ill., Urbana, 1946—, prof. econs., 1953-77; prof. emeritus dept. econs. Coll. Commerce and Bus. Adminstrn., 1977—; prof. emeritus dept. family and consumer econs. Coll. Agr., 1980—; chmn. masters research seminar, 1947-74, cons. in field. Author: Science and Social Science, 2d edit, 1962, Status of Military Personnel as Voters, 1942, Collection Rural Real Property Taxes in Illinois, 1938; co-author: Contemporary Foreign Governments, 1946, The Conceptual Framework for a Science of Marketing, 1964; contbr. numerous articles to profl. jours. Pres. Three Lakes (Wis.) Waterfront Homeowners Assn., 1969-71, dir., 1971-75, ofcl. bd., 1975—. Served to lt. col. AUS, 1942-46. Univ. fellow U. Ill., 1936-37, Yale U., 1937-39; recipient Bronze tablet U. Ill., 1931, Excellence in Teaching award, 1977. Mem. Am., Midwest econs. assns., Royal Econ. Soc., Econometric Soc., Phi Beta Kappa, Beta Gamma Sigma (chpt. pres. 1959-61), Phi Kappa Phi, Alpha Kappa Psi. Methodist (ofcl. bd.). Club: Yale (Chgo.). Home: 719 S Foley Ave Champaign IL 61820 Office: Dept Econs U Ill Urbana IL 61801

FLANDERS, EDWARD PAUL, actor; b. Mpls., Dec. 29, 1934; s. Francis Micheal Grey and Bernice (Brown) F.; children—Scott, Suzanne, Ian. Student pub. schs. Mem. Globe Theatre company, San Diego, 1952—. Appeared in numerous plays; film appearances include The Grasshopper, 1970, The Trial of the Catonsville Nine, 1972, The Ninth Configuration, 1980; also numerous TV appearances.; (Recipient Emmy awards, Tony award, Drama Desk award.). Served with U.S. Army, 1956-58. Office: care Artists Agy 190 N Canon Dr Beverly Hills CA 90210 *

FLANDERS, HENRY JACKSON, JR., religion educator; b. Malvern, Ark., Oct. 2, 1921; s. Henry Jackson and Mae (Hargis) F.; m. Tommie Lou Pardew, Apr. 19, 1943; children: Janet Flanders Mitchell, Jack III. B.A., Baylor U., 1943; B.D., So. Bapt. Theol. Sem., 1948, Ph.D., 1950. Diplomate: ordained to ministry Baptist Ch., 1941. Asst. prof., assoc. prof. Furman U., Greenville, S.C., 1950-55, prof., chaplain, chmn. dept. religion, 1955-62; pastor First Bapt. Ch., Waco, Tex., 1962-69; prof. dept. religion Baylor U., Waco, Tex., 1969—, chmn. dept. religion, prof., 1980—; chmn., trustee Golden Gate Bapt. Theol. Sem., Mill Valley, Calif., 1956-66; chaplain Tex. Ranger Commn., 1965—; mem. exec. com. Bapt. Gen. Conv. Tex., Dallas, 1966-68. Author: (with R.W. Crapps and D.A. Smith) People of the Convenant, 1963, 73, (with Bruce Cresson) Introduction to the Bible, 1973; TV speaker: weekly program Lessons for Living, WFBC-TV, 1957-62. Trustee Baylor U., Waco, Tex., 1964-68, Hillcrest Bapt. Hosp., Waco, Tex., 1963-64; chmn. Heart of Tex. Red Cross, Waco, Tex., 1967-68; narrator Waco Cotton Palace Pageant, 1970-80. Served to 1st. lt. USAAC, 1943-45; ETO. Grantee Furman U., 1960, Baylor U., 1977, 82. Mem. Assn. Bapt. Profs. Religion (pres. 1958-59), AAUP (chpt. pres. 1973), Soc. Bibl. Lit., Am. Acad. Religion, Inst. Antiquity and Christianity, Waco Bapt. Ministerial Assn. (pres. 1967-68). Lodges: Rotary; Shriners. Home: 3820 Chateau St Waco TX 76710 Office: Baylor U Waco TX 76798 *How fortunate I am that my parents, brother, wife, and children have offered only supportive encouragement across my years. Add two public school teachers and three scholarly and challenging professors to my good fortune. Above all, the experienced presence of God in Christ made the Depression, World War II, and all other unpleasant valleys bearable, edifying, and meaningful. I am an inexpressibly grateful human being.*

FLANIGAN, PETER MAGNUS, investment banker; b. N.Y.C., June 21, 1923; s. Horace C. and Aimee Magnus F.; m. Brigid Snow; children: Brigid Snow, Sheila Magnus, Timothy Palen, Megan Adams, Robert White. B.A., Princeton U. V.p. Dillon, Read & Co. Inc., N.Y.C., 1947-69, mng. dir., 1975—; asst. to pres. The White House, Washington, 1969-74; dir. Anheuser-Busch Cos. Inc., St. Louis, Thyssen Inc., N.Y.C., Kleinworth Benson Investment Mgmt. Ltd., London. Mem. Pres. Econ. Policy Adv. Bd., Washington, 1981—; trustee Cath. U. Am., Washington, 1979—, Portsmouth (R.I.) Abbey Sch., 1978—; chmn. Silon Bolivar Found., N.Y.C., 1980—. Mem. U.S. C. of C. (mem. internat. policy com. 1978—). Clubs: Links; Anglers (N.Y.C.); Blind Brook (Purchase, N.Y.); Round Hill (Greenwich, Conn.). Office: Dillon Read & Co Inc 46 William St New York NY 10577

FLANIGAN, WILLIAM JOSEPH, physician; b. Hot Springs, Ark., June 2, 1930; s. William J. and Edith Mary (Reville) F.; m. Yvonne Robinson, Apr. 29, 1983; children: Tamara, Leslie, Steven, Nancy, Patrick. B.S., U. Ark., 1953, M.D., 1955. Mem. faculty U. Ark. Med. Center, Little Rock, 1963—, prof. medicine, 1968—, dir. transplanatation, 1963—; dir. Clin. Research Center, 1963-71; chmn. council dialysis and transplanation Nat. Kidney Found., 1974-75; chmn. Ark. Kidney Commn., 1973-77. Author books, articles in field. Served as officer M.C. USAF, 1955-59. Named. Nephrologist of Yr. Am. Soc. Extracorporeal Technicians, 1977. Fellow ACP; mem. Am. Soc. Artificial Organs, Am. Soc. Nephrology, Transplanatation Soc., So. Soc. Clin. Research, S.E. Dialysis-Transplant Soc. Office: 4301 W Markham St Little Rock AR 72212

FLANNERY, JOSEPH PATRICK, manufacturing company executive; b. Lowell, Mass., Mar. 30, 1932; s. and Mary Agnes Egan F.; m. Margaret Barrows, June 1957; children: Mary Ann, Diane, Joseph, James, David, Elizabeth. B.S. in Chemistry, Lowell Tech. Inst., 1953; M.B.A., Harvard U., 1955. With Uniroyal Chem. Co., 1959-79, dir. mktg., 1972-75, pres., 1975-77; exec. v.p. Uniroyal, Inc., Middlebury, Conn., 1977, pres., 1977—, chief exec. officer, 1980—, chmn. bd., 1982—, also dir.; dir. Colonial Bank., Scovill Co., Newmont Mining Co., Colonial Bank. Mem. Am. Chem. Soc., Chem. Mfrs. Assn. (dir.). Roman Catholic. Clubs: Country of Waterbury (Conn.); Vesper Country (Lowell). Home: 435 Squire Hill Rd Cheshire CT 06410 Office: Oxford Mgmt and Research Center Uniroyal Inc Middlebury CT 06749

FLANNERY, ROBERT GENE, railroad executive; b. Washington, Ind., Sept. 14, 1924; s. Allen H. and Nellie Jane (White) F.; m. Barbara Ann Angell, Feb. 23, 1952; children: Julia Ann, Jennifer Ann, Amy Lynn. B.S. in Civil Engring, Purdue U., 1948. With N.Y.C. R.R., 1948-68, gen. mgr., Syracuse, N.Y., 1965, asst. v.p. transp., N.Y.C., 1965, v.p. systems devel., 1967-68, Penn Central Co., 1968-69, v.p. ops., Phila., 1969-70; exec. v.p. Penn Central Transp. Co., 1970, v.p. operations, 1970; exec. v.p. Western Pacific R.R. Co., San Francisco, 1971-72, pres., 1973—, chief exec. officer, 1975—; pres., chief operating officer Union Pacific/Mo. Pacific RRs, 1982—. Served with USNR, 1943-45. Mem. U.S. Ry. Assn. (dir.), Pi Kappa Alpha. Democrat. Club: Mason. Office: Missouri Pacific Railroad Missouri Pacific Bldg St Louis MO 63103

FLANNERY, THOMAS, polit. cartoonist; b. Carbondale, Pa., Dec. 16, 1919; s. James A. and Clare (Reap) F.; m. Donna Hossack, Dec. 26, 1952 (dec. June 1973); children—Shawn, Sharon, Janine, David. Student, Pratt Inst., 1939-40, U. Scranton, 1946-47. Polit. cartoonist, Lowell (Mass.) Sun, 1947-57, Balt. Sunpapers, 1957—; staff cartoonist: Yank mag, 1943-45. Served with USAAF, World War II. Decorated Bronze Star. Mem. Am. Soc. Editorial Cartoonists. Home: 518 Orkney Rd Baltimore MD 21212 Office: 500 Calvert St Baltimore MD 21203

FLANNERY, THOMAS AQUINAS, U.S. judge; b. Washington, May 10, 1918; s. John J. and Mary (Sullivan) C.; m. Rita Sullivan, Mar. 3, 1951; children: Thomas Aquinas, Irene M. LL.B., Cath. U., 1940. Bar: D.C. 1940. Practice in, Washington, 1940-42, 45-48; trial atty. Dept. Justice, Washington, 1948-50; asst. U.S. Atty., Washington, 1950-62; partner Hamilton and Hamilton Washington, 1962-69; U.S. atty for D.C., Washington, 1969-71, U.S. dist. judge for D.C., 1971—. Served as combat intelligence officer USAF, 1942-45; ETO. Fellow Am. Coll. Trial Lawyers; Mem. Am., D.C. bar assns. 20016 *

FLANSBURGH, EARL ROBERT, architect; b. Ithaca, N.Y., Apr. 28, 1931; s. Earl Alvah and Elizabeth (Evans) F.; m. Louise Hospital, Aug. 27, 1955; children: Earl Schuyler, John Conant. B.Arch., Cornell U., 1954; M.Arch., MIT, 1957; S.C.M.P., Harvard U. Sch. Bus., 1982. Job capt., designer The Architects Collaborative, Cambridge, Mass., 1958-62; partner Freeman, Flansburgh & Assos., Cambridge, 1961-63; prin. Earl R. Flansburgh & Assos., Cambridge, 1963-69, pres., dir. design, 1969—; exec. v.p. Environment Systems Internat., Inc.; vis. prof. archtl. design Mass. Inst. Tech., 1965-66; instr. art Wellesley Coll., 1962-65, lectr. art, 1965-69; cons. Arthur D. Little, Inc., Cambridge, 1964—. Archtl. works include Weston (Mass.) High Sch. Addition, 1965-67, Cornell U. Campus Store, 1967-70, Cumnock Hall, Harvard U. Bus. Sch, 1973-75, Acton (Mass.) Elementary schs, 1966-68, 69-71, Peabody High Sch, 1969-71, Wilton (Conn.) High Sch, 1968-71, Marlborough (Mass.) High Sch, 1972-76, 14 Story St. Bldg, 1970; exhibited works Light Machine I, IBM Gallery, N.Y.C., 1958, Light Machine II, Carpenter Center, Harvard, 1965, 5 Cambridge Architects, Wellesley Coll., 1969, Work of Earl R. Flansburgh and Assos, Wellesley Coll., 1969, New Architecture in New Eng, DeCordova Mus., 1974-75, Residential Architecture, Mead Art Gallery, Amherst Coll., 1976, works represented in, 50 Ville del Nostro Tempo, 1970, Nuove Ville, New Villas, Vacation Houses, Vacation Houses, 2d edit., 1977, Interior Design, 1970, Drawings by American Architects, 1973, Interior Spaces Designed by Architects, 1974, New Architecture in New England, Great Houses, 1976, Architecture Boston, Presentation Drawings by American Architects, 1977, Architecture, 1970-1980, A Decade of Change, 1980, Old and New Architecture, A Design Relationship, 25 Years of Record Houses, 1981; Author: (with others) Techniques of Successful Practice, 1975. Chmn. architecture com. Boston Arts Festival, 1964; chmn. Downtown Boston Design Adv. Com.; Bd. dirs. Cambridge Center Adult Edn.; chmn. bldgs. and properties com.; mem. exec. com., academic affairs com. bd. trustees Cornell U. Served to 1st lt. USAF, 1954-56. Recipient design awards Progressive Architecture, Record Houses, AIA, City of Boston, Mass. Masonry Inst.; spl. design citations Am. Assn. Sch. Adminstrs.; spl. 1st prize Buffalo-Western N.Y. chpt. AIA Competition.; Fulbright research grantee Bldg. Reseacch Sta., Eng., 1957-58. Fellow AIA; mem. Royal Inst. Brit. Architects, Boston Soc. Architects (chmn. program com. 1969-71, commr. pub. affairs 1971-73, commr. design 1973-74, dir. 1971-74, pres. 1980-81), Cornell U. Council, Quill and Dagger Soc., Tau Beta Pi. Home: Old County Rd Lincoln MA 01773 Office: 77 N Washington St Boston MA 02114

FLANZ, WILLIAM WINSHIP, banker; b. N.J., Sept. 25, 1944; s. G. H. and Elizabeth (Winship) F.; children: Ellen, Kenneth. B.A., N.Y. U., 1966; M.B.A., U. Mich., 1967. With Chase Manhattan Bank, N.A. (N.A.), 1967-73, asst. treas., 1969, 2d v.p., 1970, v.p. banking dept., 1972, country mgr. Japan, 1973-76; area dir. for Middle East and North Africa Chase Manhattan Bank, 1976-80, sr. v.p., 1980, area dir. for Asia-Pacific, Hong Kong, 1980—; dir. Chase Manhattan Asia Ltd. Clubs: Nautilus, American, Hong Kong., World Trade Centre. Home: 27 Barker Rd The Peak Hong Kong Office: 12th Floor World Trade 280 Centre Gloucester Rd Hong Kong

FLASCHEN, STEWARD SAMUEL, corporation executive; b. Berwyn, Ill., May 28, 1926; s. Hyman Herman and Ethel (Leviton) F.; m. Joyce Davies, Apr. 21, 1949; children: John, Sheryl, David, Evan. B.S. in Chemistry, U. Ill., 1947; M.S., Miami U., Oxford, Ohio, 1948; Ph.D. in Geochemistry, Pa. State U., 1953. Supr. research dept. Bell Telephone Labs., Murray Hill, N.J., 1952-59; dir. phys. scis., research and devel., semiconductor products div. Motorola, Inc., Phoenix, 1959-64; sr. v.p., gen. tech. dir. ITT Corp., N.Y.C., 1964—; lectr. Pace U. Grad. Sch. Bus. Author: Search and Research, 1965; also articles. Mem. Phoenix Bd. Edn., 1962-64. Served with USNR, 1944-46. Fellow Am. Inst. Chemists, IEEE; mem. Electromech. Soc. Am., Am. Ceramic Soc., AAAS, Indsl. Research Inst., N.Y. Acad. Scis. Patentee in field. Home: 592 Weed St New Canaan CT 06840 Office: 320 Park Ave New York NY 10022 *I was fortunate in my education to have had broad exposure to philosophy, the natural sciences and English. This early training in the reduction to basics of problems, concepts, and decisions, and in the skill of communicating effectively, has been of the utmost value to me professionally and personally.*

FLASKAMP, WILLIAM DAVIDSON, lawyer; b. St. Louis, May 8, 1924; s. William D. and Grace Ann F.; m. Betty Ann Dreyer, June 21, 1947; children: Ann, Jill, Meg, Thomas, Ted. B.S. in Math, U. Mich., 1947, B.A. in Speech, 1948, J.D., 1951; student, Georgetown U., 1941-43. Bar: Mich. bar 1951. Partner firm Meagher, Geer, Markham & Anderson, Mpls., 1951—; lectr. in field. Judge adv. State of Minn., 1952-62. Served with USAAF, 1943-46; now brig. gen. USAF ret. Mem. Am., Minn. bar assns., Am. Coll. Trial Lawyers, Internat. Acad. Trial Lawyers, Internat. Soc. Barristers (pres. 1981), Am. Bd. Trial Advs., Am. Judicature Soc. Republican. Presbyterian. Clubs: Mpls. Athletic, Edina Country, Ft. Snelling Officers, Masons, Shrine. Home: 5309 Minnehaha Blvd Edina MN 55424 Office: 2250 IDS Center Minneapolis MN 55402

FLASTE, RICHARD ALFRED, science editor, writer; b. Huntington, N.Y., Aug. 29, 1942; s. Irving and Beatrice (Kirshman) F.; m. Dale Judith Napolin, Dec. 25, 1966; children: Rebecca, Jordan. B.A., Pace U., 1972; M.A., NYU, 1977. Parent, child columnist, reporter N.Y. Times, N.Y.C., 1973-76, asst. style editor, 1976-80, dep. dir. sci. news, 1980-82, dir. sci. news, 1982—. Author: The New York Times Guide to Children's Entertainment, 1976, (with Pierre Franey) Pierre Franey's Kitchen, 1982. Recipient Silurians award Soc. Silurians, 1974, Disting. Contbr. Am. Psychol. Assn., 1976. Office: The NY Times 229 W 43d St New York NY 10036

FLATHMAN, RICHARD EARL, political science educator; b. St. Paul, Aug. 6, 1934; s. Gerald Martin and Agnes Joan (Gadow) F.; m. Nancy S. Wold, June 10, 1956; children: Kristen Edna, Karen Margaret, Jennifer Laura. B.A., Macalester Coll., 1956; M.A., U. Calif., Berkeley, 1958, Ph.D. (Social Sci. Research Council fellow), 1961. Asst. prof. polit. sci. and humanities Reed Coll., Portland, Oreg., 1961-64; asst. prof. polit. sci. U. Chgo., 1964-66, asso. prof., 1966-68, prof., 1969-71, U. Wash., 1971-74, chmn. dept. polit. sci., 1971-74; prof. Johns Hopkins U., Balt., 1974—. Author: The Public Interest, 1966, Political Obligation, 1972, Concepts in Social and Political Philosophy, 1973, The Practice of Rights, 1976, The Practice of Political Authority, 1980. Willett Found. fellow, 1971; Auggenheim fellow; Nat. Found. Humanities Sr. fellow, 1975; fellow Ctr. Advanced Study in Behavioral Scis. Mem. Am. Polit. Sci. Assn., AAUP, Conf. Study of Polit. Thought, Am. Soc. Legal and Polit. Philosophy, Mind Assn. Democrat. Home: 819 W University Pkwy Baltimore MD 21210 Office: Dept Polit Sci Johns Hopkins U Baltimore MD 21218

FLATLEY, GUY, writer, mag. editor; b. St. Louis, Oct. 25, 1934; s. Bernard Woodrow and June Catherine (Smith) F.; m. Dolores McCormack, Aug. 26, 1961; children—Norah, Owen. B.S., St. Louis U., 1959. Writer, editor N.Y. Times, N.Y.C., 1959-78; mng. editor, film critic Cosmopolitan mag. Mags. div. Hearst Corp., N.Y.C., 1978-82; freelance writer, 1961—. Served with AUS, 1954-56. Office: Cosmopolitan Mag Mags Div Hearst Corp 224 W 57th St New York NY 10019

FLATOW, RICHARD WILLIAM, cosmetics company executive; b. N.Y.C., May 5, 1941; s. William F.; m. Tracy Ruth Freeman; children: Pamela, Michael. B.A. in Econs., Lafayette Coll., 1963. Account supr. Benton & Bowles Advt., N.Y.C., 1967-69; dir. product mktg. Avon Products, N.Y.C., 1971-73, v.p. product mktg., 1973-77, v.p. mktg.-Pacific, 1977-82, group v.p. mkgt.-U.S., 1982-83, group v.p. planning and sales devel., 1983, group v.p. field ops., 1983—. Office: Avon Products 9 W 57th St New York NY 10019

FLATT, ADRIAN EDE, surgeon; b. Frinton, Eng., Aug. 26, 1921; came to U.S., 1956, naturalized, 1960; s. Leslie Neeve and Barbara F.; m. Carol Ann Conners; 1 son, Andrew James. B.A., Cambridge U., 1942, M.A., 1945, M.B., B. chir., 1946, M.D., 1953, M. chir., 1972. Diplomate: Am. Bd. Orthopedic Surgery. Rotating intern, then resident in gen., plastic and orthopaedic surgery London (Eng.) Hosp., 1946-54, 55-56; mem. faculty U. Iowa Med. Sch., 1956-79; prof. orthopaedic surgery and anatomy, dir. div. hand surgery, chmn. dept. surgery Norwalk (Conn.) Hosp., 1979-82; clin. prof. Yale U. Med. Sch., 1979-82; Hunterian prof. Royal Coll. Surgeons, 1962; McIlrath guest prof. Royal Prince Alfred Hosp., Sydney, Australia, 1972; cons. in hand surgery to surg. gen. U.S. Air Force, 1962—. Editor-in-chief: Jour. Hand Surgery, 1981—; author textbooks, papers in field. Served as officer RAF, 1948-50. Recipient Kappa Delta award Am. Acad. Orthopaedic Surgeons, 1972. Mem. Am. Soc. Surgery Hand, Brit. Hand Soc., Group Etude de la Main, Am. Orthopaedic Assn., Am. Acad. Orthopaedic Surgeons, Am. Soc. Plastic and Reconstructive Surgery. Patentee artificial wrist and finger joints. Office: 3707 Gaston Ave Suite 412 Dallas TX 75246

FLATT, ERNEST ORVILLE, choreographer, director; b. Denver, Oct. 30, 1918; s. Ernest Scorrow and Della May (Allen) F. Grad. high sch. Dir. Ernatt Corp.; Bd. dirs. Am. Sch. Dance. Dancer: films including Singin' in the Rain; choreographer: film Anything Goes; TV shows Your Hit Parade, 1955-58, Garry Moore Show, 1958-63, Carol Burnett Show, 1968-77; assoc. producer: TV spl. Julie and Carol at Carnegie Hall; dir.-choreographer: Broadway show Sugar Babies, 1979; (Recipient Emmy award for Garry Moore Show, for Julie and Carol at Carnegie Hall, and for Carol Burnett Show 1971). Served with AUS, 1941-45. Mem. AFTRA, Actors' Equity, Soc. Dirs. and Choreographers, Dirs. Guild Am. Home: PO Box 8478 Palm Springs CA 92262 Office: Becker & London 30 Lincoln Plaza New York NY 10023

FLATT, JANE DEE, book publisher; b. Chgo., Aug. 8, 1945; d. Oscar and Marion (Dietler) Dystel; m. S. Thomas Flatt, May 12, 1978; 1 dau., Jessica Fanny. B.A. in Polit. Sci. cum laude, N.Y. U., 1967. Mng. editor, then editor Grosset & Dunlap Pubs., N.Y.C., 1973-76; sr. editor A&W Pubs., Inc., N.Y.C., 1976-77; pub., v.p. World Almanac and Book of Facts, N.Y.C., 1977—. Cons. Multiple Sclerosis Read-a-Thon.; bd. dirs. Scripps-Howard Found. Mem. Phi Beta Kappa. Home: 1172 Park Ave New York NY 10028 Office: 200 Park Ave New York NY 10166 *I strive always to bring out the best in myself, so that I can bring out the best in others.*

FLATT, WILLIAM PERRY, university dean; b. Newbern, Tenn., June 17, 1931; s. Carl Hadley and Evelyn Inez (Kelso) F.; m. June Nesbitt, Apr. 9, 1949; children: Melynda Claire, Katherine Ann. Student, Bethel Coll., 1948-49; B.S., U. Tenn., 1952; Ph.D. (NSF fellow), Cornell U., 1955; postdoctoral studies, Rowett Research Inst., Scotland, 1967-68. Dairy cattle nutritionist, head energy metabolism lab. Agrl. Research Service, U.S. Dept. Agr., Beltsville, Md., 1956-68, asst. dir. animal husbandry research div., 1968-69; prof. animal sci., head dept. U. Ga., 1969-70, dir. agrl. expt. stas., 1970-81; dean and coordinator Coll. Agr., 1981—; mem. bd. agr. and renewable resources NRC-Nat. Acad. Scis. Contbr. articles to profl. jours. Recipient presdl. citation U.S. Dept. Agr., 1965, Superior Service award, 1968, Hoblitzelle nat. award, 1968. Mem. AAAS, Am. Soc. Animal Sci. (Hon. Fellow award 1979), Am. Dairy Sci. Assn. (Disting. Service award 1983), Am. Inst. Nutrition, So. Assn. Agrl. Scientists (pres.-elect 1983), Nat. Assn. Agrl. Expt. Stas. (chmn. 1980), So. Assn. Agrl. Expt. Stas. (chmn.). Lodge: Rotary (pres. 1983-84). Home: 110 Broomsedge Trail Athens GA 30605 *Food to feed the world. These five words summarize my goal in life. This goal can only be achieved by research and education. Research and education need the support of all who are concerned with survival of the human race.*

FLATTE, STANLEY MARTIN, physicist, educator; b. Los Angeles, Dec. 2, 1940; s. Samuel and Henrietta (Edelstein) F.; m. Renelde Marie Demeure, June 26, 1966; children: Michael, Anne. B.S., Calif. Inst. Tech., 1962; student, N.Y. U., 1960-61; Ph.D., U. Calif., Berkeley, 1966. Research particle physicist Lawrence Berkeley (Calif.) Lab., 1966-71; asst. prof. physics U. Calif., Santa Cruz, 1971-73, asso. prof., 1973-78, prof., 1978—; dir. Ctr. for Studies of Nonlinear Dynamics La Jolla Inst., 1982—; cons. phys. oceanography and underwater sound U.S. Govt.; vis. researcher, Cern, Geneva, 1975, Scripps Inst. Oceanography, 1980, Cambridge (Eng.) U., 1981. Author: (with others) Sound Transmission Through a Fluctuating Ocean, 1979; Contbr. articles profl. jours. Woodrow Wilson fellow, 1962; NSF fellow, 1962-66; Guggenheim Found. fellow, 1975. Fellow Acoustical Soc. Am.; Mem. Am. Phys. Soc., Sigma Xi. Discovered cusp phenomenon in particle physics; developed methods for probing statis, ocean processes with sound. Office: Univ Calif Santa Cruz CA 95064 *An understanding of science requires two elements: significant, individual research accomplishment, and a knowledge of the historical development of one's discipline, particularly through the personal histories of past scientists. Both are essential. I have tried to balance them in research, and in teaching the young.*

FLATTERY, THOMAS LONG, manufacturing company executive, lawyer; b. Detroit, Nov. 14, 1922; s. Thomas J. and Rosemary (Long) F.; m. Gloria M. Hughes, June 10, 1947; children: Constance Marie, Carol Dianne (Mrs. Jeffrey M. Lee), Michael Patrick, Thomas Hughes, Dennis Jerome, Betsy Ann (Mrs. Patrick M. Bagnall). B.S., U.S. Mil. Acad., 1947; J.D., UCLA, 1955; LL.M., U. So. Calif., 1965. Bar: Calif. 1955, U.S. Patent Office 1957, U.S. Customs Ct. 1969, U.S. Supreme Ct. 1974, Conn. 1983. With Motor Products Corp., Detroit, 1950, Equitable Life Assurance Soc. Am., 1951, Bohn Aluminum & Brass Co., 1952; mem. legal staff, asst. contract adminstr. Radioplane Co., Van Nuys, Calif., 1955-57; successively corp. counsel, gen. counsel, asst. sec. McCulloch Corp., Los Angeles, 1957-64; sec., corp. counsel Technicolor, Inc., Hollywood, Calif., 1964-70; successively corp. counsel, asst. sec., v.p., sec. and gen. counsel Amcord, Inc., Newport Beach, Calif., 1970-72; v.p., sec., gen. counsel Schick Inc., Los Angeles, 1972-75; counsel, asst. sec. C.F. Braun & Co., Alhambra, Calif., 1975-76; sr. v.p., sec., gen. counsel Automation Industries, Inc. (a unit of Penn Central Corp.), 1976—; lectr. continuing edn. program Calif. State Bar. Contbr. articles to various legal jours. Served to 1st lt. AUS, 1942-50. Mem. ABA, Calif. Bar Assn. (co-chmn. corp. law dept. com. 1978-79), Los Angeles County Bar Assn. (chmn. corp. law dept. com. 1966-67), Century City Bar Assn. (chmn. corp. law dept. com. 1979-80), Conn. Bar Assn., Am. Soc. Corp. Secs. (Los Angeles regional group pres. 1973-74), Patent Law Assn. Los Angeles, Fgn. Law Assn. Los Angeles, Licensing Exec. Soc. U.S., Westchester-Fairfield County Corp. Counsel Assn., West Point Alumni Assn., Army Athletic Assn., Friendly Sons St. Patrick, Phi Alpha Delta. Roman Catholic. Clubs: Los Angeles Athletic, Jonathan (Los Angeles); County of Darien (Conn.). Home: 232 W Norwalk Rd Darien CT 06820 Office: 500 W Putnam Ave Greenwich CT 06830

FLAUM, JOEL MARTIN, judge; b. Hudson, N.Y., Nov. 26, 1936; s. Louis and Sally (Berger) F.; m. Thea Kharasch, July 3, 1960; children: Jonathan, Alison. B.A., Union Coll., Schenectady, 1958; J.D., Northwestern U., 1963, LL.M., 1964. Bar: Ill. 1963. Asst. state's atty., Cook County, Ill., 1965-69, 1st asst. atty. gen., Ill., 1969-72; 1st asst. U.S. atty. No. Dist. Ill., Chgo., 1972-75; judge U.S. Dist. Ct. No. Dist. Ill., Chgo., 1975-83, U.S. Ct. Appeals 7th Cir., 1983—; lectr. Northwestern U. Sch. Law, 1967-69; mem. Ill. Law Enforcement Commn., 1970-72; cons. U.S. Dept. Justice, Law Enforcement Assistance Adminstrn. Mem.: Northwestern U. Law Rev., 1962-63; contbr. articles to legal jours. Mem. adv. bd. Loyola U. Sch. Law, 1978—; mem. vis. com. U. Chgo. Law Sch., 1983—, Northwestern U. Sch. Law, 1984—; trustee Congregation Anshe Emet, Chgo., 1978—. Served to lt. JAGC, USNR. Ford Found. fellow, 1963-64; Am. Bar Found. fellow, 1984. Mem. Fed. Bar Assn., ABA, Bar Assn. 7th Circuit, Ill. Bar Assn., Chgo. Bar Assn., Legal Club Chgo., Maritime Law Assn., Law Club Chgo., Judge Advs. Assn., Am. Judicature Soc. Jewish. Office: 219 S Dearborn St Chicago IL 60604 *

FLAUM, MARSHALL ALLEN, TV producer, writer and director; b. Bklyn.; s. Mayer and Ethel (Lamkay) P.; m. Gita Faye Miller; children—Erica, Seth Baruch. B.A., U. Iowa, 1948; D.F.A. (hon.), So. Ill. U., Edwardsville, 1974. Story editor, writer, asso. producer TV series Twentieth Century, 1957-62; producer, writer, dir. TV spls. for Wolper Prodns., 1962-65; founder Flaum-Grinberg Prodns., 1966; v.p. Metromedia Producers Corp., 1968-76; pres. Marshall Flaum Prodns., Inc., 1976—. Producer, writer, dir.: TV spls. Day of Infamy, 1963, Hollywood: The Great Stars, 1963, The Yanks Are Coming, 1964, Battle of Britain, 1964, Berlin: Kaiser to Kruschev, 1964, Let My People Go, 1965 (Ohio State award), Miss Goodall and the Wild Chimpanzees, 1966 (Edinburgh Festival award), Bogart, 1967 (Melbourne Festival award); producer, writer: Killy Le Champion, 1969; producer, writer, dir.: Hollywood: The Selznick Years, 1969 (Silver Lion award Venice Film Festival); TV spl. The Time of Man, 1969 (Silver Hugo award Chgo. Internat. Festival); exec. producer, co-writer: TV series Undersea World of Jacques Cousteau, 1970-76; Jane Goodall and The World of Animal Behavior, 1972-76, The Wild Dogs of Africa (Emmy award best documentary), 1973 (Chgo. Internat. Festival Gold Hugo award), Baboons of Gombe, 1974, Hyena, 1975, Lions of Serengeti, 1976; producer: Am. Film Inst. Salute to Bette Davis, 1977; producer, writer, dir.: TV spl. Yabba Dabba Doo! The Happy World of Hanna-Barbera, 1977, Bing Crosby: His Life and Legend, 1978 (Christopher award), Playboy's 25th Anniversary Celebration, 1979, A Bing Crosby Christmas... Like the Ones We Used To Know, 1979; producer: (co-writer) TV spls. Ripley's Believe It or Not, 1982, Bob Hope's Who Makes the World Laugh, 1983; producer, writer, dir.: TV spl. A Bing Crosby Christmas... Like the Ones We Used To Know, 1979. Recipient Emmy award as best documentary for A Sound of Dolphins, 1972, The Unsinkable Sea Otter, 1972, The Wild Dogs of Africa, 1973; Recipient George Foster Peabody award for TV spls. Let My People Go, 1965, for Miss Goodall and The Wild Chimpanzees, 1966; recipient Monte Carlo Internat. TV Festival Golden Nymph award for TV spl. The Yanks Are Coming, 1964, Silver medal Atlanta Film Festival for Wild Dogs of Africa, 1973, Octopus, Octopus, 1972, Chgo. Internat. Film Festival Silver Hugo award for Tragedy of the Red Salmon, 1971, Oscar nomination for best documentary feature for The Yanks Are Coming, 1964, Let My People Go, 1966. Mem. Writers Guild Am., Acad. Motion Picture Arts and Scis., Acad. TV Arts and Scis. Address: 301 S Rodeo Dr Beverly Hills CA 90212

FLAVIN, DAN, artist; b. N.Y.C., Apr. 1, 1933. Student, Cathedral Coll. Immaculate Conception, 1947-52, U. Md., Korea, 1954-56, New Sch. Social Research, Columbia U. Lectr. U. N.C., 1967; Albert Dorne vis. prof. U. Bridgeport, 1973. Works represented in, Met. Mus. Art, N.Y.C., Mus. Modern Art, N.Y.C., Whitney Mus., N.Y.C., Guggenheim Mus., N.Y.C., Phila. Art Mus. Commn., installations of work include, Kunstmus, Basel, Switzerland, 1975, platforms, Grand Central Sta., N.Y.C., 1976, Kröller Müller Mus., Eindhoven, Netherlands, 1977, U.S. Courthouse, Anchorage, Alaska, 1980, numerous exhbns. including, Mus. Contemporary Art, Chgo., 1967-68, Nat. Gallery Can., Jewish Mus., N.Y.C., 1969-70, Scottish Nat. Gallery Modern Art, 1976, Contemporary Arts Center, Cin., 1977, Art Inst. Chgo., Univ. Art Mus., Berkeley, Calif., 1978, Ottawa Nat. Mus., 1979. Recipient William and Norma Copley Found. award, 1968; Nat. Found. Art and Humanities award, 1966; Skowhegan medal for sculpture, 1965. *

FLAVIN, GLENNON P., bishop; b. St. Louis, Mar. 2, 1916. Grad., St. Louis Prep. Sem., Kendrick Sem. Ordained priest Roman Catholic Ch., 1941; sec. to archbishop, St. Louis, 1949-57, consecrated bishop, 1957, ordained titular bishop of Joannina and aux. bishop, St. Louis, 1957-67; bishop Diocese of Lincoln, Nebr., 1967—. Office: Chancery Office PO Box 80328 Lincoln NE 68501 *

FLAVIN, JOSEPH B., manufacturing company executive; b. St. Louis, Oct. 16, 1928; s. Joseph B. and Mary E. (Toomey) F.; m. Melisande Barillon, 1946; children: Patrick Brian, Shawn Elaine. M.S., Columbia U. Grad. Sch. Bus., 1957; LL.D. (hon.), U. Mass., 1978. Acct., Cawley Aircraft Supply Co., 1953; with IBM World Trade Corp., 1953-67, controller, 1965-67; group v.p. Xerox Corp., 1968-70, exec. v.p., 1970-75, pres. internat. ops., 1972-75, dir., 1969-75; chmn. chief exec. officer, dir. The Singer Co., 1975—; mem. Industry Policy Adv. Com. for Trade Policy Matters, Washington; trustee Northwestern Mut. Life Ins. Co., Milw.; dir. Pfizer, Inc. Mem. nat. devel. bd. Columbia U.; bd. dirs. Layman's Nat. Bible Com., Inc.; trustee Com. Econ. Devel., U.S. Council for Internat. Bus., Am. Bus. Cancer Research Found., Inc., Stamford Hosp.; mem. bus. adv. council Religion in Am. life; bd. dirs., vice-chmn. Conn. region United Way Tri-State; chmn. United Way Stamford; trustee Hartman Regional Theatre, Inc., Stamford; mem. Nat. Bus. Council for ERA; bd. dirs. Health Corp. Greater Stamford. Served with USMC. Recipient Nat. Brotherhood award NCCJ, 1978. Mem. N.A.M.,

Internat. C. of C., Southwestern Area Commerce and Industry Assn. Conn. (dir.), Conf. Bd. (mem. corp.), Elec. Mfrs. Club. Clubs: Economic (N.Y.C.); Blind Brook (Port Chester, N.Y.); Windham Mountain; Landmark (Stamford) (gov.). Office: The Singer Co 8 Stamford Forum PO Box 10151 Stamford CT 06904

FLAWN, PETER TYRRELL, university president, educator; b. Miami, Fla., Feb. 17, 1926; s. Stanley Charles and Laura Carolyn (Rotz) F.; m. Priscilla Bernice Pond, June 28, 1946; children—Tyrrell Flawn Hill, Laura. B.A., Oberlin Coll., 1947; M.S. (Cooksey fellow), Yale U., 1948; Ph.D. (Binney fellow), Yale U., 1951. Jr. geologist mineral deposits br. U.S. Geol. Survey, 1948; research scientist, geologist Bur. Econ. Geology, U. Tex., Austin, 1949-60; dir. Bur. Econ. Geology, prof. geology, 1960-70, dir. div. natural resources and environment, prof. geol. scis. and pub. affairs, 1970-73, v.p. acad. affairs, 1970-72, exec. v.p., 1972-73; pres. U. Tex.-San Antonio, 1973-78; Leonidas T. Barrow prof. mineral resources U. Tex.-Austin, 1978—; pres. univ. U. Tex., 1979—; dir. Tenneco, Inc., Gearhart Industries; mem. Tex. Interagy. Council on Natural Resources and Environment, 1969-73; served various coms. Nat. Acad. Scis.-NRC; mem. Nat. Sci. Bd., 1980—. Author: Basement Rocks of Texas and Southeast New Mexico, 1956, The Ouachita System, 1962, Mineral Resources, 1966, Environmental Geology in Landuse Planning Resource Management and Conservation, 1970; contbr. articles to profl. jours. Vice chmn. edn. com. Tex. Constl. Revision Commn.; Bd. govs., adv. trustee S.W. Found. for Research and Edn., 1973-78, bd. govs., 1974-78; trustee Southwest Research Inst., 1973—, Tex. Mil. Inst., 1974-77, St. David's Hosp., 1981—; bd. dirs. S.W. Tex. Ednl. TV Council, 1973-78. Served with USAAF, 1944-45. Mem. Nat. Acad. Engring., Am. Inst. Mining, Metall. and Petroleum Engrs., Assn. Profl. Geol. Scientists, Am. Assn. Petroleum Geologists, Assn. Am. State Geologists (hon. mem.; pres. 1969-70), Soc. Econ. Geologists (trustee 1971-76), Sociedad Geologica Mexicana, Am. Geol. Inst. (dir. 1967-70), Geol. Soc. Am. (councilor 1971-77, v.p. 1977, pres. 1978), Greater San Antonio C. of C. (dir. 1975-78). Clubs: Citadel, Headliners, Tarry House (Austin); Rotary; Cosmos (Washington). Home: 2101 Meadowbrook Dr Austin TX 78703 Office: U Tex Austin TX 78712

FLAX, ALEXANDER HENRY, administrator, aeronautical engineer; b. Bklyn., Jan. 18, 1921; s. David and Etta (Schenker) F.; m. Ida Leane Warren, Aug. 25, 1951; 1 dau., Laurel Elizabeth. B.Aero. Engring., N.Y. U., 1940; Ph.D. in Physics, U. Buffalo, 1958. Structure, vibration engr. airplane div. Curtiss-Wright Corp., 1940-44; chief aerodynamics and structures Piasecki Helicopter Corp., 1944-46; asst. head aeromechanics dept. Cornell Aero. Lab., 1946-49, head aerodynamics dept., 1949-55, asst. dir., 1955-56, v.p., tech. dir., 1956-59, 61-63; chief scientist USAF, 1959-61; asst. sec. Air Force for research and devel., 1963-69; v.p. for research Inst. Def. Analyses, Arlington, Va., 1969, pres., 1969—; mem. com. aerodynamics NACA, 1952-54, subcom. highspeed aerodynamics, 1954-58; adv. com. aircraft aerodynamics NASA, 1958-62; mem. sci. com. nat. reps. SHAPE Tech. Center, The Hague, Netherlands, 1963-69, chmn., 1965-67; U.S. del. adv. com. aero. research and devel. NATO, 1969—; mem. bd. direction Von Karman Inst., Brussels, 1969—; mem. adv. council Stanford U. Sch. Engring., 1981—. Contbr. sect. to book, numerous articles to profl. jours. Recipient Air Force Exceptional Civilian Service awards, 1961, 69; NASA Distinguished Service medal, 1968; Civilian Service medal Def. Intelligence Agy., 1974; Von Karman medal NATO Adv. Group for Aerospace Research and Devel., 1978; Medal for Disting. Pub. Service Dept. Def., 1983. Hon. fellow AIAA (Lawrence Sperry award 1949, Wright Bros. lectr. 1959); fellow Royal Aero. Soc. (Wright Bros. Meml. Lectr. 1974); mem. Nat. Acad. Engring., Sigma Xi. Club: Cosmos (Washington). Home: 9007 Belmart Rd Potomac MD 20854 Office: 1801 N Beauregard St Alexandria VA 22311

FLEAGLE, ROBERT GUTHRIE, meteorologist, educator; b. Woodlawn, Md., Aug. 16, 1918; s. Benjamin Edward and Frances Taylor (Guthrie) F.; m. Marianne Diggs, Dec. 19, 1942; children: Robert Guthrie, John B. A.B., Johns Hopkins U., 1940; M.S., N.Y. U., 1944, Ph.D., 1949. Asst. prof. U. Wash., 1948-51, asso. prof., 1951-56, prof., 1956—, chmn. dept. atmospheric scis., 1967-77; Cons. various bus., instns., govt. agys.; tech. asst. Office Sci. and Tech., Exec. Office of Pres., 1963-64; mem. Nat. Acad. Scis. Com. on Atmospheric Scis., 1962-76, chmn., 1969-73; mem. panel on oceanography Pres.'s Sci. Adv. Com., 1965-66; mem. U.S. com. Global Atmospheric Research Program, 1968-73; mem. NATO adv. panel on meteorology, 1970-73; chmn. BOMAP adv. panel, 1969-73; mem. assembly of math. and phys. scis. Nat. Acad. Scis., 1976-79. Author: (with J.A. Businger) An Introduction to Atmospheric Physics, 1963, 2d edit., 1980; editor: Weather Modification: Science and Public Policy, 1968, Weather Modification in the Public Interest, 1974; contbr. articles to sci. jours. Trustee Univ. Corp. for Atmospheric Research, 1970-78, chmn. bd., 1975-77, chmn. council mems., 1966-67. Served from pvt. to capt. AUS, 1942-46. NSF fellow Imperial Coll., London, 1958-59. Fellow Am. Geophys. Union (pres. meteorol. sect. 1967-70), AAAS (chmn. sect. atmospheric and hydrological scis. 1977-78), Am. Meteorol. Soc. (Meisinger award 1959, Cleveland Abbé award 1971, commn. sci. and technol. activities 1965-69, council 1957-60, 73-76, 80-84, pres. 1981); mem. Sigma Xi. Club: Cosmos. Home: 7858 56th Pl NE Seattle WA 98115

FLECK, ELMER EARL, aerospace co. exec.; b. Bradock, Pa., Nov. 28, 1926; s. James Homer and Amanda Jane (Swails) F.; m. Mildred Joyce Fleck, Oct. 13, 1950; children—Deborah, Susan, Laura. B.S. in Chem. Engring, Lawrence Inst. Tech., 1951, Wayne State U., 1957; M.S. in Engring, U. Detroit, 1963. Registered profl. engr., Mich. Chemist Timken Co., Detroit, 1950-51; metallurgist Ford Motor Co., Detroit, 1951-53; with Ex-Cell-O-Corp., Troy, Mich., 1954—, mgr. mfg., 1963-69, mgr. operations, 1969-79, pres. aerospace div., 1979—. Served with USAF, 1945-46. Mem. Engring. Soc. Detroit, Am. Mgmt. Assn. Presbyterian. Home: 9712 Daleview St Lyon MI 48178 Office: 850 Ladd Rd PO Box 700 Walled Lake MI 48088

FLECK, FRANCIS CLINTON, mfg. co. exec.; b. Kalamazoo, Nov. 2, 1924; s. Edward Preston and Stella Cecelia (Klausmeyer) F.; m. Joanne DeConick, May 30, 1953; children—Francis J., Christopher P., James M., Mary K. B.M.E., Gen. Motors Inst. Tech., 1949. With Gen. Motors Corp., 1942—, chief engr. parts div., 1969-72; dir. engring. and forward planning Gen. Motors Can. Ltd., Oshawa, Ont., 1972—. Bd. dirs. Traffic Injury Research Found., Ont. Safety League; mem. Govtl. Task Force Alt. Fuels. Served with USAAF, 1943-46. Mem. Soc. Automotive Engrs., Engring. Soc. Detroit, Am. Soc. Quality Control, Am. Ordnance Assn. Clubs: Elks, K.C. Patentee automotive power transmission systems, truck chassis devices. Office: 215 William St Oshawa ON L1G 1K7 Canada

FLECK, GEORGE MORRISON, chemistry educator; b. Warren, Ind., May 13, 1934; s. Ford Bloom and Deloris Magdalene (Morrison) F.; m. Margaret Dyer Reynolds, June 27, 1959; children: Margaret Morrison, Louise Elizabeth. B.S., Yale U., 1956; Ph.D., U. Wis., 1961. Asst. prof. Smith Coll., Northampton, Mass., 1961-67, assoc. prof., 1967-76, prof. chemistry, 1976—. Author: Equilibria in Solution, 1966, Chemical Reaction Mechanisms, 1971, Carboxylic Acid Equilibria, 1973, Chemistry: Molecules That Matter, 1974, Patterns of Symmetry, 1974. Fellow Danforth Found., 1956-61; Dupont fellow, 1960; Danforth assoc., 1982—; grantee NSF, NIH, U.S. Office Edn., Am. Philos. Soc. Mem. Am. Chem. Soc., Sigma Xi. Home: Village Hill Rd Williamsburg MA 01096 Office: Smith Coll Clark Sci Center Northampton MA 01063

FLECK, GUSTAV PETER, former banker, former securities firm executive; b. Amsterdam, Netherlands, 1909; came to U.S., 1941, naturalized, 1945; s. Richard and Anna (Stein) F.; m. Ruth Alice Irene Melchior, June 1, 1939; children: Ann Fleck Henderson, Andrea Fleck Clardy, Marjorie Fleck Withers. Grad., Amsterdam Lyceum, 1927, Hochschule für Welthandel, Vienna, 1928; D.H.L. (hon.), Starr King Sch. for Minstry, D.L., Meadville Theol. Sch. With Erlangers, Ltd., London, 1928-29, Banque des Pays de L'Europe Centrale, Paris, 1929-30, Bank für Auswartigen Handel, Berlin, 1930-31; with Continental Handelsbank, Amsterdam, 1931-40, v.p., 1936-40; organized Amsterdam Overseas Corp., N.Y.C., 1947, pres., 1947-67, chmn., 1967-71, New Court Securities Corp., 1968-78, chmn. exec. com., 1978-81; Chmn. adv. bd. Wesleyan Univ. Press.; hon. dir. Rothschild Inc. Decorated officer Order Orange Nassau. Mem. Council Fgn. Relations. Home: Bayhouse Quanset Rd South Orleans MA 02662 Office: 1 Rockefeller Plaza New York NY 10020

FLECK, RAYMOND ANTHONY, JR., university administrator; b. Bklyn., Mar. 9, 1927; s. Raymond Anthony and Dorothy (Canavan) F.; m. Dorothy Marie Rossow, Aug. 22, 1970; children: Andrew Jerome, Casey Thomas. Student, Manhattan Coll., 1946-48; B.S., U. Notre Dame, 1951, Ph.D., 1954. Prof. chemistry St. Edward's U., 1954-69, pres., 1957-69; assoc. research chemist dept. environ. toxicology U. Calif. at Davis, 1969-72; pres. Marygrove Coll., Detroit, 1972-79; acting dir. Food Protection and Toxicology Center, U. Calif., Davis, 1979-83; dir. research Calif. State Poly. U., Pomona, 1983—; cons. U.S. EPA. Environ. cons., State of Calif., 1971-72; dir. Monterey Basin Pilot Monitoring Project, 1971-72. Vice pres., bd. dirs. Harmony Village Home Corp. N.W., Detroit, 1971-72. Served with USNR, 1945-46. NSF fellow, 1952, 1969; recipient U. Notre Dame Centennial of Sci. medal, 1965; sci. bldg. at St. Edward's U. named Fleck Hall. Mem. Am. Chem. Soc., AAAS, Nat. Council Univ. Research Adminstrs., Sigma Xi. Club: K.C. (4 deg.). Home: 1038 S Grand Ave Diamond Bar CA 91765 Office: Research Office Calif State Poly U Pomona CA 91768

FLEESON, WILLIAM, psychiatry educator; b. Sterling, Kans., May 21, 1915; s. William H. and Eva Lynn (Seward) F.; m. Beatrice Riedel, Mar. 26, 1943; children—William, Breck, Lucinda, Peter, Elizabeth. A.B. (Summerfield scholar), U. Kans., 1937; M.D., Yale U., 1942; postgrad. Advanced Mgmt. Program, Harvard U., 1964. Diplomate: Am. Bd. Psychiatry and Neurology. Intern U. Hosps., Mpls., 1942-43; asso. psychiatrist Manhattan Project, Oak Ridge, 1945-46; asso. psychiatrist, dir. child guidance div. Minn. Psychiat. Inst., Mpls., 1946-55; staff psychiatrist Elizabeth Kenny Inst., Mpls., 1953-56; Nat. Found. fellow U. Minn., Mpls., 1956, asst. prof. psychiatry and phys. medicine, 1957-61; MEND coordinator Coll. Med. Scis., 1959-63; lectr. Law Sch., 1960-63, asso. prof. psychiatry; asst. dean Coll. Med. Scis., 1960-63; prof. psychiatry Sch. Medicine, U. Conn., Farmington, 1963-82, asso. dean, 1963-74, acting clin. dir. dept. psychiatry, 1979-80, assoc. chmn., 1980-82—, prof. emeritus, 1982—, lectr., 1967-75; acting head dept. psychiatry U. Conn., 1967-68; acting chief psychiatry VA Med. Ctr., Newington, Conn., 1983—; lectr. psychiatry Sch. Medicine, Yale, 1965-74; supr. psychotherapy Inst. for Living, Hartford, Conn., 1965-67; fellow Bur. Health Resources Devel. program Center for Ednl. Devel., U. Ill., 1974-75; vis. prof. psychiatry Free Catholic U., Lille, France, 1975-80. Contbr.: book revs. to Sci. Books. Cons. psychiatry child study div. Mpls. Bd. Edn., 1957-63. Served to capt. AUS, 1943-46. USPHS fellow child psychiatry Judge Baker Guidance Center, Boston, 1950-51. Fellow Am. Psychiat. Assn. (life); mem. Assn. Am. Med. Colls. (sec.-treas. Northeastern group for student affairs 1970-72, chmn. 1972-73), Conn. Psychiat. Soc. (council 1966-68), Hartford Med. Soc. Home: 37 Wendy Ln West Hartford CT 06117 Office: VA Med Ctr. Newington CT 06111

FLEETWOOD, MICK, musician; b. Cornwall, Eng., June 24, 1947; m. Jenny Boyd; children—Lucy, Amy. Drummer (with John Mayall), 1967; with, Fleetwood Mac, 1967—; albums include Tusk, Fleetwood Mac, Rumours *

FLEGE, JOHN BLAIN, JR., educator, cardiovascular surgeon; b. Williamstown, Ky., May 10, 1929; s. John Blain and Frances (Sea) F.; m. Allison V. Stevens, Dec. 28, 1961; children: Hartley, Elizabeth, John, William. B.S., U. Ky., 1951; J.D., U. Cin., 1954. Diplomate: Am. Bd. Surgery, Am. Bd. Thoracic Surgery. Intern Cin. Gen. Hosp., 1954-55, resident, 1959-63, Ohio State U. Hosp., Columbus, 1955-56, Hammersmith Hosp., London, 1963-65; asst. prof. surgery U. Iowa, Iowa City, 1965-69; prof., dir. div. thoracic and cardiovascular surgery U. Cin., 1982—; dir. div. cardiac surgery Jewish Hosp., Cin., 1977—; dir. dept. cardiac surgery Christ Hosp., 1969—. Served to capt. USAF, 1956-58. Mem. ACS, Central Surg. Assn., Soc. Thoracic Surgeons, Internat. Cardiovascular Soc. Club: Cin. Country.

FLEGENHEIMER, ERNEST, sugar company executive; b. Zurich, Switzerland, Jan. 30, 1927; came to U.S., 1942, naturalized, 1943; s. Albert and Helen (Stern) F.; m. Marjorie McGinn, June 7, 1952; children: Ellen, Lauren, Eric Jon, Mark Steven. Student, N.Y. U., 1946-48, Middlebury (Vt.) Coll., 1948-49, Grenoble (France) U., 1949-50. With Domestic Concentrates, Inc. (imports-exports), N.Y.C., 1950-54, Menominee Sugar Co., Green Bay, Wis., 1954-62, Bend Southall McBratnie Co. (sugar brokers), Green Bay, 1962-63; pres., chief exec. officer, dir. Mich. Sugar Co., Saginaw, 1963—; dir. 2d Nat. Bank of Saginaw, Am. Mut. Ins. Co., Wakefield, Mass. Mem. Farmers and Mfrs. Beet Sugar Assn. (dir.), U.S. Beet Sugar Assn. (trustee). Office: Mich Sugar Co 300 Plaza N Saginaw MI 48606 *

FLEISCHAKER, JOSEPH, retail electric appliance exec.; b. Louisville, Jan. 9, 1910; s. Siegfried and Sophie (Lippold) F.; m. Marie Sales, June 14, 1937 (dec. June 1973); children—Carol R. (Mrs. Alvin G. Westerman), Susan (Mrs. Eliot Lee Silbar), Joan (Mrs. Henry T. Evers III) (dec.); m. Nancy Ashley Smith, Feb. 9, 1974. B.S. in Bus. Adminstrn, U. Miami, Fla., 1932; extension courses, N.Y. U. Dist. sales mgr. Orbon Stove Co., Delaware, Ohio; v.p. Leppart Bros., Inc., St. Louis. Columnist: Jerusalem Post. Mem. treas. com. Jefferson County Republican Campaign Fund; bd. dirs. Jewish Hosp. Louisville, Hebrew Home for Aged, Old Peoples Home, St. Louis, Annie Maloney Home, St. Louis; asso. Jewish Hosp., St. Louis; trustee Children's Hosp., St. Louis. Served from lt. (j.g.) to comdr. USNR, 1941-46. Mem. Nat. Appliance Radio-TV Dealers (pres. 1958- 59), Ky. Retail Appliance Dealers (pres. 1954-56), Urban League, Am. Jewish Com., Jewish Hosp. Assn. (asso.), NCCJ, Am. Legion, Brandeis U. (asso. fellow and life mem.), Phi Epsilon Pi, Rho Beta Omicron. Jewish (temple pres. 1952-55). Clubs: Kiwanian., Standard Country (Louisville) (v.p., chmn. house com. 1954-58). Home: 4931 Lindell Blvd Saint Louis MO 63108 Office: 401 S 4th St Louisville KY 40201

FLEISCHER, ARTHUR, JR., lawyer; b. Hartford, Conn., Jan. 27, 1933; s. Arthur and Clare Lillian (Katzenstein) F.; m. Susan Abby Levin, July 6, 1958; children: Elizabeth, Katherine. B.A., Yale U., 1953, LL.B., 1958. Bar: N.Y. State 1959. Assoc. firm Strasser, Spiegelberg, Fried & Frank, N.Y.C., 1958-61; legal asst. SEC, Washington, 1961-62, exec. asst. to chmn., 1962-64; assoc. Fried, Frank, Harris, Shriver & Jacobson, N.Y.C., 1964-67, partner, 1967—; Vis. lectr. law Columbia U. Law Sch., N.Y.C., 1972-73; adviser to advisory com. Fed. Securities Code Project, Am. Law Inst., 1970-78; adviser to com. to consider new issue proposals Nat. Assn. Securities Dealers, 1973-75, mem. com. corporate financing, 1976-80; chmn. Ann. Inst. on Securities Regulation, Practising Law Inst., 1969-81; mem. indsl. issuers adv. com. SEC, 1972-73, mem. adv. com. corporate disclosure, 1976-77; bd. govs. Am. Stock Exchange, 1977-83. Author: Tender Offers: Defenses, Responses and Planning, 1978; Co-editor: Annual Institute on Securities Regulation, 1970-81; contbr. to publs. in field. Mem. adv. council Center for Study of Fin. Instns., U. Pa. Law Sch., 1969—. Served with AUS, 1953-55. Mem. Am. Bar Assn. (mem. com. on fed. regulation of securities regulation 1969—), Assn. Bar City N.Y. (mem. spl. com. on lawyers role in securities transactions 1973-77, chmn. com. securities regulation 1972-74). Home: 1050 Park Ave New York NY 10028 Office: 1 New York Plaza New York NY 10004

FLEISCHER, EVERLY BORAH, coll. dean; b. Salt Lake City, June 5, 1936; s. Arthur and Clare (Katzenstein) F.; m. Harriet Eve Perlysky, June 14, 1959; children—Deborah, Adam Joseph. B.S., Yale U., 1958, M.S., 1959, Ph.D. (NSF fellow 1959-61), 1961. Asst. prof., then asso. prof. chemistry U. Chgo., 1961-69; prof. U. Calif., Irvine, 1970-80, dean phys. sci., 1975-80; prof. chemistry, dean Coll. Arts and Scis., U. Colo., Boulder, 1980—. Author articles on metalloporphyrins, bioinorganic chemistry. Recipient Univ. Service award U. Calif., Irvine, 1980; Alfred P. Sloan fellow, 1962-66. Fellow AAAS; mem. Am. Chem. Soc., Sigma Xi, Alpha Chi Sigma. Home: 69 Wild Horse Circle Boulder CO 80302 Office: Coll Arts and Scis Univ Colo Boulder CO 80309

FLEISCHER, MICHAEL, chemist; b. Bridgeport, Conn., Feb. 27, 1908; s. Julius and Flora (Reinitz) F.; m. Helen Anna Isenberg, Aug. 5, 1934; children—Walter H., David A. B.S., Yale, 1930, Ph.D., 1933. Research fellow Yale, 1934; asst. phys. chemist, geophys. lab. Carnegie Inst., Washington, 1936-39; geochemist U.S. Geol. Survey, 1939—; dir. Am. Geol. Inst., 1951-52; pres. commn. on geochemistry Internat. Union of Pure and Applied Chemistry, 1953-56; profl. lectr. George Washington U., 1957-65. Asst. to editor: Dana's System Mineralogy, 1935; asst. editor: Chem. Abstracts, 1940—; asso. editor: Am. Mineralogist, 1941-54. Recipient Becke medal Austrian Mineral. Soc., 1976; Disting. Service medal Dept. Interior, 1978. Fellow Mineral Soc. Am. (councilor 1944-46, v.p. 1951, pres. 1952, Roebling medalist 1975), Geol. Soc. Am. (v.p. 1953), Soc. Econ. Geol.; mem. Am. Chem. Soc., mineral. socs. Britain, France, Can., Geochem. Soc. (pres. 1964), Sigma Xi. Home: 3104 Chestnut St NW Washington DC 20015 Office: 958 US Geol Survey Reston VA 22092

FLEISCHER, RICHARD O., film director; b. Bklyn., Dec. 8, 1916. B.A., Brown U.; M.F.A., Yale U. Former stage dir.; joined RKO Pathe, 1942; writer-producer Flicker Flashbacks. Writer-dir.: This is America; co-producer: Design for Death; dir.: Cinematheque Francais Retrospective Tribute, Paris, 1975, Crossed Swords, Tough Enough, Ashanti, The Jazz Singer, Amityville III-D, Conan, The Destroyer; Guardian lectr., London, 1981. Address: 169 S Rockingham Ave Los Angeles CA 90049

FLEISCHER, ROBERT LOUIS, physicist; b. Columbus, Ohio, July 8, 1930; s. Leo H. and Rosalie (Kahn) F.; m. Barbara L. Simons, June 10, 1954; children: Cathy Ann, Elizabeth Lee. A.B., Harvard U., 1952, A.M., 1953, Ph.D., 1956. Asst. prof. metallurgy Mass. Inst. Tech., 1956-60; physicist Gen. Elec. Research Lab., Schenectady, 1960—; Sr. research fellow physics Calif. Inst. Tech., 1965-66; adj. prof. physics and astronomy Rensselaer Poly. Inst., 1967-68; adj. prof. geol. sci. SUNY, Albany, 1982—; cons. U.S. Geol. Survey, 1967-70; vis. scientist Nat. Center for Atmospheric Research, also Nat. Oceanic and Atmospheric Adminstrn., 1973-74. Author: Nuclear Tracks in Solids, 1975.; Asso. editor: 1st-4th Lunar Sci. Conf. Procs, 1970-73. Pres. Zoller Sch. P.T.A., 1968-69; mem. com. on candidates Schenectady Citizens Conv. for Sch. Bd., 1969-72, 82—, chmn., 1969-70, 71-72, vice chmn. conv., 1977-78, chmn., 1978-79; mem. com. on priorities Schenectady Sch. Bd., 1974-75; Bd. dirs. Schenectady Citizens' League, Freedom Forum, Inc. Recipient awards Indsl. Research, 1964, 65, 72, Spl. award Am. Nuclear Soc., 1964, Ernest O. Lawrence award AEC, 1971, Gen. Elec. Silver medallion Inventor's award, 1971, Golden Plate award Am. Acad. Achievement, 1972, Coolidge award Gen. Electric Research and Devel. Center, 1972; NASA Exceptional Sci. Achievement award, 1973; spl. recognition, 1979. Fellow Am. Acad. Arts and Scis., Am. Phys. Soc., AAAS, Am. Geophys. Union; mem. Health Physics Soc., Am. Meterol. Soc., Sigma Xi. Research in charged particle tracks in solids and their use in several fields, including cosmic ray and meteorite sci., geochronology, nuclear physics, radiobiology, mineral exploration; defects in solids and their effects on mech. properties and superconducting properties. Publs. and patents in field. Home: 1356 Waverly Pl Schenectady NY 12308 Office: Gen Elec Research Lab Schenectady NY 12301

FLEISCHMAN, ALBERT SIDNEY, writer; b. Bklyn., Mar. 16, 1920; s. Reuben and Sadie (Solomon) F.; m. Beth Elaine Taylor, Jan. 25, 1942; children—Jane, Paul, Anne. B.A., San Diego State Coll., 1949. Newspaper reporter San Diego Daily Jour., 1949-50; freelance screenwriter; lectr. fiction writing UCLA. Author: children's books including Mr. Mysterious & Company, 1962, By the Great Horn Spoon!, 1963, The Ghost in the Noonday Sun, 1965, Chancy and the Grand Rascal, 1966, Jingo Django, 1971, Humbug Mountain, 1978, The Hey Hey Man, 1979, McBroom and the Great Race, 1980. Served with USNR, 1941-45. Recipient Spur award Western Writers Am.; Commonwealth Club award; Lewis Carrol Shelf award; Mark Twain award. Mem. Writers Guild Am., Authors Guild, Soc. Children's Book Writers. Democrat. Jewish. Home and Office: 305 10th St Santa Monica CA 90402

FLEISCHMAN, EDWARD HIRSH, lawyer; b. Cambridge, Mass., June 25, 1932. B.A., Harvard U.; LL.B., Columbia U., 1959. Bar: N.Y. 1959, U.S. Supreme Ct. 1980. Asso. Beekman & Bogue, N.Y.C., 1959-67, partner, 1968—; adj. prof. NYU Law Sch. Contbr. articles to legal jours. Mem. Am. Law Inst., ABA (chmn. ad hoc subcom. rule 144 1970-72, chmn. subcom. broker-dealer matters 1973-78, chmn. adminstrv. law com. securities, commodities and exchanges 1981—). Office: 14 Wall St New York NY 10005

FLEISCHMAN, LAWRENCE ARTHUR, art dealer, publisher, consultant; b. Detroit, Feb. 14, 1925; s. Arthur and Stella (Granet) F.; m. Barbara Greenberg, Dec. 18, 1948; children: Rebecca, Arthur, Martha. Student, Purdue U., 1942-43; B.S., U. Detroit, 1948; L.H.D. (hon.), St. John's U., 1978. Pres. Lawrence Investment Co., Detroit, 1949-66, Lawrence Advt. Agy., 1950-60; dir. Ind. Newspaper, Inc., Detroit, 1952-60, WITI, Channel 6, Milw., 1952-59; pres., owner Kennedy Galleries, N.Y.C., 1966—; dir. Hartwell Hedge Fund, N.Y.C., 1966-72; founder, pres. Archives Am. Art, 1952-66, dir., 1967—; mem. Fine Arts Commn., USIA, 1956-62; advisor Fine Arts Commn., White House, 1960-62, 64-66; pres Detroit Arts Commn., 1962-66; Treas. Soc. Arts and Crafts Sch., Detroit, 1953-66; bd. dirs. Mannes Coll. Music, N.Y.C., 1967-71, Skowhegan Sch. Painting and Sculpture, Maine and N.Y., 1968-83; v.p. Com. Religion and Art of Am., N.Y.C., 1972—; mem. president's council Met. Mus. Art, N.Y.C.; advisor NAD, N.Y.C.; nat. trustee Balt. Mus. Art. Editor Am. Art Jour., 1969—. Served with AUS, 1943-46; ETO. Recipient Spl. Resolution award City of Detroit, 1966, Art award Lotus Club,

N.Y.C., 1967; Copley medal Nat. Portrait Gallery, 1978; decorated knight Order of San Silvestre Pope Paul VI, 1978; fellow Morgan Library, N.Y.C., 1968. Mem. Pa. Acad. Fine Arts (life), Pa. Hist. Soc. (life), Art Dealers Assn. Am., Nat. Antique and Art Dealers Assn. Club: City Athletic. Office: Kennedy Galleries Inc 40 W 57th St New York NY 10019

FLEISCHMAN, MARK H., hotel and night club executive; b. N.Y.C., Feb. 1, 1940; s. Martin and Sylvia (Zausner) F. B.S., Cornell U., 1961. Exec. dir., owner Forest Hills (N.Y.) Inn, 1965-67; prin. in exec. hotel and design A Quiet Little Table in the Corner, 1967; partner Monarck Shrimp Corp., 1967-68; pres. Davos, Inc. (leisure time and foods), N.Y.C., 1968-74; prin. owner Virgin Isle Hotel, St. Thomas, V.I., Exec. Hotel, N.Y.C., John Newcombes Vacation Resort, Orlando, Fla., New Line Cinema, N.Y.C., Robata Restaurants, N.Y.C., Bonnehomme Richard Inn, Williamsburg, Va., Studio 54, N.Y.C. Served to lt. USNR, 1962-64. Mem. Cornell Soc. Hotelmen, Friars Club. Office: Studio 54 229 W 53 St New York NY 10003

FLEISCHMAN, MARVIN, chemical and environmental engineering educator; b. N.Y.C., May 19, 1937; s. Julius and Miriam (Kuropatva) F.; children: Sam, Steve, Richard. B.Ch.E., CCNY, 1959; M.S., U. Cin., 1965, Ph.D., 1968. Registered profl. engr. Research chemist Monsanto Research Corp., Miamisburg, Ohio, 1959-60; sr. asst. san. engr. USPHS, Washington and Cin., 1961-63; research engr. Exxon Co. U.S.A., Florham Park, N.J., 1968-70, Amoco Chems., Naperville, Ill., 1977-78; prof. dept. chem. and environ. engrng. U. Louisville, 1970—, chmn. dept., 1970—. Contbr. articles to profl. jours. Served to lt. USPHS, 1961-63. Grantee NSF, 1971, AID, 1975, Office Water Research Tech., 1974. Mem. Am. Inst. Chem. Engrs. (chmn. AID-Life com. 1975-77), Am. Soc. Enrng. Edn. (vice chmn. continuing edn. com. 1982—). Democrat. Jewish. Home: 6811 Greenlawn Rd Louisville KY 40222 Office: Dept Chem and Environ Engrng U Louisville Louisville KY 40292

FLEISCHMANN, ERNEST MARTIN, music administrator; b. Frankfurt, Germany, Dec. 7, 1924; came to U.S., 1969; s. Gustav and Antonia (Koch) F.; m. Elsa Leviseur, Sept. 22, 1953; children: Stephanie, Martin, Jessica. Mus.B., U. Cape Town, South Africa, 1954; postgrad., South African Coll. Music, 1954-56. Sec. London Symphony Orch., 1959-67; dir. for Europe CBS Records, 1967-69; exec. dir. Los Angeles Philharm. Orch. and Hollywood Bowl, 1969—; mem. French Govt. Commn. Reform of Paris Opera, 1967-68; steering com. U.S. nat. commn. UNESCO Conf. Future of Arts, 1975. Debut as condr., Johannesburg (South Africa) Symphony Orch., 1942; asst. condr., South African Nat. Opera, 1948-51, Cape Town U. Opera, 1950-54; condr., South African Coll. Music choir, 1950-52, Labia Grand Opera Co., Cape Town, 1953-55; music organizer, Van Riebeeck Festival, Cape Town, 1952; dir. music and drama, Johannesburg Festival, 1956; Contbr. music publs. Bd. dirs. Calif. Confedn. of Arts; co-chmn. music policy and festivals panels Nat. Endowment for Arts. Mem. Assn. Calif. Symphony Orchs. (dir.), Major Orch. Mgrs. Conf. (chmn. policy com.). Address: 135 N Grand Ave Los Angeles CA 90012 *Progress in the arts involves taking risks. Safety and blandness go hand in hand and should be banished from the artistic experience: better to stick your neck out and fail than to err on the side of correctness.*

FLEISCHMANN, GLEN HARVEY, artist, author; b. Manley, Nebr., Feb. 23, 1909; s. Frederick Ferdinand and Sarah Montgomery (Taylor) F.; m. Evelyn Grace Fitzpatrick, Feb. 10, 1931. Student, Vogue Sch. of Art, Chgo., 1929-30. From apprentice to ad creator (layout, copy, finished art) Meyer Both Advt. Co., Chgo., 1932-37; exec. artist R. H. Macy & Co., N.Y.C., 1937-39. Author; artist; contbr. to nat. mags., 1939—; including Nation's Business, Sat. Evening Post, Good Housekeeping, Collier's, Woman's Home Companion, Am. Field and Stream, Outdoor Life, Sports Afield, This Week; Author: While Rivers Flow, 1963, The Cherokee Removal, 1971 (Jr. Lit. Guild selection), The Artist: His Markets and His World, 1971. Served with Dept. Tng. Publs., C.E. AUS, 1943-45. Mem. Authors Guild, Authors League Am. Office: 1160 Midland Ave Bronxville NY 10708

FLEISCHMANN, PETER FRANCIS, mag. pub. exec.; b. N.Y.C., Jan. 27, 1922; s. Raoul H. and Ruth (Gardner) F.; m. Nancy Montgomery, 1948 (div.); children—James R., Ruth G., Stephen G.; m. Jeanne Cowles Wilson, May 1964. Grad., Hotchkiss Sch., 1940; B.A., Yale, 1944. Staff New Yorker Mag., Inc., N.Y.C., 1955—, treas., 1955-65, dir., 1953—, exec. v.p., 1965-68, pres., 1968-75, chmn. bd., 1969—. Served as capt. AUS, 1945. Office: New Yorker Magazine Inc 25 W 43d St New York City NY 10036

FLEISCHMANN, WOLFGANG BERNARD, educator; b. Vienna, Austria, July 10, 1928; came to U.S., 1940, naturalized, 1950; s. Walter and Gertrude (Furth) F. B.A., St. John's Coll., 1950; A.M., U. N.C., 1951, Ph.D., 1954. Instr. English U. N.C., 1957-59; asst. prof. comparative lit. U. Okla., 1959-61; asst. prof., asso. prof. Emory U., 1961-63; faculty U. Wis., Milw., 1963-66, prof., chmn. comparative lit. dept., 1964-66; vis. prof. Romance langs. Princeton, 1966-67; prof., chmn. comparative lit. dept. U. Mass., Amherst, 1967-70; prof. comparative lit. Montclair State Coll., Upper Montclair, N.J., 1970—, dean, 1970-80; vis. prof. comparative lit. N.Y. U., 1972, 73-84; also lectr., critic. Mem. bd. visitors and govs. St. John's Coll., Annapolis, Md. and; Santa Fe, 1967-79. Author: Lucretius and English Literature 1680-1740, 1964; gen. editor: Ency. of World Lit. in the 20th Century, vol. 1, 1967, vol. 2, 1969, vol. 3, 1971; mem. editorial bds.: Books Abroad (now World Lit. Today), 1959—, James Joyce Quar, 1964—. Served with U.S. Army, 1953-55. Inst. Research in Humanities fellow U. Wis., 1965-66. Mem. Modern Lang. Assn. (chmn. 1965, 67), Am. Comparative Lit. Assn. (editor Newsletter 1968-72). Home: 235 W 22d St Apt 5-D New York NY 10011 Office: Dept English Montclair State Coll Upper Montclair NJ 07043

FLEISHER, HAROLD, computer scientist; b. Kharkov, Russia, Oct. 12, 1921; came to U.S., 1923, naturalized, 1936; s. Morris and Yetta (Derman) F.; m. Gertrude Lozensky, Dec. 30, 1945; children—Sherry Ann, Leslie Jan, David M. B.A. in Physics, U. Rochester, N.Y., 1942; M.S., 1943; Ph.D. (Ames and AEC fellow 1947-49), Case Inst. Tech., 1951. Mem. staff radiation lab. M.I.T., 1943-45; sr. engr. Rauland Corp., Chgo., 1945-46; instr. physics Case Inst. Tech., 1946-50; with IBM Corp., Poughkeepsie, N.Y., 1950—, IBM fellow, 1974—; adj. prof. Vassar Coll. Author; editor. Mem. adv. bd. Poughkeepsie Bd. Edn., 1967; mem. Poughkeepsie City Commn. Environ. Quality, 1968-69. Recipient cert. merit OSRD, 1945; Vassar fellow, 1975. Fellow IEEE; mem. Am. Phys. Soc., AAAS, Sigma Xi. Jewish. Patentee in field. Home: 30 Wilmot Terr Poughkeepsie NY 12603 Office: PO Box 390 C14/704 Poughkeepsie NY 12602

FLEISHER, LEON, concert pianist, condr.; b. San Francisco, July 23, 1928; s. Isidor and Bertha (Mittelman) F.; m. Dorothy Druzinsky, 1951 (div. Mar. 1962); children—Deborah, Richard, Leah; m. Risselle Rosenthal, Apr. 1, 1962; children—Paula Beth, Julian. Ed. privately; pupil, Artur Schnabel, Lago di Como, Italy, N.Y.C., 1938-48. Prof. piano Peabody Conservatory, Balt., 1959—; bd. dirs. Walter W. Naumburg Found. Music dir., Theatre Chamber Players, Washington, 1968—; debut as condr., N.Y. Chamber Orch.'s Mostly Mozart Festival, 1970; condr., Annapolis (Md.) Symphony, 1970—; asso. condr., Balt. Symphony Orch., 1973-78, recs. for, Columbia Masterworks, Epic Records; First recital, San Francisco, 1935, concert debut, San Francisco Orch., 1943; soloist, N.Y. Philharm. Orch., 1944; recitalist; soloist maj. orchs. in, U.S., Can., S. Am., Europe. First Am. winner Concours Internat. Reine Elisabeth de Belgique, 1952. Mem. AAUP. Due to paralysis of right hand has performed only compositions for left hand, 1965. Office: care Columbia Artists Mgmt Inc 165 W 57th St New York NY 10019 *

FLEISHMAN, AVROM HIRSCH, educator; b. N.Y.C.; s. Louis and Sarah F.; m. Sophia Abraham, Aug. 9, 1960; children: Franz, Ilya. B.A., Columbia, 1954; M.A., Johns Hopkins, 1956, Ph.D., 1963. Asst. prof. U. Minn., Mich. State U.; now prof. English Johns Hopkins U., Balt. Author numerous lit. criticism books. Mem. MLA. Home: 1123 Bellemore Rd Baltimore MD 21210 Office: Dept English Johns Hopkins U Baltimore MD 21218

FLEISHMAN, EDWIN ALAN, psychologist, author; b. N.Y.C., Mar. 10, 1927; s. Harry E. and Sera (Weinblatt) F.; m. Pauline S. Utman, Feb. 6, 1949; children: Jeffrey B., Alan R. B.S., Loyola Coll., Balt., 1945; M.A., U. Md., 1949; Ph.D., Ohio State U., 1951; D.Sc. hon., U. Edinburgh, 1982. Dir. SKill Components Research Lab., U.S. Air Force, San Antonio, 1951-56; prof. indsl. adminstrn. and psychology Yale U., 1957-63; Guggenheim fellow, vis. prof. Israel Inst. Tech., 1962-63; sr. v.p., dir. Washington office Am. Inst. Research, 1963-75; vis. prof. Grad. Sch. Adminstrn., U. Calif.-Irvine, 1975-76; pres. Advanced Research Resources Orng., Washington, 1976—; cons. to govt., ednl. instrns. and industry, 1957—; mem. adv. panel social sci. Office Sec. Def., 1959-61; mem. adv. panel behavioral scis. Office Surgeon Gen. Army, 1964—. Author: (with others) Leadership and Supervision in Industry, 1955, (with R. Gagne) Psychology and Human Performance, 1959, Studies in Personnel and Industrial Psychology, 1961, (with A. Bass) Studies in Personnel and Industrial Psychology, 3d edit., 1974, Structure and Measurement of Physical Fitness, 1964, (with J.G. Hunt) Current Developments in the Study of Leadership, 1973, Human Performance and Productivity, 1982, (with M. Quainsarce) Taxonomies of Human Performance, 1984; contbr. numerous articles, chpts. to jours., books, encys.; assoc. editor: Personnel Psychology, 1961-63, Orgnl. Behavior and Human Performance, 1966-70; editor-in-chief: Jour. Applied Psychology, 1971-76. Served with USNR, 1945-46. Recipient Franklin Taylor award Soc. Engrng. Psychologists, 1974, Profl. Practice award Soc. Indsl. and Organizational Psychology, 1983. Fellow Am. Psychol. Assn. (pres. div. indsl. and organizational psychology 1973-74, Disting. Sci. award for applications psychology 1980, pres. div. engrng. psychology 1977-78, pres. div. evaluation and measurement 1979-80); mem. AAAS, Internat. Assn. Applied Psychology (pres. 1974-82), AAHPER, Psychometric Soc., Am. Ednl. Reserach Assn., Sigma Xi. Club: Cosmos (Washington). Home: 8201 Woodhaven Blvd Bethesda MD 20817 Office: Advanced Research Resources Orgn 4330 East West Hwy Bethesda MD 20814

FLEISHMAN, JOEL LAWRENCE, university administrator; b. Fayetteville, N.C., Apr. 15, 1934; s. Albert Maurice and Ruth (Zeighauser) F. A.B., U. N.C., 1955, J.D., 1959, M.A., 1959; LL.M., Yale U., 1960. Bar: N.C. 1959. Asst. to dir. Walter E. Meyer Research Inst. Law, 1960-61; legal asst. to gov. N.C., 1961-65; dir. Yale Summer High Sch., 1965-67; asso. provost Urban Studies and Programs, Yale U., 1967-69; asso. dir. program devel. Inst. Social Sci., 1969-71; asso. chmn. Center for Study of City, 1969-71, lectr. polit. sci., 1969-71; vice-chancellor for edn. and research in pub. policy, 1971-78, vice chancellor, 1978—; dir. Inst. Policy Scis. Duke U., 1971-82, asso. prof. law, 1971-74, prof. law and policy scis., 1974—, chmn. capital campaign for arts and scis., 1982—; cons. Alfred P. Sloan Found., Ford Found.; Pres. Ruth Z. Fleishman Found.; commr. N.C. Agy. for Public Telecommunications. Author: (with Bruce L. Payne) Ethical Dilemmas and the Education of Policymakers, 1980; co-editor: Public Duties: The Moral Obligations of Public Officials, 1981; editor: The Future of American Political Parties, 1982, The Future of the Postal Service, 1983. Bd. dirs. N.C. Sch. of Arts Found., Nat. Inst. Dispute Resolution, N.C. Center for Pub. Policy Research; trustee Urban Inst., Dillard U., John and Mary Markle Found., Center Philosophy and Pub. Policy. Served with USNR, 1955-56. Mem. Assn. for Public Policy Analysis and Mgmt. (pres. 1979-80, policy council 1979—), Nat. Acad. Public Adminstrn., N.C. Symphony Soc., Order of Golden Fleece, Century Assn., Phi Beta Kappa. Democrat. Jewish (trustee 1972-73). Clubs: Yale (N.Y.C.); Met. (Washington). Home: 205 Wood Circle Chapel Hill NC 27514 Office: 4875 Duke Sta Durham NC 27706

FLEMING, ARTHUR FAZZIN, TV host, film actor; b. N.Y.C., May 1, 1924; s. William Guy and Marie (Volk) Fazzin; m. Becky Lynn, July 4, 1977; children: Kimberly, Timothy. Student, Colgate U., 1941-42; B.S., Cornell U., 1944. Asst. mgr. Roxy Theatre, N.Y.C., 1937-41; state ambassador Pa. Lottery. Disc jockey, Sta. WEED, Rocky Mount, N.C., 1945-47, Sta. WPTF, Raleigh, N.C., 1947-48, Sta. WAKR, Akron, Ohio, 1948-50; announcer, ABC Radio and TV, 1950-54; stuntman, 1954-57; appeared as Ralph Bellamy's double in: TV show Man Against Crime, 1954-55; star: TV series The Flying Tigers, 1958-59, The Californians, 1959-60, Internat. Detective, 1960-62; host: quiz show Jeopardy, 1964, 1976-79; TV appearances include The Moneychangers; also numerous dramatic and variety programs through the years; movies include Hatful of Rain, 1961; MacArthur, 1977, Prime Time, Airplane-Two, Twilight Zone; host TV and radio host, College Bowl, 1977-81; with, Sta. KMOX, St. Louis. Trustee, Collegiate Sch., N.Y.C., 1973-75; sr. deacon Marble Collegiate Ch., N.Y.C.; active Pa. sr. citizens program. Served with AC, USN, World War II. Recipient numerous awards. Mem. Screen Actors Guild, AFTRA, Actors Equity Assn. Republican. Clubs: N.Y. Athletic (life), Lambs, Variety. *Never give up; persevere under all obstacles and think positively. You are what you think you are.*

FLEMING, BRICE NOEL, philosophy educator; b. Hutchinson, Kans., July 29, 1928; s. Augustus Brice and Anna (Noel) F.; m. Barbara Warr, Dec. 20, 1965. B.A., Harvard U., 1950; D.Phil., Oxford (Eng.) U., 1961. Asst. lectr. Manchester (Eng.) U., 1956-57; instr. Yale U., 1957-59, 1960-62; asst. prof. U. Calif. at Santa Barbara, 1962-65, assoc. prof., 1965-69, prof., 1969—. Served with AUS, 1951-53. Office: Dept Philosophy U Calif Santa Barbara CA 93106

FLEMING, CHARLES CLIFFORD, JR., retired jet aircraft sales company executive; b. Gt. Bend, Kans., Dec. 19, 1923; s. Charles Clifford and Nana Gaye (Hanson) F.; m. Barbara Inez Miller, Sept. 15, 1947; children: Charles Clifford III, John Ralph, Robert Mark, Barbara Lisabeth, Roger Andrew. Student, U. Miami, Fla., 1946-48. With Pan Am. World Airways Inc. (and subs's.), 1942-80, v.p. bus. jets div., N.Y.C., 1970-72; pres., chief exec. officer Falcon Jet Corp., Teterboro, N.J., 1972-80, Bus. Jets Internat., Inc., Cocoa, Fla., 1980—; dir. Central Brevard Nat. Bank, Cocoa, Fla. Ordained deacon Baptist Ch.; bd. dirs. United Fund, Brevard County, Fla. Served with AC U.S. Army, 1942-46; PTO. Mem. Nat. Bus. Aircraft Assn., Air Force Assn., Nat. Aviation Club. Republican. Club: Wings (N.Y.C.). Office: Cocoa FL 32922

FLEMING, DONALD HARNISH, educator, historian; b. Hagerstown, Md., Aug. 7, 1923; s. Donald Harnish and Luciphene (Beery) F. A.B., Johns Hopkins, 1943; A.M., Harvard, 1944, Ph.D., 1947. With Brown U., 1947-58, successively lectr., asst. prof., asso. prof., 1953-55, prof. history, 1955-58; prof. history of sci. Yale, 1958-59; vis. prof. Harvard, 1958-59, prof. history, 1959-70, Jonathan Trumbull prof. Am. history, 1970—; dir. Charles Warren Center for Studies in Am. History, 1973-80. Author: John William Draper, 1950 (Beveridge prize Am. Hist. Assn.), William Henry Welch and the Rise of Modern Medicine, 1954; Co-editor: Perspectives in American History, 1967-80, The Intellectual Migration: Europe and America, 1930-1960, 1969. Fellow Am. Acad. Arts and Scis.; mem. History of Sci. Soc. Home: 221 Mt Auburn St Cambridge MA 02138

FLEMING, DOUGLAS G., agribusiness and food processing company executive; b. Harvey, Ill., Apr. 28, 1930; s. Harold L. and Genevieve (Hodges) F.; m. Sara L. Waters, May 25, 1952; children: Christine J., James C. B.S., Mich. State U., 1954. With Central Soya Co., 1954—, asst. mgr. field ops., Ft. Wayne, Ind., 1963-65, v.p., dir. mktg., 1965-70, exec. v.p., 1970-76, pres., 1976-79, chmn., pres., chief exec. officer, 1979—, also dir.; dir. Ft. Wayne Nat. Bank, Midwestern United Life Ins. Co., Tokheim Corp., Arvin Industries. Bd. dirs. United Way Allen County. Served to 2d lt. AUS, 1951-53. Mem. Am. Feed Mfrs. Assn. Clubs: Ft. Wayne Country, Summit (Ft. Wayne). Home: 16817 Tonkel Rd Leo IN 46765 Office: 1300 Fort Wayne Nat Bank Bldg Fort Wayne IN 46802

FLEMING, EDWARD J., clergyman; b. Montclair, N.J., Mar. 29, 1920; s. Timothy Joseph and Agnes (Gannon) F. Student, Seton Hall Prep. Sch., South Orange, N.J., 1932-36; A.B., Seton Hall U., 1940, M.A., 1948, LL.D., 1970, Immaculate Conception Sem., Ramsey, N.J., 1936-40; S.T.L., Cath. U. Am., 1944; Ph.D., St. John's U., Bklyn., 1955; grad., Inst. Advanced Studies, N.Am. Coll., Rome, 1977. Ordained priest Roman Catholic Ch., 1944, elevated to papal chamberlain, 1963; priest St. Teresa's Ch., Summit, N.J., 1944-49; prof. ednl. psychology and religion Seton Hall U., 1949-51, dean student affairs, 1951-53, dean coll., 1953-59, exec. v.p., 1959-69, acting pres., 1969-70; pastor Our Lady of Blessed Sacrament Ch., Roseland, N.J., 1970—; archdiocesan dean, 1975—; mem. exam. bd. Archdiocesan Clergy and Seminary, 1954-64; mem. Archdiocesan Commn. Parish Visitation, 1969—; dean West Essex area Newark Archdiocese; coordinating dean Essex County, 1975—; pres. Roseland Council Chs.; mem. ethics com. N.J. Supreme Ct., 1979—; mem. Senate of Priests, Archdiocese of Newark, 1980—, Archdiocesan Sch. Bd., 1980. Contbr. articles on higher edn. to ednl. periodicals and jours. Mem. Army Adv. Panel ROTC Affairs, 1961-70; mem. Edn. Commn. U.S.; mem. pres.'s council Caldwell Coll., N.J.; trustee Assumption Coll., Mendham, N.J., Greater Newark Black and White Opera Co., Tri-Hosp. Ecumenical Chaplaincy Council No. N.J., 1979. Recipient Alpha Epsilon Mu award, 1956; Sapientiae Christianae Humanitarian award, 1958; John J. Crecca Found. Humanitarian award, 1967; Zionist Brotherhood award, 1979; named Irishman of Year Friends of Brian Boru, Inc., 1967. Mem. Eastern Assn. Coll. Deans and Advisers of Men, Nat. Cath. Edn. Assn. (pres. Eastern unit 1965-66), Middle States Accreditation Assn., N.J. Hist. Soc. (com. of 125), Cath. Theol. Soc. Am. Address: 28 Livingston Ave Roseland NJ 07068

FLEMING, EDWARD STITT, psychiatrist; b. San Diego, Apr. 11, 1930; s. Robert Walton and Emma Scott (Stitt) F.; m. Mariana Moran; children: Edward Stitt, Edith Page, Richard Bland Lee. B.A., U. N.C., 1951; M.A. in Psychology, U. Tex., 1952; M.D. cum laude, George Washington U., 1957. Intern U. N.C. Sch. Medicine, 1957-58; resident in psychiatry Yale Sch. Medicine, 1958-61; instr. psychiatry Yale U., 1961-63; also physician-in-charge psychiat. out-patient clinic Yale-New Haven Hosp., 1961-63; career tchr. NIMH, 1963-65; dir. in-patient psychiat. services George Washington U. Hosp., Washington, 1963-67; asst. prof. psychiatry George Washington U. Sch. Medicine, 1963-65, asso. clin. prof., 1965-81; postgrad. med. tng. Washington Psychoanalytic Inst., 1963-67; founder Psychiat. Inst. Washington, 1966; pres. 1966-73; founder, dir., chief exec. officer, pres. Psychiat. Insts. Am., 1969-82; founder, bd. dirs. Psychiat. Inst. Found., 1968-82; founding dir., chmn., pres., chief exec. officer First Washington Group, Inc., 1979-82. Mem. Fed. City Council, Washington. Served with USAF, 1951-53; Served with USPHS, 1955-56. Fellow Am. Psychiat. Assn.; mem. AMA, D.C. Med. Soc., Washington psychiat. socs., N.Y. Acad. Scis., Alpha Omega Alpha. Episcopalian. Clubs: George Town, 1925 F St. (Washington); Gibson Island, Army and Navy. Home: Washington DC Office: First Mgmt Group Inc 1208 30th St NW Washington DC 20007

FLEMING, ELYSE S., educator; b. N.Y.C., Aug. 3, 1927; d. Benjamin H. and Evanora Lyon Schwartz; m. David G. Fleming, Jan. 30, 1949; 1 son, Neil S. A.B., Queens Coll., 1948; M.A., U. Calif., Berkeley, 1952, Ph.D., 1956. Tchr. public schs., Oakland, Calif., 1950-52; psychologist, social worker Douglas County (Kans.) Mental Health Clinic, 1956-58; asst. prof. edn. Case Western Res. U., Cleve., 1959-63, asso. prof., 1963-72, prof., 1972-79, chairperson dept., 1972-77; prof. Cleve. State U., 1979—; dir. Center for Study of Individual Differences, 1980—. Contbr. articles to profl. jours. Recipient John S. Diekhoff award for Distinguished grad. teaching, 1978. Mem. Am. Psychol. Assn., Am. Ednl. Research Assn., Council Exceptional Children, Assn. for the Gifted, Ohio Assn. Gifted, Cleve. Psychol. Assn. Office: Coll Edn Cleve State U Cleveland OH 44115

FLEMING, JAMES SYDNEY CLARK, Canadian politician; b. Kitchener, Ont., Can., Oct. 30, 1939; s. Alexander and Alice Evelyn (McVannel) F.; m. Ilona Snepers, Nov. 30, 1971; children: Alexander, Skye F., John Robert. Student, Eastwood Coll. Inst., 1955-58; B.A., U. Toronto, 1961. Pres. Toronto Mcpl. Press Gallery, 1966; dir. Canadian Soc. Abolition Death Penalty, 1971-72; mem. House of Commons for Toronto York West, 1972—; Parliamentary Sec. to Minister of Communications, 1975, to Minister Fisheries and Environment, 1976; Minister of State for Multiculturalism, Can., 1980-84. Liberal. Presbyterian. Office: House of Commons Ottawa ON K1A 0A6 Canada *

FLEMING, JOHN GUNTHER, legal educator; b. Berlin, July 6, 1919; U.S., 1960, naturalized, 1975; m. Valerie Joyce Beall, Apr. 16, 1946; children—Anthony, Barbara, Colin, Stephen. B.A., Oxford U., 1939, M.A., 1941, D.Phil., 1948, D.C.L., 1959. Bar: English bar 1947. Lectr. in law King's Coll., London, 1946-48; prof., dean faculty law Australian Nat. U., 1949-60; prof. law U. Calif. at Berkeley, 1957-58, 60—, Shannon Cecil Turner prof. law, 1974—. Author: Law of Torts, 6th edit, 1983, Introduction to the Law of Torts, 1967; editor-in-chief: Am. Jour. Comparative Law, 1971—. Served with Royal Armoured Corps, Brit. Army, 1941-45. Hon. fellow Brasenose Coll., Oxford U.; mem. Am. Law Inst., Internat. Acad. Comparative Law, Internat. Assn. Legal Sci. (pres. 1980—). Home: 401 Western Dr Point Richmond CA 94801

FLEMING, JOHN VINCENT, humanities educator; b. Baxter County, Ark., May 20, 1936; s. Marvin Dale and Janet Elizabeth (Davidson) F.; m. Joan Elizabeth Newman, June 2, 1962; children—Richard Arthur, Katherine Elizabeth, Christopher Luke Owles. B.A., U. of South, Sewanee, Tenn., 1958, Oxford (Eng.) U., 1960, M.A., 1965; Ph.D., Princeton U., 1963. Instr. English U. Wis., 1963-65; mem. faculty Princeton, 1965—, prof. English, and comparative lit., 1971—, Louis W. Fairchild '24 prof. English, 1982—, acting chmn. dept. English, 1979—, chmn., 1981—; publisher Pilgrim Press, 1973—; Bicentennial preceptor Princeton, 1968-69; Mem. Middle States

Commn. on Higher Edn., 1982; bd. dirs. Newcombe Fellowship Awards, 1981; Mem. George Jean Nathan Prize Com., 1981—. Author: Roman de la Rose, 1969, An Introduction to the Franciscan Literature of the Middle Ages, 1977, (with Marjorie Reeves) Two Poems Attributed to Joachim of Fiore, 1978; From Bonaventure to Bellini, 1982; Author also articles.; Editor: Good Reading, 1968-74; editorial bd.: Medievalia, 1975—. Trustee William Alexander Procter Found., Assn. Advancement Mentally Handicapped, 1981, Bd. Examining Chaplains of Episcopal Ch., 1958; vis. research fellow William Morris Centre, London. Nat. Endowment for Humanities fellow William Morris Centre, 1976-77. Mem. Medieval Acad. Am., MLA, Ozark Soc., Phi Beta Kappa. Home: 39 University Pl Princeton NJ 08540 Office: Dept English Princeton U Princeton NJ 08540

FLEMING, JON HUGH, college president; b. Dallas, Oct. 8, 1941; s. Durwood and Lurlyn (January) F.; m. Ann Robinson, Apr. 17, 1961; children: Marcus, Phillip, Jon Mark, Mallory, Jonathan Robinson. B.A., So. Meth. U., 1963, Th.M., 1966; Rel.D., Sch. Theology at Claremont, 1968. Exec. asst. to dean, dir. devel. U. Tex. Med. Sch., Houston, 1970-73; dir. devel., exec. dir. health sci. center relations U. Tex. Health Sci. Center, Houston, 1973-76; lectr. dept. psychiatry, 1971-76, adj. prof. psychiatry, 1976-78; exec. v.p., prof. psychology and human devel. Tex. Woman's U., Denton, 1976-78; pres., prof. psychology Tex. Wesleyan Coll., Ft. Worth, 1978—; grad. teaching asst. Sch. Theology at Claremont, Calif., 1966-68; cons. Sadler Clinic and Doctor's Hosp., Conroe, Tex. Telemetrics Internat., 1974-75. Mem. bds. Edna Gladney Home, Ft. Worth Symphony, Arts Council t. Worth and Tarrant County, Inc.; mem. exec. com. Jr. Achievement Tarrant County, Inc.; bd. dirs. W. Tex. region NCCJ, Goodwill Industries, March of Dimes, Girls' Service League; mem. exec. com. Van Cliburn Found.; state chmn. educators for Reagan-Bush, 1980; mem. chancellor's council U. Tex. System. Mem. Council for Advancement and Support Edn., Assn. Higher Edn. North Tex. (mem. bd.), Philos. Soc. Tex. Republican. Methodist. Clubs: Ft. Worth, Colonial Country, Century II (Fort Worth); Doctor's, Ramada (Houston); Headliners (Austin, Tex.). Office: Tex Wesleyan Coll Fort Worth TX 76105

FLEMING, JOSEPH BENEDICT, newspaperman; b. N.Y.C., Jan. 29, 1919; s. Joseph Benedict and Eleanor (Kane) F.; m. Doris Fleming; children—Volker, Sabine. B.S., CCNY, 1941. Staff Portsmouth (N.H.) Herald, 1942, Stars and Stripes, 1943-45, Chattanooga Times, 1946-47; with UPI, 1948—, bur. mgr., Berlin, from 1950, now bur. mgr. Home: 50 Johannes Strasse 5300 Bonn 3 West Germany office: Heuss Allee 2-10 Pressehaus 1 5300 Bonn West Germany

FLEMING, JULIAN DENVER, JR., lawyer; b. Rome, Ga., Jan. 12, 1934; s. Julian D. and MargaretMadison (Mangham) F.; m. Sidney Howell, June 28, 1960; 1 dau., Julie Adrianne. Student, U. Pa., 1951-53; B. Chem. Engring., Ga. Inst. Tech., 1955, Ph.D, 1959; J.D., Emory U., 1967. Bar: Ga. 1966, D.C. 1967. Research engr., prof. chem. engring. Ga. Inst. Tech., 1955-67; ptnr. Sutherland, Asbill & Brennan, Atlanta, 1967—. Contbr. articles to profl. jours.; patentee in field. Bd. dirs. Mental Health Assn. Ga., 1970-80, Mental Health Assn. Met. Atlanta, 1970-80; pres. Mental Health Assn. Met. Atlanta, 1974-75; mem. council legal advisers Republican Nat. Com., 1981—. Fellow Am. Inst. Chemists; mem. ABA (council sect. sci. and tech. 1980-82, vice chmn. 1982—), Am. Inst. Chem. Engrs. Home: 2238 Hill Park Ct Decatur GA 30033 Office: 3100 First Atlanta Tower Atlanta GA 30383

FLEMING, LOUIS BROWN, journalist; b. Pitts., Apr. 16, 1925; s. Thomas and Margaret Eaton (Brown) F.; m. Jean Tarr, July 19, 1947; children: Mary Fleming Kowalski, Helen Fleming Whitehead, Sarah, Louis Brown. B.A., Stanford U., 1947. Reporter San Gabriel (Calif.) Sun, Pomona (Calif.) Progress-Bull. and; Pasadena (Calif.) Star-News; also asso. dir. Presbyterian Office Info., 1947-60; staff writer Los Angeles Times, since 1960, UN corr., 1962-68, Rome corr., 1968-71, 77-82, editorial writer, 1971-77, 83—. Served with USNR, 1943-46. Congressional fellow Am. Polit. Sci. Assn., 1954-55. Episcopalian. Home: 1579 Lombardy Rd Pasadena CA 91106 Office: 201 W 1st St Los Angeles CA 90053

FLEMING, MACK GERALD, lawyer; b. Hartwell, Ga., May 3, 1932; s. Mack Judson and Dessie Leola (Vickery) F.; m. Elizabeth McClellan, Mar. 30, 1963; children: Katharine Lee, John McClellan. B.S., Clemson (S.C.) U., 1956; J.D., Am. U., Washington, 1966. Asst. dir. prodn. control Woodside Mills, Simpsonville, S.C., 1959-60; adminstrv. asst. to mem. congress, 1960-64; dir. Congressional Liaison Office, VA, Washington, 1965-68, spl. asst. to adminstr., 1968-69; adminstrv. asst., counsel to mem. congress, 1969-70, pvt. practice law, Washington, 1970-74; chief counsel Com. on Vets. Affairs, U.S. Ho. of Reps., 1974-80, staff dir. and chief counsel, 1980—. Served to 1st lt. U.S. Army, 1956-58. Mem. D.C., S.C. bar assns. Democrat. Methodist. Home: 805 E Capitol St SE Washington DC 20003 Office: 335 Cannon House Office Bldg Washington DC

FLEMING, NED NELSON, wholesale food distbr.; b. Lyndon, Kans., Jan. 18, 1900; s. Oliver Albert and Edith May (Hollingsworth) F.; m. Marjorie Virginia Miller, Oct. 15, 1923; children—Marilyn Jean (Mrs. Richard D. Harrison), James B., Stephen M. Student, Washburn U., 1917-19, D.B.A. (hon.), 1963; B.S. in Econs, U. Pa., 1921. With Fleming Cos., Inc., Inc., Topeka, 1921—, treas., gen. mgr., 1922-33, v.p., gen. mgr., 1933-45, pres., 1945-64, chmn. bd., chief exec. officer, 1964-66, chmn. bd., 1966-81, hon. chmn., 1981—; dir. Unitog Co., Kansas City, Mo. Adv. dir. Boys Clubs, Topeka, 1969—; trustee Washburn Coll.; former mem. exec. com. Menninger Found., Topeka. Recipient Distinguished Service citation U. Kans., 1971. Mem. Phi Delta Theta. Clubs: River (Kansas City, Mo.); Topeka Country; Paradise Valley (Ariz.); Country. Home: 9347 SW 10th St Topeka KS 66604 also 5315 E Solano Dr Paradise Valley AZ 85253 Office: 2 Town Site Plaza Topeka KS 66601

FLEMING, PEGGY GALE, ice skater; b. San Jose, Calif., July 27, 1948; d. Albert Eugene and Doris Elizabeth (Deal) F.; m. Greg Jenkins; 1 son, Andy. Student, Colo. Coll., from 1966. Commentator for ABC Sports; appears in comml s. for Concord Watch. Performer with, Ice Capades, from 1968, Ice Follies; performer 7 TV spls.; guest appearance, Fantasy Island; Ambassador of goodwill, UNICEF. Nat. chmn. Easter Seals; trustee Womens Sports Found. Recipient Sports award ABC-TV, 1967; named Woman of Year Reader's Digest, 1969, Female Athlete of Year A.P., 1968; named to Colo. Hall of Fame, 1969. Mem. U.S. Figure Skating Assn. Club: Broadmoor Figure Skating (Colorado Springs, Colo.). Juvenile ice skating champion S.W. Pacific and Pacific Coast, 1960, novice champion, 1961, sr. champion, 1963, jr. champion S.W. Pacific, 1962; 2d place nat. novice champion, 1962, 3d nat. jr. champion, 1963; U.S. ladies champion, 1964-68; 2d place N.Am. competition, 1965; 3d place world championship competition, 1965; world champion, 1966, 67, 68; N.Am. ladies champion, 1967; 1st place gold medal for women's figure skating Olympic Games, 1968. Address: care William Morris Agy 151 El Camino Beverly Hills CA 90212 *

FLEMING, PHYLLIS JANE, physicist, educator; b. Shelbyville, Ind., Oct. 9, 1924; d. Russell P. and Grace (Wheeler) F. B.A., Hanover Coll., 1946; M.S., U. Wis., 1948, Ph.D., 1954. Instr. physics Mt. Holyoke Coll., 1948-50; instr. dept. physics Wellesley Coll., 1953-55, asst. prof., 1955-61, asso. prof., 1961-67, prof. physics, 1967—, dean, 1968-72, dir. Sci. Ctr., 1982-84. Contbr. articles to profl. jours. Mem. Am. Phys. Soc., Am. Assn. Physics Tchrs., AAUP, Sigma Xi. Roman Catholic. Home: 668 Washington St Wellesley MA 02181

FLEMING, REX JAMES, scientist; b. Omaha, Apr. 25, 1940; s. Robert Leonard and Doris Mae (Burrows) F.; m. Kathleen Joyce Ferry, Sept. 3, 1969; children: Thane, Manon, Mark, Noel. B.S., Creighton U., 1963; M.S., U. Mich., 1968, Ph.D., 1970. Commd. lt. U.S. Air Force, 1963, resigned commn. as capt., 1972; research scientist, Offutt AFB, Nebr., 1963-67; sci. liaison to Nat. Weather Service for Air Weather Service, Suitland, Md., 1970-72; resigned, 1972; mgr. applications mktg. advanced sci. computer Tex. Instruments, Inc., Austin, 1972-75; dir. U.S. Project Office for Global Weather Expt., NOAA, Rockville, Md., 1975-80, Spl. Research Projects Office, 1980-82, Office of Climate and Atmospheric Research, 1983—. Contbr. articles to profl. jours. Recipient Gold Medal award Dept. Commerce, 1980. Fellow AAAS; Mem. Am. Meteorol. Soc. (chmn. probability and statistics com. 1976-77), Am. Soc. Photogrammetry, Am. Geophys. Union (sec. atmospheric scis. sect. 1984), The Ocean Soc. Republican. Home: 9200 Bells Mill Rd Potomac MD 20854 Office: 6010 Executive Blvd Rockville MD 20852 *One need only be inspired by its spring-morning freshness, stimulated by its magnificent variety of color and form, and humbled by the power of its ever-present energy, to be driven to unveil the secrets of our life-sustaining atmosphere.*

FLEMING, RHONDA, actress, singer; b. Calif., Aug. 10; d. Harold Cheverton and Effie (Graham) Louis; m. Ted Mann. Student, public schs., Los Angeles, Beverly Hills, Calif. Founding mem. Hunting Hartford Theatre, The Greek Theatre, Los Angeles Music Center. Appeared in: numerous motion pictures, including Spellbound, 1945, Spiral Staircase, 1945, A Connecticut Yankee in King Arthur's Court, 1949, The Great Lover, 1949, Gunfight at OK Corral, 1957, Home Before Dark, Pony Express, 1958, The Nude Bomb, 1979; Broadway debut in The Women, 1973; appeared in: musical plays, including The Boyfriend, 1975, Marriage Go Round, 1960, Bell, Book and Candle, 1963, Kismet, 1976; sang Gershwin concert in; 10-week tour, 1963; starred, Las Vegas, Nev., 1959, one-woman concert at, Hollywood Bowl, 1960, numerous guest appearances on, TV series and talk shows; TV movies include The Last Hours Before Morning, 1975; spokeswoman for: Beecham's 2d Debut Facial Lotion. Recipient award NCCJ, Silver Angel award Religion in Media; Named Woman of Year City of Hope. Mem. Achievement Rewards for Coll. Scientists, United Cerebral Palsy/Spastic Found., Child Help (Woman of World award), Animal and Wildlife Protection Inst. Am.; Assoc. Pepperdine U.; Mem. Los Angeles Philanthropic Assn.

FLEMING, RICHARD, chemical company executive; b. N.Y.C., June 15, 1924; s. James and Caroline (Jung) F.; m. Roberta Marie Seeber, Apr. 8, 1945; children: Richard James, Robert Carleton, Kathleen Teresa Mary. B.Chem. Engring., Pratt Inst., 1944; M.Chem. Engring., N.Y. U., 1949. Devel. engr. Air Reduction Co., Stamford, Conn., 1946-48; design engr. Tex. Co.-N.Y., N.Y.C., 1948-50; devel. engr. Rohm & Haas Co., Bristol, Pa., 1950-52; asst. mgr. corp. devel. Lukens Steel Co., Coatsville, Pa., 1952-54; sect. mgr. research and devel. Sun Oil Co., Marcus Hook, Pa., 1954-59, asst. dir. research and engring., Phila., 1959-62; pres. Avisun Corp., Phila., 1962-69; group v.p., dir., mem. exec. fin. com. Air Products & Chems., Inc., Allentown, Pa., 1969-78, exec. v.p., 1978-80; pres., chief operating officer, dir. GAF Corp., 1980-81; founder Richard Fleming Assocs., Inc. (mgmt. cons.), 1981; founder, chmn. Fiscal Dynamics Inc., 1982; bd. dirs., treas. Chem. Industry Inst. Toxicology, 1975-77, chmn. bd., 1977-81. Bd. dirs. Allentown Hosp., 1976-82; pres., chmn. bd. dirs. Allentown and Sacred Heart Hosp. Center, 1978—; bd. dirs., mem. steering com., exec. com. Am. Indsl. Health Council, 1978-80; bd. dirs., mem. exec. com. Health East, 1981—. Served with USNR, 1942-46. Mem. Am. Inst. Chem. Engrs., Am. Chem. Soc., Am. Mgmt. Assn., Chem. Mfrs. Assn. (vice chmn. chem. regulations adv. com. 1979-80). Home: Windfields Zionsville PA 18092

FLEMING, RICHARD CARL DUNNE, urban planner; b. Balt., July 20, 1945; s. Winter M. and Ethel (Murphy) F. B.S. in Polit. Sci., Loyola U., Balt., 1967; M.B.A. (Carnegie-Mellon fellow), U. Pa., 1971; M. City Planning (H.B. Erhardt Found. fellow), U. Pa., 1971. Asst. devel. dir. Rouse Co., Columbia, Md., 1967-69; dir. planning Phipps Land Co., Inc., Atlanta, 1971-72; v.p. Central Atlanta Progress, Inc., 1972-76; sr. adviser to Pres.-elect Carter, 1976-77; gen. dep. asst. sec. for community planning and devel. Dept. Housing and Community Devel., Washington, 1977-80; pres., chief exec. officer Downtown Denver, Inc., 1980—, Denver Partnership, Inc., 1980—, Denver Civic Ventures, Inc., 1980—. Bd. dirs., vice chmn. Downtown Devel. Found., Inst. Urban and Pub. Policy, U. Colo.; bd. dirs. Historic Paramount Found., Big Bros. Redevel. Corp., Met. Denver Arts Alliance, Denver Family Housing Corp. Mem. Urban Land Inst. (dir.), Nat. Assn. Housing and Redevel. Ofcls., Assn. M.B.A. Execs., Internat. Downtown Execs. Assn. (bd. dirs.), Nat. Urban Coalition, Consumer Fedn. Am., Common Cause. Democrat. Home: 1843 Wazee St Lower Downtown Denver CO 80202 Office: Denver Partnership Inc 511 16th St Mall Suite 200 Denver CO 80202

FLEMING, ROBERT HENRY, former govt. ofcl.; b. Madison, Wis., Jan. 30, 1912; s. Robert H. and Mabel Clair (Scanlan) F.; m. Jean Elizabeth Heitkamp, June 27, 1936; children—Robert Henry, Frederick Heitkamp. B.A., U. Wis., 1934; Nieman fellow, Harvard, 1950. Reporter Madison Capital Times, 1931-43, Milw. Jour., 1945-53; Midwest bur. chief Newsweek mag., 1953-57; corr. ABC, 1957-61, chief Washington bur., 1961-65; dep. press sec. to Pres. U.S., 1966-68; asst. dir. USIA, 1968-69; staff Ho. of Reps., 1969-81. Contbr. to: Nieman Reports. Served as officer, inf. AUS, 1943-45. Recipient Distinguished Service award U. Wis., 1959. Presbyterian (deacon). Home: 2711 Jenifer St NW Washington DC 20015

FLEMING, ROBERT JOHN, food company executive; b. Des Moines, Dec. 7, 1921; s. John Charles Stanhope and Elizabeth Ball (Gathright) F.; m. Virginia Ann Wallace, Aug. 16, 1944; children: Robert John, III, James Wallace, Erik Lindhardt. Student, M.I.T., Iowa State U. With Nat. By-Products, Inc., Des Moines, 1947—, chmn., chief exec. officer, 1955—; dir. Fed. Co., Memphis, Pioneer Hi-Bred Internat., Equitable of Iowa Cos., Bankers Trust Co., all Des Moines. Pres. Living History Farms Found., Des Moines; chmn. Iowa Meth. Med. Ctr, Des Moines; trustee Drake U., Des Moines; past pres., trustee Des Moines Art Center. Served with F.A. AUS, 1943-46. Mem. Fats and Proteins Research Found. (past chmn.), Nat. Renderers Assn. (past pres.), Beta Gamma Sigma. Republican. Episcopalian. Clubs: Des Moines, Wakonda Country. Office: PO Box 615 Des Moines IA 50303

FLEMING, ROBERT WRIGHT, investment banker; b. Washington, Aug. 26, 1918; s. Robert Vedder and Alice Listen (Wright) F.; m. Martha Wills Schoenfeld, Nov. 21, 1942; children: Margaret Johanna, Robert Vedder II, Bruce Wright. B.A., George Washington U., 1941. Washington rep. Pan. Am. Airways, 1946-48; became v.p., sec., dir. Folger Nolan Fleming Douglas Inc., Washington, 1948, now pres., dir.; dir. Steadman Am. Industry Fund Trust, Steadman Investment Fund, Interstate Fed. Savs. & Loan Assn., Acacia Mut. Life Ins. Co., Security Storage Co.; adv. bd. Riggs Nat. Bank, Washington.; Mem. Washington Bd. Trade, N.Y., Am. stock exchanges.; Chmn. endowment and investment com. Washington Hosp. Center; chmn. adv. com. Pub. Service Commn. D.C., 1967-70. Treas. Nat. Citizens for Eisenhower Congl. Com.; Bd. dirs., treas. D.C. Crippled Children's Soc.; chmn. bd. trustees endowment fund ARC; pres. Rotary Found., 1976-78; bd. dirs. Washington Heart Assn., D.C. chpt. A.R.C.; trustee Boys Club of Washington, Washington Hosp. Center. Served as lt. comdr. USNR, 1941-46. Mem. Friendly Sons St. Patrick, Nat. Assn. Security Dealers (bd. govs.), Assn. Stock Exchange Firms, Investment Bankers Assn., Phila.-Balt. Exchange, Nat. Geog. Soc. (finance com.), Kappa Alpha, Omicron Delta Kappa. Clubs: Burning Tree (Bethesda, Md.); Chevy Chase (Md.); Metropolitan, Nat. Press, Alfalfa (Washington); Pine Valley Golf (N.J.); Rehoboth Beach Country (Del.); Rotary. Home: 5106 Cammack Dr Spring Hill Bethesda MD 20816 Office: 725 15th St Washington DC 20005

FLEMING, ROSE ANN, college president; b. Cin., Aug. 23, 1932; d. Thomas John and Mary Gertrude F. B.A., Mt. St. Joseph-on-the-Ohio, 1954; M.A. in English, U. Detroit, 1964; M.Ed., Xavier U., Cin., 1969; Ph.D., Miami U., Oxford Ohio, 1973. Joined Sisters of Notre Dame de Manur, Roman Cath. Ch., 1954; tchr. Latin, social studies, English Mt. Notre Dame High Sch., Reading, Ohio, 1954-60; mem. faculty Summit Country Day Sch., Cin., 1960-75, supr., 1967-75; pres. Trinity Coll., Washington, 1975—; mem. Washington Commn. Post-Secondary Edn., 1975—; asso. mem. Consortium Univs. and Colls., Washington, 1975—. Trustee Washington Ednl. TV Assn. Mem. Internat. Assn. Univ. Presidents (mem. steering com. of N.Atlantic com. 1981—), Kappa Gamma Pi. Address: 701 E Columbia Ave Cincinnati OH 45215

FLEMING, RUSSELL, JR., utility executive; b. New Brunswick, N.J., Aug. 20, 1938; s. Russell and Margaret Olga (Kebly) F.; children: Eileen, Russell III. A.B., Rutgers U., 1960; J.D., Columbia U., 1963. Bar: N.J. 1964. Partner firm Sailer and Fleming, Elizabeth, N.J., 1970-73; v.p., gen. counsel Elizabethtown Gas Co., 1973-80, exec. v.p., gen. counsel, 1980—; gen. atty. Elizabethtown Water Co., 1973-80; v.p., gen. counsel NUI Corp., 1975—; exec. com. Associated Gas Distbrs., 1979—; counsel boroughs of, Milltown and Middlesex, 1969, 73. Pres. Milltown Bd. Edn., 1968-69; sec. Middlesex County Charter Study Commn., 1973. Served to capt. USAR, 1963-65. Mem. Am. Gas Assn., Am. Bar Assn., N.J. Gas Assn., N.J. Bar Assn. (chmn. public utility law sect. 1975), Union County Bar Assn., Middlesex County Bar Assn. Roman Catholic. Office: 1 Elizabeththown Plaza Elizabeth NJ 07207

FLEMING, RUTH, physician, association executive; b. Poteau, Okla., Nov. 15, 1913; d. William T. and Ora Antoinette (Ellis) F. B.S., U. Ark., 1935; M.D., Washington U., St. Louis, 1939. Diplomate: Am. Bd. Surgery. Intern Children's Hosp., San Francisco, 1939-40, resident, 1940-42, St. Joseph's Hosp., San Francisco, 1942-43; preceptor Alison R. Kilgore M.D., San Francisco, 1943-48; practice medicine specializing in gen. surgery, San Francisco, 1942-81, practice medicine ltd. to breast, 1981—; mem. staff Children's, Pacific Med. Center; adminstr. Western Pacific Employees Med. Corp., San Francisco, 1963—; nat. pres. Am. Med. Women's Assn., 1973—; Bd. cooperators Med. Coll. Pa., Phila., 1973. Fellow A.C.S.; mem. AMA, Calif. Med. Assn., San Francisco Med. Soc., Am. Assn. R.R. Surgeons, Western Assn. R.R. Surgeons, Am. Med. Women's Assn. No. Calif., San Francisco Bus. and Profl. Women's Club. Home: 155 Graystone Terr San Francisco CA 94114 Office: 490 Post St San Francisco CA 94102

FLEMING, SAMUEL M., banker; b. Franklin, Tenn., Apr. 29, 1908; s. Samuel M. and Cynthia Graham (Cannon) F.; m. Josephine Cliffe, Dec. 10, 1930 (dec.); children: Joanne Cliffe (Mrs. Toby S. Wilt), Daniel Milton. Student, Battle Ground Acad., 1919-24; A.B., Vanderbilt U., 1928. Asst. credit mgr. N.Y. (City) Trust Co., 1928-31; with Third Nat. Bank, Nashville, 1931—, dir., 1947—, pres., 1950-70, chmn. bd., 1970—, chmn. trust bd., 1973-83; dir. Hillsboro Enterprises, Inc., Breeko Industries, Inc., Murray-Ohio Mfg. Co., Nashville & Decatur R.R.; adv. dir. Williamson Co. Bank, First Nat. Bank, Palm Beach, Fla. Trustee Battle Ground Acad.; past chmn. bd. trustees Vanderbilt U. Served to lt. comdr. USNR, 1942-45. Mem. Am. Bankers Assn. (pres. 1961), SAR, Sigma Alpha Epsilon (past hon. eminent supreme archon). Presbyterian (elder). Clubs: Nat. Golf (Augusta, Ga.); Cumberland, Belle Meade Country, Nashville City Richland Golf (Nashville); Links, University (N.Y.); U.S. Seniors Golf; Gulf Stream Golf, Bath and Tennis, Yacht (Delray Beach, Fla.); Everglades, Seminole Golf, Bath and Tennis (Palm Beach, Fla.); Garden of the Gods (Colorado Springs, Colo.). Home: 810 Jackson Blvd Nashville TN 37205 also 365 N Ocean Blvd Palm Beach FL 33480 Office: Third Nat Bank Bldg Nashville TN 37219

FLEMING, SCOTT, health services executive; b. Twin Falls, Idaho, Oct. 17, 1923; s. John Scott and Anna Laura (Bascom) F.; m. Alma Geneva Skinner, Mar. 5, 1954; children: India Christie, Hilari Lanice. Student, U. Nev., 1941-42, U. Chgo. Law Sch., 1946-47; A.B., U. Calif., Berkeley, 1948, J.D., 1949; grad., Advanced Mgmt. Program, Harvard U., 1964. Bar: Calif. 1949. Bus. and tax law practice, San Francisco, 1949-52; atty. Henry J. Kaiser Co., Oakland, Calif., 1952-55; with Kaiser Found. Health Plan and Kaiser Found. Hosps., Oakland, 1955-71, Portland, Oreg., 1973-76, exec. v.p., sec., 1970-71, sr. v.p., regional mgr., Oreg., 1973-76, sr. v.p., Oakland, 1977—; dep. asst. sec. health policy devel. Office Asst. Sec. Health, HEW, 1971-73. Life mem. Sierra Club, past chmn. river conservation com., past bd. dirs. legal def. fund; mem. steering com. on nat. health care strategy study Nat. C. of C. Found., 1977-78. Served to 1st lt. AUS, 1943-46. Mem. Inst. Medicine of Nat. Acad. Scis., Am. Hosp. Assn. (spl. com. on regulatory process 1976-77), Order of Coif. Democrat. Home: 2750 Shasta Rd Berkeley CA 94708 Office: Kaiser Found Health Plan One Kaiser Plaza Oakland CA 94612

FLEMING, SUZANNE MARIE, universit official, chemistry educator; b. Detroit, Feb. 4, 1927; d. Albert Thomas and Rose E. (Smiley) F. B.S., Marygrove Coll., 1957; M.S., U. Mich., 1960, Ph.D., 1963. Joined Congregation of Sisters Servants of Immaculate Heart of Mary, Roman Catholic Ch., 1945. Chmn. natural sci. div. Marygrove Coll., Detroit, 1970-75, v.p., dean, 1975-78, acad. v.p., 1978-80; asst. v.p. acad. affairs Eastern Mich. U., Ypsilanti, 1980-82, acting assoc. v.p. acad. affairs, 1982-83; provost, acad. v.p. Western Ill. U., Macomb, 1983—; pres. Mich. Coll. Chemistry Tchrs. Assn., 1975; councilor Mich. Inst. Chemists, 1973-77. Contbr. articles to profl. publs. NIH research grantee, 1966-69. Fellow Am. Inst. Chemists; mem. Am. Chem. Soc. (councilor, Detroit 1980— Petroleum Research Fund grantee 1967-76), Am. Assn. Higher Edn., AAUP (assoc.), Sigma Xi. Home: 85 Carriage Hill Macomb IL 61455 Office: Western Ill U 211 Sherman Hall Macomb IL 61455

FLEMING, THOMAS JAMES, writer; b. Jersey City, July 5, 1927; s. Thomas James and Katherine (Dolan) F.; m. Alice Mulcahey, Jan. 19, 1951; children: Alice, Thomas, David, Richard. A.B., Fordham U., 1950; postgrad., Sch. Social Work, 1950-51. Reporter Yonkers (N.Y.) Herald Statesman, 1951; asst. to Fulton Oursler, 1951-52, lit. executor estate, 1953; asso. editor Cosmopolitan mag., 1954-58, exec. editor, 1959-61; writer, 1961—. Author: Now We Are Enemies, 1960, All Good Men, 1961, The God of Love, 1963, Beat the Last Drum, 1963, One Small Candle, 1964, King of the Hill, 1966, A Cry of Whiteness, 1967, West Point, The Men and Times of the U.S. Military Academy,

1969, The Man from Monticello, 1969, Romans Countrymen Lovers, 1969, The Sandbox Tree, 1970, The Man Who Dared the Lightning, 1971, The Forgotten Victory, 1973, The Good Shepherd, 1974, 1776: Year of Illusions, 1975, Liberty Tavern, 1976, Rulers of the City, 1977, New Jersey, 1977, Promises To Keep, 1978, A Passionate Girl, 1979, The Officers' Wives, 1981, Dreams of Glory, 1983; also various TV scripts, articles, short stories.; Editor: Affectionately Yours, George Washington, 1967, Benjamin Franklin, A Biography in His Own Words, 1972, The Living Land of Lincoln, 1980. Chmn. N.Y. Am. Revolution Round Table, 1970-81. Recipient Achievement award in communication arts Fordham U., 1961, Encaenia award, 1965; Mass Media award NCCJ, 1963; Christopher award, 1970; Colonial Dames Am. ann. book award, 1970, 72; award of merit Am. Assn. for State and Local History, 1974; Fiction award Nat. Cath. Press Assn., 1974; Best Book award Am. Revolution Round Table, 1975. Fellow N.J. Hist. Soc., Soc. Am. Historians; mem. N.Y. Hist. Soc., Am. PEN (pres. 1971-73). Clubs: University, Dutch Treat, Century (N.Y.C.). Home: 315 E 72d St New York NY also Westbrook CT 06498

FLEMING, WENDELL HELMS, educator, mathematician; b. Guthrie, Okla., Mar. 7, 1928; s. James Lucian and Helen (Helms) F.; m. Florence Tatum, Apr. 4, 1948; children: Randall, Daniel, William. B.S., Purdue U., 1948, M.S., 1949; Ph.D., U. Wis., 1951. Mathematician RAND Corp., 1951-55, cons., 1960-65; asst. prof. Purdue U., 1955-58; mem. faculty Brown U., 1958—, prof. math., 1963—, prof. applied math., 1969—, chmn. dept., 1965-68, 82—; Mem.-at-large Conf. Bd. Math. Scis., 1970-73. Author: Functions of Several Variables, 1965, (with R.W. Rishel) Deterministic and Stochastic Optimal Control, 1975; Editor: SIAM Rev; Editorial cons.: Math. Reviews, 1963-65. NSF fellow, 1968-69; Guggenheim fellow, 1976-77. Mem. Am. Math. Soc. (chmn. com. on employment and ednl. policy 1975-77), Math. Assn. Am., Soc. Indsl. and Applied Math. Home: 3 Colley Ct Barrington RI 02806 Office: Div Applied Math Brown Univ Providence RI 02912

FLEMING, WILLIAM ADAM, aero. engr.; b. Battle Creek, Mich., Apr. 14, 1921; s. William and Greta Jane (Wolf) F.; m. Evelyn Alice Lasch, Oct. 20, 1945; children—Jack William, Janice Lynne. B.S., Purdue U., 1943. Engaged in jet engine and rocket research Lewis Research Center, NASA, Cleve., 1943-60, staff tech. asst. space flight program planning, coordination, Washington, 1960-61, dir. program rev. div., 1961-70, dep. dir. office analysis and evaluation, 1970-72; sr. tech. officer NASA Hdqrs., 1972-74; sr. program mgr. Systems Cons.'s, Inc., Washington, 1974-76; v.p., dir. Burns & Roe Tenn., Inc., 1977-78; ind. engrng. and mgmt. cons., 1978-79; mem. profl. staff Arthur D. Little Program Systems Mgmt. Co., Washington, 1979—. Asso. fellow AIAA (past chmn. Cleve.-Akron sect.); mem. Pi Tau Sigma, Pi Kappa Alpha. Home: 6611 Melody Ln Bethesda MD 20817

FLEMING, WILLIAM CARY, physician; b. Lee Hall, Va., Jan. 16, 1918; s. Thomas Hayes and Martha (Kirby) F.; m. Mabel Clare Green, Mar. 19, 1944; children: Martha Frances, Sharon Anne, Joan Marie. B.S. in Chemistry, U. Va., 1942, M.D., 1945. Diplomate: Am. Bd. Phys. Medicine and Rehab. Intern Del. Hosp., Wilmington, 1945-46; gen. practice, Glasgow, Va., 1948-49; mem. staff student health U. Kans., 1949-51; indsl. physician E.I. duPont de Nemours & Co., Inc., Waynesboro, Va., 1951-53; resident phys. medicine and rehab. VA Hosp.-Med. Coll. Va., Richmond, 1953-56; phys. medicine and rehab. physician VA hosps., Richmond, 1956-58, Pitts., 1959, Coral Gables, Fla., 1959-64, VA Hosp., Birmingham, Ala., 1970-78; cons. 1978—; prof. phys. medicine and rehab. U. Ala. Med. Sch., 1964—, chmn. dept., 1964-70; physiatrist in chief Univ. Hosp., Birmingham, 1964-70, now physiatrist; med. dir. Spain Rehab. Center, Birmingham, 1964-69, physiatrist, 1969—; dir. U. Ala. Rehab. Research and Tng. Center, 1966-69; med. staff, chmn. med. bd. Lakeshore Rehab. Hosp., 1973—; cons. staff Children's and St. Vincent's hosps., 1965—; dir. chronic illness project, Dade County, Fla., 1962-63; mem. med. adv. bd. Birmingham Vis. Nurse Assn., 1965—, Central Ala. chpt. Nat. Multiple Sclerosis Soc., 1966—, chmn., 1976; bd. dirs. N. Central Ala. Occupational Rehab. Center, 1966-70, 73-79, chmn. bd., 1978-79. Bd. dirs. Birmingham Civic Ballet, 1971-77. Served to capt. M.C. AUS, 1946-48. Mem. AMA, So. Med. Assn. (chmn. sect. 1966-67), Ala. Med. Assn., Am. Congress Rehab. Medicine, Am. Acad. Phys. Medicine and Rehab., So. Soc. Phys. Medicine (chmn. 1970-72), Assn. Acad. Physiatrists, Raven Soc. (v.p. 1942-43), Alpha Chi Sigma, Nu Sigma Nu. Club: Poinsettia Men's (pres. 1971-72). Lodge: Rotary. Spl. research rehab. aspects stroke, emphysema, kidney disease, heart disease, spinal cord injury, electromyography. Home: 3528 Belle Meade Way Birmingham AL 35223

FLEMING, WILLIAM DAVID, stockbroker; b. San Mateo, Calif., July 8, 1910; s. William J. and Maude (Lockie) F.; m. Barbara Trotter, Oct. 20, 1934; children—Gerald S., Richard D. Student, pub. schs. With Blyth & Co., San Francisco, Los Angeles, 1929-45; with Walston & Co., Inc., Los Angeles, 1945-52, partner, N.Y.C., 1952-57, sr. v.p., Chgo., 1957-64, pres., N.Y.C., 1964-74; with Shearson/Am. Express, Inc., Newport Beach, Calif., 1974—. Club: Big Canyon Country (Newport Beach). Home: 1633 Castle Cove Circle Corona Del Mar CA 92625

FLEMING, WILLIAM HARRISON, lawyer; b. South Bend, Ind., May 9, 1915; s. Lew and Grace (Tienken) F.; m. Jeane Alfred Gibbs, Aug. 26, 1939; children: William L., Nancy J., Lew II, Candace J. A.B., U. Mich., 1937; J.D., Harvard U., 1940. Bar: Ind. 1940, Ohio 1941. Asso. mem. firm Baker & Hostetler, Cleve., 1940-42, 45-52, partner, 1953-80, sr. partner, 1981-83; formerly sec., dir. Speed Selector, Inc.; Lincoln Co., Fifty West Broad, Inc. Trustee Forest Hill Home Owners, 1949-56; trustee, pres. Willows Assn., 1978-79, trustee, 1983—; trustee Walden Assn., 1979-81. Served to maj. AUS, 1942-45. Mem. Cleve. Bar Assn., Ohio Bar Assn., ABA, Am. Judicature Soc., Portage County Bar Assn. Republican. Presbyterian. Clubs: Walden Golf and Tennis, Kiwanis. Home: 520-18 Willow Circle Aurora OH 44202 Office: 3200 National City Center Cleveland OH 44114

FLEMING, WILLIAM JOSEPH, manufacturing company executive; b. Bklyn., Oct. 14, 1922; s. William J. and Agnes V. (Lowrey) F.; m. Anne Alice Thoet, Aug. 18, 1945; children: Herbert J., William J. B.E.E., Bklyn. Poly. Inst., 1949; M.B.A., Harvard U., 1956. Div. mgr. Westinghouse Electric Corp., Pitts., 1945-64; v.p. adminstrn. Continental Copper & Steel Co., N.Y.C., 1964-66; v.p. ops. Lehigh Valley Industries, N.Y.C., 1966-69; pres., dir. Mallory Randall Corp., N.Y.C., 1969-72; exec. v.p., dir. Gt. Am. Industries Inc., Binghamton, N.Y., 1974—; bus. and fin. cons., N.Y.C., 1972-74. Served as ensign USN (Air), 1943-45. Mem. Tau Beta Pi, Eta Kappa Nu. Republican. Roman Catholic. Clubs: Sky (N.Y.C.); Northfork Country (Cutchogue, N.Y.). Home: PO Box 556 Cutchogue NY 11935 Office: Great Am Industries Inc 1325 Franklin Ave Suite 495 Garden City NY 11530

FLEMING, WILLIAM THOMAS, JR., lawyer; b. Phila., Oct. 16, 1925; s. William Thomas F. A.B., Princeton U., 1946; LL.B., Columbia U., 1952. Bar: Tex. 1953. Ptnr. firm Vinson & Elkins, Houston, 1952—; dir. Rowan Cos. Inc., Houston, Fairmont Foods Co. Mem. ABA, Tex. State Bar (chmn. sect. on corp. banking-bus. law 1970-71), Houston Bar Assn. Home: 2111 Fulham Ct Houston TX 77063 Office: Vinson & Elkins First City Tower Houston TX 77002

FLEMING, WILLIAM WRIGHT, JR., pharmacology educator; b. Washington, Jan. 30, 1932; s. William Wright and Esme (Reeder) F.; m. Dolores D. Atchison, Sept. 1, 1952; children: Lisa Marie, Jennifer Amelia, David William. A.B. cum laude, Harvard U., 1954; Ph.D. (Procter fellow), Princeton U., 1957. Mem. faculty Med. Center W.Va. U., Morgantown, 1960—, prof. pharmacology, 1966—, chmn. dept., 1966—; vis. prof. U. Melbourne, Australia, 1969, St. George's Hosp. Med. Sch. U. London, 1978; cons. Mead Johnson Research Center, Evansville, Ind., 1970-77; mem. pharmacology-toxicology research program com. Nat. Inst. Gen. Med. Scis., NIH, 1973-77, chmn., 1975-77. Contbr. articles to profl. jours.; editorial bd.: Jour. Pharmacology and Exptl. Therapeutics, 1966—, Life Scis, 1978—. USPHS postdoctoral fellow Harvard U., 1957-60; recipient P.L. MacLachlan award excellence in teaching W.Va. U. Med. Sch., 1964, 67, 78. Mem. Am. Soc. Pharmacology and Exptl. Therapeutics (councilor 1975-78, pres. 1981-82, chmn. bd. publs. trustees 1984—), Soc. Exptl. Biology and Medicine, AAAS, Assn. Med. Sch. Pharmacology (councilor 1977-79, treas. 1977-78), Fedn. Am. Socs. for Exptl. Biology (dir. 1980—), Internat. Union Pharmacology (del. 1980-83). Home: 27 Citadel Rd Morgantown WV 26505 Office: Dept Pharm WVa U Med Center Morgantown WV 26506

FLEMISTER, LAUNCELOT JOHNSON, physiologist, educator; b. Atlanta, Dec. 11, 1913; s. Launcelot Johnson and Willie (Moore) F.; m. Sarah Elizabeth Culbreth, Dec. 25, 1941. A.B., Duke, 1935, M.A., 1939, Ph.D., 1941. Instr. Med. Sch. George Washington U., 1941-42; research asso. Sharp & Dohme, Phila., 1946-47; asst. prof. Swarthmore Coll., 1947-51, asso. prof., 1951-66, prof. zoology, 1966—; Cons. NSF, 1963-64. Served to lt. USNR, 1942-46. Fulbright fellow, Peru, 1959-60. Fellow AAAS; mem. Am. Physiol. Soc., Am. Soc. Zoologists, Sigma Xi, Delta Tau Delta. Office: PO Box F Swarthmore PA 19081

FLEMMING, WILLIAM NORMAN, sports commentator; b. Chgo., Sept. 3, 1926; s. Norman Albert and Elizabeth (Morrisson) F.; m. Barbara Alice Forster, Aug. 5, 1950; children—Lindy, William Mason. B.A., U. Mich., 1949. Sports dir. WUOM, U. Mich., 1950-53; sports dir. WWJ-TV, Detroit, 1953-59; NCAA football announcer CBS, N.Y.C., 1960-62, NBC, 1962-64; sports commentator ABC Sports, N.Y.C., 1964—; covered Olympics, Mexico City and winter games in Grenoble, France, 1968, Munich and Montreal games, 1972, 76; pres. Detroit Sports Broadcasters Assn., 1957-58; guest lectr. U. Mich., 1960. State chmn. March of Dimes, 1978. Served with USAAF, 1944-45. Hon. mem. M Club; U. Mich. letter winners; elected to Mich. Media Hall of Fame, 1980. Mem. AFTRA (past dir.), Screen Actors Guild, Nat. Assn. Sportscasters. Republican. Clubs: Bloomfield Hills Country, Bloomfield Open Hunt, Little Harbor. Office: ABC Sports 1330 6th Ave New York NY 10019

FLENNIKEN, CECIL STEPHENSON, forest products company executive; b. Chickasaw, Ala., Aug. 11, 1925; s. Warren S. and Pearle M. (Stephenson) F.; m. Alyce Quince Parrish, June 15, 1948; 1 son, Bruce Phillips. B.M.E., Ga. Inst. Tech., 1949. With Internat. Paper Co., 1949-69, mgr. pulp and paper mill, Pine Bluff, Ark. and Bastrop, La., 1965-69; with CIP Inc. (formerly Canadian Internat. Paper Co.), Montreal, Que., 1969—, v.p., 1970; exec. v.p. CIP (formerly Canadian Internat. Paper Co.), 1971; pres., chief exec. officer CIP Inc. (formerly Canadian Internat. Paper Co.), 1972—, also dir.; dir. Toronto-Dominion Bank, Facelle Co., Ltd., Toronto; chmn., pres., dir. Tahsis Co. Ltd., Vancouver, B.C. Served with USN, 1943-45. Mem. Canadian Pulp and Paper Assn. (exec. bd.), Paper Industry Mgmt. Assn. (trustee), TAPPI, Can. Mfrs. Assn. (adv. bd.). Clubs: Mt. Royal, St. James, Le Club St. Denis; Rideau (Ottawa). Home: 1321 Sherbrooke St W E-50 Montreal PQ H3G 1J4 Canada Office: Suite 1400 1155 Metcalfe St Montreal PQ H3B 2X1 Canada

FLESCH, RUDOLF, author; b. Vienna, Austria, May 8, 1911; came to U.S., 1938, naturalized, 1944; s. Hugo and Helene (Basch) F.; m. Elizabeth Terpenning, Sept. 6, 1941; children: Anne Sutherland Flesch Wares, Hugo Walter, Gillian Ruth, Katrina Woodburn, Abigail Allan Flesch Connors, Janet Amalia. Dr.Jur., U. Vienna, 1933; Ph.D., Columbia U., 1943. Cons. FTC, 1976-82. Author: The Art of Plain Talk, 1946, The Way to Write, (with A.H. Lass), 1947, The Art of Readable Writing, 1949, rev. edit., 1974, The Art of Clear Thinking, 1951, How to Make Sense, 1954, Why Johnny Can't Read, 1955, The Book of Unusual Quotations, 1957, A New Way to Better English, 1958, How to Write, Speak and Think More Effectively, 1960, How to Be Brief, 1962, The ABC of Style, 1965, The Book of Surprises, 1965, The New Book of Unusual Quotations, 1966, Say What You Mean, 1972, Look It Up: A Deskbook of American Spelling and Style, 1977, How to Write Plain English: A Book for Lawyers and Consumers, 1979, Why Johnny Still Can't Read: A New Look at the Scandal of Our Schools, 1981, LITE English: Some Popular Words that Are OK to Use, 1983. Home: 24 Belden Ave Dobbs Ferry NY 10522

FLESHER, HUBERT LOUIS, religion educator; b. Elyria, Ohio, Apr. 30, 1933; s. O. Jay and Armide Elizabeth (deSaulles) F.; m. Mary June Mosher, Apr. 3, 1965; children: Erika Anne, Jonathan Jay. B.A. magna cum laude, Pomona U., 1954; B.D., Yale U., 1958, M.A., 1960. Ordained to ministry Episcopal Ch., 1958. Asst. dean chapel Princeton U., N.J., 1956-57; instr. Episcopal Theol. Sch., Cambridge, Mass., 1963-66; chaplain Millersville State Coll., 1967-71, Lehigh U., Bethlehem, Pa., 1971—, assoc. prof. religion, 1971-80, prof., 1980—; vis. prof. Lancaster Theol. Sem., 1967-71; founder, 1st chmn. Lancaster Ind. Press, Pa.; mem. exec. com. Pa. Commn. United Ministries in Higher Edn.; lectr. in field. Honnold fellow, 1954-55. Mem. Am. Acad. Religion, Soc. Bibl. Lit. and Exegesis, Nat. Campus Ministers Assn., Pa. Campus Ministers Assn., Phi Beta Kappa, Omicron Delta Kappa. Club: Home. Home: 224 W Packer Ave Bethlehem PA 18015 Office: Lehigh U 36 Johnson Hall Bethlehem PA 18015

FLETCHER, ALAN GORDON, university dean; b. Gibson's Landing, C., Can., Jan. 2, 1925; s. William G. and Florence (Smith) F.; m. A. Irene Flynn, Aug. 6, 1949; children: Christopher Lee, Lynn Patricia, Elizabeth Joan, Anne Marie. B.Applied Sci., U. B.C., 1948; M.S., Calif. Inst. Tech., 1952; Ph.D. (Walter P. Murphy fellow), Northwestern U., 1965. Registered profl. engr., B.C. Engr.-in-tng. B.C. Electric Co., Ltd., Vancouver, 1948-52, hydraulic designer, 1952-56; supr. hydro planning B.C. Engrng. Co., Vancouver, 1956-59; asst. prof., asso. prof. civil engrng. U. Idaho, 1959-62; asso. prof. civil engrng. U. Utah, 1964-69; dean U. N.D. Sch. Engrng., Grand Forks, 1969—, dir. Engrng. Expt. Sta., 1969-83; dir. N.D. Mining and Mineral Resources Research Inst., 1979-83. Pres. bd. Vancouver-Central YMCA; bd. govs. Vancouver Met. YMCA; mem. com. on higher edn. Synod of Lakes and Prairies, United Presbyn. Ch., 1978-82; pres. N.D. Commn. for United Ministries in Higher Edn., 1980—. Danforth asso., 1965—. Mem. Am. Soc. C.E., Am. Soc. Engrng. Edn., Nat., N.D. socs. profl. engrs., N.D. Acad. Sci., Sigma Xi, Chi Epsilon, Sigma Tau, Tau Beta Pi. Presbyterian (elder). Club: Rotarian. Home: 3117 Olson Dr Grand Forks ND 58201

FLETCHER, ALBERT BYRNE, JR., judge; b. Arkansas City, Kans., Sept. 8, 1924. B.S., Kans. State U., 1948; LL.B., Washburn U., Topeka, 1951. Bar: Kans. bar 1951. Practice in, Junction City, Kans., 1951-61; judge 8th Jud. Dist. Kans., 1961-75, U.S. Ct. Mil. Appeals, Washington, 1975—, chief judge, 1975—; mem. Kans. Jud. Council, 1973-75; lectr. in field, 1961—. Mem. Am. Bar Assn., Kans. Bar Assn., Kans. Dist. Judges Assn. (pres. 1972), Nat. Conf. State Trial Judges (exec. com. 1972-76), Geary County Bar Assn. (past pres.). Office: US Ct Mil Appeals 450 E St NW Washington DC 20442

FLETCHER, ANGUS (JOHN STEWART), literature educator; b. Bronxville, N.Y., June 23, 1930; s. Angus Somerville and Helen Muir (Stewart) F. B.A., Yale U., 1950, M.A., 1952; diplome d'hautes Etudes, U. Grenoble, France, 1951; Ph.D., Harvard U., 1958. Instr. English Cornell U., 1958-62; asst. prof., then assoc. prof. Columbia U., 1962-68; vis. assoc. prof. SUNY, Buffalo, 1968-69, prof. English and comparative lit., 1969-73; vis. prof. English UCLA, 1973-74; disting. prof. English and comparative lit. Lehman Coll., N.Y.C., 1974—; Doris and Henry Dreyfuss prof. English and comparative lit. Calif. Inst. Tech., Pasadena, 1977; sr. lectr. Christian Gauss Seminars Princeton U., 1981; sr. lectr. Aston Magna Found., 1982. Author: Allegory: The Theory of a Symbolic Mode, 2d edit, 1970, The Prophetic Moment: an Essay on Spenser, 1971, The Transcendental Masque: An Essay on Milton's Comus, 1971; editor: The Literature of Fact: English Institute Essays, 1976; contbr. articles, book revs., essays, chpts. to books. Nat. Endowment for Humanities sr. research fellow, 1979-80. Mem. Renaissance Soc. Am., Modern Lang. Assn. (chmn. anthropology sect. 1977-78), Milton Soc. Am., Spenser Soc. Am., English Inst. (bd. advisers 1974-77). Home: One Lincoln Plaza New York NY 10023 Office: City Univ NY 33 W 42d St New York NY 10036

FLETCHER, HON. BETTY B., judge; b. Tacoma, Mar. 29, 1923. B.A., Stanford U., 1943; LL.B., U. Wash., 1956. Bar: Wash. 1956. Former mem. firm Preston, Thergrimson, Ellis, Holman & Fletcher, Seattle; judge U.S. Circuit Ct. for 9th Circuit, Seattle. Mem. Wash. Bar Assn., Am. Bar Assn., Order of Coif, Phi Beta Kappa. Office: 1010 Fifth Ave Seattle WA 98104 *

FLETCHER, CHARLES WILLIAM, ret. army officer; b. Mpls., May 11, 1920; s. John Wilkinson and Mary (McLaughlin) F.; m. Johnnie Dillard, Oct. 16, 1946; children—Suzanne E. (Mrs. Daniel Patrick Alexander), Charles W., Mary K. (Mrs. Paul Francis Donohue), James E., Margaret A., Anne R. B.S., U.S. Mil. Acad., 1941; M.A., George Washington U., 1963. Commd. 2d lt. F.A. U.S. Army, 1941, advanced through grades to brig. gen., 1968; served in, Europe, World War II; assigned to Office Chief of Staff U.S. Army, 1961-63; comdr. arty. units in, Europe, 1963-65, Korea, 1967-68; dir. ground ammunition Office Asst. Sec. Def., Installation and Logistics, Washington, 1968-71, dir. indsl. moblzn. planning and munitions prodn., 1971; ret., 1971; exec. dir. Com. for Purchase from the Blind and other Severely Handicapped, 1972—. Decorated D.S.M., Bronze Star, Silver Star with oak leaf cluster, Air medal, Joint Services Commendation medal. Roman Catholic. Home: 4205 Cordell St Annandale VA 22003 Office: Com for Purchase from the Blind and other Severely Handicapped 2009 14th St N Arlington VA 22201

FLETCHER, CLIFF, professional hockey executive; b. 1935; m. Donna Owens; 2 children. With Montreal Canadien Orgn., 1956-66; mgr. Verdun Jr. B team; later mgr. Jr. Canadiens; chief scout St. Louis Blues, 1966-69, asst. gen. mgr., 1969-72; v.p., gen. mgr. Atlanta Flames, Nat. Hockey League, 1972-80, Calgary (Alta., Can.) Flames, from 1980, now pres., gen. mgr. Office: Calgary Flames PO Box 1540 Station M Calgary AB T2P 3B9 Canada *

FLETCHER, COLIN, author; b. Cardiff, Wales, Mar. 14, 1922; emigrated to Kenya, 1947; s. Herbert Reginald and Margaret Elizabeth (Williams) F. Student, West Buckland Sch., North Devon, Eng. Mfr.'s rep., Nairobi, mgr. hotel, Kitale, 1947-48, farmer, nr. Nakuru, 1948-52, road builder on estate, nr. Inyanga, So. Rhodesia, 1952-53, with mining cos., Can., summers 1954-56; head janitor Polyclinic Hosp., San Francisco, 1957-58; free-lance writer, Calif., 1958—. Author: The Thousand-Mile Summer, 1964, The Man who Walked Through Time, The Complete Walker, 1968, The Winds of Mara, 1973, The New Complete Walker, 1974, The Man from the Cave, 1981, Complete Walker III, 1984; Contbr.: articles to Field and Stream, Reader's Digest; other mags. in, U.S., Can., Gt. Britain, Africa. Served to capt. Royal Marine Commandos, 1940-47. Mem. Wilderness Soc., Nat. Audubon Soc., Planning and Conservation League, Friends of the Earth, East African Wildlife Soc., Trustees for Alaska, Friends of the Sea Otter, Nature Conservancy, Sierra Club, Cousteau Soc., Environ. Def. Fund, Whale Protection Fund, Solar Lobby, Center for Law in Public Interest, Zero Population Growth, Common Cause. Club: Rift Valley Sports (Kenya). Office: care Brandt & Brandt 1501 Broadway New York NY 10036

FLETCHER, DEAN CHARLES, educator; b. Logan, Utah, June 14, 1921; s. Calvin and Susette (Ricks) F.; m. Ann Louise Barber, Apr. 5, 1944; children—Louise, Susette Barber, Ellen Jean. B.S. in Physiology, Utah State U., 1943, M.S., 1948; Ph.D. in Chemistry, U. Del., 1951. Instr. physiology Utah State U., 1943, 48-49, research, teaching asst., 1946-48; research asso. Biochem. Research Found., Franklin Inst., 1949-51; research biochemist E.I. du Pont de Nemours & Co., Inc., 1951-57; dir. research Washoe Med. Center, Reno, 1957-61; Allie M. Lee research prof. biol. scis. U. Nev., Reno, 1961-70, coordinator health scis., health physicist, 1970, also dir. student affairs; asst. clin. prof. Sch. Medicine, U. Utah, 1965-72, dir. health sci. planning, 1972-73; dir. sect. foods AMA, Chgo., 1973-76; chmn. dept. foods and nutrition Wash. State U., Pullman, 1976—; cons. biochemistry Washoe Med. Center, St. Mary's Hosp., Reno, Lamar Chem. Co., Reno VA Hosp.; Bd. dirs. Talent, Inc.; bd. dirs. Center for Learning Resources, U. Ky. Med. Center, Lexington, 1972. Mem. Gov. Nev. Com. Med. Edn.; Pres. U.S. Com. on Youth, Nev. Cancer Coordination Com., Nev. Med. Basic Sci. Bd., Gov.'s Com. Med. Edn., Gov.'s Com. Emergency Patient Care, Gov.'s Com. Title IX.; Bd. dirs. Reno Cancer Center. Served with AUS, World War II. Decorated Commendation medal. Mem. Am. Chem. Soc., N.Y. Acad. Scis., Fed. Socs. Biology and Medicine, Internat. Acad. Forensic Scis., Am. Acad. Forensic Scis., Sigma Xi, Phi Delta Kappa, Gamma Sigma Delta. Mem. Ch. of Jesus Christ of Latter-Day Saints (bishop, pres. stake). Home: SE 905 Kamiaken Pullman WA 99163

FLETCHER, DENISE KOEN, publishing and communications company executive; b. Istanbul, Turkey, Aug. 31, 1948; came to U.S., 1967, naturalized, 1976; d. Moris and Kety (Barkey) Koen; m. Robert B. Fletcher, Nov. 11, 1969; children—David, Kate. A.B. (Coll. scholar), Wellesley Coll., 1969; M.City Planning, Harvard U., 1972. Analyst Getty Oil Co. (Eastern), N.Y.C., 1972-73, sr. analyst, 1973-74, cash mgmt. and bldg. supr., 1974-76, asst. treas., 1976, N.Y. Times Co., N.Y.C., 1976-80, treas., 1980—. Mem. budget com. City of Larchmont, N.Y.; Mem. Alumni exec. Council Harvard U. Sch. Govt., 1982—. Mellon scholar, 1970. Mem. Fin. Execs. Inst., Fin. Women's Assn., Treasurers Club N.Y., Phi Beta Kappa. Club: Harvard (N.Y.C.).

FLETCHER, DOUGLAS BADEN, investment company executive; b. Pleasant Ridge, Mich., Mar. 25, 1925; s. Ernest H. and Gladys (Marthan) F.; m. Sally Wittenberg, Sept. 9, 1950; children: David, Christopher, James, Jonathan. B.A., Princeton, 1949. Security analyst Walston & Co., N.Y.C., 1949-53; mem. underwriting dept. Blyth & Co., Los Angeles, 1953-62; chmn. bd., chief exec. officer First Pacific Advisors, Inc., Los Angeles, 1968-83, Angeles Corp., 1968-83, Source Capital, Inc., Los Angeles, 1968-82; chmn. Paramount Mut. Fund, Inc., Los Angeles, 1978—. Trustee Claremont McKenna Coll. (Calif.),

1969—. Served with AUS, 1943-46. Mem. Inst. Chartered Fin. Analysts, Los Angeles Soc. Fin. Analysts (pres. 1960-61). Club: Princeton of So. Calif. (pres. 1962-64). Home: Newport Beach CA Office: 3416 Via Oporto Suite 300 Newport Beach CA 92663

FLETCHER, EDWARD ABRAHAM, educator; b. Detroit, July 30, 1924; s. Morris and Lillian (Protes) F.; m. Roslyn Silber, June 15, 1948; children—Judith Ellen, Deborah Gail, Carolyn Ruth. B.S., Wayne State U., 1948; Ph.D. (DuPont fellow, AEC fellow), Purdue U., 1952. Head propellant chemistry and flame mechanics sects. NASA, Cleve., 1952-59; asso. prof. U. Minn., Mpls., 1959-60, prof., 1960—, dir. grad. studies in mech. engring., 1965—; vis. scientist Byellorussian Acad. Scis., 1964; vis. Fulbright prof. U. Poitiers, 1968; cons. U.S. Dept. Commerce Study Waste Heat Mgmt., Minn. Energy Agy., No. States Power Co., Public Systems Research Corp.; co-chmn. com. on fire resistant hydraulic fluids NRC-Nat. Acad. Scis. Nat. Materials Adv. Bd., 1977-78; Participant adv. group for aero. research and devel. NATO Confs., 1960, 61. Editor: Isotopes, 1958-59. Bd. dirs. Minn. Com. for Technion., New Friends of Chamber Music. Served with USNR, 1943-46. Recipient NASA Spl. award, 1961; Outstanding Ski Patrolman of Western Region award Nat. Ski Patrol, 1969-70. Mem. Combustion Inst. (bd. advisers, sec. Central States sect. 1967-78, vice chmn. 1978-79, chmn. 1979—), Am. Chem. Soc., AAAS, Sigma Xi, Tau Beta Pi, Pi Tau Sigma, Phi Lambda Upsilon. Home: 3909 Beard Ave S Minneapolis MN 55410

FLETCHER, FRANK UTLEY, lawyer; b. Sparta, N.C., Feb. 7, 1912; s. Alfred J. and Elizabeth (Utley) F.; m. Elizabeth Dalrymple, 1935 (dec. 1955); children: Frank Utley, Alfred Dalrymple, Anne; m. Nelle Wood Crowell, Oct. 3, 1961. Student, N.C. State Coll., 1927-29; LL.B. cum laude, Wake Forest Coll., 1932; postgrad., Duke, 1932-34. Bar: N.C. bar 1933, D.C. bar 1939. Atty. FCC, 1934-39; asso. Spearman & Roberson, Washington, 1939-42; now sr. partner Fletcher, Heald, Rowell, Kenehan & Hildreth; pvt. practice, 1945-53; co-owner Sta. WARL, Arlington, Va., 1946-51; Chmn. communications industry com. Bus. Adv. Council on Fed. Reports; mem. planning council World Peace Through Law Center. Sec., bd. dirs. Call for Action, 1975—. Served from 1st lt. to capt., ordnance dept. AUS, 1942-45. Mem. Nat. Assn. Broadcasters, Am., Fed., D.C. bar assns., Fed. Communications Bar Assn. (pres. 1960, exec. com. 1954-55), Am. Judicature Soc., Broadcast Pioneers (bd. dirs.; chmn. D.C. chpt.). Clubs: Mason (32 deg.), International, Congressional Country, Columbia Country. Home: 5001 Van Ness St Washington DC 20016 Office: 1225 Connecticut Ave NW Suite 400 Washington DC 20036

FLETCHER, GEORGE P., legal educator; b. 1939. B.A., U. Calif.-Berkeley, 1960; J.D., U. Claif.-Berkeley, 1963; M.C.L., U. Chgo., 1965. Bar: Calif. 1970. Grad. fellow U. Freibur, W. Ger., 1964-65; asst. prof. U. Fla. Law Sch., 1965-66, U. Wash., Seattle, 1966-69; acting prof. UCLA Law Sch., 1969-70, prof., after 1971; prof. law Columbia U., N.Y.C.; vis. assoc. prof. Boston Coll., 1968-69; vis. prof. Hebrew U., Jerusalem, 1972-73, Harvard U., 1973-74, Yale U., 1977. Author: Rethinking Criminal Law, 1978; mem., U. Chgo. Law Rev. Home: 404 Riverside Dr New York NY 10025 Office: Columbia U Sch Law 435 W 116th St New York NY 10027

FLETCHER, GILBERT HUNGERFORD, radiotherapist, educator; b. Paris, Mar. 11, 1911; s. Walter Scott and Marie (Boudol) F.; m. Mary Critz, June 10, 1943; children: Walter Scott, Thomas. B.A., U. Paris, 1929, U. Louvain, Belgium, 1932; M.S. in Math., U. Brussels, 1935, M.D., 1941. Diplomate: Am. Bd. Radiology. Rotating intern U. Brussels Hosp., 1939-41; intern obstetrics French Hosp., N.Y.C., 1942-43; asst. resident radiology N.Y. Hosp., 1942-43, resident radiology, 1943-44; fellow radiotherapy Royal Cancer Hosp., London, Eng., Curie Found., Paris, France, 1947-48; head dept. radiotherapy M.D. Anderson Hosp., Houston, 1948-81, prof., 1981—; prof. radiotherapy U. Tex. Med. Sch., Houston, 1965—; cons. Baylor U. Coll. Medicine, Houston, Santa Rosa Med. Center, San Antonio; nat. cons. to surgeon gen. USAF, 7968—. Served from 1st lt. to capt. M.C. AUS, 1944-47. Fellow Am. Coll. Radiology; mem. Inter-Am. Coll. Radiology, Radiol. Soc. N.Am., Am. Soc. Therapeutic Radiologists (pres. 197-68), Am. Radium Soc. (treas. 1959-61, pres. 1962-63, Janeway lectr. 1970), Tex. Radiol. Soc., AMA, Harris County Med. Soc., Royal Soc. Medicine London, French Soc. Radiotherapists Paris. Home: 2215 Dorrington St Houston TX 77030 Office: MD Anderson Hosp and Tumor Inst Houston TX 77030

FLETCHER, HARRY GEORGE, III, editor; b. Bklyn., Mar. 25, 1941; s. Harry G. and Helen T. (Dawson) F.; m. Toni A. Owen, 1966; children: Alexandra, Thomas More. A.B., Fordham Coll., 1962, M.A., 1970; postgrad., U. Munich, 1962-63. Asst. editor Fordham U. Press, Bronx, N.Y., 1966-69, editor, 1969-81, dir., 1972—. Author: Aldus Manutius and the Aldine Press, 1985; Editor: The Heritage of New York, 1970, A Miscellany for Bibliophiles, 1979; co-editor: Paradosis, 1976; contbr. articles to profl. jours., chpts. to books. Served with AUS, 1963-66. Mem. Baker Street Irregulars. Club: Grolier. Office: Fordham U Press Bronx NY 10458

FLETCHER, HOMER LEE, librarian; b. Salem, Ind., May 11, 1928; s. Floyd M. and Hazel (Barnett) F.; m. Jacquelyn Ann Blanton, Feb. 7, 1950; children—Deborah Lynn, Randall Brian, David Lee. B.A., Ind. U., 1953; M.S. in L.S, U. Ill., 1954. Librarian Milw. Pub. Library, 1954-56; head librarian Ashland (Ohio) Pub. Library, 1956-59; city librarian Arcadia (Cal.) Pub. Library, 1959-65, Vallejo (Calif.) Pub. Library, 1965-70, San Jose, Calif., 1970—. Contbr. articles to profl. jours. Pres. S. Solano chpt. Calif. Assn. Neurol. Handicapped Children, 1968-69. Served with USAF, 1946-49. Mem. ALA (intellectual freedom com. 1967-72), Calif. Library Assn. (pres. pub. libraries sect. 1967), Phi Beta Kappa. Democrat. Mem. Christian Ch. Disciples of Christ (elder, chmn. congregation 1978-79). Club: Rotarian. Home: 7921 Belknap Dr Cupertino CA 95014 Office: 180 W San Carlos St San Jose CA 95113

FLETCHER, JAMES CHIPMAN, consulting engineer; b. Millburn, N.J., June 5, 1919; s. Harvey and Lorena (Chipman) F.; m. Fay Lee, Nov. 2, 1946; children: Virginia Lee, Mary Susan, James Stephen, Barbara Jo. A.B., Columbia U., 1940; Ph.D., Calif. Inst. Tech., 1948; D.Sc. (hon.), U. Utah, 1971, Brigham Young U., 1977; LL.D., Lehigh U., 1978. Research physicist bur. ordnance Dept. Navy, 1940-41; spl. research asso. Cruft Lab., Harvard U., 1941-42; instr. Princeton U., 1942-45; teaching fellow Calif. Inst. Tech., 1945-48; instr. U. Calif. at Los Angeles, 1948-50; dir. theory and analysis lab. Hughes Aircraft Co., 1948-54; asso. dir. guided missile lab., dir. electronics guided missile research div., later in space tech. labs. Ramo-Wooldridge Corp., 1954-58; pres., founder Space Electronics Corp., 1958; pres. Space-Gen. Corp. (merger between Space Electronics Corp. and Aerojet-Gen. Corp.), 1960; chmn. bd. Space-Gen. Corp., 1961-64; pres. U. Utah, 1964-71; adminstr. NASA, Washington, 1971-77; Whiteford prof. U. Pitts., 1977—; cons. engr., McLean, Va., 1977—; mem. subcom. on stability and control NACA, 1950-54; cons. Office Sec. Def., 1959-64; asst. sec. USAF, 1961-64, to ACDA, 1962-63, Aerojet-Gen. and Space-Gen. Corps., 1964-71; cons., then mem. Pres.'s Sci. Adv. Com., 1958-70; chmn. com. rev. Minuteman Command and Control System, 1961; mem. Air Force Sci. Adv. Bd., 1962-67; chmn. physics panel rev. com. NIH, 1962-64; mem. strategic weapons panel, 1959-61, mil. aircraft panel, 1964-67, chmn. naval warfare panel, 1967-73; mem. Pres.'s Nat. Crime Commn., 1966; mem. tech. assessment adv. council Office of Tech. Assessment; mem. Def. Sci. Bd.; chmn. safety adv. bd. Three Mile Island No. 2; governing bd. NRC, 1978—; v.p. Nat. Space Inst.; dir. Standard Oil Co. (Ind.), Burroughs Corp., COMARLO, Inc. Author classified papers, sci. papers, chpts. in books; bd. editors, Addison-Wesley Pub. Co., 1958-64. Trustee Rockefeller Found., Theodore von Karman Meml. Found., Univ. Corp. on Atmospheric Research; bd. regents Nat. Library Medicine, 1971—; bd. visitors Def. Intelligence Sch., 1970—. Recipient Disting. Service medal NASA; Exceptional Civilian Service award USAF; Dept. Energy award, 1982; John Jay award Columbia U. Fellow IEEE, Am. Acad. Arts and Sci., AIAA (hon.), Am. Astronautical Soc.; mem. Am. Phys. Soc., Nat. Acad. Engring. (council, rep. to governing bd. NRC, governing bd. 1978-81), Am. Ordnance Assn., Air Force Assn., Sigma Xi. Club: Cosmos. Home: 7721 Falstaff Rd McLean VA 22102

FLETCHER, JESSE CONRAD, university president; b. San Antonio, Apr. 9, 1931; s. Jesse N. and Ruby (Arnold) F.; m. Dorothy Jordan, Feb. 24, 1953; children: Jordan Scott, Melissa Dupree. B.B.A., Tex. A&M U., 1952; M.Div., Southwestern Baptist Theol. Sem., 1956, Ph.D., 1958; Litt.D. (hon.), Rio Grande Coll., 1979. Ordained to ministry Baptist Ch., 1951; pastor various churches, Wellborn, Tex., Kopperl, Tex., 1953-57; John Townes prof. Bible U. Tex., 1958-60; with Bapt. Fgn. Mission Bd., 1960-75, sec. missionary personnel, 1963-68, mission support div. dir., Richmond, Va., 1968-75; pastor First Bapt. Ch., Knoxville, Tenn., 1975-77; pres. Hardin-Simmons U., 1977—; moderator Meridian Bapt. Assn.; trustee Harrison-Chilhowee Bapt. Acad., Gold Gate Bapt. Theol. Sem.; bd. dirs. Ministers Life; pres. Trans Am. Athletic Conf. Author: Bill Wallce of China, 1963, Wimpy Harper of Africa, 1967, The Wimpy Harper Story, 1967, Journeyman Missionary, 1967, The Search for Blonnye Foreman, 1971, Living Sacrifices: A Missionary Odyssey, 1974, Baker James Cauthen: A Man for All Nations, 1977, Practical Discipleship, 1980. Bd. dirs. Abilene United Way. Served to capt. U.S. Army, 1952-63. Named Disting. Student Tex. A&M U., 1950, Disting. Mil. Student, 1951; recipient Disting. Alumni award Southwestern Bapt. Theol. Sem., 1978. Mem. Abilene C. of C. (dir. 1977—).

FLETCHER, JOHN ALLEN, zoo director; b. Burlington, Wash., May 7, 1919; s. Fred Allen Flethcer and Lena Augusta (Huelsdonk) F.; m. Valata Dakota Green, Oct. 23, 1942; children: Ken, Lala, Sylvia. B.Sc., U. Wash., 1946. Dir. Como Zoo, St. Paul, 1957—. Fellow Am. Assn. Zool. Parks and Aquaria. Home: 1501 Breda Ave Saint Paul MN 55108 Office: Como Zoo Hamline Ave and Midway Pkwy Saint Paul MN 55103

FLETCHER, JOHN CALDWELL, bioethicist, educator; b. Bryan, Tex., Nov. 1, 1931; s. Robert Capers and Estelle Collins (Caldwell) F.; m. Adele Davis Woodall, Sept. 4, 1954; children: John Caldwell, Page Moss, Adele Davis. B.A., U. of South, 1953; M.Div. cum laude, Va. Theol. Sem., 1956, U. Heidelberg, 1957; Ph.D., Union Theol. Sem., N.Y.C., 1969. Ordained priest Episcopal Ch., 1957; curate St. Lukes Episc. Ch., Mountain Brook, Ala., 1957-60; rector R.E. Lee Meml. Ch., Lexington, Va., 1960-64; chaplain Cornell Med. Sch.-New York Hosp., 1964-66; asso. prof. Va. Theol. Sem., 1966-71; dir. Interfaith Met. Theol. Edn., Inc., Washington, 1971—, pres., 1975-77; asst. for bioethics Clin. Center, NIH, 1977—; asso. for theol. edn. Alban Inst., Washington, 1977—; project mgr. Sem. Futures Project, 1979—. Author: (with Celia A. Hahn) Inter/Met: Bold Experiment in Theological Education, 1977, The Futures of Protestant Seminaries, 1983, Coping with Genetic Disorders, 1982; Translator: Creation and Fall, 1959; Asso. editor: Ency. of Bioethics, 1975—, Ency. of Deafness and Deaf Persons; Contbr. articles to profl. jours. Founding fellow, bd. dirs. Inst. Soc., Ethics and Life Scis., Hastings-on-Hudson, N.Y.; vice-chmn. council Coll. Preachers, Washington. Mem. Am. Assn. Christian Ethics. Home: 203 Vassar Pl Alexandria VA 22314 Office: Bldg 10 Room 1C150 NIH Bethesda MD 20205 *My personal philosophy is that responsibility is the highest achievement for a human being, and that each situation can be saved from meaninglessness by the search for responsibility.*

FLETCHER, JONATHAN MOSS, savs. and loan assn. exec.; b. Des Moines, Oct. 28, 1914; s. Clyde Beals and Jennie (Moss) F.; m. Virginia Jane Votruba, Mar. 21, 1941; children—Gary Stephen, John Wise, Virginia Ann, Katherine Jean. A.B., U. Iowa, 1935; postgrad., Drake U., 1937-38. With U.S. Dept. Agr., 1935-37; with Am. Fed. Savs. & Loan Assn. Central Iowa (formerly Home Fed. Savs. & Loan Assn.), Des Moines, 1937—, successively treas., sec. and treas., exec. v.p., sec., 1937-58, pres., 1958-73, chmn. bd., 1973—, chief exec. officer, 1949-80, dir., 1938—, Fed. Home Loan Bank Des Moines, 1964-67, vice chmn., 1967; dir. Iowa Bus. Devel. Credit Corp., Iowa Kemper Ins. Co., 1966-80, FHLB of Des Moines; Midwest adv. bd. Lumbermens Mut. Casualty Co.; Mem. savs. and loan adv. com to U.S. sec. of treasury, 1966-80. Gen. chmn. United Campaign, 1958; mem. Greater Des Moines Com., 1957—, pres., 1968; mem. City Planning and Zoning Commn., Des Moines, 1950-59, chmn., 1957; Treas. Iowa Central Com. Rep. Party, 1955-57; Bd. control athletics U. Iowa, 1960-66; bd. dirs. U. Iowa Found., 1973—, vice chmn. exec. com., 1978; bd. dirs. Iowa Meth. Med. Center, vice chmn. exec. com., 1978-80; trustee Drake U. Served to capt. AUS and USAAF, 1942-45. Recipient Des Moines Tribune Community award, 1959. Mem. Savs. and Loan Found. (trustee 1954-56), U.S. Savs. and Loan League (exec. com. 1956-58), Ia. Savs. and Loan League (pres. 1950), Des Moines C. of C. (pres. 1954, bd. dirs. 1952-80), Nat. Planning Assn. (nat. council 1970—), Delta Upsilon. Congregationalist. Clubs: Des Moines, Wakonda, Bradenton (Fla.) Country; University Athletic (Iowa City). Home: 2935 Sioux Ct Des Moines IA 50321 Office: 601 Grand Ave Des Moines IA 50307

FLETCHER, KIM, savings and loan executive; b. Los Angeles, 1927. Grad., Stanford U., 1950. Chmn. bd., chief exec. officer Home Fed. Savs. & Loan Assn., San Diego. Office: 701 Broadway San Diego CA 92101

FLETCHER, LEROY STEVENSON, engineering educator; b. San Antonio, Oct. 10, 1936; s. Robert Holton and Jennie Lee (Adkins) F.; m. Nancy Louise McHenry, Aug. 14, 1966; children: Laura Malee, Daniel, Alden. B.S., Tex. A&M U., 1958; M.S., Stanford U., 1963, Engr., 1964; Ph.D., Ariz. State U., 1968. Registered profl. engr., Ariz., N.J., Va., Tex. Research scientist Ames Research Ctr., NASA, Moffett Field, Calif., 1958-62; instr. Ariz. State U., Tempe, 1964-68; prof. aero., engring., assoc. dean Rutgers U., New Brunswick, N.J., 1968-75; prof., chmn. dept. mech. and aero. engring. U. Va., Charlottesville, 1975-80; prof. mech. engring., assoc. dean Tex A&M U., College Station, 1980—; cons. to various industries; dir. Accreditation Bd. Engring. and Tech., 1979-82. Author: Introduction to Engineering Including FORTRAN Programming, 1977, Introduction to Engineering Design with Graphics and Design Projects, 1979; editor: Aerodynamic Heating and Thermal Protection, 1978, Heat Transfer and Thermal Control Systems, 1978. Served to capt. USAF, 1958-61. Fellow ASME (bd. govs., Charles Russ Richards award 1982), AAAS, AIAA (dir. 1981-84, Aerospace Edn. Achievement award 1982); mem. Am. Soc. Engring. Edn. (dir. 1978-80, George Westinghouse award 1981, Ralph Coats Roe award 1983), Sigma Xi, Tau Beta Pi, Pi Tau Sigma, Sigma Gamma Tau. Home: 9007 Sandstone Dr College Station TX 77840 Office: Texas A&M University College of Engrineering College Station TX 77843

FLETCHER, LLOYD, judge; b. Amarillo, Tex., Jan. 5, 1915; s. Lloyd and Florence (McKenzie) F.; m. Lola Slaight, Apr. 25, 1940; 1 dau., Diane. B.B.A., U. Tex., 1936; J.D., George Washington U., 1939. Bar: D.C. 1940. Pvt. practice, Washington, 1940-59; professorial lectr. law Am. U., 1946-68; trial judge U.S. Ct. Claims, Washington, 1960—. Contbr. articles to legal jours. Served to lt. (j.g.) USCGR, World War II. Recipient Alumni Achievement award George Washington U., 1981. Mem. Am. bar assns., The Barristers (Washington), Order of Coif, Phi Kappa Psi. Club: Mason. Home: 4851 Maury Ln Alexandria VA 22304

FLETCHER, LOUISE, actress; b. Birmingham, Ala., 1936; d. Robert Capers F. B.S., N.C. State U.; D.D.L.; student acting with Jeff Corey.; TV appearances include Maverick; films include Thieves Like Us, 1974, Russian Roulette, 1975, One Flew Over the Cuckoo's Nest, 1975 (Acad. award Best Actress), Exorcist II: The Heretic, 1977, Natural Enemies, 1979, The Lucky Star, 1980, Once Upon a Time in America, 1982, Brainstorm, 1983, Firestarter, 1983, Strange Invaders, 1983

FLETCHER, MAX ELLIS, educator; b. Preston, Idaho, Aug. 23, 1921; s. Sam H. (Marian);; s. Sam H. and (Ellis) F.; m. Ann Barrows, Dec. 14, 1954; children: Coly, Justin. B.A. magna cum laude, U. Wash., 1946; M.A., U. Idaho, 1949; postgrad., London Sch. Econs., 1954-55; Ph.D., U. Wis., 1957. With Equitable Life Assurance Soc., N.Y.C., Los Angeles, 1949-52; instr. econs. Marquette U., 1955-56; asst. prof. econs. Humboldt State Coll., 1957-58; asst. prof., prof. econs. U. Idaho, Moscow, 1958—, chmn. dept. econs., 1968-72, 74—. Author: Economics and Social Problems, 1979; Contbr. articles to profl. jours. Served with USN, 1939-45, 47-48. Fulbright scholar, 1954-55; Ford Found. fellow, 1956-57. Mem. Am. Econ. Assn., Econ. Hist. Assn., Assn. Evolutionary Econs., Phi Beta Kappa, Beta Gamma Sigma. Home: 1379 Four Mile Rd Viola ID 83872 Office: Dept Econ U Idaho Moscow ID 83843

FLETCHER, NORMAN COLLINGS, architect; b. Providence, Dec. 8, 1917; s. Robert C. and Lily (Wilcock) F.; m. Jean Bodman, Sept. 23, 1944 (dec. Sept. 1965); children: Judith, Jon B., Jeremy B., Mollie H., Rebecca H., Katrina H.; stepchildren: Lucas B. Houk, Damon O. Houk; m. Marjorie Taplin, Oct. 10, 1970. B.F.A. in Architecture, Yale U., 1940. Designer Skidmore, Owings and Merrill, N.Y.C., 1943-44, Saarinen, Swanson & Assos., Washington, Birmingham, Mich., 1944-46; prin. The Architects Collaborative Inc., Cambridge, Mass., 1946—; Instr. architecture Grad. Sch. Design, Harvard, 1949-52; vis. critic Sch. Architecture, Mass. Inst. Tech., 1957-58, Sch. Architecture, Yale U., 1956—, U. Tucuman, Argentina, 1954; Thomas Jefferson prof. architecture U. Va., 1977; mem. jury Higher Edn. Facilities Design Award Program, Dept. Health, Edn. and Welfare, 1966; mem. com. Rotch Travelling Fellowship, 1964-66, mem. preliminary jury, 1969; mem. architecture com. Boston Arts Festival, 1955-57, Yale Arts Assn., 1965—, pres., 1970; mem. Fed. Res. Bank Archtl. Rev. Panel, 1975-77; sec. Rotch Travelling Scholarship, 1980—; mem. vis. com. visual and environ. studies Harvard U., 1981—; archtl. adv. cons. Dept. State Office Fgn. Bldgs. Ops., 1983—. Recipient numerous awards, including citation Progressive Architecture Design awards for Chem. Lab. Tufts U., Medford, Mass., 1963, for IBM fed. systems div., Gaithersburg, Md., 1964, 1st prize Nat. House competition, 1945, Smith Coll. dormitory competition, 1946; honor award for YMCA, Roxbury, Mass. New Eng. regional council A.I.A., 1966; nat. honor award for dormitory and dining commons Clark U., Worcester, Mass. A.I.A., 1967; dormitory and dining commons complex 2, central Mass. A.I.A., 1970; for Worcester Found. for Exptl. Biology, Shrewsbury central Mass. A.I.A., 1970; Merit award for Roxbury YMCA HUD, 1968; Architecture and Allied Arts award Tau Sigma Delta, 1970; Alice Kimball English travelling fellow, 1940. Fellow A.I.A.; mem. Nat. Acad. Design (asso. mem.), Boston Soc. Architects (pres. 1966-67), Mass. Assn. Architects (exec. com. 1963-68). Home: 36 Moon Hill Rd Lexington MA 02173 Office: 46 Brattle St Cambridge MA 02138

FLETCHER, RALPH JOSEPH, publishing company executive; b. Mass., Nov. 30, 1929; s. Ralph J. and Margaret C. F.; m. Jean Collins, Feb. 16, 1952; children: Ralph, James, Elaine, Thomas, Robert, Joseph, John, Kathleen, Carolyn. B.E., Mass. State Coll. at Bridgewater, 1953, M.Ed., 1957. Tchr. pub. schs., Marshfield, Mass., 1953-54, Scituate, Mass., 1954-57; sales rep. Laidlaw Co., New Eng., 1957-64; regional mgr. William H. Sadlier, Inc., Chgo., 1964-68, nat. sales mgr., N.Y.C., 1968-75, pres., chief exec. officer, 1975—; also dir.; pres. Sadlier/Oxford, 1975—, also dir.; dir. Sahara Co., Novo Ednl. Toys Co., Keyway Co., Arrowhead Co. Mem. Cardinal's Com. of Laity, Roman Catholic Archdiocese of N.Y., Pres's. Assn. Democrat. Club: K.C. Home: William H Sadlier Inc 38 W Islip Rd West Islip NY 11795 Office: 11 Park Pl New York NY 10007 *

FLETCHER, ROBERT, lawyer; b. Birmingham, Ala., May 4, 1920; s. Robert Hall and Beatrice (Skelding) Jones; m. Florence K. Szuba, Sept. 12, 1942; children—Andrew R., William Alan. B.F.A., Ohio U., Athens, 1943; LL.B., J.D., Case Western Res U., 1948. Bar: Ohio bar 1948. Asst. gen. counsel Cleve. Transit System, 1951-56; with firm Jamison, Ulrich, Johnson & Burt, Cleve., 1956-59, Meyers, Stevens & Rea, 1959-61; pvt. practice, Cleve., 1961—; Lectr. Am. Heart Assn. Served with AUS, World War II; Korea. Recipient Speakers Bur. award Am. Heart Assn., 1973-76. Mem. Parma Bar Assn. Republican. Presbyterian. Club: Rosicrucian Order. Home: 5801 Hollywood Dr Parma OH 44129 Office: 5875 Broadview Rd Parma OH 44134

FLETCHER, ROBERT DAWSON, meteorologist; b. Lampacitos, Mexico, Feb. 11, 1912; s. Edmond McC. and Grace (Dawson) F.; m. Elsie Walser, June 1, 1935; children—Robert Dawson, John E. B.S. in Mech. Engring, Calif. Inst. Tech., 1933, M.S. in M.E. (Aero), 1934, 1935, D.Sc., Mass. Inst. Tech., 1941. Meteorologist Am. Airlines, Inc., 1935-39; instr. meteorology U. Calif. at Los Angeles, 1940- 42; meteorologist U.S. Weather Bur., 1940-50, supervising forecaster, 1941-46, chief hydrometeorol. sect., 1946-50; with USAF Air Weather Service, 1950—, cons., 1950-52, dir. sci. services, 1952-64, dir. aerospace scis., 1964-71, chief scientist, 1971-72; sci. adviser Weather Cons., Inc., 1977—; Tech. cons. OSRD, 1944, USAAF in, CBI and Caribbean, 1944-45; U.S. del. World Meteorological Orgn. (UN), 1952—; USAF and NRC del., Manila, 1952, Bangkok, 1957, NASA adv. group aero. research and devel. NATO Conf. Polar Meteorology, Oslo, Norway, 1956, Australian Conf. Tropical Storms, Brisbane, 1956; mem. meteorology panel U.S. Nat. Com. on Internat. Geophys. Year, 1955-64; liaison rep. com. on high altitude rocket and balloon research Nat. Acad. Scis., 1963—, mem. panel on edn., 1963—. Contbr. articles to profl. jours. Pres. Bannockburn (Md.) Citizens Assn., 1951-52. Recipient USAF decoration for exceptional civilian service, 1962, 72; Robert M. Losey award Am. Inst. Aeros. and Astronautics, 1969; Charles Franklin Brooks award Am. Meteorol. Soc., 1970. Fellow Am. Meteorol. Soc. (pres. 1956-57, councillor 1972—); asso. fellow Am. Inst. Aeros. and Astronautics (chmn. tech. com. on atmospheric environment 1964-65); mem. Am. Geophys. Union, Royal Meteorol. Soc., Sigma Xi. Home: Tubac Valley Country Club Estates PO Box 2461 Tubac AZ 85640

FLETCHER, RONALD DARLING, microbiology educator; b. Foxboro, Mass., Jan. 18, 1933; s. Howard Wendel and Ada Louise (Darling) F.; m. Barbara Gunderson, Jan. 30, 1954; children: Deborah, Mark Ronald, Christopher, Gary. B.S., U. Conn., 1954, M.S., 1959, Ph.D., 1963; postgrad., U. Zurich, Switzerland, 1963-64.

Instr. U. Conn., Storrs, 1959-63; researcher Am. Cyanamid Co., Pearl River, N.Y., 1964-67; cons. U.S. Army, Frederick, Md., 1977—; dir. microbiology McKeesport Hosp., Pa., 1971-79; prof., assoc. chairperson dept. microbiology U. Pitts., 1967—; cons. Mellon Inst., Pitts., 1981, Cons. Brokerage, Mountain View, Calif., 1981. Contbr. articles on microbiology to prof. jours. Judge Internat. Sci. and Engrng. Fair, Mpls., 1980 judge Internat. Sci. and Engrng. Fair, Milw., 1981 judge Internat. Sci. and Engrng. Fair, Dallas, 1982, Nat. Jr. Sci. and Humanities Symposium, West Point, N.Y., 1983. Served to col. U.S. Army, 1954-57, 78-79. Grantee U.S. Army, Am. Cancer Soc., NIH. Fellow Am. Acad Microbiology (registered microbiologist, specialist microbiologists), AAAS; mem. Internat. Assn. Dental Research (pres. Pitts. 1979-80), Assn. Mil. Surgeons, Am. Assn. Microbiologists, N.Y. Acad. Scis., Am. Legion. Republican. Office: 645 Salk Hall Univ Pitts Pittsburgh PA 15261

FLETCHER, STEWART GAILEY, iron and steel cons.; b. Wilkinsburg, Pa., Jan. 20, 1918; s. C.T. and Ruth (Gailey) F.; m. Helen M. Bennett, June 27, 1942; children—Fred B., Nancy G. (Okonak), Sherrill A., Stewart Gailey. B.S., Carnegie Inst. Tech., 1938; Sc.D., Mass. Inst. Tech., 1943. Registered profl. engr. Research asso. Mass. Inst. Tech., 1942-45; chief metallurgist Latrobe Steel Co., Pa., 1947-58, v.p., tech. dir., 1958-73; sr. v.p. Am. Iron and Steel Inst., 1973-80; pres. Ferrotechnology, Inc., Md., 1980—; mem. NRC, 1967-70. Fellow Am. Soc. Metals (pres. 1965-66, Howe medal 1945, 49), AAAS; mem. Am. Iron and Steel Inst., AIME, Metals Soc. (London). Presbyterian (elder). Clubs: Cosmos, Congressional Country (Washington); Rolling Rock (Ligonier, Pa.). Home: 4407 Tournay Rd Bethesda MD 20816

FLETCHER, THOMAS WILLIAM, urban affairs specialist; b. Portland, Oreg., Mar. 1, 1924; s. Irving A. and Florence (Cooper) F.; m. Margerie Frances Muller, Dec. 27, 1945; children—Thomas William, Heidi, Dean. B.S. in Bus. Adminstrn, U. Calif. at Berkeley, 1951. Asst. to city mgr., San Leandro, Calif., 1951-52, city adminstr., Davis, Calif., 1952-55, asst. to city mgr., San Diego, 1955-61, city mgr., 1961-66; pres. Franchise Corp., 1966-67; dep. asst. sec. HUD, 1967; dep. mayor of, Washington, 1967-69, city mgr., San Jose, Calif., 1969-72; pres. Nat. Tng. & Devel. Service, Washington, 1972-75; asso. prof. Golden Gate U., San Francisco, 1975-77; dir. Public Policy Analysis SRI Internat., Menlo Park, Calif., 1977—; mem. Commn. on Orgn. Govt. D.C., 1970-71. Contbr. articles in field to profl. jours. Vice pres. San Diego County council Boy Scouts Am., 1959—; mem. adv. bd. San Jose State Coll.; bd. dirs. San Diego YMCA, 1961-64, San Jose YMCA. Served with AUS, 1943-46. Named Outstanding Young Man of Year in San Diego San Diego Jr. C. of C., 1960. Mem. League Calif. Cities (pres. city mgrs. dept. 1965-66, chmn. electronic data processing com. 1965-67), Western Govt. Research Assn. (pres. 1963-64), Am. Soc. Pub. Adminstrn. (pres. San Diego 1960-61), Internat. City Mgrs. Assn., Nat. Municipal League (council), Inst. Local Self Govt., Nat. Acad. Pub. Adminstrn. Clubs: Kiwanis, Rotary. Home: 2940 Emerson St Palo Alto CA 94306 Office: 333 Ravenswood Ln Menlo Park CA 94025

FLETCHER, WILLARD ALLEN, history educator; b. Johnson, Vt., Oct. 18, 1924; s. Willard Allen and Anne Marguerite (Scharlé) F.; m. Jean Elizabeth Tucker, Sept. 17, 1949; children: Ian, Colin, Hilary, Brian. B.A., U. Vt., 1949; certificat d'études, Université de Bruxelles, Belgium, 1950; M.A., U. Ark., 1952; Ph.D., U. Pa., 1956. Asst. prof. U. Vt., Burlington, 1955-58; asso. prof. U. Colo., Boulder, 1958-65, U. Tex., Austin, 1965-69; prof. U. Del., Newark, 1969—, chmn. dept. history, 1969-74; Dir. Am. Hist. Assn. microfilm project of captured German documents, 1960-61; mem. World War II Archival Commn., Luxemburg, 1964—. Author: The Mission of Vincent Benedetti to Berlin, 1864-70, 1965; also series of guides to German captured records, 1960—; Contbr. articles and revs. on modern German and European history to profl. jours. Adv. council Eleutherian Mills-Hagley Found., 1969-72; mem. U.S. Holocaust Meml. Council, 1980—. Served with AUS, 1944-46. Decorated officer Order of Oak Chaplet, Luxemburg).; Fulbright scholar, 1949-50; Harrison fellow, 1953-54; Penfield scholar, 1954-55; Guggenheim fellow, 1963-64. Mem. Am. Hist. Assn., Société d'histoire moderne, Soc. Contemporary Historians, Soc. French Hist. Studies, Institut Grand-Ducal de Luxembourg (corr.). Home: 216 Hanover Pl Newark DE 19711

FLEWELLEN, WILLIAM CRAWFORD, JR., business educator, dean; b. Eufaula, Ala., Aug. 31, 1918; s. William Crawford and Lena Kendrick (Hurt) F.; m. Tommie Sue Kendrick, Aug. 31, 1941; children: Susan, Mary Jane. B.S., U. Ala., 1940, M.S., 1947; Ph.D., Columbia U., 1956. Asst. dean, prof. accounting U. Ala., 1946-61; prof. accounting, dean Coll. Bus. and Industry Miss. State U., 1961-68; prof. accounting, dean Coll. Bus. Adminstrn. U. Ga., Athens, 1968—, univ. prof. bus. and indsl. devel., 1982—; mem. policy study com. Walter E. Heller Internat. Corp. Inst. Advancement Small Bus. Enterprises; nat. adv. council SBA, 1975-81; small bus. adv. council Treasury Dept., 1975-77; adv. group to commr. IRS, 1966-67; nat. adv. bd. Internat. Council Small Bus., 1982—. Served to maj. USAAF, 1942-46; lt. col. Res. Recipient Algernon Sidney Sullivan award U. Ala., 1961; Sr. Fulbright fellow, 1973. Mem. Nat. Assn. Accountants (chpt. pres. 1965-66), Am. Assn. Collegiate Schs. Bus. (pres. 1976-77), Accounting Careers Council (nat. chmn. 1965-66), So. Bus. Adminstrn. Assn. (pres. 1966-67), Fin. Execs. Inst. (nat. coms. edn. and taxation 1964-68), Delta Sigma Pi, Beta Alpha Psi, Omicron Delta Kappa, Blue Key, Beta Gamma Sigma, Phi Kappa Phi. Home: 140 Mal Bay Rd Athens GA 30601 Office: 346 Brooks Hall Small Bus Devel Center U Ga Athens GA 30602 *Be honest. Be considerate, place the good of the organization first. Listen carefully. Treat everyone alike in similar circumstances. Never be satisfied with average performance.*

FLEXNER, JAMES THOMAS, author; b. N.Y.C., Jan. 13, 1908; s. Simon and Helen (Thomas) F.; m. Beatrice Hudson, 1950; 1 dau., Helen Hudson. Grad., Lincoln Sch. of Tchrs. Coll., Columbia, 1925; B.S. magna cum laude, Harvard Coll., 1929. Reporter N.Y. Herald Tribune, 1929-31; exec. sec. Noise Abatement Commn., N.Y.C. Dept. of Health, 1931-32; Guggenheim fellow, 1953; cons. Colonial Williamsburg, 1956-57; adv. com. The Papers of George Washington.; Lectr. on founding fathers, history of Am. art and civilization. Author: several books including Doctors on Horseback: Pioneers of American Medicine, 1937, The Pocket History of American Painting, 1950, The Traitor and the Spy, rev. edit, 1953, American Painting: The Light of Distant Skies, 1954, Treason, 1780; TV drama, 1954, Gilbert Stuart, 1955; Mohawk Baronet: Sir William Johnson of N.Y, 1959, rev. edit., 1979, That Wilder Image: The Painting of America's Native School from Thomas Cole to Winslow Homer, 1962 (Parkman prize), George Washington: The Forge of Experience, 1732-1775, 1965, The World of Winslow Homer, 1966, America's Old Masters, rev. edit, 1980, George Washington in the American Revolution, 1968, George Washington and the New Nation, 1970, Ninteenth Century American Painting, 1970, George Washington: Anguish and Farewell, 1972 (Nat. Book award for biography, spl. Pulitzer prize citation), Washington: The Indispensable Man, 1974 (Christopher's award), (with Linda Samter) The Face of Liberty, 1975, The Young Hamilton, 1977, Steamboats Come True, rev. edit, 1978, States Dyckman, American Loyalist, 1980, An American Saga: The Story of Helen Thomas and Simon Flexner, 1983; Contbr. mags. and newspapers. Trustee emeritus N.Y. Pub. Library. Recipient Library of Congress grant-in-aid for studies history of Am. civilization, 1945; Life in America Prize, 1946. Mem. P.E.N. (pres. 1954-55, hon. v.p. 1963-66), Soc. Am. Historians (pres. 1975-77), Am. Acad. Inst. Arts and Letters (v.p. for lit. 1981—), Phi Beta Kappa. Club: Century. Address: 530 E 86th St New York NY 10028

FLEXNER, LOUIS BARKHOUSE, scientist, educator; b. Louisville, Jan. 7, 1902; s. Washington and Ida (Barkhouse) F.; m. Josefa Barba Gosé, Aug. 23, 1937. B.S., U. Chgo., 1923; M.D., Johns Hopkins, 1927; LL.D., U. Pa. Fellow medicine Johns Hopkins Hosp., 1928-29; resident physician U. Chgo. Clinics, 1929-30; instr. and asso. anatomy Johns Hopkins Med. Sch., 1930-39; with dept. physiology Cambridge (Eng.) U., 1933-34; staff mem. dept. embryology Carnegie Instn., Washington, 1939-51, research asso., 1951—; prof. anatomy Sch. Med. U. Pa., 1951—, chmn. dept., 1951-67; dir. Inst. Neurol. Scis., 1953-66. Contbr. articles to profl. jours. Sci. adv. bds. USPHS, United Cerebral Palsy, Nat. Council to Combat Blindness, Nat. Paraplegic Soc., NRC, Nat. Found. Mem. Am. Assn. Anatomists, Nat. Acad. Scis., Am. Physiol. Soc., Am. Soc. Biol. Chemists, Am. Acad. Arts and Scis., Am. Philos. Soc. Home: 4631 Pine St Philadelphia PA 19143

FLEXNER, STUART BERG, publishing executive, editor, educator; b. Jacksonville, Ill., Mar. 22, 1928; s. David and Gertrude (Berg) F.; m. Doris Louise Hurcomb, Nov. 21, 1967; children: Jennifer, Geoffrey. B.A., U. Louisville, 1948, M.A., 1949; postgrad., Cornell U., 1950-52. Exec. editor Verlan Books, Inc., N.Y.C., 1952-57; mng. editor coll. div. MacMillan Co., N.Y.C., 1957-58; pres. Jugetas, S.A., Mexico City, 1958-64; div. v.p. Random House, Inc., N.Y.C., 1964-72, editor-in-chief reference dept., 1980—; v.p. The Hudson Group, Pleasantville, N.Y., 1972-80, mem. bd., Pleasntville, N.Y., 1976-80; tchr. Cornell U., Ithaca, N.Y., 1950-52. Author: (with Harold Wentworth) The Dictionary of American Slang, 1960, I Hear America Talking, 1976, Listening to America, 1982; chief lexicographer: The Oxford American Dictionary, 1980. Named Outstanding Alumni U. Louisville, 1977. Mem. MLA, Nat. Council Tchrs. English, Dictionary Soc. N. Am., Am. Hist. Assn. Office: Random House Inc 201 E 50th St New York NY 10022

FLICK, JOHN EDMOND, newspaper publishing company executive; b. Franklin, Pa., Mar. 14, 1922; s. Edmond Leroy and Mary M. (Weaver) F.; m. Lois Anna Lange, Apr. 20, 1946; children: Gregory Allan, Scott Edmond, Lynn Ellen, Ann Elizabeth. Student, Northwestern U., 1941-44, U. Pa., 1945; LL.B., Northwestern U., 1948. Bar: Ill. 1948, Calif. 1971, fed. cts 1971, U.S. Supreme Ct 1974. Commd. 1st lt. Judge Adv. Gen. Corps U.S. Army, 1950, advanced through grades to lt. col. Res., 1968; ret., 1972; faculty U.S. Mil. Acad., 1954-57, Judge Adv. Gen. Sch., U. Va., 1960-61; counsel Litton Industries, 1963-67; sr. v.p., sec., gen. counsel, dir. Bangor Punta Corp., 1967-69; sr. v.p., sec., gen. counsel Times Mirror Co., Los Angeles, 1970—; dir. Tejon Ranch Co., Piper Aircraft Co., 1969. Chmn. Los Angeles adv. bd. Salvation Army. Recipient Am. Bar Assn. Acad. award, 1961. Mem. Am., Los Angeles County bar assns., state bars Calif., Ill., Am. Soc. Corp. Secs. Club: Wigmore (Northwestern U. Law Sch.) (life mem.). Office: Times Mirror Sq Los Angeles CA 90053

FLICK, SOL E., watch co. exec., lawyer; b. N.Y.C., May 4, 1915; s. Joseph and Anna (Mednick) F.; m. Stella Hurwitz, Jan. 14, 1940; children—Susan, Jonathan. B.A., Bklyn. Coll., 1937; LL.B., St. Lawrence U., 1939. Bar: N.Y. bar 1941. Practice in, N.Y.C.; chmn. exec. com., chief exec. officer Bulova Watch Co., Inc., 1977-79; gen. counsel N.Am. Watch Corp.; pres. N.Am. Watch Internat. Ltd. Bd. dirs. Booth Meml. Hosp., N.Y.C. Mem. Am. Bar Assn. Clubs: Nat. Lawyers (Washington); Twenty-Four Karat (N.Y.C.). Home: 55 Percheron Ln Roslyn Heights NY 11577

FLICKER, TED, writer, dir., actor; b. Freehold, N.J., June 6, 1930; s. Sidney K. and Ray (Lopatin) F.; m. Barbara Perkins, Sept. 30, 1966. Student, Bard Coll., 1948-50; diploma, Royal Acad. Dramatic Art, 1952. A founder of improvisational theatre in, U.S., 1955. Producer, dir., actor, Compass Theatre, Chgo., 1955, Compass Players, St. Louis, 1956; writer dir.: Broadway musical The Nervous Set, 1959; producer, dir., actor: The Premise, 1960-64; writer, dir.: films The Troublemaker, 1963, The President's Analyst, 1968, Up in The Cellar, 1970, Just a Little Inconvenience, 1977, Last of the Good Guys, 1978; dir.: Where The Ladies Go, 1979, Soggy Bottom U.S.A, 1980; creator, writer, dir.: TV series Barney Miller, 1974. Served with AUS, 1952-54. Recipient Obie award, 1960; Vernon Rice award, 1960. Mem. Dirs. Guild Am. (council 1970-73), Writers Guild Am. (dir. 1973-75, Best Screenplay award 1968, Best Musical award 1969), Screen Actors Guild, Actors Equity. Address: care Writers Guild Am 8955 Beverly Blvd Los Angeles CA 90048

FLICKINGER, CHARLES JOHN, anatomist, educator; b. Bethlehem, Pa., July 13, 1938; s. Wilbur James and Verna (Diehl) F.; m. Agnes Elizabeth Dickel, Feb. 23, 1963; children: Laura Jill, David Paul. A.B., Dartmouth Coll., 1960; M.D., Harvard U., 1964. Research fellow dept. anatomy U. Colo., Denver, 1964-65, Harvard Med. Sch., Boston, 1965-66; research assoc. Inst. Developmental Biology, U. Colo., Boulder, 1966-67, asst. prof., 1967-70; assoc. prof. dept. anatomy Sch. Medicine, U. Va., Charlottesville, 1971-75, prof., 1975—, Harvey E. Jordan prof. anatomy, 1982—, chmn. dept., 1982—; mem. reproductive biology study sect. NIH, 1979-83; mem. anatomy test com. Nat. Bd. Med. Examiners, 1981—. Author: (with Brown, Kutchal, Ogilvie) Medical Cell Biology, 1979; articles in cell and reproductive biology; Assoc. editor: Anatomical Record jour. Am. Assn. Anatomists, 1972-79; adv. editor: Internat. Rev. Cytology. NIH research career devel. award grantee, 1968-70. Mem. Am. Soc. Cell Biology, Am. Assn. Anatomists, Soc. Study Reprodn., Am. Soc. Andrology, Phi Beta Kappa, Alpha Omega Alpha. Home: 2009 Meadowbrook Rd Charlottesville VA 22901

FLICKINGER, HARRY HARNER, government official, personnel consultant; b. Hanover, Pa., July 27, 1936; s. Harry Roosevelt and Goldie Anna (Harner) F.; m. Hsin Yang, May 30, 1961; children: Audrey Mae, Deborah Lynn. B.S. in Psychology, U. Md., 1958. Investigator U.S. Civil Service Commn., Washington, 1962-64; personnel specialist U.S. Naval Ordinance Lab., Silver Spring., Md., 1964-66; from asst. dir. to dir. personnel U.S. OMB, Washington, 1966-73; asst. dir. personnel AEC and Dept. Energy, Washington, 1973-78; dir. personnel U.S. Dept. Justice, Washington, 1978-79, dep. asst. atty. gen. adminstrn., 1979—; adviser Nat. Acad. Pub. Adminstrn., Washington, 1981-83. Recipient Ribcoff-Percy award for excellence in civil service reform, 1980, Disting. Service award Atty. Gen. U.S., 1981, Sr. Exec. Service award U.S. Dept. Justice, 1981, 82. Mem. Internat. Personnel Mgmt. Assn. Lutheran. Home: 8730 Lochaven Dr Gaithersburg MD 20879 Office: Justice Mgmt Div Dept Justice 10th and Constitution Ave NW Washington DC 20530

FLICKINGER, THOMAS L., hospital administrator; b. Carroll, Iowa, Apr. 22, 1939; s. Leslie Winfred and Evelyn (Hanson) F.; m. Marjorie Ellen Madison, Apr. 19, 1970; children: Benjamin, Samuel. B.B.A., U. Iowa, 1961, M.A., 1963. Adminstrv. asst. Presbyn.-St. Luke's Hosp., Chgo., 1963-64; asst. adminstr. 1 Creighton Meml. St. Joseph Hosp., Omaha, 1964-66, asso. dir., 1966-68, adminstr., 1968-73; exec. dir. Creighton Omaha Regional Health Care Corp., 1973-75; asso. dir. Vanderbilt U. Hosp., 1975-77; adminstr. Routt Meml. Hosp., Steamboat Springs, Colo., 1977—. Mem. Omaha Hosp. Assn. (pres. 1971), Am. Coll. Hosp. Adminstrs., Colo. Hosp. Assn. (chmn. 1982), Health Issues Study Soc., Phi Kappa Psi. Home: PO Box 1915 Steamboat Springs CO 80477 Office: Routt Meml Hosp Steamboat Springs CO 80477

FLIEGEL, FREDERICK CHRISTIAN, sociology educator; b. Edmonton, Alta., Can., Apr. 3, 1925; came to U.S., 1928, naturalized, 1935; s. John Carl and Ruth Friedeborg (Aastrup) F.; m. Thellyn Ruth Haller, Aug. 25, 1955; children: Frederick M., Ruth E., David C., Johanna C. Student, Moravian Coll., 1942-43; B.A., U. Wis., 1949, M.A., 1952, Ph.D., 1955. Asst. prof. to asso. prof. Pa. State U., 1955-65; asso. prof. Mich. State U., 1966-67; prof. sociology U. Ill., 1968—, head dept., 1970-73; vis. prof. U. Wis., summer 1963, Tamil Nadu Agrl. U., Coimbatore, India, spring 1977. Author: (with Roy, Sen and Kivlin) Agricultural Innovations in Indian Villages, 1968, Agricultural Innovation Among Indian Farmers, 1968, Communication in India: Experiments in Introducing Change, 1968; Editor: Rural Sociology, 1970-72. Served with USMC, 1943-46. Fellow Am. Sociol. Assn.; mem. Rural Sociol. Soc. (pres. 1975-76), Midwest Sociol. Soc., AAAS, AAUP. Home: 606 W Church St Champaign IL 61820 Office: Mumford Hall Univ Illinois Urbana IL 61821

FLIEGER, HOWARD WENTWORTH, editor; b. Denver, Oct. 11, 1909; s. Sterling N. and Florence (Milliken) F.; m. Dorothy Kathryn James, Apr. 7, 1927; children: Howard Wentworth, Kenneth Hugh. Student pub. schs. Reporter, city editor Shawnee (Okla.) Morning News, 1929-33; with A.P., St. Louis, 1933-35, night news editor, Kansas City, Mo., 1935-37, bur. chief, Jefferson City, 1937-43, White House corr., Washington, 1943-45; mng. editor World Report, Washington, 1945-48; directing editor world staff U.S. News and World Report, 1948-58, asst. exec. editor, 1958- 65, asso. exec. editor, 1965-69, exec. editor, 1969-72, editor, sr. v.p., 1972-77. Mem. White House Corrs. Assn. Clubs: Nat. Press, Cosmos, F. Street (Washington). Home: 6818 Selkirk Dr Bethesda MD 20817 Office: US News and World Report Washington DC 20037

FLIER, MICHAEL STEPHEN, educator; b. Los Angeles, Apr. 20, 1941; s. Albert and Bonnie F.; (m), Dec. 8, 1973. B.A., U. Calif., Berkeley, 1962, M.A., 1964, Ph.D., 1968. Acting vis. asst. prof. Slavic langs. and lit. U. Calif., Berkeley, 1968; asst. prof. Slavic langs. UCLA, 1968-73, assoc. prof., 1973-79, prof., 1979—, chmn. dept., 1978—. Author: Aspects of nominal determination in Old Church Slavic, 1974; editor: Slavic forum: Essays in Slavic Linguistics and Literature, 1974; co-editor: Medieval Russian Culture, 1983. Internat. Reserach and Exchange Bd. travel grantee, USSR, Czecholsovakia, 1966-67, 71, 78. Mem. Linguistic Soc. Am., Am. Assn. Tchrs. Slavic and East European Langs., Am. Assn. Advancement Slavic Studes, Western Slavic Assn. Home: 5740 Etiwanda Ave 7 Tarzana CA 91356 Office: Dept Slavic Langs and Lits UCLA Los Angeles CA 90024

FLIGG, JAMES EDWARD, oil company executive; b. Sydney, N.S.W., Australia, June 1, 1936; came to U.S., 1975; s. Henry Joseph and Florence (Purvis) F.; m. May Dorothea Hunt, Apr. 18, 1959; children: Tracey, Jennifer. B.S., U. N.S.W., 1968; A.M.P., Harvard U., 1980. Mgr. product mgmt., fiber and film intermediates Amoco Chem. Corp., Chgo., 1975-78; mgr. corp. planning Standard Oil Co. (Ind.), Chgo., 1978-80; v.p. mktg. olefins and polymers Amoco Chem. Corp., Chgo., 1980-82, v.p. internat. ops., 1982—. Mem. Soc. Chem. Industry. Club: Mid.-Am. Home: 1708 Shagbark Ct Naperville IL 60565 Office: 200 E Randolph Dr Chicago IL 60601

FLINK, EDMUND BERNEY, physician; b. Isanti, Minn., Jan. 27, 1914; s. John Leonard and Huldah (Swenson) F.; m. Marian Richard, June 12, 1940; children: Charles, Alice, James, Paul. M.B., U. Minn., 1937, M.D., 1938, Ph.D., 1945. Diplomate: Am. Bd. Internal Medicine. Intern, then resident in internal medicine Univ. Hosp., U. Minn., 1937-42; from instr. to prof. medicine U. Minn. Med. Sch., 1943-60; prof. medicine, chmn. dept. W.Va. U. Med. Sch., Morgantown, 1960-76, Benedum prof. medicine, 1976—. Commonwealth Fund fellow, 1948-49. Mem. AMA, ACP (regent 1969-75), Am. Fedn. Clin. Research, Am. Soc. Clin. Investigation, Assn. Am. Physicians, Endocrine Soc., Central Soc. Clin. Research, Am. Diabetes Assn., Am. Coll. Nutrition. Lutheran. Home: 672 Bellaire Dr Morgantown WV 26505 Office: Dept Medicine WVa Univ Hosp Morgantown WV 26506

FLINK, RICHARD ALLEN, lawyer, manufacturing company executive; b. N.Y.C., Mar. 1, 1935; s. Jack and Claire (Goldberg) F.; m. Lois Gudeon, June 12, 1960; children: Andrea L., Gary R. B.A., Brandeis U., 1955; J.D., NYU, 1959, LL.M., 1962. Bar: N.Y. 1959, N.J. 1969. Individual practice law, N.Y.C., 1960-65; gen. atty. Becton Dickinson & Co., Rutherford, N.J., 1966-70; with C.R. Bard, Inc., Murray Hill, N.J., 1970—, gen. counsel, 1971—, v.p., 1973—; adj. asst. prof. indsl. adminstrn. Columbia Coll. Pharm. Scis., 1966-75; co-adj. instr. Rutgers U. Coll. Pharmacy, 1976—. Mem. Internat., Fed., Am., N.Y., N.J., Bergen County bar assns., Assn. Fed. Bar N.J., Assn. Advancement of Med. Instrumentation (dir.). Office: 731 Central Ave Murray Hill NJ 07974

FLINN, EDWARD AMBROSE, III, government research official; b. Oklahoma City, Aug. 27, 1931; s. Edward Ambrose and Marion Catalina (Prater) F.; m. Jane Margaret Bott, Dec. 29, 1962; 1 dau., Susan Katherine. B.S. in Geophysics (William Barton Rogers scholar), Mass. Inst. Tech., 1953; Ph.D. in Geophysics (NSF fellow 1953-54), Calif. Inst. Tech., 1960; postgrad. (Fulbright scholar), Australian Nat. U., 1958-59; certificat, Le Cordon Bleu Ecole de Cuisine et de Patesserie, 1971. Seismologist United ElectroDynamics Inc., Pasadena, Calif., 1960-62; chief seismologist, lab. seismic data Teledyne Geotech, Alexandria, Va., 1962-64, dir. research, 1964-68; asso. dir. Alexandria labs., 1968-74; dir. lunar programs office space sci. NASA, Washington, 1975, dep. dir., chief scientist lunar and planetary programs, 1976-77, chief scientist earth and ocean programs, 1977, chief scientist geodynamics program, 1978—; mem. joint research panel AEC-U.K. Atomic Energy Authority, 1963-74; vis. research asso. Calif. Inst. Tech., 1969, 78; vis. asso. prof. geophysics Brown U., 1970; cons. subcom. planetology steering com. space sci. and applications NASA, 1969-70, Nat. Swedish Inst. Bldg. Research, Stockholm, 1970; participant sci. exchange Nat. Acad. Sci.-Acad. Scis. USSR, 1970; mem. com. lunar and planetary exploration Nat. Acad. Scis., 1973-75, mem. com. on seismology, 1973-75, mem. com. on internat. geology, 1982—; mem. adv. com. earthquake studies U.S. Geol. Survey, 1975—. Trans., editor two books; asso. editor for gen. seismology: Geophysics, 1965-67; editor sect. earth and planetary surfaces and interiors: Jour. Geophys. Research, 1973-78. Mem. adv. bd. No. Va. br. Urban League, 1970-71; mem. Alexandria Council on Human Relations, 1970—; mem. traffic bd., Alexandria, 1972-74; mem. Alexandria Democratic Com., 1970-74, exec. bd., 1971-73. Mem. AAAS, Am. Astron. Soc., Royal Astron. Soc. (editorial bd. Geophys. Jour. 1969-74), Am. Geophys. Union (sec. sect. seismology 1970-74), Assn. Earth Sci. Editors, Internat. Union Geodesy and Geophysics (chmn. commn. planetary scis. 1976—, sec. Commn. on Internat. Coordination of Space Techniques for Geodesy and Geodynamics), Seismol. Soc. Am., Soc. Exploration Geophysicists, Inter-Assn. Com. Math. Geophysics (sec. 1971-75), Internat. Council Sci. Unions (sec.-gen. Inter-Union Commn. on Lithosphere, mem. com. on publs. and communications 1981—), 89ers Soc., Sigma Xi, Beta Theta Pi. Club: Cosmos. Research, numerous publs. on seismology, geophysics, applied maths., computer sci. Home: 3605 Tupelo Pl Alexandria VA 22304 Office: NASA Hqrs Code EE-8 Washington DC 20546

FLINNER, CHARLES FREDERICK, cons.; b. Leavenworth, Kans., Jan. 17, 1920; s. Max and Florence (Hampel) F.; m. Betty Goodwin, Oct. 26, 1946; children—Linda Charlene (Mrs. Michael Collier), Charles Frederick, Margaret Anne. B.S., U. Kans., 1941. Accountant Aetna Fed. Savs. and Loan Assn., Topeka, 1941; accountant VA, Chgo. and Washington, 1946-50; dep. chief accountant Office U.S. High Commr. for Germany, Frankfurt and Bonn, 1950-52; comptroller Det. Material Procurement Agy., London, Eng., 1952-54; with ICA, AID, 1954-79, controller, Washington, 1964-73, ROCAP, Guatemala City, 1973-79; cons. fgn. econ. assistance, 1979—. Served to capt., Finance Corps AUS, 1942-46. Mem. Fed. Govt. Accountants Assn., Internat. Com. for Accounting Coop., Alpha Kappa Psi. Club: Oconee Country (Seneca, S.C.). Home: 302 Bobolink Dr Seneca SC 29678

FLINT, C. W., JR., corporate executive. Chmn., dir. Flint Industries, Inc. Office: PO Box 490 Tulsa OK 73101§

FLINT, DANIEL WALDO BOONE, lawyer; b. Phila., Nov. 24, 1926; s. Ralph Woodberry and Laura Chapin (Schontz) F.; m. Joan Graebe, Dec. 14, 1957; children: Daniel Waldo Boone, Adam P., Charlton G. B.A., U. Pa., 1950; J.D., Temple U., 1956. Bar: Pa. 1957. Practiced law, Phila., 1960—, King of Prussia, Pa., 1972—, farmer, Perkiomenville, Pa., 1966—; sec., gen. counsel Nat. Liberty Life Ins. Co., 1967-72. Dir. Montgomery County (Pa.) Conservation Dist., 1972-76; pres. gen. Gen. Soc. SR, 1974-76, pres. emeritus, 1976; pres. emeritus King of Prussia Hist. Soc., 1968—; bd. dirs., legal counsel Freedom Forge Found., 1969-76; pres., legal counsel Soc. Preservation Am. Indian Culture, 1968-76; past pres., legal counsel, chaplain Chaplin Scudder Assn., Inc.; gen. counsel Keystone Christian Sch. Assn.; founder, v.p., counsel Valley Forge Tours, 1968-78; mem. sch. bd. Upper Bucks Christian Sch., 1975-78. Served with USNR, 1945-46. Recipient Washington Gold medal Freedoms Found., at Valley Forge, 1973; Man of Year award Patriotic Order Sons of Am., 1970; Ky. Col. Mem. Descs. Signers of Declaration Independence, Mil. Order Loyal Legion U.S., Soc. War 1812, Am., Pa., Phila. bar assns., Am. Arbitration Assn., Valley Forge Hist. Soc., Goschenhoppen Historians, Am. Vets. Assn. (pres. 1977—), Am. Legion. Baptist (deacon). Clubs: Rotary, Union League (Phila.). Home: Flintlock Farm Perkiomenville PA 18074 Office: 125 N Gulph Rd King of Prussia PA 19406

FLINT, EMILY PAULINE RIEDINGER, editor; b. N.Y.C., Apr. 1, 1909; d. Louis and Emma Therese (Schaufele) Riedinger; m. Paul H. Flint, Aug. 18, 1935; 1 son, Paul H. A.B., Barnard Coll., 1930; M.A., Tufts U., 1932; B.S., Columbia Sch. Library Service, 1935; L.H.D. (hon.), New Eng. Coll., 1967, D.Litt, Franklin Pierce Coll., 1969. Teaching fellow English Tufts Coll., 1930-32; instr. Tufts U. Writers' Workshop, summer 1954; library staff Mt. Vernon (N.Y.) Pub. Library, 1932-34, Columbia Library, 1934-35; humanities librarian Mass. Inst. Tech., 1935-44; editorial asst. Atlantic Monthly, 1945-47, research editor, 1948-51, mng. editor, 1951-70, contbg. editor, 1970-73; editor Peabody Museum, Harvard U., 1970-76; pres. Creative Editing, Inc., 1970—; asso. editor Alma Mater mag., 1971-74; instr. div. journalism Boston U., 1948-51; lectr. editorial procedures Simmons Coll., 1975, spl. instr. in communications, 1977-78. Editor: (with Edward Weeks) Jubilee: 100 Years of the Atlantic, 1957, The Lithographs of Ture Bengtz, 1978, Every Child a Wanted Child, The Work of Clarence J. Gamble, M.D. in the Birth Control Movement, 1978, Creative Editing and Writing Handbook, 1980; editorial cons.: History of the Harvard Medical Unit at Boston City Hospital, 1915-1973, 2 vols., 1982. Trustee Medford (Mass.) Pub. Library, 1954—; trustee Franklin Pierce Coll., 1972—, vice chmn. bd., 1977-79, chmn. bd., 1979—; alumna trustee Barnard Coll., 1965-69. Mem. New Eng. Women's Press Assn. (dir. 1958, 61-69, pres. 1967-69), Boston Center Adult Edn. (dir. 1948-50, 58-70, 71-74, hon. dir. 1974—, pres. 1949-50, 60-65, v.p. 1959-60). Club: Zonta (Medford). Home: 26 Edison Ave Medford MA 02155

FLINT, GEORGE SQUIRE, lawyer; b. Ft. Wayne, Ind., Oct. 28, 1930; s. A. Verne and Alberta (Minor) F.; m. Emily Gregg McLees, Nov. 23, 1968; 1 son, Alexander C.; children by previous marriage: Julia M., Melissa A., Anthony E. A.B., U. Mich., 1952, J.D., 1955. Bar: N.Y. 1956. Assoc., then sr. assoc. firm Fulton, Walter & Duncombe, N.Y.C., 1955-65, ptnr., 1983; with Tenneco Chems., Inc., 1965-82, v.p., sec., gen. counsel, 1965-82; asst. sec. Tenneco Inc., Tenneco Internat. Inc. Served with USNR, 1955-57. Mem. N.Y. State Bar Assn., Am. Arbitration Assn. (panel arbitrators), Assn. Bar City N.Y., Order of Coif. Club: Indian Harbor Yacht. Home: 114 E 90th St New York NY 10028 Office: 30 Rockefeller Plaza New York NY 10112

FLINT, JOHN E., educator, historian; b. Montreal, Que., Can., May 17, 1930; s. Alfred Edgar and Sarah (Pickup) F.; m. Nezhat Sepanj, Sept. 19, 1975; children: Helen Sarah, Richard John. B.A., U. Cambridge, 1952, M.A., 1954; Ph.D., U. London, 1957. Asst. lectr., lectr., reader colonial history King's Coll., U. London, 1954-67; vis. prof., Fulbright fellow U. Calif., Santa Barbara, 1960-61; vis. prof., head history dept. U. Nigeria, Nsukka, 1963-64; prof. history Dalhousie U., 1967—, dir. African Studies Centre; mem. acad. panel Can. Council, 1967-68, Social Scis. and Humanities Research Council Can. Author: Sir George Goldie and the Making of Nigeria, 1960, Nigeria and Ghana, 1966, Cecil Rhodes, 1974; Editor: Cambridge History of Africa, Vol. V, 1790-1870, 1977. Fellow Royal Hist. Soc., Royal Soc. Can.; mem. Canadian Assn. African Studies, Canadian Hist. Assn., Nigerian Hist. Assn., African Studies Assn. U.K. Office: Dept History Dalhousie U Halifax NS Canada

FLINT, ROBERT NELSON, utility executive; b. Eaton, Colo., May 29, 1921; s. Nelson J. and Agnes M. (Lechnor) F.; m. Marilou Bosee, Apr. 3, 1975; 1 dau., Karen Louise Flint Berry. B.A. in Econs, U. Denver, 1946; LL.B., Stanford U., 1948. Bar: Calif. bar 1949, N.Y. bar 1954. Jr. accountant comptroller's dept. Pacific Tel.&Tel. Co., San Francisco, 1948-50, staff accountant, 1950-51, accountant, 1951-53; tax atty. AT&T, N.Y.C., 1953-64, asst. comptroller, 1964-68, asst. treas., 1968-71; v.p. fin. N.Y. Telephone Co., N.Y.C., 1971, exec. v.p. fin., 1971-73, v.p., comptroller, 1973—; dir. 195 Broadway Corp., Northwestern Bell Telephone Co., Harvey Hubbell, Inc.; trustee East River Savs. Bank. Served with USNR, 1942-45. Mem. N.Y., Calif. bar assns., Fin. Execs. Research Found. (trustee), Fin. Execs. Inst., Officers Conf. Group. Republican. Presbyterian. Club: Ardsley Country. Home: Grey Rock Terr Irvington NY 10533 Office: 195 Broadway New York NY 10007

FLINTON, JENNIFER STRAIGHT, health care services executive; b. Medford, Mass., Nov. 11, 1945; d. Edgar William and Doris (Holt) F. B.A., Radcliffe Coll., 1967; M.B.A., Harvard U., 1972. Editorial asst. Addison-Wesley, Reading, Mass., 1967-69; asst. fund dir. Radcliffe Coll., Cambridge, Mass., 1969-70; with Am. Med. Internat., Beverly Hills, Calif., 1972—; sr. v.p. Am. Med.l Internat., Beverly Hills, Calif., 1983—. Mem. Orgn. Women Execs. Club: Regency. Office: 414 N Camden Dr Beverly Hills CA 90210

FLIPPO, RONNIE GENE, congressman; b. Lauderdale County, Ala., Aug. 15, 1937; s. Claude and Esther (McAfee) F.; m. Faye Cooper, Nov. 27, 1958; children—Ronnie Gene, Linda Gail, Brenda Faye, Lea Ella, Kelly Reid, Ryan Cooper. B.S. in Accounting, Florence (Ala.) State U., 1965; M.A., U. Ala., 1966; D.Sc. (hon.), Southeastern Inst. Tech., 1979. C.P.A., Ala. Ironworker in, Sheffield, Ala.; partner firm Flippo & Robbins (C.P.A.'s), Florence, 1972-76; mem. Ala. Ho. of Reps., 1971-75, Ala. Senate, 1975-76, 95th-97th Congresses from 5th Dist. Ala; past mem. faculty U. Ala., U. No. Ala. Pres. Wilson Dam Little League; active local March of Dimes, Cub Scouts; del. Democratic Nat. Conv., 1976. Named Alumnus of Year Florence State U., 1976; recipient Achievement award Ala. Rehab. Assn., 1972. Mem. Am. Inst. C.P.A.'s, Ala. C.P.A.'s Soc., Nat. Assn. Accountants, Florence Jaycees. Mem. Ch. of Christ. Club: Elks. Home: 114 Lance Ln Florence AL 35630 Office: 405 Cannon House Office Bldg Washington DC 20515

FLITCRAFT, RICHARD KIRBY, II, former chemical company executive; b. Woodstown, N.J., Sept. 5, 1920; s. H. Milton and Edna (Crispin) F.; m. Bertha LeSturgeon Hitchner, Nov. 14, 1942; children: Alyce, Anne, Elizabeth, Richard. B.S., Rutgers U., 1942; M.S., Washington U., 1948. With Monsanto Co., St. Louis, 1942—, dir. inorganic research, 1960-65, dir. mgmt. info. and systems dept., 1965-67, asst. to pres., 1967-68, group mgr. electronics enterprises, 1968-69, gen. mgr. electronic products div., 1969-71; v.p. Monsanto Research Corp., 1971-75; dir. Mound Lab., 1971-75, v.p. ops., 1975-76; pres. Monsanto Research Corp., Dayton, 1976-82, ret., 1982; dir. 3d Nat. Bank., Medam. Health Systems Corp. Bd. dirs. United Way, Dayton, Dayton Art Inst.; bd. dirs. City-Wide Devel. Corp.; mem. Dayton Devel. Council, Dayton Performing Arts Fund; chmn. bd. trustees Miami Valley Hosp.; dir. Pvt. Industry Council.; chmn. bd. Huber Heights Health Care Ctr. Mem. AAAS, Am. Chem. Soc., Am. Inst. Chem. Engrs., Am. Inst. Chemists, Am. Mgmt. Assn., N.Y. Acad. Scis., Soc. Chem. Industry, Dayton C. of C. (past dir.), Sigma Xi. Presbyterian. Clubs: Moraine Country, Dayton Racquet.

FLITTIE, CLIFFORD GILLILAND, petroleum company executive; b. Brookings, S.D., Mar. 10, 1924; s. Theodore Ignatius and Grace Eliza (Gilliland) F.; m. Dawn Marie Lee, May 22, 1954. Student, Okla. State U., 1944, Colo. Sch. Mines, 1946; B.S. (Nat. scholar Am. Inst. Mining and Metall. Engrs.), S.D. Sch. Mines and Tech., 1948. Geologist Arabian Am. Oil Co., Dhahran, Saudi Arabia, 1948-57; v.p. exploration Conorada Petroleum Corp., N.Y.C., 1958-63, dir., 1963-65; v.p., mgr. Amerada Petroleum Corp. of U.K., London, 1964-65, Amerada Petroleum Corp. of Australia, Brisbane, 1966-69; exploration supr. Amerada Hess Corp., N.Y.C., 1970-73; v.p. Shaheen Natural Resources Co., Inc., N.Y.C., 1974-75, Macmillan Oil Co., 1975-82, Natomas Co., San Francisco, 1982—; dir. Amerada Exploration Ltd., 1964-65. Served with USNR, 1944-46. Mem. Am. Assn. Petroleum Geologists, Soc. Exploration Geophysicists, Theta Tau, Sigma Tau. Episcopalian. Home: 46 San Jacinto Way San Francisco CA 94127 Office: 601 California St San Francisco CA 94108

FLITTIE, EDWIN GILBERT, sociologist; b. Brookings, S.D., Mar. 10, 1924; s. Theodore I. and Grace (Gillil) F.; m. Mary Josephine Fowler, 1949 (div. 1970). B.A. magna cum laude, U. Colo., 1946; M.A., Stanford, 1947; Ph.D., Northwestern U., 1955. Instr. sociology U. Wyo., Laramie, 1947-51, asst. prof., 1957-60, asso. prof., 1960-64; asst. dean (Coll. Arts and Scis.), 1961-63, chmn. dept. sociology, anthropology and geography, 1963-66, prof. sociology, 1964—, chmn. dept. sociology, 1966-75; program officer Inst. Inter-Am. Affairs, Bogota, Colombia, 1952-54; asst. prof. sociology San Jose (Calif.) State Coll., 1955-57. Contbr. articles profl. jours. Fellow Am. Sociol. Assn. Democrat. Home: 223 Corthell Rd Laramie WY 82070

FLITTIE, WILLIAM JORGEN, lawyer, educator; b. Brookings, S.D., Nov. 23, 1919; s. Theodore Ignatius and Grace Eliza (Gillil) F.; m. Elizabeth Lorraine Hanten, Mar. 26, 1951; 1 son, William Hanten. Student, S.D. State Coll., 1937-38, U. So. Calif., 1938-39; B.S., U. Minn., 1946; LL.B., Columbia, 1947. Bar: S.D. bar 1947, Colo. bar 1954, Tex. bar 1963. Practiced in, Huron, 1947-48, asst. atty. gen., dep. indsl. commr., State of S.D., 1948-53, ex-officio commr. labor, 1948-53; atty. Denver div. Texaco, Inc., 1953-61; prof. law So. Meth. U., 1961—. Served as lt. comdr. USNR, 1940-45. Address: Sch of Law Southern Methodist U Dallas TX 75222

FLOCH, MARTIN HERBERT, physician; b. N.Y.C., July 24, 1928; s. Samuel and Jean (Scheinman) F.; m. Gladys Wisser, Nov. 24, 1954; children: Jeffrey Aaron, Craig Lawrence, Lisa Suzanne, Neil Robert. B.A., N.Y. U., 1949; M.S., U. N.H., 1950; M.D., N.Y. Med. Coll., 1956. Diplomate: Am. Bd. Internal Medicine, Am. Bd. Gastroenterology Am. Bd. Nutrition. Intern Beth Israel Hosp., N.Y.C., 1956-57, resident in medicine, 1957-59; fellow in gastroenterology Seton Hall Coll. Medicine, South Orange, N.J., 1959-60; instr. medicine U. P.R., 1960-62; asst. attending physician Montefiore Hosp., N.Y.C., 1962-64; practice medicine specializing in gastroenterology, Norwalk, Conn., 1962—; mem. staff Norwalk Hosp., 1964—, chmn. dept. medicine, 1970—; clin. prof. medicine Yale U., New Haven, 1976—; cons. staff Griffin Hosp., Hall-Brooke Hosp., Waveny Care Center. Contbr. articles in field to profl. jours. Trustee Aspetuck Valley Health Dist., 1974-76, Norwalk Hosp., 1972-78. Served with M.C. U.S. Army, 1960-62. Conn. Digestive Disease Soc. grantee, 1974-76; NIH grantee, 1975-78; U.S. Army Med. Research grantee, 1964-67; Leslie Found. grantee, 1980. Fellow A.C.P.; mem. Am. Soc. Clin. Nutrition, Am. Inst. Nutrition, Am. Gastroenterology Assn., Am. Soc. Gastroendoscopy, Am. Soc. Internal Medicine, Am. Fedn. Clin. Research, Am. Soc. Tropical Medicine and Hygiene, Am. Public Health Assn., Fairfield County Med. Soc., Conn. Med. Soc. (pres. gastroenterology sect. 1972-74), Assn. Am. Med. Colls., Conn. Digestive Disease Soc. (pres. 1972-74). Home: 32 Woody Ln Westport CT 06880 Office: Maple St Norwalk CT 06856

FLOE, CARL FREDERICK, educator, cons. metallurgist; b. Dawson, Yukon Terr., Can., Jan. 1, 1908; s. Iver Stefan and Caroline (Ulvestad) F.; m. Margaret Proctor, Aug. 30, 1935; children—Carol Sherwood, Joan Proctor; m. Beverly Brooks, June 21, 1954; children—Charles Pennell, Jonathan Tyndall. B.S., Wash. State U., 1930, M.S, 1932; Sc.D., M.I.T., 1935. Mem. faculty Mass. Inst. Tech., 1939—, prof. phys. metallurgy, 1950—, asst. provost, 1952-56, asst. chancellor, 1956-57, administrv. vice chancellor, 1957-59, v.p. research adminstrn., 1959-69; cons. metallurgist, 1932—; dir. Indsl. Materials Tech., Inc. Fellow Am. Acad. Arts and Scis.; mem. Am. Inst. Mining and Metall. Engrs., Am. Soc. for Metals, Sigma Xi, Tau Beta Pi, Phi Kappa Phi, Sigma Tau, Phi Sigma Kappa. Clubs: St. Botolph, Boston (Boston); University (N.Y.C.). Office: Mass Inst of Tech Cambridge MA 02139

FLOM, EDWARD LEONARD, steel company executive; b. Tampa, Fla., Dec. 10, 1929; s. Samuel Louis and Julia (Mittle) F.; m. Beverly Boyett, Mar. 31, 1956; children—Edward Louis, Mark Robert, Julia Ruth. B.C.E., Cornell U., 1952. With Fla. Steel Corp., Tampa, 1954—, v.p. sales, 1957-64, pres., dir., 1964—; dir. NCNB Nat. Bank Fla., Teco Energy Inc., Gen. Portland Inc. Bd. dirs. mem. exec. com. United Fund Tampa; advisory com. St. Joseph's Hosp., Tampa; bd. dirs. Family Service Assn. Tampa, Jewish Welfare Fedn. Tampa; exec. com. Com. of 100, Tampa. Served with C.E. AUS, 1952-54. Mem. Am. Iron and Steel Inst. (dir.), Young Pres.'s Orgn., Fla. Engring. Soc. Jewish (bd. dirs. temple). Clubs: Rotary (Tampa) (bd. dirs.); University, Palma Ceia Golf and Country, Tampa Yacht, Gasparilla Krewe. Home: 4936 Saint Croix Dr Tampa FL 33629 Office: 1715 Cleveland St Tampa FL 33606

FLOM, JOSEPH HAROLD, lawyer; b. Balt., Dec. 20, 1923; s. Isadore and Fannie (Fishman) F.; m. Claire Cohen, Nov. 14, 1958; children: Peter Leslie, Jason Robert. Student, Coll. City N.Y.; LL.B. (cum laude), Harvard U., 1948. Bar: N.Y. 1949. Since practiced in, N.Y.C.; dir. William Wrigley Co., Petrie Stores Corp., 1951, 52; Spl. counsel to subcom. of Com. on Ways and Means on Adminstrn. of Internal Revenue Laws, 1951, 52; mem. com. on tender offers SEC, 1983. Editor: Harvard Law Rev, 1947-48; co-editor: Disclosure Requirements of Public Corporations and Insiders, 1967, Texas Gulf Sulphur, 1968; bd. editors: N.Y. Law Jour; chmn. bd. editors: Nat. Law Jour. Mem. N.Y.C. Mayor's Commn. on Status of Women, 1976-77; trustee Fedn. Jewish Philanthropies N.Y., N.Y. U. Med. Center, Barnard Coll., 1983—; mem. Archdiocesan Task Force on Crime Prevention and Youth, 1983—, N.Y.C. Holocaust Meml. Commn., 1983—. Mem. Assn. Bar City N.Y. (spl. com. on lawyer's role in securities transactions). Home: 31 E 79th St New York NY 10021 Office: 919 3d Ave New York NY 10022

FLOOD, ANN, actress; b. N.Y.C., Nov. 12; d. Frank J. and Ann K. (Flood) Ott; m. Herbert A. Granath, Nov. 22, 1958; children: Kevin Michael, Brian John, Peter James, Karen Mary. Appeared in: TV shows including Matinee Theatre; Broadway plays Kismet, 1953, Holiday for Lovers, 1958; appeared in: TV day time drama From These Roots, 1958-62, The Edge of Night, 1962—. Mem. AFTRA, Actors Equity Assn., Screen Actors Guild, Acad. TV Arts and Scis., Vets. Hosp. Radio and TV Guild. Office: 222 E 44th St New York NY 10017

FLOOD, AUGUSTINE JAMES, clergyman, college president; b. Hollywood, Calif., May 29, 1938; s. James Joseph and Lucille M. (Fleischer) F. B.A., St. John's Coll., 1959; S.T.B., Pontifical Coll. St. Anselm, Rome, 1962, S.T.L., 1964; Ph.D., Claremont Grad. Sch., 1975. Diplomate: ordained priest Roman Catholic Ch., 1964. Pastor Am. Mil. Chapel, Dachau, Germany, 1965-67; dir. St. Andrew's Retreat House, Valyermo, Calif., 1967-70; assoc. pastor Our Lady Assumption parish, Claremont, Calif., 1969-73; Cath. chaplain Wayside Honor Rancho, Saugus, Calif., 1974; chaplain St. Vincent Coll., Latrobe, Pa., 1975, dir. liberal arts, 1977-81, asst. prof. coll. and sem., 1978-82, dir. continuing edn., 1980-82, pres., 1982—. Dir. Latrobe C. of C.; mem. devel. com. Women's Services, Greenburg, Pa., 1982-83. Mem. Am. Acad. Religion, Pa. Assn. Coll. and Univs. Democrat. Home: St Vincent Archabbey Latrobe PA 15650 Office: St Vincent College Latrobe PA 15650

FLOOD, JAMES JOSEPH, airline executive; b. Joliet, Ill., Sept. 3, 1923; s. Joseph P. and Rose Marie (Kwasneski) Lencioni; m. Joan Lydia Dahlquist, Jan. 31, 1948; children: James W. (dec.), Janice K., Jody Ann. B.A., Beloit Coll., 1949. Pricing adminstr. Sundstrand Corp., 1952-61; pres., chief exec. officer Alaska Brick Co. Inc., 1961-76, Wien Air Alaska, Anchorage, 1976—, chmn., 1978—, also dir.; dir. Alaska Pacific Bank. Bd. dirs. YMCA Anchorage, from 1968, pres., 1971; bd. dirs. Anchorage Fine Arts Museum Assn., from 1977. Served with USAAF, 1943-45. Decorated Air medal; recipient Community Service award YMCA, 1977. Mem. Airline Transport Assn., Beloit Coll. Chapin Soc., Assn. Local Transport Airlines, Sigma Alpha Epsilon. Republican. Methodist. Clubs: Petroleum of Anchorage, Washington Athletic, Elks. Office: Wien Air Alaska Inc 4100 International Airport Rd Anchorage AK 99502 *

FLOOD, JOHN ETCHELLS, JR., software services executive; b. Sanford, Maine, Oct. 16, 1929; s. John Etchells and Bertha (Goodrich) F.; m. Dorothy Haight, Nov. 27, 1954; children: Elizabeth Ann, John Brian. A.B., U. N.C., 1952; M.B.A., Harvard U., 1957. Mktg. cons. Litton Industries, 1957-59; with Mobil Chem. Co., 1959-69, gen. mgr. films dept., plastics div., 1965-69; group v.p. Chelsea Industries, 1969-71; pres., chief exec. officer, dir. Title Ins. and Trust Co./Pioneer Nat. Title Ins. Co., Los Angeles, 1971-82; chmn. bd. ICS Software Services, 1983—; dir. ATV Systems, Antaeus Mgmt. Corp. Bd. councilors U. So. Calif.; bd. dirs. Harvard Bus. Sch. Assn. So. Calif., Los Angeles Jr. Achievement. Served to lt. (j.g.) USNR, 1952-55. Unitarian. Club: Los Angeles. Office: 24500 S Vermont Ave Harbor City CA 90710

FLORA, GEORGE CLAUDE, neurology educator, neurologist; b. Clark, S.D., Apr. 8, 1923; s. Loren and Elma (Lyngbye) F.; m. Joan Chalk, Aug. 28, 1951 (dec. 1971); children: George, Elizabeth, John. B.S., U. S.D., 1948; M.D., Temple U., 1950. Diplomate: Am. Bd. Psychiatry and Neurology. Prof. neurology U. Minn., Mpls., 1957-73, U. S.D., Sioux Falls, 1973—; cons. neurology VA Hosp., Sioux Falls, S.D., 1973—. Served to 1st lt. U.S. Army, 1950-54; Korea. Club: Minn. Alumni (Mpls.). Home: 4209 S Lewis Ave Sioux Falls SD 57103 Office: U SD Sch Medicine 2501 W 22d St Sioux Falls SD 57101

FLORA, JOSEPH M(ARTIN), English educator; b. Toledo, Feb. 9, 1934; s. Raymond D. F. and Frances (Ricica) Nuemann; m. Glenda Christine Lape, Jan. 30, 1959; children: Ronald James, Stephen Ray, Peter Joseph, David Benjamin. B.A., U. Mich., 1956, M.A., 1957, Ph.D., 1962. Instr. U. Mich., Ann Arbor, 1961-62, U. N.C., Chapel Hill, 1962-64, asst. prof., 1964-66, assoc. prof., 1966-77, prof. English, 1977—, acting chmn. dept. English, 1980-81, chmn., 1981—, asst. dean grad. sch., 1967-72, assoc. dean grad. sch., 1977-78. Author: Vardis Fisher, 1965, William Ernest Henley, 1970, Hemingway's Nick Adams, 1982 (Mayflower Cup award 1982); co-editor: Southern Writers, 1979; editorial bd.: Studies in Short Fiction, So. Lit. Jour. Mem. MLA, So. Atlantic MLA, Western Lit. Assn. (bd. dirs. 1978-81), Phi Beta Kappa, Phi Eta Sigma. Home: 505 Caswell Rd Chapel Hill NC 27514 Office: Dept English U NC Chapel Hill NC 27514

FLORANCE, COLDEN L'HOMMEDIEU RUGGLES, architect; b. Balt., Jan. 24, 1931; s. Eustace Lee and Colden (Ruggles) F.; m. Elizabeth Owens, Mar. 31, 1972; children: Hilary, Susanna, Andrew. A.B., Princeton U., 1952, M.F.A., 1955. Partner Keyes Condon Florance (Architects), Washington. Mem. D.C. Commn. on Arts and Humanities, 1981-83, D.C. Historic Preservation Rev. Bd., 1983; Washington trustee Fed. City Council. Served with USN, 1955-59. Fellow AIA; mem. Washington Met. Bd. Trade, Com. of 100. Office: 1320 19th St NW Washington DC 20036

FLOREA, JOHN TED, film producer-dir.; b. Alliance, Ohio, May 28, 1924; s. Nicholas and Elizabeth (Druga) F.; m. Evelyn Barnes, May 8, 1938; children—Gwendolyn, Melanie, John Dana. Grad. high sch. Photographer Internat. News, 1936; San Francisco Examiner, 1939, Life mag., 1942-51, Collier's mag., 1951-55; film cons. Matson Nav. Co., 1950-70. TV producer-dir., 1957-80; now film dir., MGM Studios, Warner Bros.; Contbr.: photographs to book Family of Man. Decorated for service as war corr., World War II; Recipient commendation for photographs from Winston Churchill; N.Y. Mus. Modern Art Pictorial award, 1950. Mem. Screen Actors Guild, Dirs. Guild Am., Overseas Corrs. Club, Tokyo Corrs. Club, TV Acad. (charter). Office: care Lew Sherrell Agy 7060 Hollywood Blvd Hollywood CA 90028

FLORES, FELIXBERTO C., bishop; b. Agana, Guam, Jan. 13, 1931. Student, St. John's Sem., Mass., Fordham U. Ordained priest Roman Catholic Ch., 1949. Ordained titular bishop of Stonj and apostolic adminstr. Dioces of Agana, 1970; installed second residential bishop of Agana Diocese of Agana, 1972—. Office: Bishops House Cuesta San Ramon Agana Guam 96910 *

FLORES, PATRICK F., archbishop; b. Ganado, Tex., July 26, 1929. Ed., St. Mary's Sem., Houston. Ordained priest Roman Catholic Ch., 1956; ordained titular bishop of, Itolica and aux. bishop of San Antonio, 1970, apptd. bishop of, El Paso, 1978, archbishop of, San Antonio, 1979. Office: PO Box 32648 San Antonio TX 78228 *

FLORES, THOMAS R., professional football coach; b. Fresno, Calif., Mar. 21, 1937; s. Tom C. and Nellie (Padilla) F.; m. Barbara Ann Fridell, Mar. 25, 1961; children: Mark and Scott (twins), Kim. B.A., Coll. Pacific, 1959. Quarterback Oakland Raiders, 1960-66; quarterback Buffalo Bills, 1967-68, Kansas City (Mo.) Chiefs, 1969-70; asst. coach Oakland (now Los Angeles) Raiders, 1972-78, head coach, 1979—; player rep. AFL, 1966-68. Nat. hon. chmn. Lung Assn. Named Man of Yr. No. Calif. Lung Assn., 1979; Latino of Yr. City of Los Angeles, 1981. Democrat. Roman Catholic. Coached team to Super Bowl victories 1981, 84. Office: Los Angeles Raiders 332 Center St El Segundo CA 90245 *

FLORESCUE, BARRY WILLIAM, business executive; b. N.J., Dec. 5, 1943; s. Harold and Gertrude F.; m. Renate Schlessinger, May 13, 1979; children: Gretchen, Geremy, Bryan. B.B.A. in Acctg, U. Rochester, N.Y., 1966; M.B.A., N.Y. U., 1970. C.P.A., N.Y. Accountant, then sr. accountant Peat, Marwick, Mitchell & Co. (C.P.A.s), N.Y.C., 1966-70; investment exec., securities analyst Scharson Hammill, N.Y.C., 1969-70; v.p. fin., controller Seronsonic Labs., N.Y.C., 1970-71; v.p. fin., dir. Threshold Tech. Inc., Delran, N.J., 1971-74; ptnr. Sharon Gardens Meml. Park, Broward County, Fla., 1974-80, lt. ptnr., 1980—; pres., chmn. bd. Jesson, Inc., Delray Beach, Fla., 1974—; pres. Horn & Hardart Co., Inc., N.Y.C., 1977-82, chmn. bd., 1982—; dir. Color Systems Tech., Inc, Los Angeles, Am. Homestead Inc., Mt. Laurel, N.J., NMR Centers Inc., Newport Beach, Calif.; bd. overseers food service dept. N.Y. U. Recipient U. Rochester award acctg. excellence Haskins & Sells Found., 1965. Mem. Am. Inst. C.P.A.'s, Nat. Restaurant Assn., Young Pres. Orgn. (award 1979), N.Y. State Soc. C.P.A.s, Am. Bus. Conf. Office: Horn & Hardart Co 1163 Ave of the Americas New York NY 10036

FLOREY, KLAUS GEORG, chemist, pharmaceutical company executive; b. Dresden, Germany, July 4, 1919; came to U.S., 1947, naturalized, 1952; s. Friedrich Georg and Margarethe Käthe (Pick) F.; m. Anne Major, Nov. 22, 1956; children: Peter, Andrea. Ed., U. Munich, U. Heidelberg, Germany; Ph.D., U. Pa., 1954. Research asst. Bayer, Leverkusen, Germany, 1944-45; research asso. Merck & Co., Rahway, N.J., 1949-50; research chemist Squibb Inst. Med. Research, New Brunswick, N.J., 1954-59, dir. analytical research and devel., 1959—; mem. com. revisions U.S. Pharmacopeia, 1970—; mem. WHO Expert Adv. Panel Internat. Pharmacopeia, 1976—. Editor: Analytical Profiles of Drug Substances, 11 vols., 1971—; contbr. articles to profl. jours. Fellow Acad. Pharm. Scis., AAAS; mem. Am. Chem. Soc., Soc. Nuclear Medicine, Acad. Pharm. Scis. (chmn. pharm. analysis and control sect. 1967-68, pres. 1980-81), Council Sci. Soc. Pres. (chmn. 1983). Patentee in field. Home: 151 Loomis Ct Princeton NJ 08540 Office: PO Box 191 New Brunswick NY 08903

FLORIAN, FRANK LEE, JR., planning executive; b. Washington, Pa., June 10, 1933; s. Francis Leopold and Elizabeth (Curran) F.; m. Suzanne Young, Oct. 29, 1960; children: Christopher, Suzanne, Diana, Melissa, Justine. B.S.M.E., U. Notre Dame, 1955; M.S. in Indsl. Adminstrn., Carnegie Inst. Tech., 1957. From budget analyst to dir. fin. planning Cousumer Products div. Westinghouse Electric Corp., Pitts., 1958-66; from dir. planning to corp. budget dir. Uniroyal, Inc., N.Y.C., 1966-70; from asst. gen. controller to asst. to pres. Borden, Inc., N.Y.C., 1970-79, v.p. planning, 1979—. Served with U.S. Army, 1957-58. Republican. Club: Echo Lake Country. Home: 66 Nomahegan Dr Westfield NJ 07090 Office: 277 Park Ave New York NY 10172

FLORIDA, JOHN ANTHONY, advertising executive; b. Manila, Philippines, Jan. 9, 1935; s. John Freeborn and Ana (Luling) F.; m. Charmaine Bryant, Mar. 30, 1959 (div. 1969); children: Sean, Tennyson, Tyrone; m. Laura Seoane, July 30, 1970; children: Rowena, Charisse, Sabrina. B.A. in Internat. Relations, Stanford U., 1956, M.A. in Polit. Sci., 1957; B.F.T., Am. Grad. Sch. Internat. Mgmt., Glendale, Ariz., 1962; postgrad. Advanced Mgmt. Program, Harvard U., 1977. Account exec. J. Walter Thompson Co., N.Y.C., 1962-65, account supr., Buenos Aires, 1965-69, N.Y.C., 1969-73, gen. mgr., Lima, Peru, 1973-77, chmn., chief exec. officer, regional dir., Mex. and Central Am., 1977—. Served to capt. USAF, 1958-61. Recipient Alfred Hollingsworth award Stanford U., 1957, Barton Kyle Yount award Am. Grad. Sch. Internat. Mgmt., 1962. Mem. N.Am.-Mex. Inst. Cultural Relations (dir.), Assn. Am. Chambers of Commerce Latin Am. (regional v.p. 1977-78), Am. C. of C. Mex. (assoc. dir. 1981-82). Republican. Roman Catholic. Clubs: West Side Tennis (Forest Hills, N.Y.); Club Raqueta Bosques, Cuernavaca Racquet (Mex.). Home: Monte Casucaso 1280 Lomas de Chapultepec Mexico 10DF Mexico Office: J. Walter Thompson de Mexico SA Ejercito Nacional 519 Mexico 5DF Mexico

FLORIO, JAMES J., congressman; b. Bklyn., Aug. 29, 1937. B.A. magma cum laude, Trenton State Coll., 1962; postgrad., Columbia, 1962-63; J.D., Rutgers U., 1967. Mem. law firm Florio and Maloney, 1967-74; mem. 94th-98th Congresses from 1st N.J. Dist., Energy and Commerce Com., Permanent Select Com. on Aging, Interior and Insular Affairs com. Mem. Camden City Council on Econ. Opportunity, 1966-67, Camden Civil Rights Commn., 1966-67, Camden County Council on Aging, 1968; chmn. East Camden Heart Fund Dr., 1967; v.p. bd. advisors Camden County Legal Service Program, 1968; borough solicitor for towns of, Runnemede, N.J., 1969-74,, Woodlynne, 1970-74,, Somerdale, 1972-74; mem. N.J. Gen. Assembly, 1969-74; Democratic nominee for gov. N.J., 1981. Served with USN, 1955-58; lt. comdr. USNR, 1958—. Office: 2162 Rayburn House Office Bldg Washington DC 20515

FLORIO, STEVEN T., mag. exec.; b. N.Y.C., Apr. 19, 1949; s. F. Steve and Sophia (Masciale) F.; m. Mariann McNeill, June 1, 1974; children—Steven John, Kelly Anne. A.A., N.Y. U., 1970, B.S., 1972. Researcher Esquire mag., N.Y.C., 1972-73, New Eng. mgr., 1974-76, advt. dir., 1976-79, v.p., 1979-80; pub. Gentlemen's Quar., N.Y.C., 1980—; guest speaker. Mem. Men's Fashion Assn., Mag. Pubs. Assn. Office: Gentlemen's Quar 350 Madison Ave New York NY 10017

FLORY, DAISY PARKER, ednl. adminstr.; b. Charlotte, N.C., Feb. 18, 1915; d. Julius Monroe and Daisy (Kidd) Parker; m. Claude R. Flory, Mar. 26, 1973. B.A., Fla. State Coll. Women, 1937; M.A., U. Va., 1940, Ph.D., 1959. Instr. Leon High Sch., Tallahassee, 1937-42; instr. Fla. State U., Tallahassee, 1942-47, asst. prof., 1947-57, asso. prof., 1957-65, prof. govt., 1965—, asst. v.p. academic affairs, 1969-73, dean faculties, 1974—, interim v.p. for academic affairs, 1980—. Mem. Fla. Gov.'s Study Commn. on Personnel, 1954; pres. Le Moyne Art Found., 1967-68. Mem. Fla. Hist. Soc., Tallahassee Hist. Soc. (past pres.), So. Polit. Sci. Assn. (past sec.), AAUW (pres. local chpt. 1942-43), Phi Beta Kappa, Phi Kappa Phi, Pi Sigma Alpha, Phi Alpha Theta, Mortar Bd. (editor Jour. 1950-56). Home: 1551 Crestview Ave Tallahassee FL 32303 Office: Dean Faculties Fla State U Tallahassee FL 32306

FLORY, PAUL JOHN, chemist; b. Sterling, Ill., June 19, 1910; s. Ezra and Martha (Brumbaugh) F.; m. Emily Catharine Tabor, Mar. 7, 1936; children—Susan, Melinda, Paul J. B.S., Manchester Coll., 1931, Sc.D. (hon.), 1950; M.S., Ohio State U., 1931, Ph.D., 1934, Sc.D., 1970. Engaged in research on synthetic fibers, synthetic rubber and other polymeric substances Dupont Exptl. Sta., Wilmington, Del., 1934-38, U. Cin., 1938-40, Standard Oil Devel. Co., Elizabeth, N.J., 1940-43; dir. fundamental research Goodyear Tire & Rubber Co., Akron, Ohio, 1943-48; prof. chemistry Cornell U., 1948-57; exec. dir. research Mellon Inst., Pitts., 1956-61; J.G. Jackson-C.J.Wood prof. chemistry Stanford, 1961—. Author: Principles of Polymer Chemistry and of Statistical Mechanics of Chain Molecules; Contbr. to sci. publs. Recipient Sullivant medal Ohio State U., 1945; Baekeland award Am. Chem. Soc., 1947; George Fisher Baker non-resident lectureship in chemistry Cornell U., 1948; Peter Debye award in phys. chemistry Am. Chem. Soc., 1968; Gibbs medal, 1973; Priestley medal, 1974; Cresson medal Franklin Inst., 1971; Nobel prize for chemistry, 1974; Nat. medal of sci., 1974. Fellow AAAS; mem. Am. Chem. Soc., Nat. Acad. Scis., Am. Acad. Arts and Scis., Am. Phys. Soc., Am. Philos. Soc. Pioneered research on constitution and properties of substances composed of giant molecules (rubbers, plastics, fibers, films, proteins, etc). Home: 210 Golden Oak Dr Portola Valley CA 94025 Office: Stanford U Stanford CA 94305

FLORY, WALTER S., JR., geneticist, botanist, educator; b. Bridgewater, Va., Oct. 5, 1907; s. Walter Samuel and Ella May (Reherd) F.; m. Nellie) Maude Thomas, Apr. 24, 1930 (dec. 1971); children: Kathryn Sue Flory Maier, Walter Samuel, Thomas Reherd; m. Gale Crews Gramley, June 25, 1975. A.B., Bridgewater Coll., 1928, Sc.D. (hon.), 1953; A.M. (Blandy fellow, 1928-31), U. Va., 1929, Ph.D., 1931; Nat. Research fellow biol. scis. and research assoc., Harvard U., 1935-36. In charge tech. work Shaver Bros., Inc., Jacksonville and Tampa, Fla., 1931-32; instr. in sci. Greenbrier Coll., Lewisburg, W.Va., 1932-34; prof. biology Bridgewater Coll., 1934-35; horticulturist Tex. Agrl. Expt. Sta., 1936-44, Va. Agrl. Expt. Sta., 1944-47; prof. exptl. horticulture U. Va., 1947-63; vice dir., mgr. Blandy Exptl. Farm, 1947-63, vis. prof., summer 1964; curator O.E. White Research Arboretum, 1955-63; bd. dirs. Winston-Salem (N.C.) Nature Sci. Center, 1964-69, treas., 1965-66; Babcock prof. botany Wake Forest U., Winston-Salem, 1963-80, Babcock prof. emeritus, 1980—; dir. Reynolda Gardens, 1964-76; research cons. Fairchild Tropical Garden, 1972; instnl. lectr. Piedmont U. Center, 1965-70; collaborator U.S. Dept. Agr., 1945-48; del. Internat. Botany Congress, Paris, 1954, Montreal, 1959, Edinburgh, 1964, Seattle, 1969, Sydney, 1981; mem. Internat. Genetics Congress, Montreal, 1958, Tokyo, 1968, Internat. Hort. Congress, College Park, Md., 1966, Sydney, Australia, 1978; invited lectr. Internat. Chromosome Seminar, Calcutta, 1968, 76. Contbr. articles on genetics, cytology and hort. subjects to profl. jours. and mags. Trustee, mem. exec. com. Highlands Biol. Sta.; pres., 1969-72; life trustee Bridgewater Coll. Recipient J. Shelton Horsley Research award Va. Acad. Sci., 1949; Pres. and Visitors Research prize U. Va., 1951; Bridgewater Coll. Alumni award, 1956; I.F. Lewis disting. service award Va. Acad. Sci., 1969; spl. citation Highlands Biol. Sta., 1973; Outstanding Service award Bridgewater Coll., 1981; Bicentennial hon. fellow Royal Hort. Soc. (Eng.). Fellow AAAS, Va. Acad. Sci. (pres. 1956, Hon. Life Mem. award 1981); mem. Genetics Soc. Am., Am. Genetics Assn., Soc. Study Evolution, Bot. Soc. Am. (chmn. southeastern sect. 1951-52), Assn. Southeastern Biologists (pres. 1962-63, research award 1978), Am. Boxwood Soc. (hon. life mem., co-founder, treas., editor 1961-63, dir. 1982—), Am. Assn. Bot. Gardens and Arboretums (editorial bd. 1962-64), Am. Begonia Soc. (hon.), Fairchild Tropical Garden (life), So. Appalachian Bot. Club (v.p. 1962), Am. Plant Life Soc. (Herbert medal 1978), La. Soc. Hort. Research (hon.), Am. Magnolia Soc. (v.p. 1968-79), Phi Beta Kappa (chpt. pres. 1974), Sigma Xi (chpt. pres. 1970), Tau Kappa Alpha, Phi Sigma. Democrat. Mem. Ch. of Brethren. Club: Torch (local pres. 1970). Home: 2025 Colonial Pl Winston-Salem NC 27104

FLORY, WILLIAM EVANS SHERLOCK, govt. ofcl.; b. Canton, Ohio, Apr. 25, 1914; s. Wilson Reese and Frances (Sherlock) F.; m. Anne Randolph Putney, June 4, 1938; children—William, Anne. A.B., Coll. Wooster, 1935; A.M., Duke, 1938, Ph.D., 1941. Various teaching positions, Ohio and Ga., 1935-39; analyst Princeton U. govt. surveys, 1940; dir. research N.J. Municipal Aid Adminstrn., Trenton, 1940-42; analyst N.Y. Joint Legis. Economy Commn. Albany, 1942-43, Bur. Budget, Washington, 1943-44; dep. asst. to under-sec. State, Washington, 1944-50; econ. policy adviser to sec. Interior, Washington, 1950-53; staff economist Bur. Mines and Office Minerals and Solid Fuels, Washington, 1953-61, dir., 1961-69; asso. and adj. prof. mktg. and transp. Am. U. Sch. Bus. Adminstrn., Washington, 1969-79. Author: Prisoners of War, 1941, Restoration of Historic Bel Air Plantation; Contbr. to govt. publs. Bd. dirs. Prince William County Indsl. Devel. Authority, Manassas, Va.; curator Weems-Botts Mus., Dumfries, Va. Democrat. Episcopalian. Home: Bel Air Plantation 14313 Minnieville Rd Woodbridge VA 22193

FLOSS, HEINZ G., scientist, educator; b. Berlin, Aug. 28, 1934; s. Friedrich and Annemarie F.; m. Inge Sauberlich, July 17, 1956; children: Christine, Peter, Helmut, Hanna. B.S. in Chemistry, Technische Universitat, Berlin, 1956, M.S. in Organic Chemistry, 1959, Dr. rer. nat., Technische Hochschule, Munich, W. Ger., 1961, Dr. habil. in Biochemistry, 1966. Hilfsassistent Technische Universitat, Berlin, 1958-59; hilfsassistent Technische Hochschule, Munich, 1959-61, wissenschaftlicher asst. and dozent, 1961-66; on leave of absence at dept. biochemistry and biophysics U. Calif., Davis, 1964-65; asso. prof. Purdue U., 1966-69, prof., 1969-77, Disting. prof., 1977-82, Lilly prof. medicinal chemistry, dept. head, 1968-69, 74-79; prof., chmn. dept. chemistry Ohio State U., Columbus, 1982; vis. scientist ETH Zurich, 1970. Editorial bd.: Lloydia-Jour. Natural Products, 1971—, BBP-Biochemie und Physiologie der Pflanzen, 1971—, Applied Microbiology, 1974—, Planta Medica, 1978—, Jour. Medicinal Chemistry, 1979-82. Recipient Lederle Faculty award, 1967, Mead Johnson Undergrad. Research award, 1968, Research Career Devel. award USPHS, 1969-74, Volwiler award, 1979, Humboldt Sr. Scientist award, 1980. Fellow Acad. Pharm. Scis. (Research Achievement award in natural products 1976), AAAS; mem. Am. Chem. Soc., Am. Soc. Biol. Chemists, Am. Soc. Microbiology, Am. Soc. Pharmacognosy, Phytochem. Soc. N.Am., Sigma Xi (Faculty Research award 1976). Home: 2730 Alliston Ct Columbus OH 43220 Office: Dept Chemistry Ohio State U Columbus OH 43210

FLOTO, RONALD JOHN, supermarket executive; b. Spangler, Pa., Nov. 12, 1942; s. John Lester and Frances (McCormick) F.; m. Sara Jean Albert, Jan. 6, 1968; children: Lisa, John, Mary, Patricia. B.S., U.S. Mil. Acad., 1965; M.B.A., Harvard U., 1971. Vice pres. Masa Feeding Corp., Elk Grove, Ill., 1977-78, Jewel Food Stores, Melrose Park, Ill., 1978-81, Jewel Cos. Inc., Chgo., Il, 1981-83; pres. Buttrey Food Stores, Great Falls, Mont., 1983—. Bd. dirs. Jr. Achievement of Chgo., 1978-81, Vietnam Vets. Leadership Program, Chgo., 1981-82. Served to capt. U.S. Army, 1965-73. Republican. Roman Catholic. Home: 325 Fox Dr Great Falls MT 59404 Office: PO Box 5008 Great Falls MT 59403

FLOWER, GEORGE EDWARD, university administrator; b. Montreal, Que., Can., Oct. 15, 1919; s. Herbert William and Alice Gertrude (Tabb) F.; m. Muriel Armstrong, Nov. 30, 1940; 1 dau., Judith (Mrs. Kenneth William White). B.A., McGill U., 1940, M.A., 1949; Ed.D., Harvard, 1954. Tchr. Montreal Protestant Sch. Bd., 1939-41, 1947-49; asst. dir. Center for Field Studies, Harvard Grad. Sch. Edn., 1950-52; dir. Can. Edn. Assn., Kellogg Leadership Project, Toronto, Ont., 1952-56; prof. Ont. Coll. Edn., Toronto, 1956-65; coordinator grad. studies Ont. Inst. for Studies in Edn., chmn. grad. dept. ednl. theory U. Toronto, 1965-75; dean faculty edn. McGill U., Montreal, 1975—, bd. govs., 1979-82. Author: (with F.K. Stewart) Leadership in Action: The Superintendent of Schools in Canada, 1958, How Big Is Too Big? Problems of Organization and Size, 1964. Exec. mem. Crest Theatre Found., Toronto, 1955-60; bd. govs. Ont. Inst. for Studies in Edn., 1965-75; pres. Can. Found. Econ. Edn., 1980—. Served to capt. Can. Army, 1941-45. Recipient Centennial medal Can. Govt., 1967; Can. Coll. Tchrs. fellow, 1961. Fellow Ont. Tchrs. Fedn.; mem. Can. Edn. Assn. (dir., pres. 1973-74), Can. Assn. Profs. Edn. (pres. 1961-62), Can. Ednl. Researchers Assn. (founding mem.), Am. Ednl. Research Assn., Am. Assn. Sch. Adminstrs., British Ednl. Adminstrn. Soc., Can. Soc. Study Edn. Home: 380 Olivier Ave Westmount PQ H3Z 2C9 Canada Office: Faculty of Education McGill Univ 3700 McTavish St Montreal PQ H3A 1Y2 Canada

FLOWER, JOHN ARNOLD, university administrator; b. Aberdeen, Wash., Feb. 4, 1921; s. Lloyd Edwin and Linda (Nelson) F.; m. Lenette Sheaffer, Feb. 1, 1951; children: Jill Flower Tenwick, John Arnold. B.A., U. Wash., 1948; Mus. M., U. Mich., 1951, Ph.D., 1956. Cert. Conservatoire Americaine, France, 1955. Instr. music U. Mich., Ann Arbor, 1952-62, prof. music, 1962-66, assoc. dean music, 1962-66; prof., assoc. provost Kent State U., Ohio, 1966-73; dean Blossom Festival Sch. of Cleve. Orch. and Kent State U.; v.p. acad. affairs Cleve. State U., 1973—, provost; harpsichordist U. Mich. Baroque Trio, 1963-65; cons. U.S. Office Edn.; cons. examiner N. Central Assn. Colls. Contbr. articles to profl. jours. Bd. dirs. Ohio Outdoor Theater Assn., Cleve. Ballet Guild, Peninsula Valley Heritage Assn., Western Res. Found.; pres. Cleve. Area Arts Council. Served to capt. USAAF, 1942-46. Mem. Internat. Assn. Fine Arts Deans, Pi Kappa Lambda, Pi Kappa Delta. Office: Office of Provost Cleve State U Cleveland OH 44115

FLOWERREE, ROBERT EDMUND, retired forest products company executive; b. New Orleans, Jan. 4, 1921; s. Robert E. and Amy (Hewes) F.; m. Elaine Dicks, Sept. 22, 1943; children: Robert E. III, Ann D., John H., David R. B.A., Tulane U., 1942. Vice pres. Georgia-Pacific Corp., 1956-63, exec. v.p. pulp, paper and chem. ops., 1963-75, pres., 1974-76, chmn., chief exec. officer, 1976-83, chmn., 1983-84, ret., 1984; dir. Chase Manhattan Corp. Mem. bd. adminstrs. Tulane U., New Orleans; life trustee Lewis and Clark Coll., Portland, Oreg. Served to lt. USNR, 1942-46. Recipient Disting. Alumnus award Tulane U., 1978. Clubs: Knights of Malta; Arlington, Waverley Country (Portland); Boston (New Orleans); Links (N.Y.C.). Home: 1322 SE Lava Dr Milwaukie OR 97222 Office: 900 SW 5th Ave Portland OR 97204

FLOWERS, CHARLES ELY, JR., physician, educator; b. Zebulon, N.C., July 20, 1920; s. Charles Ely and Carmen (Poole) F.; m. Juanita Bays, Nov. 23, 1944 (dec.); children: Charles Ely III, Carmen Eva; m. Jaunzetta Shoe, Sept. 25, 1972. B.S., The Citadel, 1941; M.D., Johns Hopkins U., 1944. Diplomate: Am. Bd. Ob-Gyn (asso. examiner). Intern Johns Hopkins Hosp., 1944, resident, 1945-50; instr. SUNY, 1950-51, asst. prof., 1951-53; asso. prof. U. N.C., 1953-61, prof., 1961-66; prof., chmn. dept. obstetrics and gynecology Baylor U. Med. Sch., 1966-69; prof., chmn. dept. ob-gyn U. Ala. Med. Center, Birmingham, 1969—; obstetrician and gynecologist in chief U. Ala. Hosp., 1969—; cons. NIH; mem. adv. com. oral contraceptives Internat. Planned Parenthood; mem. med. services adv. com. Nat. Found.; chmn. 6th World Congress Gynecology and Obstetrics, 1970. Mem. editorial bd.: Obstetrics and Gynecology. Served to capt. M.C., AUS, 1946-48. Recipient Disting. Service award U. N.C., 1970. Mem. AMA, Continental Gynecol. Soc., Am. Gynecol. Soc., Am., Central assns. obstetricians and gynecologists, ACS, Am. Coll. Obstetricians and Gynecologists (chmn. com. obstetrics anesthesia and analgesia, v.p. 1983), Internat. Coll. Anesthetists. Home: 3757 Rockhill Rd Birmingham AL 35223

FLOWERS, LANGDON STRONG, foods company executive; b. Thomasville, Ga., Feb. 12, 1922; s. William Howard and Flewellyn Evans (Strong) F.; m. Margaret Clisby Powell, June 3, 1944; children: Margaret Flowers Rich, Langdon Strong, Elizabeth Powell Flowers McKinney, Dorothy Howard Flowers Swinson, John Howard. B.S., MIT, 1944, M.S., 1947. Engr., Douglas Aircraft, Los Angeles, 1947; supr. Flowers Baking Co., Thomasville, 1947-50, sales mgr., 1950-58, v.p. sales, 1958-65; pres., chief operating officer Flowers Industries, Inc., Thomasville, 1965-76, chmn. bd., chief exec. officer, 1976—; dir. Am. Heritage Life Ins. Co., Ga. Power Co. Pres. Thomasville YMCA, 1958-62; past trustee Presbyn. Coll., Clinton, S.C., Archbold Meml. Hosp., Thomasville. Served as lt. (j.g.) USNR, 1943-46. Named Man of Year, Thomas County C. of C., 1974. Mem. Am. Bakers Assn. (exec. com. 1974-75, chmn. 1975-76), So. Bakers Assn. (chmn. bd. 1969-70), NAM (dir., exec. com.), Thomasville C. of C. (pres. 1953-54), Sigma Alpha Epsilon. Presbyterian (chmn. bd. deacons 1952-56, elder 1956—, rep. Gen. Assembly 1966). Club: Rotarian. Home: 819 Blackshear St Thomasville GA 31792 Office: PO Box 1338 Thomasville GA 31799

FLOWERS, VIRGINIA ANNE, college dean; b. Dothan, Ala., Aug. 29, 1928; d. Kyrie Neal and Annie Laurie (Stewart) F. B.A. (State of Fla. scholar), Fla. State U., 1949; M.Ed., Auburn (Ala.) U., 1958; Ed.D. (Delta Kappa Gamma scholar, teaching asst.), Duke U., 1963. Elem. and secondary sch. tchr., adminstr., Dothan and Dalton, Ga., 1949-61; asst. prof., then prof. edn., head dept. Columbia (S.C.) Coll., 1963-68, asso. dean, then dean, 1969-72; prof. edn. Va. Commonwealth U., 1968-69; asso. dean, asst. provost, acting dean, vice provost Trinity Coll. Arts and Scis., Duke U., 1972-74, prof. edn., chmn. dept., asst. provost ednl. program devel., 1974-80; dean Sch. Edn., Ga. So. Coll., Statesboro, 1980—; bd. dirs., exec. com. Am. Assn. Colls. Tchr. Edn., 1979-84, pres., 1983-84; bd. dirs., exec. com. Learning Inst. N.C., 1976-80. Co-author: Law and Pupil Control, 1964, Readings in Survival in Today's Society, 2 vols, 1978; editorial bd.: Jour. Tchr. Edn, 1980-82, Ednl. Gerontology, 1979—; contbr. articles to profl. jours. Adv. trustee Queens Coll., Charlotte, N.C., 1976-78; vice chmn. continuing commn. study black colls. related to United Methodist Ch., 1973-76. Recipient Star Tchrs. award Dalton. Mem. So. Assn. Colls. and Schs. (commn. on colls.), Am. Ednl. Research Assn., Nat. Orgn. Legal Problems in Edn., Nat. Soc. Study Edn., Am. Assn. Higher Edn., NEA, AAUP, Assn. Study Higher Edn., Am. Assn. Colls. Tchr. Edn. (pres. 1983), Ga. Ednl. Research Assn., Ga. Assn. Educators, Delta Kappa Gamma, Kappa Delta Pi., Phi Delta Kappa. Home: PO Box 7545 Statesboro GA 30458 Office: Ga So Coll Landrum Box 8013 Statesboro GA 30460

FLOWERS, WILLIAM HOWARD, JR., food company executive; b. Thomasville, Ga., Nov. 14, 1913; s. William Howard and Flewellyn Evans (Strong) F.; m. Fontaine Maury Tice, June 22, 1936; children: Fontaine (Mrs. E. McFadden), Maury, Daphne (Mrs. C. Martin Wood III), Taliaferro (Mrs. Robert P. Crozer). B.A. in Bus. Adminstrn, Washington and Lee U., 1933. With Flowers Baking Co. div. Flowers Industries, Inc., Thomasville, Ga., 1933-68, chmn. bd., chief exec. officer, 1965-68, Flowers Industries, Inc., Thomasville, 1968-81, chmn. exec. com., 1981—; dir. Rollins Internat., Inc., Riverside Mfg. Co.

Chmn. Thomas County Bi-Centennial/Sesqui-Centennial Commn.; Mem. spl. adv. com. on pub. opinion U.S. Dept. State, 1970-72; Mem. Thomas County Sch. Bd., 1953-58, Madeira Sch. Corp., Greenway, Va., 1960-68, Ga. Senate, 1964-68; city commr., Thomasville, 1941; Trustee William Howard Flowers Found., John D. Archbold Meml. Hosp., 1953-71, Thomasville. Named Man of Year Thomas County C. of C., 1964. Mem. N.A.M. (dir. 1962-66), Young Presidents' Orgn., Chief Execs. Forum, Ducks Unltd. (nat. trustee 1967—), Kappa Alpha. Episcopalian. Clubs: Rotarian., Lyford Cay (Nassau); Sapphire Valley Country, Wildcat Cliffs Country (Highlands, N.C.); Farmington Country (Charlottesville, Va.); Buck's (London, Eng.); Rolling Rock (Ligonier, Pa.). Address: PO Box 1338 Thomasville GA 31792

FLOYD, CARLISLE, composer, educator; b. Latta, S.C., June 11, 1926; s. Carlisle Sessions and Ida (Fenegan) F.; m. Margery Kay Reeder, Nov. 28, 1957. Mus.B., Syracuse U., 1946, Mus.M., 1949; Mus.D. (hon.), Dickinson Coll., 1983. Mem. faculty Sch. Music Fla. State U., Tallahassee, 1947-76; prof. music; M.D. Anderson prof. Sch. Music, U. Houston, 1976—. Composer: mus. play Slow Dusk, 1949, Susannah, 1954; mus. drama Pilgrimage, 1955, Sonata For Piano, 1957, Wuthering Heights, 1958, The Mystery, 1960, The Passion of Jonathan Wade, 1962, The Sojourner and Mollie Sinclair, 1963; comedy-drama Markheim, 1965; mus. drama Of Mice and Men, 1970, Flower and Hawk, 1972; monodrama Bilby's Doll, 1976, Citizen of Paradise, 1983; mus. drama Willie Stark, 1981. Recipient Citation of Merit Nat. Assn. Am. Composers and Condrs., 1957, N.Y. Music Critics Circle award, 1957, service award Nat. Opera Inst., 1983; named one of ten Outstanding Young Men U.S. Jr. C. of C., 1959; Guggenheim fellow, 1956. Mem. ASCAP, Am. Guild Mus. Artists, Pi Kappa Lambda, Phi Mu Alpha, Delta Omicron, Phi Kappa Phi. Democrat. Home: 4491 Yoakum Blvd Houston TX 77006

FLOYD, EDWIN EARL, educator; b. Eufaula, Ala., May 8, 1924; s. John Quincy and Ludie (James) F.; m. Marguerite Stahl, May 11, 1945; children—Judith L., Sally J., William J. B.A., U. Ala., 1943; Ph.D., U. Va., 1948. Instr. math. Princeton, 1948-49; mem. faculty U. Va., 1949—, prof. math., 1956—, Robert Taylor prof., chmn. dept., 1966-69, dean, 1974-81, v.p., provost, 1981—; mem. Inst. Advanced Study, 1958-59, 63-64. Author: (with P.E. Conner) Differentiable Periodic Maps, 1964; also articles. Sloan Research fellow, 1962-64. Home: Pavilion II East Lawn Charlottesville VA 22903

FLOYD, JACK WILLIAM, lawyer; b. Columbia, S.C., May 14, 1934; s. Edward Immanuel and Edith Fletcher (Herlong) F.; m. Ruth Parker Matthews, Jan. 10, 1957; children—Connie, Cindy, Jay. B.S., U. N.C., 1958, J.D. with honors, 1961. Bar: N.C. bar 1961, U.S. Supreme Ct. bar 1971. Asso. firm Smith, Moore, Smith, Schell & Hunter, Greensboro, N.C., 1961-67, partner firm, 1967—; lectr. acctg. U. N.C., 1960-61; lectr. bus. law Guilford Coll., 1962-64; speaker on jury trials Am. Bar Assn., Am. Patent Law Assn. Bd. editors: N.C. Law Rev, 1960-61. Mem. parents' bd. dirs. Meredith Coll., Raleigh, N.C., 1977-79, chmn., 1980-81. Served with USN, 1951-55. Mem. Am. Bar Assn., N.C. Bar Assn., Am. Law Inst., N.C. Assn. Trial Lawyers, Order of Coif. Democrat. Baptist. Club: Elks. Home: 1404 Valleymede Dr Greensboro NC 27410 Office: PO Box 21927 Greensboro NC 27420

FLOYD, RAYMOND, golfer; b. Ft. Bragg, N.C., Sept. 14, 1942; s. Loren B. and Edith (Brown) F.; m. Maria; children: Raymond, Robert Loran. Student, U. N.C., 1960. Profl. golfer, 1961—; mem. Ryder Cup team, 1969, 75. Named Rookie of Year Golf Mag., 1963, 77, Player of Yr., 1976. Winner PGA tournament, 1969, 82 St. Petersburg Open, 1963, St. Paul Open, 1965, Jacksonville Open, 1969, Am. Golf Classic, 1969, Kemper Open, 1975, Masters, 1976, World Open, 1976, Byron Nelson Golf Classic, 1977, Pleasant Valley Golf Classic, 1977, Brazilian Open, 1978, Greater Greensboro Open, 1979, Canadian PGA, 1981, Ryder Cup, 1969, 75, 77, 81. Office: care PGA Tour Hdqrs Ponte Vedra FL 32082 *

FLOYD, ROBERT LESTER, lawyer; b. Cin., Jan. 4, 1918; s. Paul Leslie and Margaret (Scott) F.; m. Rose Marie Norcross, Sept. 4, 1946; children: Robert Lester, Edward R., Rosemarie, James N. Student, U. Fla., 1936-37; J.D., Am. U., 1941. Bar: D.C. 1942, Fla. 1944. Spl. agt. FBI, 1941-45; pvt. practice, Miami, Fla., 1945-54, 63—; partner firm Floyd, Pearson, Richman, Greer, Weil & Brumbaugh, P.A. (and predecessor), 1963—; judge 11th Jud. Circuit Fla., 1955-63; chmn.-elect Circuit Judges Conf. Fla., 1962. Mayor of Miami, 1947-49; mem. Miami City Commn., 1949-50, Fla. Ho. Reps., 1950-54; sheriff of, Dade County, 1966. Fellow Internat. Acad. Trial Lawyers, Am. Coll. Trial Lawyers, Am. Bar Found.; mem. ABA (ho. dels. 1974-77, 79—), Dade County Bar Assn. (pres. 1966-67), Fla. Bar (gov. 1968-78, pres. 1978-79), Soc. Former Spl. Agts. FBI (pres. 1966). Democrat. Methodist. Clubs: Coral Gables (Fla.) Country; Ocean Reef (Upper Key Largo, Fla.); Shriners, Elks. Home: 6800 SW 68th St Miami FL 33143 Office: 1 Biscayne Tower 25th Floor Miami FL 33131

FLOYD, ROBERT W., computer scientist; b. N.Y.C., June 8, 1936; s. Darwin and Mary F.; (divorced); children: Susan, Michael, Sean. A.B., U. Chgo., 1953, B.S. in Physics, 1958. Elec. engr. Westinghouse Co., Elmira, N.Y., 1955-56; computer operator, programmer Armour Research Found., Chgo., 1956-62; analyst Computer Assocs., Wakefield, Mass., 1962-65; assoc. prof. computer sci. Carnegie-Mellon U., 1965-68; assoc. prof. Stanford U., 1968-70, prof., 1970—, chmn. dept. computer sci., 1974-77. Guggenheim fellow, 1976-77. Fellow Am. Acad. Arts and Scis.; mem. Assn. Computing Machinery (asso. editor Jour. 1966-67, A. M. Turing award 1978, AAAS.). Home: 895 Allardice Way Stanford CA 94305 Office: Computer Sci Dept Stanford U Stanford CA 94305

FLOYD, WALTER LAWRENCE, physician, educator; b. Asheville, N.C., Dec. 15, 1926; s. James and Nonnie (B.) F.; m. Helen Ann, Aug. 22, 1951; children—Walter L., David Bruce, Elizabeth Ann. B.S., Auburn (Ala.) U., 1949; M.D., Johns Hopkins U., 1954. Diplomate: Am. Bd. Internal Medicine. Mem. faculty Med. Center, Duke U., Durham, N.C., 1959—, now prof. medicine. Fellow A.C.P., Am. Heart Assn. (council on clin. cardiology), mem., Durham-Orange County Heart Assn., Durham-Orange County Med. Soc., N.C. Med. Soc., N.C. Soc. Internal Medicine, Am. Heart Assn., Alpha Omega Alpha. Office: Duke Medical Center Durham NC 27710 *

FLUNO, JERE DAVID, business executive; b. Wisconsin Rapids, Wis., June 3, 1941; s. Rexford Hollis and Irma Dell (Wells) F.; m. Anne Marie Derezinski, Aug. 10, 1963; children: Debbie, Julie, Mary Beth, Brian. B.B.A., U. Wis., 1963. C.P.A., Ill. Audit supr. Alexander Grant & Co., Chgo., 1963-69; controller W.W. Grainger, Inc., Skokie, Ill., 1969-74, v.p., controller, 1974-75, v.p. fin., 1975-81, sr. v.p., chief fin. officer, 1981—, dir., 1975—; mem. adv. bd. Allendale Ins. Co., Oak Brook, Ill., 1983—; dir. W.W. Grainger, Internat., Skokie, Ill., 1977—; v.p., asst. treas. Dayton Electric Mfg. Co., Chgo., 1981—; treas. Doerr Electric Corp., Cedarburg, Wis., 1979—. Mem. Econ. Club Chgo., 1979, Bascom Hill Soc. U. Wis., Madison, 1979; treas., chmn. fin. com. Holy Cross Parish, Deerfield, Ill., 1961; trustee Glenkirk Found., Northbrook, Ill., 1981 trustee Glenkirk Found., Northbrook, Ill., 1982. Mem. Am. Inst. C.P.A.s, Fin. Execs. Inst., Ill. C.P.A. Soc., U. Wis. Alumni Assn. Republican. Roman Catholic. Clubs: Lincolnshire Bath and Tennis; Knollwood (Lake Forest, Ill.). Office: W W Grainger Inc 5500 W Howard St Skokie IL 60077

FLUOR, JOHN ROBERT, manufacturing executive; b. Santa Ana, Calif., Dec. 18, 1921; s. Peter E. and Margaret (Fischer) F.; m. Lillian Marie Breaux, May 17, 1944; children: John Robert II, Peter. Grad., U. So. Calif., 1946. With Fluor Corp., 1946—, successively mgr., v.p. and gen. mgr. mfg., v.p. in charge mfg., exec. v.p., 1952-62, pres., 1962-68, chief exec. officer, 1962—, chmn., 1968—, also dir.; dir. Calif. Canadian Bank, Tex. Commerce Bancshares, Santa Anita Operating Co., Santa Anita Realty Enterprises, Hughes Aircraft. Trustee Pacific Mut.; Trustee U. So. Calif., James Irvine Found.; campaign chmn. United Way Los Angeles County, 1977, pres., 1977—, chmn., 1978—; chmn. devel. com. Boy Scouts Am., 1977—. Served as 1st lt. USAAF, 1941-45. Mem. NAM (dir.), Calif. Thoroughbred Breeders Assn. (dir.). Roman Catholic. Clubs: California, Bohemiam, San Gabriel Country; Sky (N.Y.C.); Eldorado Country, Vintage (Palm Desert, Calif.); Los Angeles Country. Home: PO Box 2387 Newport Beach CA 92663 Office: 3333 Michelson Dr Irvine CA 92730

FLUSSI, HARRY VALENTINE, former medical center administrator;; b. Hilldale, Pa., Feb. 14, 1918; s. Sam and Josephine (Baldinucci) F.; m. Mary Martha Dinis, Apr. 8, 1944; children: Diane Marie (Mrs. John W. Gittinger, Jr.), Claire Denise (Mrs. Peter Jordan). B.A., U. Scranton, 1939; postgrad., Bucknell U., 1939-42. Social worker Pa. Dept. Pub. Assistance, 1939-41; officer mgr. SSS, Plains, Pa., 1941-43; with VA, 1946—; dir. VA Ctr., Togus, Maine, 1965-70, VA Med. Ctr., Lebanon, Pa., 1970-82; high sch. tchr. St. Thomas High Sch., Scranton, 1939. Chmn. U.S. CSC Interagy. Bd., Augusta, Maine, 1966-68, Combined Fed. Campaign for Maine, 1966—; mem. action panel USDA, 1968—; mem. regional health services com. Augusta-Gardiner Area Community Council, 1966—. Served with C.E. AUS, 1943-46. Recipient citations and awards of merit Am. Legion, VFW, Am. Vets., World War II; letters of commendation VA and other govt. agencies; VA Sustained Superior Performance award manager's commendation. Mem. Nat. Inter-Agy. Inst. Fed. Hosp. Adminstrs., U.S. Postoffice Mail Users Council, Lambda Alpha Phi. Address: 905 Aspen Drive RD #8 Mountain Top PA 18707

FLYNN, BRIAN JOHN, journalist; b. Des Moines, Jan. 3, 1945; s. Edward William and Dorothy (Bolton) F.; m. Suzanne Rae Lyman, Nov. 14, 1970; 1 dau., Megan Elizabeth. B.Journalism, Drake U. Service mgr. Look Mag., Des Moines, 1968-71, Univ. Microfilms, Ann Arbor, 1971-72; asst. bus. mgr. Register and Tribune Syndicate, Des Moines, 1972-76, bus. mgr., 1976-79, gen. mgr., 1979—. Republican. Roman Catholic. Address: 10639 Ridgeview Dr Des Moines IA 50322

FLYNN, COLIN PETER, physicist, educator; b. Stockton-on-Tees, Eng., Aug. 18, 1935; came to U.S., 1960; s. Francis Johnson and Edith (Mercer) F.; m. Marilyn Louise Jacobs, July 2, 1961 (div.); 1 son, James Edward; m. Susan Kingston, June 12, 1971; children—Derek Mather, Megan. B.S., U. Leeds, Eng., 1957, Ph.D., 1960; M.A., Cambridge U., Eng., 1966. Research asso. U. Ill. at Urbana, 1960-62, mem. faculty, 1962—, prof. physics, 1968—; dir. Materials Research Lab., 1978—; fellow Christs Coll., Cambridge (Eng.) U., 1966-67; cons. Atomic Energy Research Establishment, Harwell, Eng., Argonne (Ill.) Nat. Labs. NSF Internat., Sci. Research Council Con. Author: Point Defects and Diffusion, 1972; also articles on magnetism, alloys, thermal defects, diffusion, optical phenomena. NSF Internat. Programs fellow, 1977-78. Fellow Am. Phys. Soc.; mem. Am. Soc. Metals. Home: 1810 S Vine St Urbana IL 61801

FLYNN, DAVID PAUL, actuary, underwriting company executive; b. Peckville, Pa., June 19, 1940; s. James Gerald and Winifred Aileen (O'Dowd) F.; m. Louise Cloud; children: Karen, Michael, Colleen; m. Sarah Elizabeth Larson; children: Erik, Elizabeth. A.B. in Math., San Francisco State U., 1965. Various actuarial positions Fireman's Fund Ins., San Francisco, 1965-74, v.p., actuary, 1974, Crum & Forster Underwriters, Morristown, N.J., 1974-80, sr. v.p., actuary, 1980—. Fellow Casualty Actuarial Soc. (sec. 1978-81); mem. Am. Acad. Actuaries. Office: Crum & Forster Underwriters 211 Mount Airy Rd Basking Ridge NJ 07920

FLYNN, DENNIS PATRICK, electronic security company executive, accountant; b. Danville, Ill., Feb. 12, 1944; s. Aloysius James and Alva Anne (Owen) F.; m. Carol Louise Houlihan, June 8, 1968; children: Dennis Patrick Houlihan, Molly Maureen. B.S., U. Ill., 1966; M.B.A., Harvard U., 1968. C.P.A., Calif. Sr. auditor Price Waterhouse Co., San Francisco, 1968-72; regional contriller Am. Dist. Telegraph Co., San Francisco, 1973-74, gen. mgr. Europe, London, 1975-76, v.p. Europe, 1977-78, v.p. fin., chief fin. officer, N.Y.C., 1978—; lectr. Calif. State U.-Haywood, 1972, San Francisco State U., 1973, U. Claif.-Berkeley, 1974. Chief fin. adviser City of San Francisco Bd. Suprs., 1970-72. Mem. Fin. Execs. Inst., Am. Inst. C.P.A.s, N.Y. Start Soc. C.P.A.s, Nat. Rifle Assn. Republican. Club: Windows of the World (N.Y.C.). Home: RD 1 PO Box 565 Canadensis PA 18325 Office: Am Dist Telegraph Co Suite 9200 One World Trade Ctr. New York NY 10048

FLYNN, EDWARD JAMES, chocolate co. exec.; b. Coldwater, Mich., 1906; s. Edmond and Kinney F.; m. Hilah Bloomquist, Nov. 6, 1935; one dau., Jeannine. Grad., Loyola U., 1933. With Cook Chocolate Co., Chgo., 1935—, exec. v.p., dir., 1957—; pres. Kalva Corp., Gurnee, Ill. Mem. Loyola U. Alumni Assn., Exec. Mgmt. Alumni Assn. (Columbia). Home: Post and Rail Farm Palos Park IL 60464 Office: 2521 W 48th St Chicago IL 60632

FLYNN, FRANK PATRICK, JR., prefabricated homes constrn. co. exec.; b. Des Moines, June 23, 1912; s. Frank P. and Agnes (Dohohoe) F.; m. Jenevieve E. Hanson, June 1932 (dec. May 1966); children—Patricia (Mrs. Alan Birchler), Martin J., Sheila (Mrs. Michael F. Boone), Kevin M., Caroline (Mrs. Joel Muse), Victoria (Mrs. B.C. May); m. Joanna Cory Martin, Dec. 11, 1967. LL.B., Drake U., 1935. Asst. state dir. FHA, Des Moines, 1934-40; v.p. Percey Wilson & Co., Chgo., 1940-43; mortgage loan supr. Equitable Life Iowa, Des Moines, 1946-47; pres. Nat. Homes Acceptance Corp., Lafayette, Ind., 1947-74; chmn. bd., chief exec. officer Nat. Homes Corp., Lafayette, 1974-77, chmn. bd., 1977—, also dir.; dir. Purdue Nat. Bank, Star City Fed. Savs. & Loan Assn., Lafayette; trustee Chase Manhattan Mortgage & Realty, Boston. Bd. dirs. Ind. Catholic Conf. Served with USNR, 1943-46. Mem. Fed. Nat. Mortgage Assn. (adv. bd. 1959-68). Roman Catholic. Clubs: K.C., Elks, Lafayette Country, Indpls. Athletic. Home: 2318 Ellen Dr Lafayette IN 47905 Office: Earl Ave at Wallace Lafayette IN 47902

FLYNN, JACQUES, lawyer, Can. govt. ofcl.; b. St. Hyacinthe, Que., Can., Aug. 22, 1915; s. Francis and Jeanne (Lussier) F.; m. Renee des Rivieres, Feb. 14, 1942; children—Marie (Mrs. Marc-André Pey), Francis. B.A., Laval U., 1936, LL.L., 1939. Bar: Called to bar Que 1939. Practice in, Quebec City, 1948—; partner Flynn, Rivard & Assos., 1948—; enforcement counsel Wartime Prices and Trade Bd. Eastern Que., 1942-45. Dir. St. Maurice Ins. Co., Trans-Pub. Advt. Co., Ltd., Savs. & Investments Trust Co., Savs. & Investments Group, Savs. & Investments Mut. Fund, Savs. & Investments-Am. Mut. Fund.; Mem. Ho. of Commons, 1958-62, dep. speaker, chmn. coms., 1960; minister Mines and Tech. Surveys, 1961; mem. Senate, 1962—, leader of opposition, 1967-79, 80—; minister justice, atty. gen. Govt. of Can., Ottawa, Ont., 1979-80. Roman Catholic. Clubs: Cercle Universitaire, Garrison (Quebec). Home: 1086 Thornhill Park Sillery PQ Canada Office: The Senate Ottawa ON K1A 0H8 Canada

FLYNN, JAMES ROURKE, insurance company executive; b. Jamaica, L.I., N.Y., Jan. 18, 1925; s. John Michael and Anne Theresa (Stark) F.; m. Anne Virginia Farley, Oct. 28, 1944; children: James Rourke, Anne Maureen, Christopher P., Marybeth, David. B.S., U. Dayton, 1947. With Metropolitan Life Ins. Co., 1947—, sr. v.p., officer-in-charge, Great Lakes Head Office, Aurora, Ill., 1976—. Bd. dirs. Aurora Coll.; trustee Paramount Arts Ctr. Endowment, Aurora. Served with USN, 1943-46. Mem. Ill. Life Ins. Council, Ill. Life and Health Ins. Guaranty Assn. Democrat. Roman Catholic. Home: 122 George St Wheaton IL 60187 Office: 177 S Commons Aurora IL 60505

FLYNN, JAMES THOMAS, state lieutenant governor; b. Chgo., Sept. 25, 1944; s. Thomas Edward and Ann (Davoli) F.; m. Mary Catherine Basso, Dec. 27, 1969. B.A., Marquette U., 1970, J.D., 1973. Bar: Wis. 1973. Tchr. jr. high sch., Milw., 1968-70; mem. Wis. Senate, 1972-82, chmn. com. on judiciary and consumer affairs; ptnr. firm Piaskoski & Flynn, Milw., 1973-82; lt. gov. State of Wis., Madison, 1982—; sec. Wis. Dept. Devel. Democrat. Roman Catholic. Office: Office of Lieutenat Gov State Capitol Madison WI 53702

FLYNN, JOHN EDWIN, cargo airline executive; b. Boston, Oct. 29, 1940; s. Gerald I. and Mary C. (Crowley) F.; m. Madeline (Jill) Borland, June 14, 1968; children: Alexandra, Lisa, Taylor. Student, Middlebury Coll., until 1963; LL.B., Columbia U., 1966. Bar: Ill. 1974, N.Y. 1967, Calif. 1978. Vice pres., gen. counsel No. Am. Car, Chgo., 1973-76; v.p. law Tiger Internat., Los Angeles, 1976-79; v.p. corp. affairs Flying Tiger Line, Los Angeles, 1979, sr. v.p. adminstrn., los Angeles, 1980-81, exec. v.p., Los Angeles, 1981-83, pres., 1983—. Mem. Calif. Bar Assn. Office: Flying Tiger Line Inc 7401 World Way West Los Angeles CA 90009

FLYNN, PAUL BARTHOLOMEW, newspaper publisher; b. Quincy, Mass., Sept. 17, 1935; s. Bartholomew Joseph and Katherine Marie (Coleman) F.; m. Aline Therese Nicholson, Feb. 11, 1961; children: Bonnie Marie, Laureen P., Elizabeth A., Bernadette J. A.B., Stonehill Coll., 1957. Sportswriter The Patriot Ledger, Quincy, 1955-63, community relations dir., 1963-65; dir. public relations Mass. Tchrs. Assn., Boston, 1965-66; asst. dir. pub. service Rochester (N.Y.) Democrat and Chronicle and The Times-Union, 1966-71, dir. pub. service and research, 1971-72; dir. advt. Huntington (W.Va.) Herald-Dispatch and Advertiser, 1972-74, Binghamton (N.Y.) Press and Sun-Bulletin, 1974-76; dir. mktg. services Gannett Co., Rochester, N.Y., 1976-77; gen. mgr. Jour.-News, Nyack, N.Y., 1977; pres., pub. Fort Myers (Fla.) News-Press, 1977—; S.E. regional v.p. Ganett Co., 1981-83; exec. v.p. USA Today, Washington, 1983—; v.p. Gannett Newspaper Advt. Sales, N.Y.C., 1976-77; dir. 1st Nat. Bank of Fort Myers, S.W. Fla. Banks Inc. Co-editor: Promoting the Total Newspaper, 1977. Pres. Lend-a-Hand Fund of S.W. Fla.; pres. S.W. Fla. Boy Scouts Am. Council, 1981; bd. dirs. Lee County United Way, 1978—, campaign chmn., 1981; bd. dirs. Edison Community Coll. Endowment Found., 1978—, Fla. C. of C., 1978-80, Sr. Friendship Centers, Inc., 1981—; mem. adv. bd. U. South Fla., Fort Myers. Served with U.S. Army, 1957-58. Recipient Disting. Service award B'nai B'rith of Cape Coral, Fla., 1979; Gold medal for good citizenship SAR, 1980. Mem. Am. Newspaper Pubs. Assn., Internat. Newspaper Promotion Assn. (dir. 1977-78), So. Newspaper Pubs. Assn., Fla. Press Assn., Fla. C. of C., Met. Fort Myers C. of C., Cape Coral C. of C., Stonehill Coll. Alumni Assn. Roman Catholic. Clubs: Royal Palm Yacht, Forest Country, Burnt Store Golf and Tennis, Burnt Store Marina, Fiddlesticks Country. Office: PO Box 10 Fort Myers FL 33902 Office: USA Today PO Box 500 Washington DC 20044

FLYNN, RICHARD JAMES, lawyer; b. Omaha, Dec. 6, 1928; s. Richard T. and Eileen (Murphy) F.; m. Kay House Ebert, June 28, 1975; children: Richard McDonnell, William Thomas, Kathryn Eileen, James Daniel. Student, Cornell U., 1944-46; B.S., Nothwestern U., 1950; J.D., Northwestern U., 1953. Bar: D.C. 1953, Ill. 1954. Law clk. to Chief Justices Vinson and Warren, 1953-54; assoc. Sidley, Austin, Burgess & Smith, Chgo., 1954-63, ptnr., Washington, 1963-66, Sidley & Austin, 1967—. Contbr. articles to profl. jours. Served with USN, 1946-48. Mem. ABA, Fed. Bar Assn., Fed. Energy Bar Assn., Assn. ICC Practitioners, Nat. Lawyer Club, Chgo. Bar Assn., D.C. Bar Assn., Order of Coif, Phi Beta Kappa, Phi Delta Phi, Sigma Chi. Republican. Presbyterian. Clubs: Economic of Chgo., Legal, Kenwood Golf and Country; Metropolitan (Washington). Home: 2343 S Queen St Arlington VA 22202 Office: 1722 Eye St NW Washington DC 20006

FLYNN, RICHARD JEROME, manufacturing company executive; b. Albia, Iowa, Jan. 4, 1924; s. William Alfred and Elizabeth (Mahoney) F.; m. Ellen Francis McGarty, May 3, 1952; children: Bernard M., Elizabeth A., Mark W., Mary R., Richard T., Patricia J., Matthew J. B.S., Coll. Holy Cross, Worcester, Mass., 1947; LL.B., Georgetown U., 1949. Bar: D.C. 1950. Law clk., bd. govs. FRS, 1950; assoc. Mulholland, Robie & Hickey, Washington, 1950-51; atty. Raytheon Co., Waltham, Mass., 1951-56; gen. atty., v.p. fin. subs., treas. Collins Radio Co., Dallas, 1956-62; v.p. Ling-Temco-Vought, Dallas, 1962-64; exec. v.p. Continental Electronics Mfg. Co., Dallas, 1964-69; pres., chief exec. officer, dir. Riley Stoker Corp., Worcester, Mass., 1969-73; exec. v.p. fin., dir. Norton Co., Worcester, 1974—; dir. Mechanics Bank, Fidelity Mgmt. and Research Co., Arkwright-Boston Ins. Co. Trustee Holy Cross Coll., Old Sturbridge Village. Served with USNR, 1943-46. Home: Fiske Hill Sturbridge MA 01566 Office: 1 New Bond St Worcester MA 01606

FLYNN, ROBERT EMMETT, process controls equipment company executive; b. Montreal, Que., Can., Sept. 10, 1933; came to U.S., 1957; s. Emmett Joseph and Pauline Perrier (Lupien) F.; m. Irene P. Kantor, July 28, 1960; children: Donna, Darren, Diane. B.S. in Physics, Loyola Coll., Montreal, 1955; B.E. in Engring, McGill U., 1957; M.B.A., Rutgers U., 1962. Vice pres. Carborundum Co., Niagara Falls, N.Y., 1973-76, group v.p., 1976-79, sr. v.p., 1979-81; exec. v.p. Fisher Controls Internat. Inc., St. Louis, 1981-82; pres., chief exec. officer Fisher Control Internat. Inc., St. Louis, 1982—. Trustee Foundry Edn. Found., Chgo., 1977-80; bd. dirs. United Way, Niagara Falls, 1972-81, campaign chmn., Niagara Falls, 1978. Served with USMCR, 1958. Republican. Roman Catholic. Club: St. Louis (Clayton, Mo.). Home: 70 Lake Forest Richmond Heights-Saint Louis MO 63117 Office: Fisher Controls Internat Inc 8000 Maryland Ave Clayton MO 63105

FLYNN, THOMAS J., army officer; b. Corning, N.Y., Nov. 2, 1930; s. Frank Leo and Kathryn Louise (Relihan) F.; m. Alice Gilberte Duclos, Nov. 30, 1957; children—Michael, Lisa, Mary, Timothy, Mark. B.A., St. Michael's Coll. U. Toronto, 1952; postgrad., Command and Gen. Staff Coll., 1968-69, Air War Coll., 1973-74. Enlisted as pvt. U.S. Army, 1952, commd. 2d. lt., 1954, advanced through grades to maj. gen., 1982, served in Korea, 1956, served in W. Ger., 1959-61, 74-78, served in Vietnam, 1971-72; dep. comdr. Army Intelligence and Security Command, 1979-81; spl. asst. to dir. Nat. Security Agy., 1981-82, asst. dep. dir., 1982—. Decorated Legion of Merit with 3 oak leaf clusters, Bronze Star, others; named to Inf. Officers Candidate Sch. Hall of Fame. Roman Catholic. Office: Nat Security Agy Ft Meade MD 20755

FLYNN, THOMAS JOSEPH, hospital management company executive; b. Pitts., Dec. 28, 1936; m. Elizabeth A. Gessner, May 28, 1960; children: Sean Patrick, Kelly Lynn Flynn. B.S., Mt. St. Mary's Coll., Emmitsburg, Md., 1958; LL.B., Duquesne U., Pitts., 1964. Bar:

Pa. 1964, Ky. 1976. Atty. Westinghouse Electric Corp., Pitts., 1964-74; exec. v.p., gen. counsel Humana Inc., Louisville, 1974—. Mem. Am. Bar Assn., Am. Hosp. Assn., Ky. Bar Assn., Allegheny County Bar Assn. Roman Catholic. Clubs: Jefferson, Hunting Creek Country. Address: 1800 First Nat Tower Louisville KY 40202

FLYNN, THOMAS PATRICK, state official; b. Woonsocket, R.I., Oct. 13, 1924; s. Thomas Patrick and Margaret Esther (Egan) F.; m. Jeanne Allard, Sept. 25, 1950; children: Christine Jeanne, Karen Patrice, Thomas Patrick. B.A., Providence Coll., 1945; postgrad., Am. Press Inst., Columbia U., 1968. With Providence Jour.-Bull., 1948-50; sports editor Vineland (N.J.) Times-Jour., 1950-60, polit. editor, 1960-66; asst. mng. editor Courier-Post, Camden, N.J., 1966-70, editor, 1972-75; editor N.J. edit. Phila. Evening and Sunday Bull., Cherry Hill, 1975-82; dir. communications N.J. Dept. Transp., Trenton, 1982—. Press sec. 2N.J. Gov. William T. Cahill, 1970-72; Mem. adv. com. Rutgers U. Mem. Am. Soc. Newspaper Editors, N.J. Press Assn. Home: 4 Cobblestone Rd Cherry Hill NJ 08003 Office: 1035 Parkway Ave Trenton NJ 08625

FLYNT, ALTHEA SUE, publisher; b. Marietta, Ohio, Nov. 6, 1953; d. Richard Earl and June Avonelle (Osbourne) Leasure; m. Aug. 21, 1976. Student public schs., Hamilton Twp., Ohio. Pres. Mini Clubs Am., Ohio nightclub chain, 1971-74; editorial dir. Hustler mag., Larry Flynt Publs. Inc., Los Angeles, 1974-80, Chic mag., 1976—; pres. Larry Flynt Publs., Inc., 1980—; also pres. Flynt Distbg. Co.; pub., chmn. bd. Rage Inc., Los Angeles, 1983—. Office: 2029 Century Park E Suite 3800 Los Angeles CA 90067 *

FLYNT, JOHN JAMES, JR., lawyer, former congressman; b. Griffin, Ga., Nov. 8, 1914; s. John James and Susan Winn (Banks) F.; m. Patricia Irby Bradley, Feb. 7, 1942; children: Susan, John James III, Crisp. A.B., U. Ga., 1936; postgrad., Emory U., 1937-38; LL.B., George Washington U., 1940; grad., Nat. War Coll., Command and Gen. Staff Sch., Air Corps Advanced Flying Sch., Brooks Field, Tex. Bar: Ga. 1938. Asst. U.S. atty. No. Dist. Ga., 1939-41, 45-46; mem. Ga. Ho. of Reps., 1947-48; solicitor gen. Griffin Jud. Circuit, 1949-54; mem. 83d-88th Congresses, 4th Ga. Dist., and 89th-95th Congresses from 6th Ga. Dist.; partner firm Smalley Cogburn & Flynt (P.C.), Griffin, 1979—. Served in U.S. Army, 1936-37, 41-45; ETO; col. Res. Decorated Bronze Star medal. Fellow Ga. Bar Found. (charter); Mem. ABA, Ga. Bar Assn. (pres.), Am. Legion, V.F.W., Phi Delta Phi, Sigma Alpha Epsilon. Democrat. Methodist (trustee, chmn. bd. stewards). Lodges: Masons; Kiwanis; Shriners. Home: Griffin GA 30223 Office: 115 N 6th St Griffin GA 30224

FLYNT, LARRY CLAXTON, publisher; b. Magoffin County, Ky., Nov. 1, 1942; s. Larry Claxton and Edith (Arnett) F.; m. Althea Leasure, Aug. 21, 1976; children: Tonya, Lisa, Teresa, Larry Claxton, III. Student public schs., Saylersville, Ky. Factory worker Gen. Motors, Dayton, Ohio, 1958, 64-65; owner, operator Hustler Club, Dayton, Columbus, Toledo, Akron and Cleve., 1970-74; owner, pub. Hustler and Chic mags., Los Angeles, 1974—; owner, operator Flynt Distbg. Co., Los Angeles, 1976—. Served with U.S. Army, 1958; Served with USN, 1959-64. Office: 2029 Century Park E Suite 3800 Los Angeles CA 90067 *I intend to devote my entire life to the cause of civil liberties and civil rights for all mankind in an effort to bring about peace on earth. I absolutely refuse to compromise my unorthodox strategy concerning my principles, ideas, goals, and conduct that have brought me this far.*

FOA, JOSEPH VICTOR, educator, aero. engr.; b. Turin, Italy, July 10, 1909; came to U.S., 1939, naturalized, 1944; s. Ettore and Lelia (DellaTorre) F.; m. Lucy Bouvier, June 27, 1942; children—Lelia, Sylvana, Eugenie, Gay. Dr.Ing., Politecnico di Torino, 1931, U. Rome, 1933. Cert. of appreciation Dept. Army, 1951. Project engr. Piaggio Aircraft Co., Italy, 1933-35, 37-39; chief engr. Caproni Engring. Center, Studi Caproni, Italy, 1935-37; project engr. Bellanca Aircraft Corp., 1939-40; cons., chief engr. Am. Aeromarine Co., 1942; head aero. design research Curtiss Wright Corp., 1943-45; head propulsion br. Cornell U. Aero. Lab., 1945-52; prof. aero. engring. Rensselaer Poly. Inst., 1952-70, head dept., 1958-67; prof. engring. and applied sci. George Washington U., 1970—; cons. aircraft cos. Author and co-author sci. books and articles. Recipient devel. award and cert. for exceptional service Navy Ordnance Dept., 1945. Originator of cryptosteady flow concept and theories and of new concepts in aero and marine propulsion, high-speed ground transp., heating and air-conditioning. Patentee. Home: 3404 Thornapple St Chevy Chase MD 20815

FOA, URIEL GASTON, psychologist; b. Parma, Italy, 1916; came to U.S., 1965, naturalized, 1972; s. Enea Avraham and Dora Alice (Muggia) F.; m. Edna Ben-Jacob, Aug. 14, 1962; children—Gad, Ephraim, Ora Tamar Foa Goldstein, Hagar, Yael, Michelle. J.D., U. Parma, 1939; Ph.D., Hebrew U., 1947. Exec. dir., co-founder Israel Inst. Applied Social Research, Jerusalem, 1948-65; asso. prof. chmn. psychology Bar-Ilan U., Ramat Gan, Israel, 959-62; vis. prof. U. Ill., Champaign-Urbana, 1965-67; prof. U. Mo., Columbia, 1967-71; prof. psychology Temple U., Phila., 1971—; specialist UNESCO, 1962; cons. in field. Author: (with E. B. Foa) Societal Structures of the Mind, 1974, Resource Theory of Social Exchange, 1975; contbr.: articles to profl. jours. Resource Theory of Social Exchange. Grantee Ford Found.; NIMH; NSF. Fellow Am. Psychol. Assn., AAAS, N.Y. Acad. Sci. Republican. Jewish. Home: 531 Broad Acres Rd Narberth PA 19072 Office: 505 Weiss Hall Temple U Philadelphia PA 19122

FOARD, SUSAN LEE, editor; b. Asheville, N.C., Aug. 1, 1938; d. Carson Cowan and Anne (Brown) F. A.B., Salem Coll., 1960; M.A., William and Mary Coll., 1966. Asst. editor Inst. Early Am. Hist. and Culture, Williamsburg, Va., 1961-66, asso. editor, 1966; editor U. Press of Va., Charlottesville, 1966—. Office: Box 3608 University Sta Charlottesville VA 22903

FOBES, DONALD EDWARDS, lawyer; b. Ridgewood, N.J., Sept. 23, 1910; s. Hiram and Carrie (Edwards) F.; m. Nancy W. Garoutte, Dec. 29, 1950; children—David L., Katherine F. (Mrs. Edward S. Gilfillian III), Alison F. Grad. Loomis, Sch., 1928; B.A., Yale, 1932; LL.B., Columbia, 1935. Bar: N.Y. bar 1935, Mass. bar 1972. Practiced in, N.Y.C.; asso. Cadwalader, Wickersham & Taft, 1935-36, Cravath, Swaine & Moore, 1936-42; with Asiatic Petroleum Corp., 1942-69, formerly v.p., sec., dir. Home: Main Rd Chesterfield MA 01012

FOCH, NINA, actress, educator; b. Leyden, Netherlands, Apr. 20, 1924; came to U.S., 1928; d. Dirk and Consuelo (Flowerton) F.; m. James Lipton, June 6, 1954; m. Dennis R. Brite, Nov. 27, 1959; m. Michael Dewell, Oct. 31, 1967. Grad., Lincoln Sch., 1939. Adj. prof. U. So. Calif., 1966-68, 78-80; artist-in-residence U. N.C., 1966, Ohio State U., 1967, Calif. Inst. Tech., 1969-70; mem. sr. faculty Am. Film Inst., 1973-77; founder, tchr. Nina Foch Studio, Hollywood, Calif., 1973—; a founder, actress Los Angeles Theatre Group, 1960-65; Bd. dirs. Nat. Repertory Theatre, 1967-75. Appeared in: motion pictures Nine Girls, 1944, Return of the Vampire, 1944, Shadows in the Night, 1944, Cry of the Werewolf, 1944, Escape in the Fog, 1945, A Song to Remember, 1945, My Name Is Julia Ross, 1945, I Love a Mystery, 1945, Johnny O'Clock, 1947, The Guilt of Janet Ames, 1947, The Dark Past, 1948, The Undercover Man, 1949, Johnny Allegro, 1949, An American in Paris, 1951, Scaramouche, 1952, Young Man with Ideas, 1952, Sombrero, 1953, Fast Company, 1953, Executive Suite, 1954, Four Guns to the Border, 1954, You're Never Too Young, 1955, Illegal, 1955, The Ten Commandments, 1956, Three Brave Men, 1957, Cash McCall, 1959, Spartacus, 1960, Such Good Friends, 1971, Salty, 1973, Mahogany, 1976, Jennifer, 1978, Rich and Famous, 1981; appeared in: Broadway plays including John Loves Mary, 1947, Twelfth Night, 1949, A Phoenix Too Frequent, 1950, King Lear, 1950, Second String, 1960; Am. Shakespeare Festival in Taming of the Shrew, Measure for Measure, 1956; appeared with, San Francisco Ballet and Opera in, The Seven Deadly Sins, 1966; also many regional theatre appearances including, Seattle Repertory Theatre (All Over, 1972 and The Seagull, 1973); actress on TV, 1947—, including, Playhouse 90, Studio One, Pulitzer Playhouse, Playwrights 56, Producers Showcase, Lou Grant; many other series, network spls. and TV films; TV panelist and guest on: also others The Dinah Shore Show; TV moderator: Let's Take Sides, 1957-59; asso. dir.: film The Diary of Ann Frank, 1959; dir.: nat. tour and on Broadway Tonight at 8:30, 1966-67; asso. producer re-opening, Ford's Theatre, Washington, 1968; (nominated for Emmy award for supporting performance Lou Grant 1980). Hon. chmn. Los Angeles chpt. Am. Cancer Soc., 1970. Recipient Film Daily award, 1949, 53; nominated for Acad. Award for supporting performance Executive Suite, 1954. Mem. Acad. Motion Pictures Arts and Scis. (exec. com. fgn. film award, exec. com. student film award, com. mem. spl. projects), Hollywood Acad. TV Arts and Scis. (gov. 1976-77). Address: PO Box 1884 Beverly Hills CA 90213

FOCHT, JOHN ARNOLD, JR., geotechnical engineer; b. Rockwall, Tex., Aug. 31, 1923; s. John Arnold and Fay (Goss) F.; m. Edith Rials, Aug. 8, 1950; children: John Arnold III, Judith Lynn Focht. B.S. in C.E., U. Tex., 1944, M.S., Harvard U., 1946. Soils engr. U.S. Waterways Expt. Sta., Vicksburg, Miss., 1947-50, 52-53; sr. soils engr. McClelland Engrs., Inc., Houston, 1953-55, v.p. engring., 1955-72, exec. v.p., 1972—; v.p. TERA, Inc., 1965—. Contbr. articles to tech. jours. Chmn. ofcl. bd. Grace Methodist Ch., 1960-62; bd. dirs. N.W. YMCA, 1957-59; chmn. vis. com. dept. civil engring. U. Tex., Austin, 1974. Served to capt. AUS, 1944-46, 50-52. Recipient Distinguished Engring. Alumnus award U. Tex., Austin, 1964. Fellow ASCE (nat. dir. 1980-83, nat. v.p. 1983-85, pres. Tex. sect. 1970-71, Thomas A. Middlebrooks award 1957, 76, James Laurie prize 1959, Civil Engring. State of the Art award 1971, 79); mem. Nat., Tex. socs. profl. engrs., Am. Cons. Engrs. Council, Cons. Engrs. Council Tex. (dir. 1965-67), Tex. Council Engring. Labs. (dir. 1972-75), Houston Engring. and Sci. Soc. (treas., dir. 1973-76). Methodist. Home: 12226 Perthshire Houston TX 77024 Office: 6100 Hillcroft Ave Houston TX 77081

FOCKE, THEODORE BROWN, corp. exec.; b. Cleve., Sept. 16, 1904; s. Theodore Moses and Anne (Bosworth) F.; m. Mary duPont; children—William B., H. Elizabeth, Mary L. B.S., Case Inst. Tech., 1926; D.Sc., U. Nancy, France, 1928. Engr. Perfection Stove Co., 1929-42; factory mgr., gen. mgr. Curtiss-Wright Corp., 1946-49; v.p., gen. mgr. Wright Aero. Corp., 1949-52; pres., dir. Nat. Radiator Co., 1952-55, Nat.-U.S. Radiator Corp., 1955-60; v.p., gen. mgr. plumbing, heating, air conditioning group Crane Co., 1960; v.p. finance and adminstrn. The Mitre Corp., Bedford, Mass., 1961-63; pres., dir. The Better Tire Sales Co., Johnstown, Pa., 1963—, Wm. K. Stamets Co., Pitts., 1964-74. Served with Bur. Aeros. USN, 1942-46. Mem. Am. Soc. Metals. Home: 930 Windan Lane Johnstown PA 15905 Office: 119 Roosevelt Blvd Johnstown PA 15907

FODERARO, ANTHONY HAROLDE, nuclear engineering educator; b. Scranton, Pa., Apr. 3, 1926; s. Edward and Myrtha (Bachman) F.; m. Rita Lacey, May 4, 1953; children—Anthony, John, Diana. B.S. in Physics, U. Scranton, 1950, Ph.D., U. Pitts., 1955. Supervisory scientist Westinghouse Atomic Power Div., Pitts., 1954-56; sr. nuclear physicist Gen. Motors Research, Warren, Mich., 1956-60; asso. prof. nuclear engring. Pa. State U., University Park, 1960-63, prof., 1963—; cons. on radiation protection govt. and industry. Author: The Elements of Neutron Interaction Theory, 1971, The Photon Shielding Manual, 1976; co-author: The Reactor Shielding Design Manual, 1956, The Engineering Compendium on Radiation Shielding, 1968; contbr. articles to publs. in field. Served with U.S. Army, 1944-46. Fellow Am. Nuclear Soc. (chmn. radiation protection and shielding div. 1969-70); mem. Am. Phys. Soc., Am. Assn. Physics Tchrs., Health Physics Soc. Home: 301 S Gill St State College PA 16801 Office: 231 Sackett Bldg University Park PA 16802

FODOR, EUGENE, editor, publisher; b. Léva, Hungary, Oct. 14, 1905; came to U.S., 1938, naturalized, 1942; s. Gyula Mátyás and Malvin (Kürti) F.; m. Vlasta Maria Zobel, Dec. 4, 1948. Baccalaureat, Lucenec, Czechoslovakia, 1924; Licencié ès Econ. Politique, Faculté de Droit, U. Grenoble, France, 1927; postgrad., U. Hamburg, Germany. Travel corr. Prague Hungarian Jour., 1930-33; travel editor European Travel Guides, London, 1934-38; fgn. editor Query mag., London, 1937-38; editor, pub. Fodor's Modern Guides, Inc., Paris, France, 1949-64, pres., Litchfield, Conn., 1964—; chmn. bd. Fodor's Modern Guides, Ltd., London, 1964—. Editor 66 travel books pub. annually, 1950, trans. French, German, Italian, Dutch, Spanish, Hungarian. Served to capt. AUS, 1942-47. Recipient Grand prix de Littérature de Tourisme, 1959; award Caribbean Tourist Assn., 1960; Spl. award Pacific Area Tourist Assn., Hong Kong, 1962; Austrian Govt. Honor medal, 1970; other recent awards, England, Spain, Italy; Discover Am. Travel Orgn. award New Orleans, 1975; Travel Hall of Fame award, 1978. Mem. Nat. Assn. Travel Orgns. (award 1966), Soc. Am. Travel Writers, Internat. Union Ofcl. Travel Orgns., Fedn. Internat. des Journalistes et Ecrivains de Tourisme, Pacific Area Travel Assn., S.Am. Travel Orgn., Caribbean Tourist Assn. Home: Norfolk Rd Litchfield CT 06759 Office: PO Box 784 Litchfield CT 06759 *International tourism has become the greatest mass migration in human history. Nearly 300 million travelers a year crisscross each other's boundaries in a peaceful, useful and joyful invasion. They are the most effective communicators and promoters of good will, and we in the travel industry are their prime movers.*

FODOR, EUGENE NICHOLAS, concert violinist; b. Denver, Mar. 5, 1950; s. Eugene Nicholas and Antoinette Elizabeth (Pastore) F. Student preparatory div., Juilliard Sch. Music, 1967-68; Heifetz Master Class, U. So. Cal., 1970-71; performers certificate, Ind. U., 1969-70. Made solo debut, Denver Symphony Orch.; soloist with numerous symphony orchs.; performed at, White House, 1974; rec. artist, RCA. Recipient 1st prize Merriweather Post Competition, 1967, 1st prize Internat. Paganini Competition, 1972, 5th Internat. Tchaikovsky Violin Competition, Key to N.Y.C. Office: care Kazuko Hillyer Internat Inc 250 W 57th St New York NY 10107 *

FODOR, GABOR BELA, chemistry educator, researcher; b. Budapest, Hungary, Dec. 5. 1915; came to U.S., 1969, naturalized, 1976; s. Domokos Victor and Paula Maria (Bayer) F. Cand. Ing., Poly Inst., Graz, Austria, 1934; Ph.D., Szeged U., (Hungary), 1937; D.Sc., Acad. Scis., Budapest, 1952. Univ. asst. Szeged U., (Hungary), 1935-38, assoc. prof., prof., 1945-57; research chemist Chinoin Pharm. Ltd., Budapest, Hungary, 1938-45; head stereochemistry Lab. of Acad., Budapest, Hungary, 1958-65; prof. Laval U., Que., Can., 1965-69; centennial prof. chemistry W.Va. U., Morgantown, 1969—; regional dir. Nat. Found. Cancer Research, Bethesda, Md., 1977—. Author: Organische Chemie I-II, 1966; contbr. articles to prof. jours.; patentee in field. Recipient Kossuth prize, Budapest, 1950, 54, Silver medal U. Helsinski, 1958; fellow Churchill Coll. Cambridge, Eng., 1961—. Mem. Am. Chem. Soc., Can. Inst. Chemistry, Am. Inst. Chemists, Chem. Soc. London. Calvinist. Club: Lakeview Country (Morgantown). Office: Dept Chemistry WVa U Morgantown WV 26506

FOEHR, DONALD L., automotive parts company executive, accountant; b. Portsmouth, Ohio, Sept. 1, 1930; s. Harry and Violet (Ater) F.; m. Donna L. Poole, Dec. 27, 1952; children: Danial L., Stephen L., Lora L. B.S., Mich. State U., 1952, M.A., 1957. C.P.A., Ohio, Mich. Staff acct. Price Waterhouse, Toledo, 1957-62, audit mgr., Detroit, 1962-65; controller, v.p. DAB Industries Inc., Detroit, 1965-70; v.p. Republic Automotive Parts Inc., East Detroit, 1970-79, exec. v.p., chief fin. officer, 1979—. Mgr. and officer Bloomfield Little League, Bloomfield Hills, Mich., 1964-76; com. chmn. Boy Scouts Am., 1965-70. Served to lt. U.S. Army, 1952-54. Mem. Mich. Assn. C.P.A.s, Am. Inst. C.P.A.s, Fin. Execs. Inst. Republican. Clubs: Cranbrook Tennis (Bloomfield Hills) (treas. 1970-72, pres. 1973-74. Office: Republic Automotive Parts Inc 22777 Kelly Rd East Detroit MI 48021

FOELBER, CHARLES HEPBURN, insurance company executive; b. Fort Wayne, Ind., Nov. 20, 1924; s. Herbert Jacob and Marie (Roesner) F.; m. Lois Ann Rieck, July 1, 1950; children: Charles R., John T., Susan M., Michael D. Student, U. Mich., 1947-48; B.A., Valparaiso U., 1949. With U.S. Fidelity & Guaranty Co., Balt., 1951—, sr. exec. v.p., dir., 1970—; dir. Md. Nat. Bank. Mem. exec. bd. Balt. Area council Boy Scouts Am.; trustee Deaton Med. Center, Balt.; bd. dirs. Valparaiso U. Served with AUS, 1943-44; to 2d lt. USAAF, 1944-45. Mem. Rho Lamda Tau. Republican. Lutheran. Club: Center (Balt.). Office: U S Fidelity & Guaranty Co 100 Light St Baltimore MD 21202

FOELL, EARL WILLIAM, editor; b. Houston, Sept. 21, 1929; s. Ernest W. and Margaret (Kane) F.; m. Cordelia Treanor, Sept. 20, 1962; children: David, Jonathan, Hayden. B.A., Principia Coll., 1949. Reporter, editorial writer, fgn. corr. Christian Sci. Monitor, Boston, 1953-68; UN corr. Los Angeles Times, 1968-70; mng. editor Christian Sci. Monitor, 1970-79, editor, 1979-83, editor-in-chief, 1983—. Home: 43 Black Horse Ln Cohasset MA 02025 Office: 1 Norway St Boston MA 02115

FOELL, WESLEY KAY, engineer, energy and environmental scientist, educator; b. Elgin, Ill., May 20, 1935; s. Otto William and Lillian Mae (Hari) F.; m. Anne C. Schuller, Oct. 6, 1962. B.S.E.E., Stanford U., 1958, Ph.D. in Nuclear Engring, 1964; M.S. MIT, 1959. Scientist Phillips Petroleum Co., Idaho Falls, Idaho, 1962-64, Nuclear Research Center, Karlsruhe, Germany, 1965-66; vis. asso. prof. nuclear engring. and environ. studies U. Wis., Madison, 1967-69, asso. prof., 1969-74, prof., 1974—; head, ecology environ. dept. Internat. Inst. Applied Systems Analysis, Austria, 1975-76; cons. Argonne (Ill.) Nat. Labs., Ford Found. Author: Small-Sample Reactivity Measurements in Nuclear Reactors, 1972, Resources and Decisions, 1975, (with C.J. Cicchetti) Energy Systems Forecasting, Planning and Pricing, 1975, Management of Energy/Environment Systems: Methods and Case Studies, 1979, National Perspectives on Management of Energy/Environment Systems, 1983. OECD. NSF fellow, 1959-60; AEC fellow, 1958-59. Mem. AAAS, Phi Beta Kappa, Tau Beta Pi. Home: 35 Bagley Ct Madison WI 53705 Office: Energy Research Center U Wis 1402 University Ave Madison WI 53706

FOERSTER, BERND, educator; b. Danzig, Dec. 5, 1923; U.S., 1947, naturalized, 1954; s. Joseph and Martha (Brumm) F.; m. Enell Dowling, May 13, 1950; children: Kent, Mark (dec.). Student, Columbia U., 1948-49; B.S. in Architecture, U. Cin., 1954; M.Arch., Rensselaer Poly. Inst., 1957. Worked for Govt. Netherlands, 1945-47; with various engrs. and architects offices, 1950-59, ch. bldg. cons., design cons., 1954—; instr. architecture U. Cin., 1954, Rensselaer Poly. Inst., Troy, N.Y., 1954-56, asst. prof., 1956-62, asso. prof., 1962-65, prof., 1965-71; prof., dean Coll. Architecture and Design, Kans. State U., Manhattan, 1971—; cons. archtl. and community surveys N.Y. State Council on Arts, 1962-71; chmn. Gov.'s Adv. Com. on Historic Preservation in N.Y. State, 1968-71; cons. Albany Hist. Sites Commn., 1967-71, Independence (Mo.) Heritage Commn., 1975-77; leader U.S. del. on preservation planning to China, 1982. Author: Man and Masonry, 1960, Pattern and Texture, 1961, Architecture Worth Saving in Rensselaer County, N.Y, 1965, (with others) Independence, Missouri, 1978; films Man and Masonry, 1961 (Am. Film Festival selection); film What Do You Tear Down Next?, 1964, Earth and Fire, 1964, Assault on the Wynantskill, 1967. Dir. Mohawk-Hudson Council on Ednl. TV, 1968-71, v.p., 1970-71; co-chmn. Conf. on Rensselaer County, 1966; pres. Rensselaer County Council for Arts, 1963-64, 66-67; Bd. dirs. Albany Inst. History and Art, 1967-71; trustee Olana Historic Site, 1969-71; pres. bd. trustees Riley County Hist. Mus., 1977; chmn. Manhattan Downtown Redevel. Adv. Bd., 1979—; mem. State Bldg. Adv. Commn., 1980-82. Mem. AIA (com. historic resources 1977—, state preservation coordinator 1979—); mem. AIA Coll. Fellows; Mem. Kans. Soc. Architects (sec. 1975, exec. com. 1975-80, pres. elect 1978, pres. 1979—), Nat. Trust Hist. Preservation (bd. advs. 1979-81, trustee 1981—), Nature Conservancy, AAUP (past chpt. pres.), Assn. Collegiate Schs. Architecture, The Land Inst. (dir. 1976—), Manhattan Arts Council (dir. 1973-78, pres. 1976-77), Kans. Preservation Alliance (dir. 1979—), Nat. Council Preservation Edn. (dir. 1980—, vice-chmn. 1981—), Sierra Club, Audubon Soc., Scarab, Tau Sigma Delta., Phi Kappa Phi. Club: Rotary. Home: 920 Ratone Street Manhattan KS 66502

FOERSTER, PAUL FRIEDRICH, chemical company executive; b. Grevesmuehlen, Ger., June 12, 1929; came to U.S., 1967; s. Paul Friedrich and Marie Martha (Holldorf) F.; m. Ruth Ingrid Susanne Krueger, May 9, 1953; children: Thomas Friedrich-Wilhelm F., Claus-Christoph F. M.A. with honors, U. Greifswald, W.Ger., 1953, Ph.D., German Acad. Sci., U. Greifswald, 1956. Research asst. U. Greifswald, 1950-58; research asso. German Acad. Sci., 1953-56; research mgr. mfg. mgmt., corp. staff Hoechst AG, Frankfurt, W. Ger., 1956-67; v.p. Hystron Fibers Inc., Spartanburg, S.C., 1967-74; exec. v.p. Hoechst Fibers Industries, Spartanburg, 1975—. Dir. United Way, Spartanburg, 1973-76; trustee Mary Black Meml. Hosp., 1976—; mem. ch. council St. John's Luth. Ch., Spartanburg, 1971-74. Mem. AMA, S.C. Textile Mfrs. Assn., German-Am. C. of C. (dir. 1982-84). Clubs: Piedmont, AAA Country (Spartanburg). Patentee in field. Office: PO Box 5887 Spartanburg SC 29304

FOFONOFF, NICHOLAS PAUL, oceanographer, educator; b. Queenstown, Alta., Can., Aug. 18, 1929; came to U.S., 1962; s. Paul Alexander and Anna Dimitri (Malakoff) F.; m. Mabel Beryl Hutton Deckard, June 16, 1951; children—Paul Wynn, Stephanie Anne, Timothy Wayne, Nicholas David. B.A., U. B.C., Can.), Vancouver, 1950; M.A., 1951; Ph.D., Brown U., 1955. Postdoctoral fellow Nat. Inst. Oceanography, Eng., 1955-56; scientist Fisheries Research Bd. Can., 1956-62; sr. scientist Woods Hole (Mass.) Oceanographic Instn., 1962—, chmn. dept. phys. oceanography, 1967-71, 81—; prof. practice of phys. oceanography, Harvard U., 1968—; asso. mem. Center for Earth and Planetary Physics, 1971—. Mem. AAAS. Research in dynamics of ocean circulation, phys. properties and thermodynamics of seawater, application of buoy systems to measurement of ocean currents. Home: 6 Greengate Rd Falmouth MA 02540 Office: Woods Hole Oceanographic Instn Woods Hole MA 02543

FOFT, JOHN WILLIAM, physician, educator; b. Los Angeles, May 13, 1928; s. Wilford L. and Mary E. (McMahon) F.; m. Marianne T. Deibler, Mar. 12, 1957; children—John, Christine. B.S., U. Nebr., 1951; M.D., 1954. Intern Mpls. Gen. Hosp., 1954-55; asst. prof. pathology, dep. dir. clin. chemistry U. Chgo., 1965-67; asso. prof. clin. pathology U. Ala., 1968-70, dir. pediatric-clin. pathology lab., 1968-70, dep. chmn. research clin. pathology, 1969-70, prof., chmn. dept. clin. pathology, 1970-77, clin. prof. dept. pathology, 1977—; chmn. dept. pathology Carraway Meth. Med. Center, 1977—, Norwood Clinic, 1977—. Served as capt. AUS, 1955-57; Served as capt. USAF, 1961-64. Nat. Heart Inst. fellow U. Minn. Hosps., 1959-61; Am. Cancer Soc. scholar Argonne Cancer Research Hosp., 1968. Mem. N.Y. Acad. Scis., Am. Assn. Pathologists, AAAS, Coll. Am. Pathologists, AMA, Ala. Assn. Pathologists, Jefferson County Med. Soc., Birmingham Acad. Medicine, World Assn. of Socs. of Pathology (chmn. subcom. on instrument repair Council on World Standards in Clin. Pathology), Sigma Xi, Alpha Omega Alpha. Research on clin. lab. systems in developing countries. Home: 3529 Spring Valley Ct Birmingham AL 35223

FOGARTY, JOHN THOMAS, lawyer; b. N.Y.C., Aug. 17, 1929; s. Michael T. and Marguerite (Carmody) F.; m. Anna Weidehaus, Nov. 29, 1952; children: Kathleen, Michael, Carol, Teresa. B.B.A. cum laude, CCNY, 1953; J.D., St. John's U., 1959; postgrad., N.Y. U. Sch. Law, 1960-62. Office acct. Ex-Lax, Inc., N.Y.C., 1957-61, asst. sec., controller, 1961-69, v.p., sec., controller, 1969-71; sec., hdqrs. counsel Schering Corp., Bloomfield, N.J., 1971—; sec., asso. gen. counsel Schering-Plough Corp., Madison, N.J., 1973—, staff v.p., 1980—. Mem. adv. com. Twp. of Warren. Served to lt. Supply Corps USNR, 1953-57. Mem. Am., N.Y. State, N.J. bar assns., Phi Alpha Delta. Republican. Club: Optimist (Warren, N.J.) (sec. 1971-72). Home: 22 Mountain Ave Warren NJ 07060 Office: One Giralda Farms Madison NJ 07940

FOGARTY, ROBERT STEPHEN, historian, magazine executive; b. Bklyn., Aug. 30, 1938; s. Michael Joseph and Marguerita (Carmody) F.; m. Geraldine Wolpman, Dec. 30, 1961 (div.); children: David, Suzanne. B.A., Fordham U., 1960; Ph.D., U. Denver, 1968. Instr. Mich. State U., 1963-67; asst. prof. Antioch Coll., Yellow Springs, Ohio, 1968-73, chmn. humanities area, 1973-74, 78-79, asso. prof., 1974-80, prof. history, 1980—; editor Antioch Rev., 1977—; dir. Asso. Colls. Midwest/Gt. Lakes Coll. Assn.; Program in Humanities, Newberry Library, 1978-79; cons. Nat. Endowment for Arts, 1975-81, U. Waterloo, Ont., Can., 1981—. Author: Dictionary of American Communal and Utopian History, 1980, The Righteous Remnant - The House of David, 1981. Am. Philos. Soc. grantee, 1976; Am. Council Learned Socs. grantee; NEH fellow; recipient Martha K. Cooper award for editorial achievement, 1981. Mem. Am. Studies Assn. (bibliography com. 1981—, editorial bd. Alternative Futures 1977—), Nat. Hist. Communal Sites Assn. (exec. com. 1975-80, Orgn. Am. Historians.). Office: Antioch Rev Antioch Coll Box 148 Yellow Springs OH 45387

FOGARTY, WILLIAM THOMAS, steel company executive; b. Cleve., Dec. 30, 1923; s. James Linus and Frances A. (Haley) F.; m. Helen A. LaViolette, June 12, 1948; children—Susan, Patricia, Barbara, Colleen. B.S. cum laude, Kent State U., 1949. C.P.A., Ohio. Audit mgr. Price Waterhouse & Co., Cleve., 1949-61, resident mgr., Columbus, 1961-66; asst. comptroller Youngstown Sheet & Tube Co., Ohio, 1966-71, dep. comptroller, 1971, treas., 1971-75, Lykes-Youngstown Corp., 1973-75; comptroller, New Orleans, 1975-79; dir. internal audit LTV Corp., Dallas, 1979—; ltd. service instr. accounting Youngstown State U., 1967-70. Served with USNR, 1942-46. Mem. Am. Inst. C.P.A.s, Ohio Soc. C.P.A.s. Club: Scioto Country (Columbus). Home: 6729 Regal Bluff Dallas TX 75248 Office: PO Box 22503 Dallas TX 75248

FOGEL, BERNARD J., university administrator, pediatrics educator, physician; b. N.Y.C., Nov. 30, 1936; s. Isadore and Shirley E. F.; m. Judith Ann, June 8, 1958; children: Lori, Wendy, Amy. M.D., U. Miami, 1961. Cert. Fla. Bd. Med. Examiners, Nat. Bd. Med. Examiners. Researcher Walter Reed Army Inst., Washington, 1964-66; Am. Cancer Soc. fellow U. Miami (Fla.) Sch. Medicine, 1966-69, dir. newborn services, 1966-69; dir. Birth Defects Ctr. U. Miami (FLa.) Sch. Medicine, 1966-74; assoc. dean med. edn. U. Miami (Fla.) Sch. Medicine, 1970-76, assoc. dean research, 1971-73, asst. v.p. med. affairs, 1974-81, v.p., dean, 1981—, assoc. prof. pediatrics, 1970-76; prof. U. Miami (FLa.) Sch. Medicine, 1977—; ex-officio mem. bd. dirs. Pub. Health Trust Dade County, 1981—; bd. govs. U. Miami Hosps. and Clinics, 1981—, Bascolm Palmer Eye Inst., 1981. Chmn. program Greater Miami Coalition Careers for Minorities, 1971-73; trustee Mus. Sci. Dade County, 1973—; bd. dirs. HSA Dade County, 1978-82. Served as capt. U.S. Army, 1964-66. Nat. Allergy Found. fellow, 1958. Mem. Assn. Am. Med. Colls. (council of deans 1981—), Alpha Omega Alpha. Democrat. Jewish. Home: 9240 SW 120th St Miami FL 33176 Office: U Miami PO Box 016099 R-699 Miami FL 33101

FOGEL, ROBERT WILLIAM, educator, economist, historian; b. N.Y.C., July 1, 1926; s. Harry Gregory and Elizabeth (Mitnik) F.; m. Enid Cassandra Morgan, Apr. 2, 1949; children: Michael Paul, Steven Dennis. A.B., Cornell U., 1948; A.M., Columbia U., 1960; Ph.D., Johns Hopkins U., 1963; M.A., U. Cambridge, Eng., 1975, Harvard U., 1976. Instr. Johns Hopkins U., 1958-59; asst. prof. U. Rochester, 1960-64; Ford Found. vis. research prof. U. Chgo., 1963-64, asso. prof., 1964-65, prof. econs., 1965-69, prof. econs. and history, 1970-75; prof. econs. U. Rochester, 1968-71, prof. econs. and history, 1972-75; Taussig research prof. Harvard U., Cambridge, Mass., 1973-74, Harold Hitchings Burbank prof. polit. economy, prof. history, 1975-81; Charles R. Walgreen prof. Am. instns. U. Chgo., 1981—; Pitt prof. Am. history and insts. U. Cambridge, 1975-76; chmn. com. math. and statis. methods in history Math. Social Sci. Bd., 1965-72. Author: The Union Pacific Railroad: A Case in Premature Enterprise, 1960, Railroads and American Economic Growth: Essays in Econometric History, 1964, (with others) The Reinterpretation of American Economic History, 1971, Dimensions of Quantitative Research in History, 1972, (with S.L. Engerman) Time on the Cross: The Economics of American Negro Slavery, 1974, Ten Lectures on the New Economic History, 1977, (with G.R. Elton) Which Road to the Past? Two Views of History, 1983. Gilman fellow, 1957-60; Social Sci. Research Council fellow, 1960; faculty research grantee, 1966; NSF grantee, 1967, 70, 72, 75, 76, 78; Fulbright grantee, 1968; Ford Found. faculty research fellow, 1970; recipient Arthur H. Cole prize, 1968; Schumpeter prize, 1971; co-recipient The Bancroft prize, 1975. Fellow Econometric Soc., Royal Hist. Soc., AAAS; mem. Am., Royal econ. socs., Econ. History Assn. (trustee 1972—, pres. 1977-78), Econ. History Soc., Am. Hist. Assn., Assn. Am. Historians, Social Sci. History Assn. (pres. 1980-81), Agrl. History Soc., Am. Acad. Arts and Scis., Nat. Acad. Scis., Population Assn. Am., Internat. Union for Sci. Study of Population, Phi Beta Kappa. Office: 118 Rosenwald U Chgo Chicago IL 60637

FOGEL, SEYMOUR, artist; b. N.Y.C., Aug. 25, 1911; s. Benjamin and Lillian (Jones) F.; m. Barbara Clark, Nov. 6, 1936; children: Gail, Jared Allen. Student, Art Students League, N.Y.C., 1929, NAD, 1929-32. Asst. prof. art U. Tex., 1946-54; vis. prof. Mich. State U., 1960; lectr. colls., 1948—. Artist, mural painter, 1934—; Artist one-man shows include, McNey Inst.; San Antonio, Houston, Santa Barbara and Ft. Worth mus., M. Knoedler Gallery, Duveen Graham, 1955, 81-83, Allan Stone Gallery, N.Y.C., Stamford (Conn.) Art Mus., 1981, also Can., S.Am., Eng., group shows include, Met. Mus., Whitney Mus., Mus. Modern Art, Archtl. League N.Y., Berlin, Hamburg, 1980, 81, represented in permanent collections, Whitney Mus., Dallas and Houston mus., Hirshhorn Collection, Mich. State U., U. Mo., City St. Louis Art Mus., Ft. Worth Art Center, Nat. Archives Am. Art, executed numerous stained, glass, paintings and mosaics for sch., hosps., govt. bldgs., pvt. instns., including lobby for, Social Security Bldg., Washington, 1942, Hoffmann-LaRoche Research Tower, Nutley, N.J., 1964, U.S. Fed. Bldg., Ft. Worth, 1966, Bklyn. pub. schs., 1967, U.S. Customs Ct. Bldg., N.Y.C., 1968, Gouveneur Hosp., N.Y.C., 1971, Bellevue Hosp., 1973, Sch. 383, Bklyn., 1976, New Park West High Sch., N.Y.C., 1976-77. Recipient awards U.S. Govt. sponsored competitions for mural painting, 1940-41; Silver medal Archtl. League N.Y., 1958; 1st prize Gulf Caribbean Internat., Houston, 1956, Tex. Gen. Exhbn., 1956. Mem. Archtl. League N.Y. (past v.p.). Address: Torandor 339 Georgetown Rd Weston CT 06883 Office: 1014 Madison Ave New York NY 10021

FOGELBERG, DANIEL GRAYLING, composer, recording artist; b. Peoria, Ill., Aug. 13, 1951; s. Lawrence Peter and Margaret Young (Irvine) F. Student, U. Ill., 1969-71. Founder Hickory Grove Music, Full Moon Prodns., 1971; v.p. Full Moon Prodns. Co.; free lance record producer, studio musician. Recordings Homefree, 1972, Souvenirs, 1974, Captured Angel, 1975, (with Tim Weisberg) Twin Sons of Different Mothers, 1979, Phoenix, 1980, The Innocent Age, 1981, Greatest Hits, 1982, Windows & Walls, 1983. Mem. ASCAP, AFTRA, Telstar. Office: care press relations Epic Records 1801 Century Park W Los Angeles CA 90067 *

FOGELMAN, MORRIS JOSEPH, physician; b. Chgo., Feb. 27, 1923; s. Joseph and Tillie (Schwartz) F.; children—Evan, Joe, Margo. B.A., U. Ill., 1941; M.D., 1944, M.S., 1948. Diplomate: Am. Bd. Surgery. Intern Wayne County Gen. Hosp., Eloise, Mich., 1944-45; resident Parkland Hosp., Dallas, 1948-51; research fellow dept. clin. sci. U. Ill. Coll. Medicine, Chgo., 1947-48, asst. physiology, 1947-48; asst. in physiology and pharmacology Southwestern Med. Sch., Dallas, 1948-50, fellow in surgery, 1948-52, instr. surgery, 1952-53, asst. prof. surgery, 1953, asso. prof. surgery, 1953, prof. surgery, 1954-57, clin. prof. surgery, 1957—; practice medicine, specializing in surgery, Dallas, 1952—; sr. attending surgeon Parkland Meml. Hosp., Dallas, 1953; cons. physician in surgery VA Hosp., Dallas, 1954; cons. surgeon Baylor Hosp., 1957, Parkland Meml. Hosp., 1952, Presbyn. Hosp., Dallas; pres. med. staff Presbyn. Hosp., U4Dallas, U71973, Morris J. Fogelman, M.D. & Assos., Dallas, 1972—; research dir. surgery Baylor Med. Center, 1972-78. Author: Fluid Balance; Contbr. articles to various publs. Served to capt., M.C. AUS, 1945-47. Fellow Am. Assn. Surgery of Trauma; mem. Am. Assn. History of Medicine, A.C.S., AAAS, AMA, Dallas County Med. Soc., Dallas Soc. Gen. Surgeons, Dallas County Clin. Soc., N.Y. Acad. Sci., Tex. Med. Assn., Sigma Xi. Home: 6921 Norway Pl Dallas TX 75231 Office: 8210 Walnut Hill Ln Suite 513 Dallas TX 75231

FOGELSON, DAVID, lawyer; b. Netcong, N.J., Mar. 15, 1903; s. Reuben and Sarah (Peshkin) F.; m. Gertrude Edelman, July 10, 1930; children—Ellen Fogelson Liman, James H. B.C.S., N.Y. U., 1923; LL.B., Fordham U., 1926. Bar: N.Y. bar 1928. With Nathan Burkan, N.Y.C., 1926-36; mem. firm Schwartz & Frohlich, N.Y.C., 1936-68. Pres. Joe and Emily Lowe Found. Home: 1 N Breakers Row Palm Beach FL 33480 Office: 720 Fifth Ave New York NY 10021

FOGERTY, ARTHUR JOSEPH, farm supply cooperative company executive; b. Troy, N.Y., June 1, 1938; s. Arthur Anthony and Mary Catherine (Shanahan) F.; m. Mary Jane Grindrod, Aug. 17, 1963; children: Mark, Tara, Matthew. B.A., Siena Coll., 1960. Dist. dir. N.Y. State CD Commn., Albany, 1962-71; mgr. govt. relations Agway Inc., Syracuse, N.Y., 1971-73, sr. v.p. corp. relations, 1982—; dir. Curtice-Burns Food, Rochester, N.Y.; trustee Am. Inst. Cooperation, Washington, 1982—, Agrl. Co-op. Devel. Internat., 1982—. Pres. Citizens Found, Syracuse, 1978-80; trustee Future Bus. Leaders Am., N.Y. State, 1979—; bd. dirs. Literacy Vols. N.Y.C., 1980-83. Mem. Bus. Council N.Y. State, U.S. C. of C., Syracuse C. of C. (bd. dirs. 1982—), Fertilizer Inst., Nat. Council Farmer Coops. Roman Catholic. Home: 7459 Armstrong Rd Manlius NY 13104 Office: Agway Inc PO Box 4933 Syracuse NY 13221

FOGG, RICHARD LLOYD, food products company executive; b. Boston, Jan. 22, 1937; s. Lloyd Clark and Mildred Ann (Cass) F.; m. Carolyn Ann Kane, Feb. 12, 1966; children—Amanda C., Jennifer S., Timothy L. A.B., Bowdoin Coll., Brunswick, Maine, 1959; M.B.A., Cornell U., 1961. With brand mgmt. dept. Procter & Gamble Co., Cin., 1961-66; dir. mktg. mgmt. Hunt-Wesson Foods, Fullerton, Calif., 1967-76; sr. v.p. Amfac Food Group, Portland, Oreg., 1977; pres. subs. Fisher Cheese Co., Wapakoneta, Ohio, 1978-83; group v.p., chief operating officer Land O'Lakes Foods, Mpls., 1983—. Mem. Am. Mktg. Assn. Club: Shawnee Country. Home: 16 Buffalo Rd North Oaks MN 55110 Office: PO Box 116 Minneapolis MN 55440

FOGLE, RICHARD HARTER, educator; b. Canton, Ohio, Mar. 8, 1911; s. James Underhill and Amanda (Harter) F.; m. Catherine Pace Cox, Sept. 6, 1939; children—Catherine Harter, Faith Underhill. B.A., Hamilton Coll., Litt.D., 1967; M.A., Columbia, 1936; Ph.D., U. Mich., 1944. Instr. English U. Rochester, 1939-40, U. Mich., 1943-46; asst. prof., then prof. Tulane U., 1946-54, head dept. English, 1954-63, chmn., 1957-60, 63-66; prof. English U. N.C., Chapel Hill, 1966-68, Univ. Distinguished prof. English, 1968-81, prof. emeritus, 1981—. Author: The Imagery of Keats and Shelley, 1949, John Keats, Selected Poetry and Letters, 1951, Hawthorne's Fiction, 1952, rev. edit., 1964, Melville's Shorter Tales, 1960, The Idea of Coleridge's Criticism, 1962, The Romantic Movement in American Writing, 1966, Romantic Poets and Prose Writers, 1967, Hawthorne's Imagery, 1969, The Permanent Pleasure, 1974; Mem. editorial bd.: Keats-Shelley Jour. Fellow Melville Soc. (pres. 1961); mem. MLA (exec. com. 19th century Am. lit. group 1977—), So. Atlantic MLA, Internat. Assn. Univ. Profs. English, Modern Humanities Research Assn., Keats-Shelley Assn. Home: 511 E Rosemary St Chapel Hill NC 27514

FOGLEMAN, HARRY FRANK, development company executive; b. Johnson City, Tenn., May 21, 1931; s. E. Carl F.; m. Keturah Carroll, Oct. 15, 1960. B.S.E.E., Tenn. State U. Engr. Gen. Dynamics, San Diego, 1955-57; mgr. Arnoux, Los Angeles, 1957-60; pres. Aeromarine, San Diego, 1960-69, Gremlin Industries, 1969-80; vice chmn. Sega Electronics, San Diego, 1980-83, dir., 1970—; pres. KeyOne, Inc., San Diego, 1983—; dir. Cerprobe, Phoenix, AGMA, Washington, Penduflo, Scottsdale, Ariz. Patentee temperature apparatus, solid state switch, electronic game panel, underwater release. Served with USN, 1951-55. Home: 9955 Lemonwood Ln San Diego CA 92412 Office: KeyOne Inc 1022 W Morena Blvd San Diego CA 92110

FOGLEMAN, JOHN ALBERT, lawyer, former judge; b. Memphis, Nov. 5, 1911; s. John Franklin and Julia (McAdams) F.; m. Annis Adell Appleby, Oct. 24, 1933; children: John Albert, Annis Adell (Mrs. Henry M. Rector), Mary Barton (Mrs. Charles L. Williams, Jr.). Student, U. Ark., 1927-31; LL.B., U. Memphis, (now Memphis State U.), 1934. Bar: Ark. 1934. Dep. circuit ct. clk., Crittenden County, 1933-34, pvt. practice law, 1934-44; partner Hale & Fogleman, Marion and West Memphis, 1944-66; dep. pros. atty., Crittenden County, 1946-57; assoc. justice Ark. Supreme Ct., 1967-79, chief justice, 1980; of counsel firm Gill Skokos Simpson Buford & Owen, Little Rock, 1981—; mem. State Bd. Law Examiners, 1960-63; chmn. Ark. Judiciary Commn., 1963-65; mem. Ark. Constl. Revision Study Commn., 1967, Fed.-State Jud. Council, Ark., 1971-75, Ark. Criminal Code Revision Com., 1972-74; lectr. Sch. Law, U. Ark., 1981; assoc. justice Delta Theta Phi, 1981—. Active Ark. and Crittenden County Democratic central coms., 1937-44. Served from pvt. to 1st lt. AUS, 1944-45. Fellow Am. Coll. Trial Lawyers, Am. Bar Found.; mem. Ark. Bar Assn. (past pres.), N.E. Ark. Bar Assn. (past pres.), Crittenden County Bar Assn. (past pres.). Clubs: Masons, Rotary. Home: 67 Cherry St Marion AR 72364 Office: 300 Superior Federal Bldg Capitol at Broadway Little Rock AR 72201

FOGLEMAN, JULIAN BARTON, lawyer; b. Memphis, Apr. 17, 1920; s. John Franklin and Marie Julia (McAdams) F.; m. Melba Margaret Henderson, Aug. 11, 1950; children: Margaret Elisabeth, Julian Barton, John Nelson, Jennifer Leigh, Frances Lorie. B.S., U. Ark., 1941, LL.B., 1943, J.D., 1969. Bar: Ark. 1943. Practiced in Marion, 1946-54, West Memphis, 1954—, pvt. practice, 1946-52; asso. Hale & Fogleman, 1952-66, partner, 1967-73, Hale, Fogleman & Rogers, 1974—; city atty., Marion, 1951-81, dep. pros. atty., 1957-64. Chmn. finance drive Crittenden Dist.-Chickasaw council Boy Scouts Am., 1969; mem. exec. bd. Chickasaw council, 1970-71, 75-80; bd. dirs. Ark. Good Rds. Transp. Council, 1976—; mem. Ark. Community Based Rehab. Commn., 31978—. Served with inf. AUS, 1943-45; ETO. Mem. ABA, Ark. Bar Assn. (ho. of dels. 1972-75, 81-84, exec. council 1972-75, 81—), N.E. Ark. Bar Assn. (past pres.), Crittenden County Bar Assn. (past pres.), Phi Alpha Delta, Sigma Chi. Methodist. Home: 84 Turner Ave Marion AR 72364 Office: 108 Dover Rd West Memphis AR 72301

FOGLIETTA, THOMAS MICHAEL, congressman; b. Phila., Dec. 3, 1928; s. Michael and Rose (Buttari) F. B.A., St. Joseph's Coll.; student, Temple U. Bar: Pa. bar, U.S. Supreme Ct. bar. Practice law, Phila.; mem. U.S. Ho. of Reps. from 1st Dist. Pa.; Mem. Phila. City Council. Chmn. South Philadelphia chpt. ARC, Phila. chpt. Am. Cancer Soc.; mem. Phila. Mayor's Complete Count Com. Fed. Census; Bd. dirs. St. Luke's Hosp., Guiffre Med. Center, Phila. Easter Seal Soc. Mem. Sons of Italy, Justinian Soc. Roman Catholic. Address: Dist Office William J Green Bldg 6th and Arch Sts Philadelphia PA 19106 also 1217 Longworth Office Bldg Washington DC 20006

FOIL, ROBERT RODNEY, forestry educator; b. Bogalusa, La., Aug. 12, 1934; s. Earl Odell and Rose A. (Green) F.; m. Patti Sue Thomas, Jan. 20, 1959; children: Jerry Thomas, Allison. B.S. in Forestry, La. State U., 1956, M.F., 1960; D.Forestry, Duke U., 1965. Forester Union Camp Corp., Ga., 1956; instr., then asst. prof. La. State U., 1959-67; asso. specialist, specialist Coop. Extension Service, 1967-69; prof., head dept. forestry Miss. State U., 1969—, asso. dean Sch. Forest Resources, asso. dir. Miss. Agr. and Forestry Expt. Sta., 1972-73, dean, 1974-78, dir., 1978—; cons. in field. Contbr. articles profl. jours. Pres. Jr. C. of C., Homer, La., 1967. Served with AUS, 1956-58. Named Outstanding Young Man Homer (La.), 1967. Mem. Soc. Am. Foresters (chmn. Gulfstate sect. 1969, 76, chmn. Miss. chpt. 1972, mem. council 1978), Miss. Forestry Assn., La. Forestry Assn. (dir. 1969), Sigma Xi, Xi Sigma Pi, Alpha Zeta, Gamma Sigma Delta, Phi Kappa Phi. Home: 9 Cardinal Ln Starkville MS 39759

FOISIE, JACK, journalist; b. Seattle, Apr. 21, 1919; s. Francis Patrick and Winifred Amanda (Shaw) F.; m. Florence Mildred McTighe, Apr. 8, 1944; children—Kathleen Florence, Franklin Sean, Patricia Abbie. Student, U. Wash., 1938-39, U. Calif., Berkeley, 1940-41. Sports reporter Seattle Post-Intelligencer, 1937; jr. reporter Seattle Times, 1938; reporter San Francisco Chronicle, 1940, 45-64, corr., Korean War, 1953, Vietnam War, 1962; bur. chief in Saigon Los Angeles Times, 1964-66, Bangkok, 1966-74, Cairo, 1974-76, Johannesburg, 1976—. Tech. adviser: movie story of G.I. Joe, 1944; Contbr. to: and other nat. mags. Sat. Eve. Post. Served with AUS, 1941-45. Decorated Legion of Merit for combat coverage of campaign in Sicily; Nieman fellow, 1946-47; recipient Overseas Press Club award, 1966. Home: PO Box 5660 Johannesburg South Africa Office: Los Angeles Times Fgn Bur Times Mirror Sq Los Angeles CA 90053

FOK, THOMAS DSO YUN, civil engineer, educator; b. Canton, China, July 1, 1921; came to U.S., 1947, naturalized, 1956; s D. H. and C. (Tse) F.; m. Maria M.L. Liang, Sept. 18, 1949. B.Eng., Nat. Tung-Chi U., Szechuan, China, 1945; M.S., U. Ill., 1948; M.B.A. Dr. Nadler Money Marketeer scholar, NYU, 1950; Ph.D., Carnegie-Mellon U., 1956. Registered profl. engr., N.Y., Pa., Ohio, Ill., Ky., W.Va., Ind., Md., Fla. Structural designer Lummus Co., N.Y.C., 1951-53; design engr. Richardson, Gordon & Assocs., cons. engrs., Pitts., 1956-58; assoc. prof. engring. Youngstown U., Ohio, 1958-67, dir. computing ctr., 1963-67; ptnr. Cernica, Fok & Assocs., cons. engrs., Youngstown, Ohio, 1958-64; prin. Thomas Fok & Assocs., cons. engrs., Youngstown, Ohio, 1964-65; ptnr. Mosure-Fok & Syrakis Co., Ltd., cons. Engrs., Youngstown, Ohio, 1965-76; cons. engr. to Mahoning County Engr., Ohio, 1960-65; pres. Computing Systems & Tech., Youngstown, Ohio, 1967-72; chmn. Thomas Fok and Assocs., Ltd., cons. engrs., Youngstown, Ohio, 1977—. Contbr. articles to profl. jours. Trustee Pub. Library of Youngstown and Mahoning County, 1973—, Youngstown Ednl. Found, 1975—, Youngstown State U., 1975-84; chmn. Youngstown State U., 1981-83. Recipient Walter E. and Caroline H. Watson Found. Disting. Prof.'s award Youngstown U., 1966. Fellow ASCE; mem. Am. Concrete Inst., Internat. Assn. for Bridge and Structural Engring., Am. Soc. Engring. Edn., Nat. Soc. Profl. Engrs., AAAS, Soc. Am. Mil. Engrs., Ohio Acad. Sci., N.Y. Acad. Sci., Sigma Xi, Beta Gamma Sigma, Sigma Tau, Delta Pi Sigma. Lodge: Rotary. Home: 325 S Canfield-Niles Rd Youngstown OH 44515 Office: 3896 Mahoning Ave Youngstown OH 44515

FOLCARELLI, RALPH JOSEPH, library science educator, university dean; b. Phila., Oct. 5, 1928; s. Joseph John and Mary Theresa (DiTullio) F.; m. Carol Hoiriis Field, July 20, 1952; children: Michele Folcarelli Marshall, Guy. B.S., Kutztown State Coll., 1951; M.L.S., Rutgers U., 1958; Ph.D., NYU, 1972. Head librarian Mansfield State Coll., Pa., 1959-61; library coordinator Gold Spring Harbor Schs., N.Y., 1961-65; assoc. prof. Palmer Sch. Library and Info. Sci., C.W. Post Ctr., L.I.U., N.Y., 1965-75, prof. library sci., 1975-83, asst. v.p. acad. affairs, 1976-77, dean sch., 1982—; cons. L.I. Lighting Co., 1975, Xerox U. Microfilms, Ann Arbor, Mich., 1976, Nassau County Com. Coll., 1980, N.Y.C. Bd. Edn., 1980. Author: (with J.T. Gillespie and Diana L. Spirt) Multi-Media Kit-Library Learning Lab, 1980, (with R. Ferragamo and A. Tannenbaum) Microform Connection, 1982; reviewer: book-media revs. Sch. Library Jour., 1970. Trustee L.I. Library Resources Council, Bellport, N.Y., 1977-82, Huntington Pub. Library, N.Y., 1979—. Served with AUS, 1947-49. Recipient Founders Day award NYU, 1972. Mem. ALA, Am. Library Trustees Assn., NEA (life), N.Y. Library Assn. (pres. library educators sect. 1972), Suffolk County Library Assn., Huntington Hist. Soc., Kappa Delta Pi. Clubs: New York Library, Archons of Colophon (N.Y.C.). Home: 117 Bay Dr Huntington NY 11743 Office: Office of Dean Palmer Sch Library and Info Sci C.W. Post Ctr LI Univ Northern Blvd Greenvale NY 11548 *During the more than 30 years in the dynamic library profession, I have witnessed and been a part of many* *exciting changes. As a practicing librarian, as an active member of professional associations, and as a library educator I have actively and consistently attempted to upgrade the role and image of librarianship as a service-oriented profession; I have also been a strong advocate of the newer technology toward this goal.*

FOLDI, ANDREW HARRY, singer, educator; b. Budapest, Hungary, July 20, 1926; came to U.S., 1939, naturalized, 1947; s. Alexis and Ann (Rothman) F.; children: David John, Nancy Susanne. Ph.B., U. Chgo., 1945, M.A., 1948; pvt. student singing and piano. Music critic Chgo. Times, 1947; vis. prof. voice and opera Cleve. Inst. Mus., 1978—, chmn. opera dept., 1981—; mem. faculty U. Chgo., 1947-49, dept. adult edn., 1951-61; instr., dir. opera workshop DePaul U., 1949-57; vis. instr. voice Augustana Coll., 1950-51; pvt. tchr. voice, 1949—; cantor, mus. dir. Temple Isaiah Israel, Chgo., 1948-61, English-speaking Jewish Community of Geneva, 1966-72; faculty apprentice tng. program Santa Fe Opera, 1959, 64, 76, 77, also stage dir.; stage dir. Pa. Opera Festival, 1982—. Author: recorded text An Introduction to Music, 1959; also criticism, program notes; contbr. articles to profl. publs.; Leading bass, Met. Opera, N.Y.C., La Scala, Milan, Vienna Staatsoper, Teatro San Carlo, Naples, Vienna Festival, Grand Théâtre, Geneva, Théâtre Royale de la Monnaie, Brussels, Am. Nat. Opera, Cin. Opera, Stadttheater, Zurich, Teatro Comunale, Genoa, Nederlandsche Opera, Amsterdam, San Francisco Opera Co., Lyric Opera Chgo., Santa Fe Opera, Sociedad Pro Arte Mus., Havana, Cuba; guest soloist, Vienna Festival, Bavarian State Radio, Munich, Concertgebouw Orch., Amsterdam, Orch. de la Suisse Romande, Geneva, Nat. Orch. Monte Carlo, Pitts. Symphony Orch., Clarion Concerts, N.Y., Gulbenkian Found., Lisbon, Concerti sinfonici, Genoa, Atlanta Symphony Orch., Aldeburgh, Lucerne, Lausanne, Ravina, Glyndebourne festivals, Chgo. Symphony Orch., Boston Symphony, San Francisco Symphony, Little Orch. Soc., N.Y., Rochester, Kansas City (Mo.) philharmonic orchs., Radio Sottens, Geneva, Radio Beromunster, Zurich, Grant Park Concerts, Chgo., Indpls. Symphony Orch., Internat. Soc. Contemporary Arts, also numerous recitals, radio and TV appearances, recordings for, Vanguard, Concert Hall, La Voix d'Eglise. Mem. Am. Musicological Soc., Nat. Assn. Tchrs. Singing, Soc. Am. Musicians, Internat. Soc. Contemporary Music, Am. Guild Mus. Artists. Office: Cleve Inst Music 11021 East Blvd Cleveland OH 44106 also

FOLDS, CHARLES WESTON, merchandising cons.; b. Pitts., Oct. 22, 1910; s. George Robert and Camilla (McKey) F.; m. Suzanne Lord, Apr. 10, 1948; 1 dau., Suzanne Folds McCullagh. A.B., Yale, 1932. With Marshall Field & Co., 1932-72, v.p., 1957-70, sr. v.p., gen. mdse. mgr., 1970-72; cons., 1972—. Bd. dirs. Children's Meml. Hosp. Served as comdr. Supply Corps USNR, 1941-46; supply officer Mediterranean Forces, 1945. Decorated Bronze Star. Clubs: Chicago, University, Economic, Yale (Chgo.); Glen View (Golf) (Ill.). Home: 1200 Whitebridge Hill Winnetka IL 60093

FOLEY, ADRIAN M., JR., lawyer; b. Bartlett, N.D., Jan. 16, 1922. B.S. cum laude, Seton Hall U., 1943; LL.B., Columbia, 1947. Bar: N.J. 1948. Mem. firm Connell, Foley & Geiser, Newark; dir. Kay Elemetrics Corp., Prudential Life Ins. Co. Surrogate County of Essex, 1954-58; pres. N.J. Constl. Conv., 1966. Fellow Am. Bar Found., Am. Coll. Trial Lawyers; mem. ABA (gov., mem. ho. dels., chmn. commn. on advt. 1981—, chmn. sect. on litigation 1983-84), N.J. State Bar Assn. (trustee 1957-58, treas. 1958-61, 2d v.p. 1961-62, 1st v.p. 1962-63, pres. 1964-65), Montclair-West Essex Bar Assn., Hudson County Bar Assn., Essex County Bar Assn. (mem. practice and procedure in probate cts. com. 1956-58), Am. Coll. Probate Counsel, Am. Law Inst. Office: Gateway I Newark NJ 07102

FOLEY, DONALD WEBSTER, government official; b. Kingston, Ont., Can., July 26, 1928; s. Delbert Lloyd and Evelyn Joyce (Webster) F.; m. Jane Elizabeth Thurston, May 11, 1957. B.A. with honors, Queens U., Kingston, 1951, postgrad. in indsl. relations, 1953-54. Program analyst Fed. Treasury Bd., Ottawa, Ont., 1961-66; personnel adminstr. Fed. Ministry of Transport, Ottawa, 1966-68; exec. asst. to v.p. Can. Transport Commn., Ottawa, 1968-76, v.p. law, 1976-78, sec., 1978—. Office: 15 Eddy St Hull PQ K1A 0N9 Canada *

FOLEY, DORANCE VINCENT, clergyman; b. Ryan, Iowa, Apr. 6, 1900; s. Frank M. and Lillian (Synan) F. A.B., Campion Coll., 1921; student priesthood, St. Paul Sem., Minn., to 1925; LL.D., Loras Coll., 1947, Clarke Coll., 1975. Ordained priest Roman Catholic Ch., 1925; curate Nativity Ch., Dubuque, Iowa, 1925-26; chancellor and sec. Archdiocese of Dubuque, 1926-51; vicar gen., 1944-52, officialis, 1950-51, prothonotary apostolic, 1952—, papal chamberlain, 1934, domestic prelate, 1945; irremovable rector St. Patrick's Parish, Dubuque, 1952-56; dean Dubuque Roman Cath. Clergy, 1952-56; pres. Loras Coll., Dubuque, 1956-66, spl. asst. to pres. for devel., 1972—; pastor St. Patrick's Parish, Dubuque, 1966-72; Chaplain Mercy Hosp., Dubuque, 1926-31, Mt. Loretto, Dubuque, 1931-52; Vice pres., treas. Archdiocese Dubuque, Inc., 1944-52, archdiocesan consultor, 1944-81; v.p. Cath. Charities, Archdiocese of Dubuque; dir. The Witness, Cath. Charities, Inc., 1944-52. Served Students Army Tng. Corps., World War I. Mem. Am. Legion (past chaplain Dubuque post), C.O.F., Delta Epsilon Sigma. Club: K.C. Address: Loras College Dubuque IA 52001

FOLEY, DUNCAN KARL, economics educator; b. Columbus, Ohio, June 15, 1942; s. Gerald M. and Ruth C. (Johnson) F.; m. Helene Peet, June 11, 1966; 1 son, Nicholas C.B. B.A., Swarthmore Coll., 1964; Ph.D., Yale U., 1966. Asst. prof., assoc. prof. econs. MIT, Cambridge, 1966-73; assoc. prof. econs. Stanford U., Palto Alto, Calif., 1973-79; prof. econs. Barnard Coll., Columbia U., N.Y.C., 1977—. Co-author: Book Monetary and Fiscal Policy in a Growing Economy, 1971; assoc. editor: Jour. Econ. Theory, 1975-81. Ford Found. research prof., 1969. Mem. Am. Econs. Assn., Union Radical Policy Economy. Office: Dept Econs Barnard Coll Columbia U New York NY 10027

FOLEY, GEORGE HUTCHINSON, lawyer; b. Cambridge, Mass., July 28, 1910; s. John Joseph and Ida Frances (Hutchinson) F.; m. Janina Wanda Lukomska, Mar. 5, 1939; children: Janina Helena Foley Mix, Pamela Marya, Kristina Hutchinson. A.B. magna cum laude, Harvard U., 1932, J.D., 1935. Bar: Mass. 1935, U.S. Ct. Appeals (1st cir.) 1941, U.S. Dist. Ct. Mass. 1942, U.S. Ct. Appeals (2d cir.) 1964. Sole practice, Boston, 1935-39; spl. asst. atty. gen. Dept. Justice, 1940, New Eng. regional solicitor, 1943-51; chmn. New Eng. Wage Stabilization Bd., 1952-53; sr. ptnr. Hale & Dorr, Boston, 1953—; lectr. labor relations law Northeastern U., 1948-60; lectr. various New Eng. univs.; chmn. New Eng. Govtl. Labor Relations Conf., 1950. Bd. dirs. West Suburban YMCA, 1981—. MEM. Boston Bar Assn.; mem ABA. Republican. Clubs: Lakewood Tennis (Newton); Badminton and Tennis (Boston). Home: 41 Chatham Rd Newton Highlands MA 02161 Office: Hale & Dorr 60 State St Boston MA 02109

FOLEY, J. PATRICK, hotel management company executive; b. Kelso, Wash., Feb. 12, 1932; s. James and Verna F.; m. Paula Green, June 7, 1969; children—Sean, Erin. Grad., Wash. State U., 1955. With Western Internat. Hotels Co., 1958-61; with Hyatt Hotels Corp., Rosemont, Ill., 1961—, exec. v.p., 1972-77, pres., 1977—. Served to 1st lt. U.S. Army, 1955-56. Mem. Am. Hotel and Motel Assn. (industry adv. council). Office: One Hyatt Ctr Rosemont IL 60018 *

FOLEY, JAMES THOMAS, U.S. dist. judge; b. Troy, N.Y., July 9, 1910; s. Thomas David and Mary (Malone) F.; m. Eleanor Marie Anthony, July 16, 1953; 1 dau., Mary Jude. A.B., Fordham U., 1931; LL.B., Albany Law Sch., 1934. Bar: Admitted N.Y. bar 1934. Engaged in private practice law, Troy, 1935-42; sec. to Supreme Ct. Justice William H. Murray, 1939-42, 46-49; judge U.S. Dist. Ct., No. Dist. N.Y., 1949-63, chief judge, 1963-80, sr. judge, 1980—. Served as lt. USNR, 1942-45. Mem. Am., N.Y. bar assns., VFW, Am. Legion. Clubs: K.C., Elk. Home: RFD 1 Rensselaer NY 12144 Office: Federal Post Office Bldg Albany NY 12207

FOLEY, JOAN COLEMAN, literary agent, author; b. Stafford Springs, Conn., Feb. 10, 1929; d. Francis John and Kathryn Maureen (Cummiskey) Coleman; m. Joseph J. Foley, June 7, 1952. B.A., Barry Coll., 1950. Publicity writer Burl Ives, N.Y.C., 1950-51; writer TV, radio commls. Videocast Prodns./Nat. Farm Network, N.Y.C., 1951-54; lit. agt. Donald MacCampbell Agy., N.Y.C., 1954-56, Foley Agy., 1956—. Author: (with husband) The Hangover Cookbook, 1968, The Finger and Fork Snack Book, 1970, The Grand Central Oyster Bar and Restaurant Seafood Cookbook, 1977, The Chesapeake Bay Fish and Fowl Cookbook, 1981. Address: New York NY 10016 also Madison MD 21648

FOLEY, JOHN J., business executive; b. Chgo., May 11, 1928; m. Victoire Harari, May 15, 1971; children—John Brian, Sean Stephen. Ph.B., M.B.A., U. Chgo. Materials mgr., dir. ops. staff ITT Latin Am., 1965-73; dir. Telecom projects, 1973-75, group gen. mgr., Africa and Middle East, 1976-78, exec. asst. to office chief exec., 1978-79; v.p. ITT and dir. operation staffs, 1979—. *

FOLEY, JOHN PATRICK, philosophy educator, editor; b. Darby, Pa., Nov. 11, 1935; s. John Edward and Regina Beatrice (Vogt) F. B.A. summa cum laude, St. Joseph Coll., Phila., 1957; Ph.L., U. St. Thomas Aquinas, Rome, 1964, Ph.D. cum laude, 1965; M.S. magna cum laude, Columbia U., 1966. Ordained priest Roman Catholic Ch., 1962; asst. pastor Sacred Heart Ch., Havertown, Pa., 1962-63; asst. editor Cath. Standard and Times, Phila., 1963, 67-70, Rome corr., 1963-65, editor, 1970—; asst. pastor St. John Evangelist Ch., Phila., 1966; mem. faculty Cardinal Dougherty High Sch., Phila., 1966-67; assoc. prof. philosophy St. Charles Borromeo Sem., Phila., 1967—; news sec. gen. meetings Nat. Conf. Cath. Bishops, 1969—; bd. govs. Internat. Eucharistic Congress, 1974-76; vice chmn. Pa. State Ethics Commn., 1979—; English-lang. press sec. Internat. Synod of Bishops, Rome, 1980; regional bd. dirs. NCCJ. Author: Natural Law, Natural Right and the Warren Court, 1965; author: The Eucharist and the Hungers of the Human Family, 1976, The Eucharist in Relation to the other Sacraments, 1976. Named hon. prelate by Pope Paul VI, 1976. Mem. Am. Cath. Hist. Soc., Am. Cath. Philos. Assn., Cath. Press Assn. U.S. and Can. (dir. 1979—, v.p. 1981—). Office: 222 N 17th St Philadelphia PA 19103 *My religious faith has been and remains the most important motivating force in my life, and my work as a Catholic priest has been most consoling because no task seems more important than making people aware of their purpose in life and making available the religious direction and the sacramental assistance so vitally important in achieving that purpose.*

FOLEY, PATRICK JOSEPH, lawyer; b. Wabasha, Minn., May 10, 1930; s. John R. and Ellen Monica F.; children: Brennan E., Justin I. Student, Coll. St. Thomas, 1949-53; LL.B., Cath. U. Am., Washington, 1956. Bar: Minn. 1956, D.C. 1959, Mont. 1976. Partner firm Foley & Foley, Wabasha, 1957-59; judge Probate Ct., Dodge County, Minn., 1957-59; partner firm Foley & Foley, Washington, 1959-61; asst. U.S. atty. Dist. of Minn., 1961-66, U.S. atty., 1966-69; asso. firm Rerat, Crill, Foley & Boursier, Mpls., 1969-75; partner firm Kelly, & Foley, Billings, Mont., 1975-79; asso. firm DeParcq, Anderson, Perl, Hunegs & Rudquist (P.A.), Mpls., 1979—. Served with USN, 1948-49. Mem. Minn. Bar Assn., Minn. Trial Lawyers Assn. Democrat. Office: 565 608 Bldg Minneapolis MN 55402

FOLEY, PATRICK MARTIN, computer manufacturing company executive; b. Portland, Maine, Nov. 10, 1930; s. Coleman Daniel and Anne Theresa (Foley) F.; m. E. Kay Parslow, July 9, 1955; children—Cynthia, Steven, Kevin, Brian, Gregory. B.A. in Bus. Adminstrn, U. Maine, 1952; M.E., N.Y. U., 1956. Corp. controller IBM Corp., Armonk, N.Y., 1970-74, v.p. bus. plans, 1974-76; adminstr. dir. gen. IBM Europe, v.p., 1976-79, pres., Atlanta, 1979-82; corporate v.p., exec. v.p. IBM Corp. (world trade div.), White Plains, N.Y., 1983—. Mem. Fin. Execs. Inst., ASME, Pi Tau Sigma, Phi Gamma Delta. Democrat. Roman Catholic. Office: IBM Corp 360 Hamilton Ave White Plains NY 10601

FOLEY, RAYMOND WILLIAM, advertising executive; b. Mpls., Sept. 5, 1921; s. John J. and Theresa (Shandl) F.; m. Virginia Donna Reiling, June 19, 1948; children—Greg, Mark, Tom. B.A., U. Minn., 1948. Editor employee publ. Dayton's, Mpls., 1948-52; dir. pub. relations United Fund. Hennepin County, Mpls., 1952-55; v.p. client contact Pidgeon Savage Lewis, Mpls., 1955-65; exec. v.p. Colle & McVoy, Mpls., 1965-74, pres., 1974—; dir. Custom Labs Inc. Past pres. Hennepin County chpt. Am. Lung Assn.; chmn. public relations com., dir., mem. exec. com. Indianhead council Boy Scouts Am.; bd. dirs. Minn. Arthritis Found.; councilman City of North Oaks, Minn.; mem. City Planning Commn., Police Commn.; bd. dirs. No. Suburbs Cable TV Commn. Served with AUS, 1942-46. Mem. NW Council Advt. Agys. (past pres.), Advt. Club. Minn. (past dir.), Savs. Instns. Mktg. Soc. Am. (chmn., past dir.), U. Minn. Coll. Liberal Arts Alumni Assn. (past pres.), Mpls. Jr. C. of C. (past 1st v.p.). Clubs: Mpls. Athletic, Observatory, Ticker Tape, Daybreakers Breakfast (Mpls.); North Oaks Golf (St. Paul); Quail Ridge Golf (Boynton Beach, Fla.). Home: 7 Duck Pass Rd St Paul MN 55110 Office: 1550 E 78th St Minneapolis MN 55423

FOLEY, ROGER D., judge; b. 1917; s. Roger T. and Helen (Drummond) F. LL.B., U. San Francisco. Bar: Nev. bar 1946. Former atty. gen., Nev.; chief judge U.S. Dist Ct. Nev., Las Vegas, to 1980, judge, 1980— *

FOLEY, THOMAS STEPHEN, congressman; b. Spokane, Wash., Mar. 6, 1929; s. Ralph E. and Helen Marie (Higgins) F.; m. Heather Strachan, Dec. 1968. B.A., U. Wash., 1951, LL.B., 1957. Bar: Wash. Partner Higgins & Foley, 1957-58; dep. pros. atty. Spokane County, Spokane, 1958-60; asst. atty. gen. State of Wash., Olympia, 1960-61; spl. counsel interior and insular affairs com. U.S. Senate, Washington, 1961-64; mem. 89th-98th Congresses from 5th Dist. Wash.; chmn. Com. Agr., 1975-81, vice chmn., 1981—; chmn. House Democratic Caucus, 1976-80, House majority whip, 1981—; instr. law Gonzaga U., 1958-60. Mem. Phi Delta Phi. Democrat. Office: Longworth Bldg Washington DC 20515

FOLEY, WILLIAM EDWARD, federal courts administrator; b. Danbury, Conn., Feb. 7, 1911; s. Edward L. and Hertha (Braun) F.; m. Marguerite M. Pratt, June 6, 1951; children: William, Christopher, Anne, Richard, Jonathan, David, Carl. A.B., Harvard U., 1932, LL.B., 1935, A.M., 1939, Ph.D., 1940. Bar: Mass. 1935. Practiced in, Boston, 1935-40; chief internal security fgn. agts. registration sect. Dept. Justice, 1948-54, exec. asst. internal security div., 1954-58, 1st asst. criminal div., 1958-64; dep. dir. Adminstrv. Office U.S. Cts., 1964-77, dir., 1977—, sec. com. on rules of practice and procedure; bd. dirs. Fed. Jud. Ctr., 1977—. Served to lt. comdr. USNR, 1942-46; capt. Res. Mem. Am. Law Inst., Am., Fed. bar assns., Am. Judicature Soc. Home: 5 E Melrose St Chevy Chase MD 20815 Office: Supreme Ct Bldg Washington DC 20544

FOLEY, WILLIAM JOSEPH, labor union official; b. Hamilton, Ont., Canada, June 2, 1924; s. Thomas Michael and Marion F.; m. Elizabeth Foley, 1945; 5 children. Pres. local 1053 Textile Workers Union Am., Hamilton, 1948-52; pres. local 252 United Textile Workers Am., Hamilton, 1952-53, rep., 1953-56, area dir., 1956-64, Can. dir., 1964-74, now sec.-treas., Lawrence, Mass. Bd. dirs. McMaster U. Med. Sch., 1970-72; former mem. Hamilton City Council. Served with RCAF. Recipient Can. Centennial medal, 1967. Office: United Textile Workers of Am 420 Common St Lawrence MA 01840

FOLEY, WILLIAM R., JR., photographer; b. Chgo., Dec. 12, 1954; s. William Robert and Sara (Sloan) F. Student, Ind. U. Photogapher AP, Cairo and Beirut, 1978-84, Time mag., Beirut, 1984—. Recipient Pulitzer prize for spot news photography Columbia U., 1983. *

FOLEY, WILLIAM THOMAS, physician, educator; b. N.Y.C., Oct. 30, 1911; s. Edmund Leo and Sarah (O'Loughlin) F.; m. Barbara Ball, June 29, 1946; children: Caroline Ball, Lucy L., Claire E., Laura D.; m. Regula von Muralt, Apr. 25, 1970; 1 dau., Alix E. B.A., Columbia U., 1933; M.D., Cornell U., 1937. Diplomate: Am. Bd. Internal Medicine. Instr. anatomy Hong Kong U., 1939-41; organizer Fong Pin Hosp., Canton, China, 1940; mem. pub. health survey Orient for Navy, 1941; research fellow Pekin Union Med. Coll., 1941; mem. staff N.Y. Hosp., 1946—; asso. attending physician, chief vascular clinic, clin. asso. prof. medicine emeritus Cornell U. Med. Sch.; cons. physician N.Y. Infirmary, Mary Walsh Home, Southampton, Beckman Downtown hosps., Community Hosp., Glen Cove; mem. med. bd. Doctors Hosp. Del. Internat. Cardiovascular Congress, Paris, 1950, Buenos Aires, 1952, Basel, 1954, Stockholm, 1956, Brussels, 1958, Mexico, 1962, Barcelona, 1967, London, 1970; del. European-Am. Symposium on Venous Disease, Zurich, 1978; mem. U.S. nat. commn. USPHS. Author: Vascular Diseases, 1947, Colored Atlas and Management of Vascular Diseases, 1959; co-author: Diseases of the Heart and Blood Vessels, 1964; editor: Advances in the Management of Vascular Diseases, Vol. I, 1980, Vol. II, 1981, Vol. III, 1983, also 108 articles in med. jours. Served as lt. (j.g.) USN, 1937-38; comdr., 1941-46. Decorated D.S.M. Navy, Bronze Star, Purple Heart, China War medal, 1978; recipient A.R.C. citation for heading relief work beri beri epidemic, Canton, China, 1940; named to Xavier Hall of Fame, 1973. Fellow A.C.P. (life), N.Y. Acad. Medicine, Am. Coll. Cardiology; mem. Am. Fedn. Clin. Research, A.M.A. (cons. to council pharm. and chemistry), Am. Heart Assn. (circulation bd.), N.Y. Physicians Sci. (pres.), Internat. Council Health and Travel, Harvey Soc., Beta Theta Pi. Clubs: Dutch Treat, University (N.Y.C.); Piping Rock, Seawanhaka Yacht, Beaver Dam Winter Sports, Everglades, Palm Beach Bath and Tennis. Prisoner of war Japanese, 1941-45; comdg. officer Prisoner of War Camp Sendai II. Home: 120 East End Ave New York NY 10028 Office: New York Hospital Doctors Bldg 441 E 68th St New York NY 10021

FOLGATE, HOMER EMMETT, JR., lawyer; b. Rockford, Ill., Nov. 10, 1920; s. Homer Emmett and Hazel J. (Grissinger) F.; m. Letty Rae Huber, Apr. 28, 1944; children—Randall Lind, Jill, John Ernest. J.D., U. Ill., 1948. Bar: Ill. bar 1948. Asst. states atty., Winnebago County, Ill, 1948-55; partner firm Reno, Zahm, Folgate, Lindberg & Powell, Rockford, 1955—. Chmn. Winnebago County Republican Central Com., 1955-64. Served with AUS, 1943-46. Decorated Purple Heart, Silver Star. Club: Mason (Shriner). Home: 5177 Norwich Dr Rockford IL 61107 Office: Camelot Tower Rockford IL 61108

FOLGER, LEE MERRITT, investment company executive; b. Washington, May 5, 1934; s. John Clifford and Mary Kathrine (Dulin) F.; m. Nancy McElroy, 1961 (div.); children: Neil, Peter, Nicholas; m. Juliet Campbell Birmingham, 1976. A.B., Harvard U., 1956. With Folger Nolan Fleming Douglas, Inc., Washington, 1959—, vice chmn., 1976-81, chmn., 1981—; v.p. Piedmont Mortgage Co., Washington, 1960-82; pres. Cumberland Trust Co., Knoxville, Tenn., 1962—; mng. partner H.L. Dulin Co., Knoxville, 1960—; dir. Washington Star Newspaper., Allbritton Communications. Chmn. D.C. chpt. ARC, 1971-77; bd. govs..Am. nat. ARC, 1976-82, vice chmn., 1978-82; bd. govs. St. Albans Sch., Washington, 1970-83, chmn., 1975-76; trustee, treas. Corcoran Gallery Art, Washington; vice chmn. United Way Nat. Capital area, 1975-78; mem. D.C. Arts Commn., 1972-75, Protestand Episcopal Cathedral Found., 1980—; v.p. Folger Fund, Washington, 1958—. Served to lt. j.g. USNR, 1956-58. Mem. Nat. Assn. Security Dealers (dist. com. 1971-74), vice chmn. (1973-74). Clubs: Brook, Downtown Assn. (N.Y.C.); Chevy Chase (Md.); Metropolitan, Federal City (Washington); Essex County (Boston). Home: 80 Kalorama Circle NW Washington DC 20008 Office: 725 15th St NW Washington DC 20005

FOLINSBEE, ROBERT EDWARD, geologist; b. Edmonton, Alta., Can., Apr. 16, 1917; s. Francis John and Elizabeth Irene (Woolverton) F.; m. Catherine Elizabeth Terwillegar, July 6, 1942; children—Allin, John, James, Catherine. B.Sc., U. Alta., 1938; M.S., U. Minn., 1940, Ph.D., 1942; LL.D., U. Windsor, 1972. Geologist Geol. Survey of Can., 1936-50; asst. prof. geology U. Alta., Edmonton, 1946-50, asso. prof., 1950-55, prof., 1955-78, prof. emeritus, 1978—, chmn. dept., 1955-69. Served with Royal Can. Air Force, 1941-45. Decorated officer Order of Can.; recipient Queen's Jubilee medal, 1977. Fellow Royal Soc. Can. (pres. 1977-78, recipient Willet G. Miller medal 1967); mem. Geol. Soc. Am. (pres. 1975-76), Internat. Geol. Congress (pres. 1968-72), Geol. Assn. Can., Soc. Econ. Geologists, Am. Assn. Petroleum Geologists, Assn. Profl. Engrs., Geologists and Geophysicists of Alta. (Centennial award 1974), Can. Inst. Mining and Metallurgy (recipient past pres.' medal). Anglican. Club: Mayfair Golf and Country (Edmonton). Home: 11027 87th Ave Apt 1703 Edmonton AB T6G 2P9 Canada Office: Dept Geology U of Alberta AB T6G 2E3 Canada

FOLK, JOHN WILLIAM, insurance executive; b. Reading, Pa., Sept. 5, 1920; s. Harry J. and Lydia G. (Folk); m. Jean Russell, Jan. 14, 1944; children: J. Michael, Todd R., Jennifer. Student, Franklin and Marshall Coll., Lancaster, Pa., 1938-41, George Washington U., 1941-43. C.P.C.U., 1959. From adjuster to asst. v.p. claims Liberty Mut. Ins. Co., Boston, 1945-66; with Reliance Ins. Co., Phila., 1966—, chmn. bd., chief operating officer, 1978-81, cons., 1981—, also dir. subs. cos.; chmn. Inst. Ins. Research, 1979-81, pres., 1981—, Ins. Value Added Network Services, 1983. Served with USCGR, 1943-45. Mem. Soc. Chartered Property and Casualty Underwriters. Republican. Episcopalian, Club: Waynesborough Country. Home: 729 Clovelly Ln Devon PA 19333 Office: 1 N Broadway White Plains NY 10601

FOLK, ROBERT LOUIS, geologist; b. Cleve., Sept. 30, 1925; s. George Billmyer and Marjorie Marshall (Kinkead) F.; m. Marjorie Thomas, Sept. 7, 1946; children—Robert T., Jennifer Louise, Charles Marshall. B.S., Pa. State Coll., 1946, M.S., 1950, Ph.D., 1952. Research geologist Gulf Oil Co., Houston, 1951-52; mem. faculty U. Tex., Austin, 1952—, prof. geol. scis., 1960—, J. Nalle Gregory prof. geol. scis., 1977—; vis. lectr. Australian Nat. U., Canberra, 1965, Tong-Ji U., Shanghai, China, 1980; vis. researcher Universita degli Studi, Milan, Italy, 1973. Author: Petrology of Sedimentary Rocks, 1968; Contbr. articles to sci. publs. Fellow Geol. Soc. Am.; mem. Soc. Econ.

Paleontologists and Mineralogists (hon.). Methodist. Home: 1107 Bluebonnet Ln Austin TX 78704 Office: U of Tex Dept Geol Scis Austin TX 78801 *My unique characteristic is that I run my life randomly. At home each day, I put all the things I have/want to do in a list. Then I roll dice to see which thing to do and do that immediately whether it be a painful or pleasureful choice. Since I adopted this method I get immeasurably more work done and much greater pleasure out of daily life. Try it.*

FOLKERS, KARL AUGUST, chemist; b. Decatur, Ill., Sept. 1, 1906; s. August William and Laura Susan (Black) F.; m. Selma Leona Johnson, July 30, 1932; children—Cynthia Carol, Richard Karl. B.S., U. Ill., 1928, D.Sc., 1973; Ph.D., U. Wis., 1931; postdoctoral research, Yale, 1931-34; D.Sc., Phila. Coll. Pharmacy and Sci., 1962, U. Wis., U. Uppsala (Sweden), 1969. With Merck & Co., Inc., Rahway, N.J., summer 1933, 34-63, asst. dir. research, 1938-45, dir. organic and biochem. research, 1945-63, asso. dir. research and devel., 1951-53, dir. organic and biol. chem. research, 1953-56, exec. dir. fundamental research, 1956-62, v.p. exploratory research, 1962-63; pres., chief exec. officer Stanford Research Inst., Menlo Park, Calif., 1963-68, mem. council bd. trustees, 1971-74; courtesy prof. chemistry Stanford, 1963-68; Ashbel Smith prof., dir. Inst. Biomed. Research, U. Tex., 1968—; Baker non-resident lectr. in chemistry Cornell U., 1953; Regents lectr. UCLA, 1960; lectr. vitamin chemistry U. Calif., Berkeley, 1963; F.F. Nord lectr. biochemistry Fordham U., 1971; mem. sci. adv. com. Inst. Microbiology, Rutgers; chmn. symposium chmn. 3d Internat. Congress Pure and Applied Chemistry, Boston, 1971; adv. council dept. chemistry Princeton, 1958-64; Walter Hartung lectr. U. N.C., Chapel Hill; chmn., lectr. sect. 1 Isolation, Chemistry and Radioimmunoassay Nobel Symposium on Substance P, Stockholm, 1976; lectr. Tohoku U. Sch. Medicine, Japan, 1981, Assn. Advancement Med. Instrumentation, Washington, 1981, U. Athens, 1981; plenary lectr., chmn. sect. on chemistry of hypothalamic hormones 2d European Colloquim on Hypothalamic Hormones U. Tübingen, Germany, 1976; chmn., lectr. Internat. Symposium on Coenzyme Q, Japan, 1976; Burger lectr. U. Va., 1977; Plenary lectr. 500th Anniversary U. Uppsala, 1977; organizer, chmn. Gordon Research Conf. on Chemotherapy of Exptl. and Clin. Cancer, 1978; lectr. Ferring Symposium, Munich, 1979, Internat. Brain Research Symposium, Zurich, 1979; co-chmn., lectr. Internat. Symposium on Coenzyme Q, Tokyo, 1979; Dreyfus Disting. scholar Reed Coll., Portland, Oreg., 1981. Mem. editorial bd.: Jour. Molecular Medicine; Contbr. sci. jours. on organic chemistry. Trustee Gordon Research Confs., 1971-77. Recipient Am. Chem. Soc. award in pure chemistry, 1941, Spencer award, 1959; Julius Sturmer Lecture award, 1957; Perkin medal Soc. Chem. Industry, 1960; Nichols medal N.Y. sect. Am. Chem. Soc., 1967; Robert A. Welch Internat. award and medal for research on life processes, 1972; award in pharm. and medicinal chemistry Am. Pharm. Assn. Found. and Acad. Pharm. Scis., 1974, Alexander von Humboldt-Stiftung, 1977; 2d S.W. Sci. Forum award, 1979; co-recipient Van Meter prize Am. Thyroid Assn., 1969. Mem. Nat. Acad. Sci., Am. Chem. Soc. (pres. 1962), Am. Soc. Biol. Chemistry, Am. Inst. Nutrition, Soc. Exptl. Biology, N.Y. Acad. Sci., Am. Soc. Biol. Chemistry, Am. Inst. Nutrition, Soc. Exptl. Biology and Medicine, A.A.A.S., Am. Inst. Chemists, Royal Swedish Acad. Engring. Scis. (fgn. mem.), Societa Italiana di Scienze Farmaceutiche (hon.), Sigma Xi (Phi Lambda Upsilon, hon.), Alpha Chi Sigma, Rho Chi. Methodist. Home: 6406 Mesa Dr Austin TX 78731

FOLKMAN, DAVID H., department store executive; b. Jackson, Mich., Nov. 6, 1934; s. Jerome D. and Bessie (Schomer) F.; m. Susan Kleppner, June 22, 1958; children: Louis, Sarah, Karen, Jeffrey. A.B., Harvard U., 1957, M.B.A., 1960. Mdse. mgr. Foley's, Houston, 1957-69; v.p. dir. stores Famous-Barr, St. Louis, 1969-74; sr. v.p., gen. mdse. mgr. Macy's Calif., San Francisco, 1974-82; pres., chief exec. officer Emporium Capwell, San Francisco, 1982—; lectr. U. Houston, 1965-68; instr. Washington U., St. Louis, 1970-73. Clubs: Olympic (San Francisco); Harvard (N.Y.C.). Office: Emporium Capwell Co 835 Market St San Francisco CA 94103

FOLKMAN, MOSES JUDAH, surgeon; b. Cleve., Feb. 24, 1933; s. Jerome D. and Bessie Folkman. B.A., Ohio State U., 1953; M.D., Harvard U., 1957. Intern, then asst. resident in surgery Mass. Gen. Hosp., Boston, 1957-60, sr. asst. resident in surgery, 1962-64, chief resident, 1964-65; chief resident in pediatric surgery Phila. Children's Hosp., 1969; instr. surgery Harvard U. Med. Sch., 1965-66, asso. in surgery, 1967, prof. surgery, 1967—, Julia Dyckman Andrus prof. pediatric surgery, 1968—; asst. surgeon Boston City Hosp., 1965-66; asso. dir. Sears surg. lab., 1966-67; sr. surgeon Children's Hosp. Med. Center, Boston, 1968—. Served as officer M.C. USN, 1960-62. Recipient Career Devel. award NIH, 1966; Boylston Med. prize Harvard Med. Sch., 1957; Soma Weiss award, 1957; Lila Gruber award Am. Acad. Dermatology, 1974. Fellow A.C.S.; mem. Aesculapian Club, Am. Coll. Chest Physicians, Am. Surg. Assn., Assn. Acad. Surgery, Soc. U. Surgeons, Surg. Biology Club I, Am. Acad. Pediatrics, Allen O. Whipple Soc., Am. Pediatric Surg. Assn., N.Y. Acad. Scis., Mass. Med. Soc. Office: 300 Longwood Ave Boston MA 02115

FOLKS, J. LEROY, statistician, educator; b. Hydro, Okla., Oct. 12, 1929; s. Homer Caesar and Mae Theo (Payne) F.; m. Emily Sue Martin, Sept. 9, 1956; children: Martha, Karen, Ellen, John. B.A., Okla. State U., Stillwater, 1953, M.A., 1955; Ph.D., Iowa State U., Ames, 1958. Assoc. prof. stats. Okla. State U., 1961-67, prof., 1967—, head dept. stats., 1969—. Co-author: (with Oscar Kempthorne) Probability, Statistics and Data Analysis, 1971; author: Ideas of Statistics, 1981. Served with U.S. Army, 1950-52. Fellow Am. Statis. Assn., Royal Statis. Soc.; mem. Biometric Soc., Inst. Math. Stats., Internat. Statis. Inst. Republican. Am. Baptist. Home: 5 Pecan Dr Stillwater OK 74075 Office: Okla State U Stillwater OK 74078

FOLL, LLEWELLYN EUGENE, English educator; b. Lubbock, Tex., Apr. 22, 1943; s. Merlin Eugene and Merelle Elizabeth (Wilson) F.; m. Patricia Anne McFarland, Aug. 27, 1967; 1 dau., Sarah Elizabeth. B.A., Columbia Union Coll., Takoma Park, Md., 1965; M.A., Andrews U., 1967; Ph.D., Mich. State U., 1974. Assoc. prof. Kettering Coll. Med. Art, Ohio, 1967-78; prof., chmn. dept. English Loma Linda U., Riverside, Calif., 1978—. Mem. Nat. Council Tchrs. English, MLA. Adventist. Home: 5395 Sierra Vista Ave Riverside CA 92515

FOLLESDAL, DAGFINN, philosophy educator; b. Askim, Norway, June 22, 1932; s. Trygve and Margit (Teigen) F.; m. Vera Heyerdahl, Jan. 23, 1957; children: Andreas, Inge, Benedikte, Magne, Olav, Hallvard. Cand. mag., U. Oslo, 1953; mag. art, 1956; fellow, U. Gottingen, W.Ger., 1954-55; Ph.D. in Philosophy, Harvard U., 1961. Research asst. ionospheric physics Norwegian Research Council for Sci. and Humanities, 1955-57; instr. in philosophy Harvard U., 1961-63, asst. prof. philosophy, 1963-64, Santayana fellow, 1964-65; research fellow U. Oslo, 1966-67, prof., 1967—. Stanford U., 1969—, Clarence Irving Lewis prof. philosophy, 1976—. Editor: Jour. Symbolic Logic, 1970-82; bd. editors: Synthese, 1966—, Lumen, 1967-75, Metaphilosophy, 1970—, Jour. Philos. Logic, 1972—, Behaviorism, 1972—, Monist, 1972—, Erkenntnis, 1975—, Grazer philosophische Studien, 1975—, Studia Logica, 1976—, Philosophy of Sci., 1981—, Philosophical Studies, 1977—, Phenomenology and the Human Scis, 1981—, Epistemologia, 1978—, Philos. Topics, 1981—; author: Husserl und Frege, 1958, Referential Opacity and Modal Logic, 1961. Guggenheim fellow, 1978-79; fellow Center for Advanced Study in Behavioral Scis., 1981-82; Am. Council Learned Socs. fellow, 1983-84. Mem. Assn. Symbolic Logic (council 1965-67, 70—), Inst. Internat. Philosophy (v.p. 1978-81), Norwegian Acad. Sci., Royal Norwegian Soc. Sci. and Humanities. Home: Staverhagan 7 1300 Sandvika Norway Office: Stanford U Stanford CA 94305

FOLLETT, JEAN FRANCES, artist; b. St. Paul, June 5, 1917; d. Sherman Theodore and Helen Maude (Crapsey) F.; m. Alan Shirey, Jan. 4, 1946 (div. 1949). A.A., U. Minn., 1940; postgrad., Hans Hoffman Sch. Art, 1946-51. Co-founder Hausa Gallery, N.Y.C., 1951-59. One-woman shows at, Hahsa Gallery, 1952-58, exhibited in group shows, Guggenheim Mus., N.Y.C., 1954, Leo Castelli Gallery, N.Y.C., 1960, numerous others, represented in permanent collections, Mus. Modern Art, N.Y.C., Whitney Mus. Am. Art, N.Y.C. Served with U.S. Army, 1943-46. Recipient Nat. Found. Arts and Humanities award, 1966. Unitarian. Address: 1510 English St Saint Paul MN 55106 *I was one of a prior generation of women unfairly having to choose between having a family of my own or a career. I chose the art career. I am not sorry.*

FOLLETT, KENNETH MARTIN (SYMOND MYLES), author; b. Cardiff, Wales, June 5, 1949; s. Martin D. and Lavinia C. (Evans) F.; m. Mary Emma Ruth Elson, Jan. 5, 1968; children: Emanuele, Marie-Claire. B.A., Univ. Coll., London, 1970. Music columnist South Wales Echo, 1970-73; reporter Evening News, London, 1973-74; editorial dir. Everest Books Ltd., London, 1974-76, dep. mng. dir., 1976-77. Author: Secret of Kellerman's Studio, 1976, Bear Raid, 1976, The Shakeout, 1976, Eye of the Needle, 1978, Triple, 1979, The Key to Rebecca, 1980, The Man from St. Petersburg, 1981, On Wings of Eagles, 1983; as Simon Myles: The Big Needle, 1973; author screenplays: Fringe Banking, 1978, A Football Star, 1979. Office: care Arbor House Publishing Co 235 E 45th St New York NY 100170

FOLLETT, ROBERT JOHN RICHARD, publisher; b. Oak Park, Ill., July 4, 1928; s. Dwight W. and Mildred (Johnson) F.; m. Nancy L. Crouthamel, Dec. 30, 1950; children: Brian L., Kathryn R., Jean A., Lisa W. A.B., Brown U., 1950; postgrad., Columbia U., 1950-51. Editor Follett Pub. Co., Chgo., 1951-55, sales mgr., 1955-58, gen. mgr. ednl. div., 1958-68, pres., 1968-78, Follett Internat., 1972—; chmn., dir. Follett Corp., 1979—; pres. Follett Group, Inc.; v.p. United Learning Corp.; chmn. School Pubs., 1971-73; dir. Ednl. Systems Corp.; Mem. Ill. Gov.'s Commn. on Schs., 1972; pres. Alpine Research Inst., 1968—; mem. Nat. Adv. Council on Edn. Statistics, 1975-77; chmn. Book Distbn. Task Force of Book Industry, 1978-81. Author: Your Wonderful Body, 1961, What to Take Backpacking and Why, 1977, How to Keep Score in Business, 1978, The Financial Side of Book Pub., 1982. Bd. dirs. Village Mgr. Assn., 1964—, Community Found. Oak Park and River Forest, 1959—; Community Found. Oak Park and River Forest Fund for Justice, 1974-77; trustee Inst. Ednl. Data Systems, 1965—; elected mem. Republican State Com. from 7th dist. Ill., 1982—. Served in AUS, 1951-53. Mem. Assn. Am. Pubs. (dir. 1972-79), Ill. C. of C., chmn. edn. com. (1977-79), Chgo. Pubs. Assn. (pres. 1976—), Sierra Club. Clubs: Cliff Dwellers, Tower (Chgo.); River Forest Tennis. Home: 508 N Oak Park Ave Oak Park IL 60302 also Shorewood Hills MI 49125 Office: 1000 W Washington Blvd Chicago IL 60607

FOLLEY, JARRETT HARTER, educator, physician; b. Syracuse, N.Y., Aug. 25, 1913; s. John Frederick and May (Harter) F.; m. Barbara Hope, June 3, 1938; children—Hilda Pamela (Mrs. Sidney C. Miller), Jarrett Harter, Gillian Hope (Mrs. Michael White). A.B., Hamilton Coll., Clinton, N.Y., 1934; M.D., Harvard, 1938. Diplomate: Am. Bd. Internal Medicine. Intern Mary Hitchcock Meml. Hosp., Hanover, N.H., 1938-40, mem. clin. staff, 1941—, pres. staff bd. govs., 1964—; sr. medicine New Haven Hosp., 1940-41; fellow gastroenterology Univ. Hosp., Phila., 1941; cons. VA Hosp., White River Junction, Vt., 1946—; pres. Hitchcock Clinic, Hanover, 1964-74; mem. faculty Dartmouth Med. Sch., 1941—, prof. clin. medicine, 1969-78, prof. emeritus, 1978—; med. dir. Dartmouth-Hitchcock Med. Center, 1973-76, dir. grad. and continuing med. edn., 1976—. Contbr. papers in field. Trustee Conn. & Passumpsic Ry. Assn. Med.; dir. Atomic Bomb Casualty Commn., Japan, 1950-52; Trustee Mary Hitchcock Meml. Hosp., Hitchcock Found. Fellow A.C.P. (gov. N.H. 1962-68); mem. N.H., Grafton County med. socs. Home: Main St Norwich VT 05055

FOLSE, JOHN ROLAND, surgeon; b. Beaumont, Tex., Oct. 28, 1932; s. Parker C. and Evelyn (Wynn) F.; m. Hazen Lewis, June 12, 1954; children: Gwen, John, Lynn, Dick. B.S., Southwestern U., Georgetown, Tex., 1954; M.D., John Hopkins U., 1958. Intern in surgery Johns Hopkins Hosp., 1958-59; asst. resident in surgery, then chief resident U. Wash. Affiliated Hosps., Seattle, 1961-67; asst. prof., then asso. prof. U. Wash. Med. Sch., 1967-71; prof. surgery, chmn. dept. So. Ill. U. Med. Sch., Springfield, 1971—; cons. cancer info. service Ill. Cancer Council. Contbr. numerous articles to med. jours. Served with USPHS, 1959-61. Recipient Mead-Johnson award grad. tng., 1965-68, NIH Career Devel. award, 1965-68, citation merit Alumni Assn. Southwestern U., 1973. Mem. ACS (pres. Ill. chpt. 1980), AMA, Assn. Acad. Surgery, Am. Surg. Assn., Assn. Surg. Edn., Am. Heart Assn. (council cardiovascular surgery), Henry Hawkins Surg. Soc., Ill. Med. Soc., Ill. Surg. Soc. (v.p. 1980), Midwest Surg. Soc., Midwest Vascular Soc., N. Pacific Surg. Soc., Sangamon County Med. Soc., St. Louis Surg. Soc., Soc. Surg. Chmn., Soc. Vascular Surgery, Springfield Med. Club, Sigma Xi. Club: Sangamon State U. Home: 2 Virginia Ln Springfield IL 62707 Office: 800 N Rutledge St Springfield IL 62708

FOLSOM, FRANKLIN BREWSTER, author; b. Boulder, Colo., July 21, 1907; s. Fred Gorham and Mary Elvira (Elwell) F.; m. Mary Letha Elting, Sept. 1, 1936; children: Michael Brewster, Rachel Alice Folsom Moll. Student, Dartmouth, 1924-25; B.A., U. Colo., 1928, Oxford U., 1932, M.A., 1963. Instr. Swarthmore Coll., 1928-30; editor Hunger Fighter, 1934-35; exec. sec. League Am. Writers, 1937-42, New York Council Am.-Soviet Friendship, 1943; dir. adult edn. Downtown Community Sch., 1945; staff writer Tass, 1946-47; free lance writer, 1948—; Chmn. Council on Interracial Books for Children, 1965-69. Author: America's Ancient Treasures, 1971, 3d edit., 1983, Red Power on the Rio Grande: The Native American Revolution of 1680, 1973, Life and Legend of George McJunkin: Black Cowboy, 1974, Give Me Liberty: America's Colonial Heritage, 1974, Some Basic Rights of Soviet Citizens, 1983; numerous others.; Contbr. articles to periodicals. Served with U.S. Mcht. Marine, 1945-46. Recipient Harriet Monroe poetry award, 1937, Follett award, 1974, Spur award, 1974, Norlin award Alumni U. Colo., 1974; Macdowell Colony fellow; Rhodes scholar, 1930-33. Mem. Soc. Am. Archeology, Authors Guild, Soc. Children's Book Writers, Colo. Archaeol. Soc., Colo. Hist. Soc., Colo. Authors League (Top Hand award, 1975, 79), Archeol. Soc. N.J. (v.p. 1968-72). Address: Overland Star Route Ward CO 80481

FOLSOM, JAMES KING, English educator; b. Cleve., Aug. 9, 1933; s. Frederick Kenneth and Elizabeth Edna (Yost) F.; m. Mary Katherine Fox. B.A., Northwestern U., 1955; Ph.D., Princeton U., 1959. Asst. prof. English Yale U., New Haven, 1959-68; prof. U. Colo., Boulder, 1968—. Author: Man's Accidents & God's Purposes, 1963, Timothy Flint, 1965, The American Western Novel, 1966; contbr. to: Readers Ency. of Am. Midwest. Mem. MLA, Western Lit. Assn. Home: 1447 S Foothills Hwy Boulder CO 80303 Office: Dept English Univ Colo Box 226 Boulder CO 80309

FOLSOM, JOHN ROY, savings and loan executive; b. Hartsville, S.C., Dec. 30, 1918; s. William Arthur and Flora (Newsom) F.; m. Anita Anderson, Oct. 18, 1941; children: Anita Marie (Mrs. Harold A. Boney, Jr.), Dale (Mrs. Guy M. Tate, Jr.), John William, George Anderson. B.A., Furman U., 1940. With Aiken Loan & Security Co., Florence, S.C., 1940-41, Surety Life & Liberty Life Ins. Co., Greenville and Columbia, S.C., 1941-43, 46-60; with S.C. Fed. Savs. & Loan Assn., Columbia, 1960—, pres., 1963—, chmn. bd., 1982—, also mem. exec. com., loan com., dir.; pres., dir. 1st Service Corp. S.C., 1973—; v.p., dir. S.C. Student Loan Corp., 1973-77; dir. S.C. Title Ins. Co., Investors Nat. Life Ins. Co., Seibels Bruce Group, Inc.; dir., mem. audit com. S.C. Ins. Co., 1975-81, Giant Portland & Masonry Cement Co. Mem. Richland-Lexington Airport Commn., 1973—, chmn., 1980-82; Mem. financial adv. com. Erskine Coll.; mem. Am. Heart Policy Com., 1972-73; Trustee United Fund Columbia, 1966-80; past treas., vice chmn., bd. dirs. S.C. Heart Assn., 1968-73, 75—, chmn., 1968-73; bd. dirs., campaign chmn. Musical Arts; pres. Columbia Mus. Festival; trustee, v.p. Research Devel. and, Ednl. Found. Richland County Meml. Hosp.; mem. citizens com., bd. adminstrs., Richland County, 1968—; adv. bd., co-chmn. Providence Hosp., 1974—; pres. adv. council, Columbia Coll pres. adv. council, 1974-81, trustee, 1980-81; pres. adv. council Furman U., 1975—; bd. dirs. Salvation Army, 1975-77; mem. mgmt. fin. com. Am. Heart Assn., 1976-77, 78-79, bd. dirs., 1980—, mem. audit com., 1982—, chmn. audit com., mem. budget com., 1984—; apptd. by gov. to study S.C. biennial budget. Recipient Good Egg award S.C. Heart Assn. Mem. S.C. Savs. and Loan League (pres. 1968-69, dir. 1979-80), U.S. Savs. and Loan League (dir. 1973—), S.C. C. of C. (pres. 1979, chmn. 1980-81), Columbia C. of.C (dir. 1975-78, v.p. indsl. devel.), Furman U. Alumni Assn. (pres. 1953-54, mem. athletic council 1955), Columbia Real Estate Bd., Columbia Real Estate Appraisers, Columbia Home Builders Assn., Univ. Assos. U. S.C. (pres. 1972-73, pres. Summit club 1971-76, v.p. club 1976—), Newcomen Soc. N.Am., Sigma Alpha Epsilon. Methodist (chmn. finance com., bd. dirs.). Clubs: Rotarian., Palmetto, Forest Lake (Columbia). Home: 1515 Adger Rd Columbia SC 29205 Office: 1500 Hampton St Columbia SC 29201

FOLTZ, EDWIN JOSEPH, lawyer, business executive; b. Ft. Smith, Ark., Dec. 31, 1915; s. James Arthur and Janie and Price (Foltz); m. Dorothy Deane Mitchell, Dec. 31, 1941; children—Edwin Joseph, Dorothy and Deane (twins). J.D., Washington and Lee U., 1940. Bar: Va. 1940, U.S. Supreme Ct. 1945, Ga. 1947, Ark. 1948, Ohio 1952, Pa. 1977. Pvt. practice law, 1940-41; spl. agt. FBI, 1941-50, adminstrv. asst. to dir., 1944-46, spl. agt. in charge 3 divs., 1946-50; dir. indsl. and pub. relations Pesco Products div. Borg-Warner Corp., also sec. and asst. to pres. Wooster div., 1950-53; asst. dir. personnel adminstrn. Campbell Soup Co., Camden, N.J., 1953-55, dir. personnel adminstrn., 1955-58, v.p. personnel, in charge corporate labor and personnel relations, 1958-60, v.p. internat. div., 1960-73, v.p. corp. relations, 1973-80; pres. Campbell's Soups Internat., 1960-73, Campbell Soup Fund, 1973-80; of counsel firm Hepburn Willcox Hamilton & Putnam, 1981—; condr. seminars Am. Mgmt. Assn., 1960-64, 68-73; Mem. World Council, 1960-73, v.p., 1968-70. Mem. Crime Commn. Phila., 1972—, bd. dirs., 1974—, pres., 1977-78; mem. Phila. '76 Adv. Commn., 1973-76; bd. dirs. Am. Grad Sch. Internat. Mgmt., 1964-74, Keep Am. Beautiful, 1977—; trustee Gladwyne Free Library, 1962-65, pres., 1962-63; bd. advisors Coll. Physicians Phila., 1980—; bd. mgrs. Franklin Inst., 1980—; pres., bd. dirs. Citizens Crime Commn. of Phila., 1980—; mem. pres.' adv. bd. World Affairs Council, 1978—. Recipient Disting. Service award Am. Mgmt. Assn., 1970. Mem. Conf. Bd. (internat. council 1968-73, program chmn. Internat. Mktg. Conf. 1971), Am. Mgmt. Assn. (pres.'s council 1974—), World Affairs Council Phila. (dir. 1973-78, vice chmn. 1974-78), Phila. Com. Fgn. Relations, South Jersey C. of C. (dir., exec. com. 1974-80), Washington and Lee U. Alumni Assn. (dir. 1975-77, pres. bd. dirs. 1977-79, Disting. Alumni award 1983). Episcopalian (vestryman). Clubs: Phila. Country, Union League (Phila.); Merion Cricket. Home: 917 Black Rock Rd Gladwyne PA 19035 Office: 2000 Penn Center Plaza Philadelphia PA 19102

FOLTZ, RICHARD HARRY, bus. exec.; b. Frackville, Pa., Apr. 11, 1924; s. John Boyd and Blanche (Price) F.; m. Margie Alexander, June 6, 1948 (dec.); children—Richard Gary (dec.), Karen Lynn, Terri Nan; m. Ruth M. Capper, Mar. 21, 1980. Student extension center, Pa. State Coll., 1941; B.A., Harding Coll., 1949. Chief inspector's office Glenn L. Martin Co., Balt., 1941-42; adminstrv. insp. Far East Air Forces, 1942-45; writer lectr. dept. nat. edn. Harding Coll., 1945-49; with Freedoms Found., Valley Forge, Pa., 1949—, v.p. pub. relations, 1952-62, sr. v.p., 1962-65; exec. v.p. Western region, 1965-78; asst. to pres. Hydril Co., Los Angeles, 1978—. Author articles on citizenship. Past pres. Upper Merion Twp. Sch. Bd.; mem. nat. pub. relations com., nat. uniform and insignia com. Boy Scouts Am. Republican. Mem. Ch. of Christ. Club: Jonathan (Los Angeles). Office: 714 W Olympic Blvd Los Angeles CA 90015

FOLTZ, RODGER LOWELL, organic chemist, mass spectroscopist; b. Milw., Feb. 10, 1934; s. Ross Milton and Ida Louise (Campbell) F.; m. Ruth Lynch Bilbe, June 9, 1956; children—R. Craig, Camilla M. B.S., Mass. Inst. Tech., 1956; Ph.D., U. Wis., 1961. Research chemist Battelle Meml. Inst., Columbus, Ohio, 1961-76, sr. research leader, 1976-79; adj. prof. pharmacy Ohio State U., 1972-76, adj. asso. prof. pharmacology, 1976-79; asso. dir. Center for Human Toxicology, U. Utah, Salt Lake City, 1979—, research asso. prof. dept. biochem. pharmacology and toxicology, 1980—. Contbr. articles to profl. jours.; editorial adv. bd.: Biomed. Mass Spectrometry, 1979—. Pres. N.W. Area Human Relations Council, Columbus, 1968-70; deacon First Congregational Ch., Columbus, 1971-75; trustee Denison U. Research Found., 1977-79. Mem. Am. Chem. Soc. (chmn. elect Columbus sect. 1978, Columbus sect. award 1977), Chem. Soc. (London), Am. Soc. Mass Spectrometry (chmn. nominating com. 1980, 82), Sigma Phi Epsilon. Home: 2080 Belaire Dr Salt Lake City UT 84109 Office: Center for Human Toxicology U Utah Salt Lake City UT 84112

FOLWELL, WILLIAM HOPKINS, clergyman, bishop; b. Port Washington, N.Y., Oct. 26, 1924; s. Ralph Taylor and Sara Ewing (Hopkins) F.; m. Christine Elizabeth Cramp, Apr. 22, 1949; children: Ann, Mark, Susan. B.C.E., Ga. Inst. Tech., 1947; B.D., Seabury Western Theol. Sem., 1953, D.D., 1970; D.D., U. South, Sewanee, 1970. Ordained to ministry Episcopal Ch., 1952; priest Plant City and Mulberry, Fla., 1952-55; asst. chaplain St. Martin's Sch., New Orleans, 1955-56; vicar St. Augustine Ch., New Orleans, 1955-56; rector St. Gabriel's Ch., Titusville, Fla., 1956-59, All Saints Ch., Winter Park, Fla., 1959-70; bishop Diocese Central Fla., Winter Park, 1970—; asst. traffic engr. City of Miami, 1947-49. Trustee U. South, Seabury-Western Theol. Sem., Evanston, Ill. Lt. j.g. USNR, 1943-46. Home: 458 Virginia Dr Winter Park FL 32789 Office: The Episcopal Ch 324 N Interlachen Ave PO Box 790 Winter Park FL 32789

FOMON, ROBERT M., investment banker; b. Chgo., 1925. Grad., U. So. Calif., 1947. Chmn. bd., chief exec. officer, pres., dir. E.F. Hutton & Co., Inc., N.Y.C.; dir. PSA Inc., Gt. Lakes Carbon Corp. Adv. UCLA Sch. Medicine; trustee White House Preservation Fund. *

FONDA, JANE, actress; b. N.Y.C., Dec. 21, 1937; d. Henry and Frances (Seymour) F.; m. Roger Vadim (div.); 1 dau., Vanessa; m. Tom Hayden, Jan. 20, 1973; 1 son, Troy. Student, Vassar Coll. Appeared on: Broadway stage in There Was A Little Girl, 1960; Appeared on: The Fun Couple, 1962; Appeared in: Actor's Studio prodn. Strange Interlude, 1963; appeared in: films Tall Story, 1960, A Walk on the Wild Side, 1962, Period of Adjustment, 1962, Sunday in New York, 1963, In the Cool of the Day, 1963, The Love Cage, 1963, La Ronde, 1964, Cat Ballou, 1965, The Chase, 1966, Any Wednesday, 1966, The Game Is Over, 1967, Hurry Sundown, 1967, Barefoot in the Park, 1967, Barbarella, 1968, Spirits of the Dead, 1969, They Shoot Horses, Don't They?, 1969, Klute, 1970 (Acad. award best actress), Steelyard Blues, 1973, A Doll's House, 1973, The Blue Bird, 1976, Fun With Dick and Jane, 1976, Julia, 1977, Coming Home, 1978 (Acad. award best actress), California Suite, 1978, Comes a Horseman, 1978, The China Syndrome, 1979, Electric Horseman, 1979, Nine to Five, 1980, On Golden Pond, 1981, Roll Over, 1981; Author: Jane Fonda's Workout Book, 1981. Recipient Golden Apple prize for female star of yr. Hollywood Women's Press Club, 1977, Golden Globe award, 1978. Address: PO Box 900 Beverly Hills CA 90213 *

FONDA, PETER, actor dir., producer; b. Feb. 23, 1940; s. Henry and Frances (Seymour) F.; m. Susan Brewer (div. Apr. 1974); 2 children. Student, U. Omaha. Film appearances include Tammy and The Doctor, 1963, The Victors, 1963, Lilith, 1964, The Young Lovers, 1964, The Trip, 1967, The Wild Angels, 1966, The Last Movie, 1971, Race With The Devil, 1975, 92 in the Shade, 1975, Killer Force, 1975, Fighting Mad, 1976, Futureworld, 1976, Outlaw Blues, 1977, High Ballin', 1978, Wanda Nevada, 1979; dir.: Idaho Transfer; directed and appeared in: The Hired Hand, 1971, Two People, 1973; writer, co-producer, appeared in: Easy Rider, 1969 *

FONDAHL, JOHN WALKER, civil engineering educator; b. Washington, Nov. 4, 1924; s. John Edmund and Mary (DeCourcy) F.; m. Doris Jane Plishker, Mar. 2, 1946; children: Lauren Valerie, Gail Andrea, Meredith Victoria, Dorian Beth. B.S., Thayer Sch. Engring., Dartmouth, 1947, M.S. in Civil Engring, 1948. Instr., then asst. prof. U. Hawaii, 1948-51; constrn. engr. Winston Bros. Co., Mpls., 1951-52; project engr. Nimbus Dam and Powerplant project, Sacramento, 1952-55; mem. faculty Stanford U., 1955—, prof. civil engring., 1966—, Charles H. Leavell prof. civil engring., 1977; dir. Caterpillar Tractor Co., Peoria. Author reports in field. Served with USMCR, 1943-46. Recipient Golden Beaver award Heavy Constrn. Industry, 1976. Fellow ASCE (Constrn. Mgmt. award 1977), Project Mgmt. Inst. (hon. life mem.); mem. Phi Beta Kappa, Sigma Xi, Lambda Chi Alpha. Republican. Patentee. Home: 12810 Viscaino Rd Los Altos Hills CA 94022 Office: Dept Civil Engring Stanford Univ Stanford CA 94305

FONER, ERIC, historian; b. N.Y.C., Feb. 7, 1943; s. Jack D. and Liza F.; m. Lynn Garafola, May 1, 1980. B.A., Columbia U., 1963, Oxford (Eng.) U., 1965; Ph.D., Columbia U., 1969. Prof. history City Coll., CUNY, N.Y.C., 1973-82, Columbia U., 1982—; Pitt prof. Am. history and instns. Cambridge (Eng.) U., 1980-81. Author: Free Soil, Free Labor, Free Men, 1970, Tom Paine and Revolutionary America, 1976, Politics and Ideology in the Age of the Civil War, 1980. Am. Council Learned Socs. fellow, 1972-73; Guggenheim fellow, 1975-76. Mem. Am. Hist. Assn., Orgn. Am. Historians. Home: 606 W 116th St New York NY 10027

FONER, PHILIP S., history educator; b. N.Y.C., Dec. 14, 1910; s. Abraham and Mary (Smith) F.; m. Roslyn Held, 1939; children: Elizabeth, Laura. A.B., CCNY, 1932; M.A., Columbia U., 1933, Ph.D., 1941. Began as tchr., 1933; pub., mem. firm Citadel Press, N.Y.C., 1945-66; prof. history Lincoln U., Pa., 1967-79, Rutgers U., Camden, 1981. Author: Business and Slavery, 1941, Jack London, American Rebel, 1947, The Fur and Leather Workers Union, 1950, History of Labor Movement in the United States, Vol. 1, 1947, Vol. 2, 1955, Vol. 3, 1964, Vol. 4, 1965, Vol. 5, 1980, Vol. 6, 1982, The Life and Writings of Frederick Douglass, 1949-52, Mark Twain, Social Critic, 1958, History of Cuba and its Relations with the United States, 2 vols, 1962-63, The Case of Joe Hill, 1965, The Letters of Joe Hill, 1965, The Haymarket Autobiographies, 1969, The Black Panthers Speak, 1970, W.E.B. Du Bois Speaks, 2 vols, 1970, American Labor and the War in Indochina, 1971, The Voice of Black America: Major Speeches of Negroes in the United States, 1797-1971, 1972, The Spanish-Cuban-American War and the Birth of American Imperialism, 1895-1902, 2 vols, 1973, When Karl Marx Died: Comments in 1883, 1973, Organized Labor and the Black Worker, 1619-1973, 1974, American Labor Songs of the Nineteenth Century, 1975, History of Black Americans: From Africa to the Emergence of the Cotton Kingdom, 1975, Writings of Jose Marti: Inside the Monster, 1975, Formation of the Workingmen's Party of the United States, 1976, Blacks and the American Revolution, 1976, We, The Other People, 1976, Labor and The American Revolution, 1976, The Great Labor Uprising of 1877, 1977, Frederick Douglass on Women's Rights, 1977, The Factory Girls, 1977, Our America, 1977, Essays in Afro-American History, 1978, The Black Worker: A Documentary History, vols. I, II, 1978, III, 1979, IV, 1980, V, 1981, VI, 1981, VII, 1983, Paul Robeson Speaks, 1978, Women and the American Labor Movement: From Colonial Times to the Eve of World War I, 1979, On Education, 1979; Women and the Labor Movement: From World War I to the Present 1980; On Art and Literature, 1982, Major Poems, 1982, British Labor and the American Civil War, 1982, Wilhelm Liebknecht: Letters to the Chicago Workingmen's Advocate, 1983, From the Emergence of the Cotton Kingdom to the Eve of the Compromise of 1850, 1983, From the Compromise of 1850 to the End of the Civil War, 1983; others.; Compiler writings: Frederick Douglass. Mem. Am. Hist. Assn., Phi Beta Kappa. Address: The Lenox 250 S 13th St Philadelphia PA 19107 also Rutgers U Camden NJ 08102

FONER, SIMON, research physicist; b. Pitts., Aug. 13, 1925; s. Newton F. F. B.S., Carnegie Inst. Tech., 1947, M.S., 1948, D.Sc., 1952. Research physicist Carnigie Inst. Tech., Pitts., 1952-53; staff physicist Lincoln Lab. MIT, Lexington, 1953-61, Francis Bitter Nat. Magnet Lab., MIT, Cambridge, 1961-63, project leader, 1963-77, chief scientist, head research div., 1977—; sr. research scientist dept. physics MIT, Cambridge, 1982—; dir. NATO Advanced Study Insts. in Europe, 1970, 73, 76, 80, chmn., Internat. Cryogenic Materials Conf., 1983—; mem. bd. Applied Superconductivity Conf. Inc., 1982—; cons. editor Rev. of Sci. Instruments, 1979—. Editor 4 books in magnetism, superconductivity and applications; patentee magnetometers, superconducting materials. Served with USN; 1944-46. Named Disting. lectr. for Magnetic Soc. IEEE, 1982-83. Fellow Am. Phys. Soc. (exec. com. council 1983—, mem.-at-large exec. com. condensed matter physics div. 1970-72, chmn. 1978-81, councillor 1982—). Office: Francis Bitter Nat Magnet Lab MIT 170 Albany St NW-14 Cambridge MA 02139

FONES, WILLIAM HARDIN DAVIS, state supreme court justice; b. Friendship, Tenn., Oct. 6, 1917; s. Roy Revelle and Kitty (Davis) J.; m. Rebecca Logan Barr, July 26, 1946; children: Jere, William Hardin Davis. Student, Memphis State U., 1934-37; J.D., U. Tenn., 1940. Bar: Tenn. 1942. Practiced in, Memphis, 1945-71; judge div. 3 15th Jud. Circuit Ct. Tenn., Shelby County, Memphis, 1971-73; assoc. justice Supreme Ct., Tenn., 1973-74, 76—, chief justice, 1974-76, 82—; mem. exec. council Conf. Chief Justices, 1976-79. Active local Boy Scouts Am., ARC, Shelby United Neighbors fund drives. Served with USAAF, 1942-45. Decorated Air medal with 3 oak leaf clusters. Office: Supreme Ct Tenn 1103 State Office Bldg Memphis TN 38103

FONG, BENSON, actor, business executive; b. Sacramento, Oct. 10, 1916; s. Toon and Shee (Yee) F.; m. Gloria Chin, Nov. 11, 1946; children: Cynthia, Preston, Lori, Pamela, Lisa. Student, Lingnan U., Canton, China. Owner, operator A.H. Fong's Restaurants, Los Angeles, 1946—; pres. Maylia Corp., Cinlopamlis, Prescorp of Calif.; v.p. Landsberg, Ltd., Hong Kong. Appeared in over 200 theatrical and television films, 1941—; appeared in Charlie Chan series as the Hon. Son. Recipient Public Service and Achievement awards from Hollywood Canteen, Los Angeles Chinese Community, AFL-CIO Council, Los Angeles chpt. WAIF, So. Calif. Chinese Hist. Soc., Sacramento Chinese Soc. Mem. Screen Actors Guild, AFTRA. Republican. Roman Catholic. Clubs: Los Angeles Chinese Golf, El Caballero Country, Hollywood Lakeside Golf. Home: Hollywood CA Office: 424 N Beverly Dr Beverly Hills CA 90210 *"Life is a series of little green islands in a sea of tears." One must work for every success and happiness.*

FONG, HIRAM L., former U.S. senator; b. Honolulu, Oct. 1, 1907; s. Lum Fong and Chai Ha Lum; m. Ellyn Lo; children—Hiram, Rodney, Merie-Ellen Fong Mitchell and Marvin-Allan (twins). A.B. with honors, U. Hawaii, 1930, LL.D., 1953; J.D., Harvard U., 1935; LL.D., Tufts U., 1960, Lafayette Coll., 1960, Lynchburg Coll., 1970, Lincoln U., 1971, U. Guam, 1974, St. John's U., 1975, Calif. Western Sch. Law, 1976, Tung Wu (Soochow) U., Taiwan, 1978, China Acad., Taiwan, 1978; L.H.D., L.I. U., 1968. With supply dept. Pearl Harbor Navy Yard, 1924-27; chief clk. Suburban Water System, 1930-32; dep. atty., City and County of Honolulu, 1935-38; founder, partner law firm Fong, Miho, Choy & Robinson, until 1959; founder, chmn. bd. Finance Factors, Finance Home Builders Grand Pacific Life Ins. Co., Finance Investment Co., Market City, Ltd.; chmn. bd. Hwy. Constrn. Co., Ltd.; pres. Ocean View Cemetery, Ltd.; owner, operator farm; dir. numerous firms, Honolulu; hon. cons. China Airlines. Mem. Hawaii Legislature, 1938-54, speaker, 1948-54; mem. U.S. Senate, 1959-77, Post Office and Civil Service Com., Judiciary Com., Appropriations Com., Spl. Com. on Aging; U.S. del. 150th Anniversary Argentine Independence, Buenos Aires, 1960, 55th Interparliamentary Union (World) Conf., 1966, Ditchley Found. Conf., 1967, U.S.-Can. Inter-Parliamentary Union Conf., 1961, 65, 67, 68, Mex.-U.S. Inter-Parliamentary Conf., 1968, World Interparliamentary Union, Tokyo, 1974; mem. Commn. on Revision Fed. Ct. Appellate System, 1975—; Active in civic and service orgns.; v.p. Territorial Constl. Conv., 1950; del. Rep. Nat. Conv., 1952, 56, 60, 64, 68, 72; founder, chmn. bd. Fin. Factors Found.; bd. visitors U.S. Mil. Acad., 1971—, U.S. Naval Acad., 1974—. Served from 1st lt. to maj. USAAF, 1942-44; ret. col. USAF Res. Recipient award NCCJ, 1960; Meritorious Service citation Nat. Assn. Ret. Civil Employees, 1963; Horatio Alger award, 1970; citation for outstanding service Japanese Am. Citizens League, 1970; award Am. Acad. Achievement, 1971; award outstanding service Orgn. Chinese Ams., 1973, Nat. Soc. Daus. Founders and Patriots Am., 1974; certificate Pacific Asian World, 1974; decorated Order of Brilliant Star with Grand Cordon, Republic of China; Order of Diplomatic Service Merit; Gwanghwan Medal, Republic of Korea). Mem. Am. Legion, VFW, Phi Beta Kappa. Congregationalist. Home: 1102 Alewa Dr Honolulu HI 96817

FONKALSRUD, ERIC WALTER, physician, educator; b. Balt., Aug. 31, 1932; s. George and Ella (Fricke) F.; m. Margaret Ann Zimmermann, June 6, 1959; children: Eric Walter, Margaret Lynn, David Loren, Robert Warren. B.A., U. Wash., 1953; M.D., Johns Hopkins U., 1957. Diplomate: Am. Bd. Surgery, Am. Bd. Thoracic Surgery, Am. Bd. Pediatric Surgery. Intern Johns Hopkins Hosp., Balt., 1957-58, asst. resident, 1958-59, U. Calif. Med. Center, Los Angeles, 1959-62, chief resident surgery, 1962-63, asst. prof. surgery, chief pediatric surgery, 1965-68, assoc. prof., 1968-71, prof., 1971—, chmn. dept. surgery, 1982—; resident pediatric surgery Columbus (Ohio) Childrens Hosp. and Ohio State U., 1963-65; practice medicine specializing in pediatric surgery, Los Angeles, 1965—; Mem. surg. study sect. NIH; James IV surg. traveller to, Gt. Britain, 1971. Editorial bd.: Jour. Surg. Research; Author book, chpts. in textbooks; Contbr. over 300 articles to med. jours. Recipient Mead Johnson award for grad. tng. surgery A.C.S., 1963; Golden Apple award for teaching UCLA Sch. Medicine, 1968; John and Mary R. Markle scholar in acad. medicine, 1963-68. Fellow A.C.S. (surg. forum com., bd. govs. 1978—), Am. Acad. Pediatrics (exec. bd.); mem. Soc. Univ. Surgeons (sec. 1973-76, pres. 1976-77), Assn. Acad. Surgeons (pres. 1972), AMA, Calif., Los Angeles County med. assns., Am. Surg. Assn., Pan Pacific Surg. Assn., Pacific Coast Surg. Assn. (recorder 1979—), Am. Pediatric Surg. Assn. (gov. 1975-78), Southwest, Los Angeles pediatric socs., Soc. for Clin. Surgery, Transplantation Soc., Pediatric Surgery Biology Club, Am. Thoracic Surg. Assn., Bay, Los Angeles surg. socs., Am. Acad. Sci., Sigma Xi, Alpha Omega Alpha. Methodist. Club: Pithotomy (pres.). Home: 428 24th St Santa Monica CA 90402 Office: Dept Surgery U Calif Med Center Los Angeles CA 90024

FONKEN, GERHARD JOSEPH, univ. adminstr.; b. Krefeld, Germany, Aug. 3, 1928; came to U.S., 1930, naturalized, 1935; s. Henry A. and Wilhelmina Katerina (von Eyser) F.; m. Carolyn Lee Stay, Dec. 20, 1952; children—David, Katherine, Steven, Karen, Eric. B.S., U. Calif., Berkeley, 1954, Ph.D., 1957. Chemist Procter & Gamble Co., 1957-58, Stanford (Calif.) Research Inst., 1958-59; instr. U. Tex., Austin, 1959-61, asst. prof., 1961-66, asso. prof., 1966-72, prof. chemistry, 1972—, asso. provost, 1972-75, acting v.p. acad. affairs, 1975-76, exec. asst. to pres., 1976-79, v.p. research, 1979-80, v.p. acad. affairs and research, 1980—. Contbr. articles to chemistry jours. Served with U.S. Army, 1946-49, 50-51; Korea. NIH grantee, 1961-64; Robert A. Welch Found. grantee, 1962-79. Mem. Am. Chem. Soc., Western Pharm. Soc. Home: 6800 Kings Point W Austin TX 78723 Office: Dept Chemistry U Tex Austin TX 78712

FONTAINE, ARMAND LOUIS, insurance company executive; b. Sorel, Que., Can., Apr. 24, 1924; came to U.S., 1926, naturalized, 1943; s. Louis Phillip and Angelina (Villandre) F.; m. Barbara Jones, Aug. 7, 1953; 1 son, George Robert. Student, U. Americas, 1947, McGill U., 1948; B.S., U. So. Calif., 1949; postgrad., U. Paris, 1950. Exec. v.p. Am. Bldg. Contractors Assn., from 1955; pres. Western Adminstrs., from 1955; v.p. Nat. Home Improvement Council, from 1960; now chmn. bd. Contractors Surety Co.; now pres. Western Regional Master Builders Assn. Columnist: Los Angeles Times. Dir. Calif. Compensation Ins. Fund. Served with AUS, World War II; CBI. Mem. Lambda Chi Alpha, Delta Phi Epsilon. Office: 8727 W 3d St Suite 203 Los Angeles CA 90048

FONTAINE, JOAN (BORN DE HAVILLAND), actress; b. Tokyo, Japan, Oct. 22, 1917; d. Walter and Lilian (Ruse) de H.; m. Brian Aherne, Aug. 20, 1939 (div. 1944); m. William Dozier, May 2, 1946; 1 dau., Deborah Leslie, 1 adopted dau., Martita Valentina Caideron; m. Collier Young, Nov. 10, 1952 (div. 1961); m. Alfred Wright, Jr., Feb. 1964. Lectr. univs., women's clubs. Has appeared in numerous motion pictures since, 1937; pictures include Rebecca, 1939 (N.Y. Critics award, Can. Film Critics award), Suspicion, 1940 (Acad. award), Constant Nymph, 1943, Jane Eyre, 1944, Frenchman's Creek, 1944, Ivy, 1947, You Gotta Stay Happy, 1948, September Affair, 1949, Born to be Bad, 1949, Something to Live For, 1950, Darling How Could You, 1950, Ivanhoe, 1951, Decameron Nights, 1952, Casanova, 1953, Beyond A Reasonable Doubt, 1956, Island in the Sun, 1957, Until We Sail, 1957, A Certain Smile, 1958, Voyage To The Bottom of The Sea, 1961, Tender Is the Night, 1962, The Devils Own, 1966; broadway debut in Tea and Sympathy, 1954; other theatre prodns. including Cactus Flower, Private Lives, The Marriage-Go-Round, Forty Carats, Dial "M" for Murder; TV panelist; Author: No Bed of Roses, 1978. Bd. dirs. Motion Picture Welfare Trust Fund. Recipient Eleanor Roosevelt award, 1966. Mem. Motion Picture Acad. *

FONTAINE, JOHN CLOVIS, lawyer; b. Cin., Oct. 12, 1931; s. Athanas P. and Arline (McGrath) F.; m. Elizabeth Whitney Ellis, Aug. 19, 1954; children: Anne Elizabeth, Amy Bienvenue, Alison Whitney. B.A., U. Mich., 1953; LL.B., Harvard U., 1956. Bar: N.Y. 1957. Ptnr. Hughes Hubbard & Reed, N.Y.C., 1964—; gen. counsel Knight-Ridder Newspaper, Miami, Fla., 1980—. Office: Hughes Hubbard & Reed One Wall St New York NY 10005

FONTAINE, RICHARD KERN, naval officer; b. Mpls., May 31, 1928; s. Jean Henri and Lillian (Richard) F.; m. Sara Jean Wyatt, June 8, 1951; children: Richard S., Martha J., Catherine J., Susan J., Sara J. Student, U. Minn., 1946-47; B.S., U.S. Naval Acad., 1951, Naval Postgrad. Sch., 1959. Commd. ensign U.S. Navy, 1951, advanced through grades to rear adm., 1978; spl. asst. Office Undersec. Navy, Washington, 1965-67; comdg. officer USS Hoel, USN, 1967-69; communications officer 1st Fleet, USN, San Diego, 1969-71, exec. asst., sr. aide to chief naval material, Washington, 1971-73; comdg. officer USS Reeves, USN, 1973-75; asst. chief staff for ops. U.S. Pacific Fleet, USN, 1975-78; dir. surface warfare div. Office Chief Naval Ops., USN, Washington, dep. dir. tactical-theater C3 systems. Decorated Legion of Merit, Bronze Star, others. Mem. U.S. Naval Inst. Office: Dept Navy Washington DC 20301

FONTANA, MARS GUY, engr.; b. Iron Mountain, Mich., Apr. 6, 1910; s. Dominic and Rosalie (Amico) F.; m. Elizabeth Frances Carley, Aug. 21, 1937; children—Martha Jane, Mary Elizabeth, David Carley, Thomas Edward. B.S., U. Mich., 1931, M.S., 1932, Ph.D., 1935, D.Eng. (hon.), 1975. Research asst., dept. engring. research U. Mich., 1929-34; metall. engr., group supervisor engring. dept. duPont Co., Wilmington, Del., 1934-45; prof., chmn. dept. metall. engring. Ohio State U., 1945-75, prof. emeritus, 1976, Regents prof., 1967—, Duriron prof., 1970-75; dir. Corrosion Center; supr. metall. research; dir. Worthington Industries, 1973—, mem. audit com., 1975—; research NASA, USN, USAF, Nat. Sci. Found., Alloy Casting Inst.; cons. engr. several pvt. and govtl. orgns. Author: Corrosion: A Compilation, 1957, Corrosion Engineering, 1967, 2d edit., 1978; contbr.: column Indsl. and Engring. Chemistry, 1947-56; also other tech. publs. Recipient distinguished alumnus citation U. Mich., 1953, Sesquicentennial award, 1967; Frank Newman Speller award in corrosion engring. Nat. Assn. Corrosion Engrs., 1956; Native Son award Iron Mountain (Mich.) Rotary Club, 1969; Neil Armstrong award Ohio Soc. Profl. Engrs., 1973; MacQuigg Teaching award Coll. Engring., Ohio State U., 1973; Mars G. Fontana Labs. at Ohio State U. named in his honor, 1981. Fellow Am. Soc. Metals (hon.; Gold medal 1979), Am. Inst. Mining, Metall. and Petroleum Engrs., Am. Inst. Chem. Engrs.; mem. Nat. Assn. Corrosion Engrs. (pres. 1952, editor Jour. Corrosion 1962-74), Electrochem. Soc., Materials Tech. Inst. of Chem. Process Industries (exec. dir. 1977—), Nat. Acad. Engring., Nat. Soc. Profl. Engrs., Am. Soc. Engring. Edn. (award for excellence in engring. instruction 1969), Sigma Xi, Tau Beta Pi, Alpha Chi Sigma, Iota Alpha, Phi Eta Sigma, Phi Lambda Upsilon, Sphinx, Texnikoi. Clubs: Port au Villa (Naples, Fla.) (pres. 1967-70); Faculty, Univ. Golf. Patentee on corrosion testing and recording devices, also iron ore reduction and corrosion resistant alloys. Home: 2086 Elgin Rd Columbus OH 43221

FONTANA, ROBERT EDWARD, educator, ret. air force officer; b. Bklyn., Nov. 26, 1915; s. Valentino and Secondina (Lesca) F.; m. Victoria E. Mauriello, Dec. 2, 1945; children—Robert Edward, Thomas Paul, Mary Joan. B.Elec. Engring, N.Y. U., 1939; M.S., U. Ill., 1947, Ph.D., 1949. Commd. 2d lt. USAAF, 1942; advanced through grades to col. USAF, 1959, ret., 1969; research scientist Sandia Corp., 1949-54; spl. asst. nuclear devel. Hdqrs. USAF, 1954-58; head nuclear applications (Air Research and Devel. Command), 1958-61, dir., Wright-Patterson AFB, Ohio, 1961-66, chmn. dept. elec. engring., Wright-Patterson AFB, 1966—. Pres. Honors Seminars Met. Dayton, 1966—. Decorated Legion of Merit with oak leaf cluster. Fellow IEEE (chmn. Dayton sect. 1971, editor edn. group newsletter 1970—); mem. Am. Soc. Engring. Edn. (editor elec. engring. div. newsletter 1970—, chmn. energy conversion com. 1978—), Sigma Xi, Tau Beta Pi, Eta Kappa Nu. Home: 6679 Statesboro Rd Dayton OH 45459 Office: AFIT Dept Elec Engring Wright-Patterson AFB OH 45433

FONTEYN DE ARIAS, DAME MARGOT, ballerina; b. Reigate, Surrey, Eng., May 18, 1919; d. Felix J. Hookham; m. Roberto E. Arias, 1955. Hon. degrees; Litt.D., U. Leeds; D.Mus., U. London, Oxford U.; LL.D., U. Edinburgh; D.Litt., U. Manchester. Prima ballerina Royal Ballet Co., London; pres. Royal Acad. Dancing, London, 1954—. Author: Margot Fonteyn, 1975, A Dancer's World, 1978, The Magic of Dance (BBC series), 1979, 80; films include I am a Dancer, 1972. Recipient Benjamin Franklin medal Royal Soc. Arts, 1974; Internat. Artist award, Philippines, 1976; Hamburg Internat. Shakespeare prize, 1977; decorated Order Finnish Lion, 1960, Order Estacio de Sa, Brazil, 1973, chevalier Order Merit of Duarte, Sanchez and Mella, Dominican Republic, 1975. Address: care Royal Opera House Covent Garden London England WC2 *

FOONBERG, JAY G., lawyer, accountant; b. Chgo., Oct. 29, 1935; s. Hyman J. and Esther (Leon) F.; m. Lois Alpin, Aug. 31, 1958; children: Alan Marshall, David Jeffrey Steven Mark. B.S., UCLA, 1957, J.D., 1963. Auditor Calif. Bd. Equalization, 1957-59; accountant Seidman & Seidman, C.P.A.s, Beverly Hills, Calif., 1959-60, Lever & Anker, C.P.A.s, 1960-63; pres. law corp. of Foonberg & Frandzel, Beverly Hills, 1970-79; prin. Slavitt, King & Foonberg, Los Angeles, 1979-81, Foonberg, Jampol & Gardner, 1981—; arbitrator Am. Arbitration Assn., 1965—; judge pro tem Beverly Hills Municipal Ct., 1970-71, Los Angeles Municipal Ct., 1980-81; trustee, pres. Brazil-Calif. Trade Assn.; spl. advisor for Latin Am. to Calif. sec. state. Author: How To Start and Build A Law Practice, 1976, 2d edit., 1984; Contbr. articles to profl. jours.; lectr. in field. Mem. Men's Club of Cedars-Sinai Med. Center, Speakers Bur., 1966; also dir. Speakers Bur.; mem. Los Angeles Olympics Adv. Commn., 1981—. Served with USAF, 1958-64. Decorated Order of So. Cross (Brazil), Order of Rio Branco (Brazil). Mem. Am. Assn. Atty.-C.P.A.s (charter sec., pres., dir.), Calif. Assn. Atty.-C.P.A.s (dir., pres.), Calif. Soc. C.P.A.s, Am. Bar Assn. (council econs. of law practice sect. 1975-77, Gold Key award law student div. 1977, award of highest honors law students div. 1983), Beverly Hills Bar Assn. (gov.), Century City Bar Assn. (bd. govs. 1980-81), State Bar Calif. (mem. spl. commn. for assimilation of new lawyers into the profession; chmn. econs. of law practice sect. 1977, 78), Argentine-Calif. Bus. Assn. (founder, pres. 1983), Phi Alpha Delta, Phi Epsilon Phi. Home: 716 N Rexford Dr Beverly Hills CA 90210 Office: 8500 Wilshire Blvd Suite 900 Beverly Hills CA 90211 *Whatever you do in life, do it right.*

FOOSANER, ROBERT STEPHEN, government official; b. Newark, Feb. 1, 1943; s. George and Gertrude (Rood) F.; m. Jeanne Schneider, Dec. 21, 1965; children: Eve, Matthew. B.A., Rutgers U., 1965; J.D.,

Washington Coll. Law, 1968. Bar: U.S. Dist. Ct. D.C. 1968, U.S. Ct. Appeals D.C. 1969. Atty. Broadcast Bur., FCC, Washington, 1968-73, atty. Office Gen. Counsel, 1973-77, supervisory atty., 1977-79, chief policy task force Office of Sci. and Tech., 1979-80, chief policy and mgmt. staff, 1980-81, dep. chief Pvt. Radio Bur., 1981-83; chief Pvt. Radio Bur., 1983—; U.S. del. MF Broadcasting Conf., Buenos Aires, Argentina, 1980, Mobile WARC Conf., Geneva, Switzerland, 1983. Trustee Leukemia Soc. Am., Washington, 1976-82. Mem. D.C. Bar Assn., Bar Assn. D.C. Office: Fed Communications Commn 1919 M St NW Room 5002 Washington DC 20054

FOOSE, RICHARD MARTIN, geology educator; b. Lancaster, Pa., Oct. 9, 1915; s. Leon K. and Grace (Leinbach) F.; m. Dorothy Jane Kell, Feb. 11, 1943; children: Michele Leslie, Michael Peter, Stephan, Terry. B.S., Franklin and Marshall Coll., 1937; M.S., Northwestern U., 1939; Ph.D., Johns Hopkins U., 1942; M.A. (hon.), Amherst Coll., 1964. Instr. Northwestern U., 1937-39; prof. and head dept. geology Franklin and Marshall Coll., 1946-57; sr. geologist Stanford Research Inst., 1957-63; chmn. dept. earth scis.; prof., chmn. dept. geology Amherst (Mass.) Coll., 1963—; asst. geologist Pa. Geol. Survey, 1939-42, asso. geologist, 1942-43, sr. geologist, 1943-46; geologist Pa. Turnpike Commn., 1941; cons. geologist, 1942—; Ford Found. fellow, research asso. Stanford U., 1955-56; NSF sr. postdoctoral fellow Eidg. Technische Hochschule, Zurich, Switzerland, 1962-63; Nat. Acad. Sci. fellow, USSR, 1969, 76, Bulgaria, 1972. Contbr. articles profl. jours. U.S. govt. del. Internat. Geol. Congress, 1968; mem. NRC, 1969—. Fellow AAAS, Geol. Soc. Am., Am. Geog. Soc.; mem. Soc. Econ. Geologists (councillor 1954-57), AIME (chmn. div. indsl. minerals 1950-51, vice chmn. mineral econ. div. 1953-54, del. internat. geol. congress 1952, 56, 60, chmn. council mineral econs. 1962-63, asso. editor Indsl. Minerals and Rocks 1960, 75, 81), Yellowstone Bighorn Research Assn. (v.p. 1955, 83-84), Pa. Acad. Sci. (pres. 1949-50), Am. Geol. Inst., Assn. Geol. Tchrs. (del. internat. geol. congress 1956), Am. Geophys. Union, Am. Inst. Profl. Geologists (charter; sec. 1968), Geochem. Soc., Phi Beta Kappa, Sigma Xi. Club: Torch (Lancaster). Office: Amherst Coll Amherst MA 01002

FOOTE, CALEB, legal educator; b. 1917. A.B., Harvard U., 1939; M.A., Columbia U., 1951; LL.B., U. Pa., 1953. Bar: Pa. 1956. Instr. U. Pa., 1953-54; assoc. prof. U. Nebr. Law Sch., 1956-58, prof., 1958-65; prof. law U. Calif.-Berkeley, 1965—, Elizabeth Josselyn Boalt prof.; Walter E. Meter vis. Research prof. Harvard U. Law Sch., 1960-61. Co-author: (with R.J. Levt and F.E.A. Sander) Cases and Materials on Family Law, 1966; editor: Studies on Bail, 1966; mng. editor: U. Pa. Law Rev. Legal Edn. Office: U Calif Law Sch 225 Boalt Hall Berkeley CA 94720 *

FOOTE, CHRISTOPHER SPENCER, chemist; b. Hartford, Conn., June 5, 1935; s. William J. and Dorothy (Bennett) F.; m. Judith L. Smith; children: Jonathan, Thomas. B.S. magna cum laude, Yale U., 1957; Fulbright scholar, U. Gottingen, 1957-58; A.M., Harvard U., 1959, Ph.D., 1961. NSF predoctoral fellow Harvard U., 1958-61; instr. chemistry UCLA, 1961-62, asst. prof., 1962-66, assoc. prof., 1966-69, prof., 1969—, chmn. dept., 1978-81; cons. Proctor & Gamble Co. Recipient Baeklund medal, 1975; Sloane fellow, 1965-67; Guggenheim fellow, 1967-68. Mem. Am. Chem. Soc., Chem. Soc. London, AAAS, Am. Soc. Photobiology (council 1978-81), Gesellschaft Deutscher Chemiker, Phi Beta Kappa, Sigma Xi, Phi Lambda Upsilon. Home: 766 Malcolm Ave Los Angeles CA 90024 Office: Dept Chemistry U Calif Los Angeles CA 90024

FOOTE, EDWARD THADDEUS, II, lawyer, university president; b. Milw., Dec. 15, 1937; s. William Hamilton and Julia Stevenson (Hardin) F.; m. Roberta Waugh Fulbright, Apr. 18, 1964; children: Julia, William, Thaddeus. B.A., Yale U., 1959; LL.B., Georgetown U., 1966. Bar: Mo. 1966. Reporter, Washington Star, 1963-64, Washington Daily News, 1964-65; Pennsylvania asst. Pa. Ave. Commn., 1965-66; asso. Bryan, Cave, McPheeters & McRoberts, St. Louis, 1966-70; vice chancellor, gen. counsel Washington U., St. Louis, 1970-73, dean Sch. Law, 1973-80, spl. adv. to chancellor and bd. trustees, 1980-81; pres. U. Miami (Fla.), 1981—; fed. ct.-apptd. chmn. citizens com. and desegregation monitoring com. St. Louis sch. desegregation case, 1980—. Mem. steering com. Gov.'s Conf. on Edn., 1974-76; pres. bd. New City Sch., St. Louis, 1967-73; bd. dirs. St. Louis City and County Legal Aid Soc., 1973-78; bd. advs. to pres. Naval War Coll., 1979—. Served with USMCR, 1959-62. Mem. ABA, Mo. Bar. Democrat. Office: U Miami Office of Pres Coral Gables FL 33124

FOOTE, EMERSON, retired corporation executive; b. Sheffield, Ala., Dec. 13, 1906; s. James Adonijah and Ruth (Penn) F.; m. Sabina Fromhold, Apr. 18, 1938; children: Florence Anne, Katherine Penn, James Adair, Jennifer Broughton. Student pub. schs.; D.Pub. Service, Brigham Young U., 1965. With bldg. and loan assn., automobile distbg. co., life ins. co., 1923-31, Leon Livingston Advt. Agy., San Francisco, 1931-35, Yeomans & Foote, 1935-36, J. Stirling Getchell, Inc., N.Y.C., 1936-38; with Lord & Thomas, 1938-42, exec. v.p., 1942; co-founder Foote, Cone & Belding, 1942, pres., 1942-50; with McCann-Erickson, Inc., 1951-64, pres., 1960-63, chmn. bd., 1962-64; 1st chmn. Nat. Interagy. Council on Smoking and Health, Washington, 1964-67; chmn. Campaign to Check Population Explosion, 1967-69; dir. Nat. Liberty Corp., Valley Forge, Pa., 1969-73; chmn. bd. DeMoss Assos., Inc. subsidiary, 1969-73. Mem. Pres. Johnson's Commn. on Heart Disease, Cancer and Stroke, 1964-65; adviser to Govt. India on Family Planning, 1969; mem. U.S. Senate Panel Consultants on Cancer, 1970-71, USPHS Cancer Control Adv. Com., 1972—; hon. dir. Non-Smokers' Rights Assn., Can., 1979—; Trustee or bd. dirs. numerous non-profit orgns. including Menninger Found., Am. Cancer Soc., The Environmental Fund, Population Inst.; chmn. adv. bd. Rutgers Center for Alcohol Studies, AAPC, Inc., others; bd. dirs. Putnam Hosp. Ctr., 1975-82. Recipient Clement Cleveland medal for cancer work, 1953, Nat. Vol. Leadership award Am. Cancer Soc., 1974. Address: Gipsy Trail Carmel NY 10512

FOOTE, FRANKLIN MANLEY, pub. health physician; b. Dannemora, N.Y., Apr. 15, 1908; s. Wilbur Ephraim and May Etta (Manley) F.; m. Doris Brewer Humphrey, June 24, 1933; children—Patricia Beverly, Susan Eleanor, Franklin Humphrey. B.S., Yale U., 1930, M.D., 1933, D.P.H., 1935. Physician USPHS Hosp., Norfolk, Va., 1933-34; county health officer, Tenn., 1935-37; chief div. local health administrn. Conn. State Dept. Health, 1937-41; dist. health officer, N.Y.C., 1941-46; med. dir., later exec. dir. Nat. Soc. Prevention Blindness, N.Y.C., 1946-59; asst. prof. pub. health and preventive medicine Cornell U. Med. Sch., 1941-52; commr. Conn. State Dept. Health, 1959-73; lectr. in epidemiology, pub. health Yale, 1959; med. cons. Travelers Ins. Co., 1973-77; health dir., City of Wethersfield, 1977—; sec. Nat. Health Council, N.Y.C., 1957-59. Contbr. sci. articles to publs. Served as maj. M.C. AUS, 1942-46. Recipient Fones medal Conn. Dental Assn., 1965; Winslow medal Conn. Pub. Health Assn., 1967; Decorated Army Commendation medal. Fellow Am. Pub. Health Assn.; mem. AMA, Conn. Med. Soc., Internat. Assn. Prevention Blindness, Am. Assn. State Hosp. Constrn. Authorities (pres. 1966). Home: 4 Round Hill Rd Wethersfield CT 06109

FOOTE, FRED L., architect; b. Little Rock, May 6, 1938; s. Ernest Gaston and Lucy Lee (Young) F.; m. Rosslynn Ferrier, June 2, 1962; 1 dau., Alexandra Lee. B.A., Rice Inst., 1960; B.Arch., U. Pa., 1962. Registered architect, Pa., N.Y., N.J., Conn., Australia. Apprentice Hendrick & Stanley, Ft. Worth, 1957-59; draftsman Thomas E. Stanley, Dallas, 1959-61; architect Mitchell/Giurgola, Phila., 1962-71, assoc., 1971-74, ptnr., 1974—; vis. critic U. Pa., Phila., 1972-78, Temple U., 1982. Mem. Housing Assn. Delaware Valley, Phila., 1981-82. Served with USMCR, 1960-61. Recipient Brooke medal U. Pa., 1962; Schenck-Woodman traveling fellow, 1962. Fellow AIA; mem. Pa. Soc. Architects (pres. 1980). Democrat. Methodist. Club: Racquet (Phila.). Home: Vernon Ln Rose Valley PA 19065 Office: Mitchell/ Giurgola Architects 12 S 12th St Philadelphia PA 19107

FOOTE, FREEMAN, emeritus geology educator; b. Orange, N.J., Nov. 8, 1908; s. Will Howe and Helen (Freeman) F.; m. Sally Newnham Carlton, July 22, 1939; 1 dau., Nancy Newnham. B.A., Princeton U., 1931; postgrad., Columbia U., 1931-37. Asst. Columbia U., 1933-37; mem. faculty Williams Coll., Williamstown, Mass., 1937—, prof. geology, 1956—, Edward Brust prof. geology and mineralogy, 1968-74, emeritus, 1974—, chmn. dept., 1964-67; assoc. prof. Columbia U., summers 1952, 53, Wesleyan U., Middletown, Conn., summer 1955; tchr. Mt. Greylock High Sch. Ecology Inst., Williamstown, 1967; Mem. fellowship selection panel NSF, 1964, 65, 68. Vice chmn. Williamstown Republican Com., 1952-60; Vice pres. Greylock Found., 1964—; mem. Williamstown Fin. Com., 1970-72; trustee Williamstown Pub. Library, 1982—. Served to lt. comdr. USNR, 1942-45. Fellow Geol. Soc. Am.; mem. AAAS, Nat. Assn. Geology Tchrs. (sec. 1958-60), Sigma Xi. Home: 1550 Cold Spring Rd Box 602 Williamstown MA 01267

FOOTE, GUY MYRPH, investment consultant; b. Nacogdoches, Tex., Jan. 31, 1922; s. James Burton and Clyde (Locke) F.; m. Mary Nell Taylor, Feb. 3, 1946; children—Guy Myrph, Kenneth Taylor. B.S., Stephen F. Austin State U., 1942; postgrad., So. Meth. U., 1947-49. C.P.A., Tex., Okla., N.Mex., Ga., La. C.P.A. Dranguet, Foote & Co., Dallas, 1947-60, Haskins & Sells, 1960-71, Washington, 1971-72; pres., dir. Wylain, Inc., Dallas, 1972-80; cons. Marley-Wylain, 1980-82; dir. Gulf United Corp., Jacksonville, Fla., Zale Corp., Dallas, Dallas Fed. Savs.; Active United Fund, 1960-73. Treas., bd. trustees St. Mark's Sch., Dallas, 1963-72; vice chmn. Cancer Soc., 1968; pres. Goodwill Industries, 1974; bd. dirs. Dallas chpt. ARC, 1977—. Served with USAAF, 1942-46. Mem. Am. Inst. C.P.A.'s. Democrat. Methodist. Clubs: Brook Hollow Golf, Petroleum, Northwood (Dallas); Univ. (Washington). Home: 11586 Ricks Circle Dallas TX 75230 Office: 2021 Republic Bank Tower Dallas TX 75201

FOOTE, JOEL LINDSLEY, biochemist; b. Cleve., Jan. 11, 1928; s. Joel Lindsley and Beth Eliza (Brainard) F.; m. Alice Lydia Tanner, June 16, 1951; children: Robert Lindsley, Karen Ann. B.S. in Edn, Miami U., 1952; postgrad, Ohio State U., 1955; Ph.D., Case Inst. Tech., 1960. Tchr. sci. Wilmington (Ohio) Public Schs., 1952-53; tchr. sci. and math Springfield (Ohio) Public Schs., 1953-56; NSF postdoctoral fellow U. Mich., Ann Arbor, 1960-62; instr., asst. research biochemist, 1962-65; mem. faculty Western Mich. U., Kalamazoo, 1965—, asso. prof., 1969-79, prof., 1979—. Contbr. articles to profl. jours. Originator, founding chmn. City of Kalamazoo Environ. Concerns Com., 1970-72; mem. Kalamazoo County Democratic Exec. Com., 1968-82; candidate for county commr., 1968, 70. Served with USN, 1946-48. NIH research grantee, 1966-70. Mem. Am. Soc. Biol. Chemists, Am. Chem. Soc., AAAS, AAUP, Phi Beta Kappa, Sigma Xi. Unitarian. Home: 3623 Lancaster Dr Kalamazoo MI 49007 Office: Dept Chemistry Western Mich U Kalamazoo MI 49008

FOOTE, ROBERT HUTCHINSON, animal physiology educator; b. Gilead, Conn., Aug. 20, 1922; s. Robert E. and Annie (Hutchinson) F.; m. Ruth E. Parcells, Jan. 12, 1946; children: Robert W., Dale H. B.S., U. Conn., 1943; M.S., Cornell U., 1947, Ph.D. in Animal Physiology and Biochem. Genetics, 1950. Grad. asst. Cornell U., Ithaca, N.Y., 1946-50, asst. prof. animal physiology, 1950-56, assoc. prof., 1956-63, prof., 1963—, Jacob Gould Schurman chair, 1980—; cons. Corning Glass Co., 1978—, Genetic Engring. Co., Denver, 1980—, Equi Cryotech. Co., Aitken, S.C., 1983—. Author: Animal Reproduction, 1954; mem. editorial bds. various jours., 1958—; contbr. articles to profl. jours., chpts. to books. Chmn. trustees Congregation Ch., Ithaca, 1955-60. Served to capt. inf. U.S. Army, 1943-46; ETO. Named Prof. of Merit Cornell U., 1967; recipient Sci. medal N.Y. Farmers, 1969. Fellow AAAS; mem. Soc. Study Reprodn. (bd. dirs. 1976-78, pres.-elect 1984), Am. Soc. Andrology (mem. editorial bd. 1982—), Am. Soc. Animal Sci. (editorial bd. 1958-60, Nat. Physiology and Endocrinology award 1970), Am. Soc. Theriogenology (editorial bd. 1976—), Sigma Xi, Phi Kappa Phi. Republican. Home: 70 Woodcrest Ave Ithaca NY 14850 Office: Dept Animal Sci Cornell U 201 Morrison Hall Ithaca NY 14853

FOOTE, ROBERT THADDEUS, food company executive; b. Newton Center, Mass., Oct. 25, 1917; s. Edward Thaddeus and Laura (Stedman) F.; m. Barbara Brumder, Mar. 30, 1940 (div. 1965); children: Robert Thaddeus, Barbara Chapin; m. Dorothy Bergamini, June 1972. B.S., Cornell U., 1939; D.Comml.Sci. (hon.), U. Wis.-Milw. Prodn. foreman Procter & Gamble Co., Chgo., 1939-41; with Red Star Yeast & Products Co. (name changed to Universal Foods Corp.), Milw., 1941—, exec. v.p., dir., 1957-66, pres., chief exec. officer, dir., 1966-68, chmn. bd., pres., chief exec. officer, 1968—; chmn. bd. Universal Foods Corp., 1979—; dir. Marine Bank, N.A., Marine Corp., Johnson Controls, Inc. Hon. bd. dirs. Zool. Soc. Milw. County; bd. dirs. Friends of Mus., Froedtert Meml. Lutheran Hosp., U. Wis.-Milw. Found., Greater Milw. Com.; mem. council Med. Coll. Wis., Cornell U.; corp. mem. Milw. Sch. Engring.; mem. nat. corps. com. United Negro Coll. Fund; mem. Goals for Milw. 2000; trustee, vice chmn. Nutrition Found., Inc., N.Y.C.; trustee Marquette U.; trustee, mem. exec. com. Citizens Govt. Research Bur.; corp. mem. Milw. Sch. Engring. Mem. Met. Milw. Assn. Commerce (pres. 1971—, dir.), Chi Psi. Republican. Club: Rotary (hon.). Home: 6100 N Brumder Rd Hartland WI 53029 Office: 433 E Michigan St Milwaukee WI 53201

FOOTE, SHELBY, author; b. Greenville, Miss., Nov. 17, 1916; s. Shelby Dade and Lillian (Rosenstock) F.; m. Gwyn Rainer, Sept. 5, 1956; children: Margaret Shelby, Huger Lee. Student, U. N.C., 1935-37; D.Litt. (hon.), U. of the South, 1981, Southwestern U., 1982. Novelist lectr., U. Va., 1963; playwright in residence, Arena Stage, Washington, 1963-64; writer in residence, Hollins Coll., Va., 1968; Author: novels Tournament, 1949, Follow Me Down, 1950, Love in a Dry Season, 1951, Shiloh, 1952, Jordan County, 1954, September September, 1978; history The Civil War, A Narrative: Vol. I, Fort Sumter to Perryville, 1958, Vol. II; Fredericksburg to Meridian, 1963, Vol. III, Red River to Appomattox, 1974; play Jordon County: A Landscape in the Round, 1964. Recipient Distinguished Alumnus award U. N.C., 1975; Guggenheim fellow, 1955-57; Ford Found. fellow, 1963-64. Mem. Soc. Am. Historians. MailingAddress: 542 E Parkway S Memphis TN 38104

FOOTE, TIMOTHY GILSON, editor; b. London, May 3, 1926; s. John Taintor and Jessica Florence (Todhunter) F.; m. Audrey Chamberlain, June 18, 1948; children: Colin Chamberlain, Victoria Ravenhill, Valerie Sophia, Andrew Todhunter. A.B. magna cum laude, Harvard U., 1949, A.M., 1952. Reporter-writer Life mag., 1949-51, asst. editor, 1953-54, assoc., sr. editor, 1958-62; tchr. Thomas Jefferson Sch., 1952-53; fgn. corr. Time-Life, Paris, 1954-58; book reviewer Time mag., N.Y.C., 1962-64, assoc. editor, 1968, sr. editor, reviewer, 1969-82; bd. editors Smithsonian mag., 1982—; European editor Internat. Book Soc., Paris, 1964-66; fiction judge Nat. Book Awards, 1974; vis. lectr. English composition Yale U., 1975-76; exec. bd. Nat. Book Critics Circle, 1976-83; mem. adv. bd. Sea History mag., 1977—; mem. selection com. Nat. Medal for Lit, 1980; Time fellow Duke U., 1980. Author: The World of Peter Bruegel, 1968, The Great Ringtail Garbage Caper, 1980; contbr. articles to mags. Served with USNR, 1944-46. Recipient Bowdoin prize in lit., 1949. Mem. Signet Soc., Phi Beta Kappa. Episcopalian. Office: 900 Jefferson Dr SW Washington DC

FORAN, KENNETH LAWRENCE, lawyer, government official; b. Aug. 14, 1941. A.B., Dartmouth Coll., 1963; J.D., Cornell U., 1970; M.P.A., Harvard U., 1971; Diploma in Comparative Legal Studies, Cambridge (Eng.) U., 1973. Cert. The Hague Acad. Internat. Law, 1972; cert. U.S. Naval Justice Sch., Newport, R.I., 1979, Ohio 1973, Va. 1979, N.Y. 1980, N.D. 1981, Pa. 1981, U.S. Dist. Ct. (ea. dist.) Va. 1979, U.S. Dist. Ct. (we. dist.) Va. 1979, U.S. Dist. Ct. (no. dist.) Calif. 1979, U.S. Dist. Ct. (ea. dist.) Wis. 1980, U.S. Dist. Ct. (no. dist.) Ohio 1973, U.S. Ct. Claims 1979, U.S. Tax Ct. 1979, U.S. Ct. Customs 1979, U.S. Ct. Mil. Appeals 1979, U.S. Ct. Appeals (4th Cir.) 1974, U.S. Ct. Appeals (5th cir.) 1981, U.S. Ct. Appeals (6th cir.) 1973, U.S. Ct. Appeals (8th and 9th cirs.) 1979, U.S. Ct. Appeals (11th cir.) 1982, U.S. ct. Appeals (D.S. cir.) 1979, U.S. Supreme ct. 1979. Law clk. U.S. Ct. Appeals (6th cir.), Cin., 1972-73; asst. prof. law U. Richmond, 1974-76; prof. law Potomac Sch. Law, Washington, 1976-77; minority cousel subcom. on constrn., com. on judiciary U.S. Senate, Washington, 1977-78; sole practice law, Alexandria, Va., 1979-82; dir. merit systems rev. and studies U.S. Merit Systems Protection Bd., Washington, 1982—; trial atty. Presdl. Clemency Bd., The White House, Washington, 1975; atty. mem. Va. State Bd. Accountancy, 1979-83, Va. Dept. Commerce, 1979-83. Asst. editor: Cornell Law Forum, 1969-70; assoc. editor: Cornell Internat. Law Jour., 1969-70. Served to maj. JAGC USMC, 1965-68; Vietnam. Decorated Vietnam Cross of Gallantry with palm; Rufus Choate scholar Dartmouth Coll., 1962-63; Lucius Littauer fellow Harvard U., 1970-71; Evan Lewis-Thomas law studentship Sidney Sussex Coll., Cambridge U., 1971-72. Mem. ABA (co-chmn. ethics com. Young Lawyers sect. 1973-77, editor, The Forum 1976-77), Fed. Bar Assn. (chmn. Charlottesville chpt. Law Day 1973, chmn. comparative law subcom. internat. law com. 1976-77), Va. State Bar Assn., Ohio State Bar Assn., N.D. Bar Assn., D.C. Bar Assn., N.Y. State Bar Assn., Pa. Bar Assn., Alexandria Bar Assn., Va. Trial Lawyers Assn., Akron Bar Assn., No. Va. Young Lawyers Assn., Am. Judicature Soc., Am. Soc. Internat. Law, Cornell Law Assn., Marine Corps Res. Officers Assn., Judge Advs. Assn., Phi Alpha Delta. Clubs: Oxford-Cambridge University (London); Kiwanis, Dartmouth, Harvard; Cornell (Washington). Lodge: Masons. Home: 5001 Seminary Rd Alexandria VA 22311 Office: US Merit Systems Protection Bd 1120 Vermont Ave NW Washington DC 20419

FORAN, THOMAS AQUINAS, lawyer; b. Chgo., Jan. 11, 1924; s. Francis Leo and Mary Elizabeth (Larkin) F.; m. Jean Marie Burke, Oct. 14, 1950; children: Elizabeth, John, Julie, Edmund, Stephen, Regina. Ph.B., Loyola U., Chgo., 1947; LL.B., J.D., U. Detroit, 1950. Bar: Ill. 1950. Since practiced in Chgo.; U.S. atty. No. Dist. Ill., 1968-70; partner Foran, Wiss & Schultz, 1959-68, 70—, sr. partner, 1959—; lectr. Ill. Inst. Continuing Legal Edn.; gen. counsel Chgo. Bd. Elections, 1973-79; chmn. Cook County Environ. Control Bd. Appeals, 1973-76; spl. asst. atty. Chgo. Park Dist. and Chgo. Transit Authority, 1971—. Served with USNR, 1942-46. Fellow Am. Coll. Trial Lawyers; mem. ABA, Fed. Bar Assn., Am. Trial Lawyers Assn., Ill. Bar Assn., Ill. Trial Lawyers Assn., Chgo. Bar Assn. Democrat. Roman Catholic. Clubs: Chgo. Athletic Assn., Mid-Day (Chgo.). Office: Foran Wiss & Schultz 30 N LaSalle St Suite 3000 Chicago IL 60602 *

FORBES, ALLAN LOUIS, government agency administrator, physician; b. Richmond, Va., July 28, 1928; s. John Campbell and Irene Byrd (Duval) F.; m. Janie Catherine Robb, June 12, 1954; children: Laurie Elizabeth, Ellen Irene Robb, John Campbell. B.Sc., McGill U., Can., 1949; M.D., Med. Coll. Va., 1953, M.S. in Biochemistry (A.D. Williams Meml. scholar, Mead Johnson-A.C.P. scholar), 1964; diplomate, Nat. War Coll., 1968. Rotating intern Montreal (Que., Can.) Gen. Hosp., 1953-54; resident in internal medicine Med. Coll. Va., 1954-56; chief clin. physiology br. U.S. Army Med. Research and Nutrition Lab., Denver, 1956-58; clin. investigator VA Hosp., Richmond, 1958-61; asst. dir. med. programs, interdepartmental com. on nutrition for nat. def. Nat. Inst. Arthritis and Metabolic Disease, Bethesda, Md., 1961-63; med. officer sci. analysis br. Life Sci. div. Office Chief of Research and Devel., U.S. Army Gen. Staff, Washington, 1963-70, br. chief, 1968-70; with Bur. Foods, FDA, Washington, 1970-73, 74—, dir. div. nutrition, 1972-73, 74-75, asso. dir. for nutrition and consumer scis., 1975-79, asso. dir. for nutrition and food scis., 1979—; dir. Nutrition Bur., Health and Welfare Can., 1973-74; mem., chmn. numerous nat. and internat. groups on human nutrition. Author: books, including Nutrition Survey of the Republic of Vietnam, 1960, Nutrition Survey of the Kingdom of Thailand, 1962; research, publs. on human nutrition; contbr. articles to profl. jours. Served with U.S. Army, 1956-58. Recipient William Branch Porter award in internal medicine Med. Coll. Va., 1953; Meritorious Civilian Service decoration Dept. Army, 1966; award of merit FDA, 1973; Superior Service award US PHS, 1983. Mem. Am. Soc. Clin. Nutrition (pres.-elect 1983-85), Am. Inst. Nutrition (Conrad A. Elvehjem award for pub. service in nutrition 1982), Va. Acad. Sci., Am. Fedn. Clin. Research, Acad. Medicine Washington, Nutrition Soc. Can., Alpha Omega Alpha. Republican. Presbyterian. Club: Cosmos. Home: 11312 Farmland Dr Old Farm Rockville MD 20852 Office: 200 C St SW Washington DC 20204

FORBES, BRYAN, actor, writer, director; b. London, Eng., July 22, 1926; s. William Theobald and Judith Kate Helen (Seaton) F.; m. Constance Smith, Feb. 19, 1951 (div. 1955); m. Nanette Newman, Aug. 27, 1955; children—Sarah Kate Amanda, Emma Katy. Student, Royal Acad. Dramatic Art, London, 1941-42. Entered profl. theatre, 1942; chief cons. editor King mag.; Mem. gen. adv. council BBC, 1965—. Debut in: The Corn is Green, London, 1942; other stage appearances include Flare Path, 1943, Gathering Storm, 1948, September Tide, 1948, The Holly and The Ivy, 1950, Tobias and The Angel, 1953, A Touch of Fear, 1956; dir.: Macbeth for, The Old Vic, 1980; film appearances include The League of Gentlemen, 1959, The Baby and the Battleship, 1955, The Wooden Horse, 1948, An Inspector Calls, 1954, The Key, 1957; films Whistle Down the Wind, 1961, The L-Shaped Room, 1962, Seance on a Wet Afternoon, 1963, King Rat, 1964, The Wrong Box, 1965, The Whisperers, 1966, Deadfall, 1967, The Madwoman of Chailot, 1968, The Raging Moon, 1970, The Stepford Wives, 1974; writer, dir.: The Slipper and the Rose, 1975; writer, producer dir.: International Velvet, 1978; dir.: Brit. segment The Sunday Lovers, 1980; writer, dir.: original screenplay for BBC 1, entitled Jessie, broadcast Dec. 1980; Menage à Trois (U.S. title Better Late Than Never), 1981; head prodn., mng. dir.: The Naked Face, 1983, EMI Films Ltd., 1969-71; fiction critic: Spectator, 1961-52; Author: screenplays The Angry Silence, 1959 (Brit. Acad. award), The League of Gentlemen, 1959, Only Two Can Play, 1962 (Brit. Acad. award), The L-Shaped Room, 1962 (UN award), Seance on a Wet Afternoon, 1964 (Edgar award), (with Brian Garfield) Hopscotch; short stories Truth Lies Sleeping, 1951; autobiography Notes for a Life, 1974, Ned's Girl, The Biography of Dame Edith Evans, 1977;

novels The Distant Laughter, 1972, International Velvet, 1978, Familiar Strangers (U.S. title Stranger), 1979, The Rewrite Man, 1983; That Despicable Race—a history of the British acting tradition, 1980. Served with Brit. Army, 1943-48. Mem. Brit. Screenwriters Guild (council treas. 1960-63), Brit. Actors Equity, Screen Actors Guild, Writers Guild Am., Dirs. Guild Am., Assn. Cinema Technicians. Address: care Pinewood Studios Iver Heath Buckinghamshire England *I have always lived by Flaubert's maxim that "we shall find life tolerable once we have consented to be always ill at ease" and have accepted the fact that in company with the majority of my fellows we will always be at the ultimate mercy of the entrepreneurs. I drive ever forward, Gatsby-like, boats against the current. I have never been wholly at ease with success and can embrace honourable failure with more pleasure than I can endure fame that needs to be bought at any price.*

FORBES, EDWARD COYLE, diversified company executive; b. Bangalore, India, Sept. 5, 1915; s. Sherman Guy and Bertha (Coyle) F.; m. Anne Fromm Forbes, June 28, 1980; children: Christina, Lucien, Alexandra, Edward, Alvaro. Grad., Phillips Exeter Acad., 1934; B.S. in Elec. Engring, Auburn U., 1938; M.S. in Aero. Engring, Air Force Aero. Inst., 1945. Registered profl. engr. N.J., Ohio. With Gen. Electric Co., 1939-41, Internat. Gen. Electric Co., Paris, 1946-51; pres. Gen. Electric Portugal, 1951-55; gen. mgr. Gen. Electric Argentina, 1955-63; v.p. corporate planning Worthington Corp., Harrison, N.J., 1963-64, v.p., group exec., 1964-67, chmn., chief exec. officer, 1971-74; pres., chmn. Alco Products, Inc., 1967-69; v.p., group exec. Studebaker-Worthington, Inc., 1967-74; chmn., dir. MLW-Worthington, Ltd., Can., 1967-74; pres. E.D.E.A., Inc., 1974—; pres., vice chmn. Liberia Mining Co., Ltd., 1974-78; pres., chief exec. officer Am. Ship Bldg. Co., Tampa, Fla., 1978-83, vice chmn., 1983—; pres. Sentinel Group Funding Inc., Sentinel Cash Mgmt. Fund Inc.; Mem. exec. com. Engring. Council Auburn U.; lectr. on mgmt. to profl. assns. U.S., Argentina; Bd. dirs., founder Argentine Inst. for Devel. Execs., 1953-64; bd. dirs., treas. Centro de Estudios Sobre Libertad, Argentina, 1957-63. Trustee Eaglebrook Sch., Deerfield, Mass., 1945-61. Served to maj. USAAF, 1941-46. Mem. ASME, Acad. Polit. Sci., Eta Kappa Nu. Clubs: Univ., N.Y. Yacht, Tampa Yacht, Two Rivers Hounds; American Men's (Lisbon, Portugal) (past pres.). Home: 929 Guisando de Avila Tampa FL 33612 Office: Am Ship Building Co 2502 Rocky Point Rd Tampa FL 33607

FORBES, ELLIOT, educator; b. Cambridge, Mass., Aug. 30, 1917; s. Edward Waldo and Margaret (Laighton) F.; m. Kathleen Brooks Allen, June 7, 1941; children—Diana, Barbara Anne, Susan. B.A., Harvard, 1941, M.A., 1947. Tchr. Santa Barbara (Calif.) Sch., 1941-43, Belmont Hill Sch., 1943-45; asst. prof. music Princeton, 1947-54, asso. prof., 1954-58; dir. Harvard Glee Club and Radcliffe Choral Soc., Harvard, 1958-70, prof. music, 1958-61, Fanny Peabody prof. music, 1961—. Editor: Thayer's Life of Beethoven, 1964, rev. edit., 1967. Mem. Am. Musicol. Soc., Coll. Music Soc., Am. Acad. Arts and Scis. Home: 182 Brattle St Cambridge MA 02138

FORBES, FRANKLIN SIM, lawyer, educator; b. Kingsport, Tenn., Sept. 21, 1936; s. Harvey Sim and Virginia Smith (Pooler) F.; m. Suzanne Marie Willard, June 30, 1962; children—Franklin Sim, Anne Marie. B.A., U. Hawaii, 1955; J.D., U. Iowa, 1963. Bar: Hawaii bar 1963, Nebr. bar 1964. Law clk. Hawaii Supreme Ct., 1963; mem. faculty U. Nebr. Coll. Bus. Adminstrn., Omaha, 1965—, prof. law, 1965—, chmn. dept. law and society, 1970—; pvt. practice, Omaha, 1964—. Author: Going Into Business in Nebraska: The Legal Aspects, 1983, Instructor's Resource Guide-Business Law, 1983; Contbr. articles to legal publs. Mem. integration com. Omaha Sch. Bd., 1974; mem. St. James Bd. Edn., Omaha, 1974; pres. parish council St. James Roman Catholic Ch., 1975; St. Elizabeth Ch., 1983. Recipient Real Dean award U. Hawaii, 1959, Gt. Tchr. award U. Nebr., 1978, 81, Chancellor's medal, 1977, Outstanding Achievement award U. Nebr. Coll. Bus. Adminstrn., 1983; Rotary Found. grantee, Australia, 1972. Mem. Am. Bar Assn., Am. Judicature Soc., Midwest Bus. Adminstrs. Assn., Midwest Bus. Law Assn. (pres. 1975), Omaha Bar Assn. (del. conf. Future Law 1979), Alpha Phi Omega, Phi Alpha Delta, Beta Gamma Sigma, Phi Theta Chi. Democrat. Club: Rotary. Office: Univ Nebr Omaha NE 68182

FORBES, GILBERT BURNETT, physician, educator; b. Rochester, N.Y., Nov. 9, 1915; s. Gilbert DeLeverance and Lillian Augusta (Burnett) F.; m. Grace Moehlman, July 8, 1939; children: Constance Ann (Mrs. Joseph F. Citro), Susan Young (Mrs. William A. Martin). B.A., U. Rochester, 1936, M.D., 1940. Intern Strong Meml. Hosp., Rochester, 1940-41; resident St. Louis Children's Hosp., 1941-43; practice medicine, specializing in pediatrics, Los Alamos, 1946-47, Rochester, 1954—; instr. pediatrics Sch. Medicine, Washington U., St. Louis, 1943-46, asst. prof., 1947-50; prof. pediatrics, chmn. dept. Southwestern Med. Sch., Dallas, 1950-53; assoc. prof. pediatrics Sch. Medicine, U. Rochester, 1953-57, prof., 1957-68, prof. pediatrics, prof. radiation biology, 1968—, alumni disting. service prof. pediatrics, 1978—, chmn. faculty council, 1969-70, acting co-chmn. dept. pediatrics, 1974-76; cons. Nat. Inst. Child Health and Human Devel.; mem. sci. adv. com. Nutrition Found., 1963-66; mem. Nat. Council on Radiation Protection; mem. com. infant nutrition, com. dietary allowances NRC, 1960-63; vis. research fellow U. Oxford, Eng., 1970-71. Assoc. editor: Am. Jour. Diseases Childhood, 1964-72; chief editor, 1973-82; asso. editor: Nutrition Revs, 1961-71; Contbr. numerous articles to profl. jours. Recipient Research Career award USPHS, NIH, 1962—, Borden award Am. Acad. Pediatrics, 1964, Alumni award to faculty U. Rochester, 1975; Albert David Kaiser award, Rochester Acad. Medicine, 1979. Mem. Am. Pediatric Soc. (council, v.p. 1975-76), Soc. Pediatric Research (past pres.), AMA, AAAS, Am. Acad. Pediatrics (com. on nutrition 1974-80), U. Rochester Med. Alumni Assn. (past pres., Gold medal 1982), Sigma Xi, Alpha Omega Alpha, Theta Chi. Club: Rotarian. Home: 2021 Westfall Rd Rochester NY 14618 Office: 601 Elmwood Ave Rochester NY 14642

FORBES, JAMES WENDELL, publisher, consultant; b. Evansburg, Alta., Can., Oct. 8, 1923; s. Prescott and Alvira (MacLean) F.; m. Carolyn J. Irvine; children: James Wendell, Elizabeth MacLean. B.Commerce, U. B.C., 1948. With Time Inc., 1948-70; circulation dir. Life mag., 1962-64, adminstr. book pub. div., 1964-68; asst. planning dir. Time-Life Books, 1969; asst. to mng. dir. Time-Life Records, 1970; pub. cons., Ridgefield, Conn., 1970—; cons., dep. pub. Guideposts mag.; mgr. direct response advt. Young & Rubicam Internat., Inc., 1973-74; founder Sch. Mag. Mktg., 1979; Chmn. bd. Direct Mail Mktg. Assn., 1964-65. Contbr. articles to profl. jours. Served with RCAF, 1943-45. Congregationalist (chmn. bd. missions 1976, deacon 1977, chmn. bd. deacons 1978-79). Address: 87 Peacable Hill Rd Ridgefield CT 06877

FORBES, JOHN DOUGLAS, architectural and economic historian; b. San Francisco, Apr. 9, 1910; s. John Franklin and Portia (Ackerman) F.; m. Margaret Funkhouser, Feb. 4, 1937 (dec.); children: Pamela, Peter; m. Mary Elizabeth Lewis, July 26, 1980; 1 son, Michael. A.B., U. Calif.-Berkeley, 1931; M.A., Stanford U., 1932; A.M., Harvard U., 1936, Ph.D., 1937. Accountant J.F. Forbes & Co. (C.P.A.'s), San Francisco, 1937-38, 42-43; asst. to dir. fine arts, curator paintings San Francisco World's Fair, 1938-40; chmn. dept. fine arts U. Kansas City, Mo., 1940-42; faculty history Bennington Coll., 1943-46; asso. prof. history and fine arts Wabash Coll., 1946-50, prof., 1950-54; prof. bus. history U. Va., 1954-80, prof. emeritus, 1980—, lectr. art history Div. Continuing Edn., 1982—; adv. bd. Historic Am. Bldgs. Survey, 1974-78. Author: Israel Thorndike, 1953, Victorian Architect, 1953, Murder in Full View, 1968, Death Warmed Over, 1971, Stettinius, Sr., Portrait of a Morgan Partner, 1974, J.P. Morgan, Jr. (1867-1943), 1981; editor: Jour. Soc. Archtl. Historians, 1953-58; adv. editor industry: Ency. Brit., 1956-58. Served as 2d lt. AUS, 1942. Decorated officier Ordre des Palmes Académiques, France; cavaliere Ordine al Merito (Italy). Mem. Am. Hist. Assn. (life), Coll. Art Assn. (life), Mystery Writers Am., Soc. Archtl. Historians (pres. 1962-64, life), Colonial Soc. Mass. (life), AAUP, AIA (hon.), Audubon Soc., Nat. Trust Historic Preservation, Wilderness Soc. (life), Sierra Club (life), Nature Conservancy (life), Mechanics Inst. (life), Victorian Soc., Victorian Soc. in Am., Calif. Hist. Soc., Soc. Calif. Pioneers (life), Friends of Sea Otter (life), Tamalpais Conservation Club (life), Am. Kitefliers Assn. (life), Am. Soc. Dowsers (life), Phi Beta Kappa. Clubs: Colonnade (life), Pacific-Union (San Francisco); Farmington Country (Charlottesville); Cambridge (Mass.) Boat; Tennis and Racquet (Boston). Home: Box 3607 Charlottesville VA 22903 (summer) 1250 Jones St San Francisco CA 94109

FORBES, JOHN GEORGE, lawyer; b. N.Y.C., Oct. 19, 1919; s. George and Hazel (Mavricos) F.; m. Demetra Ramos, May 6, 1950; 1 son, John George. B.S.S., Coll. City N.Y., 1940; LL.B., Harvard, 1943. Bar: N.Y. bar 1943. Since practiced in, N.Y.C.; partner firm Forbes & Sommers, 1975—; lectr. Practising Law Inst., 1959—; instr. Tax Workshop Sch., 1954-56. Editor: Harvard Law Rev, 1942-43; Contbr. articles to legal jours. Trustee, sec.-treas. Inst. Mus. Art City N.Y.; v.p., trustee Christian A. Johnson Endeavor Found.; Mem. N.Y. N.G., 1944-47. Mem. Assn. Bar City N.Y., Am. Bar Assn. Home: 111-20 73d Ave Forest Hills NY 11375 Office: 750 3d Ave New York NY 10017

FORBES, JOHN RIPLEY, naturalist; b. Chelsea, Mass., Aug. 25, 1913; s. Kenneth Ripley and Ellen Elizabeth (Barker) F.; m. Margaret Sanders, Dec. 10, 1951; children: Ripley, Anne. Spl. student, U. Iowa, 1933-34, Bowdoin Coll., 1934-35. Founder, dir. Stamford (Conn.) Mus., 1935-37; ornithologist, taxidermist Lee Mus. Biology, Bowdoin Coll., MacMillan-Arctic Expdn., Labrador and Baffin Island, 1937; founder, dir. William T. Hornaday Meml. Found., N.Y., 1938-50; organizer, dir. Kansas City (Mo.) Mus., 1939-41; founder Nashville Children's Mus., 1944, acting dir., 1945-46, trustee for life, 1975—; exec. dir. Jacksonville (Fla.) Children's Mus., 1945, Fernbank Children's Nature Mus., Atlanta, 1946; organizer, dir. Oreg. Mus. Sci. and Industry, Portland, 1947-49; founder Nat. Found. for Jr. Mus., N.Y., dir., 1951-60; founder Sacramento Jr. Mus., dir., 1951-53; co-founder, dir. ops. Nature Centers for Young Am., 1959-60; founder, pres., chmn. bd. Natural Sci. for Youth Found., Conn., 1961—; founder Big Cypress Nature Center, Naples, Fla., 1959. Founder, pres. William T. Hornaday Meml. Trust, Conn., 1961-77; founder Mid-Fairfield County Youth Mus., Westport, Conn., 1958, pres., 1963-66, trustee for life, 1966—; founder Am. Assn. Youth Mus., 1964, hon. life mem., 1976; co-founder, v.p. Aspetuck Land Trust, Fairfield County; pres. St. John's on the Lake Assn., 1963-64; pres. emeritus, trustee John and Anna Newton Porter Found., 1974; founder Outdoor Activity Center, Atlanta, chmn., 1977-80; founder Chattahoochee Nature Center, Roswell, Ga., pres., 1977-78; founder Reynolds Arboretum and Nature Preserve Morrow, Ga., 1976; founder, pres. Lakes Region Conservation Trust, Tuftonborough, N.H., 1977; founder Ragged Island Nature Center, Lake Winnipesaukee, N.H., 1979, Kimball Castle Lake Winnipesaukee Mus. Arboretum and Wildlife Sanctuary, Gilford, N.H., 1981; trustee Milford (Pa.) Reservation, 1977, pres., 1977-82; trustee Hilla Von Rebay Found., 1968. Served with M.C., USAAF, 1942-45. Recipient Am. Motors Conservation award, 1971; William T. Hornaday Gold Medal award, 1977. Mem. Am. Assn. Mus. (chmn. children's mus. sec. 1965), Nat. Audubon Soc. (life), Am. Nature Study Soc., Nature Conservancy, Wilderness Soc., Am. Ornithologist Union (life), N.Y. Zool. Soc., Am. Birding Assn. (life), Nat. Wildlife Fedn., Conn. Conservation Assn. (pres. 1969-70), Sierra Club, Audubon Soc. N.H. (pres. 1975). Clubs: Bald Peak Colony (Melvin Village, N.H.); Explorers (N.Y.C.); Mazamas (Portland, Oreg.); Campfire of America. Home: 11 Wildwood Valley NE Atlanta GA 30338 Office: 763 Silvermine Rd New Canaan CT 06840

FORBES, LORNA MIRIAM (MRS. ROBERT CHANEY), psychiatrist; b. Berkeley, Calif., Feb. 28, 1921; d. Louis Charles and Romilda (Smith) F.; m. Dr. Robert H. Chaney, June 14, 1947; children—Victor Louis, Hollis Roberta, Bradford William. B.A. in Zoology, U. Calif., Berkeley, 1942; M.D., Woman's Med. Coll. Pa., 1946. Intern Calif. Hosp., Los Angeles, 1946-47; resident in surgery New Eng. Hosp., Boston, 1947-50; resident in psychiatry Pacific State Hosp., 1951-52, dir. diganostic and preadmission service, 1952-58; pvt. practice psychiatry, Pomona, Calif., 1958—; psychiat. chief of staff Guidance Center, Exceptional Children's Found., Los Angeles; psychiat. cons. Convent of the Good Shephers, Children's Hosp., Los Angeles, Family Service Agy. of Pomona, also in Claremont, Calif., 1961-71; clin. instr. psychiatry Coll. Med. Evangelists, 1958-61; asso. clin. prof. child psychiatry U. So. Calif., 1961-74, clin. prof., 1974—; med. examiner Superior Ct., 1958—; cons., lectr. So. Calif. Sch. Theology, Claremont; cons. Riverside County Adoptions, 1973—. Author articles in profl. jours. Adv. bd. Family Service of Pomona, Dept. of Recreation, Los Angeles Dept. Edn., Bur. Vocat. Rehab. Pomona, 1971, Community Coop. Nursery Sch., Pomona, McLaren Hall, 1976-80; cons. Los Angeles County Dept. Adoptions, 1970—, San Bernardino County Welfare, 1972—. Mem. AMA, Am. Psychiat. Soc., So. Calif. Psychiat. Soc., Am. Med. Women's Assn., Am. Assn. Mental Deficiency. Home: 1890 Westwood Pl Pomona CA 91767 Office: 1842 N Garey Ave Pomona CA 91767

FORBES, MALCOLM HOLLOWAY, university administrator; b. New Haven, Aug. 20, 1933; s. Malcolm and Christine Elizabeth (Holloway) F.; m. Ingely Hansmann, Sept. 28, 1963; children: Hilary Allison, Malcolm Cameron, Garrett Andrew. B.S., Yale U., 1954; M.S., Trinity Coll., Hartford, Conn., 1958; Ph.D., U. Cambridge, Eng., 1960. Postdoctoral fellow Mass. Inst. Tech., 1960-61, 62-63; mem. staff Ednl. Services, Inc., Watertown, Mass., 1963-65; acad. dean Cazenovia (N.Y.) Coll., 1965-70; dean Coll. Arts and Scis., Millikin U., Decatur, Ill., 1970-78; v.p. academic affairs U. Evansville, Ind., 1978—; cons. Raytheon Edn. Corp., 1965-68; cons., evaluator North Central Assn., 1981—. Bd. dirs. Evansville Philharmonic Orch., pres., 1982-83. Served to capt. USNR, 1954-56, 61-62. U.S. Office Edn. grantee for Dean's Seminar in India, 1972. Mem. Am. Chem. Soc., Am. Assn. Higher Edn., N. Central Assn. Academic Deans (pres. 1978-79), Naval Res. Assn. (pres. Decatur chpt. 1971-74), Alpha Epsilon Delta, Phi Kappa Phi. Home: 852 S Alvord Blvd Evansville IN 47714

FORBES, MALCOLM STEVENSON, publisher, author, former state senator; b. N.Y.C., Aug. 19, 1919; s. Bertie Charles and Adelaide (Stevenson) F.; m. Roberta Remsen Laidlaw, Sept. 21, 1946; children: Malcolm Stevenson, Robert Laidlaw, Christopher Charles, Timothy Carter, Moira Hamilton. Grad. cum laude, Lawrenceville Acad., 1937; A.B., Princeton U., 1941; L.H.D., Nasson Coll., 1966; LL.D., Okla. Christian Coll., 1973; Litt.D., Milliken U., 1974, Ball State U., 1980; D.F.A., Franklin Pierce Coll., 1975; D.Sc. in Bus. Adminstrn, Bryant Coll., 1976; D.Journalism, Babson Coll., 1977, Central New Eng. Coll., 1981; LL.D., Am. Grad. Sch. Internat. Mgmt., 1977, Pace U., 1979, Potomac Sch. Law, 1979, Kean Coll. N.J., 1981, Westminster Coll., 1981, Seton Hill Coll., 1981, U. Vt., 1982, U. No. Colo., 1983; D.Econ. Journalism, Lakeland Coll., 1980; H.H.D. (hon.), Hofstra U., 1981, Ohio U., 1981, Southwestern at Memphis, 1983, D.B.A., Bloomfield Coll., 1982, Husson Coll., 1983; L.H.D., Lincoln Coll., 1983, U. Denver, 1983; Litt.D., Miami U., 1983. Owner, pub. Fairfield Times (weekly), Lancaster, Ohio, 1941; est. Lancaster Tribune (weekly), 1942; asso. pub. Forbes Mag. Bus., N.Y.C., 1946-54, pub., editor-in-chief, 1957—; v.p. Forbes Inc., N.Y.C., 1947-64, pres., 1964-80, chmn., chief exec. officer, 1980—; chmn. bd. 60 Fifth Ave. Corp.; pres. Forbes Trinchera Inc.; chmn. Fiji Forbes; founder, pres., pub. Nations Heritage (bi-monthly), 1948-49; chmn. bd. Sangre de Cristo Ranches Inc. Author: Fact and Comment, 1974, The Sayings of Chairman Malcolm, 1978. Campaign chmn. A.R.C., Somerset Hills, N.J., 1949; mem. Borough Council Bernardsville, N.J.; state senator, 1952-58, Republican candidate for gov., N.J., 1957, N.J. del.-at-large, 1960; N.J. del.-at-large Rep. Nat. Conv. bd. dirs., Naval War Coll., 1975-77; trustee St. Mark's Sch., 1976-80, Princeton U., 1982; bd. dirs. Coast Guard Acad. Found.; chmn. N.J. Rhodes Scholarship Com., 1976, 78, 79; mem. Princeton Art Council, 1973-79. Served with inf. AUS, 1942-45. Decorated Bronze Star, Purple Heart; Order of Merit, France; Order of Ouissam Alaoyite (Morocco); President's Medal of Achievement (Pakistan); asso. officer Order of St. John; named Young Man of Year N.J. Jr. C. of C., 1951; recipient Aeronauts trophy, Harmon award, 1975; named hon. paramount chief Nimba tribe, Liberia; recipient Eaton Corp. award Internat. Platform Assn., 1979; Image award for bus. and industry Men's Fashion Assn. Am., 1979; Bus. Leadership award Columbia U. Sch. Bus., 1980; Man of Conscience award Appeal of Conscience Found., 1980; Franklin award for disting. service Printing Industries Met. N.Y., 1981; Sacred Cat award Milw. Press Club, 1981; award for entrepreneurial excellence Yale U. Mgmt. Sch., 1982; Superstar of Yr. award Police Athletic League, 1982; Manstyle award Gentlemen's Quar., 1983; Community Service award Greenwich Village C. of C., 1983; Communicator of Yr. award Bus. Profl. Advt. Assn., 1983, 33d Ann. Enterprise award, award Council for Econ. Edn., 1983. Mem. St. Andrew's Soc., 84th Inf. Div. Assn., Def. Orientation Conf. Assn., N.J. Hist. Soc., Nat. Aero. Assn. (dir., exec. v.p.), Internat. Balloonists Assn., Balloon Fedn. Am. (dir. 1974-76), Aircraft Owners and Pilots Assn., Lighter than Air Soc., Brit. Balloon and Airship Club, Internat. Soc. Balloonpost Specialists, Confrerie des Chevaliers du Tastevin, Pilgrims of U.S. Episcopalian (vestryman). Clubs: Princeton, Essex Fox Hound, New York Racquet and Tennis, New York Yacht, Links. First person to fly coast-to-coast in U.S. in hot air balloon; set 6 world records in hot air ballooning, 1973; made 1st free flight of hot air balloon over Beijing, also 1st motorcycle tour of China, 1982. Home: Timberfield Far Hills NJ 07931 Office: 60 Fifth Ave New York NY 10011

FORBES, PETER, architect; b. Berkeley, Calif., May 22, 1942; s. John Douglas and Margaret (Funkhouser) F.; m. Patricia Ann Marsh, Aug. 27, 1965 (div. 1982); children: Alexander John, Anne deMarken. B. Arch., U. Mich., 1956; M. Arch., Yale U., 1967. Registered architect, Mass., Va., Calif., Maine, R.I., N.Y., Mich.; cert. Nat. Council Archtl. Registration Bds. Project designer Skidmore, Owings & Merrill, Chgo., 1965-66; assoc. ptnr. PARD Team, Inc., Boston, 1967-71; pres. Forbes Hailey Jeas Erneman, Inc., Boston, 1972-80, Peter Forbes and Assoc., Inc., 1980—; dir. continuing edn. Boston Archtl. Ctr., 1975-77; vis. critic U. Mich., 1980-82, Cath. U. Am., Rome, 1982; lectr., vis. critic Va. Poly. Inst. and State U., 1980-82; commr. Commn. of Mass., Spl. Commn. Concerning State and County Bldgs., 1978-81; prop. Boston Athenaeum, 1982—. Fellow AIA; mem. Mass. State Assn. Architects (pres. 1983—), Boston Soc. Architects (dir., commr. pub. affairs, chmn. ethics com.), Soc. Archtl. Historians. Clubs: Newport Reading Room, Tennis and Racquet, National Tennis, Yale. Home: 124 Myrtle St Boston MA 02114 Office: Peter Forbes and Assocs 124 Myrtle St Boston MA 02114

FORBES, RICHARD E., retired publishing company executive; b. Larchmont, N.Y., Sept. 21, 1915; s. George P. and Charlotte (Ricketson) F.; m. Phinina Gagliardi, June 22, 1946; children—Mary C., Richard E. (dec.). B.A., Williams Coll., 1936. With Macy Westchester Papers, 1937-42; appliance advt. mgr., staff cons. Gen. Electric Co., 1948-56; dir. advt. Chrysler Corp., 1956-73; regional mgr. Forbes Mag., Detroit, 1973-82. Bd. dirs. Advt. Research Found., Adcraft Club Detroit, Detroit Advt. Assn. Home: 980 Timberlake Dr Bloomfield Hills MI 48013

FORBES, RICHARD MATHER, educator; b. Wooster, Ohio, Jan. 8, 1916; s. Ernest Browning and Lydia Maria (Mather) F.; m. Mary Medlicott, Feb. 26, 1944; children—Sally Allen, Anne Mather, Stephen Harding. B.S., Pa. State Coll., 1938, M.S., 1939; Ph.D., Cornell U., 1942. Instr. biochemistry Wayne State U., 1942; research fellow Cornell U., Ithaca, N.Y., 1942-43; asst. prof. U. Ky., Lexington, 1946-49; asso. prof. U. Ill., Champaign-Urbana, 1949-55, prof. nutritional biochemistry, 1955—. Contbr. articles to profl. jours. Served to capt. U.S. Army, 1943-46. Recipient H. H. Mitchell award U. Ill., 1981. Fellow AAAS; mem. Am. Soc. Animal Sci. (Gustav Bohstedt award 1968), Am. Inst. Nutrition, Am. Chem. Soc., Sigma Xi. Republican. Mem. United Ch. of Christ. Clubs: Nat. Exchange, Izaak Walton League. Home: 2005 S Vine St Urbana IL 61801 Office: 1207 W Gregory St U Ill Urbana IL 61801

FORBES, THEODORE MCCOY, JR., lawyer; b. Atlanta, Oct. 28, 1929; s. Theodore M. and Mary (Christie) F.; m. Margaret Paty, Dec. 12, 1953; children—Theodore McCoy, Margaret Paty. B.S. in Chemistry, Ga. Inst. Tech., 1950; LL.B., U. Va., 1953. Bar: Ga. bar 1952, D.C. bar 1973. Instr. Culver (Ind.) Summer Naval Sch., 1950; practiced in, Atlanta, 1952—; assoc., then ptnr. firm Gambrell & Russell, 1953—. Bd. dirs. Travelers Aid Soc. Atlanta, 1975-83, pres., 1975-76; bd. dirs. Ga. chpt. Arthritis Found., 1961-68, Shepherd Spinal Center, 1977—. Mem. Am., Atlanta, Interam. bar assns., State Bar Ga. (chmn. adminstrv. law sect. 1967-68, chmn. internat. law sect. 1976-77), D.C. Bar, Am. Judicature Soc., Order of Coif, Alpha Tau Omega, Sigma Nu Phi, Alpha Chi Sigma. Presbyterian (deacon). Club: Capital City. Home: 1760 Marlborough Dr Dunwoody GA 30338 Office: First Atlanta Tower Atlanta GA 30383

FORBES, THOMAS ROGERS, anatomist, medical historian; b. N.Y.C., Jan. 5, 1911; s. James Bruff and Stella (Rogers) F.; m. Helen Frances Allen, June 19, 1934; children—Thomas R., William M. B.A. cum laude, U. Rochester, 1933, Ph.D., 1937; M.A. (hon.), Yale U., 1962. Fellow anatomy U. Rochester, 1933-37; asst. anatomy Johns Hopkins U., 1937-38, instr., 1938-42; instr. anatomy Yale U., 1945-46, asst. prof., 1946-51, asso. prof., 1951-62, prof., 1962-79, E.K. Hunt prof. anatomy, 1977-79, E.K. Hunt prof. emeritus, 1979—, asst. dean, 1948-60; asso. dean Sch. Medicine, 1960-69, chief sect. gross anatomy dept. surgery, 1974-78, sr. research scholar in history of medicine, 1979—, lectr. surgery, 1979—; fellow Branford Coll., Yale U., 1951—; adviser on Yale med. memorabilia, 1974—; tech. aide, div. med. scis. NRC, OSRD, 1942-45; mem. spl. study sect. med. history NIH, 1977-78. Author: The Midwife and the Witch, 1966, Chronicle from Aldgate, 1971, Crowner's Quest, 1978; bd. editors: Jour. History of Medicine, 1956-68; pres. bd. mgrs., 1958-75; acting editor, 1960-62; editor, 1962-63; contbr. research papers on endocrinology, history of medicine; producer: films John Hunter, Enlightened Empiricist, 1972, Vesalius, Founder of Modern Anatomy, 1972, Ambroise Paré, Military Surgeon, 1974, The Resurrectionists, 1977. Guggenheim fellow, 1942. Fellow AAAS, Soc. Antiquaries London, Royal Hist. Soc. (London);

mem. Am. Assn. Anatomists, Endocrine Soc., Am. Assn. History Medicine, Royal Soc. Medicine (London), Faculty Hist. and Philosophy Pharmacy and Med., Worshipful Soc. Apothecaries (London) (Gideon de Laune lectr. and medal 1975), Conn. Acad. Arts and Scis., Soc. Social History Medicine (London), Internat. Soc. History of Medicine, Phi Beta Kappa, Sigma Xi, Psi Upsilon. Club: Athenaeum. Home: 86 Ford St Hamden CT 06517

FORBIS, RICHARD GEORGE, archeologist; b. Missoula, Mont., July 30, 1924; s. Clarence Jenks and Josephine Marie (Hunt) F.; m. Marjorie Helen Wilkinson, Nov. 12, 1960; children: Michael, David, Amanda. B.A., U. Mont., 1949, M.A., 1950; Ph.D., Columbia U., 1955. Sr. archeologist Pacific N.W. Pipeline Corp., Western U.S., 1955-56; archeologist Glenbow Found., Calgary, Alta., Can., 1957-63; mem. faculty U. Calgary, 1963—, prof. archaeology, 1968—, interim chmn. dept., Killam Meml. fellow, 1977; chmn. Alta. Public Adv. Com. Hist. and Archeol. Resources, 1971-74; mem. Alta. Historic Sites Bd., 1974-78; vis. scientist Can. Nat. Museum Man, 1970. Author: Cluny: An Ancient Fortified Village in Alberta, 1977; co-author: An Introduction to the Archaeology of Alberta, Canada, 1965. Served with AUS, 1943-46. Decorated Bronze Star. Mem. AAAS, Soc. Am. Archaeology, Can. Archaeol. Assn. (Smith-Wintemberg award 1984), Am. Anthrop. Assn., Arctic Inst. N. Am., Plains Anthrop. Conf., Royal Anthrop. Inst. Gt. Brit. and Ireland, Explorers Club, Champlain Soc., Sigma Chi. Office: 2500 University Dr NW Calgary AB T2N 1N4 Canada

FORCE, ROBERT, legal educator; b. Phila., Aug. 11, 1934; s. Charles and Dora (Woloshin) F.; m. Ruth Morris, Aug. 18, 1962; children: Joshua Simon, Seth Daniel. B.S., Temple U., 1955, LL.B., 1958; postgrad., U. Adelaide, 1958-59; LL.M., NYU, 1960. Bar: Pa. 1961. Law clk. to presiding justice Pa. Ct. Common Pleas., Phila., 1960-61, U.S. Dist. Ct., 1961-62; instr. Temple U., Phila., 1960-61; assoc. Kleibard, Bell & Brecker, Phila., 1963-64; asst. prof. Ind. U. Law Sch., Indpls., 1964-67, assoc. prof., 1968; prof. Tulane U., New Orleans, 1969—, acting dean, 1977-78, Thomas Pickles prof. law, 1979—; reporter Speedy Trial Panel, 1980. Co-author: Cases and Readings on Criminal Law and Procedure, 1967; editor: (with D.M. Gallant) Legal and Ethical Issues in Human Research and Treatment-Psychopharmacological Considerations, 1978. Mem. adv. com. Mental Health Advocacy Service, 1977—. Fulbright fellow, 1958-59. Mem. ABA, Beta Gamma Sigma, Omicron Delta Kappa. Home: 1038 Flonore St New Orleans LA 70115 Office: 6801 Freret St Suite 200 New Orleans LA 70118

FORCE, ROLAND WYNFIELD, anthropologist, museum executive; b. Omaha, Dec. 30, 1924; s. Richard Erwin and Edna Fern (Collins) F.; m. Maryanne Tefft, Sept. 16, 1949. B.A., Stanford U., 1950, M.A. in Edn, 1951, 1952, Ph.D., 1958; D.Sci. (hon.), Hawaii Loa Coll., 1973. Acting instr. Stanford U., 1954; asso. in ethnology Bernice P. Bishop Mus., Honolulu, 1954-56, dir., 1962-76, dir. emeritus, 1976—, holder C.R. Bishop Disting. chair in Pacific studies, 1976-77; dir. Mus. Am. Indian, Heye Found., N.Y.C., 1977—; curator oceanic archeology, ethnology Field Mus. of Natural History, Chgo., 1956-61. Served with C.E. AUS, 1943-46. Fellow Am. Anthrop. Assn., AAAS, Pacific Sci. Assn. (hon. life, mem. council 1966-77); mem. Am. Assn. Museums, Sigma Xi. Home: 21 Rockleigh Rd Rockleigh NJ 07647

FORCHESKIE, CARL S., apparel company executive; b. Shamokin, Pa., Feb. 3, 1927; s. John A. and Helen F.; m. Geraldine Eagan, June 4, 1949 (dec. Apr. 1982); children: Carl, Gail, Caroline Karen. B.A., Pa. State U., 1951. Mgr. Coopers & Lybrand, 1951-62; cons. U.S. Dept. Treasury, 1962-63; chief fin. officer Loral Corp., 1963-69; exec. v.p. Salant Corp., N.Y.C., 1969-81, pres., chief exec. officer, 1981—. Mem. Planning Bd. Hastings-on-Hudson, N.Y. Served with AUS, 1945-46. Mem. Am. Inst. C.P.A.s, N.Y. State Soc. C.P.A.s, Fin. Execs. Inst., Am. Apparel Mfrs. Assn. Roman Catholic. Clubs: St. Andrews Golf, Union League. Home: 77 Tompkins Ave Hastings-on-Hudson NY 10706 Office: 330 Fifth Ave New York NY 10001

FORCIONE, ALBAN KEITH, language educator; b. Washington, Nov. 17, 1938; s. Eugene and Wilda (Ashby) F.; m. Renate Muhlenstedt, Sept. 4, 1964; children: Michael, Mark. A.B., Princeton U, 1960; M.A., Ph.D., Princeton U., 1968, Harvard U., 1960. Emory L. Ford prof. Spanish and comparative lit. Princeton U., N.J., 1965-82; prof. Spanish and comparative lit. Stanford U., Calif., 1983—. Author: Cervantes, Aristotle and the Persiles, 1970, Cervantes Christian Romance, 1972, Cervantes and the Humanist Vision, 1982. Woodrow Wilson fellow, 1960-61; Fulbright fellow, 1961-62; Am. Council Learned Socs. fellow, 1973-74. Office: Stanford U Stanford CA 94305

FORD, ALLEN HUNTINGTON, oil company executive; b. Cleve., July 29, 1928; s. David K. and Elizabeth (Brooks) F.; m. Constance Towson, Feb. 19, 1954; children—Hope, Sarah, James T. B.A., Yale U., 1950; M.S., Case Inst. Tech., 1964. With Pickands Mather & Co., Cleve., 1953-69, v.p. fin., 1967-69; treas. Diamond Shamrock Corp., Cleve., 1969, v.p. fin., 1969-75, exec. v.p., 1976-80; sr. v.p. Standard Oil Co., Ohio, 1981—; dir. AmeriTrust Corp., Parker Hannifin Corp., Elwell-Parker Electric Co.; trustee First Union Real Estate Investments. Trustee Case Western Res. U., Western Res. Hist. Soc., Cleve., Martha Holden Jennings Found., Mus. Arts Assn., Cleve. Orch., Univ. Hosps. Served with AUS, 1950-52. Home: 50 Mill Hollow Dr Chagrin Falls OH 44022

FORD, ANDREW THOMAS, educational administrator, consultant; b. Cambridge, Mass., May 22, 1944; s. Francis Lawler and Eleanor (Vahey) F.; m. Anne M. Monahan, July 2, 1966; 1 dau., Lauren Elizabeth. B.A., Seton Hall U., 1966; M.A., U. WIs., 1968; Ph.D., U. Wis., 1971. Asst. prof. history Stockton State Coll., Pomona, N.J., 1971-72, asst. to v.p. for acad. affairs, 1972-74; acting dir. Nat. Materials Devel. Ctr. for French and Portuguese, Bedford, N.H., 1976-77; acad. programs coordinator N.H. Coll. and Univ. Council, Manchester, 1975-78; v.p. acad. affairs R.I. Sch. Design, Providence, 1978-81; dean of coll. Allegheny Coll., Meadville, Pa., 1981—. Author: (with R. Chait) Beyond Traditional Tenure, 1982. Bd. dirs. Vis. Nurse Assn., Providence, 1979-81, Allegheny Summer Music Festival, Meadville, 1981—; bd. incorporators Spencer Hosp., Meadville, 1981—. Democrat. Roman Catholic. Home: 661 Chestnut St Meadville PA 16335 Office: Allegheny Coll Meadville PA 16335

FORD, ASHLEY LLOYD, detergent corporation executive, lawyer; b. Cin., Mar. 10, 1939; s. Starr MacLeod and Mary Lloyd (Mills) F.; m. Barbara Hill, Apr. 23, 1965; children: Christopher Ashley, Elizabeth Hill. A.B., Princeton U., 1960; J.D., Yale U., 1963. Bar: Ohio 1963. Assoc. Dinsmore, Shohl, Coates & Deupree, Cin., 1964-69; with legal div. Procter & Gamble Co., Cin., 1969—, div. counsel paper products, 1971—, coffee, 1972-73, toilet goods, 1971-79, sec., 1979—. Sec. Cin. Summer Opera Assn., 1967-74, Cin. Opera Guild, 1974-79; mem. adv. council dept. history Princeton U.; bd. dirs. Jr. Achievement, Cin. Mem. ABA, Ohio Bar Assn., Cin. Bar Assn., Am. Soc. Corp. Secs., Cin. His. Soc. (trustee), Cin. Mus. Assn. (shareholder), Phi Beta Kappa, Order of Coif. Clubs: Cincinnati Country; University (Cin.). Office: Legal Div Proctor & Gamble Co PO Box 599 301 E 6th St Cincinnati OH 45202

FORD, BARNEY, government official; b. Norton, Va., 1922. B.S. in Prodn. Mgmt. and Control, U. Calif.-Berkeley, 1948. Registered profl. engr., Calif. With Hercules Powder Co., 1941-42; postmaster, Bishop, Calif., 1951-54; exec. dir. fact-finding com. on natural resources Calif. Senate, 1959-67; dep. sec. Calif. Resources Agy., 1967-73; chmn. Calif. Occupational Safety and Health Appeals Bd., 1973-78; v.p. Calif. Inst. Industry and Govt. Relations, 1978-81; asst. sec. labor Mine Safety and Health Adminstrn., Dept. Labor, 1981-83, undersec. labor, 1983—. Served to 2d lt. AUS, 1943-46. Office: Office Undersec Dept Labor 200 Constitution Ave NW Washington DC 20210 *

FORD, BETTY (ELIZABETH) BLOOMER, wife of former Pres. U.S.; b. Chgo., Apr. 8, 1918; d. William Stephenson and Hortence (Neahr) Bloomer; m. Gerald R. Ford (38th Pres. U.S.), Oct. 15, 1948; children: Michael Gerald, John Gardner, Steven Meigs, Susan Elizabeth. Student, Sch. Dance Bennington Coll., 1936, 37; LL.D. hon., U. Mich., 1976. Dancer Martha Graham Concert Group, N.Y.C., 1939-41; model John Powers Agy., N.Y.C., 1939-41; fashion dir. Herpolscheimer's Dept. Store, Grand Rapids, Mich., 1943-48; dance instr., Grand Rapids, 1932-48. Author: autobiography The Times of My Life, 1979. Formerly active Cub Scouts Am.; program chmn. Alexandria (Va.) Cancer Fund Drive; chmn. Heart Subday, Washington Heart Assn., 1974; pres. ARC Senate Wives Club; partron Salvation Army Aux. Ann Fashion Show Luncheon; active Benefits Hosp. for Sick Children, Washington; active supporter Nat. Endowment Arts; mem. Nat. Commn. Observance Internat. Women's Year, 1977; bd. dirs. League Republican Women, D.C.; trustee Eisenhower Med. Ctr., Palm Desert, Calif.; advisory bd. Rosalind Russell Med. Research Fund; hon. chmn. Palm Springs Desert Mus.; nat. trustee Nat. Symphony Orch.; trustee Nursing Home Advisory and Research Council Inc.; mem. Golden Circle Patrons Ctr. Theatre Performing Arts; bd. dirs. The Lambs, Libertyville, Ill. Episcopalian (tchr. Sunday sch. 1961-64). Home: Rancho Mirage CA 92262

FORD, CHARLES WILLARD, university dean; b. Bloomsburg, Pa., Oct. 28, 1938; s. John Willard and Pauline Teresa (Rakocy) F.; m. Barbara Marie Hanawalt, June 6, 1959; children: Lane, Lori, Lanae, Lanette. B.A., Taylor U., 1959; B.S., Pa. State U., 1961; M.Ed., SUNY, Buffalo, 1962, Ph.D., 1970; postgrad., U. Mich., 1976-77. High sch. instr., 1961-64; faculty Erie Community Coll., 1965-70; fgn. service officer Peace Corps, Ghana, 1970-72; various positions SUNY Sch. Health Related Professions, Buffalo, 1972-75, 77-79, assoc. dean, 1978-79; with Grand Rapids (Mich.) Med. Edn. Center, 1975-77; dean U. Health Scis./Chgo. Med. Sch., 1979-80; health professions edn. cons., Clarence, N.Y., 1980-82; dean Coll. Health Scis., dean St. Francis Coll. U. New Eng., Biddeford, Maine, 1982—; cons. Author: (with M.K. Morgan) Teaching in the Health Professions, 1976, Clinical Education for the Allied Health Professions, 1978; contbr. articles to profl. jours. Mem. Aircraft Owners and Pilots Assn., Am. Assn. Higher Edn. (charter life), Am. Soc. Allied Health Professions (life), NEA (life). Mem. Ch. Brethren in Christ. Home: 35 Intervale Rd Kennebunk ME 04043

FORD, CORNELIUS WILLIAM, management consultant; b. Bingham, Utah, Oct. 16, 1918; s. John W. and Esther (Jones) F.; m. Anne Pecoraro, July 18, 1945; children: Leanna Jo, William Douglas, John Christopher. Ed. pub. schs., Bingham. Exec. v.p. Santa Maria Savs. & Loan Assn., Calif., 1947-56; pres. Central Savs. & Loan Assn., San Luis Obispo, Calif., 1956-60; exec. v.p. First Savs. & Loan Assn., Oakland, Calif., 1960-61, pres., dir., 1961-70, Gt. Western Fin. Corp., Beverly Hills, Calif., 1964-75, Gt. Western Savs. & Loan Assn., Los Angeles, 1964-75; now chmn. bd., chief exec. officer Centurion Savs. & Loan Assn., Los Angeles. Served to 1st lt. USAAF, World War II; prisoner of war. Decorated Air medal, Purple Heart. Mem. Calif. Savs. and Loan League (past dir.). Home and Office: 1632 Stradella Rd Los Angeles CA 90077

FORD, DENYS KENSINGTON, med. educator; b. Newcastle, Staffordshire, Eng., Aug. 8, 1923; s. Ronald Milne and Margaret Jessie (Coghill) F.; m. Marguerite Geraldine Stewart, Aug. 7, 1954; children—Cicely, Stewart, Nancy. B.A., Cambridge (Eng.) U., 1944, M.B., 1947, M.D., 1953. Registrar London Hosp.; fellow in arthritis N.Y. U.-Bellevue Hosp., N.Y.C.; asso. prof. U. B.C., Vancouver, Can., now prof. medicine. Mem. Can. Med. Assn., Am. Rheumatism Assn. Research on arthritis through immunology, microbiology and cell culture. Office: 895 W 10th St Vancouver BC V5Z 1L7 Canada *

FORD, DEXTER, retired insurance company executive; b. Utica, N.Y., Nov. 18, 1917; s. David E. and Anna Mae (Dexter) F.; m. Jean Brand McGowan, Nov. 1, 1944; children: David K., Dexter T., Nancy E. B.S., St. Lawrence U., 1939. With Aetna Life & Casualty Co., Hartford, Conn., 1946—, v.p. mktg., 1968-76, v.p. personal ins. dept., 1976-80. Chmn. bd. mgmt. YMCA, 1978-80. Served to lt. (s.g.) USNR, 1941-45. Recipient St. Lawrence U. Alumni citation, 1978. Mem. St. Lawrence U. Alumni Assn. (pres. 1974-75). Republican. Congregationalist. Clubs: Avon Golf (Conn.); Hartford (Conn.). Home: 20 Rosewood Dr Simsbury CT 06070

FORD, DONALD HAINLINE, lawyer; b. Chgo., Dec. 5, 1906; s. Matthew Henry and Ethel (Griffith) F.; m. Siri Ann Enegren, Aug. 22, 1934; children—Carol Ann (Mrs. Raymond D. McMullin), Barbara Jean (Mrs. Robert A. Harrington), Richard Donald. B.S., Oreg. State U., 1929; J.D., U. Mich., 1932. Bar: Calif. bar 1933. Park ranger Lassen Volcanic Nat. Park, 1931-32; asso. firm Overton, Lyman & Prince, Los Angeles, 1933-41, partner, 1941—; dir. W/W. Henry Co. Served with USAAF, 1941-46; col. USAF; Ret. Decorated Bronze Star. Presbyn. Home: 4079 Punta Alta Dr Los Angeles CA 90008 Office: 550 S Flower St Los Angeles CA 90071

FORD, DONALD HERBERT, psychologist, educator; b. Sioux City, Iowa, Aug. 15, 1926; s. Herbert Owen and Esther (Sanow) F.; m. Carol Clark, May 30, 1948; children—Russell, Martin, Douglas, Cameron. B.S., Kans. State U., 1948; M.S., 1951; Ph.D., Pa. State U., 1955. Counselor Kans. State U., 1948-52; asst. prof. psychology Pa. State U., University Park, 1955-64, asso. prof., 1964-67, asso. prof. human devel., 1967-72, prof. human. devel., 1972—; asst. dir. div. counseling, 1956-59, dir., 1959-67; dean Coll. Human Devel., 1967-77. Author: Systems of Psychotherapy; A Comparative Study, 1963; Contbr.: chpt. to Ann. Rev. Psychology, 1966—. Served with USAAF, 1944-45. Mem. AAAS, Am., Eastern psychol. assns. Home: Squirrel Dr Lemont PA 16851 Office: Coll Human Devel Pa State U University Park PA 16802 *My basic values are rooted in the "teaching by example" of my parents, serving the objectives of being of service to others as well as to self, utilizing a strong, caring family unit as the best cornerstone of psychological, social, and economic health. My basic professional goal is to help harness the fruits of technological advances, resulting from the intensive application of the principle of specialization, to the evolution of humanistic societies designed to serve people as open, living systems rather than as classical machines. This requires a new scientific model of Man as a coherent unit, enabling us to synthesize the fruits of analytical science and to put "Humpty Dumpty" back together again as a person with purposes and values as well as productive potential.*

FORD, DOUGLAS ALBERT, bishop; b. Vancouver, C., Can., July 16, 1917; s. Thomas George and Elizabeth (Taylor) F.; m. Doris Ada Elborne, June 10, 1944; children—Michael Douglas, Stephen Thomas, Kathryn Joan. B.A., U. B.C., Vancouver, 1939; L.Th., Anglican Theol. Coll., Vancouver, 1941, B.D., 1948, D.D., 1971. Ordained deacon Anglican Ch. Can., 1941, priest, 1942, consecrated bishop, 1970; curate St. Mary's Ch., Vancouver, 1941-42; priest-in-charge St. George's Ch., Vancouver, 1942-44; incumbent ch., Strathmore, Alta., Can., 1944-49, rector chs., Okotoks and Turner Valley, Alta., 1949-52, St. Saviour Ch., Vermilion, Alta., 1952-55, St. Michael and All Angels Ch., Calgary, Alta., 1955-62, St. Augustine Ch., Lethbridge, Alta., 1962-66; dean, rector St. John's Cathedral, Saskatoon, Sask., Can., 1966-70; bishop of Sask., 1970-81, parish priest, asst. to bishop of, Calgary, 1981—. Home: PO Box 1043 Cochrane AB T0L 0W0 Canada

FORD, DWAIN L., chemistry educator; b. Nevada, Iowa, Dec. 21, 1927; s. Paul Guy and Orpha (Root) F.; m. Lorraine Mabel Saline, Sept. 7, 1947; children: David Linden, Diane Lynn, Larry Dean. B.A. in Chemistry, Andrews U., Berrien, Springs, Mich., 1949; Ph.D., Clark U., 1962. Instr. sci. and math. Columbus (Wis.) Acad., 1949-58; mem. faculty Andrews U., 1962—, prof. chemistry, chmn. dept., 1963-71, dean Coll. Arts and Scis., 1971-81, prof. organic chemistry, 1981—, ombudsman, 1981—. Adminstr. Berrien County Drug Identification Center.; Mem. sci. com. Bibl. Sci. Research Inst., 1971—; bd. dirs. Gateway Center for rehab. of handicapped, 1971-80, Battle Creek (Mich.) Sanitarium and Hosp. Named Tchr. of Year Andrews U., 1968. Mem. Am. Chem. Soc., Sigma Xi. Home: Route 1 Box 14 Berrien Center MI 49102 *Serving God and others brings great reward.*

FORD, EILEEN OTTE (MRS. GERARD W. FORD), modeling agency executive; b. N.Y.C., Mar. 25, 1922; d. Nathaniel and Loretta Marie (Laine) Otte; m. Gerard William Ford, Nov. 20, 1944; children: Margaret (Mrs. Robert Craft), Gerard William, M. Katie, A. Lacey. B.S., Barnard Coll., 1943. Stylist Elliot Clarke Studio, N.Y.C., 1943-44, William Becker Studio, 1945; copywriter Arnold Constable, N.Y.C., 1945-46; reporter Tobe Coburn, 1946; co-founder, v.p. Ford Model Agy., N.Y.C., 1946—. Author: Eileen Ford's Model Beauty, Secrets of the Model's World, A More Beautiful You in 21 Days; Author: Beauty Now and Forever, 1977. Bd. dirs. London Philharmonic, 1948—. Recipient Harpers Bazaar award for promotion internat. understanding., Woman of Yr. in Advt. award, 1983. Office: 344 E 59th St New York NY 10022 *

FORD, ERNEST JENNINGS (TENNESSEE ERNIE), entertainer; b. Bristol, Tenn., Feb. 13, 1919; s. Clarence and Maude (Long) F.; m. Betty Jean Heminger, Sept. 18, 1942; children: Jeffrey Buckner, Brion Leonard. Student, Cin. Conservatory Music, 1939. Pres. BetFord Corp., San Francisco. TV show, NBC Network, 1955-61, daytime TV show, ABC, 1962-65; headliner: 1st country music show to USSR, 1974; rec. artist, Capitol Records, 1949-76; outstanding records include 16 Tons. Served to lt. USAAF, World War II. Named col. personal staff Gov. of Tenn.; recipient Presdl. Medal of Freedom, 1984. Office: care James L Loakes Betford Corp PO Box 31-552 San Francisco CA 94131

FORD, FRANKLIN LEWIS, history educator, historian; b. Waukegan, Ill., Dec. 26, 1920; s. Frank Leland and Dorothy Elsey (Lewis) F.; m. Eleanor Rose Hamm, Jan. 8, 1944; children: Stephen Joseph, John Franklin. A.B., U. Minn., 1942; M.A., Harvard U., Ph.D., 1950. Mem. faculty Bennington Coll., 1949-52; mem. faculty Harvard U., 1953—, prof. history, 1959—, McLean prof. ancient and modern history, 1968—, dean faculty arts and scis., 1962-70, acting dean, 1973; mem. Inst. for Advanced Study, 1974. Author: Robe and Sword, 1953, Strasbourg in Transition, 1958, Europe, 1780-1830, 1970; Co-editor: Traditions of Western Civilization, 1966. Served with OSS AUS, 1943-46. Fulbright research fellow, France, 1952-53; Guggenheim fellow, Germany, 1955-56; fellow Center Advanced Study Behavioral Scis., 1961-62; fellow Nat. Humanities Ctr., 1983-84. Mem. Am. Philos. Soc., Am. Hist. Assn., Mass. Hist. Soc., Phi Beta Kappa. Home: 12 Clifton St Belmont MA 02178 Office: Widener Library Harvard Univ Cambridge MA 02138

FORD, FREDERICK WAYNE, lawyer; b. Bluefield, W.Va., Sept. 17, 1909; s. George Michael and Annie Laurie (Linn) F.; m. Virginia Lee Carter, Aug. 12, 1933 (dec. Feb. 1958); 1 dau., Mary Carter; m. Mary Margaret Mahony, Oct. 11, 1959 (div. Aug. 1981); 1 son, Frederick Wayne. A.B., W.Va. U., 1931, J.D., 1934. Bar: W.Va. 1934, D.C. 1968. Jr. partner Stathers & Cantrall, Clarksburg, 1934-39; atty. FSA, 1939-42, OPA, 1942, 46-47, FCC, 1947-53, mem., 1957-65, chmn., 1960; 1st asst. to asst. atty. gen. Office Legal Counsel Dept. Justice, 1953-56; acting asst. atty. gen. Office Legal Counsel, 1956-57; asst. dept. atty. gen., U.S., 1957; pres. Nat. Community TV Assn., 1965-69; sr. ptnr. firm Lovett, Ford, & Hennessey and predecessor, 1970-81; ptnr. Pepper & Corazzini, 1981—. Editorial staff: W.Va. U. Law Quar, 1932-33. Mem. Harrison County Republican Exec. Com., 1936. Served as maj. USAAF, 1942-46. Mem. Am., Fed. Communications bar assns., W.Va. State Bar, Am. Law Inst., Alexandria Assn. (pres. 1950-53), Scabbard and Blade, Phi Delta Phi, Sigma Chi. Episcopalian. Clubs: Young Republican of Harrison County (pres. 1939), Congressional Country, Belle Haven Country. Home: 6602 10th St Alexandria VA 22307 Office: 1776 K St Washington DC 20006 *Be true to the man you shave and always do what you say you will. My word is my bond.*

FORD, GEORGE BURT, lawyer; b. South Bend, Ind., Oct. 1, 1923; s. George W. and Florence (Burt) F.; m. Charlotte Ann Kupferer, June 12, 1948; children: John, Victoria, George, Charlotte. B.S. in Engring. Law, Purdue U., 1946; LL.B., Ind. U., 1949. Bar: Ind. 1949. Since practiced in, South Bend; partner firm Jones, Obenchain, Johnson, Ford, Pankow & Lewis, 1953—; atty. Hosp. Authority St. Joseph County, South Bend Middle Sch. Bldg. Corp., Nat. Bank & Trust Co. South Bend. Bd. dirs. Robert P. and Clara I. Milton Home. Served with AUS, 1943-45. Fellow Am. Coll. Probate Counsel; mem. ABA, Ind. Bar Assn., St. Joseph County Bar Assn. (pres. 1976—), Phi Gamma Delta, Phi Delta Phi. Presbyterian (trustee 1966-68, elder 1967-70). Home: 1512 Wildflower Way South Bend IN 46617 Office: 1800 Valley Am Nat Bank Bldg South Bend IN 46601

FORD, GEORGE HARRY, educator; b. Winnipeg, Man., Can., Dec. 21, 1914; s. Harry and Gertrude (Burgess) F.; m. Patricia Murray, May 4, 1942; children: Leslie Margaret, Harry Seymour. B.A., U. Man., 1936; M.A., U. Toronto, 1938; Ph.D., Yale U., 1942. Lectr. U. Man., 1945-46; asso. prof. U. Cin., 1946-54, prof., 1954-58; vis. prof. U. Chgo., 1948, Johns Hopkins U., 1949, U. B.C., 1953; prof. English, U. Rochester, 1958—, chmn. dept., 1960-72, Joseph H. Gilmore prof., 1969. Author: Keats and the Victorians, 1945, Dickens and His Readers, 1955, Double Measure: D.H. Lawrence, 1965, The Making of a Secret Agent, 1978; editor: Dickens' David Copperfield, 1958, Hard Times, 1966, Bleak House, 1977, The Dickens Critics, 1962, The Norton Anthology of English Literature, 4th edit., 1979, Victorian Fiction, A Second Guide to Research, 1978. Served from lt. to capt. Can. Army, 1942-45. Guggenheim fellow; Huntington Library fellow; Wilbur Cross medal Yale U., 1983. Fellow Am. Council Learned Socs.; mem. Internat. Assn. Profs. English, Literary Club Cin., Dickens Fellowship (pres. 1975), N.Y. Council Humanities, Internat. Assn. Study of Time (pres. 1979), Am. Acad. Arts and Scis. Episcopalian. Home: 2230 Clover St Rochester NY 14618

FORD, GERALD RUDOLPH, JR., former pres. U.S.; b. Omaha, July 14, 1913; s. Gerald R. and Dorothy (Gardner) F.; m. Elizabeth Bloomer, Oct. 15, 1948; children—Michael, John, Steven, Susan. A.B., U. Mich., 1935; LL.B., Yale U., 1941; LL.D., Mich. State U., Albion Coll., Aquinas Coll., Spring Arbor Coll. Bar: Mich. bar 1941. Practiced law at, Grand Rapids, 1941-49; mem. law firm Buchen and Ford;

mem. 81st-93d Congresses from 5th Mich. Dist., elected minority leader, 1965; v.p., U.S., 1973-74, pres., 1974-77; del. Interparliamentary Union, Warsaw, Poland, 1959, Belgium, 1961, Bilderberg Group Conf., 1962; dir. Santa Fe Internat., GK Technologies, Shearson Loeb Rhoades, Pebble Beach Corp., Tiger Internat. Served as lt. comdr. USNR, 1942-46. Recipient Grand Rapids Jr. C. of C. Distinguished Service award, 1948; Distinguished Service Award as one of ten outstanding young men in U.S. by U.S. Jr. C. of C., 1950; Silver Anniversary All-Am. Sports Illustrated, 1959; Distinguished Congressional Service award Am. Polit. Sci. Assn., 1961. Mem. Am., Mich. State, Grand Rapids bar assns., Delta Kappa Epsilon, Phi Delta Phi. Republican. Episcopalian. Clubs: Masons, Univ., Peninsular (Kent County) *

FORD, GLENN (GWYLLYN SAMUEL NEWTON FORD), actor; b. Que., Can., May 1, 1916; s. Newton and Hannah F.; m. Eleanor Powell, Oct. 23, 1943 (div.); 1 son, Peter Newton; m. Kathryn Hays, March 27, 1966; m. Cynthia Hayward., March 27, 1966. Ed. high sch., Santa Monica, Calif. (Named Number One Box Office Star in Am., ann. poll Motion Picture Herald 1958); Acting debut at age 4 in Tom Thumb's Wedding; stage mgr., Wilshire Theater, 1934; stage mgr., actor: The Children's Hour, 1935, Golden Boy; on tour with, John Beal in, Soliloquy, 1938; actor: Heaven with a Barbed Wire Fence, Twentieth Century-Fox Studio, 1939; with, Columbia Pictures Corp., 1939-43, 45-53; free lance, 1953-55, Metro-Goldwyn Mayer, 1955—; films include Destroyer, 1943, A Stolen Life, 1946, Framed, 1947, Return of October, 1948, Interrupted Melody, 1955, Blackboard Jungle, 1955, Don't Go Near the Water, 1957, Imitation General, Cowboy, 1958, Torpedo Run, 1958, Trial, The Teahouse of the August Moon, Cimarron, 1961, Cry for Happy, 1961, The Courtship of Eddie's Father, 1963, Fate Is The Hunter, 1964, Dear Heart, 1965, The Rounders, 1965, Is Paris Burning?, 1966, The Last Challenge, 1967, A Time For Killing, 1967, The Money Trap, 1968, Rage, 1966, The Day of the Evil Gun, 1968, Heaven With a Gun, 1969, Smith!, 1969, Santee, 1973, Midway, 1976, Superman, 1978, Happy Birthday to Me and Virus, 1981; appeared in: TV series Cade's County, 1971, Jarrety, The Family Holvak, 1975; movies for TV include Punch and Jody, 1974, The Greatest Gift, 1975, The Disappearance of Flight 412, 1975, Police Story: No Margin for Error, 1978, The Gift, 1979; narrator: documentary America, 1971; host: TV series When Havoc Struck, 1978; appeared in: TV spl. Evening in Byzantium, 1978. Served with USMCR, 1942-45. Address: care Chasin-Park-Citron Agency 9255 Sunset Blvd Los Angeles CA 90069 *

FORD, HAROLD EUGENE, congressman; b. Memphis, May 20, 1945; s. Newton J. and Vera (Davis) F.; m. Dorothy Bowles, Feb. 10, 1969; children: Harold, Jake, Sir Isaac. B.S., Tenn. State U., 1967; A.A., John Gupton Coll., 1969; M.B.A., Howard U. Mem. Tenn. Ho. of Reps., 1970-74; mem. 94th-98th congresses from 9th Tenn. Dist.; mem. Ways and Means Com., Select Com. Aging. Trustee Fisk U.; Bd. dirs. Rust Coll., Mental Health Bd. Memphis, Memphis and Shelby County YMCA; mem. nat. adv. bd. St. Jude Children's Research Hosp. Named Outstanding Young Man of Year Memphis Jaycees, 1976, Tenn. Jaycees, 1977. Office: 2305 Rayburn House Office Bldg Washington DC 20515

FORD, HARRISON, actor; b. Chgo., 1942; m. Mary; children—Willard, Benjamin. Ed., Ripon Coll. Appeared: motion pictures including Dead Heat on a Mery-Go-Round, 1966, Luv, 1967, The Long Ride Home, 1967, Getting Straight, 1970, Zabriske Point, 1970, The Conversation, 1974, American Graffiti, 1974, Star Wars, 1977, Heroes, 1977, Force 10 From Navarone, 1978, Hanover Street, 1979, Frisco Kid, 1979, The Empire Strikes Back, 1980, Raiders of the Lost Ark, 1981; played in: TV movie James A. Michener's Dynasty, 1976; numerous: TV appearances including Judgement: The Court-Martial of Lt. William Calley, 1975, The F.B.I., Gunsmoke, The Virginian *

FORD, HARRY XAVIER, coll. pres.; b. Seymour, Ind., Jan. 12, 1921; s. John William and Emma (Gibo) F.; m. Celeste K.C. deVaca, Aug. 8, 1945; children—John Damian, Anthony Alexius. A.B., U. Calif. at Los Angeles, 1949; M.A., Sacramento State Coll., 1953; grad. student higher edn., U. Calif. at Berkeley, 1962-67; D.F.A. (hon.), Kansas City Art Inst., 1974. Tchr. Placer Union High Sch., Auburn, Calif., 1950-53, Stuttgart (Germany) Am. High Sch., 1953-58; chmn. dept. tchr. edn. Calif. Coll. Arts and Crafts, Oakland, 1958-59, pres., 1959—; Adv. bd. Coordinating Council Higher Edn. Calif., 1966—. One man show, State Dept. Amerika Haus, Stuttgart, 1957, exhbns. include, Kingsleey Art Show at Crocker Art Gallery, Sacramento, 1950. Chmn. Oakland-Piedmont Arts Council, 1966-68; mem. Alameda County Art Commn., 1966-69; gov. bd. Oakland Museums Assn., 1966-70, Oakland Repertory Theatre Assn., 1967-68, Museum West of Am. Craftsman Council, 1967-68; adv. bd. Paramount Theater of Arts, 1973-74; nat. com. mem. Advocates for Arts, 1975; hon. trustee Osaka U. Arts, 1973. Served to capt. USAAF, 1942-45; ETO; maj. Res. Decorated Air medal, Bronze Star; recipient 1st award watercolor AAUW competition, Auburn, Calif., 1953. Fellow Nat. Assn. Schs. Art (life mem., treas. 1975, chmn. joint commn. accreditation schs. theatre and dance). Democrat. Roman Catholic. Home: 21 Humphrey Pl Oakland CA 94610

FORD, HENRY, II, automobile manufacturing executive; b. Detroit, Sept. 4, 1917; s. Edsel B. and Eleanor (Clay) F.; m. Anne McDonnell, July 13, 1940 (div.); children: Charlotte, Anne, Edsel Bryant II; m. Maria Cristina Vettore Austin, Feb. 19, 1965 (div.); m. Kathleen DuRoss, Oct. 1980. Grad., Hotchkiss Sch., 1936; student, Yale U., 1936-40. Dir. Ford Motor Co., 1938—, with co., 1940—, v.p., 1943, exec. v.p., 1944, pres., 1945, chmn., 1960-80, chief exec. officer, 1960-79. Trustee The Ford Found., 1943-76; chmn. Detroit/Wayne Port Authority; co-chmn. Detroit Renaissance; grad. mem. Bus. Council; trustee Edison Inst. *

FORD, JAMES DAVID, clergyman; b. Sioux Falls, S.D., July 25, 1931; s. Reuben Haquin and Luella Marie (Lindquist);; s. Reuben Haquin and Luella Marie (Ford); m. Marcia Ruth Sodergren, June 25, 1954; children: Julia Ruth, Peter David, Marie Rebecca, Molly Christine, Sarah Marie. B.A., Gustavus Adolphus Coll., 1953; M.Div., Augustana Sem., 1957; postgrad., Heidelberg (Germany) U., 1957-58; D.Div., Wagner Coll., 1979. Ordained to ministry Lutheran Ch., 1958; pastor Luth. Ch., Ivanhoe, Minn., 1958-61; asst. chaplain U.S. Mil. Acad., West Point, N.Y., 1961-64, sr. chaplain, 1965-79; chaplain U.S. Ho. of Reps., Washington, 1979—; speaker colls. and univs. Trustee Gustavus Adolphus Coll. Recipient Alumni Citation for disting. service Gustavus Adolphus Coll., 1965, alumni citation for disting. service U.S. Mil. Acad., 1965, meritorious service award, 1979. Mem. Guild of St. Ansgar. Club: World Ocean Cruising. Capt. of 31 foot sailboat; sailed Atlantic Ocean, Plymouth, Eng., to N.Y. Home: 6008 Beech Tree Dr Alexandria VA 22310 Office: HB-25 The Capitol Washington DC 20515

FORD, JAMES DAYTON, lawyer, ret. moving co. exec.; b. Harrisburg, Ill., May 31, 1924; s. J. Dayton and Anna (Dorris) F.; m. Alice Maria Evans, June 9, 1944; children—Lynn Alice (Mrs. G. Personius), Katherine Anne (Mrs. Wayne E. Graham), Anna Maria, Elizabeth Ellen (Mrs. James E. Flores), Jamie LaCene. B.B.A., U. Mich., 1948, M.B.A., 1948, J.D., 1951. Bar: Ill. bar 1952, Ariz. bar 1960. Tax. atty. U.S. Steel Corp. subsidiaries in, Duluth, Minn. and Pitts., 1951-54; tax mgr. M.W. Kellogg Co., N.Y.C., 1954-58, Comml. Solvents Corp., 1958-59; partner firm Hull, Terry & Ford, Tucson, 1960-66; gen. counsel Allied Van Lines, Broadview, Ill., 1966-68, exec. v.p., 1968-71, pres., 1971-75; practice law, Tucson, 1976—. Served with AUS, 1943-46. Mem. Ariz., Pima County bar assns., Nat. Def. Transp. Assn. (life), Nat. Rifle Assn. (life), Household Goods Carriers Bur. (v.p. 1974-76), Am. Movers Conf. (dir. 1973-76), Delta Sigma Pi. Republican. Presbyterian. Clubs: Masons, Shriners, Elks, Exchange, Tucson Rod and Gun. Home: 6742 N Los Arboles Circle Tucson AZ 85704 Office: 6985 N Oracle Rd Tucson AZ 85704 *Try to lead a peaceable life, and cherish the earth and all that is in it. Keep ever in mind that no matter how heavy your burdens from time to time seem, there are those in this world to whom your circumstances would be paradise.*

FORD, JAMES HENRY, JR., hospital administrator; b. Brownfield, Miss., May 25, 1931; s. James H. and Katie Sue (Jamieson) F.; m. Peggy Simpson, Mar. 1959; children: Renee, James, Randy, Penny. B.S. in Acctg., Memphis State U., 1953; M.H.A., St. Louis U., 1969. Auditor Sears, Roebuck & Co., Memphis, 1955-60; adminstrv. asst. Meth. Hosp., Memphis, 1964-67; asst. adminstr. Druid City Hosp., Tuscaloosa, Ala., 1969-76, adminstr., 1976—; pres. W. Ala. Emergency Med. Services; past pres. W. Ala. Hosp. Council, 1974. Past pres. Phoenix House of Tuscaloosa, 1974; loaned exec. United Fund in Tuscaloosa County, 1974, 75; past chmn. adminstrv. bd. First Mehtodist Ch. of Tuscaloosa, 1973. Mem. Hosp. Fin. Mgmt. Assn. (past pres. 1975-76, William G. Follmar award 1966, Robert H. Reeves award 1975), Ala. Assn. Hosp. Execs. (past pres. 1981-82), Am. Coll. Hosp. Adminstrs., Ala. Hosp. Assn. (trustee 1978—). Office: Druid City Hosp 809 University Blvd E Tuscaloosa AL 35403

FORD, JAMES WILLIAM, finance company executive; b. Alameda, Calif., Feb. 1, 1923; s. Shelton C. and Eunice (George) F.; m. Anne Farley, June 30, 1945; children: Julian, Amy, Carol. A.B., Oberlin Coll., 1947; M.A. in Econs, Harvard U., 1949, Ph.D., 1954; postgrad. (Fulbright scholar), 1949-51, U. Chgo., 1958-59. Instr. econs. Columbia U., 1951-53; asst. prof econs. Vanderbilt U., 1953-57; asso. prof. econs. Ohio State U., 1957-59; economist to bd. govs. FRS, 1959-61; various positions including dir. Econs. Office, asst. controller fin. staff Ford Motor Co., 1961-75, v.p., 1980—; exec. v.p. ins. and spl. fin. ops. Ford Motor Credit Co., Dearborn, Mich., 1975-77, pres., 1977-80, chmn., 1980—. Corp. mem. Detroit Osteo. Hosp. Corp., 1976-83; bd. dirs. Inner City Bus. Improvement Forum, 1979-83, Youth Living Centers, Inc., 1970-83. Served with USAAF, 1943-46. Office: Ford Motor Credit Co The American Rd Dearborn MI 48121

FORD, JESSE HILL, author; b. Troy, Ala., Dec. 28, 1928; s. Jesse Hill and Lucille (Musgrove) F.; m. Lillian Pellettieri, Nov. 15, 1975; children: Charles Davis, Sarah Ann, Elizabeth. B.A., Vanderbilt U., 1951; M.A., U. Fla., 1955; postgrad. (Fulbright scholar), U. Oslo, Norway, 1961-62; Litt.D. (hon.), Lambuth Coll., 1968. Reporter The Nashville Tennessean, 1950-51; news writer U. Fla., 1953-55; dir. pub. relations Tenn. Med. Assn., 1955-56; asst. dir. pub. relations AMA, Chgo., 1956-57; vis. fellow Center for Advanced Study, Wesleyan U., Middletown, Conn., 1965. Author: Mountains of Gilead, 1961, The Liberation of Lord Byron Jones, 1965, (with Stirling Silliphant) screenplay, 1969, The Feast of St. Barnabas, 1969, The Raider, 1975; short story collection Fishes, Birds and Sons of Men, 1967; play The Conversion of Buster Drumwright, 1963; musical Drumwright, 1982. Served with USNR, 1951-53. Atlantic grantee, 1959; Guggenheim fellow, 1966; included in O. Henry Prize Collection Short Stories, 1961, 66, 67; Best Detective Stories, 1972-76; recipient Edgar award for short story The Jail Mystery Writers Am., 1976. Episcopalian. Clubs: Overseas Press; Spratt Bay (V.I.); Guadalajara Racquet. Address: 500 Plantation Ct Nashville TN 37221 *Each day I try to bear in mind that while life is short the art of fiction is long; that while death is nothing, to live without growth is to die everyday; that the God-fearing among us, who earn their bread and honor their debts, are the backbone of civilization.*

FORD, JOE THOMAS, telephone company executive, state senator; b. Conway, Ark., June 24, 1937; s. Arch W. and Ruby (Watson) F.; m. Jo Ellen Wilbourn, Aug. 9, 1959; children: Alison, Scott. B.S., U. Ark., 1959. With Allied Telephone Co., Little Rock, 1959—, v.p.-treas., 1963-77, pres., 1977—; mem. Ark. State Senate, 1967-82; dir. Comml. Nat. Bank, Little Rock, Security Savs. and Loan Assn., Conway. Trustee Baptist Med. Center, Little Rock; bd. dirs. Little Rock Boys Club. Mem. Greater Little Rock C. of C. (dir.). Baptist. Home: 2100 Country Club Ln Little Rock AR 72207 Office: PO Box 2177 Little Rock AR 72203

FORD, JOHN BAILEY, bond company executive; b. Chgo., Mar. 21, 1934; s. Kenneth Arthur and Dorothy (Bailey) F.; m. Jill Hunsberger, July 17, 1976; children: John, Sandra, Russell, Debbie, Douglas. B.A. magna cum laude, Princeton U., 1956. Govt. bond trader Bankers Trust Co., N.Y.C., 1956-62; pres. Aubrey G. Lanston & Co., Inc., N.Y.C., 1962—. Mem. Assn. Primary Dealers in U.S. Govt. Bonds. Congregationalist. Club: Lake (New Canaan, Conn.). Home: 100 Greenley Rd New Canaan CT 06840 117 Beekman St New York NY Flying Point Rd Watermill NY 11976 Office: 20 Broad St New York NY 10005

FORD, JOHN CHARLES, artist; b. Choudrant, La., Sept. 29, 1929; s. John Leon and Jessie Faye (Dugdale) F.; 1 son, John Charles. B.F.A., La. Tech. U., 1950; B.D., Austin Presbyn. Theol. Sem., 1953; M.F.A., U. Oreg., 1960. One man shows at, Neuberger Mus., Purchase, N.Y., 1977, Guggenheim Mus., N.Y.C., exhibited in group shows at, San Francisco Art Mus., Seattle Art Mus., Smithsonian Instn., Washington, Cambridge Sch. Archtl. Engrng., others; represented in permanent collections, Addison Gallery of Am. Art, Guggenheim Mus., Corcoran Gallery, many others. Address: 121 Mercer St New York NY 10012

FORD, JOHN GILMORE, interior designer; s. John Gilmore and Marian Brunner (Mainhart) F.; m. Berthe Diana Hanover, Aug. 19, 1972. B.F.A., Md. Inst. Coll. Art. Founder, 1962; since pres. John Ford Assocs., Inc., Balt.; tchr. seminars Md. Inst. Coll. Art; lectr. Indo-Asian art Johns Hopkins U., Towson State Coll. Served with USCGR. Recipient citation of merit Md. Inst. Coll. Art, 1960. Fellow Am. Soc. Interior Designers (past nat. v.p., pres. Md. chpt.; Presdl. citation); mem. Internat. Chinese Snuff Bottle Soc. (pres., co-editor jour.), Asia Soc. Club: Masons (32 deg.). Home: 3903 Greenway Baltimore MD 21218 Office: 2601 N Charles St Baltimore MD 21218

FORD, JOHN WILLIAM, government official; b. Louisville, Ky., May 19, 1920; s. John M. and Leila (Waters) F.; m. Mercedes Barreda, Jan. 13, 1945; children: John Henry, Douglas William, Walter Paul, Richard Anthony, Glen Michael, Robert James. Student, U. Louisville., 1939-40, Jefferson Law Sch., Louisville, 1940-42, 46-47; grad., Nat. War Coll., Washington, 1961. With Dept. Justice, 1939-44, 46-47; attache U.S. embassy, Caracas, Venezuela, 1947-49, Mexico City, 1949-50, Paris, France, 1950-51; asst. chief, div. chief Dept. State, 1952, office dir., 1953; attaché Am. embassy, Manila, 1954-55, 1st sec., consul, 1955-56, Mexico City, 1956- 60; assigned to Dept. State, Washington., 1960—, exec. sec. policy planning council, 1962-64; consul gen., Barcelona, Spain, 1964-67; dir. Inter-Am. polit. affairs U.S. Permanent Mission to OAS, Washington, 1967-70, minister, counselor, 1971—; dep. U.S. permanent rep., 1970-75; Alternate U.S. mem. Inter-Am. Peace Com., 1967-70; Inter-Am. com. Alliance for Progress, 1970-75; advisor to Sec. Gen. OAS, Washington, 1975—. Served with U.S. Army, 1944-46. Recipient Commendable Service award Dept. State, 1958, 61, Meritorious Service award, 1964, Outstanding Service award, 1974, 35 Yr. Govt. Service recognition, 1975, Leo S. Rowe Meml. award OAS, 1983; Cruz y Placa Defensores de la Republica y Sus Descendientes, Mexico, 1960. Home: 1588 Lake Christopher Dr Virginia Beach VA 23458

FORD, JOHNNY LAWRENCE, mayor; b. Tuskegee, Ala., Aug. 23, 1942; s. Charlie and Tennessee F.; m. Frances Baldwin Rainer, 1970; children—Johnny Lawrence, Christopher Ashley. B.S., Knoxville Coll., 1964; postgrad., Nat. Exec. Inst., 1965; M.A., Auburn U., 1977. Mgr. Hudgins Small Bus. Assn., N.Y.C., 1964, N.Y. council Boy Scouts Am., 1965-69; exec. coordinator Tuskegee Model Cities, 1969-70; v.p. Multi Racial Corp., New Orleans, 1970-71; mayor, Tuskegee, 1972—; Committeeman Carver dist. Boy Scouts Am., 1971—; mem. Gov.'s Manpower Ancillary Com., 1973—, Gov.'s Tourism Council, 1973—. Chmn. Macon County Council on Retardation and Rehab.; bd. mgmt. John Andrew Hosp.; mem. exec. com. Ala. League Municipalities. Recipient Nat. Law and Social Justice Leadership award Afro-Am. Patrolmens League, 1973; named Young Man of Yr. Boy Scouts Am., 1970, Top Recruiter, 1968. Mem. Knoxville Coll. Alumni Assn., NAACP, Nat. Conf. Black Mayors (2d v.p.), Ala. Conf. Black Mayors (pres.), Tuskegee C. of C., Kappa Alpha Psi. Democrat. Baptist. Clubs: Mason, Elk. Home: PO Box 414 Tuskegee Institute AL 36088 Office: 214 N Main St Tuskegee AL 36083

FORD, JOSEPH, superior ct. judge; b. Easton, Mass., May 18, 1914; s. Joseph L. and Margaret E. (Malloy) F.; m. Barbara Bacheller; children—Carolyn Ford Howell, Richard B. J.D., Northeastern U., 1938, LL.M., 1941. Bar: Mass. bar. Partner firm Bingham, Dana & Gould, Boston, 1941-62; superior ct. judge, mem. appellate div., Boston, 1962—; lectr. trial practice Law Schs. Boston U., Suffolk U., New Eng. Sch. Law. Mem. Mass. Crime Commn., 1953-55. Served to lt. USNR, 1944-46. Mem. Am. Law Inst. Roman Catholic. Office: Superior Ct 1109 Ct House Govt Center Boston MA 02108

FORD, JOSEPH FRANCIS, accounting educator; b. Phila., Mar. 16, 1919; s. John Joseph and Anne (Schneider) F.; m. Janet Bruce Weiler, Apr. 18, 1942; children: Emille Louise, Linda Jean. B.S. in Commerce with highest honors, Drexel Inst. Tech., 1941; M.B.A. magna cum laude, U. Pa., 1952. C.P.A., Pa. With Curtis Pub. Co., 1938, Scott Paper Co., 1939, Joseph H. McGrath & Co., C.P.A.s, Phila., 1940-41; mem. faculty Drexel U., Phila., 1946—, prof. accounting, 1952—, dir. M.B.A. program, 1951-66, asso. dean, 1966-73, 77—, acting dean, 1970-71, 76-77. Author: (with others) Principles of Accounting, 1954. Vice pres. Home and Sch. Assn. Drexel Hill Sch. Served to lt. col. AUS, 1941-46; ETO. Decorated Bronze Star. Mem. Am., Pa. insts. C.P.A.s, Res. Officers Assn., Scabbard and Blade, Phi Kappa Phi, Beta Gamma Sigma, Sigma Rho. Republican. Presbyn. (pres. trustees). Home: 1221 Cornell Ave Drexel Hill PA 19026 Office: Drexel Univ 32d and Chestnut Sts Philadelphia PA 19104 *Be honest in all that you do and be honest in all that you say. That way you never have trouble recalling what was done in the past.*

FORD, KENNETH WILLIAM, physicist, university administrator; b. West Palm Beach, Fla., May 1, 1926; s. Paul Hammond and Edith (Timblin) F.; m. Karin Stehnike, Aug. 27, 1953 (div. 1961); m. Joanne Baumunk, June 9, 1962; children: Paul T., Sarah E., Caroline, Adam, Jason, Lucas; 1 stepdau., Nina. Student, John Carroll U., 1945, U. Mich., 1945-46; A.B., Harvard U., 1948; Ph.D., Princeton U., 1953. Research asst. Los Alamos Sci. Lab., 1950-51; research asso., Princeton U., 1951-52, Ind. U., 1953-54, asst. prof., 1954-1957, asso. prof., 1957-58, Brandeis U., 1958-1961, prof., 1961-64; prof. physics U. Calif. at Irvine, 1964-70, chmn. dept., 1964-68; prof. physics U. Mass., Boston, 1970-75; pres. N.Mex. Inst. Mining and Tech., Socorro, 1975-82; exec. v.p. U. Md., Adelphi, 1982—; mem. Commn. Coll. Physics, 1968-71. Author: The World of Elementary Particles, 1963, Basic Physics, 1968, Classical and Modern Physics, 3 vols, 1972-74; bd. editors: Phys. Rev, 1960-62; contbr. articles on nuclear physics and field theory to tech. publs. Served USNR, 1944-46. Fulbright fellow Max Planck Inst., Germany, 1955-56; NSF Sr. Postdoctoral fellow Imperial Coll., London, also Mass. Inst. Tech., 1961- 62. Fellow Am. Phys. Soc. (chmn. Forum on Physics and Soc. 1981), AAAS (council del. physics electorate 1983-86); mem. Am. Assn. Physics Tchrs. (pres. 1972, Disting. Service Citation 1976), Fedn. Am. Scientists. Home: 12503 Davan Dr Silver Spring MD 20904 Office: U Md Central Adminstrn Adelphi MD 20783

FORD, LUCILLE GARBER, economist, educator; b. Ashland, Ohio, Dec. 31, 1921; d. Ora Myers and Edna Lucille (Armstrong) Garber; m. Laurence Wesley Ford, Sept. 1, 1946; children: Karen Elizabeth, JoAnn Christine. A.A., Stephens Coll., 1942; B.S. in commerce, Northwestern U., 1944, M.B.A., 1944; Ph.D. in econs., Case Western Res. U., 1967. Cert. fin. planner. Instr. Allegheny Coll., Meadville, Pa., 1945-46, U. Ala., Tuscaloosa, 1946-47; personnel dir., asst. sec. A.L. Garber Co., Ashland, Ohio, 1947-67; prof., chmn. dept. econs. Ashland Coll. (Ohio), 1970-75, dir. Gill Ctr. for Econ. Edn., 1975—, v.p., dean Sch. Bus., Adminstrn. and Econs., 1980—; dir. Ohio Edison, Nat. City Corp., A. Schulman Co., Shelby Mut. Ins. Co.; lectr. in field. Author University Economics—Guide for Education Majors, 1979; Economics: Learning and Instruction, 1981; contbr. articles to profl. jours. Candidate for lt. gov. of Ohio, 1978; trustee Stephens Coll., 1977-80; elder Presbyterian Ch.; bd. dirs. Presbyn. Found; active ARC. Recipient outstanding alumni award Stephens Coll., 1977, outstanding prof. award Ashland Coll., 1971, 75. Mem. Am. Econs. Assn., Nat. Indsl. Research Soc., Am. Artitration Assn. (profl. arbitrator), Assn. Pvt. Enterprise Edn. (pres. 1983—), Omicron Delta Epsilon, Alpha Delta Kappa. Republican. Home: 1717 Upland Dr Ashland OH 44805 Office: Ashland College Ashland Ohio 44805

FORD, MORGAN, judge; b. nr. Wheatland, N.D., Sept. 8, 1911; s. Morgan J. and Mary (Langer) F.; m. Margaret Duffy, July 30, 1955; children: William, Patrick and Michael (twins), Mary Ellen. B.A., U. North Dakota, 1935; LL.B., Georgetown U., 1938. Tchr. Dist. 102, Everest Twp., Cass Co., N.D., 1933-34; state mgr. Royal Union Fund, Des Moines, 1938-39; in gen. law practice, Fargo, N.D., 1939-49; pres. Surety Mut. Health & Accident Ins. Co., Fargo, 1939-49; v.p. 1st State Bank of Casselton, N.D., 1941-49; judge U.S. Customs Ct., N.Y.C., 1949—. City atty., Casselton, 1942-48, mem. adv. bd. for registrants in selective service, 1942. Address: US Ct of Internat Trade 1 Federal Plaza New York NY 10007

FORD, NANCY LOUISE, composer; b. Kalamazoo, Oct. 1, 1935; d. Henry Ford III and Mildred Wotring; m. Keith W. Charles, May 23, 1964. B.A., DePauw U., 1957. Composer: (off-Broadway musicals (in collaboration with Gretchen Cryer) Now Is the Time for All Good Men, The Last Sweet Days of Isaac, I'm Getting My Act Together and Taking It on the Road; also Broadway musical Shelter; performer, lectr. stage and TV. Mem. Dramatists Guild, Writers Guild, AFTRA, Actors Equity, Am. Fedn. Musicians.

FORD, PATRICK KILDEA, Celtic studies educator; b. Lansing, Mich., July 31, 1935; s. Oliver Patrick and Ina Mildred (Spence) F.; m. Carol Mae Larsen, June 20, 1959 (div. 1978); children: Anne Kristina, Paul Kildea, James Oliver; m. Chadine Pearl Bailie, Nov. 17, 1979.

B.A., Mich. State U., 1959; M.A., Harvard U., 1966, Ph.D., 1969. Asst. prof. English Stanford U., 1968-70; asst. prof. Indo-European studies UCLA, 1970-71, asst. prof. English, 1971-74, assoc. prof., 1974-79, prof. English and Celtic studies, 1979—, dir. Folklore and Mythology Ctr., 1979—, chmn. Indo-European Studies program, 1972-73, 74-75, 79-82. Author: The Poetry of Llywarch Hen, 1974, The Mabinogi and Other Medieval Welsh Tales, 1977; editor, contbr.: Celtic Folklore and Christianity: Essays in Memory of William W. Heist, 1983; co-author: Sources and Analogues of Old English Poetry: Celtic and Germanic, 1984. Served with AUS, 1956-57. NEH fellow, 1972; UCLA fellow, 1973; Skaggs Found. grantee, 1981-83. Mem. Internat. Arthurian Soc. (pres. N.Am. bd. 1981—), Medieval Assn. Pacific, MLA, Medieval Acad. Am., Am. Folklore Soc., Calif. Folklore Soc., Celtic Studies Assn. N.Am. Office: Dept English UCLA 405 Hilgrad Ave Los Angeles CA 90024

FORD, RICHARD, lawyer; b. Ypsilanti, Mich., Nov. 22, 1903; s. Richard Clyde and Grace Augusta (Cogshall) F.; m. Janet Hankinson, Sept. 21, 1931; children—Thomas Clyde, Janet Grace (Mrs. Donald J. Campbell), Mary Ainslie (Mrs. Neal A. Talbot). Student, U. Montpellier, France, 1922; A.B., Eastern Mich. U., 1923; J.D., U. Mich., 1926. Bar: Mich. bar 1926. Since practiced in, Detroit; partner firm Fischer, Franklin, Ford, Simon & Hogg, 1942—; instr. Detroit Coll. Law, 1957-78. Contbr. legal publs. Mem. ABA, Detroit Bar Assn. (bd. dirs. 1956-62), Oakland County Bar Assn., State Bar Mich., Am. Coll. Trial Lawyers. Republican. Methodist. Home: 4555 Pickering Rd Birmingham MI 48010 Office: Guardian Bldg Detroit MI 48226

FORD, RICHARD EARL, plant virologist, educator; b. Des Moines, May 25, 1933; s. Victor S. and Gertrude (Headlee) F.; m. Roberta Jean Essig, June 20, 1954; children—Nina Diane, Linda Marie, Kent Richard (dec.), Steven Earl. B.S., Iowa State U., 1956; M.S., Cornell U., 1959, Ph.D., 1961. Undergrad. research technician Iowa State U., 1952-55, undergrad. tchr. botany, 1956; grad. research asst. plant pathology Cornell U., 1956-59, grad. research asst. virology tchr., 1959-61; research plant pathologist, asst. prof. U.S. Dept. Agr. and Oreg. State U., 1961-65; prof. plant virology, virus research Iowa State U., Ames, 1965-72; prof., head dept. plant pathology U. Ill., Urbana, 1972—, cons. agrl. improvement, Europe, Asia, S.Am., others. Editor: Jour. Phytopathology; contbr. articles to profl. jours. Mem. Am. Phytopath. Soc. (sec., councilor, pres. N.C. div., nat. pres. and v.p.), Assn. Dept. Heads of Plant Pathology in U.S. (chmn.), Sigma Xi (v.p., treas. U. Ill. chpt.), Phi Kappa Phi, Phi Sigma Gamma, Gamma Sigma Delta, Gamma Gamma, FarmHouse Frat. (nat. pres., Master Builder of Men award, tres. FarmHouse Found.). Clubs: Lions, Toastmasters. Home: 11 Persimmon Circle Urbana IL 61801 *Principles guiding my life are honesty, integrity and complete openness and candor. Hard work and long, often tedious, hours on the farm taught me the value of these attributes in all jobs. My goal is to provide an atmosphere conducive for all associates to attain their pinnacle of success by honest, intelligent use of time with hard work.*

FORD, RICHARD EDMOND, lawyer; b. Ronceverte, W.Va., May 3, 1927; s. Grady Williams and Hazel Loraine (Fry) F.; m. Sally Frances Alexander, June 14, 1952; children: Richard Edmond, Sally Anne, Melinda J. Student, U. N.C., 1950; B.S. in Bus. Adminstrn., W.Va. U., 1951, LL.B., 1954. Bar: W.Va. 1954. Assoc. Holt & Haynes, Lewisburg, W.Va., 1954-55; ptnr. Haynes & Ford, Lewisburg, 1955-74; firm Haynes, Ford & Rowe, Lewisburg, 1975—; dir. Greenbrier Cable Corp. Mem. W.Va. Legislature, 1961-64; bd. dirs. W.Va. U. Found., Daywood Found., W.Va. Legal Services Plan, 1973-79; trustee Greenbrier Coll. for Women, 1960-73; mem. exec. bd. Buckskin council Boy Scouts Am.; mem. adv. bd. Greenbrier Community Coll. Center; mem. vis. com. Coll. Law, W.Va. U., 1972-74. Served as ensign U.S. Maritime Service, 1945-47. Mem. ABA (ho. of dels. 1977-80), W.Va. Bar Assn. (v.p. 1965-66, 75-76), W.Va. State Bar (pres. 1978-79), Greenbrier County Bar Assn. (pres. 1964-66, 81-82), W.Va. Law Sch. Assn. (pres. 1966-67), Nat. Conf. Commrs. Uniform State Laws, Am. Coll. Real Estate Lawyers, W.Va. U. Alumni Assn. (pres. 1971), Phi Beta Kappa, Sigma Chi, Phi Delta Phi, Order of Vandalia. Democrat. Methodist. Clubs: Masons, KT, Shriners, Lewisburg Elks. Home: Buckingham Acres Lewisburg WV 24901 Office: 203 W Randolph St Lewisburg WV 24901

FORD, RICHARD IRVING, curator, educator; b. Harrisburg, Pa., June 27, 1941; s. Frank Boyd and Alma Elizabeth (Love) F.; m. Karen Lucile Cowan, Aug. 17, 1963; children—Rebecca Ana, Nathaniel Gabriel. A.B., Oberlin Coll., 1963; M.A., U. Mich., 1965, Ph.D., 1968. Asst. prof. anthropology U. Cin., 1967-69; asst. prof. anthropology U. Mich., Ann Arbor, 1969-72, asso. prof., 1972-77, prof. anthropology and botany, 1977—; curator Mus. Anthropology, Ann Arbor, 1972—, asso. dir., 1972-75, dir., 1975—, dir. Ethnobot. Lab., 1969—. Author: (with others) Paleoethnobotany of the Koster Site, 1972, Systematic Research Collections in Anthropology, 1977, The Nature and Status of Ethnobotany, 1978; mem. editorial bd.: Jour. Ethnobiology; contbr. articles to profl. jours. Recipient Distinguished Service award U. Mich., 1971; NSF research grantee, 1970-73, 75, 76, 78, 79; Weatherhead scholar Sch. Am. Research, 1978-79; Nat. Geog. Soc. grantee, 1983. Fellow AAAS (council, nominations com.), Am. Anthrop. Assn. (fin. com.); mem. Soc. for Am. Archeology (exec. com.), Archaeol. Conservancy (bd. dirs.), Council Museum Anthropology (pres., editor), Herb Research Found. (profl. adv. bd.), Soc. for Econ. Botany (editorial bd.), Ethnobiology Conf. (steering com., editorial bd.). Office: 4045 Mus Anthropology U Mich Ann Arbor MI 48109

FORD, ROBERT NELSON, lawyer, deputy assistant attorney general U.S.; b. Washington, Jan. 20, 1929; s. Rowland H. and Osce Donna (Pratt) F.; m. Ann Graninger, Apr. 26, 1951; children: Gary W., Jeffrey R., Judith Ford Osborne. A.A., George Washington U., 1950; A.B., Geroge Washington U., 1952, J.D., 1967. Bar: Md., D.C. Mktg. mgr. Pepsi Cola Bottling Co., Cheverly, Md., 1957-67; trial atty. Dept. Justice, Washington, 1967-75, asst. U.S. atty., 1975-78, dep. assoc. atty. gen., 1978-81, dep. asst. atty. gen., 1981—. Recipient John Marshall Dept. Justice, 1976, Stanley D. Rose Meml. award Civil Div. Justice, 1982. Lutheran. Office: US Dept Justice 9th and Constitution Ave NW Washington DC 20530

FORD, RUTH, actress; b. Brookhaven, Miss.; d. Charles and Gertrude (Cato) F.; m. Zachary Scott, July 6, 1952; 1 dau., by previous marriage. B.A., U. Miss., M.A. Actress (first appearence) play, Ivoryton Playhouse, Conn., 1937, Ways and Means, Ivoryton Playhouse, Conn., 1937; Orson Welle's Mercury Theatre Co., 1938, Cyrano de Bergerac, 1946, No Exit, 1947, Hamlet, 1949, Macbeth, The Failures, A Phoenix Too Frequent, Six Characters in Search of an Author, (debut) Requieum for a Nun, Royal Ct., London, 1957, Lovely, 1965, Dinner at Eight, 1966, The Ninety-Day Mistress, 1967, The Grass Harp, 1971, Madame de Sade, 1972, A Breeze from the Gulf, 1973, The Charlatan, 1974, The Seagull, 1977, The Aspern Papers, 1978; (first appearence) film, 1941, Wilson, Dragonwyck, Keys of the Kingdom, Act One, Play It As It Lays. Mem. AFTRA, Screen Actors Guild. Democrat. Address: 1 W 72d St New York NY 10023

FORD, T. MITCHELL, corp. exec.; b. Albany, N.Y., Apr. 27, 1921; s. Clarence Edwin and Alice (Mitchell) F.; m. Mimi Parsons, Oct. 4, 1944; children: Kyle Ford Schutz, Mitchell P. A.B., Harvard U., 1943; J.D., Yale U., 1948. Bar: Conn. 1948. With firm Becket & Wagner, Lakeville, Conn., 1948-52; asst. gen. counsel CIA, 1952-55; gen. counsel Naugatuck Valley Indsl. Council, Waterbury, Conn., 1955-58; with Emhart Corp. and predecessor Am. Hardware Corp., Hartford, Conn., 1958—; gen. counsel Am. Hardware Corp., 1960-64, v.p., 1964-67, pres., 1967—, chmn., 1976—, also dir.; dir. Conn. Nat. Corp., United Techs. Corp., Travelers Ins. Corp., Conn. Natural Gas Corp. Served with AUS, 1943-45; ETO. Office: 426 Colt Hwy Farmington CT 06032

FORD, THOMAS PATRICK, lawyer; b. Wausau, Wis., Dec. 29, 1918; s. John Patrick and Matild (Flatley) F.; m. Jean Ann Smith, Fed. 6, 1943 (dec. 1969); children: Thomas Patrick, Howard Michael, John Timolthy, James J.; m. Mary Louise McGovern, Oct. 2, 1970; children: Mary Dolph Adkins, Louise C. Dolph, William McGovern Ford. Ph.B., U. Notre Damen, 1940; LL.B., Harvard U., 1947. Bar: N.Y. 1948, Fla. 1975. Assoc. Shearman & Sterling, N.Y.C., 1947-55, ptnr., 1955—; pres. and dir. W.M. Keck, Jr. Found., Calif., 1958—; dir. Forbes, Inc., N.Y.C., Coalinga Corp., (Calif.), Owen Cheatham Found., N.Y.C., W.M. Keck Found., Calif., Can. Bank of Commerce Trust Co., N.Y.C. Served to lt. comdr USNR, 1943-46. Clubs: Links, River (N.Y.C.); Everglades (Palm Beach, Fla.). Home: 555 Park Ave New York NY 10021 also: 154 Middle Beach Rd Madison CT 06443 Office: Shearman & Sterling 153 E 53d St New York NY 10022

FORD, THOMAS ROBERT, sociologist, educator; b. Lake Charles, La., June 24, 1923; s. Gervais w. and Alma (Weil) F.; m. Harriet Lowrey, Aug. 13, 1949; children: Margaret Erin, Janet Patricia, Mark Lowrey, Charlotte Elizabeth. B.S., La. State U., 1946, M.A., 1948; Ph.D., Vanderbilt U., 1951. Instr. sociology La. State U., 1948-49; asst. prof. U. Ala., 1950-53; supervisory analytical statistician (demography) USAF Personnel and Tng. Research Center, Maxwell AFB, Ala., 1953-56; faculty U. Ky., Lexington, 1956—, prof. sociology, 1960—, chmn. dept., 1966-70; dir. Center Developmental Change, 1975—; Research dir. So. Appalachian Studies, Inc., 1957-62; Mem. Pres.'s Nat. Adv. Com. on Rural Poverty, 1966-67; sr. adviser Population Council to Colombian Assn. Med. Faculties; Faculties Medicine, Bogota, 1970-72. Author: Man and Land in Peru, 1955, Health and Demography in Kentucky, 1964; Editor: The Southern Appalachian Region: A Survey, 1962, The Revolutionary Theme in Contemporary America, 1965, (with Gordon DeJong) Social Demography, 1970, Rural U.S.A.: Persistence and Change, 1978. Served with USAAF, 1943-45. Decorated Air medal with 6 oak leaf clusters.; Guggenheim fellow, 1962. Mem. AAAS, Am. Sociol. Assn., Population Assn. Am., Rural Sociol. Assn. (pres. 1972-73), So. Sociol. Assn. (pres. 1976-77), Internat. Rural Sociology Assn. (sec. 1976-80). Home: 1107 Eldemere Rd Lexington KY 40502

FORD, WENDELL HAMPTON, U.S. senator; b. Owensboro, Ky., Sept. 8, 1924; s. Ernest M. and Irene (Schenk) F.; m. Jean Neel, Sept. 18, 1943; children: Shirley Jean (Mrs. Dexter), Steven. Student, U. Ky., 1942-43. Partner Gen. Ins. Agy., Owensboro, 1959—; chief asst. to gov. Ky., 1959-61; mem. Ky. Senate, 1966-67; lt. gov. Ky., 1967-71, gov. Ky., 1971-74, U.S. senator from Ky., 1974—; mem. Energy and Resources Com., Rules Com., Commerce, Sci. and Transp. Com., Democratic steering com.; past chmn. Dem. Senatorial Campaign Com., Nat. Dem. Gov.'s Caucus; chmn. Dem. Nat. Campaign Com., 1976. Served with AUS, 1944-46, Ky. N.G., 1949-62. Baptist. Club: Elk. Home: Bethesda MD 20816 Office: US Senate Washington DC 20510

FORD, WILLIAM CLAY, automotive company executive; b. Detroit, Mar. 14, 1925; s. Edsel Bryant and Eleanor (Clay) F.; m. Martha Firestone, June 21, 1947; children: Martha, Sheila, William Clay, Elizabeth. B.S., Yale U., 1949. Sales and advt. staff Ford Motor Co., 1949; indsl. relations, labor negotiations with UAW, 1949; quality control mgr. gas turbine engines Lincoln-Mercury div., Dearborn, Mich., 1951, mgr. spl. product ops., 1952, v.p., 1953, gen. mgr., 1954; group v.p. Lincoln and Continental divs., 1955, v.p. product design, 1956-80, dir., 1948—, chmn. exec. com., 1978—, vice chmn. bd., 1980—; pres., owner Detroit Lions Profl. Football Club. Chmn. Edison Inst., Edsel B. Ford Inst. Med. Research; trustee Eisenhower Med. Center, Thomas A. Edison Found.; bd. dirs. Nat. Tennis Hall of Fame, Boys Clubs Am. Mem. Soc. Automotive Engrs. (asso.), Automobile Old Timers, Phelps Assn., Psi Upsilon. Clubs: Econ. of Detroit (dir.), Masons, K.T. Office: Ford Motor Co Dearborn MI 48121

FORD, WILLIAM DAVID, lawyer, congressman; b. Detroit, Aug. 6, 1927; s. Robert Henderson and Jean Bowie (McGhee) F.; m. Martha Ford; children: William David, Margaret, John P. Student, Nebr. Tchrs. Coll., Peru, 1946, Wayne State U., 1947-48; B.S., U. Denver, 1949, LL.B., 1951; L.H.D., Westfield State Coll., 1970; Ph.D. (hon.), Eastern Mich. U., 1976, Grand Valley State Coll. of Mich., 1979, Wayne State U., 1979, Mich. State U., 1980, No. Mich. U., 1980, Central Mich. U., 1981, U. Detroit, 1981. Bar: Mich. bar 1951. Practice law, 1951—; mem. 89th to 98th Congresses from 15th Mich. Dist.; mem. steering and policy com., chmn. com. on post office and civil service, edn. and labor com., Democratic nat. whip-at-large; justice of peace 89th to 97th Congresses from 15th Mich. Dist., Taylor, Mich., 1955-57, twp. atty., 1957-64; city atty., Melvindale, Mich., 1957-59; congressional adviser to UNESCO, 1971-74; vice-chmn. Conf. Great Lake Congressmen.; Del. Mich. Constl. Conv., 1961-62; mem. Mich. Senate from 21st Dist., 1962-64. Served with USNR, 1944-46. Recipient Distinguished Service award; Outstanding Young Man of Year award, Taylor, 1962. Mem. ABA, Mich. Bar Assn., Downriver Bar Assn. (pres. 1961-62), Am. Legion. Clubs: Masons, Shriners, Eagles, Elks, Moose, Rotary (pres. 1961-62). Home: Taylor MI 48180 Office: 239 House Office Bldg Washington DC 20515

FORD, WILLIAM DUDLEY, industrial company executive; b. Lawrence, Mass., Jan. 14, 1917; s. Edmond J. and Grace (Daly) F.; m. Helen Pidgeon, May 29, 1943. A.B., Harvard U., 1939; LL.B., Va. Law Sch., 1948. Bar: N.Y. Mem. firm Cadwalader, Wickersham & Taft, N.Y.C., 1948-51, Cravath, Swaine & Moore, 1951-61; v.p. Equity Corp., N.Y.C., 1961-63; v.p., gen. counsel, sec. Colt Industries, Inc., N.Y.C., after 1963, now sr. v.p. legal; v.p., sec., dir. numerous subs.'s; dir. Coca Cola Bottling Co. Editor: Va. Law Rev, 1947-48. Served to lt. col. USAAF, 1940-45. Decorated Legion of Merit. Clubs: Harvard, Metropolitan (N.Y.C.) (gov.); Edgartown (Mass.) Yacht.). Home: 30 Sutton Pl New York NY 10022 Office: 430 Park Ave New York NY 10022

FORD, WILLIAM F., banker; b. Huntington, N.Y., Aug. 14, 1936; s. William and Margaret (Mueller) Freithaler; m. Diane McDonald, June 11, 1960; children: Eric W., Kristin E. B.A. in Econs. summa cum laude, U. Tex., 1961; M.A., U. Mich., 1962, Ph.D., 1966; D.Sc. (hon.), Fla. Inst. Tech., 1981. Part-time teaching asst. U. Mich., 1962-63, instr., 1965-66; economist Rand Corp., 1966, cons., 1967-68, 70-71; asst. prof. econs. U. Va., 1967-69; assoc. prof. Tex. Tech. U., Lubbock, 1969-70; prof. econs., dean Transylvania Coll., Lexington, Ky., 1970-71; exec. dir., chief economist research and planning group Am. Bankers Assn., 1971-75; sr. v.p., chief economist Wells Fargo Bank, San Francisco, 1975-80; pres. Fed. Res. Bank Atlanta, 1980—; mem. faculty Stonier Grad.Sch. Banking, 1976—; mem. fed. open market com. Fed. Res. System, 1982—; speaker in field. Author: Mexico's Foreign Trade and Economic Development, 1968; also articles, revs., TV script. Trustee Marin council Boy Scouts Am., 1978-80; mem. steering com. San Francisco Bay Area council, 1977-80. Served with USN, 1954-57. Woodrow Wilson fellow, 1961; NDEA fellow, 1961-63; Ford Found. fgn. area fellow, Mex., 1964-65; Rotary Internat. fellow, Chile, 1970; co-winner Fred M. Taylor Prize U. Mich. Mem. Am. Econ. Assn., Nat. Assn. Bus. Economists, Phi Beta Kappa. Methodist. Office: first nationwide savings 700 market street san francisco ca 94102

FORD, WILLIAM FRANCIS, bank holding company executive; b. Albany, N.Y., Mar. 11, 1925; s. Patrick J. and Ellen M. F.; m. Marcia J. Whalen, Jan. 7, 1956; children: William Francis, Michael P., Timothy K., Daniel J., Cathleen A. B.A. in Acctg. with honors, St. Michaels Coll., 1950. V.p. Equitable Credit Corp., Albany, 1950-60, Am. Fin. Systems Inc., Silver Spring, Md., 1960-65, Gen. Electric Credit Corp., Stamford, Conn., 1965-74; chmn., chief exec. officer Security Pacific Fin. Corp., San Diego, 1974-81; exec. v.p., adminstr. specialized fin. services group Security Pacific Corp., Los Angeles, 1981—. Served with USN, 1943-46. Mem. Am. Fin. Services Assn. (dir. exec. com.). Club: Stone Ridge Country. Office: 10089 Willow Creek Rd San Diego CA 92131

FORDHAM, CHRISTOPHER COLUMBUS, III, med. educator; b. Greensboro, N.C., Nov. 28, 1926; s. Christopher Columbus and Frances Long (Clendenin) F.; m. Barbara Byrd, Aug. 16, 1947; children—Pamela Fordham Richey, Susan Fordham Crowell, Betsy Fordham Templeton. Cert. in medicine, U. N.C., 1949; M.D., Harvard U., 1951. Diplomate Am. Bd. Internal Medicine. Intern Georgetown U. Hosp., 1951-52; asst. resident Boston City Hosp., 1952-53; sr. asst. resident N.C. Meml. Hosp., Chapel Hill, 1953-54; fellow in medicine U. N.C. Sch. Medicine, 1954-55, instr. medicine, 1958-60, asst. prof., 1960-64, asso. prof., asst. dean, 1964-68, prof., asso. dean, 1968-69; prof. medicine, v.p. for medicine, dean Sch. Medicine, Med. Coll. Ga., Augusta, 1969-71; prof. medicine, dean Sch. Medicine, U. N.C., Chapel Hill, 1971—, prof. community medicine and hosp. adminstrn., 1978—, vice chancellor for health affairs, 1977-80; chancellor U. N.C., 1980—; practice medicine, specializing in internal medicine, Greensboro, N.C., 1957-58. Served as officer USAF, 1955-57. Fellow A.C.P.; mem. AMA, N.C. Med. Soc., So. Soc. Clin. Investigation, Am. Soc. Nephrology, Am. Fedn. Clin. Research, Soc. Health and Human Values, Am. Assn. Med. Colls. (exec. council 1975—, rep. liaison com. med. edn. 1977—), Am. Assn. Med. Coll. So. Regional Deans (chmn. 1972-73, 75-76), N.Y. Acad. Scis., Elisha Mitchell Sci. Soc., AAAS, AAUP, Order Golden Fleece, Sigma Xi, Alpha Omega Alpha. Address: Office of Chancellor U NC 103 South Bldg 005 A Chapel Hill NC 27514

FORDHAM, JAMES LYNN, chemist; b. Rodney, Ont., Can., Mar. 27, 1924; came to U.S., 1952, naturalized, 1958; s. Elmer L. and Thelma L. (Knight) F.; m. Mary H. Messerschmid, Aug. 31, 1946; children—Larry R., Dale R., Janet L. Fordham Cooney, Amy L. B.S., U. Western Ont., London, 1946. Chemist Uniroyal Co., Elmira, Ont., 1946-47; research chemist Polymer Corp., Sarnia, Ont., 1947-52; devel. chemist Monsanto Co., Springfield, Mass., 1952-55; with Diamond Shamrock Corp., 1955-80, asst. dir. research, then dir. research, Painesville, Ohio, 1965-69, corporate v.p. tech., Cleve. and Dallas, 1969-80; pres., dir. FTI, Dallas, 1981—, Bioelectric Tech., 1982—; dir. Coal Technology, Inc., Laramie, 1980—; dir. MDS Health Group Ltd., Toronto. Author. Recipient Engring. Materials Achievement award Am. Soc. Metals, 1976. Mem. Am. Chem. Soc., Indsl. Research Inst. Club: University. Patentee polymers. Home: 15810 Ranchita Dr Dallas TX 75248 Office: 17000 Dallas Pkwy Suite 219 Dallas TX 75248

FORDHAM, JEFFERSON BARNES, lawyer, educator; b. Greensboro, N.C., July 8, 1905; s. Christopher Columbus and Maggie Shepherd (Barnes) F.; m. Rebecca Jane Norwood, Sept. 6, 1930 (dec. 1962); children—Robert, William; m. Rita Ennella, Mar. 21, 1964. A.B., U. N.C., 1926, A.M., J.D. with honors, 1929, LL.D., 1953; J.S.D., Yale, 1930; LL.D., Franklin and Marshall Coll., 1960; L.H.D., U. Pa., 1970. Bar: N.Y., N.C., Ohio, Pa., Utah bars. Sterling Research fellow Yale Law Sch., 1929-30; mem. law faculty W.Va. U. and faculty editor W.Va. Law Quar., 1930-35; spl. asst. to U.S. Sec. Labor, 1935; asso. law firm Reed, Hoyt & Washburn, N.Y.C., 1935-38; rev. counsel U.S. PWA, Washington, 1938-39, counsel, chief bond atty., 1939-40; prof. law La. State U., 1940-46, Vanderbilt U., 1946-47; dean, prof. law Ohio State U., 1947-52, U. Pa., 1952-70, univ. prof. law, 1970-72, dean, prof. emeritus, 1972—; prof. law U. Utah, 1972—, distinguished prof. law, 1974—; Edward Douglass White lectr. La. State U., 1954; Benjamin N. Cardozo lectr. Assn. Bar City N.Y., 1957; William H. Leary lectr. U. Utah, 1971. Author: Local Government Law, rev. edit, 1975; co-author: Coursebook on Legislation; Contbr. legal publs. Mem. Pres.'s Adv. Panel on Conflicts of Interest and Ethics in Govt., 1961; co-chmn. Utah Joint Legis. Com. on Energy Policy, 1976. Served with USNR, 1942-45. Recipient Distinguished Service award Yale Law Alumni, 1968, U. N.C. Sch. Law, 1969, U. Pa. Law Alumni, 1970; Jefferson B. Fordham professorship established at U. Pa. Law Sch., 1973. Mem. Am. Bar Assn. (chmn. sect. municipal law 1949-51, 1st chmn. sect. individual rights and responsibilities 1966-68), Am. Law Inst. (council), Assn. Am. Law Schs. (pres. 1970), Phi Beta Kappa, Phi Kappa Phi, Order of Coif. Democrat. Club: Century Assn. (N.Y.C.). Home: 584 16th Ave Salt Lake City UT 84103

FORDHAM, LAURENCE SHERMAN, lawyer; b. Chgo., Dec. 3, 1929. B.S. cum laude, U. Ill., 1951; LL.B. magna cum laude, Harvard U., 1954. Bar: D.C. 1954, Mass. 1957. Atty. tax div. Dept. Justice, 1954; law clk. to Supreme Ct. Justice Sherman Minton, 1954-55; assoc. firm Fischer, Willis & Panzer, Washington, 1955-57; assoc., then partner firm Foley, Hoag & Eliot, Boston, 1957—, mng. partner, 1972-82; instr. law Harvard U. Law Sch., 1976-78. Editor Harvard Law Rev., 1953-54; Contbr. articles to legal publs. Trustee, exec. com. Lawyers Com. Civil Rights Under Law; mem. steering com. New Eng. com. NAACP Legal Def. Fund; mem. Lawyers Campaign United Way, 1983-84; legal counsel various local polit. campaigns.; Mem. Wayland (Mass.) Redevel. Authority, 1962-67, Wayland Sch. Com., 1967-70, Wayland Sch. Bldg. Com., 1968-70; class agt. Class of 1954, Harvard U. Law Sch. Fund, 1978—, reunion chmn., 1979. Mem. Am. Law Inst., Am. Bar Assn., Mass. Bar Assn., Boston Bar Assn. Clubs: Wightman Tennis, Harvard of Mass. Office: One Post Office Sq Boston MA 02109

FORDHAM, SHELDON LEROY, coll. dean; b. Walnut, Ill., June 1, 1919; s. Lafe L. and Alta (Miller) F.; m. Margaret Bischof, Jan. 18, 1945; 1 dau., Barbara Fordham Lubbers. BS., U. Ill., 1941, M.S., 1949; Ed.D., Mich. State U., 1963. Tchr. public schs., Ill., 1945-47; mem. faculty U. Ill., Chgo. Circle, 1947—, prof. phys. edn., dean, 1963—; cons. in field. Co author: Physical Education and Sports: An Introduction to Alternative Careers, 1978. Pres. scholarship bd. Evergreen Park (Ill.) High Sch., 1963-66. Served with USNR, 1942-45. Mem. AAHPER, Assn. Research, Adminstrn., Profl. Councils and Socs., Nat. Assn. Phys. Edn. in Higher Edn., Nat. Coll. Phys. Edn., Assn. Men (pres. 1974), Ill. Assn. Profl. Preparation in Health, Phys. Edn. and Recreation (pres. 1965). Office: Room 354-PEB Box 4348 Univ Ill Chicago Circle Chicago IL 60680

FORDTRAN, JOHN SATTERFIELD, physician; b. San Antonio, Nov. 15, 1931; s. William M. and Josephine (Bell) F.; m. Jewel Evans, July 25, 1953; children: William, Bess, Josephine, Amy. Student, U.

Tex., 1949-52; M.D., Tulane U., 1956. Diplomate Am. Bd. Internal Medicine. Internal medicine intern Parkland Meml. Hosp., Dallas, 1956-57, asst. resident internal medicine, 1957-58; research fellow gastroenterology Mass. Meml. Hosp., Boston, 1960-62; instr. internal medicine U. Tex. Southwestern Med. Sch., Dallas, 1962-63, asst. prof. internal medicine, 1963-67, assoc. prof. internal medicine, 1967-69, prof., 1969-79, chief sect. gastroenterology, 1963-79; chief dept. internal medicine Baylor U. Med. Center, Dallas, 1979—; mem. attending staff Parkland Meml. Hosp., Dallas, 1963—; cons. gastroenterology Dallas VA Hosp., 1963—. Contbr. articles to profl. jours.; editorial bd.: Jour. Clin. Investigation, 1968-73; editor: Gastroenterology, 1977-81; co-editor: Gastrointestinal Disease, 3d edit., 1983. Served with USPHS, 1958-60. Recipient King Faisal prize in medicine Saudi Arabia, 1984. Mem. A.C.P., Am. Soc. Clin. Investigation (past pres.), Am. Gastroent. Assn. (Disting. Achievement award 1971), Assn. Am. Physicians. Home: 3508 Hanover St Dallas TX 75225 Office: 3500 Gaston Ave Dallas TX 75246

FORDYCE, DONALD MICHAEL, insurance company executive; b. N.Y.C., Apr. 26, 1936; s. James Paul and Margaret (Monahan) F.; m. Ann Glascock, June 9, 1956; children: James H., Elizabeth A., Michael D. B.A., U. Notre Dame, 1958. With U.S. Life Ins. Co., N.Y.C., 1954-58, Kidder, Peabody & Co., 1958-60, Manhattan Life Ins. Co., 1960—, pres., N.Y.C., 1973-78, chmn., chief exec. officer, N.Y.C., 1973—; pres. Manhattan Life Corp., chmn. chief exec. officer, 1978—. Trustee Greater N.Y. Council Boy Scouts Am., Gilmour Acad., 1962-67; gov. Gilmour Acad., 1967-70. Mem. Am. Soc. C.L.U. (dir. 1977—), N.Y. Area Tng. Dirs. Assn. (pres. 1967), N.Y. Life Mgrs. Assn., N.Y. Life Underwriters Assn., N.Y. Bd. Trade (dir. 1973, mem. exec. com. 1973, pres. 1975), Assn. N.Y. State Life Ins. Cos. (dir. 1973, pres. 1977), C.L.U. Assn. (dir. 1967, exec. v.p. N.Y. chpt. 1975, pres. 1976), Young Pres.'s Orgn. Clubs: Wee Burn Country (Darien, Conn.); Bankers Club of P.R.; Univ. (N.Y.C.); Sky. Home: Wheat Ln Darien Ct 06820 Office: Manhattan Life Corp 111 W 57th St New York NY 10019

FORDYCE, EDWARD WINFIELD, JR., lawyer; b. St. Louis, Sept. 23, 1941; s. Edward Winfield and Jane (Nol) F.; m. Nancy Cairns Abbott, June 13, 1964; children: Edward Winfield III, Douglas A., Russell S. A.B. cum laude, Harvard Coll., 1963; LL.B., U. Va. Law Sch., 1966. Bar: Pa. 1966, Mo. 1968. Asso. firm Dechert, Price & Rhoads, Phila., 1966-68; atty. Monsanto Co., St. Louis, 1968-70; asst. to pres. New Eng. Mut. Life Ins. Co., Boston, 1970; asso., partner Fordyce and Mayne, St. Louis, 1970-75; corp. counsel Nat. Gypsum Co., Dallas, 1975-77, asst. gen. counsel, 1977-79, v.p., gen. counsel, 1979—. Chmn. trustees Parish Day Sch., 1980-81. Mem. Am. Bar Assn., Dallas Bar Assn., Am. Soc. Corp. Secs. Republican. Episcopalian (vestryman). Clubs: City Club, Bent Tree Country. Home: 6823 Hillwood Ln Dallas TX 75248 Office: 4100 Interfirst Two Dallas TX 75270

FORDYCE, PHILLIP RANDALL, univ. adminstr.; b. Lyons, Ind., May 28, 1928; s. Russell and Agnes (Fulk) F.; m. Lois Marilyn Lamb, Dec. 27, 1947; children—Deborah, Natalie, Marilyn, Kerry, Timothy. B.S., Butler U., 1951, M.S., 1954. Asst. prof. sci. edn. Fla. State U., Tallahassee, 1963-67, asso. prof., 1967-70, prof., 1970—, asst. dean, 1965-67, asso. dean, 1967-69, dean, 1969-74, provost, 1974-77, asst. chief exec. officer, 1977-80, asso. chief exec. officer, 1981—; cons. AID Sci. Edn. in India Program, summer 1964, Ford Found. Sci. Lise, Turkey, 1966. Co-author sci. text.; Contbr. articles to profl. jours. Dir. NSF-U.S. Office Edn. Grant projects, 1963-67. Fellow A.A.A.S. (council 1969-75, sec. edn. sect. 1969-75); mem. Assn. for Edn. Tchrs. in Sci., Nat. Assn. Biology Tchrs. (editor newsletter 1965-68, pres. 1963), Phi Delta Kappa, Kappa Delta Pi, Omicron Delta Kappa. Home: 2805 St Leonard Dr Tallahassee FL 32312

FORELL, GEORGE WOLFGANG, educator; b. Breslau, Germany, Sept. 19, 1919; came to U.S., 1939, naturalized, 1945; s. Frederick J. and Madeleine (Kretschmar) F.; m. Elizabeth Jean Rossing, June 14, 1945; children: Madeleine Helene (Mrs. Gary Marshall), Mary Elizabeth (Mrs. Christopher Davis). Student, U. Vienna, 1937-38; B.D., Lutheran Theol. Sem., Phila., 1941; Th.M., Princeton Theol. Sem., 1943; Th.D., Union Theol. Sem., N.Y.C., 1949; D.D. (hon.), Wartburg Theol. Sem., 1967; L.H.D., Gustavus Adolphus Coll., 1974; LL.D., Luther Coll., 1983; Litt. D., Upsala Coll., 1983. Ordained to ministry Luth. Ch., 1941; pastor in, N.J. and N.Y., 1941-47; asst. prof., then asso. prof. philosophy Gustavus Adolphus Coll., St. Peter, Minn., 1947-54; asst. prof., then asso. prof. theology U. Iowa, 1954-58; prof. systematic theology Luth. Sch. Theology, Chgo., 1958-61; prof. religion U. Iowa, 1961-73, dir., 1965-71, Carver prof. religion, 1973—; vis. prof. U. Hamburg, Germany, 1957-58, All Africa Theol. Seminar, Marangu, Tanzania, 1960, Japan Luth. Coll., Tokyo, 1968, Gurukul Theol. Research Inst., Madras, India, 1978; cons. dept. studies Luth. World Fedn., Geneva, 1981—. Author: Faith Active in Love, 1954, Ethics of Decision, 1955, The Protestant Faith, 1960, The Christian Year, 1964-65, Understanding the Nicene Creed, 1965, Christian Social Teachings, 1966, The Augsburg Confession, A Contemporary Commentary, 1968, Zinzendorf: Nine Public Lectures, 1973, The Proclamation of the Gospel in a Pluralistic World, 1973, The Christian Lifestyle, 1975, The Revolution at the Frontier: Reports from Moravian Missionaries Among the American Indians, 1976, History of Christian Ethics, Vol. I, 1979, The Luther Legacy, 1983. Mem. Am. Philos. Assn., Am. Soc. Ch. History, Am. Soc. Reformation Research (pres. 1959), Soc. Values in Higher Edn., Omicron Delta Kappa. Democrat. Lutheran. Home: 10 Bella Vista Iowa City IA 52240

FOREMAN, CAROL LEE TUCKER, business executive; b. Little Rock, May 3, 1938; d. James Guy and Willie Maude (White) Tucker; m. Jay Howell Foreman, June 13, 1964; children: Guy Tucker, Rachel Marian. A.A., William Woods Coll., 1958; A.B., Washington U., St. Louis, 1960; postgrad., Am. U. Research asst. com. on govt. ops. U.S. Senate, 1961; asso. Fed. Counsel Assos., 1961-63; instr. Am. govt. William Woods Coll., Fulton, Mo., 1963-64; press officer So. Calif. Com. to Elect Johnson and Humphrey, 1964; exec. asst. to Rep. James Roosevelt, 1964; writer-researcher Nat. Ednl. TV, 1965; dir. research and publs. Democratic Nat. Com., 1965-66; Congressional liaison aide HUD, 1967-69; chief info. liason Center for Family Planning Program Devel., Planned Parenthood-World Population, 1969-71; dir. policy coordination Commn. on Population and Am. Future, 1971-72; exec. dir. Citizens Com. on Population and Am. Future, 1972-73, Paul Douglas Consumer Research Center, 1973-77, Consumer Fedn. Am., 1973-77; asst. sec. food and consumer services Dept. Agr., Washington, 1977-81; pres. Foreman & Co., Washington, 1981—; exec. dir. Ctr. Women Policy Studies, 1983—; mem. Interdeptl. Task Force on Women, 1979-81; bd. dirs. Commodity Credit Corp., Dept. Agr., 1977-81, Nat. Consumer Coop. Bank, 1979-81, Women's Equity Action League, 1983—, Food Research and Action Council, 1982—, Alliance to Save Energy, 1983—, Pub. Voice for Food and Health Policy, 1982—; vice-chair Ctr. Nat. Policy, 1982—. Mem. D.C. Commn. on Status Women, 1973-74. Mem. Nat. Women's Polit. Caucus, Women's Nat., Pi Beta Phi. Democrat. Home: 5408 Trent St Chevy Chase MD 20815 Office: Foreman & Co 2000 P St Suite 508 Washington DC 20036

FOREMAN, DONLIN MALOY, dancer, choreographer; b. Campbellsville, Ky., July 22, 1952; s. Max Maloy and Mary (Fundaburk) F.; m. Jacqulyn Rose Buglisi, July 25, 1976. Student, U. Montevallo, Ala., 1970-73, Fla. State U., 1973, Utah, 1974. Dancer Ballet West, Salt Lake City, 1974-75; soloist Nat. Ballet of Ill., Champaign-Urbana, 1975, Cliff Kauter Dance Co., N.Y.C., 1976, Joyce Trisler Dance Co., 1976-77; prin. dancer Martha Graham Dance Co., N.Y.C., 1977-83, Elliot Feld Ballet Co., 1983—; choreographer, tchr. Burchfield Ballet Co., Mobile, Ala., 1981, Dance Theatre Workshop, Chattanooga, 1982, Dance Charlotte, N.C., 1982; choreographer Wilkes-Barre Ballet Theatre, 1983; performed for Pres. Regan at the White House, 1982. Recipient pres.'s award for outstanding achievement U. Montevallo, 1983. Office: Feld Ballet 890 Broadway New York NY 10003

FOREMAN, GENE CLEMONS, editor; b. Fremont, Ohio, Nov. 20, 1934; s. Clemons Walter and Louise Augusta (Vogel) F.; m. Jo Ann Baldwin, Dec. 14, 1957; children—Harry, Valerie, Susan, Jo Claire, Nell Rose. B.A., Ark. State Coll., 1956. Reporter Ark. Gazette, Little Rock, 1957, asst. city editor, 1958-60, state editor, 1960-62; copy editor N.Y. Times, N.Y.C., 1962; mng. editor Pine Bluff (Ark.) Commercial, 1963-68; Ark. Democrat, Little Rock, 1969-71; exec. news editor Newsday, Garden City, N.Y., 1971-73; mng. editor Phila. Inquirer, 1973—. Served as 2d lt., arty. U.S. Army, 1956-57. Mem. AP Mng. Editors Assn. (dir. 1977—). Office: 400 N Broad St Philadelphia PA 19101

FOREMAN, JAMES DAVIS, cement company executive; b. Barnesville, Ohio, Mar. 13, 1925; s. J. Harrison and Freda (Davis) F.; m. Helen Laura Bolon, Nov. 27, 1943; children—James Bolon, Barbara Jean, Helen Marie. B.S. magna cum laude, Syracuse U., 1949; M.B.A., U. Pa., 1956. C.P.A., Conn., 1954. With Arthur Young & Co. (C.P.A.'s), N.Y.C., 1950-51, Ernst & Ernst (C.P.A.'s), Hartford, Conn., 1951-55; mgr. accounting and adminstrn. Xerox Corp., 1955-60; v.p., controller, sec. Olivetti Corp., 1960-79; exec. v.p., dir. River Cement Co., St. Louis, 1980—. Home: 10 Lochhaven Ln Saint Louis MO 63011 Office: 12700 Southfork Rd Saint Louis MO 63128

FOREMAN, JAMES LOUIS, judge; b. Metropolis, Ill., May 12, 1927; s. James C. and Anna Elizabeth (Henne) F.; m. Mabel Inez Dunn, June 16, 1948; children—Beth Foreman Banks, Rhonda Foreman Riepe, Nanette. B.S., U. Ill., 1950, J.D., 1952. Bar: Ill. bar. Individual practice law, Metropolis, Ill.; partner firm Chase and Foreman, Metropolis, until 1972; Ill. state's atty., Massac County, asst. atty. gen., State of Ill., chief judge So. Dist. of Ill., East St. Louis, 1972—. Pres. Bd. of Edn., Metropolis. Served with USNR, 1945-46. Mem. Am. Bar Assn., Ill. State Bar Assn., Metropolis C. of C. (past pres.). Republican. Home: PO Box 866 Metropolis IL 62960 Office: PO Box 186 East St Louis IL 62202

FOREMAN, LAURA, multi-discipline artist, choreographer, writer; b. Los Angeles; d. Michael and Gladys (Charnas) F.; m. John Everett Watts. Mem. faculty, dir. dance dept., Foreman Dance Theatre artist-in-residence. New Sch. Social Research, N.Y.C., 1971—; Dir. Laura Foreman Dance Theatre, N.Y.C.; founder, dir. Choreographers Theatre, N.Y.C.; artist-in-residence Channel 13 TV Lab., N.Y.C., 1978; dance dir., bd. dirs. Composers and Choreographers Theatre, Inc.; commd. dances Channel 31 TV, 1966, Nat. Council Chs., 1967, CAPS, 1970, 73, Choreographers Theatre, 1970-73, Nat. Endowment Arts, 1971, 73; mem. dance panel N.Y. State Council on Arts; artist-in-residence Holographic Film Found., 1983; cons. Nat. Endowment Humanities. Dancer, Ann Halprin Workshop Group, San Francisco, 1955, Marion Scott Dance Co., N.Y.C., Tamiris-Nagrin Dance Co., N.Y.C., 1962-64; Choreography includes Memorials, Study, A Time, Perimeters, Epicycles, SkyDance, Margins, Signals, Laura's Dance, Spaces (Collage I-IV), Locrian, Performance adeax, Postludes, Monopoly, Program, Heirlooms, Entries, others.; video includes Time coded Woman I, II, III (2 silver, 1 bronze awards Houston Internat. Film Festival 1979, 80, 81); (with John Watts) conceptual work includes Wall Work, crowd-created art work, 1981, Cray-Pas Concourse, 1981, Cray-Pas, The Philadelphia Story, 1981; installations include Roomwork, 1981, WindoWork, 1982; one-woman shows, Portico Gallery, Phila., Limbo, N.Y.C., also group shows; poetry and short stories include the collection Scripts for a Small Planet, included in anthologies. Grantee CAPS, 1970, 73, N.Y. State Council Arts, 1970-74, N.Y. Dance Festival, 1975, Nat. Endowment Arts, 1971, 73, 77, 78, Off-Broadway City Junket, 1980. Home: 94 Chambers St New York NY 10011 Office: CCT 225 Lafayette St Suite 906 New York NY 10012

FOREMAN, SPENCER, pulmonary specialist, hospital executive; b. Phila., Nov. 10, 1935; s. Samuel and Freda F.; m. Sandra Lee Finkelstein, June 10, 1961; children: Corinne, Todd, Cheryl, Andrea. B.S., Ursinus Coll., 1957; M.D., U. Pa., 1961. Diplomate Am. Bd. Internal Medicine (subspecialty bd. pulmonary disease). Intern Henry Ford Hosp., Detroit, 1961-62; med. officer USPHS, San Pedro, Calif., 1962-63; resident in internal medicine USPHS Hosp., New Orleans, 1963-65; fellow in pulmonary diseases Tulane U., 1965-67; asst. chief dept. internal medicine USPHS Hosp., Balt., 1967-68, chief dept. internal medicine, 1968-73, hosp. dir., 1971-73; exec. v.p., dir. Sinai Hosp., Balt., 1973-79, pres., 1980—. Contbr. articles to med. jours. Commr. Md. Health Resources Commn. Served to med. dir. USPHS, 1962-73. Fellow ACP; mem. Am. Thoracic Soc., Md. Thoracic Soc., Assn. Am. Med. Colls. (rep. Assembly; adminstrv. bd. Council of Teaching Hosps.), Accreditation Council on Grad. Med. Edn. Office: Sinai Hosp of Balt Belvedere Ave at Greenspring Baltimore MD 21215

FORER, RAYMOND, sociologist; b. New Brunswick, N.J., Feb. 12, 1915; s. Solomon and Celia G. (Jelin) F.; m. Valeria Jean Trimble, Sept. 25, 1946; children—Susan Gretel, Alice Rebecca. B.A. U. Denver, 1947; M.A., Yale U., 1951, Ph.D., 1955. Instr. sociology and anthropology U. Conn., 1953-57; research sociologist Conn. Dept. Mental Health, 1957-60; dir. behavioral scis. program Ky. Dept. Health, 1960-61; also vis. lectr. U. Ky. Med. Center; prof. sociology, head dept. sociology and anthropology U. Maine, 1961-63; chief behavioral scis. activities Communicable Disease Center, USPHS, 1963-66; prof. sociology Emory U., 1963-66, State U. N.Y., Albany, 1966—, chmn., 1972-75; research cons., 1950—. Contbr. articles to profl. jours. Served with USAAF, 1942-45. Fellow Soc. Applied Anthropology, Royal Anthrop. Inst. Gt. Britain and Ireland; mem. Am., Eastern sociol. socs., AAAS, AAUP, Phi Beta Kappa, Pi Gamma Mu, Alpha Kappa Delta. Home: PO Box 22028 Sunya Sta Albany NY 12222

FOREST, HERBERT LEON, government official; b. Arlington, Mass., Apr. 20, 1910; s. Joseph Michel Henry and Rose Ella (Quinn) F.; m. Anna Katherine Digney, June 10, 1935; 1 dau., Anna Katherine. B.S., U. Mass., 1932; grad. student, Harvard, 1932-35. Analyst Office Fed. Milk Market Adminstr., Boston, 1935; with U.S. Dept. of Agr., 1935—, beginning as economist dairy br., successively head lend-lease and fgn. requirements div., asst. dep. dir. charge civilian activities, asst. dep. dir. dairy br., dep. dir. dairy br., dir. dairy div. agrl. marketing service, 1954-82, cons., 1982—. Recipient Superior Service award U.S. Dept. Agr., 1970, Distinguished Service award, 1976. Mem. Am., Farm econ. assns., Phi Sigma Kappa, Phi Kappa Phi. Home: 1208 Shenandoah Rd Alexandria VA 22308

FOREST, HERMAN SILVA, biology educator; b. Chattanooga, Feb. 18, 1921; s. William Hirsh Silva and Frances (Schutzer) Silver; m. Grace Marie Wyman, Apr. 5, 1963; children: Samuel, Benjamin. B.A., U. Tenn., 1942; M.S., Mich. State U., 1948, Ph.D. with honors, 1951. Instr. biology Coll. William and Mary, Williamsburg, Va., 1953-54; instr. botany U. Tenn., Knoxville, 1954-55; asst. prof. U. Okla., Norman, 1955-58; research assoc. U. Tenn. Research Ctr., Knoxville, 1958-60, U. Rochester (N.Y.), 1961-65; research asst. U. Okla. Med. Ctr., Oklahoma City, 1960-61; mem. faculty SUNY-Geneseo, 1965—, prof. biology, 1965—; SUNY exchange prof. U. Moscow, 1979; SUNY vis. scholar, 1974—; prin. scientist Environ. Resource Ctr., Geneseo, 1968-80; adviser N.Y. State Depts. Health and Environ. Conservation, 1965-74; nat. lectr. Am. Inst. for Biol. Scis., 1970; mem. Monroe County Environ. Mgmt. Council, 1971-74. Author: Handbook of Algae, 1954, The Limnology of Consensus Lake, in Lakes of New York State, 1978; contbr. articles in field to profl. jours. Served with U.S. Army, 1944-46, 51-53. Fellow Scientists Inst. for Pub. Info. (Nat. lectr.), 1974, Rochester Acad. Sci., 1981; Nat. Acad. Scis. Exchange scholar, 1964, 80. Mem. AAAS, Am. Inst. Biol. Scis., Internat. Congress Ecology, Internat. Great Lakes Research Assn. (conf. chmn. 1979), Ecol. Soc. Am., Bot. Soc. Am., Phycol. Soc. Am., Internat. Assn. Aquatic Vascular Plant Biologists. Jewish. Home: 19 Genessee Park Blvd Rochester NY 14611 Office: Biology Dept SUNY Geneseo NY 14454

FOREST, JEAN BEATRICE, university chancellor emeritus; b. Minitonas, Man., Can., July 24, 1926; d. Archibald Lloyd and Beatrice Lily (Holloway) Janz; m. Joseph H. Forest, Dec. 21, 1946; children: Richard, Leanne, Daniel, Michelle, Karen, Roslyn, Thomas. LL.D. (hon.), U. Alta, 1983. Tchr. schs. in, Man., 1943-47; tchr. Edmonton (Alta.) Roman Cath. Sch. Dist., 1947-48, trusfee, 1968-77; chmn. bd. adminstrs. Newman Theol. Coll., 1971-74; bd. govs. U. Alta., Edmonton. Mem. univ. senate, from 1972, now chancellor emeritus; Mem. Alta. Human Rights Commn., 1974-79, Unified Can. Movement. Recipient Alta. Achievement award, 1979; City of Edmonton Builder of Community award, 1979; ATA Citizen of Yr. award, 1978; Queen's Jubilee medal, 1977; DeSmet medal Gonzaga U., 1983. Home: 6503 Hardisty Dr Edmonton AB T6A 3V2 Canada

FORESTER, BERNARD I., recreational equipment company executive; b. 1928. B.S. in Bus. Adminstrn., U. Ariz., 1950. Audit mgr. Price Waterhouse & Co., 1950-64; chief fin. officer, dir. Republic Corp., 1964-66; exec. v.p., gen. mgr. Anthony Industries, Inc., City of Commerce, Calif., 1966-67, pres., 1967—, chief exec. officer, 1973—, chmn. bd., 1975—, also dir. Served with AUS, 1946-48. Office: Anthony Industries Inc 4900 Triggs St City of Commerce CA 90022 *

FORESTER, JOHN GORDON, JR., lawyer; b. Wilkesboro, N.C., Jan. 14, 1933; s. John Gordon and Mary Hope (Hendren) F.; m. Georgina Ramirez, June 26, 1957; children: John Gordon III, Robert Raoul, Georgina Yasué, Richard Alexander. B.S.; in Indsl. Relations, U. N.C., 1955; LL.B., George Washington U., 1962. Bar: D.C. 1962. Internat. economist Dept. Commerce, 1958-62; confidential asst. to asst. sec. commerce, 1962-63; law clk. to U.S. Dist. Judge L.P. Walsh, 1963-64; pvt. practice, Washington, 1964-80; ptnr. firm Pohoryles, Greenstein, Goldberg, Forester, Staton & Harris, Washington, 1980—; mem. Jud. Conf. D.C. Cir., 1981, 82. Contbr. articles to profl. jour. Pres. Friendly Citizens Assn., 1963, Gonzaga Fathers Club, 1974-76; Chmn. bd. dirs. Henson Valley Montessori Sch.; bd. dirs. Sursum Corda Neighborhood Center, 1975-77. Served to lt. comdr. USNR, 1955-58. Mem. ABA, D.C. Bar Assn.; Mem. Am. Judicature Soc., Counselors, Barrister Inn (pres. 1976-77), Order Golden Fleece, Kappa Alpha Order, Phi Delta Phi. Democrat. Roman Catholic. Home: 9810 Indian Queen Point Rd Fort Washington MD 20744 Office: 1801 K St NW Washington DC 20006

FORESTER, RUSSELL, artist; b. Salmon, Idaho, May 21, 1920; s. Alvin R. and Mary (Isley) F.; m. Marie-Christine Meymet, Feb. 2, 1968; 1 dau., Lynn. Student; Inst. Design, Chgo., 1950. Prin. Russell Forester Architect, Inc., 1948-72. Group shows include, La Jolla Mus. Contemporary Art, Guggenheim Mus., N.Y.C., Everson Mus. Art, Syracuse, N.Y., represented in permanent collections, Guggenheim Mus., Cedars-Sinai Med. Center, Los Angeles, McCrory Corp., N.Y.C., 1st Nat. Bank of Chgo. Mem. AIA, Artists Equity. *

FORGACA, OTTO LIONEL, forest products company executive; b. Berlin, Jan. 4, 1931; emigrated to Can., 1955; s. Joseph and Luise (Schick) Forgacs; m. Patricia Purdom Saunders, Sept. 24, 1960; children: Anthony, Stephen, Jonathan. B.Sc. in Tech., U. Manchester, Eng., 1955; Ph.D., McGill U., 1959. Pulp and paper research scientist Inst. Can., Montreal, 1958-63; research mgr. Domtar, Ltd., Montreal, 1963-73; research dir. Macaillan & Bloedel, Ltd., Vancouver, B.C., Can., 1973-77, v.p. research and devel., 1977-79, sr. v.p. reserach and devel., 1979—; dir. Zellstoff, Papierfabrik Frantschach, Austria, Forintek, Vancouver; councillor Can. Forestry Adv. Council, 1981—, Sci. Council B.C., 1977-83. Contbr. numerous articles tech. jours. Fellow TAPPI (chmn. resarch and devel. div.), Chem. Inst. Can.; mem. Can. Pulp and Paper Assn. (councillor, exec. council 1977-80). Club: Vancouver Lawn Tennis. Home: 1843 Acadia Rd Vancouver BC Canada V6T 1R2 Office: MacMillan Bloedel Ltd 1075 W Georgia St Vancouver BC Canada V6E 3R9

FORGATCH, JOSEPH THOMAS, savings and loan association executive; b. Orient, Ill., Mar. 10, 1920; s. Andrew and Anna (Marko) F.; m. Geraldine Swanson, Jan. 22, 1950; children: Pamela Jo, Nancy Lynn, Gregory Thomas. B.S., U. So. Calif., 1951; law degree, Woodrow Wilson Coll. Law, 1942. With FBI; acct. Touche, Ross, Bailey and Smart; with Calif. Fed. Savs. and Loan Assn., Los Angeles, exec. v.p. subs. Served with AUS. Mem. Soc. Savs. and Loan Controllers (pres. 1963-64), Fin. Execs. Inst., Calif. Soc. C.P.A.'s, Nat. Assn. Accts., Calif. Savs. and Loan League (treas. 1978-79). Lutheran. Clubs: Jonathan (Los Angeles); San Gabriel Country. Office: 5670 Wilshire Blvd Los Angeles CA 90036

FORGE, ANDREW MURRAY, artist, educator; b. Hastingleigh, Kent, U.K., Nov. 10, 1923; came to U.S., 1972; s. Sydney Wallace and Joanna Ruth (Bliss) F.; m. Ruth Miller, Dec. 24, 1974; children by previous marriage: Clair Helen, Katherine Anne, Stella. Student, Camberwell Sch. of Art, 1947-49. Lectr. painting Slade Sch., Univ. Coll., London, Eng., 1950-64; head fine art Goldsmith's Coll., London U., 1964-70; dean Sch. of Art, Yale U., New Haven, 1975-83. Author: Soutine, 1965, Rauschenberg, 1969, Monet at Giverny, 1973, Monet, 1983. Trustee Tate Gallery, London, Eng., 1964-72, Nat. Gallery, London, Eng., 1966-70.

FORGER, ROBERT DURKIN, professional association administrator; b. Norwalk, Conn., May 24, 1928; s. Alois John and Elsie Marie (Durkin) F.; m. Eleanor Marie Goddard, May 14, 1951; children: Gary Robert, Jeffrey Alois. B.S., Norwich U., Northfield, Vt., 1949; grad., U.S. Army Command and Gen. Staff Coll., 1970. Research and devel. engr., mgr. tech. publicity Dorr-Oliver Inc., Stamford, Conn., 1949-59; conf. mgr., pub., exec. dir. Soc. Plastics Engrs., Brookfield, Conn., 1959—; Chmn. Westport (Conn.) Public Housing Authority, 1959-64; treas. Plastics Edn. Found., 1971-75; bd. dirs. Norwich U. Alumni Assn., 1981—; trustee Nat. Plastics Mus., 1983—. Served to lt. col. U.S. Army. Named Conn. Assn. Exec. of Yr., 1983. Mem. Am. Inst. Chem. Engrs., Soc. Plastics Engrs., Am. Soc. Assn. Execs., Council Engring. and Sci. Soc. Execs. (dir. 1983—), Chemists Club N.Y.C. Home: 42 DeForest Rd Wilton CT 06897 Office: 14 Fairfield Dr Brookfield Center CT 06805

FORGEY, BENJAMIN FRANKLIN, architecture and art critic; b. Ashland, Ky., July 31, 1938; s. Chauncey Eaton F. and Joyce Evangeline (Shafer) Heinzen; m. Julie A. Savage, Sept. 1963 (div. 1967); 1 son, Benjamin Eric; m. 2d Gabriella A. von Joeden, Aug. 14, 1967; children: Elisa Gabriella, Martina Jane. B.A., Princeton U., 1960. Reporter, editor, art critic Washington Star, 1964-81; architecture critic Washington Post, 1981—. Contbr.: essays, revs., articles to various publs. including Art News, Art in America, Portfolio, AIA Jour.; essyas, revs., articles to various publs. including Smithsonian Mag.; essays, revs., articles to various publs. including others. Served with USAR, 1961-67. Mem. Internat. Assn. Art Critics (Am. sect.). Home: 2856 28th St NW Washington DC 20008 Office: Washington Post 1150 15th St NW Washington DC 20071

FORK, RICHARD LYNN, physicist; b. Dearborn, Mich., Sept. 1, 1935; s. Lynn Kenneth and Catherine Elizabeth (Harsch) F.; m. Patricia Alice Green, Aug. 17, 1957 (div. Aug. 1969); children—Carl Richard, Heather Elizabeth, David Kirtland; m. Shirley June Dowie, July 3, 1971; 1 dau., Katherine Lynne. B.S., Principia Coll., 1957; Ph.D., Mass. Inst. Tech., 1962. Research physicist Bell Labs., Murray Hill, N.J., 1962-69, Holmdel, N.J., 1969—. Fellow Am. Phys. Soc.; mem. Optical Soc. Am. Home: 191 Holland Rd Middletown NJ 07748 Office: Room 4D-417 Bell Labs Holmdel NJ 07733

FORKER, OLAN DEAN, agricultural economics educator; b. Kendallville, Ind., Aug. 18, 1928; s. Fred Forrest and Mary May (Butler) F.; m. Kathleen Rose Buuck, Apr. 21, 1951; children: Michael, Brent, Susan. B.S., Purdue U., 1950; M.S., Mich. State U., 1958; Ph.D., U. Calif. at Berkeley, 1962. Fieldman Halderman Farm Mgmt. Service, Wabash, Ind., 1954-58; extension economist U. Calif. at Berkeley, 1961-65; asso. prof. Cornell U., Ithaca, N.Y., 1965-70, prof., 1971—; chmn. dept. agrl. econs., 1976—; dir. Universal Foods Corp., Inc., Milw., 1974—; cons. USAID, Turkey, 1970-71, Ford Found., 1978—. Contbr. articles in field to profl. jours. Cornell campus campaign chmn. United Way, 1975; officer, council mem. Trinity Luth. Ch., Ithaca, 1967-69, 72—. Served with U.S. Army, 1950-53. Recipient award for profl. excellence for quality of discovery in pub. research Am. Agrl. Econs. Assn., 1975. Mem. Am. Agrl. Econs. Assn., N.E. Agrl. Econs. Council, AAUP, Res. Officers Assn. Home: 13 Stormy View Rd Ithaca NY 14850 Office: 102 Warren Hall Cornell U Ithaca NY 14853

FORLANO, ANTHONY, investment company executive; b. N.Y.C., Aug. 13, 1936; m. Natalie Syracuse, June 8, 1958; children—Stephen, David, Matthew. B.B.A., Bernard Baruch Sch. Bus., 1959; LL.B., N.Y. Law Sch., 1962. Bar: N.Y. 1963. Adminstrv. asst. 1st Investors Corp., N.Y.C., 1956-65, Dreyfus Corp., 1965-66; sec., asst. treas. Lehman Corp., N.Y.C., 1966—; treas. Lehman Capital Fund, Inc., N.Y.C., 1976—; v.p. Lehman Mgmt. Co., Inc., 1980—; treas. One William Street Fund, Inc., N.Y.C., 1983—. Mem. N.Y. State Bar Assn. Office: 55 Water St New York NY 10041

FORM, WILLIAM H., educator; b. Rochester, N.Y., June 2, 1917; s. Anthony and Mary (Conet) F.; children—Catherine Louise (Mrs. Sternberg), Helen (Mrs. Land). A.B. cum laude, U. Rochester, 1938, A.M., 1940; Ph.D., U. Md., 1944. Asst. prof. Kent (Ohio) State U., 1945-47; prof. Mich. State U., Lansing, 1947-71; asso. dir. research and planning Sch. Labor and Indsl. Relations, 1959-61, acting dir., 1963-64, chmn. dept. sociology, 1965-68, research prof., 1962-71; prof. sociology, labor and indsl. relations U. Ill., Urbana, 1971—; Cons. NSF, 1964—, U.S. Dept. Labor, 1965—, U.S. Dept. Health, Edn. and Welfare, 1968—. Author: Community in Disaster, 1958, Industry, Labor and Community, 1960, Industrial Sociology, 1964, Influentials in Two Border Cities, 1965, Comparative Perspectives on Industrial Society, 1969, Income and Ideology, 1973, Blue-Collar Stratification, 1976, also numerous articles. Recipient Distinguished Prof. award Mich. State U., 1965. Mem. Am. (council 1968-71, sec. 1974-77, editor Am. Sociol. Rev. 1980-81), North Central (pres. 1953), sociol. assns., Indsl. Relations Research Assn., Am. Assn. U. Profs., Internat. Sociol. Soc. Home: 1439 London Drive Columbus OH 43221

FORMAN, CHARLES WILLIAM, religious studies educator; b. Gwalior, India, Dec. 2, 1916; s. Henry and Sallie (Taylor) F.; m. Helen Janice Mitchell, Mar. 12, 1944; children—David, Sarah, Harriet. B.A., M.A., Ohio State U., 1938; Ph.D., U. Wis., 1941; B.D., Union Theol. Sem., N.Y.C., 1944, S.T.M., 1947. Ordained to ministry Presbyn. Ch., 1944; prof. N. India United Theol. Coll., Saharanpur, 1945-50; sec. program emphasis Nat. Council Chs., 1951-53; mem. faculty Yale Div. Sch., 1953—, D. Wills James prof. missions, 1961—; Chmn. theol. edn. fund World Council Chs., 1965-70, mem., 1970-77; mem. commn. ecumenical mission United Presbyn. Ch., 1962-71, chmn., 1965-71, Found. for Theol. Edn. in Southeast Asia, 1970—. Author: A Faith for the Nations, 1958, The Nation and the Kingdom, 1964, Christianity in the Non-Western World, 1967, The Island Churches of the South Pacific, 1982. Mem. bd. edn., Bethany, Conn., 1957-66; bd. dirs. Community Action Agy., New Haven, 1978-81, Overseas Ministries Study Center, Ventnor, N.J., 1979—. Office: 409 Prospect St New Haven CT 06510

FORMAN, DONALD T., biochemist; b. N.Y.C., Feb. 27, 1932; s. Jack and Fannie (Jaffee) F.; m. Florence Sporn, Aug. 22, 1953; children: Joan Diane, Steven Lawrence, Debra Helene. B.S., Bklyn. Coll., 1953; M.S., Wayne State U., 71957, Ph.D., 1959. Clin. biochemist Mercy Hosp. Med. Center, Chgo., 1959-63; dir. clin. biochemistry, asso. prof. biochemistry and pathology Evanston Hosp./Northwestern U. Med. Sch., Chgo., 1963-78; prof. pathology and biochemistry U. N.C., Chapel Hill, 1978—, dir. clin. chemistry, 1978—; cons. clin. chemist, industry and govt., 1965—. Editor: Clinical Chemistry, 1976. Served with AUS, 1953-55. Recipient Chgo. Clin. Chemists Creativity award, 1974; Mich. Heart Assn. fellow, 1957-59. Mem. Assn. Clin. Scientists (pres. 1973-74), Am. Assn. Clin. Chemistry (dir.), Am. Bd. Clin. Chemistry, Nat. Acad. Clin. Biochemistry, AAAS, AAUP, Sigma Xi, Phi Lambda Upsilon., B'nai B'rith. Jewish. Research on enzymology, tumor associated antigens, atherosclerosis. Home: 2559 Owens Ct Chapel Hill NC 27514 Office: Dept Pathology U NC Med Sch Chapel Hill NC 27514

FORMAN, H(ARRY) N(ORRIS), gas company executive. Dir. Empire, Inc., Lebanon, Mo.; cons., dir. Delaware Valley Propane Corp., subs. Bklyn. Union Gas Co., Moorestown, N.J. Club: North Hempstead Country (Port Washington, N.Y.). Home: 7 Knolls Ln Manhasset NY 11030

FORMAN, H(ENRY) CHANDLEE, art educator, architect; b. N.Y.C.; s. Horace Baker, Jr. and Elizabeth (Chandlee) F.; m. Caroline Biddle Lippincott, Sept. 28, 1929 (dec. June 5, 1975); children: Elizabeth (Mrs. Bryant Harrell, Jr.), Richard Townsend Turner, Lawrence Thorne; m. Rebecca Anthony Russell, May 26, 1978. A.B., Princeton U., 1926; M.Arch., U. Pa., 1931, Ph.D. in Fine Arts, 1942; Litt.D. St. Mary's Coll. of Md, 1981. Pvt. practice architecture as H. Chandlee Forman, Easton, Md., specializing in residences, chs., hist. restorations, 1931-35, 52-78; chief architect Jamestown (Va.) Archaeol.; Project, 1935-36; editor nat. records Historic Am. Bldgs. Survey, 1936-37; lectr. fine arts Haverford Coll., 1937-38; instr. art Rutgers U., 1939-40; lectr. history art U. Pa., 1940-41; Catherine L. Comer prof. fine arts Wesleyan Coll. of Ga., 1941-45; prof. art, head dept. Agnes Scott Coll., 1945-52; cons. architect Ga. Hist. Commn., 1952-60. Author: numerous books, including Early Manor and Plantation Houses of Maryland, 1934, 2d edit., 1982, Jamestown and St. Mary's, Buried Cities of Romance, 1938, The Architecture of the Old South, The Medieval Style, 1948, Virginia Architecture in the 17th Century, 1957, Early Nantucket and its Whale Houses, 1966, Old Buildings, Gardens and Furniture in Tidewater Maryland, 1967, The Virginia Eastern Shore and its British Origins, 1975; Art work exhibited, Library Congress, Art Inst. Chgo., Balt. Mus. Art, U. Pa., others. Adviser Md. St. Mary's City Commn., 1965-69; mem. Md. Archeol. Commn., 1968-77, chmn., 1973; sec. bd. dirs. Soc. Preservation Md. Antiquities, 1952-54; mem. corp. bd. Haverford Coll., 1975—; lectr. throughout world for State Dept., 1964. Recipient George Barnard White prize Princeton, 1926; Calvert prize for historic preservation State of Md., 1976; historic preservation award Assn. Preservation Va. Antiquities, 1982, Gov.'s citation for history and archeology State of Md., 1983; Carnegie Found. fellow creative painting, 1947. Fellow AIA (exec. com. Balt. chpt., charter mem., v.p., historian Chesapeake Bay chpt.); mem. Talbot County (Md.) Hist. Soc. (bd. dirs., co-organizer, 1st curator, librarian), Nantucket Garden Club (hon.), Townsend Soc. Am. (hon.), Archeol. Soc. Md. (hon.), Soc. Colonial Wars, Princeton Alumni Assn. Eastern Shore (pres. 1960-61, 70-72, 77-79, sec.-treas. 1974-77). Club: Explorers (fellow). Donor H. Chandlee Forman Nature Preserve to Nantucket Maria Mitchell Assn., 1973, reconstrn. of mus. and collections to Hist. Soc. of Talbot County Md., 1984. Address: PO Box 807 Easton MD 21601

FORMAN, HOWARD IRVING, lawyer, former government official; b. Phila., Jan. 12, 1917; s. Jacob and Dora (Moses) F.; m. Ada Pressman, Aug. 2, 1938; children: Kenneth J., Harvey R. B.S. in Chemistry, St. Joseph's Coll., 1937; LL.B., Temple U., 1944; M.A., U. Pa., 1949, Ph.D., 1955. Bar: D.C. 1945, Pa. 1973. Research chemist Frankford Arsenal, Dept. Army, Phila., 1940-44, patent atty., 1944-46, chief patents br., 1946-56; asst. dir. Pitman-Dunn Research Labs., 1955-56; evening lectr. polit. sci. Temple U., 1956-63; patent atty. Rohm and Haas Co., Phila., 1956-66, trademark and internat. corp. counsel, 1966-76; dep. asst. sec. U.S. Dept. Commerce, Washington, 1976-81; also dir. Office of Product Standards Policy; counsel Weiser, Stapler & Spivak, Phila., 1974-76, chmn. interagy. com. on standards policy, 1976-81; head. U.S. dels. to internat. confs., 1976-81; sec., dir. Rohm & Haas Asia, Inc., 1973-76; v.p., gen. counsel, dir. Brilliant Internat., Inc., Bala-Cynwyd, Pa., 1974-83; sec., dir. Far East Chem. Services, Inc., Wilmington, Del., 1973-76, Rohm and Haas, GmbH, Zug, Switzerland, 1975-76; dir. U.S. Pharm. Corp., 1975-83. Author: Inventions, Patents and Related Matters, 1957, Patents-Their Ownership and Administration by the U.S. Government, 1957; Editor: Patents, Research and Management, 1961, The Law of Chemical, Metallurgical and Pharmaceutical Patents, 1967; Contbr. to publs. in field. Bd. dirs. Lower Moreland Twp. Sch. Bd., Montgomery County, Pa., 1969-75; bd. dirs. Eastern Montgomery County Vocat.-Tech. Sch., 1969-75, sec., 1970-75; bd. dirs. Warminster Gen. Hosp. (Pa.), 1983—. Recipient Robert J. Painter Meml. award Standards Engring. Soc.-ASTM, 1978, Leo B. Kelly award Standards Engring. Soc., 1981. Fellow Am. Inst. Chemists; mem. ABA, Fed. Bar Assn., Phila. Bar Assn. (sec. 1973-74, com. on jurimetrics, tech. and patents, v.p. 1975), Am. Patent Law Assn. (bd. mgrs. 1970-73), Phila. Patent Law Assn. (pres. 1964-66), ASTM (life), Am. Nat. Standards Inst. (bd. dirs. 1977-80), Internat. Assn. Protection Indsl. Property, Nat. Council Patent Law Assn. (chmn. 1967-68), Am. Chem. Soc., Sci. Research Soc. Am., Am. Assn. Lab. Accreditation (dir. 1982—), AAAS, Nat. Lawyers Club, Licensing Execs. Soc., Sigma Xi. Home: 1033 Corn Crib Dr Huntingdon Valley PA 19006 Office: 1000 Connecticut Ave NW Washington DC 20036 also Albidale-Windmill Circle Huntingdon Valley PA 19006 *My life has been a slow-but-sure progression in which patience, diligence and determination, mixed with a readiness to adapt myself to each new circumstance, have enabled me to overcome numerous obstacles and forge a useful career and a happy life as a husband, father and grandfather that have been personally gratifying and rewarding. My creed consists of truth, simplicity, candor, tolerance, genuine humility, and faith in God and my fellow men and women.*

FORMAN, J(OSEPH) CHARLES, chemical engineer, association executive; b. Chgo., Dec. 22, 1931; s. Joseph O. and Marie (Smith) F.; m. Ursula Diane Weston, July 22, 1953; children: Stephen Charles, Diane Brigitte, Mary Erika. S.B., M.I.T., 1953; M.S., Northwestern U., 1957, Ph.D., 1960. Registered profl. engr., Ill. Trainee chem. engring. Dow Chem. Co., Midland, Mich., 1953-54; from sr. chem. engr. to dir. mfg. ops. agrl. vet. div. Abbott Labs., North Chicago, Ill., 1956-77; asso. exec. dir. Am. Inst. Chem. Engrs., N.Y.C., 1977-78; exec. dir., sec., pub. Jour of Am. Inst. Chem. Engrs., Internat. Chem. Engring., Energy Progress, Environ. Progress, Plant/Ops. Progress, 1978—; cons. in field, accreditation insp. chem. engring. curricula. Mem. ednl. council M.I.T., 1961-74, 78—; mem. Lake Bluff (Ill.) Bd. Edn., 1967-73, pres., 1971-73, Lake County (Ill.) Sch. Bd. Assn., 1969-71; mem. Lake Bluff Plan Commn., 1973-77, chmn., 1976-77. Served with USAF, 1954-56. Fellow Am. Inst. Chem. Engrs.; mem. Am. Chem. Soc., Am. Soc. Assn. Execs., Council Engring. and Sci. Soc. Execs. (dir. 1980-83, sec. 1983-84, v.p. 1984-85), Nat. Soc. Profl. Engrs., AAAS, Soc. Chem. Industry (U.K.), Sigma Xi, Tau Beta Pi, Phi Lambda Upsilon, Alpha Tau Omega. Club: Chemists (N.Y.C.). Patentee in field. Home: 77 Stanton Rd Darien CT 06820 Office: Am Inst Chem Engrs 345 E 47th St New York NY 10017

FORMAN, MILOS, film dir.; b. Feb. 18, 1932. Ed. film faculty, Acad. Music and Dramatic Art, Prague, Czechoslovakia. Dir. Laterna Magika, Prague, 1958-62. Mem. artistic com., Sebor-Bor Film Producing Group; dir. films: including Peter and Pavla (Czechoslovak Film Critics' award 1963, Grand Prix 17th Internat. Film Festival, Locarno 1964), A Blonde in Love, Firemen's Ball, Taking Off, Visions of Eight, One Flew Over the Cuckoo's Nest, (Acad. award direction), Hair, Ragtime. Address: care Robert Lantz 114 E 55th St New York NY 10022

FORMAN, RICHARD T.T., botany educator; b. Richmond, Va., Nov. 10, 1935; s. Henry Chandlee and Caroline (Lippincott) F.; m. Barbara J. Lee, 1963; children: Sabrina, Adrian, Brent. B.S., Harverford Coll., 1957; postgrad., Duke U., 1959-60; Ph.D., U. Pa., 1961. Vol. Am. Friends Service Com., Guatemala and Honduras, 1961-63; asst. prof. U. Wis., 1963-66; mem. faculty Rutgers U., New Brunswick, N.J., 1966—, prof. botany, New Burnswick, N.J., 1976—, dir. grad. program, Brunswick, N.J., 1979—; dir. Hutcheson Meml. Forest, New Brunswick, N.J., 1972—; instr. Pigeon Lake Field Sta., Wis., 1964, 65, Orgn. Tropical Studies, Costa Rica, 1970, W.I. Lab., St. Croix, 1973, Ft. Burgwin Research Ctr., N. Mex., 1976. Author: An Introduction to the Ecosystems and Plants of St. Croix, U.S. Virgin Islands, 1974; editor: Pine Barrens: Ecosystem and Landscape, 1970; mem. editorial bd.: Ecology and Ecol. Monographs, 1973-77, Bioscience, 1978—; contbr. articles to profl. jours. Fulbright scholar, Bogota, Columbia, 1970-71; chercheur CNRS-CEPE, Montepellier, France, 1977-78. Fellow AAAS; mem. Am. Inst. Biol. Scis., Ecol. Soc. Am. (v.p. 1982-83), Torrey Bot. Club (pres. 1980-81, editorial bd. Bull. 1967-70), Am. Bryological and Lichenological Soc., N.J. Acad. Soc. (editorial bd. Bull. 1972—), Nature Conservancy, Internat. Assn. Landscape Ecology (v.p. 1982—). Office: Dept Biol Scis Rutgers U New Brunswick NJ 08903

FORMAN, ROBERT HENRY, army officer; b. Phoenix, Feb. 17, 1930; s. Henry Theadore and Dorothy Donnan (Woods) F.; m. Hannah Jean Schooler, Feb. 9, 1952; children: Mona, Nancy, Robert. B.S., Ariz. State U., 1951; M.S., U. Okla., 1980. Commd. 2d lt. U.S. Army, 1951, advanced through grades to maj. gen., 1981; served as dir. of instrn. Field Artillery Sch., Ft. Sill, Okla., 1975-76; dep. comdg. gen. Tng. Center, Ft. Leonard Wood, Mo., 1976-79; dep. commandant Command and Gen. Staff Coll., Ft. Leavenworth, Kans., 1979-81; comdg. gen., Ft. Dix., N.J., 1981-83; chief of staff Tng. and Doctrine Command, Ft. Monroe, Va., 1983—. Recipient Jones award Am. Def. Preparedness Assn., 1982, Alumni Achievement award Ariz. State U., 1983. Mem. Assn. U.S. Army (appreciation award 1983). Methodist. Home: 51 Fenwick Rd Fort Monroe VA 23651 Office: Office Chief of Staff Hdqrs US Army Tng and Doctrine Command Fort Monroe VA 23651

FORMAN, STANLEY JOSEPH, photographer; b. Winthrop, Mass., July 10, 1945; s. David and Gertrude (Levy) F. Student, Franklin Inst., Boston, 1965-66; Nieman fellow in journalism, Harvard U., 1979-80. Campaign photographer, Sen. Edward Brooke, Mass., 1966; news photographer, Boston Record American (now Boston Herald American), 1966-82, Sta. WCUB-TV, Needham, Mass., 1983—. Recipient Pulitzer prize for spot news, 1976, 77; Recipient award for feature, 1979; Internat. Assn. Fire Fighters award, 1976-78; Golden Plate award Am. Acad. Achievement; World Press Photo award, 1976; named Photographer of Yr., Region One, Nat. Press Photographers Am., 1973, Boston Press, 1978. Mem. Boston Press Photographers Assn. (v.p., Best of Show 1976, 77), Nat. Headliners (Spot News Photography award 1976-77), Sigma Delta Chi (award 1976). Office: WCUB-TV TV Place Needham MA

FORMAN, WILLIAM N., judge; b. San Francisco, Dec. 12, 1930. B.A., U. Nev., 1952; LL.B., U. Utah, 1955. Bar: Nev. bar 1955. Practiced law, Reno, legislative bill drafter, 1957, spl. dep. atty. gen., 1959-62; judge dept. 5 2d Jud. Ct., Reno, 1973—. Mem. Am. (state chmn. jr. bar div. 1961, chmn. hard minerals com. natural resources sect. 1972-73), Washoe County bar assns., State Bar Nev., Phi Alpha Delta. Office: PO Box 11130 Reno NV 89501

FORMICOLA, ALLAN JERRY, dentist, educator; b. Mt. Vernon, N.Y., Oct. 3, 1939; s. Jerome C. and Marie F.; m. Jo Renee Gatto, Aug. 5, 1967; children—Matthew, Allison. Student, Pa. State U., 1957-59; D.D.S., Georgetown U., 1963, M.S. in Periodontics, 1965. Practice dentistry specializing in periodontics, Silver Spring, Md., 1967-68; asst. prof. periodontics Georgetown U., 1967-68; asst. prof. dentistry U. Ala., 1968-70; clin. investigator Inst. Dental Research, 1968-70; asso. prof. periodontics N.J. Dental Sch., 1970-72, prof., 1972-73, chmn. dept., 1970-73; asso. dean Coll. of Medicine and Dentistry, 1973-76, acting dean, 1976-77, prof., 1977-78; prof. dentistry Columbia U., N.Y.C., 1978—; dean Sch. Dental and Oral Surgery, 1978—. Contbr. chpts. to books and articles in field to profl. jours. Asst. pack master Morris-Sussex council Boy Scouts Am., Madison, N.J. Served with USN, 1965-67. Mem. ADA, Am. Acad. Periodontology (chmn. membership com. 1975-76), N.J. Soc. Periodontists, Internat. Assn. Dental Research, Am. Assn. Dental Research, AAAS, N.Y. Acad. Sci., Am. Coll. Dentists, Omicron Kappa Upsilon. Roman Catholic. Home: 2 N Oak Ct Madison NJ 07940 Office: 630 W 168th St New York NY 10032

FORNARA, CHARLES WILLIAM, historian, classicist, educator; b. N.Y.C., Nov. 19, 1935; s. Charles and Dorothy Mae (Stind) F.; m. Nancy Cecilia Pattison, Dec. 21, 1963; 1 son, Charles William, III. B.A., Columbia U., 1956; M.A., U. Chgo., 1958; Ph.D., UCLA, 1961. Instr. Ohio State U., Columbus, 1961-63; asst. prof. to prof. classics and history Brown U., Providence, 1963—; vis. prof. U. Tex., Austin, 1976; prof. Greek history Inst. Ancient History, Ann Arbor, Mich., summer 1977; vis. fellow Humanities Research Ctr. Australian Nat. U., Canberra, Spring 1983. Author: Herodotus, An Interpretative Essay, 1971, The Athenian Board of Generals, 1971, Archaic Times to the End of the Peloponnesian War, 1977, 2d edit., 1983, Greco-Roman Historiography, 1982, The Nature of History in Ancient Greece and Rome, 1983; contbr. articles and revs. in field to profl. jours. Mem. Am. Hist. Assn., Am. Philol. Assn., Assn. Ancient Historians, Soc. for Promotion Hellenic Studies. Republican. Home: Perryville Rd Rehoboth MA 02769 Office: Dept Classics Brown Univ Providence RI 02912

FORNES, MARIA IRENE, playwright-director; b. Havana, Cuba, May 14, 1930; came to U.S., 1945, naturalized, 1951; d. Carlos Luis and Carmen Hismenia (Collado) F. Ed. Havana pub. schs. Pres. N.Y. Threatre Strategy, 1973-80. Writer: plays Tango Palace, 1963, The Successful Life of 3, 1965, Promendade, 1965-69, The Office, 1966, A Vietnamese Wedding, 1967, The Annunciation, 1967, Dr. Kheal, 1968, The Red Burning Light, 1968, Molly's Dream, 1968, The Curse of the Langston House, 1972, Aurora, 1974, Cap-a-Pie, 1975, Lolita in the Garden, 1977, Fefu and Her Friends, 1977, Eyes on the Harem, 1979, In Service, 1978, Eyes on the Harem, 1979, Evelyn Brown (A Diary), 1980, Life is Dream, (adaptation of Calderon's play), 1981, A Visit, 1981. John Hay Whitney Found. grantee, 1961; Centro Mexicano de Escritores grantee, 1962; OADR U. Minn. grantee, 1965; recipient Obie award, 1965, 77, 79, 82; grantee Cintas Found., 1967, Creative Artists Pub. Service Program, 1972, 75; fellow Yale-ABC, 1967, Yale-Levine Found., 1968, Rockefeller Found., 1971, Guggenheim Found., 1972, Nat. Endowment for Arts, 1974. Address: 1 Sheridan Sq New York NY 10014 *

FORNEY, ROBERT CLYDE, chemical industry executive; b. Chgo., Mar. 13, 1927; s. Peter Clyde and Hildur Hoglund F.; m. Marilyn Glenn, Apr. 3, 1948; children: Gerald Glenn, Barbara Dale, Gregory Byron, Robert C. B.S. in Chem. Engring, Purdue U., 1947, M.S., 1948, Ph.D., 1950. With E.I. DuPont de Nemours, 1950—, asst. gen. mgr. textile fibers dept., 1970-75, v.p., gen. mgr., 1975-77, v.p. plastic products and resins, 1977-78, sr. v.p., Wilmington, Del., 1979-81, exec. v.p., 1981—; dir. Wilmington Trust Co.; mem. mgmt. labor textile adv. com. Dept. Commerce, 1972-77. Mem. adv. council Del. Family Services, 1969-73; bd. govs. Purdue Found., 1979—. Mem. Am. Chem. Soc., Am. Inst. Chem. Engrs., Soc. Chem. Industry, Chem. Mfrs. Assn. (dir.), Sigma Xi. Republican. Lutheran. Home: Centerville DE 19807 Office: 1007 Market St Wilmington DE 19898

FORNI, PATRICIA ROSE, nursing educator, university dean; b. St. Louis, Feb. 14, 1932; d. Harold and Glenda M. (Keay) Brown. B.S.N., Washington U., St. Louis, 1955, M.S. (USPHS trainee), 1957; Ph.D. (USPHS fellow), St. Louis U., 1965; postgrad. (USPHS scholar), U. Minn., summers 1968, 70. Staff nurse McMillan EENT Hosp., St. Louis, summer 1955, Renard Psychiat. Hosp., part-time 1955-57; research asst. Washington U. Sch. Nursing, St. Louis, 1957-59, research assoc., 1959-61, asst. prof., 1964-66, asso. dean in charge grad. edn., asso. prof. gen. nursing sci., 1966-68; asso. prof. public health nursing Wayne State U., Detroit, 1968-69; asst. dir. for manpower and edn. Ill. Regional Med. Program, Chgo., 1969-71; project dir. Midwest Continuing Profl. Edn. for Nurses, St. Louis U., 1971-75; dean, prof. nursing So. Ill. U., Edwardsville, 1975—; grant proposal reviewer U.S. Dept. Edn., 1980, Div. Nursing, USPHS, 1972-79, NSF, 1978; mem. Ill. Implementation Commn. on Nursing, 1975-77. Bd. dirs. Greater St. Louis Health Systems Agy., 1976-81, Adult Edn. Council Greater St. Louis, 1973-76. Named Outstanding Student of Italian Studies So. Ill. U., 1978. Mem. Nat. League Nursing (accreditation site visitor 1979—), Nat. League for Nursing (nominating com. Council

Baccalaureate and Higher Degree Programs 1979-81, pub. policy and legis. com. 1981—), Am. Nurses Assn. (chmn. continuing edn. publs. com. 1975-76), Mo. Nurses Assn. (chmn. edn. com. 1973-77), Greater St. Louis Soc. Health Manpower Edn. and Tng. (chmn. legis. com. 1974-75), Midwest Alliance in Nursing (1st governing bd. 1979-80, chmn. nominations com. 1980, 81), Am. Assn. Colls. Nursing (program com. 1978-82), Ill. Council Deans/Dirs. Baccalaureate and Higher Degree Programs in Nursing (chmn. 1979-81), Am. Acad. Nursing (editor Newsletter 1982—), Sigma Theta Tau (charter mem. Epsilon Eta chpt. 1980). Office: So Ill U at Edwardsville Sch Nursing Edwardsville IL 62026

FORNSHELL, DAVE LEE, educational broadcasting executive; b. Bluffton, Ind., July 9, 1937; s. Harold Christman and Mary Ann Elizabeth (Fox) F.; m. Elizabeth Slagle Clinger, Nov. 11, 1978; 1 son, John David. B.A., Ohio State U., 1959. Continuity dir. Sta. WTVN-TV, Columbus, Ohio, 1959-61; traffic dir., asst. program mgr. Sta. WOSU-TV, Columbus, 1961-69; ops. mgr. Md. Center for Pub. Broadcasting, Balt., 1969-70; exec. dir. Ohio Ednl. TV Network Commn., Columbus, 1970—; pres. Ohio Radio Reading Services; dir., mem. exec. com. Central Ednl. Network, 1972—; mem. exec. com., chmn. Postsecondary Edn. Council of Central Ednl. Network; chmn. Ohio Postsecondary Telecommunications Council. Pres. Landings Residents Assn., 1973; active March of Dimes, 4-H. Served with USAF, 1961-62. Recipient award Dayton Fedn. Women's Clubs, 1974. Mem. N.G. Assn., Ohio State U. Alumni Assn., Nat. Acad. TV Arts and Scis. (bd. govs. Columbus chpt. 1970—), Nat. Assn. Ednl. Broadcasters (chmn. state adminstrs. council), Health Scis. Communications Assn., Nat. Assn. TV Program Execs., Am. Assn. Higher Edn., Alpha Epsilon Rho, Alpha Delta Sigma, Sigma Delta Chi. Clubs: University (Columbus); Kiwanis. Home: 240 Larrimer Ave Worthington OH 43085 Office: Ohio Educational Broadcasting 2470 N Star Rd Columbus OH 43221

FORRER, GORDON RANDOLPH, physician; b. Balt., Apr. 1, 1922; s. William Gordon and Blanche (Shules) F.; m. Carol Lucille Hanke, May 26, 1951; children—Jane Elizabeth, Susan Ellen, John Gerritt. Student, State Tchrs. Coll., Towson, Md., 1939-41, Johns Hopkins, 1941-42; B.A., U. Md., 1945, M.D., 1947. Diplomate: Am. Bd. Psychiatry and Neurology. Intern U.S. Marine Hosp., Balt., 1947-48; psychiat. resident Ypsilanti (Mich.) State Hosp., 1948-50, Wayne County (Mich.) Mental Health Clinic, 1950-51; clin. dir. Northville (Mich.) State Hosp., 1954-60; pvt. practice psychiatry, Detroit, 1960—; chief psychiatry Mt. Carmel Mercy Hosp.; mem. staff St. Mary Hosp., Livonia, Mich., Detroit Rehab. Inst.; clin. asst. prof. Wayne U. Med. Sch., 1955-68. Author: Weaning and Human Development, 1969, Psychiatric Self-Help, 1973, The Technique of Psychiatric Self-Help, 1975, also articles in field. Trustee Schoolcraft Coll., Livonia, 1963-67. Served to capt. M.C. AUS, 1952-54. Mem. Mich., Wayne County med. socs., Mich. Soc. Psychiatry and Neurology (Research award 1953), Am., Pan-Am. med. assns., Am. Psychiat. Assn. Introduced atropine coma therapy for treatment psychoses, 1950; devel. psychoanalytic theory hallucination, psychoanalytic theory placebo. Home: 45995 W Main St Northville MI 48167 Office: 20141 James Couzens Hwy Detroit MI 48235

FORREST, EARL EUGENE, utility corporation executive; b. Horseheads, N.Y., Sept. 9, 1927; s. Earl and Elizabeth (Mayhood) F.; m. Margaret Moran Sebring, Aug. 31, 1951; children: Mark Eugene, Brian Francis. A.A.S., Rochester Inst. Tech., 1950; B.S., Empire State Coll., 1974. Lic. profl. engr., N.Y. Dist. mgr. N.Y. State Electric and Gas Corp., Liberty, N.Y., gen. mgr., Oneonta, NY, 1972-74, Binghamton, NY, 1974-76; v.p. N.Y.State Electric and Gas Corp., Binghamton, NY, 1976-77; sr. v.p. N.Y. State Electric and Gas Corp., Binghamton, NY, 1977—; regional dir. Bank of N.Y., Endicott, 1974—. Home: 600 Lowell Dr Endwell NY 13760 Office: NY State Electric & Gas Corp 4500 Vestal Pkwy E Binghamton NY 13903

FORREST, FREDERICK AUGUST, educator; b. Buenos Aires, Argentina, Dec. 27, 1914; came to U.S., 1940, naturalized, 1943; s. Santiago Noe and Desiderata (La Tullerie) F.; m. Alice Elizabeth Brown, June 17, 1955 (div. 1967); m. Lorain June McClintock, 1967. Bachelor Humanities, Colegio Nacional Bartolome Mitre, 1933; student, Institute de Estudios Libres; A.A., San Mateo Jr. Coll., 1942, U. Calif. at Berkeley, 1942-43; M.A. in L.S, U. Calif. at Berkeley, 1955; B.A., San Jose State Coll., 1947; M.A., Stanford, 1948, Ph. D., 1952. Playground dir., Argentina, 1934-39; teaching asst. Stanford, 1949-50; lectr. modern U.S. history Ateneo de la Juventud, 1949-50; travel fellow Inst. Internat. Edn. (for collection data on constl. history of Argentina), 1952-53; bibiliographer, social sci. cataloguer Long Beach State Coll., 1955-58, head librarian, 1958-60; asst. prof. history So. Ill. U., 1959-60; dean libraries and communication arts Inter-Am. U., San German, P.R., 1960-64; curator Hispanic Am. collections Yale, 1964-65; asso. prof. library sci. Denver U., 1965-68; chmn. dept. library sci. Queens Coll. City U. N.Y.; also spl. lectr. econs., mem. Latin Am. area studies faculty; dir. Reference Resource Center, Flushing, N.Y., 1980—; lectr. Latin Am. history peace corps, Ecuador, 1962; Mem. Hispanic Found. U.S. Library of Congress.; Bd. dirs. Eurico Corp. (mfrs. x-ray plates), Mayaguez, P.R. Research editor, Inst. Press, New Haven. Mem. Latin Am. Council. Served with USAAF, 1943-46; PTO. Mem. Latin Am. Studies Assn. Address: Queen Coll City U NY Flushing NY 11367

FORREST, HERBERT EMERSON, lawyer; b. N.Y.C., Sept. 20, 1923; s. Jacob K. and Rose (Fried) F.; m. Marilyn Lefsky, Jan. 12, 1952; children: Glenn Clifford, Andrew Matthew. B.A. with distinction, George Washington U., 1948; J.D. with highest honors, 1952; student, CCNY, 1941, Ohio U., 1943-44. Bar: Va. 1952, D.C. 1952, U.S. Supreme Ct. 1956, Md. 1959. Plate printer Bur. Engraving and Printing, Washington, 1946-52; law clk. to chief judge Bolitha J. Laws U.S. Dist. Ct., Washington, 1952-55; practice in, Washington, 1952—; mem. firm Welch & Morgan, 1955-65, Steptoe & Johnson, 1965—; chmn. adv. bd. D.C. Criminal Justice Act, 1971-74; sec. com. admissions and grievances U.S. Ct. Appeals, D.C., 1973-79; mem. Title-1 audit hearing bd. U.S. Office Edn. HEW, 1976-79; mem. edn. appeals bd. U.S. Dept. Edn., 1979-82; mem. Lawyer's Support Com. for Visitors Service Center, 1975—. Contbr. articles to legal jours.; advisory bd.: Duke Law Jour, 1969-75. Pres. Whittier Woods PTA, 1970-71. Served with U.S. Army, 1943-46. Recipient Walsh award in Irish history, 1952, Goddard award in commerce, 1952. Fellow Am. Bar Found.; Mem. George Washington Law Assn., Am. Judicature Soc., ABA (council 1972-75, 81—, chmn. com. on agy. rule making 1968-81, editor ann. reports 1973—, adminstrv. law sect., mem. communications com. public utilities law sect., mem. industry regulation com., chmn. communications subcom. antitrust law sect., internat. law sect., sect. sci. and tech.), Va. State Bar Assn., Fed. Bar Assn. (chmn. jud. rev. com. 1981—), Fed. Commn. Bar Assn. (chmn. legal aid com. 1973-81, mem. exec. com. 1976—, del. to house of dels. Am. Bar Assn. 1979-81, mem. minority legal intern program com. 1978-81, v.p. 1981-82, pres. 1982-83), D.C. Bar Assn. (past sec., exec. com.), NAM, Nat. Assn. Bar Pres., Washington Council Lawyers, Legal Aid and Pub. Defender Assn., Am. Arbitration Assn. (comml. panel 1976—), D.C. Unified Bar (bd. govs. 1976-79, chmn. com. on employment discrimination complaint service 1973-79, chmn. task force on services to public 1974-78, chmn. com. on appointment counsel in criminal cases 1978—, co-chmn. com. on participation govt. employees in pro bono activities 1977-79), Computer Law Assn., Broadcast Pioneers, Order of Coif, Phi Beta Kappa, Pi Gamma Mu., Artus, Phi Eta Sigma, Phi Delta Phi. Democrat. Clubs: Internat. of Washington, B'nai Brith. Home: 8706 Bellwood Rd Bethesda MD 20817 Office: 1250 Connecticut Ave Washington DC 20036

FORREST, HUGH SOMMERVILLE, zoology educator; b. Glasgow, Scotland, Apr. 28, 1924; came to U.S., 1951; s. Archibald and Margaret Watson (Peden) F.; m. Rosamond Scott Baker, June 12, 1953; children: Eleanor Scott, Anne Sommerville, Hugh Watson. B.S. with honors, U. Glasgow, 1944; Ph.D., U. London, 1947; D.Sc., 1970; Ph.D., U. Cambridge, 1951. Research scientist Med. Research Council Gt. Britain, 1947-51; research fellow Calif. Inst. Tech., Pasadena, 1951-54, sr. research fellow, 1954-55; research scientist U. Tex., Austin, 1955-56, asso. prof., 1956-63, prof. zoology, 1963—, chmn. dept., 1974-78. Editor: Biochemical Genetics, 1971—; Contbr. articles to profl. jours. Carnegie scholar, 1944-45; Gt. Britain Dept. Sci. and Indsl. Research fellow, 1948-51; USPHS research fellow, 1951-53; spl. research fellow, 1973; numerous research grants NSF, USPHS, Robert A. Welch Found. Fellow Royal Soc. Edinburgh, Royal Chem. Soc.; mem. Am. Chem. Soc., Soc. Gen. Physiologists, Soc. Biol. Chemists. Home: 3302 River Rd Austin TX 78703

FORREST, JOHN FRANKLIN, former army officer; b. Mexia, Tex., June 20, 1927; s. Robert Porter and Gertrude (Kluge) F.; m. Patricia Grace Smith, July 31, 1949; children: Scott, John, Robert, Diana, Michael, William, Patrick, James, Harry, Mary. B.S., U.S. Mil Acad., 1949; M.S. in Journalism, U. Wis., 1962. Commd. 2d lt. U.S. Army, 1949, advanced through grades to lt gen., 1978, platoon leader, co. comdr., staff officer, Korea, comdr. 3d Bn., 187th Inf., also staff officer, bietnam, asst. div. comdr. 82d Airborne Div., 1974-75; dir. mil. personnel policies Dept. Army, 1975-76; comdg. gen. Ft. Carson (Colo.) and 4th Inf. Mechanized Div. U.S. Army, 1976-78; dep. comdg. gen. U.S. Army Forces Command, Ft. McPherson, Ga., 1978-79; dep. comdg. chief U.S. Army Europe, 1981-83, ret., 1983; exec. dir. U.S. Space Found., 1983—. Bd. mgrs. Army Emergency Relief, 1978; mem.exec. council Atlanta Chpt. USO. Decorated Silver Star with 2 oak leaf clusters, Bronze Star with 3 oak leaf clusters, Combat Inf. badge with oak leaf cluster, Purple Heart with oak leaf cluster, Air medal with star, Legion of Merit with oak leaf cluster, Army Commendation medal with oak leaf cluster. Lodge: Rotary (Atlanta). Office: APO New York 09403

FORREST, STEVE (WILLIAM FORREST ANDREWS), actor; b. Huntsville, Tex., Sept. 29, 1925; m. Cris; 3 sons. Student, U. Calif. at Los Angeles. Film appearances include The Bad and the Beautiful, 1952, So Big, 1953, Prisoner of War, 1954, Bedevilled, 1955, Flaming Star, 1960, Heller in Pink Tights, 1960, Five Branded Women, 1960, The Longest Day, 1962, The Yellow Canary, 1963, Rascal, 1969, The Late Liz, 1971, The Wild Country, 1971, North Dallas Forty, 1979; TV movies The Hatfield and the McCoys, 1975, Wanted: The Sundance Women, 1976, The Last of the Mohicans, 1977, Testimony of Two Men, 1977, Maneaters Are Loose, 1978; regular: TV series The Baron, 1966, S.W.A.T, 1975-76; other TV appearances include Hec Ramsey; TV spl. Legend of Robin Hood, 1968. Office: care Artists Agy 190 N Canon Dr Beverly Hills CA 90210 *

FORREST, WILLIAM ALEXANDER, JR., lawyer, manufacturing company executive; b. Richmond, Va., Nov. 19, 1929. B.A., U. Va., 1951, LL.B., 1956. Bar: Va. 1956. Partner firm McGuire, Woods & Battle, Richmond, 1961-65; with A. H. Robins Co., Richmond, 1966—, sec., gen. counsel, 1969—, v.p., 1974—. Bd. govs. St. Catherine's Sch., Richmond. Mem. Am. Bar Assn., Va. Bar Assn., Richmond Bar Assn. (past chmn. jr. bar sect.), U. Va. Alumni Assn. (bd. mgrs., pres. 1978-79). Office: 1407 Cummings Dr Richmond VA 23220

FORRESTAL, MICHAEL VINCENT, lawyer; b. N.Y.C., Nov. 26, 1927; s. James Vincent and Josephine (Ogden) F. Student, Princeton U., 1949; LL.B., Harvard U., 1953. Bar: N.Y. 1954. Since practiced in N.Y.C.; partner Shearman & Sterling, 1960—; spl. asst. to Averell Harriman (dir. Marshall Plan), 1948-50; sr. mem. White House Nat. Security Staff, 1962-65; sec. tripartite Naval Commn., Berlin, 1946; asst. U.S. naval attache, Moscow, USSR, 1946-47. Chmn. Met. Opera Guild, 1967—; bd. dirs. Met. Opera Assn., 1965—, Nat. Opera Inst., 1971—; exec. sec. adv. com. Kennedy Inst. Politics, Harvard U., 1967-82; trustee Inst. Advanced Study, Princeton, N.J., 1970—, Phillips Exeter Acad., 1979—; pres. bd. trustees Phillips Exeter Acad., 1981—. Mem. ABA, Assn. Bar City N.Y., Am. Arbitration Assn. (dir. 1980-83), Council Fgn. Relations. Episcopalian. Clubs: Racquet and Tennis, Links (N.Y.C.); Metropolitan (Washington); Travellers (Paris, France). Home: 25 Central Park West New York NY 10023 Office: 153 E 53d St New York NY 10022

FORRESTAL, ROBERT PATRICK, banker, lawyer; b. N.Y.C., Oct. 31, 1931; s. Patrick A. and Lillian D. (Moran) F.; m. Wilma Anderson, Sept. 29, 1956; 1 dau., Renee Marie. B.A., St. John's U., 1953; J.D., Georgetown U., 1961. Bar: D.C. 1961, U.S. Supreme Ct. 1964. Atty. Spencer & Whalen, Washington, 1961-64, Fed. Res. Bd., 1964-68, asst. sec., 1968-70, v.p., gen. counsel, Atlanta, 1970-74; sr. v.p., gen. counsel Fed. Res. Bank of Atlanta, 1974-79, 1st v.p., 1979—. Bd. dirs. Leadership Atlanta, 1971-73, Child Services and Family Counseling Ctr., Atlanta, 1974-81, Ga. Worlds Congress Inst., 1979—; bd. sponsors Atlanta Symphony Orch., 1973-77; div. chmn. United Way, Atlanta, 1980-81; trustee Ga. State U., Atlanta, 1972—, chmn. recognition fund, Atlanta, 1975, chmn. trustees, Atlanta, 1976-78, mem. adv. com. for health, Atlanta, 1981—. Served to lt. USN, 1953. Fulbright Scholar, 1953. Mem. Robert Morris Assocs. Lodge: Rotary. Home: 3949 Vermont Rd NE Atlanta GA 30319 Office: 104 Marietta St PO Box 1731 Atlanta GA 30301

FORRESTER, ALVIN THEODORE, physicist; b. Bklyn., Apr. 13, 1918; s. Joseph D. and Rose (Kissen) F.; m. Joy Levin, 1948 (dec. 1956); children—Bruce H., Cheri J.; m. June Doris Berg, Oct. 5, 1956 (div. 1972); children—William C., Susan J. A.B., Cornell U., 1938, A.M., 1939, Ph.D., 1942. Research asso. U. Calif. at Berkeley, 1942-45; physicist RCA Labs., Princeton, N.J., 1945-46; asst. prof. physics U. So. Calif., Los Angeles, 1946-51, asso. prof., 1951-54; vis. asso. prof. physics U. Pitts., 1954-55; physicist Westinghouse Research Labs., Pitts., 1955-58; nuclear spl. Atomics Internat., Los Angeles, 1958-59; dept. mgr. Electro-Optical Systems, Pasadena, Calif., 1959-65; prof. U. Calif.- (Irvine), 1965-67, 1967—; Vis. prof. astronomy U. Utrecht, Netherlands, 1971; asso. Culham Lab., Eng., spring 1974; vis. prof. physics Technion, Haifa, Israel, fall 1977. Fellow Am. Phys. Soc., IEEE; mem. AIAA (Research award 1962, chmn. electrostatic propulsion panel 1960-61), AAAS, AAUP, Am. Assn. Physics Tchrs., Sigma Xi, Phi Kappa Phi. Research in photoelectric mixing of light, ion propulsion, isotope separation, superconductivity, plasma physics, high power neutral beams. Home: 11525 Ohio Ave Los Angeles CA 90025 Office: Room 7731 BH U Calif Los Angeles CA 90024

FORRESTER, BRUCE MILLAR, judge; b. Kansas City, Mo., Dec. 26, 1908; s. James M. and Bertha (Wilkinson) F.; m. Anne Lee Broaddus, Nov. 9, 1937; children—Anne Norris, Jean Bruce, Bruce Millar. J.D., U. Mo., 1935. Bar: Mo. bar 1935. Practiced in Kansas City, 1935-57; mem. firm Watson, Ess, Groner, Barnett & Whittaker (now Watson, Ess, Marshall & Enggas); judge U.S. Tax Ct., Washington, 1957—, sr. judge, 1976—. Hon. trustee Holton-Arms School, Washington. Served with AUS, 1944-45; instr. ROTC. Mem. Fed., Am., Mo., Kansas City bar assns., Lawyers Assn. Kansas City, Am. Law Inst., Am. Judicature Soc., Sigma Alpha Epsilon (past pres., trustee). Episcopalian. Home: 7017 Beechwood Dr Chevy Chase MD 20815 Office: US Tax Ct 400 2d St NW Washington DC 20217

FORRESTER, JAY WRIGHT, educator; b. Anselmo, Nebr., July 14, 1918; s. Marmaduke M. and Ethel Pearl (Wright) F.; m. Susan Swett, July 27, 1946; children: Judith, Nathan Blair, Ned Cromwell. B.Sc., U. Nebr., 1939, D.Eng. (hon.), 1954; M.Sc., MIT, 1945; D.Sc. (hon.), Boston U., 1969, Union Coll., 1973; D.Eng. (hon.), Newark Coll. Engring., 1971, U. Notre Dame, 1974; D.Polit.Sci. (hon.), U. Mannheim, 1979. Tchr., X-ray equipment research MIT, 1939-40, co-founder servomechanisms lab., 1940, devel. electric and hydraulic servomechanisms for gun mounts and radar, 1940-44, asso. dir. servomechanisms lab., also supr. Whirlwind I digital computer devel., 1944-51, founder Digital Computer Lab., dir., 1951-56, div. head Lincoln Lab. for Air Def., 1951-56, prof. mgmt. Sloan Sch. Mgmt., 1956—; partner Forrester Cattle Ranch, Anselmo, Nebr. Lectures and tech. papers on digital computers and indsl. mgmt.; also dynamics indsl. and econ. behavior.; author: Industrial Dynamics, 1961, Principles of Systems, 1968, Urban Dynamics, 1969, World Dynamics, 1971, Collected Papers, 1975. Recipient Inventor of Year award George Washington U., 1968; Valdemar Poulsen Gold medal Danish Acad. Tech. Scis., 1969; Outstanding Accomplishment award Systems, Man and Cybernetics Soc. of IEEE, 1972; Computer Pioneer award IEEE Computer Soc., 1982; Benjamin Franklin fellow Royal Soc. Arts, London, 1972; New Eng. award Engring. Socs. New Eng., 1973; Potts medal Franklin Inst., 1974; Harry Goode Meml. award Am. Fedn. Info. Processing Socs., 1977; Common Wealth award of Disting. Service, 1979; named to Nat. Inventors Hall of Fame, 1979. Fellow IEEE (medal of Honor 1972), Am. Acad. Arts and Scis., Acad. Mgmt.; mem. Nat. Acad. Engring., Inst. Mgmt. Scis., Soc. Mfg. Engrs. (hon.), Am. Phys. Soc., Assn. Computing Machinery, Eta Kappa Nu, Sigma Xi, Sigma Tau. Patentee servomechanisms, digital info. storage, indsl. control. Office: Building E40-294 MIT Cambridge MA 02139

FORRESTER, MAUREEN KATHERINE STEWART, contralto; b. Montreal, Que., Can., July 25, 1930; d. Thomas and Mae (Arnold) F.; m. Eugene J. Kash, July 1954; children—Paula, Gina, Daniel, Linda, Susanna. Student of, Sally Martin, Frank Rowe, Bernard Diamant; D.Mus. (hon.), St. George William U., St. Mary's U., Toronto U., McMaster U., Victoria U., Bishop's U., York U., Western U., Mt. Allison U., Wilfred Pelletier U. Debut in, Can., 1953, at Town Hall, N.Y.C., 1956, concert appearances maj. orchs. and festivals throughout world; with various cos., N. Am.; rec. artist for, RCA Victor, Decca, Westminster, Philips, Columbia, DGG, Vanguard. Decorated companion Order of Can.; recipient Molson prize. Address: care Shaw Concerts Inc 1995 Broadway New York NY 10023 *

FORROW, BRIAN DEREK, lawyer, corp. exec.; b. N.Y.C., Feb. 6, 1927; s. Frederick George and Doris (Williams) F.; m. Eleanor Reid, Mar. 8, 1952; children—Lisa Coggins, Brian Lachlan, Catherine Frances, Derek Skylstead. A.B., Princeton, 1947; J.D., Harvard, 1950. Bar: N.Y. bar 1950. Asso., then partner firm Cahill, Gordon, Sonnett, Reindel & Ohl (and predecessors), 1950-68; v.p., gen. counsel Allied Chem. Corp., 1968—, dir., 1969—. Contbr. articles to profl. publs. Served to 1st lt. USAF, 1951-53. Mem. Am., Internat., Conn., N.Y. State bar assns., Bar Assn. City N.Y., N.Y. C. of C. (com. on law reform). Republican. Episcopalian. (lay reader, past sr. warden). Home: 704 Lake Ave Greenwich CT 06830 Office: PO Box 3000 R Morristown NJ 07960

FORSBERG, EDWARD CARL ALBIN, SR., finance company executive; b. Bklyn., Dec. 2, 1920; s. Gunnar A. and Martha E. (Boehme) F.; m. Byrne E. Johnson, July 13, 1946; children: Edward Carl Albin, Cassandra Gayle. B.S., U.S. Mcht. Marine Acad., 1944. With Gulf Fin. Co., 1958—, pres., chief exec. officer, Atlanta, 1969—; dir. Delta Life Ins. Co., Delta Fire & Casualty Ins. Co.; mem. consumer adv. council Fed. Res. Bd., 1982-85. Mem. exec. com. credit mgmt. program Columbia U. Grad. Sch. Served to officer USNR, 1943-46. Mem. Nat. Consumer Fin. Assn. (chmn. bd.), Ga. Consumer Fin. Assn. (dir., exec. com.). Republican. Lutheran. Office: 4362 Peachtree Rd NW Atlanta GA 30319

FORSBERG, FRANKLIN S., communications cons., publishing co. exec.; b. Salt Lake City, Oct. 21, 1905; s. Charles E. and Anna (Olson) F.; m. Ann Rountree, Jan. 15, 1944; children—Kristin Forsberg Williams, Lars, Erik. B.S., U. Utah, 1930, LL.D., 1974; M.B.A., N.Y. U., 1931. Mem. faculty N.Y. U., Pace Coll.; research and sales analyst for Reuben H. Donelley, N.Y.C., 1936-37; gen. mgr. Street & Smith Pubs., Inc., N.Y.C., 1937-42, v.p., 1946-47; pres. Forsberg, Merritt & Harrity, Inc., N.Y.C., 1947-48; pres. and pub. Liberty mag., 1948-50; Forsberg & Church (mgmt. cons.), 1950-52; ops. v.p. Popular Mechanics Co., 1955-59; exec. v.p., dir. Holt, Rinehart & Winston, 1959-73; communications cons., 1973—; chmn. bd. Yank Publs., Inc.; Mem. bd. nat. adv. council U. Utah. Served as col. charge info. and edn. activities Yank, Army Weekly, Army News Service, Camp Newspaper Service, NEWSMAP, Fgn. Lang. Unit, Radio and Music Sects., Stars and Stripes U.S. Army, 1942-46. Decorated D.S.M., U.S.; Order Brit. Empire; Royal Order of Vasa, Sweden; Gold medal Dutch Treat Club; recipient Distinguished award pub. U. Utah. Mem. Swedish C. of C. U.S.A. (dir.), West Point Soc., Pi Kappa Alpha. Clubs: Chgo.; Dutch Treat (dir.), Lochinvar (N.Y.C.); Question; Round Hill (Greenwich, Conn.). Home: 465 Lake Ave Greenwich CT 06830 Office: 200 Park Ave New York NY 10166

FORSBERG, SHIRLEY ANN, business information services company executive; b. Concord, N.H., July 10, 1934; d. Theodore and Alva Christina (Christiansen) F. B.A., Wells Coll., Aurora, N.Y., 1955. Exec. sec., adminstrv. asst., then corp. asst. sec. Dun & Bradstreet, Inc., N.Y.C., 1955-75, corp. sec., 1975—. Mem. Am. Soc. Corp. Secs. Lutheran. Office: One Diamond Hill Rd Murray Hill NJ 07974

FORSEE, AYLESA, author; b. Kirksville, Mo.; d. Edward W. and Lena (Moore) F. B.S., S.D. State U.; Mus.B., MacPhail Coll. Music, Mpls., 1938; M.A., U. Colo., 1939. Instr. history and music, Rochester, Minn., 1939-45; tchr. history and music U. Iowa, 1945-46, U. Denver, 1946-49; mem. staff writers conf. Temple Buell Coll., 1967, 68; Mem. adv. bd. Nat. Writers Club. Author: The Whirly Bird, 1955, Miracle for Mingo, 1956, Too Much Dog, 1957, American Women Who Scored Firsts, 1958, Louis Agassiz: Pied Piper of Science, 1958, Frank Lloyd Wright: Rebel in Concrete, 1959, Women Who Reached for Tomorrow, 1960, My Love and I Together, 1961, Beneath Land and Sea, 1962, Albert Einstein, 1963, William Henry Jackson, 1964, Pablo Casals: Cellist for Freedom, 1965, Men of Modern Architecture, 1966, Headliners, 1967, Famous Photographers, 1968, Artur Rubinstein: King of the Keyboard, 1969, They Trusted God, 1980; also articles in adult and juvenile publs. Recipient Helen Fish award, 1955. Mem. Colo. Author's League. (Tophand award 1966, 69). Christian Scientist (practitioner). Address: 1845 Bluebell Ave Boulder CO 80302

FORSELL, LAWRENCE LEROY, energy company executive; b. Rockford, Ill., May 29, 1938; s. George E. and Petrona A. (Kazlauskis) F.; m. Karen Ann Nelson, Aug. 14, 1959; children: Camilla A., Michael J., David E. Student, Rockford Men's Coll., 1956-58; B.S. in Civil Engring, Valparaiso U., 1960; M.B.A., U. Chgo., 1966. Mktg. dir.

No. Ill. Gas Co., Aurora, 1969-72, dir. rates and forecasting, 1972-73, div. v.p., 1973-75, treas., 1975—, v.p., 1976—; treas. NICOR Inc., 1976—, group v.p., 1978—; dir. Barber Greene Co., NICOR Exploration Co., NICOR Drilling Co., NICOR Mining Co., Nat. Marine Service Inc., Nicor Marine Inc., Tropical Shipping and Constrn. Co. Chmn. Batavia (Ill.) Police and Fire Commn. Mem. Am. Gas Assn., Tau Beta Pi. Lutheran. Club: Economic (Chgo.). Home: 849 Mandrake Dr Batavia IL 60510 Office: PO Box 190 Aurora IL 60507

FORSLING, RICHARD ARMITAGE, cable television executive, print dealer; b. Ogden, Utah, Mar. 17, 1925; s. Clarence Luther and Lucie Vivian (Armitage) F.; m. Ludmila McGonigal, Sept. 15, 1951 (div. 1969); children: Cathy, Stephen, Lucie. B.A., Princeton U., 1947; LL.B., Yale U., 1950. Bar: N.Y. 1950. Atty. N.Y.C., 1950-53; with CBS, Inc., N.Y.C., 1953-71; chmn. bd. Viacom Internat., N.Y.C., 1971-72; chief exec. officer Cablecom-Gen., Denver, 1972-81; chmn. bd. Capital Cities Cable, Englewood, Colo., 1981—. Home: 311 Lionshead Centre Vail CO 81657 Office: Capital Cities Cable 7120 Orchard St Englewood CO 89111

FORSON, NORMAN RAY, corporation executive; b. Port Arthur, Tex., July 12, 1929; s. Hollis G. and Annie (Butler) F.; m. Nancy McAnelly, Dec. 6, 1952; children: James Hollis, Diana Nancy. B.A., Baylor U., 1952; M.B.A., U. Houston, 1961. Sales engr. Magcobar, New Orleans and Houston, 1956-57; buyer Transcontinental Gas Pipe Line, Houston, 1957-61; supr. Ernst & Whinney, Houston, 1961-65; sr. v.p. Gulf & Western Industries, Inc., N.Y.C., 1965—. Served to 1st lt. USAF, 1952-56. Mem. Am. Inst. C.P.A.s, U.S. Handball Assn. Clubs: New York Athletic.; Lake (New Canaan, Conn.). Office: 1 Gulf and Western Plaza New York NY 10023

FORST, DONALD H., magazine editor; b. Bklyn., July 3, 1932; s. Emmanuel and Frances (Moss) F.; m. Starr Ockenga, Aug. 20, 1980. B.A., U. Vt., 1954; M.S. in Journalism, Columbia U., 1955. Mng. editor news Newsday Inc., Garden City, N.Y., 1977-78; exec. editor Los Angeles Herald Examiner, 1978-79; editor Boston Herald Am., 1979-82, Boston Magazine. Mem. Am. Soc. Newspaper Editors. Jewish. Club: University. Home: 94 St Botolph St Boston MA 02116 Office: 1050 Park Square Bldg Boston MA 02116

FORST, JUDITH DORIS, mezzo-soprano; b. New Westminster, C., Can., Nov. 7, 1943; d. Gordon Stanley and Euna Jessie (Thompson) Lumb; m. Graham Nicol Forst, May 30, 1964; children: Noel Graham, Paula Judith. Mus.B., U. B.C., Vancouver, 1965. Featured lectr. U. B.C., U. Mont. Debut with, Seattle Opera Co., 1967; with, Met. Opera, 1968-74; guest artist, Met. Opera, 1977; guest artist appearances throughout U.S., including San Francisco, New Orleans, Ft. Worth, Santa Fe and Seattle opera cos.; guest artist, N.Y.C. Opera, Opera Soc. Washington, Can. Opera Co., Toronto, Ont., Miami Opera Co., Vancouver Opera Assn., Edmonton Opera Assn., Winnipeg Opera Assn., Calgary Opera Assn., Montreal Symphony, Vancouver Symphony., Balt. Opera Co., Nat. Arts Ctr., Ottawa, Ont., Can.; appeared in performance for Queen Elizabeth, Vancouver, 1983. Named Canadian Woman of Year, 1978; named Walter and Ida Olsen Young Am. Artist of Yr. Miami Opera Assn., 1980. Mem. Actors Equity, Am. Guild Musical Artists, Assn. Canadian TV Radio Artists. Winner N.W. regional finals Met. Opera auditions, 1968; Canadian Broadcasting Co. Cross-Can. Talent Contest, 1968. Home: 428 Princeton Ave Port Moody BC V3H 3L3 Canada Office: care Harold Shaw 1995 Broadway New York City NY 10023

FORST, MARION FRANCIS, clergyman; b. St. Louis, Sept. 3, 1910; s. Frank A.J. and Bertha T. (Gulath) F. Grad., Kenrick Sem., Webster Groves, Mo., 1934. Ordained priest Roman Catholic Ch., 1934; pastor St. Mary's Cathedral, Cape Girardeau, Mo., 1949-60; vicar gen. Diocese of Springfield-Cape Girardeau, 1956-60; bishop, Dodge City, Kans., 1960-76; aux. bishop Archdiocese of Kansas City, Kans., 1976—; Kan. chaplain K.C., 1964—. Served with Chaplains Corps USNR, World War II. Address: 615 N 7th St Kansas City KS 66101

FORSTER, ARNOLD, lawyer, author; b. N.Y.C., June 25, 1912; s. Hyman Lawrence and Dorothy (Turits) Fastenberg; m. May Kasner, Sept. 29, 1940; children: Stuart William, Jane E. LL.B., St. John's Coll., 1935. Bar: N.Y. 1935, U.S. Supreme Ct. 1935. Gen. practice law, 1935-40; dir. law dept. Anti-Defamation League of B'nai B'rith, 1940-46, asso. dir., 1946-78, gen. counsel, 1946—; mem. firm Shea & Gould, N.Y.C., 1979—; police justice N.Y. State, 1954-57. Author, corr.: (TV and radio program series) Dateline Israel, 1967-83; author: Anti-Semitism in the United States, 1947; Author: A Measure of Freedom, 1950, (with B.R. Epstein) The Troublemakers, 1952, Cross-Currents, 1956, Some of My Best Friends, 1962, Danger on the Right, 1964, (with Epstein) Report on the Ku Klux Klan, 1965, Report on the John Birch Society, 1966, Radical Right: Report on the John Birch Society and Its Allies, 1967, Report From Israel, 1969, The New Anti-Semitism, 1974. Mem. bd. edn., New Rochelle, N.Y., 1962-66. Recipient Emmy award for film Avenue of the Just, 1980, Zubin and the I.P.O., 1983. Home: 79 Wykagyl Terr New Rochelle NY 10804 Office: 330 Madison Ave New York NY 10017 *In one's vintage years, it becomes unarguably clear that the only true satisfaction is in understanding that one's achievements, however small or large, made others happy and this earth a better place for living.*

FORSTER, CORNELIUS PHILIP, clergyman, graduate college dean; b. N.Y.C., Oct. 27, 1919; s. Cornelius and Mary Catherine (Collins) F. A.B., Fordham U., 1941, Ph.D., 1963; M.A., Cath. U., 1951; S.T.L., S.T.Lr., Pontifical U., Washington, 1949; M.A. (hon.), Providence Coll., 1959. Ordained Dominican priest Roman Cath. Ch., 1948; instr. Providence Coll., 1949-52, asst. prof., 1952-55, assoc. prof., 1955-58, chmn. dept. history, prof., 1958—, dean Grad. Sch., 1965—, exec. v.p., 1982—. Mem. Johannine Soc., History Club (founder, moderator), Nat. Cath. Edn. Assn., Am. Hist. Assn., Cath. Hist. Assn., Am. Assn. Colls. for Tchr. Edn., Am. Assn. Univ. Adminstrs., New Eng. Assn. Grad. Schs., Delta Epsilon Sigma. Office: Providence Coll Providence RI 02918

FORSTER, DENIS, research scientist; b. Newcastle-on-Tyne, Eng., Feb. 28, 1941; came to U.S., 1965; s. Thomas Reginald and Margaret (Dobson) F.; m. Hazel Frances Onions, Apr. 18, 1964; children: Juliet, Rachel. B.Sc., Imperial Coll., London, 1962, Ph.D., 1965. Fellow Princeton U., 1965-66; sr. research chemist Monsanto Co., St. Louis, 1966-70, group leader, 1970-75, sci. fellow, 1975-80, sr. sci. fellow, 1980—. Editor: Homogeneus Catalysis, 1974; contbr. articles to profl. jours.; patentee in field. Mem. Am. Chem. Soc. (Ipatieff prize 1980), Am. Inst. Chemists (Chem. Pioneer award 1980). Club: Racquet (St. Louis). Home: 32 Woodcrest Dr Saint Louis MO 63124 Office: Monsanto Co 800 N Lindbergh St Saint Louis MO 63167

FORSTER, ERIC OTTO, physicist; b. Lemberg, Poland, Oct. 24, 1918; came to U.S., 1946, naturalized, 1951; s. Joseph and Elsa (Jchaefer) F.; m., May 23, 1954; children: Joseph D., Kenneth M., Susan A., Ronald G.N., Robert I., Judith K. B.S., Columbia U., 1949, M.S., 1950, Ph.D., 1951. With Exxon Research & Engring. Co., Linden, N.J., 1951—, sci. advisor, 1976—; prof. physics Rutgers U., Newark, N.J., 1968—. Guest editor: Jour. Electrostatics, 1978-79; contbr. articles to profl. jours. Alfred A. Hunt Meml. medal Am. Soc. Lubricating Engrs., 1960. Fellow IEEE (Disting. Service award Elec. Insulation Sec. 1983); mem. Am. Chem. Soc., Am. Inst. Physics. Office: PO Box 45 Linden NJ 07036

FORSTER, FRANCIS MICHAEL, physician, educator; b. Cin., Feb. 14, 1912; s. Michael Joseph and Louise Barbara (Schmid) F.; m. Helen Dorothy Kiley, June 15, 1937; children—Denis, Susan, Kathleen, Mark, Gabrielle. Student, Xavier U., Cin., 1930-32, LL.D., 1955; B.S., U. Cin., 1935, B.M., 1936, M.D., 1937; D.Sc. hon., Georgetown U., 1982. Diplomate: Am. Bd. Psychiatry and Neurology (dir.). Rotating intern Good Samaritan Hosp., Cin., 1936-37; house officer neurology and neurosurgery Boston City Hosp., 1937-38, resident neurology, 1939-40; fellow psychiatry Pa. Hosp., Phila., 1938-39; asst. neurology Harvard Med. Sch., 1939-40; Rockefeller Found. research fellow physiology Yale Sch. Medicine, 1940-41; instr. neurology Boston U. Sch. Medicine, 1941-43; asst. prof. neurology Jefferson Med. Sch., 1943-47, asso. prof. neurology, 1947-50; prof. neurology, dir. dept. Georgetown U. Sch. Medicine, 1950-58, dean Sch. Medicine, 1953-58; prof., chmn. dept. neurology U. Wis. Sch. Medicine, 1958-78; emeritus, 1978—; dir. Epilepsy Center, VA Hosp., Madison, Wis., 1977-82; cons. neurology. Author: Synopsis of Neurology, 1962, 66, 73, 78, Reflex Epilepsy, Behavioral Therapy and Conditional Reflexes, 1977; editor: Modern Therapy in Neurology, 1957, Evaluation of Drug Therapy, 1961. Mem. AMA (chmn. nervous and mental diseases sect. 1952-53), D.C. Med. Soc. (chmn. sect. neurology and psychiatry 1955-56, pres. 1958), Am. Acad. Neurology (chmn. survey com. 1948-51, pres. 1957-59), Am. Neurol. Assn. (chmn. com. internat. collaboration 1954-55), Am. Epilepsy League (pres. 1951-52), Assn. Research Nervous and Mental Diseases, Am. Physiol. Soc., Am. Psychiat. Assn., Am. Assn. Electroencephalographers, AAAS, Am. Assn. U. Profs. Neurology, Mass. Med. Soc., State Med. Soc. Wis., N.Y. Acad. Scis., Acad. Medicine Washington, Sigma Xi, Alpha Omega Alpha. Club: Cosmos (Washington). Home: 4020 Co M Middleton WI 53562 Office: Dept Neurology U Wis Med Sch 600 Highland Ave Madison WI 53792

FORSTER, KURT W(ALTER), art and architecture historian, educator, critic, author, lecturer; b. Zurich, Switzerland, Aug. 12, 1935; s. Walter and Margrit (Frank) F.; m. Francoise L. Hahn, July 29, 1961; children: Myriam, Stephanie. Ph.D., U. Zurich, 1961. Asst. prof. Yale U., New Haven, 1960-67; vis. asst. prof. U. Calif.-Berkeley, 1965; prof. dept. art history Stanford U., (Calif.), 1967-82; prof. dept. architecture MIT, Cambridge, 1982-84; dir. Getty Ctr. History of Art and Humanities, Santa Monica, Calif., 1984—; dir. Swiss Inst. in Rome, 1975-77; mem. scholarly council Inst. Advanced Study, West Berlin, 1980-83; mem. Centro Internazionale di Studi di Architettura, Vicenza, 1982—; dir. Stanford Study Center, West Berlin, 1980. Author: Pontormo, 1966, Palladio, 1980; editor: jour. Oppositions, 1978—. Mem. vis. com. Harvard U. Morse fellow Yale U., Rome, 1966; sr. fellow Swiss Nat. Fund, London, 1971-72. Mem. Soc. Archtl. Historians, Coll. Art Assn. Home: 85 Revere St Boston MA 02114 Office: Getty Ctr History of Art 401 Wilshire Blvd Santa Monica CA 90401

FORSTER, LESLIE STEWART, educator; b. Chgo., May 10, 1924; s. Sol and Celia (Oppenheim) F.; m. Maryalice Levy, July 28, 1946; children—Mark, Stephanie. Student, U. Calif. at Los Angeles, 1941-43; B.S., U. Cal. at Berkeley, 1947; Ph.D., U. Minn., 1951. Postdoctoral fellow U. Rochester, N.Y., 1951-52; instr. Bates Coll., Lewiston, Me., 1952-55; mem. faculty U. Ariz., Tucson, 1955—, asso. prof. chemistry, 1959-64, prof., 1964—; Cons. NIH, 1963-64. Bd. dirs. So. Ariz. br. Am. Civil Liberties Union, 1966-67. Served with AUS, 1943-45. NSF Faculty Sci. fellow, 1961-62; USPHS Spl. fellow, 1968-69. Mem. Am. Chem. Soc., Am. Phys. Soc., Am. Assn. U. Profs. (v.p. U. Ariz. chpt. 1965-66, pres. state conf. 1972-73), Sigma Xi. Home: 5615 Julius St Tucson AZ 85712

FORSTER, PETER H., power company executive; b. Berlin, Germany, May 28, 1942; s. Jerome and Margaret Hanson; m. Susan E. Forster. B.S., U. Wis., 1964; postgrad., Bklyn. Law Sch., Columbia U., 1972. Engr. trainee Wis. Electric Power Co., 1960-64; head regional planning Am. Electric Power Service Corp., 1964-73; atty. Dayton Power & Light Co., Ohio, from 1973, v.p. adminstrn., treas., 1977, v.p. fin. and adminstrn., 1977-78, v.p. energy resources, 1978-79, exec. v.p., 1980-81, exec. v.p., chief operating officer, 1981—82, pres., chief operating officer, 1982—, also dir.; dir. Citizens Fed. Savs. & Loan Assn., C.H. Gosiger Machinery Co. Trustee Wilmington Coll., Dayton Performing Arts Fund, F.M. Tait Found. Mem. Am. Bar Assn., Ohio Bar Assn., Dayton Bar Assn., Engrs. Club Dayton. Office: PO Box 1247 Courthouse Plaza SW Dayton OH 45401

FORSTER, ROBERT, history educator; b. N.Y.C., June 7, 1926; s. Theodore and Elise (Strobel) F.; m. Elborg Hamacher, July 8, 1955; children: Marc Richard, Thomas Theodore. B.A., Swarthmore Coll., 1949; M.A. in Modern European History, Harvard U., 1951; Ph.D., Johns Hopkins U., 1956. Instr. modern European history Johns Hopkins U., 1956-57; Bissing fellow U. Toulouse, France, 1957-58; asst. prof. U. Nebr., 1958-62; asso. prof. Dartmouth, 1962-65; prof. history Johns Hopkins, 1966—; fellow Inst. for Advanced Study, Princeton, N.J., 1975-76, Center for Advanced Study in Behavioral Scis., Stanford U., 1979-80; U.S. rep. Internat. Congress Hist. Scis., 1975-80. Author: The Nobility of Toulouse in the 18th Century, 1960, The House of Saulx-Tavanes: Versailles and Burgundy, 1700-1830, 1971, Seeds of Change: Peasants, Nobles, and Rural Revolution in 18th Century France, 1975; author: Merchants, Landlords, Magistrates: The Depont Family in 18th Century France, 1980; Author also articles.; Editor: (with Elborg Forster) European Society in the 18th Century, 1969, (with Jack P. Greene) Preconditions of Revolution in Early Modern Europe, 1970, (with Elborg Forster) European Diet from Pre-Industrial to Modern Times, 1975, (with Orest Ranum) Biology of Man in History, 1975, Family and Society, 1976, (with E. Carter and J. Moody) Enterprise and Entrepreneurs in 19th and 20th Century France, 1976, (with Orest Ranum) Rural Society in France, 1977, Deviants and the Abandoned, 1978, Food and Drink in History, 1979; editor: Medicine and Society in France, 1980, Ritual, Religion, and the Sacred, 1981. Served with AUS, 1944-46. French Govt. fellow, 1953-55; Social Sci. Research Council fellow, France, 1962, 64; Guggenheim fellow, Paris, 1969-70; recipient Prix Gaussail Acad. Toulouse. Mem. Soc. French Hist. Studies (pres. 1974), Phi Beta Kappa. Home: 208 Oakdale Rd Baltimore MD 21210

FORSTER, ROY PHILIP, educator, physiologist; b. Milw., Sept. 28, 1911; s. Frank M. and Adele M. (Schatz) F.; m. Dorothy F. Seegers, Aug. 31, 1935; 1 dau., Peggy (Mrs. A. Alexander Hyde). B.S., Marquette U., 1932; Ph.M., U. Wis., 1935, Ph.D., 1938; M.A. (hon.), Dartmouth, 1948. Faculty mem. Dartmouth Coll., Hanover, N.H., 1938—, prof., 1948-64, Ira Allen Eastman prof., 1964-76, research prof. biology, 1976—, chmn. zoology dept., 1950-56, chmn. sci. div., 1947-51, lectr. physiology Med. Sch., 1964-74, adj. prof., 1974—; cons. research VA Center, White River Junction, Vt., 1963—; cons. research lab. sci. medicine VA, 1964-66; dir. regulatory biology program NSF, 1959-60; dir. Mt. Desert Island Biol. Lab., summers 1940-47, trustee, 1940-72, 76—, v.p., 1960-63, pres., 1963-70; Mem. Conf. Renal Function of Josiah Macy, Jr. Found., 1949-54; mem. corp. Bermuda Biol. Sta. for Research; mem. sci. rev. com. health research facilities NIH, 1964-66, 1966-67, 1966, 1969-78; vis. prof. physiology U. Hawaii Sch. Medicine, 1973. Contbr. articles to profl. jours.; Editor kidney sect.: Biol. Abstracts, 1947—; asso. editor: Jour. Gen. Physiology, 1960-68; editorial bd.: Am. Jour. Physiology, Jour. Applied Physiology, 1960-66, 70-76, Jour. Gen. Physiology, 1968-76. John Simon Guggenheim Meml. Found. fellow Cambridge U. and various European biol. labs., 1948-49; for travel and study abroad, 1955-56. Fellow AAAS; mem. Am. Heart Assn. (council circulation), Am. Soc. Zoologists, Am. Physiol. Soc., N.H. Acad. Sci. (exec. com. 1945-48), Am., Internat. socs. nephrology, Soc. Gen. Physiologists, Sigma Xi (pres. Dartmouth chpt. 1968-69), Gamma Alpha, Alpha Sigma Nu, Delta Sigma Rho, Phi Sigma. Developed techniques for evaluation of kidney function, research on hemodynamics, cellular and comparative physiology of kidney. Home: 18 Hemlock Rd Hanover NH 03755

FORSTER, WALTER LESLIE, cons.; b. Leeds, Eng., June 30 1903; s. John Mark and Margaret (Forster) F.; m. Lorna Bonstow, Feb. 3, 1936; 1 son, John. B.Sc., Leeds U., 1924. Engr. Royal Dutch-Shell Group, Mexico, Venezuela, Rumania, Egypt, 1925-40, gen. mgr., Colombia, 1946-47, Venezuela, 1947-50; cons., 1951—; dir. various companies. Served as col. Brit. Army, 1940-46. Decorated comdr. Order Brit. Empire, Legion of Merit, U.S.). Fellow Inst. Petroleum London. Home: 61 Summit Crescent Westmount PQ H3Y 1L5 Canada

FORSTER, WILLIAM HALL, retired telephone manufacturing company executive, consultant; b. Belmar, N.J., July 11, 1922; s. Hans Walter and Edith (Hall) F.; m. Gail Daly, July 13, 1945; children: William Daly, John Marshall, Robert Walter, Susan Hall, Frances Gail. A.B., Harvard U., 1943, grad. Advanced Mgmt. Program, 1959. With Philco Corp., Phila., 1943-65, dir. research solid state electronics, 1955-59, dir. semiconductor mktg. and devel. Internat. div., 1959-61, dir. engring. and research, 1962-65; staff asst. to pres. ITT Corp., N.Y.C., 1966—, v.p., 1973—, v.p., product group mgr.-telecommunications, 1976-82; cons. telecommunications, 1982—; v.p., tech. dir. ITT Europe, Brussels, Belgium, 1967-75. Mem. John Scott Award Com., Phila., 1961-78; mem. com. on sci. and arts Franklin Inst., Phila., 1964-66; bd. corporators Med. Coll. Pa., 1956-72; bd. dirs. Am. Cancer Soc., N.Y.C.; chmn. bd. dirs. Mason's Island Fire Dist.; bd. dirs. Centers for Artsin Westerly. Fellow IEEE (chmn. Internat. Communications Conf. 1966), Phys. Soc. (U.K.), Radio Club Am.; mem. Electronic Industries Assn. (com. chmn.), Am. C. of C. in Belgium (dir. 1976), Phi Beta Kappa, Sigma Xi. Unitarian. Club: Mason's Island Yacht. Home: Mason's Island Mystic CT 06355

FORSTMAN, HENRY JACKSON, theology educator, university dean; b. Montgomery, Ala., June 15, 1929; s. Joseph Carl and Kate Gertrue (Kelley) F.; m. Shirley Marie Cronk, June 3, 1950; children: David Jackson, Valerie Marie, Paul Frederick. B.A., Phillips U., 1949, D.D. (hon.), 1982; B.D., Union Theol. Sem., N.Y.C., 1956, Th.D., 1959. Asst. prof. Randolph-Macon Woman's Coll., 1958-60, Stanford, 1960-64; mem. faculty Vanderbilt U., 1964—, prof. religion, 1968—, Charles G. Finney prof. theology, 1979—, chmn. grad. dept. religion, 1969-72, acting dean, 1970-71, dean, 1979—; Fulbright research scholar, Germany, 1973-74, 79-80; Mem. faith and order commn. World Council Chs. Author: Word and Spirit, 1962, Christian Faith and the Church, 1965, A Romantic Triangle, 1977. Kent fellow, 1957-58; postdoctoral fellow for cross disciplinary studies Soc. Values in Higher Edn., 1966-67. Mem. Soc. Religion in Higher Edn., Am. Soc. Ch. History, Am. Acad. Religion, AAUP, Assn. Disciples Theol. Discussion. Home: 3913 Kimpalong St Nashville TN 37205 Office: Divinity Sch Vanderbilt U Nashville TN 37240

FORSYTH, GEORGE HOWARD, JR., art historian; b. Highland Park, Ill., Sept. 2, 1901; s. George Howard and Sarah (Brockunier) F.; m. Eleanor Marquand, Feb. 5, 1927; children: Eleanor, Mary Blaikie, George Allan; m. Mary Isom Hayes, August 18, 1942 (dec. Nov. 1958); 1 dau., Hope Gifford; m. Ilene Eleanor Haering, June 4, 1960. A.B., Princeton U., 1923, M.F.A., 1927, mem. Inst. Advanced Study, 1935-36, 45. Instr. and later asst. prof., dept. art and archaeology Princeton U., 1927-42; prof. history of art U. Mich., 1947-72, chmn. dept., 1947-61; dir. Kelsey Mus. Archaeology, 1961-69, research prof. archeology, 1969-72; dir. survey and excavation Ch. St. Martin, Angers, France; field dir. Mich., Princeton, Alexandria univs. archeol. expdn. to Mt. Sinai, Egypt, 1958, 60, 63, 65; bd. scholars Dumbarton Oaks Research Library and Collection, Harvard U., 1957-72, hon. asso., 1972—; research asso. Freer Gallery, Smithsonian Instn., 1954, 56, 60. Author: Church of St. Martin at Angers, 1953, (with Kurt Weitzmann) Monastery of St. Catherine at Mt. Sinai, 1973, The Church and Fortress of Justinian: Vol. 1: Plates, 1973; contbr. to art publs. Served as lt. USNR, 1942-45. Recipient traveling fellowship Mediaeval Acad. Am., 1924-25, Haskins medal, 1955; Rockefeller Found. research grantee, 1946; Guggenheim fellow, 1953. Life mem. Société française d'archéologie; mem. Coll. Art Assn. (dir. 1949, 54), Royal Soc. Arts (London), Phi Beta Kappa, Phi Kappa Phi. Clubs: Century Assn. (N.Y.C.); Cosmos (Washington). Home: 5 Geddes Heights Ann Arbor MI 48104

FORSYTH, ILENE HAERING, art historian; b. Detroit, Aug. 21, 1928; d. Austin Frederick and Eleanor Marie (Middleton) H.; m. George H. Forsyth, Jr., June 4, 1960. A.B., U. Mich., 1950; A.M. (univ. fellow), Columbia U., 1955; Ph.D. (Fulbright, AAUW, Fels Found. fellow), Columbia U., 1960. Lectr. Barnard Coll., 1955-58; instr. Columbia U., 1959-61; mem. faculty U. Mich., Ann Arbor, 1961—, prof. history of art, 1974—, Arthur F. Thurnau prof., 1984—; vis. prof. Harvard U., 1980; Mellon vis. prof. U. Pitts., 1981; mem. Nat. Com. History Art, 1975—; bd. dirs. Internat. Center Medieval Art, 1970—, v.p., 1981—. Author: The Throne of Wisdom, 1972 (Charles Rufus Morey Book award 1974); also articles. Rackham research grantee and fellow, 1965-66, 75-76; grantee Am. Council Learned Socs., 1972-73; mem. Inst. Advanced Study Princeton, 1977. Mem. Coll. Art Assn. (dir. 1980—), Archaeol. Inst. Am., Medieval Acad. Am., Medieval Club N.Y., Soc. francaise d'archéologie, Soc. Archtl. Historians, Acad. Arts, Scis. et Belles Lettres Dijon (France), Centre de recherches et d'études préromanes et romanes. Home: 5 Geddes Heights Ann Arbor MI 48104 Office: Dept History Art U Mich Ann Arbor MI 48109

FORSYTH, JOSEPH, librarian; b. County Durham, Eng., Aug. 15, 1942; emigrated to Can., 1966; s. James Frederick and Maisie (Appleby) F.; m. Kay Frances Appleby, Oct. 3, 1964; children: Julian Alastair, Andrew Stuart. Asso. of Library Assn., Newcastle (Eng.) Sch. Librarianship, 1963; M.A. in Library Sci., U. London, 1976, Fellow of Library Assn., 1971. Library asst. Durham County Library, 1960-62; coll. librarian Easington (Eng.) Tech. Coll., 1962-63; regional librarian North Riding County (Eng.) Library, 1964-66; reference librarian Calgary (Alta., Can.) Public Library, 1966-70; library devel. officer Govt. Alta., Edmonton, 1970-77; dir. library services Alta. Dept. Culture, Edmonton, 1977—. Author: Government Publications Relating to Alberta, 1972. Mem. ALA, Edmonton Library Assn., Library Assn. Alta., Can. Library Assn., Library Assn. Gt. Britain, Internat. and Comparative Librarianship Group of Library Assns. Anglican. Home: 15211 83d Ave Edmonton AB T5R 3T5 Canada Office: 16214 114th Ave Edmonton AB T5M 2Z5 Canada

FORSYTHE, CARL STANFORD, lawyer; b. Jackson, Ohio, Jan. 29, 1910; s. Carl F. and Clara (Evans) F.; m. Virginia Cluff, July 6 1936; 1 son, Carl S. Student, Princeton Prep. Sch., 1927-28; A.B., U. Mich., 1932, J.D., 1935. Bar: N.Y. bar 1935. Asso. O'Connor & Farber, N.Y.C., 1935-37; partner Townley, Updike & Carter, 1937-51, Forsythe, Holbrook, Seward & Bovone, 1951—; dir. Crompton &

Knowles Corp., Worcester, Mass., 1955—, chmn. bd., 1970—. Bd. dirs., treas. Versailles Found. Served as 1st lt. OSS AUS, 1944-45. Decorated Certificate of Merit, Bronze Star, U.S., Golden medal of Vasa, Sweden). Mem. Judge Adv. Gen.'s Assn., Am. Legion, Am., N.Y. bar assns., Assn. Bar City N.Y., Sigma Delta Chi, Theta Delta Chi. Republican. Methodist. Clubs: Union League (N.Y.C.); Greenwich Country, Indian Harbor Yacht (Greenwich). Home: Dingletown Rd Greenwich CT 06830 Office: 420 Lexington Ave New York NY 10170

FORSYTHE, EARL ANDREW, lawyer, steel company executive; b. Hagerstown, Md., Dec. 24, 1904; s. Andrew Johnson and Mary Susan (Snyder) F.; m. Janet Kendall, Apr. 2, 1937; children: Elizabeth Forsythe Hailey, Gail, Judith Forsythe Sanford, Andrew. A.B., Dickinson Coll., 1928; LL.B., Yale U., 1931. Bar: Md. 1932, Tex. 1932. Of counsel Worsham, Forsythe & Sampels, Dallas, 1951—; chmn. bd. Austin Steel Co., Inc., Dallas, 1967—; dir. Cullum Cos., Inc., Dallas, 1957—. Chmn. Dallas chpt. ARC, 1963-65, hon. life bd. dirs., 1977—; founder, gen. counsel Community Chest Trust Fund (now Communities Found. of Tex., Inc.), Dallas, 1955-61; bd. dirs. United Way Met. Dallas, 1964-72; pres. Salesmanship Club Dallas, 1957-58; chmn. bd. Children's Bur., Dallas, 1951-54; bd. dirs. Dallas Child Guide Clinic, 1972-75; mem. adv. council St. Philips Sch. and Community Ctr.; mem. adv. com. U. Tex. at Dallas, 1968-69; bd. devel. So. Methodist U., 1963-66; chmn. bd., bd. dirs. Canterbury House, 1955-58; bd. dirs. Gaston Episcopal Hosp., 1972—, Dallas County Hosp. Dist., 1964-75, Episc. Sch. Dallas. Recipient J. Erik Jonsson award United Way Met. Dallas, 1980, Justinian award Dallas Lawyers Wives Club, 1982. Mem. ABA, Tex. Bar Assn., Dallas Bar Assn. (sec.), Dallas C. of C. (dir. 1965-66), Phi Alpha Delta. Episcopalian (sr. warden). Clubs: Northwood, Dallas. Home: 4309 Belclaire Dallas TX 75205 Office: 2500 2001 Bryan Tower Dallas TX 75201

FORSYTHE, HENDERSON, actor; b. Macon, Mo., Sept. 11, 1917; s. Cecil Proctor and Mary Catherine (Henderson) F.; m. Dorothea Maria Carlson, May 26, 1942; children: Eric, Jason. Student, Culver-Stockton Coll., 1935-37; B.A., State U. Iowa, 1939, M.F.A., 1940. Mem. faculty, dir. U. Iowa, summers 1953-55. Numerous Broadway and off-Broadway appearances, 1955—, numerous TV and film appearances, 1955—; sheriff in: prodns. in The Best Little Whorehouse in Texas, U.S. and London (Tony award); appears in running role in: TV series As The World Turns. Served with U.S. Army, 1941-46. Mem. Actors Equity Assn., AFTRA, Screen Actors Guild, ANTA. Presbyterian. Office: care 46th St Theater 226 W 46th St New York NY 10036

FORSYTHE, JOHN, actor; b. Penn's Grove, N.J., Jan. 29, 1918; s. Samuel Jeremiah and Blanche Materson (Blohm) Freund; m. Parker McCormick (div.); m. Julie Warren; children: Dall, Page, Brooke. Student, U. N.C., also N.Y. Actor's Studio. Motion picture debut in Destination Tokyo, 1944; other films include Escape from Fort Bravo, 1953, Trouble with Harry, 1956, Ambassador's Daughter, 1956, Madame X, 1966, In Cold Blood, 1968, Topaz, 1969, Happy Ending, 1970, And Justice for All, 1979; on tour with: play Mr. Roberts; then on Broadway; later dir.: City Center (N.Y.) revival, 1956; Broadway play Weekend, 1968; TV debut, 1947; appeared numerous dramatic shows; role: TV series Bachelor Father, 1957-62, To Rome With Love, 1971, World of Survival, 1970-82, Charlie's Angels, 1976-81, Dynasty, 1981—; TV movies include Terror on the 40th Floor, 1974, The Deadly Tower, 1975, Cruise Into Terror, 1978, The Users, 1978, A Time of Miracle, 1980, Sizzle, 1981; role: on Broadway in Yellow Jack; host: sports show Hollywood Park Feature Race, 1971-74. Office: care Aaron Spelling Prodns Inc 132 S Rodeo Beverly Hills CA 90212 *

FORSYTHE, MARGARET JEANNE, university administrator; b. Flint, Mich., May 28, 1923; d. William Ray and Genevieve (Lancashire) F. B.A., Oberlin Coll., 1945; certificate bus. adminstrn., Radcliffe Coll., 1946; M.A., Syracuse U., 1951; Ed.D., Western Res. U., 1962. Adminstrv. asst. pub. relations Central Nat. Bank Cleve., 1946-49; editor Cleve. Banker (publ. Fed. Res. Dist.), 1948-49; residence hall dir., Panhellenic adviser Kan. State Coll., Manhattan, 1951-53; faculty Kent State U., 1953-63, dean of women, 1959-63, asst. prof. spl. edn., 1962-63; dean of women U. Cin., 1963-65; dean of women Ohio Wesleyan U., Delaware, 1965—, dean student devel., 1970-76, coordinator acad. advising, 1976—; Adviser dist. 1 Alpha Lambda Delta, 1963-65. Mem. Am. Coll. Personnel Assn. (exec. council 1962-63, sec. 1963-65), Nat. Assn. Women Deans and Counselors (v.p. 1969-71), Am. Personnel and Guidance Assn., Nat. Acad. Advising Assn., AAUW, Pi Lambda Theta. Home: 175 Kensington Dr Delaware OH 43015

FORSYTHE, PETER WINCHELL, foundation executive; b. Ann Arbor, Mich., May 31, 1937; s. Franklin Cawley and Jessie Winchell F.; m. Betty Joyce Logerquist, June 28, 1956; children—David Winchell, Linda Marie, James Winchell, Martha Katherine, Paul Winchell. A.B., U. Mich., 1959; postgrad., Boston U. Sch. Theology, 1960; J.D., U. Mich., 1963; LL.D., Eastern Mich. U., 1973. Bar: Mich. bar 1963, U.S. Supreme Ct. bar 1969. Asst. pros. atty., Washtenaw County, Mich., 1963-66, asst. city atty., Ann Arbor, 1966-67, city atty., 1967-69; partner firm Forsythe, Campbell & Vandenberg (and predecessors), Ann Arbor, 1963-73; dir. Office of Youth Services, Mich. Dept. Social Services, Lansing, 1970-72; chief adminstr. social services Mich. Dept. Social Services, 1973; v.p., dir. program for children Edna McConnell Clark Found., N.Y.C., 1973—; cons. children's bur. Dept. Health and Human Services; mem. faculty Nat. Coll. Juvenile Justice. Co-founder Council on Adoptable Children, Mich., 1967, Spaulding for Children, Mich., 1968, Spaulding for Children, N.Y., 1976; bd. dirs., exec. com. Welfare Info. Services. Mem. Child Welfare League Am. (dir., exec. com.), Nat. Conf. Social Welfare (dir., v.p.), Council Social Work Edn. (treas., exec. com.), Council on Accreditation of Services to Families and Children (dir., exec. com.), Am. Public Welfare Assn., Washtenaw County Bar Assn. (pres. 1968-69). Quaker. Home: 100 Pryer Terr New Rochelle NY 10804 Office: 250 Park Ave New York NY 10017

FORSYTHE, RICHARD HAMILTON, food company executive; b. Griswold, Iowa, Dec. 9, 1921; s. Piercy and Alice (Hamilton) F.; m. Charlotte Langworthy, Mar. 20, 1943; children: Charlynn, Lesley Kay, Patricia. B.S., Iowa State Coll., 1943, Ph.D., 1949. Asst. prof. poultry products tech. Iowa State U., 1949-51, prof., head poultry sci. dept., 1960-67; asso. dir. food research Armour & Co., 1951-53; dir. central labs., v.p. Henningsen Foods, Inc., Springfield, Mo., 1953-60, v.p. tech. affairs, White Plains, N.Y., 1967-73; v.p. basic research Campbell Inst. Food Research, Camden, N.J., 1973-79; v.p. tech. adminstrn. Campbell Soup Co., Fayetteville, Ark., 1979-80, v.p. poultry research, 1980—. Contbr. articles, chpts. in books; former asso. editor: Food Tech. Recipient Mo. 4-H Alumni award, 1958; Research award Inst. Am. Poultry Industries, 1958; named Poultry Industry Man of Year, 1970. Fellow Inst. Food Technologists; Mem. Am. Chem. Soc., World Poultry Sci. Assn. (pres. U.S.A. br. 1970-74), AAAS, Am. Inst. for Nutrition, Am. Poultry Hist. Soc. (dir. 1970-71), Soc. Nutrition Edn., N.Y. Acad. Scis. Presbyn. Clubs: Mason, Rotary. Home: 2548 Golden Oaks Fayetteville AR 72701 Office: Campbell Soup Co PO Box G Fayetteville AR 72701

FORT, ARTHUR TOMLINSON, III, physician; b. Lumpkin, Ga., Sept. 724, 1931; s. Thomas Morton and Gladys (Davis) F.; m. Jane Wilmer McClelland, June 15, 1957; children: Abby Lucinda, Arthur Tomlinson, Jr., Juliana Melody, Ernest Arlington, II. B.B.A., U. Ga., 1952; M.D., U. Tenn., 1962. Diplomate: Am. Bd. Ob-Gyn, Am. Bd. Family Practice. Intern, then resident in ob-gyn U. Tenn.-City of Memphis Hosp., 1962-66; asst. prof. U. Tenn. Med. Sch., 1966-70; prof. ob-gyn, head dept. La. State U. Med. Sch., Shreveport, 1970-73; prof. maternal-child health and family planning, head program family health Tulane U. Sch. Public Health, 1973-74; practice medicine specializing in rural family medicine, Vacharie, La., 1974-79; prof. ob-gyn and family medicine, head dept. family medicine and comprehensive care La. State U. Med. Sch., Shreveport, 1980—. Author articles in field. Served with USAF, 1952-57. Recipient Golden Apple Teaching award Student AMA, 1969, Western Interstate Commn. on Higher Edn., 1973. Fellow Am. Coll. Ob-Gyn, Am. Acad. Family Practice; mem. AMA. Republican. Presbyterian. Office: PO Box 33932 Shreveport LA 71130

FORT, EDWARD BERNARD, university chancellor; b. Detroit, Apr. 14; s. Edward Clark and Inez Corrine (Baker) F.; m. Lessie Covington, Dec. 5, 1959; children: Clarke, Lezlie. B.A., Wayne State U., 1954, M.A., 1958; Ph.D., U. Calif., Berkeley, 1964. Supt. Inkster (Mich.) Schs., 1967-71; adj. prof. adminstrn./urban edn. U. Mich., Ann Arbor, 1968-71; supt., dep. supt. schs., Sacramento, 1971-74; chancellor U. Wis. Center System, Madison, 1974-81, N.C. A&T State U., Greensboro, 1981—; vis. prof. Mich. State U., East Lansing, 1974. Bd. editorial cons., Phi Delta Kappa, 1980-83. Bd. dirs. Sacramento Urban League, 1973-74, Madison Urban League, 1979—; bd. advisors Fund for Improvement Post Secondary Edn., 1979—. Served with AUS, 1954-56. Mem. Greensboro C. of C. (exec. bd. 1984—). Office: NC A&T State U Chancellor's Office E Market St Greensboro NC 27411

FORT, JAMES TOMLINSON, lawyer; b. Albany, N.Y., Apr. 12, 1928; s. Tomlinson and Beatrice (Lawson) F.; m. Judith Anne Davis, May 9, 1959; children: Edward Tomlinson, Madeline Annabelle. A.B., Allegheny Coll.; LL.B., Yale U. Bar: Supreme Ct. Assoc. Reed Smith Shaw & McClay, Pitts., 1954-62, ptnr., 1962—. Trustee Carnegie-Mellon U., Pitts., 1967-73, Allegheny Coll., Meadville, Pa., 1975—; dir. Pitts. Dance Council, 1977—. Served with usmc, 1953-54. Mem. ABA, Pa. Bar Assn., Pitts. Acad. Trial Lawyers, Bar Supreme Ct. U.S. Republican. Presbyterian. Clubs: Duquesne (Pitts.); Rolling Rock (Ligonier, Pa.). Home: 204 Woodcock Dr Pittsburgh PA 15212 Office: Reed Smith Shaw & McClay 5th and Grant Pittsburgh PA 15230

FORT, TOMLINSON, JR., chemist, chemical engineering educator; b. Sumter, S.C., Apr. 16, 1932; s. Tomlinson and Madeline A. Kean (Scott) F.; m. Martha Kirby, Oct. 13, 1956; children: Tomlinson, III, Frances Clare. B.S. in Chemistry, U. Ga., 1952; M.S., U. Tenn., 1957, Ph.D. in Phys. Chemistry, 1957; A.E. and F.A.Q. Stephens postdoctoral fellow, U. Sydney, Australia, 1957-58; cert., Inst. Ednl. Mgmt., Harvard U., 1978. Instr. surface chemistry U. Sydney, 1957-58; research chemist, then sr. research chemist and project leader duPont Co., 1958-65; mem. faculty Case Western Res. U., 1965-73, prof. chem. engring., dir. surfaces research lab., 1971-73; prof. chem. engring. and chemistry, head dept. chem. engring. Carnegie-Mellon U., 1973-80, adj. prof., 1980—; prof. chemistry and chem. engring., provost U. Mo., Rolla, 1980-82; provost Calif. Poly. State U., San Luis Obispo, 1982—, v.p. for acad. affairs, 1982-83, provost, 1983—; summer vis. prof. Nat. U. Mex., 1973, U. Copenhagen, 1978, 80; pres. Frances Fort Brown Realty Co., Chattanooga, 1970—. Author papers on surface and colloid sci. Mem. Am. Chem. Soc., Am. Inst. Chemists, Catalysis Soc., Am. Soc. Engring. Edn., Mo. Acad. Sci., Am. Inst. Chem. Engrs., AAAS, N.Y. Acad. Sci., Sigma Xi, Gamma Sigma Epsilon, Alpha Chi Sigma, Sigma Chi. Home: 1341 Ocean aire Dr San Luis Obispo CA 93401 Office: Calif Poly State U San Luis Obispo CA 93407

FORTADO, MICHAEL GEORGE, lawyer, diversified energy company executive; b. Wichita Falls, Tex., Oct. 29, 1943; s. Antonio and Flossie Juanita (Bowers) F.; m. Avis Ann Smith, Mar. 12, 1964; children: Michael Scott, Angela Avis, Shannon Michelle. B.B.A., Midwestern U., Wichita Falls, 1965; LL.B., U. Tex., Austin, 1968. Bar: Tex. 1968. Asso. atty. firm McClure & Sharpe, Houston, 1968-69; atty. ENSERCH Corp. (and predecessor), Dallas, 1969-71, corp. sec., asst. gen. counsel, 1971—. Mem. Am. Soc. Corp. Secs. (dir. 1980-83), State Bar Tex., Dallas Bar Assn., Kappa Alpha Order, Delta Sigma Pi, Phi Alpha Delta. Mem. Christian Ch. (Disciples of Christ). Club: DAC Country. Office: 300 S St Paul St Dallas TX 75201

FORTE, JOHN GAETANO, physiologist, educator; b. Phila., Dec. 23, 1934; s. Gaetano and Catherine (Cerebone) F.; m. Trudy M. Michel, June 3, 1961; children: Michele E., John G., Susan C. A.B., Johns Hopkins U., 1956; Ph.D. (Orvill Paul Phillips fellow), U. Pa., 1961. Instr. physiology U. Pa., 1961-62, asso. physiology, 1962-64; research asso. biochemistry U. So. Calif., 1964-65; asst. prof. U. Calif., Berkeley, 1965-69, assoc. prof., 1969-74, prof., 1974—, chmn. dept. physiology and anatomy, 1972-78; cons. NSF, 1970-71; chmn. physiology study sect. NIH, 1976-78. Sect. editor gastrointestinal physiology: Ann. Rev. Physiology; Contbr. articles to profl. jours. NIH grantee, 1965—. Mem. Am. Physiology Soc., Biophys. Soc., Parietal Cell Club, N.Y. Acad. Scis., Assn. Chmn. Depts. Physiology. Roman Catholic. Home: 865 Contra Costa Ave Berkeley CA 94707 Office: Dept Physiology Anatomy Univ California Berkeley CA 94720

FORTE, JOHNIE, JR., army officer; b. New Boston, Tex., Dec. 20, 1936; s. Johnie and Sadie (Ford) F.; m. Dolores Bowles Johnson, Jan. 10, 1964; children: Mitchell C. Johnson, Shermaine L. Johnson, Denise M. Forte. B.A. in Polit. Sci, Prairie View A&M U., 1956; M.A., Auburn U., 1976. Commd. 2d lt. U.S. Army, 1956; advanced through grades to brig. gen.; personnel mgmt. officer Dept. Army; dir. personnel and insp. gen., W. Ger.; now dir. personnel plans and systems Hdqrs., Dept. Army, Washington. Decorated Legion of Merit. Mem. Assn. U.S. Army (v.p. chpt. 1977-78). Methodist. Home: 8303 Terra Grande Springfield VA 22153

FORTE, WESLEY ELBERT, insurance company executive; b. Worcester, Mass., Dec. 1, 1933; s. Elbert W. and Ethel M. (Lyons) F.; m. Margaret Ellen Layman, July 29, 1961; children—Laura Jean, Scott Montgomery. B.B.A., Clark U., 1956; J.D., N.Y. U., 1959, LL.M., 1965. Bar: Pa. bar 1960, Ohio bar 1972, U.S. Supreme Ct 1972, Tex. bar 1974, D.C. bar 1975, N.Y. bar 1980. Atty. Dechert, Price & Rhoads, Phila., 1959-62; atty. corporate law dept. Standard Brands, Inc., N.Y.C., 1962-66; sr. counsel domestic ops. Borden, Inc., N.Y.C., Columbus, Ohio, 1966-72; sr. v.p. legal affairs Campbell-Taggart, Inc., Dallas, 1972-73, exec. v.p., dir., 1973-79; sr. v.p. law USLIFE Corp., N.Y.C., 1979—. Contbr. articles to profl. jours. Home: 8 Paddington Circle Bronxville NY 10708 Office: USLIFE Corp 125 Maiden Ln New York NY 10038

FORTENBACH, RAY THOMAS, lawyer; b. Chgo., Apr. 27, 1927; s. Ray J. and Mary Lee (Shively) F.; m. Marie Septer, Aug. 31, 1951; children: Karen, Karl, Kurt. B.A., U. Louisville, 1947; LL.B., U. Houston, 1954. Bar: Tex. 1954, U.S. Supreme Ct. 1971. Partner firm Childs, Fortenbach, Beck & Guyton, Houston, 1956-82, of counsel, 1982—; assoc. dir. intramural research program NIMH, 1982-83; dir. intramural research program Nat. Inst. Neurol. and Communicative Disorders and Stroke, 1983—; dir. Interfirst Bank-Greenspoint. Served with USCGR, 1945-46. Recipient Outstanding Alumnus of Yr. award U. Houston Coll. Law, 1971, Pres.'s award for meritorious service, 1976. Mem. Am., Tex., Houston bar assns., U. Houston Alumni Assn. (pres. 1974-75). Roman Catholic. Clubs: River Oaks Country, Coronado. Home: 675 Piney Point Rd Houston TX 77024 Office: 1200 Allied Bank Plaza Houston TX 77002

FORTENBAUGH, SAMUEL BYROD, JR., lawyer, bus. exec.; b. London, Eng., Mar. 2, 1902; s. Samuel Byrod and Florence (Cowden) F.; m. Katherine F. Wall, Dec. 29, 1926; children—Samuel Byrod III, William Wall. B.S., Union Coll., 1923; LL.B., Harvard, 1926. Bar: Pa. bar 1926. Since practiced, Phila.; partner Clark, Ladner, Fortenbaugh & Young; pres., dir. Devonshire Industries, Inc.; chmn. bd., treas., dir. Wall Industries, Inc., NYHM Transp. Co., Wall Rope Works, Beverly, N.J.; dir. Pub. Finance Service, Inc., Phila. Past chmn. bd. trustees Union Coll., Schenectady; dir. ednl. fund Patroni Scholastic, Phila. Mem. Am., Pa., Phila. bar assns., Phila. Maritime Soc. (past pres.), Phi Beta Kappa, Beta Theta Pi. Clubs: Harvard (N.Y.C.); Racquet (Phila.); Merion Golf (Ardmore, Pa.); Bay Head (N.J.) Yacht. Home: King of Prussia Rd Radnor PA 19087 Office: 32d Floor 1818 Market St Philadelphia PA 19103

FORTENBERRY, CHARLES NOLAN, political science educator; b. Oakvale, Miss., Sept. 18, 1908; s. John Morgan and Eliza Cornelia (Parkman) F.; m. Mae Edwards, Aug. 28, 1938; children: Charles Nolan, Joseph Edwin. B.A., M.A., U. Miss., 1931; Ph.D., U. Ill., 1937. Instr. social scis. Oakvale High Sch., 1931-32, 33-34, Clinton (Miss.) High Sch., 1932-33; grad. teaching asst. polit. sci. U. Ill., 1935-36; instr. govt. Edinburg (Tex.) Coll. (now Pan Am. U.), 1937-39, Tex. A. and M. Coll., 1939-40; asst. prof. govt. N. Tex. State Coll., 1940-42, asso. prof., 1942-46; asso. prof. polit. sci. U. Miss., 1946-49, prof., 1949-68, acting dean, 1957-58, chmn. dept. polit. sci., 1958-68; prof. polit. sci., head dept. polit. sci. Auburn (Ala.) U., 1968-79, prof. emeritus, 1979—; vis. prof. U. Ala., summer 1957. Author: A Guidebook of the Chancery Clerk, 1949, A Handbook for Mississippi Legislators, 7th edit, 1968, (with R.B. Highsaw) Municipal Government in the South, 1952, The Government and Adminstration of Mississippi, 1954; also numerous articles profl. jours.; Contbr.: Yesterday's Constitution Today, 1960, Power in American State Legislatures, 1967, Changing Politics of the South, 1972. Served to capt. USAAF, 1942-46; lt. col. Res.; ret. Mem. Am., So. polit. sci. assns. Pi Kappa Alpha, Pi Sigma Alpha, Omicron Delta Kappa, Phi Kappa Phi. Democrat. Episcopalian. Club: Rotarian. Home: PO Box 1102 Auburn AL 36831

FORTESS, KARL EUGENE, painter, lithographer; b. Antwerp, Belgium, Oct. 13, 1907; came to U.S., 1915, naturalized, 1923; s. David and Sara (Jukowska) F.; m. Lillian Fine. Student, Chgo. Art Inst., Art Students League N.Y., Woodstock Sch. of Painting; studied painting with, Y. Kuniyoshi. Faculty Art Students League, Bklyn Mus. Art Sch., La. State U., Am. Art Sch.; now prof. emeritus Boston U. Sch. Fine and Applied Arts. Contbg. author: The Funnies: An American Idiom, 1963; Contbr. articles to profl. jours.; works exhibited, Nat. Inst. Arts and Letters, Art Inst. Chgo., Carnegie Inst., Whitney Mus. Am. Art, Corcoran Gallery Art, Mus. Modern Art, N.A.D., Pa. Acad., one-man shows, Asso. Am. Artists Galleries, N.Y.C., Ganso Gallery, N.Y.C., Vose Galleries, Boston, Krasner Gallery, Mirski Gallery, also others; represented in permanent collections, Butler Inst. Am. Art, Nat. Collection Fine Arts Smithsonian Instn., Munson-Williams-Proctor Inst., Newark Mus., Bklyn. Mus., Mus. Modern Art, print collection, Hudson Walker, Wichita Art Mus., Cedar Rapids Mus. Art, Herbert F. Johnson Mus. Art, other pvt., pub. collections. Recipient E. Keith Meml. award Woodstock Artists Assn., 1935; hon. mention Carnegie Inst., 1941; Salmagundi prize NAD, 1973; Adolph and Clara Obrig prize, 1979; Guggenheim fellow, 1946. Mem. Artists Equity Assn., Coll. Art Assn., Art Students League N.Y. (life), Soc. Am. Graphic Artists, AAUP, Brit. Film Inst., Mus. Modern Art. Home: 311 Plochmann Ln Woodstock NY 12498 *Motivation and curiosity are good substitutes for talent.*

FORTIER, CLAUDE, medical scientist, physiology educator; b. Montreal, Que., Can., June 11, 1921; s. Carolus and Flore-Edith (Lanctôt) F.; m. Elise Gouin, Sept. 8, 1953; children: Anne, Michele, Nicole, Nathalie. B.A., U. Montreal, 1941, M.A. in Polit. Sci, 1941, M.D., 1948, Ph.D., 1952, D.U. (hon.), 1981, LL.D., Dalhousie U., 1977; D.U., Ottawa U., 1981. Research asst. U. Montreal Inst. Exptl. Medicine and Surgery, 1948-51; research cons. U. Lausanne, Switzerland, 1952-53; research asso. dept. neuroendocrinology U. London, 1953-55; asso. prof. physiology, dir. neuroendocrine research lab. Baylor U. Coll. Medicine, 1955-60; dir. endocrine lab. Laval U., Quebec, Que., Can., 1960—, prof. exptl. physiology, 1961—, chmn. dept. physiology, 1964—; mem. Med. Research Council Can., 1963-68, 70-72, vice chmn., 1965-67; chmn. study group on med. research, Govt. Que., 1968-70; vice chmn. med. research coordinating, adv. coms. Def. Research Bd. Can., 1967-70; chmn. Can. nat. com. Internat. Union Physiol. Scis., 1969-72; cons. physician Laval U. Med. Center, 1968—; mem. Killam com. Can. Council, 1967-72, Que. Med. Research Council, 1963-70; chmn. bd. Canadian Fedn. Biol. Socs., 1973-74; mem. neuroendocrinology panel IBRO, UNESCO, 1958—; advisory council Order of Can., 1974-75; chmn. Sci. Council Can., 1978-81, vice chmn., 1975-78, chmn. task force on research in Can., 1976-78; asso. Humanities and Social Scis. Research Council Can., 1981—. Trustee Inst. Research in Pub. Policy, 1974-75, 78-81. Decorated companion Order of Can., 1970; recipient Archambault Research award French Canadian Assn. Advancement Sci., 1972; Sci. award Govt. Que., 1972; Wightman award Gairdner Found., 1979; Marie-Victorin sci. award Govt. of Que., 1980; sci. achievement award French Can. Med. Assn., 1982. Fellow Royal Soc. Can. (pres. 1974-75), Royal Coll. Physicians Can.; mem. Can. Physiol. Soc. (pres. 1966-67), Am. Physiol. Soc., Endocrine Soc., Am. Thyroid Soc., AAAS, N.Y. Acad. Sci., Soc. Exptl. Biology and Medicine, Assn. Am. Physicians, Biomed. Engring. Soc., Peripatetic Club, Can. Soc. Clin. Investigation, Internat. Soc. Neuroendocrinology, Can. Soc. Endocrinology and Metabolism, Assn. Sci., Engring. and Tech. Communities Can. (hon.), Can. Assn. Club of Rome. Research, publs. neurohumoral control adenohypophysial functions, pituitary-thyroid-adrenocortical interactions, biostatistics, bio-control systems, role plasma steroid-binding proteins, boundaries of knowledge, science policy. Home: 1014 DeGrenoble St Quebec PQ Canada G1V 2Z9 Faculty Medicine Laval U Quebec PQ G1K 7P4 Canada

FORTIER, JEAN-MARIE, archbishop; b. Que., Can., July 1, 1920; s. Joseph and Alberta (Jobin) F. Student, Grand Sem. Que., 1940-45; L.Th., Laval U., Que., 1945; postgrad., U. Louvain, Belgium, 1946-48; Licentiate in Ch. History, Gregorian U., Rome, 1950. Ordained priest Roman Catholic Ch., 1944; sec. to bishop of, Hearst, Ont., Can., 1945-46; tchr. ch. history Grand Sem. Que., 1950-60; consecrated bishop Ste. Anne de la Pocatiere, Que., 1961-65, Gaspe, Que., 1965-68; archbishop, Sherbrooke, Que., 1968—; mem. Congregation for Sacraments and Divine Cult; v.p. Can. Cath. Conf., 1971-73, pres., 1973—. Mem. Knights Order Holy Sepulchre of Jerusalem. Address: 130 Rue de la Cathedrale Sherbrooke PQ J1H 4MI Canada

FORTIER, LOUIS YVES, lawyer; b. Quebec, Que., Canada, Sept. 11, 1935; s. Francois and Louise (Turgeon) F.; m. Carol Eaton, Sept. 26, 1959; children: Michel, Suzanne, Margot. B.A., Coll. Ste-Marie,

Montreal, Que., Can., 1955; B.C.L., McGill U., 1958; B. Litt., Oxford U., Eng., 1960.. Ptnr. Ogilvy, Renault, Montreal, Que., Can., 1961—; dir. Jannock Ltd., Mfrs. Life Ins. Co., Les Entreprises J. Rene Ouimet Ltee., Westinghouse Can. Inc., Atlantic Sugar Ltd., Maple Leaf Mills Ltd., Northgate-Patino Inc. Bd. dirs. Can. Inst. Adminstrn. Justice, Can. Olympic Assn., Can. Scholarship Trust Found. (C.S.T.Found.), Hopital Marie Enfant, Montreal Gen. Hosp., Mt. St. Hilaire Nature Conservation Centre; bd. govs. McGill U., Montreal Neurol. Inst. Rhodes scholar, 1958. Mem. Can. Bar Assn. (pres. 1982-83). Liberal. Roman Catholic. Clubs: Univ., Hermitage Golf and Country (pres. 1980-81), Montreal Badminton and Squash (Montreal, Que., Can.)). Home: 19 Rosemount Ave Westmount Montreal PQ Canada H3Y 3G6 Office: 1981 McGill Coll Suite 1100 Quebec PQ Canada H3A 3C1 (514) 286-5424

FORTIN, JACQUES, law commission administrator; b. Matane, Que., Can., Mar. 10, 1937; s. Louis-De-Gonazague and Georgette (Gregoire) F.; m. Micheline McDuff, May 30, 1964; children: Jean-Francois, Isabelle. B.A., U. Montreal, 1957, LL.M., 1961, diplome d'etudes superieures, 1963, LL.D., 1971. Bar: Que. 1962. Assoc. Cutler, Lachapelle & Lamer, Montreal, Que., Can., 1962-64; prof. law U. Montreal, 1964; project dir. Law Reform Commn. of Can., Ottawa, 1972-74, now v.p.; cons., 1974—. Author: La Preuve Penale, 1984; co-author: Traite De Droit Penal, 1982. Home: 6227 Chemin Deacon Montreal PQ Canada H3S 2P6 Office: 1010 Lagauchetiere St W Place du Canada Suite 310 Montreal PQ Canada H3C 3T1

FORTIN, LUIS HORACIO, banker; b. Buenos Aires, Argentina, Feb. 14, 1920; s. Louis Alexandre and Isabel (Garcia) F.; m. Blanca Isabel Pascual, Sept. 8, 1947. Nat. Pub. Accountant, U. Buenos Aires, 1952; M.B.A., Columbia, 1962, Ph.D., 1967. Airline capt. Argentine Airlines, 1946-61; operations dir., 1952-53; prof. finance U. Buenos Aires, 1967-68; investment officer IFC, Washington, 1968-69; minister plenipotentiary financial affairs Argentine embassy, Washington, 1969-70; sr. investment officer IFC, Washington, 1971—. Served as pilot French Air Force in RAF, 1941-45. Decorated Legion of Honor, Croix de Guerre with 3 palms, France; Distinguished Flying Cross, Eng). Club: Columbia Country (Md.). Home: 2230 47th St NW Washington DC 20007 Office: 1818 H St Washington DC 20433

FORTINBERRY, GLEN W., advertising executive; b. Monticello, Miss., Nov. 22, 1927; s. Charles Lane and Elizabeth (Magee) F.; m. Mildred Bell, Sept. 29, 1951; children—Glen, Charles, Richard. Student, Cornell U., 1945-46; B.S. in Bus. Adminstrn, Northwestern U., 1949. Account exec. Ruthrauff & Ryan, Inc., 1952-57; asst. to pres. Maxon, Inc., Detroit, 1957-60, v.p., 1963-65; also dir.; v.p. D'Arcy Advt. Co., Houston, 1960-63; with J. Walter Thompson Co., N.Y.C., 1965-80, vice chmn., 1977-80; pres., chief operating officer Ross Roy, Inc., Detroit, 1980-81, pres., chief exec. officer, 1981-83, chmn. bd., pres., 1983—. Bd. dirs. Detroit Symphony orch.; exec. com. Boy Scouts Am.; adv. bd. Detroit Inst Arts., Traffic Safety Assn. Served with A.C. U.S. Navy, 1945-46. Recipient Chgo. Tribune award, 1949. Mem. Am. Assn. Advt. Agys. (dir.), Am. Advt. Fedn., U.S. Council of Internat. C. of C., Nat. Council for Children and TV. Clubs: Detroit, Detroit Athletic; Wentworth Golf (London); Bloomfield Hills (Mich.) Country; Yale (N.Y.C.). 1056 Fifth Ave New York NY Office: 2751 E Jefferson St Detroit MI 48207

FORTNER, JOSEPH GERALD, surgical oncologist, educator; b. Bedford, Ind., May 30, 1921; s. Everett Rex and Lula Alice (Robbins) F.; m. Roberta Olson, Nov. 4, 1948; children: Kathleen, Joseph Jr. B.S., U. Ill., 1944, M.D., 1945; M.Sc. in Immunology, Birmingham (Eng.) U., 1965. Diplomate: Am. Bd. Surgery. Intern St. Luke's Hosp., Chgo., 1945-46; resident in pathology Tulane U., New Orleans, 1948-49; surg. resident Bellevue Hosp., N.Y.C., 1949-51, Meml. Hosp., 1952-54, clin. asst. surgeon, asst. to clin. dir., 1955-59, asst. attending surgeon, 1958-66, asso. attending surgeon, 1966-69, attending surgeon, 1969—, chief gastric and mixed tumor service, 1970-78, chief surg. research service, 1978—, asso. chmn. for lab. affairs dept. surgery, 1978—, chief div. surg. research, 1968-77; chief Gen. Motors Surg. Research Lab., 1977—; instr. surgery Sloan-Kettering Inst., N.Y.C., 1954-58, asst. prof. clin. surgery, 1958-64; clin. asst. prof. surgery Cornell U. Med. Coll., N.Y.C., 1964-70, asso. prof. surgery, 1970-72, prof., 1972—. Contbr. articles to profl. jours.; editor Accomplishments in Cancer Research. Pres. Gen. Motors Cancer Research Found., 1978—, also mem., trustee; mem. WHO Collaborating Center for Evaluation of Methods of Diagnosis and Treatment of Melanoma. Served with U.S. Army, 1946-48. Recipient Alfred P. Sloan award Sloan-Kettering Inst. Cancer Research, 1963. Fellow ACS, N.Y. Acad. Scis.; mem. AMA, Pan Am. Med. Assn., AAAS, Am. Assn. Cancer Research, Am. Gastroent. Assn., Am. Radium Soc., Am. Soc. Clin. Oncology, Brit. Soc. Immunology, European Soc. Exptl. Surgery, Harvey Soc., Soc. Surg. Oncology, N.Y. County, N.Y. State med. socs., Am. Surg. Assn., N.Y. Surg. Soc., Soc. Univ. Surgeons, Reticuloendothelial Soc., Am. Soc. Transplant Surgeons, Transplantation Soc., N.Y. Cancer Soc., Sigma Xi, Alpha Omega Alpha. Republican. Club: Metropolitan. Home: 131 E 66th St New York NY 10021 Office: 1275 York Ave New York NY 10021

FORTUNE, PHILIP ROBERT, metal manufacturing company executive; b. Gouverneur, N.Y., Feb. 14, 1913; s. Robert J. and Mary (Cain) F.; m. Margaret E. Burns, Apr. 15, 1944 (div. Aug. 15, 1980); children: Joanne, Terence, David, Christopher, Stephen; m. Kathryn T. Crawford, Oct. 4, 1980. B.A., St. Joseph's Coll., 1933; M.A., Niagara U., 1939. Instr. Niagara U., 1938-40; with N.Y. Air Brake Co. (merged with Gen. Signal Corp. 1967), Watertown, 1940—, gen. mgr., 1955-63, v.p., 1959-65; group exec., 1961-65, pres., 1965-67, chmn. exec. com., 1967-77, cons., 1977—, also dir.; dir. Hamworthy Hydraulics Ltd., 1963-82, chmn. bd., 1971-82; div. Burnham Corp.; trustee Watertown Savs. Bank. Served to lt. col. AUS, World War II; ETO. Home: 18 Stonehouse Rd Scarsdale NY 10583 Office: High Ridge Park Stamford CT 06904

FORTUNE, PORTER LEE, JR., university chancellor emeritus; b. Old Fort, N.C., July, 2, 1920; s. Porter and Eunice (Ross) F.; m. Mary Elizabeth Cummings, Oct. 15, 1944; children: Philip Lee, Peggy Jean, Janet Cummings, Carey Ross. B.A., U. N.C., 1941, Ph.D., 1949; M.A., Emory U., 1946. Instr. Emory U., 1946; teaching asst. U. N.C., 1946-47; faculty Miss. So. Coll., 1949-61, successively asst. prof. history, asso. prof., dean, 1948-57, prof., dean, 1957-61; nat. exec. sec. Nat. Exchange Club, 1961-68; chancellor U. Miss., 1968-84, chancellor emeritus, 1984—; dir. Miss. Bank. Civilian aide to sec. army for Miss., 1971-79; past chmn. Miss. Com. for Humanities; past pres. Southeastern Conf., So. Univ. Conf., Miss. Assn. Colls., So. Assn. Land-Grant Colls. and State Univs.; former chmn. awards jury Freedoms Found. Served as lt. (s.g.) USNR, 1942-46; advisory council Naval Affairs. Decorated Bronze Star, Navy Disting. Public Service award; recipient John R. Emens Nat. award for a Free Student Press; Gov.'s Outstanding Mississippian award; Freedoms Found. George Washington honor medal, 1966; Leadership award dist. 43 Toastmasters Club, 1974; Miss. Disting. Civilian Service medal, 1980; U.S. Disting. Civilian Service medal, 1980. Mem. NEA, Miss. Hist. Soc. (past pres.), Miss. Council Devel. Marine Resources, So. Regional Edn. Bd., So. Assn. Com. on Colls., So. Assn. Colls. and Schs. (nomination and assessment of planning com.), Miss. Art Assn. (trustee), Orgn. Am. Historians, So. Hist. Assn., C. of C., Miss. Com. for Humanities (past chmn.), Phi Alpha Theta, Pi Kappa Delta, Omicron Delta Kappa, Phi Kappa Phi, Pi Gamma Mu, Delta Theta Pi, Alpha Phi Omega, Delta Sigma Pi, Phi Delta Kappa, Pi Tau Chi, Kappa Alpha, Kappa Delta Pi, Delta Pi Epsilon. Methodist. Clubs: Masons (32 deg.), Shriners, Exchange (past pres. Hattiesburg), Exchange (past pres. Miss. chpt.), Exchange (nat. regional v.p.), Exchange (chmn. nat. edn. com.), Exchange (nat. bd. control), Exchange (past nat. pres.), Exchange (Golden award for service 1968). Address: Office of Chancellor Emeritus U Miss University MS 38677

FORTUNE, ROBERT RUSSELL, utility executive; b. Collingswood, N.J., Nov. 22, 1916; s. Colin C. and Minnie M. (Brown) F.; m. Christine E. Dent, Nov. 10, 1956. B.S. in Econs., U. Pa., 1940. C.P.A., Pa. With Haskins & Sells (C.P.A.s), 1940-42, 46-48; with Pa. Power & Light Co., Allentown, 1948—, v.p. fin., 1966-75, exec. v.p. fin., dir., 1975—; dir. Ind. Sq. Income Securities, Inc., Temp. Investment Fund, Inc., Phila. Mfrs. Mut. Ins. Co., Chestnut St. Exchange Fund, Associated Electric and Gas Ins. Services Ltd., Chancellor Tax-Managed Utility Fund, Inc., Municipal Fund for Temporary Investment, Trust for Short-Term Fed. Securities, Realty Co. Pa., Chestnut St. Cash Fund, Service Devel. Co., Safe Harbor Water Power Corp.; mem. tech. adv. com. fin. FPC, 1974-75. Treas. Allentown Sch. Dist. Authority, 1963—. Served in USN, 1942-46. Mem. Fin. Execs. Inst., Am., Pa. insts. C.P.A.s. Republican. Club: Lehigh Country. Home: 2920 Ritter Ln Allentown PA 18104 Office: 2 N 9th St Allentown PA 18101

FORTUNE, WILLIAM LEMCKE, journalist; b. Indpls., Dec. 6, 1912; s. Russell and Elinor (Lemcke) F.; m. Jane Hennessy, Nov. 26, 1938; children: Janie, Pamela, William Lemcke, Richard Hennessy. A.B., Princeton U., 1935. Reporter Ft. Wayne (Ind.) Jour. Gazette, 1936; reporter, polit. writer Indpls. Times, 1937-38; pub. Dunkirk (Ind.) News, 1938-40, Waveland (Ind.) Independent, 1941; acct. Mem. Ind. Gen. Assembly, 1947-48; treas. State of Ind., 1951-53; revenue commr., Ind., 1965-69; Spl. legis. corr. for 48 newspapers; lectr. state tax problems. Author: The Moment, 1979; Contbr. articles on state taxes and internat. trade to newspapers and mags. Campaign dir. Marion County March of Dimes, 1961-62; Bd. dirs. Indpls. Mus. Art, Indpls. Symphony Orch., Butler U., all Indpls. Served from pvt. to sgt. AUS, 1942-46. Office: 7990 Hillcrest Rd Indianapolis IN 46240

FOSBACK, NORMAN GEORGE, stock market econometrician, researcher; b. Astoria, Oreg., July 15, 1947; s. Oscar George and Lucy (Hoagland) F.; m. Myrna Liebowitz, June 13, 1982. B.S., Portland State U., 1969. Pres., research dir. Inst. Econometric Research, Ft. Lauderdale, Fla., 1971—. Author: Stock Market Logic, 1976; fin. newsletter editor: Market Logic, 1975—, New Issues, 1978—, The Insiders, 1980—, Money Fund Safety Ratings, 1981—. Mem. Am. Econ. Assn., Am. Statis. Assn., Econometric Soc., Ops. Research Soc. Am., Common Cause, ACLU. Home: 2600 NE 30th Ave Fort Lauderdale FL 33306 Office: Institute for Econometric Research 3471 N Federal Hwy Fort Lauderdale FL 33306

FOSCO, ANGELO, labor union official. Pres. Laborer's Internat. Union N.Am. Office: 905 16th St NW Washington DC 20006

FOSHOLT, SANFORD KENNETH, consulting engineer; b. Rudd, Iowa, May 11, 1915; s. Harold S. and Marie (Nubson) F.; m. Wilma I. Partington, Sept. 20, 1974; children by previous marriage: Linda Fosholt Clark, Louise Fosholt Jesson, John, Lucinda Fosholt Dyerberg. B.S. in Elec. Engring, Iowa State U., Ames, 1938. Registered profl. engr. Student engr. Stanley Engring. Co., Muscatine, Iowa, 1938-40, elec. engr., 1940-43, engr., 1944-47, head sect. mech. design, 1947-49, chief engr., 1949-50, partner, 1950-66, v.p., 1961-66; partner Stanley Consultants, Muscatine, 1966-81; sr. v.p. Stanley Consultants, Inc., 1966-73, exec. v.p., 1973-81; ret., 1981; instr. Iowa State Coll., 1943-44; Adv. bd. Coll. Engring., State U. Iowa, 1967-71. Mem. Muscatine Planning and Zoning Commn., 1954-65, chmn., 1958; bd. dirs. Muscatine United Fund, 1960-62, Vesterheim (Norwegian Am. mus.), Decorah, Iowa, 1982—, Muscatine Community Sch. Found., 1983—. Named Boss of Year Paddle Wheel chpt. Nat. Secs. Assn., 1968. Fellow ASME; mem. Soc. Am. Mil. Engrs., IEEE, Iowa Engring. Soc. (Distinguished Service award 1966), Nat. Soc. Profl. Engrs., Cons. Engrs. Council Iowa (pres. 1960), Am. Cons. Engrs. Council (pres. 1963-64), Internat. Fedn. Cons. Engrs. (U.S. del. 1965-68), Iowa State U. Alumni Assn. (Alumni of Year award 1962), Tau Beta Pi, Eta Kappa Nu. Lutheran. Club: Elks. Home: 1208 Northwood PO Box 345 Muscatine IA 52761

FOSS, CLIVE FRANK WILSON, history educator; b. London, Aug. 30, 1939; U.S., 1945, naturalized, 1980; s. Victor Albert and Jeanne Francoise (Beurton) W. A.B. magna cum laude, Harvard U., 1961, M.A., 1965, Ph.D., 1973. Instr., U. Mass., Boston, 1967, lectr., 1969, asst. prof., 1973, asso. prof., 1976, prof. history, 1980—; faculty Boston Coll., 1968-69; vis. prof. U. Lyon, France, 1977-79, U. South Africa, 1981; mem. Sardis Expdn., 1969-75, 79-83; dir. Medieval Castles Survey of Anatolia, 1982-83; asso. Ephesus Excavations, 1973-74. Author: Byzantine and Turkish Sardis, 1976, Rome and Byzantium, 1977, Ephesus after Antiquity, 1979; contbr. articles to profl. jours. Norton fellow Am. Sch. Classical Studies, Athens, 1961-62; Am. Council Learned Socs. grantee, 1974, 80; CNRS research assoc., Paris, 1983; NEH fellow, 1975-76; Guggenheim fellow, 1983-84; vis. fellow Dumbarton Oaks, 1973-74, All Souls Coll., Oxford U., 1983-84. Fellow Royal Numis. Soc.; mem. Am. Inst. Archaeology, Am. Numis. Soc., Brit. Inst. Archaeology of Ankara, South African Numis. Soc., Phi Beta Kappa. Republican. Episcopalian. Home: 15 Trowbridge St Cambridge MA 02138 Office: Dept History U Mass Boston MA 02125

FOSS, HARLAN FUNSTON, educator; b. Canton, S.D., Oct. 10, 1918; s. Hans and Thea (Hokenstad) F.; m. Beatrice Naomi Lindaas, Sept. 2, 1943; children—Richard John, Kristi Marie, Marilyn Jean. B.A., St. Olaf Coll., 1940; B.Th., Luther Theol. Sem., 1944; Th.M., Princeton Theol. Sem., 1945; Ph.D., Drew U., 1956; postgrad., Mansfield Coll. Oxford (Eng.) U., 1967, Pontifical Inst. and Gregorian U., Rome, 1974. Ordained to ministry Lutheran Ch., 1944; pastor Mt. Carmel Luth. Ch., Milw., 1944-47; mem. faculty St. Olaf Coll., Northfield, Minn., 1947—, asso. prof. religion, 1954-56, prof., 1957—, v.p., dean coll., 1979-80, pres., 1980—. Mem. Northfield Bd. Edn., 1959-66, treas., 1960-61, chmn., 1961-66. Ezra Squire Tipple fellow, 1951-52. Mem. A.A.U.P., Am. Acad. Religion, Norwegian-Am. Hist. Assn., Blue Key. Republican. Club: Lion. Home: 1215 Saint Olaf Ave Northfield MN 55057

FOSS, JOHN FRANK, mechanical engineering educator; b. Washington, Pa., Mar. 24, 1938; s. Maurice Felker and C. Catharine (Reynard) F.; m. Jacqueline Kay Voss, July 24, 1960; children: Judith Kathleen, Janette Diane. Student, Wilmington Coll., 1956-58; B.S., Purdue U., 1961, M.S., 1962, Ph.D., 1965. Mem. faculty Mich. State U., East Lansing, 1964—, asso. prof. mech. engring., 1968-75, prof., 1975—; cons. Ford Motor Co., Bd. Water and Light, Lansing, Tranter Corp. Author: (with M.C. Potter) Fluid Mechanics, 1975. Mem. Oaks Recreation Program staff, 1976-78; moderator Edgewood United Ch., 1975-77. Sloan fellow John Hopkins U., Balt., 1970-71; Alexander von Humboldt fellow U. Karlsruhe, W. Ger., 1978-79. Mem. ASME, AIAA, AAAS, Am. Soc. Engring. Edn., Am. Phys. Soc., Sigma Xi, Tau Beta Pi, Pi Tau Sigma. Mem. United Ch. of Christ. Home: 4731 Nakoma Dr Okemos MI 48864 Office: Dept Mech Engring Mich State U East Lansing MI 48824

FOSS, LUKAS, composer, conductor, pianist; b. Berlin, Germany, Aug. 15, 1922; came to U.S. from Paris, 1937, naturalized, 1942; s. Martin and Hilde (Schindler) F.; (m); 2 children. Student, Paris Lycée Pasteur, 1932-37; grad., Curtis Inst. Music, 1940; spl. study, Yale, 1940-41; pupil of, Paul Hindemith, Julius Herford, Serge Koussevitzky, Fritz Reiner, Isabelle Vengerova,. Former prof. UCLA (in charge orch. and advanced composition); faculty Harvard U., 1970-71; Founder Center Creative and Performing Arts, Buffalo U. Former condr., music dir., Buffalo Philharmonic; mus. dir., condr., Bklyn. Philharmonic, 1971—; music dir., condr., Milw. Symphony Orch., 1981—, orchestral compositions performed by many major orchs.; best known works include (opera) Griffelkin, Quintets and Night Music for John Lenon.; orch., chamber music, ballets, works commd. by, League of Composers, Nat. Endowment for Arts, N.Y. Arts Council, NBC opera on TV, Am. Choral Condrs. Assn., Ind. U., 1979 Olympics, others.; (recipient N.Y. Critic Circle citation for Prairie 1944, Soc. for Pub. Am. Music award for String Quartet in G 1948, Rome prize 1950, Horblit award for Piano concerto No. 2 1951, Naumburg Rec. award for Song of Songs 1957, Creative Music grant Inst. Arts and Letters 1957, N.Y. Music Critics Circle award for Time-Cycle orch. songs 1961, for Echoi 1963, Ditson award for condr. who has done the most for Am. music 1973, N.Y.C. award for spl. contbn. to arts 1976, ASCAP award for adventurous programming 1979, CRI rec. award for "Thirteen Ways of Looking at a Blackbird 1979). Guggenheim fellow, 1945; Creative arts award Brandeis U., 1983; Laurel leaf award Am. Composers Alliance, 1983. Mem. Nat. Acad. Arts and Letters. Address: 17 E 96th St New York NY 10128

FOSS, PHILLIP OLIVER, political scientist, educator; b. Maxbass, N.D., May 18, 1916; s. Oliver Olson and Petra (Elton) F.; m. Dorothy Marie Hansen, May 31, 1941; children: Coral Lee, Phyllis Ann, Phillip Oliver, Thorvald C. B.A., U. Wash., 1947; M.S., U. Oreg., 1953, Ph.D., 1956. Instr. U. Oreg., 1955-57; asst. prof. San Francisco State Coll., 1957-61, asso. prof., 1961-62, Colo. State U., 1962-64, prof., 1964—, chmn. dept. polit. sci., 1965-72, chmn. Natural Resources Center, 1964-67; cons. Bur. Land Mgmt., U.S. Dept. Interior, 1964-65, 69, Nat. Acad. Scis., 1969-70. Author: Politics and Grass, 1960, Federal Agencies and Outdoor Recreation, 1962, Education in Natural Resources, 1964, Politics and Policies, 1970, Public Land Policy, 1970, Outdoor Recreation, 1971, Politics and Ecology, 1972, Outdoor Recreation and Environmental Quality, 1973, Environment and Colorado, 1974, Institutional Arrangements for Effective Water Management, 1978; Contbr. articles profl. jours. Served with USAAF, 1942-46; to lt. col. USAF, 1951-53. Recipient outstanding service award San Francisco State Coll., 1960, distinguished service award Colo. State U., 1970. Mem. Am. Polit. Sci. Assn., Western Polit. Sci. Assn. (exec. council 1967-69, v.p. 1970-71, pres. 1972-73, outstanding dissertation award 1957), Am. Soc. Pub. Adminstrn. Home: 3019 Moore Ln Fort Collins CO 80526

FOSS, RICHARD WESTLEY, banker; b. Burlington, Vt., June 17, 1926; s. Cleo Justus and Vera (Fullington) F.; m. Marilyn Sias Campbell, Oct. 20, 1951; children: Deane C., Kimberly. B.A., U. Vt., 1949; LL.B., Boston U., 1951. Bar: Vt. 1951. Assoc. Lathan, Hill & Peisch, Burlington, 1951-56; trust officer Howard Nat. Bank & Trust Co., 1956-62; v.p., trust officer Marine Midland Bank, Jamestown, N.Y., 1962-67, Syracuse, Utica, 1967-69, sr. v.p., 1969-71, exec. v.p., N.Y.C., 1975-80, exec. officer trust div., 1975-80; sr. v.p. and chief trust investment officer Continental Ill. Bank & Trust Co., Chgo., 1980—; sr. v.p. Marine Midland Banks, Inc., N.Y.C., 1971-75. Bd. dirs. Charles A. Lindbergh Fund, Inc. Served with USMC, 1944-46. Recipient Distinguished Service award Greater Burlington Jr. C. of C., 1957. Fellow Fin. Analysts Fedn.; mem. N.Y. Soc. Security Analysts, Am., Vt. bar assns., N.Y. State Bankers Assn. (chmn. exec. com. trust div.), Corp. Fiduciaries Assn. (pres.), U. Vt. Alumni Assn. (exec. council). Home: 1565 Hickory Ln Winnetka IL 60093 Office: 30 N LaSalle St Chicago IL 60693

FOSS, THOMAS E., economics labortory executive; b. Litchfield, Minn., Nov. 20, 1934; s. Peter E. and Mary (Connole) F.; m. Joyce F. Hillman, Sept. 14, 1973; children: Theresa, Thomas J., Timothy. B.A., U. Minn., 1961. Acctg. trainee Economics Lab, Inc., St. Paul, 1961-63, accountant to sr. cost accountant, 1963-67, v.p. adminstrn. internat., 1967-73; v.p., treas. Economics Lab. Inc., St. Paul, 1973-76, v.p. corp. planning, 1976-80; sr. v.p. ops. Economics Lab, Inc., St. Paul, 1980—. Served with AUS, 1957-58. Republican. Roman Catholic. Home: 2899 Quadrant Ave S Hastings MN 55033 Office: Economics Lab Inc Osborn Bldg St. Paul MN 55102

FOSS, WILLIAM FRANCIS, manufacturing company executive; b. Mpls., Aug. 5, 1917; s. Peter and Lucinda (Larson) F.; m. Kathryn Bolduc, Feb. 22, 1941; children—Thomas W., Jeffrey J., Kathleen M., Timothy P., Anne Marie, William F. II (dec.). Student, St. Thomas Coll., St. Paul, 1935-36, U. Minn., 1941-42. With Mpls. Moline Inc., Hopkins, Minn., 1941-67; mng. dir. Mpls.-Moline Turk Traktor, 1954-57, controller, v.p., asst. to pres., 1957-59, v.p., treas., 1959-61, sr. v.p., treas., permanent chmn. operating com., 1961-62, pres., chief exec. officer, dir., 1962-67; v.p. White Motor Corp., 1965-67; pres., chief exec. officer, dir. Fabri-Tek, Inc., Mpls., 1967-70; pres., dir. Applied Power Inc., Milw., 1970—; dir. Apache Corp., Hill & Foss, Inc., Atlanta, Gelco Corp., Mpls. Pres., treas. William F. Foss II Meml. Found. Mem. Mpls. C. of C. (pres. 1966, dir.), Nat. Assn. Accountants. Clubs: Minneapolis; Milw. Country, University (Milw.). Home: 4154 N Lake Dr Milwaukee WI 53211 Office: Box 325 Milwaukee WI 53201

FOSSE, BOB, dir., choreographer; b. Chgo., June 23, 1927; s. Cyril K. and Sarah (Stanton) F. Choreographer, dir. musical plays, 1956—, Pajama Game, 1956, Damn Yankees, 1957, Bells Are Ringing, 1958, New Girl in Town, 1958; play Redhead, 1959, Sweet Charity, 1966; film version, 1968, Pippin; stage, 1972, Chicago, 1975, Dancin', 1978; mus. staging How To Succeed in Business Without Really Trying, 1961; choreographer, co.-dir.: Little Me, 1962; actor: Pal Joey, 1961, 63; actor, choreographer: film The Little Prince, 1974; choreographer, dir.: films Cabaret, 1972, All That Jazz, 1979; dir.: film Lenny, 1974 (Recipient Tony award for Pajama Game 1956, Damn Yankees 1957, Redhead 1959, Sweet Charity 1966, Pippin (2) 1972, Dancin 1978, Donaldson award for Pajama Game 1956, Dance Mag. and Tony award for Little Me 1963, Oscar award for Cabaret 1972, 3 Emmy awards for spl. Liza with a Z, Drama Desk award for Pippin 1972). Mem. Soc. Stage Dirs. and Choreographers (treas.). Home: 58 W 58th St New York NY 10019 Office: care Sam Cohn International Creative Mgmt 40 W 57th Street New York NY 10019

FOSSE, E(RWIN) RAY, insurance company executive; b. Marion, Ill., Dec. 3, 1918; s. Erwin Adam and Bessie (Gulledge) F.; m. Lloyd Elisabeth Alexander, Dec. 12, 1941; children: David Ray, Janet D. B.S., U. Ill., 1940, postgrad., 1948-51. Cert. tchr., Ill., Ind. Tchr. city schs., Boonville, Ind., 1940-41, Greenfield, Ill., 1945-52; mgr. farm and crop. ins. dept. CNA Ins., Chgo., 1952-67; mgr., exec. sec. Corp-Hall Ins. Actuarial Assn., Chgo., 1968-83; dir. Fed. Crop. Ins. Corp., U.S. Dept. Agr., Washington, 1981—; mem. food and agr. com. U.S. C. of C., 1979-80. Author: (with others) Reinsurnace, 1980. Served to lt. col. USAAF, 1941-45. Republican. Clubs: Union League of Chgo.; Kankakee Country (Ill.). Lodges: Masons; Lions; Kiwanis. Address: PO Box 99 Goreville IL 62939

FOSSIER, MIKE WALTER, electronics company executive; b. New Orleans, Mar. 30, 1928; s. Louis Joseph and Thelma (Titus) F.; m. Donna Scott, Apr. 16, 1953; children: Michael, Michele, Scott. B.S., La. State U., 1945; M.S., Calif. Inst. Tech., 1946, Profl. Degree, 1947. Aerodynamicist Douglas Aircraft, El Segundo, Calif., 1947-50; guidance engr. Raytheon Co., Oxnard, Calif., 1950-54, project engr., Bedford, Mass., 1954-59, chief engr. Missile System div., 1959-65, v.p., asst. gen. mgr. tech., 1965—. Contbr. articles to profl. jours.; inventor yaw damper, 1950, radome, 1953, missile guidance, 1977. Fellow AIAA (assoc.); mem. IEEE. Office: Hartwell Rd Bedford MA 01730

FOSSUM, JERRY GEORGE, electrical engineering educator; b. Phoenix, July 18, 1943; s. George Clayton and Lillian Edith (McNeilis) F.; m. Candace Rae Schaidt, Aug. 29, 1966 (div. Jan. 1984); children: Kerry Ray, Kelly Lynn. A.A., Phoenix Coll., 1963; B.S. in Elec. Engring., U. Ariz., 1966, M.S., 1969, Ph.D., 1971. Mem. tehc. staff Sandia Labs., Albuquerque, 1971-78; assoc. prof. elec. engring. U. Fla., Gainesville, 1978-80, prof., 1980—; cons. Burr-Brown Research Corp., Tucson, 1970-71, Jet Propulsion Lab., Pasadena, Calif., 1979. Contbr. articles to profl. jours.; assoc. editor: Solid-State Electronics, 1979—; patentee in field. Recipient Outstanding Reserch award Am. Soc. Engring. Edn., 1979, awards U. Fla., 1979, 81, 82. Fellow IEEE. Office: Dept Elec Engring U Fla Gainesville FL 32611

FOSTER, ALAN HERBERT, financial consultant; b. Somerville, Mass., Nov. 7, 1925; s. Herbert and Margaret J. (Griffin) F.; m. Cynthia Ann Brooks, June 26, 1954; children—Mark Brooks, Andrew Herbert. B.S., B.A., Boston Coll., 1951; M.B.A., Harvard, 1953. With Sylvania Electric Products, Inc., 1953-63; with Am. Motors Corp., 1963-77, corp. dir. financial planning and analysis, 1963-67, treas., 1967-68, v.p., treas., 1968-77; pres. A.H. Foster & Co. (Cons. in Corp. Fin.), Ann Arbor, Mich., 1977—, Trade Credit Ins. Services, Inc., Ann Arbor, 1981—, Fin. Risk Mgmt. Inc., 1983—; underwriting mem. Lloyd's of London.; commodity rep., trading adviser. Author: Practical Business Management, 1962, Treasurer's Handbook; also articles. Served with USNR, 1945-46. Mem. Commanderie de Bordeaux, Financial Execs. Inst. (pres. Detroit chpt. 1972-73), Baker Street Irregulars, Speckled Band Boston, Inst. Mgmt. Scis. (past nat. chmn. coll. planning). Clubs: Harvard (Boston); Knickerbocker, India House (N.Y.C.); Ateneo de Madrid (Spain); University (Mexico); Samuel Pepys (London). Home: 810 Earhart Rd Ann Arbor MI 48105 Office: 1327 Jones Dr Ann Arbor MI 48105

FOSTER, ARCHIBALD MCGHEE, advt. exec.; b. East Hampton, N.Y., Aug. 22, 1915; s. Albert V. and Margaret (Baxter) F.; m. Joan Bersbach, Sept. 23, 1938; 1 son, Archibald McGhee. Grad., St. Mark's Sch.; A.B., Harvard, 1938. Promotion dir. Conde Nast Publs., 1940; account exec. A.W. Lewin Co. (advt.), 1946-51; v.p. Cecil & Presbrey (advt.), 1951-54; with Ted Bates & Co., Inc., 1954-76, pres., chief exec. officer, 1965-71, chmn. bd., chief exec., 1971-73, chmn. bd., 1973-76; pres. ARJO Cons., 1976—; Mem. Nat. Bus. Council for Consumer Affairs; also vice chmn. sub-council; Mem. steering com. Nat. Advt. Rev. Bd. Served with USMCR, 1942-46. Mem. Am. Assn. Advt. Agys. (chmn. 1970-71). Home: 925 Park Ave New York City NY 10028 Office: 1 Astor Plaza New York City NY 10036

FOSTER, ARTHUR ROWE, mechanical engineering educator; b. Peabody, Mass., Apr. 22, 1924; s. Francis Joel and Helen Almira (Rowe) F.; m. Nettie Claire Pease, July 12, 1947; children: Jackson Judd, Cynthia Grace. B.S. in Mech. Engring, Tufts U., 1945, M.Engring., Yale, 1949. Registered profl. engr., Mass. Engr. material devel. lab. Pratt & Whitney aircraft div. United Aircraft Corp., 1947-48; mem. faculty Northeastern U., 1949—, prof. mech. engring., 1961—, chmn. dept., 1961-75; Latin Am. teaching fellow Escuela Politecnica Nacional, Quito, Ecuador, 1975-76; Fulbright lectr. solar engring. Colombia, summer 1979. Author: (with R. L. Wright, Jr.) Basic Nuclear Engineering, 1968, 4th edit., 1983, (with Melvin Mark) Thermodynamics: Principles and Applications, 1979. Served to ensign USNR, 1945-46. Mem. ASME (Centennial medal 1980), Am. Soc. Engring. Edn., Am. Nuclear Soc., Internat. Solar Energy Soc., Delta Tau Delta, Pi Tau Sigma, Tau Beta Pi. Home: 26 Strathmore Circle Braintree MA 02184 Office: Northeastern U Boston MA 02115

FOSTER, CHARLES HENRY WHEELWRIGHT, foundation officer; b. Boston, Mar. 18, 1927; s. Reginald Candler and Frances Helen (Hoar) F.; m. Barbara Ann Duchaine, Sept 19, 1953; children: Frances H., Jonathan R., Susan C. B.A., Harvard U., 1951; B.S.F., U. Mich., 1953, M.S., 1956; Ph.D., Johns Hopkins U., 1969; D.P.A. (hon.), Suffolk U., 1971, M.A., Yale U., 1977. Exec. sec. Wildlife Conservation Inc., Boston, 1953-55; cons. Mass. Water Resources Commn., Boston, 1956-59; commr. Mass. Dept. Natural Resources, Boston, 1959-66; pres. Nature Conservancy, Washington, 1966-67; sr. staff mem. Conservation Found., Washington, 1967-68; chmn. bd. N.E. Natural Resources Center, Boston, 1969-70; sec. Mass. Exec. Office Environ. Affairs, Boston, 1971-75; sr. staff mem. A. D. Little, Inc., Cambridge, Mass., 1975-76; prof. environ. policy U. Mass., Amherst, 1975-76; dean Yale U. Sch. Forestry and Environ. Studies, 1976-81; vis. scholar Stanford U., 1981-82; research assoc. U. Calif.-Santa Cruz, 1982; scholar in residence U. Va., 1983; pres. W. Alton Jones Found., Charlottesville, Va., 1983; chmn. Fund for New Eng., 1984; cons and lectr. in field. Trustee of numerous natural resources and ednl. orgns. Served with U.S. Army, 1945-47. Bullard fellow Harvard U., 1969-70. Fellow AAAS; mem. Soc. Am. Foresters, Ecol. Soc. AM., Soil Conservation Soc. Am., Am. Forestry Assn. Clubs: Union, Harvard (Boston); Univ. (Washington); Princeton (N.Y.C.).

FOSTER, DONALD LEE, corp. exec.; b. Bloomington, Ind., Dec. 23, 1932; s. Wayne and Marie (Butcher) F.; m. Janet Faye Lentz, Feb. 25, 1955; children—Julie Ann, Donald Lee, Thomas Gordon. B.S., Ind. U., 1954. C.P.A., Ill. Sr. accountant Arthur Young & Co., Chgo., 1954-61; gen. auditor Internat. Minerals & Chem. Corp., Skokie, Ill., 1961-64, div. controller, 1964-68, group fin. mgr., 1964-69; treas., asst. sec. Bergen Brunswig Corp., Los Angeles, 1969-71; gen. auditor Abbott Labs., North Chicago, Ill., 1971-73, asst. corporate controller, 1973—; Mem. advisory bd. Ind. U. Exec. Program. Served to 1st lt. U.S. Army, 1955-57. Mem. Fin. Execs. Inst., Kappa Delta Rho. Club: Toastmasters (Skokie) (past pres.). Office: Abbott Labs Abbott Park North Chicago IL 60064

FOSTER, EDSON L., mining/mfg. co. exec.; b. Kearny, N.J., Jan. 22, 1927; s. Edson L. and Mary Raye (Jarome) F.; m. Jean C. Slater, June 16, 1951; children—Jill, Lori, Todd, Jody, Cary. B.B.A. cum laude, Pace Coll., 1953. Pub. accountant Pogson & Peloubet, N.Y.C., 1951-57; asst. to controller Stanadyne, Inc., Chgo., 1957-61; asst. comptroller Tex. Gulf Sulphur Co., N.Y.C., 1961-67; v.p., comptroller Anaconda Co., N.Y.C., 1967-77, Phelps Dodge Industries, Inc., 1977-79, Phelps Dodge Corp., 1979—; Mem. Bd. Fin. Wilton, Conn., 1967-72, chmn. bd., 1972. Mem. Fin. Execs. Inst., Nat. Assn. Accts., Am. Inst. C.P.A.'s, N.J. Soc. C.P.A.'s, Am. Mining Congress. Clubs: Mining, Bd. Room. Home: 61 Little Fox Ln Wilton CT 06897 Office: 300 Park Ave New York NY 10022

FOSTER, EDWARD E., educational adminisrator; b. West New York, N.J., Nov. 19, 1939; s. John Conroy and Helen (Fischbach) F.; m. Jan Kennedy, June 4, 1956; children: John Conroy, James Kennedy. A.B., St. Peter's Coll., 1961; Ph.D., U. Rochester, 1965. Prof. English Grinnell Coll., Iowa, 1964-73; dean arts and sci. U. San Diego, 1973-76; chmn. humanities dept. St. Mary's Coll. of Md., St. Mary's City, 1976-79; dean faculty Whitman Coll., Walla Walla, Wash., 1979—; commr. Northwest Assn. Schs. and Colls., Seattle, 1982—. Author: Modern Lexicon of Literary Terms, 1968; contbr. articles on English lit. to profl. jours. Vice pres. Walla Walla Symphony Bd., 1982—. Mem. MLA, Medieval Acad. Am., Am. Assn. Colls., Am. Conf. Acad. Deans. Home: 220 Newell St Walla Walla WA 99362 Office: Whitman Coll Walla Walla WA 99362

FOSTER, ELIZABETH READ, historian, emeritus educator; b. Chgo., June 26, 1912; d. Conyers and Edith (Kirk) Read; m. Richard Wingate Foster, Dec. 31, 1938; children—Richard Coulson, Timothy, Benjamin Read, Daniel Wingate. A.B., Vassar Coll., 1933; A.M., Columbia, 1934; Ph.D., Yale, 1938. Instr., then asso. prof. history Ursinus Coll., Collegeville, Pa., 1953-65; asso. prof. U. Del., 1962-63; acting dir. Yale Parliamentary Diaries project Yale, 1965-66; prof. history Bryn Mawr Coll., 1966-81, prof. emeritus, 1981—, dean, 1966-73. Author: The Painful Labour of Mr. Elsyng, 1972, The House of Lords, 1603-1649, 1983; Editor: Proc. in Parliament 1610, 2 vols, 1966; editorial bd.: Am. Hist. Rev, 1979-81, Yale Center for Parliamentary History, 1966—. Mem. Royal Hist. Soc., Conf. Brit. Studies (council 1968-73, 79—), Middle Atlantic Conf. on Brit. Studies., Am. Hist. Assn. Home: 205 Strafford Ave Wayne PA 19087

FOSTER, EUGENE LEWIS, bus. exec.; b. Clinton, Mass., Oct. 9, 1922; s. George Frank and Georgie Nina (Lewis) F.; m. Mavis Estelle Howard, July 30, 1944; children—Kaye Louise, Eugene Howard, Mark Edward, Carol Anne. B.S.M.E., U. N.H., 1944, M.S., 1951; Mech. E., M.I.T., 1953, Sc.D., 1954. Research engr. Procter and Gamble, Cin., 1946-47; instr. U. N.H., 1947-49; asst. prof. mech. engring. M.I.T., Cambridge, 1950-56; pres., chmn. Foster-Miller Assos., Inc., Waltham, Mass., 1956-72; cons. Office of Sec. of Transp., Washington, 1972-73; chmn. Foster-Miller Assos., 1974—; pres., chmn. bd. UTD Corp., Alexandria, Va., 1976—; mem. U.S. nat. com. for tunneling tech. Nat. Acad. Sci., 1975-79. Author: (with W.A. Wilson) Experimental Heat Power Engineering, 1956; also articles. Mem. Recreational and Environ. Com. Fairfax County, Va., 1976-78. Served with C.E. U.S. Army, 1943-46. Mem. ASME, ASCE, N.Y. Acad. Scis., AAAS, Nat. Soc. Profl. Engrs. Home: 3316 Wessynton Way Alexandria VA 22309 Office: 8425 Frye Rd Alexandria VA 22309 *Success for me is the satisfaction of identifying needs and finding ways to fill them. Recognition, financial rewards, and the other more common measures of success seem to follow naturally, but they are peripheral to the main ingredient, satisfaction from a job well done.*

FOSTER, FRANCES HELEN, actress; b. Yonkers, N.Y., June 11, 1924; d. George Henry and Helen Elizabeth (Lloyd) Brown Davenport; m. Morton Goldsen, Sept. 11, 1982; m. Robert Standfield Foster, Mar. 29, 1941 (dec.); 1 son, Terrell Robert. Student, Am. Theatre Wing, N.Y.C., 1949-52. Artist in residence CCNY, N.Y.C., 1973-77; actress Negro Ensemble Co., N.Y.C., 1967—. Appeared in plays throughout the world including, Munich Olympics, 1972; World Theatre Festival, London, 1969, Australia, 1977. Mem. Actors Equity Assn. (councillor 1953-67), Screen Actors Guild, Am. Fedn. Radio and TV Artists. Democrat. Office: Marje Fields Inc 165 W 46th St New York NY 10036 *The gift of talent I was graced with at birth was not enough. The feeling, the knowing that I had something to offer, to share with the world, was the nucleus that enabled me to grow as an artist. The audience tells me they enjoy and appreciate my work; this is my reward.*

FOSTER, FRANCIS GREGG, JR., aluminum company executive; b. Kansas City, Mo., Fed. 8, 1936; s. Francis G. and Vivian (Pew) F.; m. Nancy R. Ingersoll, Mar. 25, 1965; children: Jennifer, Elizabeth B., Margaret. B.A., U. Mo., 1958; M.B.A., U. Chgo., 1973. Officer United Mo. Bank, Kansas City, Mo., 1959-65; grp v.p. First Nat. Bank Chgo., 1966-82; v.p. Alumaz Inc., San Mateo, Calif., 1982—. Mem. Econ. Club Chgo. Clubs: Kansas City Country (Mo.); Indian Hill Country (Winnetka, Ill.). Office: Alumax Inc 400 S El Camino Real San Mateo CA 94402

FOSTER, G. WILLIAM, JR., lawyer, educator; b. Boston, Nov. 23, 1919; s. George William and Marguerite (Werner) F.; m. Jeanette Raymond, May 26, 1950; children—Susan, Bill, Fred. Student, Antioch Coll., 1937-40; B.S. in Chemistry, Stanford U., 1947; LL.B., Georgetown U., 1951; LL.M., Yale U., 1952. Bar: Wis. bar 1972. Exec. asst. to U.S. Senator, 1949-50; spl. asst. to Sec. of State Dean Acheson, 1951; asst. prof. law U. Wis., Madison, 1952-56, asso. prof., 1956-59, prof., 1959—, asso. dean, 1969-72; reporter Wis. Long-Arm Process Statute, 1955-59; cons. sch. desegregation guidelines HEW, 1965; legal advisor Ministry of Justice, Kabul, Afghanistan, 1976. Served to lt. (j.g.) USN, 1942-46. Mem. Am. Bar Assn., Am. Ornithologists Union, State Bar Wis., Dane County Bar Assn., Am. Law Inst. Democrat. Home: 5616 Lake Mendota Dr Madison WI 53705 Office: 501 Law Bldg U Wis Madison WI 53706

FOSTER, GEORGE ARTHUR, baseball player; b. Tuscaloosa, Ala., Dec. 1, 1948. Student, El Camino Coll., Torrance, Calif. With San Francisco Giants, 1969, 70-71; outfielder with Cin. Reds, 1971-72, 73-88, N.Y. Mets, 1982—; played in All-Star Games, 1976, 77, 78, 79, 81, World Series, 1972, 75, 76. Named Nat. League Player of Year Sporting News, 1976, 77; Nat. League Most Valuable Player, 1977; Most Valuable Player in Allstar Game, 1976. Office: care New York Mets Shea Stadium Flushing NY 11368 *

FOSTER, GEORGE MCCLELLAND, JR., anthropologist; b. Sioux Falls, S.D., Oct. 9, 1913; s. George McClelland and Mary (Slutz) F.; m. Mary Fraser LeCron, Jan. 6, 1938; children: Jeremy, Melissa Bowerman. B.S., Northwestern U., 1935; Ph.D., U. Calif. at Berkeley, 1941. Instr. Syracuse U., 1941-42; lectr. UCLA, 1942-43; vis. prof. U. Calif.-Berkeley, 1953-55, prof. anthropology, 1955-79, prof. emeritus, 1979—, chmn. dept., 1958-61; acting dir. Mus. Anthropology, 1955-57; lectr. pub. health, 1955-64; anthropologist Inst. Social Anthropology, Smithsonian Instn., 1943-52, dir., 1946-1952; field research Calif. Indians, 1937, Spain, 1949-50, Mexico, 1940—; adviser AID, India-Pakistan, 1955, Afghanistan, 1957, Zambia, 1961, 62, Nepal, 1965, Indonesia, 1973-74, WHO, Sri Lanka, 1975, Malaysia, 1978, India, 1979, 80, 81, Manila, 1983, UNICEF, Geneva, 1976. Author: books including Traditional Cultures and the Impact of Technological Change, 1962, Tzintzuntzan: Mexican Peasants in a Changing World, 1967, Applied Anthropology, 1969, (with B. Anderson) Medical Anthropology, 1978; also monographs, articles. Guggenheim fellow, 1949; fellow Center for Advanced Study in Behavioral Scis., 1969-70. Fellow Am. Anthrop. Assn. (pres. 1970, Disting. Service award 1980); mem. Southwestern Anthrop. Assn. (Disting. Research award 1981), Nat. Acad. Scis., Am. Acad. Arts and Scis., Soc. Applied Anthropology (Malinowski award 1982). Club: Cosmos (Washington). Home: 790 San Luis Rd Berkeley CA 94707

FOSTER, HENRY LOUIS, veterinarian, laboratory executive; b. Boston, Apr. 6, 1925; s. Louis and Clara Friedman; m. Lois Ann Foster, June 1948; children: James C., John S., Neal R. D.V.M., Middlesex Coll., 1946. Diplomate: Am. Coll. Lab. Animal Medicine, 1961. Cons. veterinarian UNRRA, 1946-47; founder, pres. Charles river Breeding Labs., Inc., Wilmington, Mass., 1947—; dir. Century Bank & Trust Co.; chmn. vis. com. Tufts Vet. Sch.; chmn. bd. trustees Brandeis U. Contbr. numerous articles to sci. jours.; sr. editor: The Mouse in Biomedical Research, 4 vols. Trustee Boston Mus. Fine Arts, Tufts U.; mem. surgery vis. com. Mass. Gen. Hosp. Paul Harris fellow, 1972. Mem. AVMA, N.Y. Acad. Sci., Am. Assn. Lab. Animal Sci. (Charles A. Griffin award 1976), Am. Coll. Lab. Animal Medicine, Am. Inst. Biol. Scis. Home: 11 Drumlin Rd Newton MA 02159 Office: 251 Ballardvale St Wilmington MA 01887

FOSTER, HENRY WENDELL, medical educator; b. Pine Bluff, Ark., Sept. 8, 1933; s. Henry Wendell and Ivie (Hill Watson) F.; m. St. Clair Anderson, Feb. 6, 1980; children: Myrna Faye, Henry Wendell. B.S., Morehouse Coll., 1954; M.D., U. Ark., 1958. Am. Bd. Ob-Gyn. Chief ob-gyn John Andrew Hosp., Tuskegee, Ala., 1965-73; mem. faculty Meharry Med. Coll., Nashville, 1973—, prof., chmn. dept. ob-gyn; dir. maternal and infant care project Tuskegee Inst., Ala., 1970-73; sr. program cons. Robert Wood Johnson Found., Princeton, N.J., 1981—; chmn. ob-gyn exec. com. Nat. Med. Assn., 1977-79. Mem. editorial bd.: Jour. Med. Edn., 1974-77. Bd. dirs. Planned Parenthood Assn. Am., 1975-81, Alan Guttmacher Inst., N.Y.C., 1975-81. Served to capt. USAF, 1959-61. Fellow Am. Coll. Obstetricians and Gynecologists; mem. Alpha Omega Alpha. Democrat. Am. Baptist. Home: 4140 W Hamilton Rd Nashville TN 37218 Office: 1005 DB Todd Blvd Nashville TN 37208

FOSTER, HUGH WARREN, transportation company executive; b. Crooksville, Ohio, July 9, 1921; s. Frank F. and Grace Myrtle (Coleman) F.; m. Georgette Weiss, Dec. 26, 1954; 1 son, Craig Hugh. Student, Northwestern U. With Pullman Standard Co., Chgo., until 1960, again 1978—, positions held include: advt. mgr., mgr. mktg. services, and sr. v.p. mktg. freight unit, until 1960, sr. v.p. sales and mktg., 1978—; with Pullman Leasing Co., Chgo., 1960—, v.p. mktg., then v.p., gen. mgr., 1965-75, pres., 1975—, also dir.; pres., dir. Bulk Logistics, Inc., 1983—. Clubs: Arts (dir.), Racquet (Chgo.); Chikaming Country (Lakeside, Mich.) (dir.). Home: 666 N Lake Shore Drive Apt 1306 Lake Residence Chicago IL 60611 Office: 40 E Huron St Chicago IL 60610

FOSTER, JAMES HENRY, surgeon, educator; b. New Haven, June 24, 1930; children—John, Lynn, Margaret. A.B., Haverford (Pa.) Coll., 1950; M.D., Columbia U., 1954. Diplomate: Am. Bd. Surgery (dir.). Intern Barnes Hosp., St. Louis, 1954-55; resident in surgery U. Oreg.-Portland (Oreg.) VA Hosp., 1957-61, asst. dir. surgery, 1961-66; asst. prof. surgery U. Oreg., 1961-66; dir. surgery Hartford (Conn.) Hosp., 1966-78; prof. surgery, chmn. dept. U. Conn. Med. Sch., Farmington, 1978—. Co-author: Solid Liver Tumors, 1977. Served to capt. M.C. USAF, 1955-57. Mem. A.C.S., Am. Surg. Assn., Soc. Surg. Oncology, New Eng. Surg. Soc. (sec.). Office: Dept Surgery U Conn Health Center Farmington CT 06032

FOSTER, JODIE (ALICIA CHRISTIAN FOSTER), actress; b. Los Angeles, Nov. 1962; d. Lucius and Evelyn (Almond) F. Student, Yale U. Acting debut: TV show Mayberry, R.F.D, 1969; numerous other TV appearances, including My Three Sons, The Courtship of Eddie's Father, Gunsmoke, Bonanza, Paper Moon, 1974-75; TV spl. The Secret Life of T.K. Dearing, 1975; TV movies Rookie of the Year, Smile, Jenny, You're Dead; motion picture appearances Napoleon and Samantha, 1972, Menace of the Mountain, One Little Indian, 1973, Tom Sawyer, 1973, Kansas City Bomber, 1972, Alice Doesn't Live Here Any More, 1975, Taxi Driver, 1976 (Acad. award nominee Best Supporting Actress), Echoes of a Summer, 1976, Bugsy Malone, 1976, Freaky Friday, 1976, The Little Girl Who Lives Down the Lane, 1977, Candleshoe, 1977, Foxes, 1980, Carny, 1980, Hotel new Hampshire, 1984. Office: care Ufland Agy Inc 190 N Canon Dr Beverly Hills CA 90210 *

FOSTER, JOE B., oil company executive; b. Arp, Tex., July 25, 1934; s. William R. and Ruth D. (Knox) F.; m. Mary Alice Warren, Feb. 1, 1958; children: Warren, Ken, Jennifer. B.S. in Petroleum Engring., Tex. A&M U., 1957, B.B.A. in Gen. Bus., 1957. Jr. petroleum engr. Tenneco Oil Co., Oklahoma City, 1957-59, petroleum engr., Lafayette, La., 1959-62, dist. engr., 1962-66, adminstrv. asst. to exec. com., Houston, 1966-68, chief econ. planning and analysis, 1968-70, mgr. exploration, 1970-72, v.p., 1972-74, sr. v.p., 1974-76, exec. v.p., 1976-78, pres. Tenneco Oil Exploration and Prodn., 1978-81; exec. v.p. Tenneco, Inc., 1981—, dir., 1983—; dir. Tenneco Offshore Co. Served to 2d lt. U.S. Army, 1958. Mem. Soc. Petroleum Engrs. of AIME, Am. Petroleum Inst. Methodist. Clubs: Houston, The Houstonian, Met. Racquet (Houston). Office: Box 2511 Houston TX 77071

FOSTER, JOHN HORACE, cons. environ. engr.; b. Quincy, Mass., June 2, 1927; s. Horace Herbert and Alice Gertrude (Hatch) F.; m. Claire Alice Sabean, Aug. 31, 1952; children—Janet, Mark, David. B.S., Tufts U., 1952; M.S., Harvard U., 1953. Engr. Malcolm Pirnie Engrs., White Plains, N.Y., 1953-63, partner, 1963—, pres., 1970—. Contbr. articles in field to profl. jours. Served with USN, 1945-47. Recipient Distinguished Service award Dept. Civil Engring. Tufts U., 1977. Mem. Am. Acad. Environ. Engrs., Water Pollution Control Assn., TAPPI, Am. Water Works Assn., Harvard Engring. Soc., Am. Cons. Engrs. Council, ASCE. Club: Cedar Point Yacht. Home: 53 Farrell Rd Weston CT 06880 Office: 2 Corporate Park Dr White Plains NY 10602

FOSTER, JOHN STANTON, consulting engineer; b. Halifax, N.S., Can., June 14, 1921; s. Stanton Ray and Mabel Rose (Davies) F.; m. Margaret Charlotte Lane, Oct. 9, 1948; 1 dau., Margaret Anne. Dipl. Eng., Dalhousie U., 1941; B.Eng., N.S. Tech. Coll., 1943, Dr.Eng., 1967; Dr.Eng., Carleton U., 1967. With Montreal Engring. Co., Ltd., 1946-54, asst. chief mech. engr., 1952-54; head nuclear design Can. Gen. Electric Co., 1955-58; gen. mgr. power projects Atomic Energy of Can. Ltd., 1958-66, v.p., 1966-74, pres., 1974-77; v.p. Monenco Ont. Ltd., Toronto, 1978—. Served to lt. Royal Can. Navy, 1943-45. Fellow Royal Soc. Can., Engring. Inst. Can.; mem. Assn. Profl. Engrs. Ont. (mem. council 1970-73), World Energy Conf. (chmn. program com.), Can. Nat. Com. World Energy Conf. (past chmn.), Can. Nuclear Assn. (past chmn.). Clubs: Engrs., Rideau. Home: 10 Thornbury Crescent Islington ON Canada Office: 2 Saint Clair Ave E Toronto ON M4T 2T5 Canada *Faith in people has enabled me to rely on one person doing what, without it, would have required two and taken twice as long; to rely on a handshake or a single page of contract instead of a dozen or more; to look to the future with optimism; and to expect to recover a watch left in a railway station.*

FOSTER, JOSEPH W., III, industrial engineer; b. Waco, Tex., Feb. 25, 1938; s. Joseph W. F.; m. Lucille Terry, July 15, 1961; children: Nancy Karen, Joseph W. B.S. in Mech. Engring., So. Meth. U., 1961; M.S. in Indsl. Engring., Lehigh U., 1965; D.Engring., U. Okla., 1968. Registered profl. engr., Tex., Okla. Prodn. engr. Western Electric Co., Oklahoma City, 1961-63, research engr., Princeton, NJ, 1963-65, sr. computer specialist, Oklahoma City, 1965-66; instr. U. Okla., 1966-67, vis. asst. prof., 1968; mem. faculty Tex A&M U, College Station, 1968—; prof. indsl. engring. Tex. A&M U., College Station, 1975—, head indsl. engring., 1977—; mem. producability assessment space shuttle team Marshall Space Flight Ctr., Huntsville, Ala. Mem. Am. Inst. Indsl. Engrs. (sr.), Am. Soc. Quality Control (sr.), Am. Waters Works Assn. Methodist. Home: 801 Rosemary St Bryan TX 77801 Office: Dept Indsl Engring Tex A&M U College Station TX 77843

FOSTER, JULIAN FRANCIS SHERWOOD, educator; b. London, July 27, 1926; U.S., 1953; s. George Sherwood and Norah Patrickson

(Langford) F.; m. Beatrice Ingrid Joerer Lindner, Feb. 22, 1957; children—Hugh, Fiona, Jennifer. B.A. with first class honours, New Coll., Oxford, 1951, M.A. (English Speaking Union fellow, Fulbright scholar), 1955; Ph.D., UCLA, 1963. Asst. prof. polit. sci. U. Santa Clara, Calif., 1957-61; asst. prof. polit. sci. Calif. State U., Fullerton, 1963-65, asso. prof., 1965-70, prof., 1970—, chmn. faculty council, 1966-67, acad. senator, 1971-78, dept. chmn., 1978—; Am. Council on Edn. intern univ. adminstrn. Princeton, 1967-68. Author: None Dare Call it Reason, 1964; Editor and frequent contbr. to: Reason: A Review of Politics, 1965-66; editor, contbr. to: Protest: Student Activism in America, 1970. Served with Royal Navy, 1945-47. Mem. English Speaking Union, Sierra Club. Home: 12593 Vista Panorama Santa Ana CA 92634 Office: Polit Sci Dept Calif State U Fullerton CA 92634

FOSTER, LAWRENCE, opera director; b. Los Angeles, 1941. Student, Bayreuth Festival Masterclasses; studied with, Fritz Zweig. Debut as condr., Young Musicians' Found., Debut Orch., 1960; condr., mus. dir., 1960-64; assoc. condr., San Francisco Ballet, 1964-65; asst. condr., Los Angeles Philharmonic Orch., 1965-68; chief guest condr., Royal Philharmonic Orch., Eng., 1969—; guest condr., Houston Symphony, 1970-71; condr. in chief, 1971-72; music dir., 1972-78, Nat. Orch. of Monte Carlo Opera, 1979—; gen. music dir., Duisburg & Dusseldorf Opear (Ger.), 1982—; guest condr. orchs. in, U.S. and Europe. (Recipient Koussevitsky Meml. Conducting prize 1966), U.S. and Europe. (Eleanor R. Crane Meml. prize Berkshire Festival, Tanglewood, Mass. 1966). Office: care Harrison/Parrott 12 Penzance London W11 England *

FOSTER, LLOYD ELMORE, JR., furniture mfg. co. exec.; b. Hopkinsville, Ky., Sept. 28, 1917; s. Lloyd Elmore and Minnie Luella F.; m. Mary Louise Foster, Feb. 9, 1944; 1 son, Mark Lloyd. B.S., Auburn U., 1939. Salesman Armstrong Cork Co., Atlanta, 1940-41, Memphis, 1945-47, asst. dir. bur. merchandising, Lancaster, Pa., 1947-52, mgr., 1952-54, mgr. felt base sales, 1954-57, mgr. linoleum and corlon sales, mktg. mgr. floor div., 1957-61, gen. mgr. consumer products div., 1962-66; gen sales mgr. Armstrong Internat., 1967-69; exec. v.p. Thomasville Furniture Industries, Inc., N.C., 1969—; dir. Home Savs. and Loan of Thomasville. Pres. YMCA, Thomasville. Served to maj. U.S. Army, 1940-45. Decorated Bronze Star (2). Methodist. Home: 601 Valley Rd Thomasville NC 27360 Office: Thomasville Furniture Industries Inc Thomasville NC 27360

FOSTER, LUTHER HILTON, college president; b. Lawrenceville, Va., Mar. 21, 1913; s. Luther Hilton and Daisy (Poole) F.; m. Vera Chandler, Aug. 27, 1941; children—Adrienne Maria, Luther Hilton III. B.S., Va. State Coll., 1932, LL.D., 1959; B.S., Hampton Inst., 1934; M.B.A., Harvard U., 1936; M.A., U. Chgo., 1941, Ph.D., 1951; Dr. Pub. Service, Adams (Colo.) State Coll., 1957; LL.D., U. Liberia, 1958, U. Mich., 1967, Colby Coll., 1971, U. Ala., 1978, Tuskegee Inst., 1981; H.L.D., Loyola U., Chgo., 1970, Northeastern U., 1974. Budget officer Howard U., 1936-40; bus. mgr. Tuskegee Inst., 1941-53, pres., 1953-81, pres. emeritus, 1981—; dir. Norton Simon Inc.; Mem. bd. So. Regional Council; mem. Overseas Devel. Com. Bd. dirs. United Negro Coll. Fund, Coll. Retirement Equities Fund; trustee March of Dimes Birth Defects Found., Acad. Edn'l. Devel., Ga. Warm Springs Found., Coll. Retirement Equities Fund, Center Creative Leadership; mem. vis. com. Harvard U. Bus. Sch. Recipient Alumni award Hampton Inst., 1954. Mem. Phi Delta Kappa, Alpha Kappa Mu, Alpha Phi Alpha, Sigma Pi Phi Boule. Home: 309 Yoakum Pkwy Apt 1507 Alexandria VA 22304

FOSTER, MARY CHRISTINE, TV production company executive; b. Los Angeles, Mar. 19, 1943; d. Ernest A. and Mary (Quilici) F.; m. Paul Hunter, 1982. B.A. magna cum laude, Immaculate Heart Coll., 1967; M.Journalism in TV News Documentary, UCLA, 1968. Tchr. parcochial scis. (while mem. Immaculate Heart of Mary Community), Piedmont, Santa Barbara and La Puente, Calif., 1963-65; dir. tchrs. Pacific U., 1968; dir. research Metromedia Producers Corp., Los Angeles, 1968-71; dir. prodn. services and devel. Wolper Orgn., Los Angeles, 1971-76; mgr. film porgrams NBC TV Network, Burbank, Calif., 1976-77; dir. movies and longforms Columbia Pictures TV, Burbank, 1977-79, v.p. movies for TV, 1979-81, v.p. series programming, 1981; v.p. program devel. Group W. Prodns. Westinghouse Broadcasting Corp., University City, Calif., 1981—. Bd. dirs. Archdiocesan Communications Commn., 1977-80; alumnae pres., bd. dirs. Immaculate Heart High Sch., 1971-72, trustee, 1977—. Recipient Archbishop Cantwell award for gen. scholastic and service excellence, 1967, Disting. Student award Kappa Tau Alpha, 1968; named Outstanding Student of Yr. Sigma Delta Chi, 1968. Mem. Women in Film (dir. 1976-77), Cath. Press Council So. Calif., Acad. TV Arts and Scis., Kappa Gamma Phi, Delta Epsilon Sigma. Democrat. Home: 2367 W Wilver Lake Dr Los Angeles CA 90039

FOSTER, MAURICE BRYDON, Canadian legislator; b. Bloomfield, Ont., Can., Sept. 8, 1933; s. Dunam N. and Agnes Mary (Anderson) F.; m. Janet Catherine Kerr, Aug. 20, 1955; children: Peter, Andrew, Peggy, James. D.V.M., Ont. Vet. Coll., Guelph, 1957. M.P. Ho. of Commons, Ottawa, Ont., Can., 1968—, chmn. privileges and elections com., 1980—. Liberal. Mem. United Ch. Home: 3011 Linton Rd Ottawa ON Canada Office: House of Commons Ottawa ON Canada K1A 0A6

FOSTER, PAUL, playwright; b. Pennsgrove, N.J., Oct. 15, 1931; s. Elderidge M. and Mary (Manning) F. B.A., Rutgers U., 1954; LL.B., St. John's U., 1958. Pres. La Mama Theater Club, N.Y.C., 1962—; tchr. drama dept. NYU, N.Y.C., 1983. Recipient (Play award Irish Univs. 1967, 71, N.Y. Drama Critics award 1968, Tony award nominee 1973, Brit. Arts Council award 1973); Author: The Birthday Party Stories, 1962, Hurrah for the Bridge, 1963, The Recluse, 1964, Balls, 1964, Madonna In the Orchard, 1965, The Hessian Corporal, 1966, Tom Paine, 1967, Heimskringla, 1969, Satyricon, 1970, Elizabeth I, 1971, Silver Queen Saloon, 1972, Marcus Brutus, 1973-74, Murderers' Row, 1976, A Kiss is Just a Kiss, 1983; (TV) The Tragedy of the Commons, 1979, The Vampyre and Dr. Frankenstein, 1980; (film) Andrew Mellon and the National Gallery of Art, 1980, Cop and the Anthem, 1982, Smile, 1983, Cinderella Story, 1984; translator: (Horvath) Back & Forth, Faith, Hope, Charity, 1983. Served with USNR, 1955-57. Rockefeller Found. fellow, 1967-68; Creative Artists Pub. Service grantee, 1972; Nat. Endowment Creative Writing fellow, 1973; Guggenheim fellow, 1974; U.S. Dept. State lecture tour, 1975. Mem. Eugene O'Neill Meml. Theater Found., New Dramatists, Dramatists Guild. Address: 242 E 5th St New York NY 10003

FOSTER, PAUL DAVID, JR., agri-business executive; b. Greenville, Miss., Dec. 18. 1929; s. Paul David and Iva Frances (Evers) F.; m. Ida Vivian Taylor, Aug. 14, 1953; children: John Taylor, Karen Amanda. B.S. in Agrl. Adminstrn., Miss. State U., 1952. Pres., Paul D. Foster Co., Blytheville, Ark., 1953-66; regional mgr. Riverside Chem. Co., Blytheville, 1966-71, sales mgr., Memphis, 1971-73, exec. v.p., 1973-79, pres., 1979-80, also dir.; v.p. retail ops. Terra Chem. Co., 1980—; mem. Ark. Plant Bd., 1967-71; past pres. Ark. Agrl. Pesticide Assn. Mem. Blytheville City Council, 1961-71. Served with AUS, 1952-53; Korea. Mem. Nat. Agrl. Chems. Assn. (dir.), Res. Officers Assn. Republican. Presbyterian. Club: Sioux City Country. Home: 3900 Sylvian Way Sioux City IA 51104 Office: Box 1828 Sioux City IA 51102

FOSTER, PAUL MARVEL, lawyer, accountant; b. Middletown, Ohio, Mar. 13, 1926; s. Joseph Buck and Charlotte (McConnell) F.; m. Jean H. Uhland, Sept. 16, 1951; children—Judith C., Douglas P., Daniel M. B.S., Ohio State U., 1950; J.D., N.Y. U., 1968. Bar: N.Y. State bar 1968, Fla. bar 1968; C.P.A., Va. Staff SEC, 1954-65; ptnr. Main Lafrentz & Co. (C.P.A.s), N.Y.C., 1965-70, Coopers & Lybrand (C.P.A.s), 1970—. Author: Machine Accounting for Small Business, 1956, Asset Disclosure for Stockholder Decisions, 1968; co-author: Accounting for Business Lawyers, 3rd Edit., 1984. Trustee Pop Warner Jr. League Football. Recipient William H. Churchill award for excellence in acctg. lit. Nat. Assn. Accts., 1957. Mem. ABA (mem., sec. com. on law and acctg.), Assn. Bar City N.Y., Am. Inst. C.P.A.s, Order Crown of Charlemagne, Huguenot Soc. Fla. Lutheran. Club: Union League (N.Y.C.). Home: 10701 Deneale Pl Fairfax VA 22032 Office: 1251 Ave of Americas New York NY 10020

FOSTER, RICHARD, journalist; b. Chgo., Oct. 16, 1938; s. James Edward and Mary (Sebat) F. B.A., Lawrence Coll., 1963. Reporter City News Bur., Chgo., 1963-64; reporter Chgo. Sun-Times, 1964-72, editorial writer, mem. editorial bd., 1972-78; editorial writer Des Moines Register & Tribune, 1978-82, Milw. Jour., 1983—; journalist-in-residence Colo. State U., spring 1982. Served with AUS, 1958-61. Nat. Endowment for Humanities profl. journalism fellow Stanford U., 1976-77. Home: 5315 42 St NW Washington DC 20015 Office: 645 Nat Press Bldg Washington DC 20045

FOSTER, ROBERT FRANCIS, communications executive; b. Chgo., June 4, 1926; s. William John and Anna Alice (O'Farrell) F.; m. Mary D. Palella, May 4, 1963; children: Sean Terence, Nancy Marie, Patrick Daniel. Student, Cath. schs., Chgo. and Evanston, Ill. News and sports writer Sta. WGN, Chgo., 1943-55; with Chgo. Pub. Relations Counselors, 1955-60, WGN Continental Broadcasting Co., Chgo., 1960-82, news bur. chief, Springfield, Ill., 1961-63, new bur. chief, Washington, 1964-82; press sec. to Ill. Congressman Philip M. Crane, 1982—. Served with AUS, 1944-46. Decorated Combat Inf. badge; recipient award best pub. service news Am. Coll. Radio Arts, Crafts and Scis., 1961. Mem. Radio-TV Corr. Assn. Washington (pres. 1976), Broadcast Pioneers. Roman Catholic. Club: Chgo. Press. Home: 5718 Marble Arch Way Alexandria VA 22310

FOSTER, ROBERT LAWSON, judge; b. Putnam, Okla., Nov. 17, 1925; s. Mark M. and Jessie Marie (Gregory) F.; m. Mary Jo Hull, July 1, 1949; children—Candace Ann (Mrs. Mike Grey), Martha Denise (Mrs. Gerald Speed), Karen Sue (Mrs. John Greenfield), Robert L., John Michael, Cynthia Kay. B.A., U. Okla., 1949, LL.B., 1950, J.D., 1970. Bar: Okla. bar 1950. Practice in, Chandler, 1950-51, county judge, Lincoln County, Okla., 1951-69; asso. dist. judge 23d Jud. Dist., Chandler, Okla., 1969—. Chmn. dist. council Boy Scouts Am., 1968-69; chmn., an organizer Chandler Combined Appeal, 1954—; sec., pres. Lincoln County Jr. League Baseball, 1960-68; county dir. Civil Def., 1953-70; ordained deacon Catholic Ch. of Okla., 1979. Served with USAF, 1944-45. Mem. Lincoln County Bar Assn. (pres. 1965, sec. 1960-64, 67-69, 70-73), C. of C. (sec. 1964-68), Okla. Assn. County Judges (sec.-treas. 1964-67). Clubs: Lion (dir. 1964-65, pres. 1967), Lion (treas. 1968-70), Lion (zone chmn. 1973-74), Lion (dep. dist. gov. 1974—), Chandler Parents.). Home: 415 Steele St Chandler OK 74834 Office: Court House Square Chandler OK 74834

FOSTER, ROBERT WATSON, legal educator; b. Charleston, S.C., Sept. 24, 1926; s. Thomas Russell and Pamela (Watson) F.; m. Marjorie Ann O'Neil, May 22, 1953; children: Elizabeth, Marjorie, Robert, Mary, Patrick, Pamela. B.S., U.S. Mcht. Marine Acad., 1948; LL.B., U. S.C., 1950; LL.M., Duke U., 1951; Ford Found. fellow, Yale Sch. Law, 1959-60. Bar: S.C. 1950, U.S. Supreme Ct 1950, U.S. Ct. Mil. Appeals 1950. From instr. to prof. law U. Louisville, 1950-62; prof. law U. S.C., Columbia, 1962—, Am. Coll. Trial Lawyers prof., 1979-82, Strom Thurmond prof., 1982—, dean, prof. law, 1970-76; Inst. Advanced Legal Studies U. London, 1976-77, N.Y. Law Sch., 1976-77; mem. labor panel Fed. Mediation and Conciliation Service, Am. Arbitration Assn., Nat. Acad. Arbitrators (com. on profl. responsibility and grievances, com. on legislation); mem. com. bankruptcy rules Jud. Conf. U.S., 1978—; commr. Nat. Conf. Commrs. on Uniform State Laws, Am. Law Inst.; mem. S.C. Jud. Council, 1970-76. Author books on uniform comml. code.; Contbr. articles to profl. jours. Served with U.S. Mcht. Marine, 1944-48; Served with USN, 1952-54; capt. Res. Recipient Whitney North Seymour award Am. Arbitration Assn., 1979. Mem. Am. Bar Assn. (com. on uniform comml. code, labor arbitration com., com. on state regulation of securities), S.C. Bar (gov. 1974-76, com. on comml. law 1979—), Assn. Am. Law Schs. (com. on accreditation, chmn. S.E. conf.), AAUP (pres. U. S.C. chpt. 1966-67), Phi Delta Phi. Clubs: Kosmos, Forest Lake Country, Summit, Carolina Yacht. Home: 1509 Milford St Columbia SC 29206

FOSTER, RUEL ELTON, English educator; b. Springfield, Ky., Nov. 30, 1916; s. Ruel Elton and Emily Bird (Russell) F.; m. Margaret Mary O'Connor, Aug. 30, 1947; children: Russell Edward, Mary Alethaire, David Ruel, Emily Frances, Robert Joseph, Paul Thomas. A.B., U. Ky., 1938, M.A., 1939; Ph.D., Vanderbilt U., 1941. Mem. faculty W.Va. U., 1941-42, 46—, prof. English, 1956—, chmn. dept., 1967-74, Benedum prof. Am. lit., 1974—. Author: Jesse Stuart, 1969, also articles, short stories, poems; co-author: Work in Progress, 1948, William Faulkner: A Critical Appraisal, 1951, Elizabeth Madox Roberts, American Novelist, 1956; Editor: Appalachian Literature, Critical Essays, 1976. Served to 1st lt. AUS, 1942-46. Ford Found. fellow, 1952-53; W.Va. U. Found. fellow, 1960; Benedum writing grantee, 1965. Mem. AAUP, Modern Lang. Assn., Internat. Assn. U. Profs. English, Phi Beta Kappa. Republican. Roman Catholic. Home: 1100 Windsor Ave Morgantown WV 26506

FOSTER, STEPHEN KENT, banker; b. St. Louis, Dec. 14, 1936; s. John William and Josephine Fladune (Bushman) F.; m. Rosanne Pleier, Sept. 13, 1958; children: John Andrew, Stephanie Mary. B.B.A., U. Wis., 1959, M.B.A. (H.B. Earhart fellow), 1964. Asst. export mgr. Cargill, Inc., Portland, Oreg., 1959-61; with First Nat. Bank of Oreg. (now First Interstate Bank of Oreg.), Portland, 1964-81, sr. v.p. loan adminstrn., 1973-75, sr. v.p. br. and loan adminstrn., 1975-76, exec. v.p., 1976-81, First State Bank Oreg. (now Pacific Western Bank), Milwaukie, 1981-82, pres., chief operating officer, dir., 1983—; sr. v.p. Pacwest Bancorp, 1981—; dir. Medford Corp. Bd. dirs. United Cerebral Palsy of N.W. Oreg., 1967-80; bd. dirs. Oreg. Council on Econ. Edn., 1970-80, Portland Opera Assn., 1970-74, United Way of Columbia-Willamette, 1973-75, Oreg. Ind. Coll. Found., 1983—; bd. regents U. Portland, 1976—, mem. fin. com., 1976-78, mem. exec. com., 1979—, chmn. acad. affairs com., 1980—, chmn. presdl. rev. com., 1981. Served with U.S. Army, 1958, 61-62. Recipient Service to Legal Edn. award Oreg. Bar Assn., 1971, Ednl. and Service award Bank Adminstrn. Inst., 1971. Mem. Portland C. of C., Oreg. Assn. Credit Mgmt. (Leadership and Service award 1973), Am. Bankers Assn., Robert Morris Assos., Am. Fin. Assn., Nat. Assn. Accountants (Ednl. and Service award 1971), Phi Beta Kappa, Phi Kappa Phi, Phi Eta Sigma, Beta Gamma Sigma, Sigma Chi. Clubs: Arlington; University (Portland); Waverley Country. Office: 10888 SE Main St Milwaukie OR 97222

FOSTER, WILLIAM CHAPMAN, bus. exec., ret. govt. ofcl.; b. Westfield, N.J., Apr. 27, 1897; s. Jed S. and Anna Louise (Chapman) F.; m. Beulah Robinson, May 9, 1925; 1 son, Seymour Robinson. Student, Mass. Inst. Tech., 1918; LL.D., Syracuse U., 1957, Rutgers U., 1968, Bowdoin U., 1968, Yale, 1969; D.Pub. Service, George Washington U., 1963; H.L.D., Kenyon Coll., 1968. Officer, dir. Pressed and Welded Steel Products Co., Inc., 1922-46; under-sec. commerce, 1946-48; dep. U.S. spl. rep. ECA, 1948-49, dep. adminstr., 1949-50, adminstr., 1950-51; dep. sec. def., 1951-53; pres. Mfg. Chemists Assn., Inc., 1953-55; exec. v.p., dir. Olin Mathieson Chem. Corp., 1955-58, dir., v.p., sr. adviser, 1958-61; chmn. bd., pres. United Nuclear Corp., 1961; dir. U.S. ACDA, 1961-69; chmn. bd. Porter Internat. Co., 1970—; Chief U.S. rep. 18th Nation Disarmament Conf., 1962-69; U.S. del. UN, 1964-66, 68; U.S. rep. UN Disarmament Commn., 1965. Served with U.S. Army, World War I; dir. purchases div. Army Services Forces and spl. rep. Under-sec. of War on procurement for USAAF, World War II. Decorated U.S. Medal for Merit; recipient commendations for civilian service from War Dept. Def., Disting. Honor award ACDA, 1969. Mem Arms Control Assn. (chmn. bd. until 1981), Bus. Council (hon.). Clubs: Metropolitan, Cosmos, Chevy Chase (Washington). Home: 3304 R St NW Washington DC 20007

FOSTER, WILLIAM EDWIN (BILL FOSTER), basketball coach; b. Ridley Park, Pa., Aug. 19, 1930; s. Howard M. and Viola Jane (Beaston) F.; m. Shirley Ann Junkin, June 17, 1957; children: Vicki R., Debra Jo, Julia Ann, Mary K. B.S., Elizabethtown Coll., 1954; M.E.D., Temple U., 1957. Coach, tchr. Chichester (Pa.) High Sch., 1954-57, Abington (Pa.) High Sch., 1957-60; coach, instr. Bloomsburg (Pa.) State Coll., 1960-63; head basketball coach Rutgers U., New Brunswick, N.J., 1963-71, U. Utah, Salt Lake City, 1971-74; head basketball coach, asst. athletic dir. Duke U., Durham, N.C., 1974-80, U. S.C., Columbia, 1980—; co-owner Pocono All-Star Sports Resort, Inc., East Stroudsburg, Pa. Trustee Basketball Hall Fame. Served with USAF, 1951-52. Named Nat. Coach of Yr. Sporting News-Playboy Mag., 1978; S.C. Coach of Yr., 1981. Mem. Nat. Assn. Basketball Coaches (past pres., co-coach of yr. 1978), Nat. Speakers Assn. Home: 112 Southlake Rd Columbia SC 29204 Office: U SC Columbia SC 29208

FOTI, MARGARET A., association executive, editor; b. Phila., Dec. 15, 1944; d. Samuel A. and Margaret (DiBiase) F. B.A., Temple U. Tech. editor U. Pa., Phila., 1962-64, asst. to bus adminstr., 1964-65; sr. editorial asst. Cancer Research Jour., Phila., 1965-69; mng. editor Cancer Reserch Jour., Phila., 1969—; exec. dir. Am. Assn. Cancer Research, Phila., 1982—; cons. program devel. Internat. Union Against Cancer; editorial cons., lectr. in field. Contbr. articles to profl. jours. Recipient Cert. of Appreciation Am. Assn. Cancer Research, 1975. Mem. Internat. Fedn. Sci. Editors, Council Biology Editors, Soc. Sch. Publs., Assn. Sci. Editors, Am. Assn. Clin. Research, Council Engrs. and Sci. Soc. Execs., AAAS, Profl. Conf. Mgmt. Assn. Democrat. Roman Catholic. Home: 220 Locust St Apt 24A Philadelphia PA 19106 Office: Am Assn Cancer Reserch Temple Univ Sch Med West Bldg Rm 301 Broad and Tioga Sts Philadelphia PA 19140

FOUHY, EDWARD MICHAEL, TV news executive; b. Boston, Nov. 30, 1934; s. Joseph Timothy and Mary (Herlihy) F.; m. Barbara Mahoney, Apr. 15, 1961; children: Beth Anne, Mark Edward. B.A., U. Mass., 1956; M.S., Boston U., 1960. News writer sta. WBZ-TV, Boston, 1959-61, news dir., 1963-66, sta. WBZ, Boston, 1961-63; with CBS News, 1966-74, 78—, bur. chief, Washington, 1978-81, v.p., dir. news, N.Y.C., 1981-82; v.p., Washington bur. chief ABC News, 1982—; producer NBC Nightly News, 1974-76; bur. dir. NBC News, Washington, 1976-77. Served to capt. USMCR, 1956-59. Decorated Commendation medal; recipient Emmy award Nat. Acad. TV Arts and Scis., 1973, Drew Pearson award investigative reporting, 1973. Mem. Radio-TV News Dirs. Assn., Sigma Delta Chi. Roman Catholic. Club: Fed. City (Washington). Office: ABC News 1717 DeSales Street Washington DC 20036

FOULKE, WILLIAM GREEN, banker; b. Whitemarsh, Pa., Nov. 20, 1912; s. Walter Longfellow and Helen (Pardee) F.; m. Louisa Lawrence Wood, Nov. 2, 1934; children: Louisa Lawrence Foulke Newlin, Walter Longfellow, William Green. A.B., Princeton U., 1934. Asst. treas. Provident Trust Co., Phila., 1940-41, trust officer, 1945-50, v.p., 1950-57; sr. v.p. charge trust div. Provident Tradesmens Bank and Trust Co., Phila., 1957-60, exec. v.p., 1960-62, pres., 1962-64, Provident Nat. Bank, Phila., 1964-69, chmn. chief exec. officer, 1969-74; chmn., chief exec. officer Provident Nat. Corp., 1969-73, chmn., 1973-74, Pardee Mgmt. Co.; chmn. bd., dir. Pardee & Curtin Lumber Co. Gen. chmn. United Campaign, 1975. Served to lt. comdr. USNR, 1941-45. Mem. Pa. Bankers Assn. (pres. 1970-71). Episcopalian. Clubs: Racquet, Philadelphia (Phila.); Ivy (Princeton). Home: 321 Evergreen Ave Philadelphia PA 19118 Office: Pardee Co 1510 Two Girard Plaza Philadelphia PA 19102

FOULKES, LYN, artist, educator; b. Yakima, Wash., Nov. 17, 1934; m. Katie Foulkes; children—Laurey, Jenny. Student, Central Wash. Coll., 1952-53, U. Wash., 1954, Chouinard Art Inst., 1957-59. Prof. art U. Calif. at Los Angeles. Resident painter, Art Center Sch., Los Angeles. (Recipient Los Angeles County Mus. Purchase grant 1963), Art Center Sch., Los Angeles. (1st prize (gold medal) Paris Biennale 1967); Exhibited group shows, Los Angeles County Mus. Art, 1960, 61, 63, 67, 73, Pomona (Calif.) Coll., 1961, San Francisco Mus. Art, 1961, 63, 68, 76, Pasadena (Calif.) Art Mus., 1964, 68, 70, 73, São Paulo, Brazil, 1964, 66, Allan Frumkin Gallery, Chgo., 1964, N.Y. Worlds Fair, 1965, U. Mich., U. Ill., Mus. 20th Century, Vienna, Guggenheim Mus., 1966, 78, Mus. Modern Art, N.Y.C., 1966, 76, Whitney Mus., N.Y.C., 1967, 69, 70, 71, 74, 77, Robert Frazier Gallery, London, 1966, São Paulo Biennale, 1968, Paris Biennale, 1967, Mus. Modern Art, Paris, Seattle Art Mus., 1968, Portland (Oreg.) Art Mus., San Francisco Mus., 1968, 76, Brandeis U., 1968, traveling exhbn., Found. Maeght, France, 1968, Art Council London, Eng., U. Nev., 1969, Va. Mus., Richmond, 1970, Inst. Contemporary Art, Phila., 1972, Art Inst. Chgo., 1972, 74, 75, 77, Los Angeles County Art Inst., 1971, Los Angeles Municipal Art Gallery, 1973, 76, Los Angeles Inst. Contemporary Art, 1975, 76, 79, Visual Arts Mus., N.Y.C., 1975, Aldridge Mus. Contemporary Art, Ridgefield, Conn., Corcoran Gallery, Washington, Gallery Darthea Speyer, Paris, 1975, 78, U. Tex., 1977, Nat. Collection Fine Arts, Washington, others, Mus. Contemporary Arts, Chgo., 1976, 78, retrospective, 1978, one man shows, Nelson Gallery, 1963, 64, Oakland (Calif.) Art Mus., Ferus Gallery, 1961, Pasadena Art Mus., 1962, Rolf Nelson Gallery, Los Angeles, 1966, David Stuart Gallery, Los Angeles, 1969, 73, 74, Galerie Danthea Speyer, Paris, 1970, 75, Willard Gallery, N.Y.C., 1975, Gruenebaum Gallery, Ltd., N.Y.C., 1977, retrospective exhbn., Newport Harbor Art Mus., Newport Beach, Calif., 1974; represented in permanent collections, Mus. 20th Century, Vienna, LaJolla (Calif.) Mus. Art, Los Angeles County Mus. Art, Oakland Art Mus., Pasadena Art Mus. (now Norton Simon Mus.), Whitney Mus., Mus. Modern Art, N.Y.C., Mus. Modern Art, and Paris, Mus. Modern Art, Stanford, Mus. Modern Art, Palo Alto, Chgo. Art Inst., Beaubourg Mus., Paris, Mus. Boymans, Rotterdam, Guggenheim Mus., N.Y.C., Newport Harbor Art Mus., Newport Beach, Calif. Served with AUS, 1954-56. Guggenheim fellow, 1977. Address: care Gruenebaum Gallery 25 E 77th St New York NY 10021 *

FOUNTAIN, L.H., former congressman; b. Leggett, N.C., Apr. 23, 1913; s. Lawrence H. and Sallie (Barnes) F.; m. Christine Dail, May 14, 1942; 1 dau., Nancy Dail. A.B. (Wiley P. Mangum Oratorial medal), U. N.C., 1934, J.D. (Mary D. Wright Debate medal 1935), 1936, LL.D. hon., 1981. Bar: N.C. 1936. Reading clk. N.C. Senate, 1936-41; mem. 83d-97th congresses from 2d N.C. Dist., mem. fgn. affairs com., chmn. inter-govtl. relations and human relations subcom. of govt. operations com.; mem. U.S. del. 22d session UN Gen. Assembly, 1967, Presdl. Adv. Com. on Federalism. Mem. exec. com. East Carolina council Boy Scouts Am.; State senator 4th Senatorial Dist., Gen. Assembly, 1947-52; Pres. Edgecombe Young Democratic Club, 1940; eastern organizer Young Dem. Clubs of N.C., 1941; past chmn. exec. com. 2d Congl. Dist.; elder Presbyterian Ch., unbroken Bible class attendance, 1916—. Served to maj. AUS, 1942-46.; lt. col. Res. (ret.). Elected Tarboro's Man of Year, 1948; recipient citation for distinguished pub. service N.C. Citizens Assn., 1971; Distinguished Service award U. N.C. Sch. Medicine, 1973, N.C. League Municipalities, 1976; Distinguished Services to Higher Edn. and Scholarly Community award Am. Assn. Univ. Presses, 1975; Leadership and Disting. Service award Assn. Fed. Investigators, 1978; Person of Yr. award Inst. Internal Auditors, 1979. Mem. N.C. Bar Assns., Edgecombe County Bar Assn., N.C. Farm Bur., N.C. Grange, Am. Legion. Democrat. Lodges: Kiwanis (lt. gov. 6th N.C. div.,). Home: Tarboro NC 27886 Office: 1102 Panola St Tarboro NC 27886

FOUNTAIN, PETER DEWEY, JR. (PETE FOUNTAIN), clarinetist; b. New Orleans, July 3, 1930. Operator night club Pete Fountain's, New Orleans. Mem., Basin St. Six, 1949-54, Lawrence Welk Orch., 1957-60; now leader own group; appeared in: films Pete Fountain Sextet, 1962, Pete's Place, 1966, The New Orleans Jazz Museum, 1967; featured in: PBS spl. Dukes of Dixieland and Friends, 1980, Pete; featured guest with major orchs. throughout world.; Co-author: A Closer Walk: The Pete Fountain Story, 1972; rec. 84 albums. Address: As Was 2 Poydras St New Orleans LA 70140

FOUNTAIN, ROBERT ROY, JR., naval officer; b. Norfolk, Va., Jan. 25, 1932; s. Robert Roy and Hilda (Burton) F.; m. Elizabeth Whitmarsh Bean, June 4, 1955; children: Robert, Dorothy, Sally, Edwin. Student, U. Rochester, 1950-51; B.S. Engring. with distinction, U.S. Naval Acad., 1955. Commd. ensign U.S. Navy, 1955, advanced through grades to rear adm., 1980; new constrn. engr. officer U.S.S. John C. Calhoun, 1963-65; exec. officer U.S.S. Scorpion, 1965-67; program mgr. nuclear power personnel Bur. Naval Personnel, 1968-70; comdg. officer U.S.S. Sea Devil, 1970-74; dep. chief of staff for tng., staff Comdr. Submarine Force Atlantic Fleet, Norfolk, Va., 1974-76; comdr. Submarine Devel. Squadron 12, New London, Conn., 1976-78; dep. asst. chief naval ops. for submarines Attack Submarine Div., OPNAV, Pentagon, Washington, 1978-79, comdr. U.S. Naval Forces Marianas comdr. U.S. Naval Base Guam comdr. in chief Pacific rep. for, Guam and Trust Ter. Pacific Islands, 1979-81; asst. dep. chief naval sea systems command, ASW and undersea warfare systems Navy Dept., Washington, 1981—. Decorated Legion of Merit (2), Meritorious Service medal (2), Navy Commendation medal. Home: 3653 N 38th St Arlington VA 22207 Office: Asst Dep Chief Naval Sea Systems Command Navy Dept Washington DC 20360

FOURAKER, LAWRENCE EDWARD, museum executive; b. Bryan, Tex., Oct. 28, 1923; s. Leroy L. and Laura (Broach) F.; m. Patricia Orr, June 14, 1949; children: Senter Elizabeth, Lawrence Anderson. B.A., Tex. A.&M. Coll., 1947, M.S., 1948; Ph.D., U. Colo., 1951; M.A. (hon.), Harvard U., 1963. Instr. U. Wyo., 1948-49; from asst. prof. to prof. Pa. State U., 1951-61; faculty Harvard U. Bus. Sch., 1961—, prof. bus. adminstrn., 1962—, dir. div. research, 1968-70, George Fisher Baker prof. bus. adminstrn., 1970-80, dean Bus. Sch., 1970-80; chmn. Boston Mus. Fine Arts, 1983—. Author: (with S. Siegel) Bargaining and Group Decision Making, 1960, Bargaining Behavior, (with H. Bierman and R. Jaedicke) Quantitative Analysis for Business Decisions, 1961. Served with AUS, 1943-46. Home: 80 Fernwood Rd Chestnut Hill MA 02167

FOURCADE, XAVIER, art dealer; b. Paris, Sept. 20, 1926. Student, Polit. Sci. Sch., Paris, U. Paris, Sch. Oriental Langs., Paris, U. Paris Sch. Advan. Studies, Paris, Oxford U. V.p., dir. M. Knoedler & Co., Inc., N.Y.C., 1966-72; pres. Fourcade Droll Inc., N.Y.C., 1972-76, Xavier Fourcade Inc., 1976—. Mem. Art Dealers Assn. Am. Office: Xavier Fourcade Inc 36 E 75th St New York NY 10021 *

FOURNEY, MICHAEL E., engineering educator, consultant; b. Blue Jay, W.Va., Jan. 30, 1936; m. Patricia; 1 dau., Michelle. B.S., W. Va. U., 1958; M.S., Calif. Inst. Tech., 1959, Ph.D., 1963. Registered profl. engr., Wash., Calif. Engr. Gen. Electric Co., Cin., 1957, Douglas Aircraft Co., Santa Monica, Calif., 1958, Boeing Aircraft Co., Seattle, 1959, research engr., 1961, 63-64; engr. Boelkow Entwicklungen KG, Munich, W. Germany, 1963-64; asst. prof. U. Wash., Seattle, 1964-69, assoc. prof., 1969-72; dir. engring. Math. Scis. Corp., Seattle, 1965-72; assoc. prof. UCLA, 1972-76, prof., 1976—, chmn. dept. mechanics and structures, 1979-83; cons. engr. Southwest Engrs., Seattle, Rocket Research Corp., Washington, U.S. Army, N.H., USN (Port Hueneme, Army Missile Command), Ala., Math. Scis. Corp., Seattle, Seattle U., Washington. Contbr. articles to profl. publs. Recipient B.S. Lazan award Soc. for Exptl. Stress Analysis, U. Wash. faculty; fellow and research grantee NASA, NSF, U.S. Army, USAF, U. Wash., NASA Ames, Hubbes Sea World. Mem. ASME, Optical Soc. Am., Soc. for Exptl. Stress Analysis (nat. past pres.), 8th U.S. Nat. Congress Applied Mechanics (treas.), Reunion Internationale des Laboratoires d'Ensais des Materianx Com., Sigma Xi, Sigma Gamma Tau, Tau Beta Pi. Home: 32060 1/2 Pacific Coast Hwy Malibu CA 90265 Office: UCLA 405 Hilgard Ave Los Angeles CA 90265

FOURNIER, SERGE RAYMOND-JEAN, orch. condr.; b. Mayet, France, Sept. 28, 1931; came to U.S., 1961, naturalized, 1969; s. Raymond and Genevieve (Brisset) F. Grad., Conservatoire Nat. Superieur de Musique, Paris, 1956; student, Berkshire Music Center, 1961-62, Friedelind Wagner's Master Class, Bayreuth, 1963; D.F.A. (hon.), U. Toledo, 1974. Lic. comml. pilot, flight instr. Flutist, Lamoureux Orch., France, 1958-60; condr., Compagnie Madeleine Renaud and Jean Louis Barrault, Theatre de France, 1960; asst. to Leonard Bernstein, condr., N.Y. Philharmonic Orch., 1962, 63; music dir., condr., Toledo Symphony Orch., 1964-79, guest appearances, Radio Diffusion and Television Francaise, Paris, 1963, Orch. Grand Casino de Vichy, 1957, 58, Berkshire Music Festival, 1961; guest condr. in, Europe, U.S., Mexico City, Japan and, Can.; (Recipient Premiere Medaille de Solfege 1948, Premier Prix de Flute 1949, Premier Prix d'Histoire de la Musique 1951, Premier Prix d'Ensemble Instrumental 1952, Premier Prix de Direction d'Orchestre 1956, Deuxieme accessit de Contrepoint 1956, Koussevitzky Meml. Conducting prize 1961, decorated chevalier Ordre des Arts et Lettres (France). Served in French Army, 1952-54. Named One of Ten Outstanding Young Men Toledo C. of C., 1965. Club: Rotary. Home: 1454 Beacon Street Boston MA 02146

FOUSEK, PETER, banker; b. Prague, Czechoslovakia, Nov. 13, 1923; came to U.S., 1948; s. Frantisek and Helena F.; m. Adrienne Albee, Jan. 27, 1948; children: Elizabeth Kendall, John Howard, Christopher Albee. B.A., Cambridge U., (Eng.), 1946; M.A., Columbia U., 1949, Ph.D., 1959. With Fed. Res. Bank N.Y., N.Y.C., 1950—, v.p. personnel, 1968-73, equal opportunity officer, 1971-73, econ. adviser, 1973-76, v.p., 1977-78, dir. research, 1977—, sr. v.p., 1979-82, exec. v.p., 1983—; staff economist Council of Econ. Advisers, Washington, 1960-61; adj. prof. Columbia U. Grad. Sch. Bus., N.Y.C., 1974-75; lectr. in field. Author: Foreign Central Banking: The Instruments of Monetary Policy, 1957; contbr. articles to profl. jours. Mem. adv. com. N.Y. State Health Care Capital Adv. Com.; mem. Mamaroneck Human Rights Commn., (N.Y.), 1970—, chmn., (N.Y.), 1974-79; mem.tax adv. com. Mamaroneck Sch. Bd., 1970-75; coach Larchmont Little League, (N.Y.), 1968-75. Served with Czechoslovak Army, 1942-45; Western Europe. Mem. Council on Fgn. Relations, Am. Econ. Assn. Club: Larchmont Shore. Home: 21 York Rd Larchmont NY 10538 Office: Fed Res Bank NY 33 Liberty St New York NY 10045

FOUST, ALAN SHIVERS, educator; b. Dublin, Tex., June 26, 1908; s. Charles George and Carrie E. (Lattimore) F.; m. H. Elizabeth Aigler, Nov. 29, 1939 (dec. Aug. 1980); children—H. Patricia, Alan S., Carolyn E., Charles William. B.S., U. Tex., 1928, M.S., 1930; Ph.D., U. Mich., 1938. Chemist Magnolia Petroleum Co., Beaumont, Tex., 1930-32; devel. engr. Tex. Pacific Coal & Oil Co., 1932; asso. prof. chemistry Tex. Coll. Mines (now U. Tex., El Paso), 1935-36; instr. chem. engring. U. Mich., 1937-39, asst. prof., 1939-46, asso. prof., 1946-48, prof. chem. engring., 1948-52, Lehigh U., Bethlehem, Pa., 1952—, head dept., 1952-62, dean, 1962-65, McCann prof. chem. engring., 1965-77, prof. emeritus, 1977—. Author: (with G.G. Brown and others) Unit Operations, 1950, Evaporation and Crystallization, 1955, (with others) Principles of Unit Operations, 1960, 2d edit., 1980; also articles. Served to lt. col., Chem. Corps AUS, 1942-46. Decorated Legion of Merit. Fellow Am. Inst. Chem. Engrs.; mem. Sigma Xi, Delta Kappa Epsilon, Tau Beta Pi, Phi Lambda Upsilon, Phi Kappa Phi. Club: Mason (Shriner). Home: 917 Prospect Ave Bethlehem PA 18018 also Whitaker Lab 5 Lehigh U Bethlehem PA 18015 *When I chose a career of teaching, I was aware of the expected shortcomings as well as the rewards. I can't say I never wavered, but I can now look back at the many young men whom I had a chance to help in growing up, and to become good citizens. That exceeds the short-falls in a few directions.*

FOUTS, DANIEL FRANCIS, professional football player; b. San Francisco, June 10, 1951; s. Robert Oliver and Carolyn Doris (Morgan) F.; m. Juliane Mehl, Apr. 16, 1977; children: Dominic Daniel, Suzanne Marie. B.S., U. Oreg., 1973. Quarterback San Diego Chargers, 1973—. Named to NFL Pro Bowl, 1980-84. Address: San Diego Chargers San Diego Stadium PO Box 20666 San Diego CA 92120 *

FOWINKLE, EUGENE W., physician, medical center administrator; b. Memphis, Sept. 2, 1934; m. Ruby; children: Greta, Frieda, Brenda. Student, Southwestern U., 1952-55; M.D., U. Tenn., 1958; M.P.H., U. Mich., 1962. Intern City of Memphis Hosps., 1959; resident in neurosurgery Bapt. Meml. Hosp., Memphis, 1960; dir. communicable disease control Memphis and Shelby County Health Dept., 1962-65, asst. dir., 1965-66, dir., 1966-69; clin. instr. U. Tenn., 1964-65, asst. prof., 1965-74, clin. prof. community medicine, 1974-83; commr. pub. health State of Tenn., 1969-83; assoc. vice chancellor for med. affairs Vanderbilt U. Med. Center, Nashville, 1983—; mem. Nat. Adv. Com. Occupational Safety and Health, 1976—; mem. adv. com. Nat. Center for Health Statistics, 1974—. Contbr. articles to profl. jours. Mem. Milbank Meml. Fund Commn. on Higher Edn. in Pub. Health, 1972-75. Recipient Pres.'s award Tenn. Hosp. Assn., 1983, Disting. Service award Memphis Med. Soc., 1982, U. Tenn. Coll. Medicine Alumni Assn., 1982; named Physician of Yr. Tenn. Assn. for Home Health, 1983. Mem. AMA, Am. Pub. Health Assn. (governing council 1969, Charles Jordan award 1972, governing council so. br. 1965-69), Am. Coll. Preventive Medicine (regent 1974-78), Am. Assn. Pub. Health Physicians (past pres.), Assn. State and Territorial Health Officials (chmn. health reporting system adv. com. 1972-74, pres. 1975, McCormack award 1980), Tenn. Med. Assn. (ho. dels., Disting. Service award 1983), Nashville and Davidson County Med. Soc., Jaycees (named Man of Year Tenn. 1967). Office: Vanderbilt U Med Center Nashville TN 37232

FOWKE, EDITH MARGARET FULTON, author; b. Lumsden, Sask., Can., Apr. 30, 1913; d. William Marshall and Margaret (Fyffe) Fulton; m. Franklin George Fowke, Oct. 1, 1938. Student, Regina Coll., 1929-31; B.A. with high honors in English and history, U. Sask., 1933; M.A. in English, U. Sask., 1938; LL.D. (hon.), Brock U., 1974; D.Litt., Trent U., 1975, York U., 1982. Editor Western Tchr., Saskatoon, Sask., 1937-45; asso. editor Mag. Digest, Toronto, Ont., 1945-50; free lance writer CBC Radio, 1950-71; asso. prof. English York U., Downsview, Ont., 1971-77, prof., 1977—. Author: Folk Songs of Canada, 1954, Folk Songs of Quebec, 1957, Songs of Work and Freedom, 1960, Canada's Story in Song, 1960, Traditional Singers and Songs from Ontario, 1965, More Folk Songs of Canada, 1967, Lumbering Songs from the Northern Woods, 1970, Sally Go Round the Sun, 1969, Penguin Book of Canadian Folk Songs, 1974, Folklore of Canada, 1976, Ring Around the Moon, 1977, Folktales of French Canada, 1979, Sea Songs and Ballads from Nineteenth Century Nova Scotia, 1981, Bibliography of Canadian Folklore in English, 1982; editor: Songs and Sayings of an Ulster Childhood by Alice Kane, 1983, Can. Folk Music Jour, 1973—. Decorated Order Can. Fellow Am. Folklore Soc., Royal Soc. of Can.; mem. English Folk Dance and Song Soc., Assn. Can. U. Tchrs. English, Can. Assn. U. Tchrs., Can. Folk Music Soc. (exec. com.). Home: 5 Notley Pl Toronto ON M4B 2M7 Canada Office: Ross Bldg 4700 Keele St Downsview ON M3J 1P3 Canada

FOWLER, BARBARA HUGHES, classicist; b. Lake Forest, Ill., Aug. 23, 1926; d. Fay Orville and Clara (Reber) Hughes; m. Alexander Murray Fowler, July 14, 1956; children—Jane Alexandra, Emily Hughes. B.A., U. Wis., 1949; M.A., Bryn Mawr Coll., 1950, Ph.D., 1955. Instr. classics Middlebury (Vt.) Coll., 1954-56; asst. prof. Latin Edgewood Coll., Madison, Wis., 1961-63; mem. faculty U. Wis., Madison, 1963—, prof. classics, 1976—, John Bascom prof., 1980—. Contbr. articles to profl. jours. Fulbright scholar, Greece, 1951-52; Fanny Bullock Workman travelling fellow, 1951-52. Mem. Am. Philol. Assn., Archaeol. Inst. Am., Classical Assn. Middle West and South. Home: 1102 Sherman Ave Madison WI 53703 Office: 902 Van Hise Hall Univ Wis Madison WI 53706

FOWLER, BEN B., lawyer; b. Hopkinsville, Ky., Mar. 9, 1916; s. William Thomas and Ila (Earle) F.; m. Eleanor Randolph, Oct. 19, 1940. B.S. in Commerce, U. Ky., 1937; LL.B., U. Va., 1940. Bar: Ky. bar 1940. Atty. firm Fowler & Fowler, Lexington, 1940-41; asst. atty. gen., Ky., 1945-47; mem. firm Dailey & Fowler, Frankfort, Ky., 1948-71, Stites, McElwain & Fowler, Frankfort and Louisville, 1972-83, Stites & Harbison, 1983—; city solicitor, Frankfort, 1958-60; chief counsel Ky. Civil Code Com., 1953; chmn. Ct. Appeals Adv. Com. Civil Rules Procedure, 1953-73; Vice pres., gen. counsel, dir. Frankfort & Cin. R.R. Pres., dir. Community Service, Inc.; Adv. com. Ky. Ednl. TV. Fellow Am. Coll. Trial Lawyers; mem. Am. Judicature Soc., ABA (ho. of dels. 1955-60), Ky. Bar Assn. (bd. bar commrs. 1953-60, pres. 1959-60, Outstanding Service award 1954), Franklin County Bar Assn. (pres. 1969), Frankfort C. of C. (pres. 1957-58, chmn. indsl. devel. 1958-59), Ky. C. of C. (bd. dirs.), Delta Tau Delta, Phi Alpha Delta. Presbyn. (deacon 1947-53, elder 1953—). Clubs: Rotary (pres. Frankfort 1952-53), Frankfort Country (dir. 1953-56), Frankfort Country (v.p. 1955). Home: 110 Reservoir Dr Frankfort KY 40601 Office: McClure Bldg Frankfort KY 40601

FOWLER, CHARLES ALBERT, electronics engineer; b. Centralia, Ill., Dec. 17, 1920; s. Clarence J. and Bess (Maxwell) F.; m. Kathryn Elizabeth Grimes, Oct. 23, 1943; children: Patricia Ann, Mary Catherine. B.S. in Engring. Physics, U. Ill., 1942. Mem. staff radiation lab. MIT, 1942-45; head radar systems dept. Airborne Instruments Lab., Deer Park, N.Y., 1946-66; dep. dir. (tactical warfare) def. research and engring. Dept. Def., 1966-70; v.p., mgr. equipment devel. labs. Raytheon Co., Sudbury, Mass., 1970-76; v.p., gen. mgr. Bedford (Mass.) ops. Mitre Corp., 1976—; mem. sci. adv. com. Def. Intelligence Agy., 1971—, chmn. sci. adv. com., 1976-82; mem. Air Force Sci. Adv. Bd., 1971-77, Def. Sci. Bd., 1972—. Contbr. articles in field. Mem. East Norwich Sch. Bd., 1955-61, East Norwich Library Bd., 1956-62. Fellow IEEE, AAAS; assoc. fellow AAAS. Home: 15 Woodberry Rd Sudbury MA 01776 Office: Mitre Corp Bedford MA 01730

FOWLER, CHARLES ALLISON EUGENE, architectural engineer; b. Halifax, N.S., Can., Jan. 24, 1921; s. Charles Allison and Mildred (Crosby) F.; m. Dorothy Christine Graham, Aug. 30, 1947; children: Graham Allison, Beverly Anne. B.Sc., Dalhousie U., 1942; B.Eng., McGill U., 1944; B.Arch., U. Man., 1948; D.Eng. (hon.), N.S. Tech. Coll., 1975. With C.A. Fowler, Bauld & Mitchell, Ltd. (and predecessor firms), Halifax, 1946-80, sr. partner, 1950-70, pres., 1970-80, chmn., 1980-81; pres. C.A. Fowler & Co., 1981—; dir. Tidal Power Corp.; mem. standing com. energy conservation in bldgs. NRC; mem. Energy Sector and Constrn. Sector Voluntary Planning N.S. Prin. works include Miners Mus., Glace Bay, N.S., Dalhousie U. Fine Arts Center, 1970, Dartmouth Gen. Hosp., univ. centers Acadia U., St. Francis Xavier U., Acad. Center at Mt. St. Vincent U., Halifax Law Cts., Mt. St. Vincent Residential Village, Canadian Martyrs Ch., Halifax Metro Center, Stadacona Hosp., Victoria Gen. Hosp. Served with Can. Army, 1943-45. Fellow AIA (hon.), Royal Archtl. Inst. Can. (pres. 1965); mem. Engring. Inst. Can., Assn. Profl. Engrs. N.S., N.S. Assn. Architects (past pres.), Arbitration Inst. of Can., N.S. Mus. Fine Art (pres. 1971, 72, 74), Royal United Service Inst. Mem. United Ch. Clubs: Halifax (Halifax); Royal Nova Scotia Yacht Squadron. Home: 2 Hall's Rd Halifax NS B3P 1P3 Canada Office: 7001 Mumford Rd Suite 3030 II Halifax NS B3L 4R3 Canada

FOWLER, CONRAD JOHN, electronics company executive; b. Phila., Dec. 23, 1921; s. Charles Thomas and Katherine (Sauter) F.; m. Julia Basala, Nov. 24, 1945; children—Deborah Fowler Rollins, Janet Fowler Grey. B.S. in Elec. Engring, U. Pa., 1943. Lab. mgr. research dept. Moore Sch., U. Pa., Phila., 1946-50; co-founder, v.p. Am. Electronic Labs., Inc., Lansdale, Pa., 1950-65, exec. v.p., chmn. bd., 1965-82; chmn. bd. Am. Electronics Labs., Inc., 1982—. Bd. dirs. North Penn Hosp., Lansdale; trustee Abington (Pa.) Bapt. Ch., 1971—. Served to lt. USNR, 1943-46. Mem. IEEE, Nat. Security Indsl. Assn. (v.p. 1972-74, trustee 1974—), Sigma Xi, Sigma Tau. Clubs: Union League (Phila.); Mfrs. Golf and Country (Oreland, Pa.). Patentee in field. Office: PO Box 552 Lansdale PA 19446

FOWLER, CONRAD MURPHREE, manufacturing company executive; b. Montevallo, Ala., Sept. 17, 1918; s. Luther J. and Elsie (Murphree) F.; m. Virginia Evelyn Mott, June 15, 1945; children: Conrad, Randolph. B.S., U. Ala., 1941, LL.B., 1948. Bar: Ala. 1948. Practiced in, Columbiana, 1948-53; mem. firm Ellis and Fowler, 1948-53; dist. atty. 18th Jud. Circuit Ala., 1953-59; probate judge Shelby County Ct., Columbiana, 1959-77; dir. pub. affairs West Point-Pepperell, Inc., 1977—; Mem. Presdl. Adv. Commn. on Intergovtl. Relations, 1970-77. Mem. Ala. Democratic Exec. Com., 1966-77; chmn. Ala. Constl. Commn., 1970-76, Shelby County Commn., 1959-77; bd. dirs. Associated Industries Ala., 1979—, Public Affairs Council, 1979—; v.p. Am. Lung Assn., 1980-82, pres., 1982-83; mem. council Nat. Mcpl. League, 1976—. Served to col. USMCR, 1941-46. Decorated Silver Star with gold star, Purple Heart (2); named to Ala. Acad. Honor, 1981. Mem. Nat. Assn. Counties (pres. 1969-70), Assn. County Commrs. Ala. (pres. 1970-71), Probate Judges Assn. Ala. (pres. 1968-69). Club: Rotary. Home: PO Box 568 Lanett AL 36863 Office: PO Box 71 West Point GA 31833

FOWLER, DANIEL EISON, lawyer; b. Hopkinsville, Ky., Nov. 20, 1908; s. William Thomas and Ila (Earle) F.; m. Louisa Bickel, Apr. 14, 1932; 1 son, Robert Bickel. B.A., U. Ky., 1932, J.D., 1933. Bar: Ky. bar 1933. Since practiced in, Lexington; partner Fowler & Fowler, 1933-52, Fowler & Bell, 1952-54, Fowler, Bell, Cox & Hancock, 1958-59, Fowler, Rouse, Measle & Bell, 1959-77, Fowler, Measle & Bell, 1977—; Sec. F. & C. R.R. Co., 1933-60, Old Lewis Hunter Distillery Co., 1935-42; pres. Properties, Inc., 1959-80; sec. Spindletop Research, Inc., 1968-72; County judge Fayette County, 1954-58. Bd. dirs. Spindletop Hall, 1979—. Served to lt. comdr. USNR, 1942-45. Mem. Ky. Soc. S.R., Am., Ky. bar assns., Delta Tau Delta, Phi Delta Phi. Presbyn. (deacon). Clubs: Kiwanian., Thoroughbred of America (Lexington). Home: 409 Bristol Rd Lexington KY 40502 Office: 4A Citizens Bank Sq Lexington KY 40507

FOWLER, DAVID WAYNE, archtl. engr., educator; b. Sabinal, Tex., Apr. 25, 1937; s. Otis Lindley and Sadie Gertrude (Cox) F.; m. Maxine Yvonne Thomson, Mar. 31, 1961; children—Teresa, Leah. B.S. in Archtl. Engring, U. Tex., Austin, 1960, M.S., 1962; Ph.D. in Civil Engring, U. Colo., 1965. Design engr. W.C. Cotten (Cons. Engr.), Austin, Tex., 1961-62; asst. prof. archtl. engring. U. Tex., Austin, 1964-69, asso. prof., 1969-75, prof., 1975—, Taylor prof., 1981—; vis. prof Nihon U., Japan, 1981; Bd. dirs. Univ. Fed. Credit Union, 1976—. Editor procs.: 2d Internat. Congress on Polymers in Concrete, 1978; Contbr. articles to profl. jours. Ford Found. faculty devel. grantee, 1962-64; recipient Teaching award Gen. Dynamics, 1975, Amoco Found., 1978; cited by Engring.-News Record, 1975. Mem. Am. Soc. Engring. Edn. (chmn. archtl. engring. div. 1971-72), Tex. Soc. Profl. Engrs. (bd. dirs. Travis chpt. 1968), ASCE (pres. Austin br. 1976-77), Am. Concrete Inst., Tau Beta Pi, Chi Epsilon. Mem. Ch. of Christ. Home: 612 Brookhaven Trail Austin TX 78746 Office: Univ of Tex Austin TX 78712

FOWLER, EARLE CABELL, administrator, physicist; b. Bowling Green, Ky., June 10, 1921; s. William Earle and Reba (Brownfield) F.; m. Marjorie Jane Land, Oct. 25, 1950; children: Marjorie Anne, Walter Earle, Thomas Land. B.S. in Chemistry, U. Ky., 1942; A.M. in Physics, Harvard U., 1947, Ph.D., 1949. Asso. physicist Brookhaven Nat. Lab., Upton, N.Y., 1949-52, cons., 1952—; acad. staff Yale U., 1952-62; prof. physics Duke U., Durham, N.C., 1962-71, Purdue U., 1971-82, head dept., 1971-77; chief facilities ops. br. div. high energy physics U.S. Dept. Energy, Washington, 1980-82; cons. Oak Ridge Inst. Nuclear Studies, 1962-67; charter mem. high energy physics adv. panel AEC, 1967-69; Sr. Fulbright lectr., U.K., 1958-59, U. Rome, Italy, 1967-68. Author: (with Robert K. Adair) Strange Particles, 1963. Fellow Am. Phys. Soc. (sec.-treas. div. particles and fields 1974-77); mem. Phi Beta Kappa, Sigma Xi, Sigma Pi Sigma, Delta Tau Delta. Research in application electronic computers to automatic film data analysis, high energy physics, cosmic radiation and with large accelerators, neutrino physics; helped to develop 1st high pressure diffusion cloud chambers. Office: ER-223 High Energy Physics US Dept Energy Washington DC 20545

FOWLER, ELAINE WOOTTEN, historian, researcher, writer; b. N.Y.C., Mar. 22, 1914; d. Irving and Marion Bell (Wootten) Hayward; m. Gordon Fowler, June 5, 1938; children: Gordon, Terry Marion,

Eric Raymond. B.A., Wellesley Coll., 1935. Systems rep. IBM Corp., 1935-37, 39; reporter Santa Ana (Calif.) Jour., 1937; writer, newscaster sta. KGER, Long Beach, Calif., 1942; head reading room services Folger Shakespeare Library, Washington, 1955-71, assoc. editor publs., 1961-71; research assoc. of Louis B. Wright Nat. Geog. Soc., 1971-83; freelance editor, writer, cons., 1971—. Author: English Seapower in Early Tudor Period, 1965, (with Louis B. Wright) English Colonization of North America, 1968, West and By North: North America Seen Through Eyes of Its Seafaring Discoverers, 1971, The Moving Frontier, 1972, Everyday Life in the New Nation, 1972, Visual Guide to Shakespeare, 1975; author, editor, cons.: Nat. Geog. film series World of William Shakespeare, 1978; cons. (Time Life) The Armada, 1981. Mem. Virgil Soc., Internat. Shakespeare Assn. Republican. Episcopalian. Club: Army-Navy. Home: Laurel Point Route 1 Box 158D Lancaster VA 22503

FOWLER, HENRY HAMILL, investment banker; b. Roanoke, Va., Sept. 5, 1908; s. Mack Johnson and Bertha (Browning) F.; m. Trudye Pamela Hathcote, Oct. 19, 1938; children: Mary Anne Fowler Smith, Susan Fowler-Gallagher, Henry Hamill (dec.). A.B., Roanoke Coll., 1929, LL.D., 1962; LL.B., Yale U., 1932, J.S.D., 1933; LL.D., William and Mary U., 1966, Wesleyan U., 1966. Bar: Va. 1933, D.C. 1946. Counsel TVA, 1934-38, asst. gen. counsel, 1939; spl. asst. to atty. gen. as chief counsel subcom. Senate Com. Edn. and Labor, 1939-40; spl. counsel Fed. Power Commn., 1941; asst. gen. counsel O.P.M., 1941, W.P.B., 1942-44; econ. advisor U.S. Mission Econ. Affairs, London, 1944; spl. asst. to adminstr. Fgn. Econ. Adminstrn., 1945; dep. adminstr. N.P.A., 1951, adminstr., 1952, Def. Prodn. Adminstrn., 1952-53; dir. Office Def. Moblzn., mem. NSC, 1952-53; sr. mem. firm Fowler, Leva Hawes & Symington, Washington, 1946-51, 1953-61, 64-65; undersec. Treasury, 1961-64, sec. Treasury, 1965-68; gen. partner Goldman, Sachs & Co., N.Y.C., 1969-81; chmn. Goldman, Sachs Internat. Corp., 1969—; dir. Corning Glass Works, U.S. & Fgn. Securities Corp. Trustee Lyndon B. Johnson Found., Franklin D. Roosevelt Found., Atlantic Inst., Atlantic Council U.S. (vice chmn.), Inst. Internat. Edn.; co-chmn. Com. on the Present Danger, 1976—; chmn. bd. trustees Roanoke Coll. Mem. Conf. Bd. (councilor), Yale Law Sch. Assn. Washington (pres. 1955), Pi Kappa Phi, Phi Delta Phi. Democrat. Episcopalian. Clubs: Recess River, Links (N.Y.C.); Metropolitan (Washington). Home: 209 S Fairfax St Alexandria VA 22314 also 200 E 66th St New York NY 10021 Office: 55 Broad St New York NY 10004

FOWLER, H(ORATIO) SEYMOUR, educator; b. Detroit, Mar. 1, 1919; s. Horatio Seymour and Bessie Liona (Ladd) F.; m. Kathleen M. Marshall, Nov. 21, 1945 (dec.); 1 dau., Kathleen Marie Fowler Barto. B.S., Cornell U., 1941, M.S., 1946, Ph.D., 1951. Tchr. sci. McLean (N.Y.) Central Sch., 1946-47, Dryden (N.Y.) Freeville Central Sch., 1947-49; asst. prof. sci. edn. So. Oreg. Coll., Ashland, 1951-52; asst. prof. biology U. No. Iowa, Cedar Falls; also dir. Iowa Tchrs. Conservation Camp, 1952-57; prof. edn., dir. Pa. Conservation Lab. for Tchrs., Pa. State U., University Park, 1957—, chmn. sci. edn. faculty, 1969—, coordinator div. acad. curriculum and instrn., 1974-76; dir. Pa. Gov.'s Sch. for Scis., 1978-79. Author: Secondary School Science Teaching Practices, 1964, Las Ciencias en la Esquelas Secundarias, 1968, Fieldbook of Natural History, 1974; contbr. articles to profl. jours. Served with 9th inf. div. AUS, 1942-45; ETO. Fulbright lectr., Korea, 1968-69; recipient citation Pa. Dept. Edn., 1970, 83, Centre County (Pa.) Conservation award, 1973, Faculty Service award Nat. Univ. Continuing Edn. Assn., 1983, citation Pa. Ho. of Reps., 1983, Service award U.S. Army Office of Research, 1983; Paul Harris fellow Rotary Club, 1983. Fellow AAAS, Iowa Acad. Sci., Explorers Club; mem. Am. Nature Study Soc. (pres. 1967), Nat. Assn. Biology Tchrs. (v.p. 1956, dir. region II 1971-74, hon. mem. 1974), Nat. Assn. Research in Sci. Teaching, Nat. Sci. Tchrs. Assn. (Disting. Service citation 1976), Pa. Sci. Tchrs. Assn. (dir. 1971—, v.p. 1975, pres. 1976, meritorious service to sci. teaching citation 1975), Korean Sci. Tchrs. Assn., Royal Asiatic Soc., Sigma Xi, Phi Kappa Phi, Phi Delta Kappa (chpt. v.p. 1973, pres. 1974-75, Leadership award 1983), Beta Beta Beta, Phi Sigma. Clubs: Masons, Shriners, Rotary (1st v.p. 1981), Rotary (pres. 1982), Elks.). Home: 1342 Park Hills Ave W State College PA 16803 Office: Sci Edn Dept Pa State Univ University Park PA 16802

FOWLER, JAMES ALEXANDER, JR., lawyer; b. Clinton, Tenn., Feb. 27, 1897; s. James Alexander and Lucy Ellen (Hornsby) F.; m. Hilleda Thomas, July 17, 1920; children—James Alexander III, Ann Astelle (Mrs. D.L. Walters). A.B., U. Tenn., 1916; LL.B., Harvard, 1919. Bar: N.Y. bar 1920. Since practiced in, N.Y.C.; asso. firm Cahill, Gordon & Reindel, 1921—, partner, 1927—; counsel Bur. Naval Personnel, 1942-44. Nat. chmn. Harvard Law Sch. Fund, 1955-57. Fellow Am. Coll. Trial Lawyers, Am. Bar Found; mem. N.Y. Practicing Law Inst. (trustee emeritus), Am. Law Inst., Am., N.Y. bar assns., Assn. Bar City N.Y., N.Y. County Lawyers Assn., Harvard Law Sch. Assn. (pres. 1961-63). Clubs: University, Down Town Assn. Home: 5 Huyler Rd Setauket NY 11733 Office: 80 Pine St New York NY 10005

FOWLER, JOHN RUSSELL, chain dept. store exec.; b. Pontiac, Mich., Apr. 4, 1918; s. John Tasker and Amy (Hurlburt) F.; m. Dorthalene Borthwick, Oct. 5, 1924; children—John Russell, James Borthwick. B.A., Amherst Coll., 1940. With Jacobson Stores Inc., Jackson, Mich., 1946—, exec. v.p., 1962-68, pres., 1968—; dir. Nat. Bank of Jackson, Tecumseh Products Co., Mich.; Camp Realty Co., Jackson, Gerber Co., Fremont, Mich. Chmn. Torch drive, Jackson, 1956, Community Chest, 1957, City Planning Commn., 1970; Chmn. citizens com. Bd. Edn., Jackson, 1960-61; Bd. dirs. Mercy Hosp., Jackson. Served to lt. comdr. USNR, 1941-45. Decorated D.F.C., Air medal. Clubs: Town, Country of (Jackson); Otsego (Gaylord). Home: 1115 S Higby St Jackson MI 49203 Office: 1200 N West Ave Jackson MI 49202

FOWLER, MARK STAPLETON, govt. agency administrator; b. Toronto, Ont., Can., Oct. 6, 1941. B.A., U. Fla., 1966, J.D., 1969. Bar: Fla. 1970. Assoc. firm Smith & Pepper, Washington, 1970-75; partner Fowler & Meyers, Washington, 1975-81; chmn. FCC, Washington, 1981—; vice. chmn. Adminstrv. Council of U.S.; bd. dirs. U.S. Telecommunications Tng. Inst. Named Virginian of Yr. Va. Assn. Broadcasters, 1981; recipient Thomas Jefferson award U. Tex., 1982. Mem. D.C. Bar, D.C. Bar Assn., Fla. Bar Assn., Delta Theta Phi. Office: 1919 M St NW Washington DC 20554

FOWLER, NOBLE OWEN, physician, university administrator; b. Vicksburg, Miss., July 14, 1919; s. Noble Owen and Annie Lou (Robertson) F.; m. Charlotte Ruth Walters, June 13, 1942; children: Joann, Michael, Anne Stewart. Student, Memphis State U., 1936-38; M.D., U. Tenn., 1941. Diplomate: Am. Bd. Internal Medicine (examining bd. 1970-72, cardiovascular subspecialty examining bd. 1966-72, chmn. cardiovascular subspecialty bd. 1970-72). Intern Cin. Gen. Hosp., 1942-43, resident in internal medicine, 1945, 47-48, fellow in cardiology, 1948-52; resident in internal medicine Peter Bent Brigham Hosp., Boston, 1946; instr. U. Cin., 1950-51, asst. prof. medicine, 1951-52, asso. prof., 1957-64, prof., 1964—, prof. pharmacology and cell biophysics, 1980—, asso. dir. dept. medicine, 1970-79, dir. div. cardiology, 1970—; asst. prof. SUNY, 1952-54; chmn. cardiovascular research Emory U., 1954-57; mem. adv. com. on cardiovascular and renal drugs FDA, 1970-78, chmn., 1974-78; mem. sci. adv. com. Nat. Inst. Aging NIH, Balt., 1983—. Author: Cardiac Diagnosis and Treatment, 3d edit., 1980, Myocardial Diseases, 1973, Cardiac Arrhythmias; Diagnosis and Treatment, 1977. Served with M.C. AUS, 1943-44. Recipient award for contbns. to cardiology Georgetown U., 1978; Nat. Heart and Lung Inst. grantee, 1961-73. Fellow A.C.P., Am. Coll. Cardiology (Master Tchr. award 1974), Am. Heart Assn. Council on Clin. Cardiology; mem. Am. Clin. and Climatol. Assn., Am. Physiol. Soc., Am. Thoracic Soc., Central Soc. Clin. Research, Am. Fedn. Clin. Research, Assn. Univ. Cardiologists (founding mem.; pres. 1976), Am. Heart Assn. (pres. chpt. 1979—, trustee chpt., exec. com. chpt.), Sigma Xi, Alpha Omega Alpha, Phi Chi. Presbyterian. Home: 3533 Deepwoods Ln Cincinnati OH 45208 Office: U Cin Coll Medicine 231 Bethesda Ave Cincinnati OH 45267

FOWLER, RICHARD GILDART, physicist; b. Albion, Mich., June 13, 1916; s. Rufus Alexander and Ethel Alberta (Gildart) F.; m. Frances Miriam Holmes, Aug. 26, 1939; children—Lynne Carol, Nancy Barbara, Patricia Ann, Richard Gerald. A.B., Albion Coll., 1936; M.S., U. Mich., 1939, Ph.D., 1942; postgrad., Christ Ch., Oxford, Eng., 1953-54, U. Zurich, 1968-69, U. Giessen, Ger., 1971. Research asst. Dow Chem. Co., 1936-38; grad. research asst. U. Mich., 1938-42, research physicist, 1943-46; asst. prof. physics N.C. State Coll., 1942; asst. to asso. to prof. U. Okla., Norman, 1946-61, research prof., 1961-80, prof. emeritus, 1980—, chmn. dept. physics, 1955-59, 66-68, chmn., 1948-53, 55-62, v.p., 1962-64; chmn. physics fellowship panel NSF, 1959-61. Asso. editor: Physics of Fluids, 1964-68, Jour. Quant. Spect. Rad. Transfer, 1980—; physics cons.: World Book Ency, 1966—. Carroll fellow U. Sydney, Australia, 1963; Fulbright lectr., 1963; Guggenheim fellow Oxford U., 1952-53. Fellow Okla. Acad. Scis., Am. Phys. Soc. (chmn. fluid dynamics div. 1968), Inst. Physics; mem. AAAS, AAUP, Am. Inst. Physics (regional counsellor 1964-66), Phi Beta Kappa, Sigma Xi, Sigma Pi Sigma (hon.), Sigma Tau, Delta Tau Delta, Gamma Alpha. Address: Dept Physics Univ Okla 440 W Brooks Norman OK 73069

FOWLER, ROBERT ASA, oil company executive; b. Sewickley, Pa., Aug. 5, 1928; s. William Henry and Violet Lee (Baker) F.; m. Grace Ohmer Grasselli, Mar. 3, 1951; children: William Henry, Thomas Grasselli, Robert Saxton, Mary Antonia. B.A., Princeton U., 1950; M.B.A., Harvard U., 1955. With Conoco, Inc., 1955—; comml. mgr. Conch Methane Services Ltd., U.K., 1960-65; gen. mgr. adminstrv. and ops. Conoco Ltd. (U.K.), London, 1965-68; mktg. devel. mgr. Conoco Inc. (U.S.A.), Houston, 1968-73, area mgr., N.W. Europe, 1973-78; chmn., mng. dir. Conoco Ltd., U.K., 1978-81; v.p. internat. mktg. Conoco Inc. (U.S.A.), Houston, 1981—. Served to lt. USNR, 1950-53; Korea. Mem. Am. Petroleum Inst. Republican. Episcopalian. Clubs: Knickerbocker, River (N.Y.C.); Allegheny Country (Sewickley, Pa.); Chagrin Valley Hunt (Gates Mills, Ohio); Hurlingham (London). Office: PO Box 2197 Houston TX 77252

FOWLER, ROBERT GLEN, exploration company executive; b. Mart, Tex., Apr. 29, 1930; s. J.H. and Elizabeth F.; m. Bonita Faye Conner, Mar. 22, 1955; children: Becky Ann, Robert Glen. B.S. in Petroleum Engring, Okla. U., 1958; grad., Advanced Mgmt. Program, Harvard U., 1975. With Enserch Exploration, Inc. (and predecessor), 1958—, v.p., then exec. v.p., Dallas, 1972-78, pres., chief operating officer, 1978—, also dir.; dir. Reunion Bank, Dallas. Mem. Am. Petroleum Inst., Ind. Petroleum Assn. Am., Am. Petroleum Landmen's Assn., Permian Basin Natural Gas Men's Assn., Soc. Petroleum Engrs., Okla. Natural Gas Men's Assn., Dallas Petroleum Landmen's Assn., Houston Natural Gas Men's Assn., Harvard Advanced Mgmt. Assn. Baptist. Club: Dallas Petroleum. Address: 1817 Wood St Dallas TX 75201

FOWLER, ROBERT HOWARD, magazine publisher; b. Monroe, N.C., July 2, 1926; s. James Wiley and Stella (Mundy) F.; m. Beverly Jeanne Utley, June 30, 1950; children: Wade Utley, Alyce Mundy, Robert Howard, Susanna Jeanne. Student, Guilford (N.C.) Coll., 1946-48; A.B., U. N.C., 1950; M.S. in Journalism, Columbia U., 1954. Reporter Reidsville (N.C.) Rev., 1950; reporter, asst. city editor Greensboro (N.C.) Daily News, 1950-55; city editor St. Petersburg (Fla.) Times, 1955-56; editorial writer Harrisburg (Pa.) Patriot-News, 1956-60; founder, editor Civil War Times Illustrated, 1959—, Am. History Illustrated, 1966—; v.p., sec. Hist. Times, Inc., 1960-69, pres., 1968—, chmn. bd., 1980—. Author: Album of the Lincoln Murder, 1965, Jim Mundy, A Novel of the American Civil War, 1977, Jason McGee, A Frontier Novel, 1979; also articles. Dir. People-to-People book drive, 1959. Served with USNR, 1944-46. Recipient prizes for editorial and pub. service Pa. Newspaper Publ. Assn. Mem. Am. Soc. Mag. Editors, Nat. Hist. Soc. (founder). Democrat. Methodist. Clubs: Princeton (N.Y.C.); Savage (London). Home: 703 Hilltop Dr New Cumberland PA 17070 Office: Historical Times Inc. Box8200 Harrisburg PA 17105

FOWLER, TALBERT BASS, JR., legal educator, law librarian; b. Columbia, S.C., Feb. 12, 1920; s. Talbert Bass and Doris Ernestine (Blitch) F.; m. Mabel Virginia Hiatt, Dec. 7, 1941; children: Kay Charlotte, Talbert Bass III. A.A., U. Fla., 1940, B.A., 1942, J.D. with honors, 1949, student library sci., 1950-51. Bar: Fla. 1949, Ala. 1958. Asst. law librarian U. Fla., Gainesville, 1949-54; law librarian, asst. prof. law U. Ala., Tuscaloosa, 1954-57, law librarian, assoc. prof., 1957-59, law librarian, prof., 1959-69; law librarian, prof. law U. Pitts., 1969-77, dir. legal research, prof. law, 1977—, acting dir. law library, 1980. Contbr. articles to profl. jours. Served to sgt. C.E. U.S. Army, 1943-46; PTO. Mem. Am. Assn. Law Libraries, Order of Coif, Delta Theta Phi. Democrat. Mem. Christian Ch. (elder). Home: 6525 Northumberland St Pittsburgh PA 15217 Office: University of Pittsburgh School of Law 3900 Forbes Ave Pittsburgh PA 15260

FOWLER, THOMAS KENNETH, physicist; b. Thomaston, Ga., Mar. 27, 1931; s. Albert Grady and Susie (Glynn) F.; m. Carol Ellen Winter, Aug. 18, 1956; children—Kenneth, John, Ellen. B.S. in Engring, Vanderbilt U., 1953, M.S. in Physics, 1955, Ph.D., U. Wis., 1957. Staff physicist Oak Ridge Nat. Lab., 1957-65, group leader plasma theory, 1961-65; staff physicist Gen. Atomic Co., San Diego, 1965-67, head plasma physics div., 1967; group leader plasma theory Lawrence Livermore Lab., Livermore, Calif., 1967-69, div. leader, 1969—, asso. dir., 1970—. Fellow Am. Phys. Soc. (chmn. plasma physics div. 1970); mem. Sigma Xi, Sigma Nu. Home: 221 Grover Ln Walnut Creek CA 94596 Office: Lawrence Livermore Lab PO Box 808 Livermore CA 94550

FOWLER, WILLIAM ALFRED, physicist, educator; b. Pitts., Aug. 9, 1911; s. John McLeod and Jennie Summers (Watson) F.; m. Ardiane Olmsted, Aug. 24, 1940; children: Mary Emily, Martha Summers Fowler Schoenemann. B.Eng. Physics, Ohio State U., 1933, D.Sc. (hon.), 1978; Ph.D., Calif. Inst. Tech., 1936; D.Sc. (hon.), U. Chgo., 1976, Denison U., 1982; Doctorat h.c., U. Liège (Belgium), 1981, Observatoire de Paris, 1981. Research fellow Calif. Inst. Tech., Pasadena, 1936-39, asst. prof. physics, 1939-42, asso. prof., 1942-46, prof. physics, 1946-70, Inst. prof. physics, 1970—; Fulbright lectr. Cavendish lab. U. Cambridge, 1954-55; Guggenheim fellow, 1954-55; Guggenheim fellow St. John's Coll. and dept. applied math. and theoretical physics U. Cambridge, 1961-62; vis. fellow Inst. Theoretical Astronomy, summers 1967-72; vis. scholar program Phi Beta Kappa, 1980-81; asst. dir. research, sect. L NDRC, 1941-45; tech. observer, office of field service OSRD, South Pacific Theatre, 1944; sci. dir., project VISTA, Dept. Def., 1951-52; mem. nat. sci. bd. NSF, 1968-74; mem. space sci. bd. Nat. Acad. Scis., 1970-73, 77-80; chmn. Office of Phys. Scis., 1981-84; mem. space program adv. council NASA, 1971-73; mem. nuclear sci. adv. com. Dept. Energy/NSF, 1977-80; Phi Beta Kappa Vis. scholar, 1980-81, named lectr. univs., colls. Contbr. numerous articles to profl. jours. Bd. dirs. Am. Friends of Cambridge U., 1970-78. Recipient Naval Ordnance Devel. award U.S. Navy, 1945, Medal of Merit, 1948; Lammé medal Ohio State U., 1952; Liège medal U. Liège, 1955; Calif. Co-Scientist of Yr. award, 1958; Barnard medal for contbn. to sci. Columbia, 1965; Apollo Achievement award NASA, 1969; Vetlesen prize, 1973; Nat. medal of Sci., 1974; Bruce gold medal Astron. Soc. Pacific, 1979; Nobel prize for physics, 1983; Benjamin Franklin fellow Royal Soc. Arts. Fellow Am. Phys. Soc. (Tom W. Bonner prize 1970, pres. 1976), Am. Acad. Arts and Scis., Royal Astron. Soc. (asso., Eddington medal 1978); mem. Nat. Acad. Scis. (council 1974-77), AAAS, Am. Astron. Soc., Am. Inst. Physics (governing bd. 1974-80), AAUP, Am. Philos. Soc., Soc. Royal Sci. Liège (corr. mem.), Brit. Assn. Advancement Sci., Mark Twain Soc. (hon.), Sigma Xi, Tau Beta Pi, Tau Kappa Epsilon. Democrat. Clubs: Athenaeum (Pasadena); Cosmos (Washington). Research on nuclear forces and reaction rates, nuclear spectroscopy, structure of light nuclei, thermonuclear sources of stellar energy and element synthesis in stars and supernovae; study of gen. relativistic effects in quasar and pulsar models. Office: Kellogg 106-38 Caltech Pasadena CA 91125

FOWLER, WILLIAM WYCHE, JR., Congressman; b. Atlanta, Oct. 6, 1940; s. William Wyche and Emelyn (Barbre) F.; 1 dau., Katherine Wyche. B.A., Davidson Coll., 1962; J.D., Emory U., 1969. Bar: Ga. bar 1970. Chief asst. to Congressman Charles Weltner, 1965; mem. Atlanta Bd. Aldermen, 1969-73; pres. Atlanta City Council, 1973-77; mem. 95th-97th Congresses from 5th Ga. Dist.; asso. firm Smith Cohen Ringel Kohler & Martin, Atlanta. Served in U.S. Army. Recipient Myrtle Wreath award, 1972; named Outstanding Young Man Atlanta Jaycees, 1972, Ga. Jaycees, 1973. Mem. Am. Bar Assn., State Bar Ga. Democrat. Office: US Ho of Reps The Capitol Washington DC 20515

FOWLER, W(YMAN) BEALL, physics educator; b. Scranton, Pa., June 18, 1937; s. Wyman B. and Frances (Blake) F.; m. Marlene Oberkotter, June 17, 1961; children: Wyman, Virginia, Cameron, Christopher. B.S., Lehigh U., 1959; Ph.D. in Physics, U. Rochester, 1963. Research assoc. U. Rochester, N.Y., 1963; research assoc., research asst. prof. U. Ill., Urbana, 1963-66; assoc. prof. physics Lehigh U., Bethlehem, Pa., 1966-69, prof., 1969—, dept. chmn., 1978—; cons. Naval Research Lab., Washington, 1966-81, Eastman Kodak, Rochester, 1973-74, Argonne Nat. Lab., Ill., 1963-68. Editor: Physics of Color Centers, 1968; contbr. articles to publs. Active govt. study commn., Lower Saucon Twp., Pa., 1972-73. Fellow Am. Phys. Soc.; mem. AAAS, Sigma Xi. Office: Physics Dept Lehigh Univ Bethlehem PA 18015

FOWLES, JOHN, author; b. Essex, Eng., Mar. 31, 1926; s. Robert and Gladys (Richards) F.; m. Elizabeth Whitton, Apr. 2, 1954. Honours degree in French, Oxford U., 1950; D.Litt., Exeter U., 1983. Author: The Collector, 1963, The Aristos, 1964, The Magus, 1966, The French Lieutenant's Woman, 1969, Poems, 1973, The Ebony Tower, 1974, Shipwreck, 1977, Daniel Martin, 1977, Islands, 1978, The Tree, 1979, Mantissa, 1982. Address: care Jonathan Cape Ltd London WC1B 3EL England *

FOWLIE, ELDON LESLIE, library adminstr.; b. Chatham, Ont., Can., Feb. 10, 1928; s. John Gabriel and Violet May (Tucker) F. B.A. with honors, Queens U., 1954; B.L.S., U. Toronto, 1960. Asst. sec. Can. Nat. Commn. UNESCO, Ottawa, 1957-59; asst. librarian Extension Library, U. Alta., Edmonton, 1960-63; librarian Assn. Univs. and Colls. Can., Ottawa, 1963-67, Architects Collaborative, Cambridge, Mass., 1967-68; chief librarian St. Catharines (Ont.) Pub. Library, 1968-73; dir. Calgary (Alta.) Pub. Library, 1973-78; chief librarian Toronto Pub. Library, 1979—. Asst. editor: Univ. Affairs, 1963-66; editor, 1966-67, Inst. Profl. Librarians Ont. bull, 1972-73. Mem. Ont. Library Assn., Foothills Library Assn., Can. Library Assn. (treas. 1972-73), ALA, Library Assn. Alta. (pres. 1978), Inst. Profl. Librarians Ont. (pres. 1971-72), Can. Civil Liberties Assn. Office: 40 Orchard View Blvd Toronto ON M4R 1B9 Canada *

FOWLIE, WALLACE, author, lit. critic; b. Brookline, Mass., Nov. 8, 1908; s. Wallace Bruce and Helen (Adams) F. A.B., Harvard, 1930, A.M., 1933, Ph.D., 1936; Fellow, Ezra Stiles Coll., Yale. Faculty French lit. Yale, 1940-45, U. Chgo., 1945-49, Bennington (Vt.) Coll., 1950-62; James B. Duke prof. French Duke, 1964—. Author: Sleep of the Pigeon, 1948, Pantomime, 1951, Age of Surrealism, 1953, Mallarmé, 1953, Paul Claudel; Studies in Modern European Literature and Thought, 1957, A Guide to contemporary French Literature: From Valéry to Sartre, 1957, Dionysus in Paris, 1960, A Reading of Proust, 1964, André Gide: His Life and Art, 1965, Rimbaud: A Critical Study, 1965, Jean Cocteau: The History of a Poet's Age, 1965, Climate of Violence: The French Literary Tradition from Baudelaire to the Present, 1967, The French Critic: 1549-1967, 1968, Stendhal, 1969, French Literature: Its History and Its Meaning, 1973, Jour. of Rehearsals: a memoir, 1977, Translator: The Journals of Jean Cocteau, 1955, Seamarks (Saint-John Perse), 1958, Two Dramas of Claudel, 1960, Complete Works of Rimbaud, 1966, many other French works.; Fgn. editor: Poetry mag, 1950-70. Guggenheim fellow, 1948-49. Home: 17-D Valley Terr Durham NC 27707

FOX, ARTHUR CHARLES, physician, educator; b. Newark, Sept. 16, 1926; s. Jacob and Mae (Bonda) F. Student, Harvard U., 1942-44; M.D., N.Y. U., 1948. Intern, asst. resident and chief resident in medicine Bellevue Hosp., N.Y.C., 1948-52; from asst. to prof. N.Y. U. Sch. Medicine, N.Y.C., 1954—, chief cardiology sect., 1969—; cons. Manhattan VA Hosp. Contbr. articles to profl. jours. Served with M.C. USAF, 1952-54. NIH fellow, 1954-56; grantee, 1956-80. Fellow ACP (gov. region), Am. Coll. Cardiology; mem. Am. Fedn. Clin. Research, N.Y. Heart Assn. (dir.), Alpha Omega Alpha, AAAS, Sigma Xi. Jewish. Home: 330 E 33 St New York NY 10016 Office: 550 1st Ave New York NY 10016

FOX, ARTHUR JOSEPH, JR., editor; b. Bklyn., Sept. 19, 1923; s. Arthur Joseph and Mary Loretta (Foley) F.; m. Ann Marie McElroy, Sept. 7, 1946; children: Jane Ann, John Arthur. B.S. in Civil Engring, Manhattan Coll., 1947, D.Sc. (hon.), 1982. Structural designer Sanderson & Porter, N.Y.C., 1947-48; asst. editor Engring. News-Record, McGraw-Hill Publs., N.Y.C., 1948-54, asso. editor, 1954-58, sr. editor, 1956-57, sr. staff editor, 1957-60, mng. editor, 1960-64, editor-in-chief, 1964—. Mem. N.Y.C. Environ. Control Bd., 1974-77. Served with AUS, 1943-45. Decorated Bronze Star; recipient award merit Am. Cons. Engrs. Council, 1975, Met. Civil Engr. Year, 1975, Silver Shovel award Subcontractors Trade Assn., 1975. Fellow ASCE (pres. 1975-76); mem. Am. Acad. Environ. Engrs. (trustee), Engrs. Council for Profl. Devel. (dir. 1969-75), Nat. Constrn. Industry Council (exec. com. 1976-77), N.Y. Bldg. Congress (bd. govs. 1969-73, 78—), Engrs. Joint Council (dir. 1976-77, v.p. 1978-80), The Moles, Manhattan Coll. Alumni Soc. (past pres.), Chi Epsilon, Tau Beta Pi. Club: Douglaston (v.p. 1972-74). Home: 345 Warwick Ave Douglaston NY 11363 Office: 1221 Ave of Americas New York NY 10020

FOX, ARTURO ANGEL, Spanish language educator; b. Hoguin, Cuba, Aug. 2, 1935; came to U.S., 1962, naturalized, 1972; s. Arturo Roberto and Dulce Marie (Macle) F.; m. Rosa del Carmen Portilla, Jan 17, 1959; children: Franz, Alexandra. B. Letters and Scis., Friends Sch., Holguin, Cuba, 1952; LL.D., U. Havana, 1960; M.A. in Spanish, U. Minn., 1968, Ph.D., 1971. Bar: Cuba 1960. Sole practice law, Holguin, 1960-62; instr. Spanish Luther Coll., Dechorah, Iowa, 1963-66; asst. prof. Spanish Dickinson Coll., Carlisle, Pa., 1966-72, assoc. prof., 1972-79, prof., 1979—, chmn. dept. modern langs., 1972-74, chmn. depts. Spanish and Italian, 1978-79, chmn. dept. Spanish, 1981—; coodinator Latin Am. Studies program, 1968-77; dir. Columbia Semester program Central Pa. Consortium, 1977-78. Author: novel Anecdotario del Comandante, 1976; contbr. articles in field to profl. publs. Ford grantee, 1969-70; Lilly and Mellon faculty devel. grantee, 1978, 79; recipient Christain R. and F. Lindback Found. Disting. Teaching award, 1981. Mem. Am. Assn. Tchrs. Spanish and Portuguese. Home: 2800 Spring Rd Carlisle PA 17013 Office: Dept Spanish Dickinson Coll Carlisle PA 17013

FOX, BENNETT LOUIS, operations research and computer science educator; b. Chgo., Aug. 13, 1938; s. Daniel T. and Kate (Streng) F. B.A., U. Mich., 1960; M.S., U. Chgo., 1962; Ph.D., U. Calif.-Berkeley, 1965. Analyst RAND Corp., Santa Monica, Calif., 1965-71; mem. faculty U. Chgo., 1971-72; prof. ops. research U. Montreal, 1972—. Author: A Guide to Simulation, 1983; dept. editor: Mgmt. Sci., 1977-80; contbr. articles to profl. jours. Mem. Ops. Research Soc. Am. (assoc. editor Jour. Ops. Research 1977-80). Office: Dept Info and Operational Research CP 6128 Succursale A U Montreal Montreal PQ Canada H3C 3J7

FOX, CARROLL LAWSON, electric utility executive; b. Sevierville, Tenn., June 23, 1925; s. Grady Bascom and Aura (Lawson) F.; m. Mildred Grace Perryman, Sept. 1, 1951; children: Lawson Alan, Shauna Carol. B.E.E., U. Tenn., 1944. Registered profl. engr., Tenn. With Elec. Power Bd. Chattanooga, 1947—, engr. substa. design, 1947-64, asst. sec., 1964-66, sec.-comptroller, 1966-72, sec.-treas., 1972—; co-founder Employee Credit Union, pres., 1954-64. Active United Fund. Served with USNR, 1944-46. Baptist. Club: Rotarian. Home: 540 N Crest Ct Chattanooga TN 37404 Office: 537 Cherry St Chattanooga TN 37402 *Man's greatest achievement in life is to effectively reflect his faith in Christ and express this through service to his fellow being*

FOX, CHARLES EPHRAIM, management consultant; b. Bronxville, N.Y., Aug. 22, 1922; s. Charles E. and Kathryn H. (Umstad) F.; m. Rosemary Quinn, July 11, 1959; children: Elisabeth K., Charles Ephriam. B.A., Dartmouth Coll., 1946; M.B.A., Stanford U., 1948. Govt. relations specialist ARAMCO, Jeddah, Saudi Arabia, 1948-51; gen. asst. to pres. Winchester Electronics Co., Norwalk, Conn., 1951-57; internat. recruitment cons. Booz, Allen & Hamilton, Chgo., 1957-64; pres., vice chmn. Billington, Fox & Ellis, Inc., Chgo., 1964—. Vice pres., trustee Jane Addams Hull House Assn., Chgo., 1976—; trustee Ricker Coll., Houlton, Maine, 1970-75. Served with OSS AUS, 1942-45. Decorated Bronze Star. Mem. Assn. Exec. Recruiting Cons. Republican. Presbyterian. Clubs: Union League, Met. (Chgo.); Bath and Tennis (Lake Bluff, Ill.); Dartmouth Alumni, Stanford Alumni. Home: 990 N Lakeshore Dr Apt 21C Chicago IL 60611 Office: 20 N Wacker Dr Chicago IL 60606

FOX, CHARLES IRA, composer, conductor; b. N.Y.C., Oct. 30, 1940; s. Walter and Mollie F.; m. Joan Susan Redman, Sept. 9, 1962; children—Robert, David, Lisa. Student, Fontainbleau Conservatory, 1959-61; student of, Nadia Boulanger, Paris, 1959-61. Pianist, composer-condr. records, TV and films, N.Y.C., 1963-67; pianist, composer: films Barbarella, 1967, Goodbye Columbus, 1969, A Separate Peace, 1970, Pufnstuf, 1971, The Laughing Policeman, 1974, Last American Hero, 1974, The Other Side of the Mountain, 1975, The Dutchess and Dirtwater Fox, 1976, Two Minute Warning, 1976, Victory at Entebbe, 1976, One on One, 1977, Foul Play, 1978, Little Darlings, 1980, Why Would I Lie, 1980, Oh, God! Book II, 1980, Nine to Five, 1980; composer: music for TV films One on One, 1977, Our Winning Season, 1978; also numerous songs and music for TV series. (Recipient Emmy awards for composing for Love American Style 1969, 72, Grammy award for best song for Killing Me Softly 1973); Composer works for chamber orch. Mem. Composers and Lyricists Guild (gov. 1974-75), Acad. Motion Picture Arts and Scis. (exec. com. of music br. 1973-74). Office: care Am Internat Pictures Inc 9033 Wilshire Blvd Beverly Hills CA 90211 *

FOX, CYRIL A., JR., law educator; b. Pitts., Feb. 18, 1937; s. Cyril A. and Josephine (Clark) F.; m. Jane Hastings Taylor, June 24, 1961; children: Edwin T., Cyril A. III, Jane H. A.B., Coll. of Wooster, 1958; J.D., U. Pitts., 1965. Bar: Pa., U.S. Supreme Ct. Asst. city solicitor, Pitts., 1965-70, asst. sch. solicitor, 1970-71; mem. firm Ryan & Bowser, 1970-71; prof. law U. Pitts., 1971—; Bd. dirs., v.p. Eastern Mineral Law Found.; bd. dirs., treas. Pitts. Architects' Workshop, 1976—. Co-editor: Eastern Mineral Law Inst, 1980—; contbg. author: A Role for Municipalities in Controlling Strip Mining Activities, 1978; contbr. articles to legal jours. Bd. dirs., v.p. Squirrel Hill Urban Coalition, 1972-76. Served with USAR, 1960-66. Mem. Am. Law Inst., Am., Allegheny County bar assns., Order Coif. Home: 300 Maple Ave Edgewood PA 15218 Office: 521 Law Bldg U Pitts Pittsburgh PA 15260

FOX, DAVID WAYNE, banker; b. Aurora, Ill., Aug. 29, 1931; s. Wayne Stauffer and Helen Katherine (Lynch) F.; m. Mary A. Evans, Sept. 22, 1956; children: Susan E., David Wayne, Katherine A., Thomas E. B.S., U. Notre Dame, 1953; M.B.A., U. Chgo., 1958. With No. Trust Co., Chgo., 1955—, sr. v.p., 1974-78, exec. v.p., 1978-81, vice chmn., 1981—; chmn. adv. bd. Banking Research Center, Northwestern U. Trustee Village of Clarendon Hills, 1967-71; bd. govs. Hinsdale Community House, 1981—; mem. civic adv. bd. Hinsdale San. & Hosp., 1981—; mem. adv. bd. U. Notre Dame, DePaul U.; trustee Adler Planetarium. Served with USMC, 1953-55. Mem. Assn. Reserve City Bankers, Am. Bankers Assn., Bankers Club Chgo., U.S. Marine Corps Res. Officers Assn. Republican. Roman Catholic. Clubs: Econ., Chgo., Commonwealth, Mid-Day, Hinsdale Golf. Home: 428 N Lincoln St Hinsdale IL 60521 Office: 50 S LaSalle St Chicago IL 60675

FOX, DONALD THOMAS, lawyer; b. Council Bluffs, Iowa, June 12, 1929; s. Donald and Genevieve (Tinley) F.; m. Ana Clemencia Tercero-Graham; children: Mark, Matthew, Genevieve, Melissa. A.B. magna cum laude, Harvard U., 1951; LL.B., N.Y. U., 1956; Brevet de Traduction et de Terminologie Juridiques, U. Paris, 1957, Diplôme de Droit Comparé, 1960. Bar: N.Y. 1957. Assoc. firm Davis, Polk, Wardwell, Sunderland & Kiendl, N.Y.C., 1958-67; partner firm Fox, Glynn, & Melamed, N.Y.C., 1968—; instr. Inst. Comparative Law, N.Y. U., 1957-59; dir. Washington Sq. Legal Services, Inc., N.Y.C., 1974—. Author: Human Rights in Guatemala, 1979; editor: The Cambodian Incursion—Legal Issues, 1979; contbr. articles to legal jours. Trustee N.Y. U. Law Center Found., 1975—; chmn. N.Y. U. Campaign Fund, 1980—. Served to 1st lt. USAF, 1951-53. Albert Gallatin fellow, 1978—. Fellow Am. Bar Found.; mem. Am. Law Inst., Council Fgn. Relations, Am. Assn. Internat. Commn. Jurists (exec. com.), Assn. Bar City N.Y. (chmn. com. audit 1978—, chmn. fin. com. 1982—), N.Y. U. Law Alumni Assn. (pres. 1971-73), N.Y.U. Alumni Fedn. (pres. 1983—). Clubs: Century Assn., Recess. Office: One Broadway New York NY 10004

FOX, EDWARD A., business executive; b. N.Y.C., July 17, 1936; s. Herman and Ruth F.; divorced; children: Brian, Laura, Jacqueline. A.B., Cornell U., 1958; M.B.A., NYU, 1963. Pres., chief exec. officer Student Loan Mktg. Assn., Washington, 1973—. Trustee Talladega Coll.; bd. dirs. D.C. chpt. ARC, 1977—, Washington Performing Arts Soc. Mem. Potomac Appalachian Trail Club. Address: Student Loan Mktg Assn 1050 Thomas Jefferson St NW Washington DC 20007

FOX, EDWARD INMAN, educator; b. Nashville, Aug. 22, 1933; s. Herbert Franklin and Ladye (Inman) F. B.A., Vanderbilt U., 1954, M.A., 1958; student, U. Montpellier, France, 1956-57; A.M., Princeton U., 1959, Ph.D., 1961; L.H.D., Knox Coll., 1982, Monmouth Coll., 1982. Teaching asst. Vanderbilt U., 1957-58; preceptor European lit. Princeton U., 1959; asst. prof. Romance langs. Vanderbilt U., 1960-64, acting dir. admissions, 1960-61, asso. prof. Spanish, 1964-66; asso. prof. Romance langs. U. Mass., 1966-67; prof. Hispanic studies, chmn. dept. Hispanic studies Vassar Coll., 1967-74, John Guy Vassar prof. modern langs., 1972-74, acting dean faculty, 1971-72, dir. long range ednl. planning, 1972-73; pres. Knox Coll., Galesburg, Ill., 1974-82; prof. Spanish, chmn. dept. Spanish and Portuguese, Northwestern U., Evanston, Ill., 1982—; cons. Library of Congress on Spanish newspapers, NEH; exec. com. Fedn. Ill. Ind. Colls. and Univs.; chmn. bd. Asso. Colls. Midwest; chmn. Ill. Rhodes Scholarship Com., 1974-77, Gt. Lakes Rhodes Com., 1979—; bd. advisors Patterson Sch. Diplomacy and Internat. Commerce.; Bd. dirs. Internat. Inst. Spain, 1967—. Author: Azorin as a Literary Critic, 1962, La Crisis Intelectual del 98, 1976; also articles, translations poetry.; editor: La voluntad, 1969, 2d edit., 1973, 3d edit., 1981, Antonio Azorin, 1970, Articulos desconocidos de R. de Maeztu, 1977; co-editor: Spanish Thought and Letters in the Twentieth Century, 1966. Served to lt. (j.g.) USNR, 1954-56; capt. Res. Woodrow Wilson fellow, 1956-57; Fulbright scholar, France, 1956-57; Herbert Montgomery Bergen fellow, 1958-59; grantee Am. Philos. Soc., 1963, 68; Fulbright research scholar, Spain, 1965-66; Guggenheim fellow, 1970-71; NEH fellow, 1983. Mem. Assn. Princeton Grad. Alumni (bd. govs.), Internat. Assn. Hispanists, MLA (mem. exec. and nominating com. Spanish 4, 1965-68, chmn. Spanish 5, 1968, exec. com. Spanish 5, 1980—), Vanderbilt U. Alumni Assn. (dir.), Phi Beta Kappa, Omicron Delta Kappa, Sigma Alpha Epsilon. Address: 1508 Hinman Apt 4B Evanston IL 60201

FOX, ELEANOR MAE COHEN, lawyer, educator, writer; b. Trenton, N.J., Jan. 18, 1936; d. Herman and Elizabeth (Stein) Cohen; m. Byron E. Fox, Mar. 31, 1957; children: Douglas Anthony, Margot Alison, Randall Matthew. B.A., Vassar Coll., 1956; LL.B., N.Y. U., 1961. Bar: N.Y. bar 1961, U.S. Dist. Ct. bar 1964, U.S. Supreme Ct. bar 1965. Editor high sch. textbooks Cambridge Book Co., N.Y.C., 1956-57; editor labor service publ. Bur. Nat. Affairs, Washington, 1957-58; since practiced in, N.Y.C.; assoc. Simpson Thacher & Bartlett, 1962-70, partner, 1970-76. of counsel, 1976—; assoc. prof. law N.Y. U., 1976-78, prof., 1978—; dir. Root-Tilden program, 1979-81; lectr. on antitrust and competition policy, domestic, internat. and comparative; mem. Pres. Carter's Nat. Commn. Rev. Antitrust Laws and Procedures, 1978-79; mem. adv. bd. Bur. Nat. Affairs Antitrust and Trade Regulation Reporter, 1977—; trustee N.Y.U. Law Center Found. Author: novel W.L., Esquire, 1977; (with Byron E. Fox) Corporate Acquisitions and Mergers, Vol. 1, 1968, Vol. 2, 1970, Vol. 3, 1973; bd. editors: N.Y. Law Jour, 1976—; contbr. articles to profl. jours. Fellow Am. Bar Found., N.Y. Bar Found.; mem. Assn. Am. Law Schs. (chmn. sect. antitrust and economic regulation 1981-83), Am. Law Inst., ABA (chmn. merger com. antitrust sect. 1974-77, chmn. publs. com. 1977-78, chmn. Sherman Act com. 1978-79, mem. council antitrust sect. 1979-83), N.Y. State Bar Assn. (chmn. antitrust sect. 1978-79, mem. exec. com. antitrust sect. 1979—), Fed. Bar Council (trustee 1974-76, v.p. 1976-78), Assn. Bar City N.Y. (exec. com. 1977-81, chmn. trade regulation com. 1973-76, lawyer advt. com. 1976-77), N.Y. U. Law Alumni Assn. (dir. 1974-79), Am. Fgn. Law Assn. (v.p. 1979-82). Home: 69 W 89th St New York NY 10024 Office: 40 Washington Sq S New York NY 10012

FOX, FRANCIS, Canadian govt. ofcl.; b. Montreal, P.Q., Can., Dec. 2, 1939; s. Francis and Pauline (Taschereau) F. B.A., Coll. Jean de Berbeuf, 1959; law license, U. Montreal, 1962; LL.M., Harvard U., 1963; M.A. in Polit. Sci. and Econs. (Rhodes scholar), Oxford U., 1966. Bar: Queen's counsel 1976-77. Mem. firm Tansey, DeGranpre, Bergeron, Monet & O'Donnell, 1966-68; spl. asst. to minister of consumer and corporate affairs of Can., 1968; spl. asst. to Prime Minister of Can., 1969-72; M.P. for Riding of Argenteuil-Deux Montagnes, 1972—; parliament sec. to minister of justice and atty. gen., 1975-76, solicitor gen. of Can., 1976-78, sec. of state, minister of communications, 1980—. Co-chmn. Liberal Nat. Conv., 1975. Served to capt. Canadian Army Spl. Res., 1958-62. Mem. Quebec, Ont. bar assns. Office: Room 586 Confederation Bldg House of Commons Ottawa ON Canada

FOX, FRANCIS HENRY, veterinarian; b. Clifton Springs, N.Y., Mar. 11, 1923; s. Henry Sylvester and Alma (Lindner) F.; m. Mildred Genevieve Cullen, Aug. 6, 1946; children—Rosanna, Laurinda, Teresa, Henry. D.V.M., N.Y. State Veterinary Coll., 1945. Diplomate: Charter diplomate Am. Coll. Veterinary Internal Medicine. Research asst. N.Y. State Veterinary Coll.-Cornell U., 1945-46, mem. faculty, 1947—, prof. veterinary medicine and obstetrics, 1953—, chmn. dept. large animal medicine, obstetrics and surgery, 1972-77; instr. surgery Veterinary Coll., Ohio State U., 1946-47. Author articles in field. Mem. Am. Vet. Med. Assn. (exec. bd. dist. I 1966—, chmn. 1973-74, 77-78), So. Tier (sec.-treas. 1957-62), N.Y. State veterinary med. assns., N.Y.State Assn. Professions, Am. Assn. Bovine Practitioners (pres. 1971-72), Sigma Xi, Alpha Psi, Phi Zeta, Phi Kappa Phi., Omega Tau Sigma. Home: 11 Muriel St Ithaca NY 14850

FOX, GEOFFREY CHARLES, physics educator, dean; b. Dunfermline, Scotland, June 7, 1944; came to U.S., 1967; s. Eustace Neville and Joan Mary (Mole) F.; m. Rosemary Gillian Kennett; 1 son, Oliver Rupert. B.A., Cambridge U., 1964, Ph.D., 1967, M.A., 1968. Mem. Inst. for Advanced Study, Princeton, N.J., 1968; asst. prof. physics Calif. Inst. Tech., Pasadena, 1971-74, assoc. prof. physics, 1974-79, prof. physics, 1979—, exec. officer for physics, 1981-83, dean ednl. computing, 1983—. Sloan Found. fellow, 1974. Mem. Am. Phys. Soc. Home: 1074 Glen Oaks Blvd Pasadena CA 91105 Office: Calif Inst Tech 1201 E California Blvd Pasadena CA 91125

FOX, HAZEL METZ (MRS. ALLAN E. FOX), educator; b. Barton, Md., July 2, 1921; d. Jefferson and Blanche (Inskeep) Metz; m. Allan E. Fox, Jan. 6, 1951; children—Jeff, Margaret, Allan, Robert, Frank. B.A., Western Md. Coll., 1943, D.Sc., 1969; M.S., Iowa State U., 1947, Ph.D., 1954. Research asso. Children's Fund Mich., 1947-50; grad. asst. Iowa State U., 1950-54, instr., 1954-55; mem. faculty dept. food and nutrition U. Nebr. at Lincoln, 1955—, prof., 1962—, George Holmes prof., 1968—, chmn. dept., 1963—. Contbr. articles to profl. jours. Recipient Human Nutrition award Borden Co., 1969, Centennial award Iowa State U. Alumni Assn., 1971. Mem. Am. Inst. Nutrition, Am. Dietetic Assn., Am. Home Econs. Assn., A.A.A.S., Sigma Xi, Sigma Delta Epsilon. Home: 1231 N 38th St Lincoln NE 68503

FOX, JACK JAY, chemist, educator; b. N.Y.C., Dec. 21, 1916; s. Samuel and Celia (Stern) F.; m. Ruth C. Inabu, June 13, 1939; children: Dolores M. Fox Emspak, John Reed. A.B., U. Colo., 1939, Ph.D., 1950. With Sloan-Kettering Inst. for Cancer Research, N.Y.C., 1952—; mem., sect. head; prof. biochemistry Cornell U. Grad. Sch. Med. Scis., 1958—. Recipient Alfred P. Sloan award cancer research, 1956; C.S. Hudson award carbohydrate chemistry, 1977; Pap award for sci. achievement, 1983; NRC fellow, 1950-52; Damon Runyon Meml. Fund fellow, 1952-54. Mem. Am., Westchester chem. socs., Am. Soc. Biol. Chemists, Am. Assn. Cancer Research, Sigma Xi. Research, numerous publs. on synthesis and structural elucidation of compounds of biochem. importance, specific syntheses of compounds related to nucleic acid components, carbohydrate and heterocyclic chemistry. Home: 424 S Lexington Ave White Plains NY 10606 Office: Walker Lab Sloan Kettering Inst 145 Boston Post Rd Rye NY 10580

FOX, JACOB LOGAN, lawyer; b. Chgo., Apr. 20, 1921; s. Jacob Logan and Sarah (Schutz) F.; m. Mary S. Livingston, May 19, 1956; children—Jay, Katherine, Laura. B.A., U. Chgo., 1942, J.D., 1947. Bar: Ill. 1947. Practiced in, Chgo.; mem. firm Altheimer & Gray, Chgo.; chmn. bd. Republic Industries, Inc.; dir. Inlander-Steindler Paper Co., AMD Industries, Inc., Raco Steel Co. Co. Bd. dirs. Chgo. Youth Centers; chmn. bd. trustees sec. Columbia Coll., Chgo. Served with AUS, 1942-46. Mem. Am., Ill., Chgo. bar assns. Clubs: Tavern, Arts (Chgo.); Chikaming (Lakeside, Mich.). Home: 422 Arlington Pl Chicago IL 60614 Office: 333 W Wacker Dr Chicago IL 60606

FOX, JAMES FREDERICK, public relations counsel; b. Cedar Rapids, Iowa, Feb. 5, 1917; s. Samuel James and Anna L. (Pietz) F.; m. Sylvia Porter Collins, 1979. B.A., U. Iowa, 1940; LL.D., World U., San Juan, 1975. Copywriter Kohler Co., Wis., 1940-41; partner James W. Irwin Assos., N.Y.C., 1945-48; mgr. editorial services Prudential Ins. Co., Newark, 1949-52; dir. pub. relations Congoleum-Nairn, Inc., Kearney, N.J., 1953; mgr. pub. relations chem. divs. Olin Mathieson Chem. Corp., N.Y.C., 1954-56; dir. pub. relations Chase Manhattan Bank, N.Y.C., 1957-61, v.p., 1959-61, indsl. pub. relations counsel, 1961—; cons. editor Prentice-Hall, Inc., 1982—. Contbr. articles to profl. jours. Bd. visitors Guilford Coll., Greensboro, N.C., 1982—. Served to lt. USNR, 1942-45. Mem. Internat. Pub. Relations Assn., Pub: Relations Soc. Am. (chmn. counselors sect. 1970, pres. 1974, Gold Anvil award 1978), Found. Public Relations Research and Edn. (dir. 1980—, treas. 1981, v.p. 1982—), Nat. Investor Relations Inst., Sigma Delta Chi, Phi Delta Theta, Kappa Tau Alpha. Republican. Episcopalian. Clubs: Univ., Met. Opera (N.Y.C.). Home: 2 Fifth Ave New York NY 10011 Office: 2 Fifth Ave. New York NY 10011

FOX, JAMES JOSEPH, sports exec.; b. St. Louis, Sept. 18, 1944; s. Jules Anderson and Ruth Jane (Nolan) F.; m. Vicki Regina Graham, June 21, 1969; children—Kristin, James Graham. B.S. in Edn, Drake U., 1964-68. Tchr. Berkley High Sch., St. Louis, 1968-69; sports adminstr. AAU, Indpls., 1971-79, acting exec. dir., 1980; exec. dir. U.S. Amateur Boxing Fedn., Colorado Springs, 1981—; cons. U.S. Weightlifting Fedn., 1981; mem. council Amateur Basketball Assn. Served with U.S. Army, 1969-71. Home: 6520 Grey Eagle Ln Colorado Springs CO 80919 Office: 1750 E Boulder St Colorado Springs CO 80909

FOX, JOHN DAVID, educator, physicist; b. Huntington, W.Va., Dec. 8, 1929; s. David and Eleanor (Griffin) F.; m. Terese Marie Connell, Dec. 27, 1953 (div. 1974); children: Heidi Fox Roberts, Lise Fox Brady, Peter, Paul, Michelle; m. Mary Elizabeth Clark, Nov. 18, 1978. B.S., MIT, 1951; Fulbright fellow, Rijksuniversiteit, Groningen, Netherlands, 1951-52; M.S., U. Ill., 1954, Ph.D., 1960. Asst. physicist Brookhaven Nat. Lab., Upton, N.Y., 1956-59; asst. prof. physics Fla. State U., Tallahassee, 1959-63, asso. prof., 1963-65, prof., 1965—, dir. exptl. nuclear physics program, 1980—; guest scientist Max-Planck Inst. für Kernphysik, Heidelberg, Germany, 1968-69; Inst. für Kernphysik U. Köln, 1975; cons. physics div. Argonne Nat. Lab., 1982—; dir. Branchland Pipe & Supply Co., Huntington, W.Va., 1965-81. Co-editor: Isobaric Spin in Nuclear Physics, 1966, Nuclear Analogue States, 1976; Contbr. articles to sci. jours. Mem. Leon County Democratic Com., 1970-74; Bd. dirs. LeMoyne Art Found., Tallahassee, 1971-73. NSF Grad. fellow, 1955-56; Sr. postdoctoral fellow, 1968-69; sr. U.S. scientist award Alexander von Humboldt-Stiftung, 1975. Fellow Am. Phys. Soc.; mem. AAAS, Sigma Xi, Sigma Pi Sigma, Phi Sigma Kappa. Office: Physics Dept Fla State U Tallahassee FL 32306

FOX, JOHN PATRICK, JR., lawyer; b. Chgo., Dec. 14, 1918; s. John Patrick and Irene (Boyle) F. A.B., Loyola U., Chgo., 1941, J.D., 1949. Bar: Ill. 1948. Atty. law dept. Beatrice Foods Co., Chgo., 1949-65, gen. atty., chief corporate legal officer, 1965—, gen. counsel, 1969—, v.p. law, 1971-75, sr. v.p., gen. counsel, asst. to chmn., 1975-77, cons., 1977; counsel to firm Johnson, Cusack & Bell, Ltd., 1977-79, Abramson & Fox, 1979—; dir., counsel Boyle Ice Co. of Delaware, Chgo., 1950-74; underwriting mem. Lloyd's, 1979. Served to lt. USNR, 1942-46. Mem. Am., Chgo. bar assns., Alpha Delta Gamma (pres. 1949-50). Club: Evanston Golf (pres. 1981-82). Home: 201 Kedzie St Evanston IL 60202 Office: One E Wacker Dr Chicago IL 60601

FOX, JOSEPH CARTER, pulp and paper manfacturing company executive; b. Petersburg, Va., Sept. 8, 1939; s. William Tarrant and Virginia (Newell) F.; m. Carol Spaulding Fox, June 16, 1962; children: Carol Faulkner, Lucy Carter, Baylor Tarrant. B.S., Washington and Lee U., 1961; M.B.A., U. Va., 1963. With Chesapeake Corp. of Va., 1963—, controller, 1969-71, controller, asst. treas., 1971-74, v.p. corp. planning and devel., asst. treas., 1974-79, sr. v.p., asst. treas., 1979-80, pres., chief exec. officer, 1980—; dir. affiliate cos.; dir. Robertshaw Controls Co. Chmn. ann. fund Washington and Lee U., 1973-75. Episcopalian. Clubs: West Point Country (past pres.), Commonwealth). Home: PO Box 461 West Point VA 23181 Office: Chesapeake Corp PO Box 311 West Point VA 23181

FOX, KARL AUGUST, economist, educator; b. Salt Lake City, July 14, 1917; s. Feramorz Young and Anna Teresa (Wilcken) F.; m. Sylvia Olive Cate, July 29, 1940; children: Karl Richard, Karen Frances Anne. B.A., U. Utah, 1937, M.A., 1938; Ph.D., U. Calif., 1954. Economist USDA, 1942-54; head div. statis. and hist. research Bur. Agrl. Econs., 1951-54; economist Council Econ. Advisers, Washington, 1954-55; head dept. econs. and sociology Iowa State U., Ames, 1955-66, head dept. econs., 1966-72, Distinguished prof. scis. and humanities, 1968—; Vis. prof. Harvard, 1960-61, U. Calif., Santa Barbara, 1971-72, 78, vis. scholar, Berkeley, 1972-73; William Evans vis. prof. U. Otago, N.Z., 1981; Bd. dirs. Social Sci. Research Council, 1963-67, mem. com. econ. stability, 1963-66, chmn. com. areas for social and econ. statistics, 1964-67; mem. Com. Reg. Accounts, 1963-68. Author: Econometric Analysis for Public Policy, 1958, (with M. Ezekiel) Methods of Correlation and Regression Analysis, 1959, (with others) The Theory of Quantitative Economic Policy, 1966, rev. edit., 1973, Intermediate Economic Statistics, 1968, rev. edit, (with T.K. Kaul) Intermediate Economic Statistics, 1980, (with J. K. Sengupta) Economic Analysis and Operations Research, 1969, (with W.C. Merrill) Introduction to Economic Statistics, 1970, Social Indicators and Social Theory, 1974; author-editor: Economic Analysis for Educational Planning, 1972; Co-editor: Readings in the Economics of Agriculture, 1969, Economic Models Estimation and Risk Programming (essays in honor of Gerhard Tintner), 1969; contbr.

articles to profl. jours. Recipient superior service medal USDA, 1948, award for outstanding pub. research Am. Agrl. Econs. Assn., 1952, 54, 57, for outstanding doctoral dissertation, 1953. Fellow Econometric Soc., Am. Statis. Assn. (Census Research fellow 1980-81), Am. Agrl. Econs. Assn. (v.p. 1955-56, award for publ. of enduring quality 1977), AAAS; mem. Am. Econs. Assn. (research and publs. com. 1963-67), Regional Sci. Assn., Ops. Research Soc. Am., Am. Ednl. Research Assn., Phi Beta Kappa, Phi Kappa Phi. Home: 234 Parkridge Circle Ames IA 50010 Office: Econs Dept Iowa State U Ames IA 50011

FOX, KENNETH LEE, retired newspaper editor, writer; b. Kansas City, Mo., Mar. 18, 1917; s. Henry Hudson and Margaret Patience (Kiely) F.; m. Mary Harbord Manville, June 20, 1975. A.B., Washington U., St. Louis, 1938; student, U. Kansas City, 1939-40. With Kansas City Star, 1938-78, asso. editor, 1966-78; news analyst Sta. WDAF, Kansas City, 1948-53; war corr., Vietnam, 1964, corr., No. Ireland, 1973. Served to col. AUS, 1940-46. Recipient 1st place editorial div. nat. aviation writing contest, 1957, 58, 59, 60, 67; named Aviation Man of Year for Kansas City, 1959. Mem. Am. Legion, 40 and 8, Res. Officers Assn., Ret. Officers Assn., Mil. Order World Wars, Phi Beta Kappa, Beta Theta Pi, Pi Sigma Alpha, Sigma Delta Chi. Club: Kansas City Press. Home: 9796 E Ironwood Dr Scottsdale AZ 85258

FOX, LOUIS, wholesale grocery exec.; b. N.Y.C., Aug. 16, 1917; s. Pincus and Gussie (Gordon) F.; m. Dora Levin, June 18, 1939; children—Irene (Mrs. Martin Goodman), Helen (Mrs. Daniel Guckenheimer). Student, Am. U., 1950-52. Vice pres. Dist. Grocery Stores, Washington, 1948-50, pres., 1950-56; ops. mgr. Asso. Wholesale Grocers, Inc., Kansas City, Kans., 1956-57, gen. mgr., 1957-68, pres., chief exec. officer, 1968—; pres. Supermarket Ins. Agy., Supermarket Investment Co., Inc., Super Market Developers, Inc.; dir. Shurfine-Central Corp., Northlake, Ill., Golub Corp., Schenectady, N.Y., United Mo. Bank, Kansas City. Bd. dirs. Boy Scouts Am., Food Mktg. Inst., Washington, Kansas City Crime Commn.; bd. councilors Menorah Med. Center, Kansas City, Mo. Home: Prairie Village KS 66207 Office: 5000 Kansas Ave Kansas City KS 66106 *When someone gives you a lemon, learn how to make lemonade.*

FOX, MARVIN, philosophy educator; b. Chgo., Oct. 17, 1922; s. Norman and Sophie (Gershengorn) F.; m. June Elaine Trachtenberg, Feb. 20, 1944; children: Avrom Baruch, Daniel Jonathan, Sheryl Deena. B.A., Northwestern U., 1942, M.A., 1946; Rabbi, Hebrew Theol. Coll. Chgo., 1942; Ph.D., U. Chgo., 1950. Instr. philosophy Ohio State U., 1948-52, asst. prof., 1952-56, asso. prof., 1956-61, prof., 1961-73, Leo Yassenoff prof. philosophy and Jewish studies, 1973-74; Philip W. Lown prof. Jewish philosophy, dir. Lown Sch. Near Eastern and Judaic Studies Brandeis U., Waltham, Mass., 1974—; Vis. prof. Hebrew Theol. Coll. Chgo., summer 1955, Hebrew U. of Jerusalem, 1970-71, Bar-Ilan U., Ramat-Gan, Israel, 1970-71; Mem. exec. com. Conf. Jewish Philosophy, 1963-69; mem. exec. com. Inst. for Judaism and Contemporary Thought, Israel, 1971—; mem. acad. bd. Melton Research Center of Jewish Theol. Sem. Am., 1972—. Author: Modern Jewish Ethics: Theory and Practice, 1975; Editor: Kant's Fundamental Principles of the Metaphysic of Morals, 1949; cons. editor: Jour. History of Philosophy, 1970-76; editorial bd.: Library of Living Philosophers, Inc, 1946—, Judaism, 1953—, Tradition, 1956—, AJS Rev, 1976—, Daat, 1978—, Jewish Edn. Yearbook, 1979—; Contbr. articles to profl. jours. Bd. dirs. Inst. for Jewish Life, 1972-76. Served with USAAF, 1942-46. Am. Council Learned Socs. fellow, 1962-63; Nat. Endowment for Humanities sr. fellow, 1980-81; Elizabeth Clay Howald postdoctoral fellow, 1956-57. Mem. Nat. Commn. B'nai B'rith Hillel Founds. (exec. com.), Assn. Jewish Studies (dir. 1970—, v.p. 1973-75, pres. 1975-78), AAUP, Am. Philos. Assn., World Union Jewish Studies (mem. governing council), Medieval Acad. Am., Metaphys. Soc. Am., Am. Acad. Jewish Research, Conf. Jewish Philosophy. Home: 11 Ellison Rd Newton Centre MA 02159 Office: Dept Near Eastern and Judaic Studies Brandeis U Waltham MA 02254

FOX, MATTHEW IGNATIUS, publishing company executive; b. N.Y.C., Apr. 10, 1934; s. Matthew I. and Lucille V. (Reilly) F.; children: Cathleen, Matthew, Patricia. A.B., Rutgers U., 1956. Field rep. Prentice-Hall, Inc., N.Y.C., 1958-60, editor engring., 1960-67, exec. editor, asst. v.p., 1967-71, exec. editor, 1981—; pres. Reston Pub. Co., Va., 1971-81, also dir.; dir. Zachary & Co., Zachary Assos. Dep. mayor, mayor, Rivervale (N.J.), 1964-67, commr., Bergen County (N.J.), 1966-70. Mem. Assn. Am. Pubs., Am. Assn. Jr. Colls., Am. Tech. Edn. Assn., Washington, N.Y. pubs. groups. Democrat. Roman Catholic. Home: M-11-1 Liberty Street Little Ferry NJ 07643 Office: Prentice-Hall Inc Englewood Cliffs NJ 07643

FOX, MAURICE SANFORD, molecular biologist, educator; b. N.Y.C., Oct. 11, 1924; s. Albert and Ray F.; m. Sally Cherniavsky, Apr. 1, 1955; children: Jonathan, Gregory, Michael. B.S. in Meteorology, U. Chgo., 1944, M.S. in Chemistry, 1951, Ph.D., 1951. Instr. U. Chgo., 1951-53; asst. Rockefeller Inst., 1953-55, asst. prof., 1955-58, assoc. prof., 1958-62, M.I.T., 1962-66, prof., 1966-79, Lester Wolfe prof. molecular biology, 1979—. Served with USAAF, 1943-46. USPHS fellow, 1952-53; Nuffield Research fellow, 1957. Fellow AAAS; mem. Inst. Medicine of Nat. Acad. Scis. Office: Massachusetts Institute Technology Cambridge MA 02139

FOX, MICHAEL WILSON, veterinarian, animal behaviorist; b. Bolton, Eng., Aug. 13, 1937; came to U.S., 1962; s. Geoffrey and Elizabeth (Wilson) F.; m. Deborah Johnson, Aug. 1974; children by previous marriage: Michael Wilson, Camilla. B.Vet. Med., Royal Vet. Coll., London, 1962; Ph.D., U. London, 1967, D.Sc., 1975. Postdoctoral fellow Jackson Lab., Bar Harbor, Maine, 1962-64; med. research asso. State Research Hosp., Galesburg, Ill., 1964-67; asso. prof. psychology Washington U., St. Louis, 1967-76; dir. Inst. Study Animal Problems, Human Soc. U.S., Washington, 1976—; asso. professorial lectr. George Washington U. Contbg. editor: McCall's mag; author: syndicated newspaper column Ask Your Animal Doctor; Author: Canine Behavior, 1965, Canine Pediatrics, 1966, Integrative Development of Brain and Behavior in the Dog, 1971, Behavior of Wolves, Dogs and Related Canids, 1971, Understanding Your Dog, 1972, Understanding Your Cat, 1974, Concepts in Ethology: Animal and Human Behavior, 1974, Between Animal and Man: The Key to The Kingdom, 1976, The Dog, Domestication and Behavior, 1977, Understanding Your Pet, 1978; (juveniles), The Wolf, 1973 (Christopher award), Vixie, The Story of a Fox, 1973, Sundance Coyote, 1974, Ramu and Chennai, 1975 (Sci. Tchrs.' award), Wild Dogs Three, 1977; co-author: What Is Your Dog Saying?, 1977, Dr. Fox's Fables, 1980, The Touchlings, 1981; Co-author: Understanding Your Pet, 1978, The Soul of the Wolf, 1980, One Earth One Mind, 1980, Returning to Eden: Animal Rights and Human Responsibility, 1980, How to be Your Pet's Best Friend, 1981, What Is Your Cat Saying?, 1981, The Healing Touch, 1982, Love is a Happy Cat, 1982, Farm Animal Husbandry, Behavior and Veterinary Practice, 1983, The Whistling Hunters: Field Studies of the Asiatic Wild Dog (Cuon alpinus), 1984; Editor: Abnormal Behavior in Animals, 1968, Readings in Ethology and Comparative Psychology, 1973, The Wild Canids, 1975, On the Fifth Day: Animal Rights and Human Ethics, 1978, Internat. Jour. for Study of Animal Problems, Advances in Animal Welfare Sci. Mem. Brit. Vet. Assn., AVMA, Animal Behavior Soc., AAAS, Am. Assn. Lab. Animal Care, Am. Assn. Animal Sci., Am. Psychol. Assn., Writers Guild, AFTRA, Am. Massage and Therapy Assn. Office: 2100 L St NW Washington DC 20037 *My life was shaped in childhood by close contact with animals and nature. Empathy and concern for the well-being of non-human beings lead to a veterinary degree and curiousity about their behavior and inner awareness to several years research. Most influential teacher: the wolf. My philosophy: reverence for all life; mankind as steward/co-creator.*

FOX, MURIEL, public relations executive; b. Newark, Feb. 3, 1928; d. M. Morris and Anne L. (Rubenstein) F.; m. Shepard G. Aronson, July 1, 1955; children: Eric R., Lisa S. Student, Rollins Coll., 1944-46; B.A. summa cum laude, Barnard Coll., 1948. Art critic, bridal editor Miami (Fla.) News, 1946; reporter U.P.I., 1946-48; polit. speechwriter, publicist, 1949-50; with Carl Byoir & Assos., N.Y.C., 1950—, TV-radio writer, 1950-52, dir. TV-radio dept., 1952-57, v.p., 1956-74, group v.p., 1974-76, exec. v.p., 1977—; pres. subs. MediaCom Communications Tng., 1975—, By/Media Inc., 1981—; dir. Harleysville Ins. Co., Rorer Group Inc.; Co-chmn. Vice Presdl. Task Force on Women, 1968; mem. steering com. Women's Forum, 1947—, pres., 1976—; mem. Women's Econ. Adv. Com., N.Y.C., 1974—; mem. nat. adv. com. Nat. Women's Polit. Caucus; mem. nat. adv. bd. Women Today, Ethnic Woman. Bd. dirs. N.Y. Diabetes Assn., 1956-66, Holy Land Conservation Fund, United Way of Tri-State, Internat. Rescue Com., 1977—. Named one of 100 Top Corp. Women Bus. Week mag., 1976; recipient Matrix award Women in Communications, 1977, Bus. Leader of Year award ADA, 1979. Mem. Am. Women in Radio and TV (dir. 1959-61, chmn. nat. publicity com. 1955-57, chmn. nat. pub. relations com. 1957-59, Achievement award 1983), NOW (founder, v.p. 1967-70, chmn. bd. 1971-73, chmn. nat. adv. com. 1973-74, bd. dirs. Legal Def. and Edn. Fund 1974—, v.p. Fund 1977-78, pres. 1978—), Am. Arbitration Assn. (nat. comml. panel). Home: 66 Hickory Hill Rd Tappan NY 10983 Office: 380 Madison Ave New York NY 10017 *As a business executive, a founder and leader of the modern women's movement, and a fulfilled wife and mother, I hope I have helped to prove that women can enjoy success at many levels-professionally, politically and personally-without being forced to sacrifice one aspect of life for another. I also hope I've helped make such multifaceted success more attainable for other women in the present and future.*

FOX, NOEL PETER, U.S. dist. judge; b. Kalamazoo, Aug. 30, 1910; s. Charles K. and Caroline C. (Kokx) F.; m. Dorothy A. McCormick, Aug. 1, 1934; children—Maureen, Noel Joseph, Virginia Lynn. Ph.B., Marquette U., 1933, J.D., 1935. Bar: Wis. bar 1935, Mich. bar 1935, also U.S. Supreme Ct 1935. Asso. firm Bunker & Rogoski, 1935-39, Fox & Beers, 1945-49; pvt. practice, 1935-44, 46-51, asst. pros. atty., Muskegon County, 1937-39; circuit judge 14th Jud. Circuit of Mich., 1951-62; U.S. dist. judge Western Dist. Mich., 1962—, chief U.S. dist. judge, 1971-79, sr. judge, 1979—; mem. faculty Fed. Jud. Center for Seminars for Newly Apptd. Dist. Judges, 1970-72; mem. State Labor Mediation Bd., 1941-44; chmn. Mich. Mediation Bd., 1949-51; counsel to gov. Mich., 1949. Mem. Mich. Youth Commn., 1961; chmn. Gov.'s Constl. Planning Com., 1961; mem. mediation panel Nat. War Labor Bd., Detroit, 1940-44. Served with USNR, World War II. Named Man of Year Aquinas Coll., 1979; award Kent County Legal Aid and Defender Assn., 1977, K.C., 1962. Mem. Mich. Judges Assn. (past pres.), 6th Circuit Judges Assn. (pres. 1976-77), State Bar Mich. (past chmn. ct. adminstrn. com.), Nat. Jesuit Scholastic and Hon. Soc., Fed., Am., Muskegon, Grand Rapids bar assns., Jud. Conf. Com. Trial Practice and Techniques, Jud. Council Mich., Am. Judicature Soc. Office: 416 Federal Bldg Grand Rapids MI 49503

FOX, PAUL HARRIS, aluminum company executive; b. Sevierville, Tenn., Mar. 29, 1915; s. James Manker and Sarah Katherine (Walker) F.; m. Mary Frances Beasley, June 13, 1942; 1 dau., Susan Frances. B.A., Maryville (Tenn.) Coll., 1938. With Aluminum Co. Am., Alcoa, Tenn., 1934-39, Jenkins Furniture Co., Knoxville, Tenn., 1939-41; with Reynolds Metals Co. (and affiliates), 1941—, former v.p.; former exec. v.p. Reynolds Internat., Inc., also former dir., now sr. adv. to chmn. bd.; past pres., past dir. Reynolds Aluminum Export Corp.; past dir. Westeel-Rosco Co. Ltd., Toronto, Expert Candy Ltd., Montreal, Reynolds Cable Co. Ltd., Reynolds Extrusion Co. Ltd., Can., Lincoln Savs. & Loan, Richmond, Va.; dir. Eskimo Pie Corp. Bd. dirs. Richmond Symphony.; bd. dirs., mem. exec. com. Maryville Coll. (Tenn.). Clubs: Hermitage Country (Richmond); Peachtree Golf, Commerce (Atlanta). Home: 312 Saint Davids Ln Richmond VA 23221 Office: 6603 W Broad St Richmond VA 23261 *I believe that one should live each day as if it were the greatest day of life. I also believe in the adage that it is better to light a candle than to curse the darkness and finally, I believe that what one does should be done on the basis of the greatest good for the greatest number.*

FOX, PAULA (MRS. MARTIN GREENBERG), author; b. N.Y.C., Apr. 22, 1923; d. Paul Hervey and Elsie (de Sola) F.; m. Richard Sigerson (div. 1954); children: Adam, Gabriel; m. Martin Greenberg, June 9, 1962. Student, Columbia U. Condr. writing Seminars U. Pa. Author: eleven children's books, including How Many Miles to Babylon, 1966, Portrait of Ivan, 1968; 16 children's books, including Blowfish Live in the Sea, 1970; (novels) Poor George, 1967; Desperate Characters, 1970, The Western Coast, 1972, The Slave Dancer, 1974 (John Newbery medal), The Widow's Children, 1976, The Little Swineherd and Other Tales, 1978, A Place Apart, 1983 (Am. Book award). Guggenheim fellow, 1972; Recipient Arts and Letters award Nat. Inst. Arts and Letters, 1972, Hans Christian Andersen medal, 1978; Recipient fiction citation Brandeis U., 1984. Mem. P.E.N., Authors League.

FOX, RAYMOND BERNARD, educator; b. Woodstock, Minn., Feb. 8, 1926; s. Fred Joseph and Esther (Short) F.; m. Gudelia Agnes Utz, Jan. 27, 1950; 1 dau., Jacalyn Ann. B.S., Mankato State Coll., 1949; M.A., Colo. Coll., 1952; Ed.D., U. Calif. at Berkeley, 1957. Tchr., English and dramatics Springfield (Minn.) High Sch., 1949-50, Reno (Nev.) Sr. High Sch., 1950-53; tchr. social studies Pittsburg (Calif.) Sr. High Sch., 1953-57; asst. prof. edn. St. Cloud State Coll., 1957-59; prof. edn., head edn. dept. No. Ill. U., 1959-65, asso. dean, 1965-69, prof. edn., 1969—; Dir. Am. Sch. Project, Addis Ababa, Ethiopia. Contbr. articles profl. jours. Served with USNR, 1943-46. Mem. Assn. for Supervision and Curriculum Devel. (bd. dirs.), Ill. Assn. for Supervision and Curriculum Devel. (pres., dir.), Ill. Curriculum Council (exec. bd.), Am. Assn. Colls. for Tchr. Edn. (instl. rep.), Am. Ednl. Research Assn., Nat. Soc. Coll. Tchrs. Edn. Home: 102 Augusta Ave DeKalb IL 60115

FOX, RENÉE CLAIRE, sociology, educator; b. N.Y.C., Feb. 15, 1928; d. Paul Fred and Henrietta (Gold) F. A.B. summa cum laude, Smith Coll., 1949, L.H.D., 1975; Ph.D., Harvard U., 1954; M.A. (hon.), U. Pa., 1971, Sc.D., Med. Coll. Pa., 1974, St. Joseph's Coll., Phila., 1978; D. honoris causa, Katholieke U., Belgium, 1978. Research asst. Bur. Applied Social Research, Columbia U., 1953-55, research asso., 1955-58; lectr. dept. sociology Barnard Coll., 1955-58, asst. prof., 1958-64, assoc. prof., 1964-66; lectr. sociology Harvard U., 1967-69; research fellow Center Internat. Affairs, 1967-68, research assoc. program tech. and soc., 1968-71; prof. sociology, psychiatry and medicine U. Pa., Phila., 1969—, Annenberg prof. social scis., 1978—, chmn. dept. sociology, 1972-78; Sci. adviser Centre de Recherches Sociologiques, Kinshasa, Congo, 1963-67; vis. prof. sociology U. Officielle du Congo, Lubumbashi, 1965; vis. prof. Sir George Williams U., Montreal, Que., Can., summer 1968; Phi Beta Kappa vis. scholar, 1973-75; dir. humanities seminar med. practitioners Nat. Endowment Humanities, 1975-76; maitre de cours U. Liége, Belgium, 1976-77; vis. prof. Katholicke U., Leuven, Belgium, 1976-77; Wm. Allen Neilson prof. Smith Coll., Mass., 1980; mem. bd. clin. scholars program Robert Wood Johnson Found., 1974-80; mem. Pres.'s Commn. on Study of Ethical Problems in Medicine, Biomed. and Behavioral Research, 1979-81; dir. human qualities of medicine program James Picker Found., 1980-83; Fal Golden Kass lectr. Harvard U. Sch. Medicine and Radcliffe Coll., 1983. Author: Experiment Perilous, 1959, (with Willy DeCraemer) The Emerging Physician, 1968, (with Judith P. Swazey) The Courage to Fail: Essays in Medical Sociology, 1979; assoc. editor: Am. Sociol. Rev, 1963-66, Social Sci. and Medicine; mem. editorial com.: Ann. Rev. Sociology, 1975-79; mem. editorial adv. bd.: Tech. in Soc, Science, 1982-83; editorial bd.: Bibliography of Bioethics, 1979—, Culture, Medicine and Psychiatry, 1980—, Jour. of AMA, 1981—; contbr. articles to profl. jours. Bd. dirs. medicine in Public Interest, 1979—; mem. tech. bd. Milbank Meml. Fund, 1979—; mem. overseers com. to visit univ. health services Harvard Coll., 1979—; trustee Russell Sage Found., 1981—. Recipient E. Harris Harbison Gifted Teaching award Danforth Found., 1970; Radcliffe Grad. Soc. medal, 1977; Guggenheim fellow, 1962. Fellow African Studies Assn., AAAS (dir. 1977-80), Am. Sociol. Assn. (rep. to Social Sci. Research Council 1970-73, v.p. 1980-81), Am. Acad. Arts and Scis., Inst. Medicine (Nat. Acad. Scis., council 1979—), Inst. Soc., Ethics and Life Scis. (founder, gov.); mem. AAUP, AAUW, Assn. Am. Med. Colls., Social Sci. Research Council (v.p., dir.), Eastern Sociol. Soc. (pres. 1976-77), N.Y. Acad. Scis., Soc. Sci. Study Religion, Inst. Intercultural Studies (asst. sec. 1969-78, sec. 1978-81). Home: 135 S 19 St Philadelphia PA 19103

FOX, RICHARD GABRIEL, anthropologist; b. N.Y.C., Mar. 3, 1939; s. Joseph and Elizabeth (Cetron) F.; m. Judith Huff, Dec. 18, 1974; 1 dau., Sarah Sushila. A.B., Columbia U., 1960; M.A., U. Mich., 1962, Ph.D., 1965; postgrad., U. Calif., Berkeley, 1962-63. Asst. prof. Brandeis U., Waltham, Mass., 1965-68; asso. prof. Duke U., Durham, N.C., 1968-71, prof. anthropology, 1972—, chmn. dept., 1977—; mem. Inst. for Advanced Study, Princeton, N.J., 1971-72. Author: From Zamindar to Ballot Box, 1969, Kin, Clan, Raja and Rule, 1971, Urban Anthropology, 1977; Editor: Urban India - Society, Space and Image, 1970, Am. Ethnologist, 1976-79. Grantee NIMH, 1970-72, NSF, 1975-76, 80-81. Mem. Am. Anthrop. Assn. Office: Dept Anthropology Duke U Durham NC 27706

FOX, RICHARD K., manufacturing company executive; b. Celina, Ohio, Aug. 7, 1940; s. Reed F. and Mildred F. (Krugh) F.; m. Lind Lou Wiley, Sept. 16, 1961; children: Richard K., Douglas E. A.B.S. in Bus. Adminstrn., Internat. Coll., Ft. Wayne, Ind., 1960; cert. in accountancy and fin. adminstrn., Walsh Inst. Accountancy, Detroit, 1965. Acct. Kent-Moore Corp., Warren, Mich., 1960-65, corp. controller, 1973-75, treas., 1976-78, v.p., treas., asst. sec., 1978-80; pres. Robinair div. Sealed Power Corp., Montpelier, Ohio, 1980—; staff acct. R.J. Clark C.P.A., Farmington, Mich., 1965; vice chairperson values and assessories div. Air Conditioning and Refrigeration Inst., Arlington, Va., 1982—, bd. dirs., 1984—; trustee, sec., treas. Kent-Moore Found., Warren, 1977-80. Pres. Parent-Tchr. Orgn., Jackson, Mich., 1970. Mem. Nat. Assn. Accts. (dir. Jackson-Lansing chpt.). Club: Orchard Hills Country (Bryan, Ohio). Lodge: Moose. Home: 414 W South St Bryan OH 43506 Office: Robinair Div Sealed Power Corp 1 Robinair Way Montpelier OH 43543

FOX, ROBERT AUGUST, food company executive; b. Norristown, Pa., Apr. 24, 1937; s. August Emil and Elizabeth Martha (Deimling) F.; m. Linda Lee Carnesale, Sept. 19, 1964; children: Lee Elizabeth, Christina Carolyn. B.A. with high honors, Colgate U., 1959; M.B.A. cum laude, Harvard U., 1964. Unit sales mgr. Procter & Gamble Co., 1959-62; gen. sales mgr. T.J. Lipton Co., 1964-69; v.p. mktg. Can. Dry Corp., 1969-72; pres., chief exec. officer, dir. Can. Dry Internat., 1972-75; exec. v.p., dir. Hunt-Wesson Foods, Inc., 1975-78; pres., chief exec. officer, dir. R.J. Reynolds Tobacco Internat. S.A., 1978-80, Del Monte Corp., San Francisco, 1980—; dir. New Perspective Fund, Growth Fund Am., Income Fund Am., Am. Balanced Fund. Mem. San Francisco C. of C. (dir.), Colgate U. Alumni Assn. (dir.). Address: 1 Market Plaza PO Box 3575 San Francisco CA 94119

FOX, ROBERT KRIEGBAUM, manufacturer; b. Covington, Ohio, Apr. 1, 1907; s. Ammon L. and Josephine (Kriegbaum) F.; m. Dorothy Carroll Bush, Aug. 28, 1934; children: Susan, Hannah, Robert L. A.B., Ohio State U., 1929, M.A., 1930, Ph.D., 1932. Chemistry instr. Bethany Coll., W.Va., 1932-36; mem. faculty Hiram Coll., Ohio, 1936-41; partner Fox Chem. Co., Coshocton, Ohio, 1941-45; pres. Lancaster Glass Corp., 1945-76, chmn. bd., 1976—; Indiana Glass Co., 1956-74; v.p., treas. Lancaster Colony Corp., 1962-82; dir. Hocking Valley Nat. Bank, 1948-77. Mem. Sigma Xi, Phi Lambda Upsilon. Clubs: Mason, Shriner, Rotarian. Home: 1445 Cincinnati-Zanesville Rd SW Lancaster OH 43130 Office: 220 W Main St Lancaster OH 43130

FOX, ROBERT PHILLIP, manufacturing company executive; b. Duluth, Minn., June 20, 1917; s. Phillip and Christine (Peterson) F.; m. Alice Sten, Sept. 6, 1947; children—Phillip, James. B.M.E., U. Minn., 1939. Chief engr. Clyde Iron Works, Duluth, 1939-59; with Am. Hoist & Derrick Co., St. Paul, 1959—, v.p. ops., 1971-73, exec. v.p., 1973, pres., 1973, chief exec. officer, 1974—, also dir.; dir. First Trust Co. St. Paul. Trustee Minn. Mut. Ins. Co.; Bd. dirs. Dunwoody Tech. Inst., Mpls. Served to lt. (j.g.) USNR, 1944-46. Clubs: Minnesota, North Oaks Golf. Home: 7 Island Rd North Oaks MN 55110 Office: 1800 Amhoist Tower Saint Paul MN 55102

FOX, ROBERT WILLIAM, educator; b. Montreal, Que., Can., July 1, 1934; s. Kenneth and Jessie (Glass) F.; m. Beryl Williams, Dec. 15, 1962; children—David, Lisa. B.S. in Mech. Engring, Rensselaer Poly. Inst., 1955; M.S., U. Colo., 1957; Ph.D., Stanford U., 1961. Instr. mech. engring. U. Colo., Boulder, 1955-57; research asst. Stanford (Calif.) U., 1957-60; mem. faculty Purdue U., Lafayette, Ind., 1960—, assoc. prof., 1963-66, prof., 1966—, asst. head mech. engring., 1971-72, asst. dean engring. for instrn., 1972-76, acting head, 1975-76, asso. head, 1976—, chmn. univ. senate, 1971-72; cons. Owens-Corning Fiberglass Co., Edn. Services Inc., Nelson Mfg. Co., Peoria, Ill., B. Offen Co., Chgo., Agard Co., Johns-Marsville Co., Richmond, Ind., Babcox & Wilcox, Alliance, Ohio. Named Standard Oil Outstanding Tchr. Purdue U., 1967; recipient Harry L. Solberg Outstanding Tchr. award, 1978, 83. Mem. ASME, Am. Soc. Engring. Edn., Sigma Xi, Pi Tau Sigma, Tau Beta Pi, Delta Tau Delta. Home: 921 Hall Rd West Lafayette IN 47906 Office: Sch Mech Engring Purdue U Lafayette IN 47907

FOX, RONALD ERNEST, psychologist; b. Conover, N.C., May 11, 1936; s. Fred Yount and Carolyn Victoria (Weeks) F.; m. Margaret Elizabeth Smith, Dec. 27, 1956; children: Kelley Victoria, Brett Anthony, Jonathan Eric. A.B., U. N.C., 1958, M.A., 1961, Ph.D., 1962. Diplomate: Am. Bd. Profl. Psychology. Asst. prof. dept. psychiatry and psychology U. N.C., 1963-68; asso. prof. dept. psychiatry and psychology Ohio State U., 1968-74, prof., 1974—, coordinator edn. and tng. dept. psychiatry, 1968—, dir. Family Therapy Clinic, Med. Sch., 1970—; dean Sch. Profl. Psychology, Wright State U., 1977—. Author: (with others) Patients View Their Psychotherapy, 1968, Abnormal Psychology, 1972; contbr. articles to sci. jours. Fellow Am.

Psychol. Assn. (bd. dirs.); mem. Ohio Psychol. Assn., Am. Acad. Psychotherapists, Assn. Psychology Internship Centers. Home: 415 Kramer Rd Dayton OH 45419 Office: Wright State U Dayton OH 45435

FOX, SAM, conglomerate executive; b. Desloge, Mo., May 9, 1929; s. Max and Fanny (Gold) F.; m. Marilyn Widman, Oct. 25, 1953; children: Cheryl Ann, Pamela Sue, Jeffrey Lawrence, Gregory Alan, Steven Mitchell. B.B.A., Washington U., St. Louis, 1951. Pres. Fox Industries, Inc., Madison, Ill., 1952-72, Photronix., Inc., Clayton, Mo., 1965-67; pres., chief exec. officer Diversified Industries Inc., mem. N.Y. Stock Exchange, St. Louis, 1972-75; chmn. bd., chief exec. officer Synthetic Industries Internat., Clayton, 1975—; chmn. bd. Synthetic Industries (Ireland) Ltd., 1976—; chmn., chief exec. officer Synthetic Industries (Tex.), 1980—, Harbor Group Ltd., 1980—; chmn. Fibron Corp. of Tenn., 1981. Assoc. chmn. Jewish Fedn. St. Louis; mem. Commn. on Services to Older Persons, also mem. transp. subcom.; bd. dirs. Nat. Jewish Hosp. Denver, Am. Jewish Com., Camp Sabra, Jewish Community Centers Assn.; mem. alumni exec. com. Washington U. Bus. Sch. Served with USNR, 1951-55. Mem. Ill. Mfrs. Assn., Tri Cities Mfrs. Assn. (dir. 1976-80), Greenleaf Elliot Soc., Tri-Cities C. of C. (dir. 1970-74), Washington U. Bus. Sch. Alumni Assn. (pres.), Beta Gamma Sigma, Sigma Alpha Nu. Jewish (dir. temple). Clubs: Masons, St. Louis, Century, Clayton, Mo. Athletic. Home: 60 Villa Coublay Saint Louis MO 63131 Office: 7701 Forsyth Blvd Clayton MO 63105

FOX, SAMUEL, lawyer, accountant, educator; b. Chgo., Mar. 18, 1905; s. M. Bert and Sara (Nestor) F.; m. Genevieve Kubreener, Mar. 29, 1928; children—Stanley K., Lawrence Nestor, Stephen Richard. Ph.B., U. Chgo., 1924, M.B.A., 1947; J.D., Loyola U., Chgo., 1927, LL.M., 1928; Ph.D., U. Notre Dame, 1950. Bar: Ill. bar 1927; C.P.A., Wis. Practiced in, Chgo., 1927-39; atty. Luster & Luster, Chgo., 1927; partner firm Fox & Fox, 1928-39; pres., gen. mgr. Fox Shoe Co., 1931-64; U.S. regional enforcement atty., Chgo. region, 1943-46; budget accountant U.S. Rubber Co., 1940-41; inventory controller Bendix Aviation Corp., 1941-42; controller Bell & Thorn, Inc., 1942-43; mgmt. cons. H.B. Maynard & Co., Pitts., 1967; lectr. law Loyola U., Chgo., 1928-32; prof. accountancy, managerial jurisprudence U. Ill. at Chgo. Circle, 1946-73; lectr. accounting control Ill. Inst. Tech., Chgo., 1949-53; vis. prof., lectr. mgmt. Am. U., Beirut; lectr. Beirut Mgmt. Coll., 1963; Fulbright-Hayes vis. prof. Al-Hikma U., Baghdad, Iraq, 1966-67; lectr. accounting, curriculum cons. to pres. Peruvian U. Sci. and Tech., cost accounting specialist Peruvian Army and Navy AID, U.S. Dept. State, Lima, Peru, 1967; mem. accounting curriculum com. C.P.A. accreditations Wis. State U. at Eau Claire, 1967, vis. prof., acting chmn. dept. accounting, 1968; prof. accounting Roosevelt U., Chgo., 1973—; lectr. Aichi U., Toyohashi, Japan, 1970, 5th World Congress Engrs. and Architects, 1979, U. Khartoum, Sudan, 1979. Author: Law of Decedents' Estates, 1938, Fundamental Cost Accounting Stipes, 1958, Advanced Cost Accounting, 1959, Management and the Law, 1966, Workbook on Managerial Law, 1971; sports and travel editor: Park Ridge Herald, 1947-65; drama critic: Des Plaines Suburban Times, 1957-64; exec. editor: Lex et Scientia, Internat. Jour. Law and Sci, 1976—. Recipient Silver Circle award for best tchr. from students U. Ill., 1972. Fellow Internat. Inst. Community Service, Internat. Acad. Law and Sci., Intercontinental Biog. Assn.; mem. Am. Taxation Assn., Acad. Internat. Bus., Am. Inst. C.P.A.'s, Tax Inst. Am., Smithsonian Instn., Acad. Mgmt., AAAS, Am. Bus. Law Assn. (exec. v.p. 1963-64), Chgo. Bus. Law Assn. (organizer 1957, pres. 1957-59), Ill. Bar Assn., Am. Accounting Assn. (chmn. membership 1970-72), Nat. Assn. Accountants, Am. Econ. Assn., Internat. Platform Assn., Wis., Ill. socs. C.P.A.'s, Am. Assn. Atty.-C.P.A.'s, Am. Judicature Soc., Am. Soc. Engring. Edn., Umpires Assn. Chgo., Football Writers Assn. Am., Beta Gamma Sigma. Home: 175 E Delaware Pl Chicago IL 60611

FOX, SAMUEL MICKLE, III, physician, educator; b. Andalusia, Pa., Feb. 13, 1923; s. Samuel Mickle, Jr. and Francenia Allibone (Randall) F.; m. Mary Alice Vann, June 25, 1949; children: Elizabeth Mickle Fox Zimmerman, John MacRae, Samuel Mickle, Emily Randall. B.A., Haverford Coll., 1944; M.D., U. Pa., 1947. Intern, resident, fellow Hosps. U. Pa., Phila., 1947-50; commd. ensign USNR, 1942; advanced through grades to comdr. M.C. USN, 1957; acting chief gastroenterology (Nat. Naval Med. Center), Bethesda, Md., 1950-51, mem. staff, later chief cardiology service, 1953-54, mem. staff, 1951-53, head dept. clin. investigation, Cairo, 1954-56, chief cardiology, Portsmouth, Va., 1956-57; sr. staff sect. on cardiodynamics Nat. Heart Inst., NIH, Bethesda, 1957-58, co-chief, 1959-60, asst. inst. dir., 1961-62; dep. chief Heart Disease and Stroke Control Program, USPHS, 1962-65, chief, 1965-70; asst. clin. prof. medicine Georgetown U. Sch. Medicine, 1959-70, prof. medicine, 1975—, dir. preventive cardiology program, 1980—; prof. medicine George Washington U. Sch. Medicine, 1970-75; vis. prof. medicine Ein Shams and Kasr-el-Aini Faculties Medicine, Cairo, 1955-56; chief Cardiac Out-patient Clinic, D.C. Gen. Hosp., 1959-62; med. monitor project Mercury NASA, 1960-64, mem. research adv. com. on biotech. and human research, 1964-67; mem. subcom. on altitude physiology U.S. Olympic Com., 1966-68; mem. Pres.'s Council on Phys. Fitness and Sports, 1970—; organizer, mem. Nat. Research Com. on Phys. Activity and Heart Disease, 1964—; mem. adv. com. Inter-Soc. Commn. on Heart Disease Resources, 1968-72, steering com., 1973—; mem. subcom. on emergency services NRC, 1969-75; cons. USN, USAF, U.S. Army, NASA, VA, FAA, HEW, Dept. State, D.C. Gen. Hosp., Asian-Pacific Cardiol. Soc., WHO, Olympic Com., Nat. Jogging Assn., Nat. Ski Patrol. Mem. founders com. and adv. planning bd. Bethesda YMCA, 1960-62; nat. policy bd. YMCA Health Enhancement Program, 1976-84. Fellow Am. Coll. Cardiology (pres. 1972-73, Disting. fellow 1977), A.C.P., Am. Coll. Sports Medicine (v.p. 1976-77), AAAS; mem. Am. Heart Assn. (dir.), Inter-Am. Soc. Cardiology (exec. bd.), Internat. Soc. Cardiology (council), U.S. Naval Inst. Club: Edgemoor Tennis (Bethesda). Home: 7400 Fairfax Rd Bethesda MD 20814 Office: 3800 Reservoir Rd NW Washington DC 20007

FOX, SIDNEY WALTER, chemist, educator; b. Los Angeles, Mar. 24, 1912; s. Jacob and Louise (Burmon) F.; m. Raia Joffe, Sept. 14, 1937; children: Jack Lawrence, Ronald Forrest, Thomas Oren. B.A., UCLA, 1933; Ph.D., Calif. Inst. Tech., 1940. Technican Rockefeller Inst., 1934-35; research asst. Calif. Inst. Tech., 1935-37, teaching fellow, 1937-39; research chemist Cutter Labs., 1940-41, F.E. Booth Co., 1942-43; asst. prof. chemistry Iowa State Coll., 1943-46, asso. prof., 1946-47, prof., 1947-55; head chem. sect. Iowa Agrl. Expt. Sta., 1949-55; dir., prof. Oceanographic Inst., Fla. State U., 1955-61, Inst. for Space Biosci., 1961-64, Inst. Molecular and Cellular Evolution, U. Miami, Coral Gables, Fla., 1964; vis. scholar U. R.I., 1979; AAAS Chautauqua lectr., 1979-82; Chinese Acad. Sci. lectr., 1979; cons. AEC, 1947-55, Staley Mfg. Co., 1954-60, NASA, 1960—; USA-USSR interacad. lectr., 1969; chmn. subcom. nomenclature of biochemistry NRC, 1956-57; mem. adv. panel systematic biology NSF, 1958-60. Author: (with Joseph F. Foster) Introduction to Protein Chemistry, 1957, (with Klaus Dose) Molecular Evolution and the Origin of Life, 1972, rev. edit., 1977; Editor: Origins of Prebiological Systems, 1965, (with others) The Origin of Life and Evolutionary Biochemistry, 1974; asso. editor: Chem. Rev, 1956-58; editor: BioSystems, 1965—; Contbr. articles to sci. jours. Recipient Honors medal and citation as Outstanding Scientist Fla. Fla. Acad. Scis., 1968; Tex. Christian U. Disting. Scientist of Year, 1968; Iddles award, 1973; honoree Festschrift on Molecular Evolution, 1972. Mem. AAAS (nominations com. 1975-76), Am. Chem. Soc. (chmn. div. biol. chemistry 1958-59, nat. councilor 1955-58, recipient award Fla. sect. 1974), Internat. Union Biochemistry (U.S. nat. com. 1956-59, sec. 1957-59), Internat. Soc. Study of Origin Life (v.p. 1970-74), Internat. Assn. Geochemistry and Cosmochemistry, Am. Soc. Biol. Chemists, Geochem. Soc., Soc. Neurosci., Am. Soc. Cell Biologists, Sigma Xi. Home: 7721 SW 50th Ct Miami FL 33143 Office: IMCE U Miami 521 Anastasia Coral Gables FL 33134

FOX, SYLVAN, journalist; b. Bklyn., June 2, 1928; s. Louis and Sophie (Shapiro) F.; m. Gloria R. Endleman, Sept. 8, 1948; 1 dau., Erica. B.A., Bklyn Coll., 1951; M.A., U. Calif., Berkeley, 1952. Reporter Little Falls (N.Y.) Evening Times, 1954, Schenectady Union Star, 1954-55, Buffalo Evening News, 1955-59; successively rewriteman, asst. city editor, city editor N.Y. World Telegram and Sun, 1959-66; dep. police commr. for press relations, N.Y.C., 1966-67; successively rewriteman reporter, dep. met. editor, Saigon bur. chief N.Y. Times, 1967-73; Nassau editor Newsday, L.I., N.Y., 1973-77, nat. editor, then asst. mng. editor nat. and fgn. news, 1977-79, editor editorial pages, 1979—; tchr. journalism N.Y.U., 1965, L.I.U., 1967. Author: The Unanswered Questions About President Kennedy's Assassination, rev. edit., 1975. Recipient Pulitzer prize local reporting, 1963. Mem. Am. Soc. Newspaper Editors, Nat. Conf. Editorial Writers. Home: 304 Mariners Way Copiague NY 11726 Office: Newsday Long Island NY 11747

FOX, TERRY J., business executive; b. Bklyn., Jan. 1, 1938. B.S., N.Y.U., 1960; student Grad. Sch. Bus., N.Y. U., 1962, Latin Am. Inst., 1960. Registered rep. Gruntal & Co. (mems. N.Y. Stock Exchange), N.Y.C., 1959-63; sales exec. Am. Flange & Mfg. Co., N.Y.C., 1963-64; v.p. Internat. Breweries, Buffalo, 1959, chmn. bd., chief exec. officer, 1965; pres., chief exec. officer Iroquois Brands, Ltd., 1968-81, chmn., pres., chief exec., 1981-83, chmn., chief exec., 1983—; vice chmn. Lincoln Nat. Bank Buffalo, 1968-71; trustee Emigrant Savs. Bank; former mem. bd. govs. Am. Stock Exchange. Past pres., chmn. bd. Henry St. Settlement Jr. Bd.; former trustee head Polymer Lab.; former chmn. investment bankers com. Rosary Hill Coll.; regional coordinator White House Conf. on Children and Youth; trustee Marymount Coll., Tarrytown, N.Y.; bd. dirs. USO, Cath. Youth Orgn.; mem. adv. bd. Grad. Sch. Bus. Adminstrn., U. Conn.; mem. arms and armor vis. com. Met. Mus., N.Y.C. Served with AUS, 1960-61. Tower fellow U. Bridgeport. Mem. Young Pres.'s Assn. Clubs: Goldens Bridge Hunt (North Salem); Union League, Nat. Arts (N.Y.C.); Stanwich, Greenwich (Greenwich, Conn.); Palm Bay (Miami, Fla.). Inventor, designer, patentee Sam Snead hand strengthener. Office: 41 W Putnam Ave Greenwich CT 06830

FOX, THOMAS WALTON, educator; b. Pawtucket, R.I., Mar. 21, 1923; s. Thomas Mathew and May (Walton) F.; m. Jean Dorothy Manning, June 6, 1948; children—Cynthia Jean, Sandra Jane. B.S., U. Mass., 1949, M.S., 1950; Ph.D., Purdue U., 1953. Teaching fellow U. Mass. at Amherst, 1949-50, instr., 1952-53, prof., head dept. poultry sci., 1954-64, head dept. vet. and animal scis., 1964-79; research asst. Purdue U., Lafayette, Ind., 1950-52; cons. Pilch Poultry Breeding, Inc., Hazardville, Conn., 1967-70. Contbr. articles profl. jours. Mem. Amherst-Pelham Regional Sch. Com., 1963-69, chmn. region, 1968, 69; mem. Amherst Sch. Com., 1963-69. Served to sgt. AUS, 1943-45. Decorated Purple Heart with oak leaf cluster. Fellow AAAS; mem. Am. Inst. Biol. Scis., Poultry Sci. Assn., World's Poultry Sci. Assn., Am. Genetic Assn., Genetic Soc. Am., Brit. Soc. Animal Prodn., Sigma Xi, Phi Kappa Phi. Research in poultry genetics and applied poultry breeding, poultry physiology. Home: 676 E Pleasant St Amherst MA 01002

FOX, THURMAN ORVILLE, museum director; b. Oshkosh, Wis., Aug. 7, 1922; s. Orville Wesley and Francis Loraine (Smith) F.; m. Betty Lou Patch, June 17, 1950; children: James Thurman, Beth Leslie. B.S., Oshkosh State Tchrs. Coll., 1967; M.S., U. Wis., 1969. Tchr. pub. jr. high sch., Beaver Dam, Wis., 1948, West Jr. High Sch., Madison, Wis., 1949-56; coordinator officer sch. services State Hist. Soc. Wis., Madison, 1956-64, mus. dir., 1964—. Served with USAAF, 1942-46. Decorated Air medal with 5 oak leaf clusters; Ford Found. grantee, 1952. Mem. Am. Assn. Museums (chmn. accreditation team), Am. Assn. State and Local History (cons.), Midwest Museums Conf. Club: Rotary. Home: 506 Togstad Glenn St Madison WI 53711 Office: 816 State St Madison WI 53706

FOX, VERNON BRITTAIN, criminologist, educator; b. Boyne Falls, Mich., Apr. 25, 1916; s. John Lorenzo and Ethel (Hamilton) F.; m. Laura Grace Ellerby, Mar. 22, 1941; children: Karen, Vernon, Loraine. A.B., Mich. State U., 1940, cert. in social work, 1941, M.A., 1943, Ph.D., 1949. Caseworker, athletic dir. Starr Commonwealth, Albion, Mich., 1941-42; psychologist State Prison So. Mich., 1942-46, dep. warden, 1949-52; psychologist Cassidy Lake Tech. Sch., Mich. Dept. Corrections, 1946-49; prof. criminology Fla. State U., Tallahassee, 1952—, chmn. dept. criminology, 1952-71; cons. U.S. Law Enforcement Assistance Adminstrn.; bd. visitors U.S. Army Mil. Police Sch. Author: Violence Behind Bars, 1956, reprinted, 1974, Guidelines for Corrections Programs in Community and Junior Colleges, 1969, Crime and Law Enforcement, 1971, Introduction to Corrections, 1972, 2d edit., 1977, 3d edit., 1985, A Handbook for Volunteers in Juvenile Court, 1973; co-author, editor: Crime and Law Enforcement, 1971; co-author: Introduction to Criminal Justice, 1975, 2d edit., 1979, Introduction to Criminology, 1976, Russian edit., 1980, 2d edit., 1985, Community-Based Corrections, 1977, (with Burton Wright) Criminal Justice and the Social Sciences, 1978, Correctional Institutions, 1983; internat. bd. editors: Abstracts in Criminology, 1959-71; asso. editor: Criminal Justice, 1971—, Jour. Humanics, 1973—; mem. adv. bd. dirs.: Criminal Justice Rev., 1975—; bd. advisors: Internat. Jour. Comparative and Applied Criminal Justice, 1976—; abstractor: Abstracts for Social Workers, Fed. Probation. Served with AUS, 1945-46. Named Alumni Prof. of Year, Fla. State U., 1970, Outstanding Prof., Tallo-Ho, 1960, 68; Outstanding Criminal Justice Educator award So. Assn. Criminal Justice Educators, 1979; Social Sci. award Delta Tau Kappa, 1963. Mem. Am. Correctional Assn., Am. Sociol. Soc., Fla. Psychol. Assn., Omicron Delta Kappa, Delta Tau Kappa (chancellor Southeastern U.S.). Clubs: Capital City Country, Exchange (Tallahassee). Papers collected in Archive Contemporary History at U. Wyo. Home: 644 Voncile Ave Tallahassee FL 32303 Office: Sch Criminology Fla State Univ Tallahassee FL 32306

FOX, WILLIAM TEMPLETON, geologist; b. Chgo., Nov. 15, 1932; s. Edward Alexander and Mary Evelyn (Templeton) F.; m. Norma Gertrude Heinzen, Jan. 3, 1959; children—Stephen, Katherine, Amy. B.A., Williams Coll., 1954; M.A., Northwestern U., 1961, Ph.D., 1962. Faculty geology Williams Coll., 1962, prof. geology, 1974—; NSF fellow Stanford U., 1966-67; vis. prof. Sch. Oceanography, Oreg. State U., 1973-74; researcher Office Naval Research, 1969-79. Contbr. numerous articles on time series analysis, Fourier analysis and computer applications in geology and oceanography. Served with C.E. U.S. Army, 1955-57. NSF research grantee, 1962-65. Fellow Geol. Soc. Am.; mem. Am. Assn. Petroleum Geologists, Internat. Assn. Math. Geologists. Roman Catholic. Home: 51 Moorland St Williamstown MA 01267 Office: Geology Dept Williams Coll Williamstown MA 01267

FOX, WILLIAM THORNTON RICKERT, political science educator; b. Chgo., Jan. 12, 1912; s. John Sharpless and Myrtie Leah (Perrigo) F.; m. Annette Baker, Sept. 3, 1935; children: Carol Perrigo Fox Foelak, Merritt Baker. B.S., Haverford Coll., 1932; M.A., U. Chgo., 1934, Ph.D., 1940. Instr. polit. sci. Temple U., 1936-41; instr., conf. dir. Sch. Pub. and Internat. Affairs, Princeton U., 1941-43; research asso. Inst. Internat. Studies, Yale U., 1943-51, asso. prof. polit. sci., 1946-50; prof. internat. relations Columbia U., N.Y.C., 1950-68, James T. Shotwell prof. internat. relations, 1968-70, Bryce prof. history of internat. relations, 1970-80, Bryce prof. emeritus, 1980—; dir. Inst. War and Peace Studies, 1951-76; vis. research fellow Australian Nat. U., 1968, 79; Claude T. Bissell prof. Can.-Am. relations U. Toronto, 1982-83; chmn. nat. security policy research com. Social Sci. Research Council, 1953-64. Author: The Super-Powers, 1944, The American Study of International Relations, 1967; editor, co-author: Theoretical Aspects of International Relations, 1959, NATO and the Range of American Choice, 1967; co-author: American Arms and a Changing Europe, 1973; mng. editor: World Politics, 1948-53; mem. editorial bd., 1948-61, 62-78. Trustee Fund for Peace, 1978—. Fellow Am. Acad. Arts and Scis., Hudson Inst.; mem. Am. Polit. Sci. Assn. (v.p. 1965-66, council 1956-58), Internat. Studies Assn. (pres. 1972-73), Council Fgn. Relations. Home: 18 Lake Dr Riverside CT 06878 Office: Inst War and Peace Studies Columbia U 420 W 118th St New York NY 10027

FOX, WILLIAM WALTER, psychiatrist; b. Winnipeg, Man., Can., June 24, 1924; came to U.S., 1952, naturalized, 1957; s. William Joseph and Edith (MacDonald) F.; m. Margaret Elizabeth Livingston, Dec. 16, 1949; children—Tannis Lillian, Jennifer Colleen. M.D., U. Man., 1948; M.S. in Adminstrv. Medicine, Columbia, 1965. Diplomate: Am. Bd. Psychiatry and Neurology. Intern Winnipeg Gen. Hosp., 1947-48; resident Winnipeg Gen. Hosp., also Norton Psychiat. Unit, Louisville, 1949-54; practice medicine specializing in psychiatry, Winnipeg, 1950-51, Louisville, 1954-65, New Orleans, 1965-66, Mt. Pleasant, Iowa, 1966-72; staff psychiatrist Winnipeg Psychopathic Hosp., 1951-52; cons. (psychiatry); Ky. Dept. Mental Health, 1954-55, 1955; clin. dir. Central Hosp., Louisville, 1955-56, supt., 1956-65; asst. prof. dept. psychiatry Faculty Medicine, U. Louisville, 1952-65, Tulane Med. Sch., 1965-66; supt., area dir. mental health Mental Health Inst., Mt. Pleasant, 1966-72; asst. commr. for mental health Ariz. Dept. Health, Phoenix, 1972-75; dir. Camelback Hosp. Mental Health Center, Scottsdale, Ariz., 1975-78; practice medicine specializing in psychiatry, Phoenix, 1978—; lectr. dept. psychiatry U. Ariz. Sch. Medicine, 1972—; spl. cons. NIMH; mem. tech. com. health White House Conf. on Aging, 1971; field rep. Accreditation Council for Psychiat. Facilities, Joint Commn. on Accreditation of Hosps., 1973-78. Fellow Am. Psychiat. Assn.; mem. Assn. Med. Supts. Mental Hosps. (past pres.), A.M.A., Ariz. Med. Assn., Ariz. Psychiat. Soc., Maricopa County Med. Assn. Home: 5313 N 43d St Phoenix AZ 85018 Office: 5051 N 34th St Suite 6 Phoenix AZ 85018

FOXLEY, WILLIAM COLEMAN, meat packing company executive, cattleman; b. St. Paul, Jan. 7, 1935; s. William Joseph and Eileen (Conroy) F. B.A., U. Notre Dame, 1957. Pres., chmn. bd. Foxley & Co., Omaha, 1960—, also dir.; chmn. bd. Flavorland Industries, Inc., Denver, 1974—; chmn. Stagecoach Ski Corp. Served with USMCR, 1957-60. Republican. Roman Catholic. Office: Foxley & Co 10050 Regency Circle Omaha NE 68114 *

FOXWORTHY, JAMES ERNEST, univ. adminstr.; b. Los Angeles, Feb. 23, 1930; s. James Norwood and Mary (Stone) F.; m. Peggy Lou Jones, Aug. 20, 1950; children—Michael D., Paula C., John E., Maryellen, Timothy M., Stephen J., Brian J. B.E., U. So. Calif., 1955, M.S., 1958, Ph.D., 1965. Research asso. U. So. Calif., Los Angeles, 1957-58; mem. faculty, adminstrn. Loyola U. Los Angeles, 1958—, prof., chmn. dept. civil engring., 1959-69, dean engring., 1969-72, dean sci. and engring., 1972-80, exec. v.p., 1981—; cons. sanitation dists. Los Angeles County, 1960—, Allan Hancock Found., Los Angeles, U. So. Calif., 1962—, WHO, 1974—. Mem. Mayor's Council on Environmental Mgmt., Los Angeles, 1970-71, vice chmn., 1970—. Served with Engrs. AUS, 1950-52. Mem. Am. Soc. Engring. Edn., ASCE, Am. Assn. Profs. San. Engring., Am. Acad. Environ. Engrs., Sigma Xi, Phi Kappa Phi, Tau Beta Pi, Chi Epsilon, Alpha Sigma Nu. Research in marine pollution. Home: 27953 Alaflora Dr San Pedro CA 90732 Office: 7101 W 80th St Los Angeles CA 90045

FOXX, REDD (JOHN ELROY SANFORD), actor, comedian; b. St. Louis, Dec. 9, 1922; s. Fred Sanford; m. Evelyn Killibrew (div. 1951); m. Betty Jean Harris, 1955 (div.); 1 stepdau., Debraca. Ed. pub. schs., Chgo. Mem. amateur mus. group, Bon-Bons, 1939-41; performer numerous night clubs, N.Y.C., Balt., San Francisco, Los Angeles, Las Vegas, Honolulu, Miami Beach, Chgo., 1941—; performed with: Slappy White, 1947-51; film appearances include Cotton Comes To Harlem, 1970, Norman... Is That You?, 1976; TV appearances include Soul; series Sanford and Son, 1972-77, 80-81, The Redd Foxx Comedy Hour, 1977; rec. artist, Dooto Records, Loma Records.; Recs. include Laff of the Party, 1956. Address: 933 N La Brea Ave Los Angeles CA 90038 *

FOY, JOE HARDEMAN, lawyer; b. Henderson, Tenn., Aug. 16, 1926; s. C.M. and Carrie (Hardeman) F.; m. Martha Lowe Overall, May 28, 1949; children: Joe Hardeman, Melissa Haynes. Student, Freed Hardeman Coll., 1942-44, Ga. Tech. U., 1944-45; B.A., Vanderbilt U., 1948, J.D., 1950. Bar: Tenn. and Tex. 1950. City atty., San Angelo, Tex., 1951-53; partner firm Hardeman, Smith & Foy, San Angelo, 1953-65; v.p., gen. counsel Houston Nat. Gas Corp., 1965-69, sr. v.p., gen. counsel, 1969-73, vice chmn. bd. operating and corporate, 1973-74, pres., chief operating officer, 1974-80; partner firm Bracewell & Patterson, Houston, 1980—; vice chmn. Minden Oil & Gas Co., Inc.; dir. Central & S.W. Corp., Del., Lifemark Corp., Templeton Energy, Inc., Gulf Coast Savs. Assn., all Houston. Contbr. articles to profl. jours. Pres. Houston Opera Assn., 1971-73, chmn., 1973-75; chmn. Houston Am. Revolution Bicentennial Commn.; Mem. sch. bd., San Angelo, 1961-64, pres., 1964-65, mem. city council, Bunker Hill Village, Tex., 1967-71; Bd. dirs. Tex. Turnpike Authority, 1971-83, vice chmn., 1976-83. Served as ensign USNR, 1945-48. Fellow Tex. Bar Found. (charter); mem. Am. Bar Assn., Harris County Bar Assn., Tex. Bar Assn., Houston C. of C. (dir. 1977—, chmn. aviation com. 1978—), Order of Coif, Tau Beta Pi, Alpha Tau Omega, Omicron Delta Kappa, Phi Delta Phi. Democrat. Mem. Ch. Christ. Home: 2422 Inwood Dr Houston TX 77019 Office: 2900 South Tower/Pennzoil Pl Houston TX 77002

FOY, JOSEPH GERARD, food industry consultant; b. Quincy, Mass., Mar. 5, 1910; s. Robert Edward and Ellen (Hassett) F.; m. Geraldine Marie Kelly, Sept. 2, 1933; children: Joseph Gerard, Nancy Louise (Mrs. Robert A. Meisenheimer), Peter Dudley, Thomas Gerald, Judith Ellen. A.B., Holy Cross Coll., 1931; student, Boston U., 1931-33. Tchr.-coach. North Quincy High Sch., 1933-42; dir. processed foods rationing OPA, 1942-43; dir. research and edn. Nat. Assn. Retail Grocers, 1946-48; chmn. bd. Spartan Stores, Inc., Grand Rapids, Mich., 1948-73; sec., dir. Market Devel. Corp., 1961-73; pres., dir. Beaver Valley Canning Co., 1952-68; Shurfine-Central Corp., 1951, pres., 1962-65; treas., dir. United Wholesale Grocery Co., 1950-73; food industry cons., 1974—; pres. Certified Grocers Fla., 1977, now pres. emeritus; dir. Pacific Merc. Corp., Grand Rapids Coffee Co.; Chmn. Food Industry Council, 1965; dir. food ops. Cost of Living

Council, 1973. Served with USNR, 1943-46. Named Food Statesman of Year Coop. Food Distbrs. Am., 1965; recipient Distinguished Service award Western Mich. U., 1968; Hon. life mem. Nat. Assn. Retail Grocers. Mem. Coop. Food Distbrs. Am. (dir., past pres.), Super Market Inst., Mich. Food Dealers Assn. (certificate of merit 1973), Asso. Food Dealers of Mich. (Man of Year award 1973), Pa. Grocers Assn. (hon.), Food Execs. Club. Home: 1741 Clatter Bridge Rd Ocala FL 32671

FOY, LEWIS WILSON, metals executive; b. Somerset County, Pa., Jan. 8, 1915; s. George Martin and Nellie (Speicher) F.; m. Marjorie Werry, May 9, 1942; children: Susan Foy Heller, Jane Foy Karaman. Student, Duke U., 1933-34, George Washington U., 1943-44, Lehigh U., 1947-49; LL.D., Moravian Coll., 1971, Lehigh U., 1975, Valparaiso U., 1979; D.C.L., U. Liberia, 1973. With Bethlehem Steel Corp., 1936—, v.p. purchasing, 1963-70, exec. v.p., 1970, pres., 1970-74, chmn., chief exec. officer, 1974-80; chmn. Continental Metals; dir. Goodyear Tire & Rubber Co., J.P. Morgan & Co. Inc., Morgan Guaranty Trust Co. N.Y., Met. Life Ins. Co., Communications Satellite Corp. Trustee Moravian Coll., Bethlehem. Served with AUS, 1941-46. Mem. Bus. Council, Am. Iron and Steel Inst. (chmn. 1978-80). Clubs: Union League, Links, Sky (N.Y.C.); Bethlehem, Saucon Valley Country (Bethlehem, Pa.); Rolling Rock (Ligonier, Pa.); Everglades, Augusta Nat. Golf, Seminole. Home: The Elms Saucon Valley Rd RD 4 Bethlehem PA 18015 Office: 437 Main St Suite 310 Bethlehem PA 18018

FOYE, LAURANCE VINCENT, JR., physician, hospital administrator; b. Seattle, Nov. 26, 1925; s. Laurance Vincent and Sara Pauline (Given) F.; m. Laura Marian Love, June 22, 1951; children: Patricia Marian, Michael Laurance. A.B., U. Calif., Berkeley, 1949, M.D., 1952. Diplomate: Am. Bd. Internal Medicine. Intern San Francisco Gen. Hosp., 1952-53; resident in medicine VA Hosp., San Francisco, 1953-55, 56-57, Stanford U. Hosp., 1955-56; asst. chief med. service VA Hosp., San Francisco, 1958-66; chief clin. investigations br. Nat. Cancer Inst., Bethesda, Md., 1966-70; dir. edn. service VA, Washington, 1970-74; dep. chief med. dir., 1974-78; dir. VA Med. Center, San Francisco, 1978—; asso. clin. prof. medicine U. Calif. Sch. Medicine, San Francisco, 1979—; mem. adv. council Nat. Heart and Lung Inst., 1971-73. Contbr. articles on cancer research to profl. jours. Mem. governing bd. West Bay Health Systems Agy., 1978-82; mem. Fed. Exec. Bd., San Francisco, 1978—. Served with U.S. Army, 1944-46. Recipient Exceptional Service award VA, 1978. Fellow ACP; mem. Am. Soc. Clin. Oncology, Soc. Philatelic Americans, Phi Beta Kappa, Sigma Xi, Alpha Omega Alpha. Address: 4150 Clement St San Francisco CA 94121

FOYT, A(NTHONY) J(OSEPH), JR., auto racer; b. Houston, Jan. 16, 1935; m. Lucy Zarr, 1955; children: A.J. 3d, Jerry, Terry Lynn. Ed. pub. schs. Auto racer, 1953—; owner Foyt Engine Corp.; dir. Greenway Bank, Houston, SCI Corp.; profl. horse breeder and trainer, Houston. Named Racing Driver of Year, Auto Racing Frat. Greater N.Y., 1963; named outstanding performer Am. Driver of Year award, 1967. Winner Indpls. 500, 1961, 64, 67, 77; winner U.S. Auto Club championship, 1960, 61, 63, 64, 67, 75, 79; winner Twenty Four Hours of Le Mans (France), 1967, Schaefer 500, 1973, Pocono 500, 1975, 79, Daytona 500, 1972, nat. championship stock car div. U.S. Auto Club, 1968, 78, 79. Address: care USAC Publicity Dept 4910 W 16th St Speedway IN 46224 *

FRACKMAN, RICHARD BENOIT, investment banker; b. N.Y.C., Apr. 14, 1923; s. H. David and Ruth (Warren) F.; m. Noel Stern, July 2, 1950; 1 dau., Noel Dru. Grad., Pratt Sch. Bus., 1941; student, U. Pa., 1941-42, N.Y. U., 1946-48, N.Y. Inst. Fin., 1962-63. Mdse. mgr. R.H. Miller Stores, Inc., N.Y.C., 1946-49; v.p., mdse. mgr. Darling Stores Corp., N.Y.C., 1949-61; stockbroker, sr. security analyst, ltd. partner Burnham & Co., N.Y.C., 1962, v.p., corp., 1972; corp. v.p. Drexel Burnham Lambert, Inc., 1972—; mem. hearing bd. N.Y. Stock Exchange, 1978—. Pres. Greenville Community Council, 1967-70; vice chmn. Town of Greenburgh (N.Y.) Planning Bd., 1970-77; bd. dirs. N.Y. State Planning Fedn., 1975-78; mem. Westchester County Regional Plan Assn., 1970—; trustee Sarah Lawrence Coll., Bronxville, N.Y., 1979—; mem. N.Y. State Republican Com., 1976-82. Served to capt. USAAC, 1942-46. Recipient Silver Box award Greenville Community Council, 1970. Mem. N.Y. Soc. Security Analysts (sr. mem.), Fin. Analysts Fedn. Clubs: Metropolis Country (White Plains, N.Y.) (gov. 1974—, v.p. 1977-78); Metropolis Country (White Plains, N.Y.) (treas. 1979-80, pres. 1981-83); Harmonie (N.Y.C.)). Home: 3 Hadden Rd Scarsdale NY 10583 Office: 60 Broad St New York NY 10004

FRADLEY, FREDERICK MACDONELL, architect; b. Bronxville, N.Y., July 31, 1924; s. Justis Frederick and Helen Josephine (Macdonell) F.; m. Dorothy Davis Richard, Aug. 7, 1948; children—Stephen Davis, Wendy Macdonell. B.S., Brown U., 1948; M.F.A. (Lowell M. Palmer fellow), Princeton, 1954. Office engr. Turner Constrn. Co., Phila., 1948-51; project architect Vincent G. Kling, Phila., 1954-61; partner Bower & Fradley Architects, Phila., 1961-78; pvt. practice, 1978—. Important works include Market St. Transp. Mall Center, Phila., Phila. Gallery. Served with USAAF, 1942-46; PTO. Mem. Phi Delta Theta. Home: Route 1 Box 84 New Harbor ME 04554 New Harbor ME 04554

FRADON, DANA, cartoonist; b. Chgo., Apr. 14, 1922; m. Ramona Dom, Sept. 20, 1948; 1 dau., Amy. Student, Art Inst. Chgo., 1940-41, Art Students League N.Y., 1946-50. Contract cartoonist: New Yorker mag, N.Y.C., 1950—; Author: Insincerely Yours, 1978. Mem. bd. edn. Town of Newtown, Conn., 1970-75, councilman, 1976-78. Served with USAF, 1942-46. Democrat. Home: RFD 2 Brushy Hill Rd Newtown CT 06470

FRADY, MARSHALL BOLTON, television journalist, author; b. Augusta, Ga., Jan. 11, 1940; s. Joseph Yates and Jean Marshall (Bolton) F.; m. Susanne Barker, Jan. 20, 1961 (div. Oct. 1966); m. Gloria Mochel, Nov. 10, 1966 (div. 1975); children: Katrina, Carson, Shannon; m. Gudrun Barbara Schunk, May 14, 1975. B.A., Furman U., 1963; postgrad., U. Iowa, 1965-66. Corr. Newsweek mag., Atlanta and Los Angeles, 1966-67; staff writer Saturday Evening Post, Atlanta, 1968-69; contbg. editor Harper's mag., Atlanta, 1969-71; writer Life mag., Atlanta, 1971-73; chief corr. ABC News Closeup, N.Y.C., 1979—. Author: Wallace, 1968, Across A Darkling Plain, 1971, Billy Graham, 1979, Southerners, 1980. Recipient Golden Eagle Council Internat. Non-Theatrical Events, 1980, 83, Emmy Nat. Acad. TV Arts and Scis., 1981-82; named Disting. Alumnus Furman U., 1982; Woodrow Wilson fellow, 1963. Office: ABC News 7 W 66th St New York NY 10023

FRAEDRICH, ROYAL LOUIS, magazine editor, publisher; b. Weyauwega, Wis., Apr. 23, 1931; s. Clarence Otto and Libbie Clara (Trojan) F.; m. Phyllis Bohren, June 26, 1955; children—Lynn, Craig, Ann, Sarah, Paul. B.S., U. Wis., 1955. With Doane Agrl. Service, St. Louis, 1955-57; info. specialist Mich. State U., East Lansing, 1957-59; mng. editor Agrl. Pubs., Inc., Milw., 1959-64; editor Big Farmer mag., Milw., 1964-69, Frankfort, Ill., 1969-73, Farm Futures mag., Milw., 1973-81, pub., 1981—; exec. v.p. Top Farmers Am. Assn., Milw., 1973-81; pub., gen. mgr. AgriData Resources, Inc., 1981—; v.p., dir. Big Farmer Inc., 1969-73; v.p. Market Communications Inc., Milw., 1973-78. Vice pres. Grace Lutheran Ch., Menomonee Falls, Wis., 1963, mem. stewardship com., 1965-67, sec. bd. elders, 1974-77. Mem. Am. Agrl. Editors Assn. Home: N95 W16529 Richmond Dr Menomonee Falls WI 53051 Office: 205 W Highland Ave Milwaukee WI 53203

FRAENKEL, DAN GABRIEL, microbiologist; b. London, May 6, 1937; U.S., 1948, naturalized, 1957; s. Gottfried Samuel and Rachel F.; m. Margaret Duncan, Jan. 12, 1974; 1 dau., Naomi Rosamond. B.S., U. Ill., 1957; Ph.D., Harvard U., 1962. Postdoctoral fellow N.Y. U. and Einstein Coll. Medicine, 1962-65; asst., then asso. prof. microbiology and molecular genetics Harvard U. Med. Sch., 1965-73, prof., 1973—. Home: 34 Griggs Rd Brookline MA 02146 Office: Dept Microbiology and Molecular Genetics Harvard U Med Sch Boston MA 02115

FRAENKEL, GEORGE KESSLER, chemist, university administrator; b. Deal, N.J., July 27, 1921; s. Osmond Kessler and Helene (Esberg) F.; m. Johanna-Maria Herzog, June 30, 1951 (div. Aug. 1965); m. Elizabeth R. Rosen, Nov. 11, 1967. B.A., Harvard U., 1942; Ph.D., Cornell U., 1949. Research group leader National Def. Research Com., 1943-46; instr. chemistry Columbia U., N.Y.C., 1949-53, asst. prof., 1953-57, assoc. prof., 1957-61, prof., 1961—, chmn. dept. chemistry, 1966-68, dean grad. sch. arts and scis., 1968-83, v.p. spl. projects, 1983—; mem. postdoctoral fellowship com. Nat. Acad. Sci.-NSF, 1964-65; chmn. Gordon Research Conf. Magnetic Resonance, 1967; mem. Arts Coll. adv. council Cornell U., 1964-74. Asso. editor: Jour. Chem. Physics, 1962-64; Mem. adv. editorial bd.: Chemical Physics Letters, 1966-71; editorial bd.: Jour. Magnetic Resonance, 1969-70. Trustee Columbia U. Press, 1968-71, Walden Sch., N.Y.C., 1964-66. Recipient Army-Navy certificate of appreciation, 1948; Harold C. Urey award Phi Lambda Upsilon, 1972; decorated officer Ordre des Palmes Académiques. Fellow Am. Phys. Soc.; fellow AAAS; mem. Am. Chem. Soc., Assn. Grad. Schs. (exec. com. 1976-80, v.p. 1977-78, pres. 1978-79, chmn. com. policies on grad. edn. 1969-71), Phi Beta Kappa, Sigma Xi, Phi Kappa Phi. Home: 450 Riverside Dr New York NY 10027

FRAENKEL, GIDEON AUGUST, educator, chemist; b. Frankfurt, Germany, Feb. 21, 1932; came to U.S., 1948; s. Gottfried Samuel and Rachel (Sobol) F.; m. Alice Helen Messeloff, June 16, 1961; children—Peter Nicholas, Emily Alexandra. B.S., U. Ill., 1952; M.A., Harvard, 1953, Ph.D., 1957. Research asso. Calif. Inst. Tech., 1957-60; mem. faculty Ohio State U., 1960—, prof. chemistry, 1968—; guest prof. U. Lund, Sweden, 1971; vis. prof. M.I.T., 1980. Noyes fellow Calif.Inst. Tech., 1958. Mem. Am. Chem. Soc., Chem. Soc., AAAS, Sigma Xi, Phi Lambda Epsilon. Home: 3615 Romney Rd Columbus OH 43220

FRAENKEL, STEPHEN JOSEPH, engineering and research executive; b. Berlin, Germany, Nov. 28, 1917; came to U.S., 1938, naturalized, 1943; s. Max S. and Martha (Plessner) F.; m. Josephine Rubnitz, June 28, 1941; children: Richard Mark, Charles Matthew, Martha Ann. B.S. in Civil Engring. with distinction, U. Nebr., 1940, M.S., 1941; Ph.D., Ill. Inst. Tech., 1951. Registered profl. engr., Ill., registered structural engr. Engr. Pitts.-Des Moines Steel Co., 1941-44, Link Belt Co., 1944-46; with Ill. Inst. Tech. Research Inst., successively research engr., supr., dept. mgr., head dept. propulsion and structural research, 1946-55; dir. research and devel. Stanray Corp., Chgo., 1955-62; dir. research engring. Continental Can Co., 1962-64; gen. mgr. research and devel. Container Corp. Am., Chgo., 1964-75, dir. research and devel., 1975-82; pres. Tech. Services, Inc., Chgo., 1982—; Adviser effects nuclear weapons Dept. Def., 1950—; cons. space flight programs ABC. Mem. bd. editors: Research Mgmt; Contbr.: articles to profl. jours. Ency. Chem. Tech. Recipient certificate of achievement for atomic test Greenhouse, U.S. Joint Task Force Three. Mem. Soc. Exptl. Stress Analysis, Am. Ordnance Assn., Am. Mgmt. Assn., TAPPI (chmn. Chgo. sect. 1968-69, dir. 1969—, chmn. acad. adv. group 1971-73, chmn. acad. relations div. 1973-76), AIAA (pres. Chgo. sect. 1958-59, dir. 1959—), Navy League, Sigma Xi, Sigma Tau, Tau Beta Pi, Chi Epsilon. Home: 1252 Spruce St Winnetka IL 60093 Office: 209 S La Salle St Suite 575 Chicago IL 60604

FRAENKEL-CONRAT, HEINZ, research biochemist; b. Breslau, Germany, July 29, 1910; came to U.S., 1936, naturalized, 1941; s. Ludwig Fraenkel and Lili Conrat; m. Jane Opermann, July 14, 1939 (div.); children—Richard, Charles; m. Bea A. Singer, 1964. Student univs., Breslau, Munich, Vienna, Geneva; Dr. Med., U. Breslau, 1933; Ph.D. in Biochemistry, U. Edinburgh, 1936. Research in enzymatic peptide synthesis Rockefeller Inst., N.Y.C., 1936-37; crystallization of rattlesnake venom neurotoxin Inst. Butantan, Sao Paulo, Brazil, 1937-38; chemistry and biology pituitary hormones Inst. Exptl. Biology, U. Calif. at Berkeley, 1938-42; research methods protein modification Western Regional Research Lab., Dept. Agr., Albany, Calif., 1942-49; Rockefeller fellow, Eng., Denmark, 1950; staff virus lab., prof. virology U. Calif. at Berkeley, 1951—, also prof. molecular biology. Author: Design and Function at the Threshold of Life: the Viruses, 1962, the Chemistry and Biology of Viruses, 1969, Comprehensive Virology, Vol. 1, 1974, Virology, 1981. Recipient (with Schramm and Hershey) Lasker award, 1958; named Calif. Scientist of Year, 1958. Mem. Am. Soc. Biol. Chemists, Am. Chem. Soc., Nat. Acad. Scis., Am. Acad. Arts and Scis. Also research degradation and reconstitution tobacco mosaic virus, chem. research protein and nucleic acid of viruses, viral and nonviral plant enzymes, mechanism of snake venom neurotoxicity. Home: 870 Grizzly Peak Blvd Berkeley CA 94708

FRAGER, ALBERT S., retail food company executive; b. Boston, Dec. 29, 1922; s. Oscar and Anna (Polterak) F.; m. Marion Nathan, June 15, 1950; children: Owen R., Bonnie L. Frager Rubin, Laurie J. Burton, Sherri L. Student, Amos Tuck Sch. Bus., Dartmouth Coll., 1943; B.S. in Bus. Adminstrn, Northeastern U., 1944. Internal revenue agt. IRS, 1945-56; v.p., controller Stop & Shop, Inc., Boston, 1956-67, treas., 1967—, fin. v.p., 1969-79, sr. v.p., 1979—, also dir.; dir. South Shore Nat. Bank. Trustee, v.p Brookline Hosp.; trustee Combined Jewish Philanthropies; mem. corp. Northeastern U. Served with USNR, 1943-44. Mem. Am. Inst. C.P.A.s, Mass. Soc. C.P.A.s. Jewish (pres. temple). Home: 45 Ferncroft Rd Waban MA 02168 Office: PO Box 369 Boston MA 02101

FRAGER, NORMAN, stock broker; b. St. Louis, Aug. 7, 1936; s. Louis and Minnie (Eisenberg) F.; m. Deborah Berger, June 16, 1963; children—Susan, Anita. B.S., Washington U., St. Louis, 1960; M.S.C., St. Louis U., 1968. C.P.A., Mo. Pub. accountant Peat, Marwick, Mitchell & Co. (C.P.A.'s), St. Louis, 1960-65, Sidney S. Cohen & Co. (C.P.A.'s), 1965-67; stock broker, controller Burns, Stix Friedman & Co. Inc., St. Louis, 1967-69; asst. to corp. controller May Dept. Stores, St. Louis, 1969-70; v.p., treas., dir. Scherck, Stein & Franc, Inc.; allied mem. N.Y. Stock Exchange, St. Louis, 1970—; instr. finance St. Louis U. Grad. Sch., 1969-70. Served with AUS, 1954-57. Mem. Am. Inst. C.P.A.'s, Mo. Soc. C.P.A.'s. Home: 14532 Eddington Dr Chesterfield MO 63017 Office: 515 Olive St St Louis MO 63101

FRAGOMEN, AUSTIN THOMAS, capital goods co. exec.; b. Hoboken, N.J., Feb. 24, 1919; s. August and Mary (Firmin) F.; m. Ann E. Duffy, June 22, 1942; children—Austin Thomas, Ann E., Maryanne. Student, Cornell U., 1944; B.S. in Sci. and Physics, Seton Hall U., 1946; student at, Rensselaer Poly. Inst., 1945. Constrn. supt. Babcock & Wilcox Co., N.Y. area, 1942-43, supt. shop assembly mobile power plants, 1943; supt. charge constrn. Phila. Electric Southwark Sta., 1946-48, mgr. constrn., Chgo., 1950-59, mgr. constrn. dept., Barberton, Ohio, 1960-63, corp. v.p., 1963-69; dist. mgr. constrn. A.M. Lockett Co., New Orleans, 1948-49; corp. v.p. Diebold, Inc., Canton, Ohio, 1969-74; pres. BCC Mech. Inc., Washington; chmn. bd. AFCO Internat., Mantoloking; mng. dir. Kupper (Nigeria) Ltd., Kupcon (Nig.) Ltd., Kupper Int. N.V., 1977—. Trustee Area Devel. Summit County, Ohio. Served with USNR, 1943-45. Mem. Ohio Mfg. Assn. (trustee). Clubs: Brookside Country, Mantoloking (N.J.) Yacht, Bay Head (N.J.) Yacht. Home: Ocean Reef Club Key Largo FL 33037 Office: 1120 Connecticut Ave Washington DC also 1100 Ocean Ave Mantoloking NJ 08738

FRAHM, DONALD ROBERT, insurance company executive; b. Kansas City, Mo., Jan. 25, 1932; m. Jean Phyllis Appleton; children: Heather, Timothy, Mark. B.S. in Bus. Adminstrn., Washington U., St. Louis, 1953. Sr. v.p. CNA Ins., Chgo., 1955-74; v.p. Hartfold Ins. Group, Conn., 1974-76, sr. v.p., 1976-79, exec. v.p., 1979-83; pres. and chief operating officer Hartford Ins., Conn., 1983—. Served to lt. U.S. Army, 1953-55. Home: 29 Cheltenham Way Avon CT 06001 Office: Hartford Ins Group Hartford Plaza Hartford CT 06115

FRAILEY, FREDERICK WILLIAM, JR., journalist; b. Arkansas City, Kans., Feb. 13, 1944; s. Frederick William and Katherine (Getter) F.; children—Barbara Katherine, William Hughes. B.A., U. Kans., 1966. Reporter Sulphur Springs (Tex.) News-Telegram, 1961-64, Dallas Times-Herald, 1965, Chgo. Sun-Times, 1966-71; Chgo. bur. chief, asso. editor, sr. editor U.S. News and World Report, Washington, 1971-81, asst. mng. editor, 1981—. Author: Zephyrs, Chiefs and Other Orphans: The First 5 Years of Amtrak, 1977. Served with Ill. N.G., 1966-71. Presbyterian. Office: 2300 N St NW Washington DC 20037 *

FRAKES, JOHN LEWIS, advertising agency executive; b. Wayne, Mich., Oct. 28, 1934; s. George E. and Evelyn (Mott) F.; m. Kathleen A. Arnold, June 28, 1959; children: Drew, Eric, Evan, Elyse. B.A., Mich. State U., 1957. Group supr. Campbell-Ewald, Detroit, 1960-66, Young & Rubicam, 1966-70; sr. art dir. Leo Burnett, Chgo., 1970-71, Grey Advt., Detroit, 1971-72; creative dir., exec. v.p. McCann-Erickson, Detroit, 1972-82; exec. creative dir., exec. v.p. Ross Roy Inc., Detroit, 1982—, dir. Office: Ross Roy Inc 2751 Jefferson Detroit MI 48207

FRAME, CLARENCE GEORGE, banker; b. Dakota County, Minn., July 26, 1918; s. George and Helen (Hunter) F. A.B., U. Minn., 1941; J.D., Harvard U., 1947. Bar: Minn. 1947. With First Nat. Bank, St. Paul, 1947-80, asst. cashier, 1953-54, cashier, 1954-57, v.p., cashier, 1957-59, v.p., 1959-61, sr. v.p., 1961-68, exec. v.p., 1968-72, pres., 1972-80; vice-chmn. First Bank System, Inc., 1980-83, also dir., until 1983; dir. St. Paul Securities Inc., Webb Co., J.L. Shiely Co., Northland Co., MRFY Corp, Opus Corp., all Mpls., Chgo. Milw. Corp., Chgo., Courier Dispatch Group, Atlanta, Tosco Corp., Los Angeles. Trustee Walker Art Ctr., Mpls. Served from ensign to lt. comdr. USNR, 1942-46; to comdr., 1951-53. Clubs: Somerset Country, Minneapolis. Home: 334 Cherokee Ave Saint Paul MN 55107 Office: W-3070 First Bank Bldg 332 Minnesota St Saint Paul MN 55101

FRAME, JAMES H., telecommunication corporation executive; b. Chgo. B.A., St. John's Coll., Md., 1951. Various positions including dir. corp. programming devel. IBM, before 1978; dir. programming ITT, N.Y.C., 1978—, v.p., 1982—. Office: ITT Programming 320 Park Ave New York NY 10022

FRAME, JOHN TIMOTHY, bishop; b. Toronto, Ont., Can., Dec. 8, 1930; s. Duncan McClymont and Sarah Aitken (Halliday) F.; m. Barbara Alida Butters, Sept. 8, 1956; children—Alida Grace, Bronwyn Ruth, Monica Mary. B.A., Trinity Coll., Toronto, 1953, L.Th., 1957, S.T.B., 1961, D.D. (hon.), 1968. Ordained deacon, priest Anglican Ch. Can., 1957; minister Mission to Lakes Dist., Burns Lake, B.C., 1957-67; canon Diocese of Caledonia, 1965-67; bishop of, Yukon, 1967-80, sr. bishop, Province of B.C., 1971-80, acting metropolitan, 1973-75; dean of Columbia and rector Christ Ch. Cathedral, Victoria, B.C., 1980—. Home: 930 Burdett Ave Victoria BC V8V 3G8 Canada Office: 912 Vancouver St Victoria BC V8V 3V7 Canada

FRAME, RUSSELL WILLIAM, electronics executive; b. Clinton, Ind., Aug. 15, 1929; s. John Thompson and Virginia Mae (Whitted) F.; m. Dorothy Helen King, May 6, 1950; children: Russell W., Doranne Virginia (dec. 1969). A.E.E., Valaparaiso Tech. Inst., Ind., 1954. Electronics technician, project engr. Sandia Corp., Albuquerque, 1954-65; field engr. Data Instrument div. Bell & Howell, Albuquerque, 1965-66, dist. sales mgr., Huntsville, Ala., 1966-69, regional sales mgr., Dayton, Ohio, 1969-74, div. mgr. mktg. Datatape div., Pasadena, Calif., 1974-80, pres., 1980—. Served with USAF, 1948-52; Korea. Mem. Assn. Old Crows. Republican. Methodist. Club: Glendora Country. Lodge: Masons. Office: Datatape Div Bell & Howell 300 N Sierra Madre Vills Pasadena CA 91109

FRAME, RUTH RHEA, library association executive; b. Frederick, Okla., Oct. 19, 1916; d. Carl Sam and Mable Lutie (Rhea) McFall; m. Frederick William Frame, June 21, 1941. B.A., Okla. Central Coll., 1937; B.S. in L.S, Peabody Coll., 1939. Librarian U.S. Army, various locations, 1946-57; public library cons. Mich. State Library, Lansing, 1958-63, asst. state librarian, 1964-67; exec. sec. library adminstrn. div. ALA, Chgo., 1967-73, dep. exec. dir., 1973—; ALA rep. to Am. Nat. Standards Inst., N.Y.C., 1979-80. Mem. ALA (life), Freedom To Read Found., Friends of Libraries. Office: 50 E Huron St Chicago IL 60611

FRAMPTON, GEORGE THOMAS, lawyer; b. N.Y.C., Mar. 24, 1917; s. Harry Vinton and Mary Louise (Fottrell) F.; m. Margaret Anne Raup, May 2, 1941; children—George Thomas, Mary Louise. A.B., Duke U., 1938, J.D., 1941. Bar: N.Y. bar 1942, Ill. bar 1956, also U.S. Supreme Ct 1956. Assoc. firm Cravath, deGersdorff, Swaine & Wood, N.Y.C., 1941-42; with OPA, Washington, 1942-43; assoc. firm Fulton, Walter & Halley, N.Y.C., 1945-53; teaching fellow Harvard Law Sch., 1953-54; mem. faculty U. Ill. Coll. Law at Urbana-Champaign, 1954—, prof., 1957—; vice chancellor Urbana-Champaign, 1970-72; vis. summer prof. N.Y. U., 1954, Stanford U., 1957, Salzburg (Austria) Seminar Am. Studies, 1965; vis. prof. U. Calif. at Berkeley, 1959-60, N.Y. U., 1967-68; dir. Nat. Provisioner, Inc.; cons. Joint Congressional Com. Atomic Energy, 1963, Nat. Council Radiation Protection; project corp. debt financing ABA, 1963-65; AEC, 1974, ERDA, 1975, U.S. Dept. Energy, 1979-80. Author: (with E.R. Latty) Basic Business Associations, 1963. Mem. Democratic County Com., Westchester County, N.Y., 1946-53 Mem. Democratic County Com., Champaign County, Ill., 1960-70. Served with AUS, 1943-45; ETO. Mem. Am., Fed., Internat., Ill. bar assns., Assn. Bar City N.Y., Am. Arbitration Assn. (panelist), Nat. Lawyers Club. Home: 803 W Delaware Ave Urbana IL 61801 Office: U Ill Coll Law 504 E Pennsylvania Ave Champaign IL 61820

FRAMPTON, MERLE ELBERT, teacher educator; b. Smithfield, W.Va., Sept. 15, 1903; s. Clark Sylvester and Ethel Pearl (Von Betzer) F.; m. Iris Coldwell, Dec. 30, 1923; children—Scott Athearn, Iris Merle, Diane Joyce. B. Religious Edn., Boston U., 1925, A.M., 1927, M.S., 1928; A.M., Harvard, 1935, Ph.D., 1935; LL.D., Coll. of Ozarks, 1932; Litt.D., Mo. Valley Coll., 1940. Bus. asso. to dean Boston U., 1925-29; boys worker Chgo. Commons Settlement House, 1921-23;

prof. econs. Coll. of Ozarks, 1930-33, v.p., 1930-33; dir. Westminster Found., Boston, 1933-35; prof. edn. and head dept. Tchrs. Coll., Columbia, 1935-44; prof. edn. Hunter Coll., 1952—; dir. N.Y. Inst. for Edn. of Blind, 1935—; vis. prof. Hunter Coll., N.Y.C. Author: several books, including Camping for Blind Youth; The Residential School, 1954, Tragedy, 1968, Forgotten Children, 1969; Editor: Special Education for the Exceptional, Vols. I, II, III (Porter Sargent), 1956; Sec. treas.: Internat. Jour. of Blind; Contbr. articles on edn. of handicapped to jours. Dir. Am. Printing House for Blind, Soc. for Prevention Cruelty to Children, Westminster Found.; Mem. or chmn. several spl. coms. or orgns. on edn., tng. and employment of blind persons including: chmn. policy com. Nat. Com. for Employment of Handicapped; dir. of study for U.S. House Reps. Com. on Edn. and Labor, Spl. Edn. and Rehab.; mem. exec. com. Bronx Council Social Agys.; vice chmn. Pres. Com. on Employment of the Handicapped; pres. Eyes Right Found. for Handicapped Children, Inc. Commd. comdr. H.(S) USNR. Deocrated Nat. Order of Merit Republic Paraguay). Mem. N.E.A., Am. Sociol. Soc., Am. Assn. Instrs. and Workers for Blind, others. Republican. Presbyn. Clubs: Nat. Arts (Harvard); Nat. Republican, University (N.Y.C.); Rotary, N.Y. Athletic. Home: 14000 N Como Dr Route 1 Box 627 K Tucson AZ 85741

FRAMPTON, PETER, singer, musician; b. Beckenham, Kent, Eng., Apr. 22, 1950; m. Mary Lovett, 1972 (div. 1976). Former mem.: musical group The Herd; mem.: rock group Humble Pie, 1968-71; soloist, then founder: group Frampton's Camel, to 1974; soloist, 1974—; rec. artist, A & M Records, 1968—; (with Humble Pie) album's include Performance-Rockin' At the Fillmore, (with Frampton's Camel) Frampton's Camel; solo Where I Should Be; appeared in: film Sergeant Peppers Lonely Hearts Club Band, 1978. Office: care Beldock Levine & Hoffman 565 Fifth Ave Suite 600 New York NY 10017

FRANCA, CELIA, director, choreographer, dancer, narrator; b. London, Eng., June 25, 1921; m. James Morton, Dec. 7, 1960. Student, Guildhall Sch. Music, Royal Acad. Dancing; LL.D., U. Windsor, 1959, Mt. Allison U., 1966, U. Toronto, 1974, Dalhousie U., 1976, York U., 1976, Trent U., Peterborough, Ont., Can., 1977; D.C.L., Bishop's U., 1967; D.Litt., Guelph U., 1976. Mem. jury 5th Internat. Ballet Competition, Varna, Bulgaria, 1970, 2d Internat. Ballet Competition, Moscow, 1973. Debut: corps de ballet in Tudor, Mercury Theatre, London, 1936; soloist, Ballet Rambert, London, 1936-38; leading dramatic dancer, Ballet Rambert, 1938-39; guest artist, Ballet Rambert, 1950; dancer, Ballet des Trois Arts, London, 1939, Arts Theatre Ballet, London, 1940, Internat. Ballet, London, 1941; leading dramatic dancer, Sadler's Wells Ballet, 1941-46; guest artist, choreographer, Sadler's Wells Theatre Ballet, London, 1946-47; dancer, tchr., Ballets Jooss, Eng., 1947; ballet mistress, leading dancer, Met. Ballet, London, 1947-49; dancer, Ballet Workshop, London, 1949-51; founder, artistic dir., Nat. Ballet Can., Toronto, 1951-74; a prin. dancer, Nat. Ballet Can., 1951-59; co-founder, Nat. Ballet Sch., Toronto, 1959—; prin. roles include Black Queen in Swan Lake; title roles in Lady from the Sea; choreographer: ballets, including Midas, London, 1939, Cancion, London, 1942, Khadra, London, 1946, Dance of Salome, The Eve of St. Agnes, BBC-TV, 1950, Afternoon of a Faun, Toronto, 1952, Le Pommier, Toronto, 1952, Casse-Noisette, 1955, Princess Aurora, 1960, The Nutcracker, 1964, Cinderella, 1968, numerous others for CBC, Can. Opera Co.; author: The National Ballet of Canada: A Celebration, 1978. Bd. dirs. Can. Council. Decorated Order of Can.; recipient Key to City of Washington, 1955; Woman of Year award B'nai B'rith, 1958; award for outstanding contbn. to arts Toronto Telegram, 1965; Centennial medal, 1967; Hadassah award of merit, 1967; Molson award, 1974; award Internat. Soc. Performing Arts Adminstrs., 1979. Office: 250 Clemow Ave Ottawa ON K1S 2B6 Canada

FRANCE, NEWELL EDWIN, corporation executive; b. Massillon, Ohio, Sept. 30, 1927; s. Lawrence Joel and Marcella Ruth (Nelson) F.; m. Eve Elisabeth Voluter, 1953; children: Philip J., Corinne E., Anne-Claire I., Stephen C., Louise A. B.S., Northwestern U., 1953, M.S. in Hosp. Adminstrn, 1955. Adminstrv. resident Herrick Meml. Hosp., Berkeley, Calif., 1954-55; evening supt. Chgo. Wesley Meml. Hosp., 1955-56; asst. adminstr. St. Lukes Episcopal and Tex. Children's hosps., Houston, 1956-58, asso. adminstr., 1958-64, adminstr., 1964-73, exec. dir., 1973-83; exec. v.p. Burlington Am. Corp., Houston, 1983—; asso. adminstr. Tex. Heart Inst., Houston, 1958-64, adminstr., 1964-73, exec. dir., 1973—; cons. adv. council HEW and NIH; staff cons. AID, 1969—; cons. program projects rev. com. Nat. Inst. Neurol. and Communicative Disorders and Stroke; acad. planning bd. health care scis. Walden U., Naples, Fla.; mem. com. pediatrics NRC-Nat. Acad. Scis., 1975—; chmn. Greater Houston Hosp. Council, Children's Hosps. Execs. Council, 1972-73; dir. Child Care Center, Tex. Med. Center, 1967—; adj. asso. prof. Sch. Architecture, Rice U.; prof. health scis. Tex. Women's U. Bd. dirs. Met. Houston chpt. Nat. Found. March of Dimes, First City Bank Med. Center; trustee Pin Oaks Charity Horse Show Assn., Houston Bot. Soc.; mem. exec. bd. South Main Center Assn., Inc.; active Houston/Baku Sister City Assn. Served with USNR, 1946-48, 51-52. Fellow Am. Coll. Hosp. Adminstrs.; mem. Am. Hosp. Assn., Tex. Hosp. Assn. (chmn. council hosp. auxs. 1969-73, trustee 1972—, adviser, chmn. council on profl. service 1976—), Houston Area Hosp. Assn. (pres. 1968-69), Nat. Assn. Childrens Hosps. and Related Instns. (pres. 1969-70, conf. chmn. 1969, trustee 1971—, chmn. council past pres.'s 1973-74), Am. Assn. Hosp. Planning. Methodist. Clubs: Rotary Internat.; Doctors (Houston). Home: 9703 Oasis Dr Houston TX 77096 Office: 770 S Post Oak Ln #330 Houston TX 77056

FRANCE, RICHARD XAVIER, playwright, educator; b. Boston, May 5, 1938; married; 2 children. Spl. playwrighting fellow, Yale U., 1964-65; M.F.A. in Playwrighting, Carnegie-Mellon U., 1970; Ph.D. in Theatre History, Carnegie-Mellon U., 1973. Instr. English Allegheny Community Coll., Pitts., 1970-72; asst. prof. theatre arts R.I. Coll., 1972-73; vis. asst. prof. playwriting SUNY-Genesco, 1973-74; asst. prof. theatre and drama Lawrence U., Appleton, Wis., 1974-76, chmn. dept., 1976—; film and drama critic Sta. WQED-TV, Pitts., 1969-72; producer, writer, narrator sta. prodns. The Market Square Revival, 1971; writer, narrator U.S. Army Pictorial Ctr., N.Y.C., 1966-67; resident playwright U. Pitts., 1965-66, Music and Art Inst., San Francisco, 1961-63; playwright, observer Am. Conservatory Theatre, 1965-66; playwright, oberver Actors Workshop, San Francisco, 1960-62. Author: The Theatre of Orson Welles, 1977; play The Magic Shop, 1972, Fathers and Sons, 1972, The Adventure of the Dying Detective, 1974, The First Word and the Last, 1974, One Day in the Life of Ivan Denisovich, 1974, The Image of Elmo Doyle, 1976, Feathertop, 1979, Station J., 1979; articles. Grantee Ford Found., 1979, Rockefeller Found., 1979, Lawrence U., 1975, 76, Wis. Council Arts, 1975; fellow NDEA, 1969-71, Nat. Endowment Arts, 1973, 79-80; summer stipendee NEH, 1977; ind. fellow NEH, 1979; recipient Sam. S. Schubert Playwriting Fellowship, 1965, John Golden Playwriting Fellowship, 1965. Mem. Authors League, Dramatics Guild Am. (grantee 1967), Am. Theatre Assn. (theatre playwrights program 1975-77), Office Advanced Drama Research, Nat. Acad. TV Arts and Scis. Office: Dept Theatre and Drama Lawrence U Appleton WI 54911

FRANCE, ROBERT RINEHART, economist, univ. ofcl.; b. Massillon, Ohio, Aug. 12, 1921; s. Karl Anthony and Jennie (Fields) F.; m. Jean Charmion Reitsman, Jan. 31, 1948; children—Robert Karl, Virginia Grace, Cornelia Reitsman. A.B., Oberlin Coll., 1947; Ph.D., Princeton U., 1952. Asst. prof. dept. econs. Princeton U., 1952-56, research asso. indsl. relations sect., 1952-55; asso. prof. dept. econs. U. Rochester, 1956-62, prof., 1962—, asso. dean, 1962-63, asso. provost univ., 1963-70, v.p. planning, 1970—; impartial arbitrator labor-mgmt. disputes, 1953—. Contbr. articles to profl. publs. Chmn. Human Relations Commn., Monroe County.; Bd. dirs. Finger Lakes Health Service Agy.; pres. Rochester Regional Research Library Council, 1975-80, bd. dirs., 1970—. Served to capt. USAAF, 1942-46; lt. col. Res. ret. Mem. Am. Econ. Assn., Am. Arbitration Assn., Indsl. Relations Research Assn., Nat. Acad. Arbitrators. Home: 25 Hardwood Hill Rd Pittsford NY 14534

FRANCESCATTI, ZINO RENE, concert violinist; b. Marseille, France, Aug. 9, 1902; s. Fortuné and Ernesta-Feraud F.; m. Yoland de la Briere, Jan. 2, 1930. Appeared in concerts throughout Europe with leading condrs. and orchs., 1928-38, concert tour in, South Am., 1938, 47, 52, first tour in, U.S., 1939; and since appeared with leading orchs. tours of, South Am. and Mexico, 1947, 52, Europe, yearly, concert performances in, Israel, 1949-56, 58, 63, 66. Decorated commandeur De L'Ordre de la Légion d'Honneur, commandeur l'Ordre des Arts et Lettres; commandeur l'Ordre de Leopold, Belgium). Roman Catholic. Address: 165 W 57th St New York NY 10019 also 13600 La Clotat France

FRANCHOT, DOUGLAS WARNER, steel co. exec.; b. Tulsa, Mar. 27, 1922; s. Douglas Warner and Constance (Lippincott) F.; m. Maryan Smagula, Sept. 22, 1974; children by previous marriage—Douglas Warner, III, Peter van R., Michael L., Jenny Franchot Dashiell. B.A., Yale U., 1945, J.D., 1949. Bar: R.I. bar 1950, Mich. bar 1963. Asso., then partner firm Hinckley, Allen, Salisbury & Parsons, Providence, 1949-61; sr. atty. Ford Motor Co., Dearborn, Mich., 1961-65; v.p. gen. counsel various divs. Bristol-Myers Co., N.Y.C., 1965-75, v.p. devel., Cin., 1967-68; asso. gen. counsel Republic Steel Corp., Cleve., 1975-76, v.p., gen. counsel, sec., 1976—. Past bd. dirs. Lying-In Hosp., Providence, Children's Friend Service, Providence. Served as pilot USNR, 1943-45. Mem. Am., R.I., Mich. bar assns. Democrat. Episcopalian. Clubs: Mayfield Country; Yale (N.Y.C.); Cleve. Athletic. Home: 14707 Shaker Blvd Shaker Heights OH 44120 Office: Republic Steel Corp PO Box 6778 Cleveland OH 44101

FRANCIOSA, ANTHONY (ANTHONY PAPALEO), actor; b. N.Y.C., Oct. 25, 1928; s. Anthony and Jean (Franciosa) Papaleo; m. Beatrice Bakalyar, 1952 (div. Apr. 1957); m. Shelley Winters, May 5, 1957 (div. Nov. 1960); m. Judy Balaban, Jan. 1, 1962. Ed. high sch., N.Y.C.; studied drama with, Joseph Geiger; scholarship, Dramatic Workshop, New Sch. Social Research; studied, Actor's Studio. Waiter U.S.S. Pres. Cleveland. Worked with drama groups including, Off Broadway, Inc., N.Y. Repertory Theatre; on, Broadway in, End as a Man, 1953, Wedding Breakfast, 1954-55, A Hatful of Rain, 1955; motion pictures include Long Hot Summer, 1958, Naked Maja, 1959, Career Story on Page One, 1960 (Golden Globe award for best motion picture actor), Go Naked in the World, 1960, Senilita, 1961, Period of Adjustment, 1962, In Enemy Country, 1968, Across 110th Street, 1972, The Drowning Pool, 1975, Firepower, 1979; appeared in: Assault on a Queen, 1966, A Man Could Get Killed, 1966, The Swinger, 1966, A Girl Called Fathom, 1967, A Man Called Gannon, 1968, The Sweet Ride, 1968; star: TV series Valentine's Day, 1964-65, The Name of the Game, 1968-72, Search, 1972-73, Matt Helm, 1975-76. Recipient Count Volpe Di Misurata cup Venice Film Festival. Address: care Creative Artists Agency 1888 Century Park E Los Angeles CA 90067 *

FRANCIS, ARLENE (MRS. MARTIN GABEL), actress; b. Boston, Mass., Oct. 20; d. Aram and Leah (Davis) Kazanjian; m. Martin Gabel, May 14, 1946; 1 son, Peter. Student, Covent of Mt. St. Vincent, Finch Finishing Sch., and Theatre Guild Sch. Appeared in: plays The Women, 1937, Orson Welles' Mercury Theatre prodn. of Horse Eats Hat, and Danton's Death, 1938, All That Glitters, 1938, Michael Drops In, 1938, Young Couple Wanted, 1939, Journey to Jerusalem, 1940, The Walking Gentleman, 1942, The Doughgirls, 1942, The Overtons, 1945, The French Touch, 1945, The Cup of Trembling, 1948, (in translation of French play) L'Empereur de Chine, 1949, The Little Blue Light, 1951, Once More with Feeling; radio Monitor; films Stage Door Canteen, 1943, All My Sons, 1948, One, Two, Three, 1961, The Thrill of it All, 1963; appeared in: plays Mrs. Dally, 1965, Dinner at Eight, 1966, Lion in Winter, Pal Joey, Who Killed Santa Claus?; TV appearances include: Soldier Parade, 1949-55, What's My Line, 1950-67, Home, 1954-57, Arlene Francis Show, 1957-58; Author: That Certain Something, 1960, Arlene Francis - A Memoir, 1978. Mem. Am. Fedn. of Radio Artists, Actors Equity Assn., Screen Actors Guild. *

FRANCIS, BILL DEAN, university dean, artist; b. Salem, Ill., Oct. 14, 1929; s. Otto Kenoid and Louise (Shanafelt) F. B.S. in Art Edn, Ill. State (Normal) U., 1951; M.S. in Applied Art, U. Wis., 1952; postgrad., Ind. U., 1956-63. Tchr. art William Horlick High Sch., Racine, Wis., 1954-58; asst. prof. art and edn. Drake U., 1958-60; asst. prof. art U. Tex., Austin, 1960-64, asso. prof. art and edn., 1964-74, prof. art and edn., 1974—, asso. dean, 1978—; art edn. presenter White House Conf. on Children, 1970; HEW rep. Nat. Alliance for Arts in Edn., 1973-74; mem. edn. adv. panel Tex. Commn. on Arts and Humanities, 1976-80; mem. Tex. Council on Arts in Edn., 1978—, v.p., 1980—, pres., 1982-84; mem. Tex. Alliance on Arts, 1979. Author: The Humanities in Retrospect—A Cross-Comparison of Cultures from 1100 to 1972, 1973; author: Helping Children See Art and Make Art, 2 vols., 1-3, 4-6, 1982. Served with U.S. Army, 1952-54. Named Outstanding Art Educator Tex., 1978. Mem. Nat. Art Edn. Assn. (Tex. rep. 1971-73, v.p. Western region 1982-84, conv. mgr. Western arts div. 1962-67), Tex. Art Edn. Assn. (pres. 1971-73), Tau Kappa Epsilon, Phi Delta Kappa. Republican. Mem. Christian Ch. Home: 1100 Yaupon Valley Rd Austin TX 78746 *Growing up during the depression in rural, mid-America taught me to be thankful for anything good and not to complain about what was bad. Those times also taught me that honest, hard work was the most rewarding way of survival. No task has ever been beneath me even if I did not like it. I have not worked toward specific goals except to learn as much as I could about as many things as possible and do my best at whatever task was before me. The rewards came from this. Life has always been too exciting and enjoyable for me to become bored or cynical.*

FRANCIS, DALE LYMAN, publisher, columnist; b. Newark, Ohio, Mar. 8, 1917; s. Clarence Theodore and Florence (Day) F.; m. Barbara Hoole, Oct. 15, 1943 (dec. 1961); children: Guy Edward, Marianne Elizabeth; m. Margaret Alexander, Jan. 6, 1962; 1 dau., Rita Kathryn. B.A., Bluffton (Ohio) Coll., 1941; postgrad., U. Notre Dame, 1946-50; Litt.D. (hon.), St. Leo Coll., Fla., 1968. Sports writer Troy (Ohio) Daily News, 1932-35; reporter Lima (Ohio) News, 1935-36; reporter, columnist Dayton (Ohio) Jour.-Herald, 1936-38; founding editor N.C. Cath., Raleigh, 1946-47; dir. publs., founder U. Notre Dame Press, 1950-52; dir. bur. information Nat. Cath. Conf., Washington, 1952-55; dir. Def. of Faith, Matanzas, Cuba, 1955-56; founding editor Lone Star Cath., Austin, Tex., 1956-61; editor Troy Daily News, 1961-64; exec. editor Our Sunday Visitor, Huntington, Ind., 1964-68, 74-78; pub. Twin Circle, Los Angeles, 1968-70; editor, pub. Nat. Cath. Register, 1970-74; pres. Julian Press, 1974—; editor Cath. Standard, Washington, 1978-83; columnist Huntington Herald-Press, Washington, 1983—. Books include Catholic Prayer Book, 1959, Kneeling in the Bean Patch, 1960, Caring Is Living, 1978. Bd. dirs. Citizens for Ednl. Freedom, 1968—; founding bd. dirs. Cath. League for Religious and Civil Rights, 1973—. Served with USAAF, 1941-46; PTO. Mem. Cath. Press Assn. (bd. dirs. 1970-74, St. Francis de Sales award 1959), Am. Newspaper Guild, Sigma Delta Chi. Democrat. Club: Kiwanis. Home: 9 Northway Dr Huntington IN 46750 Office: Box 680 Huntington In 46750 *My life has been directed by belief in God and my conviction that belief in God compels me to care about people.*

FRANCIS, DARRYL ROBERT, former banker; b. Ridgeway, Mo., Aug. 21, 1912; s. Leonard F. and Cora (Young) F.; m. Loretta Smyth, Feb. 26, 1938; children: Darryl Robert, Linda Francis Northrip, Marilyn Francis Obermiller. B.S. in Agr, U. Mo., 1936. Research asst. dept. agrl. econs. U. Mo., 1936-39; sec.-treas. Ozark Prodn. Credit Assn., Springfield, Mo., 1939-42, St. Joseph Prodn. Credit Assn. (Mo.), 1942-44; agrl. economist Fed. Res. Bank St. Louis, 1944-49; v.p. Nat. Bank Commerce, Memphis, 1949-52, Boatmen's Nat. Bank, St. Louis, 1953; mgr. Memphis br. Fed. Res. Bank St. Louis, 1954-59, 1st v.p., 1960-66, pres., 1966-76; chmn. bd., chief exec. officer Mchts. Nat. Bank, Ft. Smith, Ark., 1979-82; dir. Baldor Electric Co., Ft. Smith, Edison Bros. Stores, Inc., St. Louis. Mem. Alpha Gamma Sigma, Gamma Sigma Delta. Home: 3509 Royal Scots Way Fort Smith AR 72903

FRANCIS, DAVID LIVINGSTON, coal co. exec.; b. Charlottesville, Va., Sept. 29, 1914; s. James Draper and Permele Crawford (Elliott) F.; m. Janine Martin, Nov. 27, 1976; children—Kathy Anne, Anna Barbour. B.A., Yale U., 1937; M.B.A., Harvard U., 1939; student mining, W.Va. U., 1937; LL.D., Davis and Elkins Coll., 1961, Marshall U., 1963. Vice pres., gen. mgr. Princess Elkhorn Coal Co., David, Ky., 1940-42, pres., 1946-59, Princess Coals, Inc. (merger Princess Elkhorn, Powellton, Sycamore and Cinderella coal cos.), 1959-63, chmn. bd., 1963—; pres. Princess Coal Sales Co., 1946-68, chmn. bd., 1968—; pres. Mallory Stores, Inc., Huntington, W.Va., 1946-63, Sycamore Coal Co., 1968—, Kathy's Farm, Inc., 1978—, Princess Coals, Inc. (merger Kathy's Farm), 1975-78, chmn. bd., 1979—; dir. Appalachian Coals, Inc. Dir. So. States Indsl. Council, 1950—; chmn. W.Va. Adv. Com. Manpower Utilization; mem. W.Va. Rehab. Adv. Council, 1961—; mem. adv. council Outdoor Recreation Resources Rev. Commn., Washington, 1962; chmn. Cancer, United Fund-ARC campaigns; pres. Tri-State area council Boy Scouts Am.; chmn. W.Va. Citizens for Constl. Conv., 1967; vice chmn. Citizens Adv. Commn. on W.Va. Legislature, 1967-70; councilman City of Huntington, 1956-61, mayor, 1960-61; chmn. Huntington Constl. Commn., 1957-61; trustee, past pres. Huntington Clin. Found.; trustee, mem. research com. Com. Econ. Devel. N.Y.C., 1958—; trustee Davis and Elkins Coll.; bd. dirs. W.Va. Found. Ind. Colls. Served to lt. comdr. USNR, 1942-45. Mem. U.S. C. of C. (dir. 1956-64, chmn. natural resources 1957-64, v.p. 1961-64), Nat. Coal Assn. (dir. 1958-, treas. 1960-61), So. Coal Producers Assn. (dir. 1958—, exec. com.), AIME, NAM, Chi Psi. Presbyterian (elder). Clubs: Masons, Engrs. (Huntington). Home: Kathy's Farm Frankford WV 24938 Office: PO Box 1210 Huntington WV 25714

FRANCIS, DICK (RICHARD STANLEY FRANCIS), author; b. Tenby, South Wales, Oct. 31, 1920; s. George Vincent and Catherine Mary (Thomas) F.; m. Mary Margaret Brenchley, June 21, 1947; children: Merrick, Felix. Student Brit. schs. Steeplechase jockey, 1946-57; racing corr. London Sunday Express, 1957-73. Author: Dead Cert, 1962, Odds Against, 1965, Flying Finish, 1966, Blood Sport, 1967, Rat Race, 1970, Slay-Ride, 1973, High Stakes, 1975, Trial Run, 1978, Whip Hand, 79, Reflex, 1980, Twice Shy, 1981, Banker, 1982, The Danger, 1983; autobiography The Sport of Queens, 1957. Served as officer RAF, 1943-45. Decorated officer Order of Brit. Empire; Champion steeplechase jockey, 1953-54. Mem. Crime Writers Assn., Detection Club, Racecourse Assn. Clubs: Press, Sportsmans. Address: Penny Chase Blewbury Oxfordshire England UK

FRANCIS, JAMES DELBERT, oil company executive; b. Orange, N.J., Jan. 8, 1947; s. Delbert Matthew and Margaret Janet (Thornley) F.; m. Alexandra Isabelle Ould; children: Elizabeth M., John A., David S., Virginia A. B.S. in Commerce, U. Va., 1970; J.D., U. Fla., 1973. Bar: Fla. 1973. Ptnr. Smith and Hulsey, Jacksonville, Fla., 1973-82; exec. v.p. Charter Oil Co., Jacksonville, 1982—. Bd. dirs. Buckner Manor Maternity Home, Jacksonville, 1976—, St. Johns Presbyterian Kindergarten, Jacksonville, 1981-83; pres. St. Johns Presbyterian Kindergarten, Jacksonville, 1983—. Mem. ABA, Fla. Bar, Jacksonville Bar Assn. Democrat. Clubs: Fla. Yacht; River, Seminole (Jacksonville). Home: 4250 Ortega Forest Dr Jacksonville FL 32210 Office: Charter Oil Co PO Box 4726 Jacksonville FL 32232

FRANCIS, JOSEPH A., clergyman; b. Lafayette, La., Sept. 30, 1923; s. Joseph and Mabel (Coc) F. B.A., Cath. U. Am., also; M.A.; postgrad., Xavier U., New Orleans, Loyola U., Mt. St. Mary's Coll. Ordained priest Roman Catholic Ch., 1950; asst. dean students St. Augustine Sem., 1951-52; asst. dir. Holy Rosary Inst., 1952-60; adminstr. Immaculate Heart of Mary Parish, 1950, Holy Cross, Austin, Tex., 1960-61; instr. Pius X High Sch., 1961-62; founder, prin. Verbun Dei High Sch., Watts, Calif., 1962-67; provincial superior, 1967-73, titular bishop of Valiposita, aux. bishop of Newark, 1976—; trustee Immaculate Conception Sem., Mahwah, N.J.; bd. overseers Harvard Div. Sch.; bd. trustees Divine Word Coll., Epworth, Iowa; bd. dirs. Am. Bd. Cath. Missions, Cath. Relief Services. Mem. Black Priests' Caucus (past pres.), Nat. Office for Black Catholics (dir.), Conf. Maj. Superiors of Men (past pres.), Nat. Cath. Conf. Interracial Justice (dir.). Address: 139 Glenwood Ave East Orange NJ 07017

FRANCIS, LLOYD CYRIL, Canadian parliament official, economist; b. Ottawa, Ont., Can., Mar. 19, 1920; s. Frederick Roland and Mary (Dyble) F.; m. Margery Elizabeth Miller, Dec. 23, 1943; children: John Paul, Donald Lyle, Mary Elaine. B.A., U. Toronto, 1940, M.A., 1945; Ph.D., U. Wis., 1955. Research economist Govt. of Can., Ottawa, 1951-60; nat. pres. Profl. Inst. Pub. Service of Can., 1958-59; alderman City of Ottawa, 1958-60, mayor, 1960-63; mem. parliament, Ottawa, 1963-65, 68-72, 74-79, 80—; dep. speaker House of Commons, Ottawa, 1980—. Trustee Ottawa Civic Hosp., 1960-63, Children's Aid Soc., 1963. Served to flying officer RCAF, 1941-45. Liberal. Unitarian. Lodge: Kiwanis. Home: 1130 Castlehill Crescent Ottawa ON Canada K2C 2A8 Office: House of Comons Room 233S Ottawa ON Canada K1A OA6

FRANCIS, MARION SMITH, lawyer; b. Slater, Mo., July 17, 1905; s. Marion L. and Annie Marian (Smith) F.; m. Jewel M. Brandenberger, May 26, 1943; 1 son, James Ashby. Student, Kemper Mil. Sch., 1923-24; A.B., U. Mo., 1927, J.D., 1929. Bar: Mo. bar 1928. Practice of law, Mexico, Mo., 1929-38; pub. adminstr. Audrain Co., Mo., 1931-33; mem. Pub. Service Commn. Mo., Jefferson City, 1938-41; asso. Bryan, Cave, McPheeters & McRoberts, St. Louis, 1942-50, partner, 1951-77, counsel, 1978—; Past trustee Mo. U. Law Sch. Found. Served from 2d lt. to maj., judge adv. gen. dept. AUS, 1943-46; served with 70th inf. div. 7th army; ETO. Mem. St. Louis, Mo. State, Am. bar assns., S.A.R., Judge Advocates Assn., Phi Gamma Delta, Phi Delta Phi. Clubs: Mo. Athletic, Bellerive Country (St. Louis). Home: 13 Nantucket Ln Saint Louis MO 63132 Office: 500 N Broadway Saint Louis MO 63102

FRANCIS, MERRILL RICHARD, lawyer; b. Iowa City, Jan. 28, 1932; s. Kenneth Victor and Blythe (White) F.; m. Nancy Humphreys, Sept. 11, 1954; children: Kerry L., David M., Robin A. B.A. magna cum laude, Pomona Coll., 1954; J.D., Stanford U., 1959. Bar: Calif. 1960. Partner firm Sheppard, Mullin, Richter & Hampton, Los Angeles, 1959—. Pres. La Canada Coordinating Council, 1973-74; mem. exec. bd. Cityhood Action Com., 1975-76; chmn. La Canada High Sch. adv. com. La Canada Unified Sch. Dist., 1978-79; bd. dirs. Family Service Los Angeles, 1980-81; treas. Fellows of Contemporary Art, 1980-81. Served to lt. (j.g.) U.S. Navy, 1954-56. Fellow Am. Bar Found.; mem. ABA (chmn. subcom.), State Bar of Calif., Los Angeles county Bar Assn. (sect. chmn.), Fin. Lawyers Conf. (pres. 1972-73), La Canada-Flintridge C. of C. and Community Assn. (pres. 1971-72), Order of Coif, Phi Beta Kappa. Club: Jonathan. Office: 333 S Hope St 48th Floor Los Angeles CA 90071

FRANCIS, PHILIP HAMILTON, engineering educator, consultant; b. San Diego, Apr. 13, 1938; s. William Samuel and Ruth Kathryn (Allison) F.; m. Regina Elizabeth Kirk, June 10, 1961 (div. Apr. 1971); children: P. Scott, Mary A.; m. Diana Maria Villarreal, July 15, 1972; adopted children: Edward P., Kenneth J. B.S., Calif. Poly. State U., 1959; M.S., U. Iowa, 1960, Ph.D., 1965; M.B.A., St. Mary's U., San Antonio, 1972. Registered profl. engr., Tex. Stress analyst Douglas Aircraft Co., Santa Monica, Calif., 1960-62; mgr. solid mechanics S.W. Research Inst., San Antonio, 1965-79; prof., chmn. dept. mech. and aerospace engring. Ill. Inst. Tech., Chgo., 1979—; cons. U.S. Gypsum Co., Chgo., 1983—, Internat. Harvester Co., 1979-82. Author: Principles of R & D Management, 1977; editor: Dynamic Problems of Thermoelasticity, 1975, Advanced Experimental Techniques in the Mechanics of Solids, 1973. Mem. Leon Valley City Council (Tex.), 1976-79. Recipient Gustas Larson award ASME and Pi Tau Sigma, 1978. Mem. ASME, Am. Acad. Mechanics Edn. (founding mem.), Am. Soc. Engring. Edn., Sigma Xi, Tau Beta Pi, Pi Tau Sigma. Home: 139 Prairie Ave Wilmette IL 60091 Office: Ill Inst of Technology 3300 S Federal St Chicago IL 60616

FRANCIS, ROBERT, author; b. Upland, Pa., Aug. 12, 1901; s. Ebenezer Fisher and Ida May (Allen) F. A.B., Harvard U., 1923, Ed.M., 1926; L.H.D., U. Mass., 1970. Author: poetry Stand With Me Here, 1936, Valhalla and Other Poems, 1938, The Sound I Listened For, 1944, The Face Against the Glass, 1950, The Orb Weaver, 1960, Come Out Into the Sun, 1965, Like Ghosts of Eagles, 1974, Robert Francis: Collected Poems, 1936-76, 1976, Butter Hill and Other Poems, 1984; fiction We Fly Away, 1948; essays The Satirical Rogue on Poetry, 1968, Pot Shots at Poetry, 1980; prose sketches and poems A Certain Distance, 1976; autobiography The Trouble With Francis, 1971, Frost: A Time to Talk, Conversations and Indiscretions Recorded by Robert Francis, 1972; interview Francis on the Spot, 1976; rec. Robert Francis Reads His Poems, 1975. Co-recipient Shelley Meml. award, 1938; recipient Golden Rose award New Eng. Poetry Club, 1942, Jennie Tane Poetry award Mass. Rev., 1962; Brandeis U. Creative Arts award in poetry, 1974; Phi Beta Kappa poet Tufts U., 1955, Harvard, 1960; Rome fellow Am. Acad. Arts and Letters, 1957-58; fellowship award Acad. Am. Poets, 1984; Amy Lowell poetry travelling scholar, 1967-68. Hon. mem. Phi Beta Kappa. Address: Fort Juniper 170 Market Hill Rd Amherst MA 01002

FRANCIS, RONALD, chemist, educator; b. Livermore Falls, Maine, Oct. 21, 1933; s. Wallace Herbert and Mabel Louise (Kenrick) F. A.B. in Physics, Colby Coll., Waterville, Maine, 1955; Ph.D. in Chemistry, M.I.T., 1964. Asso. inorganic chemist Arthur D. Little Inc., Cambridge, Mass., 1960-64; head dept. inorganic chemistry ITEK Corp., Lexington, Mass., 1964-69; electronics dept. mgr. Atlantic Electronics, Newton, Mass., 1966; head dept. photog. sci. E.G. & G., Inc., Bedford, Mass., 1966-69; prof., div. chmn. Rochester (N.Y.) Inst. Tech., 1969—; lectr. dept. chemistry Met. Coll., Boston U., 1964-69; dir. Am. Photosystems Inc., St. Johnsbury, Vt.; cons. in field. Mem. Soc. Photog. Scientists and Engrs., Am. Chem. Soc., Am. Photogrammetry Soc.

FRANCIS, SAM, artist; b. San Mateo, Calif., June 25, 1923; m. Mako Ioemitsu; 1 child, Osamu. B.A., U. Calif., Berkeley, 1949, M.A., 1950; student, Académie Fernand Leger, Paris, 1950. Works in permanent collection, Mus. Modern Art, N.Y.C., Whitney Mus., N.Y.C., Nat. Gallery, Washington, Albright-Knox Art Gallery, Buffalo, Tate Gallery, London, Mus. Nationale d'Art Moderne, Paris, Stedelyk Mus., Amsterdam, others, one-person shows include, San Francisco Mus. Art, 1958, Moderna Museet, Stockholm, 1960, Kunsthalle, Berne, Pasadena Art Mus., 1964, Stedelyk Mus., Amsterdam, 1968, Albright-Knox Art Gallery, Buffalo, 1972, Hong Kong Arts Ctr., 1981, Galerie Niepel, Dusseldorf, W. Ger., 1982; also numerous group exhbns. U.S. and abroad. Served with AUS, 1943-45. Recipient 1st prize 3d Internat. Biennial Exhibit Prints, Tokyo, 1962; Dunn Internat. prize Tate Gallery, London, 1963; Tamarind fellow, 1963. Office: Galerie Smith Anderson 200 Homer St Palo Alto CA 94301 *

FRANCISCUS, JAMES GROVER, actor; b. Clayton, Mo., Jan. 31, 1934; s. John Allen and Loraine (Grover) F.; m. Kathleen Kent Wellman, Mar. 28, 1960; children: Jamie, Kellie, Korie, Jolie. B.A., Yale U., 1957. V.p., producer Omnibus Prodns. Inc., Ltd., 1968. Appeared: TV series Naked City, 1958, Mr. Novak, 1963-65, Longstreet, 1971, Doc Elliot, 1973, Hunter, 1977; films include The Outsider, 1962, Youngblood Hawke, 1963, Hell Boats, 1968, Marooned, 1969, Beneath the Planet of the Apes, 1969, Cat and Nine Tails, 1970, The Amazing Dobermans, 1976, Puzzle, 1977, Good Guys Wear Black, 1977, The Greek Tycoon, 1977, Greed, 1978, The Concorde, 1978, City on Fire, 1978, Killer Fish, 1979, Nightkill, 1980, Butterfly, 1980, White Death, 1980, Jacqueline Bouvier Kennedy, 1981, The Courageous, 1982; prodns. include Heidi, 1969, David Copperfield, 1970, Jane Eyre, 1971, Kidnapped, 1972, The Red Pony, 1973. Office: care ICM 8899 Beverly Blvd Los Angeles CA 90048

FRANCIS-VOGELSANG, CHAREE, business executive; b. Akron, Ohio, Aug. 22, 1946; d. William John and Mary Martha (Kemp) Francis; m. Carl R. Vogelsang. Student, Ohio Paralegal Inst., 1975-76; A.A., U. Akron, 1979, B.S.B.A., 1982. With gen. office and legal dept. Diebold, Inc., Canton, Ohio, 1964-72, asst. sec., 1972-78, sec., 1978—. Mem. Am. Soc. Corp. Secs., Nat. Assn. Legal Assts. Republican. Presbyn. Home: 432 31st St NW Canton OH 44709 Office: 818 Mulberry Rd SE Canton OH 44711

FRANCK, FREDERICK SIGFRED, artist, author, dental surgeon; b. Maastricht, Netherlands, Apr. 12, 1909; came to U.S., 1939, naturalized, 1945; s. Daniel and Helen (Foyer) F.; m. Claske Berndes Franck, July 15, 1960; 1 son, Lukas van Witsen Franck. Student, U. Amsterdam, 1926-31; Chirurgien Dentiste, Antwerp Dental Sch., 1935; L.D.S., Royal Coll. Surgeons, Edinburgh, Scotland, 1937; D.M.D., U. Pitts., 1942, D.F.A. (hon.), 1963. Practice dentistry, London, 1937-39; resident oral surgery U. Pitts., 1942-44; anaesthetist Elizabeth Steel Magee Hosp.; staff Children's Hosp., Pitts., 1942-44; service cons. Netherlands East Indies govt., 1944-46; dentist, N.Y.C., 1946-66; vis. staff Albert Schweitzer Hosp., 1958-60; chief mission Med. Internat. Coop., 1958; research fellow Nanzan U., Nagoya, 1981. Author: Open Wide, Please, 1957, Au Pays du Soleil, 1958, Days with Albert Schweitzer, a Lambarene Landscape, 1959; juvenile My Friend in Africa, 1960; African Sketchbook, 1961, My Eye is in Love, 1963 (Art Am. 50th Anniversary spl. citation 1963), Au Fil de L'Eau, 1964, Outsider in the Vatican, 1965, Met Het Oog Op Het Vatican, 1965, I Love Life, 1967, Exploding Church, 1968, Open Boek, 1967, Croquis Parisiens, 1969, Tutte le Strade portano a Roma, 1969, Le Paris de Simenon, 1969, Simenon's Paris, 1970, Tussen Broek en Brooklyn, 1971, The Zen of Seeing, 1973, Pilgrimage to Now/Here, 1973; play Inquest on a Crucifixion, 1975; author: An Encounter with Oomoto, 1975; Author: The Book of Angelus Silesius, 1976, Zen and Zen Classics, 1977, EveryOne, the Timeless Myth of Everyman Reborn, 1978, The Awakened Eye, 1979, Art as a Way, A Return to the Spiritual Roots, 1981, The Buddha Eye, An Anthology of the Kyoto School, 1982, The Supreme Koan, Confessions of a Journey Inward, 1982, Messenger of the Heart, The Book of Angelus Silesius, 1982; De Zenvar het Zien, 1983; Cons. editor: Parabola Quar; research editor: Nanzan Monograph Series; Contbr. articles, drawings to various mags. and periodicals.; One-man shows, Contemporary Arts Gallery, Lilienfeld Galleries, Passedoit Gallery, Albert Landry Gallery, (all N.Y.C.), 1959, 60, Saginaw (Mich.) Mus., Doll & Richards Gallery, Boston, Ringling Mus. Art, M.H. De Young Mus., San Francisco, Waddell Gallery, Far Gallery, both N.Y.C., Foster—White Gallery, Seattle, 1976, U. Puget Sound Gallery, Seattle, 1977, Thorpe Intermedia Gallery, N.Y.C., others, shows in, Paris, Amsterdam, Geneva, London, Rotterdam, Brussels, Rome, Tokyo, Kyoto, 1971, U. Maine, 1970-72, Melbourne, Australia, 1972, Interchurch Center Gallery, Greater Middletown Arts Council, 1973, Far Gallery, group shows, Met. and Whitney museums, Corcoran Biennale, also Indpls., Mpls., Nanzan U., Nagoya, Japan, 1981; represented in permanent collections, M.H. de Young Meml. Mus., Fogg Art Mus., San Francisco Mus., U. Ill., Mus. Modern Art, Vatican, Rome, Witherspoon Gallery, Raleigh, N.C., Tokyo Nat. Mus., Nat. Collection Fine Arts, Washington, museums, Santa Barbara, Amsterdam, Eindhoven, Maastricht, N.Y. Pub. Library, Seattle Mus., Dartmouth, Cornell U., Aschenbach Found., Georgia Mus., Whitney Mus., N.Y. U., State Capitol Mus., Wash., others, traveling exhbn. to 12 univs. and colls., Midwest, 1970-72. Bd. dirs. Temple of Understanding. Recipient purchase prize U. Ill., Am. Inst. Arts Letters, Living Arts Found.; 1st prize Carnegie Inst.; prize Musees Nationaux Francais; medal for drawings Pope John XXIII, 1963. Fellow Internat. Inst. Arts and Letters, Soc. for Arts, Religion and Contemporary Culture (dir.); mem. Artists Equity Assn. (hon. dir. N.Y.), P.E.N. Built Pacem In Terris Trans-religious Sanctuary, Warwick, N.Y., 1965. Home: Route 1 Box 165 Pacem in Terris Covered Bridge Rd Warwick NY 10990 *I discovered that to defy the general trend towards specialization as a writer, painter, draughtsman, playwright, does not mean "to spread oneself thin", is only seemingly a multiple commitment, and is in my case a single-minded obedience to what my very nature bids me to express in any medium I can handle.*

FRANCK, LAWRENCE JOSEPH, lawyer; b. Vicksburg, Miss., Sept. 10, 1931; s. Charles Etienne and Angela Marie F.; m. Dorothy R. Walker, May 24, 1958; children—Alicia Ann, Angela Marie, Lawrence Walker. B.B.A., 1953; LL.B., 1958. Bar: Miss. bar 1958, U.S. Supreme Ct. bar 1971. Asso. firm Vollor & Thames, Vicksburg, 1958-62; partner firm Travis, McKee & Franck, Jackson, Miss., 1962-63, Butler, Snow, O'Mara, Stevens & Cannada, Jackson, 1963—; adj. prof. law Miss. Coll., 1976; mem. Miss. Supreme Ct. Adv. Com. on Rules of Civil Procedure, 1976-79, vice chmn., 1978. Pres. Diocesan Council Catholic Men, Diocese of Natchez-Jackson, 1965-67; bd. dirs. Nat. Council Cath. Men, 1967-72, sec., 1972-74; bd. dirs. Nat. Council Cath. Laity, 1972-74. Served to 1st lt. U.S. Army, 1953-56. Nat. Endowment for Humanities grantee, 1974. Fellow Am. Coll. Trial Lawyers, mem., Am. Bar Assn., Miss. Bar Assn., Hinds County (Miss.) Bar Assn., Miss. Def. Lawyers Assn. (pres. 1977-78), Internat. Assn. Ins. Counsel, Am. Law Inst. Office: 1700 Deposit Guaranty Plaza Jackson MS 39201

FRANCK, MICHAEL, lawyer, association executive; b. Berlin, Oct. 6, 1932; U.S., 1941, naturalized, 1950; s. Wolf and Marga (Oppenheimer) F.; m. Carol E. Eichert, May 29, 1965; children: Michele, Lauren, Rebecca, Jennifer. B.A., Columbia U., 1954, J.D., 1958. Bar: N.Y. 1958, Mich. 1970. Trial counsel Liberty Mut. Ins. Co., Bklyn., 1958-60; chief litigator com. on grievances Assn. Bar City N.Y., 1960-70; cons. spl. com. on disciplinary procedures, bd. governance Pa. Supreme Ct., 1969-72; spl. counsel Phila. Ct. Common Pleas, 1970-73; exec. dir. State Bar Mich., Lansing, 1970—; mem. Commn. on Uniform State Laws, 1975—, Mich. Malpractice Arbitration Adv. Com., 1975—; mem. coordinating council on lawyer competence Conf. Chief Justices, 1981—. Contbr. articles to bar jours. Served with U.S. Army, 1954-56. Mem. ABA (com. on nat. coordination disciplinary enforcement 1970-73, reporter, com. on evaluation of fee dispute procedures 1968-70, chmn. sect. bar activities 1975-76, mem. long range planning council 1979-81, mem. council sect. on individual rights and responsibilities 1982—, mem. com. on ethics and profl. responsibility 1982—, chmn. com. to implement model rules of profl. conduct 1983—, del. 1978, 82—, mem. ALI-ABA adv. com. on medel peer rev. 1978-79, liaison to Commn. on Evaluation Profl. Standards 1977-83, chmn. com. profl. discipline 1979-82, mem. task force on lawyer advt. 1977), State Bar Mich., N.Y. State Bar Assn., Ingham County Bar Assn. Office: 306 Townsend St Lansing MI 48933

FRANCK, THOMAS MARTIN, legal educator; b. Berlin, July 14, 1931; naturalized, 1977; s. Hugo and Ilse (Rosenthal) F. B.A., U. B.C., 1952, LL.B., 1953; LL.M., Harvard U., 1954, S.J.D., 1956. Asst. prof. law U. Nebr., 1956-57; mem. faculty NYU, 1957—, prof. law, 1960—, dir. Center Internat. Studies, 1965—; acting dir. internat. law Carnegie Endowment Internat. Peace, 1973-75, dir., 1975-79; vis. prof. Stanford U., 1963, U. East Africa, 1964, 65, York U. Osgoode Hall Law Sch., 1972-73, 74-76; dir. research UN Inst. Tng. and Research, 1980-82; cons. U.S. AID Dept. State, 1970-72; constl. adviser govts., Tanganyika, 1963, Zanzibar, 1963, 64, Mauritius, 1965; mem. Sierra Leone Govt. Commn. Legal Edn., 1964, Nat. Liberal Adv. Council Can., 1952-53. Author: Race and Nationalism, 1960, The United Nations in the Congo, 1963, East African Unity Through Law, 1965, Comparative Constitutional Process, 1968, The Structure of Impartiallity, 1968, Why Federations Fail, 1968, A Free Trade Association, 1968, Word Politics, 1971, Secrecy and Foreign Policy, 1973, Resignation in Protest, 1975, Control of Sea Resources by Semi-Autonomous States, 1978, Foreign Policy by Congress, 1979; co-author: Foreign Relations Law, 1980; editor: The Tethered Presidency, 1981, Human Rights in Third World Perspective, 1982; bd. editors: Am. Jour. Internat. Law; Contbr. to books. Served to lt. Can. Army, 1953. Guggenheim fellow, 1973-74, 82-83. Mem. Can. Council Internat. Law, African Law Assn., Assn. Am. Law Schs., Am. Soc. Internat. Law (exec. council), Internat. Law Assn. (v.p. U.S. br.), Council Fgn. Relations. Home: 15 Charlton St New York NY 10014

FRANCK, WILLIAM FRANCIS, textile company executive; b. Fayetteville, N.C., July 29, 1917; s. William Francis and Martha Elizabeth (Lawhon) F.; m. Carolyn Ann Pannill, Nov. 29, 1941; children—Martha (Mrs. Overman Rollins), William Francis III, Carolyn Ann (Mrs. Alex Gordon), John M. B.A., Duke, 1939. Salesman Belk Leggett Co., Durham, N.C., 1935-40; cost clk. DuPont Co., Martinsville, Va., 1940-43; personnel mgr. Pannill Knitting Co., Martinsville, 1946-50; v.p. gen. mgr. Sale Knitting Co., Martinsville, 1950-53; pres., chief exec. officer Tultex Corp., Martinsville, 1953—; v.p. Tulstar Factors, Inc., N.Y.C.; dir. Piedmont Bank Group, Inc., Am. Furniture Co., Martin Processing Co. Inc., all Martinsville. Bd. mem. Martinsville YMCA, 1969-78; fund chmn. Meml. Hosp. drive, 1966-67, bd. mem., 1963-77; mem. Martinsville Sch. Bd., 1956-61, Blue Ridge Airport Authority, 1962—. Served to 1st lt. Q.M.C. AUS, 1943-46; ETO. Mem. Martinsville C. of C. (1st pres. 1959-61). Presbyterian (elder 1954-76). Clubs: Kiwanis, Chatmoss Country. Home: 1105 Plantation Rd Martinsville VA 24112 Office: Box 5191A Martinsville VA 24115

FRANCKE, LINDA BIRD, journalist; b. N.Y.C., Mar. 14, 1939; d. Samuel Curtis and Janet (King) Bird; m. G.D. Mackenzie, Jan. 12, 1961; 1 son, Andrew Mackenzie; m. Albert Francke III, Oct. 7, 1967; children—Caitlin, Tapp. Student, Bradford Jr. Coll., 1958. Copywriter Young & Rubicam, Inc., N.Y.C., 1960-63, Ogilvy & Mather, Inc., 1965-67; contbg. editor N.Y. Mag., N.Y.C., 1968-72, 80—; gen. editor Newsweek Mag., N.Y.C., 1972-77; columnist N.Y. Times, 1977—; TV news commentator Spl. Edit., 1978-79; dir. New Directions; juror Am. Book Awards, 1981; Co-chmn. Writer's Resource Center, Southampton, N.Y. Works in numerous anthologies, including, The New York Spy, 1967, The Power Game, 1970, Running Against the Machine, 1969, Women: A Book for Men, 1979; author: The Ambivalence of Abortion, 1978, Growing Up Divorced, 1983. Recipient award Cannes Film Festival, 1969. Mem. Authors Guild, Women's Media Group N.Y.C. Home: Sagaponack NY 11962 *The thought on my life that consumes me these days is the glorious excitement of being a woman in contemporary America. For two-thirds of my life, I felt lesser and angrily frustrated because I was not born a male, the gender that seemed biologically destined to spawn the leaders, the movers, the producers. Now all is in the process of change and for the past twelve years, I have revelled in the joy-and the privilege-of being a woman.*

FRANCKLE, CHARLES TRAVERS, banker; b. St. Petersburg, Fla., Aug. 17, 1945; s. Cornelius Shaw and Ruth (Travers) F.; m. Mary Fox, June 21, 1971; children: Katherine Ruth, Charles Travers Jr. B.A., U. South Fla., 1970; M.A., Northwestern U., 1971; Ph.D., U. N.C., 1977. Asst. prof. fin. U. Tex., Austin, 1976-81; chief economist First City Cancorp., Houston, 1981—. Contbr. articles to profl. jours. Mem. Tex. Econ. and Demographic Assn. (pres. 1983), Nat. Assn. Bus. Economists, Am. Econ. Assn., Am. Fin. Assn., Southwest Fin. Assn., Houston C. of C. (econ. newsletter com 1982-83), Beta Gamma Sigma. Home: 16707 Sir William Dr Spring TX 77373 Office: First City Bancorp of Tex Inc 1001 Fannin St Suite 950 Houston TX 77002

FRANCO, ANTHONY M., public relations executive; b. Detroit, July 7, 1933; s. John Richard and Evelyn Louise F.; m. Lois Ann McCann, Aug. 23, 1958; children: Catherine, Suzanne, Anne, Anthony, Patricia, Michael, David. Student, U.S. Naval Acad., 1955-57; B.S., Wayne State U., 1958. Dir. public relations Dawson-Murray Advt., Detroit, 1958-60; dir. public relations Fred M. Randall Co., Detroit, 1960-62, Denman & Baker Advt., 1962-64; pres. Anthony M. Franco, Inc., Detroit, 1964—. Past Trustee Marygrove Coll., Detroit; trustee U. Detroit; corp. bd. dirs. Boys Clubs Met. Detroit, 1972—; v.p. Met. Detroit council Boy Scouts Am.; vice chmn. Channel 56. Served with U.S. Army, 1953-55. Mem. Internat. Public Relations Group of Cos. (v.p., dir.), Public Relations Soc. Am. (dir.-at-large, past pres., dir. Detroit chpt., chmn. East Central dist.), Mich. C. of C., Greater Detroit C. of C. (dir.), U.S. Naval Acad. Alumni Assn. Roman Catholic. Clubs: Detroit Athletic, Press, Bloomfield Hills Country; Wilderness Country (Noblis, Fla.). Home: 1914 Long Lake Shores Dr Bloomfield Hills MI 48013 Office: 28 W Adams Detroit MI 48226

FRANCO, JEAN, educator; b. Dukinfield, Eng., Mar. 31, 1924; d. William and Ella (Newton) Swindells; m. Juan A. Franco (div.); 1 child, Alexis Parke. B.A., U. Manchester (Eng.), 1944, M.A., 1946; B.A., U. London, 1960, Ph.D. in Spanish, 1964. Lectr. spanish Queen Mary Coll. U. London, 1960-64; reader King's Coll., 1964-68; prof. lit. U. Essex, 1968-72; prof. spanish and comparative lit. Stanford U., 1972-82; prof. Spanish Columbia U., N.Y.C., 1982—. Author: Modern Culture of Latin America, 1967, 2nd edit., 1970, Introduction to Spanish American Literature, 1969, Cesa Vallejo: The Dialectrics of Poetry and Silence, 1976; editor: (with others) Companion to World Literature; contbr.: Ency. Lit., Times Lit Supplement, Spectator; editor: Tabloid, 1980—. Mem. Soc. for Latin Am. Studies (founding, past officer), MLA, Latin Am. Studies Assn. Address: Dept of Spanish and Portuguese Columbia U New York NY 10027 *

FRANCO, JOHAN (HENRI GUSTAVE), composer; b. Zaandam, Netherlands, July 12, 1908; came to U.S., 1934, naturalized, 1942; s. S. Franco and Margaretha J.E.C. (Gosschalk) F.; m. Eloise Lavrischeff, Mar. 28, 1948. Grad., First Coll., The Hague; studied composition with, Willem Pijper, Amsterdam, 4 yrs. Entire program of his compositions was presented at Town Hall, N.Y., 1938; commd. to write opening music at Centennial of his college, 1938; collaborated with Oscar Thompson on sect. on Contemporary Dutch composers in the Cyclopedia of Music and Musicians, 1938; prin. works include 5 symphonies, 6 concerti lirici, Divertimento for Flute and Strings, 1946, many songs, 2 cello sonatas, 1 viola sonata, 6 partitas piano, 12 partitas for piano, 13 partitas and other compositions for carillon, As the Prophets Foretold (cantata), The Stars Look Down (oratorio), The Prodigal, Songs of the Spirit (for soprano and woodwind quintet), The Song of Life (for mixed chorus a cappella), Seven Biblical Sketches (for carillon and narrator), Twelve Preludes (for piano); recs. Fantasy for Cello and Orch, The Virgin Queen's Dream (for soprano and orch.), Symphony V "The Cosmos", As the Prophets Foretold (for soloists, mixed chorus, brass, and carillon), Seven Biblical Sketches (for carillon and narrator); incidental music for 5 prodns. The Tempest, The Book of Job, Romans By St. Paul, Electra; recs. The Pilgrim's Progress. Served in U.S. Army, Mar. 1942-Sept. 1943. Mem. Am. Composers Alliance (B.M.I.). Home: 403 Lake Dr Virginia Beach VA 23451 *I have learned to trust inspiration exclusively for my compositions. All else is merely scaffolding.*

FRANCO, JOHN ALBERT, ins. holding co. exec.; b. N.Y.C., Apr. 1, 1942; s. Dominick and Theresa (DiBlasi) F.; m. Mary Elizabeth Drake, May 27, 1967; children—John Albert, Susan, Margaret, Carol. A.B., Columbia, 1963; LL.B., N.Y. U., 1967. Bar: N.Y. bar 1967. With Westvaco Corp., N.Y.C., 1970-79, comptroller, 1979; exec. v.p., chief fin. officer Capital Holding Corp., Louisville, 1979—; dir. Commonwealth Fire & Casualty Co; past chmn. pension com. Am. Paper Inst. Served with U.S. Army, 1967-69; Vietnam. Decorated Bronze Star.

FRANCO, VICTOR, physics educator; b. N.Y.C., Dec. 15, 1937. B.S., NYU, 1958; M.A., Harvard U., 1959, Ph.D., 1964. Research assoc. MIT, Cambridge, 1963-65, Los Alamos Sci. Lab., 1965-67, Lawrence Radiation Lab., Berkeley, Calif., 1967-69; assoc. prof. Bklyn. Coll., 1969-72, prof., 1973—; cons. in field. Contbr. numerous articles to sci. jours. Recipient various fellowships and research grants. Fellow Am. Phys. Soc.; mem. Sigma Xi. Office: Physics Dept Brooklyn Coll Brooklyn NY 11210

FRANCOEUR, JACQUES GERVAIS, publisher; b. Montreal, Que., Can., May 15, 1925; s. Louis and Adele (Gervais) F.; m. Catherine Thompson, Oct. 8, 1956; children: Lyne, Anne, Josee, Louise. Student, St. Laurent Coll., 1938-41, Sir George Williams Coll., 1941-43. Pres., pub. UniMedia Newspapers, Montreal, 1950—; pres. Dimanche Matin, Montreal; chmn. Le Soleil, Quebec, Le Quotidien, Chicoutimi; v.p. Montreal-Granby Press, Inc., Distbn. Eclair, Montreal, Progres-Dimanche, Chicoutimi, La Parole, Drummondville; pres. Suburban Weeklies, Montreal; vice chmn. Le Droit, Ottawa, Litho-Prestige, Inc.;

past chmn. Can. Exec. Service Overseas. Former mem. City Montreal Public Safety Commn., 1961-70; pres. Federal-Provincial-Municipal Study Commn. on Civil Pro- tection, 1964-66. Mem. Can. Daily Newspapers Publishers Assn. (past pres.), Am. Newspapers Publishers Assn. (dir.), Internat. Press Inst. (mem. exec. bd.), French Weeklies Assn. (past pres.), Can. Press (past mem. exec. bd.), Que. Daily Newspaper Publishers Assn. (past pres.). Roman Catholic. Home: 65 Belvedere Pl Westmount Montreal PQ Canada Office: 5701 Christophe-Colomb St Montreal PQ Canada

FRANCOIS, EMILE ANDRE, manufacturing executive; b. Montpellier, France, July 25, 1939; came to U.S., 1980; s. Emile M. and Joaquina (Falceto) F.; m. Agnes M.A. Tourriere, Aug. 8, 1959; children: Rachel, Christine, Gilles-Olivier. Engr., Conservatoire National des Arts et Metiers, 1968; M.B.A., Institut d'Administration des Entreprises, Paris, 1969. Quality engr. Norton (S.A.), Conflans, France, 1962, works mgr., Pamplona, Spain, 1969, gen. mgr., after 1970, then mng. dir.; v.p. Norton Co., Worcester, Mass., 1979, group v.p. diversified products, Worcester, 1980-82, group v.p. engring. materials, 1982—. Served with French Air Force, 1959-61. Mem. Worcester Com. Fgn. Relations, Am. Mgmt. Assn. Club: Worcester. Home: 80 Hundreds Rd Wellesley MA 02181 Office: 1 New Bond St Worcester MA 01606

FRANCOIS, FRANCIS BERNARD, association executive, lawyer; b. Barnum, Iowa, Jan. 21, 1934; s. Rudolph John and Irene Frances (McDonough) F.; m. Eileen M. Schmelzer, Feb. 6, 1960; children: Joseph, Marie, Michael, Monica, Susan. B.S., Iowa State U.; LL.B., George Washington U. Bar: Md. 1960, U.S. Patent and Trademark Office. Chief judge Orphan's Ct. Prince George's County, Upper Marlboro, Md., 1962-66; commr. Prince George's County, Upper Marlboro, Md., 1966-71; councilman Trince George's County, Upper Marlboro, Md., 1971-80; exec. dir. Am. Assn. State Hwy. and Transp. Ofcls., Washington, 1980—; adv. com. Ctr. Transp. Studies, MIT, 1983—; mem. adv. panel White House Intergovtl. Sci. and Enging. Tech., 1976-80; mem. Washington Suburban Transit Commn., 1978-80, chmn., 1979; dir. Washington Met. Area Transit Authority, 1978-80; exec. com. Transp. Research Bd., 1980—; trchr. urban affairs Earlham Coll., Washington, 1969—; lectr. Contbr. articles to profl. jours. Mem. adv. council Nat. Community Energy Mgmt. Ctr., 1981-82; mem. local govt. energy policy adv. com. Dept. of Energy, 1979-80; vice chmn. Md. Potomac Water Authority, 1970-80; air quality control adv. council State of Md., 1975-80; chmn. Water Resources Planning Bd., 1975-77; mem. Gov.'s Interstate Water Quality Planning Com., 1973-74; v.p. Md. Com. for Fair Representation, 1962; counselor Washington Career Inst., 1963; dir. Bowie Jaycees, Bowie Fine Arts Soc., Bowie YMCA; trustee Md. Easter Seal Soc., Prince George's United Way, Md. Soc. Crippled Children and Adults. Recipient Community Service award Nat. Capital chpt. ASCE, 1980, Community Serviceaward Bowie Jaycees, 1980, Community Service award Cedar Heights Civic Assn., 1978; named Washingtonian of Yr. Washingtonian Mag., 1973. Mem. Nat. Assn. Counties (pres. 1978-80), Md. Assn. Regional Councils (pres. 1972-73), Washington Met. Council Govts. (dir. 1966-80, pres. 1971), Community Assns. Inst. (dir. 1975-80, pres. 1979-80), Am. Inst. Planners. Democrat. Roman Catholic. Lodges: K.C.; Lions. Home: 12421 Seabury Ln Bowie MD 20715 Office: Am Assn State Hwy and Transp Officials Suite 225 444 N Capitol St NW Washington DC 20001

FRANCOIS, WILLIAM ARMAND, lawyer; b. Chgo., May 31, 1942; s. George Albert and Evelyn Marie (Smith) F.; m. Barbara Ann Sala, Aug. 21, 1965; children—Nicole Suzanne, Robert William. B.A., DePaul U., 1964, J.D., 1967. Bar: Ill. bar 1967. Practiced in, Lyons, Ill., 1967-68; atty. Nat. Can Corp., Chgo., 1970—, sec., 1974—, v.p., 1978—. Served to capt. AUS, 1968-70. Mem. Am., Ill., Chgo. bar assns., Am. Soc. Corporate Secs. Home: 326 Earls Ct Deerfield IL 60015 Office: 8101 W Higgins Rd Chicago IL 60631

FRANCONERI, LOUIS JOHN, newspaper publishing executive, communications technology executive; b. Bklyn., Nov. 3, 1942; s. Angelo and Connie (Dericco) F.; 1 dau., Stacy. B.S., Rochester Inst. Tech., 1965. Asst. dir. Am. Newspaper Pubs. Assn., Reston, Va., 1965-71; v.p. ops. The Balt. Sun, 1971—; pres. Newspaper Systems Group, 1976-77, Harris Systems Users Group, Melbourne, Fla., 1975-76. Author: Harris 2500 at the Baltimore Sun, 1976; author, speech editor, pub.: Lower Costs thru Election Technology, 1976; author, paper editor, pub.: Letterpress to Offset, Baltimore Sun, 1982, Newsprint Runnability, 1983. Mem. Am. Newspaper Pubs. Assn. (mem. research and devel. com. 1982—). Office: The Balt Sun 501 N Calvert St Baltimore MD 21278

FRANGIONE, BLAS, physician; b. Buenos Aires, Argentina, Mar. 26, 1929; came to U.S., 1961; s. Juan and Filomena (Liuni) F. M.D., U. Buenos Aires, 1953; Ph.D. Molecular Research Council, Cambridge U., Eng., 1968. Intern Hosp. Militar, Buenos Aires, 1950-52, resident in clin. medicine, 1952-54; instr. medicine NYU Med. Ctr., N.Y.C., 1965-66; asst. prof. medicine NUY Med. Ctr., N.Y.C., 1969-70; assoc. prof. exptl. medicine NYU Med. Ctr., N.Y.C., 1970-75, assoc. prof. pathology, 1975-76; prof. pathology NUY Med. Ctr., N.Y.C., 1976—. Acting chmn. Irvington House Inst., N.Y.C., 1981—. Served to lt. Argentine Army, 1949-50. Mem. Am. Soc. Clin. Investigation, Am. Assn. Immunologists, Biochem. Soc., Brit. Soc. Immunology, Brit. Biochem. Soc. Roman Catholic. Club: Cambridge Soc. Office: NYU Med Ctr 550 1st Ave New York NY 10016

FRANK, ALBERT EUGENE, foreign service officer; b. Marengo, Ill., Feb. 24, 1918; s. Robert Worth and Grace (Haun) F.; m. Nancy Ballard, May 25, 1942; children: Chana, Worth, Nancy, Morley. Student, Wabash Coll., 1934-36; B.A., Coll. Wooster, 1938; M.A., U. Minn., 1941; postgrad., Woodrow Wilson Sch., Princeton, 1960-61. Instr. Highlands U., 1946, Morgan Park Jr. Coll., 1946-47; joined U.S. Fgn. Service, 1947; vice consul, Sydney, Australia, 1947-1950; 2d sec. Am. embassy, Ottawa, Can., 1950-1952; officer State Dept., 1952-56; 2d sec. Am. embassy, Rome, 1956-60; officer State Dept., 1961-65; 1st sec. Am. embassy, Mogadiscio, Somali Republic, 1965-68, Paris, France, 1968-71; adviser Dept. State Office Telecommunications, Washington, 1971-73. Chmn. Princeton unit Recording for Blind, Inc., 1979-82; chmn. bd. trustees North Princeton Devel. Ctr. Served with USN, 1941-46. Presbyterian. Home: 28 Laurel Rd Princeton NJ 08540

FRANK, BARNEY, congressman; b. Bayonne, N.J., Mar. 31, 1940; s. Samuel and Elsie (Golush) F. A.B., Harvard U., 1962, J.D., 1977. Exec. asst. to mayor of Boston, 1968-71; adminstrv. asst. to U.S. congressman, 1971-72; mem. Mass. Ho. of Reps. from Boston, 1972-80, 97th Congress from 4th Dist. Mass.; teaching fellow govt. Harvard U., 1963-67; asst. to dir. Inst. Politics, John F. Kennedy Sch., 1966-67; fellow Inst. Politics, 1971. Home: 114 Floral St Newton MA 02161 Office: US Ho of Reps Washington DC 20515

FRANK, BERNARD, lawyer; b. Wilkes-Barre, Pa., June 11, 1913; s. Abraham and Fanny F.; m. Muriel I. Levy, June 19, 1938; children: Roberta R. Frank Penn, Allan R. Ph.B., Muhlenberg Coll., Allentown, Pa., 1935; J.D., U. Pa., 1938; postgrad., N.Y. U., 1940-42. Bar: Pa. bar 1939. Since practiced in, Allentown; asst. U.S. atty. Eastern Dist. Pa., 1950-51; asst. city solicitor, Allentown, 1956-60. Author articles on ombudsmen in profl. jours. Vice chmn. B'nai B'rith Nat. Commn. Adult Jewish Edn., 1959-61, chmn., 1961-63. Served with F.A. AUS, 1943-46. Decorated comdr. Order of North Star, Sweden; recipient Disting. Service award Internat. Ombudsman Inst., 1980. Mem. Internat. Bar Assn. (chmn. com. ombudsman 1973-80), ABA (chmn. com. ombudsman 1970-76), Fed. Bar Assn. (chmn. com. ombudsman 1971-74), Pa. Bar Assn., Lehigh Bar Assn., World Assn. Lawyers, U.S. Assn. Ombudsmen (hon.), Internat. Ombudsman Inst. (dir., v.p. 1978—), Jewish Publ. Soc. Am. (dir. 1982—), 94th Inf. Div. (pres. 1953-54). Home: 745 N 30th St Allentown PA 18104 Office: 931 Hamilton Mall Allentown PA 18105

FRANK, CLINTON EDWARD, advt. exec.; b. St. Louis, Sept. 13, 1915; s. Arthur A. and Daisy Marian (Irwin) F.; m. Frances Calhoun Price, July 25, 1941 (div. 1967); children—Marcia Case, Clinton Edward, Laurie Anne, Cynthia Calhoun, Arthur A. III; m. Margaret Rathje Mullins, May 24, 1967. A.B., Yale, 1938. Account exec. Blackett-Sample-Hummert, 1938-41; Dancer-Fitzgerald-Sample, 1947-48; sales promotion mgr. E. J. Brach & Sons, Chgo., 1948-49; v.p., treas., partner Price-Robinson & Frank, Inc., 1949-53; pres. Clinton E. Frank, Inc., Chgo., 1954-67, chmn. exec. com., dir., 1967-77, chmn. bd., 1973-77, hon. chmn., 1977—; chmn. Bridlewood Corp., Chgo., 1977—; dir. Baxter Travenol Labs. Trustee Eye Research Inst., Boston; vice-chmn., trustee Brain Research Found. Served with USAAF, 1941-45; aide to Lt. Gen. James H. Doolittle; exec. officer 98th Bomb Group; Africa, Italy; ret. as lt. col. Clubs: Chicago, Yale of Chgo. (dir.), University, Commonwealth, Commercial, Indian Hill, Old Elm. Home: 28 Bridlewood Rd Northbrook IL 60062 Office: Bridlewood Corp One First Nat Plaza Suite 2530 Chicago IL 60603

FRANK, CURTISS E., lawyer, organization executive; b. N.Y.C., Nov. 13, 1904; s. Augustus A. and Mary (Fowler) F.; m. Grace Watkins, Oct. 11, 1929 (dec. Nov. 1957); children: Anne Fairfield Frank DuBois, Curtiss Ely; m. Lila Bonhus Shaw, Dec. 13, 1958. A.B., Colgate U., 1925, L.L.D., 1969; L.L.B., Columbia U., 1928. Bar: N.Y. bar 1928. Asso. firm Hughes, Schurman & Dwight, 1928-37; asst. U.S. atty. So. Dist. N.Y., 1931-32; partner firm Hughes, Hubbard & Ewing, 1937-49; v.p., gen. counsel Reuben H. Donnelley Corp., 1949-51, exec. v.p., 1952-55, pres., 1956-61, chmn. bd., chief exec. officer, 1961-66; pres. Dun & Bradstreet, Inc., 1966-67, vice chmn., 1968-69; pres. Council for Fin. Aid to Edn., N.Y.C., 1970-73, chmn. exec. com., 1974-78, mem. adv. bd., 1978—; dir. Willcox & Gibbs, Inc., Shearson Mut. Funds, Elderworks, Elderhostel; pres. Nat. Exec. Service Corps., 1977-80, vice chmn., chmn. exec. com., 1981—; mem. cons. panel to comptroller gen. U.S., 1967-69. Councilman City of Yonkers, 1942-43, mayor, 1944-49; chmn. bd. trustees Colgate U., 1969-75, trustee emeritus, 1976—; bd. visitors Columbia U. Law Sch., 1976—; bd. dirs. ACF Industries Found., Recs. for Blind; hon. bd. dirs. Assn. Governing Bds. Univs. and Colls.; mem. exec. com. Nat. Municipal League. Mem. Phi Beta Kappa. Episcopalian. Clubs: Union League, Blind Brook, Round Hill (Conn.) Country; Port Royal, Hole-in-the-Wall Golf (Naples, Fla.). Home: 3725 Fort Charles Dr Naples FL 33940 also 7 Butternut Hollow Rd Greenwich CT 06830

FRANK, DAVID D., public relations executive; b. Phila., Sept. 4, 1923; s. Arthur William and Mabel Elise (Droste) F.; m. Marcia Peaslee, Apr. 10, 1948; children: Wendy Lynn Frank Locksley, Thomas Peaslee, Mary Elise, Amy Chase. B.A. cum laude, Princeton U., 1947. Reporter, Wall Street Jour., N.Y.C., 1947-49; mgr. pub. infor. Am. Locomotive Co., Schenectady, 1949-53; dir. pub. relations Montreal Locomotive Works, Ltd., 1953-55; asso. Ivy Lee and T.J. Ross, N.Y.C., 1955-65; v.p. T.J. Ross & Assos., Inc., N.Y.C., 1965-71, exec. v.p., 1971-80, pres., 1980—; cons. UN Secretariat, 1973. Served to 1st lt. F.A., AUS, 1943-46. Mem. Pub. Relations Soc. Am. (pres. N.Y. chpt. 1973-74). Republican. Office: 405 Lexington Ave Room 1902 New York NY 10017 *

FRANK, EDGAR GERALD, financial executive; b. Cin., May 15, 1931; s. Carl F. and Marcella M. F.; m. Joy Hueber, Oct. 30, 1954; children: Thomas, Phillip, Angela, Walter. B.B.A., U. Cin., 1955. Acct. Wm. S. Merrell Co., Cin., 1960-61; asst. sec. Emery Industries, Cin., 1961-66; fin. v.p. Samuel Moore & Co., Aurora, Ohio, 1966-79; v.p. fin. Telex Corp., Tulsa, 1979—. Served with USN, 1955-58. Mem. Am. Inst. C.P.A.s, Fin. Execs. Inst. Office: PO Box 1526 Tulsa OK 74101

FRANK, EDWARD, editor; b. Binghamton, N.Y., Aug. 30, 1924; s. Leon H. and Frances (Parnagian) F.; m. Doris K. Lyon, May 16, 1959; 1 son, Stephen. B.S., Am. U., 1952. Feature writer USIA; Washington, 1951-53; reporter Binghamton Sun, 1953-59; asst. news editor Syracuse (N.Y.) Post-Standard, 1960-62, Rochester (N.Y.) Democrat and Chronicle, 1962-66; news editor Cocoa (Fla.) Today, 1966-73, Phila. Inquirer, 1973—. Served with U.S. Army, 1943-46. Office: Phila Inquirer Newspapers Inc 400 N Broad St Philadelphia PA 19101

FRANK, ELKE, foreign service officer; b. Hamburg, Germany, May 27, 1934; came to U.S., 1953, naturalized, 1965; d. Rudolf and Margarethe (Daehn) F. B.A., Fla. State U., 1957, M.A., 1959; Ph.D., Harvard U., 1964. Asst. prof. polt. sci. Fla. State U., 1961-66, Hunter Coll., 1966-68; asso. prof. Am. U., 1968-70; dean, prof. polit. sci. Mary Baldwin Coll., Staunton, Va., 1970-72; spl. student master Theol. Studies Program, Va. Theol. Sem., spring 1977; res. officer Fgn. Service, Washington, 1977—; Brookings Instn. guest scholar, 1964; guest scholar Radcliffe Inst., Cambridge, Mass., 1973. Author: Law Makers in a Changing World, 1966, John F. Kennedy, a Political Biography, 1968, A Theory of Comparative Politics, 1973, U.S. Foreign Policy: 1947-1974, 1975, Introduction to Comparative Politics, 2d edit., 1977; also articles, book revs.; mem. editorial bd.: Jour. Politics, 1969-73. Mem. So. Polit. Sci. Assns., Am. Polit. Sci. Assns., LWV, Phi Beta Kappa, Phi Kappa Phi, Pi Sigma Alpha, Phi Alpha Theta, Alpha Lambda Delta. Club: Harvard (Washington). Home: 220 N Saint Asaph St Apt 16 Alexandria VA 22314

FRANK, EUGENE MAXWELL, bishop; b. Cherryvale, Kans., Dec. 11, 1907; s. Ade W. and Emma W. (Maxwell) F.; m. Wilma A. Sedoris, June 20, 1930; children: Wilmagene Frank Noonan, Gretchen Frank Beal, Susan Frank Parsons, Thomas E. B.S., Kans. State Tchrs. Coll., 1930, Garrett Bibl. Inst., 1932; D.D., Baker U., 1947; LL.D., Central Coll., 1957; D.D., Depauw U., 1959, St. Paul Sch. Theology, Methodist, 1962. Ordained to ministry Meth. Ch., 1932; pastor, Tonganoxie, Kans., 1932, Americus, Kans., 1933-36, Olathe, Kans., 1936-42, Kansas City, Kans., 1942-48, Topeka, 1948-56, consecrated bishop, 1956, bishop of Mo., St. Louis, 1956-72, Ark. Area, Little Rock, 1972-76; vis. prof. ch. ministry Candler Sch. Theology, Emory U., 1976-79; bishop-in-residence Central United Meth. Ch., Kansas City, Mo., 1979—; pres. Council of Bishops of Meth. Ch., 1968—; mem. bd. global missions, bd. ch. and soc. Mem. Kappa Delta Pi, Pi Kappa Delta; Phi Mu Alpha Tau Kappa Epsilon. Address: 3913 W 57th Terr Shawnee Mission KS 66205

FRANK, F. ALEXANDER, retired savings and loan executive, lawyer; b. Elmhurst, N.Y., June 19, 1916; s. Daniel and Julia (Weiss) F. B.A., Amherst Coll., 1937; M. in Govt. and Internat. Relations, Columbia U., 1938, LL.B., 1941; grad., Advanced Mgmt. Program, Inst. Fin. Edn. Bar: N.Y. 1942, Pa. 1981. Practice law, N.Y.C., 1946—; counsel, dir., mem. exec. com. Citizens Savs. and Loan Assn. N.Y., 1946-65, chmn. bd., 1965-77, pres., 1969-77; dir. FHLBNY, 1976-77. Patron Met. Opera Assn.; active urban renewal work, Bklyn. and Bronx, N.Y.; chmn. bd. Woodside-on-the-Move (community devel. corp.), 1976—; pres. 71st St.-Lexington Corp. (coop. residential corp.), 1973-74, 77-80; chmn. Solebury Twp. Zoning Hearing Bd., Solebury Twp. Hist. Soc., 1980—. Served with AUS, 1942-46. Mem. Savs. Assn. League N.Y. (chmn. legis. com. 1970-77, mem. exec. com. 1973-77, dir. 1972-77, chmn. bd. 1974-75), U.S. Savs. and Loan League (mem. fin. and exec. com., dir. 1976, 77, mem. legis. policy com., legis. com.), N.Y. Real Estate Bd. (legis. com. 1979—, mortgage com. 1979—), Queens County C. of C., Am., Queens County bar assns. Home: Lumberville PA 18933

FRANK, FLOYD WILLIAM, coll. dean, vet. educator; b. Fortuna, Calif., Feb. 12, 1922; s. Seth A. and Jessie (Swortzel) F.; m. Eloise F. Flory, Apr. 3, 1948; children—John M., LeiAnn. B.S. with honors, Wash. State U., 1951, D.V.M., 1951, Ph.D. in Vet. Sci, 1963. Vet. livestock insp. U.S. Dept. Agr., Astoria, Oreg., 1951-53; vet. bacteriologist Wyo. Vet. Lab., Laramie, 1953-55; research veterinarian Caldwell Vet. Research Lab., U. Idaho, Caldwell, 1955-67; prof., head dept. vet. sci. U. Idaho, Moscow, 1967—; dean vet. medicine WOI Regional Program in Medicine, 1974—; cons. bur. vet. medicine FDA, 1972—; Mem. wild horse and burro adv. bd. sec. agr. and sec. interior, 1972-76, chmn., 1975; mem. resource com. animal health legislation Am. Vet. Med. Colls., 1974-75. Trustee Caldwell Sch. Dist. 132, 1966-67. Served with USNR, 1941-42; Served with USMCR, 1942-46. Recipient service citation Assn. Students U. Idaho, 1972. Mem. N. Idaho Vet. Med. Assn., S.W. Idaho Vet. Med. Assn. (pres. 1966), Idaho Vet. Med. Assn. (dir.), Inter-Mountain Vet. Med. Assn. (pres. 1973-74), Am. Vet. Med. Assn. (del.), Am. Soc. Microbiology, Moscow C. of C., Sigma Xi, Phi Kappa Phi (sec.-treas. 1974-77), Alpha Psi, Phi Zeta, Farmhouse. Clubs: Rotary, Elks. Home: 1395 Walenta Dr Moscow ID 83843 *Much of my limited success is attributable to others. I have emphasized service, believing that university programs must serve societal needs in order to gain public support. This emphasis on service appears to be a primary factor in the growth and development of the programs which I administer and in my own personal advancement.*

FRANK, GEORGE WILLARD, oil company executive; b. Beloit, Kans., Mar. 2, 1923; s. George Nicklas F. and Catherine Cecilia (Frank); m. Dorothy Elaine Wells, June 22, 1947; children: Barbara Beth Frank Doherty, Janis Frank Henry. Student, Ottawa U., 1941; B.S. in Petroleum Engring., U. Kans.-Lawrence, 1946; postgrad., South Tex. Law Coll., Houston, 1960. Exec. v.p. Austral Oil, Houston, 1956-78; pres. Houston Oil Internat., 1978-81, dir. and officer fgn. subs.; v.p., gen. mgr. E & P Internat. div. Tenneco Oil Co., Houston, 1981—, dir. fgn. subs. Served to lt. USNR, 1942-46. Republican. Presbyterian. Clubs: Lakeside County (pres. 1975-76); Petroleum (Houston) (pres. 1979-80). Office: E & P International Division Tenneco Oil Co 1100 Louisiana St Suite 2400 Houston TX 77002

FRANK, GEROLD, author; b. Cleve., Aug. 2, 1907; s. Samuel and Lillian (Frank) Lefkowitz; m. Lillian Cogen, Sept. 1, 1932; children: Amy (Mrs. William Rosenblum), John Lewis. B.A., Ohio State U., 1929; M.A., Western Res. U., 1933. With Cleve. News, 1933-37; with N.Y. Jour. Am., 1937-43; U.S. war corr. Overseas News Agy., Middle East, 1943-44, Europe and Middle East corr., 1946-50; sr. editor Coronet mag., 1952-58; screen writer Warner Bros., 1960; bd. dirs. Copyright Clearance Ctr.; juror Am. Book Awards, 1981. Author: Out in the Boondocks, 1943, (with James D. Horan) U.S.S. Seawolf, 1945, (with Lillian Roth and Mike Connolly) I'll Cry Tomorrow, 1954 (Christophers award), (with Diana Barrymore) Too Much Too Soon, 1957, (with Sheilah Graham) Beloved Infidel, 1958, Zsa Zsa Gabor: My Story, 1960, The Deed, 1963 (Edgar Allan Poe award), The Boston Strangler, 1966 (Edgar Allan Poe award), An American Death: The True Story of the Assassination of Dr. Martin Luther King Jr., 1972, Judy (biography of Judy Garland), 1975; panelist: Harper's Dictionary of Contemporary Usage, 1975, 83; Contbr. to: Grolier Ency.; Contbr.: articles to popular mags. Mem. chancellor's council U. Tex. Mem. Authors Guild (sec. 1970—, council 1971—), P.E.N., Authors League (treas. 1973-76, council 1971—), Overseas Press (past gov.), Am. Soc. Journalists and Authors. Club: Dutch Treat (N.Y.C.). Home: 930 Fifth Ave New York NY 10021 Office: care William Morris Agy 1350 Ave of Americas New York NY 10019

FRANK, HANS JESSE, lawyer; b. Germany, May 29, 1911; came to U.S., 1933; s. Erich and Paula (Heilbrunn) F.; m. Beatrice Brimberg, June 5, 1970; children from previous marriage: Steven, Evelyn, Susan. Dr. Law, Heidelberg U., 1933; postgrad., Law Sch., NYU, 1933-37. Bar: N.Y. 1940. With N.Y. Hanseatic Corp., N.Y.C., 1933-41; assoc. Marcus, Chaitkin & Gardner, N.Y.C., 1941-43, Fried, Frank, Harris, Shriver & Jacobson (and predecessor firms), 1943-45, partner, 1945—; dir. various cos. Chmn. United Help, Inc.; trustee-at-large, mem. distbn. com. Fedn. Jewish Philanthropies. Mem. N.Y.C. Bar Assn., N.Y. County Bar Assn. Democrat. Jewish. Office: 1 New York Plaza New York NY 10004

FRANK, HOWARD, systems company executive; b. N.Y.C., June 4, 1941; s. Herman and Tina (Sander) F.; m. Jane Steinberg, Apr. 23, 1965; children: David, Laura, Erica. B.S. in Elec. Engring., U. Miami, 1962; M.S., Northwesten U., 1964; Ph.D., Northwestern U., 1965. Asst. prof. U. Calif.-Berkeley, 1965-68, assoc. prof., 1969; exec. v.p. Network Analysis Corp., Glen Cove, N.Y., 1969, pres., 1970-81, Contel Info. Systems Inc., Great Neck, NY, 1982—; vis. cons. Exec. Office Pres. of U.S., 1968. Author: Communications, Transmission and Transportation Networks, 1971; contbr. articles to profl. jours. NASA fellow, 1963-65; Gen. Motors fellow, 1958-62. Fellow IEEE (Leonard G. Abraham 1969); mem. AAAS, Ops. Research Soc., N.Y. Acad. Scis. Office: 130 Stemboat Rd Great Neck NY 11024

FRANK, ISAIAH, educator, economist; b. N.Y.C., Nov. 7, 1917; s. Henry and Rose (Isserles) F.; m. Ruth Hershfield, Mar. 23, 1941; children—Robert E., Kenneth D. B.S.S., CCNY, 1936; M.A. in Econs, Columbia U., 1938, Ph.D., 1960. Research asso. in econs. Columbia U. Council for Research in Social Scis., 1936-39; teaching fellow, instr. econs. Amherst Coll., 1939-41; Carnegie fellow Nat. Bur. Econ. Research, 1941-42; cons. WPB, 1942; sr. economist OSS, 1942-44; various positions Dept. State, 1945-63; dir. Office Internat. Trade, 1957-59, Office Internat. Financial & Devel. Affairs, 1961-62, dep. asst. sec. for econ. affairs, 1962-63; William L. Clayton prof. internat. econs. Sch. Advanced Internat. Studies, Johns Hopkins, 1963—; Mem. Industry-Govt. Iron and Steel Mission to Europe, 1947; adviser U.S. del. Econ. Commn. of Europe, 1948; dep. dir. fgn. resources div. Pres.'s Materials Policy Commn., 1951-52; head U.S. del. Conf. on Dollar Liberalization, OEEC, Paris, 1955-56; chmn. U.S. del. GATT, Geneva, 1958; alt. U.S. rep. Fourth Meeting Devel. Assistance Group, London, 1961; chmn. U.S. del. to prep. com. UN Conf. Trade and Devel., Geneva, 1963—; U.S. rep. Spl. Trade Conf. OAS, Alta Gracia, Argentina, 1964; exec. dir. Pres.'s Commn. on Internat. Trade and Investment Policy, 1970-71; adv. com. UN Trade and Devel. Bd.; dir. internat. econ. studies Com. Econ. Devel.; mem. adv. council Inst. for Latin Am. Integration; cons. World Bank; chmn. State Dept. Adv. Com. on Internat. Investment, Tech. and Devel. Author: Foreign Enterprise in Developing Countries; co-author, editor: The Japanese Economy in International Perspective; Contbr. articles to profl. publs. Served to 1st lt.; AUS, 1944-45. Recipient Rockefeller Pub. Service award, 1959-60. Mem. Council Fgn. Relations, Am. Econ. Assn., Phi Beta Kappa. Club: Cosmos (Washington). Home: 3102 Hawthorne St NW Washington DC 20008 Office: Johns Hopkins U 1740 Massachusetts Ave NW Washington DC 20036

FRANK, JEROME B., managing editor; b. N.Y.C., May 8, 1934; s. Murray H. and Frances (Sobrin) F.; m. Louise Orcutt, Oct. 18, 1969; 1 son, Daniel P. B.S., Union Coll., 1955. Owner, mgr. Minerva Books, Bennington, Vt., 1971-75, mgr. coll. dept., 1976-77, dep. dir. mktg., 1977-79; sr. mng. editor Pergamon Press, Elmsford, N.Y., 1979—. Democrat.

FRANK, JEROME DAVID, psychiatrist, educator; b. N.Y.C., May 30, 1909; s. Jerome W. and Bess (Rosenbaum) F.; m. Elizabeth Kleeman, Jan. 4, 1948; children—Deborah, David, Julia, Emily. A.B. summa cum laude, Harvard, 1930, A.M., 1932, Ph.D. in Psychology, 1934, M.D. cum laude, 1939. Research asso. group psychotherapy research project VA, 1946-49; instr. Washington Sch. Psychiatry, 1947-49; clin. asso. prof. Howard U., 1948-49; instr. Johns Hopkins Med. Sch., 1942-46, faculty, 1949—, prof. psychiatry, 1959-74, prof. emeritus psychiatry, 1974—; psychiatrist-in-charge psychiat. out-patient dept. Johns Hopkins Hosp., 1951-64; dir. clin. services Henry Phipps Psychiat. Clinic, 1961-63, acting chief dept. psychiatry, 1960-61, 62-63; staff mem. Center Study Dem. Instns., 1966; Adv. bd. Patuxent Instn., 1954-78; mem. adv. coms. NIMH, 1951-55, 57-58, 59-61, 68-69, 74-78, mem. task force on homosexuality, 1967-69; mem. social sci. adv. bd. ACDA, 1970-73; mem. adv. com. psychiatry and neurology service Dept. Medicine and Surgery, VA Central Office, 1960-64; bd. dirs. Met. Balt. Assn. Mental Health, 1952—; Bd. dirs. SANE, Council for a Livable World, 1963—; mem. nat. adv. bd. Physicians for Social Responsibility, 1980—. Author: Persuasion and Healing; A Comparative Study of Psychotherapy, 1961, rev. edit., 1973, (with Florence Powdermaker) Group Psychotherapy: Studies in Methodology of Research and Therapy, 1953, Sanity and Survival: Psychological Aspects of War and Peace, 1967, (with others) Effective Ingredients of Successful Psychotherapy, 1978, Psychotherapy and the Human Predicament: A Psychosocial Approach, 1978, also articles. Served to maj. AUS, 1943-46. Fellow Center Advanced Study Behavioral Scis., Palo Alto, Calif., 1958-59; praelector in psychiatry Faculty Medicine, U. St. Andrews, Dundee, Scotland, 1967; H.B. Williams travelling prof. psychiatry, Australia and N.Z., 1971; Litchfield lectr. Oxford U., 1977; Recipient Emil A. Gutheil award Assn. Advancement Psychotherapy, 1970, Kurt Lewin Meml. award Soc. for Psychol. Study Social Issues, 1972, Blanche Ittleson award Am. Orthopsychiat. Assn., 1979; Spl. Research award Soc. for Psychotherapy Research, 1981; McAlpin Research Achievement award Nat. Mental Health Assn., 1981; Oskar Pfister award Am. Psychiat. Assn., 1983. Fellow Am. Psychiat. Assn., Am. Psychol. Assn., Soc. for Psychol. Study of Social Issues (pres. 1965-66), Am. Coll. Psychiatrists, Am. Group Psychotherapy Assn., Am. Assn. for Social Psychiatry (v.p. 1974), World Acad. Art and Sci., Royal Coll. Psychiatrists (hon.); mem. Am. Psychopath. Assn. (pres. 1963), AMA, Fedn. Am. Scientists (vice chmn. 1976-79, chmn. 1979), AAUP, Phi Beta Kappa, Sigma Xi, Alpha Omega Alpha. Home: 603 W University Pkwy Baltimore MD 21210 Office: Phipps Clinic Johns Hopkins Hosp Baltimore MD 21205

FRANK, JOHN PAUL, lawyer, author; b. Appleton, Wis., Nov. 10, 1917; s. Julius Paul and Beatrice (Ullman) F.; m. Lorraine Weiss, May 11, 1944; children: John Peter, Gretchen, Karen, Andrew, Nancy Jo. B.A., U. Wis., 1938, M.A., LL.B., 1940; J.S.D., Yale U., 1946; LL.D., Lawrence U., 1981. Bar: Wis. bar 1940, D.C. bar 1966, Ariz. bar 1954, U.S. Supreme Ct. bar 1954. Law clk. U.S. Supreme Ct. Justice Hugo L. Black, 1942; asst. to sec. interior, 1943, to atty. gen., 1944-45; asst. prof. law Ind. U., 1946-49; asso. prof. law Yale, 1949-54; vis. lectr. law U. Wash., 1966, U. Ariz., 1967, Ariz. State U., 1969, 72; with firm Covington & Burling, Washington, 1947, Arnold & Porter, 1948, 53; mem. firm Lewis & Roca, Phoenix, 1954—; Mem. adv. com. civil procedure Jud. Conf. U.S., 1960-70; chmn. U.S. Circuit Judge Nominating Commn.-9th Circuit Panel, South, 1977; mem. exec. com. Adv. Com. on Appellate Justice; mem. Ariz. Commn. Appellate Ct. Appointments, 1974—. Author: Mr. Justice Black, 1949, Cases on Constitutional Law, 1950, Cases on the Constitution, 1951, My Son's Story, 1952, Marble Palace, 1958, Lincoln as a Lawyer, 1961, Justice Daniel Dissenting, 1964, The Warren Court, 1964, American Law: The Case for Radical Reform, 1969, also articles. Democratic precinct committeeman, 1956—; counsel Ariz. Dem. Com., 1962-65, 79—. Fellow Am. Bar Found.; Mem. ABA, Maricopa County Bar Assn., Am. Law Inst. (council). Clubs: Arizona, University (Phoenix). Home: 5829 E Arcadia Ln Phoenix AZ 85018 Office: 100 W Washington St Phoenix AZ 85003

FRANK, JOSEPH, educator; b. Chgo., Dec. 20, 1916; s. A. Richard and Gertrude (Greenbaun) F.; m. Margery Goodkind, Feb. 1, 1941; children—Thomas, Peter, Andrew (dec.); m. Florence Stanton Clark Zartman, Jan. 24, 1969. B.A., Harvard, 1939, M.A., 1947, Ph.D., 1953. From instr. to prof. English U. Rochester, 1948-67; prof., chmn. dept. English U. N.Mex., 1967-69; prof. English U. Mass., Amherst, 1969—, head dept., 1969-75; Exchange prof. U. Kent, Canterbury, Eng., 1976-77. Author: The Levellers, 1955, The Beginnings of the English Newspaper, 1961, Hobbled Pegasus, 1968, Milton Without Footnotes, 1974, Cromwell's Press Agent, 1980; Editor: Literature From the Bible, 1963, Modern Essays in English, 1966, The New Look in Politics, 1968, You, 1972, The Doomed Astronaut, 1972. Pres. Genesee Valley, ACLU, 1965, mem. N.Mex. bd., 1967-69. Served with Am. Field Service, 1942; Served with AUS, 1943-45. Huntington Library fellow, 1955-56; Guggenheim fellow, 1958-59, 61; Folger Shakespeare Library fellow, 1962. Mem. Modern Lang. Assn., Renaissance Soc., Milton Soc., Assn. Depts. of English (exec. bd., past pres.). Home: 166 Lincoln Ave Amherst MA 01002

FRANK, JOSEPH NATHANIEL, comparative literature educator; b. N.Y.C., Oct. 6, 1918; s. William and Jennie (Garlick) F.; m. Marguerite J. Straus, May 11, 1953; children: Claudine, Isabelle. Student, NYU, 1937-38, U. Wis.-Madison, 1941-42, U. Paris, 1950-51; Ph.D., U. Chgo., 1960. Spl. researcher Am. Embassy, Paris, 1951-52; lectr. Princeton U., 1955-56, prof. dept. comparative lit., 1966—, dir. Christian Gauss Seminars in Criticism, 1966-83; asst. prof. U. Minn., Mpls., 1958-61; assoc. prof. Rutgers U., 1961-66; vis. prof. Harvard U., 1965. Author: The Widening Gyre, 1963, F.M. Dostoevsky: Seeds of Revolt, 1976; editor: A Primer of Ignorance, 1967. Grantee Am. Council Learned Socs., 1970-71, Rockefeller Found., 1979-80; recipient Phi Beta Kappa award, 1977. Mem. MLA (James Russell Lowell prize 1977), Am. Assn. Advancement of Slavic Studies, Nat. Acad. Arts and Scis. Office: Princeton U Dept Comparative Lit 327 E Pyne Princeton NJ 08544

FRANK, KAYE GOODWIN, manufacturing executive; b. Mich., Apr. 24, 1927; s. Samuel and Kate (Jacob) F.; Sept. 3, 1950; 2 daus. B.F.A., U. Mich., 1950; grad. Advanced Mgmt. Program, Harvard U., 1971. With D.A.B. Industries, Inc., Troy, Mich., 1950—, v.p., sec., 1959-68, exec. v.p., 1969-72, pres., chief operating officer, 1972—. Past pres. bd. dirs. Jewish Vocat. Service and Community Workshop, Detroit; mem. exec. com., past pres. Hist. Soc. Mich.; chmn. arts com. Am. Indian Art and Primitive Arts, Detroit; bd. dirs. Friends of Modern Art of Detroit Inst. Art; trustee Detroit Inst. Arts; mem. Joint Museums Collections Com., Detroit; bd. dirs., mem. exec. com. Jewish Home for Aged, Detroit; nat. bd. dirs. Jewish Occupational Council. Served with Mcht. Marines, 1945-47. Office: DAB Industries Inc PO Box 2801 Troy MI 48084

FRANK, LLOYD, lawyer, chemical company executive; b. N.Y.C., Aug. 9, 1925; s. Herman and Selma (Lowenstein) F.; m. Beatrice Silverstein, Dec. 26, 1954; children: Margaret Lois, Frederick. B.A., Oberlin Coll., 1947; J.D., Cornell U., 1950. Bar: N.Y. 1950, U.S. Supreme Ct. 1973. Practice law, N.Y.C., 1950—; ptnr. Parker Chapin Flattau & Klimpl; sec. Grow Group, Inc., N.Y.C., 1964—; dir. Madison Industries, Inc., N.Y.C., Pacesetter Industries, Inc., Metro-Tel Corp., Syosset, N.Y., Ketchum & McDougall, Inc., Public Art Fund, Inc., N.Y.C., Wilfred Am. Ednl. Corp.; lectr. Am. Mgmt. Assn., 1967-77, Probe Internat., Inc., 1975-77, Corporate Seminars, Inc., 1968-71. Mem. Assn. Bar City N.Y., N.Y. County Lawyers Assn. (mem. com. on corps., com. on SEC), ABA (com. affiliated and related corps. taxation sect.). Clubs: Chemists, Oberlin of N.Y. Home: 25 Central Park W New York NY 10023 Office: 530 Fifth Ave New York NY 10036

FRANK, MICHAEL M., physician; b. Bklyn., Feb. 28, 1937; s. Robert and Helen (Prakin) F.; m. Ruth Sybil Pudolsky, Nov. 5, 1961; children—Robert E., Abigail B., Brice S.H. A.B., U. Wis., 1956; M.D., Harvard U., 1960. Intern Boston City Hosp., 1960-61; resident in pediatrics Johns Hopkins Hosp., 1961-62, 64-65; vis. scientist Nat. Inst. Med. Research, London, 1965-66; with NIH, 1967—; chief lab. of clin. investigation, clin. dir. Nat. Inst. Allergy and Infectious Diseases, Bethesda, Md., 1977—. Editor: Blood. Mem. Assn. Am. Physicians, Am. Soc. Clin. Investigation, Soc. Pediatric Research, Infectious Diseases Soc., Am. Acad. Allergy, A.C.P., Soc. Hematology. Office: Room 11N232 Clin Center NIH Bethesda MD 20205

FRANK, MORTON, newspaper executive; b. Pitcairn, Pa., June 14, 1912; s. Abraham and Goldie (Friedenberg) F.; m. Agnes Dodds, June 2, 1944 (div. 1957); children: Allan Dodds, Michael Robert, Marilyn Morton; m. Elizabeth Welt Pope, Dec. 31, 1963. A.B., U. Mich., 1933; postgrad., Carnegie Inst. Tech., U. Pitts., Duquesne U.; LL.D., Alfred U., 1979. Advt. mgr. Braddock (Pa.) Daily News-Herald, 1933-34; editor Braddock Free Press, 1934-35; rotogravure mgr. Pitts. Press, 1935-42; writer, commentator Pitts. radio stas., corr. trade mags., 1935-42; v.p., bus. mgr. Ariz. Times, Phoenix, 1946; editor, pub. Canton (Ohio) Economist, 1946-58, Lorain (Ohio) Sun News, 1949-50, Inter-County Gazette, Strasburg, Ohio, 1950, Stark County Times Canton, 1950-58, Farm and Dairy, Salem, Ohio, 1952; pres. Tri-Cities Telecasting, Canton, 1953-61, Printype, 1956-58, Property Devel. Corp., 1956-58; dir. publisher relations, v.p. Family Weekly and Suburbia Today, N.Y.C., 1958-65; pub., exec. v.p. Family Weekly, 1966-71, pres., pub., 1971-75, 76-80, chmn., 1976, chmn., pub., 1980-82, chmn. emeritus, 1982—. Chmn. Commn. Corr. Ind. Higher Edn. N.Y., 1976-79, exec. com., 1980—; bd. dirs. Canton Symphony Orch., 1950-56; trustee Alfred U., 1968, Mus. Cartoon Art, 1980—. Served from ensign to lt. USN, 1942-45. Recipient 1st prize for feature writing N.E.A., 1954; community service award Accredited Hometown Newspapers Am., 1954. Mem. Tri-State Fedn. Non-Comml. Theatres (pres. 1936-38), Controlled Circulation Newspapers Am. (dir. 1948-56), Pitts. Fgn. Policy Assn. (dir. 1940-42), Newspaper Advt. Bur. (plans com. 1974-82), Am., So., Inland, Tex., Calif., N.Y. newspaper pubs. assns., Internat. Press Inst., Interam. Press Assn., Internat. Circulation Mgrs. Assn., Internat. Newspaper Promotion Assn., Internat. Newspaper Advt. Execs. Assn., Sigma Alpha Mu, Sigma Delta Chi. Clubs: Canton Advt., Players, N.Y.C. Sales Execs., Overseas Press (dir. 1983), Overseas Press (found. trustee 1983—), Deadline (pres. 1974-75), Deadline (chmn. 1975-76). Home: 534 Rock House Rd Easton CT 06425 also 115 E 67th St New York NY 10021 Office: 641 Lexington Ave New York NY 10022

FRANK, NEIL LAVERNE, meteorologist, meteorol. center adminstr.; b. Kans., Sept. 11, 1931; s. Clarence E. and Mary Violet F.; m. Velma L. Becker, Sept. 12, 1952; children—Pamela, Debra, Ron. B.A., Southwestern Coll., 1953; M.S., Fla. State U., 1959, Ph.D., 1967. Meteorologist Nat. Hurricane Center, Miami, Fla., 1961-73, dept. dir., 1973-74, dir., 1974—. Contbr. articles to profl. jours. Bd. dirs. Dade County Citizens Safety Council, Dade County ARC. Served with USAF, 1953-57. Mem. Am. Meteorology Soc. Methodist. Office: 1320 S Dixie Miami FL 33146

FRANK, PETER SOLOMON, art critic, curator; b. N.Y.C., July 3, 1950; s. Reuven and Bernice (Kaplow) F. B.A., Columbia U., 1972, M.A., 1974. Critic SoHo Weekly News, N.Y.C., 1973-76, Village Voice, 1977-79; asso. curator Ind. Curators Inc., N.Y.C. and Washington, 1974-80; co-curator Documenta VI, Kassel, W. Ger., 1976-77; asso. editor Nat. Arts Guide, Chgo., 1979-81, Art Express, N.Y.C., 1980-81; curator Exxon Nat. Exhbn. of Young Am. Artists, Guggenheim Mus., N.Y.C., 1980-81; mem. faculty New Sch. for Social Research, 1974, Pratt Inst., 1975-76, Columbia U. Sch. of Arts, 1978; bd. dirs. Franklin Assoc. Art Pubs.; mem. bd. advs. Center Book Arts. Author: The Travelogue, 1982, Something Else Press: An Annotated Bibliography, 1983; contbr. articles to art periodicals; Assoc. editor: Tracks mag, 1974-76; sr. editor: Metro, 1983—; contbg. editor: Art Economist, 1981—; Art critic: Diversion Planner, 1983. Nat. Endowment for Arts art critics travel fellow, 1978; critics project fellow, 1981. Mem. Internat. Assn. Art Critics. Home: 712 Broadway 5th Floor New York NY 10003

FRANK, REUVEN, journalist; b. Montreal, Que., Can., Dec. 7, 1920; came to U.S., 1940, naturalized, 1943; s. Moses Zebi Reichenstein and Anna (Rivenovich) F.; m. Bernice Kaplow, June 9, 1946; children: Peter Solomon, James Aaron. Student, Univ. Coll., U. Toronto, 1937-40; B.S. in Social Scis, Coll. City N.Y., 1942; M.S. in Journalism, Columbia, 1947. Reporter Newark Evening News, 1947-49, night city editor, 1949-50; mem. staff NBC News, 1950-67, exec. v.p., 1967-68, pres., 1968-72, exec. producer, 1972-82, pres., 1982-84, editorial advisor, 1984—; news editor Camel News Caravan, 1951-54; producer polit. conv., 1956, polit. convs. and elections, 1960, elections, 1962; producer Huntley-Brinkley Report, 1956-62, exec. producer, 1963-65; exec. producer polit. convs. and elections, 1964. Writer-producer: Berlin-Window on Fear, 1953, The Road to Spandau, 1954, Outlook; series, 1956-59, Time Present, 1959-60, Chet Huntley Reporting, 1960-63, Israel The Next Ten Years, 1958, The S-Bahn Stops at Freedom, 1958, The American Stranger, 1958, The Requiem for Mary Jo, 1959, The Big Ear, 1959, Our Man in the Mediterranean, 1959, Where is Abel, Your Brother?, 1960, Our Man in Hong Kong, 1961, The Land, 1961, The Many Faces of Spain, 1962, Our Man in Vienna, 1962, Clear and Present Danger, 1962, The Tunnel, 1962, A Country Called Europe, 1963, The Problem with Water is People, 1963; exec. producer: Weekend, 1974-79; exec. producer, co-writer: If Japan Can... Why Can't We?, 1980. Trustee Edwin E. Aldrin Fund State of N.J., 1970-73. Recipient Sigma Delta Chi award news writing for TV, 1955; Robert E. Sherwood award, 1958, 59; George Polk award L.I. U., 1961; Columbia Journalism Alumni award distinguished service, 1961; First Person award Inst. Edn. by Radio-TV, Ohio State U., 1963; Emmy award best news program, 1958, 59, 60, 61, 62, 64; best documentary program, 1963; program of year, 1963; Alfred I. DuPont award Columbia U., 1980; Martin R. Gainsbrugh award Fiscal Policy Council, 1980; Headliners award, 1981; others.; Poynter fellow Yale, 1970. Mem. Writers Guild Am. (organizing com. 1954-56), Am. Newspaper Guild (Newark News organizing com. 1948-50). Office: 30 Rockefeller Plaza New York NY 10020

FRANK, RICHARD CALHOUN, architect; b. Louisville, May 17, 1930; s. William George and Helen (Calhoun) F.; m. Janet Nickerson, Feb. 12, 1966; children—Richard, Scott, Elizabeth, William, Jennifer, Philip. B.Arch., U. Mich., 1953. Asso. archtl. firms, Lansing, Mich., 1953-61; pres. Frank & Stein Assos., Inc., Lansing, 1961-70; prin. Johnson, Johnson & Roy, Ann Arbor, 1971-75; pres. Preservation/Urban Design/Inc., Ann Arbor, Mich., 1975—. Life trustee Hist. Soc. Mich. Fellow AIA; mem. Nat. Trust Historic Preservation (trustee emeritus), Victorian Soc. Am. Home: 302 E Henry St Saline MI 48176 Office: 202 E Washington St Suite 710 Ann Arbor MI 48104

FRANK, RICHARD H(ARVEY), TV distbn. exec.; b. Bklyn., Nov. 4, 1942; s. Hyman and Edythe F. (Caplan) F.; m. Constance Ilona Zieger, July 29, 1964; children: Paul Stuart, Darryl Brian. B.S. in Mktg., U. Ill., 1965. Media planner/buyer Batton Barton Durstine & Osborne (advt.), 1965-67; account exec. Edward Petry Co., 1967-69; mgr. Chgo. office Telerep Inc., 1969-71, sales mgr., N.Y.C., 1971-72; nat. sales mgr. Sta. KTLA, Los Angeles, 1972-73, gen. sales mgr., 1973-74; pres. TV div., pres., gen. mgr. Sta. KCOP, Chris-Craft Co., Los Angeles, 1975-77; pres. TV distbn. Paramount Pictures Corp., Hollywood, Calif., 1977-81, pres. TV and video distbn., 1981—. Mem. Nat. Acad. TV Arts and Scis., Internat. Radio and TV Soc., Assn. Ind. TV Stas. (dir. 1975-77). Office: Paramount TV & Video 5555 Melrose Ave Hollywood CA 90038 *

FRANK, RICHARD HORTON, JR., lawyer; b. Columbia, Tenn., May 31, 1928; s. Richard Horton and Jean Delphia (Noble) F.; m. Katherine A. Barbehenn, Apr. 24, 1954; children: Richard Horton, III, Mary Delphia. B.A., Vanderbilt U., 1950, J.D., 1951; LL.M. in Taxation, N.Y. U., 1956. Bar: Tenn. 1951. Partner firm Gilbert, Frank & Milom (and predecessors), Nashville, 1956—; sr. partner Gilbert, Frank, Ludwick & Milom (and predecessors), 1966—; vis. lectr. entertainment law Vanderbilt U., 1969—; lectr. copyright YMCA Law Sch., lectr. at various profl., acad. insts., seminars. Vestryman, sr. warden Ch. of the Advent, Episcopal ch., Brentwood, Tenn., 1978—; dir. So. region Am. Daffodil Soc.; trustee Country Music Found. Served with USN, 1951-54. Mem. Am. Bar Assn. (mem. exec. steering com. Entertainment and Sports Law Forum), Tenn. Bar Assn. (trustee copyright sect.), Nashville Bar Assn., Copyright Soc. U.S. (trustee), Country Music Assn., Nashville Music Assn., Gospel Music Assn. (dir.), SAR, Huguenot Soc., Order of Coif. Anglican. Club: Masons. Home: 715 Hill Rd Brentwood TN 37027 Office: 13th Floor Third Nat Bank Bldg Nashville TN 37219

FRANK, RICHARD SANFORD, magazine editor; b. Paterson, N.J., July 28, 1931; s. David and Shirley (Dwoskin) F.; m. Margaret Schwartz, June 30, 1957; children: Daniel, Peter. B.A., Syracuse U., 1953; M.A., U. Chgo., 1956. Reporter Balt. Evening Sun, 1957-64, Phila. Bull., 1965-71; asst. to mayor City of Balt., 1964-65; reporter Nat. Jour., 1971-72, editor, 1972-76, editor-in-chief, 1976—. Served with U.S. Army, 1953-55. Mem. Am. Soc. Mag. Editors. Home: 5111 Wessling Ln Bethesda MD 20814 Office: Nat Jour 1730 M St NW Washington DC 20036

FRANK, ROBERT EDWIN, hospital adminstrator; b. St. Louis, Nov. 30, 1926; s. Edwin J. and Genevieve (Graeff) F.; m. Mary Catherine Porter, Sept. 10, 1949; children: Michael, Nancy Frank Vahldieck. B.S., St. Louis U., 1950; M.H.A., Washington U. Med. Sch., St. Louis, 1962. Intern in hosp. adminstrn. Barnes Hosp., St. Louis, 1961, asst. dir., 1961-64, assoc. dir., 1964-65, dir., pres., 1965—; asst. prof. dept. health planning and adminstrn. Washington U. Med. Sch., 1966—; dir. Blue Cross, St. Louis. Served with USAAF, 1945-46. Mem. Assn. Am. Med. Colls. (exec. council 1982—), Mo. Hosp. Assn. (chmn. 1981-82), Hosp. Assn. Met. St. Louis (pres. 1971-73). Republican. Clubs: Forest Hills (Chesterfield, Mo.); University (St. Louis). Home: 1525 Hampton Hall Dr Chesterfield MO 63017 Office: Barnes Hosp Barnes Hosp Plaza Saint Louis MO 63110

FRANK, ROBERT L., photographer; b. Zurich, Nov. 9, 1924; emigrated to U.S., 1947. Free-lance photographer for Harper's Bazaar, Fortune, Life, Look; ind. photographer, filmmaker, N.Y.C., 1956-69; vis. instr. in filmmaking U. Calif.-Davis, 1977. Films include Pull My Daisy, 1959, (with Rudi Wurlitzer) Keep Busy, 1975; books include The Americans, 1958, The Lines of My Hand, 1972, Robert Frank, 1976; one-man exhbns. include, Mus. Modern Art, N.Y.C., 1948, 62, Helmhaus, Zurich, 1955, Kunsthaus, Zurich, 1976, Inst. Contemporary Arts, London, 1980, Art Gallery of Toronto; also numerous group exhbns. Guggenheim grantee, 1955-56.

FRANK, ROBERT WORTH, JR., English educator; b. Logansport, Ind., Apr. 8, 1914; s. Robert Worth and Grace Alice (Haun) F.; m. Gladys Martine Loeb, May 11, 1940; children: Thaisa, Elizabeth Ann. A.B., Wabash (Ind.) Coll., 1934; M.A., Columbia U., 1939; Ph.D., Yale U., 1948. Instr. English Lafayette Coll., Easton, Pa., 1937-39, U. Rochester (N.Y.), 1940-42, Princeton U., 1942-44, Northwestern U., 1944-48; asst. prof., then asso. prof. Ill. Inst. Tech., 1948-58; prof. English Pa. State U., 1958-79, head dept., 1975-79, emeritus, 1979—; O'Connor prof. lit. Colgate U., 1980; editor Chaucer Rev., 1966—; Fellow Am. Council Learned Socs., 1951-52, 60-61, Fund Advancement Edn., 1955-56, Guggenheim Found., 1970-71; asso. fellow Clare Hall, Cambridge (Eng.) U., 1971, 76, vis. fellow, 1972-73. Author: Piers Plowman and the Scheme of Salvation, 2d edit, 1969, The Responsible Man: The Insights of the Humanities, rev. edit, 1965, The Critical Question, 1964, Chaucer and the Legend of Good Women, 1973. Mem. Mediaeval Acad. Am., MLA, New Chaucer Soc. (trustee 1980-84), Internat. Assn. Univ. Profs. of English. Democrat. Club: Lit. (State College, Pa.). Home: 749 W Hamilton Ave State College PA 16801 Office: 117 Burrowes Pa State Univ University Park PA 16802 *

FRANK, RONALD EDWARD, marketing educator; b. Chgo., Sept. 15, 1933; s. Raymond and Ethel (Lundquist) F.; m. Iris Donner, June 18, 1958; children: Linda, Lauren, Kimberly. B.S. in Bus. Adminstrn, Northwestern U., 1955, M.B.A., 1957; Ph.D., U. Chgo., 1960. Instr. bus. statistics Northwestern U., Evanston, Ill., 1956-57; asst. prof. bus. adminstrn. Harvard U., Boston, 1960-63, Stanford U., 1963-65; assoc. prof. mktg. Wharton Sch., U. Pa., 1965-68, prof., 1968-84, chmn. dept. mktg., 1971-74, vice dean, dir. research and Ph.D. programs, 1974-76, assoc. dean, 1981-83; dean, prof. mktg. Krannert Grad. Sch. Mgmt., Purdue U., 1984—; cons. to industry. Author: (with Massy and Kuehn) Quantitative Techniques in Marketing Analysis, 1962, (with Matthews, Buzzell and Levitt) Marketing: an Introductory Analysis, 1964, (with William Massy) Computer Programs for the Analysis of Consumer Panel Data, 1964, An Econometric Approach to a Marketing Decision Model, 1971, (with Paul Green) Manager's Guide to Marketing Research, 1967, Quantative Methods in Marketing, 1967, (with Massy and Lodahl) Purchasing Behavior and Personal Attributes, 1968, (with Massy and Wind) Market Segmentation, 1972, (with Marshall Greenberg) Audience Segmentation Analysis for Public Television Program Development, Evaluation and Promotion, 1976, The Public's Use of Television, 1980, Audiences for Public Television, 1982. Recipient pub. TV research grants John and Mary R. Markle Found., 1975-82. Mem. Am. Mktg. Assn. (dir. 1968-70, v.p. mktg. edn. 1972-73), Am. Statis. Assn., Inst. Mgmt. Sci., Assn. Consumer Research, Am. Assn. Pub. Opinion Research. Home: 144 Creighton Rd West Lafayette IN 47906 Office: Purdue U Krannert Grad Sch Mgmt Krannert Bldg West Lafayette IN 47907

FRANK, SAM HAGER, university chancellor; b. King City, Mo., July 23, 1932; s. Edward Lloyd and Louise (Hager) F.; m. Ellen Wilson Snow, June 3, 1955; 1 dau., Marian Elizabeth. B.A., Fla. State U., 1953, M.A., 1957; Ph.D., U. Fla., 1961. Prof. history, chmn. div. social scis. Tift Coll., Forsyth, Ga., 1961-65; assoc. prof. history Augusta (Ga.) Coll., 1966-67, Jacksonville (Fla.) U., 1967-72, prof. history, 1972-78, dean Coll. Arts and Scis., 1972-78; chancellor La. State U., Alexandria, 1979—; cons. Research Studies Inst., USAF U. (Maxwell AFB), Ala., 1957-58; Fulbright prof. Osmania U., India, 1965-66; participant Conf. Acad. Deans of So. States, 1973. Author: (with M. Maurer) Air Force Combat Units of World War II, 1960, American Air Service Observation in World War I, 1961; conrbr. articles on aviation, the mil. and Asia to profl. jours. Served with U.S. Army, 1954-56; korea. Mem. Am. Hist. Assn., Orgn. Am. Historians, AAUP (exec. com. Ga. sect. 1962-65), Soc. Hist. Assn., Alexandria C. of C. (dir.), Phi Mu Alpha Sinfonia, Phi kappa Phi, Phi Alpha Theta, Pi Sigma Alpha, Phi Delta Kappa. Clubs: Torch, Mensheviki. Lodge: Rotary. Home: Route 2 Box 27 Alexandria LA 71301 Office: Chancellor La State U Alexandria LA 71301

FRANK, STANLEY DONALD, publishing co. exec.; b. N.Y.C., June 30, 1932; s. Arthur and Jessie (Schwartz) F.; m. Sheila Rose, Dec, 25, 1958; children—Bradley Scott, Tracy Lynne. B.S., Coll. City N.Y., 1953, M.S., 1956; Ed.D., Columbia, 1961. Dir. mktg. Sci. Research Assos. subsidiary IBM, Chgo., 1961-68, v.p. mktg. and ops., 1968-73; pres. Holt, Rinehart & Winston, Inc. subsidiary CBS, N.Y.C., 1974-77, CBS Ednl. Pub. Div., 1975-78; exec. v.p., chief operating officer CBS Pub. Group, 1978-80, pres., 1980—. Mem. Bd. Edn. Dist. 67, Niles, Ill., 1972-73; mem. council Rockefeller U. Served with AUS, 1953-55. Andrew Wellington Cordier fellow Columbia U. Sch. Internat. Affairs. Office: 383 Madison Ave New York NY 10017 *

FRANK, THOMAS EDWARD, mfg. co. exec.; b. Pitts., Jan. 1, 1939; s. Charles R. and Lucille M. (Briscoe) F.; m. Suzanne Lewis, Dec. 30, 1960; children—Timothy, Ellen, Wendy, Frank; m. Anneliese Krohn, Aug. 5, 1973; adopted children—Angela, Tina, Frank. B.B.A., U. Pitts., 1962; M.S. in Indsl. Adminstrn. (grad. scholar 1962-64), Carnegie Inst. Tech., 1964. With brand mgmt. dept. Procter & Gamble Co., Cin., 1964-70; mktg. cons. Glendinning Cos., Westport, Conn., 1970-71; sr. v.p. mktg. Heublein, Inc., Louisville, 1972-78, sr. v.p. food group, internat. div., Farmington, Conn., 1978—. Served with USAR, 1958-60. Democrat. Home: 270 Mountain Rd West Hartford CT 06107 Office: Heublein Internat Ltd Farmington CT 06032

FRANK, WERNER LOUIS, computer consultant; b. Heilbronn, Germany, June 4, 1929; came to U.S., 1937; s. Arthur and Bertha (Weingartner) F.; m. Phoebe Mannel, Aug. 21, 1955; children: Dori, Judith, Daniel. B.S., Ill. Inst. Tech., 1951; M.S., U. ILL.-Urbana, 1955. Sr. staff TRW, Los Angeles, 1955-62; exec. v.p. Informatics Gen. Corp., Los. Angeles, 1962-82; pres. Werner Frank Computer Group, Calasbasas, Calif., 1983—; dir. Computer Processing Inst., East Hartford, Conn., 1979—, Informatics Gen., 1965-78, Sage Systems, 1983—; author column Softline, 1980-83. Served with U.S. Army, 1952-54. Mem. Assn. Computering Machinery, IEEE. Jewish. Home: 4363 Park Milano Calabasas CA 91302

FRANKE, ERNEST AUGUST, electronics company executive; b. Uvalde, Tex., Oct. 22, 1939; s. Clarence B. and Mary Lee (Fisher) F.; m. Doris Walters, Aug. 23, 1964; children—Eric, Kurt, Scott. B.S., Tex. Coll. Arts and Industries, 1961, M.S., 1963; Ph.D., Case-Western Res. U., 1967. Registered profl. engr., Tex. Instr. elec. engring. Tex. Coll. Arts and Industries, 1963; teaching fellow Case Inst. Tech., 1964-67; asso. prof. Tex. A. and I. U., Kingsville, 1967-70, prof., 1970-79, chmn. dept. elec. engring., 1969-71, dean, 1971-79; v.p. research and devel. Alpha Electronics, 1979—. Mem. Am. Soc. Engring. Edn., Instrument Soc. Am., I.E.E.E. (sec.-treas. Corpus Christi sect. 1971, vice chmn. 1972, chmn. 1973), Tau Beta Pi, Eta Kappa Nu. Home: 10687 E Black Forest Dr Parker CO 80134

FRANKE, FREDERICK RAHDE, physician; b. Pitts., Oct. 14, 1918; s. Frederick Ferdin and Louise Anna (Rahde) F.; m. Nancy Olive Digby, Mar. 22, 1943; children—Suzanne, Paula, Frederick Rahde, Paul D., John C., Virginia N. B.S., U. Pitts., 1941, M.D., 1943; M.S., U. Pa., 1950, D.Sc., 1952. Diplomate: Am. Bd. Internal Medicine (cardiovascular diseases). Intern, then resident St. Francis Hosp., Pitts., 1943-45, research asso. physiology, 1947-52, physician-in-chief charge therapeutics, 1953-56; pvt. practice, Pitts., 1952—; asst. prof. medicine Sch. Medicine U. Pitts., 1953-56; chief medicine St. Clair, South Side, St. Margaret hosps., 1955-63; mem. faculty Sch. Medicine Johns Hopkins U., 1960-61; sr. cardiologist charge cardiovascular-pulmonary lab., chief div. medicine Western Pa. Hosp., 1963-69, med. dir., 1967-73; clin. prof. pharmacology U. Pitts. Sch. Pharmacy, 1972—; Bd. dirs. Health Research Services Found.; governing com. Pa. Comprehensive Health Planning Com. Contbr. articles, chpts. in books. Served with M.C. USNR, 1945-46. Fellow A.C.P., Council Clin. Cardiology, Am. Heart Assn.; mem. Pa. Heart Assn. (past pres., com. chmn., Meritorious Service award 1962), Soc. Exptl. Biology and Medicine, Am. Therapeutic Soc., Am. Soc. Human Genetics, AMA, Sigma Xi. Republican. Presbyterian. Club: Rolling Rock (Ligonier, Pa.). Home: 19 Glen Ridge Ln Pittsburgh PA 15243 Office: 4815 Liberty Ave Pittsburgh PA 15224

FRANKE, JOHN JACOB, JR., federal official; b. Tonkawa, Okla., June 28, 1930; s. John Jacob and Golda Elaine (Peace) F.; m. Melba Jean Graul, June 17, 1950; children: Michael D., John P., Robert K. Student, Kansas City Bus. Coll., Mo., 1947-48, U. Kansas City, Mo., 1951-52, LaSalle U., 1954-55. With Franke Barber Supply, Inc., Kansas City, Mo., 1952-72; councilman City of Merriam, Kans., 1965-70, mayor, 1970-72; mem. Johnson County Bd. Commrs., 1973-81; regional adminstr. EPA, 1981-82; asst. sec. U.S. Dept. Agr., Washington, 1982—. Mem. Kans. Legis. Council League Municipalities, 1966-73, commr., 1973, chmn., 1974-77; mem. adv. bd. Nat. Park Service, 1973-76; mem. Kaw council Boy Scouts Am., 1962-76, Republican Central Com. Johnson County, 1972-81; chmn. Johnson County Library Bd., 1974-77; chmn. human resources policy com. Kans. Mcpl. League; bd. dirs., v.p. Mo.-Ark. Water Resources; bd. dirs. Greater Kansas City Resources Found.; chmn. labor mgmt. steering com. Nat. Assn. Counties. Mem. Christian Ch. Lodges: Masons; Shriners. Home: 6401 Craig Rd Merriam KS 66602 Office: Dept Agr 14th and Independence Ave SW Washington DC 20250

FRANKE, RICHARD JAMES, investment banker; b. Springfield, Ill., June 23, 1931; s. William George and Frances Marie (Brennan) F. B.A., Yale U., 1953; M.B.A., Harvard U., 1957. With John Nuveen & Co., Chgo., 1957—, v.p., 1965-69, exec. v.p., 1969-74, chief adminstrv. officer, 1970-74, pres., chief exec. officer, 1974—, also dir., 1969—. Bd. dirs. North Shore Country Day Sch., Winnetka, Ill.; mem. Social Service Devel. council U. Chgo.; bd. dirs. Gt. Books Found. Served as 1st lt. U.S. Army, 1953-55. Mem. Bond Club Chgo., Mcpl. Bond Club Chgo., Chi Phi. Clubs: Mid-Am., Attic, Carlton (Chgo.); Glenview (Ill.); Garden of the Gods (Colorado Springs, Colo.). Office: 209 S La Salle St Chicago IL 60604

FRANKE, WILLIAM AUGUSTUS, corporate executive; b. Bryan, Tex., Apr. 15, 1937; s. Louis John and Frances (Hanna) F.; m. Carolyn D. Walker, July 16, 1977; children: Catherine Anne, Paige Estelle, Brian Hanna, David Parker, Rebecca Ann Walker. B.A., Stanford, 1959, LL.B., 1961. Bar: Wash. bar 1961. Assoc. firm MacGillivray, Jones, Clark & Schiffner, Spokane, 1962-67, partner, 1967-70; v.p., sec., corporate counsel S.W. Forest Industries, Phoenix, 1970-72, sr. v.p., sec., 1972-73, exec. v.p., asst. chief exec. officer, 1973-75, pres., 1975—, chief operating officer, 1977-78, chief exec. officer, 1978—, also dir. subs. cos.; dir. Phelps Dodge Corp., Circle K Corp., Valley Nat. Bank. Trustee Combined Health Resources, Inc.; mem. dean's council Stanford U. Law Sch. Served to capt. U.S. Army, 1961-62. Mem. Am., Wash., Spokane County bar assns., NAM, Am. Mgmt. Assn., Am. Paper Inst. (dir.), Young Presidents Orgn. Episcopalian. Clubs: Stanford, Paradise Valley Country, Phoenix Country (Phoenix); Plaza. Home: 7701 N Saguaro Dr Paradise Valley AZ 85253 Office: 6225 N 24th St Phoenix AZ 85016

FRANKEL, ANDREW JOHN, corp. exec.; b. N.Y.C., Oct. 24, 1932; s. William Victor and Selma Fern (Rentner) F.; m. Anita Ruth Grutzner, Sept. 21, 1956; children—Donna, David, Pamela, Elizabeth. B.S., Columbia, 1955. Treas. Nat. Cleaning Contractors, N.Y.C., 1959-64, exec. v.p., 1964-66; exec. v.p., dir. Warner Communications, Inc., N.Y.C., 1966-71; chmn. bd., chief exec. officer Nat. Kinney Corp., N.Y.C., 1971—, pres., 1973—; chmn. bd. Uris Bldgs. Corp., N.Y.C.; pres., dir. Circle Acoustics Corp.; dir. Circle Industries Corp., Katz Parking System, Inc., Kinney System, Inc., Wachtel, Duklauer & Fein Inc. Bd. govs. grad. schs. Yeshiva U., 1972—; bd. dirs. Juvenile Diabetes Found., 1972—. Served with USN, 1955-58. Clubs: Fairview Country (Greenwich, Conn.); Boca Rio Golf (Boca Raton, Fla.). Office: Nat Kinney Corp 10 E 53d St New York NY 10022 *Be honest with yourself.* *

FRANKEL, ARNOLD J., Chemical company executive; b. N.Y.C., Mar. 17, 1922; s. Sol and Rose (Blitz) F.; m. Miriam J. Drexler, Oct. 29, 1949; children—Hinda Squires, Janet Staub, Alan. B.S. in Chem. Engring, CCNY, 1942; M.S., Bklyn. Poly. Inst., 1949. Co-founder, 1947; since chmn. dir. Aceto Chem. Co., Inc., Flushing, N.Y., also sec.-treas.; mem. Queens adv. bd. Chem. Bank, N.Y.C. Pres., bd. dirs. Queens Child Guidance Center; trustee Jewish Museum, N.Y.C.; N.Y. bd. trustees Am. Jewish Com.; chmn. chems., plastics and paint industry group United Jewish Appeal, N.Y.C.; bd. dirs. CCNY Research Found. Mem. Am. Chem. Soc., AAAS, Am. Inst. Chemists (chmn. N.Y. sect.), City Coll. Alumni Assn., Sigma Xi. Club: Chemists (N.Y.C.).

FRANKEL, DONALD LEON, manufacturing executive; b. San Francisco, May 23, 1931; s. Donald A. and Sallie A. F.; m. Donna J. Frankel; children: Michael, Pamela, Karen, Mark Steven. B.B.A., U. Okla., 1956. Vice pres. fin., treas., then v.p. internat. Gardner Denver Co., Dallas, 1956-78; also dir.; sr. v.p. fin., treas. Galveston Houston Co., 1980—; sr. v.p. fin. Geosource, Inc., Houston, 1980—; dir. Protection Mut. Ins. Co. Served with USAF, 1951-53. Republican. Presbyterian. Clubs: Houstonian, Petroleum, Lochinvar Golf. Home: 5812 Lynbrook St Houston TX 77057 Office: 2700 S Post Oak Rd Suite 2000 Houston TX 77056

FRANKEL, FRANCINE RUTH, political science educator; b. N.Y.C., Aug. 31, 1935; d. William and Dora (Tuchschneider) Goldberg; m. Douglas Vernon Verney, Nov. 28, 1975; stepchildren: Andrew, Jonathan. B.A., CCNY, 1956; M.A., Johns Hopkins Sch. Advanced Internat. Studies, 1958; Ph.D., U. Chgo., 1965. Instr. dept. polit. sci. U. Pa., Phila., 1964-65, asst. prof., 1965-70, assoc. prof., 1970-79, prof., 1979—, prof. South Asian studies, 1978—, chmn. grad. program polit. sci., 1980-83; vis. mem. Inst. Advanced Study, 1976; vis. fellow Center of Internat. Studies, Princeton (N.J.) U., 1969-73; resident scholar Bellagio Study and Conf. Center, 1975; sr. research fellow Am. Inst. Indian Studies, 1979-80; prin. investigator project on caste, class, and power in modern India Smithsonian Instn., 1983-85; cons. AID Mission, New Delhi, 1969; mem.-at-large Commn. Internat. Relations, Nat. Acad. Scis., 1973-79. Author: India's Political Economy, 1947-77, The Gradual Revolution, 1978, Chinese edit., 1982, India's Green Revolution, 1971; contbr. articles on India's polit. economy to profl. jours. Ford Found. research Grantee, 1972-73; Am. Philos. Soc. research grantee, 1976; Smithsonian Instn. grantee, 1983-85. Mem. Am. Polit. Sci. Assn., Assn. Asian Studies. Club: Univ. (Toronto). Home: 130 Spruce St Apt 35B Philadelphia PA 19106 also 64 Gilgorm Rd Toronto ON M5N 2M5 Canada Office: Stiteler Hall Dept Polit Sci U Pa Philadelphia PA 19104

FRANKEL, GENE, theatre director, producer, educator; b. N.Y.C., Dec. 23, 1923; s. Barnet and Anna (Talerman) F.; m. Pat Ruth Carter, May 1, 1963; children: Laura Ann, Ethan-Eugene. B.A., NYU, 1943. Artistic dir. Gen. Frankel Theatre, N.Y.C., 1963—, exec. dir., 1973—; founding dir. Berkshire Theatre Festival, Stockbridge, Mass., 1965-66; vis. Arena Stage, Washington, 1969-71; cultural exchange dir. U.S. Dept. State, Belgrade, Yugoslavia, 1968-69; dir. Hartman Theatres, Stamford, Conn., 1976-79; vis. prof. Boston U., 1967-69, Queens Coll., N.Y.C., 1969-71, Columbia U., 1972-73; cons. dir. Nat. Shakespeare Co., N.Y.C., 1966—; dir. various regional theaters, 1969-80. Dir.: Indians, Broadway, 1969 (Burns Mantle 1969), Emperor Jones, European tour, 1970, Oh Dad, Poor Dad, Belgrade, Yugoslavia, 1969, Lost in the Stars, 1971, The Night That Made American Famous, 1975, Cry of Players, 1967, The Blacks, Off-Broadway, 1961 (Obie award 1963), also European tour, Brecht on Brecht, Off-Broadway, 1965, Young Gifted and Black, Off-Broadway, 1970, Enemy of the People, Off-Broadway, 1969. Recipient Lola D'Annunzio award, 1958, Obie award for Volpone Village Voice, 1958, Obie award for Machinal, 1963, Vernon Rice award for Machinal Drama Desk-N.Y. Post, 1963; Ford Found. fellow, 1963. Mem. Soc. Choreographers and Dirs., Actors Equity Assn. Home: 4 Washington Sq Village New York NY 10012 Office: Gene Frankel Theatre 36 W 62d St New York NY 10023 *To acquire knowledge and insight, one must learn from others. In so doing, it can happen that a pygmy standing on the shoulders of a giant may see further than the giant. So learn-learn-learn-then teach so that you can learn some more.*

FRANKEL, GERALD ALAN, magazine publisher, editor; b. Chgo., Oct. 28, 1938; s. Jay Bernard and Dorothy (Cohen) F.; m. Janice Richter, Sept. 3, 1966. B.A., Roosevelt U., Chgo., 1960. Project editor LaSalle Extension U. subs. Crowell-Collier Pub. Co., 1963-64; asso. editor Modern Metals mag., Chgo., 1965-69; editor-in-chief Communications Industry News Service, Chgo., 1970-73; feature editor Waste Age mag., Chgo., 1974; editor Instl. Mgmt. mag., Chgo., 1975-77; exec. pub. Am. Automatic Merchandiser mag., Northfield, Ill., 1977-78; pres. Frankel & Assos., Chgo., 1979—. Writer, producer series: And So We Sang, Sta. WFMQ, Chgo., 1961-62. Mem. Am. Soc. Bus. Press Editors, Inst. Bus. Designers (press mem.). Home: 510 bush san francisco ca 94108

FRANKEL, JACOB PORTER, college president; b. Phila., Sept. 7, 1923; s. Harold Aaron and Ceil (Porter) F.; m. Helen Bruce, Jan. 27, 1946 (div. Dec. 1981); children: Martha Jean, Molly, David Alan, Deborah, Robert Aaron. M.S., U. Calif. at Berkeley, 1947; Ph.D., U. Calif. at Los Angeles, 1951. Instr., then asst. prof. engring. U. Calif. at Los Angeles, 1948-52; lead metallurgist Calif. Research and Devel. Co., 1952-54; asso. prof. Northwestern U., 1954-56; asso. prof., then prof. U. Calif. at Los Angeles, 1957-66; asso. dean, prof. Thayer Sch. Engring., Dartmouth, 1966-68; dean faculty Harvey Mudd Coll. Sci. and Engring., 1968-74; pres. Calif. State Coll., Bakersfield, 1974—; Cons. systems engring., 1956—, cons. sci. and engring. edn. to govts., India, Republic of China, 1970. Author: The Principles of the Properties of Materials, 1957, also articles. Chmn. Livermore (Calif.) Recreation Bd., 1953-54. Served to lt. (j.g.) USNR, 1944-51. Mem. Am. Soc. Engring. Edn., Soc. Hist. Tech., Phi Beta Kappa, Sigma Xi, Tau Beta Pi. Clubs: Petroleum, Rio Bravo Tennis. Address: Calif State Coll Bakersfield CA 93309

FRANKEL, MARVIN, economist, educator; b. Oakland, Calif., Mar. 28, 1924; s. Joseph and Mathilde (Sewelson) F.; m. Matilda Shoenberg, Sept. 23, 1951; children—Karen, Kenneth Alan, David Paul. A.B. in Econs, U. Calif. at Berkeley, 1947, Ph.D., 1953; student, London Sch. Econs., 1950-51. From asst. prof. to asso. prof. Bur. Econs. and Bus. Research, U. Ill., Urbana, 1952-57, asso. dean, 1963-66, prof. econs., 1961—, chmn. dept., 1967-71; Vis prof. U. Colo., summer 1966; vis. asso. prof. Stanford, 1957-58; cons. to govt. and industry, 1957—. Bd. editors: So. Econ. Jour, 1967-69; editor: Quar. Rev. Econs. and Bus, 1952-63; Contbr. articles to profl. jours. Served to 1st lt., pilot USAAF, 1943-46. Mem. Am. Econ. Assn., Am. Assn. U. Profs., Phi Beta Kappa.

FRANKEL, MARVIN E., lawyer; b. N.Y.C., July 26, 1920; s. Charles and Anne (Brody) F.; m. Betty Streich, June 20, 1945 (div. 1965); 1 dau., Eleanor; m. Alice Kross, Aug. 22, 1965; 1 dau., Mara; stepchildren: David K. Schorr, Ellen Schorr. A.B., Queens Coll., 1943; LL.B., Columbia U., 1948. Bar: N.Y. 1949, also U.S. Supreme Ct 1949. Asst. to U.S. solicitor gen., 1952-56; mem. firm Proskauer Rose Goetz & Mendelsohn, 1956-62, 78-83, Kramer, Levin, Nessen, Kamin & Frankel, N.Y.C., 1983—; prof. law Columbia U., 1962-65, vis. prof. law, 1970—; U.S. dist. judge So. Dist. N.Y., 1965-78; dir. legal def. fund Civil Rights Inst., 1964-65. Author: Criminal Sentences, 1973, (with Gary P. Naftalis) The Grand Jury-An Institution on Trial, 1977, Partisan Justice, 1980; editor-in-chief: Columbia Law Rev, 1948. Served with AUS, 1942-46. Mem. Am., N.Y. State bar assns., Bar Assn. City N.Y. Address: 919 3d Ave New York NY 10022

FRANKEL, MAX, journalist; b. Gera, Germany, Apr. 3, 1930; came to U.S., 1940, naturalized, 1948; s. Jacob A. and Mary (Katz) F.; m. Tobia Brown, June 19, 1956; children—David M., Margot S., Jonathan M. A.B., Columbia, 1952, M.A. in Polit. Sci, 1953. Mem. staff N.Y. Times, 1952—, chief Washington corr., 1968-73, Sunday editor, 1973-76, editorial pages editor, 1977—. Served with AUS, 1953-55. Recipient Pulitzer prize for internat. reporting, 1973. Mem. Council Fgn. Relations, Phi Beta Kappa. Home: 5261 Independence Ave Riverdale NY 10471 Office: 229 W 43d St New York NY 10036

FRANKEL, SANDOR, lawyer, author; b. N.Y.C., Nov. 16, 1943; s. David and Bessie (Edelson) F. B.A., N.Y. U., 1964; LL.B., Harvard U., 1967. Bar: N.Y. bar 1967, D.C. bar 1968, U.S. Supreme Ct. 1976. Staff mem. White House Task Force on Crime, 1967; counsel Nat. Commn. Reform Fed. Criminal Laws, 1968; asst. U.S. atty. for D.C., 1968-71, practice law, N.Y.C., 1971—; lectr. N.Y. U. Inst. on Fed. Taxation, 1976, 77. Author: Beyond a Reasonable Doubt, 1972 (Edgar Allan Poe award), The Aleph Solution, 1978; Contbr. articles to legal publs. Mem. Phi Beta Kappa. Office: 225 Broadway New York NY 10007

FRANKEL, SAUL JACOB, Can. govt. ofcl.; b. Montreal, Que., Can., Aug. 6, 1917; s. Moses Shaya and Rebecca (Goodman) F.; m. Freda Schneyer, Oct. 7, 1939; children—Deborah, Daniel, Naomi. B.A., McGill U., 1950, M.A., 1952, Ph.D., 1958. Mem. faculty McGill U., 1953-69; prof. polit. sci., vice dean social scis. div. McMaster U., Hamilton, Ont., Can., 1969-76; dean faculty social sci.; mem. Pub. Service Staff Relations Bd. Can., Ottawa, 1976—; Guy Drummond scholar, Paris, 1951; Can. Council sr. fellow, London, 1959-60; participant Internat. Inst. Labor Studies ILO, Geneva, 1974-75. Author: Municipal Labour Relations in Canada, 1954, Staff Relations in the Civil Service, 1962, Model of Negotiation and Arbitration for the Canadian Civil Service, 1963, Report of the Royal Commission on Employer-Employee Relation in the Public Services of New Brunswick, 1967. Chmn. Royal Commn. Employer-Employee Relations in Pub. Services N.B. Served with Canadian Army, 1943-46. Office: PSSRB PO Box 1525 Sta B Ottawa ON K1P 5V2 Canada

FRANKEL, SHERMAN, physicist; b. N.Y.C., Nov. 15, 1922; s. Harry and Rose F.; m. Ruzena Bajcsy, Oct. 22, 1981; 1 son by previous marriage, Walter. B.A., Bklyn. Coll., 1943; M.S., U. Ill., 1947, Ph.D., 1949. Mem. staff radiation lab M.I.T., 1943-46; instr. U. Pa., Phila., 1950-52, asst. prof. physics, 1952-56, asso. prof., 1956-60, prof., 1960—. Guggenheim fellow, 1957, 79. Mem. AAUP, Am. Phys. Soc., AAAS, Sigma Xi, N.Y. Acad. Sci., Pi Mu Epsilon. Home: 2320 Delancey Pl Philadelphia PA 19103 Office: Physics Dept U Pa 33d and Walnut Sts Philadelphia PA 19104

FRANKEL, STANLEY ARTHUR, corporate executive; b. Dayton, Ohio, Dec. 8, 1918; s. Mandel and Olive (Margolis) F.; m. Irene Baskin, Feb. 20, 1946; children—Stephen, Thomas, Nancy. B.S. with high honors, Northwestern U., 1940; student, Columbia U., 1940, U. Chgo., 1946-49. Reporter Chgo. News Bur., 1940; publicist CBS, 1941; asst. to pres. Esquire and Coronet mags., N.Y.C., 1946-56; pres. Esquire Club, 1956-58; with McCall Corp., N.Y.C., 1958-61, asst. to pres. and pub., 1958-61, v.p., 1959-61; v.p., dir. corporate devel. Ogden Corp., 1961—; dir. Michaelis Prodns., Inc., Rockwood Corp., Careful Office Service Inc., Western Calif. Canners Corp., Internat. Terminal Operating Co., Inc., Ogden Am. Corp.; adj. prof. Baruch Coll., CUNY, 1974—, Pace U., 1983—; guest lectr. N.Y. U., 1974; mem. Pres.'s Adv. Council on Peace Corps, 1965, Pres.'s Adv. Council on Youth Opportunity.; Mem. chancellor's panel State U. N.Y., 1970—; mem. N.Y. State Task Force on Higher Edn., 1974—; bd. mem., exec. com. Nat. Council Crime and Delinquency; bd. mem., vice chmn. Nat. Businessmen's Council; bd. dirs., officer Scarsdale Adult Sch. Author: History of 37th Division, 1947; contbr. articles to popular mags. Exec. bd. Writers for Stevenson, 1952, 56, for Kennedy, 1960, McGovern for Pres., 1972; pub. relations dir. Stevenson-for-Pres., 1956; chmn. Writers for Senator Humphrey Vice-Presdl. campaign, 1964; exec. bd. Businessmen for Humphrey-Muskie, 1968; chmn. N.Y. Writers for Humphrey-Muskie, 1968; mem. nat. exec. com. McGovern for Pres., 1972; vice chmn. N.Y. State McGovern for Pres. Com., 1972; bd. overseers Rutgers U., 1977—; chancellor's external relations com. City U. N.Y., 1977—; bd. dirs., v.p., mem. exec. com. YMCA of Greater N.Y.; founder Public Relations Bd., Inc., N.Y. and Chgo., Bedford Stuyvesant Project (T.R.Y.); mem. Vice President's Task Force on Youth Unemployment, 1979—. Served to maj. AUS, 1940-46. Decorated 2 Presdl. Citations, 3 Bronze Stars; recipient Peabody award for TV Series Adlai Stevenson Reports, 1961-63; Northwestern U. Alumni Merit award, 1964. Mem. Am. Mgmt. Assn. (chmn. pub. relations course 1971), Phi Beta Kappa, Phi Beta Kappa Assocs. (v.p., trustee), Phi Beta Kappa Assocs., Scarsdale-Westchester (pres. 1980—). Clubs: Northwestern U. of N.Y. (pres. 1964); Overseas Press (N.Y.C.); Scarsdale (N.Y.) Town (bd. govs.), Sunningdale Country.). Home: 109 Brewster Rd Scarsdale NY 10583 Office: 277 Park Ave New York NY 10017 *Peace of heart and of mind . . . among races and among nations . . . in families and in neighborhoods . . . at schools and at churches . . . in cities and in space . . . on streets and on highways . . . between you and me and between them and us.*

FRANKEL, TAMAR, lawyer; b. Israel, 1925; came to U.S., 1963, naturalized, 1972; d. Elazer and Judith Hofmann; m. Ernst Gabriel

Frankel, July 21, 1964; children—Anat Yalif, Michael E.S. Grad., Jerusalem Law Classes, 1947; LL.M., Harvard U., 1964, S.J.D., 1972. Bar: Mass. 1972, Israeli bar 1949. Asst. atty. gen. Ministry of Justice of Israel, 1949-50; practiced law, Tel Aviv, 1951-62; legal adv. State of Israel Bonds, Europe, 1962-63; assoc. Ropes & Gray, Boston, 1964-65, Arnold & Porter, Washington, 1965-66; spl. asst. to Calif. Commr. Corps., Los Angeles, 1966-67; lectr. Boston U. Sch. Law, 1967, asst. prof., 1968-70, prof., 1971—; vis. prof. Harvard Law Sch., 1979-80, Harvard Bus. Sch., fall 1980, Boalt Hall, U. Calif., Berkeley, 1982-83. Author: The Regulation of Money Managers, 4 vols, 1978-80; contbr. articles to law jours. Mem. Am. Law Inst., Israeli Bar Assn., Mass. Bar Assn., Boston Bar Assn., ABA, Am. Trial Lawyers Assn. Office: Boston U Law Sch 765 Commonwealth Ave Boston MA 02146

FRANKEL, VICTOR HIRSCH, orthopaedic surgeon; b. Wilmington, Del., May 14, 1925; s. Harry and Estelle (Hillersohn) F.; m. Elna Ruth Olsen, Feb. 15, 1958; children—Victor Hirsch, Dana G., Lars-Erik, Carl S., Paul A. B.A., Swarthmore Coll., 1946; M.D., U. Pa., 1951; D.Sc., U. Upsala, Sweden, 1960. Intern Grad. Hosp. U. Pa., 1951-52; resident Charlotte (N.C.) Meml. Hosp., 1954-55, Hosp. Joint Diseases, N.Y.C., 1955-58, attending orthopaedic surgeon, 1960-66; prof. orthopaedic surgery and bioengring. Case Western Res. U., 1966-75; prof., chmn. dept. orthopaedic surgery U. Wash. Sch. Medicine, Seattle, 1976-81; dir. orthopaedic surgery, surgeon-in-chief Hosp. Joint Diseases, Orthopaedic Inst., N.Y.C., 1981—; prof. orthopaedic surgery Mount Sinai Med. Sch., N.Y.C.; chmn. orthopaedic panel FDA Bur. Med. Devices, 1972-75. Author: Orthopaedic Biomechanics, 1970, Basic Biomechanics of Skeletal System, 1980. Served with M.C. U.S. Army, 1952-54. Recipient Klinkicht award Am. Orthopaedic Foot Soc., 1972; award of merit U.S. Ski Assn., 1972; Citation award Am. Coll. Sports Medicine, 1974; award of Merit ASTM, 1978; citation Outstanding Performance Boeing Comml. Airplane Co., 1978; Clemson award Internat. Biomaterials Symposium, 1980; Nat. Found. fellow, 1958-60; Frauenthal fellow Hosp. Joint Diseases, 1958-60; Am. Orthopaedic Assn. exchange fellow, 1965. Mem. Internat. Soc. Orthopaedic Surgery and Traumatology, Internat. Soc. Study Lumbar Spine, AMA, Am. Acad. Orthopaedic Surgeons, Can. Orthopaedic Assn., Am. Orthopaedic Assn., Hip Soc., Am. Orthopaedic Soc. Sports Medicine. Office: 301 E 17th St New York NY 10003

FRANKEN, PETER ALDEN, physicist; b. N.Y.C., Nov. 10, 1928; s. Sigmund Anthony and Rose Dorothy (Lewin) F.; m. Donna Marie Barbeau, Jan. 4, 1955 (div. Mar. 1979); children: Jessica, Lydia, Alicia.; m. Peg Stone Nash, Jan. 28, 1983. B.A., Columbia U., 1948, M.A., 1950, Ph.D. in Physics, 1952. Instr., then asst. prof. physics Stanford (Calif.) U., 1952-56; asst. prof. U. Mich., Ann Arbor, 1956-59, asso. prof., 1959-62, prof., 1962-73; dep. dir., acting dir. Advanced Research Projects Agy., Dept. Def., Washington, 1967; chmn. bd. CFC Products, Inc., Ann Arbor, 1969—; dir. Optical Scis. Ctr., U. Ariz., Tucson, 1973-83, acting dir. Ariz. Research Labs., 1983—; cons. ACDA, 1977-79; chmn. Navy Research Adv. Bd., 1975-78; task force on particle beam tech. Def. Sci. Bd., 1979-80; mem. exec. panel Chief of Naval Ops., 1974-78; cons. Los Alamos Sci. Lab., 1975-79; chmn. adversary group on survivability USAF, 1975-77. Sloan fellow, 1959-62. Fellow Optical Soc. Am. (pres. 1977, Wood prize 1979), AAAS, Am. Phys. Soc. (award 1967); mem. Am. Inst. Physics (governing bd. 1976-79), Radiol. Soc. N.Am., Sigma Xi. Club: Cosmos (Washington). Inventor metastable helium magnetometer. Home: 2105 E 4th St Tucson AZ 85719 Office: Ariz Research Labs Flandreau Planetarium 218 U Ariz Tucson AZ 85721

FRANKENBERG, DIRK, marine scientist; b. Woodsville, N.H., Nov. 25, 1937; s. Charles Henry and Patricia Edith (Smith) F.; m. Susan Alice Campbell, June 25, 1960; children—Elizabeth Alice, Eben Whitfield. A.B. in Biology, Dartmouth Coll., 1959, M.S., Emory U., 1960, Ph.D., 1962. Asst. prof. zoology, research asso. Marine Inst., U. Ga., 1962-66; adj. lectr. Dartmouth Coll., 1965-69; asst. prof. dept. biol. scis. U. Del., 1966-67; asso. prof. zoology, research asso. Marine Inst., U. Ga., 1967-72, prof. zoology, research asso., 1972-74; dir. ocean scis. div. NSF, Washington, 1978-80; dir. marine sci. program, prof. U. N.C., Chapel Hill, 1974—; mem. ocean scis. div. adv. com. NSF, 1980—; vice chmn. Univ. Nat. Oceanographic Lab. System, 1981—; mem. Duke U.-U. N.C. Oceanographic Consortium Policy Bd., 1980—, State of N.C. Marine Sci. Council, 1976—. Contbr. articles to profl. jours. Mem. AAAS, Assn. Southeastern Biologists, Am. Soc. Limnology and Oceanography, Ecological Soc. Am., Estuarine and Brackish Water Scis. Assn. Office: Univ of NC Chapel Hill NC 27514

FRANKENBERGER, JAMES GILWOOD, hotel executive; b. Hong Kong, Oct. 9, 1934; U.S., 1940; s. Homer and Patricia (King) F.; m. Sandra Lee McCurdy, Aug. 17, 1958; children: Jaemi, JoDee, Jenee, Jacques. B.S. in Acctg, U. So. Calif., 1960. Auditor Alexander Grant & Co., Honolulu, 1960-62; v.p., treas. Wheels Ltd., Honolulu, 1962-65, Harbor Fin., Blvd. Properties Inc.; sr. auditor Harris, Kerr, Forster & Co., Honolulu, 1965-67; controller Maui Hilton, Hilton Hotels, Hawaii, 1967-70, Holiday Inn-Waikiki Beach, Honolulu, 1970-71, exec. asst. mgr., 1971-73, gen. mgr., 1973-80, (Waikiki Sunset Hotel subs.); also div. mgr. Hotel Corp. of Pacific, Honolulu, 1980-83; v.p. mktg. and devel. Ironwood Resorts, Honolulu, 1983—; legis. alert chmn. Holiday Inns, Inc.; dir. mktg. com. Hawaii Visitors Bur. Pack master Aloha council Boy Scouts Am. Served with U.S. Army, 1954-56. Recipient Top Ten award Holiday Inn, 1975, hon. mention, 1976, 77, 78, Outstanding Productivity award, 1977; named Innkeeper of Year Holiday Inns, 1976. Mem. Hawaii Hotel Assn. (dir. 1976-79, pres. Oahu chpt. 1976-77), Hawaii Hotel and Motel Acctg. Assn., Navy League U.S., U.S. Yacht Racing Union, Jaycees (dir. Waikiki chpt.), Association Internationale des Skal Clubs, Skal Club Hawaii, Sales and Mktg. Execs. Honolulu, Midget Ocean Racing Club, Hawaii Pacific Handicap Racing Fleet (sec.-treas. 1980, pres. 1981). Club: Waikiki Yacht. Home: 4035 Black Point Rd Honolulu HI 96816 Office: 677 Ala Moana Blvd Suite 400 Honolulu HI 96813

FRANKENBERGER, ROBERT RUSSELL, architect; b. Freeport, Ill., July 20, 1937; s. Russell Earl and Genevieve (Evans) F.; m. Jean Marshall, Sept. 1, 1967; children: Nicole Jean, Lisa Jane. B.Arch., Ariz. State U., 1961. Registered profl. architect, Ariz. Draftsman Ralph Haver, Architect, Phoenix, 1962-64, Defial & Miller, Architects, 1964-65; draftsman, designer Bennie M. Gonzales, Architect, Phoenix, 1965-69; architect, prin. Gonzales Assocs., Inc., Phoenix, 1969-73, Frankenberger Assocs., Inc., 1973—; pres. profl. adv. council Coll. Architecture. Ariz. State U., 1982—; dir. Rosson House-Heritage Sq. Found., Phoenix, 1980—. Architect: urban design Lath House, Heritage Square, 1982 (AIA honor award 1982); co-author: Phoenix Historic Building Survey, 1980. Served to sgt. USAF, 1961-62; Germany. Recipient Honor award for archtl. design Ariz. Soc. Architects, 1980. Mem. AIA (urban design com. 1978—). Home: 1609 Palmcroft Dr SE Phoenix AZ 85007 Office: Robert R Frankenberger AIA, Inc 763 E Moreland Phoenix AZ 85006

FRANKENHEIM, SAMUEL, lawyer; b. N.Y.C., Dec. 20, 1932; s. Samuel and Mary Emma (Ward) F.; m. Nina Barbara Mennerich, Sept. 2, 1960; children—Robert Mennerich, John Frederick. B.A., Cornell U., 1954, LL.B., 1959. Bar: N.Y. bar 1959, Mass. bar 1976. Law clk. N.Y. Ct. Appeals, 1959-61; partner Shearman & Sterling (attys.), N.Y.C., 1961-69; sr. v.p., dir. Damon Corp., Needham Heights, Mass., 1969-78; sr. v.p., gen. counsel Gen. Cinema Corp., Chestnut Hill, Mass., 1979—. Trustee Newton-Wellesley Hosp., Newton, Mass., 1973—, pres., 1980-82. Served to 1st lt. USAF, 1955-57. Mem. Assn. Bar City N.Y., Am., N.Y. State, Boston bar assns. Club: Broad St. (N.Y.C.). Home: 115 Shornecliffe Rd Newton MA 02158 Office: 27 Boylston St Chestnut Hill MA 02167

FRANKENHEIMER, JOHN MICHAEL, film and stage director; b. N.Y.C., Feb. 19, 1930; s. Walter Martin and Helen Mary (Sheedy) F.; m. Carolyn Diane Miller, Sept. 22, 1954 (div. 1961); children: Lisa Jean, Kristi; m. Evans Evans, 1964. Grad., LaSalle Mil. Acad., 1947; B.A., Williams Coll., 1951. Actor, 1950-51; dir.: CBS-TV programs You Are There, Danger, Climax, Studio One, Playhouse 90, 1954-59; programs directed include For Whom the Bell Tolls; motion picture Young Stranger, RKO, 1959; Broadway play The Midnight Sun, 1959, The Browning Version, DuPont Show of the Month, 1959, Ingrid Bergman in Turn of the Screw, 1959; motion pictures The Train, 1965; Seconds, 1966, Seven Days In May, Grand Prix, The Extraordinary Seaman, The Fixer, The Gypsy Moths, I Walk the Line, Young Savages, 1961, Birdman of Alcatraz, 1962, All Fall Down, 1962, Manchurian Candidate, 1962, Horsemen, 1971, Impossible Object, 1972, The Iceman Cometh, 1973, 99 and 44/100% Dead, 1974, French Connection II, 1975, Black Sunday, 1977, Prophecy, 1979, Challenge, 1982, The Comedian, 1958 (Brotherhood award 1959, Acapulco Film Festival award 1962). Recipient of the Christopher award, 1954; grand prize for best film dir. Lacarno Film Festival, 1955; Critics award for best direction of year, 1956-59. Office: care Jeff Berg Internat Creative Mgmt 8899 Beverly Blvd Los Angeles CA 90048

FRANKENTHALER, HELEN, painter; b. N.Y.C., Dec. 12, 1928; d. Alfred and Martha (Lowenstein) F.; m. Robert Motherwell, Apr. 6, 1958. B.A., Bennington Coll., 1949; L.H.D., Skidmore Coll., 1969; D.F.A., Smith Coll., 1973, Moore Coll. Art, 1974, Bard Coll., 1976, N.Y. U., 1979; D.Art, Radcliffe Coll., 1978, Amherst Coll., 1979. Tchr., lectr. Yale U., 1966, 67, 70, Hunter Coll., 1970, Princeton U., 1971, Cooper Union, N.Y.C., 1972, Washington U. Sch. Fine Arts, 1972, Skidmore Coll., 1973, Swathmore Coll., 1974, Drew U., 1975, Harvard, 1976, Radcliffe Coll., 1976, Bard Coll., 1977, Detroit Inst. Arts, 1977, also N.Y. U., U. Pa., Sch. Visual Arts, Goucher Coll., Wash. U., Yale Grad. Sch., U. Ariz., 1978, Graphic Arts Council N.Y., 1979; U.S. rep. Venice Biennale, 1966. One-woman shows include, Tibor de Nagy Gallery, N.Y.C., 1951-58, Andre Emmerich Gallery, N.Y.C., 1959-73, 75, 77, 78, 79, 81, 82, 83, Jewish Mus., N.Y., 1960, Everett Ellin Gallery, Los Angeles, 1961, Galerie Lawrence, Paris, 1961, 63, Bennington Coll., 1962, 78, Galleria dell'Ariete, Milan, 1962, Kasmin Gallery, London, 1964, David Mirvish Gallery, Toronto, 1965, 71, 73, 75, Gertrude Kasle Gallery, Detroit, 1967, Nicholas Wilder Gallery, Los Angeles, Andre Emmerich Gallery, Zurich, 1974, 80, Swathmore (Pa.) Coll., 1974, Solomon R. Guggenheim Mus., N.Y.C., 1975, Corcoran Gallery Art, Washington, Seattle Art Mus., Mus. Fine Arts, Houston, Ace Gallery, Vancouver, B.C., Can., Rosa Esman Gallery, N.Y.C., 3d Internat. Contemporary Art Fair, Paris, 1976, 81, retrospective Whitney Mus. Am. Art, 1969, Whitechapel Gallery, London, Eng., Kongress-Halle, Berlin, Kunstverein, Hannover, Heath Gallery, Atlanta, 1971, Galerie Godard Lefort, Montreal, Fendrick Gallery, Washington, 1972, 79, John Berggruen Gallery, San Francisco, 1972, 79, 82, Portland (Oreg.) Art Mus., 1972, Waddington Galleries II, London, 1973, 74, Janie C. Lee Gallery, Dallas, 1973, Janie C. Lee Gallery, Houston, 1975, 76, 78, 80, 82, Met. Mus. Art, N.Y.C., 1973, Gallery Diane Gilson, Seattle, 1976, Greenberg Gallery, St. Louis, 1977, Galerie Wentzel, Hamburg, Germany, Jacksonville (Fla.) Art Mus., 1977-78, Knoedler Gallery, London, 1978, 81, 83, USIA exhbn., 1978-79, Atkins Mus. Fine Art, William Rockhill Nelson Gallery Art, Kansas City, Mo., 1978, 80, numerous others; exhibited in group shows including, Whitney Mus., 1958, 71, 75-79, 82, Carnegie Internat., Pitts., 1955, 58, 61, 64, Columbus Gallery Fine Arts, 1960, Guggenheim Mus., 1961, 76, 80, 82, Seattle World's Fair, 1962, Art Inst. Chgo., 1963, 69, 72, 76, 77, 82, 83, San Francisco Mus. Art, 1963, 68, Krannert Mus., U. Ill., 1959, 63, 65, 67, 80, Washington Gallery Modern Art, 1963, Pa. Acad. Fine Arts, 1963, 68, 76, N.Y. World's Fair, 1964, Am. Fedn. Arts Circulating Exhbn., U. Austin Art Mus., Rose Art Mus. Circulating Exhbn., Detroit Inst. Arts, 1965, 67, 73, 77, U. Mich. Mus. Art, 1965, Md. Inst., 1966, Norfolk Mus. Arts and Scis., Venice Biennale, Smithsonian Instn., Expo '67, Montreal, 1967, Washington Gallery Modern Art, Ga. Mus. Art, Athens, U. Okla. Mus. Art, Norman, 1968, Philbrook Art Center, Tulsa, Cin. Mus., U. Calif. at San Diego, Mus. Modern Art, N.Y.C., 1969, 75, 76, 80, 82, Met. Mus., N.Y.C., 1969-70, 76, 79, 81, Va. Mus., Richmond, 1970, 74, Balt. Mus. Art, 1970, 76, Boston U., 1970, Boston Mus. Fine Arts, 1972, 82, Des Moines Art Center, 1973, Mus. Fine Arts, Houston, 1974, 82, Smith Coll. Mus. Art, Northampton, Mass., 1974, El Instituto de Cultura Puertorriquena, San Juan, Basil (Switzerland) Art Fair, 1974, 76, Finch Coll. Mus. Art, N.Y.C., 1974, S.I. Mus., 1975, Denver Art Mus., Visual Arts Mus., N.Y.C., 1975, 76, Mus. Modern Art, Belgrade Yugoslavia, 1976, Galleria d'Arts Moderna, Rome, Grey Art Gallery, N.Y.C., 1976-78, 81, Bklyn Mus., 1976-77, 82, Edmonton Art Gallery, Alta., Can., 1977, 78, Albright-Knox Mus., Buffalo, 1978, Fogg Art Mus., Harvard U., 1978, 83, Nat. Gallery Art, Washington, 1981, St. Louis Art Mus., 1982, Phoenix Art Mus., 1980; represented in permanent collections, Met. Mus. Art; exhibited in group shows including, Chrysler Mus., Norfolk, Va., 1976; represented in permanent collections, Bklyn. Mus.; exhibited in group shows including, Everson Mus., Syracuse, N.Y., 1976, 79; represented in permanent collections, Solomon R. Guggenheim Mus.; exhibited in group shows including, Art Gallery of Ont., Toronto, 1979; represented in permanent collections, N.Y. U.; exhibited in group shows including, Hirshorn Mus. and Sculpture Garden, Washington, 1980; represented in permanent collections, Mus. Modern Art; exhibited in group shows including, Tate Gallery, London, 1981; represented in permanent collections, Whitney Mus., all N.Y.C.; exhibited in group shows including, Walker Art Ctr., Mpls., 1981, numerous others; represented in permanent collections, Albright-Knox Art Gallery, Buffalo, U. Mich., High Mus., Atlanta, Milw. Art Inst., Wadsworth Atheneum, Hartford, Newark Mus., Yale U. Art Gallery, U. Nebr. Art Gallery, Carnegie Inst., Pitts., Detroit Inst. Art, Balt. Mus. Art, Univ. Mus., Berkeley, Calif., Bennington (Vt.) Coll., Art Inst. Chgo., Cin. Art Mus., Cleve. Mus. Art, Columbus Gallery Fine Arts, Honolulu Acad. Arts, Contemporary Arts Assn., Houston, Pasadena Art Mus., William Rockhill Nelson Gallery Art, Mus. Fine Arts, Kansas City, Mo., City Art Mus., St. Louis, Mus. Art, R.I. Sch. Design, Providence, San Francisco Mus. Art, Everson Mus., Syracuse, N.Y., Smithsonian Instn., Walker Art Inst., Mpls., Washington Gallery Modern Art, Wichita Art Mus., Brown Gallery Art, Nat. Gallery Victoria, Melbourne, Australia, Australian Nat. Gallery, Canberra, Victoria and Albert Mus., London, Eng., Tokyo Mus., Ulster Mus., Belfast, No. Ireland, Elvehjem Art Center, U. Wis., Israel Mus.-Instituto Nacional de Bellas Artes, Phila. Mus. Art, Phoenix Art Mus., Corcoran Gallery Art, Boston Mus. Fine Arts, Springfield (Mass.) Mus. Fine Arts, Witte Mus., San Antonio, Abbott Hall Art Gallery, Kendal, Eng., Mus. Contemporary Art, Nagaoka, Japan, numerous others. Trustee Bennington Coll., 1967—. Fellow Calhoun Coll., Yale U., 1968—; Recipient 1st prize for painting Paris Biennale, 1959; Gold medal Pa. Acad. Fine Arts, 1968; Great Ladies award Fordham U., Thomas Moore Coll., 1969; Spirit of Achievement award Albert Einstein Coll. Medicine, 1970; Gold medal Commune of Catania, III Biennale della Grafica d'Arte, Florence, Italy, 1972; Garrett award 70th Am. Exhbn., Art Inst. Chgo., 1972; Creative Arts award Nat. Women's div. Am. Jewish Congress, 1974; Art and Humanities award Yale Women's Forum, 1976; Extraordinary Woman of Achievement award NCCJ, 1978; Alumni award Bennington Coll., 1979. Mem. Nat. Inst. Arts and Letters. Subject of film Frankenthaler: Toward a New Climate, 1978. Home: 173 E 94th St New York NY 10028 *

FRANKFORTER, WELDON DELOSS, museum dir.; b. Tobias, Nebr., May 1, 1920; s. Archie and Mary Ann (Schroder) F.; m. Laura Glea Nicholas, Sept. 12, 1943; children: Mary Glea, Nicholas Dean, Gary Don, Matthew Jason, Lori Ann. B.Sc., U. Nebr., 1944, M.Sc., 1949. Student asst., asso. curator vertebrate paleontology U. Nebr. State Mus., 1941-50; dir. Sanford Mus. and Planetarium, Cherokee, Iowa, 1951-62; asst. dir. Grand Rapids (Mich.) Public Mus., 1962-64, dir., 1965—; mem. Nat. Mus. Act adv. council Smithsonian Instn., 1971-76; adv. for Mich., Nat. Trust Historic Preservation, 1972-78, regional v.p., 1975-76; adv. council Mich. Hist. Preservation Act, 1971-78, chmn., 1975-78; mem. Kent County Council Historic Preservation, 1972—, pres., 1973-74; mem. faculty Williamsburg Seminar, 1971-73; extension instr. Mich. State U., 1973-75; mem. Grand Rapids Hist. Commn., 1973—, Gerald R. Ford Presdl. Mus. Com., 1976—, Michigan Sesquicentennial Study Com., 1982—. Author research papers in field. Mem. Am. Assn. Museums (exec. bd. 1973-75, v.p. 1977-80, chmn. mus. services com. 1978-79), Midwest Museums Conf. (pres. 1966-67), Hist. Soc. Mich. (dir. 1970-76), Mich. Museums Assn., Am. Assn. State and Local History, AAAS, Geol. Soc. Am., Soc. Vertebrate Paleontology, Soc. Am. Archaeology, Mich. Archaeol. Soc., Mich. Acad. Scis., Arts and Letters, Iowa Acad. Scis., Nebr. Acad. Scis., Sigma Xi. Episcopalian. Clubs: Rotary, Torch. Home: 4856 Fuller Ave SE Grand Rapids MI 49508 Office: 54 Jefferson Ave SE Grand Rapids MI 49503

FRANKL, DANIEL RICHARD, educator, physicist; b. N.Y.C., Sept. 6, 1922; s. William and Frances (Lerner) F.; m. Estelle Marder, Aug. 26, 1951; children—Joseph Frederick, Phyllis Gail. B.Chem.Engring., Cooper Union, 1943; Ph.D., Columbia, 1953. With U.S. Rubber Co., Detroit, 1943-50; with Gen. Telephone & Electronics Labs., Inc., Bayside, N.Y., 1953-63; vis. prof. phys. metallurgy U. Ill., Urbana; (on leave Gen. Telephone & Electronics Labs.), 1962-63; prof. physics Pa. State U., University Park, 1963—; Vis. sr. research asso. U. Sussex, 1969-70; vis. research physicist U. Calif., San Diego, 1978-79. Author: Electrical Properties of Semiconductor Surfaces, 1967. Fellow Am. Phys. Soc. Research, publs. on internal friction, electroluminescence, surface properties of solids, thermal conduction, atomic beam scattering. Home: 438 Sierra Ln State College PA 16801 Office: Dept Physics Pa State University University Park PA 16801

FRANKL, KENNETH RICHARD, communications company executive, lawyer; b. N.Y.C., May 23, 1924; s. Hugo Joseph and Sydney (Miller) F.; m. Jeanne Ritchie Silver, Aug. 6, 1972; 1 dau., Kathryn; 1 son by previous marriage, Keith E. A.B. cum laude, Harvard U., 1947, LL.B., 1950. Bar: N.Y. 1951. Asst. dist. atty. N.Y. County, 1951-56; asso. firm Liebman Eulau & Robinson, N.Y.C., 1957-60; asst. gen. atty. CBS, 1960-69; gen. counsel, asst. sec. Bishop Industries, Inc., 1969-70; v.p., gen. counsel, sec. RKO Gen., Inc. and Subs., 1970—; sec.-treas. All Industry Radio Com.; mem. All Industry TV Com. Author: Equal Justice for the Accused, 1969. Served with Signal Corps U.S. Army, 1943-46; PTO. Decorated Army Commendation medal. Mem. Am. Bar Assn. (anti-trust com.), Assn. Bar City N.Y. (communications com., chmn. legis. subcom.), FCC Bar Assn., Copyright Circle, Internat. Radio and TV Soc. Jewish. Club: Harvard. Home: Old Montauk Hwy Amagansett NY 11930 Home: 45 Christopher St New York NY 10014 Office: RKO Gen Inc 1440 Broadway New York NY 10018

FRANKL, SPENCER NELSON, dentist, univ. dean; b. Phila., Nov. 19, 1933; s. Louis and Vera F.; m. Rhoda Lee, June 12, 1955; children—Elizabeth Ann, Catherine Susan. D.D.S., Temple U., 1958; postgrad., Children's Hosp. D.C., 1958-59; M.S., Tufts U., 1961. Asst. prof. dentistry Tufts U., 1961-64; asso. prof. Boston U., 1964-67, prof., 1967—, chmn. dept. dentistry, 1964-67, asst. dean, 1970-73, asso. dean, 1973—; dean Henry M. Goldman Sch. Grad. Dentistry, 1977—; chief pedodontics Boston U. Med. Center U. Hosp., 1964; head pediatric dentistry Beth Israel Hosp., 1964; chief dental service Joseph P. Kennedy Jr. Meml. Hosp., Brighton, Mass., 1968—. Contbr. articles to profl. jours. Fellow Am. Coll. Dentists, Internat. Coll. Dentists, Am. Acad. Pedodontists; mem. Am. Soc. Dentistry for Children, Mass. Soc. Dentistry for Children (past pres.), Am. Pub. Health Assn., Internat. Assn. for Dental Research, Am. Dental Assn., Am. Bd. Pedodontics (examiner). Office: 100 E Newton St Boston MA 02118

FRANKL, VIKTOR E., psychiatrist, author; b. Vienna, Austria, Mar. 26, 1905; s. Gabriel and Elsa (Lion) F.; m. Eleonore Katharina Schwindt, July 18, 1947; 1 dau., Gabriele Vesely. M.D., U. Vienna, 1930, Ph.D., 1949; LL.D. (hon.), Loyola U., Chgo., 1970, Edgecliff Coll., 1970, L.H.D., Rockford Coll., 1972. Editor jour. Man in Everyday Life, 1927; founder, head Youth Counseling Centers, Vienna, 1928-38; staff Neuropsychiatric Univ. Hosp., 1930-38; diplomate neurology and psychiatry, 1936—; head neurol. dept. Rothschild Hosp., Vienna, 1940-42; head Neurol. Poliklinik Hosp. of Vienna, 1946-70; asso. prof. neurology and psychiatry U. Vienna, 1947-55, prof., 1955—; Distinguished prof. logotherapy U.S. Internat. U., San Diego, 1970—; vis. prof. Harvard Summer Sch., 1961, So. Meth. U., 1966, Stanford U., 1971-72, Duquesne U., 1972; founder sch. logotherapy or existential analysis. Lectr., U.S. and fgn. countries.; Chmn. bd. trustees Logotherapy Inst., 1970-72, chmn. bd. dirs., 1977—; mem. internat. council Internat. Center Integrative Studies; bd. internat. cons. Religion in Edn. Found.; hon. pres. div. logotherapy Italian Center for Psychotherapy, 1979—. Author: The Doctor and the Soul, from Psychotherapy to Logotherapy, 1955, Man's Search for Meaning, an Introduction to Logotherapy, 1962, Psychotherapy and Existentialism, 1967, The Will to Meaning, 1969, The Unconscious God, 1976, The Unheard Cry for Meaning, 1978; others pub. Portuguese, German, Polish, Japanese, Dutch, Spanish, Italian, Swedish, Norwegian, Danish, French, Chinese, Hebrew, Greek, Serbo-Croatian, Finnish, Korean, Afrikaans.; Editor: (with V.E. von Gebsattel, J. H. Schultz) Ency. of Psychotherapy (5 vols.). Recipient Austrian State prize for pub. edn., 1956; West Va. Wesleyan Coll. Founders award, 1968; citation Religion in Edn. Found., 1960, Indpls. Pastoral Counseling Center; Austrian Cross of Honor for Sci. and Art, 1969; Wash. Coll. Distinguished Lectr. award, 1970; City Vienna prize for scientific achievement, 1970; Quest medal St. Edward's U., 1976; plaque of appreciation U. Philippines and U. Santo Tomas, Manila, 1976; Donauland prize for non-fiction, 1976; Albert Schweitzer award, 1977; Cardinal Innitzer award, 1977; Theodor Billroth medal, 1980; City of Vienna Ring of Honor, 1980; World Congress of Logotherapy award, 1980; citation Order of St. John Knights of Malta, 1980; Austrian Sign of Honor for Sci., 1981; plaque U.S. Internat. U., 1983; Gt. Cross of Merit Fed. Republic Germany, 1983; named hon. citizen of Austin, Tex., 1976. Mem. Austrian Soc. for Psychotherapy (founder; pres. 1950—), Internat. Fedn. Med. Psychotherapy (exec. bd.), Austrian Soc. Psychiatry and Neurology, Acad. Human Rights (adv.), Am. Med. Soc. Vienna, Internat. Union Cultural Cooperation (adv.), Austrian Acad. Scis.; hon. mem. Brazilian Soc. Integral Psychoanalysis (hon. pres.), Argentine Soc. Med. Anthropology, Instituto di Sociopsicologia Umanistica e Psicoterapia, Peruvian Soc. Neuropsychiatry and Legal Medicine, Peruvian Soc. Geriatrics, Spanish Soc. of Clinical and Exptl.

Hypnosis, Peruvian Soc. Neurology, Psychiatry and Neurosurgery, Mark Twain Soc., Med. Soc. Vienna, Nat. Honor Soc. Philosophy, Nat. Character Lab. (hon. life). Imprisoned in concentration camps, 1942- 45. Home: Mariannengasse 1 Vienna A-1090 Austria *I have seen the meaning of my life in helping others to see in their lives a meaning.*

FRANKL, WILLIAM STEWART, physician; b. Phila., July 15, 1928; s. Louis and Vera (Simkin) F.; m. Razelle Sherr, June 17, 1951; children: Victor S. (dec.), Brian A. B.A. in Biology, Temple U., 1951, M.D., 1955, M.S. in Medicine, 1961. Diplomate: Am. Bd. Internal Medicine, Am. Bd. Cardiovascular Disease. Intern Buffalo Gen. Hosp., 1955-56; resident in medicine Temple U., Phila., 1956-57, 59-61, mem. faculty, 1962-68, dir. EKG sect. dept. cardiology, 1966-68, dir. cardiac care unit, 1967-68; research fellow U. Pa., Phila., 1961-62; prof. medicine, dir. div. cardiology Med. Coll. Pa., Phila., 1970-79; prof. medicine, assoc. dir. cardiology div. Thomas Jefferson U., Phila., 1979-84; prof. medicine, co-dir. William Likoff Cardiovascular Inst. Hahnemann U., Phila., 1984—; physician-in-chief Springfield (Mass.) Hosp., 1968-70; practice medicine specializing in cardiology, Phila., 1962-68, 70—; cons. cardiology Phila. Va Hosp., 1970-79; Fogarty Sr. Internat. fellow Cardiothoracic Inst., U. London, 1978-79; Pres. elect Pa. affiliate Am. Heart Assn. Contbr. articles to profl. jours. Served with M.C. U.S. Army, 1957-59. Recipient Golden Apple award Temple U. Sch. Medicine, 1967; award Med. Coll. Pa., 1972; Lindback award for distinguished teaching, 1975. Fellow A.C.P., Am. Coll. Cardiology, Phila. Coll. Physicians, Am. Coll. Clin. Pharmacology (regent), Council Clin. Cardiology, Am. Heart Assn. (council on arteriosclerosis); mem. N.Y. Acad. Scis., Am. Fedn. Clin. Research, AAUP, AAAS, Assn. Am. Med. Colls., Am. Heart Assn. (bd. govs. S.E. Pa. chpt. 1972—, pres. 1976), Am. Soc. Clin. Pharmacology and Therapeutic Therapeutics. Home: 536 Moreno Rd Wynnewood PA 19096 Office: William Likoff Cardiovascular Inst Broad and Vine Sts Philadelphia PA 19102 *The essence of humanity and being human is caring. When one cares, life takes on a new dimension and provides one the ability to transcend the thin veneer which separates human and animal.*

FRANKLIN, ARETHA, singer; b. Memphis, Mar. 25, 1942; d. Clarence L. and Barbara (Siggers) F.; m. Ted White (div.); m. Glynn Turman, Apr. 11, 1978. First rec. at age 12; rec. artist, Columbia Records, N.Y.C., 1961; then with, Atlantic records; now with, Arista Records; also concert tours, U.S. and Europe; films include: Blues Brothers, 1980. Named Top Female Vocalist, 1967, Number one female singer (talent deserving of wider recognition) 16th Internat. Jazz Critics Poll, 1968; recipient Grammy award for Best female rhythm and blues vocal, 1967-74, 81, Grammy award for best rhythm and blues rec., 1967, Grammy award for best soul gospel performance, 1972; Am. Music award, 1984. Address: care Reverend Cecil Franklin 8450 Linwood St Detroit MI 48206 *

FRANKLIN, BILLY JOE, university president; b. Honey Grove, Tex., Jan. 30, 1940; s. John Asia and Annie Mae (Castle) F.; m. Sonya Kay Erwin, June 1, 1958; children: Terry Daylon, Shari Dea. B.A., U. Tex., 1965, M.A., 1967, Ph.D., 1969. Asst. prof. sociology U. Iowa, Iowa City, 1969-71; chmn. Western Carolina U., Cullowhee, N.C., 1971-72, Wright State U., Dayton, Ohio, 1973-75; dean S.W. Tex. State U., San Marcos, 1975-77; v.p. acad. affairs Stephen F. Austin State U., Nacogdoches, Tex., 1977-81; pres. Tex. A&I U., Kingsville, 1981—; state rep. Am. Assn. State Colls. and Univs., 1981—; dir. Assn. Tex. Colls. and Univs., 1983—; mem. nat. agr. research com. Dept. Agr., 1982—. Co-editor: Research Methods: Issues and Insights, 1971, Social Psychology and Everyday Life, 1973; contbr. articles to profl. jours. Mem. sr. adv. bd. Tex. Lyceum, Inc., Longview, 1982—; bd. dirs. United Way of Coastal Bend, Corpus Christi, Tex., 1981—. Fellow Tex. Acad. Sci. (dir. 1981—); mem. Am. Sociol. Assn., Southwestern Social Sci. Assn., Am. Assn. Higher Edn., Kingsville C. of C. (dir. 1981—). Democrat. Presbyterian. Lodge: Rotary. Office: Tex A&I Univ Campus Box 101 Kingsville TX 78363

FRANKLIN, BONNIE GAIL, actress; b. Santa Monica, Calif., Jan. 6, 1944; d. Samuel Benjamin and Claire (Hersch) F. B.A., UCLA, 1966. Mem. regional theatres in, N.Y. Mass. and Ohio, 1972-74. Stage appearances include Your Own Thing, San Francisco, Los Angeles, N.Y.C., 1968, Dames at Sea, 1969, Applause, N.Y.C., 1970-71 (Aegis Theatre Club award 1970), N.Y.C. (Theatre Club award 1970), N.Y.C. (Outer Critics Circle award 1960-70); TV appearances in The Law, 1974, One Day at a Time, 1975—, Portrait of A Rebel: Margaret Sanger, 1980, Bonnie and the Franklins, 1982, Your Place or Mine, 1983. Mem. Actors Equity Assn., Stage Actors Guild, AFTRA. Democrat. Jewish. Address: care Creative Artist's Agy 1888 Ave of Stars Suite 1400 Los Angeles CA 90067 *To avoid criticism: say nothing, do nothing, be nothing.*

FRANKLIN, CHARLES SCOTHERN, lawyer; b. Knoxville, Tenn., Dec. 12, 1937; s. Samuel Leroy and Mildred (Gibson) F.; m. Janice Stone; children—Jill Parvin, Melissa Ann, Samuel Arthur. B.S., U. Tenn., 1958; LL.B., Vanderbilt U., 1966. Bar: Calif. bar 1967, Nev. bar 1971. Instr. econs. U. Tenn., Knoxville, 1960-61; asso. firm Kent Brookes & Anderson, San Francisco, 1966-70; gen. counsel, sec. Harrah's, Reno, 1970-79; practice law, Reno, 1980—; Ford Found. fellow in econs. U. Calif., Berkeley, 1962. Mem. Am., Washoe County bar assns., Nev. State Bar, Calif. State Bar. Clubs: Prospectors, Elks (Reno).

FRANKLIN, EDWARD WARD, controls co. exec., lawyer; b. N.Y.C., Sept. 23, 1926; s. Albert Ward and Edith (Meyers) F.; m. Joan Rice, Aug. 25, 1956; children—Caroline, Melissa, Edward Ward. A.B. magna cum laude, Harvard, 1947; LL.B., Harvard U., 1950. Bar: N.Y. 1951. Assoc. Cadwalader, Wickersham & Taft, N.Y.C., 1950-56; gen. counsel N.Y. Air Brake Co., 1956-67, v.p. internat. and legal, 1962-67; v.p., gen. counsel Gen. Signal Corp., N.Y.C., 1967-80, sec., 1969-80, sr. v.p., 1980—, also dir., mem. exec. com.; dir. Gen. Signal of Can., Ltd., Hamworthy Hydraulics, Ltd., Poole, Eng., Leeds & Northrup, Inc., Mixing Equipment Co., Inc., Regina Corp., Edwards Co., Inc., Holborn Internat. Portfolio Mgrs. Trustee, treas. Town Sch., Inc.; bd. govs. Soc. N.Y. Hosp.; trustee Trinity Episcopal Schs. Corp. Served with USAAF, 1945. Mem. ABA, Assn. Bar City N.Y., Phi Beta Kappa. Clubs: Regency Whist, Knickerbocker, Board Room, Harvard (N.Y.C.); Misquamicut (Watch Hill, R.I.). Home: 1185 Park Ave New York NY 10028 Office: Box 10010 Stamford CT 06904

FRANKLIN, GEORGE S., government commission executive; b. N.Y.C., Mar. 23, 1913; s. George Small and Elizabeth (Jennings) F.; m. Helena Edgell, June 24, 1950; children: Helena, George III, Cynthia, Sheila. Student, U. Grenoble, 1931-32; A.B., Harvard, 1936; LL.B., Yale, 1939. Law clk. Davis, Polk, Wardwell, Gardiner & Reed, 1939; asst. Nelson A. Rockefeller, 1940; div. world trade intelligence Dept. State, 1941-44; assoc. Council on Fgn. Relations, 1945-71, asst. exec. dir., 1951-53, exec. dir., 1953-71; N.Am. sec. Trilateral Commn., 1972-76, coordinator, 1977-82; pres. Trilateral Commn. N. Am., 1977—. Life trustee Internat. House, N.Y.C.; former trustee Brearley Sch., N.Y. Soc. Library, Boys Brotherhood Republic, N.Y.C., Robert Coll., Istanbul, Turkey; trustee Atlantic Council U.S., Am Ditchley Found., Commn. United World Colls., Salzburg Seminar Am. Studies, Council on Fgn. Relations, French Am. Found.; hon. chmn. Mid-Atlantic Club; past sec., trustee Am. Com. on United Europe. Presbyterian. Clubs: Century, River (N.Y.C.). Home: 1220 Park Ave New York NY 10028 also Cove Neck Rd Osyter Bay NY 11771 Office: 345 E 46th St New York NY 10017

FRANKLIN, GILBERT ALFRED, art educator, sculptor, consultant; b. Birmingham, Eng., June 6, 1919; came to U.S., 1924; s. William and Nellie (Toney) F.; m. Joyce Gertrude Swirsky; 1 dau., Nina. B.F.A., R.I. Sch. Design, 1941. Prof. sculpture R.I. Sch. Design, Providence, 1946-55, chmn. div. fine arts, 1955-69, 72-79, dean fine arts, 1979-81, Helen M. Danford Dist. Prof. art, 1982-85. (Sculpture) Harvey Meml., 1955, Orpheus Ascending, 1963, Metcalf Meml., 1968, Harry S. Truman Meml., 1976. Assoc. trustee U. Pa. Grad. Sch. Art, Phila., 1975-81; bd. overseers Boston U. Sch. Art, 1980—; trustee, dir. Truro Sch. Fine Arts, Mass., 1982—. Recipient Prix De Rome Am. Acad. Rome, 1948, Grand Prize Boston Arts Festival, 1958; named Artist in Residence Dartmouth Coll., 1975; recipient medal for Excellence in the Arts Providence Art Club, 1975. Fellow Am. Acad. Rome; mem. Providence Art Club, NAD, Century Assn. Home: 52 Angell St Providence RI 02906 Office: RI Sch of Design College Hill Providence RI 02903

FRANKLIN, JOEL NICHOLAS, educator, mathematician; b. Chgo., Apr. 4, 1930; m. Patricia Anne; 1 dau., Sarah Jane. B.S., Stanford, 1950, Ph.D., 1953. Research asso. N.Y. U., 1953-55; asst. prof. math. U. Wash, 1955; mem. faculty Calif. Inst. Tech., 1957—, prof. applied sci., 1966-69, prof. applied math., 1969—. Author: Matrix Theory, 1968, Methods of Mathematical Economics, 1980, also articles. Mem. Am. Math. Soc., Soc. Indsl. and Applied Math., Phi Beta Kappa. Home: 1763 Alta Crest Altadena CA 91001 Office: California Inst Tech (217-50) Pasadena CA 91125

FRANKLIN, JOHN HOPE, educator, author; b. Rentiesville, Okla., Jan. 2, 1915; s. Buck Colbert and Mollie (Parker) F.; m. Aurelia E. Whittington, June 11, 1940; 1 son, John Whittington. A.B., Fisk U., 1935, A.M., Harvard, 1936, Ph.D., 1941; hon. degrees, Morgan State Coll., Va. State Coll., Lincoln (Pa.) U., Cambridge (Eng.) U., Drake U., Mich. State U., U. Ill. at Chgo., Carnegie-Mellon U., Columbia U., Loyola U., Chgo., Bklyn. Coll., Wilmington, Bard Coll., Boston Coll., Brown U., Tuskegee Inst., Grand Valley Coll., Marquette U., Lincoln Coll., Ill., Princeton, Hamline U., Fisk U., R.I. Coll., Dickinson Coll., Howard U., U. Md., U. Notre Dame, Tulsa U., Morehouse Coll., Miami U., Johnson C. Smith Coll., Lake Forest Coll., Tougaloo Coll., Union Coll., Northwestern U., Whittier Coll., U. Mass., U. Mich., Seattle U., U. Toledo, Yale U., L.I. U., Catholic U. Am., Tulane U., Temple U., Kalamazoo Coll., Washington U., Trinity Coll. (Conn.), Ariz. State U., U. State N.Y., No. Mich. U., U. Utah, Coll. of New Rochelle, Governors State U., Harvard U., U. Pa., Ripon U., Atlanta U., Wayne State U., U. N.C.-Chapel Hill, Dillard U., Manhattan Coll., Roosevelt U., N.C. Central U., Ind. State U., St. Olaf Coll., Emory U., U. Miami, U. Conn., U. N.C.-Charlotte. Instr. history Fisk U., 1936-37; prof. history St. Augustine's Coll., 1939-43, N.C. Coll. at Durham, 1943-47, Howard U., 1947-56; chmn. dept. history Bklyn. Coll., 1956-64; prof. Am. history U. Chgo., 1964-82, chmn. dept. history, 1967-70, John Matthews Manly Distinguished Service prof., 1969-82; James B. Duke prof. history Duke U., 1982—; Pitt prof. Am. history and instns. Cambridge U., 1962-63; vis. prof. Harvard, U. Wis., Cornell U., Salzburg Seminar, U. Hawaii, U. Calif., Cambridge U.; Chmn. Bd. Fgn. Scholarships, 1966-69, Nat. Council on Humanities, 1976-79; dir. Ill. Bell Telephone Co., 1972-80. Author: Free Negro in North Carolina, 1943, From Slavery to Freedom: A History of Negro Americans, 5th edit, 1980, Militant South, 1956, Reconstruction After the Civil War, 1961, The Emancipation Proclamation, 1963, A Southern Odyssey, 1976, Racial Equality in America, 1976, (with others) Land of the Free, 1966, Illustrated History of Black Americans, 1970; Editor: Civil War Diary of James T. Ayers, 1947, A Fool's Errand by Albion Tourgee, 1961, Army Life in a Black Regiment by Thomas Higginson, 1962, Color and Race, 1968, Reminiscences of an Active Life by John R. Lynch, 1970; editor: (with August Meier) Black Leaders in the Twentieth Century, 1982; mem. editorial bd.: Am. Scholar, 1972-76. Bd. dirs. Salzburg Seminar, Mus. Sci. and Industry, 1968-80; trustee Chgo. Symphony, 1976-80, chmn. bd. trustees, Fisk U., 1968-74; now trustee. Fisk U. Edward Austin fellow, 1937-38; Rosenwald fellow, 1937-39; Guggenheim fellow, 1950-51, 73-74; Pres.'s fellow Brown U., 1952-53, Center for Advanced Study in Behavioral Sci., 1973-74; Sr. Mellon fellow Nat. Humanities Center, 1980-82; Fulbright prof., Australia, 1960; Jefferson lectr. in the humanities, 1976; Named to Okla. Hall of Fame, 1978. Fellow Am. Acad. Arts and Scis.; mem. Am. Hist. Assn. (pres. 1978-79), So. Hist. Assn. (pres. 1970-71), Orgn. Am. Historians (pres. 1974-75), Assn. for Study Negro Life and History, Am. Studies Assn. (past pres.), Am. Philos. Soc., AAUP, Phi Beta Kappa (senate 1966—, pres. 1973-76), Phi Alpha Theta. Home: 208 Pineview Rd Durham NC 27707

FRANKLIN, JON DANIEL, journalist; b. Enid, Okla., Jan. 13, 1942; s. Benjamin Max and Wilma Irene (Winburn) F.; m. Nancy Sue Creevan, Dec. 12, 1959 (div. 1976); children: Teresa June, Catherine Cay. B.S. with high honors, U. Md., 1970. Reporter/editor Prince Georges (Md.) Post, 1967-70; sci. writer Balt. Eve. Sun, 1970—; sr. lectr. U. Md.-Baltimore County; mem. unit council Newspaper Guild at Balt. Sunpapers. Prin. author: Shocktrauma, 1980, Not Quite a Miracle, 1983, Guinea Pig Doctors, 1984. Served as journalist U.S. Navy, 1959-67. Recipient James T. Grady medal Am. Chem. Soc., 1975, Pulitzer prize feature writing, 1979. Mem. Nat. Assn. Sci. Writers, Newspaper Guild. Clubs: Nat. Press (Washington); Md. Press (Balt.). Address: PO Box 1130 Glen Burnie MD 21061

FRANKLIN, KENNETH L(INN), astronomer; b. Alameda, Calif., Mar. 25, 1923; s. Myles Arthur and Ruth Linn (Huston) F.; m. Beverly Mattson, Nov. 29, 1949 (dec. Mar. 1956); children: Kathleen (Mrs. James R. Williams), Christine (Mrs. Russell Redding); m. Charlotte Walton, May 18, 1958; 1 adopted dau., Julie (Mrs. A.D. Jones). A.A., U. Calif.-Berkeley, 1943, A.B., 1948; Ph.D., U. Calif. at Berkeley, 1953. Sci. asst. dept. astronomy U. Calif., 1953-54; research fellow dept. terrestrial magnetism Carnegie Instn., 1954-56; asst. astronomer Am. Museum-Hayden Planetarium, N.Y.C., 1956-58, assoc. astronomer, 1958-63, astronomer, 1963—, asst. chmn., 1968-72, chmn., 1972-74; cons. aerospace firms, pubs., news media on astronomy and space sci.; mem. faculty CUNY, NYU, Cooper Union, Rutgers U.; participant Nat. Security Seminar, Army War Coll., 1975; Chmn. Mus. Council N.Y.C., 1977, 78. Numerous appearances TV, Radio.; Astronomy editor: World Almanac, 1968—; mem. editorial adv. panel: Sci. Digest, 1970—. Served with AUS, 1943-46. Fellow AAAS, Royal Astron. Soc., Explorers Club; mem. Am. Astron. Soc. (pub. info. rep. 1973-79, soc. vis. prof. 1959—), Astron. Soc. Pacific, IEEE, N.Y. Acad. Scis., Sigma Xi. Club: Trap Door Spiders. Discoverer (with B.F. Burke) radio emissions from Jupiter, 1955; devised a system for lunar-based timekeeping, 1970. Appeared CBS Sputnik Special, 1957; CBS Landing Surveyor I, 1966; NBC Apollo 8, 1968, Apollo 10, 11, 1969; CBS Eclipse Special, 1970.

FRANKLIN, LARRY DANIEL, newspaper publishing company executive; b. Commerce, Tex., July 16, 1942; s. John Asia and Annie Mae (Castle) F.; m. Charlotte Anne Walker, Aug. 18, 1962; children: Kelly Leigh, Kristi Lynn. B.B.A., East Tex. State U., 1965; M.B.A., Tex. Tech. U., 1966. Mem. audit staff Arthur Andersen Co., Dallas, 1966-67; controller, treas. Paris Milling Co., Tex., 1967-69; mem. audit staff Price Waterhouse Co., Dallas, 1969-71; asst. copr. dir. acctg. Harte-Hanks Communications Inc., San Antonio, 1971, corp. dir. fin. services, 1971-72, chief fin. officer, treas., 1972-74, v.p. fin., treas., 1974-75, v.p. fin., sec.-treas., 1975-78, sr. v.p., pres. newspaper ops., 1978-80, exec. v.p., 1980—, dir.; dir. Interfirst Bank, San Antonio. Mem. mass communication adv. com. Tex. Tech U., Lubbock; mem. mass communications adv. com. St. Thomas Episcopal Ch., San Antonio; mem. adv. council Sch. Bus. Incarnate Word Coll.; mem. program ops. com. United Way; past mem. graphic arts adv. com. Rochester Inst. Tech.; bd. dirs. East Tex. State U. Found., Commerce. Mem. Am. Inst. C.P.A.s, Fin. Execs. Inst. (founding dir., past pres. South Tex. chpt.), Am. Newspaper Pubs. Assn. (newsprint com.), So. Newspaper Pubs. Assn. (bd. dirs.), Am. Press Inst. (bd. dirs.), Tex. Daily Newspaper Assn. Home: 16451 Lost Cabin St San Antonio TX 78232 Office: Harte-Hanks Communications Inc PO Box 269 San Antonio TX 78291

FRANKLIN, MARC ADAM, legal educator; b. Bklyn., Mar. 9, 1932; s. Louis A. and Rose (Rosenthal) F.; m. Ruth E. Korzenik, June 29, 1958; children—Jonathan, Alison. A.B., Cornell, 1953, LL.B., 1956. Bar: N.Y. bar 1956. Atty. firm Proskauer Rose Goetz & Mendelsohn, N.Y.C., 1956-57; law clk to Hon. Carroll C. Hincks, New Haven, 1957-58, to Earl Warren, U.S. Supreme Ct., Washington, 1958-59; prof. law Columbia, 1959-62, Stanford, 1962—, Frederick I. Richman prof. law, 1976—. Author: Biography of a Legal Dispute, 1968, Dynamics of American Law, 1968, Cases and Materials on Tort Law and Alternatives, 1971, 3d edit., 1983, Mass Media Law, 1977, 2d edit., 1982, The First Amendment and the Fourth Estate, 1977, 2d edit., 1981. Fellow Center for Advanced Study in the Behavioral Scis., 1968-69; Fulbright research scholar Victoria U., Wellington, N.Z., 1973. Home: 2870 Pacific Ave San Francisco CA 94115 Office: Stanford Law Sch Stanford CA 94305

FRANKLIN, MERVYN, university administrator; b. Minehead, Eng., Jan. 13, 1932. B.Sc., U. Reading, 1955, 56; Ph.D. in Biochemistry, McGill U., 1959. Demonstrator McGill U., 1957-59; J.C. Child fellow microbiology Western Res. U., 1959-60; lectr. McGill U., 1960-62, asst. prof., 1962-65; asst. prof. microbiology N.Y. Med. Coll., 1965-66, assoc. prof., 1967-69; prof. biology U. N.B., 1969-78, dean faculty sci., 1969-75, acting v.p., Fredericton, 1975-76, acad. v.p., 1976-78; vice chancellor, pres. U. Windsor, Ont., Can., 1978-84; mem. Sci. Council Can., 1970-76; chmn. environ. council Province of N.B., 1972-75. Assoc. editor: Can. Jour. Microbiology, 1970-73. Mem. Can. Assn. Deans Arts and Sci., Can. Soc. Microbiologists (2d v.p. 1975-76), Am. Soc. Microbiology. Office: U Windsor Office of Pres and Vice Chancellor Sunset Ave Windsor ON N9B 3P4 Canada *

FRANKLIN, MICHAEL HAROLD, orgn. exec.; b. Los Angeles, Dec. 25, 1923; children—Barbara, John, James, Robert. A.B., UCLA, 1948; LL.B., U. So. Calif., 1951. Bar: Calif. bar 1951. Practiced in, Los Angeles, 1951-52, pvt. practice, 1951-52; atty. CBS, 1952-54, Paramount Pictures Corp., 1954-58; exec. dir. Writers Guild Am. West, Inc., 1958-78; nat. exec. dir. Dirs. Guild Am., Inc., 1978—; Mem. Fed. Cable Adv. Commn. Served with C.E. AUS, 1942-46. Mem. ACLU, Los Angeles Copyright Soc., Order of Coif. Office: 7950 Sunset Blvd Los Angeles CA 90046

FRANKLIN, MITCHELL, lawyer, educator; b. Montreal, Que., Can., Feb. 19, 1902; s. Adolphe and Emma (Franklin) F.; m. Virginia Frances Wesler, June 25, 1922. A.B., Harvard U., 1922, J.D., 1925, S.J.D., 1928; LL.D. (hon.), Tulane U., 1978. Law sec. to Supreme Jud. Ct. of Mass., 1925-28; practiced in, N.Y.C., 1928-30; W.R. Irby prof. law Tulane U., New Orleans, 1930-67; now emeritus; vis. prof. State U. N.Y. at Buffalo, 1967-68, prof. law, prof. philosophy, 1968-74, prof. emeritus, 1974—; Legal adviser UNRRA, Southwestern Europe, Middle East, hdqrs., Rome, 1946; legal officer UN Secretariat, 1948; U.S. reporter at Congresses of Comparative Law, The Hague, also; London, Paris. Contbr. articles to legal publs. Served as pvt. U.S. Army, World War I; maj. to lt. col., World War II. Recipient Franklin D. Roosevelt award, 1958; Rosenwald fellow, Paris, 1939; Guggenheim fellow, 1948-49. Mem. N.Y., La. bar assns. Home: 675 Delaware Ave Buffalo NY 14202 Office: Law Sch State Univ NY at Buffalo North Campus Buffalo NY 14260 also Tulane U New Orleans LA 70118

FRANKLIN, MURRAY JOSEPH, steel foundry executive; b. Orange, N.J., Apr. 1, 1922; s. Joseph Charles and Edna S. F.; m. Jane Modlin, Oct. 25, 1946; children: Gail Lee, Martha Ann. B.A., Ohio Wesleyan U., 1943; M.A. (univ. fellow 1946-49), U. Mich., 1947, Ph.D., 1963. With Hayes-Albion Corp., Jackson, Mich., 1968-70; v.p., gen. mgr. Westinghouse Airbrake div. Am. Standard Corp., Pitts., 1970-77; pres. transp. equipment div. Dresser Industries, Inc., DePew, N.Y., 1977—; asso. prof. bus. U. Mich., 1963-65. Bd. dirs. Better Bus. Bur. Chgo., 1966-67. Served with USMCR, 1943-46. Mem. Am. Econ. Assn., Am. Mktg. Assn., Ry. Progress Inst. (exec. com., bd. govs.). Republican. Methodist. Clubs: Buffalo, Country of Buffalo. Home: 20 Lancaster Ln Orchard Park NY 14127 Office: 2 Main St DePew NY 14043

FRANKLIN, OMER W., JR., lawyer, assn. exec.; b. Valdosta, Ga., 1914. A.B., U. Ga., 1936, LL.B., 1939. Bar: Ga. Bar 1939. Sr. partner firm Franklin, Barham, Coleman, Elliott & Blackburn, Valdosta, 1961-69; judge Superior Cts., So. Jud. Circuit, Valdosta, Ga., 1969-72; gen. counsel State Bar Ga., Atlanta, 1972—; Mem. rules com. Ga. Supreme Ct., 1961. Fellow Am. Coll. Trial Lawyers; mem. ABA, Valdosta Bar Assn. (pres. 1959-60), State Bar Ga. (chmn. com. rules of practice and procedure 1964-65, pres. 1966-67), Am. Judicature Soc., Phi Delta Phi. Office: State Bar of Georgia 11th Floor Flatiron Bldg 84 Peachtree St Atlanta GA 30303

FRANKLIN, OWEN ELLSWORTH, social service adminstr.; b. Vincennes, Ind., Oct. 27, 1924; s. Court M. and Zoe (Day) F.; m. Joyce C. Benton, Sept. 12, 1980; children—Randall M., Mark A., Jeffrey W., Rebecca A. B.S., Ind. U., 1950, M.A., 1952. Sch. social worker Indpls. Pub. Schs., 1952-55; child welfare cons. State Welfare Dept., Indpls., 1956; asst. dir. Nat. Child Welfare div. Am. Legion, Indpls., 1957-59; dir. social services Woodward (Iowa) State Hosp.-Sch., 1959-64, supt., 1969—; specialist social services to mentally retarded children and their families U.S. Children's Bur., Dept. Health, Edn. and Welfare, Washington, 1964-69; Mem. sec.'s com. on Mental retardation Dept. Health, Edn. and Welfare, Washington, 1965-67; co-chmn. com. on mental retardation U.S. Childrens Bur., 1965-68. Served with AUS, 1943-46. Decorated Bronze Star (5) with bronze arrowhead. Mem. Am. Assn. on Mental Deficiency, Nat. Assn. Social Workers. Address: Woodward State Hosp-Sch Woodward IA 50276

FRANKLIN, RICHARD EWELL, railroad exec.; b. Birmingham, Ala., Dec. 3, 1919; s. William F. and Mary (Cunningham) F.; m. Frances Stevens, Oct. 19, 1940; children—R. Miles, Elaine (Mrs. Donald E. Love), Frances Mabel (Mrs. Robert Abernathy). Student, Internat. Corr. Schs., 1937-40. With So. Ry. Co., 1937-61, 64-65, supt. maintenance equipment, Charlotte, N.C., 1952-55, asst. v.p. mech., Washington, 1956-61, chief mech. officer, 1963-64, v.p., asst. to pres., v.p. ops., 1964, sr. v.p., 1965; v.p. engring., prodn. and research Ry. Maintenance Corp., Pitts., 1961-62; dir. indsl. engring. Pa. Ry. Co., Phila., 1962-63, v.p. transp., maintenance, 1966-67; asst. pres. Central of Ga. R.R., Savannah, 1967-68, pres., 1968—, dir., 1967—; pres., dir. Ocean S.S. Co. Savannah, South Western R.R. Co., Albany Passenger Terminal Co., 1967—, Central of Ga. Motor Transport Co., 1967—, Chatham Terminal Co., 1967—; dir. Augusta & Summerville R.R. Co.,

C & S Nat. Bank adv. bd., Savannah, 1967—; Dir. So. States Indsl. Council, 1968—; mem. Savannah Regional Export Expansion Council, 1978—. Bd. dirs. ARC, Savannah, 1968—, Savannah YMCA, 1968—; chmn. Savannah area U.S. Savs. Bonds campaign, 1969; chmn. div. A United Community Appeal, 1969—; mem. Coastal Empire council Boy Scouts Am., 1968—; trustee Ga. Coll. Found., Milledgeville, 1969—, Historic Savannah Found., 1969—; mem. adv. bd. Shorter Coll., 1979. Served with AUS, 1944-46. Mem. Ga. C. of C., Savannah Area C. of C. (pres. 1969). Baptist. Clubs: Rotarian., Ogelthorpe, Savannah Golf, Savannah Yacht, Chatham. Home: 2 Woodhull Circle The Bluff Savannah GA 31404 Office: PO Box 456 Savannah GA 31402

FRANKLIN, ROBERT BREWER, journalist; b. Phila., Mar. 31, 1937; s. John Jay and Sarah Louise (Redman) F.; m. Norma Jean Belke, June 18, 1966; children: James Robert, Mary Jean. B.A. in Journalism, Pa. State U., 1959; postgrad., U. Minn. News editor Hatboro (Pa.) Public Spirit, 1959-60; reporter No. Va. Sun, Arlington, 1960-62; journalist AP, Phila., 1962, Mpls., 1962-67; reporter, then asst. city editor Mpls. Tribune, 1967-74, city editor, 1975-82, Mpls. Star and Tribune, 1982-83, state editor, 1983—. Mem. Medina (Minn.) City Council, 1971-76, chief police, 1971-73, commnr. public safety, 1974-76. Served with U.S. Army, 1960-62. Mem. Sigma Delta Chi. Lutheran. Home: 2819 Lakeshore Ave Maple Plain MN 55359 Office: 425 Portland Ave Minneapolis MN 55488

FRANKLIN, ROBERT CHARLES, transportation and communication company executive; b. Toronto, Ont., Can., July 30, 1936; s. Edward C. and Louise M. (Edwards) F.; m. Rita Mae Kelly, Oct. 3, 1959; children: Katherine Diane, Karen Kelly, Craig Robert. B.A., Queen's U., 1956; P.M.D., Harvard U., 1974. Asst. to gen. mgr. Can. Nat. Telecommunications, Toronto, Ont., 1967-72, dir. mktg., 1972-74, v.p. mktg. fin., 1974-80; v.p. fin. Can. Nat. Rys., Montreal, Ont., 1980-81, sr. corp. v.p., 1982; pres. Can. Nat. Enterprises, Can. Nat. Rys., Montreal, Ont., 1982—; chmn. bd. CN Marine Inc., 1982—, Northwestel Inc., 1982—, Terra Nova Tel Inc., 1982—; dir. CN/CP Telecommunications, 1981; chmn. dir. CN Hotels, Inc., 1983; dir. Canac Cons., Inc., 1982, CN Tower Inc. and CN Explorations, Inc., 1982, Transport Route Can. Inc., 1982. Clubs: Mt. Royal, McGill Assocs. (Montreal Que., Can.); Beaconsfield Golf, Concordia Univ. Home: 90 Prince St Beaconsfield PQ Canada H9W 3M7 Office: Can Nat Enterprises 935 Rue Lagauchetier Montreal PQ Canada H3C 3N4

FRANKLIN, STANLEY PHILLIP, mathematician, educator; b. Memphis, Aug. 14, 1931; s. Sam and Lily (Rosenblum) F.; m. Jeannie Stonebrook, Apr. 1, 1979; children—Lynn Ann, Michele Suzanne, Phillip Byron, Bruce Eric, Halli Eileen, Elena Simone. B.S., Memphis State U., 1959; M.A., UCLA, 1962, Ph.D., 1963; NSF postdoctoral fellow, U. Wash., Seattle, 1963-64. Asst. prof. math. U. Fla., 1964-65; asso. prof., then prof. Carnegie-Mellon U., 1965-72; prof. math., chmn. dept. math. scis. Memphis State U., 1972—; vis. prof. Indian Inst. Tech., Kanpur, Technion, Haifa, Israel; vis. mem. Mathematische Centrum, Amsterdam, Netherlands; condr. workshops, cons. in field. Author research papers in field. Program dir. Gateways, center human potential, 1974-78. Served with USMCR, 1951-53. Mem. Am. Math. Soc., Math. Assn. Am., Assn. Humanistic Psychology, Sigma Xi, Pi Mu Epsilon. Home: 3568 Highland Park Pl Memphis TN 38111 Office: Dept Math Sci Memphis State Univ Memphis TN 38152

FRANKLIN, THOMAS CHESTER, chemistry educator; b. Birmingham, Ala., Feb. 5, 1923; s. Chester S. and Irene (Tibbetts) F.; m. Nellie Louise Friel, June 26, 1946; children: Irene Elise, Margaret Elaine, Janice Carol, Thomas Edward. B.S., Howard Coll., 1944; Ph.D., Ohio State U., 1951. Instr. Howard Coll., 1946-48; asst. instr. Ohio State U., 1948-51; asst prof. U. Richmond, Va., 1951-54; research asso. Va. Inst. for Sci. Research, Richmond, 1951-53; faculty Baylor U., Waco, Tex., 1954—, prof. chemistry, 1964—. Author: (with John Xan) A Lab Manual for Semimicroqualitiative Analysis, 1948. Mem. Am. Chem. Soc., Electrochem. Soc., Am. Electroplaters Soc., Internat. Soc. Electrochemistry, Sigma Xi. Studies, publs. of electrochem. and catalytic properties of metal surfaces in contact with solutions using absorption of hydrogen as a measure of active area; studies of electrodeposition, catalytic and electrolytic oxidations and reductions of organic compounds. Home: 1312 Guthrie Dr Waco TX 76703

FRANKLIN, WILLIAM DONALD, government official; b. Dacula, Ga., Nov. 26, 1933; s. Thomas Kimsey and Lora Claudia (Martin) F.; m. Elizabeth Ann Giles, Nov. 25, 1970; children: Braden, Kimette, Laura, Thomas, Amy, Holly. B.S., Austin Peay State U., 1961; M.S., Tex. A&M U., 1963; Sc.D., U. London, 1972; A.M.P., Harvard U., 1973; grad. Indsl. Coll. Armed Forces, 1971, Command and Gen. Staff Coll., 1975, Air U., 1977, Nat. Def. U., 1978. Data processing mgr. Boillin-Harrison, Inc., Clarksville, Tenn., 1959-61; economist Tex. A&M U., 1961-63; asst. prof. bus. Upper Iowa U., 1963-64; transport economist Tex. Transp. Inst., 1964-69; head dept. econs., dir. mgmt. devel. Tenn. Weseleyan Coll., Athens, 1969-75; pres. Econotec Research Co., Athens, Tenn., 1969-75; dep. div. dir. trade and industry analysis div. Bur. Internat. Econ. Affairs, Dept. Labor, Washington, 1975-77; industry economist Fed. R.R. Adminstrn., Dept. Transp., Washington, 1977; div. tech. assessment Fed. Hwy. Traffic Safety Adminstrn., Dept. Transp., Washington, 1977-78; chief airport and consumer affairs br. Office Noise Control and Abatement, EPA, Washington, 1978-81, dir. plans and programs staff, 1981-82; sr. economist Office of Asst. Adminstr. for Air, Noise and Radiation, EPA, Washington, 1982-83; spl. asst. to asst. adminstr. Office of Policy, Planning & Evaluation, EPA, Washington, 1983—; fed. coordinator Emergency Transp. for State of Tenn., 1973-76; mem. bd. Am. Security Council, 1980-81; dir. Congl. Adv. Bd., 1981-82. Author: (with Doyle) Federal Emergency Transportation Preparedness, 1968, Management: Theory and Practice, 1972, Civil Affairs Personnel Survey, 1973, (with Hutson and Ryberg) Community Leadership Developement, 1975; contbr. numerous articles to profl. publs. Mem. adminstrv. bd. Keith Methodist Ch., Athens, 1974-75; mem. stewardship com. Vienna Bapt. Ch., 1983—; bd. dirs. Statewide Council Community Leadership Tenn., 1973-75, Tenn. Alcohol and Drug Abuse Higher Edn. Planning Council, 1973, Ctr. Govt. Tng. Tenn., 1973-75; mem. Presdl. Exec. Res., Office Pres. U.S., 1966-75; fed. coordinator for emergency transp. State of Tenn., 1973-76. Served col., paratroopers U.S. Army, 1953-58. Decorated Army Commendation medal; recipient cert. of acheivement Dept. Def., 1958, Outstanding Acheivement award Dept. Def., 1967, Presdl. commendation Pres. of U.S., 1983; Woodrow Wilson fellow, 1961; univ. fellow Tex. A&M U., 1961-63; grad. acad. fellow Harvard U., 1971-72. Fellow Meninger Found.; mem. Am. Econ. Assn., Am. Statis. Assn., Am. Acad. Polit. and Social Scis., AAUP, Harvard Bus. Sch. Alumni Assn., Internat. Platform Assn., Res. Officers Assn., Assn. U.S. Army, Phi Sigma Kappa, Phi Alpha Theta. Clubs: Harvard, Harvard Bus. Sch., Capitol Yacht, Officers of Mil.* Dist. Washington, Nat. Aviation. Lodges: Lions; Rotary. Home: 509 Lewis St Vienna VA 22180 Office: Office of Policy Planning & Evaluation CPM-219 EPA Washington DC 20460 *I believe that the opportunities of today grow out of the preparations of yesterday and that the sometimes casual acquaintances we make today will be the good friends of tomorrow. Gradually I have come to realize that life rewards us far better in almost every way than even we think we deserve.*

FRANKLIN, WILLIAM WEBSTER, congressman; b. Greenwood, Miss., Dec. 13, 1941; s. Webster Cromwell and Mary Elizabeth (Irby) F.; m. Edna Green Lott, June 12, 1965; children: Webster Cromwell, Melissa Lansdale. B.A., Miss. State U., 1963; J.D., U. Miss., 1966; grad., Nat. Jud. Coll., 1979. Bar: Miss. Practice law, Greenwood, Miss., 1970-82; asst. dist. atty. 4th Dist. Miss., 1972-78; judge Miss. Circuit Ct. 4th dist., 1978-82; mem. 98th Congress from 4th Miss. Dist. Served to capt. JAGC U.S. Army, 1966-70. Recipient Meritorious Service City of New Orleans, 1968; fellow Miss. Inst. Politics, 1971. Mem. ABA, Miss. Bar Assn., Leflore County Bar Assn. Republican. Episcopalian. Home: 613 River Rd Greenwood MS 38930 Office: Room 508 Cannon Office Bldg Washington DC 20515

FRANKOVICH, GEORGE RICHARD, trade association executive; b. Pitts., Aug. 17, 1920; s. George and Anna (Subasic) F.; m. Madelaine E. Ruest, Jan. 29, 1944; children: Richard E., Diane. B.A., U. Pitts, 1941. Cert. assn. exec. Indsl. engr. MJ & Silversmiths of Am., Providence, 1946-48, exec. dir., Prividence, 1948—, v.p., Providence, 1958—; dir. Silver Users Assn., Washington, 1970—, Columbus Nat. Bank, Providence, 1976—; dir., asst. treas. Jewelers Shipping Assn., Providence, 1953—; dir., treas. The Jewelry Inst., Providence, 1978—. Chmn. R.I. Apprentice Council, Providence, 1960-75; mem. Jewelry Adv. Council, Providence, 1981—, Salute to Industry Com., 1983. Served to maj. U.S. Army, 1941-46. Decorated Bronze Star, Croix de Guerre. Mem. Am. Soc. Assn. Execs., Worshipful Co. Goldsmiths (London), Internat. Precious Metals Inst. (dir. 1978-83). Roman Catholic. Clubs: Sqantum Association (East Providence); Providence Jewelers. Home: 29 Weeden Ave Rumford RI 02916 Office: Manufacturing Jewelers and Silversmiths of Am Biltmore Plaza Hotel Providence RI 02903

FRANKOVICH, MIKE J., film producer; b. Bisbee, Ariz., Sept. 29, 1910; m. Binnie Barnes. B.A., U. Cal. Producer, commentator on radio, 1934-38; mng. dir. Columbia Pictures Corp. Ltd., 1955-59, chmn., 1959-67; v.p. Columbia Pictures Internat. Corp., 1955-67; head Columbia Pictures Internat. Prodns., 1958-67; 1st v.p. charge world prodn. Columbia, until 1967; dir. BLC Films; chmn. Screen Gems Ltd.; ind. producer, 1967—. Author screenplays for, Universal Studios, 1938, Republic Pictures, 1940-49; producer: Joe Macbeth; Producer: films including Forty Carats, 1973, Report to the Commissioner, 1975, From Noon Till Three, 1976, The Shootist, 1976. Served with AUS, World War II. Club: Variety (chief banker Tent 36). Address: 733 N Kings Rd Apt 145 Los Angeles CA 90069 *

FRANKS, CHARLES LESLIE, banker; b. Columbus, Miss., Jan. 21, 1934; s. Leslie J. and Almeda (Morris) F.; m. Cecile Alice Cronovich, Feb. 7, 1959; children—Carolyn Anne, Charles Christopher. B.S. summa cum laude, Miss. State U., 1956. Certified internal auditor. Accountant Arthur Andersen & Co., Houston, 1959-61; mgr. internal audit dept. Bank of S.W., Houston, 1961-71; gen. auditor Southwest Bancshares, Inc., 1972-79; v.p., auditor Merc. Nat. Bank, Dallas, 1979-82, sr. v.p., auditor, 1982—; instr., speaker various Bank Adminstrn. Inst. seminars, meetings and convs. Served to capt. USAF, 1956-59. Mem. Tex. Soc. C.P.A.s (sec. Houston chpt. 1971-72), Bank Adminstrn. Inst. (v.p. Gulf Coast chpt. 1971-72, pres. 1973-74, dir. 1974-75, state dir. 1975-77, dir. Dallas chpt. 1980-84), Am. Inst. Banking, Inst. Internal Auditors (gov. 1973-78, pres. Houston chpt. 1974-75), Houston C. of C., Arnold Air Soc., Phi Eta Sigma, Chi Lambda Rho, Phi Kappa Phi, Alpha Kappa Psi. Roman Catholic. Home: 6022 La Cosa Dallas TX 75248 Office: PO Box 225415 Dallas TX 75265

FRANKS, LUCINDA LAURA, journalist; b. Chgo., July 16, 1946; d. Thomas Edward and Lorraine Lois (Leavitt) F.; m. Robert M. Morgenthau, Nov. 1977. B.A., Vassar Coll., 1968. Journalist specializing youth affairs, civil strife in No. Ireland UPI, London, 1968-73, N.Y. Times, N.Y.C., 1974-77; freelance writer, writing for N.Y. Times Mag., The Atlantic, N.Y. mag., The Nation, Saturday Rev.; Vis. prof. Vassar Coll., 1977-82; Ferris prof. journalism Princeton U., 1983. Author: Waiting Out A War: The Exile of Private John Picciano, 1974. Recipient Pulitizer prize for nat. reporting, 1971, N.Y. Newspaper Writers Assn. award, 1971; Nat. Headliners award, Soc. Silurians journalism award, 1976. Mem. Am. PEN Club (alumni bd.), Women's Ink, Author's League, Council on Fgn. Relations, The Writers Room Inc. (pres.). Address: 1085 Park Ave New York NY 10028

FRANKS, RICHARD HERBERT, business educator; b. Washington, Dec. 19, 1937; s. Herbert A. and Edna L. (Mathisen) F.; m. Elke Koerner, Dec. 23, 1963; children: Martin, Andrea, Erik. Student, U. Goetttingen, 1956-57; B.S. in Chem. Engring., Cornell U., 1960; postgrad., U. Hamburg, 1963-64; M.B.A., U. Pitts., 1965; Ph.D. in Mgmt., U. Rochester, 1974. Prodn. engr. in petrochems. field Union Carbide Internat. Co., Texas City and Victoria, Tex., 1960-63, Sircusa, Italy, 1960-63; research and mktg. research engr. St. Joseph Lead Co., Monaca, Pa., 1966-67; research asst. mgmt. Research Ctr. U. Rochester (N.Y.), 1968-72; research fellow Nat. Acad. Scis., Belgrade, Yugoslavia, 1972-73; asst. prof. Sch. Bus. Adminstrn. U. Wis.-Milw., 1973-78; assoc. prof. dept. mgmt. Worcester Poly Inst. (Mass.), 1978-83; prof. Sch. Bus. and Mgmt. Loyola Coll., Balt., 1983—. Editor, contbr. The Science of Productivity, 1984; contbr. articles to various publs. McMullen scholar, 1955-59; Nansen House-Cornell scholar, 1956-57; U. Pitts. fellow, 1964-65; U. Rochester fellow, 1968-72; Nat. Acad. Scis. grantee, 1972-73; Japan Found. grantee, 1979-80; nsf grantee, 1979-82. Mem. Am. Psychol. Assn., Acad. Mgmt., Am. Sociol. Assn., Am. Chem. Soc., AAAS. Office: Shc of Bus and Mgmt Loyola Coll 4501 N Charles St Baltimore MD 21210

FRANKUM, JAMES EDWARD, airlines company executive; b. Vincennes, Ind., Feb. 25, 1921; s. Hubert and Pearl (Evans) F.; m. Madalene Tharp, June 6, 1943; children: Stephanie Anne, Barbara Ellen, James Edward. Student, Vincennes U., 1940-41, Northwestern U., 1955, Stanford U., 1959, Advanced Mgmt. Program, Harvard U. Grad. Sch. Bus., 1966; LL.D., Vincennes U., 1967. With Trans World Airlines, Inc., 1942—, v.p. transp., 1961-68, v.p. flight ops., 1968-81, v.p. ops., 1981-82, sr. v.p. ops., 1982—; dir. Grand Ave. Bank, Kansas City, Mo.; trustee Hamburg Savs. Bank, Bklyn. Mem. Air Transport Assn. (exec. com.), Internat. Air Transport Assn. (chmn. tech. council), Nat. Def. Transp. Assn. (mil. airlift com.). Clubs: Wings, Pinnacle (N.Y.C.); Kansas City (Kansas City, Mo.); Innisbrook Country (Tampa, Fla.); Evergreen (Palm City, Fla.); Nassau Country, Manhasset Bay Yacht (L.I.). Home: 841 Park Ave Manhasset NY 11030 Office: 605 3d Ave New York NY 10158

FRANSIOLI, THOMAS ADRIAN, artist; b. Seattle, Sept. 15, 1906; s. Thomas Adrian and Josephine (Young) F.; m. Elizabeth McVickar, Mar. 5, 1932; 1 son, Thomas Adrian 3d. B.Arch., U. Pa., 1930; student, Art Students League, N.Y.C., 1939. Practice architecture, Warrenton, Va., 1932. One-man shows include, Margaret Brown Gallery, Boston, 1947, Farnsworth Mus., Rockland, Maine, 1954, Seattle Art Mus., Kennedy Gallery, N.Y.C., 1958, Palace of Legion of Honor, San Francisco, 1955, Milch Gallery, N.Y.C., 1961, St. Gaudens Mus., N.H., 1955, Cornwall (Conn.) Hist. Soc., 1975, group shows include, Colby Coll. and Whitney Mus., 1963, Met. Mus. Art, N.Y.C., 1950, Whitney Ann., 1948, 52, 58, Carnegie Inst., 1949-52; represented in permanent collections, Mus. Fine Arts, Boston, Farnsworth Mus., Dallas Mus. Art, Boston Public Library, Seattle Art Mus., Whitney Mus. Am. Art, N.Y.C., Brit. Embassy, Washington, others, works include: 9 paintings of Am. cities for cover Collier's mag., 1949-50; 4 paintings New York 1892 for, Univ. Club, N.Y.C.; mural for, Princeton Club, N.Y.C., 1966. Served with USAAF, 1943-46. Club: Century Assn. (N.Y.C.). Address: 55 Dodges Row Wenham MA 01984

FRANTEL, EDWARD WILLIAM, soft drink company executive; b. Wauwatosa, Wis., Mar. 18, 1925; s. Edward S. Frantl and Myrtle E. (Fischer) Frantl) Hollmann; m. Sherry Lieg, Aug. 24, 1946; 1 son, Scott. B.S. in Bus. Adminstrn, Marquette U., 1948. Field sales supr. H. J. Heinz Co., Milw., 1948-53; with Miller Brewing Co., Milw., 1953-79, dir. sales, 1972-74, v.p. sales, 1974-79; pres., chief exec. officer Seven-Up Co., Clayton, Mo., 1979—; v.p. Philip Morris, Inc.; dir. and officer Dixi Cola, Inc., Seven-Up U.S.A., Inc.; dir. Mission Viejo, Cheer Up Co., Marbert, Inc., Seven-Up Bottling of Phoenix, Inc., Seven-Up Bottling Co. of Norfolk, Inc., Seven-Up Can. Ltd., Ventura Coastal Corp., Warner-Jenkinson Co., Inc., Warner-Jenkinson Co. of Calif., Warner-Jenkinson East, Inc., Golden Crown Citrus Corp. Pres. Council of Fitness, Council of St. Louis U.; active Nat. Fitness Found., United Fund. Served with paratroops U.S. Army, World War II. Decorated Bronze Star with oak leaf cluster, Purple Heart with oak leaf cluster; recipient Gold Ring award Philip Morris, Inc., 1979. Mem. Sales and Mktg. Execs. of Milw., Bus. Adminstrn. Alumni Assn. of Marquette U. (Man of Yr. 1978), Confrerie de la Chaine des Rotisseurs. Clubs: St. Louis, Milw. Athletic. Office: 121 S Meramec Clayton MO 63105 *Nothing is work unless you'd rather be doing something else.*

FRANTZ, ANDREW GIBSON, physician; b. N.Y.C., May 22, 1930; s. Angus Macdonald and Virginia (Kneeland) F. A.B. magna cum laude, Harvard U., 1951; M.D., Columbia U., 1955. Intern Presbyn. Hosp., N.Y.C., 1955-56, resident in medicine, 1956-58; vis. fellow in medicine Columbia U., N.Y.C., 1958-60, asst. prof. medicine, 1966-68, assoc. prof., 1968-73, prof., 1973—, chief div. endocrinology, 1971—, chmn. admissions com., 1981—; assoc. in medicine Harvard U., 1962-66; asst. in medicine Mass. Gen. Hosp., Boston, 1962-66; mem. staff Presbyn. Hosp., N.Y.C.; mem. med. adv. bd. Nat. Pituitary Agy., 1970-73; prin. investigator USPHS grants, 1964—; established investigator Am. Heart Assn., 1968-73. Contbr. articles to med. and sci. jours; mem. editorial bd.: Jour. Clin. Endocrinology and Metabolism, 1971-76; asso. editor: Metabolism, 1969—. Served to lt. comdr. USNR, 1960-62. Recipient Silver Medal Coll. Physicians and Surgeons, Columbia U., 1981. Mem. Endocrine Soc., Mem. Am. Soc. Clin. Investigation, Internat. Soc. for Neuroendocrinology, Harvey Soc., Practitioners Soc., Peripatetic Club, Am. Fedn. Clin. Research, N.Y. Acad. Sci., AAAS, N.Y. Acad. Medicine, Alpha Omega Alpha. Episcopalian. Clubs: Union, Century Assn. (N.Y.C.). Home: 1185 Park Ave New York NY 10128 Office: 630 W 168th St New York NY 10032

FRANTZ, CHARLES, anthropology educator; b. Rocky Ford, Colo., Apr. 22, 1925; s. Osee Clark and Blanche (Talhelm) F. A.B., Earlham Coll., 1950; A.M., Haverford Coll., 1951; Ph.D., U. Chgo., 1958. From instr. to prof. anthropology Portland (Oreg.) State U., 1953-64, chmn. dept., 1960-64; vis. prof. U. Toronto, 1964-65; dir. African Studies program Howard U., 1965-67; exec. sec. Am. Anthrop. Assn., 1966-68; prof. anthropology SUNY-Buffalo, Amherst, 1968—; prof., head dept. sociology Ahmadu Bello U., Zaria, Nigeria, 1970-72; chmn. N.W. Anthrop. Conf., 1963. Author: (with C.A. Rogers) Racial Themes in Southern Rhodesia, 1962, The Student Anthropologist's Handbook, 1972, Pastoral Societies, Stratification and National Integration in Africa, 1975, Ideas and Trends in World Anthropology, 1981; also articles. Grantee Am. Council Learned Socs., 1964-65, Wenner-Gren Found., 1960, Am. Friends Service Com., 1956-58. Fellow Am. Anthrop. Assn., Northeastern Anthrop. Assn. (pres. 1975-76), African Studies Assn., Soc. Applied Anthropology; mem. Am. Ethnol. Soc., Internat. African Inst., Am. Sociol. Assn. Office: Anthropology Dept SUNY Amherst NY 14261

FRANTZ, JACK THOMAS, advertising executive; b. Indpls., Dec. 27, 1939; s. John Richard and Edna Louise F.; m. Georgene Mary Meyers, Aug. 18, 1962; 1 son, John Bennett. B.S. in Mktg, Ind. U., 1961. With Ted Bates & Co., N.Y.C., 1962-65, Papert, Koenig, Lois Inc., 1965-69; with Grey Advt., Inc., N.Y.C., 1969—, sr. v.p. account mgmt., 1979—. Served with USAR, 1962. Home: 571 Canoe Hill Rd New Canaan CT 06840 Office: Grey Advt Inc 777 3d Ave New York NY 10017

FRANTZ, JOHN CORYDON, librarian; b. Seneca Falls, N.Y., Aug. 25, 1926; s. John Clark and Cora May (Gilbert) F.; m. Vivien May Rowan, Dec. 31, 1947; children—Sheila Heather, Keith Hunter, Jay Corydon. A.B., Syracuse (N.Y.) U., 1950, B.S., 1951, M.S., 1952. Cons. Wis. State Library, 1954-58; dir. Green Bay (Wis.) Pub. Library, 1958-61; dir. pub. library grants U.S. Office Edn., 1961-67; dir. Bklyn. Pub. Library, 1967-70, Nat. Book Com., 1970-75; exec. chmn. Pahlavi Nat. Library, Tehran, Iran, 1975-77; librarian San Francisco Pub. Library, 1977—; bd. dirs. Reading is Fundamental, Bookmobile Services Trust, Am. Reading Council, Metro Research Libraries Council. Served with U.S. Army, 1945-47. Mem. Am., N.Y. State, Calif. library assns. Club: Coffee House (N.Y.C.). Home: 1390 Market St San Francisco CA 94102 Office: Public Library Civic Center San Francisco CA 94102

FRANTZ, PATRICK GEORGES JOSEPH EUGENE, choreographer; b. Paris, July 31, 1943; U.S., 1970; s. Jean and Monique (Louwyck) Raffy; m. Patricia Diane Davis, Dec. 30, 1977; 1 dau., Noelle Claire. Certificat d'etudes primaires, L'ecole de l'Opera de Paris. Tchr. dance Ecole internationale de mime de Marcel Marceau; tchr. music singing and dance L'armee de l'Air de France. Former artistic dir., Pitts. Ballet Theatre; freelance choreographer, tchr. Christian.

FRANTZ, RAY WILLIAM, JR., librarian; b. Princeton, Ky., Aug. 17, 1923; s. Ray William and Marjorie (Kevil) F.; m. Doris Methvin, Aug. 26, 1951; children—Katherine Kevil, Paul William. A.B., U. Nebr., 1948; M.L.S., U. Ill., 1949, M.A., 1951, Ph.D. in English, 1955. Dir. library U. Richmond, Va., 1955-60; asst. dir. Ohio State U. Library, Columbus, 1960-62; dir. libraries U. Wyo. Library, 1962-67; univ. librarian U. Va. Library, Charlottesville, 1967—; chmn. bd. dirs. Southeastern Library Network, 1975-76. Served with inf. AUS, 1943-46. Mem. Assn. Research Libraries (pres. 1977-78), Assn. Southeastern Research Libraries (chmn. 1975—), ALA, Bibliog. Soc. Am., Bibliog. Soc. U. Va. (sec.-treas. 1967—). Club: Torch Internat. Home: 1859 Fendall Ave Charlottesville VA 22903 Office: Gen Office Alderman Library Charlottesville VA 22901

FRANTZ, WELBY MARION, business executive; b. Atlanta, Ill., Oct. 27, 1912; s. Marion C. and Jennie (Brandt) F.; m. Frances C. Mitchell, Mar. 9, 1940; 1 dau., Melana Susan. Student, Ill. State U. With Brandt's Truck Line, Bloomington, Ill., 1930-33; terminal mgr. Decatur Cartage Co., Danville and Peoria, Ill., also Terre Haute, Ind., 1933-46; with Eastern Express, Inc., Terre Haute, 1946-76, exec. v.p., 1946-62, pres., 1962-70, vice chmn. bd., 1970-76; pres. Am. Movers Conf., Arlington, Va., 1976-81; dir. Terre Haute 1st Nat. Bank; life bd. govs. Regular Commo Carriers Conf., 1961—; Mem. Ind. Com. Bus. Edn.; mem. bus. adv. com. Northwestern U. Transp. Center, 1960-76; civilian adviser on transp. and distbn. to bd. dirs. Army and Air Force

Exchange Services, 1973—; Distinguished Exec.-in-Residence Ind. State U. Sch. Bus., 1976; faculty asso. Ind. U., 1960-64; bd. consultants Eno Found. for Transp. Past. bd. dirs. Terre Haute Community Chest; mem. adv. council Ind. State Univ.; bd. assos. Rose-Hulman Inst. Tech., dir., chmn. finance com., exec. com., Union Hosp., Terre Haute; pres. bd. dirs. Ind. State U. Found. Served as capt. Transp. Corps AUS, 1942-46. Named Terre Haute Man of Week, Dec. 1954, Transp. Man-of-Year, 1964, Ind. Transp. Man of Year, 1972; recipient U.S. Air Force Exceptional Service award. Mem. Ind. Motor Truck Assn. (pres. 1953-55, chmn. bd.), Am. Trucking Assns. (life past chmn., pres. 1960, chmn. bd. 1961, vice chmn. Found. 1960-75), Nat. Def. Transp. Assn. (nat. pres. 1967-70, chmn. bd. 1971, nat. transp. award 1974), A.I.M. (pres.'s council), Transp. Assn. Am. (dir. emeritus), Nat. Safety Council (v.p.), Internat. Platform Assn., Eastern Central Motor Carriers Assn. (chmn. bd. trustees 1954-64, life chmn. 1964—), U.S. C. of C. (dir., chmn. transp. com. 1969-75), Ind. C. of C. (dir. 1955, life mem.), Terre Haute C. of C. (past pres.), Am. Truck Hist. Soc. (chmn. bd. dirs. 1973—), Ind. Acad. Clubs: Masons, Shriners, Elks, Kiwanis, Terre Haute Country, N.Y. Traffic; Columbia (Indpls.); Congressional Country (Washington). Home and Office: 14 Fairway Dr Woodgate East Terre Haute IN 47802

FRANZ, FREDERICK WILLIAM, religious orgn. ofcl.; b. Covington, Ky., Sept. 12, 1893; s. Frederick Edward and Ida Louise (Krueger) F. Student, U. Cin., 1911-14. Ordained to ministry Jehovah's Witnesses, 1914, mem. internat. hdqrs. staff, 1920—; bd. dirs. Watchtower Bible and Tract Soc. N.Y., 1932—, v.p., 1949-77, pres., 1977—; bd. dirs. Watch Tower Bible and Tract Soc. Pa., 1943—, v.p., 1945-77, pres., 1977—. Address: 124 Columbia Heights Brooklyn NY 11201 *My hope is for Jehovah's kingdom to come for the blessing of all mankind.*

FRANZ, JOHN MATTHIAS, educator; b. Oak Park, Ill., May 23, 1927; s. John Edward and Lucy Marie (Mallan) F.; m. Janice Helen Howard, Aug. 18, 1951; children—Kristine, John, Kathleen, Janice. B.S. in Chemistry, U. Ill., 1950; M.S. in Biochemistry, U. Iowa, 1952, Ph.D., 1955. USPHS research fellow, 1952-55; instr. biochemistry U. Mo. at Columbia, 1955-57, asst. prof., 1957-61, asso. prof. biochemistry, 1961—, asst. chmn., 1975-76, asso. chmn., 1976-79, dir. undergrad. edn., 1979—; research asso. dept. biol. chemistry Harvard, 1965-66; wine cons. Served with AUS, 1946-47. NIH spl. fellow, 1965-66. Fellow A.A.A.S.; mem. Am. Chem. Soc., Sigma Xi, Alpha Chi Sigma, Phi Lambda Upsilon. Clubs: Oenophiles, Les Amis Du Vin, Tastevin. Research in devel. metabolic control mechanisms in neonatal mammals, hormonal control of metabolism, comparative aspects of enzyme devel. and control, use of computers in biochemistry. Home: 301 S Greenwood Ave Columbia MO 65201

FRANZ, RICHARD PETER, leasing company executive; b. Milw., Jan. 2, 1924; s. Walter A. and Lenore (Sievers) F.; m. Marjorie Elaine Mandt, Aug. 28, 1948; children: Richard Peter, Steven C., Gary M. B.B.A., U. Wis., 1948. With Arthur Young & Co., 1948-51; mgr. tax dept. Miller Brewing Co., 1951-57; with Edw. F. Jennick & Co. (pub. accountants), 1957-58; sec. treas. Johnson Service Co., Milw., 1958-73; v.p. mktg. Midland Nat. Bank, Milw., 1973-76; sec.-treas. Milw. Engine & Equipment Corp., 1976-82; v.p., gen. mgr. Hallease, Inc., Milw, 1982—. Served with USNR, 1943-46. Mem. Am. Inst. C.P.A.s, Wis. Soc. C.P.A.s, Nat. Assn. Accountants, Financial Execs. Inst. Home: 5157 N Lake Dr Milwaukee WI 53217 Office: 11011 W North Ave Milwaukee WI 53226

FRANZ, ROBERT WARREN, banker; b. Portland, Oreg., Feb. 18, 1924; s. Joseph and Elizabeth (Streib) F. B.S. in Fin., U. Notre Dame, 1948. Vice pres. First State Bank Oreg. (now Pacific Western Bank), Milwaukie, 1948-62, pres., 1962-79, chmn. bd., chief exec. officer, 1979—; chmn. bd. Pacwest Cancorp., Milwaukie, 1979—; dir. U.S. (Franz) Bakery, Portland; mem. Oreg. Banking Bd., 1972-76. Pres. Columbia Pacific Council Boy Scouts Am., 1978-79; mem. adv. bd. Providence Hosp., Portland, 1980—; chmn. bd. regents U. Portland, 1981—. Mem. Western Ind. Bankers (pres. 1959-61, exec. council 1955-69), Nat. C. of C. (monetary and fiscal affairs com. 1976-80). Republican. Roman Catholic. Office: Pacific Western Bank and Pacwest Bancorp 10888 SE Main St Milwaukie OR 97222

FRANZEN, EARL THEODORE, ret. civil engr.; b. Palisade, Minn., Jan. 7, 1915; s. Emil Ferdin and Jennie (Anderson) F.; m. Irene Helen Super, Oct. 28, 1944; children—Robert, Thomas, Jonathan. B.C.E. with high distinction, U. Minn., 1937. Asst. bridge engr. G.N. Ry., St. Paul, 1937-55; structural engr. Wis. Hwy. Dept., 1955; bridge engr. Rock Island R.R., Chgo., 1955-63; structural engr. Alfred Benesch & Assos. (cons. engrs.), Chgo., 1963-64; chief engr. M.P. R.R., St. Louis, 1964-81. Mem. ASCE, Am. Ry. Engring. Assn., Am. Ry. Bridge and Bldg. Assn., Roadmasters and Maintenance of Way Assn. Club: Mason. Home: 83 Webster Woods Webster Groves MO 63119

FRANZEN, JANICE MARGUERITE GOSNELL, magazine editor; b. LaCrosse, Wis., Sept. 24, 1921; d. Wray Towson and Anna Heldena (Renstrom) Gosnell; m. Ralph Oscar Franzen, Feb. 15, 1964. B.S. cum laude, Wis. State U., LaCrosse, 1943; M.R.E., No. Bapt. Theol. Sem., 1947. Tchr. history and social sci. Galesville (Wis.) High Sch., 1943-45; registrar Christian Writers Inst., Chgo., 1947-49, dir., 1950-63, dir. studies, 1964—; fiction editor Christian Life Mag., Wheaton, Ill., 1950-63, woman's editor, 1964-72, exec. editor, 1972—; mem. editorial bd. Creation House, Wheaton, 1972—; speaker writers confs. Author: Christian Writers Handbook, 1960, 61; editor: Christian Author, 1949-54, Christian Writer and Editor, 1955-63; contbr. articles to various mags.; compiler/contbr.: The Successful Writers and Editors Guidebook, 1977. Sec. bd. dirs., v.p. Christian Life Missions, 1971—. Home: 3N455 Mulberry St West Chicago IL 60185 Office: 396 E Saint Charles Rd Wheaton IL 60187

FRAPPIER, GILLES, librarian; b. Papineauville, Que., Can., Feb. 13, 1931; s. Romeo and Roma (Robinson) F.; m. Gertrude Mainville, Oct. 13, 1956; children: Raymond, Robert, Joanne. B.A., U. Ottawa, 1954, B.Ph., 1954, B.L.S., 1955; postgrad. in library sci, McGill U., 1957-61. Librarian Baie Comeau (Que.) Community Assn., 1955-57; br. librarian Pulp and Paper Research Inst. Can., Pointe Claire, Que., 1957-59; librarian United Aircraft Can., Ltd., Longueuil, Que., 1959-63; supr. engring. libraries Canadair Ltd., St. Laurent, Que., 1963-69; dir. sci. libraries U. Montreal, Que., 1969-70; asso. parliamentary librarian Library of Parliament, Ottawa, Ont., Can., 1970-79; dir. library, sec.-treas. bd. Ottawa Public Library, 1979—; lectr. in field. Bd. dirs. Can. Writers Found.; chmn. Council of Adminstrs. of Large Urban Public Libraries. Mem. Assn. Parliamentary Librarians in Can., Canadian Micrographic Soc. (past sec.-treas.), Library Assn. Ottawa, Spl. Libraries Assn. (past pres.), Internat. Fedn. Library Assns. and Instns. (sec. organizing com. conf. 1982), Canadian Assn. Info. Sci., Canadian Library Assn., Corp. Profl. Librarians Que., Inst. Pub. Adminstrn. Can., Montreal chpt. Spl. Libraries Assn. (past pres., sec. and bull. editor), L'Alliance francaise d'Ottawa, Chief Execs. of Large Public Libraries of Ont., L'Association des écrivains Ottawa-Hull. Roman Catholic. Home: 423 Carillon St Gatineau PQ Canada J8P 3P9 Office: Ottawa Public Library 120 Metcalfe St Ottawa ON Canada K1P 5M2

FRASCA, ROBERT JOHN, architect, urban planner; b. Niagara Falls, N.Y., May 10, 1933; s. John and Jean Marie (Delgross) F.; m. Marilyn Margaret Buys, Apr. 9, 1966; children: Jason Robert, Andrea Melina. B.Arch., U. Mich., 1957; M.City Planning, MIT, 1959. Registered architect, Oreg., Wash., Calif., N.Y. Utah, Ariz., Colo. Design award juror AIA, 1982-83; speaker Portland Art Mus., 1982, Bellevue Downtown Assn., Wash., 1982; design cons. Boise Redevel. Agy., 1977. Recipient George Booth Traveling fellowship U. Mich., 1960. Fellow AIA; mem. Assn. Portland Progress. Club: Multnomah Athletic (Portland, Oreg.). Home: 137 SW Kingston Portland ODR 97201 Office: Zimmer Gunsul Frasca Partnership 320 SW Oak St Suite 500 Portland OR 97204

FRASCONI, ANTONIO, artist, author; b. Montevideo, Uruguay, Apr. 28, 1919; came to U.S., 1945; s. Franco and Armida (Carbonai) F.; m. Leona Pierce, July 18, 1951; children—Pablo, Miguel. Student, Circulo de Bellas Artes, Montevideo; scholarship, Art Students League, N.Y.C., 1944-46, New Sch. Social Research, 1947-48. Art faculty New Sch. Social Research, 1951-57; artist-resident U. Hawaii, Honolulu, in 1964; mem. faculty State U. N.Y. at Purchase, 1974—. Author: 12 Fables of Aesop, 1954, See and Say, 1955, Frasconi Woodcuts, 1957, The House that Jack Built, 1958, Birds from My Homeland, 1958, The Face of Edgar Allen Poe, 1959, A Whitman Portrait, 1960; film The Neighboring Shore, 1960 (Grand Prix award Venice Film Festival 1960); books Known Fables, 1964, The Cantilever Rainbow, 1965 (both chosen as one of Fifty Books of Year, Am. Inst. Graphic Arts), Unstill Life, 1969, Overhead The Sun, 1969, Elijah the Slave, 1970, On the Slain Collegians, 1971, Frasconi Against the Grain, 1975; film Antonio Frasconi-Graphic Artist, 1975; one man shows, Montevideo, Mex., Bklyn. Mus., Pasadena Art Inst., Pan American Union, Va. Mus. Fine Arts, Balt. Mus. Art, Witte Meml. Mus., San Antonio, Wehye Gallery, N.Y.C., Art Alliance, Phila., others, retrospective shows, Montevideo, Uruguay, 1961, Balt. Mus. of Art, 1963, Brooklyn Mus., N.Y., 1964, group shows, Europe, S.Am., U.S., including, Nat. Acad. N.Y.C., U. Minn., Library Congress, Seattle Art Mus., Pa., Acad. Art, San Francisco Mus. Art, Memphis Acad. Art, others; represented in permanent collections, Mus. Modern Art, Cleve. Mus. Art, San Diego Mus. Art, N.Y.C. Pub. Library, R.I. Sch. Design, Newark Mus., Detroit Mus. Art, Art Inst. Chgo., several univs., others. Recipient purchase prize Bklyn. Mus., 1946, U. Nebr., 1951; prize Phila. Print Club, 1951; Erickson award Soc. Am. Graphic Arts, 1952; Yaddo scholarship, 1952; Guggenheim fellowship, 1952-53; prize Pa. Acad. Fine Arts; Nat. Inst. Arts and Letters award, 1954; winner competition to design postage stamp honoring Nat. Acad. Sci., 1963; Joseph H. Hirshorn Found. prize Soc. Am. Graphic Artists, 1963; W. H. Walker prize Print Club Phila., 1964; prize 2d Biennale d'Art Graphique, Brno, Czechoslovakia, 1966, Salon Nacional de Bellas Artes, Montevideo, 1967; Grand Premio Exposition de la Habana, Cuba, 1968; Tamarind Lithography grantee, 1962; prize 9th Internat. Biennial of Arts, Tokyo, Japan, 1975. Home: 26 Dock Rd South Norwalk CT 06854

FRASER, CAMPBELL, corporation executive; b. Dunblane, Scotland, May 2, 1923. B.Com., Dundee Sch. Econs., 1950; LL.B. (hon.), Strathclyde U., 1977, D. Univ., Stirling U., 1977. Exec. Dunlop Holdings, London. Pres. Confedn. Brit. Industry, London, 1982—. Home: 41 Silver Birches Purley Surrey England CR2 3HG Office: Dunlop Holdings Ryder St London England SW1Y 6PV

FRASER, CHARLES ELBERT, telecommunications and residential development company executive; b. Hinesville, Ga., June 13, 1929; s. Joseph Bacon and Pearl (Collins) F.; m. Mary Wyman Stone, Nov. 30, 1963; children: Mary Wyman Stone, Laura Lawton. Student, Presbyn. Coll., 1946-48; B.B.A., U. Ga., 1950; J.D., Yale U., 1953. Bar: Ga. bar 1953. Asso. firm Hull, Towill, Norman, Barrett & Johnson, Augusta, 1953-54; chmn. Sea Pines Co., Hilton Head Island, S.C., 1958-83, Digital Telecom Inc., Hilton Head Island, 1981—, Fraser Communications, 1981—, Sea Pines Assocs., Inc., 1983—; U.S. commr. gen. for 1982 World's Fair, 1980—; mem. space sta. adv. com. Office Tech. Assessment. Contbr. articles on land use, planning, leisure, recreation to various publs. Chmn. Beaufort County Bd. Dirs., 1962-66; chmn. Beaufort-Jasper Econ. Opportunity Commn., 1966; mem. Pres.'s Citizens Adv. Com. on Environ. Quality, 1968-69, Pres.'s Citizens Adv. Com. on Natural Beauty and Outdoor Recreation, 1964-68; past mem. S.C. Parks, Recreation and Tourism Commn., 1967-74; chmn. Nat. Recreation and Parks Assn., 1974-76, trustee, 1968—; bd. visitors Presbyn. Coll., 1971; chmn. Am. Golf Bicentennial Commn. Served to 2d lt. USAF, 1954-56. Recipient Certificate of Excellence in Pvt. Community Planning AIA, 1968. Mem. Am. Soc. Landscape Architects (hon.), AIA (hon.), Young Pres.'s Orgn., Chief Execs. Forum. Presbyterian elder). Clubs: Met. (N.Y.C.); Plantation (Hilton Head Island); Chatham (Savannah, Ga.); Harbour Town Yacht. Home: 25 Baynard Park Rd Sea Pines Plantation Hilton Head Island SC 29928 Office: PO Drawer One Hilton Head Island SC 29938

FRASER, DAVID WILLIAM, epidemiologist, college president; b. Abington, Pa., May 10, 1944; s. Grant Clippinger and Ella Finlaw (Ayars) F.; m. Barbara Josephine Gaines, June 25, 1966; children: Evan Grant, Leigh Robertson. B.A. (Clementine Cope fellow 1965), Haverford (Pa.) Coll., 1965; M.D., Harvard U., 1969. Diplomate: Am. Bd. Internal Medicine. Intern in internal medicine U. Pa. Hosp., Phila., 1969-70, resident, 1970-71, chief resident in internal medicine, 1973-74, fellow in infectious diseases, 1974-75; commd. officer USPHS, 1971-73, 75-82; chief spl. pathogens br., bacterial diseases div. Bur. Epidemiology, Center Disease Control, USPHS, Atlanta, 1975-80, med. epidemiologist, asst. dir. bacterial diseases div., 1981-82; pres. Swarthmore Coll. (Pa.), 1982—; epidemiologic cons. Office Mgmt. and Budget, Washington, 1980-81. Author articles in profl. jours., chpts. in books. Bd. mgrs. Haverford Coll., 1980-83; Bd. advisers Educators for Social Responsibility. Recipient Meritorious Service medal USPHS, 1978; Daland fellow Am. Philos. Soc., 1974. Fellow ACP (Richard and Hinda Rosenthal Found. award 1979), Infectious Diseases Soc. Am., Am. Coll. Epidemiology; mem. Am. Epidemiol. Soc., Aesculapian Club. Democrat. Quaker. Club: Founders (Haverford Coll.). Home: 324 Cedar Ln Swarthmore PA 19081

FRASER, DONALD MACKAY, mayor, former congressman; b. Mpls., Feb. 20, 1924; s. Everett and Lois (MacKay) F.; m. Arvonne Skelton, June 30, 1950; children: Thomas Skelton, Mary MacKay, John DuFrene, Lois MacKay, Anne T. (dec.), Jean Skelton. B.A. cum laude, U. Minn., 1944, LL.B., 1948. Bar: Minn. 1948. Practiced in, Mpls., 1948-62; partner firm Lindquist, Fraser & Magnuson (and predecessors), 1950-62; mem. Minn. Senate, 1954-62; sec. Senate Liberal Caucus, 1955-62; mem. 88th-95th congresses from 5th Dist. Minn., mem. internat. relations com., chmn. subcom. on internat. orgn., mem. budget com.; mayor of, Mpls., 1980—; mem. study and rev. com. Democratic Caucus; mem. Commn. on Role and Future Presdl. Primaries, 1976—; Vice chmn., dir. Mpls. Citizens Com. on Pub. Edn., 1950-54; Sec. Minn. del. Democratic Nat. Conv., 1960; chmn. Minn. Citizens for Kennedy, 1960; mem. platform com. Dem. Nat. Conv., 1964, mem. rules com., 1972, 76; chmn. Nat. Com. Tithing in Investment, 1964-72; vice chmn. Com. Dem. Selection Presdl. Nominees, 1968; chmn. Democratic Study Group Congress, 1969-71, Commn. on Party Structure and Del. Selection Dem. Party, 1971-72; 1st Am. co-chmn. Anglo-Am. Parliamentary Conf. on Africa, 1964; mem. U.S. del. 7th spl. session and 30th session UN Gen. Assembly, 1975; Congl. adviser to U.S. del. to UN Conf. on Disarmament, 1967-73, to U.S. del. to 3d Law of Sea Conf., 1972, to UN Commn. on Human Rights, 1974. Served as lt. (j.g.) USNR, 1944-46. Mem. Mpls. Fgn. Policy Assn. (pres. 1952-53), Citizens League Greater Mpls. (sec. 1951-54), Minn., Hennepin County bar assns., Ams. for Dem. Action (nat. chmn. 1973-76), Dem. Conf. (nat. chmn. 1976—), U. Minn. Law Alumni Assn. (dir. 1958-61), Univ. Dist. Improvement Assn. (pres.). Office: Office of Mayor City Hall Minneapolis MN 55415 *

FRASER, DOUGLAS ANDREW, labor official; b. Glasgow, Scotland, Dec. 18, 1916; s. Douglas and Sarah (Andrew) F.; m. Winifred Davis, July 28, 1967; children: Judith, Jeanne. Student pub. schs., Detroit. Pres. Local 227, UAW, Detroit, 1943-46, internat. rep., 1947-51, adminstrv. asst. to internat. pres., 1951-58, co-regional dir. Region 1A, 1959-62, mem.-at-large internat. exec. bd., 1962-70, internat. v.p., 1970-77, internat. pres., 1977-83, pres. emeritus, 1983—; mem. council AFL-CIO, 1981—; dir. Chrysler Corp.; Mem. Pres.'s Com. Employment of Handicapped. Mem. exec. com. Leadership Conf. on Civil Rights; v.p. Am. Immigration and Citizenship Conf., United Found.-Detroit; bd. dirs. Full Employment Action Council, NAACP, New Detroit; trustee Aspen Inst. Humanistic Studies. Served with U.S. Army, 1945-46. Mem. ACLU, Detroit Urban League, Ams. for Democratic Action (v.p.). Democrat. Club: Econ. (Detroit) (dir.). Office: 8000 E Jefferson Ave Detroit MI 48214

FRASER, GEORGE BROADRUP, legal educator; b. Washington, May 9, 1914; s. George B. and Florence M. (Hillyard) F.; m. Phebe E. Bandy, Dec. 20th, 1965. A.B., Dartmouth Coll., 1936; LL.B., Harvard U., 1939; LL.M., George Washington U., 1941. Bar: D.C. 1939, Okla. 1952. Practiced in, Washington, 1939-41; asso. atty. Boise (Idaho) regional office, VA, 1946; acting prof. law, then prof. law U. Idaho, 1946-49; prof. law U. Okla., 1949—, Boyd prof., 1959—, Murrah prof. law, 1981; vis. prof. George Washington U., summers 1948, 51, 58, U. Ill., 1959-60; vis. prof. law U. Mich., spring 1964, Hastings Coll. Law, U. Calif., San Francisco, 1966. Contbr. articles to profl. jours., chpts. in books. Served to lt. comdr. USNR, 1941-45. Mem. ABA, Okla. Bar Assn. (Golden Gavel award 1983), Cleveland County Bar Assn., Order of Coif, Phi Delta Phi. Address: College of Law Univ of Oklahoma Norman OK 73019

FRASER, GEORGE DUNCAN, JR., investment company executive; b. Omaha, July 5, 1941; s. George Duncan and Annette (Flannagan) F.; m. Eleanor Howe, Sept. 1, 1979; children: Charles D., F. Alexander. B.A., Parsons Coll., Fairfield, Iowa, 1964; M.A., U. Nebr., 1964. C.P.A., Nebr., Mass. Acct. Peat, Marwick Mitchell, C.P.A.s, Omaha, 1965-68; with Mass. Fin. Services Co., Boston, 1968—, treas., 1971—. Bd. dirs., treas. Big Bros. Assn. Boston; trustee, treas. Anatolia Coll., Thessaloniki, Greece. Mem. Am. Inst. C.P.A.s, Am. Acctg. Assn., Nebr. Soc. C.P.A.s, Mass. Soc. C.P.A.s. Republican. Episcopalian. Clubs: Essex County (Manchester, Mass.); University (Boston); Key Biscayne (Fla.) Yacht. Office: 200 Berkeley St Boston MA 02116

FRASER, HENRY RONALD, mining executive; b. South Africa, Oct. 5, 1920; s. Andrew Gibson and Mary Margaret (Joyce) F.; m. Betty Wyne Barnes, Dec. 26, 1944; children: Michael, Mary, John, Peter, Elizabeth. B.A., Natal (South Africa) U.; B.Econs. with honors, U. South Africa; M.B.A., Pretoria (South Africa) U. Tchr. pub. schs., South Africa; with South African Iron & Steel Indsl. Corp., 1949-54, Anglo Am. Corp. South Africa Ltd., 1954-72; pres. Anglo Am. Corp. Can. Ltd., Toronto, Ont., from 1972, chmn., 1974-80; chmn. bd. Hudson Bay Mining and Smelting Co., Ltd., Toronto, 1974-80; pres. Minerals and Resources Corp. Ltd., Hamilton, Bermuda, 1979—, Old Court Internat. Reserves, 1980—; dir. Engelhard Minerals & Chems. Corp., Minerals & Resources Corp., Zambian Anglo Am. Corp. Mem. AIME, Internat. Copper Research Assn. (chmn.). Clubs: York (Toronto); Bel Horizonte, Mid-Ocean (Bermuda). Office: Box 650 Hamilton 5 Bermuda *

FRASER, HENRY S., lawyer; b. Oswego, N.Y., July 11, 1900; s. Hector A. and Minnie (Salmon) F.; m. Myrtle Gosse, June 15, 1937; children: Bruce, Rosene, Roger. A.B., Haverford Coll., 1922; J.D., Cornell U., 1926. Bar: N.Y. State bar 1927, U.S. Supreme Ct. bar 1930. Tech. adviser League of Nations Com. Experts for Progressive Codification of Internat. Law, 1927; chief research staff N.Y. State Constl. Conv., 1938; chmn. N.Y. State Uniform Law Commn., 1948-70; chief counsel U.S. Senate, Spl. Com. Investigating Petroleum Resources, 1945-47; pvt. practice, Syracuse, N.Y., 1927—. Author various legal publs. Fellow Am. Coll. Probate Counsel; mem. Am. Law Inst. (life), ABA, N.Y. State Bar Assn., Onondaga County Bar Assn. (dir.), N.Y. City Bar Assn., Phi Beta Kappa, Chi Phi. Club: Century. Lodge: Rotary. Home: Presdl Plaza Syracuse NY 13202 Office: 499 S Warren St Syracuse NY 13202

FRASER, JOHN FOSTER, investment company executive; b. Saskatoon, Sask., Sept. 19, 1930; s. John Black and Florence May (Foster) F.; m. Valerie Georgina Ryder, June 21, 1952; children: John Foster, Lisa Ann. B.Commerce, U. Sask., 1952. Pres., chief exec. officer Empire Freightways Ltd., Saskatoon, Sask., 1952-60, Empire Oil Ltd., Saskatoon, 1960-62, Hanford Drewitt Ltd., Winnipeg, 1962-69, Norcom Homes Ltd., Mississauga, Ont., 1969-78, Fed. Industries Ltd., Winnipeg, 1978—; dir. The Investors Group, Nat. Sea Products, The Conf. Bd. Can. Progressive Conservative. Presbyterian. Clubs: Manitoba, Royal Lake of the Woods Yacht. Home: 119 Handsart Blvd Winnipeg MB Canada R3P 0C4 Office: Federal Industries Ltd 2400 One Lombard Pl Winnipeg MB Canada R3B 0X3

FRASER, KENNETH WILLIAM, JR., textile co. exec.; b. N.Y.C., Oct. 28, 1937; s. Kenneth William and Emma Kathryn (Ruch) F.; m. Susan Towne Mattison, June 20, 1959; children—John William, Elisabeth Grenell, Charles Angus, Andrea Mary. B.M.E., Cornell U., 1960; M.B.A. in Accounting, N.Y. U., 1968. Sales engr. Ingersoll-Rand, Inc., Mass., Maine, 1960-63; asst. treas. John P. Maguire & Co., Inc., N.Y.C., 1963-67, treas., 1967-70; fin. v.p., treas. Fieldcrest Mills, Inc., Eden, N.C., 1970-77, sr. v.p. fin., 1977—. Pres. Eden YMCA, 1976—; chmn. bd. trustees Morehead Meml. Hosp., Eden, 1980—. Mem. Fin. Execs. Inst. (pres. No. Carolina chpt. 1977). Methodist. Clubs: Rotary; Union League (N.Y.C.). Home: 414 Dogwood Ln Eden NC 27288 Office: Fieldcrest Gen Office Eden NC 27288

FRASER, MURRAY JUDSON, biochemist, educator; b. Yarmouth, N.S., Can., Aug. 21, 1930; s. Alexander James and Melda Fay (Pugh) F. B.Sc. with honors, Dalhousie U., Halifax, N.S., 1952, M.Sc., 1954; Ph.D., Cambridge U., 1957. Postdoctoral fellow Nat. Inst. Research in Dairying, Reading, Eng., 1957-58, McGill-Montreal Gen. Hosp. Research Inst., 1958-59; asst. prof. biochemistry U. Man., Can., 1959-63, assoc. prof., 1963-64; assoc. prof. med. biophysics U. Toronto, 1964-67; assoc. prof. biochemistry McGill U., Montreal, 1967-73, prof., 1973—; vis. scientist Stanford U., 1973-74, U. Calif., Berkeley, 1981-82. Assoc. editor: Can. Jour. Biochemistry, 1964-67; editor, 1967-72; contbr. articles to profl. jours. Guggenheim fellow, 1981-82. Mem. Am. Soc. Biol. Chemists, AAAS, Can. Biochem. Soc. Home: Apt 801 1411 Fort St Montreal PQ Canada H3H 2N7 Office: Dept Biochemistry 3655 Drummond St Montreal PQ Canada H3G 1Y6

FRASER, RAYMOND BRUCE, consumer products company executive; b. Halifax, N.S., Can., Nov. 7, 1943; s. John Phillip and Olive Margaret (Fequet) F.; m. Valerie Jean Chambers, Dec. 16, 1972; children: James William, Charles Michael. B. Comm., Dalhousie U., Halifax, 1964; M.B.A., U. Western Ont., 1966. Venture planner DuPont of Can. Ltd., Montreal, Que., 1966-68; mgr. corp. planning

Imasco Ltd., Montreal, 1968-79; v.p. corp. devel. John Labatt Ltd., London, Ont., Can., 1979—; dir. Maynard Energy Inc., Calgary, Alta., Can., Allelix Inc., Toronto. Fund raiser London Regional Art Gallery, 1983. Progressive Conservative. Club: london Hunt and Country. Office: John Labatt Ltd 451 Ridout St London ON Canada N6A 4M3

FRASER, ROBERT GORDON, diagnostic radiologist; b. Winnipeg, Man., Can., June 30, 1921; s. William Gordon and Amy Dena (Rumball) F.; m. Joanne Elsa Williams, June 15, 1974; children by previous marriage: Richard S., Merrill A., John R., Nancy L. M.D., U. Man., 1945. Resident in radiology Royal Victoria Hosp., McGill U., 1948-51; radiologist-in-chief Royal Victoria Hosp., Montreal. Que., 1964-76; prof. diagnostic radiology McGill U. Med. Sch., Montreal, 1964-76, chmn. dept., 1971-76; prof. diagnostic radiology U. Ala. Med. Sch., Birmingham, 1976—; vis. prof. U.S. and fgn. univs. Sr. author: Diagnosis of Diseases of the Chest, 4 vols, 1978-79. Served with Can. Navy, 1945-46. Recipient ann. medal Am. Coll. Chest Physicians, 1972. Fellow Royal Coll. Physicians Can., Am. Coll. Chest Physicians; mem. Fleischner Soc., Radiol. Soc. N.Am., Am. Roentgen Ray Soc., Can. Med. Assn. Office: 619 S 19th St Dept Diagnostic Radiology Birmingham AL 35233

FRASER, RUSSELL ALFRED, educator, author; b. Elizabeth, N.J., May 31, 1927; s. Roger John and Mary Louise (Narden) F.; m. Eleanor Jane Phillips, May 31, 1947 (div. 1979); children—Karen Mildred, Alexander Varennes; m. Mary Nelva Zwiep, July 5, 1980. A.B., Dartmouth Coll., 1947; M.A., Harvard U., 1949, Ph.D., 1950. Instr. English UCLA, 1950; postgrad. study, Eng., 1951-52; instr., then asst. prof. English Duke, 1952-56; asst. prof., then asso. prof. English Princeton, 1956-65, asso. dean, 1962-65; prof., chmn. English Vanderbilt U., Nashville, 1965-68; prof. English U. Mich., Ann Arbor, 1968—, chmn. dept., 1968-73, Austin Warren prof., 1983—; resident Inst. for Advanced Study, Princeton U., 1976. Author: Shakespeare's Poetics, 1962, The War Against Poetry, 1970, An Essential Shakespeare, 1972, The Dark Ages and the Age of Gold, 1973, The Language of Adam, 1977, A Mingled Yarn: The Life of R.P. Blockmun, 1982; Editor: The Court of Venus, 1955, The Court of Virtue, 1961, King Lear, 1963, Oscar Wilde, 1969, (with others) Drama of the English Renaissance, 2 vols, 1976. Served with USNR, 1944-46. Grantee Am. Council Learned Socs., 1951-52, 60, 68, Am. Philos. Soc., 1951-52, 60, 68, Dartmouth, 1951-52; jr. fellow Council Humanities, Princeton, 1960; NSF grantee, 1964-67; Guggenheim fellow, Rome, 1973-74; Rockefeller resident scholar, Bellagio, 1975; sr. Fulbright-Hays scholar, 1975; Nat. Endowment Humanities fellow, 1978-79. Mem. AAUP, Authors Guild, Renaissance Soc. Am., Shakespeare Assn. Am. Office: Dept English U Mich Ann Arbor MI 48109

FRASER, WILLIAM NEIL, association executive; b. Vancouver, B.C., Can., May 25, 1932; s. James Herbert and Katherine Baikie (Grieve) F.; m. Elizabeth Helen Bagatto, Mar. 15, 1975; children: Gordon, Alan, Katherine, Ian. Student, Banff Sch. Advanced Mgmt., 1967. Product mgr. Masonry, Deeks-McBride Ltd., Vancouver, 1952-68; gen. mgr. Masonry Contractors Assn. B.C., Vancouver, 1968-71; exec. dir. Can. Masonry Contractors Assn., Toronto, 1971—. Served with Can. Navy Res., 1953-57. Mem. Inst. Assn. Execs. (pres. Toronto chpt.), Constrn. Specifications Can., Can. Standards Assn., Council Ont. Contractors Assns., Masonry Council Can. (sec.-treas.). Clubs: Vancouver Golf, Bd. Trade Met. Toronto. Home: 500 Scarlett Rd Weston ON M9P 2S1 Canada Office: 1013 Wilson Ave Downsview ON M3K 1G1 Canada

FRASHIER, GARY EVEN, corporation executive; b. Pampa, Tex., July 2, 1936; s. Virgil G. F. and Hazel V. (Frashier); m. Sandra J., Dec. 29, 1972; children: Brian L., Kathy A., Denise L. B.S. in Chem. Engring., Tex. Tech. U., 1958; M.B.A., MIT, 1970. Registered profl. engr., Tex., La. Chem. engr. E.I. Dupont de Nemours & Co., 1958-59; research engr. Cabor Corp., Pampa, 1959-62, plant mgr., 1963-69, mgr. prodn., 1970-71, gen. mgr., 1971-72; dir. bus. planning Rockwell Internat. Corp., Pitts., 1973; v.p. mfg. Loctite Corp., Newington, Conn., 1974-75, pres., chief exec. officer indsl. products group, 1976-80; exec. v.p. Millipore Corp., Bedford, Mass., 1980—; pres., chief exec. officer Waters Assocs., Bedford, 1980—. Served as 1st lt. Chem. Corps, AUS, 1959. Mem. Am. Inst. Chem. Engrs., Young Presidents Orgn., Am. Supply and Machinery Mfg. Assn. (dir. 1980—, pres., sr.). Republican. Presbyterian. Clubs: Algonquin of Boston; Sombrero Country (Marathon, Fla.). Office: Waters Assocs Inc Maple St Milford MA 01757

FRASIER, RALPH KENNEDY, banker, lawyer; b. Winston-Salem, N.C., Sept. 16, 1938; s. LeRoy Benjamin and Kathryn O. (Kennedy) F.; m. Jeannine Quick, Aug. 1981; children: Karen D., Gail S., Ralph Kennedy, Keith L. B.S., N.C. Central U., Durham, 1962, J.D., 1965. Bar: N.C. 1965, Ohio 1976. With Wachovia Bank and Trust Co., N.A., Winston-Salem, 1965-70, v.p., counsel, 1969-70; asst. counsel, v.p. parent co. Wachovia Corp., 1970-75; v.p., gen. counsel Huntington Nat. Bank, Columbus, Ohio, 1975—, sr. v.p., 1976-83, exec. v.p., 1983—, sec., 1981—; v.p., gen. counsel Huntington Bancshares Inc., 1976—, sec., 1981—; sec., dir. Huntington Mortgage Co., Huntington State Bank, Huntington Leasing Co., Huntington Bancshares Fin. Corp., Huntington Investment Mgmt. Co., Scioto Life Ins. Co.; v.p., asst. sec. Huntington Bank N.E. Ohio. Bd. dirs. Family Services Winston-Salem, 1966-74, sec., 1966-71, 74, v.p., 1974; chmn. Winston-Salem Transit Authority, 1974-75; bd. dirs. Research for Advancement of Personalities, 1968-71, Winston-Salem Citizens for Fair Housing, 1970-74, N.C. United Community Services, 1970-74; treas. Forsyth County (N.C.) Citizens Com. Adequate Justice Bldg., 1968; trustee Appalachian State U., Boone, N.C., 1973-83, trustee endowment fund, 1973—; trustee, vice chmn. Employment and Edn. Commn. Franklin County, 1981—; mem. Winston-Salem. Forsyth County Sch. Bd. Adv. Council, 1973-74, Atty. Gen. Ohio Task Force Minorities in Bus., 1977-78. Served with AUS, 1958-60. Mem. Am. Bar Assn., Nat. Bar Assn., Ohio Bar Assn., Columbus Bar Assn. Address: 17 High St PO Box 1558 Columbus OH 43260

FRASIER, S. DOUGLAS, pediatric endocrinologist; b. Los Angeles, Nov. 29, 1932; s. Marc and Mildred F.; m. Robin D'Arvin, July 1, 1956; children—Karen Lynn, Eric Marc, Sara Leslie. B.A., UCLA, 1954, M.D., 1958. Diplomate: Am. Bd. Pediatrics (pediatric endocrinology). Intern Strong Meml. Hosp., Rochester, N.Y., 1958-59; resident UCLA Hosp., 1959-61, fellow in pediatric endocrinology, 1963-65; asst. prof. pediatrics UCLA Med. Sch., 1965-67; mem. faculty U. So. Calif. Med. Sch., 1967—, prof. pediatrics, 1974—, asso. dean student affairs years I and II, 1970-76; chief div. pediatric endocrinology Los Angeles County-U. So. Calif. Med. Center, 1967—. Author: Pediatric Endocrinology, 1980, also numerous articles. Served as officer M.C. USAR, 1961-63. Mem. Am. Acad. Pediatrics, Endocrine Soc., Soc. Pediatric Research, Am. Pediatric Soc., Lawson Wilkins Pediatric Endocrine Soc., Western Soc. Pediatric Research, Los Angeles Pediatric Soc., Alpha Omega Alpha. Office: Pediatric Pavilion 4E8 Los Angeles County-Univ So Calif Med Center 1129 N State St Los Angeles CA 90033

FRATCHER, WILLIAM FRANKLIN, lawyer; b. Detroit, Apr. 4, 1913; s. Vernon Claude and Ethel Stuart (Thomas) F.; m. Elsie Florene Briscoe, Aug. 22, 1941; 1 dau., Agnes. A.B. with distinction, Wayne U., 1933, A.M., 1938; J.D. with distinction, U. Mich., 1936, LL.M., 1951, S.J.D., 1952; grad., Command and Gen. Staff Sch., U.S. Army, 1944; spl. study, U. Paris, 1945. Bar: Mich. 1936. Asso., mem. Lewis & Watkins, 1936-41; asso. prof. law U. Mo., 1947-49, prof., 1949—, R.B. Price distinguished prof. law, 1971—, chmn. faculty com. on tenure, 1970—; research dir. spl. com. model probate code sect. real property, probate and trust law Am. Bar Assn., 1962-63; research counsel N.Y. Temporary State Commn. Estates, 1963; vis. prof. law U. Mich., summer 1952, N.Y. U., 1954-55, summer 1963, 65, U. Calif.-Hastings Coll. Law, 1976, U. Puget Sound, 1983-84; Ford Found. Law Faculty fellow Inst. Advanced Legal Studies; also hon. mem. Faculty of Laws, King's Coll., U. London (Eng.), 1963-64; research asso. U. Mich., summer 1953; chmn. joint com. on cooperation between Assn. Am. Law Schs. and Am. Assn. Law Libraries, 1969; mem. adv. com. to Sec. of State on UNIDROIT Draft Conv. to Establish Internat. Form of Will. Author: The National Defense Act, 1945, Perpetuities and Other Restraints, 1954, (with Lewis M. Simes) Cases and Other Materials on Fiduciary Administration, 1956, Trusts and Estates in England, 1968, Cases and Materials on Veterinary Jurisprudence, 1968, (with others) Landmark Papers on Estate Planning, Wills, Estates and Trusts, 1968, Planning Large Estates, 1968, Uniform Probate Code, 1970, Uniform Probate Code Practice Manual, 1972, 2d edit., 1977, Fascicle on Trust, Internat. Ency. Comparative Law, 1974, (with others) Death, Taxes and Family Property, 1977, The Law Barn: A Brief History of The School of Law, University of Missouri-Columbia, 1978, (with others) Trusts and Trust-Like Devices, 1981; editor: (pocket parts) Simes and Smith, The Law of Future Interests, 1961, 65, 67, 69, 72, 73, 75, 77, 79, 81, 83, Supplements to Scott, The Law of Trusts, 1982, 83; govt. publs. on mil. law; editorial bd.: Manual for Courts-Martial, U.S.A, 1949; reporter: Uniform Probate Code, 1963-70; gen. reporter: Internat. Ency. Comparative Law, 1966—; reporter: Mo. Probate Laws Revision Project, 1973-80, (with others) Mo. Guardianship Laws Revision Project, 1975—, Mo. Trust Laws Revision Project, 1980—; contbr. to Ency. Brit, 1974; also articles to various publs. Served as 2d lt. cavalry Civilian Conservation Corps, 1934-35; commd. capt. JAGC U.S. Army, 1941; served as chief, control br., Office JAG, War Dept., 1942; exec. to asst. judge adv. gen. in charge civil matters, 1943-44; chief, miscellaneous br., Mil. Justice div., Br. Office JAG, 1945; ETO, Paris; chief war crimes br., legal div., Office Mil. Govt. U.S., 1945-46; Berlin; U.S. commr. and chmn. Internat. Commn. for Control of Central Registry of War Criminals and Security Suspects, 1946; staff judge adv., Berlin Dist. and hdqrs. command U.S. Forces, 1946; ETO; reviewed Kronberg Castle jewel theft cases; lt. col. Res., 1947; col., 1957. Decorated Legion of Merit, Commendation medal; Acad. fellow Am. Coll. Probate Counsel, 1971; research grantee Nat. Conf. Commrs. on Uniform State Laws at U. Mich., summer 1966, Am. Bar Found. at U. Colo., summer 1967, Internat. Assn. Legal Sci. at U. Oxford, Eng., summer 1969. Mem. Am. Bar Assn. (spl. com. mil. justice 1959-61, 64-71, vice chmn. 1970-71, chmn. com. real property lit. 1953-55, vice chmn. 1975-77, vice chmn. com. probate and trust lit. 1974—), Mo. Bar (chmn. mil. law com. 1967-68, mem. council probate and trusts com. 1969—), Judge Advs. Assn., Am. Law Inst., Res. Officers Assn. U.S., Selden Soc. (Mo. corr.), Soc. Pub. Tchrs. Law (U.S. corr.), Am. Soc. Legal History, Pipe Roll Soc., Order of Coif. Presbyterian. Office: U Mo Tate Hall Columbia MO 65211 *A man's talents are bestowed upon him so that he may accomplish some purpose of God. It is each man's duty to discover God's purpose for him and to strive, to the utmost of his ability and endurance, to achieve it.*

FRATELLO, MICHAEL ROBERT, professional basketball coach; b. Hackensack, N.J., Feb. 24, 1947. Student, Montclair State Coll., U. R.I. Asst. coach U. R.I., Kingston, 1971, James Madison U., Harrisburg, Va., 1972-75, Villanova U., Phila., 1976-78, Atlanta Hawks, NBA, 1978-82, coach, 1983—; asst. coach N.Y. Knicks, NBA, 1982-83. Office: Atlanta Hawks 100 Techwood Dr NW Atlanta GA 30303 *

FRATER, ROBERT WILLIAM MAYO, surgeon, educator; b. Cape Town, South Africa, Nov. 12, 1928; came to U.S., 1964, naturalized, 1974; s. Kenneth and Ethel (Barrow) F.; m. Elaine Glynn Nagle, Aug. 27, 1954; children: Hugh R., Dirk A., Phillipa. M.B., B.Chir. (Jagger Scholar, Medalist, Anatomy, Surgery, Pathology), U. Cape Town Med. Sch., 1952; M.S. in Surgery (Minn. Heart Assn. fellow), U. Minn., 1961. Intern medicine and surgery Groote Schuur Hosp., Cape Town, 1953; resident casualty officer Lewisham Hosp., London, 1955; fellow in gen. and thoracic surgery Mayo Clinic, Rochester, Minn., 1955-61; sr. lectr. cardiothoracic surgery U. Cape Town, 1962-64; asst. prof. surgery Albert Einstein Coll. Medicine, N.Y.C., 1964-68, assoc. prof., 1968-72, prof. surgery, 1972—, chief cardiothoracic surgery, 1968—, acting chmn. dept. surgery, 1971-75, mem., 1971-74; chief cardiothoracic surgery Montefiore Hosp. and Med. Center, 1975—; mem. staff, exec. council Bronx Mcpl. Hosp. Center, Albert Einstein Coll. Hosp., 1969—; mem. staff Lawrence Hosp., Bronxville, N.Y. Assoc. editor: Quar. Jour. Cardiac Surgery. Mem. Concern for Dying Council, 1982—. Recipient award Noble Found., 1961; NIH grantee, 1965-70, 68-70, 74-78, 79-81, 82-84; Am. Heart Assn. grantee, 1966, 71. Fellow Royal Coll. Surgeons, A.C.S., Am. Coll. Cardiology; mem. Am. Assn. Thoracic Surgery, Soc. Thoracic Surgeons (postgrad. edn. com. 1978—, chmn. postgrad. program 1981), N.Y. Soc. Thoracic Surgery (pres. 1978), N.Y. Surg. Soc. (mem. council 1975-80), Thoracic Surgery Dirs. Assn. (exec. council 1982-85), Assn. Acad. Surgeons, Am. Heart Assn. (exec. com. Council on Cardiovascular Surgery 1979-84, program com. 1979-82), Sigma Xi, Alpha Omega Alpha. Club: Bronxville Field (Squash capt.). Home: 17 Gladwin Pl Bronxville NY 10708 Office: 1300 Morris Park Ave Bronx NY 10461 *The good fortune to use both mind and hand in asking questions, finding answers and healing others.*

FRATTI, MARIO, playwright, educator; b. L'Aquila, Italy, July 8, 1927; came to U.S., 1963, naturalized, 1974; s. Leone and Palmira (Silvi) F.; children: Mirko, Barbara, Valentina. Ph.D., Ca Foscari U., 1951. Tchr., 1964-65; mem. faculty Columbia U., 1965-66; mem. Adelphi Coll., 1964-65; mem. faculty Hofstra U., 1973-74; prof. lit. New Sch. Hunter Coll., N.Y.C., 1967—; drama critic. Drama critic: Paese, 1963—, Progresso, 1963—, Ridotto, 1963—, Ora Zero, 1963—; playwright: Case-Suicide, 1964, Academy-Return, 1967, Mafia, 1971, Races, 1972, Bridge, 1971, Eleven Plays in Spanish, 1977, Refrigerators, 1977; author: Eleonora Duse-Victim, 1981, Nine, 1982 (Tony), Biography of Fratti, 1982. Served to lt. Italian Army, 1951-53. Recipient awards for plays and musicals. Mem. Drama Desk, Am. Theatre Critics, Outer Critics Circle (v.p.). Democrat. Home: 145 W 55th St New York NY 10019 Office: Hunter Coll 695 Park Ave New York NY 10021

FRAUENFELDER, HANS, physicist, educator; b. Neuhausen, Switzerland, July 28, 1922; came to U.S., 1952, naturalized, 1958; s. Otto and Emma (Ziegler) F.; m. Verena Anna Hassler, May 16, 1950; children: Ulrich Hans, Kätterli Anne, Anne Verena. Diploma, Swiss Fed. Inst. Tech., 1947, Ph.D. in Physics, 1950. Asst. Swiss Fed. Inst. Tech., 1946-52; asst. prof. physics U. Ill. at Urbana, 1952-56, asso. prof., 1956-58, prof., 1958—; Cons. Los Alamos (N.M.) Sci. Lab.; Guggenheim fellow, 1958-59, 73; vis. scientist CERN, Geneva, Switzerland, 1958-59, 63, 73. Author: The Mössbauer Effect, 1962, (with E.M. Henley) Subatomic Physics, 1974, Nuclear and Particle Physics, 1975; Contbr. articles to profl. publs. Fellow Am. Phys. Soc., N.Y. Acad. Sci., AAAS; mem. Nat. Acad. Scis., Am. Acad. Arts and Sci., Acad. Leopoldina. Home: 8 Hagan Blvd Urbana IL 61801 Office: Dept Physics 1110 West Green Street U Ill Urbana IL 61801

FRAUNFELDER, FREDERICK THEODORE, ophthalmologist; b. Pasadena, Calif., Aug. 16, 1934; s. Reinhart and Freida F.; m. Yvonne Marie Halliday, June 21, 1959; children—Yvette Marie, Helene, Nina, Frederick, Nicholas. B.S., U. Oreg., 1956, M.D., 1960, postgrad. (NIH postdoctoral fellow), 1962. Intern U. Chgo., 1961; resident U. Oreg. Med. Sch., 1964-66; NIH postdoctoral fellow Wilmer Eye Inst., Johns Hopkins U., 1967; prof. ophthalmology U. Ark. Health Scis. Center, 1968-78; prof., chmn. dept. ophthalmology U. Oreg. Health Scis. Center, 1978—; dir. Nat. Registry Drug-Induced Ocular Side Effects, 1976—; vis. prof. ophthalmology Moorfields Eye Hosp., London, 1974. Author: Drug-Induced Ocular Side Effects and Drug Interactions, 1976, Current Ocular Therapy, 1980; contbr. numerous articles to profl. jours. Served with U.S. Army, 1962-64. FDA grantee, 1976—; Nat. Eye Inst. grantee, 1970-76. Mem. Am. Acad. Ophthaolmology, AMA, A.C.S., Assn. Univ. Profs. in Ophthalmology, Am. Ophthalmol. Soc., Am. Coll. Cryosurgery, Assn. Research in Ophthalmology. Lutheran. Clubs: Lions, Elks. Home: 13 Cellini Ct Lake Oswego OR 97034 Office: 3181 SW Sam Jackson Park Rd Portland OR 97201

FRAUTSCHI, STEVEN CLARK, physicist, educator; b. Madison, Wis., Dec. 6, 1933; s. Lowell Emil and Grace (Clark) F.; m. Mie Okamura, Feb. 16, 1967; children—Laura, Jennifer. B.A., Harvard, 1954; Ph.D., Stanford, 1958. Research fellow Kyoto U., Japan, 1958-59, U. Calif. at Berkeley, 1959-61; mem. faculty Cornell U., 1961-62, Calif. Inst. Tech., Pasadena, 1962—, prof. theoretical physics, 1966—; vis. prof. U. Paris, Orsay, 1977-78. Author: Regge Poles and S-Matrix Theory, 1963. Guggenheim fellow, 1971-72. Mem. Am. Phys. Soc. Research, publs. on Regge poles, bootstrap theory. Home: 1561 Crest Dr Altadena CA 91001 Office: 1201 E California Blvd Pasadena CA 91125

FRAUTSCHI, WALTER ALBERT, contract and publications printing company executive; b. Madison, Wis., Dec. 4, 1901; s. Emil John and Ida (Parman) F.; m. Dorothy Jones, Aug. 10, 1927; children: John Jones, Walter Jerome. B.A., U. Wis., 1924. Chmn. bd. Webcrafters, Inc., Madison, 1959—. Campaign chmn. Madison United Givers Fund, 1938; Trustee Wis. Alumni Research Found.; chmn. Vilas Estate Fund, 1972, Madison Civic Center Campaign, 1976; Chmn., trustee Brandenburg Found. (merged with Madison Rotary Found.). Mem. Wis. Acad. Sci., Arts and Letters, Wis. Alumni Assn. (pres. 1948), Sigma Nu, Sigma Delta Chi, Phi Kappa Phi. Presbyn. (trustee). Club: Rotarian (pres. Madison 1955). Home: 29 Fuller Dr Madison WI 53704 Office: Box 7608 Madison WI 53707

FRAWLEY, ERNEST DAVID, publisher; b. Brockton, Mass., Apr. 17, 1920; s. Arthur Henry and Viola (Morse) F.; m. Natalie Pingree, Oct. 29, 1948 (dec. Dec. 30, 1962); children: Betsy, Cynthia, Susan; m. Elizabeth von Thurn, Nov. 19, 1965. A.B., Middlebury Coll., 1942; student, Bread Loaf Grad. Sch. English, summers 1940, 41. Staff mem. N.E. regional magazine Boston Transcript, 1946; with advt. dept. Dewey & Almy Chemical Co., Cambridge, Mass., 1947-48, Green Mountain Pubs. (baseball publs.), Boston, 1948-49; pub., treas., dir. Child Life mag., 1949-56; circulation dir., asst. bus. mgr. Harvard Bus. Review, Harvard Grad. Sch. Bus. Adminstrn., 1956-63, controller, 1963-71, gen. mgr., 1971-79, pub., 1979—; trustee, adminstr. Internat. Marketing Inst., 1960-70, treas., 1961-70; dir. Comml. Bank & Trust Co., Wilmington, Mass., 1962-65, W. A. Wilde Co., Bus. Research Corp.; cons. U.S. Dept. State, 1960-70, Dept. Commerce, 1960-66; Sec. Boston Conf. on Distbn., 1961-64. Trustee Thayer Pub. Library, Braintree, 1964-79; trustee Mass. Hort. Soc., 1976-79. Served as lt. (s.g.) USNR, 1942-45. Mem. Am. Marketing Assn., Nat. Planning Assn. (nat. council 1970), Am. Arbitration Assn., Delta Kappa Epsilon. Club: Harvard. Office: Grad Sch Bus Adminstrn Harvard U Soldiers Field Boston MA 02163

FRAWLEY, PATRICK JOSEPH, JR., corporate executive; b. Leon, Nicaragua, May 26, 1923; came to U.S., 1928, naturalized, 1958; s. Patrick Joseph and Maria Theresa (Peugnet) F.; m. Gerardine Ann Clancy, Sept. 12, 1944; children: Frances Ann Frawley Swanson, Patrick Joseph, Mary Louise, Eileen Josephine Frawley Callahan, Michael Paul, Joan Theresa, Barbara Irene. Student Calif. schs. Chmn. bd. Shadel Hosp., Seattle, 1964—, Schick-Shadel Hosp., Ft. Worth, 1970—, Santa Barbara, Calif., 1979—; pres., chmn. Frawley Corp., Los Angeles, 1970—, Schick Labs., 1971—; chmn. Schick Centers for Control Smoking and Weight, 1971—, Sunn Classic Pictures, Los Angeles, 1972-80, Twin Circle Publiching Co. div. Frawley Corp.; chmn. bd. Technicolor, Inc., 1961-70, chmn. fin. com., 1968-70; chmn. Eversharp, Inc., Schick Safety Razor Co., 1958-66; founder, owner Paper Mate Pen Co., 1949-55. Trustee Freedoms Found. at Valley Forge; mem. president's bd. Pepperdine Coll., Los Angeles; bd. regents U. Santa Clara, Calif. Served with RCAF, 1942-45. Recipient Golden Plate award Am. Acad. Achievement, 1974, Free Enterprise award San Fernando Valley Bus. and Profl. Assn., 1983; decorated knight of St. Gregory, knight of Sylvester, knight of Malta, knight Order St. Brigitte.; recipient Free Enterprise award San Fernando Valley Bus. and Profl. Assn., 1983. Mem. Am. Security Council (sr. adv. bd., Best Citizen of Year award 1965). Roman Catholic. Clubs: Bel Air Bay, Los Angeles Country. Home: 539 S Mapleton Dr Los Angeles CA 90024 Office: 1901 Ave of Stars Los Angeles CA 90067

FRAWLEY, THOMAS FRANCIS, physician; b. Rochester, N.Y., June 27, 1919; s. Thomas J. and Mary (Leddy) F.; m. Marigrace Cecelia Gould, Feb. 23, 1946; children—Thomas Joseph II, Colleen, Brian. A.B., U. Rochester, 1941; M.D., U. Buffalo, 1944. Diplomate: Am. Bd. Internal Medicine, Am. Bd. Endocrinology/Metabolism. Intern St. Mary's Hosp., Rochester, 1944-45; resident Buffalo Gen. Hosp., 1945-48; research fellow Harvard Med. Sch., 1948-52; resident Peter Bent Brigham Hosp., Boston, 1948-52; chief endocrinology and metabolism Albany (N.Y.) Med. Sch., 1952-58, asso. prof. medicine, 1952-58, prof. medicine, 1960-63; research asso. NIH, 1958-60; prof. medicine St. Louis U. Sch. Medicine, 1963—, chmn. dept. internal medicine, 1963-73, chmn. emeritus, 1977—; chmn. Office of Grad. Med. Edn., St. John's Mercy Med. Center, St. Louis, 1981—; physician-in-chief St. Louis U. Hosp., 1963-73; Mem. drug efficacy study panel Nat. Acad. Scis., 1966-69; med. adv. com. Cath. Hosp. Assn., 1966-69; mem. sci. rev. com. NIH, 1970—; commr. Joint Commn. Accreditation of Hosps., 1976—. Author books in field.; Contbr. articles to profl. jours. Served to capt., M.C. AUS, 1946-47; surgeon USPHS, 1958-60. Fellow A.C.P. (gov. Mo. 1971-75, regent 1976—, pres. 1981), N.Y. Acad. Scis.; mem. Assn. Am. Physicians, Am. Fedn. Clin. Research, Endocrine Soc., Central Soc. Clin. Research, So. Soc. Clin. Investigation, Am. Thyroid Assn., Am. Diabetes Assn., Am. Clin. and Climatol. Assn., Sigma Xi, Alpha Omega Alpha. Home: 23 Williamsburg Estates Saint Louis MO 63131 Office: Office of Grad Med Edn St John's Mercy Med Center 615 S New Ballas Rd Saint Louis MO 63141

FRAYNE, JOHN PATRICK, educator; b. N.Y.C., June 13, 1931; s. Patrick John and Mary C. (Smith) F.; m. Eva Rostek, Sept. 13, 1958; children—Patrick, Henry. B.A., Fordham U., 1953; M.A., Columbia U., 1962, Ph.D., 1967. Lectr. Hunter Coll., 1961-64; preceptor Columbia Coll., 1963-65; instr. English U. Ill., 1965-66, asst. prof., 1966-71, asso. prof., 1971-77, prof., 1977—; opera critic Sta. WILL. Editor: Uncollected Prose by W.B. Yeats, vol. I, 1970, (with Colton Johnson) vol. II, 1975. Served to lt. U.S. Army, 1953-55. Mem. MLA,

Am. Com. on Irish Studies. Office: 100 English Bldg U Ill Urbana IL 61801

FRAZEE, ROWLAND CARDWELL, banker; b. Halifax, N.S., Can., May 12, 1921; s. Rowland Hill and Callie Jean (Cardwell) F.; m. Marie Eileen Tait, June 11, 1949; children: Stephen, Catherine. B.Commerce, King's Coll. and Dalhousie U., Halifax, 1948. With Royal Bank Can., 1939—, v.p. and chief gen. mgr., Montreal, 1972-73, exec. v.p. and chief gen. mgr., 1973-77, pres., 1977—, chief exec. officer, 1979—, chmn., 1980—; dir. Continental Corp., Fraser Inc., Imasco Ltd., Power Corp. Can. Bd. dirs. Roosevelt Campobello Internat. Park Commn.; chmn. Bus. Council Nat. Issues; trustee Sports Fund for Physically Disabled.; chmn. Jr. Achievement Can.; gov. McGill U. Served to maj. Can. Army, World War II. Anglican. Clubs: Toronto, Granite (Toronto); Mt. Royal, St. James's (Montreal); Mt. Bruno Country (Quebec); Manitoba; Lyford Cay. (Nassau). Home: 1955 Dumfries St Mount Royal PQ H3P 2R8 Canada Office: 1 Pl Ville Marie Montreal PQ H3B 4A7 Canada

FRAZER, ALFRED KNOX, architect; b. Birmingham, Ala., May 23, 1928; s. Sidney Arthur and Martha Jane (Park) F.; m. Margaret Elspeth English, Dec. 21, 1964; children—Martha Claudia, Zoë Sophia. B.Arch., Ala. Poly. Inst., 1949; M.A., Inst. Fine Arts, N.Y. U., 1958, Ph.D., 1964. Asst. prof. art Vassar Coll., Poughkeepsie, N.Y., 1961-66; asso. prof. Columbia U., N.Y.C., 1966-69, prof., 1969—, chmn. dept. art history and archaelogy, 1972-78; archtl. designer, N.Y.C., 1952-60. Author: Key Monuments in the History of Architecture, 1965; co-author: Corpus Basilicarum Christianarum Romae, Vol. 5, 1977; contbr. articles to profl. jours. Served with AUS, 1949-52. Am. Acad. Rome fellow, 1959-61. Mem. Soc. Archtl. Historians (dir. 1966-69, pres. N.Y.C. chpt. 1966-69), Am. Inst. Archaeology, Coll. Art Assn. (dir. 1973-77). Democrat. Home: 84 Park Ave Larchmont NY 10538 Office: Columbia U 815 Schermerhorn Hall New York City NY 10027

FRAZER, ARTHUR WATSON, economist, nurseryman; b. Wheeling, W.Va., May 28, 1913; s. Arthur W. and Evelyn L. (Myers) F.; m. Beulah L. Edmond, Aug. 1933 (div. 1944); children—Christina, Brenda; m. Anita de la Fuente, Jan. 1961. A.B., W.Va. Wesleyan Coll., Buckhannon, 1934; grad. student, Carnegie Inst. Tech., 1935, Harvard U., 1950; Ph.D., Am. U., 1953. Clk. FBI, 1936-37; economist Dept. Labor, 1938-49; intelligence specialist USAF, 1949-51; spl. asst. program coordination Nat. Prodn. Authority, 1951-53; asst. to asst. sec. Dept. Commerce, 1953-57; cons. economist GSA, 1957; fgn. service officer ICA, Israel, 1957-59; cons. economist Devel. Loan Fund, Washington, 1959-60; indsl. economist ICA, 1960-61; sr. planning assistance officer AID, 1962-65, internat. fin. economist, 1965-67, chief capital assistance policy div., 1967-68; cons. IMF, 1971; gen. mgr. Columbia Nursery, Alexandria, Va., 1970—. Author govt. monographs and bulls.; Contbr. articles to hort. and tech. publs. Mem. Am. Econ. Assn., Am. Acad. Polit. and Social Sci., Am. Rhodendron Soc., Am. Hort. Soc., Internat. Plant Propagators Soc., No. Va. Nurserymen's Assn., Nat. Capital Fedn. Garden Clubs (mem.-at-large). Club: Masons. Home: 1903 Martha's Rd Alexandria VA 22307

FRAZER, JACK WINFIELD, chemistry educator; b. Forest Grove, Oreg., Sept. 9, 1924; s. Jack Henry and Edna (Alfranc) F.; m. Juanita Maxfield, Jan. 27, 1947; children: John Christopher, Pamela, Candice. B.S., Hardin Simmons U., 1948. Chemist Los Alamos Sci. Lab., U. Calif. and AEC, 1948-52; scientist Lawrence Livermore Lab., U. Calif., 1953-82, head chemistry and materials sci. dept., 1974-78, sr. research scientist, 1978-82; chief exec. officer Keithley Instruments Inc., 1982-83; adj. prof. chemistry U. Ga., 1983—; Indsl. prof. Ind. U., 1972-77; mem. affiliate faculty Colo. State U., Fort Collins; editorial adviser Analytica Chimica Acta, Computer Techniques and Optimization, 1977; chmn. Gordon Research Conf. on Analytical Chemistry, 1979; mem. adv. com. Oak Ridge Nat. Lab., 1983—; dir., cons. Keithley Instruments, Inc.; cons. Merck, Inc., Universal Oil Products. Contbr. articles to profl. jours. Served with USAAF, 1943-45. Recipient Sargent-Welch Sci. Co. award in chem. instrumentation Am. Chem. Soc., 1973. Fellow ASTM (chmn. E-31 1970-75, award of merit 1975). Home: 6767 Alisal St Pleasanton CA 94566 Office: Lawrence Livermore Lab Livermore CA 94550

FRAZER, JAMES NISBET, lawyer; b. Cedartown, Ga., Oct. 1, 1903; s. James Newton and Willie (Nisbet) F.; m. Rebecca Young, July 7, 1937; children—James Nisbet, Rebecca Young. Student, Oglethorpe U., 1924; LL.B., Atlanta Law Sch., 1926. Bar: Ga. bar 1926. Since practiced in, Atlanta; mem. firm Powell, Goldstein, Frazer & Murphy, 1937—; dir. Citizens & So. Nat. Bank. Chmn. bd. Children's Rehab. Center. Mem. Am., Ga., Atlanta bar assns., Lawyers Club Altanta. Presbyn. (deacon, trustee). Clubs: Piedmont Driving, Capital City, Commerce (Atlanta). Home: 565 W Wesley Rd NW Atlanta GA 30305 Office: Citizens & So Nat Bank Bldg Atlanta GA 30303

FRAZER, JOHN HOWARD, manufacturing company executive; b. Cin., June 3, 1924; s. H. Howard and Amelia (Spieth) F.; m. Joann Elizabeth McEvoy, Nov. 3, 1956; children: John Howard, Victoria Spieth. B.A., U. Cin., 1948, J.D., 1950. Bar: Ohio bar 1950. V.p. H. Howard Frazer Co., Cin., 1950-62, pres., 1962-76; treas., dir. Cin. Transit Co., 1957-73; dir. Am. Controlled Industries, Cin., 1973—, pres., 1974-75, exec. v.p., 1975—; dir. Vulcan Corp., Cin., 1960—, pres., 1975—; sec., dir. Valley Industries, 1973—, Colorpac, Inc., 1973—. Chmn. men's com. Cin. Symphony Orch., 1971-73; pres. Cincinnatus Assn., 1969-70; chmn. Western Tennis Championships, Cin., 1970-73; chmn. nat. men's ranking com. U.S. Tennis Assn., 1971-73, mem. long-range planning com., 1981—; bd. dirs. Nat. Tennis Found./Tennis Hall of Fame, 1979—. Served with USAAF, 1942-45. Mem. U.S. Tennis Assn. (mem. exec. com. 1975—, chmn. sanction and schedule com. 1973—), Am. Footwear Industries Assn. (dir.), Rubber Mfrs. Assn. (dir.), Shoe Last Mfrs. Assn. (pres. 1978-79). Clubs: University, Cin. Country, Cin. Tennis, Marco Island Racquet, Naples (Fla.) Bath and Tennis. Home: 415 Bond Pl Cincinnati OH 45206 Office: 6 E 4th St Cincinnati OH 45202

FRAZER, JOHN PAUL, surgeon; b. Rochester, N.Y., Sept. 14, 1914; s. Edward and Annie Margaret (Burdick) F.; m. Doris V. Larsen, Sept. 23, 1950; children—Karin Ann, Gail Sherry. M.D., U. Rochester, 1939. Intern in pathology Cornell U. Med. Center, 1939-40; intern in surgery L.I. Coll. Hosp., 1940-41; resident in ear, nose and throat Yale-New Haven Hosp., 1941-45, instr., 1945-48; practice medicine specializing in ear, nose and throat, Honolulu, 1948-63; prof. surgery U. Rochester Sch. Medicine and Dentistry, 1963—; cons. in field. Mem. A.C.S., Am. Laryngol. Assn., Am. Bronchoesophagological Assn., Am. Laryngol-Rhinol-Otol. Soc., N.Y. State Soc. Medicine. Address: Sch Medicine and Dentistry U Rochester 601 Elmwood Ave Rochester NY 14642

FRAZER, MAURICE DOYLE, physician; b. Utica, Nebr., Apr. 3, 1911; s. David J. and June (Doyle) F.; m. Margaret Clare Underwood, Sept. 17, 1935; children—Betty Lou, Patricia Jane. B.Sc., U. Nebr., 1936, M.D., 1937. Intern Methodist Hosp., Omaha, 1937-38; practice of medicine, 1938—, specializing radiology, 1940—; asso. prof. U. Nebr. Coll. Medicine; former chmn. Nebr. Bd. Health; cons. radiologist Nebr. State Hosp.; Past mem. radiation adv. council Nebr. Dept. Health. Mem. AMA (ho. of dels.), Am. Coll. Radiology, Radiol. Soc. N.Am. (past pres.), Am. Radium Soc., Nebr. Med. Assn., Lancaster County Med. Soc. Home: 1774 S 58th St Lincoln NE 68506 Office: 5145 O St Lincoln NE 68510

FRAZER, ROBERT E., utility executive; b. 1928. B.S., Central Mich. U., 1950. Acct. Consumer Power Co., 1950-52; audit mgr. Anderson Authur & Co., 1952-61; v.p. fin. Duke Power Co., 1961-75; with Dayton Power & Light Co., Dayton, Ohio, 1975—, pres., 1976—, chief operating officer, 1978-82, chief exec. officer, 1982—, also chmn. bd., dir. Address: Dayton Power & Light Co Courthouse Plaza SW Dayton OH 45401 *

FRAZER, WILLIAM ROBERT, physicist; b. Indpls., Aug. 6, 1933; s. William Jay and Mildred (Dahlman) F.; m. Jane Zaiser, July 31, 1954; children—Bruce, Katherine. A.B., Carleton Coll., 1954; Ph.D., U. Calif. at Berkeley, 1959; postgrad., U. Utrecht, Netherlands, 1956-57. Mem. Inst. Advanced Study, Princeton, N.J., 1959-60; mem. faculty U. Calif. at San Diego, 1960—, prof. physics, 1967—, chmn. dept., 1975-77, acting provost, 1969-70, chmn. acad. senate, 1978-79, acad. v.p., 1981—. Author: Elementary Particles, 1966, also articles. Mem. Am. Phys. Soc. Research on theory of interaction of elementary particles, principally strong interactions responsible for nuclear force. Office: U Calif at San Diego La Jolla CA 92037

FRAZETTA, FRANK, artist; b. Bklyn., Feb. 9, 1928. Student, Bklyn. Acad. Fine Arts.; Former asst. to, Michael Falanga; former artist numerous comic book houses including, Baily, Pines, Fawcett, National, Eastern Color, Hillman, Avon, Western; artist: syndicated comic strip Johnny Comet (later titled Ace McCoy), 1952-53; ghosted: Flash Gordon comic strip, 1953; past asst.: Al Capp; mem. staff: L'il Abner comic strip; freelance illustrator, 1960—; also artist publicity posters for movies, book covers, record album jackets; author: Frank Frazetta, the Living Legend, 1980; created characters for animated feature: Fire and Ice, 1983. Recipient Hugo award, 1966. Mem. Nat. Cartoonists Soc. Address: Sun Litho-Prints PO Box R Marshall Creek PA 18335 *

FRAZIER, CHET JUNE, advertising agency executive; b. Wynona, Okla., May 17, 1924; s. R.C. and Alice (Terry) F.; m. Lucille Whetzel, Nov. 17, 1942; children: John, Lynette, Terry Luanna. B.S., Okla. State U., 1949, M.S., 1950. Editor Okla. News Service, Stillwater, 1949-50; product sales mgr. Ralston Purina Co., St. Louis, 1951-58, advt. mgr., 1958-63; v.p. Bozell & Jacobs Internat., Inc., N.Y.C., 1964-68, sr. v.p., 1968-71, exec. v.p., 1971-76, pres., 1976—, 1978—, also dir.; chmn. bd. Henke Machine, Inc., 1972—. Contbr. articles on agrl. advt. to profl. jours. Served with U.S. Army, 1943-46; PTO. Named Advt. Man of Year Advt. Fedn. Am., 1968. Mem. Nat. Agrl. Advt. and Mktg. Assn. (pres. 1967-68, dir. 1967-70), U.S. Feed Grains Council (bd. dirs., chmn. pub. relations com.), Am. Feed Mfg. Assn., Agrl. Council Am. (bd. dirs.), Farm Equipment Mfg. Assn., Agrl. Pubs. Assn. Methodist. Club: Kiwanis. Home: 9770 Westchester Dr Omaha NE 68114 Office: 10250 Regency Circle Omaha NE 68114 *My business philosophy has always been one of honesty, integrity, hard work and respect for the rights of those with whom I work. Coming from an agricultural background, I put great value on the land and all things that come from the land.*

FRAZIER, DALLAS JUNE, songwriter, singer; b. Spiro, Okla., Oct. 27, 1939; s. Floyd William and Eva Marie (Laughlin) F.; m. Sharon R. Carpani, June 8, 1958; children: Melody June, Robin Marie, Alison Grace. Student pub. schs., Calif. Singer, since 1952; composer, since 1950; rec. artist, Capitol, Mercury, RCA and 20th Century Fox records; composer: Alley Oop, 1960, Mohair Sam, 1965, There Goes My Everything, 1967, The Son of Hickory Hollers Tramp, 1968, All I Have To Offer You Is Me, 1970, Johnny One Time, 1971. Recipient 23 awards Broadcast Music, Inc., including, Robert J. Burton award for Elvira as most performed country song of yr. Broadcast Music, Inc., including, 1982, pop award for Fourteen Carat Mind, 1982. Mem. Country Music Assn. (Song of Yr. award 1967), Nashville Songwriters Assn. (Songwriter of Yr. award 1967, named to Internat. Hall of Fame 1976), AFTRA, Nashville Assn. Musicians. Mem. Pentecostal Full Gospel Ch. Address: Route 5 Box 149 Longhollow Pike Gallatin TN 37066

FRAZIER, HENRY BOWEN, III, government official, lawyer; b. Bluefield, W.Va., Aug. 9, 1934; s. Henry Bowen and Margaret Beale (West) F.; m. Joan McIntosh, Dec. 30, 1959. B.A. with honors, U. Va., 1956; J.D. with honors, George Washington U., 1967; LL.M. in Labor Law, Georgetown U., 1969. Bar: Va. bar 1967. Personnel adminstr. Army Dept. Washington, 1959-63, spl. projects officer, 1963-67; dep. for civilian personnel policy and civil rights Office Sec. Army, 1967-70; chief program div. Fed. Labor Relations Council, Exec. Office Pres., 1970-71, dep. exec. dir., 1971-72, exec. dir., 1973-78; mem. Fed. Labor Relations Authority, Washington, 1979-81; chmn. Employee Relations Commn., U.S. Fgn. Service, 1979-81. Served with USAF, 1961-62. Recipient W.H. Kushnick award Sec. Army, 1968, Exceptional Civilian Service award, 1970, spl. commendation award Dir. OMB, 1978. Am. Bar Assn.; Mem. Soc. Fed. Labor Relations Profs., Soc. Profs. in Dispute Resolution, Jefferson Soc., Indsl. Relations Research Assn., SAR, U. Va. Alumni Assn. (nat. v.p. 1984—), Order of Coif, Phi Beta Kappa, Phi Eta Sigma, Phi Kappa Psi. Unitarian. Home: 1605 Stonebridge Rd Alexandria VA 22304 Office: Fed Labor Relations Authority 500 C St SW Washington DC 20424 *

FRAZIER, HOWARD STANLEY, physician; b. Oak Park, Ill., Jan. 16, 1926; s. Cecil Austin and Harriet DeGolyer (Greenleaf) F.; m. Lenore Callahan, June 10, 1950; children—Mark C., Reid J., Anne K., Peter B. Ph.B., U. Chgo., 1949; M.D., Harvard U., 1953. Intern, then resident in medicine Mass. Gen. Hosp., Boston, 1953-55; postdoctoral fellow Harvard U. Med. Sch., 1955-56, Cambridge U., 1956-57, Case Western Res. U. Med. Sch., 1957-58; mem. faculty Harvard U. Med. Sch., 1958—, prof. medicine, 1978—, dir. center analysis health practices, 1975—; cons. NIH, Nat. Center Health Care Tech. Author papers in field. Served with USNR, 1943-46. Mem. Am. Soc. Clin. Investigation, Am. Physiol. Soc., Am. Soc. Nephrology, Inst. Medicine. Office: 677 Huntington Ave Boston MA 02115

FRAZIER, JOE, retired prize fighter; b. Beaufort, S.C., Jan. 17, 1944; s. Rubin and Dolly F.; m. Florence Frazier; children: Marvis, Weatta, Jo-Netta, Natasha, Jacquelyn. Prize fighter, from 1958, profl., 1965-76, 81, heavyweight champion, N.Y., Mass., Ill., Maine, 1968, World Boxing Assn. heavyweight champion, 1970-73; winner fight with Muhammad Ali, 1971; former mem. rock-blues group Knockouts and Joe Frazier's Review; owner, mgr., trainer Joe Frazier's Gymnasium, Phila., 1974—; owner, pres. Joe Frazier & Sons Limousine Service, Phila., 1974—. Recipient Olympic gold medal, 1964. Baptist. Heavyweight champion N.Y., Mass., Ill., Maine, 1968; World Boxing Assn. heavyweight champion, 1970-73; winner fight with Muhammad Ali, 1971. Address: Joe Frazier's Gym 2917 N Broad St Philadelphia PA 19132 *

FRAZIER, JOHN EARL, chemical engineer; b. Houseville, Pa., July 4, 1902; s. Chauncey E. and Mary Ellen (Gibson) F.; m. Frances Sprague Lang, June 23, 1936; children—John Earl II, Thomas Gibson. B.S., Washington and Jefferson Coll., 1922, achievement citation award, 1953; postgrad. chem. engring. practice, MIT, 1922-24, S.M., 1924; Sc.D., U. Brazil, 1938. Chemist and engr. Berney Bond Glass Co. (now Owens-Ill. Inc.), 1924-26; fuel engr. Simplex Engring. Co., 1926-28, asst. sec., asst. treas., 1928-30, sec., treas., 1930-38; v.p., treas. Frazier-Simplex, Inc., 1938-45, pres., sec., 1945-67, pres., treas., 1967—; mem. adv. bd. Pitts. Nat. Bank (Washington County br.); past pres., dir. Washington Union Trust Co., Washington County Motor Club.; Past pres. adv. bd. dept. ceramic engring. U. Ill. Author: Kilns for, Nat. Ency.; co-author: also other papers for trade and sci. publs. Glass Industry for Venezuela. Past pres. bd. trustees Western State Sch. and Hosp., Canonsburg; trustee, sec., treas. Washington Hosp. (chmn. property com.); life trustee, v.p., asst. sec. bd. Washington and Jefferson Coll.; past chmn. Glass Industry Bd. (Phoenix Com.); past pres. Ceramic Camera Club; past chmn. Pa. Economy League (Washington County br.); past pres. Washington (Pa.) C. of C., Nat. Soc. Am. Comp. Shooters. Recipient Distinguished Citizen award Washington (Pa.) City Council, 1960; named Kappa Sigma Frat. Man of Year, 1964; named to Bus. and Profl. Hall of Fame, 1966. Fellow Royal Soc. Arts Eng. (Benjamin Franklin fellow), Am. Inst. Chemists, AAAS, Am. Ceramic Soc. (Albert V. Bleininger Meml. award 1969, John Jeppson award 1976, v.p. 1967-68, treas. 1968-69, pres. 1970-71, hon. life mem. 1978, chmn. Orton Meml. lecture com. 1968), Nat. Acad. Engring. U.S.A. (life), Intercontinental Biog. Assn. (life), Soc. Glass Tech. of Eng.; mem. Pa. Ceramic Assn. (past pres., dir.), Ind. Heating Equipment Assn. Washington (past dir.), Am. Chem. Soc., Am. Soc. Mil. Engrs., Nat. Soc. Profl. Engrs., Am. Soc. Heating, Refrigeration and Air-Conditioning Engrs., ASTM, Nat. Inst. Ceramic Engrs. (PACE award judge 1962), Pa. Soc. of N.Y.C., Nat. Rifle Assn. of Am., Pictorial Photographers Am., Royal Photog. Soc. of Eng., Photog. Soc. Am., Am. Legion, Pa. Atomic Scientists, N.Y. Acad. Scis., Pa. Acad. Sci., Keramos (Greaves-Walker roll of honor), Phi Beta Kappa, Sigma Xi, Phi Chi Mu, Kappa Sigma. Republican. Presbyterian. Clubs: Mass. Inst. Tech. of Western Pa., also N.Y., Inc.; Druids, Univ. (Pitts.); Chemists (N.Y.C.); Varsity Letermen of Washington and Jefferson Coll.; Fortnightly (Washington, Pa.); Masons, Shriners, Lions (Lion of Year 1970), Elks.). Frazier-Keramos Library at Pa. State U. named in his honor. Home: 36 Morgan Ave Washington PA 15301 Office: 436 E Beau St PO Box 493 Washington PA 15301

FRAZIER, JOHN WARREN, civil engineer; b. Columbus, Ohio, May 20, 1913; s. Forrest Faye and Maybelle E. (Warren) F.; m. Edna E. Johnson, May 25, 1935; 1 dau., Mary Faye Frazier Bradley. B.S. in Civil Engring, Kans. State U., 1935. With Kans. Hwy. Commn., 1935-46; cons. engr. Finney & Turpinseed, Topeka, 1946—, mng. partner, 1968-83. Mem. Kans. State Bd. Edn., 1969-79, chmn., 1971-77, vice chmn., 1977-79; alumni rep. Kans. State U. Athletic Council, 1961—; mem. Kans. Master Planning Commn. (edn.), 1971-72, Edn. Commn. of States, 1972-79, Nat. Assn. State Bds. Edn., Bd. Examiners and Appeals, Topeka, 1967-77, Bd. Bldg. and Fire Appeals, Topeka, 1977—; trustee Kans. State U. Found., 1961—. Recipient Nat. Civil Govt. award, 1974, Edmund Friedman Profl. Engring. award ASCE, 1975, Citizenship award Kans. Engring. Soc., 1981, Disting. Service award Kans. State U. Coll. Engring., 1983. Fellow ASCE (dist. dir. 1968-70, v.p 1971-73); mem. Kans. State U. Alumni Assn. (pres. 1961-62), Topeka C. of C., C. of C. U.S., Kans. Assn. Commerce and Industry, Chi Epsilon (hon.). Home: 1646 Knollwood Dr Topeka KS 66611 Office: 603 Topeka Ave Topeka KS 66603 *Be diligent, honest and forthright. Do not hesitate to express an honest opinion, even though it might not appear to be popular. Develop a reputation of integrity and the ability to complete an assignment in a concise and efficient manner. Don't push for opportunities, but prepare for opportunities that might exist in the future. If you are prepared, have a reputation for doing your utmost on each assignment; if you have been fair and abided by high moral and ethical standards, many opportunities are in your future.*

FRAZIER, KENDRICK CROSBY, writer, editor; b. Windsor, Colo., Mar. 19, 1942; s. Francis Elliott and Sidney Lenore (Crosby) F.; m. Ruth Toelle, Sept. 10, 1964; children—Christopher, Michele. B.A. in Journalism, U. Colo., 1964; M.S., Columbia U., 1966. Reporter Greeley (Colo.) Daily Tribune, 1962; news editor Golden (Colo.) Transcript, 1963-64; newman Denver bur. UPI, 1964-65; editor News Report, Nat. Acad. Scis., Washington, 1966-69; earth scis. editor Sci. News mag., Washington, 1969-70, mng. editor, 1970-71, editor, 1971-77, contbg. editor, 1977-82; sci. writer Sandia Nat. Labs., Albuquerque, 1983—; editor The Skeptical Inquirer, 1977—; freelance sci. writer, 1977—; adj. instr. U. Mo. Sch. Journalism, 1975-77; guest lectr. George Washington U., 1974-77; mem. com. pub. affairs Am. Geophys. Union, 1976-78. Author: The Violent Face of Nature, 1979, Our Turbulent Sun, 1982; also numerous articles on sci. topics; editor: Paranormal Borderlands of Science, 1981. Boettcher Found. scholar, 1960-64; Pulitzer traveling fellow, 1966; Robert E. Sherwood scholar, 1966. Mem. Nat. Assn. Sci. Writers, Com. for Sci. Investigation of Claims of the Paranormal (editor 1977—, exec. council 1977—, dir. 1978—), Am. Astron. Soc. (hist. astronomy div.), Am. Polar Soc., Soc. South Pole, Planetary Soc., Soc. Profl. Journalists. Home: 3025 Palo Alto Dr NE Albuquerque NM 87111

FRAZIER, LEROY *See* **DYYON, FRAZIER**

FRAZIER, ROBERT G., assn. exec.; b. Oak Park, Ill., Apr. 16, 1923; s. Cecil Austin and Harriet (Greenleaf) F.; m. Ruth Ann Johnson, Nov. 25, 1950; children—Stephen, Thomas, Carolyn. Ph.B., U. Chgo., 1943; B.S., 1945; M.D., 1947. Intern Grace-New Haven Community Hosp., 1947-48; resident pediatrics U. Chgo. Clinics, 1948-50; instr. pediatrics U. Colo. Med. Sch., 1950-52; asst. prof. pediatrics State U. Iowa Med. Sch., 1954-58; sec. Am. Acad. Pediatrics, 1958-67, exec. dir., 1967-80; sr. asso. dean Stritch Sch. Medicine, Loyola U., Chgo., 1980—. Served to 1st lt. M.C. AUS, AUS, 1952-54. Home: 1226 Ashland Wilmette IL 60091 Office: 2160 S First Ave Maywood IL 60153

FRAZIER, SHERVERT HUGHES, JR., psychiatrist, educator; b. Shreveport, La., June 12, 1921; s. Shervert Hughes and Mary (Lowman) F.; m. Gloria Barger, July 20, 1947; children: Elise, Alan, Rosalie, Stephen. Student, Baylor U., 1936-39; B.S., U. Ill., Chgo., 1941, M.D., 1943; M.S. in Psychiatry, U. Minn., 1957; cert. psychoanalytic medicine, Columbia Coll. Physicians and Surgeons, 1963; M.A. (hon.), Harvard U., 1972. Diplomate: Am. Bd. Psychiatry and Neurology (dir. 1965, pres. 1972), Am. Bd. Family Practice (by-laws com. 1979-80, exam. com. 1979—, research and devel. com. 1979-80, chmn. patient mgmt. problem panel). Intern U. Ill. Research and Ednl. Hosp., 1943-44; fellow internal medicine Mayo Found., 1951-52, fellow psychiatry, asst. to staff, 1954-56; pvt. practice, Harrisburg, Ill., 1946-50, 53; adminstr. Harrisburg Med. Found., 1948-51; cons. sect. psychiatry Mayo Clinic, St. Marys Hosp., also Meth. Hosp., Rochester, Minn., 1956-58; chief research scientist internal medicine N.Y. State Psychiat. Inst., 1958-61, dep. dir., 1968-72; asst. attending psychiatrist Presbyn. Hosp., N.Y.C., 1958-63; dir. inpatient cons. service in psychiatry, 1961-62; later attending psychiatrist; dir. Houston Psychiat. Inst., 1962-65; psychiatrist in chief Ben Taub Gen. Hosp., Houston, 1962-68; cons. VA Hosp., Houston, 1962-68; sr. attending psychiatrist Meth. Hosp., Houston, 1962-68; psychiatrist-in-chief McLean Hosp., Belmont, Mass., 1972—; asso. in psychiatry Columbia Coll. Phys. and Surg., Joske asst. prof. psychiatry, 1958-62, prof., 1968-72; prof. psychiatry, chmn. dept. Baylor U. Coll. Medicine, 1962-68; prof. psychiatry Harvard, Boston, 1972—; cons. Rice U., 1963-68; commr. Mental Health and Mental Retardation for Tex., 1965-67; pres. VI World Congress Psychiatry; mem. vis. com. Yale U. Med. Sch., 1977-81. Contbr. numerous articles to profl. jours. Served as officer, M.C. USNR, 1944-46; PTO. Recipient disting. alumnus award Mayo Found., 1983. Fellow N.Y. Acad. Medicine (chmn. Salmon lecture com.); mem. AMA (council continuing physician edn. 1976-81), Mass. Med. Assn., Middlesex County Med. Soc., Am. Coll. Psychiatrists (regent 1972, v.p. 1977-79, pres. 1979-81), Am. Psychiat. Assn. (chmn. program com. 1965-68, chmn. joint commn. pub. affairs, sec. 1983—), World Psychiat. Assn. (v.p. 1977—), Central Neuropsychiat. Assn., Assn. Research Nervous and Mental Disease (pres. 1972, chmn. bd. 1976-78), Boston Psychoanalytic Soc. and Inst., Sigma Xi, Alpha Omega Alpha. Home: 115 Mill St Belmont MA 02178 Office: McLean Hosp Belmont MA 02178

FRAZIER, WARNER CARLISLE, manufacturing company executive; b. Harrisburg, Pa., Apr. 4, 1932; s. Ledwin Carlisle and Kathryn (Maeder) F.; m. Dorothy Delores Dickinson, Nov. 28, 1953; children: Barbara, Christopher. B.S. in Marine Engring., U. S. Mcht. Marine Acad., 1955; postgrad. in Bus. Adminstrn., U. Wis.-Milw., 1958, Loyola U., Chgo., 1968-69. Cert. 3d asst. engr. With Allis-Chalmers Corp., Milw., 1957-76; v.p. mktg. Simplicity Mfg. Co. div. Allis-Chalmers Corp., Port Washington, Wis., 1976-80; pres. Simplicity Mfg. Co., 1980-83, pres., chief exec. officer, 1983—; bd. dirs. Outdoor Power Equipment Inst., Washington, 1981—. Club: Rotary. Home: 1815 Woodbury Ln Milwaukee WI 53209 Office: Simplicity Mfg Inc 500 N Spring St Port Washigton WI 53074

FRAZZA, GEORGE S., lawyer, business executive; b. Paterson, N.J., Jan. 21, 1934; s. Paul T. and Myrtle Mary (Van Riper) F.; m. Marie Pollara, Sept. 17, 1955; children: Caren, Janine, Leslie, Lauren. A.B., Marietta Coll., 1955; LL.B., Columbia U., 1958. Bar: N.Y. 1959. Atty. Rogers & Wells, N.Y.C., 1958-66, Johnson & Johnson, New Brunswick, N.J., 1966, assoc. gen. counsel, 1973, corp. sec., 1975; gen. counsel, 1978—. Bd. dirs. N.J. Ballet, Morristown, 1983—. Mem. Assn. Gen. Counsel, ABA, N.Y. State Bar. Club: Roxitious. Home: Oak Knoll Rd Mendham NJ 07945 Office: 1 Johnson and Johnson Plaza New Brunswick NJ 08903

FREAS, FRANK KELLY, illustrator; b. Hornell, N.Y., Aug. 27, 1922; s. Francis Matthew and Miriam Eudora (Sylvester) K.; m. Pauline H. Bussard, Mar. 26, 1952; children—Jacqueline Deborah, Jeremy Patrick. Grad., Pitts. Art Inst., 1951. V.p. Environ. Assos., Inc., Virginia Beach, Va., 1974—; lectr., cons. colls., art schs. Free-lance illustrator book and mag. cover artist, 1950—; art dir., cons. publishers, 1952—; cover artist: Mad mag, 1955-62, Religious Art Franciscans, 1958-76; designer space posters, Smithsonian Instn., 1971, Skylab I insignia, 1974; NASA artist, 1975; pub.: Astounding Fifties, 1971, Six-to-go, 1971, Science Fiction Art Print Portfolios, 1972-79; author: Frank Kelly Freas: The Art of Science Fiction, 1977; editor, illustrator: Starblaze Editions, 1978-79; one-man show, Chrysler Mus. at Norfolk, 1977, 82, NASA, Langley, Va., 1979, GOH Spacecon 10th anniversary, GOH Baycon, 1983, GOH Moscon, retrospective exhbn., Am. Mus. Natural History, N.Y.C., 1974. Bd. govs. Internat. Star Found., Vienna, Va., 1981—. Served with USAAF, 1941-46. Recipient Hugo Achievement award World Sci. Fiction Soc., 1955, 56, 58, 59, 70, 72-76; Frank R. Paul award, 1977; Ink Pot award, 1979; Skylark award New Eng. Sci. Fiction Assn., 1981; ROVA award, 1981; Lensman award, 1982; Phoenix award, 1982; named Dean Sci. Fiction Artists, 1972; Am. Art guest Eurocon IV, Brussels, 1978; guest of honor Aggiecon Tex. A&M U., 1980, World Sci. Fiction Conv., Chgo., 1982. Mem. Sci. Fiction Writers Assn., So. Fandom Confedn., Assn. Sci. Fiction Artists. (pres. 1982, 83). Club: Masons (32 deg.). Address: 4216 Blackwater Rd Virginia Beach VA 23457

FREBERG, CARL ROGER, mechanical engineering educator; b. Hector, Minn., Mar. 17, 1916; s. Charles and Bertha (Boock) F.; m. Virginia Clawson, June 11, 1941; children: Charles Alan, Barbara Ann. B.Mech. Engring., U. Minn., 1938, M.S. in Mech. Engring, 1940; Ph.D., Purdue U., 1943. Draftsman Cereal Engring. and Constrn. Co., 1939; instr. machine design U. Minn., 1939-40; instr. mech. engring., then asst. prof. mech. and aero. engring. Purdue U., 1940-45; research engr. Carrier Corp., 1945-46; head engring. div. So. Research Inst., 1946-49; dir. equipment research U.S. Naval Civil Engring. Lab., 1949-52; asso. dir. Borg-Warner Research Center, 1952-57; prof., head mech. and aerospace engring. U. So. Calif., 1957-66, prof. mech. engring., 1966—. Author: Elements of Mechanical Vibrations, 2d edit, 1949, Aircraft Vibration and Flutter, 1944. Mem. ASME, Am. Soc. Engring. Edn., AAUP, Sigma Xi, Tau Beta Pi, Pi Tau Sigma. Home: 846 S Hudson Ave Los Angeles CA 90005

FRECCERO, JOHN, Italian language educator; b. N.Y.C., July 25, 1931; m., 1955; 3 children. A.B., Johns Hopkins U., 1952, M.A., 1953, Ph.D. in Italian, 1958. Instr. Italian Johns Hopkins U., 1959-59, asst. prof., 1959-61, assoc. prof., 1961-63; with Cornell U., 1963-69, prof., 1966-69; mem. faculty Yale U., 1969-79; Rosina Pierotti prof. of Italian lit. Stanford U., 1979—, chmn. dept. comparative lit., 1982—, dir. Italian program dept. French and Italian. Contbr. articles to profl. jours. Fulbright research scholar Florence, Italy, 1961-62; Florence fellow Harvard Ctr. Renaissance Cult, 1961-62. Mem. MLA, Am. Assn. Tchrs. Italian. Office: Dept French and Italian Stanford U Stanford CA 94305 *

FRECHE, GERHARD MARTIN, communications company executive; b. Kansas City, Mo., July 13, 1931; s. Martin and Anna Margarete (Naumann) F.; m. Norma Jean Ellis, June 16, 1951; children: Mark Alan, Steven Martin. B.B.A., Valparaiso (Ind.) U., 1955. With Ill. Bell Telephone Co., Chgo., 1955-65, 68-77, v.p. suburban ops., 1975-77; with ops. planning div. AT&T Co., 1965-68; v.p. ops., then exec. v.p. Northwestern Bell Telephone Co., Omaha, 1977-79; also dir.; v.p. Western Electric Co., N.Y.C., 1979-80, exec. v.p., 1980-82; pres. New Eng. Tel. & Tel., Boston, 1982—; dir. Equitable of Iowa Cos., 1st Nat. Bank of Boston, Bank of Boston Corp. Bd. dirs. Valparaiso U., Mass. Bus. Roundtable, United Way of Massachusetts Bay, Freedom Trail Found. Inc.; trustee Mass. Eye and Ear Infirmary, Boston; mem. corp. Babson Coll.; mem. adv. bd. Jr. Achievement of Eastern Mass. Mem. N.J. C. of C., N.J. Bus. and Industry Assn., Morris County C. of C., Chgo. Econ. Club. Club: Roxiticus Country. Home: 158 Farm St Dover MA 02030 Office: 185 Franklin St Boston MA 02107

FRECHETTE, MYLES R., ambassador; b. Santiago, Chile, Apr. 25, 1936. B.S., U. B.C., 1958; M.A. in Latin Am. Studies, UCLA, 1972. Merchandising trainee J.C. Penney Co., 1958-59; procedures analyst Boeing Co., 1960-62; internat. relations officer Office of Coordinator of Cuban Affairs Dept. State, 1963-65, consular officer, San Pedro Sula, 1965-67, polit. and econ. officer, Ft. Lamy, 1968-69; Peru desk officer Dept State, 1971-74; chief of polit. sect. Dept. State, Rio de Janeiro, 1974-76, counselor polit. affairs, Caracas, Venezuela, 1976-79; dir. Cuban Affairs Bur. Inter-Am. Affairs, Dept. State, Washington, 1979-82, spl. projects officers, 1982-83; U.S. ambassador to United Republic of Cameroon, Yaunde, 1983—. Office: US Embassy Rue Nachtigal Yaunde Cameroon *

FRECHETTE, PETER LOREN, dental products executive; b. Janesville, Wis., Aug. 15, 1937; s. Francis Michael and Gladys Jean F.; m. Patricia Jean O'Brien, June 24, 1961; children: Kathleen and Kristen (twins). B.S. in Econs., U. Wis., 1960; M.B.A., Northwestern U., 1980. With Sci. Products, 1963-82, v.p. sales, McGaw Park, Ill., 1972-74, v.p. sales/ops., 1974-75, pres., 1975-82, Patterson Dental Co., Mpls., 1982—; dir. Metatech, Inc. Served with U.S. Army, 1961-63. Mem. Am. Dental Trade Assn., Sigma Chi. Office: 1100 E 80th St Minneapolis MN 55420

FRECHETTE, VAN DERCK, ceramic engineer; b. Ottawa, Ont., Can., Jan. 5, 1916; s. Howells and Lena D. (Derick) F.; m. Sarah W. Houghton, Apr. 4, 1940; children: William G.H., Howells Van Derck, Christopher J., Margaret Kathleen, Judith L. Student, U. Toronto, 1934-36; B.S., Alfred U., 1939; M.S., U. Ill., 1940, Ph.D., 1942. Registered profl. engr., N.Y. Research physicist Corning Glass Works, N.Y., 1942-44; prof. ceramic sci. State U. N.Y. Coll. Ceramics, Alfred U., 1944—; guest prof. U. Göttingen, Germany, 1955-56, Max Planck Inst., 1965-66, U. Erlangen-Nurnberg, 1973; cons. on fractology, ceramic problems and microscopy. Pres. Alfred Delta Sig Corp., 1971-76. Author: Microscopy of Ceramics, 1955; Editor: Noncrystalline Solids, 1960, Kinetics of Reactions in Ionic Systems, 1970, Surfaces and Interfaces of Glass and Ceramics, 1974, Ceramic Engineering and Science-Emerging Priorities, 1974, Borate Glasses, 1977, Quality Assurance in Ceramic Industries, 1979, Applied Mineralogy Series, 1971-80. Recipient Gordon Research Conf. award, 1955, Western Elec. award, 1969; named Outstanding Educator Ceramic Ednl. Council, 1983; Fulbright fellow, 1955. Fellow Am. Ceramic Soc.; mem. Swedish Royal Acad. Scis., Sigma Xi, Delta Sigma Phi, Phi Kappa Phi. Home: 22 S Main St Alfred NY 14802

FREDERICK, DOYLE GRIMES, geological survey administrator; b. Holcut, Miss., Nov. 22, 1935; s. Bolivar Herman and Attie Lou (Grimes) F.; m. Betty Lois Todd, June 7, 1957; children: Michael Dale, Jeffrey Glen. Student, N.E. Miss. Jr. Coll., Booneville; B.S., Bethel Coll., McKenzie, Tenn.; postgrad., U. Cin. Tech. mgr. geodesy and geophysics group Def. Intelligence Agy., Washington, 1965-70; phys. sci. adminsr. Def. Mapping Agy., Washington, 1972-73; chief office Plans and Program Devel. Topographic div. U.S. Geol. Survey, Reston, Va., 1973-79, assoc. chief nat. mapping div., 1980, acting assoc. dir., 1980—; co-chmn. coordinating com., NOAA, 1980—; co-chmn. coordinating com. Bur. Land Mgmt., 1980—; co-chum. coordinating com. Office of Surface Mining, 1980—; mem. fed. mapping task force, Washington, 1971-72. Contbr. articles to profl. jours. Recipient outstanding performance award Def. Intelligency Agy., 1967-70, quality increase award Def. Intelligence Agy., 1967-70, outstanding performance award Def. Mapping Agy., 1972, 73, meritorious service award Dept. Def., 1973, Dept. Interior, 1976, meritorious bonus award, 1980, 81, 82, outstanding performance award U.S. Geol. Survery, 1979. Mem. Am. Congress on Surveying and Mapping. Baptist. Office: US Geological Survey National Center MS 102 12201 Sunrise Valley Dr Reston VA 22092

FREDERICK, EARL JAMES, hospital administrator; b. Canton, Ohio, May 25, 1927; s. Earl Jacob and Mary Elizabeth (Killin) F.; m. Arden Ann Hill, June 14, 1953; children: Charlotte Elizabeth, Robert Winston. B.I.E., Ohio State U., 1951, M.Sc. in Indsl. Engring, 1951. Dir. methods Cleve. Clinic Found., 1951-56; asso. Cresap, McCormick & Paget Inc., N.Y.C., 1956-64, prin., 1964-66, partner, 1966-68, v.p., 1968-74, dir. health services, 1970-74; pres. Children's Meml. Hosp., Chgo., 1974—, bd. dirs., 1974—; trustee McGaw Med. Center of Northwestern U., 1974—; bd. dirs. Hosp. Bur., Inc., 1975-82, Health Care Service Corp., 1980—. Bd. trustees Hastings-on-Hudson (N.Y.) Bd. Edn., 1963-68, pres., 1967; trustee Masters Sch., Dobbs Ferry, N.Y., 1975-81; bd. dirs. Sudden Infant Death Syndrome, 1981—. Served with USNR, 1945-46. Mem. Am. Hosp. Assn., Am. Public Health Assn., Assn. Am. Med. Colls., Ill. Hosp. Assn. (trustee), Am. Inst. Indsl. Engrs., Nat. Assn. Childrens Hosps. and Related Instns. (trustee 1977-81), Council Teaching Hosps. (adminstrv. bd. 1971—, chmn. 1983). Episcopalian. Clubs: Indian Hill, Ardsley Curling.; Commercial (Chgo.). Home: 1222 Chestnut Ave Wilmette IL 60091 Office: 2300 Children's Plaza Chicago IL 60614

FREDERICK, EDWARD CHARLES, university official; b. Mankato, Minn., Nov. 17, 1930; s. William H. and Wanda (MacNamara) F.; m. Shirley Lunkenheimer, Aug. 16, 1951; children: Bonita Frederick Treangen, Diane Frederick Labs, Donald, Kenneth, Karen Frederick Swenson. B.S. in Agrl. Edn, U. Minn., 1954, M.S. in Dairy Husbandry, 1955, Ph.D. in Anatomy and Physiology, 1957. Animal scientist, instr. N.W. Sch. and Expt. Sta. U. Minn., Crookston, 1958-64, supt., Waseca, 1964-69, provost, 1969—; Mem. Tech. Agrl. Edn. Study Team to Morocco, 1977. Contbr. articles on dairy physiology, mgmt., agrl. edn. and adminstrn. to tech. jours. and popular publs. Bd. dirs. Bob Hodgson Student Loan Fund, 1971—, Minn. Agrl. Interpretive Center, 1978—. Recipient Alumni award 4-H, 1972. Mem. Am. Dairy Assn., Am. Soc. Animal Prodn., AAAS, Nat. Assn. Colls. and Tchrs. Agr. (pres. 1976-77), Am. Assn. Community and Jr. Colls., South Central Edn. Assn. (Disting. Service award 1971), Waseca Area C. of C. (dir. 1979), Phi Kappa Phi. Roman Catholic. Club: Foresters. Lodges: Rotary (gov. dist. 596 1982-83); K.C. Home: Route 4 Box 32A Waseca MN 56093 Office: U Minn Tech Coll Waseca MN 56093

FREDERICK, JOSEPH FRANCIS, JR., hotel exec.; b. Luzerne, Pa., July 13, 1933; s. Joseph Francis and Emma (Sabatini) F.; m. Joanne Agnes Pollock, July 23, 1955; children—Joelle Ann, Joseph Francis, III. B.S., Pa. State U., 1956. Exec. trainee Waldorf-Astoria Hotel, N.Y.C., 1956-57, asst. front office mgr., 1962-63; service mgr. Statler Hilton, N.Y.C., 1963-65; dir. sales Hartford (Conn.) Hilton, 1965-68; resident mgr. Dallas Statler Hilton, 1968-69; gen. mgr. Hartford Hilton, 1969, Netherland Hilton, Terrace Hilton hotels, Cin., 1969-74, Washington Statler-Hilton Hotel, 1974-76, New Orleans Hilton, 1976—; Bd. dirs. Conv. and Visitors Bur., New Orleans; mem. exec. bd. Greater New Orleans Tourist Conv. Commn.; mem. New Orleans Pvt. Industry Council. Mem. citizens com. Internat. Assn. Chiefs of Police; mem. alumni bd. Coll. Human Devel., Pa. State U.; mem. Mayor's Task Force, City of New Orleans. Served with USAF, 1957-62. Mem. New Orleans Hotel and Motel Assn. (pres.), Pa. State U. Alumni Assn., Sigma Pi Eta, Sigma Pi. Address: New Orleans Hilton Hotel 2 Poydras St New Orleans LA 70140

FREDERICK, LAFAYETTE, botanist; b. Friarspoint, Miss., Mar. 19, 1923; s. James Davis and Ellen Marie (Johnson) F.; m. Antoinette Arlene Reed, Dec. 24, 1950; children: Lewis Reed, Karla Mae, David Warren. B.S., Tuskegee Inst., 1943; postgrad., U. Hawaii, 1946-48; M.S., U. R.I., 1950; Ph.D., Wash. State U., 1952; postgrad., U. Ill., 1960-61, U. Mich. Biology Field Sta., 1961. Archtl. draftsman U.S. Navy, 1946-48; assoc. prof. biology So. U., Baton Rouge, 1952-56, prof., 1956-62; prof., chmn. dept. biology Atlanta U., 1962-76; prof. botany, chmn. dept. Howard U., Washington, 1976—; dir. summer and acad. yr. sci. insts. NSF, 1964-73; mem. gen. research support adv. com. NIH, 1972-76, chmn., 1975-76; mem. biology achievement test com. Ednl. Testing Service, 1971-77, chmn., 1973-77; mem. Commn. on Undergrad. Edn. in Biol. Scis. Contbr. articles to profl. jours. Served with USN, 1944-46. NSF sci. faculty fellow U. Ill., 1960-61; recipient Excellence in Teaching award Atlanta U. Bd Trustees, 1964, Disting. Alumnus Tuskegee Inst., 1981. Fellow Ga. Acad. Sci.; mem. Bot. Soc. Am., AAAS, Am. Inst. Biol. Scis., Am. Soc. Plant Taxonomists, Brit. Mycol. Soc., Mycol. Soc. Am., Am. Phytopathol. Soc., Electron Microscope Soc., Assn. Southeastern Biologists, So. Appalachian Bot. Club, Ga. Conservancy, Tuskegee Nat. Alumni Assn. (pres. 1982), Sigma Xi, Phi Kappa Phi, Phi Sigma, Beta Beta Beta. Presbyterian. Office: Dept Botany Howard U Washington DC 20059

FREDERICK, PAULINE, broadcast news analyst; b. Gallitzin, Pa.; d. Matthew Phillip and Susan (Stanley) F.; m. Charles Robbins. A.B., Am. U., Washington, also A.M.; numerous hon. degrees. State Dept. corr. U.S. Daily; radio editorial asst. H.R. Baukhage, Blue Network and ABC; free-lance Western Newspaper Union, N.Am. Newspaper Alliance; also news commentator ABC, 1946-53; news corr. NBC, 1953-74; also UN corr. ABC, NBC; radio anchor Dem. and Rep. Convs. NBC, 1956; internat. affairs analyst Nat. Public Radio; moderator 2d debate Pres. Ford-Gov. Carter, Oct. 6, 1976. Bd. dirs. Am. U., Save the Children, UN Assn. U.S.A. Recipient Headliner award Theta Sigma Phi, Alfred I duPont award, George Foster Peabody award for contbn. to internat. understanding, Golden Mike award for outstanding woman in radio-TV McCall's; Paul White award for contbn. to broadcast journalism Radio and TV News Dirs. Assn.; voted radio's woman of the year Radio-TV Daily poll; U. Mo. Sch. Journalism medal; spl. citation for UN coverage Nat. Fedn. Women's Clubs; East-West Center award; Journalism Achievment award U. So. Calif.; 1st Pa. Journalism Achievment award; Carr Van Anda award Ohio U. Sch. Journalism; named to N.Y. Profl. Journalists Soc. Hall of Fame. Fellow Soc. Profl. Journalists; mem. UN Corrs. Assn. (pres.), Assn. Radio and Television Analysts, Council on Fgn. Relations.

FREDERICK, ROBERT RICE, electronics company executive; b. Elkhart, Ind., Jan. 12, 1926; s. Vard Welligton and Beryl Catherine (Rice) F.; m. Carolyn Nancy Smith, Mar. 5, 1949; children: Sara Henesey, Jane Rodas. A.B., DePauw U., 1948. With Gen. Electric Co., Fairfield, Conn., 1948-82, v.p. Home Laundry div., 1970-73, v.p., group exec. consumer group, 1973-77, sr. v.p. corp. strategic planning, 1977-79, exec. v.p. internat. sector, 1979-82; pres. RCA Corp., N.Y.C., 1982—. Office: RCA Corp 30 Rockefeller Plaza New York NY 10020

FREDERICK, STANLEY, cosmetic co. exec.; b. Bklyn., Jan. 20, 1929; s. Albert and Bertha (Kaplan) F.; m. Shirley Radzivill, Oct. 20, 1957; children—Debra Beth, Robin Gail, Steven Michael. B.A., N.Y. U., 1951, J.D., 1954, LL.M., 1960. Bar: N.Y. bar 1956. Asso. Gelfand & Shedler, N.Y.C., 1956-58; atty. Mfrs. Hanover Trust Co., N.Y.C., 1958-64, Faberge, Inc., 1964-72, corporate counsel, 1971—, asst. sec., 1971-72, corporate v.p., 1972-75, exec. v.p., 1975—, also dir. Served in U.S. Army, 1954-56. Mem. Cosmetics Toiletries and Fragrances Assn. (dir.), Am., N.Y. State bar assns., Assn. Bar City N.Y., N.Y. County Lawyers Assn. Clubs: Masons, Seaman's Neck Yacht. Home: 49 Hollywood Dr Plainview NY 11803 Office: 1345 Ave Americas New York NY 10105

FREDERICK, WILLIAM SHERRAD, manufacturing company executive; b. Canton, Ohio, Sept. 5, 1938; s. Paul Criswell and Mary Alice (Bissell) F.; m. Karen Katherine Smith, Oct. 9, 1965; children: Stephen Smith, Michael Sherrad. B.S., Kent State U., 1962; M.B.A., U. Akron, 1968. Accounting mgr. Hoover Co., North Canton, Ohio, 1962-68, controller Knapp Monarch div., St. Louis, 1969-70; controller Juvenile and Recreation Products Cos. (mem. cos. of Brown Group, Inc.), St. Louis, 1971-73, Brown Group, Inc., 1974—. Mem. Fin. Execs. Inst. Home: 13324 Kings Glen Dr St Louis MO 63131 Office: 8400 Maryland Ave Clayton MO 63105

FREDERICKS, CARLTON, nutritionist, researcher, author, educator; b. N.Y.C., Oct. 23, 1910; s. David Charles Caplan and Blanche Goldsmith; m. Betty Shachter, Oct. 26, 1946; children: Alice, April, Dana, Spencer, Rhonda. B.A., U. Ala., 1931; M.A., NYU, 1949, Ph.D., 1955. Dir. edn. Casimir Funk Lab., N.Y.C., 1939-44; nat. broadcaster local and network radio, N.Y.C., 1941-83; dir. nutrition services Atkins Med. Ctr., N.Y.C., 1982—; nutrition cons. Dr. Paul Rosch, Yonkers, N.Y., 1983—; vis. prof. edn. Fairleigh Dickinson U., Rutherford, N.J., 1974-82; bd. dirs. Am. Inst. Stress, Yonkers, N.Y., 1982—; founding fellow Internat. Coll. Applied Nutrition, La Habra, Calif., 1955—. Author: Low Blood Sugar and You, 1969 (ABA award 1970), Nutrition Guide, 1982, Program for Living Longer, 1983. Recipient Rachel Carson Found. award, 1982, citations Huxley Inst., N.Y.C., 1980, Internat. Acad. Metabology, Los Angeles, 1980, Disting. Achievement award Fairleigh Dickinson U., 1984. Fellow Internat. Acad. Preventive Medicine (hon. pres.), Internat. Acad. Metabology (hon. pres.), Royal Soc. Health, Price-Pottenger Found., Internat. Acad. Orthomolecular Psychiatry (hon. mem.); mem. Phi Beta Kappa. Home: 5 Patricia Dr New York City NY 10956 Office: Atkins Center for Alternate Therapy 400 E 56th St New York NY 10022 *The therapeutic applications of nutrition are frequently a monument to lost opportunities for prophylaxis. It is for that reason that I have devoted more than forty years to nutrition education of the public via the mass media. It has been my goal to shorten the cultural lag between findings in nutritional science and their acceptance and application by the professions and the public.*

FREDERICKS, JOHN DONNAN, clay products manufacturing company executive, lawyer; b. Los Angeles County, Calif., Sept. 7, 1900; s. John Donnan and Agnes (Blakeley) F.; children: John Donnan (dec.), Mary (Mrs. John W. Downs, Jr.) (dec.), Thomas Anthony (dec.); m. Charlotte Rayner Joyce, Mar. 31, 1934 (dec.). J.D., Stanford U., 1923. Bar: Calif. 1923. Mem. firm Fredericks & Fredericks, Los Angeles, 1923-50; pres. Pacific Clay Products, 1950-65, chmn. bd., chief exec. officer, 1965-70, chmn. bd., dir., 1970-75; former dept. chmn., dir. Fed. Res. Bank San Francisco; past dir. numerous pvt. corps. Served with USN, World War I. Mem. Mchts. and Mfrs. Assn. Los Angeles (past dir.), Los Angeles C. of C. (past dir.), Alpha Delta Phi, Phi Delta Phi. Roman Catholic. Home: 956 Mariposa Ln Santa Barbara CA 93108

FREDERICKS, MARSHALL MAYNARD, sculptor; b. Rock Island, Ill., Jan. 31, 1908; s. Frank A. and Frances Margaret (Bragg) F.; m. Rosalind Bell Cooke, Sept. 9, 1943; children: Carl Marshall and Christopher Matzen (twins), Frances Karen Bell, Rosalind Cooke, Suzanne Pelletreau. Student, John Huntington Poly. Inst., Cleve.; grad., Cleve. Sch. Art, 1930; student, Heimann Schule, Schwegerle Schule, Munich, Germany, Academie Scandinav, Paris, France; pvt. studies, Copenhagen, Rome and London, Carl Milles' Studio, Stockholm, Sweden; student, Cranbrook Acad. Art; 3 hon. doctorate degrees in fine arts. Faculty Cleve. Sch. Art, 1931, Cranbrook Sch., Bloomfield Hills, Mich., 1932-38; Kingswood Sch., Cranbrook, 1932-42, Cranbrook Acad. Art, Bloomfield Hills, Mich., 1932-42; Royal Danish consul. for, Mich. Local, nat., internat. exhbns. art since 1928 include, Carnegie Inst., Pitts., Cleve. Mus., Pa. Acad., Chgo. Art Inst., Whitney Mus. Am. Art Nat. Invitational, Detroit Art Inst., Denver Mus., Phila. Internat. Invitational, N.Y. World's Fair Am. art exhbn., Modern Sculpture Internat. Exhbn. Detroit, Internat. Sculpture Show Cranbrook Mus., A.I.A., Nat. Sculpture Soc., Archtl. League of N.Y., Mich. Acad., Brussels, Belgium, others; commns. include Vets. Meml. Bldg, Detroit, adminstrn. bldg. war meml., U. Mich., Louisville Courier-Jour. Bldg, Jefferson Sch., Wyandotte, Mich., Holy Ghost Sem., Ann Arbor, Mich.; State Dept. Fountain, Washington, Cleve. War Meml. Fountain, Milw. Pub. Mus. Sculpture, N.Y. World's Fair permanent sculpture, Fed. Bldg. sculpture, Cin., Community Nat. Bank, Pontiac, Mich., Sir Winston Churchill Meml., Freeport, Bahamas; union bldg., Freeport, Bahamas; J.L. Hudson's Eastland, Northland, and Flint (Mich.) Mall, Two Sister fountain, Cranbrook, Michigan, Dallas Library sculpture, Henry Ford Meml., Dearborn, Mich., Oakland U., Saints and Sinners Fountain, Midland Center for Arts, Crittenton Hosp., Rochester, Fgn. Ministry Copenhagen, many others; portrait commns. include Willard Dow, Midland, Mich., George G. Booth Meml., Cranbrook, Mrs. Horace Rackham Meml, Pres. John F. Kennedy, Yoshita, others; works included numerous museums, pvt., civic collections. Mem. Pres.'s Com. for Employment of Handicapped; mem. Gov.'s State Capitol Com.; co-founder, dir. DIADEM Program for Internat. Exchange of Handicapped.; Trustee Am.-Scandinavian Found., People-to-People Program, Inc. Served with C.E. U.S. Army, 1942-44; lt. col. 20th bomber command; 8th Air Force, 1944-45; Okinawa. Decorated knight Order of Dannebrog, also officer 1st class, comdr. Order Dannebrog (Denmark); knights cross 1st class Order of St. Olav (Norway); recipient of 1st prize Cleve. Mus. Art, 1931; Anna Scripps Whitcomb prize Detroit Inst. Arts, 1938; 1st prize internat. exhbn. Dance Internat., Rockefeller Center, N.Y.C., Barbour Meml. nat. competition; medal Mich. Inst. Architects; gold medal Achtl. League of N.Y.; Golden Plate award Am. Acad. Achievement; citation Mich. Assn. Professions, Nat. Soc. Interior Designers, Internat. Com. of Internat. Ctr. Disabled, U. Detroit; President's Cabinet award U. Detroit, 1973; other Am. and fgn. awards and decorations. Fellow Internat. Inst. Arts and Letters, Royal Soc. Arts, Nat. Sculpture Soc. (Henry Heriog medal, Herbert Adams Medal, bd. dirs., 1st v.p. Brookgreen Gardens); mem. Mich. Soc. Architects (hon.), Federation Internationale de la Medaille, A.I.A. (fine arts gold medal 1952), St. Dunstans Dramatic Guild, Mich. Acad. Sci., Arts and Letters (gold medal honor 1953), Nat. Acad. Design (academician), C. of C., Am. Soc. Interior Designers, Mich. Assn. Professions, Nat. Soc. Interior Designers, Beta Sigma Phi, Alpha Beta Delta. Clubs: Royal Swedish Yacht, Orchard Lake Country; Architectural League N.Y. (N.Y.C.); Prismatic (Detroit); Royal Norwegian Yacht, Royal Danish Yacht. Home: 440 Lake Park Dr Birmingham MI 48009 Studio: 4113 N Woodward Ave Royal Oak MI 48053 also East Long Lake Road Bloomfield Hills MI 48013 *There are several things concerning sculpture that I believe are extremely important. It must be wholly consistent and in harmony with the architecture involved, as well as being a beautiful entity within itself. It must embody a significance suitable to and expressive of the purpose and setting, and finally it must have aconnstructive meaning for others. I love people, for I have learned through many experiences, both happy and sad, how beautiful and wonderful they can be; therefore, I want more than anything in the world to do sculpture which will have real meaning for other people, many people, and might in some way encourage, inspire, or give them happiness.*

FREDERICKSEN, BURTON BAUM, curator; b. Mitchell, S.D., Aug. 6, 1934; s. George Edward and Delphine Alice (Baum) F.; m. Marianne Willersinn, Sept. 26, 1961; children—Andrea, Luca. B.A., UCLA, 1955, M.A., 1957. Curator J. Paul Getty Mus., Malibu, Calif., 1965-71, chief curator, 1971-73, curator of paintings, 1973—; adj. curator Renaissance and Baroque paintings Los Angeles County Mus. Art, 1969-73. Author: Census of Pre-Nineteenth-Century Italian Paintings in North American Public Collections, 1972, Giovanni di Francesco and the Master of Pratovecchio, 1975. Office: J Paul Getty Museum 17985 Pacific Coast Hwy Malibu CA 90265

FREDERICKSON, ARMAN FREDERICK, minerals co. exec.; b. Winnipeg, Man., Can., May 5, 1918; came to U.S., 1923, naturalized, 1940; s. Albert F. and Ethel M. (Wilton) F.; m. Mary Maxine Stubblefield, Sept. 23, 1943; children—Mary Christene, Clover Diane, Penny Kathlene, Kimberly Mei, Sigrid. B.S. in Mining Engring, U. Wash., 1940; M.S. in Metall. Engring, Mont. Sch. Mines, 1942; Sc.D. in Geology, Mass. Inst. Tech., 1947. Mining engr., chief geologist Cornucopia Gold Mines, Oreg., 1939-40; instr. mineral dressing Mont. Sch. Mines, 1941; research asst. Mass. Inst. Tech., 1942-43; prof. geology Washington U., St. Louis, 1947-55; organizer, supr. geol. research Pan Am. Petroleum Corp., Tulsa, 1955-60; prof. geology, chmn. dept. earth and planetary sci., dir. oceanography U. Pitts., 1960-65; sr. v.p., dir. research, mgr. petroleum prospecting and mineral programs in U.S., Middle East, Africa, Latin Am., 1965-71; pres. Global Survey, 1972—; v.p. Samoco (Panama), Challenger Desert Oil Corp., 1977—; cons. in mining and petroleum exploration, 1971—; v.p. SAMOCO, Del., 1977—, Panama, 1977—; v.p. ops. CHADOIL, 1978—; Organizer, past chmn. clay minerals com. Nat. Acad. Sci.-NRC. Author papers in field. Served with USNR, 1943-45. Fellow Geol. Soc. Am., Mineral Soc. Am.; mem. Am. Inst. Mining, Metall. and Petroleum Engrs., Am. Assn. Petroleum Geologists, Soc. Econ. Geologists, Geochem. Soc. Am., Underwater Soc. Am. Patentee fertilizer, oil and water pollution processes and products; world-wide mining and petroleum exploration; contract negotiator Middle and Far East, Latin Am. and Africa. Address: 425 Uvalde McAllen TX 78501

FREDERICKSON, ARTHUR ALLAN, publishing company executive; b. Grand Island, Nebr., May 30, 1923; s. Edmond Russell and Jeannette (Burlingame) F.; m. Joyce Meredith Walls, June 3, 1949; children: Jeannette Walls, Arthur Allan. Student, Doane Coll., 1940-42. Mng. editor Courier-News Co., Blytheville, Ark., 1950-54; state news copy editor Fla. Pub. Co., Jacksonville, 1954-60, women's news editor, 1960-67, asst. exec. editor, 1967-79, editorial research dir., 1979-83, editorial systems dir., 1983—. Served with USNR, 1942-46; PTO. Mem. Soc. Profl. Journalists (chpt. pres. 1975-76), Fla. Soc. Newspaper Editors. Democrat. Episcopalian. Home: 2918 Princeton Ave Jacksonville FL 32210 Office: Fla Pub Co 1 Riverside Ave Jacksonville FL 32202

FREDERICKSON, EVAN LLOYD, physician, educator; b. Spring Green, Wis., Mar. 1, 1922; s. Edward and Rebecca Lloyd (Jones) F.; m. Ruth Evans Murphey, Sept. 17, 1946; children—Mary Evans, Helen Lloyd, Edward Dent. B.S., U. Wis., 1947, M.D., 1950; M.S., U. Iowa, 1953. Diplomate: Am. Bd. Anesthesiology. Intern Walter Reed Army Hosp., Washington, 1950-51; resident State U. Iowa Hosps., 1951-53; practice medicine, specializing in anesthesiology, Atlanta, 1965—; instr., asst. prof. U. Kans. Med. Sch., 1953-56, prof., 1959-65; asst. prof., then asso. prof. U. Wash. Sch. Medicine, 1956-59; prof., dir. anesthesia research Emory U. Sch. Medicine, Atlanta, 1965—; dir. Computer Dynamics, Inc.; mem. anesthesiology tng. com. NIH, 1969-73; mem. adv. com. FDA, 1971-75. Asso. editor: Surveys of Anesthesiology, 1964-73, Clin. Anesthesia, 1967-70; Contbr. articles to profl. jours. Bd. dirs. Immunologic Cancer Research Fund; trustee Wood Library and Mus., Crawford W. Long Mus. Served with AUS, 1943-46, 50-51. Fellow Am. Coll. Anesthesiologists; mem. Am. Soc. Anesthesiologists, AMA, AAAS, Assn. U. Anesthesiologists, Sigma Xi, Alpha Omega Alpha. Home: 961 Castle Falls Dr NE Atlanta GA 30329

FREDERICKSON, HARRY GRAY, JR., motion picture producer; b. Oklahoma City, July 21, 1937; s. Harry Gray and Dorothy (McBride) F. B.B.A., U. Okla.; postgrad., U. Lausanne, Switzerland. Producer, asso. producer or exec. producer: films including The Good, Bad and the Ugly, 1967, Candy, 1968, An Italian in America, Run for Your Wife, 1966, America, God's Country, Little Fauss and Big Halsey, 1970, Making It, 1971, The Godfather, 1972 (Acad. award), Hit!, 1973, 1974, Godfather II, 1974; co-producer: Apocalypse Now, 1979. Mem. Sigma Chi. Episcopalian. *

FREDERICKSON, HORACE GEORGE, college president; b. Twin Falls, Idaho, July 17, 1934; s. John C. and Zelpha (Richins) F.; m. Mary Williams, Mar. 14, 1958; children—Thomas, Christian, Lynne, David. B.A., Brigham Young U., 1959; M.P.A., UCLA, 1961; Ph.D., U. So. Calif., 1967; LL.D. (hon.), Dongguk U., Korea. Intern Los Angeles County, 1960; research asst. Bur. Govtl. Research, U. Calif., Los Angeles, 1960-61; lectr. pub. adminstrn. U. So. Calif., 1962-64; lectr. govt. and politics U. Md., 1964-66; asst. prof. polit. sci. Maxwell Sch., Syracuse U., 1967-71; asso. dir. Met. Studies Program, 1970-72, asso. prof. polit. sci., 1971-72; fellow in higher edn. fin. adminstrn. U. N.C. System, 1972; chmn. Grad. Program, Sch. Pub. and Environ. Affairs, Ind. U., 1972-74, asso. dean for policy and adminstrv. studies, 1973-74; dean Coll. Pub. and Community Services, prof. regional and community affairs U. Mo., Columbia, 1974-76; pres. Eastern Wash. U., Cheney, 1976—. Author: (with David Mars) Suggested Library in Public Administration: With 1964 Supplement, (with Linda Schluter O'Leary) Power, Public Opinion and Policy in a Metropolitan Community: A Case Study of Syracuse, New York, 1973, (with Yong Hyo Cho) Measuring the Effects of Re-Apportionment in the American States, 1973, Determinants of Public Policy in the American States: A Model for Synthesis, 1973; editor: Neighborhood Control in the 70's, 1973; symposium editor: Pub. Adminstrn. Rev, 1974; research editor, 1970-77, New Public Administration, 1980; mem. editorial bd.: Policy Studies Jour, 1974—; mem. internat. editorial adv. bd.: SAGE Public Administration Abstracts, 1974—; contbr. articles to profl. jours. Haynes Found. fellow U. So. Calif., 1963-64. Mem. Am. Soc. Pub. Adminstrn. (pres.), Nat. Acad. Public Adminstrn., Cheney C. of C. Clubs: Rotary, Spokane, Empire. Home: 627 D St Cheney WA 99004 Office: Pres's Office Eastern Wash U Cheney WA 99004

FREDINE, CLARENCE GORDON, biologist, former government agency offical; b. St. Paul, Aug. 15, 1909; s. Andrew Clarence and Hulda (Anderson) F.; m. Edith Louise Handy, June 7, 1934; children: John Gordon, Patricia Ann Narrowe. B.S. in Biology, Hamline U., 1932; postgrad. in zoology, U. Minn., 1932-35, Purdue U., 1941-43. Assoc. biologist Minn. Emergency Conservation Work, St. Paul, 1935-36; chief biologist game and fish div. Minn. Conservation Dept., 1936-41; asst. prof. dept. forestry and conservation Purdue U., 1941-47; with fish and wildlife service Dept. Interior, 1947-55; prin. biologist Nat. Park Service, 1955-60, park planner mission 66, 1960-62, chief div. extension services, 1962-64, chief div. internat. affairs, 1964-71, staff dir. 2d World Conf. on Nat. Parks, 1972-73, ret. from, 1973, vol. asst. editor Parks Mag., 1975-80; exec. dir. Renewable Natural Resources Found., 1980-81; charter mem. The Wildlife Soc., 1937, exec. sec., 1960-63, hon. mem., 1963. Author govt. bulls., articles. Served to lt. USNR, 1943-46; PTO. Recipient Disting. Service award Dept. Interior, 1967, Conservation award Gulf Oil Corp., 1984. Mem. Am. Fisheries Soc. (Disting. Service award 1983), Washington Biologists Field Club (pres. 1973-76), Soc. Am. Foresters, Am. Land Forum, Nat. Inst. Urban Wildlife, Internat. Assn. Fish and Wildlife Agys., Student Conservation Assn., George Wright Soc. Home: 5921 Anniston Rd Bethesda MD 20817

FREDRICKS, RICHARD, baritone; b. Los Angeles, Aug. 15, 1933; m. Judith Anne Pennebaker, May 6, 1965; children: Shannan Leigh, Stephanie Brooke. Student, El Camino Jr. Coll., 1954-56; pvt. music studies, U. Denver, 1956-57. Engring. lab. technician Airesearch Mfg. Co., El Segundo, Calif., 1955-56; tchr. of voice. Leading baritone, N.Y.C. Opera, 1960—, Met. Opera, 1975, 76, 78, San Francisco Spring Opera, 1961-65, San Francisco Opera debut, 1965; appeared with various opera cos., U.S.; roles include: Almaviva (Marriage of Figaro); soloist with, Phila. Orch., Cleve. Orch., Boston Symphony, N.Y. Philharmonic, Los Angeles Philharmonic, also others; appeared with, Santiago (Chile) Opera, Israel Philharm., as Germont with, Hamburg Staatsoper, 1979, as Ford in Falstaff with, Belgian Opera, 1980; appeared in: Live from Lincoln Center as Lescaut in Manon; appeared on TV shows, Tonight Show, Merv Griffin Show, Mike Douglas Show. Served with Submarine Service USN, 1950-54. Clubs: Bohemian (San Francisco); Lotos, Players (N.Y.C.). Office: care Columbia Artists Mgmt Inc 165 W 57th St New York NY 10019 *

FREDRICKSEN, CLEVE JOHN, mfg. co. exec.; b. Bklyn., Aug. 24, 1917; s. John A. and Laura A. (Olsen) F.; m. Harriet Ingrid Johnsen, Dec. 7, 1940; children—Cleve Laurance, Brian Harold, Thomas Mark. Student, St. John's U., 1937-40. Asst. sec., asst. treas. AMP, Inc., Harrisburg, Pa., 1941-42, dir., 1942—, sec., asst. treas., 1942-56, sec.-treas., 1956-59, v.p., treas., 1959-68, v.p., chief fin. officer, 1968-71, chmn. fin. com., 1971-75, chmn. bd., 1975-81, chmn. exec. com. bd., 1981—; dir. Pamcor, Inc., San Juan, P.R., 1952—; sec.-asst. treas., 1952-56, sec.-treas., 1956-59, v.p., treas., 1959-68, v.p., chief fin. officer, 1968-71, chmn. fin. com., 1971-75, chmn. bd., 1975—; dir. Dauphin Deposit Trust Co., Harrisburg, Harsco Corp. Bd. dirs. Polyclinic Med. Center, Harrisburg; trustee Kline Found., Health Scis. Fund; chmn. com. Whitaker Found. Mem. Pa. Soc. Presbyn. Clubs: West Shore Country (Camp Hill); Coral Beach and Tennis (Paget, Bermuda). Home: 345 N 27th St Camp Hill PA 17011 Office: Eisenhower Blvd Harrisburg PA 17111

FREDRICKSON, DONALD SHARP, physician, scientist; b. Canon City, Colo., Aug. 8, 1924; s. Charles Arthur and Blanche (Sharp) F.; m. Henriette Priscilla Dorothea Eekhof, Sept. 5, 1950; children: Eric Henderikus, Rurik Charles. Student, U. Colo., 1942-43; B.S., U. Mich., 1946, M.D., 1949; Dr.Med. (hon.), Karolinska Institutet, 1977, D.Sc., U. Mich., 1977, Mt. Sinai Sch. Medicine, 1978, U. N.C., 1979, Georgetown U., 1981, Yeshiva U., 1981, N.J. U. Medicine and Dentistry, 1982. Intern Peter Bent Brigham Hosp., Boston, 1949-50; house staff mem., fellow Peter Bent Brigham and Mass. Gen. hosps., 1950-53; mem. sr. research staff lab. cellular physiology and metabolism Nat. Heart and Lung Inst., Bethesda, Md., 1955-61, clin. dir. inst., 1961-66, dir. inst., 1966-68, chief molecular disease br. div. intramural research, 1966, dir. div. intramural research, 1968-74; pres. Inst. Medicine, Nat. Acad. Scis., 1974-75; dir. NIH, 1975-81; scholar-in-residence Nat. Acad. Scis., 1981-83; v.p. Howard Hughes Med. Inst., Bethesda, 1983; professorial lectr. medicine George Washington U. Sch. Medicine, 1956—; lectr. preventive medicine Georgetown U. Sch. Medicine, 1963—; Jimenez Diaz lectr., 1974. Editor: (with others) The Metabolic Basis of Inherited Disease, 5th edit, 1982; Contbr. articles to profl. jours. Served with AUS, 1943-45. Recipient Internat. award James F. Mitchell Found. for Med. Edn. and Research, 1968, Distinguished Achievement award Modern Medicine, 1971; Superior Service award HEW, 1970; Distinguished Service award, 1971; McCollum award Am. Soc. Clin. Nutrition and Clin. div. Am. Inst. Nutrition, 1971; Modanina prize, 1975; Irving Cutter medal, 1978; Gairdner Found. ann. award, 1978; Purkinje medal Czechoslovakian Med. Soc., 1980; Fondazione Lorenzini medal, 1980; Disting. Pub. Service award HHS, 1981. Fellow Royal Coll. Physicians (London), Am. Coll. Cardiology (gold medal 1967, Disting. Service award 1983); life fellow A.C.P. (award); mem. AAAS, Am. Heart Assn., Am. Physiol. Soc., Am. Soc. Clin. Investigation, Am. Soc. Human Genetics, Assn. Am. Physicians, Harvey Soc. (hon.), Internat. Soc. Cardiology (exec. com.), Med. Soc. Sweden, Nat. Acad. Scis., Soc. Pediatric Research, Inst. Medicine Brit. Cardiac Soc. (corr.), Phi Beta Kappa, Phi Kappa Phi, Alpha Omega Alpha. Office: 6615 Bradley Blvd Bethesda MD 20817

FREDRICKSON, GEORGE MARSH, history educator; b. Bristol, Conn., July 16, 1934; s. George Frederickson and Gertrude (Marsh) F.; m. Helene Osouf, Oct. 16, 1956; children: Anne, Laurel, Thomas, Caroline. A.B., Harvard U., 1956, Ph.D., 1964. Instr. history Harvard U., Cambridge, Mass., 1963-66; assoc. prof. history Northwestern U., Evanston, Ill., 1966-71, prof., Evanston, 1971—, William Smith Mason prof. Am. history, 1979—. Author: The Inner Civil War, 1965, The Black Image in the White Mind, 1972 (Anisfield-Wolf award 1972), White Supremacy, 1981 (Ralph Waldo Emerson award 1981, Merle Curt award 1982); editor: A Nation Divided, 1975. Served to lt. USN, 1957-60. Guggenheim fellow, 1967-68; NEH fellow, 1973-74; Ctr. for Advanced Studies in Behavioral Scis. fellow, 1977-78; Fulbright fellow, 1983. Fellow Soc. Am. Historians, Amk. Antiquarian Soc.; mem. Am. Hist. Assn., Orgn. Am. Historians, So. Hist. Assn. Home: 1215 Judson Ave Evanston IL 60202 Office: Dept History Northwestern U Evanston IL 60201

FREDRICKSON, (LAWRENCE) THOMAS, composer, educator; b. Kane, Pa., Sept. 5, 1928; s. Eric Lawrence and Esther Linnea (Skoog) F.; m. Betty Jean Blessing, July 30, 1950; children: Lawrence Alan, Linda Kay, Gail Diane. Mus.B., Ohio Wesleyan U., 1950; Mus.M., U. Ill., Urbana, 1952, D.M.A., 1960. Mem. faculty U. Ill., Urbana, 1952—, prof. music, 1967—, dir. Sch. Music, 1970-74. Performer double bass in chamber music and jazz groups, symphony orchs. Mem. ASCAP (awards 1964—), Pi Kappa Lambda, Phi Mu Alpha, Kappa Delta Pi. Home: 1814 Robert Dr Champaign IL 61821 Office: Sch Music Univ Ill Urbana IL 61801

FREDRIK, BURRY, theatrical producer, director; b. N.Y.C., Aug. 9, 1925; d. Fredric Kreuger and Erna Anita (Burry) Gerber; m. Gerard E. Meunier, Dec. 27, 1945 (div. 1949). Grad., Sarah Lawrence Coll., 1947. Ind. theatrical dir., producer, U.S. and abroad, 1955—. Producer: Broadway play Too Good To Be True, 1964-65 (nominated Tony award 1965), Travesties, 1975-76 (Tony award 1976); off-Broadway play Thieves Carnival, 1955 (Tony award 1955), Exiles, 1956 (OBIE award 1956). Home: 51 Hillside Rd N Weston CT 06883 Office: Burry Fredrik Prodns 165 W 46th St New York NY 10036

FREE, JOHN MARTIN, architectural, engineering and planning company executive; b. Melrose, Minn., Oct. 30, 1923; s. John V. and Anne (Geyer) F.; m. Rosemary Buman, June 14, 1949; children—Wanda Ann, John George (dec.), Linda Jo, Rita Denise, Mary Ruth, James John, Ruth Ann, Paul Lee. B.S. in Archtl. Engring, Iowa State U., 1949. Diplomate: Registered profl. engr., Iowa, Utah., Registered architect, Conn., Iowa, Ill., Kans., Mass., Minn., Mo., Nebr., N.J., N.D., S.D., Tex., Wis., Wyo., Singapore. Architect, engr. Leo A. Daly, Omaha, 1949-53, assoc., 1953-60, v.p., 1960-66, sr. v.p., exec. dir. Omaha office, 1966—, mng. dir., Asia, 1970—, exec. dir. hdqrs. div., 1982—; project mgr. USAF Acad. Expansion program, 1964-67; Mem. Internat. Engring. Commn., vice chmn., 1978-82. Bd. dirs. Goodwill Industries Nebr., Met. YMCA, Omaha; chmn. adv. council Coll. Engring and Architecture, U. Nebr., 1982—; chmn. engring. adv. council Iowa State U., 1978-79; pres.'s council Creighton U.; chmn. UCS of Midlands Adv. Council Bus. and Industry; trustee Marian High Sch. Served with AUS, 1943-45; ETO. Decorated Bronze Star.; Recipient Engr. citation Iowa State U., 1974. Fellow Royal Australian Inst. Architects; Mem. AIA, Nat. Soc. Profl. Engrs., Nat. Council Archtl. Registration Bds., Architects Registration Council U.K., Nebr. Cons. Engrs. Assn., Cons. Engrs. Council U.S., Royal Inst. Brit. Architects, Nebr. Assn. Commerce and Industry, Omaha Indsl. Found., Office of Internat. Fin. (dir. 1978-81), Soc. Am. Mil. Engrs., Omaha C. of C. (dir. 1969-71, v.p. transp. council 1977-81, dir. 1981—). Republican. Roman Catholic. Clubs: K.C. (4 deg.), Rotary (Omaha)). Home: 9731 Rockbrook Rd Omaha NE 68124 Office: 8600 Indian Hills Dr Omaha NE 68114

FREEARK, ROBERT JAMES, surgeon; b. Chgo., May 14, 1927; s. Ray H. and Lizette (Stauffer) F.; m. Ruth Nelson, June 24, 1950; children: Kris, Kim. B.S., Northwestern U., 1949, M.D., 1952; grad., Oak Ridge Inst. Nuclear Studies, 1953. Diplomate: Am. Bd. Surgery, (dir. 1980—), Nat. Bd. Med. Examiners. Rotating intern, then resident in gen. surgery Cook County Hosp., Chgo., 1952-58, dir. surgery, 1958-68, attending physician, 1960-70, hosp. dir., 1968-70; research fellow Jerome D. Solomon Found., Chgo., 1953-54; mem. faculty Northwestern U. Med. Sch., 1960-70, prof. surgery, 1968-70; prof. surgery, chmn. dept. Loyola U.-Stritch Sch. Medicine, Maywood, Ill., 1970—; surgeon-in-chief Loyola U.-Foster G. McGaw Hosp., 1970—; cons. Hines (Ill.) VA Hosp., 1970—. Served with USMCR, 1945-46. Named Outstanding Clin. Prof. Stritch Sch. Medicine, 1973. Fellow ACS; mem. Am. Assn. Surgery Trauma (pres. 1982), Am. Surg. Assn., AMA, Am. Trauma Soc., Central Surg. Assn. (pres. 1980-81), Soc. Internat. de Chirurgie, Soc. Surgery Alimentary Tract, Soc. Surg. Chmn., Soc. U. Surgeons, Western Surg. Assn., Ill. Surg. Soc. (pres. 1983-84), Ill. Med. Soc., Midwest Surg. Soc. (pres. 1970), Chgo. Med. Soc., Inst. Medicine Chgo., Chgo. Surg. Soc., Alpha Omega Alpha, Omega Beta Pi. Congregationalist. Office: 2160 S 1st Ave Maywood IL 60153

FREED, AARON DAVID, architect; b. Galva, Ill., Apr. 29, 1922; s. Charles Henry and Ruth Igeborg F.; m. Mildred Alpha Magee, Mar. 30, 1946; children—Christine Diane, Joan Anita. Grad., Am. Acad. Art, Chgo., 1942; B.S., U. Ill., 1948. With Graham Anderson Probst White (Architects), 1950-52, Durham, Anderson Freed, Seattle, 1952-79, HDR, 1979—; instr. U. Ill., 1947-48, U. Wash., 1961-62. Served with C.E. AUS, 1943-46. Fellow AIA.; mem. Interfaith Forum on Religion, Art and Architecture. Presbyterian. Office: Aaron D Freed 1100 Eastlake E Seattle WA 98109

FREED, BERT, actor; b. N.Y.C., Nov. 3, 1919; s. Ely and Hannah (Fried) F.; m. Nancy Lee Waring, Feb. 12, 1956; children: Carl Robert, Jennifer. B.S., Pa. State U., 1940. Broadway debut: Johnny 2X4, 1942; subsequent appearances include Norma Rae. Pres., Brentwood Democratic Club, 1968-69; bd. dirs. Theatre Authority West, 1983—; pres. AFTRA/SAG Fed. Credit Union, 1978—. Mem. Acad. Motion Picture Arts and Scis. (mem. exec. com. fgn. films 1968—), Screen Actors Guild (v.p. 1975-77, dir. 1968—). Jewish. Home: 418 N Bowling Green Way Los Angeles CA 90049 Office: ATI 8816 Burton Way Beverly Hills CA 90211

FREED, DAVID CLARK, artist; b. Toledo, May 23, 1936; s. J. Clark and Thelma F.; m. Mary Lichtenwald, Sept. 3, 1962; children—Aaron, Michael. B.F.A., Miami U., Oxford, Ohio, 1958; M.F.A., U. Iowa, 1962; postgrad., Royal Coll. Art, 1963-64. Instr. art Toledo Mus., 1964-66; prof. printmaking Va. Commonwealth U., Richmond, 1966—. One-man shows include, Franz Bader Gallery, Washington, 1967, 70, 71, 73, 76, 79, 82, Va. Mus. Fine Arts, 1977, group shows include, World Print Show, San Francisco Mus. Modern Art, 35 Artists of the S.E., High Mus., Atlanta, Art of Poetry, Nat. Coll. Fine Arts; represented in permanent collections at, Mus. Modern Art, N.Y.C., Nat. Mus. Am. Art, Washington, Chgo. Art Inst., Victoria and Albert Mus., London. Fulbright grantee, 1963-64. Home: 1825 W Grace Richmond VA 23220 Studio: 305 S Laurel Richmond VA 23220

FREED, DEAN WINSLOW, technical manufacturing company executive; b. Oakland, Calif., 1923; s. Bayard A. and Lydia W. (Fogg) F.; m. Patrice L., 1948; children: Carol A., Kathryn G. B.S., Swarthmore Coll., 1943; M.S., Purdue U., 1948; postgrad., Columbia U., 1949-51. Indsl. engr. Sylvania Electric Co., 1943-52; mfg. mgr. Brush Instruments Co., 1952-58; group v.p. Bunker Ramo Co., 1958-70; pres., chief operating officer EGG Inc., Wellesley, Mass., 1970-1983, pres., chief exec. officer, 1983—; trustee Eastern Gas & Fuel Assos. Trustee New Eng. Aquarium; chmn. Emerson Hosp., Concord, Mass.; Trustee Opera Co. Boston, Wentworth Inst. Boston; vice chmn.

World Affairs Council. Office: EGG Inc 45 William St Wellesley MA 02181

FREED, DEBOW, coll. pres.; b. Hendersonville, Tenn., Aug. 26, 1925; s. John Walter and Ella Lee (DeBow) F.; m. Catherine Carol Moore, Sept. 10, 1949; 1 son, DeBow, II. B.S., U.S. Mil. Acad., 1946; grad., U.S. Army Command and Gen. Staff Coll., 1959; M.S., U. Kans., 1961; Ph.D., U. N.Mex., 1966, U.S. Air War Coll., 1966. Commd. lt. U.S. Army, 1946, advanced through grades to col., 1967; instr. (The Inf. Sch.), 1953-56, comdr., 1956-57, instr., 1957-58; chief nuclear br. U.S. Atomic Energy Agy., 1961-65; instr. physics dept. U.S. Mil. Acad., 1967-69, ret., 1969; dean Mt. Union Coll., 1969-74; pres. Monmouth Coll., 1974-79, Ohio No. U., Ada, 1979—; chmn. Asso. Colls. of Midwest, also officer other consortia of colls. and univs. Author: Using Nuclear Capabilities, 1959, Pulsed Neutron Techniques, 1965; contbr. articles, revs. to profl. publs.; editor: Atomic Development Report, 1962-64. Vice pres., dir. Buckeye council Boy Scouts Am., 1972-74, dir. Prairie council, 1974-78. Decorated Bronze Star, Legion of Merit, 1967, 69; Legion of Honor, Iran, 1953; recipient various civic and service awards.; Associated Western Univs. fellow, 1963-65; AEC fellow, 1963-65; Fgn. Policy Research Inst. fellow, 1966. Home: 115 W Lima Ave Ada OH 45810 Office: Office of Pres Ohio No U Ada OH 45810

FREED, JACK HERSCHEL, chemist, educator; b. N.Y.C., Apr. 19, 1938; s. Nathan and Pauline (Wolodarsky) F.; m. H. Renée Strauch, Mar. 25, 1961; children—Denise Elaine, Nadine Debra. B.E., Yale U., 1958; M.S., Columbia U., 1959, Ph.D., 1962. NSF fellow Cambridge U., 1962-63; asst. prof. chemistry Cornell U., 1963-67, asso. prof., 1967-73, prof., 1973—; vis. prof. Tokyo U., 1969, Aarhus U., 1974, U. Geneva, 1977, Delft U. of Tech., 1978. Mem. editorial bd.: Jour. Chem. Physics, 1976-78, Jour. Phys. Chemistry, 1979—; contbr. numerous articles to profl. jours. U.S. Ramsay Meml. fellow, 1962-63; A.P. Sloan Found. fellow, 1966-68; Sr. Weizmann fellow, 1970; recipient Buck-Whitney medal Eastern N.Y. sect. Am. Chem. Soc., 1981. Fellow Am. Phys. Soc. Jewish. Club: Cornell of N.Y. Home: 108 Homestead Circle Ithaca NY 14850 Office: Dept Chemistry Baker Lab Cornell U Ithaca NY 14853

FREED, JAMES INGO, architect; b. Essen, Germany, June 23, 1930; came to U.S., 1939, naturalized, 1948; s. Michael and Dora F.; m. Hermine Gerberg, May 28, 1967; 1 dau., Dara Michaella. B.Arch., Ill. Inst. Tech., 1953. Registered architect, N.Y., Washington, Ill., Ohio, Nebr., Mo., Wis. Assoc. Danforth & Speyer, Chgo., 1951-52, Michael Reese Planning Assn., 1952-53; designer Office Mies Van der Rohe, N.Y.C., 1955-56; assoc. ptnr. I.M. Pei & Ptnrs., N.Y.C., 1956-79, ptnr., 1980—; prof. architecture, dean Coll. Architecture, Planning and Design Ill. Inst. Tech., 1975-78. Exhibited designs at, Gray Gallery, Chgo., 1976, Walter Kelly Gallery, Chgo., 1977, Graham Found., Chgo., 1978, Walker Art Ctr., Mpls., 1978-79; archtl. works include, Kips Bay Plaza Apts., N.Y.C., 1962 (City Club N.Y. Albert S. Bard award 1965), NYU Towers, 1969 (Condrete Industry Bd. award 1966), NYU Towers (AIA Honor award 1967), NYU Towers (City Club N.Y. Albert S. Bard award 1967), Univ. Plaza (AIA Honor award 1967), 88 Pine Street, N.Y.C. (R.S. Reynolds Meml. award 1974), 88 Pine Street, N.Y.C. (AIA Honor award 1975), Nat. Bank Commerce, Lincoln, Nebr., 1976 (Concrete Reinforcing Steel Inst. award 1977). Bd. dirs. Creative Time, N.Y.C., from 1975, Bright New City, Chgo., 1976-78. Served with C.E. U.S. Army, 1953-55. Fellow AIA (chmn. nat. design com. 1975); mem. Archtl. League N.Y. Office: IM Pei & Partners 600 Madison Ave New York NY 10022 *

FREED, KARL FREDERICK, chemistry educator; b. Bklyn., Sept. 25, 1942; s. Nathan and Pauline (Wolodarsky) F.; m. Gina P. Goldstein, June 14, 1964; children: Nicole Yvette, Michele Suzanne. B.S., Columbia U., 1963; A.M., Harvard U., 1965, Ph.D., 1967. NATO postdoctoral fellow U. Manchester (Eng.), 1967-68; asst. prof. U. Chgo., 1968-73, assoc. prof., 1973-76, prof. chemistry, 1976—, dir. James Frank Inst., 1983—. Mem. editorial bd.: Jour. Statis. Physics, 1976-78; adv. editor: Chem. Physics, 1979—, Chem. Reviews, 1981-83; assoc. editor: Jour. Chem. Physics, 1982—; contbr. articles to profl. jours. Recipient Marlow medal Faraday div. Chem. Soc. London, 1973, Pure Chemistry award Am. Chem. Soc., 1976; fellow Sloan Found., 1969-71; Guggenheim fellow, 1972-73; fellow Dreyfus Found., 1972-77. Fellow Am. Phys. Soc.; mem. Royal Soc. Chemistry (London). Office: U Chgo 5640 S Ellis Ave Chicago IL 60637

FREED, MURRAY MONROE, physician, medical educator; b. Paterson, N.J., Oct. 9, 1924; s. Nathan and Fannie (Freedman) F.; m. Phyllis Dorothy Werlin, Dec. 19, 1948; children—Ellen Lisa, Leah Deborah, Andrea Beth, Janet Carolyn. A.B., Harvard U., 1948; M.D., Boston U., 1952; student, Va. Poly. Inst., 1942-43. Diplomate: Am. Bd. Phys. Medicine and Rehab. (mem. bd. 1974—). Intern Mass. Meml. Hosp., Boston, 1952-53; clin. fellow N.Y. U.-Bellevue Med. Center, N.Y.C., 1953-55, Mass. Gen. Hosp., Boston, 1956; mem. staff Univ. Hosp., Boston, 1956—, chief rehab. medicine, 1965—; physician in chief phys. medicine Boston City Hosp., 1964-75, vis. physician rehab. medicine, 1975—; mem. faculty Boston U. Med. Sch., 1956—, prof. rehab. medicine, 1967—, chmn. dept., 1966—; Bernard Kutner disting. lectr. Sargent Coll. of Allied Health Professions, 1980; mem. nat. peer review com. Rehab. Services Adminstrn., HEW, 1978—; cons. Newton-Wellesley, Norwood, St. Vincent, Bedford VA hosps. Contbr. articles to med. jours. Mem. corp. United Community Services, Boston, 1960-61; med. adv. bd. Mass. Multiple Sclerosis Found., 1959-79; cons. rehab. medicine Goodwill Industries Boston, 1962—; med. adv. bd. Sargent Coll., Boston U., 1960—; chmn. all univ. com. rehab. tng. Boston U., 1956-59; med. and sci. adv. bd. Mass. chpt. Arthritis Found., 1959—; mem. Gov. Mass. Com. Employment Handicapped, 1969—; med. adv. bd. Nat. Spinal Cord Injury Found., 1970-80; chmn. Mayor Boston Commn. Physically Handicapped; cons. to med. adv. com. Registry of Motor Vehicles, Commonwealth of Mass.; mem. ho. of dels. Mass. Easter Seal Soc.; Chmn. alumni fund campaign com. Boston U. Sch. Medicine, 1959-69. Served with AUS, 1943-46. Decorated Purple Heart; recipient citation Pres.'s Com. Employment Physically Handicapped, 1972, gov. Mass., 1972, Mass. Assn. Paraplegics, 1974; Centennial Alumni citation Boston U. Sch. Medicine, 1973; Herbert S. Talbot award Nat. Paraplegia Found., 1978; Alumnus award for spl. distinction Boston U., 1979; N. Neil Pike prize for service to handicapped Boston U. Sch. Law, 1980; named Man of Year Jewish War Vets., 1973. Fellow Am. Acad. Phys. Medicine and Rehab. (chmn. membership com. 1969-70, chmn. sci. program com. 1974-75, mem. bd. govs. 1977—, v.p. 1980-81, pres. 1982-83), ACP; mem. New Eng. Soc. Phys. Medicine (pres. 1964-65), New Eng. Rheumatism Soc., Am. Congress Phys. Medicine and Rehab., AMA, Mass. Med. Soc., Assn. Acad. Physiatrists (pres. 1971), Alumni Assn. Boston U. Sch. Medicine (v.p. 1975, pres. 1976), Alpha Omega Alpha (faculty adviser). Office: 75 E Newton St Boston MA 02118

FREED, STANLEY ARTHUR, museum curator; b. Springfield, Ohio, Apr. 18, 1927; s. Aaron Arthur and Belle (Kilstein) F.; m. Ruth Shelley, Sept. 12, 1955. Ph.B., U. Chgo., 1949; B.A., U. Calif. at Berkeley, 1951, Ph.D., 1957. Vis. asst. prof. anthropology U. N.C., 1959-60; mem. staff Am. Mus. Natural History, N.Y.C., 1960—, curator, chmn., 1969-76, curator, 1976—; sr. research fellow Am. Inst. Indian Studies, 1977-78. Served with AUS, 1945-46. Postdoctoral fellow Social Sci. Research Council, 1957, NSF, 1958. Mem. N.Y. Acad. Scis. (chmn. anthropology sect. 1974-75). Home: 344 W 72d St New York NY 10023 Office: American Museum Natural History Central Park West at 79th St New York NY 10024

FREEDBERG, A. STONE, physician; b. Salem, Mass., May 30, 1908; s. Hyman and Rachel Leah (Freedberg) F.; m. Beatrice Gordon, Aug. 29, 1935; children: Richard Gordon, Leonard Earl. A.B., Harvard U., 1929; M.D., U. Chgo., 1935. Diplomate: Am. Bd. Internal Medicine (cardiology). Intern Mt. Sinai Hosp., Chgo., 1934-35, Mass. Meml. Hosp., Boston, summer 1935; resident Cook County Hosp., Chgo., 1935-36; house officer pathology R.I. Hosp., 1936-37; practice medicine, specializing in internal medicine, Boston, 1946—; asst. in medicine Beth Israel Hosp., 1938-40, jr. vis. physician, 1940-46, asso. in med. research, 1940-50, asso. vis. physician, 1946-48, vis. physician, 1949-63, asso. dir. med. research, 1950-63, sr. Ziskind fellow, 1956, physician, 1964—, acting physician-in-chief dept. medicine, 1973, dir. cardiology unit, 1964-69; research fellow medicine Med. Sch. Harvard U., 1941-42, asst. in medicine, 1942-46, instr. medicine, 1946-47, asso. in medicine, 1947-50, asst. prof., 1950-57, asso. prof., 1958-69, prof., 1969-74, prof. emeritus, 1974—, adminstrv. bd. faculty medicine, 1958-62; cons., com. mem. med. div. Oak Ridge Inst. Nuclear Studies, 1955-56; spl. cons. metabolism study sect. USPHS, 1956-60; mem. sr. cons. staff Nuclear Medicine Inst., 1966-67. Mem. editorial bd.: Circulation, 1956-60, 62-67; contbr. articles profl. jours. Guggenheim fellow Oxford U., 1967-68. Fellow Am. Heart Assn. (bd. dirs.; mem. council clin. cardiology); mem. Mass. Heart Assn. (dir., past pres., com. chmn.), Am. Thyroid Assn. (v.p.), Mass., Charles River Dist. med. socs., Am. Soc. Clin. Investigation, Am. Physiol. Soc., Assn. Am. Physicians, Royal Soc. Medicine (London), New Eng. Cardiovascular Soc. (pres. 1971-72), Assn. Profs. Medicine. Home: 111 Perkins St Jamaica Plain Boston MA 02130 Office: 275 Longwood Ave Boston MA 02115

FREEDBERG, IRWIN MARK, dermatologist; b. Boston, July 4, 1931; s. Arthur Harris and Sayde Ruth (Bixby) F.; m. Irene Sybil Lisman, July 4, 1954; children—Marjorie, Kenneth, Deborah. Student, Dartmouth Coll., 1949-52; M.D., Harvard U., 1956. Intern Beth Israel Hosp., Boston, 1956-57, resident in internal medicine, 1957-59; resident in dermatology Mass. Gen. Hosp., Boston, 1959-62; instr. to prof. dermatology Harvard U. Med. Sch., Boston, 1962-77; prof., chmn. dept. Johns Hopkins Sch. Medicine, Balt., 1977-81; George Miller MacKee prof. and chmn. dept. dermatology, N.Y. U. Sch. Medicine, 1981—. Contbr. articles in field to profl. jours.; editor: Jour. Investigative Dermatology, 1972-77. Guggenheim fellow, 1969-70; NIH grantee, 1962—; Am Cancer Soc., Am. Contract Bridge League faculty research asso., 1965-70. Mem. Council Biologic Editors, Am. Soc. Biochemists, Soc. Clin. Investigation, Soc. Investigative Dermatology (pres. 1981-82), Am. Fedn. Clin. Research. Home: 333 E 68 St New York NY 10021 Office: 550 First Ave New York NY 10021

FREEDBERG, SYDNEY JOSEPH, museum curator, emeritus fine arts educator; b. Boston, Nov. 11, 1914; s. Samuel and Lillian (Michelson) F.; m. Anne Blake, Jan. 15, 1942 (div. 1950); 1 son, William Blake; m. Susan Pulitzer, April 10, 1954 (dec. June 1965); children: Kate Pulitzer, Nathaniel Davis; m. Catherine Blanton, June 24, 1967; 1 son, Sydney Joseph. A.B. summa cum laude, Harvard U., 1936, A.M., 1939, Ph.D., 1940. Mem. faculty Harvard U., 1938-40, 53—, prof. fine arts, 1960-83, Arthur Kingsley Porter prof., 1979-83, prof. emeritus, 1983—, chmn. dept., 1959-63, Walter Channing Cabot fellow, 1973-76; prof. in residence Harvard U. Ctr. Renaissance Studies, 1973-74, 80-81; mem. faculty council Harvard U., 1974-77, chmn. univ. museums council, 1977-80; chief curator Nat. Gallery, Washington, 1983—; asst. prof. art, then assoc. prof. Wellesley Coll., 1946-54; vis. lectr. Inst. Modern Art, Boston, 1947; adv. council Guggenheim Found., 1978—; spl. research 16th Century Italian art. Author: Parmigianino, His Works in Painting, 1950, Painting of the High Renaissance, 1961, Andrea del Sarto, 1963, Painting in Italy, 1500-1600, 1971, circa 1600, 1983. Vice chmn. Nat. Exec. Com. Rescue Italian Art, 1966-74; bd. dirs. Save Venice, Inc. Served to maj. AUS, 1942-46. Guggenheim fellow, 1949-50, 54-55; fellow Am. Council Learned Socs., 1958-59, 66-67; Nat. Endowment Humanities sr. fellow, 1973-74; decorated Order Brit. Empire, Grand officer Order of Star of Italian Solidarity, Grand officer Order of Merit of Italian Republic; recipient Faculty prize Harvard U. Press, 1961; Morey Book prize Coll. Art Assn., 1965. Fellow Am. Acad. Arts and Scis.; mem. Coll. Art Assn. (dir. 1962-66), Phi Beta Kappa. Home: 3326 Reservoir Rd Washington DC 20007 Office: National Gallery of Art 4th St and Constitution Ave NW Washington DC 20565

FREEDMAN, ALBERT ZURO, publishing and television company executive; b. Taunton, Mass.; s. Frank and Bessie (Kanaber) F.; m. Esther Hilda Katz, Sept. 23, 1954 (dec.); children: Mara, Lisa, Tani, Derek. Student, Boston U., 1945-46; B.A., U. So. Calif., 1948; postgrad., Inst. Hautes Etudes Cinématagraphiques, Paris, 1949-50; Ph.D., Inst. for Advanced Study Human Sexuality, San Francisco, 1981. Radio writer, Los Angeles, N.Y.C., 1950-52; TV writer, producer WOR-TV, N.Y., Los Angeles, 1952, NBC, CBS, 1952-58; playwright, Mex., 1959-60; with KTLA, ABC-TV, Los Angeles, 1961-64; free lance writer, London, 1964-66; editor Forum, Jour. Human Relations, London, 1967-75, co-pub., N.Y.C., 1975—; mng. dir. Penthouse Publs., London, 1970-75; v.p. Penthouse TV. Mem. Am. Coll. Sexologists, Assn. Sexologists, Soc. Sci. Study of Sex. Club: Friars. Home: 1049 Park Ave New York NY 10028 Office: Penthouse TV 1965 Broadway New York NY 10023

FREEDMAN, ALLEN ROYAL, business executive, lawyer; b. Suffern, N.Y., Apr. 4, 1940; s. Emiel and Lucille (Nagid) F.; m. Judith Brick, June 9, 1963; children: Evan Brick, Seth Daniel. B.A., Tufts U., 1961; LL.B., U. Va., 1964. Vice pres. Time Ins. Co., N.Y.C., 1970-75; exec. v.p. Lewis R. Eisner & Co., N.Y.C., 1975-79; pres. AMEV Holdings, Inc., N.Y.C., 1979—; chmn. bd. Time Ins. Co., Milw., 1983—; founder, 1st pres. N.Y. Capital Forum; dir. Systems & Computer Tech., Pa. Writer periodicals for ins. and investments. Mem. ABA. Office: AMEV Holdings Inc 2 World Trade Ctr Suite 9766 New York NY 10048

FREEDMAN, DANIEL X., psychiatrist, educator; b. Lafayette, Ind., Aug. 17, 1921; s. Harry and Sophia (Feinstein) F.; m. Mary C. Neidigh, Mar. 20, 1945. B.A., Harvard U., 1947; M.D., Yale U., 1951; grad., Western New Eng. Inst. Psychoanalysis, 1966; D.Sc. (hon.), Wabash Coll., 1974, Indiana U., 1982. Intern pediatrics Yale Hosp., 1951-52, resident psychiatry, 1952-55; from instr. to prof. psychiatry Yale U., 1955-66; chmn. dept. U. Chgo., 1966-83, Louis Block prof. biol. scis., 1969-83; Judson Braun prof. psychiatry and pharmacology UCLA, 1983—; career investigator USPHS, 1957-66; dir. psychiatry and biol. sci. tng. program Yale U., 1960-66; cons. NIMH, 1960—, U.S. Army Chem. Center, Edgewood, Md., 1965-66; chmn. panel psychiat. drug efficacy study Nat. Acad. Sci.-NRC, 1966; chmn. Nat. Acad. Scis.-NRC, 1977—; mem. adv. com. FDA, 1967—; rep. to div. med. scis. NRC, 1971—, mem. com. on brain scis., 1971-73, mem. com. on problems of drug dependence, 1971—; mem. com. problems drug dependence Nat. Inst. Medicine, 1971-76, com. substance abuse, and habitual behavior, 1976—; advisor Pres.'s Biomed. Research Panel, 1975-76; mem. selection com., coordinator research task panel Pres.'s Commn. Mental Health, 1977-78; mem. Jt. Commn. Prescription Drug Use, Inc., 1977—. Author: (with N.J. Giarman) Biochemical Pharmacology of Psychotomimetic Drugs, 1965, What Is Drug Abuse?, 1970, (with F.C. Redlich) The Theory and Practice of Psychiatry, 1966, (with D. Offer) Modern Psychiatry and Clinical Research, 1972; editor: (with J. Dyrud) American Handbook of Psychiatry, Vol. V, 1975, The Biology of the Major Psychoses: A Comparative Analysis, 1975; chief editor: Archives Gen. Psychiatry, 1970—. Bd. dirs. Founds. Fund for Research in Psychiatry, 1969-72, Drug Abuse Council, 1972-80; vice chmn. Drug Abuse Council Ill., 1972—. Served with AUS, 1942-46. Recipient Distinguished Achievement award Modern Medicine, 1973; William C. Menninger award ACP, 1975; McAlpin medal for research achievment, 1979; Vestermark award for edn., 1981. Fellow Am. Acad. Arts and Scis., Am. Psychiat. Assn. (chmn. commn. on drug abuse 1971—), Am. Coll. Neuropsychopharmacology (pres. 1970—); mem. Inst. Medicine Nat. Acad. Scis., A.C.P. (William C. Menninger award 1975), Ill. Psychiat. Soc. (pres. 1971-72), Social Sci. Research Council (dir. 1968-74), Chgo. Psychoanalytic Soc., Western New Eng. Psychoanalytic Inst., Am. Soc. Pharmacology and Exptl. Therapeutics, AAAS, Am. Assn. Chairmen Depts. Psychiatry (pres. 1972-73), Am. Psychiat. Assn. (v.p. 1975-77, pres.-elect 1980-81, pres. 1981-82), Group Advancement Psychiatry, Psychiat. Research Soc., Am. Psychosomatic Soc. (councillor 1970-73), Assn. Research in Nervous and Mental Disease (pres. 1974), Soc. Biol. Psychiatry, Sigma Xi, Alpha Omega Alpha. Home: 806 Leonard Rd Los Angeles CA 90049 Office: 760 Westwood Plaza Los Angeles CA 90024

FREEDMAN, DAVID NOEL, educator; b. N.Y.C., May 12, 1922; s. David and Beatrice (Goodman) F.; m. Cornelia Anne Pryor, May 16, 1944; children: Meredith Anne, Nadezhda, David, Jonathan. Student, CCNY, 1935-38; A.B., UCLA, 1939; B.Th., Princeton Theol. Sem., 1944; Ph.D., Johns Hopkins U., 1948; Litt.D., U. Pacific, 1973; Sc.D., Davis and Elkins Coll., 1974. Ordained to ministry Presbyn. Ch., 1944; supply pastor in, Acme and Deming, Wash., 1944-45; teaching fellow, then asst. instr. Johns Hopkins U., 1946-48; asst. prof., then prof. Hebrew and O.T. lit. Western Theol. Sem., Pitts., 1948-60; prof. Hebrew and O.T. lit. Pitts. Theol. Sem., 1960-61, James A. Kelso prof., 1961-64; prof. O.T. San Francisco Theol. Sem., 1964-70, Gray prof. Hebrew exegesis, 1970-71, dean of faculty, 1966-70, acting dean of sem., 1970-71; prof. O.T. Grad. Theol. Union, Berkeley, Calif., 1964-71; prof. dept. Near Eastern studies U. Mich., Ann Arbor, 1971—, dir. program on studies in religion, 1971—, Thurnau prof. Bibl. studies, 1984—; Danforth vis. prof. Internat. Christian U., Tokyo, 1967; vis. prof. Hebrew U., Jerusalem, 1977, Macquarie U., N.S.W., Australia, 1980, U. Queensland (Australia), 1982, 84, U. Calif.-San Diego, 1985; vis. Green prof. Tex. Christian U., Ft. Worth, 1981; Ann. dir. Albright Inst. Archeol. Research, 1969-70, dir., 76-77; centennial lectr. Johns Hopkins U., 1976; Dahood lectr. Loyola U., 1983; Soc. Bibl. Lit. meml. lectr., 1983, Smithsonian lectr., 1984. Author: (with J.D. Smart) God Has Spoken, 1949, (with F.M. Cross, Jr.) Early Hebrew Orthography, 1952, (with John M. Allegro) The People of the Dead Sea Scrolls, 1958, (with R.M. Grant) The Secret Sayings of Jesus, 1960, (with F.M. Cross, Jr.) Ancient Yahwistic Poetry, 1964, rev. edit., 1975, (with M. Dothan) Ashdod I, 1967, The Published Works of W.F. Albright, 1975, (with L.G. Running) William F. Albright: Twentieth Century Genius, 1975, (with B. Mazar, G. Cornfeld) The Mountain of the Lord, 1975, (with W. Phillips) An Explorer's Life of Jesus, 1975, (with G. Cornfeld) Archaeology of the Bible: Book by Book, 1976, Pottery, Poetry and Prophecy, 1980; others; co-author, editor: Anchor Bible Series Hosea, 1980; editor: (with G.E. Wright) The Biblical Archaeologist, Reader I, 1961, (with E.F. Campbell, Jr.) The Biblical Archaeologist, Reader 2, 1964, Reader 3, 1970, (with W.F. Albright) The Anchor Bible, 1964—, including, Genesis, 1964, James, Peter and Jude, 1964, Jeremiah, 1965, Job, 1965, 2d edit., 1973, Proverbs and Ecclesiastes, 1965, I Chronicles, II Chronicles, Ezra-Nehemiah, 1965, Psalms I, 1966, John I, 1966, Acts of the Apostles, 1967, II Isaiah, 1968, Psalms II, 1968, John II, 1970, Psalms III, 1970, Esther, 1971, Matthew, 1971, Lamentations, 1972, To the Hebrews, 1972, Ephesians 1-3, 4-6, 1974, I and II Esdras, 1974, Judges, 1975, Revelation, 1975, Ruth, 1975, I Maccabees, 1976, I Corinthians, 1976, Additions, 1977, Song of Songs, 1977, Daniel, 1978, Wisdom of Solomon, 1979, I Samuel, 1980, Hosea, 1980, Luke I, 1981, Joshua, 1982, Epistles of John, 1983, II Maccabees, 1983, II Samuel, 1984, II Corinthians, 1984, (with J. Greenfield) New Directions in Biblical Archaeology, 1969, (with J.A. Baird) The Computer Bible, A Critical Concordance to the Synoptic Gospels, 1971, An Analytic Linguistic Concordance to the Book of Isaiah, 1971, I, II, III John: Forward and Reverse Concordance and Index, 1971, A Critical Concordance to Hosea, Amos, Micah, 1972, A Critical Concordance of Haggai, Zechariah, Malachi, 1973, A Critical Concordance to the Gospel of John, 1974, A Synoptic Concordance of Aramaic Inscriptions, 1975, A Linguistic Concordance of Ruth and Jonah, 1976, A Linguistic Concordance of Jeremiah, 1978, (with T. Kachel) Religion and the Academic Scene, 1975, Anchor Bible Series, 1981, 82; also, Computer Bible Series publs, Am. Schs. Oriental Research publs; co-editor: Scrolls from Qumran Cave I, 1972, Jesus: The Four Gospels, 1973; asso. editor: Jour. Bibl. Lit, 1952-54; editor, 1955-59; cons. editor: Interpreter's Dictionary of the Bible, 1957-60, Theologische Wörterbuch des Alten Testaments, 1970—; contbr. numerous articles to profl. jours. Recipient prize in N.T. exegesis Princeton Theol. Sem., 1943; Carey-Thomas award for Anchor Bible, 1965; Layman's Nat. Bible Com. award, 1978; William H. Green fellow O.T., 1944; William S. Rayner fellow Johns Hopkins, 1946, 47; Guggenheim fellow, 1959; Am. Assn. Theol. Schs. fellow, 1963; Am. Council Learned Socs. grant-in-aid, 1967, 76. Fellow Explorers Club, U. Mich. Soc. Fellows (sr., chmn. 1980-82); mem. Soc. Bibl. Lit. (pres. 1975-76), Am. Oriental Soc., Am. Schs. Oriental Research (v.p. 1970—, editor bull. 1974-78, editor Bibl. Archeologist 1976-82, dir. publs. 1974—), Archaeol. Inst. Am., Am. Acad. Religion, Bibl. Colloquium. Home: P.O. Box 7434 Ann Arbor MI 48107

FREEDMAN, DONALD EVERETT, advertising executive; b. Lynn, Mass., Sept. 22, 1932; s. Joseph and Mary (Friedberg) F.; m. Linda Joan Star, Sept. 8, 1962; children: Lisa, Lori. B.S. in Bus. Adminstrn., Boston U., 1953. Store mgr. Gorins Inc., Boston, 1955-62; dir. ops. Rite-Way Dept. Stores, Toronto, Ont., Can., 1962-63; gen. mgr. discount ops. Reitman, Toronto, 1963-68; regional mgr. Bradlees, Braintree, Mass., 1968-74; prin. exec. v.p. Saffer, Cravit & Freedman Advt. Inc., Don Mills, Ont., 1974—. Served to cpl. USMC, 1953-55. Office: Saffer Cravit & Freedman Advt Inc 180 Duncan Mill Rd Don Mills ON Canada M3B 1Z6

FREEDMAN, ELISHA CHAIM, state official; b. Hartford, Conn., Aug. 12, 1926; s. Joseph D. and Dorothea (Simons) F.; m. Adeline Kaufman, Feb. 11, 1951; children: Jonathan, Noah, Jeremy, Anne. Student, U. Conn., 1946-48, Trinity Coll., summer 1947; A.B. cum laude, Syracuse U., 1949, M.P.A., 1955. With Hartford Redevel. Agy., 1952-53, Fed. Rent Control Office, Hartford, 1951-52, Conn. Employees Assn., 1951; supr. budget and research, Hartford, 1955-59, exec. sec. to city mgr., 1959-63, city mgr., 1963-71; chief adminstrv. officer Montgomery County, Md., 1971-72; head pub. sector office, exptl. research and devel. incentives program NSF, Washington, 1972-73; city mgr., Rochester, N.Y., 1974-79, commr. adminstrv. services, Hartford, State of Conn., 1979—; town controller, Manchester, Conn., 1959; mem. task force on demonstration project as a commercialization incentive ERDA, 1975-76. Mem. Conn. Temporary Commn. Study Municipal Collective Bargaining, 1963-65, Conn. Planning Com. Criminal Adminstrn., 1968-71. Recipient Louis Brownlow award for outstanding contbn. to lit. of pub. adminstrn., 1967. Mem. Am. Soc. Pub. Adminstrn. (pres. Conn. 1967, Bosworth

Meml. award Conn. chpt. 1983), Internat. City Mgmt. Assn. (pres. Conn. 1969, v.p. NE region 1976-78), Rochester Engring. Soc. (hon.). Home: 14 Visgrove Ln West Hartford CT 06117 Office: State Office Bldg 165 Capitol Ave Hartford CT 06115

FREEDMAN, FRANK HARLAN, judge; b. Springfield, Mass., Dec. 15, 1924; s. Alvin Samuel and Ida Hilda (Rosenberg) F.; m. Eleanor Labinger, July 26, 1953; children: Joan Robin, Wendy Beth, Barry Alan. LL.B., Boston U., 1949, LL.M., 1950; Ph.D. (hon.), Western New Eng. Coll., Springfield, 1970. Practiced law, 1950-68, mayor City of Springfield, 1968-72; judge U.S. Dist. Ct. Mass., 1972—. Chmn. fund raising drs. Muscular Dystrophy, Leukemia Soc.; mem. Susan Auchter Kidney Fund Raising Com., Springfield City Council, 1960-67; pres. Springfield City Council, 1962; del. Republican Nat. Conv., 1964, 68; mem. Springfield Rep. Com., 1959-72. Served with USNR, 1943-46. Mem. Hampden County (Mass.) Bar Assn., Lewis Marshall Club on Jurisprudence (pres.). Jewish. Office: US Courthouse 1550 Main St Springfield MA 01103 *

FREEDMAN, GERALD ALAN, director; b. Lorain, Ohio, June 25, 1927; s. Barnie B. and Fannie S. F. B.S., Northwestern U., 1949, M.A., 1950. Mem. faculty Theatre Juilliard Sch., N.Y.C., 1970—; vis. prof. Yale U., 1966. Dir.: Broadway plays The Creation of the World, 1972, Gay Life, 1961, Incomparable Max, 1971, Oh Dad, Poor Dad, 1961, Robber Bridegroom, 1976, The Grand Tour, 1978; off-Broadway shows include Colette, 1970, On The Town, 1959; dir.: King Lear, Lincoln Center Repertory Theatre, N.Y.C., 1968; artistic dir., N.Y. Shakespeare Festival, N.Y.C., 1966-70; world premier: Hair, 1967; co-artistic dir.: Acting Co, N.Y.C., 1972-78; dir.: School for Scandal, 1972, Love's Labour's Lost, 1965, The Robber Bridegroom, 1975; artistic dir., Am. Shakespeare Festival Theatre, Stratford, Conn., 1978-79; dir.: Twelfth Night, 1978; author, dir.: A Time for Singing, 1966, Take One Step, 1970; TV dir.: Antigone, 1972; dir.: operas, including world premier of Beatrix Cenci, Kennedy Center, Washington, 1971, Ariadne auf Naxos, Am. Opera Center, 1973; Author: The Festival Shakespeare-Love's Labour's Lost, 1968. Recipient OBIE award for The Taming of the Shrew, 1960; Silver medallion Am. Coll. Theatre Festival, 1973; Gold medallion, 1975; Disting. Alumni award Northwestern U. Alumni Merit award, 1975; President's medal Northwestern U., 1980. Mem. Soc. Stage Dirs. and Choreographers, Dirs. Guild Am., Dramatist Guild.

FREEDMAN, HARRY, composer; b. Lodz, Poland, Apr. 5, 1922; s. Max and Rose (Nelken) F.; m. Mary Louise Morrison, Sept. 15, 1951; children: Karen Liese, Cynthia Jane, Lori Ann. Student, Winnipeg Sch. Art, 1936-40, Royal Conservatory Music, 1945-50. Musician Toronto Symphony, 1946-70; dir. Canadian Music Centre. Composer: Tableau, 1952, Images, 1958, Tokaido; chorus and wind quintet, 1964; Tangents (orch.), 1967; ballet Rose Latulippe, 1966; Toccata, 1968; Debussy orchestration Piano Preludes, 1971; string quartet Graphic II, 1972; for orch. Tapestry, 1973; Romeo and Juliet Ballet, 1973; violin and piano Encounter, 1974; clarinet Lines, 1974; orch. Nocturne 2, 1975; narrator and chamber ensemble The Explainer, 1976; Celebration (saxaphone concerto for Gerry Mulligan), 1977; choir Green... Blue... White, 1978; 1-act jazz opera Abracadabra, 1979; chorus and orch. Nocturne 3, 1980; brass quintet and orch. Royal Flush, 1980; string quartet Blue, 1980; clarinet and string quartet Chalumeau, 1981; Concerto for Orch., 1982; violin and orch. Accord, 1982; Third Symphony, 1983; also many scores for, Stratford Shakespeare Festival, films, stage TV. Served with RCAF, 1942-45. Can. Council sr. arts grantee, 1960, 63, 73-74, 81; recipient Can. film awards, 1970; Composer of Yr. award Canadian Music Council, 1979; Tanglewood scholar, 1949; Royal Conservatory scholar, 1950. Mem. Canadian League Composers (pres. 1975-78). Address: 35 St Andrews Gardens Toronto ON M4W 2C9 Canada

FREEDMAN, HENRY HILLEL, pharmaceutical company executive; b. N.Y.C., Dec. 21, 1919; s. S. William and Ida (Mandel) F.; m. Barbara Wolpert, Sept. 19, 1948; 1 son, Jonathan Edward. A.B., N.Y. U., 1948, M.S., 1950, Ph.D., 1953. Research assoc. Princeton Labs., 1952-64; vis. investigator Inst. Microbiology Rutgers U., 1965; sr. research asso. Warner-Lambert Research Inst., Morris Plains, N.J., 1965-67, dir. microbiology, 1967-69, dir. microbiology and physiology, 1969-72, dir. biol. research, 1972-74; dir. biomed. research ICI Americas Inc., Wilmington, Del., 1974-76, gen. mgr. pharm. research and devel., 1976-79, v.p. pharm. research and devel., 1979—; Mem. research council U. Del. Research Found., 1976-79. Contbr. articles to profl. jours., chpts. to textbooks. Trustee Wilmington Med. Center, 1982—. Served with AUS, 1942-46. Fellow N.Y. Acad. Scis.; mem. Reticuloendothelial Soc. (pres. 1976), Am. Physiol. Soc., Am. Chem. Soc., Soc. Exptl. Biology and Medicine, Am. Soc. Microbiology, Transplantation Soc., Soc. Research Dirs. Patentee in field. Home: 138 Valley Rd Princeton NJ 08540 Office: ICI Americas Inc Wilmington DE 19897

FREEDMAN, JAMES OLIVER, lawyer, educator; b. Manchester, N.H., Sept. 21, 1935; s. Louis A. and Sophie (Gottesman) F. A.B., Harvard U., 1957; LL.B., Yale U., 1962. Bar: N.H. 1962, Pa. 1971, Iowa 1982. Prof. law U. Pa., 1964—, asso. provost, 1978, dean, 1979-82, also univ. ombudsman, 1973-76. Author: Crisis and Legitimacy: The Administrative Process and American Government, 1978; Editorial bd.: U. Pa. Press, 1974-81; chmn., 1979—; contbr. articles to profl. jours. Pres. bd. dirs. Mental Health Assn., SE Pa., 31972, bd. dirs., Pa., 1970-78; mem. Phila. Bd. Ethics, 1981-82; chmn. Pa. Legis. Reapportionment Commn., 1981; chmn. Iowa Gov.'s Task Force on Fgn. Lang. Studies and Internat. Edn., 1982-83. NEH fellow and research vis. fellow Clare Hall Cambridge (Eng.) U., 1976-77. Mem. Am. Law Inst., Am. Arbitration Assn. (nat. panel arbitrators). Office: U Iowa Office of Pres Iowa City IA 52242 *

FREEDMAN, JEFFREY CHARLES, lawyer; b. Los Angeles, Aug. 18, 1944; s. Jack and Selma F.; m. Jacqueline Leslie Dinkin, Dec. 29, 1968; children: Jonah Benjamin, Jamie Rebecca. B.A., Occidental Coll., 1966; J.D., UCLA, 1969. Bar: Calif. 1970. Dep. atty. gen. Calif. Dept. Justice, Los Angeles, 1969-74; asso., partner firm Nelson, Kirshman, Goldstein & Rexon, Los Angeles, 1974-77; partner firm Goldstein, Freedman & Klepetar, Los Angeles, 1977—; instr. dept. mgmt. labor and bus. UCLA, 1975-79; instr. Calif. Dept. Justice Peace Officers Standards and Tng., 1980-81. Mem. Century City C. of C. (mem. bd. 1981, 82—), Century City Bar Assn. (pres. 1981, gov. 1976—), Los Angeles County Bar Assn. (trustee 1982—). Office: 1880 Century Park E Los Angeles CA 90067

FREEDMAN, MERVIN BURTON, psychologist, educator; b. N.Y.C., Mar. 6, 1920; s. Eli and Rose (Weithorn) F.; m. Marjorie Ellingson, Feb. 16, 1952; children: Eric, Kristin, Rolf, Anne Marie. B.S., Coll. City N.Y., 1940; Ph.D., U. Calif. at Berkeley, 1950. Lectr. dept. psychology U. Calif. at Berkeley, 1950-53; research asso. Mellon Found. for Advancement Edn., Vassar Coll., 1953-58; dir. Mellon Found., 1958-60; research asso. Inst. for Study Human Problems, Stanford, 1962-63, asst. dean undergrad. edn., 1963-65; chmn. dept. psychology San Francisco State U., 1965-68, prof. psychology, 1968—; dean grad. sch. Wright Inst., Berkeley, 1969-79; sr. Fulbright research scholar U. Oslo, 1961-62; fellow Center for Advanced Study Behavioral Sci., 1960-61. Author: The College Experience, 1967, (with others) Search for Relevance, 1969, Academic Culture and Faculty Development, 1978, Human Development in Social Settings, 1983; Asso. editor: Polit. Psychology. Vice pres. San Francisco Am.-Scandinavian Found. Served with AUS, 1941-45. Decorated Bronze Star. Fellow Am. Psychol. Assn.; mem. Western Psychol. Assn., Internat. Soc. Polit. Psychology. Home: 866 Spruce St Berkeley CA 94707 Office: Dept Psychology San Francisco State U San Francisco CA 94132

FREEDMAN, PHILIP, educator, physician; b. London, June 25, 1926; U.S., 1963, naturalized, 1970; s. Myer and Mildred (Frankel) F.; m. Jean Kennis Cunningham, Dec. 21, 1954; children—Simon John, Marion Rose, Mark Alexander, Paul Daniel, Adam James. M.B., B.S. (honors), Univ. Coll. Hosp. Med. Sch., London, 1948, M.D., 1951. House surgeon Univ. Coll. Hosp., 1948; sr. house physician Chase Farm Hosp., 1949; med. registrar Univ. Coll. Hosp., 1953-56; research asst. professorial med. unit, 1956-57, Bilton Pollard fellow, 1957-59; 1st asst. physician St. George's Hosp., London, 1959-60; cons. to Woolwich Hosp. Group, London, also; Redhill Hosp. Group, Surrey, Eng., 1960-63; chief Chgo. Med. Sch. Service, Div. Medicine; also dir. renal unit Cook County Hosp., Chgo., 1963-66; chmn. dept. medicine Mt. Sinai Hosp. Med. Center, Chgo., 1966-79; prof., chmn. dept. medicine Chgo. Med. Sch., 1967-74; prof. dept. medicine Rush Med. Coll., Chgo., 1975—. Contbr. articles profl. jours. Bd. govs. Inst. Medicine Chgo. Served with M.C. Brit. Army, 1951-53. Fellow A.C.P., Royal Coll. Physicians; mem. Am. Soc. Nephrology, Brit. Soc. Immunology, Central Soc. Clin. Investigation, Internat. Soc. Nephrology, Med. Research Soc. London, Med. Soc. London, Soc. Med. History Chgo., Soc. Exptl. Biology and Medicine, Sigma Xi, Alpha Omega Alpha (faculty mem.). Home: 2808 Knollwood Ln Glenview IL 60025 Office: 710 S Paulina St Chicago IL 60612

FREEDMAN, RONALD, educator; b. Winnipeg, Man., Can., Aug. 8, 1917; came to U.S., 1924, naturalized, 1920; s. Isador and Ada (Greenstone) F.; m. Deborah Gail Selin, May 4, 1941; children—Joseph Selin, Jane Ilene. B.A., U. Mich., 1939, M.A., 1940; Ph.D., U. Chgo., 1947. Mem. faculty U. Mich., Ann Arbor, 1946—, prof. sociology, 1954—, Roderick D. McKenzie prof. sociology, 1979—; research asso. Survey Research Center, 1954—; dir. Population Studies Center, 1962-71; co-dir. Taiwan Populations Studies Center, 1962-64; cons. to govt., 1962—; Mem. Tech. Adv. Com. 1970 Census of Population, 1965, Pres.'s Adv. Com. on Population and Family Planning. Author: The Sociology of Human Fertility, 1960, (with others) Family Planning, Sterility and Population Growth, 1959, Principles of Sociology, 1952, Family Planning in Taiwan, 1969; also articles and monographs. Dir. Beth Israel Center, Ann Arbor, 1950-54. Served with USAAF, 1942-45. Recipient award excellence on teaching U. Mich. Class of, 1952, Distinguished Faculty Service award U. Mich., 1970; Guggenheim fellow, 1957-58; Fulbright fellow, 1957-58; fellow Center for Advanced Study in Behavioral Scis., 1970. Fellow Am. Acad. Arts and Scis., Am. Statis. Assn.; mem. Nat. Acad. Scis., Population Assn. Am. (pres. 1964-65), Internat. Union Study Population (v.p. 1966—), Am. Sociol. Assn., Sociol. Research Assn., Phi Beta Kappa. Home: 1404 Beechwood Rd Ann Arbor MI 48103

FREEDMAN, SAMUEL, judge; b. Russia, April 16, 1908; emigrated to migrated to Can., 1911; s. Nathan and Ada (Foxman) F.; m. Claris Brownie, June 29, 1934; children: Martin H., Susan R., Phyllis C. B.A. (hons.), U. Man., 1929; LL.B., Man. Law Sch., 1933; LL.D., U. Windsor, 1960, N.D. State U., 1965, U. Toronto, 1965, Hebrew U. Jerusalem, 1964, U. Man., 1968, Brock U., 1968, McGill U., 1968, Dalhousie U., 1971, Queen's U., 1969, York U., 1971, Trent U., 1972, William Mitchell Coll. Law, St. Paul, 1973, U. Winnipeg, 1983; D. Canon Law, St. John's Coll., Winnipeg, 1967; D.C.L., U. Western Ont., 1973. Bar: Canadian 1933, created Queen's counsel 1944. Mem. firm Steinkopf, Lawrence & Freedman, 1933-45, Freedman & Golden, 1946-52; judge Ct. of Queen's Bench of Man., 1952-60, Ct. of Appeal Man., 1960-83, chief justice, 1971-83; lectr. Man. Law Sch., 1941-59; chancellor U. Man., 1959-68. Pres. YMHA of Winnipeg, 1936-37, Winnipeg Lodge B'nai B'rith, 1943-44; chmn. Rhodes Scholarship Selection Com. Man., 1956-66; co-chmn. central div. Canadian Council Christians and Jews, 1955-58; chmn. Winnipeg chpt. Canadian Friends of Hebrew U., 1953-68; mem. adv. bd. Centre Criminology, U. Toronto.; Bd. dirs. Confdn. Centre of Arts, Charlottetown, P.E.I., Can., 1962-83; trustee John W. Dafoe Found., 1955-78; bd. govs. Hebrew U. Jerusalem, 1955—. Hon. pres. U. Man. Students Union, 1949-50; recipient Man of Year award Sigma Alpha Mu, 1957. Mem. Man. Bar Assn. (pres. 1952), Medico-Legal Soc. Man. (pres. 1954-55), Law Soc. Man. (bencher 1949-52). Home: 425 Cordova St Winnipeg 1 MB Canada Office: 3d Floor 333 Broadway Winnipeg 1 MB Canada R3C 0T1

FREEDMAN, SAMUEL ORKIN, university official; b. Montreal, Que., Can., May 8, 1928; s. Abraham Orkin and Elvira (Gottheil) F.; m. Norah Lee Maizel, Aug. 28, 1955; children—David Orkin, Daniel Ari, Abraham Edward, Elizabeth Vera. B.Sc., McGill U., Montreal, 1949, M.D., C.M., 1953. Intern Jewish Gen. Hosp., Montreal, 1953-54; resident in internal medicine and allergy Montreal Gen. Hosp., also Roosevelt Hosp., N.Y.C., 1954-59; mem. faculty McGill U. Med. Faculty, 1959—, prof. medicine, 1968—, dean, 1977-81, vice-prin. (acad.), 1981—; vis. prof. U. London, Eng., 1973-74; dir. div. clin. immunology and allergy Montreal Gen. Hosp., 1967-77; bd. dirs. Nat. Cancer Inst. Can., 1979—; chmn. com. immunology and transplanatation Med. Research Council Can., 1968-73, mem. program grants com., 1975-78. Editor: Clinical Immunology, 2d edit, 1976. Recipient Queen's Silver Jubliee medal, 1977; Gairdner Internat. award for outstanding med. research, 1978. Fellow Royal Soc. Can., Royal Coll. Physicians and Surgeons Can., ACP, Am. Acad. Allergy; Mem. Internat. Assn. Allergology and Clin. Immunology (v.p. 1982—); mem. Am. Soc. Clin. Investigation, Am. Assn. Immunology, Am. Thoracic Soc., Canadian Soc. Clin. Investigation. Jewish. Club: Univ. (Montreal). Co-discoverer CEA test for cancer, 1969. Home: 658 Murray Hill Ave Montreal PQ H3Y 2W6 Canada Office: 845 Sherbrooke St W Montreal PQ H3A 2T5 Canada

FREEDMAN, STANLEY MARVIN, mfg. co. exec.; b. Frederick, Md., Aug. 26, 1923; s. Jacob Menaham and Ethel (Freiman) F.; m. Lynn Maureen Katchen, Apr. 24, 1957; children—Rita, Lynn, Michael, Richard, Jon, Jack. Student, Georgetown U., 1944; A.B. in English, High Point Coll., 1946. Owner, operator retail bus., Bound Brook, N.J., 1949-63; dir. mktg. Franklin State Bank, Somerset, N.J., 1963-65; program dir. mktg. div. Am. Mgmt. Assn. N.Y.C., 1965-67; exec. dir. Internat. Bus. Forms Industries, Washington, 1967-69; dir. communications, dir. office machines group Bus. Equipment Mfrs. Assn., Washington, 1969-72; div. pres. Litton Industries, Hampton, Va., 1972-74, group v.p., paper, printing and forms group, Virginia Beach, Va., 1974—; cons. bus. planning and devel; univ. lectr.; dir. Somerset County Savs. & Loan; exec. in residence U. Wis. Grad. Sch. Bus., 1973. Mem. Bound Brook Bd. Edn., 1955-63; trustee Raritan Valley Hosp., Somerset, N.J., 1960-62; chmn. Urban Devel., Bound Brook, N.J., 1963. Served with U.S. Army, 1943-46; PTO. Mem. Am. Transfer Print Assn. (conf. bd.), Am. Mgmt. Assn. Home and office: 909 Muller Ln Virginia Beach VA 23452

FREEDMAN, THEODORE MURRAY, diversified mfg. co. exec.; b. N.Y.C., Dec. 13, 1930; s. Abraham and Betty (Levinson) F.; m. Hope Luby, Aug. 14, 1972; children by previous marriage—Michael, Robin. B.B.A., City Coll. N.Y., 1951. C.P.A., Calif. Sr. auditor Price Waterhouse & Co. (C.P.A.'s), Los Angeles, 1955-56; div. controller Paramount Pictures Corp., Los Angeles, 1956-59; v.p. fin. Royal Industries Inc., Los Angeles, 1959-77; treas. Lear Siegler, Inc., Santa Monica, Calif., 1977-79; exec. v.p. fin., treas. Wyle Labs., El Segundo, Calif., 1979—. Served with USMC, 1951-53. Mem. Am., Calif. insts. C.P.A.'s, Nat. Assn. Accountants. Club: Sunrise Racquet (Palm Springs, Calif.). Home: 2311 Roscomare Rd Los Angeles CA 90077 Office: 128 Maryland St El Segundo CA 90245

FREEDMAN, WALTER, lawyer; b. St. Louis, Oct. 30, 1914; s. Sam and Sophie (Gordon) F.; m. Maxine Weil, June 23, 1940; children—Jay W., Sandra Freedman Sabel. A.B., Washington U., 1937, J.D., 1937; LL.M., Harvard, 1938. Bar: Mo. bar, Ill. bar, D.C. bar. Atty. SEC, Washington, 1938-40, U.S. Dept. Interior, 1940-42; chief counsel Office Export Control, Foreign Econ. Adminstrn., 1942-44, dir., 1944-45; partner Freedman, Levy, Kroll & Simonds (and predecessor firm), Washington, 1946—; Fairchild fellow Harvard U. Law Sch., 1937-38. Editor-in-chief: Washington U. Law Quarterly, 1936-37; Contbr. articles to profl. jours. Decorated chevalier de l'Order de la Couronne (Belgium). Mem. Washington Bd. Trade, Am. Law Inst., Am., Fed., D.C. bar assns., Phi Beta Kappa, Omicron Delta Kappa, Phi Sigma Alpha. Jewish (trustee temple). Clubs: Internat., Woodmont Country (bd. mgrs.). Home: 4545 W St NW Washington DC 20007 Office: 1730 K St NW Washington DC 20006

FREEDMAN, WALTER S., retail co. exec.; b. N.Y.C., Sept. 13, 1925; s. Abraham and Florence (Sherman) F.; m. Jacqueline Mond, Sept. 7, 1947; 1 dau., Cathy. B.B.A., Coll. City N.Y., 1947. C.P.A., N.Y. Sr. accountant Touche, Ross, Bailey & Smart (C.P.A.'s), N.Y.C., 1951-56; controller Alexander's, Inc., N.Y.C., 1956-67, sr. v.p. finance, 1967—, also dir. Mem. Met. Controllers Assn., Controllers Congress, N.Y. State Soc. C.P.A.'s, Nat. Retail Merchants Assn. Home: 200 E 57th St New York City NY 10022 Office: Alexander's Inc 500 7th Ave New York City NY 10018

FREEH, EDWARD JAMES, chemical engineer; b. Pleasant Valley, Pa., Sept. 18, 1925; s. Charles Michael and Catherine (Jamann) F.; m. Vivian Marie Igel, Sept. 27, 1952; children—Edward James, Gerard, Vincent, George, Marianne. B. Chem.Engring, U. Dayton, 1948; M.S., MIT, 1950; Ph.D., Ohio State U., 1958. Process engr. du Pont Co., Seaford, Del., 1950-52; staff U. Dayton Research Inst., 1952-55, asso. dir., 1959-62; instr. Ohio State U., 1955-58, prof. chem. engring., 1968-75; v.p. tech. Duval Corp., Tucson, 1975—; staff Indsl. Nucleonics Corp., Columbus, 1958-59; prof. U. Ariz., 1962-68. Served with USNR, 1943-45. Mem. Am. Chem. Soc., Am. Inst. Chem. Engrs., AIME, Instrument Soc. Am., Ariz. Solar Energy Commn. Research in application of computers to mineral processing. Patentee in field. Home: 4415 N Alvernon Way Tucson AZ 85718 Office: Duval Corp 4715 E Fort Lowell Rd Tucson AZ 85712

FREEHLING, NORMAN, stockbroker; b. Chgo., Oct. 15, 1905; s. Isaac and Pearl (Eichberg) F.; m. Edna Wilhartz, Feb. 14, 1934; children—William W., Paul E. A.B., U. Mich., 1927; J.D., Chgo. Kent Coll. of Law, 1932. Mem. Chgo. Stock Exchange, 1927-49, Midwest Stock Exchange, 1949—; partner Norman Freehling & Co., 1936-47, Freehling, Meyerhoff & Co., 1947-63, Freehling & Co., 1963—; Past chmn. bd. Midwest Stock Exchange. Clubs: Standard (Chgo.); Northmoor Country (Highland Park, Ill.) (past pres.). Home: 399 Fullerton Parkway Chicago IL 60614 Office: 120 S LaSalle St Chicago IL 60603

FREEHLING, STANLEY MAXWELL, investment banker; b. Chgo., July 2, 1924; s. Julius and Juliette (Stricker) F.; m. Joan Steif, Jan. 26, 1947; children: Elizabeth, Robert Stanley, Margaret J. Student, U. Chgo., 1942-43, Ind. U., 1943-44, U. Stockholm, Sweden, 1946-47. With First Nat. Bank Chgo., 1947-52; partner Freehling & Co. (mems. N.Y. Stock Exchange), Chgo., 1960—, Freehling Bros. (real estate), 1948—; dir. G.R.I. Corp., Republic Capital Corp. Mem. Ill. Pub. Employees Pension Laws Commn., 1962-66; Chmn. Ravinia Festival Assn., 1967-71; pres. men's council Art Inst. Chgo., 1962-65, trustee, 1970—; trustee Glenwood (Ill.) Sch. for Boys, 1967—, Lake Forest Coll., 1972-83; mem. U. Chgo. citizen bd.; mem. vis. com. to arts and humanities U. Chgo., mem. Chgo. com., trustee, 1983—; mem. Council on Fgn. Relations; chmn. bd. Ill. Arts Council, 1971-73; hon. chmn. Chgo. Theatre Group; bd. dirs. Northwestern Meml. Hosp., Chgo., Nat. Corp. Theatre Fund, N.Y.C., Sadler's Wells Theatre Assn., London; chmn. bd. Goodman Theatre; treas. Cradle Soc.; chmn. Pub. Arts Adv. Com.; trustee Orchestral Assn. Mem. Northwestern U. Assos. Clubs: Casino, Arts, Bond, Commercial (Chgo.); Lake Shore Country (Glencoe, Ill.); Mid-Day. Home: 121 Belle St Highland Park IL 60035 Office: 120 S LaSalle St Chicago IL 60603

FREEHLING, WILLARD MAXWELL, stockbroker; b. Chgo., Oct. 16, 1913; s. Isaac and Pearl (Eichberg) F.; m. Elaine Stadeker, June 27, 1947; children—Susan (Mrs. Kenneth Axelrad), Patricia. Student, U. Mich., 1930-33. Partner Norman Freehling & Co., Chgo., 1934-47; partner Freehling, Meyerhoff & Co., Chgo., 1947-69, Freehling & Co., 1969—. Served with AUS, 1941-45. Clubs: Standard (Chgo.) (pres. 1974-76, dir. 1968-78); Northmoor Country (Highland Park, Ill.)). Home: 1350 Sunview Ln Winnetka IL 60093 Office: Freehling & Co 120 S LaSalle St Chicago IL 60603

FREEHLING, WILLIAM WILHARTZ, historian, educator; b. Chgo., Dec. 26, 1935; s. Norman and Edna (Wilhartz) F.; m. Natalie Paperno, Jan. 27, 1961 (div. Apr. 1970); children—Alan Jeffrey, Deborah Ann; m. Alison Goodyear, June 19, 1971; children—Alison Harrison, William Goodyear. A.B., Harvard, 1958; M.A., U. Calif. at Berkeley, 1959, Ph.D., 1964. Woodrow Wilson fellow U. Calif. at Berkeley, 1961-63; instr. history Harvard, 1963-64; mem. faculty U. Mich., 1964-72, asso. prof. history, 1967-70, prof. history, 1970-72, Johns Hopkins, Balt., 1972—. Author: Prelude to Civil War: The Nullification Controversy in South Carolina, 1816-1836, 1966. Trustee Balt. Mus. Art, Roland Park Country Sch. of Balt. Nat. Humanities Found. fellow, 1968; Guggenheim fellow, 1970; recipient Allan Nevins History prize, 1965, Bancroft History prize, 1967. Mem. Am., So. hist. assns., Phi Beta Kappa. Home: 1808 Belfast Rd Sparks MD 21152

FREELAND, JAMES M. JACKSON, lawyer; b. Miami, Fla., Feb. 17, 1927; s. Byron Brazil and Mary Helen (Jackson) F.; m. Saskia Oudgenoeg; children: Carole Leigh, Thomas Byron, James Jackson. A.B., Duke U., 1950; J.D., U. Fla., Gainesville, 1954; postgrad. fellow, Yale U. Law Sch., 1960-61. Bar: Fla. 1954. Assoc. firm Dowling & Culverhouse, Jacksonville, 1954-57; mem. faculty U. Fla. Law Sch., 1957-60, 61-62, 65—, prof. law, 1970—, dir. grad. tax law program, 1977-82; prof. law N.Y. U. Law Sch., 1963-65; vis. prof. U. Ariz. Law Sch., Tucson, 1969-70; mem. tax faculty Practicing Law Inst., 1969-76; of counsel firm Baer & McGoldrick, Palm Beach, Fla., 1975-77. Co-author: Federal Income Taxation of Estates and Beneficiaries, 1970, Fundamentals of Federal Income Taxation, 4th edit, 1982; adv. editor: Jour. Corp. Taxation, 1977—. Served with USNR, 1944-46. Named Outstanding prof. U. Fla., 1968, Outstanding Law Prof., 1970-73, 75; Designated Disting. Service Prof. Law, 1982. Mem. Am. Law Inst., Am. Coll. Tax Counsel, Fla. Bar (chmn. com. income tax estates and trusts, exec. counsel, tax sect. 1971-81, outstanding tax lawyer 1981), Blue Key, Order of Coif, Phi Kappa Phi. Democrat. Methodist. Home: 7700 NW 41st Ave Gainesville FL 32601 Office: Holland Law Center Univ Fla Gainesville FL 32611

FREELAND, T. PAUL, lawyer; b. Princeton, Ind., Sept. 26, 1916; s. Leander Theodore and Leona B. (Tryon) F.; m. Caroline Van Dyke Ransom, July 7, 1941; 1 dau., Caroline Carr (Mrs. Torrance C. Raymond). A.B., DePauw U., 1937; LL.B., Columbia U., 1940. Bar: N.Y., D.C., Mass. Assoc. firms Cravath, de Gersdorff, Swaine & Wood, N.Y.C., summer 1939, Dunnington, Bartholow & Miller, 1940-42; atty. office chief counsel IRS, 1945-48; partner firms Wenchel, Schulman & Manning, Washington, 1948-62, Sharp & Bogan, 1962-65, Bogan & Freeland, 1965-83, Sutherland, Asbill & Brennar, 1983—; lectr. various tax insts. Trustee Embry-Riddle Aero. U., 1972-82. Served as lt. USCGR, 1942-45; ETO. Mem. Am., Inter-Am., Fed., D.C. bar assns., Internat. Fiscal Assn., U.S. C. of C. (task force on internat. tax policy), Phi Delta Phi. Clubs: Met., Chevy Chase (Md.). Home: 5525 Pembroke Rd Bethesda MD 20817 Office: 1000 16th St Washington DC 20006

FREEMAN, ALAN RICHARD, med. educator; b. Atlantic City, Jan. 16, 1937; s. Morris and Sophia (Gulkin) F.; m. Margaret Louise Bechtold, Oct. 12, 1979; children—Barry David Freeman, Robin Lisa Freeman. B.Sc., Phila. Coll. Pharmacy and Sci., 1958; Ph.D., Hahnemann Med. Coll., Phila., 1962. Instr. Pharmacology Hahnemann Med. Coll., 1962-63; trainee fellow in neurophysiology and biophysics Columbia Coll. Physicians and Surgeons, N.Y.C., 1963-66; asst. prof. physiology Rutgers U. Med. Sch., N.J., 1966-68, asso. prof., 1968-71; asso. prof. psychiatry and physiology Ind. U. Med. Center, Bloomington, 1971-73, prof., 1973-74; prof., chmn. dept. physiology Temple U. Sch. Medicine, Phila., 1974—; cons. NIH. Contbr. numerous articles and revs. to sci. jours. Mem. AAAS, Am. Fedn. Clin. Research, Am. Physiol. Soc., Assn. Chairmen Depts. Physiology, Biophys. Soc., Marine Biol. Lab. Corp., N.Y. Acad. Sci., Soc. Gen. Physiology, Soc. Neurosci., Sigma Xi. Home: 220 Locust St Philadelphia PA 19106 Office: 3420 N Broad St Philadelphia PA 19131

FREEMAN, ALBERT CORNELIUS, JR., actor; b. San Antonio, Mar. 21, 1934; s. Albert Cornelius and Lottie Brisette (Coleman) F.; m. Sevara E. Clemon, Jan. 8, 1960. Student, Los Angeles City Coll., 1957; M.A., Amherst U. Actor various theatres in U.S., 1960-; appeared in: The Long Dream, 1960, Kicks & Co, 1961, Tiger Tiger Burning Bright, 1962, The Living Premise, 1963, Trumpets of the Lord, 1963, Blues for Mister Charlie, 1964, Conversations at Midnight, 1964, The Slave, 1964, Dutchman, 1965, Measure for Measure, 1966, Camino Real, 1968, The Dozens, 1969, Look to the Lilies, 1970, Are You Now Or Have You Ever Been, 1972, Medea, 1973, The Poison Tree, 1973, The Great Macdaddy, 1974; movies include Torpedo Run, 1958, Dutchman, 1967, Finian's Rainbow, 1968, The Detective, 1968, Castle Keep, 1969, The Lost Man, 1969, My Sweet Charlie, 1970; actor, dir.: A. Fable; writer: Countdown at Kusini, 1976; appearance: TV drama spl. The Chicago Conspiracy Trial, 1975; appeared in: TV series Hot L Baltimore, 1975; TV movie Roots: The Next Generation, 1978; now appearing: TV drama One Life to Live. Served with USAF. Recipient Russwurm award, Golden Gate award; Emmy award, 1979. Office: care ABC Press Relations 1330 Ave of Americas New York NY 10019 *

FREEMAN, ARTHUR J., educator; b. Lublin, Poland, Feb. 6, 1930; s. Louis and Pearl (Mandelbaum) F.; m. Rhea B. Landin, June 21, 1952; children—Jonathan, Seth, Claudia, Sarah. B.S. in Physics, Mass. Inst. Tech., 1952, Ph.D., 1956. Instr. Brandeis U., 1955-56; solid state physicist Army Materials Research Agy., Watertown, Mass., 1956-62; instr. Northeastern U., 1957-59; asso. dir., leader theory group Francis Bitter Nat. Magnet Lab., Mass. Inst. Tech., 1962-67; prof. physics, chmn. dept. Northwestern U., Evanston, Ill., 1967—; cons. Mass. Inst. Tech., Argonne Nat. Lab. Editor: Hyperfine Interactions, 1967, The Actinides: Electronic and Related Properties, Internat. Jour. Magnetism, 1970-75, Jour. Magnetism and Magnetic Materials, 1975—; Contbr. numerous articles to tech. lit. Guggenheim fellow, 1970-71; Fulbright-Hays fellow, 1970-71; Alexander von Humboldt Stiftung fellow, 1977-78. Fellow Am. Phys. Soc. Home: 824 Monticello Pl Evanston IL 60201

FREEMAN, BRADFORD MACLEAN, investment banking firm executive; b. Fargo, N.D., Mar. 11, 1942; s. Russell Otis and Louise Adams (Fuller) F. A.B., Stanford U., 1964; M.B.A., Harvard U., 1966. With Dean Witter & Co., Los Angeles, 1966—, N.Y.C., v.p., 1969-77, sr. v.p., 1977—. Mem. Beta Theta Pi. Clubs: Calif., Beach, Knickerbocker. Office: 5 World Trade Ctr. New York NY 10048

FREEMAN, CAROLYN RUTH, radiation oncologist; b. Kettering, Eng., Jan. 2, 1950; emigrated to Can., 1974, naturalized, 78; d. Ivor Thomas and Winnifred Mary (Scotney) F.; m. J.C. Negrete, July 25, 1981. Student, King's Coll. London U., 1967-69; DM.IB., B.S., Westminster Med. Sch. London U., 1972. House officer Westminster Hosp., London, 1972-73, registrar in med. and radiation oncology, 1973-74; intern McGill U., Montreal, Que., can., 1974-75, resident in radiation oncology, Montreal, Que., Can., 1975-78; asst. prof. radiation oncology McGill U. Hosps., 1978-79, chmn. dept. radiation oncology faculty Medicine, 1979—, radiation oncologist-in-chief, 1979—. Contbr. articles to med. publs. Fellow Royal Coll. Physicians (Can.); mem. Royal Coll. Physicians (Eng.), Royal Coll. Surgeons (Eng.), Can. Assn. Radiologists, Am. Soc. Therapeutic Radiologists, Can. Oncology Soc. Home: 4270 deMaisonneuve W Montreal PQ Canada H3Z 1K6 Office: 1650 Cedar Ave Montreal PQ Canada H3G 1A4

FREEMAN, CLARENCE CALVIN, fin. exec.; b. Lancaster, Pa., July 2, 1923; s. Clarence Calvin and Margaret (Hollinger) F.; m. B. Virginia Miller, Aug. 26, 1944; children—Margaret Ann, Elizabeth Ann, Martha Suzanne. A.B. cum laude, Franklin and Marshall Coll., 1951. Asst. bookkeeper Battery & Brake Service Co., Lancaster, 1941-42; supr. inventory records and receiving Armstrong Cork Co., Lancaster, 1946-48; accountant Internat. Latex Corp., Dover, Del., 1951-52, Ebasco Services, Inc., Holtwood, Pa., 1952-53; office mgr., accountant A.O. Smith Corp., Leola, Pa., 1953-54; office mgr., plant accountant Sybron-Permutit div., Lancaster, 1954-57; div. controller BCA div. Fed. Mogul Corp., Lancaster, 1957-64, controller, Southfield, Mich., 1964-74; v.p., controller Addressograph-Multigraph Corp., Cleve., 1974-78; adminstrv. v.p., controller Irvin Industries, Stamford, Conn., 1978-79; v.p. fin. Technical Tape Inc., New Rochelle, N.Y., 1979-80; v.p. fin., treas., dir. K-D Mfg. Co., Lancaster, Pa., 1980—; owner accounting service, 1953-64, Dairy Queen, 1956-60; lectr. Franklin and Marshall Coll., 1957-58, Wayne State Grad. Sch., 1966-67; guest speaker Nat. Assn. Accountants. Mem. Oakland County Planning Commn., 1967-68; adviser Jr. Achievement, 1957-58. Served with AUS, 1943-46; PTO. Mem. Nat. Assn. Accountants, Fin. Execs. Inst., Phi Beta Kappa (v.p. Detroit), Pi Gamma Mu. Republican. Presbyterian (elder, deacon). Clubs: Masons, Kiwanis, Elks. Home: 1411 Newton Rd Lancaster PA 17601 Office: K-D Mfg Co 3575 Hempland Rd Lancaster PA 17603 *To succeed in life, it is important to have faith and confidence in one's own capability but to rely on this alone is disastrous; a faith and belief in a supreme being (God) more powerful than any human being is necessary not only to sustain us in times of our own failure, but each and every day as we face life's challenges.*

FREEMAN, CORINNE, mayor; b. N.Y.C., Nov. 9, 1926; d. Bernard J. Hirschfeld and Sidonie (Daxe) Lichtenstein; m. Michael S. Freeman, Mar. 14, 1948; children: Michael L., Stephan J. Student, Adelphi Coll. Sch. Nursing, 1944-47. Registered nurse numerous hosps. in N.Y. and Mass., 1948-64, mayor, St. Petersburg, Fla., 1977—. Chmn. Social Service Allocations Com., St. Petersburg, 1972-76, City Budget Rev. Com., 1973-76, Youth Service System, Pinellas County, 1975-76, West Coast Regional Water Supply Authority; mem. community redevel. com. U.S. Conf. of Mayors; past pres. Fla. League Cities; mem. Pinellas County Mayors Council; 2d v.p. Pinellas County Industry, Council; mem. Nat. League of Cities Revenue and Fin. Task Force; pres. LWV, St. Petersburg, 1970-72, 75-76; bd. dirs. Friends of Library, St. Petersburg, 1973-76; trustee Bayfront Med. Center. Recipient Disting. Alumni award Adelphi U. Mem. Fla. Nursing Assn. Republican. Home: 2101 Pelham Rd N Saint Petersburg FL 33710 Office: Mayors Office PO Box 2842 Saint Petersburg FL 33731

FREEMAN, CYNTHIA (BEA FEINBERG), author; b. N.Y.C.; d. Albert C. and Sylvia Jeannette (Hack) F.; married; 2 children. Student public schs. Interior designer; author: A World Full of Strangers, 1974, Fairytales, 1978, Days of Winter, 1977, Portraits, 1979, Come Pour the Wine, 1980, No Time for Tears, 1981, Catch the Gentle Dawn, 1983. Office: care Arbor House Pub Co 235 E 45th St New York NY 10017 *

FREEMAN, DAVID FORGAN, foundation executive; b. Chgo., June 25, 1918; s. Halstead Gurnee and Marion Kerr (Forgan) F.; m. Hazel Sims Farr, Sept. 6, 1947; children: David Forgan, Simmie, Marion, John, Francis. A.B., Princeton U., 1940; LL.B., Yale U., 1947. Bar: N.Y. 1948. Atty. Debevoise, Plimpton & McLean, N.Y.C., 1947-50; exec. asso. Ford Found., 1950-52; sec. Fund for the Republic, N.Y.C., 1952-54, v.p., 1954-57; asso. Rockefeller Bros. Fund, N.Y.C., 1957-67; pres. Council on Founds., N.Y.C., 1968-78; exec. dir., treas. Scherman Found., N.Y.C., 1979—; pres. So. Edn. Found., Atlanta, 1965-79; bd. dirs. Fund for N.J., 1980—; exec. sec. major awards program Gulf & Western Found., 1981—. Author The Handbook on Private Foundations, 1981. Mem. Rumson (N.J.) Bd. Edn., 1952-55. Served with USNR, 1941-45. Decorated Legion of Merit. Presbyn. (com. on religion and race 1958-61). Clubs: Seabright (N.J.) Beach; Seabright Tennis (Rumson). Home: 13 Oyster Bay Dr Rumson NJ 07760 Office: 250 W 57th St New York NY 10019

FREEMAN, DAVID LYNN, lawyer; b. Pickens, S.C., Aug. 24, 1924; s. Jacob Gardner and Evelyn (Banks) F.; m. Keller Cushing; children: Caleb, David, Lynn, Katherine. A.B., U. S.C., 1945; postgrad., Columbia U., 1946-47; LL.B., Harvard U., 1949. Bar: S.C. 1949. Partner firm Watkins, Vandiver Freeman & Kirven, Anderson, 1949-64, Wyche, Burgess, Freeman & Parham, Greenville, 1964—; mem. S.C. Ho. of Reps., 1955-56, S.C. Bd. Bar Examiners, 1971-81. Contbr. articles to legal jours. Pres. Greenville Symphony Assn., 1975-76, Anderson Community Chest, 1961-62; bd. dirs. Greenville County United Way, Greenville County Found.; pres. Greenville County Found., 1983. Mem. Am. Bar Assn., S.C. Bar Assn. (past pres., chmn. exec. com.), Greenville County Bar Assn., Am. Coll. Trial Lawyers, Am. Law Inst. Presbyterian. Clubs: Rotary (past pres. Greenville and Anderson), Greenville Country, Poinsett. Home: 118 Crescent Ave Greenville SC 29605 Office: 44 E Camperdown Way Greenville SC 29603

FREEMAN, DONALD CHESTER, JR., healthcare company executive; b. Haverhill, Mass., May 15, 1930; s. Donald C. and Isabelle (Brown) F.; m. Wilhelmina Lind, June 23, 1978; children: Robert M., Christopher B., Dorian M. B.S., Brown U., 1951; Ph.D., U. Md., 1955; postgrad., Duke U., 1960-61. Dir. tech. materials system div. Union Carbide Corp., Indpls., 1968-69, gen. mgr. instrument dept., White Plains, N.Y., 1969-71, dir. new bus. devel., 1971-78; pres. Davol, Inc., Providence, 1978-80; group v.p. C.R. Bard, Inc., Murray Hill, N.J., 1980—; dir. R.I. Hosp. Trust Bank, Providence, RIHT Capital Corp. Contbr. articles to sci. jours.; patentee in field. Mem. Am. Phys. Soc., N.Y. Acad. Scis., Greater Providence C. of C. (dir. 1982), Sigma Xi, Alpha Tau Omega. Unitarian. Club: Agawam Hunt (Providence). Home: 27 William Penn Rd Warren NJ 07060 Office: CR Bard Inc 731 Central Ave Murray Hill NJ 07974

FREEMAN, ELSA S., librarian, govt. ofcl.; m. Stuart I. Freeman, 1938 (dec. 1976). B.A., Columbia U., 1939, M.S., 1940. Reference and sch. asst. N.Y.C. Pub. Library, 1940-41; jr. librarian U.S. Bur. Agrl. Econs., Washington, 1941-42; reference asst. Dept. Agr. Library, Washington, then sr. reference asst., asst. chief circulation sect., to 1949; asst. librarian Navy Dept. Bur. Ordnance, Washington, 1949-51; head librarian Office of Geography Library, Dept. Interior, Washington, 1951-56; dir. HUD Library, Washington, 1956—, mem. fed. women's com., 1970-73; mem. exec. adv. com. Fed. Library Com., 1970-71, also chmn. task force on acquisition library materials and correlation fed. library resources, chmn. panel on regional libraries, 1975—; mem. com. sci. and tech. info. and panel info. analysis centers Fed. Council for Sci. and Tech., 1970-73; librarians' tech com. Met. Washington Council Govts., 1969-76; mem. exec. adv. council Fed. Library and Info. Network, 1980—; coordinator Fed. Inter-Agy. Field Librarians Workshop, 1979, 80; lectr. in field. Editor: Progress in Science and Technology Communications, 1970; contbr. articles to mags. Mem. bd. Christian edn. Christ Episcopal Ch., Alexandria, Va., mem. vestry, 1976-80; bd. govs. Performing Arts Assn., Alexandria, 1977-80. Recipient Spl. Achievement award HUD Library, 1976, 78, 79. Mem. Little Theatre Alexandria, Spl. Libraries Assn. (editor brochures, pres. Washington chpt. 1954-55, chmn. conv. program com. 1960-62, chmn. planning bldg. and housing sect. 1965-66), ALA (chmn. bldgs. com. hosp., instn. spl. libraries 1962-64), Internat. Fedn. Library Assns. (chmn. conf. com. 1974), Assn. Coll., Research Libraries, Am. Soc. Info. Sci., Alumni Assn. Columbia, No. Va. Fine Arts Assn., Phi Beta Kappa, Beta Phi Mu. Club: Columbian Toastmistress (1st pres. 1959-60). Home: 3519 Fort Hill Dr Wilton Woods Alexandria VA 22310 Office: 451 7th St SW Room 8141 Washington DC 20410

FREEMAN, GEORGE CLEMON, JR., lawyer; b. Birmingham, Ala., Jan. 3, 1929; s. George Clemon and Annie Laura (Gill) F.; m. Anne Colston Hobson, Dec. 6, 1958; children: Anne Colston, George Clemon III, Joseph Reid Anderson. B.A., Vanderbilt U., 1950; LL.B., Yale U., 1956. Bar: Ala. 1956, Va. 1958, D.C. 1974. Law clk. Justice Hugo L. Black, U.S. Supreme Ct., 1956; practiced in, Richmond, Va., 1957—; mem. firm Hunton & Williams, 1957—, partner, 1963—. Contbr. articles to profl. jours. Pres. Va. chpt. Nature Conservancy, 1962-63; mem. sect. 301 Superfund Act Study Group Congl. Adv. Com., 1981-82; Mem. Falls of James Com., 1973—; Chmn. Richmond City Democratic Com., 1969-71; chmn. adv. council Energy Policy Studies Ctr., U. Va., 1981—; Sec., bd. dirs. Richmond Symphony, 1960-63. Served to lt. (j.g.) USNR, 1951-54. Mem. ABA (chmn. law library congress com. 1968-73, chmn. trade assns. com. 1969-75, council corp., banking and bus. law sect. 1975-79, chmn. ad hoc on Fed. Criminal Code 1979-81, chmn. program com. 1981-82, mem. coordinating group on regulatory reform 1981—), Richmond Bar Assn., Va. Bar Assn., Am. Law Inst. (council 1980—), Am. Judicature Soc., Phi Beta Kappa, Phi Delta Phi, Omicron Delta Kappa, Alpha Tau Omega. Episcopalian. Clubs: Country of Virginia (Richmond); Knickerbocker (N.Y.C.); Metropolitan (Washington). Home: 10 Paxton Rd Richmond VA 23226 Office: 707 E Main St Richmond VA 23212 also 2000 Pennsylvania Ave NW Washington DC 20036

FREEMAN, GEORGE LESTER, banker; b. Detroit, Feb. 16, 1928; s. Jasper Wooten and Marie (Lester) F.; m. Mary Grace Roderick, July 16, 1954; children: Thomas Lester, Helen Roderick, Martha. B.A., Vanderbilt U., 1951; cert. in Advanced Mgmt., U. Chgo. Indsl. Relations Center, 1974. With So. Bell Telephone Co., Jacksonville, Ft. Lauderdale and Miami, Fla., 1952-68, asst. to v.p., 1968; exec. v.p. Greater Miami C. of C., Miami, Fla., 1968-81; sr. v.p. Southeast Bank, Miami, 1981—; exec. v.p. Greater Miami Fgn. Trade Zone Inc. Mem. Orange Bowl Com., 1968—; mem. United Fund of Dade County, 1961—; mem. adv. council U. Miami Center for Law and Econs.; v.p. 3d Century U.S. Corp., 1969-76; metro dir. Nat. Alliance Businessmen, 1968-77; chmn. State Jobs Tng. Coordinating Council; mem. exec. com. Fla. C. of C.; Bd. dirs. South Fla. Community TV, Inc., 1965—, pres., 1967-68; trustee Baptist Hosp., Greater Miami Progress Found. Served with C.E. AUS, 1946-48. Recipient Civic Salesman of Year award Sales and Marketing Execs. Assn. S. Fla., 1966, commendation Pres. Ford, 1976; Humanitarian of Yr. award Nat. Asthma Center, 1980; Community Service award NCCJ, 1981. Methodist. Clubs: Miami, New World Center. Home: 2180 Brickell Ave Unit 5 Miami FL 33129 Office: 100 S Biscayne Blvd Miami FL 33131

FREEMAN, GORDON RUSSEL, chemistry educator; b. Hoffer, Sask., Can., Aug. 27, 1930; s. Winston Spencer Churchill and Aquila Maud (Chapman) F.; m. Phyllis Joan Elson, July 9, 1927; children: Mark Russel, Michèle Leslie. B.A., U. Sask., 1952, M.A., 1953; Ph.D., McGill U., 1957; D.Phil., Oxford (Eng.) U., 1957. Postdoctoral fellow Centre D'Etudes Nucleaires, Saclay, France, 1957-58; asst. prof., then assoc. prof. chemistry U. Alta. (Can.), Edmonton, 1958-65, prof., 1965—, chmn. div. phys. and theoretical chemistry, 1965-75; exec. Chem. Inst. Can., 1974-80, chmn. phys. chemistry div., 1976-78, councillor, 1978-80. Contbr. articles to jours., chpts. to books. Research grantee Nat. Research Council Can., 1959-78, Natural Scis. and Engrng. Research Council Can., 1978—, Def. Research Bd. Can., 1965-72. Mem. Chem. Inst. Can., Am. Phys. Soc., Radiation Research Soc., Can. Assn. Physicists. Office: Chemistry Dept U Alta Edmonton AB Canada T6G 2G2

FREEMAN, GRAYDON LAVERNE, publishing company executive; b. LaGrange, Ohio, Aug. 30, 1904; s. G. Simeon and Lena (Goodman) F.; m. Ruth Lazeare Sunderlin, June 22, 1929; children: James Lazeare, John Crosby, Peter Sunderlin. B.E., Cortland State Coll., 1923; B.S., Syracuse U., 1925; M.A., Cornell U., 1927, Ph.D., 1929; D.Sc., U. Chgo., 1935. High sch. prin., Marathon, N.Y., 1926-27; Sage research fellow, Edminster tutor Cornell U., 1928-29; fellow Nat. Research Found., Yale, 1930-31; successively instr., asst. prof., asso. prof., prof. psychology Northwestern U., 1932-45; lab. dir. psychophysiology, dir. gen. edn. Univ. Coll., 1937-42; vis. prof. New Sch. Social Research, 1949; pres. Century House Publishers, 1949-69; nat. syndicated lectr. Colson Leigh Bur., 1952-58; dir. retirement research USPHS; also prof. Western Res. U., 1955-57; exec. dir. Am. Life Found. and Study Inst., Watkins Glen, N.Y., 1959—; Pres. Prang Mark Soc.; vis. fellow Med. Research Council, Applied Med. Psychology Unit, Cambridge and London U., Eng., 1962-70, Cal. Retirement Centers, 1972-73. Author: Physiological Psychology, 2d edit, 1947, Energetics of Human Behavior, 2d edit, 1973, Fields of Psychology, 1948, How To Pick Leaders, 1950, Motivation and Morale in Industry, 2d edit, 1973, Self-Management for Management Men, 1958, Louis Prang of Boston, Giant of a Man, 1971, Self Fulfilment and Aging, 1973, Tension Release for Self Mastery of Nerves, 1974; other books on psychology and Childhood's Greatest Illustrator, 1977; Editor: The Am. Life quar, 1962-75, Next Horizons, 1969, Wish You Were Here: Centennial Guide to Postcard Collecting, 1978, American Pioneer Arts and Artists, 1978, Yesterdays Schools and School Books, 2 vols, 1978, Spa Fever, 1981, others. Served as comdr. USNR, 1942-45; dir. naval officer procurement, service sch. selection. Guggenheim fellow, 1945-46. Home: Manor House at Am Life's Study Inst Old Irelandville PO Watkins Glen NY 14891 Office: Watkins Glen NY 14891

FREEMAN, HARROP ARTHUR, lawyer; b. Elyria, Ohio, Nov. 7, 1907; s. Glenn and Lena (Goodman) F.; m. Ruth N. St. John, June 11, 1930; 1 son, Norman D. Student, Cortland Normal Sch., 1920-25; A.B., Cornell U., 1929, LL.B., 1930, S.J.D., 1945. Bar: N.Y. State bar 1931. Practiced as asso. with firm Cohn, Chorman & Franchot (later Franchot, Runals, Robillard & Cohen, then Franchot, Runals, Cohen, Taylor & Rickert), Niagara Falls, N.Y., 1930-42; in pvt. practice, specializing in taxation and pub. law, Phila. and Ithaca, N.Y., since 1942; Exec. dir. Pacifist Research Bur., Phila.; prof. law Coll. of William and Mary, Williamsburg, Va., 1942-45; prof. Law Sch., Cornell U., since 1945; lectr. on internat. affairs and law. Author: Road to Peace, 1947, Administrative Law of India, 1960, Dear Mr. President, An Open Letter on Foreign Policy, 1961, Legal Interviewing and Counseling, 1964, Counseling, 1965, Counseling in the United States, 1966, Clinical Training, 1972, Tax Practice Deskbook, 1973; Contbr. law reviews and mags. Candidate U.S. Ho. of Reps., 33d N.Y. Dist., 1962; Gen. Counsel Fellowship of Reconciliation Central Com. Conscientious Objectors Soc. Friends. Fellow Center Study Dem. Instns., Santa Barbara. Mem. ABA, Internat. Law Assn., Fellowship of Reconciliation, War Resisters League, Phi Beta Kappa, Order of Coif. Home: 103 Needham Pl Ithaca NY 14850 Office: Myron Taylor Hall Ithaca NY 14850 *Never exploit another person, and never permit another to exploit you, for exploitation is violence to the deepest personality. Associate with the young, and in so doing teach and learn, that you may pass on to them the beauty of the past and link yourself to the unfolding of the future.*

FREEMAN, HARRY BOIT, JR., financial executive; b. Providence, June 14, 1926; s. Harry Boit and Theodora (Hollander) F.; m. Leslie Stires, June 14, 1947; children: Tracy Clark Freeman Baldwin, Harry Boit III. Grad., Middlesex Sch., 1944; B.A., Yale U., 1949; M.B.A., N.Y.U., 1952. With City Bank Farmers Trust Co., N.Y.C., 1949-52; v.p. Tchrs. Ins. & Annuity Assn., also Coll. Retirement Equities Fund, N.Y.C., 1953-59; gen. partner Wood, Struthers & Winthrop (and predecessor), N.Y.C., 1959-67; v.p. Engelhard Hanovia, Inc., Newark, N.J., 1967-70; pres., dir. Channing Mgmt. Corp., also The Channing Funds, N.Y.C., 1970-73; with Lord, Abbett & Co., N.Y.C., 1973-80, gen. partner, 1974-80, asso mng. partner, 1977-78, mng. partner, 1978; dir. Lexington Group of Mut. Funds. Served with USMCR, 1944-45. Mem. Am. Finance Assn. Clubs: Knickerbocker (N.Y.C.); Rumson (N.J.). Home: 200 E 74th St New York NY 10021

FREEMAN, HARRY LOUIS, financial services company executive; b. Omaha, Mar. 1, 1932; s. Joseph H. and Celia (Rivonne) F.; m. Lucile Carpenter, Dec. 26, 1965; children: Bennett, Lansing, Rachel, Alexandra. A.B., U. Mich., 1953; J.D., Harvard U., 1956. Bar: Nebr. bar 1956, Calif. bar 1957, U.S. Supreme Ct. bar 1967, D.C. bar 1968. Clk. U.S. Ct. Appeals, 9th Circuit, 1956-57; mem. firm Janin, Morgan, Brenner & Freeman, San Francisco, 1957-66; dir. Ins. div. AID, Dept. State, Washington, 1966-69; v.p. corp. planning OPIC, Washington, 1969-71, v.p. fin., 1974-75; mgr. comml. projects, mgr. project fin. group Bechtel Corp., San Francisco, 1972-74; v.p. Am. Express Co., Washington, 1975-77, sr. v.p., N.Y.C., 1977-79, sr. v.p., office of chmn., 1979—; adj. prof. internat. law U. Calif., Berkeley, 1974, Georgetown U., 1975-76; Trustee World Affairs Council No. Calif., 1960-66. Contbr. articles to profl. jours. Bd. dirs. Calif. Clinic for Psychotherapy, San Francisco, 1964-66; trustee Com. Econ. Devel., 1983—. Recipient Disting. Service award AID, 1969, OPIC, 1971. Mem. Internat. C. of C. (chmn. comml. policy com. and mem. exec.

com. U.S. council), Am. Bar Assn., Calif. Bar Assn., Nebr. Bar Assn., Washington Bar Assn. Democrat. Jewish. Clubs: Internat. (Washington); Harvard (N.Y.C.); Stock Exchange (San Francisco). Home: 4708 Dorset Ave Chevy Chase MD 20815 Office: 125 Broad St 39th Floor New York NY 10004

FREEMAN, HARRY LYNWOOD, accountant; b. Los Angeles, May 5, 1920; s. Edward Church and Mildred Eaton (Noyes) F.; m. Ruth Turner (Feb. 14, 1941); children: Tracy Ruth (Mrs. Richard W. Flatow), Martin Harry. B.S., UCLA, 1942. C.P.A., Calif. With Price Waterhouse & Co., C.P.A.s, 1942-80, partner, Mexico City, 1956-73; partner-in-charge Middle Americas firm Price Waterhouse & Co. (C.P.A.s), 1973-80. Chmn. auditing com. Am. British Cowdray Hosp., 1962-68; Bd. dirs., treas. YMCA of Mexico, 1967-73; bd. dirs. Inst. Mexicano- Norteamericano de Relaciones Culturales, 1961-69. Served with AUS, 1944- 46. Mem. Am. Inst. C.P.A.s, Calif. Soc. C.P.A.s, Am. C. of C. Mexico (past pres.), Assn. Am. Chambers Commerce in Latin Am. (past pres.). Clubs: University (Mexico City); Wings (N.Y.C.); Lido Isle Yacht (Newport Beach, Calif.). Home: 208 Via Palermo Newport Beach CA 92663

FREEMAN, HERBERT, educator; b. Frankfurt-Main, Germany, Dec. 13, 1925; came to U.S., 1938, naturalized, 1943; s. Leo and Johanna (Friedmann) F.; m. Joan Sleppin, Nov. 24, 1955; children—Nancy, Susan, Robert. B.E.E., Union Coll., 1946; M.S., Columbia U., 1948, Dr. Engring. Sc., 1956. Registered profl. engr., N.Y. Teaching asst. Columbia, N.Y.C., 1946-48; project engr. Sperry Gyroscope Co., Great Neck, N.Y., 1948-57, head advanced studies and data processing depts., 1957-60; asso. prof. N.Y.U., 1960-64, prof., 1965-73, chmn. dept. elec. engring. and computer sci., 1968-73; prof. Rensselaer Poly. Inst., Troy, N.Y., 1975—; vis. asso. prof. Mass. Inst. Tech., 1958-59; vis. prof. Swiss Fed. Inst. Tech., Zurich, 1966, U. Pisa, Italy, 1973; cons. engr. Author: Discrete-Time Systems, 1965; Co-editor: Jour. Computer Graphics and Image Processing, 1971—. Chmn. program com. IFIP Congress 74, Stockholm, 1974; U.S. del. Internat. Fedn. Info. Processing, 1978-79. Guggenheim fellow, 1972-73. Fellow IEEE; mem. Assn. for Computing Machinery, Internat. Assn. Pattern Recognition (pres. 1978-80), N.Y. Acad. Sci., Soc. for Info. Display, Sigma Xi, Eta Kappa Nu. Patentee computers and computer graphics. Home: 4 Upper Ball Ct Albany NY 12204 Office: Rensselaer Polytech Inst Troy NY 12181

FREEMAN, HOWARD LEE, JR., financial executive; b. San Antonio, June 24, 1935; s. Howard Lee and Annie Frances (Bayer) F.; m. Eleanor Margaret Grohman, June 1, 1957; children: Joseph Paul, Thomas Edward. B.B.A. in Acctg., St. Mary's U., 1957, M.B.A. in Fin. Mgmt., 1972; grad. Exec. Program, Stanford U., 1980. Cadet acct. City Pub. Service Bd., San Antonio, 1959-61, internal auditor, 1961-64, supt. customer accounts, 1964-67, chief acct., 1967-72, controller, sec.-treas., 1972-76, asst. gen. mgr. fin. and adminstrn., 1976—; dir. USAA Growth Fund, 1978-81, USAA Income Fund, 1978-81, USAA Mut. Fund Inc., 1981—. Served to 1st lt. AUS, 1957-59. Mem. Fin. Execs. Inst. Club: Optimist. Home: 2710 Hopeton St San Antonio TX 78230 Office: PO Box 1771 San Antonio TX 78296

FREEMAN, IRA HENRY, author, journalist; b. N.Y.C., Aug. 12, 1906; s. Arthur J. and Rachel (Abrams) F.; m. Beatrice Oppenheim, Sept. 21, 1937. B.Litt., Columbia U., 1928. Staff writer N.Y. Times, 1928-61; now free-lance writer. Instr. journalism CCNY, 1950-51; corr. Yank (army weekly), U.S., Europe and Middle East, 1943-45. Author: White Sails Shaking, 1949, Out of the Burning, 1960, (with Beatrice Freeman) Careers and Opportunities in Journalism, 1965; Contbr. to: Yank, the GI Story of the War, 1947, Great Reading from Life, 1960, The Death Penalty in America, 1964, Detail and Pattern, 1969; also numerous articles, mainly on travel (illustrated), and short stories in nat. mags. Recipient George Polk award for nat. reporting L.I.U., 1951. Mem. Am. Newspaper Guild (charter). Harkaway Woodbury NY 11797 Oyster Pond Edgartown MA 02539

FREEMAN, J. STUART, editor; b. Bryn Mawr, Pa., Jan. 19, 1934; s. J. Stuart and Marguerite (Ellis) F.; m. Anne B. Howard, Oct. 12, 1963; children: Anne Shippen, Emily Newhall. A.B., U. Va.-Charlottesville, 1956. Editor article service N.Y. Herald-Tribune Syndicate, Paris, 1959-60; editor W.B. Saunders, Phila., 1960-66, J.B. Lippincott Co., 1966-78, editor-in-chief, 1978—; chmn. Phila. Book Show, 1975. Author: Centennial Reflections, 1976. Chmn. Juvenile Problems com. ACLU, Phila., 1968-72; trustee Friends Select Sch., Phila., 1973-79. Served with U.S. Army, 1956-59; Korea, Japan. Recipient Pres. Cup. Univ. Barge Club, 1968. Quaker. Clubs: Univ. Barge, Franklin Inn (Phila.). Home: 1304 Waverly St Philadelphia PA 19147 Office: JB Lippincott Co E Washington Square Philadelphia PA 19105

FREEMAN, JACK E., university official; b. Ft. Worth, June 15, 1931; s. Oswald Ledbetter and Osielee Ota (Wilcox) F.; m. Betty Ann Hawling, Sept. 1, 1951; children: Jack R., David M., Mark R., Melissa L. B.A., Baylor U., 1953, M.A., 1954; Ph.D., U. Pitts., 1977. Commd. 2d lt. USAF, 1954, advanced through grades to maj., 1965; spl. investigations officer, 1954-59; asst. prof. polit. sci. USAF Acad., 1959-64; politico-mil. affairs officer Hdqrs. USAF, 1964-66; asst. to dep. under sec. Air Force, 1966-67; ret., 1967; exec. asst. to chancellor U. Pitts., 1967-70, exec. asst. chancellor, 1970-71, vice chancellor for planning and budget, 1974-79, sr. vice chancellor adminstrn., 1979—; pres. U. Pitts.-Johnstown, 1971-74; dir. MPC Corp. Bd. dirs. Pace Sch., Presbyn.-Univ. Hosp., Western Psychiat. Inst. and Clinic. Mem. Soc. for Coll. and Univ. Planning (dir.). Office: U Pitts Pittsburgh PA 15260

FREEMAN, JERE EVANS, agribusiness executive; b. Martin, Tenn., Oct. 13, 1936; s. T.C. Donald and Ludie Blanche (Brooks) F.; m. Barbara Jean Magnuson, Dec. 29, 1962; children: Gregory E., Kristina L., Curtis M., J. Brent. B.S., U. Tenn.-Martin, 1958; M.S., U. Ill., 1961, Ph.D., 1962; M.B.A., U. Chgo., 1974. Research scientist CPC Internat., Inc., Argo, Ill., 1962-68, research sect. leader, 1968-76, dir. bus. environ. research, Englewood Cliffs, N.J., 1976-77, corp. dir. indsl. research and devel., 1977-78, mgr. tech. and capital planning N.Am. div., 1978-79; v.p. corp. devel. Gold Kist, Inc., Atlanta, 1979—; dir., v.p. Agra Tech Seeds Inc.; dir. Golden Poultry Co., Inc.; co-rep. Agri-Research Inst., Indsl. Research Inst. Contbr. articles to profl. publs.; patentee in field. Judge state expn. Ill. Jr. Acad. Scis., 1962-75; active Am. Cancer Soc., United Way; member steering com. indsl. interface program U. Ga.; mem. adv. bd. Sci. Research Inst., Atlanta; bd. dirs. Ga. Freight Bur. Mem. Planning Execs. Inst., Am. Soc. Agronomy, Am. Assn. Cereal Chemists, Inst. Food Technologists, Assn. Corp. Growth (v.p., dir. Atlanta chpt.). Office: Gold Kist Inc 244 Perimeter Center Pkwy NE Atlanta GA 30346

FREEMAN, JOE BAILEY, corporation executive; b. Dallas, Apr. 18, 1937; s. Joe Bailey and Beulah Gertrude (Caraway) F.; m. Teresa Adams, Apr. 1, 1984; children: Jon, James, Lisa. B.B.A., North Tex. State U., 1958; M.B.A., So. Meth. U., 1968. C.P.A., Tex. With Collins Radio Co., Richardson, Tex., 1959-67; sr. fin. analyst Tex. Instruments Co., Dallas, 1967-68; v.p., controller automotive group Maremont Corp., Chgo., 1968-73, v.p., controller corp., 1973-76, sr. v.p., 1976-80; sr. v.p., chief fin. officer, dir. Cronos Industries, 1980-81; sr. v.p., chief fin. officer Am. Internat. Inc., Chgo., 1981-82, pres., chief exec., chmn. bd., 1982-84. Served with AUS, 1958-59, 61-62. Mem. Fin. Execs. Inst., Machinery and Allied Products Fin. Council. Home: 1431 Glen Lake Chicago IL 60660 Office: 980 N Michigan Ave Chicago IL 60611

FREEMAN, JOHN MARK, pediatric neurologist; b. Bklyn., Jan. 11, 1933; s. Leon Lucas and Florence (Kann) F.; m. Elaine Kaplan, Aug. 26, 1956; children: Andrew David, Jennifer Beth, Joshua Leon. B.A., Amherst Coll., 1954; M.D., Johns Hopkins U., 1958. Intern Harriet Lane Home, Johns Hopkins U., Balt., 1958-59, resident in pediatrics, 1959-61; fellow in neurology Columbia Presbyn. Hosp., N.Y.C., 1961-64; asst. prof. pediatrics and neurology Stanford (Calif.) U., 1966-69; asso. prof. neurology and pediatrics Johns Hopkins U., Balt., 1969-82, prof., 1982—; dir. pediatric neurology Johns Hopkins, 1969—; dir. seizure clinic Johns Hopkins U., 1973—, dir. birth defects treatment center, 1969—; Pres. Epilepsy Assn. Md., 1977-82; mem. profl. adv. bd. Epilepsy Found. Am., 1975-82, sec., 1977, v.p., 1982—. Contbr. articles to profl. jours. Served with AUS, 1964-66. Named Physician of Yr. Gov.'s Com. on Employment Handicapped, 1979. Fellow Am. Acad. Neurology, Am. Acad. Pediatrics (chmn. neurology sect. 1978-80); mem. Profs. of Child Neurology (pres. 1980-82), Child Neurology Soc. (exec. com. 1979-81), Am. Acad. Pediatrics, Am. Pediatric Soc., Am. Fedn. Clin. Research, Am. Epilepsy Soc., Am. Neurol. Assn. Home: 1026 Rolandvue Rd Towson MD 21204 Office: Johns Hopkins Hosp 601 N Broadway Baltimore MD 21205

FREEMAN, KESTER ST. CLAIR, JR., hospital administrator; b. Richmond, Va., Sept. 10, 1944; s. Kester St. Clair and Anna Leigh (Hawthorne) F.; m. Caroline Rhae Hodges, June 3, 1967; children: Edward Carter, Hunter St. Clair Copley. B.A. in Econs, Coll. William and Mary, 1966; M.H.A., Duke U., 1968. Asst. adminstr. Greenville (S.C.) Gen. Hosp. (Greenville Hosp. System), 1971-72, asso. adminstr., 1972-75, adminstr., 1975-78; hosp. adminstr. Greenville Hosp. Center (Greenville Hosp. System), 1978-81; v.p./adminstr. Fairfax Hosp. Assn., Falls Church, Va., 1981-83; exec. v.p. Richland Meml. Hosp., Columbia, SC, 1983—. Served with USNR, 1968-71. Mem. Am. Coll. Hosp. Adminstrs., Am. Hosp. Assn., S.C. Hosp. Assn. (dir.). Republican. Methodist. Club: Kiawah Island. Home: 2518 Cantebury Rd Oakton VA 22124 Office: 3301 Harden St Columbia SC 29203

FREEMAN, LEE ALLEN, JR., lawyer; b. Chgo., July 31, 1940; s. Lee Allen and Brena (Dietz) F.; m. Glynna Gene Weger, June 8, 1968; children: Crispin McDougal, Clark Dietz, Cassidy Bree. A.B. magna cum laude, Harvard U., 1962, J.D., 1965. Bar: Ill. 1966, D.C. 1966, U.S. Supreme Ct. 1969. Practiced in, Washington, 1965-68, Chgo., 1968—; law clk. to Justice Tom C. Clark, Washington, 1965-66; asst. U.S. atty., 1966-68; v.p. Freeman, Rothe, Freeman & Salzman (P.C.), 1970—; spl. asst. atty. gen., Ill., W.Va., 1969-82, Mich., Wis., Minn., Colo., Ky., N.D., 1973-79, spl. dep. atty. gen., Pa., 1971-82, spl. asst. corp. counsel, Chgo., 1971-76. Pres. Chgo. Lyric Opera Guild; pres. Fine Arts Music Found., Chgo.; vis. com. dept. humanities U. Chgo. Named Outstanding Young Citizen Chgo. Jaycees, 1976. Mem. Am., Ill., Chgo. bar assns. Clubs: Arts, Tavern, Standard. Home: 232 E Walton St Chicago IL 60611 also PO Box 1295 Livingston MT 59047 Office: 2700 The Equitable Bldg Chicago IL 60611

FREEMAN, LEONARD MURRAY, radiologist, nuclear medicine physician, educator; b. N.Y.C., Apr. 20, 1937; s. Joseph and Tillie (Krutman) F.; m. Marlene Carolyn Held, Apr. 28, 1967; children: Eric Lawrence, David Robert, Joy Esther. B.A., N.Y. U., 1957; M.D., Chgo. Med. Sch., 1961. Diplomate: Am. Bd. Radiology, Am. Bd. Nuclear Medicine. Intern Beth Israel Hosp. and Med. Center, N.Y.C., 1961-62; resident in radiology Bronx Municipal Hosp. Center, 1962-65; mem. staff Bronx Municipal Hosp. Center and Hosp. of Albert Einstein Coll. Medicine, N.Y.C., 1965—, co-dir. div. nuclear medicine, 1965-83; dir. nuclear medicine Montefiore Hosp. and Med. Center, N.Y.C., 1976—, attending radiologist, 1977—; cons. nuclear medicine USPHS Hosp., S.I., N.Y., 1967—, St. Barnabas Hosp., Bronx, 1967—, Beth Israel Hosp. and Med. Center, 1974—, Maimonides Hosp. and Med. Center, 1974—; asst. instr. radiology Albert Einstein Coll. Medicine, Bronx, 1964-65, instr., 1965-67, asst. prof., 1967-72, asso. prof., 1972-77, prof., 1977—, prof. nuclear medicine, 1983—; mem. adv. com. nuclear medicine program Brookhaven Nat. Labs., Upton, N.Y., 1972—; examiner nuclear medicine Am. Bd. Radiology. Author: Clinical Scintillation Scanning, 1969, Clinical Scintillation Imaging, 1975, Freeman & Johnson's Clinical Radionuclide Imaging, 1984; co-editor: Seminars in Nuclear Medicine, 1970—, Physicians Desk Reference for Radiology and Nuclear Medicine, 1971-80; reviewer: Jour. Nuclear Medicine, 1972—; editor: Nuclear Medicine Ann, 1977, Current Concepts in Diagnostic Nuclear Medicine, 1983—; mem. editorial bd.: European Jour. Nuclear Medicine, 1979—, Jour. Nuclear Medicine and Allied Scis., 1982—; contbr. numerous articles to jours., also book chpts. Fellow Am. Coll. Radiology; fellow Am. Coll. Nuclear Physicians; mem. Soc. Nuclear Medicine (gov. local chpt. 1973—, nat. trustee 1973-77, nat. v.p. 1977-78, nat. pres. 1979-80, chmn. pub. relations com. 1981—, chmn. correlative imaging council 1982-84, chmn. awards com. 1983—), Assn. Univ. Radiologists, Am. Roentgen Ray Soc., Radiol. Soc. N.Am., N.Y. Roentgen Soc., L.I. Radiol. Soc., Soc. Gastrointestinal Radiologists, N.Y. State Med. Soc., Nassau County Med. Soc., Pan Am. Med. Assn. (hon. life), Gissellschaft für Nuklearmedizin (hon. corr.), L.I. Soc. Nuclear Med. Technologists (hon. life). Home: 65 Oak Dr East Hills NY 11576 Office: 111 E 210th St Bronx NY 10467

FREEMAN, LESLIE GORDON, anthropology educator, anthropologist; b. Warsaw, N.Y., Sept. 9, 1935; s. Leslie Gordon and Theresa Rosalie (Stanbro) F.; m. Susan Tax, Mar. 20, 1964; 1 dau., Sarah Elisabeth. A.B., U. Chgo., 1954, A.M., 1961, Ph.D., 1964. Asst. prof. anthropology Tulane U., 1964-65; asst. prof. U. Chgo., 1965-70, assoc. prof., 1970-76, prof., 1976—. Author (with J. Gonzalez) Cueva Morin, 2 vols., 1971, 73, Vida y Muerte en Cueva Morin, 1978; editor: Views of the Past, 1978; author: (with Sol Tax) Horizons of Anthropology, 1976. Corporator Internat. Inst. Spain, Madrid; bd. dirs. Inst. Prehistoric Investigations. Served with U.S. Army, 1957-59. Recipient Silver Plaque Provincial Deputation of Santander, Spain, 1973. Fellow Am. Anthropol. Assn., Royal Anthropol. Inst., AAAS; mem. Reial Academia de Belles Art de Sant Jordi Barcelona (corr.), Chgo. Acad. Scis. (trustee, 2d v.p. 1981—). Home: 5537 S Woodlawn Ave Chicago IL 60637 Office: Dept Anthropology U Chgo Haskell Hall M-135 Chicago IL 60637

FREEMAN, LINTON CLARKE, sociology educator; b. Chgo., July 4, 1927; s. Willis and Kathryn Clarke (Kieffer) F.; m. Sue Carole Feinberg, Aug. 2, 1958; children: Stacey Elizabeth, Michael Andrew. B.A., Roosevelt U., Chgo., 1952; M.A., U. Hawaii, 1953; Ph.D., Northwestern U., 1956. Asst. prof., then assoc. prof. sociology Syracuse (N.Y.) U., 1956-67; prof. sociology and computer sci. U. Pitts., 1967-69; prof. sociology and info. sci. U. Hawaii, 1969-72; Lucy G. Moses distinguished prof. sociology Lehigh U., Bethlehem, Pa., 1973-79; prof. Sch. Social Scis., U. Calif., Irvine, 1979—, dean, 1979-82; Killam lectr. sociology/anthropology Dalhousie U., Halifax, N.S., Can., 1972; Ward supr. Onondaga County (N.Y.) Bd. Suprs., 1966-68. Author: Elementary Applied Statistics, 1965, Patterns of Local Community Leadership, 1968; co-author: Residential Segregation Patterns, 1970; editor: Social Networks; contbr. to profl. jours. Served with USNR, 1944-46. Home: 2705 Temple Hills Dr Laguna Beach CA 92651 Office: Sch Social Scis U Calif Irvine CA 92717

FREEMAN, LUCY, author; b. N.Y.C., Dec. 13, 1916; d. Lawrence S. and Sylvia (Sobel) Greenbaum; m. William Freeman, Oct. 7, 1946 (div. Nov. 1948). A.B., Bennington Coll., 1938. Reporter, N.Y. Times, 1940-53. Author: Fight Against Fears, 1951, Hope for the Troubled, 1953, Before I Kill More, 1955, Hospital in Action, 1956, Search for Love, 1957, So You Want to Be Psychoanalyzed, 1958, Troubled Women, 1959, Story of Psychoanalysis, 1960, Emotional Maturity in Love and Marriage, 1961, The Abortionist, 1962, Children Who Kill, 1962, Remember Me to Tom, 1963, Chastise Me with Scorpions, 1964, The Wandering Husband, 1964, Why People Act That Way, 1965, The Two Assassins, 1965, Lords of Hell, 1967, The Mind, 1967, The Available Woman, 1968, The Cry for Love, 1969, Farewell to Fear, 1969, The Ordeal of Stephen Dennison, 1970, I Hate My Parents, 1970, The Search for Serenity, 1970, Celebrities on the Couch, 1970, The Dream, 1971, (with Dr. Walter Stewart) The Secret of Dreams, 1971, The Story of Anna O, 1972, Your Mind Can Cure Your Cold, 1972, (with Dr. Karl Menninger) Sparks, 1973, The Psychiatrist Says Murder, 1974, The Pursuit of Mental Health, 1974, The Case on Cloud Nine, 1974; editor: (anthology) Killers of the Mind, 1974; The Cycles of Sex, 1975, Betrayal, 1976, The Murderers, 1977, The Sorrow and the Fury, 1978, What Do Women Want?, 1978, Who Is Sylvia?, 1979, Freud Rediscovered, 1980, Too Deep for Tears, 1980, Freud and Women, 1981, Listening to the Inner Self, 1984; (anthology) The Murder Mystique, 1984. Recipient N.Y. Newspaper Women's Club award, 1948, N.Y. chpt. Theta Sigma Phi award, 1950, Writers award Am. Psychiat. Assn., 1976. Mem. Nat. Assn. Sci. Writers, Mystery Writers (pres.), Authors Guild, P.E.N., Nat. Assn. Journalists and Authors. Address: 210 Central Park S New York NY 10019 *Personal psychoanalysis has helped me accept myself and given me courage to face reality, with its pleasures and its pains. I hope through my writings I have enabled others who feel troubled to seek help so they too may live more serenely.*

FREEMAN, MARK, artist; b. Zaleszczyski, Austria, Sept. 27, 1908; came to U.S., 1923, naturalized, 1929; s. David and Henrietta (Schlaf) F.; m. Pauline Allen, Sept. 15, 1935; children: David, Stephen. A.B., Columbia U., 1930, M.Arch., 1932, postgrad. in fine arts, 1932-34, Sorbonne, Paris, summer 1930, NAD, 1927-30. One-man shows, Parrish Art Mus., Southampton, N.Y., 1964, Ringwood Manor Mus., N.Y., 1966, group shows include, Am. Watercolor Soc., Audubon Artists, N.Y., 1968-83, Internat. Biennial Color Lithography, Cin. Mus., 1951-53, Washington Water Color Assn., 1955-65, Soc. Am. Graphic Artists, N.Y., 1958, N.Y.C. Center Gallery, 1960-62, Knickerbocker Artists, N.Y., 1959-68, Boston Printmakers, 1950-60, Parrish Mus., N.Y., 1954-65, Portland (Oreg.) Mus., 1955-62, Wichita Art Assn., 1954-62, Print Club., Phila., 1960-64, Pa. Acad. Fine Arts, Art in U.S.A., N.Y., 1959, NAD, 1960, 64, 82, Nat. Inst. Arts and Letters, N.Y., 1968, 69, Butler Art Inst., 1970, Wichita Watercolor Centennial; represented in permanent collections, Guild Hall, East Hampton, N.Y., Norfolk Art Mus., Phila. Mus. Art, Library of Congress, Parrish Art Mus., Butler Art Inst., Holyoke Art Mus., St. Vincent Coll., Hengelose Kunstzaal, Holland, Slater Art Mus., Springfield Art Mus., pvt. colls. Trustee Artists Fellowship, 1981—. Mem. Audubon Artists (pres. 1977-79, hon. life pres.), Nat. Soc. Painters in Casein and Acrylic (pres. 1972—), Am. Soc. Contemporary Artists (pres. 1975-77), League Present Day Artists (pres. 1975), N.Y. Artists Equity (v.p. 1976-79, 81-83, editor-in-chief newsletter 1977—), Lotos Club (chmn. art chmn. 1977—), Am. Color Print Soc., Washington Water Color Assn., Boston Printmakers, Easthampton Guild Hall., Painters and Sculptors. Home: 117 E 35th St New York NY 10016 Studio: 333 Hudson St New York NY 10013

FREEMAN, MARK PRICE, JR., realty company executive; b. Memphis, Dec. 7, 1930; s. Mark Price and Ernestine (Stalons) F.; m. Martha Gene Nash, Oct. 19, 1956; children: Mark Price III, Dal, David, Wynne. B.A., La. State U., 1954; postgrad., Harvard, 1968. Cert. fin. planner. Pitcher N.Y. Yankees (and farm clubs), 1951-58, Kansas City Athletics, 1959, Chgo. Cubs, 1960; dist. mgr. Waddell & Reed, Inc., Denver, 1960-62; regional mgr. Westamerica Securities, Inc., Denver, 1963-69, exec. v.p., dir., 1969-72, pres., dir., 1972-78; exec. v.p., nat. dir. mktg. Angeles Realty Corp., 1978—. Trustee St. Mary's Acad. Served as 1st lt. inf. AUS, 1954-56. Mem. Inst. Cert. Fin. Planners, Sigma Chi, Psi Chi. Clubs: Denver Country, Denver Bronco Quarterback (pres. 1961-68), Colo. Harvard Bus. Sch., Rotary. Home: 6 Brookside Dr Littleton CO 80121 Office: 444 Sherman St Denver CO 80203

FREEMAN, MAURICE TRACY, ret. investment exec.; b. Somerville, Mass., Feb. 8, 1904; s. Maurice James and Catharine (Tracy) F.; m. Ruth Moulton, Sept. 12, 1931; children—Louise Freeman Ahearn, Elizabeth J. Freeman Spiller, Ruth M. Freeman O'Neill. Jean Tracy. B.S., Mass. Inst. Tech., 1925; M.B.A., Harvard, 1927. Staff research dept. Loomis, Sayles & Co., Inc., 1927-42, dir. investment research dept., 1942-63, exec. v.p., 1958-63, pres., 1963-68, chmn. bd., chief exec. officer, 1963-69; dir. Standard Shares, Inc.; Centennial life fellow Mus. Fine Arts. Chmn. bd. trustees Winchester Hosp., 1947-74. Home: 11 Lorena Rd Winchester MA 01890 Office: 28 Church St Winchester MA 01890

FREEMAN, MAX HERBERT, educator, author, consultant, lecturer; b. Poland, Oct. 12, 1907; s. Samuel and Ida (Potash) F.; m. Dora R. Tuchman, Aug. 25, 1934; children: Alice R., Carol J. B.S., N.Y.U., 1930, M.A., 1931, Ph.D., 1942. Tchr. bus. Somerville High Sch., N.J., 1931-36; tchr., chmn. bus. dept., Hastings-on-Hudson, N.Y., 1936-39; tchr. bus., placement dir. Westside High School, Newark, 1939-43; prof., chmn. bus. dept. Paterson (N.J.) State Coll., 1943-54; prof., chmn. bus. dept., dean grad. studies Montclair (N.J.) State Coll., 1954-75; pvt. acctg. and mgmt. cons. practice, 1924—; sr. research specialist U.S. Office of Edn., 1948; Cons. to AID (on Ohio State U. team in India), 1963-65; Pres. Sherwood Sch. Bus., Paterson, 1951-68. Co-author: Practical Bookkeeping, 1943, Medical Secretary, 1947, Methods of Teaching Business Subjects, 1949, 57, 65, Bookkeeping Simplified, 1953, 58, Briefhand, complete Course, 1957, Bookkeeping and Accounting Advanced, 1958, Gregg Bookkeeping and Accounting, 1963, Bookkeeping 1 and 2 Data Guides, 1963, Metodos Para La Ensenanza De Materias Comerciales, 1965, An Experience in Teacher Education in India, 1965, Accounting 10/12, 1968, 2d edit. series, 1973, 3d edit., 1977, Gregg Accounting Advanced Course, 1969, Matematicas en la Mercadotecinia, 1983; Editor: Fundamentals in Business Training, 1940. Mem. Delta Pi Epsilon (nat. pres. 1952-54). Home: 113 Buckingham Rd Upper Montclair NJ 07043

FREEMAN, MEREDITH NORWIN, college president; b. Elvins, Mo., June 1, 1920; s. William J. and Zelpha (McGuire) F.; m. Helen Lorene Larkin, Aug. 3, 1941 (dec. Nov. 1970); children: James Michael, Judith Ann; m. Joyce Mary Liebsch, Oct. 23, 1971; stepchildren: Mary Ann, Dawn Joy. B.S., S.E. Mo. State Coll., Cape Girardeau, 1949; M.Ed., U. Mo., 1951, Ed.D., 1955. Rural sch. tchr., St. Francis County, Mo., 1940-41, elementary tchr., also prin., New Haven, Mo., 1941-42, 46-47, high sch. sci. tchr., prin., 1947-50, supt. schs., Wright City, Mo., 1951-52, New Haven, Mo., 1952-54; tchr. chemistry and physics Hickman High Sch., Columbia, Mo., 1954-55; asso. prof. edn. Ft. Hays (Kans.) State Coll., 1955-57; dir. spl. services, prof. edn. Mankato (Minn.) State Coll., 1957-64, asst. academic dean, 1964-66, academic dean, 1966-67; pres. Black Hills State Coll., Spearfish, S.D., 1967-76, Concord Coll., Athens, W.Va., 1976—; mem. exec. com. Minn. Assn. Colls., 1964-67; sec. S.D. Council Coll. and

Univ. Pres.'s, 1967-68, chmn., 1969-70, 74-75; mem. S.D. Indian Scholarships Com., 1967-76. Mem. exec. com. Black Hills Area council Boy Scouts Am., 1968-76; mem. S.D. Gov.'s Scholarship Com., 1970-76; mem. exec. com. W.Va. Assn. Coll. Pres.'s; mem. W.Va. Adv. Council on Profl. Personnel, 1976—; bd. dirs. Appalachia Regional Lab., 1981—, Princeton Community Hosp. Served with AUS, 1942-46. Mem. NEA, Am. Assn. State Colls. and Univs. (S.D. rep. 1971-75, W.Va. rep. 1981—), Princeton C. of C. (dir.), Phi Delta Kappa (past faculty sponsor Epsilon Iota chpt.), Sigma Tau Gamma. Methodist. Clubs: Masons, Rotary. Home: President's Residence Concord Coll Athens WV 24712 *The home environment in which I was reared placed high value on honesty, fair play, and productive work as keys to a successful life. These values have always been important to me. Additionally, I have always tried to understand the rationale and motivations of persons who disagree with me or whose actions need explanation—"to walk a mile in my brothers' moccasins."*

FREEMAN, MILTON VICTOR, lawyer; b. N.Y.C., Nov. 16, 1911; s. Samuel and Celia (Gelf) F.; m. Phyllis Young, Dec. 19, 1937; children: Nancy Lois (Mrs. Gans), Daniel Martin, Andrew Samuel, Amy Martha (Mrs. Malone). A.B., Coll. City N.Y., 1931; LL.B., Columbia U., 1934. Bar: N.Y. 1934, D.C. 1946. With gen. counsel's office SEC, 1934-42, asst. solicitor, 1942-46; staff securities div. FTC, 1934; with firm Arnold & Porter, Wash., 1946—; lectr. Yale U., 1947, Georgetown U. Law Sch., 1952. Contbr. articles to profl. jours.; mem. adv. and editorial bds. legal instns. and publs. Hon. chmn. Internat. Law Inst., Georgetown U., 1977—, trustee, 1955—. Mem. Am., Fed. bar assns., Bar Assn. D.C., Am. Law Inst. Home: 3405 Woolsey Dr Chevy Chase MD 20815 Office: 1200 New Hampshire Ave NW Washington DC 20036

FREEMAN, MONTINE MCDANIEL, museum trustee; b. Forrest City, Ark., Apr. 19, 1915; d. Louis and Montine (Kirkpatrick) McDaniel; m. Richard W. Freeman, Oct. 15, 1936; children: Richard W., Louis McDaniel, Tina Louise Woollam. B. Design, Newcomb Coll., 1936; student, Tulane U., 1946-48. Bd. trustees New Orleans Mus. Fine Art (formerly Isaac Delgado Mus. Art), 1959-66, treas., 1961, sec. bd. trustees, 1964, now hon. mem. mus.; bd. dirs. La. State Mus., 1961-73, New Orleans Philharmonic Symphony, 1949-78, La. Council for Music and Performing Arts, 1970—, Pacific Topical Bot. Garden, 1975—, La. Nature Center, 1975-78. Trustee Greater New Orleans United Fund, 1956-58, sec., 1958, chmn. women's div., 1956; bd. dirs. New Orleans YWCA, 1954-60, v.p., 1959; mem. Community Vol. Service Bd., 1953-59, New Orleans Neighborhood Center Bd., 1950-60, Pre-Sch. for Blind, 1954-57; chmn. women's com. Internat. House, New Orleans, 1956-58; v.p. New Orleans Jr. League, 1953-54; bd. regents Kenmore Assn., Inc., Fredericksburg, Va.; mem. adv. bd. House of Good Shepherd, 1965-67. Mem. Garden Club Am. (dir. 1969-72, 74, v.p. 1974-76), Phi Beta Phi. Presbyterian. Clubs: Orleans, Petit Salon (New Orleans). Address: 295 Walnut St New Orleans LA 70118

FREEMAN, MORTON S(IGMUND), assn. exec., lawyer; b. Phila., Dec. 12, 1912; s. Samuel S. and Serena G. (Singer) F.; m. Mildred Hurwitz, May 31, 1942; children—Janet Freeman Miller, Roberta Freeman Tabachnick. A.B. with first honors, Pa. State U., 1934; J.D., U. Pa., 1937. Bar: Pa. bar 1937. Practiced law, Phila., 1937-42, 1966-70; spl. agt. FBI, 1942-51; partner Reynolds Shoes (retail chain), Phila., 1951-60; pres. Admiral Fin. Corp., Phila., 1959-66; dir. office publs. Am. Law Inst.-Am. Bar Assn., Phila., 1970—. Author: The Grammatical Lawyer, 1979, Pennsylvania Equity Digest, a biennial supplement, 1954—; author: column The Grammatical Lawyer in The Practical Lawyer, 1976—. Trustee Big Bros. Assn., Phila. Recipient Book of Yr. award Am. Soc. Legal Writers. Mem. Phila. Bar Assn., Am. Law Inst., Assn. Continuing Legal Edn. Adminstrs. (chmn. publs. com.). Jewish. Club: B'nai B'rith. Home: 166 Gramercy Rd Bala-Cynwyd PA 19004 Office: 4025 Chestnut St Philadelphia PA 19104

FREEMAN, NEAL BLACKWELL, communications corporation executive; b. N.Y.C., July 5, 1940; s. Malcolm T. and Virginia (Neal) F.; m. Jane Louise Metze, Mar. 19, 1966; children: Malcolm Trowbridge II, James Bragdon, Kathryn R. B.A. magna cum laude, Yale U., 1962. Asst. to pres. Washington Star Syndicate, 1965-66; asso. producer TV show Firing Line, 1966-67; exec. editor King Features Syndicate, N.Y.C., 1968-73; v.p., editor King Features div. Hearst Corp., 1973-76; pres. Jefferson Communications, Inc., 1976—; chmn. bd. Blackwell Corp., 1982—; cons. editor Washington Post Writers Group, 1977-80; exec. producer Public TV; dir. Nat. Rev., Inc.; Mem. Pres.'s Commn. on White House Fellows, 1974-77; chmn. of agts. Yale Alumni Fund; bd. dirs. Corp. for Pub. Broadcasting, 1972-75. Trustee Am. Shakespeare Theatre, Stratford, Conn., 1973-75. Mem. Nat. Cartoonists Soc., Colony Found., Sigma Delta Chi. Clubs: Yale (N.Y.C.); York (Maine) Country, Nat. Press. Office: 11730 Bowman Green Reston VA 22090

FREEMAN, ORVILLE LOTHROP, corporation executive; b. Mpls., May 9, 1918; s. Orville E. and Frances (Schroeder) F.; m. Jane C. Shields, May 2, 1942; children: Constance Jane, Michael Orville. B.A., U. Minn., 1940; LL.B., 1946; LL.B. (hon.), U. Seoul, (Korea); hon. degree, Am. U., Fairleigh Dickinson U., St. Joseph's Coll. Bar: Minn. 1947. Mem. Larson, Loevinger, Lindquist and Freeman, Mpls., 1947-55; gov., Minn., 1955-61; sec. U.S. Dept. Agr., 1961-69; pres. E.D.P. Technology Internat. Inc., 1969-70; pres., chief exec. officer Bus. Internat. Corp., N.Y.C., 1970-81, chmn. bd., 1981—; dir. Natomas Corp., Multinat. Agribus. Systems, Inc., Franklin Mint., Grumman Corp.; Mem. faculty Salzburg (Austria) Seminar, 1974, 77. Asst. charge vets. affairs to mayor Mpls., 1945-49; chmn. Mpls. Civil Service Commn., 1946-49; sec. Minn. Democratic Farmer Labor Party, 1946-48, chmn., 1948-50; mem. exec. com. Japan-U.S. Bus. Adv. Council; chmn. India-U.S. Bus. Adv. Council; mem. adv. com. Hubert H. Humphrey Inst.; chmn. U.S.-Nigerian Agrl. Consultative Com.; Bd. dirs. com. for future Worldwatch Inst.; chmn. bd. govs. UN Assn. U.S.A.; mem. Presdl. Commn. on World Hunger; past trustee Lutheran Ch. in Am. Served from 2d lt. to maj. USMCR, 1941-45; lt. col. Res. Mem. Exec. Alumni Assn., Phi Beta Kappa, Delta Sigma Rho. Home: Ardsley-on-Hudson NY Office: Business Internat Corp 1 Dag Hammarskjold Plaza New York NY 10017

FREEMAN, PAUL DOUGLAS, symphony conductor; b. Richmond, Va., Jan. 2, 1936; s. Louis H. and Louise (Willis) F.; m. Cornelia Perry; 1 son, Douglas Cornel. Mus.B., Eastman Sch. Music, 1956, Mus.M., 1957; Ph.D., 1963; Ph.D. Fulbright scholar, Hochshule für Musik, Berlin, Germany, 1957-59. Dir. Hochstein Music Sch., Rochester, N.Y., 1960-66; First v.p. Nat. Guild Community Music Schs., 1964-66; bd. dirs. N.Y. State Opera League, 1963-66, Detroit Community Music Sch.; music adv. com. San Francisco chpt. Young Audiences, 1966—; mem. Calif. Framework Com. for Arts and Humanities, 1967-68. Founder, conductor, Faculty-Community Orch.; also music dir., Opera Theatre, Rochester, 1961-66; dir., San Francisco Community Music Center, 1966-68; conductor, San Francisco Conservatory Orch., 1966-67; music dir., San Francisco Little Symphony, 1967-68; asso. conductor, Dallas Symphony, 1968-69, 69-70; conductor-in-residence, Detroit Symphony Orch., 1970-79; condr., music dir., Victoria (B.C., Can.) Symphony, 1979—; music dir., Saginaw Symphony; artistic dir., Delta Fstival Music and Art, 1977-79, numerous guest appearances with maj. orchs. in, U.S. and Europe; recording artist, Columbia Records, Vox Records, Orion Records. Recipient prize Dimitri Mitropolous Internat. Conductor's competition, 1967—; Spoleto award Festival of Two Worlds, 1968. Office: Victoria Symphony 631 Superior St Victoria BC V8V 1V1 Canada

FREEMAN, RALPH MCKENZIE, U.S. dist. judge; b. Flushing, Mich., May 5, 1902; s. Horace B. and Laura D. (McKenzie) F.; m. Emmalyn E. Ellis, Aug. 13, 1938. LL.B., U. Mich., 1926. Bar: Mich. bar 1926. Pvt. practice law, Flint, 1926-27, 33-54; mem. Freeman, Bellairs & Dean, 1953-54; pros. atty., Genesee County, Mich., 1930-32; U.S. dist. judge Eastern Dist. Mich., 1954—. Mem. Flint (Mich.) Bd. Edn., 1933-49, pres., 1938-39, 48-49. Fellow Am. Bar Found.; mem. Am. Bar Assn., State Bar Mich., Phi Kappa Tau, Sigma Delta Kappa. Clubs: Circumnavigators; Economic (Detroit); Birmingham Country. Office: US Courthouse and Federal Bldg Detroit MI 48226

FREEMAN, RAYMOND LEE, landscape architect, planning consultant; b. Earlham, Iowa, June 13, 1919; s. Frederick Leslie and Alta May (Snyder) F.; m. Marie A. Hossack, Apr. 16, 1943; children: Ronald Douglas, Lance Lee. Student, Creighton U., 1937-38; B.Landscape Architecture, Iowa State U., 1942. With Nat. Park Service, Omaha and Washington, 1946-78, dep. dir. field ops., Washington, 1971-72, asso. dir. ops., 1972-73, asst. dir. devel., 1973-78; landscape architect, planning cons., 1979—; vis. lectr. Iowa State U., Tex. A. and M. U., Syracuse U., Tex. Tech U., Cornell U., U. Va. Contbr. articles to profl. jours. Troop com. chmn. Nat. Capital Area council Boy Scouts Am., 1965; mem. adv. bd. Environic Found. Internat., Notre Dame, Ind., 1970—; mem. Fed. Council on Arts and Humanities. Served to maj. AUS, 1942-46; ETO. Recipient Distinguished Service award Dept. Interior, 1972. Fellow Am. Soc. Landscape Architects (dir. Found. 1971-74, nat. pres. 1971-73); mem. Nat. Recreation and Park Assn.; Tau Sigma Delta Phi Gamma Delta. Presbyterian. Club: Mason. Master planner nat. capital landscape Washington, 1965. Home: 8737 Susanna Ln Chevy Chase MD 20815

FREEMAN, REINO SAMUEL, parasitologist, educator; b. Virginia, Minn., Aug. 20, 1919; emigrated to Can., 1952; s. Gust Robert and Siiri Maria (Polkki) F.; m. Ellen Heatherly Beck, Aug. 19, 1950. B.S., Duluth State Coll., 1942; M.A., U. Minn., 1948; Ph.D., Duluth State Coll., 1950. Asst. prof. So. Ill. U., Carbondale, 1950-52; sr. research fellow Ont. Research Found., Toronto, Can., 1952-64, sr. research scientist, 1964-66; asst. to assoc. prof. parasitology U. Toronto, 1952-65, prof., 1965—, chmn. dept., 1971-75; panel mem. Study of Biology in Can., Ottawa, 1970; Wardle lectr. Can. Soc. Zoologists, 1981; cons. Jour. Parasitology, 1983—, mem. editorial bd., 1972-75; mem. grants panel Can. Nat. Sportsmen's Fund, 1978-80. Mem. editorial bd.: Proc. of Helminthological Socx., Washington. Served to lt. USN, 1942-45. Inter-Am. fellow La. State U., 1960; Fulbright scholar, 1963-64. Mem. Am. Soc. Parasitologists, Can. Soc. Zoologists, Am. Inst. Biol. Scis., Am. Soc. Tropical Medicine and Hygiene, Can. Soc. Tropical Medicine and Internat. Health, Sigma Xi. Home: 55 Langbourne Pl Don Mills ON Canada M3B 1B1 Office: Dept Microbiology Faculty Medicine U Toronto Toronto ON Canada M5S 1A1

FREEMAN, RICHARD BARRY, economist; b. Newburgh, N.Y., June 29, 1945; s. Herbert J. and Sylvia F. F. B.A., Dartmouth Coll., 1964; Ph.D., Harvard U., 1969. Asst. prof. econs. Yale U., 1969-70; U. Chgo., 1970-74; faculty Harvard U., Cambridge, Mass., 1974—, prof. econs., 1976—; dir. labor studies Nat. Bur. Econ. Research, Cambridge, 1978. Author: The Market for College-Trained Manpower, 1971, The Overeducated American, 1976, Black Elite, 1977, Labor Economics, 1979, (with Freeman and Wise) The Youth Labor Market Problem, 1982, (with Freeman and Medoff) What Do Unions Do?. Office: Dept Econs Littauer M-5 Harvard Univ Cambridge MA 02138

FREEMAN, RICHARD BENTON, physician; b. Allentown, Pa., July 24, 1931; s. Benton C. and Evelyn B. (Boyer) F.; m. Margaret C. McGuire, July 24, 1954; children—Richard, Charles C., Patricia Anne. B.S., Franklin and Marshall Coll., Lancaster, Pa., 1953; M.D., Thomas Jefferson U., 1957. Intern Pa. Hosp., Phila., 1957-58, resident, 1958-61; fellow in nephrology Georgetown U., 1960; clin. instr. medicine U. Pa., 1958-61, U. Calif., San Francisco, 1963; instr. medicine Georgetown U., 1964-67; asst. prof. U. Rochester, N.Y., 1967-69, asso. prof., 1969—, head nephrology unit, 1974—; cons. Contbr. articles to profl. jours. Served with USPHS, 1961-67. Fellow A.C.P.; mem. Am. Fedn. Clin. Investigation, Am. Heart Assn., Am. Soc. Nephrology, Internat. Soc. Nephrology, Am. Soc. Artificial Internal Organs, Renal Physicians Assn. (dir. 1977, v.p. 1979, pres. 1981—), AAAS, Nat. Kidney Found., Kidney Found. Upstate N.Y., Internat. Soc. Internal Organs. Home: 25 Hearthstone Rd Pittsford NY 14534 Office: 601 Elmwood Ave Rochester NY 14642

FREEMAN, RICHARD C., judge; b. Atlanta, Dec. 14, 1926. A.B., Emory U., 1950, LL.B., 1952. Bar: Ga. bar 1953. Since practiced in, Atlanta; mem. firm Haas, Holland & Blackshear, 1955-58; partner Haas, Holland, Freeman, Levison & Gibert, 1958-71; judge U.S. Dist. Ct., 1971—; Alderman City of Atlanta, 1962-71; pres. Atlanta Humane Soc., 1981. Mem. Ga., Atlanta bar assns., Lawyers Club Atlanta, Chi Phi, Phi Delta Phi. Office: 2121 US Courthouse 75 Spring St SW Atlanta GA 30303

FREEMAN, RICHARD FRANCIS, banker; b. Mt. Kisco, N.Y., Apr. 19, 1934; s. Richard Francis and Nora Frances (O'Connell) F.; m. Barbara Jean Calhoun, Nov. 30, 1957; children: Kathleen, Kevin, Kelley, Keith. B.S. in Finance and Banking, Miami U., Oxford, Ohio, 1956; grad., Stonier Grad. Sch. Banking, Rutgers U., 1973. With Central Nat. Bank, Cleve., 1956-60, No. Westchester Nat. Bank, Chappaqua, N.Y., 1960-67; with State Nat. Bank Conn., Bridgeport, 1967-78, exec. v.p., dir., 1974-78; pres., chief exec. officer The Bank Mart (formerly City Savs. Bank Conn.), Bridgeport, 1978—; dir. Conn. Energy Corp., So. Conn. Gas Co. Chmn. bd. trustees Park City Hosp., Bridgeport; bd. dirs. Bridgeport Econ. Devel. Corp., CYO Boys Homes Conn., YMCA of Greater Bridgeport, Center for Fin. Studies, Inc.-Nat. Assn. Mut. Savs. Banks.; mem. bus. adv. council Miami U. Sch. Bus. Adminstrn.; incorporator Neighborhood Housing Services, Bridgeport. Mem. Bridgeport Area C. of C. (dir.), Conn. Hosp. Assn. Home: 5 Greenfield Hill Rd Fairfield CT 06430 Office: 948 Main St Bridgeport CT 06604

FREEMAN, RICHARD MERRELL, power authority executive; b. Crawfordsville, Ind., July 2, 1921; s. F. Rider and Ruth (Merrell) F.; m. Joanne Spears, Nov. 26, 1943; children—Randy, Mark, Candy, Marcia. A.B., Wabash (Ind.) Coll., 1943; LL.B., Columbia U., 1948. Bar: Tenn. bar 1948, Ill. bar 1957. Atty. TVA, Knoxville, 1948-57, dir., 1978—; partner firm Belnap, Spencer, Hardy & Freeman, Chgo., 1957-67; v.p. law Chgo. & Northwestern Transp. Co., Chgo., 1967-78, also dir., voting trustee.; dir. Internat. Fertilizer Devel. Corp. Bd. dirs. Knoxville Symphony Soc., Helen Ross McNabb Mental Health Center. Served with USNR, 1943-46. Mem. Phi Beta Kappa. Democrat. Mem. Community Ch. Club: Econ. (Chgo.). Home: 3600 Montlake Knoxville TN 37920 Office: 400 Summit Hill Knoxville TN 37902

FREEMAN, RICHARD WEST, beverage manufacturing company executive; b. New Orleans, Jan. 4, 1913; s. Alfred Bird and Ella Moore (West) F.; m. Montine McDaniel, Oct. 15, 1936; children: Richard W. Louis, Tina. B.B.A., Tulane U., 1934, LL.D., 1983. Salesman Milw. Coca-Cola Bottling Co., 1934-35; asst. to pres. Great Lakes Coca Cola Bottling Co., 1936-38; pres. Wis. Coca Cola Bottling Co. (also plants in Mich., Ohio), 1938-42; dir. Coca Cola Co., Chgo., 1938-42, 58-61; asst. to pres. La. Coca Cola Bottling Co., Ltd., 1946-47, pres., 1947-70, chmn. bd., 1970-83, vice chmn. bd., 1983—; dir. Hibernia Nat. Bank, 1951-80, Coca Cola Co., 1958-75, Middle South Utilities, 1960-83, Delta Air Lines, Inc., New Orleans Pub. Service, Inc., 1954-83; bd. advisers Time-Picayune Pub. Corp. Mem. bd. adminstrn. Tulane U.; dir. YMCA, New Orleans.; Mem. Miss. River Bridge Commn., 1954-65; bd. La. Dept. Hwys., 1952-56; pres. New Orleans Community Chest, 1952; Trustee Alton Ochsner Med. Found.; dir. United Fund, 1953-55, La. div. Am. Cancer Soc., 1947-55, New Orleans chpt. ARC, 1948-50; mem. Bd. Liquidation City Debt, New Orleans. Served from 2d lt. to maj. Transp. Corps AUS, 1942-46; ETO. Mem. S.A.R., Sons Colonial Wars, C. of C., Phi Delta Theta. Democrat. Presbyn. Clubs: International House, Louisiana, Boston, Picwick., Stratford, New Orleans Country, Southern Yacht (New Orleans). Office: PO Box 50400 New Orleans LA 70150

FREEMAN, ROBERT H., utilities executive; b. 1922; married. With Eastern Gas and Fuel Assocs., Boston, 1949—, v.p. subs. Eastern Coal Corp., 1964-70, sr. v.p. parent co., 1970-77, exec. v.p., chief operating officer, 1977—, also trustee; pres. Eastern Assoc. Coal Corp. Served to 2d lt. USAAF, 1943-45. Mem. Nat. Coal Assn. (dir.). Office: Eastern Gas and Fuel Assocs One Beacon St Boston MA 02108 *

FREEMAN, ROBERT L., lieutenant governor Louisiana; b. Washington, Apr. 27, 1934. Grad., La. State U.; LL.B., Loyola U. Bar: bar 1965. With chem. co., 1960-61; since practiced law; partner Freeman and Pendley, Ltd., Plaquemine, La.; mem. La. Ho. of Reps., 1968-80; lt. gov. State of La., 1980—. Chmn. Plaquemine Planning and Zoning Commn., 1966-68. Served with U.S. Army, 1956-59. Mem. La. State Bar Assn., ABA. Roman Catholic. Office: Office Lt Gov State Capitol PO Box 44243 Baton Rouge LA 70804 *

FREEMAN, ROBERT MALLORY, banker; b. Richmond, Va., 1941. Grad., U. Va., 1963. Pres., chief operating officer dir. Bank of Va., Richmond. Office: Bank of Virginia 7 N 8th St Richmond VA 23219 *

FREEMAN, ROBERT MARK, financial executive; b. Cambridge, Mass., June 12, 1942; m. Margo Harmon, Sept. 6, 1969; children: Carie, Clayton, Edward. B.A., Dartmouth Coll, 1964; postgrad., Columbia U., 1965-68. Risk arbitrageur Goldman & Sachs, N.Y.C., 1970—; dir. Flexi-Van Corp., N.Y.C., 1983—. Trustee N.Y. Coll. Osteopathic Medicine, 1982—. Office: 55 Broad St New York NY 10004

FREEMAN, ROBERT TURNER, JR., insurance executive; b. N.Y.C., Apr. 25, 1918; s. Robert Turner and Eva (Boyd) F.; m. Mary Frances Jones, Nov. 28, 1942; children: Veronica (Mrs. Wisdom F. Coleman, Jr.), Robert Turner III. B.A., Lincoln (Pa.) U., 1941; student, N.Y.U. Grad. Sch., 1941-42. Econ. statistician WPB, 1942-45; v.p., actuary United Mut. Life Ins. Co., N.Y.C., 1945-55; founder, mng. dir. Ghana Ins. Co. Ltd., Accra, 1955-62, Ghana Gen. Ins. Co., Ltd., 1959-62; cons. actuary Providence Ins. Co., Monrovia, Liberia, 1958-59, Nigerian Broadcasting Corp., Lagos, 1964-65; founder, dir. Great Nigeria Ins. Co. Ltd., Lagos, 1960-63; mng. dir. Ghana State Ins. Corp., Accra, 1962-65; asso. dir. for mgmt. Peace Corps, 1965-66; cons. minority affairs USIA, 1966-68; pres. Freeman, Cole and Assos., Inc., Washington, 1966-68; dir. office capital devel. and finance Bur. Africa AID, 1968-71; ins. adviser to Govt. Ethiopia, 1971-73; pres. Consumers United Ins. Co., 1973—; dir. Ghana Nat. Investment Bank, 1962-65, First Ghana Bldg. Soc., 1958-63, Lafayette Fed. Credit Union, Washington, 1966—, Riggs Nat. Bank; mem. Washington Bd. Trade; bd. govs. Internat. Ins. Seminars Hall of Fame, 1977—. Dir. Commn. Ednl. Exchange between U.S. and Ghana, 1964-65; mem. Fulbright Scholarship Com., Accra, 1960-61, Bus. Community Scholarship Com., Accra, 1958-61; co-chmn. United Negro Coll. Fund, Bklyn., 1952; cons. Korry com. on Africa, ept. State, 1966, NAACP Task Force on Africa, 1977, World Bank, 1978; Trustee, vice chmn. Phelps-Stokes Fund; trustee Solebury Sch., New Hope, Pa., Lincoln U., 1977—; bd. dirs., 1st v.p. Nation's Capitol council Girl Scouts U.S.A., 1978—, African Am. Scholars Council, 1978—, Friends of Senghor Found., 1977—; bd. dirs., mem. corp. bd. Children's Hosp., Washington, 1978—. Mem. Lincoln U. Alumni Assn. (pres. N.Y.C. 1952-55), Alpha Phi Alpha. Club: Rotarian (pres. Ghana 1963-65). Home: 3001 Veazey Terr NW Washington DC 20008 Office: 2100 M St NW Washington DC 20037

FREEMAN, ROWLAND GODFREY, III, manufacturing executive, retired naval officer; b. N.Y.C., Feb. 11, 1922; s. Rowland Godfrey and Janet Erskine (Adriance) F.; m. Dorothy Gleason, Mar. 22, 1958; children: Rowland Godrey, Diane Adriance Freeman Armstrong; stepchildren: Christopher Gleason Gates, Geoffrey Stephen Gates. Student, U. Mass., 1940-42; M.B.A., Harvard U., 1953. Commd. ensign U.S. Navy, 1942, advanced through grades to rear adm., 1971; project mgr. F-111B aircraft, Wright-Patterson AFB, Ohio, 1966-68, dep. chief naval material for procurement and prodn., Washington, 1968-73, dir. naval enlisted occupational class system study, 1973-74, comdg. officer, China Lake, Calif., 1974-77; comdt. Def. Systems Mgmt. Coll., Ft. Belvoir, Va., 1977-79; ret., 1979; adminstr. GSA, Washington, 1979-81; staff v.p. McDonnell Douglas Corp., 1981—. Decorated Legion of Merit with oak leaf cluster, D.S.M., D.F.C. with oak leaf cluster, Air medal with 3 oak leaf clusters; recipient Pres.'s Energy award; Sec. Def. Disting. Service medal. Fellow Nat. Contract Mgmt. Assn. (certified, bd. advisers); mem. Am. Soc. Logistic Engrs. (adv., Founders medal 1980), Am. Inst. Aeronautics Astronautics. Methodist. Home: 12417 Conway Rd Creve Coeur MO 63141 Office: McDonnell Douglas PO Box 516 Saint Louis MO 63166 *An unshakeable faith in my fellow man, loyalty to my superiors, my peers and my juniors, absolute integrity - even when it hurts - dedication to God, my country and my duty.*

FREEMAN, RUSSELL ADAMS, banker; b. Albany, N.Y., July 22, 1932; s. Russell Marvin and Edith (Adams) F.; m. Elizabeth Frances McHale, June 30, 1956; children: Lynn, James. B.A., Amherst Coll., 1954; J.D., Albany (N.Y.) Law Sch., 1957; LL.M., U. So. Calif., 1966. Bar: N.Y. 1957, Calif. 1960. Practiced in, Albany, 1957-59; with Security Pacific Nat. Bank, Los Angeles, 1959—, v.p., 1968-72, counsel, 1968-74, head legal dept., 1968-74, sr. v.p., 1972-81, exec. v.p., 1981—; gen. counsel Security Pacific Corp., 1973—, exec. v.p., 1981—; bd. govs. Fin. Lawyers Conf., 1972-74; faculty Pacific Coast Banking Sch., 1980—; lectr. in field, 1965—. Contbr. articles to profl. publns. Trustee Flintridge Prep. Sch., La Canada, Calif., 1978-80. Mem. ABA, Am. Bankers Assn. (mem. govt. relations com.), Assn. Banking Holding Cos., Calif. Bankers Assn. (dir., chmn. govt. relations group 1979-81), Calif. Bankers Clearing House Assn. (chmn. public policy adv. com. 1980-81), Calif. State Bar, Los Angeles County Bar Assn. (past chmn. comml. law and bankruptcy sect.). Office: 333 S Hope St 52d Floor Los Angeles CA 90071

FREEMAN, SAMUEL RALPH, railroad executive, lawyer; b. N.Y.C., Sept. 2, 1929; s. Benjamin S. and Ethel S. (Salit) F.; m. Joyce Siegel, Dec. 21, 1958; children: Laura, Susan, Carol. LL.B., Bklyn. Law Sch., 1951. Bar: N.Y. 1951, Colo. 1954. Asst. atty. gen., Colo., 1955-58; partner firm Van Cise, Freeman, Tooley & McClearn, Denver, 1959-

72; v.p., gen. counsel Rio Grande Industries, Inc., Denver, 1973—; pres. San Marco Pipeline, Inc., 1977—, Jen Rio Grande Western R.R.; dir. Anderson Petroleum Co., 1979—; Mem. exec. com. Interstate Oil Compact, 1975—; vice chmn. Colo. Oil and Gas Conservation Commn., 1974—; bd. dirs. Regional Transp. Commn., 1973-77; judge adv. Colo. N.G., 1954-63; mem. urban transp. adv. com. Dept. Transp., 1969-74; mem. ind. adv. com. on energy Dept. Commerce, 1982—. Mem. Am., Colo., Denver bar assns., Nat. Inst. Petroleum Research (dir. 1982—). Jewish. Home: 743 S Oneida Way Denver CO 80224 Office: PO Box 5482 Denver CO 80217

FREEMAN, SIMON DAVID, government official, civil engineer, lawyer; b. Chattanooga, Jan. 14, 1926; s. Morris and Lena F.; children: Anita R. Hopkins, Stanley A., Roger L. B.S. in Civil Engring, Ga. Inst. Tech., 1948; LL.B., U. Tenn., 1956. Bar: Tenn. 1957, D.C. 1965, U.S. Supreme Ct. 1964; Registered profl. engr. Engr. TVA, Knoxville, Tenn., 1948-54, lawyer, 1956-61, dir., 1977-84, chmn. bd., 1978-81; asst. to chmn. FPC, Washington, 1961-65; head energy policy staff Office Sci. and Tech., Exec. Office of Pres., 1967-71; dir. Energy Policy Project, Ford Found., Washington, 1971-74; spl. energy and resources cons. U.S. Senate Commerce Com., Washington, 1974-76; mem. White House Energy Staff, 1976-77; bd. dirs. Electric Power Research Inst.; mem. tech. assessment adv. council Office Tech. Assessment. Author: Energy: The New Era, 1974; dir.: final report of Ford Found. Energy Policy Project, pub. as A Time To Choose, 1974. Served with U.S. Mcht. Marine, 1943-44. Mem. Order of Coif. Democrat. Jewish. Home: 1431 Cherokee Tr Number 122 Knoxville TN 37920 Office: 400 W Summit Hill Dr (E12A9) Knoxville TN 37902

FREEMAN, SUSAN TAX, anthropologist; b. Chgo., May 24, 1938; d. Sol and Gertrude Tax.; m. Leslie G. Freeman, Jr., Mar. 20, 1964; 1 dau., Sarah Elisabeth. B.A., U. Chgo., 1958; M.A., Harvard U., 1959, Ph.D., 1965. Asst. prof. anthropology U. Ill., Chgo., 1965-70, asso. prof., 1970-78, prof., 1978—, chmn., 1979—; panelist Council for Internat. Exchange of Scholars; mem. anthropology screening com. Fulbright-Hays Research Awards, 1975-78; mem. ad hoc com. on research in Spain Spain-U.S.A. Friendship Agreement, 1977, 78, 80, 81. Author: Neighbors: The Social Contract in a Castilian Hamlet, 1970, The Pasiegos-Spaniards in No Man's Land, 1979; asso. editor: Am. Anthropologist, 1971-73, Am. Ethnologist, 1974-76. Wenner-Gren Found. for Anthrop. Research grantee, 1966, 83; NIMH grantee, 1967, 68-71; Nat. Endowment Humanities grantee, 1979. Fellow Am. Anthrop. Assn. (nominating com. 1981-82), Royal Anthrop. Inst. Gt. Brit. and Ireland, AAAS; mem. Soc. Spanish and Portuguese Hist. Studies, Council for European Studies (steering com. 1980-82); hon. mem. Centro de Estudios Sorianos (Soria). Home: 5537 Woodlawn Ave Chicago IL 60637 Office: Dept Anthropology U Ill Chicago Circle Box 4348 Chicago IL 60680

FREEMAN, WILLIAM ERNEST, JR., architect; b. Greenwood, S.C., Apr. 11, 1913; s. William Ernest and Julia (Griffin) F.; m. Othella Leonard, Dec. 11, 1937; children—William Ernest III, Allen Leonard, John Thomas. B.S. in Architecture, Clemson U., 1934. Draftsman, designer William R. Ward (Architect), Greenville, S.C., 1935-39; archtl. examiner FHA, Columbia, S.C., 1939-40; owner W.E. Freeman, Jr. & Assos., Greenville, 1940-65; partner Freeman, Wells & Major (Architects), Greenville, 1965—; dir. First Fed. Savs. & Loan Assn., Greenville, So. Service Corp.; v.p., dir. Freeman's, Inc., Greenville.; Mem. S.C. Bd. Archtl. Examiners, 1954-59, Greenville; Archtl. Commn., 1967-70. Archtl. works include Hillcrest High Sch, 1957, St. Mark Meth. Ch, Seneca, 1960, 1st Bapt. Ch, Valdese, N.C., 1965, 5 dormitory bldgs., Clemson U., 1966, St. Mathew Meth. Ch, Greenville, 1967, Visitor's Center, Keowee-Toxaway Nuclear Devel, 1969, First Fed. Savs. & Loan Assn. Main Office Bldg, Greenville, 1973, Henderson Advt. Inc. Bldg, Greenville, 1978. Gov. S.C. Beautification and Community Devel. Bd., 1969-72; chmn. Greenville Planning and Zoning Bd. Adjustments, 1953-60; trustee Greenville Baptist Retirement Community, 1978—; Pres., trustee Archtl. Found., Clemson U., 1955-59, mem. engring. adv. bd., 1954-55. Fellow AIA (nat. dir. 1962-65, pres. S.C. chpt. 1951-52, regional dir. 1962-65); mem. Greenville C. of C. (dir. 1959-61), Greenville Art Assn. (pres. 1956-57). Baptist (deacon). Clubs: Rotarian., Greenville Country. Home: 22 Kenwood Lane Greenville SC 29609 Office: One McDaniel Greene Greenville SC 29601

FREEMAN, WILLIAM MISER, banker; b. Chgo., May 5, 1919; s. Gaylord Augustus and Pauline Angeletta (Miser) F.; m. Winifred Carol Stevens, Nov. 1, 1941; children: Carol Jean, James Stevens, Margaret Pauline. B.A. cum laude (Rufus Choate scholar 1941), Dartmouth, 1941; grad., Advanced Mgmt. Program, Harvard, 1958. With Chgo. Bridge & Iron Co., 1941-80, v.p., gen. mgr. Internat. div., 1964-66, v.p., gen. sales mgr., 1966-70, sr. v.p. finance, treas., 1970-80, now dir.; chmn. bd. Gary Wheaton Bank, Wheaton, Ill., Batavia Bank (Ill.); dir. L.E. Meyers, Chgo., Great Books Found., Perkins & Will. Served to lt. comdr. USNR, 1942-46. Mem. Am. Mgmt. Assn., Am. Bankers Assn. Clubs: Chgo. Golf, Commonwealth, Hinsdale Golf. Home: 219 E 7th St Hinsdale IL 60521 Office: 120 E Wesley st Wheaton IL 60521

FREESE, UWE ERNEST, physician, educator; b. Bordesholm, Germany, May 11, 1925; s. Heinrich and Frida (Lessau) F.; m. Gabriela Friederici, Oct. 11, 1961; children: Axel, Pamela. M.D., U. Kiel, W.Ger., 1951. Diplomate: Am. Bd. Obstetrics and Gynecology. Resident U. Kiel, 1954-56, U. Chgo. Lying-in Hosp., 1956-59, prof. ob-gun, 1971-75; prof., chmn. dept. ob-gyn Chgo. Med. Sch., 1975—, Cook County Hosp., 1976—. Patentee cervical cap. Mem. Soc. Gynecol. Investigation, Perinatal Research Soc. (founding mem.), Central Assn. Obstetrics and Gynecology (cert. of merit 1967), Perinatal Soc. Ill. (chmn.), N.Y. Acad. Scis., Sigma Xi. Lutheran. Home: 238 N Forest Ave Oak Park IL 60302 Office: Univ Health Scis The Chicago Med Sch 3333 Green Bay Rd North Chicago IL 60064

FREESE, WALTER EGON, JR., publishing company executive; b. Mineola, N.Y., Feb. 23, 1928; s. Walter and Kathryn Elizabeth (Irvin) F.; m. Virginia Clarie McCarthy, Aug. 23, 1952; children: Walter III, Richard, Virginia, Kathy. B.S., Hofstra U., 1951. Asst. to comptroller Doubleday and Co., Inc., N.Y.C., 1951-62, asst. to v.p. mktg., 1962-65, bus. mgr. pub., 1965-67, corp. treas., 1967-69, corp. v.p., 1969—, corp. v.p., pres. pub. div., 1982; dir. J. G. Ferguson Pub., Chgo., New York Mets, Flushing, N.Y. Chmn. Colgate Soc. Families, Hamilton, N.Y., 1974-75. Served with U.S. Army, 1947-48. Mem. Am. Assn. Pubs. (dir. 1982—). Methodist. Home: 441 Wolf Hill Rd Dix Hills NY 11746 Office: Doubleday and Co Inc 245 Park Ave New York NY 10167

FREETH, DOUGLAS DUNCAN, banker; b. Orange, N.J., Aug. 25, 1935; s. Douglas A. and Betty (Parsons) F.; m. Lucia Jean Little, Feb. 8, 1964; children: Timothy, Andrew. B.A., Princeton U., 1958. V.p. Marine Midland Bank Western, Buffalo, 1967-69, City Nat. Bank, Detroit, 1969-77, sr. v.p., 1977-79, exec. v.p., 1979—; dir. 1st Citizens Bank of Troy (Mich.). Served with USAR, 1958-59. Mem. Robert Morris Assocs. Clubs: Detroit; Country of Detroit (Grosse Pointe Farms, Mich.). Office: City Nat Bank Detroit Ford St and Griswod St Detroit MI 48226

FREEZE, JAMES DONALD, clergyman, university administrator; b. Balt., Sept. 15, 1932; s. Frank Leo and Helen Angela (Sweeney) F. A.B., Boston Coll., 1956, M.A., 1957; S.T.L., U. Innsbruck, Austria, 1964. Joined S.J., Roman Catholic Ch., 1950, ordained priest, 1963; mem. faculty dept. philosophy Wheeling (W.Va.) Coll., 1965-70, chmn. dept., 1967-70; asst. dean Coll. Arts and Scis., Georgetown U., Washington, 1971-74, asst. v.p. for acad. affairs, 1974-79, exec. v.p., provost, 1979—. Trustee Georgetown Prep. Sch., Rockville, Md., 1975-79, chmn. bd., 1978—; trustee Loyola Coll., Balt., 1982—; chmn. bd. U. Detroit, 1983—; bd. dirs. Villa Taverna Found., 1982—. Mem. Am. Cath. Philos. Assn., Am. Assn. for Higher Edn. Home: Georgetown U Washington DC 20057 Office: Office of Provost Georgetown U Washington DC 20057

FREEZE, ROY ALLAN, hydrologist, geological sciences educator; b. Edmonton, Alta., Can., May 23, 1939; s. Donald Allan and Beatrice Isobel (Anderson) F.; m. Donna Dorraine Davis, Dec. 22, 1961; children: Geoffrey, Christine, Lori, Sean. B.Sc., Queens U., Kingston, Ont., Can., 1961; M.Sc., U. Calif., Berkeley, 1964, Ph.D., 1966. Research scientist Can. Dept. Environment, Calgary, Alta., 1966-70, IBM Thomas J. Watson Research Center, Yorktown Heights, N.Y., 1970-73; prof. geol. scis. U. B.C., Can., Vancouver, 1973—. Author: (with J. A. Cherry) Groundwater, 1979; editor: Water Resources Research, 1976-80. Mem. Am. Geophys. Union (Robert E. Horton award 1970, 72, James B. Macelwane award 1973), Geol. Soc. Am. (O.E. Meinzer award 1974), Can. Geotech. Soc., Assn. Profl. Engrs. B.C. Home: 5125 Stevens Dr Delta BC V4M 1N8 Canada Office: Dept Geol Scis U BC Vancouver BC V6T 1W5 Canada

FREI, EMIL, III, physician, educator; b. St. Louis, 1924; m. Elizabeth Frei; children: Mary, Emil, Alice, Nancy, Judy. M.D., Yale U., 1948. Diplomate: Am. Bd. Internal Medicine. Intern St. Louis U. Hosp., 1948-49; resident in pathology Barnes Hosp., St. Louis, 1952-53; resident in internal medicine St. Louis U., 1953-54, VA Hosp., St. Louis, 1954-55; chief gen. medicine br. Nat. Cancer Inst., Bethesda, Md., 1955-65; head devel. therapeutics, assoc. dir. M.D. Anderson Hosp. and Tumor Inst., Houston, 1965-72; physician-in-chief Children's Cancer Research Found. (now Sidney Farber Cancer Inst.), Boston, 1972—; prof. medicine Harvard U. Med. Sch., Boston, 1972—; nat. cons. in internal medicine-oncology U.S. Air Force; mem. Eleanor Roosevelt internat. cancer fellowships com. Internat. Union Against Cancer; chmn. anti-neoplastic disease drug panel, drug efficacy study Nat. Acad. Scis. Served as lt. M.C. USNR, 1950-52. Recipient Lasker award, 1972, cancer research award Gen. Motors Corp., 1983. Fellow ACP; mem. Am. Assn. for Cancer Research (past pres.), Am. Soc. Clin. Oncology (pres. 1968-69), Am. Cancer Soc., Am. Soc. Hematology, Am. Soc. Clin. Investigation, AMA. Office: Dept Medicine Harvard U 44 Binney St Boston MA 02115 *

FREI, ROBERT REED, b. Evanston, Ill., Mar. 23, 1923; s. Russell Herken and Gracia Jewett (Reed) F.; m. Jean Albro, Sept. 15, 1956; children: Stephanie Albro, Robert Reed, Jennifer Jean, Thomas Albro. A.B., Princeton U., 1947; J.D., Harvard U., 1949. Bar: Ill. 1950, U.S. Tax Ct. 1950, U.S. Ct. Claims 1955, U.S. Dist. Ct. (no. dist.) Ill. 1957, U.S. Ct. Appeals (7th cir.) 1961. Assoc. Sidley & Austin, Chgo., 1949-57, ptnr., 1957-81; pres. Robert R. Frei, P.C., Chgo., 1981—; dir. Acme Printing Ink Co., Chgo. Contbr. articles to profl. jours.l. Vice-chmn. priorities com. United Way Met. Chgo., 1978-81; trustee Winnetka Congl. Ch., 1974-77. Served with U.S. Army, 1942-46. Fellow Am. Coll. Tax Lawyers; mem. ABA, Chgo. Bar Assn., Chgo. Fed. Tax Forum (chmn. 1980-81). Republican. Presbyterian. Clubs: Mid-day (Chgo.); Skokie Country (Glencoe). Home: 734 Lincoln Ave Winnetka Il 60093 Office: Sidley & Austin Robert R Frei PC 1 First Nat Plaza Chicago IL 60603

FREIBERGER, ROBERT H., radiologist; b. Vienna, Austria, July 1, 1922; m. Eva J. Benedict, Dec. 26, 1945; children—Peter M., Thomas G. M.D., Tufts U., 1949. Intern Reading (Pa.) Hosp., 1949-50, resident, 1950-53; dir. dept. radiology Hosp. Spl. Surgery, N.Y.C., 1955—; prof. radiology Cornell U., N.Y.C., 1971. Author: (with Kaye) Arthrography, 1979. Served with U.S. Army, 1943-46, 53-54. Fellow Am. Coll. Radiology; mem. Radiol. Soc. N. Am., Acad. Orthopaedic Surgery (asso.), Am. Rheumatism Assn., N.Y. Roentgen Soc. (pres. 1978). Office: 535 E 70th St New York NY 10021

FREIBERGER, WALTER FREDERICK, mathematics educator; b. Vienna, Austria, Feb. 20, 1924; came to U.S., 1955, naturalized, 1962; s. Felix and Irene (Tagany) F.; m. Christine Mildred Holmberg, Oct. 6, 1956; children: Christopher Allan, Andrew James, Nils Henry. B.A., U. Melbourne, 1947, M.A., 1949; Ph.D., U. Cambridge, Eng., 1953. Research officer Aero. Research Lab. Australian Dept. Supply, 1947-49, sr. sci. research officer, 1953-55; tutor U. Melbourne, 1947-49, 53-55; asst. prof. div. applied math. Brown U., 1956-58, asso. prof., 1958-64, prof., 1964—, dir. Computing Center, 1963-69; dir. Center for Computer and Info. Scis., 1969-76, chmn. div. applied math., 1976—; mem. fellowship selection panel NSF. Author: (with U. Grenander) A Short Course in Computational Probability and Statistics, 1971; Editor: The International Dictionary of Applied Mathematics, 1960, (with others) Applications of Digital Computers, 1963, Advances in Computers, Volume 10, 1970, Statistical Computer Performance Evaluation, 1972; Mng. editor: Quarterly of Applied Mathematics, 1965—; Contbr. numerous articles to profl. jours. Served with Australian Army, 1943-45. Fulbright fellow, 1955-56; Guggenheim fellow, 1962-63; NSF Office Naval Research grantee in field. Mem. Am. Math. Soc. (asso. editor Math. Reviews 1957-62), Soc. for Indsl. and Applied Math., Inst. Math. Statistics, Assn. Computing Machinery. Republican. Episcopalian. Club: Univ. (Providence). Home: 24 Alumni Ave Providence RI 02906 Office: 182 George St Providence RI 02912

FREID, JACOB, association executive, educator; b. N.Y.C.; s. Harry and Fanny (Axelrod) F.; m. Janet Glickman; 1 dau., Allison Orah (Mrs. Joseph Rosenblatt). B.A., CCNY; M.A. (Honor fellow), Columbia U., Ph.D. Successively head Moscow (USSR) desk Office War Info. U.S. State Dept.; asst. prof. Rutgers U., New Brunswick, N.J.; editor Jewish affairs pamphlets Am.Jewish Congress, N.Y.C.; now prof. polit. sci. New Sch. for Social Research, N.Y.C., past chmn. faculty; past exec. dir. Jewish Braille Inst. Am. Inc., N.Y.C.; now dir. pub. inf. Am. sect. World Zionist Orgn.; past chmn. dept. polit. sci. New Sch. Social Research, N.Y.C.; past Disting. vis. prof. CCNY. Author: Jews in the Modern World, 1962 (Most Important Jewish Book of 1962 Citation Jewish Telegraphic Agy. Ann. Book Rev.); Editor: Jews and Divorce, Judaism and the Community, Soviet World Politics. Former mem. Five Towns Community Devel., Planning Commn., L.I. N.Y.; Bd. dirs. Nat. Fedn. Blind; chmn. bd. dirs. Am. Coll. in Jerusalem (Israel); founder CORE, L.I. chpt. Recipient Newell Perry award; Recipient Disting. Service awards Nat. Assn. Visually Handicapped, Jewish Braille Inst.; award of honor Fedn. Jewish Philanthropies N.Y. Mem. AAUP, N.Y. State Fedn. Workers for Blind, Am. Assn. Workers for Blind. Home: 147 Upper Byrdcliffe Rd Woodstock NY 12498 also 1 Lincoln Plaza New York NY 10023

FREIDBERG, SIDNEY, lawyer, real estate development company executive; b. N.Y.C., Jan. 20, 1914; s. David and Tillie (Friedman) F.; children: David, Emily. B.S., N.Y. U., 1933; LL.B., Yale U., 1936. Bar: N.Y. 1936, D.C. 1945. Practice law, N.Y.C., 1936-42, 45-68; ptnr. firm Freidberg, Rich & Blue, N.Y.C., 1945-62, Posner, Fox, Arent & Freidberg, Washington, 1945-54; research and analysis div. OSS, 1942-43; counsel printing and pub. div. WPB, Washington, 1943-45; counsel Ho. of Reps. select com. on newsprint and paper supply, Washington, 1948-49; commr. Fgn. Claims Settlement Commn. U.S., Washington, 1968-70; exec. v.p., gen. counsel Nat. Corp. for Housing Partnerships, Washington, 1970-77; counsel firm Arent, Fox, Kintner, Plotkin & Kahn, Washington, 1977-84; pres. Morningside Heights Property Assn., 1960-62; dir. Preterm, Inc., 1983—. Contbr.: articles to legal jours., also to Washingtonian, Esquire, Holiday, Modern Photography. Mem. alumni bd. visitors N.Y. U., 1959-61; bd. dirs. Nat. Housing Conf., Inc., 1979—, Planned Parenthood of Met. Washington, Inc., 1979—; bd. dirs., sec.-treas. Nat. Minority Purchasing Council, Inc., 1977-81. Mem. Am., Fed., D.C., N.Y. State, City N.Y. bar assns., Am. Soc. Internat. Law, World Assembly Judges, World Peace Through Law Center, D.C. C. of C. (dir., counsel 1979-80), Phi Beta Kappa. Democrat. Clubs: Cosmos, Fed. City, Nat. Lawyers, Nat. Press, Army and Navy (Washington); Yale (N.Y.C. and Washington). Home: 1832 24th St NW Washington DC 20008

FREIDEL, FRANK BURT, JR., historian; b. Bklyn., May 22, 1916; s. Frank Burt and Edith (Heacock) F.; m. Elisabeth Margo, 1938 (div. 1955); children—Linda Beth, Dorothy Edith, David Alan, Charles Robinson; m. Madeleine Bicskey, Feb. 23, 1956; children—Philip (dec.), Paul, Christine, Irene. B.A., U. So. Calif., 1937, M.A., 1939; Ph.D., U. Wis., 1942; M.A., Oxford U., 1954, Harvard, 1955; D.H.L., Roosevelt U., 1975. Faculty, asso. prof. Shurtleff Coll., 1941-43; asst. prof. U. Md., 1943-45, Pa. State Coll., 1946-48, Vassar Coll., 1948-49, U. Ill., 1949-52, asso. prof., 1952-53, Stanford U., 1953-55; Harmsworth prof. Am. history Oxford U., 1955-56; prof. Harvard U., 1955—; Charles Warren prof. Am. history, 1972-81; Bullitt prof. Am. history U. Wash., 1981—; tchr. summers George Washington U., 1946, 49, Mich. State U., 1948, Columbia U., 1952, U. Calif., 1959; lectr. Salzburg (Austria) Seminar in Am. Studies, 1955-56; fellow Center for Advanced Study in Behavioral Scis., 1959-60; Cons. Office Naval Research, summer 1949; historian NSF, summer 1951; mem. Nat. Study Commn. Records and Documents Fed. Ofcls., 1976-77. Author: Francis Lieber, Nineteenth Century Liberal, 1947, Franklin D. Roosevelt: The Apprenticeship, 1952, Roosevelt: The Ordeal, 1954, Roosevelt: The Triumph, 1956, Roosevelt: Launching the New Deal, 1973, The Splendid Little War, 1958, America in the Twentieth Century, 196O, Over There, 1964, The Presidents of the United States, 1964, F.D.R. and the South, 1966, Our Country's Presidents, 1966; Co-author: A History of the United States, 1959, America, A Modern History of the United States, 1970, Dissent in Three American Wars, 1970, America Is, 1978; Editor: The Golden Age of American History, 1959, The New Deal and the American People, 1964, Union Pamphlets of the Civil War, 1967, American Epochs series, Franklin D. Roosevelt and the Era of the New Deal series, Modern American History series; Co-editor: Builders of American Institutions, 1963, American Issues in the Twentieth Century, 1966, Harvard Guide to American History, 1974. Served with USNR, 1945-46. Guggenheim fellow, 1964-65; Nat. Endowment for Humanities fellow, 1975-76. Fellow Am. Acad. Arts and Scis.; mem. Orgn. Am. Historians (pres. 1975-76). Office: History Dept DP-20 U Wash Seattle WA 98195

FREIDSON, ELIOT LAZARUS, educator, sociologist; b. Boston, Feb. 20, 1923; s. Joseph and Grace (Backer) F.; m. Helen Emery Giambruni, Apr. 21, 1976; children by previous marriages—Jane Beatrice, Oliver Eliot (dec.), Matthew Aaron. Student, U. Maine, 1941-42; Ph.B., U. Chgo., 1947, M.A., 1950, Ph.D., 1952. Postdoctoral fellow U. Ill., 1952-54; asst., then asso. prof. sociology Coll. City N.Y., 1956-61; mem. faculty N.Y.U., 1961—, prof. sociology, 1963—, head dept. sociology, 1975-78; dir. Études associé Ecole des Hautes Etudes en Sci. Sociales, Paris, 1978; Pitt prof. Am. history and instns. Cambridge (Eng.) U., 1979-80; cons. in field, 1956—; Adviser div. research grants NIH, 1963-66; adviser joint research program Social Security Adminstrn. and Social Rehab. Service, HEW, 1968-70; fellow Center Advanced Study in Behavioral Scis., 1974-75; Eastern Sociol. Assn. Falk Fund lectr., 1976; mem. Pres.'s Commn. on Mental Health, 1977-78. Author: Patient's Views Medical Practice, 1961, Profession of Medicine, 1970, Professional Dominance, 1970, Doctoring Together, 1976, also articles.; Editor: Student Government, Student Leaders and American Colleges, 1955, Hospital in Modern Society, 1963, Jour. Health and Social Behavior, 1966-69, The Professions And Their Prospects, 1973;. Co-editor: Med. Men and Their Work, 1972. Served with inf. AUS, 1943-46; ETO. Decorated Bronze Star; Guggenheim fellow, 1981-82. Fellow Am. Sociol. Assn. (chmn. med. sociol. sect. 1963-64, Sorokin award 1972), AAAS; mem. Soc. Study Social Problems, AAUP, Internat. Sociol. Assn. (pres. com. research med. sociology 1967-70), Inst. Medicine, Nat. Acad. Sci. Office: NY University 269 Mercer St New York NY 10003

FREIFELDER, DAVID MICHAEL, biochemist, author; b. Phila., July 19, 1935; s. Morris Leon and Florence (Levenson) F.; children: Rachel, Joshua. B.S. in Physics, U. Chgo., 1957, Ph.D. in Biophysics, 1959. Research asso. M.I.T., 1960-62, U. Copenhagen, 1962; asst. prof. med. physics U. Calif., Berkeley, 1963-66; mem. faculty Brandeis U., Waltham, Mass., 1966—, prof. biochemistry, 1976-82; vis. prof. U. Calif.-San Diego. Author textbooks, articles in field. Grantee NSF, AEC, USPHS, 1967—. Jewish. Office: Dept Biochemistry Brandeis Univ Waltham MA 02254 *I have always tried to do well those things that are my special abilities. Thus, I have recently turned from research to scientific writing. I can write and explain, but not do research, more proficiently than eager and energetic novices.*

FREIHEIT, CLAYTON FREDRIC, zoo director; b. Buffalo, Jan. 29, 1938; s. Clayton John and Ruth (Miller) F. Student, U. Buffalo, 1960. Caretaker Living Mus., Buffalo Mus. Sci., 1955-60; curator Buffalo Zool. Gardens, 1960-70; dir. Denver Zool. Gardens, 1970—. Contbr. articles to profl. jours. Named Outstanding Citizen Buffalo Evening News, 1967. Mem. Internat. Union Dirs. Zool. Gardens, Am. Assn. Zool. Parks and Aquariums (pres. 1967-68, Outstanding Service award 1975), Am. Soc. Ichthyologists and Herpetologists, Am. Soc. Mammalogists. Lodge: Rotary. Home: 3855 S Monaco St Denver CO 80237 Office: Denver Zool Gardens City Park Denver CO 80205 *

FREILICH, DENNIS BYRON, retinal surgeon; b. N.Y.C., June 1, 1934; s. Irving and Ida (Mittelpunkt) F.; m. Estelle Feld, June 10, 1962; children: Benjamin D., Jonathan M., David E., Elliot A.J. Student, NYU, 1952-54; M.D., SUNY-Bklyn., 1958; postgrad. in ophthalmology, Harvard U., 1961-62. Intern Kings County Hosp., 1958-59; resident in ophthalmology St. Luke's Hosp. Center, N.Y.C., 1962-64; fellow retina services Mass. Eye and Ear Infirmary, Boston, 1964-66; research fellow Retina Found., Boston, 1964-66; trainee Armed Forces Inst. Pathology, Washington, 1965; practice medicine, specializing in retinal diseases and surgery, N.Y.C., 1966—; clin. prof. ophthalmology, dir. retina service Mt. Sinai Sch. Medicine, CUNY, 1966—; assoc. in ophthalmology Columbia U., N.Y.C., 1974—; attending ophthalmologist, dir. retina service Mt. Sinai Hosp., N.Y.C., 1966—; assoc. attending ophthalmologist St. Luke's Hosp. Center, N.Y.C., 1965—; cons. ophthalmologist Lenox Hill Hosp., N.Y.C. Contbr. articles to profl. publs. Served to lt. comdr. USNR, 1959-61. Heed Ophthalmic Found. traveling fellow, 1964-65. Fellow A.C.S., Am. Acad. Ophthalmology; mem. N.Y. Acad. Scis., AMA, Vitreous Soc., N.Y. State, N.Y. County med. socs., Assn. Research in Ophthalmology, Instituto Barraquer, N.Y. Soc. Clin. Ophthalmology, Retina Soc., Soc. Eye Surgeons, Jules Gonin Club. Jewish. Home: 120 E 81st St New York NY 10028 Office: 20 E 68th St New York NY 10021

FREIMAN, DAVID GALLAND, pathologist, educator; b. N.Y.C., July 1, 1911; s. Leopold and Dorothy (Galland) F.; m. Ruth Schein, Sept. 2, 1949; children: Nancy, Leonard. A.B., CCNY, 1930; M.D., L.I. Coll. Medicine, (now Downstate Med. Center SUNY), 1935; A.M. (hon), Harvard U., 1962. Intern, house physician Jewish Hosp. of Bklyn., 1935-36; intern Kingston Ave. Hosp. (for Contagious Disease), Bklyn., 1938; intern, resident pathology Montefiore Hosp., 1938-43; asst. pathologist Mass. Gen. Hosp., 1944-50; attending pathologist Cin. Gen. Hosp., Drake Meml. Hosp., 1952-56; pathologist-in-chief, dir. labs. Beth Israel Hosp., 1956-79, emeritus, 1979—, spl. asst. to pres., 1979—; cons. pathologist VA, Hosps., Cin., Ft. Thomas, Ky., 1954-56, Boston, 1962—; instr. pathology Med. Sch. Tufts U., 1947-48, Med. Sch. Harvard U., 1949-50, clin. prof. pathology, 1956-62, prof., 1962—, Mallinckrodt prof. pathology, 1969-79, emeritus, 1979—; asst. prof. pathology Coll. Medicine, U. Cin., 1950-52; asso. prof. Coll. Medicine (U. Cin.), 1952-56; lectr. pathology Simmons, 1962-78; cons. pathology Cambridge Hosp., 1968—, Uniformed Services U. Health Scis., 1974-75, Children's Hosp. Med. Center, Boston, 1977—; mem. joint faculty Harvard-MIT, 1975-79. Editorial bd.: Am. Jour. Pathology, 1961-82, Circulation, 1962-67, Human Pathology, 1969-79; asso. editor, 1979—; mem. editorial adv. com.: Atlas of Tumor Pathology, 1966—; Contbr. articles to profl. jours. Recipient Stratford prize CCNY, 1931, Alumni prize L.I. Coll. Medicine, 1935; Kirstein fellow in med. edn. Harvard U., 1971-72. Mem. Am. Assn. Pathologists, Internat. Acad. Pathology, Histochem. Soc., Am. Soc. Clin. Pathologists, AAAS, Mass. Med. Soc., New Eng. Soc. Pathologists, Internat. Soc. for Haemostasis and Thrombosis, Phi Beta Kappa, Sigma Xi, Alpha Omega Alpha. Home: 182 Homer St Newton Centre MA 02159 Office: 330 Brookline Ave Boston MA 02215

FREIMARK, ROBERT, artist, art educator; b. Doster, Mich., Jan. 27, 1922; s. Alvin O. and Nora (Shinaver) F.; m. Mary Carvin (dec.); 1 son, Matisse Jon; m. Lillian Tihlarik; 1 dau., Christine Gay. B.E., U. Toledo, 1950; M.F.A., Cranbrook Acad. Art, 1951. Prof. art San Jose State U., 1964—; W.I.C.H.E. prof. Soledad State Prison, 1967. Guest artist, Harvard U., 1972-73; first Am. to make tapestries in Art Protis technique at, Atelier Vlnena, Brno, Czechoslovakia.; Contbr. to profl. publs.; Numerous one-man shows including, Minn. Inst. Arts, Toledo Mus. Art, Salpeter Gallery, Morris Gallery, N.Y.C., Des Moines Art Center, Santa Barbara Mus., Moravska Mus., Czechoslovakia, Brunel U., London, Amerika Haus, Munich, exhibited in group shows, Art Inst. Chgo., 1952, Pa. Acad. Fine Arts, 1953 (Lambert Fund prize), Detroit Inst. Arts, 1956, Mich. State U., N.A.D., Bklyn. Mus., Mus. Modern Art, others, Los Angeles, others, Boston, others, San Francisco, others, Omaha, others, Oklahoma City, others, Des Moines, others, Dallas, others, Phoenix, others, San Jose, exhbn. 50 States toured, European Mus., 1970-71, represented in collections, Pa. Acad. Fine Art, Boston Mus. Fine Arts, Fogg Mus., Butler Inst. Am. Art, Canton Art Inst., Daytona Beach Art Center, Albion Coll., Ford Motor Co., South Bend Art Assn., Joslyn Art Mus., Seattle Art Mus., Ga. Mus., Massillon Mus., U. Toledo, Marietta Coll., Colo. Coll., W.Va. Wesleyan Coll., Huntington Gallery, U. N.D., Oreg. State Coll., U. Oklahoma City, Des Moines Art Center, Smithsonian Instn., Library Congress, Los Angeles County Art Inst., Brit. Mus., Nat. Gallery, Prague, Birmingham (Eng.) Mus., Moravske Mus., Brno, Czechoslovakia, Bibliotheque Nationale, Paris, others, numerous tapestries in pub. and pvt. collections, created tapestry representing U.S. for Olympic Games, Moscow, 1980; produced film El Dia Tarasco, 1982; guest artist, Joslyn Meml. Mus., 1961; instr. painting and drawing, Ohio U., 1955-59; artist in residence, Des Moines Art Center, 1959-63; dir., Crystal Lake Art Center, Frankfort, Mich., (1955-57); guest lectr., one man show, Columbia U., 1963, cultural exchange exhibit, Northamerican Cultural Inst., Mexico City, 1963; guest artist, Riverside Art Center, 1964. Served with USNR, 1939-46. Recipient 2d award for oil Northwest Territorial exhibit, 1954, Roulet medal Toledo Mus. Art, 1957; elected to New Talent in U.S.A., 1957; recipient 1st award print exhbns., 1958; Ohio U. research grant, 1958-59; purchase award Midwest Biennial and Northwest Printmakers; Calif. State Coll. grant to create spl. edit. serigraphs; Western Interstate Commn. for Higher Edn. grant, 1967; San Jose State Coll. Found. grants, 1966, 67, 68, 69-70, 71; designated ofcl. U.S. Bicentennial Exhbn. German Houses, 1976. Home: Route 2 Box 539A Morgan Hill CA 95037 Office: Art Dept San Jose State U San Jose CA 95114 *It is the obligation of all men who have information, or power, to share it for the benefit of all men.*

FREINKEL, NORBERT, physician, educator, researcher; b. Mannheim, Germany, Jan. 26, 1926; s. Adolf and Veronika (Kahn) F.; m. Ruth Kimmelstiel, June 19, 1955; children: Susan Elizabeth, Andrew Jonathan, Lisa Ann. A.B., Princeton U., 1947; M.D., NYU, 1949; M.D. honoris causa honor's causa, Uppsala (Sweden) U., 1981. Postdoctoral tng. in medicine, endocrinology and metabolism Bellevue Hosp., N.Y.C., Boston City Hosp., Thorndike Meml. Lab., Harvard U., ARC Inst. Animal Physiology, Cambridge, Eng., 1949-56; from research fellow asst. prof. medicine Harvard Med. Sch. and Thorndike Meml. Lab., Boston City Hosp., 1952-66; chief metabolism div. Thorndike Meml. Lab., 1957-66; Kettering prof. medicine, chief sect. endocrinology, metabolism and nutrition, dir. Endocrine Clinics, Northwestern U. Med. Sch., 1966—, prof. biochemistry, 1969—; dir. Center for Endocrinology, Metabolism and Nutrition, 1973—; Mem. metabolism study sect. NIH, 1967-69, chmn. designate, 1970; mem. adv. com. on alcoholism NIMH, 1967-70; mem. subcom. on diabetes Fogarty Internat. Center, NIH, 1972—; mem. com. on renal and metabolic effects Space Flight Space Sci. Bd., Nat. Acad. Sci., 1973-74; cons. surg. gen. U.S. Army, 1962-79; mem. endocrinology and metabolism adv. com. Bur. Drugs, FDA, 1973-76, cons., 1976—; mem. career devel. com. VA, Washington, 1975-77; mem. sci. adv. com. Solomon A. Berson Fund for Med. Research, Inc., 1976—; mem. spl. study sect. DRTC NIAMDD, 1976-77; mem. nutrition coordinating com. NIH, 1978-80; dir. BioTechnica Internat. Inc., 1981—. Co-editor: Handbook of Physiology Series, Am. Phys. Soc.; Editorial bd.: Endocrinology, Jour. Developmental Physiology, Ann. Rev. Medicine, Jour. Clin. Investigation, Jour. Clin. Endocrinology, Jour. Lab. Clin. Medicine, Bull. Internat. Diabetes Fedn.; editor-in-chief: The Year in Metabolism, 1975-79, Contemporary Metabolism, 1979—; Contbr. articles to profl. jours., chpts. in textbooks. Served with USNR, 1943-45; Served with USNR AUS, 1950-52. Recipient Lilly award and medal Am. Diabetes Assn., 1966; Woodyatt award No. Ill. Diabetes Assn., 1976; Mosenthal award N.Y. Diabetes Assn., 1978; Banting Meml. medal Am. Diabetes Assn., 1978, 80; Joslin medal New Eng. Diabetes Assn., 1978; Kellion medal Australian Diabetes Assn., 1981; Am. Cancer Soc. fellow, 1953-55; Nat. Found. fellow, 1955-56. Fellow A.C.P., AAAS, Diabetes Assn. of India (hon.); mem. Assn. Am. Physicians, Am. Soc. Clin. Investigation (editorial com. 1971-76), Am. Physiol. Soc., World Med. Assn. (mem. med. bd. advisers 1975—), Endocrine Soc. (council 1969-72, chmn. meetings com. 1980-83, postgrad. program com. 1983—), Am. Thyroid Assn. (chmn. Van Meter award com. 1977-78), Am. Diabetes Assn. (dir. 1968-79, chmn. com. sci. programs 1971-75, v.p. profl. sect. 1975-76, pres. 1977-78, exec. com. 1975-79), Am. Soc. Clin. Nutrition (council 1984—), Soc. Exptl. Biology and Medicine, AAAS (mem. at large sect. med. scis.), Alpha Omega Alpha, Phi Beta Kappa, Sigma Xi; hon. mem. High Table, King's Coll., Cambridge, Eng. Home: 938 Edgemere Ct Evanston IL 60202 Office: Northwestern U Med Sch 303 E Chicago Ave Chicago IL 60611

FREINKEL, RUTH KIMMELSTIEL, dermatologist; b. Hamburg, Germany, Dec. 26, 1926; d. Paul and Lotte (Ven Biema) Kimmelstiel; m. Norbert Freinkel, June 19, 1955; children—Susan E., Andrew J., Lisa A. B.A., Randolph-Macon Coll., 1948; M.D., Duke U., 1952. Diplomate Am. Bd. Dermatology. Research fellow in biochemistry Harvard U. and Cambridge (Eng.) U., 1955-56; from research asso. to asst. prof. dermatology Harvard U. Med. Sch., Boston, 1958-66; asso. prof. Northwestern U., 1966-72, prof., 1972—; mem. adv. council Nat. Inst. Arthritis, Metabolism and Digestive Diseases, 1980—. Contbr. numerous articles, chpts. to profl. publs.; editor: Jour. Investigative Dermatology, 1977-82. NRC fellow, 1954-56. Mem. Am. Soc. Clin. Research, Soc. Investigative Dermatology (dir. 1973-75, 77-82), Am. Dermatol. Assn., Central Soc. Clin. Research, Alpha Omega Alpha, Phi Beta Kappa. Jewish. Home: 938 Edgemere Ct Evanston IL 60202 Office: 303 E Chicago Ave Chicago IL 60611

FREIREICH, EMIL J, physician, educator; b. Chgo., Mar. 16, 1927; s. David and Mary (Klein) F.; m. Haroldine Lee Cunningham, Mar. 13, 1953; children: Debra Ann, David Alan, Lindsay Gail, Thomas Jon. B.S., U. Ill., 1947, M.D. with honors, 1949. Diplomate: Am. Bd. Internal Medicine, Assn. Am. Physicians, Am. Soc. Clin. Investigation. Intern Cook County (Ill.) Hosp., Chgo., 1949-50; resident in internal medicine Presbyn. Hosp., Chgo., 1950-53; research asso. in hematology Mass. Meml. Hosp., Boston, 1953-55; sr. investigator, head Leukemia Service USPHS, Nat. Cancer Inst., Bethesda, Md., 1955-65; prof. medicine U. Tex. Health Sci. Center, Houston, 1966—; prof. medicine dept. developmental therapeutics U. Tex. System Cancer Center, Houston, 1965—, chief research hematology, 1965—, head dept. developmental therapeutics, 1972—, prof. medicine, 1973—, chief div. oncology, 1973—; mem. faculty Grad. Sch. Med., Health Scis. Center, 1965—; mem. rev. com. drug. devel. div. cancer treatment NIH, 1975-80, Ruth Harriet Ainsworth chair in devel. therapeutics, 1980—. Asso. editor: Cancer, 1976—, Cancer Research, 1977—; editorial bd.: Oncology News, 1975—, Cancer Treatment Reports, 1976-80, Leukemia Research, 1976—, Med. and Pediatric Oncology, 1974—; Contbr. numerous articles on research in hematology and oncology to profl. jours. Recipient Albert Lasker Med. Research award, 1972, Charles F. Kettering prize Gen. Motors Cancer Research Found., 1983; named Alumnus of Year for Service to Edn. or Research U. Ill. Alumni Assn., 1974. Fellow ACP; mem. Internat., Am. socs. hematology, Am. Fedn. Clin. Research, Am. Soc. Clin. Pharmacology and Therapeutics, Am. Soc. Clin. Oncology (David A. Karnofsky award 1976, pres. 1980-81), Am. Assn. Cancer Research, Am. Cancer Soc. (com. on unproven remedies), Leukemia Soc. Am. (pres. Gulf Coast chpt. 1968-70, trustee 1968-70, Robert Roesler DeVilliers award 1979), Tex. Med. Assn., AMA (editorial bd. jour. 1973—), Alpha Omega Alpha. Research in therapy of human acute leukemia and leukocyte physiology. Home: 810 Monte Cello Houston TX 77024 Office: 6723 Bertner Ave Houston TX 77030 *The search for eternal physical and mental health has been at the forefront of man's striving to understand and to control his destiny. The opportunity to investigate, to discover and to apply new remedies for major human illness is a rare privilege and must rank with man's highest callings.*

FREIS, EDWARD DAVID, physician, medical researcher; b. Chgo., May 13, 1912; 3 children. B.S., U. Ariz., 1936; M.D., Columbia, 1940. Intern, house physician Mass. Meml. Hosp., Boston, 1940-41; sr. intern, house physician Boston City Hosp., 1941-42; asst. resident Evans Meml. Hosp., 1946-47, resident fellow cardiovascular disease, 1947-49; adj. clin. prof. Georgetown U. Sch. Medicine, 1949-57, assoc. prof., 1957-63, prof., 1963—; chief cardiovascular research lab. Georgetown U. Hosp., 1949—; sr. med. investigator VA Med. Ctr., Washington, 1959—, asst. chief medicine, 1949-54, chief, 1954-59; instr. Boston U., 1947-49. Served with M.C. USAAF, 1942-45. Recipient Albert Lasker Med. Research award, 1971, Ciba award in hypertension. Address: VA Med Ctr 50 Irving St NW Washington DC 20422

FREITAG, HARLOW, computer scientist, corporate executive; b. Bklyn., Apr. 17, 1936; s. Abraham and Eva (Levine) F.; 1 son, Adam. B.S. with honors, NYU, 1955; M.S., Yale U., 1958, Ph.D., 1959. Research staff mem. IBM, Yorktown Heights, N.Y., 1961-70, asst. dir. computer sci., 1970-77, White Plains, N.Y., 1977-80, staff v.p., group exec., White Plains, NY, 1980-82, editor Jour. Research and Devel., White Plains, N.Y., 1982—. Recipient Outstanding Innovation award IBM, 1966, Francis Mills Turner award Electrochem. Soc., 1959. Fellow IEEE (editor procs. 1979-82), Yale Sci. and Engring. Assn. (exec. v.p. 1981-83, pres. 1983—). Office: IBM Corp 44 S Broadway St White Plains NY 10601

FREITAG, ROBERT FREDERICK, government official; b. Jackson, Mich., Jan. 20, 1920; s. Fred J. and Beatrice (Paradise) F.; m. Maxine Pryer, Apr. 13, 1941; children—Nancy Marie (Mrs. Stephen Sprague), Janet Louise (Mrs. Richard Wasserstrom), Fred John II, Paul Robert. B.S.E. in Aero. Engring, U. Mich., 1941; postgrad., MIT, 1941-42. Commd. ensign USNR, 1941; lt. comdr. U.S. Navy, 1946, advanced through grades to capt., 1960; dep. dir. NASA Space Sta. Task Force, 1982—; various guided missile programs, 1941-55, project officer Jupiter and Polaris intermediate range ballistic missiles, 1955-57, range planning officer, also spl. asst. to comdr., Point Mugu, Calif., 1957-59, astronautics officer, 1959-63, ret., 1963; dir. launch vehicles and propulsion NASA, 1963; dir. Manned Space Flight Field Center Devel., 1963-72, dir. manned space flight advanced programs, 1973-82; Mem. NACA Com. Propellers, 1944-46, Sec. Def. Spl. Com. Adequacy Range Facilities, 1956-58, Joint Army-Navy Ballistic Missile Com., 1955-57, NACA Spl. Com. Space Tech., 1958-59; re-adv. com. missile and spacecraft aerodynamics NASA, 1960-63; joint Def. Dept.-NASA-Astronautics Coordinating Bd. (on launch vehicles panel), 1960-64. Author tech. papers. Decorated Legion of Merit, 1959; recipient Spl. Commendation from Comdr.-in-Chief U.S. Pacific Fleet, 1953, Sec. Def., 1958; Sec. Navy Commendation medal, 1959, Distinguished Alumnus award U. Mich., 1957, Sesquicentennial medal and cert., 1967, NASA Exceptional Service medal, 1969, 81; Bronze medal Brit. Interplanetary Soc., 1979. Fellow Royal Aero. Soc., AIAA (pres. Central Calif. sect. 1958-59, dir. Washington sect. 1964-65, 69). Home: 4110 Mason Ridge Dr Annandale VA 22003 Office: 600 Independence Ave SW Washington DC 20546

FREITAS, GEORGE ERNEST, construction and development executive; b. Honolulu, Dec. 2, 1905; s. Henry and Mary (Lewis) F.; m. Flora Cabral, Aug. 6, 1938 (dec. Sept. 1973); children—Gail, Alan; m. Melinda P. Felix, July 1, 1976. B.S. in Civil Engring, U. Dayton, 1929; L.H.D., Chaminade Coll., Honolulu. Pres., chief exec. Hawaii Corp., 1962-69; founder, 1938; chmn., dir. Pacific Constrn. Co. Ltd., 1938-69; founder Pacific Contractors, 1957, chmn., dir., 1958-69, Von Hammn-Young, Inc., 1962-69, Pacific Investment Inc., 1962-69, Johnston & Buscher, Inc., 1962-69, VHY Pty. Ltd., Australia, 1964-72, Pacific-Peru Constrn. Corp., 1965-69, Amelco Engrs. Pty. Ltd., Australia, 1970-75; pres., chmn., dir. Pacific Devel. Co., Ltd., 1951—, Pacco, Ltd., 1962-69; v.p., dir. Moanalua Manor and Terrace Shopping, Inc., 1953-72, Rosalei Apts., Inc., 1954-74; dir. Hawaiian Life Ins. Co., 1957-64, 71-79; Hawaiian Western Steel, Ltd., 1959, First Hawaiian Bank, 1962-79, First Hawaiian Inc., 1979—, Amelco Corp., 1977-80. Mem. Territorial Bd. Health Civil Service Commn., 1937-40; bd. govs. Hawaii Employers Council, 1962-68; lay bd. mem. Marianist Province Pacific; patron Smithsonian Instn.; bd. dirs. Aloha United Fund, 1967-69; trustee, v.p. St. Louis-Chaminade Ednl. Ctr., 1968-79; mem. State Postsecondary Edn. Commn., 1976-77; chmn. bd. regents Chaminade Coll., 1966-73; life mem. Queens Hosp., Honolulu Acad. Arts, Bishop Mus. Assn., U. Hawaii Found. (trustee 1962-68). Recipient Outstanding Alumnus award St. Louis High Sch., 1970, Distinguished Alumnus award U. Dayton, 1974. Mem. Honolulu C. of C. (bd. dirs. 1962-64), Navy League U.S., Air Force Assn., St. Louis Coll., U. Dayton alumni assns., Gen. Contractors Assn. Hawaii (pres. 1947). Clubs: Outrigger Canoe, Oahu Country, Waialae Country (Honolulu). Home: 1010 Wilder Ave Apt 1701 Honolulu HI 96822 Office: Amfac Bldg Suite 1906 Honolulu HI 96813

FREIWALD, DAVID ALLEN, physicist, engineer; b. Cleve., June 4, 1941; s. Harry Herman and Arline Mildred F.; m. Joyce Gross, Apr. 3, 1976; children: Wesley, Todd, Christopher. B.S., Northwestern U., 1968, Ph.D., 1963. Asst. engr. Gen. Am. Transp., Niles, Ill., 1963; mem. staff Sandia Labs., Albuquerque, 1967-72, Los Alamos Sci. Lab., 1972—, asst. research dir.'s office, 1975-79, energy programs office-dir.'s office, 1979—. Author: Introduction of Laser Fusion, 1975; inventor magnetically protected laser fusion reactor cavity. Vice chmn. Com. environ. concerns City of Albuquerque, 1972; mem. Gov.'s com. to Draft N.Mex. State Subdiv. Laws, 1972; environ. com. Western Systems Coordinating Council, 1972-75; mem. Gov.'s Energy Task Force, 1972-75, N.Mex. Energy Inst. Adv. Com., 1977-79, Gov.'s Energy Research and Devel. Oversight Com., 1979—. NDEA fellow, 1963-66; recipient certs. of service State of N.Mex., City of Albuquerque, Albuquerque Environmentalist award, 1972. Mem. Am. Phys. Soc., Nat. Wildlife Fedn., AAAS. Home: 375 Cheryl Ct Los Alamos NM 87544 Office: PO Box 1663 Los Alamos NM 87545

FREIZER, LOUIS A., journalist, TV news producer; b. N.Y.C., Oct. 10, 1931; s. Morris and Celia (Blumberg) F.; m. Michelle Suzanne Orban, July 6, 1968; children: Sabine, Eric. B.S., U. Wis., 1953; postgrad., U. Heidelberg, W.Ger., 1956; M.A. (CBS Found. news fellow), Columbia U., 1964, Columbia U., 1966—. Corr. UPI, Madison, Wis., 1953-54; desk asst. CBS News, N.Y.C., 1956-59, newswriter, 1959-60, Sta. WCBS, N.Y.C., 1960-62, news editor, 1963-68, sr. news producer, 1968-73, sr. exec. news producer, 1973—; adj. prof. dept. communications Fordham U.; lectr., cons. journalism and internat. relations. Producer: pub. affairs series Let's Find Out, 1966, Internat. Briefing series, 1968-72. Served to 1st lt. U.S. Army, 1954-56; to capt. Res. Recipient Am. Legion medal, 1949; Radio Journalism award AMA, 1965, Nat. Headliners Club, 1965; Radio Journalism award nat. award for outstanding newscast UPI, 1982, 1st place award for best regularly scheduled local news program N.Y. State AP Broadcasters Assn., 1982, spl. mention for best one day news effort, 1983. Mem. Am. Polit. Sci. Assn., Acad. Polit. Sci., Am. Acad. Polit. and Social Scis., Radio-TV News Dirs. Assn., Broadcast Pioneers, Sigma Delta Chi. Home: 400 Central Park W New York NY 10025 Office: 51 W 52d St New York NY 10019

FREL, JIRI K., museum curator; b. Veselicko, Czechoslovakia, Nov. 13, 1923; s. Antonin and Marie Toman (Frel); m. Faya E. Causey, 1976; children: Alexander, Jan. Ph.D., U. Prague, 1948; postgrad., Ecole Normale Superieure, Paris, 1946-48. Mem. faculty dept. Greek and Roman art Prague U., 1948-68, prof., 1967-69; asso. curator Met. Mus. Art, N.Y.C., 1970-72; curator J. Paul Getty Mus., Malibu, Calif., 1973—; mem. Inst. for Advanced Studies, Princeton, N.J., 1969-70. Author books in field. Mem. German Archaeol. Inst. (corr. mem.). Office: J Paul Getty Mus Malibu CA 90265

FRELICH, PHYLLIS, actress; b. Devils Lake, N.D., Feb. 29, 1944; d. Phillip and Esther (Dockter) F.; m. Robert Steinberg, May 17, 1968; children: Reuben, Joshua. B.S. in L.S, Gallaudet Coll., 1967. Acting tchr. Nat. Theater of the Deaf, Waterford, Conn., 1977-79, 83, R.I. Sch. for Deaf, Providence, 1977-78, U. R.I., North Kingston, 1978. Appeared in numerous stage plays, 1965—; latest being Woyzeck, all with Nat. Theatre of the Deaf, 1979, Songs from Milkwood, Broadway, Children of a Lesser God, Broadway, 1980, Poets from the Inside, N.Y.C., Public Theater, 1980; dir. Gin Game, N.Y. Deaf Theatre. Recipient Humanitarian award Gallaudet Coll., 1980, Rough Rider award State of N.D., 1981; California's Year of Handicapped award, 1980; Critic's Circle award, 1980; Tony award, 1980. Mem. Actors Equity Assn., Nat. Assn. Deaf. Home: 139 Spring St New York NY 10012

FRELING, RICHARD ALAN, lawyer; b. N.Y.C., June 21, 1932; s. Jack C. and Natalie F.; m. Rhita Marlene Merson, Sept. 4, 1955; children: Darryl, Robert, Dana. B.B.A, U. Tex., 1954, LL.B., 1956. Bar: Tex. 1956. Partner firm Johnson & Swanson, Dallas; dir. Centex Corp., Fidelity Union Life Ins. Co., Tex. Law Rev. Publs., Inc.; bd. dirs., research fellow Southwestern Legal Found. Editor-in-chief: (1955-56) Tex. Law Rev; contbr. articles to legal jours. Trustee St. Marks Sch. of Tex., 1971-78, Greenhill Sch., 1972—; bd. govs., mem. exec. com. Southwest Outward Bound Sch.; trustee Colo. Outward Bound Sch., Pine Manor Coll.; bd. dirs. Friends of Dallas Pub. Library. Mem. Am. Law Inst., Am. Bar Assn. (council Taxation sect.), Tex. Bar Assn., Dallas Bar Assn., Chancellors, Friar Soc., Order of Coif, Phi Delta Phi, Beta Gamma Sigma. Office: Johnson & Swanson 4700 InterFirst Two Dallas TX 75270

FRELINGHUYSEN, PETER H.B., former congressman; b. N.Y.C., Jan. 17, 1916; s. Peter H. B. and Adaline (Havemeyer) F.; m. Beatrice S. Procter, Sept. 7, 1940; children—Peter, Beatrice, Rodney, Adaline, Frederick. A.B. magna cum laude, Princeton, 1938; LL.B., Yale, 1941. Investment bus., N.Y.C.; mem. 83d-93d Congresses, 5th N.J. Dist. Trustee Howard Savs. Bank, Newark.; Trustee John F. Kennedy Center for Performing Arts, Met. Mus. Art, N.Y.C. Served as lt. USNR, World War II. Republican. Episcopalian. Home: Sand Spring Ln Morristown NJ 07960

FREMONT, ERNEST HOAR, JR., lawyer; b. Glenwood, Minn., Nov. 19, 1925; s. Ernest Hoar and Olga (Ostlund) F.; m. Johanne M. Ravenholt; children: Paula Marie, Alicia Ann. B.A., U. Minn., 1950; J.D., U. Mo. at Kansas City, 1956. Bar: Mo. bar 1956. Dir. firm Popham, Conway, Sweeny Fremont & Bundschu (P.C.), Kansas City, 1956—; Chmn. Mo. Adv. Com. Free Press-Fair Trial, 1968-70; chmn. Supreme Ct. (Mo.) Com. on Profl. Ethics and Responsibility, 1969-71; vice chmn. DRI Automobile Compensation Com. Chmn. law found. U. Mo. at Kansas City, 1973-74, trustee, 1962-68; active Vols. for Council on Pub. Higher Edn. for Mo.; trustee Kansas City U. Conservatory Music. Served with USNR, 1944-46; served to 1st lt. AUS, 1951-53. Recipient Alumni Achievement award U. Mo. at Kansas City, 1965, Ann. Law Day award, 1972; named Distinguished Alumnus of Year Phi Delta Phi, 1970. Hon. fellow Harry S. Truman Library Inst.; mem. steering com. Truman Statue project.; Fellow Internat. Soc. Barristers; mem. ABA (mem. standing com. pub. relations 1965-71, chmn. 1965-68, vice chmn. trial techniques com. of ins. sect. 1973-77, Mo. del. ho. dels. 1974-80, ho. dels. hearing com. 1974-80, chmn. 1978-79, spl. com. on automobile legislation 1977—, gov. 1979-82, chmn. standing com. on mil. law 1981-83), Mo. Bar Assn. (bd. govs. 1964-73, mem. control council 1963-70, chmn. pub. info. com. 1962-64, pres. 1971-72, chmn. coordinating com. state bar pres. 1972-73, chmn. task force on mandatory continuing legal edn. 1975-77), Kansas City Bar Assn., Powell Inn (exchequer) (1952-53), Nat. Planning Assn. (mem. nat. council 1970-74), Fedn. Ins. Counsel, U. Mo. at Kansas City Alumni Assn. (dir. 1972-79, pres. 1978-79), Phi Delta Phi (Distinguished Alumnus of Year 1970). Congregationalist (trustee 1966-68, chmn. 1967-68, moderator 1982-83. Home: 6647 State Line Rd Kansas City MO 64113 Office: Commerce Bank Bldg Kansas City MO 64106

FREMONT, RUDOLPH ERIC, physician; b. Vienna, Austria, Dec. 12, 1912; came to U.S., 1938, naturalized, 1943; s. Boris and Anna (Reitman) Friedmann; m. Gloria Zegans, Jan. 15, 1967 (dec.); m. Ann Penn, Apr. 20, 1978. M.D., U. Vienna, 1936. Diplomate Am. Bd. Internal Medicine. Intern Univ. Hosp., Vienna, 1935-36, Municipal Hosp., 1936-37; resident S. Canning Child's Hosp. and Research Inst., Vienna, 1937-38; fellow and research asst. cardiology Mt. Sinai Hosp., N.Y.C., 1938-42; practice medicine specializing in cardiology, N.Y.C., 1947—; chief dept. medicine VA Hosp., 1947-68; chief cardiology sect. Halloran VA Hosp., 1947-51; chief cardiology sect., asst. chief medicine VA Hosp., Albany, N.Y., 1951-53; chief cardiovascular sect. Bklyn. VA Hosp., 1953-68, cons., 1968-70; asso. attending physician Jewish Chronic Disease Hosp., 1956-61, Maimonides Hosp., 1959-61; sr. attending cardiologist St. Barnabas Hosp., Bronx, 1966-72, dir. cardiology, 1973-80, cons. cardiology, 1980—; attending cardiologist Jewish Meml. Hosp., N.Y.C., 1969-73; dir. cardiology Midtown Hosp., N.Y.C., 1969-74; dir. cardiac rehab. NYU Med. Center, 1970-73; asso. attending rehab. physician Bellevue Hosp., 1970-73; attending cardiologist Met. Hosp. Center, N.Y.C., 1973-78, Flower 5th Ave. Hosp., 1973-78; asso. attending physician Kings County Hosp., Bklyn., 1966-73; asso. attending physician medicine Cabrini Med. Center, 1976—; asso. attending physician in medicine (cardiology) N. Westchester Health Center, Mt. Kisco, N.Y., 1978-82, cons., 1982—, Westchester County Hosp. Center, Valhalla, N.Y., 1978—; instr. Albany Med. Coll., 1951-52; asst. prof., 1952-53; clin. asst. prof. medicine Downstate Med. Center, Bklyn., 1956-61, clin. asso. prof., 1961-73; clin. prof. clin. medicine, research and surgery N.Y. Med. Coll., N.Y.C., 1973-81, clin. prof. medicine, 1981—; cons. in field; sr. aviation med. examiner, 1968—; U.S. rep. internat. council Internat. Congress on Diseases of Chest, Vienna, 1960. Contbr. articles on cardiovascular diseases to books and med. jours. Served to maj. M.C., U.S. Army, 1944-47. Fellow Am. Coll. Cardiology, ACP, Am. Coll. Chest Physicians, Am. Coll. Angiology, Internat. Coll. Angiology (v.p. 1965—), Am. Coll. Clin. Pharmacology, N.Y. Cardiology Soc., N.Y. Acad. Sci., N.Y. Acad. Medicine, Pan Am. Med. Assn., Am. Geriatric Soc.; mem. AMA, Aerospace Med. Assn., N.Y. County and State Med. Soc., AAAS, Assn. Mil. Surgeons, Am. Heart Assn., Civil Aviation Med. Assn., Pirquet Soc. Clin. Med. (pres. 1970-74), Virchow Piquet Med. Soc. (pres. 1982). Jewish. Office: 121 E 60th St New York NY 10022 also Somers Profl Park Somers NY 10589

FREMONT-SMITH, ELIOT, editor, critic; b. Cambridge, Mass., Apr. 16, 1929; s. Frank and Frances (Eliot) Fremont-S.; m. Leda C. Schwartz, June 15, 1963; 1 son, Andrew Eliot. Student, Yale U., 1952-53; B.A., Antioch Coll., 1963. Editor N.Y. Times Book Rev., N.Y.C., 1961-65; editor-in-chief Little Brown & Co., N.Y.C., 1968-71; book editor Saturday Rev., N.Y.C., 1972-73; sr. editor Village Voice and N.Y. Mag., N.Y.C., 1973—; pres., chmn. Nat. Book Critics Circle, 1975—; mem. various profl. coms., including public library coms. Book critic, N.Y. Times, 1965-68; Contbr. articles, revs. to various lit. and polit. publs. Democrat. Office: 842 Broadway New York NY 10003

FRENCH, A. JAMES, physician; b. Van Houten, N.Mex., Sept. 3, 1912; s. A. P. and Elizabeth (Williams) F.; m. Genevieve Fetter, July 19, 1937; 1 dau., Patricia Sue. A.B., U. Colo., 1933, M.A., 1936, M.D., 1936. Diplomate: Am. Bd. Pathology (trustee 1962-74, sec.-treas. 1964-74, exec. dir. 1974-78, cons. 1979-80). Intern Kansas City (Mo.) Gen. Hosp., 1936-37; resident pediatrics Children's Hosp., Denver, 1937-38; resident pathology St. Louis City Hosp., 1938-40; resident, instr. pathology U. Mich. Hosp., 1940-41, chief clin. labs., 1952—; asst. prof. pathology. Mich. Med. Sch., 1946-47, asso. prof., 1947-53, prof., 1953-80, chmn. dept., 1956-80; also editor Med. Bull., 1955-57; pathologist Surgeon Gen.'s Office, Washington and Far East, 1941-46, cons., 1947-50; cons., mem. pathology adv. council VA Hosp., Ann Arbor, also; Wayne County Gen. Hosp., 1959—; Dir. Mich. Maternal Tissue Registry, 1957—; mem. sci. adv. bd. Armed Forces Inst. Pathology, 1965-70, chmn., 1968-70; mem. etiology com. Am. Cancer Soc., 1962-65. Contbr. to med. jours. Col. AUS Res. Fellow A.C.P.; mem. Mich. Pathol. Soc. (pres. 1953, 73), Internat. Acad. Pathology (council 1957-60, pres. 1966), Am. Soc. Clin. Pathology, Am. Assn. Pathologists and Bacteriologists (mem. council 1970, sec.-treas. 1971-74, pres. 1975), Coll. Am. Pathologists (chmn. acad. sect. 1960-61, gov. 1964-70, sec.-treas. 1969-70), Am. Acad. Oral Pathology (hon. mem.; vice chmn. 1974-76, chmn. 1976—), AMA (sec. sect. council on pathology 1972—), Frederick A. Coller Surg. Soc. (hon.). Home: 356 Ausable Pl Ann Arbor MI 48104 Office: 1335 E Catherine Dr Ann Arbor MI 48109

FRENCH, ALDEN, JR., corp. exec.; b. Springfield, Mass., 1934. Grad., Harvard U., 1956, grad. Advanced Mgmt. Program, 1973. Pres., chief operating officer Courier Corp., Lowell, Mass. Office: Courier Corp 165 Jackson St Lowell MA 01852 *

FRENCH, ANTHONY PHILIP, physicist, educator; b. Brighton, Eng., Nov. 19, 1920; came to U.S., 1955; s. Sydney James and Elizabeth Margaret (Hart) F.; m. Naomi Mary Livesay, Oct. 6, 1945; children—Martin Charles, Gillian Ruth. B.A. with honors, Cambridge (Eng.) U., 1942, M.A., 1946, Ph.D., 1948. Mem. atomic bomb projects Tube Alloys and Manhattan Project, 1942-46; demonstrator, lectr. physics Cambridge U., 1948-55; fellow Pembroke Coll., 1950-55; prof. physics U. S.C., 1955-63, chmn. dept., 1956-62; vis. prof. Mass. Inst. Tech., 1962-64, prof., 1964—; vis. fellow Pembroke Coll., Cambridge, 1975; chmn. Internat. Commn. on Physics Edn., 1975-81. Author: Principles of Modern Physics, 1958, Special Relativity, 1968, Newtonian Mechanics, 1971, Vibrations and Waves, 1971, (with Edwin F. Taylor) Introduction to Quantum Physics, 1978; editor: Einstein: A Centenary Volume, 1979; contbr. articles to profl. jours. Mem. Am. Phys. Soc., Am. Assn. Physics Tchrs., Sigma Xi, Sigma Pi Sigma, Blue Key. Office: Mass Inst Tech Cambridge MA 02139

FRENCH, ARTHUR LEEMAN, JR., process control and instrumentation company executive; b. Beaumont, Tex., May 16, 1940; s. Arthur Leeman and Roberta Floy (Smith) F.; m. Susan Dianne Winston, Aug. 29, 1959; children: Laura, Arthur L. B.S. in Mech. Engring., Tex A&M U., 1963, Tex. A&M U., 1963. Process industry mgr. Fisher Controls Co., Marshalltown, Iowa, 1973-76, gen. sales mgr., 1976-77, v.p. instrumentation, 1977-79, v.p. tech. and devel., 1979-80; exec. v.p. Fisher Controls Internat., Inc., Clayton, Mo., 1980-82; exec. v.p. and chief operating officer Fisher Controls Co., Clayton, Mo., 1982—; indsl. councilor Tex. A&M Research Found., College Station, 1980—. Bd. dirs. Iowa Valley Community Coll. Dist., Marshalltown, 1975-79; county campaign dir. Charles Grassley 3d dist. U.S. Congl. Campaign, Marshall County, Iowa, 1974. Served to capt. U.S. Army, 1963-66. Mem. Instrument Soc. Am., Sci. Apparatus Makers Assn. (dir. process measurement and control div. 1975-78). Republican. Mem. Christian Ch. (Disciples of Christ). Home: 1836 Stenton Path Chesterfield MO 63107 Office: Fisher Controls Internat Inc 7711 Bonhomme Ave Clayton MO 63105

FRENCH, BEVAN MEREDITH, geologist; b. East Orange, N.J., Mar. 8, 1937; s. John Sprout and Lois Angelina (Meredith) F.; m. Mary-Hill Kueffner Childs, Dec. 23, 1967; children: James Allan Childs, William Tappan Childs, Sharon Elizabeth Childs Moore. A.B., Dartmouth Coll., 1958; M.S., Calif. Inst. Tech., 1960; Ph.D., Johns Hopkins U., 1964. Aerospace technologist NASA Goddard Space Flight Center, Greenbelt, Md., 1964-72; program dir. geochemistry NSF, Washington, 1972-75; discipline scientist planetary materials NASA, Washington, 1975—; vis. prof. Dartmouth Coll., 1968. Author: What's New on the Moon?, 1976, Mars: The Viking Discoveries, 1977, The Moon Book, 1977, A Meeting with the Universe, 1982, others. NSF fellow, 1958-61. Fellow Meteoritical Soc.; mem. Geol. Soc. Washington, Explorers Club, Phi Beta Kappa, Sigma Xi. Club: Cosmos. Home: 7408 Wyndale Ln Chevy Chase MD 20015 Office: NASA Hdqrs Washington DC 20546

FRENCH, BRUCE HARTUNG, economist, lawyer; b. Canton, Ohio, May 2, 1915; s. Garnett Bruce and Marie (Hartung) F.; m. Jeanne Adrienne Aeberhard, June 27, 1942 (div. 1969); m. Dorothy Fleming Gorman, Nov. 29, 1969; children: Robert Adrain, David Adrain. A.B., Haverford Coll., 1937; A.M., U. Pa., 1940, Ph.D., 1946; postgrad., Princeton U., 1941-42; LL.B., Rutgers U., 1945. Bar: N.J. 1948. Asst. in govt. Haverford Coll., 1937-39; instr. politics, Princeton U., 1941-42, 46-47; asst. prof. econs. U. Coll., Rutgers U., 1947-53, assoc. prof. econs., 1953-83, chmn. dept. econs., 1951-75; practice in Princeton; mem. firm French & Cook, Princeton, N.J., 1950-59; pvt. practice law, 1959-80, 82—; mem. firm French & Stockton, Princeton, 1981-82; chmn. bd. Am. Investors Services, Inc., Great Barrington, Mass., 1978—; pres. Estate Owners, Inc., Frenchlands Inc.; counsel, also exec. dir. Housing Authority Borough Princeton, 1949-58, Hightstown, 1958-75. Author: Banking and Insurance in New Jersey-A History, 1965, How to Avoid Financial Tangles, 1981. Pres. Princeton Community Chest, 1950; mem. N.J. Tercentenary Adv. Com., 1960; mem. corp. Haverford Coll.; pres. bd. trustees Princeton Meeting of Friends at Stony Brook, 1976-81; chmn. bd. trustees Am. Inst. for Econ. Research, Great Barrington, 1976—. Served to lt. comdr. USNR, 1942-46; as liaison officer with fgn. govts., officer-in-charge USN Internat. Aid Office; N.Y.C. Recipient letter commendation USN. Mem. N.J., Princeton, Mercer County bar assns., Princeton Hist. Soc. (past pres.), Huguenot Soc., Am. Econs. Assn., Soc. War of 1812, St. Nicholas Soc., Soc. Colonial Wars, First Families of Ohio, S.R. (past pres. N.J.), Phi Beta Kappa (del. to Bicentennial meeting 1976). Republican. Mem. Soc. of Friends. Clubs: Nassau (past pres.), Pretty Brook Tennis (Princeton); Union, Princeton (N.Y.C.); Athenaeum (Phila.); Pot and Kettle, Bar Harbor (Maine); Founders (Haverford Coll.). Home: 19 Winfield Rd Princeton NJ 08540 601 Ewing St Princeton NJ 08540 *My modus operandi: Carefully determine goals and give them order of priority; concentrate on one thing at a time, including details; finish what is started; persist in the face of obstacles while being considerate of others; leave unscheduled time for relaxation, exercise and hobbies.*

FRENCH, CATHERINE, assn. exec.; b. Teaneck, N.J., Nov. 13, 1946; d. Lester John and Catherine M. (Doyle) F. B.Mus., Manhattanville Coll., 1968. Exec. dir. Am. Symphony Orch., N.Y.C., 1970-72; mgr. N.J. Symphony, Newark, 1972-74; asst. dir. Am. Symphony Orch. League, Vienna, Va., 1974, exec. v.p., chief exec. officer, 1980—. Mem. Nat. Music Council (bd. dirs. 1981-82), Am. Soc. Assn. Execs., Chamber Music Am. Roman Catholic. Home: 2500 Q St NW Washington DC 20007 Office: Am Symphony Orch League PO Box 669 Vienna VA 22180

FRENCH, CHARLES EZRA, economist, institute director; b. Smithville, Mo., Apr. 7, 1923; s. Charley E. and Ruth (Downs) F.; m. Dolores Eloise Albers, Aug. 31, 1947 (div. Feb. 1976); children: Ned Carleton, Hugh Nathan, Sarasue, Judith; m. Jeanne Blair, June 2, 1979. Student, Washington U., St. Louis, 1943; B.S., U. Mo., 1948, M.A., 1949; Ph.D., Purdue U., 1951; postgrad., U. Calif. at Berkeley, 1957. Asst. prof. agrl. econs. Purdue U., Lafayette, Ind., 1951-54, assoc. prof., 1954-57, prof. agrl. econs., 1957-77, asst. head dept. agrl. econs., 1958-65, acting head dept., 1965-66, head dept., 1966-73; asst. study dir. White House food and nutrition study Nat. Acad. Scis., Washington, 1975-77; research coordinator Tech. Assistance Bur. AID, Dept. State, Washington, 1977; exec. dir. Food and Nutrition Study Pres.'s Reorgn. Project, Washington, 1978-79; food and agr. programs coordinator AID, Washington, 1979-82; dir. Inst. Agribus. U. Santa Clara, Calif., 1982—; mem. agrl. bd. NRC, Nat. Acad. Scis.; mem. bd. mgmt. Navajo Indian Nation; adv. U.S. Dept. Agr., Dept. State, HEW, Dept. Def.; cons. Ford Found., Dept. State in Latin Am. Author: (with others) Organization and Competition in Midwest Dairy Industries, 1970, Survival Strategies for Agricultural Cooperatives, 1980; Contbr.: articles to profl. jours. Survival Strategies for Agricultural Cooperatives. Served to capt. USAAF, 1943-46. Decorated Air medal with clusters. Mem. Am., Can. agrl. econs. assns., Western Farm Econs. Assn., Agrl. Mktg. Assn., AAAS, Internat. Assn. Agrl. Economists, Sigma Xi, Alpha Gamma Sigma, Alpha Zeta, Phi Eta Sigma, Gamma Sigma Delta, Alpha Phi Zeta. Home: 9806 Fosbak Dr Vienna VA 22180 Office: 309E Rosslyn Plaza C AID Washington DC 20523

FRENCH, CHARLES FERRIS, JR., banker; b. N.Y.C., Jan. 4, 1918; s. Charles Ferris and Alma (Young) F.; m. Anita Vernon, Apr. 25, 1970; 1 dau., Christie French Snow. B.A., Duke U., 1939; postgrad., Rutgers U. Sch. Banking, 1955. Vice pres. Mfrs. Trust (now Mfrs. Hanover Trust), N.Y.C., 1939-58; pres. First Nat. Iron Bank, Morristown, N.J., 1958-70; exec. v.p. Trust Co. of N.J., Jersey City, 1971—. Mem. N.J. Bankers Assn., Robert Morris Assocs. (pres. N.Y. chpt. 1957-58), Hudson County C. of C., Alpha Delta Phi, Chi Phi. Republican. Episcopalian. Club: Morristown. Home: Phalanx Farms 5 Wood Hollow Rd Colts Neck NJ 07722 Home: Journeys End 492 Ellison Dr Mantoloking NJ 08738 Home: 2860 S Ocean Blvd Palm Beach FL 33480 Office: The Trust Co of New Jersey 35 Journal Sq Jersey City NJ 07306

FRENCH, CHARLES STACY, scientist; b. Lowell, Mass., Dec. 13, 1907; s. Charles Ephraim and Helena (Stacy) F.; m. Margaret Wendell Coolidge, Dec. 10, 1938; children—Helena Stacy, Charles Ephraim. Student, Loomis Inst., Windsor, Conn., 1921-25; B.S., Harvard, 1930, A.M., 1932, Ph.D., 1934; Ph.D. (hon.), U. Göteborg, Sweden, 1974. Asst. in gen. physiology Harvard, 1930-33; research fellow Calif. Inst. Tech., 1934-35; guest worker with Otto Warburg Kaiser Wilhelm Inst., Berlin-Dahlem, Germany, 1935-36; Austin teaching fellow in biochemistry Harvard Med. Sch., 1936-38; instr. (research) in chemistry with James Franck U. Chgo., 1938-41; asst. prof. dept. botany U. Minn., 1941-45, asso. prof., 1945-47; dir. div. plant biology Carnegie Instn. of Washington at Stanford U., 1947-73, dir. emeritus, 1973—; prof. (by courtesy) Stanford. Contbr. articles on plant physiology to sci. jours. Bd. dirs. Hidden Villa Inc., 1979—. Mem. Am. Soc. Plant Physiologists (chmn. Western Sect. 1954, Charles Ried Barnes life mem.), Bot. Soc. Am. (award of merit 1973), Nat. Acad. Scis., Am. Acad. Arts and Scis., Am. Soc. Biol. Chemists, Soc. Gen. Physiologists (v.p. 1954, pres. 1955-56), AAAS, Biophys. Soc., Deutsche Akademie der Naturforscher Leopoldina, Friends of Hidden Villa (pres. 1977-79). Clubs: Am. Alpine, Harvard of Peninsula (pres. 1973-75), Explorers.). Home: 11970 Rhus Ridge Rd Los Altos Hills CA 94022 Office: Carnegie Institution Stanford CA 94305

FRENCH, CLARENCE LEVI, JR., shipbuilding company executive; b. New Haven, Oct. 13, 1925; s. Clarence L. and Eleanor (Curry) F.; m. Jean Sprague, June 29, 1946; children: Craig Thomas, Brian Keith, Alan Scott. B.S. in Naval Sci., Tufts U., 1945, 1947. Registered profl. engr., Calif. Foundry engr. Bethlehem Steel Corp., 1947-56; staff engr., asst. supt. Kaiser Steel Corp., 1956-64; supervisory engr. Bechtel Corp., 1964-67; with Nat. Steel & Shipbldg. Co., San Diego, 1967—, exec. v.p., gen. mgr., to 1977, pres., chief operating officer, 1977—, chmn., chief exec. officer, 1984—; mem. maritime transp. research bd. NRC. Bd. dirs. United Way, San Diego, YMCA, San Diego; past chmn., bd. dirs. Pres. Roundtable, San Diego; trustee Webb Inst. Served to lt. USN, 1943-53. Mem. Shipbuilders Council Am. (dir., past chmn. exec. com.), Soc. Naval Architects and Marine Engrs. (council, pres.), ASTM, Am. Bur. Shipping (bd. mgrs.), Am. Soc. Naval Engrs., U.S. Naval Inst., Navy League U.S., Propeller Club U.S. Office: 28th St and Harbor Dr Nat Steel and Shipbldg San Diego CA 92138

FRENCH, DANIEL WILLIAM, army officer; b. Portland, Oreg., Sept. 20, 1928; s. Gordon L. and Lyle F. (Fosterling) F.; m. Maribeth E. Muller, Dec. 30, 1950; children: Cynthia, Rebecca. B.S., U. Oreg., 1952; M.S., George Washington U., 1970; grad., U.S. Army Command and Gen. Staff Coll., 1964, Nat. War Coll., 1970. Commd. 2d lt. U.S. Army, 1950, advanced through grades to maj. gen., 1980, comdr. ed ROTC Region, Ft. Riley, Kans., 1977-78, dep. chief of staff for ROTC, Ft. Monroe, Va., 1978-81, comdr., Ft. Benjamin Harrison, Ind., 1981—. Bd. dirs. Cross Roads of Am. council Boy Scouts Am., 1980-83. Decorated Silver Star, Legion of Merit, Bronze Star. Mem. Assn. U.S. Army, Indpls. C. of C. (bd. dirs.). Episcopalian. Club: Indpls. Kiwanis. Home: 661 Lawton Loop Fort Benjamin Harrison IN 46216 Office: Comdr Fort Benjamin Harrison IN 46216

FRENCH, GEORGE WILLIAM, III, mfg. co. exec.; b. Melrose, Mass., Feb. 3, 1924; s. George William and Elsie Preston (Peabody) F.; m. Joan Stanley, Sept. 30, 1950; children—Charles (dec.), Elsie, Sarah, Timothy. B.S., Harvard U., 1944; M.B.A., 1948. Various positions Stanley Works, New Britain, Conn.; gen. mgr. Stanley Door Systems, Ltd., The Stanley Works, Toronto, Ont., Can., 1969-73; pres. The Stanley Works of Can., Hamilton, Ont., 1973-76, Stanley Drapery Hardware, Wallingfort, Conn., 1976-77; pres., chief exec. officer All-Steel Inc., Aurora, Ill., 1978-81; sr. v.p. Shaw Walker Co., Muskegon, Mich., 1981—. Bd. dirs. Aurora C. of C.; mem. adv. bd. Aurora Coll. Served with USAAF, 1943-46. Mem. Nat. Office Products Assn. Clubs: Muskegon (Mich.) Country, Geneva (Ill.) Golf; Harvard (Chgo.). Office: country roads inc belding MI 48809

FRENCH, GLENDON EVERETT, JR., health care services executive; b. Chgo., Mar. 11, 1934; s. Glendon Everett and Mabel (Eastman) Franch; m. Carolyn Miller, Nov. 28, 1959; children: Deborah Dalton, Glendon Everett, Catherine C. B.A. in Bus. Adminstrn, Dartmouth Coll., 1956; M.B.A., Amos Tuck Sch., Dartmouth Coll., 1959. With Am. Hosp. Supply Corp., 1959—, regional mgr., New Eng., 1964-68, mktg. planning mgr., 1968-69, mktg. services mgr., 1969-70, nat. sales mgr., v.p. mktg. Am. Critical Care div., McGaw Park, Ill., 1970-73, pres., 1973-82; pres. Health and Family Services Sector ARA Services, Inc., Phila., 1982—. Bd. dirs. Inroads, Chgo., 1976-80; mem. Dist. 106 Bd. Edn., 1977—. Served with USNR, 1956-58. Mem. No. Ill. Indsl. Assn. (dir. 1979—). Presbyterian. Club: Tennaqua (Deerfield, Ill.). Office: ARA Services Health Care Sector Independence Sq W Philadelphia PA 19106

FRENCH, HERBERT ELIOT, author; b. Tewksbury, Mass., July 5, 1912; s. Eliot Howe and Elizabeth (McCausl) F.; m. Clarissa Messer, June 18, 1949 (div. Mar. 1959); 1 son, Peter Eliot. B.A., Harvard, 1933. Editor: Holiday mag, N.Y.C., 1946-56, 61-71; Author: My Yankee Mother, 1942, My Yankee Paris, 1945, Of Rivers and the Sea, 1970, Love of Earth, 1973, (with others) The Role of the SOS in the Defeat of Germany, 1945. Mem. N.Y. Assn. Indsl. Communicators. Home: 305 1st Ave New York NY 10003

FRENCH, ISABELLE FRANCES, electronics engineer; b. Swampscott, Mass., Feb. 16, 1924; d. Abram and Grace Benton (Seward) F. B.S. in Radio Engr, Tri-State Coll, Angola, Ind., 1944; postgrad., Boston U., Northeastern U.; D.Eng. (hon.), Tri-State College, 1966. Jr. engr. Sylvania Electric Products Inc., 1944-52; engr. Capehart-Farnsworth Corp., 1952-54; assoc. mem. tech. staff Bell Telephone Labs., Allentown, Pa., 1954-82, mem. tech. staff, 1982—. Mem. East Allen Twp.-Northampton County Planning Commn., 1970-83, chmn., 1972-83; chmn. Zoning Hearing Bd., 1971-83; mem. Twp. Bd. Suprs., 1982—. Recipient Alumni Disting. Service award Tri-State Coll., 1962. Fellow Soc. Women Engrs. (treas. 1953-55, sec. 1961-63, v.p. 1963-64, pres. 1964-66), 66); mem. IEEE. Clubs: Allentown Altrusa (corr. sec. 1967-69, v.p. 1969-71), Allentown Altrusa (pres. 1971-73). Home: 5884 Old Carriage Rd East Allen Twp Bath PA 18014 Office: 555 Union Blvd Allentown PA 18103

FRENCH, JOHN DWYER, lawyer; b. Berkeley, Calif., June 26, 1933; s. Horton Irving and Gertrude Margery (Ritzen) F.; m. Annette Richard, 1955. B.A. summa cum laude, U. Minn., 1955, Oxford U., Eng., 1955-56; LL.B. magna cum laude, Harvard U., 1960. Bar: D.C. bar 1960, Minn. bar 1963. Law clk. Justice Felix Frankfurter, U.S. Supreme Ct., 1960-61; legal asst. to commr. FTC, 1961-62; asso. firm Ropes, & Gray, Boston, 1962-63, Faegre & Benson, Mpls., 1963-66, partner, 1967-75, mng. partner, 1975—; adj. faculty mem. Law Sch. U. Minn., 1965-70; mem. exec. com. Lawyers Com. for Civil Rights under Law, 1978—; co-chmn. U.S. Dist. Judge Nominating Commn., 1979; Vice chmn. adv. com., mem. dir. search com., chmn. devel. office search com. Hubert Humphrey Inst., 1979-80. Contbr. numerous articles and revs. to legal jours. Chmn. or co-chmn. Minn. State Democratic Farm Labor Party Conv., 1970, 72, 74, 78, 80; chmn. Mondale Vol. Com., 1972, treas., 1974; del. Democratic Nat. Conv., 1976, 78, 80; trustee Twin Cities Public TV, Inc., 1980—; mem. overseers com. to visit Harvard U. Law Sch., 1970-75, 77-82. Served with U.S. Army, 1955-56. Rotary Found. fellow, 1955-56. Mem. ABA (mem. editorial bd. jour. 1976-79), Minn. Bar Assn., Hennepin County Bar Assn., Jud. Council Minn., Lawyers Alliance for Nuclear Arms Control (nat. bd. dirs. 1982—), Phi Beta Kappa. Episcopalian. Office: 2300 Multifoods Tower Minneapolis MN 55402

FRENCH, JOSEPH HENRY, neurologist; b. Toledo, July 3, 1928; s. Joseph and Bertha F.; m. Marilyn Doss, Mar. 1950; children: Lenore, Mark, John, Lisa. B.A., Ohio State U., 1950, M.D., 1954. Intern, Phila. Gen. Hosp., 1954-55; resident St. Christopher's Hosp. for Children, Temple U., 1955-57, Balt. City Hosps., 1959-60; fellow in pediatric neurology Johns Hopkins Hosp., Balt., 1959-60, in neurologic medicine, 1960-61; mem. staff Montefiore Hosp., Bronx, N.Y., 1973-79; co dir. pediatric neurology fellowship tng. program Albert Einstein Med. Coll., 1964-76, asst. dean, 1970-79; dir. dept. pediatrics Norwalk (Conn.) Hosp., 1979-80; dep. dir. clin. service Inst. Basic Research in Mental Retardation, Staten Island, 1980—. Fellow Am. Acad. Pediatrics, Am. Acad. Neurology; mem. Nat. Med. Assn., Bronx County Pediatric Soc., Pediatric Research Soc., N.Y. Acad. Sci., Soc. Neurol. Sci., Child Neurology Assos., Am. Pediatric Soc., Norwalk Med. Soc. Office: 1050 Forest Hill Rd Staten Island NY 10314

FRENCH, JUDSON CULL, govt. ofcl.; b. Washington, Sept. 30, 1922; s. Morrison Brady and Ethel Haviland (Cull) F.; m. Julia A. McAllister, Aug. 1, 1951; 1 son, Judson Cull. B.S. cum laude, Am. U., 1943; M.S., Harvard U., 1949; postgrad., Bus. Sch., 1968, Johns Hopkins U., 1943-44, George Washington U., 1944-45, M.I.T., 1951. Instr. physics Johns Hopkins U., Balt., 1943-44, George Washington

U., Washington, 1944-47; sec., dir. Home Title Ins. Co., Washington, 1956-71; with Nat. Bur. Standards, Commerce Dept., Washington, 1948—, asst. chief electron devices sect., 1964-68, chief electron devices sect., 1968-73, chief electronic tech. div., 1973-78; dir. Center for Electronics and Elec. Engring., 1978—. Contbr. articles to profl. jours. Recipient Silver medal for meritorious service Commerce Dept., 1964; Gold medal for exceptional service, 1978; Edward Bennett Rosa award Nat. Bur. Standards, 1971; presdl. rank of Meritorious Exec. Sr. Exec. Service. Fellow IEEE; mem. Am. Phys. Soc., ASTM, Sigma Pi Sigma, Pi Delta Epsilon, Alpha Kappa Pi. Office: Center for Electronics and Elec Engring Nat Bur Standards Washington DC 20234

FRENCH, LYLE ALBERT, surgeon; b. nr. Worthing, S.D., Mar. 26, 1915; s. Leslie V. and Bernice M. (McKinney) F.; m. Gene F. Richmond, Sept. 13, 1941; children—Frederick E., Eldridge T., Barbara Gene. Student, Macalester Coll., 1933-35; B.S., U. Minn., 1936, M.B., 1939, M.D., 1940, M.S., 1946, Ph.D., 1947. Diplomate: Am. Bd. Neurol. Surgery. Intern U. Hosp., Mpls., 1939-40; instr. neurosurgery U. Minn., St. Paul, 1947-49, asst. prof., 1949-52, asso. prof., 1952-57, prof., 1957—, chmn. dept. neurol. surgery, 1960—, v.p. health scis., 1970—; chief staff Univ. Hosps., Mpls., 1968—; cons. neurosurgery Surgeon Gen. U.S. Army, 1962—; spl. cons. Central Office, VA, 1968—. Chmn. editorial bd.: Jour. Neurosurgery, 1973—, Yearbook of Cancer; Contbr. articles in field. Adv. council Neurol. Diseases and Stroke NIH, 1971—; mem. adv. bd. Nat. Paraplegia Found., Multiple Sclerosis Found. Served from lt. to maj. AUS, 1941-45. Mem. Am. Soc. Research in Stereoencephalotomy (pres. 1968—), Minn. Soc. Neurol. Scis. (pres. 1963), Neurosurg. Soc. Am. (pres. 1958), Minn. Soc. Neurology and Psychiatry (pres. 1962), Minn. Acad. Medicine (pres. 1973-74), Mpls. Acad. Medicine (pres. 1960), Am. Acad. Neurosurgery (pres. 1972-73), Am. Assn. Neurol. Surgery (Harvey Cushing Soc.) (pres. 1973-74). Home: 5620 W Bavarian Pass Minneapolis MN 55432

FRENCH, MARCUS EMMETT, manufacturing company executive; b. Worcester, Mass., Jan. 21, 1929; s. Emmett A. and Marion A. (Brady) F.; m. Mary M. Nugent, Sept. 25, 1954; children: Carol E. Boyle, Margaret A., Marci M. B.S. in Chemistry, Holy Cross Coll., 1952, M.S., 1953. Sect. leader Allied Chem. Corp., Buffalo, 1953-59; devel. chemist Hewitt Robbins Corp., Franklin, N.J., 1959-60; v.p. Gen. Foam div. Tenneco Chems., Inc., Hazleton, Pa., 1960-70; pres. Janesville Products unit AMCA Internat. Corp., Norwalk, Ohio, 1970—; dir. TWU Realty Co., N.Y.C. Trustee Textile Workers Pension Plan, Firelands Coll., Huron, Ohio. Served with U.S. Army, 1946-48. Mem. ASTM, Soc. Automotive Engrs., Soc. Plastics Engrs., Norwalk C. of C. (dir.). Club: Plumbrook. Patentee on methods of urethane foam in U.S. and fgn. countries. Home: 6 Hillcrest Ct Milan OH 44846 Office: PO Box 349 Norwalk OH 44857 *The awareness of the feelings of family and fellow employees helps me in my understanding of people and the interrelationship we have with each other. This interrelationship with people and our dependence on God provides challenge and meaning to my life.*

FRENCH, MARILYN, author, critic; b. N.Y.C., Nov. 21, 1929; d. E.C. and Isabel (Hazz) Edwards; m. children—Jamie, Robert. B.A., Hofstra Coll., 1951, M.A., 1964; Ph.D., Harvard U., 1972. Secretarial, clerical worker, 1946-53; lectr. Hofstra Coll., 1964-68; asst. prof. Holy Cross Coll., Worcester, Mass., 1972-76; Mellon fellow Harvard U., 1976-77; writer, lectr., 1967—. Author: (criticism): The Book as World - James Joyce's "Ulysses", 1976; author:: novels The Women's Room, 1977, The Bleeding Heart, 1980; author: (criticism): Shakespeare's Division of Experience, 1981, introductions to Edith Wharton's Summer and The House of Mirth, 1981. Mem. MLA, James Joyce Soc., Virginia Woolf Soc., Soc. for Values in Higher Edn. Office: care Summit Books 1230 Ave of the Americas New York NY 10020

FRENCH, PHILIP FRANKS, agricultural cooperative corporate executive; b. Albin, Ind., June 16, 1932; s. Charles E. and Helene Alwilda (Franks) F.; m. Jo Ann Pyle, Nov. 21, 1951 (dec. July 1979); children: Douglas G., Randall B., Deborah A., French Farmer, Rebecca L.; m. Kathleen Louise DeBaun, Mar. 22, 1980. B.S. in Commerce, Internat. Bus. Coll., 1952. Asst. mgr. Clay County Farm Bur. Coop., Brazil, Ind., 1957-62; gen. mgr. Allen County Farm Bur. Coop., New Haven, Ind., 1962-66; mgr. mem. services Ind. Far Mur. Coop., Indpls., 1966-70, asst. exec. v.p., 1970-80, exec. v.p., 1980—; mem. exec. com. CF Industries, Long Gorve, Ill., 1975—; pres. Agr-Petco Internat., Tulsa, 1977—; observer on bd. A.C. Toepfer, Internat., Hamburg, W. Ger., 1980—. Mem. U.S. Nat. Alcohol Fuels Commn., Washington, 1980-81; bd. dirs. Ind. Inst. Agr. Food and Nutrition. Mem. Nat. Council of Farmer Coops. (dir.). Republican. Methodist. Club: Columbia (Indpls.). Home: 5210 W Southport Rd Indianapolis IN 46241 Office: Ind Farm Bur Coop Assn 120 E Market St Indianapolis IN 46104

FRENCH, RAYMOND, realtor; b. Milw., June 14, 1920; s. Sydney and Mabel (Gamble) F.; m. Joan Foy, Dec. 27, 1947; children: Pamela Farquhar, Christina Chrysler, Wendy Collison. Grad., Yale U., 1943, U.S. Mcht. Marine Acad., 1946. Vice pres. Webb & Knapp, Inc., N.Y.C., 1957-62; chmn., pres., dir. Canal-Randolph Corp., N.Y.C., 1962—; pres., dir. United Stockyards Corp.; dir. Peninsula Terminal Co., Sioux Falls Stock Yards Co., Sioux City Terminal Co., Fargo, Union Stock Yards Co., Blue Ridge Real Estate Co., Big Boulder, Inc., Am. Union Ins. Co. N.Y., Mgmt. Assistance Inc. Trustee Dollar Savs. Bank. Clubs: Piping Rock; Yale (N.Y.C.); Island (Fla.). Home: Piping Rock Rd Locust Valley NY 11560 Office: 277 Park Ave New York NY 10017

FRENCH, RICHARD FREDERIC, educator; b. Randolph, Mass., June 23, 1915; s. Herbert F. and Edith (MacGregor) F. B.S., Harvard U., 1937, M.A., 1939. Asst. prof. music Harvard U., 1947-51; dir. publs., v.p. Asso. Music Pubs., 1951-59; pres. N.Y. Pro Musica, 1959-70, dir., 1959—; Robert S. Tangeman prof. sacred music Union Theol. Sem., N.Y.C., 1965-73, adj. prof. sacred music, 1973-77; prof. music Inst. Sacred Music, Yale, 1973—. Contbr. articles to books, mags. Trustee Schola Musicae Liturgicae, Bklyn. Music Sch. Served with USAAF, 1942-45. Decorated Bronze Star. Mem. Am. Musicol. Soc., Internat. Soc. Contemporary Music (treas. U.S. sect.). Clubs: Harvard, Yale, Century Assn. (N.Y.C.). Home: 95 E Rock Rd New Haven CT 06511 Office: 96 Wall St New Haven CT 06511

FRENCH, ROBERT HOUSTON, lawyer; b. Dayton, Ohio, Dec. 12, 1904; s. Edward Houston and Moile B. (Nevin) F.; m. Dorothy M. Duff, July 22, 1933; children—Mary F. Sweet, Nancy F. Pickard, Robert Houston. A.B. with honors, Ohio State U., 1927, J.D. summa cum laude, 1927. Bar: Ohio bar 1927. Since practiced in, Cin.; asst. U.S. atty. So. Dist. Ohio, 1928-31; spl. counsel to Atty. Gen., Ohio, 1938; mem. firm Pogue, Hoffheimer & Pogue, 1931-37, Pogue, Helmholz, Culbertson & French, 1937-72, French, Short, Valleau & Bratton, 1972-79, French, Marks, Short, Weiner & Valleau, 1979—; spl. counsel City of Piqua, 1948-68. Pres. Ohio Valley chpt. Arthritis Found., 1957-60, 65-66, 78; bd. govs. Nat. Arthritis Found., mem. exec. com., 1962-73, v.p., 1965-68, sec., 1970-73; budget rev. com. United Appeal, Cin. Recipient Distinguished Service award Nat. Arthritis Found., 1960, 66. Fellow Ohio, Am. bar assn. founds.; mem. Jud. Conf. U.S. Ct. Appeals 6th Circuit (life), ABA, Fed. Bar Assn., Ohio Bar Assn. (exec. com. 1964-66), Cin. Bar Assn. (v.p. 1959-63, pres. 1963-64), Legal Aid Soc. (trustee Cin. 1963-64), Am. Coll. Probate Counsel, Phi Beta Kappa, Order Coif, Phi Delta Phi. Republican. Clubs: Mason., University, Lawyers (Cin.). Home: 8862 Raiders Run Dr Cincinnati OH 45236 Office: 105 E 4th St Suite 700 Cincinnati OH 45202 *Life is a continuing choice of alternatives. In school we elect the snap course or the hard one, the easy teacher or the difficult one. In work we dodge or skirt the hard problem, situation, or job; or we elect to meet it head on. It is easy to assist a friend we like, but hard to help one who grates upon us. Early I learned the wrong choice is the easy one, the one I would rather take. The right choice is the one I didn't want to take—the hard one. In some way this self-discipline enables us to surmount the hard choice we made and sharpens our ability to meet the next difficult encounter.*

FRENCH, ROBERT WARREN, educator, writer, consultant; b. South Bend, Ind., May 8, 1911; s. Robert Warren and Lura (Keller) F.; m. Dorothy Louise Smith, July 8, 1934; children: Nancy Alice (Mrs. Neil McWhorter), Judith Kay (Mrs. Donald B. Lowe, Jr.). A.B., U. Mich., 1932, M.A., 1933, Ph.D., 1937. Fellow Brookings Instn., 1934-35; Teaching fellow econs. U. Mich., 1935-37; partner Johnson-Smith Co., 1937-41; asso. prof. internat. trade dir. bur. bus. research Coll. Commerce, La. State U., 1941-46; prof. internat. trade, dir. bur. bus. research, coll. bus. adminstrn. U. Tex., 1946-49; prof. econs., dean sch. bus adminstrn. Tulane U., 1949-55, v.p., 1953-56; dir. Port of New Orleans, 1956-60; Pres. Tax Found., Inc., 1960-63; dir. exec. programs, prof. mgmt. Grad. Sch. Bus. Adminstrn., U. So. Calif., 1963-65; staff asso. office of pres. U. Ill., Chgo., 1965-68, prof. econs. and mgmt., 1965-70, acting dean, 1966-68; asst. to pres. U. Ala., Birmingham, 1970-81, prof. econs. and bus. adminstrn., 1970-81, prof. emeritos, 1981—, interim dir. Center for Internat. Programs, 1980-81; lectr. bus. Miles Coll., 1973-76; exec. dir. Pub. Affairs Research Council La., 1950-54; Cons. Nat. Indsl. Conf. Bd., 1963, Assn. Western Rys., 1966-67, U.S. GAO, 1968-78, So. Regional Edn. Bd., 1973—, Ala.-Miss. Dist. Export Council, 1978—, Tenn. Higher Edn. Commn., 1974. Editor: La. Bus. Rev, 1941-46, Tex. Bus. Rev, 1946-49; Contbr.: Am. Peoples Ency, 1952-57, The Tax Exec., Vol. VIII, Tulane Tax Inst, 1951, Basics for Business, 1968, Living Together: Buchanan and Clark, 1904-1975, others. Trustee Dillard U.; bd. dirs. Amistad Research Center, bd. mgmt., Flint Goodridge Hosp., 1959-60; bd. councilors Grad. Sch. Bus. Adminstrn. U. So. Calif., 1961-63. Mem. Am. Soc. Pub. Adminstrn. (editorial bd. 1959-65), Am. Econ. Assn., Phi Kappa Phi, Pi Gamma Mu, Omicron Delta Kappa, Beta Gamma Sigma, Alpha Lambda Delta. Club: Pickwick. PO Box 108 Buchanan MI 49107

FRENCH, STANLEY GEORGE, university dean, philosophy educator; b. Hamilton, Ont., Can., Sept. 24, 1933; s. Reginald George and Marie (Larson) F.; m. Gwyneth E. Frayne, May 21, 1955; children: Shona, Sean, Keith, Ewan. B.A., Carleton U., 1955; M.A., U. Rochester, 1957; Ph.D., U. Va., 1959; spl. student, Oxford U., 1961, U. Nice, France, 1975-76. Assoc. prof. philosophy U. Western Ont., London, 1965-68; prof. philosophy Sir George Williams U., Montreal, Que., 1968, chmn. dept. philosophy, 1969-71; prof. philosophy, dean grad. studies Concordia U., Montreal, 1971—; mem. joint com. on programs Council of Univs., 1972-75; chmn. Westmount Sch. Commn., 1972; pres. London Council for Adult Edn., 1965-66; chmn. Bd. Edn. City of London, 1968; bd. govs. Sir George Williams U., 1969-71. Contbr. articles to profl. jours., chpts. to books; cons. editor: Humanities Research Council Can., 1970—; editorial adv.: Gnosis, 1977—; author: The North West Staging Route, 1957, Philosophers Look at Canadian Confederation, 1979, also monographs. Served as officer RCAF, 1951-56. Can. Council grantee, 1962. Mem. Soc. Philosophy and Pub. Affairs, Montreal Conf. Polit. and Social Thought, Société de Philosophie de Montreal, Société de Philosophie de Quebec, Can. Philos. Assn., Am. Philos. Assn., Am. Soc. Polit. and Legal Philosophy, Mind Assn., Can. Assn. Grad. Schs. (sec.-treas. 1980-81). Home: 256 Metcalfe Ave Montreal PQ H3Z 2J1 Canada Office: Concordia U Montreal PQ H3G 1M8 Canada

FRENCH, WILLIAM DANIEL, association executive; b. Boston, May 24, 1937; s. William Paul and Laura Elizabeth (Slattery) F.; m. Margaret Philomena Gacquin, Aug. 31, 1963; children: Daniel Bradford, Paula Marie. B.S. in Civil Engring, Northeastern U., 1962. Survey party chief Barnes Engring. Co., 1962-63; editor tech. publs. ASCE, 1963-68, exec. asst., 1968-72, dir. support services, asst. sec., 1972-76; exec. dir. Am. Soc. Photogrammetry, Falls Church, Va., 1977—. Contbr. articles to profl. jours. Chmn. pack 213 Boy Scouts Am., 1972-74; treas. troop 213, 1974-76. Mem. ASCE, Am. Soc. Assn. Execs., Am. Soc. Photogrammetry, Am. Topical Assn., Council of Engring. and Sci. Soc. Execs., Soc. Indsl. Archeology, Soc. for History of Tech., Friends of Cast-Iron Architecture. Roman Catholic. Clubs: Northeastern Alumni, K.C. Home: 2216 N Toronto St Falls Church VA 22043 Office: 210 Little Falls St Falls Church VA 22046

FRENCH, WILLIAM HAROLD, newspaper editor; b. London, Ont., Can., Mar. 21, 1926; s. Harold Edward and Isabel (Brash) F.; m. Margaret Jean Rollo, June 23, 1951; children—Jane, Mark, Paul, Susan. B.A., U. Western Ont., 1948; Nieman fellow, Harvard, 1954-55. With The Globe and Mail, Toronto, Ont., Can., 1948—, lit. editor, 1960—; instr. journalism Ryerson Poly. Inst., 1955—; asso. fellow York U., 1969-77; broadcaster Canadian Broadcasting Corp., 1964—; cons. Can. Council, 1969—. Author: A Most Unlikely Village, 1960. Recipient President's medal U. Western Ont., 1966; Nat. Newspaper award for critical writing, 1978, 79. Home: 78 N Hills Terr Don Mills ON M3C 1M6 Canada Office: 444 Front St W Toronto ON M5V 2S9 Canada

FRENI, MIRELLA, soprano; b. Modena, Italy, Feb. 27, 1935; d. Ennio and Gianna F.; m. Leone Magiera, 1955; 1 dau., Micaela. Debut as Micaela in: Carmen, Modena, 1955; since has appeared in maj. opera house throughout world, including, La Scala, Royal Opera House, Covent Garden, Met. Opera, Vienna State Opera, Paris Opera, Salzburg Festival, Glyndebourne Festival; appeared in: film Madame Butterfly and; U.S. public TV broadcast of The Marriage of Figaro; maj. roles include: Zerlina in Don Giovanni; appeared on: numerous operatic recs., including Carmen (Grammy award for best opera rec. 1964). Office: care Herbert H Breslin Inc 119 W 57th St New York NY 10019

FRENIER, JAMES FRANCIS, insurance executive; b. Montpelier, Vt., Jan. 3, 1934; s. Stanley F. and Geralda M. (Goulet) F.; m. Florence E. Emerton; children: James F., Diane M., Susan M. A.A. in Acctg., Bentley Coll., Boston, 1953; B.S. in Mgmt., Rutgers U., 1970. Acct. Gen. Motors Acceptance Corp., Burlington, Vt., 1953-60, fin. staff, N.Y.C., 1960-70; fin. and devel. staff Motors Ins. Corp., N.Y.C., 1970-79, mgr. corp. planning, 1979-81, treas., 1981—. Home: 20954 E Glen Haven Circle Northville MI 48167 Office: Motors Ins Corp 3044 W Grand Blvd Detroit MI 48202

FRENKEL, EUGENE PHILLIP, physician; b. Detroit, Aug. 27, 1929; s. David Eugene and Eva (Antin) F.; m. Rhoda Beth Smilay, Dec. 21, 1958; children: Lisa Michelle, Peter Alan. B.S., Wayne State U., 1949; M.D., U. Mich., 1953. Diplomate: Am. Bd. Internal Medicine (hematology, med. oncology; bd. govs. 1980—, chmn. subspecialty com. hematology 1980—). Intern Wayne County Gen. Hosp., Eloise, Mich., 1953-54; resident in internal medicine Boston City Hosp., 1954-55; resident in internal medicine, then instr. U. Mich. Med. Center, 1957-62; mem. faculty U. Tex. Health Sci. Center, Dallas, 1962—, prof. internal medicine and radiology, 1969—, chief div. hematology-oncology, 1962—; chief nuclear medicine, cons. hematology-oncology VA Med. Center, Dallas, 1962—; cons. com. evaluation research hematology Nat. Inst. Arthritis and Metabolic Diseases. Author numerous research papers in field. Served as officer M.C. USAF, 1955-57. Fellow A.C.P., Internat. Soc. Hematology; mem. Am. Soc. Hematology (treas. 1976—), Am. Soc. Clin. Oncology (chmn. membership com. 1982—), Am. Cancer Soc. (pres. Dallas unit 1970-71, dir. Tex. div. 1978—, sci. adv. com. on clin. investigations II—chemotherapy and hematology 1978—, Emma Freeman prof. 1981, nat. clin. fellowship com. 1978—), Assn. Am. Physicians, Am. Assn. Cancer Research, Am. Assn. Cancer Edn., Am. Soc. Biol. Chemists, Am. Soc. Clin. Investigation, So. Soc. Clin. Investigation, Soc. Nuclear Medicine, Am. Fedn. Clin. Research, Internat. Assn. Study Lung Cancer, Alpha Omega Alpha. Office: 5323 Harry Hines Blvd Dallas TX 75235

FRENKEL, JACOB AHARON, economist, educator; b. Tel-Aviv, Israel, Feb. 8, 1943; came to U.S., 1967; s. Kalman H. and Lea (Zwibaum) F.; m. Niza Yair, Sept. 3, 1968; children: Orli-Miriam, Tahl-Ida. B.A. in Econs. and Polit. Sci, Hebrew U., Israel, 1966, postgrad. (fellow), 1966-67, M.A., U. Chgo., 1969, Ph.D. in Econs. (Lilly Honor fellow), 1970. Teaching asst. dept. econs. Hebrew U., Jerusalem, 1966-67; instr. money and banking Ind. U., Gary, 1968-69; asst. prof. internat. econs. and fin. Grad. Sch. Bus., U. Chgo., 1970-71, vis. asst. prof., summer, 1972, asst. prof. dept. econs., 1973-74, assoc. prof., 1974-78, prof., 1979—, David Rockefeller prof. internat. econs., 1982—; sr. lectr. econs. Tel-Aviv U., Israel, 1971-73, vis. prof., 1980; adj. sr. lectr. econs. Hebrew U., Jerusalem, 1972-73; mem. adv. council Carnegie-Rochester Conf. Series on Public Policy, 1977—; research assoc. Nat. Bur. Econ. Research, 1978—; hon. research asso. dept. econs. Harvard U., 1978; adv. econs. Harvard U. Press, 1980—; mem. econs. adv. panel NSF, 1980-82; mem. adv. com. internat. seminar on macroecons. Maison des Scis. de l'Homme and NBER; Henry Thornton lectr. City U., London, 1981. Contbg. author: The Economics of the Sector Owned by Organized Labor, 1964, (with A. Ofer) Macroeconomics: Lecture Notes, 1965, (with H.G. Johnson) The Monetary Approach to the Balance of Payments, 1976, The Economics of Exchange Rates: Selected Studies, 1978, (with R. Dornbusch) International Economic Policy: Theory and Evidence, 1979; contbr. numerous articles on econ. theory and internat. econs. to profl. jours.; editor: Jour. Polit. Economy, 1975-82; mem. editorial bd.: Jour. Monetary Econs, 1978—; adv. editor: Econs. Letters, 1980—. Lehrman Inst. research fellow, 1981-82; Inst. Advanced Studies Tel-Aviv U. fellow, 1983-84; Ford Found. grantee, 1975-76; NSF grantee, 1978-81. Fellow Econometric Soc.; Mem. Am. Econ. Assn. Office: Univ Chicago 1126 E 59th St Chicago IL 60637

FRENKIL, VICTOR, contractor; b. Balt., Sept. 14, 1908; s. Isaac and Jennie (Goldscheider) F.; m. Margaret Panzer, Feb. 15, 1932; children: Janet, Vida, Victor, Leonard. Student, Johns Hopkins U., 1929-31; D.Eng. (hon.), Steed Coll. Tech., Johnson, Tenn. Started home improvement bus., 1931; former chmn. bd. Balt. Contractors, Inc.; now chmn. bd. BCI Contractors, Inc.; dir. Devel. & Constrn. Co., Inc., Jarvis Steel & Lumber Co., Inc. Life mem. Am. Cancer Soc., Md.; past mem. bus. adv. com. UN; mem. Selective Service Bd. 26; mem. adv. council Loyola Coll.; bd. dirs. Balt. Civic Opera Co., Greater Balt. Com.; trustee So. Sem. Coll., State Colls. State Md., N. Charles Gen. Hosp.; exec. council Boy Scouts Am. Recipient gold key for indsl. leadership Balt. Inst., 1953, certificate commendation USN, 1965, award Soc. for Preservation Md. Antiquities, 1977. Mem. Assn. Commerce, ASCE, Mil. Engrs., Moles, Phi Alpha (life). Clubs: Masons, Shriners, Rotary, B'nai B'rith, Engrs., Advt. (Balt.); Advt. (Brandeis U.) (life). Created first nat. TV play award. Office: 711 S Central Ave Baltimore MD 21202

FRENS, ARTHUR J., retired food company executive; b. Fremont, Mich., May 22, 1918; s. John B. and Johanna (Blaauw) F.; m. Geraldyne L. Bowman, July 26, 1940; children: John Arthur, Mary Jean. Student, La Salle Extension U., 1936-40. With Gerber Products Co., Fremont, 1936—, v.p., asst. to pres., 1960-61, v.p. adminstrn., 1961-64, exec. v.p., 1964-71, pres., 1971-78, chmn., chief exec. officer, 1978-83, still dir.; dir. Rubbermaid, Inc. Served to 1st lt. AUS, 1944-46. Mem. Fremont C. of C. Mem. Christian Ref. Ch. Home: 934 Clubview Dr Fremont MI 49412

FRENSDORFF, WESLEY, bishop; b. Hanover, Germany, July 22, 1926; s. Rudolph August and Erma Margarete (Asch) F.; m. Dolores C. Stoker, Nov. 1, 1953; 5 children. B.A., Columbia U., 1948; S.T.B., Gen. Theol. Sem., N.Y.C., 1951. Ordained deacon Episcopal Ch., 1951, priest, 1951; vicar St. Mary Virgin Ch., Winnemucca, Nev., St. Andrew's Ch., Battle Mountain, Nev., St. Anne's Ch., McDermitt, Nev., 1951-54; rector St. Paul's Ch., Elko, Nev. and; vicar St. Barnabas and St. Luke Ch., Wells, Nev., and; St. Martin's Ch., Upper Skagit Valley, Nev. and, Community Ch., Newhalem, Wash., 1959-62; dean St. Mark's Cathedral, Salt Lake City, 1962-72; bishop Diocese of Nev., Reno, 1972—; dir. North Pacific and Western parish tng. program Episcopal Ch., 1959-64; trustee Gen. Theol. Sem., 1965-74; priest in charge St. Francis Ch., Managua, Nicarague, 1968-69 *

FRENZEL, BILL, Congressman; b. St. Paul, July 31, 1928; s. Paul and Paula (Schlegel) F.; m. Ruth Purdy, June 9, 1951; children: Deborah, Pamela, Melissa. B.A., Dartmouth, 1950, M.B.A., 1951. Pres. Mpls. Terminal Warehouse Co., 1966-70, No. Waterway Terminals Corp., 1965-70; mem. 92d-97th Congresses from 3d Dist. Minn.; Mem. Minn. Ho. Reps., 1962-70. Hon. trustee Nat. Cystic Fibrosis Found. Served to lt. USNR, 1951-54; Korea. Republican. Clubs: Rotarian., Minneapolis. Office: Longworth House Office Bldg Washington DC 20515

FRENZER, PETER FREDERICK, insurance company executive; b. Omaha, Aug. 19, 1934; s. William J. and Ruth E. (Berliner) F.; m. Mary Virginia Yates, June 1, 1957; children: Peter, Michelle M., Christopher P., Jennifer S., Paula B. B.S. summa cum laude, Creighton U., 1956; student, Creighton U. Coll. Law, 1956-57; LL.B. cum laude, William Mitchell Coll. Law, 1961. C.P.A., Nebr. Investment analyst, cost acct. Prudential Ins. Co., Mpls., 1957-62; v.p. securities, 2d v.p., analyst United Benefit Life Ins. Co., Omaha, 1962-74; v.p. investments Heritage Securities Inc., Columbus, Ohio, 1974-81; v.p. securities investment Nationawide Ins. Cos., Columbus, 1977-81; exec. v.p. investments Nationwide Ins. Cos., Columbus, 1981—. Trustee Otterbein Coll., Westerville, Ohio, 1983—. Served to capt. U.S. Army, 1957. Mem. ABA, Nebr. Bar Assn., Minn. Bar Assn., Fin. Analysts Fedn. Roman Catholic. Office: Nation-wide Ins Cos One Nationwide Plaza Columbus OH 43216

FRENZ-HECKMAN, FAITH, broadcasting co. exec.; b. Flushing, N.Y., Sept. 17, 1934; d. Charles Henry and Elizabeth Henrietta (Frenz) Schwarz; m. Donald Joseph Heckman, Apr. 7, 1971; children—Allegra Tanaquil, Alexander Charles. Ed., Queens Coll. Program coordinator CBS-TV, Los Angeles; later asso. dir., dir., later v.p. children's programs; pres. The Londonderry Co., Burbank, Calif., 1980—; mem. Children's Film Bd. Advisors. Office: 210 N Pass Ave 206 Burbank CA 91505

FRERICHS, ERNEST SUNLEY, educator; b. S.I., N.Y., Apr. 30, 1925; s. Ernest V. and Eva (Sunley) F.; m. Sarah Hazel Cutts, Aug. 20, 1949; children—John Allen, David Sunley, Elizabeth Ann. A.B., Brown U., 1948; A.M., Harvard, 1949; S.T.B., Boston U., 1952, Ph.D., 1957. Ordained to ministry Methodist Ch., 1951; mem. faculty Brown

U., 1953—, prof. religious studies, 1965—, chmn. dept., 1964-70, asst. dean coll., 1958-59, dean grad. sch., 1976—; Bd. dirs. R.I. Council Chs., 1960-62.; Mem. region 1 and 11 selection com. Woodrow Wilson Found., 1959-68; mem. Grad. and Profl. Schs. Fin. Aid Council, 1978—; trustee Am. Schs. Oriental Research; 976—; trustee Albright Inst. Archeol. Research, Jerusalem, 1974—, pres., 1976—; trustee Hiatt Inst. of Brandeis U., 1979—, Roger Williams Gen. Hosp., Providence, 1981—; mem. Grad. Record Exam. Bd., 1980—; mem. com. on testing Council of Grad. Schs. in U.S., 1980—; mem. exec. com. Assn. Grad. Schs., 1980—. Served with inf. AUS, 1943-46. Beebe fellow Boston U., 1952-53; Lilly postdoctoral fellow Heidelberg (Germany) U., 1962-63. Mem. Soc. Bibl. Lit. (exec. com. New Eng. council 1977—), Am. Acad. Religion (pres. New Eng. 1970-71), Phi Beta Kappa (sec. Brown U. chpt. 1964-68, pres. 91975-77). Home: 32 Vassar Ave Providence RI 02906 Office: Grad Sch Box 1867 Brown U Providence RI 02912

FRESCO, JACQUES ROBERT, biochemist, educator; b. N.Y.C., May 30, 1928; s. Robert and Lucie (Asseo) F.; m. Rosalie Sarah Bernstein, Dec. 22, 1957; children—Lucille Deborah, Suzette Josie, Linda Hannah. B.A., N.Y. U., 1947, M.S., 1949, Ph.D., 1953; M.D. (hon.), U. Göteborg, Sweden, 1979. Postdoctoral fellow Sloan Kettering Inst. for Cancer Research, N.Y.C., 1952-54; instr. biochemistry N.Y. U. Coll. Medicine, 1953-54, instr. pharmacology, 1954-56; research fellow dept. chemistry Harvard, 1956-60, tutor biochem. scis., 1957-60; vis. fellow Cavendish Lab., Cambridge, Eng. and; Institut de Biologie Physico-Chimique, Paris, France, 1957; asst. prof. dept. chemistry Princeton, 1960-62, asso. prof., 1962-65, prof., 1965—, acting chmn. biochem. scis., 1965-66, prof. dept. biochem. scis., 1970—, chmn. dept., 1974-80; vis. prof. Hebrew U. of Jerusalem, 1973; dir. Nat. Cancer Inst. Basic Sci. Cancer Center, 1976—, Pfeiffer prof. life scis., 1977—; mem. adv. bd. Biopolymers, 1963-70; cons. sci. adv. com. Helen Hay Whitney Found.; vis. scientist MRC Lab. Molecular Biology, Cambridge, Eng., 1969-70. Mem. editorial bd.: Jour. Phys. Chemistry, 1963-70, Analytical Biochemistry, 1969-81. Recipient Am. Scientist Writing award AAAS, 1962; NIH fellow, 1952-54; Lalor Found. fellow, 1957; established investigator; Am. Heart Assn., 1958-63; Guggenheim fellow, 1969-70. Mem. Am. Chem. Soc., Am. Soc. Biol. Chemists, Sigma Xi. Home: 282 Hartley Ave Princeton NJ 08540

FRESE, WALTER WENZEL, publisher; b. Mt. Vernon, N.Y., Sept. 28, 1909; s. Walter Adolf and Clara (Wenzel) F.; m. Margaret Penny, June 20, 1931; children: Alan David Rogers, Frederick Wenzel, Diana Elaine. Student, Columbia U., 1927-31. With Archtl. Book Pub. Co., Inc., 1927—, v.p., 1930-53, pres., 1953—; founder, pres. Hastings House, pubs., 1936—, Archives Pub. Co. of Pa., Inc., 1945-56; partner Arnold & Frese (securities), 1936-39. Pres. Stamford (Conn.) Hills Assn., 1945-48; mem. adv. council Sch. Gen. Studies, Columbia U., chmn., 1963-71; mem. Conn. adv. com. on UN Orgn. Hdqrs. Site. Recipient Columbia Alumni Owl citation for distinguished pub. service, 1964. Mem. Am. Inst. Graphic Arts (pres. 1945-47), New Eng. Soc. City N.Y. (pres. 1976-77). Episcopalian. Clubs: Century, Coffee House, Princeton U. (N.Y.); Stamford Yacht (commodore 1971-73), Dutch Treat (sec.-treas. 1971—), Pilgrims.). Nat. sr. vets. platform tennis champion, 1969, 72, 74, 84. Home: 268 Dogwood Ln Stamford CT 06903 Office: 10 E 40th St New York NY 10016

FRETTER, WILLIAM BACHE, physics educator; b. Pasadena, Calif., Sept. 28, 1916; s. William Albert and Dorothy (Bach) F.; m. Grace Powles, Jan. 1, 1939; children: Travis D., Gretchen, Richard Brian. A.B., U. Calif. at Berkeley, 1937, Ph.D., 1946. Research engr. radar counter-measures Westinghouse Electric Co., 1941-45; mem. faculty U. Calif. at Berkeley, 1946—, prof. physics, 1955—, dean, 1962-67, v.p. of Univ., 1978-83. Author: Introduction to Experimental Physics, 1955, (with David S. Saxon) Physics for the Liberal Arts Student, 1971. Fulbright scholar, France, 1952-53, 60-61; Guggenheim fellow., 1960-61; decorated chevalier Legion of Honor, France, 1964. Fellow Am. Phys. Soc. Spl. research cosmic rays, high-energy particle physics. Home: 1120 Cragmont Ave Berkeley CA 94708

FRETTHOLD, TIMOTHY JON, lawyer; b. Berea, Ohio, Apr. 11, 1949; s. Norman C. and Ruth I. (Irwin) F.; m. Christe S. Siebenhar, June 26, 1971; children: Jocelyn C., Ashley B. B.A., Yale U., 1971; J.D., Case Western Res. U., 1975. Bar: Ohio 1975, Tex. 1980. Atty. SEC, Washington, 1975-77, Diamond Shamrock Corp., Cleve., 1977-79; asst. sec. Diamond Shamrock Corp., Cleve., 1979-81, sec., sr. counsel, Dallas, 1982—. Mem. ABA, Ohio Bar Assn., Tex. Bar Assn., Dallas Bar Assn., Am. Soc. Corp. Secs., Yale U. Alumni Assn. Office: 717 N Harwood St Dallas TX 75201

FRETWELL, ELBERT KIRTLEY, JR., university chancellor; b. N.Y.C., Oct. 29, 1923; s. Elbert Kirtley and Jean (Hosford) F.; m. Dorrie Shearer, Aug. 25, 1951; children: Barbara Alice (Mrs. Peter Cooke), Margaret Jean (Mrs. John C. Cross), James Leonard, Katharine Louise (Mrs. Robert Saul). A.B. with distinction, Wesleyan U., Middletown, Conn., 1944; M.A. in Teaching, Harvard U., 1948; Ph.D., Columbia U., 1953; hon. doctorate, Tech. U. Wroclaw, Poland, 1976; LL.D., Wesleyan U., 1981. Corr. AP, 1942-44; staff writer ARC, 1944-45; vice consul Am. embassy, Prague, Czechoslovakia, 1945-47; tchr. Brookline (Mass.) Pub. Schs., 1948, Evanston (Ill.) Twp. High Sch. and Community Coll., 1948-50; adminstrv. sec. John Hay Fellowships, John Hay Whitney Found., 1951-53; asst. prof., asst. to dean Tchrs. Coll., Columbia U., 1953-56, asso. prof., 1956; asst. commr. for higher edn. N.Y. State Dept. Edn., 1956-64; summer faculty U. Calif. at Berkeley, 1964; dean acad. devel. City U. N.Y., 1964-67; pres. State U. N.Y. Coll. at Buffalo, 1967-78; chancellor U. N.C., Charlotte, 1979—; Organizer N.Y.C. meeting White House Conf. Edn., 1955; cons. Pres.'s Com. Edn. Beyond High Sch., 1956; assisted in James B. Conant Study Edn. Am. Tchrs., 1962; mem. commn. higher instns. Middle State Assn., 1965-71; mem. Am. Council Edn. Nat. Commn. on Higher Edn. Issues, 1981-82; trustee Carnegie Found. for Advancement Teaching, 1968-77, chmn., 1975-77; mem. Carnegie Council on Policy Studies in Higher Edn., 1973-79; trustee N.C. Council Econ. Edn., 1979—; chmn. planning com. 17th Nat. Conf. Higher Edn., 1962; bd. dirs. Microelectronics Ctr. N.C., 1981—; trustee Wesleyan U., 1967-70, Nichols Sch., Buffalo, 1969-78, Canisius Coll., 1969-76; bd. dirs. Found. of N.C. at Charlotte, 1981—, Mint Mus., Charlotte, N.C.; bd. visitors Johnson C. Smith U.; exec. dir. com. on edn. N.Y. State Constl. Conv., 1967. Author: Founding Public Junior Colleges, 1954, also articles, chpts. in yearbooks. Vice chmn. N.Y. State Am. Revolution Bicentennial Commn., 1969-76; bd. dirs. Am. Assn. State Colls. and Univs., 1973-76, 77-80, pres., 1978-79; mem. del. to Peoples Republic of China, Peking, 1975, to Republic of China, Taiwan, 1976, to Cuba, 1978, to UNESCO/Paris Conf., 1979, to India, 1980; pres. Middle States Assn. Colls. and Secondary Schs., 1973-74; adv. commr. Edn. Commn. of States, 1975-76, 79-80; bd. dirs. Am. Council on Edn., 1979-82, chmn., 1980-81; v.p. Univ. Research Park, Charlotte, 1979—; bd. dirs. Mecklenburg council Boy Scouts Am., 1979, United Community Services, 1979—. Decorated Order of Cultural Merit, Poland; recipient ann. award N.Y. State Assn. Jr. Colls., 1962; Distinguished Alumnus award Wesleyan U., 1974; Carnegie Corp. grantee, 1964, 74. Mem. Am. Assn. Higher Edn. (exec. com. 1962-66, nat. pres. 1964-65), Am. Acad. Polit. Sci., Am. Soc. Pub. Adminstrn., Nat. Ry. Hist. Soc., Greater Charlotte C. of C. (dir. 1979—). Clubs: Harvard (N.Y.C.); Adirondack Mountain, Charlotte City, Charlotte Country, Rotary. Home: 3066 Stonybrook Rd Charlotte NC 28205 Office: Univ NC at Charlotte UNCC Sta Charlotte NC 28223

FREUDENBERG, BORIS, electrical equipment company executive; b. Nov. 23, 1909; S. Came to U.S., 1950, naturalized, 1952; s. Iso and Eugenie (Lichovetzer) F.; m. Selma Stembler, Dec. 17, 1948; 1 son, Gordon Yves. M.S., U. Paris, France, 1930; degree in elec. engring. Ecole Supérieure d'Electricité, Paris, 1931. Asst. gen. mgr. Microwave Lab., Thomson-Houston, Paris, 1947-50; cons. engr., N.Y.C., 1950-59; permanent rep. Compagnie Générale d'Electricité of Paris, 1974-77; pres. Cogenel Inc., N.Y.C., 1959-77, chmn. bd., 1973-77; chmn. bd. Citcom Systems, Inc., N.Y.C., 1970-77, Saft Batteries Ltd., Toronto, Ont., Can., Sediver Inc., Carlstadt, N.J., RCPC, Franklin Park, Ill., until 1977; pres. B. Freudenberg Inc., N.Y.C., 1956-80; now dir.; pres. Saft Corp. Am., N.Y.C., 1959-77; dir. Ascoe Felts, Inc., Clinton, S.C., Saft Am. Inc., Valdosta, Ga., Sylvania-Unelec Internat. Corp., Santurce, P.R., 2BFI Electronics Ltd., London, Eng. Served as officer French Army, 1939-45. Decorated Legion of Honor, France). Life mem. IEEE. Research on shortwave antennae. Home: 1801 S Flagler Dr Apt 905 West Palm Beach FL 33401

FREUDENHEIM, MILTON B., journalist; b. New Rochelle, N.Y., Mar. 4, 1927; s. Milton Benjamin and Lenore Patricia (Kroh) F.; m. Elizabeth Ege, Mar. 7, 1951; children: Jo Louise, Susan Patricia, John Milton Otto, Tom Henry. A.B., U. Mich., 1948. Reporter Louisville (Ky.) Courier-Jour., 1948-49; reporter Akron (Ohio) Beacon Jour., 1949-52, Washington corr., 1953-56; UN corr. Chgo. Daily News, 1956-66, nat. and fgn. editor, 1966-69, Paris corr., 1969-77; dir. public affairs for Region V HEW, Chgo., 1978-79; copy editor, writer N.Y. Times Week in Rev., 1979—; adv. U.S. del. UNESCO Gen. Conf., 1978; Pres. UN Corrs. Assn., 1966, Anglo-Am. Press Assn., 1975. Mem. Phi Beta Kappa, Sigma Delta Chi. Home: 123 W 74th St New York NY 10023 Office: 229 W 43d St New York NY 10036

FREUDENHEIM, TOM LIPPMANN, art museum administrator; b. Stuttgart, Germany, July 3, 1937; came to U.S., 1938, naturalized, 1943; s. Ernest Simon and Margot Ruth (Freund) F.; m. Leslie Ann Mandelson, Nov. 15, 1964; children: Alexander Darius, Adam Jeremy. A.B., Harvard U., 1959; postgrad., Hebrew Union Coll., 1959-61; M.A., Inst. Fine Arts, NYU, 1966; D.F.A. (hon.), (U. Md.), 1982. Asst. curator Jewish Mus., N.Y.C., 1962-65; asst. dir. Univ. Art Mus., U. Calif. at Berkeley, 1966-71; dir. Balt. Mus. of Art, 1971-78; dir. museum programs Nat. Endowment for Arts, Washington, 1979-82; dir. Worcester Art Mus., Mass., 1982—; lectr. U. Calif. at Berkeley, 1966-70. Contbr. articles on decorative and modern art to profl. publs. Bd. dirs. Mass. Cultural Alliance, Hand Hollow Found. USIA grantee, Romania, Czechoslovakia, 1969; State Dept. grantee, Japan, 1971, Romania, USSR, 1974. Mem. Coll. Art Assn., Art Mus. Assn. (dir.), Assn. Art Mus. Dirs. Office: Worcester Art Museum 55 Salisbury St Worcester MA 01608

FREUDENSTEIN, FERDINAND, mechanical engineering educator; b. Frankfurt, Germany, May 12, 1926; came to U.S., 1942, naturalized, 1945; s. George Gerson and Charlotte (Rosenberg) F.; m. Leah Schwarzchild, July 5, 1959 (dec. May 1970); children: David George, Joan Merle; m. Lydia Gersten, 1980. Student, N.Y.U., 1942-44; M.S., Harvard U., 1948; Ph.D., Columbia U., 1954. Devel. engr. instrument div. Am. Optical Co., 1948-50; mem. tech. staff Bell Telephone Labs., 1954; mem. faculty Columbia U., 1954—, prof. mech. engring., 1959—, Stevens prof. mech. engring., 1981—, chmn. dept., 1958-64; cons. to industry, 1954—. Served inf. AUS, 1944-46. Recipient Gt. Tchr. award Soc. Older Grads. Columbia, 1966; Guggenheim fellow, 1961-62, 67-68. Fellow N.Y. Acad. Scis., ASME (Jr. award 1955, Machine Design award 1972, Mechanisms com. award 1978); mem. Harvard Soc. Engrs. and Scientists, Columbia Engring. Soc., N.Y. Acad. Scis., Nat. Acad. Engring., Sigma Xi. Spl. research kinematics, dynamics, mechanisms, engring. design. Home: 435 W 259th St Riverdale NY 10471

FREUDENTHAL, STEVEN FRANKLIN, lawyer; b. Thermopolis, Wyo., June 8, 1949; s. Lewis Franklin and Lucille Iola (Love) F.; m. Janet Mae Mansfield, Aug. 30, 1969; children—Lynn Marie, Kristen Lee. B.A., Trinity Coll., Hartford, Conn., 1971; J.D., Vanderbilt U., 1975. Bar: Wyo. bar 1975, U.S. Supreme Ct. bar 1981. Tax acct. Conn. Gen. Life Ins. Co., Hartford, Conn., 1971-72; asst. atty. gen. Wyo., Cheyenne, 1975-77, atty. gen. Wyo., 1981-82; state planning coordinator Office Gov. Wyo., Cheyenne, 1977-78; dep. under sec. Dept. Interior, Washington, 1978-79, exec. asst. to sec., 1979-80; resident ptnr Sherman & Howard, Cheyenne, Wyo., 1980-81; solo practice, Cheyenne, 1982—; chmn. Western Interstate Energy Bd./ Western Interstate Nuclear Bd., 1978. Goodwin scholar, 1967-70; Vanderbilt Law scholar, 1972-75. Mem. Am. Bar Assn., Wyo. Bar Assn., Am. Soc. Planning Ofcls., Pi Gamma Mu. Episcopalian. Home: 757 Silver Sage Cheyenne WY 82001 Office: 314 E 21st St Cheyenne WY 82001

FREUND, CHARLES GIBSON, holding company executive; b. Chgo., Oct. 8, 1923; s. Charles and Jewl (Gibson) F.; m. Ann L. Schiera, June 8, 1947; children: Mark, Eric, Kurt, Scott, Pamela. B.S., Aero., U. Chgo., 1948; J.D., John Marshall Law Sch., 1956. Stress analyst Northrup Aircraft Co., Hawthorne, Calif., 1949; with Natural Gas Pipeline Co. of Am., Chgo., 1949—, asst. sec., 1957-61, sec., 1961-66, v.p. finance, 1966-69, sec.-treas., 1969—; v.p., sec., treas. Peoples Energy Corp., Chgo., 1969-81; sec., treas. Peoples Gas Light & Coke Co., 1969-81, North Shore Gas Co., 1969-81, Harper Oil Co. Ltd.; v.p., sec., treas. MidCon Corp., 1981—; chmn. bd. 1st Nat. Bank Lincolnshire, 1979—. Bd. dirs. United Cerebral Palsy of Chgo., 1959—, also v.p.; mem. sr. bd. NCCJ, 1965—, nat. trustee, 1969—; nat. trustee nat. gov., 1970—; bd. dirs. Lincoln Nat. Direct Placement Fund Inc., 1972, AEGIS, Girl Scouts Chgo., 1976—; mem. citizens bd., investment com. Loyola U., Chgo., 1972. Served with USAAF, 1942-45. Decorated Purple Heart, Air medal. Mem. Am., Ill., Chgo. bar assns., Am. Soc. Corp. Secs., Am. Gas Assn., Ind. Natural Gas Assn. Am., Tex. Mid-Continent Oil and Gas Assn., Am. Legion, Ill., Chgo. chambers commerce, Nat. Investor Relations Inst., Fin. Execs. Inst. Democrat. Roman Catholic. Clubs: Executives, Mid-Am., Economic, Chgo. Athletic, Pub. Utility Securities (Chgo.). Home: 30 Plymouth Ct Lincolnshire Deerfield IL 60015 Office: 122 S Michigan Ave Chicago IL 60603

FREUND, CLEMENT JOSEPH, mech. engr., coll. dean; b. Appleton, Wis., Aug. 7, 1895; s. Alois John and Ottilia (Lenz) F.; m. Mabelle Gertrude Ziegler, Aug. 21, 1926; children—Mary Elizabeth, Paul Clement (dec.), Louis James (dec.). A.B., Campion Coll., Prairie du Chien, Wis., 1916; M.E., Marquette U., 1922; D.Sc. (hon.), Catholic U. Am., 1962, D.Eng., U. Detroit, 1977. With Falk Corp., 1922-32, ednl. dir., 1926-32; instr. evening tech. courses Milw. Vocat. Sch., 1924-32, supr. same, 1926-30; spl. lectr. Coll. Engring., Marquette U., 1930-32; dean Coll. Engring. U. Detroit, 1932-62, prof., 1962—; cons. higher tech. edn., West Pakistan, 1958-60; cons. engring. edn. Pakistan Commn. on Nat Edn., 1958-60; cons. Minn. State Coll. Bd., S.W. Minn. State Coll.; Mem. conf. bd. Asso. Research Councils (Com. on Fulbright Awards in Engring.), 1955-58; Mem. Gov.'s Seaway Commn., Mich., 1954. Contbr. profl. jours. Served from 2d to 1st lt. U.S. Army, World War I. Fellow ASME (life), Engring. Soc. Detroit (distinguished mem. 1971—, past pres., Horace H. Rackham Humanitarian award 1978); mem. Am. Foundrymen's Soc. (hon.), Am. Soc. Engring. Edn. (past pres., past chmn. ethics com., rep. Am. Council on Edn. 1955-58), Engrs.' Council Profl. Devel. (chmn. com. on ethics 1955-58, engring. manpower com.), Mich. Soc. Profl. Engrs. (past chmn. long range planning com.), Mich. Engring. Soc. (hon.), Crown and Anchor, Tau Beta Pi, Alpha Sigma Nu, Pi Tau Sigma, Theta Tau. Roman Catholic. Home: 17597 Oak Dr Detroit MI 48221

FREUND, FRED A., lawyer; b. N.Y.C., June 18, 1928; s. Sidney J. and Cora (Strasser) Freund; m. Rosalie Sampo, Nov. 18, 1975 (div. Apr. 1983); m. Patricia A. Gardner, Mar. 13, 1957 (div. Jan. 1967); children: Gregory G., Kenneth B. A.B., Columbia U., 1948, J.D., 1949. Bar: N.Y. 1949, U.S. Supreme Ct. 1968. Law clk. to chief judge U.S. Dist. Ct. So. Dist. N.Y., N.Y.C., 1949-51; assoc. Kaye, Sholar, Fierman, Hays & Handler, N.Y.C., 1953-58; ptnr. Kaye, Scholar, Fierman, Hays & Handler, N.Y.C., 1959. Served to 1st lt. USAF, 1951-53. Mem. ABA, Assn. Bar City N.Y., Phi Beta Kappa. Home: 1085 Park Ave New York NY 10128 Office: Kaye Scholer et al 425 Park Ave New York NY 10022 *Balancing the quest for excellence with humility and humor.*

FREUND, GERALD, foundation administrator; b. Berlin, Germany, Oct. 14, 1930; came to U.S., 1940, naturalized, 1946; s. Kurt and Annelise (Josephthal) F.; m. Jane Bicker Shaw Trask, Sept. 29, 1956 (div. Sept. 1970); children: Jonathan Gerald, Matthew Trask, Andrew Josephthal; m. Peregrine White Whittlesey, Dec. 31, 1976. B.A. magna cum laude, Haverford Coll., 1952; D.Phil., Oxford (Eng.) U., 1955. Research fellow St. Anthony's Coll., Oxford U., 1955-56; Research asst. Inst. Advanced Study, Princeton, 1956-57; fellow Council Fgn. Relations, 1957-59; asst. prof. Haverford Coll., 1958-60; research assoc. Washington Ctr. Fgn. Policy Research, 1959-60; from asst. dir. to assoc. dir. social scis., humanities, arts Rockefeller Found., 1960-69; asst. to pres. Yale, 1969-70; exec. v.p. Film Soc. of Lincoln Center, 1970-71; dean humanities and arts, prof., dir. Hunter Arts, Hunter Coll., 1971-80; v.p., dir. Prize Fellows Program, John D. and Catherine T. MacArthur Found., Chgo., 1980-84; dir. for planning Nat. Task Force on the Individual Artist, Am. Council Arts; cons. Washington Center of Fgn. Policy Research, 1959-60, Annenberg Center, Phila., 1970-71, Performing Arts Program, N.Y. State Council on Arts, N.Y.C., 1973, Arts, Edn. and Americans Project, 1975-77, Inst. Advanced Mus. Studies, Montreux, Switzerland, 1975-77, Nat. Inst. Edn., Dartmouth Coll., 1978-79, John and Catherine MacArthur Found., 1979-80, Inst. Study World Politics, 1980, 83, Esther A. and Joseph Klingenstein Fund, Inc., 1983—, N.Y. Inst. Visual History, Nat. Found. Advancement in the Arts; lectr., TV and radio activities; Mem. Charter Revision Commn., Stamford, Conn., 1964-65, planning commn. cons., 1965-67. Author: German Russian Relations, 1917-1926, 1957, 1958, Germany Between Two Worlds, 1961; Contbg. editor: Worldview. Mem. Com. on Orgn. of Peace, 1963-77; mem. exec. com., chmn. Manhattan Theatre Club; mem. adv. resource com. New Canaan Country Sch.; Vice pres. Democratic Party, North Stamford, Conn., 1962-64; trustee Woodstock (Vt.) Country Sch., 1962-81, pres. bd., 1972-75; mem. bd. Nat. Book Com., until 1975; bd. dirs. Inst. Current World Affairs, N.Y.C., until 1975, Fund for Artists Colonies, N.Y.C.; mem. Am. Com. East-West Accord, Washington; bd. dirs. Imagination Workshop, Inc., co-chmn. bd., 1977-78. Recipient Fulbright award, 1952-54; Rockefeller Found. grantee, 1956-57, 59-60. Mem. Council Fgn. Relations (fellowship com., library com.), Phi Beta Kappa. Jewish. Clubs: Lotos, Century Assn. Home: 345 E 80th St New York NY 10021 29 Chicken St Wilton CT 06897

FREUND, JAMES COLEMAN, lawyer; b. N.Y.C., July 26, 1934; s. Sylvan and Marcella (Coleman) F.; children: Erik Hellstrom, Thomas Hagstrom. B.A. magna cum laude, Princeton U., 1956; J.D. cum laude, Harvard U., 1962. Bar: N.Y. 1962. Since practice, N.Y.C.; partner firm Skadden, Arps, Slate, Meagher & Flom, 1968—; spl. cons. SEC, 1980-81; lectr. law U. Pa. Law Sch., 1982. Author: Anatomy of a Merger: Strategies and Techniques for Negotiating Corporate Acquisitions, 1975, Lawyering—a Realistic Approach to Legal Practice, 1979, also articles.; Co-editor: Disclosure Requirement of Public Corporations and Insiders, 1967. Trustee Princeton U., 1981—, Horace Mann Sch., N.Y.C., 1980—; bd. dirs. The Beresford, 1978-80; pres. class of 1956 Princeton U. Alumni Assn., 1976-81, chmn. com. to nominate alumni trustees, 1975-76, exec. com. alumni council, 1975-76. Served to lt. (j.g.) USNR, 1956-59. Mem. Bar Assn. City N.Y. Home: 310 E 46th St Apt 21A New York NY 10017 Office: 919 3d Ave New York NY 10022

FREUND, LAMBERT BEN, engineering educator, researcher, consultant; b. McHenry, Ill., Nov. 23, 1942; s. Bernard and Anita (Schaeffer) F.; m. Colleen Jean Hehl, Aug. 21, 1965; children: Jonathan Ben, Jeffrey Alan, Stephen Neil. B.S., U. Ill., 1964, M.S., 1965; Ph.D., Northwestern U., 1967. Postdoctoral fellow Brown U., Providence, 1967-69, asst. prof., 1969-73, assoc. prof., 1973-75, prof. engring., 1975—, chmn. div., 1979—; vis. prof. Stanford (Calif.) U., 1974-75; cons. Aberdeen Proving Ground, U.S. Steel Corp. Editor-in-chief: ASME Jour. Applied Mechanics, 1983—; contbr. articles to tech. jours. NSF trainee, 1964-67; grantee NSF, Office Naval Research, Army Research Office, Nat. Bur. Standards. Fellow ASME (Henry Hess award 1974); mem. Am. Geophys. Union, Am. Acad. Mechanics. Home: 3 Palisade Ln Barrington RI 02806 Office: Brown U Providence RI 02912

FREUND, PAUL ABRAHAM, educator; b. St. Louis, Feb. 16, 1908; s. Charles and Hulda (Arenson) F. A.B., Washington U., St. Louis, 1928, LL.D., 1956; LL.B., Harvard U., 1931, S.J.D., 1932, LL.D., 1977; LL.D., Columbia U., 1954, U. Louisville, 1956, U. Chgo., 1961, Boston U., 1964, Queen's U., Ont., 1970, Brown U., 1972, Yale U., 1972, Brandeis U., 1974, Williams Coll., 1974, Clark U., 1977, U. Bologna, 1981; L.H.D., Hebrew Union Coll., 1961; Litt.D., Cornell Coll., 1968, Bates Coll., 1973, Temple U., 1973, Yeshiva U., 1975; D.C.L., Union Coll., 1968; H.H.D., Stonehill Coll., 1978. Bar: D.C. 1935, Mass. 1947. Law clerk to Mr. Justice Brandeis, 1932-33; legal staff Treasury Dept. and R.F.C., 1933-35; spl. asst to atty. gen. Office of Solicitor Gen., Justice Dept., 1935-39, 1942-46; lectr. law Harvard Law Sch., 1939-40, prof. law, 1940-50, Charles Stebbins Fairchild prof., 1950-57; Royall prof. law Harvard U., 1957-58, Carl M. Loeb U. prof., 1958-76, prof. emeritus, 1976—; Pitt. prof. Am. history and instns. Cambridge U., 1957-58; fellow Trinity Coll., 1957-58, Center for Advanced Study in Behavioral Scis., 1969-70; Jefferson lectr. Nat. Endowment for Humanities, 1975; mem. Jud. Nominating Commn. 1st Circuit.; Dir. Salzburg Sem. Am. Studies. Author: On Understanding the Supreme Court, 1949 (Rosenthal lectures, Northwestern U), The Supreme Court of the U.S, 1961, On Law and Justice, 1968; Editor: Experimentation with Human Subjects, 1970; co-editor: Cases on Constitutional Law, 1962, 4th edit., 1977; Editor-in-chief: History of Supreme Court; editorial bd.: Daedalus; Contbr.: legal periodicals. Social Sci. Trustee Washington U. Recipient Research award Am. Bar Found., 1973; Learned Hand award Fed. Bar Council, 1978; award in law Thomas Jefferson Meml. Found., 1979. Fellow Am. Acad. Arts and Scis. (past pres.), Brit. Acad. (corr.); mem. Am. Judicature Soc., Mass. Hist. Soc., Am. Philos. Soc., Am. Bar Assn., Am. Law Inst., Harvard Soc. Fellows (emeritus), Signet Soc., Phi Beta Kappa, Pi Sigma Alpha. Club: St. Botolph (Boston). Home: 1010 Memorial Dr Cambridge MA 02138

FREUND, TIBOR, artist; b. Budapest, Hungary, Dec. 29, 1910; came to U.S., 1953, naturalized, 1958; s. Dezso and Margit (Honig) F.; m.

Barbara Horvat, Feb. 23, 1938 (dec. 1962); 1 son, Alexander. Diploma in architecture, Fed. Tech. U., Zurich, Switzerland, 1932; student with, Vilmos Aba-Novak Art Sch., Budapest. Registered architect, N.Y. Originated motion paintings, 1957, one-man shows include, Galerie Norval, N.Y.C., 1960, Contemporaries Gallery, N.Y.C., 1965, 67, Bertha Schaefer Gallery, N.Y.C., 1969, 71, 74, City U. N.Y. Grad. Center, 1976, Am. Fedn. Arts traveling exhibits, 1963-65, 66-67, 71-72; represented in permanent collections, museums.; Created moving murals Univeral Dissemination of Knowledge, Seaton Falls Sch., N.Y.C., Vehicle of Progress, I. Sch. 162, N.Y.C. Recipient top prize Silvermine Guild award 19th Ann. New Eng. Exhbn., 1968. Fellow Royal Soc. Arts (London); mem. Nat. Soc. Mural Painters. Studio: 34-57 82d St Jackson Heights NY 11372 *Man has to learn to look at things from various angles, to see the other fellow's viewpoint. This will lead, through mutual understanding, to peace.*

FREUND, WILLIAM CURT, economist; b. Nuremberg, Germany, Sept. 4, 1926; came to U.S., 1937, naturalized, 1942; s. Hugo and Paula (Gruenstein) F.; m. Judith Irmgard Steinberger, Aug. 14, 1951; children: Hugo, Nancy, Sandra. B.B.A., CCNY, 1949; M.S., Columbia U., 1950, Ph.D., 1954. Economist Prudential Ins. Co. Am., 1950-59; asso. prof. fin. N.Y. U. Grad. Sch. Bus. Adminstrn., 1959-62; exec. dir., chief economist Prudential Ins. Co. Am., 1963-67; sr. v.p., chief economist N.Y. Stock Exchange, 1968—; prof. econs. Pace U. Grad. Sch., 1972—; mem. econ. policy council to gov. N.J.; mem. Tri-State Econ. Council. Author: Investment Fundamentals, 5th edit, 1981, (with E. Epstein) People and Productivity, 1984; also articles. Investment Fundamentals, 5th edit. Named Disting. Alumnus Coll. City N.Y., 1974. Mem. Am., Met. econ. assns., Am. Finance Assn., Am. Statis. Assn., Nat. Assn. Bus. Economists. Home: 64 Circle Dr Millington NJ 07946 Office: 11 Wall St New York NY 10005

FREUNDLICH, AUGUST LUDWIG, artist, university dean; b. Frankfort, Germany, May 9, 1924; s. Julius and Erni (Keller) F.; m. Lillian Grace Thomson, Dec. 26, 1948; children: Mary, Jeffrey Paul, Heidi, Christopher Thomson. B.A., Antioch Coll., 1949, M.A., 1950; Ph.D., N.Y.U., 1960. Head dept. art Eastern Mich. U., 1954-58; chmn. arts div., Sullivan prof. arts edn. George Peabody Coll., 1958-64; dir. Joe and Emily Lowe Art Gallery and; chmn. art dept. U. Miami, Coral Gables, Fla., 1964-70; dean Sch. of Art, Syracuse U., 1970-71, Coll. Visual and Performing Arts; Syracuse U., 1971-82; v.p. Syracuse U. Theatre Corp.; dean Coll. Fine Arts, U. South Fla., Tampa, 1983—; cons. higher edn. panel Arts Edn. Americans.; found. cons.; Vice pres. S.E. Mus. Conf., 1969. Author: William Gropper, 1963, Frank Kleinholz, 1966, Karl Schrag, 1970, Richard Florsheim, 1976, Federico Castellon, 1978; mem. editorial bd.: USA Today, Ednl. Perspectives; contbr. articles to profl. jours. Trustee, cons. Everson Mus.; bd. dirs. Partners of Americas-Syracuse, Trinidad-Tobago, 1979—. Served with USMCR, 1942-46. Samuel H. Kress Found. grantee, 1971. Mem. Western Arts Assn. (council 1954-62, pres. 1958-60), Mich., Tenn., Ohio, N.Y., Ark. art edn. assns., Coll. Arts Assn., Nat. Com. Art Edn. (council asso. 1951—), Nat. Council Arts Adminstrs., Internat. Council Fine Arts Deans, N.Y. State Arts Deans, S.E. Coll. Art Assn. (pres. 1969-70), Nat. Art Edn. Assn. (council 1956-62), Am. Assn. Mus., N.E. Mus. Assn. Home: 18407 Timberlan Dr Lutz FL 33549

FREW, JAMES W., packaging products manufacturing company executive. Pres., chief exec. officer Stone Container Corp. Office: Stone Container Corp 360 N Michigan Ave Chicago IL 60601§

FREY, ALBERT, architect; b. Zurich, Switzerland, Oct. 18, 1903; came to U.S., 1930, naturalized, 1941; s. Albert and Ida (Meyer) F. Diploma architecture, Kantonales Technikum, Winterhur-Zurich, 1924. With Le Corbusier (architect), Paris, 1929; with architects' offices, N.Y.C., Washington and; U.S. Dept. Agr., 1930-34, Palm Springs, Calif., 1934-37; with Philip L. Goodwin (architect on design Mus. Modern Art), 1937-39. Designer: others; Author: In Search of a Living Architecture, 1939. Fellow AIA. Office: 686 Palisades Dr Palm Springs CA 92262 *In my youth, out of necessity, I had to produce a desired result with the least material and effort. Since then I found this principle to be a stimulating challenge to create, with aesthetic possibilities and gratifying the intellect. Today, realizing that resources are limited and with populations increasing drastically, conspicuous consumption is against the common good.*

FREY, CARL, assn. exec.; b. N.Y.C., Feb. 1, 1927; s. Adolph and Lina (Heilmann) F.; m. Iris Ihde, Feb. 12, 1955; children—Thomas, Douglas, Clifford. B.M.E., N.Y. U., 1948; M.A., Columbia, 1952. Dir. Nat. Engrs. Register, N.Y.C., 1963-65; exec. sec. Engring. Manpower Commn., N.Y.C., 1965—; exec. dir. Engrs. Joint Council, N.Y.C., 1965—, Am. Assn. Engring. Socs., 1979—; mem. exec. com., treas. U.S. Nat. Com. World Energy Conf. Pub.: Engr. mag, 1965-70, Who's Who in Engring. Del. internat. energy and engring. confs.; mem. Exec. Res. Office of Pres., 1965—; affiliate rep. to UN (non-govtl. orgns.); pres. Commuters Action Com., Fairfield County, 1972-73; bd. dirs. CDS. Mem. Am. Soc. Engring. Edn., AIAA, Soaring Soc. Am., AAAS, Internat. Soc. Tech. Assessment, Am. Soc. Assn. Execs. Clubs: Union League, Engrs. (N.Y.C.). Home: 19 Harding Ln Westport CT 06880 Office: Am Assn Engring Socs 345 E 47th St New York NY 10017

FREY, CHRISTIAN MILLER, research center exec.; b. Cumberland, Md., Feb. 26, 1923; s. Christian Miller and Frances Rebecca (Jenkins) F.; m. Betty Ruth Hixson, Jan. 30, 1943; children—Christian Richard, David Lynn. B.S. in Mech. Engring, U. Md., 1951. Supr. advanced design Allegany Ballistics Lab., Hercules, Inc., Cumberland, Md., 1951-59; mgr. research dept. United Technologies Corp., Sunnyvale, Calif., 1959—; vis. lectr. Stanford U. Served with USAAF, 1943-47. Home: 1890 Newcastle Dr Los Altos CA 94022 Office: 1050 E Arques Ave Sunnyvale CA 94088

FREY, DAVID GARDNER, banker; b. Grand Rapids, Mich., Jan. 12, 1942; s. Edward J. and Frances (Taliaferro) F.; m. Judith G. Campbell Spindle, May 20, 1978; children: David Gardner, Campbell Woodward; stepchildren: William K. Spindle, Robert K. Spindle, David K. Spindle, Jennifer L. Spindle. B.A., U. N.C., 1964, J.D., 1967. Pres., chief exec. officer, dir. Union Bank & Trust Co., Grand Rapids, 1982—; pres., dir. Union Bancorp, Grand Rapids, 1982—; dir. Foremost Corp., Grand Rapids. Trustee Aquinas Coll., Grand Rapids, Kendall Sch. Design, Grand Rapids; bd. dirs. United Way, Kent County. Served to lt. (j.g.) USNR, 1967-71. Republican. Episcopalian. Clubs: Peninsular (pres., dir.); Kent Country (Grand Rapids); Indian (Irons, Mich.); River (N.Y.C.). Home: 2011 San Lu Rae SE Grand Rapids MI 49506 Office: Union Bank and Trust Co NA 200 Ottawa NW Grand Rapids MI 49503

FREY, DONALD NELSON, manufacturing company executive, engr.; b. St. Louis, Mar. 13, 1923; s. Muir Luken and Margaret Bryden (Nelson) F.; m. Mary Elizabeth Glynn, June 30, 1971; children by previous marriage, Donald Nelson, Judith Kingsley, Margaret Bente, Catherine, Christopher, Elizabeth. Student, Mich. State Coll., 1940-42; B.S., U. Mich., 1947, M.S., 1949, Ph.D., 1950, D.Sc. (hon.), 1965, U. Mo., Rolla, 1966. Instr. metall. engring. U. Mich., 1949-50, asst. prof. chem. and metall. engring., 1950-51; research engr. Babcock & Wilcox Tube Co., Beaver Falls, Pa., 1951; various research positions Ford Motor Co., 1951-57, various engring. positions, 1958-61, product planning mgr., 1961-62, asst. gen. mgr., 1962-65, gen. mgr., 1965-68, co. v.p., 1965-67, v.p. for product devel., 1967-68; pres. Gen. Cable Corp., N.Y.C., 1968-71; chmn. bd. Bell & Howell Co., Chgo., 1971—, pres., 1973-81; dir. Clark Equipment Co., Cin. Milicron, Spring Mills. Mem. devel. council U. Mich., 1963—; bd. dirs. Lyric Opera, Chgo. Served with AUS, 1943-46. Named young engr. of year Engring. Soc. Detroit, 1953; recipient Russell Springer award Soc. Automotive Engrs., 1956; named outstanding alumni Coll. Engring., U. Mich., 1957; outstanding young man of the year Detroit Jr. Bd. Commerce, 1958. Mem. Am. Inst. Mining Metall. and Petroleum Engrs. (chmn. Detroit 1954, chmn., editor Nat Symposium on Sheet Steels 1956), Am. Soc. Metals, Nat. Acad. Engring. (mem. council 1972), ASME, Soc. Automotive Engrs. (vice chmn. Detroit 1958), Detroit Engring. Soc. (dir. 1962—), Elec. Mfrs. Club, Council on Fgn. Relations, Sigma Xi, Phi Kappa Phi, Tau Beta Pi, Phi Delta Theta. Clubs: Chicago, Saddle and Cycle, Tavern (Chgo.); Ocean, Little (Gulfstream, Fla.). Home: 1500 Lake Shore Dr Chicago IL 60610 also 6767 N Ocean Blvd Ocean Ridge FL 33435 Office: 7100 McCormick Rd Chicago IL 60645

FREY, EDWARD JOHN, banker; b. Grand Rapids, Mich., July 3, 1910; s. John Edward and Stella (Reeves) F.; m. Frances Taliaferro, Nov. 7, 1936; children—Mary Caroline, John Monroe, David Gardner, Edward John. A.B., U. Mich., 1932; grad., Rutgers U. Grad. Sch. Banking, 1940; Litt.D. (hon.), Grand Valley State Coll., 1968, LL.D., Olivet (Mich.) Coll., 1974. Former pres., chmn. bd. Union Bank and Trust Co., N.A., Grand Rapids; now dir.; chmn. bd., dir. Foremost Corp. Am., Foremost Ins. Co., Grand Rapids; pres. Gt. Lakes Fin. Corp., Grand Rapids; past mem. faculty Rutgers U. Grad. Sch. Banking; past mem. Downtown Devel. Com., Grand Rapids. Bd. dirs. United Community Services of Grand Rapids and Kent County; chmn. bd. trustees Grand Rapids Found.; trustee Little Traverse Hosp.; trustee, chmn. fin. com. Grand Valley Coll., Grand Rapids. Served to lt. comdr. USNR, 1943-46; PTO. Recipient Sesquicentennial Alumni award U. Mich., 1967. Mem. Am. Bankers Assn. (state legis. com.), Mich. Bankers Assn. (exec. council), U.S. (taxation and fin. com.), Mich. (past v.p. and dir.), Grand Rapids (dir., past pres.) chambers commerce.). Episcopalian (vestryman, sr. warden). Clubs: Rotary (past pres.), Peninsular (past pres.), Kent Country (Grand Rapids); River (N.Y.C.); Kinne Creek (Baldwin, Mich.). Home: 180 Greenwich Rd NE Grand Rapids MI 49506 Office: 200 Ottawa Ave NW Grand Rapids MI 49503

FREY, FREDERICK WARD, political science educator; b. Cleve., June 16, 1929; s. Frederick H. W. and Helen (Simpson) F.; m. Patricia Ann Evans, Dec. 16, 1967 (div. May 1975); children: Ethan, Justin; m. Cecile Remick, Oct. 30, 1977. Student, Ohio Wesleyan U., 1946-47; A.B. summa cum laude, Western Res. U., 1951, Balliol Coll., Oxford (Eng.) U., 1953; Ph.D., Princeton U., 1962. Mem. faculty Mass. Inst. Tech., 1960-74, prof. polit. sci., 1966-74, sr. staff mem. Center Internat. Studies, 1960-74, dir. Behavioral Research Service, 1967-74; prof. polit. sci. U. Pa., Phila., 1974—, chmn. grad. program internat. relations, dir. Anspach Inst., 1974-80; Fellow Center for Advanced Study in Behavioral Scis., Stanford, Calif., 1971-72; treas. Am. Research Inst. in Turkey, 1978—. Author: The Turkish Political Elite, 1965; editor: Survey Research on Comparative Social Change, 1969, Handbook of Communication, 1973; contr. articles to profl. jours. Served with AUS, 1953-55. Mem. Am. Polit. Sci. Assn. (Pi Sigma Alpha award), Sociol. Assn., Assn. Pub. Opinion Research, Middle East Inst., Phi Beta Kappa (jr.), Phi Kappa Psi. Home: 537 Conshohocken State Rd Gladwyne PA 19035

FREY, GERARD LOUIS, bishop; b. New Orleans, May 10, 1914; s. Andrew and Marie Therese (DeRose) F. D.D., St. Joseph's Sem. at St. Benedict"s La., 1933; student, Notre Dame Sem., New Orleans. Ordained priest Roman Catholic Ch., 1938; asst. pastor, Taft, La., 1938-46, asst. dir., also asst., New Olreans, 1946, dir., Archdiocese New Orleans, 1946-67, also in residence, 1946-54; founding pastor (St. Frances Cabrini Ch.), New Orleans, 1952-63, pastor, Houma, La., 1963-67; clergy rep. 2d Vatican Council, 1964; dir. Diocesan Friendship Corps, New Orleans, 1966; bishop of Savannah, Ga., 1967-72, bishop of Lafayette, La., 1972—; Episcopal moderator Theresians Am., 1968—. Recipient Bishop Tracy Vocation award St. Joseph's Sem. Alumni Assn., 1959. Address: PO Drawer 3387 Lafayette LA 70502 *

FREY, GLENN, songwriter, vocalist, guitarist; b. Detroit, Nov. 6, 1948. Performed with, Bo Diddely and Linda Ronstadt; founding mem. mus. group, Longbranch Penny Whistle, mus. group the, Eagles; songs include Take it Easy; albums Eagles, Desperado, On the Border, One of These Nights, Hotel California (Grammy award for album of yr. 1977), The Long Run; founding mem. (Co-recipient Grammy award for Lyin' Eyes 1975, for New Kid in Town 1977). Office: care Front Line Mgmt 8380 Melrose Ave Suite 307 Los Angeles CA 90069 *

FREY, JAMES MCKNIGHT, government official; b. Mattoon, Ill., Dec. 7, 1932; s. Raymond Matthew and Virginia Laurel (McKnight) F.; m. Jean Meyer, June 18, 1954 (div. 1977); children—Katherine Marie Frey Glenn, Nancy Elizabeth Frey Longo; m. Nancy E. Hitt, Apr. 28, 1978. A.B., Harvard U., 1954, M.B.A., 1956. With Bur. of Budget, 1954-62, 65-70, mgmt. analyst internat. programs, 1960-62, dir. internat. programs div., 1970-75; asst. to spl. asst. to Pres. U.S.; also staff mem. Nat. Security Council, 1962-64; spl. asst. for policy coordination to asst. sec. state inter-Am. affairs, also policy planning officer Bur. Inter-Am. Affairs, State Dept., 1964-65, chief internat. programs div., 1970-75; asst. dir. for legis. reference U.S. Office Mgmt. and Budget, Washington, 1975—; Mem. President's Task Force Govt. Reorgn., 1964. Club: Harvard (Washington). Home: 8106 Inverness Ridge Rd Potomac MD 20854 Office: New Exec Office Bldg Room 7202 Office Mgmt and Budget Washington DC 20503

FREY, KENNETH JOHN, plant breeder; b. Mich., Mar. 23, 1923; s. John Walter and Alfrieda (Meyers) F.; m. Ann Dunlap, May 5, 1945; children: Teryl, Karen, Kevin. B.S., Mich. State U., 1944, M.S., 1945; Ph.D., Iowa State U., 1948. Asst. prof. field crops Mich. State U., 1948-53; asso. prof., prof. agronomy Iowa State U., Ames, 1953—, asso. dean, acting v.p. research, dean, 1967-71, C.F. Curtiss disting. prof. agr., 1970—. Editor: Plant Breeding, 1966, 80, Plant Breeding II, 1981, Plant Improvement and Somatic Cell Genetics, 1982. Fulbright fellow, Australia and Yugoslavia, 1968, 77. Fellow Am. Soc. Agronomy (pres. 1983), AAAS, Iowa Acad. Sci.; mem. Crop Sci. Soc. Am. (pres. 1980), AAAS. Office: Agronomy Dept Iowa State U Ames IA 50011

FREY, RICHARD LINCOLN, author, editor; b. N.Y.C., Feb. 12, 1905; s. Louis Joseph and Bessie Alice (Butzel) F.; m. Mabel Amy Planco, July 10, 1935; children: Steven Lewis (dec.), Stephanie Constance. Extension student, Columbia U. With Fed. Advt. Agy., 1921-25; v.p., account exec. Herald Advt. Agy., N.Y.C., 1925-27; advt. mgr. for clothing mfrs., 1928-34; propr. Triangle Bridge Club, 1933-34; nat. sales mgr. Kem Playing Cards; also asso. editor Bridge World mag., 1935-37; pres. Morehead, Frey & Whitman Advt., N.Y.C., 1938-39; freelance author, 1940-60; editor, pub. relations dir. Am. Contract Bridge League, 1959-70; editor-in-chief Ofcl. Ency. Bridge, 1964—; pres. Internat. Bridge Press Assn., 1969-80, chmn., 1980—. Author: According to Hoyle, How to Win at Contract Bridge in 10 Easy Lessons; chmn.: Goren Editorial Bd, 1970—. Named Leading Am. Bridge Player, 1934, Life Master, 1936. Mem. Am. Soc. Journalists and Authors. World championship chief bridge commentator, 1960-70. Home: 235 E 87th St New York NY 10028 Office: Goren Internat 110 E 42d St New York NY 10017

FREY, STUART MACKLIN, automobile manufacturing company executive; b. Peoria, Ill., Feb. 13, 1925; s. Muir Luken and Margaret Bryden (Nelson) F.; m. Lillian Maxine Paxton, 1951; children: Mellissa June, Muir Paxton. B.S. in Mech. Engring, U. Mich., 1949; S.M. in Indsl. Mgmt, Mass. Inst. Tech., 1961. With Budd Co., 1949-53; with Ford Motor Co., 1953—, chief car research engr., Dearborn, Mich., 1974-75, chief vehicle engr., 1975-80, v.p. car engring., 1980-83, v.p. car product devel., 1983—. Contbr. articles to profl. jours. Served as officer AUS, 1943-46, 51-52. Sloan fellow, 1960-61. Fellow Soc. Automotive Engrs., Engring. Soc. Detroit; mem. Am. Soc. Body Engrs., Tau Beta Pi, Pi Tau Sigma. Republican. Home: 3790 N Darlington St Birmingham MI 48010 Office: 17101 Rotunda Dr Dearborn MI 48121 *The key ingredient that has contributed most importantly to my success has been the understanding and employment of the principles of employee involvement and participative management.*

FREY, THOMAS LEE, agrl. economist, educator; b. Carthage, Ill., Oct. 31, 1936; s. Thomas R. and Dorothy B. (Harter) F.; m. Beverly A. Harrison, June 9, 1957; children—Stephen, David. Student, Western Ill. U., 1954-56; B.S., U. Ill., 1958, M.S., 1959, Ph.D., 1970. C.P.A., Ill.; accredited rural appraiser. Fieldman, Blackhawk Prodn. Credit Assn., Freeport, Ill., 1959-61; mgr. Fed. Land Bank Assn., Woodstock, Ill., 1961-67; asst. prof. farm mgmt. and agrl. fin. U. Nebr., 1970-73, asso. prof., 1973-79; prof. agrl. fin. U. Ill., Urbana, 1979—; agrl. specialist (on spl. leave) Arthur Andersen & Co., 1981-82; lectr. in field. Co-author: Coordinated Financial Statements for agriculture, 2d edit, 1980, Lending to Agricultural Enterprises, 1981, Farmland, 1981. Recipient Ensminger-Interstate Outstanding Teaching award Nat. Assn. Colls. and Tchrs. of Agr., 1978; disting. undergrad. teaching award Am. Agrl. Econs. Assn., 1978; Campus award for excellence in undergrad. teaching U. Ill., 1979; Darl A. Snyder award Men of Farmhouse, Ill. chpt., 1980; Pau. A. Funk award Coll. Agr. U. Ill., 1981; NDEA fellow, 1967-70; 2d Discipline fellow U. Ill., 1976-77. Mem. Am. Agrl. Econs. Assn., Nat. Assn. colls. and Tchrs. Agr., Am. Inst. C.P.A.'s, Ill. C.P.A. Soc., Am. Soc. Farm Mgrs. and Rural Appraisers, Ill. Soc. Profl. Farm Mgrs. and Rural Appraisers, Inst. Cert. Fin. Planners. Republican. Methodist. Office: 305 Mumford Hall 1301 W Gregory St U Ill Urbana IL 61801

FREY, WILLIAM CARL, bishop; b. Waco, Tex., Feb. 26, 1930; s. Harry Frederick and Ethel (Oliver) F.; m. Barbara Louise Martin, June 12, 1952; children: Paul, Mark, Matthew, Peter, Susannah. B.A., U. Colo., 1952; Th.M., Phila. Div. Sch., 1955, D.D. (hon.), 1970. Ordained to ministry Episcopal Ch.; vicar Timberline Circuit (Colo.) Missions, 1955-58; rector Trinity-on-the-Hill Ch., Los Alamos, 1958-62; missionary priest Episcopal Ch., Costa Rica, 1962-67, bishop, 1967, Diocese of Guatemala, 1967-72; chaplain U. Ark., Fayetteville, 1972; bishop Diocese of Colo., Denver, 1972—. Contbr. articles to religious mags. Office: PO Box M Capitol Hill Sta Denver CO 80218 *

FREYD, PETER JOHN, educator; b. Evanston, Ill., Feb. 5, 1936; s. Paul Robert and Pauline Margaret (Pattinson) F.; m. Pamela Parker, Jan. 1, 1957; children—Jennifer Joy, Gwendolyn Ann. A.B. magna cum laude, Brown U., 1958; M.A. (Woodrow Wilson fellow), Princeton, 1959, Ph.D., 1960. J.F. Ritt instr. math. Columbia U., N.Y.C., 1960-62; faculty U. Pa., Phila., 1962—, prof. math., 1968—; Adviser Pahlavi U., Shiraz, Iran, 1968; lectr. Canadian Nat. Research Seminar, 1974; vis. researcher U. Mex., 1975; vis. prof. U. Chgo., 1980, U. Louvain, Belgium, 1981. Author: Abelian Categories, 1964; Founder: Jour. Pure and Applied Algebra, 1970. Fulbright scholar, Australia, 1971; fellow St. John's Coll., Cambridge (Eng.) U., 1980-81. Mem. Phi Beta Kappa, Sigma Xi. Home: 2020 1 2 Addison St Philadelphia PA 19146

FREYMUTH, G. RUSSELL, hotel official; b. St. Charles, Mo., Sept. 30, 1928; s. Aloys Anthony and Catherine Elizabeth (Ross) F.; m. Dolores Ilene Wetter, Nov. 26, 1955; children: Lawrence, Terence, Christopher, Joseph, Marie, Timothy, Francis, Robert, Katherine, Stephan. Grad., Blair Bus. Coll., Colorado Springs, Colo., 1948. Gen. mgr. Broadmoor Hotel, Inc. and v.p. Broadmoor Mgmt. Co., Colorado Springs, 1975-83, v.p., 1983—. Exec. bd. dirs., chmn. Colorado Springs Better Bus. Bur.; bd. dirs. Colorado Springs Conv. and Visitors Bur. Mem. Colo.-Wyo. Hotel and Motel Assn. (dir.), Colorado Springs C. of C. (dir.), Pikes Peak Amateur Radio Assn., Am. Radio Relay League., Am. Hotel and Motel Assn. Club: Broadmoor Golf. Office: Broadmoor Hotel Colorado Springs CO 80901

FREYTAG, DONALD ASHE, management consultant; b. Chgo., Apr. 17, 1937; s. Elmer W. and Mary Louise (Mayo) F.; m. Elizabeth R. Robertson, Dec. 19, 1964; children: Donald C., Gavin K., Alexander M. B.A., Yale U., 1959; M.B.A., Harvard U., 1963. Pres. Mgmt. West, LaJolla, Calif., 1963-65; mktg. asst. Norton Simon, Inc., Fullerton, Calif., 1965-67; product mgr. Warner Lambert, Morris Plains, N.J., 1967-70; mgr., dir. advt. Pepsi Cola Co., Purchase, N.Y., 1970-72; with Beverage Mgmt. Inc., Columbus, Ohio, 1972-80, pres., 1976-79, vice chmn., 1979-80; prin. Freytag Mgmt. Co., Columbus, Ohio, 1980-82; pres. G. D. Ritzy's, Inc., Columbus, Ohio, 1982—; dir. Vision Service Plan, Inc., Cryosystems, Inc. Bd. dirs. Central Ohio Center for Econ. Edn., 1978—, pres., 1978-80, 81—; mem. exec. com. Ohio Council Econ. Edn., 1980-82; bd. dirs. Columbus Acad., 1982—. Served with AUS, 1959-61. Office: 1535 Bethel Rd Columbus OH 43220

FRI, ROBERT WHEELER, energy corporation executive; b. Kansas City, Kans., Nov. 16, 1935; s. Homer O. and Cora Ruth (Wheeler) F.; m. Jean Landon, Jan. 16, 1965; children—Perry, Sean, Kirk. B.A., Rice U., 1957; M.B.A., Harvard U., 1959. Assoc. McKinsey & Co., Washington, 1963-68, prin., 1968-71, 73-75; dep. adminstr. EPA, Washington, 1971-73, acting adminstr., 1973; dep. adminstr. ERDA, Washington, 1975-77, acting adminstr., 1977; head U.S. delegation to IAEA, 1977; pres. Energy Transition Corp., 1978—; dir. Transco Cos. Inc., Eberstadt Energy Resources Fund; mem. energy com. Aspen Inst., 1978—; lectr. Georgetown U., 1961-62. Mem. President's Commn. on Personnel Interchange, 1971-79. Trustee Scientists Inst. for Pub. Info. Served to lt. USNR, 1959-62. Baker scholar. Mem. Phi Beta Kappa, Sigma Xi. Republican. Presbyterian (pres. bd. trustees, clk. session). Home: 6001 Overlea Rd Bethesda MD 20816

FRIBOURGH, JAMES HENRY, university official; b. Sioux City, Iowa, June 10, 1926; s. Johan Gunder and Edith Katherine (James) F.; m. Cairdenia Minge, Jan. 29, 1955; children: Cynthia Kaye, Rebecca Jo, Abbie Lynn. Student, Morningside Coll., 1944-47; B.A., U. Iowa, 1949, M.A., 1949, Ph.D., 1957. Instr. Little Rock Jr. Coll., 1949-56; assoc. prof. biology Little Rock U., 1957-60, prov., chmn. div. life scis., 1960-69; vice chancellor U. Ark.-Little Rock, 1969-72, interim chancellor, 1972-73, exec. vice chancellor for acad. affairs, 1973-82, interim chancellor, exec. vice chancellor for acad. affairs, 1982, provost, exec. vice chancellor, 1983—; cons. in field. Contbr. articles to profl. jours. Mem. Ark. Gov.'s Com. on Sci. and Tech., 1969-71; bd. dirs., mem. nat. adv. bd. Nat. Back Found., 1979; vice chmn. NCCJ, 1981-82; div. rep. United Way of Pulaski County, 1980-82; bd. dirs. Ark. Dance Theatre, Little Rock, 1980-82; vestryman Good Shepherd Episcopal Ch., Little Rock; del. Episcopal Diocese of Ark. NSF fellow Hist. of Sci. Inst., 1959-60. Fellow AAAS, Am. Inst. Fishery Research

Biologists; mem. Am. Fisheries Soc. (chmn. com. on internationalism, cert. fisheries scientist), AAUP (pres. Ark. conf., Electron Microscopy Soc. Am.); mem. Am. Soc. Swedish Engrs. (corr. mem.), Ark. Acad. Sci. (pres. 1966), Ark. Dean's Assn. (pres. 1982), Am. Assn. State Colls. and Univs., Am. Swedish Inst., Sigma Xi, Phi Kappa Phi. Democrat. Clubs: Swedish (Chgo.); Vasa Order Am. Lodge: Rotary. Office: U Ark 33d and University Ave Little Rock AR 72204 *University life is an exciting and rewarding challenge. The inception and testing of ideas is essential to the proper role of a university. To fulfill this function, the university must be more than a place; it must be a way of life. I aspire to be part of that life.*

FRICANO, TOM SALVATORE, artist; b. Chgo., Oct. 28, 1930; s. Carmelo and Rose (Aiello) F.; m. Judith Holzheimer, Dec. 17, 1960; children: Fiama Marie, Alesia Marie. B.F.A., Bradley U., 1953; M.F.A., U. Ill., 1956; postgrad. (Fulbright scholar), U. Italiana per Stranieri, Perugia and Belle Arte, Florence, Italy. Instr. art U. Ill., 1955, Bradley U., 1958-63; faculty Calif. State U., Northridge, 1963—; now prof. art; vis. artist or artist in residence Chouinard Art Inst., Los Angeles, 1964, Ohio State U., 1969, U. Utah, Salt Lake City, 1971, Cranbrook Acad. Art, Bloomfield Hils, Mich., 1971, U. Mont., Bozeman, 1972, Sch. Art Inst. Chgo., 1975, Drake U., Des Moines, 1977, U. N.D., Grand Forks, 1980, U. Tex., Austin, 1982. One-man shows include, U. Ill., 1963, 64, Kans. State U., Manhattan, 1964, Ohio State U., 1969, Utah Mus. Fine Art, Salt Lake City, 1971, U. Mont., Tex. Technol. U., Lubbock, 1972, Lakeview Art Center, Peoria, Ill., 1973, Comsky Gallery, Los Angeles, 1975, Davidson Galleries, Seattle, 1976, Drake U., 1977, Fresno (Calif.) State U. Gallery, 1978, Pepperdine U., Malibu, Calif., 1979, U. N.D., 1980, Okla. Art Ctr., Oklahoma City, 1983, group shows include, Nat. Mus., Korea, Oakland Mus. Art, 1970, De Young Mus., San Francisco, Springfield (Mo.) Art Mus., 1976, Laguna Beach (Calif.) Mus. Art, Calif. State U., Northridge, Library of Congress, Washington, 1977, Mus. Assn. N. Orange County, Fullerton, Calif., Springfield (Ill.) Art Assn., Print Club, Phila., 1980, Lillian Heidenberg Gallery, N.Y.C., 1981, Los Angeles County Mus. Art; group shows include, UCLA, 1982, U. Dallas, 1981-83, Wesleyan Coll., Macon, Ga., 1983, Korean Cultural and Art Found., Seoul. Active art therapy programs for handicapped, aged, child guidance groups, others.; mem. adv. bd. Los Angeles Ctr. on Arts and Aging, 1982—. Served with AUS, 1956-58. Recipient awards in group shows for art works; Louis Comfort Tiffany grantee, 1965; Calif. State U. research grantee, 1968, 69, 71, 74, 78, 79; John Simon Guggenheim Meml. fellow, 1969-70. Mem. Los Angeles Printmaking Soc. (hon. life), Am. Color Print Soc., Boston Printmakers. Democrat. Roman Catholic. Home: 9820 Aldea Ave Northridge CA 91325

FRICK, IVAN EUGENE, college president; b. New Providence, Pa., May 19, 1928; s. Charles George and Lillie Jane (Miller) F.; m. Ruth Hudson, July 16, 1950; children: David Alan, Daniel Eugene, Susan Marie. A.B., Findlay (Ohio) Coll., 1949; B.D., Lancaster Theol. Sem., 1952; S.T.M., Oberlin Coll., 1955; Ph.D., Columbia, 1959; L.H.D. (hon.), Findlay Coll., 1976. Mem. faculty Findlay Coll., 1953-71, asst. to pres., 1963-64, pres., 1964-71, Elmhurst (Ill.) Coll., 1971—; vice chmn. Fedn. Independent Ill. Colls. and Univs., 1979-81, chmn., 1981. Bd. dirs. United Community Fund Findlay, 1965-71, Lizzadro Mus. Lapidary Art, Elmhurst, Elmhurst YMCA.; mem. non-pub. adv. com. Ill. Bd. Higher Edn. Danforth Found. fellow, 1959; recipient Distinguished Alumnus award Findlay Coll., 1964, Outstanding Young Man award Jr. C. of C., 1964, U.S. Jr. C. of C., 1964. Mem. Am. Philos. Assn., Am. Mgmt. Assn. (President's Assn.), Am. Acad. Religion, Econ. Club Chgo. Clubs: Oak Brook Exec., Breakfast. Home: 360 Cottage Hill Elmhurst IL 60126 *Mentors have played a significant role in my life; these mentors have been teachers, older friends, father figures and administrative colleagues. They have supported, challenged and stimulated me and sometimes they have presented an opposite view or role model against which I have reacted. In all, they have helped me immeasurably.*

FRICK, JOSEPH FRANCIS, naval officer; b. Corning, N.Y., Sept. 14, 1930; s. Joseph Aloysius and Kathleen Veronica F.; m. Marjorie Ruth Weeden, June 7, 1953; 1 dau., Leslee Jo. B.S., U.S. Naval Acad., 1953; postgrad., U.S. Naval Postgrad. Sch., 1960-62, George Washington U., 1965-66. Commd. ensign U.S. Navy, 1953, advanced through grades to rear adm., 1979; air wing comdr. (U.S.S. Enterprise), 1972-73, comdg. officer, 1973-75, 1975-77; chief of staff, comdr. Naval Air Force, U.S. Pacific Fleet, 1977-78; asst. chief of staff for logistics, comdr.-in-chief Allied Forces, So. Europe, 1978-80; comdr. Naval Base, Norfolk, Va., 1980—; tchr., chmn. chemistry com. U.S. Naval Acad., 1965-66. Decorated Silver Star, Legion of Merit with Combat V, D.F.C., Bronze Star, Navy Commendation medal. Mem. Phi Gamma Delta. Republican. Roman Catholic. Home: 1941 Sandee Crescent Virginia Beach VA 23454 Office: Com navbase Norfolk VA 23511

FRICK, OSCAR LIONEL, physician, educator; b. N.Y.C., Mar. 12, 1923; s. Oscar and Elizabeth (Ringger) F.; m. Mary Hubbard, Sept. 2, 1954. A.B., Cornell U., 1944, M.D., 1946; M.Med. Sci., U. Pa., 1960; Ph.D., Stanford U., 1964. Diplomate: Am. Bd. Allergy and Immunology (chmn. 1967-72). Intern Babies Hosp., Columbia Coll. Physicians and Surgeons, N.Y.C., 1946-47; resident Children's Hosp., Buffalo, 1950-51; pvt. practice medicine specializing in pediatrics, Huntington, N.Y., 1951-58; fellow in allergy and immunology Royal Victoria Hosp., Montreal, Que., Can., 1958-59; fellow in allergy U. Calif., San Francisco, 1959-60, asst. prof. pediatrics, 1964-67, asso. prof., 1967-72, prof., 1972—, dir. allergy tng. program, 1964—; fellow immunology Inst. d'Immunobiologie, Hosp. Broussais, Paris, France, 1960-62. Contbr. articles papers to profl. publs. Served with M.C. USNR, 1947-49. Mem. Am. Assn. Immunologists, Am. Acad. Pediatrics (chmn. allergy sect. 1971-72, Bret Ratner award 1982), Am. Acad. Allergy (exec. com. 1972—, pres. 1977-78), Internat. Assn. Allergologists (exec. com. 1970-73), Am. Pediatric Soc. Club: Masons. Home: 370 Parnassus Ave San Francisco CA 94117

FRICK, SIDNEY WANNING, lawyer; b. Cynwyd, Pa., July 19, 1915; s. Benjamin Otis and Harriet Downs (Wanning) F.; m. Marie P. Strickler, Jan. 7, 1956 (dec. Mar. 8, 1972); 1 son, Benjamin Charles. M.E., Cornell U., 1937; LL.B., U. Pa., 1940. Bar: Pa. bar 1941. Asso. firm Wintersteen & Williams, Phila., 1940-41; engr. Bendix Radio div. Bendix Corp., Towson, Md., 1941-43; head dept. contracts adminstrn., gen. counsel Kellett Aircraft Corp., Upper Darby, Pa., 1943-45; asso. firm Evans, Bayard & Frick, Phila., 1945-51; individual practice law, Phila., 1951-74, Haverford, Pa., 1974—; dir. Farrel Corp., Ansonia, Conn., 1954-68. Trustee Barnes Found., Merion, Pa., 1957—, pres., 1967—. Mem. Phila., Pa., Am. bar assns., Juristic Soc. Phila., ASME, Mil. Order of Loyal Legion, Beta Theta Pi. Republican. Presbyterian. Clubs: Philadelphia Country (Gladwyne, Pa.); Phila. Skating. Home: 608 Manor Rd Penn Valley Narberth PA 19072 Office: 355-C Lancaster Ave Haverford PA 19041

FRICKE, ARTHUR LEE, chemical engineering educator, researcher, consultant; b. Huntington, W. Va., Mar. 6, 1934; s. Arthur Henry and Anne Agnes (Turley) F.; m. Alice Faye Saunders, Mar. 14, 1954; children: Alice, Marsha, Arthur. B. Chem. Engring., U. Cin., 1957; M.S., U. Wis., 1959, Ph.D., 1962. Registered profl. engr., Va. Various indsl. positions Shell Co., 1961-67; asst. prof. Va. Poly. Inst., Blacksburg, 1967-76, assoc. prof., 1967-76; chmn. chem. engring. U. Maine, Orono, 1976-81, research prof., 1981—; vis. scientist Procter & Gamble Co., Cin., 1981-82. Inventor; patentee. Named Disting. Alumnus U. Cin., 1981. Mem. Am. Inst. Chem. Engrs., Am. Chem. Soc., Soc. Plastics Engrs., TAPPI, Paper Industry Mgmt. Assn., Phi Lambda Upsilon, Tau Beta Pi, Sigma Xi. Home: 11 Edgewood Dr Orono ME 04473 Office: Jenness Hall U Maine Orono ME 04473

FRICKE, HERBERT H(ENRY), chemical company executive, lawyer; b. Englewood, N.J., Sept. 25, 1939; s. Arthur and Anna (Sewtz) F.; m. Christa-Renate Schmidt, May 30, 1965; children: Christopher, Michael. B.S., Syracuse U., 1961; J.D., N.Y. Law Sch., 1964. Bar: N.J. 1965, U.S. Dist. Ct. N.J. 1965. Trial atty. Liberty Mut. Ins. Co., East Orange, N.J., 1968-70; gen. counsel Hoechst-Uhde Corp., Englewood Cliffs, N.J., 1970-73; atty. Am. Hoechst Corp., Somerville, N.J., 1973-75, sr. atty., asst. sec., 1975-77, corp. sec., 1977—; dir. Messer Griesheim Industries, Inc., Valley Forge, Pa., Sigri Corp., Somerville, Esmond Enterprises, Inc. Served to capt. U.S. Army, 1964-67; Germany, Vietnam. Mem. Bergen County Bar Assn., N.J. Bar Assn., ABA, Sigma Phi Epsilon (controller 1960-61), Phi Delta Phi. Republican. Lutheran. Office: Am Hoechst Corp 1041 Route 202-206 N Somerville NJ 08876

FRICKE, HOWARD RUDOLPH, ins. co. exec.; b. Ill., Feb. 15, 1936; s. Rudolph H. and Etta (Roegge) F.; m. Sharon Linton, Aug. 30, 1959; children—Karen, Steven, David. B.S., Ill. Wesleyan U., 1960. With depts. planning and underwriting Franklin Life Ins. Co., Springfield, Ill., 1960-63; sr. v.p. Horace Mann Educators Corp., Springfield, 1963-76; chmn. bd. Am. Health and Life Ins. Co., Balt., Am. Health and Life Ins. Co. N.Y., 1976—; sr. v.p. Comml. Credit Co., Balt., 1979—; chmn. bd. Gulf Ins. Group, 1979—; bd. dirs. Ill. Dept. Bus. and Econ. Devel., 1972-74. Chmn. Ill. Bicentennial Commn., 1974-76, Ill. Capital City Planning Commn., 1974-76. Served with U.S. Army, 1954-56. Recipient Pub. Service award State of Ill., 1974. Mem. Nat. Assn. Life Underwriters, Pres's. Assn., Am. Council Life Ins., Health Ins. Assn. Am. Lutheran. Home: 12850 Stone Eagle Rd Phoenix MD 21131 Office: 300 Saint Paul Pl Baltimore MD 21202

FRICKE, RICHARD IRVIN, ins. co. exec.; b. Buffalo, Mar. 25, 1922; s. Richard F. and Julia S. (Cooper) F.; m. Jeanne Hines, July 22, 1943 (dec.); children—Richard J., Diane L., Kathryn J. David R.; m. Ruth Byerly Tinker, March 26, 1967; children—Mark C., Michael A., Jodie P., John H. A.B., Cornell U., 1943, J.D. with distinction, 1947; grad., Advanced Mgmt. Program, Harvard U., 1965. Bar: N.Y. bar 1947. Asso. atty. Kenefick, Cooke, Mitchell, Bass & Letchworth, Buffalo, 1947-52; asst. prof., then asso. prof. law Cornell U. Law Sch., 1952-57; asso. counsel Ford Motor Co., 1957-62; v.p. gen counsel Mut. Life Ins. Co. N.Y., 1962-67, sr. v.p., 1967-69, exec. v.p., 1969-72, chmn. bd., 1972-76; vice chmn. bd. Nat. Life Vt., 1976-77, pres., chief exec. officer, 1977—; chmn. bd. Sentinel Group Funds, Inc.; dir. Monsanto Co., Equity Services, Inc.; Mem. speakers bur. Buffalo Council World Affairs, 1952; cons. N.Y. State Law Revision Commn., 1952-57; Mem. adv. council Cornell Law Sch., Cornell U. Council. Editor: Law quarterly, Cornell U., 1946-47. Dir. Laymen's Nat. Bible Com., Inc.; trustee Champlain Coll. Served with field arty. AUS and; Served with field arty. USAAF, 1943-45. Fellow Am. Bar Found.; mem. Am., Vt., N.Y., bar assns., Cornell Law Assn. (pres. 1965-67), Order of Coif, Am. Judicature Soc., Phi Kappa Phi, Phi Delta Phi. Clubs: University (N.Y.C.); Burlington Country, Ethan Allen. Office: Nat Life Dr Montpelier VT

FRICKER, PETER RACINE, composer, educator; b. London, Eng., Sept. 5, 1920; came to U.S., 1964; s. Edward Racine and Deborah (Parr) F.; m. Helen Clench, Apr. 17, 1943. Student, Royal Coll. Music, London, 1937-41; Mus.D. (hon.), U. Leeds, Eng., 1958. Dir. music Morley Coll., London, 1953-64; prof. music Royal Coll. Music, London, 1956-64; prof. music dept. U. Calif. at Santa Barbara, 1964—; condr., lectr., 1948—. Served to flight lt. RAF, 1941-46. Decorated Order of Merit, West Germany, 1965; recipient Freedom City, London, 1962. Fellow Royal Coll. Organists, asso. Royal Coll. Music; mem. Composer's Guild Gt. Britain (chmn. 1955), Royal Philharmonic Soc. London, Soc. Promotion New Music, Am. Music Center, Am. Guild Organists, AAUP, Am. Soc. Univ. Composers, Royal Acad. Music (hon.). Compositions include 5 symphonies, oratorio, 2 violin concertos, piano concerto, horn concerto, viola concerto, organ concerto, chamber music, music for piano and 2 pianos, also vocal, guitar and organ music, music for films and radio. Home: 5423 Throne Ct Santa Barbara CA 93111 Office: Music Dept U California Santa Barbara CA 93106

FRICKS, WILLIAM PEAVY, shipbuilding company executive; b. Byron, Ga., Aug. 14, 1944; s. Walker Nathaniel and Mary (Peavy) F.; m. Deanie Dudley, Aug. 27, 1966; children: Holly Anne, William Peavy, Austin Nathaniel. B.S. in Indsl. Mgmt, Auburn (Ala.) U., 1966; M.B.A. in Fin, Coll. William and Mary, Williamsburg, Va., 1970. With Newport News Shipbldg. and Dry Dock Co., Va., 1966—, adminstrv. asst. to pres., then controller and treas., 1979-80, v.p. fin., 1980-83, v.p. tech., 1983—. Bd. dirs. Christopher Newport Coll. Ednl. Found., 1982—. Mem. Va. C. of C. (bd. dirs. 1983), Navy League U.S. Office: 4101 Washington Ave Newport News VA 23607

FRIDAY, JOHN ERNEST, JR., securities company executive; b. Pitts., Oct. 24, 1929; s. John Ernest and Jane Nixon (Herron) F.; m. Judith Ann Favret, July 31, 1982; children—John Ernest III, Andrew Hansen, Richard Fuller, Elizabeth Herron. B.A., Trinity Coll., 1951; postgrad., N.Y. U., 1954. Sr. asso. Morgan Stanley & Co., N.Y.C., 1953-67; v.p., dir. Drexel Harriman Ripley, Inc., N.Y.C., 1967-73; mng. dir., co-head corporate fin. Drexel Burnham Lambert Inc., N.Y.C., 1973—. Served with USMCR, 1951-53. Mem. Bond Club N.Y., Phi Beta Kappa, Psi Upsilon. Clubs: Recess, Pine Valley Golf, Round Hill. Home: 37 Midwood Dr Greenwich CT 06830 Office: 60 Broad St New York NY 10004

FRIDAY, NANCY, author; b. Pitts., Aug. 27, 1937; d. Walter and Jane Colbert F.; m. W.H. Manville, Oct. 20, 1967. Student, Wellesley Coll. Reporter, San Juan Island Times, 1960-61; editor Islands in the Sun, 1961-63. Author: My Secret Garden, 1973; Forbidden Flowers, 1975, My Mother, My Self, 1977, Men in Love: Men's Sexual Fantasies, 1980. Office: care Simon and Schuster Inc 1230 Ave of Americas New York NY 10020 *

FRIDAY, WILLIAM CLYDE, university president; b. Raphine, Va., July 13, 1920; s. David L. and Mary E. (Rowan) F.; m. Ida Howell, May 13, 1942; children: Frances H., Mary H., Ida E. Student, Wake Forest Coll., 1937, LL.D., 1957; B.S., N.C. State Coll., 1941; LL.B., U. N.C., 1948; LL.D., Belmont Abbey Coll., 1957, Duke U., 1958, Princeton U., 1958, Elon Coll., 1959, Davidson Coll., 1961, U. Ky., 1970, Mercer U., 1977; D.C.L., U. of South, 1976. Bar: N.C. 1948. Asst. dean student U. N.C., 1948-51, asst. to pres., 1951-55, sec. of univ., 1955-56, acting pres., 1956, pres., 1956—; Mem. Am. Bd. Med. Spltys., 1975—; mem. Carnegie Commn. on Higher Edn., Commn. to Study SUNY, So. Regional Edn. Bd.; chmn. President's Task Force on Edn., 1966-67; mem. Commn. White House Fellows, 1965-68. Bd. visitors Davidson Coll.; mem. Citizen Involvement Network, 1975—, Nat. Com. for Bicentennial Era.; Trustee Howard U., 1975—. Served as lt. USNR, World War II. Mem. Assn. Am. Univs. (pres. 1971). Democrat. Baptist. Office: PO Box 2688 Univ NC Chapel Hill NC 27514

FRIDE, EDWARD THEODORE, lawyer; b. Duluth, Minn., Jan. 8, 1927; s. Edward T. and Lina (Wick) F.; m. Patricia Ann; children: Edward O., Nancy E., Mark R., Timothy S., Scott D., Gail E., William A. A.A., Duluth Jr. Coll., 1947; B.S. in Law, U. Minn., 1949, J.D., 1951. Bar: Minn. 1951, diplomate: Am. Bd. Trial Advocates. Pres. Hanft, Fride, O'Brien & Harries (P.A.), Duluth; pres. Arco Bldg. Corp.; dir. First Bank Duluth, Minn. and Man. R.R. Co., Mid-Continent Warehouse Co., Andresen-Ryan Coffee Co.; instr. bus. law U. Minn., 1951-53, now lectr. Vice pres. Duluth Bd. Edn., 1964-68; pres. Duluth Rehab. Center, 1958-60. Served with U.S. Mcht. Marine, 1944-46; Served with USNR, 1944-46. Fellow Internat. Soc. Barristers, Am. Coll. Trial Lawyers, Internat. Acad. Trial Lawyers; mem. Duluth, Minn., Am. bar assns., Nat. Assn. Rd. Trial Counsel, Internat. Assn. Ins. Counsel, Maritime Law Assn. U.S., Fedn. Ins. Counsel. Office: 1200 Alworth Bldg Duluth MN 55802

FRIDLEY, RUSSELL WILLIAM, historian; b. Oelwein, Iowa, Mar. 21, 1928; s. Lloyd and Laura (Tift) F.; m. Metta Holtkamp, Feb. 26, 1954; children—Scott, Nancy, Jane, Susan, Elizabeth, Jennifer. B.A., Grinnell Coll., 1950; M.A., Columbia U., 1953; Litt.D. (hon.), Concordia Coll., Moorhead, Minn., 1980. Asst. dir. Minn. Hist. Soc., St. Paul, 1953-54, dir., 1954—; v.p. Grinnell (Iowa) Coll., 1966; vice chmn. Nat. Adv. Council on Hist. Preservation, 1967-70; dir. Div. Edn. and Pub. Programs, Nat. Endowment for Humanities, 1968-69; chmn. Minn. Humanities Com., 1970—. Author: Minnesota: A State That Works. Mem. Nat. Museum Act Adv. Council, 1976-79; mem. council Hubert H. Humphrey Inst. Public Affairs, U. Minn., 1978—; trustee James J. Hill Reference Library, St. Paul, 1980—, Charles A. Lindbergh Fund, N.Y.C., 1981—. Served with U.S. Army, 1946-48; PTO. Mem. Am. Assn. Museums (dir. 1969-72), Am. Assn. State and Local History (pres. 1966-68), Nat. Conf. State Hist. Pres. Officers (v.p. 1977-79). Home: 740 Amber Dr Saint Paul MN 55112 Office: 690 Cedar St Saint Paul MN 55101

FRIDOVICH, IRWIN, biochemistry educator; b. N.Y.C., Aug. 2, 1929; s. Louis and Sylvia (Appelbaum) F.; m. Mollie Finkel; children: Sharon E., Judith L. B.S., CCNY, 1951; postgrad., Cornell U. Med. Coll., 1951-52; Ph.D., Duke U., 1955; hon. doctorate, U. Rene Descartes, Paris, 1980. Instr. biochemistry Duke U., Durham, N.C., 1956-58, assoc., 1958—; vis. research assoc. Harvard U., Cambridge, Mass., 1961-62; asst. prof. biochemistry Duke U., 1961-66, assoc. prof., 1966-71, prof., 1971-76, James B. Duke prof., 1976—; mem. study sect. Am. Cancer Soc., mem. adv. com. biochemistry and chem. carcinogenesis. Editorial bd.: Jour. Biol. Chemistry; contbr. articles to sci. jours. Recipient Founders' award Chem. Industry Inst. Toxicology, 1980, Herty award Ga. sect. Am. Chem. Soc., 1980, Research Career Devel. award NIH, 1959-69. Mem. Nat. Acad. Scis., Am. Acad. Arts and Scis., Am. Soc. Biol. Chemists (pres. 1982), N.C. Acad. Scis., Phi Beta Kappa, Sigma Xi. Home: 3517 Courtland Dr Durham NC 27707 Office: Duke U Med Center Durham NC 27710

FRIED, ALBERT, JR., investment banker; b. N.Y.C., Mar. 19, 1930; s. Albert and Rose (Frank) F.; m. Sigrid Walther, Sept. 13, 1964; 1 dau., Christina Elaine. B.A., Cornell U., 1952, M.B.A., 1953. Mng. partner Albert Fried & Co., N.Y.C., 1955—; Guest lectr. Grad. Sch. Bus. and Pub. Adminstrn., Cornell U. Active Police Res. Assn.; Bd. dirs. Tabor Acad.; pres. N.Y.'s Finest Found., Found. for Environ. Edn. Inc., Fried Found. Inc.; bd. dirs. Charles A. Lindbergh Fund. Served with USAF, 1953-55. Mem. Confrerie des Chevaliers du Tastevin, Thoroughbred Owners and Breeders Assn., Am. Horse Council. Clubs: Explorers (dir., 1st v.p.), Adventurers (dir.), N.Y. Stock Exchange Luncheon, Statler, Wine and Food Soc. Home: 420 E 54th St New York NY 10022 Office: 77 Water St New York NY 10005

FRIED, BURTON DAVID, physicist, educator; b. Chgo., Dec. 14, 1925; s. Albert O. and Bertha (Rosenthal) F.; m. Sally Rachel Goldstein, Aug. 17, 1947; children—Joel Ethan, Jeremy Steven. B.S., Ill. Inst. Tech., 1947; M.S., U. Chgo., 1950, Ph.D., 1952. Instr. physics Ill. Inst. Tech., 1947-52; research physicist Lawrence Berkeley Lab. of U. Calif., 1952-54; sr. staff physicist TRW Systems, Los Angeles, 1954—; dir. research lab. (Ramo-Wooldridge Computer Div.), Los Angeles, 1961-63; prof. physics U. Calif. at Los Angeles, 1963—. Served with USNR, 1944-46. Fellow Am. Phys. Soc. (chmn. plasma physics div. 1978-79); mem. Sigma Xi. Research and publs. on theoretical elementary particle and plasma physics. Home: 1119 Las Pulgas Pl Pacific Palisades CA 90272 Office: Physics Dept U Calif at Los Angeles 405 Hilgard St Los Angeles CA 90024

FRIED, BURTON THEODORE, lawyer; b. N.Y.C., Feb. 26, 1940; s. Meyer S. and Minnie (Grossberg) F.; m. Gail K. Fried, July 25, 1964; children: Marsha, Howard, Shari. B.S., NYU, 1961; LL.B., Bklyn. Law Sch., 1964. Bar: N.Y. 1964, U.S. Dist. Ct. (ea. and so. dists.) N.Y. 1971. Assoc. atty. H. Bermack, N.Y.C., 1964-66, I. Towbis, 1966-68; gen. counsel Medispas, Inc., N.Y.C., 1968-72; real estate counsel Michael Industries, Inc., N.Y.C., 1972-74, exec. v.p., gen. counsel and sec., 1974—, Lehigh Valley Industries, Inc., 1982—; dir. Culinary Co., Inc., Casserole of Ala., Inc. Vice chmn. sch. bd. Forest Hills Jewish Ctr. Religious Sch., Forest Hills, N.Y., 1983—. Lodge: K.P. (Chancellor comdr. 1972-73). Office: Lehigh Valley Industries Inc 200 E 42d St New York NY 10017

FRIED, CHARLES, lawyer, educator; b. Prague, Czechoslovakia, Apr. 15, 1935; came to U.S., 1941, naturalized, 1948; s. Anthony and Marta (Wintersteinova) F.; m. Anne Sumerscale, June 13, 1959; children: Gregory, Antonia. A.B., Princeton U., 1956; B.A. Juris, Oxford (Eng.) U., 1958, M.A., 1961; LL.B., Columbia U., 1960. Bar: D.C., Mass. Law clk. to asso. justice John M. Harlan, U.S. Supreme Ct., 1960; mem. faculty Harvard Law Sch., 1961—, prof. law, 1965—, Carter prof. gen. jurisprudence, 1981—; asso. reporter model code prearraignment procedure Am. Law Inst., 1965—; spl. cons. Treasury Dept., 1961-62; cons. White House Office Policy Devel., 1982, Dept. Transp., 1981-82, Dept. Justice, 1983. Author: An Anatomy of Values, 1970, Medical Experimentation: Personal Integrity and Social Policy, 1974, Right and Wrong, 1978, Contract as Promise: A Theory of Contractual Obligation, 1981; contbr. legal and philos. jours. Trustee Commonwealth Sch., Boston; bd. dirs. Boston Philharm. Orch.; mem. Lawyers for Ford, 1976, Reagan Task Force on Regulatory Reform, 1980. Guggenheim fellow, 1971-72. Mem. Nat. Acad. Scis., Inst. Medicine, Am. Soc. Polit. and Legal Philosophy, Phi Beta Kappa. Republican. Office: Harvard Law Sch Cambridge MA 02138

FRIED, CHARLES A., business executive, accountant; b. N.Y.C., Jan. 31, 1945; s. Jerome M. and Florence (Silverman) F.; m. Denise Helaine Krafte, Sept. 2, 1965; children: Marc Steven, Shari Lynne. B.S. in Acctg, Queens Coll., CUNY, 1965. Staff acct. Klein Hinds & Finke (C.P.A.'s), N.Y.C., 1965-67, sr. acct., 1967-69, Alexander Grant & Co., N.Y.C., 1969-70, supr., 1970-71, mgr., 1972-73; treas. Raybestos-Manhattan, Inc., Trumbull, Conn., 1974-79, v.p., 1979-80; pres. Creative Output, Inc., Milford, Conn., 1980—; instr. acctg. L.I. U., 1973, Fairfield U., 1977-81. Rep., dist. fin. chmn. Fairfield Republican Town Com., 1975-79; campaign worker United Way, 1976-77, United Jewish Way, 1976-78; v.p. exec. com. Conn. affiliate Am. Diabetes Assn., 1976—; founder, v.p. Greater Bridgeport chpt. Am. Diabetes Assn., 1977—; dir., v.p., treas. Parents and Friends of Retarded Citizens, 1975—; chmn. adv. council Fairfield U. Bus. Bur. Mem. Am. Inst. C.P.A.'s, N.Y. State Soc. C.P.A.'s, Conn. Soc. C.P.A.'s, Nat. Assn. Accts., Risk Ins. Mgrs. Soc., Conn. Bus. and

Industry Asbestos Info. Assn. Jewish. Club: Probus (dir., various offices local chpt.; nat. asst. treas. 1974—). Home: 140 Canterbury Ln Fairfield CT 06430 Office: 60 Commerce Park Milford CT 06460

FRIED, EDWARD R., govt. ofcl.; b. N.Y.C., Apr. 13, 1918. B.A., U. Mich., 1941. Economist, then chief div. research (Far East) Dept. State, 1946-54; chief econ. sect. and dep. prin. officer U.S. consulate, Hong Kong, 1955-60, counselor for econ. affairs Am. embassy, The Hague, 1960-62; mem. policy planning council Dept. State, Washington, 1962-65; exec. sec. President's Commn. on U.S. Trade Relations with Eastern European Countries and Soviet Union, 1964-65; dep. asst. sec. for econ. affairs Dept. State, 1965-67; sr. staff mem. NSC, 1967-69; exec. dir. President's Task Force on Internat. Devel., 1969-70; sr. fellow Brookings Instn., Washington, 1969-77, 80—; U.S. exec. dir. IBRD, Washington, 1977-79; cons. on internat. energy to White House, 1979-80; sr. fellow Brookings Instn., Washington, 1980—. Served in USAF, 1943-45. Office: 1775 Massachusetts Ave NW Washington DC 20036

FRIED, HERBERT DANIEL, advertising executive; b. Chgo., May 27, 1928; s. Herbert D. and Beatrice (Frank) F.; m. Ninon Connart, Mar. 7, 1953; children: Bruce M., William F. Student, U. N.Mex., 1946-48, U. Ill., 1948. Account exec. Foote, Cone & Belding, Chgo., 1948-54, Weiss & Geller, 1954-55; account exec., gen. mgr. W.B. Doner & Co., Balt., 1955-56, v.p., 1956-68, pres., 1968-73, chmn. bd., chief exec. officer, 1973—. Div. chmn. Community Chest-ARC-United Appeal, 1964, United Fund, 1977; dir. communication div. United Way, 1978-79; trustee Md. Inst. Coll. Art; bd. dirs. Sinai Hosp., Balt., Greater Balt. Com., Balt. Zool. Soc. Served with USNR, 1946. Recipient award Chgo. Federated Advt. Club, 1959. Mem. Am. Assn. Advt. Agencies (bd. govs. Chesapeake council 1960, regional dir. 1963), Advt. Club Balt., Kappa Sigma. Clubs: Center (Balt.); Suburban of Baltimore County (Pikesville, Md.). Home: 2414 Velvet Valley Way Owings Mills MD 21117 Office: 2305 N Charles St Baltimore MD 21218

FRIED, JOHN, chemist; b. Leipzig, Germany, Oct. 7, 1929; s. Abraham and Frieda F.; m. Heléne Gellen, June 29, 1955; children—David, Linda, Deborah. A.B., Cornell U., 1951, Ph.D., 1955. Steroid chemist, research asso. Merck and Co., Rahway, N.J., 1956-64; with Syntex Research, Palo Alto, Calif., 1964—, dir. inst. organic chemistry, 1967-74, exec. v.p., 1974-76, pres., 1976—; sr. v.p. Syntex Corp., 1981—. Mem. Am. Chem. Soc., Chem. Soc. (London). Office: Syntex Research 3401 Hillview Ave Palo Alto CA 94304

FRIED, JOSEF, chemist, educator; b. Przemysl, Poland, July 21, 1914; came to U.S., 1938, naturalized, 1944; s. Abraham and Frieda (Fried) F.; m. Erna Werner, Sept. 18, 1939; 1 dau., Carol Frances. Student, U. Leipzig, 1934-37, U. Zurich, 1937-38; Ph.D., Columbia U., 1941. Eli Lilly fellow Columbia U., 1941-43; research chemist Givaudan, N.Y., 1943; head dept. antibiotics and steroids Squibb Inst. Med. Research, New Brunswick, N.J., 1944-59, dir. sect. organic chemistry, 1959-63; prof. chemistry, biochemistry and Ben May Lab. Cancer Research, U. Chgo., 1963—, Louis Block prof., 1973—, chmn. dept. chemistry, 1977-79; mem. med. chem. study sect. NIH, 1963-67, 68-72, chmn., 1971; mem. com. arrangements Laurentian Hormone Conf., 1964-71; Knapp Meml. lectr. U. Wis., 1958. Mem. bd. editors: Jour. Organic Chemistry, 1964-69, Steroids, 1966—, Jour. Biol. Chemistry, 1975-81, 83—; contbr. articles to profl. jours. Recipient N.J. Patent award, 1968. Fellow AAAS, N.Y. Acad. Scis.; mem. Am. Chem. Soc. (award in medicinal chemistry 1974), Nat. Acad. Scis., Am. Acad. Arts and Scis., Am. Soc. Biol. Chemists, Swiss Chem. Socs., Brit. Chem. Socs., Sigma Xi. Patentee in field. Home: 5715 S Kenwood Ave Chicago IL 60637

FRIED, MELVIN, biochemist, educator; b. Bklyn., May 28, 1924; s. Max and Ethel (Baral) F.; m. Betty Rosemond Payne, June 7, 1947; children—Michael Gregory, Mark Robert, Myles Andrew. Student, Coll. City N.Y., 1940-42; B.S., U. Fla., 1948, M.S., 1949; Ph.D., Yale, 1952. Postdoctoral fellow Cambridge U., Eng., 1952-53; instr. Med. Sch. Washington U., St. Louis, 1953-56; asst. prof. U. Fla. Coll. Medicine, 1956-64, asso. prof., 1964-67, prof., 1967—, asst. dean for grad. edn., 1972-81; vis. research prof. Faculte des Sciences, Marseille, France, 1968-69; vis. scientist Bermuda Biol. Sta., 1963, 65. Contbr. articles to profl. jours. Chmn. City of Gainesville Capital Outlay Com., 1972-75; mem. City Plan Bd., 1977—, chmn., 1978-79. Served with AUS, 1942-46. AEC fellow, 1950-52; Jane Coffin Childs postdoctoral fellow, 1952-53; USPHS research career devel. award, 1957-62; spl. postdoctoral fellow NIH, 1967-68; U. Fla. faculty devel. award, 1968-69. Mem. Am. Soc. Biol. Chemists, Biochem. Soc. London, Am. Chem. Soc., Soc. Exptl. Biology and Medicine, Sigma Xi, Underwater Soc. Am. Home: 3205 SW 5th Ct Gainesville FL 32601

FRIED, MICHAEL, theatrical director, producer; b. N.Y.C., Apr. 25, 1948; s. Milton and Philoine (Hillman) F. Student, U. Vienna, 1966, CUNY, 1967-69, U. Tubingen, W.Ger., 1969-70. Co-founder Roundabout Theatre Co., N.Y.C., 1965, producing dir., 1965—; panelist First Am. Congress of Theatre, Princeton U., 1974. Producer: (theatrical prodns.) King Lear, 1968, Trumpets and Drum (Am. premiere), 1969, Hamlet, 1970, Uncle Vanya, The Master Builder, 1971, Conditions of Agreement (N.Y. premiere), Right You Are. . ., 1972, The Play's The Thing, Ghosts, The Father, 1973, The Seagull, The Circle, The Burnt Flowerbread (N.Y. premiere), All My Sons, 1974, The Rivals, 1975, James Joyce's Dublin (world premiere), What Every woman Knows, Summer and Smoke, 1975, The World of Sholom Aleichem, The Philanderer, The Rehearsal, 1976, John Gabriel Borkman, Endgame, Dear Liar, Naked, 1977, Othello, The promise, The Showoff, Pins and Needles, Streetsongs, Candida, 1978, Awake and Sing, Little Eyolf, Family Business, Diversions and Delights, The Dark at the Top of the Stairs, A Month in the Country, 1979, Blooknot, Heartbreak House, Look Back in Anger, The Winslow Boy, 1980, Inadmissable Evidence, Hedda Gabler, A Taste of Honey, Misalliance, 1981, The Caretaker, 1982, The Browning Version, The Chalk Garden, The Learned Ladies, The Fox; author: (with Gene Feist) James Joyce's Dublin, 1975; dir.: Alexei Arbuzoh's The Promise, 1978. Mem. Mayor's Com. for Pub. Interest, N.Y.C., 1974-77, Concerned Citizens for the Arts, Advocates for the Arts. Recipient Mayor's Cert. Appreciation, N.Y.C., 1975. Mem. League of N.Y. Theatres and Producers, Theatre Communications Groups, League of Resident Theatres, Am. Arts Alliance. Home: 351 W 24th St New York NY 10001

FRIED, WALTER JAY, lawyer; b. N.Y.C., May 27, 1904; s. Joseph and Flora V. (Shamberg) F.; m. Louise E. Goldman, June 8, 1934; 1 son, Michael W.; m. Brita Digby-Brown, July 8, 1948. B.A. magna cum laude, Harvard, 1924; LL.B., Columbia U., 1928. Bar: N.Y. 1929, D.C. 1966. Practiced in, N.Y.C., 1929—; former mem. firm, now counsel Fried, Frank, Harris, Shriver & Jacobson; mem. faculty Bklyn. Law Sch., 1931-39; dir. Salant Corp. Chmn. bd. dirs. Am. Chess Found.; hon. trustee Guild Hall, East Hampton, N.Y., chmn., 1974-78; trustee Southampton Hosp. Served to maj. AUS, 1942-45. Decorated Legion of Merit. Mem. Assn. Harvard Chemists, Phi Beta Kappa. Clubs: Maidstone, Harvard, Manhattan Chess (N.Y.C.) (hon. dir.). Home: 14 E 75th St New York NY 10021 also Lily Pond Ln East Hampton NY 11937 Office: 1 New York Plaza New York NY 10004

FRIEDAN, BETTY, author, feminist leader; b. Peoria, Ill., Feb. 4, 1921; d. Harry and Miriam (Horwitz) Goldstein; m. Carl Friedan, June 1947 (div. May 1969); children—Daniel, Jonathan, Emily. B.A. summa cum laude, Smith Coll., 1942, L.H.D., 1975. Research fellow U. Calif. at Berkeley, 1943; lectr. feminism univs., women's groups, bus. and profl. groups in, U.S. and Europe; founder N.O.W., 1st pres., 1966-70, chairwoman adv. com., 1970-72; Organizer Nat. Women's Polit. Caucas, 1971, Internat. Feminist Congress, 1973, First Women's Bank, 1973, Econ. Think Tank for Women, 1974; v.p. Nat. Assn. Repeal Abortion Laws, 1970-73; Vis. prof. sociology Temple U., 1972, Queens Coll., 1975; vis. lectr., fellow Yale, 1974. Author: The Feminine Mystique, 1963, It Changed My Life: Writings on the Women's Movement, 1976; contbg. editor: McCall's mag, 1971—; contbr.: Atlantic Monthly. Mem. N.Y. County Democratic Com. Mem. P.E.N., Soc. Mag. Writers, Assn. Humanistic Psychology, Am. Sociology Assn., Phi Beta Kappa. Address: 31 W 93d St New York NY 10025 *

FRIEDBERG, ARTHUR LEROY, educator, ceramic engr.; b. River Forest, Ill., Mar. 25, 1919; s. Oscar and Fannie (Blumenthal) F.; m. Marian Davis, Feb. 4, 1944; children—Richard Charles, Anne. B.S. in Ceramic Engring, U. Ill., 1941, M.S., 1947, Ph.D., 1952; postgrad., U. Chgo., 1943-44. Mem. faculty U. Ill., Champaign-Urbana, 1946-79, prof. ceramic engring., 1957-79, prof. emeritus, 1979—, head dept., 1963-79; adj. prof. ceramic engring. Ohio State U., 1979—. Trustee Edward Orton, Jr. Ceramic Found., 1979—. Served to lt. (s.g.) USNR, 1943-46. Mem. Am. Ceramic Soc. (exec. dir. 1979—), Nat. Inst. Ceramic Engrs. (exec. dir. 1979—). Home: 1375 Kingsgate Rd Columbus OH 43221

FRIEDBERG, M. PAUL, landscape architect; b. Bklyn., Oct. 11, 1931; s. Morris and Mary (Bennett) F.; m. Esther louise Hidary, Jan. 21, 1962; children: Mark, Alan Jeffry. B.S. in Landscape Architecture, Cornell U., 1954; LL.D., Ball State U., 1983. Landscape architect with Arthur Hoffman, Hartford, Conn., 1954, Joseph Gangemi, N.Y.C., 1954, 56-58; propr. M. Paul Friedberg and Assocs., landscape architects, N.Y.C., 1960—; vis. critic, lectr. U. Pa., 1967; vis. cirtic, lectr. Syracuse U., 1967, Carnegie Inst. Tech., 1967; vis. critic. lectr. Harvard U., 1966; vis. critic, lectr. 1st Fed. Design Assembly, Washington, 1973, others; mem. faculty Pratt Inst., Columbia U.; mem. New Sch. for Social Research; head urban landscape archtl. program CCNY, 1971—; bd. dirs. Internat. Design Conf., Aspen, Colo., chmn., 1976. Prin. works include, Carver House Plaza, N.Y.C., 1964, Riis Houses Plaza, N.Y.C., 1966, Buchanan Sch., Washington Pub. Sch. 166, N.Y.C., prin. workds include, Bklyn. Bedford-Stuyvesant Superblock, Harlem River Bronx State Park, 1972, prin. works include, Jeannette Plaza, N.Y.C.; landscape architect, Spanish Pavillion, N.Y. World's Fair, 1965, Winter Garden, Niagara Falls, N.Y., 1978, State Street Mall and Concourse, Madison, Wis., 1980, Pershing Park, Washington, 1981, Ft. Worth Cultural Dist., 1983. Del. White House Conf. Natural Beauty, 1965, N.Y. State Conf. Natural Beauty, 1966, Urban Am Conf., 1966. Recipient awards Am. Assn. Nurserymen, 1964, 71, 74, 77, 79, 81, 82, Albert S. Bard award, 1965, 67, honor award (2) HUD, 1966, award citation AIA, 1969, honor award, 1967, award Nat. Landscape Assn., 1971, AIA, 1972, N.Y.C. award for excellence, 1973, I.D.E.A. Downtown Achievement award, 1979, 1st ann. award N.Y.C. Art Commn., 1983. Fellow Am. Soc. Landscape Architects (past v.p., honor awards 1965, 68, 70, 74, Merit awards 1965, 67, 68, 69, 73, 74, 75, 82, v.p.); mem. Assn. N.Y.C., N.Y. Mcpl. Arts Soc. (dir., bronze plaque and merit award 1967, award for Policy Plaza 1974), N.Y.C. Council for Parks and Recreation (Art award 1967), Archtl. League. Home: 16 W 88th St New York NY 10024 Office: M Paul Friedberg & Ptnrs 36 W 62d St New York NY 10023

FRIEDBERG, MAURICE, educator; b. Rzeszow, Poland, Dec. 3, 1929; came to U.S., 1948, naturalized, 1954; s. Isaac and Ida (Jam) F.; m. Barbara Bisguier, Mar. 18, 1956; children—Rachel Miriam, Edna Sarah. B.S., Bklyn. Coll., 1951; A.M., Columbia U., 1953, Ph.D., 1958; certificate, Russian Inst., 1953. Lectr. Russian Bklyn. Coll., 1952, Middlebury Coll., 1960-61; asso. Russian Research Center, Harvard U., 1953; asso. prof. charge Russian div. Hunter Coll., N.Y.C., 1955-65; prof. Slavic langs. and lits. Ind. U., 1966-75, dir., 1967-71; prof. Russian lit. U. Ill., Urbana-Champaign, 1975—, head dept. Slavic langs. and lit., 1975—; Vis. asst. prof. Russian lit. Columbia U., 1961-62; lectr. Russian lit. N.Y. U., 1965; Fulbright vis. prof. Russian lit. Hebrew U., Jerusalem, 1965-66; cons. Russian lit. and Soviet affairs to pub., radio; former bd. dirs., mem. program com. Internat. Research and Exchanges Bd.; juror Nat. Book Award, 1973. Author: Russian Classics in Soviet Jackets, 1962, The Party and the Poet in the USSR, 1963, A Bilingual Edition of Russian Short Stories, Vol. I, 1964, Vol. II, 1965, The Jew in Post-Stalin Soviet Literature, 1970 (also Portuguese edit), A Decade of Euphoria: Western Literature in Post-Stalin Russia, 1977; Editor: (Leon Trotsky): The Young Lenin, 1972; Deptl. editor: Ency. Judaica, 16 vols, 1971-72; Contbr. to scholarly jours. and popular mags. Guggenheim fellow, 1971, 81-82; fellow Center for Advanced Study, 1981. Mem. Polish Inst. Arts and Scis. in U.S. (corr.), Am. Assn. Advancement Slavic Studies (dir.), Am. Assn. Tchrs. Slavic Langs., Modern Lang. Assn. Jewish. Home: 3001 Meadowbrook Ct Champaign IL 61820

FRIEDBERG, SIDNEY MYER, leisure industry executive; b. Norfolk, Va., Aug. 8, 1907; s. Solomon and Jennie (Graff) F.; m. Charlton Gillet, Mar. 7, 1983; 1 dau., Laura Friedberg Burrows. B.A., Johns Hopkins U., 1971; L.H.D., Western Md. Coll., 1983. With Fair Lanes, Inc. (and predecessor), Balt., 1926—, chmn. bd., chief exec. officer, 1958—; chmn. exec. com., dir. BTR Realty, Inc. Trustee Peabody Inst., Balt.; bd. dirs. Balt. Symphony Orch., Balt. Opera Co. Mem. Johns Hopkins U. Alumni Assn. Jewish. Clubs: Va. Mil. Inst. Alumni, Johns Hopkins, Center, Suburban. Office: 1112 N Rolling Rd Baltimore MD 21228

FRIEDBERG, SIMEON ADLOW, physicist, educator; b. Pitts., July 7, 1925; s. Emanuel B. and Lillian (Adlow) F.; m. Joan Brest, Sept. 4, 1950; children: Elizabeth B., Aaron L., Susan A. A.B., Harvard, 1947; M.S., Carnegie Inst. Tech., 1948, D.Sc., 1951. Fulbright grantee U. Leiden, Netherlands, 1951-52; research physicist Carnegie Inst. Tech., Pitts., 1952-53, mem. faculty, 1953-67, prof. physics, 1962-67, Carnegie-Mellon U., Pitts., 1967—, chmn. dept. physics, 1973-80. Contbr.: chpt. Methods of Experimental Physics, 1959. Westinghouse fellow, 1950-51; Alfred P. Sloan Found. research fellow, 1957-61; Guggenheim fellow Imperial Coll., London, Eng., 1965-66. Fellow Am. Phys. Soc., AAAS; mem. Sigma Xi, Tau Beta Pi, Phi Kappa Phi, Pi Mu Epsilon. Research, numerous publs. in low temperature solid state physics, thermal and magnetic properties of coupled spin systems, thermal and transport properties in certain metals, semi-conductors, insulators. Home: 1220 S Negley Ave Pittsburgh PA 15217

FRIEDBERG, THOMAS HAROLD, reinsurance brokerage company executive; b. N.Y.C., Aug. 25, 1939; s. Henry R. and Ursula J. (Cale) F.; m. Cynthia K. Thisius; children: Donald Henry, Sharon Elizabeth, Linda Lee. Student, Oberlin (Ohio) Coll., 1956-57, Western Res. U., 1959-61; M.B.A., U. Chgo., 1971. Asst. v.p. CNA Ins. Co., Chgo., 1961-71; v.p. worldwide automobile ins. ops. Am. Internat. Group, N.Y.C., 1971-74; pres., dir. Thurston F & C Ins. Co., Tulsa, 1974-75, Am. Inst. Mktg. Corp., Falls Church, Va., 1975-76; v.p. Hartford Ins. Group, Conn., 1976-79, sr. v.p., 1979-81, Reliance Ins. Cos., Phila., 1981-83; v.p. Intermediaries of Am., Inc., 1983—. Mem. Park Forest (Ill.) Recreation Bd., 1969, 71. Served with AUS, 1957-58. Recipient Disting. Service award Park Forest Jaycees, 1967. Mem. Am. Soc. Assn. Execs. Home: Box 200 Rural Route 4 Califon NJ 07830 Office: One World Trade Ctr Suite 8423 New York NY 10048

FRIEDE, ELEANOR KASK, editor, publisher; b. Rochester, N.Y., Nov. 12, 1920; d. John and Claire (Kassick) Kask; m. Donald Friede. B.A. cum laude, Hofstra U., 1942. Lic. pvt. pilot. Copywriter McGraw-Hill Book Co., 1942-46; asst. to pres. charge advt., promotion, publicity, editor mag. contingent books Funk & Wagnalls Co., 1946-51; with Pellegrini & Cudahy, 1951-52; in charge advt., publicity, promotion World Pub. Co., 1952-61; co-ordinator Internat P.E.N. Congress, N.Y.C., 1965-66; marketing dir. Macmillan Pub. Co., Inc., 1966-68, pub. dir. spl. projects dept., sr. editor trade dept., temporary publicity dir., part-time sr. editor, 1968-72; ind. editorial cons., 1972-73; ind. pub. Delacorte Press/Eleanor Friede, pres. Eleanor Friede, Inc., 1973-82; co-pub. aviation books Macmillan Pub. Co., 1982—. Mem. Ninety-Nines, Inc., PEN, Book Producers Assn. Home: 45 W 12th St New York NY 10011 also Office: Eleanor Friede Books 45 W 12th St New York NY 10011

FRIEDE, REINHARD LEOPOLD, neuropathologist, educator; b. Jaegerndorf, Czechoslovakia, May 12, 1926; emigrated to U.S., 1957, naturalized, 1962; s. Reinhard and Hilde (Rosner) F.; m. Editha R. Franzen, Dec. 22, 1953; children: Reinhard H., Gerd R. M.D., U. Vienna, 1951. Intern City Hosp., St. Poelten, Austria, 1951-52; resident dept. neurology U. Vienna, Austria, 1953, Clinic of Neurosurgery, Freiburg, Germany, 1953-57; mem. staff Aero. Med. Lab., Wright Air Devel. Center, Dayton, Ohio, 1957-59; faculty U. Mich., Ann Arbor, 1959-65; prof. neuropathology Case Western Res., 1965-75, U. Cleve., 1965-75, U. Zurich, Switzerland, 1975-80, U. Göttingen, Germany, 1981—. Author: A Histochemical Atlas of Tissue Oxidation in the Brain Stem of the Cat, 1961, Topographic Brain Chemistry, 1966, Developmental Neuropathology, 1975; contbr. numerous articles on histochemistry and neuropathology to med. jours. Mem. Am. Assn. Neuropathology. Home: 5754 Alte Uslarer Strasse 3414 Hardegsen Germany Office: Zentrum Neurologische Medizin Universität Göttingen Göttingen BRD Germany

FRIEDEBERG, PEDRO, painter, sculptor, designer; b. Florence, Italy, Jan. 11, 1937; s. Erwin and Gerda (Landsberg) F. Architecture degree, U. Iberomaericana, Mexico City, 1962. Exhibited in numerous one-man exhbns., including, Byron Gallery, N.Y.C., 1964, 66, 67, Souza Gallery, Mexico City, 1962, 64, 66, 68, Misrachi Gallery, Mexico City, 1970, 72, 74, Galerie Pecanins, Barcelona, 1976, Ft. Worth Art Center, 1979, Harcourts Gallery, San Francisco, 1980, Needleman Gallery, Chgo., 1981; exhibited in numerous group shows, including, Biennale of São Paulo, 1964, Biennale of Paris, Labyrinthe, Berlin, 1968, Museums of Modern Art, Toronto, Ottawa and Montreal, 1973-75, Biennales of San Juan, P.R., 1977-79, Bienal Coltejer, Medellin, Colombia, 1978; represented in numerous museums in, Am., Europe, Argentina, Israel, including, Mus. Contemporary Art, New Orleans, Worcester (Mass.) Art Mus., Brandeis U., Washington and Lee U., Toronto Sci. Mus., Museums of Contemporary Art of Jerusalem and Tel Aviv, Mus. of Modern Art of Mexico City, Mus. Modern Art, Bagdad, Iraq, Buenos Aires Mus. of Modern Art, Casa de las Americas, Havana, Cuba, Nat. Research Library, Ottawa, Library of Congress, Washington, others.; Art editor: Mexico This Month, 1960-64; subject of book: Pedro Friedeberg (Ida Rodríguez), 1972, Pedro Friedeberg (Alfonso de Neuvillate). Recipient 1st prize Biennale of Córdoba, Argentina, 1967; 2d prize Exposición Solar, Mex., 1968; 1st prize Biennale of San Juan, P.R., 1979; 2d prize Triennale of Buenos Aires, 1979. Mem. Foro de Arte Contemporáneo, Accademia Italia delle Arti de del Lavoro. Address: Apartado Postal 6-613 Mexico 6 DF Mexico Home: Recreo 48 San Miguel Allende Guanajuato Mexico

FRIEDEL, ROBERT OLIVER, physician; b. Corona, N.Y., Aug. 4, 1936; s. August W. and Denise G. (D'Aoust) F.; m. Susanne Weber, June 30, 1961; children—Christine, Scott, Karin, Linda. B.S., Duke U., 1958, M.D., 1964. Diplomate: Am. Bd. Psychiatry and Neurology. Intern Duke U. Med. Center, Durham, N.C., 1964-65, resident in psychiatry, 1967-70, asst. prof. psychiatry and pharmacology dept. psychiatry, 1970-73, asso. prof. psychiatry and asst. prof. pharmacology, 1973-74; asso. prof. psychiatry and pharmacology U. Wash. Sch. Medicine, Seattle, 1974-77, dir. div. psychopharmacology, 1974-77, vice chmn., dir. clin. services dept. psychiatry and behavioral scis., 1975-77; prof., chmn. dept. psychiatry Med. Coll. Va.-Va. Commonwealth U., Richmond, 1977—. Author: (with others) Behavioral Science: A Selective View, 1972; asso. editor: Jour. Clin. Psychiatry; mem. editorial bd.: Jour. Clin. Psychopharmacology; author articles and book chpts. Served to lt. comdr. USPHS, 1965-67. Fellow Am. Psychiat. Assn.; mem. Am. Psychopathological Assn., Soc. Biol. Psychiatry, Am. Soc. Pharmacology and Exptl. Therapeutics, Am. Fedn. Clin. Research, Am. Soc. Neurochemistry, AMA, Med. Soc. Va., Am. Coll. Neuropsychopharmacology, Alpha Omega Alpha. Home: 13722 Hickory Nut Point Midlothian VA 23113 Office: Dept Psychiatry Med Coll VA Box 710 1200 E Broad St Richmond VA 23298

FRIEDELL, GILBERT HUGO, pathologist, hospital administrators, educator; b. Mpls., Feb. 28, 1927; s. Aaron and Naomi (Kepman) F.; m. Janet Newell Nelson; children: Mark Lowry, Benjamin Newell, Anne, James Gilbert, Sarah Jane. Student, Harvard Coll., 1943-45; B.S., U. Minn., 1947, M.B., 1949, M.D., 1950. Diplomate: Am. Bd. Pathology. Intern Mpls. Gen. Hosp., 1949-50; resident in pathology Boston City Hosp., 1950; resident in Pathology Salem (Mass.) Hosp., 1955; resident in pathology Free Hosp. for Women, 1955, Pondville Hosp., 1955; pathologist Mass. Meml. Hosps., 1958-61, New Eng. Deaconess Hosp., 1967-69; chief pathology St. Vincent Hosp., Worcester, Mass., 1969-78, med. dir., 1978—; assoc.in pathology Boston U., 1958-65, assoc. prof. pathology, 1967-70; instr. Harvard U., 1962-67; prof. U. Mass., 1971—, acting chmn. dept. pathology, 1973; mem. breast cancer task force Nat. Cancer Inst., 1968-72, dir. nat. bladder cancer project, 1981—. Author: (with others) Carcinoma in Situ of the Uterine Cervix, 1960; contbr. numerous articles on cancer, cancer research and other pathologic-med. topics to sci. jours. Vice chmn. Mass. Com. on Medico-Legal Investigation, 1977—. Served with USNR, 1955-57. USPHS spl. research fellow, 1961-62; grantee Nat. Cancer Inst., Am. Cancer Soc. Mem. Mass. Soc. Pathologists (pres. 1975-76, exec. com. 1974-77), Am. Urol. Assn., new Eng. Cancer Soc. (exec. com. 1975-78), Worcester Dist. Med. Soc. (exec. com. 1980—), Mass. Med. Soc. (councillor 1980-81), Assn. Community Cancer Ctrs. (trustee 1978—). Club: Athenaeum (London). Home: 285 Salisbury St Worcester MA 01609 Office: 25 Winthrop St Worcester MA 01604

FRIEDEN, BERNARD JOEL, urban studies educator; b. N.Y.C., Aug. 11, 1930; s. George and Jean (Harris) F.; m. Elaine Leibowitz, Nov. 23, 1958; 1 dau., Deborah Susan. B.A., Cornell U., 1951; M.A., Pa. State U., 1953; M.C.P., Mass. Inst. Tech., 1957, Ph.D., 1962. Asst. prof. urban studies and planning Mass. Inst. Tech., 1961-65, assoc. prof., 1965-69, prof., 1969—; dir. Mass. Inst. Tech.-Harvard Joint Center for Urban Studies, 1971-75, mem. exec. com., 1975-82; cons. HUD, 1966-68, NIMH, 1968-70, HEW, 1968; staff Pres. Johnson's

Task Force Urban Problems, 1965; mem. Pres. Nixon's Task Force Urban Problems, 1968, White House Task Force Model Cities, 1969, Pres. Carter's Urban Policy Adv. Com., 1977-80. Author: The Future of Old Neighborhoods, 1964, Metropolitan America, 1966, (with Robert Morris) Urban Planning and Social Policy, 1968, (with William W. Nash) Shaping an Urban Future, 1969, (with Marshall Kaplan) The Politics of Neglect, 1975, 77, (with Wayne E. Anderson and Michael J. Murphy) Managing Human Services, 1977, The Environmental Protection Hustle, 1979; editor: Jour. Am. Inst. Planners, 1962-65; Contbr. to: The Metropolitan Enigma, 1970, Encyclopedia of Social Work, 1977, The Prospective City, 1980, Housing Urban America, 1980, Resolving the Housing Crisis, 1982. Bd. dirs. Citizens Housing and Planning Assn., 1966-75. Served with AUS, 1952-54. Research fellow Urban Land Inst., 1978—; Guggenheim fellow U. Calif., Berkeley, 1975-76. Mem. Am. Inst. Cert. Planners, Am. Planning Assn., Regional Sci. Assn., Ams. for Democratic Action. Jewish. Home: 245 Highland Ave West Newton MA 02165

FRIEDEN, CARL, educator, biochemist; b. New Rochelle, N.Y., Dec. 31, 1928; s. Alexander and Evelyn (Gutman) F.; m. Sari Ann Schneider, Dec. 20, 1953; children: Amy, Eric, Karen. B.A., Carleton Coll., 1951; Ph.D., U. Wis., 1955. Faculty dept. biochemistry Washington U., St. Louis, 1957—, prof. biol. chemistry, 1963—; chmn. St. Louis Biochemistry Group, 1961-62. Mem. editorial bd.: Jour. Biol. Chemistry, 1963-68, 75-80, Archives Biochemistry and Biophysics, 1973-79, Biochemistry, 1975-86. Mem. Am. Soc. Biol. Chemists, Am. Chem. Soc. (St. Louis award 1976), AAAS, Sigma Xi. Research, publs. on mechanism of enzyme action including correlation of protein structure to catalytic function; devel., application of kinetic theory with respect to enzymes; properties of actin. Home: 7452 Wellington Way Saint Louis MO 63105

FRIEDEN, EDWARD HIRSCH, biochemist, educator; b. Norfolk, Va., Jan. 4, 1918; s. Simon and Sarah (Bluestein) F.; m. Betty Barnett, June 29, 1941; children: Ray Allan, Jeanne E., Robert E., Roger S., Joyce S. A.B., UCLA, 1939, M.A., 1941, Ph.D., 1942. Joyce S. Lalor Found. fellow U. Tex., 1942-43, instr., research asso. Med. Sch., 1943-46; research fellow Harvard U., 1946-52; instr. Med. Sch. Harvard, 1948-52; faculty Tufts U. Med. Sch., 1952-64, asso. prof. biochemistry, 1962-64; research coordinator, dir. Rotch Lab., Boston Dispensary, 1957-64; prof. chemistry Kent (Ohio) State U., 1964—; research prof. molecular pathology Northeastern Ohio Univs. Coll. Medicine, 1980—; Biochem. cons. Hynson, Westcott & Dunning, Balt., 1950-70. Contbr. articles to profl. jours. Guggenheim fellow, 1953-54. Mem. Am. Chem. Soc., Am. Soc. Biol. Chemists, Endocrine Soc., Soc. Exptl. Biology and Medicine, N.Y. Acad. Sci., AAAS, Sigma Xi. Home: 359 Wilson Ave Kent OH 44240

FRIEDENBERG, EDGAR Z., teacher educator; b. N.Y.C., Mar. 18, 1921; s. Edgar M. and Arline (Zodiag) F. B.S., Centenary Coll., 1938; M.A., Stanford, 1939; Ph.D., U. Chgo., 1946. Instr., then asst. prof. U. Chgo., 1946-53; asst., then assoc. prof. Bklyn. Coll., 1953-64; prof. sociology U. Calif., Davis, 1964-67; prof. sociology and edn. SUNY at Buffalo, 1967-70; prof. edn. Dalhousie U., Halifax, N.S., Can., 1970—; R. Freeman Butts lectr. Am. Ednl. Studies Assn., 1978; Geo. M. Duck lectr. Faculty of Law, U. Windsor, 1979; Aquinas lectr. St. Thomas U., 1981; Weiner disting. visitor U. Man., 1982. Author: The Vanishing Adolescent, 1959, Coming of Age in America, 1965, The Dignity of Youth and Other Atavisms, 1965, R.D. Laing, 1973, The Disposal of Liberty and Other Industrial Wastes, 1975, Deference to Authority, 1980; Editor: The Anti-American Generation, 1971. Mem. ACLU, Canadian Civil Liberties Assn., Dalhousie U. Faculty Assn. (pres. 1980-81). Home: Conrad Rd Hubbards NS Canada Office: Dalhousie U Halifax NS Canada

FRIEDENBERG, RICHARD MYRON, medical educator, physician; b. N.Y.C., May 6, 1926; s. Charles and Dorothy (Steg) F.; m. Gloria Geshwind, Jan. 22, 1950; children: Lisa, Peter, Amy. A.B., Columbia, 1946; M.D., L.I. Coll. Medicine, 1949. Diplomate: Am. Bd. Radiology. Intern in medicine Maimonides Hosp., Bklyn., 1949-50; resident in radiology Bellevue Hosp., N.Y.C., 1950-51, Nat. Cancer fellow, 1951-52; fellow radiology Columbia-Presbyn. Hosp., 1952-53; cons. radiologist 3d Air Force, London, Eng., 1953-55; asst. prof. radiology Albert Einstein Coll. Medicine, 1955-66, assoc. clin. prof. radiology, 1966-68; dir., chmn. dept. radiology Bronx Lebanon Hosp. Center, 1957-68; prof., chmn. dept. radiology N.Y. Med. Coll., 1968-80; dir. radiology Flower Fifth Ave. Hosp., Met. Hosp. Center, Bird S. Coler Hosp., N.Y.C., Westchester County Med. Center, all 1968-80; prof., chmn. dept. radiol. scis. U. Calif., Irvine, 1980—. Author: (with Charles Ney) Radiographic Atlas of the Genitourinary System, 1966, 2d edit., 1981; Contbr. articles to profl. jours. Fellow Am. Coll. Radiology, N.Y. Acad. Medicine; mem. Assn. Univ. Radiologists, Radiol. Soc. N.Am., Am. Roentgen Ray Soc., N.Y. Acad. Scis., Assn. Am. Med. Colls., AMA, Soc. Chairmen Acad. Radiology Depts. (past pres.), N.Y. Roentgen Soc. (past pres.). Home: 18961 Castlegate Ln Santa Ana CA 92705 Office: U Calif Irvine CA

FRIEDENSOHN, ELIAS SOLOMON, artist, educator; b. N.Y.C., Dec. 12, 1924; s. Abraham and Celia F.; m. Doris Platzker, Feb. 1, 1968; children: Shola, Adam. A.B., Queens Coll., 1948. Mem. faculty Queens Coll., CUNY, 1951—, prof. art dept., 1979—. One-man shows include, Hewitt Galleries, 1955, 57, Isaacson Galleries, N.Y.C., 1958, 59, 61, Vassar Coll., 1961, Feingarten Gallery, N.Y.C., 1962, 63, Terry Dintenfass Galleries, N.Y.C., 1967, 70, 73, 76, 80, Moravian Coll., 1977, Magnes Mus., Berkeley, Calif., 1981, others, group shows include, Whitney Mus., N.Y.C., Art Inst. Chgo., Denver Art Mus., Dallas Mus. Art; represented in permanent collections, Whitney Mus. Am. Art, N.Y.C., Art Inst. Chgo., Mpls. Mus. Art, Walker Art Center, Mpls., Krannert Art Mus., Champaign, Ill., Magnes Mus., Berkeley, Jersey CityState Coll. Served with inf. U.S. Army, 1943-46. Guggenheim fellow, 1960; Fulbright grantee, 1957; PSC-BHE Univ. Found. for Research grantee, 1981; N.J. Council on Arts grantee, 1981; Magnes Mus. travel grantee, 1982. Home: 209 Hillcrest Ave Leonia NJ 07605

FRIEDENTHAL, JACK H., educator; b. Denver, Sept. 22, 1931; married; 3 children. A.B., Stanford U., 1953; LL.B., Harvard U., 1958. Bar: Calif. 1959. Sole practice, 1959—; from asst. prof. to assoc. prof. Stanford U., 1958-64, prof., 1964—, now George E. Osborn prof. law; cons. Law Revision Commn., 1964. Contbr. articles to profl. jours. Office: Stanford Univ Sch of Law Stanford CA 94305 *

FRIEDERICH, J., diversified company executive. Pres., chief exec. officer Furrs, Inc., 1979—, also dir. Office: Furrs Inc 1708 Ave G Lubbock TX 79408§

FRIEDERICI, HARTMANN H.R., physician, educator; b. Asuncion, Paraguay, Jan. 25, 1927; came to U.S., 1957, naturalized, 1960; s. H. Gerhard H. and Annaliese (Wacker) F.; m. Erica Y. Bachem, Mar. 23, 1958; children—Claudia Y., Peter G., Andrea L. B.S., Colegio de Goethe, Asuncion, 1946; M.D., U. La Plata, Argentina, 1953. Intern U. Ill. Research and Edn. Hosps., Chgo., 1960-61, resident, 1957-59, U. Bonn (Germany) Hosp., 1955-56; practice medicine specializing in pathology; asso. pathologist U. Ill. Hosps., Chgo., 1966-69; pathologist, attending physician Evanston (Ill.) Hosp., 1969-71, sr. attending physician, chmn. dept. pathology and lab. medicine, 1971—; asso. prof. pathology U. Ill., 1966-69; prof. pathology Northwestern U., 1969—, prof. biology, 1970—. Fellow Am. Heart Assn., Am. Soc. Clin. Pathologists; mem. AAAS, Internat. Acad. Pathology, Electron Microscopy Soc. Am., Assn. Am. Pathologists, Am. Soc. Cell Biology, Coll. Am. Pathologists. Research in capillary transport, cell membranes, kidney disease in diabetes, diseases of the pancreas, elemental microanalysis by electron microscopy. Home: 77 S Deere Park Highland Park IL 60035 Office: 2650 Ridge Ave Evanston IL 60201

FRIEDEWALD, WILLIAM FRANK, physician; b. St. Louis, June 3, 1912; s. William H. and Albertine (Eilers) F.; m. Mary L. Wright, May 29, 1937; children: William T., Jeannette A., James W., Richard W. B.S., St. Louis U., 1931, M.D., 1935. Intern, St. Louis City Hosp., 1935-36, asst. resident and resident in medicine, 1936-38; asst. in pathology and bacteriology Rockefeller Inst. for Med. Research, 1938-42; mem., staff Internat. Health div., Rockefeller Found., 1942-45; prof. bacteriology and immunology Emory U. Sch. Medicine, 1945-51, asso. prof. medicine, 1945—; pvt. practice internal medicine, allergy, 1951-76; profl. cons. internal medicine to Surgeon 3d U.S. Army, 1958-68; chief of staff St. Joseph's Hosp., Atlanta, 1968-79, trustee, 1969-82. Author articles on med. and bacteriol. subjects. Mem. Soc. Exptl. Biology and Medicine, AMA, Fulton County Med. Soc. Ga., Am. Soc. Exptl. Pathology. Home: 62 Fenwick Pl Atlanta GA 30328

FRIEDHEIM, ERIC ARTHUR, publisher, editor; b. London, Apr. 21, 1910; s. Arthur and Madeleine (Sander) F.; m. Elizabeth Sweeney, Dec. 31, 1951. Student, Am. U., 1928-30. Washington corr. Internat. News Service, 1931-42; combat corr. Air Force mag., 1945-46; also mng. editor Air News mag.; public relations adv. U.S. aviation industry, 1946; public relations and advance rep. Nat. Freedom Train, 1947-49; public relations dir. European Travel Commn., 1951-52; editor, pub. Travel Agt. mag., N.Y.C., 1951—; pub. Interline Reporter, 1957—, El Travel Agt. International, 1979—; travel columnist N.Y. Post, Los Angeles Times; travel adv. com. Dept. Commerce; adv. com. U.S. Travel Service, Congl. Travel and Tourism Caucus. Author: Fighters Up, an official history of World War II pilots in Europe, 1945. Co-sponsor with Kennedy Center Performing Arts of Arthur Friedheim ann. competition for best musical works by Am. composers, 1978—. Served as officer USAAF, 1942-45; col. USAFR; ret. Decorated Air medal; named to Travel Hall of Fame, 1980. Fellow Inst. Cert. Travel Agts.; mem. Am. Soc. Travel Agts., Soc. Am. Travel Writers (charter), Caribbean Tourist Assn., Pacific Area Travel Assn., Discover Am. Travel Orgns., Confederacione Organiziones Turisticas de la Am. Latina, World Tourism Orgn. Episcopalian. Clubs: Nat. Press (Washinton); Overseas Press (N.Y.C.); Skal. Home: 860 United Nations Plaza New York NY 10017 Home: 100 Worth Ave Palm Beach FL 33480 Office: 2 W 46th St New York NY 10036

FRIEDHEIM, JERRY WARDEN, newspaper association executive; b. Joplin, Mo., Oct. 7, 1934; s. Volmer Havens and Billie Alice (Warden) F.; m. Shirley Margarette Beavers, Oct. 17, 1956; children: Daniel Volmer, Cynthia Dianne, Thomas Eric. B.J., U. Mo., 1956, A.M., 1962. Reporter, editor, editorial writer Neosho (Mo.) Daily News, Joplin (Mo.) Globe, Columbia Missourian, 1956-61; instr. journalism U. Mo., Columbia, 1961-62; aide to Congressman Durward Hall from Mo., Washington, 1962-63; legis. asst., pres. sec., exec. asst. to U.S. Senator John Tower from Tex., Washington, 1963-69; dep. asst. Sec. Def. for Pub. Affairs, U.S. Dept. Def., Washington, 1969-72; asst. Sec. Def. for Pub. Affairs, 1973-74; v.p. pub. and govt. affairs AMTRAK, 1974-75; exec. v.p., gen. mgr. Am. Newspaper Publishers Assn. and ANPA Found., 1975—. Author: Where are the Voters, 1968. Served to capt. AUS, 1956-58. Congl. fellow Am. Polit. Sci. Assn. Mem. World Press Freedom Com., Internat. Newspaper Pubs. Fedn., Sigma Delta Chi. Clubs: Nat. Press, Georgetown, Met. Home: 1116 Allison St Alexandria VA 22302 Office: 11600 Sunrise Valley Dr Reston VA 22091

FRIEDHOFF, ARNOLD, medical scientist; b. Johnstown, Pa., Dec. 26, 1923; s. Abraham M. and Stella (Beerman) F.; m. Frances Wolfe, Feb. 24, 1946; children: Lawrence, Nancy, Richard. B.A., U. Pa., 1944, M.D., 1947. Diplomate: Am. Bd. Psychiatry and Neurology. Intern Western Pa. Hosp., 1947-48; resident psychiatry U.S. Army, 1952-53, Bellevue Hosp., N.Y.C., 1953-55; instr., prof. psychiatry N.Y. U. Sch. Medicine, 1956—, head psychopharmacology research unit, 1956-63, co-dir., 1963-69, dir., 1970—, 1970—; mem. clin. projects research rev. com. NIMH, 1970-74, chmn. treatment devel. and assessment research rev. com., 1979-81; Mem. Mayors Com. on Prescription Drugs, N.Y.C. Co-editor: Yearbook of Psychiatry and Applied Mental Health, 1968-80; mem. adv. bd.: Biological Psychiatry, 1969—; Contbr. numerous reports on biochem. psychiatry, psychopharmacology. Served to 1st lt. M.C. U.S. Army, 1951-53. Recipient Research Scientist award NIMH, 1967—. Fellow Am. Coll. Neuropsychopharmacology (past councillor and past pres. 1978-79), Am. Psychiat. Assn., Am. Soc. Clin. Pharmacology and Therapeutics, Royal Coll. Psychiatrists (Gt. Britain); mem. Am. Chem. Soc., Internat. Soc. Neurochemistry, Assn. for Research in Nervous and Mental Diseases (past asst. sec.-treas.), Am. Psychopath. Assn. (past pres., Samuel B. Hamilton award), Soc. Biol. Psychiatry (past pres.). Office: 550 1st Ave New York NY 10016

FRIEDKIN, JOSEPH FRANK, federal commissioner; b. Bklyn., Oct. 18, 1909; s. Jose and Irehe (Hedden) F.; m. Nellie May Berry, Mar. 21, 1937; children: Jonell, Kim. B.S. in Mech. Engring., U. Tex., 1932. Registered profl. engr., Calif., Ariz., N.M., Tex. Jr. to hydraulic engr. Internat. Boundary and Water Commn.-U.S. and Mexico, El Paso, Tex., 1934-41, resident engr., San Diego, 1947-52, prin. engr., supr., El Paso, 1952-62, commr., 1962—. Author: International Treaty, 1944, Water Treaty, 1944, Boundary Treaty, 1972, Salinity Agreement, 1972, Border Sanitation Agreement, 1979. Bd. dirs. YMCA, El Paso; mem. steering com. Goals for El. Paso; bd. dirs. El Paso United Fund. Served with C.E. U.S. Army, 1942-46. Recipient Superior Honor award Dept. State, El Paso, 1964, Outstanding Citizen El Paso Bd. Realtors, 1968; named Engr. of Yr. Engring. Socs., 1959, Pan Am. Engr. of yr. Pan Am. Fedn. Engring. Socs., 1979. Mem. Pan Am. Fedn. Engring. Socs. (U.S. dir. engrs. joint council), Nat. Soc. Profl. Engrs. Club: Lancers (El Paso, Tex.). Lodge: Rotary. Home: 3821 Hillcrest El Paso TX 79902 Office: Internat Boundary and Water Commn 4110 Rio Bravo El Paso TX 79902

FRIEDKIN, MORRIS ENTON, educator, biochemist; b. Kansas City, Mo., Dec. 30, 1918; s. Benjamin and Anna (Lapatuchin) F.; m. Roberta Vanocur, Sept. 1943; children—Noah, Susanna, Deborah. B.S., Iowa State Coll., 1940, M.S., 1941; Ph.D., U. Chgo., 1948. Chemist Penicillin project, World War II; postdoctoral research fellow U. Copenhagen, Denmark, 1948-49; instr. then asso. prof. pharmacology Washington U., St. Louis, 1949-58; prof. pharmacology, chmn. dept. Tufts U. Med. Sch., 1958-67, prof. biochemistry, chmn. dept., 1967-69; prof. biology U. Calif. at San Diego, 1969—; provost Revelle Coll., 1974-76. Mem. Nat. Acad. Sci., Am. Acad. Arts and Scis., Am. Soc. Biol. Chemists, Am. Soc. Pharmacology and Exptl. Therapeutics. Office: care Dept Biology M-001 Basic Sci Bldg Univ California San Diego La Jolla CA 92093

FRIEDKIN, WILLIAM, film director; b. Chgo., Aug. 29, 1939; s. Louis and Rae (Green) F. Dir.: films Good Times, 1967, The Night They Raided Minsky's, 1968, The Birthday Party, 1968, The Boys in the Band, 1970, The French Connection, 1971 (Acad. award for best picture 1971), The Exorcist, 1973, Sorcerer, 1977, The Brinks Job, 1979, Cruising, 1980. Mem. Dirs. Guild Am. (dir.), Acad. Motion Picture Arts and Scis. *

FRIEDL, ERNESTINE (MRS. HARRY L. LEVY), anthropologist; b. Cegled, Hungary, Aug. 13, 1920; came to U.S., 1922, naturalized, 1927; d. Nicholas and Ethel (Neudorfer) F.; m. Harry L. Levy, Sept. 27, 1942. A.B., Hunter Coll., 1941; Ph.D., Columbia, 1950. Lectr. Bklyn. Coll., 1942-44, 46-47; instr. Wellesley Coll., 1944-46, Queens Coll., 1947-55, asst. prof., 1956-60, asso. prof., 1960-64, prof., 1965-74, chmn. dept. anthropology-sociology, 1964-68; exec. officer Ph.D. program in anthropology City U. N.Y., 1969-70; prof. anthropology Duke U., Durham, N.C., 1973—, chmn. dept., 1973-78; dean faculty arts and scis. and Trinity Coll., 1980—; mem. Nat. Sci. Bd., 1979—. Author: Vasilika, a Village in Modern Greece, 1962, Women and Men, An Anthropologist's View, 1975. NSF grantee, 1963-65; recipient Fulbright Research (Greece) award, also; Research award Wenner-Gren Found., 1955-56. Fellow Am. Anthrop. Assn. (pres. 1974-75), Modern Greek Studies Assn. (exec. com. 1975—, sec. 1978—), AAAS, Am. Acad. Arts and Scis.; mem. Soc. Applied Anthropology, Am. Ethnol. Soc. (sec-treas. 1951-52, pres. 1967), Northeastern Anthrop. Assn. (pres. 1970), Phi Beta Kappa. Home: 21 Stoneridge Circle Durham NC 27705

FRIEDL, FRANCIS PETER, clergyman; b. Waterloo, Iowa, Nov. 26, 1917; s. Philip and Mary (Schares) F. B.A., Loras Coll., 1939; postgrad., Mt. St. Mary Sem., U. Notre Dame, summer 1947; M.A., Catholic U. Am., 1952, Ph.D., 1954. Ordained priest Roman Cath. Ch., 1943; curate Nativity Ch., Dubuque, Iowa, 1943; instr. Loras Acad., 1947-50; asst. prof. psychology, dir. pub. relations Loras Coll., 1954; v.p., 1956, exec. v.p., 1963—, acad. dean, 1965-71, pres., 1971-77, prof., 1970—; pastor St. Joseph Parish, Elkader, Iowa, 1977—. Club: K.C. Address: St Joseph Parish Elkader IA 52043

FRIEDLAENDER, ANN FETTER, economics educator; b. Phila., Sept. 24, 1938; d. Ferdinand Fetter Fields and Elizabeth Head; m. Stephen Friedlaender, Dec. 28, 1960; children: Lucas Ferdinand, Nathaniel Marc. B.A., Radcliffe Coll., 1960; Ph.D. (Woodrow Wilson fellow, 1960-62), MIT, 1964. Asst. prof., asso. prof., then prof. Boston Coll., 1965-74; prof. econs. MIT, Cambridge, 1974—, chmn. dept. econs., 1983—; Fulbright lectr., Helsinki, Finland, 1964-65; bd. dirs. Consol. Rail Corp., 1978-80; examining com. Econs. Grad. Record Exams., 1974-76; exec. com. Assembly of Behavioral and Social Scis. NRC, 1974-78; mem. NSF econs. panel, 1981-82. Author: The Dilemma of Freight Transportation, 1969, (with R.H. Spady) Freight Transport Regulation, 1981, (with John F. Due) Government Finance, 1981. NSF grantee, 1968, 76, 77, 79, 81, 83. Mem. Am. Econ. Assn. (chmn. com. on status of women in the econs. profession 1978-80, exec. com. 1982—), Econometric Soc. Office: Dept Econs MIT Room E52-373a Cambridge MA 02139

FRIEDLAENDER, FRITZ JOSEF, electrical engineering educator; b. Freiburg/Breisgau, Germany, May 7, 1925; came to U.S., 1947, naturalized, 1953; s. Ludwig and Frieda (Murzynski) F.; m. Gisela Triebe, Aug. 7, 1969; 2 sons. B.S., Carnegie Inst. Tech., 1951, M.S., 1952, Ph.D., 1955. Asst. prof. Columbia, 1954-55; asst. prof. Purdue U., West Lafayette, Ind., 1955-59, asso. prof., 1959-62, prof. elec. engring., 1962—; guest prof. Max-Planck Institut für Metallforschung, Tech. U. Stuttgart, Germany, 1964-65; Humboldt award and guest prof. Institut für Werkstoffe der Elektrotechnik, Ruhr-Universität, Bochum, West Germany, 1972-73; Japan Soc. Sci. fellow and guest prof. Nagoya U., summer 1980; guest prof. U. Regensburg (W.Ger.), 1981-82; cons. Gen. Electric Corp., Ft. Wayne, Ind., 1956-58, Components Corp., Chgo., 1959-61, Lawrence Radiation Lab., U. Calif. at Livermore, 1967-69, P.R. Mallory & Co., 1974-78, Oakridge Nat. Lab., 1979-82. Adv. editor: Jour. Magnetism and Magnetic Materials, 1975—; editorial bd.: Proc. IEEE, 1975-78; Contbr. articles profl. jours. Fellow IEEE (revs. editor trans. Magnetics 1965-67, editorial bd. jour. 1968—, chmn. awards Magnetics Soc. 1966-74, chmn. Intermag 1975, London, program co-chmn. Intermag 1978, Florence, Italy, v.p. 1975-76, pres. 1977-78, pres. Central Ind. sect. 1979-80); mem. Am. Phys. Soc., Am. Soc. Engring. Edn., Arbeitsgemeinschaft Magnetismus, Sigma Xi, Phi Kappa Phi, Tau Beta Pi, Eta Kappa Nu, Beta Sigma Rho. Research in magnetics, magnetic devices and memories, high gradient magnetic separation, magnetic bubble dynamics. Home: 151 Colony Rd West Lafayette IN 47906

FRIEDLAND, LOUIS N., communications executive; b. 1913; m. Billie Belenko; children: Eric, Joanne Roberts. B.S., Bklyn. Coll., 1934; M.A., N.Y. U., 1936. Instr. psychology, 1936-41; chief adminstrn. officer VA, 1946-48; gen. mgr. U.S. Microfilm Co., 1948-52; with MCA, Inc., 1952—, corp. v.p., 1968, v.p., 1953-73, pres. div. MCA TV div., distbr. Universal Studios TV programs, 1973-78, chmn. bd. MCA TV div., 1978—; Past chmn. Nat. Hemphilia Found. Served as lt. USCG, 1942-46. Office: MCA TV 445 Park Ave New York NY 10022

FRIEDLAND, WALDO CHARLES, microbiologist; b. Menasha, Wis., Dec, 18, 1923; s. Waldo C. and Luella (Spengler) F.; m. Lucille Nider, Aug. 1, 1946; children: Paul, Mary, Nancy, Elizabeth, Susan, David. B.S., Iowa State U., 1948, Ph.D., 1951. With Abbott Labs., North Chicago, Ill., 1951—, research mgr., microbiologist, until 1982. Address: 1020 Gracewood Dr Libertyville IL 60048

FRIEDLANDER, GERHART, chemist; b. Munich, Germany, July 28, 1916; came to U.S., 1936, naturalized, 1943; s. Max O. and Bella (Forchheimer) F.; m. Gertrude Maas, Feb. 6, 1941 (dec. 1966); children: Ruth Ann F. Huart, Joan Claire F. Hurley; m. Barbara Strongin, 1983. B.S., U. Calif. - Berkeley, 1939, Ph.D., 1942. Instr. U. Idaho, Moscow, 1942-43; staff Los Alamos Sci. Lab., 1943-46; research asso. Gen. Electric Co. Research Lab., Schenectady, 1946-48; vis. lectr. Washington U., St. Louis, 1948; chemist Brookhaven Nat. Lab., Upton, N.Y., 1948-52, sr. chemist, 1952-81, chmn. chemistry dept., 1968-77; Chmn. Gordon Research Conf. on Nuclear Chemistry, 1954; mem. adv. com. for chemistry Oak Ridge Nat. Lab., 1966-70; mem. program adv. com. Los Alamos Meson Physics Facility, 1971-75; chmn. vis. com. nuclear chemistry Lawrence Berkeley Lab., 1974-75; exec. sec. basic energy scis. lab. program panel Dept. Energy, 1976-80; mem. adv. com. for nuclear chemistry div. Lawrence Livermore Lab., 1977—. Author: (with J.W. Kennedy) Introduction to Radiochemistry, 1949, Nuclear and Radiochemistry, 1955, (with J.M. Miller) Nuclear and Radiochemistry, 1964, (with E.S. Macias) Nuclear and Radiochemistry, 1981; also articles.; assoc. editor: Ann. Rev. Nuclear Sci., 1958-67; editor: Radiochimica Acta, 1972-73. Recipient Alexander von Humboldt award Institut für Kernchemie, Mainz, W. Ger., 1978-79. Fellow Am. Phys. Soc.; mem. Nat. Acad. Scis. (mem. assembly math. and phys. scis. 1981—, mem. commn. phys. scis., math. and resources 1982—, chmn. ad hoc panel on future nuclear sci. 1975-76, chmn. com. on recommendations for U.S. Army basic sci. research Nat. Acad. Scis.-NRC 1977-81, mem. com. on postdoctoral and doctoral research staff NRC 1977-80), Am. Acad. Arts and Scis., Am. Chem. Soc. (chmn. div. nuclear chemistry and tech. 1967, award for nuclear applications in chemistry 1967), AAAS. Research chem. effects of nuclear transformations, properties of radioactive isotopes, mechanisms of nuclear reactions, especially those induced by protons of very high energies, solar neutrino detection. Home: 5 Lorraine Ct Smithtown NY 11787 Office: Brookhaven Nat Lab Upton NY 11973

FRIEDLANDER, PAUL JOSEF CROST, newspaperman; b. Utica, N.Y., July 17, 1910; s. Jacob and Rebecca (Crost) F.; m. Hilda Harris, Oct. 11, 1935; children—Susan Syra Friedlander Gutow, Rebecca Crost Friedlander Shaw. B.A., Hamilton Coll., Clinton, N.Y., 1931. With Utica (N.Y.) Daily Press, 1932-41, city editor, 1937-41; rewrite man, reporter N.Y. Post, 1941; feature editor-writer AP Feature Service, N.Y.C., 1941-43; Sunday mag. deskman, writer N.Y. Times, 1943-46, travel editor, 1946-70, travel columnist, 1970-74; propr., weekly travel columnist Traveler's World Syndicate, 1974—. Mem. N.Y. State Com. on Alcohol and Hwy. Safety, 1972; mem. Environ. Commn., Village of East Hills, 1971—. Decorated officer Ordre National du Merite, France; recipient awards for aviation and travel reporting, including; Trans World Airlines awards, 1961, 62, 63, 68; Strebig-Dobben Meml. award, 1967. Mem. N.Y. Travel Writers Assn. (founder, pres. 1967-69), Sigma Delta Chi. Democrat. Jewish. Home and Office: 113 Magnolia Ln East Hills NY 11577

FRIEDLANDER, RAYMOND NATHAN, lawyer, clothing co. exec.; b. Chgo., Apr. 16, 1926; s. Benjamin and Lillian (Rosenthal) F.; m. Sonia Treger, Jan. 29, 1950; children—David, Mark. Student, U. Ill., 1944, 46-48; J.D., DePaul U., 1951. Bar: Ill. bar 1951. House counsel Aldens, Inc., 1951-67, v.p., sec., gen. counsel, 1967—, also dir.; Bd. dirs. Ill. Retail Mchts. Assn. Served to 2d lt. AUS, 1944-46. Mem. Am., Fed., Ill., Chgo. bar assns., Ill. Workmen's Compensation Lawyers Assn., Decalogue Soc. Lawyers, B'nai B'rith. Home: 205 Rivershire Ln Apt 110 Lincolnshire IL 60015 Office: 2215 Sanders Rd Northbrook IL 60062

FRIEDLANDER, ROBERT LYNN, college president; b. Detroit, Nov. 9, 1933; s. Samuel D. and Esther E. (Engel) F.; m. Mary Louise Cloon, Nov. 27, 1960; children: Suzan, Rebecca. B.S. in Chemistry, Wayne State U., 1955, M.D., 1958. Diplomate: Am. Bd. Obstetrics and Gynecology. Intern Mt. Zion Hosp. and Med. Center, 1958-59; jr. asst. resident in ob-gyn. U. Chgo. Clinics, Chgo. Lying-In Hosp., 1959-60; resident in ob-gyn. Albany (N.Y.) Med. Center Hosp., 1962-63, chief resident in ob-gyn., 1964, attending obstetrician and gynecologist, 1969; assoc. prof. Albany Med. Coll., 1969-76, prof., 1976—, assoc. dean, 1976, assoc. dean acad. affairs, 1977-78, assoc. dean acad. and student affairs, 1976, exec. assoc. dean, 1978-79, acting pres., dean, 1979-80, pres., dean, 1980—; mem. State Bd. Medicine SUNY; guest lectr. various nat. soc. meetings, 1973—. Contbr. articles to various publs. Served to lt. comdr. USNR, 1960-62. Lederle Labs. fellow, 1955; NIH research fellowship, 1957; named Disting. Alumnus of Yr. Wayne State U., 1980. Mem. Assn. Am. Med. Colls., Am. Coll. Ob-Gyn., N.Y. Acad. Scis., Assn. Profs. and Gynecology and Obstetrics, Am. Fertility Soc., N.Y. Acad. Medicine, Northeastern N.Y. Ob-Gyn. Soc., Med. Soc. State N.Y., AAAS, AMA. Office: Albany Med Coll 47 New Scotland Ave Albany NY 12208

FRIEDLY, JOHN C., chemical engineering educator; b. Glen Dale, W.Va., Feb. 28, 1938; s. J. Chalmer and B. Grace (Lambert) F.; m. Lois R. Oyer, Dec. 22, 1962; children—Lauren, Jock, Michael, Janna. B.S., Carnegie Inst. Tech., 1960; Ph.D., U. Calif., Berkeley, 1965. Research engr. Gen. Electric Co., Schenectady, 1964-67; asst. prof. chem. engring. Johns Hopkins U., 1967-68; asst. prof. U. Rochester, N.Y., 1968-71, asso. prof., 1971-81; asso. dean grad. studies Coll. Engring. and Applied Sci., 1979-81, prof., chmn. dept., 1981—; cons. in field. Author: Dynamic Behavior of Processes, 1972. NATO sr. fellow Oxford (Eng.) U., 1975-76; NSF grantee; U.K. Atomic Energy Authority grantee. Mem. Am. Inst. Chem. Engrs., Am. Chem. Soc., Am. Soc. Edn. Engring. Home: 1620 Qualtrough Rd Rochester NY 14625 Office: Dept Chem Engring U Rochester Rochester NY 14627

FRIEDMAN, ALAN BARRY, accountant; b. Chgo., Oct. 16, 1940; s. Leonard R. and Helen F.; m. Judy E. Duff, June 26, 1966; children—Howard, Paula. B.S., UCLA, 1962, M.B.A., 1963. C.P.A., Calif. With Price Waterhouse & Co., Los Angeles and Century City, Calif., 1963-71; asst. sec.-treas., tax mgr. Monogram Industries, Inc., Santa Monica, Calif., 1971-83; acct. Bernstein, Fox, Goldberg Accountancy Corp., Century City, Calif., 1983—. Treas. West Valley Neighborhood Sch., 1979-83. Served with AUS, 1963-69. Mem. Am. Inst. C.P.A.s, Calif. Soc. C.P.A.s, Tax Execs. Inst. Jewish. Home: 7218 Hyannis Dr Canoga Park CA 91307 Office: 1900 Ave of Stars Century City CA 90067

FRIEDMAN, ALAN WARREN, humanities educator; b. Bklyn., June 8, 1939; s. Leon and Anne (Markowitz) F.; children: Eric Lawrence, Scot Bradley, Lorraine Eve. Student, U. Edinburgh, Scotland, 1960-61; B.A., Queens Coll., N.Y., 1961; A.M., NYU, 1962; Ph.D., U. Rochester, 1966. Grad. teaching asst. U. Rochester, 1963-64; instr. English U. Tex., Austin, 1964-66, asst. prof., 1966-69, assoc. prof., 1969-76, prof., 1976—, dir. honors program, 1972-76; Sr. Fulbright prof. U. Lancaster (Eng.), 1977-78. Author: Lawrence Durrell and The Alexandria Quartet, 1970, Multivalence: The Moral Quality of Form in the Modern Novel, 1978; editor books; contbr. essays and revs. to profl. jours. Founder, chmn. Neighborhood Assn., Austin, 1973-74. Nat. Endowment for Humanities fellow, 1970-71. Mem. MLA (mem. del. assembly 1977-79, 82-84), AAUP (pres. U. Tex. chpt. 1979-84), Tex. Assn. Coll. Tchrs., Nat. Collegiate Honors Council, Omicron Delta Kappa. Democrat. Jewish. Office: English Dept Univ of Texas Austin TX 78712

FRIEDMAN, ALBERT BARRON, educator; b. Kansas City, Mo., Aug. 16, 1920; s. Jay and Edith (Barron) F. B.A., U. Mo., 1941; M.A., Harvard U., 1942, Ph.D., 1952. Instr. Harvard U., 1952-55, asst. prof., 1955-60; asso. prof. Claremont (Calif.) Grad. Sch., 1960-62, prof., 1962-69, W.S. Rosecrans prof., 1969—. Author: Folk Ballads, 1956, The Ballad Revival, 1961, Ywain and Gawain, 1964, Creativity in Graduate Education, 1964, The Usable Myth, 1970, Myth and Ideology, 1976; Asso. editor: Jour. Am. Folklore, 1958-63; editor: Western Folklore, 1966-70, Pacific Coast Philology, 1983—; Contbr. articles to profl. jours. Served to capt. AUS, 1942-46. Decorated Legion of Merit, Silver Star, Order of George I, Order of Phoenix, Greece, Kaiser-i-Hind, India; recipient Internat. Folklore Soc. 1st prize, 1961; Guggenheim fellow, 1957-58, 65-66; Nat. Endowment Sr. fellow, 1971. Fellow Am. Folklore Soc. (life), mem., Mediaeval Acad. Am., Mediaeval Assn. (v.p.), English Inst. (supr. 1964-67), Calif. Folklore Soc. (v.p. 1965, 73), Modern Lang. Assn. (chmn. comparative lit. 1960, 68, Arthurian lit. 1971, Medieval lit. 1972), Philol. Soc. (pres. 1982-83). Home: 706 California Dr Claremont CA 91711

FRIEDMAN, ALVIN, lawyer; b. Bklyn., June 19, 1931; s. Isidor and Freda (Yanuck) F.; m. Maryann Kallison, Mar. 27, 1955; children—Alan K., Margot N. B.A. with honors in Polit. Sci, Cornell U., 1952; LL.B. cum laude (editor Law Jour. 1956-57), Yale, 1957. Bar: Tex. and D.C. bars 1957. Asso. firm Covington & Burling, 1957-63; spl. asst. to gen. counsel Dept. Def., 1962-64, spl. asst. to asst. sec. def. for def. for internat. security affairs, 1964, dep. asst. sec. def. for internat. security affairs Far East and Latin Am., 1964-66; partner Ginsburg & Feldman, Washington, 1966-67, Friedman and Medalie (and predecessors), 1967—; dir. Penn Central Corp., 1978—. Served to 1st lt. USAF, 1952-54. Mem. Am., Tex., D.C. bar assns. Home: 700 New Hampshire Ave Washington DC 20037 Office: 1899 L St NW Washington DC 20036

FRIEDMAN, ALVIN E., investment executive; b. N.Y.C., Aug. 8, 1919; s. Harry and Frances (Levin) F.; m. Pesselle Rothenberg, Feb. 2, 1943; children: Jeffrey F., Joan M. B.B.A., CCNY, 1942; M.B.A., NYU, 1949. Mng. dir., bd. dirs. Lehman Bros. Kuhn Loeb Inc. (investment bankers), N.Y.C.; dir. ITT, Avnet, Inc., all N.Y.C. Served to 1st lt. USAAF, 1944-46. Home: 176 Hemlock Rd Manhasset NY 11030 Office: 55 Water St New York NY 11041

FRIEDMAN, BARTON ROBERT, educator; b. Bklyn., Feb. 5, 1935; s. Abraham Isaac and Mazie Diana (Cooper) F.; m. Sheila Lynn Siegel, June 22, 1958; children—Arnold, Jonathan, Daniel, Esther. B.A., Cornell U., 1956, Ph.D. (univ. dissertation fellow), 1964; M.A., U. Conn., 1958. Instr. Bowdoin Coll., Brunswick, Maine, 1961-63; from instr. to prof. English lit. U. Wis., Madison, 1963-78; prof. English lit., chmn. dept. English Cleve. State U., 1978—. Author: Adventures in the Deeps of the Mind: The Cuchulain Cycle of W.B. Yeats, 1977, You Can't Tell the Players, 1979; editorial bd.: Irish Renaissance Ann, 1980—, Lit. Monographs, 1970-76. Recipient William Kiekhofer Teaching Excellence award U. Wis., 1967. Mem. MLA, Am. Com. Irish Studies, Coll. English Assn. Ohio (gov.), Phi Kappa Phi. Jewish. Home: 2916 E Overlook Rd Cleveland Heights OH 44118 Office: Dept English Cleve State Univ Cleveland OH 44115

FRIEDMAN, BEN IGNATIUS, physician, educator; b. Cin., Oct. 18, 1926; s. Ben and Ruth (Mueller) F.; m. Ruth Reinhart, Jan. 24, 1954; 1 son, Richard. M.D., U. Cin., 1948, postgrad., 1948. Diplomate: Am. Bd. Internal Medicine, Am. Bd. Nuclear Medicine. Intern Cin. Gen. Hosp., 1948-49, resident, 1949-50, Duke Hosp., 1950, 52-53; practice medicine, specializing in internal medicine and hematology, Cin., 1955-68; mem. faculty Coll. Medicine, U. Cin., 1953-68, asst. prof. radiology, 1964-68, asso. prof. medicine, 1965-68; prof. radiology Coll. Medicine, U. Tenn., Memphis, 1968-73, prof. medicine, 1968-77, prof. nuclear medicine, 1973-77, acting chmn. dept. radiology, 1971-73, chmn. dept. nuclear medicine, dir. div. radiation scis., 1973-77; attending physician City Memphis Hosps., 1968-77; active staff Morton Plant Hosp., Clearwater, Fla., 1980—. Contbr. articles to profl. jours. Served to capt. M.C. USAF, 1950-52. Fellow A.C.P., Am. Coll. Radiology, Am. Coll. Nuclear Physicians, Am. Coll. Nuclear Medicine; mem. Soc. Nuclear Medicine, Pinellas County Med. Soc., AMA, Fla. Med. Assn., Radiol. Soc. N.Am. Jewish. Home: 4 Belleview Blvd Apt 601 Belleair FL 33516

FRIEDMAN, BENJAMIN MORTON, economics educator; b. Louisville, Aug. 5, 1944; s. Norbert and Eva (Lipsky) F.; m. Barbara Allan Cook, Dec. 17, 1972; children: John Norton, Jeffrey Allan. A.B. summa cum laude, Harvard U., 1966, A.M., 1969, Ph.D., 1971; M.Sc. King's Coll., Cambridge U., 1970. Economist Morgan Stanley & Co., N.Y.C., 1971-72; asst. prof. econs. Harvard U., Cambridge, Mass., 1972-76, assoc. prof., 1976-80, prof., 1980—; dir. fin. markets and monetary econs. Nat. Bur. Econ. Research, Cambridge, 1977—; dir. Pvt. Export Funding Corp., N.Y.C.; trustee Coll. Retirement Equities Fund, N.Y.C., 1978-82. Author: Economic Stabilization Policy, 1975, Monetary Policy in the United States, 1981; editor: New CHallenges to the Role of Profits, 1978, The Changing Roles of Debt and Equity in Financing U.S. Capital Formation, 1982; assoc. editor: Jour. Monetary Econs., 1977—. Marshall sholar Cambridge U., 1966-68; Soc. Fellows jr. fellow Harvard U., 1968-71. Mem. Council Fgn. Relations, Brookings Panel Econ. Activity, Am. Econ. Assn., Am. Fin. Assn. Club: Harvard (N.Y.C.). Home: 11 Garfield Rd Belmont MA 02178 Office: Harvard U 127 Littauer Ctr Cambridge MA 02138

FRIEDMAN, BENNO, photographer; b. N.Y.C., Mar. 28, 1945; s. Arthur and Marion (Kaye) F. B.A. cum laude in Fine Arts, Brandeis U., 1966. One man exhbns. include, Light Gallery, N.Y.C., 1973, 75, 78, Photograph Gallery, N.Y.C., 1980, Yajima Gallery, group exhbns. include, George Eastman House, 1972, M.I.T., Hudson River Mus., 1973, One-of-a-Kind, Poloroid traveling show; represented in permanent collections, Mus. Modern Art, N.Y.C., Boston Mus. Fine Arts, Fogg Mus., George Eastman House, Rochester, N.Y., Vassar Coll. Mus. Office: 26 W 20th St 4th Floor New York NY 10011

FRIEDMAN, B(ERNARD) H(ARPER), writer; b. N.Y.C., July 27, 1926; s. Leonard and Madeline (Uris) F.; m. Abby Noselson, Mar. 6, 1948; children: Jackson, Daisy. B.A., Cornell U., 1948. With Cross & Brown Co., 1949-50; v.p., dir. Uris Bldgs. Corp., N.Y.C., 1950-63; lectr. creative writing Cornell U., 1966-67; staff cons., dir. Fine Arts Work Center, Provincetown, Mass., 1968-82; founding mem. Fiction Collective, 1973—; Adv. council Cornell U. Coll. Arts and Scis., 1968-83, Herbert F. Johnson Mus., 1972—. Author: novel Circles, 1962 (reprinted as I Need to Love, 1963); (with Barbara Guest) monograph Robert Goodnough, 1962; novel Yarborough, 1964; monographs Lee Krasner, 1965; Alfonso Ossorio, 1973, Salvatore Scarpitta, 1977, Myron Stout, 1980; novels Whispers, 1972; Museum, 1974, Almost A Life, 1975, The Polygamist, 1981; stories Coming Close, 1982; biography Jackson Pollock: Energy Made Visible, 1972; Gertrude Vanderbilt Whitney, 1978; editor: School of New York, 1959; adv. bd.: Cornell Rev., 1977-79; contbr. articles to mags., anthologies and reference vols. in U.S., Eng., Japan. Trustee Am. Fedn. Arts, 1958-64, Whitney Mus. Am. Art, 1961—, Broida Mus., 1983—. Served with USNR, 1944-46. Recipient awards for short stories, including Nelson Algren award, 1983. Club: Century Assn. (N.Y.C.). Home: 439 E 51st St New York NY 10022

FRIEDMAN, BERNARD SAMUEL, chemist; b. Chgo., Jan. 4, 1907; s. Nathan and Fannie (Baskin) F.; m. Estelle B. Freund, June 12, 1938; children—Richard F., Alice Joyce. A.B., U. Ill., 1930, Ph.D. in Organic Chemistry, 1936. High sch. tchr., Streator, Ill., 1930-33; asst. instr. chemistry U. Ill., 1933-36; research chemist Universal Oil Products Co., 1936-45; dir. chem. lab. QMC Research and Devel., 1947-48; asso. dir. organic research div. Sinclair Research Labs., Inc., 1948-59, research asso., 1959-69; professorial lectr. chem. dept. U. Chgo., 1969-73; cons. tech. manpower and coal utilization, conversion and environ. control tech. ERDA, 1975-77, U.S. Dept. Energy, 1977-79, Il. Inst. Natural Resources, 1981—. Author articles, chpts. in books, sci./engring. manpower reports. Mem. Chgo. Bd. Edn., 1962-77. Mem. Am. Chem. Soc. (nat. pres. 1974), Chgo. Tech. Socs. Council (pres., Merit award 1963), Am. Inst. Chemists (chmn. Chgo. 1952, Honor scroll 1958), Phi Beta Kappa, Sigma Xi, Zeta Beta Tau. Patentee in field. Home: 4800 S Chicago Beach Dr Chicago IL 60615

FRIEDMAN, DANIEL, artist, designer; b. Cleve., July 18, 1945. B.F.A., Carnegie Inst. Tech., 1967; postgrad., Hochschule fuer Gestaltung, Ulm, W.Ger., Sch. Design, Basel, Switzerland, 1968-70. Asst. prof. Yale U., 1970-73; asst. prof., chmn. bd. of study in design SUNY, Purchase, 1972-75; sr. design dir. Anspach, Grossman, Portugal, Inc., N.Y.C., 1975-77; free lance designer, N.Y.C., 1977-79; asso. Pentagram Design, N.Y.C., 1979-82; artist, 1982—. Mem. Am. Inst. Graphic Arts. Home: 2 Fifth Ave New York NY 10011

FRIEDMAN, DANIEL MORTIMER, judge, lawyer; b. N.Y.C., Feb. 8, 1916; s. Henry Michael F. and Julie (Freedman) Fiedman; m. Elizabeth Ellis, Oct. 18, 1975. A.B., Columbia U., 1937, LL.B., 1940. Bar: N.Y. 1941. Practice law, N.Y.C., 1940-42; with SEC, Washington, 1942-51, Justice Dept., Wahsington, 1951-78, asst. to solicitor gen., Washington, 1959-62, 2d asst. to solicitor gen., 1962-68, 1st dep. solicitor gen., 1968-78; judge Claims Ct. and U.S. Ct. Appeals, Washington, 1978—. Served with AUS, 1942-46. Recipient Exceptional Service award Atty. Gen., 1969. Home: 3249 Newark St NW Washington DC 20008 Office: US Ct Appeals 717 Madison Pl NW Washington DC 20439

FRIEDMAN, EDWARD ALAN, college dean, educator; b. Bayonne, N.J., Sept. 29, 1935; s. Philip Arthur and Esther (Weinstein) F.; m. Arline Joan Lederman, Jan. 13, 1963; children: Millard Timur. B.S., MIT, 1957; postgrad., Stanford U., 1957-58; Ph.D., Columbia U., 1963. Philip Kerim. Asst. prof., asso. prof. physics Stevens Inst. Tech., Hoboken, N.J., 1963-69, dean of coll., 1973—, prof., 1980—, chmn. computer tng. com., 1982; v.p. Mentor Systems, Inc., 1980—; vis. prof. Kabul U., 1965-67, dir. engring. coll. devel. program, Afghanistan, 1970-73; Cons. Hudson Inst., 1962-63, Doubleday Book Co., 1969; Chmn. Civic Affairs Com., Hoboken, 1968-69; vice chmn. bd. edn. Am. Internat. Sch. of Kabul, 1971-72; chmn. bd. dirs. N.Y. Scientists Com. for Pub. Info., 1977-78; chmn. Council for Understanding of Tech. in Human Affairs, 1979-82; sr. v.p. Afghanistan Relief Com., 1980—; mem. N.J. Commn. on Grad. Tchr. Edn., 1982-83. Co-founder, co-editor: Machine-Mediated Learning Jour., 1983. Trustee Hudson Higher Edn. Consortium, 1974; bd. dirs. Assn. Ind. Colls. and Univs. N.J., 1978-82. Recipient (with R.D. Andrews) Ottens research award Stevens Inst. Tech., 1970, 1st Class Edn. medal Govt. of Afghanistan, 1973; NSF grantee to direct elementary sch. sci. program for Orange, N.J., 01969. Mem. Am. Phys. Soc., AAAS, Am. Assn. Engring. Edn., Computer Soc., Am. Soc. Tng. and Devel. Home: Colonial House Castle Point Hoboken NJ 07030

FRIEDMAN, EDWARD DAVID, lawyer; b. Chgo.; s. Jacob C. and Bessie (Levison) F.; m. Mary Louise Melia, Nov. 1, 1947; children—Michael, Daniel, Maryel, Elizabeth. A.B. with honors, U. Chgo., 1935, J.D. cum laude, 1937. Bar: Ill. 1937, D.C. 1969, U.S. Ct. Appeals, U.S. Supreme Ct. 1969. Law clk. to fed. master in chancery, Chgo., 1937-38; firm Rosenberg, Toomin & Stern, Chgo., 1938-39; mem. gen. counsel staff SEC, 1939-42; chief counsel OPA, 1942-43; spl. asst. to dep. solicitor and solicitor Dept. Labor, Washington, 1943-48; chief law officer 5th regional office, also asst. gen. counsel NLRB, 1948-60; labor counsel to Senator John F. Kennedy, 1960-61, Senator Wayne Morse, 1961-65, U.S. Senate Labor and Pub. Welfare Com., 1961-65; counsel to majority and minority floor mgrs. Senators Clark and Case on Civil Rights Bill, 1964; spl. asst. fgn. farm labor program sec. labor, 1964, dep. solicitor of labor, 1965-69; partner firm Friedman & Wirtz, Washington; counsel CCAC, USWA, 1980—; U.S. del. to OECD, Paris, 1968. Asso. editor: U. Chgo. Law Rev, 1936-37. Mem. town council, Garrett Park, Md., 1954-58, mayor, 1960-66. James Nelson Raymond fellow, 1937. Mem. Am. Bar Assn., Fed. Bar Assn., Order Coif. Office: 1211 Connecticut Ave NW Washington DC 20036

FRIEDMAN, EDWARD LUDWIG, author, lecturer; b. Reynoldsville, Pa., Oct. 26, 1903; s. Sol and Fannie (Stein) F.; m. Bertha Leiser, Sept. 1, 1935; 1 dau., Linda Friedman Robinson. Student, U. Colo., 1922-23, U. Mo., 1923-25. Reporter Pueblo (Colo.) Chieftain, 1920-22; mem. editorial staff NEA Service, Cleve., 1925-28, Pueblo Star-Jour., 1928-31; editor Radio Features Service, 1931-34; dir. Nat. Reference Library, Cleve., 1934-77; pres. Library Asso. Services, Inc., 1959-80; Vol. White House Conf. Aging, 1981. Author: Speechmaker's Complete Handbook, 1955, Toastmaster's Treasury, 1960, Better Communication Guide and Manual, 1963, The Speaker's Handy Reference, 1967, Winning Wallops of Wit and Wisdom for Speakers and Toastmasters, 1968, Best Speeches for Every Purpose, 1969, Portfolio of Letter Forms, 1969, Speeches and Humor for, 1974, Comprehensive Speech and Humor Service for, 1976, Public Speaking: How, What, When, Where, Why, 1977, The Speakers Compendium, 1980; Lectr., condr. communication workshops. Developer Mnemonic Heart method of memory recall, also word picture communication. Home: 18700 Walker's Choice Rd Gaithersburg MD 20879

FRIEDMAN, EDWARD MACY, publishing executive; b. Chgo., Sept. 28, 1941; s. Irving Samuel and Ann (Stashkin) Berger; m. Wendy Levine, Jan. 16, 1966; Children: Ross Everett, Glenn Corbett. B.A., CCNY, 1963; postgrad., Hunter Coll., N.Y.C., 1964-65. Circulation-promotion writer Newsweek mag., N.Y.C., 1963; assoc. editor Med. World News, N.Y.C., 1964-68; editor Med.-Surg. Rev., Oradell, N.J., 1968-72, Med. Lab. Observer, Oradell, 1969-75, The Clin. Laboratorian, 1975, RN mag., Oradell, 1975-77, RN Recruiter, 1975-77, Nursing Opportunities, 1975-77; assoc. pub. Lab. Mgmt., N.Y.C., 1978, pub., 1979—; asso. pub. Lab. Animal, N.Y.C., 1978, pub., 1979—; compiler, editor Sharpening Laboratory Management Skills, 1978. Recipient Jesse H. Neal Editorial Achievement award Am. Bus. Press, 1972, 74, 76, Jesse H. Neal Certificates of Merit, 1975. Home: 46 Cedar St Cresskill NJ 07626 Office: 475 Park Ave S New York NY 10016

FRIEDMAN, ELI A., nephrologist; b. N.Y.C., Apr. 9, 1933; s. Israel and Ida (Gutman) F.; m. Mildred Barrett-Lennard, June 16, 1957; children: Amy Louise, Rebecca Alicia, Sara Jo. B.S., Bklyn. Coll., 1953; M.D., SUNY Downstate Med. Center, 1957. Intern in medicine Harvard Med. Sch., 1957-58; resident in medicine Peter Bent Brigham Hosp., Boston, 1960-61; Am. Heart Assn. research fellow Harvard U., 1958-60; mem. faculty Downstate Med. Center, Bklyn., 1963—, prof., 1972—, chief div. renal disease, 1963—; bd. dirs. Am. Bur. Med. Aid to China, 1979—, Cleve. Found., 1979—, Bklyn. Nephrology Found., 1978—. Author: Acute Renal Failure, 1973, Strategy in Renal Failure, 1978, Diabetic Renal-retinal Syndrome, 1980. Served to lt. comdr. USPHS, 1961-63. Grantee NIH, USPHS, N.Y. Kidney Found., N.Y. State Kidney Disease Inst., Am. Kidney Fund; Alumni medal Downstate Med. Coll. Mem. Am. Soc. Nephrology, Internat. Soc. Nephrology, Am. Soc. Artificial Internal Organs, A.C.P., Am. Soc. Immunology, Transplantation Soc., Assn. Am. Physicians; fellow Explorers Club. Co-inventor suitcase artificial kidney. Home: 1049 E 17th St Brooklyn NY 11230 Office: 450 Clarkson Ave Brooklyn NY 11203 *Achievement is as much a function of unswerving persistence, which is a learned behavior pattern, as it is of intellectual endowment, over which we have no control. Effective individuals, though often very bright, have learned to stick with it even after initial or repetitive failure. All of us lose some or even most of the time indicating the need to extract maximal joy from our wins no matter how infrequent the event.*

FRIEDMAN, EMANUEL, publishing company executive; b. N.Y.C., June 2, 1919; s. Abraham and Yetta (Jonas) F.; m. Carmel Abelson, July 7, 1940; 1 dau., April. B.S., CCNY, 1938; M.S., U. Md., 1940. Instr. history CCNY, N.Y.C., 1953-55; editor Collier's Ency. Crowell-Collier Pub. Co., N.Y.C., 1957—; sr. editor Macmillan Pub. Co., N.Y.C., 1958-69; editor-in-chief, v.p. Crowell-Collier Pub. Co., N.Y.C., 1971—. Served as 1st lt. Sanitary Corps, Med. Dept. U.S. Army, 1943-46. Mem. Am. Hist. Assn. Home: 486 Tenafly Rd Englewood NJ 07631 Office: Macmillan Pub Co 866 3d Ave New York NY 10022

FRIEDMAN, EMANUEL A., medical educator; b. N.Y.C., June 9, 1926; s. Louis and Pauline (Feldman) F.; m. E. Judith Salomon, June 6, 1948; children: Lynn Alice, Meryl Ruth, Lee Martin. A.B., Bklyn. Coll., 1947; M.D., Columbia U., 1951, Med. Sc.D., 1959; M.A., Harvard U., 1969. Diplomate: Am. Bd. Ob-Gyn. Intern Bellevue Hosp., N.Y.C., 1951-52; resident Columbia-Presbyn. Hosp., N.Y.C., 1952-57; instr. Columbia Coll. Physicians and Surgeons, 1957-59, asst. prof., 1960-62, asso. prof., 1962-63; prof., chmn. dept. ob-gyn Chgo. Med. Sch., 1963-69; chmn. dept. ob-gyn Michael Reese Hosp., Chgo.,

1963-69; prof. ob-gyn Harvard U., 1969—; obstetrician-gynecologist-in-chief Beth Israel Hosp., Boston, 1969—. Author: Labor: Clinical Evaluation and Management, 1967, 2d edit., 1978, Rh-Isoimmunization and Erythroblastosis Fetalis, 1969, Lymphatic System of Female Genitalia, 1971, Biological Principles and Modern Practice of Obstetrics, 1974, Blood Pressure, Edema and Proteinuria in Pregnancy, 1976, Pregnancy Hypertension, 1977, Uterine Physiology, 1979, Advances in Perinatal Medicine; author: Obstetrical Decision Making, 1982, Management of Labor, 1983, Gynecological Decision Making, 1983. Served with USNR, 1944-46. Recipient Joseph Mather Smith research prize Columbia U., 1958, Disting. Alumnus award Bklyn Coll., 1964, Bicentennial commemorative silver medallion award Columbia U., 1967. Fellow ACS, Am. Coll. Ob-Gyn, N.Y. Acad. Medicine; mem. N.Y. Acad. Scis., Soc. Exptl. Biology and Medicine, Soc. Gynecologic Investigation, AAUP, AAAS, Alpha Omega Alpha. Home: 260 Beacon St Boston MA 02116 Office: 330 Brookline Ave Boston MA 02215

FRIEDMAN, EMERICH IMRE, biologist, educator; b. Budapest, Hungary, Dec. 20, 1921; came to U.S., 1965; s. Hugo and Gisella (Singer) F.; m. Naomi Krausz, Sept. 16, 1953 (div. 1970); 1 dau., Daphna; m. Roseli Ocampo, July 22, 1974. Ph.D., U. Vienna, 1951. Instr., lectr. Hebrew U., Jerusalem, 1952-66; assoc. prof. Queens U., Kingston, Ont., Can., 1967-68, Fla. State U., Tallahassee, 1968-76, prof., 1976—; vis. prof. Fla. State U., Tallahassee, 1966-67, U. Vienna, 1975. Contbr. articles to profl. jours. Recipient Congl. Antartic Service medal NSF, 1979, resolution of commendation Gov. of Fla., 1978. Fellow Linnean Soc. London; mem. Am. Soc. Microbiology, Brit. Phychol. Soc., Indian Phycol Soc., Am. Phycol Soc., Internat. Phycol. Soc., Societe Phycologique de France, Internat. Soc. for Study of Origins of Life. Jewish. Discoverer micro-organism (cryptoendolithic lichens) living in Antarctic rocks, 1976. Home: 3042 Cloudland Dr Tallahassee FL 32312 Office: Dept Biol Sci Fla State U Tallahassee FL 32306

FRIEDMAN, EUGENE WARREN, surgeon; b. N.Y.C., Mar. 10, 1919; s. Isadore and Dora (Abramowitz) F.; m. Geraldine F. Gewirtz, Nov. 11, 1945; children: John Henry, Robert James. A.B., NYU, 1939, M.D., 1943. Diplomate: Am. Bd. Surgery. Intern, resident in surgery Morrisania City Hosp., N.Y.C., 1943-45; resident in surgery Mt. Sinai Hosp., N.Y.C., 1947-48, attending surgeon, chief div. head and neck surgery, 1952—, clin. prof. surgery Sch. Medicine, 1967—; resident and fellow in surgery Meml. Hosp., N.Y.C., 1948-52; attending surgeon tumor surgery Manhattan State Hosp., N.Y.C., 1960-72; attending surgeon, co-dir. head and neck surgery French Polyclinic Med. Ctr., N.Y.C., 1965-72; cons. head and neck surgery Bronx-Lebanon Hosp. Ctr., N.Y.C., 1960—, Peninsula Hosp. Ctr., 1960—, Bronx VA Hosp., 1960—; attending surgeon Doctors Hosp., N.Y.C., 1960—; cons. surgeon Lenox Hill Hosp., N.Y.C., 1976—; lectr. Editor: Lasers in Surgery and Medicine; contbr. chpts. to books and articles in field to profl. jours. Mem. sci. adv. bd. Chemotherapy Found., N.Y.C., Sanuel Waxman Research Fund, Israel Cancer Research Fund, N.Y.C.; bd. dirs. Am. Cancer Soc., N.Y.C., 1976—; med. dir. Greater N.Y. Area State of Israel Bonds, 1976—. Served to capt. AUS, 1945-47. Recipient 2d annaward Israel Cancer Research Fund, 1981. Fellow ACS, N.Y. Acad. Medicine, Am. Soc. Lasers in Medicine and Surgery; mem. N.Y. Surg. Soc., N.Y. Cancer Soc., N.Y. Head and Neck Soc., Soc. Head and Neck Surgeons, Soc. Surg. Oncology, Am. Soc. Clin. Oncology, Internat. Soc. Lasers in Surgery and Medicine (sec.-treas. 1980-82), N.Y. County Med. Soc., AMA, N.Y. State Med. Soc. Democrat. Jewish. Clubs: Univ.; Lotos (N.Y.C.). Home: 55 E Park Ave New York NY 10021 Office: 715 Park Ave New York NY 10021

FRIEDMAN, GERALD MANFRED, educator, geologist; b. Berlin, Germany, July 23, 1921; came to U.S., 1946, naturalized, 1950; s. Martin and Frieda (Cohn) F.; m. Sue Tyler, June 27, 1948; children: Judith Fay Friedman Rosen, Sharon Mira Friedman Azaria, Devorah Paula Friedman Zweibach, Eva Jane Friedman Scholle, Wendy Tamar. Student, U. Cambridge, Eng., 1938-39; B.Sc., U. London, Eng., 1945, D.Sc., 1977; M.A., Columbia, 1950, Ph.D., 1952. Lectr. Chelsea Coll., London, 1944-45; analytical chemist E.R. Squibb & Sons, New Brunswick, N.J., also J. Lyons & Co., London, 1945-48; asst. geology Columbia, 1950; temporary geologist N.Y. State Geol. Survey, 1950; instr., then asst. prof. geology U. Cin., 1950-54; cons. geologist, Sault Ste. Marie, Ont., Can., 1954-56; mem. research dept. Pan Am. Petroleum Corp. (Amoco), Tulsa, 1956-64, sr. research scientist, 1956-60, research asso., 1960-62, supr. sedimentological research, 1962-64; Fulbright vis. prof. geology Hebrew U., Jerusalem, Israel, 1964; prof. geology Rensselaer Poly. Inst., 1964-84, prof. emeritus, 1984—; adviser Judo Club, 1964—; research scientist Hudson Labs., Columbia, 1965, 66-69, research assoc. dept. geology, 1968-73; vis. prof. U. Heidelberg, Germany, 1967; cons. scientist Inst. Petroleum Research and Geophysics, Israel, 1967-71; lectr. Oil & Gas Cons. Internat., 1968—; pres. Northeastern Sci. Found., 1979—;; vis. scientist Geol. Survey of Israel, 1970-71, 78; mem. Com. Sci. Soc. Presidents, 1974-76. Co-author: Principles of Sedimentology, 1978, Exploration for Carbonate Petroleum Reservoirs,, 1982, Exercises in Sedimentology, 1982; editor: Jour. Sedimentary Petrology, 1964-70 (Best Paper award 1961), Northeastern Geology, 1979—, (Earth Scis. History), 1982—; sect. editor: Chem. Abstracts, 1962-69; editorial bd.: Sedimentary Geology, 1967—, Israel Jour. Earth Scis, 1970-76, Jour. of Geology, 1977—, GeoJournal, 1977—; co-editor, contbr.: Carbonate Sedimentology in Central Europe, 1968; editor, contbr.: Depositional Environments in Carbonate Rocks, 1969; co-editor: Modern Carbonate Environments, 1983; Contbr. articles to profl. jours. Mem. phys. edn. com. Tulsa YMCA, 1958-63; bd. dirs. Troy Jewish Community Council, 1966-72, 74-77. Fellow Mineral. Soc. Am. (mem. nominating com. for fellows 1967-69, awards com. 1977-78), Geol. Soc. Am. (publs. com. 1980-82), AAAS (chmn. geology and geography 1978-79, councillor 1979-80); mem. Am. Chem. Soc. (group leader 1962-63), Am. Assn. Petroleum Geologists (chmn. carbonate rock com. 1965-69, mem. research com. 1965-71, 76-82, lectr. continuing edn. program 1967—, adv. council 1974-75, disting. lectr. 1972-73, mem. disting. lectr. com. 1975-78, ho. of dels. 1977-80, 83—, sect. sec. 1979-80, sect. treas. 1980-81, sect. pres 1982-83, nat. v.p. 1984—), Soc. Econ. Paleontologists and Mineralogists (nat. v.p. 1970-71, pres. 1974-75, sect. pres. 1967-68, Best Paper award Gulf Coast sect. 1974), Am. Geol. Inst. (governing bd. 1971-72, 74-75), Internat. Assn. Sedimentologists (v.p. 1971-75, pres. 1975-78, nat. corr. U.S.A. 1971-73), Geol. Soc. Israel, Geol. Vereinigung, Assn. Geology Tchrs. (nat. treas. 1951-55, pres. Okla. 1962-63, pres. Eastern sect. 1983-84), Assn. Earth Sci. Editors (v.p. 1970-71, pres. 1971-72), N.Y. State Geol. Assn. (pres. 1978-79), U.S. Judo Fedn. (San Dan), Sigma Gamma Epsilon (nat. v.p. 1978-82, nat. pres 1982—). Home: 32 24th St Troy NY 12180

FRIEDMAN, H. HAROLD, cardiologist, internist; b. N.Y.C., July 31, 1917; s. Morris and Sarah (Rudnitsky) F.; m. Charlotte Lostfogel, Mar. 7, 1943; children: Alan Edward, Marsha Lynn, Betsy Ellen. B.S., N.Y. U., 1936, M.D., 1939. Intern Jewish Hosp., Bklyn., 1939-41, resident, 1941-42, 46, Bellevue Hosp., N.Y.C., 1947; practice medicine specializing in cardiology and internal medicine, Denver, 1948—; attending physician, dir. heart sta. Rose Med. Center, pres. med. staff, 1959; attending physician St. Joseph Hosp., Denver; fellow in medicine N.Y. U. Coll. Medicine, 1947; pres. med. staff Nat. Jewish Hosp., 1969; assoc. clin. prof. medicine U. Colo. Sch. Medicine, Denver, 1963-75, prof., 1975—; Mem. Colo. State Bd. Med. Examiners, 1962-67. Author: Outline of Electrocardiography, 1963, Diagnostic Electrocardiography and Vectorcardiography, 1971, 2d edit., 1977; Editor: Problem-Oriented Medical Diagnosis, 1975, 3d edit., 1983. Served to capt. M.C. AUS, 1942-46. Recipient Outstanding Clin. Faculty Teaching award U. Colo. Sch. Medicine, 1981-82. Fellow A.C.P., Am. Coll. Cardiology, Am. Coll. Chest Physicians, Council on Clin. Cardiology, Am. Heart Assn.; mem. AMA, Denver Med. Soc., Colo. Med. Soc., Phi Beta Kappa. Home: 442 Leyden St Denver CO 80220 Office: 2045 Franklin St Denver CO 80205

FRIEDMAN, HAL LEE, advertising agency executive, novelist; b. Bronx, N.Y., May 24, 1942; s. Manuel Meyer and May (Weinreb) F.; m. Sophia B. Midas, May 31, 1981. B.A., Rutgers U., 1964. Co-creative dir. Warren, Muller, Dolobowsky, Inc. (advt.), N.Y.C., 1968-76; sr. v.p., asso. creative supr. J. Walter Thompson, Inc., N.Y.C., 1976—. Author: Tunnel, 1979, Crib, 1981; songwriter. Recipient Clio award (4), Andy award, numerous others. Mem. ASCAP. Home: 41 W 10th St New York NY 10011

FRIEDMAN, HANS ADOLF, architect; b. Hamburg, Germany, June 10, 1921; came to U.S., 1939, naturalized, 1942; s. Sally and Erna (Samson) F.; m. Maxine Oppenheimer, May 31, 1952; children: Eric, Katy, John, Paul. B.Arch., Ill. Inst. Tech., 1950. Chief architect DeLeuw, Cather & Co., Chgo., 1951-61; sr. partner Friedman, Omarzu, Zion & Lundgoot, Chgo., 1961; pres. A.M. Kinney Assocs., Inc., Chgo., 1961—; partner A.M. Kinney Assocs.-William Rabon, Cin., 1961—; v.p. Kintech Services, Inc., 1975—; lectr. So. Ill. U., 1959. Editor: Inland Architect, 1958-64. Chmn. Evanston (Ill.) Preservation Commn. Served with AUS, 1942-46. Recipient Distinguished Bldg. awards Chemplex Co., Rolling Meadows, Ill., 1969, S.C. Johnson & Sons, Wind Point, Wis., 1969, Quaker Oats Co., Jackson, Tenn., 1973, Moore Bus. Forms, Inc., Glenview, Ill., 1973; Lab. of Yr. award Am. Critical Care, 1980. Fellow AIA; mem. Nat. Trust for Historic Preservation, Landmarks Preservation Council of Ill. Home: 1024 Judson Ave Evanston IL 60202 Office: 801 Davis St Evanston IL 60201

FRIEDMAN, HAROLD EDWARD, lawyer; b. Cleve., Apr. 7, 1934; s. Joseph and Mary (Schreibman) F.; m. Nancy Schweid, Aug. 20, 1961; children: Deborah, Jay, Susan. B.S., Ohio State U., 1956; LL.B., Case Western Res U., 1959. Bar: Ohio 1960. Since practiced in, Cleve.; partner Simon, Haiman, Gutfeld, Friedman & Jacobs, 1967-80, Ulmer, Berne, Laronge, Glickman & Curtis, 1981—. Sec., Harry K. and Emma R. Fox Charitable Found.; pres. Jewish Vocat. Services, Cleve.; v.p. Nat. Assn. Jewish Vocat. Services; pres. Cleve. Hillel Found.; vice chmn. endowment fund Jewish Community Fedn. Cleve., bd. dirs.; v.p. Cleve. Hosp. Found., Bur. Jewish Edn., Jewish Convalescence and Rehab. Center, Big Bros. Greater Cleve. Recipient Kane Leadership award Jewish Community Fedn. Cleve., 1974. Mem. Am., Ohio, Cleve. bar assns. Club: Oakwood Country. Home: 23149 Laureldale St Shaker Heights OH 44122 Office: 900 Bond Court Bldg Cleveland OH 44114

FRIEDMAN, IRVING SIGMUND, international economist; b. N.Y.C., Jan. 31, 1915; s. Sigmund and Sara (Tobor) F.; m. Edna M. Edelman, Sept. 27, 1938; children: Barbara Ellen Friedman Chambers, Kenneth Sigmund, John Stephen. A.B., Columbia U., 1935, M.A., 1937, Ph.D. (Univ. fellow 1938-39), 1940. Asst. to trade commr. Govt. of India, 1940-41; with div. monetary research U.S. Treasury, 1941-46, asst. dir., 1944, 46; acting fin. attache U.S. Embassy, Chungking, China; fin. adv. to U.S. Army Hdqrs., Chungking, also spl. missions to India and Egypt, 1944; chief U.S.-Can. div. IMF, 1946-48, policy asst. to dept. mng. dir., 1948-50, dir. exchange restriction dept., 1950-64; econ. adv. to pres. IBRD, 1964-72, chmn. econ. com., 1964-72, mem. pres.'s council, 1964-72; prof.-in-residence World Bank, 1971-74, adv. to pres., 1972-74; sr. adv. internat. ops., sr. v.p. Citibank, N.Y.C., 1974-80; sr. internat. advisor First Boston Corp., 1980—; advisor Asian Devel. Bank, 1981—, African Devel. Bank, 1982—; vis. fellow Yale U., 1970-71, Soul's Coll., Oxford, Eng., 1970-71; guest lectr. Vatican univs., 1970; vis. prof. U. Va., 1980—; spl. responsibility for staff work Nat. Adv. Council Internat. Monetary and Fin. Problems.; Chmn. Center of Concern, 1971, Population Resource Ctr.; vice chmn. North South Round Table on Money and Fin. Author: (with M.G. deVries) Post-war U.S. Economic Policy, 1948, Foreign Exchange Controls, 1959, Inflation: A Worldwide Disaster, 1973 (transl. into German, Spanish, Japanese, Turkish and Finnish), 2d edit., 1980, Emerging Role of Private Banks in the Developing World, 1978, World Debt Dilemma: Managing Country Risk, 1983; contbr. articles on fin. and econs. to profl. jours. Decorated Order of Sacred Treasure, Japan, comdr. Order of Falcon, Iceland). Mem. Am. Econ. Assn., Internat. Devel. Soc. (pres. 1974-75), Council on Fgn. Relations. 860 UN Plaza New York NY Office: 1015 18th St NW Washington DC

FRIEDMAN, JAMES WINSTEIN, economist, educator; b. Cleve., Sept. 25, 1936; s. Theodore and Gertrude (Winstein) F.; m. Marcia Sherman, Aug. 11, 1957; children: Nancy Elizabeth, Robert. B.A., U. Mich., 1959; M.A., Yale U., 1960, Ph.D., 1963. U. Instr., then asst. prof. econs. Yale U., 1962-68; mem. faculty U. Rochester, N.Y., 1968-83, prof. econs., 1972-83, prof. polit. sci., 1980-83, chmn. dept. econs., 1975-76; prof. econs. Va. Poly. Inst. and State U., Blacksburg, 1983—; mem. research staff Cowles Found., 1963-68, asst. dir., 1964-66; vis. prof. U. Bielefeld, W. Ger., 1976, Hebrew U., Jerusalem, 1979. Author: Oligopoly and the Theory of Games, 1977, The Theory of Oligopoly, 1983; co-author: An Experiment in Noncooperative Oligopoly, 1979; contbr. articles to profl. jours. Fellow Econometric Soc. (asso. editor jour. 1975-81); mem. Am. Econ. Soc. Office: Dept Econs Va Poly U and State U Blacksburg VA 24061

FRIEDMAN, JAY BENTLEY, dentist, educator; b. N.Y.C., Nov. 17, 1909; s. Louis and Anna (Friedman) F.; m. Judith Berman, Sept. 1, 1935; children—Rosalynd, Marilyn. B.S., Coll. City N.Y., 1928; D.D.S., N.Y. U., 1932. Gen. practice dentistry, Lawrence, N.Y., 1932—; faculty N.Y. U. Coll. Dentistry, 1933—; now prof. fixed prosthodontics; staff Walter Reed Inst. Dental Research, 1968; Presented clinics on diagnosis and treatment planning in mouth rehab. at every Dental Soc. in Greater N.Y., 1941—; radio speaker WNYC for Oral Health Com. Greater N.Y., 1941—. Founding mem. Nat. Hist. Soc.; asso. mem. Am. Mus. Natural History; charter mem. Franklin Mint Collectors Soc. Recipient Illuminated scroll for 25 years teaching and research N.Y. U., 1959, Bronze medallion for 35 years teaching and research, 1969. Fellow Assn. for Advancement Psychotherapy, Royal Soc. Health Gt. Brit.; mem. Am. Dental Assn. (life), AAUP, Am. Acad. Oral Medicine (founding), Nat. Rehab. Assn., Am. Soc. Dentistry for Children, Smithsonian Assos., Omicron Kappa Upsilon (life). Club: N.Y. U. (N.Y.C.) (founding mem.). Home: 124 Rand Pl Lawrence NY 11559 Office: NY U Sch Dentistry 421 1st Ave New York City NY 10010 also 124 Rand Pl Lawrence NY 11559

FRIEDMAN, JEFFREY FRANKLIN, corporation executive; b. N.Y.C., Apr. 7, 1946; s. Alvin E. and Pesselle (Rothenberg) F.; m. Helen Finegold, July 10, 1977; 1 son, Edward Joseph. B.A., Harvard U., 1967; M.A. in Physics, Princeton U., 1971; student, Fordham Law Sch. (evening div.), 1979—. Protfolio mgr. Dreyfus Corp., N.Y.C., 1971—; pres., dir. Dreyfus Spl. Income Fund; pres. Dreyfus Number Nine Fund, Dreyfus Third Century Fund; dir. S.J. Schafer Assocs., 1983—. Mem. N.Y. Soc. Security Analysts, Seldon Soc., Am. Phys. Soc. Home: 510 E 23d St New York NY 10010 Office: Dreyfus Corp 767 5th Ave New York NY 10153

FRIEDMAN, JOEL, exploration and equipment manufacturing company executive; b. Denver, Aug. 17, 1939; s. Israel and Josephine (Mandell) F.; m. Elaine Doris Greenbaum, Feb. 19, 1966; children—Edward J., Jennifer C. B.A. in History, Columbia U., 1961; postgrad., N.Y. U. Grad. Sch. Bus. Adminstrn., 1961-62. Jr. exec. trainee, account exec. Merrill Lynch, Pierce, Fenner & Smith, 1961-67; registered rep. Bear, Stearns & Co., 1967-69; founder, dir. Metrocare Enterprises, St. Petersburg, Fla., 1968-69; partner Steindecker, Friedman, N.Y.C., 1969-70, Haber-Friedman, Inc., 1970-71; founder, pres. New Am. Industries, Inc., N.Y.C., 1971-73; founder, 1973; since pres. Kenai Corp., N.Y.C.; chmn. bd. Founders Property Corp., N.Y.C., 1975—; dir. Campanelli Industries, Inc. Bd. dirs., exec. v.p. Asthmatic Children's Found.; bd. visitors Columbia Coll. Mem. Young Pres. Orgn. Office: 477 Madison Ave New York NY 10022

FRIEDMAN, JOSEPH BIVENS, lawyer; b. Caldwell, Ohio, June 30, 1911; s. Joseph Henry and Minnie (Bivens) F.; m. Mary Elizabeth Brown, Dec. 24, 1935; children—Jane, Robert Brown. A.B., Coll. Wooster, 1932; J.D., Ohio State U., 1935. Bar: Ohio bar 1935, U.S. Supreme Ct. bar 1939, D.C. bar 1946, N.Y. bar 1948. Atty. Office Gen. Counsel, U.S. Treasury, 1935-48, chief counsel Office Internat. Finance, also asst. gen. counsel treasury, 1945-48; Adviser to minister finance Republic of Ecuador, 1942-44; asst. exec. dir. War Refugee Bd., 1944; mem. U.S. del. Allied-Swiss negotiations regarding German external assets, 1946; legal adviser U.S. del. 1st and 2d ann. meetings bds. govs. IMF and IBRD, 1946, 47; cons. IMF; adviser Central Bank Philippines, 1950, spl. counsel, 1954; legal adviser U.S. Econ. Survey Mission to Philippines, 1950. Decorated Order Al Merito, Ecuador, 1943. Mem. Fed., D.C. bar assns., Phi Beta Kappa, Order of Coif. Home: 3315 Quesada St NW Washington DC 20015 Office: 3315 Quesada St NW Washington DC 20015

FRIEDMAN, JOYCE BARBARA, computer scientist, educator; b. Washington, Jan. 5, 1928; d. Harry and Eleanor (Balkind) F. B.A., Wellesley Coll., 1949; M.A., Radcliffe Coll., 1952; Ph.D., Harvard U., 1965. Mathematician, ACF Industries, Inc., Alexandria, Va., 1954-56; sr. mathematician Tech. Ops., Inc., Washington, 1956-60; mem. tech. staff MITRE Corp., Bedford, Mass., 1960-65; asst. prof. Stanford U., 1965-68; asso. prof. computer and communication scis. U. Mich., Ann Arbor, 1968-71, prof., 1971-83; prof., chair computer sci. Boston U., 1983—. Mem. Assn. Computational Linguistics (pres. 1971), Assn. Computing Machinery (Siglash chmn. 1970-73), Assn. Symbolic Logic, Am. Math. Soc. Office: 111 Cummington St Boston U. Boston MA 02215

FRIEDMAN, K. BRUCE, lawyer; b. Buffalo, Jan. 1, 1929; s. Bennett and Florence Ruth (Israel) F. A.B., Harvard U., 1950; LL.B., Yale U., 1953. Bar: N.Y. 1955, D.C. 1956, Calif. 1958. Atty. CAB, Washington, 1955-57; practiced in, San Francisco, 1958—; mem. firm Zang, Friedman & Damir, 1969-78, Cotton, Seligman & Ray, 1978-79, Friedman & Olive, 1980—; lectr. law U. Calif. Law Sch., Berkeley, 1966-76; Pres. Econ. Roundtable San Francisco, 1964. Bd. dirs. San Francisco chpt. Am. Jewish Com., 1960-76; trustee World Affairs Council No. Calif., San Francisco, 1970-76; pres. San Francisco Estate Planning Council, 1973-74; regional dir. for No. Calif. Asso. Harvard Alumni, 1981—. Served with U.S. Army, 1953-55. Fellow Am. Coll. Probate Counsel, Am. Bar Found.; mem. Bar Assn. San Francisco, State Bar Calif., Am. Bar Assn. Jewish. Clubs: Bankers, Calif. Tennis, Rotary, Commonwealth of Calif., Harvard (San Francisco) (pres. 1976-78). Office: One Maritime Plaza Suite 1430 San Francisco CA 94111

FRIEDMAN, LAWRENCE M., legal educator; b. Chgo., Apr. 2, 1930; s. I. M. and Ethel (Shapiro) F.; m. Leah Feigenbaum, Mar. 27, 1955; children: Jane, Amy. A.B., U. Chgo., 1948, J.D., 1951, LL.M., 1953; LL.D. (hon.), U. Puget Sound, 1977. Mem. faculty St. Louis U., 1957-61, U. Wis., 1961-68; prof. law Stanford U., 1968—, Marion Rice Kirkwood prof., 1976—; David Stouffer Meml. lectr. Rutgers U. Law Sch., 1969; Sibley lectr. U. Ga. Law Sch., 1976. Author: Contract Law in America, 1965, Government and Slum Housing, 1968, A History of American Law, 1973, The Legal System: A Social Science Perspective, 1975, Law and Society: An Introduction, 1977, (with Robert V. Percival) The Roots of Justice, 1981; Co-editor: (with Stewart Macaulay) Law and the Behavioral Sciences, 1969, 2d edit., 1977, American Law and the Constitutional Order, 1978; contbr. articles to profl. jours. Served with U.S. Army, 1953-54. Recipient Triennial award Order of Coif, 1976, Willard Horst prize, 1982; Center for Advanced Study in Behavioral Scis. fellow, 1974-75. Mem. Law and Soc. Assn. (pres. 1979-81), Am. Acad. Arts and Scis., Commn. on Behavioral and Social Scis. and Edn. Home: 724 Frenchman's Rd Stanford CA 94305

FRIEDMAN, LOUIS FRANK, lawyer; b. Balt., May 26, 1941; s. Dave Sylvan and Miriam (Sugarman) F.; m. Phyllis Cole, Dec. 25, 1968; 1 son, Samuel. B.S., U. Md., 1963, J.D., 1965; LL.M. in Taxation, Georgetown U., 1968. Bar: Md. bar 1965. Since practiced in, Balt.; ptnr. firm Friedman & Friedman, 1965—; prof. taxation U. Balt. Sch. Bus., 1975—. Pres. 9400 Ocean Hwy. Condominium, Ocean City, Md., 1976; chmn. young lawyers div. Asso. Jewish Charities, 1975-76. Mem. Md. Bar Assn. (tax counsel 1977-79), Order of Coif, Phi Alpha Delta. Jewish religion. Home: 3314 Old Forest Rd Baltimore MD 21208 Office: First Nat Bank Bldg Baltimore MD 21202

FRIEDMAN, MALCOLM, laywer, business executive; b. Bklyn., Apr. 10, 1936; s. David and Bee (Kisver) F.; m. Joyce Danin, Aug. 12, 1962; children: Hal Daniel, Vicki Lea, Eric Scott. B.S., NYU, 1957; J.D., N.Y. Law Sch., 1962. Bar: N.Y. 1963, Ky. 1969, D.C. 1979, Ind. 1982. Law clk., N.Y.C., 1962-63, pvt. practice law, 1963-64; asst. gen. counsel Youngs Drug Products Corp. and Holland Rantos Co. Inc., N.Y.C., 1964-69; asst. counsel, asst. sec. Nat. Industries Inc., Louisville, 1969-72, v.p., sec., house counsel, 1973-75, v.p.-legal, sec., 1975-78; mem. firm Handmaker, Weber, Meyer & Rose, Louisville, 1978—. Served with AUS, 1957-59. Mem. N.Y. State Bar Assn., Ky. Bar Assn., Louisville Bar Assn., ABA, D.C. Bar Assn.; Mem. Phi Delta Phi. Lodges: K.P.; Masons. Home: 728 Waterford Rd Louisville KY 40207 Office: Suite 2307 Citizens Plaza Louisville KY 40202

FRIEDMAN, MARK WILLARD, hotel and real estate developer; b. Chgo., Aug. 30, 1924; s. Percy S. and Florence (Josephson) F.; m. Anne Worbioff, May 15, 1952 (div. 1967); children—Peter Lee, Matthew; m. Joanna Young, June 11, 1973 (div. Jan. 1976). Student, U. Ill., 1942, DePaul U., 1945-46. Pres. Transam Properties, Chgo., 1962—; pres. Mark IV Mgmt. & Realty, Friedman Enterprises, Inc.; chmn. Metroam. Hotels Corp. including (Knickerbocker Hotel),,,,,, all Chgo.; owner Blackstone Hotel, Aruba-Sheraton Hotel and Casino, 1978—; pres., dir. Elgin Gas & Power Co.; chmn. Interam. Communications, Inc.; dir. Sheraton Inns, Inc., Fed. Bake Co., Internat. Savs. & Loan Assn. Contbr. articles to periodicals. Chmn. hotel div. Chgo. March of Dimes, 1968, real estate div. Chgo. Combined Jewish Appeal, 1967, hotel-restaurant div. Heart Fund Assn., 1966-69; active Mt. Sinai Med. Center. Named to Hospitality Mags. Hall of Fame. Mem. Greater Chgo. Hotel and Motel Assn. (dir.), Chgo. Real Estate Bd. (dir.), Greater N. Mich. Ave. Assn. (dir.),

Miami Beach C. of C. (hon. life 1978—), Chgo. Conv. Bur., B'nai B'rith. Jewish. Clubs: Covenant, Variety (Chgo.); Young Pres.'s, Grove Isle, Jockey (Miami); Turnberry Isle (North Miami Beach). Home: 5185 N Bay Rd Miami Beach FL 33140 Office: 1301 N State Pkwy Chicago IL 60610

FRIEDMAN, MARTIN, museum administrator; b. Pitts., Sept. 23, 1925; s. Israel and Etta (Louik) F.; m. Mildred Shenberg, Sept. 3, 1949; children: Lise, Ceil, Zoe. Student U. Pa., 1943-45; B.A., U. Wash., 1947; M.A., UCLA, 1949; postgrad., Columbia, 1956-57, U. Minn., 1958-60. Instr. art, curriculum cons. Los Angeles City Schs., 1949-56; instr. art U. Calif. Extension, Los Angeles, 1950-51; fellow Bklyn. Mus., 1956-57; grantee Belgian-Am. Ednl. Found., Brussels, 1957-58; fellow Am. art U. Minn., 1959-60; curator Walker Art Center, Mpls., 1958-60, dir., 1961—; Am. fine arts commr. Sao Paulo Bienal, 1963; mem. Nat. Collection Fine Arts Commn., Commn. on Founds. and Pvt. Philanthropy; hon. mem. commn. Nat. Mus. Am. Art; mem. adv. bd. on environ. planning Bur. Reclamation, 1965-69; art adv. com. Japan House Gallery; arts adv. group Bus. Com. for Arts, 1970; adv. Ind. Curators Inc. Author catalogues on internat. contemporary art, also books, articles; Dir. numerous mus. exhbns. Trustee Spring Hill Found., Minn., 1970-81; trustee Am. Fedn. Arts, 1972—, mem. internat. exhbns. com., 1976—; mem. mus. adv. panel Nat. Endowment for Arts, 1973-78, Nat. Council Arts, 1978—. Served with USNR, 1943-46. Ford Found. fellow, 1961-62; artist fellow Aspen Inst. Humanistic Studies, 1980; intellectual interchange fellow, Japan, 1982. Mem. Coll. Art Assn., Assn. Art Mus. Dirs. (pres. 1978-79, trustee 1979—), Internat. Com. for Museums and Collections of Modern Art. Clubs: Mpls., Century Assn. Home: 1505 Mount Curve Ave Minneapolis MN 55403 Office: Walker Art Center Vineland Pl Minneapolis MN 55403

FRIEDMAN, MARTIN BURTON, chem. co. exec.; b. N.Y.C., June 21, 1927; s. William L. and Ella (Holstein) F.; m. Rita Fleischman, Mar. 19, 1950; children—Jay Edward, Ellen Jane. Student, St. Mary's Coll., 1943-44, Cornell U., 1944-45; B.A., Pa. State U., 1949. Mgr. advt. and promotion chems. group Sun Chem. Corp., N.Y.C., 1949-54; mgr. advt. and promotion textile chems. dept. Am. Cyanamid Co., N.Y.C., 1954-58, mgr. advt. and promotion, organic chems. div., 1958-60, gen. merchandising mgr., mgr. fibers div., 1961-64, dir. sales, 1964-65, dir. mktg., 1965-69, asst. gen. mgr. fibers div., 1969-72; v.p. IRC Fibers Co. (subs.), 1969-72; exec. v.p. Formica Corp., Cin., 1972-73, pres., 1973-80; pres. fibers div. Am. Cyanamid, 1980—; chmn. bd. 4th Dist. Fed. Res. Bank, Cin. Contbr. articles to textile and tech. publs. Served with USNR, 1945-46. Mem. Am. Chem. Soc., Am. Assn. Textile Chemists and Colorists. Club: Chemists (N.Y.C.). Home: 777 Butternut Dr Franklin Lakes NJ 07417 Office: Wayne NJ *It has been the American business enterprise making products and profit that has given society the jobs to make it affluent, the leisure time to make it exciting, and the medical, nutritional and sanitary advances that enable life to be enjoyed in good health. It has been our business and economic success, in great measure that has spawned new demands and expectations in our society.*

FRIEDMAN, MARTIN JAY, advertising agency executive; b. Bklyn., Apr. 8, 1929; s. Milton and Doris (Greenfield) F.; m. Pamela Margaret Green, Dec. 13, 1959; children: Mark Andrew, Adam Michael. A.B., Syracuse U., 1950; M.B.A., NYU, 1964. Mdsg. account exec. Benton & Bowles, 1953-59; with Dancer-Fitzgerald-Sample, 1959-74, sr. v.p. mktg. services, 1967-74; editor New Product News; columnist Ad Week New Product Watch; mktg. cons., 1974—; vis. advt. profl. dept. advt. Mich. State U., 1977; advt. adv. council U. Fla., 1982—. Served with AUS, 1951-53. Republican. Jewish. Home: 1710 Daytonia Rd Miami Beach FL 33141

FRIEDMAN, MELVIN JACK, educator; b. Bklyn., Mar. 7, 1928; s. Julian and Edith (Block) F.; m. H. Judith Zervitz, Oct. 12, 1958; children—Jennifer, James. A.B., Bard Coll., 1949; M.A., Columbia, 1951; Ph.D. (Am. Council Learned Socs. fellow 1953, Jr. Sterling fellow 1953-54), Yale, 1954. Instr. English U. Md., 1956-59, assoc. prof. English and comparative lit., 1962-66; instr., asst. prof. English U. Wis.-Madison, 1959-62; prof. comparative lit. and English U. Wis.-Milw., 1966—; guest prof. U. Hannover, W. Ger., 1977; Assisted in establishing programs in Am. studies in India for State Dept., 1960; mem. fellowship com. Nat. Endowment for Humanities, 1973. Author: Stream of Consciousness: A Study in Literary Method, 1955, (with others) Calepins de Bibliographie Samuel Beckett, 1971, William Styron, 1974 (French transl. in Fer de Lance 1977-78); Editor: Configuration Critique de Samuel Beckett, 1964, (with Lewis A. Lawson) The Added Dimension: The Art and Mind of Flannery O'Connor, 1966, 2d edit., 1977, (with August J. Nigro) Configuration Critique de William Styron, 1967, (with John B. Vickery) The Shaken Realist: Essays in Modern Literature in Honor of Frederick J. Hoffman, 1970, Samuel Beckett Now: Critical Approaches to His Novels, Poetry and Plays, 1970, 2d edit., 1975, (with Irving Malin) William Styron's The Confessions of Nat Turner: A Critical Handbook, 1970, The Vision Obscured: Perceptions of Some Twentieth-Century Catholic Novelists, 1970, (with Rosette C. Lamont) The Two Faces of Ionesco, 1978, Samuel Beckett sect. of Critical Bibliography of French Literature: The Twentieth Century, 1980; assoc. editor: Yale French Studies, 1951-53; editor: Wis. Studies in Contemporary Literature, 1960-62, Comparative Literature Studies, 1962-66; asst. mng. editor: Modern Lang. Jour, 1963-70; mem. editorial bd.: Jour. of Popular Culture, 1970—, Renascence, 1972—, Studies in the Novel, 1973—, Fer de Lance, 1976—, Jour. Am. Culture, 1978—, Studies in American Fiction, 1979—, Contemporary Lit., 1981—, Jour. Beckett Studies, 1982—; contbr. (with Rosette C. Lamont) articles to profl. jours. Served with U.S. Army, 1954-56. Fulbright fellow to Lyon, France, 1950-51; vis. sr. fellow U. East Anglia, 1972; Fulbright sr. lectr. U. Antwerp, 1976. Mem. MLA (sec., chmn. Comparative Lit. 5 group 1964-66, sec., chmn. English 11 group 1972-74, sec., chmn. 20th century English lit. div. 1977-78), Internat. Comparative Lit. Assn., Am. Comparative Lit. Assn., Brecht Soc., Popular Culture Assn., Am. Com. for Irish Studies, PEN Am. Center, Phi Kappa Phi. Home: 1211 E Courtland Pl Milwaukee WI 53211

FRIEDMAN, MEYER, physician; b. Kansas City, Kans., July 13, 1910; s. Joseph and Eva (Werby) F.; m. Mary Alicia Campbell, Sept. 5, 1942; children: Joyce, Joseph, Mark. A.B., Yale, 1931; M.D., Johns Hopkins, 1935. Intern Kansas City (Mo.) Gen. Hosp., 1935-36; resident Michael Reese Hosp., Chgo., 1936-38, U. Wis. Gen. Hosp., Madison, 1938-39; dir. Harold Brunn Inst., Mt. Zion Hosp., San Francisco, 1939—; cons. Riker Labs. of 3M Co., St. Paul; mem. Wilton Park Conf. Center, Wiston House, Sussex, Eng.; Cecil H. and Ida Green vis. prof. Tex. Christian U., 1977; speaker T.W. Samuels Meml. Lecture Series Millikin U. Author: Functional Cardiovascular Disease, 1947, Pathogenesis of Coronary Artery Disease, 1969, (with Dr. Ray Rosenman) Type A Behavior and Your Heart, 1974; Contbr. articles to profl. jours. Served with M.C. AUS, 1942-45; PTO. Recipient Disting. Diploma of Honor Pepperdine U., 1982. Mem. Am. Soc. for Clin. Investigation, Western Assn. Physicians, Calif. Acad. Medicine, Am. Physiol. Soc., Am. Heart Assn., Soc. for Exptl. Biology and Medicine, Yale Alumni Assn. of San Francisco (dir.), Harold Brunn Soc. for Med. Research. Clubs: Villa Taverna, Il Cenacolo, Roxburghe, 100 (dir.), Family, Rotary. Home: 160 San Carlos Ave Sausalito CA 94965 Office: Mt Zion Hosp and Med Center PO Box 7921 San Francisco CA 94120

FRIEDMAN, MICHAEL PETER, physician, educator; b. Bklyn., Jan. 17, 1934; s. Morris H. and Ida (Topkin) F.; m. Patricia Anne McCaffrey, Sept. 1, 1963; children: Michael Peter, Daniel Thomas. Student, Western Md. Coll., 1955-58; M.D., U. Md., 1962. Intern U. Md. Hosp., 1962-63, resident, 1963-65; postdoctoral fellow U. Pa., 1965-68, asst. prof. microbiology, 1968-69; asst. prof. medicine Cardeza Found. Hematol. Research, 1969-73; dir., chmn. dept. medicine St. Francis Med. Center, Trenton, N.J., 1973—; prof. medicine Hahnemann Med. Coll., Phila., 1973—, dir. div. hematology/oncology, 1978—. Served with U.S. Army, 1953-55. Mem. Leukemia Soc. (pres. Central N.J., trustee), N.J. Med. Soc., AAAS, Phila. Hematol. Soc., Am. Soc. Hematology, Am. Soc. Clin. Investigation, Phila. Med. Assn. Clubs: Wedgewood Swim, Haddonfield Tennis. Home: 920 Washington Ave Haddonfield NJ 08033

FRIEDMAN, MILTON, economist; b. Bklyn., July 31, 1912; s. Jeno Saul and Sarah Ethel (Landau) F.; m. Rose Director, June 25, 1938; children: Janet, David. A.B., Rutgers U., 1932, LL.D., 1968; A.M., U. Chgo., 1933; Ph.D., Columbia, 1946; LL.D., St. Paul's (Rikkyo) U., 1963, Kalamazoo Coll., 1968, Lehigh U., 1969, Loyola U., 1971, U. N.H., 1975, Harvard U., 1979, Brigham Young U., 1980, Dartmouth Coll., 1980, Gonzaga U., 1981; Sc.D., Rochester U., 1971; L.H.D., Rockford Coll., 1969, Roosevelt U., 1975, Hebrew Union Coll., Los Angeles, 1981; Litt.D., Bethany Coll., 1971; Ph.D. (hon.), Hebrew U., Jerusalem, 1977, D.C.S., Francisco Marroquín U., Guatemala, 1978. Asso. economist Nat. Resources Com., Washington, 1935-37; mem. research staff Nat. Bur. Econ. Research, N.Y., 1937-45, 1948-81; vis. prof. econs. U. Wis., 1940-41; prin. economist, tax research div. U.S. Treasury Dept., 1941-43; asso. dir. research, statis. research group, war research div. Columbia, 1943-45; asso. prof. econs. and statistics U. Minn., 1945-46; asso. prof. econs. U. Chgo., 1946-48, prof. econs., 1948-62, Paul Snowden Russell Distinguished Service prof. econs., 1962-82, prof. emeritus, 1983—; Fulbright lectr. Cambridge U., 1953-54; vis. Wesley Clair Mitchell Research prof. econs. Columbia, 1964-65; fellow Center for Advanced Study in Behavioral Sci., 1957-58; Mem. Pres.'s Commn. All-Vol. Army, 1969-70, Pres.'s Commn. on White House Fellows, 1971-74, Pres.'s Econ. Policy Adv. Bd., 1981—; vis. scholar Fed. Res. Bank, San Francisco, 1977; sr. research fellow Hoover Instn., Stanford U., 1977—. Author: (with Carl Shoup and Ruth P. Mack) Taxing to Prevent Inflation, 1943, Income from Independent Professional Practice, (with Simon S. Kuznets), 1946, Sampling Inspection, (with Harold A. Freeman, Frederic Mosteller, W. Allen Wallis), 1948, Essays in Positive Economics, 1953, A Theory of the Consumption Function, 1957, A Program for Monetary Stability, 1959, Price Theory: A Provisional Text, 1962, (with Rose D. Friedman) Capitalism and Freedom, 1962, (with Anna J. Schwartz) A Monetary History of the United States, 1867-1960, 1963, Inflation: Causes and Consequences, 1963, The Great Contraction, 1965, Monetary Statistics of the United States, 1970, (with Robert Roosa) The Balance of Payments: Free vs. Fixed Exchange Rates, 1967, Dollars and Deficits, 1968, The Optimum Quantity of Money and Other Essays, 1969, (with Walter W. Heller) Monetary vs. Fiscal Policy, 1969, A Theoretical Framework for Monetary Analysis, 1972, (with Wilbur J. Cohen) Social Security, 1972, An Economist's Protest, 1972, There Is No Such Thing As A Free Lunch, 1975, Price Theory, 1976, Milton Friedman's Monetary Framework, 1974, Tax Limitation, Inflation and the Role of Government, 1978, (with wife) Free To Choose, 1980, (with Anna J. Schwartz) Monetary Trends in the U.S. and the United Kingdom, 1982, Bright Promises, Dismal Performance, 1983, (with wife) Tyranny of the Status Quo, 1984; Editor: Studies in the Quantity Theory of Money, 1956; Bd. editors: Am. Econ. Rev, 1951-53, Econometrica, 1957-69; adv. bd.: Jour. Money, Credit and Banking, 1968—; columnist: Newsweek mag, 1966-84; contbg. editor, 1971-84; contbr. articles to profl. jours. Recipient John Bates Clark medal Am. Econ. Assn., 1951; Nobel prize in econs., 1976; named Chicagoan of Year Chgo. Press Club, 1972, Educator of Year Chgo. United Jewish Fund, 1973; recipient Pvt. Enterprise Exemplar medal Freedoms Found., 1978. Fellow Inst. Math. Stats., Am. Statis. Assn., Econometric Soc.; mem. Nat. Acad. Scis., Am. Econ. Assn. (mem. exec. com. 1955-57, pres. 1967), Am. Enterprise Inst. (adv. bd. 1956-79), Western Econ. Assn. (pres. 1984-85), Royal Economic Soc., Am. Philos. Soc., Mont Pelerin Soc. (bd. dirs. 1958-61, pres. 1970-72). Club: Quadrangle. Office: Hoover Instn Stanford U Stanford CA 94305

FRIEDMAN, MORTON LEE, lawyer; b. Aberdeen, S.D., Aug. 4, 1932; s. Philip and Rebecca (Feinstein) F.; m. Marcine Lichter, Dec. 20, 1955; children—Mark, Philip, Jeffrey. Student, U. Mich., 1950-53; A.B., Stanford U., 1954, LL.B., 1956. Bar: Calif. bar 1956. Mem. firm Kimble, Thomas, Snell, Jamison & Russell, Fresno, 1957, Busick & Busick, Sacramento, 1957-59; sr. partner firm Friedman, Collard, Poswall & Thompson, Sacramento, 1959—; dir. Capitol Bank of Commerce; lectr. various law schs. and seminars; mem. Calif. Bd. Continuing Edn. Pres. Mosaic Law Congregation, 1977-80; v.p. Sacramento Jewish Fedn., 1980—; chmn. Sacramento campaign United Jewish Appeal, 1981. Served to 1st lt. USAF, 1956. Fulbright candidate Stanford Law Sch., 1956. Fellow (Am. Coll. Trial Lawyers); mem. ABA, Calif. Bar Assn., Sacramento County Bar Assn. (pres. 1976), Am. Trial Lawyers Assn., Calif. Trial Lawyers Assn. (v.p. 1973-75), Capitol City Lawyers Club (past pres.), Am. Bd. Trial Advocates (adv., pres. 1977), West Sacramento C. of C. (dir.), Order of Coif. Democrat. Club: Kiwanis. Home: 1620 McClaren Dr Carmichael CA 95608 Office: 7750 College Town Dr Suite 300 Sacramento CA 95826

FRIEDMAN, MYLES IVAN, educator; b. Chgo., Apr. 5, 1924; s. Max Edward and Ethel (Goldman) F.; m. Betty Ann McDowell, July 4, 1978; children: Gregg Alan, Myles Ivan. M.A., U. Chgo., 1957, Ph.D., 1959. Real estate, home builder, 1946-58; asst. prof. edn. Northwestern U., 1958-60, asso. prof., 1960-64; prof. edn. U. S.C., 1964—; vis. prof. U. Calif., Berkeley, summer 1968; cons. in field. Bd. dirs. Head Start Evaluation and Research Center; dir. research Regional Edn. Lab., Carolinas and Va. Author: Rational Behavior, 1975, Teaching Reading and Thinking Skills, 1979; sr. author: Improving Teacher Education, 1979; Contbr. articles to profl. jours. Served with USAAF, 1942-46. Mem. Am. Psychol. Assn., Am. Ednl. Research Assn. (com. to study research edn.). Home: 1709 Seay Ct Columbia SC 29206 Office: Coll Edn Univ SC Columbia SC 29208 *The harder I work, the luckier I get.*

FRIEDMAN, PAUL JAY, radiologist, educator; b. N.Y.C., Jan. 20, 1937; s. Louis Alexander and Rose (Solomon) F.; m. Elisabeth Clare Richardson, June 20, 1960; children: Elizabeth Ruth, Deborah Anne, Matthew Alexander, Rachel Clare. B.S., U. Wis., 1955; postgrad., Oxford (Eng.) U., 1957-58; M.D., Yale U., 1960. Intern Einstein Med. Sch., N.Y.C., 1960-61; resident in radiology Columbia-Presbyn. Hosp., N.Y.C., 1961-64; fellow in pulmonary pathology Yale U. Hosp., 1966-68; mem. faculty U. Calif. Med. Sch., San Diego, 1968—, prof. radiology, 1975—, vice chmn. dept., 1979-81, assoc. dean acad. affairs, 1982—; cons., VA. Editorial bd.: Investigative Radiology, 1976—; contbr. articles med. jours. Served as lt. comdr. M.C. USNR, 1964-66. Markle scholar acad. medicine, 1969-74; Picker Found. advanced acad. fellow and scholar, 1966-69. Fellow Am. Coll. Radiology; mem. Am. Thoracic Soc., Assn. Univ. Radiologists, Am. Assn. Med. Colls., AAUP, Fleischner Soc., Calif. Radiology Soc., San Diego Radiology Soc., Phi Beta Kappa, Alpha Omega Alpha. Home: 5644 Soledad Rd La Jolla CA 92037 Office: 225 Dickinson St San Diego CA 92103

FRIEDMAN, PHILMORE H., pharmaceutical company executive, lawyer; b. N.Y.C, Sept. 6, 1925; s. Leslie and Rose (Abelson) F.; m. Patricia Schaeffer, Nov. 24, 1949; children: Lawrence, Jonathan, Carla. B.B.A. in Acctg., CCNY, 1949; LL.B., Bklyn. Law Sch., 1953. Bar: N.Y.; C.P.A., N.Y. With various C.P.A. firms, N.Y.C., 1949-57; tax mgr. Authur Young & Co., N.Y.C., 1957-64, Pfizer Inc., 1964-67, v.p. corp. tax, 1974—; tax mgr. Pfizer Internat., N.Y.C., 1968, dir. taxes, 1969-74. Served to yeoman 2d class USN, 1943-46. Mem. N.Y. State Soc. C.P.A.'s (chmn. N.Y. state tax com.), Tax Execs. Inst. (chmn. internat. tax com. 1966-68), Internat. Tax Assn. (past pres.), U. S.C. of C. (tax com. 1979-83), Pharms. Mfrs. Assn. (past chmn. tax com.), Internat. Fiscal Assn., Com. on State Taxation. Jewish. Home: 14 Ulster Dr Jericho NY 11753 Office: Pfizer Inc 235 42d St New York NY 10017

FRIEDMAN, RALPH, financial executive; b. N.Y.C., Jan. 11, 1904; s. Uri Mark and Mary (Behrman) F.; m. Ruth J. Ehrich, Feb. 11, 1933 (dec. July 1981); children: Peter R., Robert E. Student, CCNY, 1921, N.Y. U., 1922-24. Sr. gen. partner Friedman & Co.; mem. N.Y. Stock Exchange, 1933-46; chmn. bd. dirs. Met. Body Co., 1940-48, Standard Milling Co., Kansas City, Mo., 1951-63; dir. Bank Leumi Le Israel, Tel Aviv and N.Y., 1963-79; chmn. exec. com., dir. Bank Leumi Trust Co., N.Y., 1968-79; chmn. finance com., dir. Eastern Life Ins. Co., N.Y., until 1971. Trustee Friedman Found., N.Y.C.; bd. dirs. Holy Land Conservation Fund, Inc.; mem. council com. Yale Sch. Forestry and Environ. Studies; mem. cave expdn. to Mex. for N.Y. Zool. Soc., 1940; mem. Friedman-Anthony Alaska Expdn. for Am., Mus. Natural History, U.S. Nat. Park Service, 1948, Friedman-Mozambique Expdn. for Am. Mus. of Natural History, 1968, S.W. Africa Expdn. for Am. Mus. Natural History, 1970; chmn. Am. Jewish Com., 1964-66; dir. Nat. Park Found., 1968-70. Mem. N.Y. Acad. Scis., Linnean Soc., Am. Mus. of Natural History (patron), N.Y. Zool. Soc. (life), N.Y. State Forestry Assn., Am. Acad. Polit. Sci., Explorers Club. Home: 14 E 75th St New York NY 10021 Office: 564 Fifth Ave New York NY 10036

FRIEDMAN, RAYMOND, fire protection co. exec.; b. Portsmouth, Va., Feb. 9, 1922; m. Myra Weiner, June 26, 1945. B.S. chem. engring, Va. Poly. Inst., 1942; Ph.D., U. Wis., 1948. Research scientist Westinghouse Electric Co., Pitts., 1943-46, 48-55; research mgr., v.p. Atlantic Research Corp., Alexandria, Va., 1955-69; v.p., mgr. research div. Factory Mut. Research Corp., Norwood, Mass., 1969—. Contbr. articles to profl. jours. Mem. Am. Chem. Soc., Am. Inst. Chem. Engrs., Soc. Fire Protection Engrs., AAAS, Combustion Inst. (pres. 1978-82). Club: Cosmos. Patentee in field. Home: 126 Kings Grant Rd Weston MA 02193 Office: Factory Mutual Research Corp Norwood MA 02062

FRIEDMAN, ROBERT ALAN, investment banker; b. Albany, N.Y., Apr. 21, 1941; s. Louis F. and Evelyn (Hershkowitz) Friedman; m. Linda S. Shulman, Dec. 20, 1964; children: David, Lori. B.E.E., CCNY, 1962, M.B.A., 1967. C.P.A., N.Y. Mgmt. cons. Coopers & Lybrand, N.Y.C., 1965-68; fin. analyst Goldman, Sachs & Co., N.Y.C., 1968—, v.p., controller, 1977-80, ptnr., 1980—; trustee Instl. Liquid Assets, Instl. Tax Exempt Assets, Chgo., Asset. Mgmt. Portfolios, Exempt Assets Portfolios, Internat. Money Market Fund. Bd. dirs., exec. v.p. Greater N.Y. council Boy Scouts Am., N.Y.C. Served with U.S. Army, 1962-63. Mem. Pub. Securities Assn., Am. Inst. C.P.A.s, N.Y. State Soc. C.P.A.s, Securities Industry Assn., Fin. Execs. Inst. Clubs: Broad Street, Brae Burn Country. Office: 85 Broad St New York NY 10004

FRIEDMAN, ROBERT SIDNEY, educator; b. Balt., Mar. 1, 1927; s. Harry N. and Eva (Cohen) F.; m. Renee Cohen, Aug. 11, 1953; children-Helene, David. B.A., Johns Hopkins, 1948; M.A., U. Ill., 1950, Ph.D., 1953. Research asst. Bur. Govt. Research, Md., 1953-55; instr. govt. and politics U. Md., 1955-56; from instr. to asso. prof. govt. La. State U., 1956-61; research asso. Inst. Pub. Adminstrn., U. Mich., 1961-67, acting dir., 1967-68; asso. prof. polit. sci. U. Mich., 1961-66, prof., 1966-68; prof., head dept. polit. sci. Pa. State U., 1968-78; dir. Center for Study Sci. Policy, Inst. for Policy Research and Evaluation, 1978—. Co-author: Local Government in Maryland, 1955, Government in Metropolitan New Orleans, 1959, Political Leadership and the School Desegration Crisis in New Orleans, 1963; author: The Michigan Constitutional Convention and Adminstrative Organization: A Case Study in the Politics of Constitution-Making, 1963, Professionalism: Expertise and Policy Making, 1971; Contbr. to: Politics in the American States, 1965, 2d edit., 1971, also jours. in field. Mem. bd. Pa. Civil Liberties Union, 1969-72; mem. State College (Pa.) Zoning Hearing Bd., 1976-79; mem. sci. adv. bd. Three Mile Island-2 Cleanup, 1981—. Served with AUS, 1945-46. Recipient McKay Donkin award for disting. service, 1980. Mem. Am., N.E., Midwest, So. polit. sci. assns., Am. Soc. for Pub. Adminstrn., Pi Sigma Alpha. Home: 1136 Westerly Pkwy State College PA 16801 Office: Burrowes Bldg Pa State U University Park PA 16802

FRIEDMAN, SIDNEY A., financial services executive; b. Bklyn., Mar. 7, 1935; s. Benjamin and Celia (Jacobs) F.; m. Sue Helen Mansbach, May 2, 1965; children: Lori Beth, Wendi Ellen. B.S., NYU, 1957; student, Bklyn. Law Sch., 1958. C.L.U., fin. cons.; registered health underwriter. Pres. Corp. Fin. Services, Phila., 1970-81; pres., chmn. bd. Innovative Fin. Services, Phila., 1981—; past pres. Phoenix Mut. Adv. Council; motivational speaker, cons. life ins. orgns. Author: Be Careful What You Wish For, 1981, If It Ain't Broke, Don't Fix It, 1982. Bd. dirs. Fight for Sight, 1983, Phila. Variety Club, 1983. Mem. Million Dollar Round Table, Top of the Table, 10 Million Dollar Forum; recipient Nat. Quality award, 1983. Mem. Am. Coll. Life Underwriters (pres. 1971-72), Health Underwriters, Nat. Assn. Security Dealers (registered investment advisor), Assn. Advanced Underwriters, Phila. Assn. Life Underwriters, Gen. Agts. and Mgrs Assn. So. N.J. (past pres.), C.L.U.s So. N.J. (past pres.), Gen. Agts and Mgrs. Assn. Democrat. Home: 536 Heartwood Rd Cherry Hill NJ 08003 Office: Innovative Financial Services Inc 1510 Walnut St Philadelphia PA 19102

FRIEDMAN, STANLEY, manufacturing company executive; b. Worcester, Mass., Jan. 1, 1928; s. Hyman Julius and Edith Annette (Morin) F.; m. Sharon May Bercovitz, Nov. 4, 1951; children: Steven Z., Bruce L., Clayton S. B.S., Worcester Poly. Inst., 1950; M.S., Purdue U., 1951; Sloan fellow, Stanford U. Grad. Sch. Bus., 1960-61. With RCA, 1957-63; from asst. to gen. mgr. to gen. mgr., div. v.p. Lockheed Electronics Co., 1963-70; pres. Spaulding Fibre Co., Tonawanda, N.Y.; also v.p. Monogram Industries, 1970-78; group gen. mgr., v.p. ITT Corp., N.Y.C., 1979—; dir. Mennen Med. Co., Clarence, N.Y., 1976-79; adv. bd. M&T Bank, Buffalo, 1972-78; mem. industry adv. bd. Coll. Bus. Adminstrn., Niagara U., 1977-78; bd. dirs. Buffalo-Erie County Labor-Mgmt. Council, 1976-78. Served with AUS, 1945-46. Sr. mem. IEEE; mem. Nat. Elec. Mfrs. Assn. (div. chmn. 1978), Sigma Xi, Tau Beta Pi (fellow 1950-51), Eta Kappa Nu. Republican. Jewish. Home: 18 Danebury Downs Up Saddle River NJ 07458 Office: ITT 320 Park Ave New York NY 10022

FRIEDMAN, STANLEY, insect physiologist, educator; b. N.Y.C., Dec. 11, 1925; s. Nathan and Eva (Rothstein) F.; m. Frances Ray Shapiro, May 21, 1955; children—David, Douglas, Catherine, Matthew. Student, CCNY, 1941-43; B.A., U. Ill., 1948; Ph.D., Johns Hopkins U., 1952. Research asso. U. Ill., 1953-56; biochemist NIH, 1956-58; asst. prof. entomology Purdue U., 1958-62; research fellow London Sch. Hygiene and Tropical Medicine, 1962-63; asso. prof.

entomology Purdue U., 1963-64, U. Ill., Urbana, 1964-68, prof., 1968—, head dept. entomology, 1975—. Served with USN, 1943-46. Mem. Am. Soc. Zoology, Am. Soc. Biol. Chemists, Biochem. Soc., Entomol. Soc. Am., AAAS, Federated Socs. Exptl. Biology and Medicine, Sigma Xi. Office: 320 Morrill Hall 505 S Goodwin St Urbana IL 61801

FRIEDMAN, STEPHEN, motion picture producer; b. N.Y.C., Mar. 15, 1937; s. Irving and Dorothy (Lipsious) F. B.S., U. Pa., 1957; LL.B., Harvard U., 1960. Bar: N.Y. 1958. Atty. Herzfeld & Rubin, N.Y.C., 1958-59, Columbia Pictures, 1960-63, Ashley Famous Agy., 1963-67, Paramount Pictures, Los Angeles, 1967-69; chmn. bd. Kings Road Prodns., Burbank, Calif., 1979—. Producer: Last Picture Show, 1971, Lovin Molly, 1973, Slap Shot, 1980, Fast Break, 1977, Little Darlings, 1978, Hero at Large, 1980, Bloodbrothers, 1978, Eye of the Needle, 1982. Mem. Acad. Motion Picture Arts and Scis., Bar Assn. State N.Y. Office: Kings Road Prodns 1901 Ave of the Stars Los Angeles CA 90067

FRIEDMAN, THOMAS LOREN, foreign correspondent; b. Mpls., July 20, 1953; s. Harold Abraham and Margaret (Phillips) F.; m. Ann Louise Bucksbaum, Nov. 23, 1978. B.A., Brandeis U., 1975; M.Phil., St. Anthony's Coll., Oxford U., 1978. Staff corr. UPI, London, 1978-79, Middle East corr., Beirut, 1979-81; reporter Bus. Day. sect. N.Y. Times, N.Y.C., 1981-82, Beirut bur. chief, 1982—. Recipient Pulitzer prize, 1983, George Polk award L.I. U., 1982, Livingston award Livingston Found., 1983, Overseas Press Club award, 1980. Jewish. Home: PO Box 113-6964 Beirut Lebanon

FRIEDMAN, WILBUR HARVEY, lawyer; b. N.Y.C., May 2, 1907; s. Isador Peter and Zara (Sloat) F.; m. Frances Margolis, May 21, 1943. A.B., Columbia, 1927; LL.B., Columbia U., 1930. Bar: N.Y. 1931. Law sec. U.S. Supreme Ct. Justice Harlan F. Stone, 1930-31; atty. office U.S. solicitor gen., 1931-32; mem. firm Proskauer, Rose, Goetz, & Mendelsohn, N.Y.C., 1932-40, partner, 1940—, sr. partner, 1955—; dir., sec. The Charter Corp.; Lectr. N.Y. U. insts. on fed. taxation, 1943-65, N.Y. U. Sch. Gen. Edn., 1955-60; Bd. dirs., sec. Lawrence M. Gelb Found.; chmn. exec. com. bd. visitors Columbia U. Law Sch.; bd. dirs., v.p. Erwin S. Wolfson Found. Contbr. articles to profl. jours. Mem. N.Y. County Lawyers Assn. (pres. 1975-77, exec. com. 1977-79, chmn. com. on group ins. 1960-74, chmn. spl. com. on consumers agreements 1977-83), ABA. (ho. of dels. 1978—), N.Y. Bar Assn. (exec. com. sect. taxation 1968-76), N.Y.C. Bar Assn. (chmn. com. on mgmt. and operation profl. practice 1981—), Phi Beta Kappa, Tau Delta Phi. Clubs: Lotos, Harmonie, Princeton U. (N.Y.C.). Home: 1016 Fifth Ave New York NY 10028 Office: 300 Park Ave New York NY 10022

FRIEDMAN, WILLIAM FOSTER, pediatrician, cardiologist, educator; b. N.Y.C., July 24, 1936; s. and Lillian (Cohen) F.; m. Judith Serwer, Dec. 1957; children: Michael Ross, Jonathan Todd; m. Denise Willett, July 1976. A.B., Columbia Coll., 1957; M.D., State U. N.Y., Downstate, 1961. Intern, resident pediatrics Johns Hopkins Hosp., Balt., 1961-64; commd. med. officer USPHS, 1964; clin. asso. cardiology br. Nat. Heart and Lung Inst., Bethesda, Md., 1964-66, sr. investigator, pediatric cardiologist, 1966-68; prof. pediatrics and medicine, chief pediatric cardiology U. Calif., San Diego Sch. Medicine, La Jolla, 1968-79; J.H. Nicholson prof. pediatrics UCLA Sch. Medicine, 1979—, chmn. dept., 1979—; also staff UCLA Hosps. and Clinics, 1979—. Mem. editorial bd.: Heart Bull, 1968-72, Circulation, 1970-75, European Jour. Cardiology, 1972—, Pediatric Research, Cardiovascular Medicine, Am. Jour. Cardiology; guest editor various med. jours. Fellow Am. Acad. Pediatrics (mem. young investigators award com.), Am. Coll. Cardiology; mem. Am. Heart Assn. (council on clin. cardiology), Am. Physiol. Soc., Am. Soc. Pharmacology and Exptl. Therapeutics, Soc. Nuclear Medicine, Am. Soc. Clin. Investigation, Am. Fedn. for Clin. Research, Internat. Study Group for Research in Cardiac Metabolism, Soc. for Pediatric Research (councillor, program chmn. cardiology sect., v.p. 1981), Am. Pediatric Soc., Am. Inst. Higher Studies (adv. bd.), Alpha Omega Alpha. Home: 12050 Rose Marie Ln Los Angeles CA 90049 Office: UCLA Center for Health Scis Los Angeles CA 90024

FRIEDMAN, WILLIAM HERSH, otolaryngologist, educator; b. Granite City, Ill., Aug. 14, 1938; s. Joseph and Lily May (Brody) F.; m. Hillary Lee, Aug. 9, 1974; children: Joseph Morgan, Alexander Lawrence. A.B., Washington U., St. Louis, 1960, M.D., 1964. Diplomate: Am. Bd. Otolaryngology. Intern Jackson Meml. Hosp., Miami, Fla., 1964-65; resident in surgery and otolaryngology Mt. Sinai Hosp., N.Y.C., 1965-70, NIH fellow, 1966-67, asso. prof. otolaryngology, 1974-76, asso. attending physician, 1973-76; dir. otolaryngology City Hosp. Center, Elmhurst, N.Y., 1971-76; practice medicine specializing in otolaryngology, Beverly Hills, Calif., 1976, Boston, 1977; pres. Head & Neck Surgery Group, Inc., St. Louis; prof. otolaryngology, chmn. dept. St. Louis U. Sch. Medicine, 1977—; chief otolaryngology Firmin Desloge Hosp., Cardinal Glennon Meml. Hosp. for Children; pres. Auditory Health Care; v.p. Domestic Oil Corp. Contbr. articles to books and profl. jours. Fellow ACS, Am. Acad. Ophthalmology Otolaryngology, Am. Acad. Facial Plastic and Reconstructive Surgery (Ira J. Tresley Meml. award 1978), Am. Soc. Head and Neck Surgery, Am. Laryngol. Rhinol. Otol. Soc.; mem. AMA (Hektoen gold medal 1978), Med. Soc. County of N.Y., Soc. Univ. Otolaryngologists, Centurion Club of Deafness Research Found., N.Y. State Soc. Surgeons, Assn. Academic Depts. Otolaryngology, Mo. Ear, Nose and Throat Assn., St. Louis Ear, Nose and Throat Club, Phi Beta Kappa, Sigma Alpha Mu. Clubs: Westwood Country, Mo. Athletic Assn. Inventor surg. instruments, including facial plastic instrumentarium. Home: 15 Lake Forest St Saint Louis MO 63117 Office: Dept Otolaryngology 1325 S Grand Blvd Saint Louis MO 63104

FRIEDMANN, HERBERT, educator, museum dir., ornithologist; b.; b. Bklyn., Apr. 22, 1900; s. Uriah M. and Mary (Behrmann) F.; m. Karen Juul Vejlo, 1937; 1 dau., Karen Alice (Mrs. J.N. Beall). B.Sc., Coll. City N.Y., 1920; Ph.D., Cornell U., 1923. Instr. in zoology Cornell U., summer, 1922, U. Va., summer 1923; NRC research fellow in zoology Harvard, 1923-26; instr. biology Brown U., 1926-27, Amherst Coll., 1927-29; curator of birds U.S. Nat. Museum, 1929-57, head curator zoology, 1957-61; dir. Los Angeles County Mus. Natural History, 1961-70; asst. prof. exptl. embryology Grad. Sch., Howard, 1931-33; Lida Scott Brown lectr. U. Calif., Los Angeles, 1957; adj. prof. biology U. So. Calif., 1962—; research asso. zoology U. Calif. at Los Angeles, 1962, prof.-in-residence zoology, 1963-70, prof.-in-residence history of art, 1968. Author: books including The Cowbirds, 1929, Birds of North and Middle America, Part IX, 1941, Part X, 1946, Part XI, 1950, the Parasitic Cuckoos of Africa, 1948, The Symbolic Goldfinch, 1946, Birds of Mexico, Part I, 1950. Part II 1957, The Honeyguides, 1955, The Parasitic Weaverbirds, 1960, Host Relations of Parasitic Cowbirds, 1963, A Bestiary for St. Jerome, 1980; Contbr. on sci. and art subjects. Guggenheim research fellow, 1950-51; recipient Leidy medal Acad. Nat. Sci. Phila., 1955, Elliot medal Nat. Acad. Sci., 1959; Brewster medal Am. Ornith. Union, 1964. Fellow AAAS (sect. pres. 1939), Am. Ornithologists Union (pres. 1937-39); mem. Am. Soc. Zoologists, Am. Soc. Naturalists, Washington Acad. Sci. (hon. diploma in biology 1940, v.p. 1957), Biol. Soc. Washington (pres. 1957-58), Cooper Ornith. Soc. (div. pres. 1967), Nat. Acad. Sci., Paleobiol. Soc. Washington (pres. 1938), Deutsche Ornith. Gesellschaft (hon.), S. African Ornith. Union (hon.). Participated in expdns. to Argentina, the Mexican border, S. and E. Africa. Home: 350 S Fuller Ave Los Angeles CA 90036

FRIEDMANN, NORMAN ERNEST, database publishing company executive; b. Los Angeles, Mar. 18, 1929; s. Joseph and Estelle (Jonas) F.; m. Sarelle R. Riave, June 22, 1952; children: Marc, Lance, Keyla. B.S., UCLA, 1950, M.S., 1952, Ph.D., 1957. Vice pres. ITT Fed. Labs., San Fernando, Calif., 1962-64; pres. (ITT Data and Info. Systems div.), Paramus, N.J., 1964-65; chmn. bd., chief exec. officer Cordura Corp., Los Angeles, 1965—, chmn. bd., pres., 1965; mem. def. sci. bd. U.S. Dept. Def. Contbr. articles to profl. publs. Regional dir. United Way Inc.; bd. dirs. City of Hope. Recipient award Calif. Scholastic Fedn.; named Alumnus of Year U. Calif. at Los Angeles Engring. and Applied Sci., 1973. Mem. Newcomen Soc., Sigma Xi. Office: Cordura Corp 2029 Century Park E Suite 3210 Los Angeles CA 90067

FRIEDRICH, OTTO ALVA, writer, editor; b. Boston, Feb. 3, 1929; s. Carl Joachim and Lenore (Pelham) F.; m. Priscilla Boughton, Apr. 13, 1950; children: Elizabeth Charlotte, Margaret Emily, Nicholas Max, Amelia Anne, Charles Anthony. A.B. magna cum laude, Harvard, 1948. Mem. copy desk Stars & Stripes, 1950-52; with United Press in Paris and London, 1952-54; with telegraph desk N.Y. Daily News, 1954-57; mem. fgn. dept. Newsweek, 1957-62, asst. fgn. editor, 1959-62; fgn. editor Sat. Eve. Post, 1962-63, asst. mng. editor, 1963-65, mng. editor, 1965-69; free lance writer, 1969-71; sr. editor TIME, 1971-80, sr. writer, 1980—. Author: novels The Poor in Spirit, 1952, The Loner, 1964; non-fiction Decline and Fall, 1970 (George Polk Meml. award); Before the Deluge, 1972, The Rose Garden, 1972, Going Crazy, 1976, Clover, 1979, The End of the World, 1982; (with wife) juveniles The Easter Bunny That Overslept, 1957; Clean Clarence, 1959, Sir Alva and the Wicked Wizard, 1960, The Marshmallow Ghosts, 1960, The Wishing Well in the Woods, 1961, Noah Shark's Ark, 1961, The Christmas Star, 1962, The April Umbrella, 1963, The League of Unusual Animals, 1965; also numerous articles and short stories. Home: 569 Bayville Rd Locust Valley NY 11560

FRIEDRICH, PAUL, anthropologist, linguist, poet; b. Cambridge, Mass., Oct. 22, 1927; s. Carl Joachim and Lenore Louise (Pelham) F.; m. Lore Bucher, Jan. 6, 1950 (div. Jan. 1966); children: Maria Elizabeth, Susan Guadalupe, Peter Roland; m. Deborah Joanna Gordon, Aug. 9, 1975; 1 dau., Katherine Ann. B.A., Harvard Coll., 1950; M.A., Harvard U., 1951; Ph.D., Yale U., 1957. Instr. U. Conn., Storrs, 1956-57; asst. prof. Harvard U., Cambridge, Mass., 1957-58; jr. linguistic scholar Deccan Coll., Poona, India, 1958-59; asst. prof. anthropology U. Pa., Phila., 1959-62; assoc. prof. anthropology U. Chgo., 1962-67, prof. anthropology and linguistics, 1967—. Author: Proto-Indo-European Trees, 1970, Agrarain Revolt in a Mexican Village, 1970, The Mean of Aphrodite, 1978, Bastard Moons, 1979, Language, Context and the Imagination, 1979. Served to pfc. U.S. Army, 1946-47; Germany. Grantee Wenner-gren Found., 1955, NIMH, summers 1961-62; fellow Social Sci. Research Council, 1966-67; Guggenheim fellow, 1982-83. Mem. Linguistic Soc. Am. (chmn. program com. 1972, chmn. nominating com. 1975, mem. exec. com. 1981—). Home: 5550 S Dorchester Apt 609 Chicago IL 60637 Office: U Chgo Dept Anthropology 1126 E 59th St Chicago IL 60637

FRIEDRICH, STEPHEN MIRO, human resources company executive; b. Paterson, N.J., Oct. 13, 1932; s. Miroslav and Jarmila (Lier) F.; m. Barbara Elizabeth Kissock, Aug. 14, 1954; children: Joanne Elizabeth, Barbara Ann, Jennifer Anne, Stephanie Jean, Susan Maria. B.S. in Indsl. Engring, Lehigh U., 1954; postgrad., Northeastern U., 1961-62. Asst. dir. sales Craig Systems, Inc., Lawrence, Mass., 1956-60; asst. gen. mgr. radar div. Sanders Assos., Bedford, Mass., 1961-68; group dir. environ. scis. KDI Corp., Cin., 1969-71; v.p., gen. mgr. ITT Service Industries, Cleve., 1971-73; pres. ITT Aetna Corp., St. Louis, 1973-75; chmn. bd., pres., chief exec. officer, dir. LLC Corp., St. Louis, 1975-83; chmn., treas., sec., dir. The Crown Group, Inc., Atlanta, 1983—. Served to 1st lt. USAF, 1954-56. Episcopalian. Home: 11 Ocean Dr Jupiter FL 33458 Office: 3825 Presidential Pkwy Atlanta GA 30340 *Success will result from persistence tempered by a belief in basic moral absolutes.*

FRIEDRICHS, GEORGE SHELBY, investment banker; b. New Orleans, Aug. 23, 1911; s. Camille Jerome and Marguerite (Shelby) F.; m. Virginia Gore, Oct. 8, 1935; children: Mary Virginia Gore (Mrs. Peter G. Burke), George Shelby, Joseph Maybin Gore. B.B.A., Tulane U., 1933. With Woolfolk, Huggins & Shober, New Orleans, 1936-46, partner, 1942-46; with SEC, 1935-36; partner Howard, Weil, Labouisse, Friedrichs & Co., New Orleans, 1946-71; chmn. bd., chief exec. officer Howard, Weil, Labouisse, Friedrichs, Inc., New Orleans, 1971-77, chmn., 1978—; Chmn. Nat. Assn. Securities Dealers, 1965; gov. Assn. Stock Exchange Firms, 1963-70, Securities Industry Assn., 1972; past bd. dirs. Bur. Govtl. Research, New Orleans, Internat. House. Past mem. Met. Area Com., New Orleans; emeritus trustee Tulane U.; trustee U.S. Internat. Sailing Assn. Named Alumnus of Yr. Tulane U., 1982. Home: 204 Mulberry Dr Metairie LA 70005 Office: 211 Carondelet St New Orleans LA 70130

FRIEDRICHS, ROBERT WINSLOW, educator; b. Bath, Maine, Feb. 16, 1923; s. Hans William and Gladys (Donnelly) F.; m. Pauline E. Carlson, June 16, 1951; children—Robin, Paul, Carl. Student, Antioch Coll., 1941-43; B.A., Oberlin Coll., 1946; M.A., U. Wis., 1952, Ph.D., 1957; postdoctoral studies, Oxford U., 1964, Princeton, 1970, Cambridge U., 1970, 77-78, London Sch. Econs., 1971. Instr. Ming Hsien Middle Sch. and Coll., China, 1946-48; instr. sociology Columbia, 1953-54; asst. prof., chmn. sociology dept. Elmira Coll., 1954-57; vis. prof. grad. program in sociology Bklyn. Coll., 1967; prof., chmn. dept. sociology Drew U., 1957-70; prof., chmn. anthropology and sociology Williams Coll., 1971—; vis. prof. Iliff Sch. Theology, 1974, U. N.C. at Chapel Hill, 1976, 77; cons. Victoria Found., Newark Bd. Edn. Author: A Sociology of Sociology, 1970; Contbr. articles to profl. jours. Vice chmn. Madison-Florham Park ARC, 1959-60; chmn. human relations com. Morris County Community Chest and Council, 1958-59; Co-chmn. Citizens for Kennedy and Johnson, Morris County, 1960. Named man of year Morris County Urban League, 1959. Mem. Internat. Sociol. Assn., Am. Sociol. Assn. (Sorokin award 1971), Soc. Values in Higher Edn., AAUP, AAAS, Eastern Sociol. Soc., Soc. Sci. Study Religion, Danforth Assos. Address: 33 Whitman St Williamstown MA 01267 *Do not say what others can say; do not do what others can do.*

FRIEL, BRIAN, author; b. Omagh, County Tyrone, No. Ireland, Jan. 9, 1929; emigrated to U.S., 1963; s. Patrick and Christina (MacLoone) F.; m. Anne Morrison, Dec. 27, 1955; children: Paddy, Mary, Judy, Sally, David. Student, St. Joseph's Tng. Coll., Belfast, Ireland, 1959-60; Litt.D. (hon.), Rosary Coll., Chgo. Tchr. various schs., 1950-60. Writer, 1960—; with, Tyrone Guthrie Theatre, Mpls., 1963; Author: short stories A Saucer of Larks, 1964, The Gold in the Sea, 1966; The Diviner: Brian Friel's Best Short Stories, 1983; plays Philadelphia, Here I Come, 1966, The Loves of Cass McGuire, 1966, Lovers, 1967, Crystal and Fox, 1968, The Mundy Scheme, 1969, The Gentle Island, 1970, The Freedom of the City, 1972, Volunteers, 1975, Living Quarters, 1977, Faith Healer, 1979, 80, transl., 1981, Aristocrats, 1979, Three Sisters, 1981; The Communication Cord, 1983; Contbr.: short stories to New Yorker. Recipient Macauley fellow Irish Arts Council, 1963, Ewart-Biggs Meml. prize Brit. theatre Assn. Address: Ardmore Muff Lifford County Donegal Ireland *

FRIELING, GERALD HARVEY, JR., specialty steel company executive; b. Kansas City, Mo., Apr. 29, 1930; s. Gerald Harvey and Mary Ann (Coons) F.; m. Joan Lee Bigham, June 14, 1952; children: John, Robert, Nancy. B.S. in Mech. Engring, U. Kans., 1951. Application engr. Westinghouse Elec. Corp., Pitts., 1951-53; mfg. mgr. Madison-Faessler Tool Co., Moberly, Mo., 1956-60; gen. mgr. wire and tubing Tex. Instruments Inc., Attleboro, Mass., 1960-69; v.p. Air Products & Chems. Co., Allentown, Pa., 1969-79; pres., chief exec. officer, chmn. bd. dirs. Nat.-Standard Co., Niles, Mich., 1979—; dir. Pacesetter Bank & Trust Co.-S.W., Niles, Brockway Glass, CTS, Protection Mut. Ins. Co.; adv. bd. Liberty Mut. Ins. Co.; instr. Brown U., 1965-68. Author. Pres. bd. Kutztown (Pa.) Coll., 1974-78; bd. dirs. Allentown YMCA, 1975-79, Allentown Salvation Army, 1976-79, Swain Sch., Allentown, 1973-77; v.p. Allentown-Leigh County C. of C., 1974-79. Served to lt. USNR, 1953-56; Korea. Recipient Wire Assn. medal, 1966. Mem. Am. Welding Soc., Am. Soc. Metall. Engrs. Republican. Presbyterian. Clubs: Union League (Chgo.); Point Woods, Signal Point Country, Pickwick, Summit. Patentee in field. Office: Terminal Rd Niles MI 49120

FRIEND, EDWARD MALCOLM, JR., lawyer; s. Edward Malcolm and May (Gusfield) F.; m. Hermione Frances Curjel, Sept. 22, 1938; children: Ellen Friend Elsas, Edward M. A.B., U. Ala., 1933, LL.B., 1935. Bar: Ala. 1935. Practice in Birmingham; pres. Legal Aid Soc., Birmingham, 1954-55, Jefferson County (Ala.) Family Counseling Assn., 1958-59. Hon. editor: Ala. Law Rev. Gen. co-chmn. Jefferson County United Fund, 1959; trustee Ala. Law Sch. Found., pres., 1969-71; trustee Children's Hosp., Meth. Hosp.; bd. dirs. Jefferson County chpt. ARC; nat. bd. dirs. NCCJ, 1969-71; pres. Birmingham Area council Boy Scouts Am., 1980-81; mem. pres.'s cabinet U. Ala., 1975—, chmn., 1982, 83; mem. distbn. com. Greater Birmingham Found.; bd. govs. The Club. Served with AUS, 1941-45; Normandy; brig. gen. Res. ret. Decorated Legion of Merit, Bronze Star with cluster; Croix de Guerre with palm, France; recipient Daniel J. Meador Outstanding Alumnus award U. Ala. Law Sch., 1971; Outstanding Civilian Service award U.S. Army; Disting. Eagle award Boy Scouts Am.; Silver Beaver award, 1978; Brotherhood award NCCJ, 1981; Man of Yr. award Young Men's Bus. Club Birmingham, 1982; Outstanding Civic Leader award Nat. Assn. Fund Raising Execs., Ala. Chpt., 1983. Fellow Am. Bar Found.; mem. Ala. State Bar Assn. (chmn. joint coml lawyers and interested citizens to study Ala. correctional instns. and procedures 1975), Birmingham Bar Assn. (v.p. 1970, pres. 1971), Order of Coif, Phi Beta Kappa, Omicron Delta Kappa, Zeta Beta Tau. Club: Rotary (pres. Birmingham 1974-75). Home: 22 Woodhill Rd Birmingham AL 35213 Office: 2222 Arlington Ave S Birmingham AL 35205

FRIEND, IRWIN, economics educator; b. Schenectady, July 10, 1915; s. Solomon and Dina (Ryzowy) F.; m. Corinne Vernon, Nov. 5, 1941; children: Peter Sayre, Leslie Andrea. B.S., Coll. City N.Y., 1935; Ph.D., Am. U., 1953. Asst. dir. trading and exchange div. SEC, 1937-47; chief bus. structure div. Dept. Commerce, 1947-53; Richard K. Mellon and Edward J. Hopkinson prof. finance and econs. U. Pa., Phila., 1953—; vis. Frederick R. Kappel Prof. govt. and bus. U. Minn., 1970; cons. U.S. govt. agys., congressional coms., Portugal, India, Greece, Italy, China, Argentina, Brazil, Japan, Israel, UN and bus. orgns.; mem. exec. com. Conf. on Income and Health, 1960-63; dir. Rodney L. White Center for Financial Research, Dean Witter/Sears. Author: Impediments to Capital Formation, 1981, The Changing Role of the Individual Investor, 1978, Financial Effects of Capital Tax Reforms, 1978, The Consequences of Competitive Commissions on the New York Stock Exchange, 1972, Study of the Savings and Loan Industry, 1970, Mutual Funds and Other Institutional Investors: A New Perspective, 1970, Investment Banking and The New Issues Market, 1967, Private Capital Markets, 1964; A Study of Mutual Funds, 1962, Consumption and Saving, 1960, The Over-The-Counter Securities Market, 1958, Consumer Expenditures, Inc. and Savings, 1957, Individual Savings: Volume and Composition, 1954; Editorial bd.: Am. Econ. Rev, 1968—. Recipient research fellowship, research grants Ford Found. and NSF. Fellow Econometric Soc., Am. Statis. Assn. (chmn. bus. and econ. statis. sect. 1961-62, bd. editors jour. 1968—); mem. Am. Econ. Assn., Am. Fin. Assn. (pres. 1972), Phi Beta Kappa. Home: 706 Argyle Rd Wynnewood PA 19096 Office: Wharton Sch Finance and Commerce Philadelphia PA 19174

FRIEND, THEODORE WOOD, III, historian, former college president; b. Wilkinsburg, Pa., Aug. 27, 1931; s. Theodore Wood and Jessica (Holton) F.; m. Elizabeth Groesbeck Pierson, Feb. 20, 1960; children: Theodore Porter, Pierson, Elizabeth Robinson. Grad., St. Paul's Sch., 1949; B.A., Williams Coll., 1953, LL.D. (hon.), 1978; Ph.D., Yale U., 1958. Asst. instr. Yale U., 1955-57; mem. faculty SUNY, Bufalo. 1959-73, prof. history, 1966-73, faculty advisor to pres., 1968-69, exec. asst. to pres., 1969-70; pres. Swarthmore (Pa.) Coll., 1973-82. Author: Between Two Empires; The Ordeal of the Philippines, 1929-46, 1965; also articles.; Editor: The Philippine Polity, A Japanese View, 1968. Trustee Phila. Savs. Fund Soc., 1975—; Mem. exec. com. Pa. Commn. for Ind. Colls. and Univs., 1976-82; mem. govt. relations adv. council Nat. Assn. Ind. Colls. and Univs., 1977-81; mem. Acad. Commn., Am. Council on Edn., 1980-81, com. on confidentiality, 1981-82. Fulbright grantee, in Philippines, 1957-59; Rockefeller Found. fellow internat. relations, 1961-62; Nat. Def. Fgn. Lang. postdoctoral fellow, 1966-67; Guggenheim Found. fellow, Indonesia, Philippines, Japan, 1967-68; Woodrow Wilson Internat. Center fellow, 1983-84; recipient Bancroft prize in Am. History, 1966. Mem. Am. Hist. Assn., Assn. Asian Studies, Soc. Historians of Am. Fgn. Relations, Asia Soc., Phila. Com. on Fgn. Relations, NAACP, Phi Beta Kappa. Presbyterian. Clubs: Pundit (Buffalo); Sunday Breakfast (Phila.). Home: 1257 Upper Gulph Rd Radnor PA 19087 *I agree with Samuel Johnson, that the proper end of all human endeavor is to be happy at home. There remain, however, things to be done in order to come home happy: working for a world in which there is less want, the chance of war is reduced, and the willfulness of particular interests is diminished. Education is where I begin, and continue.*

FRIEND, WALTER WILLIAM, JR., investment banker; b. Allenhurst, N.J., June 25, 1920; s. Walter William and Helen E. (Butcher) F.; m. Doris Eleanor Schwanhausser, Dec. 20, 1947; children—Walter William III, Eleanor Provost. Grad., Polytech. Prep. Country Day Sch., 1938; B.A., Dartmouth, 1942; postgrad. in law, Yale, 1942, 46. With Pressprich Corp., N.Y.C., 1948-76, partner, 1962-68, exec. v.p., 1968-69, pres., 1969-76; 1st v.p. Blyth Eastman Dillon & Co., N.Y.C., 1976-80; sr. v.p. Blyth Eastman Paine Webber, Inc., N.Y.C., 1981—; trustee Greater N.Y. Savs. Bank. Trustee Low-Haywood Sch., Stamford, Conn. Served to 1st lt. AUS, 1942-46. Mem. Municipal Fin. Officers Assn. U.S. and Can., Municipal Forum N.Y., Municipal Analysts N.Y. (pres. 1950-53). Home: Valley Rd Wilson Point South Norwalk CT 06854 Office: 1221 Ave of Americas New York NY 10020

FRIENDLY, ED, television producer; b. N.Y.C., Apr. 8, 1922; s. Edwin S. and Henrietta (Steinmeier) F.; m. Natalie Coulson Brooks, Jan. 31, 1952; children—Brooke H., Edwin S. III. Grad., Manlius Sch., 1941. Radio exec., dir. BBD&O, N.Y.C., 1946-49; sales exec. ABC-TV, N.Y.C., 1949-53; ind. producer and packager, N.Y.C., 1953-56; producer, program exec. CBS-TV, N.Y.C., 1956-59; v.p. spl. programs NBC-TV, N.Y.C., 1959-67; pres. Ed Friendly Prodns., Los Angeles, 1967—; co-chmn. steering com. Caucus for Producers, Writers and

Dirs. Exec. producer: film Little House on the Prairie; Laugh-In; producer: film Peter Lundy and the Medicine Hat Stallion (Emmy nomination); Young Pioneers; mini-series Backstairs at the White House (11 Emmy nominations); also producer motion pictures and TV spls.; exec. producer/producer: Barbara Cartland's The Flame Is Love. Served with inf. U.S. Army, 1942-45; PTO. Recipient Spl. award Internat. Film and TV Festival N.Y., 1967; Emmy award for Laugh-In, 1968; Producer of Yr. award Producers Guild of Am., 1968; Golden Globe award Hollywood Fgn. Press, 1968; Gold medal of honor Internat. Radio and TV Soc., 1970; Christopher award for motion picture, 1975; Western Heritage award Nat. Cowboy Hall of Fame and Western Heritage Center, for Little House on the Prairie, 1975, for Peter Lundy and the Medicine Hat Stallion, 1978; Scout awards for best weekly series and show of yr. for Laugh-In, 1969. Office: 1041 N Formosa Ave Hollywood CA 90046

FRIENDLY, FRED W., educator, journalist; b. N.Y.C.; m. Ruth W. Mark; children (by previous marriage)—Andrew, Lisa, David; stepchildren—Jon Mark, Michael Mark, Richard Mark. Student, Cheshire Acad., Nichols Jr. Coll.; L.H.D., Grinnell Coll., U. R.I. Pres. CBS News, N.Y.C., 1964-66; Edward R. Murrow prof. broadcast journalism Columbia U.; adviser on communications Ford Found. Began career in radio, 1938; wrote, produced and narrated: radio series Footprints in the Sands of Time, later at, NBC, Who Said That; quiz based on quotations of famous people; collaborated (with Edward R. Murrow), in presenting oral history of 1932-45 (recorded by Columbia Records under title I Can Hear It Now); (with Walter Cronkite) Vol. IV, I Can Hear It Now-The Sixties; formerly with: CBS radio series Hear It Now; also CBS TV Series See It Now; past exec. producer: CBS TV show CBS Reports; (Recipient George Peabody awards for TV prodn.); Author: Due to Circumstances Beyond Our Control, 1967, The Good Guys, The Bad Guys, The First Amendment, 1975, Minnesota Rag, 1981. Served with AUS, 1941-45; CBI. Decorated Legion of Merit and 4 battle stars; recipient DeWitt Carter Reddick award, 1980. Mem. Am. Assn. U. Profs., Assn. for Edn. in Journalism. Home: Riverdale NY 10471 Office: Columbia U Grad Sch Journalism New York NY 10027

FRIENDLY, HENRY JACOB, judge; b. Elmira, N.Y., July 3, 1903; s. Myer H. Leah and Hallo (Friendly); m. Sophie M. Stern, Sept. 4, 1930; children—David, Joan, Ellen. A.B., Harvard, 1923, LL.B., 1927; D.H.L., Hebrew Union Coll.; LL.D., Syracuse U., Bklyn. Law Sch., Jewish Theol. Sem., Western Res. U., Brandeis U., U. Cin., U. Chgo., Harvard, Columbia, Northwestern U., N.Y. U. Bar: N.Y. bar 1928, D.C. bar 1947. Law clerk to Mr. Justice Brandeis, Washington, 1927-28; asso. law firm Root, Clark, Buckner & Ballantine, N.Y.C., 1928-36, partner, 1937-45; own firm of Cleary, Gottlieb, Friendly & Hamilton, 1946-59; dir. v.p., gen. counsel Pan Am. World Airways System, 1946-59; U.S. judge Ct. Appeals, 2d Circuit, 1959—, chief judge, 1971-73; presiding judge spl. ct. under Rail Reorgn. Act, 1974—; Overseer Harvard U., 1964-69. Author: The Need for Better Definition of Standards, 1962, Benchmarks, 1967, Federal Jurisdiction: A General View, 1973; Contbr. articles to law periodicals. Recipient Louis Stein award Fordham Law Sch.; Presdl. medal of Freedom, 1977; Thomas Jefferson Meml. award in law, 1978. Mem. Am., N.Y. State, N.Y.C. bar assns., Assn. Bar City of N.Y. (hon., Am. Law Inst., council, mem. exec. com.), Harvard Alumni Assn. (pres. 1960-61). Clubs: Harmonie, Century, Mchts.

FRIERSON, JOHN BURTON, JR., retired textile processing executive; b. Shelbyville, Tenn., Aug. 26, 1903; s. John Burton and Lissie Mai (Ransom) R.; m. Rowena Kruesi, June 9, 1934; children: John Burton, III, Paul Kruesi, Thomas Cartter, Daniel Kennedy, James William. Grad., Sewanee (Tenn.) Mil. Acad., 1919; student, U. South, Sewanee, 1919-21. With First Nat. Bank Chattanooga, 1922-28; treas. Dixie Mercerizing Co. (now Dixie Yarns, Inc.), 1928-33, v.p., 1933-47, pres., 1947-63, chmn., 1963-79, now dir. and chmn. exec. com.; dir., mem. exec. com. Am. Nat. Bank and Trust Co, Chattanooga, 1942-80, Monumental Corp., Balt., 1968-77; Vice pres. Nat. Cotton Council, 1969, 70. Chmn. sch. bd. Lookout Mountain, Tenn., 1944-52, mayor, 1952-56; Trustee, exec. com. U. Chattanooga Found.; trustee Baylor Sch. for Boys, 1950—; bd. dirs. Louisville Presbyn. Theol. Sem., 1959-72. Mem. Am. Textile Mfrs. Inst. (pres. 1966), Tenn. Taxpayer Assn. (bd. dirs.), Phi Delta Theta. Presbyterian (elder). Clubs: Mountain City, Fairyland (Lookout Mountain). Home: 515 E Brow Rd Lookout Mountain TN 37350 Office: Dixie Yarns Inc Chattanooga TN 37401

FRIES, JAMES LAWRENCE, trade association executive; b. Wichita, Kans., Dec. 18, 1932; s. Leon F. and Edith (Gould) F.; m. June Elizabeth Fisher, Mar. 7, 1959; children: Thomas Blake, Dana Elizabeth. A.B., William Jewell Coll., Liberty, Mo., 1955. Asst. to nat. sales mgr. H.D. Lee Co., Kansas City, Mo., 1957-58; dir. pub. relations U. Kansas City, 1958-65; assoc. mgr. Livestock Mktg. Assn., Kansas City, 1967-81, gen. mgr., 1982—; exec. dir. Livestock Merchandising Inst., Kansas City, 1970—; gen. mgr. Livestock Mktg. Services Corp., Kansas City, 1982—; dir. U.S. Meat Export Fedn., Denver, 1982—. Chmn. Kansas City Commn. on Agribus., 1981—. Mem. Agribus. Council of Kansas City C. of C., Internat. Agribus. Club (pres. 1979-80), Am. Soc. Assn. Execs. Republican. Club: Carriage (Kansas City, Mo.). Home: 109 W 65th Terr Kansas City MO 64113 Office: Livestock Mktg Assn 301 E Armour Blvd Kansas City MO 64111

FRIES, RAYMOND SEBASTIAN, manufacturing company executive; b. St. Paul, June 19, 1919; s. Jacob H. and Christine Fries; m. Lillian Meredith, Dec. 24, 1968; children: Raymond B., John A., Christine. B.S., U. Minn., 1948. Vice pres. Honeywell, Mpls., Los Angeles and Phila., 1944-65; v.p. Varian Assos., Palo Alto, Calif., 1965-67; pres. Esterline Angus, Indpls., 1967-71; v.p. Esterline Corp., N.Y.C., 1969-71; pres. Dietzgen Corp., Chgo., 1971-73; v.p. Allegheny Ludlum Industries, Pitts., 1973-80; exec. v.p. Allegheny Internat., Pitts., 1980—, also dir.; pres. Chematron Corp., Chgo.; dir. Liquid Air N.Am., Midwest Carbide, Allegheny Ludlum Steel Corp. Contbg. author: Industrial Engineering Handbook. Mem. ASME. Clubs: Duquesne, Pitts. Athletic Assn. Office: Alleghany International 15760 Ventura Blvd Suite 1727 Encino CA 91436

FRIES, ROBERT FRANCIS, educator, historian; b. LaCrosse, Wis., Dec. 16, 1911; s. William James and Laura Merlinda (Olsen) F.; m. Frances Katherine Clements, Jan. 2, 1936 (dec. Jan. 1972); children: Mary Ann, Margaret Frances; m. Elizabeth Zevnik Dunne, Dec. 16, 1972. B.E., LaCrosse State Tchrs. Coll., 1933; Ph.M., U. Wis., 1936, Ph.D., 1939. Social sci. tchr. Cashton (Wis.) High Sch., 1933-35; asst. in history U. Wis., 1936-38; asst. prof. history De Paul U., Chgo., 1939-43, asso. prof., 1943-45, prof. history, 1945-80, emeritus prof., 1980—, chmn. dept., 1945-56, 67-76, dean univ. coll., 1955-71; Fellow in history U. Wis., 1938-39. Contbr. to hist. jours.; author: Empire in Pine, the Story of Lumbering in Wisconsin, 1951; Author: Crown and Parliament in Tudor-Stuart England, 1959, European Civilization: Basic Historical Documents, 1965; editor: Readings in European Civilization, 1956. Recipient Via Sapientiae award, 1980. Mem. AAUP (chpt. sec. 1947-48), Am. Hist. Assn., Orgn. Am. Historians, Wis. Hist. Soc. Home: 2817 Wilmette Ave Wilmette IL 60091

FRIES, VOLLMER WALTER, manufacturing executive; b. Pleasant Valley, N.Y., July 17, 1902; s. William Christian and Lona A. (Vollmer) F.; m. Ruth Dudley Wick, July 17, 1928; children: William Vollmer, Carole Wick. E.E., Rensselaer Poly. Inst., 1924; D.Eng. (hon.), Fenn Coll., 1965. With The White Motor Co., Cleve., 1924-56, v.p., dir., then exec. v.p., dir., 1944-55; chmn. bd., chief exec. officer White Consol. Industries, Inc. (formerly White Sewing Machine Corp.), Cleve., 1955-69, chmn. exec. com., 1969-70, dir., 1954—; With conservation div. WPB, 1940-41; mem. W. Averell Harriman mission, Am. embassy, London, 1942-43. Trustee Fenn Ednl. Found., Rensselaer Poly. Inst., Troy, N.Y. Clubs: Union, Fifty (Cleve.); Ocean Reef, Ocean Reef Yacht, Card Sound Golf, Key Largo Anglers (Key Largo, Fla.). Home: 8 Sunset Cay Rd Ocean Reef Key Largo FL 33037 Office: 11770 Berea Rd Cleveland OH 44111

FRIESE, GEORGE RALPH, manufacturing and retailing company executive, lawyer; b. Chgo., Feb. 15, 1936; s. George R. and Marie (Pilz) F.; m. Patricia Brown, Aug. 24, 1957; children: Christine Carol, Kurt Michael. B.A., Monmouth Coll., 1956; LL.B. (Chgo. Title & Trust scholar 1959), Chgo. Kent Coll. Law, 1960. Bar: Ill. 1961. Asst. gen. counsel, v.p. Banner Mut. Ins. Cos., Chgo., 1959-63; ptnr. Madsen & Friese, Park Ridge, Ill., 1963-68; assoc. corp. counsel, asst. sec. SCOA Industries, Inc., Columbus, Ohio, 1968-71, sec., 1971—, corp. counsel, 1971—, v.p. legal, 1974-79, sr. v.p. legal, 1979-80, exec. v.p., 1980-81, pres., 1981—. Bd. dirs. Columbus Symphony Orch.; bd. dirs. Greater Columbus Arts Council. Mem. Am., Ill., Chgo. bar assns., Tau Kappa Epsilon, Phi Delta Phi. Club: Athletic (Columbus). Home: 2770 E Broad St Bexley OH 43209 Office: 33 N High St Columbus OH 43215

FRIESEN, GILBERT BRYAN, record and film prodn. co. exec.; b. Pasadena, Calif., Mar. 10, 1937; s. Ted and Rose (Bartel) F.; 1 son, Tyler. B.A., UCLA, 1957. Asst. local promotion man Capitol Records, Hollywood, Calif., 1958-60; promotion man Kapp Records, Los Angeles, 1961-62; personal mgr. various artists, 1963-64; gen. mgr. A&M Records, Inc., Hollywood, 1964-70, sr. v.p., 1971-76, pres., 1976—, A&M Films, Hollywood, 1981—. Bd. dirs. Found. Violence in Am., 1981—, Los Angeles Olympic Com., 1980—. Recipient T.J. Martel Leukemia Meml. Found. for Leukemia Research Humanitarian award, 1979. Office: 1416 N La Brea Ave Hollywood CA 90028

FRIESEN, GORDON ARTHUR, health care consultant; b. Rosthern, Sask., Can., Jan. 21, 1909; emigrated to U.S., 1951, naturalized, 1962; s. Abraham James and Eliza (Friesen) F.; m. Jane Helen Fuller, July 25, 1947; children: Mary Jane, Sarah Elizabeth. LL.D., George Washington U.; D. Adminstrn. (hon.), Northland Open U., Toronto, Ont., Can. Bus. mgr. Saskatoon City Hosp., 1929-37; adminstr. Belleville (Ont., Can.) Gen. Hosp., 1937-41, Kitchener-Waterloo (Ont.) Hosp., 1946-51; prin. cons. sr. hosp. adminstr. United Mine Workers Hosps. in Appalachia, 1951-54; founder Gordon A. Friesen Internat., Inc., Washington, 1954—; vis. lectr. Sch. Hosp. Adminstrn., St. Louis U., Health Services Planning and Design Program, Columbia George Washington U. Grad. Sch., C.W. Post U., U.S. Army Med. Field Service Sch., U.S. Naval Sch. Hosp. Adminstrn., Nat. Naval Center; cons. surgeon gen. U.S. Navy.; Mem. adv. council, lectr. Xavier U., Cin. Contbr. articles to profl. jours. Served with RCAF, 1941-46. Recipient numerous Modern Hosp. of Month awards, Gerard B. Lambert 1st prize award for accomplishments in improved patient care and reduced hosp. costs; Gold medal Govt. of Costa Rica. Fellow Am. Coll. Hosp. Adminstrs., Royal Soc. Arts, Royal Soc. Health; hon. fellow Am. Acad. Med. Adminstrs.; hon. mem. Costa Rican Hosp. Assn. (hon. pres.); mem. Internat. Hosp. Fedn., Am. Assn. Hosp. Planning, Am. Hosp. Assn., Canadian Coll. Health Service Execs.; life mem., founder Sask. Hosp. Assn. (hon. life), Luther Rice Soc. Club: Cosmos. Address: 24 Croydon Pl Box 45 Arva ON Canada NOM 1CO

FRIESEN, HENRY GEORGE, endocrinologist, educator; b. Morden, Man., Can., July 31, 1934; s. Frank Henry and Agnes (Unger) F.; m. Joyce Marylin Mackinnon, Oct. 12, 1967; children—Mark Henry, Janet Elizabeth. B.Sc., U. Man., 1958, M.D., 1958. Diplomate: Am. Bd. Internal Medicine. Intern Winnipeg (Man.) Gen. Hosp., 1958-60; resident Royal Victoria Hosp., Montreal, Que., 1961-62; research asso. New Eng. Centre Hosp., Boston, 1962-65; prof. exptl. medicine McGill U., Montreal, 1965-73; prof. physiology and medicine U. Man., 1973—, head dept. physiology, 1973—. Contbr. numerous articles to profl. jours. Recipient Gairdner award, 1977; Killam scholar, 1979. Fellow Royal Soc. Can., Royal Coll. Physicians and Surgeons; mem. Am. Physiol. Soc., Endocrine Soc., Can. Soc. Clin. Investigation, Can. Physiol. Soc., Am. Fedn. Clin. Research, AAAS, Am. Soc. Clin. Investigation, Can. Soc. Endocrinology and Metabolism, Internat. Soc. Neuroendocrinology. Mennonite. Office: 770 Bannatyne Ave Winnipeg MB Canada R3E 0W3

FRIETZSCHE, ARTHUR H., educator; b. San Francisco, 1922; s. Clarence Harrell and Anna (Johnson) F. A.A., San Francisco Jr. Coll., 1942; B.A., U. Calif., Berkeley, 1944, M.A., 1945, Ph.D., 1949. Lectr. English U. Calif., Berkeley, 1949-51; supr. tech. publs. Hanford Atomic Works, Richland, Wash., 1952-56; asst. prof. English Utah State U., Logan, 1956-59, asso. prof., 1959-65; asst. prof. English Calif. Poly. State U., San Luis Obispo, 1965-67, asso. prof., 1967-72, prof., 1972—. Author: The Monstrous Clever Young Man: The Novelist Disraeli and His Heroes, 1959, Disraeli's Religion, 1961; Contbr. articles to profl. jours. Mem. MLA, Am. Soc. Engring. Edn., Soc. Tech. Communications. Home: PO Box 83 San Luis Obispo CA 93406

FRIGON, HENRY FREDERICK, diversified company executive; b. Bridgeport, Conn., Nov. 16, 1934; s. Henry Xavier and Veronica Anne (Beloin) F.; m. Anne Marie McCarthy, Sept. 20, 1965; children: Megan, Michele, Henry, Scott, Mark, Stephanie. B.S.C.E., Tufts U., 1957; postgrad., U. Pa., 1958-59; M.B.A., N.Y. U., 1962. With Gen. Foods Corp., 1960-68, various fin. and mktg. positions, 1960-66, chief fin. officer, internat. ops., White Plains, N.Y., 1966-68; v.p. fin., sec., treas. Gen. Housewares Corp., N.Y.C., 1968-70, pres., Stamford, Conn., 1970-74; also dir. parent co.; group v.p. Masco Corp., Taylor, Mich., 1974-81; exec. v.p., chief fin. and adminstrv. officer Batus Inc., Louisville, 1981—; dir. Batus, Inc., B.A.T. Capital Corp., Appleton Papers Co., Marshall Field & Co.; dir. Louisville br. Fed. Res. Bank of St. Louis. Served with USNR, 1957-65. Mem. Young Pres.'s Orgn., Fin. Execs. Inst. Home: 4008 Woodstone Way Louisville KY 40222 Office: 2000 Citizens Plaza Louisville KY 40202

FRIIS, ERIK JOHAN, editor, publisher; b. Oslo, Norway, Apr. 5, 1913; came to U.S., 1929, naturalized, 1937; s. Ingvard E. and Sigrid E. (Erichsen) F.; m. Sylvia Katharina Schouw, May 6, 1955; children: Erik Schouw, Elin Sylvia. B.S., St. John's U., 1938; M.A., Columbia, 1946. With Am.-Scandinavian Found., N.Y.C., 1946-78; dir. publs., editor Am.-Scandinavian Rev., 1951-75, editor emeritus, 1976—; editor, pub. Scandinavian-Am. Bull., 1966—. Author: The American-Scandinavian Foundation, 1910-1960, 1961; Contbg. author, co-editor: Scandinavian Studies, 1965; editor: The Scandinavian Presence in North America, 1976, Norwegian Trade Bull., 1983—; Translator: Body and Clothes (R. Broby-Johansen), 1968, The Red Guards (Hans Granquist), 1967, Westward to Vinland (Helge Ingstad), 1969, The Secret Transmitter (O. Rynning-Tonnesen), 1965, The Lost Musicians (William Heinesen), 1971, Cleng Peerson (Alfred Hauge), 1975, The Moment of Truth (K. Arne Blom), 1977, Red Harvest (Olav Nordrå), 1978, Wooden Boat Designs (C. Nielsen), 1980; co-translator: Changing (Liv Ullmann), 1977; contbr., translator: Nordic Democracy, 1982; Gen. editor: Library of Scandinavian Literature, 1967-78, Library of Scandinavian Studies, 1974-78, The Scandinavian Scene; reprint series; Library of Nordic Literature, 1983—; mem. editorial bd.: Norwegian-Am. Hist. Assn, 1965—; contbg. editor: World Press Rev, 1978—, Explorers Jour, 1979—; editor-compiler: The Norwegian Club, 1904-1964, 1964, The Society of Norwegian American Engineers, 1975, They Came from Norway—A Sesquicentennial Review, 1975; gen. editor series: The Scandinavian Scene. Vice chmn. Norwegian Immigration Sesquicentennial Commn., N.Y.C., also sec.-treas. nat. coordinating com. Decorated knight 1st class Norwegian Order St. Olav, 1967; knight Icelandic Order Falcon, 1968; knight Swedish Order N. Star, 1972; knight Danish Order Dannebrog, 1974; knight 1st class Finnish Order of Lion, 1976; recipient U.S. Medal for Antarctica service, 1965; Author award Newark Coll. Engring., 1973; Arts and Letters award Finlandia Found., 1974; named to Hall of Honor Norwegian-Am. Mus., Decorah, Iowa, 1954. Fellow Explorers Club; mem. P.E.N., Societas Heraldica Scandinavica, Am. Polar Soc., Scandinavian-Am. Bus. Assn. (v.p. 1976—), Scandinavian-Am. Heritage Soc. (dir. 1979—), Scandinavian Collectors Club. Clubs: Norway Ski (pres. 1942-46), Norwegian (v.p. 1961-78), Norwegian (N.Y.C.) (pres. 1978-82); Gjoa Sporting (Bklyn.) (pres. 1951-52). Home: 19 Shadow Ln Montvale NJ 07645 Office: 8104 Fifth Ave Brooklyn NY 11209

FRILEY, WILLIAM ALVA, petroleum co. exec.; b. Hubbard, Tex., Mar. 20, 1917; s. Charles E. and Nina Lynn (Wood) F.; m. Josephine Skillman, Nov. 4, 1939; children—Katy Jo (Mrs. Ray Sebastian), Shannon (Mrs. T.R. Palmer), William Alva, Joel S., Charles Dana. Student, U. Colo., 1936; B.S., Iowa State U., 1938. With Carter Oil Co., Tulsa, 1938-41, 45-50; mgr. land dept. Imperial Oil Co., Calgary, Alta., Can., 1950-51; pres., dir. Selbay Exploration, 1951-54; v.p., dir., gen. mgr. Bailey Selburn Oil & Gas Ltd., 1952-62; v.p., dir. Gt. No. Oil Co., 1962-70; pres., dir. Skyeland Oils Ltd., Calgary, 1965—; pres., dir. Skyeland Holdings, Skyeland Ranches; past dir. Petrogas Processing Ltd., Bow River Pipe Lines Ltd., Trident Drilling Co., Can. Australian Oil & Gas Co., Saddle and Sirloin Ranches Ltd.; dir. Buttes Resources Cascade Ltd. Mem. senate U. Calgary, 1968, chmn. exec. com., 1969-70, chancellor, 1970-74, chancellor emeritus, 1974—; Active United Fund, YMCA, Cancer Soc., U. Calgary fund raising campaigns.; Pres. McMahon Stadium Soc.; bd. dirs., exec. com. Calgary Philharmonic Soc., pres., 1975-76; trustee Inst. Research Into Pub. Policy; Can. Past pres. Jr. Achievement of Calgary. Served to maj. AUS, 1941-45. Mem. Independent Petroleum Assn. Can. (dir. 1965-66), Canadian Petroleum Assn. (past chmn. pub. relations com. Alta. div.), Sigma Alpha Epsilon. Baptist. Clubs: Optimist Internat., Calgary Petroleum (dir.), Calgary Golf and Country, Glencoe. Home and office: 3-3315 Rideau P SW Calgary AB Canada

FRIOU, GEORGE JACOB, immunologist, physician, educator; b. Bklyn., Oct. 5, 1919; s. George Dyson and Lillian Edna (Ackerman) F.; m. Carolyn Anderson Bower, Jan. 18, 1947; children: Deborah, Linda, Sally, George; m. Hortense Joan Nichol, Mar. 29, 1972. B.S., Cornell U., 1940, M.D., 1944. Intern New Haven Hosp., 1945-46, asst. resident, 1946, chief resident in medicine, 1949-50; asst. prof. medicine Yale U., 1951-60; asso. prof. U. Okla., 1960-64, U. So. Calif., 1964-68, prof., 1968-78; prof. medicine, dir. clin. immunology and rheumatic diseases U. Calif. at Irvine, 1978—; cons. Arthritis Found., N.Y., 1962-64, Council Mid-Winter Conf. Immunologists, 1965-70; mem. steering com. Calif. Gov.'s Conf. on Arthritis, 1967; mem. med. and sci. com. So. Calif. chpt. Arthritis Found., 1966—, chmn. med. and sci. com., 1977-78, bd. govs., 1977-78; cons. VA, mem. merit review bd. in immunology, 1972-74. Editorial bd.: Arthritis and Rheumatism, 1967-69. Served with M.C. USNR, 1946-47, 52-53. Fellow Infectious Disease Soc.; mem. Am. Soc. Clin. Investigation., Asociacion Rheumatologia de Columbia, A.C.P., Am. Assn. Immunologists, Heberden Soc. (Brit.), Brit. Soc. Immunology, Western Assn. Physicians, So. Calif. Rheumatism Soc. (pres. 1970), Ohio Rheumatism Soc. (hon. mem.), Los Angeles Acad. Medicine. Office: U Calif Dept Medicine Med Scis Bldg 1 Irvine CA 92717

FRISBEE, DON CALVIN, utilities executive; b. San Francisco, Dec. 13, 1923; s. Ira Nobles and Helen (Sheets) F.; m. Emilie Ford, Feb. 5, 1947; children: Ann, Robert, Peter, Dean. B.A., Pomona Coll., 1947; M.B.A., Harvard U., 1949. Sr. investment analyst, asst. cashier investment analysis dept. 1st Nat. Bank Oreg. (name now 1st Interstate Bank Oreg., N.A.), Portland, 1949-52, now dir.; with Pacific Power & Light Co., Portland, 1953—, treas., 1958-60, then v.p., exec. v.p., pres., 1966-73, chmn., chief exec. officer, 1973—; dir. Lucky Stores, Inc., Dublin, Calif., Weyerhaeuser Co., Standard Ins. Co., Portland., Precision Castparts Corp. Trustee Whitman Coll., Reed Coll., Com. for Econ. Devel.; cabinet mem. Columbia Pacific council Boy Scouts Am. Served to 1st lt. AUS, 1943-46. Clubs: Arlington, University, Multnomah Athletic. Office: 851 SW 6th St Portland OR 97204

FRISBY, JAMES CURTIS, agricultural engineering educator; b. Bethany, Mo., Oct. 22, 1930; s. Jackson Carey and Gladys (Selby) F.; m. Hazel M. Kallenbach, Dec. 19, 1969. B.S. in Edn., U. Mo., 1952, B.S.A.E., 1956; M.S., Iowa State U., 1963, Ph.D., 1965. Registered profl. engr., Mo. Classromm instr., tech. writer, market analyst Caterpillar Tractor Co., Peoria, Ill., 1956-60; acting mgr. farm services dept. Iowa State U., Ames, 1961-63, instr., 1963-65; asst. prof. agrl. engring. U. Mo., Columbia, 1966-69, assoc. prof., 1969-74, prof., 1974—. Served to 1st lt. U.S. Army, 1952-54. Recipient award of merit Gamma Sigma Delta, 1976, cert. of appreciation U. Mo. Coll. Engring., 1983. Mem. Am. Soc. Agrl. Engrs. (sr.; chmn. Mid-Central Region 1982-83, dir. Mid-Central Region 1984-86), Am. Soc. Engring. Edn., Nat. Assn. Colls. and Tchrs. Agr. Mem. Ch. of Christ. Home: 1113 Falcon Dr Columbia MO 65201 Office: 100 Agricultural Engineering Bldg Columbia MO 65211

FRISCH, HARRY LLOYD, educator, chemist; b. Vienna, Austria, Nov. 13, 1928; s. Jacob J. and Clara F. (Spondre) F.; m. Margaret Dampman Allen, Dec. 19, 1970; children—Benjamin, Michael. B.A., Williams Coll., 1947; Ph.D., Poly. Inst. Bklyn., 1952. Research asso. physics Syracuse U., 1952-54; instr. U. So. Calif., 1954-55, asst. prof., 1955-56; mem. tech. staff Bell Telephone Labs., Inc., Murray Hill, N.J., 1956-67; prof. chemistry SUNY, Albany, 1967-78, disting. prof. chemistry, 1978—; asso. dean Coll. Arts and Sci., 1969-71; vis. asso. prof. physics Yeshiva U., 1963-65, Inst. Study Metals, U. Chgo., 1960; asst. to dean Belfer Grad. Sch. Yeshiva U., 1963-65; cons. in field. Editor: (with J. Lebowitz) The Equilibrium Theory of Classical Fluids, 1964, (with Z. Salsburg) Simple Dense Fluids, 1968; Asso. editor: Jour. Chem. Physics, 1964-66, Jour. Statis. Physics, 1970-75; editorial bd.: Jour. Phys. Chemistry, 1976-80, Jour. Polymer Sci. (Physics edit.), 1976—, Jour. Membrance Sci, 1976—, Jour. Adhesion, 1970—; Contbr. articles to profl. jours. NSF grantee, 1968—. Fellow Am. Phys. Soc.; mem. Am. Chem. Soc., Sigma Xi. Democrat. Jewish. Club: Cosmos. Office: 1400 Washington Ave Albany NY 12222

FRISCH, IVAN THOMAS, computer and communications company executive; b. Budapest, Hungary, Sept. 21, 1937; came to U.S., 1939, naturalized, 1941; s. Laszlo and Rose (Balog) F.; m. Vivian Scelzo, June 6, 1962; children: Brian, Bruce. B.S., Queens Coll., N.Y., 1958, Columbia U., 1958, M.S., 1958, Ph.D., 1962. Asst. prof. elec. engring. and computer sci. U. Calif., Berkeley, 1962-65, asso. prof., 1965-69; Ford Found. resident engring. practice Bell Labs., Holmdel, N.J., 1965-66; founding mem. Network Analysis Corp., Great Neck, N.Y., 1969—, sr. v.p., 1971—, gen. mgr., 1978—; adj. prof. computer sic.

SUNY, Stony Brook, 1975—, Columbia U., N.Y.C., 1977—; cons. in field. Author: (with Howard Frank) Communication, Transmission and Transportation Networks, 1971; Founding editor-in-chief: Networks, 1971—; contbr. articles to profl. publs. Guggenheim fellow, 1969. Fellow IEEE; mem. N.Y. Acad. Scis., Cable TV Assn. Am., Phi Beta Kappa, Tau Beta Pi, Eta Kappa Nu. Office: Contel Info Systems 130 Steamboat Rd Great Neck NY 11024

FRISCH, ROBERT A., financial planning co. exec.; b. Schenectady, July 22, 1922; s. Harry and Ann (Hirschman) F.; m. Leona A. Abbey, Sept. 9, 1951; children—Dana R., Randi. B.S., Western Mich. U., 1947; postgrad., Wharton Sch. of Bus., 1956-57. Founder, chief exec. officer The ESOT Group, Inc., Los Angeles; fin. cons.; lectr. on corp. fin. and devel., fringe benefits, exec. benefit planning, perpetuation of closely held corp. Author: ESOP's for the Eighties. Active Boy Scouts Am. Served with USAF, World War II; CBI. Mem. Am. Mgmt. Assn. (chmn. employee stock ownership plan seminars), Am. Soc. C.L.U.'s (past pres. Phila. chpt.), Nat. Assn. Security Dealers (prin.). Home: 17146 Margate St Encino CA 91316 Office: 3701 Wilshire Blvd Suite 300 Los Angeles CA 90010

FRISCH, ROBERT EMILE, lawyer; b. Chgo., Aug. 18, 1925; s. Emile Leopold and Lillian Laverne (Ward) F.; m. Dolly Hemphill, Jan. 26, 1952; children: Kathy W., Robert P., Peter O. A.B., Harvard U., 1946, LL.M., 1950. Bar: N.Y. 1951, U.S. Supreme Ct. 1959, U.S. Tax Ct. 1954, U.S. Claims Ct. 1954. Teaching fellow Harvard Law Sch., Cambridge, Mass., 1950-51; asst. counsel U.S. Senate Crime Com., N.Y.C., 1951; assoc. firm Rogers & Wells, N.Y.C., 1951-57, ptnr., 1957—. Mem. ABA, N.Y. Bar Assn., Assn. Bar City N.Y. Republican. Episcopalian. Clubs: Sky, Am Yacht. Office: 200 Park Ave New York NY 10166

FRISCHKNECHT, LEE CONRAD, broadcasting executive; b. Brigham City, Utah, Jan. 4, 1928; s. Carl Oliver and Geniel (Lund) F.; m. Sara Jean McCulloch, Sept. 3, 1948; children: Diane Frischknecht Etherington, Jill, Ellen, Amy. B.S. in Speech, Utah State U., 1951; M.A. in Radio-TV, Mich. State U., 1957. Announcer sta. KID Radio, Idaho Falls, Idaho, 1951-52; producer-dir. sta. WMSB-TV, East Lansing, Mich., 1955-58, producer, program mgr., 1959-61, gen. mgr., 1962-63; dir. sta. relations Nat. Ednl. TV, N.Y.C., 1964-68; dir. univ. relations Utah State U., 1969-70; dir. network affairs Nat. Pub. Radio, Washington, 1971, v.p., 1972, pres., 1973-77; communications cons. Atlantic Research Corp., 1978—; mgr. telecommunication services Ariz. State U., Tempe, 1980—; assoc. prof. radio-TV Mich. State U., 1962-63; assoc. prof. speech Utah State U., 1969-70. Bd. dirs. Pub. Service Satellite Consortium, 1982—, Consortium for Lifelong Learning in Ariz. through Instructional Media, 1981; treas. Consortium for Lifelong Learning in Ariz. through Instructional Media, 1982, chmn., 1983—. Served with AUS, 1946-48; Japan. Recipient Meritorious Service award in communications Brigham Young U., 1973, Outstanding Alumnus award in communications Mich. State U., 1974. Mem. Ch. of Jesus Christ of Latter-day Saints. Home: 338 E Palmcroft Dr Tempe AZ 85282 Office: Stauffer Hall Ariz State U Tempe AZ 85287

FRISELL, WILHELM RICHARD, biochemist, educator; b. Two Harbors, Minn., Apr. 27, 1920; s. Olof Wilhelm and Thyra Magnina (Falk) F.; m. Margaret Jane Fleagle, Mar. 6, 1948; children William Richard, Robert Benjamin. B.A., St. Olaf Coll., Minn., 1942; M.A., Johns Hopkins U., 1943, Ph.D., 1946, postdoctoral, 1946-49. Instr. physiol. chemistry Johns Hopkins U. and Sch. Medicine, Balt., 1950-51; asst. prof. biochemistry U. Colo. Sch. Medicine, Denver, 1951-58, asso. prof., 1958-64, prof., 1964-69; prof., chmn. dept. biochemistry N.J. Med. Sch., Newark, 1969-76; acting dean Grad. Sch. Biomed. Sci., Coll. Medicine and Dentistry N.J., Newark, 1971-73; prof., chmn. dept. biochemistry East Carolina U. Sch. Medicine, also asst. dean grad. affairs, Greenville, N.C., 1976—; mem. fellowships com. Fogarty Internat. Center, NIH, 1962-66, 67-71, 81—, chmn., 1968-71, 81, chmn. sr. fellowship com., 1981—. Author: Acid-Base chemistry in Medicine, 1968, Human Biochemistry, 1982; also articles and revs. NDRC fellow, 1943-44; Am. Scandinavian Found. fellow, Uppsala, Sweden, 1949-50. Fellow AAAS; mem. Am. Chem. Soc., Am. Soc. Biol. Chemists, Am. Soc. Microbiology, Soc. Exptl. Biology and Medicine, N.Y. Acad. Scis., Harvey Soc., Phi Beta Kappa, Sigma Xi (pres. Colo. chpt. 1968-69). Home: 209 Fairlane Rd Greenville NC 27834 Office: Sch Medicine E Carolina U Greenville NC 27834 *As a first generation American who has been given so many opportunities, I can never forget the sacrifices of my immigrant parents and their compatriots. The likes of them may never pass this way again.*

FRISON, PAUL M., health care executive; b. 1937; married. Grad., Occidental Coll., 1958. With Am. Hosp. Supply Corp., 1962-75, Lifemark Corp., Houston, 1975—, pres., chief operating officer, dir. Served with USCG, 1959-62. Office: Lifemark Corp Box 3448 Houston TX 77001 *

FRISQUE, ALVIN JOSEPH, chemical company executive; b. Wis., Jan. 27, 1923; s. Henry Louis and Angeline (Thayse) F.; m. Jaye Anzak, June 1, 1950; children: Susan, Alice. B.S., U. Wis., 1948, Ph.D., 1954; M.S., U. Iowa, 1951. Sr. scientist Standard Oil Co. Ind., 1954-61; group leader and research mgr., then v.p. div. research Nalco Chem. Co., 1961-73, corp. v.p. research and devel., Oak Brook, Ill., 1973-82, dir. corp. tech., 1982—. Author. Trustee Ill. Benedictine Coll. Served with USAAF, 1943-46. Decorated Air medal; Croix de Guerre, France). Mem. Indsl. Research Inst., Am. Chem. Soc., Sigma Xi, Phi Lambda Upsilon. Patentee in field. Home: 6476 Sioux Trail Indianhead Park IL 60525 Office: 2901 Butterfield Rd Oak Brook IL 60521

FRIST, THOMAS FEARN, internist; b. Meridian, Miss., Dec. 15, 1910; m. Dorothy Cate, 1935; children: Thomas Fearn, Robert Armistead, William Harrison, Dorothy Frist Boensch, Mary L. Frist Barfield. B.S., U. Miss., 1929; M.D., Vanderbilt U., 1933. Diplomate: Am. Bd. Internal Medicine. Intern U. Iowa, 1933-35; asst. clinician Vanderbilt U., 1935-37; sr. mem. Frist-Scoville Med. Group, Nashville, 1940—; past pres. staff Nashville Gen. Hosp.; past pres., mem. exec. com. St. Thomas Hosp.; co-founder, past pres. Hosp. Corp. Am., 1968-71; now vice chmn. bd., chief med. services; dir. Nashville City Bank & Trust Co.; founder, vice chmn. bd. Am. Retirement Corp.; Past chmn. Pres.'s Com. on Aging, Washington. Founder, past chmn. bd. Park Manor Presbyn. Apts. for Elderly, Cumberland Heights Found. for Rehab. Alcoholics; founder, bd. dirs. Med. Benevolence Found.; bd. dirs. Montgomery Bell Acad., Nashville; hon. trustee Southwestern U., Memphis. Served to maj. USAAF, World War II. Fellow A.C.P.; mem. Southeastern Clin. Club (past pres.), Tenn. Heart Assn. (past pres.), Nashville Soc. Internal Medicine (past pres.), Royal Soc. Internal Medicine (London), Sigma Alpha Epsilon. Clubs: Belle Meade Country (Nashville); Lago Mar Golf Country (Ft. Lauderdale, Fla.). Office: 345 24th Ave N Park Plaza Med Bldg Nashville TN 37203

FRISWOLD, FRED RAVNDAHL, investment banker; b. Mpls., Jan. 21, 1937; s. Ingolf Oliver and Derrice Ernestine (Anderson) F.; m. C. Marie Martin, Sept. 14, 1957; children—Cynthia, Steven, Barry, Michelle (dec.), Benjamin. B.B.A. with distinction in Fin, U. Minn., 1958. Chartered fin. analyst. With J.M. Dain & Co. (now Dain, Bosworth, Inc.), Mpls., 1958—, exec. v.p., 1976-82, pres., 1982—. Trustee Met. Med. Center, Mpls., 1978—. Mem. Twin City Soc. Security Analysts, Securities Industry Assn. Methodist. Clubs: Decathlon Athletic, Mpls., Rotary. Home: 7033 Comanche Ct Edina MN 55435 Office: 100 Dain Tower Minneapolis MN 55402

FRITCHMAN, HARRY VERNON, coal co. exec.; b. McDonald, Pa., Nov. 27, 1907; s. Frank Markle and Margaret (Crilley) F.; m. Ethel Rendleman, Oct. 14, 1933; 1 son, Vernon N. A.B., Pa. State U., 1929; postgrad., U. Pa. Law Sch., 1929-30; LL.B., U. Pitts., 1932. Bar: Pa. bar 1933. Practice in, Indiana, Pa., 1933-37; with Rochester & Pitts. Coal Co., Indiana, 1937—, gen. counsel, 1948—, exec. v.p., 1959-70, pres., dir., 1970-73, dir., 1973—. Mem. Nat. Coal Assn. (dir.), Beta Theta Pi, Phi Delta Phi, Pi Lambda Sigma. Presbyterian. Clubs: Elk, Mason., Hare Law (U. Pa.); Oakmont Country (Pitts.); Indiana Country. Home: 549 Chestnut St Indiana PA 15701 Office: 655 Church St Indiana PA 15701

FRITH, JAMES ROBERT, educator; b. Galeton, Pa., Aug. 24, 1917; s. Ward Kilbourne and Mabel (Krebs) F.; m. Catherine Roddey Jones, Oct. 10, 1942; children: Catherine, Eleanor, Martha, Jane, Nancy, Rebecca, James, Robert. B.A., M.A., Bucknell U., 1939; Ph.D., Cornell U., 1950; D. Litt. (hon.), 1974. Lang. tchr. high sch., Danville, Pa., 1939-41; instr. French Cornell U., 1948-50, acting asst. prof., 1950-51; adviser Air Force Lang. Program, 1951-53; supr., chief lang. tng. br. Air Force Inst. Tech., 1953-57; adviser lang. tng. Dept. Def., 1953-57; mem. Inter-Agy. Coordinating Com. on Govt. Lang. Tng., 1955-57; mem. evaluation team Middle States Accrediting Commn., 1956; fgn. service officer, dir. Dept. State French Lang. Sch., Nice, France, 1957-59, lang. tng. supr. for North Africa, 1958-59; asst. dean Sch. Langs., Fgn. Service Inst., dir. overseas lang. tng. for Fgn. Service, 1959-62, asso. dean School Langs., 1962-66, dean, 1966-80. Editor: Measuring Spoken Language Proficiency, 1980; author articles on lang. learning. Pres. Skyline Evergreen Farms, Inc., 1979—. Served to lt. comdr. USNR, 1941-47. Decorated DFC; recipient Meritorious Civilian Service award, 1956, Leadership award Northeast Conf. Fgn. Lang. Tchrs., 1983. Mem. Linguistic Soc. Am., Phi Beta Kappa, Sigma Alpha Epsilon. Methodist. Home: 4919 N 14th St Arlington VA 22205 Office: Foreign Service Inst State Dept Washington DC 20520

FRITH, MARGARET, publishing company executive. Formerly exec. editor dept. children's books Coward, McCann & Geoghegan, N.Y.C.; with G. P. Putnam's Sons, N.Y.C., 1973—, co.-dir. dept. children's books, 1974-79; editor-in-chief Books for Young Readers, 1979—, v.p., assoc. pub., 1982—. Office: G P Putnams Sons 51 Madison Ave New York NY 10010

FRITSCHE, ERNEST GARFIELD, developer, builder; b. Westerville, Ohio, Aug. 5, 1916; s. Garfield Helmuth and Clara (Dickey) F.; m. Neva Clyde Lilly, Dec. 1, 1945; children: Nevalyn Anne, Roberta Kay, William Carl. Student, Otterbein Coll., 1934-36, LL.D., 1965, Franklin U., evenings 1937-41. Real estate salesman George W. Fritsche & Co., Columbus, Ohio, 1946-49; organized Ernest G. Fritsche & Co. (comml. and residential builders), Columbus, 1949, pres., 1949-81, chmn. bd., 1972-77; Trustee Nat. Housing Center, Washington, 1962-65, Bldg. Research Adv. Bd., 1969-72; mem. U.S. housing study delegation to USSR, 1956. Pres., chmn. bd. Citizens Research, Inc., Columbus, 1959-64; chmn. Columbus United Appeals, 1964, Columbus YMCA, 1962-63; trustee Devel. Com. Greater Columbus, 1950-77; 1st v.p. Big Bros. Am., 1963-66; pres. United Appeal of Columbus, 1969, 70; bd. dirs. Otterbein Coll., 1958-83, Nat. Bldg. Research Adv. Bd., Washington, 1969-72. Served to lt. col. C.E. AUS, 1941-46. Mem. Nat. Assn. Home Builders (life dir. 1962—, elected to Hall of Fame 1979), Nat. Assn. Real Estate Bds., Urban Land Inst., Columbus C. of C., Columbus Symphony Orch. Home: 5800 Clover Ln Westerville OH 43081 Office: 6245 Sunderland Dr Columbus OH 43229

FRITTS, EDWARD, communications association executive; b. Cape Girardeau, Mo., Feb. 21, 1941; m. Martha Dale; children: Kimberly, Timothy, Jennifer. Exec. Nat. Assn. Broadcasters, Washington. Office: Nat Assn Broadcasters 1771 N St NW Washington DC 20036

FRITTS, HARRY WASHINGTON, JR., physician, educator; b. Rockwood, Tenn., Oct. 4, 1921; s. Harry Washington and Hyder (Smith) F.; m. Helen Dyer Goodwin, Aug. 25, 1949; children: John Goodwin, Benjamin Carroll, Patricia Louise. Student, Vanderbilt U., 1941; B.S., Mass. Inst. Tech., 1943; M.D., Boston U., 1951. Diplomate: Am. Bd. Internal Medicine (mem.). Mem. research staff Mass. Inst. Tech., 1946-47; intern, then resident Univ. Hosp., Boston, 1951-53; vis. fellow Columbia Coll. Physicians and Surgeons, 1953-56, mem. faculty, 1956-73, prof. medicine, 1967-73, Dickinson W. Richards prof. medicine, 1972-73; prof., chmn. dept. medicine Sch. Medicine, State U. N.Y. at Stony Brook, 1973—; vis. physician Bellevue Hosp., 1957-68, Presbyn. Hosp., N.Y.C., 1961-73; vis. physician, cons. Manhattan VA Hosp., 1957-68; vis. prof. U. London, 1982; bd. dirs., adv. council research N.Y. Heart Assn.; mem. sci. council Parker Francis Found.; mem. physiology study sect., mem. cardiovascular tng. com. USPHS; mem. council Nat. Heart, Lung and Blood Inst. Contbr. articles to profl. jours.; asso. editor: Jour. Clin. Investigation; editorial bd.: Am. Rev. Respiratory Diseases. Served to lt. (j.g.) USNR, 1943-46. Guggenheim fellow, 1959-60. Fellow A.C.P.; mem. Am. Physiol. Soc., Am. Soc. Clin. Investigation, Assn. Am. Physicians, Am. Clin. and Climatol. Soc., Alpha Omega Alpha. Home: 79 Bevin Rd Northport NY 11768 Office: Dept Medicine State U NY at Stony Brook Stony Brook NY 11790

FRITTS, JOHN FREDERICK, lawyer; b. Morristown, N.J., Dec. 11, 1934; s. Frank and Mary (Graham) F.; m. Anne Henderson, Dec. 17, 1960; children: Katherine Henderson, Jean Graham, Louis M., Frank. A.B., Princeton U., 1956; LL.B., Harvard U., 1959. Bar: N.Y. 1960. Assoc. firm Cadwalader Wickersham & Taft, N.Y.C., 1960-67, ptnr., 1968—. Trustee The Peck Sch., Morristown, N.J., 1977—. Served with U.S. Army, 1959. Mem. Assn. Bar City N.Y., ABA. Episcopalian. Club: Downtown. Home: Pleasantville Rd New Vernon NJ 07976 Office: Cadwalader Wickersham & Taft 1 Wall St New York NY 10005

FRITTS, ROBERT ELLERY, home builder; b. Beatrice, Nebr., Sept. 17, 1936; s. Clay and Irene Brazille (Fouchek); m. Bix Blankenship, Dec. 30, 1977; children by previous marriage: Robert Clayton, Jon Martin. B.S. in Engring, UCLA, 1963. Tech. dir., then v.p. fgn. bus. devel. Litton Industries, 1958-70; pres. Cerro Devel. Co., N.Y.C., 1970-73; exec. v.p. Leadership Housing Inc., Ft. Lauderdale, Fla., 1973-76; pres., chief exec. officer, dir. The Housing Group, Irvine, Calif., 1976-83; pres. White Hart Devel. Co., Newport Beach, Calif., 1983—. Served with USNR, 1954-58. Republican. Club: Big Canyon. Home: 32 Rue Grand Vallee Newport Beach CA 92660 Office: 32 Rue Grand Vallee Newport Beach CA 92660

FRITZ, BRUCE MORRELL, photographer; b. Madison, Wis., Aug. 13, 1947; s. Marvin Joseph and Jeannette Irene (Morrell) F. Student, U. Wis., 1965-69. Staff photographer Capital Times, Madison, Wis., 1969-77; instr. photojournalism U. Wis., 1976-78. One man exhbns. include, 8th Ave. Gallery, Kenosha, Wis., 1972, Focal Point Gallery, Madison, 1974, Madison Art Center, 1975, Sunprint Gallery, Madison, 1977; photographs pub. in Nat. Geog. World; many others. Served with USN, 1967-68. Recipient Disting. Service award in field of news photography Sigma Delta Chi, 1976; named News Photographer of Yr. Madison Press Club, 1974, 75. Mem. Nat. Press Photographers Assn., Wis. News Photographers Assn., Soc. Photographers in Communication, Profl. Photographers Am. Address: 124 Vista Rd Madison WI 53705 *I try to remain open and receptive to everything around me. I never compromise when image making; I strive for perfection. I've learned to respect the dignity and wonder of every person and all creatures of Nature. I try to convey that wonder and to capture the awesome beauty of Nature. Photography is my life.*

FRITZ, CECIL MORGAN, investment company executive; b. Modoc, Ind., July 30, 1921; s. Kenneth M. and Ruby (Howell) F.; m. Lucile Johnson, June 9, 1946; children: John, Susan, Marcia. B.S., Ind. U., 1948, M.B.A., 1949. With City Securities Corp., Indpls., 1949—; now pres., dir.; v.p., dir. City Discount Corp., Indpls.; dir. Eagle Magnetic Co. Inc., Indpls., Bioanalytical Systems Inc., West Lafayette, Ind. Served to capt. USAAF, 1940-46. Mem. Indpls. Soc. Fin. Analysts, Indpls. Bond Club. Republican. Methodist. Clubs: Mason (32 deg.), Columbia (Indpls.)). Home: 765 Forest Blvd Zionsville IN 46077 Office: 400 Circle Tower Indianapolis IN 46204

FRITZ, HARRY GARLAND, athletics assn. adminstr.; b. Wheelersburg, Ohio, June 13, 1920; s. Clarence E. and Mary G. (Hartman) F.; m. Edwina Marie Stone, Aug. 31, 1946; children—Harry Garland, Betty, Edwin, Grace, William, John, Richard. Student, Rio Grande Coll., 1938-40; B.A., Transylvania Coll., 1946; M.A. in Edn, U. Ky., 1947; D. Phys. Edn., Ind. U., 1954. Dean of men Transylvania Coll., Lexington, Ky., 1946-48, baseball coach, intramural dir., 1946-48; asso. prof. phys. edn. Central Mo. State U., Warrensburg, Mo., 1948-53; dir. athletics Bemidji (Minn.) State U., 1954-64, chmn. div. health, phys. edn. and recreation, 1954-64, head basketball coach, 1954-58, asst. football coach, 1955-64; dir. athletics Western Ill. U., Macomb, 1964-70, dean Coll. of Health, Phys. Edn. and Recreation, 1964-70; dean Sch. Health Edn., SUNY, Buffalo, 1970-76; rep. U.S. Olympic Com., Internat. Olympic Acad., Olympia, Greece, summer 1978; exec. dir. Nat. Assn. of Intercollegiate Athletics, Kansas City, Mo., 1976—; cons. intercollegiate and amateur sport, 1974—; lectr., cons. Mexican Sport Confedn., 1974-81. Author: An Evaluation of the Boys' Health and Physican Education Program in Selected Secondary Schools of Missouri, 1954; contbg. author: Administration of Athletics in Colleges and Universities, 1971, Drugs and the Coach, 1972, The Winning Edge, 1974; contbr. articles on phys. edn. and sports to profl. publs. Bd. dirs. Greater Kansas City Sports Commn., 1976—, James A. Naismith Peachbasket Com., Kansas City, Mo., 1976—. Served with USN, 1942-45; ETO. Recipient Atwood Achievement award Rio Grande Coll., 1976; Disting. Alumnus award Ind. U., 1978, Transylvania Coll., 1980. Mem. Nat. Assn. for Sport and Phys. Edn. (pres. 1975-76), Nat. Assn. Collegiate Dirs. of Athletics (exec. com. 1968-72), AAHPER (bd. govs. 1975-76), Sports Safety and Health Care Soc. (trustee 1976-80), Nat. Track and Field Hall of Fame (dir. 1976—), AAU (bd. govs. 1976—), U.S. Collegiate Sports Council (dir. 1974—), Naismith Meml. Basketball Hall of Fame (dir. 1976—), Greater Kansas City C. of C., Phi Delta Kappa, Pi Kappa Alpha, Phi Epsilon Kappa. Republican. Methodist. Home: 12511 W 70th St Shawnee KS 66216 Office: 1221 Baltimore St Kansas City MO 64105

FRITZ, IRVING BAMDAS, scientist; b. Rocky Mount, N.C., Feb. 11, 1927; s. Henry Norman and Rose (Bamdas) F.; m. Helen Bridgman, Aug. 20, 1950 (dec. 1971); m. Angela McCourt, Oct. 21, 1972; children: David Bamdas, Jonathan Bridgman, Winston Romaine, Rachel Bamdas, Zoë McCourt, Daniel William. D.D.S., Med. Coll. Va., 1948; Ph.D., U. Chgo., 1951. Instr., Harvard U., 1951; asst. dir. metabolism and endocrinology Michael Reese Hosp., Chgo., 1954-56; asst. prof. physiology U. Mich., Ann Arbor, 1956-60, asso. prof., 1960-64, prof., 1964-68, Banting and Best Dept. Med. Research, U. Toronto, 1968—, chmn. dept., 1968-78; vis. scholar dept. biochemistry, U. Wash., 1963-64; vis. prof. U. B.C., 1970. Editor: Insulin Action, 1971; editorial bd.: Jour. Lipid Research, 1962-67, Can. Jour. Biochemistry, 1969-72, Molecular and Cellular Endocrinology, 1974-82, Am. Jour. Physiology, 1976-81; contbr. articles to profl. jours. Served with U.S. Army, 1951-53. Recipient Gairdner award, 1980; USPHS fellow U. Copenhagen, 1953-55; Guggenheim fellow, 1978-79. Mem. Am. Physiol. Soc., Am. Biochem. Soc., Am. Soc. Cell Biology, Can. Biochem. Soc., Endocrinology Soc., Soc. Reproductive Biology, Can. Med. Research Council (chmn. metabolism grants com. 1969-72). Jewish. Office: 112 College St Toronto ON M5G 1L6 Canada

FRITZ, JACK WAYNE, communications and marketing company executive; b. Battle Creek, Mich., Apr. 22, 1927; s. Charles Lewis and Ruth Marie (Lieb) F.; m. Marilyn Joyce Shingleton, Aug. 26, 1950; children—Jack Wayne II, Dain Thomas, Susan Lynne. B.A., U. Mich., 1949. Sales staff Lever Bros., Mich., 1949-51; with sales staff ABC-owned AM and TV stas., Mich. and Ohio, 1951; product mgr. Pepsodent div. Lever Brothers, N.Y.C., 1951-54; salesman, v.p., sales mgr. v.p., gen. mgr. Blair TV div., N.Y.C., 1954-68; with John Blair & Co., N.Y.C., 1954—, dir., 1968—, v.p., gen. mgr. broadcasting, 1968-72; pres., chief exec. officer, 1972—, chief exec. officer, 1972—; mem. adv. bd. Mfrs. Hanover Trust. Hon. sponsor Children of Alcoholics Found. Inc. Served with AUS, 1945-47. Mem. Internat. Radio and TV Soc. (past dir.), Broadcast Pioneers. (past dir.). Republican. Episcopalian. Clubs: Univ. (N.Y.C.); Woodway Country (Darien, Conn.). Office: John Blair & Co 1290 Ave of the Americas New York NY 10104

FRITZ, JEAN GUTTERY, author, consultant; b. Wuhan, China, Nov. 16, 1915; d. Arthur and Myrtle (Chaney) Guttery; m. Michael Fritz, Nov. 1, 1941; children: David, Andrea. B.A., Wheaton Coll., 1937; D.Lit., Washington and Jefferson U., 1982. Research asst. Silver Burdett Co., N.Y.C., 1938-41; children's librarian Dobbs Ferry Library, N.J., 1954-56; leader writers workshop, Katonah, N.Y., 1963-71; cons. Nat. Park Assn., Washington, 1976—. Author: The Cabin Faced West, 1958, Brady, 1960, Early Thunder, 1967, George Washington's Breakfast, 1969, And Then What Happened Paul Revere?, 1973, Why Don't You Get a Horse Samadams?, 1979, Stonewall, 1979, Traitor, 1981, Homesick: My Own Story, 1982, The Double Life of Pocahontas, 1982. Recipient Non-Fiction award Washington D.C. Book Guild, 1978; named Author of Yr. Pa. Sch. Library Assn., 1978. Mem. Author's Guild. Home: 50 Bellewood Ave Dobbs Ferry NY 10522

FRITZ, JOHN WAYNE, government executive, lawyer; b. Winston-Salem, N.C., Aug. 27, 1948; s. Eugene and Ethel Jennette (Snow) F.; m. Mary Kristine Hansen, May 31, 1969 (div. 1981); m. Carolyn Jane Woodcock, Sept. 11, 1982. B.S., S.D. State U., 1970; J.D., U. Minn., 1973. Bar: Minn. 1973, U.S. Dist. Ct. Minn. 1975. Atty. 3M Co., St. Paul, 1973-76, div. atty., 1976-81, sr. atty., 1981; dep. asst. sec. Dept. Interior, Washington, 1981—; dir. Minn. Bd. Law Examinters, 1978—, Minn. Bd. Adv. Com., 1979—. Bd. dirs. A. Indian Lawyer Tng. Program, Oakland, Calif. Served to 1st lt. U.S. Army, 1973. Am. Indian Law Ctr. scholar, 1970-73. Mem. ABA, Minn. Bar Assn., Am. Legion. Republican. Presbyterian. Club: St. Paul Pool and Yacht (Lilydale, Minn.). Home: 3050 Federal Hill Dr Falls Church VA 22044 Office: Dept Interior Bur Indian Affairs 18th and C Sts NW Washington DC 20240

FRITZ, MICHAEL HENRY, hospital administrator; b. Cass City, Mich., Oct. 19, 1940; s. Edwin Clare and Doris Grace (Amundson) F.; m. Margaret Jean Battin, Oct. 12, 1963; children: Sarah Beth, Amanda Anne. B.A., Albion Coll., 1962; M.H.A., U. Mich., 1964. Adminstrv. resident Harper Hosp., Detroit, 1963-64, adminstrv. asst., 1964-65, asst. adminstr., 1965-72, asso. adminstr., 1972-77, sr. asso. adminstr., 1977-78, adminstr., 1978-80; v.p., adminstr. Harper div. Harper-Grace Hosps., Detroit, 1980—. Trustee Detroit Med. Center Shared Services Coop., Inc. Mem. Am. Coll. Hosp. Adminstrs., Am. Hosp. Assn., Mich. Hosp. Assn. Methodist. Club: Detroit Rotary. Office: 3990 John R St Detroit MI 48201

FRITZ, ROGER JAY, management consultant; b. Browntown, Wis., July 18, 1928; s. Delmar M. and Ruth M. (Sandley) F.; m. Kathryn Louise Goddard, Oct. 13, 1951; children: Nancy Goddard, Susan Marie. B.A. in Polit. Sci, Monmouth (Ill.) Coll., 1950; M.S. in Speech, U. Wis., 1952; Ph.D. in Ednl. Counseling, U. Wis., 1956. Asst. dean men, asst. prof. Purdue U., 1953-56; mgr. pub. relations Cummins Engine Co.; also sec. Cummins Engine Found., 1956-59; sec. John Deere Found.; also mem. pub. relations staff Deere & Co., 1959-65, dir. mgmt. devel. and personnel research; also dir. John Deere Found., 1965-69; pres. Willamette U., 1969-72, Orgn. Devel. Cons., Naperville, Ill., 1972; dir. Intelligent Electronics, Inc. Author: A Handbook for Resident Counselors, 1952, The Argumentation of William Jennings Bryan and Clarence Darrow in the Tennessee Evolution Trial, 1952, How Freshmen Change, 1956, The Power of Professional Purpose, 1974, MBO Goes to College, 1975, Practical Management by Objectives, 1976, What Managers Need to Know-A Practical Guide for Management Development, 1978, Performance Based Management, 1980, Productivity and Results, 1981, People Compatability System, 1983; also articles, papers. Mem. edn. com. Taxpayers' Fedn. Ill., 1962-69; mem. bd. edn. Central Ill. conf. Meth. Ch., 1962-67; co-chmn. finance com. Econ. Edn. Workshop, Augustana Coll., Rock Island, Ill., 1965-67; mem. Midwest Coll. Placement Assn., 1965-69; mem. com. preparation coll. tchrs. Ill. Bd. Higher Edn., 1965-67, mem. com. med. edn., 1967-68; edn. com. N.A.M., 1967-69; founder Quad-Cities Council Grad. Edn., 1967-69; mem. Iowa-Ill. Indsl. Devel. Group, 1964-69; council contbr. Nat. Indsl. Conf. Bd., 1960-65, council devel., edn. and tng., 1966-69; adv. com. solicitations Nat. Better Bus. Bur., 1964-69; v.p. Oreg. Ind. Colls. Assn., 1969-72; mem. Pres. Johnson's Citizens Adv. Bd. on Youth Opportunity, 1968-69, Gov.'s Personnel Grievance Panel, Ill., 1974-77; Trustee Monmouth Coll., 1957-79, chmn., 1961-69; trustee Oreg. Colls. Found., 1969-72, Ind. Coll. Funds Am., N.Y.C., 1972, Internat. Coll. Commerce and Econs., Tokyo, 1970-72, U. Chgo. Cancer Research Found., 1973—. Mem. Phi Eta Sigma, Omicron Delta Kappa, Tau Kappa Epsilon, Phi Alpha Theta, Sigma Tau Delta, Pi Kappa Delta. Republican. Methodist. Club: Naperville (Ill.) Country. Home: 1113 N Loomis St Naperville IL 60540 Office: 552 S Washington St Naperville IL 60540

FRITZ, THOMAS VINCENT, accountant; b. Pitts., July 6, 1934; s. Zeno and Mary M. (Briley) F.; m. Barbara L. Jacob, Jan. 31, 1959; children: William T., James Z., Juliann. B.B.A. in Accounting, U. Pitts., 1960; J.D., Duquesne U., 1964; LL.M., N.Y. U., 1966. Bar: Pa. 1964; C.P.A. With Arthur Young & Co., Pitts., N.Y.C., Washington, 1960—, partner, 1970—, East Region Mng. Partner, 1977—, mem. mgmt. com., 1977—; adj. prof. Sch. Law, Duquesne U., 1967—. Pres. assos. program council U. Pitts.; Active Century Club, Duquesne U. Served with U.S. Army, 1955-57. Mem. Am. Bar Assn., Am. Inst. C.P.A.s, D.C. Inst. C.P.A.s, Va. Soc. C.P.A.s, Pa. Inst. C.P.A.s. Clubs: Duquesne, Rolling Rock., Capitol Hill, Edgewood Country. Home: 6303 Long Meadow Rd McLean VA 22101 Office: 1100 Blake Bldg 1025 Connecticut Ave NW Washington DC 20036

FRITZSCHE, HELLMUT, educator, physicist; b. Berlin, Germany, Feb. 20, 1927; came to U.S., 1952, naturalized, 1966; s. Carl Hellmut and Anna (Jordan) F.; m. Sybille Charlotte Lauffer, July 5, 1952; children—Peter Andreas, Thomas Alexander, Susanne Charlotte, Katharina Sabine. Diploma, U. Göttingen, Germany, 1952; Ph.D., Purdue U., 1954. Instr., then asst. prof. physics Purdue, 1954-56; mem. faculty U. Chgo., 1957—, prof. physics, 1963—, dir. materials research lab., 1973-77, chmn. dept. physics, 1977—; v.p., dir. Energy Conversion Devices, Inc., 1968—; mem. adv. bd. Ency. Brit., 1968—, Office Naval Research, 1976-79; mem. materials scis. panel Nat. Acad. Scis., 1975-80; bd. dirs. Bull. Atomic Scientists, 1981—. Editorial bd.: Jour. Applied Physics, 1975-80. Fellow Am. Phys. Soc. (chmn. div. condensed matter physics 1979-80); mem. N.Y. Acad. Scis., Am. Arbitration Assn. Home: 5801 Blackstone Ave Chicago IL 60637

FRIZZELL, KENT, lawyer, educator; b. Wichita, Kans., Feb. 11, 1929; s. Elton Sanderson and Irma A. (Hays) F. B.A., Friends U., 1953; J.D., Washburn U., 1955. Bar: Kan. bar 1955. Pvt. practice, Wichita, 1955-63; partner firm McCarter, Frizzell & Wettig, 1963-68; mem. Kans. Senate, 1965-69; atty. gen. Kan., 1969-71; asst. atty. gen. Land and Natural Resources div. U.S. Dept. Justice, Washington, 1972-73; solicitor Dept. Interior, 1973-75, undersec., 1975-76; dir. Nat. Energy Law and Policy Inst. U. Tulsa, 1976—. Pres. Bd. of Edn., Wichita, 1959-65; mem. Kans. Municipal Accounting Bd., 1961-64; Precinct committeeman County Republican Central Com., Kans., 1950-64. Served with USMCR, 1948-52. Mem. Am. Bar Assn., Am. Legion, Phi Alpha Delta, Phi Kappa Psi. Home: Route 5 Box 82 Claremore OK 74017

FRIZZELL, WILLIAM KENNETH, architect; b. Knox City, Tex., Dec. 10, 1928; s. Thomas Paul and Kelphia (Williams) F.; m. Patricia Callender, Dec. 24, 1959; children: Jane, John Callender. B.A. magna cum laude in Architecture, Princeton U., 1950; M.A., U. Okla., 1954. Prin. Frizzell-Hill-Moorhouse-Beaubois, Santa Barbara and San Francisco. Works this country, abroad.; Works include Camelback Inn, Scottsdale, Ariz, Loews Paradise Valley Resort, Paradise Valley, Ariz., Sheraton Hammamet Hotel, Tunisia, Yves St Laurent Boutique, N.Y.C., N.Y.C., Becton-Dickenson-Endevco Electronics Factory, San Juan Capistrano, Calif., Marriott Hotel, Newport Beach, Calif., Omar Kahyam Hotel, Cairo, Dysan Corp. Bldgs, Santa Clara, Calif., Monarch Hotel, San Francisco. Served to lt. (j.g.) USNR. Mem. AIA. Home: 802 Ayala Ln Santa Barbara CA 93108 Office: 527 San Ysidro Rd Santa Barbara CA 93108 also 170 Maiden Ln San Francisco CA 94108

FROCK, EDMOND BURNELL, former fabricated metal products company executive, banker; b. Hanover, Pa., Nov. 26, 1910; s. Edmond A. and Vivian (Huff) F.; m. Rebecca Black, Apr. 24, 1936; children: Edmond Burnell Jr., J. Daniel, Judith A., James W. (dec.). A.B., Catawba Coll., 1933. Mdse. mgr. Atlantic & Pacific Tea Co., Hanover, Pa., 1933-45; pres. Hanover Wire Cloth, 1945-81; v.p. Continental Copper & Steel Industries, Inc., N.Y.C., 1948-74, exec. v.p., 1974-81; ret., 1981; chmn. bd. Bank of Hanover & Trust Co., 1963—, pres., 1970-77, Hanover Bancorp, Inc.; pres., dir. Downtown Hanover Inc.; Past pres. Wire Weavers Assn., Indsl. Wire Cloth Inst., Hanover Pub. Library. Fin. com. Hoffman Home for Youth; past pres. Hanover Dist. Sch. Bd.; bd. dirs. Hanover Gen. Hosp.; trustee Catawba Coll., Hanover YMCA.; chmn. adv. com. York County Earn It Ct. Program; mem. York chpt. S.C.O.R.E. Mem. Hanover Area Indsl. Mgmt. Club (founder), Mfrs. Assn.• York (past pres. dir.), Hanover Area C. of C. (past pres.), Indsl. Mgmt. Club York County (past pres.), The Pennsylvanians. Clubs: Pine Valley Golf (Clementon, N.J.); Seaview Country (Absecon, N.J.); Hanover Country, Masons, Shriners. Home: 7 Oak St Hanover PA 17331 Office: 500 E Middle St Hanover PA 17331 also 25 Carlisle St Hanover PA 17331

FROCK, ROGER J., investment company executive; b. Detroit, Oct. 6, 1936; s. Ivan Cleveland and Anne (Walsh) F.; m. Linda Gail Wise, Aug. 15, 1981; children by previous marriage: Gregory Eric, Karen Joy, James Roger. B.S., U. Mich., 1958, M.B.A., 1959. Prin. A.T. Kearney Co., Chgo., 1960-72; sr. v.p., gen. mgr. Fed. Express Corp., Memphis, 1972-82; pres. Bus. Services Internat., Annapolis, 1983—; dir. Independent Power of N.Am., Manchester, N.H. Served with USN, 1960-66. Address: Business Services Internat 852 St Edmonds Pl Annapolis MD 21401

FROEHLICH, HAROLD VERNON, judge, former congressman; b. Appleton, Wis., May 12, 1932; s. Vernon W. and Lillian and (Wohlfeil) F.; m. Sharon F. Ross, Nov. 20, 1970; children: Jeffrey Scott, Michael Ross. B.B.A., U. Wis., 1959, LL.B., 1962. Bar: Wis. 1962. Staff acct. Ruschlien and Stortreon (C.P.A.s), Madison, Wis., 1958-62; practiced in Appleton, 1962-81, judge Circuit Ct., 1981—; mem. Wis. Ho. of Reps., 1963-73, speaker, 1967-71, minority floor leader, 1971-73; mem. 93d Congress from 8th Dist., Wis.; v.p. Black Creek Improvement Corp., Outagamic County Family Ct. Commn., 1975-78. Republican precinct committeeman 19th Ward, Appleton, 1956-62; chmn. Outagamie County Rep. Statutory Com., 1958-62, Assembly Rep. Caucus, 1965-66. Served with USN, 1951-55. Mem. Am., Wis., Outagamie County bar assns., Am. Inst. C.P.A.s, Am. Legion, VFW (judge adv. 1963-75, 82—), Midwest Council State Govts. (vice-chmn. 1968-69, chmn. 1969-70), Council State Govts. (mem. nat. exec. com. 1970-72), Phi Alpha Delta. Home: 1008 E Marnie Ln Appleton WI 54911 Office: 410 S Walnut St Appleton WI 54911

FROEHLICH, JOACHIM WILLIAM, coll. pres.; b. Waterbury, Conn., June 27, 1944; s. George Thomas and Anna Catherine (Praines) F. A.B., St. Anselm Coll., 1967; M.A., SUNY, Buffalo, 1971; Ph.D., Catholic U. Am., 1977. NSF trainee SUNY, Buffalo, 1969-70; teaching asst. Cath. U., 1972-73; asst. prof. econs. St. Anselm Coll., Manchester, N.H., 1970-79, chmn. dept. econs., 1975-79, pres., 1979—. Mem. Am. Econ. Assn., Eastern Econ. Assn. Roman Catholic. Office: St Anselm Coll Manchester NH 03102

FROEHLICH, S. CHARLES, trust co. exec.; b. Balt., Feb. 14, 1922; s. Milton S. and Anna (Reif) F.; m. Charlotte M. Woelper, Mar. 22, 1946; 1 son, Charles L. B.B.S., U. Balt., 1943. C.P.A., Md. With Union Trust Co. Md., Balt., 1946—, asst. sec., asst. treas., 1949-55, asst. v.p., 1955-60, v.p., 1960-71, sr. v.p., 1971—, also dir. Treas. Buddies Inc. Served with USMCR, 1942-46. Mem. Am. Inst. Banking (pres. Balt. chpt. 1952-53), Robert Morris Assos. (pres. Chesapeake chpt. 1953-54), Balt. Assn. Credit Mgmt. (pres. 1966-67), Md. Assn. C.P.A.'s, Am. Inst. C.P.A.'s. Lutheran. Club: Kiwanian. Home: 10021 Carrigan Dr Ellicott City MD 21043 Office: Baltimore and St Paul Sts Baltimore MD 21203

FROEHLKE, ROBERT FREDERICK, insurance company executive; b. Neenah, Wis., Oct. 15, 1922; s. Herbert O. and Lillian (Porath) F.; m. Nancy Jean Barnes, Nov. 9, 1946; children: Bruce, Jane, Anne, Scott. LL.B., U. Wis., 1949. Bar: Wis. 1949. Assoc. firm McDonald & MacDonald, Madison, 1949-50; mem. faculty U. Wis. Law Sch., 1950-51; with Sentry Ins. Co., 1951-69, resident v.p., Boston, 1968-69; asst. sec. def. for adminstrn., Washington, 1969-71, sec. of army, 1971-73; pres. Sentry Corp., 1973-75, Health Ins. Assn. Am., 1975-80; chmn. bd. Equitable Life Assurance Soc. U.S., 1982—; dir. Rexnord, Inc., Milw., Square D Co., Palatine, Ill., Phillips Petroleum, Oklahoma City. Mem. bd. Laird Youth Leadership Found., Nat. Fund for Med. Edn.; bd. dirs. N.Y.C. Partnership, Ethics Resource Ctr., Inc., Washington; trustee Inst. for Def. Analyses, Washington., Tchr.'s Coll., Columbia U., Coll. of Ins., Morehouse Med. Sch.; mem. Com. for Econ. Devel., Nat. Exec. Service Corps, Mayor's Com. Meml. for Vietnam Vets. Served to capt. AUS, 1943-46. Mem. Am. Bar Assn., Am. Council Life Ins. (pres. 1980-82), N.Y. C. of C. and Industry, U. Wis. Alumni Assn., Order of Coif, Psi Upsilon. Republican. Presbyterian. Home: 1010 Fifth Ave Apt 4C New York NY

FROEMMING, HERBERT DEAN, food and drug exec.; b. Alexandria, Minn., Aug. 19, 1936; s. Herbert Edward and Bertha Anna (Hink) F.; m. Mary Louise Gapinski, Sept. 2, 1961; children—Mark, Traci, Scott. B.B.A., U. Minn., 1959; M.B.A., U. Mo. C.P.A. Fin. exec. The Kroger Co., various locations, 1960-69; exec. v.p. E.F. MacDonald Shopping Bag, Los Angeles, 1969-73; also dir.; v.p., treas., dir. Western Auto Supply Co., Kansas City, Mo., 1973-78; sr. corp. v.p., controller Gamble-Skogmo Co., Mpls., 1978-80; exec. v.p. Red Owl Food Stores, Inc., 1980—; dir. City Bank and Trust. Served with AUS, 1955-57. Mem. Fin. Execs. Inst., Am. Inst. C.P.A.'s. Home: 5713 Parkwood Ln Edina MN 55436 Office: 215 E Excelsior Ave Hopkins MN 55343

FROEMSDORF, DONALD HOPE, college dean; b. Cape Girardeau, Mo., Mr. 4, 1934; s. Rudolph Fred F. and Marie (Mammon) Foremsdorf; m. Joy Lou Kasten, May 29, 1954; 1 dau., Dawn Elaine. B.S., S.E. Mo. State U., Cape Girardeau, 1955; Ph.D., Iowa State U., 1959. Asst. project chemist Standard Oil Co. (Ind.), Whiting, 1959-60; assoc. prof. chemistry S.E. Mo. State U., 1960-66, prof. chemistry, 1966—, chmn. div. scis., 1970-76, dean Coll. Scis., 1976—. Contbr. articles to profl. jours. DuPont Research fellow, 1958; Petroleum Research Fund grantee, 1962-72; NSF grantee, 1964-71, 75-76. Mem. Am. Chem. Soc., AAAS, Mo. Acad. Sci. Club: Lions. Office: Coll Scis Southeast Mo State U Cape Girardeau MO 63701

FROHLICH, EDWARD DAVID, physician; b. N.Y.C., Sept. 10, 1931; s. William and May (Zneimer) F.; m. Sherry Linda Fine, Nov. 1, 1959; children—Marjorie, Bruce, Lara. B.A., Washington and Jefferson Coll., 1952; M.D., U. Md., 1956; M.S., Northwestern U., 1963. Diplomate: Am. Bd. Internal Medicine. Intern, resident D.C. Gen. Hosp., 1956-58; fellow in cardiovascular research Georgetown U. Hosp., Washington, 1958-59, resident in internal medicine, 1959-60; clin. investigator VA Research Hosp., Chgo., 1962-64; asso. in medicine Northwestern U., 1963-64; staff mem. research div. Cleve. Clinic, 1964-69; faculty medicine, physiology, Biophysics, dir. div. hypertensive diseases U. Okla., Oklahoma City, 1969-76, George Lynn Cross research prof., 1975-76; v.p. edn., research Alton Ochsner Med. Found., New Orleans, 1976—; staff mem. div. hypertensive diseases Ochsner Clinic, 1976—; prof. medicine, physiology La. State U., 1976—; prof. medicine, adj. prof. pharmacology Tulane U., 1976—; cons. FDA, 1971-74, VA, 1972—, NIH, 1972—, WHO, 1975-82, U.S. Pharmacopeia, 1975—. Contbr. many chpts. to books, numerous articles in field to profl. jours.; Editor: Pathophysiology - Altered Regulatory Mechanisms in Disease, 1972, 76, Rypins' Medical Licensure Examinations, 1981; editor.: Jour. Lab. and Clin. Medicine, 1974-76, Am. Jour. Cardiology, 1977—, Archives of Internal Medicine, 1978—, Modern Medicine, 1980—, Hypertension, 1980—. Served to capt. M.C. AUS, 1960-62. Recipient Honors Achievement award Angiology Research Found., 1964, Disting. Faculty award U. Okla., 1970, So. Med. Assn. Ann. award, 1971. Fellow A.C.P., Am. Coll. Cardiology, AAAS; mem. Am. Soc. for Clin. Investigation, Am. Soc. for Clin. Pharmacology and Therapeutics (pres. 1973-74), Internat. Soc. Hypertension (sci. council 1974—, treas. 1980—), Am. Heart Assn. (dir. La. 1979—), Am. Physiol. Soc., Am. Soc. Nephrology, Central Soc. for Clin. Research, Chi Epsilon Mu, Phi Sigma, Alpha Kappa Alpha. Jewish. Home: 5353 Marcia Ave New Orleans LA 70124 Office: Alton Ochsner Med Found 1516 Jefferson Hwy New Orleans LA 70121

FROHLING, EDWARDS S., minerals company executive, engineer; b. Princeton, N.J., Mar. 26, 1942; s. Edward A. and Agnes (Odend-hal) F.; m. Irma Jean Grathwol, Jan. 30, 1947 (div. 1961); children: Edward S., Laura; m. Diane C. Corse, Sept. 28, 1961; 1 son, Matthew. B.S. in Metallurgy, MIT, 1948. Metallurgist Climax Moly Co. (Colo.), 1948-54; mill supt. Fluorspar Co., Wilmington, Del., 1954-57; regional sales mgr. Western Machinery Co., Sacramento, 1957-62; v.p., mgr. bus. devel. Parsons Jurden Co., N.Y.C., 1962-67; pres., chmn. bd., chief exec. officer Mountain State Mineral Enterprises, Tuscon, 1969—; chmn. bd., dir. A.H. Ross & Assocs., Toronto, 1982—, Mountain States Synfuels Corp., Tucson, 1982—; v.p., co-owner Tucson Toros, 1976—; chmn. bd., dir. Min Seps Corp., Tucson, 1975—; co-chmn. World Symposium on Lead and Zinc, 1970. Contbr. articles to profl. jours. Served to cpl. Combat Engrs., U.S. Army, 1942-46; ETO. Named Man of Yr. Tucson C. of C., 1975; recipient Disting. CitizenAward Coll. Mines U. Ariz., 1975. Mem. Soc. Mining Engrs. (Charles Rand Meml. award 1982), AIME, Am. Mining Congress (dir. 1982), Associated Builders and Contractors (pres. 1983). Republican. Espiscopalian. Clubs: Mining; University (N.Y.C.); Mining of Southwest, Tucson Golf and Country, Old Pueblo; Baseball (Tucson). Home: 3220 N San Sebastian Pl Tucson AZ 85715 Office: Mountain State Mineral Enterprises 1-10 and Vail Rd Tucson AZ 85641

FROHMAN, LAWRENCE ASHER, endocrinology educator, scientist; b. Detroit, Jan. 26, 1935; s. Dan and Rebecca (Katzman) F.; m. Barbara Hecht, June 9, 1957; children: Michael, Marc, Erica, Rena. M.D., U. Mich., 1958. Diplomate: Am. Bd. Internal Medicine. Intern Yale-New Haven Med. Ctr., 1958-59, resident in internal medicine, 1959-61; asst. prof. medicine SUNY, Buffalo, 1965-69, assoc. prof., 1969-73; prof. medicine U. Chgo., 1973-81; dir. endocrinology Michael Reese Hosp., Chgo., 1973-81; prof. medicine, dir. div. endocrinology and metabolism U. Cin., 1981—; mem. sci. rev. com. NIH, Bethesda, Md., 1972-76; mem. sci. rev. bd. VA, Washington, 1979-82; mem. endocrine adv. bd. FDA, Washington, 1982—. Editor: (with others) Endocrinology and Metabolism, 1981; editorial bd. 6 med. and sci. jours., 1970—; contbr. articles to profl. jours. NIH research grantee, 1967—. Mem. Endocrine Soc. (council), Assn. Am. Physicians, Am. Soc. Clin. Investigation, Am. Diabetes Assn., Internat. Soc. Neuroendocrinology. Office: Div Endocrinology and Metabolism Univ of Cincinnati College of Medicine 231 Bethesda Ave Cincinnati OH 45267

FROHNMAYER, DAVID BRADEN, state attorney general; b. Medford, Oreg., July 9, 1940; s. Otto J. and Marabel (Fisher) B.; m. Lynn Diane Johnson, Dec. 30, 1970; children: Kirsten, Mark, Kathryn. A.B. magna cum laude, Harvard U., 1962; B.A., Oxford (Eng.) U., 1964, M.A., 1971; J.D., U. Calif., Berkeley, 1967. Bar: Calif. 1967, Oreg. 1971. Assoc. firm Pillsbury, Madison & Sutro, San Francisco, 1967-69; asst. to sec. Dept. HEW, 1969-70; prof. U. Oreg. Law Sch., 1971-81, spl. asst. to pres., 1971-79; atty. gen. State of Oreg., 1981—; mem. Oreg. Gov.'s Task Force Conflict of Interest Legislation, 1973-74; Mem. Oreg. Ho. of Reps., 1975-81. Recipient awards Weaver Constl. Law Essay competition Am. Bar Found., 1972, 74. Mem. ABA (Ross essay winner 1980), Oreg. Bar Assn., Calif. Bar Assn., Round Table Eugene, Order of Coif, Phi Beta Kappa. Republican. Presbyterian. Club: Rotary. Home: 8275 Baker St Eugene OR 97403 Office: 100 State Office Bldg Salem OR 97310

FROHRIB, DARRELL ALBERT, biomedical engineering educator; b. Oshkosh, Wis., June 25, 1930; s. Albert August and Caroline Irene (Yorty) F.; m. Betty Jane Eserhut, Sept. 12, 1955; children: Ellen Marie, Sandra Jean, Paul Darrell. B.S., MIT, 1952, M.S., 1953; Ph.D., U. Minn., 1966. Engr., Sperry Gyroscope Co., Great Neck, N.Y., 1953-59; lectr. mech. engring. U. Minn., Mpls., 1959-66, asst. prof., 1966-68, asso. prof., 1968-74, prof., 1974—, grad. faculty in bioengring., 1968—, dir. grad. program in biomed. engring., 1978—; cons. in field. Mem. Minn. Gov.'s Commn. on Handicapped, 1974-75. Contbr. articles to profl. jours. Adv. com. Courage Center, Golden Valley, Minn., 1979—. Fulbright fellow, 1970; NIH grantee, 1973-77. Mem. ASME, Sigma Xi, Tau Beta Pi, Pi Tau Sigma. Lutheran. Patentee in field. Home: 2144 Princeton Ave Saint Paul MN 55105 Office: Rm 325 Design Center Mech Engring Dept U Minn Minneapolis MN 55455 *Thinking of biomedical engineering in 1953, when there was no such profession, I remained in mechanical engineering. When design education returned as an active force in curriculum in the early '60s, I moved to academia. The fusion of biomedical engineering and engineering design finally identified me with the former, and augmented the meaning of the latter. Similarly, the concerns for innovation now raise the meaning of the human force in engineering.*

FROHRING, PAUL ROBERT, food, drug and chemical manufacturer; b. Cleve.; s. William E. and Martha L. (Bliss) F.; m. Maxine A. Prince, Mar. 7, 1941; children: Martha Louise, Paula Christine. Student, Ohio State U., 1921-22; B.S. in Chem. Engring, Case Inst. Tech., 1926. With research labs. S.M.A. Corp. (formerly Lab. Products Co.), 1926-34, v.p., 1942-44; pres. Eff Labs., Inc., 1940-61; gen. mgr. Gen. Biochems., Inc., Chagrin Falls, Ohio, 1940-61, Emdee Labs., 1942-44; pres. Life Products, Inc., 1942-45; dir. Cleve. Machine Controls, Inc., Irvin & Co., Shaker Heights, Ohio, Alco Standard, Inc., Phila., Am. Home Products Corp., N.Y.C., Newbury Industries, Inc., Ohio, Horsburg & Scott, Cleve.; Mem. pharm. mfrs. adv. com. WPB, 1942; del. Pres.'s Conf. Indsl. Safety, 1954. Trustee, hon. chmn. Cleve. Health Edn. Mus.; trustee Hiram (Ohio) Coll., John Cabot Coll., Rome, Italy, Fla. Zool. Soc.; overseer Case Western Res. U.; mem. corp. Planned Parenthood, Cleve.; bd. dirs. Mercy Hosp. Found., Miami. Recipient Gold medal award for achievement Case Alumni Assn. Fellow Garfield Soc., N.Y. Acad. Scis.; mem. Ohio Acad. Sci., Am. Chem. Soc., Am. Dairy Sci. Assn., Am. Oil Chemist Soc., AAAS, Navy League (life), Newcomen Soc., Ohio Soc. (N.Y.), Alpha Chi Sigma. Clubs: Chagrin Valley Hunt (Gates Mills, Ohio); Union (Cleve.); Key Biscayne Yacht (Key Biscayne, Fla.); Commodore Club of Key Biscayne (dir.). Home and Office: Box 428 Chagrin Falls OH 44022

FROIX, MICHAEL FRANCIS, physical chemist, polymer physicist; b. Trinidad, West Indies, Jan 27, 1942; came to U.S., 1962; s. Arthur C. and Lorna E. (Lopez) F.; m. Elizabeth Moran, 1979; children: Cherie-Ann, Renee. B.S., Howard U., 1966, M.S., 1968, Ph.D., 1971. Chemist Texaco Research Labs., Beacon, N.Y., 1966, Gillette Research Inst., Washington, 1968; scientist Xerox Corp., Rochester, N.Y., 1971-77; sr. research chemist Celanese Corp., Summit, N.J., 1977-78, research supr., 1978-79; group leader Ray Chem. Corp., Menlo Park, Calif., 1979-80, dept. mgr., 1980-81, sect. dir. physics, corp. research and devel., 1981—; vis. prof. Beep Program, Nat. Urban League, 1976-77, 77-78; instr. community edn. div. U.D.C., 1970-71. Contbr. articles to profl. jours. Mem. Am. Phys. Soc., Am. Chem. Soc., N.Y. Acad. Scis., AAAS. Home: 1350 Channing Ave Palo Alto CA 94301 Office: Raychem Corp 300 Constitution Dr Menlo Park CA 94025

FROMKES, SAUL, lawyer, insurance company executive. LL.B., St. Johns U. Sch. Law, 1928, LL.D. (hon.), 1968, D.C.S., Pace U., 1973, L.H.D., N.Y. Med. Coll., 1983. Bar: N.Y. 1930, U.S. Supreme Ct. 1964. Mem. firm Fromkes Brothers, N.Y.C., 1930—; founder, pres. City Title Ins. Co., N.Y.C., 1929—; vice chmn. legis. com. Real Estate Bd. N.Y.; mem. Ins. Bd. State of N.Y., 1980—; arbitrator Small Claims Ct. Part, Civil Ct. City of New York, 1967-77; treas., dir. 1128 Park Ave. Corp.; dir. Empire Mut. Ins. Co.; guest lectr. Yale U. Law Sch., Cornell U. Law Sch., Harvard U. Law Sch., St. Johns U. Sch. of Law; Mem. N.Y. State Com. of Adv. Panel Experts on Real Estate and Condominiums, 1969, Task Force Health and Hosps., Diocese of New York, 1974—; com. on character and fitness Supreme Ct. Appellate Div., First Dept., 1977; chmn. seminars, moderator St. Johns U. Sch. Law Homecomings, 1959—; also chmn. alumni fund drive, chmn. law library fund campaign; chmn. bd. regents N.Y. State Adv. Com. on Higher Edn. Facilities Planning, 1968. Guest columnist: New York World Telegram; Hon. editor: St. Johns Law Rev, 1973. V.p., trustee Old Met. Opera House; vice chmn. bd. trustees St. Johns U.; trustee Inner-City Scholarship Fund, 1972; trustee, mem. exec. com. N.Y. Med. Coll., 1978—, chmn. com. on affiliations; bd. govs. N.Y.C. Nat. Shrines Assn.; mem. adv. com. N.Y. State Commn. on Estates; mem. hon. adv. bd. Nat. Real Estate Show; mem. hon. com. March of Dimes Man of Year, 1964, N.Y.C. Baseball Fedn., Navy Yard Boys Club, Catholic Interracial Council. Recipient certificate of merit St. Johns Alumni Fedn., 1960-61, Pietas medal St. Johns U., 1961, also medal of honor, 1978, Pres.'s medal, 1970, certificate of merit Selective Service System, 1947, certificate of recognition Bklyn. Acad. Music, 1967; named Hon. Brother Phi Delta Phi, 1970, Man of Year, 1971; Ky. Col. Mem. ABA (Merit award 1972), N.Y. State Bar Assn., Assn. Bar City N.Y., Am. Land Title Assn. (chmn. legis. com.), Pa. Land Title Assn., N.Y. Land Title Assn. (chmn. com. to confer with N.Y. State Bar Assn., pres. 1967-68), Am. Land Title Ins. Assn., N.J. Land Title Ins. Assn. (dir.), St. Johns U. Sch. of Law Alumni Assn. (pres. 1957-58, dir.), Lawyers Club (v.p., bd. govs. 1972—), Bankers Club Am. Clubs: Circus Saints and Sinners, Metropolis Country, Golf Soc. Gt. Britain, Profl. Golfers Assn. Am., The Club at World Trade Center. New Law Sch. of St. Johns U. on Jamaica campus named Fromkes Hall; Law Library of St. Johns U. Law Sch. dedicated in his honor, 1964; personally chaired 239 St. Johns U. Law Sch. alumni luncheons. Home and Office: 1130 Park Ave New York NY 10028 *What I spent I had; what I kept I lost; what I gave I have.*

FROMKIN, VICTORIA ALEXANDRIA, linguist, phonetician, educator; b. Passaic, N.J., May 16, 1923; d. Henry and Rose Lillian (Ravitz) Landish; m. Jack Fromkin, Oct. 24, 1948; 1 son, Mark. B.A., U. Calif.-Berkeley, 1944; M.A., UCLA, 1963, Ph.D., 1965. Asst. prof. dept. linguistics UCLA, 1966-69, assoc. prof., 1969-73, prof., 1973—, chmn. dept. linguistics, 1974-77, dean grad. div., vice chancellor grad. programs, 1979—; mem. communication scis. study sect. NIH, 1981—; mem. com. on basic research behavior and social sci. Nat. Acad. Sci./NRC, 1982—; vis. fellow Wolfson Coll., Oxford, 1983. Author: (with R. Rodman) An Introduction to Language, (1973); editor: Speech Errors as Linguistic Evidence, 1973, Tone: A Linguistic Survey, 1978, Errors in Linguistic Performance: Slips of the Tongue, Ear, Hand, and Pen, 1980; mem. editorial bd.: Applied Psycholinguistics, Brain and Language, Studies in African Linguistics. Recipient Disting. Tchrs. award UCLA, 1974, Profl. Achievement award UCLA Alumni Assn., 1984. Fellow Acoustical Soc. Am.; mem. Linguistic Soc. Am. (exec. com., sec.-treas. 1979-83, v.p., pres.-elect 1984), Internat. Phonetics Assn., Internat. Assn. Phonetic Scis., Am. Assn. Phonetic Sci. (councillor 1982-84), West African Linguistics Soc., Assn. Grad. Schs. (exec. com. 1981-84), Comite Internat. Permanent de Linguistes (U.S. del. 1983-86). Home: 8508 Lookout Mountain Ave Los Angeles CA 90046

FROMM, ALFRED, distbg. co. exec.; b. Kitzingen, Germany, Feb. 23, 1905; came to U.S., 1936, naturalized, 1943; s. Max and Mathilda (Maier) F.; m. Hanna Gruenbaum, July 5, 1936; children: David George, Carolynn Anne. Student, Viticultural Acad., 1920; L.H.D. (hon.), St. Mary's Coll., 1974, D.Public Service, U. San Francisco. Export dir. N. Fromm, Bingen, Germany, 1924-33; v.p. Picker-Lintz Importers, Inc., N.Y.C., 1937-44; exec. v.p. Fromm & Sichel, Inc., N.Y.C., also San Francisco, 1944-65, pres., 1965-73, chmn. bd., chief exec. officer, 1973—; dir. Joseph E. Seagram & Sons, Inc.; Dir. Calif. Med. Clinic for Psychotherapy, San Francisco, 1964—. Contbr. articles profl. jours. Mem. nat. council Eleanor Roosevelt Meml. Found., N.Y.C.; trustee San Francisco Conservatory Music; regent St. Mary's Coll., Moraga; v.p. Jewish Nat. Fund; bd. dirs. San Francisco Opera Assn.; founder, pres. Wine Mus., San Francisco. Clubs: Concordia, Commonwealth (San Francisco). Home: 850 El Camino del Mar San Francisco CA 94121 Office: 655 Beach St San Francisco CA 94109

FROMM, ARNO HENRY, physician; b. Elkhart Lake, Wis., May 5, 1902; s. Ferdinand F. and Adeline (Miller) F.; m. Emily A. Kramp, Jan. 26, 1934 (dec.); children—Barbara Gale, Kathleen Ann (Mrs. Philip Lane); m. Constance Crafts, Aug. 30, 1962. Student, U. Wis., 1920-24; M.D., Marquette U., 1929; postgrad., Columbia U., 1937, U. Minn., 1940, Cook County (Ill.) Postgrad. Sch. Medicine, 1944. Intern St. Mary's Hosp., Milw., 1928-29; resident Univ. Hosp., Madison, Wis., 1950-52; instr., research asst., dept. anatomy Marquette U., Milw., 1929-32, 33-36; practice medicine, 1932-50; resident instr. U. Wis., 1950-52; cons. Mendota (Wis.) State Hosp., 1954-56, internist, 1952-60; field rep. Joint Commn. on Accreditation of Hosps., 1962—, research dir., 1966—; asso. med. dir. Interstate Blood and Plasma Center, Milw., 1974—; staff Howard Young Med. Center, Inc., Woodruff, Wis.; cons. Eagle River (Wis.) Meml. Hosp.; Dir., trustee dept. hematology Ed K. Holz Research Fund, 1957—. Recipient citation Med. Coll. Wis., 1978. Fellow Royal Soc. Health; mem. AMA, Wis. Med. Soc., Civitan Club (charter). Clubs: Mason (32 deg.), Shriner). Home and Office: 8 Westbrook Circle Madison WI 53711

FROMM, DAVID, surgeon; b. N.Y.C., Jan. 21, 1939; s. Alfred and Hanna F.; m. Barbara Solter, June 13, 1961; children—Marc, Kenneth, Kathleen. B.S., U. Calif., Berkeley, 1960, M.D., 1964. Intern U. Calif. Hosp., San Francisco, 1964-65; resident in surgery U. Calif., San Francisco, 1965-71; asst. prof. surgery Harvard Med. Sch., Boston, 1973-77, asso. prof., 1977-78; prof. chmn. dept. surgery SUNY-Upstate Med. Center, Syracuse, 1978—. Author: Complications of Gastric Surgery, 1977; Contbr. articles to profl. jours. Served with M.C. U.S. Army, 1971-73. NIH career devel. awardee, 1976-79; grantee, 1974—. Fellow A.C.S. (gov. 1978—); mem. Soc. Univ. Surgeons, Am. Gastroent. Assn., Soc. Clin. Surgery, Assn. Acad. Surgery, Am. Physiol. Soc., Am. Surg. Assn. Office: 750 E Adams Syracuse NY 13210

FROMM, ERIKA (MRS. PAUL FROMM), clinical psychologist; b. Frankfurt, Germany, Dec. 23, 1910; came to U.S., 1938, naturalized, 1944; d. Siegfried and Clementine (Stern) Oppenheimer; m. Paul Fromm, July 20, 1938; 1 dau., Joan (Mrs. Greenstone). Ph.D. magna cum laude, U. Frankfurt, 1933; postgrad. child care program, Chgo. Inst. for Psychoanalysis, 1949-51. Diplomate: Am. Bd. Examiners in Profl. Psychology, Am. Bd. Examiners Clin. Hypnosis. Chief psychologist Apeldoorn State Hosp., Holland, 1935-38; chief psychologist Francis W. Parker Sch., 1944-51; supervising psychologist Inst. for Juvenile Research, 1951-53; asst. prof. to asso. prof. Northwestern U. Med. Sch., 1954-61; prof. U. Chgo., 1961-76, prof. emeritus, 1976—. Author: (with L.D. Hartman) Intelligence-A Dynamic Approach, (with Thomas M. French) Dream Interpretation: A New Approach, 1964, (with Ronald E. Shor) Hypnosis: Developments in Research and New Perspectives, 1972, 2d edit., 1979; also numerous articles in profl. jours.; Mem. editorial bd.: Jour. Clin. and Exptl. Psychopathology, 1951-59; clin. editor: Internat. Jour. Clin. and Exptl. Hypnosis, 1968—; assoc. editor: Bull. Brit. Soc. Exptl. and Clin. Hypnosis, 1982—; mem. bd. cons. editors: Psychoanalytic Psychology, 1982—; mem. adv. bd. editors: Imagination, Cognition and Personality: Sci. study of Consciousness, 1981—. Fellow Am. Psychol. Assn. (pres. div. 30 1972-73), Am. Orthopsychiat. Assn. (dir. 1961-63), AAAS, Soc. Clin. Exptl. Hypnosis (sec. 1965-67, fellow, v.p. 1971-75, Fellow, pres. 1975-77); mem. Am. Bd. Psychol. Hypnosis (pres. 1971-74), Ill. Psychol. Assn. (council 1951-53, 55-57, bd. examiners 1959-62, v.p. bd. examiners 1960-61), Soc. Projective Techniques, Sigma Xi. Home: 5715 S Kenwood Ave Chicago IL 60637 Office: Dept Behavioral Sciences U Chicago Chicago IL 60637

FROMM, HENRY GORDON, business executive; b. Burlington, Iowa, June 10, 1911; s. Henry Carl and Lillian (Lohmann) F.; m. Elizabeth H. Orthner, July 15, 1936; children—Dan G., Allan P., Martha E., Mark H., Eric C., Lynne M. B.S. in Chem. Engring, Iowa State U., 1933; M.S. (Sloan fellow), Mass. Inst. Tech., 1950. Gen. plant mgr. Manhattan Soap Co., Bristol, Pa., 1937-44; prodn. mgr. Johnson & Johnson, 1944-55; v.p. ops. Internat. Latex Corp., 1955-61; v.p., gen. mgr. ops. Sun Chem. Corp., N.Y.C., 1961-63; gen. mgr. Crown Cork & Seal Co., Phila., 1963-64; v.p. ops. Marathon Electric Co., Wausau, Wis., 1964-69; pres. Bell & Howell Communications Co., Waltham, Mass., 1969, Bell & Howell Electronics & Instruments Group, Pasadena, Calif., 1969-71; group v.p. Bell & Howell, Chgo., 1971-77; pres. Fromm Services, Inc., Green Bay, Wis., 1973—, Eau Claire T.A.S., Wis., 1973—, Gordon Fromm & Assos., Lake Forest, Ill., 1979—; chmn. bd. Ditto, Inc., Chgo., 1977-79; pres., chief exec. officer Templeton, Kenly & Co., 1979—, Miller Fluid Power, 1981—. Mem. gen. council Am. Baptist Conv.; mem. Dover (Del.) City Council, 1958-62; chmn. Dover City Planning Commn., 1960-62. Mem. Midwest Indsl. Mgmt. Assn. (dir.), Am. Mgmt. Assn. (v.p.), Am. Inst. Chem. Engrs. Club: Univ. (Chgo.). Home: 255 Ravine Forest Dr Lake Bluff IL 60044 Office: Templeton Kenly & Co 7N015 York Road Bensenville IL 60106

FROMM, JOHN ABBOTT, financial company executive; b. Compton, Calif., July 28, 1935; s. James William and Constance (Abbott) F.; m. Dolores Sue Rossi, Sept. 6, 1956 (div. 1967); m. Jo Ann K. Underwood; children: Camie, Krista, Holly, Lara, Amy. B.S. in Bus. Mgmt., U. Calif.-Long Beach, 1959; student, Los Angeles Inst. Fin., 1962, Investment Bankers Inst. U. Chgo., 1963. Acct. Hughes Aircraft, Fullerton, Calif., 1959-61; systems design analyst Babcock Electronics, Costa Mesa, Calif., 1961-62; ptnr., br. office mgr. Crowell Weedon & Co., Laguna Hills, Calif., 1962—. Served to lt. USN, 1953-56. Republican. Republican. Home: 171 Monarch Bay South Laguna CA 92677 Office: Crowell Weedon & Co PO Box 2248 Laguna Hills CA 92677

FROMM, JOSEPH, magazine editor; b. South Bend, Ind., Jan. 6, 1920; s. Michael M. and Ethel (Mentzel) F.; m. Gloria M. Josi, Dec. 10, 1956; children: Margot, Lisa; 1 stepson, Erik. Student, U. Chgo., 1937-38, Northwestern U., 1938-39. Reporter S. Bend Tribune, 1935-37, Southtown Economist, Chgo., 1937-39; writer UP, Chgo., 1939-40; radio news bur. chief AP, Chgo., 1940-42; mng. editor air edit. Chgo. Sun, 1942; fgn. corr. U.S. News and World Report, 1946-74, dep. editor, Washington, 1974-79, asst. editor, 1979—; lectr. on strategy and internat. relations. Served with Brit. and Indian armies, 1942-45. Decorated Order Brit. Empire. Mem. Internat. Inst. Strategic Studies (gov. council), Overseas Writers, Mid-Atlantic Club, Fgn. Corr. Club Japan (pres. 1950), Assn. Am. Corr. in London (pres. 1967), Fgn. Press Assn. London (dir. 1972-74), Arms Control Assn., Am. Soc. Mag. Editors. Clubs: Cosmos (Washington); Garrick (London). Office: US News & World Report 2300 N St NW Washington DC 20037

FROMM, PAUL, foundation executive; b. Kitzingen, Germany, Sept. 28, 1906; came to U.S., 1938, naturalized, 1944; s. Max and Matilde (Maier) F.; m. Erika Oppenheimer, July 2O, 1938; 1 dau., Joan. Ed. high sch.; Dr.Music (hon.), New Eng. Conservatory Music, Boston, Mass., Mus.D., U. Cin. Established Great Lakes Wine Co., Chgo., 1940; founder Fromm Music Found., Harvard U., 1952, since dir.; pres. Fromm Mgmt. Corp., Chgo., Kenwood Corp.; dir. Am. Music Center. Mem. citizens com. U. Ill.; adv. council Princeton U.; vis. com. humanities and music U. Chgo.; vis. com. music dept. Harvard U.; bd. overseers Boston Symphony Orch.; bd. visitors Boston U. Recipient Ill. Gov.'s award for the Arts, 1978, Peabody medal Peabody Conservatory, 1983. Home: 5715 S Kenwood Ave Chicago IL 60637 Office: 1028 W Van Buren St Chicago IL 60607

FROMMER, PETER LESLIE, physician; b. Budapest, Hungary, Feb. 13, 1932; came to U.S., 1941, naturalized, 1947; s. Joseph Charles and Magda F.; m. Ellen Mills, June 27, 1953; children: Donald, Ann Frommer Ames, David, Stephen. B.S. in Elec. Engring, U. Cin., 1954; M.D., Harvard U., 1958. Intern, then resident in internal medicine U. Cin. Med. Center, 1958-59, 61-63; commd. officer USPHS, 1959-61, 73—, asst. surg. gen., 1981—; mem. staff Nat. Heart, Lung and Blood Inst., NIH, Bethesda, Md., 1959-61, 63—, asso. dir. cardiology div. heart and vascular diseases, 1972-78, acting chief devices and tech. br., 1973-75, cardiac diseases br., 1975-78, dep. dir. inst., 1978—, acting dir., 1981-82. Author. Recipient Disting. Alumnus award U. Cin. Coll. Engring., 1969. Fellow ACP, Am. Coll. Cardiology; mem. Am. Physiol. Soc., Am. Fedn. Clin. Research, Am. Heart Assn., Am. Soc. Artificial Internal Organs, Biomed. Engring. Soc., AAAS, IEEE (chmn. joint com. engring. in medicine and biology 1964), Internat. Fedn. Med. and Biol. Engring. (v.p. 1969-71), Sigma Xi, Eta Kappa Nu, Tau Beta Pi. Patentee in field. Home: 3 Old Club Dr Rockville MD 20852 Office: Nat Heart Lung and Blood Inst Bethesda MD 20205

FROMMER, ROBERT, real estate executive; b. Phila., Mar. 11, 1935; s. Meyer William and Bessie (Spiegelman) F.; m. Joy Katzen, Mar. 23, 1959; 1 dau., Jill Ann Carpenter. B.S. in Econs, U. Pa., 1957; J.D., Yale U., 1960. Bar: Pa. 1961. Project dir. Webb & Knapp, Inc., Phila., 1961-65; asst. real estate mgr. Levitt & Sons, Inc., Lake Success, N.Y., 1965-67; exec. v.p. L'Enfant Plaza Corp., Washington, 1967-72, Urban Investment & Devel. Co., Chgo., 1972—; dir. Ritz-Carlton Hotel; mem. part-time faculty Chgo.-Kent Coll. Law, 1980; Vice chmn. bd. Anacostia Econ. Devel. Corp., Washington, 1969-72. Mem. Phila. Bar Assn. Club: Carlton (Chgo.). Office: 333 W Wacker Dr Chicago IL 60606

FROMMHOLD, LOTHAR WERNER, physicist; b. Wurzburg, Germany, Apr. 20, 1930; came to U.S., 1964, naturalized, 1971; s. Walter Karl and Karolina (Bernhardt) F.; m. Margareta Mercedes Benz, May 3, 1959; children—Sebastian, Caroline. Diplom-phys., U. Hamburg, Germany, 1954, Ph.D., 1960, Dr. habil, 1964. Research scientist, instr. U. Hamburg, Germany, 1954-64; vis. prof. U. Pitts., 1964-66; mem. faculty U. Tex., Austin, 1966—, prof. physics, 1968—. Contbr. articles to profl. jours. Fulbright travel fellow, 1964; various research grants, 1967-78. Fellow Am. Phys. Soc. Home: 4706 Ridge Oak Dr Austin TX 78731 Office: Dept Physics Univ Tex Austin TX 78712

FRONK, WILLIAM JOSEPH, machinery company executive; b. Spring Green, Wis., Apr. 14, 1925; s. Joseph Edward and Irene (Caspers) F.; m. Jeanne Gillon, Apr. 18, 1953; children: James, Nancy, Robert. B.B.A., U. Wis., 1950. C.P.A., Wis. With Haskins & Sells (C.P.A.s), Chgo., 1950-54, Ford Motor Co., Dearborn, Mich., 1954-66; pres., dir. Hyster Co., Portland, Oreg., 1966—; dir. Esco Corp., Orbanco. Trustee Linfield Coll., St. Vincent Med. Found. Served with AUS, 1943-46. Mem. Am. Inst. C.P.A.s, Beta Alpha Psi, Alpha Kappa Psi, Sigma Phi Epsilon. Clubs: Arlington (dir.), Waverly Country (Portland)). Home: 6128 SW Riverpoint Ln Portland OR 97201 Office: 700 NE Multnomah St Portland OR 97232

FRONTERHOUSE, GERALD WAYNE, banker; b. Ada, Okla., May 22, 1936; s. Victor and Austa (McClintock) F.; m. Gretchen A. Gover, Jan. 27, 1959; children: Jennifer Anne, Jeffry Scott.; M.B.A., Harvard U., 1962. With Republic Nat. Bank of Dallas, 1962-78, asst. cashier, 1964-65, asst. v.p., 1967-70, sr. v.p., 1970-74, exec. v.p., 1974-78; pres. Republic Bank Corp. (formerly Republic of Tex. Corp.), Dallas, 1978—. Group leader United Fund Campaign, 1967-68; group leader sustentation campaign So. Meth. U., 1967; group leader Am. Cancer Soc. Campaign, 1968; bd. dirs. Methodist Hosp.; trustee Lamplighter Sch. Lt. (j.g.) C.E. USNR, 1959-60. Mem. Am. Bankers Assn., Beta Theta Pi. Methodist. Club: Harvard U. Bus. Sch. (Dallas) (pres. 1969-70). Office: Republic Bank Corp 1800 Republic Bank Dallas Bldg Dallas TX 75222

FRONTIERE-ROSENBLUM, GEORGIA, professional football team executive; m. Carroll Rosenblum, July 7, 1966 (dec.); children: Dale, Carroll, Lucia. Pres. Los Angeles Rams, NFL, 1979—. Bd. dirs Los Angeles Boys and Girls Club; bd. dirs. Los Angeles Orphanage Guild, Los Angeles Blind Youth Found. Named Headliner of Yr. Los Angeles Press Club, 1981. Office: Los Angeles Rams 2327 W Lincoln Ave Anaheim CA 92801 *

FROOM, WILLIAM WATKINS, banker; b. Chgo., Nov. 21, 1915; s. Edgar Albright and Gladys (Watkins) F.; m. Anne Celich, Apr. 20, 1940; children: Pamela Froom Siegert, Gail Froom MacKenzie, Joan Froom Sensenbrenner. Student, Sch. Commerce, Northwestern U., 1933-37. Sales mgr. soybean div. Swift & Co., Champaign, Ill., 1937-47; partner I.H. French & Co., Champaign, 1947-64, pres., 1965-74, chmn. bd., 1974-75; pres., chmn. bd. City Bank of Champaign, 1975-80; dir. F & T Bldg. Corp.; v.p. Commodity Investment Fund Mgmt. Corp. Enterprises, Cable Communications, Inc., Champaign Nat. Bank; pres., chmn. bd. Champaign-Urbana Communications Inc., 1974-81. Mem. Ill. Citizens Edn. Council, 1964—; cons. U. Ill. Instl. Rev. Bd.; chmn. bd. dirs. Parkland Coll. Found., 1970—. Presbyterian. Club: Champaign Country (bd. dirs.). Home: 1402 Waverly Dr Champaign IL 61820 Office: 303 W Kirby St Champaign IL 61820

FROSCH, AARON R., lawyer; b. N.Y.C., July 9, 1924; m. Marjorie MacMillan, Jan. 17, 1955; children: Juliana, Phoebe, Suzanna. B.A., Bklyn. Coll., 1944; LL.B., Bklyn. Law Sch., 1947. Bar: N.Y. 1948. Gen. counsel, dir. Marilyn Monroe Prodns., 1962-72, Elizabeth Taylor Prodns., 1964—, Harkness Found., 1962-69, also Richard Burton Prodns., Rex Harrison Prodns. Ltd. Chmn. Mayor's Com. for N.Y. Shakespeare Festival, 1967; trustee N.Y. Shakespeare Festival, 1963—; founder Hardecker Lab. and Children's Clinic, Nassua, Bahamas. Mem. Am. Judicature Soc., Am., N.Y. State, N.Y.C. bar assns., N.Y. County Lawyers Assn. Democrat. Jewish. Home: 300 Central Park W New York NY 10024 Office: 950 3d Ave New York NY 10022

FROSCH, ROBERT ALAN, physicist, automobile manufacturing executive; b. N.Y.C., May 22, 1928; s. Herman Louis and Rose (Bernfeld) F.; m. Jessica Rachael Denerstein, Dec. 22, 1957; children: Elizabeth Ann, Margery Ellen. A.B., Columbia U., 1947, A.M., 1949, Ph.D., 1952; D. Engring (hon.), U. Miami, 1982, Mich. Technol. U., 1983. Scientist Hudson Labs. Columbia U., 1951-53, asst. dir. theoretical div., 1953-54, asso. dir., 1954-56, dir., 1956-63; dir. nuclear test detection Advanced Research Projects Agy., Office Sec. Def., 1963-65; dep. dir. Advanced Research Projects Agy., 1965-66; asst. sec. navy for research and devel., Washington, 1966-73; asst. exec. dir. UN Environment Programme, 1973-75; asso. dir. for applied oceanography Woods Hole (Mass.) Oceanographic Instn., 1975-77; adminstr. NASA, Washington, 1977-81; pres. Am. Assn. Engring. Socs., N.Y.C., 1981-82; v. p. in charge Research Labs. Gen. Motors Corp., N.Y.C., 1982—; chmn. U.S. del. to Intergovtl. Oceanographic Commn. meetings UNESCO, Paris, 1967, 70. Research and publs. numerous sci. and tech. articles. Recipient Arthur S. Flemming award, 1966, NASA Disting. Service award, 1981. Fellow AAAS, AIAA, Acoustical Soc. Am., Am. Astronautical Soc. (John F. Kennedy astronautics award 1981), IEEE; mem. Am. Geophys. Union, Seismol. Soc. Am., Soc. Exploration Geophysicists (Spl. Commendation award 1981), Marine Tech. Soc., Nat. Acad. Engring., Am. Phys. Soc., Soc. Naval Architects and Marine Engrs., Soc. Automotive Engrs., Engring. Soc. Detroit. Office: Gen Motors Research Labs Warren MI 48090

FROST, DAVID (PARADINE), author, producer, columnist; b. Tenderdon, Eng., Apr. 7, 1939; s. W.J. and Paradine F.; m. Lynne Frederick, Jan. 1981 (div. 1982); m. Carina Fitzalan Howard, 1983. M.A., Gonnville and Caius Coll., U. Cambridge (Eng.). TV appearances include That Was the Week That Was, 1962-63, Not So Much a Programme, More a Way of Life, 1964-65, The Frost Report, 1966-67, Frost Over England, 1967, David Frost at the Phonograph, 1966, The Frost Programme, 1966-68, David Frost's Night Out in London, 1966-67, The Nixon Interviews, 1977; series Headliners with David Frost, 1978; now star: theatrical appearances include An Evening with David Frost, 1966; joint founder, London Weekend TV; chmn., mng. dir., David Paradine Prodns.; exec. producer: James A. Michener's Dynasty, 1976 (Decorated Order Brit. Empire, recipient Golden Rose of Montreaux 1967, Roy, TV Soc. silver medal 1967, Richard Dimbleday award 1967, Emmy award (2), Guild of TV Producers award, named TV Personality of Yr. award.); Author: That Was the Week that Was, 1963, How to Live Under Labour, 1964, Talking with Frost, 1967, To England with Love, 1967, The Presidential Debate, 1968, The Americans, Whitman and Frost, I Gave Them a Sword, I Could Have Kicked Myself, 1982. Recipient Emmy award, 1970, 71, Religious Heritage Am. award, 1971, Albert Einstein award, 1982. Address: 46 Egerton Crescent London SW 3 England *

FROST, DOUGLAS VAN ANDEN, nutritionist; b. Pitts., Oct. 31, 1910; s. Donald Karne and Amy (Craig) F.; m. Muriel Louise Newkirk, Aug. 10, 1940; children: Nancy Newkirk (Mrs. James Kroening), Melodie Louise (Mrs. Peter Cooey), Roy Craig, Constance Manning Frost. B.A. in Chemistry, U. Ill., 1933; M.A. in Biochemistry, U. Wis., 1938, Ph.D., 1940. Petr. Analytical and research chemist Chappel Bros. Co., Pacini Labs., also Rival Packing Co., 1936; grad. asst. U. Wis., 1936- 39, research and teaching asst., 1938-40; with Abbott Labs., 1940-66, head nutrition research, 1946-59, research specialist nutrition, 1959-66; research assoc. Dartmouth Med. Sch. Trace Element Lab. at Brattleboro Hosp., 1966-69; cons. nutrition-biochemistry Selenium-Tellurium Devel. Assn.; Mem. com. on selenium in nutrition Nat. Acad. Sci.-NRC, 1968—; chmn. Animal Nutrition Research Council, 1960; mem. amino acids adv. com. U.S. Pharmacopeia XIV, 1950; cons. USPHS Drinking Water Standards Com., also Industry Task Force Agrl. Arsenical Pesticides, 1970; vice chmn. OST Subpanel on Arsenic, 1970-72; chmn. EPA PAX Co. arsenic adv. com., 1973; mem. diet-nutrition-cancer workshop Nat. Cancer Inst., 1975-76. Recipient Friedrich Schiller U. medal and scroll for research on arsenic and selenium, 1983. Fellow N.Y. Acad. Scis., AAAS; mem. Assn. Vitamin Chemists (pres. 1953), Am. Inst. Nutrition (treas. 1962-65), Agrl. Research Inst. (v.p. 1965-66), Metric Assn. (pres. 1969-70), Poultry Sci. Assn., Soc. Animal Sci., Am. Feed Mfg. Assn. (nutrition council), Sigma Xi, Gamma Alpha, Phi Eta Sigma, Alpha Chi Sigma, Delta Tau Delta. Presbyterian (elder). Spl. research vitamin role nicotinic acid; devel. first i.v. fibrin hydrolysate, vitamin K source for poultry; anti-cancer and health value of selenium; safe uses of arsenicals. Home and Office: 17 Rosa Rd Schenectady NY 12308 *Being a contrarian is not enough. One must look with extreme care at all facets of prejudice vs. what research can really show to be so. Dedication to the repeatable experiment and what it can prove unequivically is one way man can serve Nature and have Nature serve him.*

FROST, ELLEN LOUISE, electrical manufacturing company executive; b. Boston, Apr. 26, 1945; d. Horace Wier and Mildred (Kip) F.; m. William F. Pedersen, Jr., Feb. 2, 1974; 1 son by previous marriage, Jai Kumar Ojha; children: Mark Francis Pedersen, Claire Ellen Pedersen. B.A. magna cum laude, Radcliffe Coll., 1966; M.A., Fletcher Sch. Law and Diplomacy, 1967; Ph.D., Harvard U., 1972. Teaching fellow, instr. Harvard U., Wellesley Coll., 1969-71; legis. asst. Office of Senator Alan Cranston, Washington, 1972-74; fgn. affairs officer Dept. Treasury, Washington, 1974-77; dep. dir. Office of Internat. Trade Policy and Negotiations, 1977; dep. asst. sec. of def. for internat. econ. and tech. affairs Dept. Def., Washington, 1977-81; dir. govt. programs Westinghouse Electric Corp., Washington, 1981—. NSF trainee, 1967-69. Mem. Internat. Inst. Strategic Studies, Council Fgn. Relations, Radcliffe Alumnae Assn. (dir. 1968-71), Phi Beta Kappa. Office: 1801 K St NW 9th Floor Washington DC 20006

FROST, FRANCIS DANIEL, lawyer; b. Berkeley, Calif., Feb. 2, 1922; s. Francis Daniel and Alice (Rickey) F.; m. Camilla Chandler, Mar. 22, 1975; children: Daniel B., Polly. J.D., U. Ariz., 1948. Bar: Ariz. 1948, Calif. 1949. Ptnr. Gibson, Dunn & Crutcher, Los Angeles, 1956—, chmn. mgmt. com., 1979—, mem. exec. com., 1962—; dir. Times Mirror Co., Los Angeles, Avery Internat., Parsons Corp., Tejon Ranch Co. Pres., bd. dirs. Music Ctr. Found., Los Angeles, 1977—; vice-chmn., bd. dirs. Performing Arts Council, Los Angeles, 1967—; vice-chmn., gov. Claremont U. Ctr., Los Angeles, 1967-78. Mem. Assn. Tax Counsel (chmn. 1975-76), State Bar Calif. (chmn.Tax com. 1963-64), U. So. Calif. Tax Inst. (mem. planning com. 1962-72), Los Angeles County Bar Assn. (chmn. tax sect. 1961-62). Office: 333 S Grand St 49th Floor Los Angeles CA 90071

FROST, FRANK L., utility executive, lawyer; b. Crescent, Iowa, July 12, 1898. LL.B., U. Omaha, 1923. Bar: Nebr. 1923. Ptnr. firm Frost & Meyers, Omaha; chmn. bd. Met. Utilities Dist., Omaha. Chmn. bd. dirs. 1st Christian Ch.; pres. Travelers Protective Assn. Named Dad Order of Rainbow, Order of DeMolay. Mem. Omaha C. of C. (big chiefs Tribe of Yessir). Clubs: Downtown Optimist (pres.), Business and Prof. Men's Breakfast Omaha (pres.). Home: 11624 Burt St Omaha NE 68154 Office: Metropolitan Utilities Dist 1723 Harney St Omaha NE 68102

FROST, HAROLD MAURICE, physician; b. Boston, May 21, 1921; s. Harold M. and Lucy (Church) F.; m. Elsa Claudius, Oct. 21, 1956; children—Harold Maurice III, Mary Jean, Michael, Patricia, Robert, Eric. B.A., Dartmouth, 1943; M.D., Northwestern U., 1945. Intern Mary Hitchcock Meml. Hosp., Hanover, N.H.; resident Worcester (Mass.) City Hosp., 1948-50, Buffalo Gen. Hosp., 1950-52, Buffalo Children's Hosp., 1952-53; clin. instr. orthopedic surgery Buffalo U. Med. Sch., 1953-55; asst. prof. orthopaedic surgery Yale U. Sch. Medicine, 1955-57; asso. orthopaedic surgeon Henry Ford Hosp., Detroit, 1957-73, dir. orthopedic research lab., 1957—, chmn. dept. orthopedic surgery, 1966-72; clin. prof. surgery U. Mich., Ann Arbor, 1970-73. Author: Clinical Fundamentals of Orthopaedic Surgery, 1953, Bone Remodeling Dynamics, 1963, Mathematical Elements of Bone Remodeling, 1964, Laws of Bone Structure, 1964, Bone Biodynamics, 1964, Dynamics in Osteoporosis and Osteomalacia, 1966, Introduction to Biomechanics, 1966, Orthopedic Surgery in Spasticity, 1972, Physiology of Cartilaginous, Fibrous and Bony Tissue, 1972, Bone Remodeling and Its Relationship to Metabolic Bone Disease, 1972, Bone Modeling and Skeletal Modeling Errors, 1973, Orthopaedic Biomechanics, 1973; Asso. editor: Clin. Orthopaedics; Contbr. over 300 articles to profl. jours. Served to lt. (j.g.), M.C. USNR, 1946-48. Mem. AMA (Hektoen gold medal award basic research 1963), Am. Acad. Orthopaedic Surgeons, Orthopaedic Research Soc., Am. Geriatric Soc., Am. Gerontol. Soc., Am. Rheumatism Soc., Detroit Physiol. Soc., Detroit Surg. Soc., Detroit Acad. Orthopaedic Surgery, Assn. Bone and Joint Surgeons, Mich. Orthopaedic Soc., Am. Acad. Cerebral Palsy, Clin. Orthopaedic Soc., N.Y. Acad. Scis., Soc. for Cerebral Palsy, Sigma Xi. Spl. research on biomechanics bone physiology and cell dynamics. Address: Southern Colorado Clinic 2002 Lake Ave Pueblo CO 81004

FROST, JERRY WILLIAM, religion and history educator, library administrator; b. Muncie, Ind., Mar. 17, 1940; s. J. Thomas and Margaret Esther (Meredith) F.; m. Susan Vanderlyn Kohler; 1 son, James. B.A., DePauw U., Greencastle, Ind., 1962; postgrad., Yale Div. Sch., 1962-63; M.A., U. Wis.-Madison, 1965, Ph.D., 1968. Instr. Vassar Coll., 1967-68, asst. prof. history, 1968-73; assoc. prof. religion Swarthmore Coll., 1973—, prof. religion, 1979—, Howard M. and Charles F. Jenkins prof. of Quaker history and research, 1980—. Author: The Quaker Family in Colonial America, 1973, Connecticut Education in Revolutionary Era, 1974; editor: George Keith and The Quakers in Early Pennsylvania, 1980, Quaker Origins of Antislavery, 1981, Pa. Mag. of History and Biography, 1981—. Bd. dirs. Friends Hist. Assn., 1973—, Phila. Ctr. for Early Am. Studies, 1978—. John Carter Brown Library fellow, 1970; Eugene M. Lang fellow, 1980-81. Mem. Friends Hist. Assn. (bd. dirs. 1973—). Quaker. Home: 3 Whittier Pl Swarthmore PA 19081 Office: Friends Hist Library Swarthmore Coll Swarthmore PA 19081

FROST, JOHN LAWRENCE, consumer goods co. exec.; b. Valley Falls, Kans., Jan. 31, 1935; s. Lawrence Lacy and Esther Lenore (Moltz) F.; m. Elizabeth June Raasch, Jan. 17, 1957; children—Kelly John, Cheryl Jean, Robert James. A.A., Austin Jr. Coll., 1957; B.S., Macalester Coll., 1959; J.D. cum laude, William Mitchell Coll. Law, 1966. Bar: Minn. bar. With Gen. Mills, Inc., Mpls., 1959—, labor relations atty., dir. benefits, dir. personnel, now sr. v.p. employee relations. Chmn., bd. dirs. Dist. 281 Sch. Bd., 1972-79; bd. dirs. Mpls. Aquatennial Assn., 1973-77, Guthrie Theater, 1980—. Served with AUS, 1954-55. Mem. Mpls. Bar Assn., Hennepin County Bar Assn., Am. Soc. Personnel Adminstrs., Twin City Personnel Assn. Republican. Methodist. Office: 9200 Wayzata Blvd Minneapolis MN 55440

FROST, JONAS MARTIN, congressman; b. Glendale, Calif., Jan. 1, 1942; s. Jonas Martin and Doris (Marwil) F.; m. Valerie Hall, May 9, 1976; children: Alanna Shaw, Mariel Jeanne, Camille Faye. B.A., U. Mo., 1964, B.J., 1964; J.D., Georgetown U., 1970. Bar: Tex. 1970. Law clk. Judge Sarah T. Hughes, U.S. Dist. Ct., Dallas, 1970-71; individual practice law, Dallas, 1972-79; legal commentator Sta. KERA-TV, Dallas, 1971-72; mem. 96th-98th Congresses from 24th Tex. Dist.; mem. rules and budget coms., majority whip at large 98th Congress. Del. Democratic Nat. Conv., 1976, 84; coordinator N. Tex. Carter-Mondale campaign, 1976. Office: 1238 Longworth House Office Bldg Washington DC 20515

FROST, NORMAN COOPER, telephone company executive; b. Nashville, Feb. 6, 1923; s. Norman and Anna Martha (Cooper) F.; m. Katherine McDonald Shapard, Nov. 25, 1948; children: Kathy, Norman Cooper. B.A., Vanderbilt U., 1943, J.D., 1948. Bar: Tenn. 1946, Ga. 1954, N.Y. State bar 1964, D.C. bar 1965. Practiced in, Nashville, 1948-50; trust officer Nashville Trust Co., 1952-53; atty. So. Bell Telephone Co., Atlanta, 1953-61, gen. atty., 1961-62; atty. Am. Tel. & Tel. Corp., N.Y.C., 1962-66, asst. gen. atty., 1966-67; v.p., gen. counsel South Central Bell Telephone Co., Birmingham, Ala., 1968-83, Southeast Bell Region, Atlanta, 1983—. Served with USMCR, 1943-46, 50-52. Mem. Am., Ga., Tenn., N.Y., D.C. bar assns., Order of Coif. Methodist. Home: 9955 Huntcliff Trace Atlanta GA 30338 Office: 4509 Southern Bell Atlanta GA 30375

FROST, ORMOND, otolaryngologist, educator; b. Ireland, May 18, 1927; came to U.S., 1952, naturalized, 1963; s. James Patrick and Margaret (O'Loughlen) F.; m. Rita Robert, Oct. 1, 1955; 1 dau., Roberta. M.B.B.Ch., Univ. Coll. Dublin, 1952. House officer Mater Hosp., Duplin, Ireland, 1952; intern Loyola U. Mercy Hosp., Chgo., 1953; resident, asst., assoc. prof. Sch. Medicine NYU, N.Y.C., 1953-74, prof. clin. otolaryngology, 1974—. Mem. AMA, N.Y. Otologic Soc., ACS, Am. Acad. Otolaryngology, Gallatin Soc. NYU, Am. Irish Hist. Soc. Roman Catholic. Club: Nat. U. Ireland. Office: 530 First Ave New York NY 10016

FROST, OTIS LAMONT, JR., ins. co. exec.; b. Wynnewood, Okla., May 26, 1917; s. Otis L. and Viola (Knight) F.; m. Nelle Edwards, June 14, 1942; 1 son, Otis Lamont, III. B.A., Vanderbilt U., 1938; J.D., U. Calif., Berkeley, 1941; LL.M., U. So. Calif., 1947. Bar: Calif. bar 1947. Agt. IRS, Treasury Dept., Los Angeles, 1946-48; with Transam. Occidental Life Ins. Co., Los Angeles, 1948—, v.p., 1965-75, exec. v.p., gen. counsel, 1975—; also dir.; v.p. Transam. Corp., Los Angeles, 1968-73; sr. v.p., gen. counsel dir. Transam. Ins. Corp., Los Angeles, 1969—; dir. Direct Mktg. Internat. Ltd., 1975—; dir., gen. counsel Occidental Internat. Enterprises, 1975—; dir., v.p., gen. counsel Transam. Assurance Co., 1981—; gen. counsel Transam. Life Ins. and Annuity Co., 1977—, dir., 1981—; Mem. Calif. Constn. Revision Commn., 1967—. Bd. dirs., treas. Coro Found., Los Angeles; bd. dirs. Los Angeles Taxpayers Assn. Served to lt. USNR, 1941-46. Mem. Assn. Calif. Life Ins. Cos. (dir. 1961—, chmn. exec. com. 1977—), Health Ins. Assn. Am. (Calif. State chmn., mem. govt. relations com.), Calif. Ins. Fedn. (v.p., dir. 1960—), Nat. Assn. Ins. Commrs., Assn. Life Ins. Counsel (bd. govs.), Am. Council Life Ins. (Calif. v.p., mem. legis. com.), Am., Calif. State, Los Angeles County bar assns., Los Angeles Area C. of C., Calif. C. of C. Home: 2740 Monte Mar Terr Los Angeles CA 90064 Office: Transam Occidental Life Ins Co 1150 S Olive St Los Angeles CA 90015

FROST, ROBERT EDWIN, educator; b. Gowanda, N.Y., Feb. 1, 1932; s. Sidney Mauthe and Mary Theresa (Bollinger) F.; m. Janice Ruth Young, May 31, 1958; children—Elizabeth Ann, Nancy Lynn, Barbara Jean. B.S., Allegheny Coll., 1953; A.M., Harvard, 1955, Ph.D., 1957. Research chemist B.F. Goodrich Research Center, Brecksville, Ohio, 1957-61; asso. prof. State U. N.Y. at Albany, 1961-64, prof. chemistry, 1964—; Kettering vis. lectr. U. Ill., Urbana, 1965-66. Mem. Am. Chem. Soc., Phi Beta Kappa, Sigma Xi. Home: 329 Highland Dr Schenectady NY 12303 Office: Dept Chemistry State U NY Albany NY 12222

FROST, SHIRLEY DAVID (DAVE FROST), retired naval officer; b. Southard, Okla., Apr. 21, 1930; s. Chester William and Martha Leah (Weber) F.; m. Dolores Marie Radja, Oct. 17, 1953; children—Kathleen D., David J., Karen T., Mary C. B.S., U.S. Naval Acad., 1953; M.B.A., Stanford U., 1961; student, Naval War Coll., 1964-65. Commd. officer USN, 1953, advanced through grades to rear adm., 1977; jr. officer (USS Menrico), 1953-55, with, Cleve., 1956-58, supply officer, 1958-59, asst. planning officer, Mechanicsburg, Pa., 1961- 64, with, 1965-68, supply officer, 1968-70, exec. asst. asst. sec. def. (comptroller), Washington, 1970-74, exec. officer, Norfolk, Va., 1974-75, comdg. officer, Athens, Ga., 1975-77; dep. comdr. plans, policy and systems devel. Navy Dept., Washington, 1977-78; dep. comptroller of the Navy, 1978-80, comptroller, 1980-81, dep. comptroller, 1981-83; staff dir. for mgmt. Bd. Govs. Fed. Res. System, 1983—. Pres. Civic League, Va. Beach, Va., 1969; bd. dirs. N.E. Ga. council Boy Scouts of Am., 1976-77. Decorated Disting. Service Medal, Legion Merit, Vietnamese Gallantry cross. Mem. Athens C. of C., Phi Delta Theta. Roman Catholic. Club: Athens Rotary. Home: 2323 Riviera Dr Vienna VA 22180 Office: Management Board of Govenors of the Federal Reserve Washington DC 20551 *My life, both personal and professional, has been guided by allegiance to three primary areas: family, Christian faith, and the nation. My family has provided purpose and support. Christian principles furnished the most useful code of ethics. The Navy, and thereby the Country, has made sacrifice and service not only tolerable, but rewarding.*

FROST, THOMAS CLAYBORNE, banker; b. San Antonio, Oct. 29, 1927; s. Thomas Clayborne and Ilse (Herff) F.; m. Patricia Holden, June 9, 1951; children: Thomas Clayborne III, William, Donald, Patrick. B.S. in Commerce summa cum laude, Washington and Lee U., Lexington, Va., 1950; LL.D., Austin Coll. With Frost Nat. Bank, San Antonio, 1950—, pres., 1962-71, chmn. bd., 1971-81, sr. chmn. bd., 1981—; chmn. bd. Cullen/Frost Bankers, Inc., 1973—; dir. Elsinore Cattle Co., La Quinta Motor Inns, Inc., Southwestern Bell Telephone Co., Tesoro Petroleum Corp., Cullen Center Bank & Trust, Houston; past dir. San Antonio br. Fed. Res. Bank; mem. fed. adv. council Fed. Res. System; 1st chmn. regional adv. com. to comptroller of currency. Trustee U. Americas Found., San Antonio Med. Found., S.W. Research Inst., McNay Art Inst., Austin Coll.; hon. Trustee S.W. Tex. Meth. Hosp.; Trustee emeritus Washington and Lee U.; Trustee Morrison Trusts; past exec. chmn., bd. trustees Tex. Mil. Inst.; past chmn. Tex. Ind. Coll. Fund; mem. devel. bd. U. Tex. Health Sci. Center; bd. dirs. San Antonio Econ. Devel. Found. Served with AUS, 1946-47. Named Outstanding Young Man San Antonio Jr. C. of C., 1961; Mr. South Tex. Laredo (Tex.) George Washington Birthday Celebration Assn., 1974; First Outstanding Alumnus Tex. Mil. Inst., 1974; San Antonio Man of Year Exchange Club, 1974. Mem. Tex. Bankers Assn. (past pres.), San Antonio Clearing House Assn. (past pres.), Tex. Assn. Bank Holding Cos. (past dir.), Assn. Res. City Bankers (pres. 1977), Philos. Soc. Tex., Tex. Cavaliers, Sons Republic of Tex. (hon.), Order of Alamo, Phi Beta Kappa, Beta Gamma Sigma, Alpha Kappa Psi, Phi Eta Sigma, Sigma Chi. Clubs: San Antonio Country, San Antonio German, Plaza, Argyle St. Anthony. Home: 234 Rosemary St San Antonio TX 78209 Office: Cullen/Frost Bankers PO Box 1600 San Antonio TX 78296

FROTHINGHAM, A. MICHAEL, advertising executive; b. London, Eng., Oct. 4, 1921; s. Robert and Elinor (Shiff) F.; m. Sara Struthers, July 31, 1948; children: Christen, Andrew, Victoria, Eric. A.B., Dartmouth Coll., 1943; LL.B., Yale U., 1948. Bar: N.Y., Conn. Assoc. firm Coudert Bros., N.Y.C., 1948-58; v.p., sec., gen. counsel Ted Bates & Co., Inc., N.Y.C., 1958-68, sr. v.p., sec., dir., 1968-76, sr. v.p., sec., gen. counsel, chmn. exec. com., 1976—. Served to lt. USNR, 1943-46. Mem. Am., N.Y. State bar assns., Assn. Bar City N.Y., Phi Beta Kappa. Home: Rye NY 10580 Office: 1515 Broadway New York NY 10036

FROTHINGHAM, THOMAS ELIOT, pediatrician; b. Boston, June 21, 1926; s. Channing and Clara Morgan (Rotch) F.; m. Phyllis Mary Steiner, June 12, 1954; children—Phyllis Eliot, Thomas Dean, Benjamin Rotch, David Griffith. Student, Harvard U., 1944-46, M.D., 1951. Intern Bellevue Hosp., N.Y.C., 1951-52; resident also research fellow in infectuous diseases Children's Hosp., Boston, 1955-59; asst. prof. epidemiology, Tulane U. Med. Sch., 1959-60; asso. mem. Public Health Research Inst. City N.Y., 1960-61; asst. prof., then asso. prof. tropical pub. health Harvard U. Sch. Pub. Health, 1961-69; pediatrician Corvallis (Oreg.) Clinic, 1969-73; prof. pediatrics, family and community medicine Duke U. Med. Center, 1973—; mem. Child Advocacy Commn., Durham, 1978—. Contbr. articles profl. jours. Served with USNR, 1944-46, 52-55. Mem. Am. Soc. Tropical Medicine and Hygiene, Am. Acad. Pediatrics, AMA, N.C. Med. Soc. Home: 2604 McDowell St Durham NC 27705 Office: Box 3937 Duke Hosp Durham NC 27710

FRUCHTMAN, LEONARD, corporate executive. Pres. Central Steel Tube Co. Office: Central Steel Tube Co PO Box 551 Clinton IA 52732§

FRUCHTMAN, MILTON ALLEN, film and television producer-director; b. N.Y.C.; s. Benjamin M. and Fanny (Ryan) F.; m. Eva Sternberg; children: Eleanor, Jordan. B.S., Columbia U.; M.S., Sch. Bus., Columbia U. Producer, dir. TV programs and films, 1956—, dir., N.Y.C., 1956—, exec. producer, 1960-74, pres., 1958-60, Banff, Alta., Can., 1974—; tchr. grad. seminar Yale U., Adelphi U., Banff Sch. Fine Arts; cons. TV cos. Producer, dir.: High Adventure, 1st color series, CBS, 1957; 1st worldwide electronic news program Verdict for Tomorrow, 1961 (Peabody award 1962); The Secret of Michaelangelo-Every Man's Dream, ABC, 1968 (Peabody award 1969), Dance Theater of Harlem, Public Broadcasting System, 1973, Those Who Sing Together, CBS, 1979; including (Peabody award U. Ga. 1962, 69, Emmy award Nat. Acad. TV Arts and Scis. 1962, Gold Hugo award Chgo. Film and TV Festival 1973, N.Y. Film Festival award 1974, 77, Martin Luther King Festival award 1974, award Ohio State U. 1974, Am. Film Festival award 1974). Recipient awards for TV work including; Peabody award U. Ga., 1962, 69; Emmy award Nat. Acad. TV Arts and Scis., 1962; Gold Hugo award Chgo. Film and TV Festival, 1973; N.Y. Film Festival award, 1974, 77; Martin Luther King Festival award, 1974; award Ohio State U., 1974; Am. Film Festival award, 1974. Mem. Media Inst. (pres.), Dirs. Guild Am., Columbia U. Alumni Assn. Address: PO Box 1979 Banff AB Canada T0L 0C0

FRUDAKIS, EVANGELOS WILLIAM, sculptor; b. Rains, Utah, May 13, 1921; s. William and Christina (Legerakis) F.; children—Anthony, Jennifer. Student, Greenwich Work Shop, N.Y.C., 1935-39, Beaux Arts Inst. Design, N.Y.C., 1940-41, Pa. Acad. Fine Arts, 1941-42, 45-49, Am. Acad. in Rome, 1950-52. (Recipient 2 1st prizes Greenwich Work Shop 1939, Beaux Art Inst. 1941, lst Julian B. Slevin prize Pa. Acad. Fine Arts 1941, Stimson prize 1947, Stewardson prize 1947, Cresson European scholarship 1947, spl. citation achievement 1948, 1st hon. mention fellowship 1948, Fellowship gold medal 1949, 55, 56, Henry Scheidt Meml. scholarship 1949, lst hon. mention Prix de Rome 1942, Prix de Rome 1950, 51, Helen Foster Barnett prize N.A.D. 1948, Thomas R. Proctor prize 1957, Eben Demarest Trust Fund prize 1949, Louis Comfort Tiffany scholarship 1949, Sculpture House award Allied Artists Am. 1959, best portrait sculpture award Nat. Sculpture Soc.-Nat. Art Club 1961, John Gregory award Nat. Sculpture Soc. 1963, Nat. Fountain Competition award Little Rock 1965, Elizabeth N. Watrous gold medal N.A.D., N.Y.C. 1968, Dessie Greer prize N.A.D., N.Y.C. 1970, Artists Fund prize 1975, 77, Therese and Edwin H. Richards prize Nat. Sculpture Soc., N.Y. 1972, Gold medal 1972, Francis Keally prize 1974, Herbert Adams Meml. medal 1976), One-man shows include, Atlantic City Art Center, 1956, 61, Woodmere Art Gallery, 1957, 62, Phila. Art Alliance, 1958, Pa. Acad. Fine Arts, 1962, Briarcliff Coll. Mus. Art, 1975, numerous group shows, 1940—, including, Pa. Acad. Fine Arts anns., N.A.D. anns., Am. Acad. in Rome, Audubon Artists, Phila. Mus. Art, Allied Artists Am., Nat. Arts Club; represented in permanent collections, Pa. Acad. Fine Arts, Lehigh Valley Art Alliance, Woodmere Art Gallery, also pvt. collections; tchr., demonstrator sculpture, Nat. Acad. Fine Art, N.Y.C., 1941—; sculptor, John F. Kennedy meml. monument Atlantic City Conv. Hall, 1964, Statesmen in Medicine Awards; portrait works Brian Brewer Blades, 1969, Melvin R. Laird, 1970, Barnes Woodhall, 1971, Aharon Katzir and Ephraim Katzir for, Weizmann Inst., Israel, 1978; coins and medals Ted Shawn and Ruth St. Denis medal, Jacobs Pillow, Mass., Gemini Space Flights Nat. Commemorative Soc, 1966, Dacron medallion, Dupont, Wilmington, Del., Capt. James Cook medal, Hawaii Festival, Dolly Madison coin, medal Sociéte Commemorative de Femmes Celebres, 1967, Joseph Brant coin, Internat. Fraternal Commemorat Soc., 1968, Paul Lawrence Dunbar medal, Am. Negro Commemorative Soc., 1969, St. Damasus I medal, Cath. Commemorative Soc., Life of Christ series 12 coin medals, 1968-70, Alfred the Great medal, Britannia Commemorative Soc., 1970, Prince of Peace medal, Cath. Commemorative Soc., Scapular medal, Cath. Art Guild, 1970, St. John the 4th Apostle 12 Apostle series, Cath. Commemorative Medal Soc., 1970, John Quincy Adams and Lillian Wald medals, Hall of Fame for Great Ams., 1971, Brian Brewer Blades award medal Statesmen in Medicine, 1970, Richardson Dilworth Meml. Plaque, Phila., 1978, Fishing Bear fountain, Phila. Zool. Gardens.; Mem., Art Commn., Atlantic City, N.J. Served with AUS, World War II; ETO. N.A. Fellow Pa. Acad. Fine Arts, Am. Acad. in Rome, Nat. Sculpture Soc. (council, Meiselman prize 1981); founding mem. Acad. Scis. Phila.; mem. Allied Artists Am.; hon. men. Am. Inst. Commemorative Art. Address: 10 S Oxford Ave Ventnor NJ 08406

FRUHBECK DE BURGOS, RAFAEL, conductor; b. Burgos, Spain, Sept. 15, 1933; s. Wilhelm and Stefanie Ochs Fruhbeck; m. Maria Carmen Martinez, 1959; 2 children. Attended, Bilbao Conservatory, Madrid Conservatory, High Sch. for Music, Munich, Germany, U. Munich, U. Madrid. Formerly chief condr., Mcpl. Orch., Bilbao; music dir. and chief condr., Spanish Nat. Orch., Madrid; music dir., Dusseldorf (W.Ger.) and; chief condr., Dusseldorf Symphony; music dir. and prin. condr., Montreal (Que., Can.) Symphony Orch.; now prin. condr., Yomiuri Symphony, Tokyo; prin. guest condr., Nat. Symphony, Washington. (Decorated Orden de Alfonso X, Orden de Isabel la Católica, Gran Cruz al Mérito Civil.). Office: care Vitoria Alcalá 30 Madrid 14 Spain

FRUIN, ROBERT CORNELIUS, physician, hosp. adminstr.; b. El Paso, Ill., Nov. 10, 1925; s. Mark and Ella (Hayes) F.; m. Joan Harriet Haninger, Sept. 24, 1955; children—Mark Edward, Kevin Robert, Kathleen Ann Marie, David James, Maria Teresa, Peter Sean. Student, U. Ill., Urbana, 1943-45, B.S., 1947, M.D., 1949. Intern Milwaukee County Gen. Hosp., 1949-50; resident internal medicine VA Hosp., Hines, Ill., 1952-55, asst. chief gastroenterology sect., 1955-57, chief, 1957-64, chief of staff, 1964-74, dir., 1974-76, asst. chief, 1976-79, chief spinal cord injury service, 1979—; attending physician Cook County Hosp. and U. Ill. Hosp., 1958-67; asso. prof. medicine U. Ill. Coll.

Medicine, 1960-67; prof. medicine Loyola U. Stritch Sch. Medicine, 1967—; cons. council on med. edn. AMA. Contbr. articles to profl. jours. Pres. St. Eulalia Bd. Edn., 1971-73; Bd. dirs. Proviso br. YMCA, 1968-72. Served as lt. M.C. USNR, 1949-52. Fellow A.C.P.; mem. Am. Gastroent. Assn. Home: 700 Acorn Hill Ln Oak Brook IL 60521 Office: VA Hosp Hines IL 60141

FRUIT, MELVYN HERSCHEL, lawyer, management consultant; b. Buffalo, June 17, 1937; s. Morris and Ella Helen (Pertzon) F.; m. Beverly Ann Kessler, Apr. 1, 1967; children: Lori Anne, Andrew Josef. B.S., Cornell U., 1959; J.D., U. Mich., 1962. Bar: N.Y. 1962, D.C. 1963, Wash. 1970. Trial atty. FTC, Washington, 1962-69; asst. counsel Paccar, Inc., Bellevue, Wash., 1969-70; asst. sec., asso. gen. counsel Sav-A-Stop Inc., Jacksonville, Fla., 1970-75, v.p., gen. counsel, sec., 1975-82; mgmt. cons., 1982—. Pres. Los Prados Condominium No. 1, Inc., 1974—. Mem. Am. Soc. Corp. Secs. (pres. regional group 1983-84), Am., N.Y. State, D.C., Wash. bar assns., Fla. Retail Fedn. (dir.). Democrat. Jewish. Home: 7626 Las Palmas Way Jacksonville FL 32216 Office: 1914 Beachway Rd Jacksonville FL 32207

FRUMER, LOUIS RESHIN, publisher; b. Shreveport, La., Feb. 8, 1918; s. Isidor Wolf and Jennie (Reshin) F.; m. Elaine R. Doret, July 14, 1953; children: Nancy, John. Student, Tulane U., 1933-34; B.A., U. Tex., 1939, J.D., 1939; LL.M., Harvard, 1946. Bar: Tex. bar 1939, N.Y. bar 1954. Practiced in, Kilgore, Tex., 1939-42; faculty So. Methodist U. Law Sch., 1946-47, Syracuse U. Sch. of Law, 1947-56; editor-in-chief, vice chmn. bd. Matthew Bender & Co., N.Y.C., 1956—; adj. prof. law N.Y. U., 1969—. Author: (with Friedman) Products Liability, 10 vols, 1960 (rev. ann), Bender's Federal Practice Forms, 12 vols, 1951 (rev. ann); Co-editor: Personal Injury Annual, 1961—. Served with USAAF, 1942-45. Mem. Am., Internat., N.Y. State bar assns., Assn. Bar City N.Y., Fed. Bar Council, Order of Coif. Club: Harvard. Home: 110 East End Ave New York NY 10028 Office: 235 E 45th St New York NY 10017

FRUMKIN, ALLAN, art dealer; b. Chgo., July 5, 1926; s. Joseph and Libbie F.; m. Jean Martin; children: Robert, Peter. Ph.B., U. Chgo., 1946. Owner and dir. Allan Frumkin Gallery, Chgo., 1952-80, N.Y.C., 1959—; ptnr. Frumklin Gallery Photogrphs, Chgo., 1972—, Frumkin and Struve, 1980—. Recipient U. Chgo. ALumni Assn. Profl. Achievement award, 1981. Home: 1185 Park Ave New York NY 10028 Office: Allan Frumkin Gallery 50 W 57th St New York NY 10019

FRUMKIN, PAUL, TV producer; b. Omaha, Aug. 20, 1914; s. Louis and Anna (Dubnoff) F. Student, Omaha U., 1932-34. Advt. mgr. M.L. Rothschild, Chgo., 1936-42; v.p. W.H. Altice Advt. Agy., 1947-51. Producer: Mike Douglas Hi Ladies, WGN-TV, 1952-55; producer-writer: At Random, Susie's Show, CBS-TV, Chgo., 1956-62; producer: Kup's Show, ABC-TV, Chgo., 1962-68, NBC-TV, Chgo., 1968-77, PBS-WTTW-TV, 1977-79; creative cons.: The Mike Douglas Show, Los Angeles, 1979—. Mem. Chgo. Unltd., 1960—, Council Fgn. Relations, 1958—; adviser Am. Vets. from Vietnam; bd. dirs. Clarence Darrow Center. Served with AUS, 1942-46; ETO. Recipient Emmy award for best producer, 1966, 68, Peabody award, 1967. Mem. Nat. TV Hall of Fame, Acad. TV Arts and Scis. (life, pres. Chgo.), Press Club, Broadcast Advt. Club, Broadcast Pioneers, Hollywood Radio/TV Soc., Sigma Delta Chi. Club: Headline. Office: Creative Brooding Prodns 153 S Hayworth Blvd Los Angeles CA 90028 *Work is an act of love.*

FRUTON, JOSEPH STEWART, biochemist; b. Czestochowa, Poland, May 14, 1912; s. Charles and Ella (Eisenstadt) F.; m. Sofia Simmonds, Jan. 29, 1936. B.A., Columbia U., 1931, Ph.D., 1934; M.A. (hon.), Yale U., 1950, D.Sc., Rockefeller U., 1976. Asst. in chemistry Rockefeller Inst. for Med. Research, 1934-38, asso., 1938-45; with Yale U., 1945—, successively asso. prof. physiol. chemistry, prof. biochemistry, 1951-57, Eugene Higgins prof. biochemistry, 1957-82, prof. emeritus, 1982—, prof. history of medicine, 1980-82, prof. emeritus, 1982—, chmn. dept. biochemistry, 1951-67, dir. div. sci., 1959- 62; spl. fellow Rockefeller Found., 1948, Commonwealth Fund, 1962-63, Guggenheim Found., 1983-84; Mem. div. chemistry and chem. tech. NRC, 1950-52, chem. biol. coordination center, 1946-51, fellowship bd., 1951-53, 55-58, panel on enzymes, chmn. com. on growth, 1946-49, exec. com., div. med. scis., 1961-64; sci. advisor NIH, 1951-52, Anna Fuller Fund, 1951-72; vis. prof. Rockefeller U., 1969. Author: Molecules and Life, 1972, Selected Bibliography of Biographical Data for the History of Biochemistry Since 1800, 1974, 2d edit., 1977, A Bio-Bibliography for the History of the Biochemical Sciences, 1982; co-author: (with S. Simmonds) General Biochemistry, 1953, 2d edit., 1958; Mem. editorial bd.: Jour. Biol. Chemistry, 1948-58, Biochemistry, 1962-72. Recipient Lilly Award in biol. chemistry, 1944; Benjamin Franklin fellow Royal Soc. Arts. Fellow AAAS; mem. Internat. Commn. Biochem. Nomenclature, Am. Soc. Biol. Chems. (mem. council 1959-62), Am. Chem. Soc., Chem. Soc. Gt. Britain, Biochem. Soc. (Gt. Britain), Harvey Soc., N.Y. Acad. Sci., History Sci. Soc. (council 1951-54, Pfizer award 1973, Sarton lectr. 1976), Am. Philos. Soc. (council 1972-74, 78-81), Nat. Acad. Sci., Am. Acad. Arts and Sci., Sigma Xi, Phi Beta Kappa. Home: 123 York St New Haven CT 06511 Office: 508 Kline Biology Tower Yale U New Haven CT 06520

FRY, ALBERT JOSEPH, educator; b. Phila., May 12, 1937; s. Russell Mayne and Margaret (McCann) F.; m. Melissa Grant Betton, July 30, 1966; children: Anne Margaret, Peter, Jonathan. B.S., U. Mich., 1958; Ph.D., U. Wis., 1963; M.A., Wesleyan U., 1978. Postdoctoral fellow Calif. Inst. Tech., Pasadena, 1963-64, Wesleyan U., Middletown, Conn., 1964-65, asst. prof., 1965-72, assoc. prof., 1972-77, prof. chemistry, Middletown, Calif., 1977—. Author: Synthetic Organic Electrochemistry, 1972; contbr. articles to profl. jours. Fellow Chem. Soc. London; mem. Am. Chem. Soc., Conn. Acad. Sci. and Engring., Sigma Xi, Alpha Chi Sigma, Phi Lambda Upsilon. Roman Catholic. Home: 116 Maple Shade Rd Middletown CT 06457 Office: Wesleyan Univ Dept Chemistry Middletown CT 06457

FRY, ARTHUR JAMES, chemistry educator; b. Dodson, Mont., Mar. 10, 1921; s. Sidney Wilbert and May Lenora (Brown) F.; m. Lois Marie Gunning, Nov. 16, 1947; children: Gene Richard, Brian Douglas, Marian Gail. B.S. in Chemistry, Mont. State Coll., 1943; Ph.D., U. Calif. at Berkeley, 1951. Asso. chemist Oak Ridge Nat. Lab., 1946-48; faculty U. Ark., Fayetteville, 1951—, prof. chemistry, 1959—, chmn. dept., 1956-57, 64-67; With Coll. Chemistry Cons. Service, 1967—; evaluation panelist various NSF programs; vis. prof. U. Auckland (N.Z.), 1969-70, 78, U. Adelaide (Australia), 1970, Monash U. (Australia), 1977. Contbr. articles to profl. jours., textbooks. Active various conservation and local sch. and civic coms. Served with USNR, 1944-46. Recipient Faculty research award Ark. Alumni Assn., 1969. Fellow AAAS; mem. Am. Chem. Sec. (pres. local sect., nat. councillor, mem. council policy com., chmn. com. on publs.), Chem. Soc. London, Ark. Acad. Sci. (past pres.), AAUP, Sigma Xi, Alpha Chi Sigma, Phi Kappa Phi, Phi Eta Sigma. Home: 1508 Wedington Dr Fayetteville AR 72701 Office: Dept Chemistry Chem Bldg U Ark Fayetteville AR 72701

FRY, BERNARD MITCHELL, librarian; b. Ind., Oct. 24, 1915; s. Francis Earl and Veva V. (Mitchell) F.; m. June Foster, June 19, 1943; children: David, Richard, Douglas, Donald, Bernard. A.B., Ind. U., 1937, M.A., 1939; M.L.S., Catholic U., 1952; postgrad., Am. U., 1963-66. Librarian, instr. Mary Washington Coll., U. Va., Fredricksburg, 1939-40; chief bibliographer legis. reference service Library of Congress, Washington, 1941-42; mem., dir. tech. info. service AEC, Washington, 1947-58; dir. Clearinghouse for Fed. Sci. and Tech. Info., U.S. Dept. Commerce, 1963-67; dep. head Sci. Info. Service, NSF, Washington, 1959-62; dean Grad. Library Sch., Ind. U., Bloomington, 1967-80, dir. Research Center, prof. Sch. Library and Info. Sci., 1980—; cons. in field. Editor: Info. Processing and Mgmt, 1967—, Govt. Publs. Rev, 1974—; co-author: Publishers and Libraries, 1977; author: Role of Government Publications in National Program, 1979. Active Boy Scouts Am. Served with C.E. U.S. Army, 1942-46. Mem. Am. Soc. Info. Sci. (pres. 1967, gen. conf. chmn. 1977), ALA (council), Spl. Libraries Assn., AAAS, Civitan, Phi Delta Kappa., Beta Phi Mu. Unitarian. Office: Ind U Sch Library and Info Sci Bloomington IN 47405

FRY, C. HERBERT, retail executive; b. Pottstown, Pa., June 27, 1926; s. Clarence H. and Rosa B. (Savage) F.; m. Barbara Ruth McGuire, Aug. 28, 1950; children: James Nathan, David Andrew, Joel Timothy, Ann Elizabeth. B.S. magna cum laude, Syracuse U., 1950. C.P.A., Pa. Accountant Peat, Marwick, Mitchell & Co., Phila., 1950-56, supr., 1956-60, mgr., 1960-69; controller Acme Markets, Inc. (now Am. Stores Co.), Phila., 1969-73; chief accounting officer Am. Stores Group Services, Inc., Phila., 1974—, controller, 1974-75, v.p., 1975—; v.p., controller Am. Stores Co., Wilmington, Del., 1979; v.p. controller Skaggs Cos., Inc. (name changed to Am. Stores Co.), Wilmington, 1979-80; v.p., controller Acme Markets, Inc. subs. Am. Stores Co., Phila., 1980—, sr. v.p., treas., controller, 1983—. Served with 69th Inf. Div. AUS, 1944-46. Mem. Am., Pa. insts. C.P.A.'s. Presbyterian. Home: 519 Daventry Rd Berwyn PA 19312 Office: 124 N 15th St Philadelphia PA 19101

FRY, DONALD OWEN, broadcasting company executive; b. Headlee, Ind., Mar. 5, 1921; s. George Mason and Nima E. (Ulrey) F.; m. Phyllis Amy McMillan, Feb. 2, 1947. B.S., Calif. Coll. Commerce, 1953. Chief acct. Philco Dist., Inc., Los Angeles, 1953-58, Pacific Ocean Park (Calif.), 1958-59; controller Eleven-Ten Broadcasting, Pasadena, Calif., 1959-63, Los Angeles Standard, 1963-69; treas. Oak Knoll Broadcasting Corp., Pasadena, 1969—, v.p., gen. mgr., 1976-82, pres., chmn. bd., 1982—, dir., 1974—. Trustee, pres., chmn. bd. Broadcast Found. of Calif., Pasadena. Served with U.S. Army, 1940-45. Decorated Bronze star (2). Clubs: Masons, Scottish Rite, Shriners. Home: 966 Regent Park Dr Flintridge CA 91011 Office: 1401 S Oak Knoll Ave Pasadena CA 91109

FRY, DORIS HENDRICKS, museum curator; b. Bristol, Pa., Jan. 20, 1918; d. John Reading and Mary Cordelia (Mariner) Hendricks; m. Wayne Franklin Fry, Aug. 30, 1944; children: Christine Mariner Bode, David Whiteley, Janet Margaret. Student, Temple U. Sch. Music, 1936-40. Cert. tchr. Hist. Soc. Early Am. Decoration, Inc. Art tchr. home studio, Delmar, N.Y., 1957—; art tchr. The Arts Ctr., Albany, DN.Y., 1972-76, Albany Inst. History and Art, 1972-76; tchr. Mus. Hist. Soc. Early Am. Decoration, Albany, 1982—, dir., curator, 1981—, trustee, 1976—, dir. Sch., 1979-81, chmn. tchr. cert. com., 1979-80; class coordinator Albany Inst. History and Art, 1972-76; lectr. Hitchcock kMus., Conn., Conn. Valley Mus., Mass., 1981-82. Contbr. articles to profl. jours. Mem. Delmar Progress Club, 1963—. Recipient awards Hist. Soc. Early Am. Decoration. Mem. Fedn. Services. Club: PEO (Delmar, Albany) (sec., v.p.). Office: 19 Dove St Albany NY 12210

FRY, EDWARD IRAD, anthropology educator; b. Long Branch, N.J., Jan. 7, 1924; s. Wallace Cordiner and Abigail Elizabeth (Hidden) F.; m. Peggy June Crooke, Dec. 23, 1950. B.A., U. Tex., 1949, M.A., 1950; Ph.D., Harvard U., 1958. Cons. to U.S. Air Force; also asst. prof. Antioch Coll., 1955-56; asso. prof. U. Nebr., Lincoln, 1956-66; prof. anthropology So. Meth. U., Dallas, 1966—. Author numerous publs. and papers on growth, body composition and forensic anthropology. Served with USAAF, 1942-45. N.Z. fellow, N. Z. and South Pacific, 1953-54; Fulbright fellow Hong Kong U., 1963-64. Fellow AAAS (chmn. sect. anthropology 1980), Am. Anthrop. Assn.; mem. Soc. for Study Cranio-facial Biology, Internat. Assn. Human Biologists, Human Biology Council, Soc. for Study Human Biology, Am. Assn. Phys. Anthropologists (exec. com., sec.-treas., pres. 1973-75), Sigma Xi. Research on child growth and human biology especially skeletal aging. Home: 3004 Fondren Dr Dallas TX 75205

FRY, GUY, artist; b. Milton, Pa., Aug. 5, 1903; s. William H. and Sarah (Mauger) F.; m. Carol Pyle Jones, 1978. Student, Phila. Coll. Art, 1922-26. Free lance artist, 1926—, exhibited one man show, Phila. Art Alliance, exhibited group shows, Pa. Acad. Fine Arts, Phila. Art Alliance, Nat. Acad. Design, Am. Watercolor Soc.; Past chmn. bd., Phila. Coll. Art; past trustee, Phila. Mus. Art. (Recipient Zimmerman award Phila. Water Color Club 1959), Phila. Mus. Art. (Dana award Phila. Water Color Club 1960), Phila. Mus. Art. (Albert Dorne award N.A.D. 1970), Phila. Mus. Art. (Silver medal Art Dirs. Club Phila. 1971), Phila. Mus. Art. (Antoinette Graves Goetz award Am. Watercolor Soc. 1973), Phila. Mus. Art. (Gold medal Franklin Mint Gallery Am. Art 1974), Phila. Mus. Art. (John Young Hunter award Allied Artists Am. 1975). Mem. Phila. Art Dirs. Club (past pres.), Nat. Soc. Art Dirs. (past pres.). Address: Box 211 West Grove RD2 PA 19390

FRY, JAMES LAWRENCE, Canadian government official; b. Hartney, Man., Can., July 6, 1927; s. James Arthur and Marjorie (McLeish) F.; m. Julie Margaret Locke, Dec. 6, 1952; children: Julie Anne, James Michael. B.A., U. Man., 1948; M.A., U. Toronto, 1950. Asst. sec. Treasury Bd., Ottawa, Ont., Can., 1969-71; asst. dep. minister Nat. Health and Welfare, Ottawa, 1971-75, dep. minister, 1980—; dep. receiver gen. for Can., dep. minister Supply and Services, Ottawa, 1975-80; chief statistician Statistics Can., Ottawa, 1980. Bd. dirs. United Way Can., Ottawa, Ont., 1976—. Mem. Inst. Pub. Adminstrn. Anglican. Office: Nat Health and Welfare Tunney's Pasture Ottawa ON K1A OK9

FRY, JOHN, editor; b. Montreal, Can., Jan. 22, 1930; s. J. Stevenson and Beatrice (Pratt) F.; m. Marlies Strillinger, Feb. 19, 1965; children—Leslie, William, Nicole. Student, Lower Can. Coll., Montreal, 1936-47; B.A., McGill U., 1951. Writer Forster McGuire & Co. Ltd., Montreal, 1951-57; asso. editor to mng. editor Am. Metal Market, 1957-63; editor-in-chief Ski mag., N.Y.C., 1964-74, editorial dir., 1975-79, Ski Bus., 1964-79, Golf mag., 1968-71, 77-79, Outdoor Life, 1975-79, Cross Country Ski mag., 1975—; dir. publs. devel. Times Mirror Mags., 1979—; Mem. World Cup com. Internat. Ski Fedn.; chmn. future of skiing com. Am. Ski Fedn., 1977. Mem. Am. Soc. Mag. Editors. Founder Nat. Standard Ski Race. Home: 23 E Lake Dr Katonah NY 10536 Office: 380 Madison Ave New York NY 10017

FRY, MALCOLM CRAIG, clergyman; b. Detroit, June 6, 1928; s. Dwight Malcolm and Josephine (Craig) F.; m. Myrtle Mae Downing, June 5, 1948; children: Pamela Mae, Malcolm Craig, Rebecca Fry Gwartney, Matthew Dwight. Student, Bible Bapt. Sem., 1950; Th.B., Am. Div. Sch., Chgo., 1959, McNeese State Coll., Lake Charles, La., 1958-61; B.S., Austin Peay State Coll., 1962; M.Ed., U. Ariz., 1969; D. Laws and Letters (hon.), Clarksville Sch. Theology, 1974; D.Ministry, Luther Rice Sem., 1978. Asst. jewelery store mgr. Sonne Bros., Norwich, N.Y., 1948-50; ordained to ministry Free Will Bapt. Ch., 1955; pastor in, Lake Charles, La., 1955-58, 59-61, Bryan, Tex., 1958-59, Ashland City, Tenn., 1961-62, asst. pastor in, Royal Oak, Mich., 1962-64; pastor First Free Will Bapt. Ch., Tucson, 1964-71; dir. curriculum and research Bd. Ch. Tng. Service Nat. Assn. Free Will Baptists, Nashville, 1971-72; gen. dir., treas. Bd. Ch. Tng. Service, 1972-78; dir. Nat. Youth Conf., 1972-83, asst. dir. Bd. Sunday Sch. and Ch. Tng., 1978-83; pastor Unity Free Will Bapt. Ch., Smithfield, N.C., 1983—; program writer adult and teen tng. mag. Nat. Assn. Free Will Baptists, 1963—, clk., 1965-67, chmn. stewardship commn., 1962-67; moderator Ariz. Assn. Free Will Baptists, 1965-67, 69-71. Author: Total Involvement, 1964, Why Worry?, 1967, Precepts for Practice, 1971, Discipling and Developing, 1971, The Teacher-in-Training, 1972, Contemporary Topical Studies, 1973, The Ministry of Music, 1974, Balancing Christian Education, 1977, Leader's Guide Discipling and Developing, 1979, Leader's Guide the Ministry of Ushering, 1980. Served with AUS, 1946-48; with USAF, 1951-57; Korea. Mem. Evang. Philos. Soc., Phi Delta Kappa. Clubs: Kiwanis, Civitan. Home: 722 S 2d St Smithfield NC 27577 Office: 104 W Langdon Ave Smithfield NC 27577

FRY, MICHAEL GRAHAM, educator; b. Brierley, Eng., Nov. 5, 1934; s. Cyril Victor and Margaret Mary (Copley) F.; m. Anna Maria Fulgoni; children—Michael Gareth, Gabrielle, Margaret Louise. B.Sc. with honors, U. London, 1956, Ph.D., 1963. Dir. Norman Paterson Sch. Internat. Affairs, Carleton U., Ottawa, Ont., 1973-77; dean, prof. internat. relations Grad. Sch. Internat. Studies, U. Denver, 1978-81; dir., prof. Sch. Internat. Relations, U. So. Calif., Los Angeles, 1981—; vis. prof. Middle East Center, U. Utah, 1979, U. Leningrad, 1976. Author: Illusions of Security: North Atlantic Diplomacy, 1918-1922, 1972, Lloyd George and Foreign Policy, Vol. I, The Education of a Statesman, 1890-1916, 1977. NATO research fellow, 1970-71; Can. Council grantee. Mem. Internat. Studies Assn. (v.p.), Am. Hist. Assn., Soc. Historians Am. Fgn. Relations, Can. Hist. Assn. Roman Catholic. Home: 480 S Orange Grove Pasadena CA Office: U So Calif Sch Internat Relations Los Angeles CA 90007

FRY, NENAH ELINOR, college president; b. Chgo., Nov. 5, 1933; d. August Jether and Gladys Alberta (Bobcock) F. B.A., Lawrence Coll., 1955; M.A., Yale U., 1957, Ph.D., 1964; D.Litt., Wilson Coll., 1980. Instr. Lawrence Coll., Appleton, Wis., 1959-61; asst. prof., then assoc. prof. history Wilson Coll., Chambersburg, Pa., 1963-75; dean of coll. Wells Coll., Aurora, N.Y., 1975-83; pres. Sweet Briar Coll., Va., 1983—; evaluator Middle States Assn., Phila., 1970—; mem. nat. identification com. Am. Council on Edn., Washington, 1975—. Bd. dirs. Women's Hall of Fame, Seneca Falls, N.Y., 1982—. Woodrow Wilson fellow, 1955. Mem. Am. Hist. Assn., Soc. for French History, Berkshire Conf. Women Historians, Phi Beta Kappa. Office: Sweet Briar Coll Office of the Pres Sweet Briar VA 24595

FRY, ROBERT PAUL, physician, lawyer; b. Chgo., May 2, 1924; s. John George and Mabel (Rohrbaugh) F.; m. Arline Edythe Saylin, June 27, 1953; children—Robert Paul, Cynthia Denise, Eric. Student, Georgetown U., 1943-45; M.D., Temple U., 1949; J.D., U. So. Calif., 1965. Intern Luth. Hosp. So. Calif., Los Angeles, 1949; mem. staff Med. Center Hosp., El Monte, Calif., St. Luke Hosp., Pasadena, Calif., Meth. Hosp. So. Calif., Arcadia; mem. firm Robert P. Fry, atty. at law, Arcadia, 1966-78, Butler, Jefferson & Fry, Los Angeles. Trustee La Verne (Calif.) U. Served in U.S. Army, 1943-46; capt. M.C., 1949-52. Fellow Am. Coll. Anesthesiologists, Am. Coll. Legal Medicine; mem. Trial Lawyers Assn. Los Angeles (gov. 1970-71), ABA, Los Angeles County Bar Assn. (mem. law schs. com. 1969-70), Calif. Med. Assn. Home: 234 W Orange Grove Ave Arcadia CA 91006 Office: 150 N Santa Anita St Suite 560 Arcadia CA 91006

FRY, THOMAS ALBERT, JR., clergyman; b. Cleve., Apr. 23, 1919; s. Thomas Albert and Bertha (Wiggs) F.; m. Louise Sullivan, May 15, 1942; children—Thomas Albert III, Charles Sullivan. B.A., Davidson Coll., 1940; B.D., Union Theol. Sem., Richmond, Va., 1943, Th.M., 1949; D.D., King Coll., 1952. Ordained to ministry Presbyn. Ch., 1943; pastor in, Blackstone, Va., 1943-46, Red Springs, N.C., 1946-50, Bristol, Tenn., 1950-56, Atlanta, 1956-59, Dallas, 1959-72, Memphis, 1972, pastor on radio programs; v.p. Henry Miller Realtors, Dallas, 1973—. Author: Get Off the Fence-Morals for Moderns, 1964, Doing What Comes Supernaturally, 1966, Change, Chaos and Christianity, 1967, They Dared To Dream, 1972. Bd. dirs. Children's Med. Center, Dallas, Presbyn. Village, Dallas, Gen. Council Presbyn. Ch. U.S. Recipient Freedom Found. award, 1960. Mem. UN Assn. (pres. Dallas 1970-71). Home: 4411 Hockaday Dallas TX 75229 Office: Henry Miller Realtors Bryan Tower Dallas TX 75201

FRY, WILLIAM FREDERICK, physics educator; b. Carlisle, Iowa, Dec. 16, 1921; s. William C. and Flossie (Parsons) F.; m. Virgie Eastburn, June 14, 1943 (div.); children: David A., Diane E.; m. Sigrid L. B.S. in Elec. Engring, Iowa State Coll., 1943, Ph.D. in Physics, 1951. AEC postdoctoral fellow U. Chgo., 1951-52; faculty U. Wis., 1952—, prof. physics, 1956—. Served with USNR, 1944-45. Fulbright lectr., Italy, 1956-57; Guggenheim fellow, 1956-57. Research in high-energy physics, high energy astrophysics acoustics of musical instruments, high energy astrophysics. Office: Dept Physics U Wis Madison WI 53706

FRY, WILLIAM JAMES, surgeon, educator; b. Ann Arbor, Mich., Mar. 21, 1928; s. Lynn W. and Inez (Hayes) F.; m. Martha Earl, June 18, 1949; children: Richard E., William R. M.D., U. Mich., 1952. Diplomate: Am. Bd. Surgery (examiner 1974—, dir. 1976—, chmn. 1980-82). Intern, U. Minn. Hosp., 1952-53; resident U. Mich. Hosp., 1953-54, 56-59; instr. surgery U. Mich. Med. Sch., Ann Arbor, 1959-61, asst. prof. surgery, 1961-64, asso. prof., 1964-67, prof., 1967-76, head sect. gen. surgery dept. surgery, 1967-74, F.A. Coller prof. surgery, 1974-76; attending physician Ann Arbor VA Hosp., 1960-61, chief of surgery, 1961-64, cons., 1964-76, Wayne County (Mich.) Gen. Hosp., Eloise, 1967-76; chmn. dept. surgery Southwestern Med. Sch., Dallas, 1976—, Lee Hudson-Robert Penn prof. surgery, 1976—; sr. active med. staff Parkland Meml. Hosp., 1976—; cons. VA Hosp., Dallas, 1976—, Baylor U. Med. Center, 1976—, St. Paul Hosp., 1977—. Contbr. articles on surgery and vasular diseases to book chpts. and profl. jours. Served with USNR, 1954-56. Fellow A.C.S. (pres. Mich. chpt. 1970-71); mem. Soc. Clin. Vascular Surgery, Soc. Univ. Surgeons, Soc. for Surgery of Alimentary Tract, Am., Western surg. assns., Internat. Soc. of Surgery, Assn. for Acad. Surgery, Soc. Vascular Surgery, Internat. Cardiovascular Soc. (pres. 1983), Frederick A. Coller Surg. Soc. (pres. 1977-78), Central Surg. Assn. (pres. 1974-75), Collegium Internat. Chirurgiae Digestivae, So. Assn. Vascular Surgery, Dallas Soc. Gen. Surgeons. Home: 500 San Juan Ct Irving TX 75062 Office: 5323 Harry Hines Blvd Dallas TX 75235

FRYBURGER, VERNON RAY, JR., advertising and marketing educator; b. Cin., June 9, 1918; s. Vernon Ray and Florence Rose (Steding) F.; m. Marjorie Anne Clarke, June 19, 1948; 1 dau., Candace. B.S. in Bus. Adminstrn., Miami U., Oxford, Ohio, 1939; Ph.D. in Econs., U. Ill., 1950. Salesman, U.S. Printing & Lithograph Co., 1940-41; instr. mktg. Miami U., 1941-43; asso. research dir. Nat. Assn. Broadcasters, 1946; asst. prof. journalism U. Ill., 1947-53; faculty Northwestern U., 1953—, prof. advt. and mktg., chmn. dept. advt., 1959—; vis. prof. mktg. U. Hawaii, 1965—; Ednl. dir. Inst. Advanced Advt. Studies, 1963—; nat. asso. dean Am. Acad. Advt., 1964-65, nat. dean, 1965-66, chmn. bd.; cons. to bus., 1954—; adviser

Advt. Ednl. Found., 1972—; dir. Bell Fed. Savs. & Loan. Author: (with C.H. Sandage and K. Rotzoll) Advertising Theory and Practice, 1963, 11th edit., 1983, (with Boyd and Westfall) Cases in Advertising Management, 1964; editor: (with C.H. Sandage) The Role of Advertising, 1960. Bd. dirs. Lake Forest Library. Served to lt., submarines USNR, 1943-46; PTO. Mem. Am. Mktg. Assn., Internat. Advt. Assn. (edn. com.), Assn. Edn. Journalism, Beta Gamma Sigma, Kappa Tau Alpha, Delta Tau Delta, Delta Sigma Pi, Artus. Presbyn. Home: Shoreacres Rd PO Box 62 Lake Bluff IL 60044 Office: Northwestern Univ Evanston IL 60201

FRYE, GILBERT CHAPPELLE, advertising agency executive; b. Denver, June 4, 1924; s. Robert W. and Martha (Springsteen) F.; m. Mary Elizabeth Corey, Dec. 28, 1952; children: Christopher, Cynthia, Caren, Charles. Student, Colo. State U., 1942; B.S., U. Denver, 1949. Pres., chief exec. officer Frye-Sills, Inc., Denver, 1953-75; chmn. bd. Frye-Sills/Young,Rubicam, Denver, 1975—; founder, chmn. bd. Colo. Communications, 1977—. Contbr. articles to profl. jours. Trustee Colo. Outward Bound Sch., Denver, 1978—; chmn. Swedish Wellness Systems, Denver, 1981—; v.p. Denver Area council Boy Scouts Am., 1977-81. Recipient Silver Beaver award Boy Scouts Am., 1977, Internat. Leo award Lions, 1978. Mem. Denver Advt. Fedn. (v.p.), Am. Assn. Advt. Agys. (chmn. 1976-80), Denver C. of C. (dir. 1974-77, pres. award 1979), others. Home: 5645 S Monaco Blvd Englewood CO 80111 Office: 5500 S Syracuse St Englewood CA 80111

FRYE, HELEN JACKSON, U.S. dist. judge; b. Klamath Falls, Oreg., Dec. 10, 1930; d. Earl and Elizabeth (Kirkpatrick) Jackson; m. Perry Holloman, July 10, 1980; children—Eric, Karen, Heidi. B.A. in English, U. Oreg., 1953, M.A., 1960, J.D., 1966. Bar: Oreg. bar 1966. Public sch. tchr., Oreg., 1956-63, pvt. practice, Eugene, 1966-71; circuit ct. judge State of Oreg., 1971-80; U.S. dist judge Dist. Oreg., Portland, 1980—. Mem. Am. Bar Assn., Oreg. Bar Assn., Lane County Bar Assn. Office: US Courthouse Portland OR 97205

FRYE, HENRY E., state supreme court justice; b. Ellerbe, N.C., Aug. 1, 1932; s. Walter A. and Pearl Alma (Motley) F.; m. Edith Shirley Taylor, Aug. 25, 1956; children: Henry Eric, Harlan Elbert. B.S. in Biol. Scis., A & T U., N.C., 1953; J.D. with honors, U. N.C., 1959. Bar: N.C. 1959. Asst. U.S. atty. (middle dist.), N.C., 1963-65; prof. law N.C. Central U., Durham, 1965-67; sole practice, Greensboro, N.C., 1967-83; rep. N.C. Gen. Assembly, 1969-80; assoc. justice N.C. Supreme Ct., Raleigh, 1983—; organizer, pres. Greensboro Nat. Bank, 1971—; dir. N.C. Mut. Life Ins. Co. Deacon tchr. youth Sunday Sch. Providence Baptist Ch. Served to capt. USAF, 1953-55. Mem. ABA, N.C. Bar Assn., Greensboro Bar Assn., Nat. Bar Assn., Kappa Alpha Psi. Office: North Carolina Supreme Ct Justice Bldg PO Box 1841 Raleigh NC 27602 *

FRYE, JOHN H., JR., metallurgical engineering educator; b. Birmingham, Ala., Oct. 1, 1908; s. John H. and Helen (Mushat) F.; m. Helen Lewis Johnston, Sept. 21, 1935; children—John H., III, Helen (Mrs. Grant Van Siclen Parr), Kathleen (Mrs. Walter T. Woods, Jr.). B.A. with honors, Howard Coll., 1930; M.S., Lehigh U., 1934; D.Phil., Oxford (Eng.) U., 1942. Asst. prof. metallurgy Lehigh U., 1937-40, asso. prof. metallurgy, 1940-44; civilian employee Office Sci. Research and Devel., 1944; research engr. Bethlehem Steel Co., 1944-48; dir. metals and ceramics div. Oak Ridge Nat. Lab., Tenn., 1948-73; lectr. U. Tenn. Grad. Sch., 1950-73; hon. adj. prof. U. Ala. Coll. Engring., 1964-67, prof. metall. engring., 1973—; dir. Bank Oak Ridge, 1956-74; Tech. adviser on U.S. del. to 2d Internat. Conf. on Peaceful Uses Atomic Energy, Geneva, Switzerland, 1958. Editorial adv. bd.: Jour. Less-Common Metals, 1962-78; Contbr. articles to profl. jours. Fellow AAAS, Am. Soc. for Metals (mem. handbook com. 1969-72), AIME, Metall. and Petroleum Engrs. (exec. com. inst. metals div. 1959-60); mem. Sigma Xi. Episcopalian. Clubs: Indian Hills Country, University. Lodge: Rotary. Home: 69 High Forest Tuscaloosa AL 35406

FRYE, JOHN WILLIAM, III, judge; b. Pensacola, Fla., Apr. 20, 1929; s. John William, Jr. and Louise Frances (Bennett) F.; m. Renee Delores Lintz, Dec. 26, 1952. J.D., U. Fla., 1957, B.A., 1978; grad., Nat. Coll. for State Judiciary, 1967, postgrad., 1970-71, 75. Bar: Fla. 1958. Practiced in Pensacola, 1958-67; states atty. 1st Jud. Circuit of Fla., Pensacola, 1961-67, circuit judge, 1967—; adminstrv. judge Circuit Ct., Escambia County, 1976-82; Mem. evening faculty Pensacola Jr. Coll., 1964, Okaloosa-Walton Jr. Coll., 1968-70; guest lectr., adj. prof. U. West Fla.; mem. faculty Fla. Jud. Coll., 1980-83. Pres. West Fla. Council on Crime and Delinquency, 1966-68; mem. Fla. Gov.'s Council on Criminal Justice, 1971-75; chmn. Region I, Fla. Gov.'s Commn. on Criminal Justice, 1971-74, Ct. Task Force, 1974; faculty adviser Nat. Coll. State Judiciary, 1973; mem. Fla. Jud. Coll., 1980, 81; Pres. Young Democratic Clubs of Fla., 1964-65, Met. Pensacola YMCA, 1978, 79; pres. Pensacola Rose Soc., 1981. Served with USAF, 1948-52. Named One of 5 Outstanding Young Men of Fla. Jr. C. of C., 1964, Outstanding Young Man of Escambia County Jr. C. of C., 1965, Pensacola Sports Assn. Hall of Fame. Mem. Am., Fla., Pensacola bar assns., Circuit Judges Conf. of Fla., Blue Key, Phi Alpha Delta, Sigma Phi Epsilon. Methodist. Clubs: Elks, Optimist. Home: 615 Bayshore Dr Apt 105 Pensacola FL 32507 Office: 1800 St Mary's St Pensacola FL 32501

FRYE, KEITH NALE, government official; b. Salem, Ind., June 13, 1941; s. Haskel Arthur and Imogene (Nale) F.; m. Betty Jane Lloyd, Nov. 1959 (div. 1980); children: Timothy Kirk, Sherrine Kim.; m. Karen Joy Coleman, Dec. 1982. B.A., Ind. U., 1965, postgrad., 1965; postgrad., U. Louisville, 1965-66, U. Mich., 1968, U. So. Calif., 1970-72, Fed. Exec. Inst., 1977. With IRS, 1966-69; program analyst Naval Air Systems Command, 1969-73; budget examiner Office Mgmt. and Budget, 1973-75; with ERDA, 1975-77; dep. dir. Office Program Planning and Budget, asst. adminstr. nuclear energy, 1977; dir. energy tech. Office Resource Mgmt. and Acquisition Dept. Energy, 1977-79; dir. fossil energy Office Project Overview and Support, 1979-81, Office Coal Processing, 1981; dep. asst. sec. Office Oil, Gas, Shale and Coal Liquids, 1982—. Home: 19922 Waterloo Ct Germantown MD 20874 Office: MS D119 Germantown Bldg Dept Energy 1000 Independence Ave SW Washington DC 20686

FRYE, NORTHROP, English educator, author; b. Sherbrooke, Que., Can., July 14, 1912; s. Herman and Catharine and (Howard) F.; m. Helen Kemp, Aug. 24, 1937. B.A., U. Toronto, 1933; M.A., Oxford U., 1940,. Lectr. English Victoria Coll., U. Toronto, 1939—, prof., 1947—, chmn. dept. English, 1952, prin. coll., 1959-67; Univ. prof. U. Toronto, 1967—; editor Canadian Forum, 1948-52; Chancellor Victoria U., 1978—; Ordained to ministry United Ch. Can., 1936; adviser curricular planning and English teaching, Can. and U.S.; mem. adv. com. Am. Council Learned Socs., 1965; adv. mem. Can. Radio and TV Commn., 1968-77. Author: Fearful Symmetry, 1947, Anatomy of Criticism, 1957; also 19 other books. Decorated companion Order Can.; Hon. fellow Merton Coll., Oxford, 1973. Fellow Brit. Acad. (corr.); mem. MLA (exec. council 1958-61, pres. 1976), Am. Acad. Arts and Scis. (hon. fgn.), Am. Acad. and Inst. Arts and Letters (hon.). Home: 127 Clifton Rd Toronto ON Canada M4T 2G5 Office: 4 Devonshire Pl Toronto ON Canada M5S 2E1

FRYE, ROBERT EMMET, producer; b. Syracuse, N.Y., Dec. 20, 1939; s. Christopher Wilson and Elaine (Rudick) F.; m. Doris E. Tortorelli, June 8, 1964; children: Deborah D., Robert E. Student, Hobart Coll., 1957-62. Dir. communications Appalachian Regional Commn., Washington, 1972-73; Washington producer ABC Evening News, 1976-78; sr. producer ABC News-Europe, London, 1978-82; exec. producer This Morning-GMA News, N.Y.C., 1982-83, World News Tonight, 1983—; exec. producer TV news spl. program America Held Hostage-The Secret Negotiations, 1981; sr. news producer TV spl. FDR, 1982. Served with U.S. Army, 1958-61. Recipient George F. Peabody award U. Ga., 1981, Columbia-Dupont award Columbia U., 1981, Christopher award The Christophers, 1982. Episcopalian. Clubs: Royal Automobile (London); N.Y. Athletic (N.Y.C.). Office: ABC News 7 W 66th St New York NY 10023

FRYE, ROLAND MUSHAT, literary historian; b. Birmingham, Ala., July 3, 1921; s. John and Helen Elizabeth (Mushat) F.; m. Jean Elbert Steiner, Jan. 11, 1947; 1 son, Roland Mushat. A.B., Princeton U., 1943, M.A., 1950, Ph.D., 1952, student Theol. Sem., 1950-52. Instr. English Samford U., 1947-48; asst. prof. to prof. Emory U., 1952-61; research prof. Folger Shakespeare Library, Washington, 1961-65; L.P. Stone Found. lectr. Princeton Theol. Sem., 1959, vis. prof., 1963; prof. U. Pa., Phila., 1965—, Felix E. Schelling prof. English, 1978—; curator H.H. Furness Shakespeare Library, 1980—; mem. adv. com. Computerized World Shakespeare Bibliography, 1978; trustee, mem. adv. com. Center Theol. Inquiry, 1979. Author: God, Man and Satan: Patterns of Christian Thought and Life in "Paradise Lost", "Pilgrim's Progress" and the Great Theologians, 1960, Perspective on Man: Literature and the Christian Tradition, 1961, Shakespeare and Christian Doctrine, 1963, Shakespeare's Life and Times: A Pictorial Record, 1967, Shakespeare: The Art of the Dramatist, 1981, Milton's Imagery and the Visual Arts: Iconographic Tradition in the Epic Poems, 1978; editor: A Narrative: Selections from the King James Version, 1978; contbr. articles to profl. jours.; mem. editorial bd.: Shakespeare Quar., 1973—, Theology Today, 1961—. Served to maj. AUS, 1943-46. Decorated Bronze Star.; Guggenheim fellow, 1956-57, 73-74; mem. Inst. Advanced Study Princeton, N.J., 1973-74, 79; Nat. Endowment for Humanities grantee, 1973-74; Am. Council Learned Socs. grantee, 1966, 71, 78; Am. Philos. Soc. grantee, 1968, 71, 78; vis. scholar Am. Acad. in Rome, 1971; Nat. Endowment for Humanities-Huntington Library fellow, 1980-81. Mem. Am. Acad. Arts and Scis., Milton Soc. Am. (pres. 1977-78, James Holly Hanford award 1979), Am. Philos. Soc. (sec. 1978—, John Frederick Lewis prize 1979), Acad. Lit. Studies, AAUP, Modern Humanities Research Assn., MLA, Renaissance Soc. Am., Seventeenth Century Soc., Shakespeare Assn. Am. Presbyterian. Clubs: Century (N.Y.C.); Cosmos (Washington). Home: 226 W Valley Rd Wayne PA 19087 Office: English Dept D1 U Pa Philadelphia PA 19104

FRYE, THEODORE RAYMOND, foundation executive; b. Wellsville, Ohio, Aug. 21, 1921; s. Leroy B. and Edys (Culnon) F.; m. Martha Elizabeth Kissane, June 28, 1947 (div. 1977); children: Michael, Susan M., Margaret R., Dorothy, Raymond. Student, Ohio U., Athens, 1941-43; A.B., Oberlin Coll. (Ohio), 1947; postgrad., George Washington U., 1954-57; M.B.A., NYU, 1967. With Dept. State and Fgn. Service, 1947-63, assignments in India, 1950-53, assignments in Israel, 1958-62, assignments in Washington, 1947-50, 54-58, 62-63; asst. treas. Rockefeller Found., N.Y.C., 1963-67, treas., 1967—; coordinator Workshop in Bus. Opportunities, 1968-70; dir. Investor Responsibility Research Ctr., 1974—. Chmn. bd. Am. Internat. Sch., Tel Aviv, Israel, 1960-62; treas. Scarsdale Fair Housing Group, 1962-68. Served with AUS, 1943-46. Mem. N.Y. Soc. Security Analysts, Phi Beta Kappa. Home: 313 Woodlands Hills White Plains NY 10603 Office: Rockefeller Found 1143 Ave of the Americas New York NY 10036

FRYE, WILLIAM RUGGLES, journalist; b. Detroit, Dec. 15, 1918; s. William Caleb and Anna Mildred (Ruggles) F.; m. Joan Bogert Ripperger, June 6, 1953; children—John Randall, Nancy Bogert. B.S. cum laude, Harvard, 1940. Local reporter Christian Sci. Monitor, Boston, 1941-42, copy reader, asst. to fgn. editor, 1946-50, UN corr., 1950-63; dir., editor World in Focus, newspaper syndicate, 1957-76; self-syndicated diplomatic corr. and travel writer, 1963—; pres., editor Frye Syndicate and News Service, 1976—; lectr. world affairs, 1948—. Author: In Whitest Africa, 1968, A United Nations Peace Force, 1957; Contbr.: Arms Control, Disarmament and National Security, 1961. Served with AUS, 1942-46; mem. staff Stars and Stripes. Co-recipient Deadline Club N.Y.C. UN award, 1963; recipient citation Overseas Press Club, 1955. Mem. Council Fgn. Relations, Soc. Profl. Journalists, UN Corr. Assn., Soc. Am. Travel Writers. Mem. Christian Sci. Ch. Home and Office: 2 Tudor City Pl New York NY 10017

FRYER, JOHN STANLEY, university dean; b. Park City, Ky., July 12, 1937; s. John Harvey and Carrie Enola (Beckner) F.; m. Sara Lee Coleman, June 18, 1960; children: Mark Edward, David Joseph. B.S. in E.E, U. Evansville, 1959; M.B.A., Ind. U., 1969, D.B.A., 1971. Electronics engr. U.S. Naval Ordnance Lab., Silver Spring, Md., 1959; with U.S. Naval Avionics Facility, Indpls., 1962-67, chief satellite systems engring. br., 1965-66; dep. program mgr. Walleye Weapons System, 1966-67; asso. instr. mgmt. Ind. U., 1968-70, vis. faculty lectr., 1970, vis. asst. prof., 1971; asst. prof. mgmt. U. S.C., Columbia, 1971-73, assoc. prof., 1973-76, prof., 1976-78, program dir. mgmt., 1975-78, prof. mgmt. sci., 1978—, dir. div. research, 1978-83, assoc. dean for devel., 1983—; lectr. in field. Reviewer books and articles; contbr. articles to profl. jours. Chmn. evaluation criteria com. United Way of Midlands, 1978-79, mem. planning div., 1978—, performance evaluation com., 1980-81, chmn. data and stats. com., 1981—; bd. dirs., treas. Columbia Swimming League, 1977-79. Served with USAF, 1959-62. Mem. Acad. Mgmt., Inst. Mgmt. Sci., Am. Inst. Decision Scis., Am. Prodn. and Inventory Control Soc., Ops. Mgmt. Assn. (bd. dirs., v.p., sec. 1981—), Assn. for Univ. Bus. and Econ. Research, Alpha Iota Delta, Beta Gamma Sigma, Sigma Iota Epsilon, Omicron Delta Epsilon, Phi Beta Chi, Sigma Pi Sigma. Office: College Business Administration University of SC Columbia SC 29208

FRYER, MINOT PACKER, surgeon; b. Willimantic, Conn., Mar. 16, 1915; s. Minot Samuel and Mary (Packer) F.; children: Edwin Samuel, Minot Packer; m. Luise R. Whiting, 1973. A.B., Brown U., 1936; M.D., Johns Hopkins U., 1940; D.Sc. (hon.), Brown U., 1971. Diplomate: Am. Bd. Surgery, Am. Bd. Plastic Surgery (mem. 1962-68, sec.-treas. 1963-67, vice chmn. 1967-68, sr. examiner 1977—). Intern Johns Hopkins Hosp., 1940-41; resident Barnes Hosp., St. Louis, 1941-44, fellow in plastic surgery, 1946-48, asst. surgeon, 1948-67; assoc. prof. clin. surgery Washington U. Med. Sch., St. Louis, 1957-67, prof. clin. surgery, 1967—; assoc. prof. clin. maxilo-facial surgery Washington U. Dental Sch. (Dental Sch.), 1957-67, prof. clin. maxilo-facial surgery, 1967—; surgeon emeritus St. Louis Children's Hosp.; assoc. surgeon emeritus Barnes Hosp.; hon. staff DePaul Hosp., 1948—, chief surgery, 1962-64. Author: (with J. Brown) Surgery of Face, Mouth and Jaws, 1954, Postmortem Homografs, 1960; Cons. editor: Surgery, Gynecology and Obstetrics, 1960-65; Contbr. articles to sci. jours. Served to lt., M.C. USNR, 1944-46. Fellow A.C.S. (past chmn. council plastic surgery), Am. Assn. Surgery Trauma; mem. AMA, Am. Surg. Assn., St. Louis Med. Soc., Assn. Mil. Surgeons, Am. Soc. Plastic and Reconstructive Surgery, Am. Assn. Plastic Surgeons (pres. 1967-68), Central Surg. Assn., Soc. Head and Neck Surgeons, Western Surg. Assn., Halsted Soc. Home: PO Box 3907 Evansville IN 47737

FRYER, ROBERT GORDON, ins. co. exec.; b. Kansas City, Mo., Oct. 8, 1926; s. Harley Homer and Opal (Smith) F.; (married); children—Lyn, Amy Jean. B.S. in Bus. Adminstrn, Washington U., St. Louis, 1949. Gen. agt., then regional v.p. Continental Assurance Co., 1958-76; sr. v.p. Lincoln Liberty Life Ins. Co., 1976-80; pres. Gt. Nat. Life Ins. Co., Dallas, 1980—. Home: 4109 Prospect Ln Plano TX 75075 Office: 1360 Riverbend Dr Dallas TX 75247

FRYER, ROBERT SHERWOOD, theatrical producer; b. Washington, Nov. 18, 1920; s. Harold and Ruth (Reade) F. B.A., Western Res. U., 1943. Asst. to mng. dir., Theatre Inc., 1946; casting dir., 1946-48; asst. to exec., CBS, 1949-51; casting dir., 1951-52; Broadway co-producer: A Tree Grows in Brooklyn, 1951, By the Beautiful Sea, 1954; producer: Wonderful Town, 1953, The Desk Set, Shangri-La, Auntie Mame, Redhead, There Was a Little Girl, Advise and Consent, A Passage To India, Hot Spot, Roar Like a Dove, Sweet Charity, Mame, 1966, Chicago, 1975; Broadway producer: The Norman Conquests, 1976, California Suite, 1976, On the Twentieth Century, 1977, Sweeney Todd, 1978, Merrily We Roll Along, The West Side Waltz, 1981, Brighton Beach Memoirs, Noises Off, 1983; producer: films Abdication, 1973, Great Expectations, 1974, Voyage of the Damned, 1976, The Boys from Brazil, 1978; artistic dir., Ahmanson Theatre, Center Theatre Group; Author: Professional Theatrical Management New York City, 1947. Served as capt. AUS, 1941-46; maj. Res. Decorated Legion of Merit.; Rockefeller Found. fellow. Mem. Episcopal Actors Guild (v.p.), League of N.Y. Theatres (bd. govs.). Office: 135 N Grand Ave Los Angeles CA 90012 *I am grateful for all God has given me, and I feel an obligation to Him to return goodness and kindness to my fellowman.*

FRYER, THOMAS WAITT, JR., coll. adminstr.; b. Martinsville, Va., Oct. 6, 1936; s. Thomas Waitt and Wilma Pauline (Harp) F.; m. Mary Margaret Allshouse, Jan. 5, 1980; children—Laura Elizabeth, Matthew Thomas, John Anderson. A.A., Mars Hill Coll., 1956; B.A., Wayland Coll., 1958; M.A. (Ford Found. fellow), Vanderbilt U., 1959; Ph.D. (Kellogg Found. fellow), U. Calif., Berkeley, 1968. Instr. in English Daytona Beach Jr. Coll., 1959-61; asso. dean instrn. Chabot Coll., 1965-67; v.p., chief campus adminstr. Miami-Dade Community Coll., 1967-73; chancellor Peralta Colls., 1973-78; chancellor, dist. supt. Foothill-De Anza Community Coll. Dist., 1978—; vice chmn. bd. dirs. Am. Council on Edn., 1979-80; pres. Fla. Assn. Community Colls., 1971-73. Mem. New Oakland Com., 1975-78, Oakland Council for Econ. Devel., 1976-78. Recipient Communication and Leadership award Toastermasters Internat., 1977; selected a Young Leader of Acad., 1978. Mem. Western Assn. Schs. and Colls. (commr.), Nat. Soc. Study Edn., Am. Assn. Higher Edn. (dir. 1975-78), Phi Delta Kappa. Clubs: Rotary (Palo Alto, Calif.); Kenna, Commonwealth of Calif. Office: 12345 El Monte Rd Los Altos Hills CA 94022

FRYKENBERG, ROBERT ERIC, historian; b. India, June 8, 1930; s. Carl Eric and Doris Marie (Skoglund) F.; m. Carol Enid Addington, July 1, 1952; children: Ann Denise, Brian Robert, Craig Michael. B.A., Bethel Coll., Minn., 1951; M.A., U. Minn., 1953; M.Div., Bethel Theol. Sem., 1955; Ph.D. (Rockefeller fellow 1958-61), London U., 1961. Research asst. U. Calif., Berkeley, 1955-57; instr. Oakland (Calif.) Jr. Coll., 1957-58; Ford and Carnegie research and teaching fellow U. Chgo., 1961-62; mem. faculty U. Wis., Madison, 1962—, prof. history and S. Asian studies, 1971—, chmn. dept., dir. Center S. Asian Studies, 1970-73; vis. prof. U. Hawaii, summer 1968. Author: Guntur District, 1978-1848: A History of Local Influence and Central Authority in South India, 1965; editor: Land Control and Social Structure in Indian History, 1969, Land Tenure and Peasant in South Asia: An Anthology of Recent Research, 1977; contbr. articles, revs. profl. publns. Trustee Am. Inst. Indian Studies, 1971-81; dir. summer seminar NEH, 1976. Research fellow Am. Council Learned Socs.-Social Sci. Research Council, 1962-63, 67, 73-74, 77-78, 83-84; Guggenheim fellow, 1968-69; HEW Fulbright Hays sr. fellow, 1965-66; NEH fellow, 1975; fellow Wis. Inst. Research Humanities, 1975; named Alumnus of Year, Bethel Coll., 1975. Fellow Royal Hist. Soc., Royal Asiatic Soc.; mem. Internat. Conf. and Seminars, Soc. S. Indian Studies (pres. 1968-70, 82-84), Am. Hist. Assn. (pres. conf. faith and history 1970-72), Assn. Asian Studies, Inst. Hist. Studies India, Inst. Asian Studies India, Assn. S. Asian Studies Australia, Inst. Advanced Christian Studies (dir. 1979-83, pres. 1981-83). Office: 4134 Humanities Bldg Univ Wis Madison WI 53706

FRYLING, GEORGE RICHARD, manufacturing company executive; b. St. Marys, Pa., Mar. 24, 1901; s. George Percy and Emma Elisabeth (Spratt) F.; m. Florence K. McCauley, Sept. 22, 1927; children: Florence Elisabeth, George Percy II, Richard McCauley, Mary Patricia. Student, Mercersburg Acad., 1917-18, Rensselaer Poly. Inst., 1918-23; LL.D., Gannon Coll., 1957. Salesman Speer Carbon Co., St. Marys, Pa., 1923-26; v.p., gen. mgr. Elk Graphite Milling Co., St. Marys, 1926- 32; pres. Erie Technol. Products, Inc. (formerly known as Erie Resistor Corp.), Pa., 1928-62, chmn. bd., treas., 1962-64, chmn. bd., pres., 1964-72, chmn., chief exec. officer, 1966-72, chmn. bd., 1972—; chmn. Fryling Mfg., Inc., Electron Research, Inc., Tech. Materials Div., Erie Technol. Products Can., Ltd., Erie Technol. Products, Ltd., London, all until 1972; chmn. bd., pres. Fryling and Co., Inc., Erie, Pa., 1972—; chmn. bd. Preferred Fin. Services, Inc., Erie, 1973—; dir. Security Peoples Trust Co., Keithley Instruments, Inc., Cleve.; v.p. Pa. Mfrs. Assn. Casualty & Fire Ins. Co. Mem. Pa. Planning Bd., 1948-55; Bd. mgrs. Hamot Hosp., Erie; mem. bd. Gannon Coll., 1960—. Mem. Pa. Mfrs. Assn. (dir.), NAM (dir.), Mfrs. Assn. Erie (dir., past pres.), Pa. C. of C. (dir., pres. 1957-59), Theta Chi. Republican. Episcopalian. Clubs: Erie (dir., past pres.), Kahkwa Country (Erie)). Home: 1950 S Shore Dr Erie PA 16505 Office: 162 W 6th St Erie PA 16507

FRYXELL, DAVID ALLEN, newspaper columnist; b. Sioux Falls, S.D., Mar. 8, 1956; s. Donald Raymond and Lucy (Dickinson) F.; m. Lisa Duaine Forman, June 16, 1978; 1 dau., Courtney Elizabeth. B.A., Augustana Coll., 1978. Assoc.-sr. editor TWA Ambassador, St. Paul, 1978-80, mng. editor, 1980-81; sr. editor Horizon, Tuscaloosa, Ala., 1981-82; circuit writer Telegraph Herald, Dubuque, Iowa, 1982—; contbg. editor Horizon mag., 1982—; chief judge mags. Golden Quill awards, Pitts., 1980. Contbr.: articles to mags. including Travel & Leisure, Playboy, Passages, AAA World, Savvy, Databar, Diversion, Easy Living, others. Chief writer Anderson for Pres. Com., Minn., 1978. Mem. Iowa Newspaper Assn. (2d award master columnist 1983, 2d award best feature writing 1983, 2d award best series 1983), Chgo. Art Dirs. Club (merit award editing 1981), Augustana Coll. Fellows, Augustana Alumni Assn. (Decades of Leadershp award 1978), Blue Key. Democrat. Unitarian. Home: 2192 St Celia Dubuque IA 52001 Office: Telegraph Herald 8th and Bluff Dubuque IA 52001

FTHENAKIS, EMANUEL JOHN, electronics and space executive; b. Greece, Jan. 30, 1928; came to U.S., 1952, naturalized, 1956; s. John and Evanthia (Magoulakis) E.; m. Hermione Jane Coates, 1972; children: John, Basil. Diploma mech. and elec. engring., Tech. U. Athens, 1951; M.S. in Elec. Engring., Columbia U., 1953; postgrad., U. Pa., 1961-62. Mem. tech. staff Bell Telephone Labs., 1952-57; dir. engring. missile and space div. Gen. Electric Co., Phila., 1957-61; v.p., gen. mgr. space and re-entry div. Philco-Ford Co., Palo Alto, Calif., 1961-69; pres. ITT Aerospace Co., Los Angeles, 1969-70; pres., dir. Am. Satellite Corp., Germantown, Md., 1971-80, chmn. bd., 1971—; also dir.; v.p. Fairchild Industries, Germantown, 1971-80, sr. v.p.,

1980—; dir. Spacecom Inc.; adj. prof. U. Md. Author. Trustee Md. Acad. Scis., 1982—; mem. Pres.'s Nat. Security Telecommunications Adv. Council, 1982—. Recipient Bicentennial award Columbia U., 1954. Fellow IEEE; mem. AIAA, Armed Forces Communications and Electronics Assn. (chmn. fin. com. 1979—). Greek Orthodox. Patentee in field. Office: Fairchild Industries Germantown MD 20874

FU, KING-SUN, electrical engineer; b. China, Oct. 2, 1930; s. Tzao-jen and Tzao-wen (Hsiang) F.; m. Viola Ou, Apr. 7, 1958; children: Francis, Thomas, June. B.S., Nat. Taiwan U., 1953; M.A.Sc., U. Toronto, 1955; Ph.D., U. Ill., 1959. Research engr. Boeing Airplane Co., 1959-60; mem. faculty Purdue U., 1960—, prof. elec. engring., 1966—, Goss disting. prof., 1975—. Author: Sequential Methods in Pattern Recognition and Machine Learning, 1968, Syntactic Methods in Pattern Recognition, 1974, Statistical Pattern Classification using Contextual Information, 1980, Syntactic Pattern Recognition and Applications, 1982. Guggenheim fellow, 1972. Fellow IEEE; mem. Nat. Acad. Engring., Academia Sinica, Am. Soc. Engring. Edn., Assn. Computing Machinery. Home: 132 Rockland Dr West Lafayette IN 47906 Office: Sch Elec Engring Purdue U West Lafayette IN 47907

FUBINI, EUGENE GHIRON, business consultant; b. Turin, Italy, Apr. 19, 1913; naturalized, 1945; s. Guido and Anna (Ghiron) F.; m. Jane Elizabeth Machmer, May 5, 1945; children—Sylvia, Sandra, Carol, Laurie, David, Susan. Student, Poly. Turin, 1929-31; D. Physics summa cum laude, U. Rome, 1933; D.Sc., Rensselaer Poly. Inst.; D.Eng., Pratt Inst., 1967, Bklyn. Poly. Inst., 1968, George Washington U., 1972. Research asso. Nat. Inst. Electrotechnics, Rome, 1935-38; engr. charge microwave and internat. broadcasting CBS, 1938-42; research asso. devel. electronic countermeasures, radio research lab. Harvard U., 1942-44; intelligence reconnaissance and radar countermeasure missions U.S. Army, U.S. Navy, USAAF, 1944; radar countermeasures 8th Air Force, Eng., 1944-45; attached War Dept., 1945; with Airborne Instruments Lab., 1945-61, div. head to v.p., 1960-61; with Office Sec. Def., 1961-65; asst. sec. def., dep. dir. def. research and engring.; v.p., group exec. IBM, N.Y., 1965-69, cons., 1969—; gen. dir. Tex. Instruments, Inc., 1969-83; dir. BDM; cons. President's Sci. Adv. Com., 1957-61, 69-71; mem. USAF Sci. Adv. Bd., 1958-61, 65-69, Adv. Council Advancement Sci. Research and Devel. N.Y. State, 1958—; mem. panel sci. adv. bd. Nat. Security Agy., 1958-61, mem. sci. adv. bd., 1978—; chmn. electromagnetic warfare adv. group Air Research and Devel. Command, 1958-61; adv. group spl. projects Dept. Def., 1958-61; mem. Pres.'s Commn. Law Enforcement, 1965-67; mem. sci. adv. com. Def. Intelligence Agy., 1965—, chmn., 1965-69; mem. Def. Sci. Bd., 1966-69, 74—, chmn., 1977-80, vice chmn., 1980—; mem. sci. adv. com. Am. Newspaper Pubs. Assn., 1969-78, Def. Communications Planning Group, 1970-72, Bd. Narcotics Dangerous Drugs, 1972-74; mem. Soviet-Am. Sci. and Tech. Com., 1972-77; mem. adv. bd. Dept. Energy Research, 1977—; mem. sci. adv. bd. Gould Inc., 1976-81; lectr. Harvard U., 1956, Calif. Inst. Tech., 1974, 75. Author. Trustee Urban Inst., 1965, 82; mem. vis. com. Harvard U. Computing Center, 1972-76, Stanford U. Sch. Engring., 1972-78, George Washington U. Sch. Engring. Recipient Presdl. certificate of Merit, 1946; Def. medal for distinguished service, 1966, 80; Exceptional Service medal Def. Intelligence Agy., 1970. Fellow IEEE; mem. Nat. Acad. Engring., N.Y. Acad. Scis. Club: Cosmos (Washington). Patentee in field. Home: 2300 Hunter Mill Rd Vienna VA 22180 Office: 1901 N Fort Myer Dr Arlington VA 22209

FUCHS, ALFRED HERMAN, psychologist, coll. dean; b. Englewood, N.J., Nov. 29, 1932; s. Herman and Wilhemine Katharine (Dielng) F.; m. Phyllis Elizabeth Rocke, Aug. 27, 1955; children—Christopher Frederick, Jeffrey Alfred, Lisa Marie, Eric William. A.B., Rutgers U., 1954; M.A., Ohio U., 1958; Ph.D., Ohio State U., 1960. Psychologist, scientist Gen. Dynamics/Electric Boat Co., 1961-62; asst. prof. psychology Bowdoin Coll., 1962-66, asso. prof., 1966-72, prof., 1972—, chmn. dept. psychology, 1965-75, dean faculty, 1975—; summer research participant NSF, 1963, 64. Contbr. articles to profl. jours. NSF grantee, 1963-64, 64-65. Mem. Am. Psychol. Assn., AAAS, Psychonomic Soc., Internat. Soc. History Behavioral Scis., Sigma Xi. Democrat. Home: 5 Longfellow St Brunswick ME 04011 Office: Bowdoin Coll Brunswick ME 04011

FUCHS, FRITZ, physician, educator; b. Denmark, Nov. 27, 1918; came to U.S., 1964; s. Josef and Sofie (Petersen) F.; m. Seere Anna-Rita Olsson, May 19, 1948; children—Anneli, Martin, Peter Erik, Lars Frederik. M.D., U. Copenhagen, 1944, D. Med. Scis., 1957; Postgrad. tng. obstetrics and gynecology, also surgery in, Danish and Swedish hosps., 1945-58. Gynecologist-in-chief Kommunehospital, Copenhagen, 1958-65; obstetrician, gynecologist-in-chief N.Y. Hosp., 1965-78, attending obstetrician, gynecologist, 1979—; prof. obstetrics and gynecology Cornell U. Med. Coll., 1965—, Given Found. prof., chmn. dept., 1965-78, Uris prof. reproductive biology, 1977-80; cons. Rockefeller U., 1968—, WHO, 1972-73, 78—; vis. prof. Chulalongkorn U., Bangkok, Thailand, 1972-73. Author articles, chpts. in books. Mem. bd. Found. for Child Devel., 1970-76. Served with Danish Brigade, 1945. Decorated knight of Dannebrog. Mem. N.Y. Obstetrical Soc. (pres. 1981-82), Am. Gynecol. and Obstetrical Soc., Endocrine Soc. Home: 1130 Park Ave New York NY 10128 Office: 530 E 70th St New York NY 10021 *I have devoted my life to Obstetrics because nothing in medicine compares with the joy of delivering a healthy baby.*

FUCHS, HANNO, advt. agy. exec.; b. Karlsruhe, Germany, Dec. 23, 1928; came to U.S., 1941, naturalized, 1950; s. William Werner and Marianne (Hirsch) F.; m. Carol Runyan, Dec. 15, 1962; children—Andrew W., Jessica M., Daniel R., Michael J. B.S. in Journalism, Syracuse U., 1949; student, Columbia Grad. Sch. Bus. Adminstrn., 1950, N.Y. U. Coll. Law, 1961. With Young & Rubicam, Inc., 1952-69, creative exec., v.p., 1961-69; exec. v.p. Richard K. Manoff, Inc., N.Y.C., 1969-70, pres., 1970-71; v.p. Grey Advt. Inc., N.Y.C., 1971-74; sr. v.p. Needham, Harper & Steers, Inc., 1974-75, Young & Rubicam Inc., N.Y.C., 1975—. Served with AUS, 1951-53. Mem. Sales Execs. Club N.Y., Adcraft Club Detroit, Creative Advt. Club Detroit., Alpha Delta Sigma, Beta Gamma Sigma. Democrat. Jewish. Home: 1 Scott Ln Purchase NY 10577 Office: 285 Madison Ave New York NY 10017

FUCHS, JACOB, educator; b. N.Y.C., May 7, 1923; s. Alexander and Irma (Radocy) F.; m. Rose Lochansky, June 15, 1946; children—Tara Ellen, Gary Allan. B.A. in Chemistry, N.Y.U., 1944, M.S., U. Ill., 1947, Ph.D., 1950; Post-doctoral research asst., U. Ill. at Urbana, 1950-52. Asst. prof. chemistry Ariz. State U. at Tempe, 1952-56, asso. prof. chemistry, 1956-59, prof. chemistry, 1959—, exec. officer dept., 1961-75, dir. ann. summer programs in applied molecular spectroscopy, modern indsl. spectroscopy, 1956—; vis. prof. chemistry U. Colo. at Boulder, 1965 (summer). Prin. tympanist, Phoenix Symphony Orch., 1952-79. Served with AUS, 1944-45. Fellow Am. Inst. Chemists; mem. Ariz. Acad. Sci., Am. Chem. Soc., Soc. Applied Spectroscopy, Sigma Xi, Phi Kappa Phi, Phi Lambda Upsilon, Pi Mu Epsilon. Research in X-ray spectroscopy and X-ray diffraction. Home: 2035 S College Ave Tempe AZ 85282 *Enjoy whatever it is that you are doing, not only for the moment, but for a lifetime if necessary. It is easy to be happy on the day when a difficult research problem is finally solved, or a great symphony is performed before an appreciative audience. But what about the countless days when experiment after experiment proves fruitless, or the hours of repetitious rehearsal necessary to perfect the final concert performance? Also, work to satisfy yourself. Of course it is possible to set low standards for yourself, but, if you are truly honest with yourself, it will likely be much more difficult to perform up to your own expectations than those of others.*

FUCHS, JOSEPH LOUIS, mag. publisher; b. Bklyn., Nov. 23, 1931; s. Sol and Yetta (Stein) F.; m. Carol Polner, Feb. 7, 1955; children—Beth, Randy, Sheryl. B.A., Baruch Sch., City Coll. N.Y., 1954. Advt. dir. House and Garden mag., N.Y.C., 1958-73; asso. publisher House and Garden Guides, N.Y.C., 1973-75; publisher Brides mag., N.Y.C., 1975-77, Mademoiselle mag., 1977—. Served with AUS, 1956-58. Mem. Alpha Delta Sigma. Clubs: Atrium, Engrs. Country. Office: 350 Madison Ave New York NY 10017

FUCHS, ROLAND JOHN, geography educator; b. Yonkers, N.Y., Jan. 15, 1933; s. Alois L. and Elizabeth (Weigand) F.; m. Gaynell Ruth McAuliffe, June 15, 1957; children: Peter K., Christopher K., Andrew K. B.A., Columbia U., 1954, postgrad., 1956-57; postgrad., Moscow State U., 1960-61; M.A., Clark U., 1957, Ph.D., 1959. Asst. prof. to prof. U. Hawaii, Honolulu, 1958—, chmn. dept. geography, 1964—, asst. dean to assoc. dean, 1965-67, dir. Asian Studies Lang. and Area Center, 1965-67; adj. research assoc. East-West Population Inst., 1980—; Vis. prof. Clark U., 1963-64, Nat. Taiwan U., 1974; asst. editor Econ. Geography, 1963-64; mem. editorial adv. com. Soviet Geography; Review and Translation, 1966—; Mem. U.S. nat. commn. for Internat. Geog. Union, 1969-80, chmn., 1973-80; v.p. Internat. Geog. Union, 1980—; mem. bd. internat. orgns. and programs Nat. Acad. Scis., 1976—, chmn., 1980—, mem. bd. sci. and tech. in devel., 1980—. Author, editor: Theoretical Problems of Geography, Geographical Perspectives on the Soviet Union, Population Distribution Policies in Development Planning. Ford Found. fellow, 1956-57; Fulbright Research scholar, 1966-67. Mem. AAAS, Assn. Am. Geographers, Internat. Union Sci. Study Population, Population Assn. Am., Am. Assn. Advancement Slavic Studies (dir. 1976-81), Pacific Sci. Assn. (council 1978—). Home: 5136 Maunalani Circle Honolulu HI 96816

FUCHS, VICTOR ROBERT, educator; b. N.Y.C., Jan. 31, 1924; s. Alfred and Frances Sarah (Scheiber) F.; m. Beverly Beck, Aug. 29, 1948; children: Nancy, Fredric, Paula, Kenneth. B.S., NYU, 1947; M.A., Columbia U., 1951, Ph.D., 1955. Internat. fur broker 1946-50; lectr. Columbia, 1953-54, instr., 1954-55, asst. prof. econs., 1955-59; asso. prof. econs. N.Y. U., 1959-60; program asso. Ford Found. Program in Econ. Devel. and Adminstrn., 1960-62; prof. econs. Grad. Center, City U. N.Y., 1968-74; prof. community medicine Mt. Sinai Sch. Medicine, 1968-74; prof. econs. Stanford U. and Stanford Med. Sch., 1974—; v.p. research Nat. Bur. Econ. Research, 1968-78, mem. sr. research staff, 1962—; fellow Center Advanced Study Behavioral Scis., Palo Alto, Calif., 1972-73, 78-79; mem. Pres.'s Com. on Mental Retardation, 1968-71, Nat. Acad. Sci. Inst. Medicine, 1971—; dir. Bankers Life Co. Author: The Economics of the Fur Industry, 1957, (with Aaron Warner) Concepts and Cases in Economic Analysis, 1958, Changes in the Location of Manufacturing in the United States Since 1929, 1962, The Service Economy, 1968, Production and Productivity in the Service Industries, 1969, Policy Issues and Research Opportunities in Industrial Organization, 1972, The Economics of Health and Medical Care, 1972, Who Shall Live? Health, Economics, and Social Choice, 1975, (with Joseph Newhouse) The Economics of Physician and Patient Behavior, 1978, Economic Aspects of Health, 1982; contbr. articles to profl. jours. Served with USAAF, 1943-46. Mem. Am. Econ. Assn., Am. Pub. Health Assn., Am. Statis. Assn., Sigma Xi, Beta Gamma Sigma. Home: 796 Cedro Way Stanford CA 94305 Office: 204 Junipero Serra Blvd Stanford CA 94305

FUCHS, WOLFGANG HEINRICH, mathematics educator; b. Munich, Germany, May 19, 1915; came to U.S., 1950, naturalized, 1957; s. Martin Erich and Alice (Manasse) F.; m. Dorothee Julie Rausch von Traubenberg, Sept. 25, 1943; children: Ann, John, Claudia. B.A., Cambridge U. (Eng.), 1936, Ph.D., 1941. Asst. lectr. U. Swansea, Wales, 1944-47; lectr. U. Liverpool, Eng., 1947-50; assoc. prof. math. Cornell U., Ithaca, N.Y., 1950-58, prof. math., 1958—. Author: Topics in the Theory of One Complex Variable, 1967. Guggenheim fellow, 1956-57; Fulbright fellow, 1973-74; recipient Humboldt Found. prize, 1979-80. Home: 109 Oak Hill Rd Ithaca NY 14850 Office: Dept Math Cornell U Ithaca NY 14853

FUCIK, EDWARD MONTFORD, consulting civil engineer; b. Chgo., Jan. 25, 1914; s. Edward James and Agnes May (Montford) F.; m. Margaret G. Reinig, Sept. 28, 1943; children: Edward Montford, Margaret Ann, Jane (Mrs. George Allendorph III). B.S. in Civil Engring, Princeton, 1935; M.S., Harvard, 1937. Registered profl. engr., Ill., Ind. and 9 other states. With HARZA (cons. engrs.), Chgo., 1938-40; found. engr., Panama Canal, 1940-42; with Harza Engring. Co., Chgo., 1945—, pres., 1963-74, chmn. bd., 1963-77, chmn. emeritus, 1977—. Bd. mgrs. Highland Park (Ill.) Hosp., 1966-69; adv. council Ill. Inst. Tech., 1971—. Served to lt. comdr. USNR, 1943-45. Mem. Nat. Acad. Engring., ASCE (nat. dir. 1968-71, Thomas Fitch Rowland prize 1953, Chgo. Civil Engr. of Year award 1976), Western Soc. Engrs. (pres. 1972-73), Soc. Am. Mil. Engrs. (Gt. Lakes Region Pub. Service award 1976), Nat. Soc. Profl. Engrs., Phi Beta Kappa. Republican. Clubs: Exmoor Country (Highland Park); Tower, Union League (Chgo.). Home: 57 S Deere Park Dr Highland Park IL 60035 Office: 150 S Wacker Dr Chicago IL 60606

FUELLHART, DAVID CLARK, broadcasting executive; b. Pitts., Oct. 16, 1938; s. William Clarke and Katherine Modiset (Marsh) F.; m. Patricia Ann O'Reilley, Sept. 9, 1961 (div.); children: David Clark, Elizabeth Ann; m. Judith Sandra MacFarland, Oct. 31, 1969 (div.); 1 son, Mathew Scott. B.S., Ithaca Coll., 1963. Staff announcer WNAE-WRRN, Warren, Pa., 1958-59; disc jockey, sportscaster WTKO, Ithaca, N.Y., 1960-61; program dir. N.E. Radio Network, Ithaca, 1961-62; account exec. Cogan Advt., Ithaca, 1962-63; exec. producer Sun Dial Films, Washington, 1967-68; regional sales mgr. WPIK-WXRA, Alexandria, Va., 1968-70; gen. mgr. WPST, Trenton, N.J., 1970-74, WPOC, Balt., 1974—; instr. sales and mktg. Broadcast Inst. Md., 1979-81; pres. adv. bd. ABC Radio Direction Network Affiliates. Past mem. public relations subcom. Johns Hopkins Children's Center; past bd. dirs. Am. Lung Assn., Trenton, N.J.; past chmn. broadcast skills bank Balt. Urban League. Served with USN, 1963-67. Recipient Ann. award Aviation Adv. Council N.J., 1972-73, citation and Merit award Mayor of Balt., 1982, Silver award, 1984. Mem. Broadcast Pioneers, Md.-D.C.-Del. Broadcasters Assn. (past pres.), Advt. Assn. Balt. (past pres.), Radio Execs. Balt. (pres. 1984), Balt. Broadcasters Coalition (past pres.), Greater Trenton Execs. Assn. (past v.p.). Presbyterian. Clubs: Hunt Valley Golf, Downtown Athletic (Balt.). Office: 711 W 40th St Baltimore MD 21211

FUENTEALBA, VICTOR WILLIAM, labor union ofcl.; b. Balt., Sept. 1, 1922; s. Manuel Lagos and Antonia (Lengler) F.; m. Viola J. Henderson, Jan. 26, 1951; children—Victoria, Mary Lee, Donna Jean, Patricia. Student, Loyola Coll., 1946-47; LL.B., U. Md., 1950. Bar: Md. bar 1950. Practiced law, Balt., 1950-78; v.p. Musicians Assn. Met. Balt., Am. Fedn. Musicians, 1951-53, sec.-treas., 1953-56, pres., 1956-78; mem. internat. exec. bd. Am. Fedn. Musicians, N.Y.C., 1967-70, v.p., 1970-78, pres., 1978—. Bd. dirs. Hearing and Speech Agy., Balt., 1973-78. Served with inf. U.S. Army, World War II. Decorated Purple Heart. Mem. Am. Bar Assn., Md. State Bar Assn., Delta Theta Phi. Democrat. Roman Catholic. Office: 1500 Broadway New York NY 10036

FUENTES, CARLOS, author, former ambassador; b. Mexico City, Nov. 11, 1928; s. Rafael Fuentes Boettiger and Berta Macías Rivas; m. Rita Macedo, 1959 (div. 1969); 1 dau., Cecilia; m. Sylvia Lemus, 1973; 2 children. Ed., U. Mex., Institut des Hautes Etudes Internationales, Geneva; hon. degrees, Columbia Coll., Chgo. State U. Mem. Mexican del. ILO, Geneva, 1950-52; asst. head press sect. Mexican Ministry Fgn. Affairs, 1954; asst. dir. cultural dissemination U. Mex., 1955-56; head dept. cultural relations Mexican Ministry Fgn. Affairs, 1957-59; fellow Woodrow Wilson Internat. Center for Scholars, Washington, 1974; former Mexican ambassador to, France. Author: Los dias enmascarados, 1954, La region mas transparente, 1958, Las buenas conciencias, 1959, Aura, 1962, The Death of Artemio Cruz, 1962, Cantar de Ciegos, 1964, Zona sagrada, 1967, Cambio de piel, 1967 (Biblioteca Breve prize Barcelona), La Nueva Novela Hispanoamericana, 1969, Cumpleaños, 1969, Casa con dos puertas, 1970, Todos los Gatos son pardos, 1970, El Tuerto es Rey, 1971, Tiempo Mexicano, 1971, Don Quixote or the Critique of Reading, 1974, Terra Nostra, 1974 (Rómulo Gallegos prize), La cabeza de hidra, 1978, Una familia lejana, 1980, Agua Quemada, 1981, Distant Relations, 1982; play Orchids in the Moonlight, 1982; also contbns. to mags. and newspapers including Los Angeles Times; Editor: Rivista Mexicana de Literatura, 1954-58, Siempre and Politica, 1960—; co-editor: El Espectador, 1959-61.

FUERBRINGER, ALFRED OTTOMAR, clergyman, educator; b. St. Louis, Aug. 11, 1903; s. Ludwig Ernst and Anna (Zucker) F.; m. Carolyn Kuhlman, June 1, 1934; children: Kenneth Paul, Max Robert, Marian Ruth, Jane Carolyn. Student, Concordia Coll., Ft. Wayne, Ind., 1918-21; M.Div., Concordia Sem., St. Louis, 1925, S.T.M., 1927, D.D., 1953; L.H.D., Valparaiso U., 1959; Litt.D., Concordia Tchrs. Coll., Seward, Nebr., 1969. Ordained to ministry Luth. Ch., 1927; pastor Trinity Luth. Ch., Norman, Okla., 1927-34, Okmulgee, Okla., 1934-37, St. Paul's Luth. Ch., Leavenworth, Kans., 1937-41; pres. Concordia Tchrs. Coll., Seward, Nebr., 1941-53, Concordia Sem., St. Louis, 1953-69, prof., 1969-74, dir. continuing edn., 1969-74; prof. Concordia Sem. in Exile (Seminex), St. Louis, 1974-77, Christ Sem.-Seminex, 1977-83, matching gifts coordinator, 1979-83; commr. Luth. Church-Mo. Synod, Europe, 1948, 57, 58, 63, 66, Australia, Asia, 1957-58, Latin Am., 1957, 59, 61; mem. commn. on theology and ch. relations, 1950-69; bd. dirs. Gt. Rivers Synod, Assn. Evang. Luth. Chs., 1976-79; pres. Found. for Reformation Research, 1957-64, exec. dir., 1965-66, bd. dirs., 1967-69; v.p. Nat. Luth. Edn. Conf., 1963, pres., 1964. Editorial bd.: Concordia Theol. Monthly, 1953-74. Trustee Clayton Pub. Library, 1960-70. Mem. Am. Mgmt. Assn. (theologians adv. council 1960-70), State Hist. Soc. Mo. (trustee 1953—). Home: 1249 Kortwright Saint Louis MO 63119

FUERMANN, GEORGE MELVIN, editor; b. Buffalo, Aug. 25, 1918; s. Walter John and Viola Irene (Bishop) F.; m. Ruth Wagner Owens, July 9, 1970; children—Julie Anne, Walter. Student, Tex. A. and M. U., 1937-41. Columnist Houston Post, 1950-70, editor editorial page, 1971—. Author: Houston: Land of the Big Rich, 1951, Reluctant Empire: The Mind of Texas, 1957, Houston: The Feast Years, 1962, The Face of Houston, 1963, Houston Recalled: Six Miniatures, 1968, Houston: The Once and Future City, 1971. Chmn. Houston Municipal Art Commn., 1965-67, Houston Municipal Art Found., 1966-67; Mem. Houston Com. on Fgn. Relations, chmn., 1977; mem. Houston Am. Bicentennial Commn. Served to capt. AUS, 1946. Decorated Bronze Star medal. Episcopalian. Address: 4747 Southwest Freeway Houston TX 77001

FUERSTENAU, DOUGLAS WINSTON, materials science educator; b. Hazel, S.D., Dec. 6, 1928; s. Erwin Arnold and Hazel Pauline (Karterud) F.; m. Margaret Ann Pellett, Aug. 29, 1953; children: Lucy, Sarah, Stephen. B.S., S.D. Sch. Mines and Tech., 1949; M.S., Mont. Sch. Mines, 1950; Sc.D., MIT, 1953; Mineral Engr., Mont. Coll. Mineral Sci. and Tech., 1968. Asst. prof. mineral engring. MIT, 1953-56; sect. leader, metals research lab. Union Carbide Metals Co., Niagara Falls, N.Y., 1956-58; mgr. mineral engring. lab Kaiser Aluminum & Chem. Corp., Permanente, Calif., 1958-59; asso. prof. metallurgy U. Calif. at Berkeley, 1959-62, prof. metallurgy, 1962—, Miller research prof., 1969-70, chmn. dept. materials sci. and mineral engring., 1970—; dir. Homestake Mining Co.; Chmn. Engring. Found. Research Conf. on Comminution, 1963; Mem. adv. bd. Sch. Earth Scis., Stanford, 1970-73; mem. Nat. Mineral Bd., 1975—; Am. rep. Internat. Mineral Processing Congress Com., 1978—. Editor: Froth Flotation-50th Anniversary Vol, 1962; co-editor-in-chief: Internat. Jour. of Mineral Processing, 1972—; Mem. editorial adv. bd.: Jour. of Colloid and Interface Sci, 1968-72, Colloids and Surfaces, 1980—; Contbr. articles to profl. jours. Recipient Distinguished Teaching award U. Calif., 1974; Fellow Instn. Mining and Metallurgy, London. Mem. Nat. Acad. Engring., Am. Inst. Mining and Metall. Engrs. (chmn. mineral processing div. 1967, Robert Lansing Hardy Gold medal 1957, Rossiter W. Raymond award 1961, RobertH. Richards award 1975, Antoine M. Gaudin award 1978, Mineral Industry Edn. award 1983), Soc. Mining Engrs. (dir. 1968-71, Distinguished mem.), Am. Chem. Soc., Am. Inst. Chem. Engrs., Sigma Xi, Theta Tau. Congregationalist. Home: 1440 LeRoy Ave Berkeley CA 94708

FUESS, HAROLD GEORGE, retired religious organization executive; b. Belleville, Ill., Sept. 29, 1910; s. Arthur Garfield and Catherine Charlotte (Wehrung) F.; m. Lorrean W. Essenpreis, Mar. 20, 1937; 1 dau., Karen Ann. Student pub. schs., Belleville. Profl. baseball player, 1929-32; with Kroger Co., 1934-55, mdse. mgr., Little Rock, 1950-52, buyer, Cin., 1953-55; mktg. supr. Needham, Louis & Brorby, Chgo., 1956-59; sr. v.p., adminstrv. mgr., account dir. McCann-Erickson, Chgo., 1960-73, ret., 1973; v.p. Nat. Council Community Chs., Worthington, Ohio, 1975-77, pres., 1977-80, pres. emeritus, 1981—; dir. printing co.; cons. Commn. on Religion in Appalachia. Chmn. drive United Fund, Park Ridge, Ill., 1969; chmn. congregation Park Ridge Community Ch., 1967-68. Served with USAAF, 1943-47; ETO. Recipient citation Chgo. Crusade of Mercy, 1972; named hon. citizen City of Sarasota, Fla., 1979. Mem. Nat. Council Chs. (governing bd.), Consulation on Ch. Union (del.), World Council Chs. (rep.), C. of C. Republican. Clubs: Playboy, Mktg. Execs., Elks. Home: 31 Bray Wood Williamsburg VA 23185 Office: 900 Ridge Rd Homewood IL 60430

FUGATE, DOUGLAS BROWN, civil engineer; b. Reed Island, Va., Aug. 6, 1906; s. Jesse Honnaker and Elizabeth Gertrude (Brown) F.; m. Mary Addison Lathan, June 15, 1940 (dec.); 1 son, Douglas B.; m. Emma Stimson Reed, July 7, 1973. B.S. in Civil Engring., Va. Mil. Inst., 1927. Civil engr. Va. Dept. Hwys. and Transp., 1927-42, asst. chief engr., 1947-59, chief engr., 1959-60, asst. chief engr., 1961-64; commr. Va. State Hwys. and Transp., 1964-76; cons. engr., Richmond, Va., 1976—; Chmn. Elizabeth River Tunnel Commn., 1964-74; Mem. Va. Gov.'s Council on Transp., 1976-80. Bd. dirs. Va. Outdoor Recreation Commn., 1964-76, Keep Va. Beautiful, 1964-76. Served to lt. col. AUS, 1942-46. Mem. ASCE (hon., past pres. Va. sect.), Am. Assn. State Hwy. and Transp. Ofcls. (past pres.), Southeastern Assn. State Hwy. and Transp. Ofcls. (past pres.), Am. Rd. and Transp. Builders Assn. (past sr. v.p.), Hwy. and Transp. Research Bd. (past exec. com.), Automobile Club Va. (treas., dir. 1976-82, dir. emeritus 1982—). Episcopalian. Address: 102 Portland Pl Richmond VA 23221

FUGATE, IVAN DEE, banker, lawyer; b. Blackwell, Okla., Dec. 9, 1928; s. Hugh D. and Iva (Holmes) F.; m. Lois Unita Rossow, June 3, 1966; children: Vickie Michelle, Roberta Jeanne, Douglas B., Thomas P. A.B., Pittsburg (Kans.) State U., 1949; LL.B., U. Denver, 1952, J.D., 1970. Bar: Colo. 1952. Exec. sec., mgr. Jr. C. of C. of Denver, 1950-52; also sec. Colo. Jr. C. of C.; individual practice law, Denver, 1954—; chmn. bd., pres. Green Mountain Bank, Lakewood, Colo., 1975-82, Western Nat. Bank of Denver; pres., chmn. exec. com. North Valley State Bank, Thornton, Colo.; chmn. bd. Ind. State Bank of Colo., 1978—; dir. Kit Carson State Bank, Colo.; sec. 1st Nat. Bank, Burlington, Colo.; owner, farms, ranches, Kans., Colo.; instr. U. Denver Coll. Law, 1955-60; mem. Colo. Treas's. Com. Investment State Funds, 1975—. Treas. Republic Assos., Colo., 1959-61, trustee, 1959-64. Served to 1st lt. AUS, 1952-54. Mem. ABA, Colo. Bar Assn., Denver Bar Assn. (trustee 1962-65), Colo. Bankers Assn. (dir.), Ind. Bankers Colo. (founder, chmn. bd. 1973—), Ind. Bankers Assn. Am. (pres. 1978, adminstrv. com., exec. council 1976—), Denver Law Club, Phi Alpha Delta. Methodist. Clubs: Petroleum, Denver Athletic, 26 (Denver); Lakewood Country. Home: 12015 W 26th Ave Lakewood CO 80215 Office: Bldg 52 5350 South DTC Pkwy Englewood CO 80111

FUGATE-WILCOX, TERRY, artist; b. Kalamazoo, Nov. 20, 1944; m. Valerie Shakespeare, Nov. 1, 1962. Represented in permanent collections, Solomon R. Guggenheim Mus., N.Y.C., Australia Nat. Gallery, Canberra, Mus. Modern Art, N.Y.C., Western Mich. U., J. Hood Wright Park, N.Y.C., J. Patrick Lannan Found. Mus., Palm Beach, Fla., Nat. Shopping Ctrs., Harrisburg, Pa., Prudential Ins. Co., Newark, Damson Oil Co., N.Y.C., N.Y.C. Dept. Parks and Recreations; sculpture, 7th Ave and Waverly, N.Y.C., sculptrue, City Wall Holland Tunnel Entrance, N.Y.C. Address: 7 Worth St New York NY 10013 *Actual art includes in its statement the long-suppressed dimension of time, in the context of the naturally occuring changes that are part of the life of any material and should be part of the life of the work of art incorporating that material.*

FUGAZY, WILLIAM DENIS, travel and transp. co. exec.; b. Wyndham, N.Y., Aug. 17, 1924; s. Italo and Irene (Cronin) F.; m. Joan Boggiano, May 24, 1947; children: William Denis, John, Daria, Roy. Student, Fordham U., 1942-43, Cornell U., 1943-45. Chmn. Fugazy Internat., Inc., 1947—; chmn. bd. Fugazy Continental Limousine Corp.; dir. Carvel Corp., Yonkers, N.Y. Chmn. All-Am. Collegiate Golf Found., 1965—; chmn. Day With All Ams. Golf Tournament for Coll. Scholarships, 1967—; Chmn. bd. John V. Mara Meml. Fund Cancer Research; bd. dirs. Nat. Cath. Youth Orgn., St. Vincent's Hosp., N.Y.C., Discover America. Served with USNR, World War II. Decorated knight Equestrian Order Holy Sepulchre, 1950, knight grand cross, 1963; Gold medal honor Boys Town Italy. Mem. Hotel Sales Mgmt. Assn., Sales Execs. Club N.Y.C. Clubs: N.Y. Athletic (N.Y.C.); Winged Foot Golf (Mamaroneck, N.Y.). Home: Sunnyridge Rd Harrison NY 10528 Office: 767 Third Ave New York NY 10017

FUHRMAN, BENHAM, brokerage company executive, financial planner, money manager; b. Phila., May 31, 1931; s. Joseph H. and Anne F. (Freilick) F.; m. June L. Stein, Feb. 3, 1953; children: Susan, Robert, Judith, Steven. B.S. in Metall. Engring., U. Pa., 1953. Cert. fin. planner. Prin. Fuhrman-Levitt Inc., Camden, N.J., 1965-68; registered rep. Herzfeld & Stern, Phila., 1968-73, ptnr., 1973—. Chmn. endowment Fedn. Jewish Charities, Cherry Hill, N.J., 1978-80, v.p., Cherry Hill, N.J., 1979. Served to lt. USN, 1953-56. Mem. Internat. Assn. Fin. Planners (bd. dirs. Delaware Valley chpt. 1975-79). Club: Variety (Phila.) (bd. dirs. 1977-78). Home: 1901 Walnut St Apt 21E Philadelphia PA 19103 Office: Herzfeld & Stern 1760 Market St Philadelphia PA 19103

FUHRMAN, CHARLES ANDREW, real estate management executive, lawyer; b. Milw., June 14, 1933; s. Harry H. and Gertrude (Wynn) F.; m. Ann Marie Brott; children: Anthony Andrew, Nicolas Andrew, Michelle Heather. B.S., U. Wis., 1955, LL.B., 1957. Bar: Wis. 1957, Ohio 1958, Mich. 1964. Pvt. practice, Toledo, 1958-62; partner Fuhrman, Gertner, Britz & Barkan, 1963-72; Partner Varsity Sq. Apts. Co., Alexian Co., Dundee Co., Tamaron Country Club, Tamaron Mgmt. Co. Served to 2d lt. Transp. Corps, U.S. Army, 1958. Mem. Am., Wis., Mich., Ohio, Toledo bar assns., Phi Delta Phi, Pi Lambda Phi. Republican. Clubs: Masons, Shriners, Jesters, Desert Caballeros. Home: 4778 Springbrook Toledo OH 43615 Office: 2162 W Alexis Toledo OH 43613

FUHRMAN, FREDERICK ALEXANDER, educator; b. Coquille, Oreg., Aug. 13, 1915; s. Cyrus Jacob and Josie (Lyons) F.; m. Geraldine Jackson, Nov. 12, 1942. B.S., Oreg. State Coll., 1937, M.S., 1939; postgrad., Universität Freiburg im Breisgau, 1937-38, U. Wash., 1939-41; Ph.D., Stanford, 1943. Univ. fellow in pharmacology U. Wash., 1939-41; research asso. in physiology Stanford, 1941-45, instr., 1945-49, asst. prof., 1949-52, asso. prof., 1952-57, prof. physiology, 1957-61, dir. basic med. scis. labs., 1959—, prof. exptl. medicine, 1961-72, prof. physiology, 1972-80, emeritus, 1981—; physiologist Hopkins Marine Sta., Pacific Grove, Calif., 1972-79; dir. Max C. Fleischmann Labs. of the Med. Scis., 1961-70. Author: Multidiscipline Laboratories for Teaching the Medical Sciences; Asso. editor: Ann. Review of Psysiology, 1954-62; Contbr. articles on metabolism, frostbite, hypothermia and marine pharmacology to profl. jours. Guggenheim fellow, labor of zoophysiology U. Copenhagen, 1951-52; sr. postdoctoral fellow NSF, Inst. Biol. Chemistry, U. Copenhagen and Donner Lab., U. Calif., 1958-59; Commonwealth Fund fellow, 1966-67. Fellow AAAS, N.Y. Acad. Scis.; mem. Am. Physiol. Soc., Am. Soc. Pharmacology and Exptl. Therapeutics, Sigma Xi, Phi Kappa Phi. Active in med. research OSRD, World War II. Home: PO Box 313 Pebble Beach CA 93953 Office: Dept Physiology Stanford U Stanford CA 94305

FUHRMAN, HAROLD GEORGE, newspaper exec.; b. Edgeley, N.D., Sept. 20, 1921; s. George Milton and Clara Barton (Spitzer) F.; m. Florence Elizabeth Crerar, June 4, 1948; children—Janet Kay, Scott Harold. Ed., U. N.D., U. Colo. Accountant The Seattle Times, 1946-53, asst. chief accountant, 1953-58, asst. labor relations mgr., 1958-60, labor relations mgr., 1960-69, asst. gen. mgr., 1969-70, v.p., gen. mgr., 1970-79, sr. v.p., gen. mgr., 1979—. Served with AUS, 1943-46. Clubs: Rainier (Seattle); Wash. Athletic, Masons, Rotary. Office: Seattle Times Fairview Ave N & John St PO Box 70 Seattle WA 98111

FUHRMAN, RALPH EDWARD, civil and environ. engr.; b. Kansas City, Kans., Sept. 6, 1909; s. Ralph William and Olga (Woinova) F.; m. Josephine Ackerman, Jan. 1, 1935; children—William Edward, Anne Louise. B.S. in Civil Engring, U. Kans., 1930; M.S. in San. Engring, Harvard, 1937; D.Eng., Johns Hopkins, 1954. Asst. pub. health engr. Mo. Dept. of Health, 1931, 37; city san. engr., Springfield, Mo., 1931-36; asst. supt. D.C. Water Pollution Control Plant, 1937-42, supt., 1942-53; dep. dir. san. engring. D.C. Govt., 1953-55; exec. dir. Water Pollution Control Fedn., 1955-69, pres., 1950-51; asst. dir. Nat. Water Commn., 1969-71; spl. asst. to dir. municipal wastewater systems div. EPA, 1972-73; mgr. Washington regional office Black & Veatch (Cons. Engrs.), Kansas City, Mo., 1973-78, rep., 1979—; lectr. civil engring. George Washington U., 1941-60. Fellow Am. Pub. Health Assn., ASCE (chmn. exec. com. san. engring. div. 1954-55), Inst. Water Pollution Control (Brit., hon.), Instn. Pub. Health Engrs. (Brit., hon.); mem. Chesapeake Water Pollution Control Assn., Am. Water Works Assn., Am. Acad. Environ. Engrs. Episcopalian. Club: Cosmos (Washington). Home: 2917 39th St NW Washington DC 20016 Office: 7315 Wisconsin Ave Bethesda MD 20014

FUHRMAN, ROBERT ALEXANDER, aerospace company executive; b. Detroit, Feb. 23, 1925; s. Alexander A. and Elva (Brown) F.; m. Nan McCormick, Sept. 16, 1949; children: Lee Anne, Richard, William. B.S., U. Mich., 1945; M.S., U. Md., 1952; student, Stanford U., 1964, U. Calif., San Diego, 1958. Project engr. Naval Air Test Center, Patuxent River, Md., 1946-53; chief tech. engring. Ryan Aero. Co., San Diego, 1953-58; v.p., asst. gen. mgr. missile systems div. Lockheed Missiles & Space Co., Sunnyvale, Calif., 1958-69, v.p., gen. mgr., 1969, exec. v.p., 1973-76, pres., 1976—, chmn., 1979—; v.p. Lockheed Corp., Burbank, Calif., 1969-76, sr. v.p., 1976-83, group pres. Missiles, Space & Electronics System, 1983—; also dir., pres. Lockheed Ga. Co., Marietta, 1970-71; pres. Lockheed Calif. Co., Burbank, 1971-73; chmn. bd. Ventura Mfg. Co., 1970-71; dir. Bank of the West; mem. FBM Steering Task Group, 1966-70. Mem. adv. bd. Sch. Bus., U. Santa Clara; bd. govs. Federated Employees of Bay Area; trustee United Way of Santa Clara County, 1975—; bd. dirs. Atlanta Jr. Achievement; mem. adv. council Sch. Engring., Stanford U.; mem. adv. bd. Coll. Engring., U. Mich., 1981—; mem. adv. council Coll. Engring. Found. U. Tex.-Austin, 1983—; mem. Def. Sci. Bd., chmn. task force on indsl. responsiveness, 1980; mem. exec. com. San Jose Mgmt. Task Force; mem. sci. adv. com. Ala. Space and Rocket Center; bd. dirs. Bay Area Council. Served to ensign USNR, 1944-46. Recipient Silver Knight award Nat. Mgmt. Assn., 1969, John J. Montgomery award, 1964; award Soc. Mfg. Engrs., 1973; Disting. Citizen award Boy Scouts Am., 1983; Donald C. Burnham award Soc. Mfg. Engrs., 1983, Eminent Engr. award Tau Beta Pi, 1983. Fellow AIAA (dir.-at-large, Von Karman 1978); mem. Nat. Acad. Engring., Am. Astron. Soc. (sr.), Nat. Aero. Assn., Ga. C. of C. (dir.), Am. Def. Preparedness Assn. (dir., exec. com.), Navy League U.S. (life), Air Force Assn., Assn. U.S. Army, Soc. Am. Value Engrs. (hon.), Santa Clara County Mfrs. Group (past chmn.), Beta Gamma Sigma. Clubs: Sainte Claire (San Jose, Calif.); Burning Tree (Bethesda, Md.). Office: 1111 Lockheed Sunnyvale CA 94086

FUHS, ALLEN EUGENE, engineer, physicist, educator; b. Laramie, Wyo., Aug. 11, 1927; s. Michael Allen and Grace Emeline (Terrill) F.; m. Emily Ann Large, Dec. 22, 1951; 1 dau., Susan Elizabeth. B.S.M.E., U. N.Mex., 1951; M.S.M.E., Calif. Inst. Tech., 1955, Ph.D., 1958. Owner service sta., Gallup, N.Mex., 1944-46; asst. prof. Northwestern U., Evanston, Ill., 1958-59; mem. tech. staff TRW Systems, El Sequndo, Calif., 1959-60; staff scientist Aerospace Corp., El Segundo, Calif., 1960-66; prof., chmn. aeros. Naval Postgrad. Sch., Monterey, Calif., 1966-68, Disting. prof., 1970—, chmn. dept. mech. engring., 1975-78; chief scientist Air Force Aeropropulsion Lab., Dayton, Ohio, 1968-70; cons. TRW Systems, Aerospace Corp., others. Author: Instrumentation for High Speed Plasma Flow, 1965; editor 4 books; editor-in-chief: Jour. of Aircraft, 1974-79; contbr. articles to profl. jours. Served with USN, 1951-54; Korea. Guggenheim fellow, 1957-58; recipient SAE Ralph R. Teetor award. Fellow AIAA (v.p. publs. 1979-81, dir. 1982—), ASME; mem. Am. Phys. Soc., Am. Soc. Naval Engrs., Soc. Naval Architects and Marine Engrs., Am. Optical Soc., Sigma Xi. Patentee in field. Office: Naval Postgrad Sch Monterey CA 93943

FUJITA, SHIGEJI, physicist, educator; b. Oita City, Japan, May 15, 1929; came to U.S., 1964, naturalized, 1974; s. Shigeto and Makio (Eyama) F.; m. Sachiko Fujise, Sept. 30, 1958; children—Michio, Isao, Yoshiko, Eriko. B.S., Kyushu U., 1953; Ph.D., U. Md., 1960. Research asso. Northwestern U., 1958-60; sr. research asso. Universite Libre de Bruxelles, 1960-64; vis. asso. prof. physics Pa. State U., 1964-65, U. Oreg., 1965-66; asso. prof. physics State U. N.Y., Buffalo, 1966-68, prof. physics, 1968—. Author: Introduction to Non-Equilibrium Quantum Statistical Mechanics, 1966; editor: The Ta-you Wu Festschrift: Science of Matter, 1978. Mem. Am. Phys. Soc., AAUP, Phys. Soc. Japan. Research on kinetic theory of gases and plasmas, solid-state theory and polymer physics. Developed statis. mech. theory which treats transport and optical properties of matter on rigorous basis. Home: 247 Cimarand Ct Getzville NY 14068 Office: Dept Physics State U NY at Buffalo Amherst NY 14260

FUJITA, TETSUYA THEODORE, educator, meteorologist; b. Kitakyushu City, Japan, Oct. 23, 1920; came to U.S., 1953, naturalized, 1968; s. Tomojiro and Yoshie (Kanesue) F.; m. Sumiko Yamamoto, June 13, 1969; 1 son, Kazuya. B.S.Eq. in Mech. Engring, Meiji Coll. Tech., Kitakyushu City, 1943; Dr.Sci., Tokyo (Japan) U., 1953. Asst. prof. Meiji Coll. Tech., Kitakyushu, 1943-49; asst. prof. Kyushu Inst. Tech., Kitakyushu, 1949-53; sr. meteorologist U. Chgo., 1953-62, asso. prof., 1962-65, prof., 1965—. Recipient Okada award Japan Meteorol. Soc., 1959; Kamura award Kyushu Inst. Tech., 1965; Meisinger award Am. Meteorol. Soc., 1967; Aviation Week and Space Tech. Distinguished Service award Flight Safety Found., 1977; Adm. Luis de Florez Flight Safety award, 1977; Ann. award Nat. Weather Assn., 1978; Disting. Public Service award NASA, 1979; Losey Atmospheric Sci. award AIAA, 1982. Mem. Am., Japan meteorol. socs., Am. Geophy. Union, Am. Optical Soc., Sigma Xi. Specialized research on severe weather phenomena and satellite meteorology. Discovered suction vortex in tornado, 1970; originated Fujita Tornado Scale, 1971; directed NASA tornado cloud overflight, 1971-77; patentee omni-directional windspeed detector. Home: 5727 Maryland Ave Chicago IL 60637 Office: Dept Geophys Sciences U Chicago 5734 Ellis Ave Chicago IL 60637

FUKUI, HATSUAKI, electrical engineer; b. Yokohama, Japan, Dec. 14, 1927; came to U.S., 1962, naturalized, 1973; s. Ushinosuke and Yoshi (Saito) F.; m. Atsuko Inamoto, Apr. 1, 1954 (dec. 1973); children: Mayumi, Nioki; m. 2d Kiku Kato, Dec. 12, 1975. Diploma, Miyakojima Tech. Coll. (now Osaka City U.), 1949; D.Eng., Osaka U., 1961. Research assoc. Osaka City U., 1949-54; engr. Shimada Phys. and Chem. Indsl. Co., Tokyo, 1954-55; sr. engr. to supr. Sony Corp. semi-condr. div., Tokyo, 1955-61; mgr. engring. div. Sony Corp., 1961-62; mem. tech. staff Bell Telephone Labs., Murray Hill, N.J., 1962-69, supr., 1969-73; v.p. Sony Corp. Am., N.Y.C., 1973; asst. to chmn. Sony Corp., Tokyo, 1973; staff mem. Bell Labs., Murray Hill, N.J., 1973-83; supr. AT&T Bell Labs., Murray Hill, 1984—; lectr. Tokyo Met. U. (part-time), part-time 1962. Author: Esaki Diodes, 1963, Solid-State FM Receivers, 1968; contbr. to: Semiconductors Handbook, 1963; editor: Low-Noise Microwave Transistors and Amplifiers, 1981; contbr. articles to profl. jours.; patentee in field. Fellow IEEE (standardization com. 1976-82, editorial bd. IEEE Transactions on Microwave Theory and Techniques 1980—, Microwave prize 1980); mem. Inst. Electronics and Communication Engrs. Japan (Inada award 1959), Inst. TV Engrs. Japan (tech. com. 1973-75). Home: 53 Drum Hill Dr Summit NJ 07901 Office: 600 Mountain Ave Murray Hill NJ 07974

FUKUYAMA, KIMIE, dermatologist, educator; b. Tokyo, Japan, Dec. 11, 1927; came to U.S.; d. Fukutaro and Nami F. M.D., Tokyo Women's Med. Coll., 1949, Ph.D., 1964; M.S., U. Mich., Ann Arbor, 1958. Intern, resident in dermatology Tokyo Med. Sch., 1949-56; research assoc. U. Mich., 1958-61; clin. asst. Tokyo Women's Med. Coll., 1961-63, lectr., 1964-65, U. Calif., San Francisco, 1965-67, asst. prof. in residence, 1967-72, asso. prof. in residence, 1972-78, prof., 1978—, vice-chmn., 1978—. Asst. editor: Archives Dermatology, 1974-78; mem. editorial bds., 1974—, Jour. Investigative Dermatology, 1981—; contbr. over 100 articles to med. jours. Barbour scholar, 1956-58; Japan Soc. fellow, 1958-59; Fulbright grantees, 1956-61, 65-67. Mem. Am. Acad. Dermatology, Soc. Investigative Dermatology, Am. Fedn. Clin. Research, Pacific Dermatol. Assn., Japanese Dermatol. Assn., Soc. Tokyo Women's Med. Coll., Japanese Women's Med. Assn., Am. Dermatol. Assn., Soc. Cutaneous Ultrastructure Research. Office: 1092 HSE U Calif San Francisco CA 94143

FULBRIGHT, JAMES WILLIAM, former U.S. senator; b. Sumner, Mo., Apr. 9, 1905; s. Jay and Roberta (Waugh) F.; m. Elizabeth Williams, June 15, 1932; children—Elizabeth (Mrs. John Winnacker), Roberta (Mrs. Edward Thaddeus Foote II). A.B., U. Ark., 1925; B.A., Oxford (Eng.) U., 1928, M.A., 1931; LL.B., George Washington U., 1934. Bar: D.C. bar 1934. Spl. atty. Anti-Trust Div. U.S. Dept. Justice, 1934-35; instr. in law George Washington U., 1935-36; lectr. in law U. Ark., 1936-39, pres., 1939-41; mem. 78th congress from 3d Dist. Ark.; U.S. senator from, Ark., 1945-74; mem. com. on finance, mem. joint econ. com., chmn. com. on fgn. relations; of counsel firm Hogan & Hartson, Washington, 1975—; Del. 9th Gen. Assembly UN, 1954. Mem. Sigma Chi. Democrat. Mem. Disciples of Christ Ch. Club: Rotarian. Home: Fayetteville AR 72701 Office: 815 Connecticut Ave Washington DC 20006

FULCHER, MARTIN CLAY, air force officer; b. Bryant, Ark., Jan. 7, 1929; s. Bernice Connally and Theo Bernice (Martin) F.; m. Frances Marie Prankunas, Mar. 3, 1957; 1 son, Richard C.; 1 stepdau., Melissa Frances Mueller. B.A., Coll. of Pacific, 1950; grad., Armed Forces Staff Coll., 1967, Nat. War Coll., 1971; M.A., George Washington U., 1971. Served as enlisted man U.S. Air Force, 1951-52, commd. 2d lt., 1952, advanced through grades to maj. gen., 1978; aircraft comdr. and instr. pilot, 1952-58; a.d.c. to comdr. 8th Air Force, 1958-62, Tactical Air Command, 1962-63; instr. pilot, wing plans officer, 1963-66; flight comdr. and squadron ops. officer Da Nang Air Base, Vietnam, 1967-68; chief regular and res. div., asst. for gen. officer matters Hdqrs USAF, Washington, 1968-69, asst. exec. officer to chief of staff, 1969-70; vice comdr. Bomb Wing, Beale AFB, Calif., 1971-72, Air Div., Andersen AFB, Guam, 1972-73; comdr. (Bomb Wing), Fairchild AFB, Wash., 1973-74, 1974-75; asst. dep. chief of staff for logistics Hdqrs. SAC, Offutt AFB, Nebr., 1975-77, dep. chief staff for logistics, 1977-79; asst. dep. chief staff for logistics and engring. Hdqrs. USAF, 1979—. Decorated D.S.M. with oak leaf cluster, D.F.C. with 2 oak leaf clusters, Meritorious Service medal with oak leaf cluster, Air medal with 14 oak leaf clusters, Air Force Commendation medal with oak leaf cluster. Home: 7305 Burtonwood Dr Alexandria VA 22307 Office: Hdqrs USAF (AF/LE) Washington DC 20330

FULCO, ARMAND JOHN, biochemist; b. Los Angeles, Apr. 3, 1932; s. Herman J. and Clelia Marie (DeFeo) F.; m. Virginia Loy Hungerford, June 18, 1955; children—William James, Lisa Marie, Linda Susan, Suzanne Yvonne. B.S. in Chemistry, UCLA, 1957, Ph.D. in Physiol. Chemistry, 1960. Research fellow dept. chemistry Harvard U., Cambridge, Mass., 1961-63; biochemist, prin. investigator Lab. Nuclear Medicine and Radiation Biology, UCLA, 1963-80, asst. prof. dept. biol. chemistry, 1965-70, assoc. prof., 1970-76, prof., 1976—, prin. investigator, lab. biomed. and environ. scis., 1981—; cons. biochemist VA, Los Angeles, 1968—. Author: (with J.F. Mead) The Unsaturated and Polyunsaturated Fatty Acids in Health and Disease, 1976; contbr. over 60 articles to sci. jours. Served with U.S. Army, 1952-54. Mem. Am. Chem. Soc., Am. Soc. Biol. Chemists, Am. Oil Chemists Soc., AAAS, Am. Soc. Microbiology, Harvard Chemists Assn., Sigma Xi. Home: 3000 Stoner Ave Los Angeles CA 90066 Office: U Calif Lab Biomed and Environ Scis 900 Veteran Ave Los Angeles CA 90024

FULCO, JOSE ROQUE, physicist, educator; b. Buenos Aires, Argentina, Dec. 5, 1927; s. Jose Roque and Teresa (Padula) F.; m. Edith Perez Andrich, Sept. 8, 1949; children: Jorge Daniel, Monica Edith, Ana Maria Luz, Jose Miguel, Rosemarie. B.S. in Chem. Engring, Argentine Army Engring. Sch., 1955; postgrad., U. Calif., Berkeley, 1957-59; Ph.D. in Physics, U. Buenos Aires, 1962. Commd. officer Argentine Army, 1943, advanced through grades to lt. col., 1945; ret., 1964; vis. fellow Lawrence Radiation Lab., Berkeley, Calif., 1958-60; prof. physics U. Buenos Aires, 1960-62, U. La Plata, 1961-62; asst. research physicist U. Calif., San Diego, 1962-64, asso. prof., Santa Barbara, 1964-69, prof., 1969—, chmn. dept. physics, 1978-83, assoc. dir. edn. abroad program univ. wide, 1970, 76; cons. Gen. Atomics Co., Gen. Research Co., OAS. Contbr. chpts. to books; contbr. articles to profl. jours. NSF grantee, 1964. Fellow Am. Phys. Soc. Office: Dept Physics Univ of Calif Santa Barbara CA 93106

FULD, JAMES JEFFREY, lawyer; b. N.Y.C., Feb. 16, 1916; s. Gus and Blanche (Weill) F.; m. Elaine Gerstley, Sept. 14, 1942; children: Joan, James, Nancy Neff. A.B., Harvard U., 1937, LL.B., 1940. Bar: N.Y. 1940. Mem. firm Proskauer Rose Goetz & Mendelsohn, N.Y.C., 1940—, mng. ptnr., 1974—. Author: The Book of World Famous Music, 1966. Bd. dirs. United Jewish Appeal-Fedn. Jewish Philanthropies of N.Y., N.Y.C., 1974—, Am. Jewish Com., 1956-60; mem. N.Y. State Bd. Social Welfare, Albany, 1973-76; advisor Toscanini Meml. Archives, N.Y. Pub. Library, N.Y.C., 1970—. Served to maj. U.S. Army, 1942-46. Recipient War Dept. citation U.S. Army, 1945. Mem. N.Y. County Lawyers Bar Assn. (dir. 1974-77), ABA, N.Y. State Bar Assn., N.Y.C. Bar Assn., Phi Beta Kappa. Republican. Jewish. Club: Sunningdale Country (pres. 1956-58). Home: 1175 Park Ave New York NY 10128 Office: Proskauer Rose Goetz and Mendelsohn 300 Park Ave New York NY 10022

FULD, STANLEY H., lawyer; b. N.Y.C., Aug. 23, 1903; s. Emanuel I. and Hermine (Frisch) F.; m. Florence Geringer, May 29, 1930 (dec. Feb. 1975); children: Hermine (Mrs. Maurice N. Nessen), Judith (Mrs. Frank Miller); m. Stella F. Rapaport, Jan. 4, 1976. A.B., CCNY, 1923; LL.B., Columbia U., 1926, LL.D., 1959; LL.D., Hamilton Coll., 1949, Union Coll., 1961, Yeshiva U., 1962, N.Y. Law Sch., 1962, NYU, 1963, Jewish Theol. Sem. Am., 1964, Syracuse U., 1967, St. John's U., 1970, CUNY, 1972. Bar: N.Y. 1926, U.S. Supreme Ct. 1933. Pvt. practice, N.Y.C., 1926-35, 44-46; Counsel legal div. Nat. Recovery Adminstrn., Washington, 1935; asst. dist. atty., N.Y. County, 1935-44, spl. asst. atty. gen., liaison counsel, state investigations, N.Y. State, 1944-45; apptd. asso. judge Ct. of Appeals, 1946; elected for full term, beginning 1947, 61; chief judge State of N.Y. and Ct. of Appeals, 1967-73; spl. counsel firm Kaye, Scholer, Fierman, Hays & Handler, N.Y.C., 1974—; dir. Greater N.Y. Mut. Ins. Co., 1974—, Petrie Stores Corp., 1978-82; chmn. adminstrv. bd. Jud. Conf. State N.Y., 1967-73; mem. N.Y. State Ct. Facilities Task Force, 1980-82; Chmn. N.Y. Fair Trial Free Press Conf., 1967-73, hon. chmn., 1974—; chmn. Nat. Commn. on New Technol. Uses of Copyrighted Works, 1975-78, Fellows of N.Y. Bar Found., 1978-83, Greater N.Y. Health Care and Health Facilities Commn., 1979-80. Bd. editors: N.Y. Law Jour, 1976—. Commr. Nat. Hillel Commn., 1947-56; chmn. bd. visitors City Coll., CUNY, 1973-81; bd. dirs. Phi Beta Kappa Assos., 1949-80, hon. dir., 1980—; bd. visitors Columbia Law Sch., 1951—; chmn. bd. dirs. Jewish Theol. Sem. Am., 1966-74; mem. exec. com., bd. dirs., 1966—; pres. Inst. for Religious and Social Studies, 1974—; trustee Beth Israel Med. Center, 1971—; mem. N.Y.C. Charter Revision Commn., 1982-83; chmn. Nat. News Council, 1974-76; bd. dirs. Hunter Coll. Student Social, Community and Religious Clubs Assn., 1948—, chmn., 1974—; bd. dirs. Empire State Report, 1974—, World Union for Progressive

Judaism, 1981—, Benjamin N. Cardozo Sch. Law of Yeshiva U., 1976-81; hon. dir. Benjamin N. Cardozo Sch. Law of Yeshiva U., 1981—; bd. govs. Daytop Village, 1978-81. Recipient Joseph M. Proskauer medal lawyers div. Fedn. Jewish Philanthropies, 1959; Cardozo award K.P., 1951; Harlan Fiske Stone award Assn. Trial Lawyers City N.Y., 1966; medal for excellence Columbia Law Sch. Alumni Assn., 1967; Gold medal for distinguished service in the law N.Y. State Bar Assn., 1971; John Peter Zenger award N.Y. State Soc. Newspaper Editors, 1970; Gold medallion for distinguished pub. service Nassau County Bar Assn., 1971; John H. Finley award for distinguished service to N.Y.C. City Coll. Alumni Assn., 1971; award of merit Lotos Club, 1972; Earl Warren medal for distinguished contbns. to humanity and civilization Jewish Theol. Sem. Am., 1972; Martin Luther King medal City Coll. N.Y., 1974; Torch of Learning award Am. Friends of Hebrew U., 1977; Stanley H. Fuld Professorship in law established at Columbia Law Sch., 1977. Fellow Acad. Am. Arts and Scis.; hon. mem. Bar Assn. City N.Y., N.Y. County Lawyers Assn.; mem. N.Y. State, Am. bar assns., Coll. City N.Y. Alumni Assn. (v.p.), Columbia Law Alumni Assn. (dir.), Am. Law Inst. (life), Order of Coif, Phi Beta Kappa, Columbia Law Rev. Assn. (dir.). Republican. Jewish (trustee synagogue). Home: 211 E 70th New York NY 10021 Office: 425 Park Ave New York NY 10022

FULGHAM, JOHN RAWLES, JR., banker; b. Windsor, Va., July 29, 1927; s. John Rawles and Gypsie (Matthews) F.; m. Betty Berger, Dec. 2, 1950; children: Emily Ann McCullough, Janie Rawles Bel, John Rawles III. B.A., Va. Mil. Inst.; B.B.A. in Money and Banking, So. Methodist U. With First Nat. Bank, Dallas, 1954-82, sr. v.p., controller, head adminstrv. services, pres., chief adminstrv. officer, then pres., until 1982, also dir.; now exec. dir. Merrill Lynch Pvt. Capital Inc.; vice-chmn., chief adminstrv. officer 1st Internat. Bancshares, Inc., Dallas; dir. Earth Resources Co., NCH Corp., Banc Tec, Inc., Republic Fin. Services, Inc., Dorchester Gas Corp., Dresser Industries, Inc.; mem. faculty Southwestern Grad. Sch. Banking; lectr. Am. Inst. Banking, Fed. Savs. and Loan Inst.; mem. exec. com. Pres.'s Pvt. Sector Survey on Cost Control of Fed. Govt. Leader fund raising campaigns Wadley Research Inst., Dallas Goodwill Industries, United Fund Dallas, Presbyn. Hosp., Dallas.; Trustee Tex. Presbyn. Found.; bd. dirs., vice chmn. Children's Med. Center of Dallas. Served to capt. USMCR, 1950-53. Mem. Dallas Salesmanship Club, Fin. Execs. Inst., Va. Mil. Inst. Alumni Assn. (pres. N. Tex. chpt. 1959), Kappa Alpha. Presbyn. (deacon). Clubs: Dallas Country (bd. govs.), Dallas Petroleum., Preston Trail Golf. Office: Merrill Lynch 4625 Thanksgiving Tower Dallas TX 75201

FULHAM, GERARD AQUINAS, business executive; b. Winthrop, Mass., Mar. 7, 1920; s. John N. and Mary E. (Maloney) F.; m. Barbara Ann McGoldrick, Feb. 22, 1944; children: John Bernard, Trudy Deane Fulham Sullivan, Gerarda Marie, Gerard Aquinas, Barbara Ann, Maura Jude. A.B., Harvard U., 1942. With Estabrook & Co., Boston, 1946-47; pres., treas. Fulham Bros., Inc., Boston, 1947-57; fin. v.p. Cleve. Pneumatic Co., 1958-61; sr. v.p., dir. Pneumo Corp., Boston, 1961-69, chmn. bd., chief exec. officer, 1969—; pres. LaTouraine Coffee Co., Boston, 1961—, vice chmn. bd. dirs., 1963—; dir. Aeronca, Inc., Pineville, N.C. Served to lt. (s.g.) USNR, 1942-46. Mem. Woods Hole Oceanographic Instn. Clubs: Union (Cleve.); Engrs., Mchts., Harvard (Boston); Oyster Harbors (Osterville, Mass.). Home: 84 Windswept Way Osterville MA 02655 Office: 4800 Prudential Tower Boston MA 02199

FULK, ROSCOE NEAL, accountant; b. Lebo, Kans., June 23, 1916; s. Roscoe Lloyd and Maude (Calvert) F.; m. Marie Therese Rabbitt, June 15, 1946; children: Thomas, Janet, David, Robert, Kenneth, Howard. B.S., U. Ill., 1940. With Ernst & Ernst (C.P.A.s), Chgo., 1940-76, partner, 1957-76; mem. Ill. Bd. Examiners in Accountancy, 1976-79; treas. Exec. Service Corps, Chgo. Treas. Winnetka (Ill.) Caucus Com., 1956, vice chmn., 1962; chmn. accountants group United Republican Fund Ill., 1958, Met. Crusade of Mercy, 1970; pres. Civic Fedn. Chgo., 1968-70; Pres. New Trier Twp. Citizens League, 1961-65, now mem. bd.; mem. Gov.'s Adv. Council, 1969-73; mem. adv. com. to Coll. Commerce and Bus. Administrn., U. Ill., 1970-76; pres., dir. Juvenile Protective Assn., 1970-73; v.p., bd. govs. Chgo. Met. Housing and Planning Council, 1970-75; chmn. Winnetka Zoning Bd. Appeals, 1968-71; mem. Parking Adv. Council Chgo., 1970-74; mem. grand council Am. Indian Center, 1973-76; chmn. pres.'s council bus. assos. Elmhurst Coll., 1969-70; bd. dirs. U. Ill. Found., 1973-79, State Equity Council, 1969-72; pres. United Charities Chgo., 1973-75; v.p. Catholic Charities Chgo., 1973-75, Met. Easter Seal Soc. Chgo., 1973-77; pres.' council U. Chgo., 1973-76; treas. Exec. Service Corps. Chgo.; bd. dirs. St. Francis Hosp., Evanston, Ill.; trustee, treas. Chgo. Orchestral Assn., 1977-80. Served to lt. USNR, 1942-46. Mem. Am. Inst. C.P.A.s (mem. council 1968-72), Ill. Soc. C.P.A.s (dir. 1963-64, pres. 1969-70), Chgo. Assn. Commerce and Industry (dir. 1975-77). Clubs: Sunset Ridge Country (Winnetka) (dir. 1961-65, treas. 1965-66); Mid-Am., Economic (dir. 1967-79), Comml. (Chgo.); Paradise Valley Country (Phoenix). Home: 227 Church Rd Winnetka IL 60093 Office: 150 S Wacker Dr Chicago IL 60606

FULKERSON, WILLIAM MEASEY, JR., college president; b. Moberly, Mo., Oct. 18, 1940; s. William M. and Edna Frances (Pendleton) F.; m. Grace Carolyn Wisdom, May 26, 1962; children: Carl Franklin, Carolyn Sue. B.A., William Jewell Coll., 1962; M.A., Temple U., 1964; Ph.D., Mich. State U., 1969. Asst. to assoc. prof. Calif. State U.-Fresno, 1966-73, asst. to pres., 1971-73; assoc. exec. dir. Am. Assn. State Colls., Washington, 1973-77; acad. v.p. Phillips U., Enid, Okla., 1977-81; pres. Adams State Coll., Alamosa, Colo., 1981—. Author: Planning for Financial Exigency, 1973; contbr. articles to profl. jours. Commr. North Central Assn., Chgo., 1980—; bd. dirs. Acad. Collective Bargaining Info. Service, Washington, 1976, Office for Advancemnet Pub. Negro Colls., Atlanta, 1973-77. Named Disting. Alumni William Jewell Coll., 1982. Mem. Am. Assn. State Colls. and Univs. (parliamentarian), Am. Council on Edn., Alamosa C. of C. (dir., pres 1984, Citizen of Yr. award 1983). Lodge: Rotary. Address: Office of President Adams State Coll Alamosa CO 81102

FULLAGAR, WILLIAM WATTS, lawyer; b. Chgo., July 3, 1914; s. William Watts and Grace (Wilson) F.; m. Doris Virginia Olson, Feb. 11, 1956 (dec. Oct. 29, 1979). B.S., Northwestern U., 1937; LL.B., Chgo. Kent Coll., 1942. Bar: Ill. bar 1942. With loan dept. First Nat. Bank & Trust Co., Evanston, Ill., 1938-43; partner firm Rooks, Pitts, Fullagar & Poust, Chgo.,; instr. comml. law Am. Inst. Banking, Chgo., 1947-51. Mem. Am., Ill., Chgo. bar assns., Alpha Delta Phi. Republican. Presbyterian. Club: Union League (Chgo.). Home: 2320 Isabella St Evanston IL 60201 Office: 55 W Monroe St Chicago IL 60603

FULLANGAR, PAUL DAVID, geology educator, geochemical consultant; b. Fort Edward, N.Y., Dec. 19, 1938; s. William Alfred and Evelyn Louise (Hoyt) Fullagar; m. Patricia Ann Kelley, June 6, 1959; children: Scott David, Eric Craig. A.B., Columbia U., 1960; Ph.D., U. Ill, 1963. Asst. prof. Old Dominion Coll., Norfolk, Va., 1963-67, U. N.C., Chapel Hill, 1967-69, assoc. prof., 1969-73, prof. dept. geology, 1973—, chmn. dept., 1979—; analytical geochemist Goddard Space Flight Ctr., Greenbelt, Md., 1964-69. Contbr. articles to profl. jours. Gen. Motors scholar Columbia U., 1956-60; fellow U. Ill., 1961; Shell fellow, 1962-63; research grantee NSF, 1964—; grantee N.C. Bd. Sci. and Tech., 1968, So. Regional Ednl. Bd., 1982. Fellow Geol. Soc. Am., Geochem. Soc.; mem. Am. Geophys. Union, AAAS, AAUP, Nat. Assn. Geology Tchrs. Democrat. Home: 312 Glenwood Dr Chapel Hill NC 27514 Office: Dept Geology U NC Chapel Hill NC 27514

FULLENWEIDER, DONN CHARLES, lawyer; b. Milw., Jan. 25, 1935; s. Russell Charles and Anne Mae (Murphy) F.; m. Jerrie Rabon, June 23, 1962; 1 son, Keith Rabon. B.S., U. Houston, 1957, J.D., 1958. Bar: Tex. bar 1958; Cert. in family law and civil trials Tex. Bd. Legal Specialization. Asso. law firm with Fred Parks, Houston, 1958-65; partner Haynes & Fullenweider, Houston, 1965—; Adj. asso. prof. law U. Houston Bates Coll. Law, 1972-74. Mem. 43d Joint Civilian Orientation Conf., 1973; mem. Tex. Bd. Legal Specialization, 1977-81. Fellow Tex. Bar Found. (dir. 1973-76), Am. Acad. Matrimonial Lawyers (pres. Tex. chpt. 1979-81); mem. ABA, Houston Bar Assn. (treas. 1961-62, 2d v.p. 1962-63, dir. 1971, 73, 1st v.p. 1970-73, outstanding service award 1974), State Bar Tex. (dir. 1973-76, chmn. bd. 1975-76, exec. com. 1976-77, chmn. litigation sect. 1979-81), Am. Trial Lawyers Assn., Houston Trial Lawyers Assn. (v.p. 1971), Def. Orientation Conf. Assn., Houston C. of C., Sigma Chi, Phi Delta Phi. Club: River Oaks Country. Home: 3821 Del Monte Houston TX 77019 Office: 2701 Fannin St Houston TX 77002

FULLER, ANNE ELIZABETH HAVENS, educator, university official; b. Pomona, Calif., Jan. 20, 1932; d. Paul Swain and Lorraine Elizabeth (Hamilton) Havens; m. Martin Emil Fuller, II, June 17, 1961; children: Katharine Hamilton, Peter David Takashi. A.B., Mount Holyoke Coll., 1953; B.A. (Fulbright scholar), Somerville Coll., Oxford U., 1955, M.A., 1959; Ph.D. (Univ. fellow), Yale U., 1958. Instr. English, Mount Holyoke Coll., 1957-59, instr., Pomona Coll., 1959-61; asst. prof. U. Fla., Gainesville, 1961-63; lectr. U. Denver, 1964-68, 71-73; asso. prof., chmn. center for lang. and lit. Prescott (Ariz.) Coll., 1968-70; tchr. Colo. Rocky Mountain Sch., 1970-71; dean of faculty Scripps Coll., Claremont, Calif., 1973-80, prof. English, 1973-80; spl. asst. to pres., sec. to corp. Claremont U. Center, 1981-83; v.p. for acad. affairs Austin Coll., Sherman, Tex., 1983—; mem. SW dist. Rhodes Scholar Selection Com., 1975-83. Bd. dirs. Am. Council on Edn., 1979-81. Mem. Assn. Am. Colls. (dir. 1977—, chmn. 1980-81), Am. Conf. Acad. Deans (dir. 1976-79), Commn. on Women in Higher Edn., Am. Assn. Higher Edn., Modern Lang. Assn. Am., Coll. English Assn., Modern Humanities Research Assn., Nat. Council Tchrs. English. Democrat. Episcopalian. Home: 823 N Grand Ave Sherman TX 75090 Office: Austin College Sherman TX 75090

FULLER, BENJAMIN FRANKLIN, physician, educator; b. St. Paul, Aug. 7, 1922; s. Benjamin Franklin and Luella Amelia (Pfaff) F.; m. Carol Marie Myre, Sept. 24, 1945; children—Constance J., Benjamin F., Geraldine A., Lynn M. B.A., U. Minn., 1942, B.S., 1943, M.D., 1946, M.S. in Internal Medicine, 1950. Intern U. Minn. Hosp., Mpls., 1945-46; also resident in medicine; fellow in internal medicine Mayo Found., 1947-50; practice medicine specializing in internal medicine, St. Paul, 1951-66; prof., head dept. family practice and community health U. Minn., Mpls., 1968-71, prof. dept. internal medicine, head primary care sect., 1972—; chief of staff United Hosps. of St. Paul, 1983—. Author: Physician or Magician?, 1978. Served with USAF, 1946-47, 53. Fellow A.C.P., Am. Coll. Angiology; mem. Ramsey County Med. Soc., Minn. Acad. Medicine, Minn. Med. Assn., AMA, Assn. Minn. Internists (pres.), St. Paul Soc. Internal Medicine (pres.), Sigma Xi, Alpha Omega Alpha. Methodist. Home: 2641 S Shore Blvd White Bear Lake MN 55110 Office: 3615 Grand Ave White Bear Lake MN 55110 *A variety of hero figures, both real (e.g. Abraham Lincoln) and fictional (e.g. Martin Arrowsmith) have exerted a major influence on my life. I am disturbed by the gradual destruction of heroes in our current society.*

FULLER, CHARLES, playwright; b. Phila., Mar. 5, 1939; s. Charles Henry and Lillian (Anderson) F.; m. Miriam A. Nesbitt, Aug. 4, 1962; children—Charles III, David. Student, Villanova U., 1956-58, hon. degree, 1983, LaSalle Coll., 1965-67, hon. degree, 1982. Plays include Perfect Party, 1968, Candidate, 1974, The Brownsville Raid, 1976, Zooman and the Sign, 1980, A Soldier's Play, 1982 (Pulitzer prize, Drama Critics award, Outer Circle Critics award, Theatre Club award 1982). Served with AUS, 1959-62. Creative Artists in Public Service grantee, 1975; Nat. Endowment Arts grantee, 1976; Rockefeller Found. grantee, 1976; Guggenheim Found. fellow, 1977-78; recipient Obie award, 1981, Audelco award as best playwright, 1982. Mem. Writers Guild Am. East, Dramatists Guild. Roman Catholic. Office: Esther Sherman care William Morris Agy 1350 6th Ave New York NY 10019 *I have always sought wisdom and humility, using one to counterbalance the other.*

FULLER, CRAIG L., Presidential assistant; b. Pasadena, Calif., Feb. 16, 1951; s. Robert D. and Alta L. (Herring) F. B.S. in Polit. Sci, UCLA, 1973; M. Urban Affairs, Occidental Coll., 1974. Mem. task force on local govt. reform Gov. Office State of Calif., Sacramento, 1973; mgr. public affairs Pacific Mut. Life Ins. Co., Los Angeles, 1974-77; v.p., sec. Deaver & Hannaford, Inc., Los Angeles, 1977-81; asst. for cabinet affairs Pres. of U.S., Washington, 1981—. Chmn. Calif. Adv. Comn. on Youth, 1973-74. Mem. Aircraft Owners and Pilots Assn. Republican. Club: Jonathan (Los Angeles). Office: The White House Washington DC 20500

FULLER, DEREK JOSEPH HAGGARD, educator, mathematician; b. London, Eng., June 17, 1917; came to U.S., 1965; s. Brian Maitland and Olive (Haggard) F. B.S. in Engring, U. Witwatersrand, Johannesburg, S. Africa, 1950; M.Sc., U. S.Africa, 1960; A.M., Ph.D., UCLA, 1963. Lectr. Pius XII Coll., Basutoland, Africa, 1950-59; sr. lectr. U. Basutoland, 1963-65; prof. math. Creighton U., 1965—. Served with RAF, 1941-46. Mem. Vatican Philatelic Soc. Home: 5050 Grover St Apt 10 Omaha NE 68106

FULLER, GILBERT AMOS, manufacturing company executive; b. Salt Lake City, Jan. 23, 1941; s. Noel A. and Matilda T. F.; m. Lynda Merle Caldwell, June 27, 1967; children: Brittany, Brandon, Scott, Cambrey. B.S., U. Utah, 1966, M.B.A., 1967. Sr. auditor Coopers Lybrand, Salt Lake City, 1969-70; controller Boyles Bros. Drilling Co., Salt Lake City, 1970-72; asst. treas. Christensen, Inc., Salt Lake City, 1972-74, treas., 1974-78, asst. v.p. fin., 1978-80, v.p. fin., treas., 1980—; v.p. fin. Transp. Safety Systems, Salt Lake City, 1974-78; dir. Modern Alloys, Inc., Stanton, Calif., Winder Dairy, Inc., Salt Lake City. Mem. Am. Inst. C.P.A.s, Utah Assn. C.P.A.s, Nat. Assn. Corp. Treas. Republican. Mormon. Office: Norton/Christensen Inc PO Box 26185 Salt Lake City UT 84126

FULLER, HARRY LAURANCE, oil company executive; b. Moline, Ill., Nov. 8, 1938; s. Marlin and Mary Helen (Ilsley) F.; m. Nancy Lawrence, Dec. 27, 1961; children: Kathleen, Laura, Randall. B.S. in Chem. Engring., Cornell U., 1961; J.D., DePaul U., 1965. Bar: Ill. 1965. With Standard Oil Co. (and affiliates), 1961—, sales mgr., 1972-74, gen. mgr. supply, 1974-77, exec. v.p., Chgo., 1977-78; pres. Amoco Oil Co., 1978—; exec. v.p., dir. Standard Oil, Ind., 1981-83, pres., 1983—; mem. internat. adv. council Chase Manhattan Corp. Bd. dirs. Chgo. Rehab. Inst., Central DuPage Hosp.; vis. com. DePauw U.; trustee Northwestern U.; bd. dirs. central area com. Chgo. United. Mem. Ill. Bar Assn. Republican. Presbyterian. Clubs: Mid-Am., Chgo. Golf, Chicago. Office: 200 E Randolph Dr Chicago IL 60601

FULLER, JACK GLENDON, JR., plastics engineer; b. Ft. Lewis, Wash., Feb. 25, 1923; s. Jack Glendon and Matilda Margaret (Kindschi) F.; m. Nancy Dorr Tatnall, May 14, 1945; children: Jack Glendon III, Margaret Tatnall, Pamela Dorr, Joellen Swift, Charlotte Mahaffy. B.S., Dickinson Coll., 1947; postgrad. in high polymer chemistry, U. Del., 1947-48. Prodn. engr. Master Plastics, Wilmington, Del., 1946-48; research chemist Hercules Powder Co., Parlin, N.J., sr. tech. rep., Boston and Wilmington, mgr. plastics sales, Los Angeles, 1948-58; v.p. sales and gen. mgr. Chemtrol div. Rexall Drug & Chem. Co., 1958-60; nat. sales mgr. Ankerwerk Internat., 1960-62; pres. Polymer Machinery Corp., Berlin, Conn., 1962-82, chmn. bd., 1983-84; pres., dir. Wilmington Terminal Co., Inc., Wilmington, Del., 1967-75; exec. v.p., dir. Molding Systems, Inc., Berlin, 1968-82; chmn. bd. dirs. Plastics Edn. Found., 1973-74. Author numerous tech. papers. Served to 1st lt. AUS, 1943-46. Mem. Soc. Plastics Engrs. (disting. mem.; nat. council 1959, 60, treas. 1962, internat. pres. 1963), Soc. Plastics Industry (nat. dir. at large 1976-79, 80-82, exec. com. machinery div. 1973-84, chmn. machinery div. 1980-82), Plastic Pioneers. Home: 993 Mountain Rd Cheshire CT 06410 Office: 154 Woodlawn Rd Berlin CT 06037

FULLER, JACK WILLIAM, journalist; b. Chgo., Oct. 12, 1946; s. Ernest Brady and Dorothy Voss (Tegge) F.; m. Alyce Sue Tuttle, June 2, 1973; 1 son, Timothy. B.S., Northwestern U., 1968; J.D., Yale U., 1973. Bar: Ill. 1974. Reporter Chgo. Tribune, 1973-75, Washington corr., 1977-78, editorial writer, Chgo., 1978-79, dep. editorial page editor, 1979-82, editorial page editor, 1982—; spl. asst. to atty. gen. U.S. Dept. Justice, Washington, 1975-77. Author: Convergence, 1982 (Cliff Dwellers award 1983), Fragments, 1984. Served with U.S. Army, 1969-70. Recipient Gavel award ABA, 1979. Mem. Am. Soc. Newspaper Editors, Nat. Conf. Editorial Writers. Office: Chicago Tribune 435 N Michigan Ave Chicago IL 60611

FULLER, JACKSON FRANKLIN, electrical engineering educator; b. Salt Lake City, Oct. 1, 1920; s. James Emmett and Mary Wesley (Williams) F.; m. Jean Ruth Moulton, June 6, 1942; children: John B., Bruce E., Stephen T., Hilary A. B.S. with honors in Elec. Engring., U. Colo., 1944. Registered prof. engr., Colo., N.Mex. Text engr. Gen. Electric Co., Lynn, Mass., test engr., Fort Wayne, Ind., 1941, systems engr., Sechenectady, 1941-45, systems application engr., Denver, 1945-69; prof. elec. engring. U. Colo., Boulder, 1969—, prof., assoc. chmn. dept. elec. engring., 1979—. Patentee in field. Bd. dirs. Denver Parks and Recreation, 1961-65, Denver War-on-Poverty, 1965-67, Denver Bd. Edn., 1961-67; trustee La Foret Camps, Denver, 1956-71. Recipient Community Service award Elfun Soc., 1963, teaching Recognition award U. Colo., 1972, Disting. Engr. Alumnus award, 1974, Power Educator award Edison Electric Inst., 1977. Fellow IEEE; mem. Tau Beta Pi, Sigma Tau, Eta Kappa Nu. Republican. Presbyterian. Home: 2891 Ellison Pl Boulder CO 80302 Office: Dept Elec Engring U Colo Boulder CO 80309

FULLER, JAMES CHESTER EEDY, chem. co. exec.; b. Toronto, Can., June 5, 1927; came to U.S., 1968; s. James Clifford and Marion Winifred (Eedy) F.; m. Doris Shirley Johnson, June 16, 1951; children—Hilary, John. B.S.A., U. Toronto, 1948; M.B.A., U. Western Ont., 1955. Sales and mktg. ofcl. Uniroyal Chem. Co., 96414and Ont., Can., 1948-53, 55-64; with Armak Co. and affiliates, 1964—; gen. mgr. Armour Indsl. Chems., Ltd., Toronto, 1964-68, nat. sales mgr., asst. to pres., internat. dir., Chgo., 1968-70; mng. dir. Armour Hess Chems., Ltd., Harrogate, Yorkshire, Eng., 1970-73; exec. v.p. Armak Co., Chgo., 1973-74, pres., 1975—. Mem. Chem. Inst. Can. Clubs: Farmers (London); Chgo. Athletic; Univ. (N.Y.C.). Office: 300 S Wacker Dr Chicago IL 60606

FULLER, JOHN GARSED CAMPBELL, food and drug co. exec.; b. Phila., Dec. 16, 1930; s. William Duncan and Katherine Harper (Campbell) F.; m. Elizabeth Ann Dobbins, Nov. 29, 1969; 1 dau., Sarah. A.B., Harvard, 1952, M.B.A., 1958. Engaged in marketing and distbn. Acme Markets, Inc., Phila., 1958-66, asst. treas., 1966-69, treas., 1969-73; v.p. finance, treas. Am. Stores Co., 1973—. Trustee, Treas. Germantown Hist. Soc. Served with Naval Intelligence USNR, 1952-56. Republican. Episcopalian. Clubs: Harvard, Cricket (Phila.). Home: 3910 Vaux St Philadelphia PA 19129 Office: 175 Strafford Ave Wayne PA 19087

FULLER, JOHN GRANT, author, columnist, documentary film producer-dir.; b. Phila., Nov. 30, 1913; s. John Grant and Alice (Jenkins) F.; m. Elizabeth Brancae, Nov. 17, 1976; children (by previous marriage)—Judd Wheatley, John Grant III, Geoffrey Tousley. A.B., Lafayette Coll., 1936. Engaged in pub. and industry, 1936-49; sales promotion mgr. NBC, 1949-53. Producer: TV series Road to Reality, 1960-61; writer, dir.: Twentieth Century, 1958-59, Conquest, 1957, du Pont Show of the Week, 1962, writer: Home Show, 1953-55, Garry Moore Show, 1956, Candid Camera staff, 1957, others; producer: Great Am. Dream Machine (Emmy award 1971), Nat. Ednl. TV, 1971; columnist: Trade Winds in Sat. Rev, 1957-67; contbr. to: Reader's Digest; also documentary film producer and dir.; producer, writer, dir. documentaries for, USIA, NBC-TV, ABC-TV, CBS-TV, Nat. Ednl. TV.; Author: plays The Pink Elephant, 1953, Love Me Little, 1959; books Gentlemen Conspirators, 1962, The Money Changers, 1962, Incident at Exeter, 1966, Interrupted Journey, 1966, Games for Insomniacs, 1966, The Day of St. Anthony's Fire, 1968, Aliens in The Skies, 1969, The Great Soul Trial, 1969, 200,000,000 Guinea Pigs, 1972, Fever: The Hunt for a New Virus Killer, 1973 (N.Y. Acad. Scis. award), Arigo, 1974, We Almost Lost Detroit, 1975, The Ghost of Flight 401, 1976, The Poison That Fell From the Sky, 1978 (ALA award), The Airmen Who Would Not Die, 1979. Recipient award Nat. Assn. Improvement Mental Health, 1961, Nat. Assn. Womens Clubs for Road to Reality, 1961; Sigma Delta Chi award for Light Across the Shadow (TV documentary), 1966; Distinguished Alumnus award Lafayette Coll., 1972. Mem. Author's League, Dramatist's Guild, WGA, Director's Guild Am., Delta Kappa Epsilon, Pi Delta Epsilon. Democrat. Mem. Soc. of Friends.

FULLER, JOHN JOSEPH, financial executive, consultant; b. N.Y.C., June 23, 1931; s. John and Elizabeth C. (Finn) F.; m. Patricia M. Costanzo, Oct. 30, 1970; children by previous marriage: Audrey M., Kathy A., John E., George A. B.B.A., Pace U., 1958, postgrad., 1959; postgrad., Wabash Coll., 1967-69. Asst. v.p. Equitable Life, N.Y.C., 1968-70, regional v.p., 1971-72, v.p., 1973-79, sr. v.p., 1980-83; pres. Fuller Assocs., Fort Lee, N.J., 1983—. Chmn. bd. dirs. Palisades Gen. Hosp., North Bergen, N.J., 1981—; mem. pres.'s adv. council Pace U., N.Y.C., 1981—. Served with U.S. Army, 1951-53; Korea. Roman Catholic. Home: 54 Claremont Rd Fort Lee NJ 07024 Office: Fuller Assocs 54 Claremont Rd Fort Lee NJ 07024

FULLER, JOHN LANGWORTHY, ret. psychobiologist; b. Brandon, Vt., July 22, 1910; s. John H. and Joyce (Langworthy) F.; m. Ruth I. Parsons, Sept. 2, 1933; children: Mary Jean, Sarah Ann. B.S., Bates Coll., 1931; Ph.D., Mass. Inst. Tech., 1935. Instr. biology Sarah Lawrence Coll., 1935-36, Clark U., 1936-37; instr. zoology U. Maine, 1937-41, asst. prof., 1941-45, asso. prof., 1945-47; staff scientist Jackson Lab., Bar Harbor, Maine, 1947-58, sr. staff scientist, 1958-70, asst. dir. tng., 1958-63, asso. dir., 1963-70; prof. psychology SUNY, Binghamton, 1970-78, emeritus, 1978—; vis. lectr. Harvard U., 1964-65, AID-NSF India Program, 1968. Author: (with W.R. Thompson) Foundations of Behavior Genetics, 1978, Nature and Nurture, 1954,

Motivation, 1962, (with J. P. Scott) Genetics and Social Behavior of the Dog, 1965; contbr. sci. articles to profl. jours. Guggenheim fellow, 1955-56. Fellow Am. Psychol. Assn.; mem. Behavior Genetics Soc. (pres. 1973-74), Soc. for Study Social Biology (pres. 1982-84), Phi Beta Kappa, Sigma Xi. Democrat. Episcopalian. Home: PO Box 543 York ME 03909

FULLER, KEITH, newspaperman; b. Arlington, Kans., Jan. 10, 1923; s. Daniel Eugene and Sylvia (Glasgow) F.; m. Mattisue Scott, Aug. 10, 1946; children: Barbara Jean, Geoffrey Scott, Andrew Clayton. Student, Lamar Coll., Beaumont, Tex., 1940-41, So. Methodist U., 1945-47. Reporter Dallas Morning News, 1947-49; with Associated Press, 1949—, chief bur., Denver, 1959-64, asst. gen. mgr., N.Y.C., 1964-74, exec. v.p., dep. gen. mgr., from 1974, now pres., gen. mgr. Supervisory editor: The Torch is Passed, 1964. Served to capt. USAAF, World War II. Decorated Air medal; recipient William Allen White award, 1981. Mem. Phi Delta Theta. Episcopalian. Prisoner of war in Germany. Office: 50 Rockefeller Plaza New York NY 10020

FULLER, LAWRENCE JOSEPH, army officer, lawyer; b. Everett, Wash., Dec. 20, 1914; s. Harry J. and Lila (Lawrence) F.; m. Mary Elizabeth Matthews, Aug. 27, 1944; children—Patricia (Mrs. Harry C. Brundick), Victoria (Mrs. James V. Kelly, Jr.), Laureen (Mrs. Roy S. Payne), Mariel (Mrs. S. Douglas Roberts), Chan. A.A., Grand Rapids (Mich.) Jr. Coll., 1935; B.S., U.S. Mil. Acad., 1940; J.D., U. Mich., 1951; M.A., Stanford, 1957; student, Soochow U. Law Sh., 1958-59, Nat. War Coll., 1959-60; LL.M., George Washington U., 1962. Bar: Mich. bar 1951, Va. bar 1978, also U.S. Supreme Ct 1978. Commd. 2d lt. C.E. U.S. Army, 1940, advanced through grades to maj. gen., 1967; co. officer (3d Engr. Regt.), Schofield Barracks, Hawaii, 1940-42, comdg. officer, Camp Abbott, Ore., 1943, Europe, 1944-45; instr. Command and Gen. Staff Coll., Ft. Leavenworth, Kans., 1945-48; with Office Judge Adv. Gen., 1951-55, 60-63; student Chinese lang. and Chinese law, Taiwan, 1955-59; staff judge adv. UN Command, U.S. Forces Korea and U.S. 8th Army, 1963-64; asst. judge adv. gen. for civil law, 1963-67, dep. judge adv. gen., 1967-71; dep. dir. Def. Intelligence Agy. (attache affairs), 1971—; Mem. Presdl. Econ. Mission to Republic of Korea, 1952. Author: Country Law Study of China, 1959, Criminal Code of the Republic of China, 1960, Code of Criminal Procedure of the Republic of China, 1960, Police Law of the Republic of China, 1960, Examination of the Judicial System of Okinawa, 1961, Country Law Study of Thailand, 1962. Decorated D.S.M. (2), Legion of Merit, Army Commendation medal. Mem. Am., Fed., Inter-Am., Mich., Va. bar assns., Am. Soc. Internat. Law, Inst. Jud. Adminstrn., Washington Fgn. Law Soc., Internat. Legal Soc. Korea, Royal Asiatic Soc., Judge Advs. Assn., Assn. U.S. Army, Order of Coif. Home: 1122 Trotting Horse Ln Great Falls VA 22066 Office: Dept of Army Pentagon Washington DC 20310

FULLER, LAWRENCE ROBERT, newspaper publisher; b. Toledo, Sept. 9, 1941; s. Kenneth M. and Marjory A. F.; m. Suzanne Hovik, May 7, 1967; children—Elizabeth, Michael. B.J., U. Mo., 1963. Reporter Mason City (Iowa) Globe-Gazette, 1963-67; successively reporter, asst. city editor, city editor Mpls. Star, 1967-75; exec. editor Owensboro (Ky.) Messenger-Inquirer, 1975-77, Argus Leader, Sioux Falls, S.D., 1977-78, publisher, 1978—. Bd. dirs. Sioux Falls United Way, Sioux Falls YMCA, Childrens Inn, Sioux Falls, Sioux Falls Downtown Devel. Corp., Zool. Soc. Sioux Falls. Served with USAR, 1965-71. Mem. AP Mng. Editors Assn. (dir.), Am. Newspaper Pubs. Assn., S.D. Press Assn., Inland Daily Press Assn., Sioux Falls C. of C. (chmn. mktg. adv. council 1980—). Club: Minnehaha Country. Home: 2008 S Phillips Ave Sioux Falls SD 57105 Office: 200 S Minnesota Ave Sioux Falls SD 57102

FULLER, MARK ADIN, JR., forest products company executive; b. Cin., Jan. 1, 1933; s. Mark Adin and Ellen Dudley (Webb) F.; m. Julia Dula Van Patten, June 9, 1956; children: Mark Adin, Ellen McClain, Mallory McKnight. B.A., Princeton U., 1954. With Champion Papers Corp., 1957—, v.p. sales, 1971-79, v.p., gen. mgr., 1979—, exec. v.p., 1980—,. Served with USN, 1954-57. Mem. Am. Paper Inst. Clubs: Princeton (N.Y.C.); Muirfield Village Golf., Woodway Country. Office: One Champion Plaza Stamford CT 06921

FULLER, MARVIN DON, former army officer, banker; b. Aberdeen, S.D., Dec. 10, 1921; s. Don Foster and Florence Mary (Nelson) F.; m. Myrtle May Starr, Dec. 11, 1943; children: Michael Brian, Marcia Marie. A.A., Sioux Falls Coll., 1941; A.B., Dakota Wesleyan U., 1946; postgrad., U. Minn., 1947-49; M.A., U. N.D., 1957, Harvard Bus. Sch., 1970. Served from aviation cadet to capt., A.C. U.S. Army, 1943-45; commd. (Regular Army), 1949, advanced through grades to lt. gen., 1976, served in inf. command and staff positions, U.S., Austria, Korea, Germany, Vietnam, 1949-71, asst. div. comdr., Ft. Riley, Kans., 1971-73; dep. chief staff for personnel Forces Command, Ft. McPherson, Ga., 1973-74; comdr. 1st Inf. Div., Ft. Riley, 1974-76; dir. mgmt. Office Chief Staff, U.S. Army, 1976; insp. gen. U.S. Army, 1976-77; comdg. gen. III Corps, Ft. Hood, Tex., 1977-80; ret., 1980; pres. Ft. Riley Nat. Bank, 1980—. Bd. dirs. Travelers Aid, Atlanta, 1973; chmn. Fed. Exec. Bd., Atlanta, 1974; bd. dirs. Coronado Area council Boy Scouts Am., 1975-76. Decorated D.S.M., Silver Star, Legion of Merit, D.F.C., Bronze Star medal, Air medal, Army Commendation medal. Mem. Assn. U.S. Army. (v.p. 5th region, treas. Ft. Riley chpt.). Lodge: Rotary (v.p. Junction City). Home: 1005 Lockstone Ct Junction City KS 66441 Office: Ft Riley Nat Bank PO Box 2446 Fort Riley KS 66442

FULLER, MARY MARGARET STIEHM, editor; b. Lincoln, Nebr., Apr. 23, 1914; d. Ewald Ortwin and Marie Daisy (Douglass) Stiehm; m. Curtis Gross Fuller, Sept. 24, 1938; children—Nancy Abigail Fuller Abraham, Michael Curtis. B.A., U. Wis., 1938. Free-lance writer, 1940-52; asst. editor FATE mag., 1952-54, exec. editor, 1954-56, editor, 1956-77, editor, asso. pub., 1977—; pres. Clark Pub. Co., Highland Park, Ill., 1949—; v.p., sec. Woodall Pub. Co., Highland Park, 1965—. Mem. Ill. Soc. Psychic Research (pres. 1966-68), Theta Sigma Phi, Alpha Phi. Home: 815 Deerpath Rd Lake Forest IL 60045 Office: 500 Hyacinth Pl Highland Park IL 60035

FULLER, MAURICE DELANO, lawyer; b. Eveleth, Minn., Oct. 3, 1898. A.B., U. Calif.-Berkeley, 1921, J.D., 1923. Bar: Calif. 1923. Assoc. firm Pillsbury, Madison & Sutro, San Francisco, 1923-40, ptnr., 1940—; chmn. Com. Bar Examiners of Calif., 1950. Mem. Calif. State Bar Assn., San Francisco Bar Assn. Home: Apt 9 2240 Hyde St San Francisco CA 94019 Office: Pillsbury Madison & Sutro Standard Oil Bldg 225 Bush St San Francisco CA 64104

FULLER, MELVIN STUART, botany educator; b. Livermore Falls, Maine, May 5, 1931; s. George Raymond and Hilda Gordon (Pike) F.; m. Barbara Paul Newman, Apr. 2, 1955; children: Erica Ann, Scott Eliot, Amy Elizabeth. B.S., U. Maine, 1953; M.S., U. Nebr., 1955; Ph.D., U. Calif., 1959; Master's ad eundum, Brown U., 1963. Instr. Brown U., 1959, asst. prof., 1960-63, assoc. prof., 1963-64; asst. prof. U. Calif., 1964-65, assoc. prof., 1965-68; prof. botany U. Ga., 1968—, head dept., 1968-73; vis. agrl. research biologist Sandor Ltd., Basel, Switzerland, 1983; mem. editorial bd. for publs. in biology McGraw Hill.; Sec. 2d Internat. Mycol. Congress. Author: The Science of Botany, 1962, Lower Fungi in the Laboratory, 1978. Mem. Bot. Soc. Am., Mycol. Soc. Am. (counselor 1966-68, 70-72, pres. 1975), Soc. Study of Growth and Devel. Research on growth and devel. aquatic fungi, ultrastructure. Home: 190 Spruce Valley Rd Athens GA 30605

FULLER, REGINALD HORACE, clergyman, educator; b. Horsham, Eng., Mar. 24, 1915; came to U.S., 1955; s. Horace and Cora L. (Heath) F.; m. Ilse Barda, June 17, 1942; children: Caroline Fuller Sloat, Rosemary Fuller Bazuzi, Sarah. B.A. with 1st class honours in Classics and Theology, Peterhouse Coll., Cambridge U., 1937, M.A., 1942; S.T.D., Gen. Theol. Sem., N.Y.C., 1960, Phila. Div. Sch., 1962; D.D., Seabury-Western Theol. Sem., Evanston, Ill. Ordained deacon Ch. of Eng., 1940, priest, 1941; curate in, Bakewell, Eng., 1940-43, Ashbourne-w-Mapleton, Eng., 1943-46, Birmingham, Eng., 1946-50; lectr. theology Queen's Coll., Birmingham, 1946-50; prof. theology St. David's Coll., Lampeter, Wales, 1950-55; exam. chaplain to Bishop of Monmouth, 1950-55; prof. N.T. lit. and langs. Seabury-Western Theol. Sem., Evanston, Ill, 1955-66; Baldwin prof. sacred lit. (N.T.) Union Theol. Sem., N.Y.C., 1966-72; adj. prof. Columbia U., 1969-72; prof. N.T., Va. Theol. Sem., 1972—, canon theologian of Brit. Honduras, also Bishop's commissary for U.S.A., 1968—; vis. prof. Grad. Theol. Union, Berkeley, 1975, Coll. Emmanuel and St. Chad, Saskatoon, Sask., Can., 1978; mem. study commn. World Council Chs., 1957-61; mem. Episcopal-Lutheran Conversations, 1969-72, 77-80, Anglican-Luth. Conversations, 1970-72, Luth.-Cath. Dialogue (U.S.A.) Task Force, 1971-73, 75-78, Rev. Standard Version Bible Com., 1981—. Author: (with R. Hanson) A Dissuasive, 1948, The Mission and Achievement of Jesus, 1954, (with G. Ernest Wright) The Book of Acts of God, 1957, What is Liturgical Preaching?, 1957, Luke's Witness to Jesus Christ, 1958, The New Testament in Current Study, 1962, Interpreting the Miracles, 1963, The Foundations of New Testament Christology, 1965, A Critical Introduction to the New Testament, 1966, (with B. Rice) Christianity and Affluence, 1966, Lent with the Liturgy, 1969, The Formation of the Resurrection Narratives, 1971, Preaching the New Lectionary, 1974, The Use of the Bible in Preaching, 1981, (with Phame Perkius) Who is This Christ?, 1983; contbr. books, encys.; translator: (D. Bonhoeffer) The Cost of Discipleship, 1948, Prisoner for God, 1954, (H.W. Bartsch, editor) Kerygma and Myth I, 1953, (R. Bultmann) Primitive Christianity, 1956, (J. Jeremias) Unknown Sayings of Jesus, 1957, (W. von Loewenich) Modern Catholicism, 1959, Kerygma and Myth II, 1962, (H. Flender) St. Luke Theologian of Redemptive History, 1967, (J. Moltmann and J. Weissbach) Two Studies in the Theology of Bonhoeffer, 1967, (A. Schweitzer) Reverence for Life, 1969, (T. Rendtorff) Church and Theology, 1971, (G. Bornkamm) The New Testament, A Guide to Its Writings, 1973, (E. Schweizer) The Holy Spirit, 1980. Recipient Schofield prize and Crosse studentship, 1938; fellow Am. Assn. Theol. Schs., 1961-62. Mem. Studiorum Novi Testamenti Societas (pres. 1983-84, editorial com. 1978-81), Chgo. Soc. Bibl. Research, Soc. Bibl. Lit. (com. hon. membership 1978-81). Home: Post Office Seminary Alexandria VA 22304

FULLER, RICHARD HARRISON, electronics co. exec.; b. San Francisco, Mar. 15, 1928; s. Harry Samuel and Elizabeth (Tatom) F.; m. Lorna Appel, Dec. 15, 1972; children—Dana Appel Valentine, Diane Joan. B.E.E., Calif. Inst. Tech., 1952; S.M., Mass. Inst. Tech., 1954; Ph.D., U. Calif., Los Angeles, 1963. Mgr. info. tech. research, then program mgr. plated wire memories Gen. Precision Inc., 1963-68; dir. engrng. devel. def. systems div. Univac Co., 1968-70; gen. mgr. Sperry Research Center, Sperry Corp., 1970-77; v.p. corporate tech. Emerson Electric Co., St. Louis, 1977-80; v.p. digital communications Gen. Instrument, N.Y.C., 1980—; lectr. engrng. U. Calif., Los Angeles, 1958-68. Author; Tech. editor: IEEE Computer mag, 1966-68; contbg. editor computer trans., 1963-68. Served with USNR, 1946-47. Ampex Telemeter Magnetics fellow, 1961. Fellow IEEE (chmn. Boston computer group 1971-72); mem. Sigma Xi, Tau Beta Pi. Patentee electronic circuits, digital computer tech. Home: 100 W 57th St New York NY 10019 Office: 1775 Broadway New York NY 10019

FULLER, ROBERT FERREY, lawyer; b. St. Paul, Aug. 11, 1929; s. Robert Garfield and Gwendolen (Ferrey) F.; m. Marcelle McIntosh, June 6, 1953; children—Julie, Gordon McIntosh. A.B. magna cum laude, Harvard, 1950, J.D., 1953. Bar: N.Y. bar 1956. Practiced in N.Y.C. with firm Patterson, Belknap & Webb, 1955-66; sec., gen. counsel Reuben H. Donnelley Corp., 1966-68; mng. dir. R.H. Donnelley Internat. Ltd., London, Eng., 1970-73; asst. sec., internat. counsel Am. Can Co., Greenwich, Conn., 1973—; underwriting mem. Lloyd's. Served to lt. (j.g.) USCGR, 1953-55; lt. comdr. Res.; ret. Mem. Inst. Dirs. (U.K.), Am., Internat. bar assns., Assn. Bar City N.Y., Westchester-Fairfield Corp. Counsel Assn. Republican. Presbyn. Clubs: Harvard (N.Y.C.); St. George's Hill Tennis (Weybridge, Eng.); Camp Fire (Chappaqua, N.Y.); Greenwich Country. Home: Pheasant Ln Greenwich CT 06830 Office: American Can Co American Ln Greenwich CT 06830

FULLER, SAMUEL, writer-director films, novelist; b. Worcester, Mass., Aug. 12, 1912; m. Christa, July 25, 1967; 1 dau., Samantha. Formerly reporter various newspapers including N.Y. Evening Jour., N.Y. Graphic, San Diego Sun, others. Writer-dir.: films I Shot Jesse James, 1948, The Baron of Arizona, 1949, The Steel Helmet, 1950, Fixed Bayonets, 1951, Park Row, 1952, Pickup on South Street, 1952, Hell and High Water, 1953, House of Bamboo, 1955, Run of the Arrow, 1956, China Gate, 1957, Forty Guns, 1957, Verboten, 1958, The Crimson Kimono, 1959, Underworld U.S.A., 1960, Shock Corridor, 1963, The Naked Kiss, 1963, Dead Pigeon on Beethoven Street, 1973, The Big Red One, 1980, White Dog, 1981, Merrill's Marauders, 1962; author: novels Crown of India, 1966, 144 Picadilly St, 1971, Dead Pigeon on Beethoven Street, 1973, The Big Red One, 1980, The Rifle, 1981. Served with inf. U.S. Army, World War II. Decorated Silver Star, Bronze Star. Office: care Chasin-Park-Citron 9255 Sunset Blvd Los Angeles CA 90069 *

FULLER, SAMUEL ASHBY, lawyer; b. Indpls., Sept. 2, 1924; s. John L.H. and Mary (Ashby) F.; m. Betty Winn Hamilton, June 10, 1948; children—Mary Cheryl Fuller Hargrove, Karen E. Fuller Wolfe, Deborah R. B.S. in Gen. Engring, U. Cin., 1946, LL.B., 1947. Bar: Ohio bar 1948, Ind. bar 1951. Cleve. claims rep. Mfrs. and Mchts. Indemnity Co., 1947-48; claims supr. Indemnity Ins. Co. N.Am., 1948-50; with firm Stewart, Irwin, Gilliom, Fuller & Meyer (formerly Murray, Mannon, Fairchild & Stewart), Indpls., 1950—; Pres., dir. Irsugo Consol. Mines, Ltd., 1953-80; dir. Ind. Pub. Health Found., Inc.; staff instr. Purdue U. Life Ins. and Mktg. Inst., 1954-61; instr. Am. Coll. Life Underwriters, Indpls., 1964-74. Bd. dirs. Southwest Social Centre, Inc., 1965-70; pres., dir. Westminster Village North, Inc. Mem. ABA, Ind. State Bar Assn., 7th Circuit Bar Assn., Indpls. Bar Assn. (treas. 1961-62), Am. Coll. Probate Counsel, Estate Planning Council Indpls. (pres. 1966), Internat. Assn. Ins. Counsel, Research Inst., Mil. Order Loyal Legion U.S. (recorder 1970-76, comdr. 1977), Ind. Pioneer Soc., Central Ind. Bridge Assn., Inc. (pres. 1969), Brookshire Homeowners Assn. (pres. 1973), English Speaking Union (treas. Indpls. br. 1974-79), Beta Theta Pi, Phi Delta Phi. Republican. Mem. Disciples of Christ. Clubs: Mason., Lawyers, Meridian Hills Country, Woodland Country (Indpls.) (pres. 1958). Home: 8543 Quail Hollow Rd Indianapolis IN 46260 Office: Mchts Bank Bldg Indianapolis IN 46204

FULLER, SAMUEL SPENCER, banker; b. Suffield, Conn., July 12, 1923; s. William S. and Amy F.; m. Jane Purtill; children: Thomas, James, Benjamin, Abigail. B.S., Williams Coll., 1947. Treas. Fuller-Griffin Tobacco Co., Suffield, 1947-55; adminstrv. asst. Hartford Nat. Bank & Trust Co., Conn., 1957, asst. trust officer, 1958-62, trust officer, 1962-67, v.p., 1967, sr. v.p., 1967-68, exec. v.p. in charge trust div., 1968—; dir. Ensign-Bickford Corp., Simsbury, Conn. Corporator Conn. Inst. for Blind, Hartford Hosp., Mt. Sinai Hosp.; pres. Ray Sch. Corp.; trustee Knox Found., Suffield Acad.; sec., trustee Bushnell Meml. Hall Corp. Served with USNR, 1943-46. Mem. Am. Bankers Assn. (exec. com. trust div.). Baptist. Clubs: Hartford, Williams. Office: 777 Main St Hartford CT 06115

FULLER, STEPHEN HERBERT, business educator; b. Columbus, Ohio, Feb. 4, 1920; s. Josiah Allen and Mary Ellen (Quinn) F.; m. Frances Gertrude Mulhearn, June 23, 1951; children: Teofilo M. (adopted), Mark Benton, Joseph Barry. A.B., Ohio U., 1941, Ph.D. (hon.), 1977; postgrad., Harvard U. Law Sch., 1941-42, I.A., 1943, M.B.A., 1947, D.C.S., 1958; Ph.D. (hon.), Ateneo De Manila U., 1964, De La Salle Coll., 1971, Ohio U., 1977, Lawrence Inst. Tech., 1978. Instr. econs. and labor relations Ohio U., 1947; with Harvard U., 1947-71, successively research asst., instr. Bus. Sch., 1947-61, asst. prof., assoc. prof., prof. Bus. Sch., 1961-71, dir. internat. tchrs. program Bus. Sch., 1959-60, 82—, asso. dean external affairs Bus. Sch., 1964-71; on leave to serve as pres. Asian Inst. Mgmt., Manila, 1969-71, now bd. govs.; v.p. in charge personnel adminstrn. and devel. staff Gen. Motors Corp., 1971-82; dir. Owens-Ill. Co., Scott Fetzer Co., Info. Sci., Inc. Author: (with others) Problems in Labor Relations, rev. edit, 1958. Mem. vis. com. on adminstrn. Harvard U., 169-78; mem. corp. Babson Coll., 1974-79; mem. trustees fund Ohio U., 1976—; trustee Loyola U., Chgo., 1971-74, Children's Hosp., Detroit; vice chmn. United Negro Coll. Fund Mich.; vice chmn. bd. trustees Gen. Motors Inst. Served to capt. AUS, 1943-46. Recipient Presdl. medal of Merit Republic of Philippines, 1971. Fellow Internat. Acad. Mgmt.; mem. Am. Arbitration Assn., Nat. Mgmt. Assn., Garfield Soc. of Hiram Coll., Philippine-Am. Soc., Phi Beta Kappa, Phi Eta Sigma, Omicron Delta Kappa, Beta Gamma Sigma, Delta Tau Delta. Home: Harvard University School of Business Administration Boston MA 02163

FULLER, SUE, artist; b. Pitts.; d. Samuel Leslie and Carrie (Cassedy) F. B.A., Carnegie Inst. Tech., 1936; M.A., Columbia U., 1939. Producer: movies String Composition, 1970, 74; one-woman shows, Bertha Schaefer Gallery, One-woman shows, McNay Art Inst., San Antonio, Norfolk Mus. Currier Gallery, Corcoran Gallery, Smithsonian Instn., others; exhibited in group shows, Aldrich Mus., Corcoran Gallery, Phila. Mus., Mus. Modern Art, Whitney Mus., Bklyn. Mus., others; represented in permanent collections, Addison Gallery Am. Art, Larry Aldrich Mus., Chgo. Art Inst., Des Moines Art Center, Ford Found., Met. Mus., Guggenheim Mus., Whitney Mus. Am. Art, Tate Gallery London, Library of Congress, others; commd. works include, Unitarian Ch. All Souls, N.Y.C., 1980, Tobin Library, McNay Art Mus., San Antonio, 1984. Recipient Alumni Merit award Carnegie Mellon U., 1974; Louis Comfort Tiffany fellow, 1948; Guggenheim fellow, 1949; Nat. Inst. Arts and Letters grantee, 1950; Eliot Pratt Found. fellow, 1966-68; Mark Rothko Found. grantee, 1973. Home: PO Box 1580 Southampton NY 11968 Office: Chalette Internat 9 E 88th St New York NY 10028

FULLER, THOMAS R., manufacturing executive; b. Cedar Rapids, Iowa, 1927; married. B.A., U. Wis. With Thomas Industries Inc., 1950—, v.p. sales residential lighting div., then corp. exec. v.p., 1958-72, pres., 1972—, chief exec. officer, 1979—, also dir.; dir. First Ky. Nat. Bank. Mem. Nat. Assn. Mfrs. (state dir.). Office: Thomas Industries Inc 207 E Broadway Box 35120 Louisville KY 40232

FULLER, WALLACE HAMILTON, research scientist, educator; b. Old Hamilton, Alaska, Apr. 15, 1915; s. Henry Ray and Bessie (Gaines) F.; m. Winifred Elizabeth Dow, Dec. 23, 1939; 1 dau., Pamela Elizabeth. B.S., Wash. State U., 1937, M.S., 1939; Ph.D., Iowa State U., 1942. Research asst. Wash. State U., Pullman, 1937-39; soil surveyor U.S. Dept. Agr., Lancaster, Wis., Neosho, Mo., 1939-40, bacteriologist, Beltsville, Md., 1945-47, soil scientist, 1947-48; research asso. Iowa State U., Ames, 1940-45; asso. prof., biochemist U. Ariz., Tucson, 1948-56, prof., biochemist, head dept. agrl. chemistry and soils, 1956-72, prof., biochemist soils, water and engrng. dept., 1972—; cons. Fellow Am. Soc. Agronomy and Soil Sci., AAAS, N.Y. Acad. Sci.; mem. Am. Chem. Soc., Am. Soc. Biol. Sci., Am. Soc. Plant Physiologists, Sigma Xi, Phi Kappa Phi, Phi Lambda Upsilon, Gamma Sigma Delta, Alpha Zeta. Presbyterian. Home: 5674 W Flying Circle Tucson AZ 85713 *Those heritages, disciplines, and experiences gained from my parents and grandparents provide invaluable guidelines for achieving humanitarian-oriented life-goals.*

FULLER, WILLIAM RICHARD, mathematics educator; b. Indpls., Oct. 27, 1920; s. Cyrus Holbrook and Gladys Beulah (Whelan) F.; m. Louella Myers Peterson, Apr. 23, 1943; children: William Richard, Theodore Daniel, James Holbrook. B.S., Butler U., 1948; M.S., Purdue U., 1951, Ph.D., 1957. Instr. Butler U., Indpls., 1948-49; mathematician U.S. Naval Ordnance Plant, Indpls., 1951-54; mem. faculty Purdue U., 1954—, prof. math., 1961—, asso. dean sci., 1965-76, chancellor North Central Campus,, 1978-82; cons. U.S. Navy, 1958-60, RCA Service Co., Patrick AFB, Fla., 1959. Author: FORTRAN Programming-A Supplement for Calculus Courses, 1977. Bd. dirs. Lafayette Symphony Orch., 1971-83. Served with AUS, 1942-45. Decorated Bronze Star; recipient Meritorious Civilian Service award U.S. Navy, 1955; Undergrad. Teaching award Amoco Found., 1976; named to Sagamore of Wabash, 1982. Mem. AAAS, Am. Math. Soc., Math. Assn. Am., Am. Soc. Engring. Edn. Office: Dept Math Purdue U West Lafayette IN 47907

FULLER, WILLIAM SAMUEL, state ofcl.; b. Rockford, Ill., June 2, 1926; s. William Arthur and Loyda Mae (Wylam) F.; m. Marjory LaVerne Thomas, June 11, 1950; children—Heidi, Grant, Thomas, Dirck. B.Mus., Westminster Choir Coll., Princeton, N.J., 1950; M.Mus., N. Tex. State Coll., Denton, 1951; Ed.D., Ind. U., 1960. Supr. choral music El Dorado (Ark.) public schs., 1951-54; research asso. adminstrv. studies and instl. relations Ind. U., 1956-58; specialist coll. and univ. facilities U.S. Office Edn., 1958-61; dir. Bur. Phys. Facilities Studies, Ind. U., 1961-64, Office Planning in Higher Edn., N.Y. State Dept. Edn., Albany, 1964-71, asst. commnr. higher edn., 1973-76. Dir. N.Y.C. Regents Adv. Council, 1971-73; exec. dir. Nebr. Coordinating Commn. Postsecondary Edn., Lincoln, 1976—; trustee Westminster Choir Coll. Served with USNR, 1944-46. Recipient Alumni Merit award Westminster Choir Coll., 1969. Mem. Assn. Instl. Research, Am. Assn. for Higher Edn., Soc. Coll. and United Planning, State Higher Edn. Exec. Officers Assn., Adult and Continuing Edn. Assn. Nebr. Methodist. Home: 3004 Stratford Ave Lincoln NE 68502 Office: Box 95005 301 Centennial Mall S Lincoln NE 68509

FULLER, WILLIAM SIDNEY, lawyer; b. Auburn, Ala., Aug. 9, 1931; s. William Melton and Ernestine (Tolbert) F.; m. Joyce Jeffrey, Nov. 5, 1953; children: Jeffrey Melton, Barbara Rush. A.B., Auburn U., 1953; LL.B., U. Ala., 1956. Bar: Ala. 1956. Student asst. to dean U. Ala. Law Sch., 1952-53; law clk. to U.S. dist. judge, Montgomery, Ala., 1956-57; practice law, Andalusia, 1957—; mem. firm Tipler & Fuller, 1957—; lectr. Southeastern Trial Inst.; Mem. grievance com. Ala. State Bar, 1968-71, mem. bd. commrs., 1979-81; Mem. law and contemporary affairs adv. council Auburn U. Author: Personal Injury Treatises. Mem. Am., Ala., Covington County bar assns., Am. Trial

Lawyers Assn., Ala. Plaintiff Lawyers Assn., Ala. Trial Lawyers Assn. (pres. 1968), Phi Delta Phi, Kappa Alpha, Alpha Phi Omega. Presbyterian (elder, trustee, past chmn. bd. deacons Sunday sch. tchr.). Club: Andalusia (dir., pres. 1972). Home: 100 South Ridge Rd Andalusia AL 36420 Office: Tipler Bldg Andalusia AL 36420

FULLERTON, BILL JUNIOR, ednl. adminstr.; b. Burlington, Okla., Mar. 21, 1926; s. William B. and Ethel G. (Bagenstos) F.; m. Jeannine A. Cohoe, Aug. 10, 1950; children—Billie Jean, Bobbi Lea. B.S., Northwestern Okla. State Coll., 1951; Ed.M., U. Okla., 1953, Ed.D., 1956. Tchr. Hazelton (Kans.) Pub. Schs., 1948-53; tchr. Norman (Okla.) Pub. Schs., 1953; grad. asst. U. Okla., 1953-54; dir. secondary edn. Southwestern Okla. State Coll., 1954-58; chmn. secondary edn. dept. Ariz. State U., Tempe, 1958-66, prof. edn., 1967—, dir. profl. field experiences, 1968-71; asso. dean Coll. Edn., 1971-78; dean Coll. Edn., Wichita (Kans.) State U., 1966-67; cons. U.S. Office Edn., Bur. Indian Affairs Schs., Danforth Found. Contbr. articles to profl. publs. Served with USNR, 1944-46. Am. Legion scholar, 1939-40. Mem. Nat. (exec. com. 1965-68, pres. 1972-73, Disting. mem. 1979), Ariz. assns. tchr. educators, North Central Assn., Nat. Council for Accreditation Tchr. Edn. Evaluation Bd. and Visitation Teams, Phi Delta Kappa, Kappa Delta Pi. Clubs: Mason, Rotarian. Home: 331 E Broadmor Dr Tempe AZ 85282

FULLERTON, CHARLES GORDON, astronaut; b. Rochester, N.Y., Oct. 11, 1936; s. Charles Renwick and Grace (Sherman) F.; m. Marie Jeanette Buettner, July 6, 1968. B.S., Calif. Inst. Tech., 1957, M.S. in Mech. Engring, 1958. Commd. 2d lt. USAF, 1958, advanced through grades to col., 1979; completed pilot tng., 1959, bomber pilot, Davis-Monthan AFB, Tucson, 1960-64, completed aerospace research pilot sch., Edwards AFB, 1965, bomber flight test pilot, 1966, astronaut, 1966-69, Houston, 1969—. Decorated DFC, NASA Exceptional Service medal, USAF Commendation medal, Meritorious Service medal, Outstanding Unit award, Nat. Def. Service medal. Assoc. fellow Soc. Exptl. Test Pilots; Mem. Tau Beta Pi. Office: Astronaut Office NASA Johnson Space Center Houston TX 77058 *

FULLERTON, CHARLES WILLIAM, insurance company executive; b. Columbus, Ohio, May 18, 1917; s. Paul O. and Marvina (Groom) F.; m. Anne Hoddy, Jan. 21, 1940; children—Gary, Lynn Fullerton Johnson. B.S., Ohio State U., 1938. C.P.A., Ohio. Dist. financial dir. FSA, Columbus, 1938-40; office mgr. Goodyear Tire & Rubber Co., Huntington, W.Va., 1940-41; chief accountant to v.p. finance Landmark Farm Bur., Columbus, 1941-66; v.p., sec., treas. Nationwide Devel. Co., Columbus, 1966-71; with Nationwide Ins. Affiliates, Columbus, 1971—, exec. v.p., 1972-73, pres., 1973—; v.p. Nationwide Ins. Co., 1973—; dir. Nationwide Devel. Co., Nationwide Communications, Inc., Nationwide Consumer Services, Inc., Heritage Securities, Inc.; bd. govs. Investment Co. Inst., Washington. Mem. steering com. Devel. Com. for Greater Columbus, 1977-79; bd. dirs. Greater Columbus Arts Council, Ohio Dominican Coll., Players Theatre of Columbus; active Downtown Action Com., Capitol Sq. Com. Mem. Am. Inst. C.P.A.'s, Ohio Soc. C.P.A.'s, Treas. Club of Columbus (past pres.), Nat. Soc. Accountants for Coops. (past pres.), Ohio Council Farmer Coops. (v.p.), Columbus Controllers Club. Methodist. Club: Masons. Home: 6861 Hardwood Dr Galloway OH 43119 Office: One Nationwide Plaza Columbus OH 43216 *To achieve the goals and objectives established for a business enterprise, I strive to set tasks and priorities in concert with the persons responsible for the results. This process is carried on in a manner that assists those persons to grow as individuals while the organization becomes stronger through the successful performance of those goals and objectives.*

FULLERTON, GAIL JACKSON, university president; b. Lincoln, Nebr., Apr. 29, 1927; d. Earl Warren and Gladys Bernice (Marshall) Jackson; m. Stanley James Fullerton, Mar. 27, 1967; children by previous marriage—Gregory Snell Putney, Cynde Gail Putney. B.A., U. Nebr., 1949, M.A., 1950; Ph.D., U. Oreg., 1954. Lectr. sociology Drake U., Des Moines, 1955-57; asst. prof. sociology Fla. State U., Tallahassee, 1957-60, San Jose (Calif.) State U., 1963-67, asso. prof., 1968-71, prof., 1972—, dean grad. studies and research, 1972-76, exec. v.p. univ., 1976-78, pres., 1978—; Bd. dirs. EUDUCOM/Nat Commn. Co-op. Edn. Author: Survival in Marriage, 2d edit, 1977, (with Snell Putney) Normal Neurosis: The Adjusted American, 2d edit, 1966. Carnegie fellow, 1950-51, 52-53; Doherty Found. fellow, 1951-52. Mem. Am., Internat. sociol. assns., Western Coll. Assn. (pres. 1982—), San Jose C. of C., Phi Beta Kappa. Home: 226 Wave Crest Ave Santa Cruz CA 95060 Office: San Jose State U San Jose CA 95192 *Our lives are the summations of the choices we make, one at a time, by intention or by default. I have tried to choose by deliberate and rational intent, so that even when the choice proves wrong, it is clear to me that I am responsible for myself.*

FULLERTON, WILLIAM D., health policy consultant, health educator; b. Mars, Pa., Dec. 9, 1927; s. Dean Melvin and June Audrey (Steele) F.; m. Julia Cordelia Cooper, Nov. 14, 1958; children: Catherine, Scott, James, Dirk. B.A., U. Rochester, 1951. Div. chief Social Security Adminstrn., Balt., 1960-66; specialist Library of Congress, Washington, 1966-70; staff health policy Com. Ways and Means, Washington, 1970-76; dep. adminstr. Health Care Fin. Adminstrn., Washington, 1977-78; pres. Health Policy Alternatives Inc., Washington, 1978—; adj. assoc. prof. U. N.C., Chapel Hill, 1982—. Contbr. articles to profl. jours. Served with U.S. Army, 1945-47. Recipient Ralph D. McGill award in govt. U. Rochester, 1951, Superior Service award HEW, 1966, 67, 78. Mem. Inst. Medicine. Democrat. Home: Route 1 Box 20-D Morrisville NC 27560 Office: Health Policy Alternatives Inc. 545 8th St SE Washington DC 20003

FULLMAN, JOHN PATRICK, U.S. judge; b. Gardenville, Pa., Dec. 10, 1921; s. Thomas L. and Mary (Nolan) F.; m. Alice Hilliar Freiheit, Apr. 15, 1950; children: Nancy, Sally, Thomas, Jeffrey. B.S. in Edn., Villanova U., 1942; LL.B., Harvard U., 1948. Bar: Pa. 1949. With firm Eastburn, Begley & Fullam, Bristol, Pa., 1948-60; judge Ct. Common Pleas, Bucks County, Pa., 1960-66, U.S. Dist. Ct. ea. dist. Pa., 1966—. Mem. Del. River Joint Toll Bridge Commn., 1955-60, chmn., 1958; Democratic candidate for Congress, 1954-56; trustee Bucks County Community Coll., 1964-76, 1st chmn., 1964-67; bd. dirs. New Sch. Music, 1975—. Home: Wrightstown PA 18940 Office: US Dist Ct US Courthouse Philadelphia PA 19106

FULLMER, CHARLES CURTIS, opera co. exec.; b. St. Paul, Jan. 27, 1926; s. Harry Buell and Hazel (Willis) F.; m. Beverly Constance Howey, Oct. 18, 1952; children—Constance, Charles Curtis, Lisa. B.A., Hamline U., St. Paul, 1950; postgrad., U. Minn., 1950. Vice pres. Pryor-Menz Concerts, Council Bluffs, Iowa, 1959-64; dir. devel. Minn. Orch., Mpls., 1964-72; exec. dir. Upper Midwest Regional Arts Council, St. Paul, 1972-74; gen. mgr. Minn. Opera Co., St. Paul, 1974—; bd. dirs. Opera Am., Nat. Opera Inst. Served with USN, 1943-46. Club: St. Paul Rotary (dir.). Office: 850 Grand Ave Saint Paul MN 55105

FULLMER, DANIEL WARREN, educator, psychologist; b. Spoon River, Ill., Dec. 12, 1922; s. Daniel Floyd and Sarah Louisa (Essex) F.; m. Janet Satomi Saito, June 1980; children: Daniel William, Mark Warren. B.S., Western Ill. U., 1947, M.S., 1952; Ph.D., U. Denver, 1955. Post-doctoral intern psychiat. div. U. Oreg. Med. Sch., 1958-61; Mem. faculty U. Oreg., 1955-66; prof. psychology Oreg. System of Higher Edn., 1958-66; faculty dept. edn. U. Hawaii, Honolulu, 1966—, now prof., 1974—; pvt. practice psychol. counseling; cons. psychologist Grambling State U., 1960-81; founder Free-Family Counseling Ctrs., Portland, Oreg., 1959-66, Honolulu, 1966-74; co-founder Child and Family Counseling Ctr., Waianae, Oahu, Hawaii; pres. Human Resources Devel. Ctr., Inc., 1974—; chmn. Hawaii State Bd. to License Psychologists, 1973-78. Author: Counseling: Group Theory & System, 2d. edit., 1978; co-author: Principles of Guidance, 2d. edit., 1977; author six counselor/cons. training manuals; editor: Bulletin, Oreg. Coop Testing Service, 1955-57, Hawaii P&G Jour., 1970-76; assoc. editor: Educational Perspectives, U. Hawaii Coll. Edn. Served with USNR, 1944-46. Recipient Francis E. Clark award Hawaii Personnel Guidance Assn., 1972, Governor's Award State of Hawaii, 1980. Mem. Am. Psychol. Assn., Am. Personnel and Guidance Assn. (Nancy C. Wimmer award 1963). Methodist. Office: 1750 Kalakaua Ave 809 Honolulu HI 96826 *I grew up along Spoon River. The people of Spoon River had a principle of life: Improve on what you are. The purpose is to be able to help others help themselves. From here, it is like stepping into a river of life; the deeper you got, the stronger the current. Then, suddenly, here you are nearing the delta. Just ahead lies a beautiful ocean.*

FULLMER, HAROLD MILTON, dental educator; b. Gary, Ind., July 9, 1918; s. Howard and Rachel Eva (Tiedge) F.; m. Marjorie Lucile Engel, Dec. 31, 1942; children: Angela Sue, Pamela Rose. B.S., Ind. U., 1942, D.D.S., 1944; hon. doctorate, U. Athens (Greece), 1981. Diplomate: Am. Bd. Oral Pathology. Intern Charity Hosp., New Orleans, 1946-47, resident, 1947-48, vis. dental surgeon, 1948-53; instr. Loyola U., New Orleans, 1948-49, asst. prof., 1949-50, assoc. prof. gen. and oral pathology, 1949-53; cons. pathology VA hosps., Biloxi and Gulfport, Miss., 1950-53; asst. dental surgeon Nat. Inst. Dental Research, NIH, Bethesda, Md., 1953-54, dental surgeon, 1954-56, sr. dental surgeon, 1956-60, dental dir., 1960-70; chief sect. histochemistry Nat. Inst. Dental Research, 1967-70, chief exptl. pathology, 1969-70, cons. to dir., 1971-72; mem. dental caries program adv. com. HEW, 1975-79, chmn., 1976-79; dir. Inst. Dental Research; Prof. pathology, prof. dentistry, asso. dean Sch. Dentistry, U. Ala. Med. Center, Birmingham, 1970—, sr. scientist cancer research and tng. program, sci. adv. com., 1977—; mem. med. research career devel. com. VA, 1977-81. Editor: (with R. D. Lillie) Histopathologic Technic and Practical Histochemistry, 1976, Jour. Oral Pathology, 1972—, Tissue Reactions, 1976—; assoc. editor: Jour. Cutaneous Pathology, 1973—, Oral Surgery, Oral Medicine, Oral Pathology, 1970. Mem. U.S. Congl. Adv. Bd. Served to capt. AUS, 1944-46. Recipient Isaac Schour award for outstanding research and teaching in anat. scis. Internat. Assn. Dental Research, 1973, Fulbright grantee, 1972; Disting. Alumnus of Year Ind. U. Sch. Dentistry, 1978, Ind. U., 1981. Fellow Am. Coll. Dentists, Am. Acad. Oral Pathology, AAAS (chmn. sect. 1976-78, sec. sect. 1979-87); mem. ADA (cons. Council Dental Research 1973-74), Internat. Assn. Dental Research (v.p. 1974-75, pres. 1976-77), Am. Assn. Dental Research (pres. 1976-77), Internat. Assn. Pathologists, Histochem. Soc., Nat. Soc. Med. Research (dir. 1977-79), Biol. Stain Commn. (trustee 1977—), Commd. Officers Assn., Internat. Assn. Oral Pathologists (co-founder, 1st pres., 1st editor 1978—). Club: Exchange (Birmingham) (pres. New Orleans 1952-53). Home: 3514 Bethune Dr Birmingham AL 35223

FULMER, HUGH SCOTT, physician, educator; b. Syracuse, N.Y., June 18, 1928; s. Herbert C. and Emily (Price) F.; m. Zola M. Jones, July 12, 1952; children: James, Kim, Scott. A.B., Syracuse U., 1948; M.D., SUNY-Syracuse, 1951; M.P.H., Harvard U., 1961. Intern R.I. Hosp., 1951-52; resident internal medicine SUNY-Syracuse, 1954-57; asst. dir., research asso. Navajo-Cornell Field Health Research Project, 1958-60; asst. prof. community medicine U. Ky. Coll. Medicine, 1960-64; asso. prof., 1964-66, prof., 1966-68; tech. cons. health Peace Corps, Malaysia, 1968-69; prof., chmn. dept. community and family medicine U. Mass. Med. Sch., 1969-77, asso. dean for clin. edn. and primary care, 1975-79, chief sect. gen. medicine, dept. medicine, 1978-83; dir. ambulatory and community services Carney Hosp., Boston, 1983—; clin. prof. medicine Boston U. Sch. Medicine and Pub. Health, 1983—. Served with M.C., USAF, 1952-54. Mem. Worcester Dist. Med. Soc., Mass. Med. Soc., AMA, Am. Soc. Internal Medicine, Am. Pub. Health Assn., Assn. Tchrs. Preventive Medicine (past pres.), Am. Inst. Community Health (v.p.), Am. Coll. Preventive Medicine, Am. Acad. Med. Dirs. Democrat. Presbyterian. Research on chronic disease, med. care, med. edn. Home: 61 Cherlyn Dr Northboro MA 01532 Office: 55 Lake Ave N Worcester MA 01605

FULMER, ROBERT M., bus. educator, author; b. Florence, Ala., Oct. 6, 1939; s. Robert and Reba I. (Smith) F.; m. Patsy Cohen Wallace, July 9, 1977; children from previous marriage: Robert Jeffrey, James Burton. B.A., David Lipscomb Coll., 1961; M.B.A., U. Fla., 1962; Ph.D., UCLA, 1965. Mem. advt. staff Procter and Gamble, 1962-63; chmn. dept. bus. adminstrn. Pepperdine Coll., 1963-66; research asso. Nat. Indsl. Conf. Bd., 1965; asso. prof. mgmt. Fla. State U., 1966-68; prof. mgmt. Ga. State U., 1968-73; George R. Brown prof. bus. Trinity U., 1973-76; Disting. prof. mgmt. Memphis State U., 1976-79; prof. mgmt., dir. exec. edn. Sch. Bus., Emory U., Atlanta, 1979—; exec. dir. Nat. Inst. Cert. Profl. Mgrs., 1974-76; dir. Acad. Mgmt., 1971-72, Exec. Counsel, Inc., 1968—. Author: The New Marketing, 1976, Practical Human Relations, 1977, 2d edit., 1982, The New Management, 3d edit., 1982, Exploring the New Management, 3d edit., (with Ted Herbert) A Practical Introduction to Business, 1975, 4th edit., 1984. Fellow Acad. Mgmt.; Mem. So. Mgmt. Assn. (pres. 1971, dir. 1968-72), Am. Mktg. Assn., World Future Soc., Am. Soc. Tng. and Devel. Republican. Office: Sch Bus Emory U Atlanta GA 30322

FULMER, VINCENT ANTHONY, university official; b. Alliance, Ohio, Oct. 23, 1927; s. Anthony and Catherine (Long) F.; m. Mary Alma Pineau, Dec. 27, 1950; children: Kevan, Kristine, David, Amy, Charles, Alma Leigh. A.B. cum laude, Miami U., Oxford, Ohio, 1949; postgrad., Harvard U., 1950; S.M., Mass. Inst. Tech., 1963; LL.D., Suffolk U., 1971; D.Sc., Fla. Inst. Tech., 1982. Mem. staff Mass. Inst. Tech., 1951—, exec. asst. office chmn., 1960-63, v.p., 1963-73, sec. inst., 1963—; sec. M.I.T. Corp., 1979—; v.p. adminstrn. William Underwood Co., 1973-75; instr. econs. Williams Coll., 1952; dir. Moleculon Research Corp., Polyform Corp., Questar Corp. Contbr. chpts. to books and mags. Bd. dirs. Planning Office for Urban Affairs Archdiocese Boston; trustee Suffolk U., 1972—, chmn., 1976-81; trustee Hawthorne Coll., 1982—, vice chmn., 1983—. Served with USNR, 1944-46. Mem. Am. Econ. Assn., AAAS, Ops. Research Soc. Am., Inst. Mgmt. Scis., Phi Beta Kappa, Sigma Chi, Omicron Delta Kappa. Home: 26 Kimball Rd Arlington MA 02174 Office: 77 Massachusetts Ave Cambridge MA 02139 *While we may as individuals address ourselves exclusively to high personal attainments within the existing framework of our institutions, or devote prodigious efforts to improve or restructure those institutions, in the end it is our lifetime example that counts more heavily than all else.*

FULOP, MILFORD, physician; b. N.Y.C., Nov. 7, 1927; s. Herman and Adele (Karl) F.; m. Christine Lawrence, Aug. 4, 1957; children: Michael Alain, Tamara Ann. A.B., Columbia U., 1946, M.D., 1949. Intern, then resident in medicine Presbyn. Hosp., N.Y.C., 1949-51, 53-55; practice medicine specializing in internal medicine, N.Y.C., 1955—; mem. faculty Albert Einstein Coll. Medicine, Bronx, N.Y., 1956—, prof. internal medicine, 1968—, acting chmn. dept. medicine, 1975-80, vice chmn. dept. medicine, 1980—; mem. staff, dir. med. service Bronx Mcpl. Hosp.; mem. staff Hosp. of Einstein Coll. Medicine. Served with M.C. USAF, 1951-53. Recipient Commendation medal. Mem. A.C.P., Assn. Am. Physicians, Phi Beta Kappa, Alpha Omega Alpha. Home: 630 W 246th St New York NY 10471 Office: 1300 Morris Park Ave New York NY 10461

FULTON, ALBERT ANDREW, insurance company executive; b. N.Y.C., Nov. 13, 1923; s. Theodore Cuyler and Esther (Ring) F.; m. Marie Cornell Free, July 30, 1948; children: Dorian Forrest, Deidre Emily, Mark, Damian, Tiffany, Marie. B.S., UCLA, 1951, M.S., 1971. Adminstrv. service mgr. Farmers Group, Inc., Los Angeles, 1958-64, adminstrv. sales mgr., 1964-69, bond analyst, 1969-75, dir. fixed income, 1975-81, v.p., treas., Los Angelese, 1981—. Served with USAAF, 1943-46. Recipient E.F. Hutton award Farmers Group, Inc., 1978. Mem. Los Angeles Soc. Fin. Analysts. Republican. Home: 30 Rainbow Falls Irvine CA 92715 Office: Farmers Group Inc 4680 Wilshire Blvd Los Angeles CA 90010

FULTON, CHARLES B., judge; b. 1910. Grad., Washington and Lee U.; J.D., U. Fla. Bar: Fla. 1935. Judge U.S. Dist. Ct. So. Dist. Fla., now sr. judge. Address: Federal Bldg 701 Clematis St West Palm Beach FL 33401 *

FULTON, EDMUND DAVIE, barrister, solicitor; b. Kamloops, B.C., Can., Mar. 10, 1916; s. Frederick John and Winifred M. (Davie) F.; m. Patricia Mary Macrae, Sept. 7, 1946; children: C. Mary, Patricia Fulton Lockwood, Cynthia A. B.A., U. B.C., 1936, St. John's Coll., Oxford (Eng.) U., 1939; LL.D., U. Ottawa, 1960, Queen's U., 1963. Bar: Called to bar 1940, Queen's counsel 1957. Partner firm Fulton, Morley, Verchere & Rogers, Kamloops, 1945-68, Fulton, Cumming, Richards & Co., Vancouver, to 1973; mem. Can. House of Commons, 1945-63, 65-68; minister justice, atty. gen., Can., 1957-62, acting minister citizenship and immigration, 1957-58, minister of pub. works, 1962-63; judge Supreme Ct. of B.C., 1974-81. Chmn. Can. del. Can.-U.S.A. Columbia River Treaty, Wash., 1961; Pres. Young Progressive Conservatives of Can., 1946-49; leader Progressive Conservative Party B.C., 1963-66; chmn. Law Reform Commn. B.C., 1969-73; Mem. senate U. B.C., 1948-57, 69-75. Served with Can. Army, 1940-45; overseas. Mentioned in despatches. Hon. mem. Fellows Am. Bar Found. Roman Catholic. Clubs: Vancouver; Shaughnessy Golf and Country (Vancouver); Rideau (Ottawa). Office: 1300 1090 W Georgia St Vancouver BC Canada V6E 3X9

FULTON, ETHEL MARGARET, university president; b. Birtle, Man., Can.; d. Ernest Bain and Ethel Mary (Futers) F. Teaching cert., Winnipeg Normal Sch.; phys. edn. cert., U. Minn.; B.A., U. Man., 1955; English specialist teaching cert., U. Toronto, 1956, Ph.D., 1968; M.A., U. B.C., 1963; D.Sc. (hon.), U. Moncton. William P. Huffman scholar-in-residence U. Miami, Oxford, Ohio; tchr. pub. secondary schs.; head dept. English Collegiate Inst., Thunder Bay, Ont.; asso. prof. Wilfred Laurier U.; asso. prof., dean of women U. B.C.; pres. Mt. St. Vincent U., Halifax, N.S.; dir. Fireman's Fund Ins. Co. of Can., North-South Inst. Contbr. articles to various jours. Ont. grad. fellow; named hon. class pres. Wilfred Laurier U., 1973; hon. fellow Ryerson Poly. Inst. Mem. Can. Assn. Univ. Tchrs., Assn. Can. Univ. Tchrs. English, Assn. Univs. and Colls. of Can., Assn. of Commonwealth Univs., Assn. of Atlantic Univs., Assn. Can. and Que. Lit., Can. Council Tchrs. of English, Can. Soc. for Study of Edn., Victoria Studies Assn., Can. Research Inst. for Advancement of Women, Am. Assn. for Higher Edn. Mem. United Ch. of Can. Office: Mt St Vincent U 166 Bedford Hwy Halifax NS B3M 2J6 Canada

FULTON, GEORGE PEARMAN, JR., biology educator; b. Milton, Mass., June 3, 1914; s. George P. and Lottie (Fulton) F.; m. Miriam Alice Hunt, Aug. 1942 (div. 1964); children: Margaret, Susan, Peter Herrick, George Pearman III; m. Mary D. Shanks, Mar. 1970. B.S., Boston U., 1936, M.A., 1938; Ph.D., 1941. Instr. biology Boston U., 1941-42, asst. prof. biology, 1947-49, assoc. prof., 1949-53, prof., 1953—, chmn. dept., 1956-74, chmn., 1956-74, Shields Warren prof., 1959—; indsl. physiologist Arthur D. Little, Inc., Boston, 1946-47; staff mem. Children's Cancer Research Found., 1964-73; vis. prof. Stanford Med. Sch., 1958; asst. dir. health affairs S.C. Commn. Higher Edn., 1974-82, spl. asst. to exec. dir., 1982—; Cons. div. nursing Pub. Health Services; mem. sci. adv. bd. New Eng. Aquarium; mem. adv. bd. on marine sci. and oceanography Mass. Bd. Higher Edn.; trustee Sea Edn. Assn., Shared Ednl. Experiences; mem. sci. adv. bd. Sea Farms, Inc.; chmn. S.C. Hall of Sci. and Tech. Founding editor: Microvascular Research; Author numerous papers on vascular physiology, also motion picture films. Served to capt. USAAF, 1942-46; lt. col. USAF Res. Fellow Am. Acad. Arts and Scis., Am. Coll. Angiology, Gerontology Soc., Explorers Club; mem. Am. Physiol. Soc., Soc. Exptl. Biology and Medicine, Am. Assn. Anatomists, Am. Soc. Zoologists, Radiation Research Soc., Microcirculatory Soc., Sigma Xi, Phi Beta Kappa. Home: 4740 Cedar Springs Rd Columbia SC 29206 Office: 1429 Senate St Columbia SC 29201

FULTON, JAMES FRANKLIN, designer; b. Cin., Apr. 13, 1930; s. A. Franklin and and Martha D. (Hurst) F.; m. Mary Sherman Walbridge, Sept. 12, 1953; children: Martha W., James Franklin, Jr., Laurel C. Grad., Pratt Inst., 1951. Designer Towle Silver Co., Newburyport, Mass., 1951; designer Owens-Corning Fiberglas Co., Toledo, 1952; sr. designer Harley Earl, Inc., Detroit, 1953-58; design dir., mgr. Compagnie de l'Esthetique Indsl., Paris, 1958-60; v.p., dir. product design Transp. Housing Components-Lowey/Snaith (Cons.), N.Y.C., 1960-66; pres. Fulton & Partners, Inc., N.Y.C., 1966—; chmn. Design Publs., Inc.; dir. Endt-Fulton & Partners, Paris.; Trustee Pratt Inst., Dime Savs. Bank of New York. Recipient Dean's medal Pratt Inst., 1951, Contemporary Achievement award, 1967. Mem. Am. Soc. Indsl. Designers. Clubs: N.Y. Yacht, Toledo. Patentee in field. Office: 330 W 42d St New York NY 10036

FULTON, LEN, publisher; b. Lowell, Mass., May 15, 1934; s. Claude E. and Louise E. (Vaillant) F.; 1 son, Timothy. B.A., U. Wyo., 1961; postgrad., U. Calif., Berkeley. Pub. Tourist Topic, Kennebunkport, Maine, also Weekly News, Freeport, Maine, 1957-59; biostatistician Calif. Dept. Public Health, 1962-68; editor, pub. Dustbooks, Paradise, Calif., 1963—; chmn. Com. Small Mag. Editors and Pubs., 1968-71, 73; cons. small presses ALA. Author: The Grassman, 1974, Dark Other Adam Dreaming, 1975; co-author: American Odyssey, 1975. Panelist Calif. Arts Commn., 1975; supr. Butte County (Calif.). Served with AUS, 1953-55. Grantee NEA, 1959-61, Coordinating Council Lit. Mags., 1970-73, Nat. Endowment Arts, 1974, 75. Mem. PEN. Address: PO Box 100 Paradise CA 95969

FULTON, RICHARD, lecture bureau exec.; b. N.Y.C., July 5, 1921; s. Phillip and Yves (Green) F.; m. Helen Evans, May 16, 1942; children—Linda, Jo Ann. Mus.B., N.Y. Coll. Music, 1944; B.S. in Music, Hebrew Union Coll., N.Y.C., 1944. Pres. Richard Fulton Inc., N.Y.C., 1957—; Mem. Nassau County (N.Y.) Democratic Finance Com., 1957-59. Singer, Boston Opera Co., 1944-49, Trenton (N.J.) Opera Co., 1949-53, Marlboro (Vt.) Music Festival, 1956. Candidate for councilman, Town of Oyster Bay, N.Y., 1972. Mem. Hebrew Union Coll. Alumni Assn. Clubs: Masons, K.P. Address: 101 W 57th St New York NY 10019 *As I get older and look back on past events I realize that everything that happened in my life could not have happened any other way. We must, of course, try to perform only noble deeds and* *pray that they make for a better world for those whom we have brought into it. Having rethought the above after a number of years I am ever more so convinced that each person gets his due, ultimately, as a result of the good work or the evil deeds which he performs in his lifetime.*

FULTON, RICHARD ALSINA, lawyer, broadcasting co. exec.; b. N.Y.C., Feb. 27, 1926; s. Robert B. and Consuelo (Alsina) F.; m. Susan Breakefield, 1971. A.B., U. Fla., 1949; J.D., Tulane U., 1957; LL.D. (hon.), N.H. Coll., 1981. Bar: La. bar 1957, D.C. bar 1977. Practiced in, Baton Rouge, 1957-63; asst. gen. counsel La. Dept. Hwys., 1957-58, La. Dept. Revenue, 1959-60; asst. to U.S. Senator Allen J. Ellender, 1961; partner firm Sachs, Greenebaum & Tayler, Washington, 1977-83; mem. White, Fine & Verville, Washington, 1983—; exec. dir., gen. counsel Assn. Ind. Colls. and Schs., 1962-76; pres. Fulton Broadcasting Co., WRCV-FM, Mercersburg, Pa.; Mem. commn. in acad. affairs Am. Council on Edn., 1972-75; mem. task force on post secondary edn. Edn. Commn. States. Author: You Career as a Secretary, 1963, Accounting for Your Future, 1966; Editor in chief: The Compass, 1962-76; Contbg. editor: Ency. Ednl. Research, 1969, Nat. Bus. Edn. Yearbook, 1969, Ency. Edn, 1971; Contbr. articles to profl. jours. Trustee Nat. Licensed Practical Nurse Edn. Found., 1970-73; adv. com. research projects Ednl. Testing Service, Am. Insts. Research in Behavioral Scis.; public mem. exec. bd. Assn. Theol. Schs., U.S. and Can., 1980-82; mem. Commn. on Nat. Devel. in Postsecondary Edn., 1981—. Served with U.S. Mcht. Marine, World War II; Korea. Mem. Am., Fed., D.C., La. bar assns., Sigma Chi, Phi Delta Phi. Democrat. Episcopalian. Club: Univ. Lodge: Masons. Home: 3813 Garrison St NW Washington DC 20016 Office: 1156 15th St NW Washington DC 20005

FULTON, RICHARD HARMON, mayor; b. Nashville, Jan. 27, 1927; s. Lyle Houston and Labina (Plummer) F.; m. Jewel Simpson, Dec. 23, 1945 (dec.); children: Richard, Michael, Barry (dec.), Donna, Linda; m. Sandra Fleisher; stepchildren: Cynthia Fleisher, Charles Fleisher. Student, U. Tenn., 1946-47. Real estate broker Fulton & Riddle Realty Co., Nashville; mem. Tenn. Senate, 1959-60, 88th-94th Congresses from 5th Tenn. Dist.; mayor City of Nashville, 1977—. Served with USNR, 1945-46. Democrat. Methodist. Clubs: Masons, Shriners. Office: Metropolitan Courthouse Nashville TN 37201 *

FULTON, ROBERT EDWARD, state agency administrator; b. St. Louis, Sept. 8, 1931; s. Hadley James and Gleta (Miinch) F.; m. Norma Maxine Heitman, May 10, 1952; children: Robin Edward, Colin Scott Cole, Kenton Wade. A.B., B.S. in Edn., Southeast Mo. State U., 1956; J.D., Am. U., 1960; M.S. in Bus. Adminstrn, George Washington U., 1965. Tchr. elem. schs., Patton, Mo., 1948-52; mgmt. analyst U.S. Navy Dept., Washington, 1956-59, AEC, Germantown, Md., 1959-66, nuclear cooperation specialist, 1966-67, U.S. State Dept., 1967-68; community action adminstr. U.S. OEO, Chgo., 1968-70, regional dir., Boston, 1970-73, HEW, 1973-76; adminstr. Social and Rehab. Service, HEW, Washington, 1976-77; minority counsel U.S. Senate Budget Com., Washington, 1977-81, chief counsel, 1981-83; dir. Okla Dept. Human Services, Oklahoma City, 1983—. Mem. Bd. Social Services County of Montgomery, Md., 1978-81; chmn. council on ministries Damascus (Md.) Methodist Ch., 1978-80. Served with U.S. Army, 1952-54. Recipient Meritorious award for Achievement in Public Adminstrn. William A. Jump Meml. Found., 1967; Sec.'s Spl. citation HEW, 1977. Mem. Am. Bar Assn., Am. Public Welfare Assn. Republican. Office: Sequoyah Office Bldg State Capitol Complex PO Box 25352 Oklahoma City OK 73125

FULTON, ROBERT LESTER, educator; b. Toronto, Can., Nov. 30, 1926; s. Edgar John and Mary Grace (Ouderkirk) F.; m. Patricia Alma Brown, July 29, 1948 (div.); children—David, Richard; m. Julie Ann Rockman, June 13, 1964; 1 son, Regan. A.B. cum laude, U. Ill., 1951; M.A., U. Toronto, 1953; Ph.D., Wayne State U., 1959. Instr. U. Wis., 1957-58; from asst. prof. to prof. sociology Calif. State U., Los Angeles, 1958-66; prof. sociology U. Minn., Mpls., 1966—; dir. Center for Death Edn. and Research, 1969—; vis. prof. U. Minn., 1963, 65, U. Osmania, India, 1967, U. Calif. at Irvine, 1975, U. Calif., San Diego, 1979. Author: Death and Identity, 1965, Education and Social Crisis, 1967, Death, Grief and Bereavement: Bibliography 1845-1975, 1977, Death and Dying: Challenge and Change, 1978; asso. editor: Omega, 1970-73. Served with Royal Canadian Navy, 1944. Fellow Am. Sociol. Assn.; mem. AAUP, Acad. Psychosomatic Medicine, Societe de Thanatologie de Langue Francaise. Home: 25 E Minnehaha Pkwy Minneapolis MN 55419

FULTON, SANDY MICHAEL, forest products company executive; b. Comox, B.C., Can., Nov. 15, 1943; s. Russell Clyde and Muriel Maggie (Swan) F.; m. Thelma Diane Wiig, July 8, 1967; children: Michael Colby, Kristen Wade, Treva Diane. B.S., U. B.C., 1966; M.B.A., Simon Fraser U., Burnaby, B.C., Can., 1975. Vice pres. MacMillan Bloedel Bldg Material, Atlanta, 1979-81; pres. Atlantic Forest Products, Atlanta, 1979-81; sr. v.p. bldg. products BC Timber Ltd., Vancouver, 1981-83, exec. v.p. ops., 1983—, dir.; dir. Babine Forest Products, Burns Lake, B.C., Can., ILMA, Penticton, B.C., NCFLRA, Prince George, B.C., Can., Compucon Service Ltd., Vancouver, B.C. Timber Ltd. Home: 1491 Devonshire Crescent Vancouver BC Canada V6H 2G5 Office: BC Timber Ltd 1176 W Georgia St Vancouver BC Canada V6B 4B7

FULTON, THOMAS BENJAMIN, bishop; b. St. Catharines, Ont., Can., Jan. 13, 1918; s. Thomas Francis and Mary Catharine (Jones) F. Student, St. Augustines Sem., Toronto, 1935-41; D. Canon Law, Cath. U. Am., 1948. Ordained priest Roman Catholic Ch., 1941; asst. pastor in, Toronto, 1941-51; sec. Toronto Tribunal, 1948-51; chancellor Archdiocese, Toronto, 1952-69, aux. bishop, 1969-78; 2d bishop of St. Catharines, 1978—; nat. dir. Soc. for Propagation Faith, 1977—. Author: The Prenuptial Investigation, 1948. Home: 122 Riverdale Ave Saint Catharines ON L2R 4C2 Canada

FULTZ, CLAIR ERVIN, former banker; b. nr. Jeffersonville, Ohio, Nov. 23, 1911; s. Roy Bertis and Addis (Ervin) F.; m. Isabelle Eichelberger, Aug. 18, 1935; children: Robert Edward, Karen Lynn, Pamela Jane. B.S., Ohio State U., 1934; grad., Rutgers U. Grad Sch. Banking, 1946. With Huntington Nat. Bank, Columbus, Ohio, 1934-72, v.p., 1953-57, dir., 1956-77, pres., 1958-67, chmn., chief exec. officer, 1967-72; pres. Huntington Bancshares, Inc., 1966-73, chmn., 1973-83; Mem. fed. adv. council Fed. Res. System, 1973-75. Chmn., trustee Battelle Meml. Inst., 1963—; past pres. Children's Hosp.; Past chmn. Devel. Com. Greater Columbus. Mem. Ohio Bankers Assn. (past pres.), SAR, Soc. Mayflower Descs., Ohio State Med. Assn. (hon. mem.), Ohio State U. Pace Setters (hon.), Newcomen Soc. N.Am., Beta Gamma Sigma, Alpha Kappa Psi, Phi Alpha Kappa. Clubs: Washington Country, Presidents (Ohio State U.). Home: 15726 SR 729 NW Jeffersonville OH 43128

FULWEILER, HOWARD WELLS, educator; b. Media, Pa., Aug. 26, 1932; s. Howard Wells and Mary Louise (Boyles) F.; m. Sally Starr Nichols, Dec. 28, 1953; children—Peter, John, Mary, Ann. Grad., Kent Sch., 1950; B.A., U. S.D., 1954, M.A., 1957; Ph.D., U. N.C., 1960. Teaching fellow U. S.D., 1956-57, U. N.C., 1957-59, 59-60; asst. prof. U. Mo. at Columbia, 1960-64, asso. prof., 1964-70, prof. English, 1970—, chmn. dept., 1967-71. Author: Letters from the Darkling Plain, 1972; Contbr. articles profl. jours. Chmn. bd. Ecumenical Ministry for Higher Edn., Columbia, Mo., 1966-68. Served to lt. AUS, 1954-56. Mem. Modern Lang. Assn. Am., Midwest Modern Lang. Assn., AAUP. Democrat. Episcopalian. Home: 601 S Greenwood St Columbia MO 65201

FULWILER, ROBERT NEAL, oil company executive; b. Belton, Tex., Nov. 5, 1937; s. Charles Calvin and Luella (Smith) F.; m. Sylvia Jean Marshall, Dec. 26, 1959; 1 son, Roger Neal. A.A., Temple Jr. Coll., 1959; B.B.A., U. Tex., 1961. Statis. asst. Tex. Eastern Transmission Corp., Houston, 1961-62; adminstrv. asst. subs. LaGloria Oil and Gas, Houston, 1969-76, v.p., 1976; exec. v.p. La Jet, Inc., Houston, 1976-81, pres., 1981—; chmn. bd., dir. EnJet Inc.; dir. CalJet Energy Inc. Author: Competition and Growth in American Energy Markets, 1947-1985, 1968. Republican. Mem. Ch. of Christ. Clubs: Lochinvar Golf (Houston); Fairway Oaks Golf and Racquet (Abilene, Tex.). Office: 2425 West Loop S Houston TX 77027

FUMAGALLI, BARBARA MERRILL, artist, printmaker; b. Kirkwood, Mo., Mar. 15, 1926; d. Harold C. and Mary Louise (Fitch) Ellison; m. Orazio Fumagalli, Aug. 15, 1948; children: Luisa, Piera, Elio. B.F.A., State U. Iowa, 1948, M.F.A., 1950; student, Mauricio Lasansky, Iowa City, 1945-50, Garo Antreasian, John Summers, Albuquerque, 1980-81. One man shows, Tweed Gallery, U. Minn., Duluth, 1955, 82, U. Minn., St. Paul, 1964, U. Minn., Mpls., 1965, Concordia Coll., Moorhead, Minn., Suzanne Kohn Gallery, St. Paul, 1967, Hamline U., St. Paul, 1969, Paine Art Center and Arboretum, Oshkosh, Wis., 1973; represented in permanent collecions, Mus. Modern Art, N.Y.C., Nelson A. Rockefeller Collection, N.Y.C.; included in: Drawing on Dance, Cork Gallery, Lincoln Ctr., N.Y.C., 1982; Illustrator: Swing Around the Sun (Barbara J. Esbensen), 1965. Address: Route 4 Box 282-A Menomonie WI 54751

FUNARI, JOHN H., university dean; b. Connellsville, Pa., Apr. 6, 1929; s. Fred Joseph and Anna (Dowling) F.; m. Barbara J. Burriss, Apr. 4, 1959; children: Tracey Anne, Jonathan Daniel, Victoria Celeste. B.A., U. Va., 1950; postgrad., Princeton U., 1950-51, Queen's Coll., Oxford U., 1951-54, U. Pitts., 1957-59. Exec. asst. to chancellor U. Pitts., 1958-62; exec. asst. to adminstr. AID, Dept. of State, 1962-63, coordinator legislative presentation, 1963-65, dir. Office Nr. Eastern Affairs, 1965-67, dir. AID Mission in Jordan, 1967-68, dep. and acting dir. AID Mission in India, 1968-70; Ford Found. rep., Mex., 1970-74; dean Grad. Sch. Pub. and Internat. Affairs U. Pitts., 1974—. Served to lt. USNR, 1954-57. Rhodes scholar, 1951-54. Mem. Council on Fgn. Relations, Raven Soc., Phi Beta Kappa. Democrat. Home: 307 S Dithridge St Apt 514 Pittsburgh PA 15213 Office: Dean Grad Sch Pub Internat Affairs U Pitts Pittsburgh PA 15260

FUNDERBURK, DAVID B., ambassador; b. Langley Field, Va., Apr. 28, 1944; (married); 2 children. B.A., Wake Forest Coll., 1966; M.A., Wake Forest U., 1967; Ph.D., U. S.C., 1974. Instr. Wingate (N.C.) Coll., 1967-69, U. S.C., Columbia, 1969-70; assoc. prof. history Hardin-Simmons U., Abilene, Tex., 1972-78; prof. history Campbell U., Buies Creek, N.C., 1978-81; U.S. ambassador to Romania, Bucharest, 1981—. Office: Am Embassy Strada Tudor Arghezi 7-9 Bucharest Romania

FUNG, YUAN-CHENG BERTRAM, bioengineering educator, author; b. Yuhong, Changchow, Kiangsu, China, Sept. 15, 1919; came to U.S., 1945, naturalized, 1957; s. Chung-Kwang and Lien (Hu) F.; m. Luna Hsien-Shih Yu, Dec. 22, 1949; children: Conrad Antung, Brenda Pingsi. B.S., Nat. Central U., Chungking, China, 1941, M.S., 1943; Ph.D., Calif. Inst. Tech., 1948. Research fellow Bur. Aero. Research China, 1943-45; research asst., then research fellow Cal. Inst. Tech., 1946-51, mem. faculty, 1951-66; prof. aeros. Calif. Inst. Tech., 1959-66; prof. bioengring. and applied mechanics U. Calif.-San Diego, 1966—; cons. aerospace indsl. firms, 1949—. Author: The Theory of Aeroelasticity, 1956, Foundations of Solid Mechanics, 1965, A First Course in Continuum Mechanics, 1969, 77, Biomechanics, 1972, Biomechanics: Mechanical Properties of Living Tissues, 1980; also papers.; Editor: Jour. Biorheology, Jour. Biomech. Engring. Recipient Achievement award Chinese Inst. Engrs., 1965, 68; Landis award Microcirculatory Soc., 1975; von Karman medal ASCE, 1976; Guggenheim fellow, 1958-59. Fellow AIAA, ASME (Lissner award 1978); mem. Nat. Acad. Engring, Soc. Engring. Sci., Microcirculatory Soc., Am. Physiol. Soc., Nat. Heart Assn., Basic Sci. Council, Sigma Xi. Home: 2660 Greentree Ln La Jolla CA 92037

FUNK, CYRIL REED, JR., agronomist, educator; b. Richmond, Utah, Sept. 20, 1928; s. Cyril Reed and Hazel Marie (Jensen) F.; m. Donna Gwen Buttars, Feb. 2, 1951; children: Bonnie Arlene, David Christopher, Carol Jean. B.S. (Scholarship A 1955), Utah State U., 1952, M.S., 1955; Ph.D., Rutgers U., 1961. Mem. faculty Rutgers U., New Brunswick, N.J., 1956—, research prof. turfgrass breeding soils and crop dept., 1969—, also instr. grad. faculty. Author, patentee in field. Served to 1st lt. AUS, 1952-54. Recipient Green Sect. award U.S. Golf Assn., 1980, Achievement award Lawn Inst., 1977. Mem. AAAS, Am. Soc. Agronomy (research award N.E. sect. 1979), Crop Sci. Soc. Am., Am. Genetic Assn., Am. Sod Producers Assn., Golf Course Supts. Assn., Am. Turfgrass Assn. (hon. mem.; Disting. Service award 1979), N.J. Turfgrass Assn. (Achievement award 1976), N.J. Golf Course Supts. Assn. (hon.), N.Y. Acad. Scis., Sigma Xi, Phi Kappa Phi. Mormon. Developer numerous turfgrasses. Home: 4 Delaware Dr East Brunswick NJ 08816 Office: Cook Coll Rutgers Univ New Brunswick NJ 08903

FUNK, FRANK E., university dean; b. Jersey City, Feb. 21, 1923; s. Frank and Elsa A. (Bohne) F.; m. Ruth Christy, Feb. 3, 1977; children—Steven Eric, Karen Christine. B.S., Syracuse (N.Y.) U., 1949, M.S., 1952; Ph.D. in Bus. and Indsl. Communication, Purdue U., 1956. Instr. speech, dir. radio workshop Lehigh U., Bethlehem, Pa., 1949-52; grad. teaching asst., then instr. speech Purdue U., 1952-56; mem. faculty Syracuse U., 1956—, assoc. prof. speech, 1974—, chmn. dept. pub. address, 1962-65, dean, 1970—, dir. continuing edn., 1973—; pres. Syracuse U. Theatre Corp., 1973—, Univ. Council Edn. Pub. Responsibility, 1972-73; adv. bd. WAER, campus FM sta., 1972-73. Author articles. Adv. bd. Hendricks Chapel, 1978-83, chmn., 1980—; Bd. dirs. PEACE, Inc., 1969-72; bd. dirs., chmn. coms. Syracuse United Way.; v.p. planning allocation's Syracuse United Way, 1981—; bd. visitors U. Pitts., 1981—. Served as officer USAAF, 1943-45; ETO. Decorated Air medal.; Fellow Creative Problems-Solving Inst., 1958, Found. Econ. Edn. Bus., summer 1957. Mem. Assn. Continuing Higher Edn. (dir. 1973-76), Nat. Assn. Continuing Higher Edn. (regional chmn. 1973-74, chmn. nominating com. 1978, nat. program chmn. 1979, pres. 1981), Nat. Univ. Continuing Edn. Assn. (chpt. com. chmn.), Adult Edn. Assn., NEA, Am. Assn. Adult and Continuing Edn., Syracuse U. Alumni Assn. Democrat. Home: 133 Edwards Dr Fayetteville NY 13066 Office: 610 E Fayette St Syracuse NY 13202

FUNK, JAMES (ELLIS FUNK), chemical engineer, research director; b. Cin., Nov. 8, 1932; s. Nicholas J. and Agnes S. F.; m. Janet Neimer, May 21, 1955; children: Lynn, Lori, Jimmy, Lisa, John. C.M.E. Engr., U. Cinn., 1955; M.S.Ch.E. (Westinghouse fellow), U. Pitts., 1958, Ph.D., 1960. Registered profl. engr., Ohio, Ky. Co-op. student Hilton Davis Chem. Co., Cin., 1951-54; sr. engr. naval nuclear program Westinghouse Bettis Atomic Power Lab., Pitts., 1955-63; group leader, energy depot project Allison div. Gen. Motors Corp., Indpls., 1963-64; asso. prof. mech. engring. U. Ky., 1964-68, prof., 1968—, asso. dean, 1968-71, dean, 1971-79, dir., 1971-81, asso. v.p. for acad. affairs, coordinator energy research and edn., 1979-81; dir. Advanced Tech. Center, Allis-Chalmers Corp., Milw., 1981-82; prof. mech. engring., spl. asst. to sec. Ky. Energy Cabinet, 1982—; dir. tech. activities, indsl. group Combustion Engring., Inc., Windsor, Conn., 1970-71. Chmn. Ky. Bd. Registration for Profl. Engrs. and Land Surveyors, 1975-78; mem. Ky. Gov.'s Policy Adv. Com. on Energy; reviewer NSF; mem. U.S. team Internat. Energy Agy.; condr. profl. seminars, U.S., Europe, Asia., S. Am. Contbr. articles to profl. jours. Recipient Disting. Alumnus award U. Cin. Coll. Engring., 1973; U. Ky. research fellow, summer 1965; Sr. Fulbright-Hays scholar, 1972-73. Mem. Internat. Assn. Hydrogen Energy (founding mem.; chmn. publs. com., editorial bd. Internat. Jour. Hydrogen Energy 1975—), Am. Inst. Chem. Engrs., Am. Nuclear Soc. (sec. Pitts. sect. 1958, Outstanding Service award 1958), AAAS, Sigma Xi, Tau Beta Pi, Phi Lambda Upsilon, Pi Tau Sigma. Office: Ky Center for Energy Research PO Box 11888 Lexington KY 40578

FUNK, JAMES ELLIS, chemical engineer, educator; b. Cin., Nov. 8, 1932; s. Nicholas J. and Agnes S. F.; m. Janet Neimer, May 21, 1955; childen: Lynn, Lori, Jim, Lisa, John. C.M.E. Engr., U. Cin., 1955; M.S.Ch.E. (Westinghouse fellow), U. Pitts., 1958, Ph.D., 1960. Registered profl. engr., Ky., Ohio. Co-op. student Hilton Davis Chem. Co., Cin., 1951-54; sr. engr. naval nuclear program Westinghouse Bettis Atomic Power Lab., Pitts., 1955-63; group leader energy depot project Allison div. Gen. Motors Corp., Indpls., 1963-67; assoc. prof. mech. engring. U. Ky., 1964-68, prof., 1968—, assoc. dean, 1968-71, dean. Coll. Engring., 1971-79, dir. Inst. Mining and Minerals Research, 1971-81, assoc. v.p. for acad. affairs, coorinator energy research and edn., 1979-81; dir. tech. activities, indsl. group Combustion Engring., Inc., Windsor, Conn., 1970-71. Contbr. articles in field to profl. jours. Chmn. Ky. Bd. Registration for Profl. Engrs. Land Surveyors, 1975-78; mem. Ky. Gov.'s Policy Adv. Com. on Energy; reviewer NSF; mem. U.S. team Internat. Energy Agy.; condr. profl. seminars U.S., Europe, Asia, S.Am. Recipient Disting. Alumnus award U. Cin. Coll. Engring., 1973; U. Ky. research fellow, 1965; Sr. Fulbright-Hays scholar, 1972-73. Mem. Internat. Assn. Hydrogen Energy (founding mem., chmn. publs. com., editorial bd. internat. Jour. Hydorgen Energy 1975—), Am. Inst. Chem. Engrs., Am. Nuclear Soc. (sec. Pitts. sect. 1958, Outstanding Service award 1958), AAAS, Sigma Xi, Tau Beta Pi, Phi Lambda Upsilon, Pi Tau Sigma. Home: 1845 Blairmore Ct Lexington KY 40502 Office: Dept Mech Engring U Ky Lexington KY 40506

FUNK, PAUL EUGENE, advertising and marketing executive; b. Coshocton, Ohio, Mar. 13, 1920; s. Abraham Bantam and Helen (Kaiser) F.; m. Betty Jane Walter, Sept. 28, 1940 (div. July 1951); 1 son, Karl E.; m. Joan Anna Cornish, Dec., 1964 (div. July 1969); stepchildren: Douglas Cornish, Joyce Cornish. Cert. in graphic reprodn. arts, Sorbonne, Paris, 1945; B.S. in Sociology and Psychology, SUNY, 1983. Mgr., sign and decal div. Dura-Products Mfg. Co., Canton, Ohio, 1938-41; dir. advt. and pub. relations Maguire Industries, Canton, 1945-47; dir. pub. relations Norman Malone Assos., Akron, Ohio, 1947-49; account exec. Fuller & Smith & Ross, Inc., Cleve., 1949-54; account supr. McCann-Erickson, Inc., N.Y.C., 1954-66, v.p., 1957-66, exec. v.p., gen. mgr. indsl., tech. and sci. marketing div., 1962-66; pres. McCann/ITSM, Inc., 1967-68; chmn., chief exec. officer Pritchard Wood Assos., Inc., N.Y.C., 1968-70; chmn. Scenario Resources, Inc., 1970-79; pres. Paul E. Funk Assos.; mgmt. cons. Faculty creative workshop Advt. Age, 1963, 69, 70. Mem. editorial adv. bd.: Indsl. Marketing mag, 1967-70. Bd. dirs. Epilepsy Found., Epilepsy Assn. Am.; 1st v.p. Epilepsy Found., 1964-68, pres., 1969-70, exec. v.p., 1970-76, exec. v.p. emeritus, 1977—; tchr. public relations No. Va. Community Coll., Alexandria.; Mem. fin. com. Future Homemakers Am., Washington. Served with AUS, 1941-45. Mem. Internat. Advt. Assn., Interior Design Soc., Internat. Execs. Assn., Pub. Relations Soc. Am., AIM (pres.'s council), Bus. and Profl. Advt. Assn. (cert.), Am. Mktg. Assn., Am. Soc. Assn. Execs., Am. Assn. Mental Deficiency, Internat. Platform Assn., Am. Soc. Interior Designers (affiliate), Nat. Soc. Fund Raisers, Am. Pub. Health Assn. Clubs: Nat. Press (Washington); Athletic, Advt. (N.Y.C.); Lone Palm Golf (Lakeland, Fla.); Dorado Del Mar Country (Dorado, P.R.). Home: 801 N Pitt St Alexandria VA 22314 also 004 Calle Marlin Dorado PR Office: 1828 L St NW Washington DC 20036

FUNK, SHERMAN MAXWELL, government official; b. N.Y.C., Nov. 13, 1925; s. Bernard and Dorothy (Arkin) F.; m. Elaine Myrl Bayer, Mar. 6, 1953 (dec. 1977); children: Katherine Sara, Bernard Eugene; m. Sylvia M. Straka, June 6, 1978; children Eric, Marc, Paul. A.B., Harvard U., 1950; postgrad., Columbia U., 1956; A.M., U. Ariz., 1958. Salesman, sales exec. Bernard Funk Co., N.Y.C., 1950-54; history tchr. Catskill High Sch., (N.Y.), 1954-57; polit. sci. teaching asst. U. Ariz., Tucson, 1957-58; mgmt. intern USAF Hdqrs., Washington, 1958, war planning officer, mgmt. analyst, 1958-63, chief Air Force Mgmt. Improvement Programs office, 1963-67, chief Air Force Cost Reduction Office, 1967-70; White House detail Office Minority Bus. Enterprise, 1970; chmn. Washington Minority Bus. Opportunity Com., asst. dir. adminstrn. and program devel., dir. research and program devel. USAF Hdqrs., 1972-76, asst. dir. planning and evaluation, 1976-79; spl. asst. for small bus. Dept. Energy, 1979-81; insp. gen. Dept. Commerce, 1981—. Contbr. articles to profl. jours. Mem. Bowie City Council, (Md.), 1963-65, chmn. human relations com., (Md.), 1964-65, chmn. charter rev. com., (Md.), 1968; pres. Bowie Area Library, 1966-68; bd. dirs. local synagogue. Served with inf. AUS, 1943-46. Decorated Purple Heart; recipient spl. award Sec. Air Force, 1968, prizes Washington-Md.-Del Press Assn., 1970, 71, 73, 75, Silver medal Commerce Dept., 1972. Mem. Nat. Rifle Assn., Assn. Fed. Investigators, Inst. Internal Auditors. Office: Office of Insp Gen Commerce Dept Washington DC 10130 *My twenty-five years in government are marked by paradox: I have worked with some extraordinarily able people and with important and challenging programs. Yet I increasingly doubt the ability of federal programs to solve national ills. Too many of these programs are subverted externally by political pork and internally by waste, fraud, incompetence and don't-rock-the boat mediocrity. As an Inspector General, I now have more ammunition to fight such abuse, and to help change the image of federal service which scares off exactly the kind of bright and aggressive talent needed in government.*

FUNK, WILLIAM HENRY, civil engineer, educator; b. Ephraim, Utah, June 10, 1933; s. William George and Henrietta (Hackwell) F.; m. Ruth Sherry Mellor, Sept. 19, 1964; 1 dau., Cynthia Lynn. B.S. in Biol. Sci, U. Utah, 1955, M.S. in Zoology (USPHS trainee), 1966. Tchr. sci., math. Salt Lake City Schs., 1957-60; research asst. U. Utah, Salt Lake City, 1961-63; head sci. dept. N.W. Jr. High Sch., Salt Lake City, 1961-63; mem. faculty Wash. State U., Pullman, 1966—, asso. prof. civil engring., 1971-75, prof., 1975—, chmn. environ. sci./regional planning program, 1979-81; dir. Environ. Research Center, 1980-83, State of Wash. Water Research Ctr., 1981—; cons. Harstad Engrs., Seattle, 1971-72, Boise Cascade Corp., 1971-72, U.S. Army C.E., Walla Walla, Wash., 1970-74, ORB Corp., Renton, Wash., 1972-73, State Wash. Dept. Ecology, Olympia, 1971-72, U.S. Civil Service, Seattle, Chgo., 1972—. Author publs. on water pollution control and lake restoration. Served with USNR, 1955-57. NSF Summer Inst. grantee, 1961; Office Water Resources Research grantee, 1971-72, 73-76; EPA grantee, 1980-83. Mem. Naval Res. Officers Assn. (chpt. pres. 1969), Res Officers Assn. (U.S. Naval Acad. info. officer 1973-76), Pacific

N.W. Pollution Control Assn. (editor 1969-77, pres.-elect 1982-83), Water Pollution Control Fedn. (Arthur S. Bedell award Pacific N.W. assn. 1976, nat. dir. 1978—), Am. Soc. Limnology and Oceanography, Am. Micros. Soc., N.W. Sci. Assn., Sigma Xi, Phi Sigma. Home: SW 330 Kimball Ct Pullman WA 99163

FUNKE, LEWIS B., drama editor; b. Bronx, N.Y., Jan. 25, 1912; s. Joseph and Rose (Keimowitz) F.; m. Blanche Bier, July 5, 1938; children: Phyllis Ellen, Michael Jeffrey. A.B., N.Y. U., 1932. Free-lance writer, sports dept. N.Y. Times, 1928-32, staff sports writer, 1932-44, gen. news staff, movie dept., 1944, drama editor, 1944-73, asst. cultural news editor, 1970-73; former adj. lectr. Queens Coll., N.Y.C.; also distinguished vis. prof. Sch. Theater, Fla. State U., Tallahassee, 1973—; public relations cons. Eugene O'Neill Meml. Theater Center, 1973—. Author articles various nat. mags.; co-author: Actors Talk About Acting, 1962, Max Gordon Presents, 1963, A Gift of Joy, 1965; author: The Curtain Rises, 1971, Playwrights Talk About Playwriting, 1975, Actors Talk About Theater, 1977; contbg. editor: The Exec. Jeweler, 1980-83. Address: 5 Linden Trail Monroe NY 10950 also 13777-D Via Aurora Delray Beach FL 33445 *It is essential that ambition is backed by ability. To aspire is, of course, healthy; not to be able to deliver when the possibility to achieve is at hand can be disastrous.*

FUNKHOUSER, A. PAUL, transportation holding company executive; b. Roanoke, Va., Mar. 8, 1923; s. Samuel King and Jane Harwood (Cocke) F.; m. Eleanor Rosalie Gamble, Feb. 4, 1950; children: John Paul, Eleanor Kent (Mrs. Michael Doar). B.A., Princeton U., 1945; LL.B., U. Va., 1950. Bar: Va. 1951. With firm Hunton, Williams, Anderson, Gay and Moore, Richmond, 1950-51; with N. & W. Ry., 1952-63, asst. gen. counsel, 1960-63; asst. v.p. Pa. R.R., 1963-65, v.p. coal and ore traffic, 1965-68, Penn Central Transp. Co., 1968-70, v.p. pub. affairs, 1970-71, sr. v.p. sales and mktg., 1971-75; exec. v.p. Seaboard Coast Line Industries, Inc., Jacksonville, Fla., 1975-78, pres., dir., 1978-80; pres. and chief exec. officer SCL R.R. and L&N R.R. Family Lines Rail System, 1980-82; pres., dir. CSX Corp., 1982—, Seaboard System R.R., 1982—, Chessie System R.R., 1982—; dir. Universal Leaf Tobacco Co., Chem. Bank, Chem. N.Y. Corp. Chmn. bd. trustees Hollins Coll.; trustee Va. Found. Ind. Colls. Served to 2d lt. AUS, 1943-46. Mem. Order of Coif, Phi Beta Kappa, Omicron Delta Kappa, Delta Psi, Phi Delta Phi. Episcopalian. Clubs: Laurel Valley Golf (Ligonier, Pa.); Princeton, Union League (N.Y.C.); Met. (Washington); Ponte Vedra (Fla.); Country of Va., Commonwealth (Richmond, Va.). Home: 214 Berkshire Dr Richmond VA 23226 Office: CSX Corp 1500 Fed Res Bldg Richmond VA 23219

FUNKHOUSER, ELMER NEWTON, JR., university official; b. Hagerstown, Md., Nov. 23, 1916; s. Elmer Newton and Nellie Evelyn (Spielman) F.; m. Gladys Elizabeth McFeeley, Apr. 8, 1940; children: Elmer Newton III, Richard Nelson II, Susan Lynn, Lois Erica, David Kirsten. B.S., Otterbein Coll., 1938, LL.D., 1963; M.B.A., Harvard, 1941. With Dewey and Almy Chem. Corp., 1940-54, gen. mgr. cryovac div., 1950-54; with W.R. Grace & Co., 1954-62; exec. v.p. Cryovac div., 1956-62; exec. v.p., dir. Am. Metal Climax, Inc., N.Y.C., 1962-66; sr. v.p. Am. Can Co., 1966-72; spl. asst. to dean Harvard Bus. Sch., 1972—; dir. Alleghany Corp, N.Y., L.G. Balfour, Attleboro, Mass., TBS, Inc., Wellesley, Mass., RSR Corp., Dallas, TSC Corp., Cambridge, Mass., Intermagnetics Gen. Corp., Guilderland, N.Y., Arkwright-Boston Mfrs.; Mut. Ins. Co., Waltham, Mass., Martin Veneer Co., Hagerstown, Md., Cotuit Corp., Wellesley, West Chem. Products Co., N.Y.C., Fusion Systems Corp., Rockville, Md., Internat. Horizons, Inc., Atlanta, Meritape, Inc., Concord, Mass., Charles T. Main Co., Boston, Saxon Industries, N.Y.C. Trustee Otterbein Coll., Jordan Hosp., Plymouth, Mass. Mem. Am. Inst. Mining, Metall. and Petroleum Engrs. Clubs: Concord Country, Duxbury Yacht; River (N.Y.C.). Home: 81 Beacon St Boston MA 02108 also 389 King Caesar Rd Duxbury MA 02332 Office: Soldiers Field Rd Boston MA 02163

FUNKHOUSER, RICHARD NELSON, tennis ct. mfg. co. exec.; b. Hagerstown, Md., Dec. 3, 1917; s. Elmer N. and Nellie E. (Spielman) F.; m. Janet A. Kunkel, Jan. 26, 1946; children—Richard Nelson, Marsha Jill, Linda Jane. Grad., Mercersburg (Pa.) Acad., 1936; A.B., Dartmouth Coll., 1940. Vice pres. Funkhouser Co., Hagerstown, 1946-58; v.p., gen. mgr. roofing granule div. Ruberoid Co., 1959-67; pres., dir. Har-Tru Corp. (mfrs. tennis courts), 1956—; dir. Martin Veneer Corp. Regent Mercersburg Acad. Served to maj. USAAF, 1941-46. Mem. Quiet Birdmen, Sigma Alpha Epsilon. Methodist. Clubs: Winged Foot Golf (Mamaroneck, N.Y.); Canadian (N.Y.C.); Fountain Head Country (Hagerstown); West Side Tennis (Forest Hills, N.Y.); Ocean Reef (North Key Largo, Fla.). Home: 1880 Fountain Head Rd Hagerstown MD 21740

FUNKHOUSER, ROBERT BRANE, advertising executive; b. Hagerstown, Md., Oct. 25, 1926; s. Elmer Newton and Nellie Evelyn (Spielman) Funkhouser; m. Margaret Ann Crissman, Sept. 19, 1953; children: Lise K., Robert Brane, Kristen N. B.A., Dartmouth Coll., 1950. With McCann-Erickson, Inc., N.Y.C., 1951-52; account exec. Ketchum MacLeod & Grove, Pitts., 1953-57; v.p. BBDO, Pitts., 1957-70, v.p., regional mgr., Los Angeles, 1970-74; v.p. advt. and pub. relations Carnation co., Los Angeles, 1974—; instr. account mgmt. Inst. for Advanced Advt. Studies, U. So. Calif., 1972-73. Served with USAF, 1945-46. Mem. Am. Advt. Fedn. (dir.), Assn. Council (dir. 1979-82), Nat. Advt. Rev. Bd. (dir.), Advt. Edn. Found. (dir.). Republican. Presbyterian. Clubs: Los Angeles Country, Advt. of Los Angeles. Home: 2346 Mandeville Canyon Rd Los Angeles CA 90049 Office: 5045 Wilshire Blvd Los Angeles CA 90036

FUNSETH, ROBERT LLOYD ERIC MARTIN, foreign service officer; b. International Falls, Minn., May 10, 1926; s. Martin Emmanuel and Agnes (Guibault) F.; m. Marilyn Ann Schuelke, Mar. 23, 1957; 1 son, Eric Christian. B.A., Hobart Coll., 1948, postgrad., 1950-51; postgrad., Cornell U., 1950,51, Sch. Advanced Internat. Studies, Johns Hopkins U., 1951-52; M.S., George Washington U., 1969; LL.D, Hobart and William Smith Colls., 1978. Editor Coachella Desert Barnacle, (Calif.), 1948; mng. editor Anaheim Gazette, (Calif.), 1948-50; corr. AP, 1950; resident tutor Hobart Coll., 1950-51; info. officer U.S. Mut. Security Agy., 1952-53; editor USIA, 1953-54; joined U.S. Fgn. Service, 1954; advanced to rank of minister Career Sr. Fgn. Service; vice consul U.S. Fgn. Service, Tabriz, Iran, 1954-56; 3d sec. Am. embassy, Beirut, 1957-59; polit. affairs officer UN, 1959-61; Am. consul (Bordeaux), France, 1961-64; Portuguese desk officer Dept. State, Washington, 1964-66; mem. U.S. del. 20th UN Gen. Assembly, 1965; dep. dir. Iberian affairs Dept. State, 1966-68; assigned to Nat. War Coll., 1968-69; dir. mgmt. U.S. diplomatic and consular posts Dept. State, Mex. and Central Am., 1969-70, coordinator Cuban affairs, 1970-72, sr. fgn. service insp., 1972-73; counselor Am. embassy, Ottawa, Ont., Can., 1973-74; dep. dept. spokesman and dir office of press relations Dept. State, Washington, 1974-75, dept. spokesman and spl. asst. to sec. for press relations, 1975-77, dir. office No. European affairs, 1977-82; dep. asst. sec. for refugee resettlement, 1982-83; sr. dep. asst. sec. Bur. Refugee Programs, Dept. State, 1983; vis. Disting. alumnus scholar in residence Hobart and William Smith Colls., 1978; lectr. Am. studies U. Tabriz, 1955-56. Served to lt. (j.g.) USNR, 1943-46; PTO. Recipient Outstanding Service commendation Am. Forces Spl. Command, Middle East, 1958, Superior Honor Group award Dept. State, 1961, 70, Superior Honor award, 1977, Sesquicentennial award Hobart Coll., 1972. Mem. Am. Fgn. Service Assn., Hobart Coll. Alumni Assn., Johns Hopkins Alumni Assn. (exec. council 1968-70), Sch. Advanced Studies Alumni Assn. (pres., mem. adv. council 1969-70), Phi Sigma Kappa. Clubs: Am. Fgn. Service; Hobart (Washington). Office: State Dept Washington DC 20520

FUOSS, RAYMOND MATTHEW, chemist, educator; b. Bellwood, Pa., Sept. 28, 1905; s. Jacob Zachariah and Bertha May (Zimmerman) F.; m. Rose E. Harrington, July 25, 1926; 1 dau., Patricia Rose; m. Ann M. Stein, Mar. 1, 1947. Sc.B., Harvard U., 1925; Ph.D., Brown U., 1932; M.A. (Hon.), Yale U., 1945. Sheldon research fellow, Munich, 1925-26; Austin teaching fellow Harvard U., 1926-27; cons. Skinner, Sherman & Esselen, Boston, 1927-30; student with C.A. Kraus, Brown U., 1930-32; research instr. Brown U., 1932-33, asst. prof., 1933-36; Internat. research fellow (on leave from Brown U.) Leipzig, Jena and Cambridge univs., 1934-35; research chemist Gen. Electric Co., Schenectady, 1936-45; Sterling prof. chemistry Yale U., 1945-74, emeritus, 1974—; Priestley lectr. Pa. State Co., 1948. Contbr. about 300 articles on electrolytes, polymers and dielectrics in various sci. jours. Mem. Am. Chem. Soc. (award in pure chemistry 1935), Nat., N.Y., Conn. acads. sci., Am. Acad. Arts and Scis., Sigma Xi, Alpha Chi Sigma, Phi Beta Kappa. Home: 200 Leeder Hill Dr Apt 542 Hamden CT 06517

FUQUA, CHARLES JOHN, educator; b. Paris, France, Oct. 5, 1935; s. John Howe and Gillian Elynor (Quennell) F.; m. Mary Louise Morse, Aug. 26, 1961; children—Andrew Morse, David Reed, Gillian Quennell. B.A. magna cum laude, Princeton, 1957; M.A., Cornell U., 1962, Ph.D., 1964. Instr. classics Dartmouth Coll., Hanover, N.H., 1964, asst. prof., 1965-66; asso. prof. classics, chmn. dept. classics Williams Coll., Williamstown, Mass., 1966-72, Garfield prof. ancient langs., chmn. dept. classics, 1972—; Mem. adv. council Am. Acad. in Rome, 1966, chmn. exec. com., 1974. Served to lt. (j.g.) USNR, 1957-60. Mem. Am. Philol. Assn., Classical Assn. New Eng., Classical Assn. Mass., Vergilian Soc., Phi Beta Kappa, Phi Kappa Phi. Home: 96 Grandview Dr Williamstown MA 01267

FUQUA, DON, congressman; b. Jacksonville, Fla., Aug. 20, 1933. B.S. in Agrl. Econs., U. Fla., 1957. Mem. Fla. Ho. of Reps. from Calhoun County, 1958-62; mem. 88th-98th Congresses from 2d Dist. Fla., chmn. com. on sci. and tech., subcom. on energy devel. and application. Former trustee Fla. Sheriffs Boys Ranch, Rodeheaver Boys Ranch. Served with AUS. Mem. Future Farmers Am. (pres. Fla. 1950-51), Jaycees, Red Cross Constantine, Am. Legion, Fla. Blue Key, Fla. Gold Key, Alpha Gamma Rho. Presbyterian (elder). Clubs: Elks, Woodmen of the World, Masons (32 deg.), Shriners, Jesters, Rotary. Home: Altha FL 32421 Office: 2269 Rayburn House Office Bldg Washington DC 20515 *

FUQUA, JOHN BROOKS, conglomerate executive; b. Prince Edward County, Va., June 26, 1918; m. Dorothy Chapman, Feb. 10, 1945; 1 son, Rex. Ed. pub. schs.; LL.D. (hon.), Hampden-Sydney Coll., 1972, Duke U., 1973, Fla. Meml. Coll., 1982. Chmn. bd., chief exec. officer Fuqua Industries, Inc.; chmn. Triton Group Ltd., Fuqua Nat. Inc.; dir. GA Fed. Bank, Kaneb Services Inc.; Past mem. Augusta Aviation Commn., 1945-67. Past mem., fin. chmn. Augusta Hosp. Authority; past mem. Ga. Sci. and Tech. Commn.; mem. Ga. Ho. of Reps., 1957-63, Ga. Senate, 1963-64; chmn. Democratic Exec. Com. Ga., 1962-66; former bd. visitors Emory U.; former mem. adv. council Ga. State U.; former trustee Ga. State U. Found.; trustee Duke U., Hampden-Sydney Coll. Named Broadcaster-Citizen of Year Ga. Assn. Broadcasters, 1963, Broadcast Pioneer of Yr., 1979; Boss of Yr. Augusta Jr. C. of C., 1960; Horatio Alger award, 1984; Duke U. Bus. Sch. named in his honor, 1980. Mem. Augusta C. of C. (pres. 1962), Atlanta C. of C. (past dir.), World Bus. Council, Chief Exec. Orgn., Conf. Bd., Bus.-Higher Edn. Forum, Young Pres. Orgn. (past v.p.). Home: 3574 Tuxedo Rd NW Atlanta GA 30305 Office: Fuqua Industries Inc 1st Atlanta Tower Atlanta GA 30383

FURBACHER, STEPHEN A., pollution control equipment co. exec.; b. St. Louis, July 19, 1920; s. Henry and Theresa (Hora) F.; m. Geraldine Ball, Oct. 26, 1973; children—Ann Elizabeth, Stephen Arthur, Richard John, Susan Margaret, Marcy. B.S. in Bus. Adminstrn, U. Mo., 1944; M.S., U. Chgo., 1955. Sales engr. Corning Glass Works, N.Y., 1944-48; exec. v.p. Kawneer Co., Niles, Mich., 1948-62; v.p. Amax, Inc.; pres. Amax Aluminum Co., Greenwich, Conn., 1962-71; pres., chief exec. officer, dir. Neptune Internat. Corp., Atlanta, 1971-79; exec. v.p. Wheelabrator Frye, Inc., Hampton, N.H., 1979—; dir. Amerace Corp., Indsl. Nat. Corp. Served with AUS, 1942. Lutheran. Clubs: Atlanta, Athletic, University (N.Y.C.). Home: 25 Mooregate Sq NW Atlanta GA 30327

FURBAY, JOHN HARVEY, educator, author; b. Mt. Gilead, Ohio, Sept. 23, 1903; s. William LeRoy and Caroline Talbott (Wood) F.; m. Elizabeth Jane Dearmin, Dec. 19, 1930 (dec. 1946); children: John Talmadge, Judith Alison; m. Mauri Heinrichsmeyer, Sept. 29, 1951. Student, Otterbein Coll., 1921-23, LL.D., 1959; B.S., Asbury Coll., Wilmore, 1924, Ohio State U., 1925-26; M.A., NYU, 1927; Ph.D., Yale U., 1931, Sorbonne, Paris, summer 1930, U. Chgo., summer 1934; studies of colonial edn., U. London, 1935; Ed.D., Hillsdale Coll., 1966; D.Litt., Salem Coll., 1967. Prof. biology and edn. Taylor U., Upland, Ind., 1927-29, 31-33; prof. edn. and biology Coll. of Emporia, Kans., 1933-35; pres. Coll. West Africa, Monrovia, Liberia, 1935-39; lectr. on Liberia and other African subjects, 1939-40; prof. edn. Mills Coll., 1939-44, dir. Summer Session and Casa Pan-Americana, 1942, 43; specialist in internat. edn. U.S. Office Edn. and cultural attache U.S. embassies, Costa Rica and Colombia, 1943-45; U.S. del. UNESCO, Mexico City, 1947, Beirut, 1948, Paris, 1949, Florence, Italy, 1950; ednl. missions to various countries, 1948—, India, Siam, Formosa, 1953-54, Iran, Iraq, Lebanon, 1955, Ethiopia and Kenya, 1956, Viet Nam, 1964, aviation mission, Russia, 1962, trade mission, Outer Mongolia, 1963, tourism and trade mission, Liberia, 1983; dir. cultural and ednl. service Trans World Airlines, Inc., 1945-80, cons. cultural affairs, 1970—; ednl. cons. Gen. Motors, 1957-81. Author: numerous books, latest being World Without Strangers, 1955, Aviation and the Cold War, 1955, Shifting Sands in Arab Lands, 1956, The Shape of Things to Come, 1961, Spotlight on Africa, 1960, Why Study Abroad, 1964; contbg. editor: Facing the Iron Curtain, 1952, Education in a Divided World, 1952; feature writer: Phila. Public Ledger, also mags.; creator: syndicated features Know Thyself; syndicated radio program Holiday World, 1970—, Voice of Am, 1971—; 5 record albums. Pres. Internat. Scholarship Fund, 1960—, John Furbay Assos., Inc., 1970—; staff lectr. Def. Intelligence Sch., 1960-72; lectr. I.A.T.A., 1973-74; mem. collecting staff Am. Mus. Natural History. Col. USAF-CAP. Recipient Brewer aviation trophy, 1955; PAPA trophy Internat. Platform Assn., 1965; Freedoms Found. medal, 1972; Discover Am. Honor award, 1973; George Washington medal Freedoms Found., 1974; Discover Am. trophy, 1975; Am. Soc. Travel Agts. award, 1977. Fellow AAAS, Nat., Royal geog. socs., Royal Anthrop. Soc.; mem. NEA, Phi Kappa Phi. Republican. Mem. Soc. of Friends. Home: La Jolla Townehouse 5346 N 20th St Phoenix AZ 85016 Office: Broadcast House 155 Greenway South Forest Hills NY 11375

FUREDY, JOHN JULIUS, psychologist; b. Budapest, Hungary, June 30, 1940; s. Bela and Magda (Gardos) F.; m. Christine Roche, 1966. B.A., U. Sydney, Australia, 1963, M.A., 1964, Ph.D., 1965. Tutor U. Sydney, 1962-65; from vis. lectr. to asst. prof. Ind. U., 1965-67; asst. prof. psychology U. Toronto, 1967-69, asso. prof., 1969-75, prof., 1975—, Can. travelling prof., 1977; Can.-Hungary interchange vis. prof., 1980. Asso. editor: Biol. Psychology, 1976—; editorial bd.: Commentators, Brain and Behavioral Sci, 1978—, Internat. Jour. Pychophysiology; contbr. articles to profl. jours. Fulbright scholar, 1965-67; recipient award for research excellence Pavlovian Soc., 1982. Fellow Internat. Coll. Psychosomatic Medicine, Am. Psychol. Assn., Can. Psychol. Assn., Australian Psychol. Soc., Internat. Orgn. Psychophipiology. Clubs: Rosedale Tennis, Jackrabbit Cross Country Ski, Prince Arthur Bridge. Home: 24 Astley Ave Toronto ON Canada M4W 3B4 Office: Dept Psychology U Toronto ON Canada *I try to examine issues on the basis of logic and evidence and to resist the temptation to pay more attention to the status of the people making a claim than to what is being claimed.*

FURER, SAMUEL HENRY, lawyer; b. Louisville, Jan. 4, 1915; s. Abe and Alice (Barnett) F.; m. Gertrude Gooten, Oct. 12, 1947; children—Jerald A., Barbara A. B.A., Ohio State U., 1937; J.D., U. Cin., 1939; M.B.A., U. Wash., 1944. Bar: Ohio bar 1939. Practice law, Cin., 1939—; ptnr. firm O'Brien and Furer, 1951-63; sr. ptnr. firm Furer, Moskowitz, Siegel and Mezibov, 1979—; pres. Findlay Market Assn., Cin., 1963-64; instr. U. Wash., 1943. Pres. Federated Civic Assns., Hamilton County, Ohio, 1963-64, exec. sec., 1965-66. Served with JAGC U.S. Army, 1943-46. Mem. ABA, Ohio State Bar Assn., Cin. Bar Assn., Alpha Epsilon Pi. Club: Lawyers (Cin.). Home: 6765 Beechlands Dr Cincinnati OH 45237 Office: Suite 714 36 E 4th St Cincinnati OH 45202

FUREY, FRANCIS JAMES, bishop; b. Summit Hill, Pa., Feb. 22, 1905; s. John and Anna (O'Donnell) F. Student, St. Charles Sem., Overbrook, Pa., 1920-24; Ph.D., Pontificio Seminario Romano, Rome, 1926, S.T.D., 1930; LL.D., La Salle Coll., Phila., 1944, St. John's U., Bklyn., 1946, Villanova U., 1947, St. Joseph's Coll., Phila., 1949. Ordained priest Roman Catholic Ch., 1930; pvt. sec. to Cardinal Dougherty, 1930-36; pres. Immaculata (Pa.) Coll., 1936-46; rector St. Charles Sem., 1946-58, St. Helena's Parish, Phila., 1958-63; consecrated bishop, 1960, aux. bishop, Phila., titular bishop, Temnus, 1960-63, bishop of, San Diego, 1963-69, archbishop of, San Antonio, 1969—; Dir. Cath. Charities Appeal, Phila., 1958; Bd. dirs. Misericordia Hosp., Phila., St. Joseph Hosp., Ravenhill Acad., Germantown, Pa. Trustee Roman Cath. High Sch., Phila. Named Domestic Prelate by Pope Pius XII, 1947; knight comdr. Legion Cedars Lebanon. Mem. Nat., Pa. Cath. ednl. assns., Assn. Coll. Presidents Pa., John Henry Newman Soc.

FUREY, VINCENT EDWARD, JR., banker; b. Phila., Nov. 21, 1939; s. Vincent E. and Martha E. (Schroeder) F.; m. Peggy J. Tate, Aug. 15, 1965; children: Stephanie, Vincent, Kristin. B.A., Holy Cross Coll., 1961; M.B.A., U. Pa., 1969. Credit officer Girard Bank, Phila., 1969-74, v.p. nat. div., 1974-76, sr. v.p. nat. lending group, 1976-78, exec. v.p. comml. banking dept., 1978-81, exec. v.p. regional banking dept., 1981—. Bd. dirs. Phila. Urban Coalition, Pa. Economy League. Served as naval aviator USN, 1961-66, 68. Decorated Air medals. Mem. Robert Morris Assos. (pres. Phila. chpt.). Home: Old Fox Hollow Cherry Hill NJ 08003 Office: Girard Plaza Philadelphia PA 19101

FURGASON, ROBERT ROY, univ. exec.; b. Spokane, Wash., Aug. 2, 1935; s. Roy Elliott and Margaret (O'Halloran) F.; m. Gloria L. Althouse, June 14, 1964; children—Steven Scott, Brian Alan. B.S., U. Idaho, 1956, M.S., 1957; Ph.D., Northwestern U., 1961. Registered profl. engr., Idaho. Successively instr., asst. prof., asso. prof., prof. U. Idaho, Moscow, 1957—, acting head dept. chem. engring., 1964-65, head dept., 1965-74; dean Coll. Engring., 1974-78, v.p. acad. affairs and research, 1978—; engr. Phillips Petroleum Co., Bartlesville, Okla., 1957; research engr. Martin-Marietta Co., Denver, 1958; cons. J.R. Simplot Co., Minute Maid Corp., Ida. Potato Processors Assn., TRW.; Profl. cons. B.F. Goodrich Chem. Co. Devel. Center, Avon Lake, Ohio, 1969-70; adviser for NSF to Escuela Politecnica Nacional, Quito, Ecuador, 1973-74, 76. Recipient Outstanding Tchr. award U. Idaho, 1966, Idaho's Outstanding Young Engr. award, 1967. Mem. Am. Inst. Chem. Engrs., Am. Chem. Soc., Am. Soc. Engring. Edn., Nat. Soc. Profl. Engrs., Idaho Soc. Profl. Engrs. (pres. 1980-81), Sigma Xi, Phi Kappa Phi, Phi Eta Sigma, Sigma Tau, Kappa Sigma. Club: Lion. Home: 1443 Sunnyside St Moscow ID 83843

FURGIUELE, GUY, engineer; b. Beaver Falls, Pa., July 25, 1926; s. Eugene and Frances F.; m. Dorothy Jean De Young, Aug. 7, 1946; children: Terry, Patricia, Susan, Judy, Cindy. B.S.M.E., U. Houston, 1951; grad., Advanced Mgmt. Program, Harvard Bus. Sch., 1980. Registered profl. engr., Tex., Pa., Fla., Ill., Mich., Ind. Engr. Michael Baker, Jr., Beaver, Pa., 1951-53; pres., chief exec. officer Bovay Engrs., Inc., Houston, 1953—. Div. chmn. United Fund, Houston, 1975. Served with inf. U.S. Army, 1944-46; ETO. Fellow ASHRAE; mem. Nat. Soc. Profl. Engrs. (chpt. pres. 1968-69), Engring. and Sci. Soc. Houston (pres. 1977-78). Roman Catholic. Club: Warwick (Houston). Lodge: Rotary (Houston). Home: 3154 Lake Crescent Dr Houston TX 77339 Office: Bovay Engrs Inc 5619 Fannin Houston TX 77004

FURGURSON, ERNEST BAKER, JR., journalist; b. Danville, Va., Aug. 29, 1929; s. Ernest Baker and Passie Durham (Ferguson) F.; m. Mary Louise Stallings (div.); children—Ernest Baker III, Elisabeth Glyn; m. Cassie Woodward Thompson, Apr. 21, 1973. Student, Averett Coll., 1948-50; A.B., Columbia, 1952, M.S., 1953; postgrad., Georgetown U., 1961. Reporter Danville Comml. Appeal, 1948-51; sports editor radio sta. WDVA, 1949-50; reporter Roanoke (Va.) World-News, 1952, Richmond (Va.) News Leader, 1955-56; reporter, Washington corr. Balt. Sun, 1956-61, chief Moscow bur., 1961-64, White House corr., nat. polit. corr., Saigon corr., nat. affairs columnist, 1964—, chief Washington bur., 1975—; syndicated by Los Angeles Times Syndicate, 1970—. Author: Westmoreland: The Inevitable General, 1968. Trustee Averett Coll., 1978—. Served to 1st lt. USMC, 1953-55. Clubs: Gridiron, Nat. Press, Overseas Writers. Home: 4805 Sedgwick St NW Washington DC 20016 Office: 1627 K St NW Washington DC 20006

FURIGA, RICHARD DANIEL, government official; b. New Eagle, Pa., June 20, 1935; s. Joseph and Edith (Cain) F.; m. Kerry Helene Keel, July 20, 1957 (div. 1974); children: Christiann, R. Colin, Merewyn; m. Janet Marie Pietroboni, Feb. 1, 1975. B.S., U.S. Naval Acad., 1957; M.S., U. Kans., 1970. Logistics officer Strategic Petroleum Res. Dept. Energy, Washington, 1977-79, dep. dir., 1979-81, dep. asst. sec., 1982—. Served to comdr. USN, 1957-77. Mem. Soc. Petroleum Engrs. Republican. Lutheran. Home: 7823 Water Valley Ct Springfield MA 22153 Office: Dept Energy 1000 Independence Ave Washington DC 25058

FURINO, ANTONIO, economist, educator; b. Rome, Italy, May 7, 1931. J.D., U. Rome, 1955; M.A., U. Houston, 1965, Ph.D., 1972. Asst. prof. to asso. prof. econs. St. Edwards U., Austin, Tex., 1967-70; dir. regional analysis Alamo Area Council Govts., San Antonio, 1970-73; prof. econs. U. Tex., San Antonio, 1973—, dir. Center for Studies in Bus., Econs. and Human Resources,, 1973-78, dir. human resource mgmt. and devel. program, 1978-82; sr. partner, dir. Devel. Through Applied Sci., San Antonio, 1972—; cons. Cattedra di Techniche di Richerche di Mercato, U. Rome, 1972—; econ. cons. others. Mem. Am. Econ. Assn. Home: 8915 Data Point 48-D San Antonio TX 78229

FURLAUD, RICHARD MORTIMER, diversified pharmaceutical company executive, lawyer; b. N.Y.C., Apr. 15, 1923; s. Maxime Hubert and Eleanor (Mortimer) F.; children: Richard Mortimer, Eleanor Jay, Elizabeth Tamsin. Student, Institut Sillig, Villars, Switzerland; A.B., Princeton, 1943; LL.B., Harvard, 1947. Bar: N.Y. bar 1949. Asso. Root, Ballantine, Harlan, Bushby & Palmer, 1947-51; legal dept. Olin Mathieson Chem. Corp., 1955-56, asst. to exec. v.p. for finance, 1956-57, asst. pres., 1957-59, v.p., 1959-64, gen. counsel, 1957-60, gen. mgr., v.p. internat. div., 1960-64, exec. v.p., 1964-66; now dir.; pres., dir. E. R. Squibb & Sons, Inc., 1966-68; pres., chief exec., dir. Squibb Beech-Nut, Inc. (renamed Squibb Corp. 1971), 1968-74, chmn., chief exec., dir., 1974—; dir. Mut. Benefit Life Ins. Co., Am. Express Co. Mem. profl. staff Ho. of Reps. Com. Ways and Means, 1954; Trustee Rockefeller U.; bd. mgrs. Meml. Sloan-Kettering Cancer Center. Served as 1st lt., Judge Adv. Gen. Corps U.S. Army, 1951-53. Mem. Assn. Bar City N.Y., Pharm. Mfrs. Assn. (dir. 1965—), Council on Fgn. Relations. Clubs: Links, River (N.Y.C.). Home: 644 Pretty Brook Rd Princeton NJ 08540 Office: PO Box 4000 Princeton NJ 08540

FURLEY, DAVID JOHN, classics educator; b. Nottingham, Eng., Feb. 24, 1922; came to U.S., 1966; s. Athelstane Willis and Dorothy (Bee) F.; m. Diana Dill Armstrong, Aug. 28, 1948; children: Athelstane John Dill, William David; m. Phyllis Mary Huntley, Sept. 11, 1967. B.A., Jesus Coll., Cambridge (Eng.) U., 1943; M.A., 1947. Successively asst. lectr., lectr., reader Greek and Latin Univ. Coll., London, 1947-66; prof. classics, Princeton U., 1966-75, Charles Ewing prof. Greek lang. and lit., 1975—; vis. lectr. U. Minn., 1960-61; mem. Inst. Advanced Study, Princeton, 1964; Sr. fellow Center for Hellenic Studies, Washington, 1971—. Author: Aristotle: on the Cosmos, 1955, Two Studies in the Greek Atomists, 1967; also articles; Editor: Phronesis, 1968—, (with R.E. Allen) Studies in Presocratic Philosophy I, 1970, II, 1975. Served to capt. Royal Arty., 1942-45; CBI.

FURLONG, GEORGE MORGAN, JR., naval officer; b. Muskogee, Okla., Nov. 23, 1931; s. George M. and Anna (Moore) F.; m. Ryland Hagood Blakey, June 5, 1956; children: Morgan, William. B.S. in Naval Sci., U.S. Naval Acad., 1956, U.S. Naval Postgrad. Sch., 1963. Commd. ensign U.S. Navy, 1956, advance through grades to rear adm., 1981; comdg. officer USS Poncantoula, Pearl Harbor, Hawaii, 1975-76, USS Independence, Norfolk, Va., 1977-78; chief of staff U.S. Sixth Fleet, Gaeta, Italy, 1978-80; dir. Air Warfare Systems Analysis Staff, Office Chief of Naval Ops., Washington, 1980-81; comdr. Fighter Airborne Early Warning Wing. U.S. Pacific Fleet, Naval Air Sta., Mirawar, San Diego, 1981-83; dep. chief Chief Naval Edn. and Tng., Pensacola, Fla., 1983—; F-14 program mgr. Comdr. Naval Air Forces, U.S. Pacific Fleet, Naval Air Sta., North Island, Calif., 1973-74; wing comdr. Attack Carrier Air Wing 14, USS Enterprise, 1974-75. Deocorated Legion of Merit; recipient John Paul Jones award Nat. Navy League Assn., 1971. Office: Dep Chief Naval Edn and Tng Naval Air Sta Pensacola FL 32508

FURLONG, NADINE MARY, nursing administrator; b. Detroit, Mar. 7, 1945; d. William Garfield and Violet Melinda (Herford) F.; m. Jan Frederick Miller, Oct. 1980. R.N., Henry Ford Hosp., Detroit, 1966; B.S. in Nursing magna cum laude, U. Mich., 1976; M.S. in Psychiat. Nursing, U. Mich., 1978. Staff nurse William Beaumont Hosp., Royal Oak, Mich., 1966; spl. edn. nurse teaching asst. Hawthorn Children's Psychiat. Ctr., Northville, Mich., 1966-70; head nurse inpatient unit York Woods Children's Psychiat. Ctr., Ypsilanti, 1970-73; dir. Ann Arbor program Browndale Group Home, Mich., 1973; instr. inservice nursing edn., then nursing edn. dir. Ctr. Forensic Psychiatry, Ann Arbor, Mich., 1974-78; dir. nursing Met. Regional Psychiat. Hosp., Eloise, Mich., 1978-79; exec. dir. Mich. Nurses Assn., 1979—; treas. Washtenaw County Staff Devel. Com. in Nursing, 1977-78, chmn., 1978-79; cons. mental health tech. program Washtenaw Community Coll., 1976-77; adj. asst. prof. U. Mich. Sch. Nursing, 1979-80. Bd. dirs. ARC, 1976—, exec. bd., 1977—, 1st v.p., 1979-80, pres., 1981-82; instr., trainer CPR. James B. Angel scholar, 1976; recipient A.J. Brown Pub. Health Nursing award, 1976. Mem. Am. Nurses Assn. (adv. council), Mich. Nurses Assn., Sigma Theta Tau. Home: 2934 Northlawn St Ypsilanti MI 48197 Office: 120 Spartan Ave E Lansing MI 48823

FURLONG, RICHARD WILSON, engineering educator, researcher, association executive; b. Norwalk, Ohio, Mar. 30, 1929; s. Norman Burr and Dorothy (Wilson) F.; m. Helen Corinne Prince, Sept. 7, 1951; children: John Norman, Sara Catherine. B.S. in Civil Engring., So. Meth. U., 1952, M.S., Washington U., 1957; Ph.D., U. Tex., 1963. Registered profl. engr., Tex. Engr. McDonnell Aircraft, St. Louis, 1952-53; draftsman, checker Petroleum Equipment Co., St. Louis, 1953-55; design engr. F. Ray Martin, St. Louis, 1955-58; prof. civil engring. U. Tex.-Austin, 1958—; cons. engr. Richard Furlong, P.E., San Antonio, 1965—. Erskine fellow Canterbury U., Christchurch, N.Z., 1973. Fellow Am. Concrete Inst. (bd. dirs. 1978-82); mem. ASCE (exec. sec. Tex. sect. 1979—), Structural Stability Research Council, Can. Soc. Civil Engrs., Concrete Reinforcing Steel Inst., Nat. Soc. Profl. Engrs. Presbyterian. Home: 9014 Luzita Ln San Antonio TX 78230 Office: U Tex Grad Engring Program San Antonio TX 78285

FURLOW, MACK VERNON, JR., gen contracting and comml. real estate devel. co. exec.; b. Summit, Miss., Aug. 20, 1931; s. Mack Vernon and Trudie Dena (Ratcliff) F.; m. Barbara Elaine Rolfs, Mar. 20, 1954; children—David Wayne, Kevin Rolfs. B.S., La. State U., 1953; grad., advanced mgmt. program Harvard, 1968. Financial and systems analyst Humble Oil & Refining Co., Baton Rouge, 1957-61; asst. controller Skyland Internat. Corp., Chattanooga, 1961-65; v.p., corp. controller Blount, Inc., Montgomery, Ala., 1965-71; pres. Pipeco Steel Co., Inc., Wilmington, Del., 1971-73; v.p. fin., treas. Huber, Hunt & Nichols, Inc., Indpls., 1973—, dir., 1977—; Asst. treas. 54th Advanced Mgmt. Program class Harvard Bus. Sch., 1968—. Served to 1st lt. AUS, 1953-57. Mem. La. State U. Alumni Assn. (mem. adv. com. Montgomery chpt. 1967-71), Nat. Assn. Accts., Fin. Execs. Inst. Republican. Lutheran. Home: 8949 Sourwood Ct Indianapolis IN 46260 Office: 2450 S Tibbs Ave Indianapolis IN 46206 *The creation of a management climate or environment which causes people to want to excel and to perform to their fullest capabilities is a far superior approach than is a management style which causes people to perform because they are constantly afraid of the consequences of failing to perform.*

FURMAN, DAVID DICKSON, judge; b. N.Y.C., Nov. 22, 1917; s. Walter F. and Gertrude (Workman) F.; m. Alice McDowell, Mar. 5, 1942. Grad., Phillips Exeter Acad., 1935; A.B., Harvard, 1939; LL.B., N.Y.U., 1950. Bar: N.J. bar 1951. Legal sec. to Judge Nathan L. Jacobs, 1950-51; asso. firm Stryker, Tams & Horner, Newark, 1951-54; dep. atty. gen. N.J., 1954-58, atty. gen., 1958-62; judge Superior Ct. of N.J., 1962—; instr. Rutgers U. Sch. Law, 1952-53, N.Y. U. Sch. Law, 1956-58. Mem. Nat. Assn. Attys. Gen. (past pres.). Democrat. Home: Far Hills NJ 07931 Office: Middlesex County Ct House New Brunswick NJ 08901

FURMAN, DEANE PHILIP, parasitologist; b. Richarton, N.D., June 4, 1915; s. Raymond Walter and Estelle Me (O'Harrow) F.; m. Katherine McKeehan, Dec. 17, 1938; children: Philip Deane, Bryan Dale, Lynne Anne, Furman Ladwig. B.S., U. Calif.-Berkeley, 1937; Ph.D., U. Calif.-Davis, 1942. Entomologist USPHS, Washington, 1946; mem. faculty U. Calif.-Berkeley, 1946—, prof. parasitology, 1960—, entomologist, 1960-82, emeritus, 1982, chmn. div. parasitology, 1963-72, chmn. div. entomology and aprasitology, 1973-75, chmn. interdisciplinary grad. group parasitology, 1969-82; mem. fellowship rev. panel NIH, 1963-66; trustee Alameda County Mosquito Abatement Dist., 1961-64. Author manuals, papers in field, chpts. to books; mem. editorial bds. profl. jours. Served to maj. AUS, 1942-46. Decorated Bronze Star; NIH spl. fellow, 1964-65. Fellow AAAS; mem. Entomol. Soc. Am., Am. Soc. Parasitologists, Am. Soc. Tropical Med. and Hygiene, Wildlife Disease Assn., Acarological Soc. Am. (chmn. 1962-63), North Calif. Parasitologists Assn. (pres. 1973-74), Pacific Coast Entomol. Soc. Home: 235 Lake Dr Berkeley CA 94708 Office: Entomological Scis Univ Calif Berkeley CA 94720

FURMAN, JAMES MERLE, foundation executive; b. Kansas City, Mo., Apr. 3, 1932; s. James Merle and Andrey Eldena (Phillips) F.; m. Carol Ann McGhee, June 10, 1977; children: Mark Carter, Douglas Walter. B.A., Ohio State U., 1954; LL.D., Ill. Coll., 1976; L.H.D. (hon.), Nat. Coll. Edn., 1978, Ed. D., So. Ill. U., 1981, L.H.D., Govs. State U., 1981. Research asso. Ohio Legis. Service Commn., Columbus, 1955-61; dir. Community Research, Inc., Dayton, 1962-64; exec. officer Ohio Bd. Regents, Columbus, 1964-70; dir., exec. coordinator Wash. State Council on Higher Edn., Olympia, 1970-74; exec. dir. Ill. Bd. Higher Edn., Springfield, 1975-80; v.p. MacArthur Found., Chgo., 1980-81, exec. v.p., 1981—; mem. exec. com. State Higher Edn. Planning Commns., U.S. Office Edn.; bd. advisors Fund for the Improvement of Postsecondary Edn.; mem. student fin. assistance study group HEW. Trustee Loyola U.; chmn. Gov.'s Com. on Tax Reform. Mem. Edn. Commn. of States, Western Interstate Commn. on Higher Edn., State Higher Edn. Exec. Officers (pres. 1979-80), Nat. Center for Higher Edn. Mgmt. Systems (chmn.). Office: 140 S Dearborn St Suite 700 Chicago IL 60603

FURMAN, JOHN ROCKWELL, lumber company executive; b. Wellsville, N.Y., June 25, 1917; s. Harry Brennan and Helen (Rockwell) F.; m. Mary Hale Sutton, Aug. 2, 1941; children: John Rockwell II, Margery, Harry. B.A., Cornell U., 1939. New Eng. mgr. Dant & Russell, Inc., Portland, Oreg., 1948-56; founder, pres. Furman Lumber, Inc., Boston, 1956—, now chmn. chief exec. officer; trustee Boston 5-cent Savs. Bank. Mem. lumber industry area New Eng. area Nat. Def. Emergency Res., 1978—; Trustee Tilton (N.H.) Sch.; mem. corp. New Eng. Bapt. Hosp., Boston. Served to lt. comdr. USNR, 1941-46. Mem. Nat. Am. Wholesale Lumber Assn. (dir. 1967—), Sigma Nu. Clubs: Federal, Commercial (Boston); Brae Burn Country. Home: 21 Deerfield Rd Wellesley Hills MA 02181 Office: 108 Massachusetts Ave Boston MA 02115

FURMAN, MARTIN WILLIAM, automotive parts co. exec.; b. Balt., June 16, 1930; s. Max B. and Ruth (Marowitz) F.; m. Norma Rejas, July 15, 1969; children—Ronald C., Laurie A., Kenneth E., Jennifer L. B.S., Franklin and Marshall Coll., 1952; postgrad., U. Balt. Law Sch., 1952-54. With RPS Products, Inc., Balt., 1953—, pres., 1968-74, chmn. bd., chief exec. officer, 1974—. Office: 1700 S Caton Ave Baltimore MD 21227

FURMAN, ROBERT HOWARD, pharmaceutical company executive; b. Schenectady, Oct. 23, 1918; s. Howard Blackall and Jane Blessing (MacChesney) F.; m. Mary Frances Kilpatrick, Feb. 10, 1945; children: Carol K. Furman Friedman, Jane C. Furman Dougherty, Robert Howard, Hugh Patrick. A.B. (Allison prize 1939), Union Coll., Schenectady, 1940; M.D., Yale U., 1943. Diplomate: Am. Bd. Internal Medicine. Intern, then asst. resident in medicine New Haven Hosp., 1944-45; asst. in medicine Yale U. Med. Sch., 1944-45; asst. resident physician, then resident physician Vanderbilt U. Hosp., 1948-50; from research asst. in medicine to asst. prof. Vanderbilt U. Med. Sch., 1946-52; asso. prof., then prof. research medicine U. Okla. Med. Sch., 1952-70; prof. medicine Ind. U. Med. Sch., 1970—; head cardiovascular sect. Okla. Med. Research Found. and Hosp., 1952-70, asso. dir. found., 1957-70; exec. dir. clin. research Eli Lilly and Co., Indpls., 1970-73, v.p. corp. med. affairs, 1976—; v.p. Lilly Research Labs., 1973-76; mem. vis. staff Wishard Meml. Hosp., Indpls., 1971; pres. Okla. Heart Assn., 1967-68; mem. cardiovascular study sect. Nat. Heart Inst., NIH, 1960-63, heart spl. projects com., 1963-66; bd. mgrs., sci. adv. com. Wistar Inst., 1972-78; sci. adv. com. Hormel Inst., Austin, Minn., 1973—; mem. clin. scis. panel NRC, 1978—; mem. clin. pharmacology adv. com. PMAF, 1977—. Contbr. to med. jours.; mem. editorial bds. jours. Mem. council Inst. Adminstrn. and Mgmt.; mem. adv. bd. Union Coll., trustee, 1982; bd. dirs. Cathedral Arts, Indpls.; asso. trustee U. Pa. Served to comdr., M.C. USNR, 1945-46, 55-57. Fellow Am. Coll. Cardiology, A.C.P., N.Y. Acad. Scis., Royal Soc. Medicine; mem. Am. Assn. World Health (dir. 1974—), AAAS, Am. Clin. and Climatol. Assn., Am. Fedn. Clin. Research (fellow council arteriosclerosis, nat. bd. dirs., exec. and central coms.; chmn. research com. 1964-65), Ind. (dir.), Marion County heart assns.), Am. Physiol. Soc., Am. Soc. Clin. Pharmacology and Therapeutics, Am. Soc. Internal Medicine, Assn. Yale Alumni in Medicine, Central Soc. Clin. Research (council 1963-66), Endocrine Soc., Ind., Marion County med. assns., Soc. Exptl. Biology and Medicine, So. Soc. Clin. Research, Southwestern Soc. Naturalists, Wilson Ornithol. Soc., Nat. Audubon Soc., Sigma Xi, Alpha Omega Alpha, Delta Upsilon. Clubs: Cosmos, Capitol Hill (Washington); Confrerie des Chevaliers du Tastevin; Mohawk (Schenectady); Garden of the Gods (Colorado Springs). Home: 7651 Washington Blvd Indianapolis IN 46240 Office: 307 E McCarty St Indianapolis IN 46285

FURMAN, ROY LANCE, brokerage firm exec.; b. N.Y.C., Apr. 19, 1939; s. Joseph M. and Frances L. (Kurlander) F.; m. Frieda Anne Bueler, Nov. 7, 1965; children: Jill Tracy, Stephanie Gail. A.B., Bklyn. Coll., 1960; LL.B., Harvard U., 1963. Atty. Western Electric Co., N.Y.C., 1964-67; v.p. Continental Tel. Supply Co., N.Y.C., 1967-68; pres., sec., dir. Seiden & de Cuevas, Inc., N.Y.C., 1968-73; dir. Seiden & de Cuevas Internat., 1971-73; pres., chief exec. officer dir. Furman Selz Mager Dietz & Birney Inc., N.Y.C., 1973—; mem. Boston Stock Exchange, Phila. Stock Exchange; former chmn. splty. firms adv. com. N.Y. Stock Exchange.; dir. Kings Road Prodns.; bd. advs. Excelsior Fund. Pres. bd. dirs. Phoenix Theatre, N.Y.C.; bd. dirs. Film Soc. of Lincoln Ctr. Mem. N.Y. Bar Assn., N.Y. Soc. Securities Analysts., Assocs. of Mt. Sinai Hosp. Club: Friars. Office: Furman Selz Mager Dietz & Birney Inc 110 Wall St New York NY 10005

FURNAS, DAVID WILLIAM, plastic surgeon; b. Caldwell, Idaho, Apr. 1, 1931; s. John Doan and Esther Bradbury (Hare) F.; m. Mary Lou Heatherly, Feb. 11, 1956; children: Heather Jean, Brent David, Craig Jonathan. A.B., U. Calif.-Berkeley, 1952, M.S., 1957, M.D., 1955. Diplomate: Am. Bd. Surgery, Am. Bd. Plastic Surgery (dir. 1979—). Intern, U. Calif. Hosp., San Francisco, 1955-56, asst. resident in surgery, 1956-57; asst. resident in psychiatry, NIMH fellow Langley Porter Neuropsychiat. Inst., U. Calif., San Francisco, 1959-60; resident in gen. surgery Gorgas Hosp., C.Z., 1960-61; asst. resident in plastic surgery N.Y. Hosp., Cornell Med. Center, N.Y.C., 1961-62; chief resident in plastic surgery VA Hosp., Bronx, N.Y., 1962-63; registrar Royal Infirmary and Affiliated Hosps., Glasgow, Scotland, 1963-64; asso. in hand surgery U. Iowa, 1965-68, asst. prof. surgery, 1966-68, asso. prof., 1968-69; asso. prof. surgery, chief div. plastic surgery U. Calif., Irvine, 1969-74, prof., chief div. plastic surgery, 1974-80, clin. prof., chief div. plastic surgery, 1980—; surgeon East Africa Flying Doctors Service, African Med. and Research Found., 1973-74, 76, 77, 78, 79, 81, 82, 83; plastic surgeon S.S. Hope, Nicaragua, 1966, Ceylon, 1968, Sri Lanka, 1969; mem. Balakbayan med. mission, Mindanao and Sulu, Philippines, 1980, 81, 82. Contbr. chpts. to textbooks, articles to med. jours.; author/editor 3 textbooks. Served to capt. M.C., USAF, 1957-59. Recipient Golden Apple award for teaching excellence U. Calif.-Irvine Sch. Medicine, 1980, Kaiser-Permanente award U. Calif.-Irvine Sch. Medicine, 1981; named Orange County Press Club Headliner of Yr., 1982. Fellow ACS, Royal Coll. Surgeons Can., Royal Soc. Medicine, Explorers Club, Royal Geog. Soc.; mem. AMA, Calif., Orange County med. assns., Am. Soc. Plastic and Reconstructive Surgeons, Soc. Head and Neck Surgeons, Am. Cleft Palate Assn., Am. Soc. Surgery of Hand, Soc. Univ. Surgeons, Am. Assn. Plastic Surgeons (trustee 1983), Am. Soc. Aesthetic Plastic Surgery, Am. Soc. Maxillofacial Surgeons, Assn. Surgeons East Africa, Pacific Coast Surg. Assn., Internat. Soc. Aesthetic Plastic Surgery, Internat. Soc. Reconstructive Microsurgery, Pan African Assn. Neurol. Scis., Phi Beta Kappa, Alpha Omega Alpha. Home: 2501 Blue Water Dr Corona del Mar CA 92625 Office: 1310 Stewart Dr Suite 610 Orange CA 92668 *A crisis, at the outset, usually augurs nothing but ill. In the long run, however, my crises have more often than not marked a new course for my life, which is more fulfilling, and more exciting than anything in the past. Yes, a bit of good luck is needed, but the special feature of a crisis is that you are suddenly cut off from past patterns, habits, and interdependencies. Along with the distress and pain is freedom! Freedom to build again, with a new foundation and modern structure, using wisdom you didn't have the last time you built.*

FURNAS, JOSEPH CHAMBERLAIN, writer; b. Indpls., Nov. 24, 1905; s. Isaiah George and Elizabeth (Chamberlain) F. A.B., Harvard, 1927. Author: The Prophet's Chamber, 1937, Many People Prize It, 1938, So You're Going to Stop Smoking, 1939, Anatomy of Paradise, 1948 (Anisfield-Wolff non-fiction award), Voyage to Windward; The Life of Robert Louis Stevenson, 1951; Collaborator: (with Ernest M. Smith) Sudden Death and How to Avoid It, 1935, How America Lives, (with editorial staff of Ladies' Home Jour.), 1941; author: Goodbye to Uncle Tom, 1956, The Road to Harpers Ferry, 1959, The Devil's Rainbow, 1962, The Life and Times of the Late Demon Rum, 1955, Lightfoot Island, 1968, The Americans, 1969, Great Times, 1974, Stormy Weather, 1977, Fanny Kemble, 1981 (George Freedley award 1982). Mem. Phi Beta Kappa. Clubs: Harvard, Century Assn. Address: care Brandt & Brandt 1501 Broadway New York NY 10036

FURNESS, BETTY, broadcast journalist, consumer adviser, actress; b. N.Y.C., Jan. 3, 1916; d. George Choate and Florence (Sturtevant) F.; m. John Waldo Green, Nov. 27, 1937 (div. Aug. 1943); 1 dau., Barbara Sturtevant; m. Hugh B. Ernst, Jr., Jan. 3, 1945 (dec. Apr. 1950); m. Leslie Midgley, Aug. 15, 1967. Student, Brearly Sch., N.Y.C., Bennett Sch., Millbrook, N.Y.; LL.D. (hon.), Iowa Wesleyan Coll., 1968, Pratt Inst., Bklyn., 1978, Marymount Coll., 1983; D.C.L. (hon.), Pace U., 1973, Marymount Coll. Manhattan, 1976. Movie actress, 1932-37; appeared: stage plays Doughgirls; commls. for, Westinghouse Corp., 1949-60; appeared on, CBS-radio in, Dimension of a Woman's World, Ask Betty Furness, 1961-67; spl. asst. to, Pres. U.S., for consumer affairs, 1967-69; chmn., Pres.'s Com. Consumer Interests, 1967-69; columnist: McCall Mag, 1969-70, 72; chmn., exec. dir., N.Y. State Consumer Protection Bd., 1970-71; commr., N.Y. Dept. Consumer Affairs, 1973; now with, NBC News, N.Y.C.; Bd. dirs., Consumers Union, 1969—, Common Cause, 1971-75. Office: NBC News 30 Rockefeller Plaza New York NY 10020

FURRER, JOHN RUDOLF, business executive; b. Milw., Dec. 2, 1927; s. Rudolph and Leona (Peters) F.; m. Annie Louise Waldo, Apr. 24, 1954; children: Blake Waldo, Kimberly Louise. B.A., Harvard U., 1949. Spl. rep. ACF Industries, Madrid, 1949-51; asst. supr. Thermo nuclear Devel. and Test-Los Alamos, Eniwetok Atoll, 1952-53; dir. product devel. ACF Industries, N.Y.C., 1954-59; dir. machinery, systems group, central engring. labs. FMC Corp., San Jose, Calif., 1959-68, gen. mgr. engineered systems div., San Jose, 1968-70, v.p. in charge planning dept., central engring. labs. an engineered systems div., Chgo., 1970-71, v.p. material handling group, 1971-77, v.p. corp. devel., 1977—. Patentee in field. Served with USN, 1945-46. Mem. ASME. Clubs: Harvard (N.Y.C. and Chgo.); Glen View Country (Golf, Ill.); Economic, Mid-America (Chgo.). Home: 1242 N Lake Shore Dr Chicago IL 60610 Office: FMC Corp 200 E Randolph St Chicago IL 60601

FURST, ARTHUR, toxicologist, educator; b. Mpls., Dec. 25, 1914; s. Samuel and Doris (Kolochinsky) F.; m. Florence Wolovitch, May 24, 1940; children: Carolyn, Adrianne, David Michael, Timothy Daniel. A.A., Los Angeles City Coll., 1935; A.B., UCLA, 1937, A.M., 1940; Ph.D., Stanford U., 1948; Sc.D., U. San Francisco, 1983. Mem. faculty, dept. chemistry San Francisco City Coll., 1940-47; asst. prof. chemistry U. San Francisco, 1947-49, asso. prof. chemistry, 1949-52; asso. prof. medicinal chemistry Stanford Sch. Medicine, 1952-57, prof., 1957-61; with U. Calif. War Tng., 1943-45, San Francisco State Coll., 1945; research asso. Mt. Zion Hosp., 1952—; clin. prof. pathology Columbia Coll. Physicians and Surgeons, 1969-70; dir. Inst. Chem. Biology; prof. chemistry U. San Francisco, 1961-80, Disting. Univ. prof., 1980—, dean grad. div., 1976-79; Vis. fellow Battelle Seattle Research Center, 1974; Michael vis. prof. Weizmann Inst. Sci., Israel, 1982; cons. on cancer WHO; mem. com., bd. mineral resources NRC. Contbr. numerous articles to profl. and ednl. jours. Fellow AAAS, N.Y. Acad. Scis.; mem. Am. Soc. Pharmacology and Exptl. Therapeutics, Am. Chem. Soc., Am. Assn. Cancer Research, Soc. Toxicology, Am. Coll. Toxicology (nat. sec.), Sigma Xi, Phi Lambda Upsilon. Research activities on organic synthesis, chemotherapy cancer, carcinogenesis of metals and hydrocarbons. Home: 3736 La Calle Ct Palo Alto CA 94306 Office: U San Francisco Inst Chem Biology San Francisco CA 94117

FURST, LILIAN RENEE, educator; b. Vienna, June 30, 1931; came to U.S., 1971, naturalized, 1977; d. Desiderius and Sarah Freda (Neufeld) F. B.A. with honors, Manchester (Eng.) U., 1952; Ph.D., Girton Coll., Cambridge, Eng., 1957. Asst. prof. Queen's U., Belfast, Ireland, 1955-59, asso. prof., 1959-66; asso. prof., head dept. Manchester U., 1966-71; vis. prof. Dartmouth Coll., Hanover, N.H., 1971-72; prof., dir. grad. program U. Oreg., Eugene, 1972-74; prof. comparative lit. U. Tex., Dallas, 1975—; Mather vis. prof. Case Western Res. U., Cleve., 1978-79; vis. prof. Stanford U., 1981-82, Harvard U., 1983-84. Author: Romanticism in Perspective, 1969, rev. edit., 1979, Romanticism, 1969, rev. edit., 1976, Naturalism, 1971, The Anti-Hero, 1976, Counterparts, 1977, Contours of European Romanticism, 1979, European Romanticism: Self-Definition, 1980, Fictions of Romantic Irony, 1984. Am. Council Learned Socs. fellow, 1974-75; Guggenheim fellow, 1982-83; Marta Sutton Weeks fellow Stanford Humanities Ctr., 1982—. Mem. Modern Lang. Assn. Am., Am. Comparative Lit. Assn., Internat. Comparative Lit. Assn., Modern Humanities Research Assn. Home: 7654 Royal Ln Dallas TX 75230 Office: University of Texas at Dallas PO Box 688 Richardson TX 75080

FURST, STEPHEN J., JR., retail executive; m. Joan Louise Muth; children: Steve, Todd, Jennifer. B.A. in Bus. Adminstrn. With Hess's, Inc., Allentown, Pa., 1961—, div. mdse. mgr. fashion accessories, 1964-66, dir. customer services, 1966-69, asst. v.p., dir. personnel, 1969-71, v.p., 1971-75, sr. v.p. consumer and co-worker relations, 1975-76, exec. v.p. adminstrn., asst. sec., asst. treas., 1976—, also dir.; dir. parent co. Crown Am.; mem. adv. bd. Vocat. and Tech. Schs. Bd. dirs. Allentown

Credit Bur., Allentown Kiwanis Found., Lehigh County Blind Assn., ARC, Allentown Bus. Sch.; past pres. Allentown Center City Assn.; mem. Pa. State Adv. Bd. Distributive Edn. Mem. Am. Retail Fedn. (mem. employee relations com.), Nat. Retail Mchts. Assn. (mem. govt. and legal affairs com., employee relations com., consumer affairs com.), Pa. Retailers Assn. (mem. polit. action bd., tax com., tele communications com., public relations com.), Am. Soc. Tng. and Devel., Soc. Consumer Profls., Am. Soc. Personnel Adminstrs., Pa. Consumer Council, C. of C. (dir.). Office: Hess's Inc 9th and Hamilton Sts Allentown PA 18101

FURSTE, WESLEY LEONARD, II, surgeon; b. Cin., Apr. 19, 1915; s. Wesley Leonard and Alma (Deckebach) F.; m. Leone James, Mar. 28, 1942; children—Nancy Dianne, Susan Deanne, Wesley Leonard III. A.B. cum laude (Julius Dexter scholar 1934-35); Harvard Club scholar 1933-35), Harvard U., 1937, M.D., 1941. Diplomate: Am. Bd. Surgery. Intern Ohio State U. Hosp., Columbus, 1941-42; fellow surgery U. Cin., 1945-46; asst. surg. resident Cin. Gen. Hosp., 1946-49; sr. asst. surg. resident Ohio State U. Hosps., 1949-50, chief surg. resident, 1950-51; limited practice medicine specializing in surgery, Columbus, 1951—; instr. Ohio State U., 1951-54, clin. asst. prof. surgery, 1954-66, clin. assoc. prof., 1966-74, clin. prof. surgery, 1974—; mem. surg. staff Mt. Carmel Med. Center, chmn. dept. surgery, 1981—, dir. surgery program, 1981-82; mem. surg. staff Children's, Grant, Univ., St. Anthony, Riverside, Meth. hosps., all Columbus; surg. cons. Dayton (Ohio) VA Hosp., Columbus State Sch., Ohio State Penitentiary, Mercy Hosp., Benjamin Franklin Hosp., Columbus; regional adv. com. nat. blood program ARC, 1951-68, chmn., 1958-68; invited participant 2d Internat. Conf. on Tetanus, WHO, Bern, Switzerland, 1966, 3d Internat. Conf., São, Paulo, Brazil, 1970, 5th Internat. Conf., Ronneby Brunn, Sweden, 1978; invited rapporteur 4th Internat. Conf., Dakar, Sénégal, 1975; mem. med. adv. com. Medic Alert Found. Internat., 1971-73, 76—, bd. dirs., 1973-76; Douglas lectr. Med. Coll. of Ohio, Toledo; founder Digestive Disease Found. Prime author: Tétanos; Tetanus: A Team Disease; contbg. author: Advances in Military Medicine, 1948, Management of the Injured Patient; contbr. articles to profl. jours. Mem. Ohio Motor Vehicle Med. Rev. Bd., 1965-67; bd. dirs. Am. Cancer Soc. Franklin County, pres., 1964-66. Served to maj., M.C. AUS, 1942-46; CBI. Recipient 2 commendations for surg. service in China U.S. Army; Cert. of Merit Am. Cancer Soc. Mem. Central Surg. Assn., Soc. Surgery of Alimentary Tract, AAAS, A.C.S. (gov.-at-large, chmn. Ohio com. trauma; nat. subcom. prophylaxis against tetanus in wound mgmt., chmn. com. for selection Ohio Disting. Service award; Ohio adv. com.), Am. Assn. Surgery of Trauma, Ohio, Columbus surg. assns., AMA, Am. Trauma Soc. (founding mem., dir.), Ohio Med. Assn., Acad. Medicine Columbus and Franklin County (Award of Merit for 17 yrs. service), Acad. Medicine Cin., Am. Public Health Assn., Am. Med. Writers Assn., Grad. Surg. Soc. U. Cin., Robert M. Zollinger Club, Mont Reid Grad.Surg. Soc., Am. Geriatrics Soc., N.Y. Acad. Scis., Assn. Physicians State of Ohio, Collegium Internationale Chirurgiae Digestivae, Assn. Am. Med. Colls., Am. Med. Golfing Assn., Internat. Brotherhood Magicians, Soc. Am. Magicians. Presbyterian. Clubs: Scioto Country, Ohio State Univ. Golf, Ohio State Faculty (Columbus); Univ. (Cin.); Harvard (Boston). Invited guest of Pres. Johnson for signing of Community Health Act, 1965. Home: 3125 Bembridge Rd Columbus OH 43221 Office: 3545 Olentangy River Rd Columbus OH 43214 *When in China as a United States Army surgeon during World War II, I was most impressed by (1) the effectiveness of tetanus toxoid in preventing tetanus (lockjaw) in our wounded men and (2) the development of tetanus with a high mortality rate in Chinese soldiers who did not have such toxoid immunization. Ever since then, I have endeavored to emphasize the best possible surgical care of wounds including tetanus toxoid immunization so that, in the U.S. by 1985, and in the entire world by 2000, tetanus will, indeed, have become a disease of only historical significance. Participants at the 1981 International Tetanus Conference believed such tetanus elimination history is possible.*

FURTER, WILLIAM FREDERICK, chemical engineer, college dean; b. North Bay, Ont., Can., Apr. 5, 1931; s. Alfred Frederick and Eva Margaret (Stinson) F.; m. Pamela Margaret Cooper, Aug. 6, 1966; children: Lesley Margaret, Jane Elizabeth, Pamela Catharine. Grad. (Dominion scholar), Royal Mil. Coll., 1953; B.A.Sc., U. Toronto, 1954, Ph.D. (NRC Can. scholar), 1958; S.M. (scholar), MIT, 1955, Nat. Def. Coll. Can., 1970. Registered profl. engr., Ont. Research engr., research devel. dept. DuPont Can. Ltd., 1958-59, sr. tech. investigator, 1959-60; asst. prof. Royal Mil. Coll., Kingston, Ont., 1960-61, asso. prof., 1961-66, prof. chem. engring., 1966—, sec. grad. sch., 1967-80, head chem. engring. div., 1960-80, acting dean grad. studies and research, 1978-79, 82; dean Can. Forces Mil. Coll. and chmn. Extension Div., 1980-84; dean grad. studies and research Can. Forces Mil. Coll., 1984—; cons. Hexcel Corp., San Francisco, Air Liquide Can. Ltd., Montreal, Union Carbide Corp., Charleston, W.Va. Contbr. chpts. to books, research papers to profl. jours. Recipient Bronze medal Gov. Gen. of Can., 1960, Silver medal, 1951; Silver medal Lt. Gov. of Ont., 1952; Engring. Inst. Can. prize, 1952; Royal Canadian Sch. Mil. Engring. prize, 1951; grantee Def. Research Bd. Can., 1963—. Fellow Chem. Inst. Can.; mem. Assn. Profl. Engrs. Ont., Canadian Soc. Chem. Engring. (dir. 1979-82), Interam. Confedn. Chem. Engring., Canadian Nuclear Assn., Am. Nuclear Soc., Ont. Council Grad. Studies. Mem. United Ch. Can. Clubs: Royal Mil. Coll. Can. (pres. Kingston br. 1967-68, exec. com Found. exec. com. parent club 1972-75. Home: 406 Elmwood St Kingston ON K7M 2Z3 Canada Office: Royal Military College Kingston ON K7L 2W3 Canada

FURTH, ALAN COWAN, business executive, lawyer; b. Oakland, Calif., Sept. 16, 1922; s. Victor L. and Valance (Cowan) F.; m. Virginia Robinson, Aug. 18, 1946; children: Andrew Robinson, Alison Anne. A.B., U. Calif. at Berkeley, 1944, LL.B., 1949; grad., Advanced Mgmt. Program, Harvard U., 1959. Bar: Calif., U.S. Supreme Ct. With S.P. Co., 1950—, gen. counsel, 1963—, v.p., 1966, exec. v.p. law, 1976-79, pres., 1979—, also dir. and mem. exec. com.; dep. chmn., dir. Fed. Res. Bank; dir. So. Pacific Land Co., Indsl. Indemnity Co., Ticor, Fed. Res. Bank of San Francisco. Trustee Merritt Hosp., Oakland, Calif.; trustee Pacific Legal Found.; bd. dirs. U. Calif. at Berkeley Found. Served to capt. USMCR, 1944-46, 51-52. Mem. Am. Bar Assn., Calif. State Bar Assn. Clubs: Bohemian, Pacific-Union, San Francisco Golf (San Francisco); Met., Burning Tree (Washington). Office: So. Pacific Bldg One Market Plaza San Francisco CA 94105

FURTH, EUGENE DAVID, physician, educator; b. Phila., Jan. 25, 1929; s. Jacob and Olga B. F.; m. Mary Dickinson, July 19, 1952; children—David Louis, Anne Crowell. B.A., Wesleyan U., 1950; M.D., Cornell U., 1954. Diplomate: Cert. Am. Bd. Internal Medicine. Intern Cornell U. Med. Coll., 1954-55, asst. resident internal medicine, 1957-58, research fellow, 1958-59, resident in endocrinology, 1959-60, USPHS fellow, 1960-62, instr. medicine, 1961-62, asst. prof. radiology, 1962-67, asst. prof. medicine, 1963-67; asso. prof. Albany (N.Y.) Med. Coll., 1967-70, prof., 1970-76; attending physician, endocrinologist, dispensary physician, 1967-76; prof., chmn. dept. medicine East Carolina U., 1976—; chief medicine Pitt County (N.C.) Meml. Hosp., 1976—. Served to capt. AUS, 1955-57. Fellow A.C.P.; mem. Am. Thyroid Assn., Endocrine Soc., Am. Fedn. Clin. Research, N.Y. Acad. Scis., AAAS, AMA, N.C. Med. Soc., Pitt County Med. Soc. Office: Department of Medicine East Carolina University School of Medicine Greenville NC 27834

FURTH, GEORGE, actor, playwright; b. Chgo., Dec. 14, 1932; s. George R. and Evelyn (Tuerk) Schweinfurth. B.S. in Speech, Northwestern U., 1954; postgrad., Sch. Dramatic Arts, Columbia U., 1955. Mem. faculty drama dept. U. So. Calif. Actor both off and on Broadway, N.Y.C., 1956—; appeared in approximately 20 feature films, 3 TV series, also all major TV shows; writer: Broadway musicals Company (Antoinette Perry (Tony) award, N.Y. Drama Critics Circle award, Drama Desk award, Outer Critics Circle award 1970), The Act, 1977; comedy Twigs, 1971. Served with USNR, 1958-62. Mem. Actors Studio. Address: care Artists Agency 190 N Canon Dr Beverly Hills CA 90210 *

FURTH, HANS GERHARD, psychologist; b. Vienna, Austria, Dec. 2, 1920; came to U.S., 1955, naturalized, 1961; s. Hugo and Julia (Schindler) F.; m. Madeleine B. Steen, May 22, 1954; children: Sonia, Peter, Julia, Daniel, David, Paul, Catherine. L.R.A.M. in Piano, Royal Acad. Music, London, 1940; B.A. in Philosophy, Charterhouse, Sussex, Eng., 1950; M.A. in Clin. Psychology, U. Ottawa, Ont. Can., 1954; Ph.D. in Exptl. Psychology, U. Portland, 1960. Research psychologist mental health project for deaf N.Y. State Psychiat. Inst., N.Y.C., 1955-57; sch. psychologist Oreg. State Sch. for Deaf, Salem, 1958-60; asst. to prof. dept. psychology Cath. U. Am., Washington, 1960—, chmn. dept. psychology, 1967-71; Research asso. Children's Hearing and Speech Center, Washington, 1960-66; prof. social psychology U. Sussex, 1973-75. Author: Thinking without Language, 1966, Piaget and Knowledge, 1969, Piaget for Teachers, 1970, Deafness and Learning, 1973, Thinking Goes to School, 1974, The World of Grown-Ups, 1980. Research and publs. on knowledge development, particularly of deaf persons with edn. implications; concluded that language is not necessary or intrinsic to intellectual devel. Office: Youth Research Center Cath U Washington DC 20064

FURTH, HAROLD PAUL, physicist, educator; b. Vienna, Austria, Jan. 1930; came to U.S., 1941, naturalized, 1947; s. Otto and Gertrude (Harteck) F.; m. Alice May Lander, June 19, 1959 (div. Dec. 1977); 1 son, John Frederick. Grad., Hill Sch., 1947; A.B., Harvard U., 1951, Ph.D., 1960; postgrad., Cornell U., 1951-52. Physicist U. Calif. Lawrence Radiation Lab., Livermore, 1956-65, group leader, 1965-67; prof. astrophys. scis. Princeton U., 1967—; dir. Plasma Physics Lab., 1981—. Bd. editors: Physics of Fluids, 1965-67, Nuclear Fusion, 1964—, Revs. Modern Physics, 1975-80; Contbr. articles to profl. jours. Recipient E.O. Lawrence award AEC, 1974. Fellow Am. Phys. Soc. (J. C. Maxwell prize 1983); mem. Nat. Acad. Scis. Patentee in field. Home: 36 Lake Ln Princeton NJ 08540

FURTH, HELMUT JULIUS FREDERICK, lawyer, government official; b. Vienna, Austria, Sept. 12, 1930; came to U.S., 1939, naturalized, 1945; s. Joseph Herbert and Emma Paula (Kaan) F.; m. Natalie Jane Stang, Apr. 14, 1956; children: John Frederick, Allen Joseph, Robert Herbert. A.B., Harvard U., 1952, LL.B., 1955. Bar: N.Y. 1956. Assoc. Donovan Lesure Newton & Irvine, 1955-66, ptnr., 1966-78; of counsel Sullivan & Cromwell, 1978-82; dep. asst. atty. gen. antitrust div. Dept. Justice, Washington, 1982—. Home: 149 North Carolina Ave SE Washington DC 20003 Office: Dept Justice 10th and Constitution Sts NW Washington DC 20530

FURY, KATHLEEN DUNIGAN, writer, editor; b. N.Y.C., June 18, 1941; d. John Raymond and Virginia Elizabeth (Barrows) Dunigan; m. Leonard Wayne Fury, Dec. 26, 1965. Student, Ohio Wesleyan U., 1959-61; B.A., Purdue U., 1964. Assoc. editor Redbook mag., 1964-67; editorial cons. Jasmin mag., Munich, Germany, 1968; sr. writer, articles editor Ladies' Home Jour, 1974-77; founding editor-in-chief Your Place mag., McCall Pub., 1978; free lance writer, 1968-74, 78—; cons. editor Savvy mag., 1979—; articles editor Family Circle mag., 1981—; lectr. diploma in mag. pub. program N.Y.U., 1981—. Contbr. articles to mags. Mem. Am. Soc. Mag. Editors, N.Y. Women in Communications, Women's Media Group (pres. 1982). Office: Family Circle 488 Madison Ave New York NY 10022

FUSARO, RAMON MICHAEL, dermatologist; b. Bklyn., Mar. 6, 1927; s. Angelo and Ida F.; m. Lavonne Johnsen, Nov. 6, 1972; children—Lisa Ann, Toni Ann. B.A., U. Minn., 1949, B.S., 1951, M.D., 1953, M.S., 1958, Ph.D., 1965. Diplomate: Am. Bd. Dermatology. Intern Mpls. Gen. Hosp., 1953-54, resident, 1954-58; instr. U. Minn., 1957-65, asst. prof., 1965-66, asso. prof., 1966-70, dir. outpatient dermatology clinic, 1962-70; prof., chmn. dept. dermatology U. Nebr. Med. Center, Omaha, 1970—, Creighton U., 1975—; dir. dermatology program Creighton-Nebr. Univs. Health Found., 1975—. Contbr. articles to profl. publs. in field. Active Beaver Lake Property Owners' Assn. Served with USN, 1944-45. Mem. AMA, Am. Acad. Dermatology, AAUP, Assn. Am. Med. Colls., Soc. Investigative Dermatology, N.Y. Acad. Scis., Dermatology Found., Internat. Leprosy Assn., Internat. Soc. Tropical Dermatology, Am. Soc. Photobiology, Sigma Xi. Home: 639 Beaver Lake Blvd Plattsmouth NE 68048 Office: Univ Nebraska Medical Center 42nd and Dewey St Omaha NE 68105

FUSELIER, LOUIS ALFRED, lawyer; b. New Orleans, Mar. 26, 1932; s. Robert Howe and Monica (Hanemann) F.; m. Eveline Gasquet Fenner, Dec. 27, 1956; children: Louis Alfred, Henri de la Claire, Elizabeth Fenner. B.S., La. State U., 1953; LL.B., Tulane U., 1959. Bar: La. 1959, Miss. 1964, U.S. Supreme Ct. 1965. Trial atty. NLRB, New Orleans, 1959-62; pres. firm Fuselier, Ott & McKee, P.A., and predecessors, Jackson, Miss. Served as pilot and squadron comdr. USAF, 1953-56. Mem. ABA (practice and procedure com. of labor law sect.), La. Bar Assn. (past chmn. labor law sect.), New Orleans Bar Assn., Miss. Bar Assn., Hinds County Bar Assn., Fed. Bar Assn., Miss. Bar Found., Miss. Def. Lawyers, Am. Law Inst., Am. Hosp. Attys. Assn., Miss. Wildlife Fedn. (pres. 1975-77), Newcomen Soc., Am. Judicature Soc., Am. Soc. Personnel Adminstrs. (accredited personnel diplomate), Jackson C. of C. Clubs: Round Table, Boston (New Orleans); Country, Capital City Petroleum, Rotary, University (Jackson). Home: 3804 Old Canton Rd Jackson MS 39216 Office: 2100 Deposit Guaranty Plaza Jackson MS 39201

FUSFELD, HERBERT IRVING, research management and public policy executive; b. Bklyn., Feb. 13, 1921; s. Harry and Fanny (Stitch) F.; m. Ruth Lachman, July 11, 1943; children: Alan Roy, Warren Edward. B.A., Bklyn. Coll., 1941; M.A., U. Pa., 1945, Ph.D., 1950. Research physicist, head physics, math. div. Frankford Arsenal, Phila., 1941-53; sr. physicist Am. Machinery & Foundry Co., Stamford, Conn., 1953-55; dir. Central Research Lab., 1955-59, dir. research, 1959-63, Kennecott Copper Corp., N.Y.C., 1963-78; dir. Center for Sci. and Tech. Policy, N.Y. U., 1978—; dir. Hazeltine Corp.; vis. lectr. physics of metals Grad. Sch. U. Pa., 1952-53; chmn. Internat. Temperature Symposium, 1954; mem. numerical data adv. bd. NRC, 1970-75; mem. Nat. Materials Adv. Bd., 1975-79; adv. group on transnat. enterprises U.S. Dept. State, 1975—, expert cons., 1976—; chmn. adv. com. Inst. Materials Research, Nat. Bur. Standards, 1976—; mem. expert group sci. and tech. OECD, 1976-80; adv. council NSF, 1977—; mem. adv. com. corp. assos. Am. Chem. Soc.; mem. U.S.-USSR Joint Commn. on Sci. and Tech. Cooperation, 1974-79; chmn. nonferrous subcom. on energy conservation Am. Mining Congress; adv. com. Sch. Materials Research, U. Pa. Bd. editors: Research Mgmt; Co-editor: Science and Technology Policy: Perspectives for the 1980's, 1979; book series Technology Policy and Economic Growth; Contbr. articles in field to profl. jours. Fellow AAAS; mem. Indsl. Research Inst. (dir., pres. 73-74, comn. fed. sci. and tech. com. 1974—), Am. Phys. Soc., Am. Ordnance Assn., Am. Inst. Physics (governing bd.), Am. Inst. Mining and Metall. Engrs., Am. Mgmt. Assn. (trustee, v.p. research and devel. council). Club: Sky (N.Y.C.). Home: 45 Mohawk Trail Stamford CT 06903 Office: 114 Liberty St Rm 501 New York NY 10006

FUSSELL, PAUL, educator, author; b. Pasadena, Calif., Mar. 22, 1924; s. Paul and Wilhma Wilson (Sill) F.; m. Betty Ellen Harper, June 17, 1949; children: Rosalind, Samuel. B.A., Pomona (Calif.) Coll., 1947, Litt.D. (hon.), 1981; M.A., Harvard U., 1949, Ph.D., 1952; M.A. (hon.), U. Pa., 1983. Instr. English, Conn. Coll., 1951-55; mem. faculty Rutgers U., 1955—, John DeWitt prof. English lit., 1976-83; Donald T. Regan prof. English lit. U. Pa., Phila., 1983—; Fulbright lectr. U. Heidelberg, Ger., 1957-58; cons. editor Random House, 1963-64; lectr. Am. univs., 1965—. Author: The Rhetorical World of Augustan Humanism, 1965, Poetic Meter and Poetic Form, 1965, rev., 1979, Samuel Johnson and The Life of Writing, 1971, The Great War and Modern Memory (Nat. Book Critics Circle award 1975, Nat. Book award 1976), Abroad: British Literary Traveling Between the Wars, 1980, The Boy Scout Handbook & Other Observations, 1982, Class: A Guide through the American Status System, 1983; contbg. editor: Harper's, 1979—, The New Republic, 1979—. Served with AUS, 1943-46. Decorated Purple Heart (2), Bronze Star; recipient James D. Phelan award Phelan Found., 1964; Lindback Found. award, 1971; Ralph Waldo Emerson award Phi Beta Kappa, 1976; sr. fellow Nat. Endowment Humanities, 1973-74; Guggenheim fellow, 1977-78; Rockefeller Found. fellow, 1983-84. Fellow Royal Soc. Lit.; mem. MLA, Acad. Lit. Studies. Home: 2101 Chestnut St Philadelphia PA 19103 Office: Dept English U Pa Philadelphia PA 19104

FUSSLER, HERMAN HOWE, library science educator; b. Phila., May 15, 1914; s. Karl Hartley and Irene Graham (Howe) F.; m. Gladys Otten, 1937; 1 dau., Lynn Fussler Padgett. A.B., U. N.C., 1935, B.A. in L.S, 1936; A.M., U. Chgo., 1941, Ph.D., 1948. Asst. sci. and tech. div. N.Y. Pub. Library, 1936; head dept. photog. reprodn. U. Chgo. Library, 1936-46, sci. librarian, 1943-47, asst. and asso. dir., 1947-48, dir., 1948-71; instr. to asst. prof. Grad. Library Sch., U. Chgo., 1942-48, prof. library sci., 1948—, Martin A. Ryerson disting. service prof., 1974—; acting dean Grad. Library Sch., 1961-63; asst. dir. info. div. and librarian Metall. Project, Chgo., 1942-45; head demonstration of microphotog. Paris Internat. Expn., 1937; vis. prof. Monash U., Australia, 1977; del. to World Documentation Congress, Paris, 1937; 4th Internat. Conf. on Documentation, Oxford and London, 1938, 1st Japan-U.S. Conf. on Libraries in Higher Edn., Tokyo, 1969; mem. bd. dirs. Center for Research Libraries, 1950-67, vice chmn., 1954-55, 59-60, chmn., 1960-61; cons. Ford Found., Paris, 1960, 63, Brazil, 1961; mem. bd. regents Nat. Library Medicine, 1963-67; bd. dirs. Assn. Research Libraries, 1961-64, 70-71; mem. Nat. Adv. Commn. on Libraries, 1966-67; cons. Council on Library Resources, 1974-77. Author: Photographic Reproduction for Libraries, 1942, Characteristics of the Research Literature Used by Chemists and Physicists in the U.S, 1949; co-author: Patterns in the Use of Books in Large Research Libraries, 1969, Research Libraries and Technology, 1973, Current Research Library Issues, 1978; editor: Library Buildings for Library Service, 1947, The Function of the Library in the Modern College, 1954, The Research Library in Transition, 1957, Management Education: Implications for Libraries and Library Schools, 1973; asso. editor: Library Quar, 1949—. Fellow Am. Acad. Arts and Scis., AAAS; mem. ALA (former mem. council, Melvil Dewey medal 1954, Ralph Shaw award 1976, chmn. com. civil rights 1960-61), Assn. Coll. Research Libraries. Home: 5844 Stony Island Ave Chicago IL 60637

FUTIA, LEO RICHARD, insurance company executive; b. Buffalo, Aug. 27, 1919; s. Carl and Helen (Dicianne) F.; m. Marie Grace Giangreco, July 16, 1947; children: Carl, Mary, Leo J., Charles, Elaine, Anne Marie. B.B.A., Canisius Coll., 1940; M.B.A., U. Pa., 1941. C.L.U. With Guardian Life Ins. Co. of Am., N.Y.C., 1941—, field rep., 1946-65, gen. agt., 1965-67, sr. v.p., 1967-70, dir., 1970—, exec. v.p., 1970, pres., 1977—, chmn. bd., 1980—; chmn. bd., chief exec. officer Guardian Ins. and Annuity Co., Inc., 1983—; instr. ins. Canisius Coll., 1947-50; dir. Park Ave. Fund., Value Line Mut. Funds, Guardian Investors Services. V.p., dir. GLICOA Assos., Inc., N.Y.C., 1968—; bd. dirs., chmn. Med. Info. Bur., 1982—; trustee Cabrini Med. Ctr., 1984—. Served to lt. (s.g.) USCG, 1942-46. Mem. Am. Soc. C.L.U.s (dir. 1959-61, 64-68, pres. 1966-67, chpt. pres. 1953-54), Buffalo Life Underwriters Assn. (pres. 1963-64), Health Ins. Assn. Am. (bd. dirs. 1983—), Million Dollar Round Table. Roman Catholic. Clubs: Greenwich (Conn.) Country; Union League (N.Y.C.); Guardian Life Leaders (pres. 1955). Home: 18 Interlaken Rd Greenwich CT 06830 Office: 201 Park Ave S New York NY 10003

FUTRELL, JOHN WILLIAM, institute executive, lawyer; b. Alexandria, La., July 6, 1935; s. J.W. and Sarah Ruth (Hitesman) F.; m. Iva Macdonald, Aug. 13, 1966; children: Sarah, Daniel. B.A., Tulane U., 1957; postgrad., Free U. Berlin, 1958; LL.B., Columbia U., 1965. Bar: La. 1966. Atty. Lemle & Kelleher, New Orleans, 1966-71; prof. law U. Ala., 1971-74, U. Ga., 1974-80; pres. Environ. Law Inst., Washington, 1980—; lectr. Dept. State in Japan and India, 1978; Woodrow Wilson fellow Smithsonaian Instn., Washington, 1979-80. Pres. Sierra Club, San Francisco, 1977-78, nat. bd. dirs., San Francisco, 1971-81; del. UN Conf. on Water, 1977, White House Conf. Inflation, 1974. Served as officer USMC, 1957-62. Fulbright scholar, 1958. Mem. ABA, AAAS, Phi Beta Kappa, Order of Coif. Office: Environmental Law Inst 1346 Connecticut Ave NW Washington DC 20036

FUTTER, ELLEN VICTORIA, college president; b. N.Y.C., Sept. 21, 1949; d. Victor and Joan Babette (Feinberg) F.; m. John A. Shutkin, Aug. 25, 1974; 1 dau., Anne Victoria. A.B., Barnard Coll., 1971; student, U. Wis.-Madison, 1967-69; J.D., Columbia U., 1974. Bar: N.Y. 1975. Atty. Milbank, Tweed, Hadley & McCloy, N.Y.C., 1974-80; acting pres. Barnard Coll., N.Y.C., 1980-81, pres., 1981—, trustee, 1972—; dir. Squibb Corp., Milbank Meml. Fund. Mem. N.Y. Stae Gov's Com. of Coll. and Univ. Pres.'s Concerning Fin. Aid; trustee Commn. on Ind. Colls. and Univs., N.Y. State; mem. exec. com. Women's Coll. Coalition; bd. dirs. Regional Plan Assn.; mem. Helsinki Watch, N.Y. State Gov.'s Council on State Priorities, 1982; friend N.Y.C. Commn. on Status of Women, 1982. Mem. Assn. Bar City of N.Y., N.Y. State Bar Assn., ABA, Nat. Inst. Social Scis., Phi Beta Kappa. Club: Cosmopolitan. Office: 606 W 120th St New York NY 10027

FUTTER, VICTOR, corporate executive, lawyer; b. N.Y.C., Jan. 22, 1919; s. Leon Nathan and Merle Caroline (Allison) F.; m. Joan Babette Feinberg, Jan. 26, 1943; children: Jeffrey Lee Sam, Ellen Victoria Shutkin, Deborah Gail. A.B. with honors in Govt, Columbia U., 1939, J.D., 1942. Bar: N.Y. bar 1942, U.S. Supreme Ct 1948. Asso. firm Sullivan & Cromwell, 1946-52; with Allied Corp., Morristown, N.J., 1952—, asso. gen. counsel, 1976-78, v.p., sec., 1978—; dir. Allied Chem. Nuclear Products, 1977—; sec. Allied Chem. Found.; spl. prof. law Hofstra Law Sch., 1976-78. Editor: Columbia Law Rev; contbr. articles to profl. jours. Trustee, dep. mayor Village of Flower Hill, N.Y., 1974-76; mem. senate Columbia U., 1970-76; mem. devel. council Hofstra Law Sch., 1976—; chmn. bd. dirs. Columbia Coll. Fund, 1970-72; pres. Flower Hill Assn., 1968-70; bd. dirs. N.Y. Young Democrats, 1946-52; co-chmn. fund drive Port Washington

Community Chest, 1964, bd. dirs., 1964—; trustee Port Washington Civic Council, 1969-70. Served to maj. AUS, 1942-46. Recipient medal Columbia U. Alumni Fedn. Mem. Am. Soc. Corp. Secs. (pres. N.Y. region 1983—, chmn. nat. conf. program 1984), Am. Bar Assn., Am. Law Inst., Assn. Bar City N.Y. (nuclear tech. com., com. on internat. human rights 1983—), Assn. Corp. Counsel N.J., N.Y. State Bar Assn. (com. on legal edn. and admission to bar 1982—), Stockholder Relations Soc. N.Y., Phi Beta Kappa, Columbia Coll. Alumni Assn. (pres. 1972-74). Office: PO Box 4000R Morristown NJ 07960

FYE, PAUL MCDONALD, oceanographer; b. Johnstown, Pa., Aug. 6, 1912; s. Orlando G. and Jennie (McDonald) F.; m. Ruth Elizabeth Heym, Apr. 26, 1942; children—Kenneth Paul, Elizabeth Ruth. B.S., Albright Coll., 1935, D.Sc., 1955; Ph.D. in Phys. Chemistry, Columbia U., 1939; D.Sc., Tufts U., 1970, Southeastern Mass. U., 1970, Fla. Inst. Tech., 1973, L.I. U., 1978; LL.D. (hon.), Northeastern U., 1975. Asst. prof. Hofstra Coll., 1939-41; research asso. Carnegie Inst. Tech., 1941-42; research supr., research dir. underwater explosives research lab. Woods Hole Oceanographic Instn., 1942-47; asso. prof. chemistry U. Tenn., 1947-48; div. chief, then chief explosives research dept. U.S. Naval Ordnance Lab., 1948-56, asso. dir. research, 1956-58; dir. Woods Hole Oceanographic Instn., 1958-77, pres., 1961—; dir. Arthur D. Little, Inc., Lord Abbett Mut. Funds; dir., mem. exec. com. Textron, Inc.; mem. Polaris steering task group, 1956-58, 1960-65, Undersea Warfare Research and Devel. Planning Council, 1959-73; mem. com. oceanography Nat. Acad. Scis., 1961-70, ocean affairs bd., 1970-72; U.S. rep. to sci. com. nat. reps. SACLANT ASW Research Centre, Spezia, Italy, 1968-73; mem. Pres.'s Task Force on Oceanography, 1969; sci. adv. com. Internat. Atlantic Salmon Found., 1970—; mem. marine sci. sect., ocean affairs adv. com. Dept. State, 1971—, law of sea adv. com., 1972—. Mem. adv. bd. Cape Cod Community Coll., 1961—, Fla. Inst. Tech., 1973—, Mass. Maritime Acad., 1973—; Trustee Bermuda Biol. Sta. for Research, 1960—; mem. corp. Marine Biol. Lab., 1958—; trustee State Colls. Mass., 1966, Internat. Fedn. Insts. Advanced Study, Mass. Maritime Acad., 1981—; mem. exec. com. Internat. Fedn. Insts. Advanced Study, 1971—. Recipient Devel. award Bur. Ordnance, 1946; Presdl. Certificate of Merit, 1948; Meritorious Service award U.S. Navy, 1961; also Disting. Public Service award, 1977; cert. of commendation Sec. Navy, 1960, 66; Distinguished Alumni award Albright Coll., 1951. Mem. Am. Chem. Soc., Am. Geophys. Union, U.S. Naval Inst. (asso.), Am. Phys. Soc., Am. Soc. Limnology and Oceanography, AAAS, Marine Tech. Soc., Sigma Xi, Phi Lambda Upsilon, Epsilon Chi, Pi Tau Beta. Clubs: Univ. (N.Y.C.); Cosmos (Washington); Edgartown (Mass.) Yacht. Office: Woods Hole Oceanographic Instn Woods Hole MA 02543

FYFE, WILLIAM SEFTON, geochemist, educator; b. N.Z., June 4, 1927; s. Colin Alexander and Isabella Fifee; m. Patricia Walker, Feb. 27, 1981; children: Christopher, Catherine, Stefan. B.Sc., U. Otago, N.Z., 1948, M.S., 1949, Ph.D., 1952. Prof. chemistry in, N.Z., 1955-58; prof. geology U. Calif., Berkeley, 1958-66; research prof. Manchester Coll. and Imperial Coll., London, 1966-72; chmn. dept. geology Western Ont. U., 1972—. Mem. Nat. Sci. and Engring. Research Council Can.; Fellow Royal Soc. London; hon. life fellow Geol. Soc. Am., Mineral. Soc. Am.; mem. Acad. Sci. Brazil. Brit. Chem. Soc., Explorers Club. Home: 1197 Richmond London ON Canada N6A 3L3 Office: Dept Geology U Western Ontario London Canada N6A 5B7

FYFFE, WILLIAM CLARENCE, TV executive; b. Great Falls, Mont., Mar. 11, 1929; s. Clarence Don and Valene (Stapleton) F.; m. Nancy Callaway, Dec. 6, 1980. B.S. in Speech, Northwestern U., 1954. Reporter, newscaster Sta. WJIM-TV, 1955-57, Sta. WJRT, 1957-59, Sta. WWJ-TV, 1959-64; news dir. Sta. WXYZ-TV, 1964-68, Sta. WLS-TV, 1968-70, Sta. KTLA, 1970-71, Sta. KABC-TV, 1971-78; v.p. news ABC-TV, 1978-79; v.p., sta. mgr. WLS-TV, 1979-80; v.p., gen. mgr. WABC-TV, N.Y.C., 1981—. Served with USN, 1946-48. Mem. Radio-TV News Dirs. Assn., Sigma Delta Chi. Office: 7 Lincoln Sq New York NY 10023

GAAFAR, SAYED MOHAMMED, veterinary parasitologist; b. Tanta, Egypt, Jan. 18, 1924; came to U.S., 1947, naturalized, 1956; m. Mohammed Hegab and Bahia Ahmad (Salama) G.; m. Irma Eileen Bird, Aug. 30, 1949; children: Joseph Omar, Wayne Samir, Daniel Sherief, Gail Magda. B.V.Sc., Cairo U., 1944; D.V.M., Tex. A&M U., 1955; M.S., Kans. State U., 1949, Ph.D., 1950. Veterinarian Egyptian Ministry Agr., 1944-46, parasitologist vet. diagnostic lab., 1950-51; instr. Cairo U. Med. Sch., 1946-47; veterinarian Rutherford Vet. Hosp., Dallas, 1952-54; instr., then asst. prof. Tex. A&M U., 1954-58; mem. faculty Purdue U., 1958—, prof. vet. parasitology, 1963—; vis. prof. Royal Vet. Coll., London, Baghdad U., Tripoli U., Kasetsart U., King Saud U.; mem. expert adv. zoonosis WHO; cons. in parasitology. World Bank. Editor: Pathology of Parasitic Diseases, 1970; editor-in-chief: Vet. Parasitology, 1974. Career devel. fellow, 1964; grantee NIH, 1968-69. Mem. Am. Soc. Parasitologists (trustee Stoll-Stunkard Endowment Fund 1979), Conf. Research Workers in Animal Diseases, Internat. Vet. Med. Assn., Am. Assn. Vet. Parasitologists, Am. Soc. Tropical Medicine and Hygiene, World Fedn. Parasitologists, Am. Assn. Pathology, Council Biology Editors, World Assn. for Advancement of Vet. Parasitology, Sigma Xi, Phi Zeta, Gamma Sigma Delta. Clubs: Lions, Optimists, Masons. Home: 2620 Newman Rd West Lafayette IN 47906 Office: Vet Pathology Bldg Purdue U West Lafayette IN 47907 *In spite of what most of us think, under most circumstances and taking everything in consideration, our lives are the best we could have had. Biologically we have little control on the laws of nature, and our inner harmony should come from liking what we do rather than doing what we like.*

GAAL, STEVEN ALEXANDER, scientist; b. Budapest, Hungary, Feb. 22, 1924; came to U.S., 1950, naturalized, 1963; s. Istvan and Aranka (Gaspar) G.; m. Ilse Lisl Novak, Aug. 24, 1952; children—Barbara Sandra, Dorothy Janet. Ph.D., U. Budapest, 1947. Asst. Inst. Tech. Budapest, 1947; attache de recherche U. Paris, 1948-50; mem. Inst. Advanced Study, Princeton, 1950-52; asst. prof. Cornell U., 1952-58; research asso. Yale, 1958-60; prof. math. U. Minn., Mpls., 1960—; Chief investigator Army Research Office, 1959; dir. research project NSF, 1963-70; research asso. Office Naval Research, 1958; adviser AID, India, 1966. Researcher point set topology, number theory and representation theory. Home: Route 1 Box 152 Cokato MN 55321

GABARO, JOHN JOSEPH, organizational behavior and business administration educator; b. Worcester, Mass., Aug. 29, 1939; s. Rafael and Joaquina (Canet) Gabarro-Llobel; m. Marilyn Ann Peters, Nov. 18, 1967; children: Jana Palar, Jordi-Carlos. B.S., Worcester Poly. Inst., 1961; M.B.A., Harvard U., 1967, D.B.A., 1972. Plant process engr. Gen. Foods Corp., Orange, Mass., 1961; devel. engr., project leader Corning Glass Works, Bradford, Pa., 1963-65; research fellow Harvard Bus. Sch., Boston, 1970-72, asst. prof., 1972-75, assoc. prof., 1975-79, prof. organizational behavior and bus. adminstrn., 1979—; cons. govtl. agys., founds., bus. orgns., U.S., Europe. Co-author: Interpersonal Behavior, 1978, Teaching Interpersonal Behavior, 1978, Managing Behavior in Organizations, 1983. Dist. commr. Boy Scouts. Am., Bradford, Pa., 1964. Served to 1st lt. U.S. Army, 1961-63. Foote, Cone and Belding fellow Harvard U., 1967; Harvard Dissertation fellow, 1969. Mem. Acad. Mgmt. (mem. steering com. on careers and socilaization 1983—), Orgaizational Behavior Teaching Soc. (dir. 1977-80), Am. Sociol. Assn. Unitarian-Universalist. Clubs: Pennhills, Harvard Faculty. Home: 8 Monadnock Rd Arlington MA 02174 Office: Harvard U Grad Sch Bus Adminstrn Soldiers Field Boston MA 02163

GABBARD, FLETCHER, physicist, educator; b. Sand Gap, Ky., Sept. 13, 1930; s. Moss and Delta (Cook) G.; m. s. Anne Louise Verner, June 20, 1957; children—Fletcher William, Gregory Scott, Sarah Elizabeth. B.S., U. Ky., 1951; M.S., Rice U., Houston, 1957, Ph.D., 1959. Jr. scientist Naval Ordnance Lab., White Oak, Md., 1951-52; physicist Nat. Bur. Standards, Washington, 1952-53; research asst. Rice U., 1956-59; mem. faculty U. Ky., Lexington, 1959—, prof. physics, 1970—, chmn. dept. physics and astronomy, 1973—; vis. scientist Oak Ridge Nat. Lab., 1960, Nat. Bur. Standards, 1972. Author research papers in field. Councilor Oak Ridge Asso. Univs.; trustee Lees Jr. Coll.; past pres. Scientists and Engrs. for Applachia. Served with AUS, 1953-55. NSF grantee; Dept. Energy grantee. Mem. Am. Phys. Soc., Am. Assn. Physics Tchrs., AAAS, Ky. Assn. Physics Tchrs., Sigma Xi, Sigma Pi Sigma. Republican. Presbyterian. Home: 217 Barberry Ln Lexington KY 40503 Office: Dept Physics and Astronomy Univ Ky Lexington KY 40506

GABEL, W. CREIGHTON, anthropologist, educator; b. Muskegon, Mich., Apr. 5, 1931; s. Kenneth Alonzo and Edith Myrtle (Creighton) G.; m. Jane Whitfield, Sept. 6, 1952; children: James, Anne, Molly. B.A., U. Mich., 1953, M.A., 1954; Ph.D., U. Edinburgh, Scotland, 1957. Instr. Northwestern U., 1956-58, asst. prof., 1958-63; asso. prof. Boston U., 1963-69, prof., 1969—; research asso. Boston U. African Studies Center, 1963—, chmn. anthropology dept., 1970-72, 76-79. Author: Stone Age Hunters of the Kafue, 1965, Analysis of Prehistoric Economic Patterns, 1967; editor: Man Before History, 1964; Editor: Reconstructing African Culture History, 1967. NSF grantee, 1960-61, 66-67; Fulbright grantee, 1973; Social Sci. Research Council grantee, 1963-64. Mem. Soc. Am. Archaeology, South African Archaeol. Soc., Soc. Africanist Archaeologists in N.Am. Office: 270 Bay State Rd Boston MA 02215

GABELMAN, IRVING JACOB, consulting engineer, retired government official; b. Bklyn., Nov. 12, 1918; s. William and Mary (Blumenfeld) G.; m. Leah Levitt, Feb. 13, 1949; children: Alan, Philip. B.A. in Physics, Bklyn. Coll., 1938; B.E.E., Coll. City N.Y., 1945; M.E.E., Poly. Inst. Bklyn., 1948; Ph.D. in Elec. Engring, Syracuse U., 1961. Radio engr. U.S. Army Engr. Office, N.Y.C., 1941-45; electronics engr. Watson Labs., USAF, Eatontown, N.J., 1945-51; electronic scientist Rome Air Devel. Center, Griffiss AFB, N.Y., 1951-59, dir. advanced studies, 1959-69, chief plans, 1969-71, chief scientist, 1971-75; pres. Tech. Assocs., 1975—; Chmn. avionics panel, adv. group electronic research and devel. NATO, 1971-76, U.S. nat. coordinator, 1971-76; mem. council Upper Div. Coll. Utica/Rome State U. N.Y., 1974—; adviser Div. Adv. Group Electronic Systems Div. Air Force Systems Command, 1974-76. Editor: Displays for Command and Control Centers, 1969, Techniques for Data Handling in Tactical Systems, 1969, Storage and Retrieval of Information—A User-Supplier Dialogue, 1969, Data Handling Devices, 1970; Contbr. articles tech. jours. Recipient Air Force Exceptional Civilian Service award, 1974. Fellow IEEE (chmn. systems com. nat. group on computers 1966), AAAS. Patentee air traffic control device. Address: 225 Dale Rd Rome NY 13440

GABER, GEORGE JOSEPH, music educator; b. N.Y.C., Feb. 24, 1916; s. Rachmiel and Dvora (Wexler) G.; m. Esther F. Feinberg, Dec. 8, 1940; children: Robert, Deborah. Student, Cooper Union, 1930-34, Juillard Sch., 1934-37, New Sch., 1943-45, Manhattan Sch. Music, 1954-46; degree with honors, Allegro Mocidade, Sao Paulo, Brazil, 1972. Musician Ballet Russe, N.Y.C., 1937-40, Pitts. Symphony, 1939-43, ABC, N.Y.C., 1943-60; Disting. prof. music Ind. U., Bloomington, 1960—; musician Los Angeles Symphony, 1968, Capital Records, N.Y.C., 1943-60, Israel Philharm. Orch., 1969, Aspen Festival, 1957-72. Mem. AAUP, Coll. Musicians Soc., Am. Fedn. Musicians. Clubs: Bohemians, Masons. Home: 1909 Arden Dr Bloomington IN 47401 Office: Ind U Bloomington IN 47401

GABHART, HERBERT CONWAY, college chancellor; b. Morganfield, Ky., Aug, 19, 1914; s. Riley C. and Betty (Conway) G.; m. Helen Ashburn, Aug. 7, 1942; children—Diana Ruth, Betty Fay, Jo Ellen. B.S., Carson-Newman Coll., 1934; Th.M., So. Bapt. Theol. Sem., 1940, Th.D., 1943. Bus. mgr. Bapt. Messenger, 1935-37; ordained to ministry Baptist Ch., 1938; pastor in, Williamsburg, Ky., 1943-51, Memphis, 1951-59; pres. Belmont Coll., Nashville, 1959-82, chancellor, 1982—. Author: Thinking With Youth, 1947, Introduction to a Study of the Bible and Its Central Figure, Jesus Christ, 1958; mem. adv. bd.: Advantage Mag. Mem. Assn. So. Bapt. Colls., Affiliated Independent Colls. Tenn. Club: Kiwanis (pres. 1973-74). Home: 2425 Bear Rd Nashville TN 37215

GABIANELLI, VINCENT JAMES, mus. curator; b. Bridgeport, Conn., July 8, 1932; s. Joseph Charles and Emily (Gabianelli) G.; m. Allene Jane Caise, Aug. 14, 1954; children—Mary Emily, Kathy Ann, Vincent James, Laura Ann. A.B. in Zoology, U. Vt., 1954; M.Ed., U. Miami, 1959. Sci. tchr., Norwalk, Conn., 1955-57; curator edn. Mus. Sci., Miami, Fla., 1957-60, dir., 1960-66, Mus. Sci. and Space Transit Planetarium, Miami, 1966-68; chmn. interpretation dept. Fla. State Mus., Gainesville, 1968-69, 71—; dir. Ocean Space Center, Internat. Oceanographic Found., Miami, 1969-71; affiliate prof. history and joint prof. edn. U. Fla., 1979—; pres. Mus. Services, Inc.; mem. adv. com. Hotel Thomas, 1977—. Mem. Morningside Nature Center Commn., 1975—; bd. govs. Fla. Zool. Soc., Tropical Audubon Soc.; Mem. Southeastern Museums' Conf., Alachua County Hist. Commn., Gainesville Cultural Commn.; adviser Com. on Bldgs., Exhbns. and Design Fla. Bicentennial Commn. Named Man of Year Miami Jr. C. of C., 1966. Fellow AAAS; mem. Am. Assn. Museums (publs. com. 1976-78, energy com. 1977—, S.E. regional rep. to council 1979-82), S.E. Museums Conf. (pres. 1976-78), Fla. Defenders of Environment. Clubs: K.C., Rotarian. Conducted spl. tng. program in STP instrument for Spitz Labs. Home: 1303 NW 28th St Gainesville FL 32605 Office: Fla State Mus U Fla Gainesfille FL 32611

GABINET, LEON, lawyer, educator; b. Ostrow, Poland, June 1, 1927; C.H. and Sarah G.; m. Laille Schutz, Dec. 19, 1948; children—Sarah, Kathryn, Arthur. Ph.B., U. Chgo., 1950, J.D., 1953. Bar: Oreg. bar 1955. Asso. firm firm Davies, Biggs, Strayer, Stoel & Boley, Portland, Oreg., 1956-61; partner firm Krause, Lindway & Nahstoll, Portland, 1961-68; prof. law Franklin T. Backus Sch. Law, Case Western Res. U., Cleve., 1968—. Served with USN, 1944-46. Mem. Am. Law Inst., Am. Bar Assn. (tax sect.). Office: 11075 East Blvd Cleveland OH 44106

GABLE, FRED BURNARD, pharmacist, author; b. Phila., June 30, 1929; s. Samuel and Mollie (Rayfield) G.; married; children: Tracy, Dana, Jack. B.S., Temple U., 1951, M.S., 1953, M.A. in Sociology, 1959. Mem. faculty Temple U., Phila., 1955-80, prof. pharmacy, 1974-80, asst. dean, 1968-80; mem. pub. edn. com. Am. Cancer Soc., 1964-76. Author: Opportunities in Pharmacy Careers, 1964, revised edits., 1969, 74, 1984 (a new book), Psychosocial Pharmacy: The Synthetic Soc, 1974; editor: The Temple Apothecary, 1959-80; contbr. articles to pharm. jours. Served with M.C. U.S. Army, 1953-55. Mem. Pa. Prison Soc., Phila. Mus. Art, Pa. Acad. Fine Arts, Rho Chi. Home: 1901 JFK Blvd Suite 2703 Philadelphia PA 19103

GABLE, G. ELLIS, lawyer; b. Kerens, Tex., Mar. 7, 1905; s. George Warren and Sue Ethel (Collins) G.; m. Frances Doyle, Dec. 30, 1933; children: Richard Warren, Thomas Doyle. Life tchrs. certificate, Northeastern Okla. State U., Tahlequah, 1922; J.D., Okla U., 1926. Bar: Okla. 1926. Since practiced in, Tulsa; now mem. Gable & Gotwals; judge pro-tem, Tulsa County, 1938-39. Past mem. Tulsa Bd. Edn., pres., 1956-57; mem. Okla. State Regents for Higher Edn., 1958-76. Mem. ABA (mem. fellows), Okla. Bar Assn. (pres. 1954), Tulsa County Bar Assn. (pres. 1949), Phi Delta Phi. Methodist. Clubs: Mason (Shriner, Jester), Petroleum, Rotary (pres. 1961-62), Southern Hills Country.). Home: 5813 S Indianapolis Ave Tulsa OK 74135 Office: 2000 Fourth National Bank Bldg Tulsa OK 74119

GABLE, RICHARD WALTER, educator; b. Joliet, Ill., Nov. 16, 1920; s. Walter Emmanuel and Matilda (Endres) G.; m. Myra Ann Kagen, June 16, 1946; children: Cyrel Lee, Richard Siroos, Carl Walter. B.S., Bradley U., 1942; M.A., U. Chgo., 1948, Ph.D., 1950. Mem. faculty Ohio State U., 1948-50, Stanford U., 1950-53, U. So. Calif., 1954-66; mem. faculty U. Calif. at Davis, 1966—, chmn. dept. polit. sci., 1969-71; vis. faculty U. Tehran, ICA/U. So. Calif. contract, 1955-57, U. Panjab, AID/ U. So. Calif. contract, 1962-63; Mem. Calif. Gov.'s Council on Intergovernmental Relations, 1971-74; mem. AID/Ralph M. Parsons contract team, India, 1969; dir. devel. studies program U.S. AID, 1975; faculty Fed. Exec. Inst., U.S. CSC, 1975-76; mem. World Bank Basic Econ. Mission to Syria, 1977, AID evaluation team to, Egypt; mgmt. needs survey team for AID, North Yemen, 1978; mem. AID team to decentralization conf., Lesotho, 1980, AID mgmt. constraints study team, Pakistan, 1982. Author: (with H. Koontz) Public Control of Economic Enterprise, 1955, (with F.P. Sherwood) The California System of Governments, 1967, (with J.F. Springer) Administering Agricultural Development in Asia, 1976; Editor: (with J. Finkle) Political Development and Social Change, 1971; Contbr. articles to profl. jours. Served with AUS, 1942-46. Haynes Found. grantee, 1967-68; S.E. Asia Devel. Adv. Group grantee, 1969-73; sr. fellow East-West Center, Honolulu, 1972-73. Mem. Am. Soc. Pub. Adminstrn. (pres. Sacramento chpt. 1967-68), Am., Western polit. sci. assns., Soc. Internat. Devel., AAUP, Internat. Studies Assn., Internat. Inst. Adminstrv. Sci., Eastern Regional Orgn. on Pub. Adminstrn. Home: 1210 Colby Dr Davis CA 95616

GABLER, ROBERT EARL, geography educator; b. Lodi, Ohio, Nov. 22, 1927; s. Earl Raymond and Carrie (Geisinger) G.; m. Mary Ellen Johnston, Aug. 19, 1950; children: Robert Allen, Janet Ann, Mary Elizabeth (dec.). B.S. with honors, Ohio U., 1949; M.S., Pa. State U., 1951; Ed.D., Columbia U., 1957. Social studies tchr. Canton (Ohio) pub. schs., 1950-55; lectr. geography Hunter Coll., N.Y.C., 1955-57; mem. faculty Western Ill. U., Macomb, 1957—, prof. geography, chmn. dept. geography, 1965-73; Dir. NDEA Title XI Insts. Geography, 1965-67, 1968, 1977. Author: (with others) Follett Intermediate Social Studies Textbook Series, 1980, Introduction to Physical Geography, 1975, Essentials of Physical Geography, 1977, 2d edit., 1982; Editor: Bull. Ill. Geog. Soc, 1958-65, (with others) Handbook for Geography Tchrs, 1966; mem. editorial bd.: Jour. Developing Areas, 1965—. Served with C.E. AUS, 1946-47. Mem. Assn. Am. Geographers, AAUP, Nat. Council Geog. Edn. (dir. coordinators, exec. bd. 1963-68, 1st v.p., program chmn. 1972-73, pres. 1973-74), Phi Kappa Tau, Gamma Theta Upsilon, Phi Sigma Epsilon. Home: 711 E Piper St Macomb IL 61455

GABOR, EVA, actress; b. Budapest, Hungary, Feb. 11; d. Vilmos and Jolie G.; m. Eric Drimmer, 1939 (div. 1942); m. Charles Isaacs, 1942 (div. 1950); m. John E. Williams, Apr. 8, 1956 (div.); m. Richard Brown, Oct. 4, 1959 (div.); m. Frank Jamieson, 1973. Student, Forstner Inst., Budapest. Appeared in: films Forced Landing, 1939, A Royal Scandal, Song of Surrender, The Last Time I Saw Paris, 1954, Artists and Models, 1955, My Man Godfrey, 1957, Don't Go Near the Water, 1957, The Truth About Women, 1958, Gigi, 1958, Youngblood Hawke, 1964; play appearances include Arsenic and Old Lace; co-star: TV series Green Acres, CBS-TV, 1965-71; Author: Orchids and Salami, 1954. Office: care Katz-Gallin-Morey Enterprises 9255 Sunset Blvd Los Angeles CA 90069

GABOR, ZSA ZSA (SARI GABOR), actress; b. Budapest, Hungary, d. Vilmos and Jolie G.; m. Jack Ryan, 1975; 1 dau. by previous marriage, Francesca Hilton. Ed. in, Budapest and Lausanne, Switzerland. Chmn. bd. Zsa Zsa Ltd. (cosmetic co.). Author: Zsa Zsa's Complete Guide to Men, 1969, How to Get a Man, How to Keep a Man, How to Get Rid of a Man, 1971; Stage debut, Europe; motion pictures include Lovely To Look At, We're Not Married, The Story of Three Loves, Lili, Moulin Rouge, Three Ring Circus, Death of a Scoundrel, Girl in the Kremlin, For the First Time, Boys Night Out, 1962, Picture Mommy Dead, 1966, Jack of Diamonds, 1967, Won Ton Ton, the Dog Who Saved Hollywood, 1976, Hollywood, Here I Come, 1980; star: stage prodn. Arsenic and Old Lace, 1975. Address: care Robert Hussong Agy Inc 8721 Melrose Ave Suite 108 Los Angeles CA 90046 *

GABRIEL, ASTRIK LADISLAS, educator, scholar; b. Pécs (Fünfkirchen), Hungary, Dec. 10, 1907; came to U.S., 1948, naturalized, 1953; s. Alois and Mary (Boross) G. Student, Hautes Etudes, Paris, 1932-34, Ecole des Chartes, Paris, 1935-36; Ph.D., U. Budapest, Hungary, 1936, privat-dozent, 1941; Dr. honoris causa, Ambrosiana Library, Milan, 1967. Dir. French Coll., Hungary, 1938-47; privat-dozent prof. U. Budapest, 1941-47; guest prof. Pontifical Inst. Mediaeval Studies, Toronto, Ont., Can., 1947-48; mem. Inst. Advanced Study, Princeton, N.J., 1950-51, 80; prof. U. Notre Dame, 1948-74, emeritus, 1974; dir. Medieval Inst., 1953-74; Charles Chauncey Stillman guest prof. Harvard U., 1963-64; hon. fellow Pontifical Inst. Medieval Studies, Toronto, 1977. Author: Index Romain et Literature Française à l'Epoque Romantique, Tongerloo, 1936, Les Rapports Dynastiques Franco-Hongrois au Moyen-Age, 1944, Die Heilige Margarethe von Ungarn, 1944, English Masters and Students in Paris during the XIIth Century, 1949, Student Life in Ave Maria College, Mediaeval Paris History and Chartulary of the College (Mediaeval Studies 14), 1955, The Educational Ideas of Vincent of Beauvais (History of Mediaeval Education No. IV), 1956, Skara House at the Mediaeval University of Paris (History of Mediaeval Education No. IX), 1960, Auctarium Chartularii universitatis Paris, Vol. VI, 1964, Catologue of Microfilms of One Thousand Manuscripts in the Ambrosiana, 1968, The Mediavel Universities of Pécs and Pozsony, 1969, Garlandia: Studies in the History of Mediaevel Universities, 1969, Summary Bibliography of the History of the Universities of Great Britain and Ireland up to 1800, 1974, Petrus Cesaris Wagner and Johannes Stoll: 15th Century Printers at the University of Paris, 1978, The Decorated Initials of the IXth-XIth Century Manuscripts from Bobbio, in the Ambrosiana Library Milano, 1982; also numerous articles, chpts. on mediaeval subjects. Recipient Prix Thorlet French Academie des Inscriptions, 1956; Prix Dourlans, 1965; officier Légion d'Honneur, Palmes Academiques, France; decorated comdr. Order Merit Italy; Fulbright scholar and lectr., Luxembourg, 1959, Germany, 1972. Fellow Internat. Acad. Arts and Letters (Paris), Société de l'Histoire de France (Paris), Royal Hist. Soc. (London), Mediaeval Acad. Am.; corr. fellow Inst. de France, Bavarian Acad. Scis.; mem. Am. Catholic Hist. Assn. (pres. 1973), MLA, Hist. Com. on Canons of Prémontré, Internat. Com. Hist. Scis. (pres. internat. commn. for history of univs. 1961—). Home: Box 578 U Notre Dame Notre Dame IN 46556

GABRIEL, EARL A., osteopathic physician; b. Phila., Aug. 13, 1925; s. John and Rose (Cohen) G.; m. Fredelle, Feldman, Dec. 19, 1948; children: Debra Mae, Barbara Lynn, Sheri Ann, Michael David. B.S., Muhlenberg Coll., 1950; D.O., Phila. Coll. Osteo. Medicine, 1954. Gen. practice osteo. medicine, Allentown, Pa., 1955-78; chief of staff Allentown Osteo. Hosp., 1967-68, chmn. intern tng., 1956-58; prof., chmn. family practice medicine, assoc. dean clin. affairs Coll. Osteo. Medicine of Pacific, Pomona, Calif., 1978—, assoc. dean clin. affairs for postdoctoral tng., 1983—; mem. Pa. Gov.'s Sci. Adv. Com. on Health Care Delivery, 1970, 71; preceptor in gen. practice Phila. Coll. Osteo. Medicine; mem. ad hoc profl. group FDA, HEW, 1976-77; mem. Pa. Profl. Services Rev. Orgn. Council, 1977. Editorial adviser: Family Practice News, 1976—, Aches and Pains, 1980—. Fire surgeon Allentown Fire Dept.; trustee Community Services of Pa., Lehigh Valley Cancer Soc. Served with USNR and USMCR, 1943-46; PTO, CBI. Recipient Alumni Achievement award Muhlenberg Coll., 1983. Fellow Am. Coll. Gen. Practice in Osteo. Medicine and Surgery (pres. div. 1959, Disting. Service award, life mem. Pa. div. 1978); mem. Lehigh Valley Osteo. Soc. (pres. 1959-60), Pa. Osteo. Med. Assn. (pres. 1970, Distinguished Service award 1975), Am. Osteo. Assn. (ho. dels. 1966—, trustee 1970—, pres. 1975-76), Osteo. Physicians and Surgeons of Calif. (trustee 1981—), Phi Epsilon Pi (pres. 1950), Sigma Sigma Phi. Republican. Jewish. Clubs: Masons, Shriners, Jester, Lions, Lehigh Valley. Address: 1551 N Marjorie Ave Claremont CA 91711

GABRIEL, KUNO RUBEN, statistician, educator; b. Berlin, Mar. 24, 1929; U.S., 1976; s. Ernst and Ilse (Saaro) G.; m. Ayala Langerman, July 16, 1965; children: Orna, Osnat, Shira. B.S., London Sch. Econs., 1950; Ph.D., Hebrew U., Jerusalem, 1957. Asst. prof. to prof. dept. chmn. Hebrew U., Jerusalem, 1952-76; prof. U. Rochester (N.Y.), 1975—, chmn. dept. stats., 1981—; cons. Israeli Rainfall Augmentation Expts., 1961-69; mem. weather modification adv. bd. Exec. Office of Pres., 1980-81; cons. Ill. State Water Survey; chmn. Statis. Working Group Operational Weather Modification, 1979-80. Contbr. articles to profl. publs. Grantee Nat. Inst. Health Stats., 1969-72, NSF, 1979—, Nat. Weather Service, 1977-78, Office Naval Research, 1980—. Fellow Royal Statis. Soc., Am. Statis. Assn., Inst. Math. Stats.; mem. Internat. Statis. Inst. *I enjoy the interaction of mathematical abstractions and logic with empirical data. My Biplot multivariate display requires a mix of statistics, geometry, algebra, approximations, computing and graphics; it facilitates the analysis of data from medicine, political science, meteorology and other areas. I have been involved with the statistics of weather modification in several countries; it is gratifying to realize that, as a statistician, I can make some contribution to issues of wider human concern.*

GABRIEL, MICHAEL, psychology educator; b. Phila., May 5, 1940; s. Michael and Josephine (Alesio) G.; m. Linda Prinz, June, 1967 (div.); 1 son, Joseph Michael. A.B. in Psychology, St. Joseph's Coll., 1962; M.A., U. Wis.-Madison, 1965, Ph.D., 1967. Asst. prof. Pomona Coll., Claremont, Calif., 1967-70; staff psychologist Pacific State Hosp., Pomona, Calif., 1968-70; NIMH sr. postdoctoral fellow U. Calif.-Irvine, 1970-72; asst. prof. U. Tex.-Austin, 1973-77, assoc. prof., 1977-82; prof. psychology U. Ill., Urbana, 1982—; ares chmn. Biol. Psychology Program. U. Tex., Austin, 1979-82. Author: (with Brent A. Vogt) Neural and Behavioral Biology of the Cingulate Cortex, 1983. NIMH fellow, 1979-82; NIMH grantee, 1978—. Mem. Psychonomic Soc., Soc. for Neurosci., Sigma Xi. Office: Dept Psychology U Ill 603 E Daniel St Champaign IL 61820

GABRIEL, MORDECAI LIONEL, educational administrator; b. N.Y.C., Mar. 18, 1918; s. Joseph and Bertha (Fram) G.; m. Elinor Rosenstein, Nov. 11, 1945; children—Alisa, Jessica. A.B., Yeshiva U., 1938; M.A., Columbia, 1938, Ph.D., 1944. Instr. genetics U. Conn., 1943-45; mem. faculty Bklyn. Coll., 1945—, prof. biology, 1963—, chmn. dept., 1965-71, dean, 1971-76, acting v.p. for acad. affairs, 1981-82, assoc. provost, 1982—; vis. prof. Columbia, 1956; Fulbright lectr., vis. prof. U. Tel Aviv, 1959-60; mem. Marine Biol. Lab., Woods Hole, Mass., 1950—. Author: (with S. Fogel) Great Experiments in Biology, 1956. Ford Found. faculty fellow, 1955-56. Fellow AAAS; mem. Am. Soc. Zoologists, Am. Assn. Anatomists, N.Y. Acad. Scis., Soc. Study Evolution, Vertebrate Paleont. Soc., AAUP (pres. Bklyn. Coll. chpt. 1964-66), Phi Beta Kappa, Sigma Xi. Home: 120 Old Mill Rd Great Neck NY 11023 Office: Brooklyn Coll Brooklyn NY 11210

GABRIEL, PETER PAUL, corporate executive; b. Halle, Germany, July 11, 1929; came to U.S., 1960; s. Paul and Eva (Wernecke) G.; m. Linea Elizabeth Larson, Sept. 9, 1950; children: Paul Lawrence, John Peter, Kathryn Anne, Christina Eva. Student, Bach Schule, Germany, 1946-47; M.B.A., Harvard U., 1962, Dr. Bus. Adminstrn., 1965. Various adminstrv. positions, Germany and France, 1947-51; asst. to gen. mgr. Comestibles La Rosa S.A., Pereira, Colombia, 1951-52; asst. gen. mgr. Indsl. Cons. Orgn. S.A., Caracas, Venezuela, 1953-54, gen. mgr., 1954-60, 64-66; asso. McKinsey & Co., Inc., N.Y.C., 1966-69, partner, 1969-73; prof. mgmt., dean Sch. Mgmt., Boston U., 1973-76; corporate adviser, Boston, 1976-83; pres., chief exec. officer Codart Communications, Inc., Novato, Calif., 1983—. Author: The International Transfer of Corporate Skills, 1967; contbr. articles on internat. fin. and econ. devel. to profl. jours. Recipient G.M. Loeb award for distinguished writing in bus. and fin. U. Conn., 1967. Mem. Am. Econ. Assn. Clubs: Algonquin, Harvard Rhein-Ruhr (Duesseldorf, Ger.). Home: 8 Oakmount Circle Lexington MA 02173

GABRIELE, ORLANDO FREDERICK, radiologist, educator; b. North Providence, R.I., June 6, 1927; s. Federico and Rita (Caccia) G.; m. Marguerite St. John, July 30, 1960 (div. 1982); children: Frederick, Marguerite, Michael, Peter. B.A., Brown U., 1950; M.D., Yale U., 1954. Intern Phila. Gen. Hosp., 1954-55; resident Yale U. Med. Center, New Haven, 1955-58; asst. prof. Yale U., 1958-66; asso. radiologist Hosp. of St. Raphael, New Haven, 1959-66; asso. prof. U. N.C., 1967-70, prof., 1970-72; prof., chmn. dept. radiology W.Va. U., Morgantown, 1972—. Contbr. articles to profl. jours. Served with U.S. Army, 1945-47. Mem. Radiol. Soc. N. Am., Am. Roentgen Ray Soc., Assn. Univ. Radiologists, Soc. Chmn. Acad. Radiol. Depts., Soc. Nuclear Medicine. Roman Catholic. Office: Department of Radiology West Virginia Medical Center Morgantown WV 26506

GABRIELLI, DOMENICK L., judge; b. Rochester, N.Y., Dec. 13, 1912; s. Rocco and Veronica (Battisti) G.; m. Dorothy Louise Hedges, July 2, 1938; children: Veronica A. Gabrielli Dumas, Michael E. B.S., St. Lawrence U., 1936, LL.D. (hon.), 1973; LL.B., Albany Law Sch., 1936, J.D., 1968; LL.D. (hon.), Union Coll., 1973; H.L.D., Siena Coll., 1974; LL.D., Bklyn. Law Sch., 1975, Nazareth Coll., 1980. Bar: N.Y. 1937. Corp. counsel Village of Bath, N.Y., 1939-53; dist. atty. Steuben County, N.Y., 1953-57; judge Steuben County Ct. and Family Ct., Bath, 1957-61; justice Supreme Ct. N.Y., Albany, 1961-67, asso. justice appellate div., 1967-73; asso. judge Ct. of Appeals N.Y. State, Bath, 1973—; sr. counsel firm Nixon, Hargrave, Devans & Doyle, Rochester; presiding judge Extraordinary Spl. and Trial Term, Erie County, 1965-67; past dir. Bath Nat. Bank, Prattsburg (N.Y.) State Bank. Served to lt. USN, 1942-45; NATOUSA. Decorated comdr. Order of Merit Pres. of Italy, 1975; invested as knight Mil. Order Malta, 1974; Recipient 1st Hall of Fame award Steuben County, 1976, gold medal Albany Law Sch., 1983. Mem. ABA, N.Y. Bar Assn. (past pres., gold medal 1983), Steuben County Bar Assn. (past pres.), Bath Bar Assn. (past pres.), Am. Law Inst., Am. Judicature Soc., N.Y. State County Judges Assn. (pres. 1961), N.Y. State Children's Ct. Judges Assn., Juvenile Ct. Found., Internat. Assn. Jewish Lawyers and Jurists, Am. Justinian Soc. Jurists (chmn. appellate cts. com.). Republican. Roman Catholic. Home: 120 W Washington Blvd Bath NY 14810 Office: 2200 Lincoln First Tower Rochester NY 14603

GABRIELSON, IRA WILSON, physician, educator; b. N.Y.C., Nov. 27, 1922; s. Benjaim and Lily (Baran) G.; m. Mary Putnam Oliver, Sept. 4, 1948; children: Deborah Anne, David Dwight, Hugh Wilson, Carl Oliver. B.A., Columbia U., 1944, M.D., 1949; M.P.H., Johns Hopkins U., 1959. Diplomate: Am. Bd. Pediatrics, Nat. Bd. Med. Examiners. Adminstrv. asst., asst. dir. Johns Hopkins U., 1953-57; dir. community program retarded children, New Haven, 1959-61; asst. attending pediatrician Yale-New Haven Community Hosp., 1959-68; asst. prof. public health Yale, 1961-68, exec. officer dept epidemiology and public health, 1962-67; clin. prof. U. Calif., Berkeley, 1968-71; prof., chmn. dept. community and preventive medicine Med. Coll. Pa., 1971—; cons. in field. Served with AUS. Fellow Nat. Found., 1958. Fellow Am. Acad. Pediatrics, Am. Public Health Assn.; mem. Coll. Physicians Phila., Sigma Xi, Delta Omega. Club: Phila Skating,/ Appalachian Mountain. Home: 1639 Monk Rd Gladwyne PA 19035 Office: 3300 Henry Ave Philadelphia PA 19129

GABRILOVE, JACQUES LESTER, physician; b. N.Y.C., Sept 21, 1917; s. Benjamin and Pauline (Levine) G.; m. Hilda R. Weiss, May 19, 1946; children: Sandra Leslie Saltzman, Dr. Janice Lynn. B.S. magna cum laude, Coll. City N.Y., 1936; M.D. (Alpha Omega Alpha prize), N.Y.U., 1940. Diplomate: Am. Bd. Internal Medicine. Intern Mt. Sinai Hosp., N.Y.C., 1940-41, rotating intern, 1941-43, vol. radiology, 1943, resident medicine, 1943-44, Blumenthal fellow medicine, 1946-48, research asst. medicine, 1949-51, asst. attending physician, 1952-60, asso. attending physician, 1960-68, attending physician, 1969—; cons. endocrinology, 1953—; chief endocrine clinic, also clin. prof. medicine Mt. Sinai Sch. Medicine, 1969-82, Baumritter prof. medicine, 1982—; Libman fellow medicine Yale, 1945; clin. asst. prof. medicine State U. N.Y. Coll. Medicine N.Y.C., 1957-59, clin. asso. prof., 1959-66, clin. prof., 1966-69, professorial lectr., 1969—; cons. endocrinology VA Hosp., East Orange, N.J., 1958-66, Elizabeth A. Horton Hosp., Middletown, N.Y., 1961—, VA Hosp., Bronx, N.Y., 1969—, Norwalk (Conn.) Hosp., 1974—, Elmhurst City Hosp., N.Y., St. Francis Hosp., Port Jervis, N.Y.; Mem. panel on metabolic and rheumatoid diseases U.S. Pharmacopeia, 1956—; mem. spl. com. research tng. grants in diabetes, endocrinology and metabolism NIH, 1976-79, mem. com. on diabetes research and tng. centers, 1977-79; Saltzman lectr. Mt. Sinai Hosp., Cleve., 1974. Author, contbr. books in field, also articles in med. jours.; Editorial bd. jour., Mt. Sinai Hosp. Pres. Mt. Sinai Alumni Assn., 1970. Recipient Jacobi medallion Mt. Sinai Alumni Assn.; Globus prize Mt. Sinai Jour. Medicine. Fellow A.C.P., N.Y. Acad. Medicine; mem. N.Y. County Med. Soc., AMA, N.Y. Acad. Sci., AAAS, N.Y. Diabetes Assn., Endocrine Soc., Am. Diabetes Assn., Harvey Soc., Royal Soc. Medicine, Peruvian Endocrine Soc. (hon.), Pan Am. Med. Assn. (v.p. N.Am. endocrinology), Phi Beta Kappa, Alpha Omega Alpha. Jewish (trustee synagogue). Club: Lotos. Home: 25 E 86th St New York NY 10028 Office: 79 E 79th St New York NY 10021

GABURO, KENNETH LOUIS, composer, condr., educator, publisher; b. Somerville, N.J., July 5, 1926. Mus.B., Mus.M., Eastman Sch. Music; ed., Conservatorio di Santa Cecelia, Rome; Mus.D., U. Ill., also pvt. study. Former mem. faculty Kent State U., McNeese State U., U. Ill., Urbana, U. Calif. at San Diego; now composer-at-large, dir. New Music Choral Ensemble IV; editor-founder Lingua Press. Composer operas, chamber music, choral music, linguistic compositions, dramatic works, video, film and electronic music, linguistic theater works; recorded compositions include 4 Sacred Motets. Recipient numerous awards for compositions, including ASCAP Serious Music awards, UNESCO Creative Arts award, commns. Fromm and Koussevitzky founds., research grants in composition/linguistics U. Ill., U. Calif., Rockefeller Found.; Fulbright fellow; Guggenheim fellow. Address: PO Box 481 Ramona CA 92065

GADDES, RICHARD, opera company administrator; b. Wallsend, Northumberland, Eng., May 23, 1942; s. Thomas and Emilie Jane (Rickard) G. L.T.C.L. in piano,; G.T.C.L., Trinity Coll. Music, London, 1964; D. Mus. Arts (hon.), St. Louis Conservatory, 1983, D.F.A., U. Mo.-St. Louis, 1984. Founder, mgr. Wigmore Hall Lunchtime Concerts, 1965; dir. Christopher Hunt and Richard Gaddes Artists Mgmt., London, 1965-66; bookings mgr. Artists Internat. Mgmt., London, 1967-69; artistic adminstr. Santa Fe Opera, 1969-78; gen. dir. Opera Theatre of St. Louis, 1975—; cons., bd. dirs. William Matheus Sullivan Found.; cons. Nat. Opera Inst., Nat. Endowment Arts. Recipient Lamplighter award, 1982, Mo. Arts award, 1983, St. Louis award, 1983. Office: Opera Theatre of St Louis PO Box 13148 Saint Louis MO 63119

GADDIS, PAUL OTTO, university administrator; b. Muskogee, Okla., Mar. 20, 1924; s. Paul James and Ida Rose (Oerter) G.; m. Martha Louise Rinker, June 28, 1948; children: Paul James, David Charles, Holly. B.S., U.S. Naval Acad., 1946; M.S., Rensselaer Poly. Inst., 1949; M.B.A., Sloan Sch. Mass. Inst. Tech., 1961. Mgr. computer systems and finance Westinghouse Electric Corp., Pitts., 1954-68, v.p., corporate devel., 1968-72; cons. corporate devel., prof. mgmt. Wharton Sch.; sr. v.p. U. Pa., Phila., 1972-79; dean Sch. Mgmt. and Adminstrn., U. Tex. at, Dallas, 1979—; chmn., dir. Globe Ticket Co., Phila., 1975-79; mem. exec. com., dir. Western Savs. Bank, Phila., 1976-79; chmn. exec. com., dir. UNI-COLL Corp., Phila., 1974-79; dir., mem. exec. com. Energy Res. Group, Inc., Wichita, Kans.; dir. HEI Corp., Houston. Author: Corporate Accountability, 1964; contbr.: articles to Harvard Bus. Rev. Pres. La Napoule Art Found., France, 1979—. Served with USN, 1946-54. Mem. Soc. Info. Mgmt., Planning Execs. Inst. Clubs: Dallas; Union League (Phila.). Office: U Tex-Dallas Richardson TX 75080

GADDIS, WILLIAM, writer; b. N.Y.C., 1922. Student, Harvard U. Author: novels The Recognitions, 2d edit., 1962, J R, 1975 (Nat. Book award for fiction 1976). Nat. Inst. Arts and Letters grantee, 1963; Nat. Endowment for the Arts grantee, 1967; Guggenheim fellow, 1981; MacArthur Prize fellow, 1982. Mem. Am. Acad. and Inst. Arts and Letters. Address: care Candida Donadio & Assos 111 W 57th St New York NY 10019

GADDIS ROSE, MARILYN, comparative literature educator, translator; b. Fayette, Mo., Apr. 4, 1930; d. Merrill Elmer and FlorenceGeorgia (Lyon) Gaddis; m. James Leo Rose, Dec. 23, 1956 (div. 1966); m. Stephen David Ross, Nov. 16, 1968; 1 son, David Gaddis. B.A., Central Meth. Coll., 1952; M.A., U. S.C., Columbia, 1954-55; Ph.D., U. Mo., 1958. Instr. Stephens Coll., Columbia, Mo., 1958-68; assoc. prof. Ind. U., Bloomington, 1968; prof. comparative lit. SUNY, Binghamton, 1968—, dir. translation program, 1973—. Translator: Eve of the Future Eden, 1981; editor, contbr.: Translation Spectrum, 1981; contbr. articles in field to profl. jours. Fulbright fellow U. Lyon, France, 1953-54; Humanities Research Centre sr. fellow Australian Nat. U., 1977. Mem. Am. Lit. Translators (sec.-treas. 1981-83), Am. Translators Assn. (translation studies chmn. 1981-83), MLA (del. assembly 1974-78, 84-87), PEN N.Y., N.E. MLA (pres. 1975-76). Home: 4 Johnson Ave Binghamton NY 13905 Office: Comparative Lit SUNY Binghamton NY 13905

GADDY, JAMES LEONA, chemical engineer, educator; b. Jacksonville, Fla., Aug. 16, 1932; s. Leoma Ithoma and Mary Elizabeth (Edwards) G.; m. Betty Maricella, Sept. 7, 1952; children: James, Teresa. B.S. in Chem. Engring., La. Poly. U., 1955, M.S., U. Ark., 1968, Ph.D., U. Tenn., 1972. Registered profl. engr., Ark. Process engr. Ethyl Corp., Baton Rouge, 1955-60; project mgr., engring. supr. Ark.-La. Gas, Shreveport, La., 1960-66; assoc. prof. chem engring. U. Mo.-Rolla, 1972-79, prof., 1979, dir. research ctr., 1980; prof., head chem. engring. U. Ark., Fayetteville, 1980—; dir. Biosyn Corp., Mpls., Banyan Tech., Dallas; cons. UN, Pritchard Corp., Kansas City, Mo.; tchr. short courses in chem. engring. for industry. Contbr. articles to tech. jours. Faculty fellow Swiss Fed. Inst. Tech., Zurich, 1978. Mem. Am. Inst. Chem. Engrs. (speakers bur.), Am. Chem. Soc., Am. Soc. Engring. Edn., AAAS, Tau Beta Pi (Eminent Engr. 1976). Baptist. Home: 964 Arlington Pl Fayetteville AR 72701 Office: U Ark 227 Engineering Bldg Fayetteville AR 72701

GADDY, MERCER GORDON, insurance company executive; b. Atlanta, Sept. 14, 1936; s. Mercer Fain and Martha Alice (Cravens) G.; m. Janice Sue Meador, Dec. 31, 1955; children: Ginger, Scott, Robyn. B.B.A., Ga. State U., 1960, M.B.A., 1960; Exec. M.B.A., Stanford U., 1980. Cert. fin. planner; chartered life underwriter, registered prin. NASD. Controller United Family Life, Atlanta, 1964-68; v.p. Fireman's Fund Am. Life Ins. Co., San Rafael, Calif., 1968-76, sr. v.p., 1973-76, exec. v.p., sr. operating officer, 1976-77, pres., chief operating oficer, 1977—. Trustee Marin Gen. Hosp. Found., Greenbrae, Calif, 1983; mem. bd. pensions Evang. Covenant Ch., Chgo., 1983—. Mem. Pub. Relations Com., Health Ins. Assn. Am., Life Office Mgmt. Assn., Nat. Assn. Life Underwriters. Home: 2473 Vineyard Rd Novato CA 94947 Office: 1600 Los Gamos Rd San Rafael CA 94911

GADDY, ROBERT JOSEPH, lawyer; b. St. Joseph, Mo., Aug. 10, 1924; s. Joseph Vernon and Austa (Gibson) G.; m. Martha Dunbar, Sept. 16, 1949; children—Virginia Hess, Helen Gibson Turner. Student, Westminster Coll., Fulton, Mo., 1946-47; LL.B., Washington U., St. Louis, 1950. Bar: Mo. bar 1950. Partner firm Dunbar and Gaddy, St. Louis, 1953-58; v.p., gen. counsel Tower Grove Bank and Trust Co., St. Louis, 1958-60, pres., 1959-75, chmn., 1970-75; also dir.; pres. Am. Nat. Bank, St. Louis, 1976-79; of counsel firm Shifrin, Treiman, Barken, Dempsey & Ulrich, St. Louis, 1980—; pres. St. Louis Clearing House; dir. Gen. Grocer Co., St. Louis. Commr. Tower Grove Park; former trustee St. Louis Children's Hosp., Bethesda Gen. Hosp.; bd. dirs. Episcopal-Presbyn. Found. for Aging; bd. advisers South Side YMCA. Served to 1st lt. USAAF, 1943-45. Recipient alumni achievement award Westminster Coll., Mo., 1968. Mem. Am. Bankers' Assn., Mo. Bankers' Assn. (pres. 1969-70), Am. Inst. Banking (chmn. adv. bd. St. Louis chpt.), Asso. Bankers St. Louis and St. Louis County (pres. 1958). Home: 500 Oak Valley Dr Saint Louis MO 63131

GADE, MARVIN FRANCIS, paper company executive; b. Clinton, Iowa, Nov. 10, 1924; s. Bernhardt Henry and Anna Mae (Jessen) G.; m. Lorraine F. McDonald, Dec. 2, 1944; children: Michael David, Patricia Ann Gade Conn, Steven Dennis, Laura Jean Gade Stevens, Mary Kay Gade McIntyre, Karen Lynn Gade Smith, Jeffrey Scott. B.S. in Engring, U. Iowa, 1952; postgrad. exec. program, UCLA, 1960-61. Process instrumentation engr. Standards Brands Co., Clinton, 1946-50; with Kimberly-Clark Corp. (hdqrs.), Neenah, Wis., 1952—, sr. v.p., group exec., 1974-77, exec. v.p., Coosa Pines, Ala., 1977—, also dir.; pres. Kimberly Clark Health Care, Paper and Spltys. Cos., 1981—, vice chmn. bd., 1983—; dir. First Bank of Childersburg, Ala. Bd. dirs. Calif. Water Quality Control Bd., 1964-67, S.C. Tech. Edn. Bd., 1968-70; chmn. bd. adv. com. St. Jude's Hosp., Fullerton, Calif., 1962-67. Served as aviator USNR, 1943-46. Home: 3800 Old Alabama Dr Alpharetta GA 30201 Office: Kimberly-Clark Corp 1400 Holcomb Bridge Rd Roswell GA 30076

GADEN, ELMER LEWIS, JR., chemical engineering; b. Bklyn., Sept. 26, 1923; s. Elmer Lewis and Gertrude Estelle (McClellan) G.; m. Jennifer Marie Soley, Mar. 28, 1964; children: David Andrew, Paul Alexander; 1 dau. by previous marriage, Barbara Joan. B.S., Columbia U., 1944, M.S., 1947, Ph.D., 1949. Research engr. Charles Pfizer and Co., 1948-49; mem. faculty Columbia, 1949-74, prof. chem. engring., 1958-74, chmn. dept., 1960-69, 71-74; dean Coll. Engring. Math. and Bus. Adminstrn., U. Vt., Burlington, 1975-79; Wills Johnson prof. chem. engring. U. Va., Charlottesville, 1979-83. Editor: Jour. Biotech. and Bioengring, 1959-83. Served with USNR, 1943-46. Mem. Nat. Acad. Engring., Am. Chem. Soc., Am. Inst. Chem. Engrs., Am. Soc. Engring. Edn. Home: 1438 Grove Rd Charlottesville VA 22901 Office: Dept Chem Engring Thornton Hall U Va Charlottesville VA 22901

GADSDEN, RICHARD HAMILTON, biochemistry educator; b. Denver, June 30, 1925; s. Paul Hamilton and Ellen Theresa (Page) G.; m. Emily Anne Mercer, June 20, 1953; children: Judith G., Richard Hamilton, Frank McC., Phillip E., Ellen L.A., Johnathan C.M. B.S., Coll. of Charleston, 1950; M.S., Med. Coll. S.C., 1952, Ph.D., 1956. Teaching fellow Coll. of Charleston, S.C., 1949-50; instr. Med. U. S.C., Charleston, 1954-56, asst. prof., 1956-65, asso. prof., 1965-68, prof. biochemistry and lab. medicine, 1968—, dir. div. clin. chemistry, 1970—; cons. biochemistry VA Hosp., Charleston, 1967—; cons. transp., food products Am. Bar Assn., 1973—, NIH, 1973; authority on toxicology Nat. Library Sci.; dir. N.C. Warehouse Corp., Charleston. Editor: Annals of Clin. and Lab. Sci, Clin. Chemistry; contbr. to publs. in field. Trustee Coll. of Charleston, 1969-71. Served with USNR, 1943-46. Fellow AAAS, Assn. Clin. Scientists, Am. Inst. Chemists (pres. 1983, dir. 1983—); mem. S.C. Inst. Chemists (pres. 1971-72), S.C. Acad. Scis. (pres. 1966-67), Am. Assn. Clin. Chemists (nat. council, chmn. S.E. sect. 1977, dir. 1983—), Assn. Clin. Scientists (v.p. 1981), Nat. Acad. Clin. Biochemistry (treas. 1981-83), Charleston Symphony Assn. (pres. 1972-73), Coll. of Charleston Alumni Assn. (pres. 1967-68, Alumnus of Yr. award 1983), Med. U. S.C. Alumni Assn. (pres. 1975-76), Soc. of Cincinnati, Sigma Xi, Omicron Delta Kappa (hon.). Episcopalian. Home: 544 Sweetbay Rd Charleston SC 29412

GAENG, PAUL AMI, foreign language educator; b. Budapest, Hungary, Aug. 17, 1924; came to U.S., 1948, naturalized, 1955; s. Hans Peter and Therese (Brule) G.; m. Joan Elisabeth Gallagher, Apr. 6, 1967. Grad., U. Geneva, 1948; M.A., Columbia U., 1950; Ph.D. (Woodbridge hon. fellow), 1965. Fgn. editorial asst. McGraw Hill Book Co., N.Y.C., 1951-54; translator-interpreter Guaranty Trust, N.Y.C., 1954-56; fgn. lang. tchr. Montclair (N.J.) Acad., 1957-63; asst., asso. then full prof., chmn. dept. fgn. langs. Montclair State Coll., Upper Montclair, N.J., 1964-69; asso. prof. Romance philology U. Va., Charlottesville, 1969-72; head dept. Romance lang. and lit. U. Cin., 1972-76; head dept. French, U. Ill., Urbana, 1976—, assoc. Ctr. for Advanced Studies, spring 1983; vis. lectr. Hofstra Coll., Hempstead, N.Y., 1963, Queens Coll., N.Y.C., 1966, Columbia U., 1967-69. Author: Introduction to the Principles of Language, 1971, An Inquiry into Local Variations in Vulgar Latin, 1968, Studies in Honor of Mario Pei, 1972, A Study of Nominal Inflection in Latin Inscriptions, 1977, (with Mario Pei) The Story of Latin and the Romance Languages, 1976; contbr. articles on lang. teaching and philology to profl. jours. Decorated chevalier Ordre des Palmes Académiques. Mem. AAUP, MLA, Société de linguistique romane, Am. Soc. Geolinguistics (treas. 1965-68). Home: 2009 Peach St Champaign IL 61820 Office: Dept French Univ Ill Urbana IL 61801

GAERTNER, JOHANNES ALEXANDER, art history educator; b. Berlin-Lichterfelde, Germany, Apr. 26, 1912; came to U.S., 1945, naturalized, 1952; s. Carl Eugen and Fanny (Horwitz) G.; m. Gerda Meyer, May 31, 1941; 1 dau., Susanna Barbara. Student, U. Berlin, 1930-33; Th.D., U. Heidelberg, 1936. Asst. mgr. Libreria Internacional del Peru, Lima, 1939-45; researcher, editor Frederick Ungar Pub. Co., N.Y.C., 1945-47; instr. Lafayette Coll., Easton, Pa., 1947-48, asst. prof., 1948-58, assoc. prof., 1958-66, prof. art history, head dept. art and music, 1966-77. Author: Vox Humana, 1954, Prisma der Demokratie, 1961, Diapason, 1961, Cantus Firmus, 1966, Zur Deutung des Junius-Bassus-Sarkophages in Jahrbuch des Deutschen Archaeol. Instituts, 1968; Contbr. articles profl. jours. Mem. Medieval Acad., Coll. Art Assn., Am. Soc. Aesthetics, Archeol. Inst., AAUP. Home: 409 Clinton Terr Easton PA 18042 *"Mediam per desperationem prorumpere convenit".*

GAERTNER, RICHARD FRANCIS, research exec.; b. Pitts., Aug. 10, 1933; s. John William and Alma Louise (Heimbuechner) G.; m. Nancy Lawlor Keary, Sept. 29, 1962; children—Barbara, Richard, Linda, Catherine. B.S. in Chem. Enring, W.Va. U., 1955, M.S. in Chem. Engring, 1957; Ph.D., U. Ill., 1959. With Gen. Electric Co., 1959-77, mgr. laminated products dept., 1971-74, mgt. tech. resources planning chem. and metall. div., 1974-77; research dir. Tech. Center Owens-Corning Fiberglas Corp., 1977-79, dir. strategic tech. planning, 1979—. Dow Chem. Co. fellow. Mem. Am. Inst. Chem. Engrs., Sigma Xi, Tau Beta Pi, Phi Lambda Upsilon. Patentee in field. Office: Owens-Corning Fiberglas Corp Granville OH 43023

GAERTNER, WOLFGANG WILHELM, research company executive; b. Vienna, Austria, July 5, 1929; came to U.S., 1953, naturalized, 1961; s. Wilhelm and Maria (Schuetz) G.; m. Marianne L. Weber, Feb. 22, 1955; children: Marianne P., Karin C., Christopher W. Ph.D. in Physics, U. Vienna, 1951; Dipl.Ing., Technische Hochschule, Vienna, 1955. Research physicist Siemens Halske, Vienna, 1951-53, U.S. Army Signal Research and Devel. Lab., Ft. Monmouth, N.J., 1953-60; v.p. CBS Labs., Stamford, Conn., 1960-65; pres. W.W. Gaertner Research, Inc., Stamford, Conn., 1965—; cons. NATO. Author: Transistors: Principles, Design and Applications, 1960, Adaptive Electronics, 1973; contbr. articles to profl. publs. Fellow IEEE; mem. Am. Phys. Soc. Office: 100 Regent St East Norwalk CT 06855

GAFFEY, THOMAS MICHAEL, JR., consumer products executive; b. Elmira, N.Y., Mar. 1, 1934; s. Thomas Michael and Alice (Faul) G.; m. Constance R. Watkins, May 23, 1964. B.S. in Acctg., Syracuse (N.Y.) U., 1956. C.P.A., N.Y. Auditor, cons. Lybrand Ross Bros. & Montgomery (C.P.A.s), N.Y.C., 1956, 58-64; with Liggett Group Inc., 1964-83, asst. controller, then controller, 1969-76, treas., Durham, N.C. and Montvale, N.J., 1976-80, v.p., treas., 1980-82, sr. vp., chief fin. officer, dir., 1982-83; sr. v.p., chief fin. officer, dir. GrandMet USA, Inc. (formerly Liggett Group Inc., 1983—; dir. Durham City bd. N.C. Nat. Bank, 1972-76; mem. adv. bd. Arkwright-Boston Ins. Co. Mem. N.Y. County Republican Com., 1965-67. Served with U.S. Army, 1956-58. Mem. Am. Inst. C.P.A.s, Fin. Execs. Inst. (pres. N.C. chpt. 1977-78, chmn. admissions com. 1983-84), N.Y. State Soc. C.P.A.s. Roman Catholic. Clubs: Ridgewood (N.J.) Country; Union League (N.Y.C.). Home: 15 Deerhill Dr Ho-Ho-Kus NJ 07423 Office: 100 Paragon Dr Montvale NJ 07645

GAFFNEY, EDWARD J., mfg. co. exec.; b. Manistique, Mich., June 5, 1929; s. Bernard Farrell and Lora D. (Leonard) G.; m. Elizabeth Dundon, Apr. 14, 1956; children—Thomas, Ann, Bridget, Patricia, Timothy, Joan, Claire, Shaila. B.S.M.E., Mich. Tech. U., 1951. Engr. Allis Chalmers, 1951-56; with Neodyne Corp., 1956-63, pres., to 1963; pres., founder, chmn. bd. Ortho-Kinetics, Inc., Waukesha, Wis., 1963—. Mem. White House Conf. Task Force on Internat. Trade; del. White House Conf. on Small Bus., 1980; mem. nat. adv. council SBA; mem. Wis. Legis. Council Spl. Com. on Small Bus.; chmn. capital formation task force Wis. Gov.'s Conf. on Small Bus., 1981; dir. Public Expenditure Research Found., Inc.; mem. Sch. of Bus. adminstrn. adv. council U. Wis.; mem. corp. Milw. Sch. Engring. Served with USN, 1951-53. Named U.S. Small Bus. Person of the Year SBA, 1978. Mem. Ind. Bus. Assn. Wis. (dir., pres. 1980-81), Nat. Fedn. Ind. Bus., Nat. C. of C. Roman Catholic. Clubs: Rotary, Pewaukee Yacht. Patentee in field. Office: W220 N507 Springdale Rd Waukesha WI 53186

GAFFNEY, JAMES J., company executive; b. N.Y.C., Sept. 14, 1940; s. Thomas and Mary Agnes (Carroll) G.; m. Eileen McCarthy, Nov. 27, 1964; children: Mary Ellen, Charles. B.B.A., St. John's U., 1963; M.B.A., NYU, 1967. Acct., internal auditor Molycorp, Inc., N.Y.C., 1966-70, corp. controller, 1970-76, v.p., chief acct. office, 1976-79; v.p., chief fin. officer Creusot Loire Steel Corp., Bloomfield, N.J., 1979-81; exec. v.p. fin. Gen. Refractories Co., Bala Cynwyd, Pa., 1981-82, v.p., treas., dir., 1982. Mem. Fin. Exec. Inst. Republican. Roman Catholic. Clubs: Metropolitan (N.Y.C.); Westchester Country (Rye, N.Y.); Beach (Palm Beach, Fla.). Home: Hickory Pass Bedford NY 10506

GAFFNEY, MASON, educator, economist; b. White Plains, N.Y., Oct. 18, 1923; s. Matthew Page and Laura (Clarke) G.; m. Estelle Pao An Lau, Mar. 8, 1952 (div. 1968); children—Bradford Clarke, Ann Reed, Stuart Morgan; m. Ruth Letitia Atwood, Sept. 22, 1973; children—Laura Atwood, Patricia Mason, Matthew Rollin. Student, Harvard, 1941-42; B.A., Reed Coll., 1948; Ph.D., U. Calif. at Berkeley, 1956. Asst. prof. econs. N.C. State Coll., Raleigh, 1954-58; asso. prof., then prof. agrl. econs. U. Mo., 1958-62; prof. econs. U. Wis.-Milw., 1962-71; vis. prof. U. Calif. at Los Angeles, 1967; vis. scholar Resources for Future, Washington, 1969-71, sr. research asso., 1971-73; exec. dir. B.C. (Can.) Inst. for Analysis Econ. Policy, Victoria, 1973-76; cons. State of Alaska, 1976-77; prof. Grad. Sch. Adminstrn., U. Calif. at Riverside, 1976-78, chmn. dept. econs., 1978—; cons., speaker in field, 1959—. Author: Land Rent, Taxation and Public Policy, 1968, Urban Expansion, 1958, Diseconomies in Western Water Law, 1960, Containment Policies for Urban Sprawl, 1964, Extractive Resources and Taxation, 1967, The Property Tax Is a Progressive Tax, 1971, Tax Reform to Release Land, 1973, Agenda for Strengthening the Property Tax, 1973, Full Employment with Limited Land and Capital, 1975, Capital Needs for Full Employment, 1976, Oil and Gas Leasing Policy: Alternatives for Alaska, 1977, The Synergistic City, 1978, Two Centuries of Economic Thought on Taxation of Land Rents, 1981. Mem. Com. on Taxation, Resources and Econ. Devel., 1961—. Served to 1st lt. USAAF, 1943-46. Ford fellow, 1957-58; co-recipient Jesse Neal award bus. journalism Asso. Bus. Publs., 1960. Mem. Am. Econ. Assn., Nat. Tax Assn., Canadian Econs. Assn., Phi Beta Kappa. Home: 3040 Tyler St Riverside CA 92503 *The world often rewards us better for injuring than helping it; and we may injure ourselves in wasting the rewards. We can still serve the world's real needs, and fulfill ourselves by seeking reason, community and justice. There is community on the way, and fulfillment in knowing that good example encourages others.*

GAFFNEY, MAUREEN, media center executive; b. Houston, July 9, 1943; d. Arthur Thomas and Alice (Meany) G. Student, Cath. U. Am., 1961-62, Marymount Manhattan Coll., 1965-67. Customer service rep., 1962-63; readers corr. Am. Home mag., 1963-64; elementary sch. tchr. Marymount Sch., Bogota, Colombia, 1964; producer Thomas Sand Enterprises, N.Y.C., 1968-69; freelance ednl. media writer, dir., producer, cons., N.Y.C., 1970-74; festival coordinator Am. Film Festival, N.Y.C., 1974-75; dir. children's film theater project Center for Understanding Medica, N.Y.C., 1975-76; exec. dir. Media Center for Children, N.Y.C., 1976—; tchr. media prodn. New Sch. Social Research; tchr. classroom and mus. media Bank St. Coll. Edn.; juror CINE screenings. Co-author: What to Do When the Lights Go On, 1981; Editor: Young Viewers quar, 1977—; editor, compiler: More Films Kids Like, 1977. Mem. Nat. Art Educators Assn., Am. Assn. Mus., Mus. Educator's Roundtable, Ednl. Film Library Assn. (festival com.), Assn. for Care Children's Health. Office: Media Center for Children 3 W 29th St New York NY 10001

GAFFNEY, PAUL COTTER, physician; b. DuBois, Pa., May 12, 1917; s. John Charles and Anna Catherine (Cotter) G.; m. Lois G. Brown, Oct. 14, 1944; children: Louise A., Paul Cotter, William J., Maureen E., Mary Ellen, Frances J., Michael B. B.S. magna cum laude, U. Pitts., 1940, M.D., 1942. Intern St. Francis Hosp., Pitts., 1942-43, resident in pathology, 1946-48; resident in pediatrics Children's Hosp., Pitts., 1948-50, mem. staff, 1951—, med. dir., 1978—; fellow hematology Children's Hosp., Detroit, 1950-51; practice medicine specializing in pediatrics and hematology, Pitts., 1951-63; mem. med. faculty U. Pitts., 1961—; asso. dean, dir. admissions U. Pitts. Sch. Medicine, 1977-78; exec. dir. Med. Alumni Assn. Sch. Medicine U. Pitts Sch. Medicine, 1980—; mem. staff Magee-Women's Hosp., Pitts., 1951-80; mem. med. adv. com. Comprehensive Health Planning Assn. Allegheny County, 1968-76; bd. dirs. Central Blood Bank Pitts., 1969-76. Served to maj., M.C. U.S. Army, 1943-46. Decorated Bronze Star with oak leaf cluster; Named Man of Yr. in Medicine Pitts. Acad. Medicine, 1978; recipient Phillip S. Hench Disting. Alumnus award U. Pitts. Sch. Medicine, 1980. Fellow Am. Acad. Pediatrics; mem. AMA, Pa. Med Soc., Allegheny Med. Soc. (dir. 1973-76, 81—), Am. Pediatric Soc. (Golden Apple teaching award 1967, 71, 75), Phi Beta Pi. Republican. Roman Catholic. Research on treatment of childhood leukemia. Home: 5540 Elgin Ave Pittsburgh PA 15206 Office: Children's Hosp 125 De Sota St Pittsburgh PA 15213

GAFFNEY, THOMAS, banker; b. San Francisco, Sept. 22, 1915; s. John and Hannah (Doherty) G.; m. Claire Bastian, Dec. 15, 1945; children: Bruce Edward, Bryan Keith. Certificate, Am. Inst. Banking, 1940. Bank insp. Bank of Am., 1935-50; asst. cashier First Nat. Trust and Savs. Assn., Santa Barbara, Calif., 1950-51; asst. cashier, asst sec. Oakland Central Bank, Calif., 1951-53; chief insp. Transamerica Corp., San Francisco, 1953-55; v.p., auditor First Western Bank, San Francisco, 1955-61, New First Western Bank, Los Angeles, 1961-74, Lloyds Bank Calif., 1974—; pres. Golden Gate chpt. Bank Adminstrn Inst., San Francisco, 1961, nat. bd. dirs., 1965-67, gen. chmn. conv., Los Angeles, 1967, speaker conv., Portland, Oreg., 1966; chmn. crime deterrant com. Calif. Bankers Assn., 1977-79. Club: Elks (dir. Locker Room 67 club San Francisco 1960). Home: Montebello CA Office: 548 S Spring St Los Angeles CA 90013

GAFFNEY, THOMAS EDWARD, physician; b. East St. Louis, Ill., Nov. 5, 1930; s. John V. and Leola (Heisner) G.; m. Edith Ann Heitholt, June 12, 1954; children—John, David, Michael. A.B., U. Mo., 1951, M.S., 1953; M.D., U. Cin., 1957. Intern Harvard Med. Service of Boston City Hosp., 1957-58; resident medicine Mass. Gen. Hosp., 1958-59; instr. pharmacology, asst. medicine U. Cin., 1959-60; clin. asso. Nat. Heart Inst., 1960-62; asso. prof. pharmacology U. Cin., 1962-67, asst. prof. medicine, 1962, dir. div. clin. pharmacology, 1962-72, prof. pharmacology, 1967-72, prof. medicine, 1969-72; prof., chmn. dept. basic and clin. pharmacology, prof. medicine Med. U. S.C., 1972—; dir. Drug Sci. Found., 1978—; vis. scientist Karolinska Inst., Stockholm, 1969-70; mem. cardiovascular panel Nat. Acad. Scis. Drug Efficacy Study, 1967-70; mem. pharmacology and exptl. therapeutics study sect. Nat. Heart Inst., 1967-69; mem. med. adv. bd. Council High Blood Pressure Research, 1969—; mem. Council on Basic Scis. of Am. Heart Assn., 1969—, mem. cardiovascular A study sect., 1972—; mem. program rev. com. pharmacology and toxicology Nat. Inst. Gen. Med. Scis., 1971-75, chmn., 1973-75; mem. hypertension task force S.C. Heart Assn., 1974—; mem. cardiovascular/renal adv. com. FDA, 1977—. Mem. editorial bd.: Jour. Pharmacology and Exptl. Therapeutics, 1965-77; contbr. articles to profl. jours. Served with USPHS, 1960-62. Recipient research career devel. award Nat. Heart Inst., 1962, 67, 72. Mem. Am. Fedn. Clin. Research, Am. Soc. Pharmacology and Exptl. Therapeutics (exec. com. clin. pharmacology 1965—), Central Soc. Clin. Research, Am. Soc. Clin. Investigation, So. Soc. Research, Assn. Am. Physicians, Alpha Omega Alpha. Home: 303 Sumter Ave Summerville SC 29483

GAFFNEY, THOMAS FRANCIS, life insurance company executive; b. Bethlehem, Pa., July 21, 1931; s. Thomas F. and Mary M. (Glancy) G.; m. Dorothy A. Jacober, May 5, 1972; children: Thomas Francis, III, Elizabeth Ann, Susan Lynn, Jody Lynn, Kelly Ann. B.S., Pa. State U., 1957; grad. Advanced Mgmt. Program, Harvard U., 1979. With Life Ins. Co. N.Am., 1962—, sr. v.p., then exec. v.p., Phila., 1973-77, pres., 1977—, also dir.; pres. Membership Services Corp., Master Life Ins. Co., INA Life Ins. Co. N.Y. Served with U.S. Army, 1952-54. Recipient various salesmanship awards. Mem. Sigma Nu. Address: CIGNA Corp 1600 Arch St Philadelphia PA 19101

GAGE, AVERY ODELL, former corporate executive; b. South Wayne, Wis., Mar. 29, 1919; s. John R. and Lela M. (Stites) G.; m. Helen Evans, Aug. 22, 1942; children: John, Mary (Mrs. Robert Miller). B.A., Beloit Coll., 1939. Field rep. Browns Bus. Coll., Rockford, Ill., 1940-41; office mgr. mechanics univ. joint div. Borg-Warner, Rockford, 1941-53; with J.L. Clark Mfg. Co., Rockford, 1953-79, asst. sec., 1961-62, sec., 1962-79; ret., 1979. Trustee, chmn. Swedish Am. Hosp., Rockford, 1966—, Clark Found., 1962-79. Served to capt. USAAF, 1942-44. Decorated D.F.C., Air medal with 3 oak leaf clusters. Mem. C. of C. (pres., bd. dirs. 1973—). Lodge: Elks. Home: 5895 Inverness Dr Rockford IL 61107

GAGE, CALVIN WILLIAM, advt. agy. exec.; b. Mpls., Feb. 14, 1929; s. Robert Percy and Rachel (Green) G.; m. Margaret Borchmann, Sept. 6, 1958; children—Andrew William, Carolyn Elizabeth. A.B., Cornell U., 1951; M.A., U. Minn., 1953. Food and drug field auditor A.C. Nielsen Co., Chgo., 1954-55; with Leo Burnett Co., Inc., Chgo., 1955—, v.p., 1972-79, group research dir., 1977-79, dir. research, sr. v.p., 1979—. Mem. Am. Mktg. Assn., Advt. Research Found. Home: 235 W Blodgett Ave Lake Bluff IL 60044 Office: Leo Burnett Co Inc Prudential Plaza Chicago IL 60601

GAGE, FRED KELTON, lawyer; b. Mpls., June 20, 1925; s. Fred K. and Vivian L. G.; m. Dorothy Ann, Sept. 7, 1974; children: Deborah, Penelope, Fred, Amy, Lawrence. B.S. in Law, U. Minn., 1948, LL.B., 1950. Bar: Minn. 1950. Assoc. firm Wilson, Blethen & Ogle, Mankato, 1950-55; partner firm Blethen, Gage, Krause, Blethen, Corcoran, Berkland & Peterson (and predecessor firm), Mankato, 1955—; mem. State Bd. Profl. Responsibility, Minn. Supreme Ct., 1974-82; dir. Northwestern Nat. Bank of Mankato. Mem. Mankato Sch. Bd., 1957-66, Minn. State Coll. Bd., 1960-64; mem. Minn. Senate from 11th Legis. Dist., 1966-72; Mem. Minn. Sports Facilities Commn. Served with USN, 1943-46. Named Mankato Outstanding Young Man of Yr., 1956, Outstanding Man of Minn. Mankato Jr. C. of C., 1958. Fellow Am. Bar Found.; mem. Am. Bar Assn. (state del.), Minn. Bar Assn. (chmn. tax sect. 1956-66, pres. 1977-78), Order Coif. Republican. Methodist. Office: 127 S 2d St Mankato MN 56001

GAGE, GEORGE H., telephone company executive; b. Portland, Oreg., 1925; married. Grad., U. Calif.-Santa Barbara. V.p., gen. staff Gen. Telephone Co. of Calif., 1947-62; v.p. telephone ops. GTE Service Corp., 1962-71; pres., chief exec. officer Gen. Telephone Co. of Fla., Tampa, 1971—; dir. Gen. Telephone co. of Fla., Tampa; dir. Adams-Russell Co. Inc., 1st Nat. Bank Fla., Freedom Mortgage Co.; chmn. Fla. State Savs. Bond Commn.; vice chmn. Freedom Fed. Savs. and Loan Assn. Office: Gen Telephone Co of Fla Inc 610 Morgan St Box 110 Tampa FL 33601 *

GAGE, JOHN, opera company executive; b. Grand Rapids, Mich., Nov. 25, 1937; s. John McKay and Frances Charlotte (Hulswit) Criner. B.A., Wayne State U., 1965, M.A., 1969. Instr. speech and theatre Heidelberg Coll., 1966-70; mem. faculty speech and theatre Hamline U., 1971-73; gen. mgr. Friar's Theatre, Mpls., 1971-72; artistic dir. Chimera Theatre Co., St. Paul, 1971-73; stage mgr. St. Paul Opera, 1972-74; gen. mgr. Theatrical Rigging Systems, Mpls., 1974-77; prodn. stage mgr. Dallas Civic Opera, also Miami Opera, 1977-80; gen. mgr. Florentine Opera Co., Milw., 1980—, Opera America. Served with USAF, 1956-60. Office: 750 N Lincoln Memorial Dr Milwaukee WI 53202

GAGE, NATHANIEL LEES, psychologist, educator; b. Union City, N.J., Aug. 1, 1917; s. Hyman and Rose (Lees) Gewirtz; m. Margaret Elizabeth Burrows, June 27, 1942; children: Elizabeth Gage Verbeek, Thomas Burrows, Sarah, Anne. A.B. magna cum laude, U. Minn., 1938; Ph.D., Purdue U., 1947, Litt.D. (hon.), 1978. Asst. prof. div. ednl. reference Purdue U., 1947-48; prof. edn. and psychology U. Ill., Urbana, 1948-62, Stanford U., 1962—, Margaret Jacks prof. edn., 1981—; Sachs vis. prof. Tchrs. Coll., Columbia U., 1977; lectr. U. Hamburg, W. Ger., 1978; vis. fellow Brasenose Coll., Oxford U., 1983; visitor Harvard U., 1984; Mem. research adv. com. Am. Council Edn., 1967-73, chmn., 1972-73; mem. Nat. Adv. Com. on Edn. Labs., 1966-69; cons. Internat. Inst. Ednl. Planning, Paris, 1973-74; chmn. exec. bd. Stanford Center Research and Devel. in Teaching, 1968-76, co-dir., 1965-68; also dir. program on teaching effectiveness Center for Ednl. Research, Stanford, 1972—; vis. scholar, chmn. planning conf. on studies in teaching Nat. Inst. Edn., 1974; chmn. project council Internat. Classroom Environ. Study, 1979-81. Author: Teacher Effectiveness and Teacher Education, 1972, Scientific Basis of the Art of Teaching, 1978; co-author: Educational Measurement and Evaluation, 1943, 55, A Practical Introduction to Measurement and Evaluation, 1960, 65, Educational Psychology, 1975, 79, 84; editor: Handbook of Research on Teaching, 1963, Mandated Evaluation of Educators, 1973, Psychology of Teaching Methods, 1976; co-editor: Readings in the Social Psychology of Education, 1963; cons. editor: Jour. Ednl. Psychology; numerous other jours. Served with USAAF, 1943-45. Recipient Creative Leadership award Sch. Edn., N.Y. U., 1980; Fellow Center Advanced Study in Behavioral Scis., 1965-66; USPHS fellow, 1965-66; Guggenheim fellow, 1976-77. Fellow Am. Psychol. Assn. (pres. div. ednl. psychology 1961-62); mem. Am. Ednl. Research Assn. (pres. 1963-64), AAAS, Nat. Soc. Study Edn. (chmn. bd. dirs. 1972, 74, 78), Nat. Acad. Edn., Phi Beta Kappa, Sigma Xi, Phi Delta Kappa (award for meritorious contbns. to edn. 1981). Home: 845 Cedro Way Stanford CA 94305

GAGE, TOMMY WILTON, pharmacologist, educator; b. Stamford, Tex., Oct. 6, 1935; s. Carl and Mildred (Hughes) G.; m. Loyce M. Voss, June 2, 1956; children—Sharon, Stephen, Susan, Stacey. B.S., U. Tex., Austin, 1957; D.D.S., Baylor U., 1961, Ph.D., 1969. Gen. practice dentistry, Munday, Tex., 1963-66; mem. faculty Baylor Coll. Dentistry, Dallas, 1969—, prof. pharmacology, 1972—, chmn. dept., 1969—. Author papers in field, chpts. in books. Served with USAR, 1961-63. Nat. Inst. Dental Research postdoctoral fellow, 1966-69. Mem. Am. Soc. Pharmacology and Exptl. Therapeutics, ADA, Internat. Assn. Dental Research, Am. Assn. Dental Schs., Tex. Dental Assn. (Cooley Trophy 1976), S.W. Soc. Oral Medicine, Dallas County Dental Assn., Sigma Xi, Rho Chi, Omicron Kappa Upsilon. Methodist. Office: 3302 Gaston Ave Dallas TX 75246

GAGGE, ADOLF PHARO, educator; b. Columbus, Ohio, Jan. 11, 1908; s. Axel Christian Pharo and Edith (Smith) G.; m. Edwina Winter Mead, Dec. 23, 1936; children: Peter Mead, Eleanor (Mrs. James St. John Martin), John Pharo, Ann (Mrs. Gerry H. Vogt). B.A., U. Va., 1929, M.A. in Physics, 1930, Ph.D., Yale, 1933. Biophysicist Lab. Hygiene, John B. Pierce Found., New Haven, 1933-41, fellow, 1963-78, dep. dir., 1970-78, cons., fellow emeritus, 1978—; mem. faculty Yale U., 1933-41, 63—, prof. environ. physiology, 1969-77, emeritus prof. epidemiology, 1977—; chief biophysics, dir. research Aeromed. Lab., Wright Field, 1941-50; with Research and Devel. Hdqrs. USAF, Washington, 1950-55, Air Force Office Sci. Research, 1955-60, Office Sec. Def. Advanced Research Projects Agy., 1960-63; Chmn. com. hearing, bioacoustics and biomechanics Nat. Acad. Scis.-NRC, 1967-68, mem. council, 1965-69. Asso. editor, sect. editor: Jour. Applied Physiology, 1970—. Served to col. USAF, 1941-63. Decorated Legion of Merit with oak leaf cluster, Army Commendation ribbon, Def. Commendation ribbon. Fellow Aerospace Med. Assn., AAAS, ASHRAE (chmn. tech. com. physiology and human comfort 1968-79); mem. Am. Phys. Soc., Nat. Acad. Engring., Am. Physiol. Soc. Club: Cosmos (Washington). Home: 57 Island View Ave Branford CT 06405 Office: 290 Congress Ave New Haven CT 06519

GAGGIOLI, RICHARD ARNOLD, university dean, mechanical engineering educator; b. Highwood, Ill., Dec. 3, 1934; s. Gustavo and Constantina Lucille (Mordini) G.; m. Anita Catherine Sage, Nov. 9, 1957; children: Catherine Anne, Michael James, Daniel Richard, Edward Thomas, Mary Esther. B.M.E., Northwestern U., 1957, M.S. (NSF fellow), 1958; 2Ph.D. (Gen. Electric, NSF fellow), U. Wis., 1961. Registered profl. engr., Wis. Coop. student engr. Abbott Labs. (pharms.), N. Chicago, Ill., 1954-58; asst. prof. mech. engring. U. Wis.-Madison, 1962-66, asso. prof. mech. engring., 1966-69; prof., chmn. dept. mech. engring. Marquette U., Milw., 1969-72, prof., 1969-81; dean engring. and architecture Cath. U. Am., Washington, 1981—; mem. U.S. Army Math. Research Ctr., Madison, 1964-66; NSF-Soc. Indsl. and Applied Math. vis. lectr., 1969-72, engring. cons., 1970—. Author: (with E.F. Obert) Thermo-dynamics, 1963; editor: Thermodynamics-Second Law Analysis, Vol. 1, 1980, Vol. 2, 1983; contbr. articles to profl. jours. Bd. dirs. Inst. for Family Devel., Marblehead, Mass. Recipient Emil H. Steiger Meml. Teaching award U. Wis., 1965; Pere Marquette award for faculty excellence Marquette U., 1976; NSF postdoctoral fellow chem. engring. U. Wis., 1961-62; vis. fellow Battelle Meml. Inst., 1968-69. Mem. ASME, Am. Soc. Heating, Refrigerating and Air Conditioning Engrs., Sigma Xi, Pi Tau Sigma, Tau Beta Pi. Roman Catholic. Home: 6425 Western Ave NW Washington DC 20015 Office: Cath U Am Washington DC 20064

GAGLIANO, FRANK JOSEPH, playwright; b. Bklyn., Nov. 18, 1931; s. Francis Paul and Nancy (La Barbera) G.; m. Sandra Renee, Jan. 18, 1958; 1 son, Francis Enrico. B.A., U. Iowa, 1954; M.F.A., Columbia U., 1957. Free-lance copywriter, N.Y.C., 1958-61; promotion copywriter text-film div. McGraw-Hill Co., N.Y.C., 1962-65; asso. prof. drama Fla. State U., 1969-72; lectr. in playwriting, dir. E. P. Conkle Workshop for Playwrights, U. Tex., Austin, 1972-75; Benedum prof. theatre W.Va. U., 1975—; Disting. Vis. Alumni prof. U. R.I., 1975. Plays include Conerico Was Here to Stay, 1965, Night of the Dunce, 1966, Father Uxbridge Wants to Marry, 1967, In the VooDoo Parlour of Marie Laveau, 1974, The Resurrection of Jackie

Cramer, 1976, Congo Square, 1979, The Total Immersion of Madeleine Favorini, 1981. Served with U.S. Army, 1954-56. Wesleyan U.-O'Neill Found. fellow, 1967; Guggenheim fellow, 1975; Rockefeller grantee, 1965, 66; Nat. Endowment for Arts grantee, 1973. Mem. Dramatists Guild, Writers Guild Am., East, New Dramatists, Am. Theatre Assn., AAUP. Office: Creative Arts Center WVa U Morgantown WV 26506

GAGLIARDI, FRANK JOSEPH, publishing company sales executive; b. N.Y.C., June 26, 1933; s. Gina and Maria Emma (Iraldi) G.; m. Suzanne Lee Wickman, Dec. 27, 1958; children: Marylee, Laura, Ellen, Gail, Caroline. B.A., Gettysburgh Coll., 1956. Tchr. history Neptune High Sch., N.J., 1958-59; pres. sales div. World Book, Inc., World Book-Childcraft, Chgo., 1959—. Club: Atlanta Country (Marietta, Ga.) (dir. 1974-76). Home: 610 Signal Hill Rd Barrington IL 60010 Office: World Book Inc Merchandise Mart Chicago IL 60654

GAGLIARDI, LEE PARSONS, judge; b. Larchmont, N.Y., July 17, 1918; s. Frank M. and Mary F. (DeCicco) G.; m. Marian Hope Selden, Aug. 5, 1943; children—Elizabeth G. (Mrs. Charles J. Tobin III) Marian S. (dec.). Grad., Phillips Exeter Acad.; B.A., Williams Coll., 1941; J.D., Columbia U., 1947. Bar: N.Y. bar 1948. Asst. to gen. atty. N.Y. Central R.R. Co., N.Y.C., 1948-55; partner Clark, Gagliardi, Gallagher & Smyth, N.Y.C., 1955-72; judge U.S. Dist. Ct., So. Dist. N.Y., 1972—. Chmn. Bd. Police Commrs., Mamaroneck, N.Y., 1970-72; Sec. Westchester County Caddie Scholarship Com., 1964-72; Bd. govs. New Rochelle (N.Y.) Hosp. Med. Center. Club: Skytop (Pa.) (bd. govs.). Office: US Courthouse New York City NY 10007

GAGLIARDI, UGO OSCAR, computer engineering educator; b. Naples, Italy, July 23, 1931; came to U.S., 1956; s. Edgardo and Lina (Valenzuela) G.; m. Anna Josehine Italiano, July 7, 1954 (div. May 1972); children: Oscar Marco, Alex Piero. Diploma in Math. and Physics, U. Naples, Italy, 1951, Dr. Engring., 1954. Sr. scientist U.S. Air Force, Hanscom AFB, Mass., 1966-67; v.p. tech. ops. Interactive Scis., Inc., Braintree, Mass., 1968-70; dir. engring. Honeywell Info. Systems, Waltham, Mass., 1970-75; lectr. Harvard U., Cambridge, Mass., 1967-74, prof. practice, 1974—; pres. Gen. systems Groups, Inc., Salem, N.H., 1975—. Fulbright scholar, 1955-56. Home: 51 Main St Salem NH 03079 Office: Harvard U 33 Oxford St Cambridge MA 02138

GAGNE, FRANCOIS, pathologist; b. Quebec City, June 22, 1923; s. Jules Arthur and Evangeline (Garneau) G.; m. Francoise Potvin, Oct. 21, 1952; children—Louise, Isabelle, Charles and Richard (twins). B.A., Petit Seminaire de Que., 1943; M.D., Laval U., Quebec, 1948. Intern Hotel-Dieu Hosp., Quebec City, 1947-48, resident, 1951-52, Enfant-Jesus Hosp., Quebec City, 1948-50, 52-53, Institut du Cancer, Villejulf, France, 1950-51; pathologist Enfant-Jesus Hosp., 1953—; assoc. prof. dept. pathology Laval U., 1953-69, prof., 1969—, head residency program, 1974-82, chmn. dept. pathology, 1982—. Contbr. articles in field to med. jours. Mem. Que. Assn. Pathologists, Can. Assn. Pathologists, Internat. Acad. Pathology, Que. Med. Assn. Office: Department of Pathology Laval University Faculty of Medicine Quebec PQ G1K 7P4 Canada

GAGNÉ, ROBERT MILLS, educator; b. North Andover, Mass., Aug. 21, 1916; s. Alphonse F. and Alice E. (Mills) Gagne; m. Harriet N. Towle, Nov. 26, 1942; children: Samuel T., Ellen D. A.B., Yale, 1937; Ph.D., Brown U., 1940. Instr. psychology Conn. Coll., for Women, 1940-41, asst., then asso. prof. psychology, 1946-49; asst. prof. psychology Pa. State U., 1945-46; research dir. perceptual and motor skills lab. Air Force Personnel and Tng. Research Center, Air Research and Devel. Command, 1949-53, tech. dir. maintenance lab., 1953-58; prof. psychology Princeton, 1958-62; cons. Dept. Def., 1958-61; dir. research Am. Inst. Research, Pitts., 1962-65; prof. ednl. psychology U. Calif., Berkeley, 1966-69; prof. dept. ednl. research Fla. State U., Tallahassee, 1969—; Fellow Center for Advanced Study in Behavioral Scis., 1972. Author: (with E.A. Fleishman) Psychology and Human Performance, 1959, The Conditions of Learning, 1965, 2d edit., 1970, 3d edit., 1977, (with L.J. Briggs) Principles of Instructional Design, 1974, 2d edit., 1979, Essentials of Learning for Instruction, 1974; Editor: Psychological Principles in System Development, 1962, (with L.J. Briggs) Learning and Individual Differences, 1966, (with W.P. Gephart) Learning Research and School Subjects, 1968. Served from pvt. to 1st lt. USAAF, 1941-45. Mem. Am. Psychol. Assn. (fellow div. 3, 15 and 19), Nat. Acad. Edn., Am. Ednl. Research Assn. Home: 1456 Mitchell Ave Tallahassee FL 32303

GAGNEBIN, ALBERT PAUL, mining executive; b. Torrington, Conn., Jan. 23, 1909; s. Charles A. and Marguerite E. (Huguenin) G.; m. Genevieve Hope, Oct. 26, 1935; children: Anne Hope Gagnebin Coffin, Joan DeVere Gagnebin Wicks. B.S. in Mech. Engring., Yale U., 1930, M.S., 1932. With Internat. Nickel Co., Inc., 1932-74, successively staff research lab., research ferrous metallurgy, devel. ductile iron, staff devel. and research div., 1932-55, mgr. nickel sales dept., 1956-61, v.p., 1958-64, exec. v.p., 1964-67, pres., 1967-72, also dir., mem. exec. com.; v.p. Internat. Nickel Co. Can., Ltd., 1960-64, exec. v.p., 1964-67, pres., 1967-72, chmn. bd., 1972-74, ret., 1974, mem. exec. com.; trustee Atlantic Mut. Ins. Co.; mem. adv. bd. Inco Ltd.; dir. Abex Corp., Centennial Ins. Co., Am.-Swiss Assos., Inc.; dir. emeritus Ill. Central Industries; former dir. Ingersoll-Rand Co., Schering-Plough Corp., Bank of N.Y.; mem. N.Am. adv. bd. Swissair; cons. Stauffer Chem. Co. Author: The Fundamentals of Iron and Steel Castings. Decorated Ordre National du Merite, France; recipient ann. award Ductile Iron Soc., 1965; Grande Medaille d'Honneur L'Association Technique de Fonderie, 1967. Mem. ASME (Charles F. Rand Meml. Gold medal 1977), AIME, Am. Soc. Metals, Am. Foundrymen's Soc. (hon. life, Peter L. Simpson gold medal award 1952), Nat. Acad. Engring., Mining and Metall. Soc. Am., Yale Engring. Assn. (dir.), Sigma Xi. Clubs: Seabright (N.J.) Beach; Down Town Assn., Univ., Yale (N.Y.C.); Rumson Country. Co-inventor ductile iron. Home: 143 Grange Ave Fair Haven NJ 07701 Office: 1 New York Plaza New York NY 10004

GAGNON, ALFRED JOSEPH, vineyardist, former management consultant; b. Waterbury, Conn., Sept. 9, 1914; s. John and Amelia (L'Heureux) G.; m. Mary Perry, Dec. 9, 1939; children: Marianne Gagnon Palmer, Susanne Gagnon Burrill, Thom, Joanne Gagnon Janca; m. Edith Morrison, Feb. 3, 1977. B.S., Yale U., 1936. Plant indsl. engr. U.S. Steel Corp., 1936-43; mfg. engr. Sperry Gyroscope Co., 1943-45; with Booz, Allen and Hamilton, N.Y. and San Francisco, 1945-70, formerly exec. v.p. charge Central and Western regions, also dir.; gen. partner Tepusquet Vineyards, Santa Maria, Calif.; pres. Booz, Allen and Hamilton Can., Ltd., PAR Tech. Inc., Stanwich Devel. Co.; v.p., dir. Greenwich Acad.; dir. Olympia Brewing Co., Tumwater, Wash., A.C. Gilbert Co., New Haven. Pres. Millbrook Owners Assn. Mem. Calif. Vintage Wine Soc., Calif. Assn. Winegrape Growers (dir.), Vintners Club San Francisco, Sigma Xi, Tau Beta Pi, Phi Gamma Delta. Clubs: Burlingame Country; San Francisco Golf, Stock Exchange (San Francisco); Pine Valley Golf (Clementon, N.J.); California (Los Angeles); Chicago, World Trade; Pacific (Honolulu); U.S. Seniors' Golf Assn., Internat. Seniors' Amateur Golf Assn. Home: 745 Chiltern Rd Hillsborough CA 94010

GAGNON, JEAN-JACQUES, aluminum products company executive; b. Montreal, Can., 1918. Grad., U. Montreal, 1938, Trinity Coll., Eng., 1940. Sr. exec. v.p., dir. Aluminum Co. of Can., Ltd., Montreal. Mem. Can. Mfrs. Assn. (chmn.). Office: Aluminum Co of Canada Ltd 1 Place Ville Marie Montreal PQ Canada H3C 2H2 *

GAGNON, JOHN HENRY, sociologist, educator; b. Fall River, Mass., Nov. 22, 1931; s. George and Mary (Murphy) G.; m. Patricia A. Orlikoff, Mar. 20, 1955 (div. Jan. 1979); children: Andrée Giselle, Christopher Hans. B.A., U. Chgo., 1955, Ph.D., 1969. Adminstrv. asst. to sheriff Cook County, Ill., 1955-58; clin. asst. dept. neurology and psychiatry Northwestern U. Med. Sch., Chgo., 1958-59; lectr. Ind. U., Bloomington, 1959-67; trustee Inst. for Sex Research, 1959-68, sr. research sociologist, 1959-68; asso. prof. State U. N.Y., Stony Brook, 1968-70, prof. sociology, 1970—, prof. dept. psychology, 1973—, dir. lab. for social relations, 1968-70; dir. Center for Continuing Edn., 1970-72; prof. dept. psychiatry Health Sci. Center, 1972-74; vis. scientist Inst. Criminology, U. Copenhagen, 1976; vis. prof. Lab. Human Devel. Grad. Sch. Edn., Harvard U., 1978-80; vis. prof. dept. sociology U. Essex (Eng.), 1983-84. Author: Sex Offenders: An Analysis of Types, 1965, Sexual Deviance, 1967, The Sexual Scene, 1970, Sexuelle Aussenseiter, 1970, Sexual Conduct, 1973, Human Sexualities, 1977, Life Designs: Individuals, Marriages and Families, 1978, Human Sexuality in Today's World, 1977. Recipient Spl. Achievement award Nat. Hemophilia Found., 1977, award for career contbn. to sex research Soc. for Sci. Study of Sex, 1980; Overseas fellow Churchill Coll. U. Cambridge, Eng., 1972-73; Spl fellow NIMH, 1972-73. Fellow Internat. Acad. Sex Research; mem. Am. Sociol. Assn., AAAS, Soc. for Study Social Problems, Sex Info. and Edn. Council U.S. (dir. 1967-70, mem. steering com. biol. scis. curriculum study 1969-72). Research in social and cultural change, environ. studies, social biology, human sexual conduct. Address: Dept Sociology State U NY Stony Brook NY 11794

GAGUINE, BENITO, lawyer; b. Paris, Apr. 28, 1912; U.S., 1920, naturalized, 1926; s. Silvio Alexander and Rose (Braun) G.; m. Frances Cass Crouse, July 15, 1944; children—John Benedict, Bruce Alexander. A.B., Columbia, 1932, LL.B., 1934; LL.M., George Washington U., 1940. Bar: N.Y. bar 1934. Atty., adminstrv. law judge various U.S. Govt. agencies, Washington, 1935-53; partner firm Fly, Shuebruk, Blume & Gaguine, Washington, 1953—; Adviser U.S. dels. internat. confs.; mem. juridical com. Interam. Broadcasters Assn. Contbr. articles to legal jours. Served to lt. col. AUS, 1943-47. Mem. Am., Fed., Fed. Communications, D.C. bar assns. Democrat. Club: University (Washington). Home: 3628 Appleton St NW Washington DC 20008 Office: 1211 Connecticut Ave NW Washington DC 20036

GAHAGAN, JAMES EDWARD, JR., artist; b. Bklyn., Sept. 20, 1927; s. James Edward and Anna (Biondi) G.; m. Patricia De Gogorza, Apr. 18, 1963; children: Paulo, Sharon. B.A., Goddard Coll., 1951; student, Hans Hofmann Sch. Fine Art, N.Y.C., 1952-58. Asst. dir. Hans Hofmann Sch. Fine Arts, 1954-58; art tchr. Adult Workshop, SUNY, Great Neck, L.I., 1955-62; tchr. painting, drawing Pratt Inst., Bklyn., 1965-71; lectr. arts Columbia U. Grad. Sch. Arts, N.Y.C., 1968-71; mem. art faculty, chmn. faculty, acting dean, art dept. chmn. Goddard Coll., Plainfield, Vt., 1971-79; tchr. Lesley Coll. Grad. Sch., Cambridge, Mass., 1981; field faculty grad. program Vt. Coll., Montpelier, 1983—; Mem. Artist Tenants Assn., N.Y.C., 1960-71, pres., 1960-62, 65-66. Co-pub./editor: N.Y. Element newspaper, 1968-71; 18 one-man shows, 1954-81, including, James Gallery, N.Y.C., 1954, Tirca Karlis Gallery, Provincetown, Mass., 1983; exhibited numerous group shows; represented in permanent and pvt. collections; chief asst. to, Hans Hofmann on, 2 Mosaic-mural projects, N.Y.C., 1956, 57. Mem. N.Y.C. Mayor's Com. on Cultural Affairs, 71965-66; health officer, Woodbury, 1975—, justice of peace, Woodbury, Vt., 1975-77, 80—. Served with USNR, 1945-47. Longview Found. grantee, 1958; recipient Cape Cod Art Assn. award, 1957. Mem. Art Resource Assn. Vt. (chmn. bd. dirs. 1975—), AAUP, Am. Fedn. Tchrs., Printmaking Workshop N.Y.C., Artworkers Found. for Community of Artists N.Y.C., Provincetown (Mass.) Art Assn., Vt. Council Arts, ACLU. Democrat. Address: RFD 1 Box 116 East Calais VT 05650 *If I had my life to live over, I would again choose to spend it as a creative, visual, fine artist. It is a constructive, non-violent, life-affirming commitment to explore reality.*

GAHR, H. JAMES, b. Monticello, Minn., May 10, 1927; s. Harry Albert and Agnes Mary (Conlin) G. B.A., St. John's U., Collegeville, Minn., 1953; student, U. Vienna, 1950-51; LL.B., Georgetown U., 1956. Bar: N.Y. 1959. Clk. Simpson Thacher & Bartlett, N.Y.C., 1956-59, assoc., 1960-70, ptnr., 1970—. Office: Simpson Thacher & Bartlett One Battery Park Plaza New York NY 10004

GAIGE, FREDERICK HUGHES, univ. adminstr.; b. Quincy, Mass., Mar. 4, 1937; s. William Clement and Beatrice Emily (Farrell) G.; m. Austra Ozols, June 23, 1962; children—Karina Alexandra, Amity Weller. B.A., Oberlin Coll., 1959; M.A.T., Brown U., 1962; Ph.D., U. Pa., 1970. Tutor history Wilson Coll., U. Bombay, 1961-63; grad. research historian Inst. Internat. Studies, U. Calif., Berkeley, 1968-69; instr., asst. prof. Davidson Coll., 1969-74; v.p. for profl. devel. Kansas City Regional Council for Higher Edn., Kansas City, Mo., 1974-77; dean Coll. Arts and Scis. Fairleigh Dickinson U., Madison, N.J., 1977—. Author: Search for National Unity in Nepal, 1975. NDEA fellow, 1964-66; Fulbright-Hays fellow, 1966-67. Mem. Nepal Studies Assn., So. Atlantic States Assn. for African and Asian Studies, Profl. and Organizational Devel. Network in Higher Edn. Democrat. Unitarian. Office: Fairleigh Dickinson U Madison NJ 07940

GAIL, BRIAN JOHN, advertising executive; b. Phila., Nov. 30, 1946; s. John F. and Mary Eileen (Murray) G.; m. Joan Mary Kain, Sept. 20, 1969; children: Kelly Ann, Jennifer, Michelle, Mary Kate, Joan Elizabeth, Patrick John, Brian Charles. B.A., LaSalle Coll., 1969, M.B.A., 1979. Copywriter RCA, Cherry Hill, N.J., 1971-72; writer producer N.W. Ayer, Phila., 1972-74; v.p. Montgomery & Assocs., Phila., 1974-79; sr. v.p. Ted Bates, N.Y.C., 1979—. Author: Cable Marketing, 1982. Mem. presdl. adv. council LaSalle Coll., Phila., 1982—; dir. Eternal World Cable TV Network, Birmingham, 1982—. Recipient Ann. Best of TV award Bank Mktg. Assn. Am., 1976, Best Consumer Package Goods TV Comml. award Advt. Club of Phila., 1975, Effie award Am. Mktg. Assn., 1978. Mem. Cable TV Advt. and Mktg. Assn. Republican. Roman Catholic. Office: 1515 Broadway New York NY 10036

GAIL, MAXWELL TROWBRIDGE, JR., actor, director, musician; b. Detroit, Apr. 5, 1943; s. Maxwell Trowbridge and Mary Elizabeth (Scanlon) G. B.A., Williams Coll., Williamstown, Mass., 1965; M.B.A., U. Mich., 1969. Tchr. ancient history and English Grosse Pointe (Mich.) Univ. Sch., 1965-67; pres. Full Circle Prodns. Appeared in motion pictures and TV shows; appeared as Detective Sgt. Wojehowicz on: television series Barney Miller, 1975—; appeared in, San Francisco and; One Flew Over the Cuckoo's Nest, 1971, Jesse James, 1973, D.C. Cab, 1983; rec. album Do Something Beautiful, 1983. Active Am. Indian Movement. Mem. Dirs. Guild Am., AFTRA, Screen Actors Guild. Office: care Artists Agy 190 N Cannon Dr Beverly Hills CA 90210 *The truth may get the better part of beauty but there is always beauty left and that's the beauty of the truth. When Americans come to terms with the history of native peoples and the contribution of these traditions to the advancement of humanity then the true richness of our heritage is revealed and the path is clear.*

GAILEY, FRANKLIN BRYAN, biology educator; b. Atlanta, Oct. 18, 1918; s. James Herbert and Edna (Bryan) G.; m. Sara Helen Clark, July 31, 1948; children: David Clark, Carol Bryan, Patricia Lowe, Mark Alan. B.S. in Chemistry, Ga. Inst. Tech., 1940; M.S., U. Wis., 1942, Ph.D. in Biochemistry, 1946. Instr. biology, chemistry Lees Jr. Coll., Jackson, Ky., 1946-48; mem. faculty Berea (Ky.) Coll., 1948—, prof. biology, 1957—, chmn. dept., 1957-82; Research participant Oak Ridge Inst. Nuclear Studies, summers 1954, 55, U. Ill., summer 1966, U. Ky., 1966-67. Fellow AAAS; mem. Am. Inst. Biol. Scientists, Sigma Xi, Phi Kappa Phi. Mem. Ch. of Christ, Union, also Berea Friends Meeting. Home: Route 2 CPO 2312 Berea KY 40404 *I believe in the guidance of the Inner Light or Spirit of God, the value of silent meditation as well as dialogue in the spirit of love and logic, and the strengthening fellowship of kindred believers who are sensitive, concerned, and humble servants of social progress.*

GAILLARD, JOHN FRIERSON, lawyer; b. Jacksonville, Fla., July 28, 1934; s. Henry Frierson and Martha L. (Tillman) G.; m. Patricia Eskew, June 26, 1965; children: Martha, John, Rachel. B.S.C., U. Fla., 1957, J.D., 1962. Bar: Fla. 1962, U.S. Dist. Ct. Fla., U.S. Supreme Ct. Asst. county solicitor, Duval County, Fla., 1962-65; mem. firm MacLean, Baxter, Ragsdale, Gaillard & Brooke, Jacksonville, 1966-68; atty. Duval County delegation to Fla. Legislature, 1967; gen. counsel Fla. Dept. Health, Jacksonville, 1968-71; counsel Stockton, Whatley, Davin & Co., Jacksonville, 1971-74; v.p. legal and public affairs Fla. Pub. Co., Jacksonville, 1974—; dir. Area Communications, Inc., Clay Video, Inc. Pres. Jacksonville Mental Health Assn., 1963-74, Mental Health Assn. Fla., 1965-73; pres. Mental Health Clinic Jacksonville, 1968-75, N.E. Fla. Dist. Mental Health Bd., 1971, 75, Jacksonville Art Mus., 1968—, Daniel Meml. Home for Children, 1976-78; mem. Children's Home Soc., 1966; vice chmn. Hope Haven Children's Hosp., 1978; sec. Health Systems Agy., 1976; mem. Jacksonville Exptl. Health Delivery System, Inc., 1973-76, Found. Med. Care, 1972—, Legal Aid Assn., 1974-77, Community Edn. Council, 1975-77, Easter Seal Soc. Crippled Children and Adults N.E. Fla., Inc., 1974—, Fla. Alliance for Arts in Edn., 1975—; pres. Arts Assembly, 1979-80, Jacksonville Symphony, 1978—; mem. Buckner Found., 1977—, Consortium to Aid Neglected and Abused Children, 1976—. Mem. Am. Bar Assn., Jacksonville Bar Assn. Democrat. Episcopalian. Clubs: Fla. Yacht, Ponte Vedra Country, River, Timuquana Country. Home: 4396 McGirts Blvd Jacksonville FL 32210 Office: 1775 Cassat Ave Jacksonville FL 32210

GAILLARD, JOHN PALMER, JR., govt. ofcl.; b. Charleston, S.C., Apr. 4, 1920; s. John Palmer and Eleanor Ball (Lucas) G.; m. Lucy Huguenin Foster, July 15, 1944; children—John Palmer III, William Foster, Thomas Huguenin. LL.D., The Citadel, 1975. Alderman City of Charleston, 1951-59, mayor, 1959-75; dep. asst. sec. for res. affairs Dept. Navy, Washington, 1975-77; v.p. Ruscon Corp., Charleston, S.C., 1977—; dir. Home Fed. Savs. & Loan Assn., Charleston. Pres. Mcpl. Assn. S.C., 1964-65. Served to lt. USNR, 1941-45. Mem. C. of C., St. Andrews Soc., U.S. Conf. Mayors (adv. bd. 1969, trustee), Am. Legion. Episcopalian. Clubs: Carolina Yacht, Hibernian, Charleston, Charleston Country, Carolina Motor (dir.), Elks, Charleston Rotary. Home: 77 Montagu St Charleston SC 29401 Office: 149 East Bay St Charleston SC 29401

GAILYS, JOHN M., retail co. exec.; b. Pitts., June 29, 1941; s. John M. and Lillian G.; m. Doreen Erickson, Apr. 14, 1973; children—Greg, Mark, John Matthew. B.B.A., U. Pitts., 1963. Auditor Arthur Andersen & Co., Chgo., 1963-69; v.p. ops. and fin. Reliance Trading Co., Chgo., 1969-73; v.p., controller J.L. Hudson Co., Detroit, 1973-78; exec. v.p. fin., constrn. and ops. Neiman-Marcus, Dallas, 1978—. Served with AUS, 1963. Office: Neiman-Marcus Main and Ervay Sts Dallas TX 75201

GAINER, RONALD LEE, lawyer; b. Lansing, Mich., Aug. 7, 1934; s. Asher Leroy and Gladys Irene (Harvey) G.; m. Alice Louise Sherwood, June 15, 1957; children—Gregory Sherwood, Geoffrey Scott. B.A., Mich. State U., 1956; J.D., U. Mich., 1959. Bar: N.Y. bar 1960, D.C. bar 1963, U.S. Supreme Ct 1963. Atty. appellate sect., criminal div. Dept. Justice, Washington, 1963-69, dep. chief legis. and spl. projects, 1969-73, chief legis. and spl. projects, 1973-75, dir. Office of Policy and Planning, 1975-77; dep. asst. atty. gen. Office for Improvements in Adminstrn. of Justice, 1977-81, Office of Legal Policy, 1981—; U.S. expert mem. UN Com. on Crime Prevention and Control, 1979—; mem. adv. bd. Bur. Justice Stats., 1980-81. Served to capt. U.S. Army, 1960-63. Recipient Disting. Service award U.S. Atty. Gen., 1973; Guggenheim fellow Yale U. Law Sch., 1973-74. Mem. Am. Law Inst., Internat. Assn. Penal Law, Am. Judicature Soc., Am. Bar Assn., Fed. Bar Assn., D.C. Bar Assn. Home: 3000 N Monroe St Arlington VA 22207 Office: Dept Justice 10th St and Constitution Ave Washington DC 20530

GAINES, ALAN MCCULLOCH, educator, government official; b. Asheville, N.C., Nov. 13, 1938; s. Edward McCulloch and Dorothy (Hougland) G.; m. Margaret Shepherd, 1958 (div. 1972); children: Sean Frederick, Fredericka Victoria; m. Ruth L. Norman, 1975; children: Eric Edward, Lindsay Norman. B.S., U. Chgo., 1960, M.S., 1963, Ph.D., 1968. Lectr. U. Ill. at Chgo., 1960-62; lectr. U. Chgo., 1962-64, research asso., 1968-69; asst. prof. U. Pa., 1969-76; asso. program dir. geochemistry NSF, 1976-79, program dir. geochemistry, 1979—. Fellow AAAS (council 1971-72); mem. Geochem. Soc., Mineral. Soc. Am., Am. Geophys. Union, Internat. Assn. Geochemistry and Cosmochemistry, Sigma Xi. Research geochemistry of carbonate minerals; kinetics of mineral reactions; geochem. and petrologic applications in archaeology. Home: 9110 Brink Rd Gaithersburg MD 20879

GAINES, ALEXANDER PENDLETON, lawyer; b. Atlanta, May 27, 1910; s. Lewis M. and Virginia Ethel (Alexander) G.; m. Mary Delia Upchurch, Oct. 2, 1937 (dec. Nov. 1975); children: Mary (Mrs. William F. Ford), Alexander Pendleton, Delia (Mrs. Charles C. Thompson III); m. Mary Cobb Gardner, June 27, 1976. A.B., U. Ga., 1932; LL.B., Emory U., 1935. Bar: Admitted Ga. 1935, D.C. 1967. Asso Jones, Fuller and Clapp, 1935-41; asst. regional counsel OPA, 1942; partner Clapp and Gaines, 1945-50, Gaines and deGive, 1951-53, Hurt, Gaines and Baird, 1954-62; mem. firm Alston, Miller and Gaines, Atlanta, 1962-82, Alston and Bird, 1982—; sec., dir. George Muse Clothing Co., 1947-81; dir. Genuine Parts Co., 1950-81. Trustee Charles Loridans Found., Vassar Wooley Found., John Bulow Campbell Found., 1958-80; trustee U. Ga. Found., 1964-81, trustee emeritus, 1982—; trustee Berry Schs., 1964-81, trustee emeritus, 1982—; trustee J.M. Tull Found., 1964-81, Agnes Scott Coll., 1959-84; trustee emeritus Agnes Scott Coll., 1984—; trustee Piedmont Hosp. Found., 1971-83, So. Acad. Letters, Arts and Scis., 1971-83. Served with USAAF, 1942-45. Fellow Am. Coll. Probate Counsel; mem. Am., D.C., Ga., Atlanta bar assns., Atlanta C. of C., Phi Delta Theta, Phi Delta Phi. Presbyterian (elder). Clubs: Commerce, Atlanta Lawyers, Piedmont Driving. Home: 3506 Paces Pl NW Atlanta GA 30327 Office: C and S Nat Bank Bldg Atlanta GA 30335

GAINES, ERNEST J., author. D.Litt. (hon.), Denison U., 1980. Prof. and resident writer U. Southwestern La., Lafayette. Author: Catherine Carmier, 1964, Of Love and Dust, 1967, Bloodline, 1968, The Autobiography of Miss Jane Pittman, 1971, A Long Day in November, 1971, In My Father's House, 1978, A Gathering of Old Men, 1983.

Recipient gold medal Commonwealth Club of Calif., 1972, 84; La. Library Assn. award, 1972; Black Acad. Arts and Letters award, 1972; award for excellence of achievement in field of lit. San Francisco Arts Commn., 1983. Address: care Dorothea Oppenheimer 435 E 79th St New York NY 10021

GAINES, ERVIN JAMES, librarian; b. N.Y.C., Dec. 8, 1916; s. Ervin J. and Helen (Hennessy) G.; m. Martha Zirbel, Feb. 11, 1938; children: Colleen Joy (Mrs. John Clark), Sanford Ervin. B.S., Columbia U., 1942, A.M., 1947, Ph.D., 1952; L.H.D. (hon.), Cleve. State U., 1983. Instr. Columbia U., N.Y.C., 1946-53; chief tng. Radio Liberation, 1953-56, Teleregister Corp., 1956-57; free-lance cons., 1957-58; asst. dir. Boston Pub. Library, 1958-64; dir. Mpls. Pub. Library, 1964-74, Cleve. Pub. Library, 1974—. Mem. A.L.A. Home: 12700 Lake Ave Lakewood OH 44107 Office: 325 Superior Ave Cleveland OH 44114

GAINES, FRANCIS PENDLETON, JR., university dean; b. State College, Miss., Sept. 7, 1918; s. Francis Pendleton and Sadie (Robert) G.; m. Dorothy Ruth Bloomhardt, Oct. 10, 1942; children—Francis Pendleton III, Paul Randolph, Sallie du Vergne; m. Marjorie Anne Hurt, Mar. 25, 1975. Grad., Woodberry Forest Prep. Sch., 1935; student, Washington and Lee U., 1935-37; A.B. summa cum laude, U. Ariz., 1942; M.A., U. Va., 1946; Ph.D. (DuPont fellow), U. Va., 1950; L.H.D., Coll. Artesia, 1968. Engr. on, Miss. River, War Dept., 1937-39; dean of men, asst. to pres. Birmingham So Coll., 1946-48; supt. Gulf Coast Mil. Acad., 1948; dir. pub. relations and devel. U. Houston, 1950; dean of students So. Meth. U., 1951-52; pres. Wofford Coll., 1952-57; v.p. Piedmont Nat. Bank, Spartanburg, S.C., 1957-58; dir. research study Fund for Advancement Edn., 1958-59; dean continuing edn. and summer session U. Ariz., Tucson, 1959-73, dean adminstrn., 1973—, also prof. ednl. adminstrn.; sec. Assn. Summer Session Deans and Dirs., 1961-62. Editorialist: Spartanburg Herald-Jour; Contbr. profl. publs. Pres. Conf. Ch.-related Colls. South, 1956-57; ofcl. del. to jurisdictional, gen. and world confs. of Meth. Ch., 1956; mem. Council for Basic Edn, Woodrow Wilson Regional Selection com.; treas. S.C. Found. Ind. Colls.; citizens adv. council U.S. Senate Com. to P.O. and Civil Service; adv. com. Robert A. Taft Inst. Govt.; mem. Ariz. Civil War Centennial Commn. Served as capt. AUS, War Dept., Gen. Staff, M.I., 1942-45. Named S.C. Young Man of Year Jr. C. of C., 1954; Outstanding Faculty Mem. U. Ariz., 1971; recipient Ariz. Civil Def. award, 1971. Fellow Nat. Univ. Extension Assn.; mem. U. Ariz. Alumni Assn. (dir. 1967—), Washington and Lee U. Alumni Assn. (pres. Tucson chpt. 1981—), Newcomen Soc., Phi Beta Kappa, Omicron Delta Kappa, Phi Kappa Phi, Pi Delta Epsilon, Phi Kappa Sigma, Raven Soc. Methodist (mem adminstrv. bd.). Clubs: Davis-Monthan Officers; Old Pueblo (Tucson); Country (Spartanburg). Former holder regional tennis championships. Home: 3919 E Cooper St Tucson AZ 85711 Office: Slonaker Alumni Bldg Room 112 Univ Arizona Tucson AZ 85721

GAINES, GENE FRANKLIN, association executive; b. St. Louis, Jan. 2, 1941; s. Eugene Franklin and Emma Edna (Myers) G.; m. Patricia Axelson, Aug. 28, 1965; children—Elizabeth, Patricia Kathleen. B.S., U. Kans., 1963, M.S., 1967. Salesman Armstrong Cork Co., Oklahoma City, 1964-65; regional sales mgr. Celotex Corp., Dallas, 1966; with Republic Nat. Bank, Dallas, 1967-71; v.p. 1st Nat. Bank Cin., 1971-78; exec. v.p. So. Ohio Bank, Cin., 1978-80; pres. Greater Cin. C. of C., 1981—. Trustee Dan Beard council Boy Scouts Am., 1981—, Seven Hills Sch., 1980—, Urban League Cin., 1981—, Greater Cin. Center Econ. Edn., 1981—, Paul I. Hoxworth Center, 1981—. Mem. Am. C. of C. Execs., C. of C. Execs. Ohio. Clubs: Queen City, Cin. Country, University. Office: 120 W 5th St Cincinnati OH 45202

GAINES, HOWARD CLARKE, lawyer; b. Washington, Sept. 6, 1909; s. Howard Wright and Ruth Adeline-Clarke Thomas G.; m. Audrey Allen, July 18, 1936; children: Clarke Allen, Margaret Anne Gaines Munsey. J.D., Cath. U. Am., 1936. Bar: D.C. bar 1936, U.S. Supreme Ct. bar 1946, U.S. Ct. Claims bar 1947, Calif. bar 1948. Individual practice law, Washington, 1938-43, 46-47, Santa Barbara, Calif., 1948-51; asso. firm Price, Postel & Parma, Santa Barbara, 1951-54, partner, 1954—; chmn. Santa Barbara Bench and Bar Com., 1972-74. Chmn. Santa Barbara Police and Fire Commn., 1948-52; mem. adv. bd. Santa Barbara Com. on Alcoholism, 1956-67; bd. dirs. Santa Barbara Humane Soc., 1958-69; bd. trustees Santa Barbara Botanic Garden, 1960—, v.p., 1967—; bd. trustees Cancer Found. Santa Barbara, 1960-77; dir. Santa Barbara Mental Health Assn., 1957-59, v.p., 1959; pres. Santa Barbara Found., 1976-79, trustee, 1979—. Fellow Am. Bar Found.; mem. Santa Barbara County Bar Assn. (pres. 1957-58), ABA, Bar Assn. D.C., State Bar Calif. (gov. 1969-72, v.p. 1971-72, treas. 1971-72), Am. Judicature Soc., Am. Bar Found. Republican. Episcopalian. Clubs: Santa Barbara, Birnam Wood Golf, Channel City. Home: 1306 Las Alturas Rd Santa Barbara CA 93103 Office: 200 E Carrillo St Santa Barbara CA 93101 *The selection and satisfactory maintenance of desired goals require an honest and continuing evaluation of our capabilities. It is essential to appraise constantly our levels of achievement if we are to earn the respect of others, without which there can be no lasting accomplishment.*

GAINES, LUDWELL EBERSOLE, financial executive; b. Charleston, W.Va., Apr. 21, 1927; s. Ludwell Ebersole and Elizabeth (Chilton) G.; m. Sheila Kellogg, Nov. 24, 1956; children: L. Ebersole, Leith Mitchell, Kellogg Chilton, Audrey Noyes. A.B., Princeton U., 1951. Tribunal clk. Am. Arbitration Assn., N.Y.C., 1951-53; sales mgmt. exec. Plax Corp.-Monsanto Chem. Corp., West Hartford, Conn., 1953-60; sales mgmt. exec., asst. to pres. Continental Can Co., Chgo. and N.Y.C., 1960-65; mktg. mgr. Nationwide Paper div. U.S. Plywood Champion, 1965-67; exec. v.p., dir. Diversa-Graphics, Inc., Chgo., 1969-72; exec. v.p. Overseas Pvt. Investment Corp., Washington, 1981—. Chmn. bd. trustees Ketchum-Sun Valley Community Schs., Sun Valley, Idaho, 1974-77; vice chmn. Idaho Park Found., Sun Valley, 1974-81; Idaho State fin. chmn. George Bush for Pres., mem. nat. central com.; Republican chmn., Blaine County, Idaho. Served with USN, 1945-46; PTO. Clubs: Cypress Point (Pebble Beach, Calif.); Princeton, Links (N.Y.C.); Chevy Chase (Washington). Home: 4369 Westover Pl NW Washington DC 20016 Office: Overseas Pvt Investment Corp 1129 20th St NW Washington DC 20527

GAINES, WILLIAM MAXWELL, publishing executive; b. N.Y.C., Mar. 1, 1922; s. Max C. and Jessie K. (Postlethwaite) G.; m. Hazel Grieb, Oct. 21, 1944 (div. Dec. 9, 1948); m. Nancy Siegel, Nov. 17, 1955 (div. Mar. 1, 1971); children: Cathy, Wendy, Chris. Student, Poly. Inst. Bklyn., 1939-42; B.S. in Edn, N.Y. U., 1948. Pres. E. C. Publs. Inc. (pub. MAD Mag.), N.Y.C., 1948—. Served with AUS, 1942-46. Mem. Wine and Food Soc., Chaine des Rotisseurs, Les Amis du Vin, Phi Alpha. Office: 485 Madison Ave New York NY 10022

GAINEY, ROBERT MICHAEL, hockey player; b. Peterborough, Ont., Can., Dec. 13, 1953. Hockey player Montreal Canadiens, 1973—. Recipient Frank J. Selke award as Best Defensive Forward, 1977-78, 78-79, 79-80; Conn Smythe trophy as Most Valuable Player Nat. Hockey League Playoffs, 1978-79. Office: Montreal Canadiens 2313 Saint Catherine St W Montreal PQ H3H 1N2 Canada *

GAINOR, THOMAS EDWARD, banker; b. St. Paul, Oct. 13, 1933; s. Joseph Paul and Teresa Cecilia (Whelan) G.; m. Janan Rose Nolan, Aug. 8, 1964; children: Mary, Michael, John, Daniel. B.S., Marquette U., 1955; postgrad., Stonier Grad. Sch. Banking, Rutgers U., 1965-67, Stanford U. Exec. Program, 1977. With Fed. Res. Bank of Mpls., 1958—, asst. v.p., 1967-72, v.p., 1972-75, sr. v.p. ops., 1975-78, 1st v.p., 1978—. Bd. dirs. Mpls. United Way, 1974-83, v.p., 1974-77; bd. dirs. Visiting Nurse Service, 1967-75, pres., 1971-72; trustee Visitation Sch., 1983—. Served as officer USNR, 1955-58. Mem. Stanford Alumni Assn., Marquette U. Alumni Assn., Naval Res. Assn. Roman Catholic. Club: Six o'Clock (pres. 1982). Office: 250 Marquette Ave Minneapolis MN 55480

GAINSBURGH, SAMUEL CORONNA, lawyer; b. New Orleans, Nov. 22, 1926; s. Isadore Bernard and Rosalie Minnie (Coronna) G.; m. Edel Florette Zeve, Apr. 1, 1951; children: Judith Ann, Amy Beth, Alan Irwin. B.A., U. SW La., 1949; J.D., Tulane U., 1949. Bar: La. 1949. Sr. partner Kierr, Gainsburgh, Benjamin, Fallon & Lewis, New Orleans. Served with USN, 1944-46. Mem. ABA, La. Bar Assn. (gov. 1976-78), Am. Coll. Trial Lawyers, Am. Judicature Soc., Assn. Trial Lawyers Am. (gov. 1969-72), La. State Law Inst. (council 1980—), La. Trial Lawyers Assn. (pres. 1967-68), Maritime Law Assn. U.S., New Orleans Bar Assn. (v.p. 1965-66), Scribes. Office: 1718 First Nat Bank Commerce Bldg New Orleans LA 70112

GAIRDNER, JOHN SMITH, investment dealer; b. Toronto, Ont., Can., July 25, 1925; s. James A. and Norma Ecclestone (Smith) G.; m. Ivy Jane Brothwell, Nov. 30, 1946; children—John Lewis, Robert Donald, Brenda Leigh. Grad., Appleby Coll., Oakville, Ont., 1942; student, U. Toronto, 1942-43. Clk. Gairdner & Co., Ltd. (name changed to Security Trading Ltd. 1974), Toronto, 1945-48, dir., 1948-55, v.p., dir., 1955-58, pres., 1958-66, chmn. bd., dir., 1965-74, chmn., pres., 1974—; pres., dir. Gairdner Internat., Ltd.; v.p., dir. Trafalgar Investments Co., Ltd. Bd. govs. Appleby Coll.; vice chmn., trustee Gairdner Found., Toronto. Served with RCAF, 1943-45. Mem. Zeta Psi. Home: 1502 Lakeshore Rd E Oakville ON L6J 1M1 Canada Office: Suite 4706 Manulife Centre 44 Charles St W Toronto ON M4Y 1R8 Canada

GAITHER, BILL, gospel songwriter, performer; s. George and Lelah G.; m. Gloria Sickal, 1962. Grad., Anderson Coll. English tchr. Alexandria (Ind.) High Sch.; co-owner Pinebrook Studio; owner Gaither Music Co., Alexandria House Inc., Printers Zink. Gospel and country music songwriter and performer with, Bill Gaither Trio, New Gaither Vocal Band; songs include I Am a Promise; albums include Let's Just Praise the Lord, 1973 (Grammy award), Jesus, We Just Want to Thank You, 1975 (Grammy award), Alleluia—A Praise Gathering for Believers (Gold album). Named Gospel Songwriter of Year Gospel Music Assn., 1972-77; recipient Dove award, 1978. Mem. ASCAP. Office: PO Box 300 Alexandria IN 46001 *

GAITHER, JOHN STOKES, chemical company executive; b. Boston, Apr. 20, 1944; s. Perry Stokes and Elizabeth (Hamlin) G. B.A. in Econs, U. Pa., 1967; M.B.A., European Inst. Bus. Adminstrn., Fountainebleau, France, 1973. With Reichhold Chems., Inc., 1967—; v.p. internat. sales and mktg., White Plains, N.Y., 1978-79, sr. v.p. internat., 1980—. Republican. Episcopalian. Home: 625 Ridgebury Rd Ridgefield CT 06877 Office: 525 N Broadway White Plains NY 10603

GAITHER, ROBERT BARKER, educator; b. N. Bay, Ont., Can., Aug., 12, 1929; s. Edwin Hampton and Loyola (Barker) G.; m. Renate- Konstanze Zielke, Dec. 11, 1954; children—Patricia, Vivienne, Francesca. B. Mech. Engring., Auburn U., 1951; M.S. in Mech. Engring, U. Ill., 1957, Ph.D., 1962. Instr. U. Ill., 1957-62; asso. prof. mech. engring. U. Fla., Gainesville, 1962-65, prof., 1965—, chmn. dept., 1965—; cons. in field, 1956—. Chmn. bd. Fla. Found. Future Scientists, 1973. Served to lt. USNR, 1951-54. Ford Found. fellow, 1959-62. Mem. ASME (chmn. mech. engring. dept. heads 1971-72, v.p. edn. 1976-80, pres. 1981-82), Am. Soc. Engring. Edn. (chmn. energy conversion com. 1971-72), Sigma Xi, Tau Beta Pi, Pi Mu Epsilon, Pi Tau Sigma. Research in electron gas in plasma flow systems. Home: 2100 NW 63d Terr Gainesville FL 32605

GAITHER, WILLIAM SAMUEL, university president; b. Lafayette, Ind., Dec. 3, 1932; s. William Marcius and Susan Frances (Kirkpatrick) G.; m. Robin Cornwall McGraw, Aug. 1, 1959; 1 dau., Sarah Curwen. Student, Purdue U., 1950-51; B.S. in Civil Engring, Rose Poly. Inst., 1956; M. Sci. Engring., Princeton, 1962; M.A. (Arthur Le Grand Doty fellow), Princeton, 1963; Ph.D. (Ford Found. fellow), Princeton, 1964. Engr. Dravo Corp. (marine constrn.), Pitts., 1956-60; supt. Myer Corp., Neenah, Wis., 1960-61; supervising engr., chief engr. port and coastal devel., pipeline div. Bechtel Corp., San Francisco, 1965-67; asso. prof. coastal engring. dept. U. Fla. at Gainesville, 1964-65; mem. faculty U. Del. at Newark, 1967-84, assoc. prof. civil engring., 1967-70, prof. civil engring., 1970, prof., dean, 1970-84, also dir. sea grant coll. program; prof., pres. Drexel U., Phila., 1984—; dir. Roy F. Weston Inc.; mem. marine bd. NRC, 1975-81. Chmn. Gov.'s Oil Transp. Study Com., 1971-73; mem. Gov.'s Task Force Marine and Coastal Affairs, 1970-72, Gov.'s Council Sci. and Tech., Del., 1970-72; mem. ocean affairs adv. com. U.S. Dept. State; chmn. adv. council dept. civil engring. Princeton U., 1973-84. Served as pvt. C.E. AUS, 1953. Recipient Distinguished Achievement award Rose Poly. Inst., 1975. Fellow ASCE (chmn. offshore policy com. 1979-84); mem. Del. Acad. Sci. (pres. 1971-72), Soc. Naval Architects and Marine Engrs., Marine Tech. Soc., Am. Geophys. Union, Assn. Sea Grant Program Instns. (pres. 1973-74). Club: Cosmos (Washington). Home: 240 Beverly Rd Newark DE 19711 Office: Drexel Univ 32d and Chestnut St Philadelphia PA 19104

GAJDUSEK, DANIEL CARLETON, pediatrician, research virologist; b. Yonkers, N.Y., Sept. 9, 1923; s. Karl A. and Ottilia D. (Dobroczki) G.; children: Ivan Mbagintao, Josede Figirliyong, Jesus Raglmar, Jesus Mororui, Mathias Maradol, Jesus Tamel, Jesus Salalu, John Paul Runman, Yavine Borima, Arthur Yolwa, Joe Yongorimah Kintoki, Thomas Youmog, Toni Wanevi, Toname Ikabala, Magame Prima, Senavayo Anua, Igitava Yoviga, Luwi Ikavara, Iram'bin'ai Undae'mai, Susanna Undapmaina, Steven Malrui. B.S., U. Rochester, 1943; M.D., Harvard U., 1946; NRC fellow, Calif. Inst. Tech., 1948-49; D.Sc. (hon.), U. Rochester, 1977, Med. Coll. Ohio, 1977, Washington & Jefferson Coll., 1980, Harvard U., 1982, Hahnemann U., 1983; D.H.L., Hamilton Coll., 1977, U. Aix-Marseille, France, 1977; LL.D. (hon.), U. Aberdeen, Scotland, 1980. Diplomate: Am. Bd. Pediatrics. Intern, resident Babies Hosp., Columbia Presbyn. Med. Center, N.Y.C., 1946-47; resident pediatrics Children's Hosp., Cin., 1947-48; pediatric med. mission, Germany, 1948; resident, clin. and research fellow Childrens Hosp., Boston, 1949-51; research fellow pediatrics and infectious diseases Harvard U., 1949-52; with Walter Reed Army Inst. Research, Washington, 1952-53, Institut Pasteur, Teheran, Iran and dept. medicine U. Md., 1954-55; vis. investigator Nat. Found. Infantile Paralysis, Walter and Eliza Hall Inst. Med. Research, Melbourne, Australia, 1955-57; dir. program for study child growth and devel. and disease patterns in primitive cultures and lab. slow, latent and temperate virus infections Nat. Inst. Neurol. and Communicative Disorders and Stroke, NIH, Bethesda, Md., 1958—; chief Central Nervous System Studies Lab., 1970—; chief scientist research vessel Alpha Helix expdn. to, Banks and Torres Islands, New Hebrides, South Solomon Islands, 1972. Author: Hemorrhagic Fevers and Mycotoxicoses in the USSR, 1951, Journals, 35 vols., 1954-82, Hemorrhagic Fevers and Mycotoxicoses, 1959, Slow Latent and Temperate Virus Infections, 1965, Correspondence on the Discovery of Kuru, 1976, (with Judith Farquhar) Kuru, 1980. Recipient E. Meade Johnson award Am. Acad. Pediatrics, 1963, Superior Service award NIH, HEW, 1970, Disting. Service award HEW, 1975, Prof. Lucian Dautrebande prize in pathophysiology, Belgium, 1976, Nobel prize in physiology and medicine, 1976; Gudakunst lectr. U. Mich., 1973; Dyer lectr. NIH, 1974; Heath Clark lectr. U. London, 1974; B.K. Rachford lectr. Children's Hosp. Research Found., Cin., 1975; Langmuir lectr. Center for Disease Control, Atlanta, 1975; Withering lectr. U. Birmingham, Eng., 1976; Cannon Elie lectr. Boston Children's Med. Center, 1976; Zale lectr. U. Tex., Dallas, 1976; Bayne-Jones lectr. Johns Hopkins Med. Sch., Balt., 1976; Harvey lectr. N.Y. Acad. Medicine, 1977; J.E. Smadel lectr. Infectious Disease Soc. Am., 1977; Burnet lectr. Australasian Soc. Infectious Disease, 1978; Mapother lectr. U. London, 1978; Disting. lectr. in medicine Mayo Clinic, 1978; Kaiser Meml. lectr. U. Hawaii, 1979; Eli Lilly lectr. U. Toronto, 1979; Payne lectr. Children's Hosp. D.C., 1981; Ray C. Moon lectr. Angelo State U., Tex., 1981; Silliman lectr. Yale U. Sch. Medicine, 1981; Blackfan lectr. Children's Hosp. Med. Ctr., Boston, 1981; Hitchcock Meml. lectr. U. Calif.-Berkeley, 1982; Nelson lectr. U. Calif.-Davis, 1982; Derick-MacKerres lectr. Queensland Inst. Med. Research, 1982; Bicentennial lectr. Harvard U. Sch. Medicine, 1982; Cartwright lectr. Columbia U., 1982; lectr. Chinese Acad. Med. Sci., 1983. Mem. Nat. Acad. Scis., Am. Acad. Arts and Scis., Am. Philos. Soc., Soc. Pediatric Research, Am. Pediatric Soc., Am. Soc. Human Genetics, Am. Acad. Neurology (Cotzias prize 1979), Soc. Neurosci., Am. Epidemiol. Soc., Infectious Diseases Soc. Am., Société des Oceanistes, Paris, Papua and New Guinea Sci. Soc., Micronesian Acad. Sci., Slovak Acad. Scis., Academia Nacional de Medicina de Mexico, Phi Beta Kappa, Sigma Xi. Home: Prospect Hill 6552 Jefferson Pike Frederick MD 21701 Office: NIH Bethesda MD 20205

GAL, LASZLO, illustrator; b. Budapest, Hungary, Feb. 18, 1933; emigrated to U.S., 1956, naturalized, 1961; s. Istvan and Anna (Gemes) G.; m. Armida Romano Gargarella, Jan. 20, 1962; children: Anna Maria, Raffaella. Student, Acad. Dramatic Arts, 1951, Superior Sch. Pedgogy, 1952. Graphic designer CBC, 1958-65, Toronto, Ont., 1977—; illustrator Arnoldo Mondadori Editore, Verona, Italy, 1965-69; freelance illustrator, Toronto, 1969-77. Illustrator: books including El Cid, 1965, Chançon de Roland, 1966, Illiad, 1968, Odyssey, 1968, Aeneid, 1969, Fables of Andersen, 1969, Twelve Dancing Princesses, 1979, The Little Mermaid, 1983. Served with Hungarian Army, 1952-54. Recipient awards Imperial Order Daus. of Empire, 1979, Can. Library Assn., 1980, Can. Council, 1980. Roman Catholic. Office: 101 Mutual St Toronto ON Canada

GALAND, RENÉ (REUN AR C'HALAN), foreign language educator; b. Chateauneuf-du-Faou, France, Jan. 27, 1923; came to U.S., 1947, naturalized, 1953; s. Pierre and Anna (Nédélec) G.; m. Françoise Texier, Dec. 23, 1959; children: Joel, Caroline. Licence ès Lettres, U. Rennes, France, 1944; grad., Ecole Spéciale Militaire de Saint-Cyr, 1945; Ph.D., Yale, 1952. Instr. French Yale, 1949-51; mem. faculty Wellesley Coll., 1951, prof. French, 1963, chmn. dept. French, 1968-72. Author: Saint-John Perse; Levr ar Blanedenn; author: Baudelaire: Poétiques et Poésie; contbr. articles, short stories, poems and revs. to publs. Served with French Army, 1944-46. Decorated chevalier Ordre des Palmes Académiques; recipient Xavier de Langlais prize in Breton lit., 1979. Home: 8 Leighton Rd Wellesley MA 02181

GALANE, MORTON ROBERT, lawyer; b. N.Y.C., Mar. 15, 1926; s. Harry J. and Sylvia (Schenkelbach) G.; m. Rosalind Feldman, Dec. 22, 1957; children: Suzanne Galane Duvall, Jonathan A. B.E.E., CCNY, 1946; LL.B., George Washington U., 1950. Bar: D.C. 1950, Nev. 1955, Calif. 1975. Patent examiner U.S. Patent Office, Washington, 1948-50; spl. partner firm Roberts & McInnis, Washington, 1950-54; practice as Morton R. Galane, P.C., Las Vegas, Nev., 1955—; spl. counsel to Gov. Nev., 1967-70. Contbr. articles to profl. jours. Chmn. Gov.'s Com. on Future of Nev., 1979-80. Fellow Am. Coll. Trial Lawyers; mem. Am. Law Inst., IEEE, Am. Bar Assn. (council litigation sect. 1977-83), State Bar Nev., State Bar Calif., D.C. Bar. Home: 2019 Bannies Ln Las Vegas NV 89102 Office: 1st Interstate Bank Bldg Suite 1100 Las Vegas NV 89101

GALANIS, JOHN WILLIAM, insurance executive; b. Milw., May 9, 1937; s. William and Angeline (Koroniou) G.; m. Patricia Caro, Nov. 29, 1969; children: Lia, William, Charles, John. B.B.A. cum laude, U. Wis., 1959; J.D., U. Mich., 1963; postgrad. (Ford Found. grantee), London Sch. Econs., 1964. Bar: Wis. 1965; C.P.A., Wis. Assoc. firm Whyte & Hirschboeck S.C., Milw., 1964-68; sr. v.p., gen. counsel, sec. MGIC Investment Corp. and Mortgage Guaranty Ins. Corp., Milw., 1968—; dir. Citizens North Shore Bank. Asso. editor: Mich. Law Rev, 1962-63. Trustee Milw. Found., Milw. Boy's Club; pres. bd. trustees Internat. Inst., Milw.; trustee S.E. Wis. chpt. Nat. Multiple Sclerosis Soc., 1975—, chmn. bd., 1976-77; bd. dirs. Milw. Council on Alcoholism. Served with Mil. Police U.S. Army, 1959-60. Mem. Am. Bar Assn., Wis. Bar Assn., Milw. Bar Assn., Internat. Assn. Ins. Counsel, Am. Coll. Mortgage Attys., Order of Coif. Greek Orthodox. Clubs: Milw. Athletic, Western Racquet. Home: 1200 Woodlawn Circle Elm Grove WI 53122 Office: MGIC Plaza Milwaukee WI 53201

GALANOS, JAMES, designer; b. Phila., Sept. 20, 1924; s. Gregory D. and Helen (Gorgoliatos) G. With Hattie Carnegie, 1944; asst. to designer Columbia Pictures Corp., Hollywood, Calif., 1946-47; trainee Robert Piguet, Paris, France, 1947-48; founder, designer Galanos Originals, Beverly Hills, 1951—. Recipient award for distinguished service in field of fashion Neiman-Marcus, 1954; Am. Fashion Critics award Met. Mus. Art, Costume Inst., 1954; Return award, 1956; Hall of Fame, 1959; Creativity award Internat. Achievements Fair, 1956; Filene's Young Talent design award, Boston, 1958; Cotton Fashion award, 1958. Office: 2254 S Sepulveda Blvd Los Angeles CA 90064

GALANT, HERBERT LEWIS, lawyer; b. N.Y.C., Oct. 16, 1928; s. Charles A. and Bertha (Rosenberg) G.; m. Fern Judith Laikin, Feb. 10, 1957; children: Peter B., John M., Amy E. B.A. cum laude, U. Wis., 1949, LL.B., Harvard U., 1952; LL.M., NYU, 1960. Bar: N.Y. 1955, U.S. Dist. Ct. (so. dist.) N.Y. 1956, U.S. Ct. Appeals (2d cir.) 1959. Assoc. Fried, Frank et al, N.Y.C., 1955-61, ptnr., 1962—. Editor: Harvard Law Rev., 1950-52. Mem. Tenafly Twp. Bd. Ethics, (N.J.), 1978—. Served to lst lt. USAF, 1952-54. MEM. ABA; mem. Assn. Bar City N.Y. Democrat. Jewish. Club: Harvard (N.Y.C.). Home: 150 Tekening Dr Tenafly NJ 07670 Office: Fried Frank et al One New York Plaza New York NY 10004 *The practice of law has given me the opportunity to deal with some of the more stimulating issues of our economy in an environment of excellence and integrity. Although frequently made great contributions to order, progress and equality in our society!*

GALANTER, EUGENE, educator, psychologist; b. Phila., Oct. 27, 1924; s. Max and Sarah (Honigman) G.; m. Patricia Anderson, Dec. 22, 1962; children: Alicia, Gabrielle, Michelle. A.B., Swarthmore Coll., 1950; A.M., U. Pa., 1951, Ph.D., 1953. From instr. to prof. psychology U. Pa., 1952-62; research fellow Harvard U., 1955-56, Center Advanced Study Behavioral Scis., 1958-59; chmn. dept. psychology U. Wash., 1962-64, prof., 1964-66; Joseph Klingenstein vis. prof. social psychology Columbia U., N.Y.C., 1966-67, prof. psychology, 1967—; Cons. NIH, NSF, also to industry; mem. Council for Biology in Human Affairs; chmn. commn. on biology, learning and behavior Salk Inst. Author: Plans and Structure of Behavior, 1960, New Directions in Psychology, 1962, Textbook of Elementary Psychology, 1966, Kids & Computers: The Parents' Microcomputer Handbook, 1983, Kids & Computers: Elementary Programming for Kids in BASIC, 1983; Editor: Handbook of Mathematical Psychology, 3 vols., 1963-64, Readings in Mathematical Psychology, 2 vols., 1963-65. Served with AUS, 1942-46. Fellow AAAS; mem. Eastern Psychol. Assn., Acoustical Soc. Am., N.Y. Acad. Scis., Assn. Aviation Psychologists (pres. 1970-71), Am. Psychol. Assn., Human Factors, Sigma Xi. Office: 324 Schermerhorn Hall Columbia U New York NY 10027

GALATI, FRANK JOSEPH, actor, stage and opera director, educator; b. Highland Park, Ill., Nov. 29, 1943; s. Frank Joseph and Virginia Frances (Cassel) G. B.S., Northwestern U., 1965, M.A., 1966, Ph.D., 1971. Asst. prof. speech U. South Fla., Tampa, 1965-67; instr. interpretation Northwestern U., Evanston, Ill., 1970-71, asso. prof., 1973—; instr. theater Roosevelt U., Chgo., 1971-72; instr. acting Goodman Sch. Drama, Chgo., 1971-72; profl. acting, dir., Chgo., 1965—; dir. Chgo. Opera Theater, 1976—. Author: (play) Winnebago, 1974; (screenplays) The Living End, 1979, There's No Tomorrow, 1980; co-author: (textbook) Oral Interpretation, 1977. Recipient Tchr. of Year award U. South Fla., 1967, Joseph Jefferson Best New Play award, Chgo., 1973, Jefferson award for best actor, 1980. Mem. Actors Equity Assn., Speech Communication Assn. Home: 933 Maple St Evanston IL 60202 Office: Northwestern U Theatre Interpretation Center Evanston IL 60201

GALAZKA, JACEK M., publishing company executive; b. Wilno, Poland, Apr. 28, 1924; s. Michal J. and Zofia G.; m. Jacoba J.M. Jansen, July 22, 1958. B.Com., U. Edinburgh, 1947. Dir. sales and promotion St. Martin's Press, N.Y.C., 1955-63; mgr. reference dept. Charles Scribner's Sons, N.Y.C., 1963-67, dir. mktg., 1967-74, dir. trade pub., 1974—, exec. v.p., 1978-83, pres., 1983—. Translator 2 books. Served with Polish Forces, 1942-45. Home: Warren Hill Rd Cornwall Bridge CT 06754 Office: 597 Fifth Ave New York NY 10017

GALBRAITH, EVAN GRIFFITH, ambassador; b. Toledo, July 2, 1928; s. Evan Griffith and Nina (Allen) G.; m. Nancy Burdick, July 23, 1955 (div. 1962); 1 dau., Alexandra; m. Marie Helene Rockwell, Dec. 4, 1964; children: Evan, Christina, John. B.A., Yale U., 1950; LL.B, Harvard U., 1953. Bar: D.C. 1953, N.Y. 1957. Assoc. firm Shearman & Sterling, N.Y.C., 1957-60; spl. asst. to sec. Dept. Commerce, Washington, 1960-61; v.p. internat. and fin. Morgan Guaranty Trust Co., N.Y.C., 1961-63; dir. Morgan & Co., Paris, 1963-68; v.p. Morgan Guaranty Trust, N.Y.C., 1968-69; chmn. Bankers Trust Internat., London, 1969-75; mng. dir. Dillon, Read & Co., London and N.Y.C., 1975-81; U.S. ambassador to France, Paris, 1981—; dir. Nat. Rev., N.Y.C., 1957-81. Co-author: The German Stock Corp., 1966; contbr. articles to fin. jours. Gen. counsel Young Republicans, N.Y., 1958-60; chmn. Citizens for Goldwater (Europe), France, 1964. Served with USNR, 1953-57. Mem. Council on Fgn. Relations. Republican. Clubs: Capitol Hill (Washington); Field (Greenwich, Conn.); The Brook (N.Y.); Yale of N.Y.C.; Travellers (Paris). Home: 41 Rue Faubourg St Honore Paris France Office: Am Embassy 2 Ave Gabriel Paris France

GALBRAITH, JAMES GARBER, physician, educator; b. Anniston, Ala., May 28, 1914; s. Samuel L. and Sarah (Garber) G.; m. Marguerite Stabler, June 6, 1942; children: Ann, Jane, Mary Kay, Laura. Student, U. Notre Dame, 1930-32; B.S., St. Louis U., 1936, M.D., 1938; L.H.D., St. Bernard Coll., 1976. Diplomate: Am. Bd Neurol. Surgery (chmn. 1972-74). Intern Loyd Noland Hosp., Fairfield, Ala., 1938-39, resident gen. surgery, 1939-40; resident neurol. surgery Neurol. Inst., Columbia Presbyn. Med. Center, N.Y.C., 1940-43, instr. neurology, 1942-43; practice medicine, specializing in neurol. surgery, Birmingham, Ala., 1946—; assoc. prof. surgery Med. Coll. Ala., 1946-54, prof. surgery, 1954—, prof., chmn. div. neurosurgery, 1965-79; Mem. Ala. Bd. Mental Health, 1974-76; mem. Ala. State Bd. Health, 1970-76. Served to lt. M.C. USNR, 1943-46. Fellow A.C.S. (gov. for Ala. 1974-80); mem. AMA, So. Med. Assn. (pres. 1965), Med. Assn. State of Ala. (pres. 1974-75), Jefferson County Med. Soc. (pres. 1960), Soc. Neurol. Surgery (pres. 1974), So. Neurosurg. Soc. (pres. 1956), Am. Assn. Neurol. Surgeons, Assn. Research Mental and Nervous Diseases, Birmingham C. of C. (past dir.), Ala. Acad. Honor, Alpha Omega Alpha., Alpha Sigma Nu. Home: 2515 Crest Rd Birmingham AL 35223 Office: U of Ala Medical Center Birmingham AL 35294

GALBRAITH, JAMES MARSHALL, lawyer, business executive; b. Iowa City, Oct. 4, 1942; s. John Semple and Laura (Huddleston) G.; m. Margaret Rodi, Aug. 19, 1966; children: Margaret Laura, Katherine Lou, Robert James. A.B., Pomona Coll., 1964; J.D., Stanford U., 1967. Bar: Calif. bar 1967. Asso. Gibson, Dunn & Crutcher, Los Angeles, 1967-68; partner Rodi, Pollock, Pettker, Galbraith & Phillips, Los Angeles, 1968—; pres. Bell Helmets Internat., Inc., San Marino, Calif., 1980—; pres., dir. Palm Properties, Inc., 1979—; mem. White House Advance Staff, 1975-76. Author: The Datax Conspiracy, 1977, The Money Tree, 1982; Mem.: Stanford Law Rev. Bd. dirs. San Marino Men's Republican Club, 1971-80, pres., 1973-74; trustee Polytech. Sch., Pasadena, Calif., 1977-81. Mem. State Bar Calif., ABA, Los Angeles County Bar Assn., Phi Beta Kappa, Sigma Tau (alumni pres. 1971). Episcopalian. Clubs: San Marino (Calif.) City; California, Valley Hunt, Pomona College Men's (Los Angeles) (v.p., dir. 1970-71). Home: 1640 Oak Grove Ave San Marino CA 91108 Office: 611 W 6th St Los Angeles CA 90017

GALBRAITH, JOHN KENNETH, economist; b. Iona Station, Ont., Can., Oct. 15, 1908; s. William Archibald and Catherine (Kendall) G.; m. Catherine Atwater, Sept. 17, 1937; children: Alan, Peter, James. B.S., U. Toronto, 1931; M.S., U. Calif., 1933, Ph.D., 1934; postgrad., Cambridge (Eng.) U., 1937-38; LL.D., Bard Coll., U. Calif., Miami U., U. Mass., U. Mysore, Brandeis U., U. Toronto, U. Guelph, U. Sask., U. Mich., U. Durham, R.I. Coll., Boston Coll., Hobart and William Smith Colls., Albion Coll., Tufts U., Adelphi Suffolk Coll., Mich. State U., Louvain U., Cambridge U., U. Paris, Carleton Coll., U. Vt., Queens U., others. Research fellow U. Calif., 1931-34; instr. and tutor Harvard, 1934-39; asst. prof. econs. Princeton, 1939-42; econ. adviser Nat. Def. Adv. Commn., 1940-41; asst. adminstr. in charge price div. OPA, 1941-42, dep. adminstr., 1942-43; mem. bd. of editors Fortune Mag., 1943-48; lectr. Harvard, 1948-49, prof. econs., 1949-75, Paul M. Warburg prof. econs., 1959-75, ret., 1975; fellow Trinity Coll., Cambridge U.; hon. prof. U. Geneva; A.E. and P., India, 1961-63. Author: numerous books including American Capitalism, 1952, A Theory of Price Control, 1952, The Great Crash, 1955, The Affluent Society, 1958, The Liberal Hour, 1960, Economic Development, 1963, The Scotch, 1964, The New Industrial State, 1967, Indian Painting, 1968, The Triumph, 1968, Ambassador's Journal, 1969, Economics, Peace and Laughter, 1971, A China Passage, 1973, The Age of Uncertainty, 1977, Economics and the Public Purpose, 1973, Money: Whence It Came, Where It Went, 1975, (with Nicole Salinger) Almost Everyone's Guide to Economics, 1978, Annals of an Abiding Liberal, 1979, The Nature of Mass Poverty, 1979, A Life in Our Times, 1981, The Anatomy of Power, 1983; contbr. to econ. and sci. jours. Dir. U.S. Strategic Bombing Survey, 1945; dir. Office of Econ. Security Policy, State Dept., 1946. Fellow Social Sci. Research Council, 1937-38; Recipient Medal Freedom, 1946. Fellow Am. Acad. Arts and Scis.; mem. Nat. Inst. of Arts and Letters, Am. Econ. Assn. (pres. 1972), Am. Agrl. Econ. Assn., Ams. for Democratic Action (chmn. 1967-68). Clubs: Century (N.Y.); Federal City (Washington); Saturday (Boston). Home: 30 Francis Ave Cambridge MA 02138 Office: 207 Littauer Center Harvard U Cambridge MA 02138 *

GALBRAITH, JOHN SEMPLE, history educator; b. Glasgow, Scotland, Nov. 10, 1916; came to U.S., 1925, naturalized, 1931; s. James M. and Mary (Marshall) G.; m. Laura Huddleston, Aug. 22, 1940; children: James M., John H., Mary P. B.A., Miami U., Oxford, Ohio, 1938; M.A., U. Iowa, 1939, Ph.D., 1943; LL.D., Mt. Union Coll., 1968. Asst. prof. Ohio U., 1947-48; prof. Brit. Empire history UCLA, 1948-64, chmn. dept., 1954-58, prof. history, 1969-84; chancellor U. Calif.-San Diego, 1964-68, prof. history, 1984—; Smuts vis. fellow Cambridge (Eng.) U., 1968-69. Author: The Establishment of Canadian Diplomatic Status in Washington, 1951, The Hudson's Bay Company as an Imperial Factor, 1957, Reluctant Empire, 1963, MacKinnon and East Africa, 1972, Crown and Charter, 1974, The Little Emperor, 1976. Served as officer AUS, 1943-46. Mem. Royal Hist. Soc., Am. Hist Assn. (pres. Pacific Coast br. 1965), Canadian Hist. Assn., Soc. Am. Historians, African Studies Assn., AAUP, Phi Beta Kappa. Home: 221 Loma Corta Dr Solana Beach CA 92075

GALBRAITH, JOHN WILLIAM, securities executive; b. Kansas City, Mo., Aug. 8, 1921; s. Harvey C. and Honora E. (Coughlin) G.; m. Rosemary P. Loveless, Sept. 11, 1948; children: Rachel Leah Galbraith Watson, Rebecca Louise. B.S.B.A., U. Mo., Columbia, 1941. C.P.A., Kans. V.p. United Internat. Fund Inc., Hamilton, Bermuda, 1961-63, United Funds Mgmt., Toronto, Ont., Can., 1963-69, Waddell & Reed Inc., Kansas City, Mo., 1969-70; pres. Lexington Mgmt. Corp., Englewood, N.J., 1970-74, Securities Fund Mgmt., Saint Petersburg, Fla., 1974—. Bd. govs. Contractual Plan Sponsors, N.Y.C., 1971-74; chmn. adminstrn. com. Can. Mut. Fund Assn., Toronto, 1964-67; councilman Borough of Saddle River, N.J., 1977; trustee Eckerd Coll., St. Petersburg, 1983. Mem. Am. Inst. C.P.A.s, Nat. Assn. Securities Dealers (investment cos. com. 1980-84). Republican. Roman Catholic. Clubs: St. Petersburg Yacht; Yale (N.Y.C.). Office: Securities Fund Mgmt Inc 405 Central Ave Saint Petersburg FL 33701

GALBRAITH, MATTHEW WHITE, life insurance executive; b. N.Y.C., Nov. 23, 1927; s. Matthew White and Rose Marie (Howes) G.; m. Susan E. Herbig, Sept. 21, 1957; children: Susan, Peter W., Steven M. B.S. in Econs., Bucknell U., Lewisburg, Pa., 1950; postgrad., NYU, U. Pitts., Columbia U. With Met. Life Ins. Co., 1950—, v.p. charge group pensions, then chief mktg. officer group ins., N.Y.C., 1971-76, sr. v.p., office charge New Eng. head office, Warwick, R.I., 1976—; dir. Bus. Devel. Co., Trinity Personna Co.; bd. dirs. R.I. Group Health Assn.; adv. bd. Old Stone Bank, R.I. Mem. Gov. R.I. Com. Long Range Planning; bd. dirs. R.I. Fedn., Close-Up Found. R.I., United Way Southeastern New Eng., United Negro Colls., NCCJ, R.I. Philharm.; trustee YMCA. Served with C.E., AUS, 1945-47. Mem. Am. Pension Conf., Western Pension Conf., Can. Pension Conf., Greater R.I. C. of C. (dir.). Clubs: Hope, R.I. Country. Home: 52 Nayatt Rd Barrington RI 02806 Office: 700 Quaker Ln Warwick RI 02887

GALBRAITH, RUTH LEGG, university dean, home economist; b. Lecompte, La., Nov. 5, 1923; d. Byron S. and Dora Ruth (Lindley) Legg; m. Harry W. Galbraith, June 16, 1950; 1 son, Allan Legg. B.S., Purdue U., 1945, Ph.D., 1950. Chemist E.I. duPont de Nemours, Waynesboro, Va., 1945-46; textile chemist Gen. Electric Co., Bridgeport, Conn., 1946-47; teaching asst. Purdue U., 1947-48, research fellow, 1948-50; prof. textiles and clothing U. Tenn., Knoxville, 1950-55; asso. prof. U. Ill., Urbana, 1956-64, prof., 1964-70, chmn. textiles and clothing div., 1962-70; prof., head consumer affairs dept. Auburn (Ala.) U., 1970-73; dean Sch. Home Econs., head home econs. research, 1973—; mem. task force on quality of living Dept. Agr., 1967-78; mem. nat. adv. com. Flammable Fabrics Act, 1971-73; mem. U.S. Dept. Agr. Com. of Nine, 1981-83, chmn., 1983. Mem. editorial bd.: Research Jour. Home Econs., 1973-77; chmn. policy bd., 1978-80; contbr. articles to profl. jours. Recipient Disting. Alumni award Purdue U., 1970. Fellow Am. Inst. Chemists; mem. Am. Home Econs. Assn. (chmn. agy. mem. unit 1975-76, chmn. research sect. 1978-80), Ala. Home Econs. Assn. (pres. 1983-84), Am. Assn. Textile Chemists and Colorists, Am. Chem. Soc., ASTM (3d v.p. com. D-13 textiles 1975-79), Assn. Adminstrs. Home Econs., Nat. Council Adminstrs. Home Econs., AAUW, Sigma Xi, Omicron Nu, Phi Kappa Phi, Delta Kappa Gamma. Home: 368 Singleton St Auburn AL 36830 Office: Sch Home Econs Auburn U Auburn University AL 36849

GALBREATH, DANIEL MAUCK, real estate executive, professional baseball team executive; b. Columbus, Ohio, June 15, 1928; s. John Wilmer and Helen (Mauck) G.; m. Elizabeth Lind, July 17, 1954; children: Laurie Lind, Lizanne, John Wilmer II. B.A., Amherst Coll., 1950; M.B.A., Ohio State U., 1952. Assoc. John W. Galbreath & Co., Columbus, 1950—; pres. Pitts. Pirates Baseball Club, 1970—; dir. Banc One Corp., Columbus, Bank One, Ohio Bell Telephone Co., Cleve. Chmn. emeritus Columbus Zoo Assn.; bd. dirs. Boys Club of Columbus, Columbus chpt. ARC, Grand Central Art Gallery, N.Y.C., Cleve. Zool. Soc.; trustee Ohio State U., Springfield (Mass.) Coll. Named Conservationist of Year Ohio League of Sportsmen, 1973, Sportsman of Year Pitts. Variety Club, 1973. Mem. Ohio C. of C. (dir.), Ohio Thoroughbred Breeders and Owners (dir.), Battelle Commons Co. Clubs: Masons (33 deg.), Columbus Rotary (past pres.), Jockey, Coaching. Home: 2772 Clarion Ct Columbus OH 43220 Office: 180 E Broad St Columbus OH 43215

GALE, GEORGE ALEXANDER, retired Canadian chief justice; b. Quebec, Can., June 24, 1906; s. Robert Henry and Elma Gertrude (Read) G.; m. Hilda Georgina Daly, Dec. 29, 1934; children—Robert, Peter, David. B.A., U. Toronto, 1929; grad., Osgoode Hall Law Sch., Toronto, 1932; LL.D. (hon.), McMaster U., 1968, York U., 1969, Windsor U., 1980. Bar: created King's counsel 1945. Read law with firm Donald, Mason, White and Foulds, Toronto, 1929; partner firm Mason, Foulds, Davidson and Gale, Toronto, 1944-46; justice Supreme Ct. Ont., 1946, Ct. of Appeal Ont., 1963-64; chief justice High Ct. Justice Ont., 1964-67, Ont., 1967-76; vice chmn. Ont. Law Reform Commn., 1977-81; hon. lectr. Osgoode Law Sch.; also faculty medicine U. Toronto; chmn. Com. Rules of Practice for Ont., 1941-76, Jud. Council Provincial Judges, 1968-76; mem. exec. com. Canadian Jud. Council, 1972-76. Co-editor: Practice and Procedure in Ontario. Former chmn. Rhodes Scholarship Selection Com.; Bd. govs. Wycliffe Coll., U. Toronto, Ecumenical Found. Can.; past mem. bd. govs. Upper Can. Coll., Toronto; mem. Ont. Adv. Com. on Confedn. Decorated companion Order of Can. Mem. Canadian Bar Assn. (council), Bar of Ga. (hon.), Ont. Curling Assn. (hon. pres.), Delta Kappa Epsilon (pres. local chpt. 1932, internat. sec. 1932), Can. Corps Commissionaires (hon.), Phi Delta Phi. Anglican. Clubs: Lawyers (pres. 1940, hon. pres. 1968), University (v.p. 1959), Toronto Curling (hon. pres.), York (hon. mem., Toronto); Chippewa County (Southampton, Ont.)). Home: 2 Brookfield Rd Willowdale ON M2P 1A9 Canada Office: Osgoode Hall Toronto 1 ON Canada

GALE, ROBERT L(EE), educational association executive; b. St. Cloud, Minn., Jan. 13, 1927; s. John Henry and Helen (Andrews) G.; m. Barbara Joan Carr, Oct. 19, 1951; children: Jennifer Merritt Dunkin, Robert L., Morgan Andrews. Student, Gustavus Adolphus Coll., 1944-45, U.S. Naval Acad., 1945-46; B.A., Carleton Coll., 1948. Mgmt. trainee J.F. Anderson Lumber Co., Mpls., 1948-49; mem. editorial staff This Week mag., N.Y.C., 1949-53; asst. mng. editor Argosy mag., N.Y.C., 1953-54; editor-in-chief Maco Mag. Corp., N.Y.C., 1954-57; v.p. for public relations and devel. Carleton Coll., 1957-63, trustee, 1970—; dir. recruiting Peace Corps, Washington, 1963-65; dir. public affairs EEO Commn., Washington, 1965-66; chmn. bd. Gale Assos., Inc., Washington, 1966-74; pres. Assn. Governing Bds. of Univs. and Colls., Washington, 1974—; mem. adv. bd. Nat. Exec. Service Corps, N.Y.C., 1978—; chmn. bd. Acad. Collective Bargaining Info. Service, Washington, 1979—; mem. adv. bd. Inst. for Mgmt. Lifelong Edn., Harvard U. Grad. Sch. Edn., 1979—; mem. project bd. Presdl. Search Consulatation Service, Washington, 1979—. Vestryman St. George's Episcopal Ch., N.Y.C., 1967-74; pres. Eberhard Sch. Found., Washington, 1972-76; mem. exec. com. Washington Urban League, 1975—, United Negro Coll. Fund, Washington, 1975—; pres. Dance in Bethany Found., Inc., Bethany Beach, Del.; bd. dirs. Shakinah Bible Garden, St. Cloud, Minn.; mem. corp. Constance Bultman Wilson Center, Faribault, Minn., 1977—; mem. nat. fine arts com. XIII Olympic Winter Games of 1980, Lake Placid, N.Y., 1979—. Served with USN, 1944-46. Mem. Am. Assn. Higher Edn., Am. Soc. Assn. Execs., Higher Edn. Secretariat. Democrat. Home: 1625 Q St NW Apt 201 Washington DC 20009 Office: One Dupont Circle NW Suite 400 Washington DC 20036

GALE, THOMAS MARTIN, univ. dean; b. Green Bay, Wis., May 16, 1926; s. Thomas Griswold and Carrie (Danz) G.; m. Mary Margaret Hardman, May 28, 1960; children—Thomas Hardman, John Martin. B.A., U. Calif. at Berkeley, 1949, M.A., 1950; Ph.D., U. Pa., 1958. Dean Coll. Arts and Scis. N.Mex. State U., 1971—; cons. in field. Chmn. N.Mex. Humanities Council Nat. Endowment for Humanities, 1972—. Served with AUS, 1944-46. Social Sci. Research fellow, 1952-53, 53-54; Huntington Library fellow, 1959; Fulbright fellow, Peru, 1960. Mem. Latin Am. Studies Assn., Conf. Latin Am. History, Phi Beta Kappa, Phi Alpha Theta. Club: Rotarian. Home: 3115 E Majestic Ridge Las Cruces NM 88001

GALE, WILLIAM HENRY, artist; b. Yonkers, N.Y., May 3, 1905; s. William Henry and Edith (Jackson) G.; m. Floriene Ellsworth, Apr. 14, 1932; children—Bruce Ellsworth, Donald William. Student, Nat. Acad. Sch., 1928-30, Columbia, 1930-32, Art Students League, 1931-34; pvt. study with, John Pike, Charles Kinghan. Art dir. Batten, Barton, Burstine & Orborn, N.Y.C., 1940-68; artist, 1935—. 22 one-man exhbns. including, Grand Central Gallery, N.Y.C., 1958, Jasper Rand Mus., Westfield, Mass., 1973, So. Vt. Art Center, Manchester, 1966, 68, 70, Am. Internat. Coll., 1974, Holyoke (Mass.) Mus., 1976, Rockport (Mass.) Art Assn., 1977, 81, group exhbns. include, Nat. Acad., Nat. Arts Club, Springfield (Mass.) Mus. Fine Art, Berkshire Mus., Pittsfield, Mass., Salmagundi Club, Hartwick (N.Y.) Coll., Carver (Ala.) Mus., Holyoke (Mass.) Mus., Smith Mus., Worcester Mus., Butler Mus.; rep. permanent collections, Springfield Fine Arts Mus., Jasper Rand Mus., Wistariahurst Mus., Holyoke, Valley Bank, AT&T, Milton Bradley Co., Mass. Mut. Ins. Co., others. Recipient over 70 awards including gold medal award Hudson Valley Art Assn., 1967, Quimby award Smithsonian Art Mus., 1966, Acad. Artists award, 1971-72, 78, 79, Salmagundi Club award, 1968. Mem. Am. Watercolor Soc., Acad. Artists, Am. Artists Profl. League, So. Vt., Hudson Valley, Rockport, Berkshire, Deerfield art assns. Clubs: Salmagundi (N.Y.C.); Copley Soc. (Boston). Home: 14 Hunting Ln Box 156 Wilbraham MA 01095 Studio: 311 Main St Wilbraham MA 01095

GALEA, JOHN HENRY, lawyer; b. Albany, N.Y., Jan. 18, 1924; s. John Fortune and Virginia (Sterling) G.; m. Helen Flynn Conway, Aug. 14, 1948; children: Michelle Galea Jeter, Mark C., Mary Ellen, Monica, Madeleine. A.B. cum laude, Holy Cross Coll., 1947; LL.B., Harvard U., 1951. Bar: Ohio 1952, Ky. 1953, Va. 1959. Asso. firm Grossman Schlesinger & Carter, Cleve., 1951-53; with Reynolds Metals Co., Richmond, Va., 1953—, asst. gen. counsel, 1964-72, gen. atty., 1972-76, v.p. and gen. counsel, 1976—, also dir. subs.'s; mem. exec. com. Worsley Alumina Joint Venture; dir. Worsley Alumina Pty. Ltd., Australia, Manicouagan Power Co., Can. Served in USAAF, 1943-45; ETO. Decorated D.F.C., Air medal with three oak leaf clusters. Mem. Aluminum Assn. (legal audit com.), Am. Corp. Counsel Assn., Assn. Gen. Counsel, Am. Bar Assn., Va. Bar Assn., Ky. Bar Assn., Richmond Bar Assn., NAM (legal adv. com.). Republican. Roman Catholic. Clubs: Internat. (Washington); Harvard of Va. Office: 6601 W Broad St Richmond VA 23261

GALEENER, FRANK LEE, physicist; b. Long Beach, Calif., July 31, 1936; s. Floras Frank and Daisy Elizabeth (Lee) G.; m. Janet Louise Trask, June 7, 1959. S.B., MIT, 1958, S.M., 1962; Ph.D. in Physics, Purdue U., 1970. Physicist Lincoln Lab. MIT, Cambridge, 1959-61, physicist Nat. Magnet Lab., 1961-64; scientist Xerox, Palo Alto (Calif.) Research Ctr., 1970-73, mgr. semicondr., research, 1973-77, prin. scientist, 1977—; mem. com. on recommendations U.S. Army Basic Sci. Research, 1976-79; co-chmn. adv. panel on amorphous materials div. materials sci. Dept. Energy, 1980; mem. adv. panel solid state physics Office Naval Research, 1980. Editor: (with G. Lucovsky) Structure and Excitations of Amorphous Solids, 1976, (with Lucovsky and S.T. Pantelides) The Physics of MOS Insulators, 1980. Mem. Am. Phys. Soc., Am. Ceramic Soc., Optical Soc. Am., Sigma Xi, Sigma Pi Sigma. Home: 4035 Orme St Palo Alto CA 94306 Office: 3333 Coyote Hill Rd Palo Alto CA 94304

GALELLA, RONALD EDWARD, photojournalist; b. Bronx, N.Y., Jan. 10, 1931; s. Vincenzo and Michelina (Marinaccio) G.; m. Betty Burke, Apr. 21, 1979. B.A., Art Center Coll. Design, Pasadena, Calif., 1957. Freelance mag. and newspaper photographer, 1958—; contbr. photographs Life, Esquire, Cosmopolitan, People, Newsweek, other mags.; lectr. U. Miami, Fla. Author: Jacqueline, 1974, Offguard, 1976; one-man exhbns. include, Soho Gallery, N.Y.C., 1973, Nikon House Gallery, N.Y.C., 1974, Rizzoli Art Gallery, N.Y.C., 1976, William M. Lyons Gallery, Coconut Grove, Fla., 1980. Served with USAF, 1951-55. Recipient 1st prize Cigar Inst. Am., 1967. Mem. Nat. Soc. Lit. and Arts. Roman Catholic. Address: 17 Glover Ave Yonkers NY 10704
With imagination to conceive and the will to do, just about anything is possible in this world. The greatest tools are not the cameras or the hammers but the individual's mind, heart and eyes. If only each human being would use some of the inherit talent in each of us, we could build a world based on a firm foundation of peace.

GALENSON, WALTER, educator, economist; b. N.Y.C., Dec. 5, 1914; s. Louis Peter and Libby (Mishell) G.; m. Marjorie Spector, June 25, 1940; children: Emily, Alice, David. A.B., Columbia U., 1934, Ph.D., 1940. Prin. economist OSS, 1942-44, U.S. Fgn. Service, 1944-46; asst. prof. econs. Harvard, 1946-51; prof. econs. U. Calif., Berkeley, 1951-66, Cornell U., Ithaca, N.Y., 1966—; Pitt prof. Cambridge U., 1970-71. Author: Rival Unionism in the United States, 1940, Labor in Norway, 1944, The Danish System of Labor Relations, 1952, Labor Productivity in Soviet and American Industry, 1955, The CIO— Challenge to the AFL, 1960, The Quality of Labor, 1964, A Primer on Employment and Wages, 1966, The Chinese Economy Under Communism, 1968, The Labor Force and Labor Problems in Europe, 1975, Economic Growth and Structural Change in Taiwan, 1979, The International Labor Organization: An American View, 1981, The United Brotherhood of Carpenters: The First Hundred Years, 1983. Mem. Am. Econs. Assn., Assn. for Comparative Econ.

Studies (pres. 1973). Address: Sch Indsl Relations Cornell Univ Ithaca NY 14850

GALES, ROBERT SYDNEY, physicist; b. Boston, Dec. 12, 1914; s. Robert Joseph and Grace Risley (Moore) G.; m. Dorothea Frances Yocum, Aug. 29, 1942; children—Robert Timothy, Patricia Frances, Michael Jeffery. A.B., U. Calif. at Los Angeles, 1938, M.A., 1942. Asso. physicist U. Calif. Div. War Research, San Diego, 1942-45; physicist Navy Electronics Lab., San Diego, 1946-69; supervisory physicist Naval Undersea Center (now Naval Ocean Systems Center), San Diego, 1969-80, Computer Scis. Corp., 1981—; acoustical cons. Contbr. to books, also articles to profl. jours. Fellow Acoustical Soc. Am. (councilman 1967, pres. 1975); mem. Fed. Profl. Assn. (chmn. San Diego chpt. 1963, 65). Presbyterian (elder). Clubs: Alamitos Bay Yacht (commodore Long Beach, Calif. 1942), Mission Bay Yacht (commodore San Diego 1948), Coronado 25 Sailing Assn. (nat. pres. 1975). Patentee in field. Home: 1645 Los Altos Rd San Diego CA 92109

GALIARDO, JOHN WILLIAM, lawyer, diversified health care company executive; b. Elizabeth, N.J., Dec. 28, 1933; s. Joseph A. and Genevieve A. (Luxich) G.; m. Joan A. DeTurk, Aug. 26, 1961; children: Richard C., Christopher D., Elizabeth A. B.S., U. Md., 1956; LL.B., Columbia U., 1962. Bar: N.Y. 1962. Asso. firm Dewey, Ballantine, Bushby, Palmer & Wood, N.Y.C., 1962-71; asst. gen. counsel E.R. Squibb & Sons, Inc., Princeton, N.J., 1971-77; v.p., gen. counsel Becton Dickinson and Co., Paramus, N.J., 1977—. Treas. Charter Commn. Scotch Plains, N.J., 1970-71; mem. Joint Consol. Com. Princeton, 1973-76. Served with AUS, 1956-58. Mem. Am. Bar Assn., N.Y. State Bar Assn., Assn. Bar City N.Y. Home: 56 Crooked Tree Ln Princeton NJ 08540 Office: Becton Dickinson & Co Mack Centre Dr Paramus NJ 07652

GALIMIR, FELIX, violinist, music educator; b. Vienna, Austria, May 20, 1910; came to U.S., 1938, naturalized, 1943; s. Mosco and Elsa (Russo) G.; m. Suzanne Hirsch, Feb. 18, 1945. Diploma, Vienna Conservatory Music, 1928; student, Carl Flesch in Berlin and Baden-Baden, 1929-30. Mem. faculty Juillard Sch. Music, 1962—, Marlboro Music Sch. and Marlboro Music Festival, 1953—, Curtis Inst. Music, Phila., 1972—, Mannes Coll. Music, 1976—. Founder: Galimir String Quartet, Vienna, 1929; travelled, concertized, throughout Europe and Near East, 1929-36; reorganized: Galimir String Quartet in, N.Y.C., 1938—; with, NBC Symphony Orch., 1939-53; rec. artist for, Vanguard Columbia, Decca, Period Records. Address: 225 E 74th St New York NY 10021

GALIN, MILES A., physician; b. N.Y.C., Jan. 6, 1932; s. Albert and Freda (Simkowitz) G.; m. Glenda Goldenberg, June 27, 1953; children—Amy, Elizabeth, Scott, Jonathan. A.B. cum laude, N.Y. U., 1951, M.D., 1955. Diplomate: Nat. Bd. Med. Examiners, Am. Bd. Ophthalmology. Intern Mt. Sinai Hosp., 1955-56; resident surgery N.Y. Hosp., N.Y.C., 1956-58, resident surgeon, 1958-59, surgeon to out-patients, 1959-61, asst. attending surgeon, 1961-64, asso. attending surgeon, 1964-66; practice medicine, specializing in ophthalmology, N.Y.C., 1959—; cons. ophthalmology Meml. Hosp., 1960-66; attending ophthalmologist Flower and Fifth Ave., Met., Bird S. Coler, Cath. Med. Center of Bklyn. and Queens, Cabrini Med. Center,, N.Y., Westchester County Med. Center; asst. in surgery ophthalmology Cornell U. Med. Coll., N.Y.C., 1956-58, instr. surgery, 1958-61; clin. asst. prof., 1961-63, asst. prof., 1963-66; prof. N.Y. Med. Coll., 1966-80, chmn. dept. ophthalmology, 1966-73, dir. research, also dir. planning dept. ophthalmology, 1973—; adj. prof. polymer sci. U. Lowell (Mass.), 1982—; exchange scientist to USSR, U.S.-Soviet Health Exchange, 1969, 71, 74; cons. FAA, Mt. Vernon Hosp., Nat. Multiple Sclerosis Found.; tech. cons. Regional Med. Program; mem. med. adv. com. Quality Vision Care; tech. adv. com. ophthalmology Bur. for Handicapped Children; mem. spl. mediation panel Supreme Ct. Appellate Div. 1st Dept.; mem. adv. bd. govs. Internat. Glaucoma Congress; bd. dirs. Better Vision Inst.; Prin. investigator and co-investigator Nat. Soc. for Prevention Blindness, Cornell U., 1959-66, N.Y. Med. Coll., 1966-67, Nat. Council to Combat Blindness, Cornell U., 1955-66, N.Y. Med. Coll., 1966-67, USPHS, Cornell U. Med. Coll., 1959-66, N.Y. Med. Coll., 1966-73, NIAID, N.Y. Med. Coll., 1968—; career scientist Health Research Council, N.Y.C., 1963-66; Rayner Found. lectr. U.K. Intraocular Implant Soc., 1979. U.S. editor: Annali de Ottalmologia, 1967—; mem. editorial bd.: Metabolic Ophthalmology; Contbr. articles to profl. jours. Recipient Borden award N.Y. U., 1955; William Warner Hoppin award N.Y. Acad. Medicine, 1959; award of merit Am. Acad. Ophthalmology and Otolaryngology, 1967; Dr. Henry Balconi Meml. lectr., Rochester, N.Y., 1967; Culler Meml. lectr., Columbus, Ohio, 1967; Edward A. Weisser Meml. lectr., Pitts., 1976; Binkhoust award Am. Intra-Ocular Implant Soc., 1978. Fellow Internat. Coll. Surgeons; mem. Am. Acad. Ophthalmology and Otolaryngology, AAAS, Am. Inst. Ultrasound in Medicine, Am. Soc. Microbiology, N.Y. Acad. Medicine, N.Y. Acad. Scis., N.Y. Soc. for Clin. Ophthalmology, Royal Soc. Health, Royal Soc. Medicine, Surg. Soc. N.Y. Med. Coll., AMA, Assn. Career Scientists N.Y.C., Assn. U. Profs. Ophthalmology, Assn. for Research in Vision and Ophthalomology, Am. Intra-Ocular Implant Soc. (chmn. intra-ocular lens fellowship com., chmn. sci. adv. bd., v.p., pres.), Internat. Glaucoma Congress (charter), Internat. Soc. Metabolic Diseases, Metabolic Ophthalmology Soc., Internat. Strabismological Assn., French, Israel ophthalmol. socs., Instituto Barraquer, N.Y. State Soc. Med. Research, Ophthalmol. Soc. U.K., Oxford Congress, Pan-Am. Assn. Ophthalmology (hon.), Argentine, Peruvian assns. ophthalmology, Colo. Ophthalmol. Soc., Ga. Soc. Ophthalmology and Otolaryngology, Oklahoma City Clin. Soc., Pacific Coast Oto-Ophthalmology Soc., Pa. Acad. Opthalmology and Otalaryngy, Plastics and Rubber Inst., Phi Beta Kappa, Alpha Omega Alpha. Home: 180 East End Ave New York NY 10028 Office: 115 E 39 St New York NY 10016

GALINSKI, THOMAS PAUL, hospital administrator; b. Sayerville, N.J., Feb. 7, 1939; s. Edward John and Mary (Gorka) G.; m. Lesley Werner, Sept. 12, 1970; children: Todd Werner, Gregg Werner. B.A., Johns Hopkins U., 1961; M.S., U. Pitts., 1968. Fin. requirements coordinator Am. Hosp. Assn., Chgo., 1969-71, dir. div. planning, 1971-72; corp. dir. planning Samaritan Health Service, Phoenix, 1972-74; assoc. adminstr. Good Samaritan Hosp., Phoenix, 1975-76, sr. adminstr., chief operating officer, 1976-80; adminstr. City of Hope Nat. Med. Ctr., Duarte, Calif., 1980—. Bd. dirs. Maricopa County Community Health Network, 1974, Paradise Valley Bd. Adjustments, 1975-80. Served to lt. USN, 1962-65. Advanced fellow Am. Hosp. Assn.-Blue Cross Assn., 1968-69. Mem. Am. Coll. Hosp. Adminstrs., Am. Hosp. Assn., Ariz. Hosp. Assn., Hosp. Council So. Calif. Home: 1435 Oaklawn Rd Arcadia CA 91006 Office: City of Hope Nat Med Ctr 1500 E Duarte Rd Duarte CA 91010

GALINSKY, GOTTHARD KARL, classicist, educator; b. Strassburg, Alsace, Feb. 7, 1942; came to U.S., 1961, naturalized, 1971; s. Hans Karl (Edith);; s. Hans Karl and (Margenburg) G.; m. Susan Elizabeth Plume, Sept. 17, 1976; children by previous marriage—Robert Charles, John Anthony; children: Robert Charles, John Anthony. B.A., Bowdoin Coll., 1963; M.A., Princeton U., 1965, Ph.D., 1966. Instr. classics Princeton U., 1965-66; mem. faculty U. Tex., Austin, 1966—, prof. classics, 1972—, chmn. dept., 1974—, chmn. grad. assembly, 1977-79; dir. summer seminars Nat. Endowment Humanities, 1975, 76, dir. residential seminar, 1977-78, cons., 1976-78, 80—, summer grantee, 1967; Classicist-in-residence Am. Acad. Rome, 1972-73; adv. council Classical Sch., 1967—, chmn., 1982—, mem. Classical jury, 1970-71; lectr. U.S.-U.K. Edn. Commn., 1973; regional dir. Mellon human fellowship's, 1982—. Author: Aeneas, Sicily and Rome, 1969, Tibulli Carmina, 1971, The Herakles Theme, 1972, Perspectives of Roman Poetry, 1974, Ovid's Metamorphoses, 1975; editorial bd.: Classical World, 1973-76, Vergilius, 1973—. Bd. dirs. Tex. Fathers for Equal Rights, 1977-79. Fellow Am. Council Learned Socs., 1968-69; recipient Fulbright and Guggenheim Found. awards, 1972-73; Teaching Excellence award U. Tex., 1970, 76. Mem. Am. Philol. Assn. (Teaching Excellence award 1979, dir. 1980-83), Archaeol. Inst. Am., Classical Assn. Midwest and South (pres. 1980-81), Vergilian Soc. Am. (trustee 1972-76, v.p. 1976-77), Assn. Depts. Fgn. Langs. (exec. com. 1980-83, pres. 1983). Home: 2729 Trail of Madrones Austin TX 78746 Office: Waggener Hall 123 U Tex Austin TX 78712

GALKIN, ELLIOTT WASHINGTON, educator, musician; b. Bklyn., Feb. 22, 1921; s. Samuel and Ethel (Heifetz) G.; m. Jean R. Dubois, Jan 2, 1958. B.A., Bklyn. Coll., 1943; diplome de Direction d'Orchestre, Conservatoire Nat. de Paris, France, 1948; certificate Equivalentà la Licence de Concert, L'Ecole-Normale de Musique de Paris, 1948; M.A., Cornell U., 1955, Ph.D., 1960. Asso. condr. L'Orch. Philharmonique internat., 1949; instr. music Saranac Lake Rehab. Guild, 1949-52; apprentice condr. Vienna (Austria) Staatsoper, 1955-56; faculty Goucher Coll., 1956-77, chmn. dept. music, 1960-77, prof., 1964-77; faculty Peabody Conservatory, 1957—, condr. orch., 1957-64, chmn. music history and lit. dept., 1964—; dir. mus. activities, prof. Johns Hopkins U., 1968—; dir. Peabody Inst., 1977-82; guest condr. Balt. Symphony Orch., 1965—; dir. Rockefeller Found.-Balt. Symphony Orch. Am. Composers Project at Goucher Coll., 1965, 66, 67; condr. Balt. Chamber Orch., 1960—; music editor, critic Balt. Sun, 1962-77; vis. lectr. Tanglewood Music Festival, 1965, 66, chmn. music critics projects, 1968—; dir. Fromm Found. fellowship program in music criticism, 1969, 70, Music Critics Insts., Aspen, Kennedy Center, Cin., Ravinia, U. Md., Santa Fe, 1967—. Contbr. articles to profl. jours. Mem. Md. Adv. Council Arts, 1966-70; mem. music adv. planning panel Nat. Endowment for Arts, 1977-80, mem. profl. tng. panel, 1980—. Served with USAAF, 1943-46. Recipient Deems Taylor award ASCAP, 1972, 75, George Peabody medal for outstanding contbns. to music in Am., 1982. Mem. Internat., Am. musicol. socs., Coll. Music Soc., Am. Fedn. Musicians, Music Critics Assn., Am. Newspaper Guild, Phi Beta Kappa. Club: Cosmos. Home: 2211 Midridge Rd Timonium MD 21093 Office: Peabody Inst Johns Hopkins U Baltimore MD 21202

GALL, DONALD DUANE, telephone company executive; b. Baraboo, Wis., Feb. 4, 1924; s. Emil and Lila (Meyers) G.; m. Val I. Zimmerman, June 1, 1946; children: Scott, Kim, Becky. Student, U. Wis., 1942. With Gen. Telephone Co.; formerly comml. dir. Gen. Telephone Ind.; pres. Gen. Telephone of Midwest, Gen. Telephone Wis., Gen. Telephone Ill., Bloomington; dir. First Wis. Nat. Bank, Madison, First Fed. Savs. & Loan, Bloomington. Trustee Mennonite Hosp., Bloomington. Served with Armed Forces, 1943-46. Mem. Wis. Telephone Assn. (dir.), Ill. Telephone Assn. (dir.). Republican. Lutheran. Club: Rotary. Office: 1312 E Empire St Bloomington IL 61701

GALL, JOSEPH GRAFTON, biologist, researcher; b. Washington, Apr. 14, 1928; s. John Christian and Elsie (Rosenberger) G.; m. Dolores Marie Hogge, Sept. 17, 1955 (div. 1982); children: Lawrence, Barbara.; m. Diane Marie Dwyer, July 17, 1982. B.S., Yale, 1949, Ph.D., 1952. Faculty U. Minn., 1952-63, prof., 1963; prof. biology and molecular biophysics Yale, 1963-83; staff dept. embryology Carnegie Instn., Balt., 1983—; Mem. cell biology study sect. NIH, 1963-67, chmn., 1972-74. Contbr. articles profl. jours. Mem. AAAS, Am. Soc. Cell Biology (past pres.), Genetics Soc. Am., Am. Soc. Zoologists, Nat. Acad. Scis., Am. Acad. Arts and Scis. Home: 81 North Lake Dr Hamden CT 06517 Office: Dept Embryology Carnegie Instn 115 W University Pkwy Baltimore MD 21210

GALL, LAWRENCE HOWARD, lawyer; b. Leesville, S.C., Dec. 17, 1917; s. John J. and Bertha (Smyer) G.; m. Winifred Belle Nelson, Dec. 18, 1948; children: Sally Patricia, Linda, Constance. A.B., U. S.C., 1939, LL.B., 1941. Bar: S.C. bar 1941, D.C. bar 1948, U.S. Supreme Ct. bar 1952, Tex. bar 1966. Mem. legal dept. E.I. duPont de Nemours & Co., Inc.; asst. to gen. counsel Remington Arms Co., Bridgeport, Conn., 1941-43; assoc., then partner Disney & Gall, Washington, 1946-52; research dir., gen. counsel Ind. Natural Gas Assn. Am., Washington, 1952-61, exec. dir., 1961-65; v.p., gen. counsel Transcontinental Gas Pipe Line Corp., 1965-74; v.p., gen. atty. Transco Energy Co., 1974-80, v.p. govtl. affairs, 1980-83. Houston Met. dir. Nat. Alliance Businessmen, 1971; Bd. dirs. Tex. Mfrs. Assn., 1971-73, Tex. Research League, 1975-83. Served to lt. (s.g.) USNR, 1943-46. Mem. Am., Fed. Energy, Tex., Houston bar assns. Clubs: Petroleum (Houston); Congressional Country (Washington). Home: 643 Shartle Circle Houston TX 77024

GALLACCI, ROBERT JOHN, banker; b. Port Angeles, Wash., Apr. 5, 1928; s. James John and Gladys Marie (Long) G.; m. Amelia E. Catania, May 27, 1960; children—Deborah, Jeffrey, Larry, Richard, Lynn. Student, U. Wash., 1947-50; grad., U. Wis., 1966. Chartered bank auditor; certified internal auditor. With Pacific Nat. Bank, Seattle, 1950—, asst. auditor, 1959-64, auditor, 1964-70, v.p., sr. auditor, 1970—. Served with USMCR, 1945-47, 50-52. Mem. Bank Adminstrn. Inst. (pres. Puget Sound chpt. 1963-64). Home: 1648 180th St NE Bellevue WA 98008 Office: 900 2d Ave Seattle WA 98111

GALLAGHER, ANNE TIMLIN, banker; b. Wilkes-Barre, Pa., Mar. 21, 1943; d. James Joseph and Ruth Brandon (MacGuffie) G. A.B., Bucknell U., 1964. Presentation analyst A.C. Neilsen, N.Y.C., 1964-65; research asso. Gen. Electric Co., N.Y.C., 1965-67, sr. sales rep., computer time sharing, 1967-69; mgr. fin. services Rapidata Co., N.Y.C., 1969-70; mgr. fin. markets Computer Scis. Corp., N.Y.C., 1970-73; mgmt. cons. Arthur Young & Co., N.Y.C., 1973-77; mgr. mktg. communications, v.p. Bankers Trust Co., N.Y.C., 1978—; Chmn. bd. N.Y. Pro Arte Chamber Music Orch.; bd. dirs. Solaris Dance Theatre; cons. Arts and Bus. Council, Project Bus. Mem. Am. Statis. Assn. (asst. chmn. ann. forecast conf. N.Y. 1966, 67, past chmn. bus./econs. sect. N.Y. chpt.), Nat. Assn. Bus. Economists, Met. Econ. Assn., Assn. Timesharing Users (treas. 1975), N.Y. Jaycees. Home: 227 E 66th St New York NY 10021 Office: 280 Park Ave New York NY 10006

GALLAGHER, BERNARD PATRICK, editor, publisher; b. N.Y.C., Feb. 25, 1910; s. Bernard A. and Mary Helen (Fitzsimmons) G.; m. Harriet Denning, Oct. 17, 1942; 1 dau., Jill. Student, Columbia U., 1928-29, Akron U., 1941-44. Single-copy sales mgr. Crowell Pub. Co., 1932-34; sales mgr. charge sales tng. Stenotype Co., Inc., Chgo., 1934-39; pres. Stenotype Co. Ohio, Inc., Cleve., 1939-44, World Wide Publs., Inc., N.Y.C., 1945—, Gallagher Communications, Inc., 1972—; editor-in-chief pub. The Gallagher Report, 1952—, The Gallagher Presidents' Report, 1965—, Gallagher Med. Report, 1983—; pres. Gallagher Found., 1978—. Served with AUS, 1944-45. Mem. Cath. Press Assn. Clubs: Canadian, Met., Marco Polo.

GALLAGHER, CHARLES PATRICK, mfg. co. exec.; b. Toledo, Mar. 22, 1938; s. Francis J. and Dorothy D. (Shadle) G.; m. s. Diane Bertling, Sept. 8, 1962; children—Shaun P., Kelly Ann, Kevin C., Michael A. B.S. in Econs, Xavier U., 1960. With Owens-Corning Fiberglas Co., 1960-79, gen. mgr. residential insulation div., 1970-75, v.p., gen. mgr. fiberglas reinforced plastics div., 1975-79; pres., chief exec. officer, dir. Susquehanna Corp., Englewood, Colo., 1980—. Chmn. corp. fund raising Public Broadcasting Co., 1976-77; pres. bd. Gesu Sch., Toledo, 1976-78; v.p. North Shores Assn., Monroe, Mich., 1977-79. Served as officer AUS, 1960-61. Republican. Roman Catholic. Clubs: Toledo (past dir.), Cherry Hills Country.). Home: 4612 S Vine Way Englewood CO 80110 Office: 7400 S Alton Ct Englewood CO 80112

GALLAGHER, EDWARD STEPHEN, physician, state ofcl.; b. Oakland, Calif., Feb. 17, 1939; s. Bernard S. and Lillian (Doig) G.; m. Mary Jo Dowell, June 20, 1964; children—Matt, Barney, Megan, Marisa. B.S., U. Santa Clara, 1960; M.D., Marquette U., 1964; M.P.H., U. Calif., Berkeley, 1973. Diplomate: Am. Bd. Pediatrics, Assn. State Territorial Health Officers. Intern Children's Hosp. Med. Center, Oakland, 1964-65; resident in pediatrics Los Angeles Children's Hosp., 1965-67; practice medicine specializing in pediatrics, Berkeley, Calif., 1969-72; pvt. health program planning cons. Lester Gorsline Assos., Terra Linda, Calif., 1973-74; dist. health officer Washoe County Dist. Health Dept., Reno, Nev., 1974-77; pvt. practice pediatrics, community medicine, Santa Cruz, Calif., 1977-79; State health officer State of Idaho, Boise, 1979—; mem. clin. faculty U. Nev. Sch. Med. Scis., 1974-77, U. Calif., Davis, 1977-79. Bd. dirs. Greater Nev. Health Systems Agy., 1976-77; mem. Idaho Gov.'s Project Independence Task Force, 1979-80. Served with USAF, 1967-69. Mem. U. Santa Clara Alumni Assn. (pres. 1976-77), Am. Public Health Assn., Idaho Med. Assn., Idaho Public Health Assn.; Fellow Am. Acad. Pediatrics. Office: 450 W State St Boise ID 83720

GALLAGHER, GERALD RAPHAEL, retail executive; b. Easton, Pa., Mar. 17, 1941; s. Gerald R. and Marjorie A. G.; m. Ellen Anne Mullane, Aug. 8, 1964; children: Ann Patrice, Gerald Patrick, Megan Ann. B.S. in Aero. Engring, Princeton U., 1963; M.B.A. (Exec. Club Chgo. fellow 1969), U. Chgo., 1979. Dir. strategic planning Metro-Goldwyn-Mayer, N.Y.C., 1969; v.p. Donaldson, Lufkin & Jenrette, N.Y.C., 1969-77; v.p. planning and control, then sr. v.p. planning and control Dayton Hudson Corp., Mpls., 1977-79; exec. v.p., chief adminstrv. officer subs. Mervyn's, Hayward, Calif., from 1979; now vice chmn., chief adminstrv. officer. Bd. regents St. John's U., Collegeville, Minn., 1978—. Served with USN, 1963-67. Mem. N.Y. Soc. Security Analysts, Beta Gamma Sigma. Roman Catholic. Clubs: Princeton (N.Y.C.); Minneapolis; Peninsula Golf and Country (San Mateo, Calif.). Office: 25001 Industrial Blvd Hayward CA 94545

GALLAGHER, HUBERT R., governmental consultant; b. Salida, Colo., Jan. 8, 1907; s. Hugh and Margaret (Dinsmore) G.; m. Luthera Wakefield, July 29, 1930; children: Hugh, Janet. A.B., Stanford U., 1929; M.S., Syracuse U., 1930. Instr. Syracuse (N.Y.) U., 1930; asst. prof. Stanford U., 1932; research cons., later asso. dir., council of state govts., 1933-50; asso. dir. state div. Nat. Def. Commn., 1940-41; chmn. Internat. Bd. of Inquiry for Great Lakes Fisheries, 1940; office dir. OCDM and Office Emergency Planning (Exec. Office of Pres.), 1950-69; spl. cons. Nat. Gov.'s Conf. and Council State Govts., 1969—; v.p. Wakefield Farm Co., 1976—; alt. del. NATO Civil Emergency Com., 1962-64. Author: Crime Prevention, Syracuse U., 1930, Report of International Board of Inquiry for the Great Lakes Fisheries, U.S. Govt., Dept. of State, 1943; Editor: The Book of the States, Council of State Govts., 1943; Contbr. articles to profl. mags. Mem. Am. Soc. Pub. Adminstrn. (past pres. Washington), Acad. Polit. Sci., Delta Tau Delta, hon. scholastic frats. Presbyn. Home: 5416 Burling Rd Bethesda MD 20814

GALLAGHER, JAMES JOHN, research center administrator, educator; b. Pitts., June 11, 1926; s. Martin and Anne Mae (Walsh) G.; m. Gertrude Cunningham, Sept. 10, 1949; children: Kevin, Sean, Shelagh, Brian. B.S., U. Pitts., 1948; M.S., Pa. State U., 1960, Ph.D., 1951. Dir. psychol. services Dayton (Ohio) Hosp. for Disturbed Children, 1951-52; asst. prof., asst. dir. psychology clinic Mich. State U., East Lansing, 1952-54; with U. Ill., Urbana, 1954-68; asso. prof., asso. dir. Inst. for Research on Exceptional Children; vis. adj. prof. Duke U., Durham, N.C., 1966-67; asso. commr. edn. Office Edn., Bur. Edn. for Handicapped, HEW, Washington, 1967-69, dep. asst. sec. for planning, research, and evaluation, 1969-70; Kenan prof. edn. U. N.C., Chapel Hill, 1970—; dir. Frank Porter Grapham Child Devel. Center, 1970—; chmn. N.C. Competency Test Commn., 1977-80; mem. Commn. on Presdl. Scholars. Author: Teaching the Gifted Child, 1975, (with S. Kirk) Educating Exceptional Children, 1983; editor: The Application of Child Development Research to Exceptional Children, 1975, (with R. Haskins) Models of Policy Analysis, 1982. Bd. dirs. Am. Dance Festival, N.C. Sch. Sci. and Math. Served with USN, 1943-45. Recipient John Fogarty award for Govt. Service, 1972. Mem. Am. Assn. on Mental Deficiency (v.p. for edn. 1975-77, award 1976), Assn. for Gifted (pres. 1970), Council for Exceptional Children (past pres., J.E. Wallace Wallin award 1968), Assn. Children for Learning Disabilities (award 1976-77). Home: 603 Rock Creek Chapel Hill NC 27514 Office: Frank Porter Graham Child Development Center Hwy 54 Bypass West Chapel Hill NC 27514

GALLAGHER, JAMES STEPHEN, stock exchange executive; b. N.Y.C., Mar. 7, 1943; s. John James and Catherine (McGinness) G.; m. Veronica Redding, May 13, 1967; children: Sean, Geoffrey, Marc. B.A., Fordham U., 1965; M.B.A. summa cum laude, St. John's U., 1976. Asst. v.p. facilities upgrade N.Y. Stock Exchange, 1978, v.p. operating systems, 1979-80; v.p. market ops. N.Y. Futures Exchange, 1980; pres. Pacific Stock Exchange, 1981—. Mem. exec. council Regis High Sch., 1971-80. Served with U.S. Army, 1967-69. Republican. Roman Catholic. Clubs: Stock Exchange, Bankers (San Francisco). Office: Pacific Stock Exchange 618 S Spring San Francisco CA 90014

GALLAGHER, JAMES WES, journalist; b. San Francisco, Oct. 6, 1911; s. James and Chispa (Howard) G.; m. Betty L. Kelley, June 1, 1946; children—Brian, Jane, Christine. B.A., U. San Francisco, 1931; ed., La. State U., 1935. Reporter Baton Rouge State Times, 1935; reporter Rochester (N.Y.) Democrat and Chronicle, 1935-36; with A.P., 1937-76, editor, Buffalo, 1937-39, Albany, 1939, N.Y.C., 1939, became fgn. corr., 1940, chief mil. staff African invasion, 1942, chief invasion staff for, France, 1944, acting chief, 1945, chief bur. in, Germany, 1945-51, gen. exec., N.Y.C., 1951-54, asst. gen. mgr., 1954-62, gen. mgr., 1962-76, pres., 1972-76; chmn. A.P., Ltd.; pres. Press Assn., Inc., La Prensa Asociada, City News Assn., A.P. Can., World Wide Photos, Inc.; dir. A.P. Norway, A.P. Belgium, pres., gen. mgr., 1972-76; ret., 1976; dir. Gannett Co., 1976—, chmn. mgmt. continuity com. Author: Back Door to Berlin, 1943. Pres. Santa Barbara Boy's Club, 1981—. Recipient William Allan White award, 1967; George Polk award L.I. U., 1969; Carr Van Anda award Ohio U., 1969; Peter Zenger award Ariz. U., 1969; Medal of Honor U. Mo., 1976; named One of Outstanding Young Men in U.S. U.S. C. of C., 1945. Fellow Sigma Delta Chi (Deadline Club Hall of Fame 1975). Clubs: Overseas Press; Birnam Wood (Santa Barbara, Calif.). Home: 116 Conejo Rd Santa Barbara CA 93103

GALLAGHER, JOHN CHARLES, manufacturing company executive; b. Phila., June 25, 1923; s. William G. and Doyle (Gallagher); m. Geneva Williams, Nov. 22, 1946; 1 dau., Georgina. B.A., Mount Saint Mary's Coll., 1946; M.A., U. Wis., 1948. With Rockwell Mfg. Co., Pitts., 1948-61, v.p., 1955-61, Nat. Steel, Pitts., 1961-68;; exec. v.p. Rockwell Mfg. Co., Pitts., 1968-78, Dart Industries Inc., Los Angeles, 1978—, also dir.; dir. Cin. Milacron Inc., Am. Precision Industries, Inc. Served with U.S. Army, 1942-45. Mem. Machinery and Allied Products Inst., Elec. Mfrs. Club. Republican. Presbyterian. Club: Duquesne (Pitts.). Home: Werik Apts 2215 Brownsville Rd Pittsburgh PA 15210 Office: 622 Beachland Blvd Vero Beach FL 32960

GALLAGHER, JOHN JOSEPH, cardiologist; b. Bklyn., Mar. 3, 1943. B.S. in Physics, Coll. of Holy Cross, 1964; M.D. cum laude, Georgetown U., 1968. Diplomate: Am. Bd. Internal Medicine. Intern Duke U. Med. Center, Durham, N.C., 1968-69, resident in medicine, 1969-70, fellow in cardiology, 1972-74, asst. prof. medicine, 1974-77, asso. prof., 1977-80, Edward S. Orgain prof. medicine, 1980—; dir. Clin. Electrophysiology Lab., 1974—; practice medicine specializing in cardiology, Durham, 1974—; cons. cardiopulmonary div. USPHS Hosp., S.I., N.Y., 1974—. Mem. editorial bd.: Jour. of Pacing and Clin. Electrophysiology; contbr. over 125 articles on cardiology and electrophysiology to profl. jours. Served with USPHS, 1970-72. Recipient Ray C. Fish award for sci. achievement in cardiovascular disease Tex. Heart Inst., 1979. Fellow Am. Coll. Cardiology, Am. Heart Assn. (council on Clin. cardiology); mem. Am. Soc. Clin. Investigation, N.Y. Heart Assn., Am. Fedn. Clin. Research, Alpha Omega Alpha. Office: PO Box 3816 Duke Univ Medical Center Durham NC 27710 *

GALLAGHER, JOHN PATRICK, oil corporation executive; b. Winnipeg, Man., Can., July 16, 1916; s. James Gallagher Constance and Constance Mary (Burdett) G.; m. Kathleen M. Stewart, Aug. 20, 1949; children: James Stewart, Thomas Patrick, Fredrick Michael. B.Sc. in Geology, U. Man., Can., 1937, D.Sc. (hon.), 1983, LL.D., U. Calgary, 1979. Field geologist Shell Oil Co., Calif., Egypt, 1938-39, Standard Oil (N.J.), Egypt, Middle East, South and Central Am., 1939-49, Imperial Oil Co. (Exxon), 1949-50; exec. v.p. Dome Petroleum Ltd., Calgary, Alta., Can., 1950-53, chmn., chief exec., 1974-83, Dome Can. Ltd., 1981—; dir. Dome Mines Ltd., Trans Can. Pipe Lines, Can. Imperial Bank Commerce, Cyprus Anvil Mining Corp., Texasgulf Inc. Decorated Order Can., 1983. Mem. Am. Petroleum Inst., Am. Assn. Petroleum Geologists, Ind. Petroleum Assn. Can. (pres. 1966), Arctic Inst. N.Am. Clubs: Calgary Golf and Country, U. Calgary Chancellor's. Office: Dome Can Ltd PO Box 200 700 2d St SW Calgary AB Canada T2P 2H8

GALLAGHER, JOHN PIRIE, corporation executive; b. Chgo., Oct. 12, 1916; s. Edward and Elsie (Pirie) G.; m. Penny Boyer, Sept. 13, 1940; children: David A., Kathe L. Gallagher Pasters, Laurie S. Gallagher Stone, Steven R. Student, Northwestern U., 1934-40; M.B.A., U. Chgo., 1947; LL.D. (hon.), Elmhurst Coll., 1975. With Commonwealth Edison Co., Chgo., 1934-46; partner, v.p. Booz, Allen and Hamilton, Inc., Chgo., 1946-63; dir. McKinsey and Co., Chgo., 1963-68; pres., chmn., chief exec. officer Chemetron Corp., Chgo., 1968-77; pres., dir. Chemetron subs. Allegheny Ludlum Industries, Inc., 1977-78; exec. cons. to Chemetron Corp., 1978-81; dir. IC Industries, Inc., Am. Nat. Bank & Trust Co., Pet Inc., UNR Industries, Inc., Harnischfeger Corp., Heller Internat., Stone Container Corp.; sr. lectr. Grad. Sch. Bus., U. Chgo., 1979. Mem. Chgo. Crime Commn.; mem. exec. com. bus. alumni council Grad. Sch. Bus., U. Chgo.; v.p. Bd. for Homeland Ministries United Ch. of Christ; vice chmn., trustee Glenwood Sch. for Boys; bd. dirs. Protestant Found. Greater Chgo., Chgo. Theol. Sem.; mem. bus. adv. council Chgo. Urban League; vis. com. Divinity Sch. U. Chgo.; bd. govs. U. Chgo. Mem. Council on Fgn. Relations (Chgo. com.), Chgo. Com., Beta Gamma Sigma. Mem. Hinsdale Union Ch. Clubs: Chgo., Quadrangle, Comml. (Chgo.); Hinsdale (Ill.) Golf, Walloon Lake (Mich.) Country. Home: 420 E 3d St Hinsdale IL 60521 Office: 1101 E 58th St Chicago IL 60637

GALLAGHER, JOSEPH FRANCIS, marketing executive; b. N.Y.C., May 15, 1926; s. Joseph O'Neil and Nora (Shea) G.; m. Anne Decker, June 17, 1950; children: June, Virginia, Aline. Student, U. Va., 1947-50. Pres., dir. Erwin Wasey, Inc., Los Angeles, 1968-80; pres. JFG, Inc., Santa Monica, Calif., 1981—. Served with USNR, 1944-46. Mem. Phi Gamma Delta, Delta Sigma Rho. Home: 1166 Tellem Dr Pacific Palisades CA 90272 Office: JFG Inc Pacific Palisades CA 90272

GALLAGHER, MARIAN GOULD, librarian, educator; b. Everett, Wash., Aug. 29, 1914; d. John H. and Grace (Smith) Gould; m. D. Wayne Gallagher, Oct. 1, 1942 (dec. 1953). Student, Whitman Coll., 1931-32; A.B., U. Wash., 1935, LL.B., 1937, M.L.S., 1939. Law librarian, instr. law U. Utah, Salt Lake City, 1939-44; law librarian U. Wash., Seattle, 1944-81, asst. prof. law, 1944-48, asso. prof., 1948-53, prof., 1953-81, prof. emeritus, 1981—, adj. prof. Sch. of Librarianship, 1944-81, 82; vis. prof. law and disting. law librarian Sch. of Librarianship, Hastings Law Sch., San Francisco, 1982; cons. various law schs. and govt. law libraries. Mem. Gov.'s Conf. on Status of Women, 1964-71, Pres.'s Nat. Adv. Com. on Libraries, 1967-68; mem. adv. com. White House Conf. on Library and Info. Services, 1976-80; mem. council sect. on legal edn. and admissions to bar Am. Bar Assn., 1979-83. Named Disting. Alumna U. Wash. Sch. of Librarianship, 1970, U. Wash. Sch. Law, 1980, Whitman Coll., 1981. Fellow Am. Bar Found.; mem. Am. Bar Assn., Am. Assn. Law Libraries (pres. 1954-55, Disting. Service award 1955), Wash. State Bar Assn., Seattle-King County Bar Assn., PEO, Mortar Bd., Order of Coif, Delta Delta Delta, Phi Alpha Delta. Presbyterian. Home: 1000 8th Ave Seattle WA 98104 Office: U Wash Law Library Condon Hall 1100 NE Campus Pkwy Seattle WA 98105

GALLAGHER, PATRICIA CECILIA, author; b. Lockhart, Tex.; d. Frank Joseph and Martha Leona (Rhody) Bienek; married; 1 son, James Craig. Student, Trinity U., 1951. Novels include The Sons and the Daughters, 1961, Answer To Heaven, 1964, The Fires of Brimstone, 1966, Shannon, 1967, Shadows of Passion, 1971, Summer of Sighs, 1971, The Ticket, 1974, Castles in the Air, 1976, Mystic Rose, 1977, No Greater Love, 1979, All For Love, 1981, Echoes and Embers, 1983. Mem. Women in Communications, San Antonio Mag. Council. Office: care Scott Meredith Lit Agy Inc 845 3d Ave New York NY 10019

GALLAGHER, RICHARD HUGO, university official and dean, engineer; b. N.Y.C., Nov. 17, 1927; s. Richard Anthony and Anna (Langer) G.; m. Therese Marylyn Doyle, May 17, 1952; children: Marylee, Richard, William, Dennis, John. B.C.E., NYU, 1950, M.C.E., 1955; Ph.D., SUNY, Buffalo, 1966. Field engr. CAA, Dept. Commerce, Jamaica, N.Y., 1950-52; structural designer Texaco, N.Y.C., 1952-55; asst. chief engr. Bell Aerospace Co., Buffalo, 1955-67; prof. civil engring. Cornell U., 1967-78, chmn. dept. structural engring., 1969-78; dean Coll. Engring., U. Ariz., 1978-84; v.p., dean faculty Worcester (Mass.) Poly. Inst., 1984—; cons. in field. Author: Finite Element Analysis, 1975, Matrix Structural Analysis, 1979; editor: Internat. Jour. Numerical Methods in Engring, 1969—. Served with USNR, 1945-47. Fulbright fellow, Australia, 1973; Sci. Research Council fellow U. Wales, 1974. Fellow ASCE, ASME; mem. AIAA, Am. Soc. Engring. Edn., Nat. Acad. Engring., Soc. Exptl. Stress Analysis, Sigma Xi, Chi Epsilon, Tau Beta Pi. Roman Catholic. Home: 15 Regent St Worcester MA 01609 Office: Worcester Poly Inst Worcester MA 01609

GALLAGHER, ROBERT FRANCIS, engring. and design co. exec.; b. Bklyn., Apr. 9, 1934; s. Richard Anthony and Anna Theresa (Langer) G.; m. Joan Frances Davin, Nov. 19, 1955; children—Robert M., Brendan, Christine, Brian. B.B.A., Manhattan Coll., 1956. Auditor S.D. Leidesdorf & Co. (C.P.A.'s), N.Y.C., 1956-61; sponsor Stone & Webster Mgmt. Cons., Inc., N.Y.C., 1961-64; asst. treas. Stone & Webster, Inc., N.Y.C., 1966-70, treas., 1970—. Clubs: Broad St. (N.Y.C.); Wheatley Hills Golf. Home: 366 Mineola Blvd Mineola NY 11501 Office: 90 Broad St New York NY 10004

GALLAGHER, TERRENCE VINCENT, editor; b. Phila., Nov. 22, 1946; s. Harold John and Marie Elizabeth (Kershaw) G.; m. Eileen Rose Small, Dec. 26, 1971; children: Sean Terrence, Elizabeth I. B.S. in Journalism, Temple U., 1971. Asst. editor Product Design and Devel. mag. Chilton Co., Radnor, Pa., 1971-73, mng. editor Internat. Product Digest, Radnor, 1973-74, editor-in-chief Instrument and Apparatus News mag., 1974—, editor-in-chief Hardware Age mag., 1984—, chmn. editorial bd., 1980-83; contbg. editor Tennis U.S.A., 1974-75. Served to 1st lt. U.S. Army, 1966-69; Vietnam. Decorated Bronze Star with 2 V devices. Home: 6 Calvert Circle Paoli PA 19301 Office: Chilton Co Chilton Way Radnor PA 19089

GALLAGHER, THOMAS ANTHONY, advt. exec.; b. Westmeath, Ireland, July 3, 1929; s. Francis and Margaret (Byrne) G.; m. Victoria Lea, Oct. 1, 1976; 1 dau., Tara; children by previous marriage—Michelle, Siobhan. Grad. with honors, Rockwell Coll., Ireland, 1947. Trainee indsl. soaps div. Unilever, Eng., 1949-50; copywriter Lintas, Eng., 1950-59; asso. dir. Erwin Wasey Ltd., Eng., 1959-61; dir. Crane/NCK, Eng., 1961-64; chmn. bd., mng. dir. Gallagher Smail Ltd., London, 1965-71; mng. dir. Doyle Dane Bernbach Ltd., Eng., 1971-74; pres., dir. Doyle Dane Bernbach Inc., N.Y.C., 1974-78, dir., mem. exec. com., 1978—. Fellow Inst. Practioners Advt.; mem. Am. Assn. Advt. Agys. Clubs: Chelsea Arts, Landsdowne, Irish Rugby (London); Kent (Eng.) Rugby, Racquet and Tennis. Home: Paget Hall Harbour Rd Paget Bermuda Office: 437 Madison Ave New York NY 10022

GALLAGHER, WALTER EDWARD, lawyer; b. New Haven, Feb. 11, 1910; s. Lawrence James and Margaret Agnes (Donlon) G.; m. Nancy Lee Cooley, June 28, 1963; children—Janet (Mrs. Charles S. Linning, Jr.), Linda D. B.A., Georgetown U., 1931, LL.B., 1934, LL.M., 1935. Bar: D.C. bar 1934. Spl. asst. to U.S. Atty. Gen., U.S. Dept. Justice, Washington, 1934-39; practiced in, Washington, 1939—; partner firm Gallagher, Boland, Meiburger & Bosnan, 1945—. Author: (with F. Vinson Roach) Legislative History of Natural Gas Act, 1938-68, 2 vols., 1968, Legislative History of the Department of Energy Organization Act, 6 vols., 1978; Contbg. author: Legislative History of the National Energy Acts, 6 vols., 1978. Served as lt. (j.g.) USNR, 1944-45. Mem. Am. Bar Assn., Phi Alpha Delta. Roman Catholic. Clubs: Congressional Country (pres. 1965-67), Burning Tree (Bethesda, Md.)). Home: 5053 Sedgwick St NW Washington DC 20016 Office: 821 15th St NW Washington DC 20005

GALLAGHER, WILLIAM FRANCIS, foundation executive; b. Maynard, Mass., Oct. 30, 1922; s. William D. and Mary (Ryan) G.; July 25, 1961. Grad., Perkins Sch. for Blind, Watertown, Mass., 1945; B.S., Holy Cross Coll., 1948; M.S.W., Boston Coll., 1950, postgrad., 1951. Child welfare social worker City of Boston, 1950-54; Social worker Cath. Guild for All the Blind, Newton, Mass., part-time 1950-54; supr. social services St. Paul's Rehab. Center for Newly Blinded, Cath. Guild, Newton, 1954-59, chief guild's profl. services, 1959-61; asst. dir., dir. rehab. center Greater Pitts. Guild for Blind, Bridgeville, Pa., 1961-65; dir. rehab. services N.Y. Assn. for Blind, N.Y.C., 1965-72; dir. program planning dept. Am. Found. for Blind, N.Y.C., 1972-78, asso. dir. advocacy, 1978-80, exec. dir., 1980—; instr. grad. program in spl. edn. U. Pitts., 1962-65; guest lectr. Cornell U. Sch. Nursing, N.Y.C., 1972-79; Gov.'s appointee N.Y. State Commn. for Blind and Visually Handicapped, 1978—, chmn. bd. commrs., 1981—; mem. peer rev. team Rehab. Services Adminstrn., Dept. HEW; mem. U.S. del. World Council for Welfare of Blind, bd. dirs. nat. assembly, vice chmn. N.Am.-Oceania region, 1981—. Contbr. chpts. to books.; Editor: Guidelines on the Selection, Training and Placement of Qualified Blind Teaching Positions at the Elementary and Secondary Levels of Public School Systems N.Y.C, 1969. Recipient Founders award Mass. Council Orgns. for Blind, 1960, citation as Citizen of Week, Pitts., 1962, President's award Greater Pitts. Guild for Blind, 1982, Presdl. award Assn. for Edn. of Visually Handicapped, 1982. Mem. Am. Assn. Workers for Blind (pres. N.Y. State chpt., George Keane award for 20 years outstanding service 1974, nat. treas.), Nat. Rehab. Assn. (citation Met. N.Y. chpt. 1971, Profl. Worker of Yr. award), Am. Assn. for Edn. of Blind, Nat. Assn. Social Workers, Acad. Cert. Social Workers. Office: Am Found for Blind 15 W 16th St New York NY 10011

GALLAHER, ART, JR., university chancellor; b. Duncan, Okla., Mar. 22, 1925; s. Art Edward and Mildred Beatrice (Dunaway) G.; m. Dixie Ann Clower, June 6, 1950; children: Erin Brynn, Kell Darren. B.A., U. Okla., 1950, M.A., 1951; Ph.D. in Social Anthropology; Wenner Gren Predoctoral fellow, U. Ariz., 1956. Asst. prof. to assoc. prof. anthropology and sociology U. Houston, 1956-61; vis. lectr. Rice U., 1961; assoc. prof. anthropology U. Nebr., 1962-63, U. Ky., Lexington, 1963-67, prof., 1967—; acting dir. Center for Devel. Change, 1964-65, dep. dir., 1966-70; chmn. dept. anthropology U. Ky., 1970-72, dean Coll. Arts and Scis., 1972-80, v.p. acad. affairs, 1981—, chancellor, 1982—. Author: Plainville Fifteen Years Later, 1961, Perspectives in Developmental Change, 1969, (with H. Padfield) The Dying Community, 1980. Bd. dirs. Witter Bynner Found. for Poetry. Served with USCGR, 1943-46. NSF grantee, 1965-66. Fellow Am. Anthrop. Assn. (exec. bd. 1980—), Soc. Applied Anthropology (sec.-treas. 1966-76, pres. 1977—); mem. Am. Ethnol. Soc. (councilor), Alpha Kappa Delta, Omicron Delta Kappa. Democrat. Unitarian. Home: 3167 Roxburg Dr W Lexington KY 40503

GALLAND, RICHARD I., oil company executive, lawyer; b. Denver, Oct. 13, 1916; s. Raymond F. and Mabel (Wilson) G.; m. Alice Halstead, July 21, 1941; children: Richard I., Holley, John H. A.B., Yale U., 1937, LL.B., 1940. Bar: N.Y. 1940. Assoc. Cravath, deGersdorff, Swaine and Wood, N.Y.C., 1940-43, Cravath, Swaine & Moore, 1946-50; chief counsel Mathieson Chem. Corp., 1950-55; v.p., gen. counsel Colo. Oil and Gas Corp., 1955-58; pres. Am. Petrofina Co. of Tex., 1958-76, Am. Petrofina, Inc., 1969-76, chief exec. officer, 1976-83, chmn. bd., 1976—; dir. Republic of Tex. Corp. Served as lt. (j.g.) USNR, 1943-46. Office: PO Box 2159 Dallas TX 75221 *

GALLANT, (JEAN-PIERRE) EDGAR, Canadian government official; b. Egmont, Bay, P.E.I., Can., Sept. 19, 1924; s. Cyrus P. and Edna (Arsenault) G.; m. Annette-Louise Perras, June 3, 1949; children: Pierre, Louise, Marie, Christel. B.A., U. Montreal, 1946; M.S., Laval U., 1949; LL.D., U. P.E.I., 1981, U. Moncton (N.B.). With Fedn. Treasury Bd., 1949-51, Dept. Def. Prodn., 1951-53, NATO Internat. Secretariat, Paris, 1953-55, Dept. Finance, 1955-59, Canada's Mission to European Communities, Brussels, Belgium, 1959-63; sec. Econ. Council of Can., 1964-65; dir. fed.-province div. Dept. Finance, Ottawa, Ont., 1965-68; sec. Constitutional Conf., 1968-69; dep. sec. to cabinet, 1969-71; sec. Council Maritime Premiers, 1971-73; chmn. Nat. Capital Commn., 1973-76, Pub. Service Commn., Ottawa, Ont., 1976—. Bd. govs. Ottawa U. Decorated officer Ordre de la Pleiade. Mem. Inst. Pub. Adminstrn. Can. (Vanier medal 1978). Roman Catholic. Home: 2257 Bowman Rd Ottawa ON K1H 6V4 Canada Office: 300 Laurier Ave W Ottawa ON K1A 0M7 Canada

GALLANT, MAVIS, author; b. Montreal, Que., Can., Aug. 11, 1922. Hon. doctoral degree, U. Ste. Anne, N.S., Can., 1984. Writer-in-residence U. Toronto, 1983-84. Author: Green Water, Green Sky, 1959, 60, A Fairly Good Time, 1970; short stories The Other Paris, My Heart Is Broken: 8 Stories and a Short Novel (Brit. title An Unmarried Man's Summer), 1964, The Affair of Gabrielle Russier; introductory essay, 1971; The Pegnitz Junction, a Novella and Five Short Stories, 1973, The End of the World and Other Stories, 1974; short stories From the Fifteenth District, 1979, Home Truths, 1981; play What Is To Be Done? (produced Toronto 1982), 1984; contbr. to: New Yorker, 1951—. Decorated Order of Can.; recipient Gov.-Gen.'s award for lit., 1982. Home: 14 rue Jean Ferrandi Paris VI France

GALLANT, WADE MILLER, JR., lawyer; b. Raleigh, N.C., Jan. 12, 1930; s. Wade Miller and Sallie Wesley (Jones) G.; m. Sandra Kirkham, Sept. 15, 1979. B.A. summa cum laude, Wake Forest U., Winston-Salem, N.C., 1952, J.D. cum laude, 1955. Bar: N.C. 1955. Since practiced in, Winston-Salem; partner firm Womble, Carlyle, Sandridge & Rice, 1963—; chmn. bd., dir. Caymen Reef Devel. Co., Ltd., EuroCaribe Bank & Trust Co. Ltd.; dir. Brenner Cos., Inc., Thomas Built Buses, Inc.; lectr. continuing edn. N.C. Bar Found., 1966—. Contbr. articles to legal publs. Pres. Forsyth County Legal Aid Soc., 1963-67, Assoc. Family and Child Service Agy., Winston-Salem, 1962-65, Winston-Salem Symphony Assn., 1965-66, Forsyth Mental Health Assn., 1972-73, N.C. Mental Health Assn., 1974-75; dir.-at-large Nat. Mental Health Assn., 1978—, v.p., 1981-82; bd. dirs., exec. com. Blumenthal Jewish Home for the Aged Inc. Mem. Internat. Bar Assn., ABA, Am. Counsel Assn. (hon.), Am. Law Inst., N.C. Bar Assn., Forsyth County Bar Assn., Phi Beta Kappa, Omicron Delta Kappa, Phi Delta Phi; fellow Am. Bar Found. Democrat. Episcopalian. Clubs: Old Town, Twin City (Winston-Salem). Home: 2534 Warwick Rd Winston-Salem NC 27104 Office: 2400 Wachovia Bldg Winston-Salem NC 27101

GALLANTZ, GEORGE GERALD, lawyer; b. N.Y.C., Apr. 23, 1913; s. Samuel and Gussie (Safir) G.; m. Lillian Kolko, Nov. 12, 1939; children—Michael, Judith Coven. B.S., CCNY, 1932; LL.B. cum laude, Bklyn. Law Sch., 1935. Bar: N.Y. 1935. Atty. N.Y.C. Corp. Counsel's Office, 1939-42; clk. to judge N.Y. State Ct. Appeals, 1943-45; asso. firm Simpson Thacher & Bartlett, N.Y.C., 1946-56; partner firm Colton, Gallantz & Fernbach, N.Y.C., 1958-63; Proskauer Rose Goetz & Mendelsohn, 1963—. Trustee Bklyn. Law Sch., 1983—. Mem. Am. Bar Assn., N.Y. State Bar Assn. (ho. dels. 1974-76), Assn. Bar City N.Y. (chmn. exec. com. 1974-75). Club: University (N.Y.C.). Home: 37 W 12th St New York NY 10011 Office: 300 Park Ave New York NY 10022

GALLARDO GARCIA, RAFAEL, bishop; b. Yuriria, Mex., Oct. 8, 1927. Ordained priest Roman Cath. Ch., 1950. Named bishop of Linares, Mex., 1974. Address: Obispado Apartado 70 Linares NL Mexico

GALLAWAY, LOWELL EUGENE, economist, educator; b. Toledo, Jan. 9, 1930; s. Leroy and Bessie Marguerite (Hiteshew) G. Means; m. Gladys Elinor McGhee, Dec. 19, 1953; children: Kathleen Elizabeth Gallaway Searles, Michael Scott, Ellen Jane. B.S., Northwestern U., 1951; M.A., Ohio State U., 1955, Ph.D., 1959. Asst. prof. Colo. State U., Fort Collins, 1957-59; asst. prof. San Fernando Valley State Coll., Northridge, Calif., 1959-62; vis. asso. prof. U. Minn., Mpls., 1962-63; chief analytic studies sect. Social Security adminstrn., Balt., 1963-64; asso. prof. U. Pa., Phila., 1964-67; prof. econs. Ohio U., Athens, 1967-74, disting. prof., 1974—; vis. prof. U. Lund, Sweden, 1973, U. Tex., Arlington, 1976, U. New South Wales, Australia, 1978, U. N.C., Chapel Hill, 1980; staff economist Joint Econ. Com. U.S. Congress, 1982. Author: The Retirement Decision, 1965, Interindustry Labor Mobility in the United States 1957-1960, 1967, Geographic Labor Mobility in the United States 1957-1960, 1969, Manpower Economics, 1971, Poverty in America, 1973, The "Natural Rate" of Unemployment, 1982; contbr. articles to profl. jours. Served with USN, 1951-54. Ford Found. faculty fellow, 1960; Gen. Electric Found. fellow, 1962; Ford Rockefeller Population policy research grantee, 1974-75; Fulbright-Hays sr. scholar, Australia, 1978; Liberty Fund fellow Inst. Humane Studies, 1983. Mem. Phi Beta Kappa, Beta Gamma Sigma. Home: 33 Longview Heights Rd Athens OH 45701

GALLEN, RICHARD THEODORE, publishing company executive; b. New Haven, Mar. 3, 1933; s. Milton Conrad and Mildred (Lowenthal) G.; m. Jill Marshall, June 3, 1959; children: Jonathan, David. B.A., Yale U., 1954, LL.B., 1957. Bar: N.Y. 1958. Assoc. Wier, Lane, Klein & Purcell, N.Y.C., 1957-61; gen. counsel Dell Pub. Co., N.Y.C., 1961-65; pub. Parallex Pub. Co., N.Y.C., 1965-68; pres. Creative Sci. and Devel. Corp., N.Y.C., 1968-70; chmn. bd. Hal Roach Studios, N.Y.C., 1971-73; pres. Richard Gallen & Co., Inc., N.Y.C., 1977—. Author: Wives' Legal Rights, 1963, (with others) Unmarried Couples Guide to Legal Rights, 1981. Trustee Poly. Prep. Country Day Sch., Bklyn., 1982. Mem. Phi Beta kappa. Jewish. Home: 7 W 81st St New York NY 10024 Office: Richard Gallen & Co Inc 810 W 36th St New York NY 10018

GALLER, SIDNEY ROLAND, business executive; b. Balt., Nov. 9, 1922; s. Samuel D. and Ann (Brownstone) G. Grad., Balt City Coll., 1940; Ph.D., U. Md., 1948. Cons. ecology Office Naval Research, 1948-50, head biology br., 1950-65; asst. sec. sci. Smithsonian Instn., 1965-70; dep. asst. sec. commerce for environ. affairs Dept. Commerce, Washington, 1970-80; pres. Sidney R. Galler, Inc. and Assos., 1980—; charter mem. Sr. Exec. Service U.S., 1979. Contbr. articles profl. jours. Recipient Navy Civilian Service award, 1963, Disting. Civilian Service award Sec. Navy, 1965, Smithsonian Exceptional Service award, 1970, Apollo Achievement award NASA, 1971; Spl. Achievement award Sec. Commerce, 1975. Fellow AAAS, Washington Acad. Scis., Am. Inst. Biol. Scis.; mem. Am. Soc. Limnology and Oceanography, Research Soc. Am., Sigma Xi. Club: Cosmos (Washington). Designer oceanographic research ships of opportunity, center for short-lived phenomena, orbitting satellite biol. expt., animal tracking systems, marine test panels for measuring thermal pollution. Home: 6242 Woodcrest Ave Baltimore MD 21209 *The humane utilization of technology is the key to an enhanced society.*

GALLERANO, ANDREW JOHN, chain retail store executive; b. Houston, Dec. 2, 1941; s. Andrew H. and Victoria J. (LaNasa) G.; m. Evelyn Cornelius, June 6, 1964; children: Kelly Lynn, Wendy Michelle. B.A., U. Tex., Austin, 1964; J.D., S. Tex. Coll. Law, 1968. Bar: Tex. 1968, U.S. Supreme Ct. 1973. Asst. atty. gen., State of Tex., 1968-71; regional atty. Montgomery Ward & Co., 1971-72; v.p. Foley's, div. Federated Dept. Stores Inc., 1972-79; v.p., gen. counsel, sec. Nat. Convenience Stores Inc., Houston, 1979—; adj. prof. S. Tex. Coll. Law. Pres. S. Tex. Hosp. Fin. Agy., 1979—; mem. devel. bd. U. Tex. Health Sci. Center, Houston, 1978—; bd. dirs. YMCA, Houston, 1973—, Assn. Community TV, Houston, 1974-80. Served with USNR,

1959-65. Mem. Am. Soc. Corp. Secs., State Bar Tex., Houston Bar Assn., U. Tex. Ex-Students Assn. Clubs: Houston; Headliner's (Austin). Home: 13515 St Mary's Ln Houston TX 77079 Office: 100 Waugh Dr Houston TX 77007

GALLETTI, PIERRE MARIE, university executive, medical science educator; b. Monthey, Switzerland, June 11, 1927; s. Henri and Yvonne (Chamorel) G.; m. Sonia Aiden, Dec. 31, 1959; 1 son, Marc-Henri. B.A. in Classics, St. Maurice Coll., Switzerland, 1945; M.D., U. Lausanne (Switzerland), 1951, Ph.D. in Physiology and Biophysics, 1954. Asst. prof. physiology Emory U., 1958-62, assoc. prof., 1962-66, prof., 1966-67, vis. prof., 1967-68; prof. med. sci. Brown U., 1967—, chmn. div. biol. sci., 1968-72, acting dean medicine, 1980-81, v.p. biology and medicine, 1972—; mem. acad. rev. bd. Exxon; mem. polymer adv. panel Johnson and Johnson; chmn. sci. adv. council pulmonary SCOR in adult respiratory failure Mass. Gen. Hosp.; chmn. Consensus Devel. Conf. NIH, chmn. devices and tech. br. task force; plenary lectr. World Biomaterials Conf., 1980; Hasting lectr. NIH, 1979; McNeil Pharm. Spring Sci. lectr., 1982. Author: Heart-Lung Bypass: Principles and Techniques of Extracorporeal Circulation, 1962; contbr. chpts. to books, articles, abstracts to profl. jours. Recipient John H. Gibbonaward Am. Soc. Extracorporeal Technology, 1980; grantee NIH, 1969—. Fellow Am. Coll. Cardiology; mem. AAAS, Biomed. Engrng. Soc., Am. Physiol. Soc. Office: Box G 97 Waterman St Providence RI 02912 *

GALLIANO, VERNON FREDERICK, university president; b. Cut Off, La., Apr. 26, 1923; s. Emile D. and Josephine (Vega) G.; m. Josephine Bennett, Apr. 13, 1945; children: Vernon Frederick, Timothy, Gregory, Jonathon. B.S. (Univ. acad. scholar), U. Southwestern La., 1947; M.S., La. State U., 1954, Ph.D. (Univ. fellow), 1960. Tchr. vocat. agr. Larose-Cut Off High Sch., Lafourche Parish, La., 1947-54; supervising tchr. Southwestern La. Inst. (now U. Southwestern La.), Lafayette, 1948-54, prof. agrl. edn., dir. tchr. tng., 1954-60; dean edn. Nicholls State Coll., Thibodaux, La., 1960-63; pres. Nicholls State U., Thibodaux, 1963—; Dir. Citizens Bank & Trust Co., Thibodaux.; Mem. adv. com. La. State Supt. Edn., 1965-66; chmn. adv. council for vocat. and tech. edn. La. Bd. Edn., 1969-72; mem. adv. council for federally assisted programs La. Dept. Edn., 1967-72; mem. La. Gov.'s Legislative Com. Study Coordination Higher Edn., 1968-69, La. Indsl. Adv. Com., 1968-69, Council for Devel. French-Speaking La., 1968—. Contbr. articles to ednl. jours. Dist. finance campaign chmn. Boy Scouts Am., 1965; v.p. La. Sci. Found., 1967-68, pres., 1969-70; mem. com. community action and crime La. Commn. Law Enforcement and Adminstrn. Criminal Justice, 1968-69; citizens adv. com. Greater Lafourche Port Commn., 1969—; adv. com. Lafourche Parish Airport Dist., 1964-65; chmn. St. Charles-St. John the Baptist Bridge and Ferry Authority, 1968-70; mem. So. Regional Edn. Bd., 1972—, La. Sea Grant Adv. Council, 1974—; adv. bd. Nat. Ocean Industries Assn., 1974—; bd. dirs. Thibodaux Gen. Hosp.; bd. advisers St. Joseph Sem., St. Bendict, La.; bd. commrs. Hosp. Service Dist. 3 Lafourche Parish; trustee Gulf S. Research Inst. Served to lt. USNR, 1943-45, 61-62. Recipient Hon. State Farmer degree La. Assn. Future Farmers Am., 1955, commendation Houma-Terrebonne C. of C., 1966. Mem. So. Educators Corp. (bd. govs. 1968—), Gulf S. (Athletic) Conf. (pres. 1971—), Am. Assn. State Colls. and Univs. (dir., environ. com. 1970—), So. Assn. Colls. and Schs. (commn. on colls., com. on standards and reports for instns. at levels II-V), La. State Colls. and Univs. Presidents Council (chmn. 1964-66), La. Tchrs. Assn. and Dept. Higher Edn. (trustee tchrs. retirement system), Thibodaux C. of C., Am. Legion, V.F.W., John Henry Cardinal Newman Hon. Soc., Blue Key, Phi Kappa Phi, Phi Kappa Delta, Delta Tau Alpha. Democrat. Roman Catholic. Clubs: K.C., Rotarian (pres. Thibodaux 1966-67), Propeller of the U.S. (Port of Orleans)). Home: 103 Betty St Thibodaux LA 70301 Office: Box 1278 Thibodaux LA 70302

GALLIGAN, JOHN DONALD, chemist; b. Washington, Oct. 9, 1932; s. Joseph Donald and Mary Theresa (Flaherty) G.; m. Audrey Field, Dec. 27, 1958; children: Martin, Dorothy, Monica, Thomas, Charles. B.S., Georgetown U., 1952, Manhattan Coll., 1955; postgrad., Emory U., 1956. Sr. chemist Harris Research Labs., Washington, 1957-61; project chemist Gillette Safety Razor Co., Boston, 1962-65; v.p. Gillette Research Inst., Rockville, Md., 1966-72; v.p. research and devel. Gillette Co., 1973-83, corp. group dir. research and devel., Boston, 1983—. Sec. D.C. Welfare Council, 1970-72; bd. dirs. Confrat. Christian Doctrine, 1962-64, 71-73. Mem. Soc. Cosmetic Chemists, Am. Chem. Soc., AAAS, Pi Alpha. Club: Sakonnet Yacht. Patentee in field. Office: Gillette Park S Boston MA 02106 *

GALLIGAN, THOMAS JOSEPH, JR., utility company executive; b. Watertown, Mass., Sept. 13, 1919; s. Thomas Joseph and Winifred C. (McKeon) G.; m. Lauretta E. Durkin, Feb. 9, 1944; children: Thomas, John, Christopher, Martin, Peter. A.B., Boston Coll., 1941; M.B.A., Harvard, 1943. With Lybrand, Ross Bros. and Montgomery (C.P.A.s), Boston, 1945-53; dir. stores and service Boston Edison Co., 1953-57, asst. to pres., 1957-58, v.p., 1958-60, exec. v.p., 1960-67, pres., 1967-79, 83—, chmn., 1979—, chief exec. officer, 1970—, also dir.; dir. Pub. Utilities Reports, Inc., Cabot Corp., New Eng. Mut. Life Ins. Co.; Dir. Electric Council New Eng.; dir. Assn. Edison Illuminating Cos.; mem. Utilities Publ. Com.; mem. U.S. nat. com. World Energy Conf. Chmn. Boston Citizen Seminar Planning Com.; vice chmn. bd. dirs. Mass. Bus. Roundtable; chmn. bd. dirs. Edison Electric Inst.; bd. dirs. Jobs for Mass.; trustee Com. Econ. Devel., Plimoth Plantation, Civic Found. Boston. Served as officer USNR, 1943-46. Mem. Mass. Soc. C.P.A.s, Nat. Assn. Accts., Mass Electric and Gas Assn. (dir.), Am. Inst. C.P.A.s, Harvard Bus. Sch. Assocs. (bd. dirs.). Office: 800 Boylston St Boston MA 02199

GALLIVAN, JOHN WILLIAM, publisher; b. Salt Lake City, June 28, 1915; s. Daniel and Frances (Wilson) G.; m. Grace Mary Ivers, June 30, 1938; children—Gay, John, William, Michael D., Timothy. B.A., U. Notre Dame, 1937. With Salt Lake Tribune, 1937—, promotion mgr., 1942-48, asst. pub., 1948-60, pub., 1960—; pres. Kearns-Tribune Corp., 1960—; v.p., dir. Telemation, Inc., 1963—, Tele-Communications, Inc., 1965—; pres. Silver King Mining Co., 1960—. Pres. Utah Symphony, 1964-65; exec. com. Pro-Utah, 1964—. Mem. Sigma Delta Chi. Clubs: Nat. Press (Washington); Alta, Salt Lake Country, Rotary (Salt Lake City). Home: 17 S 12th E Salt Lake City UT 84102 Office: Tribune Bldg Salt Lake City UT 84111

GALLO, ERNEST, vintner. Co-owner E & R Gallo Winery, Modesto, Calif. Office: E & R Gallo Winery 600 Yosemite Blvd Modesto CA 95354

GALLO, FRANK, sculptor; b. Toronto, Jan. 13, 1933; (married). B.F.A., Toledo Mus. Sch. Art; postgrad, Granbrook Acad. Art, 1955; M.F.A., U. Iowa, 1959. Formerly asso. prof. sculpture U. Ill., Urbana, now program chmn., prof. One man shows, Toledo Mus. Art, 1955, Gilman Galleries, Chgo., 1964, 65, 68, U. Wis. Madison, 1966, Bernard Danenberg Gallery, N.Y.C., 1972, group shows include, Des Moines Art Center, 1958, 59, Krannert Art Mus., Urbana, 1963, 64, Art Inst. Chgo., 1964, Whitney Mus. Am. Art, N.Y.C., 1964, 65 (twice), 66, 67, Biennial Venice, Italy, 1968, Fogg Art Mus., Cambridge, Mass., 1972; toured, USA; represented in permanent collections, Whitney Mus. Am. Art, N.Y.C., Art. Inst. Chgo., Hirshhorn Mus., Washington, and, numerous other pub. and pvt. collections. Commd. for Commerative Medal civil engrng. U. Ill.; Recipient prize Interior Valley competition, Cin., 1961. Office: Dept Art Univ of Illinois 142 Fine Art Bldg Urbana IL 61804 *

GALLO, JULIO, vintner. Co-owner E & R Gallo Winery, Modesto, Calif. Office: E & R Gallo Winery 600 Yosemite Blvd Modesto CA 95354§

GALLO, ROBERT CHARLES, research scientist; b. Waterbury, Conn., Mar. 23, 1937; s. Francis Anton and Louise Mary (Ciancuilli) G.; m. Mary Jane Hayes, July 1, 1961; children—Robert Charles, Marcus. B.A., Providence Coll., 1959, D.Sc. (hon.), 1974; M.D., Jefferson Med. Coll., 1963. Clin. asso. med. br. Nat. Cancer Inst., NIH, Bethesda, Md., 1965-68, sr. investigator human tumor cell biology br., 1968-69, head sect. cellular control mechanisms, 1969-72, chief lab. tumor cell biology, 1972—; adj. prof. genetics George Washington U.; adj. prof. microbiology Cornell U.; cons. M.D. Anderson Hosp. and; Tumor Inst., Roswell Park Meml. Inst., U. S.C., Georgetown U. Cancer Center, Internat. Inst. Genetics, Naples, Italy, Hahnemann Med. Sch. Cancer Center; U.S. rep. to world com. Internat. Comparative Leukemia and Lymphoma Assn., 1981—. Served with USPHS, 1965-68. Recipient Dameshek award Am. Hematol. Soc., 1974, CIBA-GEIGY award in biomed. sci., 1977, USPHS Superior Service award, 1979, F. Stohlman lecture award, 1979. Mem. Internat. Soc. Hematology, Am. Soc. Clin. Investigation, Am. Soc. Biol. Chemists, Am. Microbiology Soc., Am. Soc. Pharmacology and Explt. Therapeutics, Biochem. Soc., Am. Assn. Cancer Research, Am. Fedn. Clin. Research, Fedn. for Advanced Edn. in Scis., Alpha Omega Alpha. Research on viruses, biochemistry and leukemia. Home: 8513 Thornden Terr Bethesda MD 20034 Office: Nat Cancer Inst 9000 Rockville Pike Bethesda MD 20014

GALLO, WILLIAM VICTOR, cartoonist; b. N.Y.C., Dec. 28, 1922; s. Francisco and Henrietta (Caballero) G.; m. Dolores Rodriguez, Mar. 13, 1950; children: Gregory, William. Ed., Columbia Extension, Cartoonists and Illustrators. With N.Y. Daily News, 1941—, sports cartoonist, sports columnist, 1960—, assoc. sports editor, 1984—. One-man show, Spectrum Fine Arts Gallery, N.Y.C., 1981, works represented in permanent collection, Baseball Hall of Fame, Cooperstown, N.Y., Syracuse U. archives. Served with USMC, 1942-45. Recipient 16 Page One awards N.Y. Newspaper Guild, 1965, 68, 69, 71; Elzie Segar award as outstanding cartoonist, 1976; Alumni Achievement award Sch. Visual Arts, 1977; Power of Printing award, 1977; named best sports cartoonist Nat. Cartoonist Soc., 1969, 70, 71, 72, 73, 84; named to Yonkers Hall of Fame, 1984, Westchester Hall of Fame, 1984. Mem. N.Y. Boxing Writers (pres.), Nat. Cartoonists Soc. (pres.), Baseball Writers, Profl. Football Writers, Turf Writers, N.Y. Press Assn., Soc. Silurians. Home: 1 Mayflower Dr Yonkers NY 10710 Office: 220 E 42d St New York NY 10017 *Everything has to start with a dream. First the dream, and then the chasing of it. I pity the person who doesn't own a dream.*

GALLOP, RICHARD CHARLES, lawyer; b. N.Y.C., Nov. 15, 1938; s. M. Robert and Sally G.; m. Ann McEldowney, Sept. 30, 1961; children: Jeffrey, James. B.A., Williams Coll., 1960; J.D., Harvard, 1963. Bar: N.Y. Partner firm Milbank, Tweed, Hadley & McCloy, N.Y.C., 1963-79; firm Caplin & Drysdale, Washington, 1979-81; sr. v.p., gen. counsel Columbia Pictures Industries, Inc., N.Y.C., 1981, now pres., chief operating officer. Mem. fin. com. Williams Coll.; bd. overseers Pace U. Law Sch. Mem. Am. Bar Assn., Assn. Bar City N.Y. Clubs: Sleepy Hollow Country, Wall St.; Univ. (Washington). Home: Nichols Pl Briarcliff NY 10510 Office: 711 Fifth Ave New York NY 10022

GALLOPO, CHARLES PETER, manufacturing company executive; b. Passaic, N.J., Oct. 1, 1941; s. Nicholas A. and Jean (Saletto) G.; m. Carole J. Wollmuth, Apr. 4, 1964; children: Christie Anne, Todd Nicholas. B.S. in Commerce, Rider Coll., Trenton, N.J., 1963. C.P.A., N.Y. Comml. staff auditor Arthur Andersen & Co. (C.P.A.s), N.Y.C., 1963-65; sr. auditor Johnson & Johnson, New Brunswick, N.J., 1965-68; fin. analyst Walter Kidde & Co., Clifton, N.J., 1968-69; acctg. mgr., asst. to fin. v.p. Richton Internat. Corp., N.Y.C., 1969-72; controller, sec. Milw. Western Corp., West Palm Beach, Fla., 1972-80, Steego Corp., West Palm Beach, 1972-77, treas., sec., 1975-80; pres. Stuart McGuire Co., Inc., Salem, Va., 1980-82; chief fin. officer, dir. Versachem Corp., West Palm Beach, 1982—; dir. Stuart McGuire Co., Inc. Bd. dirs. United Way Palm Beach County, 1977-80; mem. exec. bd. YMCA of Palm Beach County, 1977-80. Mem. Am. Inst. C.P.A.s; mem. Ky. Inst. C.P.A.s; Mem. Tau Kappa Epsilon. Roman Catholic. Home: 6630 42d Terr West Palm Beach FL 33407 Office: Versachem Corp West Palm Beach FL

GALLOWAY, DON, actor; b. Brooksville, Ky., July 27, 1937; s. Paul Smith and Malee (Poe) G.; m. Linda Robinson, Sept. 27, 1963; children—Tracy Dale, Jennifer Malee. B.A., U. Ky., 1961. Appeared as sgt. Brown in: Ironside, NBC-TV, series, 1967-75; appeared in numerous other TV shows; also appeared in movies, plays, radio shows and commls. Active March of Dimes, Spl. Olympics, Am. Heart Assn., Actors and Others for Animals. Served with U.S. Army, 1955-57. Office: care Beakel and Jennings 427 N Canon Dr Suite 205 Beverly Hills CA 90210

GALLOWAY, ETHAN CHARLES, chemical company executive; b. Howell, Mich., Oct. 31, 1930; s. Almon Fred and Rose Marie (Hodkinson) G.; m. Patricia Winner, Dec. 23, 1973. B.S.C., Mich. State Coll., 1951; Ph.D., U. Calif., Berkeley, 1954. With Dow Chem. Co., Midland, Mich., 1954-61; dir. research plastics div. Nopco Chem. Co., North Arlington, N.J., 1962-65; with Stauffer Chem. Co., Westport, Conn., 1965, now exec. v.p.-technical. Fellow Poly. Inst. N.Y.; mem. Am. Chem. Soc., Indsl. Research Inst. (past dir., past pres. 1978-79), Chem. Industry Inst. Toxicology (past dir.), Food Safety Council (former trustee), Council for Chem. Research (dir.), Conn. Acad. Sci. and Engrng., Sigma Xi. Clubs: Patterson, Southport Racquet. Home: 9 Salem Ln Westport CT 06880 Office: Stauffer Chem Co Westport CT 06881

GALLOWAY, GALE LEE, oil and gas company executive; b. Pearsall, Tex., Jan. 10, 1930; s. Gerald Gleen and Vida Olga (Tate) G.; m. Connie Bird, July 30, 1965; children: Georgia Gayle, Michael W., Tara Lee. B.A. in Econs., Baylor U., 1952; postgrad., Tex A&I U., 1953-54, South Tex. Law Sch., 1960-63. Fin. analyst, landman gas contracts, rep., mgr. gas supply Tenn. Gas Transmission Co., Houston, 1954-65; sr. v.p. Coastal States Gas, Houston, 1964-73; chmn., pres., chief exec. officer Celeron Corp., Lafayette, La., 1973—; dir. Rapides Bank and Trust, Alexandria, La.; commr. La. Energy Commn.; bd. dirs., adv. com. U.S. Senator J. Bennett Johnson Commn. Oil and Gas; mem. Interstate Oil Compact Commn. Bd. dirs. Evangeline council Boy Scouts Am., La. Assn. Bus. and Industry; council trustees Gulf South Research Inst. Recipient Carnegie Hero Fund commn. Life Saving award, 1982, W.R. White Meritorious Service award, 1982; named Baylor U. Hall of Fame, 1983. Mem. La. Ind. Producers and Royalty Owners, Mid-Continental Oil and Gas Assn., Nat. Petroleum Refiners Assn., Natural Gas Men Houston, Greater Lafayette C. of C. (bd. dirs.), Natural Gas Men New Orleans. Clubs: City, Petroleum; Town House (Lafayette); City (New Orleans). Home: 100 Shannon Rd Lafayette LA 70503 Office: Celeron Corp 666 Jefferson St Suite 601 Lafayette LA 70501

GALLOWAY, HARVEY SCOTT, JR., insurance company executive; b. Middletown, Ohio, Jan. 30, 1934; s. Harvey Scott and Clara (Sherman) G.; m. Virginia Lee Williams, June 13, 1953; children: Jill, Julie, Scott. B.A., Olivet Coll., Kankakee, Ill., 1955; postgrad., Drake U., 1955-57. With Southland Life Ins. Co., Dallas, 1957-69, asst. v.p., assoc. actuary, 1957-69; group actuary Nationwide Ins. Co., Columbus, Ohio, 1969-71; actuary Nat. Services Inc., Columbus, 1971-72; v.p. Nationwide Corp., Columbus, 1972-81; v.p. chief acturary Nationwide Life-Nationwide Corp.-Nationwide Variable, Columbus, 1981-83, sr. v.p., chief actuary, 1983—; v.p., chief life actuary Farmland Life Ins. Co., Des Moines, 1982—; dir. Nationwide Funding, Columbus, Hickey-Mitchell Ins. Agy., St. Louis, Pacific Life Ins. Co., Columbus, PEBSCO and PEBSCO Mcpl. Employees Services Corp. Served with USAR, 1958. Fellow Soc. Actuaries (chmn. credit ins. com. 1979-83); mem. Am. Acad. Actuaries, Tri-State Actuarial Club, S.W. Actuaries Club (sec. 1968-69), U.S. Power Squadron. Home: 4417 Norwell Dr Columbus OH 43220 Office: Nationwide Insurance Company One Nationwide Plaza Columbus OH 43216

GALLOWAY, MITCHELL OLIN, airline executive; b. Hosford, Fla., June 28, 1928; s. Jesse Olin and Velma (Mitchell) G.; m. Doris M. Pollard, Mar. 23, 1958; children: David Alan, Mitchell Glen. B.B.A. cum laude, Ga. State U., 1958. With Delta Air Lines, Inc., Atlanta, 1945—, dir. financial analysis and control, 1963-67, asst. v.p., comptroller, 1967-69, v.p., comptroller, 1969-78, v.p. fin., 1978—. Served with Fin. Corps AUS, 1950-52. Mem. Fin. Execs. Inst., Airline Fin. and Accounting Conf., East Point (past dir.), South Fulton chambers commerce. Episcopalian. Club: Washington Colonies Civic (East Point, Ga.) (past v.p.). Home: 3 Hawthorne Dr Newnan GA 30263 Office: Delta Air Lines Inc Gen Offices Atlanta Airport Atlanta GA 30320

GALLOWAY, ROBERT LEE, manufacturing executive; b. Hastings, Nebr., June 28, 1926; s. Harvey J. and Eloise M. (Brown) G.; m. Elizabeth J. Sparkes, June 12, 1949; children: Jack Alan, Jeffrey L., Nancy Elizabeth. B.S. in Engrng., U. Nebr., 1949. Mgr. br. plants Trane Co., La Crosse, Wis., 1949-68; pres. Mammoth div. LSI, Mpls., 1968-72; pres., chief exec. officer Pako Corp., Mpls., 1972-83; exec. v.p. Photo Control, Mpls., 1983—. Bd. govs. Methodist Hosp., Mpls.; trustee Dunwoody Inst., Mpls. Served with USNR, 1944-46. Mem. Nat. Assn. Photo Mfrs. (dir., officer). Republican. Episcopalian. Club: Wayzata Country. Office: 4800 Quebec Ave N Minneapolis MN 55428

GALLOWAY, WILLIAM JEFFERSON, former fgn. service officer; b. Throckmorton, Tex., Oct. 21, 1922; s. James Thomas and Ottis Virgil (Marrs) G.; m. Elizabeth Alice Cox, June 3, 1950; children—Jeff, Mary Elizabeth. B.S., Tex. A. and M. U., 1943. Fgn. affairs officer Dept. State, 1948-50; spl. asst. to U.S. ambassador to NATO, London, Paris, 1950-53; spl. asst. to counselor Dept. State, 1953-56; 1st sec., Vienna, 1956-59; spl. asst. to dir. gen. fgn. service Dept. State, Washington, 1959-64; assigned Nat. War Coll., 1964-65; 1st sec., counselor polit. affairs Am. embassy, London, Eng., 1965-74; exec. asst. to under sec. state Dept. State, Washington, 1974-80, cons., 1980—. Served to capt. AUS, 1943-48. Home: 1430 Colleen Ln McLean VA 22101 Office: Dept State Washington DC 20520

GALLUN, ROBERT LOUIS, research entomologist; b. Milw., Feb. 21, 1924; s. George O. G. and Viola C. (Paul) Gullun; m. Geraldyne Marie Dexter, June 25, 1949; children: Christine, Marie, Robert Craig. B.S., Mich. State U., 1948, M.S., 1950; Ph.D., Purdue U., 1960. Entomologist U.S. Dept. Agr., Minot, N.D., 1950-52; mem. faculty Purdue U., West Lafayette, Ind., 1952—, entomologist, 1952-62, research entomologist, 1962-64, project leader, 1964-69, research entomologist, research leader, 1970—; lectr., cons. Contbr. articles to various publs. Served with inf. U.S. Army, 1943-45. Decorated Bronze Star; Fulbright scholar, 1980. Mem. Entomol. Soc. Am., Crops Sci. Soc., Am. Soc. Agronomy, Am. Genetic Assn., Am. Registry Prof. Entomologists, Sigma Xi. Lodge: Optimist. Office: Rm 3 Agr Adminstrn Bldg Purdue U West Lafayette IN 47907

GALLUP, DONALD CLIFFORD, educator; b. Sterling, Conn., May 12, 1913; s. Carl Daniel and Lottie Elizabeth (Stanton) G. A.B., Yale U., 1934, Ph.D., 1939; Litt.D., Colby Coll., 1971. Instr. English So. Meth. U., Dallas, 1937-40, 41-42; cataloguer library Yale U., 1940-41; asst. prof. bibliography, curator collection Am. lit., editor Library Gazette; fellow Jonathan Edwards Coll., 1947-80. Author: Ezra Pound Bibliography, 1983, T.S. Eliot Bibliography, 1969, T. S. Eliot & Ezra Pound, 1970, On Contemporary Bibliography, 1970, A Curator's Responsibilities, 1976; Editor: The Flowers of Friendship, 1953, Eugene O'Neill, Inscriptions, 1960, Eugene O'Neill, More Stately Mansions, 1964, Thornton Wilder, The Alcestiad, 1977, Eugene O'Neill, Poems, 1979, Thornton Wilder, American Characteristics, 1979, Eugene O'Neill, Work Diary, 1981, Eugene O'Neill, The Calms of Capricorn, 1981, Kathryn Hulme, Of Chickens and Plums, 1982. Served as lt. col. AUS, 1941-46. Guggenheim fellow, 1961, 68. Mem. Bibliog. Soc. Am. Clubs: Elizabethan, Grolier, Yale (N.Y.C.); Grad. (New Haven). Home: 216 Bishop St New Haven CT 06511

GALLUP, GEORGE HORACE, public opinion statistician; b. Jefferson, Iowa, Nov. 18, 1901; s. George Henry and Nettie (Davenport) G.; m. Ophelia Smith Miller, Dec. 27, 1925; children: Alec Miller, George Horace, Jr., Julia Gallup Laughlin. B.A., State U. Iowa, 1923, M.A., 1925, Ph.D., 1928, LL.D., 1967; LL.D., Northwestern U., Drake U., Boston U., Chattanooga U.; D.Sc., Tufts Coll.; H.H.D., Colgate U.; D.C.L., Rider Coll., 1966, Pepperdine Coll., Okla. Christian Coll., Georgian Ct. Coll., Beaver Coll., Coe Coll. Head dept. journalism Drake U., 1929-31; prof. journalism and advt. Northwestern U., 1931-32; dir. research Young & Rubicam Advt. Agy., N.Y.C., 1932-47; prof. Pulitzer Sch. Journalism, Columbia U., 1935-37; pres. Market Research Council, 1934, 35, Nat. Municipal League, 1954-56, Internat. Insts. Pub. Opinion, 1947—; chmn. emeritus Gallup and Robinson, Inc. (advt. and mktg. research); chmn. bd. Gallup Orgn., Inc. (mktg. and attitude research); made editorial surveys of many newspapers, also many editorial and advt. surveys of Liberty, Sat. Eve. Post, Ladies Home Jour. and; Colliers; Founder Am. Inst., 1935, Brit. Inst. Pub. Opinion, 1936; founder and pres. Audience Research Inst., Inc., 1939; founder Quill and Scroll (internat. honor soc. for high sch. journalists), now chmn. bd. trustees. Author: The Sophisticated Poll Watcher's Guide, 1972, 2d edit., 1976, also numerous articles on pub. opinion. Recipient ann. advt. award, 1935, award for distinguished achievement Syracuse U., 1950; Distinguished Citizen award Nat. Municipal League, 1962; Parlin award Am. Mktg. Assn., 1965; Christopher Columbus Internat. prize for outstanding achievement in communications, 1968; Distinguished Achievement award N.J. chpt. Am. Mktg. Assn., 1975; award Nat. Assn. Secondary Sch. Prins., 1975; named to Hall of Fame in Distbn., 1962; elected to Advt. Hall of Fame, 977; Market Research Hall of Fame, 1978. Mem. World Assn. Pub. Opinion Research, Am. Assn. Pub. Opinion Research (advt. Gold medal 1964, pres. 1954-55), Am. Acad. Arts and Scis., Council Fgn. Relations, Sigma Alpha Epsilon, Sigma Delta Chi, Sigma Xi, Nat. Press Club. Episcopalian. Originator of method to measure comparative interest of readers in news features and advertising in newspapers and mags., also a method for measuring radio audiences of individual radio programs. Address: 53 Bank St 2d Floor Princeton NJ 08542

GALLUP, GEORGE HORACE, III, research organization executive; b. Evanston, Ill., Apr. 9, 1930; s. George Horace and Ophelia Smith (Miller) G.; m. Kingsley Mead Hubby, Feb. 7, 1959; children: Alison, George, Kingsley. A.B. in Religion, Princeton U., 1954; LL.D., Georgian Ct. Coll., 1975, Rider Coll., 1977; D.Litt., Glassboro State Coll., 1976; D.Sc., Rockford Coll., 1981. Pres. Gallup Poll, Princeton, N.J.; vice chmn. Gallup Orgn., Inc. Contbr. articles on religion, politics, various issues of the day to mags.; Author: (with David Poling) America's Search for Faith, 1980, (with Art Linkletter) My Kid on Drugs?, 1981, (with William Proctor) Adventures in Immortality, 1982. Bd. advisers Stuart Country Day Sch. Sacred Heart, 1969—, chmn., 1971-72; mem. council Citizens Forum Nat./Mcpl. League; bd. dirs. Roper Pub. Opinion Center, Volunteer; mem. adv. council dept. sociology Princeton U., also mem. adv. council dept. religion; exec. dir. Princeton Religion Research Center; pres. Living Ch. Assocs.; trustee Episcopal Radio-TV Found., Nat. Council for Children and TV; Mem. Market Research Council, N.Y.C.; Bd. dirs. Religion in Am. Life, Inc., Religion Research Assn., Quill and Scroll Soc., Alcohol Disease Found.; chmn. bd. trustees Nat. Coalition for Children's Justice. Hon. Ky. Col. Mem. Am., World assns. public opinion research, Nat. Council for Children and TV. Episcopalian. Home: Box 346 Princeton NJ 08540 Office: 53 Bank St PO Box 628 Princeton NJ 08540

GALLUP, JOHN GARDINER, paper company executive; b. Bridgeport, Conn., Oct. 31, 1927; s. Prentiss Brownell and Evelyn (Crocker) G.; m. Paula Burgee, June 10, 1951; children: Susan, Paula, Bruce. A.B., Dartmouth Coll., 1949. Dept. mgr. J.B. White Co., Greenville, S.C., 1951, Castner Knott Dept. Store, Nashville, 1951-52; asst. store mgr. A.T. Gallup, Inc., Holyoke, Mass., 1952-55; with Strathmore Paper Co., Westfield, Mass., 1955—, prodn. mgr., 1968-70, pres., div. mgr., 1970—; dir. Third Nat. Bank, Springfield, Mass., 1979—. Mem. George Bush Campaign Com., 1979; vice chmn. Baystate Med. Center, Springfield, 1979—; chmn. Baystate Health Systems, Inc., Springfield; bd. dirs. Jr. Achievement Western Mass., 1979, Springfield Orch. Assn., 1979—; trustee Springfield Coll., 1979—. Served with USMC, 1945-47. Mem. Boston Paper Trade Assn. (pres. 1979), Asso. Industries of Mass. (vice chmn. Boston chpt. 1979—), Am. Paper Inst. (exec. com. cover and test paper group 1979—). Episcopalian. Club: Longmeadow (Mass.) Country. Home: 64 Cambridge Circle Longmeadow MA 01106 Office: S Broad St Westfield MA 01085

GALLUZZI, NICHOLAS JOSEPH, health adminstr.; b. Bklyn., Mar. 18, 1923; s. Charles F. and Gertrude (Santora) G.; m. Eileen M. McGlone, Sept. 22, 1945; children—Katherine, Margaret, Patricia. B.S., U. Mich., 1944; M.D., U. Chgo., 1948. Diplomate: Am. Bd. Internal Medicine. Research asst. U. Chgo. Med. Sch., 1948-49; rotating intern USPHS Hosp., S.I., N.Y., 1949-50, resident internal medicine, 1950-53; with USPHS, 1953—; dir. USPHS Hosp., S.I., 1967-75; regional health adminstr. USPHS, HEW, N.Y.C., 1975-79; ret., 1979; med. dir. Richmond Meml. Hosp., S.I., 1979—; asso. clin. prof. medicine N.J. Coll. Medicine, 1966-73. Served with AUS, 1943-46. Recipient Meritorious Service medal USPHS, 1966. Fellow A.C.P.; mem. Alpha Omega Alpha. Home: 160 Nixon Ave Staten Island NY 10304 Office: Richmond Meml Hospital Staten Island NY 10309

GALPERN, ANTHONY H., communications company executive; b. N.Y.C.; 5 children. B.A., UCLA, 1955. Successively with Leach Corp., Gen. Dynamics Corp., Ford Motor Co.; with ITT Corp., 1968—, ast. dir. materials-subcontracts ITT Gilfallen, Van Nuys, Calif., from 1968, v.p., dir. contracts, until 1972, pres., gen. mgr. ITT Aerospace/Optical Div., Ft. Wayne, Ind., from 1972, then group gen. mgr. Telecommunications Equipment Group N.Am., now pres. Bus. and Consumer Group. Served with USAF, 1951-52. Recipient Harold S. Geneen Creative Mgmt. award, 1979. Office: ITT Corp 320 Park Ave New York NY 10022 *

GALPHIN, BRUCE MAXWELL, writer; b. Tallahassee, Aug. 11, 1932; s. Lawrence Tatum and Helen (Hoskins) G. A.B., Fla. State U., 1954. With Atlanta Constn., 1954-69, editorial asso., 1963-69; Atlanta bur. chief Washington Post, 1969-70; mng. editor Atlanta Mag., 1971-77, exec. editor, 1977-78; spl. projects adminstr. Perry Communications Co., 1978-80; pub. WINEWS, 1980—; syndicated wine columnist, 1970-75; writer, editorial cons. Nieman fellow Harvard, 1962-63; exec. dir. Atlanta Internat. Wine Festival, 1983—. Author: The Riddle of Lester Maddox, 1968, Atlanta: A Celebration, 1978, 500 Things To Do in Atlanta for Free, 1981; co-author: Atlanta: Triumph of a People, 1982; Author: also articles. 500 Things To Do in Atlanta for Free. Named Outstanding Young Man in Professions Atlanta Jr. C. of C., 1967. Club: Atlanta Press (pres. 1968). Address: 217 Westminster Dr NE Atlanta GA 30309

GALSTON, ARTHUR WILLIAM, biology educator; b. N.Y.C., Apr. 21, 1920; s. Hyman and Freda (Saks) G.; m. Dale Judith Kuntz, June 27, 1941; children: William Arthur, Beth Dale. B.S., Cornell U., 1940; M.S., U. Ill., 1942, Ph.D., 1943. Research plant physiologist emergency rubber project Calif. Inst. Tech., 1943-44, sr. research fellow, 1947-50, asso. prof. biology, 1951-55; instr. Yale U., 1946-47, prof. plant physiology, 1955-65, prof. biology, 1965-72, Eaton prof. botany, 1973—, dir. div. biol. scis., 1965-66, chmn. dept. botany, 1961-62; cons. central research dept. E. I. duPont de Nemours & Co., 1956-78; mem. div. biology and agr. NRC, 1963-66; Einstein prof. Faculty Agriculture, Hebrew U. Jerusalem, 1980; vis. scientist Plant Breeding Inst., Cambridge, Eng., 1983; vis. fellow Wolfson Coll., Cambridge U., 1983. Author: Life of the Green Plant, 1961, 3d edit. (with Peter J. Davies and Ruth L. Satter) 1980, (with James Bonner) Principles of Plant Physiology, 1952, (with Peter J. Davies) Control Mechanisms in Plant Development, 1970, Daily Life in People's China, 1973, Green Wisdom, 1981; also sci. articles; editorial adv. bd.: World Book Science Year, 1976-78, Pesticide Physiology and Biochemistry, 1978—, Chem. Engring. News, 1977-78, Environment, 1979—. Served as ensign USNR, 1944-46; mil. govt.; Okinawa. Guggenheim fellow, Stockholm, Paris, Sheffield, Eng., 1950-51; Fulbright fellow, Canberra, Australia, 1960-61; Sci. Faculty fellow NSF, 1967-68. Fellow AAAS (chmn. com. on meetings 1956-59); mem. Am. Soc. Plant Physiologists (sec. 1955-57, v.p. 1957-58, pres. 1963-64), Internat. Assn. Plant Physiology (sec.-treas. 1961-67), Bot. Soc. Am. (editorial bd. 1959-61, 72-76, pres. 1967-68), Fedn. Am. Scientists (council 1973-76), Am. Soc. Biol. Chemists, Am. Soc. Photobiology, Am. Inst. Biol. Scis. Home: 307 Manley Heights Orange CT 06477 Office: Yale University New Haven CT 06520

GALSTON, CLARENCE ELKUS, lawyer; b. Cedarhurst, N.Y., June 5, 1909; s. Clarence G. and Estelle (Elkus) G.; m. Constance Matthiessen, May 18, 1937 (div. 1952); children: Virginia (Mrs. John J. Walsh, Jr.), John Wood, Linda Jane (Mrs. Richard J. Fates); m. Nina Moore Shields, Feb. 17, 1955; 1 stepson, William Shields III. A.B. magna cum laude, Harvard, 1930; LL.B., 1933. Bar: N.Y. bar 1933. Asso., then mem. firm Spence, Hotchkiss, Parker & Duryee, N.Y.C., 1933-42, 45- 47; pres., chief exec. officer Motor Haulage Co., N.Y.C., 1947-55; v.p. U.S. Trucking Corp., N.Y.C., 1955-59; trustee Welfare and Pension Funds of N.Y.C. Trucking Industry, Local 807, 1948-63; v.p., gen. counsel, sec. then exec. v.p. Tchrs. Ins. & Annuity Assn. Am., also Coll. Retirement Equities Fund, N.Y.C., 1960-73; exec. v.p. Assn. N.Y. State Life Ins. Cos., N.Y.C., 1974-77. Trustee Assn. for Protection of the Adirondacks. Served from 1st lt. to col. USAAF, 1942-45. Decorated Legion of Merit. Fellow Am. Bar Found.; mem. Am. Bar Assn., Bar Assn. City N.Y. (treas. 1978—), Assn. Life Ins. Counsel, Am. Arbitration Assn. Republican. Clubs: Ausable (trustee), Cold Spring Harbor Beach; Winter (Huntington, N.Y.); Harvard (N.Y.C.); Piping Rock. Home: 338 Woodbury Rd Huntington NY 11743 Office: 475 Park Ave S New York NY 10016

GALT, BARRY J., diversified company executive; b. Ardmore, Okla., Dec. 14, 1933; s. Monroe S. and Ethelyn (Barry) G.; m. Mary Kathryn Moore, Aug. 14, 1954; children: Terri Kathryn, Carol Ann, Gayle Lyn. B.A. Naval ROTC scholar, U. Okla., 1955, LL.B., 1960. Bar: Okla. 1960. Research asst. to dean Law Sch., U. Okla., 1959-60; asso. firm Conner, Winters, Ballaine, Barry & McGowen (and predecessor firm), Tulsa, 1960-65, partner, 1966-75; sr. v.p., gen. counsel The Williams Companies, Tulsa, 1975-77, exec. v.p., 1977-78, pres., chief operating officer, 1979-82; trustee Nucorp Energy, Inc., San Diego, 1983—; dir. Bank of Okla., Econ. Therm Energy Systems, Inc.,, Mpls. Editor: Okla. Law Rev, 1959-60. Trustee U. Okla. Found.; trustee Gilcrease Art Mus., St. John Med. Ctr., Tulsa; Chmn. Tulsa Area United Way, 1982-83. Served to lt. USNR, 1955-58. Mem. Am., Okla., Tulsa County bar assns., Order of Coif, Phi Delta Theta, Phi Alpha Delta. Presbyn. (elder 1973-75). Clubs: Southern Hills Country, Tulsa; Eldorado Country (Indian Wells, Calif.); La Quinta (Calif.) Hotel Golf; Castle Pines Golf (Denver). Home: 6730 S Evanston St Tulsa OK 74136 Office: One Williams Center Tulsa OK 74172

GALT, JOHN KIRTLAND, physicist, laboratory administrator; b. Portland, Oreg., Sept. 1, 1920; s. Martin Happer and Elsie (Lee) G.; m. Marguerite VanNest, Dec. 30, 1949; children: James Michael (dec.), Lloyd Anthony. A.B., Reed Coll., 1941; Ph.D., MIT, 1947. Mem. tech. staff Bell Labs., Murray Hill, N.J., 1948-57, head solid state and plasma physics dept., 1957-61, dir. solid state electronics lab., 1961-74; dir. solid state scis. research orgn. Sandia Nat. Labs., Albuquerque, 1974-78, v.p., 1978—; mem. Air Force Studies Bd., Nat. Acad. Sci., 1971-76, Air Force Sci. Adv. Bd., 1975-82. Cons. editor: McGraw-Hill Ency. Sci. and Tech., 1965—. NRC fellow, Bristol, Eng., 1947-48. Fellow Am. Phys. Soc., IEEE, AAAS. Office: Orgn 1000 Sandia Nat Lab PO Box 5800 Albuquerque NM 87185

GALT, THOMAS MAUNSELL, insurance company executive; b. Winnipeg, Man., Can., Aug. 1, 1921; s. George F. Galt and Muriel Julyan (Maunsell) Gemmel; m. Helen W. Hyndman, June 15, 1942; children: Lesley Maunsell (Mrs. S. R. Brown), George Hyndman. Student, Queen's U.; B.Commerce, U. Man., 1948. With Sun Life Assurance Co. Can., Montreal, Que., 1948—, successively actuary, chief actuary, v.p. and chief actuary, exec. v.p., 1961-68, pres., chief operating officer, 1972, pres., chief exec. officer, 1973-78, chmn., chief exec. officer, 1978—, dir., 1970—; chmn., dir. Sun Life Assurance Co. Can. (U.K.) Ltd., Sun Life Assurance Co. Can., U.S.; dir. Bank of Montreal, Mass. Fin. Services Co., Textron Can. Ltd., Canron Inc., Can. Pacific Enterprises Ltd., Stelco Inc. Bd. dirs. Can. Opera Co., Lakefield Coll. Sch., Wellesley Hosp. Research Found. Served as flight lt. RCAF, 1941-45. Fellow Soc. Actuaries, Can. Inst. Actuaries; mem. Can. Life and Health Ins. Assn. (pres.). Clubs: Mt. Bruno Country, Toronto Golf, The York, Mt. Royal, Toronto (Toronto, Ont.). Home: 297 Russell Hill Rd Toronto ON Canada M4V 2T7 Office: PO Box 4150 Sta A Toronto ON Canada M5W 2C9 *

GALUSHA, BRYANT LEROY, physician, medical education consultant; b. Morgantown, W.Va., Nov. 28, 1927; s. Harold Leroy and Edna (Sines) G.; m. Shirley McCann, July 8, 1950; children: Janice, Sherlyn, Catherine. B.A., W. Va. U., 1948; M.D., Western Res. U., 1952. Diplomate: Am. Bd. Pediatrics. Intern Univ. Hosps. of Cleve., 1952-53, resident, 1953-54, Cleve. City Hosp., 1954-55, Charlotte Meml. Hosp. (N.C.), 1956-57, dir. med. edn., 1962—; practice medicine specializing in pediatrics, Charlotte, N.C., 1957-62; dir. Charlotte Area Health Edn. Ctr., U. N.C. Sch. Medicine, Chapel Hill, 1972—, clin. prof. pediatrics, 1972—; med. edn. cons., 1965—; dir. bd. dirs. Sun Health, Inc., Charlotte, 1983—; clin. prof. nursing U. N.C., 1981—; mem. N.C. Bd. Med. Examiners, Raleigh, 1968-80, pres., 1970-72. Served to capt. U.S. Army, 1954-56. Recipient N.C. Recognition award, 1982. Mem. Fedn. State Med. Bds. of U.S. (pres. 1981-82, recognition award 1982), Nat. Bd. Med. Examiners, Assn. Hosp. Med. Educators, AMA, Am. Acad. Pediatrics. Democrat. Presbyterian. Home: 3308 Ferncliff Rd Charlotte NC 28211 Office: Charlotte Meml Hosp and Med Center PO Box 32861 Charlotte NC 28232

GALVAN LOPEZ, FELIX, Mexican army officer and govt. ofcl.; b. Valle de Santiago, Guanajuato, Mex., Jan. 20, 1913; s. Felix Galvan Coria and Aurea Lopez; m. Elisa Juarez de Galvan; 3 children. Ed., Heroic Mil. Coll., Cavaley Sch. Adj. to pres., Mex., 1946-52, to mil. and air force attache at embassy in, U.S., 1953; gen. adj. and chief spl. inspection com. Army and Air Force Gen. Inspectorate, 1959-65; pvt. sect to sec. nat. def., 1965-69, chief nat. def. staff, 1969-70, comdt, 1971-73, 1973-74, 1974-76, sec. nat. def., 1976—. Decorated Order Mil. Tech. Merit, Mexican Legion of Honor; comdr. Order of Mayo, Argentina; Order of Abdon Calderon, Ecuador).

GALVANY, MARISA, soprano; b. Paterson, N.J., June 19, 1938; d. Samuel and Tillie Genis; m. H. George Kornbluth, June 28, 1959; 1 dau., Sally. Debut as Tosca, Seattle Opera, 1969; N.Y.C. Opera debut in Maria Stuarda, 1972; Met. Opera debut as Norma, 1979; appeared in leading roles with opera cos. of, Mexico City, 1972, Barcelona, Spain, 1974, Rouen, France, 1975, Caracas, Venezuela, Strasbourg, France, 1976, Toronto, Ont., Can., Frankfurt, W.Ger., 1977, also maj. U.S. cos.; film appearance as Lady Macbeth in Macbeth, CBC, 1973; rec.: Medea in Corinto. Mem. Am. Guild Mus. Artists, Can. Actors' Equity. Office: care Herbert Barrett Mgmt 1860 Broadway New York NY 10023 *The prime point I have always held, is the responsibility as a performer to never give less than 100% of myself to the audience, to have complete commitment to my art.*

GALVIN, CHARLES O'NEILL, legal educator; b. Wilmington, N.C., Sept. 29, 1919; s. George Patrick and Marie (O'Neill) G.; m. Margaret Edna Gillespie, June 29, 1946; children: Katherine Marie, George Patrick, Paul Edward, Charles O'Neill, Elizabeth Genevieve. B.S., So. Meth. U., 1940; M.B.A., Northwestern U., 1941, J.D., 1947; S.J.D., Harvard U., 1961. Bar: Ill. 1947, Tex. 1948; C.P.A., Tex. Practice law, Dallas, 1947-52; asso. prof. So. Meth. U., Dallas, 1952-55, prof., 1955-83, dean Sch. Law, 1963-78; Centennial prof. law Vanderbilt U., Nashville, 1983—; vis. prof. Duke U., 1979-80, Pepperdine U., 1979-80. Served to lt. comdr. USNR, 1942-46. Mem. Am., Tex., Dallas bar assns., Am. Law Inst., Am., Tex. bar founds., Am. Judicature Soc., Tex. Soc. C.P.A.s, Am. Inst. C.P.A.s, Phi Delta Theta, Beta Gamma Sigma. Home: 6384 Chickering Circle Nashville TN 37215 *Deal with others as you want them to deal with you—the Golden Rule. Be candid and open—if you stay with the truth, you don't have to remember what you said.*

GALVIN, JOHN MILLER, insurance company executive; b. Richmond, Ind., Sept. 16, 1932; s. John Lloyd and BlancheM. (Miller) G.; m. Linda Lee Baird, June 13, 1953; children: Gregory John, Robert Michael. B.S., Ind. U., 1954. Dir. fin. Chrysler Corp., Buenos Aires, Argentina, 1966-68, controller Amplex Div., Detroit, 1968, dir. fin., Madrid, Spain, 1968-69; corp. officer Am. Standard Inc., N.Y.C., 1969-71; pres., chief exec. officer A-S Devel., Inc., Newport Beach, Calif., 1971-74; sr. v.p. Aetna Life & Casualty, Hartford, Conn., 1974—; dir. Samuel Montagu & Co., London, 1982—, The Irvine Co., Newport Beach, 1982—, Global Marine Inc., Houston, 1979—; controller Badger Northland, Kaukauna, Wis., 1961-64; mem. ptnrs. com. Satellite Bus. Systems, McLean, Va., 1975; partnership com. Twentiety Century Fox-Urban Diversified Properties, Chgo. Mem. Com. on Can.-U.S. Relations, Washington, 1982; trustee Hartford Eastern Seal Rehab. Ctr., 1976; regent U. Hartford, 1976-82, 83—; bd. dirs. Hartford Inst. Criminal and Social Justice, 1981; corporator Inst. of Living, Hartford, 1981, St. Francis Hosp., Hartford, 1976. Served to capt. USAF, 1955-57. Fellow Aspen Inst. Republican. Roman Catholic. Home: 20 Balfour Dr West Hartford CT 06156 Office: 151 Farmington Ave Hartford CT 06156

GALVIN, JOHN ROGERS, army officer; b. Melrose, Mass., May 13, 1929; s. John James and Mary Josephine (Logan) G.; m. Virginia Lee Brennan, June 5, 1961; children—Mary Jo, Elizabeth Ann, Kathleen Mary, Eric Elizabeth. B.A., U.S. Mil. Acad., 1954; M.A., Columbia U., 1961-62; postgrad., U. Pa., 1963-65; grad., Command & Gen. Staff Coll., 1966. Commd. 2d lt. U.S. Army, advanced through grades to lt. gen., mil. asst. to Supreme Allied Comdr., Europe, 1974-76; comdr. DISCOM, chief of staff 3d Infantry Div., Germany, 1976-78, asst. div. comdr. 8th Infantry div., 1978-80, asst. dept. chief of staff for tng. U.S. Army Tng. and Doctrine Commd., Ft. Monroe, Va., 1980-81, comdg. gen. 24th Infantry div., also post comdr., Ft. Stewart, Ga., from 1981, now comdg. gen. 8th Army Corps, Stuttgart, W. Ger. Author: The Minute Men, 1967, Air Assault, 1969, Three Men of Boston, 1974. Chmn. Rhineland council Boy Scouts Am., 1978-80. Decorated Silver Star, Legion of Merit, D.F.C., Bronze Star, Air medal. Mem. Assn. U.S. Army, Authors Guild, Authors League Am., Inc. Roman Catholic. Home: Kelly Barracks Stuttgart Federal Republic of Germany Office: Comdg Gen 8th Army Corps USAREUR APO New York NY 09107

GALVIN, ROBERT W., electronics executive; b. Marshfield, Wis., Oct. 9, 1922. Student, U. Notre Dame, U. Chgo.; LL.D. (hon.), Quincy Coll., St. Ambrose Coll., DePaul U., Ariz. State U. With Motorola, Inc., Chgo., 1940—, exec. v.p., 1948-56, pres., 1956—, chmn. bd., chief exec. officer, 1964—, also dir. Former mem. Pres.'s Commn. on Internat. Trade and Investment.; chmn. industry policy adv. com. to U.S. Trade Rep.; mem. Pres.'s Pvt. Sector Survey; trustee Ill. Inst. Tech., U. Notre Dame; bd. dirs. Jr. Achievement Chgo. Served with Signal Corps, AUS, World War II. Named Decision Maker of Year, Chgo. Assn. Commerce and Industry-Am. Statis. Assn., 1973. Mem. Electronic Industries Assn. (pres. 1966, dir., Medal of Honor 1970, Golden Omega award 1981). Office: 1303 E Algonquin Rd Schaumburg IL 60196 *

GALVIN, RUTH MEHRTENS, journalist; b. New Haven, Jan. 14, 1922; d. Behrend and Pauline Clara (Gademann) Mehrtens; m. Roderick Allen McManigal, Sept. 9, 1947 (div.); m. John Thomas Galvin, Apr. 20, 1968. A.B., Smith Coll., 1942. Letters corr. Life mag., 1945-46; researcher, then contbg. editor Time mag., 1946-51; U.S. and Canadian corr., then chief Boston bur. Time-Life, 1951-66; fgn. corr., London; then nat. corr. Time mag., 1966-74, sr. corr., 1974—; adv. com. Grad. Program Mgmt., Simmons Coll., Boston, 1975-77. Editorial bd.: Smith Alumnae Quar., 1968-70. Recipient Smith Coll. medal, 1974, Robert T. Morse Writers award Am. Psychiat. Assn., 1978, O'Reilly-Conway medal The Pilot, 1982; TIME-Duke U. fellow, 1980. Fellow Mass. Hist. Soc.; mem. Nat. Assn. Sci. Writers. Club: Overseas Press. Home: 770 Boylston St Boston MA 02199 Office: Time News Service 277 Dartmouth St Boston MA 02116

GALVIN, THOMAS FRANCIS, architect; b. N.Y.C., Oct. 18, 1926; s. Thomas J. and Ruth (Cronin) G.; m. Margaret Rowland, Sept. 6, 1948; children: Susan Hall Davis, Stephen; m. Gladys Lozano, Aug. 1974; children: Thomas Francis, Andrew. B.Arch., Pratt Inst., 1950. Registered architect, N.Y., Conn., N.J., Md., Maine, Tex.; certified Nat. Council Archtl. Registration Bd. With Kokkins & Lyras (architects), 1950-60, asso., 1956-60; also sec. Kolyer Constrn. Corp., N.Y.C.; partner Lyras, Galvin & Anaya (architects), N.Y.C., 1960-63; also exec. v.p. Lyras-Adams Ltd. Investment Builders, N.Y.C.; pvt. practice Thomas F. Galvin, AIA, N.Y.C., 1963-64; partner Brown Guenther Battaglia Galvin (architects), N.Y.C., 1965-70; chmn. Bd. Standards and Appeals, City N.Y., 1970-72; exec. v.p. N.Y.C. Conv. and Exhbn. Center Corp., 1972-74; sr. v.p., chief operating officer Battery Park City Authority, N.Y.C., 1974-80; sr. v.p. Olympia & York Equity Corp., N.Y.C., 1980-81; pres. Bramalea Tex. Inc., Dallas, 1981-83; dir. Bramalea Inc.; adj. prof. architecture Coll. City N.Y., 1971-76; pres., chief exec. officer N.Y. Conv. Ctr. Devel. Corp., N.Y. Conv. Ctr.; cons. on utilization air rights over govt. owned real property N.Y. Legislature, 1964; mem. archtl. adv. com. U. City N.Y., 1967-70, chmn., 1970. Republican candidate Ho. of Reps., 1962, N.Y. Senate, 1965; Rep.-Conservative candidate for Pres. of City Council N.Y.C., 1973; Rep.-Conservative candidate Queens Borough Pres., 1977; trustee Manhattan Coll., N.Y.C.; mem. strategic issues com. North Tex. Commn.; mem. exec. com. Dallas-Ft. Worth Planning Conf.; mem. cornerstone campaign council, Dallas Symphony; mem. steering com. Austin Street Corridor Devel.; bd. dirs. N.Y. Conv. and Visitors Bur. Served submarine service with USNR, 1944-46. Fellow AIA (pres. N.Y. chpt. 1972-73), N.Y. State Assn. Architects of AIA (pres. 1971-72); mem. N.Y. Bldg. Congress (gov. 1968-73, 76-80), Dallas Central Bus. Dist. Assn. (dir., mem. transp. com.). Roman Catholic. Home: 15 Whitson St Forest Hills NY 11375 *For a free society to continue to exist, it requires active participation upon the part of its citizenry in government, politics and community affairs. Those individuals possessing particular expertise, whether by native skill or acquired through education and experience, have a particular obligation to contribute their fair share of time and effort for the public good. For this reason, I have accepted nominations and campaigned for public office. Although not successful in being elected I have managed to articulate key issues thereby impacting the course of some governmental proposals and have seen some of the ideas I have initiated enacted into law.*

GALVIN, THOMAS JOHN, university dean; b. Arlington, Mass., Dec. 30, 1932; s. Thomas John and Elizabeth (Rossiter) G.; m. Marie C. Schumb, Nov. 24, 1956; 1 dau., Siobhan Marie. A.B., Columbia U., 1954; S.M., Simmons Coll., Boston, 1956; Ph.D., Case Western Res U., 1973. Reference librarian Boston U., 1954-56; dir. Abbot Pub. Library, Marblehead, Mass., 1956-59; asst. dir. Simmons Coll. Library, 1959-62; asso. dir., prof. Sch. Library Sci., 1962-74; dean, prof. Sch. Library and Info. Sci., U. Pitts., 1974—; grad. fellow Case Western Res U., 1965-66; bd. visitors Sch. Library Sci., 1975—; external examiner U. Ibadan, Nigeria, 1976-78; trustee Thayer Pub. Library, Braintree, Mass., 1973-74. Author: Library Resource Sharing, 1977, Problems in Reference Service, 1965, Current Problems in Reference Service, 1971, The Case Method in Library Education, 1973, The On-Line Revolution in Libraries, 1978, The Structure and Governance of Library Networks, 1979, Excellence in School Media Programs, 1980, Information Technology, 1982, Priorities for Academic Libraries, 1982; also articles. Chmn. United Way, U. Pitts., 1975-76; mem. U.S. Nat. Commn. for UNESCO, 1980—. Recipient Alumni Achievement award Simmons Coll. Sch. Library Sci., 1978; Disting. Alumnus award Case Western Res. U., 1979. Mem. ALA (pres. 1979-80, exec. bd., council; past pres. library edn. div., Isadore Gilbert Mudge citation 1972), Spl. Libraries Assn., Assn. Am. Library Schs., Phi Beta Kappa,

Beta Phi Mu. Democrat. Roman Catholic. Home: 962 Summer Pl Pittsburgh PA 15243 Office: LIS Bldg Univ Pitts Pittsburgh PA 15260

GALVIN, WILLIAM WALTER, III, financial public relations executive; b. Hartford, Conn., Sept. 2, 1942; s. William Walter, Jr. and Helen Mary (Soboleski) G.; m. Mary Joanne Coakley, Feb. 5, 1967; children: William Walter IV, James Ryan, Timothy Coakley, Joanna Frances. B.A., Yale U., 1964; M.B.A., Columbia U., 1966. Mktg. specialist Oxford Paper Co., N.Y.C., 1966-68; corp. finance asso. Blyth & Co., N.Y.C., 1968-69; asst. to chmn. Booke & Co., N.Y.C., 1969-70, v.p., 1970-73, sr. v.p., 1973-76, exec. v.p., 1976-80; partner; exec. v.p. Newsome & Co., N.Y.C., 1980-82; sr. v.p. Carl Byoir & Assocs., N.Y.C., 1982—. Mem. Bd. Social Services, Greenwich, Conn. Served with Conn. Air N.G., 1966. Mem. Nat. Investor Relations Inst. Roman Catholic. Club: Yale of N.Y.C. Home: 111 Valley Dr Greenwich CT 06830 Office: 380 Madison Ave New York NY

GALWAY, JAMES, flutist; b. Belfast, No. Ireland, Dec. 8, 1939; s. James Galway and Ethel Stewart (Clarke) G. Student, Royal Coll. Music, Guildhall Sch. Music, London, Conservatoire National Superieur de Musique, Paris; M.A. (hon.), Open U., Eng., 1979, Mus.D., Queen's U., Belfast, 1979, New Eng. Conservatory Music, 1980. Flutist, Wind Band of Royal Shakespeare Theatre, Sadler's Wells Orch., Royal Opera House Orch., BBC Symphony Orch.; prin. flutist, London Symphony Orch., 1966, Royal Philharm. Orch., 1967-69; prin. solo flutist, Berlin Philharm. Orch., 1969-75; now solo performer U.S. debut, 1978; rec. artist.; Author: James Galway: An Autobiography, 1978, Flute, 1982. Decorated officer Order Brit. Empire; recipient Grand Prix du Disque. Office: care London Artists 73 Baker St London W1M 1AH England

GAM, RITA ELENORE, actress; b. Pitts.; d. Ben and Belle (Faley) G.; m. Sidney Lumet, 1950 (div.); m. Thomas Guinzburg, 1956 (div.); children: Kate, Michael. Student, Columbia U., 1948-51. Appeared in: Broadway plays A Flag is Born, 1948, Monserrat, 1949, The Insect Comedy, The Young and the Fair, 1950, There's a Girl in My Soup, 1967; starred in: films The Thief, 1952, Saadia, 1953, Night People, 1954, Mohawk, 1955, Attila the Hun, 1955, Hannibal, 1953, Magic Fire, 1956, No Exit, 1962 (winner Berlin Best Actress Silver Bear award), Klute, 1971, Shootout, 1971, Such Good Friends, The Gardner, 1972; played opening year at, Tyrone Guthrie Theatre, Minn., 1964; played Masha in: Three Sisters, Seattle Repertory Co., 1972; producer: documentary film The Woman in the Army, Israel, 1976; appeared on TV series: The Rockford Files, Tales of the Unexpected, Tucker's Witch, McMillan & Wife; Author: The Beautiful Woman, 1969. Mem. Actors Studio.

GAMBAL, DAVID, educator; b. Old Forge, Pa., Dec. 16, 1931; s. Evan and Alice (Witiak) G.; m. Frances Anne Warfield, May 7, 1960; children—Mark, Scott, Todd. B.S., Pa. State U., 1953, M.S., 1955; Ph.D., Purdue U., 1957. Army research contract fellow Johns Hopkins, 1957-59; asst. prof. biochemistry Iowa State U., 1959-63, asso. prof., 1963-65; asso. prof. biochemistry Creighton U. Sch. Medicine, Omaha, 1965-68, prof., 1969—, chmn. dept. biochemistry, 1976-80. Contbr. articles sci. jours. NIH grantees, 1960—. Mem. Am. Chem. Soc., Soc. Exptl. Biology and Medicine, AAAS, Sigma Xi, Phi Kappa Phi, Phi Lambda Upsilon. Republican. Episcopalian (sr. warden 1968-70, 76-78). Home: 5726 Willit St Omaha NE 68152

GAMBET, DANIEL G(EORGE), college president, clergyman; b. June 9, 1929. Student, DeSales Hall Sch. Theology, 1953-57; A.B. in Latin and Greek, Niagara U., 1954, M.A., Cath. U. Am., 1957; Ph.D. in Classical Studies, U. Pa., 1963; postgrad. in higher edn. adminstrn, U. Pa., 1964. Ordained priest Roman Catholic Ch. (Order of Oblates of St. Francis de Sales), 1957; tchr. Latin Father Judge High Sch., Phila., 1957-58; dean of men. instr. Latin, French and German Salesianum Sch., Wilmington, Del., 1958-61; instr. history Oblate Coll., Childs, Md., 1962-64, St. Mary's Coll., Wilmington, 1962-64; acad. dean, instr. Latin and history Allentown Coll. of St. Francis de Sales, 1965-70, v.p., acad. dean, instr. Latin, 1970-72, v.p., 1972-78, pres., 1978—; provincial Eastern Province Oblates of St. Francis de Sales, 1972-78; mem. Allentown Diocesan Bd. Edn., 1978—, chmn., 1968-70, 79-81; pres. bd. trustees DeSales Hall Sch. Theology, 1972-77; pres. bd. dirs. Salesianum Sch., 1972-77; chmn. vis. com. dept. classics Lehigh U., 1977—; mem. instl. survey com. Commn. for Ind. Colls. and Univs. in Pa., 1977-81, chmn. instl. survey com., 1980-81, exec. com., 1980—. Trustee Allentown Coll. of St. Francis de Sales, 1972—; bd. dirs. Better Bus. Bur. of Eastern Pa., 1978—, United Way of Lehigh County, 1979—; exec. com. Minsi Trails council Boy Scouts Am., 1980—; mem., vice chmn. bd. dirs. Lehigh Valley Hosp. Ctr., 1983—. Mem. Am. Philol. Assn., Classical Assn. Atlantic States, Lehigh Valley Assn. Ind. Colls. (bd. dirs. 1978—, chmn. 1980-81), Classical Assn. Pa., Assn. Governing Bds. Univs. and Colls., Allentown-Lehigh County C. of C. Office: Office of Pres Allentown Coll St Francis de Sales Center Valley PA 18034

GAMBILL, JOHN RANDOLPH, physician, mental health adminstr.; b. Harrisonburg, Va., Apr. 21, 1918; s. John Randolph and Alice (Filler) G.; m. Wilmer Peters, Apr. 26, 1946; children—John David, Sarah Frances, Martha Sue, Paul William. B.A., Bridgewater Coll., 1940; Th.B., So. Bapt. Theol. Sem., Louisville, 1943; M.D., U. Louisville, 1946; LL.B., Blackstone Sch. Law, Chgo., 1958. Diplomate: Am. Bd. Psychiatry and Neurology. Intern Louisville Gen. Hosp., 1946-47; sr. physician, chief female service Taunton (Mass.) Hosp., 1948-51; clin. dir., dir. tng. Norwich (Conn.) State Hosp., 1951-59; clin. dir., dir. tng. and research Madison (Ind.) State Hosp., 1959-62; dep. commr. Ind. Dept. Mental Health., Indpls., 1962-67, acting commr., 1966-67; supt. Mental Health Inst., Clarinda, Iowa, 1967-76; staff psychiatrist VA Hosp., Des Moines, 1976—; clin. instr. psychiatry Yale Med. Sch., 1957-59; asst. prof. psychiatry Med. Center Ind. U., 1962-67. Served with USPHS, 1947-48. Named Sagamore of Wabash. Fellow Am. Psychiat. Assn., Am. Geriatrics Soc.; mem. AMA, AAAS, Iowa Psychiat. Soc. (pres. 1977), Assn. Mil. Surgeons U.S. Baptist (deacon). Clubs: Mason, Rotarian., Sycamores (Indpls.) (past dir.). Address: 4118 Lynner Dr Des Moines IA 50310

GAMBLE, J. CARR, JR., manufacturing and retail company executive; b. St. Louis, Mar. 1, 1919; s. J. Carr and Edna (Idler) G.; m. Dorothy Lee Wharton, Sept. 29, 1951; children—Claire Lee, J. Carr, III, Anne Carlisle. A.B., Amherst Coll., 1940. With Ely-Walker div. Burlington Industries, St. Louis, 1946-65, v.p., 1955-62, pres., 1962-65; exec. v.p., operating head Whitmans Chocolates div. Pet, Inc., Phila., 1965-67, pres., 1967-70, J and R div. Brown Group, Inc., St. Louis, 1971-74; corp. sr. v.p. Brown Group Inc., Clayton, Mo., 1974-79, exec. v.p., 1979—, also dir. Trustee John Burroughs Sch., Ladue, Mo., 1974-77, pres. bd. trustees, 1975-77; trustee, sec. St. Luke's Hosps., St. Louis, 1978—. Served to lt. col. Signal Corps and Gen. Staff Corps U.S. Army, 1941-46. Decorated Bronze Star. Presbyterian. Clubs: Univ. (dir. 1977—), St. Louis Country (St. Louis)). Home: 2722 N Geyer Rd Saint Louis MO 63131 Office: 8400 Maryland Ave Clayton MO 63105

GAMBLE, JOHN ROBERT, physician; b. Boise, Idaho, Nov. 3, 1921; s. Clement William and Claire Elizabeth (Thomas) G.; m. Olive Wilbur, Aug. 10, 1949; children—Priscilla, •Lea. B.S., U. Wash., Seattle, 1943; M.D., U. Pa., 1951. Diplomate: Am. Bd. Internal Medicine. Intern, then resident in medicine U. Mich. Hosp., 1951-55; practice medicine specializing in internal medicine, San Francisco, 1955-73; chmn. dept. medicine Pacific Med. Center, San Francisco, 1973—; mem. mgmt. com. PSRO, 1973-76; prof. medicine U. Pacific Sch. Med., Med. Scis., also bd. regents, 1970—. Author: Chemistry of Digestive Diseases, 1961; editor: Current Concepts of Clinical Gastroenterology, 1965. Served with USNR, 1943-46. Fellow A.C.P. (master; chmn. bd. govs. 1971-73), ACP (v.p. 1977); mem. Inst. Medicine, Am., Calif. med. assns., San Francisco Med. Soc., Am. Fedn. Clin. Research, Am. Bd. Clin. Research, Am. Bd. Clin. Engring., Am. Gastroenterol. Assn., Pacific Interurban Club, Clin. and Climatol. Assn., Assn. Program Dirs. Internal Medicine (pres.), council Med. Splty. Socs. (pres.), Wine and Food Soc. San Francisco. Address: PO Box 7999 San Francisco CA 94120

GAMBLE, JOSEPH GRAHAM, JR., life insurance company executive; b. Des Moines, June 12, 1926; s. Joseph Graham and Ella Theolian (Hildreth) G.; m. Jane E. Wilkinson, Sept. 20, 1974. A.B., U. Fla., 1948; LL.B., U. Ala., 1950. Bar: Ala. 1950. Asso. firms in, Birmingham, 1950-60; with Liberty Nat. Life Ins. Co., Birmingham, 1960-83, asst. gen. counsel, 1973-83, sec., 1976-83; asst. gen. counsel Torchmark Corp. and affiliates, 1983; sec. Liberty Nat. Ins. Holding Co., Birmingham, 1980—. Bd. dirs. Birmingham Travelers Aid Soc., 1976—, pres., 1979—. Fellow Life Office Mgmt. Assn.; mem. Am., Ala., Birmingham bar assns., Phi Gamma Delta, Phi Alpha Delta. Republican. Episcopalian. Club: Mountain Brook Swim and Tennis (Birmingham). Address: PO Box 2612 Birmingham AL 35202

GAMBLE, PHILIP LYLE, economist; b. Amesbury, Mass., Sept. 25, 1905; s. Fred Keightley and Sarah Olive (Lord) G.; m. Elisabeth Davis Scales, Aug. 7, 1939; children—Ruth Scales, Philip Lyle, Richard Andrew. B.S. cum laude, Wesleyan U., 1928; A.M. (Rich fellow in econs.), 1929; Ph.D. (N.Y. State Tax Commn. fellow), Cornell U., 1935. Instr. in econs. Cornell U., 1929-32, Wesleyan U., 1932-35; vis. instr. econs. Mt. Holyoke Coll., 1934-36; asst. prof. econs. Mass. State Coll., 1935-42; asso. prof. Tulane U., summer 1939; vis. prof. Amherst Coll., 1942, Clark U., 1960, 61; prof., head dept. econs., govt. U. Mass., 1942-50, acting chmn. dept. bus. administrn., 1947, acting dean sch. bus. adminstrn., 1947-52, prof. econs., 1942-71, head dept., 1942-64; Theodore Roosevelt prof. econs. Naval War Coll., 1968-70, 71-74; prof. Sweetbriar Coll., 1977—; Fulbright lectr. Tunghai U. China, 1964, 65. Author: The Taxation of Insurance Companies, 1937; State corr. and contbr. to: The Municipal Yearbook, 1937-40, 43-50. Pub. panel mem. War Labor Bd., 1943-44; mem. consumers council Atty.-Gen.'s Office. Mem. Consumers Union (mem. nat. ednl. adv. council), Am. Arbitration Assn., AAUP, Pioneer Valley Assn. (pres. 1962-64), Am. Econ. Assn., Tax Research Found., Phi Kappa Phi, Sigma Chi. Home: 2 Mary Jane Ln Newport RI 02840

GAMBLE, WILLIAM CASHEN, multi-industry company executive; b. Ithaca, N.Y., Aug. 28, 1926; s. Dean Lafever and Dorothea E. (Lippert) G.; m. Ann Sanford, Aug. 28, 1948; children: James S., Thomas W. B.A., U. Rochester, 1950, hon. degree, 1960. Vice-pres. sales Ward's Natural Sci., Rochester, N.Y., 1956-61, chmn. bd., 1980—; pres. Establishment, Inc., Rochester, 1962-80, chmn. bd., rochester, 1980—; exec. v.p. KDI Corp., Cin., 1981—. Editor: Ward's Bull., 1950-60. Mem., pres. Penfield Sch. Bd., N.Y., 1964-70; trustee, pres. Rochester Mus. Sci., 1955-78; pres. Com. for Better Schs., Rochester, 1959; Republican committeeman, Rochester, 1978-80. Served in USN, 1944-46; PTO. Assoc. fellow Buffalo Mus., 1981; recipient Contbn. award N.Y. State Sci. Tchrs. Assn., 1980, Service award Central Western chpt. N.Y. State Sci. Tchrs. Assn., 1979. Mem. Am. Inst. Biology (life), Nat. Inst. Investor Relations (v.p. 1981—). Republican. Episcopalian. Clubs: Rochester Tennis; Bankers (Cin.). Home: 823 Indian Trace Ct Cincinnati OH 45230 DOffice: KDI Corp 5721 Dragon Way Cincinnati OH 45227 *Given enough time, the human race might fulfill our dreams. . . .*

GAMBLIN, RODGER LOTIS, research company executive; b. St. Louis, Sept. 18, 1932; s. Granville Lotis and Opal Ora (Taylor) G.; children: Anne W., Rodgers W.B., Lawrence R., Sarah A., Amanda T. B.S., Princeton U., 1954, M.A., 1963, Ph.D., 1965; M.B.A., Wright State U., 1981. Foreman Phelps Dodge Co., Fort Wayne, Ind., 1954-55; research staff Princeton (N.J.) U., 1955-59; area mgr. IBM, Boulder, Colo., 1959-76; v.p. research and devel. Mead Corp., Dayton, Ohio, 1976-80; pres. Dayton Tinker Corp., 1980—; dir. Yellow Springs Instrument Co., Inc., Ohio, Bradford Chem. Corp. Contbr. articles to profl. jours. Mem. Am. Phys. Soc., AAAS, Mensa, Sigma Xi, Beta Gamma Sigma. Republican. Presbyterian. Patentee in field. Home: 8 Springhouse Rd Dayton OH 45409 Office: Dayton Tinker Corp 143 Westpark Rd Dayton OH 45459 *The attainment of a goal is a pleasure and brings rewards. It seems to me, however, that there is much greater pleasure in finding the goal and in undergoing the process of getting there.*

GAMBRELL, DAVID HENRY, lawyer; b. Atlanta, Dec. 20, 1929; s. E. Smythe and Kathleen (Hagood) G.; m. Luck Coleman Flanders, Oct. 16, 1953; children: Luck Coleman, David Henry, Alice Kathleen Hagood, Mary Latimer. B.S., Davidson Coll., 1949; LL.B. cum laude, Harvard U., 1952. Bar: Ga. 1951. Pvt. practice, Atlanta, 1952-54, 56—; teaching fellow Harvard Law Sch., 1954-55; partner firm Gambrell & Stolz, 1963—; U.S. senator from Ga. to succeed Richard B. Russell, 1971-72. Bd. editors: Am. Bar Assn. Jour, 1969-70. Chmn. Ga. Gov.'s Com. on Postsecondary Edn., 1978-79; trustee Met. Atlanta Crime Commn., 1966-68, gen. counsel, 1970; bd. dirs. Nat. Legal Aid and Defender Assn., 1965—; chmn. Democratic Party Ga., 1970-71. Mem. ABA., Atlanta Bar Assn. (pres. 1965-66), State Bar Ga. (bd. govs. 1964-66, pres. 1967-68), Lawyers Club Atlanta, N.C. Soc. Cin., Sigma Alpha Epsilon, Omicron Delta Kappa. Democrat. Presbyterian. Clubs: Metropolitan (Washington); Piedmont Driving, Atlanta Country, Capital City (Atlanta). Home: 3820 Castlegate Dr NW Atlanta GA 30327 Office: 3900 First Atlanta Tower Atlanta GA 30383

GAMBRELL, JAMES BRUTON, lawyer, educator; b. Rochester, Minn., Jan. 17, 1926; s. James Bruton and Martha Judson (Corley) G.; m. Helen Jeanette Roddy, Aug. 12, 1950; children: Jamey, Gretchen, James Bruton IV. Student, UCLA, 1943-44; B.S. in Mech. Engring, U. Tex., 1949; M.A. in Econs, Columbia U., 1950; LL.B., N.Y. U., 1957. Bar: D.C. bar 1957, Okla. bar 1958, Calif. bar 1961, N.Y. bar 1967, Tex. bar 1976. Mem. staff Tex. Legis. Council, Austin, 1950; instr. econs. Baylor U., Waco, Tex., 1950-51; mem. tech. staff (engr.) Bell Telephone Labs., Murray Hill, N.J., 1951-53, mem. patent staff, N.Y.C., 1953-57; admitted to practice before U.S. Patent Office, 1954; asst. patent atty. Well Surveys, Inc., Tulsa, 1957-59; asso. firm Townsend & Townsend, San Francisco, 1959-61; spl. asst. to commr. patents, dir. office legis. planning U.S. Patent Office, Washington, 1961-63; ptnr. firm Fowler, Knobbe & Gambrell, Santa Ana, Calif., 1963-66; prof. law N.Y. U., N.Y.C., 1966-76, patent counsel, 1967-76; prof. law U. Houston, 1976-83, adj. prof. law, 1983—; ptnr. firm Pravel, Gambrell Hewitt, Kirk & Kimball, Houston, 1976—; cons. to Practising Law Inst., N.Y.C., 1966-71, Commn. Revision Fed. Ct. Appellate System, 1974, Energy and Research Adminstrn., 1976; commr. patents Patent Adv. Com., 1968-72. Author: (with Donald R. Dunner, Martin J. Adelman and Charles E. Lipsey) Patent Law Perspectives, 2d edit., 6 vols. 1970—; editor: Orange County Bar Bull, 1965-66; mem. adv. bd.: Patent, Trademark and Copyright Jour, 1972—. Served to lt. (j.g.) USNR, 1943-46. Mem. Am. Bar Assn., Calif. Bar Assn., Tex. Bar Assn., Assn. Bar City N.Y., Am. Intellectual Property Law Assn. (bd. mgrs. 1977-80), N.Y. Patent Law Assn., Houston Patent Law Assn., Licensing Execs. Soc., U.S. Trademark Assn. Home: 6200 Haskell St Houston TX 77007 Office: 1177 W Loop S 10th Floor Houston TX 77027

GAMELIN, FRANCIS CLIFFORD, educational administrator; b. South St. Paul, Sept. 13, 1917; s. Francis W. and Elsie (Oesterreich) G.; m. Ruth Vikner, Oct. 8, 1938; children—Theodore, Daniel, Timothy, Steven, Quentin, Lili. B.A., Gustavus Adolphus Coll., 1938; M.A., U. Minn., 1946, Ph.D., 1953; L.H.D., Gettysburg Coll., 1966. Instr. Luther Coll., Decorah, Iowa, 1938-40; instr. Gustavus Adolphus Coll., 1940-43, registrar, 1943-47; instr. U. Minn., 1947-50, sr. student personnel worker, 1953-55; acting dir. mental health services Minn. Dept. Health, 1951-52; co-ordinator psychol. services Austin (Minn.) Pub. Schs., 1955-58; asst. dist. supt. pub. schs., Robbinsdale, Minn., 1958-62; sec. coll. edn. Luth. Ch. in Am., N.Y.C., 1962-64; exec. sec. Bd. Coll. Edn., 1964-67; v.p., dean faculty Augustana Coll., 1967-69; exec. dir. Central States Coll. Assn., Rock Island, Ill., 1969-72; pres. Higher Edn. Council St. Louis, 1972—; dir. Higher Edn. Center St. Louis, 1979—. Mem. dist. sch. bd., Robbinsdale, 1954-55; mem. Minn. Adv. Bd. Exceptional Children, 1959-62; Bd. dirs. Search Inst., Mpls., Endicott Coll., Beverly, Mass., Internat. Inst., St. Louis. Served with USNR, 1945. Home: 7244 Forsyth Blvd Saint Louis MO 63105 Office: 928 N McKnight Rd Saint Louis MO 63132

GAMELIN, THEODORE WILLIAM, mathematics educator; b. Decorah, Iowa, Sept. 24, 1939; s. Francis Clifford and Ruth Mathilda (Vikner) G.; m. Helen Dorothy Kuehn, Aug. 24, 1961; children: Michelle, Andre, Daniel, David. B.S., Yale U., 1960; Ph.D., U. Calif., Berkeley, 1963. C.L.E. Moore instr. M.I.T., Cambridge, 1963-65, asst. prof. math., 1967-68; prof. math. U. Nacional de La Plata, Argentina, 1965-66; mem. faculty UCLA, 1968—, prof. math., 1971—. Author: Uniform Algebras, 1969, Uniform Algebras and Jensen Measures, 1978. Mem. Am. Math. Soc., Math. Assn. Am., Inst. Math. Stats. Office: Math Dept U Calif Los Angeles CA 90024

GAMER, SAUL RICHARD, ret. judge, lawyer; b. New Haven, Mar. 27, 1906; s. Samuel and Bertha (Resnik) G.; m. Ethel Huchberger, June 28, 1934; children—Janet G. (Mrs. T.S.L. Perlman), Susan J. (Mrs. William B. Blacklow). Ph.B., Yale, 1927, LL.B., 1929. Bar: Conn. bar 1929, N.Y. bar 1931, D.C. bar 1939, U.S. Supreme Ct 1935. Faculty research asst. Yale Law Sch., 1929-30; charge investigations for Report Nat. Commn. on Law Observance and Enforcement (Wickersham Commn.), on Lawlessness in Law Enforcement, 1930-31; pvt. practice law, N.Y.C.; asso. Engelhard, Pollak, Pitcher & Stern, 1931-34; atty. NRA, USDA, REA, 1934-37; practice law, New Haven, 1938; supervisory loan atty. REA, chief ct. claims sect., civil div. Dept. Justice, 1939-58; trial judge U.S. Ct. Claims, Washington, 1958-74, chief, trial div., 1972-74, sr. trial judge (ret.), 1974—. Bd. editors: Yale Law Jour, 1928-29; Contbr. legal periodicals. Recipient merit citation Nat. Civil Service League, 1958. Mem. Am., Fed., D.C. bar assns., Am. Arbitration Assn. (nat. panel arbitrators 1974—), Phi Beta Kappa. Home: 2818 Kanawha St NW Washington DC 20015

GAMM, GARY L., banker; b. Canton, Ill., May 21, 1947; s. Clarence J. and Harriet G.; m. Connie F., June 18, 1968; children: Emily, Matthew. B.B.A., Wichita State U.; grad. with honors, Southwestern Grad. Sch. Banking. Exec. v.p. Fourth Nat. Bank, Wichita, Kans., 1969—; cons.; dir. Harper Trucks Inc., Wichita. Bd. dirs. Project Concern Internat., NCCJ; treas. Accent on Kids. Office: Fourth Nat Bank Wichita PO Box 1090 Wichita KS 67201

GAMMON, JAMES ALAN, lawyer; b. Keokuk, Iowa, Jan. 30, 1934; s. Tench Temme and Helen D. (Joyce) G.; m. Joanne Mott, Aug. 31, 1957; children—Daniel, Thomas, Matthew, Kelly, Timothy. B.S. in Commerce cum laude, U. Notre Dame, 1956; LL.B., Georgetown U., 1959. Bar: D.C. bar 1959. Since practiced in, Washington; partner Gammon & Grange, 1978—; pres. Gammon, Camfield & Ninowski (media brokers), 1981—. Mem. Am. Bar Assn., Fed. Communications Bar Assn., Christian Legal Soc. Charismatic Catholic. Home: 3521 Glenmoor Dr Chevy Chase MD 20015 Office: 1925 K St NW Washington DC 20006

GAMMON, SAMUEL RHEA, III, assn. exec., former U.S. ambassador; b. Tex., Jan. 22, 1924; m. Mary Renwick. B.A., Tex. A. and M. U., 1946; A.M., Princeton U., 1948, Ph.D., 1953. Instr. Princeton U., 1948-49, Emory U., 1952-54; joined Fgn. Service, Dept. State, 1954; visa and polit. officer, Palermo, Italy, 1954-55, adminstrv. and econ. officer, Milan, Italy, 1955-59, personnel officer, Washington, 1959-60, supervisory placement specialist, 1960-61, supervisory fgn. affairs officer, 1961-62, officer-in-charge Italian affairs, 1962-63; detailed fgn. affairs aide to Vice Pres. Lyndon Johnson, 1963; consul gen., Asmara, Ethiopia, 1963-67, counselor for polit. affairs, Rome, 1967-70; detailed dep. asst. dir. for Europe to USIA, Washington, 1970-73; dep. exec. sec. State Dept., 1973-75; minister counselor Am. Embassy, Paris, 1975-78; ambassador to Mauritius, Port Louis, 1978-80; exec. dir. Am. Hist. Assn., 1981—. Served to capt. AUS, 1943-46, 50-52. Office: 400 A St SE Washington DC 20003

GAMMONS, ROBERT FRANKLIN, corporate exec.; b. Taunton, Mass., July 1, 1920; s. Philip A.M. and Ida F. (Smith) G.; m. Lois H. Bugbee, Nov. 9, 1947; children—Marjorie, Douglas, Richard. B.A. in Elec. Engring, U. R.I., 1942; postgrad., Alexander Hamilton Inst., 1949-52, N.Y. U. Mgmt. Inst., 1956-59. With Westinghouse Elec. Corp., 1942, Kellex Corp., Vitro Corp., 1946-55, Am. Machine & Foundry Co., 1955-65; asst. to pres. Internat. Tel. & Tel. Co., 1965-70; v.p. Laird Enterprises, N.Y.C., 1970; pres., chief exec. officer S.S. Pierce Co., Boston, 1970-73; pres. Consolidated Tube & Fabricating Co., Waterbury, Conn., Wire Form, Inc., Mildale, Conn., 1974—; group v.p. Handy & Harman, N.Y.C., 1975-76; v.p., gen. mgr. MICA Products Am., Wingdale, N.Y., 1977-79; founder R.F. Gammons and Assos., Westport, Conn., 1979—; dir. Atlas Quaranty, London. Bd. dirs. Midfairfield Youth Hockey Assn. Served to capt. USAAF, World War II. Club: Saugatuck Harbor Yacht (treas.). Home and Office: 23 Tupelo Rd Westport CT 06880

GAMSON, BERNARD WILLIAM, aluminum co. exec.; b. Chgo., Aug. 18, 1917; s. Max Nathan and Fannie Sarah (Shere) G.; m. Deborah Sobel, Dec. 14, 1952; children—Mark N., Michael M., Miriam R., Alan S. B.S. Chem. Engr, Armour Inst. Tech., 1938; M.S., U. Mich., 1939; Ph.D., U. Wis., 1943. Devel. engr. Socony Mobil Oil Co., 1939-41; with War Prodn. Bd./U. Wis., 1942-43; chief process engr., dir. research and devel. Gt. Lakes Carbon Corp., 1943-54; mgr. nuclear Fuel dept. Gen. Electric Co., 1955-56; asso. dir. research Borg-Warner Corp., 1956-60, v.p., 1960-65, cons. chem. engr., 1965-70, v.p. engring., 1970-71, v.p. raw materials, 1971-72; v.p. primary products Martin Marietta Aluminum Corp., Bethesda, Md., 1972-79, exec. v.p., 1980, pres., 1980—. Contbr. articles to profl. jours. Mem. Am. Chem. Soc., Am. Inst. Chem. Engrs., Sci. Research Soc. Am., Sigma Xi, Phi Lambda Upsilon, Iota Alpha, Phi Mu Epsilon, Tau Beta Pi. Office: Martin Marietta Aluminum Corp 6801 Rockledge Dr Bethesda MD 20034

GAMSON, WILLIAM ANTHONY, educator, sociologist; b. Phila., Jan. 27, 1934; s. Edward and Blanche (Weintraub) G.; m. Zelda Finkelstein, July 1, 1956; children: Jennifer Lisa, Joshua Paul. B.A., Antioch Coll., 1955; M.A., U. Mich., 1956, Ph.D., 1959. Research assoc. social psychology Harvard U., 1959-62; mem. faculty U. Mich.,

1962-82, prof. sociology, 1966-82, Boston Coll., 1982—. Author: Power and Discontent, 1968 (Sorokin prize 1969), Simsoc (Simulated Society), rev. edit., 1972, 1978, (with A. Modigliani) Untangling the Cold War, 1971, (with Modigliani) Conceptions of Social Life, 1974, The Strategy of Social Protest, 1975, (with B. Fireman and S. Rytina) Encounters with Unjust Authority, 1982. Recipient Socio-Psychol. award AAAS, 1962; Guggenheim fellow, 1978-79. Mem. Am. Sociol. Assn., AAUP, ACLU. Home: RFD 1 Box 11A Chilmark MA 02535

GANAS, PERRY SPIROS, physicist; b. Brisbane, Australia, June 20, 1937; came to U.S., 1968, naturalized, 1975; s. Arthur and Lula (Grivas) G. B.S., U. Queensland, Australia, 1961; Ph.D., U. Sydney, 1968. Postdoctoral research asso., instr. U. Fla., 1968-70, vis. asst. research prof., 1972, vis. asso. prof. physics, 1978, vis. asso. research prof., 1979-80; prof. physics Calif. State U., Los Angeles, 1970—; referee Phys. Rev., Phys. Rev. Letters. Contbr. articles to profl. jours. Mem. AAUP, Congress of Faculty Assns., Am. Phys. Soc., Sigma Xi. Home: 11790 Radio Dr Los Angeles CA 90064 Office: Physics Dept Calif State U Los Angeles CA 90032

GANCZARCZYK, JERZY JOZEF, civil engineering educator, wastewater treatment consultant; b. Tarnow, Poland, May 25, 1928; emigrated to Can., 1969; s. Kazimierz G. and Franciszka (Adamczyk) Ganczarcyk; m. Elisabeth B. Sawczynska, Aug. 7, 1956; 1 dau., Magdalena-Lynn. Habilitation, Warsaw Tech. U., Poland, 1962; M.A. Sci. in English, Silesian Tech. U., Gliwice, Poland, 1950, D.Sc., 1956. Diplomate: registered profl. engr., Ont. Research engr. Silesian Tech. U., 1951-56, sr. lectr., 1956-63; head tech. lab. Hydroproject Cons., Gliwice, 1956-63; v.p., research prof. Water Mgmt. Research Inst., Warsaw, 1964-69; prof. civil engring. U. Toronto, 1969—; cons. Bio-San Cons., Warsaw, 1968-69; mem. panel of experts WHO, Geneva, 1966-72; pres. J. Ganczarczyk & Assocs., Toronto, 1975—. Author: Activated Sludge Treatment, 1966, 1969, 1983; inventor utilization of desulfurization slag, 1983. Recipient award Ministry of Constrn., Warsaw, 1968, Polish State award Award Com., Warsaw, 1969. Fellow Royal Soc. Health; mem. Water Pollution Control Fedn., Internat. Assn. Water Pollution Research, Internat. Assn. Gt. Lakes Research, Assn. Environ. Engring. Profs. Roman Catholic. Club: Faculty (Toronto). Home: 83 Edenbridge Dr Islington ON Canada M9A 3G5 Office: U Toronto Dept Civil Engring Toronto ON Canada M5S 1A4

GANDER, JOHN EDWARD, biochemistry educator; b. Roundup, Mont., Mar. 9, 1925; s. Loren Dwight and Blanche Lenore (Mackay) G.; m. Dorothy Alice Hoffman, Jan. 1, 1951; children: Sharon Lee, Peggy Corinne, Linda Kay. B.S. in Agr, Mont. State U., 1950; M.S. in Biochemistry, U. Minn., 1954, Ph.D., 1956. Asst. prof. chemistry Mont. State U., Bozeman, 1955-58; asst. prof. agrl. biochemistry Ohio State U., Columbus, 1958-62, asso. prof., 1962-64, U. Minn., St. Paul, 1964-68, prof. biochemistry, 1968—. Contbr. chpts. to books, articles to profl. jours. and encys. Served with USAAF, 1943-46. Recipient Research Career award NIH, 1966-71; research grantee USPHS, 1960-69, 74—, NSF, 1957-75, 80-84. Mem. Am. Soc. Biol. Chemists, Am. Chem. Soc., AAAS, Phytochem. Soc. N.Am., Am. Soc. Plant Physiology, Sigma Xi, Alpha Chi Sigma. Presbyterian. Lodge: Masons. Home: 1743 Skillman Ave W Saint Paul MN 55113

GANGEL, KENNETH OTTO, seminary professor; b. Paterson, N.J., June 14, 1935; s. Otto John and Rose Marie (Schneider) G.; m. Elizabeth Blackburn, Sept. 1, 1956; children: Jeffrey Scott, Julie Lynn. B.A. in Bus. Adminstrn, Taylor U., 1957; M.Div. cum laude, Grace Theol. Sem., 1960; M.A. in Christian Edn, Fuller Sumner Sem., 1960; S.T.M., Concordia Sem., 1963; Ph.D. in Coll. Adminstrn, U. Mo.-Kansas City, 1969; postgrad. in coll. finance, Fla. State U., 1973. Ordained to ministry Baptist Gen. Conf.; mem. faculty Calvary Bible Coll., Kansas City, Mo., 1960-70, dir. Christian service, 1960-63, registrar, 1963-66, acad. dean, 1966-69, acad. v.p., 1969-70; adminstrv. asst. for acad. affairs Kansas City (Mo.) Regional Council for Higher Edn., 1968-69; prof., dir. Sch. Christian Edn., Trinity Evang. Div. Sch., Deerfield, Ill., 1970-74; pres. Miami (Fla.) Christian Coll., 1974-82; prof., chmn. dept. Christian edn. Dallas Theol. Sem., 1982—; Speaker, lectr. to numerous chs., schs., seminars throughout U.S. and fgn. countries, 1960—. Author: Understanding Teaching, 1968; biography of Walter L. Wilson Beloved Physician, 1970; Leadership for Church Education, 1970, The Family First, 1972, So You Want To Be A Leader!, 1973, Between Christian Parent and Child, 1974, Competent To Lead, 1974, 24 Ways to Improve Your Teaching, 1974, You and Your Spiritual Gifts, 1975, Thus Spake Qoheleth, 1983, Unwrap Your Spiritual Gifts, 1983, Toward a Harmony of Faith and Learning, 1983, Christian Education: Its History and Philosophy, 1983; Contbg. editor: Jour. Psychology and Theology; Contbr. numerous articles to ch. publs. Bd. dirs. Ft. Wayne Bible Coll., Scripture Press Ministries, Evang. Tchr. Tng. Assn. Named Distinguished Alumnus of Year Grace Theol. Sem., 1973, Alumni Achievement award U. Mo. at Kansas City, 1975; Chamber of Achievement award Taylor U., 1976; Am. Assn. Theol. Schs. postdoctoral research grantee, 1972-73. Mem. NEA, Am. Assn. Higher Edn., Nat. Christian Sch. Edn. Assn., Nat. Assn. Evangelicals, Nat. Assn. Profs. Christian Edn. (past pres., 1st v.p.), Fla. Bd. Ind. Colls. and Univs. Office: Dallas Theol Seminary 3909 Swiss Ave Dallas TX 75204 *My life has found its meaning in the search for and communication of a distinctively Christian philosophy of higher education.*

GANGWERE, GEORGE HENRY, JR., lawyer; b. Pitts., July 5, 1917; s. George Henry and Pauline (Brown) G.; m. Blanche M. Gregory, June 30, 1946; children: George Henry III, Margaret, Robert. Student, Youngstown Coll., 1935-37; A.B., U. Mich., 1940, LL.B., 1947. Bar: Mo. 1948. Since practiced in, Kansas City; partner firm Swanson, Midgley, Gangwere, Clarke & Kitchin (and predecessors), 1952—; gen. counsel Nat. Collegiate Athletic Assn.; pres. Estate Planning Council Kansas City., Mo., 1966; dir. Mo. Bank & Trust Co. Served to capt. AUS, 1941-46; ETO. Decorated Bronze Star. Mem. Lawyers Assn. Kansas City (sec. 1964-66, treas. 1960, v.p. 1976-77, pres. 1980-81), ABA, Mo. Bar Assn. (bd. govs. 1970-72), U. Mich. Alumni Assn. (dir. 1962-64), Am. Legion (past post comdr.), VFW, Kansas City (Mo.) C. of C., Kansas City Real Estate Bd., Friends of Kansas City (Mo.) Zoo (pres. 1978-80, dir. 1977-81), Alpha Sigma Phi. Clubs: U. Mich. (pres. 1955), Kansas City, Rotary, Blue Hills Country (Kansas City) (pres. 1969). Home: 6940 Edgevale Rd Kansas City MO 64113 Office: Commerce Bank Bldg Kansas City MO 64106

GANI, JOSEPH MARK, statistics educator, administrator, researcher; b. Cairo, Dec. 15, 1924; U.S., 1981; s. Mark Joseph and Lucie (Israel) G.; m. Ruth Stephens, Sept. 3, 1955; children: Jonathan, Miriam, Matthew, Sarah. B.Sc., Inperial Coll. London U., 1947; diploma, Imperial Coll., 1948; Ph.D., Australian Nat. U., Canberra, 1955; D.Sc., London U., 1970. Lectr. math stats. U. Western Australia, Perth, 1953-57, sr. lectr., 1957-59, reader, 1959-60; sr. fellow Australian Nat. U., 1961-64; prof. U. Sheffield, Eng., 1965-74; chief div. math. and stats. Commonwealth Sci. and Indsl. Research Orgn., Canberra, 1974-81; prof. stats., chmn. dept. U. Ky., Lexington, 1981—. Author: The Condition of Science in Australian Universities, 1963; editor: Perspectives in Probability and Statistics, 1975, The Making of Statisticians, 1982; editor in chief: Applied Probability Jours., 1964—; advisor: Springer-Verlag Series in Statistics, 1976—. Gov. High Storrs Sch., Sheffield, 1971-74; founder mem. South Yorkshire Family Housing Assn., Sheffielf, 1972. Nuffield Found. fellow, 1956; Australian Acad. Sci. fellow, 1976. Fellow Inst. Math. Stats., Royal Statis. Soc.; mem. Am. Math. Soc., Internat. Statis. Inst., Australian Math. Soc. (pres. 1978-80). Office: Dept of Statistics U of Ky Lexington KY 40506 Office: Grove Manufacturing Company PO Box 21 Shady Grove PA 17256

GANLEY, BARRY S., data processing executive; b. Cleve., June 6, 1942; s. Paul and Fay (Corbe) G.; m. Barbara Simmons, June 10, 1977; children: Jason Keith, Carri Dawn. B.A. in Math., Calif. State U.-Northridge, 1966, B.S. in Bus., 1972, M.S. in Bus. Adminstrn., 1974. Pres., v.p. US Life Systems Corp., Pasadena, Calif., 1972-76; dir. info. systems Cedars-Sinai Med. Ctr., Los Angeles, 1976-82; sr. v.p. Nat. Med. Enterprises Inc., Los Angeles, 1982—; pres. Productive Data Mgmt., Los Angeles, 1982—. Served with USMC. Office: Nat Med Enterprises Inc 11920 Wilshire Blvd Los Angeles CA 90025

GANLEY, JAMES FRANCIS, banker; b. Bklyn., Dec. 21, 1935; s. John Joseph and Mae (Hannon) G.; m. Geraldine Curtin, May 11, 1963; children: Sheila, James P. B.S. in Econs, NYU. With Irving Trust Co., N.Y.C., 1956—, asst. v.p., then v.p., mgr. record services, 1969-75, sr. v.p., div. mgr., 1975-80, exec. v.p. banking ops. group, 1980—; dir. Depository Trust Co., N.Y.C.; mem. steering com. N.Y. Clearing House. Office: 1 Wall St New York NY 10015

GANLEY, OSWALD HAROLD, university official; b. Amsterdam, Holland, Jan. 28, 1929; U.S., 1947, naturalized, 1952; s. Eric Harold and Emily (Auerbach) G.; m. Gladys Dickens, Sept. 3, 1950; children: Robert C., Delia A. A.B., Hope Coll., 1950; M.S., Ph.D., U. Mich., 1953; M.P.A., Harvard U., 1965. Research asst. Walter Reed Inst., 1953-55; research assoc. Merck Inst. Therapeutic Research, Rahway, N.J., 1955-60; asst. dir. internat. relations Merck, Sharp and Dohme Research Labs., Rahway, 1960-64; head tech. div. Bur. Internat. Sci. and Tech. Affairs, State Dept., 1965-66, head European affairs, 1966-69; sci. attaché Am. Embassy, Rome and Bucharest, 1969-73; dir. Soviet and Eastern European sci. and tech. affairs State Dept., Washington, 1973-75, dep. asst. sec. for tech. affairs, 1975-78; research assoc. John F. Kennedy Sch. Govt., Harvard U., Cambridge, Mass., 1978-80; exec. dir. Harvard Program Info. Resources Policy, 1980—. Contbr. articles to sci. jours. Dir. Jaycees, 1958-60; dir. pub. relations Civil Def., Plainfield, N.J., 1962-64; Bd. dirs. Am. Hosp., Rome, Fullbright Commn. Served with AUS, 1953-55. Sci. and Pub. Policy fellow Harvard U., 1964-65. Fellow Am. Acad. Microbiology; mem. Am. Physiol. Soc., Am. Soc. Microbiology, Sigma Xi. Clubs: Circolo Catoniere Tevereremo (Rome); Cosmos; Harvard (N.Y.C.). Office: 200 Aiken Harvard U Cambridge MA 02138

GANN, ERNEST KELLOGG, author; b. Lincoln, Nebr., Oct. 13, 1910; s. George Kellogg and Caroline (Kupper) G.; m. Eleanor Michaud, Sept. 18, 1933 (div.); children: George Kellogg (dec.), Steven Anthony, Polly Wing; m. Dodie Post, May 20, 1966. Student, Culver Mil. Acad., Yale U. Sch. Fine Arts. Author: Island in the Sky, Blaze of Noon, Fiddler's Green, Benjamin Lawless, The High and the Mighty, Soldier of Fortune, Twilight for the Gods, Trouble with Lazy Ethel, Fate is the Hunter, Of Good and Evil; In the Company of Eagles, Song of the Sirens, The Antagonists, Band of Brothers, Flying Circus, Hostage to Fortune; Author also many short stories. Served as capt. Air Transport Command AUS, 1942-46. Home: Red Mill Farm San Juan Island WA 98250 *"Success" is an elusive quantity, but whatever recognition I have received is due to the free and wonderful American society which has allowed me to think and live as I please.* *

GANN, GENE E., retired steel manufacturing company executive; b. New Castle, Ind., Mar. 5, 1917; s. John C. and Lilah (Gary) G.; m. Jessie C. Torrence, Aug. 7, 1936; 1 dau., Patricia Sampson. Grad. high sch. Supr. Ford Motor Co., Dearborn, Mich., 1940-44; v.p., gen. mgr. Gaylord Mfg. Co., Mich., 1946-54; exec. v.p. McLouth Steel Corp., Detroit, 1954-73, pres., chief operating officer, 1973-75, chmn. bd., chief exec. officer, 1975-82, ret., 1982; pres., dir. Ashland Mining Corp., 1968-82; v.p., dir. Empire Mining Co., 1963-82; chmn. bd. Jackson Gear Co., Brooklyn, Mich., 1982—. Served with USMCR, 1944-46. Clubs: Detroit Athletic, Recess, Oakland Hills Country, Detroit (Detroit); Otsego Ski (Gaylord, Mich.); Bloomfield Hills Country. Home: 27277 Rackham Dr Lathrup Village MI 48076 Office: Jackson Gear Co Brooklyn MI

GANNON, SISTER ANN IDA, philosophy educator, former college president; b. Chgo., 1915; d. George and Hanna (Murphy) G. A.B., Clarke Coll., 1941; A.M., Loyola U., Chgo., 1948, LL.D., 1970; Ph.D., St. Louis U., 1952; Litt.D., DePaul U., 1972; L.H.D., Lincoln Coll., 1965, Columbia Coll., 1969, Luther Coll., 1969, Marycrest Coll., 1972, Ursuline Coll., 1972, Spertus Coll. Judaica, 1974, Holy Cross Coll., 1974, Rosary Coll., 1975, St. Ambrose Coll., 1975, St. Leo Coll., 1976, Mt. St. Joseph Coll., 1976, Stritch Coll., 1976, Stonehill Coll., 1976, Elmhurst Coll., 1977, Manchester Coll., 1977, Marymount Coll., 1977, Governor's State U., 1979, Seattle U., 1981, St. Michael's Coll., 1984. Mem. Sisters of Charity, B.V.M.; tchr. English St. Mary's High Sch., Chgo., 1941-47; residence, study abroad, 1951; chmn. philosophy dept. Mundelein Coll., 1951-57, pres., 1957-75, mem. faculty philosophy dept., 1975—; Dir. S.F.N. Cos., Inc., NICOR, Inc. Contbr. articles philos. jours. Mem. Adv. Bd. Sec. Navy, 1975-80, Chgo. Police Bd., 1979—; bd. dirs. Am. Council on Edn., 1971-75, chmn., 1973—; nat. bd. dirs. Girl Scouts U.S.A., 1966-74, nat. adv. bd., 1976—; trustee St. Louis U., 1974—, Ursuline Coll., Cath. Theol. Union, 1983—; bd. dirs. Newberry Library, 1976—, WTTW Pub. TV, 1976—, Parkside Human Services Corp., 1983—. Recipient Laetare medal, 1975; LaSallian award, 1975; Aquinas award, 1976; Chgo. Assn. Commerce and Industry award, 1976; Hesburgh award, 1982. Mem. Am. Cath. Philos. Assn. (exec. council 1953-56), Assn. Am. Colls. (dir. 1965—, chmn. 1969-70), Religious Edn. Assn. Am. (pres. 1973, chmn. bd. 1975-78), N. Central Assn. (commn. on colls. and univs. 1971-78, chmn. exec. bd. 1975-77, dir.), Assn. Governing Bds. Colls. and Univs. (dir. 1979—), AAUW, Metaphys. Soc. Am. Address: 6363 Sheridan Rd Chicago IL 60660

GANNON, JAMES PATRICK, newspaper editor; b. Mpls., July 6, 1939; s. Lawrence Patrick and Nora G.; m. Joan Dorothy Ring, Aug. 12, 1961; children: Julia, Michael, Elizabeth, Virginia, Christopher, Marcella. B.A., Marquette U., Milw., 1961. With Wall St. Jour., 1961-78, chief econ. writer, 1973-76, polit. writer, 1976-78; exec. editor, v.p. Des Moines Register and Tribune, 1978-82, editor, 1982—. Mem. Am. Soc. Newspaper Editors. Roman Catholic. Office: 715 Locust St Des Moines IA 50309

GANNON, JOHN A., labor union official. Pres. Internat. Assn. Fire Fighters. Office: 1750 New York Ave NW Washington DC 20006§

GANNON, JOHN DEANE, consulting editor; b. Madison, Wis., Mar. 2, 1907; s. Thomas C. and Anna (Welsh) G.; m. Doretha V. Schoman, Aug. 29, 1936; children: James T., John D. A.B., U. Wis., 1930. Spl. agt. Aetna Life Ins. Co., 1931-33; bank examiner Wis. State Banking Dept., Madison, 1933-38, securities examiner, 1938-39, supr. credit union div., 1939-53; dir. bur. fed. credit unions HEW, 1953-70; dep. adminstr. Nat. Credit Union Adminstrn., Washington, 1970-73; cons., asso. editor Report on Credit Unions, 1974—. Staff mem. Pres.'s Com. on Financial Instns., 1963. Recipient Presdl. citation, 1964, Exceptional Service award Nat. Credit Union Adminstrn., 1983. Club: Exchequer (Washington) (chancellor 1969-70). Home: 4806 Dover Rd Bethesda MD 20816 Office: Reports Inc 700 Orange St Wilmington DE 19801

GANNON, PHILIP JEROME, college president; b. New Baltimore, Mich., July 23, 1922; s. John and Martha Rebecca (Forrest) G.; m. Lois Ann Lange, July 22, 1950; children: Michael, Kathleen, Thomas. B.A., Albion Coll., 1947; M.A., Mich. State U., 1954, Ph.D., 1979. Lab. instr. zoology Duke U., 1948-49; sci. tchr. Battle Creek (Mich.) Pub. Schs., 1949-53; research cons. Mich. State U., 1955-56; spl. asst. to supt. Lansing (Mich.) Pub. Schs., 1956-57; dean Lansing Community Coll., 1957-64, pres., 1964—; dir. Bank of Lansing. Mem. Lansing Human Relations Com., Mich. Higher Edn. Facilities Commn., 1968—; chmn. govt. and edn. com. United Community Chest, 1969—; pres. Capitol Area United Way, Inc., 1974-75, Ednl. Ptnrs. for Internat. Cooperation, Inc.; mem. Gov.'s Task Force on Governance and Coordination; leader goodwill missions to Shiga, Japan, 1981, 83; trustee Detroit Inst. Tech.; chmn. local-state relations subcom. Legis. Task Force; spl. cons. Tech. Edn. Research Inst., Korean Ministry Edn., 1980-81; Bd. dirs., pres. Lansing Gen. Hosp., Econ. Devel. Corp.; mem. govtl. relations com. Am. Council on Edn. Served to capt. USNR. Recipient Disting. Alumni award Albion Coll., 1971; Community Service award Lansing Regional C. of C., 1975; Gov.'s Minuteman award, 1978. Mem. North Central Assn. Colls. and Secondary Schs. (commr. 1967-71, govtl. relations com.), Mich. Community Coll. Assn. (Disting. Service award 1965, pres.), Mich. Assn. Higher Edn. (pres.), Am. Assn. Community and Jr. Colls. (commn. on govtl. affairs), Kappa Delta Pi, Phi Delta Kappa. Club: Rotary. Home: 2107 Holiday Ln Lansing MI 48917 Office: 419 N Capitol St PO Box 40010 Lansing MI 48901

GANNON, THOMAS MICHAEL, sociology educator; b. Chgo., Oct. 19, 1936; s. Thomas Michael and Bernice Day (Pouk) G. A.B., Loyola U., Chgo., 1959, M.A., 1961, Ph.L., 1961; S.T.L., Jesuit Sch. Theology, 1968; Ph.D., U. Chgo., 1972. Asst. prof. Loyola U. Chgo., 1972-74, assoc. prof., 1974-77, prof., 1978-82, chmn. dept. sociology, 1972-82; cons. Ill. Youth Commn., Chgo., 1965-68; research cons. Chgo.-Cook County Criminal Justice Commn., 1968-71; chmn. Jesuit Conf. Commn. on Formation, 1975-81; cons. Office of Pastoral Research, N.Y.C., 1979—; dir. Woodstock Theol. Ctr. Georgetown U., 1983—, prof. siciology, 1983—. Author The Desert and the City, 1968; editor The Jesuits in the U.S., 1971, Military Ethics and Civilian control, 1975. NIMH grantee, 1974; Mellon Found. grantee, 1980; named Faculty Mem. of Year Loyola U. Chgo., 1983. Fellow Religious Research Assn. (pres. 1970-73), Assn. for Sociology of Religion (pres. 1977-78), Am. Sociol. Assn.; mem. Internat. Conf. Sociology of Religion (U.S. sec. 1971—). Address: Woodstock Theol Ctr Georgetown U. Washington DC 20057

GANO, JOHN, lawyer; b. Dallas, Sept. 26, 1924; s. John Thomas and Olga Lucie (Lightfoot) G.; m. Betty Jeanne McIver, Dec. 21, 1948; 1 son, Stephen McIver. Student, Tex. Christian U., 1942-43, 46; LL.B., U. Tex., 1950, U. Maine, 1943-44, Georgetown U., 1943. Bar: Tex. 1950; Cert. personal injury trial specialist. Partner firm Gano & Gano, Dallas, 1950-51; asst. city atty., Fort Worth, 1953-59, sr. asst. city atty., Houston, 1959-64; partner firm Jamail & Gano, Houston, 1964-78; sr. partner firm Gano & Donovan, Houston, 1979—. Served with 77th Inf. Div. AUS, 1943-46; to 1st lt. F.A. AUS, 1952-53; Philippines, Okinawa, Germany. Mem. Tex., Houston bar assns., Am., Tex. trial lawyers assns., Am. Arbitration Assn., Phi Kappa Psi. Home: 715 Cinnamon Oak Ln Houston TX 77079 Office: 2500 West Loop South Suite 595 Houston TX 77027

GANOE, CHARLES STRATFORD, banker; b. Abington, Pa., July 16, 1929; s. Robert L. and Leonette (Rehfuss) G.; m. Frances-Sue Williams, Apr. 2, 1960; children: F. Hemsley, Alice N. B.A., Princeton U., 1951; M.B.A., U. Pa., 1952. With Fidelity-Phila. Trust Co. (now Fidelity Bank), 1952—, asst. treas., 1956-60, asst. v.p., 1960-61, v.p. 1961-66, sr. v.p., 1966-69, exec. v.p. charge internat. dept., 1969-75, exec. v.p., dir., 1975-79; exec. v.p. N.Y. Bank for Savs. (name now Goldome Bank), N.Y.C., 1979-82; sr. v.p. Am. Express Internat. Banking Corp., N.Y.C., 1982—; v.p. Co. for Investing Abroad (became Fidelity Internat. Corp., merged into Fidelity Internat. Bank 1972), 1963-65, pres., dir., 1965-72; dir., chmn. exec. com. Fidelity Internat. Bank, N.Y.C., 1970-79; mem. adv. com. Export-Import Bank U.S., 1973-74. Co-author: Offshore Lending by U.S. Commercial Banks; Contbr. articles to profl. jours. Class agt. Class of 1951 Princeton U., 1954-56, treas., 1956-61, v.p., 1981—; bd. dirs. Phila. Council for Internat. Visitors, 1963-69, chmn., 1969-73; mem. Phila. Dist. Export Council, 1966-75. Recipient Duning Meml. awards Robert Morris Assos., 1962, 65, 68. Mem. Bankers Assn. for Fgn. Trade (dir. 1969—, v.p. 1971-72, exec. v.p. 1972-73, pres. 1973-74), Council Fgn. Relations, Robert Morris Assos. (past pres. Phila. chpt.), Greater Phila. C. of C. (sec. 1960-64, treas. 1960-70, dir. 1960-73, mem. adminstrv. com.), Wharton Grad. Sch. Alumni Assn. (past pres.), Delta Psi. Clubs: Princeton (Phila.) (past gov.); Merion Cricket (Haverford, Pa.); Princeton (N.Y.C.); Princeton (N.J.) Elm; Ausable (St. Huberts, N.Y.). Home: 458 The Great Rd Princeton NJ 08540 Office: 125 Broad St New York NY 10004

GANONG, WILLIAM F(RANCIS), physician, physiologist; b. Northampton, Mass., July 6, 1924; s. William Francis and Anna (Hobbet) G.; m. Ruth Jackson, Feb. 22, 1948; children: William Francis, Susan B., Anna H., James E. A.B. cum laude, Harvard U., 1945, M.D. magna cum laude, 1949. Intern, jr. asst. resident in medicine Peter Bent Brigham Hosp., Boston, 1949-51, asst. in medicine and surgery, 1952-55; research fellow medicine and surgery Harvard U., 1952-55; asst. prof. physiology U. Calif., San Francisco, 1955-60, asso. prof., 1960-64, prof., 1964-82, Jack D. and Deloris Lange prof., 1982—, faculty research lectr., 1968, vice chmn. dept., 1963-68, chmn., 1970—; cons. Calif. Dept. Mental Hygiene. Author: Review of Medical Physiology, 11th edit., 1983; editor: (with L. Martini) Neuroendocrinology, vol. I, 1966, vol. II, 1967, Frontiers in Neuroendocrinology, 1969, 71, 73, 76, 78, 80, 82, 84; editor-in-chief: Neuroendocrinology, 1979—. Served with U.S. Army, 1943-46; served to capt. M.C., 1951-52. Recipient Boylston Med. Soc. prize Harvard U., 1949. Fellow AAAS; mem. Am. Physiol. Soc. (pres. 1977-78), Assn. Chairmen Depts. Physiology (pres. 1976-77), Am. Soc. Zoologists, Soc. Exptl. Biology and Medicine, Endocrine Soc., Chilean Endocrine Soc. (corr.), Internat. Brain Research Orgn., Nat. Soc. Med. Research, Soc. for Neurosci., Internat. Soc. Neuroendocrinology (v.p. 1976-80). Home: 710 Hillside Ave Albany CA 94706 Office: Dept Physiology U Calif San Francisco CA 94143

GANS, CARL, zoologist; b. Hamburg, Ger., Sept. 7, 1923; came to U.S., 1939, naturalized, 1945; s. Samuel S. and Else Hubertine (Leeser) G.; m. Kyoko Andow, Nov. 18, 1961. B.M.E., N.Y. U., 1944; M.S., Columbia U., 1950; Ph.D. in Biology, Harvard U., 1957. Contract and service engr. Babcock & Wilcox Co., 1947-55; from asst. prof. to prof. biology, chmn. dept. biology State U. N.Y., Buffalo, 1958-71; prof. zoology U. Mich., Ann Arbor, 1971—, chmn. dept., 1971-75; research scientist Mus. Zoology, 1971—; research asso. Carnegie Mus., 1953—, Am. Mus. Natural History, 1958—; sec., bd. dirs. Zool. Soc. Buffalo, 1961-71; med. adv. council Detroit Zool. Park, 1973—; cons. in field, vis. prof. univs. and colls. Author: Biomechanics, 1974, Reptiles of the World, 1975; co-author: Photographic Atlas of Shark Anatomy, 1964; Gen. editor: Biology of the Reptilia, 13 vols., 1969-82; mng. editor: Jour. Morphology, 1968—. Served with AUS, 1944-47. Guggenheim fellow, 1953, 77; NSF predoctoral fellow, 1956-57; postdoctoral fellow U. Fla., Gainesville, 1957-58; grantee NSF, NIH, others. Fellow N.Y. Zool. Soc., Zool. Soc. London, AAAS, Zool. Soc. India, Acad. Zoology India; mem. Am. Soc. Zoologists (pres. 1977), ASME, Soc. Study Evolution (v.p. 1971), Am. Soc. Ichthyology and Herpetology (gov. 1961, 70, 76, pres. 1979), Am. Inst. Biol. Scis. (gov. bd. 1975-78), Soc. Study Amphibians and Reptiles (pres. 1983), Am. Assn. Anatomists, Soc. Exptl. Biology, Am. Physiol. Soc., Senckenberg. Naturforsch. Gesellschaft (corr.). Home: 2811 Park Ridge Dr Ann Arbor MI 48103 Office: 2127 Natural Scis Bldg Univ Mich Ann Arbor MI 48109

GANS, HERBERT J., sociology educator; b. Cologne, Germany, May 7, 1927; came to U.S., 1940, naturalized, 1945; s. Carl M. and Elise (Plaut) G.; m. Louise Gruner, Mar. 19, 1967; 1 son, David. Ph.B., U. Chgo., 1947, M.A., 1950; Ph.D., U. Pa., 1957. Planner pvt. and pub. planning agys., Chgo. and Washington, 1950-53; from lectr. to asso. prof. urban studies and planning U. Pa., 1953-64; from asso. prof. to adj. prof. sociology Tchrs. Coll., Columbia, also sr. staff scientist Center Urban Edn., 1964-69; prof. sociology and planning Mass. Inst. Tech., also Mass. Inst. Tech.-Harvard Joint Center for Urban Studies, 1969-71; prof. sociology Columbia (Ford Found. Urban chair), 1971—; sr. research asso. Center for Policy Research, 1971-80; film critic Social Policy mag., 1971-78; cons. Ford Found., HEW, Nat. Adv. Commn. Civil Disorders; dir. Trans-action, Inc. Author: The Urban Villagers, 1962, 2d edit., 1982, The Levittowners, 1967, 82, People and Plans, 1968, More Equality, 1973, Popular Culture and High Culture, 1974, Deciding What's News (Theatre Library Assn. award 1979), 1979 (1980 Book award Nat. Assn. Ednl. Broadcasters); co-editor: On the Making of Americans, 1979; adv. editor: Jour. Am. Inst. Planners, 1965-75, Urban Life, 1971—, Am. Jour. Sociology, 1972-74, Society, 1971-76, Social Policy, 1971—, Pub. Opinion Quar., 1972—, Jour. Communications, 1974—, Ethnic and Racial Studies, 1977—, Internat. Ency. Communications, 1984—. Bd. dirs. Ams. For Democratic Action, 1969-75, Met. (formerly Suburban) Action Inst., 1974—. Served with AUS, 1945-46. Guggenheim fellow, 1977-78; German Marshall Fund research fellow, 1984. Fellow Am. Sociol. Assn. (exec. council 1968-71), Am. Acad. Arts and Scis.; mem. Soc. Study of Social Problems (exec. com. 1968-71), Eastern Sociol. Soc. (pres. 1972-73), Sociol. Research Assn. Home: 435 Riverside Dr New York NY 10025 Office: 404 Fayerweather Hall Columbia U New York NY 10027

GANS, HIRAM SELIG, lawyer; b. N.Y.C., July 13, 1905; s. Joseph and Delia (London) G.; m. Ethelyne P. Holzman. B.S., Harvard U., 1926; J.D., NYU, 1929. Bar: N.Y. 1929. Mng. clk. Root, Clark, Buckner & Ballantine, N.Y.C., 1928-31; mem. firm Amen, Gans & Butler, N.Y.C. and, Amen, Gans, Butler & Hardy, Washington, 1948-58, Gans, Davis & O'Neill Ltd.; dir. trustee, gen. counsel Spanish-Am. Bd. Trade, Inc.; chmn., chief exec. officer Universitech, Inc.; chmn. Republic Realty Cos. Inc., Varied Ventures Inc.; chmn. bd. Cinedine Inc.; counsel for Protective Com. Mortgage Bonds, Hudson & Manhattan R.R. Co., Third Ave. Transit System in reorgn. N.Y., Westchester & Boston Ry., N.Y., N.H. & H. reorgn., Fonda, Johnstown & Gloversville Ry., Nat. Rys. of Mexico, Philippine Ry., Brockway Motors, Army and Navy Investment Trust Co., Eng., Bankers Investment Trust Co.; reorgn. mgr. Eastern Paper & Pulp Co.; spl. counsel U.S. Atty. Gen. for enemy alien corps taken over by Office Alien Property U.S. Dept. Justice. Trustee, mem. exec. com. Children's Cancer Research Found., Boston; life trustee Dana-Farber Cancer Inst., Boston; bd. dirs., sec., counsel Just One Break, Inc.; bd. dirs., pres., chmn. N.Y.C. Symphony, 1958-65, pres., 1966-74; mem. bd. edn. Tuxedo (N.Y.) Pub. Sch. Dist., 1966-80; chmn. planning com. mil. govt. finance U.S. Zone, Germany, 1945; chief fgn. exchange controls br. SHAEF. Served to maj. U.S. Army, 1942-46; with Signal Corps, 3d Inf. Div.; N. Africa and Sicily; instr. Am. Sch. Center; Shrivenham, Eng.; chief Fin. Instns. br. G-5 SHEAF; dep. dir. Div. Investigation of Cartels, U.S. Group Control Council for Germany; editor Finance and Property Control Tech. Manual for Mil. Govt. in Germany; U.S. mem. quadripartite coms. on central banking, financial instns., fgn. exchange in Allied Control Council for Germany, 1945. Decorated Bronze Star medal, Invasion Arrowhead, Expert Combat Inf. badge. Mem. Mil. Govt. Assn. (pres., chmn. exec. com. and bd. dirs.), Am., Fed., N.Y. State, Internat. bar assns, Am. Judicature Soc., Am. Soc. Internat. Law., AIM (pres.'s council), Clarion Music Soc. (chmn. 1960-64). Clubs: Harvard, City Midday, Harvard Varsity, City, Lotos (N.Y.C.); United Hunts (London, Eng.); Nat. Lawyers (Washington). Address: PO Box 728 Tuxedo Park NY 10987

GANT, DONALD ROSS, investment banker; b. Long Branch, N.J., Oct. 5, 1928; s. Raymond LeRoy and Evelyn (Ross) G.; m. Jane Harriet Taylor, Sept. 12, 1953; children: Laura R., Christopher T., Sarah R., Alison A. B.S., U. Pa., 1952; M.B.A., Harvard U., 1954. Assoc. Goldman, Sachs & Co., N.Y.C., 1954-64, ptnr., 1965—; dir. Diebold, Inc., Canton, Ohio, 1977—, Liquid Air Corp., San Francisco, 1973—, United Brands Co., N.Y.C., 1972—. Mem. exec. council Harvard Grad. Sch. Bus. Adminstrn., Cambridge, Mass., 1981-84. Served with U.S. Army, 1946-48. Republican. Presbyterian. Home: Young's Rd New Vernon NJ 07976 Office: Goldman Sachs & Co 85 Broad St New York NY 10004

GANT, GEORGE ARLINGTON LEE, chemist; b. Wilson, N.C., Dec. 5, 1941; s. George William and Georgia (Cooke) G.; m. Ruth Jacqueline Jeffers, Dec. 5, 1964; children: Jon Patrick, Jeannine Patricia. B.S., N.C. Agrl. and Tech. State U., 1962, M.S., 1965; M.B.A., Central Mich. U., 1973; P.M.D., Harvard U., 1980. Chemist Down Corning Corp., Midland, Mich., 1965-66, research chemist, 1966-72, research group leader, 1972-75, sr. supr. tech. service and devel., 1975-77, sect. mgr. tech. service and devel., 1977-79, mgr. elastomers tech. service and devel., 1979-83, program mgr., 1983—; instr., lectr. in field. Contbr. articles to profl. jours.; patentee in field. Mem. Mich. Multiple Sclerosis Soc., 1974—, v.p., 1977-78, pres., 1978-81, chmn. bd. trustees, 1983—; mem. adv. bd. Lake Huron Area Council Boy Scouts Am., 1970-73, Salvation Army, 1973-77, Adhesives and Sealants Council, 1982—; pres. Midland Black Coalition. Mem. Am. Chem. Soc., Sigma Xi, Iota Epsilon (past pres. Central Mich. U. chpt.), Alpha Phi Alpha. Mem. Ch. of God. Club: KiWassee Midland (pres., lt. gov. 1979-80). Lodge: Kiwanis. Home: 1604 W Sugnet St Midland MI 48640 Office: Dow Corning Corp S Saginaw St Midland MI 48640

GANT, NORMAN FERRELL, JR., obstetrician and gynecologist; b. Wichita Falls, Tex., Feb. 16, 1939; s. Norman Ferrell and Eleanor (Taylor) G. B.A., North Tex. State U., Denton, 1962; M.D., U. Tex., 1964. Diplomate: Am. Bd. Obstetrics and Gynecology. Intern Parkland Meml. Hosp., Dallas, 1964-65, resident, 1965-68; mem. faculty U. Tex. Southwestern Med. Sch., Dallas, 1968—, prof. obstetrics and gynecology, 1976—, chmn. dept., 1977-83. Contbr. med. jours. Fellow Am. Coll. Obstetricians and Gynecologists; mem. Soc. Gynecologic Investigation (pub. affairs rep. 1976—), Am., Tex., Dallas County med. assns., Tex. Assn. Obstetricians and Gynecologists, Dallas-Ft. Worth Obstet. and Gynecol. Soc. Address: 5323 Harry Hines Blvd Dallas TX 75235

GANT, WILLIAM MILTON, judge; b. Ownesboro, Ky., Nov. 25, 1919; s. Archibald Stuart and Mattie Ellis (Sloane) G.; m. Mary Ellen Price, Dec. 27, 1952; children: Stuart Price, Walter Sloane. A.B., Transylvania U., 1940; LL.B., U. Ky., 1947. Bar: Ky. 1947, fed. cts. 1947, U.S. Supreme Ct. 1966. Commonwealth atty. 6th Jud. Dist., Owensboro, 1962-76; judge Ky. Ct. Appeals, Frankfort, 1976-83; justice Supreme Ct. Ky., Frankfort, 1983—. Curator Transylvania U., Lexington, Ky., 1968—. Served to 1st lt. USAAF, 1942-45. Recipient Disting. Service award Ky. Med. Assn., 1972, Ky. Council on Crime and Delinquency, 1973. Mem. ABA, Am. Judicature Soc., Ky. Bar Assn., U. Ky. Alumni Assn. (nat. pres. 1958-59, 64-65, Disting. Service award 1969). Democrat. Mem. Christian Ch. Home: 1643 Sherwood Dr Ownesboro KY 42301 Office: Supreme Ct Ky State Capitol Frankfort KY 40601

GANTCHER, NATHAN, financial services company executive; b. Boston, July 17, 1940; m. Alice Landes; children: Joel, Michael, Kimberly. B.A., Tufts Coll., 1962; M.B.A., Columbia U. Account exec. Young & Rubicam; gen. ptnr. Oppenheimer & Co., N.Y.C., pres., 1983—; bd. dirs. Mercantile House FLC; exec. v.p., dir. Oppenheimer Holdings, Inc.; pres., dir., mem. exec. com. Oppenheimer & Co., Inc.; dir. Oppenheimer & Co., Ltd.; bd. dirs., exec. com. HEM Assocs.; gen. ptnr. Iliad Ptnrs.; chmn., chief exec. officer Oppenheimer/Rouse Futures. Mem. Wall St. Planning Group, The Bond Club. Clubs: Quaker Ridge Golf, Quaker Ridge Dads (pres.), Quaker Ridge Assn. (exec. v.p.). Office: Oppenheimer & Co 1 New York Plaza New York NY 10004 *

GANTER, BERNARD J., bishop; b. Galveston, Tex., July 17, 1928; s. Bernard J. and Marie L. (Bozka) G. Grad., Tex. A&M Coll., St. Mary's Sem., LaPorte, Tex., Catholic U. Am., Washington. Adminstr., Sacred Heart Parish, Conroe, Tex., 1955-56; ordained priest Roman Catholic Ch.; sec. to Bishop W.J. Nold; asst. pastor Sacred Heart Co-Cathedral, Houston, 1956-58, rector, 1969-73; officialis Diocesan Matrimonial Tribunal, 1958-64; chancellor Diocese of Houston, 1964-69, elevated to rev. monsignor, 1969; bishop Diocese of Tulsa, 1973-77, Diocese of Beaumont, Tex., 1977—; organizer Diocesan PreCana Confs.; moderator Post Cana Club Houston; chmn. Diocesan Senate Priests. Office: Chancery Office PO Box 3948 Beaumont TX 77704 *

GANTNER, GEORGE EUGENE, JR., pathologist; b. St. Louis, June 7, 1927; s. George Eugene and Dorothy (Andrews) G.; m. Genevieve Timm, June 16, 1951; children: George Eugene III, Christine, Jeanne Marie, Thomas, Robert, Michael, Stephen. B.S., St. Louis U., 1949, M.D., 1953. Diplomate: Am. Bd. Pathology. Intern in surgery St. Mary's Group of Hosps., St. Louis, 1953-54; fellow pathology St. Louis U. Sch. Medicine, 1954-57; practice medicine, specializing in pathology, St. Louis, 1957—; asst. pathologist St. Mary's Group Hosps., 1957-58; patholoist, dir. labs. St. Louis U. Hosps., 1958—; assoc. prof. pathology St. Louis U. Sch. Medicine, 1962—, acting chmn. dept. pathology, 1965-66, prof., 1969—; coroner's pathologist, St. Louis County, 1958-68, chief med. examiner, 1969—. Author: A Practical Manual of Clinical Chemistry, vols. 1-6, 1966, Data Processing Methods for Diagnostic Codes: Systemized Nomenclature of Pathology, 1969, also articles. Served with USNR, 1945-46. Fellow Am. Acad. Forensic Scis. (gov. 1975—, pres. 1983-84), Am. Soc. Clin. Pathologists, Coll. Am. Pathologists; mem. Nat. Assn. Med. Examiners (sec.-treas.), AMA, Mo. Med. Assn., St. Louis Med. Soc., Mo. Soc. Pathologists, St. Louis Path. Soc. (pres. 1962), AAAS, Internat. Acad. Pathology, Internat. Assn. Coroners and Med. Examiners. Home: 233 Woodbourne Dr Saint Louis MO 63105 Office: 1402 S Grand Ave Saint Louis MO 63104

GANTT, JOHN W., banker; b. Atlanta, Jan. 10, 1925; s. Benjamin J. and Ruth (Wing) G.; m. Helen Conroy, July 7, 1947; children: John W., Sarah G. A.B., Harvard U., 1947; postgrad., Amos Tuck Sch. Bus. Adminstrn., Dartmouth Coll., 1957. Dist. sales mgr. Reynolds Aluminum Corp., 1947-54; with First Nat. Bank Cin., 1954—, pres., 1972-80, chmn., 1982—; pres. holding co. First Nat. Cin. Corp., 1974—; dir. William Powell Co., Cin., Cin., New Orleans & Tex. Pacific Ry. subs. So. Ry. System. Trustee Elizabeth Gamble Deaconess Home Assn., Cin., U. Cin. Found., Cin. Med. Ctr. Fund; past pres. Dan Beard council Boy Scouts Am.; active United Appeal Greater Cin., Fine Arts Fund, Community Improvement Corp. Served with Naval ROTC, 1943-46. Mem. Assn. Res. City Bankers, Am. Bankers Assn., Cin. C. of C. Clubs: Comml., Commonwealth, Queen City, Cin. Country (Cin.); Camagro. Office: First Nat Bank Cin Fifth & Walnut Sts Cincinnati OH 45201 *

GANTZ, CARROLL MELVIN, industrial design executive, consumer product designer; b. Sellersville, Pa., Sept. 9, 1931; s. Melvin Charles G. and Leona Alberta (Hornberger) Barner; m. Lorraine Sachs, Mar. 5, 1955; children: Erika Christine, Mitchell Allen. B.F.A., Carnegie Mellon U., 1953. Head indsl. design Hoover Co., North Canton, Ohio, 1956-72; mgr. indsl. design Back & Decker, Inc., Towson, Md., 1972-81; mgr. indsl. design Household Products Group Black & Decker (U.S.), Inc., Easton, Md., 1981—; designer canal boat St. Helena II, Canal Fulton, Ohio, 1967-70; dir. Am. Canal Soc., York, Pa., 1974-79. Patentee designs for consumer products. Bd. dirs. Stark County Hist. Soc., 1970. Served with Security Agy. U.S. Army, 1953-56. Recipient Design award Indsl. Designers Inst., 1961; Brashear scholar, 1949. Fellow Indsl. Designers Soc. Am. (pres. 1979-80, chmn. bd. 1981-82); mem. SAR, Omicron Delta Kappa, Tau Sigma Delta. Republican. Office: Black & Decker (US) Inc 515 Glebe Rd Easton MD 21601

GANTZ, MARVIN EVERETT, JR., aluminum co. exec.; b. Denver, Oct. 28, 1918; s. Marvin Everett and Mary Elizabeth (Miller) G.; m. Mary Esther Ivey, Dec. 20, 1941. Metall. Engring. degree, Colo. Sch. Mines, 1940. With Alcoa Co., 1940—, exec. v.p. mill products, Pitts., 1975-81, vice chmn., dir., 1981—. Bd. dirs. Allegheny Trails council Boy Scouts Am.; nat. bd. dirs. Jr. Achievement. Mem. NAM (dir.). Clubs: Duquesne, Lone Pine Golf, Latrobe Country, Laurel Valley Golf. Home: 102 Saxon Dr McMurray PA 15317 Office: Aluminum Company America 1501 Alcoa Bldg Pittsburgh PA 15219 *

GANTZ, WILBUR HENRY, III, health care company executive; b. York, Pa., Dec. 5, 1937; s. Wilbur Henry and Flora Shaw (Kashner) G.; m. Linda Theis, Mar. 22, 1962; children: Matthew John, Leslie Shaw, Caroline Ruhl. A.B., Princeton U., 1959; M.B.A., Harvard U., 1964. With Aetna Life Ins. Co., Hartford, Conn., 1959-62, 64-66; asst. to pres. Internat. div. Baxter Travenol Labs., Inc., Deerfield, Ill., 1967-69, asst. gen. mgr., Mexico City, 1967-69, v.p. Europe, Brussels, 1969-75, pres. Internat. div., Deerfield, Ill., 1976-79, group v.p. Internat. div., 1979, exec. v.p., dir. Internat. div., 1979-83, chief operating officer Internat. div., 1983—; dir. Harris Bankcorp, Harris Trust and Savs. Bank. Trustee, mem. pres.'s council Nat. Coll. Edn.; trustee Evanston Hosp. Corp. Clubs: Chicago, Commonwealth, Economic, Commercial (Chgo.); Sunset Ridge Country. Home: 930 Pontiac Rd Wilmette IL 60091 Office: 1 Baxter Pkwy Deerfield IL 60015

GANUS, CLIFTON LOYD, JR., clergyman, coll. pres.; b. Hillsboro, Tex., Apr. 7, 1922; s. Clifton Loyd and Martha Jewel (Bearden) G.; m. Louise Nicholas, May 27, 1943; children—Clifton Loyd III, Deborah Lynn, Charles Austin. B.A., Harding Coll., 1943; M.A., Tulane U., 1946, Ph.D., 1953; profl. diploma, Tchrs. Coll., Columbia, 1956. Ordained ministry Ch. of Christ, 1943; minister, Charleston, Miss., 1943-45; prof. history Harding Coll., Searcy, Ark., 1946—; dean Sch. Am. Studies, 1952-65, v.p., 1956-65, pres., 1965—; Dir. Finest Foods, Inc., New Orleans, First Security Bank, Searcy, Ark. Author: History of the Freedmans Bureau in Mississippi, 1953. Treas., bd. dirs. Johnnie Donaghey Wallace Found.; pres. Ark. Found. Asso. Colls.; bd. dirs. Quapaw Area council Boy Scouts Am. Recipient medals Freedoms Found., 1955, 56, 57, 58, 59, 67, 71, 77. Mem. Am. Studies Assn., So. Hist. Assn., Ark. Acad. Scis., Phi Alpha Theta, Psi Delta Sigma, Alpha Chi. Club: Lion. Home: 208 S Cross St Searcy AR 72143

GANZ, ERWIN M., consumer and industrial products executive; b. Frankfurt, Ger., Aug. 22, 1929; s. Joseph and Anna G.; m. Rosalee Rosenman, July 19, 1959 (dec.); children: Peter J., Eric L. B.S. in Acctg., Seton Hall U., South Orange, N.J., 1956. With Ronson Corp., 1962—, operating v.p. hydraulic units, Charlotte, N.C., 1970-75, exec. v.p. aerospace and indsl., Bridgewater, N.J., 1975—, also dir. Mem. Am. Ordnance Assn. Club: B'nai B'rith. Home: 20 Lenape Trail Warren NJ 07060 Office: 1 Ronson Rd Bridgewater NJ 08807

GANZ, LEO, psychology educator; b. Antwerp, Belgium, Apr. 2, 1931; U.S., 1940; s. Osias and Rose (Roisen) G.; m. Dyane N. Sherwood, June 3, 1979; m. Varda Peller, June 18, 1953 (div. 1976); children: Eric David, Karen Jennifer. B.A., CCNY, 1952; Ph.D., U. Chgo., 1959. Postdoctoral fellow Brown U., Providence, 1959-62; asst. prof. U. Calif., Riverside, 1963-66; asso. NYU, N.Y.C., 1966-67; prof. psychology Stanford U., Calif., 1967—; prof. Temple U., Phila., 1975—. Mem. Am. Psychol. Assn., Assn. Research in Vision and Ophthlamology, Psychonomic Soc., Neuroscis. Soc. Office: Stanford U Bldg 420 Stanford CA 94305

GANZ, MICHAEL JOSEPH, corporate executive; b. N.Y.C., June 18, 1928; s. Michael and Anna (Schuch) G.; m. Rita F. Klie, June 9, 1951; children: Christine Ganz McHeffey, Karen Ganz Rauch, Michael, Eric. B.S., L.I. U., 1955. Various acctg. positions Dun & Bradstreet, to 1951; with ITT, N.Y.C., 1951—, asst. treas., 1962-68, asso. treas., from 1968, v.p., 1973—; dir. ITT Financial Corp., ITT Consumer Services Corp., ITT Credit Corp., others. Served in U.S. Army, 1946-47. Office: ITT Corp 320 Park Ave New York NY 10022 *

GANZ, SAMUEL, service orgn. exec.; b. Bklyn., Nov. 12, 1911; s. Emanuel and Dora (Zahalsky) G.; m. Helen Lichtig, June 26, 1938; children: Edward, Jeffrey. B.S., CCNY, 1932, M.S., 1932; postgrad., NYU, 1941-43. Exec. in men's clothing industry, 1932-36; with N.Y. State Dept. Labor, 1936-40, U.S. Dept. Labor, Washington, 1940-66, asst. to adminstr. wage and hour and pub. contracts div., 1947-57, asst. adminstr., 1957-62; asst. dir. manpower, automation research and devel. Office Manpower, Automation and Tng., 1962-64; dep. manpower adminstr. Manpower Adminstrn., 1964-66; commr. Manpower and Career Devel. Agency, City of N.Y., 1966-69; pres. Econ. & Manpower Corp., N.Y.C., 1969—; mem. faculty New Sch. for Social Research; adj. prof. Pace U., N.Y.C., 1971-74; prof. C.W. Post Center, L.I. U., 1974-76; exec. com. Inst. Econ. Action; faculty adviser Iranian Students Forum; prof. N.Y. Inst. Tech., from 1977; mem. advisory council Ctr. for Labor and Indsl. Relations, N.Y. Inst. Tech., from 1977; adj. prof. human resources, dir. coop. edn. N.Y. Inst. Tech.; cons. in field. Contbr. articles to profl. publs. Mem. research sub-com. Nat. Manpower Adv. Com. to Secs. of Labor, and HEW, 1966-69; mem. N.Y. Gov.'s Com. on Manpower, Com. on Youth and Work, Gov.'s Task Force on Manpower and Unemployment, Task Force on Econ. Devel.; chmn. Gov.'s Subcom. on Pub. Service, Gov.'s Com. on Human Resources; mem. adv. com. Corsi Inst. Labor-Mgmt. Relations Pace U.; trustee, chmn. manpower com. Am. Found. for the Blind, 1976-79; dir., v.p. Greater N.Y. Safety Council, 1976-79. Recipient Distinguished Service award U.S. Dept. Labor, 1962, 66; commendation Mayor of N.Y.C., 1966; joint award U.S. Depts. HEW, Commerce and Labor, 1973; Superior Pub. Service award Sec. Commerce, 1974; cert. merit Minority Bus. Enterprise. Mem. Indsl. Relations Research Assn., Am. Soc. for Pub. Adminstrn., Am. Econ. Assn., Am. Vocat. Assn., N.Y. C. of C. and Industry (mem. spl. com. on environment 1971, mem. manpower devel. com. 1970-75, chmn. subcom. employment service 1974-75), N.Y. State Coop. and Experiential Edn. Assn. (v.p., pres.-elect 1982—); mem. Coop. Edn. Assn. Jewish. Home: 6700 192d St Fresh Meadows NY 11365 *As a humanist in our pluralistic society, I believe each human being should be helped to reach his or her optimum potential in a free democratic society, in a peaceful world in which our total resources and environment are preserved while progress accelerates. These goals can be achieved best through a harmonious, cooperative relationship between the public and private sectors.*

GAPEN, DELORES KAYE, librarian, educator; b. Mitchell, S.D., July 1, 1943; d. Lester S. and lena F. G. B.A., U. Wash., 1970, M.L.A., 1971. Gen. cataloger Coll. William and Mary, Williamsburg, Va., 1971-72; instr., asst. head Quick Editing Ohio State U., Columbus, 1972-74, head, 1974-77; asst. dir. tech. services Iowa State U., Ames, 1977-81; dean, prof. univ. libraries U. ALa., University, 1981—; cons. Northeast Mo. State U., 1980, Assn. Research Libraries task force on bibliog. control, 1981, Pa. State U., 1982, Conn. Coll., 982. Contbr (articles to profl. publs.). Mem. AAUP, ALA, Southeastern Library Assn., Ala. Library Assn., Bus. and Profl. Women's Assn., Beta Phi Mu, Alpha Lamba Delta. Democrat. Roman Catholic. Home: 4801 Cypress Creek Ave Tuscaloosa AL 35405 Office: University of Alabama Libraries University AL 35486

GAPLES, HARRY SERAPHIN, computer service company executive; b. St. Cloud, Minn., Feb. 11, 1935; s. Harry K. and Kalleope (Zafercke) G.; m. Rita Jean Klingbeil, June 3, 1961; children: Anthony Alexander, Rebecca Lee. B.A., U. Minn., 1957, M.A., 1960; M.B.A., U. Chgo., 1974. Instr. St. Thomas Coll., St. Paul, Minn., 1959-60; pres. Croname, Inc. subs. Control Data Corp., Chgo., 1968-70, Melabs, Inc. subs. SCM Corp., Palo Alto, Cal., 1970, Kleinschmidt SCM Corp., Deerfield, Ill., 1970—. Home: 960 North Ave Deerfield IL 60015 Office: Kleinschmidt div SCM 450 Lake-Cook Rd Deerfield IL 60015

GAPP, PAUL JOHN, journalist; b. Cleve., June 26, 1928; s. Bernard Leonard and Florence (Ganley) G.; m. Mary Joan Finch, May 16, 1970. B.S., Ohio U., 1950. Reporter, editor Columbus (Ohio) Dispatch, 1950-56; reporter, editorial page writer, feature editor Chgo. Daily News, 1956-66; exec. dir. Chgo. chpt. and Ill. council AIA, 1967; account exec. Dale O'Brien & Co., Chgo., 1968-69; dir. spl. projects, office of v.p. pub. affairs U. Chgo., 1969-72; architecture critic Chgo. Tribune, 1972—; mem. communications com. Met. Housing and Planning Council, 1968-70; bd. dirs. Nat. Building Mus., 1980-83. Contbr. articles to U.S. and fgn. newspapers, mags., profl. publs. Co-recipient Ill. AP award for best news reporting, 1965, 77; recipient Pulitzer prize for criticism, 1979; Orchid award AIA, 1980; Disting. Alumnus medal Ohio U., 1980; award for feature writing UPI, 1981. Mem. Am. Philatelic Soc., South African Philatelic Frat. (hon.), S. Allan Taylor Soc. (founder 1963, pres. 1963-76), Architects Club Chgo. (hon.), Pi Kappa Alpha. Home: 2500 N Lakeview Ave Chicago IL 60614 Office: care Chicago Tribune 435 N Michigan Ave Chicago IL 60611

GARABEDIAN, PAUL ROESEL, mathematics educator; b. Cin., Aug. 2, 1927; s. Carl A. and Margaret (Roesel) G.; m. Gladys Rappaport, Oct. 22, 1949 (div. 1963); m. Lynnel Marg, Dec. 31, 1966; children: Emily, Catherine. A.B., Brown U., 1946; A.M., Harvard U., 1947, Ph.D., 1948. Asst. prof. math. U. Calif.-Berkeley, 1949-50, Stanford U., Calif., 1950-52; assoc. prof. U. Calif.-Berkeley, 1952-56; prof. Stanford U., 1956-59; prof. math. Courant Inst. Math. Scis., NYU, 1959—; dir. Courant Math. and Computing Lab. Dept. Energy, 1972-78, dir. div. computational fluid dynamics, 1978—. Editorial bd.:

Applicable Analysis, Complex Variables and Applications; contbr. articles to profl. jours. Nat. Research Council fellow, 1948-49; Sloan Found. fellow, 1961-63; Guggenheim fellow, 1966; Fairchild Disting. scholar Calif. Inst. Tech., 1975; Guggenheim fellow, 1981-82; recipient Pub. Service Group Achievement award NASA, 1976, Cert. of Recognition Pub. Service Group Achievement award, 1980, Boris Pregal award N.Y. Acad. Scis., 1980. Mem. Nat. Acad. Scis., Am. Acad. Arts and Scis., Am. Math. Soc. (Birkhoff prize 1983), Soc. Indsl. and Applied Math., Am. Phys. Soc., AIAA. Home: 110 Bleekr St New York NY 10012 Office: New York University 251 Mercer St New York NY 10012

GARAGIOLA, JOE, radio-TV personality; b. St. Louis, Feb. 12, 1926; s. John and Angelina (Garavaglia) G.; m. Audrie Dianne Ross, Nov. 5, 1949; children: Joseph, Stephen, Gina. Ed. parochial schs. Profl. baseball player with St. Louis Cardinals, Pitts. Pirates, Chgo. Cubs and N.Y. Giants, 1946-54; engaged in radio-TV, 1955—. Broadcaster: All Star Baseball games and Game of The Week; N.Y. Yankee games; appeared on: Jack Paar show; regular mem. cast: Today Show, to 1973; broadcaster: NBC Sports, 1961—; host for Monitor programs, own radio, TV show, from 1963; author: Baseball is a Funny Game, 1960. Served with AUS, World War II. Recipient George Foster Peabody award for TV show The Baseball World of Joe Garagiola, 1974. Address: care FSM Inc One Rockefeller Plaza New York NY 10020

GARAHAN, PETER THOMAS, mining company executive; b. Queens, N.Y., Sept. 6, 1946; s. Thomas Hugh and Catherine Amelia (Slavin) G.; m. Kathy Padgett, July 15, 1972. B.A. in History and Polit. Sci, SUNY, Stony Brook, 1971; M.B.A., Cornell U., 1977. Real estate salesman Martin Assocs., Killington, Vt., 1972-75; asst. to pres., asst. to bd. dirs. United Nuclear Corp./UNC Resources, Falls Church, Va., 1977-79, treas., 1979—, v.p., 1983—. Bd. dirs. Falls Church Jr. Achievement, 1980—. Served with USNR, 1965-67. Home: 1013 Riva Ridge Dr Great Falls VA 22066 Office: 7700 Leesburg Pike Falls Church VA 22043

GARANCE, DOMINICK (D.G. GARAN), lawyer, author; b. Varaklani, Latvia, Oct. 14, 1912; came to U.S., 1950, naturalized, 1955; s. John and Virginia (Cakuls) Garans. LL.M., U. Riga, Latvia, 1935; J.U.D., U. Freiburg, Germany, 1945; LL.D., U. Paris, France, 1947; Ph.D., U. London, Eng., 1949. Bar: N.Y. 1958. Atty.-at-law, legal counsel Ministry of Welfare, Riga, 1936-42; law sec. French Mil. Govt. in Germany, Freiburg, 1945-46; documentary officer Harvard Law Sch. Internat. Program of Taxation, 1952-57; pvt. practice law, N.Y.C., 1958—. Author: The Paradox of Pleasure and Relativity, 1963, Relativity for Psychology, A Causal Law for the Modern Alchemy, 1968, The Key to the Sciences of Man, 1975, Against Ourselves: Disorders from Improvements under the Organic Limitedness of Man, 1979. Mem. ABA, N.Y. State Bar Assn., N.Y. State Trial Lawyers Assn., N.Y. Acad. Sci., Philosophy of Sci. Assn., Lacuania. Address: 2926 E 196th St New York NY 10461 *All our positive motivations and capacities, like love and interests, are satisfactions or pleasures. But satisfaction can come only from an equal need, that is nonsatisfaction; and pleasure release without equal restrictions leads to exhaustion or stress—because of our organic limitedness.*

GARAS, KAZIMER SAUL, actor, director, photographer; b. Kaunas, Lithuania, Mar. 4, 1940; came to U.S., 1949, naturalized, 1955; s. Pranas and Julia (Urbis) Gaizutis; m. Nancy Hausman, Sept. 2, 1962; children: Alexander, Katrina. B.A., U. Conn., 1962; pvt. studies in acting with, M. Katselas, S. Meisner, H. Clurman, H. Berghof. Actor in theater, films, TV, 1962—; actor, APA/Phoenix Repertory Co., 1966; appeared in: Broadway prodns. War and Peace; in off-Broadway prodns. La Mama; lead actor: The Last Safari, Paramount Pictures, 1977, Love Is a Funny Thing, United Artists, 1971; TV series Strange Report, Eng., 1968-69; actor with, Francis Ford Coppola's Zoetrope Picture Co.; appeared in numerous TV shows; producer: numerous TV shows, including Bongo Wolf's Revenge; mem. South Coast Repertory; appeared in world premier play Closely Related. Mem. Acad. Motion Pictures, Arts and Scis., Screen Actors Guild. Office: care ACM 9157 Sunset Blvd Los Angeles CA 90069 *Through my work and talents, I attempt to accentuate, emphasize, and champion the positive, the good, the noble of life's experiences, and to entertain by inspiring understanding, compassion and awareness of and for one's fellow man.*

GARAVAGLIA, BROTHER ABDON LEWIS, educational administrator; b. Detroit, Dec. 16, 1915; s. Amadeo and Rose (Ray) G. B.A., Cath. U. Am., 1942; M.A. in French Lit, Manhattan Coll., 1947; postgrad., St. John's U., 1947-50, Columbia, 1952-55; Litt.D., Coll. Mt. St. Vincent, 1970. Joined Brothers of Christian Schs., 1936; prof. world lit. and theology Manhattan Coll., Bronx, N.Y., 1950-62, dean, 1962-70, dir. grad. div., 1970—; Asso. univ. seminar higher edn. Columbia, 1962-71; spl. research Japanese culture and civilization. Contbr. articles profl. jours. Trustee Manhattan Coll., 1965-68; Ford Found. fellow Harvard, 1951-52. Decorated 2d Order Sacred Treasure (Japan). Mem. Cath. Renascence Soc. Am. (adv. bd. 1955-63), Am. Council Edn., Assn. Am. Colls., Assn. Higher Edn., Am. Conf. Acad. Deans, Modern Lang, Assn., Renaissance Soc. Am., Nat. Cath. Edn. Assn., Eastern Assn. Deans, Phi Beta Kappa. Address: Manhattan Coll Riverdale NY 10471

GARB, SOLOMON, clinical pharmacologist; b. N.Y.C., Oct. 19, 1920; s. Gerson and Fanny (Smith) G.; m. Hildreth Rose, May 21, 1954. A.B., Cornell U., 1940, M.D., 1943. Intern Beth Israel Hosp., Boston, 1944; resident in medicine Montefiore Hosp., N.Y.C., 1948; asst. prof. clin. pharmacology Cornell U. Med. Ctr., 1951-56; assoc. prof. pharmacology Albany Med. Coll., 1957-61; prof. pharmacology, assoc. prof. community health U. Mo., 1961-70; sci. dir. AMC Cancer Ctr., 1970-80; clin. coordinator Colo. Regional Cancer Ctr., Denver, 1980—; mem. panel cons. on conquest of cancer U.S. Senate, 1970, 71; chmn. Citizens Com. for Conquest of Cancer, 1970—. Author: Pharmacology and Patient Care, 3 edits, 1962-70, Cure for Cancer A National Goal, 1968, Undesirable Drug Interactions, 1974; contbr. articles to med. jours.; articles Saturday Rev. Served with AUS, 1944-46. Recipient Henry M. Moses prize Montefiore Hosp., 1949; N.Y. Heart Assn. fellow, 1949-51; Am. Heart Assn. fellow, 1952-56; recipient Career Research Devel. award NIH, 1962. Fellow ACP, Am. Coll. Clin. Pharmacology; mem. Soc. Clin. Oncology, Am. Assn. Cancer Research. Home: 7159 S Franklin Way Littleton CO 80122 Office: 234 Columbine St Denver CO 80206

GARBA, EDWARD ALOYSIUS, advertising executive; b. Newark, Sept. 26, 1921; s. Edward Victor and Ludmila (Krcah) G.; m. Martha Rheinlander, Aug. 29, 1953; 1 dau., Darina (Mrs. Gerald Kreitschitz). Diploma Engr., U. Commerce, Bratislava, Czechoslovakia, 1946; M.S., Columbia U., 1953. Mgr. Slovak Textile Works, Czechoslovakia, 1946-48; treas. Alltex Service Corp., N.Y.C., 1949-53; pub. accountant Peat, Marwick, Mitchell & Co., 1953-57; chief accountant internat. operations McCann-Erickson, Inc., 1957-60, asst. to treas., 1960-62; treas. McCann-Erickson Corp. (Internat.), hdqrs. internat. operations Interpub.), Geneva, Switzerland, 1962-65; v.p., treas. internet. operations Interpub. Group McCann-Erickson Corp. Internat., 1965-67; v.p., asst. treas. Interpub. Group Cos., Inc., N.Y.C., 1967-73, sr. v.p., treas., 1973—. Chmn. Slovak-Am. Cultural Center, N.Y.C. Mem. N.Y. Credit and Financial Mgmt. Assn. Roman Catholic. Club: New York Athletic. Home: 125 Carleon Ave Larchmont NY 10538 Office: 1271 Ave of the Americas New York NY 10020

GARBACZ, GERALD GEORGE, chemical products company executive; b. San Francisco, Oct. 12, 1936; s. George and Violette (Derbeck) G.; m. Jane E. Snyder, July 1, 1961; children: Geoffrey, Gregory. Student, Dartmouth Coll., 1954-55, M.B.A., 1965; B.S., U.S. Naval Acad., 1959; postgrad., U.S. Naval War Coll., 1978. Asst. to v.p. corp. planning Cummins Engine Co., Columbus, Ind., 1965-66, exec. dir. fin. planning and analysis, 1967-69; asst. to sec. defense (White House fellow), 1968-69; dir. corp. planning Boise Cascade Corp., Idaho, 1970-72; v.p. finance, treas. Phillips Industries, Dayton, Ohio, 1972-74; ops. asst. W.R. Grace & Co., N.Y.C., 1974-75, v.p., 1975-80, pres. Baker & Taylor div., 1980-83, sr. v.p., 1983—; instr. Ind. U., 1967-68, U. Calif., Los Angeles, 1972-74; cons. Dept. Def., 1969-70. Chmn. Idaho steering com. Common Cause, 1972; Bd. overseers Amos Tuck Sch. Bus. Adminstrn., Dartmouth, 1970-76; mem. regional selection panel Pres.'s Commn. on White House fellows, 1971, 72, 79-81. Served to maj. USMCR, 1959-82. Mem. U.S. Naval Acad. Alumni Assn. Presbyn. (elder 1967-69, 71-72, 78-81). Club: Dartmouth (N.Y.). Office: WR Grace & Co 1114 Ave of the Americas New York NY 10036

GARBARINI, EDGAR JOSEPH, civil engineer, engineering company executive; b. Jackson, Calif., Aug. 1, 1910; s. Henry Casamero and Elvira (Gardella) G.; m. Lillian Rosemarie Arata, Nov. 14, 1936; children—Paul Henry, Ann Elisabeth. B.S., U. Calif. at Berkeley, 1933. Registered profl. engr., several states. Jr. research engr. U. Cal. at Berkeley, 1933-34, research engr., 1934-38; field engr. W.A. Bechtel & Six Cos. Calif., San Francisco, 1934; civil engr. Calif. Commn., Golden Gate Internat. Expn., 1938-39, Dewell & Earl (cons. engrs.), San Francisco, 1939, Pacific Gas & Electric Co., 1939-40; with Bechtel Group of Cos., San Francisco, 1940—, now sr. exec. cons. Fellow ASCE; mem. Nat. Acad. Engring., Structural Engrs. Assn. No. Calif., Mining and Metall. Soc. Am., Order of Golden Bear, U. Calif. Alumni Assn., Sigma Xi, Tau Beta Pi, Chi Epsilon. Clubs: Family, World Trade, Pacific Union (San Francisco). Office: PO Box 3221 San Francisco CA 94119

GARBARINI, J(OSEPH) P(ETER), banker; b. Memphis, Apr. 23, 1932; s. Joseph and Ida (Vescovi) G.; m. Imelda H. Hartz, Fed. 18, 1952; children: Joseph, Michael, Carol, Robert, Catherine, Joanna. B.S., Christian Bros. Coll., 1960. Bank clk. Nat. Bank of Commerce, Memphis, 1949-57; sec.-treas. Russann Lumber, Memphis, 1957-60; asst. cashier Memphis br. Fed. Res. Bank St. Louis, Memphis, 1960-68, asst. v.p., St. Louis, 1968-71, v.p., sr. v.p., 1971-77, controller, 1977-83, fin. v.p., St. Louis, 1983—. Served with U.S. Army, 1954-56. Home: 11808 Featherwood Dr Saint Louis MO 63146 Office: Federal Res Bank of St Louis PO Box 442 Saint Louis MO 63166

GARBARINI, ROBERT F., corp. exec., mech. engr.; b. Woodside, N.Y., Dec. 31, 1918; s. Anthony M. and Adeline (Regalia) G.; m. Mary Eileen Driscoll, June 15, 1946; children—Laura Marie, Frances Mary, Virginia Ann, Helen Marita, John Michael. M.E. with distinction, Stevens Inst. Tech., 1940, M.S., 1945. Engr., later div. chief engr. Sperry Gyroscope Co., 1941-63; dep. asso. adminstr. for engring. Office Space Sci. and Applications, NASA, 1963-67; sometime tech. cons. Dept. Def.; adviser sci. adv. bd. USAF, 1960-67; v.p. Western Union Telegraph Co., N.Y.C., 1967-76, 80—; pres. Western Union Space Communications, Inc., 1977-80. Recipient Exceptional Service medal NASA, 1967, 69, Aerospace Communications award Am. Inst. Aeros. and Astronautics, 1976; named to Aviation Week and Space Tech. Honor Roll for work on Surveyor moon landing program, 1966. Mem. AIAA. Patentee in field; implemented first U.S. domestic satellite communications system. Home: Port Washington NY 11050 Office: Western Union Telegraph Co 1 Lake St Upper Saddle River NJ 07458

GARBARINO, JOSEPH WILLIAM, economics and business educator; b. Medina, N.Y., Dec. 7, 1919; s. Joseph Francis and Savina M. (Volpone) G.; m. Mary Jane Godward, Sept. 18, 1948; children: Ann, Joan, Susan, Ellen. B.A., Duquesne U., 1942; M.A., Harvard U., 1947, Ph.D., 1949. Faculty U. Calif., Berkeley, 1949—, prof., 1960—, dir. Inst. Bus. and Econ. Research, 1962—; cons. in field; vis. lectr. Cornell U., 1959-60, UCLA, 1949, SUNY, Buffalo, 1972; Fulbright lectr. U. Glasgow, Scotland, 1969; vis. scholar U. Warwick; mem. staff Brookings Instn., 1959-60; vis. lectr. U. Minn., 1978; labor arbitrator. Author: Health Plans and Collective Bargaining, 1960, Wage Policy and Long Term Contracts, 1962, Faculty Bargaining: Change and Conflict, 1975. Served with U.S. Army, 1942-45, 51-53. Decorated Bronze Star. Mem. Am. Econs. Assn., Indsl. Relations Research Assn. Democrat. Roman Catholic. Home: 7708 Ricardo Ct El Cerrito CA 94530 Office: 350 Barrows Hall Sch Bus Adminstrn U of Calif Berkeley CA 94720

GARBER, PAUL EDWARD, aeronautical historian, retired museum curator; b. Atlantic City, N.J., Aug. 31, 1899; s. Paul Greenwood and Margaret (Sithens) G.; m. Irene Tusch Reece, May 10, 1952; children by previous marriage: Paul James, Edward Williams, Barbara Jane. Student, McKinley Tech. Sch., Washington, 1917, U. Md., 1918; student aero. engring., Research U., Washington, 1920-21; nat., Aviation Sch., Washington, 1927-28, U.S. Grad. Sch., 1939-40, 47-48, 52; D.Eng. (hon.), U. Dayton, Ohio, 1979, D.Aero. Sci., Salem (W.Va.) Coll., 1981. Joined Postal Aviation Service, 1918; with Smithsonian Instn., 1920; served as asso. curator div. engring., curator Nat. Air Mus., Washington, 1946, head curator, 1952-65, asst. dir. aeros., 1965-69, sr. historian, 1958-69, historian emeritus, 1969—, now Ramsey fellow. Author: Building and Flying Model Aircraft, 1928, Kites, 1931, Navy Target Kites, 1944, The National Aeronautical Collections, 1956; also handbooks, pamphlets, ency. and mag. articles on aeros. Served as sgt. U.S. Army, World War I; comdr., spl. devices div. Br. Aero. USNR, World War II. Recipient Washington Air Derby Assn. trophy, 1954, Air Line Traffic Assn. citation, 1955; Frank G. Brewer Trophy for air-youth edn., 1959; Elder Statesman of Aviation award, 1964; Trasvolata Atlantica medal, Italy, 1964; Santos Dumont medal of Merit, Brazil, 1966; Tissandier diplome F.A.I., 1968; Gold medal Smithsonian Instn., 1969; Order Rio Branco, 1969; Merito Aeronautico medal, Brazil, 1974; named hon. pilot Brazilian Air Force, 1982; recipient Medalha Merito Tamandare, Brazil, 1983; named to Aviation Hall of Fame Ox-5 Club of Aviation Pioneers, 1974; Laskowitz gold medal N.Y. Acad. Scis., 1979. Mem. Nat. Aero Assn., Air Mail Pioneers, Early Birds of Aviation (pres. 1968, 76-77, archivist, historian), Conn. Aero. Hist. Soc. Episcopalian. Clubs: Nat. Aviation, Nat. Space, OX-5. Home: 310 N Jackson St Arlington VA 22201 Office: National Air and Space Museum 6th and Jefferson Dr Washington DC 20560

GARBER, STANLEY THOMAS, physician; b. Cin., May 19, 1908; s. Frederick W. and Alice (Woodward) G.; m. Frances Davis, 1935; children—Frances (Mrs. John E. Pepper, Jr.), Thomas, David, Helen. B.S., Princeton U., 1930; M.D., Harvard U., 1934. Diplomate: American Bd. Obstetrics and Gynecology. Intern Christ Hosp., Cin., 1934-35; resident obstetrics Cin. Gen. Hosp., 1935-37; house surgeon gynecology Free Hosp. for Women, Boston, 1937-38; practice of medicine specializing obstetrics and gynecology, Cin., 1938—; faculty U. Cin., 1938—, prof., chmn. obstetrics, 1947-66, prof. obstetrics and gynecology, 1966-78, prof. emeritus, 1978—. Editor: Stedman's Med. Dictionary, 1942-49, other obstet.-gynecol. publs. Mem. Am. Soc. Sterility, Am. Coll. Obstetricians and Gynecologists (charter), Am. Assn. Profs. Obstetrics and Gynecology (charter). Home: 1206 Hayward Ave Cincinnati OH 45226 Office: 104 William H Taft Rd Cincinnati OH 45219

GARBERDING, LARRY GILBERT, utility executive; b. Albert City, Iowa, Oct. 29, 1938; s. Gilbert D. and Lavern Marie (Specketer) G.; m. Elizabeth Ann Hankens, Aug. 20, 1961; children: Scott Richard, Kathryn Ann, Michael John. B.S., Iowa State U., 1960. C.P.A., Nebr. Partner Arthur Andersen & Co., C.P.A.s, Chgo., 1960-71; v.p. fin., controller Kans.-Nebr. Natural Gas Co., Inc., Hastings, Nebr., 1971-80; sr. v.p., chief fin. officer Tenn. Gas Transmission, Houston, 1981-83, exec. v.p., chief fin. officer, 1983—. Served with U.S. Army, 1961. Mem. Am. Inst. C.P.A.s, Tex. Soc. C.P.A.s. Republican. Lutheran. Office: Tenneco Bldg PO Box 2511 Houston TX 77001

GARBIS, MARVIN JOSEPH, lawyer; b. Balt., June 14, 1936; s. Samuel A. and Adele E. (Warshaw) G.; m. Phyllis Lorraine Zaroff, Aug. 27, 1961; children: Kendall Rose, Jason Anders, Kerri Jill. B.E.S., Johns Hopkins U., 1958; J.D., Harvard U., 1961; LL.M., Georgetown U., 1962. Bar: D.C. 1961, Md. 1962. Trial atty. Tax Div., Dept. Justice, Washington, 1962-67; pvt. practice law, Balt., 1967-71; mem. firm Garbis & Schwait, Balt., 1971—; lectr. U. Md. Law Sch., 1970—, N.Y. U. Fed. Tax Inst., 1970, 74, 79; adj. prof. Georgetown U. Law Sch., 1976-80; adviser on tax procedure study, judiciary com. U.S. Senate, 1969-70; mem. adv. commr. to commr. internal revenue, 1982; mem. adv. council U.S. Claims Ct., 1982—; v.p. Md. Inst. for Continuing Profl. Edn. for Lawyers, 1978-80, pres., 1980—. Author: (with Frome) Procedures in Federal Tax Controversy, 1968, (with Schwait) Tax Refund Litigation, 1971, Tax Court Practice, 1974, (with Struntz) Cases and Materials on Federal Tax Procedure, Civil and Criminal, 1981; contbr. articles to profl. jours. E. Barrett Prettyman fellow Georgetown Law Sch., 1961-62. Mem. Fed. Bar Assn. (pres. Balt. chpt. 1972-73, nat. vice chmn. tax com. 1974-76), Md. Bar Assn. (chmn. tax sect. 1970-71, chmn. continuing legal edn. 1973-80), ABA (chmn. ct. procedure com., tax sect. 1975—), Balt. Bar Assn. (bd. govs. 1974-79), Am. Law Inst., Md. Inst. Cert. Profl. Educator Lawyers (pres. 1981-82). Club: Merchants (Balt.). Home: 2015 Greenberry Rd Baltimore MD 21209 Office: 1001 Keyser Bldg Baltimore MD 21202

GARBO, GRETA, actress; b. Stockholm, Sweden, Sept. 18, 1905; came to U.S., 1925, naturalized, 1951; d. Sven and Louvisa Gustaffson. Ed., Royal Dramatic Acad., Stockholm. (Won her first film recognition in Goesta Berling, 1924, through work in Royal Acad.); came to U.S. and appeared in: The Temptress, 1926, The Torrent, 1926, Love, 1927, Flesh and the Devil, 1927, Anna Christie, 1930, Susan Lenox, 1931, Mata Hari, 1931, Grand Hotel, 1932, As You Desire Me, 1932, Queen Christina, 1933, The Painted Veil, Anna Karenina, 1935, Camille, 1936, Conquest, 1937, Ninotchka, 1939, Two Faced Woman, 1941 (Recipient Spl. Acad. award 1954) *

GARBO, NORMAN, author, artist, lecturer; b. N.Y.C., Feb. 15, 1919; s. Max W. and Fannie (Deitz) G.; m. Rhoda Ivy, Apr. 15, 1942; 1 son, Mickey. Student, Coll. City N.Y., 1935-36; B.F.A., Acad. Fine Art, N.Y.C., 1940. Lectr., throughout U.S., 1956—. Author syndicated art column, Chgo.-Tribune-N.Y. News Syndicate, 1954-61; portraits exhibited in galleries, throughout U.S., also, Met. Mus. of Art, N.Y.C., Phila. Mus. of Art.; Author: Pull Up An Easel, 1955, (with H. Goodkind) Confrontation, 1966, The Movement, 1969, To Love Again, 1977, The Artist, 1978, Cabal, 1979, Spy, 1980, Turner's Wife, 1983; also short stories. Spy. Address: 161 Sands Point Rd Sands Point NY *It is all pretty much reduced to its essence for me by a character in my latest novel. "Love me, I'm dying," he says, "is the unspoken plea we all too often fail to heed in time. If once in a while, in all the confusion, anguish and degraded clowning through which we must pass, we are able to accept and carry out the terms of our contracts, if we are able to share what we feel with those we love while they are still there to share it, and if they are able, occasionally, to do the same for us, then that, finally, is the truth of it, and loneliness and regret are just words that fly past in the night."*

GARBUTT, EUGENE JAMES, lawyer; b. Janesville, Wis., Feb. 10, 1925; s. Earl Thomas and Genevieve Regina (Cassidy) G.; m. Mitzi Miller, June 29, 1962; children—Jeffrey Aleck, Marilyn Elizabeth. B.S., U. Wis. at Madison, 1950; LL.B., George Washington U., 1956. Bar: Ill. bar 1957. Ins. trainee Gen. Accident Fire & Life Assurance Group Ltd., Chgo., 1950-51; spl. agt. FBI, Miami, Fla. and Washington, 1951-57; since practiced in, Chgo.; mem. firm Garbutt Jacobson and Lee Asso., 1957—. Sec. Cook County (Ill.) Sheriff's Police and Corrections Merit Bd., 1969-81, mem., 1979—. Served with AUS, 1943-46. Mem. Chgo., Ill., Am. bar assns., Am. Arbitration Assn. (arbitrator), Ill. Def. Counsel, Soc. Trial Lawyers, Chgo. Trial Lawyers Club, Soc. Former Spl. Agts. of FBI. Clubs: Oak Park (Ill.) Country, Oak Park Tennis (dir.), Oak Park-River Forest Tennis.). Home: 1139 N Oak Park Ave Oak Park IL 60302 Office: 1 N LaSalle St Chicago IL 60602

GARCEAU, OLIVER, educator; b. Boston, Nov. 22, 1911; s. Dr. Edgar and Sally Holmes (Morse) G.; m. Iris Virginia Thistle, Aug. 18, 1934; 1 son, Laurence. A.B., Harvard, 1933, M.B.A., 1935, A.M., 1939, Ph.D., 1940; student, Oxford (Eng.) U., 1933, U. Chgo., 1943-44. Instr., asst. prof. Harvard, 1935-41, 45-46; asso. prof. U. Maine, 1946-47; staff asso. Social Sci. Research Council, 1947-48; prof. govt. Bennington (Vt.) Coll., 1948-59; research prof. govt. Harvard, 1959-60, research cons. polit. economy and polit. behavior, 1960—; exec. asso., cons. Ford Found., 1955-58; exec. bd. Inter-univ. Case Program, 1952-58. Author: Political Life of American Medical Association, 1941, Public Library in the Political Process, 1949; Author, editor: Political Research and Political Theory, 1968; Asso. editor: Human Organization, 1956-66. Mem. Gov.'s Task Force on State Govt. Reorgn., 1967-69. Served to lt. comdr. USNR, 1941-45. Fellow Social Sci. Research Council (mem. com. on polit. behavior 1950-64); mem. Am. Polit. Sci. Assn. (exec. council 1951-53), Phi Beta Kappa. Home: Box 8 Sedgwick ME 04676

GARCIA, ALEXANDER, orthopaedic surgeon; b. N.Y.C., July 3, 1919; s. Alexander and Pilar (Prieto) G.; m. Helen Ann Proskey, June 12, 1943; 1 son, Alexander, III. B.S., CCNY, 1940; M.D., L.I. Coll. Medicine, 1943. Diplomate: Am. Bd. Orthopaedic Surgery. Intern Syracuse (N.Y.) U. Med. Center, 1944, asst. resident in gen. surgery, 1944-45, chief resident, 1945-46; resident in gen. surgery Nassau Hosp., Mineola, N.Y., 1948; asst. resident in orthopaedic surgery N.Y. Orthopaedic Hosp., N.Y.C., 1948-50, resident, jr. Annie C. Kane fellow, 1950-51, acting dir. orthopaedic service, 1976-77, hosp. dir., 1977—; chief orthopaedic surg. sect. North Shore Hosp., Manhasset, N.Y., 1957-70, cons., 1970—; mem. faculty Columbia U. Coll. Phys. and Surg., 1952—, prof. orthopaedic surgery, 1972—, chmn. dept., 1977—, Frank E. Stinchfield prof., 1978—; cons. numerous area hosps. Mem. editoral bds. profl. jours. Served as officer M.C. AUS, 1946-48. Mem. Internat. Soc. Orthopaedic Surgery and Traumatology, A.C.S., AMA, Am. Acad. Orthopaedic Surgeons, Am. Assn. for Surgery of Trauma, Pan Am. Med. Assn., Assn. Bone and Joint Surgeons, Am. Orthopaedic Assn., N.Y. State Med. Soc., N.Y. Acad. Medicine, N.Y. Acad. Scis., N.Y. State Soc. Orthopaedic Surgeons, Soc. Ortopedia y Traumatologia Dominicana. Democrat.

GARCÍA, CELSO-RAMÓN, physician, educator; b. N.Y.C., Oct. 31, 1921; s. Celso García Ondina and Oliva Menendez (del Valle) G.; m. Shirley Jean Stoddard, Oct. 14, 1950; children—Celso-Ramón, Sarita Stoddard. B.S., Queens Coll., 1942; M.D., State U. N.Y. Downstate Med. Center, 1945; M.A. (hon.), U. Pa. Intern Norwegian Hosp., Bklyn., 1945-46; resident Cumberland Hosp., Bklyn., 1948-53; asst. prof. obstetrics and gynecology U. P.R., San Juan, 1953-55; co-dir. Rock Reproductive Study Center; asst. obstetrician and gynecologist Boston Lying-In Hosp.; asso. surgeon Free Hosp. for Women, Brookline, Mass., 1955-65; sr. scientist, dir. tng. program in physiology reprodn. Worcester Found. for Exptl. Biology, Shrewsbury, Mass., 1960-62; asst. surgeon, chief Infertility Clinic, Mass. Gen. Hosp.; clin. asso. obstetrics and gynecology Harvard Med. Sch., 1962-65; prof. obstetrics and gynecology U. Pa., Phila., 1965—, William Shippen, Jr. prof. human reprodn., 1970—, also vice chmn. dept. obstetrics-gynecology, 1975; extraordinary prof. U. San Luis Potosi, Mex., 1974; Mem. sci. adv. bd. Inst. Human Reprodn. and Fetal Devel., U. Tel Aviv Med. Sch., 1970; rapporteur com. of experts on clin. aspects oral gestogens WHO, Geneva, Switzerland, 1965; mem. ad hoc adv. com. contraceptive devel., contract program Nat. Inst. Child Health and Human Devel., 1971-75; cons. Pa. Hosp., 1973—. Chmn. nat. med. adv. com. Planned Parenthood World Population, 1971-74; mem. nat. adv. child and human devel. council Nat. Inst. Child Health and Human Devel., 1981. Served with AUS, 1946-48. Recipient Carl G. Hartman award Am. Soc. Study Sterility, 1961; Sidney Graves fellow in gynecology Harvard Med. Sch., 1955. Fellow A.C.S., Royal Soc. Health, Coll. Physicians Phila., Am. Coll. Obstetricians and Gynecologists; mem. Am. Physiol. Soc., Am. Obstet. and Gynecol. Soc., AMA, Boston, Phila. obstet. socs., Assn. Planned Parenthood Physicians (pres.), Am. Fertility Soc. (dir., past pres.), Fedn. Columbian Socs. Obstetrics and Gynecology (hon.), Cuban Soc. Obstetrics and Gynecology (in exile, hon.), Sigma Xi, Alpha Epsilon Delta. Republican. Presbyn. Club: Mason. Mem. original team developing application of progestagen-estrogen combinations for oral contraception (the Pill); developer, dir. 1st formal tng. program in physiology of reprodn. in U.S.; innovator surg. approach to infertility of women. Home: 109 Merion Rd Merion PA 19066 Office: 3400 Spruce St Philadelphia PA 19104

GARCIA, HIPOLITO FRANK, fed. judge; b. San Antonio, Dec. 4, 1925; s. Hipolito and Francisca G. LL.B., St. Mary's U., San Antonio, 1951; LL.D., U. Tex., 1969. Bar: Tex. bar 1952. With Dist. Atty's Office, San Antonio, 1952; judge County Ct. at Law, 1964-74, Tex. Dist. Ct. Dist. 144, 1975-79, U.S. Dist. Ct. Western Dist., San Antonio, 1980—. Recipient cert. of Merit Am. Legion. Mem. San Antonio Bar Assn., Am. Bar Assn., Delta Theta Phi. Democrat. Office: US Dist Ct Hemisfair Plaza 655 E Durango Blvd San Antonio TX 78206 *

GARCIA, JERRY (JEROME JOHN GARCIA), guitarist, composer; b. San Francisco, Aug. 1, 1942; m. Sarah Garcia (div.); m. Carolyn Adams. Played guitar, banjo in folk music duo with, Sarah Garcia; musician various groups, 1959-65; founding mem.: rock group The Warlocks, 1965, The Grateful Dead, 1966—; composer: songs China Cat Sunflower; albums include Go to Heaven, Garcia, Hooteroll, Reflections, Run for the Roses; Co-author: Garcia: Signpost to a New Age. Served with U.S. Army, 1959. Office: care Grateful Dead PO Box 1065 San Rafael CA 94902 *

GARCIA, JULIO HERNAN, pathology educator; b. Armenia, Colombia, Dec. 22, 1933; naturalized, 1970; s. Ernesto and Isabel (Munoz) G.; m. Irene Murray, Feb. 25, 1965; children: David Allen, Lawrence Thomas. B.S., Coll. St. Bartholomew, Bogota, Colombia, 1951; M.D., Nat. U., Columbia, 1958. Diplomate: Am. Bd. Pathology. Trainee in pathology State U. N.Y., Downstate Med. Center, Bklyn.; asst. prof. pathology Med. Coll. Va., Richmond, 1964-66; assoc. prof. pathology and neurology U. Tenn. Med. Coll., Memphis, 1967-70, Baylor Coll. Medicine, Houston, 1970-71; prof., head div. neuropathology U. Md., Balt., 1971-79, also dir. anatomic pathology; cons. VA Hosps., Richmond, 1964-66, Houston, 1970-71, Balt., 1971-79; prof. pathology and neurology, dir. anatomic pathology U. Ala. Med. Center, Birmingham, 1979—; co-dir. U. Ala. in Birmingham Stroke Center; vis. prof. Free U. Berlin, 1977-78. Mem. editorial bd.: Stroke-A Jour. of Cerebral Circulation, 1975—, Ala. Jour. Med. Scis, 1980, Jour. Neuropathology and Exptl. Neurology, 1981—. Recipient Humboldt award Govt. of W. Ger., 1978. Fellow Coll. Am. Pathologists; mem. Md. Neurol. Soc. (pres. 1976-77), Am. Heart Assn. (fellow stroke council), AAAS, N.Y. Acad. Scis., Am. Assn. Neuropathologists (v.p. 1975-76), AAUP, Am. Soc. Exptl. Pathology, Assn. for Research Nervous and Mental Diseases, Am. Neurol. Assn., Am. Assn. Pathologists and Bacteriologists., Am. Acad. Neurology. Developed exptl. model for electron microscope study of cerebral infarction. Home: 3733 Dover Dr Birmingham AL 35223 Office: Dept Pathology 509 LHR U Ala Med Center Birmingham AL 35294

GARCIA, ROBERT, Congressman; b. Bronx, N.Y., Jan. 9, 1933; s. Rafael and Rosa (Rodrigues) G.; children: Rosalind, Robert, Kenneth. E.E., RCA Inst., 1957; B.A., CCNY. Formerly with IBM, Control Data Corp.; asst. to Congressman James H. Scheuer, 1965-66; mem. N.Y. State Assembly, 1966-67, N.Y. State Senate, 1967-78, dep. minority leader, 1975-78; mem. 95th-98th Congresses from 21st N.Y. Dist., elected to Congress in spl. election, 1978; mem. N.Y. State Temp. Commn. to Evaluate Drug Laws. Mem. Democratic Charter Commn., 1974; del. Dem. Nat. Conv., 1976. Served with U.S. Army, 1951-52; Korea. Decorated (2) Bronze Star. Mem. NCCJ, NAACP, Urban League, Aspira, Puerto Rican Forum, Puerto Rican Nat. Assn. Civil Rights. Office: 223 Cannon House Office Bldg Washington DC 20515 *

GARCIA, WALTER MANUEL, educator; b. N.Y.C., Aug. 16, 1926; s. Joseph Emanuel and Frances Margaret (Campbell) G.; m. Doris Gesine Robbert, Aug. 19, 1951 (div. May 1977); children—Amy Frances, Jane Anne. A.B., Coll. City N.Y., 1950; A.M., Harvard, 1951, Ed.D., 1955; L.H.D., Whittier Coll. Research asst. Rutgers U., 1954; instr. Harvard, 1955-57; asst. prof. Stanford, 1957-60; pres. Modesto (Calif.) Jr. Coll., 1960-64; supt. Yosemite Jr. Coll. Dist., 1964-67; supt., pres. Rio Hondo Coll., Whittier, Calif., 1967-77, prof. English, 1977—; Panelist White House Conf. Edn., 1965; participant White House Conf. Food, Nutrition and Health, 1969. Pres. Stanislaus Area United Crusade, 1964-66, Family Service Agy. Stanislaus County, 1965-66; commr. Los Angeles County Bicentennial. Served with AUS, 1944-46. Mem. No. Calif. Council Chs., Phi Beta Kappa, Am. Assn. Jr. Colls. (dir.), Calif. Community and Jr. Coll. Assn. (pres. 1975-76). Club: Rotarian. Home: 5427 Pioneer Blvd Whittier CA 90601

GARCIA GONZALEZ, RAFAEL, bishop; b. Guadalajara, Mex., May 10, 1926; s. Jose Garcia Calderon and Carmen Gonzalez Chavez. Ed., Marist Bros. Sch., 1931-37; license theology, Pio Latino Americano, Rome, 1949; license canon law, Gregorian U., Rome, 1952. Ordained priest Roman Catholic Ch., 1949; tchr., Guadalajara, 1952-67; founder, dir. Mex. Nat. Secs. Priestly Vocations, 1955-67; spiritual dir. Mex. Pontifical Sem., Rome, 1967-70; bishop, Urbisaglia, 1972, residential bishop, Tabasco, Mex., 1974—; mem. 6th Roman Cath. World Synod of Bishops, Rome, 1980. Mem. Paul VI Soc., Red Cross Soc. Club: K.C.

GARCIA-MENENDEZ, ALBERTO AUGUSTO, history educator; b. Cienfuegos, Cuba, Aug. 15, 1923; naturalized, 1970; s. Augusto C. Garcia-Castro and Josefina L. (Menendez-Palacios). Licenciate Diplomatic and Consular Law, Havana U., 1943, LL.D., 1946, D.Philosophy and Letters, 1953; M.A. in History, U. P.R., 1978. Bar: Cuba 1946. Sole practice, Cienfuegos, Cuba, 1946-60; prof. principals of econs., fgn., and domestic trade Profl. Bus. Coll., Cienfuegos, 1955-60; prof. bus. and criminal law Masonic U. Jose Marti br., Cienfuegos, 1956-58; prof. econs. and bus. adminstrn. Interam. U., Barranquitas, P.R., 1961-67; prof. history Met. Campus, Interam. U., Hato Rey, P.R., 1967—; lectr. Latin Am. history U.P.R., 1970-72; adv. council Latin Fortaleza Lecture Series Office Cultural Affairs of Gov. P.R., 1978-80. Contbr. articles in field to profl. jours. Nat. Endowment for Humanities summer grantee, 1975; reviewer for grant proposals Nat. Endowment Humanities, 1978-80. Mem. AAUP, Grupo Cubano de Estudios Historicos, Assn. Caribbean Historians (editorial com. 1978-79), Caribbean Studies Assn., Sociedad Bolivariana de P.R. (sec.), Latin Am. Studies Assn., UNESCO P.R., Academia Interamericana de P.R., Phi Alpha Theta. Roman Catholic. Home: 16 Bajos Ruiz Belvis St Floral Park PR Hato Rey 00917 Office: Interam U Special Scis Dept 117 Eleanor Roosevelt St Halo Rey PR 00919

GARCÍA OLLER, JOSÉ LUIS, neurosurgeon; b. San Juan, P.R., Mar. 17, 1923; s. José Leocadio García and Laura Oller; m. Mary Ann Balsley, Oct. 1, 1949; children—María, José, Ana, Antonio, Teresita, Margarita. B.S. with high honors, U. P.R., 1942; M.D. (Anatomy prize 1943), Jefferson Med. Coll., Phila., 1945; M.M.Sc., Tulane U., 1951. Rotating intern Jefferson Med. Coll. Hosp., 1945-46; preceptorship in gen. surgery with Drs. Devine and Devine, Lynchburg, Va., 1946-47; fellow neurosurgery Ochsner Clinic, New Orleans, 1947-50, Yale U., 1949-50; chief resident in neurosurgery Charity Hosp., New Orleans, 1950-51, head ind. neurosurgery service, 1952-63; practice medicine specializing in neurosurgery, New Orleans, 1950—; head intensive care and neurosurgery, EEG, EMG and neuroradiology Mercy Hosp., 1958-75, chief staff, 1968; founder, 1968, since exec. pres. Private Doctors of America, New Orleans; instr. physiology Tulane U. Med. Sch., 1951-59; bd. dirs. New Orleans Area Health Planning Council, 1969-76; lectr. in field. Author. Served to 2d lt. USAR, 1938-45; to comdr. M.C. USNR, 1954-56. Recipient Ochsner award, 1950. Mem. Am. Assn. Neurosurgeons, Congress Neurosurgeons, Am. Acad. Neurology, Am. Assn. Electromyography and Electrodiagnosis, Am. Soc. Assn. Execs., So. Neurosurg. Soc., So. Med. Assn., So. Electroencephalography Soc., La. State Med. Soc. (Sci. Exhibit award 1961), Orleans Parish Med. Soc. Patentee in field. Address: 3422 Bienville St New Orleans LA 70119 *As the attorney is the advocate of individual rights, and the priest of our spiritual identity, the private physician is the guardian of the patient's unique physical, spiritual and familial integrity during illness. Hence, privacy, dignity and individualized care are the hallmark of the private doctor. The doctor is the conscience of society. Avoid conflicts of interest. Accept reward only from the patient. Thus be free to exercise our full measure of skill and judgment. That is why I have chosen to dedicate my life to the freedom of private medical practice.*

GARCIA-PALMIERI, MARIO RUBEN, physician, educator; b. Adjuntas, P.R., Aug. 2, 1927; s. Rafael Garcia-Borregon and Mercedes (Palmieri-Ferri) G.-P. B.S. magna cum laude, U. P.R., 1947; M.D., U. Md., 1951. Diplomate: Am. Bd. Internal Medicine. Intern Fajardo (P.R.) Dist. Hosp., 1951-52, head dept. med., 1955-56; resident in medicine Bayamon (P.R.) Dist. Hosp., 1952-53, cons., 1953—; resident in medicine San Juan VA Hosp.; asst. in medicine U. P.R. Sch. Medicine, San Juan, 1953-54, Nat. Heart Inst. fellow in cardiology, 1954-55, instr. medicine, 1955-56, asso. in medicine, 1956-58, asst. prof., 1958-60, asso. prof., 1960, prof., head dept. medicine, chief sect. cardiology, 1961-66, 68—, prof., chief sect. cardiology, 1967-68, lectr. cardiovascular epidemiology, 1968—; head dept. medicine and sect. cardiology Univ. Hosp., San Juan, 1961-66, 67—; sec. health of P.R., 1966-67; pres. bd. dirs. P.R. Med. Center, 1966-67; cons. Presbyn., San Jorge, San Juan City, Auxilio Mutuo, Drs., Tchrs. hosps.; vis. prof. Seton Hall Coll. Medicine, 1963, U. Fla. Sch. Medicine, 1963, N.Y. Med. Coll., 1971, Downstate Med. Center Sch. Medicine, Bklyn., 1971, U. Ala. Sch. Medicine, Birmingham, 1981-82; vis. lectr. Ind. U. Sch. Medicine, 1963, Bklyn. Jewish Hosp., 1964, Central U. Venezuela, 1964, Autonomous U. Barcelona, Spain, Universidad Complutense, Madrid, 1975; guest lectr. U. Md., 1965; lectr. Postgrad. Course on Adminstrn. Med. Care Services, Dominican Republic, 1966, 68. Author: (with R.C. Rodriguez and C. Girod) The Electrocardiogram and Vectorcardiogram in Congenital Heart Disease, 1965; Mem. bd. advisers: Buhiti; Contbr. numerous articles to med. jours.; past mem. editorial bd. various jours. in field. Mem. Pres.'s Commn. on Ethical Aspects of Biomed. and Behavioral Research, 1979—; mem. nat. adv. council Nat. Inst. on Aging, 1980—. Recipient certificate of merit Fajardo Dist. Hosp., 1965, certificate of distinction Associacion de Hospitales de P.R., 1970; Internat. Achievement award Am. Heart Assn., 1980. Fellow A.C.P., Am. Coll. Cardiology (gov. P.R. chpt. 1966-69), Royal Soc. Health; mem. Am. Heart Assn. (fellow council clin. cardiology, council on epidemiology, editorial bd. Jour. 1965-70), Internat. Soc. Cardiology (dir. 1964-68, v.p. 1968-72, founder, mem. sci. council on epidemiology and prevention 1968—), Interam. Soc. Cardiology (pres. 1980—), P.R. Soc. Cardiology (pres. 1968-69), Dominican (hon. mem.), Pan. Am. Med Assn. (Latin Am. v.p. sect. cardiovascular diseases 1967—), P.R. Med. Assn. (editor Bull. 1960-66, pres. sect. cardiology 1968-69, certificate of merit 1965, recognition award 1972), AAAS, Am. Fedn. Clin. Research, Am. Soc. Tropical Medicine and Hygiene, Assn. Am. Med. Colls., Am. Soc. Internal Medicine, Am., P.R. public health assns., Soc. Epidemiologic Research, Assn. Univ. Cardiologists, Assn. Am. Physicians, Soc. Clin. Investigation, P.R. Acad. Arts and Scis., Alpha Omega Alpha. Home: Box DG Caparra Heights Sta San Juan PR 00922 Office: Dept Medicine PR Medical Sciences Campus Box 5067 San Juan PR 00936

GARD, CURTIS ELDON, banker; b. Ravenwood, Mo., Oct. 19, 1921; s. Herbert Lee and Pearl (West) G.; m. Annaleene Jones, Aug. 21, 1946; children—Lowell Curtis, Phillip Nils, Jennifer Kellogg (Mrs. Mark W. Kellogg), Joel Carroll. B.A., B.S., Northwest Mo. State Coll., Maryville, 1947. Gen. auditor City Nat. Bank & Trust Co., Kansas City, Mo., 1947-63; comptroller, cashier Exchange Nat. Bank, Atchison, Kans., 1963-64; v.p., comptroller First Nat. Bank Omaha, 1965—. Served with AUS, 1942-45. Mem. Bank Adminstrn. Inst. (past pres. local chpts.). Mem. Disciples of Christ Ch. (elder). Home: 5110 Chicago St Omaha NE 68132 Office: PO Box 3128 Omaha NE 68103

GARD, ROBERT GIBBINS, JR., educational administrator, retired army officer; b. West Point, N.Y., Jan. 28, 1928; s. Robert Gibbins and Ruth Whiteman G.; m. Lucy Marcus, Oct. 14, 1950 (div.); children: Robert G., Linda M., Susan W. B.S., U.S. Mil. Acad., 1950; M.P.A., Harvard U., 1956, Ph.D., 1962. Commd. 2d lt. U.S. Army, 1950, advanced through grades to lt. gen., 1977; asst. prof. nat. security policy U.S. Mil. Acad., 1957-60; comdr. 5th Bn., 81st F.A., 1963-64; spl. asst. to asst. sec. def. for internat. security affairs, 1966, mil. asst. to sec. def., 1966-68, comdr. div. arty., chief staff, Vietnam, 1968-69; dir. human resources devel. Office Dep. Chief Staff for Personnel, Dept. Army, 1971-73; comdr., Fort Ord, Calif., 1973-75, U.S. Army Mil. Personnel Center, Alexandria, Va., 1975-77; pres. Nat. Def. U., Washington, 1977-81; dir. Bologna (Italy) Center Johns Hopkins U. Sch. Advanced Internat. Studies, 1981—. Decorated D.S.M. Dept. Def.; Decorated Silver Star, Legion of Merit, D.F.C., Bronze Star with V, Air medal, others. Mem. Council Fgn. Relations, Internat. Inst. for Strategic Studies. Office: Johns Hopkins SAIS Via Belmeloro 11 Bologna Italy 40126

GARD, SPENCER AGASSIZ, lawyer, former judge; b. Iola, Kans., June 24, 1898; s. Samuel Arnold and Louisa (Irel) G.; m. Marjorie P. Garlinghouse, Sept. 27, 1924; 1 dau., Amy Lou (Mrs. Jack Brazil). LL.B., U. Kans., 1922. Bar: Mo. bar 1922, Kans. bar 1942. Practiced in, Kansas City, 1922-42, Iola, 1942-50; judge 37th Kans. Jud. Dist., Iola, 1950-69; county atty., Allen County, Kans., 1943-47; faculty Nat. Coll. State Trial Judges U. Colo., 1964. Author: Jones on Evidence, 6th edit, 1972, Illinois Evidence Manual and Kansas Code of Civil Procedure Annotated, 2d edit, 1979, Florida Evidence Manual, 2d edit, 1979; Contbr. profl. jours. Vice pres. Kansas City Area council Boy Scouts Am., 1941; mem. Nat. Conf. Commrs. on Uniform State Laws, 1947-62; chmn. spl. com. which drafted Kans. Code Civil Procedure, 1963; Mem. Kan. Ho. of Reps., 1947, Kans. Senate, 1949; nominated for Kans. Supreme Ct., 1964, spl. commr., 1972-76. Recipient Disting. Alumnus citation U. Kans. Sch. Law, 1968, Disting. Service in Adminstrn. of Justice award Kans. Judges Assn., 1974; Disting. Service award Kans. Bar Assn., 1975; Justinian award Johnson County Bar Assn., 1978. Mem. Am. Bar. Assn., Order of Coif, Scribes. Methodist. Home and office: 9007 Salem Dr Apt 4 Lenexa KS 66215 *I take pride in being adaptable to change, not being emotionally tied to places or things. I see frustrations as blessings in disguise. Things I have so eagerly sought, have, in their being denied me, turned me to more satisfying achievements and recognition.*

GARDENIA, VINCENT, actor; b. Naples, Italy, Jan. 7, 1923. Appeared on: stage in others; films include Death Wish; TV appearances include Mary Tyler Moore; TV series Breaking Away, 1980-81 (Recipient Tony award for Prisoner of Second Avenue 1971, Obie awards for Machinal, Passing Through from Exotic Places.). Office: care William Morris Agy 151 El Camino Beverly Hills CA 90212 *

GARDINER, DONALD ANDREW, statistician, consultant; b. Buffalo, Feb. 2, 1922; s. Andrew and Bertha Johanna (Kruger) G.; m. Marie Abigail Tropman, Dec. 4, 1943; children: Ellen Gardiner Morgan, Andrew Donald, Kathryn Abigail. B.S., U. Buffalo, 1943, M.B.A., 1948; Ph.D., N.C. State U., 1956. Instr. U. Buffalo, 1946-48; faculty U. Tenn., Knoxville, 1948-51, 64-83, prof. math., 1973-83; with Oak Ridge Nat. Lab., 1956-73, 83—, asst. dir. math. div., 1967-73, sr. staff cons. Y-12 plant, 1983—; head math. and stats. research dept. computer scis. div. Nuclear div. Union Carbide Corp., Oak Ridge, 1973—; vis. prof. Fla. State U., Tallahassee, 1966-67. Editor: Technometrics, 1972-74. Served with USNR, 1943-46, 51-53. Fellow Am. Statis. Assn., AAAS; mem. Internat. Statis. Inst., Am. Soc. Quality Control, Bernoulli Soc. Math. Stats. and Probability, Sigma Xi, Phi Kappa Phi. Lodge: Masons. Home: 108 Mason Ln Oak Ridge TN 37830 Office: Union Carbide Corp PO Box Y Oak Ridge TN 37830

GARDINER, JOHN ELIOT, conductor; b. Shaftesbury, Eng., Apr. 20, 1943; s. Henry Rolf and Mariabella Honnor (Hodgkin) G.; m. Elizabeth Suzanne Wilcock, Apr. 18, 1981. B.A. with 2d class honors in History, King's Coll., Cambridge U., Eng., 1965; M.A. with 2d class honors, 1968; cert. advanced musical studies, King's Coll., London U., 1966; student, Nadia Boulanger, Paris, 1966-68. Founder, musical dir. Monteverdi Choir, London, 1964—, Monteverdi Orch., 1968—, English Baroque Soloists, 1978—, Orchestre de l'Opera de Lyon; prin. condr., musical dir. CBD, Vancouver, B.C., Can., 1980-83; artistic dir. Gottingen Handel Festival, W. Ger., 1981—; guest condr. English Nat. Opera, Covent Garden; Philharmonia Royal Philharmonic Orch., BBC Symphony Orch., Nouvel Orchestre; Philharmonique Nat. Orch. Monte Carlo, Dusseldorfer, Symphoniker, Dresdener Staatskapelle, U.S. orchs. including Dallas Symphony Orch., San Francisco Symphony Orch.; numerous recitals BBC, Radio France, West German Radio, CBC, European Broadcasting Union; numerous recs including Acis & Galatea (Handel), Gramaphone Early Music prize, 1978, Israel in Egypt (Handel), Grand Prix du Disque, 1978, Bach Motets, Edison Prize, 1982, Fairy Queen (Purcell), Grand Prix du Disque, 1982, L'Allegro, il Penseraso ed il Moderato, Gramaphone Choral award, 1981. Editor numerous oratorios (Handel); editor numerous oratirios (Rameau); editor state works (Purcell) others; editor (L'Orfeo (Monteverdi), 1982, (Helas) Mon Dieu (Claude Le Jeune), 1971; contbr. (articles to musical jours.), (chpts. to books). King's Coll. scholar, 1962-65; French Govt. scholar, 1966-68; recipient Prix Caecilia, 1982, Internat. Record LCritics award, 1983. Mem. Inc. Soc. Musicians (U.K.), Musicians Assn. Office: 1 Surrey St London WC2UK Office: care DOpera de Lyon PLlace de la Comedie Lyon France 69001

GARDINER, JOHN WILLIAM, ins. co. exec.; b. Newark, Feb. 16, 1931; s. Frank and Alice G.; m. C. Joan Matthews, Sept. 15, 1951; children—Timothy, Glenn, Nancy, Jacquelynn. Student pub. and pvt. schs. Agt. John Hancock Mut. Life Ins. Co., 1954-58, agency mgr., 1958-60, gen. agt., 1960-66, v.p. gen. agencies, 1966-67, sr. v.p. field mgmt. and marketing, 1967-70; pres., chief exec. officer, dir. All Am. Life & Casualty Co., Chgo., 1970-77; pres. Holding Corp. Am., Denver, 1977—. Served with U.S. Army, 1949-50, 51-54. Home: 4505 S Yosemite Denver CO 80237 Office: 7730 E Belleview Ave Englewood CO 80111

GARDINER, JOSEPH WILLIAM FAWSITT, hotel executive; b. London, Mar. 8, 1928; U.S., 1945; s. Leonard Hailey and May Laura (Fawsitt) G.; m. Marianne Whiting, Sept. 12, 1945. B.A., Cambridge U., Eng., 1939. Dir. catering Conrad Hilton Hotel, Chgo., 1952-60; dir. food and beverage Palmer House, Chgo., 1960-66; asst. v.p. central region Hilton Hotels, Beverly Hills, CA, 1966-69, asst. v.p. east, 1969-74, sr. v.p., 1974—. Bd. dirs. Century Towers Assn., Los Angeles, 1977—, pres., 1982; vestryman All Saints Episcopalian Ch., Beverly Hills, 1982—. Served to lt. Brit. Royal Navy, 1939-45. Recipient Silver Plate Internat. Food Mfrs Assn., 1983. Mem. Internat. Gold and Silver Plate Soc., Nat. Restaurant Assn. (dir. Chgo. 1983), Culinary Int. Am. (trustee 1976—), Am. Hotel and Motel Assn. (v.p. food and beverage com. 1981—). Club: Corinthain Yacht (dir.) (1961-63). Office: Hilton Hotels Corp 9880 Wilshire Blvd Beverly Hills CA 90210

GARDINER, PETER ALEXANDER JACK, agribusiness executive; b. Edinburgh, Scotland, Nov. 22, 1935; came to U.S., 1976; s. Peter G.W. and Nancy (Aitkin) G.; m. Jill Mackenzie, Sept. 7, 1968; 1 son, Holt. Diploma indsl. fermentation, Heriot Watt U., Edinburgh, 1956. With Arthur Guinness Son & Co. Ltd., London, 1959-62, PE Cons. Group, 1962-67, Unilever Ltd., 1967-70; mng. dir. Atcherley & Co., Liverpool, Eng., 1970-72, Goldwell Ltd., Kent, Eng., 1972-73, Asso. Brit. Malsters Ltd., Newark, Eng., 1973-76; pres., chief exec. officer Dalgety, Inc., San Mateo, Calif., 1976—; adv. Scottish Devel. Agy., 1980; dir. Dalgety PLC, London, 1982—. Served as lt. Royal Navy, 1956-59. Mem. Young Pres. Orgn., Brit.-Am. C. of C. (dir.), World Trade Club. Mem. Ch. of Scotland. Clubs: San Francisco Golf, Stock Exchange; Caledonian (U.K.). Home: 310 Family Farm Rd Woodside CA 94062 Office: 3055 Clearview Way San Mateo CA 94402

GARDINER, ROBERT HALLOWELL, banker; b. Needham, Mass., Sept. 29, 1914; s. Robert Hallowell and Elizabeth (Denny) G.; m. Frances Weld, June 7, 1941; children: Alison, Robert Hallowell, Holly, Nathaniel S., Phyllis. Grad., Groton Sch., 1933; A.B., Harvard U.,

1937, LL.B., 1940. With Fiduciary Trust Co., Boston, 1946—, pres., 1957-79, chmn. bd., 1979-84, dir., 1948—; dir. Putnam Funds. Bd. dirs. Greater Boston Legal Services Corp., New Eng. Forestry Found.; bd. dirs., treas. Action for Boston Community Devel., Inc. Served to lt. USNR, 1941-45. Club: Tavern (Boston). Office: Fiduciary Trust Co 175 Federal St Boston MA 02110

GARDINER, ROBERT M., investment company executive; b. Denver, 1922. Grad., Princeton U., 1944. Pres., chief exec. officer, dir. Dean Witter Reynolds, Inc., San Francisco; pres., dir. Dean Witter Reynolds Orgn., Inc., San Francisco; chmn. Dean Witter Reynolds Inc., N.Y.C.; vice chmn., dir. N.Y. Stock Exchange, Inc. Office: Dean Witter Reynolds Inc 45 Montgomery St San Francisco CA 94106 *

GARDINER, WILLIAM CECIL, JR., chemist; b. Niagara Falls, N.Y., Jan. 14, 1933; s. William Cecil and Annie Charlotte (Hicks) G.; m. Gertraut Schimanski, July 28, 1959; children—Grace, Charlotte, Amy Louise. A.B., Princeton U., 1954; postgrad., U. Heidelberg, 1954-55, U. Göttingen, 1955-56; Ph.D., Harvard U., 1960. Instr. chemistry U. Tex., Austin, 1960-62, asst. prof., 1962-66, asso. prof., 1966-72, prof., 1972—; cons. on chemistry of combustion reactions to govtl. agencies. Contbr. articles on rates of chem. reactions to tech. jours. Fulbright fellow, 1954-55, 75-76; Guggenheim fellow, 1975-76; Humboldt fellow, 1979. Mem. Am. Chem. Soc., Am. Phys. Soc., Chem. Soc. London, AAAS, Combustion Inst., Solar Energy Soc., Phi Beta Kappa, Sigma Xi. Home: 2612 Maria Anna Rd Austin TX 78712 Office: WEL 3.324 University of Texas Austin TX 78712

GARDINER, WILLIAM DOUGLAS HAIG, financial executive; b. Chatham, Ont., Can., Apr. 21, 1917; s. William Henry and Elsie May (Armstrong) G.; m. Jean Elizabeth Blatchford, Sept. 5, 1945; children: Donald W. B., Campbell D., Gregory F. Grad., Kennedy Collegiate Sch., Windsor, Ont. Asst. gen. mgr. Royal Bank of Can., Montreal, 1961-64, Vancouver, 1964-67, v.p., dist. gen. mgr., 1967-73, dep. chmn., exec. v.p., Toronto, 1973-77, vice chmn., dir., 1977-80, now dir.; chmn. bd., dir. Reed Stenhouse Cos. Ltd.; pres. W.D.H.G. Fin. Assocs. Ltd., Vancouver; dir. B.C. Forest Products Ltd., Drummond Petroleum Ltd., East Asiatic Co. (Can.) Ltd., Fed. Pioneer Ltd., Galaxy Minerals, Inc., Hastings West Investment Ltd., Interprovincial Pipe Line Ltd., Mancal Ltd., Ni-Cal Devels. Ltd., Phoenician Holdings Ltd., Scott Paper Ltd., Shipping Corp. N.Z. Ltd., Woodward Stores Ltd. Pres. Boys Girls Clubs of Can., 1976. Served to lt. comdr. RCNVR. Presbyterian. Clubs: Toronto, Rosedale Golf (Toronto); Vancouver., Shaughnessy Golf and Country, Capilano Golf and Country. Home: 3115 W 49th Ave Vancouver BC V6M 3T3 Canada Office: Suite 1600 PO Box 11141 1055 W Georgia St Vancouver BC V6E 3S5 Canada

GARDINIER, DAVID ELMER, history educator; b. Syracuse, N.Y., Oct. 13, 1932; s. Kenneth Welles and Velma G. (Colyer) G.; m. Josefina Sevilla y Zialcita, July 2, 1966; children—Kenneth Raymond, Annemarie Cecile, Lourdes Marie. A.B., SUNY-Albany, 1953; M.A., Yale, 1954, Ph.D., 1960. Fulbright fellow U. Paris, France, 1958-59; instr. history U. Del., Newark, 1959-60; asst. prof. Bowling Green State U., 1960-65; asso. prof. history Marquette U., 1966-69, prof. history, 1969—, chmn. dept., 1969-75; research asso. Center Internat. Studies, Ohio U., Athens, 1965-66; sr. Fulbright scholar, Paris, fall 1979. Author: Cameroon, 1963, Historical Dictionary of Gabon, 1981; editor: Africa sect. Am. Hist. Rev, 1964—. Minister music St. Helen's Ch., Milw., 1982—. Mem. African Studies Assn., Am. Hist. Assn., French Colonial Hist. Soc. (v.p. 1976-78, pres. 1978-80, sec.-treas. 1980-82), Am. Guild Organists., Choristers Guild. Home: 21845 Gareth Ln Brookfield WI 53005

GARDNER, ALVIN FREDERICK, oral pathologist, government official; b. Chgo., Mar. 22, 1920; s. Leon William and Sarah (Kanter) G.; m. Ruth Myra Moskovitz, May 2, 1981; 1 dau., Ava Lee. A.A., U. Fla., 1940; D.D.S., Emory U., 1943; postgrad. certificate, U. Kansas City, 1946; postgrad. (NIH fellow), State U. Ia., 1954-55, M.S., U. Ill., 1957, Ph.D., Georgetown U., 1959. Diplomate: Internat. Bd. Applied Nutrition. Staff dentist AEC, Richland, Wash., 1944-45; chief dental staff Stockton (Calif.) State Hosp., 1945-46; pvt. practice dentistry, 1946-54; resident in oral pathology, mem. dental staff Armed Forces Inst. Pathology, Walter Reed Army Med. Center, Washington, 1957-59, mem. research staff, 1954—; asso. prof. pathology U. Md., Balt., 1959-63; dental officer Bur. of Medicine, FDA, HEW, 1963—; Vis. scientist Nat. Bur. Standards, 1957-59; cons. in oral pathology Stedmans Med. Dict., USPHS, VA. Author: Oral Pathology, Oral Roentgenology and Periodontics, 1963, Pathology in Dentistry, 1968, Differential Oral Diagnosis in Systemic Disease, 1970, Pathology of Oral Manifestations of Systemic Diseases, 1971, Dental Examination Review Book, 1983; also monographs, numerous articles in profl. jours.; Editor: American Lectures in Dentistry, 1968, Dental Postgraduate Handbook Series, 1976, Allied Health Handbook Series, 1983, Nursing Monograph Series, 1983; corr. editor: El Salvador Dental Jour; sci. editor: Jour. of Conn. Dental Assn. Served to capt., Dental Corps AUS Res., 1942-51. Grantee U.S. Army Research and Devel. Command, Surg. Gen.'s Office, 1962-63, NIH, USPHS, 1961-64, Sigma Xi, New Haven, 1962-63, Md. div. Am. Cancer Soc., 1962-63; recipient 3d prize Am. Soc. Oral Surgeons, 1962, Schering essay award, 1957. Fellow AAAS, Internat. Assn. Anesthesiologists, Internat. Coll. Applied Nutrition, Internat. Coll. Dentists, Am. Soc. Advancement Gen. Anesthesia in Dentistry, Am. Pub. Health Assn., Am. Med. Writer's Assn.; mem. A.M.A. (asso.), Am. Dental Assn., Md. Dental Assn. (asso. editor Jour. 1977), Calif. (hon. mem.), Conn. Dental Assns., So. Md. Dental Soc., Am. Assn. Dental Editors, Am. Acad. Oral Pathology, Am. Acad. Dental Medicine, Internat. Assn. Dental Research, Fedn. Dentaire Internationale, Am. Nutrition Soc., Am. Assn. Endodontists, Royal Soc. Health (Eng.), Am. Soc. Cytology, N.Y. Acad. Arts and Scis., Georgetown U., U. Ill., Emory U. alumni assns., Sigma Xi. Home: 2000 Hidden Valley Ln Silver Spring MD 20904 Office: Nat Ctr for Drugs and Biologics FDA Dept Health and Human Services Washington DC 20201 *A profession is an ever-changing field of endeavor. The professional man seldom examines the roots of a tree once he eats its fruit. The professional man is a continuous student throughout his life.*

GARDNER, ARNOLD BURTON, lawyer; b. N.Y.C., Jan. 3, 1930; s. Harry P. and Ruth G. (Gutfreund) G.; m. Sue Shaffer, Aug. 24, 1952; children—Jonathan H., Diane R. B.A. summa cum laude, U. Buffalo, 1950; LL.B., Harvard U., 1953. Bar: N.Y. State bar 1954. Assoc. firm Kavinoky & Cook (and predecessor), Buffalo, 1953-58; partner Kavinoky, Cook, Sandler, Gardner, Wisbaum & Lipman, 1958—, sr. partner, 1977—; chmn. bd. Algonquin Broadcasting Corp., Buffalo. Mem. Buffalo Bd. Edn., 1969-74, pres., 1971-72; mem. nat. bd. govs. Am. Jewish Com., 1972—; chmn. N.Y. State Edn. Dept. Task Force on Tchr. Edn. and Certification, 1975-77; trustee SUNY, 1980—; bd. govs. Hebrew Union Coll., Jewish Inst. Religion, Cin., 1981—. Served with U.S. Army, 1954-56. Recipient Community Service award NCCJ, 1974. Mem. Erie County Bar Assn., N.Y. State Bar Assn., ABA, Am. Law Inst. Club: Buffalo. Home: 89 Middlesex Rd Buffalo NY 14216 Office: 120 Delaware Ave Buffalo NY 14202

GARDNER, AVA, motion picture actress; b. Smithfield, N.C., Dec. 24; d. Jonas B. and Mary Elizabeth G.; m. Mickey Rooney, Jan. 10, 1942; m. Artie Shaw, 1945; m. Frank Sinatra, 1951. Student, Atlantic Christian Coll. Motion picture debut in We Were Dancing, 1942; other motion pictures include Earthquake, 1974, Devil's Widow, 1971, Life and Times of Judge Roy Bean, 1972, The Sentinel, 1976, Permission to Kill, 1976, The Bluebird, 1976, The Cassandra Crossing, 1977, City on Fire, 1978, The Kidnapping of the President, 1979, Priest of Love, 1980, Regina, 1982. Address: care Wm Morris Agy 151 El Camino Beverly Hills CA 90212 *

GARDNER, BERNARD, surgeon, educator; b. Bklyn., Oct. 1, 1931; s. Charles and Selma (Lovenberg) G.; m. Joan E. Mann., Dec. 18, 1954; children: Karen A., Pamela D., Robert A. A.B. cum laude, NYU, 1952, M.D., 1956. Intern Bellevue Hosp. Center, N.Y.C., 1956-57; resident Mt. Sinai Hosp., N.Y.C., 1957-58, U. Calif. Med. Center, San Francisco, 1961-65; asst. prof. surgery SUNY (Downstate Med. Center), Bklyn., 1965-68, asso. prof., 1968-72, prof., 1972; prof. surgery, dir. Bklyn. Cancer Center, Bklyn., 1973—; prof. surgery U. Medicine and Dentistry of N.J., 1983—; dir. dept. surgery Hackensack Med. Ctr., 1983—; cons. VA Hosp., Luth. Med. Center, Swedish Hosp., Meth. Hosp., Kingsbrook Med. Center, all Bklyn.; dir. div. surg. oncology Kings County Hosp., 1971; mem. study sect. cancer edn. Nat. Cancer Inst., 1981-83. Author: Emergency Surgery, 1974, Basic Surgery: Patient Oriented Text, 1978, Principles of Cancer Surgery, 1981. Served to capt. USAF, 1958-60. Fellow Am. Cancer Soc., 1965-68; Markle fellow, 1968-73; recipient numerous grants, 1962—. Fellow ACS; mem. Soc. U. Surgeons, Assn. Acad. Surgery (chmn. com. on issues 1971—), N.Y. Surg. Soc., N.Y. Cancer Soc., Soc. Exptl. Medicine and Biology. Research in metabolic effects of cancer, mechanism of gall stone dissolution. Home: 1 N Saddlebrook Dr Hohokus NJ 07423 Office: Dept Surgery Hackensack Med Ctr Hackensack NJ 07601

GARDNER, BERT ERWIN, manufacturing company executive; b. Los Angeles, Sept. 13, 1928; s. HillebertWilliam and Corris Vivian (Thaxter) Smith Gardner; m. Betty Joan Reese, Feb. 18, 1956; children: Laura Katherine, Barbara Lynne. B.S. in Bus. Adminstrn., U. Calif.-Berkeley, 1954. C.P.A., Pa. Supply officer Mil. Sea Transport Service, San Francisco, 1948-52; ptnr. Arthur Andersen & Co., Balt., 1956-72; sr. v.p. fin. Grove Mfg. Co., Shady Grove, Pa., 1972—; officer subs. Kidde, Inc. Bd. dirs. Day Care Ctr., Waynesboro, Pa.; trustee Waynesboro Hosp. Authority. Served with U.S. Army, 1954-56. Mem. Am. Inst. C.P.A.s, Pa. Inst. C.P.A.s, Machinery and Allied Products Inst., Am. Mgmt. Assn., Greater Wynesboro C. of C. (dir.). Home: 123 Clayton Ave Waynesboro PA 17268

GARDNER, BURDETT HARMON, English educator; b. Ashland, Maine, Aug. 14, 1917; s. Wesley Isaiah and Addie Vince (Nevers) G.; m. Rachel Margaret Cohen, Jan. 8, 1964; children: Benjamin, Daniel. Student, Colby Coll., 1935-36, La. State U., 1937-39; B.A., Boston U., 1940; M.A., Harvard, 1946; Ph.D. (Univ. fellow), Harvard, 1954. Instr. English U. Minn., 1947-48, U. Idaho, 1949-50, Fla. State U., 1950, Ga. Inst. Tech., 1950-52; asst. prof. English Heidelberg U., 1954-55, Elmira Coll., 1956-60; asso. prof. English Bloomsburg State Coll., 1961-62; asso. prof. English, chmn. dept. Park Coll., Parkville, Mo., 1962-63; prof. English, chmn. dept. Ky.-Wesleyan Coll., Owensboro, 1963-64; prof. English Monmouth Coll., West Long Branch, N.J., 1964—, chmn. dept., 1965-71; lectr. English Harvard, 1955-56. Served with Signal Intelligence AUS, 1942-46. Mem. Modern Lang. Assn. Home: 27 Elmwood Ave West Long Branch NJ 07764

GARDNER, BURLEIGH BRADFORD, consumer research company executive; b. Galveston, Tex., Dec. 4, 1902; s. William A. and Mary (Bradford) G.; m. Mary Ruby, July 1, 1933; children—Andrew, Stephen, Thomas. B.A., M.A. in Anthropology, U. Tex., 1930; Ph.D. in Social Anthropology, Harvard U., 1936. Charge sociol. survey of N.Mex. for Soil Conservation Service, 1936-37; research and devel. personnel counseling Western Electric Co., 1937-42; prof. Sch. Bus., U. Chgo., also exec. sec. com. on human relations in industry of univ., 1942-46; pres. Social Research, Inc., Chgo., 1946-72, chmn., 1972—; pres. Social Research Internat., Ltd., 1957-73; sec.-treas. Inst. for Social and Psychol. Studies, 1960-72. Author: (with D.G. Moore) Human Relations in Industry, 1955, (with A. Davis, Mary R. Gardner) Deep South-a Social Anthropological Study of Caste and Class, 1941, A Conceptual Framework for Advertising, 1982. Active Winnetka (Ill.) Village Caucus, Winnetka Schs.; Bd. dirs. Duncan Med. Center, YMCA. Mem. Am. Mktg. Assn. (chmn. publs. policy and rev. bd.), Soc. Applied Anthropology, N.Y. Acad. Scis. Home: 875 Burr Ave Winnetka IL 60093 Office: Social Research Inc 230 N Michigan Ave Chicago IL 60601

GARDNER, DALE ALLAN, astronaut, naval officer; b. Fairmont, Minn., Nov. 8, 1948; s. William Rex and Alic Bertha (Boehne) G.; m. Sue Grace Ticusan, Feb. 19, 1977; children: Lisa Amanda, Todd Allan. B.S. in Engring. Physics, U. Ill., 1970. Commd. naval flight officer U.S. Navy, 1970, advanced through grades to comdr., 1984; naval flight officer, Pensacola, Fla., 1970-71, Patuxent River, Md., 1971-73, Miramar, Calif., 1973-76, Point Mugu, Calif., 1976-78; astronaut NASA, Houston, 1978—; support crew astronaut for STS-4, 1982; mission specialist on STS-8, launched from, Kennedy Space Ctr., Fla., Aug. 30, 1983, (3d flight for Orbier Challenger), Aug. 30, 1983, completed 98 orbits of Earth in 145 hours, Aug. 30, 1983; mission specialist for Space Shuttle mission launch, Oct. 1984. Decorated Space Flight medal NASA, 1983. Mem. Phi Eta Sigma, Tau Beta Pi, Sigma Tau. Republican. Episcopalian. Office: Johnson Space Ctr CB Houston TX 77058

GARDNER, DAVID MORGAN, business administration educator; b. Des Moines, Sept. 29, 1936; s. Homer William and Ethel Louise (Morgan) G.; m. Lois K. Fritz, Dec. 31, 1958; children: Anne, John. B.S.C., U. Iowa, 1958; M.S., U. Minn., 1964, Ph.D., 1966. With J.C. Penney Co., 1958-63; prof. dept. bus. adminstrn. U. Ill., Urbana, 1966—; with FTC, 1972-73. Mem. Am. Mktg. Assn. (Harold Maynard award 1976), Assn. Consumer Research (nat. pres. 1976), Am. Psychol. Assn., Small Bus. Inst. Dirs. Assn. Home: 1003 Hollycrest Champaign IL 61821 Office: 1206 S 6th St Champaign IL 61820

GARDNER, DAVID PIERPONT, university president; b. Berkeley, Calif., Mar. 24, 1933; s. Reed S. and Margaret (Pierpont) G.; m. Elizabeth Fuhriman, June 27, 1958; children: Karen, Shari, Lisa, Marci. B.S., Brigham Young U., 1955; M.A., U. Calif. at Berkeley, 1959, Ph.D., 1966. Dir. Calif. Alumni Found., U. Calif. at Berkeley, 1962-64; asst. chancellor U. Calif. at Santa Barbara, 1966-69, vice chancellor, exec. asst., prof. higher edn., 1969-71; v.p. U. Calif. System, Berkeley, 1971-73; pres., prof. higher edn. U. Utah, Salt Lake City, 1973-83; pres. U. Calif. System, 1983—; vis. fellow Clare Hall, Cambridge U., 1979, asso., 1979—. Author: The California Oath Controversy, 1967. Dir. Utah Power & Light Co., Salt Lake City br. Fed. Res. Bank of San Francisco, First Security Corp.; Chmn. pres.'s council Western Athletic Conf., 1973; chmn. nat. bd. courses by newspaper Nat. Endowment Humanities; mem. study group on post-secondary edn. Nat. Inst. Edn.; founding trustee and chmn. Tanner Lectures on Human Values. Mem. Am. Council on Edn. (dir. 1977—), Am. Assn. Higher Edn., AAUP, Phi Kappa Phi. Clubs: Rotarian. Clubs, Alta, Timpanogos, Ft. Douglas. Office: Office of Pres U Calif 2200 University Ave Berkeley CA 94720 *

GARDNER, DONALD JOHN, forest products company executive; b. Cleve., June 15, 1927; s. John and Albina (Moser) G.; m. Norma Eileen Keyser, Mar. 17, 1951; 1 son: Mark David. B.A., Case Westren Res. U., 1951. Personnel mgr. Champion Internat., Cleve., 1962-66, gen. supr. labor relations, Canton, N.C., 1966-70, mgr. indsl. relations, Hamilton, Ohio, 1970-71, dir. employee relations, 1971-74, v.p. employee relations, Stamford, Conn., 1974—. Bd. dirs. United Way of Stamford, 1978; vol. Mgmt. Assistance Program, Stamford, 1983. Served with USN, 1945-46. Mem. Am. Soc. Personnel Adminstrn. Office: 1 Champion Plaza Stamford CT 06921

GARDNER, DONALD LAVERE, development company executive; b. Winfield, Kans., Aug. 1, 1930; s. Lindell L. and Eva (Robinson) G.; m. Dolores E. Willson, Dec. 27, 1952; children: Theresa L., Michelle M., Blake R. B.S., U. Kans., 1952; M.B.A., U. Chgo., 1956. Div. asst. No. Trust Co., Chgo., 1954-57; v.p. Security Pacific Nat. Bank, Riverside, Calif., 1957-63; pres., gen. mgr. G.T. Wolfe Mobile Homes, Inc., Corona, Calif., 1963-66; exec. v.p. Evans Products Co., Corona, 1966-71; pres. U.S. Homes, Inc., Anaheim, Calif., 1971-72; chmn., pres. DLG Devel. Corp., Santa Ana, Calif., 1972—; vice chmn. McCombs Corp., Irvine, Calif., 1979—; Instr. Valley Coll., San Bernardino, Calif., 1959-63, Riverside (Calif.) City Coll., 1960-64. Active United Fund; water commr., Corona, 1965. Served with arty. AUS, 1952-54. Named Citizen of Yr. City of Riverside, 1960. Mem. Corona C. of C. (dir.), Beta Gamma Sigma. Club: Rotarian (pres. 1964). Home: 180 S Lakeview Ave Anaheim CA 92807 Office: 2392 Morse Ave Irvine CA 92713

GARDNER, ERIC FREEMAN, psychology educator; b. Brooklyn, N.S., Can., Mar. 16, 1913; came to U.S., 1913, naturalized, 1917; s. Clayton E. and Elizabeth E. (Taylor) G.; m. Catherine Smalley-Smith, June 24, 1939; 1 dau., Elizabeth Holdsworth. A.B., Harvard U., 1935, Ed.D., 1947; M.Ed., Boston Tchrs. Coll., 1936; cert. naval architecture, U. Mich., 1944. Tchr. math. pub. and pvt. schs., Mass., R.I., Vt., 1936-41; instr. Harvard U., 1946-47; faculty Syracuse U., 1947-79, prof. psychology and edn., 1952-79; dir. grad. studies Sch. Edn. (Syracuse U.), 1952-60, chmn. psychology dept., 1960-76, dir. Psychol. Services and Research Center, 1960-78, now Margaret O. Slocum prof. edn. and psychology emeritus; chmn. bd. trustees Test Research Service, Inc., 1960-68; adv. com. exptl. programs N.Y. State Edn. Dept., also adv. com. coll. proficiency exams. Author: Tomorrow's Graduate School of Education, 1958; co-author: Stanford Achievement Test, rev. edit., 1982, Syracuse Scales of Social Relations, 1959, Educational Psychology, 1959, Social Relations and Moral in Small Groups, 1956, Stanford High School Achievement Tests, 1966, Stanford Diagnostic Reading Tests, 1968, 76, Stanford Diagnostic Mathematics Tests, 1976, Adult Basic Learning Examinations, 1968, Stanford Modern Mathematics Concepts Test, 1967, Classification and Placement Examination, 1966, Aptitude for Learning Potential Tests, 1971, Stanford Test of Academic Skills, 1982, Syracuse Environmental Awareness Tests, 1973, Stanford Early School Achievement Test, 1982; content editor: Library of Education, 100 vols., 1962. Trustee Manlius-Pebble Hill Sch., 1968-75, Syracuse Symphony. Served to lt. USNR, 1942-46. Fellow Am. Psychol. Assn.; mem. Am. Statis. Assn., Inst. Math. Stats., Psychometrics Soc., Biometrics Soc., AAUP, Nat. Council Measurement in Edn., Inst. Nuclear Power Ops. (chmn. com. selection of nuclear reactor ops.). Home: 103 Draycott St Fayetteville NY 13066 Office: Psychology Dept Huntington Hall 150 Marshall St Syracuse NY 13210

GARDNER, FREDERICK CALKIN, ins. co. exec.; b. Pawling, N.Y., Aug. 1, 1910; s. John C. and Elizabeth (Calkin) G.; m. Nancy Lewis, Dec. 29, 1949. A.B., Columbia, 1932, LL.B., 1934. With Office Gen. Counsel USN, 1946-47; v.p., sec. Chubb Corp., N.Y.C., 1967—, Chubb & Son, Inc., 1965—, Fed. Ins. Co., N.Y.C., 1960—; sec. Vigilant Ins. Co., 1960—, Gt. No. Ins. Co., 1971—, Bellemead Devel. Corp., 1971—; sec., dir. Chubb Ins. Co. Ill., 1972—. Served with AUS, 1941-42, 44-45. Decorated Bronze Star medal. Clubs: India House, Metropolitan (N.Y.C.). Home: Pecksland Rd Greenwich CT 06830 Office: 100 William St New York NY 10038

GARDNER, GEORGE PEABODY, JR., investment banker; b. Newton, Mass., Sept. 2, 1917; s. George Peabody and Rose (Grosvenor) G.; m. Tatiana Stepanova, June 21, 1947; children: George Peabody 3d, Alexandra, Tatiana. Grad., St. Mark's Sch., 1935; A.B., Harvard U., 1939. Mem. expdn. to Peru Mus. Comparative Zoology, 1939-40; with advt. dept. Boston Herald Traveler, 1947-48; account exec. Batton, Barton, Durstine & Osborn (advt.), 1948-51; with Paine, Webber, Jackson & Curtis, Boston, 1952—, partner, 1955-71; sr. v.p., dir. Paine, Webber, Jackson & Curtis, Inc., 1971-79; mng. dir. Blyth Eastman Paine Webber, 1979-82, adv. dir., 1983—; dir. Paine Webber, Inc., Stanley Home Products, Inc., Barry Wright Corp., W.R. Grace & Co. Life mem. corp. M.I.T.; trustee Boston Mus. Sci., Inst. Def. Analyses, Washington, Children's Hosp. Med. Center, Escuela Agricola Panamericana, Honduras. Served from ensign to lt. comdr. USNR, 1940-46; PTO. Fellow Am. Acad. Arts and Scis. Clubs: A.D. (Cambridge, Mass.); Tavern (Boston); Union League, Links (N.Y.C.). Home: 130 Warren St Brookline MA 02146 Office: 100 Federal St Boston MA 02101

GARDNER, HOWARD ALAN, travel marketing executive; b. Rockford, Ill., June 24, 1920; s. Ellis Ralph and Leanor (Roseman) G.; m. Marjorie Ruth Klein, Sept. 29, 1945; children: Jill, Jeffrey. B.A., U. Mich., 1941. With advt. dept. Chgo. Tribune, 1941-43; mgr. promotion dept. Esquire mag., 1943-46; advt. mgr. Mrs. Klein's Food Products Co., 1946-48; pres. Sales-Aide Service Co., 1948-56, Gardner & Stein, 1956-59, Gardner, Stein & Frank, Inc., Chgo., 1959-83, Fun-derful World, 1983—. Mem. Confrerie de la Chaine des Rotisseurs (officer), Connoisseurs Internat. (dir.), Phi Beta Kappa. Clubs: International, East Bank. Home: 100 Bellevue Pl Chicago IL 60611 Office: 20 N Wacker Dr Chicago IL 60606

GARDNER, HOYT DEVANE, surgeon; b. Paragould, Ark., Aug. 2, 1923; s. Hoyt Landis and Grace Ruth (Grady) G.; m. Rose Brakmeier, Mar. 31, 1945; children: Hoyt Devane, Thomas George, Nicholas George. Student, Westminster Coll., 1942-43; A.B., U. Louisville, 1946, M.D., 1950; M.Surgery, U. Mich., 1955. Diplomate: Am. Bd. Surgery. Intern Receiving Hosp., Detroit, 1951; resident in surgery Henry Ford Hosp., Detroit, 1953-57; practice medicine specializing in surgery, Louisville, 1958—; prof. surgery U. Louisville; trustee Ky. Blue Shield Assn.; mem. U.S. del. World Health Assembly, Geneva, 1977; chmn. Louisville and Jefferson County Bd. Health; mem. Ky. Comprehensive Health Planning Com.; chmn. Ky. Ednl. Med. Polit. Action Com.; bd. dirs. Am. Med. Polit. Action Com. Mem. Ky. Republican Central Com.; chmn. bd. trustees, mem. bd. overseers U. Louisville; mem. Louisville Mayor's Citizens Adv. Com. Served with USN, World War II; with USAF; Korea. Named Outstanding Alumni Westminster Coll., 1977, Outstanding Med. Alumni U. Louisville, 1978; recipient Outstanding Citizen award Louisville Jr. C. of C., 1978. Fellow A.C.S.; mem. Jefferson County Med. Soc. (past pres.), Ky. Med. Assn. (past pres., past chmn. nat. affairs, legis. com.), AMA (pres.-elect 1978, trustee 1974—), Southeastern Surg. Soc., Ky. Surg. Soc., U. Louisville Med. Alumni Assn. (past pres.), Delta Tau Delta, Alpha Kappa Kappa, Omicron Delta Kappa, Alpha Omega Alpha. Presbyterian. Clubs: Big Springs Country, Jefferson (Louisville); Internat. (Chgo.); Rotary. Office: 304 Baptist E Doctors Bldg 3950 Kresge Way Louisville KY 40207 *

GARDNER, HY, columnist, TV-radio performer, writer, producer; b. N.Y.C., Dec. 2, 1908; s. John Jacob and Sarah (Guilden) G.; m. Marilyn Boshnick, Apr., 1958; 1 son, Jeffrey Scott; 1 son by previous marriage, Ralph Richard. Student, Columbia U. Sch. Journalism. Syndicated Broadway columnnist: N.Y. Herald Tribune, 15 years; editor: Trib TV mag.; star: TV and radio Broadway and Hollywood Hy Gardner's Celebrity Party, Miami, Fla.; producer, performer, Miami TV-WCIX, nat. syndicate; formerly on NBC-TV series and; panelist: CBS-TV series Hy Gardner Calling; Cast, produced: Hi-Yank; made: movie The Girl Hunters; Author: So What Else is New, 1960, Tales Out of Night School, Off-Beat Guide to New York, Glad You Asked That; column pub., News America Syndicate (formerly Field Syndicate). Served as capt. AUS, 1942-45; ret. maj. Res. Recipient Freedoms Found. award in Journalism. Office: News America Syndicate 1703 Kaiser Ave Irvine CA 92714 *

GARDNER, JAMES ALBERT, college president; b. Marietta, Ohio, July 22, 1943; s. George Albert and Vernah (Stewart) G.; m. Carol Wik-Lentz, Sept. 18, 1971; 1 child, Jay Morgan. B.A. cum laude, Harvard U., 1965; J.D., Yale U., 1968. Tutor, law and social sci., asst. dir. admissions Harvard Coll., 1968-69; asst. to rep. Ford Found., Brazil, 1969-71, program officer, asst. to head for Latin Am., N.Y.C., 1971-73, rep., Caribbean, 1974-76, Brazil, 1976-81; vis. scholar Harvard U. Law Sch., 1973-74; pres. Lewis and Clark Coll., Portland, Oreg., 1981—. Author: Urbanization in Brazil, 1971, Legal Imperialism: American Lawyers and Foreign Aid in Latin America, 1980. Mem. exec. bd. Pacific council Boy Scouts Am.; bd. dirs. Fulbright Commn., Brazil, Oreg. Ind. Coll. Found. Mem. Am. Soc. Internat. Law, Oreg. Ind. Colls. Assn. (dir.), Law and Soc. Assn., Latin Am. Studies Assn., Caribbean Studies Assn., Young Pres.'s Orgn., Inst. Internat. Edn. Presbyterian. Clubs: University, Waverley Country (Portland); Windermere Island (Eleuthera, Bahamas). Office: 0615 SW Palatine Hill Rd Portland OR 97219

GARDNER, JOHN CRAWFORD, newspaper publisher; b. Emory University, Ga., Apr. 19, 1935; s. James Watts and Mary Jane (McCoy) G.; m. Ann S. Lindsay, Mar. 24, 1956; children: Ellen, Elizabeth, Paul, John, Matthew. B.J., Northwestern U., 1956; postgrad., Columbia, 1956-57. Writer A.P., N.Y.C., 1956-57; reporter Charlotte (N.C.) Observer, 1957-59, So. Illinoisan, Carbondale, 1959-61, city editor, 1961-62, mng. editor, 1962-64, editor, gen. mgr., 1964-76, pub., 1977—; pres. So. Illinoisan Inc., 1966-79; lectr. journalism Medill Sch. Journalism, Northwestern U., 1972-79; vis. lectr. Sch. Journalism, So. Ill. U., Carbondale, 1977—. Mem. Am. Soc. Newspaper Editors, So. Ill. Editorial Assn., Ill. A.P. Editors Assn. (pres. 1974-75), Inland Daily Press Assn. (chmn. edn. com. 1975-80), Ill. Humanities Council, Sigma Delta Chi. Episcopalian. Home: Drury Church Rd Route 3 Box 42C Carbondale IL 62901

GARDNER, JOHN HALE, physicist; b. Logan, Utah, Aug. 24, 1922; s. Willard and Rebecca Viola (Hale) G.; m. Olga Dotson, July 23, 1943; children—Helen, John, Kristin, Rebecca, Robert, Eric, Ann, Margaret. B.S. with honors, Utah State U., 1943; A.M., Harvard, 1947, Ph.D., 1950. Mem. staff Mass. Inst. Tech. Radiation Lab., 1943-46; teaching fellow Harvard, 1946-49; asst. prof. physics Brigham Young U., Provo, Utah, 1949-52, asso. prof., 1952-58, prof., 1958—, chmn. dept., 1961-72, chmn. univ. curriculum council, 1968-78; Mem. tech. staff Ramo-Wooldridge Corp., 1955-57; cons. Space Tech. Labs., 1957-65, mem. tech. staff, 1963-64. Contbr. articles to profl. jours. Fellow Inst. Physics London, Utah Acad. Sci., Arts and Letters (v.p. 1966-67, pres. 1967-68, mem. council 1968-69, mem. bd. fellows 1973, Distinguished service award 1972), Am. Phys. Soc.; mem. Am. Assn. Physics Tchrs., Sigma Xi (chpt. pres. 1961-62), Phi Kappa Phi (chpt. pres. 1958-59). Republican. Mem. Ch. of Jesus Christ of Latter-day Saints. Patentee on microwave antennas, plasma physics devices. Home: 1140 Aspen Ave Provo UT 84601

GARDNER, JOHN RIDGELY, retired banker; b. St. Louis, Mar. 16, 1920; s. Russell E. and Enid (Simpkins) G.; m. Virginia Shell, Dec. 31, 1959; children: John Ridgely, William Edmund Scripps, Elizabeth, Katherine, Russell Eugene II, Enid Ridgely. Grad., Princeton U., 1943. Account exec. St. Louis Union Trust Co., 1946-49; ptnr. Reinholdt & Gardner, St. Louis, 1950-79; v.p. Mark Twain Banks, 1979-82; Bd. govs. Am. Stock Exchange, 1967-70. Served with USNR, World War II. Republican. Episcopalian. Clubs: Cottage (Princeton, N.J.); St. Louis Country. Home: 9885 Conway Rd Saint Louis MO 63124

GARDNER, JOHN WILLIAM, advocate, writer, consultant; b. Los Angeles, Oct. 8, 1912; s. William and Marie (Flora) G.; m. Aida Marroquin, Aug. 18, 1934; children: Stephanie Gardner Trimble, Francesca Gardner Reese. A.B., Stanford U., 1935; Ph.D., U. Calif., 1938, LL.D., 1959; hon. degrees from various colls., univs.; hon. fellow, Stanford, 1959. Teaching asst. in psychology U. Calif., 1936-38; instr. psychology Conn. Coll., 1938-40; asst. prof. psychology Mt. Holyoke Coll., 1940-42; head Latin-Am. sect. FCC, 1942-43; mem. staff Carnegie Corp. of N.Y., 1946-47, exec. asso., 1947-49, v.p., 1949-55, pres., 1955-65, cons., 1968-77; pres. Carnegie Found. Advancement of Teaching, 1955-65; sec. HEW, 1965-68; chmn. Urban Coalition, 1968-70; founder and chmn. Common Cause, 1970-77; chmn. Pres.'s Commn. on White House Fellowships, 1980-83, Independent Sector, 1980-83; sr. fellow Aspen Inst. Humanistic Studies, 1981—; cons. United Way Am., 1977—; vis. prof. MIT, 1968-69; fellow Kennedy Inst. Politics, Harvard U., 1968-69; Mem. Pres. Kennedy's Task Force on Edn., 1960; chmn. U.S. Adv. Commn. Internat. Ednl. and Cultural Affairs, 1962-64, Pres. Johnson's Task Force on Edn., 1964, White House Conf. Edn., 1965; dir. N.Y. Telephone Co., 1961-65, Shell Oil Co., 1962-65, Am. Airlines, 1968-71, Time, Inc., 1968-72. Author: Excellence, 1961, rev. edit., 1984, Self-Renewal, 2d edit, 1981, No Easy Victories, 1968, The Recovery of Confidence, 1970, In Common Cause, 1972, Know or Listen to Those Who Know, 1975, Morale, 1978, Quotations of Wit and Wisdom, 1980; Editor: To Turn the Tide (John F. Kennedy). Trustee N.Y. Sch. Social Work, 1949-55, Met. Mus. Art, 1957-65, Stanford U., 1968-82, Rockefeller Bros. Fund, 1968-77, Jet Propulsion Lab., 1978-82. Served with USMC, 1943-46. Recipient USAF Exceptional Services award, 1956; Presdl. Medal of Freedom, 1964; Nat. Acad. Scis. Pub. Welfare medal, 1966; U.A.W. Social Justice award, 1968; Democratic Legacy award Anti-Defamation League, 1968; AFL-CIO Murray Green medal, 1970; Christopher award, 1971. Fellow Am. Acad. Arts and Scis., Nat. Acad. Edn.; mem. AAAS (past dir.). Clubs: Bohemian (San Francisco); Century Assn., Coffee House, Cosmos, Fed. City (Washington). Office: 1828 L St NW Washington DC 20036

GARDNER, JOSEPH ARTHUR FREDRICK, forestry scientist, university dean; b. Nakusp, C., Can., Aug. 17, 1919; s. GeorgeHunter and Maude (Williams) G.; m. Joyce Harper, June 3, 1944; children: Joseph William, Mary Lee. B.A., U. B.C., Vancouver, 1940, M.A., 1942; Ph.D., McGill U., Montreal, Que., Can., 1944. Research asso. McGill U., 1944-45; research chemist Howard Smith Paper Mills, 1945-47; head wood chemistry Western Forest Products Lab., Vancouver, B.C., 1947-63, lab. dir., 1963-65; prof. wood chemistry, dean Faculty of Forestry, U. B.C., 1965—; dir. Forintek, 1979—. Contbr. numerous articles on wood chemistry to profl. jours. Fellow Chem. Inst. Can., Internat. Acad. Wood Sci.; mem. Can. Inst. Forestry, Soc. Am. Foresters, Forest Products Research Soc., Soc. Wood Sci. and Tech., TAPPI, Can. Pulp and Paper Assn., Phytochem. Soc., Assn. B.C. Profl. Foresters (hon.). Home: 5537 Wallace St Vancouver BC V6N 2A1 Canada Office: Faculty of Forestry UBC Vancouver BC V6T 1W5 Canada

GARDNER, JOSEPH LAWRENCE, editor; b. Willmar, Minn., Jan. 26, 1933; s. Elmer Joseph and Margaret Eleanor (Archer) G.; m. Sadako Miyasaka, Feb. 25, 1967; children: Miya Elise, Justin Lawrence. Student, U. Portland, Oreg., 1951-52; B.A. summa cum laude, U. Oreg., 1955; M.A. (Woodrow Wilson fellow), U. Wis., 1956. Researcher, writer, asst. editor, mng. editor Am. Heritage Books div. Am. Heritage Pub. Co., Inc., N.Y.C., 1959-65; editor Am. Heritage Jr. Library and Horizon Caravel Books, 1965-68; mng. editor Newsweek Books div. Newsweek Inc., N.Y.C., 1968-70, editor, 1971-76; sr. staff editor Reader's Digest Gen. Books, N.Y.C., 1976-81, group editor gen. reference, 1982—. Author: Labor on the March, 1969, Departing Glory, Theodore Roosevelt as ex-President, 1973; Editor: series Newsweek Condensed Books, 1971-76, The World's Last Mysteries, 1978, Reader's Digest Wide World Atlas, 1979, Reader's Digest Atlas of the Bible, 1981; Eat Better, Live Better, 1982. Mem. Town Club, Scarsdale, N.Y., 1974—; bd. dirs. Friends of Scarsdale Library, 1976-81, v.p., 1979-81; trustee Scarsdale Adult Sch., 1978—, treas., 1981—; trustee Scarsdale Pub. Library, 1983—. Served with AUS, 1956-58. Mem. P.E.N., Phi Beta Kappa, Sigma Delta Chi, Phi Kappa Psi. Club: Coffee House (N.Y.C.). Home: 17 Cohawney Rd Scarsdale NY 10583 Office: Reader's Digest 750 3d Ave New York NY 10017

GARDNER, JOSEPHT., wholesale grocery distributing company executive; b. 1917. A.B., Duke U., 1940. Advt. Tip Top Grocery Co., 1945-54; prin. Gardner's Super Market Inc., 1954—; dir. Associated Grocers Fla., Miami, 1956—, v.p., 1962-63, pres., 1971—, also chmn. bd. Served to capt. USN, 1941-45. Address: Associated Grocers Fla 6695 NW 36th Ave Miami FL 33147 *

GARDNER, KEITH, editor; b. Des Moines, Nov. 8, 1930; s. Arthur E. and Edith D. (McConnell) G. Student, Coll. City San Francisco, 1948-50; A.B. in Journalism, San Jose (Calif.) State Coll., 1952. Reporter Daly City (Calif.) Record, 1952-53; with Ford Motor Motor Co., Long Beach, Calif., 1955-56; copy boy N.Y. Mirror, 1956-57; messenger Benton & Bowles (advt.), N.Y.C., 1957; staff Travel mag., 1957-69, asso. editor, 1958-69; editor Fishing World mag., 1969—. Served with AUS, 1953-55. Office: 51 Atlantic Ave Floral Park NY 11001

GARDNER, LEONARD BURTON, II, industrial automation engineer; b. Lansing, Mich., Feb. 16, 1927; s. Leonard Burton and Lillian Marvin (Frost) G.; m. Barbara Jean Zivi, June 23, 1950; children: Karen Sue, Jeffrey Frank. B.Sc. in Physics, UCLA, 1951; M.Sc., Golden State U., 1953, Sc.D. in Engring, 1954; M.Sc. in Computer Sci, Augustana Coll., Rock Island, Ill., 1977. Registered profl. engr.; cert. mfg. engr. Instrumentation engr. govt. and pvt. industry, 1951—; prin. engr. computerized systems Naval Electronic Systems Engring. Center, San Diego, 1980-82; founder, dir. Automated Integrated Mfg., San Diego, 1982—; prof. and dir. Center for Automated Integrated Mfg., San Diego State U.; cons. govt. agys. and industry, lectr., adj. prof. vaious univs. and colls., sci. advisor state and nat. legislators, 1980—, speaker in field. Contbg. author: Instrumentation Handbook, 1981; contbr. numerous articles to tech. jours. Recipient award U.S. Army. Fellow IEEE; sr. mem. Soc. Mfg. Engrs.; mem. ASTM, Nat. Soc. Profl. Engrs., Sigma Xi. Office: PO Box 1523 Spring Valley CA 92077 *I believe in professional development through continuing education and participation in technical societies. I am committed to do my fair share and believe if everyone discharged this responsibility, no one person would become burdened and mankind would benefit immeasurably.*

GARDNER, LLOYD CALVIN, JR., history educator; b. Delaware, Ohio, Nov. 9, 1934; s. Lloyd Calvin and Hazel Belle (Grove) G.; m. Nancy Jean Wintermute, June 3, 1956; children: Rebecca, Erin, Timothy. B.A., Ohio Wesleyan U., 1956; M.S., U. Wis., 1957, Ph.D., 1960. Instr. Lake Forest (Ill.) Coll., 1959-60; faculty history dept. Rutgers U., New Brunswick, N.J., 1963—, asst. prof., 1963-64, asso. prof., 1964-67, prof., 1967—, chmn. history dept., 1970-73, prof. II, 1977—; adv. com. Franklin D. Roosevelt Library, Hyde Park, N.Y., 1972-73, Fgn. Relations U.S. publ. State Dept., 1975—, chmn., 1977-78; Fulbright prof., Eng., 1975-76, Fulbright Bicentennial prof., Helsinki, 1983-84. Author: Economic Aspects of New Deal, 1964, Architects of Illusion, 1970, (with William O'Neill) Looking Backward, 1972, Imperial America, 1976, A Covenant with Power, 1983. Served with USAF, 1960-63. Social Sci. Research Council fellow, 1965-66; Guggenheim fellow, 1973-74. Mem. Am. Hist. Assn., Orgn. Am. Historians, Soc. Historians of Am. Fgn. Relations, Pacific Hist. Assn., AAUP. Home: 15 Redcoat Dr East Brunswick NJ 08816 Office: History Dept Rutgers U New Brunswick NJ 08903

GARDNER, LUCIEN DUNBIBBIN, JR., lawyer; b. Troy, Ala., Mar. 1, 1903; s. Lucien and Henrietta (Wiley) G.; m. Amy Cothran Young, Jan. 11, 1930; 1 son, William Fenwick; m. Ann G. Goodall, Nov. 27, 1974. B.A., U. Ala., 1922; LL.B., Harvard, 1925. Bar: Ala. bar 1925. Practice in, Birmingham, 1925-42, 46—; mem. firm Cabaniss, Johnston, Gardner, Dumas & O'Neal (and predecessor firms), 1933-42, 46-78, of counsel, 1979—; gen. counsel, dir. Protective Life Ins. Co., 1958-72; v.p., trust officer First Nat. Bank Montgomery, Ala., 1945-46. Trustee, hon. trustee Children's Hosp., Birmingham, 1952—; past asso. mem. Neighborhood House, Birmingham. Served to lt. col. USAAF, 1942-45. Fellow Am. Coll. Trial Lawyers; mem. ABA, Ala. Bar Assn., Birmingham Bar Assn. (pres. 1959, disting. service award 1979), Newcomen Soc., Assn. Life Ins. Counsel, S.R., Sigma Nu. Episcopalian (vestry, sr. warden 1961). Clubs: Mountain Brook (bd. govs., pres. 1960), Redstone (past bd. govs.), The Club.). Home: 34 Fairway Dr Birmingham AL 35213 Office: First Nat-Southern Natural Bldg Birmingham AL 35203

GARDNER, MCDONALD DOZIER, financial executive; b. b. St. Louis, June 29, 1933; s. Dozier Lee and Carol (McDonald) G.; m. Margaret Butler, Sept. 9, 1961; children: Dozier L., Grace M., Diana S. A.B., Princeton U., 1955; M.B.A., Harvard U., 1959. Bar: chartered fin. analyst. Research asst. Harvard Bus. Sch., Cambridge, Mass., 1959-63, assoc., instr., 1963; investment officer Mass. Investors Trust, Boston, 1963-68; v.p. Vance Sanders & Co., Boston, 1968—; pres., dir. Eaton Vance Corp., 1979—; incorporator Brookline Savs. Bank, 1973—. Vice chmn. Wheelock Coll., 1975-76, trustee, 1965-76; chmn. The Park Sch., Brookline, Mass., 1974-77, trustee, 1970-77; chmn. Dana-Farmer Cancer Inst., Boston, 1982—, trustee, 1976—. Mem. Boston Security Analysts of CFA. Office: 24 Federal St Boston MA 02110

GARDNER, MURRAY BRIGGS, pathologist, educator; b. Lafayette, Ind., Oct. 5, 1929; s. Max William and Margaret (Briggs) G.; m. Alice E. Danielson, June 20, 1961; children: Suzanna, Martin, Danielson, Andrew. B.A., U. Calif., Berkeley, 1951, M.D., 1954. Intern Moffitt Hosp., San Francisco, 1954-55; resident in gen. practice Sonoma County Hosp., Santa Rosa, Calif., 1957-59; resident in pathology U. Calif. hosps., San Francisco, 1959-63; faculty U. So. Calif. Sch. Medicine, Los Angeles, 1963-81, prof. pathology, 1973-81, U. Calif., Davis Sch. Medicine, 1981—, chmn. dept. pathology, 1982—; dir. anat. pathology U. Calif., Davis Med. Center, Sacramento, 1981—. Contbr. chpts. to books, numerous articles in field to profl. jours. Served to lt. M.C. USNR, 1957-59. NIH grantee, 1968—. Mem. Coll. Am. Pathologists, Internat. Acad. Pathology, Los Angeles Acad. Medicine. Home: 8313 Maxwell Ln Dixon CA 95620 Office: U Calif-Davis Med Sch MS-1 Davis CA 95620

GARDNER, PETER D., chemist; b. Salt Lake City, Jan. 17, 1927; s. Pete D. and Margaret (Rasmason) G.; m. Arlene Thomas, Aug. 6, 1950; children—Mark S., Connie J., Stephen P. B.S., U. Utah, 1949, M.S., 1950, Ph.D., 1953. Chemist Merck & Co., Rahway, N.J., 1951-52; faculty U. Tex., Austin, 1953-65, prof. chemistry, 1962-65, U. Utah, Salt Lake City, 1965—, prof. biology, 1977—, dean sci., 1970-73, acad. v.p., 1973-77. Served with AUS, 1945. Home: 2200 S 2300 E Salt Lake City UT 84109

GARDNER, R. H. (RUFUS HALLETTE III), drama and film critic; b. Mayfield, Ky., July 25, 1918; s. Rufus Hallette and Kathleen (Moorman) G. A.B., Tex. Christian U., 1941. Aircraft engr. Glenn L. Martin Co., 1941-49; reporter, feature writer Balt. Sun, 1951-54, drama critic, 1954—, film critic, 1954-81; Vis. lectr. Goucher Coll., 1968; lectr. Humanities Inst., 1976-77; film critic WMAR-TV, 1976-77, drama critic, 1976-80; drama and film critic WBJC Pub. Radio, 1981—. Author: plays I.O.U. Jeremiah, 1950, Christabel and the Rubicon, 1968; book The Splintered Stage: The Decline of the American Theatre, 1965. Bd. dirs. Balt. Internat. Film Festival, 1975-81. Mem. Am. Theater Critics Assn., Authors League, Dramatists Guild, Am. Newspaper Guild. Office: 1222 St Paul St Baltimore MD 21202

GARDNER, RALPH DAVID, advertising executive; b. N.Y.C., Apr. 16, 1923; s. Benjamin and Myra (Berman) G.; m. Nellie Jaglom, Apr. 9, 1952; children: Ralph David, John Jaglom, Peter Jaglom, James Jaglom. Diploma in journalism, NYU, 1942; diploma in mil. adminstrn., Colo. State Coll., 1943. With N.Y. Times, 1942-55, copy boy, city desk, fgn. corr., started internat. edit., Paris, 1949, bur. mgr. for Germany and Austria, Frankfurt, 1950, resigned, 1955; pres. Ralph D. Gardner Advt., N.Y.C., 1955—; dir. Gardner Internat. Corp.; Quality Irish Food Export (Dublin) Ltd.; dir. various other U.S. and fgn. corps.; writer, book reviewer, lectr., bibliographer 19th Century Am. lit.; Mary C. Richardson lectr. SUNY-Geneseo, 1974; vis. lectr. U. Wyo., others; mem. faculty Georgetown U. Writers Conf., 1976, 80; Hess research fellow U. Minn., 1979; book reviewer, host Ralph Gardner's Bookshelf, WVNJ-N.Y., other radio stas. Author: Horatio Alger, or The American Hero Era, 1964, 78, Road to Success: The Bibliography of the Works of Horatio Alger, 1971, Introduction to Silas Snobden's Office Boy, 1973, Introduction to Cast Upon the Breakers, 1974, History of Street & Smith, in Publishers for Mass Entertainment in 19th Century America, 1980, Introduction to a Fancy of Hers, 1981, The Disagreeable Woman, 1981, Struggling Upward, 1984, others; contbr. to: N.Y. Times Book Rev., Sat. Eve. Post, other newspapers and nat. mags. Mem.-at-large Greater N.Y. council Boy Scouts Am., 1950-60; bd. dirs. Fresh Air Council, 1964-66; mem. hon. exec. com. Nat. Citizens for Public Libraries. Served as newswriter with inf. AUS, 1943-46; ETO.; field Corr. Yank Mag. Recipient award for lit. Horatio Alger Soc., 1964, 72, 81; spl. citation scroll Horatio Alger Awards Com., 1978. Mem. Manuscript Soc., Bibliog. Soc. Am., Childrens Lit. Assn., Friends of Princeton U. Library, Syracuse U. Library Assos. (hon.), Brandeis U. Bibliophiles (hon.), Overseas Press Club of Am., Frankfurt Press Club (Germany), Nat. Book Critics Circle, Soc. of Silurians, PEN, Alpha Epsilon Pi. Clubs: Grolier; Baker St. Irregulars (N.Y.C.). Home: 135 Central Park West New York NY 10023 Office: 745 Fifth Ave New York NY 10022

GARDNER, REECE ALEXANDER, lawyer; b. Columbia, Mo., Oct. 6, 1911; s. Glenn Warner and Hazel (Straight) G.; m. Jean Clare McKeen, July 15, 1939; 1 dau., Ann Morton. A.B., Harvard U., 1933, J.D., 1936. Bar: Mo. 1936, Kans. 1941. Partner Stinson, Mag & Fizzell, Kansas City, Mo., 1939-83; dir. Mojaba Corp.; City clk., Mission Hills, Kans., 1959-70. Lectr., author in field. Pres. Andrew Drumm Inst., 1955-78, treas., 1978—; trustee The Villages, Inc., Mag Found., Park Found., H.O. Peet Found., Stinson, Mag, Thomson, McEvers & Fizzell Found.; hon. bd. dirs. Rockhurst Coll. Served to capt. AUS, 1942-46. Mem. Am., Fed., Kansas City bar assns., Am. Law Inst., Am. Judicature Soc., Judge Advocates Assn., Lawyers Assn. Kansas City, Mil. Order World Wars. Republican. Episcopalian. Clubs: Kansas City (Kans.) Country; Nat. Lawyers (Washington); University (Kansas City). Home: 5049 Wornall Rd Kansas City MO 64112

GARDNER, RICHARD ALAN, psychiatrist, author; b. Bronx, N.Y., Apr. 28, 1931; s. Irving and Amelia (Weingarten) G.; m. Lee Robbins, Apr. 14, 1957; children: Andrew Kevin, Nancy Tara, Julie Anne. A.B., Columbia U., 1952; M.D., State U. N.Y. Downstate Med. Center, 1956; certificate psychoanalysis, William A. White Psychoanalytic Inst., 1966. Diplomate: in psychiatry and child psychiatry Am. Bd. Psychiatry and Neurology. Intern Montefiore Hosp., N.Y.C., 1956-57; resident psychiatry Columbia-Presbyn. Med. Center, N.Y.C., 1957-59, resident child psychiatry, 1959-60, 62-63; dir. child psychiatry U.S. Army Hosp., Frankfurt, Germany, 1960-62; mem. attending staff Presbyn. Hosp., N.Y.C., 1963—, N.Y. State Psychiat. Inst., 1967—; pvt. practice medicine, specializing in psychiatry, child psychiatry and psychoanalysis, Cresskill, N.J., 1963—; instr. child psychiatry Columbia U. Coll. Physicians and Surgeons, 1965-70, asso. child psychiatry, 1970-72, asst. clin. prof. child psychiatry, 1972-76, asso. clin. prof., 1976-83, clin. prof. psychiatry, 1983—; mem. faculty William A. White Psychoanalytic Inst., 1967—; vis. prof. child psychiatry Cath. U. Louvain, Belgium, 1980-83. Author: The Child's Book about Brain Injury, 1966, The Boys and Girls Book about Divorce, 1970, Therapeutic Communication with Children: The Mutual Storytelling Technique, 1971, Dr. Gardner's Stories about the Real World, Vol. I, 1972, Vol. II, 1983, MBD: The Family Book about Minimal Brain Dysfunction, 1973, The Talking, Feeling, and Doing Game, 1973, Understanding Children—A Parents Guide to Child Rearing, 1973, Dr. Gardner's Fairy Tales for Today's Children, 1974, Psychotherapeutic Approaches to the Resistant Child, 1975, Psychotherapy with Children of Divorce, 1976, Dr. Gardner's Modern Fairy Tales, 1977, The Parents Book About Divorce, 1977, Gardner Steadiness Tester, 1978, The Boys and Girls Book About One-Parent Families, 1978, Reversals Frequency Test, 1978, Adoption Storytelling Cards, 1978, The Objective Diagnosis of Minimal Brain Dysfunction, 1979, Dorothy and the Lizard of Oz, 1980, Dr. Gardner's Fables for Our Times, 1981, Family Evaluation in Child Custody Litigation, 1982; editor-in-chief Internat.: Jour. Child Psychotherapy, 1972-73. Mem. internat. adv. bd. Parents Without Partners, 1973—. Served to capt. M.C. U.S. Army Res., 1960-62. Fellow Am. Acad. Psychoanalysis, Am. Acad. Child Psychiatry, Am. Psychiat. Assn.; mem. William A. White Psychoanalytic Soc. Home: 54 Forest Rd Tenafly NJ 07670 Office: PO Box R Cresskill NJ 07626

GARDNER, RICHARD HARTWELL, oil co. exec.; b. Cambridge, Mass., Oct. 9, 1934; s. Richard Hosmer and Marjorie Georgine (Pierce) G.; m. Helen Carolyn McIntyre, Oct. 11, 1957; children—Pamela, Hartwell. A.B., Colgate U., 1956; M.B.A., Harvard U., 1961. Treas. Mobil Latin Am. Inc., N.Y.C., 1964-66, asst. treas. internat. div., 1966-68; treas. Mobil Europe Inc., London, 1968-70, N. Am. div., N.Y.C., 1970-72, dep. treas., 1972-73; corp. treas. Mobil Oil Corp., 1974—; treas. Mobil Corp., 1976—. Trustee Am. Sch. London, 1968-70, Danbury Hosp. Served to 1st lt. USAF, 1956-59. Mem. Am. Petroleum Inst., Fin. Execs. Inst. (treas.). Democrat. Office: Mobil Corp 150 E 42d St New York NY 10017

GARDNER, RICHARD NEWTON, lawyer, educator; b. N.Y.C., July 9, 1927; s. Samuel I. and Ethel (Elias) G.; m. Danielle Luzzatto, June 10, 1956; children: Nina Jessica, Anthony Laurence. A.B. magna cum laude, Harvard U., 1948; J.D., Yale U., 1951; Ph.D. (Rhodes scholar), 1951-53, 1954. Bar: N.Y. 1952. Corr. UP, 1946-47, AP, 1948; teaching fellow internat. legal studies Harvard Law Sch., 1953-54; with Coudert Bros., N.Y.C., 1954-57; assoc. prof. law Columbia U., 1957-60, prof., 1960-61, 65-66, Henry L. Moses prof. law and internat. orgn., 1967-77, 81—; of counsel Coudert Bros., 1981—; U.S. ambassador to, Italy, 1977-81; dep. asst. sec. state internat. orgns. Dept. State, 1961-65; vis. prof. U. Istanbul, 1958, U. Rome, 1967-68; dep. U.S. rep. UN Com. on Peaceful Uses of Outer Space, 1962-65; U.S. alt. del. 19th UN Gen. Assembly; sr. adviser U.S. del. to 20th and 21st UN Gen. Assemblies; rapporteur UN Com. Experts on Econ. Restructuring, 1975; mem. Pres.'s Commn. on Internat. Trade and Investment Policy, 1970-71, U.S. Adv. Com. on Law of Sea, 1971-76; cons. to sec.-gen. UN Conf. on Human Environment, 1972. Author: Sterling-Dollar Diplomacy, 1956, New Directions in U.S. Foreign Economic Policy, 1959, In Pursuit of World Order, 1964, Blueprint for Peace, 1966, (with Max F. Millikan) The Global Partnership: International Agencies and Economic Development, 1968; note editor: Yale Law Jour, 1950-51. Bd. dirs. Freedom House. Served with AUS, 1945-46. Harvard Club scholar N.Y.C., 1944; recipient Detur prize for distinguished scholarship Harvard U., 1948, Arthur S. Flemming award, 1963. Mem. Am., N.Y. State bar assns., UN Assn. (dir.), Fgn. Policy Assn. (dir.), Assn. Bar City N.Y., Council Fgn. Relations, Am. Econ. Assn., Am. Acad. Arts and Scis., Phi Beta Kappa, Order of Coif. Clubs: Century Assn. (N.Y.C.); Met. (Washington). Home: 1150 Fifth Ave New York NY 10028

GARDNER, ROBIN PIERCE, engineering educator; b. Charlotte, N.C., Aug. 17, 1934; s. Robin Brem and Margaret (Pierce) G.; m. Linda Jean Gardner, Oct. 21, 1976. B.Ch.E., N.C. State U., 1956, M.S., 1958; Ph.D., Pa. State U., 1961. Scientist Oak Ridge Inst. Nuclear Studies, 1961-63; research engr., asst. dir. measurement and controls lab. Research Triangle Inst., Research Triangle Park, N.C., 1963-67; research prof. nuclear engring. and chem. engring., dir. Center Engring. Applications of Radioisotopes, N.C. State U., 1967—; Cons. Oak Ridge Inst. Nuclear Studies, Research Triangle Inst., Oak Ridge Nat. Lab., Internat. Atomic Energy Agy., NASA, AEC. Author: (with Ralph L. Ely, Jr.) Radioisotope Measurement Applications in Engineering, 1967; Contbr. articles to sci. jours. Served to 1st lt. AUS, 1956. Mem. Am. Nuclear Soc., Am. Inst. Chem. Engrs., Sigma Xi, Phi Kappa Phi, Phi Lambda Upsilon. Home: 805 Ivanhoe Dr Raleigh NC 27609 Office: Dept Nuclear Engring NC State U Raleigh NC 27695-7909

GARDNER, ROMAINE LUVERNE, college administrator, lawyer; b. Wallingford, Iowa, Aug. 19, 1933; s. Lloyd Gilbert and Olivia Agnes (Berge) G.; m. Jane Elder Andrews, June 16, 1956; children: Sibyl Kimberley, Nicholas Berge. B.A. cum laude, St. Olaf Coll., 1955; M.Div., Luth. Theol. Sem., 1958; Ph.D., Columbia U., 1966; J.D. cum laude, Bklyn. Law Sch., 1979. Bar: N.Y. 1980. Prof. Wagner Coll., S.I., N.Y., 1963-79; assoc. Cadwalader, Wickersham & Taft, N.Y.C., 1979-82; dean coll. Gustavus Adolphus Coll., St. Peter, Minn., 1982—; dir. Kalvar Corp., Mpls. Mem. ABA. Lutheran. Clubs: Mpls.; Athletic (Mpls.).

GARDNER, RUSSELL, JR., psychiatrist, educator; b. Granton, Wis., Mar. 19, 1938; s. Russell Robert and Ella Amelia (Haines) G.; m. Mary Louise Braatz, June 1960; children: Rebecca Claire, Martha Naomi, Benjamin Glen. Pre-med., Wis. State Coll., Stevens Point, 1958; M.D., U. Chgo., 1962. Rotating intern Henry Ford Hosp., Detroit, 1962-63; resident in psychiatry Albert Einstein Coll. Medicine, 1963-66, instr., then asst. prof. psychiatry, 1968-74; clin. research fellow Montefiore Hosp. Med. Center, N.Y.C., 1968-70, research psychiatrist, 1970-74; candidate N.Y. Psychoanalytic Inst., 1968-74, grad., 1974; prof. psychiatry, chmn. div. psychiatry-behavioral sci. U. N.D. Med. Sch., Fargo, 1974—; surgeon grants program specialist, clin. research br. NIMH, 1966-68, cons. psychiatry edn. br., 1976—, mem. psychiat. edn. rev. com., 1979-83, chmn., 1980-83. Co-editor: Psychotropic Drugs and Dysfunctions of the Basic Ganglia; contbr. articles to profl. jours. USPHS fellow, 1959-60; Interdeptl. fellow Albert Einstein Med. Coll., 1964-66; recipient Research Scentist Devel. award Montefiore Hosp. Med. Center, 1970-74. Mem. Am. Aging Assn., AAAS, Am. Assn. Chairmen Depts. Psychiatry, Am. Coll. Psychiatry, AMA, N.D. Med. Assn., Am. Psychiat. Assn., Assn. Acad. Psychiatrists (pres.-elect 1982-84), Am. Psychoanalytic Assn., Am. Psychosomatic Soc., Assn. Dirs. Undergrad. Psychiat. Edn., Assn. Psychophysiol. Study of Sleep, N.D. Acad. Sci., Internat. Neuropsychology Soc., Gerontol. Soc. Home: 1919 No Elm St Fargo ND 58102 Office: 1919 N Elm St Fargo ND 58102

GARDNER, WALTER, artist; b. Liverpool, Eng., May 7, 1902; s. Herman G. and Lily (Cuddy) G.; m. Emilie Roland, Nov. 1, 1937 (dec. June 1947); m. Jane Beckwith, Aug. 1948. Elementary edn., Eng.; student, Pa. Acad. Fine Arts, 1921-25. Phila. Cresson traveling scholar, 1924. Exhibited at, Whitney Mus., N.Y.C., Artists for Victory Show, Met. Mus., N.Y.C., Corcoran Gallery, Washington, Chgo. Art Inst., Detroit Inst. Art, Va. Mus. Fine Arts, Richmond, Pa. Acad.; Executed murals, post offices at, Honesdale, Pa., post offices at, Phila. (Sta. O), post offices at, Berne, Ind., Municipal Ct. Phila. Recipient purchase prize Wanamaker Regional Art Exhibit, 1934; fellowship prize Pa. Acad., 1938. Home: 2991 Schoolhouse Ln Hawthorne E 34 Germantown Philadelphia PA 19144 *If human beings were to be divided into two groups, the Gropers and the Gripers, I should like to be one of those who grope their way toward the light at the end of the tunnel, rather than gripe about the state of the tunnel walls.*

GARDNER, WARNER WINSLOW, lawyer; b. Richmond, Ind., Sept. 25, 1909; s. Frank Karl and Camilla (Winslow) G.; m. Henrietta Gertrude Tucker, Sept. 10, 1940; children—Hannah Winslow, William Tucker, Richard Randolph, Frances Winslow. A.B., Swarthmore Coll., 1930; M.A., Rutgers U., 1931; LL.B., Columbia, 1934. Law clk. Justice Stone, U.S. Supreme Ct., 1934-35; atty. and spl. asst. to atty. gen. Office Solicitor Gen., Dept. Justice, 1935-41; solicitor U.S. Dept. Labor, 1941-42, U.S. Dept. Interior, 1942-46, asst. sec., 1946-47; mem. firm Shea & Gardner, Washington, 1947—; Dir. Natomas Co., 1971-76; Spl. counsel Fed. Maritime Bd., 1957; chmn. informal action com. Adminstrv. Conf. U.S., 1968-76. Author: Building and Loan Liquidity, 1931, Taxation of Government Bondholders and Employees, 1938; Contbr. articles to mags. Served with AUS, 1943-45. Decorated Legion of Merit; Croix de Guerre. Mem. Phi Beta Kappa. Mem. Soc. of Friends. Clubs: Metropolitan, Cosmos. Home: 4219 50th St NW Washington DC 20016 Office: 1800 Massachusetts Ave NW Washington DC 20036

GARDNER, WILFORD ROBERT, physicist, educator; b. Logan, Utah, Oct. 19, 1925; s. Robert and Nellie (Barker) G.; m. Marjorie Louise Cole, June 9, 1949; children: Patricia, Robert, Caroline. B.S., Utah State U., 1949; M.S., Iowa State U., 1951, Ph.D., 1953. Cert. profl. agronomist-soil scientist. Physicist U.S. Salinity Lab., Riverside, Calif., 1953-66; prof. U. Wis., Madison, 1966-80; physicist, prof., head dept. soil, water and engring. U. Ariz., Tucson, 1980—. Author: Soil Physics, 1972. Served with U.S. Army, 1943-46. NSF sr. fellow, 1959; Fulbright fellow, 1971-72; Soil Sci. Soc. Am. Research awardee, 1962; Nat. Acad. Scis. fellow, 1983. Fellow AAAS, Am. Soc. Agronomy; mem. Internat. Soil Sci. Soc. (pres. physics commn. 1968-74). Office: Soils Water and Engring Dept U Ariz Tucson AZ 85721

GARDNER, WILLIAM ALBERT, JR., pathologist; b. Sumter, S.C., Aug. 2, 1939; s. William A. and Betty Lee (Kennedy) G.; m. Kathryn Ann Medlin, June 30, 1960; children: Mary Elizabeth, Kathryn Lee, William Dylan. B.S., Wofford Coll., 1960; M.S. in Anatomy, Med. Coll. S.C., 1963, M.D., 1965. Diplomate: Am. Bd. Pathology. Intern John Hopkins Hosp., Balt., 1965-66; asst. resident Johns Hopkins Hosp., Balt., 1966-67, fellow in pathology, 1965-67; asst. resident Duke U., Durham, N.C., 1967-68, chief resident, 1968-69, instr. pathology, 1968-69; chief lab. service VA Hosp., Charleston, S.C., 1969; asst. prof. pathology Med. U. S.C., 1969-72, assoc. prof., 1972-76; prof. pathology Vanderbilt U., Nashville, 1976-81, vice chmn. dept. pathology; chief lab. service VA Hosp., Nashville, 1976-81; prof., chmn. dept. pathology U. South Ala., Mobile, 1981—. Contbr. articles on oncology and pathology to profl. jours. Recipient Outstanding Teaching award Med. U. S.C., 1975. Fellow Am. Soc. Clin. Pathologists, Coll. Am. Pathologists (del. for govtl. pathology); mem. Internat. Acad. Pathology, Acad. Clin. Lab. Physicians and Scientists, AMA, Ala. Med. Assn., Alpha Omega Alpha. Methodist. Home: 1565 Fearnway St Mobile AL 36604 Office: 2451 Fillingim St Mobile AL 36617

GARDNER, WILLIAM EARL, university dean; b. Hopkins, Minn., Oct. 11, 1928; s. William Henry and Ida (Swenson) G.; m. Marcia Frances Anderson, Nov. 4, 1950; children: Mary Gardner Fenwick, Bret, Anne Gardner Smith, Eric. B.S., U. Minn., 1950, M.A., 1959, Ph.D., 1961. Tchr. pub. schs., Balaton, Rockford, New Ulm, Minn., 1950-54; instr. Univ. High Sch., U. Minn., Mpls., 1954-61; prof. edn. U. Minn., 1961—, assoc. dean, 1970-76, dean, 1976—; dir. Minn. Curriculum Lab., 1965-67; vis. prof. U. York, Eng., 1967-68; Mem. Bd. Edn., St. Louis Park, Minn., 1971-77; mem. Tchr. Standards and Certification Commn., 1973-80. Author: (with others) Education and Social Crisis, 1967, Social Studies in Secondary Schools, 1970, Selected Case Studies in Am. History, 1971, The Education of Tchrs. Mem. Nat. Council Social Studies, Am. Ednl. Research Assn., Assn. Supervision and Curriculum Devel., Luth. Human Relations Assn., Phi Delta Kappa. Lutheran. Home: 2631 Burd Pl Saint Louis Park MN 55426 Office: U Minn Coll Edn Minneapolis MN 55455

GARDNER, WILLIAM FREDERICK, professional baseball manager; b. New London, Conn., July 19, 1927; s. Lesley B. and Eva M. (Maynard) G.; m. Barbara Carnaroli, July 18, 1952; children: Gwen, Shelly A., William F. Jr. Grad., Chapman Tech. High Sch., New London. Second baseman N.Y. Giants, 1954-55, Balt. Orioles, 1955-59, Washington Senators, 1960-61, N.Y. Yankees, 1961-62, Boston Red Sox, 1962-63, coach, 1965-66, Montreal Expos, 1977-78; field mgr., coach Minn. Twins, 1981—. Served with AUS, 1947-48. Democrat. Roman Catholic. Address: 35 Dayton Rd Waterford CT 06385

GARDNER, WILLIAM MICHAEL, secretary state N.H.; b. Manchester, N.H., Oct. 26, 1948; s. William and Mildred (Claus) G. B.A., U. N.H., 1970; postgrad., London Sch. Econs., 1972; M.E., U. N.C., 1973. Mem. N.H. Ho. of Reps. from Hillsborough County Dist. 30, 1973-76; sec. of state, N.H., 1976—.

GARDNER, WILLIAM MICHAEL, library adminstr.; b. Cleve., Dec. 16, 1932; s. William Michael and Rosemary (Jansing) G.; m. Betty Jane Krug, July 23, 1960; children—Amy, Daniel, Robert. B.S., John Carroll U., 1955; M.S. in Library Sci, Case Western Res. U., 1960. Asst. librarian Albert R. Mann Library, Cornell U., 1960-64; agr. librarian U. Ky., 1965-66; asst. dir. U. Ky. Libraries, 1966-74; dir. libraries Marquette U., Milw., 1975—. Served with Security Agy. AUS, 1955-57. Mem. ALA, Am. Soc. Info. Services. Home: 13380 W Graham St New Berlin WI 53151 Office: Marquette U Meml Library 1415 W Wisconsin Av Milwaukee WI 53233

GARDOM, GARDE BASIL, Can. govt. ofcl.; b. Banff, Alta., Can., July 17, 1924; s. Basil and Gabrielle Gwladys (Bell) G.; m. Theresa Helen Eileen Mackenzie, Feb. 11, 1956; children—Kim Gardom Meredith, Karen, Edward, Brione, Brita. B.A., U. B.C., Vancouver, 1949, LL.B., 1949. Bar: called to bar 1949, created Queen's Counsel 1975. With Campbell, Brazier & Co., 1949; sr. partner firm Gardom & Volrich, Vancouver, 1960-75; atty. gen. of, B.C., 1975-80, minister intergovtl. relations, 1980—; mem. B.C. Legis. Assembly for Vancouver Point Grey, 1966—. Mem. Can. Bar Assn., B.C. Law Soc., Phi Delta Theta. Anglican. Clubs: Vancouver Lawn Tennis and Badminton, Union. Home: 1738 Angus Dr Vancouver BC V6J 4H5 Canada Office: Parliament Bldgs Victoria BC VHV 1X4 Canada

GARDON, JOHN LESLIE, paint research company executive; b. Budapest, Hungary, June 5, 1928; U.S., 1958; s. Louis and Clara (Poppes) G.; m. Berta Rost, Dec. 26, 1951; children: Jessica Joan, Frederic Paul. B.S., Swiss Fed. Inst. Tech., 1951; Ph.D., McGill U., 1955. Chemist Ca. Internat. Paper Co., Hawkesbury, Ont., Can., 1955-58; sr. chemist, group leader, research assoc., mgr. Rohm and Haas Co., Springhouse, Pa., 1958-68; dir. research and devel. M & T Chems. (Rahway N.J.), Southfield, Mich., 1969-80; v.p. reserch and devep. Sherwin Williams Co., Chgo., 1981—; trustee Pain Research Inst., Kent, Ohio, 1972-81; chmn. Fordon Research Conf. of Adhesion, New Hampton, N.H., 1976. Editor Non-Polluting Coatings and Processes, 1973, Emulsion Polymerization, 1976; contbr. (articles to profl. jours.); patentee (in field). Mem. Am. Chem. Soc. (chem. organic coatings and plastics div. 1980), Fedn. of Soc. for Paint Tech. (Roon award 1966), Chem. Inst. Can., Soc. Plastics Engrs., Soc. Mfg. Engrs., N.Y. Acad. Scis., Sigma Xi. Office: Sherwin Williams Co 10909 Cottage Grove Ave Chicago IL 60628

GAREK, MORRIS DANIEL, dept. store exec.; b. Columbus, Ohio, Jan. 25, 1913; s. Louis and Ida (Bloom) G.; m. Rose Lee Cohen, June 17, 1934; children—Lois (Mrs. Harry Greenbott), Robert, Diane (Mrs. David Romanoff). Grad. high sch. With F. & R. Lazarus Co., Columbus, 1935—, exec. v.p., 1966-70, vice chmn. bd., 1970—; owner M. Garek Assos. (mgmt. cons. firm), Columbus, 1973—. Bd. dirs. Goodwill Industries, Heritage House. Mem. Better Bus. Bur. (trustee), Asso. Merchandising Corp. (chmn. gen. mdse. mgrs. 1966-68), Am. Mgmt. Assn., AIM, Columbus C. of C., Nat. Retail Mchts. Assn. Jewish. Club: Winding Hollow Country. Home: 2721 Bryden Rd Columbus OH 43209 Office: M Garek Assos 88 E Broad St Columbus OH 43215

GARELICK, MARTIN, transportation executive; b. Rochester, N.Y., May 18, 1924; s. Samuel and Esther (Gerber) G.; m. Betty J. Mann, Jan. 18, 1951. B.S.C.E., Purdue U., 1947. With Milw. Rd. R.R., 1947-78, asst. v.p. mktg. devel. and planning, Chgo., 1973-76, v.p. ops., 1976-78; exec. v.p., chief operating officer AMTRAK, Washington, 1978-80; v.p. Wyer, Dick & Co., Chgo., 1980-82; v.p., gen. mgr. N.J. Transit Rail Ops., Newark, 1982—. Served with U.S. Army, 1943-46. Mem. Am. Soc. Traffic and Transp. (dir.), Am. Assn. R.R. Supts., Am. Ry. Devel. Assn., Tau Epsilon Phi. Jewish. Home: 20876 Del Luna Dr Boca Raton FL 33433 Office: PO Box 720 Newark NJ 07101

GARFIAS, ROBERT, ethnomusicologist; b. San Francisco, Sept. 22, 1932; s. Adolfo and Alice (Gonzalez) G. B.A., San Francisco State Coll., 1956; M.A., UCLA, 1958, Ph.D. (Ford Found. fellow 1958-60), 1965. Mem. faculty U. Wash., Seattle, 1962-82, prof. music, 1973-82, former vice provost faculty affairs; now dean fine arts, prof. music U. Calif.-Irvine; lectr., radio broadcaster in field. Author: Music of a Thousand Autumns, the Togaku Style of Japanese Court Music: An Analysis of Theory in Practice, 1976, Spanish American Music and Its Roots, 1975. Grantee Dept. State to Burma, 1973-74, Internat. Research and Exchange to Romania, 1977. Mem. Soc. Ethnomusicology, Nat. Acad. Rec. Arts and Scis., Nat. Fedn. Community Broadcasters. Office: Univ of Calif Irvine School of Fine Arts Irvine CA 92717

GARFIELD, BERNARD HOWARD, musician, composer; b. Bklyn., May 27, 1924; s. Maurice and Sarah (Hoffman) Garfinkel; m. Beatrice A. Hutton, May 2, 1954; children—David A., Robert B., Lawrence E., John M. Founder. Asso. diploma, Royal Coll. Music, London, 1945; B.A., N.Y. U., 1948; M.A., Columbia U., 1950. Dir. N.Y. Woodwind Quintet, 1946-57; prin. bassoonist Little Orch. Soc., N.Y.C., 1949-57, N.Y. Ballet Orch., 1950-57, Phila. Orch., 1957—; mem. Phila. Woodwind Quintet, 1962—; adj. prof. music Temple U. Coll. Music, Phila., 1957—; mem. faculty Curtis Inst. Music, Phila., 1975-80. Rec. artist, Columbia Records; composer works for piano, bassoon, woodwinds, voice and quartet for bassoon, violin, viola and cello. Served with AUS, 1943-46. Recipient Hartman Kuhn award Phila. Orch., 1975. Home: 871 Wayside Ln Haddonfield NJ 08033 Office: care Phila Orch Acad Music Philadelphia PA 19102

GARFIELD, BRIAN WYNNE, author; b. N.Y.C., Jan. 26, 1939; s. George and Frances (O'Brien) G.; m. Virve Sein, 1962 (div. 1965); m. Shan Willson Botley, 1969. B.A., U. Ariz., 1959, M.A., 1963. Instr. English U. Ariz., 1962-63; founder, pres. Shan Prodns. Co., Inc. (film prodn.), 1975—. Mem. dance bands, The Casuals, 1958-59, The Palisades, 1959-60; Author: Range Justice, 1960, The Arizonans, 1961, (under name Frank Wynne) Massacre Basin, 1961, Justice at Spanish Flat, 1961, (under name F. Wynne) The Big Snow, 1962, (under name Frank O'Brian) The Rimfire Murders, 1962, Act of Piracy, 1975, (under name Bennett Garland) Seven Brave Men, 1962, The Lawbringers, 1962, Trail Drive, 1962, (under name F. Wynne) Arizona Rider, 1962, Rio Concho, 1963, Lynch-Law Canyon, 1964, Call Me Hazard, 1964, The Lusty Breed, 1966, The Wolf Pack, 1967, Dragoon Pass, 1963, (under name Brian Wynne) Mr. Sixgun, 1965, The Night It Rained Bullets, 1966, The Bravos, 1967, The Proud Riders, 1967, Brand Of The Gun, 1968, A Badge For A Badman, 1969, Gundown, 1969, Big Country, Big Men, 1970, The Thousand-Mile War, 1969, Sliphammer, 1970, Valley of the Shadow, 1970, The Hit, 1970, The Villiers Touch, 1970, Sweeny's Honor, 1971, Gun Down (also title The Last Hard Men), 1971, What of Terry Conniston?, 1971, Deep Cover, 1971, Relentless, 1972, Line of Succession, 1972, Death Wish, 1972, Tripwire, 1973, (in collaboration with Donald E. Westlake) Gangway!, 1973, Kolchak's Gold, 1974, The Threepersons Hunt, 1974, The Romanov Succession, 1974, Hopscotch, 1975 (Edgar Allen Poe best novel award Mystery Writers Am.), Death Sentence, 1975, Recoil, 1977, Wild Times, 1979, The Paladin, 1980, Checkpoint Charlie, 1981, numerous others; screen stories for films Death Wish, 1974, The Last Hard Men, 1976, Relentless, 1977, Wild Times, 1980; story and screenplay for Hopscotch, 1979. Served with AUS, 1957-65. Mem. Western Writers Am. (pres. 1967-68), Tucson Fedn. Musicians, Authors Guild, Authors League, Dramatists Guild, Writers Guild Am. (East), Crime Writers Assn. (U.K.), Mystery Writers Am. (dir. 1974—). Home: Box 376 Alpine NJ 07620

GARFIELD, EUGENE, information scientist; b. N.Y.C., Sept. 16, 1925; s. Ernest and Edith (Wolf) Garofano; m. Faye Byron, 1945 (div.); 1 son, Stefan; m. Winifred Koziolek, 1955 (div.); children: Laura, Joshua, Thea.; m. Catheryne Stout, 1983. B.S., Columbia U., 1949, M.S., 1954; Ph.D., U. Pa., 1961. Research chemist Evans Research & Devel. Corp., 1949-50, Columbia U., 1950-51; mem. staff machine index project Johns Hopkins U., 1951-53; pres. Eugene Garfield Assos., Phila., 1954-60; pres., founder Inst. Sci. Info., Phila., 1960—; adj. prof. U. Pa., 1974—; Mem. council Rockefeller U., 1978—. Inventor: sci. info. service Current Contents, 1956; weekly columnist: Current Comments in Current Contents, 1956—; Author: Essays of an Information Scientist, 2 vols., 1977, vol. 3, 1980, vol. 4, 1981, vol. 5, 1983 (Book of Year, Am. Soc. Info. Sci.), Citation Indexing: Its Theory and Application in Science, Technology and Humanities, 1979, Transliterated Dictionary of the Russian Language, 1980; editor-in-chief: Scientometrics; mem. editorial bd.: Progress in Info. Sci. and Tech; contbr. articles to profl. jours.; Founder, inventor: Sci. Citation Index, 1961—, Index Chemicus, 1960—. Served with AUS, 1943-45. First Grolier Soc. fellow, 1953-54. Fellow AAAS (chmn. sect. T), Inst. Info. Scientists London; sr. mem. IEEE; corp. mem. Info. Industry Assn. (past chmn. bd., past pres., Hall of Fame award); mem. Spl. Libraries Assn., Assn. Computing Machinery, Authors League Am., Med. Library Assn., Am. Soc. Info. Sci. (award of merit 1975, past pres. Delaware Valley chpt.), Am. Chem. Soc. (Chem. Info. div. award 1977), Drug Info. Assn., Fedn. Am. Scientists. Patentee in field. Office: ISI 3501 Science Center Philadelphia PA 19104

GARFIELD, SOL LOUIS, psychologist, educator; b. Chgo., Jan. 8, 1918; s. Julius and Rebecca (Friedman) G.; m. Amy Nusbaum, Dec. 25, 1945; children: Ann, Joan, Stanley, David. B.S., Northwestern U., 1938, M.A., 1939, Ph.D., 1942. Teaching fellow Northwestern U., 1941-42; chief clin. psychology VA Hosp., Mendota, Wis., 1946-47; asso. prof. psychology U. Conn., 1947-49; chief clin. psychologist VA Mental Hygiene Clinic, Milw. and dir. tng. State of Wis., 1949-51; chief clin. psychol. tng. unit VA Hosp., Downey, Ill., 1951-57; chief clin. psychology div., asso. prof. Nebr. Psychiat. Inst., U. Nebr. Med. Coll., Omaha, 1957-59, prof., 1959-63; prin. research scientist Mo. Inst. Psychiatry; research prof. Washington U., St. Louis, 1963-64; prof. psychology, dir. clin. psychology program Columbia U., 1964-70; prof. psychology, dir. clin. psychology Washington U., 1970-78, prof. psychology, 1978—; cons. clin. psychology VA, 1963—, Peace Corps, 1964-70; mem. com. clin. drug evaluation NIMH, 1960-63, mem. treatment devel. and assessment research rev. com., 1982—; mem. Suicide Prevention Center Rev. Com., 1967-68. Author: Introductory Clinical Psychology, 1957, Clinical Psychology, 1974, 2d edit., 1983; editor: (with A.E. Bergin) Handbook of Psychotherapy and Behavior Change, 1971, 2d edit., 1978, Psychotherapy: An Eclectic Approach, 1980; cons. editor: Am. Jour. Mental Deficiency, 1964-66, Jour. Abnormal Psychology, 1964-70, 73-75, Profl. Psychology, 1976—, Cognitive Therapy and Research, 1979-83, Brit. Jour. Clin. Psychology, 1980—, Clin. Psychology Rev., 1981—; adv. editor: Jour. Cons. and Clin. Psychology, 1964-78; now editor; contbr. articles to profl. jours. Served with AUS, 1942-46. Fellow AAAS, Am. Psychol. Assn. (council of reps. 1955-58, 60-63, 65-67, 72-75, sec. treas. div. clin. psychology 1960-63, pres. div. clin. psychology 1964-65, disting. contbg. to clin. psychology award 1976, disting. profl. contbn. to knowledge award 1979); mem. Ill. Psychol. Assn. (pres.-elect 1957), Midwestern Psychol. Assn., Soc. for Psychotherapy Research (pres. 1977), AAUP, Sigma Xi. Home: 7030 Waterman Ave University City MO 63130 Office: Dept Psychology Washington U Saint Louis MO 63130 *In a field where beliefs and theories are abundant and empirical research data relatively limited, I have always felt it was important to have a critical perspective and to evaluate the prevailing views. This has provided a consistent pattern to my work and has kept me from following the latest fads or adhering to outmoded views.*

GARFIN, ALVIN, publisher; b. Bronx, N.Y., July 27, 1931; s. George David and Miriam (Weiner) G.; m. Dale Etzler, Sept. 8, 1956; children—Susan Michele, Jeffrey David. B.B.A., Coll. City N.Y., 1952.

Circulation mgr. Surg. Bus. mag. and Nursing Home Adminstr., 1955-57; circulation dir. Cantor Publs., 1957-61; with Art News mag., N.Y.C., 1961-72, publisher, 1968-72; gen. mgr. Newsweek Books, 1972-76, pub., 1975—, editor, 1977—; v.p. Newsweek, Inc., N.Y.C., 1978—. Served with USCGR, 1953-55. Home: 240 E 79th St New York NY 10021 Office: 444 Madison Ave New York NY 10022

GARFIN, LOUIS, actuary; b. Mason City, Iowa, June 7, 1917; s. Sam and Etta (Larner) G.; m. Clarice Fagen, Apr. 11, 1943; children: Eugene Arthur, Erica. Student, Mason City Jr. Coll., 1934-36; B.A., State U. Iowa, 1938, M.S., 1939, Ph.D., 1942. Instr. USAAF, Scott Field, Ill., 1942-43; instr. math. Ill. Inst. Tech., Chgo., 1943, U. Minn., 1943-44; actuary Oreg. Ins. Dept., Salem, 1946-52; asso. actuary Pacific Mut. Life Ins. Co., Los Angeles, 1952-62, actuary, 1962-64, v.p., chief actuary, 1964-82, cons. actuary, 1982—. Served from ensign to lt. (j.g.) USNR, 1944-46. Fellow Soc. Actuaries; mem. Am. Acad. Actuaries (v.p. 1976-78), Internat. Congress Actuaries (dir. 1977-80), Actuarial Club Pacific States (pres. 1967-68), Los Angeles Actuarial Club (pres. 1959-60), Am. Math. Soc., Am. Risk and Ins. Assn., Phi Beta Kappa, Sigma Xi. Home: 371 Dartmoor St Laguna Beach CA 92651 Office: 371 Dartmoor St Laguna Beach CA 92651

GARFINKEL, BARRY HERBERT, lawyer; b. Bklyn., June 19, 1928; s. Abraham and Shirley (Siegel) G.; m. Gloria Lorenz, Feb. 16, 1969; children—David, James, Paul. B.S.S., CCNY, 1950; LL.B., Yale U., 1955. Bar: N.Y. State bar 1955, U.S. Supreme Ct. bar 1959. Law clk. Judge Edward Weinfeld, U.S. Dist. Ct., N.Y.C., 1955-56; asso. firm Skadden, Arps, Slate, Meagher & Flom, N.Y.C., 1956—, ptnr., 1962—; trustee Practising Law Inst., Law Center Found. of N.Y. U. Sch. Law, Legal Aid Soc.; chmn. program com. 2d. Circuit Jud. Conf. Mng. editor: Yale Law Jour. Served to lt. USCG, 1953-55. Fellow Am. Coll. Trial Lawyers, Am. Bar Found.; mem. Am. Arbitration Assn., Nat. Choral Council (pres.), Assn. Bar of City of N.Y. (exec. com., past chmn. fed. cts. com.), Am. Bar Assn., N.Y. State Bar Assn., Am. Law Inst. Club: Yale (N.Y.C.). Home: 211 Central Park W New York NY 10024 Office: 919 3d Ave New York NY 10022

GARFINKEL, HARMON MARK, glass company executive; b. Bklyn., May 20, 1933; s. Samuel and Elsie (Schwartz) G.; m. Lorraine Plawsky, Mar. 4, 1956; children—Elyse, Michelle. B.A., Bklyn. Coll., 1957; Ph.D., Iowa State U., 1960; postgrad. program for mgmt. devel., Harvard U. Bus. Sch., 1973. Dir. bio-organic tech. Corning Glass Works, N.Y., 1973-74, dir. applied chemistry and biology, 1974-75, dir. biomed. and chem. tech., 1975-78, dir. research, 1978—; dir. Diagnostic Research, Inc.; instr. math. Elmira Coll., 1964. Mem. Am. Chem. Soc., Am. Phys. Soc., Am. Inst. Chemists. Republican. Jewish. Patents publs. in field. Home: 111 Country Estate Dr Horseheads NY 14845 Office: Sullivan Pk Corning NY 14831

GARFINKEL, HERBERT, univ. ofcl.; b. N.Y.C., June 16, 1920; s. Julius Louis and Gertrude (Goldstone) G.; m. Evelyn Epstein, Sept. 3, 1940; children—Laura, Paul. M.A., U. Chgo., 1950, Ph.D., 1956. Instr. polit. sci. Ill. Inst. Tech., 1948-51; research asst. Nat. Opinion Research Center, U. Chgo., 1950-51; instr. Mich. State U., 1951-53; asst. prof. Dartmouth, 1953-59; faculty Mich. State U., East Lansing, 1959—, prof. polit. sci., 1964-73; dean James Madison Coll., 1966-73; provost, vice chancellor acad. affairs U. Nebr., Omaha, 1973-78, interim chancellor, 1977-78; v.p. acad. affairs U. Louisville, 1978—; NATO prof. Inst. Social Studies, The Hague, Netherlands, 1965-66. Author: When Negroes March, 1959, (co-author) The Democratic Republic, 2d edit., 1970, The Constitution and The Legislature, 1961; Contbr. articles to profl. jours. Served as officer U.S. Mcht. Marine, 1943-45. Center for Advanced Study Behavioral Scis. fellow, 1958-59; research fellow Social Sci. Research Council, 1960-61. Mem. Am. Polit. Sci. Assn. Home: 7405 Springvale Dr Louisville KY 40222 Office: U Louisville Louisville KY 40292

GARFINKEL, MARVIN, lawyer, real estate developer; b. Phila., Mar. 23, 1929; s. Simon L. and Theresa (Brier) G.; m. Marian Schwartz, Apr. 6, 1963; 1 son, Simson Leon. B.A., Pomona Coll., 1951; LL.B. magna cum laude, U. Pa., 1954; LL.M. in Taxation, NYU, 1962. Bar: Pa. 1955. Law clk. to Curtis Bok, Gerald F. Flood and Louis E. Levinthal, Phila., 1954-55, W.H. Kirkpatrick, 1957-58; dep. atty. gen. Pa., 1955-57; sr. partner Garfinkel and Volpicelli; faculty, program chmn. Am. Bar Assn.-Am. Law Inst. on Profl. Edn., Com., 1971—; lectr. post admission program Law Sch., Temple U.; cons. real estate. Editorial bd.: Practical Lawyer; contbr. articles to legal jours. Mem. Internat. Bar Assn. (real estate com.), ABA (real estate sect., chmn. comml. leasing com.), Fed. Bar Assn., Phila. Bar Assn., Pa. Bar Assn., Am. Law Inst., Am. Soc. Internat. Law, Am. Coll. Real Estate Lawyers, Internat. Law Assn., Order of Coif. Club: Locust (Phila.). Home: Cobble Ct Haverford PA 19041 Offices Phenox of London House 308 Walnut St Philadelphia PA 19106 also Cobble Ct Haverford PA

GARFINKLE, MYRON, retail/food service executive, consultant; b. N.Y.C., Sept. 24, 1946; s. Henry and Anne (Levine) G.; m. Barbara Vreeland, Dec. 25, 1978. Student, Boston U., 1964-68. Pres. Greater Boston Distbrs., Manhattan News Co., 1969-73; pres., chmn. bd. Am. News Co., N.Y.C., 1973-80, Ancorp Nat. Services Co., 1973-80; pres. Garfield of Can., Toronto, Ont., 1971—, Advance Cons., Inc., 1980—. Bd. dirs. Boy Scouts Am., 1976-80. Republican. Jewish.

GARFUNKEL, ART, singer, actor; b. Forest Hills, N.Y., Nov. 1941. B.A., Columbia, 1965, M.A., 1967. Former mem. team, Simon and Garfunkel; recs. with Simon include Bridge Over Troubled Water, Sounds of Silence, Dangling Conversation, Homeward Bound, I Am a Rock, Mrs. Robinson, others; now soloist: albums as soloist include Angel Clare, 1973, Breakaway, 1975, Watermark, 1978, Fate For Breakfast (Doubt for Dessert), 1979, Art Garfunkel, 1979, Scissors Cut, 1981; films include Catch-22, 1970, Carnal Knowledge, 1971, Bad Timing. . .A Sensual Obsession, 1980. Recipient Grammy awards for Mrs. Robinson, 1969; 6 Grammy awards for Bridge Over Troubled Water, 1970. *

GARG, DEVENDRA PRAKASH, mech. engr., educator; b. Roorkee, India, Mar. 22, 1934; came to U.S., 1965; s. Chandra Gopal and Godawari (Devi) G.; m. Prabha Govil, Nov. 19, 1961; children—Nisha, Seema. B.Sc., Agra (India) U., 1954; B.S. in Mech. Engring, U. Roorkee, 1957; M.S. (Tech. Coop. Mission Merit scholar), U. Wis.-Madison, 1960; Ph.D., N.Y. U., 1969. Lectr. mech. engring. U. Roorkee, 1957-62, reader, 1962-65, vis. prof., 1978; instr. N.Y. U., 1965-69; asst. prof. Mass. Inst. Tech., 1969-71, asso. prof., 1971-72, chmn. engring. projects lab., 1971-72, lectr., 1972-75; prof. Duke U., 1972—, dir. undergrad. studies dept. mech. engring. and materials sci., 1977—; cons. in field. Author: An Introduction to the Theory and Use of the Analog Computer, 1963, A Textbook of Descriptive Geometry, 1964; asso. editor: Jour. Interdisciplinary Modeling and Simulation, 1978—; contbr. numerous articles to profl. jours. Recipient Founder's Day award N.Y. U., 1969. Mem. IEEE (reviewer), Instrument Soc. Am. (reviewer), ASME (reviewer, co-guest editor spl. issues on ground transp. 1974, also socioecon. and ecol. systems 1976, sec. dynamic systems and control div. 1980—), Sigma Xi (sec. chpt. 1970-72). Home: 2815 DeKalb St Durham NC 27705 Office: Sch Engring Duke Univ Durham NC 27706

GARGALLI, CLAIRE W., banker; b. Phila., Dec. 3, 1942; d. Robert and Kathryn Emma (LaPish) Waterhouse. B.A., Middlebury Coll., 1964. Credit analyst Fidelity Bank, Phila., 1964-68, asst. treas., 1968-70, asst. v.p., 1970-73, v.p., 1973-74; gen. mgr. Fidelity Internat. Bank, N.Y.C., 1974-75; sr. v.p. Fidelity Bank, Phila., 1975—; dir. Gen. Coal Co., Phila. Bd. dirs. Internat. House, Phila., 1980—, World Affairs Council, Phila., 1983—; mem. adv. bd. U. Pa. Com. Women's Concerns, 1978—. Republican. Office: Fidelity Bank Broad and Walnut Sts Philadelphia PA 10109

GARGANA, JOHN JOSEPH, JR., mutual funds executive; b. Jersey City, May 31, 1931; s. John Joseph and Mary Catherine (Fritschy) G.; m. Louise Mary Carroll, Nov. 27, 1954; children—Donna Marie, Karen Lynn, Mary Louise, John Joseph. B.S., St. Peters Coll., Jersey City, 1952. C.P.A., N.Y., N.J. Auditor Haskins & Sells, N.Y.C., 1955-65; v.p. fin. Affiliated Fund, Inc., N.Y.C., 1965—, Lord Abbett Income Fund, Lord Abbett Bond Debenture Fund, Lord Abbett Developing Growth Fund, Lord Abbett Cash Res. Fund, Lord Abbett Value Appreciation Fund, Inc.; mem. acctg. and ops. coms. Investment Co. Inst. Served with AUS, 1952-54. Mem. Am. Inst. C.P.A.'s, N.J. Soc. C.P.A.'s. Home: 2 Ware Pl Middletown NJ 07748 Office: 63 Wall St New York NY 10005

GARGETT, GEORGE GRANT, insurance company executive; b. Alma, Mich., Sept. 28, 1917; s. Ford William and Emily (Slocum) G.; m. Josephine Besancon, Nov. 25, 1944; children: Frederick Ford, John Besancon, Mark George. B.A., Mich. State Coll., 1940. Diplomate: registered health underwriter. Asst. gen. mgr. Mut. of Omaha Ins. Co., Indpls., 1957-60, dir. market research, Omaha, 1960-63, gen. mgr., Seattle, 1963-72, dir. agys. west, Los Angeles, 1972-73; v.p. div. office sales Mut. of OmahaIns. Co., Omaha, 1973-81; sr. exec. v.p. mktg. Mut. of Omaha Ins. Co., Omaha, 1981—. Active Boy Scouts Am., Omaha, 1958—; mem. Com. on Fgn. Relations, Omaha, 1980—. Republican. Home: 500 S 37th St Apt 506 Omaha NE 68105 Office: Mut of Omaha Ins Co Mut of Omaha Plaza Omaha NE 68175

GARGUS, JAMES LEON, biologist; b. Dalton, Ark., Oct. 27, 1922; s. Simon Newton and Mattie (Atkinson) G.; m. Mary Boccabella, Dec. 11, 1943; children: James, George, John, Jacqueline, Judith. B.S., George Washington U., 1950, M.S., 1954; postgrad., Rutgers U. Research asst. Warwick Cancer Inst., Washington, 1950-54; Inst. Microbiology, Rutgers U., New Brunswick, N.J., 1954-55; lab. supr. Hazleton Labs., Vienna, Va, 1955-69, dept. dir., 1969—. Contbr. articles to sci. jours. Served in U.S. Army, 1943-45. Mem. N.Y. Acad. Sci., Soc. Toxicology, Washington Acad. Sci., Am. Assn. Cancer Research, Sigma Xi. Roman Catholic. Office: 9200 Leesburg Turnpike Vienna VA 22180 *

GARIBALDI, JAMES JOSEPH, assn. exec.; b. N.Y.C., Mar. 17, 1926; s. John J. and Jane Mary (Tracey) G.; m. Katherine McSpedon, June 5, 1949; children—Karen Garibaldi Love, Colleen, James. B.S., U.S. Naval Acad., 1949; M.S. with distinction, Air Force Inst. Tech., 1966. Supply Corps officer, commd. ensign USN, 1949, advanced through ranks to comdr.; ret., 1971; asso. exec. dir. Nat. Assn. Ins. Brokers, 1971-72; asso. exec. dir. fin. and bus. mgmt. Am. Occupational Therapy Assn., 1972-75, exec. dir., 1975—; chmn. Coalition Ind. Health Professions, 1978-79; Pres. Grandview Condominium Assn.; mem. nat. adv. com. Scouting for Handicapped; mem. Pres.'s Com. Employment Handicapped; 1st vice chmn. and mem. exec. com. Nat. Voluntary Orgn. Ind. Living for Aging. Mem. U.S. Naval Acad. Alumni Assn., Am. Soc. Assn. Execs., Washington Soc. Assn. Execs., Ret. Officer Assn. Roman Catholic. Clubs: Mil. Dist. Washington Officers, K.C. Home: 4648 N 20th St Arlington VA 22207 Office: 1383 Piccard Dr Rockville MD 20850

GARIBALDI, MARIE LOUISE, state supreme court justice; b. Jersey City, Nov. 26, 1934; d. Louis J. and Marie (Servente) G. B.A., Conn. Coll., 1956; LL.B., Columbia U., 1959; LL.M. in Tax. Law, NYU, 1963; LL.D., Drew U., 1983, St. Peter's Coll., Jersey City, 1983. Atty. Office of Regional Counsel, IRS, N.Y.C., 1960-66; assoc. McCarter & English, Newark, 1966-69; ptnr. Riker, Danzig, Scherer & Hyland, Newark, 1969-82; assoc. justice N.J. Supreme Court, Newark, 1982—. Contbr. articles to profl. jours. Trustee St. Peter's Coll.; co-chmn. Thomas Kean's campaign for Gov. of N.J., 1981, mem. transition team, 1981; mem. Gov. Byrne's Commn. on Dept. of Commerce, 1981. Recipient Disting. Alumni award NYU Law Alumni of N.J., 1982, Columbia U., 1982. Fellow Am. Bar Found.; mem. N.J. Bar Assn. (pres. 1982), Columbia U. Sch. Law Alumni Assn. (bd. dirs.). Home: 34 Kingswood Rd Weehawken NJ 07087 Office: NJ Supreme Ct 520 Broad St 12th Floor Newark NJ 07102

GARIBAY-GUTIERREZ, LUIS, physician, educator; b. Zamora, Mexico, Sept. 28, 1916; s. Ignacio Garibay Zamora and Sara Gutierrez Macias; children: Luis, Jorge, Bertha (Mrs. Oscar Soria), Teresa (Mrs. Antonio Rivero), Gabriela (Mrs. Ramon Escobar), Martha (Mrs. Fernando Torres), Cristina, Patricia, Fernando; m. Bertha Bagnis Flores, Jan. 20, 1940 (div. 1965); m. Rita Sawicki, Sept. 9, 1966 (div. 1982); m. Annie Pemberton McNeill, Feb. 20, 1984. B.A., Inst. Scis., Guadalajara, 1931; med. studies U. Guadalajara, 1932-33; Dr. Surgery and Obstetrics, Nat. Autonomous U. Mexico, 1934, 1940; M.Ed., Autonomous U. Guadalajara/U. Houston, 1977; 9 hon. doctorates. Intern Ramón Garibay Hosp., 1938-40; resident in pediatrics Children's Hosp. of Mexico, 1945-46; prof. Sch. Nursing, Uruapan, 1941; founder, dir., prof. Secondary Sch., Uruapan, 1942; prof. pediatrics, head dept. Autonomous U. Guadalajara, 1947-62, sec. faculty medicine, 1947-49, dean faculty medicine, 1949-52, bd. dirs., 1948—, vice rector, 1955-57, rector, 1957—; founder, pres. Exam. Bd. Pediatrics; adviser Ministry Edn. and Culture Brazil; dir. Nat. Inquiry into Nutrition, Nat. Inquiry into Infantile Diarrhea; adviser Council Rectors Brazilian U.; lectr. univ. adminstrn., Ecuador, 1968, Brazil, 1966, others; founder, bd. dirs. Mexican Pvt. Higher Edn. Instns. Fedn., 1981; v.p. Inter Am. Council Econ. and Social Devel., 1982—; mem. Internat. Council Ednl. Devel., 1983—. Author: La Trampa, 1972, Reforma Universitaria, 1972, Financiamiento de la Universidad, 1973, Juventude em Trance, 1974, Programas de Educatión en la Comunidad, 1979, others; contbr. articles to med. and ednl. jours. Dir. U.S. Seminar on Improvement Univ. Curriculum; co-organizer Conf. Edn. Nutrition, UNICEF; pres. 4th Congress Pediatricians Latin Nations; 1st pres. Congress Latin Am. Pediatricians; pres. Jalisco Inst. Spanish Culture, 1950-52. Decorated knight Order Isabel the Catholic; comdr. Nat. Order Cruzeiro do Sul; grand officer Nat. Order Ednl. Merit, Brazil; Order Andres Bello, Venezuela; medal Koeler, Brazil, 1975; medal of Honor, IAUP, 1981; Disting. Son and Guest of Honor,, City of Zamora (Mex.), 1981; medal of Honor, Kyung Hee U., Korea, 1983. Mem. Soc. Profls. Uruapan (pres.), Internat. Assn. Univ. Pres. (v.p. 1981), Jalisco Soc Pediatrics (pres. 1958), Nat. Assn. Pediatrics Mexico (pres. 1959-63), Latin Am. Assn. Pediatrics (pres. 1963-66), Latin Am. Study Group for Improvement and Reform of Edn. (founder, pres. 1965-67, v.p. 1977), numerous others. Club: Rotary (pres. Uruapan 1944-45). Home: 5016 Paseo de Loma Larga Guadalajara Jalisco Mexico Office: 1201 Avenida Patria Guadalajara Jalisco Mexico

GARINGER, LOUIS DANIEL, educator; b. Johnson City, Tenn.; s. Merrion X. and Hilda (Gasteiger) G.; m. Joanne Mazna, June 21, 1958. A.B., U. Tenn., 1947, J.D., 1949; M.A. in Govt, Harvard, 1957. Staff writer Christian Sci. Monitor Youth Forums, Boston, 1949-51; teaching fellow, tutor govt. Harvard, 1955-58; asso. dir. Salzburg Seminar in Am. Studies, 1958-60; editorial writer Christian Sci. Monitor, 1965-67, religious affairs editor, 1967-71; research, 1971-72; asso. prof. polit. sci. and religion Principia Coll., Elsah, Ill., 1973—; vis. scholar Boston U. Sch. Theology, 1980, Grad. Theol. Union, Berkeley, Calif. Contbr. articles to profl. jours. Served with AUS, 1951-53. Recipient Religious Pub. Relations Council merit award, 1969; William E. Leidt award for religious reporting, 1970. Mem. Am. Polit. Sci. Assn., Am. Acad. Religion, Soc. Christian Ethics, Scarabbean, Pi Kappa Phi, Phi Kappa Phi, Phi Eta Sigma, Sigma Delta Pi, Phi Alpha Eta. Christian Scientist. Home: Principia Coll Elsah IL 62028

GARLAND, CARL WESLEY, chemist, educator; b. Bangor, Maine, Oct. 1, 1929; s. Cecil G. and Blandena Couillard (Wadell) G.; m. Joan A. Donaghy, July 30, 1955; children: Leslie J., Andrew E. B.S., U. Rochester, 1950; Ph.D., U. Calif.-Berkeley, 1953. Instr. chemistry U. Calif.-Berkeley, 1953; faculty MIT, 1953—, assoc. prof. chemistry, 1959-68, prof. chemistry, 1968—; vis. prof. U. Rome, 1974, Cath. U. Louvain (Belgium), 1977, Ben Gurion U., Israel, 1980, U. Paris, 1981, 82; chmn. Gordon Research Conf. Orientational Disorder in Crystals, 1984. Author: (with D.P. Shoemaker, J.W. Nibler, J.I. Steinfeld) Experiments in Physical Chemistry, 4th edit., 1981; editor: Optics and Spectroscopy, 1960-81; contbr. numerous articles to profl. jours. A.P. Sloan fellow, 1954-60; Guggenheim fellow, 1963. Fellow Am. Acad. Arts and Sci.; mem. Am. Phys. Soc. Research infrared spectra chemisorbed molecules, low temperature elastic constants, lattice dynamical calculations of properties solids, ultrasonic and thermodynamic studies order-disorder phenomena in solids at high pressures, calorimetric studies liquid crystals. Home: 4 Edward St Belmont MA 02178 Office: Mass Inst Tech Dept Chemistry Room 6-237 Cambridge MA 02139

GARLAND, CHARLES RALEIGH, educator; b. Potter, Nebr., June 10, 1917; s. Charles R. and Pearl (Finchum) G.; m. Shirley Winifred White, Sept. 9, 1945; 1 dau., Susan. Student, Carson-Newman Coll., 1935; B.S., U. Ky., 1939, Eastman Sch. Music, 1939-40; M.A., U. Iowa, 1942, Ph.D., 1945; postdoctoral studies, U. Ind., 1951. Tchr. Morningside Coll., 1945-51, U. Mo., 1951-62; mem. faculty Roosevelt U., 1962—, now prof. music. Composer opera, songs, sonata. Mem. AAUP, Music Tchrs. Nat. Assn., Coll. Music Soc. Club: Cliff Dwellers (Chgo.). Home: 828 W George St Chicago IL 60657

GARLAND, CHARLES STEDAM, JR., financial executive; b. N.Y.C., Sept. 17, 1927; s. Charles S. and Aurelia (Stoner) G.; m. Joan Burns Cardwell, Sept. 17, 1954; children: Margaret, Elizabeth, Charles S. B.A., Yale U., 1949. Investment rep. Merrill Lynch Pierce Fenner & Smith, N.Y.C., Louisville, 1950-54, Alex Brown & Sons, Balt., 1954-64; gen. ptnr. Alwx Brown & Sons, 1964—. Bd. dirs. Balt. City Hosps., Balt. Opera Co. Served with USNR, 1945-46. Mem. Pub. Securities Assn. (bd. dirs.). Republican. Episcopalian. Clubs: Ellridge Mchts.; Maryland (Balt.); Yale (N.Y.C.). Office: Alex Brown & Sons 135 E Baltimore St Baltimore MD 21202

GARLAND, JAMES CALLAWAY, physics educator; b. Columbia, Mo., Aug. 11, 1942; s. James Clifford G. and Marcella (Garland); m. Marhta McMackin, June 25, 1965 (div. 1983); children: Elizabeth, James. A.B., Princeton U., 1964; Ph.D., Cornell U., 1969. Prof. physics Ohio State U., Columbus, 1970—, acting v.p. research Lab., 1982-83, dir. Materials Research Lab., 1982—. NSF postdoctoral fellow, 1969. Mem. Am. Phys. Soc. Office: Dept Physics Ohio State 174 18th W Ave Columbus OH 43210

GARLAND, PHYLLIS TWYLA JEAN (PHYL GARLAND), author, journalist, educator; b. McKeesport, Pa., Oct. 27, 1935; d. Percy Andrew and Hazel Barbara Maxine (Hill) Garl. B.S.J., Northwestern U., 1957. Writer, feature editor Pitts. Courier, 1958-65; asst., then asso. editor Ebony mag., 1965-69, N.Y. editor, 1969-71, contbg. editor, 1971-77, Stereo Rev. mag., 1977—; music commentator Sta. WNET-TV, 1978-80; asst. prof. Black studies State U. N.Y. at New Paltz, 1971-73, acting chmn. dept., 1973; asst. prof. journalism Grad. Sch. Journalism, Columbia, 1973-79, asso. prof., 1979—. Author: The Sound of Soul: The Story of Black Music, 1969; Contbr. articles to books, mags. Mem. adv. bd. Columbia Journalism Rev.; mem. jazz panel Nat. Endowment for Arts, 1977-80. Recipient Golden Quill award for feature writing Western Pa., 1962, award for pub. service reporting N.Y. chpt. Pub. Relations Soc. Am., 1974. Mem. Women in Communications (Nat. Headliner award 1971), Delta Sigma Theta (commn. on arts and letters 1974—). Home: 60 E 8th St Apt 23-P New York NY 10003 Office: Grad Sch Journalism Columbia New York NY 10027 *One should pursue a course without an eye to the obstacles that appear to block one's way. This might even mean preparing for opportunities that do not exist at the moment. The main difference between winners and losers is that the former know how to turn handicaps into advantages.*

GARLAND, ROBERT FIELD, transportation executive; b. St. Paul, Aug. 25, 1934; s. Donald Field and Anne Clara (Merrill) G.; m. Karen Kay Mikaelsen, Mar. 14, 1969. B.B.A., U. Minn., 1956; postgrad., Program for Mgmt. Devel., Harvard U., 1970. Programmer, Gt. No. Ry. Co., St. Paul, 1959-60, systems analyst, 1961-62, acct., 1963-64, auditor, 1964-66, asst. controller, 1967-69; asst. v.p. acctg. Burlington No., Inc., St. Paul, 1970-75, v.p., controller, 1976-80; sr. v.p. planning and fin. Burlington No. R.R. Co., St. Paul, 1981—. Author: Derfflinger, 1979; contbr. articles to tech. jours. Mem. exec. bd. Indianhead council Boy Scouts Am.; active St. Paul United Way. Served with U.S. Army, 1956-58. Mem. Nat. Assn. Accts., Inst. Mgmt. Acctg. (Beyer gold medal 1973), Fin. Exec. Inst., St. Paul C. of C., Beta Gamma Sigma. Clubs: St. Paul Athletic, Southview Golf. Office: 176 E 5th St Saint Paul MN 55101

GARLID, KERMIT LEROY, educator; b. Ellsworth, Wis., May 10, 1929; s. Emil Peter and Inga Ovidia (Knutson) G.; m. Barbara Joyce Cunningham, Sept. 18, 1954; children: Peter, Jeffrey, Jonathan, Steven. B.S., U. Wis., 1950, U. Minn., 1956, Ph.D., 1961. Asst. prof. nuclear engring. and chem. engring. U. Wash., Seattle, 1960-66, assoc. prof., 1966-71, prof., 1971—, assoc. dean, 1973-82, acting dean, 1976, 80-81, vice provost, 1982—; vis. prof. Technische Hochschule Munchen, Germany, 1968-69; sr. sci. fellow, Norway, Germany, Switzerland, 1979-80, Cons. to bus. and govt. Served with Ordnance Corps AUS, 1951-53. Mem. Am. Inst. Chem. Engrs., Am. Nuclear Soc., AAAS, Sigma Xi, Phi Lambda Upsilon, Tau Beta Pi. Researcher in dynamics of two-phase flow, nuclear fuel cycle. Home: 2829 10th Ave E Seattle WA 98102

GARMENDIA, FRANCISCO, bishop; b. Lozcano, Spain, Nov. 6, 1924. Ordained priest Roman Catholic Ch., 1947. Ordained titular bishop Limisa and aux. bishop., N.Y.C., 1977—; vicar for Spanish pastoral devel. N.Y. Archdiocese. Office: 1900 Crotona Pkwy Bronx NY 10460 *

GARMEZY, NORMAN, psychologist; b. N.Y.C., June 18, 1918; s. Isadore and Laura (Weiss) G.; m. Edith Linick, Aug. 8, 1945; children: Kathy, Andrew, Lawrence. B.B.A. in Econs, CCNY, 1939; M.A. in Guidance and Counseling, Columbia U., 1940; Ph.D. in Clin. Psychology, State U. Iowa, 1950. USPHS fellow in clin. psychology Worcester (Mass.) State Hosp., 1947-48; from asst. prof. to prof. psychology Duke U., Durham, N.C., 1950-61, dir. undergrad. studies,

1951-56, dir. clin. psychology tng. program, 1957-60; tng. specialist in psychology NIMH, Bethesda, Md., 1956-57; sr. research psychologist Worcester State Hosp.; prof. U. Minn., Mpls., 1961—; dir. Center for Personality Research, 1962-67; clin. prof. psychiatry dept. U. Rochester (N.Y.) Sch. Medicine, 1969-79; vis. prof. U. Copenhagen, 1965-66, Cornell U., 1969-70; vis. colleague Inst. Psychiatry, Maudsley Hosp., London, 1975-76; vis. prof. psychiatry Stanford U. Med. Sch., 1979—; NIMH lectr. Staff Coll., 1983; mem. com. on schizophrenia research Scottish Rite, Boston, 1968-82; cons. NIMH, also past mem. grants com.; spl. rev. cons. Nat. Inst. Drug Abuse, 1974-78; mem. task force on research Presdl. Commn. on Mental Health, 1977-78; dir. Founds. Fund for Research in Psychiatry, 1976-82; mem. overall adv. com. to health com. McArthur Found., chmn. research network on risk and protective factors in major mental disorders. Author: (with G. Kimble and E. Zigler) Principles of General Psychology, 5th edit, 1980; editor: (with Rutter) Stress, Coping and Development in Children, 1983; mem. internat. adv. editorial bd.: Schizophrenia Bull, 1974—, Psychol. Medicine, 1976—; corr. editor: Jour. Child Psychology and Psychiatry, 1975—; adv. editor, MCGraw-Hill Book Co., 1969—; mem. editorial adv. bd.: Sci. Reports, Sci. Monographs, 1979—, Psychiatry and Social Sci, 1981-83, Ann. Rev. Psychology; contbr. articles to profl. jours. Served with U.S. Army, 1943-45. Recipient Lifetime Research Career award NIMH, 1962—; co-recipient Stanley Dean award for basic research in schizophrenia, 1967; fellow Center for Advanced Studies in Behavioral Scis., Palo Alto, Calif., 1979-80. Fellow Am. Psychol. Assn. (Disting. Scientist award sect. 3 1974, Master lectr. 1975, pres. div. clin. psychology 1977-78), Am. Psychopath. Assn.; mem. AAUP, AAAS, Psychonomic Soc., Soc. Research in Child Devel., Assn. Advancement Psychology (chmn. bd. trustees 1977-78), Sigma Xi. Club: Cosmos (Washington). Home: 5115 Lake Ridge Rd Edina MN 55436 Office: N419 Elliott Hall Univ Minn Minneapolis MN 55455

GARN, EDWIN JACOB, Senator; b. Richfield, Utah, Oct. 12, 1932; s. Jacob Edwin and Fern (Christensen) G.; m. Hazel Rhae Thompson, Feb. 2, 1957 (dec. 1976); children: Jacob Wayne, Susan Rhae, Ellen Marie, Jeffrey Paul; m. Kathleen Brewerton, Apr. 8, 1977; children: Matthew Spencer, Christopher Brook, Jennifer Kathleen. B.S., U. Utah, 1955. Spl. agt. John Hancock Mut. Life Ins. Co., Salt Lake City, 1960-61; asst. mgr. Home Life Ins. Co. N.Y., Salt Lake City, 1961-66; gen. agt. Mut. Trust Life Ins. Co., Salt Lake City, 1966-68; city commr., Salt Lake City, 1968-72, mayor, 1972-74; dir. Met. Water Dist., 1968-72; mem., U.S. Senate from Utah, 1974—. Chmn. joint bd. commrs. Salt Lake Model Cities Agy., 1973—; Bd. dirs. Salt Lake Community Action Program, 1968—; pres. Salt Lake County unit Am. Cancer Soc., 1970-72, chmn. county crusade, 1967, bd. dirs. Utah div., 1968—; mem. advisory bd. Salvation Army; bd. dirs. Utahns for Effective Govt., Columbus Community Center; Mem. Utah Republican party fin. com., 1965-68; chmn. Rep. voting dist., 1960-64, Rep. legis. dist., 1962-66; bd. dirs. Salt Lake County Young Reps., 1960-66; co-chmn. Coalition Peace Through Strength. Served to lt. (s.g.) USNR, 1956-60; col. Utah Air N.G., 1963-79. Recipient Tom McCoy award Utah League Cities and Towns, 1972. Mem. Utah League Cities and Towns (pres. 1971-72, dir. 1968—), Nat. League Cities (1st v.p. 1973-74, hon. pres. 1975), Sigma Chi. Mormon. Club: Kiwanian. Office: 505 Dirksen Bldg Washington DC 20510

GARN, STANLEY MARION, physical anthropologist, educator; b. New London, Conn., Oct. 27, 1922; s. Harry and Sadie Edith (Cohen) G.; m. Priscilla Crozier, Apr. 8, 1950; children: Barbara, William David. A.B., Harvard U., 1942, A.M., 1947, Ph.D., 1948. Research assoc. chem. engring. Chem. Warfare Service Devel. Lab., Mass. Inst. Tech., 1942-44; tech. editor Polaroid Co., 1944-46; cons. applied anthropology, 1946-47; research fellow cardiology Mass. Gen. Hosp., Boston, 1946-50; instr. anthropology Harvard U., 1948-52; anthropologist Forsyth Dental Infirmary, Boston, 1947-52; dir. Forsyth face size project Army Chem. Corps, 1950-52; chmn. dept. growth and genetics Fels Research Inst., Yellow Springs, Ohio, 1952-68; fellow Center Human Growth and Devel., U. Mich., Ann Arbor, also prof. nutrition and anthropology, 1968—. Author: Human Races, 1970, Gain and Loss of Compact Bone, 1970; also numerous articles; editorial bds. numerous jours. Recipient Disting. Service award U. Mich. Fellow Am. Acad. Pediatrics (hon. asso.); fellow Am. Anthrop. Assn., AAAS; Fellow Am. Acad. Arts and Scis.; mem. Nat. Acad. Scis., Am. Assn. Phys. Athropologists, Internat. Assn. Dental Research, Internat. Orgn. Study Human Devel., Am. Inst. Nutrition, Am. Soc. Naturalists, Sigma Xi. Home: 2410 Londonderry Rd Ann Arbor MI 48104 Office: 300 N Ingalls Bldg U Mich Ann Arbor MI 48109

GARNEAU, E(DOUARD) H(ENRI) PIERRE, assn. exec.; b. Quebec City, Que., Can., Nov. 27, 1922; s. Frank Joseph Gerard and Andree (deVarennes) G.; m. Lucille Woods, July 14, 1945; children—Françoise, Suzanne, Roger. Student, U. Ottawa, 1938-43. Commd. 2d lt. Can. Army, 1943, advanced through grades to maj., 1959; served in, Korea, 1952, Congo, 1962-63, asst. mil. attache, Paris, 1967-69, ret., 1970; exec. sec. Royal Soc. Can., Ottawa, 1970—. Mem. Can. Corps of Commissionnaires (bd. govs. Ottawa div.). Roman Catholic. Clubs: Hyland Golf, Men's Can. (Ottawa). Office: 344 Wellington St Ottawa ON K1A 0N4 Canada

GARNER, ALTO LUTHER, educator; b. Dothan, Ala., Dec. 10, 1916; s. Albert Early and Martha (DeBardeleben) G.; m. Katie Mae Sanders, Oct. 5, 1945 (div. 1980); 1 son, Robert Edward Lee. Student, Howard Coll., 1940-43; A.B., U. Ala., 1944; postgrad., So. Bapt. Theol. Sem., 1944-45, U. Tex., Austin, 1947; M.A., N.Y. U., 1947; Ed.D., U. Ky., 1954. Ordained to ministry Bapt. Ch., 1942; instr. history and polit. sci. Georgetown Coll., 1947-49, asst. prof., 1949-53; asso. prof. edn. Howard Coll., 1953-54; prof. edn. Samford U., Birmingham, Ala., 1954—, chmn. div. tchr. edn., head dept. edn. and psychology, 1964-66, dean, 1966-80, prof., 1980—, Disting. prof. edn., 1981; Ala. regional ednl. cons. State Farm Ins. Cos., 1955-73. Served with AUS, 1941. Named hon. lt. a.d.c. Ala. Militia, 1972, hon. adm. Ala. Navy, 1978. Mem. Kappa Phi Kappa, Kappa Delta Pi, Phi Alpha Theta, Phi Kappa Phi. Home: 417B Honey Locust Ln Birmingham AL 35209 Office: 800 Lakeshore Dr Birmingham AL 35209

GARNER, CHARLES WILLIAM, educator; b. Pine Grove Mills, Pa., Apr. 18, 1939; s. Adam Krumrine and Blanche Ella (Gearhart) G.; m. Karyl J. Packer, Sept. 8, 1962; children: Ronald Adam, Juliet Paige. Student, U.S. Navy Electronics Airborne Sonar Sch., 1959; B.S. in Bus. Edn., Pa. State U., 1965; M.Ed. in Higher Edn. Adminstrn., Pa. State U., 1968; Ed.D. in Vocat. Indsl. Edn., Pa. State U., 1974. Adminstrv. asst. dept. psychology Pa. State U., 1965-75; asst. prof., site adminstr. March AFB, Calif. for So. Ill. U., 1975-77; asst. prof., coordinator Ft. Knox Ctr.- U. Louisville, 1977-78; assoc. prof., acting vice dean Rutgers U., Camden, N.J., 1978-79, assoc. prof. urban edn., chmn. dept. edn. Univ. Coll., New Brunswick, N.J., 1978-81, assoc. prof. vocat. tech. edn. Grad. Sch. Edn., 1981—, chmn. dept. vocat. tech. edn. Grad. Sch. Edn., 1982—; mem. adv. com. 15th Air Force Noncommd. Officer Leadership Sch., Strategic Air Force Command, 1976-77; mem. N.J. state leadership team Leadership Tng. Inst.-Vocat. and Spl. Edn., 1980-81; mem. adv. council Vocat. Tng. Project, Eastern European Coalition Am., Perth Amboy, N.J., 1981-82; cons. alt. edn. program South Brunswick (N.J.) High Sch. Contbr. articles to profl. jours.; co-editor: Occupational Edn. Forum, 1979—; editorial reader: Jour. Indsl. Tchr. Edn., 1981; producer, host talk show pilot for public TV, 1979; producer, host: TV tape series Rutgers U.: Current Issues in Vocat. Edn., 1979. Elder Sands Hill Presbyterian Ch., Kendall Park, N.J. Served with USN, 1959-62. Grantee N.J. Dept. Edn. Div. Vocat. Edn., 1978-84, HEW, 1979-80. Mem. AAUP, Am. Vocat. Assn. (editorial bd. Jours. Gen. and Related Instrn. 1982), Eastern Bus. Edn. Assn. (1982), Nat. Assn. Vocat. Edn. (1982), Nat. Assn. Indsl. and Tech. Tchr. Educators (1982), N.J. Assn. Vocat. Edn. (1982), Iota Lambda Sigma (1982), Spl. Needs Personnel (exec. council 1980-81, pres. 1981-82), Nat. Bus. Edn. Assn., N.J. Bus. Edn. Assn., N.J. Vocat. Tchr. Edn. Assn., Vocat. Edn. Assn. N.J., Phi Delta Kappa, Omicron Tau Theta, Epsilon Pi Tau. Lodge: Elks (exalted ruler 1972-73). Home: 12 James Ave Kendall Park NJ 08824 Office: Dept Vocat Tech Edn Grad Sch Edn Rutgers U New Brunswick NJ 08903 *Our influence in life is determined by the good deeds we do rather than by the emotions that we feel.*

GARNER, CICERO, lawyer; b. Waynesboro, Ga., Dec. 1, 1936; s. Cicero and Bernice (Welch) G.; m. Laurie Geiger, Mar. 17, 1975; children: Caroline Belle, Evan Cicero. A.B., Emory U., 1959; J.D. cum laude, U. Ga., 1961. Bar: Ga. bar 1961. Law asst. to chief justice Supreme Ct. Ga., 1961; practiced in, Atlanta, 1962—; mng. partner firm Hurt, Richardson, Garner, Todd & Cadenhead (and predecessor.). Mem. Am. Bar Assn., Am. Law Inst., State Bar Ga., Atlanta Bar Assn., Lawyers Club Atlanta (pres. 1979-80). Methodist. Clubs: Buckhead Lions, Commerce, Capital City, World Trade (Atlanta) (dir.). Office: 1100 Peachtree Center Harris Tower 233 Peachtree St NE Atlanta GA 30043

GARNER, HARVEY LOUIS, elec. engr.; b. Lake, Colo., Dec. 23, 1926; s. Homa and Violet (Thuelin) G.; m. Yvonne Lillian King, Aug. 7, 1949; children-Susan Ann, Harvey Thomas. B.S., U. Denver, 1949, M.S., 1951; Ph.D., U. Mich., 1958. Engr. with devel. computers U. Mich., 1951-55, instr. elec. engring., 1955-58, asst. prof., 1958-60, asso. prof., 1960-63, prof., 1963-70; dir. Information Systems Lab., 1960-64, Systems Engring. Lab., 1964-66, acting chmn. dept. communications scis., 1965-67, prof. computer and communications scis., 1967-70; prof. elec. engring., dir. Moore Sch. Elec. Engring., 1970—; Cons. in field; appt. nat. lectr. Assn. Computing Machinery, 1965; Gen. chmn. 1st Nat. Computer Conf. and Exhbn., N.Y.C., 1973; gen. chmn. Islands Applications Conf., Tokyo, Japan, 1972. Contbr. articles to profl. jours. Trustee Charles Babbage Inst., 1979—. Served with USNR, 1945-46. Fellow IEEE; mem. Am. Soc. Engring. Edn., Assn. Computing Machinery, AAAS, Sigma Xi, Eta Kappa Nu, Sigma Pi Sigma. Home: 498 Meadow Ln King of Prussia PA 19406 Office: Moore Sch Elec Engring U Pa Philadelphia PA 19104

GARNER, JAMES (JAMES SCOTT BUMGARNER), actor; b. Norman, Okla., Apr. 7, 1928; m. Lois Clarke, Aug. 17, 1956; children: Kimberly, Gretta, Scott. Student, N.Y. Berghof Sch., U. Okla. Worked as salesman, oil field worker, carpet layer, lifeguard, truck driver, numerous others; pace car driver Indpls. 500, 1975, 77. Toured with road cos.; appeared: TV series Maverick, 1957-62, Nichols, 1971-72, Rockford Files, 1974-79; appeared on: motion picture debut in Toward the Unknown; other films include Sayonara, 1957, Shoot-out at Medicine Bend, 1957, Darby's Rangers, 1958, Up Periscope, 1959, Cash McCall, 1960, The Children's Hour, 1962, The Great Escape, 1963, The Americanization of Emily, 1964, 36 Hours, 1964, The Art of Love, 1965, A Man Could Get Killed, 1966, Duel at Diablo, 1966, Mister Buddwing, 1966, Grand Prix, (co-producer), 1966, Hour of the Gun, 1967, Marlowe, 1969, Support Your Local Sheriff, 1971, Support Your Local Gunfighter, 1971, Skin Game, 1971, They Only Kill Their Masters, 1972, One Little Indian, 1973, Health, 1979, The Fan, 1980; star: TV movie Rockford Files, 1974; (recipient Emmy award.). Joined U.S. Mcht. Marine; served with AUS, Korea. Decorated Purple Heart. Address: care Robinson Luttrell & Assos Inc 141 El Camino Dr Suite 110 Beverly Hills CA 90212 *

GARNER, JAMES PARENT, lawyer; b. Madison, Wis., Jan. 22, 1923; s. Harrison Levi and Mary (Parent) G.; m. Georgia Ann Trebilcock, Oct. 12, 1946; children: Gail G., Ann G., Thomas W., Mary F. B.A., U. Wis., 1947; LL.B., Harvard U., 1949. Bar: Wis. 1949, Ohio 1950. Assoc. firm Baker & Hostetler & Patterson, Cleve., 1949-58; ptnr. Baker & Hostetler, Cleve., 1959—. Served to capt. inf. U.S. Army, 1943-46. Mem. ABA, Ohio Bar Assn., Greater Cleve. Bar Assn. (trustee 1969-71), Selden Soc. Republican. Clubs: Union (N.Y.C.); Harvard. Home: 31000 Shaker Blvd Pepper Pike OH 44124 Office: 3200 National City Ctr. Cleveland OH 44114

GARNER, JOHN MICHAEL, banker; b. Miami, Fla., July 17, 1935; s. James Geston and Mary Alberta (Willis) G.; m. Beatrice Marie Keep, Apr. 5, 1958; children: John Michael, Mary Elizabeth. A.B., Washington and Lee U., 1957, LL.B., 1960. Bar: Fla. 1960. Since practiced in Miami; v.p. Garner Ins. Agy., Inc., Miami, 1960-71, pres., 1971—; v.p. Garner Mortgage Co., Miami, 1960-71, pres., 1971—; with First State Bank of Miami (formerly Little River Bank & Trust Co.), 1963-81, exec. v.p., 1971-72, pres., chief exec. officer, 1972-78, chmn., chief exec. officer, 1979-81; chmn. Barnett Mortgage Co. subs. Barnett Banks Fla., 1982—, Tele-Link Communications, Inc., 1983—; exec. v.p., dir. First State Banking Corp.; dir. Barnett Bank of S. Fla., N.A., State Mut. Ins. Co. Pres. Crippled Children's Soc. Dade County, 1965-67; mem. Fla. Crippled Children's Commn., 1969-70; trustee Barry Coll., Miami Country Day Sch. Served with AUS, 1958. Mem. Young Pres. Orgn., Phi Alpha Delta, Sigma Chi. Democrat. Presbyterian. Clubs: Kiwanis, Committee 100, LaGorge Country, Miami, University (Miami); Ocean Reef, Key Largo Anglers (Largo, Fla.); Bath, Palm Bay, Rod and Reel (Miami Beach, Fla.); Chub Cay (Bahamas); Coral Gables Yacht. Home: 2517 NE 135th St North Miami FL 33181 Office: 7900 NE 2d Ave Miami FL 33138

GARNER, MILDRED MAXINE, educator; b. nr. Liberty, N.C., Mar. 15, 1919; d. Robert Monroe and Maize (Kimrey) G. B.A., Woman's Coll. of U. N.C. at, Greensboro, 1939; M.A., Union Theol. Sem., N.Y.C., 1946; Ph.D., U. Aberdeen, Scotland, 1952. Tchr. English, history, journalism, Roanoke Rapids, N.C., 1939, 41-42; asst. editor Bibl. Recorder, Raleigh, N.C., 1940; dir. religious activities Woman's Coll., U. N.C. at Greensboro, 1942-50; asso. prof. religion Meredith Coll., Raleigh, 1952-58; prof. religion Sweet Briar (Va.) Coll., 1958—, Wallace Eugene Rollins prof. religion, 1969—, chmn. dept., 1961-62, 63-72, 74-78, 81—; Fellow summer seminar history and culture India U. Va., 1964, summer seminar history and culture China, 1965; summer inst. S. Asia Duke U., 1966; summer seminar Banaras Hindu U., Varanasi, India, 1977; Fulbright scholar U. Aberdeen, 1950-51, 51-52; program advanced religious studies fellow Union Theol. Sem., 1955-56; Am. Inst. Indian Studies fellow, Poona, India, 1962-63, Inst. Judaism, Vanderbilt Div. Sch., Nashville, 1979. Mem. Phi Beta Kappa. Republican. Baptist. Home: 123 N Asheboro St Liberty NC 27298 Office: Sweet Briar Coll Sweet Briar VA 24595 *My unschooled parents taught and practiced sharing and integrity. A lifetime of studying religious traditions in this country, in a Scottish university, and in India confirms what they knew without leaving our country village.*

GARNER, ROBERT DALE, banker; b. Lititz, Pa., Sept. 22, 1933; s. Albert S. G.; m. H. Pauline Gehman, Aug. 23, 1952; children: Sally Ann, Kathleen Jo, Robert Dale, Scott David. Student, pub. schs., Lititz, Pa. Teller Farmer Nat. Bank, Lititz, Pa., 1951-52; supervisory position East Petersburg State Bank, (Pa.), 1952-55, Fulton Nat. Bank., East Petersburg, Pa., 1955-57; asst. cashier Fulton Nat. Bank, East Petersburg, Pa., 1957-64, br. mgr., 1964-66, supervisory mgr., 1966-67, asst. v.p., Lancaster, Pa., 1967-71, exec. v.p., 1971-73, 73-80, pres., dir., 1980-82, chmn. bd., 1983—; chmn. Lancaster County div. Banking for Series E Bonds, Pa.; mem. fed. relations com. Fed. Res. Bank of Phila. Chmn. Assocs. in Downtown Lancaster; bd. dirs. YMCA, Am. Heart Assn., Luther Acres, Lititz, Pa.; bd. dirs., treas. Credit Bur. Lancaster County; residential chmn. Lancaster chpt. Am. Cancer Soc.; area compaign leader Lancaster County WITF Capital Campaign; mem. campaign Found. for Ind. Colls.; chmn. budget com. United Way of Lancaster County. Mem. Pa. Bankers Assn., Lancaster County Bankers Assn. (pres.), Robert Morris Assocs.; Mem. Lancaster C. of C. (bd. dirs.). Republican. Lutheran. Clubs: Lancaster Country, Hamilton. Home: 30 E Woods Dr Lititz PA 17543 Office: Fulton Bank 1 Penn Sq Lancaster PA 17604

GARNER, ROBERT F., bishop; b. Jersey City, Apr. 27, 1920. Student, Seton Hall U., Immaculate Conception Sem., N.J. Ordained priest Roman Catholic Ch., 1946. Ordained titular bishop Blear and aux. bishop, Newark, 1976—. Office: 311 Prospect St Midland Park NJ 07432 *

GARNER, SAMUEL PAUL, accounting educator, author; b. Yadkinville, N.C., Aug. 15, 1910; s. Samuel W. and Ila Jane (Hoots) G.; m. Ruth Bailey, Aug. 25, 1934; children: Thad Barclay, Walter Samuel, Sarah Jane. A.B., Duke U., 1932, A.M., 1934; postgrad., Columbia U., 1936; Ph.D., U. Tex., 1940; D.Ec. (hon.), Busan Nat. U., 1966; LL.D., U. Ala., 1971. C.P.A., Ala., Tex. Faculty Duke U., 1934-35, Miss. State Coll., 1935-37, U. Tex., 1937-39; assoc. prof. accounting U. Ala., University, 1939-43, prof., 1943-71, head dept. accounting, 1949-55, dean, 1954-71; Mem. Knight & Garner (C.P.A.s, University), 1942-49; dir. First Fed. Savs. & Loan Assn., Hardins Bakery, Inc., O. Bowers Co., Tide Clean, Inc., Tuscaloosa, Ala.; Cons. edn. to comptroller gen. U.S., 1955-61; cons. grad. edn. U.S. Office Edn., 1965-70; cons. mgmt. edn. U.S. Dept. Def., 1965-70; Comer lectr. U. Ga., 1957; Price Waterhouse Found. lectr. Ga. State U., 1964; Distinguished Faculty lectr. Tex. Western Coll., 1963, U. S.D., 1963, E. Carolina Coll., 1965, Va. Poly. Inst., 1966, Tex. Tech. U., 1970, Tex. A&M U., U. Tenn., 1972, Ala. A&M U., 1973, Fla. Atlantic U., 1975, Fla. Internat. U., 1973, Western Carolina U., 1976, Appalachian State U., 1975, Judson Coll., 1977, Santa Clara U., 1978, Wollongong U., 1980, others; U.S. del. internat. mgmt. and accounting congresses, 1957—; condr. spl. ednl. assignments U.S. State Dept. and other agys. in, Turkey, 1958, Far East, 1960, 66, 68, 69, 72, 80, Europe, 1957, 60, 61, 63-83, S.Am., 1962, 65, 75, 81, Africa, 1964, 73, 82; adv. bd. Internat. U. Contact for Mgmt., Holland, 1964-72; U.S. Council Internat. Exchange Commerce Students. Author: (with G.H. Newlove) Elementary Cost Accounting, 1941, rev. edit., 1949, Spanish edit., 1952, Advanced Accounting, vol. I, 1951, vol. II, 1950, Advanced Accounting Problems, Book I, 1951, Advanced Accounting Problems, Book II, 1950, Handbook of Modern Accounting Theory, 1955, Education for the Professions, 1955, Readings in Cost Accounting, Budgeting and Control, 1955, rev. edit., 1960, Evolution of Cost Accounting to 1925, 1954, Japanese edit., 1956; Co-editor: (with Ken Berg) Readings in Accounting Theory, 1966, Readings on Accounting Development, 1978; editorial adv. bd.: Mgmt. Internat. mag, 1964-70; editorial bd.: Accounting Rev, 1968-70, Essays in International Business; annual, 1967-70; Contbr. articles to profl. jours. Recipient Dow-Jones award, 1976. Fellow Acad. Internat. Bus. (historian 1974—); Mem. Am. Acctg. Assn. (life, pres. 1951, exec. com. 1948, 51-54, chmn. com. internat. relations 1966-67), Am. Inst. C.P.A.s (chmn. com. profl. statistics 1960-62), Nat. Assn. C.P.A. Examiners (chmn. com. accounting edn. 1960-61), Am. Coll. C.L.U.s (council ednl. advisers 1961-69), U.S. Council Internat. Progress in Mgmt. (nat. bd. dirs. 1960-69), Acad. Acctg. Historians (life, trustee 1975-78), Fed. Govt. Accts. Assn. (adv. com. relations with univs.), Fin. Execs. Inst. (nat. com. edn. 1956-70), Am. Assn. Collegiate Schs. Bus. (pres. 1964-65), Soc. Expert Accts. France, Nat. Assn. Accts., Ala. Soc. C.P.A.s (sec.-treas. 1949-58), Sigma Alpha Epsilon, Phi Beta Kappa, Beta Gamma Sigma (nat. exec. com. 1961-66), Beta Alpha Psi (Distinguished Service award 1975), Omicron Delta Kappa, Pi Tau Chi, Omicron Delta Epsilon, Alpha Kappa Psi (trustee found.; Found. award 1962), Pi Gamma Mu. Baptist. Club: University. Home: 1016 Indian Hills Dr Tuscaloosa AL 35406 Office: Box J University AL 35486

GARNER, STANTON BERRY, educator, author; b. Corning, N.Y., Sept. 1, 1925; s. Edward Samuel and Helen (Berry) G.; m. Lydia Magalhaes Nunes, Mar. 28, 1969; 1 son, Edward Charles; children by previous marriage: Stanton Berry, George Francis. Grad., Manlius Sch., 1943; B.S., U.S. Naval Acad., 1948; A.M., Brown U., 1960, Ph.D., 1963. From instr. to assoc. prof. English Brown U., 1963-70; prof. English U. Tex., Arlington, 1970—, chmn. dept., 1970-71; prof. colaborador U. Sao Paulo, Brazil, 1968-69; Fulbright-Hays spl. lectr., Buenos Aires and Cordoba, Argentina, 1969; vis. prof. U. Federal do Rio Grande do Sul, Brazil, 1975-76; disting. vis. prof. U.S. Naval Acad., 1980. Author: Harold Frederic, 1969; Editor: The Captain's Best Mate-The Journal of Mary Chipman Lawrence on the Whaler Addison, 1856-1860, 1966, A Bibliography of Writings by and about Harold Frederic, 1975, The Correspondence of Harold Frederic, 1977, The Market Place by Harold Frederic, 1981; gen. editor: Works of Harold Frederic; Contbr. articles to profl. jours. Mem. R.I. Commn. on Arts, 1965-67. Served with AUS, 1943-44; Served with USN, 1948-58; comdr. Res. (ret.). Mem. MLA, Melville Soc., Poe Studies Assn., Nathaniel Hawthorne Soc., Thoreau Soc., Am. Studies Assn. (Am. lit. sect.), South Central MLA. Home: 1016 Live Oak Ln Arlington TX 76012

GARNER, WENDELL RICHARD, psychology educator; b. Buffalo, Jan. 21, 1921; s. Richard Charles and Lena Belle (Cole) G.; m. Barbara Chipman Ward, Feb. 18, 1944; children: Deborah Ann, Peter Ward, Elinor. A.B., Franklin and Marshall Coll., 1942, D.Sc., 1979; A.M., Harvard U., 1943, Ph.D., 1946; D.H.L., Johns Hopkins U., 1983. Teaching fellow Harvard U., 1942-43, research assoc., 1943-46; instr. Johns Hopkins U., 1946; asst. prof. Johns Hopkins, 1947-51; assoc. prof. Johns Hopkins U., 1951-55, prof., 1955-67; dir. Psychol. Lab. Inst. Coop. Research, 1949-55, chmn. dept. psychology, 1954-64; James Rowland Angell prof. psychology Yale U., 1967—, dir. social scis., 1972-73, 81—, chmn. dept. psychology, 1974-77, dean, 1978-79; Paul M. Fitts Meml. lectr. U. Mich., 1973. Author: Uncertainty and Structure as Psychological Concepts, 1962, Processing of Information and Structure, 1974; editor: Ability Testing, 1982. Recipient alumni citation and award Franklin and Marshall Coll., 1975. Fellow Am. Psychol. Assn. (Distinguished Sci. Contbn. award 1964, pres. div. exptl. psychology 1974), AAAS (v.p. psychology 1967—), Acoustical Soc. Am.; mem. Soc. Exptl. Psychologists (chmn. 1959, 75, Warren medal 1976), AAUP, Md. Psychol. Assn. (pres. 1961-62), Eastern Psychol. Assn., Nat. Acad. Scis., Sigma Xi. Home: 48 Yowago Ave Branford CT 06405 Office: Yale U New Haven CT 06520

GARNETT, E.N., food products company executive. Pres., dir. Flav-O-Rich, Inc., Louisville. Office: Flav-O-Rich Inc 10140 Linn Station Rd Louisville KY 40223§

GARNETT, KEITH JAY, consulting engineering firm executive; b. Sheboygan, Wis., Aug. 4, 1938; s. Darrell Eldred and Elsie (Bobbe) G.; m. Elaine Anne Deblack, Aug. 26, 1961; children: Leslie, Craig. B.S. in Civil Engring., U. Wis., 1962; M.S. in Engring. Mgmt., U. Alaska,

1966. Registered profl. engr., Ill., Ind., Iowa., Mich., Minn. Engr. Charmin Paper Co., Green Bay, Wis., 1966-67; pres., chief exec. officer Donohue and Assocs., Inc., Sheboygan, Wis., 1967—; dir. Citizens Bancorp., Sheboygan, 1981—. Served to capt. U.S. Army, 1962-66. Mem. ASCE (sect. pres.), Nat. Soc. Profl. Engrs., Water Pollution Control Fedn., Am. Water Works Assn., Sheboygan C. of C. (dir. 1982—), Soc. Mil. Engrs. Lutheran. Home: Route 1 Box 144A Sheboygan WI 53081 Office: Donohue and Assocs Inc 4738 N 40th St Sheboygan WI 53081

GARNETT, WILLIAM, photographer; b. Chgo., 1916. Student, Art Center Sch. of Los Angeles, 1937-38. Free-lance advt. and mag. photographer, including aerial photography, 1938—. Exhibited in one-man shows, including, George Eastman House, Rochester, N.Y., 1955, numerous group shows in, U.S. and abroad, Mus. Modern Art, N.Y.C., Met. Mus. Art, San Francisco Mus. Art, White House, 1979, Smithsonian Instn. Air and Space Museum of Aerial Photography, Washington, also at several world fairs; represented in permanent collections, George Eastman House, Mus. Modern Art, Smithsonaisn Instn., Polaroid Collection, Cambridge, Mass., Gilman Paper Co., N.Y.C.; exhibited in works include: photo mural for, Wrigley Stadium, Los Angeles, 1938, two essays on beauty of America as seen from the air for, Life Mag., 1965; prof. design, U. Calif., Berkeley, 1968-80; fellow, Center for Advanced Visual Studies, M.I.T., 1967; appeared on: TV programs The Pursuit of Happiness, NBC, 1976, From Here to There, CBS, 1980, Evening Mag, CBS, 1981, CBS, 1981; Illustrator, collaborator: The American Aesthetic (Nathanial Owings), 1968; author, photographer: The Extraordinary Landscape, 1982; subject of illustrated mag. articles. Home: 1286 Congress Valley Rd Napa CA 94558

GARNETT, WILSON BLANTON, telephone co. exec.; b. Prince Edward County, Va., Apr. 27, 1922; s. Edward Clarke and Martha Anderson (Blanton) G.; m. Doris Lohr, Sept. 21, 1952; children: Pamela, Blanton, Clarke. Student, Maryville (Tenn.) Coll., 1939-42, Sch. Bus., U. Va., 1958, Sch. Bus., U. Kans., 1960. With Centel Corp., 1942—, v.p., regional mgr., Charlottesville, Va., 1966, v.p. telephone ops., Lincoln, Nebr., 1967-71, exec. v.p., Chgo., 1971—; also dir. Central Telephone & Utilities Corp.; pres. Central Telephone Co., Chgo., 1982—; dir. Woodmen Accident & Life Co., Lincoln. Mem. bus. adv. council U. Ill.; mem. adv. council Inst. Pub. Utilities, Mich. State U. Served with F.A. AUS, 1943-45. Mem. U.S. Ind. Telephone Assn. (dir.), Ind. Telephone Pioneer Assn. (dir.), Chgo. Assn. Commerce and Industry (dir.). Republican. Clubs: Meadow (Rolling Meadows, Ill.); Biltmore Country (Barrington, Ill.). Lodges: Masons; Shriners. Home: 25770 W Timberlake Rd Barrington IL 60010 Office: Central Telephone Co 5725 E River Rd Chicago IL 60631

GARNIER, ROBERT CHARLES, management consultant; b. Gary, Ind., June 6, 1916; s. Edward Jacob and Rose (Peters) G.; m. Katherine Mary Sulich, Aug. 17, 1940; children: Robert Charles, Katherine Rosa Garnier Kavemeier, Elizabeth Ann Garnier Moschea, John Edward. B.S. in Pub. Service Engring., Purdue U., 1939; postgrad., U. Chgo., 1940. Cert. accredited exec. in personnel Personnel Accreditation Inst. Life. Mem. staff Am. Pub. Works Assn., Chgo., 1939-41; classification officer, personnel staff officer TVA, Knoxville, Tenn., 1941-46; 1st classification examiner, then 1st chief labor negotiator City of Milw., 1946-65; city personnel dir., sec. City Service Commn., 1958-81; mgmt. cons., 1982—; pres. Fastback Ltd.; mem. Wis. Statutory Joint Study Com. Civil Service, 1965-66. Author articles, chpt. in book. Mem. Am. Pub. Works Assn. (life; exec. council Inst. Adminstrv. Mgmt. 1978-83), Internat. Personnel Mgmt. Assn. (pres. 1977; hon. life), Indsl. Relations Research Assn. (pres. Wis. 1965-66, sec.-treas. 1971-81), Internat. City Mgmt. Assn., Am. Soc. Personnel Adminstrn., Milw. Area Soc. Pub. Adminstrn. (pres. 1954-55), Purdue U. Alumni Assn. Roman Catholic. Home: 9611 W Lorraine Pl Milwaukee WI 53222 *My value judgements have undergone considerable development and change during my life. The experiences, challenges and climates, especially during my married years, have strengthened my views on what is fair and what is rational. With God's help I try to carry out my responsibilities and subject hard decision issues to two tests—the test of appearance as I think others perceive the best process of arriving at a decision, and the more important test of being right as I perceive right to be in making the decision.*

GARNSWORTHY, LEWIS SAMUEL, Archbishop; b. Edmonton, Alta., Can., July 18, 1922; m. Jean Valance Allen, Aug. 7, 1954; children—Peter, Katherine. B.A., U. Alta., 1943; L.Th., Wycliffe Coll., Toronto, Ont., Can., 1945, D.D. (hon.), 1968, Trinity Coll., Toronto, 1973, Huron Coll., London, Ont., 1976. Ordained deacon Anglican Ch. Can., 1945, priest, 1946; curate, then rector chs. in, Ont., 1946, 68; suffragan bishop Anglican Ch. Can. Diocese Toronto, 1968-72, bishop, 1972-79, archbishop of Toronto, met. of Ont., 1979—. Fellow Coll. Preachers. Clubs: Albany, York. Address: 135 Adelaide St E Toronto ON M5C 1L8 Canada

GAROUTTE, BILL CHARLES, neurophysiologist; b. Absarokee, Mont., Mar. 15, 1921; s. Bernard Clark and Anna Kosir G.; m. Sally Jeter, July 18, 1948; children—Brian, Susanna, David, Katherine. Student, San Diego State Coll., 1939-42; A.B., U. Calif., Berkeley, 1943, M.D., 1945, Ph.D., 1954. With U. Calif. Med. Sch., San Francisco, 1949—, successively lectr., instr., asst. prof., asso. prof. anatomy and neurology, 1949-66, prof. anatomy and neurology, 1966—; vis. asst. prof. U. Indonesia, Djakarta, 1956-57; electromyography and electroencephalography U. Calif., San Francisco, 1953—; vis. investigator Brain Research Inst. U. Tokyo, 1963; external examiner anatomy Nat. U. Malaysia, 1978. Author: Survey of Functional Neuroanatomy, 1981. Served as lt. (j.g.), M.C. USNR, 1946-47. Fulbright scholar London, 1950-51. Mem. Western Inst. on Epilepsy (pres. 1962), Am. Assn. Anatomists, Am. Acad. Neurology, Am. Electroencephalography Soc., Western Electroencephalography Soc. (pres. 1961-62), Hist. Soc. Pa., San Francisco Neurol. Soc. (pres. 1969-70). Research on elec. activity of central nervous system. Home: 105 Molino Ave Mill Valley CA 94941 Office: U Calif San Francisco CA 94143

GARR, CARL ROBERT, manufacturing company executive; b. Olean, N.Y., Apr. 4, 1927; s. Frederick H.J. and Mary Magdalene (Zimmerman) G.; m. Arlene Crawford, Dec. 20, 1947; children: Christine Garr Weber, Anne H., Elizabeth Garr Reese. B.S. in Physics, Kent State U., 1950, M.S., Case Inst. Tech., 1953, Ph.D. in Metall. Engring, 1957. Engring. supr. Bettis plant Westinghouse Co., 1956-58; supt. tech. services, nuclear fuel ops. Olin Mathieson Chem. Corp., 1958-62; dir. engring. and research Albuquerque div. ACF Industries Inc., 1962-68, v.p. research and devel., N.Y.C., 1968-70; pres., chief exec. officer Polymer Corp. (subs. ACF Industries, Inc.), Reading, Pa., 1970-76; v.p. ACF Industries, Inc., N.Y.C., 1976-82; pres., chief exec. officer Empire Steel Castings, Inc., Reading, Pa., 1982—; dir. Bank of Pa., Reading, Carpenter Tech. Corp. Served with USN, 1944-46. Mem. Am. Soc. Metals, AIME, Newcomen Soc. N.Am., Sigma Xi. Clubs: Union League (N.Y.C.); Berkshire Country (Reading). Home: 7 Bobolink Dr Wyomissing PA 19610 Office: PO Box 139 Reading PA 19603

GARR, TERI, actress. Appeared in: movies, including The Conversation, 1974, Won Ton Ton, The Dog Who Saved Hollywood, 1976, Oh God!, 1977, Close Encounters of the Third Kind, Mr. Mike's Mondo Video, 1979, The Black Stallion, 1979; regular on TV series The Sonny Comedy Review, 1974; other TV appearances include Law and Order. Office: care Press Relations William Morris Agy 151 El Camino Beverly Hills CA 90212 *

GARRAHY, JOHN JOSEPH, governor Rhode Island; b. Providence, Nov. 26, 1930; s. John and Margaret (Neylon) G.; m. Margherite DePietro, 1956; children: Colleen, John, Maribeth, Sheila, Seanna. Student, U. Buffalo, 1952, U. R.I., 1953. Mem. R.I. Senate, 1962-68, dep. majority leader, 1963-68; also mem. Senate fin. com., judiciary com.; lt. gov. R.I., 1968-77; gov. R.I., 1977—; Chmn. Gov.'s Council on Youth Opportunities, 1969—, chmn. screening com. Author: Rhode Island in the Year, 1975, 1969, Campaign Spending and Practices-A Direction to Pursue, 1971, Financial Aid Information-A Guide for Rhode Island High School Students, 1974. Co-chmn. Cancer Control Program R.I., Econ. Devel. Program; mem. New Eng. adv. com. N.E. Regional Kidney Program, 1970; chmn. Democratic State Com., 1967; bd. dirs. Nat. Council Vocat. Rehab. Served with USAF, 1953-55. Office: State House Providence RI 02903 *

GARRARD, DON, opera singer; b. Vancouver, C., Can; 2 children. Ed., Brentwood Coll., Royal Conservatory Music, Toronto, Music Acad. of West, Santa Barbara, Calif., Opera Sch., Milan, Italy. Prin. soloist, Canadian Opera Co., Sadler's Wells, 1961, Glyndebourne, Covent Garden, Scottish Opera, Welsh Nat. Opera, Hamburg State Opera, others, over 60 roles from; Sarastro in The Magic Flute to Motan in the Ring; internat. appearances in both opera and concerts throughout world; recs. include Roberto Devereax; also appearances TV, radio, motion pictures. Address: The Bont Teffont Evias Salisbury Wilts SP3 5RG England also care Tony Hartmann Assos 250 W 57 St Suite 1120 New York NY 10107 *To be true to oneself. To do only that which is consistent with one's own personal and professional integrity. This is increasingly a very lonely and hard road but the only honest one which still affords any man a measure of self-respect.* *

GARRARD, JOHN GORDON, educator; b. London, Aug. 28, 1934; U.S., 1962, naturalized, 1977; s. John Harold and Ella Veronica (Rudman) G.; m. Carol Elizabeth Hamersen, Oct. 27, 1979; children: Michelle Elizabeth, Alison Veronica; children by previousmarriage: Richard Gordon, Alexander John. B.A., Oxford U., 1958; M.A., Columbia U., 1963; cert., Russian Inst., 1964, Ph.D., 1966. Lectr. in Russian lang. and lit. Carleton U., Ottawa, Ont., Can., 1958-62; asst. prof. Russian lit. Dartmouth Coll., Hanover, N.H., 1964-69, assoc. prof., 1969-71; vis. assoc. prof. Ind. U., Bloomington, 1970-71; prof. Russian lit. U. Va., Charlottesville, 1971—, chmn. dept. Slavic langs. and lit., 1971-76, dir. Ctr. for Russian and East European Studies, 1972-83; cons. Nat. Endowment for Humanities-Nat. Humanities Ctr., 1977; dir. Summer Seminar for Coll. Tchrs. NEH, 1976, 77. Editor: Vladimir Tendryakov: Three Novellas, 1967, The Eighteenth Century in Russia, 1973, The Russian Novel from Pushkin to Pasternak, 1983; author: Mixail Culkov: An Introduction to His Prose and Verse, 1970, Mikhail Lermontov, 1982; editorial bd.: Slavic Rev., 1978-80; contbr. articles to profl. jours. Served with Brit. Army, 1952-54. St. Antony's Coll., Oxford Assoc. fellow, 1967-68; sr. research fellow Russian Inst., Columbia U., 1975; scholar-in-residence Bellagio, 1976; sr. scholar exchanges USSR Acad. Sci., 1980. Mem. So. Conf. Slavic Studies (pres. 1979-80), MLA (nominating com. 1979-81, adv. com. publs. 1975-79), Am. Assn. Advancement of Slavic Studies, Assn. Internationale des Langues et Litteratures Slaves (treas. 1972—). Office: Dept Slavic Langs Cocke Hall U Va Charlottesville VA 22903

GARRELS, ROBERT MINARD, geology educator; b. Detroit, Aug. 24, 1916; s. John C. and Margaret A. (Gibney) G.; m. Jane M. Tinen, Dec. 21, 1940 (div. 1969); children: Joan F., James C., Katherine G.; m. Cynthia A. Hunt, 1970. B.S., U. Mich., 1937, Sc.D. (hon.), 1980; M.S., Northwestern U., 1939, Ph.D., 1941; M.A. (hon.), Harvard U., 1955, Sc.D., U. Brussels, 1969, U. Louis Pasteur, Strasbourg, France, 1976. From instr. to assoc. prof. geology Northwestern U., Evanston, Ill., 1941-52, prof. geology, 1965-69, 72-80, Scripps Instn. Oceanography, 1969-71; prof. U. South Fla., 1980—; geologist U.S. Geol. Survey, 1952-55; assoc. prof. geology Harvard U., 1955-57, prof., 1957-65, chmn. dept. geol. scis., 1963-65; Henri Speciael prof. sci. U. Brussels, Belgium, 1962-63; Capt. James Cook prof. oceanography U. Hawaii, Honolulu, 1972-74. Author: Textbook of Geology, 1951, Mineral Equilibria, 1959, (with C.L. Christ) Solutions, Minerals and Equilibria, 1965, (with F.T. Mackenzie) Evolution of Sedimentary Rocks, 1971, (with C.A. Hunt) Water, The Web of Life, 1972, (with F.T. Mackenzie, C. Hunt) Chemical Cycles and the Global Environment, 1975. Recipient Wollaston medal Geol. Soc. London, 1981. Fellow AAAS, Geol. Soc. Am. (Arthur L. Day medal 1966, Penrose medal 1978), Mineral. Soc. Am.; mem. Geochem. Soc. (pres. 1962, V.M. Goldschmidt award 1973), Nat. Acad. Scis., Soc. Econ. Geologists, Am. Acad. Arts and Sci., Am. Chem. Soc., Sigma Xi. Office: Dept Marine Sci U South Fla Saint Petersburg FL 33701

GARRETSON, DONALD EVERETT, manufacturing company executive; b. Elizabeth, N.J., Nov. 22, 1921; s. James W. and Helen (Crane) G.; m. Adele F. Anderson, Sept. 17, 1949; children—James Robert, Katherine Crane, Donald Everett, Peter Andrew, Andrea Drew. A.B. in Commerce, Washington and Lee U., 1943; M.B.A., Harvard U., 1947; student, Northwestern U., 1942, 48. With Arthur Andersen & Co. (C.P.A.'s), Chgo., 1947-50; with Minn. Mining & Mfg. Co., St. Paul, 1950—, asst. treas., 1963-67, treas., 1967—, v.p., 1972-77, v.p. fin., chief fin. officer, 1977-82; corporate v.p., pres. 3M Found., 1982—. Dir., past pres. Liberty Plaza Corp.; dir. First Mchts. State Bank, both St. Paul; Past chmn. bd. trustees Macalester Coll., St. Paul; bd. dirs. Minn. Orchestral Assn., St. Paul Chamber Orch.; past pres., dir. various coms. St. Paul United Way; nat. bd. dirs. Jr. Achievement; chmn. Jr. Achievement of Twin Cities, 1982—; chmn. Western region Jr. Achievement, 1983—; bd. dirs. Com. for Econ. Devel., Upper Midwest Council, Hill Reference Library, Minn. Pvt. Coll. Fund; hon. trustee Minn. Ind. Sch. Fund; mem. endowment investment com. Sci. Mus. Minn. Served to lt. USNR, 1943-46. Mem. Conf. Bd. (council fin. execs.), Machinery and Allied Products Inst. (accounting council). Presbyn. (elder). Clubs: St. Paul Tennis, Lilydale Tennis, Pool and Yacht. Home: 709 Linwood Ave St Paul MN 55105 Office: 3 M Center St Paul MN 55144

GARRETSON, HENRY DAVID, neurosurgeon; b. Woodbury, N.J., June 8, 1929; s. O.K. and Mary Marjorie (Davis) G.; m. Marianna Schantz, July 4, 1964; children—John, Steven. B.S., U. Ariz., 1950; M.D., Harvard U., 1954; Ph.D., McGill U., 1968. Diplomate: Am. Bd. Neurol. Surgery (mem. 1981—). Surg. intern Royal Victoria Hosp., Montreal, 1954-55; resident Montreal Neurol. Inst., 1959-63; asst. prof. neurosurgery McGill U., Montreal, 1966-71; prof., dir. neurol. surgery U. Louisville Sch. Medicine, 1971—, asso. dean clin. affairs, 1975-79, dir. neuroscis. programs, 1979—; individual practice medicine, specializing in neurosurgery, Montreal, 1963-71; asso. with Dr. William Feindel, Montreal, 1963-71; with Granthan & Garretson, Louisville, 1971—; mem. staff Louisville Gen., Norton Children's, VA, Surburban, Ky. Baptist hosps., all Louisville; staff Inst. Phys. Medicine and Rehab. Contbr. numerous articles, abstracts, editorials, presentations in field. Served with USNR, 1955-58. Fellow ACS; mem. AAAS, AMA, Congress Neurol. Surgeons, Am. Assn. Neurol. Surgeons, Am. Acad. Neurol. Surgery, Ky. Neurosurg. Soc., Ky. Surg. Soc., Louisville Surg. Soc., Ky. Med. Assn., Soc. Neurol. Surgeons, Soc. U. Neurosurgeons, Jefferson County Med. Soc., Phi Beta Kappa, Phi Kappa Phi, Sigma Xi. Home: 517 Tiffany Ln Louisville KY 40207 Office: Dept Surgery Health Sci Center Louisville KY 40201

GARRETT, ARTHUR SELLERS, lawyer; b. Drexel Hill, Pa., Jan. 19, 1938; s. George Sellers and Elva Dorothy (Cope) G.; m. Helen L. Schwingle, June 30, 1962; children: Arthur S., Schuyler W., Stuart A. B.Ch.E., Rensselaer Poly. Inst., 1959; LL.B., George Washington U., 1963. With Am. Cyanamid Co., Washington, 1959-64; asso. firm William Steell Jackson & Sons, Phila., 1964-66; asso. to partner firm Finnegan, Henderson, Farabow, Garrett & Dunner, Washington, 1966—. Mem. D.C., Phila., Am. bar assns., Bar Assn. D.C., Phila., Am. patent law assns., Licensing Execs. Soc. (former trustee), Internat. Fedn. Patent Agts., Delta Theta Phi, Delta Tau Delta. Clubs: Chevy Chase, Metropolitan, Internat., Little Egg Harbor Yacht. Home: 616 Boyle Ln McLean VA 22102 Office: 1775 K St NW Washington DC 20006

GARRETT, BERNARD ROBERT, business executive; b. N.Y.C., Feb. 23, 1926; s. Max and Gussie (Pachter) G.; m. Carolyn Morgenstern, June 6, 1982; children: Mitchel, Lisa. Student, Princeton U., 1942-43; B.S.E.E., NYU, 1948. Project engr. Reeves Inst., N.Y.C., 1948-53; program mgr. Arma Co., N.Y.C., 1954-57; v.p., engr. Loral Corp., N.Y.C., 1958-64; pres. Instruments Systems, N.Y.C., 1965-78; chmn. A.P.X. Group, Toledo, 1981-82, dir.; chmn., dir. Hampshire Nat., Los Angeles, 1983—; dir. Instrument Systems. Developer electronic and anti submarine warfare systems, 1957-78, multiplex systems for comml. aviation, 1969-78. Served with U.S. Army, 1942-44. Mem. N.Y. Acd. Scis. Home: 1509 San Remo Dr Pacific Palasades CA 90272 Office: 8575 Hiquera St Culver City CA 90230

GARRETT, DAVID CLYDE, JR., airline executive; b. Norris, S.C., July, 1922; s. David Clyde and Mary H. G.; m. Lu Thomasson, Sept. 11, 1947; children: David, Virginia, Charles. B.A., Furman U., 1942; M.S., Ga. Inst. Tech., 1955. With Delta Air Lines, Inc., Atlanta, 1946—, pres., 1971—, chief exec. officer, 1978—, also dir.; dir. Travelers Corp., U.S. Steel, Nat. Service Ind. Served with USAAF, 1943-46. Office: Delta Air Lines Atlanta Airport Atlanta GA 30320

GARRETT, DONALD EVERETT, research and devel. co. exec.; b. Long Beach, Calif., July 5, 1923; s. Walter E. and Dorothy M. Marriam; m. JoAnne Brown, Sept. 17, 1946 (div. 1973); children—Mark Calvert, DiAnn, Carolyn Anne, David Donald. B.S. in Chemistry, U. Calif. at Berkeley, 1947; M.S. in Chem. Engring, Ohio State U., 1948, Ph.D., 1950. Research and devel. engr., group leader Dow Chem. Co., Pittsburg, Calif., 1950-52, Union Oil Co., Brea, Calif., 1952-55; mgr. research Am. Potash & Chem. Co., Trona, Calif., 1955-60; pres. Garrett Research & Devel. Co., LaVerne, Calif., 1960-75; exec. v.p. research, engring. and devel. Occidental Petroleum Corp., Los Angeles, 1968-75; pres. Garrett Energy Research & Engring., Inc., Ojai, Calif., 1975—, Saline Processors, Inc., 1975—, Liquid Chem. Corp., Hanford, Calif., 1979—; Mem. gen. tech. adv. com. Fossil Fuel div. ERDA, 1969-78; engring. adv. council U. Calif., 1970—. Recipient Distinguished Alumni award Ohio State U., 1971; Lamme medal, 1976; Kirkpatrick Chem. Engr. achievement awards, 1963, 71; personal achievement award in chem. engring., 1976. Mem. Am. Inst. Chem. Engrs. (pres. Mojave Desert sect. 1957, Engr. of Year Los Angeles sect. 1964), Am. Chem. Soc., Sigma Xi, Tau Beta Pi. Home: 110 Bristol Rd Ojai CA 93023 Office: 911 Bryant Pl Ojai CA 93023

GARRETT, EDWARD ROBERT, pharmaceutical scientist, educator; b. N.Y.C., Apr. 9, 1920; s. Murray and Stella (Abrams) G.; m. Irene Brewer, July 31, 1941; children: Jan Edward, Terry Lee, Kurt Lane. B.S., Mich. State U., 1941, M.S., 1948, Ph.D. (Hinman fellow), 1950, D.Sc. (hon.), 1974; Dr. rerum nat. honoris causa, U. Berlin, 1979. Asst. foreman Gen. Chem. Co., Claymont, Del., 1941-42; supr. TNT prodn. Keystone Ordnance Works, Meadville, Pa., 1942-43; chem. process engr. synthetic rubber Gen. Tire & Rubber Co., Baytown, Tex., 1943-45; asst. plant mgr. sulfuric acid prodn. Stauffer Chem. Co., Hammond, Ind., 1945-46; grad. asst. Mich. State U., 1946-49; sr. research scientist, group leader Upjohn Co., 1950-61; grad. research prof. U. Fla. Coll. Pharmacy, Gainesville, 1961—; chmn. grad. studies, 1968-70; vis. prof. U. Wis., 1958, U. Buenos Aires, 1965; cons. Smith Kline & French Labs., 1963-75; vis. scientist U. Calif. at San Francisco, 1964; pres. symposium indsl. pharmacy and biochemistry Latin Am. Congress Chemistry, Buenos Aires, 1962; mem. com. revision, mem. subcoms. organic and inorganic compounds, gen. tests U.S. Pharmacopeia XIX, 1970-75. Author: Drug Fate and Metabolism, Vol. I, 1977, Vol. II, 1978, Vol. III, 1980, Vol. IV, 1983; transl. editor: Analytical Metabolic Chemistry, 1971; contbr. numerous articles to profl. jours.; editor: Internat. Jour. Clin. Pharmacology, 1967—; editorial bd.: Jour. Pharm. Scis, 1966-72, Chemotherapy, 1976—; cons. editor: Jour. Pharmacokinetics, 1972—; co-editor: Clinical Pharmacology and Pharmacotherapy, 2d edit., 1973, 3d edit., 1976; editor: series Drug Fate and Metabolism, Vol. 1, 1977, Vol. 2, 1978, Vol. 3, 1979. Recipient Lawson Essay prize Mich. State U., 1938; Upjohn award Upjohn Co., 1959; medal Italian Soc. Pharm. Scis., 1967; J.E. Purkyne medal Czechoslovakian Med. Soc., 1971; chevalier d'Armagnac, France, 1977; Volwiler Gold medal award for research excellence in pharm. scis., 1980. Fellow Acad. Pharm. Scis., Internat. Soc. Clin. Pharmacology (senator, Am. v.p. 1972-74), AAAS; hon. mem. Argentine, Chilean socs. indsl. pharmacy and biochemistry; mem. N.Y. Acad. Scis., Am. Chem. Soc., Am. Pharm. Assn. (Ebert prize 1962, Research Achievement award phys. chem. in pharm. scis. 1963, Research Achievement award in drug standards and assay 1969, Indsl. Pharm. Tech. award 1976, Stimulation of Research award 1981), Am. Soc. Microbiology, Am. Soc. Clin. Pharmacology and Therapeutics (v.p. sect.), Sigma Xi, Pi Mu Epsilon, Sigma Pi Sigma, Rho Chi, Rho Pi Phi, Alpha Chi Sigma. Democrat. Unitarian. Home: 1826 NW 26th Way Gainesville FL 32605 *The function of the scientist is to establish modes which quantitatively link interdependencies and permit prediction of results under conditions that have not yet been studied. Such models are presumed reflections of reality and not reality itself. There are no shibboleths in science; sanctified and immutable dogmas must be reserved for faith and religion.*

GARRETT, ETHEL SHIELDS, civic worker; b. Pitts., May 7, 1896; d. Peter and Cora (Lewis) Shields; m. Harry Darlington, Jr., Jan. 31, 1917 (dec. Jan. 1931); children: Harry III, McCullough, Elaine Darlington (Mrs. Anderson Fowler); m. George Angus Garrett, 11, 1935. Grad., Miss Spence Sch., N.Y.C., 1915. Mem. exec. com. Nat. Symphony Orch. Assn.; nat. council Met. Opera; mem.-at-large Garden Club Am.; mem. Nat. Cathedral Assn.; Hon. trustee John F. Kennedy Centre for Performing Arts. Episcopalian. Home: 2030 24th St NW Washington DC 20008

GARRETT, GEORGE PALMER, JR., educator, writer; b. Orlando, Fla., June 11, 1929; s. George Palmer and Rosalie (Toomer) G.; m. Susan Parrish Jackson, June 14, 1952; children: William, George, Rosalie. Grad., Hill Sch., 1947; A.B., Princeton U., 1952, M.A., 1956. Asst. prof. English Wesleyan U.; writer-in-residence, resident fellow in creative writing Princeton U., 1964-65; former assoc. prof. U. Va.; prof. English Hollins Coll. Va., 1967-71; prof. U. S.C., Columbia, 1971-73, Princeton U., 1974-78, U. Mich., 1979-80, 83-84; Hoyns prof. creative writing U. Va., Charlottesville, 1984—; prof. Bennington Coll., 1980. Author: The Reverend Ghost: Poems (Poets of Today IV), 1957, King of the Mountain, 1958, The Sleeping Gypsy and Other

Poems, 1958, The Finished Man, 1959, Which Ones Are the Enemy, 1961; poems Abraham's Knife, 1961; In the Briar Patch, 1961; play Sir Slob and the Princess, 1962; Cold Ground Was My Bed Last Night, 1964; screenplay The Young Lovers, 1964; Do, Lord, Remember Me, 1965, For a Bitter Season, 1967, A Wreath for Garibaldi, 1969, Death of the Fox, 1971, The Magic Striptease, 1973, Welcome to the Medicine Show, Postcards/Flashcards/Snapshots, 1978, To Recollect a Cloud of Ghosts: Christmas in England 1602-03, 1979, Luck's Shining Child: Poems, 1981, The Succession: A Novel of Elizabeth and James, 1983, The Collected Poems of George Garrett, 1984, James Jones, 1984; editor: The Girl in The Black Raincoat, 1966, The Sounder Few, 1971, The Writer's Voice, 1973, Botteghe Obscure Reader, 1975, Intro 8: The Liar's Craft, 1977, Intro 9: Close to Home, 1978. Served in occupation of; Trieste, Austria and Germany. Recipient Rome prize Am. Acad. Arts and Letters, 1958-59, Sewanee Rev. fellow poetry, 1958-59; Ford Found. grantee in drama, 1960; Nat. Found. of Arts grantee, 1966; Guggenheim fellow, 1974. Fellow Am. Acad. in Rome; Mem. MLA, Author's League. Democrat. Episcopalian. Home: 1853 Fendall Ave Charlottesville VA 22903 Office: Dept English Univ Virginia Charlottesville VA 22903

GARRETT, GORDON MERRILL, marketing executive; b. Johnson City, Tenn., Mar. 13, 1937; s. Osmer Merrill and Margaret Lee (Dyer) G.; m. Peneolpe Anne Boudreau, Apr. 9, 1960; children: Timothy Michael, Gregory Scott. B.A., Denison U., 1959; M.A., U. Tenn.-Knoxville, 1960. Vice-pres. product mgmt. Am. Chicle div. Warner-Lambert, Morris Plains, N.J., 1970-72, v.p. sales, 1972-74, v.p. mktg., 1974-78; pres. Household div. Am. Cyanamid Co., Wayne, N.J., 1978-81; mem. mgmt. bd. Eckerd Drug Co., Clearwater, Fla., 1981-83; pres., chief operating officer, dir. Chock Full O'Nuts Corp, N.Y.C., 1983—; chmn. trade relations Nat. Confectionees Assn., Washington, 1976-77. Bd. dirs. Morris County Heart Assn., Morristown N.J., 1974. Served to capt. USAF, 1960-63. Republican. Methodist. Club: Mountain Lakes (N.J.) (dir.). Office: Chock Full O'Nuts Corp 370 Lexington Ave New York NY 10017

GARRETT, GUY THOMAS, JR., newspaper executive; b. Peekskill, N.Y., June 7, 1932; s. Guy Thomas and Anna Lee (Day) G.; m. Constance; children: Lynn Allyson, Guy Thomas, III. B.A., Howard U., 1954; postgrad., CCNY, 1961-62; grad., Advanced Mgmt. Program, Harvard U., 1977. Br. mgr. Household Fin. Corp., N.Y.C., 1957-62; tchr. N.Y.C. Bd. Edn., 1962-63; dir. personnel L.I. Lighting Co., 1963-67; with N.Y. Times Co., 1974—, v.p. personnel, 1976—. Bd. dirs. N.Y.C. chpt. March of Dimes, 1980. Served with U.S. Army, 1955-57. Mem. N.Y. Personnel Mgmt. Assn. (past dir.). Office: 229 W 43d St New York NY 10036

GARRETT, JAMES HAROLD, JR., editor; b. N.Y.C., July 2, 1940; s. James H. and Mary G.; m. Frances Gery, Sept. 5, 1964; children: Caroline, Jay. Student, St. John's U., N.Y.C., 1963-65. Staff photographer New York News, 1965-79, asst. night picture editor, 1979-80, picture editor, 1980—. Mem. N.Y. Press Photographers Assn. (sec. 1973-75, v.p. 1975-77), N.Y. Press Club. Roman Catholic.

GARRETT, JOSEPH BERNARD, business services executive; b. N.Y.C., Mar. 8, 1936; s. James P. and Helen G.; m. Regina Marie Gross, Aug. 13, 1966; children—Joseph G., James W., Brian P. B.B.A. cum laude, U. Miami, Fla., 1960. C.P.A., N.J. Auditor Price Waterhouse & Co. (C.P.A.'s), N.Y.C., 1960-66; controller Nat. Distillers & Chem. subs., 1966-67, Am. Express Co. divs., 1967-76; v.p. fin. Dun & Bradstreet, Inc., N.Y.C., 1976-80, sr. v.p. fin., 1980—. Served with AUS, 1954-56. Mem. Am. Inst. C.P.A.'s, N.J. Soc. C.P.A.'s. Roman Catholic. Club: Canoe Brook Country (Summit, N.J.). Home: 198 Sagamore Rd Millburn NJ 07041 Office: One Diamond Hill Rd Murray Hill NJ 07974

GARRETT, LUTHER WEAVER, JR., consulting engineering company executive; b. Corsicana, Tex., Apr. 26, 1925; s. Luther Weaver and Lauren (Jewell) G.; m. Evelyn Elaine Dirks, Sept. 13, 1947; children: L. Douglas, Linda L. B.S., U. Tex., 1947; postgrad., Poly. Inst. Bklyn., 1947-50. Registered profl. engr. Chem. engr. M.W. Kellogg Co., N.Y.C., 1947-50, process design engr., asst. to mgr., acting mgr., 1951-58, chief operating engr., 1958-61, mgr. iron and steel dept., 1961-63; mgr. projects dept. Contract Ops. Group (Swindell-Dressler div. Pullman, Inc.), 1963-66, v.p. ops., Pitts., 1966-69; engring. mgr. Bechtel Corp., San Francisco, 1969-74; sr. v.p. Flor Utah, Inc., San Mateo, Calif., 1974-76, exec. v.p., 1976-77, pres., 1977-78, Garrett Assos., Inc., San Mateo, 1978—. Served with USNR, 1944-45. Mem. Am. Inst. Chem. Engrs., Am. Chem. Soc., Am. Inst. Mining Engrs., Am. Inst. Chemists, Calif. Inst. Chemists (past pres.), Tau Beta Pi, Omega Chi Upsilon, Phi Lambda Epsilon, Phi Eta Sigma. Clubs: Olympic, Coyote Point Yacht, World Trade. Patentee catalytic processing of oil and iron ore reduction. Home: 537 Virginia Ave San Mateo CA 94402 Office: 1650 S Amphlett Blvd Suite 311 San Mateo CA 94402

GARRETT, ROBERT AUSTIN, physician, educator; b. Indpls., Jan. 25, 1919; s. John Dempsey and Mary Susan (Pierson) G.; m. Elizabeth Ramge Steiner, Feb. 13, 1946; children—Mary Alice, Robert Austin, Susan Elizabeth, John Dempsey II. A.B., Miami U., 1940; M.D., Ind. U., 1943. Diplomate: Am. Bd. Urology. Intern Cin. Gen. Hosp., 1943, surg. res., 1944-46; genito-urinary surgery Ind. U. Med. Center, 1947-48; instr. urology Ind. U. Med. Sch., 1949-50, asst. prof. dept. urology, 1951-52, asso. prof., 1953, prof., 1954—. Served with AUS, 1946. Mem. A.M.A., Am. Urologic Assn., Mont Reid Surg. Soc., Am. Urologic Assn. North Central Sect., Am. Assn. Genito-Urinary Surgeons, A.C.S., am. Acad. Pediatrics, Soc. for Pediatric Urology (past pres.), Soc. Univ. Urologists, Phi Beta Kappa, Alpha Omega Alpha, Omicron Delta Kappa, Sigma Chi. Episcopalian. Club: Meridian Hills. Home: 7912 Ridge Rd Indianapolis IN 46240 Office: 1100 W Michigan St Indianapolis IN 46223

GARRETT, ROBERT YOUNG, JR., insurance executive; b. Balt., May 24, 1903; s. Robert Young and Anne (Hanson) G.; m. Margaret S. Ruff, Oct. 24, 1925 (dec. June 1970); 1 son, Robert Young III.; m. Vivian M. Brown, Oct. 6, 1973. Student, Am. Inst. Banking; grad., Rutgers U. Grad. Sch. Banking, 1945. With Central Nat. Bank Phila., 1921-35, Farmers Bank and Trust Co., Lancaster, Pa., 1935-63, pres., 1961-63; pres. merged bank Lancaster County Farmers Nat. Bank, 1963-70; vice chmn. Nat. Central Bank, Lancaster, Pa., 1970-73, ret., 1973; pres. Donegal Mut. Ins. Co., 1972—, chmn. bd., 1974—; dir. Watt & Shand, Lancaster.; mem. adv. com. banking policies and practices 3d Nat. Bank Region, 1965-68. Treas. Lancaster Gen. Hosp., 1952—, vice chmn. bd., 1972, chmn. bd., 1973-77; pres. bd. Lancaster br. Pa. Assn. for Blind, 1963-80, N. Milton Woods Home for Ret. Presbyn. Ministers of Donegal Presbytery, 1958—; mem. bd. nat. missions Presbyn. Ch. U.S.A., 1955-61; mem. distbn. com. Lancaster County Found. Recipient Benjamin Rush award Lancaster County Med. Assn., 1979. Mem. Pa. Soc., Lancaster C. of C. Presbyterian (elder). Clubs: Lancaster Country, Hamilton (dir., treas. 1976—), University (Lancaster)). Lodge: Lions (pres. Lancaster 1949-50). Home: Williamson Apts 1111 Wheatland Ave Apt 4-A Lancaster PA 17603

GARRETT, SNUFF *See* **GARRETT, THOMAS LESLIE**

GARRETT, STEPHEN GEORGE, architect, former museum director; b. Ashtead, Eng., Dec. 26, 1922; s. Howard George and Ida (King-Harman) G.; m. Petronella Jones, 1952; children: Carey, Georgia; m. Jean Mackintosh, 1964; children: Rebecca, Jason. M.A., Trinity Coll., Cambridge (Eng.) U., 1950. Pvt. archtl. practice, London, 1952-73; dep. dir. J. Paul Getty Mus., Malibu, Calif., 1973-77, dir., trustee, 1977-82; lectr. architecture Poly. Central London. Author booklets, articles arch. and design projects. Assoc. Royal Inst. Brit. Architects. Served with Brit. Navy, 1941-46. Mem. Assn. Art Mus. Dirs. Address: 400 Aderno Way Pacific Palisades CA 90272

GARRETT, SYLVESTER, arbitrator; b. Elkins Park, Pa., Dec. 15, 1911; s. Sylvester S. and Mary (Thompson) G.; m. Mary Alexander Yard, Aug. 30, 1938; children—Joan Hickcox, James Yard, John Sharpless. A.B., Swarthmore Coll., 1933; LL.B., U. Pa., 1936. Chmn. Regional War Labor Bd., Phila., 1942-45; vice chmn. Nat. Wage stblzn. Bd., Washington, 1946; coordinator labor relations Libbey-Owens-Ford Glass Co., Toledo and Pitts. Plate Glass Co., 1946-49; prof. law Stanford U., 1949-51; chmn. bd. arbitration U.S. Steel Co. and United Steelworkers, 1951-79; impartial chmn. U.S. Postal Service and Postal Workers Unions, 1974-79; chmn. Iron Ore Industry Bd. of Arbitration, 1979—; chmn. arbitration panel Newport News Shipbldg. and United Steelworkers, 1980—. Author: (with L. Reed Tripp) Management Management Problems Implicit in Multi-Employer Bargaining, 1950. Mem. citizens assembly Health and Welfare Assn. Allegheny County, 1963-69; Trustee Community Services Pa. Mem. Nat. Acad. Arbitrators (gov. 1956-58, pres. 1963, exec. com. 1964-65, chmn. com. on ethics and grievances 1965-68), Am., Pa. bar assns., Indsl. Relations Research Assn. (counsel 1953-57), Am. Arbitration Assn. (panel arbitrators). Home: Box 158 Stahlstown PA 15687 Office: 1832 Gateway No 3 Pittsburgh PA 15222

GARRETT, THOMAS LESLIE (SNUFF GARRETT), music company executive; b. Dallas, July 5, 1938; s. Thomas Leslie and Lila (Ables) G.; children by previous marriage: Gwen, Gretchen; m. Yolanda Salas, Sept. 9, 1966; children: Dawn, Lesslie. Disk jockey radio stas., Lubbock, Tex., 1957-58, Wichita Falls, Tex., 1958-59; record producer Liberty Records, Hollywood, Calif., 1959-65; pres. Snuff Garrett Prodns. (record producers), Hollywood, 1965-70, Viva Music, pub. co., 1965-70, Amigo Studios, rec. studio, 1966-70, Garrett Music Enterprises, Hollywood, 1970—. Office: 6255 Sunset Blvd Suite 1019 Hollywood CA 90028 *

GARRETT, WILBUR EUGENE, editor; b. Kansas City, Mo., Sept. 4, 1930; s. Clay Dean and Cecil Zora (Melton) G.; m. Lucille Hall, Dec. 26, 1950; children: Michael Dean, Kenneth Lewis. B.J., U. Mo., 1954. Photographer Hallmark Greeting Card Co., 1948-50; picture editor, then assoc. illustrations editor, sr. asst. editor, assoc. editor illustrations Nat. Geog. mag., from 1954, editor, 1980—, also trustee; faculty photojournalism workshop U. Mo., 1963, 64, 69, 70, 73, 74, 75, 77, 78, 79, 80; designer photog. exhbn. People-to-People lounge U.S. Pavilion, N.Y. World's Fair, 1965; originator, producer Angkor Wat Exhibit Nat. Geog. Soc.-UNESCO, 1982; lectr. univs. Alaska, Boston, Md., Miami, Minn., Mo., N.C., So. Ill., Harvard U.; mem. adv. council Textile Mus.; mem. graphic evaluation panels Nat. Endowment for Arts; bd. dirs. Internat. Center Photography. Designer-producer, Nat. Geog. Soc.; exhbns. 23d, 24th, 25th Picture of Year Competition; contbr.: Smithsonian-Charles Eames's Photography and City Exhibit, 1968; Editor: Photojournalism 76. Trustee W. Eugene Smith Meml. Fund, Partners for Livable Places. Served with USNR, 1950-52. Recipient Newhouse citation U. Syracuse, 1963; 14 awards Pictures of Year competition, including Mag. Photographer of Year, 1968; Disting. Service in Journalism award U. Mo., 1978; Outstanding Environ. Leadership medal UN Environment Programme, 1982. Mem. Nat. Press Photographers Assn. (Joseph A. Sprague Meml. award 1977), White House News Photographers Assn., Washington Press Club, Asia Soc. Club: Cosmos (Washington). Home: 209 Seneca Rd Great Falls VA 22066 Office: Nat Geog Soc 17th and M Sts NW Washington DC 20036

GARRIOTT, OWEN K., astronaut, scientist; b. Enid, Okla., Nov. 22, 1930; m. Helen Mary Walker; children: Randall O., Robert K., Richard A., Linda S. B.S. in Elec. Engring., U. Okla., 1953; M.S., Stanford U., 1957, Ph.D., 1960; D.Sc. (hon.), Phillips U., Enid, 1973. NSF fellow Cambridge (Eng.) U., Radio Research Sta., Slough, Eng., 1960-61; asst. and assoc. prof. electronics, electro-magnetic theory, ionospheric physics Stanford U., 1961-65; now cons. prof.; astronaut, scientist Johnson Space Center, Houston, 1965—; sci. pilot Skylab-3, 1973, dep. dir. sci. and Applications Directorate, 1974-76, dir., 1976, Asst. dir. for space and life scis., 77-78; mission specialist on first Spacelab flight, 1983. Former regional editor: Planetary and Space Sci. Served with USN, 1953-56. Recipient Distinguished Service medal NASA, 1973; Gold medal City of Chgo., 1974; Robert J. Collier trophy, 1974; V.M. Komarov diploma Fedn. Aeronautique Internationale, 1974; Robert H. Goddard Meml. trophy, 1975. Fellow Am. Astronautical Soc.; mem. Am. Geophys. Union, IEEE, AAAS, Internat. Sci. Radio Union, Internat. Acad. Astronautics, Sigma Xi, Tau Beta Pi. Address: Johnson Space Center Houston TX 77058 *

GARRISH, THEODORE JOHN, lawyer; b. Detroit, Jan. 6, 1943; s. Theodore and Adella Beatrice (Kimball) G.; m. Joy Ann Ziegler, Aug. 4, 1967 (div. 1979); children: Theodore John, Amelia Sutter. A.B., U. Mich., 1964; J.D. cum laude, Wayne State U., 1968. Bar: Mich. 1969, D.C. 1972. Trial atty. U.S. Dept. Justice, Washington, 1969-72; pub. opinion analyst Com. for Reelection of Pres., Washington, 1972; chief advt. substantiation Fed. Trade Commn., Washington, 1973-74; asst. spl. counsel to Pres., Washington, 1974; asst. to sec. U.S. Dept. Interior, Washington, 1975-76, legis. counsel, 1981-82; gen. counsel Consumer Product Safety Commn., Washington, 1976-78; ptnr. Deane, Snowdon, Shutler, Garrish & Gherardi, Washington, 1978-81; gen. counsel Dept. Energy, Washington, 1983—; mem. U.S. Adminstrv. Conf., Washington, 1976-78, 83. Del. Mich. Republican Conv., 1966; asst. to group dir. Presdl. Inaugural Com., 1973, dep. exec. dir., 1981; mem. adv. com. on human concerns Rep. Nat. Com., 1979. Mem. Fed. Bar Assn., Mich. Bar Assn., D.C. Bar Assn., Alpha Delta Phi. Congregationalist. Club: Peninsular Soc. (Ann Arbor, Mich.). Home: 1770 Preston Rd Alexandria VA 22302 Office: Dept Energy Office of Gen Counsel 6A-245 Forrestal Bldg Washington DC 20585

GARRISON, CLAYTON, university dean; b. Independence, Kans., Dec. 27, 1921; s. Emery and Blanche (Cook) G.; children: Jacqueline, Michelle, Mark, Suzanne. B.A., U. So. Calif., 1947; Ph.D., Stanford U., 1956. Prof. drama Palos Verdes Coll., 1949-58, Calif. State U. at Long Beach, 1955-60; dir. drama dept. U. Calif., Berkeley, 1960, chmn. drama dept., Riverside, 1960-64; dean Sch. Fine Arts, U. Calif. at Irvine, 1964—, dir. plays, musicals, operas, 1966—; cons. Nat. Found. Arts and Humanities, 1966—, Arts and Humanities Inst., 1967—. Dir. operas, U.S. and Europe, Teatro Olimpico, Teatro Accademico, Stockholm Philharm., Lincoln Center, 6th Internat. Verdi Congress, Instituto Nacional de Bellas Artes, Mexico; Contbr. articles to profl. jours. Served with USAAF, 1943-46. Mem. Internat. Council Fine Arts Deans. Home: 26701 Quail Creek Rd Laguna Hills CA 92653 Office: Sch Fine Arts U Calif Irvine CA 92717

GARRISON, GUY GRADY, librarian, university dean; b. Akron, Ohio, Dec. 17, 1927; s. Grady and Emma (Dodson) G.; m. Joanne Ruth Sergeant, Mar. 22, 1964; 1 dau., Anne Olivia. B.A., Baldwin-Wallace Coll., 1950; M.S., Columbia U., 1954; Ph.D., U. Ill., 1960. Mem. staff Oak Park (Ill.) Pub. Library, 1954-58; head reader services Kansas City (Mo.) Pub. Library, 1960-62; prof., dir. library research center Grad. Sch. Library Sci., U. Ill., 1962-68; prof., dean Coll. Info. Studies, Drexel U., 1968—. Contbr. articles to profl. jours. Served with AUS, 1950-52. Mem. ALA, Am. Soc. Info. Sci., Assn. for Library and Info. Sci. Edn., Beta Phi Mu. Home: 731 Limehouse Rd King of Prussia PA 19406

GARRISON, JOHN RAYMOND, organization executive; b. Bridgeton, N.J., Jan. 30, 1938; s. Raymond Wilson and Clara Ella (Moore) G.; m. Sally Anne Woodruff, Sept. 10, 1960; children: Glenn Thomas Wilson, Matthew Moore. A.B., Harvard U., 1960; M.P.A. (scholastic award), NYU, 1964. Adminstrv. asst. N.Y. State Banking Dept., 1962-63; planner N.J. Dept. Econ. Devel. and Conservation, 1963-64; sr. planner N.Y. State Office Regional Devel., 1964-66; mem. staff Gov. N.Y. State Exec. Chamber, 1966-71; program sec. Office of Lt. Gov., N.Y. State, 1971-73; dep. commr. adminstrn. N.Y. State Health Dept., 1973-75; exec. v.p. Hosp. Assn. N.Y. State, 1975-78; exec. dir. Nat. Easter Seal Soc., 1978—; mem. exec. com. President's Com. on Employment Handicapped, 1978—; bd. dirs. nat. Health Council. Served with USAR, 1960-62. Mem. Easter Seal Execs. Assn. Clubs: Harvard (N.Y.C.); Metropolitan (Chgo.). Office: 2023 W Ogden Ave Chicago IL 60612 *One's integrity is a major determinant as to how an individual's career will develop. We all deal extensively with people and it is through integrity that one gives the credibility which is vital to moving into positions of responsibility and, therefore, trust.*

GARRISON, LAWRENCE DUANE, air force officer; b. Altadena, Calif., May 12, 1930; s. Clarence Cecil and Edna Ione (Bill) G.; m. Evelyn Smith, Oct. 19, 1955; children—Lawrence D., Kenneth A., Julie K. B.Mgmt., Ind. U., 1957; postgrad., Air Force Command and Staff Coll., 1965—, Indsl. Coll. of Armed Forces, 1968. Commd. U.S. Air Force, 1950, advanced through grades to maj. gen., 1980; squadron pilot, asst. prof. aerospace studies (U. N.C.), Chapel Hill, 1962-65, insp., Langley AFB, Va., 1971-72, squadron comdr., U.K., 1975-77, wing comdr., Laughlin AFB, Tex., 1980-81, dir. maintenance and supply hdqrs., Washington, 1981—, air dep. to comdr., NATO), No. Europe, Oslo. Decorated D.S.C., D.F.C. with 2 oak leaf clusters, Legion of Merit, Air medal (6). Mem. Air Force Assn., Airpower Hist. Assn., Smithsonian Assos., Daedalians. Methodist. Home: PO Box 1 APO NY 09084 Office: Allied Forces AF North Air Deputy Box 1 APO NY 09084

GARRISON, LLOYD LEE, business educator; b. Shelby County, Mo., Mar. 24, 1920; s. Homer Austin and Ona Lee (Harland) G.; m. Irene Joy Nelson, June 16, 1946 (div. Oct. 1973); 1 dau., Jill Kay. B.S., N.E. Mo. State U., Kirksville, 1940; M.Ed., U. Mo., 1942, Ed.D., 1951. Tchr. bus. Brashear and Shelbina High Sch. (Mo.), 1940-41, 46-47; assoc. prof., head dept. bus. Missouri Valley Coll., Marshall, Mo., 1947-49; prof. bus. edn. Okla. State U., Stillwater, 1951-79, Regents service prof., 1979—, dean Coll. Bus. Adminstrn., 1959-66, head dept. adminstrn. services and bus. edn., 1966-79; cons., mem. accreditation com. Assn. Ins. Schs. and Colls., Washington, 1970—. Author: A Syllabus for Teaching Economics in the High School General Business Course, 1964; co-author: A Teacher's Guide to Economics in the Business Education Curriculum, 1963; contbr. (articles to profl. jours.). Recipient Outstanding Tchr. award Coll. Bus.-Okla. State U., 1961. Mem. Nat. Bus. Edn. Assn. (treas. 1964-66, mem. exec. bd. 1963-66-, 67-68, chmn. com. to develop nat. action plan for bus. edn. 1980-82, Disting. Service award 1979), Mountain Plains Bus. Edn. Assn. (pres. 1967-68, mem. exec. bd. 1953-56, 59-62, 62-65, Leadership award 1972), Okla. Bus. Edn. Assn. (pres. 1955-56, Outstanding Okla. Bus. Educator award 1977), Am. Vocat. Assn., Am. Acctg. Assn., Phi Kappa Phi, Phi Delta Kappa, Delta Pi Epsilon. Home: 2010 W 3rd Ave Stillwater OK 74074 Office: Coll Bus Adminstrn Okla State U Stillwater OK 74078

GARRISON, MARION AMES, mechanical engineer, oil tool company executive; b. Indpls., July 20, 1907; s. Charles C. and Ella J. (Hilligoss) G.; m. Meriam Kathleen Goode, Aug. 23, 1933; 1 dau., Charlotte Ann. M.E., U. So. Calif., 1929. Pvt. practice bottom hole oil tool design, Los Angeles, 1945-55; chief engr. Eastman Oil Well Survey Co., Denver, 1955-57; pres., chief engr. Empire Oil Tool Co., Denver, 1957—; pres. Garrison Pneumatic Products Co. Mem. Am. Inst. M.E., Delta Sigma Rho, Sigma Phi Epsilon. Patentee in fluid mechanics, bottom hole oil tools; inventor linkage type automotive power steering. Address: 104 Crownpoint Rd Williamsburg VA 23185 *As a man who has devoted a lifetime to the invention, research and development of new products, processes, tools, etc. for industry, the steadfast encouragement of my dear wife has been the source of strength and determination to carry on, many times in the face of deep discouragement. She deserves most of the credit for whatever success these efforts have achieved. She is the business manager of our enterprises.*

GARRISON, MARK JOSEPH, educator, former diplomat; b. Kokomo, Ind., May 27, 1930; s. Mark and Nora Lucile (Ogborn) G.; m. Elizabeth Ann Myers, 1949; children: Elizabeth, Mark Edward, Eric, Sarah. A.B., Ind. U., 1953, M.A. (Woodrow Wilson fellow), 1954, Columbia U., 1955; postgrad. (Dept. State fellow), Stanford U., 1970-71. Commd. fgn. service officer Dept. State, 1955, served in, Washington, 1955-57, Hong Kong, 1957-59, Sofia, Bulgaria, 1960-62, Washington, 1962-67, Prague, Czechoslovakia, 1968-70; polit. counselor U.S. embassy, Moscow, 1971-74, minister counselor, 1978-80; dir. Office Soviet Union Affairs, Dept. State, Washington, 1974-78. Mem. faculty Sch. Advanced Internat. Studies Johns Hopkins U., 1966-67; dir. Center for Fgn. Policy Devel., Brown U., 1981—. Recipient Superior Honor award Dept. State, 1970, John Jacob Rogers award, 1980. Mem. Council on Fgn. Relations. Office: Center for Fgn Policy Devel Brown U Box 1948 Providence RI 02912

GARRISON, RICHARD CHRISTOPHER, advertising agency executive; b. Dover, N.H., May 24, 1948; s. Herbert H. and Elizabeth (Coreille) G.; m. Louisa Hammond, July 15, 1972; children: Daniel Bradford, Thomas Gardner, Nicholas Lee. B.A., Princeton U., 1970. Copywriter Quinn & Johnson, Boston, 1977-80, creative dir., 1980, pres., 1982—; dir. Berlyn Corp., Worcester, Mass. Served to lt. USN, 1970-74. Mem. Am. Assn. Advt. Agys. (sec.-treas. Northeast chpt. 1982, vice chmn. 1983). Clubs: University (Boston); Ivy (Princeton, N.J.). Office: 535 Boylston St Boston MA 02116

GARRISON, TRUITT B., architect; b. Lubbock, Tex., Apr. 6, 1936; s. Miles Elash and Iva J. (Greenway) G.; m. Joyce Ann Ward, June 27, 1959; children: Todd Michael, Craig Mitchell. B.Arch., Tex. Tech U., 1962; postgrad., Grad. Sch. Design Exec. Program, Harvard U., 1971. With Welton Becket & Assocs., Houston, 1962-63; sr. v.p. Caudill Rowlett Scott, Houston, 1963—, also dir.; exec. v.p. Internat. div. CRS Group. Bd. dirs. St. Lukes Methodist Ch., 1970-71; dir. Epernay Homeowners Assn., 1977—, pres. bd., 1978. Served with U.S. Army, 1958-59. Named Officer of Yr. Caudill Rowlett Scott, 1980. Mem. AIA, Tex. Soc. Architects. Democrat. Home: 1314 Chardonnay Dr Houston TX 77077 Office: 1111 W Loop St S Houston TX 77027

GARRISON, WALTER R., corporate executive, technical school president; b. St. Louis, July 7, 1926; s. Walter Raymond and Esther Elizabeth (Kohlhepp) G.; m. Rose Faye Wilson, Aug. 10, 1946 (dec.); children; Bruce, Susan Garrison Mayer, Mark, Pamela Garrison

Phelan, C. Jeffrey; m. Jayne Bacon, Apr. 15, 1973; stepchildren: James, Jack. B.S.A.E., U. Kans., 1948, M.S.A.E., 1950. Registerd profl. engr., Pa., N.J.,Fla., Ill. Structural engr. Boeing Airplane Co., Seattle, 1950-53, cons. engr., 1953-56; staff engr. CDI Corp. and predecessor Comprehensive Designers, Inc., Phila., 1956-58, v.p., 1958-61, pres., chmn. bd., 1961—; dir. Modern Engring. Co., Detroit, Mgmt. Recruiters Internat., Cleve., CDI Temporary Services, Phila., Stubbs Overbeck & Co., Houston, The M & T Co., King of Prussia, Pa. Trustee, pres. Pa. Inst. Tech., Media, 1953—; mem. Upper Providence Twp. Environ. Adv. Council, 1977-82, Pa. Bd. Pvt. Schs., 1965-71. Mem. Phila. Pres.' Orgn. (treas.), Phila. Pres.' orgn. (dir.), Young Pres.' Orgn., Nat. Soc. Profl. Engrs., Tau Beta Pi, Sigma Tau. Republican. Presbyterian. Clubs: Chukker Valley Golf (Gilbertsville, Pa.) (dir.); Urban (Phila.)). Home: 288 Sycamore Mills Rd Rose Tree PA 19063 Office: CDI Corp Ten Penn Center Philadelphia PA 19103

GARRITY, DONALD LEE, univ. pres.; b. LaJunta, Colo., Oct. 29, 1927; s. Fred and Rosalie (Morris) G.; m. Virginia Early, June 29, 1951; children—Michael S., Craig M. B.A., Colo. State Coll., 1950; M.A., U. Wash., Seattle, 1953, Ph.D., 1956. Instr. U. Wash., 1955-56; mem. faculty San Francisco State U., 1956-78, prof. sociology, 1964-78, chmn. dept., 1960-66, provost, 1966-78; pres. Central Wash. U., Ellensburg, 1978—; researcher, cons. in field., 1959—. Author reports, articles in field; asso. editor: Pacific Sociol. Law, 1960-63. Mem. San Francisco Crime Commn., 1970—. Served with AUS, 1945-46. Decorated comdr. Order Star Africa, Liberia).; Ford Found. vis. fellow Home Office Research Unit, London, 1961-62. Mem. Am. Sociol. Assn., Am. Correctional Assn., Soc. Study Social Problems, Am. Assn. Higher Edn., Pacific Sociol. Assn. Office: Bouillon Hall Central Wash Univ Ellensburg WA 98926

GARRITY, KEITH R., metal products company executive. Pres. Fansteel, Inc., North Chicago, ILL., until 1983, chmn., chief exec. officer, North Chicago, Ill., 1983—; chmn., chief exec. officer H. K. Porter Co., Inc., Mo. Portland Cement Co. Office: Fansteel Inc One Tantalum Pl North Chicago IL 60064§

GARRITY, ROBERT ALEXANDER, printing machine company executive; b. Kansas City, Mo., Oct. 11, 1931; s. Stanley and Marguerite Angeline (Crumpley) G.; m. Elaine Heymann, Mar. 9, 1958; children—Lisa, Lori. B.S., U. Kans., 1953, J.D., 1956. Bar: Mo. bar 1956, Kans. bar 1956; C.P.A., Kans. Mem. tax. and audit staffs Arthur Young & Co. (C.P.A.'s), Wichita, Kans. and Tulsa, 1958-63; asst. sec. Nat. Bellas Hess Co., Kansas City, Mo., 1963-69; v.p. fin. Tech. Resources Corp., Kansas City, 1969-70; v.p. taxes CNA Fin. Corp., Chgo., 1970-74; v.p. corp. acctg. St. Paul Cos., Inc., St. Paul, 1974-82; v.p. fin. and adminstrn. Check Tech. Corp., 1982—. Served with AUS, 1956-58. Mem. Fin. Execs. Inst., Am. Inst. C.P.A.'s, Minn. Soc. C.P.A.'s, Mo., Kans. bar assns. Republican. Lutheran. Home: 44 E Pleasant Lake Rd North Oaks MN 55110 Office: 385 Washington St St Paul MN 55102

GARRITY, RODMAN FOX, psychologist, educator; b. Los Angeles, June 10, 1922; s. Lawrence Hitchcock and Margery Fox (Pugh) G.; m. Juanita Daphne Mullan, Mar. 5, 1948; children—Diana, Daphne, Ronald Fox. Student, Los Angeles City Coll., 1946-47; B.A., Calif. State U., Los Angeles, 1950; M.A., So. Meth. U., Dallas, 1955; Ed.D., U. So. Calif., 1963. Tchr. elem. sch. Palmdale (Calif.) Sch. Dist., 1952-54; psychologist, prin. Redondo Beach (Calif.) City Schs., 1954-60; asst. dir. ednl. placement lectr., ednl. adviser U. So. Calif., 1960-62; asso. prof., coordinator credentials programs Calif. State Poly. U., Pomona, 1962-66, chmn. social sci. dept., 1966-68, dir. tchr. preparation center, 1968-71, coordinator grad. program, 1971-73, prof. tchr. preparation center, 1968—; cons. psychologist, lectr. in field. Pres. Redondo Beach Coordinating Council, 1958-60; mem. univ. rep. Calif. Faculty Assns., 1974-76. Served with Engr. Combat Bn. AUS, 1942-45. Mem. Prins. Assn. Redondo Beach (chmn. 1958-60), Nat. Congress Parents and Tchrs. (hon. life), Am. Psychol. Assn., Calif. Tchrs. Assn. Democrat. Office: Calif State U Pomona CA 91768 *Empathetic reaching out to others transcends the obvious importance of achievement and intellectual ability. This has been a basic guide for my endeavors in the helping professions.*

GARRITY, W. ARTHUR, JR., judge; b. Worcester, Mass., June 20, 1920; s. W. Arthur and Mary B. (Kennedy) G.; m. Barbara A. Mullins, May 24, 1952; children: W. Arthur III, Charles, Anne, Jean. A.B., Holy Cross Coll., 1941; LL.B., Harvard U., 1946. Bar: Mass. 1956. Asst. U.S. atty. for Mass., 1948-50; U.S. atty. for Mass., 1961-66; judge U.S. Dist. Ct. Mass., 1966—. Office: US Dist Court Boston MA 02109 *

GARRY, FREDERICK WILTON, electrical manufacturing company executive; b. Stratford, Conn., July 12, 1921; s. Frederick Truman and Nellie M. (Flint) G.; m. Mary Elizabeth Griswold, June 28, 1948; children: Diana E., Kenneth G. B.S. in Mech. Engring, Rose-Hulman Inst., 1951, D. Engring. (hon.), 1968. Mgr. engring. programs Gen. Electric Co., Cin., 1951-67, v.p., 1967-70, 1970-73; v.p. tech. plans Aircraft Engine Group, 1973-74; pres. Rohr Industries Inc., Chula Vista, Calif., 1974-75, chmn., chief exec. officer, 1976-80; v.p. corp. engring. and mfg. Gen. Electric Co., 1981—. Bd. mgrs. Rose-Hulman Inst.; trustee Clarkson Coll. Served with USMCR, 1943-46. Mem. Conn. Assn. Scientists and Engrs.; Mem. Air Force Assn., Nat. Acad. Engring., Aircraft Owners and Pilots Assn., Navy League, USAF Assn., Assn. U.S. Army, Am. Helicopter Soc. Home: 480 Hemlock Rd Fairfield CT 06430 Office: General Electric Co Fairfield CT 06431

GARRY, RALPH JOSEPH, educator, psychologist; b. San Francisco, Aug. 10, 1916; s. Joseph Athanatious and Ida Scott (Smith) G. B.A., Stanford, 1946, M.A., 1950, Ph.D., 1950. Dir. Psychol. Cons., San Francisco, 1947-50; prof. ednl. psychology Boston U., 1950-69; chmn. curriculum dept. Ont. (Can.) Inst. Studies Edn., Toronto, 1969-73, prof. curriculum dept., 1973—; v.p. Ednl. Research Corp., 1962-65; dir. project Found. Character Edn., Boston, 1954-69; dir. natural sci. research project, Boston, 1958-62, dir. research, modern lang. project, 1959-64. Author: (with H. Kingsley) Nature and Conditions of Learning, 1963, Guidance Techniques for Elementary Teachers, 1963; editor: Television for Children, 1955, 3d edit., 1971. Cons. U.S. Senate Subcom. Juvenile Delinquency, 1961-63, OECD, 1971-73, Halton Primary Task Force, 1973-76; mem. sci. team Prix Jeunesse Found., Munich, 1975-83. Recipient George Peabody award, 1963; Fulbright sr. lectr. Chung-Ang U., Seoul, Korea, 1975. Mem. Am., Canadian psychol. assns., Am. Edn. Research Assn., Ednl. Bridgers Internat. (v.p.), Soc. Psychoceramicists (pres.), Sigma Xi. Home: Heinestrasse 30 Wedel Federal Republic Germany

GARSAUD, MARCEL, JR., lawyer, educator; b. New Orleans; s. Marcel and Beatrice (Deffarge) G.; m. Fleta Roubieaux, Aug. 19, 1961; 4 children. B.B.A., Loyola U., 1954, LL.B., 1959; LL.M., Yale U., 1967. Bar: La. 1959, N.Y. State 1960. Tax atty. Standard Oil (N.J.), N.Y.C., 1959-63; asst. prof. law Loyola U., New Orleans, 1963-69, asso. prof., 1969-72, prof., 1972-82, dean, 1970-82; ptnr. Gordon Arata McCollam & Stuart, New Orleans, 1982—; judge pro tempore Ct. of Appeals, 4th Circuit, La., 1977-78; chmn. CSC New Orleans, 1977-81; sec. New Orleans Legal Assistance Corp., 1968-72; pres., bd. dirs. New Orleans Release on Recognisance Program, 1968-72; mem. adv. com. to La. Legis. Com. to Investigate Effect of Organized Crime on State Govt., 1969-70; vis. prof. Tulane U. Sch. Law, 1968, La. State U., summer 1974, 75. Served with U.S. Army, 1954-56. Mem. La. State Bar Assn. (bd. govs. 1965-66, 69-70, mem. law reform com. 1973-79), ABA, Am. Judicature Soc., La. State Law Inst. (mem. council), Am. Law Inst. Democrat. Roman Catholic. Home: 1667 Soniat St New Orleans LA 70115 Office: 601 Poydras St New Orleans LA 70130

GARSH, THOMAS BURTON, publisher; b. New Rochelle, N.Y., Dec. 12, 1931; s. Harry and Matilda (Smith) G.; m. Beatrice J. Schmidt; children: Carol Jean, Thomas Burton, Janice Lynn. B.S., U. Md., 1955. Edn. rep. McGraw Hill Book Co., N.Y.C., 1959-68; mktg. mgr. D.C. Heath & Co., Boston, 1969-71; dir. mktg. Economy Co., Oklahoma City, 1971-72; sr. v.p. Macmillan Pub. Co., N.Y.C., 1972-78; pres. Am. Book Co., N.Y.C., 1978—; founder, pres., dir. Am. Ednl. Computer, Inc., Palo Alto, Calif., 1982—. Mem. county council Boy Scouts Am., 1963-65; mem. ch. council on Interracial Affairs, 1966-68, pres., 1967; vice-chmn. Madison County Democratic Party, 1967. Mem. Assn. Am. Pubs., Profl. Bookman's Assn., Omicron Delta Kappa, Sigma Alpha Epsilon. Club: Cazenovia Country (founder). Home: 401 Old Spanish Trail Portola Valley CA 94025

GARSIDE, BETTIS ALSTON, relief executive, educator; b. Stringtown, Okla., Nov. 22, 1894; s. Joseph and Sarah Emeline (Alston) G.; m. Margaret Helen Cameron, Sept. 10, 1921 (dec. Dec. 1981); 1 dau., Jean Alston Garside Barth Jr. A.B., U. Okla., 1913; postgrad., Kennedy Sch. Missions, 1916-17, N. China Union Lang. Sch., 1922-23; M.A., Columbia U., 1922; L.H.D., Coll. Ozarks, 1935. Prin. high sch., Pittsburg, Okla., 1913-16, Stringtown, 1920-21; missionary to China, Presbyn. Bd., U.S.A., 1922-26; asso. prof. edn. Cheeloo U., Tsinan, China, 1923-26; sec. China Union Univs. Central Office, N.Y.C., 1927-32; exec. sec. Asso. Bds. Christian Colls. China, N.Y.C., 1932-41; exec. dir. United China Relief, Inc., N.Y.C., 1941-42, v.p., sec., 1942-45; exec. v.p., sec., United Service to China, Inc., N.Y.C., 1946-67; exec. dir. Am. Bur. Med. Aid to China, N.Y.C., 1950-79, Aid Refugee Chinese Intellectuals, 1952-70; exec. vice chmn. Am. Emergency Com. Tibetan Refugees, 1959-70; dir. Tibetan Found., 1970—; vice chmn. Am. Com. Non Participation in Japanese Aggression, 1938-41; treas. com. One Million Against Admission of Communist China to UN, 1962-70; treas. Am.-Asian Ednl. Exchange, 1957—. Author: One Increasing Purpose, the Life of Henry Winters Luce, 1948, Memoirs, Within the Four Seas, 1984; articles, stories ednl. jours. Mem. nat. adv. bd. Com. for a Free China, 1972—. Served from seaman to warrant officer USN, 1917-19. Decorated Order of Brilliant Star with ribbon and collar, also with splicravat, Order of Propitious Clouds, China). Mem. Phi Gamma Delta. Mem. Riverside Ch. Clubs: Masons, Shanghai Tiffin (pres. 1942-43). Home: 720 West End Ave New York NY 10025 *The greatest success is not measured in terms of fame, power, or wealth; but only in terms of friendships earned, useful work done well, and assistance so given that the beneficiaries gain new strength and share that strength with others.*

GARSIDE, JOHN RUSHFORTH, II, hotel co. exec.; b. N.Y.C., Feb. 3, 1935; s. Herbert Rushforth and Josephine (DeSelding) G.; m. Barbara Dalziel, Dec. 28, 1968; children—Leslie Joan, John Rushforth. Student, U. Cin., 1952-54, Georgetown U., 1955. With Sheraton Corp., 1953-68; gen. mgr. Realty Hotels, N.Y.C., 1969-72, Sheraton-Cleve., Sheraton-Chgo., Sheraton Corp., 1972-75, v.p, regional dir. ops., Boston, 1976-79, area mgr., St. Louis, 1979—. Served with U.S. Army, 1954-56. Mem. Am. Hotel and Motel Assn., Hotel Sales Mgrs. Assn. Episcopalian. Home: 2133 Heather Glen Chesterfield MO 63017 Office: Sheraton St Louis Hotel 910 N 7th St Saint Louis MO 63101

GARSON, BARNETT, foods corporation executive; b. Cleve., Nov. 19, 1914; s. Herman Abraham and Bella G.; m. Ester Bertha Garson, Aug. 10, 1941; children: Barry, Renee. Stuart, Nancy. Grad., Glenville High Sch., Cleve. Ptnr. Economy Cash & Carry Co., Cleve., 1932-57; treas. Seaway Foods, Cleve., 1957-79; pres. Am. Seaway Foods, 1979—. Served to 1st lt. U.S. Army, 1942-46; ETO. Decorated Purple Heart; recipient Centerite of Yr. award Park Synagogue, 1980, City of Peace award Israel Bonds, 1982, Cert. of Recognition, 1969. Democrat. Jewish. Home: 31649 Gates Mills Blvd Pepper Pike Cleveland OH 44124 Office: Am Seaway Foods Inc 22801 Aurora Rd Bedford Heights OH 44146

GARSTANG, ROY HENRY, astrophysicist, educator; b. Southport, Eng., Sept. 18, 1925; came to U.S., 1964; s. Percy Brocklehurst and Eunice (Gledhill) G.; m. Ann Clemence Hawk, Aug. 11, 1959; children—Jennifer Katherine, Susan Veronica. B.A., U. Cambridge, 1946, M.A., 1950, Ph.D., 1954, Sc.D., 1983. Research asso. U. Chgo., 1951-52; lectr. astronomy U. Coll., London, 1952-60; reader astronomy U. London, 1960-64, asst. dir., 1959-64; prof. astrophysics U. Colo., Boulder, 1964—; chmn. Joint Inst. for Lab. Astrophysics, 1966-67; cons. Nat. Bur. Standards, 1964-73; v.p. commn. 14 Internat. Astron. Union, 1970-73, pres., 1973-76; Erskine vis. fellow U. Canterbury, New Zealand, 1971; vis. prof. U. Calif., Santa Cruz, 1971. Editor: Observatory, 1953-60; Contbr. numerous articles to tech. jours. Fellow Am. Phys. Soc., AAAS, Optical Soc. Am., Brit. Inst. Physics, Royal Astron. Soc.; mem. Am. Astron. Soc., Royal Soc. Scis. Liege (Belgium). Research on atomic physics and astrophys. applications. Home: 830 8th St Boulder CO 80302 Office: Joint Inst for Lab Astrophysics U Colo Boulder CO 80309 *It is a privilege to help others to learn about the wonderful universe in which we live.*

GARSTIN, MICHAEL EDWARD, entertainment company financial executive; b. Paris, Jan. 2, 1949; s. Norman Anthony and Colette Maria (Robinet) G.; m. Annemarie Cairns, June 12, 1976; children: Patrick Cairn, Dominique Olivia. Student, Beaumont Coll., Old Windsor, Berks., U.K., 1962-67; B.Sc. in Econs, London Sch. Econs., 1970; M.B.A., London Bus. Sch., 1973. With Chase Manhattan Bank, N.Y.C., 1973-80; sr. v.p., chief fin. officer, treas. Orion Pictures Corp., N.Y.C., 1980—. Club: Doubles (N.Y.C.). Home: 1220 Park Ave New York NY 10028 Office: Orion Pictures Corp 711 Fifth Ave New York NY 10022

GARSTON, GERALD DREXLER, artist; b. Waterbury, Conn., May 3, 1925; s. Leonard Alexander and Rose Sarah G.; m. Lois Muriel Freed, July 12, 1948; children—Priscilla Blythe, Joanne Hope. B.A., Johns Hopkins U., 1951. Tchr. Paier Sch. Art, Hamden, Conn., 1974-81, Creative Arts Workshop, New Haven, 1969-81. One-man shows include, Pucker Safrai Gallery, Boston, 1970, 71, 72, 74, 76, 78, 80, Freedman Art Gallery of Albright Coll., Reading, Pa., 1977, Kendall Gallery, Wellfleet, Mass., 1973, Graham Gallery, N.Y.C., 1967, Winfisky Gallery of Salem (Mass.) State Coll., 1970, group shows include, Sport Mus., N.Y.C., 1967, Boston Mus. Fine Arts, 1966, A. M. Sachs Gallery, N.Y.C., 1965, Stable Gallery, N.Y.C., 1964, Betty Parsons Gallery, N.Y.C., 1960, represented in permanent collections, Harvard U. Fogg Mus., Los Angeles County Mus., William Rockhill Nelson Gallery Art, Kansas City, Mo., New Britain (Conn.) Mus. Am. Art, Phila. Mus. Art, Bradeis U. Rose Mus., Waltham, Mass., Wadsworth Athenaeum, Hartford, Conn., Worcester (Mass.) Art Mus., DeCordova Mus., Lincoln, Mass. Served with USNR, 1943-46. Decorated D.F.C., air medal with 3 oak leaf clusters. Mem. Artists Equity Assn., Phi Beta Kappa. Address: 131 Oliver Rd New Haven CT 06515

GART, MURRAY JOSEPH, journalist, newspaper editor; b. Boston, Nov. 9, 1924; s. John and Frieda (Fisher) G.; m. Jeanne Brooks, Feb. 26, 1950; children: Mitchell Brooks, Marcia Anne. B.A. in Econs, Northeastern U., 1949. Reporter Honolulu Star-Bull., 1949-50; editor Weekly Ind. Record, Cape May County, N.J., 1950-51; reporter, city editor Wichita Beacon, 1951-53; reporter, news editor Wichita Eagle, 1953-55; bur. chief Time-Life mag. News Service, Toronto, Can., 1955-57, Boston, 1957-59; chief Midwest corr. Time mag., 1959-61, bur. chief, Chgo., 1961-64, London, 1964-66; asst. mng. editor Fortune mag., N.Y.C., 1966-69; chief Time-Life News Service, 1969-78; asst. mag. editor Time mag., 1972-78; editor The Washington Star, 1978-81, Time Inc., 1981-82, cons., 1982—; assoc. Johns Hopkins Fgn. Policy Inst., Washington, 1982—. Served with AUS, 1943-46. Mem. Council on Fgn. Relations., Am. Soc. Newspaper Editors. Clubs: Century Assn. (N.Y.C.); Cosmos (Washington); The Garrick (London). Home: 2126 Connecticut Ave NW Washington DC 20008 Office: Time Inc 888 16th St NW Washington DC 20006

GARTENBERG, SEYMOUR LEE, broadcasting company executive; b. N.Y.C., May 27, 1931; s. Morris and Anna (Banner) G.; m. Anna Stassi, Feb. 18, 1956; children: Leslie, Karen, Mark. B.B.A. cum laude, CCNY, 1952. Asst. controller Finlay Straus, Inc., N.Y.C., 1950-56; controller Tappin's Inc., Newark, 1956; exec. v.p. Columbia House div. CBS, N.Y.C., 1956-73; pres. CBS (Toys div.), Cranbury, N.J., 1973-78; v.p. CBS/Columbia Group, N.Y.C., 1978—; sr. v.p. CBS Records Group, 1979—. Bd. dirs. City Coll. Fund. Mem. Mill Island Civic Assn., Nat. Assn. Accts., Am. Mgmt. Assn. Office: 51 W 52d St New York NY 10019

GARTENHAUS, SOLOMON, physicist; b. Kassel, Germany, Jan. 3, 1929; came to U.S., 1937, naturalized, 1943; s. Leopolt and Hanna (Brandler) G.; m. Johanna Lore Weisz, Aug. 30, 1953; children: Michael M., Kevin M. B.S., U. Pa., 1951; M.S., U. Ill., 1953, Ph.D., 1955. Instr. Stanford U., 1955-58; faculty physics Purdue U., Lafayette, Ind., 1958—, prof., 1963—; asst. dean Grad. Sch., 1972-77, sec. of faculties, 1980—; disting. vis. prof. USAF Acad., Colo., 1977-78; dir. Purdue-Ind. Studienprogram, U. Hamburg, W. Ger., 1979—; cons. Lockheed, summers 1958-60; officer, dir. Advanced Research Corp., 1961-65. Author: Elements of Plasma Physics, 1964, Physics-Basic Principles, 1975; contbr. articles to profl. jours. Fellow Am. Phys. Soc.; mem. N.Y. Acad. Scis., Am. Assn. Physics Tchrs., Phi Beta Kappa, Sigma Xi. Theoretical research in nuclear physics, plasma physics, many-particle systems, nuclear interactions based on meson fields and condensation phenomena at low temperatures. Home: 444 Littleton St West Lafayette IN 47906 Office: Dept Physics Purdue U Lafayette IN 47907

GARTH, DAVID, political consultant; b. Woodmere, N.Y., 1930; s. Leo and Beulah (Jagoda) Goldberg. B.S., Washington & Jefferson U., 1952. Producer, broadcaster high sch. football games, 1957-60, polit. cons., campaigner, N.Y.C., 1960—; involved in elections of Hugh Carey, John Tunney, John V. Lindsay, Tom Bradley, Edward Koch, Walter Mondale; Edward Koch; pres. Garth Group Inc., N.Y.C., 1964—. Office: Garth Group Inc 745 Fifth Ave New York NY 10151

GARTH, LEONARD I., judge; b. Bklyn., Apr. 7, 1921; s. Frank A. and Anne F. (Jacobs) Goldstein; m. Sarah Miriam Kaufman, Sept. 6, 1942; 1 dau., Tobie Gail Garth Meisel. B.A., Columbia U., 1942; postgrad., Nat. Inst. Pub. Affairs, 1942-43; LL.B., Harvard U., 1952. Bar: N.J. bar 1952. Mem. firm Cole, Berman & Garth (and predecessors), Paterson, N.J., 1952-70; judge U.S. Dist. Ct. for Dist. N.J., Newark, 1970-73; U.S. Circuit judge Ct. Appeals for 3d Circuit, 1973—; lectr. Inst. Continuing Legal Edn.; lectr., coadj. mem. faculty Rutgers U. Law Sch., 1978—, Seton Hall Law Sch., 1980—; mem. N.J. Bd. Bar Examiners, 1964-68; mem. com. on revision gen. and admiralty rules Fed. Dist. Ct. NJ. Served as 1st lt. AUS, 1943-46. Mem. ABA, Fed. Bar Assn., N.J. Bar Assn., Passaic County (N.J.) Bar Assn. (pres. 1967-68), Harvard Law Sch. Assn. (nat. v.p. 1963-64), Am. Law Inst. Home: 17 Greenview Way Upper Montclair NJ 07043 Office: US PO and Courthouse Newark NJ 07101 also 20316 US Courthouse Philadelphia PA 19106

GARTLAND, WILLIAM JOSEPH, JR., research institute administrator; b. N.Y.C., Apr. 15, 1941; s. William Joseph and Mary (Klik) G. B.S., Holy Cross Coll., 1962; Ph.D., Princeton U., 1967. Asst. research scientist N.Y. U. Med. Center, N.Y.C., 1967-69; postgrad. research biologist U. Calif., San Diego, 1969-70; grants asso. div. research grants NIH, Bethesda, Md., 1970-71; program adminstr. genetics program Nat. Inst. Gen. Med. Scis., 1971-76; exec. sec. Recombinant DNA Adv. Com., 1975—; dir. Office Recombinant DNA Activities, 1976—; U.S. rep. European Sci. Found. Liaison Com. on Recombinant DNA Research, 1976-81; NIH rep. Recombinant DNA Com. of U.S. Dept. Agr., 1978—; mem. NIH Exec. Recombinant DNA Com., 1976—; U.S. rep. U.S.-Japan Coop. Program for Recombinant DNA Research, 1982—; mem. faculty CSC exec. seminar program, advanced study program Brookings Instn. Co-author articles in field. Mem. AAAS, Am. Soc. Human Genetics. Clubs: Sierra, Washington Ski. Home: 804 New Mark Esplanade Rockville MD 20850 Office: 9000 Rockville Pike Bethesda MD 20205

GARTNER, ALAN P., educational administrator, author; b. N.Y.C., Apr. 4, 1935; s. Harold J. and Mary G.; m. Audrey S. Joseph, July 7, 1957; children: Jonathan, Rachel, Daniel. B.A., Antioch Coll., 1956; M.A., Harvard U., 1960; Ph.D., Union Grad. Sch., 1973. Dir. New Careers Tng. Lab., N.Y.C., 1968-81; prof. Queens Coll., 1972-76, Grad. Sch., CUNY, 1976-81, 83—, dir. Ctr. for Advanced Study in Edn. Grad. Sch., 1978-81, dir. Office of Sponsored Research, Grad. Sch., 1983—; exec. dir. Div. Spl. Edn., N.Y.C. Pub. Schs., 1981-83; pub. Social Policy mag., N.Y.C., 1971—. Author: Paraprofessionals and their Performance, 1971; co-author: Children Teach Children, 1971, What Nixon is Doing to Us, 1973; author: The Service Society & Consumer Vanguard, 1974, Self Help in the Human Services, 1977, Help: A Working Guide to Self-Help Groups, 1979, What Reagan is Doing to Us, 1982; co-editor: The Preparation of Human Services Professionals, 1976, After Deschooling, What?, 1973, Public Service Employment, 1973, The New Assault on Equality, 1974; others. Bd. dirs. N.Y. Civil Liberties Union, 1973—, Antioch Coll., 1974-75; treas. Congress Racial Equality, N.Y.C., 1962-64, chairperson, Boston, 1960-64. Ford Found. fellow, 1956-58; Florina Lasker fellow, 1961-62; Poynter fellow, 1976. Home: 20 Sailfish Pl Northport NY 11768 Office: Grad Sch and Univ Ctr CUNY 33 W 42d St New York NY 10036

GARTNER, LAWRENCE MITCHEL, pediatrician, med. coll. adminstr.; b. Bklyn., Apr. 24, 1933; s. Samuel and Bertha (Brimberg) G.; m. Carol Sue Blicker, Aug. 12, 1956; children—Alex David, Madeline Hallie. A.B., Columbia U., 1954; M.D., Johns Hopkins U., 1958. Intern pediatrics Johns Hopkins Hosp., 1958-59; resident pediatrics Albert Einstein Coll. Medicine, 1959-60, chief resident, 1960-61, instr. pediatrics, 1962-64, asst. prof., 1964-69, asso. prof., 1969-74, prof., 1974-80, dir. div. neonatology, 1967-80, dir. div. pediatric hepatology, 1967-80; dir. clin. research unit Rose F. Kennedy Center, 1972-80; attending physician Hosp. Albert Einstein Coll. Medicine; prof., chmn. dept. pediatrics U. Chgo. Pritzker Sch. Medicine, 1980—; dir. Wyler Children's Hosp., U. Chgo. Med. Center, 1980—; med. dir. Gail I. Zuckerman Found., 1967—. Contbr. articles to med. jours. and textbooks. Mem. adv. bd. Children's Liver Found.; Trustee Home for Destitute Crippled Children, La Rabida Children's Hosp. Recipient award NIH, 1967-74; Appleton Century Crofts prize,

1956; Mosby book award, 1958; NIH grantee, 1967—. Mem. Am. Pediatric Soc., Soc. Pediatric Research, Perinatal Research Soc., Am. Assn. Study Liver Disease, N.Y. Pediatric Soc., Am. Acad. Pediatrics, Harvey Soc., N.Y. Acad. Sci., AAAS, N.Am. Soc. Pediatric Gastroenterology (pres. 1974- 75), LaLeche League Internat., Chgo. Pediatric Soc., Phi Beta Kappa, Alpha Omega Alpha. Office: U Chgo Pritzker Sch Medicine 950 E 59th St Chicago IL 60637

GARTNER, MICHAEL GAY, editor; b. Des Moines, Oct. 25, 1938; s. Carl David and Mary Marguerite (Gay) G.; m. Barbara Jeanne McCoy, May 25, 1968; children: Melissa, Christopher, Michael. B.A., Carleton Coll., 1960; J.D., NYU, 1969; Litt. D. (hon.), Simpson Coll., 1984. Bar: N.Y., Iowa. With Wall St. Jour., N.Y.C., 1960-74, page one editor, 1970-74; Exec. editor Des Moines Register and Tribune, 1974-76, editor, 1976-82, editorial chmn., 1982—, v.p., 1975-76, exec. v.p., 1977, pres., chief operating officer, 1978—; also dir. co. Author Syndicated column on lang. Trustee Simpson Coll.; bd. dirs. Living History Farms Mus.; mem. Pulitzer Prize Bd. Mem. Assn. Bar City N.Y., ABA, Iowa Bar Assn., Am. Press Inst. (dir.), Am. Soc. Newspaper Editors (dir.). Clubs: Embassy, Wakonda Des Moines, Bohemian (Des Moines); Garden of Gods (Colorado Springs, Colo.). Home: 5315 Waterbury Rd Des Moines IA 50312 Office: 715 Locust St Des Moines IA 50304

GARTNER, MURRAY, lawyer; b. N.Y.C., Sept. 23, 1922; s. Leo and Celia (Orner) G.; m. Anne Ellis Thompson, June 9, 1961; children—Marion Moreau, Thomas Murray. A.B., N.Y. U., 1942; LL.B., Harvard, 1945. Bar: N.Y. bar 1946, Calif. bar 1948. Law clk. U.S. Supreme Ct. Justice Robert H. Jackson, 1945-47; asso. firm Pillsbury, Madison & Sutro, San Francisco, 1947-51; lectr. law Hastings Coll. Law, San Francisco, 1948; asst. to gen. counsel U.S. rep. in Paris, ECA-Mut. Security Adminstrn., 1951-53; asso. firm Roosevelt, Freidin & Littauer, N.Y.C., 1953-59; partner firm Poletti, Freidin, Prashker & Gartner (and predecessors), N.Y.C., 1959—. Trustee Children's Aid Soc. Home: 520 E 86th St New York NY 10028 Office: 1185 Ave of Americas New York NY 10036

GARVER, LEONARD LEE, electric power engr.; b. Columbus, Ohio, Sept. 11, 1932; s. Lester Wayne and Katherine Taylor (Leonard) G.; m. Nancy Bradford, Sept. 1, 1959; children—Andrew Stephen, Mary Elizabeth. B.S.E.E., Northwestern U., 1956, M.S.E.E., 1958, Ph.D., 1961. Application engr. electric utility engring. operation Gen. Electric Co., Schenectady, 1961-68; sr. application engr. advanced system planning (electric utility systems engring. dept.), 1968—; adj. prof. indsl. adminstrn. Union Coll., 1964-72. Contbr. articles to profl. jours. Mem. ch. bds. trustees and session Presbyn. Ch., 1963-81, pres., 1968-69, treas., 1975-77. Fellow IEEE; mem. Inst. Mgmt. Sci., Tau Beta Pi, Eta Kappa Nu, Triangle. Clubs: Post Stroke Patients Assn., Nat. Ry. Hist. Soc. Office: 1 River Rd Schenectady NY 12345

GARVER, ROBERT WRIGHT, banker; b. Evanston, Ill., Nov. 17, 1933; s. George Parkhurst and Susan Gillespie (Wright) G.; m. Judith Corwin, May 12, 1956; children: Linda Williams, Robert Corwin, Charlotte Ann. B.A., Dartmouth Coll., 1955; M.B.A., Harvard U., 1960. Second v.p. Continental Ill. Nat. Bank, Chgo., 1960-68; exec. v.p., trustee Neworld Bank for Savs., Boston, 1968-74, pres., trustee, 1974—, chief exec. officer, 1978—; dir. Savs. Bank Investment Fund. Bd. dirs. Easter Seal Soc. Mass. Served to lt. (j.g.) USN, 1955-58. Mem. Nat. Assn. Mut. Savs. Banks (dir.), Mass. Savs. Banks Officers Club (pres.), Greater Boston C. of C. (dir.), Urban League Eastern Mass. (dir.). Home: 8 Wayside Rd Wayland MA 01778 Office: 55 Summer St Boston MA 02110

GARVER, THEODORE MEYER, lawyer; b. Buffalo, July 29, 1929; s. John Newton and Dorothy M. (Lamay) G.; m. Emily Martha, Aug. 12, 1977; children: Douglas, Robin, Theodore, John, Benjamin, Peter. B.A., Williams Coll., 1951; LL.B., Cornell U., 1954. Bar: N.Y. 1954, Ohio 1957. Spl. asst. to atty. gen. tax div. U.S. Dept. Justice, Washington, 1954-56; mem. firm Jones, Day, Reavis & Pogue, Cleve., 1956-83, of counsel, 1983—; chmn. bd. Fostoria Corp., Cleve., 1983—. Mem. ABA, Cleve. Bar Assn. Home: 12998 Lake Ave Cleveland OH 44107 Office: 735 Citizens Federal Tower Cleveland OH 44115

GARVER, THOMAS HASKELL, art museum director, writer, lecturer, consultant; b. Duluth, Minn., Jan. 23, 1934; s. Harvie Adair and Margaret Hope (Foght) G.; m. Natasha Nicholson, Apr. 13, 1974. B.A., Harverford Coll., 1956; M.A., U. Minn., 1965. Asst. to dir. Krannert Art Mus., U. Ill., Urbana, 1960-62; asst. dir. fine arts dept. Seattle World's Fair, 1962, Rose Art Mus., Brandeis U., Waltham, Mass., 1962-68; dir. Newport Harbor Art Mus., Calif., 1968-72, 77-80; curator exhbns. Fine Arts Mus. of San Francisco, 1972-77; dir. Madison Art Ctr., Wis., 1980—; asst. prof. Calif. State U., 1970-71, 79-80; visual arts panelist Nat. Endowment Arts, Washington; art cons. Author: Twelve Photographers of The American Social Landscape, 1967, Just Before the War: Urban America from 1935-41, 1968; exhbn. catalogues. Trustee U.S.S. Mass. Meml. Commn., Fall River, 1965-68, South Coast Repertory Co., Costa Mesa, Calif., 1970-72; mem. Newport Beach Art Commn., 1978-79; mem. steering com. Archives Am. Art, San Francisco, 1977-80. Mem. Western Assn. Art Mus. (pres. 1970-71, trustee), Art Mus. Assn. Am. (pres. 1979-82, trustee), Internat. Inst. Conservation Historic and Artistic Works, Assn. Art Mus. Dirs. Lodge: Rotary. Office: Madison Art Center 211 State St Madison WI 53703

GARVEY, EDWARD ROBERT, lawyer, state official; b. Burlington, Wis., Apr. 18, 1940; s. Edward C. and June (Lockhart) G.; m. Elizabeth Miller; children: Pamela, Kathleen, Elizabeth. B.S., U. Wis., 1961, J.D., 1969. Bar: Wis. 1969, Minn. 1969. Pres. Nat. Student Assn., 1961-62; sec.-gen. Internat. Student Conf., Leiden, Holland, 1965-66; asso. firm Lindquist & Vennum, Mpls., 1969-71; exec. dir. Nat. Football League Players Assn., Washington, 1971-82; dep. atty. gen. State of Wis., Madison, 1982—; dir. seminars, lectr. in field. Comment editor: Wis. Law Rev, 1968-69. Served to 1st lt. AUS, 1963-65. Mem. Am., Wis., Minn. bar assns., Order of Coif. Democrat. Roman Catholic. Office: State Capitol Atty Gen's Office Madison WI 53702

GARVEY, GERALD THOMAS, physicist; b. N.Y.C., Jan. 21, 1935; s. John Thomas and Anne Elizabeth (Williams) G.; m. Doris Carol Burmester, June 5, 1959; children—Deirdre, Gerald Thomas, Victoria. B.S., Fairfield U., 1956; Ph.D. (NSF fellow), Yale U., 1962. Research asso. Yale U., New Haven, 1962-63, asst. prof., 1964-65; instr. Princeton (N.J.) U., 1963-64, asst. prof., 1966-67, asso. prof., 1967-69, prof., 1969-76; dir. physics div. Argonne (Ill.) Nat. Lab., 1976-79, asso. lab. dir. for phys. research, 1979-81; prof. U. Chgo., 1979—; vis. fellow Oxford U., 1969; program officer-nuclear NSF, 1973-74. Editor: Physics Reports, 1974-79. A.P. Sloan Found. fellow, 1968-70. Fellow Am. Phys. Soc. (chmn. div. nuclear physics 1981—). Roman Catholic. Home: 773 Crescent Blvd Glen Ellyn IL 60137 Office: Physics Div (203 Argonne Nat Lab)t Argonne IL 60439

GARVEY, JOANNE MARIE, lawyer; b. Oakland, Calif., Apr. 23, 1935; s. James M. and Marian A. (Dean) G. A.B. with honors, U. Calif., Berkeley, 1956, M.A., 1957, J.D., 1961. Bar: Calif. bar 1962. Asso. firm Cavaletto, Webster, Mullen & McCaughey, Santa Barbara, Calif., 1961-63, Jordan, Keeler & Seligman, San Francisco, 1963-67, partner, 1968—; bd. dirs. Mexican-Am. Legal Def. and Ednl. Fund; chmn. Law in a Free Soc., Continuing Edn. of Bar; mem. bd. councillors U. So. Calif. Law Center. Recipient Paul Veazy award YMCA, 1973, Internat. Women's Yr. award Queen's Bench, 1975, honors Advs. for Women, 1978. Fellow Am. Bar Found.; mem. Am. Bar Assn., Calif. State Bar (v.p., gov., Jud Klein award, tax sect.), San Francisco Bar Assn. (pres., pres. Barristers), Am. Law Inst., Calif. Women Lawyers (founder), Order of Coif, Phi Beta Kappa. Democrat. Roman Catholic. Home: 16 Kensington Ct Kensington CA 94707 Office: Suite 1400 1 Maritime Plaza San Francisco CA 94111

GARVEY, JOHN CHARLES, violist, conductor, music educator; b. Canonsburg, Pa., Mar. 17, 1921; s. Frank Sherwood and Esther (Gegenheimer) G.; m. Evelyn Ficarra, Mar. 13, 1947; children: Deborah, Frank, Deirdre. Student, Temple U., 1940-43. Prof. music Sch. Music, U. Ill., Urbana, 1948—. Violinist, violist, Jan. Savitt and Jerry Wald Jazz orchs., 1943-45; prin. violist, Columbus Philharmonic Orch., 1945-48, Aspen Festival Orch., 1964; condr., NIRTV Chamber Orch., Iran, 1973; founder, dir., Jazz Band, 1959, Chamber Orch., 1964, Russian Folk Orch., 1974; violist, Walden Quartet, 1948-69, State Dept. Jazz Tours, 1968-69; condr., Harry Partch Ensemble, 1959-63 (Winner Nat. Coll. Jazz Band championships 1967-69), Harry Partch Ensemble (Russian Center grantee for study balalaika in Moscow 1970, 72), Harry Partch Ensemble (Center for Advanced Studies grantee for study ethnic music 1972-73); (recipient Ill. Gov.'s award in arts 1980). Balinese Gamelan study grantee K.O.K.A.R., Bali, 1979. Mem. Nat. Assn. Jazz Educators, Am. Fedn. Musicians (Local 196), Soc. for Ethno-musicology. Democrat. Home: 1739 Westhaven Dr Champaign IL 61820 Office: Room 2136 Sch Music U Ill Urbana IL 61801

GARVEY, JOHN LEO, lawyer, educator; b. Covington, Ky., Mar. 22, 1927; s. Charles Francis and Anna G.; m. Virginia Ann Hinzman, Sept. 13, 1952; children—John Gerard, Lawrence Charles. B.A., Xavier U., Cin., 1945, LL.D. (hon.), 1978; LL.B., Catholic U. Am., 1948; S.J.D., U. Mich., 1967. Bar: Ky. bar 1948. Individual practice law Erlanger, 1948-51; instr. Cath. U., Washington, 1951-57, asst. prof., 1957-61, asso. prof., 1961-65, prof. law, 1965—, dean Law Sch., 1977—. Contbr. to: Probate Court Practice in the District of Columbia, 1960, 62, 65, 67, 70, 72, 75, 77; Mem. editorial adv. com. jour.: Legal Edn, 1976-79. Mem. Am. Law Inst., Am. Bar Assn. (real property, probate and trust law sect.), Ky. Bar Assn., Am. Coll. Probate Counsel. Home: 9744 Hedin Dr Silver Spring MD 20903 Office: 4th and Michigan Ave NE Washington DC 20064

GARVEY, RICHARD CONRAD, newspaper editor; b. Northampton, Mass., May 23, 1923; s. Michael Edward and Lucy (Bradford) G.; m. Anne Elizabeth Vanasse, May 18, 1957; children: Philip Michael, John Bradford, Mary Agnes, Margaret Anne Garvey Gardell. Student, U. Mass., 1941-42, L.H.D., 1974; D. Humanics, Springfield Coll., 1982; LL.D., Coll. Our Lady of Elms, 1982. Reporter Daily Hampshire Gazette, Northampton, 1943-44; reporter Springfield (Mass.) Daily News, 1944-51, asst. mng. editor, 1951-66, mng. editor, 1966-69, editor, 1969—; corporator Springfield Instn. for Savs., 1967—, also trustee. Dir. Westmass Area Devel. Corp.; Trustee Springfield Coll., chmn. bd., 1976-80; trustee Mercy Hosp.; mem. U.S. Cath. Bishops Adv. Council, 1980-84. Mem. Am. Soc. Newspaper Editors, New Eng. Soc. Newspaper Editors (v.p. 1970-71, pres. 1971, past bd. govs.), Am. Cath. Hist. Assn. Home: 84 Fuller St Ludlow MA 01056 Office: 1860 Main St Springfield MA 01101

GARVEY, ROBERT ROBEY, JR., government official; b. Elkin, N.C., Feb. 16, 1921; s. Robert Robey and Rose Edna (Brown) G.; m. Nancy Douglas Maclay, June 15, 1945; children: Robert Michael, Jean Maclay, Lee Beasley, William Sinclair. Student, Davidson Coll., 1938-41; sr. exec. program, Fed. Exec. Inst., 1975. Gen. mgr. Dennis, Inc., Winston-Salem, N.C., 1945-54; exec. dir. Old Salem, Inc., Winston-Salem, 1955-60, Nat. Trust for Historic Preservation, Washington, 1960-67; exec. sec. Adv. Council on Historic Preservation, 1967-76, exec. dir., 1976—; asst. sec. Nat. Park Found., 1968-71; Nat. Park Service liaison officer Am. Revolution Bicentennial Commn., 1968-71; mem. internat. com. Nat. Assn. Housing and Redevel. Ofcls., 1963—; v.p. Internat. Council of Monuments and Sites, 1965-75; cons. on cultural property UNESCO; mem. U.S. nat. commn. for UNESCO, 1974-79, vice chmn., 1976-79; mem. landscape and archaeologists com. on Philae project Govt. of Egypt. Served to maj. USMCR, 1942-45. Decorated D.F.C.; recipient N.C. Public Service award, 1978, Disting. Alumnus award Davidson Coll., 1982, Presdl. rank of Meritorious Exec., 1981. Mem. Explorers Club. Address: 1722 S Arlington Ridge Rd Arlington VA 22202

GARVEY, STEVEN PATRICK, professional baseball player; b. Tampa, Fla., Dec. 22, 1948; s. Joseph Patrick and Mildred Emma (Winkler) G.; m. Cynthia Ann, Oct. 29, 1971; children: Krisha Lee, Whitney Alyse. B.S., Mich. State U. First baseman Los Angeles Dodgers, 1970—, asst. player rep., 1972-76; mem. Nat. League All-Star Team, 1974-81; pub. relations for Pepsi-Cola Bottling Co., Los Angeles, 1974—, Allegretti Co., 1976—, Head Shampoo Co., 1977—. Trustee Multiple Sclerosis Soc. Named Most Valuable Player Nat. League, 1974, Most Valuable Player, All Star Game, 1974, 78, Outstanding Young Man of Calif., 1976. Mem. Baseball Players Assn. Am., North Hills Jr. C. of C. Democrat. Roman Catholic. Address: San Diego Padres PO Box 2000 San Diego CA 92120 *

GARVIN, ANDREW PAUL, information company executive, author, consultant; b. N.Y.C., July 24, 1945; s. Gene G. and Nora (Sheldon) London; m. Sandra Kremnitzer, June 13, 1976 (div. 1980); m. 2d Linda Gail Bernstein, Oct. 1, 1983. B.A., Yale U., 1967; M.S., Columbia U., 1968. Corr. Newsweek, N.Y.C., 1967-68; v.p. Four Elements, Inc., N.Y.C., 1968-69; pres., co-founder FIND SVP, N.Y.C., and Info. Clearing House, Inc., 1970—; dir. Packaged Facts, Inc. Author: How to Win With Information, 1980. Chmn. Nat. Info. Conf. and Expn., Washington, 1979. Mem. Info. Industry Assn. (dir. 1979-82, Product of Yr. award 1975), Assn. Info. Mgrs. (dir. 1978-82), Am. Mktg. Assn., Am. Mgmt. Assn., Spl. Libraries Assn., St. Elmo Soc. (treas. 1974-81). Home: 315 E 72d St New York NY 10021 Office: FIND SVP 500 Fifth Ave New York NY 10110

GARVIN, CLIFTON CANTER, JR., oil company executive; b. Portsmouth, Va., Dec. 22, 1921; s. Clifton Canter and Esther (Ames) G.; m. Thelma E. Volland, Mar. 15, 1943; children: James C., Carol Ann, Sandra Louise, Patricia Lynn. B.S. in Chem. Engring, Va. Poly. Inst., 1943, M.S., 1947; D.S.C. (hon.), NYU, 1978, D.Eng., Stevens Inst. Tech., 1982. With Esso Standard Oil Co., Baton Rouge, 1947-59; with Humble Oil & Refining Co., 1960-64, v.p. central region, 1963-64; exec. asst. to pres. Exxon Corp. (formerly Standard Oil Co. N.J.), 1964-65, v.p., 1968, exec. v.p., 1968-72, pres., 1972-75, chmn. bd., chief exec. officer, 1975—; dir. Citicorp, Citibank (N.A.), Pepsico, Inc., Johnson & Johnson. Mem. Nat. Petroleum Council, Bus. Com. for Arts; mem. Bus. Roundtable; bd. dirs. Am. Petroleum Inst.; chmn. Bus. Council; vice chmn. bd. mgrs. Sloan-Kettering Inst. for Cancer Research; trustee Com. for Econ. Devel.; sr. mem. Conf. Bd.; v.p. bd. of trust Vanderbilt U.; bd. dirs. United Way of Tri-State, Council for Fin. Aid to Edn., Inc., Com. for Responsible Fed. Budget; bd. govs. United Way of Am.; mem. adminstrv. bd. Lab. Ornithology, Cornell U.; nat. assoc. White Burkett Miller Ctr. Pub. Affairs, U. Va.; mem. com. of 100 Coll. Engring. Corp. Devel. Council, Va. Poly. Inst. and State U. Mem. Am. Chem. Soc., Am. Inst. Chem. Engrs., Soc. Chem. Industry, Council on Fgn. Relations, Beta Gamma Sigma. Congregationalist. Home: Greenwich CT Office: 1251 Ave of Americas New York NY 10020

GARVIN, JAMES WILLIAM, JR., lawyer; b. Phila., Sept. 20, 1937; s. James William and Mary Margaret (Ward) G.; m. Elizabeth A. Dougherty, June 13, 1964; children—James Patrick, Shawn Michael, Megan Elizabeth, Dennis Paul. B.S., U. Del., 1960; J.D., Temple U., 1969. Bar: Del. bar 1970. Chief dep. register of wills, New Castle County, Wilmington, Del., 1969; dep. atty. gen. Atty. Gen.'s Office, Wilmington, Del., 1970-72; mem. firm Sobolewski and Garvin, Newark, Del., 1972-77; U.S. atty. Dist. of Del., Wilmington, 1977—. Mem. All Star Com., Del. Found. for Retarded Children, 1970—; chmn. Del. Found. for Retarded Children, 1977. Served with U.S. Army, 1956. Mem. Del. Bar Assn. Democrat. Roman Catholic. Home: 11 Fairfield Dr Newark DE 19711 Office: 844 King St Wilmington DE 19801

GARVIN, JOHN SAMUEL, neurologist; b. Windsor, Ill., Feb. 23, 1921; s. Bruce G. and Ora L. Stivers; m. Elizabeth Harding Stone; 1951 (dec.); children: Mary Grigsby, Bruce Peters, Elizabeth Randall; m. Suzanne Spencer Faurot, Nov. 25, 1978. B.A., U. Ill., 1942, B.S., 1943, M.D., 1944. Intern, then resident in neurology U. Ill. Hosp., 1944-46, research asso. in electroencephalography, 1948-49, resident in neuropathology, 1950; clin. clk. neurology Nat. Hosp. Nervous and Mental Disorders, London, 1949-50; mem. faculty U. Ill. Med. Center, 1951—, prof. neurology, head dept., 1972—; sr. neuropsychiatrist Presbyn.-St. Luke's Hosp., 1962—, dir. electroencephalography, 1954-64; cons. Mcpl. Contagious Disease Hosp., Chgo., 1952-60, Chgo. State Tb Hosp., 1957-70, VA Westside Hosp., 1971—. Asso. editor: Clin. Electronecephalography, 1970—; author articles, revs. in field. Served to capt. M.C., AUS, 1946-48. Fellow Inst. Medicine Chgo.; mem. Am. Acad. Neurology (councillor 1977-81), AMA, Am. Epilepsy Soc., Am. Assn. Neurol. Surgeons (asso.), Assn. Research Nervous and Mental Diseases, Am. Electroencephalographic Soc., Soc. Clin. Neurologists, Am. Med. Electroencephalographic Assn. (pres. 1970-71), Central Electrencephalographic, Central Neuropsychiat. Assn. (pres. 1978), Ill. Med. Socs., Chgo. Med. Soc., Chgo. Neurol. Soc. (pres. 1968). Clubs: University, Literary (Chgo.); Indian Hill. Office: 912 S Wood St Chicago IL 60612

GARWIN, RICHARD LAWRENCE, physicist; b. Cleve., Apr. 19, 1928; s. Robert and Leona (Schwartz) G.; m. Lois Levy, Apr. 20, 1947; children: Jeffrey L., Thomas M., Laura J. B.S. in Physics, Case Inst. Tech., 1947, Ph.D., U. Chgo., 1949. Mem. faculty U. Chgo., 1949-52; with IBM, 1952—; dir. applied research IBM Thomas J. Watson Research Center, Yorktown Heights, N.Y., 1965-66; dir. IBM Watson Lab., Columbia U., 1966-67; fellow Thomas J. Watson Research Center, 1967—, mem. corp. tech. com., 1970-71; prof. public policy Kennedy Sch. Govt., Harvard U., 1979-81; Andrew D. White prof.-at-large Cornell U., 1983—; adj. prof. Columbia U.; adj. research fellow Harvard U., 1982—; congl. witness on nat. security, transp., energy policy, tech; cons. to industry and govt.; mem. Pres.'s Sci. Adv. Com., 1962-65, 69-72; mem. Def. Sci. Bd., 1966-69. Co-author: Nuclear Weapons and World Politics, 1977, Nuclear Power Issues and Choices, 1977, Securing the Seas, 1979, Energy: The Next Twenty Years, 1979, The Dangers of Nuclear War, 1979, Nuclear Energy and Nuclear Weapons Proliferation, 1979, The Genesis of New Weapons, 1980, Science Advice to the President, 1980; contbr. numerous articles to profl. publs. Ford Found. fellow CERN, 1959-60. Fellow Am. Phys. Soc. (chmn. panel on public affairs 1978-79), Am. Acad. Arts and Scis.; mem. Nat. Acad. Scis. (council 1983-85), Inst. Medicine, Nat. Acad. Engring., Council Fgn. Relations, Inst. for Strategic Studies (London) (council), Am. Philos. Soc. Jewish. Patentee in field. Office: PO Box 218 Yorktown Heights NY 10598

GARWOOD, JOHN DELVERT, former college administrator; b. Carroll, Nebr., Mar. 20, 1915; s. Harvey and Forrest (Hill) G.; m. Kathleen Marie Schnoor, Aug. 6, 1943; children: Jan Dierks, Shelley Hill. A.B., Wayne (Nebr.) State Coll., 1936; Ph.M., U. Wis., 1940; postgrad., U. La., 1940-41, U. So. Calif., 1947; Ph.D. in Econs, U. Colo., 1951. Supt. schs., Lindsay, Nebr., 1936-38; teaching fellow U. La., 1940-41, U. Colo., 1949-51; instr. Moringside Coll., Sioux City, 1941- 42; prof. econs. Ft. Hays (Kans.) State Coll., 1947- 49, 51-62, dean faculty, 1962-79, v.p. for acad. affairs, 1979-80. Author: Back to the Basics, 1978. Mem. exec. com. Kans. Council Econ. Edn., 1961—, Danforth asso., 1957—. Served with AUS, 1942-46. Recipient Disting. Service award Ft. Hays State U., 1982. Mem. NEA, Kans. Tchrs. Assn. (pres. 1969-70), Am. Econ. Assn., Phi Kappa Phi, Sigma Phi Sigma, Pi Gamma Mu, Phi Delta Kappa, Lambda Delta Lambda, Kappa Mu Epsilon. Lutheran. Home: 458 Leisure World Mesa AZ 85206

GARWOOD, VICTOR PAUL, educator; b. Detroit, Sept. 13, 1917; s. Paul J. and Helen (Garwood) Schultz; m. Dorothy Ann Olson, Mar. 13, 1942; children: Don P., Martha Hill. B.A., U. Mich., 1939, M.S., 1948, Ph.D., 1952. Teaching fellow, head exam. div. Speech-Hearing Clinic, U. Mich., 1946-50; instr., asst. prof., asso. prof., prof. dept. speech U. So. Calif., Los Angeles, 1950-67, prof., chmn. grad. program in communication disorders, 1967-71; on leave as sr. ednl. audiologist Los Angeles Unified Sch. Dist., 1972-76; prof. speech communication and otolaryngology, 1964—; cons. audiology Childrens Hosp., Los Angeles, Los Angeles County-U. So. Calif. Med. Center; cons. audiology and speech pathology Medi-Cal Benefits div. and com. on employees with disabilities Dept. Health Services, State of Calif., 1970—; Mem. profl. adv. com. on speech and hearing Welfare Planning Council Los Angeles, 1966-68; mem. hearing aid dispensers examining com. Bd. Med. Quality Assurance State Calif., 1971-79, chmn., 1977—. Contbr. articles to profl. jours. Postdoctoral fellow NIH, 1957-58; Spl. Research fellow NIH, 1960-63. Fellow Am. Speech and Hearing Assn.; mem. Am., Western psychol. assns., Psychonomic Soc., Acoustical Soc. Am., Acad. Rehabilative Audiology, Calif. Speech and Hearing Assn. (Honors of Assn. 1983), AAUP, Sigma. Xi. Home: 1240 Chautauqua Blvd Pacific Palisades CA 90272 Office: 734 W Adams Blvd Los Angeles CA 90007

GARWOOD, WILLIAM LOCKHART, lawyer, federal judge; b. Houston, Oct. 29, 1931; s. Wilmer St. John and Ellen Burdine (Clayton) G.; m. Merle Castlyn Haffler, Aug. 12, 1955; children: William Lockhart, Mary Elliott. B.A., Princeton U., 1952; LL.B. with honors, U. Tex., 1955. Bar: Tex. 1955, U.S. Supreme Ct. 1959. Law clk. to judge U.S. Ct. Appeals for 5th Circuit, 1955-56; mem. firm Graves, Dougherty, Hearon, Moody & Garwood (and predecessor firms), Austin, Tex., 1959-79, 81, partner, 1961-79, 81; asso. justice Supreme Ct. Tex., Austin, 1979-80; judge U.S. Ct. Appeals, 5th circuit, Austin, 1981—; dir. Anderson, Clayton & Co., 1976-79, 81, exec. com., 1977-79, 81. Pres. Child and Family Service of Austin, 1970-71, St. Andrew's Episcopal Sch., Austin, 1972; bd. dirs. Community Council Austin and Travis County, 1968-72, Human Opportunities Corp. Austin and Travis County, 1966-70, Mental Health and Mental Retardation Center Austin and Travis County, 1966-69, United Fund Austin and Travis County, 1971-73; mem. adv. bd. Salvation Army, Austin, 1972—. Served with U.S. Army, 1956-59. Fellow Am. Bar Found.; mem. Am. Law Inst., Tex. Bar Found. (life mem.), ABA, Am. Judicature Soc., Order of Coif, Chancellors, Phi Delta Phi. Episcopalian. Office: U.S. Courthouse 200 W 8th St Austin TX 78701

GARWOOD, WILMER ST. JOHN, lawyer, former judge; b. Bastrop, Tex., Dec. 15, 1896; s. Hiram M. and Hettie (Page) G.; m. Ellen

Clayton, July 11, 1927; children—Wilmer St. John, William Lockhart. A.B., Georgetown U., 1917; postgrad., U. Tex., 1919; LL.B., Harvard, 1922. Bar: Tex. bar 1919, N.Y. bar 1923. Atty. legal dept. Texas Co., N.Y.C., 1922-23, Baker, Botts, Parker & Garwood, Houston, 1924-28; resident Am. counsel Standard Oil Co. (N.J.), Buenos Aires, 1929-33; mem. law firm Andrews, Kelley, Kurth & Campbell, Houston, 1934-41; pvt. practice, Houston, 1945-47; vice chmn. Houston Civil Service Commn., 1945-46; apptd. to Supreme Ct. of Tex., 1948, asso. justice, 1948-58; of counsel firm; Graves, Dougherty, Hearon, Moody & Garwood (and predecessor), Austin, 1958—; prof. law U. Tex., 1961; dir. Austin Nat. Bank. Mem. U.S. delegation to Atlantic Congress, London, 1959; pres. Tex. Civil Jud. Council, 1964-71; A founder St. John's Sch., Houston, 1945; trustee U. Tex. Law Sch. Found. Served as 1st lt. Cav., 1918-23; Tex. N.G.; from lt. to lt. comdr., naval intelligence USNR, 1942-45. Decorated Orden al Merito, Chile; hon. consul Poland for Tex., 1937-39. Fellow Am. Bar Found.; Mem. Am. Bar Assn., Am. Law Inst., Austin C. of C., Philos. Soc. Tex. (pres. 1960), English Speaking Union, Am. Judicature Soc. (dir. 1963-68), Order of Coif (hon.), Phi Delta Phi (hon.), Phi Delta Theta. Republican. Episcopalian (vestryman). Clubs: Kiwanis, Headliners. Home: 1802 San Gabriel St Austin TX 78701 Office: 2300 Austin Nat Bank Tower Austin TX 78701 *A true liberal is not a congenital crusader for change but a person who can see both sides of a question.*

GARY, BENJAMIN WALTER, JR., landscape architect; b. Richmond, Va., July 9, 1934; s. Benjamin Walter and Annie May (LaFoon) G.; m. Toby Sima Freedman, June 22, 1980; children by previous marriage—Brian Taylor, Melaney Anne, Heather Leigh. Student, Davidson Coll., 1950-51, N.C. State U., 1955; M.L.A., Harvard U., 1957. Pres. Moriece & Gary, Inc., Cambridge, Mass., 1957—; instr. Grad. Sch. Design, Harvard U., 1957-61; Mem. planning bd., Wayland, Mass., 1971-74; mem. Historic Dist. Commn., Wayland, 1972-74; chmn. Urban Design Commn., Gloucester, Mass., 1975-77. Tech. editor: Landscape Architects' Handbook of Professional Practice, 1977. Fellow Am. Soc. Landscape Architects (treas. 1971-73, v.p. 1974-75, pres. 1976-77); mem. Mass. Garden Club Fedn., Landscape Architecture Found. (dir. 1973-77). Democrat. Quaker. Office: 25 Mt Auburn St Cambridge MA 02138

GARY, CHARLES LESTER, educator, consultant; b. Cin., Nov. 2, 1917; s. Frank Lester and Beulah (Merrick) G.; m. Louise Mary Levermann, June 7, 1947; children—Curt Louis, Rob Lawrence. B.A., Yale U., 1939, postgrad., 1939-40; student, Cin. Coll. Music, 1940-41, Cin. Conservatory Music, 1949-50; M.Ed., U. Cin., 1947, Ed.D., 1951. Tchr. music Cin. Pub. Schs., 1941-42, Camden (Ohio) Schs., 1946-47; prof. music Austin Peay State Coll., Clarksville, Tenn., 1947-58, head dept., 1951-58; mem. staff Music Educators Nat. Conf., Washington, 1958-76, exec. sec., 1968-76; coordinator Arts and HEW project, 1976-77; copyright cons. Nat. Music Pubs. Assn., 1976—; cons. Va. Council Arts.; dir. choirs Trinity Episcopal Ch., Clarksville, 1956-58, St. John's Episcopal Ch., McLean, Va., 1959-70; vis. prof. dept. creative arts Purdue U., 1976; adj. prof. Am. U.; prof. Cath. U. Am., 1982—. Author: Career in Music Education, 1962, Vignettes of Music Education History, 1964, (with K.D. Ernst) Music in General Education, 1965, Arts Education Advocacy, 1976, Music Educator's Guide to the New Copyright Law, 1976, The New Copyright Law and Education, 1977, Flower Fables, 1978, Try a New Face, 1979; Editor: Music Buildings, Rooms and Equipment, 1966, The Study of Music in the Elementary School, 1967; Mng. editor: Jour. Research Music Edn, 1960-68; exec. dir.: Music Educators Jour, 1968-76; mem. editorial bd.: Ednl. Forum, 1979—. Mem. edn. com. John F. Kennedy Center Performing Arts; dir. Center Ednl. Assns., Reston, Va. Served with AUS, 1942-45. Recipient Distinguished Alumnus award U. Cin. Conservatory Music, 1971, Yale Band Disting. Alumnus award, 1981. Mem. Music Educators Nat. Conf., Alliance Assns. Advancement Edn. (pres. 1974-75), Internat. Soc. Music Edn., Kappa Delta Pi, Phi Mu Alpha. Republican. Episcopalian. Clubs: University, Yale (Washington). Home: 7024 Santa Maria Ct McLean VA 22101

GARY, JAMES FREDERICK, business executive; b. Chgo., Dec. 28, 1920; s. Rex Inglis and Mary Naomi (Roller) G.; m. Helen Elizabeth Gellert, Sept. 3, 1947; children: David Frederick, John William, James Scott, Mary Anne. B.S., Haverford (Pa.) Coll., 1942. With Wash. Energy Co., and predecessors, Seattle, 1947-67; v.p. Wash. Energy Co., 1956-67; pres. Pacific Resources Inc., and predecessor, Honolulu, 1967-79; chmn., chief exec. officer Pacific Resources Inc., 1979—, also dir.; dir. Bancorp. Hawaii, Inc., Bank of Hawaii, Brewer Pacific Agronomics Co., Castle & Cooke, Inc., Wash. Energy Co., Seattle, Airborne Freight Corp., Seattle, GDC, Inc., Chgo., Research Corp. of U. Hawaii, 1971-77, chmn., 1974-77. Pres. Chief Seattle council Boy Scouts Am., 1966-67, Aloha council, 1973-74; mem. Nat. council, 1964—, v.p. western region, 1978—, mem. exec. bd.; chmn. Aloha United Way, 1978, pres., 1979, chmn., pres., 1980; dir., officer or trustee Oahu Devel. Conf., Hawaii Employers Council, Hawaii Loa Coll., Friends of East-West Center, Honolulu Symphony Soc. Served to capt. AUS, 1942-46. Recipient Distinguished Eagle award Boy Scouts Am., 1972, Silver Beaver award, 1966, Silver Antelope award, 1976. Mem. Am. Gas Assn. (dir. 1970-74), Pacific Gas Assn. (pres. 1974, Basford trophy 1960), Nat. LP-Gas Assn. (dir. 1967-70), Hawaii C. of C. (chmn. 1979), Inst. Gas Tech., Chgo. (trustee 1975—), Nat. Petroleum Council, Hawaii Dist. Export Council, Japan-Calif. Assn., Japan-Hawaii Econ. Council, Pacific Basin Econ. Council, Japan-Am. Soc. Honolulu, Pacific Forum. Episcopalian. Clubs: Pacific Union (San Francisco); Rotary, Oahu Country, Waialae Country, Outrigger Canoe, Pacific, Plaza (Honolulu); Seattle Tennis, Wash. Athletic (Seattle). Office: 733 Bishop St PO Box 3379 Honolulu HI 96842

GARY, JAMES HUBERT, chemical engineer, college research institute official; b. Victoria, Va., Nov. 18, 1921; s. James Edward and Jessie (DuPriest) G.; m. Jane Zerbee, July 18, 1945; children: Jane Lynne, Sue Ellen, Robert James, John Stephen. B.S., Va. Poly. Inst., 1942, M.S., 1946; Ph.D., U. Fla., 1951. From jr. engr. to group engr. tech. service div. Standard Oil Co., Ohio, 1946-52; asst. prof. chem. engring. U. Va., Charlottesville, 1952-56, research dir. engring. expt. sta., 1952-56; asso. prof. U. Ala., 1956-59, prof., 1959-60; chem. engr. So. Research Lab., U.S. Bur. Mines, 1957-60; prof., head chem. and petroleum-refining engring. dept. Colo. Sch. Mines, Golden, 1960-72, v.p. acad. affairs, 1972-79, dean faculty, 1977-79; dir., trustee Research Inst., 1970-72, 81—. Author: (with G. Handwerk) Technology and Economics, 1975; contbr. articles to profl. jours. Mem. tech. adv. com. Regional Air Pollution Control Adminstrn., Denver, 1967-74; mem. supply/delivery panel com. on nuclear and alt energy systems, chmn. subcom. on subecon. resources-shale oil NRC, 1976-78; mem. materials adv. com., chmn. oil shale tech. adv. com. Office Tech. Assessment, 1977-80; mem. adv. consortium U. Petroleum and Minerals, Saudi Arabia, 1975—; mem. Colo. Gov.'s Sci. and Tech. Adv. Council, 1980—. Served to maj. CAC AUS, 1942-46. Decorated Bronze Star. Fellow Am. Inst. Chem. Engrs. (sect. vice-chmn. 1962, chmn. 1963, Halliburton award for profl. achievement 1981); mem. Am. Chem. Soc., Am. Soc. for Engring. Edn. (sect. chmn.-elect 1978), Am. Inst. Mining Engring., Sigma Xi, Tau Beta Pi. Patentee in field. Home: 1021 18th St Golden CO 80401

GARY, RICHARD NEEL, steel company executive; b. Los Angeles, May 27, 1943; s. Gordon Neel and Kathryn Ann (Bell) G.; children: Mary Kathryn, John Carleton. A.B. in Econs, U. Calif., Berkeley, 1965; J.D., 1968. Bar: Calif. 1968. Asso. firm Hill, Farrer & Burrill, Los Angeles, 1969-72, Thelen, Marrin, Johnson & Bridges, San Francisco, 1972-78; with Kaiser Steel Corp., Oakland, Calif., 1978—, v.p., gen. counsel, sec., 1980-82, exec. v.p., 1982, pres., 1982—. Mem. Am. Bar Assn., State Bar Calif. Office: 300 Lakeside Dr Oakland CA 94604

GARY, WYNDHAM LEWIS, textile company executive; b. N.Y.C., Feb. 29, 1916; s. Irving Curtis and Marguerite (Case) G.; m. Shirley Davis Spaulding, Aug. 6, 1948; 1 son, Wyndham Bradford. B.A., Yale U., 1938, LL.B., 1941. Bar: N.Y. 1941. Assoc. mem. firm Breed, Abbott & Morgan, 1941-42, 46-60; with alien enemy control unit Dept. Justice, Washington, 1942-43; asst. gen. counsel J.P. Stevens & Co., Inc., 1961-64, asst. treas., 1965-68, treas., 1969-81, dir., mem. exec. com., 1974-81, cons., 1981—; adv. bd. Mfrs. Hanover Trust Co., N.Y.C. Mem. Rumson (N.J.) Boro Council, 1956-58; chmn. design com. Middletown (N.J.) Planning Bd., 1960-65; Bd. dirs., pres. J.P. Stevens & Co. Found. Served to capt. AUS, 1943-46. Mem. Am. Bar assn., Delta Kappa Epsilon, Phi Delta Phi. Episcopalian (sr. warden). Clubs: Rumson (N.J.) Country, Seabright (N.J.) Beach (bd. govs.); Princeton, Treasurers (N.Y.C.) (sec.-treas.). Home: 37 Highland Ave Fair Haven NJ 07701 Office: 1185 Ave of Americas New York NY 10036

GARZA, REYNALDO G., judge; b. Brownsville, Tex., July 7, 1915; s. Ygnacio and Zoila (Guerra) G.; m. Bertha Champion, June 9, 1943; children: Reynaldo G., David C., Ygnacio Daniel, Bertha Victoria, Monica Bernadette. B.A., LL.B., U. Tex.; LL.D. (hon.), U. St. Edwards, Austin, Tex., 1965. Bar: Tex. 1939. Pvt. practice, 1939-42, 46-50; partner firm Sharpe, Cunningham & Garza, 1950-60, Cunningham, Garza & Yznaga, 1960-61; U.S. dist. judge Dist. Tex., Brownsville, from 1961, U.S. dist. chief judge, 1974-79; judge U.S. Ct. Appeals (5th cir.), 1979—. Treas. Cameron County Child Welfare Bd., 1950-52; mem. Tex. Good Neighbor Commn., 1957-61; Commr. City Brownsville, 1947-49; Trustee Brownsville Ind. Sch. Dist., 1941-42. Served with USAAF, 1942-45. Recipient Pro Ecclesia et Pontifice medal Pope Pius XII, 1952; decorated knight Order St. Gregory the Great e Pius XII, 1954. Mem. Am., Cameron County bar assns., State Bar Tex. Office: PO Box 1129 Brownsville TX 78520

GARZIA, SAMUEL ANGELO, lawyer; b. Highland Park, Mich., July 7, 1920; s. Angelo and Josephine G.; m. Josephine Lupo, June 6, 1946; children: Sanuel Angelo, Sandra Jo, Frank. J.D., Wayne State U., Detroit, 1943. Bar: Mich. 1943. Asst. friend of ct., Wayne County, Mich., 1946-48, practice law, Detroit, 1948—; sr. ptnr. Vandeveer, Garzia, Tonkin, Kerr & Heaphy, 1960—. Served with AUS, 1943-45; ETO. Decorated Bronze Star; Croix de Guerre, Luxembourg). Mem. ABA, Mich. Bar Assn., Detroit Bar Assn. (dir. 1976-83), Oakland Bar Assn., Assn. Def. Counsel Mich. (1st pres. 1966-67), Internat. Assn. Ins. Counsel, Am. Coll. Trial Lawyers, Am. Legion (judge advocate Mich. 1958). Roman Catholic. Home: 5229 Greenbriar Ct West Bloomfield MI 48033 Office: 333 W Fort St Detroit MI 48226

GASCH, OLIVER, judge; b. Washington, May 4, 1906; s. Herman E. and Marie (Manning) G.; m. Sylvia Meyer, Oct. 17, 1942; 1 son, Michael Barrett. A.B., Princeton, 1928; LL.B., George Washington U., 1932. Bar: D.C. bar 1931. Asst. corp. counsel for D.C., 1937-53; prin. asst. U.S. atty. for D.C., 1953-56; U.S. atty. for D.C., Washington, 1956-61; partner Craighill Aiello, Gasch & Craighill, 1961-65; judge U.S. Dist. Ct. for D.C., 1965—; gen counsel Interstate Commn. on Potomac River Basin, 1940-60; chmn. Council on D.C. Law Enforcement, 1958-62; mem. Jud. Conf. D.C. Circuit; co-chmn. Commrs. Crime Council, 1962-63. Mem. dean's council Georgetown U. Law Center, 1960-65. Served as lt. col. Judge Adv. Gen. Dept. AUS, 1942-46; PTO; Served as lt. col. Judge Adv. Gen. Dept. U.S. Army Res.; ret. Fellow Am. Coll. Trial Lawyers, Am. Bar Found.; mem. Fed. Bar Assn. (chmn. of com. of gen. counsel of fed. govt. 1960-61), ABA, D.C. (dir. 1961-63, pres. 1964-65) bar assns., Am. Law Inst., Barristers of Washington (pres. 1962-63), Res. Officers Assn. (past pres. D.C. dept.), Inst. Mil. Law, Judge Adv.'s Assn., Mil. Order Fgn. Wars (comdr. D.C. 1956), Law Alumni George Washington U. (pres.), Selden Soc. (London, Eng.), Phi Delta Phi. Republican. Episcopalian (vestryman, chancellor, v.p. exec. council diocese of Washington 1961-64, dep. to gen. conv. 1961, 64). Clubs: University, Lawyers, Princeton (Washington); Counsellors; Princeton (N.Y.C.); Chevy Chase. Office: US Courthouse 3d and Constitution Aves NW Washington DC 20001

GASCON, ANDRE, pulp and paper company executive; b. Montreal, Apr. 4, 1939; s. Joseph and Juliette (Gadbois) G. B.A., Coll. Brebeuf, Monteal, 1959; LL.B., U. Montreal, 1962. Bar: Que. 1963. Legal counsel Halperin & Moris, Montreal, 1963, Domtar Inc., 1963-67, asst. sec., legal counsel, 1967-75, asst. sec., gen. counsel, 1975-78, v.p., gen. counsel, sec., 1978—. Mem. Can. Bar Assn., ABA, U.S. Salt Inst., Assn. des SEc. et chefs de contentieux du Que.

GASIOROWICZ, STEPHEN GEORGE, physics educator; b. Gdansk, Poland, May 10, 1928; came to U.S., 1946, naturalized, 1952; s. Alexander A. and Maria K. (Landau) G.; m. Hilde E. Fromm, Apr. 4, 1953; children: Nina E., Catherine A., Mara E. B.A., UCLA, 1948, M.A., 1949, Ph.D., 1952; postgrad., U. Delhi, 1945-46. Physicist Lawrence Radiation Lab., U. Calif. at Berkeley, 1952-60; assoc. prof. physics U. Minn., 1960-63, prof., 1963—; NSF fellow Bohr Inst., Copenhagen, Denmark, 1957-58; vis. scientist Max Planck Inst. Physics and Astrophysics, Munich, Germany, 1959-60, Nordita, 1964, Deutsches Elektronen Synchrotron, Hamburg, Germany, 1968-69, 80, Tokyo U., 1982; cons. Argonne Nat. Lab., 1961-70. Author: Elementary Particle Physics, 1966, Quantum Physics, 1974, Structure of Matter, 1979. Trustee Aspen Center for Physics, 1980—. Fellow Am. Phys. Soc. Home: 2786 Dean Pkwy Minneapolis MN 55416

GASIOROWSKA, XENIA, Slavic literature educator; b. Kiev, Russia; came to U.S., 1945, naturalized, 1964; d. Grzegorz and Magdalena (Olszewska) Zytomirski; m. Zygmunt J. Gasiorowski, Mar. 3; 1949. Ph.D. in Slavic Langs. and Lit, U. Calif.-Berkeley, 1949. Mem. faculty U. Wis., Madison, 1949—, prof. Slavic lit., 1965-81, prof. emerita, 1981—; Vis. asso. prof. Wellesley Coll., 1958-59. Author: Women in Soviet Fiction, 1917-1964, 1968, The Image of Peter the Great in Russian Fiction, 1979; also 3 vols. verse and a novel in Polish. Nat. Endowment for Humanities fellow, 1980-81. Mem. AAUP, Am. Assn. Tchrs. Slavic and E. European Langs., Polish Acad. Scis. in Am. Office: Slavic Dept Univ Wis Madison WI 53706 Mailing Address: 1608 Adams St Madison WI 53711

GASKELL, CHARLES THOMAS, bishop; b. St. Paul, Oct. 23, 1919; s. Chester Welles and Gertrude Pauline (Michaud) G.; m. Mabel Harriet Armitage, June 1, 1944; 3 children. B.A., U. Minn., 1940; B.D., Seabury Western Theol. Sem., Ill., 1944; D.D. (hon.), 1967. Ordained deacon Episcopal Ch., 1944, priest, 1944; priest-in-charge Holy Trinity Ch., International Falls, Minn. and St. Peters Ch., Warroad, Minn., 1944-48; curate St. Matthews Ch., Evanston, Ill., 1948-49; rector Trinity Ch., Rock Island, Ill., 1949-57, St. Mark's Ch., Milw., 1958-66, St. Lukes Ch., Evanston, Ill., 1966-70; dean St. Lukes Cathedral, Orlando, Fla., 1971-74; bishop Diocese of Milw., 1974—. Office: 804 E Juneau Ave Milwaukee WI 53202 *

GASKELL, JAMES SHIELDS, JR., banker; b. Evergreen, Ala., Nov. 12, 1921; s. James Shields and Annie Lois (Wiggins) G.; m. Dorothy Dale, Sept. 6, 1947; children: Dale, Barbara Ann, Lauri. B.S., U. Ala., 1943; postgrad., Sch. Banking of South, La. State U., 1957. With VA, 1946-47, Dun & Bradstreet, 1947-50; pres., chmn. bd. First Nat. Bank (now First Ala. Bank of Montgomery), 1951—; dir. Jenkins Brick Co. Served with inf. AUS, 1943-46. Decorated Silver Star, Bronze Star. Mem. Ala. Bankers Assn. (exec. com.), Montgomery Area C. of C. (1st v.p.). Baptist. Clubs: Kiwanis, Montgomery Country, Capitol City. Office: First Alabama Bank of Montgomery 8 Commerce St Montgomery AL 36104 *

GASKELL, ROBERT EUGENE, mathematician, educator; b. Grelton, Ohio, Jan. 18, 1912; s. Eugene R. and Effie (Fish) G.; m. Jane Ardith Weyand, Aug. 22, 1940; children—Ellen Gaskell Alcock, Robert Weyand. A.B., Albion Coll., 1933; Ph.D., U. Mich., 1940. Instr. math. U. Ala., 1940-42; research asso. Brown U., 1942-46; asst. prof., then asso. prof. math. Iowa State U., 1947-51; supr. math. services unit Boeing Airplane Co., 1951-59; prof. math. Oreg. State U., 1959-66, Naval Postgrad. Sch., Monterey, Calif., 1966-80, chmn., 1966-72, prof. emeritus, 1980—; cons. in field, 1944—. Author: Engineering Mathematics, 1958; contbr. articles to profl. jours. Fellow AAAS; mem. Am. Soc. Engring. Edn. (chmn. math. div. 1966, 73-75), Soc. Indsl. and Applied Math. (council 1959-63), Math. Assn. Am. (chmn. vis. lectrs. com. 1963-67, chmn. corp. mems. com. 1972-75), Phi Beta Kappa, Sigma Xi. Home: 1207 Sylvan Rd Monterey CA 93940

GASKILL, ROBERT CLARENCE, retired army officer; b. Yonkers, N.Y., Apr. 12, 1931; s. John Clement and Armania Drucilla (Jones) G.; m. Erotida Maria Ponce, June 19, 1954; children: Robert Clarence, Vivienne Renee, Juli Anne Gaskill Henderson, Cheryl Lynn. B.A. cum laude, Howard U., 1952; M.B.A., George Washington U., 1960; grad. various army schs. Commd. 2d lt. U.S. Army, 1952, advanced through grades to maj. gen., 1977; service in, Korea, Vietnam and, Europe, comdr. Letterkenny Army Depot, Chambersburg, Pa., 1974-75, comdg. gen. 1st Support Brigade, Kaiserslautern, Ger., 1975-76, dep. comdg. gen. 21st Support Command, 1976-77, dep. comdt. Army War Coll., Carlisle Barracks, Pa., 1977-78, dep. dir. Def. Logistics Agy., Cameron Sta., Va., 1978-81, ret., 1981; cons., assoc. professorial lectr. bus. and public adminstrn. No. Va. Community Coll., Woodbridge, 1981—; instr. acctg. U. Va., Ft. Lee, 1962; lectr. in field. Author essays, book reports in field. Dist. commr. Boy Scouts Am., W. Ger., 1975-77; founding mem. Woodbridge High Sch. Choral Boosters Club, 1979—. Decorated D.S.M., Legion of Merit, Meritorious Service medal with oak leaf cluster, Army Commendation medal with oak leaf cluster; Honor medal 1st class, (Republic of Vietnam). Mem. Assn. U.S. Army, Am. Def. Preparedness Assn., Am. Mgmt. Assn., NAACP, Omega Psi Phi. Office: No Va Community Coll 15200 Smoketown Rd Woodbridge VA 22191 *God is—and cares; He controls—but shares and spares. Be at peace with Him. Find needs worth filling—and fill them well. There is great success-fulfillment value in service, constructive teamwork and helping others succeed. Strive, with God's help, for self-dependence, integrity, charity and balance—in perspective and activity. Family and friends are anchor in a storm. Be part of the anchor—not the storm.*

GASKILL, WILLIAM JOHN, public relations executive; b. Trenton, N.J., June 5, 1910; s. William Richard and Jane (McCarran) G.; m. Mary Alice Duggan, June 5, 1936; children: Patricia, Jo-ann. A.B., Rutgers U., 1937, LL.D. (hon.), 1978; postgrad., Pa. State U., 1938-42. Reporter Trenton State Gazette, 1934-38; instr. Pa. State U., 1938-42; editor Am. Inst. Pub. Opinion (Gallup Poll), 1942-47; exec. v.p. Hawaiian Econ. Found., Honolulu, 1947-49; dir. pub. relations Hawaiian Pineapple Co., Honolulu, 1949-54; partner Ivy Lee & T.J. Ross, N.Y.C., 1954-62; exec. v.p. T.J. Ross & Assos., Inc., N.Y.C., 1962-65, pres., 1965-71, chmn. bd., 1971-80; Faculty asso. Ind. U. Grad. Sch. Bus., 1963-66. Trustee Rutgers U., 1965-71, chmn. bd. trustees, 1971-74, bd. govs., 1974—, chmn. bd. govs., 1976-77; mem. council Rutgers U. Press, 1974—; mem. Rutgers U. Found., 1972—, pres. found., 1972-75; bd. dirs. Roper Research Center, Williams Coll., Willamstown, Mass. Mem. Am. Sociol. Soc., Am. Statis. Assn., Acad. Polit. Sci., Am. Assn. Pub. Opinion Research, Pub. Relations Soc. Am. (treas., dir. 1966-67, mem. accreditation bd. 1965—, chmn. 1968-70), Phi Beta Kappa, Delta Kappa Epsilon. Clubs: Cloud (N.Y.C.) (bd. govs., pres. 1972-73); Whippoorwill Country (Armonk N.Y.)). Home: 17 Briarwood Ln Pleasantville NY 10570 Office: 405 Lexington Ave New York NY 10017

GASPARRO, FRANK, sculptor; b. Phila., Aug. 26, 1909; s. Bernard and Rosa G.; m. Julia Florence Johnston, Nov. 11, 1939; 1 dau., Christina Julia. Ed., Phila. Indsl. Arts, Pa. Acad. Fine Arts. With U.S. Mint, Phila., 1942—, asst. chief engraver-sculptor, 1962-65, chief-sculptor engraver, 1965-81; instr. sculpture Fleisher Art Meml., Phila., Pa. Acad. Fine Arts, 1981. Designer: Am. coinage including Lincoln Meml. cent reverse, 1959, John F. Kennedy half-dollar reverse, 1964, Eisenhower dollar, 1972, Susan B. Anthony dollar, 1979, Phila. Medal of Honor, 1955; FAO medals Lillian Carter and Shirley Temple Black; Presdl. medals Congl. Medal of Honor; George Washington bicentennial medal, fgn. coinage including, Philippine Islands, 1967, Panama, 1971, 75, Guatemala, 1943. Recipient Order of Merit Italian Republic, 1973, United Vets. Am. Distinguished Citizen award of Phila., 1975, Outstanding Achievement award Da Vinci Art Alliance, 1967; Cresson Traveling scholar, 1930, 31. Fellow Pa. Acad. Fine Arts (Percy Owens award 1979); mem. Le Club Francais de la Medaille of Paris. Home: 216 Westwood Park Dr Havertown PA 19083 *Every day is a challenge to me: to plan, to approach my problems and to solve them. In my execution of my art work the ultimate goal is for its appreciation and enjoyment by my fellow man. I do not consider what I have done in the past but look forward to the next project, I always feel that the great ones are looking over my shoulder to see how I perform and what the results are. The challenge to me is what makes my day worthwhile.*

GASS, CLINTON BURKE, mathematics educator; b. Lake Wilson, Minn., Jan. 9, 1920; s. Frederick G. and Elvira A. (Burke) G.; m. Myrtle Brewer, Oct. 18, 1941; children: Frederick S., Kenneth B., Glenn C. A.B. magna cum laude, Gustavus Adolphus Coll., 1941; M.A., U. Nebr., 1943, Ph.D., 1954. Instr. math. U. Nebr., 1942-43; asso. prof. math. Nebr. Wesleyan U., 1943-46, prof., 1946-47, 53-54, prof., dean of men, 1947-53; asso. prof. math. DePauw U., Greencastle, Ind., 1954-56, prof., 1956-64, John T. and Margaret Deal prof. math., 1964—, head dept. math. and computer sci., 1960—; resident dir. DePauw Program in Freiburg, Germany, 1977; Asso. program dir., tchr. edn. sect. NSF, 1965-66; cons. Dept. Def. Overseas Schs. in Europe, 1969-70; lectr. Challenge Program Dept. Def., 1978-83. Served with AUS, 1944-46. Decorated knight York Cross of Honour; recipient Disting. Alumni award in edn. Gustavus Adolphus Coll., 1968; cited for heroism by Nat. Ct. of Honor of Boy Scouts Am. Mem. Am. Math. Soc., Math. Assn. Am. (chmn. Neb. 1949-50, Ind. 1957-58), Sigma Xi, Phi Kappa Phi, Pi Mu Epsilon, Sigma Pi Sigma. Clubs: Masons, Shriners. Home: 707 Highridge Ave Greencastle IN 46135

GASS, MANUS M., accountant; b. Montreal, Que., Can., June 28, 1928; came to U.S., 1948, naturalized, 1953; s. Maurice and Bertha (Silverberg) G.; m. Estella L. Gass; children: Thomas Evan, Winifred Caitlyn. Student, McGill U., 1945-48; B.B.A. cum laude, CCNY, 1953. C.P.A., N.Y. Pres., dir. Buitoni Foods Corp., South Hackensack, N.J., 1966—; dir. Buitoni Perugina Inc., N.Y.C., Perugina Chocolates & Confections Inc., Little Ferry, N.J.; acct. Am. Jewish Tercentenary Com., 1953-54. Chmn. River Edge-Oradell United Jewish Appeal,

1964-65, 67-76; mem. Shade Tree Commn., River Edge, 1974-77; bd. govs. Hackensack Med. Center. Mem. Am. Inst. C.P.A.s, N.Y. State Soc. C.P.A.s, Fin. Execs. Inst. Home: 184 Woodland Ave River Edge NJ 07661

GASS, RAYMOND WILLIAM, lawyer, meat packing company executive; b. Chgo., Apr. 6, 1937; s. William Frederick and Clara Gertrude (Grotman) G.; m. Patricia Ann Thomas, Apr. 20, 1968; children: Elizabeth Ann, Katharine Patricia, Christina Susanne. A.B., Purdue U., 1959; LL.B., U. Ill., 1962. Bar: Ill. Patent examiner U.S. Patent Office, Washington, 1962-63; atty. Armour and Co., Chgo., 1963-70; sr. atty. Greyhound Corp., Chgo., 1970-71; sr. v.p., gen. counsel, sec. John Morrell & Co., Chgo., 1971—; dir. Am. Chemet Corp., Chgo. Mem. ABA, Chgo. Bar Assn. (chmn. com. corp. law depts. 1975-77). Office: 191 Waukegan Rd Northfield IL 60093

GASS, WILLIAM H., author, educator; b. 1924. A.B., Kenyon Coll., 1947, L.H.D. (hon.), 1973, 82; Ph.D., Cornell U., 1953. Prof. philosophy Purdue U., U. Ill.; Disting. Univ. prof. in humanities Washington U., St. Louis, 1980—. Author: Omensetter's Luck, 1966, In the Heart of the Heart of the Country and Other Stories, 1968, Willie Masters' Lonesome Wife, 1968, Fiction and the Figures of Life, 1970, On Being Blue, 1976, The World Within the Word, 1978, The Habitations of the Word, 1984. Address: Washington U Saint Louis MO 63130

GASSER, HENRY MARTIN, artist; b. Newark, Oct. 31, 1909; s. William Henry and Mary Teresa (Jansus) G.; m. Joane Rone, May 27, 1930. Student, Fawcett Art Sch., 1924-25, Newark Sch. Fine and Indsl. Art, 1928-34, Grand Central Art Sch., 1935, Art Students League, 1938-41. Dir. Newark Sch. Fine and Indsl. Art, 1946-54; past. pres. N.J. Art Council; lectr. Am. Water Color Soc., Nat. Acad. Audubon Artists, Allied Artists Am., Mobile Art League, Shreveport Art Club, Art Assn. Guild New Orleans. Has exhibited in most well known museums and art galleries, throughout U.S.; represented in: collections of numerous museums and galleries, including Nat. Collection of Fine Arts at, Smithsonian Instn., Met., Phila., Boston, Newark museums; Author: motion picture Exploring Casein, 1962; Casein Painting Methods and Demonstrations, Oil Painting Methods and Demonstrations, Water color—How to Do It, Techniques of Painting, Techniques of Painting the Waterfront, Techniques of Picture Making, How to Draw and Paint. Served with inf. AUS, 1944-45. Recipient many honors and awards, The most recent Am. Watercolor Soc., 1980, Nat. Art Club, 1981. Mem. N.A.D., Nat. Arts Club (life), Am. Water Color Soc. (past v.p.), N.J. Water Color Soc., past pres.), Cal. Water Color Soc., Allied Artists Am., Conn. Acad., Audubon Artists, Artists and Craftsmen Asso., Acad. Artists Assn., Am. Artists Profl. League, Royal Soc. Art London. Clubs: Philadelphia Water Color, Baltimore Water Color, New Haven Paint and Clay. Address: 654 Varsity Rd South Orange NJ 07079

GASSERE, EUGENE ARTHUR, lawyer, bus. exec.; b. Beaumont, Tex., Oct. 20, 1930; s. Victor Eugene and Althea June (Haight) G.; m. Mary Alice Engelhard, Aug. 4, 1956; children—Paul, John, Anne. B.S., U. Wis., 1952, J.D., 1956; postgrad., Oxford U., 1956-57. Bar: Wis. bar 1956. Asst. counsel Wurlitzer Co., Chgo., 1958-61, Campbell Soup Co., Camden, N.J., 1961-65; asst. to pres. Thilmany Pulp & Paper Co., Kaukauna, Wis., 1966-68; with Skyline Corp., Elkhart, Ind., 1968—, v.p., gen. counsel, asst. sec., 1973—. Pres., bd. dirs. Elkhart Urban League, 1972-73, Elkhart Symphony, 1975-76, Elkhart Concert Club, 1976-77. Served with U.S. Army, 1952-54. Mem. Am. Bar Assn., Wis. Bar Assn., Am. Soc. Corp. Secs., Phi Mu Alpha. Home: 420 Aspin Dr Elkhart IN 46514 Office: 2520 Bypass Rd Elkhart IN 46515

GASSERT, ROBERT GEORGE, university administrator; b. Milw., July 6, 1921; s. Joseph C. and Emily (Bier) G. B.A., St. Louis U., 1945, M.A., 1948, Ph.L., 1948; S.T.L., St. Mary's (Kans.) Coll., 1955; S.T.D., Gregorian U., Rome, 1958. Joined S.J., Roman Catholic Ch., 1941; ordained priest Roman Catholic Ch., 1954; tchr. Campion High Sch., Prairie du Chien, Wis., 1949-51; mem. faculty Marquette U., 1958-79, dean, 1963-79, prof. theology, 1975—, v.p., 1979—. Author: (with Bernard H. Hall) Psychiatry and Religious Faith. Theol. fellow Menninger Found., 1962-63. Mem. Assn. Higher Edn., Assn. Am. Colls., Jesuit, Nat. Cath. edn. assns., N. Central Assn. Home: 1404 W Wisconsin Ave Milwaukee WI 53233

GASTIL, RUSSELL GORDON, geologist, educator; b. San Diego, June 25, 1928; s. Russell Chester and Frances (Duncan) G.; m. Emily Janet Manly, Sept. 13, 1958; children—Garth Manly, Mary Margaret, George Christopher, John Webster. A.B, U. Calif. at Berkeley, 1950, Ph.D., 1954. With Shell Oil Co., 1954, Canadian Javelin Co., 1956-58; lectr. U. Calif. at Los Angeles, 1958-59; faculty San Diego State U., 1959—, prof. geology, 1965—, chmn. dept., 1969-72. Publisher: We Can Save San Diego, 1975; Contbr. papers to profl. lit. Democratic candidate U.S. Ho. of Reps., 1976; mem. Calif. Dem. Central Com., 1977-78; coordinator 41st Congl. dist. Common Cause, 1977; pres. Grossmont-Mt. Helix Improvement Assn., 1978-80; mem. San Diego County Air Pollution Hearing Bd., 1977-80. Fellow Geol. Soc. Am. (vice chmn. Cordilleran sect. 1967); mem. AAAS, Soc. Econ. Mineralogists and Paleontologists, Am. Geophys. Union. Home: 9435 Alto Dr La Mesa CA 92041 Office: San Diego State U San Diego CA 92182

GASTINEAU, CLIFFORD FELIX, physician; b. Pawnee, Okla., Dec. 18, 1920; s. Felix Thomas and Grace Lucille (Rice) G.; m. Patricia Murphey, Mar. 16, 1951; children—Dennis Arthur, John Edward. B.A., U. Okla., 1941, M.D. with honors, 1943; Ph.D. in Medicine, U. Minn., 1950. Intern U. Colo. Hosps., Denver, 1943-44; resident in medicine Mayo Found., Rochester, Minn., 1944-50; mem. staff Mayo Clinic, 1950—; cons. in internal medicine, endocrinology and nutrition, 1950—; Endicott prof. medicine Mayo Med. Sch., 1977—. Co-author: Obesity, 1949; editor: Diabetes Forecast, 1965-74; co-editor: Fermented Food Beverages in Nutrition, 1979. Served as officer M.C. AUS, 1953-55. Fellow A.C.P.; mem. Am. Diabetes Assn., AAAS, AMA, Am. Soc. Clin. Nutrition, Central Soc. Clin. Research, Sigma Xi, Phi Beta Kappa. Presbyterian. Office: Mayo Clinic 200 1st St SW Rochester MN 55901

GASTLER, HAROLD LEE, railroad executive; b. Wellsville, Mo., May 16, 1927; s. Leo J. and Thelma L. (Oliver) G.; m. Joyce D. Isman, Sept. 13, 1952; 1 son, Kim Leigh. B.S. in Engring., U. Mo., 1951; grad., Advanced Mgmt. Program, Harvard U., 1962. With Frisco R.R., 1951-66, v.p. staff, 1962-63, gen. mgr., 1963-66; pres. Toledo, Peoria & Western R.R., Peoria, Ill., 1966-67; v.p. ops. Chgo. & Northwestern R.R., Chgo., 1968-73; pres., chief operating officer Missouri-Kansas-Texas R.R. Co., Dallas, 1973—. Served to ensign USN, 1945-46. Democrat. Lutheran. Office: Mo.-Kans-Tex RR Katy Bldg Dallas TX 75202 *

GASTON, DAVID AIKEN, lawyer; b. Waynesville, N.C., Aug. 21, 1903; s. Arthur Lee and Virginia Carolina (Aiken) G.; m. Reubie Holliday, May 9, 1931; children: Virginia Aiken (Mrs. Julian Hennig), Arthur Lee. A.B., U. S.C., 1924, M.A., 1926, LL.B., 1926; student, Columbia. Bar: S.C. 1926. Since practiced in, Chester; partner firm Gaston, Gaston & Marion, P.A., 1948—; pres. Chester Bldg. & Loan Assn., 1970-76, also dir. Author: Chester County Economic and Social, 1924. Mem. S.C. Hwy. Commn., 1956-60, chmn., 1959-60; chmn. Chester dist. Boy Scouts Am., 1955; mem. exec. bd. Palmetto area council, 1955—; pres. Chester Area United Fund, 1957-58; Mem. S.C. Ho. of Reps. from Chester County, 1941-44; del. Democratic Nat. Conv., 1960; Trustee U. S.C., 1955-56; trustee Presbyn. Home S.C., vice chmn., 1970-76. Mem. ABA., S.C. Bar Assn. (pres. 1961-62), Chester County Bar Assn. (pres. 1955-57), S. Caroliniana Soc., Chester County Hist. Soc., Chester County C. of C. (pres. 1937-38), Kappa Alpha. Presbyn. (chmn. deacons 1948-49, 60-61, elder 1973-78). Club: Rotarian (pres. Chester County 1953-54). Home: Pinckney Rd Chester SC 29706 Office: Southern Bank & Trust Bldg Chester SC 29706

GASTON, GERALD NICHOLAS, insurance executive; b. Houma, La., Aug. 16, 1932; s. Nicholas Joseph and Helen (Voison) G.; m. Anita Houdek, Feb. 28, 1959; 1 son, Matt James. B.S., Nicholls State U., 1959; M.B.A., Loyola U., New Orleans, 1965. With Indsl. Fin. & Thrift Corp., New Orleans, 1959-73, coordinator, 1959-63, treas., 1963-71, sr. v.p. ops., 1971-73; pres., chief exec. officer La. Gulf Industries, Inc., Houma, 1973-77; vice chmn., exec. v.p., chief fin. officer Am. Bankers Ins. Group, Am. Bankers Life Assurance Co. Fla., Miami, 1977—; asso. prof. data processing Loyola U. of South, 1965-70. Served with USAF, 1952-56. Named Outstanding Alumnus, Nicholls State U., 1971. Mem. Greater Miami C. of C., Nat. Assn. Accts., Nat. Consumer Fin. Assn. Republican. Roman Catholic. Club: Coral Reef Yacht (Miami). Office: Am Bankers Ins Group 600 Brickell Ave Miami FL 33134 *

GASTON, WILLIAM W., agricultural products company executive; b. Fayetteville, N.C., 1926; married. B.S., Clemson U., 1949. With Gold Kist Inc., Atlanta, 1950—, sr. v.p., mem. mgmt. exec. com., 1972-77, exec. v.p., mem. mgmt. exec. com., 1977-78, pres., chmn. mgmt. exec. com., 1978—, chief exec. officer; dir. Central Bank Coops., Ga. No. Ry. Co., Cotton States Life and Health Ins. Co., Cotton States Mut. Ins. Co., Nat. Council Farmer Coops., So. Bell Te. & Tel. Co., Trust Co. Ga. Office: Gold Kist Inc 244 Perimeter Center Pkwy NE Box 2210 Atlanta GA 30301 *

GASTWIRTH, JOSEPH LEWIS, educator; b. N.Y.C.; s. Paul and Tillie (Scheinert) G. B.S. summa cum laude, Yale U., 1958; Ph.D., Columbia U., 1963. Research assoc. Stanford U., 1963-64; asst. prof., then assoc. prof. stats. Johns Hopkins U., 1964-70; vis. assoc. prof. Harvard U., 1970-71; vis. faculty adviser Office Mgmt. and Budget, 1971-72; prof. stats. and econs. George Washington U., 1972—; vis. prof. MIT, 1979; cons. Bur. Labor Statistics, 1972-74; panelist grad. student fellowship com. NSF, 1973; cons. Office Mgmt. and Budget, 1974-77, 81—; cons. law firms, 1974—. Author papers in field.; Assoc. editor: theory sect. Jour. Am. Statis. Assn, 1978-79; application sect., 1980-81, book rev. sect., 1983—. Bd. dirs. Monroe House Tenant Assn., 1979-84. Fellow Am. Statis. Assn. (chmn. com. on privacy and confidentiality 1975-77), Inst. Math. Stats. (fellows com. 1980-82, nominating com. 1980), AAAS; mem. Econometric Soc., Am. Econ. Soc., Internat. Statis. Inst., Wash. Statis. Soc. (pres. 1982-83). Home: 522 21st St NW Washington DC 20006 Office: 2201 G St NW Washington DC 20052

GATCHELL, SETH COLE, life insurance company executive; b. Kansas City, Mo., Aug. 26, 1926; s. James Whittier and Nellie Dean (Campbell) G.; m. Mary Margaret Greene, Jan. 26, 1951; children: Seth Cole, Sarah Jane, Jeffrey Holmes. B.S., U.S. Naval Acad., 1947; B.A., U. Mo., 1951. With pub. relations dept. Sta. WQED, Pitts., 1953-54; asst. mgr. Pitts. Symphony Soc., 1954-56; agt. Union Mut. Life Ins. Co., Pitts., 1956-59; supr., tng. dir., gen. agt. Pan-Am. Life Ins. Co., New Orleans, 1959-67; successively v.p., agy. dir., sr. v.p., pres. and chief exec. officer Lincoln Liberty Life Ins. Co., Nebr., 1967-80, also dir., Nebr.; pres. Consol. Programs, Inc., 1967-80; pres., chief exec. officer Midwest Life Ins. Co. Nebr., 1979-80; exec. v.p. USLife Corp., 1980-81; pres., chief exec. officer All Am. Life Ins. Co., 1981-83, vice chmn., 1984—; dir. 6 subs. life ins. cos. Served with USN, 1947-50, 51-53; Korea. Mem. Am. Coll. C.L.U.s, Nebr. Assn. Life Underwriters. Republican. Episcopalian. Office: 8501 W Higgins Rd Chicago IL 60631

GATELL, FRANK OTTO, educator; b. N.Y.C., July 28, 1931; s. Francisco Tomás and Ana María (Gutiérrez) G.; m. Kay Tapper, Feb. 10, 1956 (div. 1969); children—Susan, Lisa; m. Gabriela Fernández, Mar. 14, 1970; 1 son, Frank. B.A., Coll. City N.Y., 1956; A.M., Harvard U., 1958, Ph.D., 1960. Instr. U. Md., College Park, 1959-61, asst. prof., 1961-64; asso. prof. U. Calif. at Los Angeles, 1965-70, prof. history, 1970—; vis. prof. Stanford U., 1964-65, Universidad de Chile, Santiago, 1968. Author: John Gorham Palfrey and the New England Conscience, 1963, (with others) USA: An American Record, 1972, Freedom and Crisis, 3d edit, 1981; co-editor: American Themes, 1968, American Negro Slavery, 3d edit, 1979. Served with AUS, 1952-53. John Hay Whitney Found. fellow, 1958; Guggenheim Found. fellow, 1967-68; Fulbright prof. U. Buenos Aires, Argentina, 1972. Mem. Am., So. hist. assns., Orgn. Am. Historians. Democrat. Home: 810 California Ave Santa Monica CA 90403 Office: Dept History U Calif Los Angeles CA 90024

GATELY, GEORGE (GALLAGHER GATELY), cartoonist; b. Queens Village, N.Y., 1928. Attended, Pratt Inst., N.Y. Worked in advt., 11 yrs. Began cartooning, 1957; cartoons appeared in: This Week, others; created: Hapless Harry, 1964, Heathcliff, 1973—; numerous Heathcliff collections published. Address: McNaught Syndicate Inc 537 Steamboat Rd Greenwich CT 06830 *

GATES, CHARLES BERNARD, JR., banker; b. Charleston, W.Va., Apr. 20, 1921; s. Charles Bernard and Harriet Koplin (Hostetter) G.; m. Katherine Ann Hall, Nov. 6, 1945; children—Ione Gates Hardy, Charles Bernard III, Ann Katherine Gates Westmoreland. B.S., Harvard, 1942, J.D., 1949. Bar: bar 1949. Asso. mem. firm Steptoe & Johnson, Charleston, 1949-56, partner, 1956-63; with Charleston Nat. Bank, 1962—, exec. v.p., 1968-71, pres., 1971-75, chmn., chief exec. officer, 1975—, also dir.; dir. Bellemead Coal Co., Ravencliff, W.Va., Little Coal Land Co., Charleston, Ravencliffs Devel. Co., Pfaff & Smith Bldg. Supply Co., Charleston. Pres. United Fund Kanawha Valley, Inc., 1962-63, treas., 1969-72; asst. treas. Charleston Area Med. Center, 1972—; chmn. finance com. Davis and Elkins Coll., 1958-73; Bd. dirs. Sunrise, Inc., 1969—; treas. St. Francis Hosp., Charleston, 1971—; chmn. Charleston Regional Chamber of Commerce and Devel., 1979-80; trustee U. Charleston. Served to capt., inf. AUS, 1942-46. Mem. Am., W.Va. bar assns., W.Va. State Bar, Kanawha County Bar, Am. Bankers Assn., W.Va. Bankers Assn. (pres. trust div. 1967-68), Sigma Alpha Epsilon. Republican. Presbyn. Clubs: Elk, Rotarian., Edgewood Country. Office: Charleston Nat Plaza Charleston WV 25301

GATES, CHARLES CASSIUS, rubber company executive; b. Morrison, Colo., May 27, 1921; s. Charles Cassius and Hazel LaDora (Rhoads) G.; m. June Scowcroft Swaner, Nov. 26, 1943; children: Diane, John Swaner. Student, MIT, 1939-41; B.S., Stanford U., 1943; D.Eng. (hon.), Mich. Tech. U., 1975. With Copolymer Corp., Baton Rouge, 1943-46; with Gates Rubber Co., Denver, 1946—, v.p., 1951-58, exec. v.p., 1958-61, pres., chmn. bd., 1961—; chmn. bd. Gates Learjet Corp., Wichita, Kans.; dir. Fed. Res. Bank Kansas City, Hamilton Bros. Petroleum Corp., Denver, Robinson Brick & Tile Co., Denver. Pres., trustee Gates Found.; bd. dirs. Mountain States Employers Council, Colo. Pub. Expenditure Council; pres. bd. trustees Denver Mus. Natural History. Recipient Community Leadership and Service award Nat. Jewish Hosp., 1974; Mgmt. Man of Year award Nat. Mgmt. Assn., 1965. Mem. NAM (dir.), Rubber Mfrs. Assn. (dir.), Colo. Assn. Commerce and Industry, Conquistadores del Cielo. Clubs: Denver Country, Cherry Hills Country, Denver, Outrigger Canoe, Waialae Country, Boone and Crockett, Club Ltd., Country Club of Colo., Roundup Riders of Rockies, Shikar-Safari Club Internat. (dir.), Augusta Nat. Golf, Castle Pines Golf. Home: 444 S University Blvd Denver CO 80209 Office: 900 S Broadway Denver CO 80209

GATES, CRAWFORD MARION, conductor, composer; b. San Francisco, Dec. 29, 1921; s. Gilbert Marion and Leila (Adair) G.; m. Georgia Lauper, Dec. 19, 1952; children: Stephen Randall, Kathryn, Elizabeth, David Wendell. B.A., San Jose State Coll., 1944; M.A., Brigham Young U., 1948; Ph.D., Eastman Sch. Music, 1954. Grad. asst. music theory Eastman Sch. Music, 1948-50; faculty Brigham Young U., 1950-66, prof. music, chmn. dept., 1960-66; artist-in-residence Beloit (Wis.) Coll., 1966—, chmn. dept. music, 1982—; owner Pacific Publs. (music pubs.), Provo, Beloit, 1948—. Free-lance orchestrator, 1946—; orchestrator radio, sta. KSL, Salt Lake City, 1946-47; music dir., condr., Beloit Symphony Orch., 1963-64, 66—; music dir., Quincy Symphony Orch., 1969-70, Rockford Symphony Orch., 1970—; asst. to music dir.: Broadway prodn. Redhead, 1958; guest condr., Utah Symphony, numerous others.; Composer: Utah Centennial mus. play Promised Valley, 1947; Hill Cumorah Pageant, Palmyra, N.Y., 1957, commns. for religious ednl. films and Utah Symphony, U. Utah, numerous others.; Author: Catalog of Published American Choral Music, rev. edit. Mem. gen. bd. Mut. Improvement Assn., Ch. Jesus Christ of Latter-day Saints, 1949-66, mem. gen. music com., 1960-73. Served with USNR, World War II; PTO. Recipient Max Wald Meml. Fund award, N.Y.C., 1955; ASCAP standard award annually, 1965—. Mem. Nat. Fedn. Music Clubs (nat. choral chmn. 1951-55, 69-73), ASCAP. Club: Timpanogos (Salt Lake City). Home: 911 Park Ave Beloit WI 53511 Office: Rockford Symphony Orch 401 S Main St Rockford IL 61101 *The premises on which I have based my life are: (1) That God and Christ and the Holy Spirit are real and concerned. (2) That Christ's Kingdom and its true principles have been restored to earth in this period.*

GATES, DARYL FRANCIS, police chief; b. Aug. 30, 1926. B.S. in Pub. Adminstrn., U. So. Calif., also postgrad. With Dept. Police City of Los Angeles, 1949—, lt., 1959-63, capt., 1963-65, comdr., 1965-68, dep. chief, 1968-69, asst. chief, 1969-78, chief, 1978—. Bd. councilors U. So. Calif. Inst. Saftey and Systems Mgmt.; bd. dirs. YMCA, Los Angeles; mem. Children's Village Adv. Bd. Served with USN, World War II. Mem. Calif. Peace Officers Assn., Internat. police Assn., Calif. Police Chief Assn., Internat. Assn. Chiefs of Police, Women's Peace Officers Assn. Calif., Los Angeles C. of C. Lodge: Rotary. Office: PO Box 30158 Los Angeles CA 90030 *

GATES, DAVID MURRAY, botany educator; b. Manhattan, Kans., May 27, 1921; s. Frank Caleb and Margaret Henry (Thompson) G.; m. Marian Francis Penley, June 4, 1944; children: Murray Penley, Julie Mary, Heather Margaret, Marilyn Joan. B.S., U. Mich., 1942, M.S., 1944, Ph.D., 1948. Faculty, U. Denver, 1947-57; sci. dir. Office Naval Research, Am. embassy, London, 1955-57; cons. to dir., asst. chief upper atmosphere and space physics div. Boulder Labs., Nat. Bur. Standards, Colo., 1957-64; prof. natural history U. Colo., 1964-65; prof. biology Washington U., dir. Mo. Bot. Garden, St. Louis, 1965-71; prof. botany U. Mich.; dir. Biol. Sta., Ann Arbor, 1971—; dir. Detroit Edison Corp.; mem. nat. sci. bd. NSF, 1970-76; chmn. environ. studies bd. Nat. Acad. Scis. and Nat. Acad. Engring., 1970-73; mem. panel sci. and tech. Com. Sci. and Astronautics, U.S. Ho. of Reps., 1970-74. Author: Energy Exchange in the Biosphere, 1962, Atlas of Energy Exchange for Plant Leaves, 1971, Man and His Environment: Climate, 1972, Perspectives of Biophysical Ecology, 1975, Biophysical Ecology, 1980; contbr. numerous articles to profl. jours. Bd. dirs. Conservation Found., Washington, 1970—, Nat. Audubon Soc., 1972-78, Cranbrook Inst. Sci. Recipient Gold Seal award Nat. Council State Garden Clubs, 1971; Recipient Disting. Faculty Achievement award U. Mich., 1982. Mem. Am. Inst. Biol. Scis. (dir. 1970-76, pres. 1975, Outstanding Achievement in Bioclimatology award), Am. Meteorol. Soc. Club: Cosmos (Washington). Home: 442 Huntington Pl Ann Arbor MI 48104

GATES, DILLARD HERBERT, govt. rangeland scientist, ednl. adminstr.; b. Gates, Nebr., Jan. 23, 1925; s. Howe P. and Mary Ethel (Westbrook) G.; m. Anastasia Mohatt, Jan. 27, 1946; children—Dillard Howe, Charles Herbert. Student, Nebr. State Coll., 1949-50; B.S., U. Nebr., 1952, M.S., 1953; Ph.D., Utah State U., 1955. Cert. range mgmt. cons., profl. agronomist, soil specialist. Range scientist Agrl. Research Service, USDA, Woodward, Okla., 1955-57, Pullman, Wash., 1957-62; range specialist Oreg. State U., Corvallis, 1962-70, dir. rangeland resources program, 1971-74; natural resources specialist Bur. Land Mgmt., U.S. Dept. Interior, Sacramento, 1970-71; range scientist AID, Washington, 1974-80; dir. Yemen program Oreg. State U., Corvallis, 1980—; Cons. FAO, Iraq, 1969, Devel. Resources Corp., Sacramento, 1970-73, NASA, 1970-74, AID, 1973-74. Contbr. articles to profl. and ednl. jours. Served with USCGR, 1943-45. Mem. Soc. Range Mgmt. (pres. 1975), Sigma Xi, Xi Sigma Phi, Gamma Sigma Delta. Clubs: Elk, Mason. Home: 3514 NW McKinley Dr Corvallis OR 97330 Office: Yemen Program Oregon State U Corvallis OR 97331

GATES, EDWIN WILDER, physician; b. Nashua, N.H., May 18, 1900; s. Edwin Lewis and Alice (Wilder) G.; m. Agnes Jessie Cameron, Dec. 22, 1922; 1 son, Edwin Wilder. B.S., Colby Coll., 1922, D.Sc. (hon.), 1968; M.D., Harvard, 1926. Intern U.S. Marine Hosp., S.I., N.Y., 1926-27, resident, 1927-29; chief medicine Mt. St. Mary's Hosp., 1947-50, chief staff, 1950-54, hon. cons. diabetes, 1966—; chief medicine Niagara Falls (N.Y.) Meml. Hosp., 1950-67, head div. diabetes, 1959-69, hon. chief medicine, 1967—; dir. Katherine Nye Bartlett Diabetic Teaching Unit, 1966—; instr. medicine Niagara U. Sch. Nursing, 1947-50; Established Niagara Falls Diabetes Assn., 1954; continuous gen. med. audit Niagara Falls Meml. Hosp., 1955; pub. med. forums Niagara Falls Meml. Hosp. and Mt. St. Mary's Hosp., 1957, div. diabetes Niagara Falls Meml. Hosp., 1959, Dr. Charles H. Best Birthplace Trust, Inc., 1959. Author: (with others) Diabetes Mellitus: Diagnosis and Treatment, 1964; also articles. Treas. Niagara Falls Community Chest, 1946-49; Bd. dirs. Children's Aid Soc., 1933-35, Niagara Falls YMCA, 1933-39. Served with U.S. Army, 1918. Recipient Colby Coll. gavel Colby Coll. Alumni Assn., 1968. Fellow ACP; mem. Am. Diabetes Assn. (bd. dirs. 1955-69, pres. 1967-68, Banting medal 1968), AMA, Buffalo Acad. Medicine, Niagara County Med. Soc., N.Y. State Med. Soc. (chmn. subcom. diabetes 1951), Am., Western N.Y. socs. internal medicine, Phi Beta Kappa. Home: 509 College Ave Niagara Falls NY 14305 Office: 625 6th St Niagara Falls NY 14301

GATES, ELMER D., business executive; b. Blue Mountain Lake, N.Y., Dec. 12, 1929; s. Arthur and Hazel (Coon) G.; m. Betty Gates, July 4, 1953; children: Patti Smith, Jodi. B.Mech. Engring., Clarkson Coll. Mgr. employee relations Gen. Electric Co., Erie, Pa., 1969-71, mgr. mfg., 1971-78, gen. mgr., Schenectady, 1978-82; pres. Fuller Co., Bethlehem, Pa., 1982—. Pres. Fairview (Pa.) Sch. Bd., 1978—; div. chmn. United Way of Lehigh and Bethelhem (Pa.), 1983. Served to 1st lt. U.S. Army, 1951-53; Korea. Mem. Bethlehem C. of C. (dir. 1983). Republican. Lutheran. Clubs: Saucon Valley Country (Bethlehem);

Bethlehem. Lodges: Masons; Rotary. Home: 840 Yorkshire Rd Bethlehem PA 18017 Office: Fuller Co 2040 Ave C Bethlehem PA 18001

GATES, ERNEST EDGAR, textile scientist; b. Norwich, Conn., June 11, 1927; s. Theodore Louis and Emeline G.; m. Gertrude A. Bussiere, Jan. 27, 1957; children—Karen Ann, Waring Wade. B.A., U. Conn., 1951, Ph.D. in Phys. Chemistry, 1957. Sr. research chemist nylon div. Dupont de Nemours & Co., Inc., Chattanooga, 1957-60, sr. supr., 1963-65, asst. tech. service mgr. textile fibers dept., 1969-73, mktg. tech. mgr. indsl. fibers, Wilmington, Del., 1974-78, lab. dir. textile research, 1978—. Served in USN, 1945-46. Roman Catholic. Office: Dupont de Nemours & Co Inc Wilmington DE 19898 *

GATES, HARRY IRVING, painter, sculptor, educator; b. Elgin, Ill., Dec. 8, 1934; s. Harry Max and Verna Grace (Lutz) G.; m. Elaine Behling, 1958; children: Claire, Patti; m. Ortrun Armgard-Wenzel, July 20, 1979. B.F.A., U. Ill., 1958, M.F.A., 1960. One man shows Rochester Inst. Tech., Goucher Coll., Corcoran Gallery Art, Balt. Mus., Washington County Mus.; exhibited in over 40 group shows U.S. and fgn. countries; represented in permanent collections Corcoran Gallery Art, Washington County Mus., Balt. Mus. Art, Chase Manhattan Bank; assoc. prof. sculpture George Washington U. Home: 118 E Church St Frederick MD 21701 Office: George Washington Univ Washington DC 20052

GATES, JAMES DAVID, association executive; b. East Cleveland, Ohio, July 9, 1927; s. James Adelbert and Margaretta (Voigt) G.; m. Carol Marie Schreiber, June 9, 1956; children: David, Keith, Robert. A.B., Hiram (Ohio) Coll., 1951; M.A., Columbia, 1956; Ed.D., George Washington U., 1975. Tchr. Maple Heights (Ohio) City Schs., 1951-61; profl. asst. Nat. Council Tchrs. Math., Reston, Va., 1961-63, exec. sec., 1963-76, exec. dir., 1976—; mem. faculty U. Va., 1963-66, George Washington U., 1966-75. Served with AUS, 1945-47. Mem. Nat. Council Tchrs. Math., Math. Assn. Am., AAAS, NEA. Club: Rotarian. Home: 11303 Fieldstone Ln Reston VA 22091 Office: 1906 Association Dr Reston VA 22091

GATES, JAY RODNEY, museum administrator; b. Kansas City, Mo., Nov. 21, 1945; s. William Russell and Kathleen Lorraine (Hagie) G.; m. Susan Jerkins. B.A., Coll. of Wooster, 1968; postgrad, U. Vienna, 1966-67; M.A., U. Rochester, 1970, U. Pitts., 1970-71. Instr. art Coll. of Wooster, Ohio, 1971-73, curator, 1972-73; asst. curator dept. art history and edn. Cleve. Mus. Art, 1973-76; adj. inst. art Case Western Res. U., 1973-76; curator edn. St. Louis Art Mus., 1976-78; dir. Brooks Meml. Art Gallery, Memphis, 1978-81; asst. dir., curator Am. art William Rock Nelson Gallery of Art, Kansas City, Mo., 1981—. Mem. NAACP, Am. Assn. Museums. Episcopalian. Home: 6709 Kenwood Kansas City MO 64131 Office: William Rockhill Nelson Gallery Art and Atkins Mus 4525 Oak St Kansas City MO 64111

GATES, LARRY, actor; b. St. Paul, Sept. 24, 1915; s. Lloyd Roland and Marion Douglas (Wheaton) G.; m. Tania Wilkof, Aug. 2, 1959 (dec. Sept. 1961); m. Judith Seaton, Apr. 11, 1963. Student, U. Minn., 1933-38. Mem. Barter Theatre, Abingdon, Va., 1946-47; mem Webster Shakespeare Co., N.Y.C., 1950-51; councillor Actors' Equity Assn., N.Y.C., 1952-62. Appeared in: Broadway play Bell, Book and Candle, 1951, The Love of Four Colonels, 1952, The Teahouse of the August Moon, 1953, First Monday in October, 1979, Poor Murderer, 1976, A Case of Libel, 1963 (nominated for Tony award); mem.: nat. tour The Gin Game, 1982; appeared in: The Missiles of October, The Lou Grant Show, Backstairs at the White House; films The Invasion of the Bodysnatchers, Cat on a Hot Tin Roof, Some Came Running; appeared: The Sand Pebbles; appeared in: In the Heat of the Night. Vice chmn. Democratic Town Com., Cornwall, Conn., 1958-81; Democratic candidate for Conn. senate, 1972; chmn. Cornwall Recreation Commn., 1966-77; vice chmn. Housatonic River Commn., Warren, Conn., 1978. Served to maj. C.E. AUS, 1941-49; PTO. Recipient Outstanding Achievement award U. Minn., 1976. Mem. Screen Actors guild, AFTRA, Soc. Stage Dirs. and Choreographers, Episcopal Actors' Guild (councillor N.Y.C. 1977—). Democrat. Club: Players (N.Y.C.). Home: West Cornwall CT

GATES, LESLIE CLIFFORD, civil engr.; b. Dorothy, W.Va., Nov. 17, 1918; s. Lauren Adolphus and Lillian (Sandburg) G.; m. Martha Rose Shrewsbury, Dec. 21, 1940; children—Ellen (Mrs. James G. Anderson III), Leslie Allen. B.S., Va. Poly. Inst. and State U., 1940. Registered profl. engr., W.Va., Ky., Ohio, Pa., Ill., Tenn., Wyo., Utah, Va., Mont., Ind., Ariz., Colo., Wash., N.Mex., N.D., Okla. Mem. field party Solvey Process Co., Hopewell, Va., 1940-41; asso. Ferguson-Gates Engrng. Co. (name changed to Gates Engrng. Co. 1961), Beckley, W.Va., also Charleston, W.Va., Pitts., Chgo., Denver, Sydney, Australia, 1946-54, partner, 1955-58, owner, 1958-61; pres., 1962-78, chmn. bd., chief exec. officer, 1978—; dir. Cardinal State Bank; trustee Engrng. Index, Inc.; Mem. W.Va. Bd. Registration for Profl. Engrs., 1965-80. Pres. Beckley Bus. Devel. Corp., 1965; campaign chmn. Raleigh County United Fund, 1962-63, pres., 1965; pres. Raleigh County Citizens Scholarship Assn., 1966, Flat Top Lake Assn., 1965; adv. bd. W.Va. U., 1970—. Served from 2d lt. to maj. C.E. AUS, 1951-45; ETO. Fellow ASCE; mem. Nat. Soc. Profl. Engrs. (pres. 1974-75), W.Va. Soc. Profl. Engrs. (pres. 1951) socs. profl. engrs.), Am. Rd. Builders Assn., Am. Inst. Mining, Metall. and Petroleum Engrs. (chmn. Central Appalachian sect. 1965-66), Am. Mining Congress (resolutions com. 1981), Am. Water Works Assn., W.Va. Coal Mining Inst., Hwy. Research Bd., W.Va. C. of C. (pres.-elect), Beckley-Ralegh County C. of C. (pres. 1953), Colo. Mining Assn., Ill. Mining Inst., Am. Concrete Inst., Am. Arbitration Assn., Nat. Coal Assn., Am. Soc. Engrng. Edn. Presbyn. (elder). Club: Rotarian. Office: PO Drawer AF Beckley WV 25801 *

GATES, MAHLON EUGENE, applied research executive, former government official and army officer; b. Tyrone, Pa., Aug. 21, 1919; s. Samuel Clayton and Elsie (Nieweg) G.; m. Esther Boone Campbell, July 4, 1972; children by previous marriage: Pamela Townley, Lawrence Alan. B.S., U.S. Mil. Acad., 1942; M.S., U. Ill., 1948; postgrad., Command and Gen. Staff Coll., 1957, Army War Coll., 1962, Harvard U., 1965. Commd. 2d lt. U.S. Army, 1942, advanced through grades to brig. gen., 1966; area engr., Iran, Gulf Dist., 1960-61; chief, engr. br., officer Personnel Directorate, Dept. Army, 1963-64; gen. staff Dept. Army, 1964-66; comdg. gen., Cam Ranh Bay, Vietnam, 1966-67, dir. constrn., Vietnam, 1967; dir. research, devel. and engring. Army Materiel Command, Washington, 1971; ret., 1972; mgr. Nev. ops. office AEC now Dept. Energy, Las Vegas, 1972-82; with S.W. Research Inst., San Antonio, 1982—. Past pres. Boulder Dam Area council Boy Scouts Am.; past chmn. adv. bd. Clark County Community Coll. Decorated D.S.M., Legion of Merit, Bronze Star, Air medal; Army Distinguished Service Order 1st class Govt. Vietnam; Meritorious Service award; named Meritorious Exec. ERDA. Home: 210 Country Wood San Antonio TX 78216 Office: SW Research Inst 6220 Culebra Rd San Antonio TX 78284 *Cherish the past; do not worship it.*

GATES, MARK THOMAS, JR., lawyer; b. Santa Monica, Calif., Jan. 13, 1937; s. Mark Thomas and Margaret (Woods) G.; m. Elizabeth B. Wilson, June 18, 1960; children: Mark Thomas III, Stephanie L., Whitney E. B.A., Dartmouth Coll., 1959; LL.B., Stanford U., 1962. Bar: Calif. 1963. Practiced law, Los Angeles, 1962-78; mem. firm Wilson & Gates, San Bruno, Calif., 1964-78; prin. real estate mgmt. and devel. co., 1978-82, real estate cons., 1983—. Chmn. Los Angeles County Republican gubernatorial campaign, 1970; Mem. Calif. State Bd. Edn., 1971-75, chmn. legal compliance com., 1975. Mem. Am., Calif., Los Angeles County bar assns. Club: California. Office: Gates Land Company 3000 Sand Hill Rd Bldg 4 Suite 175 Menlo Park CA 94025

GATES, MARSHALL DEMOTTE, JR., chemistry educator emeritus; b. Boyne City, Mich., Sept. 25, 1915; s. Marshall DeMotte and Virginia (Orton) G.; m. Martha Louise Meyer, Sept. 9, 1941; children—Christopher David, Catharine Louise, Marshall DeMotte III, Virginia Alice. B.S., Rice Inst., 1936, M.S., 1938; Ph.D., Harvard, 1941; D.Sc. (hon.), MacMurray Coll., 1963. Asst. prof. chemistry Bryn Mawr Coll., 1941-43; vis. prof. Harvard, 1946; asso. prof., 1947-49, Max Tishler lectr., 1953; tech. aid NDRC, 1943-46; lectr. chemistry U. Rochester, 1949-52, part-time prof., 1952-60, prof., 1960-68, Charles Frederick Houghton prof. chemistry, 1968-81, prof. emeritus, 1981—; Welch Found. lectr., 1960; adv. bd. Chem. Abstracts Services, 1974-76; vis. prof. Dartmouth Coll., 1982. Mem. com. on drug addiction and narcotics, div. med. scis. NRC, 1956-70, also com. on organic nomenclature div. of chemistry; mem. Pres.'s Com. on Nat. Medal of Sci., 1968-70. Recipient Edward Peck Curtis award for excellence in undergrad. teaching, 1967; Armed Services certificate Appreciation, 1946. Fellow Am. Acad. Arts and Scis., N.Y. Acad. Scis.; mem. Am. Chem. Soc. (editor Jour. 1963-69), Nat. Acad. Scis. Home: 41 W Brook Rd Pittsford NY 14534 Office: U Rochester Rochester NY 14627

GATES, RICHARD DANIEL, manufacturing company executive; b. Trenton, Mo., Mar. 27, 1942; s. Daniel G. and Effie Wright (Johnson) G.; m. Jean Gates, Jan. 26, 1966; 1 son, Daniel Wright. B.S., U. Mo., 1964; M.C.S., Rollins Coll., Winter Park, Fla., 1968; postgrad., Harvard U., 1976. Mgmt. assoc. Western Electric Co., N.Y.C., 1964-66; bus. mgmt. adminstr. Martin Marietta Aerospace Co., Orlando, Fla., 1966-68, chief indsl. engring., 1968-69; fin. analyst Martin Marietta Co., N.Y.C., 1969-70, sr. acct., 1970-71; controller Dragon Cement Co., div. Martin Marietta Co., 1971-72, N.E. div. Martin Marietta Aggregates Co., 1972-73; asst. controller, then asst. treas. Rubbermaid, Inc., Wooster, Ohio, 1973-79, treas., 1979-80, v.p., treas., 1980—. Mem. Wooster City Fin. Task Force, 1979—; active local Cub Scouts.; adviser Art Center; chmn. maj. indsl. capital campaign Boy Scouts Camp. Mem. Beta Gamma Sigma, Omicron Delta Kappa. Clubs: Harvard Bus. Sch., Wooster Country. Address: Rubbermaid Inc 1147 Akron Rd Wooster OH 44691

GATES, SAMUEL EUGENE, lawyer; b. Lagro, Ind., Feb. 9, 1906; s. Eugene Franklin and Fannie (Miller) G.; m. Philomene Asher, Apr. 26, 1941; children—Gilda (Mrs. Cecil Wray, Jr.), Sharon (Mrs. Richard B. Stearns, Jr.), Mary Kathe (Mrs. Edwin D. Williamson). A.B., U. So. Calif., 1926, M.A., 1929, LL.B., 1933; postgrad., Harvard U., 1929-30; diplome, U. Paris, France, L'Institut des Hautes Etudes Internationales, 1931. Bar: Calif. bar 1933, N.Y. bar 1948. Tchr. pub. schs., Long Beach, Calif., 1927-29; fellow Carnegie Found., 1930-31; asso. atty. Haight, Trippet & Syvertson, Los Angeles, 1933-35; partner Gates & Inch, Los Angeles, 1936-38; internat. counsel CAB, Washington, 1938-42; partner Douglas, Proctor, MacIntyre & Gates, Washington, 1946-48, Debevoise, Plimpton, Lyons & Gates (and predecessor firms), N.Y.C., 1948—; Mem. Comite Internat. Technique des Experts Juridiques Aerien (Am. sec.), 1939-46; mem. U.S. commn. Permanent Am. Aero. Commn., 1941-44, Am. delegations U.S.-Can. Civil Aviation Confs., 1939-40; adviser Am. delegation Internat. Civil Aviation Conf., Chgo., 1944; Anglo-Am. Civil Aviation Conf., Bermuda, 1946, 1st Gen. Assembly Provisional Internat. Civil Aviation Orgn., Montreal, 1946, Internat. Civil Aviation Orgn. Montreal, 1947. Bd. dirs. Goodwill Industries N.Y. Served as col. Air Transport Command USAAF, 1942-46. Decorated D.S.M. Mem. Am., Internat., N.Y. State bar assns., State Bar Calif., Bar Assn. N.Y.C., Am. Law Inst., Am. Coll. Trial Lawyers (regent 1973-78, pres.-elect 1978—), Am. Judicature Soc., Am. Soc. Internat. Law. Clubs: University (N.Y.C.); Metropolitan (Washington); Westhampton Country, Quantuck Beach (Westhampton Beach, N.Y.); Nat. Golf Links of Am. Home: 1112 Park Ave New York NY 10028 Office: 299 Park Ave New York NY 10017

GATES, THEODORE ROSS, economic consultant; b. Milw., May 22, 1918; s. W. Ross and Mary (Balcom) G.; m. Dorothy P. Kaiser, Dec. 17, 1942; children—C. Parker, Mary M. A.B., Dartmouth Coll., 1940; student, Yale Sch. Law, 1940-41; M.A., Harvard U., 1948. Economist Guaranty Trust Co., 1948-50; internat. economist Nat. Indsl. Conf. Bd., 1950-63; chief economist Office Spl. Rep. for Trade Negotiations, Exec. Office of Pres., 1963-67, asst. spl. rep., 1967-73; v.p., dir. econ. research Internat. Bus. & Econ. Research Corp., Washington, 1973-74; pres. Theodore R. Gates Assos., Inc., 1975—. Author: other books, articles on econ. subjects. Costs and Competition. Served with AUS, 1942-46. Mem. Phi Beta Kappa. Democrat. Home: 7827 Overhill Rd Bethesda MD 20814

GATEWOOD, BUFORD ECHOLS, ret. educator, aero. and astronautical engr.; b. Byhalia, Miss., Aug. 23, 1913; s. Robert P. and Irene (Echols) G.; m. Margaret Murphy, June 28, 1939; 1 dau., Marianne. B.S. in Mech. Engring, La. Poly. Inst., 1935; M.S., U. Wis., 1937, Ph.D., 1939. Faculty La. Poly. Inst., 1939-42, Air Force Inst. Tech., 1947-60; with McDonnell Aircraft Corp., 1942-46, Beech Aircraft Corp., 1946-47; prof. aero. and astronautical engring. Ohio State U., Columbus, 1960-78; Cons. on structural design and analysis, structural fatigue, problems in dynamics, thermal Problems to various cos., 1949—. Author: Thermal Stresses, 1957. Mem. Am. Inst. Aeros. and Astronautics, Soc. Exptl. Stress Analysis, Math. Assn. Am., ASME, Am. Soc. Engring. Edn., Sigma Xi. Research, publs. on thermal stresses and inelastic structures for flight vehicle structures. Home: 2150 Waltham Rd Columbus OH 43221

GATEWOOD, WILLARD BADGETT, JR., historian; b. Pelham, N.C., Feb. 23, 1931; s. Willard Badgett and Bessie Lee (Pryor) G.; m. Mary Lu Brown, Aug. 9, 1958; children—Willard Badgett, Elizabeth Ellis. B.A., Duke U., 1953, M.A., 1954, Ph.D., 1957. Asst. prof. history East Tenn. State U., 1957-58, East Carolina U., 1958-60; asso. prof. N.C. Wesleyan Coll., 1960-64; prof. U. Ga., 1964-70; Alumni Disting. prof. history U. Ark., 1970—. Author: books including Theodore Roosevelt and the Art of Controversy, 1970; Smoked Yankees, 1971, Black Americans and the White Man's Burden, 1975, Slave and Freeman, 1979, Free Men of Color, 1982; bd. editors: books including Ga. Rev, 1968-70, Jour. Negro History, 1972-74. Recipient Parks Excellence in Teaching award Phi Alpha Theta, 1970, Michael Research award, 1967; Outstanding Teaching award Omicron Delta Kappa, 1979; research award U. Arik. Alumni Assn., 1980; Gingles award Ark. Hist. Assn., 1982; Truman Library fellow, 1963; Acad. Arts and Scis. grantee, 1962. Mem. Am. Hist. Assn., So. Hist. Assn., Ark. Hist. Assn., Orgn. Am. Historians, Assn. Study Afro-Am. Life and History, Phi Beta Kappa. Presbyterian. Home: 1651 Cleveland St Fayetteville AR 72701 Office: Ozark Hall U Ark Fayetteville AR 72701

GATHANY, VAN R., banker; b. Evanston, Ill., July 16, 1926; s. William Vandervoort and Isabel (Risser) G.; m. Hilda Lang Denworth, Oct. 13, 1951; children: Virginia Lynn (Mrs. Henry Page, Jr.), Douglas Vandervoort, Robin Elizabeth (Mrs. Kevin Shea). B.A., Swarthmore Coll., 1950; M.B.A., U. Chgo., 1953. Vice pres. No. Trust Bank, Chgo., 1963-67, sr. v.p., 1967—; dir. No. Trust Co. Ariz., Top Star, Inc., Lake Forest Book Store, Inc.; pres. NorTrust Farm Mgmt., 1970-77; now dir., instr. Lake Forest (Ill.) Coll. Advanced Mgmt. Inst. Mem. adv. council U. Chgo. Grad. Sch. Bus.; mem. Lake Forest Elementary Sch. Bd., 1963-70; pres. Chgo. Home for Incurables; bd. dirs. Johnson R. Bowman Health Center; chmn. bd. regents Northwestern U.; trustee Nat. Coll. Edn., Evanston. Served with AC USNR, 1944-46. Mem. Am. Bankers Assn. (chmn. trust div.), Ill. Bankers Assn. (pres. trust div.). Presbyn. (elder). Clubs: Lake Forest (past pres., dir.), Exmoor Country; University (Chgo.). Home: 786 Longwood Dr Lake Forest IL 60045 Office: 50 S LaSalle St Chicago IL 60690

GATHERUM, GORDON ELWOOD, forestry educator; b. Salt Lake City, Oct. 22, 1923; s. James Elwood and Jessie Margaret (Robertson) G.; m. Patricia Jeanne Brandley, July 31, 1947; children: Laurie Patricia, Mark Gordon, Kristin Lee. B.S. in Forest Mgmt., U. Wash., 1949; M.S. in Range Mgmt., Utah State U., 1951; Ph.D., Iowa State U., 1959. Mem. faculty dept. forestry Iowa State U., 1953-69; chmn. dept. forestry Ohio State U., also Ohio Agrl. Research and Devel. Center, 1969-75; dir. Sch. Natural Resources, asso. dean Coll. Agr., Ohio State U. and Ohio Agrl. Research and Devel. Center, 1975—; AID cons., Brazil. Contbr. articles to profl. jours. NSF grantee. Mem. Nat. Assn. Profl. Forestry Schs. and Colls. (regional chmn.), Soc. Am. Foresters, Sigma Xi, Phi Eta Sigma, Xi Sigma Pi. Home: 5710 Strathmore Ln Dublin OH 43017

GATI, LASZLO, symphony conductor; b. Timisoara, Rumania, Sept. 25, 1925; s. Ignatie and Veronica (Grosz) Osterreicher; children: Suzanne, Kathleen. Diploma in Violin, Conservatory of Music, 1945; student, Ferencz Liszt Acad. Music, Budapest, 1946-49; degree in Violin, Conducting, Nat. Conservatory Music, Budapest, 1949; diploma, Pan Am. Orch. Condrs. Course, Mexico, 1958, Academie Internationale D'Eté, Nice, 1964. Condr. choir and orch. U. Econs., 1950-56; prof. violin Mus. Sch. Budapest, 1953-54; head symphonic and chamber music dept. and internat. music programe exchange dept. Hungarian Radio, 1954-56. Violinist, State Philharmonic Orch. (formerly Capital's Orch.), 1946-53; condr., Nat. State Philharmonic, 1953-56; asst. solo viola, Montreal Symphony, 1957-64; acting asst. condr., Zubin Mehta, Montreal, 1960-64; condr., Philharmonia Orch. Montreal, 1958-61; founder, condr., Montreal Chamber Orch., 1959—; music dir., condr., Victoria Symphony Orch., 1967-78, Windsor (Ont.) Symphony Orch., 1979—; artistic and exec. dir., Victoria Summer Festival, 1972-77; regular guest condr. with numerous, Can., U.S., Mexican, European, N.Z. orchs.; (sr. Art fellow Can. Council 1964). Recipient Queen's Silver Jubilee award. Mem. Zoltan Kodaly Acad. (hon.). Home: PO Box 831 Sta A Windsor ON N9A 6P2 Canada Office: 586 Ouellette Ave Suite 307 Windsor ON N9A 1B7 Canada

GATJE, ROBERT FREDERICK, architect; b. Bklyn., Nov. 27, 1927; s. Frederick Christopher and Erna Henrietta (Kelting) G.; m. Barbara Mansfield Wright, Oct. 20, 1956 (div. Aug. 1981); children: Alexandra Lord, Marianna Sherwood, Margot Kim. B.Arch., Cornell U., 1951; Fulbright scholar, Archtl. Assn. Sch. Architecture, London, 1951-52. With Marcel Breuer and Assos., architects (name now Gatje, Papachristou, Smith), N.Y.C., 1953—; asso. Marcel Breuer and Assos., 1956—, partner, 1965—, dir. Paris office, 1964-66. Architect: Broward County Main Library, 1980; co-architect: IBM France Research Center, 1962, Ski Town, Flaine, France, 1969, IBM Mfg. Center, Boca Raton, Fla., 1969, Armstrong Rubber Co. Hdqrs, New Haven, 1969, Baldegg (Switzerland) Convent, 1972, Mundipharma GmbH Hdqrs, Limburg, Ger., 1975. Trustee Deep Springs Coll., Calif., 1974-82; pres. Telluride Assn., 1953-55. Served with C.E. AUS, 1946-47. Telluride scholar, 1947-51; Skidmore, Owings and Merrill scholar, 1950-51; recipient Clifton Beckwith Brown medal Cornell U. Coll. Architecture, 1951, Charles Goodwin Sands medal, 1951. Fellow AIA (pres. N.Y. chpt. 1975-76, Sch. medal 1951); mem. Ordre des Architectes Français, Am. Arbitration Assn. Democrat. Clubs: University, Bedford Golf and Tennis. Home: Hopp Ground Ln Bedford Village NY 10506 Office: 114 Fifth Ave New York NY 10011

GATLIN, LARRY WAYNE, singer, songwriter; b. Seminole, Tex., May 2, 1948; s. William Wayne and Billie Christine (Doan) G.; m. Janis Gail Moss, Aug. 9, 1969; children—Kristin Kara, Joshua Cash. Student, U. Houston, 1966-70. Country music singer, since 1971; songwriter.; (Recipient Grammy Songwriter award for Broken Lady 1976, Broadcast Music Inc. award for Broken Lady, 1976, for Delta Dirt 1975, Best Album, Best Single and Top Male Vocalist awards Acad. Country Music 1980). Mem. Country Music Assn. Baptist. *

GATOF, NORMAN, jewelry company executive; b. N.Y.C., Oct. 29, 1929; s. Herbert and Frances (Vogel) G.; m. Judith Segal; children: Wendy Gatof Malina, Mark S. B.S., U.S. Mcht. Marine Acad, 1951. Ops. mgr. Monet Jewlers, N.Y.C., 1952-56, salesman, 1956-62, staff product devel. and mfrg., 1962-73, exec. v.p., gen. mgr., N.Y.C., 1973-76, pres., N.Y.C., 1976-79, chmn. bd., chief exec. officer, 1979—; v.p. Gen. Mills, Inc., Mpls., 1977—. Patentee in field. Bd. dirs. Nat. Med. Fellowships, Inc., N.Y.C., 1980—. Served to lt. USN, 1952-54. Mem. Mfg. Jewlers and Silversmiths Am. (dir. 1979—). Office: Monet Jewelers 16 E 34th St New York NY 10016

GATOS, HARRY CONSTANTINE, educator; b. Greece, Dec. 27, 1921; came to U.S., 1946, naturalized, 1955; s. Constantine B. and Paraskevi (Merinztos) G.; m. Dawn Spiropoulos, July 15, 1950; children—Pamela Dawn, Niki Ann, Constantine Harry. Diploma in chemistry, U. Athens, Greece, 1945; M.A. in Chemistry, Ind. U., 1948; Ph.D., MIT, 1950; D.Sc., Ind. U., 1983. Instr. U. Athens, 1943-46; mem. research staff MIT, 1948-52; from sect. leader to div. head solid state div. Lincoln Lab., 1955-64; prof. materials sci. and elec. engring. MIT, Cambridge, 1962—; research engr. E.I. duPont de Nemours & Co., Inc., 1952-55; Cons. to industry, govt., 1962—. Contbr. articles to profl. jours.; Editor-in-chief: Surface Sci. Trustee Longy Sch. Music, Cambridge, Mass. Decorated golden cross Order of Merit, Poland; recipient medal for exceptional sci. achievement NASA, 1974; Solid State Sci. and Tech. award Electrochem. Soc., 1975; Acheson medal Electrochem. Soc., 1982. Fellow AAAS; mem. Electrochem. Soc. (hon. mem.; pres. 1967-68), Materials Research Soc. (pres. 1972-75), Am. Phys. Soc., Am. Inst. Metall. Engrs., Nat. Acad. Engring., Am. Acad. Arts and Scis., Acad. Athens (corr.), Cambridge Soc. for Early Music (trustee). Home: 20 Indian Hill Rd Weston MA 02193 Office: Mass Inst Tech Cambridge MA 02139

GATSKI, ROBERT LAWRENCE, physician; b. West Hazelton, Pa., May 27, 1919; s. Peter Paul and Estella (Schlacky) G.; m. Betty Eileen Carey, June 29, 1942; children—Robert Lawrence, Charles P., Marsha E., Mark. Student, Bucknell U., 1942-44; M.D., Jefferson Med. Coll., 1948. Diplomate: Am. Bd. Psychiatry, Nat. Bd. Med. Examiners. Intern St. Josephs Hosp., Lancaster, Pa., 1948-49; resident Danville (Pa.) State Hosp., 1949-53; acting clin. dir. Gov. Bacon Health Center, Delaware City, Del., 1954-55; clin. dir. Danville (Pa.) State Hosp., 1954-55, supt., adminstr., 1955-77; ret., 1977, practice medicine specializing in psychiatry, Danville, 1977—; acting supt. Retreat State Hosp., 1965-67; psychiat. cons. Geisinger Med. Center, Bloomsburg (Pa.) Hosp., Muncy (Pa.) State Indsl. Home, Eastern Fed. Penitentiary, Lewisburg, Pa. Editor: Pa. Psychiat. Quar, 1959-63; cons.

editor, 1963—. Mem. council on stroke Susquehanna Valley Regional Med. Program, 1971-72; mem. Pa. Drug Standardization Com. Recipient Alumni award Bucknell U., 1971. Mem. AMA, Am. Psychiat. Assn., Am. Acad. Neurology, Am. Coll. Hosp. Adminstrs. Research mental disorders. Address: 310 E Market St Danville PA 17821

GATTI, RICHARD ANTHONY, pediatrician, pathology educator; b. Hoboken, N.J., Jan. 12, 1937; s. Attilio and Esther (Picco) G.; m. Patricia Lees, Apr. 19, 1969; children—Tana Felice, Allegra Noelle, Ilana Pilar. B.A., Columbia Coll., 1958; M.D., St. Louis U., 1962. Diplomate: Am. Bd. Pediatrics. Intern, resident in pediatrics Children's Meml. Hosp., Northwestern U., Chgo., 1962-65, research trainee fellow in biochem. genetics, 1965-66; research trainee fellow dept. immunobiology U. Minn., 1968-69; USPHS fellow, 1969-71, USPHS career devel. awardee, tumor immunology, 1971-72, Karolinska Inst. dept. tumor biology, Stockholm, 1972-74; prof. pediatrics UCLA, 1974-80, prof. pathology, 1980—; dir. pediatric hematology, oncology and immunology Cedars-Sinai Med. Center, Los Angeles, 1974-80. Asso. editor: Am. Jour. Reproductive Immunology; co-editor: Tissue Typing and Organ Transplantation, 1972; Contbr. articles to med. jours. Served to capt., M.C. U.S. Army, 1966-68. Guggenheim fellow, 1972-73. Fellow Am. Acad. Pediatrics; mem. Am. Fedn. Clin. Research, Soc. Pediatric Research, Am. Assn. Immunologists, Brit. Soc. Immunologists, European Soc. Pediatric Hematology and Immunology, Western Soc. Pediatric Research, AAAS, Am. Pediatric Soc., Brit. Transplantation Soc., Am. Soc. Clin. Oncology, Am. Soc. Zoologists, Fedn. Am. Socs. Exptl. Biology, Am. Assn. Clin. Histocompatibility Testing, Internat. Assn. Comprehensive Research on Leukemia, Am. Assn. Cancer Research, Internat. Soc. Devel. and Comparative Immunology, Scandinavian Soc. Immunologists. Presbyterian. Office: Dept Pathology UCLA Los Angeles CA 90024

GATTO, LOUIS CONSTANTINE, college president; b. Chgo., July 4, 1927; s. Louis S. and Marie (Bacigalupo) G.; m. Kathleen M. Paquette, July 7, 1951; children: Christine Gatto Swickard, Beth, Mark, Gregory, Janine Gatto Bass, Sandra. Student, Amherst Coll., 1945-46; B.A., St. Mary's Coll., Minn., 1950; postgrad, U. Minn., 1950-51; M.A., DePaul U., 1956; Ph.D., Loyola U., Chgo., 1965. Speech asst. St. Mary's Coll., 1949-50; staff artist TV Times, Mpls., 1950-51; chmn. dept. English Zion (Ill.)-Benton High Sch., 1951-56; tchr. New Trier High Sch., Winnetka, Ill., 1956-57; instr. English St. Josephs Coll., Rensselaer, Ind., 1957-58, asst. prof., 1958-63, assoc. prof. Medieval and Renaissance lit., 1963-66, prof., 1966-71, asst. acad. dean, dir. summer session, 1967, acad. dean, 1968, v.p. acad. affairs, 1969-71; pres., prof. English Marian Coll., Indpls., 1971—; Mem. Ind. Northwest Consortium Pvt. and Pub. Instns., 1968-71; selection com. Ind. Fulbright Found., 1968-70; mem. community adv. council Indpls. Pub. Schs., 1976-77; mem. policy adv. council parent/child devel. project Bank Street Coll. Edn.; mem. Hist. Landmarks Found. Ind., 1973—; mem. adv. com. Alcohol Safety Action Project, 1972-75; mem. exec. com., adv. bd. Center for Econ. Edn., Ind. U.-Purdue U., Indpls.; mem. exec. com. Ind. Conf. on Higher Edn., 1973-75, 78-81, pres., 1979-80; chmn. council of presidents Consortium for Urban Edn., 1974-75, pres., 1975—. Contbr. articles to profl. jours. Bd. dirs. Greater Indpls. Progress Com., Catholic Social Services, sec., 1978-80; bd. dirs. WYFI-TV, Ind. Health Careers, Inc., ARC; vice-chmn. Ind. Health Careers, Inc., 1979-81, chmn.-elect, 1981-82, chmn., 1982-83; bd. dirs., treas. Associated Colls. Ind., 1976-78, pres., 1984—; bd. dirs. Hosp. Audiences, Indpls., 1974-76, Independent Colls. and Univs. Ind.; chmn. Independent Colls. and Univs. Ind., 1979-80; adv. bd. Sta. WIAN. Served with AUS, 1945-46. Mem. Am., Ind., confs. on higher edn., Nat. Cath. Edn. Assn., MLA, Renaissance Soc. Am., Medieval Acad. Am., Ind. Coll. English Assn. (bus. mgr. Associator 1965-66), Indpls. C. of C., Indpls. Mus. Art, Alpha Phi Omega. Club: Indpls. Athletic. Lodge: Kiwanis. Home: 3024 Cold Spring Rd Indianapolis IN 46222

GATZKE, HANS WILHELM, history educator; b. Duelken, Germany, Dec. 10, 1915; came to U.S., 1937, naturalized, 1944; s. Wilhelm and Else (Schwab) G. Student, U. Munich, Germany, 1935, U. Bonn, 1936; A.B., Williams Coll., 1938; M.A., Harvard U., 1939, Ph.D., 1947; M.A. (hon.), Yale U., 1964. Teaching fellow, tutor history Harvard U., 1939-41, 42-44, 46-47; Sheldon traveling fellow, 1941-42; asst. sr. tutor Eliot House, 1942-43; instr. history Williams Coll., 1942; asst. prof. history Johns Hopkins U., 1947-51, assoc. prof., 1951-56, prof., 1956-64; prof. history Yale U., 1964—; fellow Timothy Dwight Coll., 1964—; mem. Inst. Advanced Study, Princeton U., 1951-52. Editor, translator: (Carl von Clausewitz) Principles of War, 1942, Germany's Drive to the West, 1950, Stresemann and the Rearmament of Germany, 1954, The Present in Perspective, 1957, European Diplomacy between Two Wars, 1972, Germany and the U.S.: A "Special Relationship"?, 1980, The Mainstream of Civilization, 1984; editorial bd.: Jour. Modern History, 1954-57, Current History; U.S. editor in chief: (Carl von Clausewitz) Documents on German Foreign Policy, 1969—. Served as 2d lt. AUS, 1944-46. Guggenheim fellow, 1956-57; Rockefeller grantee, 1962-63. Mem. Am. Hist. Assn. (Herbert Baxter Adams prize 1950), Phi Beta Kappa, Delta Kappa Epsilon. Home: 56 Farrell Rd Weston CT 06883 Office: Dept History Yale U New Haven CT 06520

GAUCH, EUGENE WILLIAM, JR., former air force officer; b. Newark, Dec. 6, 1922; s. Eugene William and Wilhelmina Katrina (Beiswenger) G.; m. Beryl Merle Walker, Jan. 15, 1947; children: Kathryn A. (Mrs. Jerry T. Stansfield), Tracey L. Student, Syracuse U.; grad., Nat. War Coll., 1969. Enlisted as pvt. USAAF, 1942; advanced through grades to brig. gen. USAF, 1972; assigned, Okinawa, World War II and Korean War; tng. and standardization officer SAC, Offutt AFB, Neb., 1955-59; ops. staff officer 72 Bombardment Wing, Ramey AFB, P.R., 1959-63; asst. exec. sec. to air staff bd. Office Vice Chief Staff Air Force, Washington, 1963-67; asst. chief staff, exec. to comdr. 7th Air Force, Vietnam, 1967-68; faculty Nat. War Coll., 1969; exec. to comdr. Hdqrs. Tactical Air Command, Langley AFB, Va., 1969-70, chief staff, 1970-72; comdr. 834th Air Div., Little Rock AFB, 1972-74; dir. automated mobility requirements DSC/Plans and Ops., Hdqrs. USAF, Washington, 1974-76. Decorated Legion of Merit with 3 oak leaf clusters, D.F.C., Air medal with 4 oak leaf clusters, Air Force Commendation medal. Home: 628 Owl Way Sarasota FL 33577

GAUDAUR, JACOB GILL, football league exec.; b. Orillia, Ont., Can., Oct. 5, 1920; s. Jacob Gill and Alice Grace (Hemming) G.; m. Isabel Grace Scott, Apr. 16, 1943; children—Jacqueline, Diane, Janice. Grad., Orillia, Collegiate Inst., 1940. Mem. Hamilton (Ont.) Tigers Football Team, 1940, 48-49; mem. Toronto (Ont.) Argonauts Football Team, 1941, Toronto Indians, 1945-46, capt., 1945-47; mem., co-capt. Montreal (Que., Can.) Alouettes, 1947; mem., capt. Hamilton Tiger-Cats Football Team, 1950-51, dir., 1952, mem. team, 1953, pres., gen. mgr., 1954-68; pres. Eastern Football Conf., Can. Football League, 1959, pres. league, 1962, commr., 1968—; pres., owner Gaudaur Motor Co. (Gen. Motors dealership), Burlington, Ont., 1956-62; pres. JayGil Ltd. (mgmt. cons.), Hamilton, 1963—; chmn. bd. dirs. Can. Football Hall of Fame; chmn. adv. bd. Can. Football Players Pension Fund. Served with RCAF, 1942-45. Anglican. Clubs: Albany (Toronto); Burlington (Ont.) Golf and Country, Variety Internat., Masons. Can. Sr. One-Mile Rowing Champion, 1941. Office: 11 King St W Suite 1800 Toronto ON M5H 1A3 Canada *

GAUDETTE, HENRI EUGENE, geochemist, educator; b. Boston, Jan. 26, 1932; s. Eugene Octave and Marion (Reed) G.; m. Alice M. Connors, Sept. 1, 1960; children—Eugene H. B.A., U. N.H., 1959; M.S. (Univ. fellow), U. Ill., 1962, Ph.D., 1963. Research asso. U. Ill., 1963-65; asst. prof. U. N.H., Durham, 1965-68, asso. prof. dept. earth scis., 1968-78, prof., 1978—; cons. geology and geochemistry. Contbr. articles to sci. jours. Served as 1st lt. U.S. Army, 1953-57. NSF grantee, 1975—; Sea Grant grantee, 1977—. Fellow Geol. Soc. Am.; mem. Geochem. Soc., Mineral. Soc. Am., Sigma Xi. Roman Catholic. Office: Dept Earth Sci U NH Durham NH 03824

GAUDIERI, ALEXANDER V.J., museum executive; b. 1940; married; 1 child. B.A., Ohio State U., 1962; Diploma, Sorbonne U. Paris, 1962; postgrad., Colgate U., 1963; M.B.A. in Internat. Fin., Grad. Sch. Internat. Mgmt., 1965; M.A., Inst. Fine Arts, NYU, 1976. Internat. banking officer Marine Midland Bank, N.Y.C., 1965-71; with Sotheby Parke Bernet, 1972—. Chmn. nat. coucil Young Concert Artists, N.Y.C.; mem. bd. sponsors Attingham Park Program, Eng. Barton Kyle Yount scholar. Mem. Assn. Art Mus. Dirs., Am. Assn. Mus. (accreditation commn.), Brit. Nat. Trust, Soc. Archtl. Historians. Address: Telfair Sq PO Box 10081 Savannah GA 31412

GAUDION, DONALD ALFRED, former diversified manufacturing executive; b. Buffalo, July 10, 1913; s. William Thomas and Orpha (Gascoyne) G.; m. Gertrude Margaret McKie, Aug. 3, 1940; children: Sharon Margaret Sanford, Jacquelyn Elaine McClelland, Donald Alfred. A.B. cum laude, U. Rochester, 1936; M.B.A. with high distinction, Harvard U., 1938; D.H.L. (hon.), Keuka Coll., 1972, Ithaca Coll., 1974. Asst. to v.p. charge sales and advt. Eastman Kodak Co., 1938-45; v.p. Kryptar Corp., 1945-48; with Sybron Corp., Rochester, N.Y., 1948-78, exec. v.p., 1955-59, pres., 1959-71, chmn. bd., chief exec. officer, 1971-75, chmn. bd., 1975-78; dir. Rochester Telephone Corp., Schlegel Mfg. Co., Rochester, Brown & Sharpe, Providence, Security Trust Co. of Rochester, Security N.Y. State Corp.; trustee Monroe Savs. Bank, Rochester.; chmn. N.Y. State Econ. Devel. Bd., 1975-77; mem. exec. com. Machinery and Allied Products Inst., Washington, Conf. Bd. N.Y.C. Chmn. emeritus bd. trustees Rochester U.; trustee Center for Govtl. Research; past pres. Rochester Jobs Inc.; past chmn. United Negro Coll. Fund. Recipient Prime Minister's medal State of Israel, 1978. Mem. Rochester Soc. Investment Analysts, Indsl. Mgmt. Council (trustee, past pres.), Rochester C. of C. (past pres., bd. trustees, award 1969), NAM (chmn. 1974, hon. vice-chmn. 1983, now dir.), Harvard Bus. Sch. Assn. (exec. council), Phi Beta Kappa, Beta Gamma Sigma. Presbyterian. Clubs: City (past pres.), University, Rochester Country (Rochester); Genessee Valley; Harvard (N.Y.C.); Harvard Business School (past pres.), Philosophers). Home: 30 Golfside Pkwy Rochester NY 14610 also 2121 N Ocean Blvd Boca Raton FL 33432 293 East Lake Rd Canandaigua NY 14424

GAUDRAULT, ROBERT JOSEPH, former food service executive; b. Holyoke, Mass., 1917; s. Joseph Arthur and Bernadette (Lamontagne) G.; m. Shirley Greenhalgh, Apr. 20, 1942; children: Betsy Gaudrault McNerney, Sandra Gaudrault Hartnett, Judith Gaudrault Higgins. Student, Am. Internat. Coll., 1946-47. With Friendly Ice Cream Corp., Wilbraham, Mass., 1946-82, v.p., then exec. v.p., 1951-70, pres., 1970-79, chief exec. officer, 1974-80, chmn. bd., 1979-82; dir. Bank of New Eng.-West, Milton Bradley Co., Mass. Mut. Life Ins. Co., all Springfield, Mass. Bd. corporators Springfield Girls Club, Springfield Boys Club, Baystate Med. Center; trustee Am. Internat. Coll. Served to 1st lt. AUS, 1940-46. Clubs: Colony (Springfield); Longmeadow (Mass.) Country; Ekwanok (Manchester, Vt.); Dorset (Vt.) Field. Home: 2601 Gulfshore Blvd N Naples FL 33940 *Learning how to work with and through others, with integrity and determination, is a sure formula for success.*

GAUDREAU, JOSEPH MICHAEL, insurance company executive; b. Quincy, Mass., Sept. 23, 1921; s. Victor Eli and Mary Veronica (Golden) G.; m. Alicia Margaret Golden, Apr. 10, 1948; children: J. Michael, Elise M., William P., Robert V. B.S. in Physics, Boston Coll., 1944. Sales rep. Liberty Mut. Ins. Co., Boston and Providence, 1947-50, city sales mgr., 1950-53, dist. mgr., New Haven, 1953-60, div. sales mgr., Boston, 1960-66, v.p. New Eng. div., Weston, Mass., 1966-79, sr. v.p. field ops., Boston, 1979—; dir. Mass. Coop. Bank, Boston. Served with U.S. Army, 1943-46. Republican. Roman Catholic. Clubs: Algonquin (Boston); Weston Golf (Mass.). Home: 44 Westgate St Wellesley MA 02181 Office: Liberty Mut Ins Co 175 Berkeley St Boston MA 02117

GAUDRY, ROGER, chemist, university official; b. Quebec, Que., Can., 1913. B.A., Laval U., 1933, B.Sc. in Chemistry, 1937, D.Sc. in Organic Chemistry, 1940; postgrad. (Rhodes scholar), Oxford (Eng.) U., 1937-39. Faculty medicine Laval U., Quebec, 1940-54; asst. dir. research labs. Ayerst, McKenna Harrison Ltd., Montreal, Que., 1954-57, dir., 1957-65, v.p., 1963-65; bd. govs., mem. exec. com. U. Montreal, 1961-65, rector, 1965-75, now conseiller du recteur; Dir. Bank of Montreal, CDC Life Scis., Connaught Labs., Corby Distilleries Ltd., Alcan Aluminum Ltd., Can. Hoechst Ltd., S.K.W. Can., Ltd. Contbr. sci. papers to profl. lit. Mem. Def. Research Bd. Can., 1962-68, Bd. Trust Gen. Can., 1970-75; mem. council UN U., 1974-80, chmn., 1974-76. Decorated companion Order Can.; recipient Pariseau medal Assn. Canadienne Francaise pour l'Avancement des Scis., 1958. Fellow Royal Soc. Can.; mem. Chem. Inst. Can. (pres. 1955-56), Societe de Chimie Industrielle de France (mem. bd. 1960), Sci. Council Can. (vice chmn. 1966-72, pres. 1972-75), Assn. Univs. and Colls. Can. (pres. 1969-71), Academie du Monde Latin Paris (life), Can. Geriatrics Research Soc. (dir.), Corp. Profl. Chemists Can., Assn. Univs. Partiellement ou Entierement de Langue Francaise (v.p. 1973-75), Internat. Assn. Univs. (pres. 1975-80), Conf. Rectors and Prins Que. Univs. (pres. 1970-72). Address: U Montreal 2910 Blvd Edouard-Montpetit Montreal PQ Canada H3C 3J7

GAUDY, ANTHONY FRANCIS, JR., educator, sanitary engineer; b. Jamaica, N.Y., June 16, 1925; s. Anthony Francis and Catherine (Ford) G.; m. Elizabeth Thomas, June 11, 1955. B.S. in Civil Engring. cum laude, U. Mass., 1951; M.S. in San. Engring., MIT, 1955; Ph.D., U. Ill., 1959. Registered profl. engr., Ill., Okla., Del.; cert. Nat. Council Engring. Examiners. Civil engr. E.F. Carlson, Inc., Springfield, Mass., 1951-52, Capuano Constrn., Inc., West Springfield, 1952-53; research asst., san engr. Sedgewick Labs., MIT, 1953-55; research engr. Nat. Council Stream Improvement, Va. Poly. Inst., 1955; regional engr. West coast Oreg. State U., 1955-57; USPHS grad. fellow san. engring. dept. U. Ill., Urbana, 1957-59, asst. prof. san. engring., 1959-61; asso. prof. civil engring. Okla. State U., Stillwater, 1961-63, prof. civil engring., 1963-79, Edward R. Stapley prof., 1968-79, dir. center for water research in engring., 1965-79, acting head Sch. Civil Engring., 1966-67; H. Rodney Sharp prof., chmn. dept. civil engring. U. Del., Newark, 1979—; research cons. indsl. wastes, 1959—; prin. Thomas-Gaudy & Taylor, Inc., engring. cons., Memphis; mem. task force on pollution control NRC, 1972-77, also com. on army basic research, 1976-79. Editorial bd.: Environ. Sci. and Tech, 1967-69, Jour. Applied and Environ. Microbiology, 1967-73, Biotech. and Bioengring., 1971—; co-author textbook; contbr. articles to profl. jours. Served with USAAF, 1943-46. Recipient Harrison Prescott Eddy award Water Pollution Control Fedn., 1967. Fellow ASCE; mem. Am. Soc. Engring. Edn. (chmn. environ. engring. div. 1966-67, 70-71), Am. Soc. Microbiology, Am. Chem. Soc., Am. Water Works Assn., AAAS, Am. Inst. Chem. Engrs., Nat. Soc. Profl. Engrs., Water Pollution Control Fedn. (dir. 1962-65), Assn. Environ. Engring Profs. (dir. 1972-75), Am. Acad. Environ. Engrs. (trustee 1977-82), Internat. Assn. Water Pollution Research. Club: Newark Rotary (dir. 1982-83). Home: 111 Bridleshire Ct Newark DE 19711 *Carefully weigh the facts as you see them, make a decision, and strike out in the direction you've determined is right. If others follow, you are a leader; if they do not, you are a loner. Either way you're your own man*

GAUDY, ELIZABETH THOMAS, microbiology educator, consultant; b. Clarksville, Tenn., Mar. 23, 1924; d. Carlyle and Irene Elizabeth (Farrar) Thomas; m. Anthony Francis Gaudy, Jr., June 11, 1955. B.S., Austin Peay State Coll., 1947; M.S., U. Ill., 1960, Ph.D., 1962. Research asst. microbiology U. Ill., Urbana, 1960-62; asst. prof. microbiology Okla. State U., Stillwater, 1962-65, asso. prof., 1965-70, prof., 1970-79, chmn. faculty council and gen. faculty, 1976-77, chmn. women's council, 1977-78; mem. NRC advisory com., steering com. U.S. Army Basic Research, 1979—. Co-author textbook.; Contbr. articles to profl. jours. Ford Found. fellow, 1959-60. Mem. Am. Soc. Microbiology, Genetics Soc. Am., Soc. Gen. Microbiology, AAAS, Am. Inst. Biol. Scis., Assn. Women in Sci., Sigma Xi. Democrat. Methodist. Home: 111 Bridleshire Ct Newark DE 19711

GAUER, CHARLOTTE EDWINA, assn. exec.; b. Balt., Jan. 16, 1912; d. Charles E. and Lucinda D. (Smith) G. B.S., U. Ill., 1932, LL.B., 1935. Bar: Ill. bar 1935. Legal editor Commerce Clearing House, Chgo., 1935-42; legal staff Montgomery Ward & Co., 1942-50, Pub. Housing Adminstrn., 1951-54; exec. dir. Am. Patent Law Assn., Arlington, Va., 1954-79; Nat. bd. Med. Coll. Pa., from 1953, now ret. Served with Am. Women's Vol. Services, 1942- 45. Mem. Women's Bar Assn. Ill. (pres. 1942-43), Nat. Assn. Women Lawyers (v.p. Ill. 1943-44, pres. 1947-49), Am. Bar Assn., Delta Delta Delta, Alpha Alpha Alpha, Kappa Beta Pi, Mortar Bd. Republican. Conglist. Home: 80 N Los Olmos Green Valley AZ 85614

GAUL, GILBERT MARTIN, newspaper reporter; b. Jersey City, May 18, 1951; s. Albert Joseph and Jane (Daughton) G.; m. Cathryn Lou Candy, May 30, 1953. B.A., Fairleigh Dickinson U., 1973; tchr.'s cert., Montclair (N.J.) State Coll., 1974. Reporter Lehighton (Pa.) Times-News, 1976-78, Pottsville (Pa.) Republican, 1978-80, investigative reporter, 1981-83, Phila. Inquirer, 1983—; reporter Phila. Bull., 1980-81. Recipient Pulitzer prize spl. local reporting, 1979, Edward J. Meeman award Scripps-Howard Found., 1979, Silver Gavel award ABA, 1979. Mem. Investigative Reporters and Editors Assn. Office: 111-117 Mahantongo St Pottsville PA 17901 *

GAULIN, JEAN, gas distribution company executive; b. Montreal, July 9, 1942; s. Paul and Berthe (Lariviere) G.; m. Andree LeBoeuf; children: Marie-Claude, Philippe, Mathieu. Chem. Engr. and B.A.Sc., Montreal U., 1967. Dir. Que. Refinery of Canadian Ultramar Ltd., 1976-79; v.p. supply and refining Canadian Ultramar Ltd., Toronto, 1979-80; pres. Nouveler Inc., Montreal, 1980-82; pres., chief exec. officer Gaz Metropolitain, Inc., Montreal, 1982—; dir. Sceptre Resources Ltd. Bd. dirs. Internat. Centre for Research and Studies in Mgmt., Montreal, 1982—, Foundation de l'Universite du Quebec a Montreal, 1982—, Institut de Cardiologie de Montreal, 1983—. Served with Canadian Navy, 1958-62. Mem. Canadian Gas Assn. (dir. 1982—), Am. Gas Assn., Ordre des Ingenieurs du Que. Club: St. Denis. Office: 1155 Dorchester Blvd W Montreal PQ Canada H3B 3S7

GAULINI, CARLO MARIA, conductor; b. Barletta, Italy, May 9, 1914; m. Marcella Giulini. Student, Accademia Santa Cecilia, Rome, Chigiana Acad., Siena, Italy. Asst. condr. Rome Radio Orch., 1944-46, prin. condr., 1946-50, Orch. of Radio Milan, Italy, 1950-54, La Scala, Milan, 1954-58; prin. guest condr. Chgo. Symphony Orch., 1969-72; music dir. Los Angeles Philharm., 1978—. Recipient Grammy award Nat. Acad. Rec. Arts and Scis., 1971, Gold medal Bruckner Soc., 1978, Internat. Mahler Soc., 1978. Mem. Gesellschaft der Musikfreunde(hon.). Office: Los Angeles Philharmonic 135 N Grand Ave Los Angeles CA 90012

GAULKE, RAMON GEORGE, advt. exec.; b. Oak Park, Ill., Jan. 21, 1934; s. Walter George and Ann (Jaraback) G.; children—Mark, Ann, Peter. B.A., Elmhurst Coll., 1955. Advt. mgr. Ekco-Alcoa Packaging Co., Wheeling, Ill., 1959-63; creative dir. Lows, Inc., Chgo., 1963-65; pres., dir. Marsteller, Inc., N.Y.C., 1965-80; chief exec. officer Intermarco Advt., N.Y.C., 1980—. Trustee Elmhurst (Ill.) Coll. Served with USNR, 1955-59; capt. Res. (ret.). Mem. Advt. Council (dir.). Office: 4 W 58th St New York NY 10022

GAULL, GERALD EDWARD, pediatrician, scientist, educator; b. Boston, Sept. 17, 1930; s. Samuel and Alice Charlotte (Berkowitz) G.; children: Erik, Stephen. B.A. with honors in Philosophy, U. Mich., 1951; M.D., Boston U., 1955. Junior and sr. resident in pathology Peter Bent Brigham Hosp., Boston, 1955-57; NIH postdoctoral research fellow Harvard, 1957-60, NIH research fellow in pediatrics, 1963-64; research asso. Columbia, 1965-67; jr. resident pediatrics Babies Hosp., N.Y.C., 1960-61, attending pediatrician, 1965-67; chief pediatric research N.Y. Inst. Research in Devel. Disabilities, S.I., N.Y., 1967—; chief Div. Human Devel. and Nutrition, dep. dir. N.Y. Inst. Research in Mental Retardation, 1976—; asso. prof. pediatrics Mt. Sinai Sch. Med., 1967-74, prof., 1974—; asso. attending, then attending pediatrician Mt. Sinai Hosp., 1967—. Author: Biology of Brain Dysfunction, 1973-75, Natural Sulfur Compounds, 1980; contbr. articles to profl. jours. Served with U.S. Army, 1961-62. Recipient Borden award Am. Acad. Pediatrics, 1978, St. Ambrosiano gold medal City of Milan (Italy), 1983; Med. Research Council fellow, 1964. Mem. Am. Soc. Biol. Chemists, Am. Soc. Neurochemistry, Soc. Pediatric Research, Am. Inst. Nutrition, Am. Soc. Clin. Nutrition, Internat. Soc. Neurochemistry, Am. Pediatric Soc., Internat. Brain Research Orgn., Soc. Neurosci., Am. Soc. Human Genetics, Perinatal Research Soc., Soc. Inherited Metabolic Inherited Disorders. Home: 420 E 51st St Apt 5B New York NY 10022 Office: 1050 Forest Hill Rd Staten Island NY 10314

GAULT, N.L., JR., physician, educator; b. Austin, Tex., Aug. 22, 1920; s. N.L. and Pauline (Johnson) G.; m. Sarah Jane Dickie, June 28, 1947; children—Elizabeth Jean, John Dickie, Paul Alan. Student, U. Tex., 1938-42, Baylor U. Med. Sch., 1946-48; B.A., U. Tex., 1950; M.B., U. Minn., 1950, M.D., 1951, student Grad. Sch., 1951-54. Intern Mpls. Gen. Hosp., 1950-51; resident internal medicine Mpls. VA Hosp., 1951-52; chief resident internal medicine Ancker Hosp., St. Paul, 1952, U. Minn. Hosp., 1953-54; faculty U. Minn. Med. Sch., Mpls., 1953-67, 72—, asso. prof. internal medicine, asso. dean, 1962-67, prof. medicine, dean, 1972—; prof. medicine U. Hawaii, asso. dean, 1967-72; chief adviser Seoul (Korea) Nat. U. Coll. Medicine, 1959-61; med. edn. cons. China Med. Board, N.Y.C., 1963, 71, AID, 1964-68; dir. postgrad. med. edn. program for, Ryukyu Islands, 1967-69; cons. Mpls. VA Hosp., 1956-67. Sec.-treas. Minn. Med. Found., 1956-67. Served to capt. AUS, USAAF, 1942-46. Decorated Commendation medal.; Recipient Supreme award Japan Med. Assn., 1969. Mem. AMA, Assn. Am. Med. Colls. (exec. council 1974-80, chmn. council deans MidWest-Gt. Plains region 1974-76), Minn. Med. Assn., Hennepin County Med. Soc. Address: Medical Sch U Minn Minneapolis MN 55455

GAULT, ROBERT KRUGER, JR., zoological park and aquarium executive; b. San Diego, Mar. 29, 1944; s. Robert Kruger and Ruth Addie (Johnson) G.; m. Claudia Ann Stalder, June 24, 1966; children: Stacy, Michelle, Tobin, Robert. Student, San Diego State U., 1962-66. Ops. mgr. Sea World Inc., San Diego, 1964-66, dir. ops., 1966-73, Orlando, Fla., 1973-75, asst. gen. mgr., 1975-79, v.p., gen. mgr., Aurora, Ohio, 1979—. Dir., mem. exec. com. Conv.-Visitors Bur. Greater Cleve., 1981-83; sec. Community Improvement Corp., Aurora, 1981—. Named Kiwanian of Year, 1983. Fellow Am. Assn. Zool. Parks and Aquariums; mem. Am. Mgmt. Assn., Aurora C. of C. (dir. 1979—, Citizen of Yr. award 1982). Republican. Episcopalian. Lodge: Kiwanis. Office: Sea World Inc 1100 Sea World Dr Aurora OH 44202

GAULT, STANLEY CARLETON, manufacturing executive; b. Wooster, Ohio, Jan. 6, 1926; s. Clyde Carleton and Aseneth Briton (Stanley) G.; m. Flo Lucille Kurtz, June 11, 1949; children: Stephen, Christopher, Jennifer. B.A., Coll. Wooster, 1948. With Gen. Electric Co. (and subs.), 1948-79, v.p. and group exec. maj. appliance bus. group, Louisville, 1970-77, v.p. and sector exec. consumer products and services sector, Fairfield, Conn., 1977, sr. v.p., sector exec., 1977-79; vice chmn. bd. Rubbermaid Inc., Wooster, Ohio, 1980, chmn. bd., chief exec. officer, 1980—; dir. Internat. Paper Co., PPG Industries, Inc.; mem. exec. bd. Nat. Bus. Council for Consumer Affairs, from 1972, vice chmn. subcouncil for product safety, 1972. Trustee Coll. of Wooster. Served with USAAF, 1944-46. Mem. NAM (dir.). Republican. Methodist. Office: Rubbermaid Inc 1147 Akron Rd Wooster OH 44691

GAULT, WILLIS MANNING, stringed-instrument maker, performer, composer; b. Showell, Md., June 10, 1908; s. James E. and Essel May (Campbell) G. Student violin and harmony with, Anton Nimmerrichter, Anton Kasper, Dudley Clark. Dir. Gault Sch. Bowed Instrument Making, 1950—. Violinist, Globe Theatre, Berlin, Md., 1927-29; organizer, dir., Chamber Music Workshop, Washington, 1946-66; performer on viola d'amore.; Composer: various other works for viola d'amore. Suite in A Major for viola d'amore and orch. Home: 35-A Ridge Rd Greenbelt MD 20770 Office: 5502 Kenilworth Ave Riverdale MD 20737

GAULTNEY, JOHN ORTON, life insurance agent, consultant; b. Pulaski, Tenn., Nov. 7, 1915; s. Bert Hood and Grace (Orton) G.; m. Elizabethine Mullette, Mar. 30, 1941; children: Elizabethine (Mrs. Donald H. McClure), John Mullette, Walker Orton, Harlow Denny. Student, Am. Inst. Banking, 1936; diploma, Life Ins. Agy. Mgmt. Assn., 1948, Little Rock Jr. Coll., 1950; C.L.U., 1948; Mgmt. C.L.U. diploma, 1952; grad. sales mgmt. and mktg., Rutgers U., 1957. With N.Y. Life Ins. Co., 1935—, regional v.p., Atlanta, 1956-64, v.p., N.Y.C., 1964-67, v.p. in charge group sales, 1967-68, v.p. mktg., 1969-80, agt., 1980—; life ins. cons., 1981—; v.p. N.Y. Life Variable Contracts Corp., 1969-80; hon. dir. Bank of Frankewing (Tenn.), 1984—. Chmn. Downtown YMCA, Atlanta, 1963-65; mem. Bd. Zoning Appeals Bronxville, N.Y., 1970-80; mem. pub. relations com. Nat. Council YMCAs, 1965-80; mem. internat. world service com. YMCA, 1968-80; chmn. Vanderbilt YMCA, 1974-76, Bd. dirs., N.Y.C., 1966-76; Bd. dirs. Memphis YMCA, 1939-40, Little Rock YMCA, 1941-55, Atlanta YMCA, 1959-65, Greater N.Y. YMCA, 1975-80, Nashville YMCA, 1981—. Served to capt., inf. AUS, 1942-45; MTO. Decorated Bronze Star with 3 clusters, Silver Star, Purple Heart with 2 clusters.; Recipient Devereux C. Josephs award N.Y. Life Ins. Co., 1954; named Ark. traveler, 1955; hon. citizen Tenn., 1956; Tenn. ambassador, 1981—; Ky. col., 1963. Mem. Am., Tenn. socs. C.L.U.'s, Nat., Tenn. assns. life underwriters, Tenn. Gen. Agts. and Mgrs. Conf., Sales and Mktg. Execs. Internat., Heritage Found., Carnton Assn., N.Y. So. Soc. (trustee 1965-80), Williamson County Hist. Soc. (pres. 1983—), 361st Inf. Assn. World War II (pres. 1967-70), SAR (N.Y. state dir. 1970-80), St. Nicholas Soc. City N.Y., Soc. Colonial Wars, Tenn. Sons of Revolution, Tenn. Soc. in N.Y. (pres. 1971-74, trustee 1980—), Am. Risk and Ins. Assn., Newcomen Soc. in Am. Presbyterian (elder). Clubs: Rotarian., Capital City (Atlanta); Siwanoy (Bronxville, N.Y.); Brentwood Country., Nashville City. Lodges: Masons; Shriners. Home: 6109 Johnson Chapel Rd Brentwood TN 37027 Office: Parkway Towers Suite 2012 Nashville TN 37219 *The harder one works and the more one gives toward assisting others, the greater his success and happiness in life.*

GAUSMAN, EDITH MARIE, retired foundation executive; b. N.Y.C., Jan. 17, 1919; s. George and Eliza (Heuermann) G. Fiduciary acct. Sage Gray Todd & Sims, N.Y.C., 1950-64; asst. v.p. Scudder, Stevens & Clark, N.Y.C., 1964-72; asst. treas. Commonwealth Fund, N.Y.C., 1972-75, treas., 1975-81. Vice pres. bd. trustees Riverside Ch., N.Y.C., 1976-78; bd. dirs. Westside Ecumenical Ministry to the Elderly, Inc., 1979—. Mem. Bus. and Profl. Women's Club. Home: 11 Riverside Dr New York NY 10023

GAUSTAD, EDWIN SCOTT, historian; b. Rowley, Iowa, Nov. 14, 1923; s. Sverre and Norma (McEachron) G.; m. Helen Virginia Morgan, Dec. 19, 1946; children—Susan, Glen Scott, Peggy Lynn. B.A., Baylor U., 1947; M.A., Brown U., 1948, Ph.D., 1951. Instr. Brown U., 1951-52, Am. Council Learned Socs. scholar in residence, 1952-53; dean Shorter Coll., 1953-57; prof. humanities U. Redlands, 1957-65; asso. prof. history U. Calif., Riverside, 1965-67, prof., 1968—. Author: The Great Awakening in New England, 1957, Historical Atlas of Religion in America, 2d edit, 1976, A Religious History of America, rev. edit, 1974, Dissent in American Religion, 1973, Baptist Piety: The Last Will and Testimony of Obadiah Holmes, 1978, George Berkeley in America, 1979; editor books, most recent being: Documentary History of Religion in America, 2 vols., 1982, 83; editor: Arno Press, 1970-79; editorial bd.: Jour. Ch. and State, 1970—; contbr. articles to profl. publs. Served to 1st lt. USAAC, 1943-45. Decorated Air medal; Am. Council Learned Socs. grantee, 1952-53, 72-73; Am. Philos. Soc. grantee, 1972-73. Mem. Am. Hist. Assn., Am. Acad. Religion, Am. Soc. Ch. History (pres.), Phi Beta Kappa. Democrat. Baptist. Office: Dept History Univ Calif Riverside CA 92521

GAUSTAD, JOHN ELDON, astronomy educator; b. Mpls., May 23, 1938; s. Leonard Nicholas and Anne (Hewett) G. A.B., Harvard U., 1959; Ph.D., Princeton U., 1962, Research asso., 1962-63; Research asso., Calif. Inst. Tech., 1963-64. Lectr. U. Nigeria, Nsukka, 1964-67; asst. prof. astronomy U. Calif., Berkeley, 1966-70, asso. prof., 1970-75, prof., 1975-82, chmn. dept., 1976-79, asst. dean, 1980-82; prof. astronomy Swarthmore (Pa.) Coll., 1982—, chmn. dept., 1982—, dir. Sproul Obs., 1982—. Contbr. articles to profl. jours. Mem. Am. Astron. Soc., Internat. Astron. Union, Astron. Soc. Pacific, AAAS, Am. Assn. Variable Star Observers, Phi Beta Kappa, Sigma Xi. Office: Dept Astronomy Swarthmore College Swarthmore PA 19081

GAUT, NORMAN EUGENE, environmental consulting firm executive; b. Gilman, Colo., Sept. 20, 1937; s. Marvin Joseph and Margaret Elmo (Carl) G.; m. Madeleine Suzanne Dupuy, Aug. 29, 1964; children: Christopher Carl, Eric Kerwin, Jeffrey Gareth. B.S. in Physics, UCLA, 1959; S.M. in Meteorology, M.I.T., 1964, Ph.D., 1967. Pres. Environ. Research and Tech., Inc., Concord, Mass., 1968—. Served with USAF, 1959-62. NASA grantee, 1963-67. Mem. Am. Meteorol. Soc., Am. Geophys. Union, AAAS. Home: 25 Marrett St Lexington MA 02173 Office: 696 Virginia Rd Concord MA 01742

GAUTHIER, CLARENCE JOSEPH, utility executive; b. Houghton, Mich., Mar. 16, 1922; s. Clarence A. and Muriel V. (Beesley) G.; m. Grayce N. Wicall, July 25, 1941; children: Joseph H., Nancy M. B.S. in Mech. Engring, U. Ill., 1943; M.B.A., U. Chgo., 1960. Registered profl. engr., Ill. With Pub. Service Co. No. Ill., 1945-54; with No. Ill. Gas Co., 1954—, v.p. finance, 1960-62, v.p. ops., 1962-64, exec. v.p., 1965-69, pres., 1969-76, chmn., 1971—, chief exec. officer, 1971-81; dir. 1965; chmn., pres., chief exec. officer, dir. NICOR Inc., 1976—; dir. GDC, Inc., Bank of Yorktown, Lombard, Ill., GATX Corp., Nalco Chem. Co., Sun Electric Corp., Chgo. and NorthWestern Transp. Co.; vice chmn., dir. AEGIS, Ltd., 1978—. Contbr. articles to profl. jours. Trustee Council Energy Studies, 1977—; bd. dirs. Gas Research Inst., 1977-82; mem. Northwestern U. Assos., 1977—; citizens bd. U. Chgo., 1972—; chmn. devel. campaign Good Samaritan Hosp., Downers Grove, Ill., 1974-77; trustee George Williams Coll., Downers Grove, 1968-77, Ill. Inst. Tech., 1976—, IIT Research Inst., 1976-80; bd. dirs. Mid-Am. chpt. ARC, 1962-78; trustee Met. Crusade of Mercy, Chgo., 1965-77; mem. Ill. Savs. Bond Com., 1975—, U. Ill. Presidents Council, 1978—, U. Ill. Adv. Council, 1981—, U. Ill. Found.; bd. sponsors Evangel. Hosp. Assn., Oak Brook, Ill., 1977—. Served to capt. C.E. AUS, World War II; PTO. Decorated Silver Star, Bronze Star with V; recipient Distinguished Alumnus award, 1971, Alumni Honor award U. Ill., 1974, Loyalty award, 1977. Mem. Internat. Gas Union (council 1970-75, chmn. Com. Gas Utilization 1970-73), Am. Gas Assn. (dir. 1970-76, chmn. bd. 1975, Disting. Service award 1976), Midwest Gas Assn. (dir. 1964-67), So. Gas Assn. (dir. 1966-69), Ind. Natural Gas Assn. Am. (dir. 1972-73), Inst. Gas Tech. (trustee 1964-70, 71-78, chmn. bd. trustees 1976-78), AAAS, Am. Finance Assn., Am. Mgmt. Assn., Presidents Assn., U. Chgo. Grad. Sch. Bus. Alumni Assn. (pres. 1964-65), Ill. C. of C., Chgo. Council on Fgn. Relations (Chgo. com. 1974—), Chgo. Assn. Commerce and Industry (dir. 1966-71, 73-79), ME-IE Alumni Assn. U. Ill. (pres. 1976-77, dir. 1973—), Sigma Pi, Pi Tau Sigma, Tau Beta Pi, Beta Gamma Sigma, Tau Nu Tau. Clubs: Chicago, Commercial, Economic, Mid-America (Chgo.); Butler Nat. Golf (Oak Brook, Ill.). Home: 15 Lochinvar Ln Oak Brook IL 60521 Office: PO Box 200 Naperville IL 60566

GAUTHIER, JEAN-ROBERT, member Canadian parliament, chiropractor; b. Ottawa, Ont., Can., Oct. 22, 1929; s. Georges and Beulah G.; m. Monique Lemieux, Feb. 25, 1957; children: Jean-Francois, Pierre, Vincent, Nathalie. Student, Academie de La Salle, Coll. St Alexandre, Limbour, Que., Chiropractic Coll. of Toronto. Pvt. practice chiropractor; elected to House of Commons, 1972—, sec. to Minister of Urban Affairs, 1975, now chmn. com. miscellaneous pvt. bills and standing orders. Bd. dirs. Richelieu Day Camp and Sch. of Natural Scis. for Ottawa; mem. sch. bd. Mcpl. of Gloucester Adminstrn. Unit, 1961-66, chmn., 4 yrs.; mem. Coll. Bd. Ottawa, vice chmn. mgmt. com., 1969; mem. Ottawa Bd. edn., 1969; vice chmn. Ottawa Bd. Edn., 1971. Named Man of Yr. Jr. C. of C. of Ottawa-Vanier, 1970. Mem. Ont. Chriopractic Assn. Club: Richelieu (Ottawa). Address: 1741 Dorset Dr Ottawa ON Canada *

GAUTHIER, JOSEPH DELPHIS, clergyman; b. Hartford, Conn., Aug. 23, 1909; s. Victor Adélard and Marie Alexandrine (Domingue) G. B.S., Trinity Coll., Hartford, 1930; A.B., Weston Coll., 1940, A.M., 1941, S.T.L., 1945; D. ès L., U. Laval, 1948; D.H.L., Boston Coll., 1981. Spl. agt. Hartford Accident & Indemnity Co., 1930-35; entered Soc. of Jesus, 1935; ordained priest Roman Cath. Ch., 1944; asst. prof., chmn. Romance lang. dept. Boston Coll., 1948-52, chmn. dept., 1952-61, asso. prof. French lit., until 1966, prof., 1966—; editorial adviser, cons. Brit. World Lang. Dictionary, 1955; Mem. Mass. adv. com. fgn. lang. cons.; steering com. for Mass., Nat. Def. Edn. Act. Author: Le Canada français et le roman americain, 1948, Nouvelle Promenade littéraire, 1959, Variétés, 1960, (with Lewis A. Sumberg) Les Grands Ecrivains Francais, 1965, Douze voix Francaises, 1969, (with Vera G. Lee) La Vie des Lettres, 1970. Decorated chevalier Palmes Académiques, 1951, officer, 1958. Mem. N.E. Modern Lang. Assn. (pres. 1958), Modern Lang. Assn., Renaissance Soc. Am., Cath. Commn. Cultural and Intellectual Affairs, Am. Assn. Tchrs. French, Franco-Am. Hist. Soc., Am. Assn. Tchrs. German, Am. Assn. Tchrs. Spanish and Portuguese, Am. Assn. Tchrs. Italian. Address: Boston Coll Chestnut Hill MA 02167

GAUTHIER, VICTOR ARTHUR, JR., public administration consultant, former government official; b. Bklyn., May 21, 1917; s. Victor Arthur and Martha Louise (Cantrell) G.; m. Mary Faison Richardson, Sept. 8, 1943; children: Robert Cantrell, Richard Faison, Mary Dixon, Frank Raymond. B.A. cum laude, St. Lawrence U., 1939; postgrad., Columbia U., NYU, Johns Hopkins U., Am. U. Inst. Pub. Adminstrn., N.Y.C. Prin. orgn. and planning analyst ECA, 1948-52; Far East industry adviser Mut. Security Adminstrn., 1953-55; chief Near East-S. Asia industry div. ECA, 1955-59; acting dep. sec. gen. econ. also tech. asst. adviser CENTO, Ankara, Turkey, 1959-62; with AID, 1962—73, dir., Washington, 1962-64, 1964-67; U.S. dep. econ. coordinator for CENTO affairs, Ankara, Turkey, 1967-68; econ. coordinator for CENTO affairs AID, 1968-69; program officer (AID), Washington, 1969-73;, cons. in pub. adminstrn., 1973—; U.S. del. CENTO Econ. Com., Karachi, 1963, CENTO Ministerial Council, 1964. Served to capt. AUS, 1942-46. Mem. Soc. Internat. Devel., Soc. Pub. Adminstrn. Home: 1200 N Nash St Apt 846 Arlington VA 22209

GAUTIER, DICK, actor, writer; b. Los Angeles, Oct. 30, 1937; s. Aldoma Napoloeon and Marie Antionette G.; m. Barbara Stuart, Mar. 8, 1967; children: Christine Horta, Rand, Denise. Student pub. schs., Los Angeles. Comedian, hungry i, San Francisco; appeared in N.Y.C. supper clubs, including, Blue Angel and, Bonsoir; supper clubs, including Coconut Grove; starred on Broadway as Conrad Birdie in: Bye Bye Birdie, 1960-62 (Tony award and Most Promising Actor nominee); appeared in: motion pictures including Billy Jack Goes to Washington, Divorce, American Style, Ensign Pulver, Manchu Eagle, Fun with Dick and Jane; played Hymie in: series Get Smart; starred in: TV series Mr. Terrific, CBS, It's Your Bet, NBC, Can You Top This?, Here We Go Again, ABC; star as Robin Hood in: When Things Were Rotten, ABC, from 1975; Author: screenplays Uncle Sam; Contbg. writer to numerous TV situation comedies; composer numerous songs. Active in Thalians Charity. Served with Spl. Services br. USNR. Mem. Actors Equity Assn., AFTRA, Screen Actors Guild, ASCAP, Am. Guild Variety Artists. Office: Irv Schechter Co 9300 Wilshire Blvd Suite 410 Beverly Hills CA 90212 *

GAUTREAUX, MARCELIAN FRANCIS, JR., chemical company executive; b. Nashville, Jan. 17, 1930; s. Marcelian Francis and Mary Eunice (Terrebonne) G.; m. Mignon Alice Thomas, Apr. 26, 1952; children—Marcelian, Marian, Kevin, Andrée. B.S.Ch.E. magna cum laude, La. State U., 1950, M.S.Ch.E., 1951, Ph.D. in Chem. Engring, 1958. With Ethyl Corp., Baton Rouge, 1951-55, 58—, gen. mgr. dept. research and devel., 1968-69, v.p., 1969-74, sr. v.p., 1974—, advisor to exec. com., 1981—, also dir.; instr. La. State U., 1955-56, asst. prof. chem. engring., 1956-58; mem. sci. adv. com. Biotech Research Lab., Inc., 1982—. Bd. dirs. Baton Rouge Community Concerts Assn., 1974—, pres., 1981—; trustee La. Arts and Sci. Center, Baton Rouge, 1974-77; mem. La. State U. Found.; chmn. adv. com. dept. chem. engring. La. State U. Recipient (charter) Personal Achievement in Chem. Engring. award Chem. Engring. Mag., 1968; Charles E. Coates Meml. award Am. Chem. Soc./Am. Inst. Chem. Engrs., 1976; Ann. Meml. award Chem. Mktg. Research Assn., 1978; Best Paper award, 1980; charter mem. La. State U. Engring. Hall of Distinction, 1979. Fellow Am. Inst. Chem. Engrs. (Best Presented Paper award 1952); mem. Nat. Acad. Engring., Soc. Chem. Industry, Soc. Engring. Sci. (past dir.), Inst. Amorphous Studies (sci. adv. com. 1982—). Roman Catholic. Clubs: Baton Rouge Country, Baton Rouge City, Baton Rouge Camelot. Patentee and author in field. Home: 1662 Pollard Pkwy Baton Rouge LA 70808 Office: 451 Florida Blvd Baton Rouge LA 70801 *Any successes I have had are no more or less than the composite result of a supportive and loving wife and children, professional associates who have never let me down, a corporation whose ethics are the highest, a religious heritage from my parents and early schooling, and some God-given talents for chemistry and engineering.*

GAUVIN, WILLIAM HENRY, chem. engr.; b. Paris, Mar. 30, 1913; emigrated to Can., 1930, naturalized, 1937; s. Hectore Gustave and Albertine Marie (VanHalle) G.; m. Dorothy Strong, Aug. 23, 1965; children—Suzanne, Robin, Christopher, Ian, Geoffrey, Stephanie. B.Eng., McGill U., Montreal, 1941, M.Eng., 1942, Ph.D. in Phys. Chemistry, 1945; D.Eng. (hon.), U. Waterloo, Ont., 1967. Lectr. chem. engring. McGill U., 1942-44, asso. prof., 1947-62, research asso., 1961-72, sr. research asso., 1972—; plant supt. F.W. Horner Ltd., Montreal, 1944-46; cons., then head chem. engring. div. Pulp and Paper Research Inst. Can., Montreal, 1951-61; research mgr. Noranda Research Centre, Pointe Claire, Que., 1961-70; del. gen. policy and planning Nat. Research Council Can., 1970-71; dir. research and devel. Noranda Mines Ltd., Pointe Claire, 1970—; mem. council Nat. Research Council Can., 1964-70; pres. adv. com. Indsl. Materials Research Inst., 1978—; mem. Sci. Council uan., 1966-70, 73-76; bd. dirs. Institut National de Productivité, Que., 1979—; hon. pres. 2d World Congress Chem. Engring., Montreal, 1981; mem. Can. council Weizman Inst. Sci., 1966—. Author. Bd. govs. McGill U., 1972—. Decorated companion Order Can.; recipient Archambault medal ACFAS, 1966; Gold medal Société d'Encouragement pour la Recherche et l'Invention, 1979. Fellow Royal Soc. Can., Chem. Inst. Can. (pres. 1977-78, Palladium medal 1966), Inst. Chem. Engring. U.K. (Sr. Moulton medal 1964), Am. Inst. Chem. Engring.; mem. Interam. Confedn. Chem. Engring. (pres. 1979-81), Assn. de la Recherche Industrielle du Quebec (pres. 1980—), Can. Inst. Mining and Metallurgy (Alcan award 1970, Disting. Lectr. award 1972, v.p.), Can. Soc. Chem. Engring. (pres. 1966-67, award 1968, R.S. Jane Meml. Lectr. award 1963), Can. Pulp and Paper Assn. (I.H. Weldon medal 1958), Corp. Profl. Engrs. Que., Am. Mgmt. Assn. (research and devel. planning council 1968—), Conseil de la Politique Sci. Que., Acad. Sci. Can., Engring. Inst. Can., Can. Nuclear Soc., Internat. Centre Heat and Mass Transfer, Am. Inst. Chem. Engrs., Am. Inst. Mining and Metall. Engrs., Can. Research Mgmt. Assn., Indsl. Research Inst., Instn. Chem. Engrs., Brit. Non-Ferrous Metals Research Assn., TAPPI, Dechema, Soc. de Chimie Industrielle (hon.), Soc. des Ingenieurs Civils de France, Soc. Chem. Industry, AAAS, Montreal Bd. Trade. Clubs: Royal St. Lawrence Yacht; University, Faculty (Montreal). Patentee in field. Home: 7 Harrow Pl Beaconsfield PQ H9W 5C7 Canada Office: Noranda Research Centre 240 Hymus Blvd Pointe Claire PQ H9R 1G5 Canada

GAVALAS, GEORGE R., chemical engineering educator; b. Athens, Greece, Oct. 7, 1936; s. Lazaros R. and Belouso A. (Matha) G. B.S., Nat. Tech. U., 1958; M.S., U. Minn., 1962, Ph.D., 1964. Asst. prof. chem. engring. Calif. Inst. Tech., 1964-67, asso. prof., 1967-75, prof., 1975—; cons. in field. Author: Nonlinear Differential Equations of Chemically Reacting Systems, 1968, Coal Pyrolysis, 1983; contbr. articles to profl. jours. Mem. Soc. Petroleum Engrs., Am. Inst. Chem. Engrs. (Tech. award 1968, Wilhelm award 1983), Am. Chem. Soc. Home: 3439 N Marengo Altadena CA 91001 Office: Caltech 208-41 Pasadena CA 91125

GAVAN, JAMES ANDERSON, anthropologist, educator; b. Ludington, Mich., July 17, 1916; s. James B. and Mary (Anderson) G.; m. Margaret Sheninger, Dec. 17, 1945; children—Margaret Jean, James Charles. B.A., U. Ariz., 1939; M.A., U. Chgo., 1949, Ph.D., 1953. Research staff Yerkes Labs. Primate Biology, Orange Park, Fla., 1950-53; asst. prof. anatomy Med. Coll. S.C., 1953-60, asso. prof., 1960-62; asso. prof. anatomy, anthropology U. Fla., 1962-67; prof. anthropology U. Mo. at Columbia, 1967—, chmn. dept. anthropology, 1968-71, 75-78; Mem. dental study sect. NIH, 1970-74; mem. anthropology rev. panel NSF, 1976-78. Author: Paleoanthropology and Primate Evolution, 1976; Editor: The Non-Human Primates and Human Evolution, 1955; Contbr. articles to profl. jours. Fellow AAAS, Am. Anthrop. Assn.; mem. Am. Assn. Phys. Anthropology (sec.-treas. 1972-76, pres. 1976-78), Sigma Xi. Home: RD 1 Box 253 Clark MO 65243 Office: Dept Anthropology 210 Switzler Hall Univ Mo Columbia MO 65211

GAVAZZI, ALADINO A., med. center adminstr.; b. Exeter, Pa., July 24, 1922; s. Guido and Ambrozina (Santoni-O'Brien) G.; m. Nancylee Ray, June 21, 1958; children—William A., Ann Marie, Lisa Kathryn, Alan Lee, Michael J. B.S., Columbia, 1953, M.S., 1955; Ph.D., U. Chgo., 1959. Adminstrv. officer VA br.-dist. office, N.Y.C., 1946-50; med. adminstrv. officer VA hosps., Bklyn., Bronx, N.Y., 1950-53; hosp. adminstrv. resident Bronx, Beth Israel and Presbyn. hosps., N.Y.C., 1953-54; hosp. adminstr. VA Hosps., Hampton, Va., 1955-57, Chgo. Research Hosp., 1957-59, Dwight, Ill., 1960-62, Mt. Alto VA Hosp., Washington, 1963-64, asso. dir. hosp. constrn., 1964-65, center dir., Martinsburg, W.Va., 1965-68; exec. asst. to chief med. dir. dept. medicine and surgery VA, 1968-70, exec. dir. for adminstrn. dept. medicine and surgery, 1970-71; dir. VA Med. Center, Washington, 1971—; professorial lectr. health care adminstrn. George Washington U.; Guest lectr. hosp. adminstrn. Med. Coll. Va., Richmond, Northwestern U., Chgo., U. Fla., U. Ala., Duke U., Cornell U., Columbia U., U. Sao Paulo, Brazil; adj. prof. in internat. health Georgetown U. Dist. chmn. Boy Scouts Am., W.Va., 1967-68; chmn. Combined Fed. Campaign for W.Va. for all fed. agys., 1966-68. Served to 1st lt. Armored Div. AUS, 1940-45; col. Res. Recipient Outstanding Performance awards VA, 1952, 56, 59, 63, 65, 70, 74, 80, Exceptional Service award, 1981; Nat. Civil Servant of Year-Silver Helmet award Amvets, 1974. Fellow Am. Coll. Hosp. Adminstrs. (regent for D.C. 1977-80, mem. various commns.), Royal Soc. Health (London), Am. Hosp. Assn.; mem. Fed. Exec. Inst. Alumni Assn. (pres. 1974-75). Home: 1541 Dahlia Ct McLean VA 22101

GAVENDA, J(OHN) DAVID, physicist; b. Temple, Tex., Mar. 25, 1933; s. Edward and Rose Katherine (Machalek) G.; m. Janie Louise Yeoman, Dec. 22, 1952; children—Victor Joseph, Philip Martin. Student, U. Chgo., 1950-51; B.S., U. Tex., Austin, 1954, M.A., 1956; Ph.D., Brown U., 1959. Asst. prof. physics U. Tex., Austin, 1959-62, asso. prof., 1962-65, asso. prof. physics and edn., 1965-67, prof., 1967—; sr. phys. scientist Ginn Sci. Program, 1968—; chmn. steering com. Tech Physics Project, 1972-76. Contbr. artices on physics of metals to profl. jours. Sr. research fellow Inst. Study of Metals, U. Chgo., 1963; NATO sr. fellow in sci. U. Oslo, Norway, 1969. Fellow Am. Phys. Soc., Tex. Acad. Sci.; mem. Am. Assn. Physics Tchrs., AAUP, AAAS, Phi Beta Kappa, Sigma Xi. Democrat. Baptist. Home: 5709 Bullard Dr Austin TX 78731 Office: Dept of Physics University of Texas Austin TX 78712

GAVENUS, EDWARD RICHARD, banker; b. Kingston, Pa., June 13, 1932; s. Edward A. and Bertha (Bellas) G.; m. Ruth Madeline James, Apr. 30, 1954; children: Gary, Edward, Paul, James. Student, Wharton Sch., U. Pa., 1951-54, Wilkes Coll., 1954-61. With First Eastern Bank

N.A., Wilkes-Barre, 1950—, asst. cashier, 1959-62, asst. v.p., 1962-67, v.p., 1967-72, sr. v.p., cashier, 1972—; instr. Am. Inst. Banking, 1963-82; cons. Wilkes-Barre Area Voc-Tech. Sch. Automation Com., 1962—. Bd. dirs. Luzerne-Wyoming County Mental Health Center, 1976—; mem. Luzerne County Police Automation Com., 1980—. Recipient Wesley A. Kuhn Math. award Wyo. Sem. Dean Sch. Bus., 1950. Mem. Am. Inst. Banking (chpt. pres. 1961-62, nat. pres. 1972-73), Data Processing Mgmt. Assn., Am. Bankers Assn. (ops. and automation ednl. com. 1977-81), Pa. Bankers Assn. (chmn. data processing com. 1969-70), Third Dist. Automated Clearinghouse Assn. (dir. 1980—), C. of C. Republican. Methodist. Club: Mason. Home: 373 Rutter Ave Kingston PA 18704 Office: 11 W Market St Wilkes-Barre PA 18768 *One should be honest in all things at all times. To deviate from the truth, even in the slightest, is to lie.*

GAVER, KENNETH DARREL, state official, physician; b. Santa Barbara, Calif., Jan. 12, 1925; s. Morris Fred and Nina Annis (McEwen) G.; m. Dona Loree Averill, Aug. 6, 1969; children—Linda, Paul, Jananne. B.A., U. Calif., Berkeley, 1946; M.D., U. Tenn., 1948. Intern U.S. Naval Hosp., Oakland, Calif., 1949-50; resident Ind. U. Med. Center, 1956; dir. edn. Oreg. State Hosp., Salem, 1956-58; pvt. practice psychiatry, Salem, 1959-65; adminstrn. Oreg. Mental Health Div., Salem, 1965-71; dir. Ohio Dept. Mental Health and Mental Retardation, Columbus, 1971-74; commr. Tex. Dept. Mental Health, Mental Retardation, Austin, 1974-78; med. dir. Del Amo Hosp., Torrance, Calif., 1978—; prof. psychology U. Oreg., 1956-57, asst. prof. psychiatry, 1958-59, assoc. clin. prof. psychiatry, 1956-71; Councillor Accreditation Council for Psychiat. Facilities Joint Commn. Accreditation of Hosps., 1975-78. Served with USNR, 1943-45, 49-53. Fellow Am. Coll. Mental Health Adminstrn.; Mem. Nat. Assn. State Health Program Dirs. (pres. 1973-75), Am. Psychiat. Assn. (pres. Oreg. dist. br. 1960-61), Nat. Assn. Pvt. Psychiat. Hosps. (trustee 1983). Office: Del Amo Hosp 32700 Camino del Sol Torrance CA 90505

GAVIN, AUSTIN, lawyer; b. Phila., Feb. 6, 1909; m. Helen A. Blaisdell; children—Austin III, Susan. A.B., Ursinus Coll., 1930, LL.D., 1974; LL.B., U. Pa., 1933. Bar: Pa. bar 1933. Jr. counsel Pa. Dept. Revenue, 1934-35; law clk. to justice Pa. Supreme Ct., 1935-36; with Pa. Power & Light Co., Allentown, 1936-74, gen. counsel, 1958-60, v.p., gen. counsel, 1960-65, v.p. mgmt. services, 1965-69, exec. v.p., 1969-74; exec. cons. Lehigh U., 1974—; Chmn. Lehigh County Charter Study Commn., 1974-76. Bd. dirs. Minsi Trails council Boy Scouts Am., pres., 1966-71; trustee Allentown YWCA. Served as 1st sgt. AUS, World War II. Decorated Silver Star, Purple Heart. Mem. Am. Pa., Lehigh County bar assns., Am. Arbitration Assn. (nat. panel arbitrators). Home: RD 1 Macungie PA 18062 Office: Lehigh Univ Bethlehem PA 18015

GAVIN, HERBERT JAMES, cons., ret. air force officer; b. nr. Winterset, Ia., Nov. 15, 1921; s. John Joseph and Catherine Mary (Gallagher) G.; m. Doris M. Brown, July 20, 1946; children—Michael J., Stephanie L., Patrick H., Ann Maureen. B.S., U. Md., 1964; grad., USAF Air War Coll., 1966; M.S., George Washington U., 1969. Aero. Engr. Northrop Inst. Tech., 1949; Commd. 2d lt. USAAF, 1943; advanced through grades to maj. gen. USAF, 1971; ret., 1978, various assignments in flight test, tactical fighter ops., logistics, research and hdqrs. staff in U.S., China, India and Japan, to 1965, dep. comdr. ops., vice comdr., Bergstrom AFB, Tex., 1966-68, dep. comdr. operations, Republic South Vietnam, 1968-69, asst. dep. chief of staff logistics, Langley AFB, Va., 1969-70, comdr., Nellis AFB, Nev., 1970-71, dep. chief of staff logistics, Langley AFB, 1971-75, comdr., McClellan AFB, Calif., 1975-78. Decorated D.S.M. with oak leaf cluster, Silver Star, Legion of Merit, D.F.C., Bronze Star, Meritorious Service medal, Air medal with 7 oak leaf clusters, Air Force Commendation medal with oak leaf cluster; Nat. Order Merit, Korea; Gallantry Cross with palm, Vietnam). Mem. Air Force Assn., Exptl. Aircraft Assn. Roman Catholic. Club: Sutter.

GAVIN, JAMES JOHN, JR., corp. exec.; b. Phila., July 18, 1922; s. James John and Mary E (Ludlow) G.; m. Zita C. Kabeschat, Aug. 23, 1952; children—William, James, Kevin, Steven, Peter. B.S. in Econs, U. Pa., 1949. Sr. accountant Peat, Marwick, Mitchell & Co. (C.P.A.'s), Phila., 1949-53; chief accountant Indian Head Mills, Inc. (name changed to Indian Head Inc.), N.Y.C., 1953, asst. treas., 1953-56, controller, 1956-61, treas., v.p., 1961-66, v.p. finance, 1966-68; v.p. finance, controller Borg-Warner Corp., Chgo., 1968-75, sr. v.p. finance, 1975—. Served with USNR, 1943-46. Mem. Pa. Inst. C.P.A.'s, Delta Sigma Pi, Beta Alpha Psi, Beta Gamma Sigma. Club: K.C. Home: 161 Thorn Tree Ln Winnetka IL 60093 Office: 200 S Michigan Ave Chicago IL 60604

GAVIN, JAMES M., corp. cons.; b. N.Y.C., Mar. 22, 1907; s. Martin Thomas and Mary (Terrel) G.; m. Jean Emert Duncan, July 31, 1948; children—Caroline, Patricia, Aileen, Chloe; 1 dau. (by previous marriage), Barbara Margaret. B.S., U.S. Mil. Acad., 1929; grad., Inf. Sch., officers course, 1933, Command and Gen. Staff Sch. Parachute Sch. Enlisted as pvt. U. S. Army, 1924; commd. 2d lt. inf., 1929, advanced through grades to lt. gen., 1944, service included World War II in, ETO, ret., 1958; chmn. bd. Arthur D. Little, Inc., 1964-77; U.S. ambassador to, France, 1961-62, 62-63. Author: Airborne Warfare, 1947, War and Peace in the Space Age, 1958, France and The Civil War in America, 1962, Crisis Now, 1968, On to Berlin, 1978. Trustee Mus. Fine Arts, Boston; bd. dirs. Harry Frank Guggenheim Found. Decorated grand officer Legion of Honor, Croix de Guerre with palm, France; D.S.C. with oak leaf cluster; Purple Heart; Silver Star, U.S.; Distinguished Service Order, Eng.). Mem. Am. Battle Monuments Commn. Office: 25 Acorn Park Cambridge MA 02140

GAVIN, JOHN, actor, business executive, diplomat; b. Los Angeles, Apr. 8, 1932; s. Herald Ray and Delia Diana (Pablos) G.; m. Constance Mary Towers; children—Cristina Miles, Maria Della, Maureen Ardath, Michael Ford. B.A. in Econ. History of Latin Am, Stanford, 1952. Spl. adviser to sec. gen. OAS, 1961-74; pres. Gamma Services Corp., 1968—; ambassador to, Mexico, 1981—. Trustee Villanova Prep. Sch. Served from ensign to lt. comdr. USNR, 1952-55. Mem. Screen Actors Guild (pres. 1971-73), Stanford Alumni Assn., Omicron Delta Kappa, Chi Psi. Club: Sunset (Los Angeles). Office: Box 961 Beverly Hills CA 90213 also US Embassy Box 3087 Laredo TX 78041

GAVIN, JOHN JOSEPH, biologist; b. New Brunswick, N.J., Oct. 21, 1922; s. John Joseph and Mildred Veronica (Donahue) G.; m. Margaret Shirley Fieger, May 30, 1945; children: Michael, Terrence, Christopher, John Joseph III, Timothy, Mary, Judith, Margaret, Paul. B.S., Rutgers U., 1949, M.S., 1950, Ph.D., 1964. Head biol. control Smith, Kline & French Labs., Phila., 1950-55; chief microbiologist Food and Drug Research Labs., Maspeth, N.Y., 1955-57; research asso. Fund for Research Therapeutics, Wayne, Pa., 1957-64; group leader bacteriology research group Norwich Pharmacal Co., N.Y., 1964-66; head dept. allergy/immunology Dome Labs. div. Miles Labs., Inc., West Haven, Conn., 1966-70, dir. biol. product devel., 1968-70; dir. molecular biology research lab. Miles Labs., Inc., Elkhart, Ind., 1970-75, dir. allergy research affairs, corp. research, 1975-80; dir. allergy research affairs Hollister-Stier, Spokane, Wash., 1980-81, dir. research, 1981—; adj. asso. prof. dept. microbiology U. Notre Dame., 1978-81; adj. prof. dept. biology Eastern Wash. U. Contbr. sci. articles to profl. jours. Bd. dirs. Devel. Evaluation and Adjustment Facilities, 1979-80, Assn. for Disabled of Elkhart County, 1979-80; trustee Deaf Services Center, Spokane, 1981—; mem. Gov.'s Com. on Employment of Handicapped, 1983; chmn. Spokane Community Partnership Com. on Handicapped, 1983—. Served with AUS, 1943-45. Recipient Chmn.'s Commendation award Pres.'s Com. on Employment of Handicapped, Washington, 1977, Sidney S. Kramer award for meritorious service to handicapped Ind. Rehab. Services Bd., Indpls., 1977; Handicapped Hoosier of Yr. award Ind. Commn. for Handicapped, 1979; Handicapped Citizen of Yr., Region V HEW, 1979; fellow Can. Med. and Bioengring. Soc., 1981. Mem. AAAS, Am. Acad. Microbiology, Am. Inst. Chemists, Am. Soc. Microbiology, Am. Chem. Soc., Soc. Indsl. Microbiology, Nat. Assn. Deaf, Found. for Sci. and Handicapped (pres. 1978-80, chmn. bd. dirs. 1980—), Ind. Acad. Scis., N.Y. Acad. Scis., Sigma Xi. Roman Catholic. Patentee in field. Home: E 1525 Kaywood Way Spokane WA 99208 Office: Box 3145 Terminal Annex Spokane WA 99220

GAVIN, JOSEPH GLEASON, JR., aerospace company executive; b. Somerville, Mass., Sept. 18, 1920; s. Joseph Gleason and Elizabeth (Tay) G.; m. Dorothy Dunklee, Sept. 1943; children: Joseph Gleason III, Tay Anne (Mrs. Peter B. Erickson), Donald Lewis. B.S., M.S. in Aeros, MIT, 1942. With Grumman Aerospace Corp., Bethpage, N.Y., 1946—, chief missile and space engr., 1957-62, v.p., 1962-70, dir., 1953-72, sr. v.p., 1970-72, pres., 1972-76, chmn. bd., 1973-76, also dir.; pres., chief operating officer, dir. Grumman Corp., Bethpage; chmn. bd. Grumman Data Systems Corp.; dir. Grumman Houston Corp., Grumman Internat., Inc., Grumman Allied Industries, Inc., Grumman Credit Corp., Calldata Systems, Inc., Grumman St. Augustine Corp., Grumman Tech. Services, Inc., European Am. Banking Corp., Call Data Fed. Services, Inc., ISI Systems, Inc., Charles Stark Draper Lab., Inc., Pine St. Fund. Mem. corp. vis. com. dept. aeros. and astronautics M.I.T.; former pres. Harborfields Bd. Edn., Central Sch. Dist. 6, Huntington, N.Y., 1960-64; chmn. United Fund, 1978; trustee Huntington Hosp., Poly. Inst. N.Y.; mem. MIT Corp., 1983—; mem. policy adv. com., adv. panel on fusion energy Dept. Def. Served with USNR, 1942-46. Recipient Leadership award C.W. Post Coll. of L.I. U.; Distinguished Pub. Service medal NASA, 1971. Fellow AIAA (past pres.), Am. Astronautical Soc.; mem. Aerospace Industries Assn., Nat. Acad. Engring. Home: 6 Endicott Dr Huntington NY 11743 Office: 1111 Stewart Ave Bethpage NY 11714

GAVIN, LAWRENCE RICHARD, retail executive; b. Chgo., May 13, 1927; s. Frederick Richard and Ruth (Brauner) G.; m. Rita Grace Wolcott, Aug. 4, 1974; children: Richard, Ronald, John. Warehouse mgr. Ace Hardware Corp., Oak Brook, Ill., 1958-73, v.p. ops., Oak Brook, 1973-82, exec. v.p., 1982, pres., 1983—. Served with U.S. Army, 1945-47. Clubs: Ruth Lake Country (Hinsdale, Ill.); Central States Hardware. Home: 8473 Kimberly Ct Burr Ridge IL 60521 Office: Ace Hardware Corp 2200 Kensington Ct Oak Brook IL 60521

GAVIN, ROBERT MICHAEL, JR., coll. provost; b. Coatesville, Pa., Aug. 16, 1940; s. Robert Michael and Helen Regina (Finnegan) G.; m. Charlotte Marie Dugan, June 2, 1962; children—Anne, Patricia, Robert, Charles, Sean. B.A., St. John's U., Collegeville, Minn., 1962; Ph.D., Iowa State U., 1966. Mem. faculty Haverford (Pa.) Coll., 1966—, prof. chemistry, 1975—, dir. computing, 1979-80, provost, dean faculty, 1980—. Author papers in field. Pres. Haverford Twp. Sch. Bd., 1975. Recipient Dreyfus Tchr.-Scholar award, 1973; NSF fellow, 1969-70. Mem. Am. Chem. Soc. Democrat. Roman Catholic. Home: 635 Ardmore Ave Ardmore PA 19003 Office: Haverford Coll Haverford PA 19041

GAVOOR, RICHARD HAIG, food company financial executive; b. Watertown, Mass., Dec. 7, 1930; s. Aram and Agnes (Asoian) G.; m. Priscilla Deborah Perkins, Apr. 21, 1959; children: Susan, Robin, David. A.B. cum laude, Tufts U., 1958; student, Advanced Mgmt. Program, Harvard U., 1980. Mgr. cost analysis Nabisco, Inc., N.Y.C., 1965-68, asst. controller, 1968-73, controller, 1973—, corp. v.p., 1978-81, v.p. fin., 1981—; v.p. corp. devel. Nabisco Brands Inc., 1982—; sr. v.p. fin. Nabisco Brands Ltd., U.K., 1983—. Served with C.E. AUS, 1952-54. Mem. Fin. Execs. Inst. (dir. N.J. chpt., com. on corp. reporting), Nat. Assn. Accountants (N.Y. chpt.), Grocery Mfrs. Am. (wage and price task force com.). Clubs: Summit (N.J.) Tennis; Canoe Brook (Summit); Crestview Swim (New Providence, N.J.). Home: 59 Blackburn Pl Summit NJ 07901 Office: Nabisco Brands USA River Rd East Hanover NJ 07936

GAVRITY, JOHN DECKER, insurance company executive; b. S.I., N.Y., Oct. 26, 1940; s. John S. and Eleanor R. (Decker) G.; m. Jacqueline M. Cerami, Dec. 4, 1965; children: John, Joseph. B.S., Wagner Coll., 1963. With U.S. Life, N.Y.C., 1963-69, asst. actuary, 1970-71, assoc. actuary, 1972-74; actuary USLIFE Corp., N.Y.C., 1975-76, 2d v.p., actuary, 1977, v.p., chief actuary, 1978, sr. v.p., chief actuary, 1979-84, exec. v.p., chief actuary, 1984—. Fellow Soc. Actuaries; mem. Am. Acad. Actuaries. Republican. Roman Catholic. Home: 190 Maybury Ave Staten Island NY 10308 Office: 125 Maiden Ln New York NY 10038

GAWF, JOHN LEE, foreign service officer; b. Salida, Colo., July 22, 1922; s. John and Gertrude (Bondurant) G.; m. Elizabeth Laflin, Dec. 31, 1950; children: Mary Anne, Katherine, Matilda, Anthony, Margaret, John Alan. B.S., U.S. Naval Acad., 1945; M.S., George Washington U., 1969. Instr. U. Colo., 1947-48; elec. engr. Bechtel Corp., San Francisco, 1948-50, TVA, Knoxville, Tenn., 1950-52; with Fgn. Service, State Dept., 1954—, vice consul, Guadalajara, Mexico, 1954-56; policy info. officer, Washington, 1956-58, internat. relations officer, 1958; officer-in-charge El Salvadoran affairs, 1958-59, Honduran affairs, 1958-60; consul, Genoa, Italy, 1960-63, 1st sec., Caracas, Venezuela, 1963-65, Ottawa, Ont., Can., 1965-68; detailed to Nat. War Coll., Washington, 1968-69, congl. relations officer, 1969-70; internat. relations officer, Naples, Italy, 1970-74, consul gen., Belize City, Belize, Brit. Honduras, 1974-78; counselor Am. Embassy, Rome, 1978-81, minister counselor, 1981-83; detailed to Stanford U. Ctr. for Internat. Security and Arms Control, 1983—. Served to lt. comdr. USNR, 1945-47, 52-54. Office: Stanford U Ctr for Internat Security and Arms Control Stanford CA 94305

GAY, E. LAURENCE, lawyer; b. Bridgeport, Conn., Aug. 10, 1923; s. Emil D. and Helen (Mihalich) G.; m. Harriet A. Ripley, Aug. 2, 1952; children: L. Noel, Peter C., Marguerite S., Georgette A. B.S., Yale U., 1947; J.D., Harvard U., 1949. Bar: N.Y. 1950, Conn. 1959, Calif. 1981. Atty. Root, Ballantine, Harlan, Bushby & Palmer, N.Y.C., 1949-51; legal staff U.S. High Commr. for Germany, 1951-52; law sec., presiding justice appellate div. 1st dept. N.Y. Supreme Ct., 1952-53; atty. Debevoise, Plimpton & McLean, 1953-58; v.p., sec.-treas. Hewitt-Robins, Inc., Stamford, Conn., 1958-65; pres. Litton Gt. Lakes Corp., N.Y.C., 1965-67; sr. v.p. finance AMFAC, Inc., Honolulu, 1967-73, vice chmn., 1974-78; fin. cons., Burlingame, Calif., 1979-82; of counsel Pettit & Martin, San Francisco, 1983—; dir. Orrox Corp. Pres. Honolulu Symphony Soc., 1974-78; trustee Loyola Marymount U., 1977-80, San Francisco Chamber Soloists. Served to 2d lt. AUS, 1943-46. Mem. Phi Beta Kappa. Roman Catholic. Home: 199 Ridgeway Rd Hillsborough CA 94010 Office: 101 California St 35th Floor San Francisco CA 94111

GAY, HELEN, biologist; b. Pittsfield, Mass., Aug. 30, 1918; d. Ulrich and Alice (Gonnet) G. B.A., Mt. Holyoke Coll., 1940; M.A., Mills Coll., 1942; Ph.D. (Lalor fellow), U. Pa., 1955. Research asst. dept. genetics Carnegie Instn., Cold Spring Harbor, L.I., N.Y., 1942, 43, 45-51, asso. in research, 1954-60; asso. cytogeneticist, 1960-62, cytogeneticist, 1962-71, charge, 1963-71; prof. zoology U. Mich., 1962-75, prof. biol. scis., 1975—; lectr. cytology, biology dept. Adelphi Coll., Garden City, N.Y., 1959-62; jr. profl. asst. NIH, Bethesda, Md., 1943-45, mem. genetics study sect. div. research grants, 1979-82; mem. discipline adv. com. life scis. Council Internat. Exchange of Scholars, 1980-83. Asso. editor: cytology sect. Biol. Abstracts; Contbr. to sci. jours. Asso. chmn. dept. zoology, 1973-75. Fellow AAAS; mem. Am. Soc. Zoologists, Internat., Am. socs. cell biology, Genetics Soc. Am., Am. Soc. Naturalists, Soc. for Developmental Biology, Sigma Xi. Home: 2650 Heather Way Ann Arbor MI 48104

GAY, J. EDWIN, lawyer; b. Jacksonville, Fla., Nov. 19, 1909; s. Gracey David and Callie (Beard) G.; m. Dorothy Dyrenforth, Apr. 25, 1946; 1 son, Rhodes. B.S. in Bus. Adminstrn, U. Fla., 1928-31, J.D., 1951. Bar: Fla. 1951. Mgr. Credit Assn. No. Fla., 1931-33; asst. to pres. Am. Investment & Mortgage Co., 1935-41; plant supt., dist. salesman Sun Oil Co., 1933-35; div. mgr. N. Fla. div. Can. Dry Bottling Co. Fla., 1946-48; with firm Bedell & Bedell, Jacksonville, 1951, 52; asst. U.S. dist. atty. So. Dist. Fla. (Jacksonville div.), 1951-53; adminstrv. asst. to Gov. LeRoy Collins, 1955-56; partner firm Rogers, Towers, Bailey, Jones & Gay, Jacksonville, 1962-; Lectr. U. Fla., 1951—. Mem. Fla. Racing Commn., 1957-58, 4th Circuit Jud. Nominating Commn. State Fla. Served to lt. comdr. USNR, 1941-46; rear adm. Res. ret. Fellow Am. Coll. Trial Lawyers; mem. Fla. Bar, Jacksonville Bar Assn. (pres. 1967), Kappa Alpha, Phi Delta Phi (past pres.). Clubs: Steppers (past pres.), Bachelors (past pres.), Friars (past pres.), Fla. Yacht (Jacksonville) (past commodore). Home: 4804 Apache Ave Jacksonville FL 32210 Office: 1300 Gulf Life Dr Jacksonville FL 32207

GAY, KENNETH BREWSTER, mfg. co. exec.; b. Belle Fourche, S.D., June 25, 1919; s. Alford C. and Ruth (Layton) G.; m. Janice Lucille Jennings, Aug. 30, 1941; 1 dau., Cynthia Louise. Student, U. Colo., 1937-40; LL.B. magna cum laude, Southwestern U., 1953. Bar: Calif. bar 1954; Cert. purchasing mgr. With N. Am. Aviation, Los Angeles, 1941-56, v.p. purchasing, 1967; dir. material Atomics Internat. Co., Los Angeles, 1956-61, dir. space adminstrv. div., 1961-62, exec. dir. material, 1962-67; v.p. purchasing Rockwell Internat. Corp., Pitts., 1967—; tchr. univ. courses in field. Served with USNR, 1944-46. Mem. Nat. Assn. Purchasing Mgmt. (life), Purchasing Mgmt. Assn. Pitts., Aerospace Industries Assn. (exec. com. material mgmt. com. 1970—), Am. Def. Preparedness Assn. (pres. Pitts. chpt. 1980-81), Electronics Industries Assn., State Bar Calif. Republican. Clubs: Duquesne, Edgeworth (Pitts.). Home: Box 162X RD 3 Witherow Rd Sewickley PA 15153 Office: 600 Grant St Pittsburgh PA 15129

GAY, PETER, history educator, author; b. Berlin, Germany, June 20, 1923; came to U.S., 1941, naturalized, 1946; s. Morris Peter and Helga (Kohnke) G.; m. Ruth Slotkin, May 30, 1959; stepchildren: Sarah Khedouri, Sophie Glazer, Elizabeth Glazer. B.A., U. Denver, 1946; M.A., Columbia, 1947, Ph.D., 1951. Faculty Columbia, 1947-69, prof. history, 1962-69, William R. Shepherd prof. history, 1967-69; prof. comparative European intellectual history Yale, 1969—, Durfee prof. history, 1970—. Author: The Dilemma of Democratic Socialism: Eduard Bernstein's Challenge to Marx, 1952, Voltaire's Politics: The Poet as Realist, 1959, The Party of Humanity: Essays in the French Enlightenment, 1964, A Loss of Mastery: Puritan Historians in Colonial America, 1966, The Enlightenment: An Interpretation, vol. I, The Rise of Modern Paganism, 1966 (Nat. Book award 1967, Melcher Book award 1967), Weimar Culture: The Outsider as Insider, 1968 (Ralph Waldo Emerson award Phi Beta Kappa 1969), The Enlightenment, vol. II, The Science of Freedom, 1969, The Bridge of Criticism: Dialogues on the Enlightenment, 1970, (with R.K. Webb) Modern Europe, 1973, Style in History, 1974, Art and Act, 1976, Freud, Jews, and Other Germans, 1978. Fellow Am. Council Learned Soc., 1959-60; fellow Center Advanced Study Behavioral Scis., 1963-64; Guggenheim fellow, 1967-68, 77-78; Overseas fellow Churchill Coll., Cambridge, 1970-71; Rockefeller Found. fellow, 1979-80. Mem. Am., French hist. socs., Phi Beta Kappa. Home: 105 Blue Trail Hamden CT 06518

GAY, ROBERT DERRIL, county health department administrator; b. Savannah, Ga., June 23, 1939; s. Roscoe Degomar and Mollie Ann (Jones) G. B.A., Oglethorpe U., 1962; M.A., Emory U., 1966. Dep. dir. Div. Mental Health and Mental Retardation Ga. Dept. Human Resources, Atlanta, 1975-77, asst. commr., 1977-78, dir. Div. Mental Health and Mental Retardation, 1978-81; dep. dir. DeKalb County Health Dept., Decatur, Ga., 1981—; vis. instr. Oglethorpe U., 1966, 69, Emory U. Sch. Nursing, 1972; mem. Ga. Gov.'s Council on Devel. Disabilities, 1978-81, Ga. Gov.'s Council on Mental Health and Mental Retardation, 1978-81, DeKalb County Council on Devel. Disabilities, 1981—. Mem. Am. Sociol. Assn., So. Sociol. Soc. Home: 2295 I Dunwoody Crossing Atlanta GA 30338 Office: 440 Winn Way Decatur GA 30030

GAY, WILLIAM ARTHUR, JR., physician, educator; b. Richmond, Va., Jan. 16, 1936; s. William Arthur and Marion Harriette (Taylor) G.; m. Frances Louise Adkins, Dec. 17, 1960; children—William Taylor, Mason Arthur. B.A., Va. Mil. Inst., 1957; M.D., Duke, 1961. Asst. prof. surgery Cornell U. Med. Coll., N.Y.C., 1971-74, assoc., prof., 1974-78, prof., 1978—; cardiothoracic surgeon-in-chief N.Y. Hosp., 1976—. Contbr. articles to profl. jours. Served with USPHS, 1963-65. Recipient Career Scientist award Irma T. Hirschl Charitable Trust, 1972. Mem. A.C.S., Assn. for Acad. Surgery, N.Y. Cardiovascular Soc., N.Y. Surg. Soc., Am. Assn. Thoracic Surgery, Am. Surg. Assn., Soc. Univ. Surgeons (treas. 1977-80). Office: 525 E 68th St New York City NY 10021

GAY, WILLIAM INGALLS, veterinarian, health science administrator; b. Sussex, N.J., Jan. 25, 1926; s. William David and Dorothy Julia (Ingalls) G.; m. Millicent Ruth Chapman, June 10, 1948. D.V.M., Cornell U., 1950; grad., Fed. Exec. Inst., 1972. Pvt. practice vet. medicine, Richmond Hill, N.Y., 1950-52; chief animal hosp. sect. lab. aids br. div. research services NIH, Bethesda, Md., 1954-63, asst. chief lab. aids br. div. research services, 1962-63, asst. chief animal resources br. div. research facilities and resources, 1964-65; program dir. comparative medicine Nat. Inst. Gen. Med. Scis., NIH, 1966-67, program adminstr. radiology and physiology tng. programs, 1966, chief research grants br., 1967-70, acting asso. dir., 1970; asso. dir. extramural programs Nat. Inst. Allergy and Infectious Diseases, NIH, 1970-80, dir. animal resources program, div. research resources, 1981—; mem. com. on primates Inst. Lab. Animal Resources, NRC, 1961-63, chmn. subcom. on cat standards, 1963-64, mem. standards com., 1965-66; program chmn. Internat. Symposium on Lab. Animals, 1969. Author numerous papers on expt. surgery and lab. animal research.; editor: Methods of Animal Experimentation, 6 vols. Mem. sci. adv. bd. Mark L. Morris Found., 1966-71, trustee, 1971—; mem. grants adv. council The Seeing Eye, 1971-74. Served as lt. Vet. Corps, AUS, 1952-54. Recipient Superior Service award USPHS, 1975, NIH Dir's. award, 1983. Fellow Am. Coll. Lab. Animal Medicine (sec.-treas. 1964, 65); mem. Am. Assn. Lab. Animal Sci. (dir. 1961-69, program chmn. 1962-64, exec. bd. 1963, 66, nat. pres. 1968, chmn. awards com. 1969, Griffin award 1971, pres. Washington br. 1962), AVMA (sec.-treas. D.C. chpt. 1957-58, v.p. 1962, pres. 1963), AAAS, Phi Zeta. Club: Cosmos (Washington). Office: Div Research Resources NIH Bethesda MD 20205

GAY, WILSON A., chemical company executive; b. Freeland, Mich., June 30, 1928; s. Harry H. and Kittie Gay (Wilson) G.; m. Kathleen Conley, Apr. 9, 1977; children: James W., David S. B.A., Mich. State U., 1952. With Dow Chem. Co., Midland, Mich., 1957—, staff asst., then asst. treas., 1967-76, treas., 1976—; treas. Dow Chem. Internat. Inc., Dow Chem. Internat. Ltd., Dow Chem. Inter-Am. Ltd., Dow Chem. Overseas Capital N.V.; fin. dir. Dow Chem. A.G.; dir. Chem. Bank & Trust Co., Midland; dir. Bank Mendes Gans N.V., Amsterdam, Dow Banking Corp., Zurich, Midland Pipeline Co., Dorintal Reins. Ltd., Dorinco Reins. Co., Dow Chem. Overseas Mgmt. Co., Dow Chem. Overseas Capital N.V., Dow Chem. Internat. Inc., Del. Mem. Freeland (Mich.) Sch. Bd., 1974-75. Served to lt. comdr. USNR, 1952-55. Home: 1124 Holyrood St Midland MI 48640 Office: 2030 Dow Center Midland MI 48640

GAYDA, JOSEPH NORBERT, food co. exec.; b. Chgo., June 6, 1929; s. Joseph Frank and Anna Catherine (Duray) G.; m. Jeanette Wolf, May 12, 1956; children—Joseph Norbert, John, Jerome. B.S., Tri State U., 1956. With Arthur Andersen & Co., Chgo., 1956-60; controller Super Food Services, Inc., Chgo., 1960-62; treas. Nachman Corp., Chgo., 1962-68; v.p. fin., sec. Ind. Grocers Alliance, Chgo., 1968-72; sr. v.p. Booth Fisheries Corp., Chgo., 1973—. Served with U.S. Army, 1951-53. Office: Booth Fisheries Corp 2 N Riverside Plaza Chicago IL 60606

GAYDOS, JOSEPH MATTHEW, Congressman; b. Braddock, Pa., July 3, 1926; s. John and Elona (Magella) G.; m. Alice Ann Gray, Nov. 26, 1955; children: Joseph Matthew, Colleen, Kathleen, Kelly, Tammy. Student, Duquesne U.; LL.B., U. Notre Dame, 1951. Bar: Pa. 1953. Mem. Pa. Senate for 45th Dist., 1967-68; dep. atty. gen., Pa., 1955, asst. solicitor, Allegheny County, Pa.; gen. counsel dist. 5 United Mine Workers Am.; then legal counsel dist. 50; mem. 90th-98th Congresses from 20th Dist., Pa. Served with USNR, World War II; PTO. Mem. Allegheny County Bar Assn., Am. Legion, Cath. War Vets., VFW, Sons of Italy, McKeesport Am.-Slovak Club, Croatin Fraternal Union, Jednota, Polish Nat. Alliance, U. Notre Dame Alumni Soc. Democrat. Roman Catholic. Office: 2366 Rayburn House Office Bldg Washington DC 20515 *

GAYLE, CRYSTAL, singer; b. Paintsville, Ky.; d. Melvin Ted and Clara Marie (Ramey) Webb; m. Vassilios Gatzimos, June 3, 1971; 1 dau., Catherine Claire. Student pub. schs., Wabash, Ind. Recorded for, MCA Records, 1970-72, United Artists Records, 1973-79, Columbia Records, 1979-82, Warner Bros. Records, 1982—; country hits include Beyond You, 1975; Wrong Road Again, 1974, This is My Year for Mexico, 1975, Somebody Loves You, 1975, One More Time, 1976, I'll Do It All Over Again, 1977, Never Miss a Real Good Thing, 1976, I'll Get Over You, 1976, Don't It Make My Brown Eyes Blue, 1977 (Gold record), Ready for the Times to Get Better, 1978, Talking in Your Sleep, 1978, Why Have You Left Me for the One You Left Me For, 1978, When I Dream, 1979, Half the Way, 1979, The Blue Side, 1980, It's Like We Never Said Goodbye, 1980, If You Ever Change Your Mind, 1980, Take It Easy, 1981, Too Many Lovers, 1981, The Woman in Me, 1981, You Never Gave Up On Me, 1982, 'Til I Gain Control Again, 1982, (with Eddie Rabbit) You and I, 1982, Our Love is on the Faultline, 1983, Baby What About You, 1983, The Sound of Goodbye, 1983, I Don't Wanna Lose Your Love, 1984; albums include Crystal Gayle, 1975; Somebody Loves You, 1975, Crystal, 1976, We Must Believe in Magic, 1977 (Platinum record), When I Dream, 1978 (Platinum record), Miss the Mississippi, 1979 (Gold record), Classic Crystal, 1979 (Gold record), We Should Be Together, 1979, These Days, 1980, Favorites, 1980, A Woman's Heart, 1980, Hollywood, Tennessee, 1981, True Love, 1982, (with Tom Waits) One from the Heart, 1982, Cage the Songbird, 1983; starred in: The Crystal Gayle Spl., CBS-TV, 1979, Crystal, CBS-TV, 1980, Crystal Gayle in Concert, HBO, 1982. Recipient Outstanding Female Vocalist award Acad. Country Music, 1977, 78, 80; recipient award Country Music Assn., 1977, 78, Grammy award Outstanding Female Country Vocalist, 1978, Am. Music award as favorite female country vocalist, 1979, 80; Recipient AMOA Jukebox award, 1978, award Most Played Country Female Artist, 1979. Address: care Paul Shefrin 800 S Robertson Blvd Los Angeles CA 90038

GAYLE, GIBSON, JR., lawyer; b. Waco, Tex., Oct. 15, 1926; s. Gibson and Elsie (Little) G.; m. Martha Jane Wood, May 29, 1948; children: Sally Ann, Alice, Gibson III, Jane, Philip. A.B., LL.B., Baylor U., 1950. Bar: Tex. 1950. Since practiced in, Houston; sr. partner, chmn. exec. com. Fulbright & Jaworski.; Instr. U. Houston Law Sch., 1951-55; Bd. govs. Harris County Center for Retarded, 1956-76; bd. dirs., pres. Am. Bar Endowment, 1978-79. Bd. editors: Am. Bar Assn. Jour, 1967-72. Trustee M.D. Anderson Found., Tex. Med. Center Inc., Leon Jaworski Found.; chmn. bd. trustees Baylor Coll. Medicine. Served to 2d lt. F.A. AUS, 1945-47. Fellow Am. Bar Found. (dir. 1978-79), Tex. Bar Found. (chmn. 1968-69); mem. ABA (chmn. jr. bar conf. 1959-60, ho. of dels. 1960-62, ho. of dels. 63—, sec. 1963-67), Internat. Bar Assn. (council), Houston Bar Assn., State Bar Tex. (dir. 1966-69, pres. 1976-77), Houston C. of C. (dir.). Home: 11727 Broken Bough Circle Houston TX 77024 Office: Bank of Southwest Bldg Houston TX 77002

GAYLES, JOSEPH NATHAN WEBSTER, JR., college president; b. Birmingham, Ala., Aug. 7, 1937; s. Joseph Nathan Webster and Ernestine Williams G.; m. Gloria Jean Wade, Aug. 24, 1967; children: Jonathan Ifeanyi Chukw, Monica Saliyeka. A.B. summa cum laude, Dillard U., 1958; Ph.D., Brown U., 1963; postgrad., Oreg. State U., 1962-63, U. Uppsala, Sweden, 1965. Asst. prof. chemistry Oreg. State U., 1962-63; Woodrow Wilson teaching asso., asst. prof. chemistry Morehouse Coll., 1963-66, asso. prof. chemistry, 1969-71, program dir. med. edn. project, 1971-75; program dir. Sch. Medicine, 1975-77, prof., 1971-77; pres. Talladega (Ala.) Coll., 1977—; staff scientist, project dir. IBM Research Lab., San Jose, Calif., 1966-69. Contbr. articles to profl. jours. Bd. dirs. Woodrow Wilson Nat. Fellowship Found., 1978—; bd. overseers Sch. Medicine, Morehouse Coll., 1977-81; bd. dirs. Donoho Sch., Anniston, Ala., 1979—, Camp Cosby, YMCA, 1978-80, Met. Atlanta Council on Alcohol and Drug Abuse, 1972-74, Council for Internat. Exchange Scholars, 1979—; mem. Indsl. Devel. Com., Talladega, 1979—; mem. exec. bd. Choccolocco council Boy Scouts Am.; trustee Talladega Coll., 1977—, Morehouse Med. Coll., 1981—; mem. nat. adv. council, dir. research resources NIH, 1980—. Woodrow Wilson fellow, 1958-59; Dreyfus Found. Tchr.-scholar, 1972—; Recipient Tchr. of Yr. award Morehouse Coll., 1976; Alumnus of Yr. award Dillard U., 1977. Mem. Am. Phys. Soc., Am. Chem. Soc., Am. Assn. Polit. and Social Scientists, Nat. Assn. Equal Opportunity in Higher Edn. (bd. dirs. 1979—), Sigma Xi, Beta Kappa Chi, Alpha Phi Alpha. Home: 702 W Battle Talladega AL 35160 Office: Talladega Coll Talladega AL 35160

GAYLIN, NED L., psychology educator; b. Cleve., May 2, 1935; s. Harry C. and Fay I. G.; m. Rita Atran, June 30, 1957; children: Hilarie C., Ann E., Jed J., Daniel S. B.A., U. Chgo., 1956, M.A., 1961, Ph.D., 1965. Staff psychologist Inst. Juvenile Research, Chgo., 1965-68; counselor Bellefaire Children's Home, Cleve., 1953, Sonja Shankman Orthogenic Sch., Chgo., 1954-56; group worker, supr. Jewish Community Centers of Chgo., 1957-60; grad. research asst. Com. Human Devel., U. Chgo., 1959-60; intern Inst. Juvenile Research, Chgo., 1960-61, Counseling and Psychotherapy Research Center, U. Chgo., 1961-63; grad. teaching asst. dept. psychology U. Chgo., 1961-63; psychol. cons. State Ill., Rockford, 1961-64; psychotherapist, cons. Counseling and Psychotherapy Research Center, U. Chgo., 1963-65, psychol. cons., lectr., 1965; lectr. dept. social sci. S.E. Jr. Coll., Chgo., 1965-66; staff psychologist Inst. Juvenile Research, Chgo., 1965-68; psychol. cons. Peace Corps, No. Ill. U., DeKalb, 1966-68; chief psychologist S.W. Suburban Mental Health Assn., LaGrange, Ill., 1966-68; psychol. cons. Virginia Frank Child Devel. Center, Chgo., 1966-68; child clin. research psychologist NIMH, Bethesda, Md., 1968-70; lectr., cons. Washington Sch. Psychiatry, 1968-72; chmn. dept. family and community devel. Coll. Human Ecology, U. Md., College Park, 1970-77, prof., dir. family therapy tng., 1977—; mem. research com. Md. Community Coordinated Child Care, 1970-75. Contbr. articles in field to profl. jours. USPHS grantee, 1961-63; U. Chgo. fellow and scholar, 1954-56, 58-60; State Ill. edn. and tng. grantee, 1963-65. Mem. Nat. Council on Family Relations, Am. Psychol. Assn., Am. Assn. Marriage and Family Therapy, Groves Conf. on the Family, Sigma Xi. Home: 4617 Norwood Dr Chevy Chase MD 20815 Office: U Md College Park MD 20742

GAYLIN, WILLARD, physician, educator; b. Cleve., Feb. 23, 1925; s. Harry C. and Fay (Baumgard) G.; m. Betty Schofer, June 15, 1947; children: Joan Deborah, Ellen Andrea. A.B., Harvard U., 1947; M.D., Western Res. U., 1951. Intern Cleve. City Hosp., 1951-52; resident psychiatry Bronx VA Hosp., 1952-54; faculty Columbia Psychoanalytic Sch., 1956—, clin. prof. psychiatry, 1972—; adj. prof. psychiatry Union Theol. Sem.; adj. prof. psychiatry and law Columbia Sch. Law, 1970; pres., founder The Hastings Ctr., Hastings-on-Hudson, N.Y., 1970—; Cons. A.M.A. Jud. Council, Inst. de La Vie, U. Paris; vis. prof. Harvard U. Med. Sch., 1978; Mem. exec. bd. Com. for Pub. Justice, 1971. Author: (with H. Hendrin and A. Carr) Psychoanalysis and Social Research, 1965, The Meaning of Despair, 1968, In The Service of Their Country: War Resisters in Prison, 1970, Partial Justice: A Study of Bias in Sentencing, 1974, Caring, 1976, (with others) Doing Good: The Limits of Benevolence, 1978, Feelings: Our Vital Signs, 1979, The Killing of Bonnie Garland: A Question of Justice, 1982; Contbr. (with others) articles to profl. jours. Bd. dirs. Helsinki Watch., Field Found. Served with USNR, 1943-45. Recipient George E. Daniels medal of Merit for contbns. to psychoanalytic medicine, 1973; Elizabeth Cutter Morrow lectr. Smith Coll., 1970; Chubb fellow Yale, 1972. Fellow Am. Psychiat. Assn.; mem. Am. Psychoanalytic Assn., N.Y. Psychiat. Soc. Home: 108 Circle Dr Hastings-on-Hudson NY 10706 Office: Hastings Center Hastings-on-Hudson NY 10706

GAYLOR, DONALD HUGHES, surgeon; b. Bklyn., Apr. 17, 1926; s. Norman Hunter and Frances (Hughes) G.; m. Joan Winifred Power, Apr. 3, 1948; children: David, Christopher, Steven, Susan, Timothy. Student, Queen's Coll., 1943; A.B., U. Rochester, 1946, M.D., 1949. Diplomate: Am. Bd. Surgery, Am. Bd. Thoracic Surgery. Commd. lt. (j.g.) USN, 1949; advanced through grades to capt. M.C., 1966; intern U.S. Naval Hosp., Phila., 1949-50; student flight surgeon (Sch. Aviation Medicine), Pensacola, Fla., 1950-51, flight surgeon, U.S. Naval Sta., Trinidad, B.W.I., 1951-53, resident gen. surgery U.S. Naval Hosp., St. Albans, N.Y., 1953-57; postgrad. fellow surgery Royal Victoria Hosp., McGill U., Montreal, Can., 1957; resident thoracic surgery U.S. Naval Hosp., St. Albans, 1957-59; resident cardiovascular surgery St. Francis Hosp., Roslyn, L.I., N.Y., 1958; staff thoracic surgeon U.S. Naval Hosp., Portsmouth, Va., 1959-64; surgeon U.S.S. Enterprise, 1964; staff thoracic surgeon U.S. Naval Hosp., Nat. Naval Med. Center, Bethesda, Md., 1964-65, chief thoracic and cardiovascular surgery, 1965-68; chief surgery, exec. officer U.S.S. Repose, 1968-69; exec. officer Naval Med. Sch., Nat. Naval Med. Center, Bethesda, Md., 1969-72; ret., 1972; chief of surgery Allentown (Pa.) Hosp., 1972—, Sacred Heart Hosp., 1973-76, Allentown and Sacred Heart Hosp. Center, 1974—. Contbr. articles to profl. jours. Fellow ACS; mem. AMA, Am. Thoracic Soc., Soc. Thoracic Surgeons (a founder), Pa. Assn. Med. Edn. (pres. 1983—), Pa. Med. Soc., Assn. for Hosp. Med. Edn., Pa. Assn. for Thoracic Surgery, Assn. Mil. Surgeons U.S., Am. Trauma Soc. (a founder). Roman Catholic. Home: RD 2 Devonshire Rd Allentown PA 18103 Office: Lehigh Valley Hospital Ctr 1200 S Cedar Crest Blvd Allentown PA 18103

GAYLOR, JAMES LEROY, educator; b. Waterloo, Iowa, Oct. 1, 1934; s. David P. and Lena (Livingston) G.; m. Marilyn Louise Gibson, Mar. 25, 1956; children—Douglas, Ann, Robert, Kenneth. B.S., Iowa State U., 1956; M.S., U. Wis., 1958, Ph.D., 1960. Asst. prof. Cornell U., 1960-63, asso. prof. biochemistry, 1963-69, prof., 1969—, chmn. biochemistry, molecular and cell biology sect., 1970-76; prof., chmn. dept. biochemistry U. Mo., 1977-80; asso. dir. life scis. research E.I. duPont, 1981—; vis. prof. U. Ill., summers, 1964-65; sabbatical leave U. Oreg. Sch. Medicine, 1966-67, U. Osaka (Japan), 1973-74; vis. lectr. La Molina, summer 1962. Mem. various editorial bds.; contbr. numerous research articles to sci. jours. NIH fellow, 1958-60; spl. fellow, 1966-67; Guggenheim fellow, 1973-74. Mem. Am. Chem. Soc., Am. Soc. Biol. Chemists, Am. Inst. Nutrition. Developer health sci. research programs. Home: 18 Kent Dr Foxmeadow Hockessin DE 19707

GAYLORD, CLAYTON R., milling machine company executive; b. Rockford, Ill., Jan. 18, 1919; s. Robert March and Mildred (Ingersoll) G.; m. Gail Gartz, Aug. 8, 1942 (dec. July 1967); children: Jeannette (Mrs. Charles B. Lorch), Holly (Mrs. Bernard Windon), March (dec.), Russell; m. Joan Ryan Zulfer, Dec. 20, 1968. Grad., Phillips Exeter Acad., 1937; B.A., Princeton U., 1941. With Ingersoll Milling Machine Co., Rockford, 1946—, pres., 1958-71, chmn. bd., 1971-72, chmn. fin. com., treas., 1972—; dir. Ill. Bank & Trust Co. Trustee Rockford Meml. Hosp., pres., 1955; trustee Keith Country Day Sch., chmn., 1957-61; trustee Found. for Econ. Edn., N.Am. Wildlife Found; bd. dirs. Ams. for Effective Law Enforcement; chmn. bd. Rockford Inst. Home: 2310 Stoneridge Close Rockford IL 61107 Office: 707 Fulton Ave Rockford IL 61101

GAYLORD, DONALD ANDREW, air force officer; b. Chgo., Apr. 18, 1920; s. Andrew S. and Louise (Horn) G.; m. Verona Clay, Apr. 27, 1940; children—Jeraldine L., Victoria A., Eric A. Student, Fla. State U., 1950, George Washington U., 1962-63, Indsl. Coll. Armed Forces, 1963. With Nat. Cash Register Co., 1939-42; commd. officer USAAF, 1942, advanced through grades to brig. gen., 1969; bomber and tanker command pilot, 1942—, logistician, 1958-72, comdr., Hawaii, 1972—. Decorated D.S.M., Legion of Merit with 2 oak leaf clusters, D.F.C. with 3 oak leaf clusters, Air medal with 3 oak leaf clusters. Mem. Air Force Assn., Nat. Def. Transp. Assn., Order Daedalians. Home: 3221 Murchison Way Carmichael CA 95608

GAYLORD, EDSON INGERSOLL, machine tool company executive; b. Rockford, Ill., Feb. 18, 1922; s. Robert March and Mildred (Ingersoll) G.; m. Jane Wanzer, May 22, 1954; children: William Bradley, Charles Ingersoll, Susan Starr, John Wanzer, Mary March. B.A., Princeton U., 1945. Chmn., pres. Ingersoll Milling Machine Co., Rockford, Ill., 1971—. Served to capt. U.S. Army, 1942-46. Republican. Clubs: Chgo.; Univ. (N.Y.C.). Home: 2811 Country Club Terr Rockford IL 61103

GAYLORD, EDWARD LEWIS, publishing company executive; b. Denver, May 28, 1919; s. Edward King and Inez (Kinney) G.; m. Thelma Feragen, Aug. 30, 1950; children: Christine Elizabeth, Mary Inez, Edward King II, Thelma Louise. A.B., Stanford U., 1941; LL.D., Oklahoma City U., Okla. Christian Coll. Chmn., pres., dir. Gaylord Broadcasting Co.; WKY, Oklahoma City, WTVT, Tampa-St., Petersburg, KTVT, Dallas-Ft. Worth, KHTV, Houston, WVTV, Milw., KSTW-TV, Seattle-Tacoma, WVUE-TV, New Orleans, WUAB-TV, Cleve.-Lorain; chmn. bd., dir. Mistletoe Express Service; pres., gen. mgr., dir. Okla. Pub. Co.; editor, pub. Daily Oklahoman, Oklahoma City Times, Sunday Oklahoman; Pubs. Petroleum, Okla. Graphics; pres. Colorado Springs Sun, Sun Resources, Inc., Greenland (Colo.) Ranch, OPUBCO Resources, Inc., OPUBCO Devel. Co.; chmn. bd. Gayno, Inc., Denver, Farmer-Stockman, Dallas, Gaylord Prodn. Co. Calif.; partner Cimarron Coal Co., Denver, Lazy E Ranch, Saint Jo, Tex. Chmn., trustee Okla. Industries Authority; chmn. bd. govs. Okla. Christian Coll.; bd. dirs. Okla. State Fair, pres., 1961-71; bd. dirs., pres. Nat. Cowboy Hall of Fame and Western Heritage Center; bd. dirs. Okla. Eye Found.; vice chmn. bd. govs. Am. Citizenship Center; trustee S.W. Research Inst., San Antonio; past trustee Casady Sch., Oklahoma City U. Served with AUS, 1942-46. Recipient Brotherhood award Nat. Conf. Christians and Jews; named to Okla. Hall of Fame, 1974. Mem. Oklahoma City C. of C. (dir., past pres.), So. Newspaper Pubs. Assn. (past pres.). Conglist. Home: 1506 Dorchester Dr Oklahoma City OK 73120 Office: PO Box 25125 Oklahoma City OK 73125

GAYLORD, JAMES FREDERICK, JR., banker; b. Springfield, Mass., June 15, 1926; s. James F. and Helen S. (Jones) G.; m. Nancy G. Walton, Sept. 6, 1947; children: Barrie E., Susan W., James F. III, Nancy S. B.A., Dartmouth Coll., 1950; M.B.A. with highest distinction, Amos Tuck Sch., 1951. With Scott Paper Co., 1957-75, dir. adminstrn. personnel, Phila., 1965-71; staff v.p. Scott Paper Co., 1971-75; v.p. Fed Res. Bank, Phila., 1975-82; sr. v.p. Fed. Res. Bank, 1982—; mem. subcom. on personnel Fed Res. System, 1976—, chmn. subcom. on personnel, 1977-78, chmn. task force on employee benefits, 1981—. Bd. dirs. community Arts Ctr., Wallingford Pa., 1975; elder Firest Prsbyterian Ch., Swarthmore, Pa., 1978; mem. personnel com. United Way of Southeastern Pa. Served with USN, 1944-46. Mem. Phila. C. of C. (chmn. personnel com. 1971-74), Indsl. Relations Assn., Am. Soc. Personnel Adminstrn. Office: Fed Res Bank Phila 10 Independence Mall Philadelphia PA 19106

GAYLORD, THOMAS KEITH, electrical engineering educator; b. Casper, Wyo., Sept. 22, 1943; s. Earl Frederick and Vesta Jane (Kinsley) G.; m. Janice Lynn Smith, June 5, 1966; 1 dau., Grace May. B.S. in Physics, U. Mo.-Rolla, 1965, M.S. in Elec. Engring., 1967; Ph.D., Rice U., 1970. Registered profl. engr., Tex. Research assoc. Rice U., Houston, 1970-72; asst. prof. Ga. Tech. Inst., Atlanta, 1972-76, assoc. prof., 1976-80, prof. elec. engring., 1980—. Contbr. numerous articles to profl. jours.; editor: IEEE Transactions on Edn., 1979-82; reviewer jour. articles, 1975—. Recipient Curtis W. McGraw Research award Am. Soc. Engring Edn., 1979, Outstanding Young Engr. of Yr. award Ga. Soc. Profl. Engrs., 1977, research awards Sigma Xi, 1976-83. Fellow IEEE (Centennial medal 1984), Optical Soc. Am.; mem. AAUP, AAAS, Soc. Photo-Optical Instrumentation Engrs. Home: 3180 Verdun Dr NW Atlanta GA 30305 Office: Sch Elec Engring Ga Inst Tech Atlanta GA 30322

GAYNER, ESTHER K., artist; b. Trenton, Feb. 3, 1914; d. Leon and Ida Gootl (Morris) Kasman; m. Irving C. Gayner, Mar. 17, 1946; children: Stephen Hersh, Jay David. Student, Trenton Sch. for Indsl. Arts, 1929-31; B.S., N.J. State Tchrs. Coll., 1935; postgrad., Ednl. Alliance Art Sch., 1938-39, New Sch. for Social Research, 1958-73, Mus. of Modern Art Sch., 1966, 67. One woman show at, New Sch. Assos. Gallery, N.Y.C., 1964; two-woman show, Jewish Community Center Gallery, Wilmington, Del., 1974; group shows include, Audubon Artists Nat. Exhbn., Lever Bros., N.Y.C., Albany (N.Y.) Inst. History and Art, Cayuga Inst. History and Art, Auburn, N.Y., Jesse Besser Mus., Alpena, Mich., Bergen County (N.J.) Mus., Mus. of S.W., Midland, Tex., Oshkosh (Wis.) Pub. Mus., Okla. Art Center, Oklahoma City, Pallazzo Vecchio, Florence, Salvator Rose Pub. Gardens, Naples, Italy, travelling exhbn. in 5 cities in, Israel, also Cairo, Egypt; represented in permanent collections, Jesse Besser Mus., Butler Inst. Am. Art, Youngstown, Ohio, Slater Meml. Mus., Norwich, Conn., numerous pvt. collections in, U.S., Eng., and Israel. Mem. Nat. Assn. Women Artists (recipient, Nat. Medal of Honor 1972, Paula Kapp award 1969, Georgi Meml. award 1975, Gehner prize 1979, pres. 1974-76), Artists Equity N.Y., Am. Soc. Contemporary Artists (exec. bd., Graphics award 1981, Winsor and Newton award for collage painting 1982). Address: 78-03 Austin St Forest Hills NY 11375

GAYNOR, JOSEPH, chem. engr., cons.; b. N.Y.C., Nov. 15, 1925; s. Morris and Rebecca (Schnapper) G.; m. Elaine Bauer, Aug. 19, 1951; children—Barbara Lynne, Martin Scott, Paul David, Andrew Douglas. B.Ch.E., Polytechnic Inst. Bklyn., 1950; M.S., Case-Western Res. U., 1952, Ph.D., 1955. Research asst. Case Inst., Cleve., 1952-55; with Gen. Engring. Labs., Gen. Electric Co., Schnectady, N.Y., 1955-66, sect. mgr., 1962-66; group v.p. research Bell & Howell Co., 1966-72; mgr. comml. devel. group Horizons Research, Inc., Cleve., 1972-73; pres. Innovative Tech. Assos., Sierra Madre, Calif., 1973—; chmn. conf. com. 2d internat. conf. on bus. graphics, 1979, program chmn. 1st internat. congress on advances in non-impact printing technologies, 1981. Served with U.S. Army, 1944-46. Fellow AAAS, Am. Inst. Chem. Engrs.; mem. Am. Chem. Soc., Soc. Photographic Scientists and Engrs. (gen. chmn. 2d internat. conf. on electrophotography 1973, chmn. bus. graphics tech. sect. 1976—, chmn. edn. com. Los Angeles chpt. 1978—), Am. Soc. Photobiology, Sigma Xi, Tau Beta Pi, Phi Lambda Upsilon, Alpha Chi Sigma. Patentee in field. Home: 1407 Oaklawn Pl Arcadia CA 91006 Office: PO Box 637 Sierra Madre CA 91024

GAYNOR, MITZI (FRANCESCA MITZI VON GERBER), actress; b. Chgo., 1930; m. Jack Bean. Dancer with, Los Angeles Light Opera Co.; acting roles include South Pacific, Fortune Teller, Song of Norway, Louisiana Purchase, Naughty Marietta; motion pictures include For Love or Money, My Blue Heaven, Anything Goes, The Joker, Les Girls, South Pacific, Happy Anniversary, Surprise Package, Anniversary Waltz, Birds and the Bees, There's No Business Like Show Business, Bloodhounds of Broadway, Take Care of My Little Girl, Golden Girl, The I Don't Care Girl, We're Not Married; Dancer with concert tour, U.S., 1972-73, made TV comedy-variety appearance. *

GAZELEY, HAROLD JAMES, manufacturing company executive; b. Wisconsin Rapids, Wis., May 19, 1923; s. Arthur A. and Bessie Helen (Shearier) G.; m. Janis E. Peterman, Sept. 3, 1947; children: Gail Ann, Jill Lynn. B.B.A., U. Wis., 1949. C.P.A., Wis. Mem. comml. audit staff Arthur Andersen & Co., Milw., 1949-53; chief accountant Trane Co., LaCrosse, Wis., 1953-60, mgr. long-range corporate planning, 1960-65; treas. Duriron Co., Inc., Dayton, Ohio, 1965-68, v.p. fin., 1968-76, pres., 1976—, chief exec. officer, 1979—, also dir.; dir. 1st Nat. Bank Dayton, Reynolds & Reynolds Co., Transmission, Inc. Trustee, mem. investment com. Dayton YMCA.; Trustee Miami Valley Hosp. Served to capt. USAF, 1942-45. Decorated D.F.C., Air medal, Purple Heart. Mem. Am. Inst. C.P.A.'s, Dayton Area C. of C. (dir.). Clubs: Dayton Rotary, Masons, Shriners. Home: 330 Wellesley Way Dayton OH 45459 Office: Duriron Co PO Box 1145 Dayton OH 45401

GAZES, PETER CHRISTOPHER, cardiologist; b. St. Matthews, S.C., Oct. 10, 1921; s. Christopher Demetrious and Elpis (Voutsinas) G.; m. Athena Critikos, June 1947; children—Hope Gazes Crayson, Catherine Gazes Baker, Joanne Gazes Ellison. B.S., Coll. of Charleston, S.C., 1941, hon. degree, 1978; M.D., Med. U. S.C., 1944. Diplomate: Am. Bd. Internal Medicine, Am. Bd. Cardiovascular Disease. Rotating intern Jersey City Med. Center, 1944-45; resident in medicine Phila. Gen. Hosp., 1946-48, research fellow in cardiology, 1948-49; teaching fellow in cardiology and pharmacology Med. U. S.C., Charleston, 1949-50, mem. faculty, 1950—, prof. medicine, dir. cardiovascular div., 1967—, Disting. Univ. prof. cardiology, 1982—; Mem. Nat. Heart, Lung and Blood Adv. Council, 1979-83. Author, editor numerous med. textbooks. Served to lt. (j.g.) M.C. USNR, 1945-46. Peter C. Gazes Cardiology Soc. founded, 1980. Mem. AMA, Am. Heart Assn., So. Med. Assn., S.C. Med. Assn., Charleston County Med. Assn., S.C. Heart Assn. (pres. 1968), Assn. Univ. Cardiologists, Med. U. S.C. Assn., Council on Clin. Cardiology of Am. Heart Assn. (exec. com. 1982). Office: 171 Ashley Ave Charleston SC 29425

GAZOULEAS, PANAGIOTIS, journalist; b. Thessaloniki, Greece, Oct. 3, 1927; came to U.S., 1957, naturalized, 1960; s. John Panagiotis and Eva S. (Papanastasiou) G.; m. Patricia Tuttle, Aug. 26, 1956; children—John, Edward, Mary-Elizabeth. B.A., Hunter Coll., 1964, M.A. in Soviet Affairs, 1967. Journalist, Greece, 1950-56; reporter Atlantis, N.Y.C., 1957-59; editor Monthly Illus. Atlantis; editor in chief daily Atlantis, 1959-71; pub., editor Orthodox Observer, N.Y.C., 1971—. Author: poetry Destinies, 1956; fiction Chronicles 76, 1976. Served to lt. Greek Army, 1950-53. Mem. Asso. Ch. Press, Overseas Press Club. Home: 10 Brooklands Bronxville NY 10708 Office: 8 E 79th St New York NY 10021

GAZZARA, BEN, actor; b. N.Y.C., Aug. 28, 1930; s. Antonio and Angelina (Cusumano) G.; m. Louise Erickson, 1952 (div. 1956); m. Janice Rule; 1 dau.; 1 stepdau.; m. Elke Kriwat. Student, CCNY, 1947-48, Erwin Piscator Dramatic Workshop of New Sch. for Social Research, 1948-49; mem., Actors Studio, from 1951. Actor: stage appearances include Jezebel's Husband, 1952, End As a Man, 1953, Cat on a Hot Tin Roof, 1955, Hatful of Rain, 1955, The Night Circus, 1959, Epitaph for George Dillon, 1959, Two for the Seesaw, 1960, Strange Interlude, 1963, Traveller Without Luggage, 1964, Hughie, 1974, Who's Afraid of Virginia Woolfe, 1975; motion pictures include The Strange One, 1957, Anatomy of Murder, 1959, Joy of Laughter, 1960, The Passionate Thief, 1960, The Young Doctors, 1961, Convicts Four, 1961, A Rage to Live, 1964, Husbands, 1969, Al Capone, 1974, High Velocity, 1976, Killing of a Chinese Bookie, 1976, Voyage of the Damned, 1976, Opening Night, 1977, Bloodline, 1978, Inchon, 1979, They All Laughed, 1980, Tales of Ordinary Madness, 1981; TV series Arrest and Trial, 1963-64, Run for Your Life, 1965-68; appeared: TV dramas including DuPont Show of the Month (Recipient Drama Critics award for role in End As a Man 1953, Theatre World award 1953). Office: care J Julien 1501 Broadway New York NY 10036

GEANAKOPLOS, DENO JOHN, history educator; b. Mpls., Aug. 11, 1916; s. John Christ and Helen (Economou) G.; m. Effie Vranos, Aug. 23, 1953; children: John, Constance. Diploma in violin, Juilliard Sch. Music, 1939; B.A., U. Minn., 1941, M.A., 1946; Litt.D., U. Pisa, Italy, 1946; Ph.D., Harvard U., 1953; M.A. (hon.), Yale U., 1967, D.Litt., Hellenic Coll. Violinist, Mpls. Symphony Orch., 1939-42, 46; teaching fellow Harvard U., 1951-53; fellow Dumbarton Oaks, Washington, 1949-50; instr. history Brandeis U., 1953-54; prof. Greek Theol. Sch., Boston, 1953-54; from asst. prof. to prof. Western medieval and Renaissance history U. Ill., Urbana, 1954-67; prof. depts. history and religious studies Yale U. and Yale Div. Sch.; teaching Byzantine and Renaissance history, history Eastern Orthodox Ch., 1967—; lectr. univs., Athens, Greece, 1961, Paris, 1964, Salonika, Greece, 1964, Rome, 1964, Oxford, Eng., 1967, U. Ill., Chgo., 1967, Cini Found., Venice, Italy, 1962-68; lectr. on Orthodoxy, Rosary Coll., Chgo., 1959; speaker Brit. Eccles. History Soc., Oxford, 1975, Cambridge U., 1973; attended Vatican II Council, 1962, Council of Chalcedon conf. World Council Chs., Geneva, 1969, Greek Orthodox-Jewish Colloquium, N.Y.C., 1972; ann. lectr. Inst. Balkan Studies, Salonika; mem. U.S. Com. Byzantine Studies. Author: Emperor Michael Palaeologus and the West, 1959 (Greek edit. 1967), Erasmus and the Aldine Academy, 1960, Greek Scholars in Venice in the Renaissance, 1962 (repub. as Byzantium and the Renaissance, 1975), Byzantine East and Latin West, 1966, Bisanzio e il Rinascimento, 1967, Western Civilization, 1975, (with others) Byzantium, in Perspectives on the Past, 1971, Byzantium and the Later Crusades, in a History of the Crusades, 1975, Interaction of the Sibling Byzantine and Western Cultures in Middle Ages and Italian Renaissance, 1976, Medieval Western Civilization and the Byzantine and Islamic Worlds, 1979, Byzantium: Church, Society and Civilization Seen through Contemporary Eyes, 1984; editor: Europe and the Wider World, Jour. Greek and Roman Byzantine Studies, 1962-79; editorial bd.: Greek Orthodox Theol. Rev.; contbr. articles, revs. to profl. jours. Trustee Hellenic Coll. Served to capt. Q.M.C., AUS, 1942-46. Recipient award Am. Council Learned Socs., 1960, 61, 68, 72; Griswold award, 1978, 79; decorated gold cross Order King George (Greece), 1966, Order St. Andrew by Patriarch Constantinople, 1970, title Archon Didaskalos tou Genous, 1972; Fulbright scholar, 1960-61; Guggenheim fellow, 1964; grantee Am. Philos. Soc., 1962, 66, 72; Yale concilium, 1973; Nat. Humanities Inst., summer 1974. Mem. Am. Hist. Assn., Medieval Acad., Ch. History Soc. (exec. com. 1967-72, pres.-elect 1983-84), Renaissance Soc. Am. (exec. com. 1979—), Cretan Hist. Soc., Soc. Byzantine Studies (Athens), Soc. Macedonian Studies (Salonika), Modern Greek Studies Assn., Greek Hist. Soc., G. Palamas Soc. (Milan), Orthodox Theol. Soc. Am. Office: History Dept Hall Grad Studies Yale U New Haven CT 06520

GEANNOPULOS, NICK GEORGE, association executive; b. Chgo., Mar. 12, 1930; s. George Nick and Alice E. (Doulogeris) G.; m. Maryann E. Satterlee, Sept. 4, 1954; children: Kerry, Tim, Lisa, Sara, Lindsey. B.S., Northwestern U., 1951. Asst. editor Popular Mechanics, 1952-55; account exec. public relations Holtzman & Kain Advt. Co., Chgo., 1963-70; asst. dir. public relations Am. Osteo. Assn., Chgo., 1957-63; editorial dir. Golf Course Supts. Assn. Am., Chgo., 1970-74; asst. sec. communications Kiwanis Internat., Indpls., 1974—. Contbr., editor: Picture History of American Transportation, 1955, World Book Ency., Brit. Jr. Ency. Served with CIC AUS, 1955-57. Recipient numerous awards for art work, photography Soc. Publs., Designers, Communications Collaborative and N.Y. Art Dirs. Club. Greek Orthodox. Home: 572 Hawthorne St Elmhurst IL 60126 Office: Kiwanis International 3636 Woodview Trace Indianapolis IN 46268

GEARHART, MARVIN, oil company executive; b. Erie, Kans., May 13, 1927; s. Charles Herman and Marjorie Catherine (Hudson) G.; m. Jan Olson, Feb. 14, 1947; children: Dee Ann Gearhart Stenberg, Dale Alan, Jill Sue Gearhart Johnston, Janice Kay. B.S. in Mech. Engring., Kans. State U., 1949. Logging engr. Welex, 1949-53; chief field engr. Security Engr. div. Dresser, 1953-55; co-founder, chmn., pres. Go Oil Well Services (now Gearhart Industries Inc.), Ft. Worth, 1955—, dir. subs.; dir. Tex. Am. Bank, Ft. Worth, Justin Industries Inc. Contbr. tech. papers in field. Trustee Tex. Christian U., Ft. Worth, 1978—; bd. dirs. Am. Paralysis Assn., Dallas, 1979; div. chmn. United Way Campaign, Ft. Worth, 1979; dir. Tex. Assn. Taxpayers, 1979-81. Served with USAF, 1944-46. Recipient Ike Harrison award Tex. Christian U. Mgmt. Alumni Assn., 1979; named Hon. Alumnus Tex. Christian U. Mgmt. Alumni Assn., 1982, Bus. Exec. of Yr. Tex. Wesleyan Coll., Ft. Worth C. of C., 1982. Mem. Soc. Petroleum Engrs. (disting. lectr. 1981-82), Soc. Profl. Well Log Analysts (pres. Dallas-Ft. Worth chpt. 1969), Am. Petroleum Inst. Clubs: Nomads (bd. regents) (1971-72); Petroleum, Ft. Worth, Wildcatters (chmn. exec. com. 1983). Office: Gearhart Industries Inc 1100 Everman Rd Ft. Worth TX 76101

GEARHART, THOMAS LEE, newspaper editor; b. Toledo, Nov. 23, 1942; s. Edwin Lewis and Genevieve Vera G.; m. Barbara Jones, July 1, 1972; 1 dau., Elizabeth Jane. Student, U. Toledo, 1965-66. Reporter, asso. editor, mng. editor Toledo Monitor, 1965-67; reporter, asst. city editor Toledo Blade, 1967-77; editor Toledo mag., 1977-82; entertainment editor Toledo Blade, 1982—. Served with USN, 1961-65. Recipient 1st pl. award for feature writing Ohio Asso. Press, 1967. Democrat. Roman Catholic. Club: Toledo Press. Home: 2810 Cheltenham Rd Toledo OH 43606 Office: Toledo Mag Toledo Blade Co 541 Superior St Toledo OH 43660

GEARON, JOHN MICHAEL, professional basketball executive; b. Englewood, N.J., May 6, 1934; s. C.P. and Elizabeth (Asburg) G.; m. Patricia Smith, Jan. 1, 1960; children: Tierney, Michael, Tim. Pres., gov. Atlanta Hawks Profl. Basketball, 1983—; owner Gearon & Co., Atlanta, 1983—. Home: 368 Camden Rd NE Atlanta GA 30309

GEARTY, EDWARD JOSEPH, lawyer; b. Mpls., Mar. 17, 1923; s. John Edward and Elletta Winnifred (Newton) G.; m. Lorraine M. Breher, Aug. 7, 1965; 1 dau., Ann Therese. B.A., St. Thomas Coll., St. Paul, 1952; LL.B., Georgetown U., 1955. Commnr. Mpls. Park Bd., 1959-62; mem. Minn. Ho. of Reps., 1963-70, Minn. Senate, 1971-80, pres., 1977-80. Served with USN, 1942-48. Home: 3810 Xerxes Ave N Minneapolis MN 55412 Office: 1102 W Broadway Minneapolis MN 55411

GEARY, JOHN DANIEL, inland waterways transportation executive; b. Boston, Jan. 16, 1927; s. John Maurice and Bernice Catherine (Crowley) G.; m. Audrey Palmer, Oct. 17, 1959. B.S. in Nautical Scis, Mass. Maritime Acad., 1947, Boston U., 1952; M.B.A., Harvard U., 1954. With Eastern Gas and Fuels Assos. subsidiaries, 1954—; dispatcher Boston Tow Boat Co., 1954-57; asst. operating mgr. Mystic Steamship Co., Boston, 1957-60, mgr. ops., 1960-64; asst. to pres. Ohio River Co., Cin., 1964-66, v.p. ops., 1966-74; pres. Ohio River Co. and Midland Enterprises Inc., Cin., 1974—, sr. v.p. and trustee parent co., Boston, 1974—; dir. Fifth Third Bank, Cin., Fifth Third Bancorp. Bd. visitors Mass. Maritime Acad.; trustee Mt. St. Joseph Coll. on Ohio.; bd. dirs. Jr. Achievement of Greater Cin. Mem. Am. Waterways Operators (chmn. 1976, dir. 1974-80), Water Transport Assn. (chmn. exec. com.), Ohio Valley Improvement Assn. (trustee 1975-83), Am. Bur. Shipping, Boston Marine Soc., Greater Cin. C. of C. (v.p. govt. affairs). Clubs: Hyde Park Country, Queen City (Cin.); Harvard (Boston).

GEBALLE, RONALD, univ. dean, physicist; b. Redding, Calif., Feb. 7, 1918; s. Oscar and Alice (Glaser) G.; m. Marjorie Louise Cohn, Oct. 31, 1940; children—Margaret (Mrs. Howard Gilbert), Thomas R., Leslie (Mrs. Richard Mackay), Daniel T., Robert O., Jonathan L., Emily R., Anthony J. B.S., U. Calif. at Berkeley, 1938, M.S., 1940, Ph.D., 1943. Teaching asst. physics U. Calif. at Berkeley, 1938-42, physicist radiation lab., 1943; physicist Applied Physics Lab., U. Wash., 1943-46; mem. faculty U. Wash., 1946—, prof., 1959—, chmn. dept. physics, 1957-73; asso. dean Coll. Arts and Scis., 1973-75, acting dean, 1975-76, vice provost for research, also dean of grad. sch., 1976-81, dean emeritus, 1981—; Guest scientist Lab. for Atomic and Molecular Physics, Amsterdam, 1964-65; cons. NSF, Army Research Office; mem. research adv. com. electro-physics NASA, 1962-64; Mem. com. atomic and nuclear physics Nat. Acad. Scis., 1970-72; mem. Nat. Acad. Scis.-NRC evaluation panels for Nat. Bur. Standards panel on Inst. for Basic Standards, 1973-75, chmn. panel on lab. astrophysics, 1973-75; mem. Nat. Acad. Scis.-NRC exec. com. for evaluation panels for Nat. Bur. Standards, 1975-78; also adv. bd. to Office Phys. Scis., Assembly Math. and Phys. Scis., 1975-77; sec. Internat. Conf. on Physics of Electronic and Atomic Collisions, 1967-77; mem. adv. com. grants Research Corp., 1967-73; mem. Commn. on Coll. Physics, 1966-71; mem.-at-large U.S. Nat. Com. for Internat. Union of Pure and Applied Physics, 1974-76; Solomon Katz disting. lectr. humanities, 1978; mem. Grad. Record Exams. Bd., 1978-79. Mem. citizens com. edn. Wash. State Legislature, 1960; trustee Pacific Sci. Center, 1977—. Fellow Am. Phys. Soc. (chmn. div. electron and atomic physics 1968), AAAS; mem. AAUP, Am. Assn. Physics Tchrs. (pres. 1969-70, Distinguished Service citation 1973), Fedn. Am. Scientists, ACLU, Pacific N.W. Assn. Coll. Physics (chmn. bd. dirs. 1965-70), Am. Inst. Physics (governing bd., exec. com. 1968-71), Assn. Grad. Schs. (sec.-treas. 1977-80, v.p. 1980—), Phi Beta Kappa, Sigma Xi. Home: 4201 N E 92d St Seattle WA 98115

GEBALLE, THEODORE HENRY, educator; b. San Francisco, Jan. 20, 1920; s. Oscar and Alice (Glaser) G.; m. Frances C. Koshland, Oct. 19, 1941; children—Gordon, Alison, Adam, Monica Ruth, Jennifer, Ernest. B.S. in Chemistry, U. Calif. at Berkeley, 1941, Ph.D., 1950. Research asso. Low Temperature Lab., U. Calif. at Berkeley, 1949-51; mem. staff Bell Telephone Lab., Murray Hill, N.J., 1952—, head low temperature physics dept., 1958-67, research cons., 1967—; prof. applied physics Stanford, 1967—. Served to capt. AUS, 1941-46. Guggenheim fellow, 1974-75. Fellow Am. Phys. Soc. (Oliver E. Buckley solid state physics prize 1970); mem. Nat. Acad. Scis., Am. Acad. Arts and Scis., Am. Chem. Soc., Phi Beta Kappa, Sigma Xi. Home: 259 Kings Mountain Rd Woodside CA 94062 Office: Dept Applied Physics Stanford Univ Stanford CA 94305

GEBELEIN, RICHARD STEPHEN, former attorney general Delaware; b. Upper Darby, Pa., June 8, 1946; s. Walter C. and Margaret E. (Stratton) G.; m. Anna Grace Thomason.; children: R. Zachary, Lauren E. V. B.S. in Math., U. Pitts., 1967; J.D., Villanova U., 1970. Bar: Pa. 1971, Del. 1971, U.S. Supreme Ct. bar 1975. Justice of peace, Kennett Twp., Pa., 1967-70; dep. atty. gen. State of Del., 1971-74, state solicitor, 1974-75, chief dep. public defender, 1975-76; partner firm Wilson & Whittington, Wilmington, Del., 1976-79; atty. gen., Del., Wilmington, 1979-83; adj. prof. Del. Law Sch., Widener Coll.; instr. U. Del.; Mem. Bench-Bar Press Conf. Del., Del Gov.'s Sentencing Reform Commn. Republican. Roman Catholic. Clubs: Univ., Whist (Wilmington). Home: 509 N Washington St Wilmington DE 19801 Office: One Rodney Sq Wilmington DE 19899

GEBEL-WILLIAMS, GUNTHER, animal trainer; b. Schweidnitz, Ger., Sept. 12, 1934; came to U.S., 1968; s. Max and Elfriede (Koch) Gebel; m. Sigrid Elisabeth Neubauer, Apr. 10, 1968; children—Tina, Oliver Marc. Ed., Pestalozzi Sch., Ger. With Circus Williams, European tours, 1947-68; animal trainer Ringling Bros. Barnum & Bailey Circus, Venice, Fla., 1968—. Appeared: TV spls. including Gunther William: The Lord of the Ring, 1977. Recipient award German Assn. Raising and Breeding Horses, 1970; Granx prize Fedn. du Cirque France, 1962; Ernst Renz plaque, Ger., 1967; Entertainer of Yr. award AGVA, 1973; grand prize Fedn. Internat. dur Cirque, 1974; named Miss. Col., Ky. Col. Address: care Ringling Bros Barnum Bailey Combined Shows inc 320 New Mexico Ave NE Washington DC 20016

GEBHARD, DAVID, museum director, educator; b. Cannon Falls, Minn., July 21, 1927; s. Walter J. and Ann (Olson) G.; m. Patricia Peeke, July 7, 1954; children: Ellen Jean, Tyra Ann. B.A., U. Minn., 1949, M.A., 1951, Ph.D., 1957. Curator, instr. art U. N.Mex., 1953-55; dir. Roswell (N.Mex.) Mus., 1955-61; prof. art, dir. art galleries U. Calif. at Santa Barbara, 1961-80; curator archtl. drawing collection Art Mus., 1980—; field research in archeology, summers 1949-57; Fulbright prof. Tech. U. Istanbul, Turkey, 1960-61; cons. hist. preservation, 1970—. Author: Prehistoric Cave Paintings of the Diablo Region of Texas, 1960, A Guide to the Architecture of Purcell and Elmslie, 1960, A Guide to Architecture in Southern California, 1964, R.M. Schindler: Architect; Architecture in California, 1868-1968, 1968, Kem Weber and the Moderene, 1969, The Richfield Building, 1928-1968, 1969, Charles F.A. Voysey, Architect, 1970; co-author: Lloyd Wright, Architect, 1972, A Guide to Architecture in San Francisco and Northern California, 1973, Indian Art of the Northern Plains, 1974, Los Angeles in the 30's; Bay Area Houses, 1976, A Guide to Architecture in Los Angeles and Southern California, 1977, A Guide to Architecture in Minnesota, 1977, 200 Years of American Architectural Drawing, 1977, A View of California Architecture, 1960-1976, 1977, Picturesque California Homes, 1978, The Architecture of Samuel and J.C. Newsom, 1878-1908, 1979, The Architecture of Gregory Ain, 1980, California Crazy, 1980, Tulsa Art Deco, 1980, Santa Barbara, the Creation of a New Spain in America, 1980, Legacy of Minneapolis, 1983; contbr. articles to profl. jours. Pres. Citizens Planning Assn. Santa Barbara County, Inc., 1970-76; vice chmn. Historic Landmark Commn., Santa Barbara, 1973—, Citizens Planning Assn., 1980—; Bd. dirs. Regional Plan Assn., So. Calif., Western Found. Served with AUS, 1945-47. Research grantee NSF, NEA, Nat. Endowment Humanities; Nat. Park Service grantee; Ford found. grantee study Turkish architecture, 1965; Guggenheim Found. fellow, 1980-81. Mem. AIA (hon.), Soc. Am. Archaeology, Am. Anthrop. Assn., Coll. Art Assn., Soc. Archtl. Historians (pres. 1980-81, dir). Home: 895 E Mountain Dr Santa Barbara CA 93103 Office: Archtl Drawing Collection U Calif Santa Barbara CA 93106

GEBHARD, PAUL HENRY, anthropologist, educator; b. Rocky Ford, Colo., July 3, 1917; s. Paul Adam and Eva (Baker) G.; m. Agnes E. West, May 19, 1939 (div. 1965); children: Mark West, Jan Cynthia, Karla Lynn.; m. Joan Huntington, July 24, 1983. B.S. cum laude, Harvard, 1940, M.A., 1942, Ph.D., 1947. Asso. Inst. for Sex Research, Ind. U., Bloomington, 1946-55, exec. dir., 1956-82, curator, 1982—, instr. dept. anthrolology, 1947-52, asst. prof., 1953-60, asso. prof., 1961-66, prof., 1967—. Author: (with A. Kinsey) Sexual Behavior in the Human Female, 1953; sr. author: Pregnancy, Birth and Abortion, 1958, Sex Offenders, 1965, Kinsey Data, Marginal Tabulations, 1979. Fellow Am. Anthrop. Assn., Am. Sociol. Assn., Ind. Acad. Sci.; mem. Soc. Am Archaeology. Home: Route 1 Box 214 Nashville IN 47448 *I have tried to be reasonably diligent and useful because I believe that being born is not sufficient justification for continued existence. I have tried to be honest, except in those instances where honesty would cause needless pain to others, because honesty is the basis for the human interaction upon which we all ultimately depend. I have tried to be objective because objectivity is the essence of science. I have tried, but I have not succeeded to the extent I wished. Fortunately we humans are adept at devising exculpatory rationalizations.*

GEBHARDT, JAMES B(RUCE), airline executive; b. Moline, Ill., May 18, 1936; s. James B. and Lucielle E. (Priebe) G.; m. Patricia A. Ray, Sept. 29, 1962; children: Cynthia, Kristen. B.S.C., U. Iowa, 1955; M.B.A., Loyola U., Chgo., 1972. Dir. market research Club Aluminum Products Co., LaGrange Park, Ill., 1960-65; v.p. mktg. United Airlines, Chgo., 1965-79, Pacific Intermountain Express, Walnut Creek, Calif., 1979-82; v.p. cargo Pan Am. World Airways, N.Y.C., 1982—; dir. Hale Kamole, Maui, Hawaii. Served with U.S. Army, 1958-60; Korea. Mem. Nat. Council Phys. Distbn. Mgmt. Club: Wings (N.Y.C.). Lodge: Masons. Office: Pan American World Airways Inc 200 Park Ave New York NY 10166

GEBHART, CARL GRANT, security broker; b. Santa Monica, Calif., Jan. 24, 1926; a. Carl V. and Hazel (Grant) G.; m. Margaret Mary del Bondio, Nov. 29, 1952; children—Elizabeth G., Margaret H., Julia Ann. B.A. in Journalism, U. So. Calif., 1947; M.B.A. in Fin, Harvard U., 1949. Registered rep. Mitchum, Jones & Templeton, Inc., Los Angeles, 1949-56, gen. partner, 1956-62, sr. v.p., sec., dir., 1962-73; account v.p. Paine, Webber, Jackson & Curtis, Inc., Los Angeles, 1973—; financial reporter radio sta. KABC, Los Angeles, 1968-73. Mem. Los Angeles Soc. Fin. Analysts (v.p. 1959), Spring St. Forum (pres. 1962), Phi Beta Kappa, Phi Kappa Phi, Phi Eta Sigma, Chi Phi, Sigma Delta Chi. Republican. Methodist. Club: Stock Exchange (Los Angeles). Home: 749 Amalfi Dr Pacific Palisades CA 90272 Office: 700 S Flower St Los Angeles CA 90017

GECHT, MARTIN LOUIS, banker; b. Chgo., July 12, 1920; s. Max and Sarah (Rolnick) G.; m. Francey Ann Heytow; children: Lauren Paula Gecht Kramer, Susan Ellen Gecht Rieser, Robert David. B.A., U. So. Calif., 1941; M.D., U. Health Scis./Chgo. Med. Sch., 1945. Intern Brookdale Med. Center, N.Y.C., 1944-45; resident in dermatology Cook County Hosp., 1955-58; gen. practice medicine, 1946-59, practice medicine specializing in dermatology, 1959—; organized Allport Med. Group, 1948, now pres.; chmn. bd. Met. Bank and Trust Co., Chgo., 1964—; chmn. Amalgamated Trust & Savs. Bank, Chgo., 1966—, now chmn. exec. com., 1978—; chmn. bd. Albany Bank & Trust Co. N.A., 1976—. Pres. Aristocrat Inns Am.; Mem. State St. Council; trustee, mem. exec., fin. coms., chmn. bldg. devel. com. U. Health Scis./Chgo. Med Sch.; participant numerous activities Jewish Fedn. Chgo.; Chgo. com. Weizmann Inst. Sci.; mem. adv. on prints and drawings com. Art Inst. Chgo. Recipient Disting. Service award Anti-Defamation League, B'nai B'rith, 1975, 83. Mem. Am., Ill. bankers assns., AMA, Ill., Chgo. med. socs., Am. Acad. Dermatology (asso.), Soc. Indsl. Medicine and Surgery. Jewish. Club: Metropolitan. Home: 1110 N Lake Shore Dr Apt 37 Chicago IL 60611 Office: 1 W Monroe St Chicago IL 60603

GECHTOFF, SONIA, artist; b. Phila., Sept. 25, 1926; d. Leonid and Etya (Freedman) G.; children—Susannah Kelly, Miles Kelly. B.F.A., Phila. Mus. Sch. Art, 1950. Instr. painting, drawing Calif. Sch. Fine Art, 1956-57; adj. asst. prof. art NYU, 1966-70; lectr. art Queens Coll., N.Y.C., 1970-74; assoc. prof. art U. N.Mex., 1974-75. One-woman shows, DeYoung Mus., San Francisco, 1957, Ferus Gallery, Los Angeles, 1957, 59, Poindexter Gallery, N.Y.C., 1959, 60, Cortella Gallery, N.Y.C., 1976, 78, Gruenebaum Gallery, N.Y.C., 1979, 80, 82, 83; group shows include, Guggenheim Mus., N.Y.C., 1954, San Francisco Mus. Art, 1953-58, Brussels World's Fair, 1958, 1st Paris Biennale, 1959, Whitney Mus., N.Y.C., 1959, 60, Sao Paulo (Brazil) Biennale, 1961, Mus. Modern Art, N.Y.C., 1977, Aldrich Mus. Contemporary Art, Ridgefield, Conn., 1981; represented in permanent collections, San Francisco Mus. Modern Art, Guggenheim Mus., Mus. Modern Art, Met. Mus., N.Y.C., Balt. Mus. Art, also pvt. and corp. collections. Ford Found. fellow Tamarind Inst., Los Angeles, 1963; recipient Purchase awards San Francisco Mus. Art, 1955-59. Mem. Artists Equity N.Y. Address: 421 Hudson St New York NY 10014 *I have, since my early twenties, always thought of myself as a painter. As* *the mother of two children (now adults), I was able to work on my paintings and to develop my art continuously. My life is my work.*

GECKLE, GEORGE LEO, III, English language educator; b. Danbury, Conn., Dec. 2, 1939; s. George Leo and Dorothy Marian (Hill) G.; m. Justine Virginia Carroll, Aug. 19, 1961; children: George, Richard. A.B., Middlebury Coll., 1961; M.A., U. Va., 1962, Ph.D., 1965. Asst. prof. English U. Wis., Madison, 1965-68, U. S.C., Columbia, 1968-70, assoc. prof. English, 1970-74; prof. English U S.C., Columbia, 1974—; dir. honors program U. S.C., Columbia, 1970-73, dir. English grad. studies, 1974-76, 77-78, assoc. head English dept., 1973-76, chmn. English dept., 1978—. Author: John Marston's Drama, 1980; editor: Twentieth Interpretations of Measure for Measure, 1970. Mem. Internat. Assn. Univ. Profs. English, MLA, South Atlantic MLA, Southeastern Renaissance Conf., South Atlantic Assn. Depts. English (pres. 1983-84). Home: 303 Southwood Dr Columbia SC 29205 Office: U South Carolina Dept English Humanities Bldg Columbia SC 290208

GECKLE, JEROME WILLIAM, bus. services co. exec.; b. Balt., June 16, 1929; s. George Francis and Rose Catherine (Katzenberger) G.; m. Mary Margaret Trageser, June 9, 1951; children—Timothy James, Teresa Ann, Stephen Lawrence, Karen Joy. Student public schs. Supr. Internat. Harvester Co., Balt., 1949-52; mgr. machine acctg. Lever Bros. Co., Balt., 1952-55; with PHH Group, Inc., Balt., 1955—, chmn. bd., pres., 1980—; dir. First Md. Bancorp., Balt. Gas & Elec.; Bd. dirs. Econ. Devel. Council Greater Balt., 1979—; mem. Greater Balt. Com., 1979—. Trustee Villa Julie Coll., 1973—, Goucher Coll., 1981—. Served with USMC, 1946-48, 50-51. Mem. Data Processing Mgmt. Assn. Democrat. Roman Catholic. Club: Balt. Country. Office: PHH Group Inc 11333 McCormick Rd Hunt Valley MD 21931 *

GECKLER, RICHARD DELPH, metal products company executive; b. Toledo, Nov. 4, 1918; s. Maurice T. and Edith (Payne) G.; m. Elaine Mary Campbell, June 27, 1965; children: Elaine Demian, Sharon Jean (Mrs. Alex Bellehumeur); 1 dau. by previous marriage, Carole Faye (Mrs. Gene Hendrix). A.B., DePauw U., 1939. Chem. engr. Standard Oil Co., Ind., 1939-45; with Aerojet-Gen. Corp., 1945-68, v.p., mgr. solid rocket plant, Sacramento, 1956-63, corp. v.p., El Monte, Calif., 1963-68; chmn. bd., chief exec. Aerojet Delft Corp., 1968-69; exec. v.p. Anellux Systems Corp., El Segundo, Calif., 1970-71; pres. Marquardt Co., 1972-73, Geckler Industries, Inc., 1972—, Pitter Metal Products, Inc., 1972—, J.L. Mallard Co., 1972—; asst. dir. strategic weapons Office Sec. Def., 1964-66. Recipient Meritorious Pub. Service citation Navy Dept., 1961. Fellow Am. Inst. Aeros. and Astronautics; mem. Am. Chem. Soc., Am. Math. Soc., Phi Beta Kappa. Home: 135 Belday Rd Pasadena CA 91105 Office: 10580 Silicon Ave Montclair CA 91763

GEDDA, NICOLAI H. G. (BORN NICOLAI H.G. USTINOV), tenor; b. Stockholm, July 11, 1925; s. Michael and Olga (Gedda) Ustinov; 1 dau. by; m. marriage, Titiana; m. Anastasia Caraviotis, Feb. 21, 1965. Studied with, Karl-Martin Oehman, Stockholm; attended opera sch., Stockholm Conservatory. Opera debut in: Le Postillon de Longjumea, Stockholm Opera, 1952; La Scala debut in: Trionfo di Afrodite, 1953; Paris Opera debut in: Faust, 1954; Covent Garden debut in: Rigoletto, 1954; Am. debut with, Pitts. Opera in, Faust, 1957; Met. Opera debut in; appeared with opera cos. in, Europe and N.Am., including, Vienna State Opera, Hamburg (W. Ger.) Opera, Munich (W. Ger.) Opera, Budapest (Hungary) Opera, Rome Opera, Monte Carlo (Monaco) Opera, Edinburgh (Scotland) Festival, Met. Opera, La Scala, Paris Opera; rec. artist, beginning with, EMI, 1952; apptd. (royal ct. singer of Sweden.). Decorated Order of Vasa Litteris et Artibus, Sweden; comdr. Order Danneborg, Denmark; winner Christine Nilsson award. Mem. Royal Acad. Stockholm (hon. mem.). Office: care Shaw Concerts Inc 1995 Broadway New York NY 10023 *

GEDDES, FRANK MICHAEL, JR., business and financial consultant; b. Chgo., Aug. 11, 1939; s. Frank Michael and Marjorie Mary (Creevy) G.; m. Sheila Patricia Shanahan, June 10, 1962; children: Daniel Patrick, Timothy Brian. B.S. in Accounting with honors, U. Notre Dame, 1961; M.B.A. with distinction, Harvard U., 1963; D.C.S. (hon.), U. So. Colo., 1974. With Ariz.-Colo. Land & Cattle Co. (name changed to AZL Resources, Inc.), Phoenix, 1964-78, pres., 1969-71, chmn. bd., 1971-78, chief exec. officer, 1969-78; pres. Geddes & Co., 1978—; chmn. bd., chief exec. officer Remuda Oil and Gas Corp., Midland, Tex., Coe and Van Loo Cons. Engrs., Inc., Phoenix, ADG Engring., Inc., Englewood, Colo.; dir. Valley Nat. Corp., Valley Nat. Bank of Ariz., Phoenix, Questor Corp., Tampa, Fla., NuWest, Inc., Phoenix. Past bd. dirs. Jr. Achievement Ariz.; past mem. dean's adv. com. Ariz. State U. St. Patrick's scholar, 1959-60; U.S. Rubber Co. scholar, 1960-61; Ralph P. Sayles Meml. fellow, 1961-63; recipient Golden Plate award Am. Acad. Achievement, 1974. Mem. U.S., Phoenix chambers commerce, Ariz. Acad., Phoenix Together. Republican. Roman Catholic. Clubs: Notre Dame, Harvard Bus. Sch., Paradise Valley Country, Kiva, K.M. Home: 6725 N Tatum Blvd Paradise Valley AZ 85253 Office: 2930 E Camelback Rd Suite 110 Phoenix AZ 85016

GEDDES, LESLIE ALEXANDER, bioengr., physiologist, educator; b. Scotland, May 24, 1921; s. Alexander and Helen (Humphrey) G.; m. La Nelle E. Nerger, Aug. 3, 1962; 1 son, James Alexander. B.E.E., M.S., Sc.D., McGill U.; Ph.D. in Physiology, Baylor U. Demonstrator in elec. engring. McGill U., 1945, research asst. dept. neurology, 1945-52; cons. elec. engring. to various indsl. firms, Que., Can.; biophysicist dept. physiology Baylor Med. Coll., Houston, asst. prof. physiology, 1956-61, asso. prof., 1961-65, prof., 1965—; dir. Lab. of Biophysics, Tex. Inst. Rehab. and Research, Houston, 1961-65; prof. physiology Coll. Vet. Medicine, Tex. A. and M. U., College Station, 1965—, prof. biomed. engring., 1969—; Showalter Distinguished prof. bioengring. Purdue U., West Lafayette, Ind., 1974—; cons. NASA Manned Spacecraft Center, Houston, 1962-64, USAF, Sch. Aerospace Medicine, Brooks AFB, 1958-65. Author: (with H.E. Hoff) Experimental Physiology, 1967, (with others), 5 books, also numerous articles on bioengring.; Cons. editor: Med. and Biol. Engring, 1969—, Med. Research Engring, 1964—, Med. Electronics and Data, 1969—; editorial bd.: Jour. Electrocardiology, 1968—. Served with Canadian Army. Fellow Am. Coll. Cardiology, Australasian Coll. Physicists in Biology and Medicine; mem. IEEE, Tex., Nat. socs. profl. engrs., Houston Engring. and Sci. Soc., Biomed. Engring. Soc., Am. Inst. Biol. Scis., Assn. for Advancement Med. Instrumentation, Am. Physiol. Soc., N.Y. Acad. Scis., Neuroelectric Soc., Sigma Xi, Tau Beta Pi. Home: 400 N River Rd Apt 1724 West Lafayette IN 47906 Office: APEC Bldg Purdue Univ West Lafayette IN 47907

GEDDES, ROBERT, architect, educator; b. Phila., Dec. 7, 1923; s. Louis J. and Kay (Malmed) G.; m. Evelyn Basse, June 15, 1947; children: David, Ann. Student, Yale U., 1941-46; M.Arch., Harvard U., 1950. Sr. partner Geddes-Brecher Qualls Cunningham (architects), Phila., 1954—, Princeton, 1965—; prof. architecture and civic design U. Pa., 1951-65; prof. architecture, dean Sch. Architecture Princeton U., 1965-82, William Kenan prof., 1968—; univ. lectr. U. London, 1972; dir. Manville Corp., Butler Mfg. Co.; Chmn. adv. bd. design Redevel. Authority Phila., 1959-66; bd. dirs. Citizens Council City Planning, Phila., 1961-63, Urban America, Inc. Contbr. articles on architecture to Ency. Brit., 1974-79; prin. works include Penn's Landing Plan, Phila., 1959-65, Rockville (Md.) Town Center, 1965—, Moore Sch. Elec. Engring, U. Pa., 1958, Police Hdqrs, Phila., 1962, resident hall groups, U. Del., 1966, U. Pa., 1967, housing projects, Westchester, Pa., also, Phila. and, Trenton, 1966-77, U. Pa. Med. Sch. and Hosp., 1978-84, sci. bldg., Beaver Coll., 1971, dining hall and acad. bldg., Inst. for Advanced Study, Princeton, 1971, humanities and social scis. bldg., So. Ill. U., Carbondale, 1968-74, Stockton State Coll, 1971-75, Corning (N.Y.) Downtown Renewal, 1975; master plan and design Liberty State Park, N.J., 1975-77; cloister gallery Dock St. theaters and shops; master plan Miami Downtown Govt. Center, 1978—; Lab. bldgs., Mobil Corp., 1981, J. B. Speed Art Mus., Louisville, 1982, State of N.J. Commerce Bldg., Trenton, 1983. Served with AUS, 1942-45. Appleton Traveling fellow Harvard U., 1950-51; recipient 6 Design awards Progressive Architecture, First Design award, 1958; 2d prize Nat. Opera House, Sydney, Australia, 1958; first prize Internat. Town Planning Competition for Expansion of Vienna, Austria, 1971; award for Excellence in Archtl. Edn. ACSA-AIA, 1984. Fellow for design AIA (dir. edn. research project 1965-67, Nat. First Honor award 1960, 77, Archtl. Firm award 1979, Gold medals Phila. chpt., Silver medals Pa. Soc., medals N.J. Soc.); mem. Harvard Grad. Sch. Design Alumni Assn. (past pres.). Clubs: Century Assn., Princeton (N.Y.). Home: 229 Mercer St Princeton NJ 08540 also 140 Riverside Dr New York NY 10024

GEDGAUDAS, EUGENE, radiologist, educator; b. Lithuania, Oct. 7, 1924; came to U.S., 1963, naturalized, 1968; children—Kristina, Nora, Sandra. M.D., U. Munich, 1948. Diplomate: Am. Bd. Radiology. Intern St. Boniface Hosp., Winnipeg, Man., Can., resident in radiology, Winnipeg, U. Minn. Hosp., Mpls.; chmn. cardiac unit, asso. radiologist St. Boniface Gen. Hosp., Winnipeg, 1958-63; also dir. dept. radiology Mericordia Gen. Hosp., Winnipeg; asst. prof. radiology U. Minn., Mpls., 1963-67, asso. prof., 1967-69, prof., 1969—, head radiology, 1969—; chmn. council clin. scis. Med. Sch. Med. Sch., 1975—, mem. dean's adv. council, 1975—. Contbr. articles to profl. jours. Fellow Royal Coll. Physicians and Surgeons Can., Am. Coll. Radiology, Internat. Coll. Surgery; mem. AMA, Radiol. Soc. N. Am., Am. Roetgen Ray Soc., Minn. Radiology Soc., Minn. Acad. Medicine, Assn. Univ. Radiologists; Soc. Chmn. Acad. Radiology Depts. Home: 26 Evergreen Rd North Oaks St Paul MN 55110 Office: Box 292 Radiology 420 Delaware St SE Minneapolis MN 55455

GEE, EDWIN AUSTIN, chemical company executive; b. Washington, Feb. 19, 1920; s. Edwin S. and Marie (Junghans) G.; m. Genevieve Riordan, Aug. 26, 1944; children: J. Michael, William S., David S. B.S., George Washington U., 1941, M.S., 1944; Ph.D., U. Md., 1948. Asst. chemist Naval Research Lab., Washington, 1941-42; chemist U.S. Bur. Mines, 1942-44, engr., 1945-46, asst. chief metallurgist, 1947-48; with E.I. duPont de Nemours & Co., Inc., Wilmington, Del., 1948-78, with devel. dept., 1960-68, photo products dept., 1968-69, v.p., mem. exec. com., from 1970, sr. v.p., dir., until 1978; pres. Internat. Paper Co., N.Y.C., 1978-80, chmn., chief exec. officer, 1980—. Mem. Nat. Acad. Engring. Home: Box 362 Buck Hill Falls PA 18323 Office: Internat Paper Co 77 W 45th St New York NY 10036

GEE, ELWOOD GORDON, university president; b. Vernal, Utah, Feb. 2, 1944; s. Elwood A. and Vera (Showalter) G.; m. Elizabeth Dutson, Aug. 26, 1968; 1 dau., Rebekah. B.A., U. Utah, 1968; J.D., Columbia U., 1971, Ed.D., 1972. Asst. dean U. Utah, Salt Lake City, 1973-74; jud. fellow U.S. Sup. Ct., Washington, 1974-75; assoc. dean Brigham Young U., Provo, Utah, 1975-79; dean W.Va. U., Morgantown, 1979-81, pres., 1981—. Author: Education Law and Public Schools, 1978, Law and Public Education, 1980, Violence, Values and Justice in American Education, 1982, Fair Employment Practice, 1982. W.K. Kellogg fellow, 1971-72; Mellon fellow, 1977-78. Mem. ABA, Adminstrv. Conf. U.S., Phi Delta Kappa, Phi Kappa Phi. Mormon. Home: 948 Riverview Dr Morgantown WV 26505 Office: W Va U Office of Pres Stuart Hall Morgantown WV 26506

GEE, GEORGE DUVALL, savings association executive; b. Kansas City, Mo., June 16, 1915; s. Herbert H. and Lillian (Walz) G.; m. Lillian E. Johnson, May 25, 1940; children: Donald A., Gordon D. B.S., U. Kans., 1935. With Interstate Securities Co. (now ISC Fin. Corp.), Kansas City, 1935-78, v.p., 1953-58, exec. v.p., 1958-60, pres., 1960-62, chmn. bd., 1962-78, Anchor Savs. Assn., 1974—. Bd. dirs. Jr. Achievement, 1965-78, v.p., 1968-70; bd. dirs. Heart of Am. council Boy Scouts Am., 1962—, v.p., 1979-83; bd. dirs. Trinity Luth. Hosp., 1955—, pres., 1961-67; bd. dirs. Trinity Luth. Manor, Inc., 1977—, pres., 1977-82; bd. dirs. Oxford Park Acad., 1976—. Recipient Silver Beaver award Boy Scouts Am., 1968. Mem. Fin. Execs. Inst. (chpt. pres. 1957-58, nat. dir. 1970-73), Nat. Assn. Accts. (past nat. v.p., nat. pres. 1976-77, nat. dir. 1958-59, 67-69, 73—). Lutheran. (trustee 1941-57). Clubs: Mission Hills Country (Shawnee Mission, Kans.); Scandinavian (Kansas City) (pres. 1981-83). Home: 2803 W 66th Terr Shawnee Mission KS 66208

GEE, RONALD DAVENPORT, business executive; b. Manchester, Eng., May 16, 1925; s. Fred Davenport and Ena Mary (Hoff) G.; m. Marianne Margaret Julie Kalbeck, Dec. 6, 1950; children: Pamela Davenport Tapolcai, Jennifer Davenport. Grad., Balliol Coll., Oxford, 1949, Vienna Acad. Music, 1951. With AMAX RST Group, N.Y.-London, 1952-78; sr. v.p., dir. Drexel Burnham Lambert Inc., N.Y.-London, 1978—; chmn., chief exec. officer Drexel Burnham Lambert Holdinigs, London, 1978-83; dir. BICC Cables Lte., London, London Metal Exchange; chmn. London Gold Futures Market, 1983. Served to lt. Fleet Air Army, 1942-45. Clubs: Vincents (Oxford); Cresham (London); Sunningdale Golf. Office: Drexel Burnham Lambert Inc 77 London Wall London UK EC2N 1BE

GEE, THOMAS GIBBS, fed. judge; b. Jacksonville, Fla., Dec. 9, 1925; s. James Gilliam and Cecile (Gibbs) G.; m. Nola Smith, July 20, 1979; children by previous marriage—Jennifer Gee Updegraf, John Christopher, Mary Cecile, Thomas Gibbs. Student, The Citadel, 1942-43; B.S., U.S. Mil. Acad., 1946; LL.B., U. Tex., 1953. Bar: Tex. bar 1953. Asso. firm Baker & Botts, Houston, 1953-54, Graves, Dougherty, Gee, Hearon, Moody & Garwood (and predecessors), Austin, Tex., 1954, partner, 1955-73; judge U.S. Ct. Appeals, 5th Circuit, Austin, 1973—. Contbr. articles to profl. jours., publs.; editor-in-chief: Tex. Law Rev, 1952-53. Served with USAAF, 1946-47; Served with USAF, 1947-50. Mem. Am. Law Inst., Am. Bar Assn., Am. Judicature Soc., Tex. Bar Found., Order of Coif. Home: 16301 Fitzhugh Rd Austin TX 78736 Office: US Courthouse Room 105 200 W 8th St Austin TX 78701

GEEHAN, ROBERT WILLIAM, consulting mining engineer; b. Yakima, Wash., Dec. 12, 1909; s. Michael and Susan (Stratton) G.; m. Iria Alanne, June 11, 1932; children: Roberta (Mrs. Robert Horton), David, Patrick. E.M., U. Minn., 1932; student, Am. U., 1954, U. Colo., 1959. Mining engr. Winston Bros. Co., Helena, Mont., 1932-34, Cripple Creek Mining Co., Folger and Anchorage, Alaska, 1934-39; designing engr. Alaska R.R., Anchorage, 1939-42; with U.S. Bur. Mines, 1942-72; successively mining engr., Nev. and Va., commodity specialist tungsten and molybdenum, Washington, asst. chief ferrous metals and alloys br., asst. chief div. minerals, chief div. mineral tech., Rolla, Mo., 1956-59, chief div. resources, Denver, 1959, regional dir., 1960-63, area dir., then program mgr., 1964-72; now cons. mining engr.; U.S. rep. for tungsten and molybdenum Internat. Materials Conf., Washington, 1952-53; mem. manganese ore com. Am. Standards Assn.-Internat. Standards Orgn. (meetings in), Leningrad, USSR, 1954, 56; cons. tungsten and molybdenum NATO, Paris, 1954; mem. tungsten raw materials panel Nat. Acad. Scis.-NCR, 1958-60; vol. exec. Internat. Exec. Service Corps, Brazil, 1973, El Salvador, 1974, Colombia, 1977. Contbr. articles to profl. jours., bulls. Mem. Am. Inst. Mining and Metall. Engrs., Denver Mining Club, Sigma Xi, Tau Beta Pi. Unitarian. Club: Teknik (Denver). Home and Office: 12423 St Andrew Dr Sun City AZ

GEEKER, NICHOLAS PETER, lawyer; b. Pensacola, Fla., Dec. 15, 1944. B.A. in English, La. Poly. Inst., 1966; J.D., Fla. State U., 1969. Bar: Fla. 1969, U.S. Dist. Ct. 1970. Assoc. firm Merritt & Jackson, Pensacola, 1969; law clk. U.S. Dist. Judge D.L. Middlebrooks, Tallahassee, 1970-73; asst. state atty. Fla. 1st Jud. Circuit, 1973; asst. U.S. atty. No. Dist. Fla., 1973-76, U.S. atty., 1976-82; sole practice, Pensacola, Fla., 1982—; mem. Fed.-State Joint Com. on Law Enforcement. Mem. Fla. Bar Assn., Fla. Trial Lawyers Assn. (editor Newsletter 1975), Phi Delta Phi. Office: PO Box 12009 Pensacola FL 32589

GEER, JACK CHARLES, pathology educator; b. Galesburg, Ill., Sept. 19, 1927; s. John Charles and Ruth Helen (McGee) G.; m. Sara Kathleen Williamson, Feb. 16, 1951; children: Charles Robert, Richard John, John Michael, Cynthia Jane, Michael James. B.S., La. State U., 1950, M.D., 1956.. Research asst. prof. La. State U., Baton Rouge, 1954-66; prof. U. Tex.-San Antonio, 1966-67; prof., chmn. Ohio State U., Columbus, 1967-72; assoc. pathologist Davidson Labs., Columbus, 1972-75; prof. pathology U. Ala., Birmingham, 1975—, chmn. dept., 1975—; cons. nutrition study sect. Nat. Heart, Lung and Blood Inst., Bethesda, Md., 1965-69, cons., chmn. pathology study sect., 1976-80; mem. research com. Am. Heart Assn., 1968-82, pres. Ala. affiliate, 1983—. Author: Smooth Muscle Cells in Atherosclerosis, 1972; mem. editorial bd.: Jour. Exptl. and Molecular Pathology, 1967—, Am. Jour. Pathology, 1969-80; contbr. articles to profl. jours. Mem. Ala. region ARC Blood Services, 1979—. Served with USN, 1945-47; ATO. USPHS research career devel. award, 1959-66; recipient Disitng. Faculty citation La. State U., 1964, Disting. Service award Am. Heart Assn., 1972-75, Outstanding Vol. Achievement award ARC, 1981; named to ALumni Hall of Distinction La. State U., 1982. Fellow Coll. Am. pathologists; mem. AMA, Am. Registry Pathologists (exec. mem., prs.). Home: 3744 Wimbleton Dr Birmingham AL 35223 Office: Dept Pathology Univ Ala Birmingham AL 35294

GEER, JAMES HAMILTON, ret. broadcasting co. exec.; b. Ft. Oglethorpe, Ga., June 25, 1924; s. Joseph White and Katharine Ellis (Hamilton) G.; m. Patricia O'Sullivan, Mar. 17, 1973; children—Christopher Potter, Michael Danforth; children by previous marriages—James Hamilton, Penelope Echo. A.B. cum laude, Williams Coll., 1949; M.B.A. with distinction, Harvard U., 1951. Asst. control supt. E.I. duPont de Nemours & Co., Camden, S.C., 1951-52; cons. Price Waterhouse & Co., N.Y.C., 1952-54, asso. dir., Cleve., 1954-56; asst. controller ACF Industries, Inc., N.Y.C., 1956-59; controller CBS Television Network Div., N.Y.C., 1959-70, CBS Inc., 1970-71, v.p., controller, 1971-72, v.p. fin., 1972-78, chief fin. officer, 1974-78; sr. v.p. CBS/Broadcast Group, N.Y.C., 1978-81, ret., 1981. Trustee Citizens Budget Commn., Inc. Served with inf. AUS, 1942-46; ETO. Mem. Nat. Assn. Accountants, Fin. Execs. Inst., Internat. Radio and TV Soc., Phi Beta Kappa, Phi Beta Kappa Assos., Delta Psi. Clubs: Power Squadron, Harvard Bus. Sch. (N.Y.C.); Fla. West Coast. Home: 1582 MacCharles Ct Dunedin FL 33528

GEER, JOHN FARR, diversified company executive; b. N.Y.C., Oct. 15, 1930; s. William Montague and Edith Jaffray (Farr) G.; m. Carolyn Boston, June 25, 1954; children: Jennifer, Evelyn, John Farr. B.A., Princeton U., 1952; LL.B., Columbia U., 1957. Bar: N.Y. State 1957. Asso. firm Sullivan & Cromwell, N.Y.C., 1957-65, Whitman & Ransom (and predecessor firms), 1965-67, partner, 1967-73; v.p., gen. counsel, sec. Am. Standard Inc., N.Y.C., 1973—. Trustee Protestant Episcopal Soc. for Promoting Religion and Learning in State N.Y., 1960-82, treas., 1968-82; trustee Gen. Theol. Sem., 1980—; mem. Corp. for Relief Widows and Children of P.E. Clergymen in State N.Y., 1960—, treas., 1967—. Served to 1st lt. F.A. AUS, 1952-54; Korea. Mem. Phi Delta Phi. Episcopalian. Club: Princeton (N.Y.C.). Home: 151 Central Park W New York NY 10023 Office: 40 W 40th St New York NY 10018

GEER, RODERICK LELAND, association executive; b. Syracuse, May 12, 1928; s. Laverne and Gertrude (Driscoll) G.; m. Mynema June Birnie, Oct. 27, 1944; children: Stewart, Lila Lee, Cheryl Lynn. B.S., Syracuse U., 1950. Exec. dir. Ind. Mut. Agts. of N.Y., 1950-59, Ind. Mut. Agts. Assn. of N.J., 1959-60; dir. Ind. Mut. Agts. Assn. Conn., 1960-64; sec., mgr. IM Inc., 1964-71; exec. v.p. Million Dollar Round Table, Des Plaines, Ill., 1971—. Mem. Am. Soc. Assn. Execs. (trustee Found. 1971, edn. com. 1973-75, bd. dirs. 1974-77), Chgo. Soc. Assn. Execs., Am. Mgmt. Assn. Republican. Methodist. Office: Million Dollar Round Table 2340 River Rd Des Plaines IL 60018

GEER, RONALD LAMAR, mech. engr., oil co. exec.; b. West Palm Beach, Fla., Sept. 2, 1926; s. Marion Wood and Bertha (Lightfoot) G.; m. Geneva Yvonne Chappell, Dec. 24, 1951; children—Ronald Lamar, Mark Randall. B.M.E., Ga. Inst. Tech., 1951. With Shell Oil Co., 1951—, sr. staff mech. engr., head office, Houston, 1969-71, cons. mech. engr., 1971—; mem. various govt., univ. adv. coms. Contbr. articles on petroleum drilling and prodn. to profl. jours. Mem. Nat. Acad. Engring., NRC (marine bd.), Nat. Security Indsl. Assn. (petroleum panel, research and engring. adv. com.), ASME, Marine Tech. Soc., Am. Petroleum Inst., Model-A Ford Club Am., Classic T-Bird Club Internat., Thistle Class Assn., Pi Tau Sigma. Republican. Patentee petroleum drilling and prodn. equipment; mem. Shell Oil Co. team recognized in Offshore Tech. Conf. Disting. Achievement award to co., 1971. Home: 14723 Oak Bend Dr Houston TX 77079 Office: One Shell Plaza Houston TX 77001

GEER, STEPHEN DUBOIS, journalist; b. Mt. Kisco, N.Y., Aug. 20, 1930; s. Solon and Eve (DuBois) G.; m. Elizabeth White, Jan. 2, 1953 (div.); children: William Joseph, Catherine Anne, Stephen Michael, Thomas White (dec.), Nancy Ellen; m. Laura Palmer, Apr. 26, 1980; 1 dau., Sabrina Palmer. Student, Grinnell Coll., 1946-48; B.A., Columbia U., 1951. Broadcast newsman radio stas. in Conn. and Va., 1952-55, WHEN-TV, Syracuse, N.Y., 1955-59, WBEN-TV, Buffalo, 1959-63, WTOP-TV, Washington, 1963-69; corr. ABC-News, Washington Bur., 1969-74, Los Angeles Bur., 1974-84, ABC News, N.Y.C., 1974—. Reporter-narrator: documentary The Right to Die, ABC News; Recipient (Emmy award Nat. Acad. Television Arts and Scis. 1966-67). Mem. Radio and Television Corrs. Assn. Office: 7 W 66th St New York NY 10023

GEER, WILLIAM DUDLEY, univ. dean; b. Augusta, Ga., Dec. 25, 1922; s. William Fred and Ida (Fuller) G.; m. Elizabeth Durner, Dec. 18, 1949; children—John William, Deborah Elizabeth, Margaret Ruth. B.S., Stetson U., 1948, M.A., 1950; D.Bus. Adminstrn., Ind. U., 1963. C.L.U. Instr. Mars Hill (N.C.) Coll., 1950-52; asso. prof. Miss. Coll., Clinton, 1953-56; asst. prof. Stetson U., Deland, Fla., 1956-59; prof. bus. adminstrn. Samford U., Birmingham, Ala., 1959-66; dean Sch. Bus., 1966—; Faculty Sch. Banking of South, La. State U.; cons. to bus. Contbr. articles to profl. jours. Bd. mgrs. Five Point YMCA; trustee annuity bd. So. Bapt. Conv., chmn. exec. com., vice chmn. bd. Served with Signal Corps AUS, 1943-45. Mem. Ala. Acad. Sci. (v.p.),

So. Bus. Adminstrn. Assn. (pres.), Am. Econ. Assn., Am. Finance Assn., Am. Risk and Ins. Assn., Am. Soc. C.L.U.'s, Alpha Kappa Psi, Beta Gamma Sigma, Phi Alpha Theta. Baptist (deacon). Club: Rotarian. Home: 2703 Lakeland Trail Birmingham AL 35243

GEERDES, JAMES (DIVINE GEERDES), chemical company executive; b. Davenport, N.D., Apr. 13, 1924; s. William A. and Martha (Buchholz) G.; m. Patricia Seney, July 6, 1968; children: Andrew, John, Laura, Margaret. B.S., N.D. State U., 1949, M.S., 1950; Ph.D., U. Minn., 1953. Instr. biochemistry U. Minn., 1950-53; research chemist E.I. duPont de Nemours & Co., Inc., Richmond, Va. and Seaford, Del., 1954-58, group supr., 1958-60, tech. supr., 1960-62, research asso., 1962-64; dir. research Entoleter, Inc., Hamden, Conn., 1964-65, exec. v.p., 1965-66, pres., 1966-67; asst. to v.p. fibers div. Allied Chem. Corp., N.Y.C., 1967, asst. to pres., 1967-68, exec. v.p., 1968, pres., 1968-71; pres., dir. Alrac Corp., Stamford, Conn., 1971-73, Geerdes Industries, Richmond, Va., 1971—; pres. GGB Enterprises, Inc., Cocoa Beach, Fla.; pres., dir. Geerdes Internat., Richmond, pres., U.K.; pres., dir. Creative Iron, Inc., Ashland, Va.; dir. Photo Chem Industries, Inc., Meriden, Conn. Contbg. editor jour.: Fiber World; contbr. articles to profl. jours. Bd. dirs. Richmond Children's Museum. Served to 1st lt. C.E. AUS, 1943-46. Mem. Textile Inst., Del. Acad. Sci., Am. Chem. Soc., AAAS, Textile Research Inst., Fiber Soc., Sigma Xi, Phi Kappa Phi, Gamma Sigma Delta, Gamma Alpha. Patentee in field. Home: 3223 Hawthorne Ave Richmond VA 23222 Office: Geerdes Industries Richmond VA 23222

GEERLINGS, GERALD KENNETH, architect, etcher; b. Milw., Apr. 18, 1897; s. Jacob and Cattalina (Geerlings); m. Elizabeth Filby Edmunds, Sept. 2, 1924; children: Barbara Filby (Mrs. Merrill Soldier), Gillian (Mrs. David D. Brown III). B.A. in Architecture, U. Pa., 1921, M.A., 1922; student, St. John's Coll. (Cambridge U.), Eng., Royal Coll. Art, London. Employed as a newspaper reporter, Milw.; 2 yrs. a head designer York & Sawyer, also Starrett & Van Vleck (architects), N.Y.; own archtl. practice in, N.Y., 1926—. Author several books.; Contbr.: articles to mags. Ency. Brit; Etchings exhibited in, Europe, also in Am.; collection entitled Contemporary Etching, frequently, 1929—; and in Fine Prints of the Year, London; etchings in permanent collection, Victoria and Albert Mus., London, Congl. Library, Met. Mus., N.Y.C., Nat. Collection Fine Arts, Washington, Bklyn. Mus., Chgo. Art Inst., Boston Pub. Library, Phila. Mus. Art. (Awards include 1st prize for best etching Chgo. Century of Progress 1933), others. Served from pvt. to 2d lt. F.A. AEF, World War I; Served from capt. to col. USAAF, World War II; spl. civilian cons. USAF, 1949-55. Decorated Legion of Merit with oak leaf clusters; Army Commendation medal.; recipient Gold medal Phila. Acad. Fine Arts. Mem. AIA, Archtl. League N.Y., Am. Soc. Graphic Artists, Pastel Soc. Am., Theta Xi, Tau Sigma Delta. Home: 26 Gower Rd New Canaan CT 06840 *In retrospect it seems to me it was important to disregard the possibility of not surviving both wars and the dismal effects of the Depression, and to have faith in the future.*

GEERTSMA, ROBERT HENRY, psychologist, educator; b. Chgo., July 22, 1929; s. Henry George and Ruth (Wren) G.; m. Nobuko Sakamoto, Apr. 8, 1956; children: Martin Alex, Phillip R., Francesca Ruth. A.B., U. Chgo., 1950, Ph.D., 1956. Diplomate: clin. psychology Am. Bd. Profl. Psychology. From instr. to asst. prof. psychiatry U. Calif. Med. Sch., Los Angeles, 1956-62; assoc. prof. med. communication U. Kans. Med. Sch., 1962-69, chmn. dept., 1964-69; prof., chmn. dept. med. edn. and communication, prof. psychiatry, also prof. Coll. Edn., U. Rochester (N.Y.) Sch. Medicine and Dentistry, 1969—. Home: 912 Mendon Center Rd Pittsford NY 14534 Office: Univ Rochester Sch Medicine and Dentistry Rochester NY 14642

GEERTZ, CLIFFORD JAMES, anthropology educator; b. San Francisco, Aug. 23, 1926; s. Clifford James and Lois (Brieger) G.; m. Hildred Storey, Oct. 30, 1948 (div. 1981); children: Erika, Benjamin. A.B., Antioch Coll., 1950; Ph.D., Harvard U., 1956, LL.D. (hon.), 1974, L.H.D., No. Mich. U., 1975, U. Chgo., 1979, Bates Coll., 1980, Knox Coll., 1982, Brandeis U., 1984, Swarthmore Coll., 1984. Asst. prof. to prof. dept. anthropology U. Chgo., 1960-70; prof. dept. social sci. Inst. for Advanced Study, Princeton, N.J., 1970—; Eastman prof. Oxford U., 1978-79. Author: The Religion of Java, 1960, Peddlers and Princes, 1963, Agricultural Involution, 1963, The Social History of an Indonesian Town, 1965, Islam Observed, 1968, The Interpretation of Cultures, 1973, (with H. Geertz) Kinship in Bali, 1975, (with L. Rosen and H. Geertz) Meaning and Order in Moroccan Society, 1979, Negara: The Theatre State in Nineteenth-Century Bali, 1980, Local Knowledge, 1983. Served with USNR, 1943-45. Nat. Acad. Scis. fellow, 1973—. Fellow Am. Philos. Soc., Am. Acad. Arts and Scis., AAAS; mem. Am. Anthrop. Assn., Assn. for Asian Studies, Middle East Studies Assn. Home: 5 Newlin Rd Princeton NJ 08540 Office: Institute for Advanced Study Princeton NJ 08540

GEERTZ, HILDRED STOREY, anthropologist; b. N.Y.C., Feb. 12, 1927; d. Walter Rendell and Helen (Anderson) S.; m. Clifford Geertz, Oct. 30, 1948 (div. Sept. 1981); children—Erika Storey, Benjamin Warren. B.A., Antioch Coll., 1948; Ph.D., Radcliffe Coll., 1956. Lectr. Smith Coll., 1956-57, Coll. of U. Chgo., 1962-63, 65-66, 68-70; lectr. Princeton U., 1970-71, asso. prof. anthropology, 1971-74, prof., 1974—, chmn. dept. anthropology, 1973-78. Author: The Javanese Family, 1961, (with C. Geertz) Kinship in Bali, 1975, Cultures and Communities of Indonesia, 1963, (with others) Meaning and Order in Moroccan Society, 1979; editor: Letters of A Javanese Princess, 1968. Fellow Am. Anthrop. Assn.; mem. Assn. Asian Studies (exec. bd. 1975-78). Office: Dept Anthropology 100 Aaron Burr Hall Princeton U Princeton NJ 08540

GEFFE, PHILIP REINHOLD, electrical engineer; b. Napa, Calif., Oct. 22, 1920; s. Eugene Carl and Mary Rebecca (Woliston) G.; m. Barbara Ann Wean; children: Bethann, Philip, Timur. Student, Calif. Inst. Tech., 1947-49. Chief filter engr. Triad Transformer Corp., Venice, Calif., 1952-56; dir. engring. Hycor, Inc., Sylmar, Calif., 1957-60; sr. staff engr. Axel Electronics Inc., Jamaica, N.Y., 1962-65; fellow engr. Westinghouse Electric Corp., Balt., 1965-74; staff engr. Lynch Communication Systems, Inc., Reno, 1974-80, Scientific-Atlanta, Inc., Atlanta, 1980—. Author: Simplified Modern Filter Design, 1963; contbr. articles to profl. jours.; patentee in field. Master U.S. Chess Fedn. New Windsor, N.Y., 1968. Fellow IEEE; mem. AAAS. Home: 709 Willow Creek Dr Sandy Springs GA 30328 Office: Sci-Atlanta Inc 3845 Pleasantdale Rd Atlanta GA 30340

GEFFEN, DAVID, recording company executive; b. 1944. Agt. with William Morris; founder agy. with Elliott Roberts; founder Asylum Records, 1970; pres. Eleka-Asylum Records, 1973-76, Geffen Records, 1980—; vice-chmn. Warner Brothers Pictures, 1975; exec. asst. to chmn. Warner Communications, 1977; producer Master Harold . . . and the Boys, 1982; Producer Cats, 1982; producer Good, 1982; mem. music faculty Yale U., 1978. Address: care Geffen Records 9126 Sunset Blvd Los Angeles CA 90069 *

GEFKE, HENRY JEROME, lawyer; b. Milw., Aug., 4, 1930; s. Jerome Henry and Frances (Daley) G.; m. Caroline Ann Lawrence, June 25, 1955 (div. Jan. 1968); children: Brian Lawrence, David Jerome; m. Mary Clare Nuss, Aug. 28, 1976; children: Lynn Marie, James Scott. B.S., Marquette U., 1952, LL.B., 1954; postgrad., Ohio State U., 1955-56. Bar: Wis. 1954, Tax Ct. U.S 1969; C.P.A., Wis. Accountant-auditor John G. Conley & Co. (C.P.A.s), Milw., 1956-59; with J.I. Case Co., Racine, Wis., 1959-68, corp. sec., asst. gen. counsel, 1965-68; asso. Maier & Mulcahy, S.C., Milw., 1968-69; prin. Mulcahy, Gefke & Wherry, S.C., Milw., 1969-73; individual practice law, Milw., 1973—; Corp. officer, dir. various bus. corps. Bd. dirs. Racine County Mental Health Assn., 1963-67; pres., bd. dirs. Big Bros., Greater Racine, 1965-67; trustee Racine County Instns., 1960-63; bd. dirs., sec., legal counsel Racine Transitional Care, Inc., 1973-76; bd. dirs., legal counsel Our Home Found., Inc., 1978—; bd. dirs., treas. Ballet Found., Milw., 1979-82. Served with AUS, 1954-56. Mem. Wis., Milw. bar assns., Delta Sigma Pi, Delta Theta Phi. Home: 5740 N Kent Ave Whitefish Bay WI 53217 Office: 759 N Milwaukee St Milwaukee WI 53202

GEFTER, WILLIAM IRVIN, physician, educator; b. Phila., Jan. 29, 1915; s. Samuel and Pauline (Bulmash) G.; m. Winnie Neiman, June 17, 1939; children: Sharon Gefter Greene, Ellen Gefter Rodriguez, Warren, Gail Gefter Simon. A.B., U. Pa., 1935, M.D., 1939. Diplomate: Am. Bd. Internal Medicine. Intern, then resident medicine Phila. Gen. Hosp., 1939-43; mem. faculty Med. Coll. Pa., 1943-66, Mullen prof. medicine, 1959-66; prof. medicine Temple U. Sch. Medicine, 1966-74; chief medicine Phila. Gen. Hosp., 1959-66; dir. dept. medicine Episcopal Hosp., Phila., 1966-74, pres. med. bd., 1970-72; dir. profl. services St. Joseph Hosp., Stamford, Conn., 1974-77, dir. med. edn., 1977-82; clin. prof. medicine N.Y. Med. Coll., 1975—. Author: Synopsis of Cardiology, 1965; also numerous articles. Served to capt. M.C., USAAF, 1943-46. Recipient Disting. Service citation Med. Coll. Pa., 1966, Phila. Gen. Hosp., 1964; named to Cultural Hall of Fame, So. High Sch., Phila., 1983. Fellow ACP, Coll. Physicians Phila., Am. Coll. Cardiology; mem. Am., Conn., Fairfield County med. assns. Home: West Ln and Toilsome Brook Rd Stamford CT 06905

GEHLING, JOHN ADAM, mfg. co. exec.; b. Cambridge, Mass., July 23, 1920; s. Daniel C. and Hazel A. (Dyson) G.; m. Madelyn V. Brown, July 25, 1943; children—Nancy, Martha, John, William, James, Tim and Virginia (twins), Jane. B.S. in Mech. Engring, Tufts U., 1943; M.B.A., Harvard U., 1947. Vice pres. Harris Intertype, Bklyn., 1961-67; staff exec. White Consol. Industries, Cleve., 1968-69; v.p. mfg. Kelvinator, Grand Rapids, Mich., 1969-70; exec. v.p. Gibson Refrigerator Co., Greenville, Mich., 1970-72; pres. Greenville Products Corp., 1972—; group v.p. W.C.I., Cleve., 1979—; lectr. Western Res. U., Cleve. Coll., 1948-54. Served with USNR, 1943-46. Mem. Assn. Home Appliance Mfrs., Tau Beta Pi. Club: Cascade Hills. Home: 7314 Cascade Rd Grand Rapids MI 49508 Office: 634 W Charles Greenville MI 49508

GEHLSEN, NORBERT J., express lines company executive; b. Clinton, Iowa, May 23, 1921; s. Herman Leon and Alta Louise (Klinge) G.; m. Anne Marie Walsh, Sept. 17, 1949; children: Robert, Marilyn, James, William Kathleen. B.B.A., U. Minn. Sr. v.p. Red Star Express Lines of Auburn Inc., Auburn, N.Y. Home: PO Box 534 Skaneateles NY 13152 Office: Red Star Express 24-50 Wright Ave Auburn NY 13021

GEHR, MARY, illustrator, printmaker; b. Chgo.; d. Francis Lycett and Ruth Nettie (Mead) G.; m. Bert Ray, Oct. 14, 1950. Student, Smith Coll., Art Inst. Chgo., 1946-53, Inst. Design, Ill. Inst. Tech., summer 1962. Designer, book illustrator, 1954—; lectr. Art Inst. Chgo., 1979-82. One-man shows include, Joseph Faulkner-Main St. Galleries, Chgo., 1964, 65, 67, 69, 70, Helenic Am. Union, Athens, Greece, 1971, Jacques Baruch Gallery, Chgo., 1973, 75, Art Rental and Sales Gallery, Art Inst. Chgo., 1980, group exhbns. include, Best Books of Midwest, 1954-55, 66-67, Art Inst. Chgo., Galerie Schwarze, Vienna, 1975, others; represented in permanent collections, Art Inst. Chgo., Bklyn. Mus., Phila. Mus., Free Library Phila., Library of Congress, many pvt., corp. collections; Author, illustrator: The Littlest Circus Seal, 1952; illustrator numerous others. Recipient prizes for etchings. Mem. Soc. Typographic Arts. Democrat. Episcopalian. Club: Arts of Chgo. Address: 1829 Orleans St Chicago IL 60614 *Much of my work is taken from sketch books of extensive and in-depth travel, a keen interest in the natural world, archaeology, and the myriad cultures I seek out and enjoy.*

GEHRIG, LEO JOSEPH, physician; b. Mapleton, Minn., Apr. 25, 1918; s. Paul P. and Marcella (Hund) G.; m. Marillyn May Nelson, June 10, 1944; children: Gregory Paul, Mark Nelson. B.S., U. Minn., 1942, B.Medicine, 1944, M.D., 1945. Diplomate: Am. Bd. Surgery, Am. Bd. Thoracic Surgery. Intern Salt Lake County Gen. Hosp., Salt Lake City, 1944-45; resident New Eng. Deaconness Hosp., Boston, 1947-50; with USPHS, 1950—; chief chest surgery unit S.I., N.Y., 1950-52, resident, 1952-55, chief surgery, Seattle, 1955-57; asst. chief div. hosps., Washington, 1957-59, dep. chief, 1959-60, program officer bur. med. services, Washington, 1960-61; med. dir. Peace Corps, 1961-62; asst. surgeon gen., dep. chief Bur. Med. Services, 1962-64, chief bur., 1964-65, dep. surgeon gen., 1965-68; dir. office internat. health Dept. Health, Edn. and Welfare, 1968-70; asso. dir. Washington service bur. Am. Hosp. Assn., 1970-72, v.p., 1972-75, sr. v.p., 1975-80; dir. Washington office, 1972-80. Recipient U.S. Disting. Service medal. Fellow ACS; mem. AMA, Am. Heart Assn., Assn. Mil. Surgeons, USPHS Clin. Soc., Am. Pub. Health Assn., Alpha Omega Alpha. Home: 4535 Alton Pl NW Washington DC 20016

GEHRING, BENJAMIN ROBERT, mgmt. cons.; b. Chillicothe, Ohio, Feb. 26, 1915; s. Louis C. and Jennie (Rector) G.; m. Ellen R. Payne, Nov. 6, 1937; children—Julie, Barbara Lee, Susan Jane. Student, Ohio State U., 1936. C.P.A., Ohio. With Kent & Rector, 1940-49; pres. Andre Wood Products, Inc., 1949-59; pres., dir. Kilgore, Inc., Westerville, Ohio, 1951-56; pres. Am. Gen. Corp.; dir., sec. Timmons Metal Products Co., Stardust Lanes, Inc., Eastern Enterprises Corp., Columbus, Ohio, Zipf Lock Co.; mgmt. cons. Mem. Am. Inst. C.P.A.'s, Am. Accounting Assn., Am. Mgmt. Assn., Ohio Soc. C.P.A.'s. Clubs: Mason, Rotarian., Scioto Country, Athletic. Home: 4090 Bayberry Ct Columbus OH 43220 Office: 3040 Riverside Dr Columbus OH 43221

GEHRING, FREDERICK WILLIAM, mathematician, educator; b. Ann Arbor, Mich., Aug. 7, 1925; s. Carl E. and Hester McNeal (Reed) G.; m. Lois Caroline Bigger, Aug. 29, 1953; children: Kalle Burgess, Peter Motz. B.S.E. in Math, U. Mich., 1946, M.A., 1949; Ph.D. (Fulbright fellow) in Math, Cambridge U., Eng., 1952, Sc.D., 1976; Ph.D. (hon.), U. Helsinki (Finland), 1977. Benjamin Peirce instr. Harvard U., Cambridge, Mass., 1952-55; instr. math. U. Mich., Ann Arbor, 1955-56, asst. prof., 1956-59, asso. prof., 1959-62, prof., 1962—, T.H. Hildebrandt prof. math., 1984—, chmn. dept. math., 1973-75, 77-84; vis. prof. Harvard U., 1964-65, Stanford U., 1964, U. Minn., 1971, Inst. Mittag-Leffler, Sweden, 1972. Editor: Duke Math. Jour, 1963-80, D. Van Nostrand Pub. Co., 1963-69, North Holland Pub. Co., 1970—, Springer-Verlag, 1974—; editorial bd., Procs. Am. Math. Soc., 1962-65, Ind. U. Math. Jour., 1967-75, Math. Revs., 1969-75, Bull. Am. Math. Soc., 1979—, Complex Variables, 1981—; contbr. numerous articles on research in pure math. to sci. jours. Served with USNR, 1943-46. NSF fellow, 1959-60; Fulbright fellow, 1958-59; Guggenheim fellow, 1958-59; Sci. Research Council sr. fellow, 1981; Humboldt fellow, 1981. Mem. Assn. Women in Math., Math. Assn. Am., Am. Math Soc. (council 1980-83, trustee 1983—), Inst. for Math. and Its Applications (gov. 1981-84), Swiss Math Soc., Swedish Math. Soc., Finnish Math Soc., London Math. Soc., Finnish Acad. Sci. Home: 2139 Melrose Ave Ann Arbor MI 48104

GEHRING, PERRY JAMES, pharmacologist; b. Yankton, S.D., Mar. 15, 1936; s. Rinold Lou and Bertha (Reiger) G.; m. Barbara Tennis, Aug. 8, 1959; children: Daniel, Matthew, Elizabeth, Heidi. B.S., D.V.M., U. Minn., 1960, Ph.D. in Parmacology, 1965. Research asso. Iowa State U., 1960-61; with Dow Chem. Co., Midland, Mich., 1965-68, 1978—, dir. toxicology, 1974-78, dir. health and environ. sci., v.p. agrl. chems. research and devel., dir. health and environ. sci., 1981—; asso. prof. pharmacology Mich. State U., 1968-70, adj. prof., 1970—; vis. lectr. U. Mich., 1978—; trustee Nutrition Found., 1981; chmn. sci. adv. panel Chem. Industry Inst. Toxicology, 1976-80; mem. safe drinking water subcom. organic contaminants Nat. Acad. Scis., 1975-76, mem. nat. center toxicol. research rev. com., 1976-77; participant internat. meetings. Asso. editor: Toxicology and Applied Pharmacology Jour., 1977-80; mem. editorial bds. profl. jours.; contbr. articles to profl. publs. NIH fellow, 1961-65; recipient Founders award Chem. Industry Inst. Toxicology, 1983. Mem. Am. Indsl. Hygiene Assn. (trustee), Soc. Toxicology (pres. 1980-81, council 1975-77, Frank R. Blood award 1979, Merit Award 1983), Am. Soc. Pharmacology and Exptl. Therapeutics. Presbyterian (trustee 1983—). Clubs: Midland Country, Elks. Home: 2101 Sylvan Ln Midland MI 48640 Office: Dow Chem Co 2020 Dow Center Midland MI 48640

GEHRING, RICHARD LEO, computer company executive; b. Mpls., Jan. 25, 1924; s. Leo Charles and Clara (Ames) G.; m. Kathryn J. Brown, June 12, 1946; children: Randolph, Bruce, Don. B.S. in Naval Sci., U.S. Naval Acad., 1946; B.A., U. Minn., 1956, postgrad., 1957-63. Salesman, Black & Decker, 1949-53; mgr. parts dept. Electric Machinery Mfg. Co., 1953-55; with Sperry Univac div. Sperry Rand Corp., Phila., 1955-83, v.p., gen. mgr. def. systems div., 1971-73, group v.p., 1974-81; exec. v.p. corp., pres. Sperry Univac, exec. v.p. corp., to 1983; pres., chief exec. officer Automated Transp. Systems, Inc., St. Paul, 1983—; mem. mgmt. bd. Franklin Inst. Mem. Internat. Gyro Club. Home: 8044 Pennsylvania Rd Bloomington MN 55438 Office: 310 Cedar St Saint Paul MN 55101

GEHRKE, ALLEN CHARLES, corporation executive; b. Milw., Sept. 29, 1934; s. Earl F. and Angeline (Pasdirtz) G.; m. Roberta K. Bohrer, July 23, 1955; children: Christine K., Lynda F., Mark A. With Midwest Contractors, Milw., 1952-60; designer Godfrey Co., Waukesha, Wis., 1960-68, constrn. mgr., 1968-70, dir. design and constrn., 1970-76, v.p. store devel., 1976-80, sr. v.p. corp. devel., 1980—. Served with USNR, 1951-59. Mem. Wis. Food Dealers Assn. Republican. Roman Catholic. Clubs: Woodland Sportsmens (pres. 1970-73), Gt. Lakes Sport Fishermen). Office: Godfrey Co 1200 W Sunset Dr Waukesha WI 53186

GEHRKE, CHARLES WILLIAM, biochemistry educator; b. N.Y.C., July 18, 1917; s. Henry Edward and Louise (Mader) G.; m. Virginia Dorothy Horcher, Dec. 25, 1941; children: Charles William, Jon Craig, Susan Gay. B.A. in Biochemistry, Ohio State U., 1939, B.S. in Edn, 1941, M.S. in Biochemistry and Bacteriology, 1941, Ph.D. in Agrl. Biochemistry, 1947. Prof., head dept. chemistry Missouri Valley Coll., Marshall, Mo., 1942-49; instr. agrl. chemistry Ohio State U., Columbus, 1945-46; assoc. prof. agrl. chemistry U. Mo., Columbia, 1949-54, prof. biochemistry, 1954—, mgr. Expt. Sta. Chem. Labs.,, 1954—; chmn. bd. dirs. Analytical Biochemistry Labs., 1968-84; co-investigator lunar samples NASA, 1969-75; lectr., Japan, China, Taiwan, Philippines, Hong Kong, 1982. Author: 75 Years of Chromatography-A Historical Dialogue; mem. editorial bd.: Jour. Chromatographic Sci, Jour. Chromatography; Contbr. 225 articles to sci. jours. Recipient Faculty Alumni Gold medal award U. Mo., 1975, Chromatography Meml. medal Sci. Council on Chromatography of USSR Acad. Scis., 1980. Fellow Am. Inst. Chemists, Assn. Ofcl. Analytical Chemists (Harvey W. Wiley award 1971, chmn. Magruder standard sample subcom. 1958-79, bd. dirs., mem. editorial bd. 1979—, pres.-elect 1983, pres. centennial yr. 1984); mem. Am. Soc. Biol. Chemists, Am. Chem. Soc. (pres. Mo. sect. 1958-59, 78-79, Spencer award 1980), Am. Dairy Sci. Assn. (chmn. com. on protein nomenclature 1961-62), Fedn. Am. Socs. Exptl. Biology, AAAS, Internat. Soc. Study of Origin of Life, N.Y. Acad. Sci., Sigma Xi. Club: Cosmopolitan Luncheon. Home: 708 Edgewood Ave Columbia MO 65201 Office: Room 4 Agr Bldg Univ Mo Columbia MO 65211

GEHRZ, ROBERT GUSTAVE, retired railroad executive; b. Milw., July 9, 1915; s. Gustave Gerhardt and Paula (Frey) G.; m. Mary Gilbert Laubscher, Feb. 12, 1944; children: Robert Douglas, Richard Campbell, William Rolfe, Elizabeth Hart, Thomas Frank, James Charles. B.A., U. Wis., 1938, LL.B., 1941. Bar: Wis. 1941. Legal editor West Pub. Co., St. Paul, 1947-52; atty. Soo Line R.R. Co., Mpls., 1952-57, gen. atty., 1957-59, gen. solicitor, 1959-79, v.p., gen. counsel, 1979-80, ret., 1980. Served with USNR, 1942-46. Mem. State Bar Assn. Wis., Minn. Bar Assn., Ramsey County Bar Assn. Club: St. Paul Athletic. Home: 2251 Princeton Ave Saint Paul MN 55105

GEIB, PHILIP OLDHAM, physician, former naval officer; b. Verona, N.J., Oct. 6, 1921; s. Amos Philip and Ada Mae (Oldham) G.; m. Frances Parker, Nov. 5, 1949; children: Melanie, Philip John. B.S., Franklin and Marshall Coll., 1942; M.D., Temple U., 1945. Diplomate: Am. Bd. Surgery. Commd. lt. U.S. Navy, 1945, advanced through grades to rear adm., 1972; intern (Naval Hosp.), Chelsea, Mass., 1945-46, med. officer, Leyte and Samar, Philippines, 1946-47, mem. staff, Portsmouth, Va., 1947-48, resident, 1953-54, Phila., 1948-51, mem. staff Naval Hosp., Corpus Christi, Tex., 1950-51, Pearl Harbor, Hawaii, 1951-53, Annapolis, Md., 1954-57, mem. staff, 1957-58, mem. staff Naval Hosp., Pensacola, Fla., 1962-64, chmn. dept. surgery Naval Hosp., Great Lakes, Ill., 1964-68, comdg. officer Naval Hosps., Yokosuka, Japan, 1968-71, Camp Lejeune, N.C., 1971-72, asst. chief research and mil. med. spltys. Bur. Medicine and Surgery, Navy Dept., Washington, 1972-74, fleet surgeon CINCLAN Fleet, Norfolk, Va., 1974-76, med. tng. and readiness officer COMTRALANT, Norfolk, 1976-77, ret., 1977; med. dir. Norfolk Shipbldg. and Drydock Corp., 1977—; mem. surg. staff Med. Center Hosps., Norfolk; asst. prof. Eastern Va. Med. Sch., Norfolk. Fellow ACS; mem. Am. Coll. Chest Physicians, Am. Occupational Med. Assn., AMA, Va. Occupational Med. Assn. (sec.-treas.), Pan Am. Surg. Soc. Home: 4309 Duke Dr Portsmouth VA 23703 Office: PO Box 2100 Norfolk VA 23501

GEIBERGER, ALLEN L., profl. golfer; b. Red Bluff, Calif., Sept. 1, 1937; m. Lynn Butler; children—Lee Ann, John, Robby, Brent, Bryan. B.S. in Bus, U. So. Calif., 1959. Profl. golfer, 1959—; with PGA Tour, 1960—; mem. Ryder Cup Team, 1967, 75. Winner Caracas Open & Ont. Open, 1962, Almaden Open, 1963, Am. Golf Classic, 1965, PGA Championship, 1966, Sahara Invitational, 1974, Tournament of Champions and Tournament Players Championship, 1975, Greater Greensboro Open and Western Open, 1976, Danny Thomas-Memphis Open 1977, (with Dave Stockton), CBS Classic, 1969, 70, Colonial Nat. Invitational, 1979; holder record for lowest 18 hole score in profl. golf, 1977. Office: care PGA Tour Ponte Vedra FL *

GEIER, GEORGE, chemical engineering consultant; b. N.Y.C., Feb. 2, 1918; s. George Jakob and Frieda (Marbach) G.; m. Isabel Lillian Brandt, Oct. 15, 1944; children: George Jeffrey, William Stuart. B.Chem.Engring., Cooper Union, 1939; M.S., Stevens Inst. Tech.,

1942. With research and devel. dept. Keuffel & Esser Co., Morristown, N.J., 1940-81, dir. dept., 1968-81; cons., 1981—. Author articles. Mem. Optical Soc. Am., Soc. Photog. Instrumentation Engrs., Am. Soc. Photogrammetry, Am. Congress Surveying and Mapping. Clubs: Lake Mohawk Golf., Pelican Bay Golf. Patentee in field. Home and Office: 43 Whippoorwill Ln Sparta NJ 07871 also: 9 Skimmer Circle Daytona Beach FL 32019

GEIER, JAMES AYLWARD DEVELIN, manufacturing executive; b. Cin., Dec. 29, 1925; s. Frederick V. and Amey (Develin) G.; children: Deborah Anne, James Develin, Aylward Whittier. Attended, Williams Coll., 1947-50. With Cin. Milacron Inc., 1951—, became v.p., 1964, dir., 1966, exec. v.p., 1969, pres., chief exec. officer, 1970, also chmn.; dir. Clark Equipment Co., Central Bancorp., Central Trust Co., Marathon Oil Co. Pres. Cin. Museum Natural History; mem. adv. bd. Cin. Council on World Affairs; mem. Kenton County Airport Bd.; trustee Children's Home of Cin. Served with USAAF, 1944-46. Mem. Am. Mgmt. Assn. (council), NMTBA Conf. Bd., Engring. Soc. Cin. Republican. Clubs: Commercial, Commonwealth, Queen City, Camargo. Office: Cin Milacron Inc 4701 Marburg Ave Cincinnati OH 45209 *

GEIER, PHILIP HENRY, JR., advertising executive; b. Pontiac, Mich., Feb. 22, 1935; s. Philip Henry and Jane (Gillen) G.; m. Faith Power, children—Hope, Johanna Geier. B.A., Colgate U., 1957; M.S., Columbia U., 1958. With McCann-Erickson, Inc., Cleve., 1958-60, N.Y.C., 1960-68; chmn. McCann-Erickson Internat. U.K. Co., London, 1969-73; exec. v.p. McCann-Erickson Europe, 1973-75; vice chmn. internat. ops. McCann Worldwide, London, 1973-75; vice chmn. internat. Interpublic Group of Cos., Inc., N.Y.C., 1975-77, pres., chief operating officer, 1977-80, chmn., chief exec. officer, 1980—; dir. EAC Industries, Inc. Trustee Marymount Manhattan Coll., N.Y. Mem. Am. Assn. Advt. Agys. Clubs: Racquet and Tennis, River (N.Y.C.); Hurlingham (London). Office: 1271 Ave of Americas New York NY 10020 *

GEIGER, GENE EDWARD, educator; b. Castle Shannon, Pa., Oct. 27, 1928; s. Harry and Jessie Jane (Lee) G.; m. Virginia Ann Miller, Jan. 24, 1959; children—Gregg, Amy. B.S., Carnegie-Mellon U., 1950; M.S., U. Pitts., 1955, Ph.D., 1964. Registered profl. engr., Pa. Instr. mech. engring. U. Pitts., 1951-55, asst. prof., 1955-65, asso. prof., 1965-71, prof., 1971—; Cons. to various cos. Contbr. articles to profl. publs. Ford Found. grantee, 1962-64. Mem. Pa. Soc. Profl. Engrs., ASME, Sigma Xi, Pi Tau Sigma. Home: 113 Grienbrier Dr Carnegie PA 15106 Office: 645 Benedum Hall Univ Pitts Pittsburgh PA 15261

GEIGER, GEORGE RAYMOND, philosophy educator; b. N.Y.C., May 8, 1903; s. Oscar Harold and Nina Cecelia (Daly) G.; m. Julia Louise Jarratt, Dec. 25, 1934. A.B., Columbia U., 1924, B.Lit., 1925, M.S., 1926, Ph.D., 1931. Asst. prof. philosophy Bradley Poly. Inst., Peoria, Ill., 1928-30, 35-37; asso. prof. philosophy U. N.D., 1930-34, U. Ill., 1934-35; prof. philosophy Antioch Coll., Yellow Springs, Ohio, 1937-68, John Dewey prof. humanities, 1968—; vis. prof. philosophy U. Wis., 1947-48, U. Calif.-Santa Barbara, 1963. Author several books, 1933—; including Philosophy and the Social Order, 1947; John Dewey in Perspective, 1958, Science, Folklore and Philosophy, 1966, The Philosophy of Henry George, new edit, 1976; contbr.: The Philosophy of John Dewey, 1939, Value: A Cooperative Inquiry, 1949, The Cleavage in Our Culture, 1952, Modern Philosophies and Education, 1955; bd. editors: Am. Jour. Econ. and Sociology. Mem. Am. Philos. Assn. (sec.-treas. Western div. 1944-47, nat. sec.-treas. 1947-53), Phi Beta Kappa. Home: 131 W Center College St Yellow Springs OH 45387

GEIGER, HOMER KENT, sociology educator; b. Bluffton, Ohio, June 23, 1922; s. Homer Harvey and Flora Alberta (Gottshall) G.; m. Mildred Sharpe Shade, Aug. 17, 1950 (div.); children: Martha Ellen, Daniel William; m. Elinor C. Schnore, Jan. 23, 1970 (div.). A.B., Princeton U., 1947; A.M., Harvard U., 1950, Ph.D., 1955. Teaching and research in sociology Tufts U., 1954-61, Ohio State U., 1961-63, U. Calif. at Berkeley, 1963-64; prof. sociology U. Wis., Madison, 1964-84, prof. emeritus, 1984—; research fellow Russian Research Center, Harvard, 1954-55, 58-59; research asso. New Eng. Bd. Higher Edn., 1957-58. Author: The Family in Soviet Russia, 1968, National Development 1776-1966, 1969. Served with AUS, 1943-46. Home: 241 Langdon St Madison WI 53703

GEIGER, LOUIS GEORGE, historian, emeritus educator; b. Boonville, Mo., Mar. 21, 1913; s. George Victor and Dorothea Elizabeth (Hoflander) G.; m. Helen Margery Watson, Dec. 20, 1946; 1 son, Mark Watson. Student, Elmhurst Coll., 1929-30; B.S., Central Mo. State U., 1934; M.A., U. Mo., 1940, Ph.D., 1948. Tchr. pub. sch., Mo., 1930-31, 34-39; grad. asst., instr. U. Mo., 1939-42; asst. prof. history U. N.D., 1946-55, asso. prof., 1955-58, prof., 1958-60; prof. history, chmn. dept. Colo. Coll., 1960-70, prof., 1971-72; prof. history Iowa State U., Ames, 1972-79, prof. emeritus, 1979—, chmn. dept., 1972-77; vis. prof. U. Mo., 1960, Jadavpur U., 1963-64, Miami U., Ohio, 1967, Ariz. State U., 1970-71; Fulbright lectr. U. Leningrad, 1978-79; chmn. N.D. Com. Social Sci. Curricular Revision, 1959-60. Author: From Apennines to Po, 1948, Joseph W. Folk of Missouri, 1953, University of the Northern Plains, 1958, Higher Education in a Maturing Democracy, 1963, Voluntary Accreditation: History of North Central Association, 1970; Contbr.: Muckrakers and American Society, 1968; author articles and revs. Served to 1st lt. AUS, 1942-46. Fellow Fund for Advancement Edn. Harvard and Stanford, 1953-54; Fulbright lectr. U. Helsinki, 1954-55; recipient research award Social Sci. Research Council, 1963. Mem. Western Social Sci. Assn. (v.p. 1965-66, v.p. 68-69), N.D. Social Sci. Assn. (pres. 1959-60), AAUP, Am. Hist. Assn., Am. Studies Assn., History Edn. Soc., Agr. History Soc., Orgn. Am. Historians. Club: Rotarian. Home: 975 Terrace Circle Colorado Springs CO 80904

GEIGER, ROBERT KEITH, aerospace executive; b. White Cloud, Kans., Oct. 27, 1923; s. William Stephen and Kathryn Frances (Prebble) G.; m. Sibyl Vincent Godfrey, Sept. 2, 1949; children: Barbara Kathryn Geiger Toohill, Robert Vincent. B.S., U.S. Naval Acad., 1947, U.S. Naval Postgrad. Sch., 1955; M.S. in Aero. Engring, M.I.T., 1956. Commd. ensign U.S. Navy, 1947, advanced through grades to rear adm., 1973; ops. tours on ship, flight tng., ops. tours as aviator in squadrons, various assignments in research and devel., space projects; project mgr. (Navy Space Project), Arlington, Va., 1971-75; dir. space and command support div. Office Chief Naval Ops., Arlington, 1973-75; chief of naval research, Arlington, 1975-78; dir. devel. Martin Marietta Aerospace Co., Bethesda, Md., 1978-80; asst. v.p. Sci. Applications Inc., Falls Church, Va., 1980—; dir. adv. group for aerospace research and devel. NATO (AGARD/NATO), 1982—. Decorated Legion of Merit (2) D.S.M. Mem. AIAA, Sigma Xi, Sigma Gamma Tau, Phi Eta Sigma, Beta Theta Pi. Home: 2067 Hopewood Dr Falls Church VA 22043 Office: AGARD/NATO APO New York NY 09777

GEIRINGER, KARL, educator, musicologist; b. Vienna, Austria, Apr. 26, 1899; came to U.S., 1940, naturalized, 1945; s. Ludwig and Martha (Wertheimer) G.; m. Irene Steckel, Apr. 19, 1928; children—Martin Frederick, George Karl. Student, U. Berlin, 1920-21; Ph.D., U. Vienna, 1923. Curator archives Soc. of Friends of Music, Vienna, 1930-38; vis. prof. Royal Coll. Music, London, 1939-40, Hamilton Coll., Clinton, N.Y., 1940-41; prof. music Boston U. Sch. Fine Arts, chmn. dept. history and theory of music. and div. grad. studies, 1941-62; prof. music charge grad. studies in music U. Calif. at Santa Barbara, 1962-70, prof. emeritus, 1971—. Author: Musical Instruments, 1943, rev. edit, Instruments in the History of Western Music, 1978, Haydn, 1946, 3d edit., 1982, Brahms, 3d edit, 1981, Bach Family, 1954, reprinted, 1981, Music of the Bach Family, 1955, 80; Symbolism in the Music of Bach, 1956; reprinted The Small Sacred Works by Haydn; The Structure of Beethoven's Diabelli Variations, 1964; reprinted Johann Sebastian Bach, 1966; Editor: J. Haydn: 100 Scottish Songs, 1961, J. Haydn-Orlando Paladino (opera), 1971, Chr. W. Gluck: Telemaco (opera), 1971, Isaac Posch: Harmonia Concertans (cantiones sacrae), 1972; Gen. editor: U. Calif. at Santa Barbara Series of Early Music, 1970—, The Harbrace History of Musical Forms, 1973—; Contbr. to: Grove's Dictionary Music and Musicians, Ency. Brit. Recipient Austrian Cross of Honor 1st class, 1969; Studies in 18th Century Music, a tribute to Karl Geiringer on his 70th birthday, edited by H.C.R. Landon and R. Chapman, 1970. Fellow Am. Acad. Arts and Scis.; mem. Am. Musicological Soc. (hon. mem., pres. 1955-56, exec. bd. 1954, exec. bd. 57-58, exec. bd. 64, exec. bd. 68-69), Internat. Musicological Soc., Austrian Musicological Soc. (hon. mem.), New Bach Soc. (hon. mem. Am. chpt.), Am. Brahms Soc (dir. 1983), Coll. Music Soc. (exec. bd. 1965-67), Music Library Assn. Methodist. Home: 1823 Mira Vista Ave Santa Barbara CA 93103

GEIS, BERNARD, book publisher; b. Chgo., Aug. 30, 1909; s. Harry M. and Bessie (Gesas) G.; m. Darlene Stern, Mar. 28, 1940; children: Peter, Stephen. B.A., Northwestern U., 1931. Newspaper reporter, contbr. mags., 1931-33; editor Apparel Arts mag., 1933-38; asst. editor Esquire mag., 1938-45; editor Coronet mag., 1939-45; war corr., ETO for Coronet and Esquire mags., 1942-43; editor-in-chief Grosset & Dunlap Pub. Co., 1945-53, v.p., 1949-53; editor Prentice-Hall Pub. Co., 1954-57; pres., dir. Bernard Geis Assocs., N.Y.C., 1958—; pres. subsidiary Ampersand Press Inc., 1963—; pres. Capricon Press, Inc., 1984—; chmn. bd. Casino Press, Inc., 1984—. Chmn. pubs. group N.Y.C. Salvation Army ann. appeal, 1960-66; bd. dirs. council N.Y. Heart Assn.; Bd. dirs. Ams. for Democratic Action, mem. exec. com., 1965—. Home: 1385 York Ave New York NY 10021 Office: 128 E 56th St New York NY 10022

GEIS, DUANE VIRGIL, investment banker; b. Okeene, Okla., Apr. 16, 1923; s. Harry H. and Margareth (Tieman) G.; m. Lois Blakey, Mar. 11, 1944; children—Duane Gregory, Paul Geoffrey. B.A., Okla. State U., 1947. Accounting machine salesman IBM Corp., 1948-54; with Rotan Mosle Dallas Union, Inc., Houston, 1954-59, partner, 1959-66, 1st sr. v.p., 1966-70; also dir.; partner Paine, Webber, Jackson & Curtis, 1970—. Bd. dirs. Star of Hope Mission; trustee annuity bd. So. Bapt. Conv.; Vice chmn. Houston Ednl. Found., 1967—. Mem. Houston C. of C. (life), Financial Analysts Soc., Phi Kappa Phi, Phi Eta Sigma (pres. 1942-43), Beta Alpha Psi (pres. 1946-47), Kappa Sigma, Blue Key (v.p. 1946-47). Republican. Baptist. Clubs: Houston Country, Coronado (Houston). Home: 522 Shadywood St Houston TX 77057 Office: ENTEX Bldg Houston TX 77002

GEIS, GILBERT LAWRENCE, sociology educator; b. Bklyn., Jan. 10, 1925; s. Joseph and Ida (List) G.; m. Ruth Steinberg, Apr. 4, 1948; children: Ellen Dagney, Jean Marit; m. Robley Huston, Dec. 17, 1966. A.B., Colgate U., 1947; student, U. Stockholm, 1947; M.S., Brigham Young U., 1949; Ph.D., U. Wis., 1953. Instr., then asst. prof. sociology U. Okla., 1952-57; faculty Calif. State U. at Los Angeles, 1957-71, prof. sociology, 1963-71; fellow law and sociology Harvard Law Sch., 1964-65; vis. prof. criminal justice State U. N.Y. at Albany, 1969-70; prof. social ecology U. Calif. at Irvine, 1971—; vis. fellow Inst. Criminology, Cambridge (Eng.) U., 1976-77; vis. prof. Inst. Criminology, Sydney, Australia, 1978-79; disting. vis. prof. Pa. State U., 1981. Author: (with H. Bloch) Man, Crime and Society, 1962, 2d edit., 1970, (with W. Bittle) Longest Way Home, 1964, Juvenile Gangs, 1966, Not the Law's Business?, 1972, (with H. Edelhertz) Public Compensation to Victims of Crime, 1974; Editor: White Collar Criminal, 1968, (with Robert Meier) White Collar Criminal, 1977, (with Duncan Chappell and Robley Geis) Forcible Rape, 1977, (with Arnold Binder) Research in Criminology and Criminal Justice, 1982. Adv. Pres.'s Com. on Narcotic and Drug Abuse, 1963-64; cons. Pres.'s Commn. on Law Enforcement and Adminstrn. Justice, 1966-67, Joint Commn. on Correctional Manpower and Tng., 1967-69, Nat. Commn. on Causes and Prevention Violence, 1968-70; mem. narcotic addiction and drug abuse rev. com. Nat. Inst. Mental Health, 1970-74. Served with USNR, 1943-46. Fulbright and Social Sci. Research Council fellow, Oslo, 1952-53. Mem. Am. Sociol Soc. (chmn. sect. criminology 1970-71), Pacific Sociol. Soc., Soc. Study Social Problems (chmn. criminal and delinquency sect. 1964-66), Am. Soc. Criminology (pres. 1975-76). Home: 31461 Alta Loma Dr South Laguna CA 92677

GEIS, NORMAN WINER, lawyer; b. St. Paul, July 13, 1925; s. Alexander and Shirley (Magid) Winer; m. Dorothy Bockman, Oct. 17, 1954; children: Deborah, Nancy, Carolyn (dec.), Sarah. A.B. with honors, U. Chgo., 1947, J.D., 1951. Bar: Ill. 1950. Mng. editor U. Chgo. Law Review, 1949-50; practice in, Chgo., 1951—; mem. firm Greenberger, Krauss & Jacobs; adv. Nat. Conf. Commrs. Uniform State Laws spl. drafting coms. for Uniform Condominium Act, 1976-77, Uniform Planned Community Act, 1978-80, Uniform Real Estate Coop. Act, 1979-80, Uniform Common-Interest Ownership Act, 1982. Mem. joint editorial bd.: Uniform Real Property Acts; Contbr. articles on condominium and homeowner assn. law to legal jours. Chmn. Highland Park (Ill.) Bd. Zoning Appeals. Served with inf. AUS, 1943-45. Decorated Purple Heart, Bronze Star medal. Mem. ABA (chmn. com. condominiums, coops. and homeowner assns. 1978-80, sec. real property div., sect. of real property probate and trust law 1981-83), Ill. Bar Assn. (real estate sect.), Chgo. Bar Assn. (chmn. real property law com. 1970-71, chmn. condominium subcom. 1966-68), Am. Coll. Real Estate Lawyers (gov. 1980-83, sec. 1983-84), Anglo-Am. Real Property Inst., Pi Lambda Phi. Club: Mid-Day (Chgo.). Home: 1530 Green Bay Rd Highland Park IL 60035 Office: 180 N LaSalle St Chicago IL 60601

GEISEL, CAMERON MEADE, JR., banker; b. Harrisburg, Pa., Oct. 7, 1937; s. Cameron Meade and Dorothy Mae G.; m. Martha L. Frohring, Sept. 3, 1977; children: Melissa Ellen, Gregory Stuart, Andrew Frohring, Hariha Bliss. B.A., Bucknell U., Lewisburg, Pa., 1960; grad., Sch. Credit and Fin. Mgmt., Harvard U., 1970. With Phila. Nat. Bank, 1961—, asst. v.p., then v.p., 1965-77, sr. v.p., 1977—. Served to 2d lt., inf. U.S. Army, 1960-61. Mem. Robert Morris Assos., U.S. Council Internat. Bus. (trustee, exec. com.). Republican. Episcopalian. Clubs: Merion Golf, Merion Cricket; Racquet (Phila.); University (N.Y.C.). Home: 1814 Old Gulph Rd Villanova PA 19085 Office: Phila Nat Bak Broad and Chestnut Sts Philadelphia PA 19101

GEISEL, HAROLD WALTER, diplomat; b. Chgo., May 11, 1947; s. Gustav and Stefi S. (Siegel) G. B.A. in History, Johns Hopkins U., 1968; M.B.A., U. Va., 1970. Commd. fgn. service officer Dept. State, 1970, adminstrv. officer, Washington, 1973-75; first sec. U.S. embassy, Bern, Switzerland, 1975-78, Bamako, Mali, 1978-80; adminstrv. officer Dept. State, Washington, 1980-82; consul gen. U.S. Consulate Gen., Durban, South Africa, 1982—. Jewish. Home: 20 Monteith Pl Durban North Natal South Africa 4051 Office: US Consulate Gen 2901 Durban Bay House Durban Natal South Africa 4001

GEISEL, THEODOR SEUSS (DR. SEUSS), author, artist, TV producer, publisher; b. Springfield, Mass., Mar. 2, 1904; s. Theodor Robert and Henrietta (Seuss) G.; m. Helen Marion Palmer, Nov. 29, 1927 (dec. Oct. 1967); m. Audrey Stone Dimond, Aug. 6, 1968. Grad., Dartmouth Coll., 1925; postgrad., Lincoln Coll., Oxford (Eng.) U., 1925-26; L.H.D., Dartmouth Coll., 1955, Am. Internat. Coll., 1968, Whittier Coll., Lake Forest Coll.; Litt.D., John F. Kennedy U. Began career as humorist, illustrator for: publs. including Liberty mags; advt. illustrator, 15 yrs; creator of humorous advt. campaigns for, Standard Oil of N.J., including, Quick Henry the Flit!; series; mural painter, author and illustrator of children's books; editorial cartoonist: PM newspaper, N.Y.C.; now pres., pub., editor-in-chief, Beginner Books, Inc. div. Random House, Inc.; Author: If I Ran the Zoo, 1950, Scrambled Eggs Super, 1953, Horton Hears a Who, 1954, On Beyond Zebra, 1955, If I Ran the Circus, 1956, How the Grinch Stole Christmas, 1957, The Cat in the Hat, 1957, The Cat in the Hat Comes Back, 1958, Yertle the Turtle, 1958, Happy Birthday, 1959, One Fish Two Fish Red Fish Blue Fish, 1960, Green Eggs and Ham, 1960, The Sneetches and Other Stories, 1961, Dr. Seuss's Sleep Book, 1962, Hop on Pop, 1963, Dr. Seuss's ABC Book, 1963, Fox in Socks, 1965, I had Trouble in Getting to Solla Sellew, 1965, The Cat in the Hat Songbook, 1967, The Foot Book, 1968, I Can Lick 30 Tigers Today and Other Stories, 1969, My Book About Me, 1969, I Can Draw it Myself, 1970, Mr. Brown Can Moo! Can You?, 1970, And to Think That I Saw It on Mulberry Street, The 500 Hats of Bartholomew Cubbins, The Seven Lady Godivas, The King's Stilts, Horton Hatches the Egg, McElligot's Pool, Thidwick the Big-Hearted Moose, Bartholomew and the Oobleck, The Lorax, Marvin K. Mooney, Will You Please Go Now!, Did I Ever Tell You How Lucky You Are?, The Shape of Me and Other Stuff, There's a Wocket in my Pocket, Great Day for Up, Oh, The Thinks You Can Think!, The Cat's Quizzer, I Can Read With My Eyes Shut, Oh, Say Can You Say?, Hunches in Bunches; Motion Pictures Hitler Lives (Acad. award documentary short 1946), Design for Death (Acad. award documentary feature 1947), (with Helen Palmer Geisel) Gerald McBoing Boing, (Acad. award cartoon 1951); designer, producer: amimated cartoons for TV How the Grinch Stole Christmas (Peabody award), Horton Hears a Who, (Peabody award), The Cat in the Hat, The Lorax, (Critics' award Internat. Animated Festival, Zagreb), Dr. Seuss on the Loose, The Hoober Bloob Highway, Halloween is Grinch Night, (Emmy award), Pontoffel Pock Where Are You?; animated cartoons for TV The Grinch Grinches the Cat in the Hat (Emmy award). Served to lt. col. Signal Corps and Information and Edn. Div. AUS, 1943-46; ETO; lt. col. Res. Decorated Legion of Merit for edn. and information film work; recipient Laura Ingalls Wilder award ALA, 1980, Spl. Pulitzer Prize, 1984.

GEISER, ELIZABETH ABLE, publishing company executive; b. Phillipsburg, N.J., Apr. 28, 1925; d. George W. and Margaret I. (Ross) G. A.B. magna cum laude, Hood Coll., 1947. Promotion mgr. coll. dept. Macmillan Co., N.Y.C., 1947-54; promotion mgr. R.R. Bowker, N.Y.C., 1954-60, sales mgr., 1960-67, dir. mktg., 1967-70, v.p., 1970-73, sr. v.p., 1973-75; dir., adj. prof. U. Denver Pub. Inst., 1976—; sr. v.p. Gale Research Co.; cons. Excerpta Medica, Elsevier, 1976-82; lectr. pub. procedures Radcliffe Coll., 1966-75; lectr. schs. library sci. U. Wash., U. So. Calif.; panel mem. TV series Living Library, 1970. Contbr.: Manual of Bookselling, 1969. Mem. Assn. Am. Pubs. (adv. council Frankfurt book fair 1971, sch. and library promotion and mktg. com. 1972—, bd. dirs. 1982—), ALA (pres. exhibits roundtable 1968-70, dir. exhibits roundtable 1968). Presbyterian. Home: 24 Forest Dr Springfield NJ 07081 Office: 150 E 50th St New York NY 10022

GEISER, KARL FREDERICK, lawyer; b. New Hampton, Iowa, June 6, 1903; s. Mathias Edgar and Belle (Rowe) G.; m. Jane Schoentgen, June 6, 1928; children: Karl Frederick, Gretel (Mrs. George E. Stephens, Jr.). Student, Oberlin Coll., 1921-22; A.B., State U. Iowa, 1925, J.D., 1927. Bar: Iowa 1927, Calif. 1946, U.S. Supreme Ct. 1946. Ptr.firm Geiser, Donohue & Geiser, New Hampton, 1927-29; exec. v.p. E.H. Lougee, Inc., 1929-30; partner firm Tinley, Mitchell, Rosa Everest & Geiser, Council Bluffs, Iowa, 1930-42; pvt. practice, Beverly Hills, Calif., 1945-78, ret., 1978. Served to comdr. USNR, 1942-45. Mem. Am., Iowa, Calif. bar assns., Order of Coif, Phi Delta Phi, Sigma Alpha Epsilon. Republican. Home: 1219 Montana Ave Apt 103 Los Angeles CA 90049

GEISERT, WAYNE FREDERICK, college president; b. Elmo, Kans., Dec. 20, 1921; s. Frederick Jacob and Martha E. (Lauer) G.; m. Ellen Maurine Gish, July 2, 1944; children: Gregory Wayne, Bradley Kent, Todd Wilfred. A.B., McPherson (Kans.) Coll., 1944; Ph.D. in Econs, Northwestern U., 1951. Instr. Hamilton (Kans.) High Sch., 1946-48; part-time instr. Kendall Coll., Evanston, Ill., 1948-50; grad. asst. Northwestern U., 1950-51; asso. prof., later prof. and head dept. econs. and bus. Manchester Coll., North Manchester, Ind., 1951-57; dean coll. McPherson Coll., 1957-64; pres. Bridgewater (Va.) Coll., 1964—; dir. Planters Bank Bridgewater., Smith Cattleguard Co.; cons. in field; Pres. Assn. Va. Colls., 1970-71; mem. exec. com. Church-related Colls. and Univs. in the South, 1973-74. Bd. dirs. Univ. Center in Va., 1964-78; Council Ind. Colls. Va.; bd. dirs. Shenandoah Valley Ednl. TV, chmn. bd., 1979—; bd. dirs. Va. Found. Ind. Colls., v.p., 1974-76, pres., 1976-78; moderator Ch. of Brethren, 1973-74, chmn. rev. and evaluation com., 1975-77, mem. gen. bd., 1977-82, vice chmn., 1977-78, chmn. gen. services commn., 1979-82, chmn. pension bd., 1979-82; chmn. United Way campaign, 1979-80. Served with USNR, 1944-46; PTO. Mem. Am. Econ. Assn., Harrisonburg-Rockingham County C. of C. (dir. 1977—, pres. 1980-81), Pi Kappa Delta, Alpha Psi Omega. Club: Rotary. Home: 409 E College St Bridgewater VA 22812

GEISINGER, ROBERT NELSON, retired titanium sponge and mill products executive; b. Dover, Ohio, Jan. 11, 1925; s. Nelson Omer and Helen Alvena G.; m. Catherine E. Buzzelli, Aug. 7, 1966; children: Cynthia Ann, Robert Paul, Robert Gregory. B.S. in Bus. Adminstrn. cum laude, Kent (Ohio) State U., 1949. Chief acct. Dominion Ekectric Corp., Mansfield, Ohio, 1949-58; plant acct. RMI Co., Ashtabula, Ohio, 1958-60, sec.-treas., Niles, Ohio, 1960-76, v.p. fin., sec., 1976-82; officer, dir. Titanium Research & Devel. Co., Titanium Mill Products Co., Ashco, Inc., Nati Gas Co. Served with USNR, 1943-46. Republican. Methodist. Home: 296 Bradford Dr Canfield OH 44406

GEISINGER, WILLIAM ROBERT, economist-business forecaster, management consultant; b. Fredricksburg, Va., Oct. 21, 1908; s. William Morris and Glada Belinda (Hawthorne) G.; m. Verna E. Cragg, June 20, 1931 (div. 1946); children: Harry Clifford, William Robert. A.B. in Econs., Dartmouth Coll., 1930; postgrad., Cin. Art Acad., 1950-51; Ph.D. in Bus. Adminstrn., Hamilton State U., 1973; cert. stats., George Washington U. Credit analyst trust dept. Central Trust Bank, Cin., 1930-40; economist budgets Montgomery Ward Co., Chgo., 1940-49; forecast exec. Kroger Co., Cin., 1949-54; mktg. and distbn. specialist State Dept., Hicog, Germany, 1955; mgmt. cons. Geisinger Indicator, Troy, Ohio, 1965—; lectr. fin. U. Miami, Oxford, Ohio, 1939-40, Northwestern U., Evanston, Ill., 1948, others; tchr. investments and analyzing fin. statements U. Cin., 1937-40, Am. Inst. Banking, 1938-40. Author: Pub. Forecasting Bus. Letter for Geisinger Indicator, 1963-83. Examiner for RFC, Cleve., 1938-39; chief of food and rest Office Price Stabilization, Washington, 1952; organizer Am. Coalition Patriotic Socs. Seminar, 1954; mem. Transatlantic council Boy Scouts Am. in Germany for Europe, N. Africa and Near East,

1955. Mem. Am. Econ. Assn., Am. Mgmt. Assn., Am. Statis. Assn., Found. for Study of Cycles, AAAS, Waco Hist. Soc. (founder). Lodges: Lions; Masons. Home and Office: 108 S Monroe St PO Box 279 Troy OH 45373

GEISLER, RICHARD MARCUS, manufacturing company executive; b. Abilene, Kans., May 14, 1925; s. August E. and Clare E. (Taylor) G.; m. Barbara J. Bernas, Aug. 4, 1971; children: Debra, Michael, Michelle. B.S. in Acctg., Kans. State Tchrs. Coll., 1951; M.B.A., Tex. Christian U., 1964. Pres. Am. LaFrance div. A.T.O., Elmira, N.Y., 1969-71, Spaulding div. Questor, Chicopee, Mass., 1971-79; pres., chief exec. officer Champion Products, Inc., Rochester, N.Y., 1979-81, chmn. bd., chief exec. officer, 1981—. Trustee Springfield Coll.; bd. dirs. Jr. Achievement, 1974-79, Basketball Hall of Fame. Served with U.S. Army, 1946-48. Mem. Sporting Goods Mfg. Assn., Athletic Inst. Nat. Sporting Goods Assn., Nat. Knitwear Mfrs. Assn. (dir. 1981—), Rochester Area C. of C. (dir. 1981—). Home: 107 Knollwood Dr Rochester NY 14618 Office: Champion Products Inc 3141 Monroe Ave Rochester NY 14618

GEISMAR, RICHARD LEE, communications company executive; b. Paterson, N.J., Aug. 22, 1927; s. Sylvan and Marjorie (Leeser) G.; m. Patricia Willard, Nov. 27, 1954; children—John, Elisabeth, Nancy. B.Mgmt. Engring., Rensselaer Poly. Inst., 1949; M.B.A., Harvard, 1951. With DuMont TV Network, 1951-55; with Metromedia, Inc. (and predecessors), N.Y.C., 1955-69, treas., 1958-68, v.p., 1961-68; also dir.; pres., dir. Reeves Telecom Corp., 1969-70; communications cons. BGW Assos., Inc., 1970—; chmn. Broad St. Communications Corp., 1971—; asso. dir. Union Trust Co., New Haven. Bd. dirs., treas. Greenwich chpt. ARC. Served with USNR, 1945-46. Mem. Sigma Xi. Republican. Conglist. (trustee 1971-73; chmn. 1973). Clubs: Riverside Yacht; Internat. (Washington). Home: 37 Tower Rd Riverside CT 06878 Office: Box 151 Riverside CT 06878

GEISMAR, THOMAS H., graphic designer; b. Glen Ridge, N.J., July 16, 1931; s. Arthur D. and Adeline (Caro) G.; m. Joan Hyams, Nov. 9, 1958; children: Peter, Kathryn, Pamela. B.A., Brown U., 1953; M.F.A., Yale U., 1958. Founder Brownjohn, Chermayeff & Geismar, N.Y.C., 1957; founder Chermayeff & Geismar Assos., N.Y.C., 1960, prin., 1960—, Cambridge Seven Assos. (Architects), 1963; founder, partner MetaForm, Inc., N.Y.C., 1980—; lectr. Chmn. com. signs and symbols Dept. Transp.; mem. council Yale U. Served with U.S. Army, 1955-57. Mem. Am. Inst. Grphic Arts (Gold medal 1979), Alliance Graphique Internationale, Indsl. Designers Soc. Am. Office: 15 E 26th St New York NY 10010 *

GEISMER, ALAN STEARN, lawyer; b. Cleve., May 10, 1917; s. Eugene L. and Mollie (Stearn) G.; m. Barbara Peck, Aug. 2, 1942; children: Alan Stearn, Martha Geismer Ostrum, Mollie Rose Geismer Kross. A.B. magna cum laude, Harvard U., 1938, LL.B., 1941. Bar: Ohio 1941. Clk. to justice Supreme Ct. Ohio, 1941-42; with firm Hahn, Loeser, Freedheim, Dean & Wellman, Cleve., 1946-51, 52—, partner, 1955—, of counsel, 1970—. Sec., dir. Child Welfare League Am., 1954-62; hon. life trustee, past pres. Jewish Children's Bur. Cleve. and Bellefaire, Ohio; mem. Shaker Heights (Ohio) Bd. Edn., 1957-67, pres., 1964-66; hon. life trustee, past sec. Musical Arts Assn.; operating Cleve. Orch.; past trustee Cleve. Welfare Fedn.; past trustee, v.p. Cleve. Guidance Center. Served to capt. CIC, AUS, 1942-46, 51-52. Mem. Am., Ohio, Cleve. bar assns., Phi Beta Kappa. Home: 14620 Shaker Blvd Shaker Heights OH 44120

GEISSBUHLER, STEPHAN, graphic designer; b. Zofingen, Kanton Aargau, Switzerland, Oct. 21, 1942; came to U.S., 1967; s. Theodor and Ruth (Schneider) G.; m. Elissa Beth Feuerman, June 26, 1983; children by previous marriage: Marc Phillip, Christopher Luke. M.A., Sch. Design Basel, 1964. Designer J.R. Geigy A.G., Basel, Switzerland, 1964-67; assoc. prof., dept. chmn. Phila. Coll. Art, 1967-73; design cons. Murphy-Levy-Wurman Architects, Phila., 1968-71; designer/assoc. Anspach-Grossman-Portugal, Inc., N.Y.C., 1973-75; assoc. ptnr. Chermayeff & Geismar Assocs., N.Y.C., 1975-79, ptnr., 1979—; v.p., dir. Am. Inst. Graphic Arts, N.Y.C., 1980-83; mem. Faculty for Improvement of Fed. Graphics, Washington, 1976—; vis. lectr. in field. Served with Swiss Army, 1962-67. Recipient nat. prize for applied art Fed. Govt. Switzerland, 1966, 67, others. Mem. Am. Inst. Graphic Arts, Group for Environ. Edn., Alliance Graphique Internationale. Methodist. Office: Chermayeff and Geismar Assocs 15 E 26th St New York NY 10010 *I do what I enjoy doing, and, having the privilege to contribute to abetter understanding and appreciation of visuals by creating and designing givesme see, listen and to keep learning while darling to try the new.*

GEISSER, SEYMOUR, educator; b. Bronx, N.Y., Oct. 5, 1929; s. Leon and Rose (Kielmanowicz) G.; m. Mary Lee George, Jan. 30, 1955 (div. Apr. 1977); children—Mindy Sharon, Dan Levi, Georgia Lynn, Adam Dov.; m. Anne S. Flaxman, Mar. 21, 1982. B.A., Coll. City N.Y., 1950; M.A., U. N.C., 1952, Ph.D., 1955. Mathematician NIMH, Bethesda, Md., 1955-61; chief biometry sect. Nat. Inst. Arthritis and Metabolic Diseases, Bethesda, 1961-65; prof. statistics State U. N.Y. at Buffalo, 1965-70, chmn., 1965-70; prof., dir. Sch. Statistics, U. Minn., 1971—; professorial lectr. George Washington U., 1960-65; vis. asso. prof. Iowa State U., Ames, 1960; vis. prof. U. Wis., Madison, 1964, U. Tel-Aviv (Israel), 1971, U. Waterloo (Can.), 1972, Stanford U., 1976, Carnegie-Mellon U., Pitts., 1976, U. Orange Free State, Bloemfontein, South Africa, 1978, Harvard U. Sch. Public Health, 1981; mem. biometric and epidemiological methodology adv. com. FDA, 1976-78, mem. arthritis adv. com., 1978—. Assoc. editor: Jour. Am. Statis. Assn, 1968-70; contbr. articles to profl. jours. Fellow Inst. Math. Statistics (council 1978-80), Royal Statis. Soc., Am. Statis. Assn. (bd. dirs. 1964-65); mem. Biometric Soc., Math. Assn. Am., Internat. Statis. Inst., Psychometric Soc., Sigma Xi. Home: 1770 Summit Ave Saint Paul MN 55105

GEISSINGER, JAMES DONOVAN, lawyer; b. Spirit Lake, Iowa, Aug. 3, 1911; s. John Dewalt and Ellen Josephine (Anderson) G.; m. Martha Dollena Cooper, Dec. 23, 1956; children: James Donovan, Richard Clifton, Gary Adams. Student, U. Minn., 1928-30; B.A., U. Colo., 1932, J.D., 1935; postgrad., Harvard U., 1932-33. Bar: Colo. 1935. Dep. dist. atty., Pueblo, Colo., 1937-42, practiced law, Pueblo, 1942-44, Denver, 1948-53; asst. atty. gen. State of Colo., 1946-48, 62-68, spl. asst. atty. gen. for water matters, 1969-76; spl. asst. to solicitor Dept. Interior, Washington, 1953-54, regional solicitor, Denver region, 1954-61; mem. Bowman, Shambaugh, Geissinger & Wright, Denver, 1962-82; of counsel Bowman, Wright & Gower, Denver, 1982—; spl. water counsel City of Englewood (Colo.), 1975-81; dir. recodification Colo. Water Law, 1968-69. Served as lt. USNR, 1944-46. Mem. Denver, Colo. bar assns. Republican. Episcopalian. Lodge: Masons (33d deg.). Home: 13190 W 21st Ave Golden CO 80401 Office: 730 Equitable Bldg Denver CO 80202

GEISSINGER, JOHN BLANK, superintendent schools, association executive; b. Bethlehem, Pa., Aug. 27, 1906; s. John Benner and Sadie (Blank) G.; m. Amy Helen Findon, June 21, 1928 (dec.); children: Amy Diane, John Brent (dec.); m. Eve C. Nevard, June 25, 1977. A.B., Muhlenberg Coll., 1927; M.A., U. Pa., 1929, Ph.D., 1945. Tchr. Jenkintown (Pa.) High Sch., 1927-30; prin. high sch., supervising prin. Springfield Twp., Bucks County, Pa., 1930-40; supervising prin., North Wales, Pa., 1940-46, supt. schs., Palmyra, N.J., 1946-52, Somerville, N.J., 1952-58, Tenafly, N.J., 1958-76; instr., lectr. Pa. State Coll., 1949, U. Del., 1950-51, Lehigh U., 1952-58; Temple U., 1957-58; cons. Overseas Schs., U.S. Dept. State; exec. sec. Nat. Assn. Sch. Affiliates, Alexandria, Va., 1977; cons. Robert Strauss Assos., 1978—; ednl. cons. New Horizons Corp., 1981—; Mem. N.J. Scholarship Commn., 1961-68; adv. bd. Channel 13 Ednl. TV; adv. com. N.J. Tercentary, 1961-64. Editorial bd.: The Clearing House, 1966—; Contbr. articles to profl. jours. Mem. awards jury Am. Freedom Found., 1972; Trustee Tenafly Pub. Library, 1958-76, pres., 1977—; trustee Center Urban Edn., N.Y.C.; Englewood (N.J.) Hosp. and Sch. of Nursing Com. Upsala Coll., East Orange, N.J.; N.J. bd. dirs. Save the Children Fedn., People to People Program, 1976-77. Mem. Am. Assn. Sch. Adminstrs. (mem. exec. com. 1965-71, pres. 1971-72), N.J. Sch. Supts. Assn. (pres. 1958-59), Nat. Council Accreditation Tchr. Edn. (evaluation com., appeal bd.), N.J. Sch. Devel. Council (pres. 1957-58), NEA (life), N.J. State Interscholastic Athletic Assn. (mem. exec. com. 1959), Am. Inst. Fgn. Study (adv. bd.), Alpha Tau Omega, Phi Delta Kappa, Kappa Phi Kappa. Republican. Lutheran. Clubs: Mason (Shriner), Knickerbocker Country (Tenafly, N.J.)). Home: 83 Woodland Park Dr Tenafly NJ 07670

GEIST, GLEN OTTO, rehabilitation couselor educator, rehabilitation psychologist; b. Buffalo, June 11, 1943; s. Harold Jacob and Dorothy Anna (Marshall) G.; m. Melinda Gehron, Sept. 18, 1965 (div. Dec. 1977); children: Steven, Lori; m. 2d Chrisann Schiro, Aug. 10, 1978. B.A., Allegheny Coll., Meadville, Pa., 1965; postgrad., McCormick Theol. Sem., Chgo., 1965-66; M.S., SUNY-Buffalo, 1968, Ph.D., 1971. Registered psychologist, Ill.; cert. rehab. counselor. Rehab. counselor Gowanda State Hosp., Helmuth, N.Y., 1968-70; asst. prof. psychology Ill. Inst. Tech., 1971-75, assoc. prof., 1975-80, prof., 1980—, chmn. dept., 1981—; psychologist Geist Assocs., Chgo., 1973—; exchange scientist Poland Nat. Acad. Sci., 1980. Contbr. in field. Bd. trustees Goodwill Industries of Chgo., 1978—. Mem. Nat. Council on Rehab. Edn. (pres. 1978-79), Nat. Rehab. Assn., Nat. Rehab. Counseling Assn. (recipient Disting. Service award 1979), Am. Rehab. Counseling Assn., Am. Psychol. Assn. Club: Lincolnshire Country (Crete, Ill.). Home: 1843 Cornell Rd Flossmoor IL 60422 Office: Ill Inst Tech Chicago IL 60616

GEIST, JACOB MYER, chemical engineer; b. Bridgeport, Conn., Feb. 2, 1921; s. David and Anne Rose (Steinschreiber) G.; m. Sandra Levy, Nov. 17, 1972; children by previous marriage—Eric D., Ellen A., David C. B.S. in Chem. Engring, Purdue U., 1940; M.S., Pa. State U., 1942; Ph.D., U. Mich., 1951. Instr. Pa. State U., 1943-44; teaching fellow, part-time instr. U. Mich., 1946-48; instr., then asst. prof. Mass. Inst. Tech., 1950-52; sr. lectr. Technion, 1952-55; with Air Products and Chems., Inc., Allentown, Pa., 1955-82, assoc. dir. research and devel., 1961-63, assoc. chief engr., 1963-69, chief engr., 1969-82; pres. Geist Tech., 1982—; lectr., adj. prof. Lehigh U., Bethlehem, Pa., 1960—. Author. Served to 2d lt. AUS, 1944-46. Hon. fellow Indian Cryogenic Soc., 1975. Fellow Am. Inst. Chem. Engrs. (award chem. engring. practice 1976); mem. Nat. Acad. Engring., Am. Chem. Soc., AAAS, Internat. Inst. Refrigeration (v.p.), Cryogenic Engring. Conf. (dir.), Nat. Soc. Profl. Engrs., Sigma Xi, Tau Beta Pi, Phi Lambda Upsilon. Patentee in field. Home and Office: 2720 Highland St Allentown PA 18104

GEIST, JAMES EUGENE, telephone company executive; b. Louisville, Nebr., Oct. 14, 1929; s. Alex M. and Elsie (Zelenka) G.; m. Eleanor Richards, Feb. 7, 1954; 1 son, Alec James. B.S. with high distinction, U. Nebr., 1960. Personnel dir. Lincoln Telephone Co., Nebr., 1967-72, asst. to v.p. ops., 1972-73; v.p. ops. Lincoln Telphone Co., 1973-76; exec. v.p. Lincoln Telephone Co., Nebr., 1976-83; pres. Lincoln Telecommunications Co., 1983—; dir. Basic Telecommunications, Ft. Collins, Colo. Trustee Bryan Hosp., 1983, U. Nebr. Found., 1983; mem. Gov.'s Task Force, 1983—, Mayor's Businessmen's Round Table, 1983—. Served to staff sgt. USAF, 1950854. Mem. U.S. Ind. Telephone Assn. (pres. 1980-81, dir.), Lincoln C. of C. (pres. 1979), Am. Legion, Beta Gamma Sigma. Democrat. Methodist. Clubs: Lincoln Country; Univ. (Lincoln). Lodge: Kiwanis (pres. 1972). Office: Lincoln Telecommunications Co 1440 M St Lincoln NE 68508

GEIST, JERRY DOUGLAS, electric utility company executive; b. Raton, N.Mex., May 23, 1934; s. Jacob D. and Jessie Kathleen (Wadley) G.; m. Sharon Ludell Kaemper, June 9, 1956; children: Douglas, Bruce, Robert. Student, U. Mo., 1952-54; B.E.E., U. Colo., 1956. Registered profl. engr., N.Mex. With Pub. Service Co. N.Mex., Albuquerque, 1960—, v.p. engring. and ops., 1970-71, v.p. corporate affairs, 1971-73, exec. v.p., 1973-76, pres., 1976-82, chmn., pres., 1982—, also dir., mem. exec. com.; sr. v.p. Western Coal Co., 1972—; dir. Lectrosonics Inc., Reddy Communications, Inc., Bank Securities, Inc.; mem. Western Regional council Asso. Electric & Gas Ins. Ltd. Bd. dirs. Resources for the Future, S.W. Community Health Services; chmn. adminstrv. bd. First United Meth. Ch. Served with USN, 1952-59. Mem. Colo. River Water Users Assn. (dir.), Albuquerque C. of C. (pres. 1972-73), Tau Beta Pi, Sigma Tau, Eta Kappa Nu, Pi Mu Epsilon. Clubs: Four Hills Country, Tanoan Country, Albuquerque Country, Albuquerque Petroleum. Home: 1312 Cuatro Cerros Trail SE Albuquerque NM 87123 Office: Pub Service Co N Mex Alvarado Sq Albuquerque NM 87158

GEITGEY, DORIS ARLENE, nursing educator, dean; b. Monroe, Mich., Nov. 3, 1920; d. Harry and Nellie Love (Richardson) C. B.A., U. Toledo, 1942; diploma, Los Angeles County Gen. Hosp., 1948; M.S., Immaculate Heart Coll., 1951; Ed.D., UCLA, 1966. Asst. prof. nursing San Diego State Coll., 1957-62; specialist nursing edn. UCLA, 1962-66; assoc. prof. U. Wash. Sch. Nursing, 1966-73, assoc. dean, 1970-75, prof., 1973-75; prof., dean U. Kans. Sch. Nursing, 1975—. Author: The Art and Science of Nursing, 1954, 59, A Handbook for Head Nurses, 1961. Capitation grantee. Fellow Am. Acad. Nursing; mem. Am. Nurses Assn., Sigma Theta Tau. Office: Rainbow Blvd at 39th St Kansas City KS 66103

GEITZ, WILLIAM DANIEL, oil and gas company executive; b. Woodbury, N.J., Sept. 14, 1923; s. William Daniel and Margaret M. G.; m. Laura Rainey, Dec. 28, 1943; 1 son, Michael. B.S. cum laude, Washington Coll., 1950; M.S. in Chemistry, U. Del., 1951. Sr. process engr. Mobil Oil Co., Paulsboro, N.J., 1951-57; supr. planning, N.Y.C., 1957-60, gas liquids adminstr., 1961-63, mgr. planning and devel., Houston, 1963-65; asst. to sr. v.p. Union Tex. Petroleum Div., Allied Corp., Houston, 1965-66, dir. mktg., 1966-68, v.p. mktg., 1968-72; exec. v.p. Specialty Chems. div., Morristown, N.J., 1972-74, pres., 1974-75; group v.p. corp. office Allied Corp., 1975-83, exec. v.p., pres. oil and gas sector, 1983—; pres. Union Tex. Petroleum Corp., 1979-81, chmn., chief exec. officer, 1981—. Served with USN, 1943-45. Mem. Am. Petroleum Inst. (dir. 1978—), Nat. Petroleum Refiners Assn. (dir. 1978—). Episcopalian. Club: Houstonian (Houston). Office: PO Box 3000R Morristown NJ 07960

GEJDENSON, SAM, congressman; b. Eschwege, Germany, May 20, 1948; s. Szloma and Julia G.; m. Karen Fleming; children: Mia, Ari. A.S., Mitchell Coll., 1968; B.A., U. Conn., 1970. Mem. Conn. Ho. of Reps., 1974-78; coal broker, 1978-79; legis. liaison Conn. Office Policy and Mgmt., Hartford, 1979-80; mem. 97-98th congresses from 2d Conn. Dist. Office: 1404 Longworth House Office Bldg Washington DC 20515

GEKIERE, MADELEINE, artist, filmmaker; b. Zurich, Switzerland, May 15; came to U.S., 1940, naturalized, 1945; d. Richard and Erna (Blum) Wormser; m. Rene Gekiere, July 20, 1946. Student, Art Students League, N.Y.C., Bklyn. Mus. Art Sch., N.Y. U. Asst. prof. painting N.Y. U., 1958-67; asso. prof. CCNY, 1967-78, prof., 1978—; vis. prof. painting U. Ga., 1967. Author, illustrator: Who Gave Us, 1953, The Princess and the Frilly Lilly, 1960; illustrator: Switch on the Night, 1957, The Reason for the Pelican, 1960; Exhbns. include, U. Ga., 1967, Western Carolina U., 1972, Audubon Artists, N.Y.C., N.Y. U. Loeb Center; represented in permanent collections, Worcester (Mass.) Art Mus., Fogg Mus. Art, N.Y. U. Collection, Bklyn. Mus., Currier Gallery Art, Manchester, N.H., and others. Recipient Best Illustrated Book of Year award N.Y. Times, 1957, 59, 63; Audubon medal of honor, 1969. Mem. Artists Equity Assn. Address: 427 W 21st St New York NY 10011

GEKS, FRANZ T., pharmaceutical company executive. Pres. Miles Labs., Elkhart, Ind., 1983—. Office: Miles Labs Inc 1127 Myrtle St Elkhart IN 46515§

GELATT, CHARLES DANIEL, manufacturing company executive; b. LaCrosse, Wis., Jan. 4, 1918; s. Philo Madison and Clara (Johnson) G.; m. Jane Leicht, Mar. 6, 1942 (div. 1972); children: Sarah Jane Gelatt Gephart, Charles D., Philip Madison; m. Paula Jo Evans, Aug. 22, 1973 (div. 1978); m. Sue Ann Jimieson, Dec. 11, 1983. B.A., M.A., U. Wis., 1939. Vice pres. Gelatt Corp., La Crosse, 1940-52, pres., 1952—, No. Engraving Corp., 1958-67, chmn., 1967—. Trustee Northwestern Mut. Life Ins. Co., Milw., 1960—, also mem. exec. com., 1961-77; Bd. regents U. Wis., 1947-74, pres. bd., 1955-57, v.p., 1964-68, pres., 1968-69; mem. Wis. Coordinating Com. for Higher Edn., 1955-59, 64-69, chmn., 1956; chmn. Assn. Governing Bds. Univs. and Colls., Washington, 1971-72; trustee Carroll Coll., Waukesha, Wis., 1971-79, Viterbo Coll., La Crosse, 1972—, Gundersen Found., La Crosse, 1973—; pres. Gundersen Found., 1977—. Mem. Phi Beta Kappa. Home: 1326 Cass St LaCrosse WI 54601 Office: Box 1207 LaCrosse WI 54601

GELB, ARTHUR, research company executive; b. Bklyn., Sept. 20, 1937; s. Charles and Rose (Bulkin) G.; m. Linda Lewis, Aug. 24, 1958; children: Ronald C., Caren R., Laurie I. B.E.E., CCNY, 1958; S.M., Harvard U., 1959; Sc.D., MIT, 1961. Engr. Am. Distr. Telegraph Co., N.Y.C., 1957-58, MIT Instrumentation Lab., Cambridge, 1959-60; mgr. systems analysis dept. Dynamics Research Corp., Stoneham, Mass., 1961-66; pres. TASC (The Analytic Sciences Corp.), Reading, Mass., 1966—. Editor, co-author: Applied Optimal Estimation, 1974; author: (with W. E. Vander Velde) Multiple Input Describing Functions, 1968. Mem. Mass. Gov.'s Mgmt. Task Force, 1974-75; bd. dirs. Mass. Port Authority, 1976—. NSF fellow, 1958-60; named Outstanding Young Engr. CCNY, 1969. Fellow IEEE; mem. Am. Mgmt. Assn., Mensa. Patentee in field. Home: 38 Meriam St Lexington MA 02173 Office: TASC 1 Jacob Way Reading MA 01867

GELB, ARTHUR, editor; b. N.Y.C., Feb. 3, 1924; s. Daniel and Fanny G.; m. Barbara Stone, June 2, 1946; children—Michael, Peter. B.A., N.Y. U., 1946. Mem. staff N.Y. Times, 1944—, asst. drama critic, 1958-61, chief cultural corr., 1961-63, met. editor, 1967-76, dep. mng. editor, 1976—; lectr. on theatre, also Eugene O'Neill, 1961—. Author: (with Mrs. Gelb) O'Neill, 1962, (with Dr. Salvatore Cutolo) Bellevue is My Home, 1956, (with A.M. Rosenthal) One More Victim, 1967; Editor: The Pope's Journey to the United States, 1965, The Night the Lights Went Out, 1965. Mem. Am. Soc. Newspaper Editors, A.P. Mng. Editors. Address: care NY Times 229 W 43d St New York NY 10036

GELB, BRUCE S., pharmaceutical consumer goods company executive; b. N.Y.C., Feb. 24, 1927; s. Lawrence M. and Joan Friedman (Hewett) G.; m. Lueza Denise Thirkield, June 6, 1953; children: John T., Joan H., Richard E., Mary C. B.A., Yale U., 1950; M.B.A., Harvard U., 1953. With Clairol Inc., 1950-51, 58—, exec. v.p., 1961-65, pres., from 1965; brand mgr. Procter & Gamble, 1953-57; pres. Charter Corp.; now exec. v.p. Bristol Myers Co. Bd. dirs. Madison Sq. Boys Club; chmn. bd. trustees Choate Rosemary Hall Sch. Office: 345 Park Ave New York NY 10154

GELB, HAROLD SEYMOUR, investor; b. N.Y.C., Apr. 26, 1920; s. Daniel and Fanny (Gelb) G.; m. Sylvia M. Miller, Sept. 24, 1942; children: Richard, Alan. B.B.A., CCNY, 1941. C.P.A., N.Y. With S.D. Leidesdorf & Co. (C.P.A.s), N.Y.C., 1943-78, mng. partner, 1969-78; sr. ptnr. Ernst & Whinney, N.Y.C., 1978-82, cons., 1982—, vice-chmn., 1984—; trustee Citizens Budget Commn., N.Y.C., 1969—; mem. N.Y. State Bd. Pub. Accountancy, 1977—. Pres. Bronx-Lebanon Hosp. Center, 1977; bd. dirs., v.p. S.D. Leidesdorf Found., 1969-80; trustee Accts. Found., 1973-80; bd. overseers Albert Einstein Med. Coll., 1977-79; bd. dirs., sec. Benjamin Cardozo Law Sch., 1977—; mem. nat. council Am. Jewish Com.; mem. N.Y.C. Mayor's Com. on Taxi Regulatory Issues. Recipient Disting. Community Service award Brandeis U., 1978. Mem. N.Y. State Soc. C.P.A.s (past v.p. dir.), Am. Inst. C.P.A.s (mem. council 1970-76). Clubs: Metropolis (White Plains); City Athletic, Accountants, Sky, City, Economic (N.Y.C.); Town (Scarsdale); International (Bolton, Mass.); Boca Woods Country (Boca Raton, Fla.). Home: 181 Fox Meadow Rd Scarsdale NY 10583 Office: 153 E 53 St New York NY 10022 Office: 45 Rockefeller Plaza New York NY 10111

GELB, IGNACE JAY, Assyriologist, linguist, educator; b. Tarnow, Poland, Oct. 14, 1907; came to U.S., 1929, naturalized, 1939; s. Salo and Regina (Issler) G.; m. Hester Mokstad, May 13, 1938; children: Walter, Alexander, John Vincent. Student, U. Florence, (Italy), 1925-26; Ph.D., U. Rome, 1929. Travelling fellow, research assoc. U. Chgo., 1929-41; asst. prof. Assyriology U. Chgo, 1941-43; assoc. prof. U. Chgo., 1943-47, prof., 1947-65, Frank P. Hixon Sisting. Service prof., 1965-78; vis. prof. U. Mich., 1956-67; mem. archaeol. expdns. to Nr. East, 1932, 35, 47, 65, 66; sci. collaborator Polish Acad. Scis., Cracow. Author: Hurrians and Subarians, 1944, Study of Writing, 1952, Sargonic Texts From the Diyala Region, 1952, Old Akkadian Writing and Grammar, 1952, Glossary of Old Akkadian, 1955, Sequential Reconstruction of Proto-Akkadian, 1968, Computer-Aided Analysis of Amorite, 1980, (others); contbr. articles to profl. jours.; editor: Chicago Assyrian Dictionary, 1947—. Served with AUS, 1943-45. Fellow Am. Acad. Arts and Scis, Brit. Acad.; hon. mem. Societe Asiatique (Paris), Finnish Oriental Soc.; mem. Am. Philos. Soc., Accademia Nazionale dei Lincei (Italy), Am. Oriental Soc. (br. pres. 1959-60, nat. pres. 1965-66), Am. Schs. Oriental Research, Linguistic Soc. Am., Internat Linguistic Assn., Am. Name Soc. (pres. 1963-64), Archaeol. Inst. Am., Societe Hittiete (Paris), Inst. Asian Studies (hon. mem. Hyderabad, Italy). Clubs: Quadrange; Nr. East (Chgo.) (pres. 1942-43). Home: 5454 Woodlawn Ave Chicago IL 60615 Office: U Chgo Oriental Inst 1155 E 58th St Chicago Il 60637

GELB, LESLIE HOWARD, journalist, lectr.; b. New Rochelle, N.Y., Mar. 4, 1937; s. Max and Dorothy (Klein) G.; m. Judith Cohen, Aug. 2, 1959; children—Adam, Caroline, Alison. A.B. magna cum laude in Govt. and cum laude in Philosophy, Tufts U., 1959; M.A., Harvard U., 1961, Ph.D., 1964. Teaching fellow govt. and social scis., non-resident tutor Winthrop House, Harvard U., 1962-64, asso. def. studies program, 1963-64; asst. prof. govt. Wesleyan U., Middletown, Conn., 1964-65; exec. asst. to U.S. Senator Jacob K. Javits, 1966-67; dep. dir. policy planning staff Dept. Def., Washington, 1967-68, dir., 1968, acting dep. asst. sec. def. for policy planning and arms control staff, 1968-69; dir. sec. def. Vietnam task force, 1967-68; sr. fellow Brookings Instn., Washington, 1969-73; corr. N.Y. Times, Washington, 1973-77. Author: The Irony of Vietnam: The System Worked, 1979; contbr. numerous articles to mags. Dir. Bur. Politico-Mil. Affairs, Dept. State, Washington, 1977-79; sr. asso. Carnegie Endowment for Internat. Peace, Washington, 1979-81; chmn. Carnegie Endowment Panel on Future U.S. Security and Arms Control, 1980-81; nat. security corr. N.Y. Times, 1981—. Recipient Woodrow Wilson award, 1980. Mem. Internat. Inst. Strategic Studies, Council on Fgn. Relations. Home: 2405 Elba Ct Alexandria VA 22306 Office: NY Times 1000 Connecticut Ave NW Washington DC 20036

GELB, RICHARD LEE, pharmaceutical corporation executive; b. N.Y.C., June 8, 1924; s. Lawrence M. and Joan F. (Bove) G.; m. Phyllis L. Nason, May 5, 1951; children: Lawrence N., Lucy G., Jane E., James M. Student, Phillips Acad., 1938-41; B.A., Yale, 1945; M.B.A., Harvard, 1950. Joined Clairol, Inc., N.Y.C., 1950, pres., 1959-64; exec. v.p. Bristol-Myers Co., 1965-67, pres., 1967—, chief exec. officer, 1972—, chmn. bd., 1976—; dir. Charter Corp., Bankers Trust Co., Bankers Trust N.Y. Corp., Cluett Peabody & Co., N.Y. Times Co., N.Y. Life Ins. Co. Mem. N.Y. Urban Coalition; chmn. Crime Control Planning Bd., State of N.Y.; Mem. N.Y. City Police Found.; trustee Com. Econ. Devel.; charter trustee Phillips Acad.; bd. dirs. Lincoln Center for Performing Arts. Mem. Council on Fgn. Relations (dir.), Bus. Council, Bus. Roundtable. Home: 1060 Fifth Ave New York NY 10028 Office: Bristol Meyers Co 345 Park Ave New York NY 10154

GELB, VICTOR, company executive; b. Cleve., Oct. 15, 1926; s. Charles and Lena Regina (Katz) G.; m. Joan Marie Freeman, June 16, 1948; children: Kathy Lee (Mrs. Dana deWindt), Robert James, Cynthia Ellen Gelb Grabner, Leslie Ann. Student, Western Res. U., 1948-51. Exec. v.p. Ohio Advt. Agy., 1949-53; sales mgr. to pres., chief exec. officer Woodhill Permatex Corp., Cleve., 1953-79; pres., chief exec. officer Cole Consumer Products, 1980—; pres. Victor Gelb Inc., 1980-81; dir., v.p. Cook-United; chmn. Capital Am. Life Ins. Co.; dir. Pioneer-Standard Electronics, Cardinal Fed. Savs. & Loan Assn. Nat. pres. Big Bros. of Am., 1970-74; pres. Bellefaire Child Care Center, Jewish Children's Bur., 1969-72, Greater Cleve. Neighborhood Settlements Assn., 1967-69; chmn. Mayor's Council Youth Activities, 1970-71; Bd. dirs., v.p. United Way Services; trustee Jewish Community Fedn.; nat. vice chmn. United Jewish Appeal, 1981—. Served with U.S. Mcht. Marine, 1944-47. Recipient Baker award Cleve. Jewish Community Fedn., 1960. Mem. Automotive Parts and Accessories Assn. (chmn. 1973-74). Jewish. Club: Cleve. City (dir. 1966-68). Home: 33845 Chagrin Blvd Moreland Hills OH 44022

GELBAND, HENRY, pediatric cardiologist; b. Austria, Aug. 31, 1936; U.S., 1941, naturalized, 1951; s. Herman and Charlotte (Rubin) G.; m. Ellen Brooke Charin, Aug. 26, 1962; children—Craig Harris, Mark Evan, Todd David. B.A., Washington (Pa.) and Jefferson Coll., 1958; M.D., Jefferson Med. Coll., Phila., 1962. Intern Beth Israel Hosp., Newark, 1962-63; resident in pediatrics Mt. Sinai Hosp., N.Y.C., 1965-67; fellow in pediatric cardiology Columbia U. Coll. Phys. and Surg., 1967-69, spl. research fellow in pharmacology, 1969-71; mem. faculty U. Miami (Fla.) Med. Sch., 1971—, prof. pediatrics, dir. div. pediatric cardiology, 1976—, prof. pharmacology, 1977—; prin. investigator NIH grants, 1976—; Vice pres. Ronald McDonald House, South Fla., Miami, 1978—. Co-author: Infant and Child, 1977; contbr. articles to med. jours. Served as officer M.C. USNR, 1963-65. Mem. Am. Physiol. Soc., Soc. Pediatric Research, Am. Soc. Pharmacology and Exptl. Therapeutics, Internat. Study Group Research Cardiac Metabolism, Am. Acad. Pediatrics, Am. Heart Assn., Am. Coll. Cardiology, Internat. Coll. Pediatrics, Am. Coll. Chest Physicians, Fla. Assn. Pediatric Cardiology. Democrat. Jewish. Home: 15020 SW 69th Ct Miami FL 33158 Office: Univ Miami Med Sch PO Box 016820 Miami FL 33101

GELBAND, STEPHEN LAURENCE, lawyer; b. N.Y.C., Feb. 13, 1931; s. Sol Lawrence and Martha Ruth (Dossick) G.; m. Carla Dena Shapiro, Aug. 21, 1955; children—Scott Lee, Joanna Susan. A.B., Yale U., 1952; J.D., Harvard U., 1955. Bar: N.Y. bar 1955, D.C. bar 1961. Atty. Office U.S. Atty., So. Dist. N.Y., N.Y.C., 1955; legal assistance advisor, Ft. Myer, Va., 1956-57; trial atty. Bur. Econ. Regulation, CAB, Washington, 1957-60; ptnr. Hewes, Morella, Gelband & Lamberron P.C., Washington, 1981—; Councilman, Somerset, Md., 1967-70. Served with AUS, 1955-57. Mem. Am., Fed. bar assns., D.C. Bar, Bar Assn. D.C. Clubs: Internat., Nat. Aviation (Washington). Home: 6510 River Rd Bethesda MD 20034 Office: 1010 Wisconsin Ave NW Washington DC 20007

GELBART, ABE, mathematics educator; b. Paterson, N.J., Dec. 22, 1911; s. Wolf and Pauline (Landau) G.; m. Sara Goodman, July 2, 1939; children: Carol Marie (Mrs. Ivan P. Auer), Judith Sylvia (dec.), William Michael, Stephen Samuel. B.Sc., Dalhousie U., 1938, LL.D. honoris causa, 1972; Ph.D. in Math, Mass. Inst. Tech., 1940. Asst. Mass. Inst. Tech., 1939-40; instr. math. N.C. State Coll., 1940-42; research asso. Brown U., 1942; asso. physicist NACA, Langley Field, Va., 1942-43; asst. prof. to prof. math. Syracuse U., 1943-58; dir. Inst. Math., Yeshiva U., 1958-59; dean Belfer Grad. Sch. Sci., 1959-70, dean emeritus, 1970—, distinguished univ. prof. math., 1968—; vis. Disting. prof. math. Bard Coll. and fellow Bard Coll. Center, 1979—, David and Rosalie Rose Disting. prof. natural sci. and math., 1983—; lectr., Sorbonne, Paris, 1949; vis. prof. U. So. Calif., 1951; Mem. Inst. Advanced Study, Princeton, 1947-48, 77—; Fulbright lectr., Norway, 1951-52; Mem. directorate math. scis. USAF Office Sci. Research.; vice chmn. bd. dirs., chmn. sci. adv. bd. Daltex Med. Scis., Inc., 1983—. Editor: Scripta Mathematica, 1957—. Trustee, chmn. acad. sci. com. Bar-Ilan U., Israel, 1982—. Recipient Bard medal, 1981. Mem. Am. Math. Soc., Math. Assn. Am. Co-developer theory of pseudo-analytic functions. Home: 140 West End Ave New York NY 10023

GELBART, LARRY, TV producer; b. Chgo., Feb. 25, 1928; s. Harry and Frieda (Sturner) G.; m. Pat Marshall, Nov. 25, 1956; children: Cathy, Gary, Paul, Adam, Becky. Writer: for radio Duffy's Tavern, 1945-48, Jack Paar, 1947, Jack Carson, 1947-48, Bob Hope, 1947-51, for TV, 1949-51, Red Buttons, 1951-52, Sid Caesar, 1953-55, Art Carney, 1960; for theatre My L.A, 1950, The Conquering Hero, 1960, A Funny Thing Happened on the Way to the Forum, 1961; for films The Notorious Landlady, 1960, (also co-producer) The Wrong Box, 1966, Not With My Wife You Don't, 1966, Little Me, 1968, The Ecstacy Business, 1968, Oh, God, 1977, Sly Fox, 1976, Movie, Movie; Neighbors, 1981, Tootsie, 1982; Writer, exec. producer: Blame It on Rio, 1984; producer: (also co-producer) TV shows MASH, 1972, Karen, 1975; composer songs; (Recipient Sylvania award 1960, Emmy award 1960, 74, Antoinette Perry award 1962). Served with AUS, 1945-46. Mem. Dramatists Guild, Writers Guild Am. (award 1972, 74), ASCAP, Writers Guild Gt. Britain, Dirs. Guild Am. Office: care Howard Rothberg Suite 609 9255 Sunset Blvd Los Angeles CA 90069 *

GELBAUM, BERNARD RUSSELL, mathematics educator; b. N.Y.C., Feb. 26, 1922; s. Harry and Regina (Kratka) G.; m. Beatrice Lerner, Nov. 14, 1942; children: Daniel, David, Martin, Ethan. A.B., Columbia U., 1943; M.A., Princeton U., 1947, Ph.D. (NRC Predoctoral fellow), 1948. Instr. Princeton U., 1947; mem. faculty U. Minn., Mpls., 1948-64, prof., 1957-64; prof., chmn. dept. math. U. Calif. at Irvine, 1964-68; asso. dean Sch. Phys. Scis., 1968-71; v.p. acad. affairs state SUNY at Buffalo, 1971-74, prof., 1974—; vis. mem. Inst. Advanced Study, Princeton, 1960; cons. Inst. Def. Analyses, Washington, 1962-67; cons. editor W. B. Saunders Co., Phila., 1964-68. Author: (with J.M.H. Olmsted) Counterexamples in Analysis, 1964, (with J.G. March) Mathematics for the Social and Behavioral Sciences, 1969; Editor: Functional Analysis, 1967; Contbns. to functional analysis, study of topological groups, theory of games. Pulitzer scholar, 1939; NSF research grantee, 1959—. Mem. Am. Math. Soc., Math. Assn. Am., Phi Beta Kappa. Home: 127 Ruskin Rd Buffalo NY 14226 Office: 139 Diefendorf State U New York Buffalo NY 14214

GELBER, ARTHUR, arts advocate; b. Toronto, Ont., Can., June 22, 1915; s. Louis and Sara Leah (Morris) G.; m. Esther Gelber, June 17, 1941; children: Nancy Joan Gelber Bjarnason, Patricia Susan Gelber Rubin, Judith Ann Gelber Weintrob. Student, Upper Can. Coll., Toronto, Ont., 1934; LL.D., Brock U., 1982. Pres. Argel Holdings Ltd. Chmn. Nat. Arts Centre Corp., Ottawa Ont., Can., 1977-81; chmn. adv. council Ont. Cabinet Bi-Centenary Com., Can.; past pres. Can. Conf. Arts; mem., past chmn. Ont. Arts Council, Can., 1979-82; past pres. Nat. Ballet, St. Lawrence Centre, Toronto Arts Prodns.; bd. dirs. Am. Council for Arts, N.Y.; gov. Nat. Theatre Sch. of Can., MontrealQue.; chmn. Shakespeare Three com. and tng. program com./Stratford Festival, Que., Can.; hon. dir. Centre Stage, Toronto, Ont. Can.; hon. chmn. Performing Arts Devel. Fund; former gov. York U.; bd. dirs. Can. Jewish Congress. Decorated Order of Can.; recipient Centennial medal, 1967, Diplome d'Honeur, 1978, award of Merit City of Toronto, Queen's Jubilee medal. Club: Arts and Letters. Home: 166 Roxborough Dr Toronto ON Canada M4W 1X8 Office: 203 Richmond St W Toronto ON Canada M5V 1V5

GELBER, JACK, writer; b. Chgo., Apr. 12, 1932; s. Harold and Molly (Singer) G.; m. Carol Westenberg, Dec. 23, 1957; children: Jed, Amy. B.S. in Journalism, U. Ill., 1953. Adj. asso. prof. Columbia U., N.Y.C., 1967-72, prof., 1967-72, Bklyn. Coll., 1972—. Author: plays The Connection, 1959, The Apple, 1961, Square in the Eye, 1965, The Cuban thing, 1968, Sleep, 1972, Rehearsal, 1976; novel On Ice, 1964, Barbary Shore, 1974, Rehearsal, 1976. Recipient Best Play award for The Connection Village Voice, 1959-60, Vernon Rice award for outstanding contbn. to off-Broadway, 1959-60, Directing award Village Voice, 1972-73; Guggenheim fellow, 1963-64, 66-67; Rockefeller grantee, 1972; Nat. Endowment Arts fellow, 1974; CBS fellow Yale U., 1974-75. Office: care Grove Press 169 W. Houston New York NY 10014 *

GELBOIN, HARRY VICTOR, biochemist; b. Chgo., Dec. 21, 1929; s. Herman and Eva (Jurkowsky) G.; m. Marlena Maisels, Apr. 1, 1962; children: Michele Ida, Lisa Rebecca, Sharon Anna, Tamara Rachel. A.B., U. Ill., 1951; M.S., U. Wis., 1956, Ph.D., 1958. Devel. chemist U.S. Rubber Co., 1952-54; research asst. McArdle Meml. Lab. Cancer Research, U. Wis., 1954-58; biochemist NIMH, 1958-61; supervisory biochemist Nat. Cancer Inst., 1962-64, head chemistry sect., 1964-66; chief Lab. Molecular Carcinogens div. cancer cause and prevention, 1966—; adj. prof. Mt. Vernon Jr. Coll., Washington, Georgetown U., 1978; cons. Am. Cancer Soc., EPA, Nat. Acad. Sci., Fedn. Am. Soc. Exptl. Biology, others.; Predoctoral fellow Nat. Cancer Inst., 1957-58; keynote speaker Gordon Research Conf. Cancer, 1965; Franz Bielschowsky Meml. lectr., Dunedin, New Zealand, 1966, Smith, Kline and French hon. lectr., 1974, 76. Author articles, chpts. in books.; Asso. editor: Chem.-Biol. Interactions; assoc. editor: Cancer Research, 1983-86; editor: Environmental Health Sciences, 1976. Recipient Claude Bernard award U. Montreal, 1970; New Horizons award lectr. Radiol. Soc. N.Am., 1970; Superior Service award NIH, 1970. Mem. AAAS, Am. Assn. Cancer Research Am., Soc. Biol. Chemists, Am. Soc. Pharmacology and Exptl. Therapeutics. Jewish religion (trustee congregation 1972—). Club: Mem. B'nai B'rith. Home: 2806 Abilene Dr Chevy Chase MD 20015 Office: Nat Insts Health Bethesda MD 20014

GELDARD, FRANK ARTHUR, psychologist; b. Worcester, Mass., May 20, 1904; s. Arthur and Margaret Hardy (Gordon) G.; m. Jeannette Manchester, June 20, 1928; 1 dau., Deborah Rea. A.B., Clark U., 1925, A.M., 1926, Ph.D., 1928, Sc.D. (hon.), 1978, Washington and Lee U., 1969. Asso. prof. psychology U. Va., 1928-37, prof. psychology, dir. psychol. lab., 1937-60, chmn. dept., 1946-60; dean Grad. Sch. Arts and Scis., 1960-62; Stuart prof. psychology Princeton, 1962-72, prof. emeritus, 1972—, sr. research psychologist, 1972—; Green Honors prof. Tex. Christian U., 1977; Served as col. U.S. Army Air Corps, chief field service and liaison sect., psychol. br. Office of Air Surgeon, hdqrs. Army Air Forces, 1942; chief psychol. sect. Office of Surgeon, hdqrs. Army Air Forces Tng. Command, 1942-45; comdg. officer, psychol. mission to P.I. and Japan, 1945; col. USAF Res., 1946-57; Cons. research and devel. bd. Nat. Mil. and Office of Naval Research, U.S. Navy Dept., 1947-58; research chief human resources div., research and devel. directorate Hdqrs. USAF, 1949-50; chmn. human resources com. Office Sec. of Def., 1950-56; sci. liaison officer Office Naval Research, London br., 1956-57. Author: The Human Senses, 2d edit, 1972, Fundamentals of Psychology, 1962, Sensory Saltation, 1975; Editor: Defense Psychology, 1962, Communication Processes, 1965, Cutaneous Communication Systems and Devices, 1974; Contbr. numerous articles to psychol. and ednl. jours. Chmn. NATO Adv. Group on Human Factors, 1959-65; chmn. Mil. Psychology Comm.; mem. Com. Internat. Relations in Psychology; NRC Vision Com., com. on biol., med. scis. NSF, 1953-59. Decorated Legion of Merit; recipient Distinguished Teaching award Am. Psychol. Found., 1974; Disting. Contbn. to Psychology award Va. Psychol. Assn., 1979. Fellow Am. Psychol. Assn. (past pres. div. exptl. psychology and div. mil. psychology), Royal Soc. Medicine (Gt. Brit.), AAAS (v.p. sect. I 1957-58); mem. AAUP, Soc. Exptl. Psychologists, So. Soc. for Philosophy and Psychology (past pres.), Internat. Brain Research Orgn., UNESCO, Eastern Psychol. Assn., Raven, Gryphon, Phi Beta Kappa, Sigma Xi, Phi Sigma, Kappa Phi, Omicron Delta Kappa. Democrat. Clubs: Colonnade, Nassau (Princeton); Cosmos (Washington); Princeton (N.Y.C.). Home: 551 Lake Dr Princeton NJ 08540

GELDMACHER, ROBERT CARL, software corporation executive; b. Elgin, Ill., Apr. 22, 1917; s. Walter Carl and Emma (Goers) G.; m. Theresa Julia Swanberg, Sept. 27, 1941; children: Ann Marie (Mrs. Peter A. Alicandri), Cecily Louise, Mary Ellen. B.E., No. Ill. U., 1942; M.S., Purdue U., 1946; Ph.D., Northwestern U., 1959. Tchr. physics and math. Chadwick (Ill.) High Sch., 1942-43; instr. Naval Tng. Sch., Purdue U., 1943-45, research asst., 1945-47, from asst. prof. to assoc. prof. engring. sci., 1947-60; prof. engring. sci., assoc. dean sch. Engring. and Sci., NYU, 1960-66; Anson Wood Burchard prof. Stevens Inst. Tech., 1966-83, head dept. elec. engring., 1966-76; pres., chief exec. officer Sundale Software Corp., 1983—; cons. to govt., 1952—. Mem. Am. Soc. Engring. Edn., Am. Phys. Soc., AAAS, IEEE, Math. Assn. Am., Soc. Indsl. and Applied Math., AAUP, Sigma Xi, Tau Beta Pi. Research in magneto-elasto-dynamics, graph theory. Home: 831 Hudson St Hoboken NJ 07030 Office: Burchard Bldg Stevens Inst Tech Hoboken NJ 07030

GELFAND, DAVID H., biologist, genetic research adminstr.; b. N.Y.C., June 9, 1944; s. Sidney J. and Gigi P. (Levinson) G.; m. Ellen Daniell, Dec. 29, 1980; 1 dau., Duskie Lynn. A.B., Brandeis U., 1966; Ph.D. in Biology, U. Calif., San Diego, 1970. Research asst. biochemistry Brandeis U., Waltham, Mass., 1965; research asso. biology U. Calif.-San Diego, 1966; NIH trainee molecular genetics U. Calif., 1966-70, staff research biochemist, 1970-72; asst. research prof. U. Calif.-San Francisco, asst. research biochemist and lab. mgr., 1972-76; dir. recombinant molecular research Cetus Corp., Berkeley, Calif., 1977-81, v.p. sci. affairs, 1979—; mem. sci. adv. council NSF, 1980—. Contbr. articles on molecular research in genetics to sci. jours. Mem. Am. Soc. Biol. Chemists, Am. Soc. for Microbiology, AAAS. Office: 1400 53rd st Emeryville CA 94608

GELFAND, IVAN, investment advisor, columnist; b. Cleve., Mar. 29, 1927; s. Samuel and Sarah (Kruglin) G.; m. Suzanne Frank, Sept. 23, 1956; children: Dennis Scott, Andrew Steven. B.S., Miami U., Oxford, Ohio, 1950; postgrad., Case-Western Res. U., 1951; grad., Columbia U. Bank Mgmt. Program, 1968; certs., Am. Inst. Banking, 1952-57. Acct. Central Nat. Bank Cleve., 1950-53, v.p., mgr. bank and corp. investments, 1957-75; chief acct. Stars & Stripes newspaper, Darmstadt, Germany, 1953-55; account exec. Merrill, Lynch, Pierce, Fenner & Smith, Inc., Cleve., 1955-57; chmn., chief exec. officer Gelfand, Quinn & Assos., Inc., Cleve., 1975-83; v.p., mng. dir. Prudential-Bache Securities, Inc., 1983—; pres. Lindow, Gelfand and Quinn, Inc., 1976—; co-editor Gelfand-Quinn/Liquidity Portfolio Mgr. Newsletter, 1978-81, Gelfand-Quinn Analysis/Money Market Techniques, 1981—; money market columnist Nat. Thrift News, 1976-78, guest money market columnist, 1982—; instr. investments adult div. Cleve. Bd. Edn., 1956-58, Am. Inst. Banking, 1958-68; guest lectr., speaker nat. and local TV and radio stas.; lectr. in econs., fin. instn. portfolio mgmt., cash mgmt., 1972—. Mem. investment com. United Torch Cleve., 1972-74; study-rev. team capt. Lake Erie Regional Transp. Authority, 1973-77; chmn. Bus. in Action, 1979-82; mem. bond com. Jewish Community Fedn., Cleve., 1979—, mem. fin. com., Cleve., 1981—; mem. Cuyahoga County Republican Fin. Com., 1978-82; mem. exec. com. Cuyahoga County Rep. Orgn., 1982—; asst. sec. Cleve. chpt. Am. Men's Orgn. for Rehab. and Tng., 1970-72. Served with AUS, 1945-47. Mem. Greater Cleve. Growth Assn., Cleve. Soc. Security Analysts, Les Politiques. Republican. Clubs: Mid-day, Commerce, City (Cleve.); Oakwood, Masons. Home: 2900 Alvord Pl Pepper Pike OH 44124 Office: Leader Bldg Cleveland OH 44114

GELFAND, LAWRENCE EMERSON, historian, educator; b. Cleve., June 20, 1926; s. Maurice Hirsch and Rachel S. (Shapiro) G.; m. Miriam J. Ifland, June 14, 1953; children: Julia M., Daniel B., Ronald S. B.A., Western Res. U., 1949, M.A., 1950; Ph.D., U. Wash., 1958. Asst. prof. history U. Hawaii, 1956-58; acting asst. prof. history U. Wash., 1958-59; asst. prof. history U. Wyo., 1959-62, U. Iowa, Iowa City, 1962-64, asso. prof., 1964-66, prof., 1966—; vis. prof. U. Oreg., summer 1966, U. Mont., summer 1970, U. Wash., 1974. Author: The Inquiry: American Preparations for Peace 1917-1919, 1963; Editor: A Diplomat Looks Back (Memoirs of Lewis Einstein), 1968, Essays on the History of American Foreign Relations, 1972, Herbert Hoover: The Great War and Its Aftermath 1914-1923, 1979. Bd. curators State Hist. Soc. Iowa, 1970-72; mem. adv. bd. Nat. Archives for Region VI, 1968-74. Served with AUS, 1944-46. Decorated Purple Heart.; Am. Council Learned Socs. grantee in Korean studies, summer 1951; Rockefeller Found. grantee, 1964-65. Mem. Am. Hist. Assn., Orgn. Am. Historians, Soc. for Historians of Am. Fgn. Relations (v.p. 1981, pres. 1982). Home: 1437 Oakcrest Iowa City IA 52240

GELFAND, LEONARD, elec. mfg. co. exec.; b. Cleve., Oct. 30, 1927; s. Max and Tillie (Raider) G.; m. Barbara Joan Goodrich, July 16, 1965; 1 son, Craig. B.S., Case Western Res. U., 1950. With Erico Products Inc., Cleve., 1950—, v.p. research and devel., 1963-77, pres., chief exec. officer, 1977—, also dir.; dir. Harco Corp., Medina, Ohio.; Mem. orthopedic resources com. Univ. Hosp., Case-Western Res. U. Med. Sch., since 1979. Served with USNR, 1945-46. Mem. ASCE, Am. Ry. Engrs. Assn., Am. Concrete Inst., AIME. Republican. Jewish. Clubs: Temple Men's, Cleve. Racquet. Home: 2742 Lander Rd Pepper Pike OH 44124 Office: 34600 Solon Rd Solon OH 44139

GELFAND, MORRIS ARTHUR, librarian; b. Bayonne, N.J., June 1, 1908; s. Joseph Samuel and Sadie (Schneider) G.; m. Beatrice Margaret Traube, Feb. 1, 1948; children: James Munn, Lisa Jay. B.S., NYU, 1933, M.A., 1939, Ph.D., 1960; B.S. in Library Service, Columbia U., 1934. Supr. res. reading room Washington Sq. Library, NYU, 1931-37; library asst. Queens Coll. Library, Flushing, N.Y., 1937-41, asst. librarian, 1941-42, librarian, 1946-59, prof. librarian, 1959-70; chmn. dept. library sci. Queens Coll., 1970-76; Fulbright lectr., cons. U. Rangoon, Burma, 1958-59; mem. visitation coms., commn. instns. higher edn. Middle States Assn. Colls. and Secondary Schs., 1949-69, 74—; cons. AID, Venezuela, 1970; UNESCO library expert, Thailand, 1962; vis. prof., library cons. U. Delhi, India, 1966; library cons. Ford Found., Brazil, 1964, 66, 67, 69; UNESCO cons. Hacettepe (Turkey) U., 1976; pres. Roslyn (N.Y.) chpt. Am. Field Service, 1964-65; trustee Council on Research in Bibliography, Inc., Bryant Library, Roslyn, Nassau Library System, N.Y. Met. Reference and Research Library Agy., pres. bd. trustees, 1973-79; chmn. chancellor's task force on libraries City U. N.Y., 1979-81. Author: University Libraries for Developing Countries, 1968; editor: N.Y. Library Club Bull., 1940-41, 51-52; contbr. to library publs. Served with U.S. Army, 1942; 2d lt. to maj., A.C., 1942-45; statis. officer, adj.; ETO; library officer U.S. Army Forces, 1945-46; Pacific. Mem. AAUP (pres. Queens Coll. 1952-53), ALA (rep. to UN Orgn. 1962-65); mem. Am. Printing History Assn. (pres. 1982-83); Mem. Assn. Coll. and Reference Libraries (chmn. program com., coll. sec. 1949-50), Bibliog. Soc. Am., N.Y. Library Club (pres. 1947-48), Steering Com. on Library Cooperation in Met. N.Y. (sec. 1949), Sigma Soc. of NYU (pres. 1928), Phi Delta Kappa, Alpha Lambda Phi. Clubs: Archons of Colophon, Grolier (N.Y.C.). Home: The Stone House Post Dr Roslyn Harbor NY 11576

GELFAND, NEAL, oil company executive; b. Bronx, N.Y., Nov. 8, 1944; s. Daniel and Faye (Frank) G.; m. Jane Auerbach, Sept. 11, 1982. B.S., CCNY, 1968; M.S., Western Mich. U., 1967; Ph.D., U. Houston, 1972. Lic. Psychologist, Pa. Ptnr. Hay Assocs., N.Y.C., 1972-80; sr. v.p. human resources Amerada Hess Corp., N.Y.C., 1980—. Mem. Am. Psychol. Assn. Office: Amerada Hess Corp 1185 Ave of Americas New York NY 10036

GELFMAN, ROBERT WILLIAM, lawyer; b. N.Y.C., Jan. 22, 1932; s. Irving and Lillian (Meltzer) G.; m. Phyllis Trustman, Dec. 18, 1955; children—Lisa Jane, Peter Trustman. B.S., U. Pa., 1953; LL.B., Harvard U., 1956. Bar: N.Y., Mass. bar 1956. Partner firm Battle, Fowler, Jaffin and Kheel, N.Y.C.; dir. Edward Gray Corp.; past chmn. bd. dirs. Arrow Lock Corp. Former trustee, v.p. Jewish Bd. Guardians; past chmn. bd. Hawthorne Cedar Knolls Sch.; past pres. bd. edn. Served to capt. USAF, 1957-60. Mem. Am. Law Inst., Am. Arbitration Assn., Am. Bar Assn., Assn. bar of City of N.Y., N.Y. County Lawyers Assn. Jewish. Clubs: Harvard (N.Y.C.); Metropolis Country (White Plains, N.Y.). Home: 17 Eton Rd Scarsdale NY 10583 Office: 280 Park Ave New York NY 10017

GELINAS, GRATIEN, playwright, actor; b. St.-Tite, Quebec, Can., Dec. 8, 1909; s. Mathias and GENève (Davidson) G. Student, Ecole des hautes etudes commerciales de Montreal; hon. degrees, U. Toronto, 1951; hon. degrees, U. Sask., 1966, McGill U., 1968, U. N.B.,

1969, Trent U., 1970, Mt. Allison U., 1973. Chmn. Can. Film Devel. Corp., 1969-78; Mem. Can. Nat. Film Bd., 1950-53; vice chmn. Greater Montreal Arts Council, 1957-63; pres. Can. Theatre Center, 1959. Co-founder, La Troupe des Anciens du Coll. de Montreal, 1929-33; mem., Montreal Repertory Theatre, 1933, radio debut, 1934; creator radio series; actor: Le Carrousel de la Gaieté, 1937; creator, actor: revue Fridolinons, 1938-46; plays include Tit-Coq, 1948, Bousille et les Justes (Can. record for number of profl. performances), 1959, Hier les enfants dansaient, 1966; founder, dir., Comédie-Canadienne, Montreal, 1957; founding mem., Nat. Theatre Sch. Can., 1960; screenwriter, producer, co-dir.: Tit-Coq, 1952 (Film of Yr. award Can. Film awards); appeared with, Stratford (Ont.) Shakespeare Festival in, Merry Wives of Windsor, Henry V; dir., actor numerous plays. Named Most Popular Comedian of Yr. Radiomonde, 1939; recipient Grand prix de Theatre Victor-Morin, Soc. St. Jean Baptiste de Montreal, 1967; Order of Can. medal, 1967; spl. award Concert Soc. Jewish People's Schs., 1969. Mem. Union des Artistes de Montreal (past v.p.). Address: 316 Girouard C P 207 Oka PQ J0N 1E0 Canada

GELINAS, JOHN GERALD, public affairs consultant; b. Stroudsburg, Pa., Feb. 24, 1929; s. Anthony J. F. and Margaret E. (Morris) G.; m. Barbara Ann Link, Sept. 6, 1958; children: Cynthia A., John Gerald, Amy Elizabeth, Gregory J., Garrick M. A.A., Keystone Jr. Coll., 1951; B.S. in Public Communication, Boston U., 1953; M.S. (fellow), Boston U., 1954. Public relations intern Alleghany-Young-Kirby Ownership Bd., N.Y.C., 1954; public relations staff asst. N.Y. Central R.R., 1955-56, Mobil Corp., 1956-58; public relations advisor Mobil Oil Nigeria Ltd. and Mobil Exploration Nigeria, Inc., Lagos, 1958-62; sr. public relations advisor Mobil Internat., 1962; account exec. Thomas J. Deegan Co., Inc., 1962-65, asst. v.p., 1965, v.p., 1965-67; dir. corp. communication Nat. Union Electric Corp., 1967-68, exec. asst. to chief exec. officer, cons. public relations, 1968-71; exec. v.p., chief ops. officer Thomas J. Deegan Co., Inc., 1971-73, vice chmn., 1973; sr. v.p., dir. fin. services Edward Gottlieb & Assos., N.Y.C., 1973-76; internat. public affairs cons., pres. John G. Gelinas Assos., Inc., N.Y.C., 1976—; adv. and asst. in various capacities to Govt. of Guyana, several internat. confs., 1981, 82, 83. Contbr. articles to profl. jours. Mem. planning bd. Town of Eastchester, N.Y., 1975-78; exec. bd. Westchester-Putnam council Boy Scouts Am., 1977—, chmn. quality program com. of long range planning com., 1978; mem. exec. council Greater N.Y. Councils, chmn. public relations com., 1967-72; mem. nat. alumni council Boston U., 1971—. Served with U.S. Army, 1947-48. Recipient Robert R. Young-Boston U. award, 1954; PR News Gold Key award, 1970. Mem. Investors Relations Inst. (charter), Internat. Inst. Communications, Nat. Press Club Nigeria (life), Soc. Internat. Devel. (past v.p., exec. bd. N.Y. chpt.), Explorers Club, Classic Car Club Am. (former dir.), Tau Mu Epsilon. Home: 96 Puritan Dr Scarsdale NY 10583 Office: 576 Fifth Ave New York NY 10036

GELINAS, WILLIAM PAUL, assn. exec.; b. Bklyn., Aug. 30, 1930; s. William Joseph and Catherine (Rae) G.; m. Rita Ann Zielinski, May 1, 1954. B.S. in Bus. Adminstrn, U. Hartford, Conn., 1958; M.A. in Adminstrn. and Supervision, Central Mich. U., 1975; M.P.A., Nova U., Fla., 1976, D.P.A., 1980. With Am. Heritage Agy., West Hartford, Conn., 1954—, chmn. bd., 1980—; exec. sec. Am. Assn. Profl. Bridal Cons.'s, West Hartford, 1962—; dir. Heritage Gen. Contractors, Guaranty Bank & Trust Co. Justice of peace, West Hartford, 1960-66, chmn. dist. com., mem. town com., 1960-66. Served to col. U.S. Army, 1956-75. Mem. Am. Soc. Public Adminstrn., Res. Officers Assn. Republican. Roman Catholic. Home: 42 Woodridge Circle West Hartford CT 06107 Office: 104 Park Rd West Hartford CT 06119

GELINEAU, LOUIS EDWARD, clergyman; b. Burlington, Vt., May 3, 1928; s. Leon and Juliette (Baribault) G. Student, St. Michael's Coll., Winooski, Vt., 1946-48; B.A., B.Phil., St. Paul's U., Ottawa, Ont., Can., 1950, L.S.T., 1954; Licentiate Canon Law, Catholic U. Am., 1959; D.R.E., Providence Coll., 1972. Ordained priest Roman Catholic Ch., 1954; asst. chancellor Diocese Burlington, 1959-61, chancellor, 1961-71, vicar gen., 1968-71; bishop of, Providence, 1971—. Office: One Cathedral Sq Providence RI 02903 *

GELLER, ESTHER (BAILEY GELLER), artist; b. Boston, Oct. 26, 1921; d. Harry and Fannie (Geller) G.; m. Harold Shapero, Sept. 21, 1945; 1 dau., Hannah. Diploma, Sch. Boston Mus. Fine Arts, 1943. Tchr. Boston Mus. Sch., 1943, Boris Mursk Sch., 1945-49; art cons. Leonard Morse Hosp., Natick, Mass. One-woman shows, Boris Mirski Art Gallery, Boston, 1945-47, 49, 52, 61, Addison Gallery Am. Art, Children's Art Centre, Andover, Mass., 1953-55, Mayo Gallery, Provincetown, Mass., 1958, Marion (Mass.) Art Centre, 1966, St. Mark's Sch., Southboro, Mass., 1969, Decenter Gallery, Copenhagen, Regis Coll., Weston, Mass., 1970, Am. Acad. Gallery, Rome, (1971), Newton (Mass.) Library, 1973, Newton Art Centre, 1978, Artworks of Wayne, Providence, 1979, group shows include, San Francisco Mus., Va. Mus. Art, Chgo. Art Inst., Worcester Art Mus., U. Ill., Smith Coll., Inst. Contemporary Art, DeCordova Mus., USIA traveling show, USIS circulating exhbn., Far East, Boston Mus. Cabot fellow, 1949; Studios Am. Acad. fellow, 1949-50, 70-71, 75; MacDowell Colony-Yaddo fellow, 1945, 67, 69. Mem. Boston Visual Arts Union, Arts Wayland Assn. Home: 9 Russell Circle Natick MA 01760 Office: Loker Studios 47 Loker St Wayland MA 01778

GELLER, RONALD GENE, physiologist, inst. adminstr.; b. Peoria, Ill., Jan. 15, 1943; s. Harold H. and Rose G.; m. Lois S. Geller, Sept. 5, 1971; children—Andrea, Steven, Lauren. B.S. in Zoology, U. Wis., 1964, Ph.D. in Physiology, 1969. Spl. research fellow Nat. Heart Inst., NIH, 1969-71; sr. staff fellow Nat. Heart, Lung and Blood Inst., NIH, Bethesda, Md., 1971-72; grants asso. NIH, 1972-73; asst. chief, chief hypertension and kidney diseases br. Nat. Heart, Lung and Blood Inst., 1973-78; asso. dir. extramural and collaborative programs Nat. Eye Inst., NIH, 1978—; instr. Found. for Advanced Edn. in Sci.; USPHS trainee, 1966-67. Contbr. articles to profl. jours. Wis. Heart Assn. fellow, 1967-69. Mem. Am. Heart Assn. (mem. med. adv. bd. council for high blood pressure research), Am. Physiol. Soc., Soc. Exptl. Biology and Medicine. Home: 14109 Blazer Ln Silver Spring MD 20906 Office: Nat Inst Health Bethesda MD 20205

GELLERMANN, HENRY, journalist; b. Munich, Ger., Nov. 18, 1912; came to U.S., 1929, naturalized, 1929; s. Max Solomon and Bertha Rosa (Lightman) G.; m. Sylvia Solal, Dec. 8, 1961. Ed., Columbia U., 1934. Fin. reporter UP, 1935-41; partner charge public relations Bache & Co. (investments), N.Y.C., 1964-77; pres. Overseas Press Club Am., N.Y.C., 1977—. Author: Advertising with a Smile, 1954, How to Make Money Make Money, 1959, also articles. Trustee Edward R. Murrow Found.; mem. Overseas Press Club Found.; Past bd. dirs. USO, Knickerbocker Hosp., N.Y.C. Served with maj. AUS, World War II; Korea. Decorated Bronze Star; recipient Honor award Ohio U., 1968, also various commendations. Mem. Public Relations Soc. Am., Soc. Silurians, Comite International des Arts de France (conseilleur, hon. mem.). Club: Nat. Press (Washington). Address: 1111 Park Ave New York NY 10028

GELLERT, GEORGE GEZA, food importing co. exec.; b. N.Y.C., Apr. 15, 1938; s. Imre and Martha (Tessler) G.; m. Barbara Rubin, July 21, 1963; children—Andrew, Amy, Thomas. B.S., Cornell U., 1960, M.B.A., 1962, LL.B., 1963. Bar: N.Y. State bar 1963. Atty. SEC, Washington, 1963-64; v.p., exec. v.p., pres. Atalanta Corp., N.Y.C., 1966—, chmn. bd., 1978—; chmn. U.S.-Rumanian Econ. Council. Served to 1st lt. Office Staff Judge AUS, 1964-66. Decorated Army Commendation medal. Mem. Am. Importers Assn. (dir., exec. com. meat product group), Young President's Orgn. Home: 625 Briarwood Ct Oradell NJ 07649 Office: 17 Varick St New York NY 10013

GELLERT, MICHAEL ERWIN, investment banker; b. Prague, Czechoslovakia, June 15, 1931; s. Oswald Rudolf and Grete (Petschek) G.; m. Mary Ellen Crombie, Jan. 11, 1969; children: John Matthew, Catherine Ann. B.A., Harvard U., 1953; M.B.A., Wharton Sch. Fin. and Commerce, U. Pa., 1955. With Burnham & Co. (name changed to Drexel Burnham Lambert, Inc. 1977), N.Y.C., 1958—, exec. v.p., 1972-73, exec. dir., 1974—; gen. partner Windcrest Partners, N.Y.C.; chmn. bd., dir. Alaska Basic Industries, Anchorage; dir. Coordinated Apparel Inc., N.Y.C., Devon Corp., Oklahoma City, Harvey Group Inc., Woodbury, N.Y., Humana Inc., Louisville, Worldwide Securities Ltd., Bermuda, Worldwide Spl. Fund N.V., Curacao, Syncsort Inc., Englewood Cliffs, N.J., Tierco Group, Inc., Oklahoma City, Bus. Solutions, Inc., Kings Park, N.Y., Drexel Burnham Fund, N.Y.C., Drexel Burnham Lambert Group, Irwin Magnetics, Inc., Ann Arbor, Mich., Irwin Internat., Inc., PC Technologies, Inc., Tab Books, Inc., Blue Ridge Summit, Pa., NAD Electronics, Norwood, Mass. Served with U.S. Army, 1955-57. Clubs: Burning Tree Country (Greenwich, Conn.); Harvard (N.Y.C.). Home: 75 Round Hill Rd Greenwich CT 06830 Office: 60 Broad St New York NY 10004

GELLES, HARRY, executive recruiter; b. N.Y.C., Feb. 23, 1934; s. Paul Phillip and Jeanne (Peterzell) G.; m. Carolyn Stockley Humphreys, June 18, 1956; children: Paul Humphreys, Carolyn Cranston, Harrison Humphreys. A.B. in Govt., Harvard U., 1956, M.B.A., 1958. Syndication mgr. Lee Ackerman Investment Co., Phoenix, 1958; leasing agt., dir. corp. planning and fin., v.p. fin. Del Webb Corp., Phoenix, 1959-66; exec. v.p. MCA Devel. Co., Universal City, Calif., 1966; v.p. Goldman Sachs & Co., Los Angeles, 1967-77; sr. v.p. White Weld, Los Angeles, 1978; mng. dir. Dean Witter Reynolds, Los Angeles, 1979-81; mng. dir., mgr. Los Angeles office Russell Reynolds Assocs., Inc., 1981—; dir. Trico Industries Inc., Crest Steel Corp, Clark Metals, Inc. Treas. Rolling Hills Community Assn., (Calif.), 1978-80; trustee So. Calif. chpt. Nat. Multiple Sclerosis Soc., 1972—, pres., 1977-78, chmn., 1979-80; mem. tech. adv. bd. Dept. commerce, 1974, 76; mem. Citizens' Adv. Com. Los Angeles Olympic Organizing Com. Mem. Newcomen Soc. N.Am. Republican. Clubs: California, Las Caballeros, Portuguese Bend, Harvard. Home: 3 Runningbrand Rd Rolling Hills CA 90274 Office: Russell Reynolds Assocs Inc 333 S Grand Ave 42d Floor Los Angeles CA 90071

GELLES, ROBERT WILLIAM, communications company executive; b. Anchorage, July 12, 1923; s. Gustav A. and Wanda M. (Nowacki) G.; m. Cecile M. Burke, Aug. 13, 1952 (div. 1970); children: Laura, Amalie; m. 2d Sheila N. Zangwill, Oct. 20, 1970; 1 dau., Lesli. B.S., U. Ill., 1948; J.D., St. John's U., 1954. C.P.A., N.Y., N.Y. 1955. Acct. Price, Waterhouse, Arthur Anderson and other cos., N.Y.C., 1948-56; sec. and asst. treas. Pepsi-Cola United Bottlers, N.Y.C., 1956-61; treas. Bernard Relin & Assocs., N.Y.C., 1956-61; assoc. legal counsel Hudson Pulp and Paper Corp., N.Y.C., 1961-63; controller Capital Cities Communications Inc., N.Y.C., 1963-80, treas., 1980—, v.p., 1982—; treas. All-Industry TV Sta. Music License Commn., 1977—. Served with U.S. Army, 1943-45. Democrat. Home: 167 E 67th St New York NY 10021 Office: Capital Cities Communications Inc 24 E 51st St New York NY 10022

GELLHORN, ERNEST ALBERT EUGENE, law school dean; b. Oak Park, Ill., Mar. 30, 1935; s. Ernst and Hilde Betty (Obermeier) G.; m. Jaquelin Ann Silker, Feb. 1, 1958; children: Thomas Ernest, Ann Lois. B.A. cum laude, U. Minn., 1956, LL.B. magna cum laude, 1962. Bar: Ohio bar 1962, Va. bar 1975, Ariz. bar 1976. With firm Jones, Day, Cockley & Reavis, Cleve., 1962-66; prof. law Duke Law Sch., 1966-70, U. Va. Law Sch., 1970-75; dean Coll. Law, Ariz. State U., Tempe, 1975-78, Law Sch., U. Wash., Seattle, 1978-79; T. Munford Boyd prof. U. Va. Law Sch., Charlottesville, 1979-82; dean, Galen J. Roush prof. Case Western Res. U. Sch. Law, Cleve., 1982—; sr. counsel Commn. CIA Activities Within U.S., 1975; cons. in field. Author: Antitrust Law and Economics, 2d edit, 1981; co-author: Administrative Law and Process, 2d edit, 1981, The Administrative Process, 2d edit, 1980. Served to lt. USNR, 1956-59. Mem. Am., Ariz., Va., Ohio bar assns., Phi Beta Kappa, Order of Coif. Home: 3119 Courtland Blvd Shaker Heights OH 44122 Office: Law School Case Western Res U Cleveland OH 44106

GELLHORN, MARTHA, author, fgn. corr.; b. St. Louis; d. George and Edna (Fischel) G.; 1 son, George Alexander. Student, John Burroughs Sch., St. Louis, and, Bryn Mawr Coll. War corr. for Collier's Weekly in, Spain, 1937-38, Finland, 1939, China, 1940-41, Eng., Italy, France and Germany, 1943-45, Java, 1946; war corr. for The Guardian, London, Eng., in Vietnam, 1966, and in Israel, 1967. Author: The Trouble I've Seen, 1936, A Stricken Field, 1940, The Heart of Another, 1941, Liana, 1943, Wine of Astonishment, 1948, The Honeyed Peace, 1953, Two by Two, 1958, The Face of War, 1959, His Own Man, 1961, Pretty Tales for Tired People, 1965, The Lowest Trees Have Tops, 1967, The Weather in Africa, 1978, Travels with Myself and Another, 1978; Contbr. to mags. Address: 72 Cadogan Sq London England SW1

GELLISE, SISTER MARY YVONNE, health system executive, former hospital executive; b. Bay City, Mich., Aug. 21, 1934; d. Levi Joseph and Regina (Savage) G. B.S. in Accounting, U. Detroit, 1960; M.Hosp. Adminstrn., St. Louis U., 1965. Jr. accountant Tripp & Laine, C.P.A.s, Bay City, Mich., 1952-55; joined Sister of Mercy, 1955; bus. mgr. Mercy Med. Center, Dubuque, Iowa, 1960-63; adminstrv. resident Providence Hosp., Seattle, 1964-65; adminstr. Villa Elizabeth, Grand Rapids, Mich., 1965-67; asso. adminstr. St. Joseph Mercy Hosp., Clinton, Iowa, 1967-68; exec. dir. St. Joseph Mercy Hosp., Ann Arbor, Mich., 1968-76; corp. v.p., trustee Sisters of Mercy Health Corp., Farmington Hills, Mich., 1976—; lectr. hosp. adminstrn. Sch. Pub. Health, U. Mich., 1969-76; Dir. Ann Arbor Bank. Pres. Mich. Conf. Cath. Health Care Facilities, 1976; bd. dirs. Mercy Sch. Nursing, Detroit. Named Boss of Year Arbor Charter chpt. Am. Bus. Women's Assn., 1969. Fellow Am. Coll. Hosp. Adminstrs.; mem. Mich. Hosp. Assn. (trustee 1975-79, Homminga award 1981), Ann Arbor C. of C. (bd. dirs. 1971-72), Southeast Mich. Hosp. Council (physician/hosp. relations com. 1983—). Address: 28550 Eleven Mile Rd Farmington Hills MI 48018

GELLMAN, ISAIAH, assn. exec.; b. Akron, Ohio, Feb. 19, 1928; s. Meyer and Pearl (Milker) G.; m. Lola Malkis, Dec. 27, 1947; children—Paula, Judith. B.S. in Chem. Engring, CCNY, 1947; M.S., Rutgers U., 1950, Ph.D., 1952. Research asso. Rutgers U., 1948-52; process engr. Abbott Labs., 1952-56; mem. staff Nat. Council Paper Industry for Air and Stream Improvement, N.Y.C., 1956—, tech. dir., 1969-77, exec. v.p., 1977—; lectr. Johns Hopkins U., 1961-65. NIH fellow, 1948-52. Fellow TAPPI; mem. Water Pollution Control Fedn., Air Pollution Control Assn., Am. Inst. Chem. Engrs., N.Y. Acad. Scis., Sigma Xi. Address: 260 Madison Ave New York NY 10016

GELLMAN, WILLIAM, emeritus rehabilitation administration educator; b. N.Y.C., Sept. 30, 1911; s. Benjamin and Lena (Eisenberg) G.; m. Rhoda Honig, July 31, 1934; 1 dau., Laura Susan. B.S., Columbia U., 1931; M.A., NYU, 1934; Ph.D., U. Chgo., 1955. Dir. Jewish Vocat. Service, Chgo., 1946-78; mem. faculty DePaul U., Chgo., 1969—, adj. prof., 1969-78, prof., chmn. dept. rehab. adminstrn., 1978-81, prof. emeritus, 1981—; dir. Easter Seal Research Found., 1956-82; Bd. dirs. Nat. Easter Seal Soc. Crippled Children and Adults, Inc., Chgo., 1981-83, cons., 1983—; Bd. dirs. Options, Inc., 1976-81; cons. Ill. Dept. Mental Health, 1980-82, rehab. agys., Australia, Gt. Britain, India, Israel, Pakistan, Sweden, Yugoslavia; mem. Ability Based Upon Long Experience, Inc., 1976-81, Ill. Epilepsy, 1977-80; mem. long-range planning com. Roosevelt U., 1969-75; mem. Nat. Adv. Com. Vocat. Edn., 1971-73. Contbr. articles to various publs. Served with U.S. Army, 1943-44. Recipient W. F. Faulkes award Nat. Rehab. Assn., 1958; Rehab. Services Adminstrn. Commr.'s award, 1975; Disting. Service award Nat. Rehab. Counseling Assn., 1978; Disting. Career award Nat. Assn. Rehab. Facilities, 1983; fellow World Rehab. Fund Internat. Exchange of Experts, 1982-83. Fellow Am. Psychol. Assn.; mem. Am. Personnel and Guidance Assn., Nat. Assn. Social Workers, Acad. Cert. Social Workers, Am. Rehab. Counseling Assn., Sigma Xi. Home: 3500 Lake Shore Dr Chicago IL 60657 Office: Council Rehab Affiliates 8 S Michigan Ave Suite 1408 Chicago IL 60603

GELL-MANN, MURRAY, theoretical physicist; b. N.Y.C., Sept. 15, 1929; s. Arthur and Pauline (Reichstein) Gell-M.; m. J. Margaret Dow, Apr. 19, 1955 (dec. 1981); children: Elizabeth, Nicholas. B.S., Yale, 1948; Ph.D., Mass. Inst. Tech., 1951. Mem. Inst. for Advanced Study, 1951; instr. U. Chgo., 1952-53, asst. prof., 1953-54, asso. prof., 1954, Calif. Inst. Tech., Pasadena, 1955-56, prof., 1956—, now R.A. Millikan prof. physics.; Mem. Pres.'s Sci. Adv. Com., 1969-72. Author: (with Y. Ne'eman) Eightfold Way. Regent Smithsonian Instn., 1974—; bd. dirs. J.D. and C.T. MacArthur Found., 1979—. NSF post doctoral fellow, vis. prof. Coll. de France and U. Paris, 1959-60; Recipient Dannie Heineman prize Am. Phys. Soc., 1959; E.O. Lawrence Meml. award AEC, 1966; Franklin medal, 1967; Carty medal Nat. Acad. Scis., 1968; Research Corp. award, 1969; Nobel prize in physics, 1969. Fellow Am. Phys. Soc.; mem. Nat. Acad. Scis., Royal Soc. (fgn.), Am. Acad. Arts and Scis. Club: Cosmos. Research theory of weak interactions, research dispersion relations. Developed eightfold way theory and Quark scheme developed strangeness theory. Office: Dept Physics Calif Inst Tech Pasadena CA 91125

GELMAN, DAVID GRAHAM, journalist; b. Bklyn., Nov. 1, 1926; s. George and Rose (Shulman) G.; m. Elaine Edith Rodkinson, Apr. 6, 1952; children: Eric Adam, Andrew Seth, Amy Miriam. Student, Bklyn. Coll., 1947-55. Reporter, writer N.Y. Post, 1943-62; evaluation officer, dir. spl. projects Peace Corps, Washington, 1962-66; asso. editor nat. affairs and spl. projects Newsweek, N.Y.C., 1966-68; v.p. for edn. U.S. Research & Devel., N.Y.C., 1968-69; editor editorial pages, chief corr., nat. editor Newsday, Garden City, N.Y., 1969-75; gen. editor Newsweek, N.Y.C., 1975-78, sr. writer, 1978—. Served with USNR, 1944-46. Recipient Nat. Mag. award, 1968; Overseas Press Club citation for excellence, 1973; Newspaper Guild Page One award, 1978. Home: 229 W 78th St New York NY 10024 Office: 444 Madison Ave New York NY

GELMAN, FRANK HERMAN, lawyer; b. Phila., May 11, 1912; s. Samuel and Fannie (Perchin) G.; m. Rivie Perlmutter, Mar. 17, 1940; children—Norris E., Marcia. A.B., Temple U., 1932; J.D., U. Pa., 1935. Bar: Pa. bar 1935. Since practiced in, Phila.; mem. firm Mesirov, Gelman, Jaffe, Cramer & Jameison, 1959—; lectr. Am., Pa. law insts.; also legal edn. program Pa. Bar. Assn.; counsel, chief negotiator Phila. Sch. Bd. in collective bargaining, 1966-69; pub. employer collective bargaining cons. to Northampton Sch. Dist. Author: course materials Pennsylvania Leases, 1958, Pennsylvania Mortgages and Their Enforcement, 1965, The Real Estate Transaction, 1964. Served with USNR, 1943-46. Mem. Am., Pa., Phila. bar assns. Clubs: Union League, Philadelphia Lawyers. Home: 2401 Pennsylvania Ave Philadelphia PA 19130 Office: Fidelity Bldg Philadelphia PA 19109

GELMAN, LARRY, actor; b. Bklyn., Nov. 3, 1930; s. Frank and Dorothy (Slepakoff) G. Student, CCNY, 1954-55. Appeared on numerous television shows, 1965—, including, The Odd Couple, Bob Newhart Show, Maude, Mary Tyler Moore Show, Eight Is Enough, Kojak, Raid On Entebbe, Triangle Factory Fire, Barney Miller; appeared in: feature films Super Dad, O'Hara's Wife, Dreamscape; short subject, live action film A Different Approach (nominated for Motion Picture Acad. award 1979); (Nominated Acad. TV Arts and Scis. award for outstanding single performance by a supporting actor in a comedy or drama series 1977-78). Served with USMC, 1951-53. Mem. Screen Actors Guild, Am. Guild Variety Artists, Actors Equity Assn., AFTRA, Acad. TV Arts and Scis. Jewish.

GELMIS, JOSEPH STEPHAN, film critic, author; b. Bklyn., Sept. 28, 1935; s. Steve Andrew and Tillie (De Pietro) G.; m. Deborah Dobski, Nov. 21, 1973; children by previous marriage—Steven Keith, Susan Valerie. B.A., Bklyn. Coll., 1956; M.S. in Journalism, Columbia, 1960. With Newsday, 1960—, film critic, 1964—; syndicated columnist, 1971—; coll. lectr.; asst. prof. theater arts dept. State U. N.Y. at Stony Brook. Host radio and TV shows; Author: The Film Director as Superstar, 1970. Served with USAF, 1956-59. Recipient Polk award for journalism, 1961. Mem. N.Y. Film Critics Circle (chmn. 1969-70, 73-74), Nat. Soc. Film Critics. Office: NY Bur Newsday 1500 Broadway Suite 2207 New York NY 10036

GELPI, ALBERT JOSEPH, educator, literary critic; b. New Orleans, July 19, 1931; s. Albert Joseph and Alice Marie (Delaup) G.; m. Barbara Charlesworth, June 14, 1965; children: Christopher Francis Cecil, Adrienne Catherine Ardelle. A.B., Loyola U., New Orleans, 1951; M.A., Tulane U., 1956; Ph.D., Harvard U., 1962. Asst. prof. Harvard U., 1962-68; asso. prof. Stanford U., 1968-74, prof. Am. lit., 1974—, Wm. Robertson Coe prof. Am. lit., 1978—, chmn. Am. studies program, 1980-83, asso. dean grad. study and research, 1980—. Author: Emily Dickinson: The Mind of the Poet, 1965, The Tenth Muse: The Psyche of the American Poet, 1975; editor: The Poet in America: 1650 to the Present, 1974, (with Barbara Charlesworth Gelpi) Adrienne Rich's Poetry, 1974, Cambridge Studies in American Literature and Culture. Served with U.S. Army, 1951-53. Guggenheim fellow, 1977-78. Mem. MLA. Democrat. Roman Catholic. Home: 870 Tolman Dr Stanford CA 94305 Office: Dept English Stanford U Stanford CA 94305

GELSEY, STEPHEN IAN, fin. exec.; b. Budapest, Hungary, Jan. 22, 1925; came to U.S., 1949, naturalized, 1955; s. Eugene and Melanie (Lazar) G.; m. Elinor Anne Harris, Mar. 21, 1959; children—Andrew, Peter, Jonathan. Ph.D., Tech. U., Budapest, Hungary, 1947; M.B.A., U. Colo., 1950. Staff accountant Price Waterhouse & Co., Chgo., 1950-52; staff accountant Touche Ross & Co., Los Angeles, 1952-55; div. mgr., controller United Piece Dye Works, Los Angeles, 1955-59; treas. Good Humor Co. Calif., Los Angeles, 1960-62; v.p., treas. Benson-Lehner Corp., Van Nuys, Calif., 1962-67; v.p. finance and adminstrn. Ebsco Industries, Inc., Birmingham, Ala., 1967-69; v.p. finance Nat. Convenience Stores, Inc., Houston, 1969-80; pres. Bunker Hill Co.

Inc., Houston, 1980—. Vice pres. Westwood Young Republicans, 1957-58. Mem. Financial Execs. Inst., Am. Inst. C.P.A.'s. Office: 5 Powderhorn Ln Houston TX 77024

GELSTHORPE, EDWARD, cheese manufacturing company executive; b. Phila., 1921. Student, Hamilton Coll., 1942. With Gelsthrope assocs., 1945-48; v.p., dir. mktg. Bristol Myers, 1948-60; v.p. Colgate Palmolive Co., 1960-62; pres., chief exec. officer Ocean Spray Cranberries, 1962-68; pres. Hunt Wesson Foods, 1968-72, Gillett Co., 1972-74; exec. v.p. United Brands Co., 1975-77; pres., dir. H.P. Hood Inc., 1975-77; dir. Clearfield Cheese, Inc., Curwensville, Pa., 1977, pres., dir., 1979—. Address: Clearfield Inc PA Cooper Rd Curwensville PA 16833 *

GELTZER, HOWARD E., public relations executive; b. Hazleton, Pa., Oct. 23, 1936; s. Nathan and Sally (Harris) G.; m. Shelia Simon, Sept. 10, 1967; children: Jeremy, Gabriel. B.S., Northwestern U., 1958, M.S., 1959. Advt. pub. relations staff Gen. Electric Co., Plainville, Conn., 1960-66, Litton Industries, Mount Vernon, N.Y., 1966-67; mgr. advt. pub. relations McGraw-Hill, N.Y.C., 1967-68, Family Health Mag., 1969-72; pub. relations mgr., pres. Geltzer & Co., N.Y.C., 1972—; ad hoc asst. prof. mktg. NYU Sch. Continuing Edn., N.Y.C., 1968-77. Club: Gipsy Trail (Camel, N.Y.) (v.p. 1978-80). Office: Geltzer & Co Inc 1700 Broadway New York NY 10019

GEMERY, HENRY ALBERT, economics educator; b. Shelton, Conn., Sept. 5, 1930; s. John and Mary (Benco) G.; m. Pamela Joyce Malcolm, Aug. 30, 1958; childen: John Malcolm, Pamela Ann. B.S., So. Conn. State Coll., 1952; M.B.A., Harvard U., 1958; Ph.D., U. Pa., 1967; M.A. hon., Colby Coll., 1977. Asst. dir. admissions Colby Coll., Waterville, Maine, 1958-61, instr., asst. prof., assoc. prof. Dana prof. econs., 1961—. Contbg. author, co-editor: The Uncommon Market, 1979; author: monograph Emigration from the British Isles, 1980. Served to 1st lt., C.E. U.S. Army, 1953-56. NDEA fellow U. Pa., 1963-65, NIH postdoctoral fellow, 1968-69; Charles Warren fellow Harvard U., 1982-83. Mem. Am. Econs. Assn., Royal Econ. Soc., Econ. History Assn., Internat. Union for Sci. Study of Population. Home: RFD 1 Oakland ME 04901 Office: Colby Coll Mayflower Hill Waterville ME 04963

GEMIGNANI, MICHAEL CAESAR, computer scientist, lawyer, clergyman; b. Balt., Feb. 23, 1938; s. Hugo J. and Dorothy G.; m. Carol A. Federico, June 30, 1962; children: Stephen, Susan. B.A., U. Rochester, 1962; M.S., U. Notre Dame, 1964, Ph.D., 1965; J.D., Ind. U., 1980. Asst. prof. math. SUNY, Buffalo, 1965-68; asso. prof. Smith Coll., 1968-72; prof., chmn. dept. math. scis. Ind. U.-Purdue U. at Indpls., 1972-81; dean Coll. Scis. and Humanities, Ball State U., Muncie, Ind., 1981—; ordained to ministry Episcopal Ch., 1973; vicar St. Francis Episcopal Ch., Zionsville, Ind., 1974-79; pres. Met. Indpls. Campus Ministry, 1975-76, bd. dirs., 1974-81; mem. adv. bd. Ind. Office Campus Ministry, 1983-84. Author: books, including Elementary Topology, 1967, 2d rev. edit., 1972, Introductory Real Analysis, 1970, Law and the Computer, 1981; composer. Mem. Am. Math. Soc. (chmn. N.E. sect. 1970-71, chmn. Ind. sect. 1975-76), AAAS, ABA, Scribes, Sigma Xi, Kappa Sigma. Research, publs. in math. Home: 3556 Johnson Circle Muncie IN 47304 Office: NQ 112 Ball State U Muncie IN 47304

GEMMELL, JOSEPH P., banker; b. Bklyn., July 23, 1935; s. Joseph and Rose (McCarrol) G.; m. Diane Kormanik, Sept. 7, 1957; children: Joseph, Donald, Dennis, Barbara. B.B.A. in Finance, Pace U., 1967. With First Nat. City Bank, N.Y.C., 1953-57; auditor Fed. Res. Bank N.Y., 1957-64; auditing officer S.I. Savs. Bank, 1964-69; v.p. planning Savs. Bank Trust Co., N.Y.C., 1969-74; sr. v.p. Independence Savs. Bank, 1974-83; pres., chief exec. officer Perth Amboy Savs. Instn. (N.J.), 1983—; dir. Institutional Group Info. Corp. Treas. Mariners Family Home, 1968-69; mem. Bay Terrace Civic Assn., 1964—. Served with AUS, 1958-60. Mem. Savs. Banks Auditors-Controllers N.Y. State, Nat. Assn. Mut. Savs. Banks, Bank Adminstrn. Inst. Club: Great Kills Yacht (S.I.). Lodge: Rotary. Home: 103 Bay Terr Staten Island NY 10306 Office: Perth Amboy Savings Instn Smith and Maple St Perth Amboy NJ 08861

GEMMETT, ROBERT JAMES, university dean, English educator; b. Schenectady, Mar. 11, 1936; s. A James and Dorothy M. (MacFarlane) G.; m. Kendra B. Baxter, Jan 24, 1964; children: Stephen, Scott, David, Kerry. B.A. cum laude, Siena Coll., 1959; M.A., U. Mass., 1962; Ph.D., Syracuse U., 1967. Instr. Clarkson Coll. Postdam, N.Y., 1964-65; assoc. prof. English SUNY, Brokport, 1965-70, prof., 1970—, chmn. dept., 1975-79, Dean Humanities, 1979-82, dean letters and scis., 1982—. Author: William Beckford, 1977; editor: Biographical Memoirs of Extraordinary Painters, 1969, Dreams, Waking Thoughts and Incidents, 1971; author: Poets and Men of Letters, 1975. Served as 2d lt. U.S. Army, 1959. Recipient Chancellor's Excellence in Teaching award SUNY, 1975; fellow, research grantee SUNY, 1967-69, recipient, 1971, fellow, research grantee, 1977. MEM. Am. Assn. for Higher Educators; mem. Assn. Am. Colls., Am. Studies Assn. Office: Coll Letters and Sci SUNY Brookport NY 14420

GEMMILL, ELIZABETH H., lawyer, banker; b. Phila., Dec. 7, 1945; d. Kenneth W. and Helen H. G.; m. Douglas B. Richardson, July 15, 1977; 1 dau., Katherine Preston Richardson. A.B., Bryn Mawr Coll., 1967; J.D., Boston U., 1970. Bar: Mass. bar 1970, Pa. bar 1973. Asso. firm vom Baur, Coburn, Simmons & Turtle, Boston, 1970-71; staff atty. Cape Cod Legal Services, Inc., Hyannis, Mass., 1971-73; asst. dist. atty. City of Phila., 1973-74; atty., asst. sec. Girard Bank, Phila., 1974-75, sec., treas., counsel, 1975-76, v.p. customer services, 1976-78, v.p., gen. auditor, 1979-81, sr. v.p. personnel dept., 1981-83, sr. v.p., regional banking group head, 1983—; dir. Am. Water Works, Inc. Active Children's Country Week Assn., Com. of 70, United Way, Contact Phila.; treas. Butera for Gov. Com.; bd. dirs. Met. YMCA Phila. and Vicinity, 1979—, Presbyn.-U. Pa. Med. Center, 1982—; Trustee United Way Eastern Pa., 1977—, Exec. com., 1981—; Bd. dirs. WHYY Inc., 1981—, Zool. Soc. Phila., 1982—. Mem. ABA, Pa., Phila. bar assns., Am. Soc. Corp. Secs. (pres. Middle Atlantic group), Nat. Investors Relations Inst., Forum for Exec. Women, Phila. Coll. Textiles and Sci., Greater Phila. Fedn. Settlements, Pa. Bankers Assn. (governing council 1982—), Third Dist. Automated Clearing House, Nat. Found. Women's Health. Home: 3817 The Oak Road Philadelphia PA 19101 Office: Girard Bank Girard Plaza Philadelphia PA 19101

GEMMILL, ROBERT ANDREW, lawyer; b. Marion, Ind., Sept. 12, 1911; s. Willard B. and Florence (Jones) G.; m. Lottie Wine Lugar, Apr. 25, 1970. A.B., Ind. U., 1932, J.D., 1934. Bar: Ind. bar 1934. Since practiced in, Marion; sr. partner firm Gemmill Browne Torrance Spitzer & Herriman (and predecessors), 1935-74; of counsel Browne Torrance Spitzer Herriman & Browne, 1975—; Mem. bd. law examiners Ind. Supreme Ct., 1956-60, pres., 1958-59; mem. Gov. Ind. Probate Study Commn., 1956-64; vis. com. Ind. U. Sch. Law, 1964-74; bd. dirs. Ind. Bar Found., 1961-75, pres., 1965-66. Served to lt. comdr. USNR, 1942-45; comdr. Res. Decorated Navy Commendation medal. Fellow Am. Bar Found., Ind. Bar Found. (charter); mem. ABA (ho. dels. 1962-64), Ind. Bar Assn. (bd. mgrs. 1954-56, bd. mgrs. 61-65, bd. mgrs. 69-70, pres. 1963-64, chmn. ho. of dels. 1969-70), Grant County Bar Assn. (pres. 1951-52), Fifth Dist. Bar Assn. (pres. 1935-36), Indpls. Bar Assn., Nat. Conf. Bar Pres. (council 1964-65), Am. Judicature Soc. (dir. 1967-71), Am. Legion, Delta Upsilon, Phi Delta Phi. Republican. Episcopalian. Clubs: Mason (33 deg., Shriner), Mecca, Meshingomesia Country (Marion); Columbia (Indpls.). Home: Shadeville Farm 5760 S Strawtown Pike PO Box 927 Marion IN 46952 Office: 122 E 4th St PO Box 927 Marion IN 46952

GENDELL, GERALD STANLEIGH, consumer products company executive; b. Stamford, Conn., June 14, 1929; s. Irving and Henrietta (Lund) G.; m. s. Marion F. Belvin, July 28, 1952; children: Carin Gaye, Danna Joyce, Adrian Leigh, Jeffrey Lund, David Blake, Marc Steven, Bradley Howard. B.S., N.Y. U., 1949. With Procter & Gamble Co., Cin., 1954—, dir. community affairs and contbns., 1976-80, mgr. external affairs div., 1980, mgr. public affairs div., 1981—, v.p., trustee Procter & Gamble Fund,. Trustee Glen Manor Home, 1978-80; trustee Queen City Housing Corp., Cin., 1981—; bd. dirs. Ohio Council on Econ. Edn.; trustee Cin. Local Initiative Support Corp.; mem. met. adv. council U. Cin.; mem. Cin Mayor's Com. on Econ. Devel. Served to 1st lt. U.S. Army, 1950-53. Mem. Public Affairs Council Am. (dir. 1981—), Greater Cin. C. of C. (v.p., trustee), Conf. Bd. Clubs: Bankers, Wyoming. Office: 301 E 6th St Cincinnati OH 45201 *

GENDLIN, FRANCES O., magazine editor; b. N.Y.C.; d. Julius A. and Juliet (Neustadtl) Oshlag; (div.)children: Judith Ann, Gerry. Ed., U. Chgo., 1956. Mng. editor Psychotherapy: Theory, Research and Practice, 1964-69; prodn. editor Bull. Atomic Scientists, 1969-73; environ. editor The Hyde Parker, 1972-73; exec. asst. to pres. Aspen (Colo.) Inst. Humanistic Studies, 1973-74; research coordinator N.Y. State Council Environ. Advisers, 1974-75; editor Sierra, San Francisco, 1975—; dir. public affairs Sierra Club, 1977—. Editor: Against Breaking and Entering: Let's Stand Together, 1972. Recipient certificate appreciation EPA, 1975. Mem. Sigma Delta Chi. Home: 405 Davis Ct San Francisco CA 94111 Office: 530 Bush St San Francisco CA 94108

GENDRON, EDWARD CHARLES, steel company executive; b. Uxbridge, Mass., July 1, 1928; s. Charles L. and Grace E. (Wilmot) G.; m. May P. Gagnon, Sept. 6, 1948; children—Judy, Jay. Student, Coll. of Holy Cross, 1945-47; B.B.A., U. Detroit, 1959. Mgr. mktg. adminstrn. RCA, Needham, Mass., 1962-64; pres., treas. AcraMation, Inc., North Adams, Mass., 1964; plant controller Internat. Tel. & Tel. Corp., Clinton, Mass., 1965-66, divisional controller, Morton Grove, Ill., 1966; v.p. Crucible Steel Co., Pitts., 1967-68, pres., 1968-69, Midland Ross Corp., Cleve., 1969—. Home: 421 Darbys Run Bay Village OH 44140 Office: 20600 Chagrin Blvd Cleveland OH 44122

GENDRON, JOHN WILBROD, oil executive; b. Washington, July 30, 1919; s. Ulric Joseph and Louise M. (Nash) G.; m. Mary Sullivan, Mar. 5, 1946; children: John Michael, Robert Patrick, David Andrew. B.A., U. Oreg., 1940; postgrad., U. San Francisco Law Sch., 1946-48, Georgetown U. Law Sch. With Tidewater Oil Corp., 1946-59, asst. gen. mgr. Eastern div., N.Y.C., 1958-59; gen. mgr. transp. and supply Richfield Oil Corp. (merger Atlantic Refining Co. and Richfield into Atlantic Richfield Co. 1966), Los Angeles, 1959-62, v.p., gen. mgr. mfg. and transp., 1962-66, sr. v.p. public affairs, 1966—, also dir. Bd. dirs. Am. Heart Assn.; bd. govs. Arthritis Found.; bd. dirs., chmn. allocations com. U. So. Calif. Bldg. Funds. Served to lt. comdr. USN, 1942-46. Mem. Western Oil and Gas Assn. (pres.), Petroleum Club Los Angeles, Am. Petroleum Inst., Twenty-Five Year Club Petroleum Industry, Delta Upsilon. Clubs: Calif. (Los Angeles); Internat., Pisces (Washington). Office: Atlantic Richfield Co 515 S Flower St Suite 5037 Los Angeles CA 90071 *

GENDRON, ODORE JOSEPH, bishop; b. Manchester, N.H., Sept. 13, 1921; s. Francis and Valida (Rouleau) G. Student, St. Charles Borromeo Sem., Can., U. Ottawa, 1942-47. Ordained priest Roman Catholic Ch., 1947; asso. pastor Angel Guardian Ch., Berlin, N.H., 1947-52, Sacred Heart Ch., Lebanon, N.H., 1952-60, St. Louis Ch., Nashua, N.H., 1962-65; pastor Our Lady of Lourdes Ch., Pittsfield, N.H., 1965-67, St. Augustine Ch., Manchester, N.H., 1967-71; monsignor, 1970, consecrated bishop of, Manchester, 1975—, episcopal vicar for religious, 1972-74, episc. vicar for clergy, 1974—. Office: 153 Ash St PO Box 310 Manchester NH 03105 *

GENEEN, HAROLD SYDNEY, communications company executive; b. Bournemouth, Eng., Jan. 22, 1910; came to U.S., 1911, naturalized, 1918; s. S. Alexander and Aida (DeCruciani) G.; m. June Elizabeth Hjelm, Dec. 1949. B.S. in Accounting and Fin, NYU, 1934; grad., Advanced Mgmt. Program, Harvard; LL.D. (hon.), Lafayette Coll., PMC Colls. C.P.A., N.Y., Ill. Accountant and analyst Mayflower Assos., 1932-34; sr. accountant Lybrand, Ross Bros. & Montgomery, 1934-42; chief accountant Am. Can Co., 1942-46; controller Bell & Howell Co., Chgo., 1946-50, Jones & Laughlin Steel Corp., Pitts., 1950-56; exec. v.p., dir. Raytheon Mfg. Co., Waltham, Mass., 1956-59; pres. ITT, 1959-73, chief exec., 1959-77, dir., 1959-83, chmn. bd., 1964-79, chmn. exec. com., 1974-80, chmn. emeritus, 1980—, also dir. fgn. subs., affiliated cos.; adv. com. Uptown br. Bankers Trust Co. Bd. dirs. Internat. Rescue Con.; mem. nat. council Salk Inst. Biol. Studies, 1977—; treas. Voice Found. Decorated grand officer Order of Merit, Peru; comdr. Order of the Crown, Belgium; Grand Cross of Civil Merit; Grand Cross of Isabella Cath. Mothers of the Americas, Spain; co-recipient 5th Ann. Communications award ICD Rehab. and Research Center, 1976. Mem. Am. Inst. C.P.A.'s, Financial Execs. Inst., Soc. C.P.A.'s N.Y., Internat. C. of C. (trustee U.S. council). Episcopalian. Clubs: Duquesne (Pitts.); Oakmont Country, Braeburn Country, The Links, Oyster Harbors, Union League (N.Y.C.); Harvard (Boston). *

GENEL, MYRON, pediatrics educator; b. York, Pa., Jan. 6, 1936; s. Victor and Florence (Mowitz) G.; m. Phyllis Norman Borkman, Aug. 25, 1968; chidlren: Eliabeth, Jennifer, Abby. Grad., Moravian Coll., 1957; M.D., U. Pa., 1961; M.A. hon., Yale U., 1983. Diplomate: Am. Bd. Pediatrics. Intern Mt. Sinai Hosp., N.Y.C., 1961-62; resident in pediatrics Children's Hosp. Phila., 1962-64; trainee pediatric endocrinology Johns Hopkins Hosp., Balt., 1966-67; instr. pediatrics U. Pa. Sch. Medicine, 1967-71; spl. postdoctoral fellow NIH, assoc. physician Children's Hosp. Phila., 1967-68, 1969-71; mem. faculty Yale U. Sch. Medicine, New Haven, 1971—, prof., 1981—; attending physician Yale-New Haven Hosp., 1971—; program dir. Children's Clin. Research Ctr., 1971—, dir. pediatric endocrinology, 1971—; cons. Newington Children's Hosp., Hosp. St. Raphael, also Milford, Norwalk, Stamford hosps.; Robert Wood Johnson Health Policy fellow Inst. Medicine, Nat. Acad. Scis., Washington, 1982-83; mem. genetic adv. bd. State of Conn.; mem. med. adv. bd. New Eng. Congenital Hypothyroidism Collaborative; cons. subcom. investigations and oversight com. sic. and tech. U.S. Ho. of Reps., 1982-84; dir. Com. Organ Donation Edn. Contbr. articles to profl. jours. Served as capt. U.S. Army, 1964-66. Recipient ann. award Conn. Campaign Against Cooley's Anemia, 1979. Mem. AAAS, Am. Acad. Pediatrics (task force organ transplants), Am. Diabetes Assn. (co-recipient Jonathan May award 1979), Am. Fedn. Clin. Research, Am. Pub. Health Assn., Am. Pediatric Soc., Am. Soc. Bone and Mineral Research, Assn. Program Dirs., Conn. Endocrine Soc., Endocrine Soc. (pub. affairs com.), Lawson Wilkins Pediatric Endocrine Soc., Soc. Pediatric Research, Sigma Xi. Democrat. Jewish. Home: 30 Richard Sweet Dr Woodbridge CT 06525 Office: PO Box 3333 New Haven CT 06510

GENEST, JACQUES, physician, research administrator, educator; b. Montreal, Que., Can., May 29, 1919; s. Rosario and Annette (Girouard) G.; m. Estelle Deschamps, Oct. 3, 1953; children: Paul, Suzanne, Jacques, Marie, Helene. B.A., Coll. Jean de Brebeuf, Montreal, 1937; M.D., U. Montreal, 1942; LL.D. (hon.), Queen's U., 1966, U. Toronto, Ont., Can., 1970, U. Ottawa, Ont., Can., 1983, D.Sc., Laval U., Quebec, Que., 1973, Sherbrooke U., 1974, Meml. U. Nfld., 1978, St. Xavier U., 1983. Intern Harvard Med. Sch., Boston, 1938, 39; resident Hôtel-Dieu Hosp., Montreal, 1942-45, Johns Hopkins Hosp., Balt., 1945-48, Harvard Sch. Chemistry, Boston, 1948, Rockefeller Hosp. Med. Research, N.Y.C., 1948-51; cons. practice medicine specializing in nephrology, endocrinology and internal medicine, dir. clin. research physician Hôtel-Dieu Hosp., Montreal, 1952—; prof. medicine U. Montreal, 1965—; prof. exptl. medicine McGill U., Montreal, 1960—; sci. dir. Clin. Research Inst. Montreal, 1965—; dir. Merck & Co., Rahway, N.J., Montreal Trust Co. Editor: (with Erich Koiw) Hypertension, 1972, (with Erich Koiw and Otto Kuchel) Hypertension: Physiopathology and Treatment, 1977, 2d edit., 1983. Decorated companion Order of Can.; recipient award Gairdner Found., 1963; Archambault medal Can. Assn. Advancement of Sci., 1965; Stouffer prize Am. Heart Assn., Cleve., 1969; Marie-Victorin Sci. prize Govt. Que., Que., 1977; Royal Bank award, 1980; Sims Commonwealth travelling prof., 1970. Fellow Royal Coll. Physicians and Surgeons Can., A.C.P., Royal Soc. Can. (Flavelle medal and award 1968); mem. Peripatetic Club U.S.A., Assn. Am. Physicians, Am. Clin. and Climatol. Assn., Am. Heart Assn. Roman Catholic. Clubs: St.-Denis (Montreal); Century Assn. and Club (N.Y.C.). Home: 1171 Mont-Royal Blvd Montreal Canada PQ H2V 2H6 Office: 110 Pine Ave W Montreal Canada PQ H2W 1R7

GENG, EDWARD JOSEPH, banker, former government official; b. Queens, N.Y., Feb. 9, 1931; s. William and Vera (Scanlan) G.; m. Arlene Fuchs, Sept. 7, 1957; children—Alan Edward, Glenn William, Scott Matthew. Student, Manhattan Coll., 1948-49, Fordham U., 1949-51; B.B.A., St. Johns U., 1957; M.B.A., N.Y. U., 1962; grad., Stonier Grad. Sch. Banking, 1966. With Gt. A & P Tea Co., N.Y.C., 1949-57; with Fed. Res. Bank of N.Y., 1957-69, asst. sec., 1966-67, asst. v.p. open market ops., 1968-69, 70-71; spl. asst. to sec. for debt mgmt. Treasury Dept., Washington, 1969-70; v.p. govt. securities Paine, Webber, Jackson & Curtis, Inc., N.Y.C., 1971-77; asso. Hilliard Farber & Co., Inc., N.Y.C., 1977-79; sr. v.p., treas. Baer Am. Banking Corp., N.Y.C., 1979-82; sr. v.p. Fed. Res. Bank, N.Y.C., 1982—. Served with AUS, 1951-53. Recipient Money Marketeers award for U.S. Treasury bills N.Y. U., 1962. Home: 1632 Demott Ct North Merrick NY 11566 Office: Fed Res Bank 33 Liberty St New York NY 10045

GENGE, WILLIAM HARRISON, advertising executive, writer; b. Warren, Pa., May 7, 1923; s. Valleau Francis and Beatrice (Badger) G.; m. Beverly Ann Milway, June 23, 1945; children: Deborah Ann, William Dean. B.A., U. Pitts., 1948; grad., Internat. Mktg. Inst., Harvard U., 1967. Writer, Bull. Index, Pitts., 1947-48; editor Gulf Oil Corp., 1948-53; with Ketchum, MacLeod & Grove, Inc., 1953—, sr. v.p., 1965-68, exec. v.p., 1968-70, pres., 1970—, chmn., 1979—, also dir. Bd. dirs. Citizens Choice, U.S. C. of C. Found., United Way of Allegheny County, Allegheny Gen. Hosp., Health Research and Services Found., Pitts. Ballet Theatre; pres. Pitts. Youth Symphony; bd. dirs., v.p. Pitts. Symphony Soc. Served to 1st lt. USAAF, 1942-46. Decorated Purple Heart, D.F.C. with oak leaf cluster. Mem. Phi Gamma Delta. Republican. Presbyn. (elder). Clubs: Pitts. Golf, Duquesne, University, Fox Chapel, Rolling Rock (Pitts.); Laurel Valley (Ligonier, Pa.); River Oaks Country (Houston). Prisoner of war, 1944-45. Home: 725 Devonshire St Pittsburgh PA 15213 Office: 4 Gateway Center Pittsburgh PA 15222 *I'm not sure that I am a success. I'd say that whatever degree of achievement I've attained is due to unflagging optimism, perseverance and effort, a Christian outlook at least 50% of the time, and recognition that no man can do it alone. You need friends and supporters all along the way.*

GENGER, ARIE, retail and industrial company executive; b. Tel Aviv, July 10, 1945; U.S., 1967, naturalized, 1978; s. Shraga and Dora (Menkes) G.; m. Dalia Cohen, July 23, 1967; 1 child, Sagi. B.B.A. in Econs, Bernard Baruch Sch., CCNY, 1971, M.B.A. in Fin, 1972. Asst. to chmn. bd. Rapid-Am. Corp., 1972-76, v.p., exec. asst. to chmn., 1976-80, exec. v.p., 1980—, McCrory Corp., N.Y.C., 1976-80, pres., 1980—; also dir.; exec. v.p. Rapid-Am. Corp., 1980—; dir. Kenton Corp., J.J. Newberry Co.; sr. advt. Econ. Ministry of Israel, 1982-83. Served with Israeli Army, 1963-66. Address: McCrory Corp 888 7th Ave New York NY 10019

GENGERELLI, JOSEPH ANTHONY, psychologist, ret. educator; b. Glouster, Ohio, Feb. 2, 1905; s. Nugent and Filomena (Leonetti) G.; m. Carmen Noguero y Cierco, Aug. 27, 1942; 1 dau., Carmen Anna Maria. A.B., Ohio U., 1925; M.A., U. Wis., 1927; Ph.D., U. Pa., 1928. Research fellow Nat. Research Council, Yale, 1928-29; instr. U. Calif., Los Angeles, 1929-32, asst. prof. psychology, 1932-42, asso. prof., 1942-49, prof., 1949-72, chmn. dept., 1950-55. Served with planning staff O.S.S., 1942-44; Washington; chief psychol. warfare br., 1944-45; Naples, Italy; chief intelligence officer USIS, 1945; Am. Zone, Austria. Mem. Am. Psychol. Assn., Sigma Xi. Research areas physiol. psychology, exptl. psychology, psychometrics, learning theory. Devel., dir. constrn. miniature transmitter for radio broadcasting of brain waves; designer method for stimulation brain of waking animal while in process of learning in order to study learning process. Home: 2001 Linda Flora Dr Los Angeles CA 90024

GENGLER, SISTER M. JEANNE, hosp. adminstr.; b. Mackville, Wis., Feb. 10, 1912; d. Jacob Joseph and Jeannette (Mullen) G. R.N., Marquette U., 1937, B.S. in Pub. Health, 1957. Took vows in Roman Cath. Ch.; staff nurse St. Anthony Hosp., St. Louis, 1937-40; supr. nursing St. Mary Hosp., Racine, Wis., 1940-50; also ednl. dir. ARC aids; nursing service, personnel dir., Waterloo, Ia., 1950-54; also coordinator disaster program; dir. out-patient comprehensive family clinic St. Michael Hosp., Milw., 1953-58, adminstr., 1958-64, dir., 1958—; pres., dir. St. Joseph's Hosp., Milw., 1965-80, constrn. program coordinator, 1965-68; Outreach program asst. St. Anthony Hosp., Milw., 1981—; dir. hosp. bldg. project Milw. Hosp. Council.; Developer psychiat. in-patient unit St. Michael Hosp., 1958, re-organizer out-patient clinic, 1958. Mem. United Community Service Greater Milw., 1954—, Area Planning Bd., 1965-70; mem. Provincial Council-Motherhouse, Wheaton, Ill., 1975-76; Bd. dirs. Wis. Cath. Conf. Fellow Am. Coll. Hosp. Adminstrs.; mem. Wis. Hosp. Assn. (bd. dirs. 1970—), Mental Health Assn., Coll. Hosp. Adminstrs. Address: 5241 N 25th St Milwaukee WI 53209

GENN, NANCY, artist; b. San Francisco; d. Morley P. and Ruth W. Thompson; m. Vernon Chathburton Genn; children: Cynthia, Sarah, Peter. Student, San Francisco Art Inst., U. Calif., Berkeley. Lectr. on art and papermaking Am. Centers in, Osaka, Japan, Nagoya, Japan, Kyoto, Japan, 1979-80; guest lectr. various univs. and art museums in U.S., 1975—. One woman shows of sculpture, paintings include, De Young Mus., San Francisco, 1955, 63, Gumps Gallery, San Francisco, 1955, 57, 59, San Francisco Mus. Art, 1961, U. Calif., Santa Cruz, 1966-68, Richmond (Calif.) Art Center, 1970, Oakland (Calif.) Mus., 1971, Linda/Farris Gallery, Seattle, 1974, 76, 78, 81, Los Angeles Inst. Contemporary Art, 1976, Susan Caldwell Gallery, N.Y.C., 1976, 77, 79, 81, Nina Freudenheim Gallery, Buffalo, 1977, 81, Annely Juda

Fine Art, London, 1978, Inoue Gallery, Tokyo, 1980, Toni Birckhead Gallery, Cin., 1982, Kala Inst. Gallery, Berkeley, Calif., 1983, group exhbns. include, San Francisco Mus. Art, 1971, Aldrich Mus., Ridgefield, Conn., 1972-73, Santa Barbara (Calif.) Mus., 1974, 75, Oakland (Calif.) Mus. Art, 1975, Susan Caldwell, Inc., N.Y.C., 1974, 75, Mus. Modern Art, N.Y.C., 1976, traveling exhbn. Arts Council Gt. Britain, 1983-84, Inst. Contemporary Arts, Boston, 1977; represented in permanent collections, Mus. Modern Art, N.Y.C., Albright-Knox Art Gallery, Buffalo, Nat. Collection Fine Arts, Smithsonian, Washington, McCrory Corp., N.Y.C., Mus. Art, Auckland, N.Z., Aldrich Mus., Ridgefield, Conn., Internat. Center Aesthetic Research, Torino, Italy, Cin. Art Mus., San Francisco Mus. Modern Art, Oakland Art Mus., City of San Francisco Hall of Justice, Harris Bank, Chgo., Chase Manhattan Bank, N.Y.C., various mfg. cos., also numerous pvt. collections; commd. works include, Bronze lectern and 5 bronze sculptures for chancel table, 1st Unitarian Ch., Berkeley, Calif., 1961, 64, bronze fountain, Cowell Coll., U. Calif., Santa Cruz, bronze menorah, Temple Beth Am, Los Altos Hills, Calif., 1981, 17, murals and 2 bronze fountain sculptures, Sterling Vineyards, Calistoga, Calif., 1972, 73, fountain sculpture, Expo 1974, Spokane, Wash. U.S./Japan Creative Arts fellow, 1978-79; recipient Ellen Branston award, 1952; Phelan award De Young Mus., 1963; honor award HUD, 1968. Home: 1515 La Loma Ave Berkeley CA 94708

GENNARO, PETER, dancer, choreographer; b. Metairie, La.; s. Charles and Conchetta (Sabella) G.; m. Jean Kinsella, Jan. 24, 1948; children—Michael, Liza. Ed. pub. schs.; student, Am. Theatre Wing. Danced professionally at, San Carlo Opera, 1949; in Broadway prodns. including Make Mine Manhattan, 1949, Subway Circuit, 1949, Kiss Me Kate, 1950, Guys and Dolls, 1950, Arms and the Girls, 1950, Pajama Game, 1954, Bells Are Ringing, 1956; choreographer: Broadways prodns. Seventh Heaven, 1955, Fiorello, 1959, Mr. President, 1963, Bajour, 1964; film Unsinkable Molly Brown, 1960; co-choreographer: Broadway prodn. West Side Story, 1957, Annie, 1977; TV choreographer, performer: Polly Bergen Show, 1958, Andy Williams Show, 1960, Bob Crosby Show, 1960, Perry Como Show, 1961-63, Judy Garland Show, 1964, Bing Crosby Show, 1964, 1965, Acad. Awards, Ed Sullivan Show, 1966, 67, 68; choreographer various TV spls., 1967—, Ed Sullivan's Tribute to Irving Berlin, 1968; Broadway prodn. Miss Am. pageants, 1973, 74, 75, Kraft Music Hall, 1967-71; producer, Radio City Music Hall; appeared on: nightclub debut A.M. America, N.Y.C., 1974, Barmitzvah Boy, London, 1978; (Tony award for Annie 1977, nominated for Emmy award for spl. choreography Brigadoon.). Recipient Dance Educators Am. award, 1957, 73, Ann. Dance Mag. award, 1965, Boston Dance Assn. award, 1963, Eleanor Roosevelt Humanitarian award N.Y. League Hard of Hearing, 1974. Address: care William Morris Agency 1350 Ave of Americas New York NY 10019 *

GENOVESE, EUGENE DOMINICK, educator, historian; b. Bklyn., May 19, 1930; s. Dominick F. and Lena (Chimenti) G.; m. Elizabeth Fox. B.A., Bklyn. Coll., 1953; M.A., Columbia U., 1955, Ph.D. (Richard Watson Gilder fellow), 1959. Asst. prof. Poly. Inst. Bklyn., 1958-63; asso. prof. Rutgers U., 1963-67; prof. history Sir George Williams U., Montreal, Can., 1967-69; Social Sci. research fellow, 1968-69; prof. history U. Rochester, 1969—; vis. prof. Columbia, 1967, Yale, 1969; Pitt prof. Am. history and instns. U. Cambridge, Eng., 1976-77. Author: The Political Economy of Slavery, 1965, The World the Slaveholders Made, 1969, In Red and Black, 1971, Roll, Jordan, Roll, 1974, From Rebellion to Revolution, 1979, (with Elizabeth Fox-Genovese) Fruits of Merchant Capital, 1983; also articles, revs.; mem. editorial bd.: Dialectical Anthropology. Served with AUS, 1953-54. Fellow Center for Advanced Study in Behavioral Scis., Stanford, Calif., 1972-73. Fellow Am. Acad. Arts and Scis.; mem. Am. Hist. Assn. (exec. council 1970-75), Orgn. Am. Historians (pres. 1978-79). Address: 115 E Upland Rd Ithaca NY 14850

GENOVESE, FRANCIS (FRANK) CHARLES, economist, consultant; b. Toronto, Ont., Can., Feb. 16, 1921; came to U.S., 1946, naturalized, 1960; s. Francis A. and Florence M. (Ferguson) G.; m. Candace E. Moorhouse, June 17, 1944; children: Margaret, Steven, Jeremy, Anne, Michael. B.A., U. Toronto, 1942, M.A., 1946; Ph.D., U. Wis., 1953. Mem. faculty Babson Coll., Babson Park, Mass., 1955—, dean Grad. Sch., 1962-73, prof. econs., 1962—; pres. Pleiad Corp., 1974—; advisor Central Bank Jordan, 1975; vis. prof. N.Y.U., 1960-62; vis. faculty Brown U. Grad. Sch. Banking, 1962-64, Wellesley Coll., 1962; cons. Brown U. Grad. Sch. Banking, 1962-64, Wellesley Coll., 1962. Editor: Lombard Street; contbr. articles to profl. jours., newspapers. Mem. Democratic Town Com., 1978—, Nelson Small Bus. Task Force; bd. dirs. Mass. Higher Edn. Loan Corp., 1978-81; corp. mem. Mass. Goodwill Industries, 1973—. Served with Can. Army, 1944-45. Fellow U. Wis., 1946-47. Mem. Am. Econ. Assn., Am. Fin. Assn., Can. Econ. Assn. Unitarian. Club: Wellesley. Home: 21 Appleby Rd Wellesley MA 02181 Office: Babson Coll Babson Park MA 02157

GENOVESE, THOMAS LEONARDO, lawyer; b. Flushing, N.Y., Feb. 28, 1936; s. Robert Pasquale Sisto and Jean Laura (Lundari) G.; m. Linda Luella Le Maire, Nov. 30, 1980; children: Torene Lucia, Andrea Lisa. A.B., U. Va., 1957; J.D., Fordham U., 1960. Bar: N.Y. 1961. Atty. FAA, Jamaica, N.Y., 1961-65, NBC, N.Y.C., 1965-66, Grumman A/C Engring. Co., Bethpage, N.Y., 1966-70; gen. counsel Grumann Data Systems Co., Bethpage, N.Y., 1970-73, Grumman Corp., 1979—, v.p., 1981—; dir. Paumanock Ins. Ltd., Hamilton, Bermuda; adj. prof. SUNY-Stony Brook, 1976-78. Contbr.: legal articles to Fordham Law Rev. Chmn. United Way Grumman corp., 1983. Mem. ABA, Am. Corp. Counsel Assn. Episcopalian. Office: Grumman Corp 1111 Stewart Ave Bethpage NY 11714

GENT, ALAN NEVILLE, physicist, educator; b. Leicester, Eng., Nov. 11, 1927; came to U.S., 1961, naturalized, 1972; s. Harry Neville and Gladys (Hoyle) G.; m. Jean Margaret Wolstenholme, Sept. 1, 1949; children: Martin Paul Neville, Patrick Michael, Andrew John. B.S., U. London, Eng., 1946, 1949, Ph.D. in Sci, 1955. Lab. asst. John Bull Rubber Co., Leicester, Eng., 1944-45; research physicist Brit. (now Malaysian) Rubber Producers' Research Assn., 1949-61; prof. polymer physics U. Akron, Ohio, 1961—, dean grad. studies and research, 1978—; vis. prof. dept. materials Queen Mary Coll., U. London, 1969-70; cons. Goodyear Tire & Rubber Co., 1963—, Gen. Motors, 1973—. Contbr. articles to profl. publs. Served with Brit. Army, 1947-49. Recipient Mobay award, cellular plastics div. Soc. of Plastics Industry, 1963, Colwyn medal Plastics and Rubber Inst. Gt. Brit., 1978, adhesives award Com. F-11, ASTM, 1979, internat. research award Soc. Plastics Engrs., 1980. Mem. Soc. of Rheology (v.p. 1979-81, Bingham medal 1975), Adhesion Soc. (pres. 1978-80), Am. Phys. Soc. (chmn. div. high polymer physics 1977-78). Democrat. Home: 2969 Harriett Rd Cuyahoga Falls OH 44224 Office: Inst of Polymer Science U Akron Akron OH 44325

GENTHER, CHARLES BOOHER, architect; b. Savannah, Mo., May 27, 1907; s. Carl Marshall and Mattie Martha (Selecman) G.; m. Shirley Claire Babcock, Mar. 17, 1932; 1 son, Gene Halliday. B.S. in Archtl. Engring, U. Okla., 1939; postgrad., Armour Inst., 1939-40, Ill. Inst. Tech., 1942-43. Architect Skidmore, Owings & Merrill (Architects & Engrs.), Chgo., 1942-44; designer/draftsman Holabird & Root (Architects & Engrs.), Chgo., 1945; co-founder, partner Pace Assos. Planners Architects (Cons. Engrs.), Chgo., 1946-68; prof. architecture U. Ill., Chgo., 1966—. Architect of record: Promontory Apts, Chgo., Toll Hwy. Restaurants and Service Area and 22 Toll Plazas No. Ill. Toll Hwy. Fellow AIA (First Honor award for Gen. Telephone Co. Office Bldg., San Angelo, Tex. 1955). Episcopalian. Clubs: Arts of Chgo., Cliff Dwellers (Chgo.). Home: 121 Valley Dr Santa Fe NM 87501

GENTILE, ARTHUR CHRISTOPHER, university dean; b. N.Y.C., Nov. 24, 1926; s. Leo and Grace (Leone) G.; m. Gloria Lenore Ennevor, Jan. 22, 1949; 1 dau., Flora. B.S., CCNY, 1948; M.S., Brown U., 1951; Ph.D., U. Chgo., 1953. Plant physiologist U.S. Forest Service, Lake City, Fla., 1955-56; mem. faculty U. Mass., Amherst, 1956-72, prof. botany, 1964-72, asso. dean, 1965-72; dean Grad. Coll., v.p. research adminstrn. U. Okla., 1972-74; v.p. for acad. affairs U. Nev., Las Vegas, 1974-79; exec. dir. Am. Inst. Biol. Scis., 1979-83; dean acad. affairs Ind. U.-Kokomo, 1983—; Bd. dirs. Midcontinent Environ. Council Assn., 1972-74; mem. Sci. Manpower Commn., 1980-83; trustee Am. Type Culture Collection, 1980-83, Bioscis. Info. Service, 1981—. Author: Plant Growth, 1971. Served with AUS, 1945-46. USPHS research fellow Nat. Cancer Inst., 1954-55. Mem. Am. Soc. Plant Physiologists, AAUP, AAAS, Sigma Xi, Alpha Epsilon Delta. Office: Ind U-Kokomo 2300 S Washington St Kokomo IN 46902

GENTILE, GLORIA IRENE, artist, actress, educator; b. N.Y.C., Jan. 4, 1929; d. Pasquale Francesco and Giusepinna (Dittore) G. Grad., Cooper Union Art Sch., 1950; B.F.A., Yale U., 1952, M.F.A., 1954. Instr. Sch. Visual Arts, N.Y.C., 1967—, Gentille Mini Sch., 1968—, Parsons Sch. Design, 1972—, Cooper Union, 1974—; Queens Coll., 1977, Fashion Inst. Tech., 1980, Pratt Inst., 1981; founder, dir. Gentille Sch. Graphics, N.Y.C., 1975—; lectr., U.S.A. and Europe, 1973—. Designer promotion-collateral, 1955—; conceptual art dir., French Curve Studio, N.Y.C., 1966—; book designer, Harcourt Brace Jovanovich, N.Y.C., 1965-67; mag. designer, United Bus. Publs., 1975—; design supr., Holt, Rinehart & Winston, 1981; seven one-woman sculpture shows, 1967-72; devel. articulated bronze sculpture; conceptualist happening: Impromptu, Mus. Modern Art, 1972; radio and TV appearances. (Recipient Desi award 1978); Author: Kinaesthetics: Analysis of Cat Drawings by Famous People, 1971, Kinaesthetics: Cats Tell Tales, 1972; Contbr.: sculpture and story to New Worlds of Reading, 1969. Designed, developed only live hybrid Rumpie Persian-Manx cat. Address: 333 E 46th St New York NY 10017

GENTILE, JOSEPH F., lawyer, educator; b. San Pedro, Calif., Jan. 15, 1934; s. Ernest B. and Icy Otie (Martin) G.; m. Kathleen McMahon, Aug. 11, 1976; children—Kim Yvonne, Kevin James, Kelly Michele, Kristien Elyse, Kerri Nicole. B.A. cum laude, San Jose State U., 1955; J.D., U. San Fernando Valley, 1966; certificate in Indsl. Relations, U. Calif., Los Angeles, 1959; Teaching credential, Calif. Community Coll., 1972; M.Pub. Adminstrn., U. So. Calif., 1976. Bar: U.S. Supreme Ct. bar 1972. Mem. indsl. relations staff Kaiser Steel Corp., Fontana Works, 1957-62; labor relations counsel Calif. Trucking Assn., Burlingame, Calif., 1964-68; acting dir. indsl. relations, labor relations counsel McDonnel Douglas Corp., Santa Monica, Calif., 1968-70; sr. partner Nelson, Kirshman, Goldstein, Gentile & Rexon, Los Angeles, 1970-76; individual practice, 1976—; Evening instr. bus. econs., indsl. relations U. Calif., 1969—; evening instr. personnel and indsl. relations San Bernardino Valley Coll., 1969-72; evening instr. transp. Mt. San Antonio Coll., 1972-74; lectr. labor law Loyola U., 1973-74; lectr. Grad. Sch. Pub. Adminstrn., U. So. Calif., 1975—; adj. prof. law Pepperdine U., 1979—; Mem. Employee Relations Commn., Los Angeles County, 1979—; mem. arbitration panel Fed. Mediation and Conciliation Service, Calif. Counciliation Service. Contbr. articles to profl. jours. Served with AUS, 1955-57. Mem. ABA, Calif. Bar Assn., Los Angeles County Bar Assn. (former chairperson exec. com. labor law sect.), Am. Arbitration Assn. (chairperson regional adv. council, arbitration panel), Phi Sigma Alpha, Phi Alpha Delta. Office: 11620 Wilshire Blvd Suite 540 Los Angeles CA 90022

GENTLE, KENNETH WILLIAM, physicist; b. Oak Park, Ill., Oct. 27, 1940; s. William and Cathryn Mary (Spence) G. B.S., MIT, 1962, Ph.D., 1966. Asst. prof. dept. physics U. Tex., Austin, 1966-69, assoc. prof., 1970-75, prof. physics, 1976—. Sloan fellow, 1973-75. Mem. Am. Phys. Soc. Home: 212 Buckeye Trail Austin TX 78746 Office: Dept Physics Univ Tex Austin TX 78712

GENTLES, ROY ALLAN, aluminum manufacturing company executive; b. Toronto, Ont., Can., June 21, 1921; came to U.S., 1973; s. Charles Allan and Berta (Roy) G.; m. Margaret Louise Alexander, Sept. 6, 1945; children: Gail Gentles Smiley, Gary, Brian, Terry. M.B.A., Harvard U., 1949. Sales mgr. Alcan Sales Inc., N.Y.C., 1950-59; mng. dir. Alcan U.K. Ltd., London, 1959-62; exec. v.p. dir. Alcan Internat. Ltd., Montreal, Que., Can., 1962-70; v.p., planning coordinator Alcan Aluminum Ltd., Montreal, 1970-72; exec. v.p. Alcan Aluminum Corp., Cleve., 1973-78, pres., chief exec. officer, 1978—; also dir.; exec. v.p., dir. Aluminum Co. Can.; dir. Alcan Can. Products, Toronto. Served with Canadian Armed Forces, 1940-45. Mem. Zeta Psi. Clubs: Pepper Pike, Country, Cleve., Racquet (Cleve.); St. James (Montreal); Toronto (Toronto). Home: 2837 N Park Blvd Cleveland Heights OH 44118 Office: Alcan Aluminum Corp 100 Erieview Plaza Cleveland OH 44114

GENTRY, BERN LEON, SR., minority consulting company executive; b. Goldsboro, N.C., Sept. 9, 1941; s. Theodore Alfonso and Ruth Ester (Taylor) G.; m. Jane A. Price, Nov. 11, 1965; children: Michelle Lorraine, Bern Leon. Student, Rutgers U., 1959-61, Temple U., 1961-63, Cornell U., 1966-67, U. Okla., 1971. Tax acct. IRS, Phila., 1965-66; collection mgr., credit mgr., appliance store mgr., soft goods mdse. mgr. Sears, Roebuck & Co., Phila., 1966-71; program mgr., dir. nat. urban affairs U.S. Jr. C. of C., 1971-73, cons., 1973—; pres. Together, Inc., Tulsa, 1973—. Contbr. articles to profl. jours. Mem. nat. adv. bd. Boys Clubs Am., 1971—; mem. nat. Black alliance for grad. level edn. U. Mich.; past pres., bd. dirs. Tulsa Econ. Opportunity Task Force; pres. Community Service Agy.; bd. dirs. Jr. Achievement. Recipient award of accomplishment Sears Staff Sch., 1967; award of appreciation Black Peoples Unity Movement Econ. Devel. Corp., 1971; George Washington Honor medal Freedoms Found., 1974, 76; Keys to cities of, Roanoke, Va., Baton Rouge, La., New Orleans; named Outstanding Young Man, Camden, 1970; Outstanding Chpt. Pres. N.J. Jaycees; Outstanding Jaycee. Mem. Nat. Urban League, NAACP, Am. Mgmt. Assn., Nat. Assn. Human Rights Workers, Assn. Black Found. Execs., Nat. Assn. Pub. Relations Execs., Nat. Civil Service League, Nat. Assn. Community Devel., Nat. Assn. Vol. Services Coordinator, Camden Jaycees (pres. 1970-71), Tulsa Met. C. of C. Office: Box 52528 Suite 2901 University Club Tower Tulsa OK 74152

GENTRY, DONALD WILLIAM, college dean; b. St. Louis, Jan. 18, 1943; s. William Henry and Roberta Elizabeth (Bardelmeier) G.; m. Sheila Carol Schuepbach, Aug. 21, 1965; children: Tara Cassandre, Chad Ryan. B.S.E., U. Ill., 1965; M.S., U. Nev., 1967; Ph.D., U. Ariz., 1972. Registered profl. engr., B.C. Asst. prof. mining engring. Colo. Sch. Mines, Golden, 1972-74, assoc. prof., 1974-77, asst. to dean faculty, assoc. prof., 1977-78, asst. to dean faculty, 1978-79, prof. mining engring., 1978-83, dean undergrad. studies, 1983—. Contbr. articles to profl. jours. Mem. Soc. Mining Engrs. of AIME (vice chmn. ednl. activities com. 1981-83, chmn. ednl. activites com. 1983), AIME dir. Colo. sect. (1982-83), Sigma Tau, Sigma Gamma Epsilon. Republican. Lutheran. Home: 6590 Ridgeview Dr Morrison CO 80465 Office: Dean Undergrad Studies Colo Sch Mines Golden CO 80401

GENTRY, HUBERT, JR., lawyer; b. Sonora, Tex., Oct. 3, 1931; s. Hubert and Julia (Killin) G.; m. Patsy Lynn Bullington, Dec. 27, 1953; children: Julia Ruth, Chester Lindsey, Beth Marie, Hubert Michael, Patsy Jean. B.A., Tex. Tech. U., 1952; J.D., So. Meth. U., 1955. Bar: Tex. 1955. Mem. firm Fulbright & Jaworski, Houston, 1955-72, partner, 1967-72; exec. v.p., then chief operating officer, pres. Southwest Bancshares, Inc., Houston, 1973-76, vice chmn., 1976-77; partner firm Tita, Phillips, Jensen & Gentry, Houston, 1977-78; sr. v.p., gen. counsel Entex, Inc., Houston, 1978—; mem. faculty Southwestern Grad. Sch. Banking So. Meth. U., 1972; chmn. consumer credit law sect. State Bar Tex., 1969-70, chmn. banking laws com. of corp., banking and bus. law sect., 1970-71, mem. counsel, pub. utility law sect., 1980-83, sec. pub. utility law sect., 1983-84. Mem. Am. Bar Assn., Tex. Bar Assn., Houston Bar Assn., So. Meth. U. Alumni Law Assn. (pres. 1963-64), Tex. Assn. Bank Holding Cos. (v.p. 1976, dir. 1976-77). Methodist. Clubs: River Oaks Country, Coronado. Office: Entex Inc 1200 Milam St Houston TX 77001

GENTRY, RICHARD STERLING, steel manufacturing executive; b. Carmel, Ind., Sept. 1, 1932; s. Otha and Grace (Wenfred) G.; m. Mardell Lois Newquist, Sept. 20, 1958; children: Bryan, Gail, Andrew, Kirk. B.S., Ball State U., 1957. Salesman Jones and Laughlin Steel Co., Detroit, 1957-60, 1960-62, mgr. flat roll products, 1962; salesman Marsh Steel and Aluminum Co., Denver, 1963, Carpenter Tech. Corp., South Bend, Ind., 1964-65, br. mgr., Milw., 1966, mgr. north central dist., 1967, dist. sales mgr., Chgo., 1968-70, mgr. western dist., Los Angeles, 1971-72; gen. mgr. distbn. Carpenter Steel div., Reading, Pa., 1973-75, gen. mgr. mktg. and distbn. steel div., 1976, asst. v.p. comml. steel div., 1978, group v.p. fabricated products, 1979, group v.p. fabricated products and engring., 1980, v.p. corp. services, 1982—. Mem. Hawk Mt. council Boy Scouts Am.; active United Way of Berks County, Pa.; trustee Lutheran Home at Topton, Pa., mem. devel. com.; active greater Berks Devel. Fund. Mem. Am. Iron and Steel Inst., Steel Service Center Inst., Berks County C. of C. (solid waste task force). Berkshire Country. Office: Carpenter Tech Co 101 Bern St Reading PA 19603

GENTRY, ROBERT VANCE, physicist; b. Chattanooga, July 9, 1933; s. Vance Ault and Sara Frances (Northington) G.; m. Patricia Ann Gentry, Jan. 20, 1953; children—Patricia, Michael, David. B.S. in Physics, U. Fla., 1955, M.S., 1956; D.Sc. (hon.), Columbia Union Coll., Takoma Park, Md., 1977. Nuclear engr. Gen. Dynamics Co., Ft. Worth, 1956-58; sr. engr. Martin Co., Orlando, Fla., 1958-59; instr. math. U. Fla., Gainesville, 1959-61, Walla Walla (Wash.) Coll., 1961-62; instr. physics Ga. Inst. Tech., 1962-64; research physicist Archeol. Research Found., Atlanta, 1965-66; mem. faculty Columbia Union Coll., 1966—, asso. prof. physics, 1977—; guest scientist chemistry div. Oak Ridge Nat. Lab., 1969-82; hon. prof. physics U. Tenn.-Knoxville, 1982—. Contbr. articles to profl. jours. Fellow NSF, 1962; grantee, 1971-77, NASA, 1970-72. Mem. AAAS, Am. Phys. Soc., Am. Geophys. Union, N.Y. Acad. Scis., Sigma Xi. Seventh-day Adventist. Home: 6321 Cate Rd Powell TN 37849 *To recognize that success in any field is not the result of chance or destiny but instead the reward of faithfully developing those talents endowed by the Creator provides the highest possible incentive for achieving that station in life for which each individual is uniquely fitted.*

GENTSKI, ROBERT JAMES, banker, economist; b. N.Y.C., Dec. 26, 1942; s. Alex and Helen (Turbek) Genetski. B.S., Eastern Ill. U., 1964; M.A., NYU, 1968, Ph.D., 1972. Tchr. English St. Procopius Acad., Lisle, Ill., 1965-66; research analyst Nat. Econ. Research Assn., N.Y.C., 1967-68; lectr. econs. NYU, N.Y.C., 1969-70; econ. analyst Morgan Guaranty Trust Co., N.Y.C., 1969-71; v.p., economist Harris Trust & Savs. Bank, Chgo., 1971—; lectr. bus. econs. U. Chgo., 1973. Author: (with Beryl Sprinkel) Winning with Money, 1977. Chmn. ednl. com. Sch. Bd. Dist. 25, West Chicago, Ill., 1973-79. Mem. Am. Statis. Assn., Am. Econ. Assn., Nat. Assn. Bus. Economists (editor Newsletter 1978), Western Econ. Assn., Am. Bankers Assn. (econ. adv. com. 1980-83). Office: Harris Trust & Savs Bank Suite 6E 111 Monroe St Chicago IL 60603

GEOFFREY, IQBAL (SYED MOHAMMED JAWAID IQBAL JAFREE), reformer; b. Chiniot, Pakistan, Jan. 1, 1939; s. Syed Iqbal Hussain and Shahzadi Mumtazjehan Shah; m. Regina Wai-ling Cheng, 1967 (div. 1978); children—Syed Hussain Haider, Shahzadi Zohra Elinoi. B.A. with distinction, Punjab U. Govt. Coll., 1957, LL.B. summa cum laude, 1959; LL.M., Harvard U., 1966; A.I.C.E.A., London, 1961; A.M.B.I.M., London, 1969; Ph.D., Read Coll., 1970; also LL.D.; M.A., Sangamon State U., 1973. Bar: Pakistan 1959, U.S. Supreme Ct. 1975. Partner, sr. counsel firm Geoffrey & Khitran (internat. lawyers), 1960-76; lectr., art critic, cons. urban affairs and aesthetics; human rights officer UN, 1966-67; drafted Establishment of Office of Ombudsman Order, Pakistan, 1982. Author: Qose-Qizah, 1957, Justice is the Absence of Dictatorial Prerogative, 1965, Human Rights in Pakistan, 1966, A Critical Study of Moral Dilemmas, Iconographical Confusions and Complicated Politics of XX Century Art, 1967, The Concept of Human Rights in Islam, 1981; Editor: Law Rev, 1958-59; grad. editor: Harvard Art Rev, 1965-66; One-man shows include, Hyde Park, London, 1960-62, Hull (Eng.) U., Birmingham (Eng.) U., Queens U., Arts Council, No. Ireland, Los Angeles Mcpl. Art Gallery, Pakistan Arts Council, Grand Central Moderns, Swetzoff Gallery, Ward-Nasse Gallery, Pakistan Arts Council, Lahore, Henri Gallery, Washington, St. Mary's Coll., Ind., Franklin Coll., Miami (Fla.) Mus. Modern Art, Mus. Art Cornell U., Everson Art Mus., Syracuse, N.Y., other exhbns. include, Kinetic reliefs, superscluptures, biennials, Paris, Sao Paulo, Brazil, Tokyo, Ljubljana, Yugoslavia, Arts Council Gt. Britain touring exhbts., world fairs, N.Y.C., world fairs, Montreal and, world fairs, Tokyo; represented in permanent collections, Herbert Johnson Mus. Cornell U., Philips Collection, Washington, Boston Mus. Fine Arts, Pasadena (Calif.) Art Mus., Everson Art Mus., Worcester (Mass.) Mus., Arts Council Gt. Britain, Tate Gallery, London, Eng., Brit. Mus., London, Chase Manhattan Bank, N.Y.C., also pvt. collections. Recipient Paris Biennial award, 1965; pub. tribute by Pakistan Pres. Sir Ayub Khan, 1964; Arts Council Gt. Britain Sir Philip Hendy and Lord Goodman award, 1969; Distinguished Community Service award L.A.W., 1970; Huntington Hartford II and John D. Rockefeller III fellow, 1962-65; Aug. 14 designated Syed Iqbal Jafree Day by Gov., Ill., 1977; Outstanding New Citizen Citizenship Council Met. Chgo., 1979; Fellow Royal Soc. Arts, London, 1961. Address: 3410 W McLean Ave Chicago IL 60647 also Sul Sabeel Shahrah-e Iqbal Gulberg 3 Lahore Pakistan also 128 Saint Pancras Way London NW1 9NB England *Creativity in ethics is triggered by conscious descaffolding of faits accompli. An artist endeavors to abrogate the gap that segregates an idea. Easier said than done! Inevitably, picturization processes confronting future metaphysics disturb status quo.*

GEOFFROY, CHARLES HENRY, retail executive; b. Longford, Ireland, Sept. 24, 1926; came to U.S., 1927, naturalized, 1945; s. Francis Louis and Kathleen Elizabeth (Fetherston) G.; m. Alida Baird McClenahan, Apr. 24, 1954; children: Evan Lloyd, Mark Lee, Douglas Baird. B.A., Haverford Coll., 1949; postgrad., U. Pa., 1950. With Gen.

Motors Ins. Corp., Phila., 1950-51; mgr. research dept. Ward Wheelock Co., Phila., 1951-54; asso. research dir., account exec. Lennen & Newell, Inc., N.Y.C., 1954-59; account exec. Young & Rubicam, Inc., N.Y.C., 1959-64, v.p., Los Angeles, 1965-67; pres., mng. dir. Young & Rubicam, Ltd., Toronto, Ont., Can., 1968-74; pres., dir. J.K. Gill Co. Ltd., Portland, Oreg., 1974-80; pres., chief operating officer Grantree Corp., Portland, 1980—. Served with AUS, 1945-46. Fellow Inst. Canadian Advt. Clubs: Riverside (Conn.); Yacht, Waverley Country, University. Office: Grantree Corp 2501 SW 1st Ave Portland OR 97201 *

GEOFFROY, KEVIN EDWARD, educator; b. Milford, Mass., Nov., 1932; s. Frank Anthony and Dorothy Veronica (Cahill) G.; m. Shirley Jo Chilcoat, Apr. 17, 1959; children: Leigh-Ann, Mark. B.A., Tufts U., 1955; M.Ed., Boston U., 1960; Ed.D., Ariz. State U., 1966. Counselor Littleton (Mass.) High Sch., 1961-63; prof. edn. Coll. William and Mary, Williamsburg, Va., 1965—, div. chairperson, 1979—; vis. prof. U. Miami, 1968-69; cons. in field. Editor: Va. Personnel and Guidance Jour, 1973-75, Jour. for Specialists in Group Work, 1975-79. Bd. dirs. Eastern State Hosp., Williamsburg. NDEA fellow, 1963-65; Breeden fellow Rolle Coll., Eng. Mem. Am. Personnel and Guidance Assn. (mem. editorial bd. jour. 1973-79), Assn. Specialists in Group Work, Assn. Counselor Edn. Suprs., Va. Personnel and Guidance Assn., Peninsula Personnel and Guidance Assn. Home: 106 Little John Rd Williamsburg VA 23185 Office: School of Education College of William and Mary Williamsburg VA 23185

GEOGHEGAN, ELMO LEON, restaurant co. exec.; b. Kirksville, Mo., Mar. 24, 1927; s. Luke and Katherine Elizabeth (Weber) G.; m. Wilma Rebecca Green, Jan. 26, 1949; children—Elmo Leon, David Lee. Student public schs. With Big Boy Restaurants Am., 1942—, exec. v.p., Glendale, Calif., 1968—; v.p. Marriott Corp. Served with USCGR, 1945-46. Mem. Calif. Restaurant Assn. (dir.). Office: 1001 E Colorado St Glendale CA 91205 *

GEOGHEGAN, JOHN JOSEPH, retired publisher; b. Phila., Mar. 14, 1917; s. John Joseph and Kathryn Genevieve (Landers) G.; m. Margaret Anna Chittick, June, 1940 (div. 1974); children—Michael, Peter, Margaret Kathryn, John Joseph III; m. Carole Magner De Cordova, Feb. 1980. Student, Columbia U. Extension Sch., 1942, U.S. Air Force Sch. Engring. and Ops., 1943. Publishers rep. J.B. Lippincott Co., 1945-48; pub. rep. Doubleday & Co., 1948-53, trade advt. mgr., 1953-55, West Coast editorial rep., dist. sales mgr., 1955-58; v.p., mgr. trade dept. Coward-McCann, Inc. (became Coward-McCann & Geoghegan 1970), N.Y.C., 1959, editor-in-chief, 1959-60, pres., 1960-80, chmn., 1980—; editor-at-large Wm. Morrow & Co., N.Y.C., 1981—; dir. G.P. Putnam's Sons, Berkeley Pub. Co. N.Y. Author short stories. Served with USAAF, 1942-45; China. Decorated Battle Stars. Clubs: Aspetuck Country (Weston); Century Assn. (N.Y.C.); Publishers Lunch. Home: Box 1036 Weston CT 06880 *It is a happy man who chooses a field or profession requiring a lifetime to chart its regions. Such undertakings ensure challenge, provide opportunities for personal growth, and can ultimately culminate in a reasonable portion of knowledge about oneself and one's fellow man.*

GEOGHEGAN, WILLIAM DAVIDSON, clergyman, educator; b. Wilmington, Del., July 16, 1922; s. Presley Downs and Mildred (Davidson) G.; m. Sarah Elizabeth Phelps, Oct. 5, 1946; children—Grace Elizabeth, Andrew Phelps, Emily Bernice, William Davidson II. B.A., Yale U., 1943; student, Harvard Div. Sch., 1943-44; M.Div., Drew Theol. Sem., 1945; Ph.D., Columbia-Union Theol. Sem., 1951. Ordained to ministry Methodist Ch., 1947; pastor in, Christiana, Del., 1944-47, tchr. jr. high sch., New Castle, Del., 1945-46; chaplain, Asst. prof. religion U. Rochester, 1950-54; prof. religion, chmn. dept. Bowdoin Coll., 1954—. Author: Platonism in Recent Religious Thought, 1958. Recipient Bowdoin Coll. Alumni Council Faculty and Staff award, 1981. Mem. Am. Acad. Religion, AAUP, Am. Philos. Assn., Phi Beta Kappa, Zeta Psi. Republican. Home: 40 Federal St Brunswick ME 04011 also PO Box 336 Wolfeboro NH 03894

GEORGE, ALBERT RICHARD, mech. and aerospace engr., educator; b. N.Y.C., Mar. 12, 1938; s. Albert Richard and Tekla (Kovtoun) G.; m. Carol Mae Frerichs, June 21, 1959; children—Albert Frederick, David Kovtoun, Amy Margaret. B.S.E., Princeton U., 1959, M.A., 1961, Ph.D., 1964. Vis. asst. prof. U. Wash., Seattle, 1964-65; asst. prof. Cornell U., 1965-69, asso. prof., 1969-77, prof., 1977—, asst. dir. mech. and aerospace engring. dept., 1972-77, dir., 1977—; vis. sr. fellow U. Southampton, Eng., 1971-72; cons. in field. Contbr. articles to profl. jours. Mem. AIAA (asso. fellow), ASME, Soc. Automotive Engrs., Am. Helicopter Soc., AAUP, Sigma Xi. Congregationalist. Home: 119 Pine Tree Rd Ithaca NY 14850 Office: 105 Upson Hall Cornell U Ithaca NY 14853

GEORGE, ALEXANDER LAWRENCE, political scientist, educator; b. Chgo., May 31, 1920; s. John and Mary (Sargis) G.; m. Juliette Lombard, Apr. 20, 1948; children—Lee Lawrence, Mary Lombard. A.M., U. Chgo., 1941, Ph.D., 1958. Research analyst OSS, 1944-45; dep. chief research br. Info. Control Div., Office Mil. Govt. for Germany, 1945-48; specialist study decision-making and internat. relations RAND Corp., Santa Monica, Calif., 1948-68, head dept. social sci., 1961-63; prof. polit. sci. Stanford, 1968—; Lectr. U. Chgo., 1950, Am. U., 1952-56. Author: (with Juliette L. George) Woodrow Wilson and Colonel House: A Personality Study, 1956, Propaganda Analysis, 1959, The Chinese Communist Army in Action, 1967, (with others) The Limits of Coercive Diplomacy, 1971, (with Richard Smoke) Deterrence in American Foreign Policy: Theory and Practice, 1974 (Bancroft prize for Deterrence in Am. Fgn. Policy 1975), Towards A More Soundly Based Foreign Policy: Making Better Use of Information, 1976, Presidential Decisionmaking in Foreign Policy, 1980; author: Managing U.S.-Soviet Rivalry, 1983, (with Gordon Craig) Force and Statecraft, 1983. Center for Advanced Study Behavioral Scis. fellow, 1956-57, 76-77; Founds. Fund for Research in Psychiatry grantee, 1960; NIMH spl. fellow, 1972-73; NSF research grantee, 1971-73, 75-77. Mem. Am. Acad. Arts and Scis., Council on Fgn. Relations, Am. Polit. Sci. Assn., Internat. Studies Assn. (pres. 1973-74), AAUP, Phi Beta Kappa. Home: 944 Lathrop Pl Stanford CA 94305

GEORGE, BEAUFORD JAMES, JR., lawyer, educator; b. Kansas City, Mo., Oct. 16, 1925; s. Beauford James and Elizabeth (Pope) G.; m. Grace Isabella Loucks, June 17, 1950; children—Paul, Andrew, Nancy. B.A., U. Mich., 1949, J.D. with honors, 1951. Asst. prof. law U. Mich., Ann Arbor, 1952-55, asso. prof., 1955-58, prof., 1958-68; lectr. law Kyoto U., 1956-57; lectr. fgn. law Tokyo U., 1962-63; asso. dir. Practicing Law Inst., N.Y.C., 1968-71; adj. prof. law N.Y. U., 1968-71; prof. law, dir. Center for Adminstrn. Justice, Wayne State U., Detroit, 1971-77; pres. Southwestern Legal Found., Richardson, Tex., 1977-79; vis. prof. law Baylor U., 1979-80; prof. N.Y. Law Sch., 1980—. Editor-in-chief: Am. Jour. of Comparative Law, 1966-68. Mem. Gov. Mich. Commn. on Criminal Justice, 1966-68, 71-77, Mich. Corrections Commn., 1976-77. Served with inf. AUS, 1943-46. Mem. Am. Law Inst., Am. Bar Assn., State Bar Mich., State Bar Tex., Internat. Penal Law Assn. (past pres. Am. chpt.), Order of Coif. Office: NY Law Sch 57 Worth New York NY 10013

GEORGE, CHARLES, corporation executive; b. Williamsport, Pa., Mar. 17, 1920; s. George and Helen (Mitchell) G.; children—Charles, Christopher Corey. B.S. in Metall. Engring, Columbia U., 1943; M.B.A., N.Y. U., 1945. Former chmn. bd., pres. Telerad Mfg. Corp., Flemington, N.J., 1948-61, dir., 1948-62; pres. govt. support div. Lionel Corp., Hillside, N.J., 1961-62; chmn. bd., pres. Oral Books, Inc., N.Y.C., 1961—; also dir.; chmn. bd., chief exec. officer, dir. Internat. Breweries, Inc., Buffalo, 1965; chmn. Lee Myles Corp.; pres. Lee Myles Assos. Corp., TPM Corp.; dir. Mardon Realty, Hunterdon Finance Co.; cons. Lionel Corp., Servo Corp. Am. Named Ky. col., 1965. Mem. Young Pres.'s Orgn. (co-chmn. Eastern area conf. 1967), Met. Pres.'s Orgn., Am. Soc. Metals, IEEE. Episcopalian. Clubs: Englewood (N.J.) Country, Capri Yacht (Manorhaven); Explorers (N.Y.C.). Home: 5 Tudor City Pl New York NY 10017 Office: 325 Sylvan Ave Englewood Cliffs NJ 07632

GEORGE, CHARLES WILLIAM, aerospace business management consultant; b. Shenandoah, Pa., July 9, 1914; s. Robert and Martha (Eberhard) G.; m. Helen Marie Brengel, Sept. 30, 1944; children: Nancy George Hamberger, Kathryn George Schnur, William. B.S., Ursinus Coll., 1935; M.S., Duke U., 1940. Instr. physics Pa. State Coll., 1941-42; with Gen. Electric Co., 1946-80, mgr. control systems engring., 1951-55, mgr. nuclear reactor engring., 1955-59, mgr. gas turbine engring., 1959-63, gen. mgr. radio guidance dept., 1963-64, gen. mgr. aerospace electronics dept., Utica, N.Y., 1964-67, v.p., gen. mgr. def. electronics div., 1967-68, v.p., gen. mgr. aircraft equipment div., 1968-80; now aerospace business mgmt. cons.; dir. Marine Midland Bank Central, Syracuse, N.Y. Chmn. Greater Utica United Fund Campaign, 1971-72; met. dir. Nat. Alliance Businessmen, 1971-73; bd. dirs. Greater Utica Community Chest and Planning Council, 1972; chmn. nat. fund drive Ursinus Coll., Collegeville, Pa., 1972-74, bd. dirs., Collegeville, Pa., 1977—; Trustee SUNY Coll. Tech., Utica-Rome, 1973-81, chmn. council, 1978-81. Served to lt. USNR, 1942-45. Named Indsl. Man of Yr. Indsl. Mgmt. Club, Utica, 1972, Alumnus of Yr. Ursinus Coll., 1975. Mem. Nat. Security Indsl. Assn. (trustee 1968-80, hon. life mem.), Greater Utica C. of C. (v.p. 1968-76, 1st Disting. Exec. award 1979), Air Force Assn., Assn. U.S. Army, U.S. Naval Inst., IEEE, AIAA, Armed Forces Mgmt. Assn., Asso. Industries N.Y. State (dir., regional v.p., exec. com.). Home: 42 Lynacres Blvd Fayetteville NY 13066 Office: Aircraft Equipment Div Gen Electric Co 5794 Widewaters Pkwy Box 605 DeWitt NY 13214

GEORGE, CLAUDE SWANSON, JR., educator; b. Danville, Va., June 4, 1920; s. Claude Swanson and Myrtle Ann (Dillard) G.; m. Eleanor Anthony, Dec. 22, 1960. B.S., U. N.C., 1942, M.S., 1951; Ph.D., State U. Iowa, 1953. Mem. mgmt. staff Western Electric Co., 1946-50; instr. State U. Iowa, 1951-53; asso. prof. mgmt. U. Tex., 1953-54; prof. mgmt. U. N.C., 1954—, asso. dean, 1958-77. Author: Management in Industry, 3d edit., 1982, The History of Management Thought, 2d edit, 1972, Management for Business and Industry, 1970, Action Guide for Supervisors, 1981, Supervision in Action, 3d edit., 1982. Fellow Acad. Mgmt.; mem. Soc. Advanced Mgmt., So. Mgmt. Assn., Phi Beta Kappa, Beta Gamma Sigma, Order Artus, Sigma Iota Epsilon, Delta Sigma Pi. Home: 926 Coker Dr Chapel Hill NC 27514

GEORGE, DEVERAL D., journalist; b. Dallas, Nov. 23, 1939; s. Jack Weldon and Lleen Lelia (Hume) G. Student, U. Tex., 1958-61; B.A., N. Tex. State U., 1964; P.B.A., U. Houston, 1974. Copywriter advt. agys., Houston, Dallas, 1964-70, free lance journalist, 1970-73, 75-76; copy and creative dir. Scheny Advt., Houston, 1973, Bruce Advt., 1973-75; editor-in-chief, v.p. Bus. and Energy Internat., Houston, 1976-80; editor Ultra mag., 1980-81; free lance journalist, Houston, 1981-83; editor Saudi Bus. Mag.; cons. Saudi Research and Mktg. Inc., Houston, Washington, and Jeddah, Saudi Arabia, 1983—. Author: Cathedrals of Mexico, and Other Poems, 1963, The Erratic Pilgramage, 1973, The Whole World Cookbook, 1976; (screenplays) The Monument, 1980, Armageddon, 1981. Del. Democratic Conv., 1972. Mem. Soc. Internat. Devel., N.Am. Congress on Latin Am., Amnesty Internat., Internat. Platform Assn., Ctr. for Study of Dem. Instns., Asia Soc., World Expeditionary Assn., Soc. Profl. Journalists-Sigma Delta Chi. Club: Houston Press. Home: 230 W Alabama St Apt 910 Houston TX 77006 Office: 2100 West Loop S Suite 1000 Houston TX 77027

GEORGE, EARL, composer, critic; b. Milw., May 1, 1924; s. Adolph Robert and Eleanore Lilly (Werle) G.; m. Margaret Heidner, Sept. 11, 1948; 1 son, Stephen Hubbard. B.M., Eastman Sch. Music, Rochester, N.Y., 1946, M.M., 1947, Ph.D., 1958. Instr. Julius Hartt Music Found., Hartford, Conn., 1948; asst. prof. composition U. Tex., Austin, summer 1948; instr. theory and composition U. Minn., Mpls., 1948-56; Fulbright lectr. U. Oslo, Norway, 1955-56; prof. Syracuse (N.Y.) U., 1959—; music critic Syracuse Herald-Jour., 1961—. Orchestral works performed by major orchs. include, N.Y. Philharmonic, 1947, Mpls. Symphony, 1950, 54, 56, Symphony of the Air, N.Y.C., 1957. Recipient George Gershwin Meml. prize, 1947, Koussevitzky Music Found. commn., 1947, James Millikin U. Choral prize, 1947, Nat. Fedn. Music Clubs prize, 1950; Guggenheim fellow, 1957. Mem. Am. Music Center, ASCAP. Democrat. Home: 21 Sewickley Dr Jamesville NY 13078 Office: 216 Crouse Coll Syracuse Univ Syracuse NY 13210

GEORGE, EDWIN ORDELL, utility executive; b. Petoskey, Mich., Feb. 9, 1905; s. Edward Daley and Ethel (Brott) G.; m. Florence E. Watchpocket, June 6, 1931; 1 dau., Julie Ann George Pope. Student, Alma Coll., 1925; A.B., Knox Coll., 1928; M.A., U. Ill., 1929; postgrad., Wayne U., 1938; LL.D., No. Mich. U., 1966. With Detroit Edison Co., 1929—, comml. office clk., supr. tng., asst. supr. comml. office div., supr. comml. office div., asst. comml. mgr., comml. mgr., mgr. sales, 1929-56, v.p., 1956-65, sr. v.p., 1965-67, exec. v.p. for mktg., 1967, pres., 1967-70, dir., 1967—; dir. First Fed. Savs. Detroit, Panax Corp. Bd. dirs., past pres. Detroit Ednl. TV Found.; pres. Traffic Improvement Assn. Oakland County; bd. dirs., v.p. Overseas Adv. Assn., Inc.; bd. dirs., past pres. Detroit Area council Boy Scouts Am.; trustee Detroit Sci. Center, Oakland U. Found., United Hosp.; trustee, mem. exec. com. Alma Coll.; trustee, mem. bd. control, past chmn. No. Mich. U.; mem. exec. bd., past pres. Greater Mich. Found. Mem. World Soc. Ekistics, Newcomen Soc. N.Am., Pi Kappa Delta, Pi Gamma Nu. Presbyterian (trustee). Clubs: Rotary (past pres.), Detroit Athletic (past pres., dir.), Detroit (Detroit); Circumnavigators (past pres. Mich. br.), Oakland Hills Country.). Home: 352 Barden Rd Bloomfield Hills MI 48013

GEORGE, EMERY EDWARD, educator; b. Budapest, Hungary, May 8, 1933; came to U.S., 1946, naturalized, 1954. A.B., U. Mich., 1955, M.A., 1959, Ph.D., 1964; doctoral student, U. Tübingen (Ger.) and Hölderlin-Archiv der Württembergischen Landesbibliothek, 1961-62. Instr. U. Ill., Champaign-Urbana, 1964-65, asst. prof. German, 1965-66, U. Mich., Ann Arbor, 1966-69, asso. prof., 1969-75, prof., 1975—, faculty program in comparative lit., 1969—, faculty program Center for Russian and East European Studies, 1975—. Author: Hölderlin's Ars Poetica, 1973, Mountainwild: Poems, 1974, Black Jesus, 1974, A Gift of Nerve: Poems, 1966-77, 1978, Kate's Death, 1980; Editor: Friedrich Hölderlin: An Early Modern, 1972, (with L.T. Frank) Husbanding the Golden Grain, 1973, Contemporary East European Poetry: An Anthology, 1983; also transls.; Contbr. poetry, transls., articles, revs. to scholarly jours., lit. pubs.; founding editor: Mich. Germanic Studies; assoc. editor: Russian Lit. Triquar; bd. editorial advisors: Germano-Slavica, 1973-77; editorial bd.: Mich. Monographs in the Humanities, 1979—. Served with M.I. U.S. Army, 1957-58. Ger. Recipient Avery and Jule Hopwood award in poetry U. Mich., 1960; Ottendorfer Meml. fellow, 1961; Am. Council Learned Socs. Publs. award, 1964; Rackham Publ. award U. Mich., 1973, 80. Fellow Internat. Acad. Poets; mem. MLA, Hölderlin-Gesellschaft, Poetry Soc. Am., Shelley Soc. N.Y. Home: 8 Dickinson St Princeton NJ 08540 *To listen carefully to language, to words; to try to write each day. To make no separation between writing and scholarship, between old and new literature. To monitor not fashion, zeitgeist, obsolescence, but the eternal present; to be concerned with style, shape; to try to achieve newness, a sense of experiment from within. In pursuing the art of the translator, to listen to both languages. In ethical conduct, to eschew the exile syndrome; to feel oneself enriched, rather than deprived, by the sea-change of an adoptive culture; to feel privileged to be an heir of American English, with no apologies.*

GEORGE, GRAHAM ELIAS, composer, educator; b. Norwich, Eng., Apr. 11, 1912; emigrated to Can., 1928, naturalized, 1930; s. Alfred Robert and Ethel Elizabeth (Graham) G.; m. Tjot Coster, Sept. 5, 1945; children: Charles Robert Brian, Paul Philip Graham, Jan Michael, Derek Norman. Student, McGill U., 1932-33; B.M., U. Toronto, 1936; D.M., 1939; D.M. postdoctoral studies, Yale U., 1952-53. Ch. musician, Montreal, Sherbrooke, Que., Kingston, Ont., Gananoque, Ont., 1932—; dir. music West Hill High Sch., Montreal, 1940-41; prof. music Queen's U., Kingston, 1946-77, prof. emeritus, 1977—. Condr. orchs. and choral groups; Author: Tonality and Musical Structure, 1970, Twelve-Note Tonal Counterpoint, 1976; Composer: operas Evangeline, 1948, Way Out, 1960, A King for Corsica, 1975; ballets Jabberwocky, 1947, Peter Pan, 1948, The Queen's Jig, 1950; also composer incidental music, choral, orchestral, chamber, organ and piano works. Served with Canadian Army, 1941-45. Can. Council Sr. Arts fellow, 1966-67; Can.-France exchange grantee, 1972; Can. Council Arts grantee, 1983. Fellow Royal Can. Coll. Organists (pres. 1972-74, hon. 1975); mem. Internat. Folk Music Council (sec. gen. 1969-80), Coll. Music Soc. (mem. council 1966-69), Can. Folk Music Soc. (pres. 1965-68), Am. Musicological Soc. Home: 151 Earl St Kingston ON K7L 2H3 Canada

GEORGE, JEAN CRAIGHEAD, author-illustrator; b. Washington, July 2, 1919; d. Frank Cooper and Carolyn (Johnson) Craighead; m. John L. George, Jan. 28, 1944 (div. Jan. 1964); children: Twig Craighead, John Craighead, Thomas Lothar. B.A., Pa. State U., 1941. Reporter Washington Post, 1943-44; artist Pageant mag., 1945; reporter United Features, 1945-46; roving editor Reader's Digest, 1973-80; continuing edn. tchr., Chappaqua, N.Y., 1960-68. Author, illustrator: Summer of the Falcon, 1962, Gull Number 737, 1964, The Thirteen Moons, 1967-69, Coyote in Manhattan, 1968, River Rats, Inc, 1968, Who Really Killed Cock Robin, 1971, Julie of the Wolves, 1972, American Walk Book, 1978, Cry of the Crow, 1980, Journey Inward, 1982, The Talking Earth, 1983, One Day on an Alpine Tundra, 1984, Survival Filmstrips, 1984; film My Side of the Mountain, 1959, Nature Filmstrips, 1978-80. Recipient Aurrainne award, 1957; Newberry Honor Book award, 1961; medal, 1973; Hans Christian Andersen Honor List award, 1964; Pa. State Woman of Yr. award, 1968; World Book award, 1971; Kerlan award, 1982. Address: 20 William St Chappaqua NY 10514

GEORGE, LYNDA DAY, actress; b. San Marcos, Tex., 1946; m. Christopher George, May 15, 1970; 1 son by previous marriage, Nicky. Formerly model, motion picture actress; actress: TV series Silent Force, 1970-71, Mission Impossible, 1966-73, Rich Man, Poor Man; numerous other TV appearances; TV film Cruise into Terror, Casino, 80, Quick & Quick, 1981; motion pictures The Gentle Rain, The Junkman. Mormon. Office: Artists Agy 10000 Santa Monica Blvd Los Angeles CA 90067 *

GEORGE, MARCUS BENJAMIN, television executive; b. New Braunfels, Tex., Sept. 16, 1923; s. Bennett Hollis and Hedwig Clara (Engel) G.; m. Ruby Lee Wiley, Sept. 30, 1945; children: Susan Kay, Karen Lee, Mark Engel. B.J., U. Tex., 1947. Editor, v.p., treas. Ark.-Democrat, Little Rock, 1947-74; v.p., treas. Ark. Democrat Co., 1974-79; pres., treas., dir. Ark. TV Co. (KTHV); co-owner ComputerLand of Little Rock; pres. ComputerLand of Little Rock, Fort Smith and Fayetteville, Nolan-Marcus, Inc. Served with USAAF, 1943-45. Decorated Air medal. Mem. Sigma Delta Chi. Club: Rotary. Home: 5327 Southwood Rd Little Rock AR 72205 Office: 8th and Izard Sts Little Rock AR 72203

GEORGE, M(ERTON) BARON T(ISDALE), research company executive; b. Pope, Man., Can., Oct. 24, 1920; s. Baron and Elizabeth (Leith) G.; m. Kathleen Cousens, Aug. 25, 1945; children: Heather Kathleen, Penelope Karen. B.Engring. with honors, McGill U., 1949; Ph.D., Cornell U., 1953. Group leader, draftsman Noorduyn Aviation and Canadiar Ltd., Montreal, 1941-49; aerodynamics engr. Douglas Aircraft Co., Santa Monica, Calif., 1953-55; prin. research scientist Everett (Mass.) Research Lab., 1955-58; v.p. plans and programs AVCO Corp. (Govt. Products Group), 1958-76; v.p. planning AVCO Everett Research, 1976—; corp. rep. Aerospace Industries Assn., 1965—. Bd. dirs. Am. Nat. Metric Council, 1978-80, Melrose Orchestral Assn., 1981—. Asso. fellow AIAA. Conglist. Patentee in field. Home: 177 Upham St Melrose MA 02176 Office: 2349 Revere Beach Pkwy Everett MA 02149

GEORGE, NEWELL A., lawyer; b. Kansas City, Mo., Sept. 24, 1904; s. Adolphus K. and Ida (Scobee) G.; m. Jean Hannan, Apr. 16, 1934. Student, Park Coll., Parksville, Mo., Kansas City U.; LL.B., Nat. U., 1934, M.P.L., LL.M., 1935. Bar: D.C. 1935, Kans. 1943. Mem. staff U.S. Senator George McGill of Kans., 1933; regional atty. Bur. Employment Security, also FSA, 1935-52; chief legal counsel War Manpower Commn., 1942-44; pvt. practice law, Kansas City, Kans., 1943—, 1st asst. atty., Wyandotte County, Kans., 1952-58; mem. 86th Congress, 2d Dist. Kans.; U.S. atty. for Kans., 1961-68; Mem. Gov.'s Com. on Criminal Adminstrn., Interstate Oil Compact Commn., Kans. Govt. Ethics Commn., Gov.'s Criminal Justice Adv. Panel; mem. commn., mem. rules and personnel coms. Kans. Govtl. Commn. (name now Kans. Pub. Disclosure Commn.). Author: articles Kans. Law Rev. Trustee U. Mo. at Kansas City Law Found.; mem. Kansas City (Kans.) CSC; pres. Kans. Assn. Hi-12 Clubs; bd. dirs. for Kans., Nat. Multiple Sclerosis Soc. Recipient Outstanding Service award Am. Assn. Criminology; Law Enforcement Man of Year Rockne Club Am.; named adm. Nebr. Library, 1960; others. Hon. fellow Harry S. Truman Library; Mem. Am., Kans., Wyandotte County bar assns., Am. Judicature Soc., Am. Acad. Polit. and Social Sci., Supreme Ct. Hist. Soc., Nat. Ctr. for State Cts., L.B. Johnson Library, John F. Kennedy Meml. Library, Kansas City (Kans.) C. of C., Assn. U.S. Army, Delta Theta Phi. Democrat. Presbyn. Clubs: Mason (Kansas City, Kans.) (past master, trustee, Shriner); Optimist, Hi-12, Top O'the Morning (Kansas City, Kans.) (past pres.). Sponsor legislation to create Agr. Hall of Fame, Wyandotte County, Kans. Home: 1831 New Jersey Ave Kansas City KS 66102 Office: Huron Bldg Kansas City KS 66101

GEORGE, ORLANDO JOHN, state representative, college adminstrator; b. Wilmington, Del., Dec. 14, 1945; s. Orlando John and Lena (Ficca) G.; m. Linda Mary Krystopolski, July 29, 1967; children: Melanie Lynn, Leana Marie, Natalie Rae, Olivia Julene. B.A. in Math., U. Del., M.Ed. Math. instr. Del. Tech. and Community Coll., Wilmington, 1969-75, chmn. math. dept., 1975-79, asst. to campus dir., 1979-82, dean instrn., 1982-83, asst. campus dir., 1983—; city councilman, chmn. edn. com., sch. tax commr., Wilmington, 1972-74; mem. Del. Ho. of Reps., chmn. fin. com., 1974-80, minority leader, 1980-82, speaker, 1982—; mem. state econ. and fin. adv. com. Recipient Com. 39 Good Govt. award, 1979; named U.S. Jaycees Outstanding Man of Yr., 1981. Mem. Nat. Council Tchrs. Math., Big Bros. Assn., Port Wilmington Maritime Soc. Club: Cityside (Wilmington). Home: 2707 Baynard Blvd Wilmington DE 19802 Office: House of Representatives Legislative Hall Dover DE 19901

GEORGE, PETER JAMES, economist, educator; b. Toronto, Sept. 12, 1941; s. Ralph Langlois and Kathleen May (Larder) G.; m. Gwendolyn Jean Scharf, Oct. 19, 1962; children—Michael James, Katherine Jane. B.A. with honors, U. Toronto, 1962, M.A., 1963, Ph.D., 1967. Lectr. McMaster U., 1965-67, asst. prof., 1967-71, asso. prof., 1971-80, prof. econs., 1980—, asso. dean grad. studies, 1974-79, dean social scis., 1980—; spl. lectr. U. Toronto, 1967; vis. lectr. U. Cambridge, 1974; economist Govt. of Ont., 1963; project mgr. Tanzania Tourist Corp., 1970-71. Author: Government Subsidies and the Construction of the Canadian Pacific Railway, 1981; author: The Emergence of Industrial America: Strategic Factors in American Economic Growth Since 1970, 1982. Mem. Can. Econs. Assn., Can. Hist. Assn., Am. Econ. Assn., Econ. History Assn., Econ. History Soc. Home: 91 South St W Dundas ON L9H 4C7 Canada Office: 1280 Main St W Hamilton ON L8S 4M4 Canada

GEORGE, PHYLLIS, sports broadcaster, wife of former gov. of Ky.; b. Denton, Tex., June 25, 1949; d Robert and Louise G.; m. Robert Evans, Apr. 14, 1977 (div.); m. John Y. Brown, Jr., Mar. 17, 1979; 1 son, Lincoln Tyler George. Student, North Tex. State U., Tex. Christian U.; studied dance with Peter Gennaro, Ron Poindexter, Luigi; studied drama under Darryl Hickman, Charles Conrad, Warren Robinson. Joined CBS Sports, 1975; sportscaster CBS NFL Today Show, 6 yrs., Super Bowl, 1979, 80, 81; co-host Miss America Pageant, 1971-79, Candid Camera, People, Tournament of Roses Parade, 1978-82; guest host Good Morning America Show; appeared on Muppets Ann. Award Night, Charlie Brown's 30th Birthday Show, NBC's Tonight Show, CBS's Celebrity Challenge of Sexes, Hour Magazine, Mike Douglas Show, PM Magazine, Merv Griffin Show, Dinah Shore Show; lectr. Author: (with Bill Adler) I Love America Diet Book. Hon. chmn. Ky. Arts and Crafts Found., Save the Mansion, Inc.; charter mem. Com. of 200; chmn. Ky. Film Found.; bd. dirs. Appalachian Community Service Network, 1980-82; house tour chmn. Mus. Am. Folk Art, 1982; chmn. community affairs Spl. Olympics, 1977, 78, 79; hon. trustee United World Coll.; originator Ky. Salute to Women of 80's Rally; sponsor Phyllis George Scholarships at U. Ky. and North Tex. State U. Named Texan of Yr., 1971; Named Miss America, 1971; recipient Ky. Gov.'s Disting. Service medal, 1982, Jack Quinlan award Notre Dame Club Chgo., 1983, Ida Lee Willis Preservation Project award, 1983; named Sportscaster of Yr. Washington Football Club, 1975; co-recipient Emmy award for NFL Today. Mem. Zeta Tau Alpha. Home: Cave Hill Place Lexington KY Office: care Gov's Office State Capitol Frankfort KY 40601

GEORGE, RAYMOND EUGENE, JR., banker; b. Oak Park, Ill., July 22, 1930; s. Raymond Eugene and Irene (Salb) G.; m. Carol Elaine Blumenschein, May 7, 1960; children: Renee Elaine, Melissa Martin, Raymond Eugene III. B.A., Williams Coll., 1952; M.B.A., U. Chgo., 1959. With No. Trust Co., Chgo., 1953—, sr. v.p., 1970—. Treas., dir. Community Fund, Northfield, Ill., 1966-74; Treas. Village of Northfield, 1965-67; commr., pres. Northfield Park Dist., 1970-77; Bd. dirs. Child Care Assn. Ill., 1967-73, Presbyn. Home, Evanston, Ill. Mem. Am. Inst. Banking, Corp. Fiduciaries Ill. (exec. com. 1978—, pres. 1981—), Williams Coll. Alumni Assn. (past pres., dir. Chgo. chpt. 1972—). Republican. Clubs: Economic, University (Chgo.); Indian Hill (Winnetka, Ill.). Home: 703 Prospect Ave Winnetka IL 60093 Office: Northern Trust Co 50 S LaSalle St Chicago IL 60690

GEORGE, RONALD BAYLIS, physician; b. Zwolle, La., Nov. 17, 1932; s. Ronald Lee and Theodora Virginia (Baylis) G. B.A., U. Ala., 1954; M.D., Tulane U., 1958. Diplomate: Am. Bd. Internal Medicine. Intern Charity Hosp., New Orleans, 1958-59, resident internal medicine, 1959-60, 62-64; fellow pulmonary diseases Tulane U., New Orleans, 1964-66; chief inhalation therapy and emphysema sect. VA Hosp., New Orleans, 1966-71; asso. prof. medicine, head pulmonary diseases sect. La. State U. Med. Center, Sch. Medicine, 1972-74, prof. medicine, 1974—, dep. head dept. medicine, 1978—, med. dir. respiratory care and med. ICU, 1983—; chief med. service Shreveport VA Med. Center, 1978-82. Served to capt. M.C. USAF, 1960-62. Fellow Am. Coll. Chest Physicians, A.C.P.; mem. Am. Thoracic Soc., Alpha Omega Alpha. Home: 1821 Willow Point Shreveport LA 71119 Office: PO Box 33932 Shreveport LA 71130

GEORGE, SCOTT, fgn. service officer; b. Mantee, Miss., July 30, 1920; s. Allie Cross and Lena Elvira (Scott) G.; m. Margaret Dean Crain, July 15, 1940; children—Lois Margaret, Rosemary. B.A., Vanderbilt U., 1940, M.A., 1941, Ph.D., 1943; postgrad., U. Mich., 1944-45. Asst. prof. English Vanderbilt U., 1943; joined U.S. Fgn. Service, 1947; assigned successively, Taipei, Hong Kong, Tel Aviv, Bonn, Berlin, Washington, 1st sec. embassy, Oslo, Norway, from 1960, Washington, 1964, counselor embassy, Tokyo, 1967; then dir. Office No. European Affairs, Dept. State, Washington; U.S. minister, dep. comdt., West Berlin, 1975-78; internat. affairs advisor Nat. War Coll., Washington, 1978—; Lectr. English George Washington U., Am. U., 1957-60. Served to 2d lt. AUS, 1945-47. Mem. Am. Fgn. Service Assn., Phi Beta Kappa, Omicron Delta Kappa, Phi Kappa Psi. Address: 7616 Edenwood Ct Bethesda MD 20817

GEORGE, THOMAS, artist; b. N.Y.C., July 1, 1918; s. Rube and Irma (Seeman) Goldberg; m. Laverne Burton, July 16, 1951; children: John R., Geoffrey T. B.A., Dartmouth Coll., 1940. One-man exhbns. include, Feragil Gallery, N.Y.C., 1951, 53, Korman Gallery, N.Y.C., 1954, one-man exhbns. include, Dartmouth Coll., 1965, Contemporaries Gallery, N.Y.C., 1956, Bridgestone Mus., Tokyo, 1957, Betty Parsons Gallery, N.Y.C., 1959, 63, 65, 66, 68, 70, 72, 74, 76, 78, 81, Reid Gallery, London, 1962, 64, Esther Bear Gallery, Santa Barbara, Calif., 1969, Del. Mus., 1971, Henie-Onstad Art Mus., Oslo, Trane Garden Gallery, Copenhagen, Jefferson Pl. Gallery, 1973, Princeton U. Art Mus., 1975, Nat. Collection Fine Arts, 1977, Dartmouth Coll., 1979, Nat. Gallery, Oslo, 1980, Maxwell Davidson Gallery, N.Y.C., 1983, Riis Gallery, Oslo, 1982, 84, group exhbns. include, Met. Mus. Art, N.Y.C., Am. Fedn. Arts, Mus. Modern Art, N.Y.C., Whitney Mus. Ann., N.Y.C., Carnegie Internat., Pitts., Pa. Acad., Japan Internat Biennial Art, Tokyo, White House, Lausanne (Switzerland) Mus.; represented in permanent collections, Whitney Mus., Mus. Modern Art, N.Y.C., Bklyn. Mus., Tate Gallery, London, Nat. Coll. Fine Arts at Smithsonian Instn., Washington, Chase Manhattan Coll., N.Y.C., Library of Congress, Bridgestone Mus., Dartmouth Coll., Lausanne Mus. Art, Mus. Fine Arts, Houston, U. Calif. Art Mus., Berkeley, Santa Barbara Mus. Fine Arts, Okla. Art Center, U. Calif. Mus., Santa Clara, Yale U. Art Gallery, Flint (Mich.) Inst., N.J. State Mus., Rose Art Mus., Brandeis U., Heine-Onstad Art Mus., San Francisco Mus. Art, Del. Art Mus., Nat. Gallery, Oslo, Princeton Art Mus., many corp. collections; vis. painter, Edward MacDowell Colony, 1956; vis. artist, U. Tex., 1978; artist-in-residence, Dartmouth Coll., 1979 (Recipient purchase prize Bklyn. Mus. 1955), Dartmouth Coll. (Ford Found. 1961), Dartmouth Coll. (Whitney Mus. Ann. Am. Painting 1962), Dartmouth Coll. (N.J. State Mus. 1971), Dartmouth Coll. (Purchase prize N.J. State Mus. 1971), Dartmouth Coll. (Olympic games Poster/Print Commn. 1974). Served with USNR, 1942-45. Grantee Rockefeller Found., 1957. Address: 20 Greenhouse Dr Princeton NJ 08540 *In the modern world artists remain among the few individuals who can still control their work from beginning to end. This independence carries a unique and critical responsibility.*

GEORGE, THOMAS FREDERICK, chemistry educator; b. Phila., Mar. 18, 1947; s. Emmanuel John and Veronica Mather (Hansel) G.; m. Barbara Carol Harbach, Apr. 25, 1970. B.A. in Chemistry and Math, Gettysburg (Pa.) Coll., 1967, M.S., Yale U., 1968, Ph.D., 1970. Research asso. M.I.T., 1970; postdoctoral fellow U. Calif., Berkeley, 1971; mem. faculty U. Rochester, N.Y., 1972—, prof. chemistry, 1977—; disting. vis. lectr. dept. chemistry U. Tex., Austin, 1978; disting. speaker dept. chemistry U. Utah, 1980; disting. lectr. Air Force Weapons Lab., Kirtland AFB, N.Mex., 1980; mem. com. recommendations U.S. Army Basic Sci. Research, 1978-81; vice chmn. 6th Internat. Conf. Molecular Energy Transfer, Rodez, France, 1979; chmn. Gordon Research Conf. Molecular Energy Transfer, Wolfeboro, N.H., 1981; cons., lectr. in field. Sloan fellow, 1976-80. Mem. adv. editorial bd.: Chem. Physics Letters, 1979-81; mem. adv. bd.: Jour. Phys. Chemistry, 1980—; co-author 160 papers in field. Tchr.-scholar Camille and Henry Dreyfus Found., 1975-82. Guggenheim fellow, 1983-84. Mem. Am. Chem. Soc. (exec. com. phys. div. 1979-82), Am. Phys. Soc., N.Y. Acad. Scis., Soc. Photo-Optical Instrumentation Engrs., Royal Soc. Chemistry (Marlow medal and prize Faraday div. 1979), Phi Beta Kappa, Sigma Xi. Democrat. Episcopalian. Office: Dept Chemistry U Rochester Rochester NY 14627

GEORGE, WALTER EUGENE, JR., architect; b. Wichita Falls, Tex., Oct. 28, 1922; s. Walter Eugene and Mamie Alta (Evans) G.; m. Mary Carolyn Hollers Jutson, May 20, 1980. B.Arch., U. Tex., 1949; M.Arch., Harvard, 1950. Designer Wiltshire and Fisher (architects), Dallas, 1950-51; partner Pendley, George and Bowman (architects and engrs.), Austin, 1952-57; asst., then asso. prof. architecture U. Tex., 1956-62; prof. architecture, chmn. dept. U. Kans., 1962-67; dean Coll. Architecture, U. Houston, 1967-69; practice of architecture, Austin, 1969-71, 74—, resident architect, Colonial Williamsburg, Va., 1971-73. Served as pilot USAAF, 1943-46; ETO. Decorated Air medal with oak leaf cluster, Purple Heart; recipient Mont San Michele and Chartres award AIA, 1949; 2d award 1st ann. Southwestern furniture competition Dallas Mus. Fine Arts; award for teaching excellence U. Tex., 1960. Mem. AIA, Archaeol. Inst. Am., Soc. Archtl. Historians, Tau Sigma Delta. Episcopalian. Office: PO Box 4426 Austin TX 78765

GEORGE, WILLIAM ARTHUR, dentist, educator; b. Pitts., Jan. 29, 1910; s. Arthur G. and Edith E. (Hall) G.; m. Wilma M. Mackey, Aug. 29, 1936; children—Ruth Ann, William Arthur, Richard Allan. B.S., U. Pitts., 1932, D.D.S., 1932. Gen. practice dentistry, Pitts., 1932-43, 46-58; dentist Sewickley (Pa.) Child Health Assn., 1938-39; part-time instr., then asst. prof. Sch. Dentistry U. Pitts., 1947-58, prof., head dept. prosthodontics, chmn. postgrad. edn., mem. exec. and curriculum coms., 1958—, asst. dean, 1965-68, asso. dean, 1968—; dir. grad. edn.; chmn. bd. Pa. Dental Service Corp., 1973-75; cons. VA Central Office; cons. dentistry VA Hosp., Pitts.; cons. Vietnam edn. project ADA, 1970, 73. Pres. bd. health O'Hara Twp., Allegheny County, Pa., 1958-63. Served from lt. (j.g.) to lt. (s.g.) USNR, 1943-46; capt. Res. Recipient letters of commendation from U.S. Navy, 1955; Plaque award E. Liberty YMCA, Pitts., 1956. Fellow Am. Coll. Dentists; mem. Internat. Assn. Dental Research, ADA (chmn. council on dental research 1965-67, 2d v.p. 1972-73), Pa. Acad. Gen. Dentistry (pres. 1970), East End Dental Soc. (past pres.), Pa. Dental Assn. (pres. 1971-72, trustee, Annual award 1981), Chgo. Dental Soc. (asso.), Odontological Soc. Western Pa. (pres. 1963, del.), Allied Dental Assn. Vietnam, Am. Prosthodontic Soc. (exec. com.), Internat. Coll. Dentists, U. Pitts. Dental Alumni Assn. (past pres.), Res. Officers Assn., Sigma Xi, Pi Kappa Alpha, Psi Omega, Omicron Kappa Upsilon, Omicron Delta Kappa. Presbyn. (elder). Club: Mason (32 deg., Shriner). Home: 110 N Oak Hill Rd Pittsburgh PA 15238

GEORGE, WILLIAM DOUGLAS, JR., consumer products company executive; b. Chgo., Nov. 21, 1932; s. William D. and Kathryn (McWhinney) G.; m. Elinor A. Elsing, June 20, 1964; children: David W., Douglas E., Stephen J. B.A., Depauw U., 1954; M.B.A., Harvard U., 1959. With Gen. Mills, Mpls., 1959-70; dir. corp. devel. Brown Group, Inc., St. Louis, 1970-74, v.p., 1974-81; exec. v.p. S.C. Johnson & Son, Inc., Racine, Wis., 1981—. Bd. dirs. The Prairie Sch., Racine, 1982—. Served with U.S. Army, 1955-57. Office: S C Johnson & Son Inc 1525 Howe St Racine WI 53403

GEORGE, WILLIAM LEO, JR., plant geneticist, educator; b. Riverside, N.J., June 1, 1938; s. William L. and Edna F. G.; m. Marilyn Richard, May 21, 1960; children: Jeffrey, Deborah. B.S., Delaware Valley Coll., 1960; M.S., Rutgers U., 1962, Ph.D., 1966. Research asst. Rutgers U., New Brunswick, N.J., 1960-66; asst. geneticist Conn. Agrl. Expt. Sta., New Haven, 1966-71; asso. prof. dept. horticulture and Lab. for Environ. Studies Ohio State U. and Ohio Agr. Research and Devel. Center, Columbus, 1971-76, prof., 1976-77; prof., head dept. horticulture U. Ill., Urbana, 1977—; vis. prof. U. Fla., Bradenton, 1983; sci. advisor Ill. Apple and Peach Mktg. Bd. Contbr. articles to profl. jours. Mem. Am. Soc. Hort. Sci. (research dir. 1977-78, dir.), Am. Genetic Assn., Bot. Soc. Am., Genetics Soc. Am., Sigma Xi, Gamma Sigma Delta (pres. Ill. chpt. 1981-82). Developer hybrids of vegetable crops. Home: 401 Pond Ridge Ln Urbana IL 61801 Office: 1301 W Gregory St Urbana IL 61801

GEORGE, WILLIAM WALLACE, manufacturing company executive; b. Muskegon, Mich., Sept. 14, 1942; s. Wallace Edwin and Kathryn Jean (Dinkeloo) G.; m. Ann Tonnlier Pilgram, Sept. 6, 1969; children: Jeffrey, Jonathan. B.S. with honors in Indsl. Engring. (Alfred P. Sloan scholar), Ga. Inst. Tech., 1964; M.B.A. with high distinction (J. Spencer Love fellow), Harvard U., 1966. Asst. to asst. sec. Dept. Def., Washington, 1966-68; spl. civilian asst. to sec. Navy, Washington, 1968-69; with Litton Industries, 1969-78, dir. long range planning, Cleve., 1969-70, v.p., 1976—; with Litton Microwave Cooking Products, 1970-78, v.p., Mpls., 1970-71, exec. v.p., 1971-73, pres., 1973-78; v.p. corp. devel., Honeywell, Mpls., 1978-80, exec. v.p., 1983—; pres. Honeywell Europe (S.A.), 1980-82. Bd. dirs. Minn. Symphony Orch., 1976-80, United Way, 1976-79; nat. chmn. United Way, Belgium, 1982-83; bd. dirs., pres., treas. Guthrie Theater, 1977—; vice chmn. bd. United Theol. Sem., 1977-80. Recipient Meritorious Civilian Service Award Sec. Navy, 1969. Sigma Chi (Internat. Balfour award 1964, trustee 1971-77). Episcopalian. Clubs: Minneapolis, Minikahda, Harvard Bus. Sch. (dir. 1971-78), Harvard Bus. Sch. (pres. 1975-76). Home: 2284 W Lake of Isles Blvd Minneapolis MN 55405 Office: Honeywell Plaza Minneapolis MN 55408

GEORGEN, W. DONALD, accountant; b. Chgo., June 1, 1929; s. Michael A. and Lauretta M. G.; m. Eleanor J. Hays, Sept. 15, 1956; children: Susan M., Lauretta M., Catherine J., Sarah A., William D. B.S. in Acctg., U. Notre Dame, 1951; J.D., Northwestern U., 1953. Bar: Ill. 1953. With Touche Ross & Co., 1953—, ptnr., Chgo., 1966-69, dir. audit ops., 1969-72, nat. dir. acctg. and auditing, 1972-79, ptnr.-in-charge, 1979—, vice chmn. bd. dirs., 1979—. Served with AUS, 1954-56. Mem. Am. Inst. C.P.A.s (exec. com SEC practice div.), Ill. Soc. C.P.A.s, N.Y. Soc. C.P.A.s, N.J. Soc. C.P.A.s, Beta Alpha Psi. Roman Catholic. Clubs: Spring Brook Country, Essex, Baltusrol Golf. Home: Morristown NJ 07960 Office: Gateway 1 Newark NJ 07102

GEORGES, JOHN A., paper company executive; b. El Paso, Feb. 24, 1931; s. John A. and Opal (Biffle) G.; m. Zephera M. Givas, June 15, 1952; children: Mark, Andrew, Elizabeth. B.S., U. Ill., 1951; M.S. in Bus. Adminstrn, Drexel U., 1957. Asst. gen. mgr. DuPont Co., 1974-77, gen. mgr., 1977-79; exec. v.p. internat. and wood products and resources Internat. Paper Co., N.Y.C., 1979, vice chmn., 1980, pres., chief operating officer, 1981—, also dir.; dir. Warner Lambert Co. Mem. Joint Council Econ. Edn.; dir. Bus. Council N.Y. State. Served with U.S. Army, 1953-55. Club: N.Y. Yacht. Office: 77 W 45th St New York NY 10036 *

GEORGES, PAUL GORDON, artist, educator; b. Portland, Oreg., June 15, 1923; s. Thomas Theseus and Daisy G.; m. Lisette Georges, Jan. 23, 1950; children: Paulette, Yvette. Student, U. Oreg., Fernand Leger U., Paris. Hans Hofman prof. fine arts Brandeis U., Waltham, Mass., 1977—; vis. artist U. Pa., Phila., Queens Coll., Bklyn., Boston U., Yale U., Dartmouth U. Recipient Hallmark award Carol Beck Gold medal, award Longview Found.; grantee CAPS. Mem. Artists Choice Mus. (bd. chmn.), NAD. Home: 85 Walker St New York NY 10013

GEORGESCU, PETER ANDREW, advertising executive; b. Bucharest, Rumania, Mar. 9, 1939; came to U.S., 1954, naturalized, 1954; s. V.C. Rica and Lygia (Bocu) G.; m. Barbara Anne Armstrong, Aug. 21, 1965; 1 son, Peter Andrew. A.B. cum laude, Princeton U., 1961; M.B.A., Stanford U., 1963. With Young & Rubicam, Inc., N.Y.C., 1963—, dir. mktg., 1977-79, exec. v.p.; dir., Chgo., 1979-82, pres. Young & Rubicam Internat., N.Y.C., 1982—, also corp. dir. Clubs: River (N.Y.C.); Racquet (Chgo.). Home: 901 Lexington Ave New York NY 10021 Office: 285 Madison Ave New York NY 10017

GEORGI, CARL EDUARD, microbiologist, educator; b. Milw., Feb. 18, 1906; s. Herman Emil and Ottilie (Memmler) G.; m. Marjorie Clare Womelsdorff, Aug. 20, 1936 (dec. Sept. 1980); children: Liesl Andrea (Mrs. Leonard Turnus), Todd Anthony. B.S., U. Wis., 1930, M.S., 1932, Ph.D. (Frasch Found. fellow), 1934; Fulbright scholar, U. Paris, 1951-52; student, Inst. Nuclear Studies, Oak Ridge, summer 1950, Cornell U., summer 1960. Diplomate: Am. Bd. Microbiology. Chemist Pfister & Vogel Leather Co., Milw., 1924-26; asst. instr. chemistry U. Wis., 1934-35; mem. faculty U. Nebr., 1935-74, prof. bacteriology, 1947-74, chmn. dept., 1953-71, Regents. prof. microbiology, 1964-71; mem., staff dept. biochemistry, nutrition; research microbiologist Nebr. Agrl. Expt. Sta., 1949-64; lectr., cons. Mem. numerous internat. sci. congresses. Author: (with G.L. Peltier and L.F. Lindgren) Laboratory Manual for General Microbiology; Editorial bd.: Applied Microbiology, 1953-58; Contbr. articles to profl. jours. Trustee Lincoln Gen. Hosp., 1962-75. Recipient Seaman award N.Y. Acad. Medicine, 1951; Sterling fellow Yale U., 1935. Charter fellow Am. Acad. Microbiology; fellow AAAS; mem. Am. Inst. Biol. Scis. (vis. coll. lectr. 1960-70), Am. Soc. Microbiology (pres. Mo. Valley br. 1942-43, chmn. nat. div. gen. microbiology 1966), Nebr. Acad. Sci. (past pres.), Electron Microscope Soc. Am., Am. Soc. Cell Biology, Soc. Exptl. Biology and Med., Soc. Gen. Microbiology of Gt. Britain, AAUP (pres. Nebr. chpt. 1968-69), Am. Soc. Biol. Chemists, Sigma Xi (pres. Nebr. 1948-49), Alpha Chi Sigma, Phi Lambda Upsilon, Gamma Alpha, Phi Beta Kappa (hon., chpt. pres. 1972-73). Episcopalian. Spl. research biochemistry, physiology of thermophilic bacteria, microbial utilization agrl. products. Home: 3033 Georgian Ct Lincoln NE 68502

GEORGI, HOWARD MASON, III, physicist, educator; b. San Bernardino, Calif., Jan. 6, 1947; s. Howard Mason and Mary Alice (Mack) G.; m. Ann Rutledge Blake, June 14, 1969; children: Geoffrey Barnes, Justin Avery. B.A., Harvard U., 1967; Ph.D., Yale U., 1971. Mem. faculty Harvard U., Cambridge, Mass., 1976—, prof. physics, 1980—. Contbr. articles on theoretical particle physics to profl. jours.; author Lie Algebras in Particle Physics. NSF postdoctoral fellow, 1971-73; Sloan Found. fellow, 1976-80. Mem. Am. Phys. Soc., Harvard Soc. of Fellows.; fellow Am. Acad. Arts and Scis. Episcopalian. Office: Physics Dept Harvard U Cambridge MA 02138

GEORGIADE, NICHOLAS GEORGE, physician; b. Lowell, Mass., Dec. 25, 1918; s. George Nicholas and Stephanie (Englisch) G.; m. Ruth Katherine Sauer, Sept. 21, 1942; children—Gregory Stephen, Robert Charles, Nancy Jeanne. Student, Fordham U., 1937-40; D.D.S., Columbia U.; M.D., B.S. in Medicine, Duke U., 1950. Diplomate: Am. Bd. Plastic Surgery (vice chmn. 1974-75), Am. Bd. Oral Surgery. Intern Kings County Hosp., N.Y.C., 1944; intern Med. Center, Duke U., Durham, N.C., 1949-50, resident, 1950-54, mem. faculty, 1953—, asso. prof. plastic, maxillofacial, oral surgery, 1957-61, prof., 1961—; chmn. div. plastic, maxillofacial and oral surgery; mem. staff Duke Hosp.; cons. VA Hosp., Durham, 1954—, Surgeon Gen. of USAF, 1960—, Surgeon Gen. (of U.S. Army), 1958—, NIH, 1963—; dir. Liberty Bank & Trust Co., Durham. Co-author: Textbook of Plastic and Reconstructive Surgery, 1964, Textbook on Burns, 1965; Editor: Plastic and Maxillofacial Trauma Symposium, 1969, Aesthetic Breast Surgery, 1983, Cleft Lip-Palate Symposium, 1973, Reconstructive Breast Surgery, 1976, Reconstructive Surgery Following Mastectomy, 1979; co-editor: Pediatric Plastic Surgery, 1983; Internat. editor: Cleft Palate Jour, 1970—; Contbr. articles to profl. jours. Served with AUS, 1944-46. Nat. Cancer Inst. clin. fellow, 1952-54. Fellow A.C.S. (chmn. plastic and maxillofacial adv. com. 1972-73), So. Surg. Assn.; mem. Am. Soc. Maxillofacial Surgeons (pres. 1962-63), AMA (vice chmn. sect. plastic and maxillofacial surgery), Am. Assn. Plastic Surgeons (v.p., nat. sec., pres. 1977-78), Am. Soc. Plastic and Reconstructive Surgeons (exec. com., chmn. postgrad. edn. com. Ednl. Found.), Am. Soc. Plastic Surgeons (recipient jr. research award 1955, 1st prize sr. research paper 1972), Soc. Head and Neck Surgeons, Plastic Surgery Research Council, Internat. Surg. Soc., Internat. Soc. Aesthetic Surgery (sec. N.Am. 1979—), So. Surg. Assn., Am. Burn Assn., Tissue Culture Assn., Sigma Xi, Alpha Omega Alpha. Patentee in field. Office: Box 3098 Duke U Med Center Durham NC 27710

GEORGIADES, WILLIAM DEN HARTOG, university dean; b. Chgo., May c630, c71925; s. George and Alice (Den Hartog) G.; children: Sheldon Franklin, Beverly Jo. A.B., Upland (Calif.) Coll., 1946; M.A., Claremont (Calif.) Grad. Sch., 1949; Ed.D., U. Calif. at Los Angeles, 1956. Tchr. Whittier (Calif.) High Sch., 1947-49; teaching asst. UCLA, 1950-51; dean Upland Coll., 1951-53; chmn. dept. English Whittier High Sch., 1953-56; prof. edn., chmn. dept. curriculum and instrn. U. So. Calif., 1956-79, asso. dean edn. program devel., 1973-74; dean Coll. Edn., U. Houston, 1979—; Fulbright lectr., Cyprus and Greece, 1962, vis. lectr. in, U.S., Eng., Netherlands, Iraq, Pakistan, India, Iran, Japan, Saudi Arabia; asso. dir. Danforth Found.-Nat. Assn. Secondary Sch.; Prins. model sch. project, 1968—, cons. in field. Author: Models for Individualized Instruction, 1974, New Schools for a New Age, 1977, How Good Is Your School? Program Evaluation for Secondary Schools, 1978, How to Change Your School, 1978, Take Five: A Methodology for the Humane School, 1979; Editor bulls.; Contbr. to research and edn. jours. Pres. La Cresta PTA, 1966; Sr. Danforth asso., 1962. Mem. AAUP, Assn. Higher Edn., Assn. Supervision and Curriculum Devel. (bd. dirs.), Nat. Soc. Study Edn., World Curriculum Council, Doctoral Alumni Assn.

(Disting. Leadership award 1982), Phi Delta Kappa (Research award 1978). Presbyn. (elder 1959—). Home: 204 Sugarberry Circle Houston TX 77024 Office: Coll Edn U Houston Houston TX 77004 *I believe that education is the greatest tool humans have yet discovered to bring about the betterment of humankind everywhere. If the peace dreams of the centuries are ever to become a reality, it will be necessary for those of us who live in this century to commit ourselves as never before to the education of our young.*

GEORGINE, ROBERT A., union official; b. Chgo., July 18, 1932; s. Silvio G. and Rose Gerorgine; m. Rita Greener; 4 children. Student, DePaul U., 1950-54, U. Ill., 1954-56. With Wood, Wire & Metal Lathers Internat. Union, 1953-71, apprentice Local 74, Chgo., 1953, officer, 1956-64, internat. rep., Washington, 1964, asst. to gen. pres., 1966-70, gen. pres., 1970-71; sec.-treas. Bldg. and Constrn. Trades Dept., AFL-CIO, Washington, 1971-74, pres., 1974—. Served with U.S. Army, 1955-57. Office: Bldg and Constrn Trade Dept Room 603 AFL CIO Bldg 815 16th St NW Washington DC 20006 *

GEPHARDT, RICHARD ANDREW, congressman; b. St. Louis, Jan. 31, 1941; s. Louis Andrew and Loreen Estelle (Cassell) G.; m. Jane Ann Byrnes, Aug. 13, 1966; children—Matthew, Christine, Katherine. B.S., Northwestern U., 1962; J.D., U. Mich., 1965. Bar: Mo. bar 1965. Partner firm Thompson & Mitchell, St. Louis, 1965-76; alderman 14th ward, St. Louis, 1971-76; mem. 96th-97th Congress from 3d Mo. Dist.; Pres. Children's Hematology Research Assn., St. Louis Children's Hosp., 1973-76; Democratic committeeman 14th ward St. Louis, 1968-71. Mem. Mo., St. Louis bar assns., Am. Legion, Young Lawyer's Soc. (chmn. 1972-73). Clubs: Mid-Town (St. Louis); Kiwanis. Home: 4121 Fairview St Saint Louis MO 63116 Office: 218 Cannon House Office Bldg Washington DC 20515

GEPHARDT, THOMAS STEUBER, editor; b. Anderson, Ind., May 23, 1927; s. Ralph Andrew and Clara Charlotte (Steuber) G.; m. Deborah Ann Rotruck, Oct. 15, 1960; children—Andrew David Ellis, Clare Deborah Rotruck. Student, U. Chgo., 1947-49; A.B., George Washington U., 1950; M.S. in Journalism, Columbia, 1951. Editor Anderson Herald, 1951-60; editorial writer Cin. Enquirer, 1960, editor editorial page, 1960-72, asso. editor, 1972—. Served with AUS, 1945-47. Mem. Am. Soc. Newspaper Editors, Nat. Conf. Editorial Writers, Sigma Chi. Home: 851 Clifton Hills Terr Cincinnati OH 45220 Office: 617 Vine St Cincinnati OH 45202

GERALD, REX ERVIN, anthropologist, educator; b. Lenorah, Tex., Mar. 18, 1928; s. Cecil Leroy and Mary Elnora (Donelson) G.; m. Elgie Zaiz, Feb. 14, 1961; children: Elgie Lisette, Rex Ervin II, Lorenzo Xocotzin, Camille Nenetzin; children from previous marriage: Rosemary Elaine, Eric Campbell. B.A., U. Ariz., 1951; A.M. (Amerind Found. fellow), U. Pa., 1957; Ph.D. (fellow), U. Chgo., 1975. Anthropometrist Wilton M. Krogman Center for Study Child Growth and Devel., Phila., 1954-55; dir. El Paso Centennial Mus., 1958-80; asst. prof. anthropology U. Tex., El Paso, 1958-75, assoc. prof., 1975—, dir. Archeology Lab., 1977—; cons. archeologist, 1959—. Contbr. articles to profl. jours. Mem. Tex. Bd. Rev., Nat. Register Historic Places, 1974-80. Served with AUS, 1946-48, 51-54; Germany, Korea. Recipient grants U. Tex. El Paso, 1963-65, U. Chgo., 1964-66. Fellow AAAS; mem. Am. Anthropol. Assn., Soc. Am. Archeology, Soc. Profl. Archeologists, N.Mex. Archeology Council, Council Tex. Archeology, Ariz. Archeology Council, Sociedad Mexicana de Geografia y Estadistica, Sigma Xi, Phi Delta Theta. Roman Catholic. Office: Dept Anthropology U Tex El Paso TX 79968

GERALDSON, RAYMOND I., lawyer; b. Racine, Wis., Oct. 7, 1911; s. Gerald and Christina (Johnson) G.; m. Evelyn A. Thorpe, Aug. 5, 1939; children: Raymond I., Mary Nelson Vice, Martha G. Driscoll. B.A., U. Wis., 1933, J.D., 1935; LL.M. (Grad. fellow), Columbia U., 1936; LL.D. (hon.), American U., 1983. Bar: Wis. 1935, Ill. 1945, U.S. Supreme Ct. 1965, D.C. 1972. Practiced in, Racine, 1937-45, Chgo., 1945—; partner firm Seyfarth, Shaw, Fairweather & Geraldson, Chgo.; Dir. Ilg Industries, Easy Up, Inc., Superior Racine, Inc., Precision Gears, Inc. Mem. Midwest Pension Conf., 1958-80, chmn., 1965-66; del. No. Ill. Conf., United Methodist Ch., 1961-75; Trustee Am. U., 1963—, mem. exec. com., 1965-76, chmn. bd. trustees, 1970-76; bd. govs. Am. Nat. Red Cross, 1972-78, mem. exec. com., 1975-78, vice chmn., 1976-78, chmn. nat. planned giving com., 1978-82, mem. nat. fin. devel. com., 1981—, chmn. subcom. on United Way relationships, 1981—; bd. dirs. Mid-Am. chpt. A.R.C., 1963—; bd. dirs., sec. YMCA, Racine, 1943-45, Curtis P. Kendall Found., Evanston, Ill., 1950-71; bd. dirs. Protestant Found. Greater Chgo., 1976—; trustee Kendall Coll., Evanston, 1947—, chmn. bd. trustees, 1952-68; trustee Chgo. Home Missionary and Ch. Extension Soc., 1949—, pres., 1957-61; trustee Met. Crusade of Mercy, Chgo., 1971—. Mem. Am., Ill., Chgo., D.C. bar assns., Am. Judicature Soc. (dir. 1978-82, investment com. 1978-82, chmn. 1979-82), Order of Coif, Phi Beta Kappa, Phi Kappa Phi. Republican. Methodist (steward, trustee, chmn. various commns. and com., chmn. adminstrv. bd. 1970-72). Club: Union League (Chgo.). Home: 1410 Sheridan Rd Wilmette IL 60091 Office: 55 E Monroe St Chicago IL 60603

GERARD, EMANUEL, communications co. exec.; b. Bklyn., Dec. 30, 1932; s. Samuel N. and Sophie (Altschuler) G. B.A. magna cum laude, Brown U., 1954; M.B.A., Harvard U., 1956. Security analyst Wood, Struthers & Co., N.Y.C., 1957-61; partner Roth, Gerard & Co., N.Y.C., 1961-74; mem. office of the pres. Warner Communications Inc., N.Y.C., 1975—, also dir. Home: 10 Gracie Sq New York NY 10028 Office: 75 Rockefeller Plaza New York NY 10019

GERARD, JEAN BROWARD SHEVLIN, ambassador, lawyer; b. Mar. 9, 1938; m. James Watson Gerard; children: James W., Harriet C. A.B., Vassar Coll., 1959; J.D., Fordham U., 1977; LL.M., NYU, 1977; LL.D. hon., U. S.C., 1983. Bar: D.C., Fla., N.Y. Atty. firm Cadawalader, Wickersham & Taft, N.Y.C., 1977-81; ambassador, permanent rep. of U.S. UNESCO, Paris, 1981—. Editor: Fordham Internat. Law Forum, 1977. Bd. govs. Women's Nat. Republican Club, 1967-73, 74-80, pres., 1971-73; hon. del. Rep. Nat. Conv., N.Y.C., 1972; alt. del. 18th Congl. Dist. N.Y. N.Y.C., 1980. Recipient SAR medal, 1970, medal of honor VFW, 1982. Mem. N.Y. County Lawyers Assn., Assn. Bar City of N.Y. Roman Catholic. Clubs: Colony; City Midday (N.Y.C.); Capitol Hill (D.C.). Office: US Mission to UNESCO 1 rue Miollis Paris France 75015

GERARD, ROBERT A., investment banker; b. N.Y.C., Oct. 19, 1944; s. Michael A. and Loti G. (Falk) G.; m. Elizabeth Collidge Gallatin, Oct. 15, 1969; children: Celia Coolidge, Robert Gallatin, William Alexander. B.A. cum laude, Harvard U., 1966; J.D. magna cum laude, Columbia U., 1969. Bar: D.C. 1970. Law clk U.S. Ct. Appeals, Washington, 1969-70; assoc. Wilmer, Cutler & Pickering, Washington, 1970-74; asst. sec. U.S. Dept. Treasury, Washington, 1974-77; mng. dir. Dillon, Read & Co. Inc., N.Y.C., 1977-83, Morgan Stanley & Co., Inc., 1983—. Trustee Episcopal Sch., N.Y.C., 1981—; mem. Bi-State Panel on Port Authority, N.Y., N.J., 1982; mem. Gov.'s Panel on World Trade Ctr., N.Y.C., 1980. Home: 133 E 64th St New York NY 10021 Office: Morgan Stanley & Co Inc 1251 Ave of America New York NY 10020

GERARD, ROY JOSEPH, physician; b. Bay City, Mich., Dec. 18, 1924; s. Roy Joseph and Grace Q. (Reed) G.; m. Patricia Beckett, Apr. 6, 1947; children—Patrice, Michele, Timothy, Thomas, Suzette, Celeste, Elice, Juliette, Marianne, Roy Joseph. A.A., Bay City Jr. Coll., 1945; B.S., U. Mich., 1949, M.D., 1953. Diplomate: Am. Bd. Family Practice. Intern St. Luke's Hosp., Saginaw, Mich., 1953-54; resident Saginaw Gen. Hosp., 1954; practice medicine, Saginaw, 1955-71; dir. Family Practice Residency Program, Saginaw, 1971-75; prof., chmn. dept. family practice Mich. State U., East Lansing, 1975—; med. dir. St. Francis Home for Aged, Saginaw, 1960-70. Contbr.: chpt. to Family Practice, 1978. Bd. dirs. Mich. Blue Cross/Blue Shield.; Physician coordinator Vis. Nurses Assn. Home Care Project, Saginaw, 1965-75; Physician rep., project coordinator Robert Wood Johnson Health Team devel. grant, 1974-76. Served with inf. AUS, 1943-45. Decorated Bronze Star, Purple Heart. Fellow Am. Acad. Family Physicians; mem. AMA, Mich. Med. Soc. (cert. of commendation 1975), Ingraham County Med. Soc., Mich. Acad. Family Physicians, Soc. Tchrs. Family Medicine, Royal Soc. Medicine, Assn. Depts. Family Medicine. Home: 1117 Portage Path East Lansing MI 48823 Office: Dept Family Practice Mich State U B-100 Clinical Center East Lansing MI 48824

GERARD, W. GENE, corporate executive; b. Decatur, Ill., Dec. 10, 1932; s. William A. and Pauline (Brown) G.; m. Georgette S. Gerard, Sept. 30, 1960; children: Jennifer, Lisa, Kathleen. B.A., Dartmouth Coll., 1955; M.B.A., Northwestern U., 1957. Ptnr. White & Co., Saint Louis, 1961-68; v.p. fin. Liberty Loan, St. Louis, 1970-74; sr. v.p. and treas. ITT Fin., St. Louis, 1975—; dir., pres. Genedon Investment Corp., St. Louis, 1961—; chmn. bd. trustees AFSA Execs. Inst., Boulder, Colo., 1981—. Mem. Fin. Execs. Inst., Soc. Fin. Analysts. Club: St. Louis (Clayton, Mo.). Office: ITT Fin Corp 700 Community Federal Center Saint Louis MO 63131

GERARDIA, HELEN, artist, educator; b. Ekaterinislov, Russia, Dec. 25, 1903; d. Jacob and Sophie (Lipshitz) Goldberg. Student, N.Y. Tng. Sch. for Tchrs., Art Students League, Hans Hoffman, Bklyn. Mus. Art Sch. Tchr., N.Y. Tng. Sch. Tchrs., 1921-23. Tchr. pub. schs., N.Y.C., 1924—; Adv. bd. Marquis Biog. Library Soc., 1969—. Artist in oil, watercolor, casein, lithography, etching, drawing media; one-man shows include, Research Studio Art Center, Maitland, Fla., 1953, 57, Rudolph Galleries, Woodstock, N.Y., 1953, 55, Albany Inst. History and Art, 1955, U. Maine, Orono, 1957, exhbn. oils, Bodly Gallery, N.Y.C., 1957, 59, 61, 63, 65, 68, 72, Fairleigh Dickinson U., 1960, Fordham U., 1967, Ga. Mus., Athens, Ga., 1968, Carver Mus., 1969, Abilene Fine Arts Mus., Tex., 1971, Fla. Gulf Coast Art Center, 1973, Mobile (Ala.) Art Gallery, 1974, Lincoln U., Jefferson City, Mo., Central Wyo. Art Mus., 1975, Keokuk (Iowa) Arts Center, 1976, Purdue U., 1978, SUNY, Alfred, 1979, 83, Central Mo. State U., 1980, Loyola U., New Orleans, U. Portland, Oreg., 1981, Niles Twp. Media Ctr., Ill., 1982, U. Minn., Bemidji, Anderson Coll., Ind., group shows, Art U.S.A., 1958, 59, Corcoran Gallery, 1959, 60, Provincetown Art Assn., 1958, 59, Soc. Am. Graphic Artists, 1959, print retrospective at, Marist Coll., 1968, France, also exhibits in, Europe, Africa, Japan, Greece; exhibited oil painting, Athens, Greece, 1957; many traveling shows, U.S. and abroad, one-man traveling show of caseins, U.S., 1957—, one-man traveling show of graphics, U.S., 1957, one-man traveling show of paintings and graphics, U.S., 1969; represented in collections, NYU, Fogg Mus., Cin. Mus., Butler Art Inst., Met. Mus., Bklyn. Mus., Dartmouth, Lincoln Center, N.Y.C., Tampa Art Center, Library of Congress, Wichita Art Mus., Abilene Fine Arts Mus., Fayette Mus., Ala., Tyler Mus., Tex., Meridian Mus., Miss., Albany Inst. History and Art, N.Y., Portland Art Mus., Oreg., Lyman Allen Mus., New London, Conn.; Demonstrator casein technique, 64th and 65th ann. Nat. Assn. Woman Artists; represented in collections, Schumacher Gallery, Columbus, Ohio; juror, 6th Ann. Nat. Portsmouth Seawall Art Show, 1976; represented in collections, Columbus Mus. Art, Ohio; juror, 21st Nat. Print Show, Hunterdon Art Center, Clinton, N.J., 1977; represented in collections, Kearney State Coll., Nebr., Everson Mus. Art, Syracuse, N.Y., Miss. Mus. Art, Jackson, Downey Mus. Art, Calif., Mus. Fine Arts, Springfield, Mass., Asheville Art Mus., N.C., Albright-Knox Art Gallery, Buffalo, Reading Pub. Mus., Pa. Recipient purchase prize award Boston Soc. Independents, 1951, 56, Abraham Lincoln Graphics Exhbn. fellowship Research Studio Art Center, 1952, 53, Yaddo, Saratoga Springs, 1955, Maganini award for an oil Silvermine Guild 8th N.E. Ann., 1957, award Painters and Sculptors Soc., N.J., 1961, Joel Landres prize oil Bklyn. Soc. Artists, 1957, 2d Grumbacher award Nat. Soc. Painters in Casein, 1960, award, 1963, 66, Lempert award N.J. Painters and Sculptors, 1960; also Robert Boardman prize, 1968; Paris Meml. prize Am. Soc. Contemporary Artists, 1968; Watson Guptill award, 1979; Harry N. Abrams award in graphics, 1976; 2d pl. award Oil Painters and Sculptors N.J., 1978; Andrew Nelson Whitehead award, 1981; Elizabeth Erlanger Meml. prize for painting Nat. Assn. Women Artists, 1982; Stauffer award Pen and Brush, 1983. Mem. Nat. Soc. Painters in Casein (v.p. 1968-69, award juror 1968 Ann), Soc. Am. Graphic Artists (corr. sec. 1966—, exec. bd. 1968-72, del. Internat. Assn. Art 1962, Japan 1966, Holland 1969, Bulgaria 1973, corr. sec. 1970—, treas. 1974-84), Bklyn. Soc. Artists (past bd. govs., juror in all mediums), League of Present Day Artists (past chmn.), Vectors, Internat. Assn. Artists (treas. U.S. com. 1975-84, U.S. del. to 10th Internat. Congress, Finland 1983, treas. 1979-82), Am. Soc. Contemporary Artists (award 1963-66, pres. 1965-66, exec. bd. 1967, v.p. 1968—, permanent hon. adv. bd. 1970—), Silvermine Guild Artists, Artists Equity N.Y. (corr. sec. 1964—, exec. bd., dir. 1974-78, rec. sec. 1979-82), Nat. Assn. Woman Artists (medal of Honor, Markell prize 1961, 64, award 1962, 63, Berne Meml. prize 1966, Dr. Holzinger Meml. award 1969, Grumbacher award 1972, Buell Meml. prize 1973, permanent adv. bd. pres. 1972-74), Woodstock Artists Assn. (bd. govs., past chmn.), Creative Assos., Soc. Young Am. Artists, Print Club, Color Print Soc., Audubon Artists Inc. (pub. relations chmn. 1964-68, juror selection Ann. in Graphics 1968, treas. 1969—, dir. in oil 1974-76, chmn. ways and means com. 1979-81). Home: 490 West End Ave Apt 4C New York NY 10024

GERATHY, E. CARROLL, former insurance executive, real estate developer; b. Long Island City, N.Y., June 25, 1915; s. Joseph Hewson and Emma E. (Donady) G.; m. Julia F. Gill, Sept. 7, 1942; children: Nancy, John; m. Joyce K. Baker, Dec. 31, 1972; children: Stephen Baker, Nancy Baker. M.B.A., U. Chgo., 1962. C.L.U. With McKesson & Robbins, Inc., 1933-48; with Prudential Ins. Co. Am., 1948-78, sr. v.p., 1964-78; project dir. Hilton Hawaiian Village, Hilton Hotels Corp., 1979-81, Third Newark Gateway Urban Renewal Assn., 1981—. Mem. N.J. C. of C. Club: Canoe Brook (N.J.) Country. Home: 42 Knob Hill Dr Summit NJ 07901 Office: Third Newark Gateway Urban Renewal Assn Newark NJ 07102

GERBER, BARBARA ANN WITTER, university dean, educator; b. Buffalo, May 28, 1934; d. Leslie Martin and Erma Anna (Euller) Witter; m. W.J. Gerber, Jan. 29, 1955 (div. 1964); 1 dau., Jaime Ann. A.B., Syracuse U., 1955, M.S., 1959, Ed.D., 1964. Lic. psychologist, N.Y. Tchr. Lafayette (N.Y.) Central Sch., 1955-57; counselor, guidance dir. Cheektowaga (N.Y.) Central Sch., 1958-61; lectr. Syracuse (N.Y.) U., 1963-64, asst. prof., 1964-66; asst. prof. counseling and sch. psychology SUNY, Oswego, 1965-67, asso. prof., 1967-75, prof., 1975—, acting dean grad. studies, 1974-75, assoc. dean profl. studies, 1978-80, dean profl. studies, 1980—; pvt. practice psychology, Syracuse, 1964—. Bd. dirs. Central N.Y. council Girl Scouts U.S.A., 1973-76, 81—; mem. Nat. Ski Patrol, 1967-80, asst. patrol leader for first aid tng., 1973-77, sect. chief, Syracuse, 1977-79; trustee May Meml. Unitarian Soc., 1972-75. Mem. Am. Psychol. Assn., Am. Personnel and Guidance Assn., Nat. Women's Studies Assn. (treas. 1982-84), Nat. Assn. Women Deans, Adminstrs. and Counselors. Unitarian. *Being trustworthy, honest but kind, open to ideas from self and others, and loyal, along with a belief that everyone is capable of change, has characterized my adult life.*

GERBER, DAVID, television producer; b. Bklyn.; m. Loraine Stephens. Ed., U. Pacific. Former TV supr. Batten, Barton, Durstine & Osborn; former sr. v.p. Gen. Artists Corp.; v.p. charge TV sales 20th Century Fox TV, 1965. Entered ind. prodn. with: TV series The Ghost and Mrs. Muir, 1968-70; became ind. producer for, Columbia Pictures TV, 1972; exec. v.p. for worldwide prodn., 1974-76; ind. producer, David Gerber Prodns., N.Y.C., 1976—; exec. producer: TV series including Nanny and the Professor, 1970-71, Ghost and Mrs. Muir, 1970, Cade's Country, 1971-72, Needles and Pins, 1973, Born Free, 1974, Police Story, 1973—, Police Woman, 1974—, Joe Forrester, 1975-76, The Quest, 1976, Gibbsville, 1976; TV movies including The Return of Joe Forrester, 1975, John O'Hara's Gibbesville, 1976, The Lindbergh Kidnapping Case, 1976, To Kill A Cop, 1978, Power, 1979, Medical Story, Born Free, 1979, Beulah Land, 1980, The Night the City Screamed, 1981, Follow the North Star, 1981 (Christopher award); others. (Recipient Emmy award Nat. Acad. TV Arts and Scis. 1976)

GERBER, DOUGLAS EARL, educator; b. North Bay, Ont., Can., Sept. 14, 1933; s. Earl Jacob and Bertha (Cox) G.; m. Shirley Mildred Baker, Aug. 31, 1957; 1 dau., Allison S. B.A., U. Western Ont. (Can.), London, 1955, M.A., 1956; Ph.D., U. Toronto, 1959. Lectr. Greek U. Toronto, 1958-59; mem. faculty dept. classics U. Western Ont., London, 1959—, asso. prof., 1964-69, prof., 1969—, chmn. dept., 1969—, W.S. Fox chair of classics. Author: A Bibliography of Pindar, 1513-1966, 1969, Euterpe: An Anthology of Early Greek Lyric, Elegiac and Iambic Poetry, 1970, Emendations in Pindar, 1513-1972, 1976, Pindar's Olympian One: A Commentary, 1981. Mem. Classical Assn. Canada (treas. 1960-62), Am. Philol. Assn. (editor trans. 1974-82), Classical Assn. Middle West and South, Classical Assn. (Gt. Britain). Home: 105 Cherryhill Blvd Apt 1004 London ON Canada N6H 2L7 Office: Dept Classics U Western Ontario London ON Canada N6A 3K7

GERBER, ELLA, theatre director, actress; b. N.Y.C., Aug. 25, 1916; d. Isadore and Esther (Treisman) G.; m. Sam Kasakoff, May 29, 1943. Student, Columbia U., 1943, Am. Theatre Wing, 1948-49, U. Birmingham, Eng., 1955, Actors Studio, 1960-61, 74-76, N.Y. U., 1963, Fordham U., 1979-80. With Army Spl. Services, Hawaii, Japan, Korea, 1946-47; adjudicator Alaska State Community Theatre Assn., Haines, 1979, Festival of Community Theatres, 1983; mem. faculty Studio of the Theatre, Hollywood, Calif., 1947-48, Am. Acad. Dramatic Arts, N.Y.C., 1957-59, 66-67, 76, Am. Mus. and Dramatic Acad., 1967-68; guest faculty London Opera Center, 1968; artistic dir. Youngstown (Ohio) Playhouse, 1964-65; dir.-tchr. for arts Six Theatre Program, Mass., 1969-72. Appeared in: plays Pins and Needles on Broadway and U.S. and Can. tours, 1938-41, Inside Emily Payne, 1959, The Laundry, 1963; appeared in: film Barabbas, Rome, 1961; dir.: Broadway show Design for a Stained Glass Window, 1950; Off Broadway plays Homecoming, 1950, Tiger Rag, 1961; dir. for, Equity Theatre, Dark of the Moon, 1949, Primrose Path, 1950, All God's Chillun, 1952, Flight Into Egypt, 1958, Dial M for Murder, 1958, Lost in the Stars, 1968; dir.: Dark of the Moon, Rome, Italy, 1961; Porgy and Bess, N.Z., 1965; plays, Australia, 1965-66, Israel, 1966, Portugal, 1973, 75, Carousel, Johannesburg, S. Africa, 1968; Love and Conflict, Theatre-in-Edn. Tour, U.S., 1973, Madwoman of Chaillot, Duke U., 1972, The Crucible, St. Lawrence U., N.Y., 1976, S.C. Open Road Ensemble, 1973, The Skin of Our Teeth, E. Carolina U., Greenville, N.C., 1977; also on univ. faculty; dir., mus. theatres in, Tex., N.J., Pa., Ohio. Can., Fla., Mo.; Conn., R.I., Md, N.Y., Mass, 1958-67, summer stock, 1949-71; Porgy and Bess in, Eastern U.S. and Can., 1958, 65, S.C. Tri-Centennial Celebration, 1970, Los Angeles Civic Light Opera Co., Los Angeles, 1974, Theatre of Stars, Atlanta, Mich. Opera Theatre, 1975, U. Utah, 1981, Children's Hour, Harvard U., 1978, Thread of Scarlet, N.Y.C., 1978, A Doll's House, 1980, The Three Sisters, 1980, The Miser, Vanderbilt U.; Author: (with Howard Richardson) Thread of Scarlet, 1980, Glory for Me. Bd. dirs. Found. for Extension and Devel. of Am. Profl. Theatre, 1968. MacDowell Colony fellow, 1966-67. Mem. Dramatist Guild Soc. Stage Dirs. and Choreographers (past exec. bd.), Actors Equity Assn., AFTRA. Address: 329 E 58th St New York NY 10022 *My life in the theatre has been very rewarding and challenging. My adage has always been "Dare to Do"—whether I'm teaching or directing. Without courage one cannot hope to make creative contributions—and it takes guts to stick to what you believe in. If I had it to do all over again, I'd still choose a life in the theatre. It's been glorious and fabulous and painful and divine.*

GERBER, EUGENE J., bishop; b. Kingman, Kans., Apr. 30, 1931; s. Cornelius John and Lena Marie (Tiesmeyer) G. B.A., St. Thomas Sem., Denver; B.S., Wichita State U.; B.S.Th., Catholic U. Am.; S.T.L., Angelicum, Rome. Ordained priest Roman Catholic Ch., 1959; asst. chancellor Wichita Diocese, 1963, sec. to bishop, 1964, vice chancellor, 1967, mem. diocesan bd. adminstrn., 1973, diocesan cons., 1973, chancellor, 1975; chaplain, mem. governing bd. Holy Family Center for Mentally Retarded; bd. dirs. Cursillo; pastor Blessed Sacrament Parish, Wichita, bishop of, Dodge City, Kans., 1976—. Office: Chancery Office 910 Central Ave PO Box 849 Dodge City KS 67801 *

GERBER, HADASSA, advertising agency executive; b. N.Y.C., Mar. 15, 1952; s. Benjamin and Rosalyn (Pollack) G. Student, Pratt Inst., 1973-74, postgrad., 1977. Media planner Ted Bates & Co., N.Y.C., 1972-74; asst. media dir. Grey Advt. Inc., N.Y.C., 1975-78; v.p., asst. media dir. BBDO, N.Y.C., 1978-80; sr. v.p., dir. media info. and new technologies McCann-Erickson Inc., N.Y.C., 1981—; lectr., instr. Bernard Baruch, Coll., 1979-80, Parson Sch. Design, 1980—, NYU, 1982. Mem. Videotex Industry Assn. (dir. 1982—), Am. Assn. Advt. Agys. (new tech. com. 1982—). *To remove from life as many ifs as possible, so that in advance years I will not look back sadly and say, "if only I had done this"*

GERBER, JOHN CHRISTIAN, English educator; b. New Waterford, Ohio, Jan. 31, 1908; s. Christian G. and Leonora (Hauptmann) G.; m. Margaret E. Wilbourn, Sept. 3, 1941; children: Barbara Page Barrett, Ann Wilbourn Gerber Sakaguchi. A.B., U. Pitts., 1929, M.A., 1932; Ph.D., U. Chgo., 1941; D.Letters (hon.), Morningside Coll., 1979. Instr. English U. Pitts., 1931-36; instr. English U. Chgo., 1938-42, pre-meteorology, 1942-44; asst. prof. English U. Iowa, 1944-47; asso. prof., 1947-49, prof., 1949-76, Carpenter prof. emeritus, 1976—, chmn. dept. English, 1961-76, dir. Sch. Letters, 1967-76; prof. English State U. N.Y. at Albany, 1976-84, chmn. dept., 1976-81; vis. asso. prof. English U. So. Calif., summer 1949; vis. prof. U. N.Mex., summers 1952, 57, Trinity Coll., summers 1960, 63, U. Calif. at Berkeley, 1960-61, U. Colo., summer 1965, Am. U. at Cairo, 1970, Korean univs., summer; 1972, Chinese univs., summer 1979; cons. English U.S. Office Edn., 1964-65. Author: (with Walter Blair) Factual Prose, 1945, Literature, 1948, Writers Resource Book, 1953, (with Fleece and Wylder) Toward Better Writing, 1958, (with Arnold and Ehninger) Repertory, 1960, Twentieth Century Interpretations of the Scarlet Letter, 1968, Studies in Huckleberry Finn, 1971; also chpts. in Toward General Education,

1948; editorial bd.: Coll. English, 1947-48, 65-71, Am. Quar, 1963-68; editorial adviser: Philol. Quar, 1951-57; editorial adv. bd.: Resources for American Literary Study, 1971—; chmn. editorial bd.: Windhover Press, 1968-72; mem. editorial bd.: U. Iowa Press, 1963-67; chmn. editorial bd.: Iowa-California Edit. of the Works of Mark Twain, 1965-83; hist. editor: Tom Sawyer vol., 1980; editor: Teaching Coll. English, 1965, Scott-Foresman Key Edits; contbr. articles to profl. jours.; author intros. several books. Recipient Distinguished Service award Iowa Council Tchrs. English, 1972. Mem. Nat. Council Tchrs. English (Hatfield award 1964, Exec. Com. award 1974, trustee of research found. 1962-65, pres. 1955), Conf. Coll. Composition and Communication (chmn. 1950, Founders award 1976), Modern Lang. Assn. (chmn. Am. lit. sect. 1969, mem. exec. council 1972-75, mem. nominating com. 1981-83), Midwest Modern Lang. Assn. (pres. 1966), N.E. Modern Lang. Assn., Assn. Depts. English (chmn. 1964), Phi Beta Kappa. Address: 359 Magowan Ave Iowa City IA 52240

GERBER, JOHN JAY, pub. relations exec.; b. Morton, Ill., Nov. 26, 1914; s. John E. and Anna (Mosiman) G.; m. Gladys Eittreim, Sept. 20, 1941; children—Jay T., Julia Ann, Stephen E. A.B., U. Utah, 1935; student, Northwestern, 1937-39. Salesman Keystone Steel & Wire Co., Peoria, Ill., 1935-37; pub. relations dept. Northwestern U., 1937-42, 46-52, dir., 1947, v.p. pub. relations, 1949-52; partner Gonser-Gerber-Tinker-Stuhr, Chgo., 1952-80, cons., 1980—; spl. agt. FBI, 1942-46; vice chmn., dir. Bank of Westmont, Ill.; chmn. Bank of Naperville, Ill.; dir. Bank Lisle, Ill.; vice chmn. bd., dir. 1st Security Bank Glen Ellyn, Ill., Bank of Lockport; chmn. 1st Security Bank of Fox Valley, Aurora, Ill.; Past alumni regent Northwestern U. Author: (with Thomas A. Gonser) Gonser and Gerber on College Development, 1961. Recipient Alumni Service award Northwestern U., 1961. Mem. Phi Beta Kappa, Beta Gamma Sigma. Republican. Mem. United Ch. of Christ. Club: Economic. Home: 25 W 8th Ave Naperville IL 60540 Office: 105 W Madison St Chicago IL 60602

GERBER, JOSEPH NEWTON, coll. dean; b. Bloomington, Ill., Jan. 1, 1910; s. Elmer Joseph and Mary Edna (Hilton) G.; m. Gertrude Palmer, Aug. 9, 1942; children—John (dec.), Barbara Hilton. B.A., Ill. State U., 1934; M.S., U. Ill., 1935; Ph.D., George Peabody Coll., 1941. High sch. tchr. and prin. Witt, Ill., 1935-39; coordinator workshop activities George Peabody Coll., summer 1951; dir. student personnel Northwestern State Coll., Natchitoches, La., 1941-50; dean jr. div. Stephen F. Austin State Coll., Nacogdoches, Tex., 1950-55, dean of coll., 1955-59, acting pres., 1958, dean of coll., dean, 1959-67, dean, dir. research, 1967-80; workshop cons. U. Fla., also Fla. State U., summers 1948-49; Mem. Tex. Commn. on Guidance; bd. So. Bd. Tchr. Edn.; chmn. Tex. Statewide Com. on Common Calendar for Colls. and Univs.; coordinator sch. and coll. calendars; mem. exec. com., pres. Conf. So. Grad. Schs., 1974—. Contbr. articles profl. jours. Mem. exec. com. Council of Grad. Schs. in, U.S., 1974-77; Bd. dirs. Nacogdoches County United Fund, Nacogdoches Community Hotel Corp.; exec. com. Attoyac area council Boy Scouts Am. Served to lt. comdr. USNR, 1942-45; comdr. Res. Mem. Assn. Tex. Colls. and Univs. (chmn. commn. standards and classification 1965-68, v.p. 1968-69), Am. Psychol. Assn., AAAS, Am. Assn. Sch. Adminstrs., Am. Coll. Personnel Assn., Nacogdoches C. of C. (dir.), Phi Delta Kappa, Kappa Delta Pi, Kappa Phi Kappa, Gamma Theta Upsilon. Methodist (steward). Club: Rotarian (past pres. Nacogdoches, Tex.). Home: 3307 N Raguet St Nacogdoches TX 75961

GERBER, MYRON DANE, retail executive; b. Balt., 1922. Ed., U. Fla. With Drug Fair Inc., 1938—, chmn. bd., chief operating officer, dir., 1970—. Address: Drug Fair Inc 6295 Edsall Rd Alexandria VA 22321 *

GERBER, ROGER ALAN, lawyer, business executive; b. Bklyn., Jan. 27, 1939; s. Edward and Anne (Rothstein) G.; m. Jane E. Satlow, Sept. 20, 1964; children—Dina, Deborah, Tamar. B.A. magna cum laude (Rufus Choate scholar), Dartmouth Coll., 1959; J.D., Harvard U., 1962. Bar: N.Y. 1963. Assoc. firm Kaye, Scholer, Fierman, Hays & Handler and other law, real estate atty. ABC, Inc., 1965-68; v.p., sec., gen. counsel, dir. Meyers Parking System, Inc., N.Y.C., 1975—; v.p., gen. counsel ISS Internat. Service System, Inc., N.Y.C., 1975-83; pres. Meyers Realty Co., N.Y.C., 1982—; abritrator Am. Arbitration Assn., 1973—. Treas. Scarsdale (N.Y.) Democratic Com., 1977—; v.p., exec. com. Bd. Jewish Edn., Greater N.Y., 1977—; bd. dirs. Conf. Jewish Social Studies, 1975—, Jewish Conciliation Bd., N.Y.; class agt. Dartmouth Coll. Mem. N.Y. State Bar Assn., Phi Beta Kappa. Democrat. Club: Harvard (N.Y.C.). Office: 330 W 42d St New York NY 10036

GERBER, SANFORD EDWIN, audiologist; b. Chgo., June 16, 1933; s. Leon and Rose (Ely) G.; children: Howard M., Michael B., Naomi R., Sharon R. B.A., Lake Forest Coll., 1954; M.S., U. Ill., 1956; Ph.D., U. So. Calif., 1962. Sr. human factors specialist System Devel. Corp., Santa Monica, Calif., 1958-60; head speech and hearing research Hughes Aircraft Co., Fullerton, Calif., 1960-65; asst. prof. audiology U. Calif., Santa Barbara, 1965-69, assoc. prof., 1969-75, prof., 1975—, coordinator speech and hearing scis., 1974-79, chmn. dept. speech and hearing scis., 1979—; mem. sci. bd. Audio-Metric Labs. Inc., Stamford, Conn.; cons. CBS Tech. Center, Stamford. Author: Introductory Hearing Science, 1974, Audiometry in Infancy, 1977, Early Diagnosis of Hearing Loss, 1978, Auditory Dysfunction, 1980, Early Management of Hearing Loss, 1981, The Development of Auditory Behavior, 1983, The Multiply-Handicapped Hearing-Impaired Child, 1983; contbr. numerous articles to profl. jours. Pres. Congregation B'nai B'rith, Santa Barbara, 1972-74; pres. Univ. Religious Conf., 1974-76; trustee Santa Barbara Council for Retarded, 1973-78, treas., 1983—; trustee Santa Barbara Jewish Fedn., 1974—. Fellow Soc. Ear, Nose, Throat Advances in Children (pres. 1976-77), Am. Acad. Otolaryngology (asso.), Am. Speech-Lang.-Hearing Assn.; mem. Internat. Audiology Soc. (exec. com. 1982—), Acoustical Soc. Am., Am. Assn. Phonetic Scis., AAUP, Sigma Xi. Clubs: Channel City, B'nai B'rith. Home: 3856 Crescent Dr Santa Barbara CA 93110 Office: Dept Speech U Calif Santa Barbara CA 93106 *While I may be able to comment upon my own standards of conduct, I cannot say if these standards have led to "success" in another's view. I have endeavored to find and say truth in my scholarly activity and in my daily life; perhaps this is a form of integrity. As a teacher, I hope to help find my students' integrity. I don't believe that I have "created" my students, but maybe sometimes I have helped them create themselves.*

GERBER, SEYMOUR, publishing company executive; b. Chgo., Feb. 19, 1920; s. Hyman and Fannie (Walton) G.; m. Rose Kaminker, Dec. 25, 1941; children: Ila Barrie Gerber Richter, Avis Hope Gerber Jones, Larry Alan. Grad., U. Ill. Pres. Graphic Advt., Inc., Chgo., Graphic Arts Inc., Halsey Pub. Co., Miami, Fla. Served to capt., Ordnance Dept. AUS, 1941-45. Recipient awards from various assns. Mem. Fla. Mag. Assn. Clubs: Art Dirs. Miami; Emerald Hills Country (Hollywood, Fla.); La Costa Country (Carlsbad, Calif.). Office: Halsey Publishing Co 12955 Biscayne Blvd North Miami FL 33169 *If in the space of my lifetime, I can as a communicator, contribute to an understanding among all people for a peaceful coexistence and eliminate at least a modicum of bigotry, my efforts will have been worthwhile.* *

GERBER, THOMAS WILLIAM, retired newspaper editor; b. Portland, Oreg., May 2, 1921; s. Thomas W. and Mary Anne (Smith) G.; m. Gail L. Graham, Jan. 20, 1951 (div. Jan. 1970); children: Cheryl Ann, Linda Lee; m. Electra Bilmazes, Dec. 26, 1971. A.B., Dartmouth, 1948. Reporter U.P.I., Boston, 1948-51, mgr. Providence bur., 1952-53; rewriteman, spl. assignment reporter Boston Herald and Traveler, 1953-56, chief, 1956-61; gen. mgr. Concord (N.H.) Monitor, 1961-67, editor, asst. pub., 1967-83, ret., 1983; dir., sec. Monitor Pub. Co., 1962-78; dir. TeleCable, Inc., Concord, 1968-73, Concord br. Bank of N.H., 1962—. Mem. adv. com. N.H. Tech. Inst., 1966-70; chmn. air quality com. N.H. Environmental Council, 1970; mem. Citizens Task Force, 1969, N.H. Jud. Council, 1972-74; vice chmn. N.H. Council for Humanities, 1972-74; Bd. dirs. Concord YMCA, 1962-71, N.H. Council World Affairs, N.H. Council Better Schs., 1965-72, Concord Hosp., 1962-73; adv. bd. Dartmouth Pub. Affairs Center, 1974—; pres. bd. Bishop Brady High Sch., Concord, 1969-73; vice chmn. N.H. Free Press-Fair Trail Com., 1976—; mem. Pulitzer Prize Jury, 1978-79. Served with USAAF, 1942-45; Served with USAF, 1951-52. Decorated Air medal with two oak leaf clusters; recipient Heywood Broun award Am. Newspaper Guild, 1955. Mem. New Eng. Newspaper Assn., Am. Soc. Newspaper Editors, New Eng. Soc. Newspaper Editors (pres. 1967), Sigma Delta Chi (Yankee Quill award 1973). Home: RFD 7 Carter Hill Rd Concord NH 03301

GERBER, WILLIAM, writer; b. Phila., July 12, 1908; s. Samuel and Fanny (Kramer) G.; m. Sylvia R. Wigdor, Aug. 6, 1933; 1 son, Louis M.W. B.A. with honors, U. Pa., 1929; M.A., George Washington U., 1932; student, Johns Hopkins U., 1932-33, 35-37; Ph.D., Columbia, 1945. Tchr. secondary sch., 1929-30; staff Office Hist. Adviser, Div. Research and Publ., Hist. div. Dept. State, 1930-57, fgn. service officer, 1957-60; staff div. fgn. labor conditions Dept. Labor, 1958-65, dep. chief, 1965- 68; cons. Harvard U. Program on Tech. and Society, 1968-69; fgn. affairs writer Editorial Research Reports, Washington, 1968-71; writer Congl. Quar. Service, Washington, 1972-73; instr. philosophy and world lit. Washington Hall Jr. Coll., 1955-57, acting dir. humanities div., 1956-57; lectr. philosophy U. Md., 1959-60, 63-72, Am. U., 1962. Author: The Department of State of the United States, 1942, The Domain of Reality, 1946, (with Letitia A. Lewis) Freedom of Information in American Policy and Practice, 1948, (with Edwin S. Costrell) The Department of State, 1930-55, 1955, The Mind of India, 1967, paperback edit., 1977, American Liberalism, 1975; Contbr. to: Am. Brit. periodicals. Program participant Internat. Congress Philosophy, Mexico City, Mexico, 1963 Program participant Internat. Congress Philosophy, Vienna, Austria, 1968 Program participant Internat. Congress Philosophy, Varna, Bulgaria, 1973, Inter-Am. Congress Philosophy, Washington, 1957, Inter-Am. Congress Philosophy, Tallahassee, 1982, Internat. Congress Philosophy, Montreal, 1983. Mem. Am. Philos. Assn., Phi Beta Kappa, Eta Sigma Phi (editor nat. jour. 1928-29). Jewish. Home: 3077 Chestnut St NW Washington DC 20015

GERBERDING, WILLIAM PASSAVANT, university president; b. Fargo, N.D., Sept. 9, 1929; s. William Passavant and Esther Elizabeth Ann (Habighorst) G.; m. Ruth Alice Albrecht, Mar. 25, 1952; children: David Michael, Steven Henry, Elizabeth Ann, John Martin. B.A., Macalester Coll., 1951; M.A., U. Chgo., 1956, Ph.D., 1959. Congl. fellow Am. Polit. Sci. Assn., Washington, 1958-59; instr. Colgate U., Hamilton, N.Y., 1959-60; research asst. Senator E.J. McCarthy, Washington, 1960-61; staff Rep. Frank Thompson, Jr., Washington, 1961; faculty UCLA, 1961-72, prof., chmn. dept. polit. sci., 1970-72; dean faculty, v.p. for acad. affairs Occidental Coll., Los Angeles, 1972-75; exec. vice chancellor ULCA, 1975-77; chancellor U. Ill., Urbana-Champaign, 1978-79; pres. U. Wash., Seattle, 1979—; dir. Wash. Mut. Savs. Bank, Pacific N.W. Bell, Seattle, Safeco Corp.; cons. Def. Dept., 1962, Calif. Assembly, 1965. Author: United States Foreign Policy: Perspectives and Analysis, 1966; co-editor, contbg. author: The Radical Left: The Abuse of Discontent, 1970. Trustee Macalester Coll., 1980-83. Served with USN, 1951-55. Recipient Distinguished Teaching award U. Calif., Los Angeles, 1966; Ford Found. grantee, 1967-68. Mem. Am. Polit. Sci. Assn. Address: 808 36th Ave E Seattle WA 98112

GERBERICH, WILLIAM WARREN, educator; b. Wooster, Ohio, Dec. 30, 1935; s. Harold Robert and Clarissa Thelma (Ross) G.; m. Susan Elizabeth Goodwin, Aug. 15, 1959; children—Bradley Kent, Brian Keith, Beth Clarice. B.S. in Engring. Adminstrn, Case Inst. Tech., 1957; M.S. in Indsl. Engring, Syracuse U., 1959; Ph.D. in Materials Sci. and Engring, U. Calif., Berkeley, 1971. Registered profl. engr. Calif. Research engr. Jet Propulsion Lab., Calif. Inst. Tech., Pasadena, Calif., 1959-61; research scientist Aeronutronic, Newport Beach, Calif., 1961-64; engring. research specialist Aerojet Gen., Sacramento, 1964-67; lectr., research metallurgist U. Calif. and Lawrence Radiation Lab., Berkeley, 1967-71; dir. materials sci. U. Minn., Mpls., 1972—, asso. prof., dept. chem. engring. and materials sci., 1971-75, prof., 1975—, asso. head dept., 1980—; cons. accident prevention div. Minn. Dept. Labor and Industry, also steel, constrn. and aerospace cos. Contbr. articles to tech. jours. Recipient Teleen English prize Case Inst. Tech., 1959, William Spraragen award Welding Jour., 1968. Mem. AIME, ASTM, Am. Soc. Metals, Sigma Xi, Tau Beta Pi, Pi Delta Epsilon, Phi Delta Theta. Republican. Home: 8016 Ridgeway Rd Golden Valley MN 55426 Office: Chem Engring and Materials Sci Bldg U Minn Minneapolis MN 55455

GERBIE, ALBERT BERNARD, obstetrician, gynecologist, educator; b. Toledo, Nov. 20, 1927; s. Louis and Fay (Green) G.; m. Barbara Hirsch, June 29, 1952; children: Gail Diane, Stephen Ralph. M.D., George Washington U., 1951. Intern Michael Reese Hosp., Chgo., 1951-52; preceptorship in Ob-Gyn under Drs. R.A. Reis, J.L. Baer, E.J. DeCosta, Chgo., 1952-55; practice medicine specializing in Ob-Gyn, Chgo., 1955—; mem. faculty Northwestern U. Med. Sch., Chgo., 1952—, prof. Ob-Gyn, 1972—, dir. continuing grad. edn., 1975—; mem. staff Northwestern Meml. Hosp., 1955—; chief div. ob-gyn. Children's Meml. Hosp.; v.p., dir. Am. Bd. Ob-Gyn, 1978—. Assoc. editor: Surgery, Gynecology, and Obstetrics, Am. Jour. Ob-Gyn; author textbooks; contbr. articles to profl. jours., chpts. to textbooks. Served with U.S. Army, 1946-47. Mem. Am. Gynecol. Soc., Am. Assn. Obstetricians and Gynecologists, A.C.S., Am. Coll. Obstetricians and Gynecologists, Central Assn. Ob-Gyn, Soc. Human Genetics, AMA, Chgo. Gynecol. Assn. (pres. 1977-78). Office: 707 Fairbanks Ct Chicago IL 60611

GERBINO, JOHN, advt. co. exec.; b. N.Y.C., Mar. 28, 1941; s. John and Pauline (Valenti) G.; m. JoAnna LoPresti, Jan. 20, 1962 (div.); 1 son, John Paul; m. E. Randall McConahy, Aug. 14, 1976; 1 son, Christopher Laughlin. Student, N.Y. Community Coll., 1959; student design, Sch. Visual Arts, 1963-66. Designer Lashe and Driscoll Studio, N.Y.C., 1959-61, Dell Pub. Co., 1961-64; asst. art dir. Harper's Bazaar mag., 1964-66; art dir. New York mag. and Book Week mag. of World Jour. Tribune Co., 1966-67; asst. to editorial dir. Condé Nast Publs., 1967-69; art dir., designer U.S. Mag.; art dir. Essence Mag., 1969, New Woman Mag., 1969-72; formed John Nicholas Gerbino Advt., Inc., Ft. Lauderdale, Fla., 1973—; cons. art dir. to mags., 1964—; work rep. Art Dirs. Show, 1966. Designed, illustrated: 1st edit. Nixon Poems; freelance book jacket designer, 1962—; (Recipient 2 awards Sch. Visual arts Show 1965, Certificate of Merit, Art Dirs. Show 1966). Mem. N.Y. N.G., 1966-70. Home: 901 SE 11 St Deerfield Beach FL 33441 Office: 2000 W Commercial Blvd Fort Lauderdale FL 33309

GERBNER, GEORGE, communications educator, university dean; b. Budapest, Hungary, Aug. 8, 1919; came to U.S., 1939, naturalized, 1944; s. Arpad and Margaret (Muranyi) G.; m. Ilona Kutas, Oct. 8, 1946; children: John C., Thomas J. Student, U. Budapest, 1937-38, UCLA, 1940-41; B.A., U. Calif.-Berkeley, 1943; M.S., U. So. Calif., 1951, Ph.D., 1955; L.H.D. (hon.), LaSalle Coll., Phila., 1980. Reporter, asst. fin. editor The Chronicle, San Francisco, 1942-43; engaged in free-lance publicity, 1947-48; instr. Pasadena (Calif.) Jr. Coll., 1948-51, El Camino Coll., Los Angeles, 1951-56; asst. prof., then asso. prof. U. Ill., Urbana, 1956-64; prof. communications, dean Annenberg Sch. Communications, U. Pa., 1964—. Author numerous articles and books in field.; Editor: Jour. of Communication, 1974—. Served to 1st lt. inf. AUS; Served to 1st lt. inf. OSS, 1943-46; NATOUSA ETO. Decorated Bronze Star; grantee U.S. Office Edn., 1959, NSF, 1962, 80, 83, NIMH, 1958, 71—, Internat. Sociol. Assn., 1963, UNESCO, 1963, 83, Nat. Commn. Causes and Prevention Violence, 1969, Surgeon Gen.'s Sci. Adv. Com., 1970, White House Office Telecommunications Policy, 1977, U.S. Adminstrn. on Aging, 1978, AMA, 1979; grantee Com. on Religious Research, 1983. Fellow Internat. Communication Assn.; Mem. Am. Sociol. Assn., Internat. Assn. Mass Communication Research, Assn. Edn. Journalism. Home: 234 Golf View Rd Ardmore PA 19003 Office: Annenberg Sch Communications Univ Pa Philadelphia PA 19104 *Promise nothing, deliver everything.*

GERBODE, FRANK LEVEN ALBERT, surgeon, research executive; b. Placerville, Calif., Feb. 3, 1907; s. Frank A. and Anna Mary (Leven) G.; children: Maryanna Gerbode Shaw, Frank Albert, Penelope Ann, John Philip. B.A. cum laude in Physiology, Stanford U., 1932, M.D., 1936; M.D. (hon.), U. Thessaloniki, Greece, 1964, U. Uppsala, Sweden, 1965, M.Surgery, Nat. U. Ireland, 1961. Diplomate: Am. Bd. Surgery, Am. Bd. Thoracic Surgery (founding mem. 1951). Intern Highland Hosp., Oakland, Calif., 1935-36; asst. in pathology U. Munich (Germany), 1936-37; asst. resident in surgery Stanford U. Hosps., 1937-38, 38-39, asst. in surg. research, 1938, resident in surgery, 1939-40; practice medicine specializing in surgery and cardiovascular surgery, San Francisco, 1945—; instr. surgery Stanford U., 1940-42, asst. clin. prof. surgery, 1947-50, asso. clin. prof., 1950-54, asso. prof., 1954-59, clin. prof., 1959-71, clin. prof. emeritus, 1971—; dir. Heart Research Inst., Med. Research Inst., Pacific Med. Center, San Francisco, 1959—; chief dept. cardiovascular surgery Heart Research Inst., Inst. Med. Scis., Pacific Med. Center, 1959-79; mem. staffs Children's Hosp., Presbyn. Hosp., both San Francisco; cons. Letterman Army Hosp., San Francisco; guest prof. surgery to univs., hosps., 1953-74; clin. prof. U. Calif., San Francisco, 1964-75; mem. surgery tng. com. USPHS NIH, 1960-67. Editorial bd.: Annals of Surgery. Mem.-at-large San Francisco Bay Area council Boy Scouts Am., 1971—. Served to lt. col. M.C. U.S. Army, World War II; ETO, Africa. Decorated knight Brit. Order St. John of Jerusalem; hon. perpetual student St. Bartholomew's Hosp., London; recipient Disting. Civilian Service award U.S. Army, 1978. Fellow Royal Coll. Surgeons (Eng.) (hon.), Royal Coll. Surgeons (Edinburgh) (hon.); mem. Am. Coll. Cardiology, A.C.S., Am., Calif., San Francisco heart assns., AMA, Calif., San Francisco, Pan Am. med. assns., Am. Surg. Assn., Pacific Coast Surg. Assn., Pan Pacific Surg. Assn. (pres. 1966-69), Western Surg. Assn., Argentine Surg. Assn., Am., Calif. thoracic socs., Calif., Hollywood acads. medicine, Calif. Acad. Sci., Excelsior, So. surg. socs., Halsted Soc., James IV Assn. Surgery, Internat. Soc. Cardiovascular Surgery (pres. N.Am. chpt. 1961-62), Internat. Soc. Surgery (pres. N.Am. chpt. 1971-74, pres. congress 1973-75, pres. 1975-77), Am. Assn. Thoracic Surgery (pres. 1972-73), Samson Thoracic Surg. Soc., Soc. Thoracic Surgeons, Soc. Univ. Surgeons, Soc. Vascular Surgery (pres. 1958-59), Soc. Clin. Surgery, AAAS, Deutsche Gesselschaft für Chirurgie, Soc. Thoracic and Cardiovascular Surgeons Gt. Britain and Ireland, Assn. Thoracic and Cardiovascular Surgeons Asia, Panhellenic Surg. Soc., La Sociedad Mexicana de Cardiologia, Societa Italiana di Chirurgia, Société de Chirurgie Thoracique de Lange Francaise, 38th Parallel Med. Soc. (Korea), Sigma Xi, Alpha Omega Alpha. Clubs: St. Francis Yacht, Stanford, Pacific-Union, Bohemian, Chit Chat (San Francisco); Univ. (N.Y.C.). Home: 2560 Divisadero St San Francisco CA 94115 Office: 2200 Webster St San Francisco CA 94115

GERBOSI, WILLIAM A., bus. cons.; b. Chgo., Feb. 6, 1909; s. Paul and Mary (Palermo) G.; m. Celia Gambardella, July 13, 1929; 1 dau., Maryann. Ph.C., U. Ill., 1928. With Jewel Tea Co., Inc., 1930—, v.p., gen. mgr. routes dept., 1945-55, dir., 1948-73, exec. com., 1951-55; cons., 1955-59; asst. to pres. Salerno Megowen Biscuit Co., 1959-65; v.p. Boden Products, Inc., 1962—; v.p., dir. Safeway Trucking Co., 1962-67; v.p., chmn. exec. com. Ramo, Inc., until 1967; chmn. exec. com., dir. Jet X Corp., 1970-75; chmn. Picture Master Color Lab. Inc., 1970—; dir. Resco, Inc., 1st Nat. Bank of Barrington, Navajo Freight Lines, Matthews Realty Co. Inc., 1980—; treas. Hydro-Wash Inc., 1980. Trustee Village of Arlington Heights, 1952-54. Decorated Star of Solidarity, Italy). Mem. Nat. Retail Tea and Coffee Mchts. Assn. (past pres., dir.). Club: Hiwan Country. Home: 2523 S Thunderbird Ln Evergreen CO 80439

GERBRACHT, RICHARD EDWIN, marketing company executive; b. Erie, Pa., Jan. 2, 1932; s. Edwin Jacob and Ursula (Schulze) G.; m. Shirley Ann Dillon, Jan. 22, 1955; children: Robert, Thomas, Elizabeth, John, Patrick, Kathleen, Richard. B.A., U. Notre Dame, 1954; postgrad., Advanced Mgmt. Program, Harvard U. With Interpub. Group of Cos., 1954-74; exec. v.p., gen. mgr. Marschalk Co., Cleve., 1967-73; v.p. Interpub., N.Y., 1973; sr. v.p., area mgr. McCann-Erickson Europe, 1974; chmn., chief exec. officer Griswold-Eshleman Co., Cleve., 1974-83; prin. Gerbracht & Co., Cleve., 1983—. Trustee St. John Hosp., 1980—; also treas.; bd. dirs. Cleve. Ballet, 1979—; trustee Old Stone Ch. Mem. Greater Cleve. Growth Assn. (dir. 1972-82). Clubs: Union, Chagrin Valley Hunt; Harvard (N.Y.C.). Home: PO Box 232 Fox Hill Dr Gates Mills OH 44040 Office: Gerbracht & Co 1801 E 12th St Suite 218 Cleveland OH 44114

GERCKENS, LAURENCE CONWAY, regional planning educator; b. Passaic, N.J., Mar. 30, 1934; s. Henry and Anna Estelle (Conway) G.; m. Louise Edith Graupp, Nov. 19, 1955; children: Krista Dorothy, Ann Estelle, Jeffrey Laurence, Kim Marie, Timothy Joseph, Jon Andrew. Certificate in art, Cooper Union, 1954; B.S. in Architecture, U. Cin., 1956; M. Regional Planning, Cornell U., 1958. Instr. architecture Mont. State U., 1958-60; inst., asst. prof. architecture Ariz. State U., 1960-63; asso. prof. city and regional planning Ohio State U., Columbus, 1963-69, prof., 1969—, chmn. div. city and regional planning, 1968-70, dir. Sch. Architecture, 1970-78, mem. exec. com., 1970-77, mem. Univ. Senate, 1974-76, council on acad. affairs, 1975-78, co-chmn. council on acad. affairs, 1976-77, mem. rules com., council on acad. affairs, 1974-76, chmn. rules com., council on acad. affairs, 1975-76, mem. computer-based edn. com., council on acad. affairs, 1977-79; Fulbright distinguished vis. scholar U. Chile, 1977, Pontificia U. Javeriana; U. Nacional, U. de Los Andes, Bogota, Colombia, 1979, U. Nacional, U. Bolivariana, Medellin, Colombia, 1979; guest lectr. Am. city planning history at over 40 Am. and fgn. colls. and univs.; pvt. practice urban devel. cons., 1958—; mem. nat. adv. com. Fulbright Sr. Scholar's Council for Internat. Exchange of Scholars, 1982—; U.S. rep. Internat. Conf. on the Future of the City, Medellin, Colombia, 1982. Author: A Primer in Architectural Drawing and Composition, 1963, Programmed Annual Course Manuals in City Planning History-Computer Aided Instruction, 1970—; Contbr.: chpts. to The World of Construction, 1968, The Practice of Local Government Planning, 1979; The American Planner: Biographies and Recollections, 1982. Bd. dirs. Center for Exptl. Research in Arts, 1965-

67, Columbus Urban Environment Workshop, 1968-71, Ohio Planning Conf., 1968-70. Recipient Nat. Design Merit award FHA, 1964; recipient Award of Achievement Ohio Planning Conf., 1981, MacQuigg Award for Outstanding Teaching Coll. of Engring. Ohio State U., 1981. Mem. Am. Inst. Cert. Planners (charter mem., dir. Columbus sect. 1966, pres. Ohio Valley chpt. 1967-69, medal for significant service to Inst. 1971, chmn. program com. Nat. Conf. 1970, bd. govs. 1973-76), Am. Planning Assn., Town Planning Inst. Gt. Britain (hon. corr.), Coll. Architects Chile (hon.), Orgn. Am. Historians, Fulbright Alumni Assn., Phi Kappa Phi, Epsilon Pi Tau, Alpha Rho Chi., Texnikoi. Democrat. Home: 3655 Darbyshire Dr Columbus OH 43220 Office: Room 392 Brown Hall 190 W 17th Ave Ohio State U Columbus OH 43210

GERDEMANN, JAMES WESSEL, plant pathologist, educator; b. Warrenton, Mo., Nov. 13, 1921; s. Carl Edward and Cora Wilhelmina (Wessel) G.; m. Janice Mae Olbrich, July 2, 1949; children—Stephen, Dale, Glenn. B.A., U. Mo., 1945, M.A., 1946; Ph.D., U. Calif., Berkeley, 1948. Teaching asst. U. Mo., Columbia, 1945-46; research asst. U. Calif., Berkeley, 1946-48; prof. plant pathology U. Ill., Urbana, 1948-81, prof. emeritus, 1981—. Author: Taxonomy of the Endogonaceae, 1974; condr. research in field; contbr. writings to publs. Recipient Ruth Allen award, 1977, Funk award, 1977, excellence in undergrad. teaching award U. Ill., 1976. Fellow Am. Phytopathol. Soc.; mem. Am. Mycol. Soc. Home: PO Box 391 Yachats OR 97498

GERDES, INGEBORG, photographer; b. Merseburg, Germany, July 20, 1938; d. Guenter and Gertrud Klein. M.F.A., San Francisco Art Inst., 1970. Photography instr. extension program U. Calif., San Francisco, 1976-78, San Francisco Art Inst., 1978, U. Calif., Santa Cruz, 1981-83; freelance photographer, San Francisco, 1970—. Nat. Endowment for Arts fellow, 1975, 77; photography survey grantee, 1978; Seattle Arts Commn./Nat. Endowment for Arts photography survey grantee, 1980. Home: 3025 21st St San Francisco CA 94110

GERDES, NEIL WAYNE, library director; b. Moline, Ill., Oct. 19, 1943; s. John Edward and Della Marie (Ferguson) G. A.B., U. Ill., 1965; B.D., Harvard U., 1968; M.A., Columbia U., 1971; M.A. in L.S., U. Chgo., 1975. Ordained to ministry Unitarian Universalist Assn., 1975. Copy chief Little, Brown, 1968-69; instr. Tuskegee Inst., 1969-71; library asst. Augustana Coll., 1972-73; editorial asst. Library Quar., 1973-74; librarian Meadville Theol. Schs., Chgo., 1973—; library program dir. Chgo. Cluster Theol. Schs., 1977-80; dir. Hammond Library, 1980—; prof. Chgo. Theol Sem., 1980—. Mem. ALA, Am. Theol. Library Assn., Chgo. Area Theol. Library Assn., Phi Beta Kappa. Office: Hammond Library Chgo Theol Seminary 5757 S University Ave Chicago IL 60637

GERDES, ROBERT H., foundation executive; b. Oakland, Calif., July 4, 1904; s. Robert Anton and Anna (Banks) G.; m. Narendra Blair, June 1, 1935; children: Sally Wray, Anne Vietmeyer, Barbara Brandes. B.S., U. Calif., 1926, J.D., 1928. Bar: Calif. 1928. Assoc. Hugh Goodfellow, atty., 1928-29; atty. law dept. Pacific Gas & Electric Co., 1929-35; ptnr. Earl, Hall & Gerdes, 1935-43; asst. gen. counsel Pacific Gas & Electric Co., 1943-45, gen. counsel, 1945-53, v.p. and gen. counsel, dir., 1953-55, exec. v.p., dir., 1955-63, pres., 1963-65, chmn. bd., chief exec. officer, 1965-69, chmn. exec. com., 1969-77; v.p., trustee James Irvine Found., San Francisco. Mem. Edison Electric Inst. (pres. 1968-69), San Francisco Bar Assn., State Bar Calif., Pacific Coast Elec. Assn. (past pres.), Kappa Alpha, Phi Delta Phi. Republican. Clubs: Bohemian, Pacific-Union, Claremont Country. Home: 61 King Ave Piedmont CA 94611 Office: James Irvine Found 1 Market Plaza Staurt St Suite 2305 San Francisco CA 94105

GERDINE, LEIGH, university president; b. Sheyenne, N.D., June 22, 1917; s. O. E. and Margaret E. (Mattson) G.; m. Alice Strauch Meyer, Nov. 21, 1961. A.B., U. N.D., 1938; Mus. B. (Rhodes scholar), Oxford U., Eng., 1941, postgrad., 1946-48; Ph.D., U. Iowa, 1941; H.H.D. (hon.), Washington U., St. Louis, 1979. Asst. prof. music Miss. State Coll. for Women, Columbus, 1941-42; asso. prof. music, exec. sec. dept. music, Miami U., 1948-50; prof., chmn. dept. music Washington U., St. Louis, 1950-70; pres. Webster U., St. Louis, 1970—; chmn. bd. Block Partnership, Inc., 1967-70; Program annotator St. Louis Symphony Orch., 1950-66, acting mgr., 1965-67. Translator: Phrasing and Articulation (by Hermann Keller), 1965, The Well-Tempered Clavier (by Hermann Keller), 1976, New Music With Thirty-One Notes (by Adriaan Fokker), 1975; pub. orchestrations Brahms sonatas, realizations of Handel violin sonatas, Bach flute sonatas. Bd. dirs. Greater St. Louis Arts and Edn. Council, St. Louis Symphony Soc., Loretto-Hilton Repertory Theatre, Inc., Opera Theatre St. Louis. Served with USAAF, 1942-46; ETO. Decorated Bronze Star medal; Croix de Guerre, France. Home: 6244 Forsyth Blvd Saint Louis MO 63105 Office: Webster Coll 470 E Lockwood St Saint Louis MO 63119

GERDING, THOMAS GRAHAM, health care co. exec.; b. Evanston, Ill., Feb. 11, 1930; s. Louis Henry and Helen Frances (Graham) G.; m. Beverly Ann Starnes, June 18, 1955; children—Mark, David, Gail, Gene Ann. Student, U. Notre Dame, 1948-49; B.S., Purdue U., 1952, M.S., 1954, Ph.D., 1960. Tech. dir. Glenbrook Labs. div. Sterling Drug Inc., N.Y.C., 1964-66; dir. product devel. Sterling-Winthrop Research Inst. div., Rensselaer, N.Y., 1966-71; v.p. research and devel. Calgon Consumer Products div. Merck & Co., Inc., Rahway, N.J., 1971-77; v.p., dir. research div. Johnson & Johnson Products Inc., New Brunswick, N.J., 1977—. Served with U.S. Army, 1954-56. Mem. Am. Chem. Soc., Am. Pharm. Assn., Soc. Chem. Industry, Am. Mgmt. Assn., Assn. Research Dirs. Republican. Roman Catholic. Clubs: Union League (Chgo.); Shrewsbury River Yacht. Office: 501 George St New Brunswick NJ 08903

GERE, JAMES MONROE, educator; b. Syracuse, N.Y., June 14, 1925; s. William S. and Carol (Hixson) G.; m. Janice M. Platt, June 1, 1946; children—Susan M., William P., David S. B.S., Rensselaer Poly. Inst., 1949, M.S., 1951; Ph.D., Stanford, 1954. Registered profl. engr., Calif., N.Y. Instr. Rensselaer Poly. Inst., 1949-51; faculty, Stanford, 1954—, prof. civil engring., 1962—; asso. dean Sch. Engring., 1960-67, exec. head dept. civil engring., 1967-72; cons. and lectr. in field, 1954—. Author 7 textbooks in field, also tech. papers. Served with USAAF, 1943-46; ETO. Fellow ASCE; mem. Am. Soc. Engring. Edn., Earthquake Engring. Research Inst., Sigma Xi, Tau Beta Pi. Home: 932 Valdez Pl Stanford CA 94305

GERE, RICHARD, actor; b. Phila., Aug. 31, 1949. Attended, U. Mass. Played trumpet, piano, guitar and bass and composed music with various musical groups acting appearances with, Provincetown Playhouse; plays include Great God Brown; Camino Real, Rosencrantz and Guildenstern are Dead; off-Broadway prodn. Killer's Head, in; London and Broadway prodn. Taming of the Shrew, Midsummer Night's Dream; Broadway prodns. Habeas Corpus, Bent; appeared in and composed music for: Volpone at, Seattle Repertory Theatre; film debut in Report to the Commissioner, 1975; other films include Baby Blue Marine, 1976, Looking for Mr. Goodbar, 1977, Days of Heaven, 1978, Blood Brothers, 1978, Yanks, 1979, American Gigolo, 1980, An Officer and a Gentleman, 1982, Breathless, 1983, Beyond the Limit, 1983. Office: Care Pickwick Maslansky Koenigsberg 545 Madison Ave New York NY 10022

GERETY, PETER LEO, archbishop; b. Shelton, Conn., July 19, 1912; s. Peter Leo and Charlotte (Daly) G. Student, St. Thomas Sem., Bloomfield, Conn., 1934, Seminaire St. Sulpice, Paris, France, 1939. Ordained priest Roman Catholic Ch., 1939; asst. pastor, New Haven, 1939-42; dir. Blessed Martin de Porres Interracial Center, 1942-56; pastor, New Haven, 1956-66, coadjutor bishop, Portland, Maine, 1966—, apostolic adminstr., Portland, 1967—, bishop, 1969-74, archbishop of, Newark, 1974—. Address: 31 Mulberry St Newark NJ 07102

GERFEN, HENRY JAMES, advertising executive; b. Chgo., Ill., Apr. 24, 1940; s. John and Alma Anna (Schwager) G.; m. Constance Heyland McCurdy, Dec. 10, 1961 (div. 1968); 1 son, Henry James; m. 2d Margaret Agnes Mihalko, July 24, 1971. B.A., Dartmouth Coll., 1961; M.B.A., Tuck Sch. Bus. Admintrn., 1962. Sales rep. Scott Paper Co., Chgo, Ill., 1962-63; assoc. product mgr. Gen. Foods Corp., White Plains, N.Y., 1963-66; v.p., mgmt. supr. Warren Muller, Dolobowsky, N.Y.C., 1966-72; v.p. mktg. Mennen Co., Morristown, N.J., 1972-73; pres. Mathieu, Gerfen & Bresner, N.Y.C., 1973-83; chmn. bd. Bloom Agy., Inc. (formerly Mathieu, Gerfen & Bresner), N.Y.C., 1983—, dir.; dir. Mathiew, Gerfen & Bresner, Toronto, Marenwood Mgmt., Inc. Mem. Am. Assn. Advt. Agys., Nat. Advt. Agy. Network. Lutheran. Club: Spring Brook Country. Office: 304 E 45th St New York NY 10017

GERGEN, DAVID RICHMOND, former government official; b. Durham, N.C., May 9, 1942. B.A., Yale U., 1963; J.D., Harvard U., 1967. Staff asst. Nixon Adminstrn., Washington, 1971-72; spl. asst. to Pres., chief White House writing/research team, Washington, 1973-74; spl. counsel to Pres. Ford, dir. White House Office Communications, Washington, 1975-77; resident fellow Am. Enterprise Inst.; mng. editor Am. Enterprise Inst. Public Opinion mag., Washington, 1977-81; asst. to Pres., staff dir. White House, Washington, 1981, asst. to Pres. for communications, 1981-83; resident fellow Inst. Politics, John F. Kennedy Sch. Govt., Cambridge, Mass, 1983—. Office: Inst Politics John F Kennedy Sch Govt Cambridge MA 02138 *

GERGEN, KENNETH JAY, psychology educator; b. Rochester, N.Y., Dec. 9, 1934; s. John Jay and Aubeign (Lermond) G.; m. Mary Kathryn McCanney, Oct. 4, 1969; children by previous marriage: Laura Lynne, John Stanford. B.A., Yale U., 1957; Ph.D., Duke U., 1963. Research assoc. Duke U., 1962-63; asst. prof. social psychology Harvard U., 1963-67; assoc. prof. psychology Swarthmore (Pa.) Coll., 1967-71, chmn. dept., 1967-77, prof. psychology, 1971—; sr. research scientist Eastern Pa. Psychiat. Inst., 1972-81; cons. Nat. Acad. Sci., Nat. Planning Assn., Arthur D. Little, Inc., NSF, NIH. Author: (with C. Gordon) The Self in Social Interaction, 1968, (with R. Bauer) The Study of Policy Formation, 1968, The Psychology of Behavior Exchange, 1969, (with D. Marlowe) Personality and Social Behavior, 1970, The Concept of Self, 1971, (with others) Social Psychology in Transition, 1977, Social Exchange, 1980, Self Concept, 1981, (with M. Gergen) Social Psychology, 1981, Toward Transformation in Social Knowledge, 1982. Com. Internat. Exchange. Served to lt. USNR, 1957-59. Guggenheim fellow, 1967-69; Fulbright fellow 1971-72, 76-77. Fellow Am. Psychol. Assn., Soc. Exptl. Psychology. Home: 331 Roger's Ln Wallingford PA 19086 Office: Swarthmore Coll Dept Psychology Swarthmore PA 19081 *At one time I considered very carefully the guiding principles, goals, and standards of conduct that would be most worthwhile to follow in life. As time has passed, I have found such issues of increasingly less relevance to the process of living. Goals, principles, and standards now seem to be static, arbitrary and misleading abstractions from life rather than of life itself. They stand as remote simulacres rather than as vital and vibrant guides. Increasingly I have come to trust my continuously emerging intuitions as a basis for my own conduct, but to question these intuitions as guides for anyone else's behavior, and to question the process of translating these intuitions with fidelity to other persons.*

GERHARD, LANG HALLETT, investment analyst; b. Montclair, N.J., Dec. 28, 1945; s. William Howard and Harriett King (Dreckmeier) G.; m. E. Melissa Fairgrieve, May 21, 1978. B.A. in Acctg, Miami U., Ohio, 1967; M.B.A., U. Wis., 1968. Security analyst Dreyfus Corp., N.Y.C., 1968-72; mut. fund mgr. Channing Mgmt. Corp., N.Y.C., 1972; pension fund mgr. Mfrs. Hanover Trust Co., N.Y.C., 1972-78; mut. fund mgr. Oppenheimer Mgmt. Corp., N.Y.C., 1979—; dir. Gordon Corp., Farmington, Conn. Active Big Bros., N.Y., 1970—. Mem. N.Y. Soc. Security Analysts, Fin. Analysts Fedn., Sierra Club, Soho Photo Found. Club: Appalachian Mountain. Office: New York NY

GERHARD, LEE CLARENCE, geologist, educator; b. Albion, N.Y., May 30, 1937; s. Carl Clarence and Helen Mary (Lahmer) G.; m. Darcy LaFollette, July 22, 1964; 1 dau., Tracy Leigh. B.S., Syracuse U., 1958; M.S., U. Kans., 1961, Ph.D., 1964. Exploration geologist, region stratigrapher Sinclair Oil & Gas Co., Midland, Tex. and Rosewell, N.Mex., 1964-66; asst. prof. U. So. Colo., Pueblo, 1966-69, asso. prof., 1969-72; asso. prof., asst. dir. West Indies Lab., Fairleigh Dickinson U., Rutherford, N.J., 1972-75; asst. state geologist N.D., Grand Forks, 1975-77, state geologist 1977-81; prof., chmn. geology dept. U. N.D., Grand Forks, 1977-81; Rocky Mountain div. mgr. Supron Energy Corp., Denver, 1981-82; owner, pres. Gerhard & Assocs., Cons. Geologists, Englewood, Colo., 1982—; prof. petroleum geology Colo. Sch. Mines, Denver, 1982—. Contbr. articles to profl. jours. Served to 1st lt. U.S. Army, 1958-60. Danforth fellow, 1970-72. Mem. Am. Assn. Petroleum Geologists, Geol. Soc. Am., Am. Inst. Profl. Geologists, Rocky Mountain Assn. Geologists, Colo. Sci. Soc., N.D. Geol. Soc., Sigma Xi, Sigma Gamma Epsilon. Home: 10093 E Lake Dr Englewood CO 80111 Office: Suite 201 7373 S Alton Way Englewood CO 80112

GERHARDT, LILLIAN NOREEN, magazine editor; b. New Haven, Sept. 28, 1932; d. Victor Herbert and Lillian (Beecher) G. B.S., So. Conn. State Coll., 1954; postgrad., U. Chgo., 1961-62. Asst. in reference New Haven Pub. Library, 1954-55; first asst. reference dept. Meriden (Conn.) Pub. Library, 1955-58, head reference dept., 1958-61; asso. editor Kirkus Service, Inc., 1962-66; exec. editor Sch. Library Jour. Book Rev., R.R. Bowker Co., Juvenile Projects, N.Y.C., 1966-71; editor-in-chief Sch. Library Jour., 1971—; Lectr. Columbia U. Sch. Library Service, 1969-72. Sr. editor: Best Books for Children, 1967-70; sr. editor, project coordinator: SLJ Book Review Cumulative, 1969, Children's Books in Print, 1969, Subject Guide to Children's Books in Print, 1970. Judge Juvenile Nat. Book Award.; Recipient Disting. Alumnus award So. Conn. State Coll., Div. Library Sci., 1978. Mem. A.L.A. (mem.-at-large council 1976-80, Mildred Batchelder award com. 1970, Newberry-Caldecott award com. 1970), Women's Nat. Book Assn., Assn. Library Services to Children (pres. 1978-79). Home: 39 Gramercy Park N New York NY 10010 Office: 205 E 42d St New York NY 10017

GERHARDT, PHILIPP, microbiologist, educator; b. Milw., Dec. 30, 1921; s. Philipp W. and Agnes (Daigh) G.; m. Vera Mary Armstrong, Feb. 24, 1945; children: Ellen Daigh, Stephen Philipp, Doris Mary. Ph.B. with honors, U. Wis., 1943, M.S., 1947, Ph.D., 1949. Diplomate: Am. Bd. Med. Microbiology. Faculty microbiology Oreg. State U., 1949-51, U. Mich. Med. Sch., 1953-65; prof., chmn. dept. microbiology and pub. health Colls. Natural Sci., Human Medicine, Osteo. Medicine, Vet. Medicine and Agr. Expt. Sta., Mich. State U., 1965-75; prof., asso. dean for research and grad. study Coll. Osteo. Medicine, Mich. State U., 1975—; cons. various univs. and corps.; mem. U.S. nat. com. Internat. Union Biol. Scis. Editor: Manual of Methods for General Bacteriology, 1981. Served with AUS, 1943-46, 51-52. Wis. Alumni Research Found. fellow, 1946-47; NIH research fellow, 1947-49. Fellow AAAS; mem. Am. Soc. for Microbiology (sec. 1961-67, v.p. 1973-74, pres. 1974-75), Am. Acad. Microbiology (charter fellow, bd. govs. 1970-76), Brit. Soc. Gen. Microbiology, Internat. Union Microbiol. Socs. (pres. 1982—), Phi Beta Kappa, Sigma Xi. Research and publs. on microbial endospores, permeability, fermentations. Home: 529 Woodland Dr East Lansing MI 48823

GERHART, EUGENE CLIFTON, lawyer; b. Bklyn., Apr. 7, 1912; s. Herman Eugene and Mary Elizabeth (Hamilton) G.; m. Mary Richardson Schreiber, Mar. 30, 1939; children: Catherine Gerhart Landon, Virginia Gerhart Mason. A.B., Princeton U., 1934; LL.B., Harvard U., 1937. Bar: N.J. 1938, N.Y. 1945. Practiced in, Newark, 1938-43, Binghamton, N.Y., 1946—; sr. partner firm Coughlin & Gerhart, Binghamton; sec. to Judge Manley O. Hudson, Secretariat League of Nations, Geneva, 1934; lectr. bus. law U. Newark, 1942-43, Triple Cities Coll., 1946-48, Harpur Coll., Endicott, N.Y., 1953-55; lectr. indsl. and labor relations Cornell U., Ithaca, N.Y., 1946; dir., gen. counsel Columbian Mut. Life Ins. Co., 1949-83, acting pres., 1969-70, chmn. bd., 1970-82; dir. McIntosh Lab., Inc., Stickley Corp.; mem. nat. panel Am. Arbitration Assn., N.Y. State Mediation Bd. Arbitration Panel.; Mem. council SUNY, Cortland, 1967-77, chmn., 1971-77; mem. Select Task Force on Ct. Reorgn. N.Y. State Senate; mem. jud. nominating com. 3d Jud. Dept., State of N.Y. Author: Arthur T. Vanderbilt: The Compleat Counsellor; editor: The Lawyer's Treasury; spl. contbg. author: Law Office Econs. and Mgmt, 1962—; mem. editorial bd.: Quarterly Report of Conf. on Personal Fin. Law, 1965—; contbr. articles to legal, other publs. Served as lt. USNR, 1943-46. Fellow Am. Bar Found., Am. Coll. Probate Counsel; mem. Assn. Bar City N.Y., N.Y. State Bar Assn., Am. Law Inst., ABA (editor Jour. 1946-67, Ross Essay award 1946), N.Y. State Bar Assn. (editor in chief jour. 1961—), Broome County Bar Assn. (pres. 1961-62), Selden Soc., Internat. Assn. Ins. Counsel, Assn. Life Ins. Counsel, Am. Judicature Soc., Broome County Princeton Alumni Assn., Harvard Law Sch. Assn. Upstate N.Y. (pres. 1955-57), Scribes (pres., dir. 1966-67), St. Andrew's Soc. Republican. Clubs: Rotary (pres. 1969-70), Cosmos, Oteyokwa Lake (pres. 1971-73), Nassau, Harvard of N.Y., Princeton of N.Y. Home: 34 West End Ave Binghamton NY 13905 Office: One Marine Midland Plaza Binghamton NY 13901

GERHART, JAMES BASIL, educator; b. Pasadena, Calif., Dec. 15, 1928; s. Ray and Marion (van Deusen) G.; m. Genevra Joy Thomesen, June 21, 1958; children: James Edward, Sara Elizabeth. B.S., Calif. Inst. Tech., 1950; M.A., Princeton, 1952, Ph.D., 1954. Instr. physics Princeton, 1954-56; asst. prof. physics U. Wash., Seattle, 1956-61, asso. prof., 1961-65, prof., 1965—; Exec. officer Pacific Northwest Assn. for Coll. Physics, 1972—, bd. dirs., 1965—, chmn., 1970-72; governing bd. Am. Inst. Physics, 1973-76, 78-81. Recipient Disting. Teaching award U. Wash. Regents and Alumni Assn. Fellow Am. Phys. Soc, AAAS; mem. Am. Assn. Physics Tchrs. (sec. 1971-77, v.p. 1977, pres.-elect 1978, pres. 1979). Home: 2134 E Interlaken Blvd Seattle WA 98112

GERHOLZ, ROBERT PAUL, home builder; b. Merrill, Wis., June 25, 1896; s. Robert and Bertha (Degener) G.; m. Freda Clark, Sept. 15, 1923; children: Robert Charles, Barbara Lee, Janyce Allyn. Grad., Ferris Inst., Big Rapids, Mich., 1916, LL.D., 1957; student, U. Wis., 1919-21; D.Adminstrn. (hon.), Limestone Coll., Gaffney, S.C., 1979. Organizer Robert P. Gerholz Co. (homebuilders, realtors), 1922; pres. Gerholz Ins. Service, 1940-59, Gerholz Community Homes, Inc., 1947—, Gerholz Realty, Inc., 1954—, Gerholz Supply Co., 1949—, Robert P. Gerholz Orgn., 1952—, Gerholz Agy., Inc., 1959-68; treas. Gerholz-Healy Co., 1941-47, Bassett Park Homes, Inc., 1943-47; dir. Mich. Nat. Bank of Flint; central bd. Mich. Nat. Bank, Lansing, 1952-74, Mack Trucks, Inc., Mich. Nat. Corp., The Wickes Corp., 1966-72. Active YMCA, Boy Scouts; mem. Mich. Gov.'s Exec. Com. State Unemployment Compensation, 1932, Civil Service Commn., 1944-49; mem. industry adv. com. FHA, 1957-61; mem. Gov.'s Commn. on Higher Edn., 1973-74; Sec.-treas. Genesee County Real Estate Bd., 1927, pres., 1928, now mem.; pres. Citizens Civic League, 1929; treas. Flint Light Opera Co., 1944; dir. Am. Real Property Fedn., 1956; mem. adv. com. U. Wis. Sch. Bus., 1966-68; mem. bd. control Ferris State Coll., 1967—, vice chmn., 1969-71, chmn. bd., 1972-79; mem. exec. com. Religious Heritage Am., 1969—, chmn. bd., 1976—; mem. exec. com. Campus Crusade for Christ Internat.-Here's Life; mem. nat. exec. com. Horatio Alger Awards Com., 1978—; gen. chmn. capital fund campaign AutoWorld Found., Flint, 1981. Served to lt., F.A. U.S. Army, 1917-19. Named Flint Realtor of Year, 1966, Mich. Realtor of Year, 1966; recipient Wisdom award of honor, 1970; Mich. Minutemen award, 1972; Bus. Man of Year award Religious Heritage Am., Inc., 1971; George Washington award Freedoms Found., 1975; Horatio Alger award, 1977; named to Housing Hall of Fame, 1977; C.S. Mott Citizen of Year award, 1978; Realtor Emeritus award, 1977; named in his honor Robert P. Gerholz Inst. Life-long Learning Ferris State Coll., 1983. Mem. Mich. Real Estate Assn. (pres. 1931), Nat. Assn. Home Builders (pres. 1944, chmn. Research Inst. 1961; dir), U.S. C. of C. (dir.-at-large 1960-65, chmn. Can.-U.S. com. U.S. sect. 1963-64, pres. 1965-66, chmn. bd. 1966-67, chmn. exec. com. 1967-68, F. Stuart Fitzpatrick Meml. award 1968), Mich. C. of C. (dir. 1968—, chmn. bd. 1972-73), Urban Land Inst. Am. (trustee 1946-69, 1st v.p. 1953-54), Nat. Assn. Real Estate Bds. (dir.; pres. 1950), Flint Fedn. Chs. (pres. 1932), Beta Gamma Sigma (hon. Alpha chpt.), Omicron Delta Kappa. Presbyn. (elder). Club: Rotarian (pres. 1932). Home: 1704 Crescent Dr Flint MI 48503 Office: 4020 Hammerberg Rd Flint MI 48507

GERICKE, PAUL WILLIAM, clergyman, librarian; b. St. Louis, Apr. 8, 1924; s. Orville Herman and Irma Rose (Reinhart) G.; m. Jean Fisher, Feb. 18, 1953; 1 son, Michael Paul. B.S. in Elec. Engring, Washington U., St. Louis, 1949; B.D., So. Bapt. Theol. Sem., 1960; Th.D., New Orleans Bapt. Theol. Sem., 1964; M.A., U. New Orleans, 1972. Instr. electronics USAF, 1949; calibration engr. Emerson Electric Co., St. Louis, 1950; asst. pastor Calvary Bapt. Ch., St. Louis, 1951-53; ordained to ministry Baptist Ch., 1952; pastor First Bapt. Ch., Marceline, Mo., 1954-56, New Hope Bapt. Ch., St. Louis, 1957, Summit Park Bapt. Chapel, Louisville, 1959-60, Logtown (Miss.) Bapt. Ch., 1960-64; asst. prof., dir. library services New Orleans Bapt. Theol. Sem., 1965-73, asso. prof., dir. library, 1973—. Author: The Preaching of Robert G. Lee, 1967, The Ministers Filing System, 1971, Sermon Building, 1973, Crucial Experiences in the Life of D.L. Moody, 1978. Served with AC USNR, 1942-46. Mem. Am. Theol. Library Assn., Nat. Religious Broadcasters, Am. Radio Relay League, Theta Xi. Home: 1321 Aris Ave Metairie LA 70005 Office: 3939 Gentilly Blvd New Orleans LA 70126 *My life has been completely changed by a personal encounter with Jesus Christ in 1951. Through faith in Him as Savior and Lord, I received a new life, a new sense of values, a new purpose in life, and a new hope both for this life and the life to come. My purpose now is to seek first the kingdom of God and all the other things I need will be given unto me.*

GERIG, JARED FRANKLIN, clergyman; b. Allen County, Ind., June 29, 1907; s. Jonas F. and Clara Mae (Miller) G.; m. Mildred Grace Eicher, Dec. 22, 1928; children—Wesley Lee, Gwendolyn Grace (Mrs. Arthur Riewald), William Dean. Diploma, Fort Wayne (Ind.) Bible

Coll., 1929; Th.B., Malone Coll., Canton Ohio, 1938; A.B., Cleve. State U., 1941; M.A., Ariz. State U., 1946; D.D., Wheaton Coll., 1958; postgrad., Ind. U., U. Calif. at Los Angeles. Ordained to ministry Missionary Ch., 1931; minister in, Ind., Ohio, Ariz., 1929-45; dean Ft. Wayne Bible Coll., 1945-50, Azusa Pacific Coll., Cal., 1950-52; pres. Missionary Ch., Ft. Wayne, 1952-58, Ft. Wayne Bible Coll., 1958-71, chancellor, 1971—; sr. pastor Missionary Ch. Van Nuys (Calif.), 1973-76, Grace Bible Ch., Sun City, Ariz., 1978—; Vis. prof. Am. Inst. Holy Land Studies, Jerusalem, Israel, fall 1964, bd. dirs., 1962-71; Pres. Nat. Assn. Evangelicals, 1964-66; also chmn. bd. adminstrn. and exec. com.; mem. exec. com. Am. Assn. Bible Colls., 1959-60, 62-73, pres., 1970-73; mem. gen. bd. Missionary Ch., 1948-50, 52-68; bd. dirs. Winona Lake (Ind.) Christian Assembly, 1962-67. Co-author: The Missionary Church Association, Its Origin and Development, 1950. Mem. Delta Epsilon Chi. Home: 6620 Butler Dr Apt 31 Glendale AZ 85302 *Success in my life, in whatever measure it has come, had been rooted in the high standards, Biblical principles, and righteous example of generations of forebears. Recognition of God, supreme dedication, honesty and integrity, respect for authority, and appreciation of others achievements have been principles woven into the fabric of life. One must not overlook the fundamental hope and basic trust in the Christian way of life. This adds a dimension to life which is inescapably important.*

GERING, WILLIS G., banker; b. Freeman, S.D., Aug. 29, 1926; s. Arthur C. and Lydia (Schwartz) G.; m. Marilyn J. Foley, Dec. 25, 1946; children: Robert, Marla, Steven, Paul, Linda. Asst. cashier First State Bank, Richey, Mont., 1946-50; asst. cashier Wash. State Bank, Bellevue, 1951-56; sr. v.p., mgr. data processing div. Seattle First Nat. Bank, 1956-79, sr. v.p. data processing, 1979-82, exec. v.p. ops. group, 1982—. Served with AUS, 1943-45. Office: Seattle First Nat Bank PO Box 3586 Seattle WA 98124

GERJUOY, EDWARD, physicist, lawyer; b. Bklyn., May 19, 1918; s. Abraham and Clara (Hirsch) G.; m. Clark Jacqueline Reid, Aug. 26, 1940; children: Neil, David Leif. B.S. cum laude, CCNY, 1937; M.A., U. Calif., Berkeley, 1940, Ph.D., 1942; J.D. magna cum laude, U. Pitts., 1977. Bar: Calif. 1977, Pa. 1978. Asso. dir. sonar analysis group Div. War Research, Columbia, 1942-46; mem. faculty U. So. Calif., Los Angeles, 1946-51; vis. asso. prof. N.Y. U., 1951-52; mem. faculty U. Pitts., 1952-58, 64-82, prof. physics, 1964-82, prof. emeritus, 1982—; mem. Pa. Environ. Hearing Bd., 1982—; mem. research staff Gen. Atomic div. Gen. Dynamics Corp., San Diego, 1958-62; dir. plasma and space applied physics RCA Labs., Princeton, N.J., 1962-64; cons. Westinghouse Research Labs., 1952-58; mem. adv. com. health physics div. Oak Ridge Nat. Labs., 1967-71, chmn. com., 1971-74; asso. firm Tucker Arensberg Very & Ferguson, Pitts., 1978-80; vis. fellow Joint Inst. Lab. Physics, U. Colo., Boulder, 1970; cons. EPA, 1977-81; hearing examiner Pa. Environ. Hearing Bd., 1980-81. Author: (with A. Yaspan) Reverberation, in series The Physics of Sound in the Sea, 1968; Editor: Physics Text Series, 1960-62, Jour. Comments on Atomic and Molecular Physics, 1971-74, Jurimetrics Jour. of Law Sci. and Tech, 1980—; Contbr. chpts. and numerous articles to tech. and legal lit. Bd. dirs. Pitts. ACLU, 1975-80. Fellow Am. Phys. Soc. (mem. panel on public affairs 1976-79, chmn. 1981), AAAS, Inst. Physics, Phys. Soc. (Eng.); mem. Am. Bar Assn. (chmn. phys. scis. com., sect. sci. and tech. 1976-77, mem. council sect. sci. and tech. 1977-80), AAUP, Phi Beta Kappa, Sigma Xi, Order Coif. Home: 400 Richland Ln Pittsburgh PA 15208 Office: Pa Environ Hearing Bd 300 Liberty Ave Pittsburgh PA 15222 *I have tried to avoid overspecialization, while not letting myself descend into dilettantism. I believe I have succeeded in these endeavors. The last phase of my career, embarking on a law degree at age 56, earning the degree and passing the bar at 59, and now being employed full time as a judge in environmental disputes, probably is an extreme example of career restlessness. I am not sorry to have strayed from a straight line career path, and it has kept me feeling young in my so-called golden years. Nevertheless— and this is more a comment about the present world than about me— I do not believe I would advise young men today to be guided by me.*

GERKEN, WALTER BLAND, insurance company executive; b. N.Y.C., Aug. 14, 1922; s. Walter Adam and Virginia (Bl) G.; m. Darlene Stolt, Sept. 6, 1952; children—Walter C., Ellen M., Beth L., Daniel J., Andrew P., David A. B.A., Wesleyan U., 1948; M., Pub. Adminstrn., Maxwell Sch. Citizenship and Pub. Affairs, Syracuse, 1958. Supr. budget and adminstrv. analysis, Wis., Madison, 1950-54; mgr. investments Northwestern Mut. Life Ins. Co., Milw., 1954-67; v.p. finance Pacific Mut. Life Ins. Co., Los Angeles, 1967-69, exec. v.p., 1969-72, pres., 1972-75, chmn. bd., 1975—, also dir.; dir. Whittaker Corp., Carter Hawley Hale Stores, So. Calif. Edison Co., Times Mirror Co. Bd. Dirs. Los Angeles World Affairs Council; trustee Occidental Coll., Los Angeles, Wesleyan U., Middletown, Conn.; chmn. United Way, Los Angeles, Calif. Round Table. Served to capt. USAAF, 1942-46. Decorated D.F.C., Air medal. Clubs: California, Stock Exchange (Los Angeles); Pacific Union (San Francisco); Balboa Bay (Newport Beach, Calif.); Dairymen's Country (Boulder Junction, Wis.); Metropolitan (Washington). Office: 700 Newport Center Dr Newport Beach CA 92660

GERKING, SHELBY DELOS, JR., zoologist, educator; b. Elkhart, Ind., Nov. 16, 1918; s. Shelby Delos and Fezon (Churchill) G.; m. Louisa B. Pfretzschner, Dec. 28, 1943; children: Shelby Delos III, Timothy Churchill, Andrew Alfred. A.B., DePauw U., 1940; student, U. Mich., 1939, 41; Ph.D., Ind. U., 1944. Research asso. physiology Ind. U., 1944-46, faculty zoology, 1946-67, prof., dir. Biol. Sta., 1959-67; prof. zoology Ariz. State U., Tempe, 1967—, chmn. dept., 1967-74; dir. Ind. Aquatic Research Unit, 1959-67; research asso. lake and stream survey Ind. Dept. Conservation, 1946-53; asso. dir. Water Resources Research Center; mem. freshwater productivity com. Internat. Biol. Program, mem. U.S. nat. com.; cons. fisheries Dept. Agr. France, 1972, Czechoslovakian Acad. Scis.; guest (fisheries) Govt. Hungary; mem. ecology adv. com. Sci. Adv. Bd. EPA, 1973-79, cons., 1979—, Lake Ohrid project, Yugoslavia, Commonwealth Edison, Chgo.; participant jubilee symposium 500th anniv. founding U. Uppsala, 1977; Council Sci. and Indsl. Research cons. and lectr. U. Cape Town (South Africa). Author: Laboratory Manual for Man and the Biological World, 1958, 4th edit., 1974, Biological Systems, 1969, 2d edit., 1974; editor: Biological Basis of Fresh Water Fish Production, 1967, rev. edit., 1978; asso. editor: Environ. Biology of Fishes, Jour. Fish Biology, Marine Ecology Progress Reports; contbr. articles profl. jours. Fellow AAAS, Ind. Acad. Sci., Am. Inst. Fishery Research Biologists; mem. Ecol. Soc. Am., Am. Inst. Biol. Scis., Internat. Assn. Limnology, Am. Fisheries Soc. (Silver medal No. Central div.), Am. Soc. Limnology and Oceanography, Am. Soc. Ichthyologists and Herpetologists, Am. Soc. Zoologists, Wildlife Soc., Internat. Assn. for Ecology, Sigma Xi. Home: 418 E Alameda St Tempe AZ 85282

GERLACH, G. DONALD, lawyer; b. Toledo, July 13, 1933; s. Werner George and Marian (Peiter) G.; m. Betty Lou Smith, Dec. 19, 1959 (dec.); children: Lisa A., Gregory D., Jeffrey S.; m. Diane Bonfigli, July 30, 1983. B.A., Princeton U., 1955; LL.B., Harvard U., 1960. Bar: Pa. 1961. Assoc. firm Reed Smith Shaw & McCaly, Pitts., 1960-66, ptnr., 1967—, dir. legal personnel, 1980-82, asst. mng. ptnr., mng. panr.-elect, 1983. Served to capt. U.S. Army, 1955-60. Fellow Am. Coll. Probate Counsel; mem. ABA (real property, probate and trust sect.), Pa. Bar Assn. (chmn. real property, probate and trust sect. 1977-78). Republican. Episcopalian. Clubs: Duquesne, Harvard, Yale, Princeton; Fox Chapel Golf (Pitts.). Office: Reed Smith Shaw & McClay PO Box 2009/747 Union Trust Bldg Pittsburgh PA 19230

GERLACH, GARY GENE, newspaper publisher; b. Osage, Iowa, June 8, 1941; s. Gene Wayne and Norma Linda (Rosel) G.; m. Karen Ann Conner, June 21, 1980. B.A., U. Iowa, 1964; M.S., Columbia U., 1965; J.D., Harvard U., 1970, M.P.A., 1972. Reporter copy editor Miami Herald, 1964; staff writer Nat. Observer, Washington, 1965-67; legal asst. Commr. Nicholas Johnson, FCC, Washington, 1970-71; atty. Arnold & Porter, Washington, 1972-74; exec. v.p., gen. counsel dir. Des Moines Register and Tribune Co., 1974-82, exec. v.p., dir., 1982—; pres., pub. Des Moines Newspapers, 1982—; bd. editors Nat. Media Law Reporter, Washington, 1978—. Pres. Des Moines Met. Opera, 1981, Iowa Freedom of Info. Council, 1978; v.p. Des Moines Met. YMCA, 1979-81; trustee Civic Center Greater Des Moines, 1975—; bd. dirs. U. Iowa Found., Iowa City, 1978—. Mem. ABA, Am. Newspaper Pub. Assn. (dir. press-bar com.), Bar Commonwealth Mass., D.C. Bar, Iowa State Bar, Phi Beta Kappa. Lutheran. Clubs: Des Moines; Prairie (Des Moines); Harvard (N.Y.C.). Office: Des Moines Register and Tribune Co 715 Locust St Des Moines IA 50309

GERLACH, HORST W.A., microwave electronics engineer, writer; b. Dresden, Germany, June 23, 1912; came to U.S., 1955; s. Walter Edward and Marie Henriette (Hoentsch) G.; m. Hildegard Margarete Strietzel, Sept. 9, 1939; children: Ulrich, Detlef. M.E.E., Technische Hochschule, Sewaswn, Germany, 1938; postgrad., Tech. U. Berlin, 1939-41, George Washington U./U. Md., Washington, 1959-63; student mgmt. seminars, Dept. Army, Washington, 1960-68. Staff mem., group leader Telefunken, Berlin, 1938-45, sr. staff mem., Ulm, Germany, 1952-55; tech. sr. mem. Diamond Ordnance Fuze Labs., Washington, 1956-61; research and devel. supr. Harry Diamond Labs., Dept. Army, Adelphi, Md., 1961-80, br. chief, 1980-81, cons., 1981-82; freelance tech. writer, York, Pa., 1983—. Patentee microwave electronics. Recipient medal of Merit German Dept. Def., 1944, Spl. award Harry Diamond Labs., 1973, citations, 1977, 78, 82, Dept. Def., 1982. Fellow IEEE (chmn. electron devices chpt. 1973-74, sect. chmn. 1978-79, ADCOM/EXCOM Patron award 1980, Auto Test Conf. citation 1980, Internat. Electron Devel. Conf. citation 1982, Centennial medal 1983). Home: 545 Eton Ln York PA 17402

GERLACH, JOHN B., business executive; b. Columbus, Ohio, Jan. 28, 1927; s. John Joseph and Pauline (Pollitt) G.; m. Dareth Axene, Sept. 30, 1949; children: John B., David P., Susan. Student, Ohio State U., 1945-47, Ohio U., 1947-49. Ptnr. John Gerlach & Co., Columbus, 1949—; pres. Lancaster Glass Corp. (Ohio), 1958—, dir.; pres. Ind. Glass Co., Dunkirk, 1952—, dir.; pres. Lancaster Colony Corp., 1963—, dir.; sec.-treas., dir. Pretty Products Inc., Coshocton, Ohio, Nat. Glove Inc.; dir. Columbus Dental Mfg. Co., Mills Inc., Columbus, Jackson Corp. (Ohio), Beverage Mgmt. Inc., Columbus. Trustee Columbus Gallery Fine Arts. Clubs: Univ., Columbus, Scioto Country, Coshocton Country. Home: 2320 Onandaga Dr Columbus OH 43215 Office: 37 Broad St Columbus OH 43215

GERLACH, JOHN J., diversified company executive; b. Columbus, Ohio, 1902. Grad., Ohio State U., 1923. Ptnr. John Gerlach & Co., Columbus; chmn., sec. Lancaster Colony Corp., N.Y. Frozen Foods, Molded Products Inc.; v.p., sec., dir. Lancaster Glass Co., Ind. Glass Co.; sec., dir. Am. Mat. Co., August Barr Inc., Candle Lite Inc., Christian & Co., Inc., Enterprise Aluminum Co., Loma Corp., Nelson McCoy Pottery Co., Nat. Glove Inc., Jackson Corp., I. Marzetti Co., Barr Inc., Koneta Rubber Co. Office: John Gerach & Co 37 W Broad St Columbus Ohio 43215 *

GERLACH, JOHN THOMAS, restaurant chain executive; b. McAdoo, Pa., Oct. 24, 1932; s. John A. and Mary (Meshinsky) G.; m. Pamela Ann Wester, May 16, 1964; children: John Thomas, Audrey, David. B.S., Drexel U., 1955; M.B.A., U. Pa., 1961. Assoc. Booz Allen & Hamilton, Chgo., 1961-67; v.p. Gen. Mills, Inc., Mpls., 1967-77; pres. Consumer Growth Capital, Mpls., 1977-82; pres., chief operating officer Horn & Hardart Co., N.Y.C., 1982—; dir. SAFE, Mpls., Consumer Growth Capital, Am. Woodmark Corp., Berryville, Va., Creighton Shirtmakers Inc., Reidsville, N.C., CPT Corp., Mpls. Author: Successful Management of New Products, 1968. Mem. vis. com. Drexel U., Phila., 1978; bd. regents St. Johns U., Mpls., 1981. Club: Mpls. Office: Horn & Hardart Co 1163 Ave of Americas New York NY 10036

GERLACH, LUTHER PAUL, anthropologist; b. Oct. 25, 1930; married; 3 children. B.A., U. Minn., 1952; Ph.D., U. London, 1961. Vis. lectr. anthropology U. Minn., 1961-71, assoc. prof., 1965-71, prof., 1971—, adj. prof. Hubert Humphrey Inst. Pub. Affairs, 1983—; asst. prof. anthropology and sociology Lafayette Coll., 1961-63; vis. assoc. Calif. Inst Tech., 1971-72; sr. cons. Aspen Inst. Humanistic Studies, 1972-73. Author: (with Virginia H. Hine) People, Power, Change: Movements of Social Transformation, 1970, Lifeway Leap: The Dynamics of Change in America, 1973; Contbr. chpts. to books, articles to profl. and popular jours.; contbg. editor Cultural Futures Research; Producer: films and filmstrips including Zanj-Africa, 1970, People Eco-Action, 1970, Systemic Thinking, 1973, Grassroots Energy, 1978; TV series Lifeway Leap, Energy, Resource Use and System Change. Served with AUS, 1952-54. Fulbright jr. fellow, 1958-60; Northwest Area Found. grantee, 1967-80; Rockefeller Found. research grantee, 1969-70; OWRR grantee, 1969-72, 75-78; Solar Energy Research Inst. grantee, 1978-79; Bush fellow, 1983-84. Mem. Am. Anthropol. Assn., Soc. Applied Anthropology, African Studies Assn, Internat. African Law Assn. Address: Dept Anthropology U Minn 225 Ford Hall Minneapolis MN 55455

GERLITS, FRANCIS JOSEPH, lawyer; b. Chgo., Mar. 29, 1931; s. John T. and May (Cameron) G.; m. Suzanne Long, June 20, 1953; children: Kathleen, Karen, Mary Cameron, Francis Jr. Ph.B., U. Notre Dame, 1953; J.D., U. Chgo., 1958. Bar: Ill. 1958. Ptnr. Kirkland & Ellis, Chgo., 1964—; gen. counsel Internat. Harvester Co., Chgo., 1983—. Mem. ABA, Order of Coif. Clubs: Tavern, Chicago (Chgo.). Office: Kirkland & Ellis 200 E Randolph Dr Chicago IL 60601

GERMAIN, JEAN-PAUL, designer; b. Paris, Mar. 31, 1944; s. Paul and Germaine (Germain) Carbone; m. Wendy Gropper; 1 dau., Stephanie. Pres. Jean-Paul Germain Ltd. and Jean-Paul Germain, N.Y.C. (Recipient Oscar award for exportation masculine clothing, Coty award 1976). Mem. Fashion Designers Am. (council). Office: Jean-Paul Germain Ltd 1 E 57th St New York NY 10022 *

GERMAN, JOHN GEORGE, transportation consultant; b. Devils Lake, N.D., Sept. 22, 1921; s. George and Dorothy Florence (Stenson) G.; m. Mary Alice Chambers, Sept. 15, 1973; 1 son, John R. B.S.M.E., Case Sch. Applied Sci., Cleve., 1943. With Gt. No. Ry. Co., 1943-61; with Mo. Pacific R.R. Co., 1961-83, chief mech. officer, 1961-66, asst. v.p. engring., 1966-75, v.p. engring., St. Louis, 1975-83; pres. John German Ry. Engring. Cons. Inc., 1983—. Fellow ASME; mem. Air Brake Assn., Am. Ry. Bridge and Bldg. Assn., Am. Ry. Engring. Assn., Car Dept. Officers Assn., Locomotive Maintenance Officers Assn., Railway Fuel and Operating Officers Assn., Assn. Am. Railroads, Roadmasters and Maintenance of Way Assn. Republican. Lodges: Masons; Shriners; Scottish Rite. Home and Office: 1776 Lynkirk Ln Kirkwood MO 63122

GERMAN, WILLIAM, newspaper editor; b. N.Y.C., Jan. 4, 1919; s. Sam and Celia (Norack) G.; m. Gertrude Pasenkoff, Oct. 12, 1940; children: David, Ellen, Stephen. B.A., Bklyn. Coll., 1939; M.S., Columbia U., 1940, Harvard U., 1950. Reporter, asst. fgn. editor, news editor, mng. editor, exec. editor San Francisco Chronicle, 1940—; editor Chronicle Fgn. Service, 1960-77; mng. editor KQED, Newspaper of the Air, 1968; lectr. U. Calif., Berkeley, 1946-47, 68-70. Editor: San Francisco Chronicle Reader, 1962. Served with AUS, 1943-45. Mem. Am. Soc. Newspaper Editors, A.P. Mng. Editors Assn. Home: 150 Lovell Ave Mill Valley CA 94941 Office: San Francisco Chronicle 901 Mission St San Francisco CA 94103

GERMANE, GAYTON ELWOOD, educator; b. Iowa, Aug. 1920; s. Charles E. and Edith N. (Gayton) G.; m. Janet Claire Reinertson, June 1949; 1 dau., Charlotte. A.B., U. Mo., 1941; M.B.A., Harvard U., 1946, A.M. in Econs., 1948, Ph.D., 1949. Teaching fellow in econs. Harvard U. Grad. Sch. Arts and Sci., 1946-49, asst. prof. Grad. Sch. Bus., 1950-52; mem. faculty Stanford U. Grad. Sch. Bus., 1952—, former prof. transp. and mgmt., now 1907 Found. prof. logistics Grad. Sch. Bus., also courtesy prof. indsl. engring. Sch. Engring.; (on leave) former dir. transp. policy U.S. Dept. Def.; former dir. transp. planning and research U.S. Steel Corp.; former adj. prof. bus. adminstrn. U. Pitts. Grad. Sch. Bus.; former mem. adv. com. Transp. Center, Northwestern U.; former vis. Ryder prof. mgmt. and logistics U. Miami (Fla.); also former mem. faculty Can. Nat. Rys. Staff Coll.; former moderator, dir., chmn. coordinating com. Transp. Assn. Am.; faculty prin. Mgmt. Analysis Center, Inc.; dir. Guild Wineries & Distilleries Co.; cons. to industry and govt. Co-author: Case Problems in Transportation Management, 1957, Top Management, 1968; sr. author: A New Concept of Transportation Movement, 1959, Highway Transportation Management, 1963, Logistics of Furniture Distribution, 1975; author: Transportation Policy Issues for the 1980's, 1983; editor: Management for Growth, 1957; asso. editor: Logistics and Transp. Rev. Served with AUS, 1943-46. Recipient John Drury Sheehan award Nat. Council Phys. Distbn. Mgmt., 1971. Mem. Soc. Logistics Engrs., Transp. Research Forum (past pres.). Home: 28168 Radcliffe Ln Los Altos Hills CA 94022 Office: Grad Sch Bus Stanford Univ Stanford CA 94305

GERMANY, DANIEL MONROE, aerospace engineer; b. Lake Village, Ark., Sept. 14, 1937; s. Jones Harry and Sara (Farrar) G.; m. Grace Jizmejian, Oct. 25, 1974; children: Cheryl Germany, Brian Bentti. B.S.M.E., Miss. State U., 1959. Aerospace systems engr. NASA Marshall Space Flight Center, Huntsville, Ala., 1960-78; tech. exec. asst. to asso. adminstr. of shuttle transp. systems NASA Hdqrs., Washington, 1978-79, dir. orbiter programs, 1979-81; asst. mgr. Orbiter Project Office Johnson Space Ctr., Houston, 1982, mgr. Flight Equipment Project Office, 1983—. Republican. Office: Johnson Space Center Houston TX 77058

GERNREICH, RUDI, designer; b. Vienna, Austria, Aug. 8, 1922; came to U.S., 1938, naturalized, 1943; s. Siegmund and Elisabeth (Mueller) G. Student, Los Angeles City Coll., 1938-41, Los Angeles Art Center Sch., 1941-42. Founder, pres. GR Designs, Inc. (name changed to Rudi Gernreich, Inc. 1964), Los Angeles, 1960—; mem. internat. designer adv. council Montgomery Ward, 1967—. Modern dancer, Lester Horton Dance Theatre, 1942-48; free-lance designer, N.Y.C., Los Angeles, 1948-51; designer, Walter Bass, Inc., Beverly Hills, Calif., 1951- 59, swimwear designer, Westwood Knitting Mills, Los Angeles, 1953-59, shoe designer, Genesco Corp., 1958-60, underwear and sleepwear for, Lily of France, 1975-77, decor and costumes for, Bella Lewitzky Dance Co.'s Inscape, 1976-77, dance wear for, Capezio-Ballet Makers, 1977, swimwear for, Berlei-Hestia, U.K., 1977 (Recipient Designer of Year award Sports Illustrated mag. 1956), Berlei-Hestia, U.K. (Sporting Look award 1963), Berlei-Hestia, U.K. (spl. award for swimming design Coty Am. Fashion Critics 1960), Berlei-Hestia, U.K. (Winnie award 1963), Berlei-Hestia, U.K. (award for creative achievement women's knitwear industry Wool Knit Assos. 1960, 62), Berlei-Hestia, U.K. (Hall of Fame award 1964), Berlei-Hestia, U.K. (Am. Fortnight trophy Nieman-Marcus Co. 1961), Berlei-Hestia, U.K. (London Sunday Times Internat. Spl. award 1965), Berlei-Hestia, U.K. (Filene's Design award 1966), Berlei-Hestia, U.K. (Coty Am. Fashion Critics Return award 1966), Berlei-Hestia, U.K. (named to Hall of Fame 1967), Berlei-Hestia, U.K. (Fenit-Industria Textil Trophy, San Paolo, Brazil 1967), Berlei-Hestia, U.K. (Mare Moda-Tiberio D'Oro award (Italy) 1967), Berlei-Hestia, U.K. (Production Design award for bedspreads and pillows Am. Resources Council Inc. 1972), Berlei-Hestia, U.K. (Knitted Textile Assn. Design award 1975), Berlei-Hestia, U.K. (Robinson's Creative Spirit award 1976); knitwear, swimwear designer, Harmon Knitwear, Marinette, Wis., 1960-72, Quilts for Knoll Internat., 1972. Office: 371 3/4 N La Cienega Blvd Los Angeles CA 90048

GERNSBACK, MARCELLUS HARVEY, editor, publisher; b. N.Y.C., May 31, 1912; s. Hugo and Rose (Harvey) G.; m. Elizabeth Ann Sandt, Sept. 25, 1943 (div. Jan. 1970); children: Mark, Wendy; m. Carol Ann Roth, Nov. 7, 1970 (div. Nov. 1976). B.A., Columbia, 1935. Assoc. editor Short Wave and TV mag., 1938-40; cons. editor Radio-Electronics Mag., N.Y.C., 1946—, editor, 1961-70, pub., 1967-80, editor-in-chief, 1970—; pub., editor-in-chief Merchandising 2-Way Radio, 1975-77; pres. Gernsback Pub., Inc., N.Y.C., 1954—, SXO Corp., 1967-80, Luz Mag., Inc., 1967-80; pub., editor-in-chief Sexology, also Luz mag., 1970-78. Served to maj. AUS, 1941-45. Fellow Radio Club Am.; hon. mem. Vet. Wireless Operators Assn. Office: 200 Park Ave S New York NY 10003

GEROLD, NICOLAS JOHN, former educator; b. N.Y.C., Jan. 1, 1919; s. Nicolas Jean and Cecilia (Schwarz) G.; m. Patricia Kenyon, June 25, 1949; children—Nicolas John, Alison Louise. B.A., Brown U., 1942, M.A., 1948; Ph.D., Cornell U., 1951. Asst. prof. biology Hamilton Coll., Clinton, N.Y., 1951-58, asso. prof., 1958-64, prof., 1964-81, ret., 1981, chmn. dept. biology, 1966-72. Served with AUS, 1942-46. Mem. Am. Inst. Biol. Scis., Am. Soc. Zoologists, AAAS, Nat. Assn. Biol. Tchrs., Am. Assn. Med. Colls., N.Y. Acad. Scis., Sigma Xi. Research in histochemistry of cell division. Home: 13 Griffin Rd Clinton NY 13323

GEROW, EDWIN MAHAFFEY, educator; b. Akron, Ohio, Oct. 16, 1931; s. Adolphus Denton and Alice Corinne (Mahaffey) G.; m. Cheryl Ann Chevis, Nov. 18, 1976; children from previous marriage—Matthew, Aaron. B.A., U. Chgo., 1952, Ph.D., 1962; postgrad., U. Paris, 1954-56, 59-60, U. Madras, 1960-61. Asst. prof. Sanskrit U. Rochester, 1962-64; lectr. in Sanskrit Columbia U., 1963-64; asst. prof. U. Wash., Seattle, 1964-67, assoc. prof., 1967-73, assoc. dir., 1969-73; Frank L. Sulzberger prof. Civilizations, prof. Sanskrit dept. S. Asian langs. and civilizations U. Chgo., 1973—; vis. prof. history and lit. of religions Northwestern U., 1980. Author: A Glossary of Indian Figures of Speech, 1971, Indian Poetics, 1977, others; editor: (with Margery Lang) Srih; Studies in the Language and Culture of South Asia, 1974, (with Dimock and van Buitenen) The Literatures of India, an Introduction, 1974. Ford Found. fellow, 1959-61; Am. Inst. Indian Studies fellow, 1967-68, 75. Mem. Am. Oriental Soc. (exec. com. Sanskrit council), Société Asiatique, Philol. Assn. Pacific Coast. Home: 901 S Plymouth Ct Chicago IL 60605 Office: 1116 E 59th St Chicago IL 60637

GERRARD, ROBERT WILKIN, banker; b. Austin, Tex., Sept. 4, 1927; s. Oswald and Marie Cage (Hickman) G.; m. Myrtle Lucille Watkins, June 14, 1952; children: Celia, Jann, Robert, Sheri. Student, Tex. A&M U., 1944-45, U. Houston, 1948-50; B.B.A., U. Tex., 1952; cert. Stonier Grad. Sch. Banking, Rutgers U., 1961. Credit analyst Tex. Commerce Bank, Houston, 1952-56, asst. cashier, 1956-58, asst. v.p., 1958-61, v.p., 1961-66, sr. v.p. and sr. loan officer, 1966-68, exec. v.p. and sr. loan officer, 1968-71; dep. chmn. Barston and Tex. Commerce Ltd., London, 1969-71; chmn. bd. Continental Nat. Bank, Ft. Worth, 1971—; dir. S.W. Bamcshares Inc., Houston, Bank S.W., 1st Nat. Bank Euless, Tex., Keller-Hyden Co., Ft. Worth, 1st Denton Nat. Bank, Tex.-N. Mex. Power Co., Ft. Worth. Past chmn., dir. North Tex. Commn.; trustee All Saints Hosp., Ft. Worth, Tex. Christian U., Ft. Worth, Tarrant County United Way, Ft. Worth; dir., past chmn. Ft. Worth C. of C. Served with USN, 1945-48. Recipient Ike Harrisonaward Tex. Christian U., 1981, Sales and Mktg. Assn. Ft. Worth Salesman of Yr. award, 1980. Mem. Assn. Reserve City Bankers, Robert Morris Assocs. Clubs: Ft. Worth Exchange, Rivercrest Country, Shady Oak Country, Ft. Worth, Petroleum, Ft. Worth Boys. Home: 3806 Montecello Dr Ft Worth TX 76107 Office: Continental Nat Bank 777 Main St Ft. Worth TX 76101

GERRAUGHTY, ROBERT JOSEPH, educator, univ. dean; b. Newton, Mass., Aug. 30, 1928; s. John Joseph and Dorothy (Moran) G.; m. G. June Wheatley, Sept. 18, 1953; children—David R., Andrew M., Susan J. Matthew E., Samuel W. B.S., Mass. Coll. Pharmacy, 1950, M.S., 1952; Ph.D., U. Conn., 1958. Asst. prof. pharmacy Rutgers U., 1958-60; prof., chmn. dept. pharmacy U. R.I., 1960-72, dir. tng. course drug inspectors, 1964-72; dean Sch. Pharmacy, Creighton U., Omaha, 1972-77, asso. v.p. health scis., 1977-79, adminstrv. v.p., 1979—; cons. pharm. cos. Author: Pharmacy Examination Review Book, 1964—. Chmn. Heart Fund Narragansett, R.I., 1966, Narragansett Democratic Com., 1969. Served to capt. USAF, 1952-55. Mem. Am., R.I., Nebr. pharm. assns., Sigma Xi, Rho Chi, Phi Lambda Upsilon, Phi Sigma, Kappa Psi. Office: Creighton U Omaha NE 68178

GERRIE, ROBERT BRUCE, manufacturing company executive; b. Oak Park, Ill., Feb. 28, 1924; s. Archibald Munro and Frances Irene (O'Connor) G.; m. Janice M. Gamble, Sept. 1, 1949; children: Alison S. Lindsey, Nancy S. B.S., Northwestern U., 1948, J.D., 1951. Bar: Ill. 1951. Asso. McBride, Baker, Wienke & Schlosser, Chgo., 1951-57, partner, 1958-73; v.p. legal affairs, gen. counsel Morton Thiokol, Inc., Chgo., 1974—, sec., 1974-76. Commr. Wilmette Park Dist., 1965-77, pres., 1967-71; pres. New Trier Citizens League, 1969-73; chmn. New Trier Twp. Com. on Youth, 1972-75. Served to 1st lt., inf. AUS, 1943-46. Mem. Am., Ill., Chgo. bar assns., Law Club Chgo., Legal Club Chgo., Phi Delta Phi. Republican. Episcopalian. Clubs: Skokie Country (Glencoe, Ill.); Mill Reef (Antigua); Royal Poinciana (Naples, Fla.); Metropolitan, Mid-America. Home: 630 Park Dr Kenilworth IL 60043 Office: 110 N Wacker Dr Chicago IL 60606

GERRISH, BRIAN ALBERT, clergyman, educator; b. London, Eng., Aug. 14, 1931; s. Albert and Doris (King) G.; m. Millicent June Warburton, June 25, 1955; children—Carolyn, Paul. B.A., Queens' Coll., Cambridge, Eng., 1952, M.A., 1956; certificate, Westminister Coll., Cambridge, 1955; S.T.M., Union Theol. Sem., N.Y.C., 1956; Ph.D., Columbia, 1958. Asst. pastor West End Presbyn. Ch., N.Y.C., 1956-58; tutor philosophy of religion Union Theol. Sem., N.Y.C., 1957-58; instr. ch. history McCormick Theol. Sem., Chgo., 1958-59, asst. prof., 1959-63, asso. prof., 1963-65; asso. prof. hist. theology U. Chgo., 1965-68, prof., 1968—. Author: Grace and Reason: A Study in the Theology of Luther, 1962 (Japanese transl. 1974), reprinted, 1979, Tradition and the Modern World: Reformed Theology in the Nineteenth Century, 1978, The Old Protestantism and the New: Essays on the Reformation Heritage, 1982; Editor: The Faith of Christendom: A Source Book of Creeds and Confessions, 1963, Reformers in Profile, 1967, Reformatio Perennis: Essays on Calvin and the Reformation in Honor of Ford Lewis Battles, 1981; co-editor: Jour. Religion, 1972—; Contbr. articles to profl. jours. Am. Assn. Theol. Schs. faculty fellow, 1961; Guggenheim fellow, 1970; Nat. Endowment Humanities fellow, 1980. Mem. Am. Acad. Religion, Am. Soc. Ch. History (pres. 1979), Am. Soc. for Reformation Research, Am. Theol. Soc. (Midwest Div.) (pres. 1973-74). Home: 18541 Klimm Homewood IL 60430 Office: Swift Hall U Chgo Chicago IL 60637

GERRITSEN, HENDRIK JURJEN, physics educator, researcher; b. The Hague, Netherlands, Jan. 19, 1927; came to U.S., 1957; s. Hendrik Pieter and Augusta (Koopmans) G.; m. Lida Buitelaar, June 13, 1955 (dec.); children: Robert, Steven, Albert, Leon; m. Heide Robertson Hoppe, Dec. 28, 1978. A.B in Physics and Chemistry, U. Leiden, 1948, Ph.D., 1955. Scientist RCA Labs., Zurich, Switzerland, 1955-57, 57-67, Princeton, N.J., 1955-5,, 57-67, cons., 1967-68, Zurich, Switzerland, 1967-68; lectr. electrophysics Chalmers U., Gothernburg, Sweden, 1961-62; prof. physics Brown U., Providence, 1967—, U. Utrecht, Netherlands, 1974, U. Karlsruhe, W. Germany, 1981-82; cons. Polaroid Corp., Cambridge, Mass., 1968-70; prin. investigator U.S. Bur. Mines, Brewster, Pa., 1970-76, Honeywell, Mpls., 1980-83. Contbr. sci. articles to profl. jours.; patentee. Mem. Fedn. Am. Scientists, Union of Concerned Scientists, Profl. Photographers Soc. Am. (hon.), Am. Optical Soc., Sigma Xi. Office: Physics Dept Brown U Providence RI 02912

GERRITY, EDWARD JOSEPH, JR., communications company executive; b. Scranton, Pa., Jan. 3, 1924; s. Edward Joseph and Helen T. (Walton) G.; m. Katharine Casey, Sept. 22, 1956; children: Katharine, Edward Joseph III. B.S., U. Scranton, 1946, LL.D.; M.S., Columbia, 1948. Editorial staff, columnist Scranton Times; with Internat. Tel. & Tel. Corp., 1958—, v.p., dir. pub. relations, 1961-64, sr. v.p., dir. corporate relations and advt., 1964—, dir. subsidiaries; dir. Bank of Commerce. Bd. dirs. Fifth Ave. Assn. Served with AUS, 1942-45; ETO. Decorated Silver Star, Bronze Star with cluster.; Named PR Profl. of Year Pub. Relations News, 1971. Mem. Pub. Relations Soc. Am., Internat. Pub. Relations Assn., Am. Mgmt. Assn., Pa. Soc., Internat. Econ. Policy Assn. (dir.), Sigma Delta Chi. Clubs: Overseas Press (N.Y.C.); Metropolitan, Federal City, Nat. Press (Washington); Westchester Country (Rye, N.Y.); Knight of Malta, Knight Order Holy Sepulchre. Office: ITT World Hdqrs 320 Park Ave New York NY 10022 *

GERRITY, JAMES ROBERT, diversified company executive; b. Saskatoon, Sask., Can., Oct. 1, 1941; came to U.S., 1963; s. James Garnet and Helen Doris (Evans) G.; m. Susan Bogovitz, Dec. 1, 1972; children—James Robert, Scott Cameron, Robert Bradley. B.Comm., U. Sask., 1963; M.B.A., U. Calif., Berkeley, 1965. Audit supr. Touche, Ross & Co., Saskatoon, 1959-63; mgr. fin. control Boise Cascade Corp., Idaho, 1965-67, group controller tech. equipment group, 1967-70; sr. v.p. fin. and adminstrn. Dyneer Corp., Westport, Conn., 1970—, also dir. Johnson Wax Fund scholar, 1965; U. Calif., Berkeley Bus. Sch. research grantee, 1964-65. Mem. Can. Inst. Chartered Accts., Fin. Execs. Inst., Beta Alpha Psi, Beta Gamma Sigma. Office: 33 Riverside Ave Westport CT 06880

GERRY, ELBRIDGE THOMAS, banker; b. N.Y.C., Nov. 22, 1908; s. Robert L. and Cornelia (Harriman) G.; m. Marjorie Kane, May 21, 1932; children: Elbridge T., Peter G., Marjorie K. A.B., Harvard U., 1931. With Hanover Bank, 1931-36; with Brown Brothers Harriman & Co., N.Y.C., 1936—, partner, 1956—; dir., chmn. exec. com. Union Pacific Corp.; dir. Doubleday & Co., Inc., Biltmore Dairy Farms, Inc. Chmn. bd. N.Y. Soc. Prevention of Cruelty to Children; trustee Am. Mus. Natural History. Home: Delhi NY 13753 Office: 59 Wall St New York NY 10005

GERRY, JOSEPH JOHN, priest, college chancellor; b. Millinocket, Maine, Sept. 12, 1928; s. Bernard Eugene and Blanche Agnes (McManemon) G. A.B. summa cum laude, St. Anselm's Coll., Manchester, N.H., 1950; postgrad., St. Anselm's Sem., 1954; M.A., U. Toronto, 1955; Ph.D., Fordham U., 1959. Joined Order of St. Benedict, Roman Catholic Ch., 1948; ordained priest: Roman Catholic Ch., 1954. Asst. dean studies St. Anselm's Coll., 1958-59, dean studies, 1971-72, chancellor. Office: Office of Chancellor St Anselm Coll Manchester NH 03102

GERSCHEFSKI, EDWIN, music educator, composer; b. Meriden, Conn., June 10, 1909; s. Otto J. and Josephine (Sturmer) G.; m. Ina Magnuson, June 18, 1931; children: Jo Ellen, Peter, Martha, Michael, John. Ph.B., Mus.B., Yale, 1931,; diploma (Jeffrey Reynolds scholar), Matthay Pianoforte Sch. London, 1932; postgrad. study piano with, Artur Schnabel. Mem. piano faculty Yorkville Music Sch., N.Y.C., 1933-37, Turtle Bay Music Sch., 1937-40; dir. music dept. Home Thrift Assn., N.Y.C., 1938-40; tchr. piano, theory and composition Converse Coll., Spartanburg, S.C., 1940—, dir., 1942-45, dean, 1945-59; tchr. piano and composition Cummington Sch., summer 1943; guest faculty Appalachian State Tchrs. Coll., Boone, N.C., summer 1956; chmn. dept. music U. N.M., 1959-60; mem. faculty U. Ga., Athens, 1960—, head music dept., 1960-72; Mem. bd. New Music Recs., 1938-43; judge Young Artists contest Nat. Fedn. Music Clubs, 1954, 1961; mem. founders bd. Southeastern Composers League, 1952—; mem. scholarship com. Presser Found; participant Danforth Found. Workshop, Sarah Lawrence Coll., summer 1957. Composer, radio performer recs. and motion picture scores; Contbr. articles to publs.; Composer: Classic Symphony, 1944, Half Moon Mountain (women's chorus, baritone), 1948, Song of the Mountains (for piano), 1957, Saugatuck Suite (orch.), 1958, Salutation of the Dawn (mixed chorus), 1964, 100th Psalm (mixed chorus), 1965, also numerous manuscripts.; Regional editor: Jour. Music Theory, 1957—. Recipient invitation to spend 2 summers Yaddo Found., Saratoga Springs, N.Y., 1936-37; award radio commn. League Composers, 1937; winner band music competition N.Y. World's Fair, 1939; Carnegie grantee, 1947; Fund for Advancement Edn. grantee, 1952; gold medal Arnold Bax Soc. for musicial composition in Harriet Cohen Internat. awards, 1963. Mem. Nat. Assn. Schs. Music (regional v.p. 1953-55, examiner 1955—, chmn. library com. 1962-65), Music Tchrs. Nat. Assn., Ga. Composers (pres. 1961-63), Ga. Music Council (pres. 1962-64), Phi Beta Kappa, Phi Kappa Phi, Pi Kappa Lambda, Phi Mu Alpha, Sinfonia. Home: 765 Riverhill Dr Athens GA 30601

GERSHANIK, JUAN JORGE, neonatologist, educator; b. Concepcion del Uruguay, Argentina, Nov. 20, 1941; came to U.S., 1966, naturalized, 1974; s. Marcos and Sophia (Schwarzbein) G.; m. Ana Ester Garfinkel, June 14, 1966; children: Alex, Viviana, Esteban. M.D., U. Rosario, Argentina, 1963. Diplomate: Am. Bd. Pediatrics. Intern in pediatrics Univ. Hosp., Gran, Baig, 1965-66, Variety's Children's Hosp., Miami, 1966-67; resident in pediatrics U. Ky. Med. Ctr., Lexington, 1967-69; fellow in neonatology Med. U. S.C., Charleston, 1969-70; instr. biology U. Rosario, 1966; instr. pediatrics Med. U. S.C., Charleston, 1970-81, assoc. in pediatrics, 1971; asst. prof. pediatrics La. State U., Shreveprot, 1971-73, assoc. prof., Shreveport, 1973-78, dir. newborn services, 1971-79, prof. pediatrics, 1978-79; dir. neonatology So. Baptist Hosp., New Orleans, 1979—; clin. prof. pediatrics Tulane U., 1979—. Contbr. articles to profl. jours. Mem. La. Commn. of Perinatal Care, 1978—. Grantee in field. Fellow Am. Acad. Pediatrics; mem. So. Soc. Pediatrics Research, Greater New Orleans Pediatric Soc., So. Perinatal Assn., La. State Med. Soc., Orleans Parish Med. Soc. Jewish. Home: 1303 Henry Clay Ave New Orleans LA 70118

GERSHENSON, HARRY, lawyer; b. St. Louis, July 8, 1902; m. Dorothy Rose Lupfer; children—Harry, Dorothy (Mrs. Ralph Clock). LL.B., Benton Coll. Law, 1924. Bar: Mo. bar 1923. Practiced in St. Louis, 1923—; sr. partner firm Gershenson & Gershenson; lectr. law St. Louis U., 1948-57. Adv. bd. Salvation Army. Fellow Am. Coll. Probate Counsel (v.p. life bd. regents, pres. 1965-66); mem. Fed. Bar Assn. (life), Am. Bar Found. (life), Scribes Law Writers Assn. (past pres.), Bar Assn. St. Louis (pres. 1946-47, past mem. exec. com.), Practising Law Inst. (past dir.), Mo. State Bar (pres. 1957-58, bd. govs., Pres.'s Distinguished Service award 1966), Am. Bar Assn. (ho. of dels. 1948-66, bd. govs. 1962-64, com. on profl. ethics, past chmn. Lawyers Title Guaranty Fund, lawyers referral), Am. Judicature Soc. (past dir.), Mo. Bar Found. (pres. 1965-70, mem. bd. 1970—), Am. Trial Lawyers Assn., Phi Alpha Delta. Clubs: Mason (33 deg., grand orator, grand lodge 1963-64), Mo. Athletic, Lawyers (St. Louis). Home: 542 Warder Ave University City MO 63130 Office: 7733 Forsyth Blvd Saint Louis MO 63105 *To strive mightily for worthwhile endeavors for my fellowman and myself.*

GERSHINOWITZ, HAROLD, chemist, former oil company executive; b. Bklyn., Aug. 31, 1910; s. Louis and Mamie (Leibowitz) G.; m. Mary Piesman, June 14, 1935. B.S., CCNY, 1931; A.M., Harvard U., 1932, Ph.D., 1934. Research asso. Columbia U., 1935-36, Harvard U., 1936-38; research technologist Shell Oil Co., 1938-40, dir. mfg. research, 1940-45, dir. exploration, prodn. research div., 1945-50, v.p. in charge exploration, prodn. tech. div., 1950-52, cons. to pres., 1965-66; pres., dir. Shell Devel. Co., 1953-62; research coordinator, chmn. research council, dir. Royal Dutch Shell Group of Cos., 1962-65; cons. Orgn. for Econ. Cooperation and Devel., 1966-70; Chmn. environ. studies bd. Nat. Acad. Scis-Nat. Acad. Engring., 1967-70; affiliate mem. faculty Rockefeller U., 1967-78, adj. prof., 1979-82. Mem. exec. bd. Council on Environment of N.Y.C., 1973-76. Fellow AAAS; mem. N.Y. Acad. Scis., Am. Chem. Soc., Phi Beta Kappa, Sigma Xi. Clubs: Explorers, Harvard of N.Y., Princeton of N.Y. Address: 25 Sutton Pl S New York NY 10022

GERSHMAN, CARL SAMUEL, government official; b. N.Y.C., July 20, 1943; s. Joseph Saul and Josephine (Cohen) G.; m. Laurie Gay Pfeffer, Jan. 25, 1970; children: Sarah, Joseph, Jacob. B.A. magna cum laude, Yale U.; M.Ed., Harvard U., 1968. VISTA vol., Pitts., 1965-67; mem. staff research dept. Anti-Defamation League, B'nai B'rith, N.Y.C., 1968; research dir. A. Philip Randolph Inst., N.Y.C., 1969-71; exec. dir. Youth for Peace in Middle East, N.Y.C., 1971-74, Social Democrats, U.S.A., 1974-80; resident scholar Freedom House, N.Y.C., 1980-81; counselor to U.S. permanent rep. to UN, N.Y.C., 1981—; lead cons. Nat. Bipartisan Commn. on C.Am., 1983. Author: The Foreign Policy of American Labor, 1975; co-editor: Israel, The Arabs, and the Middle East, 1972; contbr.: essays, articles to N.Y. Times Mag., Commentary, Wall St. Jour. Bd. dirs. Internat. Rescue Com. Smith Richardson Found. grantee, 1980. Jewish. Office: 799 UN Plaza New York NY 10017

GERSHON, ELLIOT SHELDON, psychiatrist; s. David and Ann (Pohorille) G.; m. Faye Deborah Saltman, Nov. 4, 1967; children: Ari Andrew, Ethan Daniel. A.B., Harvard U., 1961, M.D., 1965. Intern Mt. Sinai Hosp., N.Y.C., 1965-66; teaching fellow psychiatry Harvard U. Med. Sch.; also resident in psychiatry Mass. Mental Health Center, Boston, 1966-69; cons. Peter Bent Brigham Hosp., Boston, 1968-69, Prince George's County (Md.) Health Dept., 1969-70; clin. asso. lab. clin. sci. NIMH, Bethesda, Md., 1969-71, unit chief, sect. psychogenetics, biol. psychiatry br., 1974—, sect. chief, 1978—, mem. faculty staff coll., 1977—; dir. research Jerusalem (Israel) Mental Health Center, 1971-74; mem. faculty Washington Sch. Psychiatry, 1976—; sci. adv. bd. Israel Center Psychobiology, 1972-74; sr. surgeon USPHS, 1969-71, 75-80, med. dir., 1980—; Mem. sci. adv. bd. Am. Friends of Jerusalem Mental Health Center, 1978—. Author: Impact of Biology on Modern Psychiatry, 1977, Genetic Research Strategies for Psychobiology and Psychiatry, 1981; also articles; editorial bd.: Jour. Affective Disorders, 1978—, Psychiatry Research: An Internat. Jour. for Rapid Communications, 1978—, Psychiat. Devels., 1982—, Jour. Psychiat. Research, 1983. Recipient Anna Monika Found. prize, 1979; USPHS Commd. Officer's Commendation medal, 1979. Mem. AAAS, Am. Psychiat. Assn., Am. Psychopath. Assn., Psychiat. Research Soc., Am. Coll. Neuropsychopharmacology, Soc. for Neurosci. Jewish. Address: Bldg 10 Room 3N218 NIMH 9000 Rockville Pike Bethesda MD 20205

GERSHON, MICHAEL DAVID, anatomist, educator; b. N.Y.C., Mar. 3, 1938; s. Murray Huda and Juliette (Levinson) G.; m. Elda Anne Angen, June 10, 1961; children: Perry, Timothy, Dana. B.A., Cornell U., 1958, M.D., 1963. Fellow, instr. Cornell U. Med. Coll., N.Y.C., 1963-65, asst. prof., 1965-69, assoc. prof. anatomy, 1969-74, prof., 1974-75; research assoc. Oxford (Eng.) U., 1965-66; prof. anatomy and cell biology, chmn. dept. Columbia U. Coll. Phys. and Surgeons, 1975—; mem. neurol. disorders program project rev. com. NIH, 1972-75, Neurology A study sect., 1980—. Contbr. med. jours.; Editorial bd.: Neurochemistry Internat., Jour. Histochemistry, Anat. Record, Jour. Comparative Neurology and Anatomy and Embryology. Recipient Borden Undergrad. research prize, 1963; N.Y.C. Health Research Council Career Scientist award, 1971; Markle Found. scholar acad. medicine, 1968; grantee NIH. Mem. Am. Assn. Anatomists, Am. Gastroenterol. Assn., Am. Soc. Cell Biology, Am. Physiol. Soc., AAAS, Endocrine Soc., Soc. Neurosci., N.Y. Soc. Electron Microscopists (pres. 1977-78), N.Y. Acad. Sci., Internat. Soc. Devel. Neurosci., Phi Beta Kappa, Sigma Xi, Alpha Epsilon Delta, Phi Kappa Phi. Club: Cajal. Office: 630 W 168th St New York NY 10032

GERSON, IRWIN CONRAD, advertising executive; b. N.Y.C., Mar. 18, 1930; s. Leon and Charlotte (Steinhause) G.; m. Lenore Greenblatt, Nov. 29, 1953; children: Jill Beth, Matthew Ted. B.S., Fordham U., 1953; M.B.A., N.Y. U., 1959. Ter. mgr. Wyeth Labs. div. Am. Home Products, 1956-58; account exec., supr. William Douglas McAdams, Inc., N.Y.C., 1958-66, v.p., 1966-68, sr. v.p., 1969-70, exec. v.p., 1971-74, pres., 1974—; instr. sales mgmt. Columbia Coll. Pharm. Scis., 1967-77. Editorial adv. bd.: U.S. Jour. Drug and Alcohol Dependence, 1977-83. Trustee, bd. dirs. Chemotherapy Found., 1971—; bd. dirs. Nutritional Research Found., 1977—. Served with AUS, 1954-56. Mem. Pharm. Advt. Club (dir. 1974—, treas. 1976-77, v.p. 1979—), Alpha Zeta Omega. Republican. Clubs: Mason., Elmwood Country (White Plains, N.Y.). Home: 35 Sutton Pl New York NY 10022 Office: 110 E 59th St New York NY 10022

GERSON, LOUIS LIEB, educator; b. Tomaszow, Lubelski, Poland, Nov. 10, 1921; came to U.S., 1938, naturalized, 1942; s. Morris and Ann (Berger) G.; m. Elizabeth Shanley, June 24, 1950; children—Elliot, William, Ann. B.A. with high distinction, U. Conn., 1948; M.A., Yale U., 1950, Ph.D., 1952. Mem. faculty U. Conn., Storrs, 1950—, prof. polit. sci., 1963—, head dept., 1967-78; research fellow Yale U., 1953-54; research asso. Inst. War and Peace, Columbia U., 1964-66; Fulbright vis. prof. U. Bombay, India, 1966-67; vis. research prof. Nat. Taiwan U., 1974-75. Author: Woodrow Wilson and the Rebirth of Poland, 1953, The Hyphenate in Recent American Politics and Diplomacy, 1964, John Foster Dulles, 1967. Adv. bd. John Foster Dullas Oral History Project, Princeton U.; Chmn. Mansfield Democratic Town Com., 1969-72; Trustee Inst. Mediterranean Studies, 1957—; mem. bd. Conf. on European Problems. Rockefeller fellow, 1963-64; Ford fellow, 1952-53; Guggenheim fellow, 1956-57; NATO fellow, 1975-76. Mem. Am. Hist. Assn., Am. Polit. Sci. Assn., Phi Beta Kappa, Pi Sigma Alpha, Phi Alpha Theta, Phi Kappa Phi. Home: Ball Hill Rd Storrs CT 06268

GERSON, NOEL BERTRAM, author; b. Chgo., Nov. 6, 1914; s. Samuel Philip and Rosa Anna (Noel) G.; children: Noel Anne (Mrs. Brennan), Michele (Mrs. Schechter), Margot (Mrs. Burgett), Paul; m. Marilyn A. Hammond. A.B., U. Chgo., 1934, M.A., 1935. Reporter, rewriteman Chgo. Herald-Examiner, 1931-36; exec. Sta. WGN, Chgo., 1936-41. Radio and TV scriptwriter over 10,000 scripts for nat. networks, 1936-51; Author numerous fiction and non-fiction books under own name and various pseudyonyms; books include The Golden Lyre, 1961, The Land is Bright, 1961, The Naked Maja, 1962, Queen of Caprice, 1963, The Slender Reed, 1964, Old Hickory, 1963, Sex and the Mature Man, 1964, Kit Carson, 1964, Lady of France, 1965, Yankee Doodle Dandy, 1965, Give Me Liberty, 1966, Sex and the Adult Woman, 1965, Light-Horse Harry Lee, 1966, The Swamp Fox, The Anthem, 1967, Sam Houston, 1968, Jefferson Square, 1968, The Golden Ghetto, 1969, P.J., My Friend, 1969, TR, 1969, Mirror, Mirror, 1970, Warhead, 1970, The Divine Mistress, 1970, Because I Loved Him, 1971, Island in the Wind, 1971, Victor Hugo, 1971, Double Vision, 1972, The Prodigal Genius, 1972, George Sand, 1972, Daughter of Earth and Water, 1973, State Trooper, 1973, Peter Paul Rubens, 1973, Rebel-Thomas Paine, 1974, The Exploiters, 1974, All That Glitters, 1975, The Caves of Guernica, 1975, Special Agent, 1976, Harriet Beecher Stowe, 1976, Liner, 1977, The Vidocq Dossier, 1977, The Smugglers, 1977, Trelawny's World, 1977, Wagons West, 1979, White Indian, 1980; also numerous articles. Bd. dirs. Goodspeed Opera House Found., Haddam, Conn., Conn. Advocates of Arts. Fellow Internat. Inst. Arts and Letters; mem. Authors Guild Am., Western Writers Am., Mystery Writers Am., Miss. Valley hist. assns., Am. Acad. Polit. and Social Sci., Centro Studi E Scambi Internat., Phi Beta Kappa, Kappa Alpha. Clubs: Players (N.Y.C.); Liguanea (Jamaica, W.I.). Home: 7946 Palacio del Mar Dr Boca Raton FL 33433 *Both Thornton Wilder and Sinclair Lewis, who taught me so much about my craft, stressed the same thing. Writing, they said, was the application of the seat of the pants to the seat of the chair. So, I suppose, I could claim that the old-fashioned American-hard-work-ethic is responsible for whatever success I've enjoyed. But, on the days when the words won't flow, when the ideas dissipate and the concepts atrophy, I'm afraid I must agree with Dorothy Parker, and would rather dig ditches.*

GERSON, SAMUEL JOSEPH, retail store executive; b. Boston, Dec. 14, 1941; s. Michael and Edythe G.; m. Geraldine Elaine Bohn, Mar. 22, 1964; children: Dana Ann, Michelle Jill. A.B. in Econs., Boston Coll.; M.B.A., Boston U. Vice pres., gen. mdse. mgr. William Filene's, Boston, 1968-77; pres., chief exec. officer Denver Co., 1977-78; pres., chief operating officer The Gap, San Bruno, Calif., 1979—. Served with USN, 1963-66. Address: Gap Stores Inc 900 Cherry Ave San Bruno CA 94066

GERSONY, WELTON MARK, pediatric cardiologist, educator; b. Syracuse, N.Y., Nov. 19, 1931; s. Irving and Ann (Cohen) G.; m. Susan Mirsky; children: Neal, Anne, Richard, Deborah. A.B., Syracuse U., 1954; M.D., SUNY, Syracuse, 1958. Diplomate: Am. Bd. Pediatrics, Sub Bd. Pediatric Cardiology (mem. Sub-Bd. Pediatric Cardiology 1976-83, chmn. 1981-83). Intern Cleve. Met. Gen. Hosp., 1958-59, resident in pediatrics, 1959-61, Babies and Childrens Hosp.,

Cleve., 1959-61; fellow in cardiology Harvard U., 1963-65; asst. prof. pediatrics U. Tex., Dallas, 1965-68, Columbia U., 1968-71, asso. prof., 1971-74, prof., 1974—; dir. div. pediatric cardiology Columbia-Presbyn. Med. Center. Mem. editorial bd.: Pediatric Cardiology, 1978; contbg. author: Nelson's Textbook of Pediatrics, 1983; contbr. numerous articles, and revs. to profl. jours., chpts. in books. Prin. investigator NIH grants. Served as capt. M.C. U.S. Army, 1961-63. Fellow Am. Coll. Cardiology, Am. Acad. Pediatrics; mem. Soc. Pediatric Research, Am. Pediatric Soc., Am. Heart Assn., Am. Fedn. Clin. Research, Harvey Soc., Am. Contract Bridge League (life master). Research on cardiovascular disease in infants and children, natural history of congenital heart disease in children; patent ductas arteiosus in premature infants; persistence of the fetal circulation. Office: 630 W 168th St New York NY 10032

GERST, IRVING, educator, applied mathematician; b. N.Y.C., May 30, 1912; s. Nathan and Jeny (Jacobs) G.; m. Gussie Siegal, Feb. 14, 1937; children: Cynthia Harriet, Adrienne Sari. B.S., Coll. City N.Y., 1931; M.A., Columbia U., 1932, Ph.D., 1947. Tchr. math. high sch., N.Y.C., 1937-41; instr. USAAF, Miss., 1942-44; cons. Transp. Corps, U.S. Army, N.Y.C., 1944-46; research mathematician, head applied analysis group Burroughs Corp., N.Y.C., 1946-58; head network group RCA, N.Y.C., 1958-61; prof. math., chmn. dept. applied analysis State U. N.Y. at Stony Brook, 1961-70, prof. math., chmn. dept. applied math., statistics, 1970-72, prof. applied math. and stats., 1972-82, prof. emeritus, 1982—; lectr. City U., N.Y.C., 1958-61; cons. Sperry Rand Corp., 1961-63. Contbr. articles to profl. jours.; Assoc. editor: SIAM (jour. applied math.), 1959-80, SIAM Rev., 1959—. Mem. Am. Math. Soc., Math. Assn. Am., Phi Beta Kappa, Sigma Xi. Address: State U NY Stony Brook NY 11794

GERST, PAUL HOWARD, physician; b. Sept. 24, 1927; s. David and Hilde (Werbel) G.; m. Elizabeth Carlsen, Aug. 3, 1957; children—Steven R., Jeffrey C., Andrew L. A.B., Columbia U., 1948, M.D., 1952. Diplomate: Am. Bd. Surgery, Am. Bd. Thoracic Surgery. Intern Columbia Presbyn. Med. Center, N.Y.C., 1952-53, resident, 1956-62, mem. staff, 1962—; instr. physiology U. Pa., 1955-56; practice medicine specializing in surgery, N.Y.C., 1962—; asst. clin. prof. surgery Columbia U., 1964-72; prof. surgery Albert Einstein Coll. Medicine, 1972—; dir. surgery Bronx-Lebanon Hosp. Center, N.Y.C., 1964—. Contbr. articles to profl. jours. Served to 1st lt. U.S. Army, 1953-55. USPHS postdoctoral fellow, 1955-56; Recipient Research Career Devel. award, 1964-65. Fellow A.C.S.; mem. Am. Physiol. Soc., N.Y. Soc. for Thoracic Surgery, N.Y. Surg. Soc., N.Y. Soc. for Cardiovascular Surgery, Am. Heart Assn. Home: 141 Tekening Dr Tenafly NJ 07670 Office: Bronx Lebanon Hospital Center 1650 Grand Concourse New York NY 10457

GERSTACKER, CARL ALLAN, former chemical company executive; b. Cleve., Aug. 6, 1916; s. Rollin Michael and Eda (Uhinck) G.; m. Jayne Harris, Oct. 22, 1950 (div.); children: Bette Mignon, Lisa Jayne; m. Esther Schuette, Mar. 8, 1975. B.S., U. Mich., 1938; LL.D., Central Mich. Coll. Edn., 1957, Northwood Inst., 1977, Alma Coll., 1982; Sc.D. Albion Coll, 1972; L.H.D., Waynesburg Coll., 1980. Accounting dept. Dowell, Inc., 1938-40; chem. engr. Dow Chem. Co., 1946-48, dir., 1948-81, treas., 1949-59, v.p., 1955-60, mem. exec. com., 1957-76, chmn. finance com., 1959-81, chmn. bd., 1960-76; dir. Chem. Fin. Corp., Midland, Mich., Chem. Bank & Trust Co., Midland, Consol. Foods Corp., Dundee Cement Co., Eaton Corp., K Mart Corp., Spence Engring. Co. Bd. dirs. Rollin M. Gerstacker Found., Elsa U. Pardee Found.; mem. adv. bd. New Perspective Fund Inc.; trustee Albion Coll., Rockefeller U. Council. Decorated Order of Rising Sun 2d class, Japan; recipient Ohio Gov.'s award, 1966; U.S. Pres.'s E award, 1971; Soc. Chem. Industry medal, 1974; Silver Tower award, Korea, 1976. Mem. Synthetic Organic Chem. Mfrs. Assn. (pres. 1960-61), Mfg. Chemists Assn. (chmn. 1968-69), Japan-U.S. Friendship Commn., Theta Xi, Beta Alpha Psi, Sigma Iota Epsilon. Presbyn. Clubs: Mason (33 deg.), Rotarian., Exchange, Midland Country. Home: Box 226 Midland MI 48640 Office: 127 Townsend St Midland MI 48640

GERSTEIN, DAVID BROWN, hardware manufacturing company executive; b. N.Y.C., Jan. 30, 1936; s. Frank and May G.; m. Jane Ellen Gerstein, May 4, 1963; children: Mark, James. Student, Columbia U., 1951-58, postgrad., 1958; B.S., Seton Hall U., 1958. With Thermwell Products Co., Paterson, N.J., 1958—, sales mgr., 1965-68, v.p., 1968-74, pres., 1974—; owner N. J. Nets basketball team, 1978—; v.p. Lever Mfg. Co., Paterson; pres. Woodlowe Realty, Paterson, Wait Assos., Dim Assos., Mahwah, N.J. Chmn. adv. council energy and conservation State of N.J. Home: 432 Long Hill Dr Short Hills NJ 07078

GERSTELL, A. FREDERICK, cement manufacturing company executive; b. 1939. Vice pres. mktg. Alpha Portland Cement Co., 1960-75; v.p. Calif. Portland Cement Co., Los Angeles, 1975-81, pres., chief operating officer, 1981—. Office: Calif Portland Cement Co 800 Wilshire Blvd Los Angeles CA 90017 *

GERSTEN, JEROME WILLIAM, physician; b. N.Y.C., Apr. 20, 1917; s. Louis and Bessie (Abrams) G.; m. Rhoda Rich, Nov. 8, 1941; children: Steven, Wendy, Christopher, Dennis, Madeleine. B.S., CCNY, 1935; M.D., N.Y. U., 1939; M.S. in Physiology, U. Minn., 1949. Diplomate: Am. Bd. Phys. Medicine and Rehab. Intern Morrisania City Hosp., N.Y.C., 1939-40; resident in internal medicine Montefiore Hosp., N.Y.C., 1940-41; fellow M.I.T., 1946, Columbia U. Coll. Phys. and Surg., 1946-47; resident in phys. medicine Mayo Clinic, Rochester, Minn., 1947-49; mem. faculty U. Colo. Med. Sch., 1949—, prof. phys. medicine and rehab., 1957—, chmn. dept., 1955-81. Editorial bd.: Am. Jour. Phys. Medicine; contbr. numerous articles med. jours. Served as officer M.C. AUS, 1941-46. Mem. Am. Inst. Ultrasonics in Medicine (pres. 1956-59), Am. Assn. Electromyography (pres. 1959), Am. Congress Rehab. Medicine (pres. 1969), Am. Physiol. Soc., Am. Acad. Phys. Medicine and Rehab., Soc. Exptl. Biology and Medicine, Am. Assn. Electromyography and Electrodiagnosis, Am. Heart Assn., Phi Beta Kappa, Sigma Xi, Alpha Omega Alpha. Home: 1370 Forest St Denver CO 80220 Office: 4200 E 9th Ave Denver CO 80262

GERSTENBERGER, DONNA LORINE, humanities educator; b. Wichita Falls, Tex., Dec. 26, 1929; d. Donald Fayette and Mabel G. A.B., Whitman Coll., 1951; M.A., U. Okla., 1952, Ph.D., 1958. Asst. prof. English, U. Colo., Boulder, 1958-60; prof. U. Wash., 1960—, chmn. undergrad. studies, 1971-74, assoc. dean Coll. Arts and Scis., dir. Coll. Honors and Office Undergrad. Studies, 1974-76, chmn. dept. English, 1976-83, vice chmn. faculty senate, 1984-85; cons. in field; bd. dirs. Am. Lit. Classics; mem. grants-in-aid com. Am. Council Learned Socs.; chmn. region VII, Mellon Fellowships in Humanities, 1982-84. Author: J.M. Synge, 1964, The American Novel: A Checklist of Twentieth Century Criticism, vols. I and II, 1970, Directory of Periodicals, 1974, The Complex Configuration: Modern Verse Drama, 1973, Iris Murdoch, 1974; editor: Microcosm, 1969, Richard Hugo, 1983, Swallow Series in Bibliography, 1974—; assoc. editor: Abstracts of English Studies, 1958-68. Bd. dirs. N.W. Chamber Orch., Seattle, 1975-78. Am. Council Learned Socs. grantee, 1962; Am. Philos. Soc. grantee, 1963. Mem. MLA, Am. Com. Irish Studies. Office: English Dept GN-30 U Wash Seattle WA 98195

GERSTENMAIER, JOHN HERBERT, rubber company executive; b. St. Paul, Aug. 24, 1916; s. Walter and Alma (Lindenberg) G.; m. Lois Rolfing, Dec. 28, 1939; children: John Herbert, Jan Lee McClennan. B.M.E., U. Minn., 1938; M.Indsl. Mgmt., MIT, 1952. With Goodyear Tire & Rubber Co., Akron, Ohio, 1938-63, 67—, plant mgr., Logan, Ohio, 1963, exec. v.p., dir., Akron, 1971-74, pres., 1974-78, chief operating officer, 1974—, vice chmn., 1978—; pres. Motor Wheel Corp., Lansing, Mich., 1964-67. Mem. Soc. Automotive Engrs., Sigma Nu. Lutheran. Club: Portage Country (Akron). Home: 431 St Andrews Dr Akron OH 44303 Office: Goodyear Tire & Rubber Co 1144 E Market St Akron OH 44316

GERSTER, ROBERT GIBSON, composer; b. Chgo., Oct. 13, 1945; s. Robert Heer and Betty Lou (Gibson) G.; m. Pamela Daneal Ward, Aug. 24, 1968; children: David Ward, James William, Sara Jeanne. B.Mus., Ohio State U., 1967, M.Mus. (fellow), 1968; D.M.A., U. Wash., 1976. Teaching asst. U. Wash., 1968, 71-73; lectr. Calif. State U., Fresno, 1974—, Fresno City Coll., 1981; organist, choir dir. Good Shepherd Luth. Co., 1977—; exec. dir. Orpheus, 1981-83. Composer: Fanfare, 1966, Ten Pieces, 1966, Cantata, 1967, West-Running Brook, 1968, Cycles, 1968, Woodwind Trio, 1968, Music for Brass and Percussion, 1971, Mobiles, 1971, Bird in the Spirit, 1972, Synchromy, 1972, Chance Dance Game, 1973, Flowers, 1974, Music for Organ Pedals and Brass, 1975, Music for Cello and Piano, 1976, Visalia Fanfare, 1977, Cantata for Woodwind Quartet, 1977, Fantasy-Variations for Piano, 1978, The Temple of Fire and Ice, 1979, Christmas Suite, 1979, The Silver Palace of Night, 1980, Fowl Play, 1981, Visions of a Golden Phoenix, 1981, The Range of Light, 1982, Oh, Blest the House, 1982, Visions of a Celestial Cathedral, 1983. Served with U.S. Army, 1969-70. Charles E. Ives scholar Nat. Inst. Arts and Letters, 1973; composition fellow Nat. Endowment for Arts, 1979. Mem. Am. Soc. Univ. Composers, Coll. Music Soc., Broadcast Music, Am. Guild Organists, Pi Kappa Lambda. Home: 2850 E Santa Ana Fresno CA 93726 Office: Dept Music Calif State U Fresno CA 93740

GERSTLEY, JAMES MACK, ret. indsl. exec.; b. London, Eng., Nov. 11, 1907; naturalized, 1939; s. James and Adele (Mack) G.; m. Elizabeth Lilienthal, Sept. 7, 1934; children—James Gordon, Ann. L. (Mrs. G. R. Pieper). Student, Cheltenham Coll., Gloucester, Eng., 1919-24, Cambridge U., Eng., 1926-28; studied with, Mr. Weber, Bonn, Germany, 1924-25, Mme. de la Rive, St. Avertin, France, 1925-26. With Gt. Western Electro Chem. Co. (now Dow Chem. Co.), 1930-33; with Pacific Coast Borax Co. div. Borax Consol., Ltd. (became U.S. Borax & Chem. Corp. 1956), 1930—, pres., 1950-61, vice chmn. bd., 1961-78; dir. Haas Bros., San Francisco. Vice chmn. Asian Art Commn., San Francisco; vice chmn., treas. Asian Art Found., San Francisco.; Trustee Pomona Coll.; bd. dirs. Heritage Found., San Francisco; mem. Council Friends Bancroft Library, Berkeley. Mem. Cheltonian Soc., Peterhouse Soc., Museum Assn. Los Angeles County, Save the Redwoods League, Brandeis U. Assos. Home: 160 Farm Rd Woodside CA 94062

GERSTNER, LOUIS VINCENT, JR., financial services executive; b. N.Y.C., Mar. 1, 1942; s. Louis Vincent and Marjorie (Rutan) G.; m. Elizabeth Robins Link, Nov. 30, 1968; children—Louis, Elizabeth. B.A., Dartmouth Coll., 1963; M.B.A., Harvard U., 1965. Dir. McKinsey & Co., N.Y.C., 1965-78; exec. v.p. Am. Express Co., N.Y.C., 1978-81, vice chmn. bd., 1981—, also dir., chmn. exec. com.; dir. Warner/Amex Cable Communications, Shearson/Am. Express, Jewel Cos., Inc., Fireman's Fund Ins. Co. Bd. mgrs. Meml. Sloan Kettering Hosp., 1978—; mem. exec. com., bd. trustees Joint Council on Econ. Edn., 1975—; chmn. Joint Council Econ. Edn., 1983—; bd. dirs. Council U.S. and Italy, Greenwich Boys' Club Assn. Mem. Internat. Golf Assn. (dir.), Council Fgn. Relations. Clubs: Round Hill, Links, Sky. Office: 125 Broad St New York NY 10004

GERSTNER, ROBERT WILLIAM, structural engineering educator; b. Chgo., Nov. 10, 1934; s. Robert Berty and Martha (Tuchelt) G.; m. Elizabeth Willard, Feb. 8, 1958; children: Charles Willard, William Mark. B.S., Northwestern U., 1956, M.S., 1957, Ph.D., 1960. Registered structural and profl. engr., Ill. Instr. Northwestern U., Evanston, Ill., 1957-59, research fellow, 1959-60; asst. prof. U. Ill., Chgo., 1960-63, asso. prof., 1963-69, prof. structural engring., architecture, 1969—; structural engr. cons., 1959—. Contbr. articles to profl. jours. Pres. Riverside Improvement Assn., 1973-77, 79-82. Fellow ASCE; Mem. Am. Concrete Inst., Am. Soc. for Engring. Edn., AAAS, AAUP, ACLU. Home: 2628 Agatite Ave Chicago IL 60625

GERSTNER, WILLIAM CARL, utility company executive; b. Detroit, June 3, 1924; s. William Carl and Mamie Marie (Schneider) G.; m. Anna Fredrikke Bertun, Mar. 17, 1945; children: Jan Steven, William Carl. Certs., Internat. Corr. Schs., 1949, 52, 56. Registered profl. engr., Ill. With Ill. Power Co., 1945—, mgr. energy supply, Decatur, 1971-72, v.p., 1972-76, exec. v.p., 1976—, dir. Mem. Galesburg (Ill.) Electric Commn., 1958-66; dir. Elec. Energy Inc., 1976—; bd. dirs. Galesburg Prairie council Boy Scouts Am., 1961-66. Served with USNR, 1942-45. Decorated Air médal. Mem. Edison Electric Inst. (chmn. air quality subcom. environment and energy com. 1973-75, mem. adv. com. environment and energy div. 1975—, chmn. PCB task force 1976—). Republican. Home: 535 N Country Club Rd Decatur IL 62521 Office: 500 S 27th St Decatur IL 62525

GERT, GERARD MARTIN, retired government official; b. Free City of Danzig, Feb. 4, 1920; U.S., 1937; s. Samuel and Martha (Levy) G. Student, Lebanon Valley Coll., 1937-39; B.S., N.Y. U., 1942, New Sch. Social Research, 1942, Nat. War Coll., 1965-66. Pub. affairs work U.S. Dept. State, 1949-53; fgn. service info. officer USIA, Germany, Austria, Yugoslavia, Laos, Vietnam, 1953-68; dir. RIAS, Berlin, Germany, 1968-80, ret., 1980. Served to lt. col., inf. AUS, 1942-46; CBI. Recipient Meritorious Honor award (2) USIA, 1975, 80; awarded German Fed. Order of Merit, 1st class, 1980. Mem. World Affairs Council No. Calif., Beta Gamma Sigma. Club: Commonwealth (San Francisco). Home: 688 Joliet Way Napa CA 94559

GERTH, DONALD ROGERS, university president; b. Chgo., Dec. 4, 1928; s. George C. and Madeleine (Canavan) G.; m. Beverly J. Hollman, Oct. 15, 1955; children: Annette Gerth Childs, Deborah A. B.A., U. Chgo., 1947, A.M. in Polit. Sci, 1951, Ph.D., 1963. Admissions counselor U. Chgo., 1956-58; asso. dean students, admissions and records, mem. dept. polit. sci. Calif. State U., San Francisco, 1958-63; asso. dean instnl. relations and student affairs Calif. State Univs. and Colls., 1963-64; dean of students Calif. State U., Chico, 1964-68, prof. polit. sci., 1964-76; co-dir. Danforth Found. Research Project, 1968-69; coordinator Inst. Local Govt. and Public Service, 1968-70; asso. v.p. for acad. affairs, dir. internat. programs Calif. State U., Chico, 1969-70, v.p. acad. affairs, 1970-76, pres., prof. polit. sci. and public adminstrn., Dominguez Hills, 1976-84; pres., prof. govt. and polit. sci. Calif. State U.-Sacramento, 1984—; chmn. commn. on extended edn. Calif. State U. and Colls., 1977—; asso. West Coast coordinator Higher Edn. Exec. Assos. of Chgo., 1967-71; bd. dirs. Ombudsman Found., Los Angeles, 1968-71; com. continuing edn. Calif. Coordinating Council for Higher Edn., 1963-64; lectr. Claremont Grad. Sch. and Univ. Center, 1965-69. Contbr. articles to profl. jours. Mem. personnel commn. Chico Unified Sch. Dist., 1969-76, chmn., 1971-74; adv. com. on justice programs Butte Coll., 1970-76. Served to capt. USAF, 1952-56. Mem. Soc. Coll. and Univ. Planning, Town Hall of Los Angeles, Am. Polit. Sci. Assn., Am. Soc. Public Adminstrn., Western Govtl. Research Assn., World Affairs Council Los Angeles, Calif. Assn. Public Adminstrn. Edn. (chmn. 1973-74), Nat. Assn. Schs. Public Affairs and Adminstrn. Home: 404 Palos Verdes Blvd Redondo Beach CA 90277 Office: Pres's Office Calif State U 6000 J St Sacramento CA 95819

GERTLER, ALFRED MARTIN, public relations executive; b. N.Y.C., Nov. 15, 1922; s. Harry and Peggy L. (Weinberg) G.; m. Claire O. Gruenberg, Oct. 19, 1951; children: Eric, Jonathan, Richard. B.S. in Journalism, U. Ill., 1947. With Harshe-Rotman & Druck, Inc. (now Ruder Finn & Rutman Inc.), Chgo., 1948—, sr. exec. v.p., 1973-82, chief operating officer, 1977-82, pres., 1979-82, vice chmn., pres.-Chgo., 1982—, also dir.; reporter, editor Peoria (Ill.) Star, 1947; account exec. Ridings & Ferris, Inc., Chgo., 1948; lectr. U. Ill., 1975, counselor, 1974-75. Contbr. articles to profl. jours. Served with USAAF, 1942-45. Decorated D.F.C., Air medal with 5 oak leaf clusters. Mem. Pub. Relations Soc. Am. (accredited), Publicity Club Chgo., Sigma Delta Chi. Democrat. Jewish. Home: 1450 Ridge Rd Highland Park IL 60035 Office: 444 N Michigan Ave Chicago IL 60611

GERTLER, MAYNARD, editor, publisher; b. Montreal, Que., Can., Dec. 1, 1916; s. Karl H. and Gertrude (Slover) G.; m. Ann-Elizabeth Straus, Sept. 20, 1942; children: Michael Eden, Jeffrey Lee, Alfred Stieglitz, Franklin Straus, Edward Hart. B.A. with honors, Queen's U., 1939; postgrad., Columbia U., 1939-43, Cambridge (Eng.) U., 1953-58. Economist to U.S. Army, 1943-46; tchr. econs. and govt. N.Y. U., 1948-51; tchr. Am. history Queens and Clare colls. Cambridge U., 1955-58; research dir., sec.-treas., pres. World Today Inc., documentary films, N.Y.C., 1946-48; engaged in farming, Va., Pa., Ont., 1945—; pres. Harvest House Ltd. Publishers, Montreal, 1960—; v.p. Montreal Internat. Book Fair, 1977—; corr. sec. Can. centre PEN, 1978-79, v.p., 1983—. Mem. statutory com. Civil Liberties Union, Montreal, 1963, bd. dirs., 1968-72; bd. dirs. Can. Human Rights Found., 1973—; pres. Can. sect. Amnesty Internat., 1979-80. Ont. Fedn. Agr. Club: Montreal Amateur Athletic Assn. (Montreal). Home: 482 Strathcona Ave Montreal PQ H3Y 2X1 Canada Office: 2335 Sherbrooke St W Montreal PQ H3H 1G6 Canada

GERTLER, MENARD M., physician; b. Saskatoon, Sask., Can., May 21, 1919; came to U.S., 1947, naturalized, 1953; s. Frank and Clara (Handelman) G.; m. Anna Paull, Sept. 4, 1943; children—Barbara Lynn, Stephanie Jocelyn, Jonathan Paull. B.A., U. Sask., 1940; M.D., McGill U., 1943, M.Sc., 1946; D.Sc., N.Y. U., 1959. Intern Royal Victoria Hosp., Montreal, Que., Can., 1943-44; resident Mass. Gen. Hosp., Boston, 1947-50; also research fellow in medicine Mass. Gen. Hosp., Harvard Med. Sch., 1947-50; dir. cardiology Francis Delafield div. Columbia Presbyn. Med. Center, N.Y.C., 1950-54; spl. research fellow NIH, N.Y. U. dept. biochemistry, 1954-56; prof. Sch. Medicine, dir. cardiovascular research Inst. Rehab. Medicine N.Y. U. Med. Center, 1958—; sr. med. examiner FAA, 1975; med. dir. Sinclair Oil Corp., 1958-68; Dir. Washington Fed. Savs. & Loan Assn.; internat. cons. cardiovascular diseases, social and rehab. services HEW, Washington, 1968—. Author: Coronary Heart Disease in Young Adults, 1954, Coronary Heart Disease, 1974; Contbr. articles to profl. jours. Served with M.C. Royal Canadian Army, 1940-43. Recipient Founders Day award N.Y. U., 1959. Clubs: Cosmos (Washington); Harvard (Boston); University (N.Y.C.). Home: 1000 Park Ave New York NY 10028 Office: 400 E 34th St New York NY 10016

GERTY, FRANCIS JOSEPH, physician; b. Chgo., Nov. 17, 1892; s. Frank K. and Josephine (Vincent) G.; m. Ursula Mitchell, Dec. 21, 1922 (dec. 1968); children: John Mitchell, Josephine (dec.), Mary Frances (Mrs. William C. Taylor, Jr.), Helen Joan (Mrs. Brian Owens), Frank J. Grad., Chgo. Tchrs. Coll., 1912; student, U. Chgo., 1912-17; B.S., Loyola U., 1920; M.D., 1921; D.Sc. (hon.), 1957, U. Ill., 1976. Diplomate: Am. Bd. Psychiatry and Neurology (pres. 1959). Tchr. pub. schs., Chgo., 1912-16; intern, resident physician Cook County Hosp., 1920-22; supt. Cook County Psychopathic Hosp. and county physician, 1922- 41; attending neurologist Cook County Hosp., 1932-41; asst. and asso. prof. nervous and mental diseases Loyola U. Med. Sch., 1923-30, prof., head dept., 1931-41; prof. psychiatry, head dept. U. Ill. Coll. Medicine, 1941-61; now prof. emeritus; prof. emeritus Rush Med. Coll., 1974—; dir. psychiat. div. Ill. Neurophychiat. Inst., 1941-61; attending specialist in neuropsychiatry Edward Hines Jr. Hosp., 1940-61, 63—; chmn. neuropsychiatry dept. Presbyn. St. Luke's Hosp., 1958-60; dir. Dept. Pub. Welfare, State of Ill., 1961, Dept. Mental Health, State of Ill., 1961-63; psychiatrist-in-chief Riveredge Hosp., Forest Park, Ill., 1963-77, sr. cons., 1977—. Contbr. articles to profl. jours. Mem. psychiat. adv. council State Ill., 1933-61, mem. psychiat. tng. and research authority, 1957- 63; mem. adv. council in neuropsychiatry U.S. Vets. Bur., 1955-61; mem. profl. adv. com. Nat. Assn. Mental Health, 1956-65; mem. Nat. Mental Health Inst., 1951-55; chmn. dean's com. for psychiatry VA Hosp., Hines, Ill., 1946-60; mem. Med. Center Commn. Chgo., 1961-67; chmn. profl. adv. com. Ill. Assn. for Mental Health, 1965-70; chmn. constrn. grants commn. Ill. Dept. Mental Health, 1965-70. Served with Med. R.C., 1917-18, lt. comdr. USNR, 1933-51. Decorated knight St. Gregory, 1957; recipient George Howell Coleman award Inst. Medicine Chgo., 1961; Stritch medal Stritch Sch. Medicine, 1964. Fellow Am. Coll. Psychiatrists (Bowis award 1968); mem. AMA (chmn. sect. on nervous and mental diseases 1948, mem. council on mental health 1954-57), Ill., Chgo. med. socs., Chgo. Neurol. Soc., Am. Psychiat. Assn. (council 1952-55, chmn. com. on med. edn. 1951-52, pres. 1958-59, disting. service award 1984), Soc. Biol. Psychiatry, Inst. Medicine Chgo., Central Neuro-Psychiat. Assn. (pres. 1956), Ill. Psychiat. Soc., Blue Key, Phi Chi, Sigma Xi, Alpha Omega Alpha. Roman Catholic. Address: 1150 Laurie Ln Burr Ridge IL 60521

GERTZ, ELMER, lawyer, author, educator; b. Chgo., Sept. 14, 1906; s. Morris and Grace (Grossman) G.; m. Ceretta Samuels, Aug. 16, 1931 (dec.); children: Theodore, Margery Ann Hechtman; m. Mamie L. Friedman, June 21, 1959; 1 son, Jack M. Friedman. Ph.B., U. Chgo., 1928, J.D., 1930. Bar: Ill. bar 1930. Since practiced in, Chgo.; formerly asso. firm McInerney, Epstein & Arvey, Chgo.; asst. to masters in chancery Jacob M. Arvey, Samuel B. Epstein, 1930-43; atty. for Nathan Leopold in successful parole procs., 1957-58; atty. various censorship litigations including Tropic of Cancer, 1961—, atty. for Jack Ruby in setting aside death sentence; counsel commn. to investigate disorders in Chgo. during, spring, summer 1968; prof. John Marshall Law Sch., 1970—. Author: (with A.I. Tobin) Frank Harris: A Study in Black and White, 1931, The People vs. The Chicago Tribune, 1942; play Mrs. Bixby Gets a Letter, 1942; Joe Medill's War, 1946, American Ghettos, 1946, A Handful of Clients, 1965, Moment of Madness: The People vs. Jack Ruby, 1968; foreword The Tropic of Cancer On Trial, 1968; To Life, 1974 (Friends of Lit. award), Short Stories of Frank Harris, 1975, Henry Miller: Years of Trial and Triumph: The Letters of Henry Miller and Elmer Gertz, 1978, German edit., 1980, Odyssey of a Barbarian, 1979, (with Joseph Pisciotte) Charter for a New Age, 1980, others; Contbr. to: Henry Miller and the Critics, 1963, Mass Media and the Law, 1969, For the First Hours of Tomorrow, 1971; Author articles in various periodicals and encys. Dir. pub. relations Ill. Police Assn., 1934; mem. exec. com. Ill. Com. Equal Job Opportunity; mem. nat., Chgo. adv. bd. commn. on law and social action Am. Jewish Congress; chmn. soldier vote com. Profl. and Bus. People, 1944; mem. law and order com. Chgo. Commn. on Human

Relations, 1945—; v.p. Ill. Freedom to Read Com.; chmn. Vets. Housing Com., 1945-47; mem. Mayor's Housing Com., 1946-48, legal chmn., 1946-47; mem. Chgo. Com. on Housing Action, 1947-49; adv. com. Chief Justice Municipal Ct. Chgo., 1950-51; pres. Greater Chgo. council Am. Jewish Congress, 1959-63; del. 6th Ill. Constl. Conv., 1969-70; chmn. conv. Bill of Rights com., 1969-70; bd. dirs. Jackson Park Hosp.; exec. v.p. Blind Service Assn.; trustee Belefaire; nat. bd. trustees City of Hope. Recipient Golden Key award City of Hope, 1966; award Ill. div. A.C.L.U., 1963, 74, U. Chgo. Alumni Assn., 1959; State of Israel Prime Minister's medal, 1972; selected for Chicagoland honor roll Chgo. Council Against Discrimination, 1946, 47, Hadassah, 1975, Educator of Year award, 1975, numerous others. Mem. Pub. Housing Assn. (founder, counsel, pres. 1943-49), Civil War Round Table (founder, exec. com., pres., hon. life), Adult Edn. Council Chgo. (sec., pres.), Shaw Soc. (founder, pres., exhibit chmn. Shaw Centennial 1956, Darrow Centennial 1957), ABA., Fed. Bar Assn., Chgo. Bar Assn. (chmn. legal edn. com. 1970-71, chmn. civil rights com. 1978-79, chmn. civil rights com. 1979-80), Bar Assn. 7th Circuit, Am. Judicature Soc., Decalogue Soc. Lawyers (mgr., pres., editor Jour.), First Amendment Lawyers Assn. (pres. 1978-79, chmn. 1979-80), Soc. Midland Authors (award 1969, sec. 1976), Authors Guild, Appellate Lawyers Assn. Ill. Clubs: Chicago Literary (v.p. 1968-69, 1978-79, pres. 1979-80), Cliff Dwellers, City. Home: 6249 N Albany Ave Chicago IL 60659 Office: 315 S Plymouth Ct Chicago IL 60604 *Now that I have reached the magical age of 75, I look upon it as the beginning of a new youthfulness, rather than second childhood or senility. I am challenged by new ideas and new tasks.*

GERULAITIS, VITAS KEVIN, tennis player; b. Bklyn., July 26, 1954; s. Vitas and Aldona G. Student, Columbia U. Became profl. tennis player, 1974; player for Pitts. Triangles (World Team Tennis), 1974-76; mem. Davis Cup team, 1977-79, BP Cup team, 1973. Established Vitas Gerulaitis Found., 1977. Winner U.S. Clay Ct. Amateur Doubles Championship, 1973, Men's Amateur Grass Doubles, 1971, Australian Open, 1977, 79, Italian Open, 1977, 79, Forest Hills Invitation, 1978, Austrian Grand Prix, 1979, Wimbledon Doubles, 1975, South African Singles, 1981-82, Can. Singles, 1982. Office: care US Tennis Assn 51 E 42d St New York NY 10017 *

GERVAIS, SISTER GENEROSE, hospital administrator; b. Currie, Minn., Sept. 18, 1919; d. Philip Frederick and Elizabeth Eleanor (Sandgathe) G. B.S., Stout State U., Menomonie, Wis., 1945; M.Hosp. Adminstrn., U. Minn., 1954. Joined Sisters of St. Francis, Roman Catholic Ch., 1938; adminstrv. dietitian St. Marys Hosp., Rochester, Minn., 1948-50, adminstrv. asst., 1951-52, asst. adminstr., 1954-63, asso. adminstr., 1963-71, hosp. adminstr., 1971-81, exec. dir., 1981—, also mem. and sec. bd. dirs.; cons. dietitian Mercy Hosp., Portsmouth, Ohio, 1950-51; dir. 1st Nat. Bank, Rochester, 1975-78, Fed. Res. Bank of Mpls., 1978—. Bd. dirs. St. Francis Med. Ctr., LaCrosse, Wis., 1979—, S.E. Minn. Health Systems Agy., 1978-83, S.E. Minn. Health Council, 1983—. United Way of Olmsted County, 1968-73. Mem. Cath. Health Assn. U.S. (trustee, chmn. 1982-83, Speaker membership assembly 1983-84), Am. Coll. Hosp. Adminstrs., Am. Hosp. Assn., Minn. Public Health Assn., Minn. Hosp. Assn., Minn. Conf. Cath. Health Facilities, Minn. Citizens Concerned for Life, Rochester Area C. of C. (past dir.). Republican. Address: 1216 SW 2d St Rochester MN 55902

GERVAIS, MARCEL ANDRE, clergyman; b. Elie, Man., Can., Sept. 21, 1931; s. Fredrick Pierre and Marie-Louise (Beaudry) G. B.A. in Philosophy with honors, St. Peter's Sem. U. Western Ont., London, 1954; licentiate sacred theology, Angelicum U., Rome, 1959, Pontifical Biblical Inst., Rome, 1960, Ecole Biblique Jerusalem, 1961. Ordained priest Roman Catholic Ch., 1958. Prof. sacred scripture St. Peter's Sem., 1962-76; dir. Divine Word Internat. Centre of Religious Edn., London, 1974-79; aux. bishop Diocese of London, 1980—; titular bishop, Rosemarkie, Scotland, 1980—. Author, gen. editor: Journey: 40 Lessons on the Bible, 1977-80.

GERVASI, FRANK, artist; b. Palermo, Italy, Oct. 5, 1895; came to U.S., 1908, naturalized, 1919; s. Angelo and Elizabeth (Bottone) G.; m. Leonilda Isabella Sansone, Dec. 23, 1933. Student, N.Y. Sch. Indsl. Design, Art Students League of N.Y. Works exhibited nat. exhbns., Nat. Acad. Design, Allied Artists Am., Audubon Artists, Am. Watercolor Soc., Albany Inst. History and Art, Balt., Watercolor Club, So. Vt. Artists, works in collections, Brueckner Mus., Albion, Mich., Mus. of Lubbock, Tex., Okla. Mus. Art, Oklahoma City, Permian Basin Petroleum Mus., Midland, Tex., also pvt. collections. Served with U.S. Army, World War I. Recipient bronze medal for painting Allied Artists Am., 1st prize for painting Salmagundi Club Hudson Valley Art Assn., Balt. Water Color Club. Mem. Allied Artists Am. (past pres.), Audubon Artists (past v.p.), Am. Watercolor Soc., N.A.D., Art Students League N.Y. Clubs: Baltimore Watercolor; Salmagundi (N.Y.C.). Home: PO Box 415 Marfa TX 79843

GERVIN, GEORGE, basketball player; b. Detroit, Apr. 27, 1952. Student, Eastern Mich. U. Basketball player Va. Squires, Am. Basketball Assn., 1972-74, San Antonio Spurs, Nat. Basketball Assn., 1974—; mem. Nat. Basketball Assn. All-Star team, 1976-84. Named Most Valuable Player NBA All-Star Game, 1980. Scoring leader Nat. Basketball Assn., 1977-78, 78-79, 79-80. Office: San Antonio Spurs PO Box 530 San Antonio TX 78292 *

GERWICK, BEN CLIFFORD, JR., construction engineer, educator; b. Berkeley, Calif., Feb. 22, 1919; s. Ben Clifford and Bernice (Coultrap) G.; m. Martelle Louise Beverly, July 28, 1941; children: Beverly (Mrs. Robert A. Brian), Virginia (Mrs. Roy Wallace), Ben Clifford III, William. B.S., U. Calif., 1940. With Ben C. Gerwick, Inc., San Francisco, 1939-70, j1pres, 1952-70; exec. v.p. Santa Fe-Pomeroy, Inc., 1968-71; prof. civil engring. U. Calif. at Berkeley, 1971—; sponsoring mgr. Richmond-San Rafael Bridge substructure, 1953-56, San Mateo-Hayward bridge, 1964-66; lectr. constrn. engring. Stanford U., 1962-68; cons. major bridge and marine constrn. projects; cons. constrn. engr. for ocean structures, also concrete offshore structures in, North Sea, Arctic Sea, Japan, Australia, Indonesia, Arabian Gulf; mem. exec. com., past chmn. marine bd., mem. polar research bd. NRC; mem. Nat. Acad. Engring., Norwegian Acad. Tech. Scis. Author: (with Peter V. Peters) Russian-English Dictionary of Prestressed Concrete and Concrete Construction, 1966, Construction of Prestressed Concrete Structures, 1971, (with John C. Woolery) Construction and Engineering Marketing for Major Project Services; Contbr. articles to profl. jours. Served with USNR, 1940-46; comdr. Res. ret. Recipient Lockheed award Marine Tech. Soc., 1977. Fellow ASCE (Karp award 1976), Am. Concrete Inst. (dir. 1960, hon. mem., Turner award 1974, Corbetta award 1981); mem. Federation Internationale de la Precontrainte (pres. 1974-78, now hon. pres., Freyssinet medal 1982), Prestressed Concrete Inst. (pres. 1957-58, hon.), Deutscher Beton Verein (hon., Emil Mörsch medal 1979), Concrete Soc. U.K. (hon.), Association Francaise du Beton (hon.), Moles, Soc. Naval Architects and Marine Engrs. (Blakely Smith award 1981), Beavers (Engring. award 1975), Phi Beta Kappa, Tau Beta Pi, Sigma Xi, Chi Epsilon, Kappa Sigma. Conglist. Clubs: Bohemian (San Francisco); Claremont Country (Oakland). Home: 5874 Margarido Dr Oakland CA 94618 Office: 217 McLaughlin Hall U Calif Berkeley CA 94720 also 500 Sansome St San Francisco CA 94111

GESCHWIND, NORMAN, physician, educator; b. N.Y.C., Jan. 8, 1926; s. Morris and Anna (Blau) G.; m. Patricia Dougan, Sept. 8, 1956; children: Naomi, David, Claudia. B.A., Harvard U., 1946, M.D., 1951; LL.D. (hon.), Northwestern U., 1981; D.h.c., U. Lyon, 1981. Moseley Travelling fellow Nat. Hosp., London, 1952-53, USPHS research fellow, 1953-55; resident in neurology Boston City Hosp., 1955-56; research fellow MIT, 1956-58; staff neurologist Boston VA Hosp., 1958-62, chief neurology service, 1962-66; asso. prof. neurology Boston U., 1962-66, prof., chmn. dept., 1966-68; James Jackson Putnam prof. neurology Harvard Med. Sch., 1969—. Fellow Am. Acad. Neurology; mem. Am. Acad. Arts and Scis., Acad. Aphasia, Am. Neurol. Assn., Royal Belgian Acad. Medicine (corr.). Research, publs. on anat. basis higher functions nervous system, biological foundations of cerebral dominance, brain and emotion. Office: 330 Brookline Ave Boston MA 02215

GESELL, GERHARD ALDEN, judge; b. Los Angeles, June 16, 1910; s. Arnold Lucius and Beatrice (Chandler) G.; m. Marion Holliday Pike, Sept. 19, 1936; children—Peter Gerhard, Patricia Pike. A.B., Yale, 1932, LL.B., 1935. Bar: Conn. 1935, D.C. 1941. With SEC, Washington, 1935-40, tech. adviser to chmn., 1940-41; acted for Commn. as spl. counsel Temporary Nat. Econ. Com., study legal res. life ins. cos.; mem. Covington & Burling, Washington, 1941-67; judge U.S. Dist. Ct. D.C., 1968—; designated mem. Temporary Emergency Ct. Appeal, 1983; chief asst. counsel Joint Congl. Com. on Investigation Pearl Harbor Attack, 1945-46; Chmn. Pres.'s Com. on Equal Opportunity in the Armed Forces, 1962-64; chmn. com. on adminstrn. of justice D.C. Jud. Council, 1965-67; jud. mem. D.C. Commn. on Jud. Disabilities and Tenure, 1976-81. Co-author: Study of Legal Reserve Life Insurance Cos, 1940, Families and Their Life Insurance, 1940. Mem. Am. Bar Assn., Am. Law Inst., Am. Coll. Trial Lawyers, Phi Delta Phi, Zeta Psi. Clubs: Lawyers, Met. (Washington); Casino (North Haven, Maine). Home: 3304 N St Washington DC 20007 Office: US Courthouse Washington DC 20001

GESELOWITZ, DAVID BERYL, bioengineering educator; b. Phila., May 18, 1930; s. Sidney W. and Fannie (Charny) G.; m. Lola Wood, June 21, 1953; children: Daniel, Michael, Ari. B.S. in E.E, U. Pa., 1951, M.S., 1954, Ph.D., 1958. Asst. prof., asso. prof. U. Pa., Phila., 1951-71; vis. asso. prof. elec. engring. M.I.T., Cambridge, 1965-66; cons. to med. dir. Provident Mut. Life Ins. Co., Phila., 1959-71; vis. prof. Duke U., Durham, N.C., 1978-79; prof., head bioengring. Pa. State U., University Park, 1971—. Editor: (with C. V. Nelson) Theoretical Basis of Electrocardiography, 1976, IEEE Transactions on Biomed. Engring, 1967-72; mem. editorial bd.: Jour. Electrocardiology, 1974—, CRC Critical Revs., 1979—; contbr. articles to various publs. Chmn. com. electrocardiography Am. Heart Assn., 1976-81. J.S. Guggenheim fellow, 1978-79. Fellow Am. Coll. Cardiology, IEEE; mem. Biophys. Soc., Biomed. Engring. Soc., Am. Assn. Physics Tchrs., AAAS. Office: Pa State Univ University Park PA 16802

GESSNER, CHARLES HERMAN, consumer products executive; b. Escanaba, Mich., Nov. 26, 1938; s. Charles and Ruth (Weinberger) G.; m. Susanne Thone, Dec. 18, 1971; 1 dau., Ayala Lenore. B.S. in Indsl. Engring, U. Mich., 1961, M.B.A., 1963. Mgmt. cons. Swissair, Zurich, Switzerland, 1961-63; sales mgr. Oomphies, Inc., Lawrence, Mass., 1964-72, exec. v.p., 1973, pres., 1974-78; chief exec. officer consumer group, corp. v.p. U.S. Industries, Inc., N.Y.C., 1978-80, chief exec. officer consumer segment, corp. exec. v.p., 1981—. Home: 339 Oenoke Ridge New Canaan CT 06840 Office: One Cummings Point Rd Stamford CT 06904

GESSNER, IRA HAROLD, physician, educator; b. Rockville Center, N.Y., June 23, 1931; s. Murray M. and Grace Z. (Gorlin) G.; m. Geraldine Engles, June 28, 1959; children: Michele Lynn, Bradford David, Jennifer Ann. A.B., U. Iowa, 1952; M.D., U. Vt., 1956. Intern Ohio State U. Hosps., 1956-57; resident in pediatrics U. Fla., Gainesville, 1960-62, fellow in pediatric cardiology, 1962-65, mem. faculty dept. pediatrics, 1965—, prof. pediatrics, chief div. pediatric cardiology, 1970—; fellow in pediatric cardiology U. Stockholm, 1962-65. Author: Handbook of Pediatric Cardiology, 1969; contbr. articles to profl. jours. Served with USAF, 1957-60. Recipient research career devel. award Nat. Heart, Lung and Blood Inst., NIH, 1967; research grantee Am. Heart Assn., Fla. Heart Assn., 1965-71. Fellow Am. Acad. Pediatrics, Am. Coll. Cardiology; mem. Soc. Pediatric Research, Am. Pediatric Soc., Teratology Soc., Fla. Pediatric Soc. Office: Dept Pediatrics J Hillis Miller Health Center Gainesville FL 32610

GESSOW, ALFRED, aerospace engineer, educator; b. Jersey City, Oct. 1922; s. Morris Samuel and Emma (Levovsky) G.; m. Elaine E. Silverman, Nov. 23, 1947; children: Laura Gessow Goldman, Lisa Gessow Michelson, Miles Jory, Andrew Jody. B.C.E., CCNY, 1943; M.Aero. Engring., N.Y. U., 1944. Aero. research scientist, nat. adv. com. on aeros. Langley Research Center, Va., 1944-59; chief fluid physics research NASA, Washington, 1959-66, asst. dir. research div., 1966-70, dir. for aerodynamics, 1970-79; prof., chmn. dept. aerospace engring. U. Md., College Park, 1979—; lectr. U. Va., Va. Poly. Inst.; adj. prof. N.Y. U., Cath. U. Am.; vis. prof. Korean Inst. Advanced Sci.; cons. NATO; chmn. aerospace div. adv. council Pa. State U.; mem. Nat. Acad. Sci/NRC bd. Army Sci. and Tech., 1982—. Sr. author: Aerodynamics of the Helicopter, 3d edit, 1967; contbr. articles to encys. and profl. jours. Recipient medal for exceptional service NASA, 1974. Fellow Am. Helicopter Soc., AIAA. Jewish. Home: 7308 Durbin Terr Bethesda MD 20817 Office: U Md College Park MD 20742 *The human psychology is such as to require and respond to an awards system which is made up of many factors—challenge, variety, peer recognition and economic benefits. The young generally place more importance on the first two, while the last two are more significant in later years. The chances of achieving such rewards are enhanced by starting early to develop expertise in a specialty area, to be interested and knowledgeable in one or more allied areas, and to take on challenging tasks which are not required but are self motivated. If these steps are followed, success and satisfaction will follow.*

GEST, HOWARD, microbiologist, educator; b. London, Oct. 15, 1921; m. Janet Olin, Sept. 8, 1941; children: Theodore Olin, Michael Henry, Donald Evan. B.A. in Bacteriology, UCLA, 1942; postgrad. in biology (Univ. fellow), Vanderbilt U., 1942; Ph.D. in Microbiology (Am. Cancer Soc. fellow), Washington U., St. Louis, 1949. Instr. microbiology Western Res. U. Sch. Medicine, 1949-51, asst. prof. microbiology, 1951-53, asso. prof., 1953-59; USPHS spl. research fellow in biology Calif. Inst. Tech., 1956-57; prof. Henry Shaw Sch. Botany, Washington U., 1959-64, dept. zoology, 1964-66; prof. Ind. U., Bloomington, 1966-78, Disting. prof. microbiology, 1978—, adj. prof. history and philosophy of sci., 1983—, chmn. dept. microbiology, 1966-70; NSF sr. postdoctoral fellow Nat. Inst. Med. Research, London, 1965-66; Guggenheim fellow Imperial Coll., London, U. Stockholm, U. Tokyo, UCLA; vis. prof. dept. biophysics and biochemistry U. Tokyo, 1970; mem. study sect. bacteriology and mycology NIH, 1966-68, chmn. study sect. microbial chemistry, 1968-69; mem. com. microbiol. problems of man in extended space flight Nat. Acad. Scis.-NRC, 1967-69. Office: Dept Biology Ind U Bloomington IN 47405

GEST, KATHRYN WATERS, editor; b. Boston, Mar. 20, 1947; d. Mendal and Anna Hilda (Black) Waters; m. Theodore O. Gest, May 28, 1972; 1 son, David Mendal. B.S., Northwestern U., 1969; M.S., Columbia U., 1970. Reporter The Patriot-Ledger, Quincy, Mass., 1968; writer Europe desk Voice of Am., Washington, 1969; reporter St. Louis Globe-Democrat, 1970-77, Congl. Quar., Washington, 1977-78, news editor, 1978-80, asst. mng. editor, 1980-83, mng. editor, 1983—; St. Louis corr. Time Mag., 1975-77, The Christian Sci. Monitor, 1976-77. Recipient award for investigative reporting Inland Daily Press Assn., 1975. Mem. Soc. Profl. Journalists, Washington Press Club. Home: 6221 Western Ave NW Washington DC 20015 Office: Congressional Quar 1414 22d St NW Washington DC 20037

GESTELAND, ROBERT CHARLES, neurophysiologist; b. Madison, Wis., July 1, 1930; s. Elmer Raymond and Bernice Jeanette (Elver) G.; m. Jean Smitherman, June 9, 1961; children—Matthew Warren, Wendy Kristen, Caroline Quenby. B.S. in Elec. Engring, U. Wis.-Madison, 1953; S.M., Mass. Inst. Tech., 1957; Ph.D., in Neurophysiology, 1961. Engr. Gen. Radio Co., Cambridge, Mass., 1953-54; mem. research staff Sci.-Engring. Inst., Waltham, Mass., 1962-65; prof. neurobiol. physiology Northwestern U., 1965—, chmn. neurosci., 1977—; pres. Taste and Smell Cons. Group, Inc., 1979—. Home: 320 Davis St Evanston IL 60201

GETIS, ARTHUR, geography educator; b. Phila., July 6, 1934; s. Samuel J. and Sophie (Zeitzew) G.; m. Judith M. Marckwardt, July 23, 1961; children: Hilary Hope, Victoria Lynn, Anne Patterson. B.S., Pa. State U., 1956, M.S., 1958; Ph.D., U. Wash., 1961. Asst. instr. geography U. Wash., 1960-61; asst. prof. Mich. State U., 1961-63; faculty Rutgers U., New Brunswick, N.J., 1963-77, prof. geography, 1969-77, dir. grad. programs in geography, 1970-73, chmn. New Brunswick geography dept., 1971-73; prof. geography U. Ill., Urbana-Champaign, 1977—, head dept., 1977-83, dir. Sch. Social Scis., 1983—; vis. lectr. Bristol U., Eng., 1966-67, UCLA, summers 1968, 74, U. B.C., summer 1969; vis. prof. Princeton U., 1971-74; mem. Regional Sci. Research Group, Harvard U., 1970; panelist NSF, 1981-83. Author: (with B. Boots) Models of Spatial Processes, (with J. Getis and J.D. Fellmann) Geography; contbg. editor, asso. editor: Jour. Geography, 1972-74; contbr. monographs and articles to profl. lit. Mem. Urbana Zoning Bd. Appeals, 1980—; co-pres. Univ. High Sch. Parent-Faculty Orgn., 1982-83. Rutgers U. faculty fellow, 1970; East-West Center sr. fellow, 1974. Mem. Assn. Am. Geographers (grantee 1964-65, vis. scientist 1970-72), Regional Sci. Assn. (pres. N.E. sect. 1973-74), Inst. Brit. Geographers, Sigma Xi. Home: 309 W Indiana St Urbana IL 61801 Office: Sch Social Scis U Ill Urbana-Champaign Urbana IL 61801

GETMAN, FRANK NEWTON, bus. cons.; b. Ilion, N.Y., Nov. 5, 1910; s. George B. and Bertha (Myers) G.; m. Dorothy D. Etheridge, Nov. 4, 1941 (dec. July 20, 1979); 1 son, Willard E. A.B., Cornell U., 1932, J.D., 1934. Bar: N.Y. bar 1934. With firm Alfeld, Sowers & Herrick, N.Y.C., 1934-37; atty. Vick Chem. Co., N.Y.C., 1937-42; atty., sec. William S. Merrell Co., Cin., 1946-49, v.p., asst. gen. mgr., 1949-55, pres., gen. mgr., 1957-62; exec. v.p. Hess & Clark, Inc., Ashland, O., 1955-56, pres., 1956-57, 60-61; v.p. Richardson-Merrell, Inc. (formerly Vick Chem. Co.), N.Y.C., 1959-61, exec. v.p., 1961-75; dir. Fifth Third Union Trust Co., Cin., 1959-65. Mem. Cornell U. Council, 1963-69; Bd. dirs. Nat. Multiple Sclerosis Soc., 1975-80, mem. nat. adv. council, 1980—. Served as maj. USAAF, 1942-46. Mem. Lambda Chi Alpha. Presbyn. Clubs: Wee Burn, Country (Darien, Conn.); Landmark (Stamford, Conn.); Quail Ridge Golf and Tennis, Delray Dunes Country (Delray Beach, Fla.). Home: Holly 17 Delray Dunes Boynton Beach FL 33436 *An executive is no better nor any worse than the people who work under his supervision.*

GETMAN, JULIUS G., legal educator, lawyer. J.D., Harvard U., 1958, LL.M., 1963. Bar: D.C. 1959, Ind. 1970. Atty. NLRB, Washington, 1959-61; from asst. prof. to prof. law Ind. U., Bloomington, 1963-75; prof. Stanford U., Calif., 1975-77; William K. Townsend prof. law Yale U., New Haven, 1977—; cons. legal edn. Ford Found.; vis. prof. Benares Hindu U., 1967-68, Indian Law Inst., 1967-68; chief negotiator Conn. State Police, 1978—; spl. inst. for labor and mgmt. groups, arbitrator, 1963—; mem. editorial com. and exec. com. Labor Law Group; gen. conusel AAUP, 1980-82. Author: (with Sneve Goldberg and Jeanne B. Herman) Union Representation Elections: Law and Reality, 1976, Labor Relations: Law, Practice and Policy, 1978; editor: (with John Blackbourn) Employment Discrimination Casebook, 1979. Mem. Nat. Acad. Arbitrators. Office: Yale U Law Sch 127 Wall St New Haven CT 06520

GETMAN, MORTON JEROME, chamber of commerce executive; b. N.Y.C., June 29, 1933; s. Murray and Sylvia (Siegel) G.; (div.)1 dau., Risa F. Student, N.Y. U., 1954; J.D., N.Y. Law Sch., 1956. Bar: N.Y 1956. Pvt. practice, N.Y.C., 1956-63; spl. asst. atty. gen. N.Y. State, 1963-66, exec. asst. to atty. gen., 1967-71; asst. to v.p. govt. relations Consol. Edison Co., N.Y.C., 1971-75, asst. v.p. employee relations, 1975-77; exec. v.p., gen. counsel N.Y. C. of C. and Industry, 1977—; pres. N.Y. C. of C. Ednl. Found., 1977-82. Bd. dirs. N.Y. Found. Sr. Citizens; bd. dirs. United Neighborhood Houses; mem. dental bd. advisers Group Health Ins.; mem. adv. bd. Manhattan Coll., Rider Coll. Office: 200 Madison Ave New York NY 10016

GETTE, WARREN ANDREWS, physician, former hosp. administrator; b. Phillipsburg, Pa., Apr. 17, 1910; s. Claude Anthony and Anna Margaret (Hamer) G.; m. Doris Fitzgibbon, July 8, 1944; 1 dau., Gladys Ruth. A.B., U. Pa., 1932, M.D., 1943. Intern U. Pa. Hosp., 1944; resident Dixon Hosp., South Mountain, Pa., 1944-45, Tb physician, 1945-51, chief med. staff, 1951-59, med. dir., 1959, clin. dir., until 1970. Pres. corp. South Mountain Ch. of God, 1960—. Fellow Am. Coll. Chest Physicians; mem. AMA, Franklin County (pres. 1962), Pa. med. socs., Pa. Assn. Chest Physicians, Am. Thoracic Soc., Am. Assn. Tb Physicians. Lutheran. Address: 890 Bird Bay Way Venice FL 33595

GETTING, IVAN ALEXANDER, aerospace company executive; b. N.Y.C., Jan. 18, 1912; s. Milan Alexander and Hermina (Almasy) G.; m. Dorothea Louise Gracy, Oct. 2, 1937 (dec. Sept. 1976); children: Nancy Louise Getting Resch, Ivan Craig, Peter Alexander; m. Helen A. Griggs, Jan. 9, 1977. B.S., MIT, 1933; D. Phil., Oxford (Eng.) U., 1935; D.Sc. (hon.), Northeastern U. Edison scholar Mass. Inst. Tech., 1929-33; Rhodes scholar Oxford U., 1933-35; Soc. Fellows Harvard U., 1935-40; with radiation lab. Mass. Inst. Tech., 1940-45, asso. prof., 1945-46, prof. elec. engring., 1946-51; on leave, 1950-51; to serve USAF; asst. for devel. planning Dep. Chief of Staff for Devel.; v.p. research and engring. Raytheon Co., 1951-60; pres. Aerospace Corp., El Segundo, Calif., 1960-77, cons., dir., 1977—. Author sci. articles, chiefly in publs. of Am. Phys. Soc. Decorated medal for Merit, Exceptional Civilian Service award USAF; recipient Naval Ordnance award. Fellow Am. Phys. Soc., Am. Inst. Aeros. and Astronautics, IEEE (Pioneer award, pres. 1978), Am. Acad. Arts and Scis.; mem. Nat. Acad. Engring., Am. Assn. Rhodes Scholars. Clubs: Cosmos, Calif. Yacht. Home: 312 Chadbourne Ave Los Angeles CA 90049

GETTLER, BENJAMIN, lawyer, manufacturing company executive; b. Louisville, Ky., Sept. 16, 1925; s. Herbert and Gertrude (Cohen) G.; m. Deliaan Angell, Mar. 1972; children: Jorian, Thomas, Gail, John, Benjamin. B.A. with high honors, U. Cin., 1945; J.D. (Frankfurter scholar), Harvard U., 1948. Bar: Ohio 1949. Partner firm Brown & Gettler, Cin., 1951-73, Gettler & Katz, 1973—; chmn. bd., dir., sec.

Cin. Transit Inc., 1957-73; chmn. bd. Am. Controlled Industries Inc., Cin., 1973—; chmn. exec. com. Vulcan Corp., Cin., 1976—; chmn. bd. Colorpac Inc., Cin., 1973—; chmn. exec. com. Valley Industries, Inc., Cin., 1973—; spl. counsel U. Cin., 1975-77. Mem. Ohio, Ky. and Ind. Mass Transit Policy Com., 1970-75; pres. Cin. Jewish Community Relations Council, 1978-80; vice chmn. bd. dirs. Jewish Hosp., 1978—; chmn. Cin. Coalition for Reagan, 1980. Served to capt. U.S. Army, 1955-56. Mem. Am., Cin. bar assns., Phi Beta Kappa, Omicron Delta Kappa. Club: Coldstream Country. Office: 6 E 4th St Suite 1300 Cincinnati OH 45202

GETTY, GORDON PETER, philanthropist; b. 1933; s. J. Paul and Ann Rork (Light) G.; m. Ann Getty; 4 children. Former cons. Getty Oil Co., dir.; chmn. LSB Leakey Found., Pasadena, Calif. Office: LSB Leaky Found 1201 E California Blvd Pasadena CA 91106

GETZ, GEORGE FULMER, JR., business executive; b. Chgo., Jan. 4, 1908; s. George Fulmer and Susan Daniel (Rankin) G.; m. Olive Cox Atwater, Jan. 17, 1933 (dec. Sept. 22, 1980); children: George Fulmer, III (dec.), Bert Atwater. Pres. Eureka Coal & Dock Co., 1935-45; chmn. bd., chief exec. officer Globe Corp.; chmn. bd. Getz Coal Co., 1939-48, pres., 1948-53; dir. Chgo. Nat. League Ball Club, 1940-72; mem. exec. com., dir. A.T. & S.F. Ry., 1955-80, Sante Fe Industries, Inc., 1968-80; dir. Upper Ave. Nat. Bank, Chgo., 1936-74, Chgo. Transit Authority, 1945-47. Mem. United Republican Fund Ill.; mem. citizens bd. U. Chgo., 1956-71; bd. dirs. Jr. Achievement Chgo., 1939—, v.p., 1947-49; v.p. Met. Jr. Achievement, 1942-44; mem. Pres.'s Commn. White House Fellowships, 1982, 83; bd. dirs. Getz Found., Ind. U. Found.; pres., dir. Arthur R. Metz Found.; hon. trustee Chgo. Zool. Soc.; past v.p. finance, treas. Nat. Safety Council; pres. Geneva Lake Water Safety Com., Inc., 1949-54, bd. dirs., 1949-69, hon. dir., 1969—; mem. Ill. Com. Crusade for Freedom, Inc., 1957, 58; pres., dir. Nat. Hist. Fire Found., Globe Found.; bd. dirs. Ariz. Zool. Soc., 1966-81, 84—, show dir., 1966-81; trustee Am. Grad. Sch. Internat. Mgmt., vice chmn. bd., 1976-78; mem. organizing com., mem. Chgo. Rotary Found., 1936-45; mem. Nat. Republican Finance Com., 1976—; trustee Grand Central Art Galleries, N.Y.C., 1982—. Mem. Chgo. Assn. Commerce and Industry (com. mem. govtl. affairs council); emeritus mem. Phoenix 40. Episcopalian. Clubs: Executives Kiva (Phoenix); Chicago, Tavern, Chicago Yacht (Chgo.); Economic; Los Rancheros Visitadores (Santa Barbara, Cal.); Paradise Valley Country (Ariz.); Circumnavigators, Phoenix Symphony Assn. 400; Valley Field Riding and Polo (Ariz.); Balboa (Mazatlan, Mexico). Home: 120 Mountain Shadows W Scottsdale AZ 85253 Office: Globe Corp 3634 Civic Center Plaza Scottsdale AZ 85251 also 16555 W Hwy 120 Libertyville IL 60048

GETZ, LOWELL LEE, zoology educator; b. Chesterfield, Ill., sept. 21, 1931; s. Carl C. and Evelyn (Dowland) G.; m. Mary Ruth Clardy, July 5, 1953; children: Colleen Marie, Allison Lynn. B.S., U Ill., 1953; M.S., U. Mich., 1959, Ph.D., 1960. Research asso. U.Mich., 1959-61; asst. prof., then asso. prof. zoology U. Conn., 1961-69; prof. zoology U. Ill., Urbana, 1969—, head ecology, ethology and evolution, 1975-80; Hon. fellow zoology U. Wis.-Madison, 1967-68. Author papers in field. Served to 1st lt. AUS, 1953-55. Mem. Am. Soc. Mammalogists, Ecol. Soc. Am., Brit. Ecol. Soc., Animal Behavior Soc., Phi Beta Kappa, Sigma Xi, Phi Eta Sigma, Phi Kappa Phi, Phi Sigma (editor Biologist 1967-81). Home: 2113 Lynwood Dr Champaign IL 61820

GETZ, STAN, saxophonist; b. Phila., Feb. 2, 1927; s. Alexander and Goldie G.; m. Monica Silfveskiold, 1956; children—Steven, David, Beverly, Pamela, Nicholas. Mem. bands led by, Jack Teagarden, Stan Kenton, Jimmy Dorsey, Benny Goodman, Woody Herman; leader own group, 1949—; film appearances: The Benny Goodman Story, 1955, Get Yourself a College Girl, 1964, The Hanged Man, 1964, Mickey One, 1965 (Recipient Grammy awards for recs. Desafinado 1962), Jazz Samba, 1962, Big Band Bossa Nova, 1962, Getz/Gilberto, 1964, Mickey One, 1965, Sweet Rain, 1967 (numerous Down Beat, Metronome and Playboy Jazz polls and mag. awards.). Address: care Jack Whittemore 80 Park Ave New York NY 10016

GETZELS, JACOB WARREN, psychologist, educator; b. Bialystok, Poland, Feb. 7, 1912; came to U.S., 1921, naturalized, 1933; es. Hirsch and Frieda (Solon) G.; m. Judith Nelson, Dec. 24, 1949; children: Katharine, Peter, Julia. B.A., Bklyn. Coll., 1936; M.A., Columbia U., 1939; Ph.D., Harvard U., 1951. Instr. ednl. psychology U. Chgo., 1951, asst. prof. ednl. psychology, 1952-54, asso. prof., 1955-57, prof., 1957—, now R. Wendell Harrison Disting. Service prof. edn. and behavioral scis.; vis. prof. psychology U. P.R., summer, 1962, Stanford U., summer, 1963; mem. U.S. Office Edn. Mission to Soviet Russia, 1960, mem. research adv. council, 1964-70; mem. council of scholars Library of Congress, 1980—. Author: (with A. Coladarci) The Use of Theory in Educational Administration, 1955, (with P.W. Jackson) Creativity and Intelligence: Explorations with Gifted Students, 1962, (with J.M. Lipham and R.F. Campbell) Educational Administration as a Social Process, 1968, (with I. Taylor) Perspectives in Creativity, 1975, (with M. Csikszentmihalyi) The Creative Vision: A Longitudinal Study of Problem Finding in Art, 1976; contbr. articles to profl. jours. Mem. bd. visitors Learning Research and Devel. Center, U. Pitts., 1973-79; bd. dirs. Spencer Found., 1971—. Recipient Research award Am. Personnel and Guidance Assn., 1959; Tchrs. Coll. medal, 1977; Nicholas Murray Butler medal for theory or philosophy of edn. Columbia U., 1980; Center for Advanced Study in Behavioral Scis. fellow, 1960-61; Center for Policy Study (U. Chgo.) fellow, 1967-75. Mem. Am. Psychol. Assn., Am. Sociol. Assn., Nat. Acad. Edn. (1st. v.p. 1972-76), Nat. Soc. for Study Edn. (dir. 1975-77), Am. Ednl. Research Assn. Office: 5835 S Kimbark Ave Chicago IL 60637

GETZENDANNER, SUSAN, U.S. dist. ct. judge; b. Chgo., July 24, 1939; d. William B. and Carole S. (Muehling) O'Meara; children—Alexandra, Paul. B.B.A., Loyola U., 1966, J.D., 1966. Bar: Ill. bar 1966. Law clk. to Judge Julius J. Hoffman U.S. Dist. Ct., 1966-68; asso. firm Mayer, Brown & Platt, Chgo., 1968-74, partner, 1974-80; judge U.S. Dist. Ct., Chgo., 1980—. Recipient medal of excellence Loyola U. Law Alumni Assn., 1981. Mem. Am. Bar Assn., Ill. Bar Assn., Chgo. Council Lawyers. Office: 219 S Dearborn St Chicago IL 60604

GEVANTMAN, LEWIS HERMAN, chemist, govt. ofcl.; b. N.Y.C., Sept. 12, 1921; s. Benjamin and Ida (Goldberg) G.; m. Leatrice Black, Aug. 22, 1948; children—Sandra Cay, Janis Mara. B.Engring., Johns Hopkins, 1942; Ph.D. in Phys. Chemistry, U. Notre Dame, 1951. Chem. operator Bethlehem Steel Co., 1942-43; research chemist Clinton Labs., Manhattan Project, 1943-46; supervisory research chemist U.S. Naval Radiol. Def. Lab., San Francisco, 1951-56, acting head applied research br., 1956-59, head radiation chemistry br., 1959-61, sci. research adminstr., head chem. tech. div., 1961-64; sr. sci. adviser U.S. mission IAEA, 1964-67; coordinator nuclear material safeguard program U.S. Dept. Commerce, 1967-74; program mgr. Office Standard Reference Data, 1967—; coordinator AEC-Nat. Bur. Standards, 1970-74; sr. analyst Program Office, 1972-73; coordinator environ. programs Nat. Bur. Standards, 1972; Cons. Nuclear Sci. & Engring. Corp., 1956-59; mem. Bd. Civil Service Examiners, 1958-61, Nat. Com. on Chem. Disaster, 1970—. Contbr. articles to profl. jours. Mem. Am. Chem. Soc. (chmn. civil def. com. No. Calif. sect. 1961-64), ASTM (ad hoc com. dosimetry, com. D19.07 1977—), IUPAC (sec. commn.), AAAS, Sigma Xi. Patentee in field. Address: Nat Bur Standards Washington DC 20234

GEWARTOWSKI, JAMES WALTER, electrical engineer; b. Chgo., Nov. 10, 1930; s. Joseph Walter and Irene Dorothy (Dziekanowski) G.; m. Marion Ruth Wakeman, June 23, 1956; children: Marion, Diane, Patricia, John, Karen. B.S. in Elec. Engring., Ill. Inst. Tech., 1952; S.M., MIT, 1953; Ph.D., Stanford U., 1958. Research asst. Stanford Electronics Lab., Calif., 1954-57; supr. microwave and lightware subsystems AT&T Bell Lab., Inc., Allentown, Pa., 1957—. Co-author: Principles of Electron Tubes, 1965, Fundamentals of Electron Tubes, 1969; contbg. author: Microwave Semiconductor Devices and Their Circuit Applications, 1969; contbr. articles to profl. jours. Fellow IEEE (Browder J. Thompson Meml. prize 1960); mem. Sigma Xi, Tau Beta Pi, Eta Kappa Nu. Republican. Roman Catholic. Home: 2908 Edgemont Dr Allentown PA 18103 Office: AT&T Bell Labs Inc 555 Union Blvd Allentown PA 18103

GEWIRTH, ALAN, philosopher, educator; b. Union City, N.J., Nov. 28, 1912; s. Hyman and Rose (Lees) G.; m. Marcella Tilton, Mar. 18, 1956; children: James, Susan; by former marriage), Andrew Alan, Daniel Tilton, Letitia Rose. B.A. with honors in Philosophy, Columbia, 1934, Ph.D. (Rockefeller Found. fellow), 1947; postgrad. (Sage fellow in philosophy), Cornell U., 1936-37. Teaching, research asst. philosophy U. Chgo., 1937-41, faculty, 1947—, prof., 1960-75, Edward Carson Waller Distinguished Service prof., 1975—; vis. prof. Harvard, 1957, U. Mich., 1959-60, Johns Hopkins, 1966-67; lectr. Humanities Conf., Ohio State U., 1958; Cooper Found. lectr. Swarthmore Coll., 1961; Niebuhr lectr. Elmhurst Coll., 1969; Distinguished guest lectr. Iowa Philos. Soc., 1969; Lindley lectr. U. Kans., 1972; vis. philosopher Ind. U., South Bend, 1972; Perspectives lectr. U. Notre Dame, 1975; Mellon Found. lectr. Marquette U., 1975, Colby Coll., 1978; Marsilius of Padua lectr. U. Padua, Italy, 1980; Hannah Arendt Meml. lectr. New Sch. Social Research, N.Y.C., 1981; mem. com. rev. and evaluate grad. programs in philosophy SUNY, Buffalo, 1971, Marquette U., 1975, So. Ill. U., 1975; judge dissertation essay competition Philosophy Edn. Soc., 1972; judge essay contest John Dewey Found., 1983; mem. various panels Nat. Endowment Humanities. Author: Marsilius of Padua and Medieval Political Philosophy, 1951, Moral Rationality, 1972, Reason and Morality, 1978, Human Rights: Essays on Justification and Applications, 1982; monograph Ethics, 1974; co-author: Social Justice, 1962, The Forward Movement of the Fourteenth Century, 1961; Editor: Political Philosophy, 1965; Translator: Marsilius of Padua: Defensor Pacis, 1956, 67, 79; adv. bd. editors: Ethics, Nomos. Served from pvt. to capt. AUS, 1942-46. Recipient Woodbridge prize Columbia U., 1948, Nicholas Murray Butler medal, 1975; Gordon Laing prize U. Chgo. Press, 1980; Rockefeller Found. fellow, 1957-58; Nat. Endowment for Humanities sr. fellow, 1974-75; Guggenheim Found. fellow, 1975-76. Fellow Am. Acad. Arts and Scis.; mem. Am. Philos. Assn. (chmn. program com. 1953-54, 70-71, pres. 1973-74, mem. com. lectures, publs. and research 1972-76), Am. Soc. Polit. and Legal Philosophy (pres. 1983-84), Internat. Soc. for Legal and Social Philosophy, ACLU, Phi Beta Kappa. Home: 1365 E Park Pl Chicago IL 60637

GEWIRTZ, GERRY, editor; b. N.Y.C., Dec. 22, 1920; d. Max and Minnie (Weiss) G.; m. Eugene W. Friedman, Nov. 11, 1945; children: John Henry, Robert James. B.A., Vassar Coll., 1941. Editor Package Store Mgmt., 1942-44, Jewelry Mag., 1945-53; freelance editor promotion dept. McCall's Mag., Esquire, 1953-56; free-lance fashion and gifts editor Jewelers Circular Keystone, N.Y.C., 1955-71; editor, pub., The Fashionables, 1971-74, The Forecast, 1974—, Nat. Jeweler, Ann. Fashion Guide, 1976-80; editor, asso. pub. Exec. Jeweler, 1980-83; editor The Gerry Gewirtz Report, N.Y.C., 1983—. Mem. exec. com. Citizens Com. N.Y.; exec. com. Inner City Council of Cardinal Cooke, N.Y.; chairperson women's task force United Jewish Appeal Fedn.; bd. govs. Israel Bonds; trustee Israel Cancer Research Fund, Central Synagogue. Honored guest Am. Jewish Com., 1978; Israel Cancer Research Fund. Mem. N.Y. Fashion Group, Nat. Home Fashions League, Women's Jewelry Assn. (pres. 1983—, named editor who has contbd. most to jewelry industry 1984), Phi Delta Epsilon. Clubs: N.Y., Vassar, Overseas Press. Home and Office: 55 E 86th St New York NY 10028 Office: 505 5th Ave New York NY 10017

GEYELIN, PHILIP LAUSSAT, journalist; b. Devon, Pa., Feb. 27, 1923; s. Emile Camille and Cecily (Barnes) G.; m. Cecilia Sherman Parker, Jan. 28, 1950; children—Mary Sherman, Emile Camille, Philip Laussat, Cecily Parker. Grad., Episcopal Acad., Overbrook, Pa., 1940; B.A., Yale, 1944. With Washington bur. A.P., 1946-47; mem. staff Wall St. Jour., 1947-66, diplomatic corr., 1960-67; mem. editorial staff Washington Post, 1967—, editor editorial page, 1968-79, syndicated columnist, 1980—; editor-in-residence Fgn. Policy Inst., Sch. Advanced Internat. Studies, Johns Hopkins U., 1980—. Author: Lyndon B. Johnson and the World, 1966. Bd. dirs. Alliance Francaise, Washington, 1964—; pres. bd. trustees Georgetown Day Sch., 1971-74. Served to 1st lt. USMCR, 1943-46. Fellow Inst. Politics Harvard Sch. Govt., 1967; recipient Pulitzer prize for editorial writing, 1969. Mem. Council on Fgn. Relations (dir. 1977—). Clubs: Gridiron, Overseas Writers, Federal City (Washington). Office: 1740 Massachusetts Ave NW Washington DC 20036

GEYER, CHARLES EDGAR, musician; b. Joliet, Ill., Nov. 25, 1944; s. Harry Chase and Eunice Luella (Smith) G.; m. Barbara Lorraine Butler. B.Music Edn., Northwestern U., 1966, M.Mus., 1969. Asso. prof. trumpet Eastman Sch. Music, Rochester, N.Y., 1980—. Trumpet soloist, Chgo. Little Symphony, 1964, 66; 1st trumpet, Chgo. Lyric Opera, 1964-66, Grant Park Orch., 1967-78, Chgo. Brass Quintet, 1962-78, Music of the Baroque, Chgo., 1975-81; 2d trumpet, Chgo. Symphony Orch., 1966-78; prin. trumpet, Houston Symphony, 1978-81. Mem. Phi Mu Alpha Sinfonia. Home: 7093 Boughton Hill Rd Victor NY 14564 Office: 26 Gibbs St Rochester NY 14604

GEYER, GEORGIE ANNE, syndicated columnist, educator, author; b. Chgo., Apr. 2, 1935; d. Robert George and Georgie Hazel (Gervens) G. B.S., Northwestern U., 1956; postgrad. (Fulbright scholar), U. Vienna, Austria, 1956-57; Litt. D. (hon.), Lake Forest Coll., (Ill.), 1980. Reporter Southtown Economist, Chgo., 1958; soc. reporter Chgo. Daily News, 1959-60, gen. assignment reporter, 1960-64, Latin Am. corr., 1964-67, roving fgn. corr. and columnist, 1967-75; syndicated columnist Los Angeles Times Syndicate, 1975-80; columnist Universal Press Syndicate, 1980—; Lyle M. Spencer prof. journalism Syracuse U., 1976; steering com. Aspen Inst. Latin Am. Governance Project, 1981-82; convenor Iran Com. for Democratic Action and Human Rights. Author: The New Latins, 1970, The New 100 Years War, 1972, The Young Russians, 1976; Autobiography Buying the Night Flight, 1983. Active Orgn. for S.W. Community Chgo., 1960-64; trustee Am. U., Washington, 1981—. Recipient 1st prize Am. Newspaper Guild, 1962; 2d prize Ill. Press Editors Assn., 1962; award for best writing on Latin Am. Overseas Press Club, 1966; Merit award Northwestern U., 1968; Nat. Headliner award Theta Sigma Phi, 1968; Maria Moors Cabot award Columbia, 1970; Hannah Solomon award Nat. Council Jewish Women, 1973; Ill. Spl. Events Commn. Woman's award, 1975; Northwestern U. Alumnae award, 1981; Woodrow Wilson fellow Rollins Coll., Winter Park, Fla., 1982; Disting. fellow Mortar Bd. Nat. Sr. Honor Soc., Am. U., 1982. Mem. Mortar Bd., Women in Communications, Chgo. Council on Fgn. Relations (dir.), Inst. Internat. Edn. (dir.), Midland Authors, Internat. Inst. Strategic Studies, Sigma Delta Chi. Subjects of interviews include Prince Sihanouk of Cambodia, Yassar Arafat, Anwar Sadat, King Hussein of Jordan, Pres. Khaddafy of Libya, the Ayatollah Khomeini, Sultan Qaboos of Oman, Argentine pres. Juan Peron, Pres. Siad Barre of Somalia, Prime Minister Mauno Koivisto of Finland, Anastasio Somoza, Jerzy Urban, Janusz Onyszkiewicz, Prime Minister Eclwárd Seaga of Jamaica, others; discovered and had first interview with second most-wanted Nazi, Walter Rauff in Tierra del Fuego, Chile, 1966; found Dominican pres. Juan Bosch in hiding in P.R. during Dominican revolution, 1965; held by Palestinians as Israeli spy, 1973; imprisoned in Angola for writing about revolutionary government, 1976. Home and office: 800 25th St NW Washington DC 20037 *I have never compromised seriously on any ethical or moral principle, and I truly believe that the women of my generation can bring a new and cleansing element to American public life. Whatever I have accomplished I could not have done it without profoundly analyzing myself—but I also find that in professional life the old injunction to "Know Thyself" reaches women more than men. It has been a constant struggle, often with little personal approval or backing, which I feel also adds to a woman's inner strength.*

GEYER, HAROLD CARL, artist, writer; b. Cold Spring, N.Y., Aug. 16, 1905; s. Harold Carl and Mary Brindsmaid (de Camp) G.; m. Ina Helen Doane, July 29, 1943. B.A., Yale U., 1926, B.F.A., 1930. Exhibited one-man shows, Aux Arcades, Troyes, France, 1984, group shows, Library of Congress, Soc. Am. Etchers, NAD, N.Y.C.; represented permanent collections, Library of Congress, Bibliotheque, Paris; author, artist: All Men Have Loved Thee, 1941, The Long Way Home, 1949. Recipient 3d Purchase prize Library of Congress, 1945. Mem. NAD, Soc. Am. Graphic Artists. Home: Middle Rd PO Box 113 Chilmark MA 02535

GEYER, JOHN CHARLES, educator, engr.; b. Neosho, Mo., Aug. 11, 1906; s. Harold G. and Nina (Dorman) G.; m. Dorothy Anderson, July 19, 1933; 1 dau., Joellen Armitage. Student, Drury Coll., 1925-27, D.Sci., 1969; B.S. in C.E, U. Mich., 1931; M.S., Harvard, 1933; D.Engring., Johns Hopkins U., 1942. Asst. prof. san. engring. U. N.C., 1934-37; faculty Johns Hopkins U., 1937—, asst. dept. civil engring., 1937-42; on leave as asst. chief engr., health and sanitation div. Office Inter-Am. Affairs, Washington, 1942-43, asso. prof. san. engring., 1946-48, prof., 1948—, chmn. dept. san. engring. and water resources, 1957-70; prin. investigator AEC waste disposal projects, 1948-65; cons. WHO, U. Chile Sch. Public Health, Santiago, 1955-56; commr. Md. Geol. Survey, 1956—; dir. survey Textile Found., Washington, 1935-36; mem. adv. com. Spl. Weapons Def., 1951-55; mem. com. on ednl. objectives NRC, 1957—; dir. Low-Flow Augmentation for Stream Pollution Abatement, 1958-63, Residential Water Use Project, 1959-66; dir. san. sewage research project FHA, 1959-66; dir. cooling water research Edison Electric Inst., 1961-75; mem. adv. com. on reactor safeguards AEC, 1961-64; mem. environ. pollution panel PSAC, 1964-71; mem. study sect. san. engring. and occupational health NIH, 1959-63; cons. Md. State Planning Commn., 1949-70, Bur. Water Supply, Balt., 1952—, Balt. Regional Planning Council, 1958-59, Phila. Electric Co., 959-75, Interstate Commn. on Potomac River Basin, 1956-57, AEC-Atomic Safety and Licensing Bd. Panel, 1966-76. Author: latest book Ground Water in Baltimore Industrial Area, 1944; co-author: Water Supply and Waste-Water Disposal, 1954, Water and Wastewater Engineering, vol. 1, Water Supply and Waste water Removal, 1966, vol. 2, Water Purification and Wastewater Treatment and Disposal, 1968, Elements of Water Supply and Waste water Disposal, 1971. Served from lt. to lt. comdr. USNR, 1943-46. Recipient Harrison Prescott Eddy medal, 1952. Fellow AAAS, Am. Pub. Health Assn., ASCE (hon. mem.); mem. Am. Water Works Assn. (utilities com. Cheseapeake sect. 1958-75), Fedn. Sewage Works Assns., Am. Geophys. Union, Md.-Del. Water and Sewerage Assn., Am. Acad. Environ. Engrs., Nat. Acad. Engring., Phi Beta Kappa, Sigma Xi, Tau Beta Pi, Phi Kappa Phi, Delta Omega. Home: 710 Bosley Rd Cockeysville MD 21030 Office: Johns Hopkins U Baltimore MD 21218

GEYMAN, JOHN PAYNE, physician, educator; b. Santa Barbara, Calif., Feb. 9, 1931; s. Milton John and Betsy (Payne) G.; m. Emogene Clark Deichler, June 9, 1956,; children: John Matthew, James Caleb, William Sabin. A.B. in Geology, Princeton U., 1952; M.D., U. Calif., San Francisco, 1960. Diplomate: Am. Bd. Family Practice. Intern Los Angeles County Gen. Hosp., 1960-61; resident in gen. practice Sonoma County Hosp., Santa Rosa, Calif., 1961-63; practice medicine specializing in family practice, Mt. Shasta, Calif., 1963-69; dir. family practice residency program Community Hosp. Sonoma County, Santa Rosa, 1969-71; asso. prof. family practice, chmn. div. family practice U. Utah, 1971-72; prof., vice chmn. dept. family practice U. Calif., Davis, 1972-77; prof., chmn. dept. family medicine U. Wash., 1977—. Author: The Modern Family Doctor and Changing Medical Practice, 1971, Family Practice: Foundation of Changing Health Care, 1980; editor: Content of Family Practice, 1976, Family Practice in the Medical School, 1977, Research in Family Practice, 1978, Preventive Medicine in Family Practice, 1979, Profile of the Residency Trained Family Physician in the U.S, 1970-79, Funding of Patient Care, Education and Research in Family Practice, 1981, The Content of Family Practice: Current Status and Future Trends, 1982, Archives of Family Practice, 1980, 81, 82; founding editor: Jour. Family Practice, 1973—; co-editor: Behavioral Science in Family Practice, 1980; editor: Family Practice: An International Perspective in Developed Countries, 1983. Served to lt. (j.g.) USN, 1952-55; PTO. Recipient Gold-headed Cane award U. Calif. Sch. Medicine, 1960. Mem. Am. Acad. Family Physicians, AMA, Soc. Tchrs. Family Medicine. Republican. Unitarian. Home: 2325 92d Ave NE Bellevue WA 98004 Office: Dept Family Medicine RF 30 U Wash Sch Medicine Seattle WA 98195

GFELLER, JOHN CHARLES, publishing company executive; b. N.Y.C., Apr. 2, 1937; s. Charles C. and Sylvia A. G.; m. Lorraine Ann Jaccarino, June 25, 1960; children: Lisa Ann, John Charles, Ann-Marie, Kathryn. B.S., Syracuse U., 1960; P.M.D., Harvard U., 1969. Sales trainee Maxwell House div. Gen. Foods Corp., White Plains, N.Y., 1960-64; dir. sales E.R. Squibb & Sons, N.Y.C., 1964-70; v.p. sales Liggett & Myers, Inc., N.Y.C., 1970-72; sr. v.p. sales and mktg. Consol. Cigar Corp., N.Y.C., 1972-78; v.p. mktg. Madison Sq. Garden Corp., N.Y.C., 1978-80; pres. Silhouette Books div. Simon & Schuster, N.Y.C., 1980—. Author: 5 Keys to Better Salesmanship, 1978. Bd. regents Fairfield Prep. Sch., 1978. Recipient Kolodny Young Exec. award, 1976; named Tobacco Industry Man of Year, 1976. Mem. Am. Mgmt. Assn., Sales Execs. Club of New York (pres. 1978). Clubs: Burning Tree Country (pres. 1978), Winged Foot Golf; Urban League (N.Y.C.). Home: 68 Sherwood Ave Greenwich CT 06830 Office: 1230 Ave of Americas New York NY 10001

GHADIALLY, FEROZE NOVROJI, pathologist, educator; b. Bombay, India, Nov. 13, 1920; s. Novroji Bomanji and Testarbanoo (Panday) G.; m. Edna May Bryant, Aug. 14, 1950; 4 children. M.B., B.S., London Hosp., London U., 1947, M.D., St. Thomas Hosp., London U., 1949, Ph.D., 1955, D.Sc., 1962. Lectr. pathology U. Sheffield, Eng., 1951-59, sr. lectr. exptl. pathology, 1959-66, reader in neoplastic diseases, 1966-68; prof. dept. pathology U. Sask., Saskatoon, Can., 1968—, head div. electron microscopy, 1968—, W.S. Lindsay prof., 1981—; pathologist Univ. Hosp. Author: Ultrastructure of Synovial Joints in Health and Disease, 1969, Diagnostic Electron Microscopy of Tumours, 1980, Ultrastructural Pathology of the Cell and Matrix, 1982; mem. sci. com.: Jour. Submicroscopic Cytology;

mem. editorial bd.: Ulstrastructural Pathology; contbr. articles to profl. jours. Recipient Izaak Walton Killam Meml. award Can. Council, 1981. Fellow Royal Coll. Pathologists (U.K.), Royal Coll. Physicians and Surgeons (Can.). Office: Dept Pathology Health Scis Bldg U Sask Saskatoon SK S7N 0W0 Canada

GHANDHI, SORAB KHUSHRO, electrical engineering educator; b. Allahabad, India, Jan. 1, 1928; came to U.S., 1947, naturalized, 1960; s. Khushro S. and Dina (Amroliwalla) G.; children: Khushro, Rustom, Behram. B.Sc. in Elec. and Mech. Engring, Benares (India) Hindu U., 1947; M.S., U. Ill., 1948, Ph.D., 1951. Mem. electronics lab. Gen. Electric Co., 1951-60; mgr. electronic components and functions lab., research div. Philco Corp., 1960-63; prof. elec. engring. Rensselaer Poly. Inst., Troy, N.Y., 1963—, chmn. electrophysics and electronic engring. div., 1968-74, prof. electrophysics, elec. and systems engring. dept., 1975—; Cons. to industry, 1963—. Author: (with R. F. Shea editor) Principles of Transistor Circuits, 1953, Transistor Circuit Engineering, 1957, Amplifier Handbook, 1966, The Theory and Practice of Microelectronics, 1968, Semiconductor Power Devices, 1977, VLSI Fabrication Principles: Silicon and Gallium Arsenide. J.N. Tata fellow, 1947-50. Fellow IEEE; mem. Electrochem. Soc., Am. Standards Assn., Sigma Xi, Eta Kappa Nu, Pi Mu Epsilon, Phi Kappa Pi. Home: 7 Linda Ln Schenectady NY 12309 Office: Rensselaer Poly Inst Troy NY 12181

GHAUSI, MOHAMMED SHUAIB, engineering educator, university dean; b. Kabul, Afghanistan, Feb. 16, 1930; came to U.S., 1951, naturalized, 1963; s. Mohammed Omar and Homaira G.; m. Marilyn Buchwold, June 12, 1961; children: Nadjya, Simine. B.S. summa cum laude, U. Calif.-Berkeley, 1956, M.S., 1957, Ph.D., 1960. Prof. elec. engring. NYU, 1960-72; head elec. scis. sect. NSF, Washington, 1972-74; prof., chmn. elec. engring. dept. Wayne State U., Detroit, 1974-77; John F. Dodge prof. Oakland U., Rochester, Mich., 1978—, dean Sch. Engring., 1978-83; dean Coll. Engring., U. Calif.-Davis, 1983—. Author: Principles and Design of Linear Active Circuits, 1965, Introduction to Distributed-Parameter Networks, 1968, Electronic Circuits, 1971, Modern Filter Design: Active RC and Switched Capacitor, 1981, also numerous articles.; Cons. editor, Van Nostrand Rinehold Pub. Co., 1968-71. Mem. disting. alumni rev. panel EECS programs U. Calif., Berkeley, 1973; mem. external bd. visitors U. Pa., 1974—. Fellow IEEE; mem. Circuits and System Soc. (v.p. 1970-72, pres. 1976), N.Y. Acad. Scis., Engring. Soc. Detroit, Sigma Xi, Phi Beta Kappa, Tau Beta Pi, Eta Kappa Nu. Home: 3195 Ayrshire Rd Bloomfield Hills MI 48013 Office: Dean's Office Sch Engring U Calif Davis CA 95616

GHERLEIN, GERALD LEE, diversified manufacturing company executive, lawyer; b. Warren, Ohio, Feb. 16, 1938; s. Jacob A. and Ruth (Matthews) G.; m. Joycelyn Hardin, June 18, 1960; children: David, Christy. Student, Ohio Wesleyan U., 1956-58; B.S. in Bus. Adminstrn, Ohio State U., 1960; J.D., U. Mich., 1963. Bar: Ohio 1963. Asso. firm Taft Stettinius & Holister, Cin., 1963-66; corp. atty. Eaton Corp., Cleve., 1966-68, European legal counsel, Zug, Switzerland, 1968-71, asst. sec., asso. counsel, Cleve., 1971-76, v.p., gen. counsel, 1976—. Trustee Citizen's League Greater Cleve., 1971—, v.p., 1977-79, pres., 1979-81; trustee Cleve. Ballet, 1983—. Mem. Greater Cleve. Bar Assn. (trustee), Am. Bar Assn., Ohio Bar Assn., Am. Soc. Corp. Secs. (pres. Ohio regional group 1977). Clubs: Cleve. Athletic, Mayfield Country. Home: 3679 Greenwood Dr Pepper Pike OH 44124 Office: 100 Erieview Plaza Cleveland OH 44114

GHIARDI, JAMES DOMENIC, lawyer, educator; b. Gwinn, Mich., Nov. 10, 1918; s. John B. and Margaret M. (Trosello) G.; m. Phyllis A. Lindmeier, Sept. 5, 1945; children—Catherine, Jeanne, Mary. Ph.B., Marquette U., 1940, LL.B., 1942, J.D., 1968. Bar: Wis. bar 1942. Prof. law Marquette U. Law Sch., Milw., 1946—; research dir. Def. Research Inst., Milw., 1962-72; of counsel firm Kluwin, Dunphy, Hankin & McNulty, Milw., 1972—. Author: Personal Injury Damages, Wisconsin, 1964, Punitive Damages, 1981; contbr. articles to profl. jours. Served to capt. Med. Adminstrv. Br. U.S. Army, 1942-45. Recipient award for teaching excellence Marquette U. Faculty, 1971; award for excellence in teaching Edward A. Uhrig Found., 1971; Alumni of Yr. award Marquette U. Law Sch., 1971. Fellow Am. Bar Found.; mem. Am. Bar Assn. (mem. ho. of dels. 1967-80), State Bar Wis. (gov. and mem. exec. com. 1962-72, pres. 1970-71), Am. Judicature Soc., Am. Law Ins., Wis. Bar Found., Am. Legion. Club: Milw. Athletic. Office: Marquette U Law Sch 1103 W Wisconsin Ave Milwaukee WI 53233

GHIARDI, JOHN FELIX LINUS, govt. ofcl.; b. Negaunee, Mich., Mar. 6, 1918; s. Martin and Catherine (Chiabotto) G.; m. Lucille Torreano, Apr. 7, 1947; children—Christopher, Giancarlo. B.A., Sacred Head Sem., Detroit, 1939; M.A. in Econs, Catholic U. Am., 1942, doctoral student, 1946-48. Economist VA, 1946-48; with Treasury Dept., 1948-66; sr. rep. Am. embassy, Italy, 1953-66; dir. Office Developing Nations, 1966; dep. asst. sec. state for internat. monetary affairs State Dept., 1966-68; dir. Office Econ. Research, 1972-74; adviser fin. devel. Inter-Am. Devel. Bank, Washington, 1974—; adviser internat. fin. to bd. govs. FRS, 1968-72. Served to 2d lt. AUS, 1942-46. Decorated Bronze Star, Purple Heart. Mem. Am. Econ. Assn. Roman Catho. Home: 12 Park Overlook Ct Bethesda MD 20817 Office: 808 17th St NW Washington DC 20577

GHIAUROV, NICOLAI, opera singer; b. Velingrad, Bulgaria, Sept. 13, 1929; m. Zlatina; 2 children. Attended, Acad. Music, Sofia, Bulgaria, Moscow Conservatory. Debut at, Sofia Opera House in, Barber of Seville, 1955; has appeared in maj. opera house throughout world, including, La Scala, Lyric Opera Chgo., Met. Opera, Phila. Lyric Opera, London Royal Opera, Bolshoi Opera. Recipient 1st prize Internat. Singin Contest, Paris, 1955. Office: care Columbia Artists Mgmt 165 W 57th St New York NY 10019 *

GHIGLIA, OSCAR ALBERTO, classical guitarist; b. Livorno, Italy, Aug. 13, 1938; s. Paulo and Guiliana (Folena) G.; m. A-M Boulet d'Hauteserre, Dec. 1, 1966; 1 dau., Thalia Emmanuelle. Grad. with honors, Conservatory Santa Cecilia, Rome, 1962. Instr. summers Aspen (Colo.) Music Festival, 1969—, Academia Musicale Chigiana, Siena, Italy, 1976—, Banff (Can.) Music Festival, 1978—; artist-in-residence Hartt Sch. Music, 1981. Debut in, Europe Two World Festival, Spoleto, Italy, 1961, concert tours, N. Am., 1966—; performed with, Juillard String Quartet, Tokyo String Quartet; records include Oscar Ghiglia plays Scarlatti and other Baroque Masters; Author: transcription Bach's 3d Lute Suite, 1976, Bach's Suite in E Major, 1979. Recipient grant to study Segovia, 1958-63, with Jacques Chailly, Paris, 1963-64; unanimous winner Internat. guitar competition ORTF, Paris, 1963. Home: BP 1795 Papeete Tahiti French Polynesia Office: Colbert Artists Mgmt Inc 111 W 57th St New York NY 10019

GHISELIN, BREWSTER, author, educator; b. Webster Groves, Mo., June 13, 1903; s. Horace and Eleanor (Weeks) G.; m. Olive F. Franks, June 7, 1929; children: Jon Brewster, Michael Tenant. A.B., UCLA, 1927; M.A., U. Calif.-Berkeley, 1928, student, 1931-33; student, Oxford U., Eng., 1928-29. Asst. in English U. Calif., Berkeley, 1931-33; instr. English U. Utah, 1929-31, 34-38, lectr., 1938-39, asst. prof., 1939-46, assoc. prof., 1946-50, prof., 1950-71, prof. emeritus, 1971, Distinguished Research prof., 1967-68; dir. Writers' Conf., 1947-66; poetry editor Rocky Mt. Rev., 1937-46; assoc. editor Western Rev., 1946-49; lectr. creativity, cons. Inst. Personality Assessment and Research, U. Calif., Berkeley, 1957-58; editorial adv. bd. Concerning Poetry, 1968—. Author: Against the Circle, 1946, The Creative Process, 1952, The Nets, 1955, Writing, 1959, Country of the Minotaur, 1970, (with others) The Form Discovered: Essays on the Achievement of Andrew Lytle, 1973, Light, 1978, Windrose: Poems, 1929-1979, 1980. Bd. advisors Silver Mountain Found. Ford Found. fellow, 1952-53; recipient award Nat. Inst. Arts and Letters, 1970; Blumenthal-Leviton-Blonder prize Poetry mag., 1973; Levinson prize, 1978; William Carlos Williams award Poetry Soc. Am., 1981; Gov.'s award for arts Utah Arts Council, 1982. Mem. MLA, Utah Acad. Scis., Arts and Letters (Charles Redd award), Phi Beta Kappa, Phi Kappa Phi. Home: 1747 Princeton Ave Salt Lake City UT 84108 Office: U Utah Salt Lake City UT 84112 *To be human is to be a user of the basic resources of society, those modes and forms of vision and action that by determining the character and quality of men's experience shape everything men do and are.*

GHISTA, DHANJOO N., biochemical engineering educator. Ph.D., Stanford U., 1964. Research assoc. theoretical and applied mechanics Nat. Acad. Scis., 1964-66; with NASA, Ames Research Ctr., Moffett Field, CA, 1966-69; sr. scientist NASA Ames Research Ctr., Moffett Field, CA, 1975-77; assoc. prof. Washington U., St. Louis, 1969-71; prof., head biomed. engring. Indian Inst. Tech., Madras, 1971-75; sr. biomed. and rehab. research engr. Spinal Cord Injury Ctr., VA Hosp., Palo Alto, Calif., 1977-78; prof. Mich. Technol. U., Houghton, 1978-80; dir. biomed. engring., prof. McMaster U., Hamilton, Ont., 1980—. Author, editor 10 books on physiol. mechanics and biomed. engring.; editor: Automedica; contbg. author (in field); contbr. articles to profl. jours.; patentee (in field). Mem. Internat. Panel Biomed. Engring., Med. Bioengring. Soc., Internat. Soc. Biomechanics, Soc. Math. Biology, ASME, Am. Acad. Mechanics, Sigma Xi. Office: Dept Medicine McMaster U Hamilton ON Canada L85 4L7

GHOLSON, CECIL JACK, diversified energy company executive; b. Haskell, Tex., Sept. 25, 1927; s. Jesse White and Beulah Harriet (Foy) G.; m. Bettye Jo Lynch, Sept. 16, 1956; 1 dau., Twyla Lynn. B.B.A. with highest honors, Tex. Tech. U., Lubbock, 1949. C.P.A., Tex. With Pioneer Corp. (and predecessors), Amarillo, Tex., 1949—, v.p. fin., 1969—, also dir. subsidiaries and non-affiliated companies; mem. Amarillo Area Fin. and Econ. Council. Treas. Trinity Baptist Ch., Amarillo; bd. dirs. Bible Studies, Inc., Panhandle Bapt. Found. Served with U.S. Army, 1947-48, 50-53. Mem. Am. Inst. C.P.A.s. Clubs: Amarillo, Amarillo Country. Home: 1508 Bowie St Amarillo TX 79102 Office: 301 Taylor St Amarillo TX 79163

GHORMLEY, RALPH MCDOUGALL, naval officer; b. Boston, July 10, 1927; s. Ralph Kalb and Jean Kennedy (McDougall) G.; m. Sara Herd McKnight, July 11, 1953; children: Ruth Walker, Ralph McKnight. B.S., U.S. Naval Acad., 1949; postgrad., U.S. Naval Postgrad. Sch., 1955-57; grad., U.S. Naval Nuclear Power Sch., 1961. Commd. ensign U.S. Navy, 1949, advanced through grades to rear adm., 1973; service in submarines; comdr., U.S. Naval Base, Guantanamo Bay, Cuba, 1973-75; dep. comdr. Naval Electronics System Command, 1975-76; dep. dir. Def. Communications Agy., Washington, 1976-79; asst. logistics dep. chief naval ops. Dept. Navy, 1979; comdr. Naval Telecommunications Command, 1980-83. Decorated Legion of Merit, Meritorious Service medal, Def. Superior Service medal, Navy Commendation medal (2). Mem. U.S. Naval Inst., Armed Forces Communications Electronics Assn., Ret. Services League, Mil. Order Carabao. Club: Army-Navy (Washington). Home: 6138 Lee Hwy Arlington VA 22205 Office: CSC 803 W Broad St Falls Church VA 22046

GHORMLEY, WILLIAM KERR, former army officer; b. Hutchinson, Kan., Sept. 29, 1905; s. Davis Wilbert and Sarah Lansing (Dales) G.; m. Margaretta Elizabeth Clark, Aug. 31, 1929. Student, Coll. Emporia, Kan., 1923-24; B.S., U.S. Mil. Acad., 1929. Commd. 2d lt. U.S. Army, 1929, advanced through grades to maj. gen., 1959; chief tank, vehicle sect. (Office Chief Ordnance), Detroit, 1942-43, staff ordnance officer, Western Base, Channel Base Sects. ETO, 1944-45, staff, 1945-46, chief staff, 1946-47; chief service br. logistics group N.G. Bur., 1947-49; comdg. officer (Phila. Ordnance Dist.), 1950-52, chief automotive br. indsl. operations indsl. div., 1952-53, dep. chief indsl. div., 1954; asst. staff dir. purchasing, contracting policies Office Sec. Defense, 1954-55, staff dir., 1956-57; comdg. gen. U.S. Army Ordnance Weapons Command, Rock Island, Ill., 1957-59, U.S. Army Ordnance Spl. Weapons-Ammunition Command, Dover, N.J., 1959-61, U.S. Army Munitions Command, Dover, 1962; ret., 1962; asst. to exec. v.p. Am. Def. Preparedness Assn., Arlington, Va., 1963, exec. v.p., 1964-71, sr. staff cons., 1972—. Decorated D.S.M., Bronze Star medal; Croix de Guerre with palm, France; Belgian Order de Couronne. Mem. West Point Assn., Assn. U.S. Army, Nat. Rifle Assn. Home: 3604 Massachusetts Ave NW Washington DC 20007 Office: 1700 N Moore St Arlington VA 22209

GHOSE, RABINDRA NATH, electrical engineer; b. Mowrah, India, Sept. 1, 1925; came to arrived U.S., 1951, naturalized, 1960; s. Phatick Chandra and Bimala (Bala) G.; m. Dorothy Stewart, 1964; 1 son—Geoffrey. B.E.E., Jadavpur U., Calcutta, 1946; D.I.I.Sc., U. Bangalore, 1948; M.S., U. Wash., 1950; M.A., U. Ill., 1954, Ph.D., 1954, E.E., 1956, LL.B., 1975. Instr. elec. engring. Jadavpur U., Calcutta, India, 1946-49; research fellow U. Wash., 1951-52, U. Ill., 1952-54; mem. tech. staff RCA Corp., Camden, N.J., 1954-56, Los Angeles, 1956-59; dir. research, advanced devel. Space-Gen. Corp., El Monte, Calif., 1959-63; pres., chmn. bd. dirs., chief scientist Am. Nucleonics Corp., Westlake Village, Calif., 1983—. Author: Microwave Circuit Theory and Analysis, 1963, EMP Environment and System Hardness, 1983; contbr. numerous articles to tech. jours. Fellow AAAS, IEEE, Instn. Elec. Engrs. (London), Instn. Physics (London), Am. Phys. Soc., Wash. Acad. Scis.; mem. Am. Bar Assn. (patent com.), Calif. State Bar, Sigma Xi, Eta Kappa Nu, Pi Mu Epsilon. Patentee in field. Home: 8167 Mulholland Terrace Los Angeles CA 90046

GIACCO, ALEXANDER FORTUNATUS, diversified chemical company executive; b. St. John, Italy, Aug. 24, 1919; s. Salvatore J. and Maria Concetta (de Maria) G.; m. Edith Brown, Feb. 16, 1946; children: Alexander Fortunatus, Richard John, Mary P. Giacco Walsh, Elizabeth B., Marissa A. B.S. in Chem. Engring, Va. Poly. Inst., 1942; postgrad. in mgmt., Harvard U., 1965; D.B.A. (hon.), William Carey Coll., Hattiesburg, Miss., 1980. With Hercules Inc., Wilmington, Del., 1942—, gen. mgr. polymers dept., 1968-73, dir., 1970—, gen. mgr. operating dept., 1973, v.p. parent co., 1974-76, mem. exec. com., 1974—, exec. v.p., 1976-77, pres., chief exec. officer, chmn. exec. com., 1977—, chmn. bd., 1980, Himont Inc., 1983; dir. Texasgulf Inc., Montedison S.p.A. and Erbamont, N.V.; mem. U.S. Com. on New Initiatives in East-West Co-op., 1976—. Hon. chmn., mem. nat. bd. dirs. Jr. Achievement Del., 1975; trustee, bd. dirs., mem. exec. com. Wilmington Med. Center, 1975—; trustee, bd. visitors Va. Poly. Inst., 1979; bd. dirs. Greater Wilmington Devel. Council; chmn. bd. Grand Opera House, Wilmington. Named One of Ten Outstanding Chief Exec. Officers Fin. World, 1980, Best Chief Exec. Officer in Chem. Industry Fin. World, 1981, Outstanding Chief Exec. Officer in the Chem. Industry Wall Street Transcript, 1983, 84. Mem. Chem. Mfrs. Assn. (dir.), Soc. Plastics Industry, Soc. Chem. Industry, Soc. Automotive Engrs., Man-Made Fiber Producers Assn., Am. Ordnance Assn. (past dep. chmn.), Del. Roundtable (chmn. econ. devel. com.). Clubs: Wilmington, Wilmington Country, Vicmead Hunt, Bidermann Golf, Hercules Country, Rehoboth Beach Country. Patentee in field. Home: Greenville DE 19807 Office: Hercules Plaza Wilmington DE 19894

GIACCONI, RICCARDO, astrophysicist; b. Genoa, Italy, Oct. 6, 1931; came to U.S., 1956, naturalized, 1967; s. Antonio and Elsa (Canni) G.; m. Mirella Manaira, Feb. 15, 1957; children: Guia Giaconni Chmiel, Anna Lee, Marc A. Ph.D., U. Milan, Italy, 1954; Dr.Sci. hon., U. Chgo., 1983; hon. degree in astronomy, U. Padua, 1984. Asst. prof. physics U. Milan, 1954-56; research assoc. Ind. U., 1956-58, Princeton U., 1958-59; exec. v.p., dir. Am. Sci. & Engring. Co., Cambridge, Mass., 1959-73; prof. astronomy Harvard U.; also assoc. dir. high energy astrophysics div. Center Astrophysics, Smithsonian Astrophys. Obs./Harvard Coll. Obs., Cambridge, 1973-81; dir. Space Telescope Sci. Inst., Balt., 1981—; prof. astrophysics Johns Hopkins U.; mem. space sci. adv. com. NASA, 1978-79, mem. adv. com. innovation study, 1979—, astronomy adv. com., 1979—; mem. high energy astronomy survey panel Nat. Acad. Scis., 1979-80, mem. Space Sci. Bd., 1980—. Co-editor: X-ray Astronomy, 1974; Author numerous articles, papers in field. Fulbright fellow, 1956-58; recipient Röntgen prize astrophysics Physikalish-Medizinische Gesellschaft, Wurzburg, Germany, 1971; Exceptional Sci. Achievement medal NASA, 1971, 80; Disting. Public Service award, 1972; Space Sci. award AIAA, 1976; Elliott Cresson medal Franklin Inst., 1980; Gold medal Royal Astron. Soc., 1982; A. Cressy Morrison award N.Y. Acad. Sci., 1982; also Bruce medal; Heinneman award; Russell lectr. Mem. Am. Astron. Soc. (Helen B. Warner award 1966, chmn. high energy astrophysics div. 1976-77, councilor 1979-82), Italian Phys. Soc. (Como prize 1967), AAAS, Internat. Astron. Union (Nat. Acad. Scis. astron. rep. 1979-82), Nat. Acad. Scis., Am. Acad. Arts and Scis., Md. Acad. Sci. (sci. council 1982—). Club: Cosmos (Washington). Inventor x-ray telescope, discovered x-ray stars. Home: 4205 Underwood Rd Baltimore MD 21218 Office: Space Telescope Sci Inst Homewood Campus Baltimore MD 21218

GIACOMANTONIO, ARCHIMEDES ARISTIDES MICHAEL, sculptor; b. Jersey City, Jan. 17, 1906; s. Gaetano and Rosina (Fanelli) G.; m. Muriel Rose Ruoff, Aug. 10, 1935. Student, Leonardo da Vinci Art Sch., N.Y.C.; grad., Royal Acad. Art, Rome, 1929; pvt. student, Onorio Ruotolo, Vincenzo Gemito. Asso. dir. (under name Jock Manton) ABC-TV, 1951-71. (Recipient 1st prize 6th Ann. N.J. Exhbn., Montclair Mus. 1936, Maynard prize NAD 1940, Allied Artist award religious sculpture, 1976, Bronze Sculpture 1977, Mass. Realistic Art award 1977), Prin. works: bust Mohammed Riza Pahlevi; heroic size bronze Christopher Columbus; granite fountain, Journal Sq., Jersey City, Columbus monument, Hazelton, Pa.; bronze bust Dr. Harry A. Sprague, Sprague Library, Montclair (N.J.) State Coll.; bust Harry S. Truman and; bronze statuette Woodrow Wilson for, Truman Library, Independence, Mo.; bust Robert Kinter, Gen. Eisenhower for, West Point Acad., Leonard Goldenson, Martin Luther King, Jr, Dr. King Sch., Jersey City; bronze bust Milton Cross, Met. Opera House, Madonna of Assumption Shrine, North Arlington, N.J.; designed: Ann. Spirit medal, Cath. Poetry Soc. Am.; bronze Grandma, Royal Palace, Rome, Italy; terra cotta Mediterranean Flower; bronze Vincenzo Gemito, Mus. Modern Art, Valle Giulia, Rome; commemorative coin-medal of Pearl S. Buck for, La Société de Femmes Celebres. Exec. dir. Sussex County (N.J.) Arts Council, 1971-77; trustee Mus. Jersey City, Internat. Inst. Jersey City. Technician; M.C., 42d Div. (Rainbow); Technician; overseas. Named Accademico of Italy, 1980. Fellow Nat. Sculpture Soc.; mem. NAD (Daniel Chester French Gold medal 1980), Nat. Acad. TV Arts and Scis., Allied Artists. Am. Roman Catholic. Clubs: Kiwanian., Lotos (N.Y.C.); Carteret (Jersey City). Office: 42 W 67th St New York NY 10023

GIACOMINI, GIUSEPPE, tenor; b. Monselice (Padua), Italy, Sept. 7, 1940; m. Liliana; children: Giovanna, Giacomo. Debut in: Madame Butterfly, 1970; appeared with, Met. Opera, 1975—, La Scala, 1974, Vienna State Opera, Berlin Opera, 1972, Hamburg State Opera, 1973, Chgo. Symphony, 1979, Cleve. Orch. (Recipient First prizes Conc d. Adria 1968), Cleve. Orch. (San Carlo 1973), Cleve. Orch. (Viotti Competition 1970), Cleve. Orch. (Conc della Scala 1970). *

GIAEVER, IVAR, physicist; b. Bergen, Norway, Apr. 5, 1929; came to U.S., 1957, naturalized, 1963; s. John A. and Gudrun (Skaarud) G.; m. Inger Skramstad, Nov. 8, 1952; children: John, Anne Kari, Guri, Trine. Siv. Ing., Norwegian Inst. Tech., Trondheim, 1952; Ph.D., Rensselaer Poly. Inst., 1964. Patent examiner Norweigian Patent Office, Oslo, 1953-54; mech. engr. Can. Gen. Electric Co., Peterborough, Ont., 1954-56; applied mathematician Gen. Electric Co., Schenectady, 1956-58, physicist, 1958—. Served with Norwegian Army, 1952-53. Recipient Nobel Prize for Physics, 1973; Guggenheim fellow, 1970. Fellow Am. Phys. Soc. (Oliver E. Buckley prize 1965); mem. IEEE, Norwegian Profl. Engrs., Nat. Acad. Sci., Nat. Acad. Engring. (V.K. Zworykin award 1974), Am. Acad. Arts and Scis., Norwegian Acad. Sci., Norwegian Acad. Tech. Office: Gen Electric Co Research and Devel Center PO Box 1088 Schenectady NY 12301 *

GIALANELLA, PHILIP THOMAS, newspaper publisher; b. Binghamton, N.Y., June 6, 1930; s. Felix and Frances (Demuro) G.; m. Marie Amelia Davis, May 1, 1953; 1 son, Thomas Davis. B.A., Harpur Coll., 1952; M.A., State U. N.Y., 1955. Promotion dir. Evening Press and Sta. WINR-TV, Binghamton, 1957-62; v.p., gen. mgr. Daily Advance, Dover, N.J., 1962-66; v.p. Hartford (Conn.) Times, 1966-70; pres., pub. Newburgh (N.Y.) News, 1970-71; exec. v.p. Hawaii Newspaper Agy., Honolulu, 1971-73, pres., 1974—; pub. Honolulu Star-Bull., 1975—; pres. Gannett S.W. & Pacific Newspaper Group; v.p., dir. Gannett Pacific Corp.; dir. Capital Investment Co., Hawaii Newspaper Agy., Inc., Tucson Newspapers, Inc., Guam Publs.; sec., asst. treas. Newspaper Printing Corp., El Paso, Tex., Newspaper Realty Corp., El Paso. Past chmn., exec. com. mem. Nat. Alliance Businessmen for Hawaii and Micronesia; pres. Hawaii Newspaper Agy. Found.; bd. dirs. Aloha United Way, AP Assn., Calif., Ariz., Hawaii and Nev.; mem. Japan Hawaii Econ. Council; bd. govs. Pacific Asian Affairs Council. Served with U.S. Army, 1952-54. Mem. Am. Newspaper Pubs. Assn., Hawaii Pubs. Assn. Roman Catholic. Office: Hawaii Newspaper Agy Inc Honolulu HI 96801 *

GIAM, CHOO-SENG, college dean, educator; b. Singapore, Apr. 2, 1931; U.S., 1964, naturalized, 1970; s. Chong-Hing and Eng-Keow (Tan) G.; m. Mun-Yung Ng, Feb. 25, 1956; children: Benny Y.B., Patrick Y.Y., Michael Y.K. M.Sc., U. Sask, 1961, Ph.D., 1963. Research chemist Imperial Oil, Sarnia, Can., 1963-64; postdoctoral fellow Pa. State U., State College, 1964-65; research assoc. U. Calif.-Irvine, 1965-66; asst. prof. Tex A&M U., College Station, 1966-70, assoc. prof., 1970-72, prof. dept. chemistry, 1972-81, prof. chemistry and oceanography, chmn. dept. chemistry, 1982—; dean Coll. Sci., prof. chemistry and geol. scis. U. Tex., El Paso, 1981-82. Contbr. articles to profl. jours.; patentee in field. Mem. Am. Chem. Soc., Can. Chem. Soc., Royal Inst. Chemistry, N.Y. Acad. Scis., Sigma Xi, Phi Lambda Upsilon. Home: 425 Hollydale St El Paso TX 79912 Office: U Tex Coll Sci El Paso TX 79968

GIAMATTI, A. BARTLETT, university president, English educator; b. Boston, Apr. 4, 1938; (m), 1960; 3 children. B.A., Yale U., 1960, Ph.D. in Comparative Lit, 1964; LL.D., Princeton U., 1978, Harvard

U., 1978, Notre Dame U., 1982, Coll. of New Rochelle, 1982, Dartmouth Coll., 1982; Litt.D., Am. Internat. Coll., 1979, Jewish Theol. Sem. Am., 1980, Atlanta U., 1981. Instr. in Italian and comparative lit. Princeton U., 1964-65, asst. prof., 1965-66; asst. prof. English Yale U., 1966-68, asso. prof., 1968-71, prof. English and comparative lit., 1971—, master Ezra Stiles Coll., 1970-72, Frederick Clifford Ford prof. English and comparative lit., 1976-77, John Hay Whitney prof. English and comparative lit., 1977-78, pres. univ., 1978—; vis. prof. comparative lit. N.Y. U., summer 1966; mem. faculty Bread Loaf Sch. English, summers 1972, 73, 74. Author: The Earthly Paradise and the Renaissance Epic, 1966, Play of Double Senses: Spenser's Faerie Queene, 1975, The University and the Public Interest; editor: (with others) The Songs of Bernart de Ventadorn 1962, Ludovico Ariosto's Orlando Furioso, 1968, A Variorum Commentary On the Poems of John Milton, Vol. 1, 1970, Western Literature, 3 vols, 1971. Decorated comdr. Order of Merit, Italy; Guggenheim fellow, 1969-70. Fellow Am. Acad. Arts and Scis.; mem. MLA, Am. Philos. Soc., Dante Soc. Am., Am. Comparative Lit. Assn., Council for Fin. Aid to Edn., Commn. on Humanities, Mediaeval Soc. Am., Council on Fgn. Relations, Nat. Commn. on Excellence in Edn. Office: Office of Pres Yale U New Haven CT 06520

GIANACAKES, PETER JAMES, corporation executive; b. Louisville, May 2, 1924; s. James C. and Maniatis G.; m. Mimi Bacas; children: James P., Anne. B.Ch. E., U. Louisville, 1947, M.Ch.E., 1976. Chmn. bd. chief exec. officer Research-Cottrell, Inc., Somerville, N.J., 1982—; dir. 1st Nat. Bank Central Jersey. Leader Boy Scouts Am.; bd. dirs. United Fund; mem. Boston Pub. Welfare Adv. Bd., 1979-81. Named Disting. Alumnus Speed Sci. Sch., U. Louisville, 1982. Office: PO Box 1500 Somerville NJ 08876

GIANELLI, WILLIAM R., government official; b. Stockton, Calif., Feb. 19, 1919. B.S., U. Calif., 1941. Registered profl. engr., Calif., Nev. Dist. engr. Engrs. Office and Dept. Water Resources Calif., until 1960; sr. partner firm Gianelli and Murray (Cons. Engrs.), 1960-67; dir. Calif. Dept. Water Resources, 1967-73; cons. engr., from 1973; mem. Nat. Commn. Water Quality, 1973-76; asst. sec. Dept. Army, 1981—. Mem. ASCE, Calif. C. of C. (dir.). Address: Pentagon Washington DC 20310 *

GIANELLY, ANTHONY ALFRED, educator; b. Boston, Aug. 19, 1936; s. Eugene and Pasquelena (Carideo) G.; m. Ernestine Painter, May 27, 1960; children—Lisa Lawrence, Anthony Todd. A.B., Harvard U., 1957, D.M.D., 1961; Ph.D., Boston U., 1967, M.D., 1974. Orthodontic certificate, 1963. Research fellow orthodontics Harvard Sch. Dental Medicine, 1961-63; research fellow Nat. Inst. Dental Research, Boston U., 1964-67, prof. orthodontics, chmn. dept., 1967—, research prof. biochemistry, 1968—, head orthodontic sect., 1967—; Mem. adv. council Mass. Med. Assistance Program, 1970—. Author: Biologic Basis of Orthodontics, 1971. Named One of Outstanding Educators in Am., 1970. Mem. Am. Assn. Orthodontics, Am. Dental Assn., Angle Orthodontic Soc., Tweed Found. Orthodontic Research, Mass. Dental Soc. (chmn. continuing edn. sect.), Sigma Xi. Home: 92 Windsor Rd Waban MA 02168 Office: 100 E Newton St Boston MA 02118

GIANINNO, SUSAN MCMANAMA, research psychologist; b. Boston, Dec. 25, 1948; d. John Carroll and Barbara (Frances) Magner; m. Lawrence John Gianinno, June 7, 1970; 1 dau., Alexandra Christin. B.A. in English Lit. and Psychology cum laude, Boston Coll., 1970; M.A. in Ednl. Psychology, Northwestern U., 1973; postgrad. in behavioral scis., U. Chgo. Psychiat. asst. Quinn Psychiat., Pavilion St Elizabeth's Hosp., Brighton, Mass., 1967-70; research assoc. com. human devel., dept behavioral scis. U. Chgo., 1973-79; resident adv. U. Chgo. Housing Systems, 1979—; research assoc., then research supr. Needham, Harper and Steers Advt. Inc., Chgo., 1979-80, dir. spl. projects, Chgo., Il, 1981—; cons. in field. Contbr. papers, reports to profl. jours. Univ. scholar U. Chgo., 1975-77. Mem. Am. Psychol. Assn., Assn. Consumer Research, Nat. Council Family Relations, Am. Mktg. Assn., Midwest Assn. Pub. Opinion Research, Mass. Tchrs. Assn. Home: 5454 South Shore Dr Chgo. Il. 60615 Office: Needham Harper and Steers Advt Inc 3 Illinois Ctr 303 E Wacker Dr Chgo. Il 60601

GIANNETTI, LOUIS DANIEL, film educator, film critic; b. Natick, Mass., Apr. 1, 1937; s. John and Vincenza (Zappitelli) G.; m. Justine Ann Gallagher, Sept. 7, 1963 (div. 1980); children: Christina, Francesca. B.A., Boston U., 1959; M.A., U. Iowa, 1961, Ph.D., 1967. Asst. prof. English Emory U., Atlanta, 1966-70; prof. English and film Case Western Res. U., Cleve., 1970—. Author: Understanding Movies, 1972, 1976, 1982, Godard and Others, 1975, Masters of the American Cinema, 1981. Mem. Soc. Cinma Studies, Univ. Film Assn. Democrat. Office: Case Western Res U Euclid Ave Cleveland OH 44106

GIANNINI, VALERIO LOUIS, investment banker; b. N.Y.C., Feb. 7, 1938; s. Gabriel M. and Luisa M. (Casazza) G.; m. Linda Martin, Oct. 6, 1979. B.S.E., Princeton U., 1959. With Kidder Peabody & Co., N.Y.C., 1961-64; sr. cons. IIT Research Inst., Chgo., 1964-66; sec. Giannini-Voltex, Los Angeles, 1966-68; pres. V.L. Giannini, Los Angeles, 1968-76; chmn. Namco Chems., Inc., 1975; dir. White House Operations, Washington, 1977-78; dep. spl. asst. to the Pres. for Adminstrn. The White House, Washington, 1979-80; dir. Office Productivity and Product Tech., Dept. Commerce, Washington, 1980-81; prin. Cumberland Investment Group, N.Y.C., 1981—. Served to lt. USN, 1959-61. Club: N.Y. Yacht. Home: 94 Lyons Plains Rd Weston CT 06883

GIANTURCO, DELIO E., business executive; b. Washington, Sept. 28, 1940; s. Elio and Valentine (McGillycuddy) G.; m. Mary Elizabeth Jordan, Jan. 31, 1961; children: Lisa, Grace Maria, Mark. B.S. in Fgn. Trade, Georgetown U., 1963; M.A., George Washington U., 1967. Staff asst. to Rep. Robert J. Corbett of, Pa., 1960-62; legis. asst. to Rep. Robert L.F. Sikes of, Fla., 1962-63; dep. v.p. for project devel., dep. sr. v.p. for guarantees and ins., sr. v.p. for guarantees, ins. and exporter credits, exec. v.p., vice chmn., 1st v.p. Export-Import Bank, Washington, 1963-77; pres. First Washington Assocs., 1978—. Home: 6338 Waterway Dr Falls Church VA 22044 Office: 1819 H St NW Washington DC 20006

GIANTURCO, MAURIZIO ANTONIO, beverage co. exec.; b. Potenza, Italy, Dec. 2, 1928; s. Giulio and Lisa G.; m. Rita Cacciapuoti, Oct. 7, 1954; children—Giulio Mark, Luca Francesco. Grad., U. Rome; Fulbright postdoctoral research fellow, U. Ill., 1952-53, sr. research asso., 1953-56. Asst. prof. chemistry U. Rome, 1951-52; research chemist Tenco div. Coca-Cola Co., 1956-61, head research sect., 1961-63; head tech. research and devel. sect. Coca-Cola Co., Atlanta, 1963-68, dir. corp. research and devel., 1968-73, asst. to v.p., 1973-75, asst. to sr. vp., 1975-76, v.p. for sci., 1976-81, sr. v.p. for sci., 1981—. Author: also articles. Interpretive Spectroscopy; The Chemistry and Physiology of Flavor. Donegani Research Found. fellow. Mem. N.Y. Acad. Scis., AAAS, Am. Chem. Soc., Chem. Soc. (London), Am. Inst. Chemists, Am. Inst. Food Technologists, Gamma Alpha. Roman Catholic. Club: Commerce (Atlanta). Office: PO Drawer 1734 Atlanta GA 30301 *

GIARDINO, ALFRED A., lawyer; b. Bklyn., May 1, 1913; s. Joseph and Lucy (Tasca) G.; m. Lucie Veulliez; 2 children. A.B., Bklyn. Coll., 1934; J.D., Columbia, 1937; student, Inst. Internat. Affairs, Geneva, 1946. Bar: N.Y. 1937. Trial atty., exec. sec. N.Y. State Labor Relations Bd., 1937-48; mem. firm Lambos Flynn Nyland & Giardino, N.Y.C., 1948—; arbitrator Fed. Mediation and Conciliation Service, N.Y. State Mediation Bd., Am. Arbitration Assn.; former tchr. Bklyn. Coll., Columbia, N.Y. U. Grad. Sch., Cornell U. Extension; dir. research Gov. N.Y. Spl. Commn. Illegitimacy, 1936-37; pub. mem. Internat. Commn. Labor Experts to Bolivia, 1943; spl. rep. State Dept. and Labor Dept. in, Brazil, Chile, Argentina, and Uruguay, 1942-43; vice chmn. com. character and fitness Jud. Dept., 1st Dept. N.Y., 1961—; mem. N.Y.C. Bd. Edn., 1964-68, pres., 1967-68; chmn. N.Y.C. Bd. Higher Edn., 1974-76. Served as officer AUS, World War II. Mem. Am. Bar Assn., Assn. Bar City N.Y., Internat. Soc. Labor and Social Legis. (sec.). Home: 4600 Fieldston Rd New York NY 10471 Office: 29 Broadway New York NY 10006

GIARRUSSO, GIOVANNI, stock exchange exec.; b. Montreal, Que., Can., Mar. 22, 1939; s. Michele and Maria (Ciarlo) G.; m. Suzanne L'Ecuyer, Sept. 1, 1962; children—Nathalie, Gian-Carlo. B.Commerce, Sir George Williams U., Montreal, 1961; chartered accountant, McGill U., Montreal, 1967. Student in accounts Touche, Rosse, Bailey & Smart (chartered accountants), Montreal, 1961-63; with Montreal Stock Exchange, 1963—, v.p., sec., 1969-72, exec. v.p., 1973—; exec. v.p. Trans Can. Options Inc. Bd. dirs. Royal Victoria Hosp. Centre, Can. Council Christians and Jews. Mem. Order Chartered Accountants Que., Montreal Bd. Trade, Chambre de commerce française du Can., Italian C. of C. (pres., dir.). Club: Stock Exchange (Montreal) (pres.). Address: 800 Victoria Sq PO Box 61 Montreal PQ H4Z 1A9 Canada

GIAUDRONE, ANGELO, assn. exec.; b. Cle Elum, Wash., Oct. 6, 1912; s. Joseph and Caterina (Aimone) G.; m. Marie Swap, June 18, 1939; children—John, Kathleen Giaudrone Allen. B.A., Wash. State Coll., 1935, M.A., 1948; Ed.D., Harvard, 1953. Tchr. sci., Naches, Wash., 1935-38, prin. high sch., Granger, Wash., 1938-41, Sunnyside, Wash., 1941-44, supt. pub. schs., Sunnyside, 1944-49, Ellensburg, Wash., 1949-52; lectr. edn. Harvard, 1952-55; supt. schs., Concord, Mass., 1955-56, Tacoma, 1956-74, ednl. cons., 1974-75; exec. dir. SW Wash. Multiple Sclerosis Soc., 1978—; Mem. adv. com. U.S. Office Edn., 1952; mem. Fulbright Comparative Edn. Seminar, Norway and Italy, 1960; mem. steering com., biol. scis. curriculum study NSF; participant White House Conf. Edn., 1965; mem. Wash. State Legislature Interim Com. on Edn., Wash. Gov.'s Commn. Ednl. TV. Editorial bd.: Music Educators Jour. Recipient Williston Acad. citation, 1965, Lamplighter award NAACP, 1972; named Outstanding Citizen Municipal League Tacoma-Pierce County, 1974. Mem. Wash. Sch. Supts. Assn. (pres. 1951-52), NEA (life), Wash. Assn. Sch. Adminstrs. (exec. bd.). Club: Rotarian (pres. 1944). Address: 2722 SW 327th St Federal Way WA 98003

GIBALA, RONALD, metallurgical engineering educator; b. New Castle, Pa., Oct. 3, 1938; s. Steve Anthony and June Rose (Frank) G.; children: Maryellen, Janice, David, Kristine. B.S., Carnegie Inst. Tech., 1960; M.S., U. Ill., 1962, Ph.D., 1964. Engrng. technician Crane Co., New Castle, Pa., 1956-59; engr. U.S. Steel Research Labs., Monroeville, Pa., 1960; research asst. U. Ill., Urbana, 1960-64; asst. prof. metallurgy Case Western Res. U., Cleve., 1964-69, assoc. prof., 1969-76, prof. metallurgy and materials sci. and macromolecular sci., 1976—, co-dir. materials research lab., 1981—. Contbr. articles to profl. jours.; editor: Hydrogen Embrittlement and Stress Corrosion Cracking: A Troiano Festschrift, 1983. Recipient Alfred Noble prize ASCE, 1969; named Outstanding Young Mem. Cleve. chpt. Am. Soc. Metals, 1971; Tech. Achievement award Cleve. Tech. Socs. Council, 1972; vis. research fellow C.E.N.G. Labs., Grenoble, 1973-74. Mem. AIME (dir. 1981—), Am. Soc. Metals (chpt. chmn. 1975-76), AAAS, Sigma Xi, Tau Beta Pi. Democrat. Club: Suburban Ski (pres. 1981-82). Home: 4072 Lambert Rd South Euclid OH 44121 Office: Dept Metallurgy Case Western Res Univ Cleveland OH 44106 *Leo Durocher was wrong. Good guys don't finish last. Do your work as well as you can. Do more than is expected. Take advantage of all opportunities without hurting others. Be fair and logical, and make sensible decisions. And you won't finish last—by a long shot.*

GIBALDI, MILO, univ. adminstr.; b. N.Y.C., Dec. 17, 1938; s. Ignatius and Angela G.; m. Florence D'Amato, Dec. 26, 1960; 1 dau., Ann Elizabeth. B.S., Coll. Pharmacy, Columbia U., 1960, Ph.D., 1963. Asst. prof. pharmacy Columbia U., N.Y.C., 1963-66; asst. prof. pharmaceutics SUNY, Buffalo, 1966-67, asso. prof., 1967-70, prof., 1970-78, chmn. dept., 1970-78; prof. pharmaceutics U. Wash., Seattle, 1978—, dean, 1978—; cons. Bur. Drugs, FDA, 1970-72, VA, Washington, 1971-72; vis. prof. U. Rochester, 1972-74; program dir. clin. pharmacokinetics and biopharmaceutics NIH, 1973-78, mem. pharmacology study sect., 1976-80; mem. sci. adv. bd. G.D. Searle & Co., 1978—. Author: (with Donald Perrier) Pharmacokinetics, 1976; contbr. articles to profl. jours. Fellow Acad. Pharm. Scis., AAAS; mem. Am. Chem. Soc., Am. Pharm. Assn., Acad. Soc. Clin. Pharmacology, Am. Soc. Pharmacology and Exptl. Therapeutics, N.Y. Acad. Scis., Am. Assn. Colls. Pharmacy, Sigma Xi, Rho Chi. Office: Univ of Wash Health Scis Center Seattle WA 98195

GIBB, BARRY, vocalist, songwriter; b. Manchester, Eng., Sept. 1, 1946; s. Hugh and Barbara G.; m. Lynda Gray; children: Stephen, Ashley. Performed in: (with bros. Robin and Maurice as group) amateur shows The Blue Cats, Manchester, in 1950's; formed: (with bros.) The Bee Gees, 1958; disbanded, 1969; reunited, 1971; appeared in local clubs, Brisbane, Australia; released: 1st single record Three Kisses of Love, Australia, 1963; appeared on own weekly TV show, Australia, in 1960's; returned to, Eng., 1967; signed with, NEMS Enterprises; made: 1st U.S. TV appearance on Am. Bandstand, 1967; former rec. group for, Robert Stigwood Orgn., 1973—; composer: (with bros.) music and lyrics for film Saturday Night Fever, 1977; title song of film Grease, 1978; appeared in: film Sgt Pepper's Lonely Hearts Club Band, 1978; albums include Bee Gees First, 1967, Horizontal, 1968, Idea, 1968, Rare, Precious and Beautiful, Volume I, 1968, Odessa, 1969, Best of the Bee Gees, 1969, Rare, Precious and Beautiful, Volume II, 1970, Cucumber Castle, 1970, Two Years On, 1971, Trafalgar, 1971, To Whom It May Concern, 1972, Life in a Tin Can, 1973, Best of Bee Gees, Volume II, 1973, Mr. Natural, 1974, Main Course, 1976, Children of the World, 1976, Bee Gees Gold Volume I, 1976, Odessa, 1976, Here At Last. . .Bee Gees. . .Live, 1977, Saturday Night Fever, 1977, Sgt Pepper's Lonely Hearts Club Band, 1978, Spirits Having Flown, 1978, Bee Gees Greatest Hits, 1979, Living Eyes, 1979; wrote, sang, co-produced album for, Barbra Streisand, Guilty (Named Composer of Yr.). Recipient Top Talent award Radio Adelaide KA, Australia, 1965; named Pop Stars of Yr., Holland, 1967; recipient Grammy award, 1971, 78, 81; citation of achievement BMI, 1971, 75, 76, 77; Record of Yr. award Stereo Rev., 1973; Trendsetter award Billboard, 1977; Best Movie Soundtrack award Italian Record Reviewers, 1978; Ampex Golden Reel award; numerous RIAA Gold and Platinum albums and singles, numerous gold and platinum albums and singles from various locations, including Can., South Africa, Germany, Belgium, Holland, Australia, N.Z., France, Hong Kong.; Hon. Citizens of Man. (Can.), City of Winnipeg, 1975; Hon. Citizens State of Fla., 1978, Nat. 2UE award, Australia, 1966, Golden Lion award Radio Luxemburg, 1967, Carl-Allan award, Eng., 1967, Valentine award, Eng., 1968, Ivor Novello award, 1968-69, 76-77, 77-78, John Stephen Fashion award, 1969. Office: care Middle Ear 1801 Bay Rd Miami Beach FL 33139 *

GIBB, MAURICE, vocalist, songwriter; b. Manchester, Eng., Dec. 22, 1949; s. Hugh and Barbara; m. Yvonne; children: Adam, Samantha. Performed in: (with bros. Barry and Robin as group) amateur shows The Blue Cats, Manchester, in 1950's; formed: (with bros.) The Bee Gees, 1958; disbanded, 1969; reunited, 1971; appeared in local clubs, Brisbane, Australia; released: 1st single record Three Kisses of Love, Australia, 1963; appeared on own weekly TV show in, Australia, in 1960's; returned to, Eng., 1967; signed with, NEMS Enterprises; made 1st U.S. TV appearance on: Am. Bandstand, 1967; former rec. group for, Robert Stigwood Orgn.; composer (with bros.); music and lyrics for film Saturday Night Fever, 1977; title song of film Grease, 1978; appeared in film; appeared in film Sgt Pepper's Lonely Hearts Club Band, 1978; albums include Bee Gees First, 1967, Horizontal, 1968, Idea, 1968, Rare, Precious and Beautiful, Volume I, 1968, Odessa, 1969, Best of the Bee Gees, 1969, Rare, Precious and Beautiful, Volume II, 1970, Cucumber Castle, 1970, Two Years On, 1971, To Whom It May Concern, 1972, Life in a Tin Can, 1973, Best of Bee Gees, Volume II, 1973, Mr. Natural, 1974, Main Course, 1976, Children of the World, 1976, Bee Gees Gold Volume I, 1976, Odessa, 1976, Here At Last. . .Bee Gees. . .Live, 1977, Saturday Night Fever, 1977, Sgt Pepper's Lonely Hearts Club Band, 1978, Spirits Having Flown, 1978, Bee Gees Greatest Hits, 1979, Living Eyes. Recipient Grammy award, 1971, 78; citation of achievement BMI, 1971, 75, 76, 77; Record of Yr. award Stereo Rev., 1973; Trendsgtter award Billboard, 1977; Best Movie Soundtrack award Italian Record Reviewers, 1978; Ampex Golden Reel award; numerous RIAA Gold and Platinum albums and singles, numerous gold and platinum albums and singles from various locations, including Can., South Africa, Germany, Belgium, Holland, Australia, N.Z., France, Hong Long.; Named Pop Stars of Yr., Holland, 1967, Hon. Citizens of, Man. (Can.), City of Winnipeg, 1975, Hon. Citizens State of, Fla., 1978; recipient Nat. 2UE award, Australia, 1966, Golden Lion award Radio Luxemburg, 1967, Carl-Allan award, Eng., 1967, Valentine award, Eng., 1968, Iver Novello award, 1968-69, 76-77, 77-78. Office: care Middle Ear 1801 Bay Rd Miami Beach FL 33139 *

GIBB, RICHARD DEAN, university president; b. Smithshire, Ill., Dec. 6, 1928; s. Edward Dale and Anna Marie (Anderson) G.; m. Betty G. Epperson, Dec. 22, 1951; children: Richie William, Connie Marie. Student, Western Ill. U., 1947-50; B.S., U. Ill., 1951, M.E., 1955; Ph.D., Mich. State U., 1958. Faculty agrl. econs. Western Ill. U., Macomb, 1958-68, prof., 1965-68, adminstrv. asst. to pres., 1964-67, dean adminstrn., 1967-68, acting coordinator internat. programs, 1964-65; S.D. commr. for higher edn., Pierre, 1968-74, Ind. commr. for higher edn., Indpls., 1974-77; pres. U. Idaho, 1977—. Served with AUS, 1952-53. Mem. Am. Assn. Higher Edn., Statewide Higher Edn. Assn., Am. Agrl. Econs. Assn., Delta Sigma Phi. Home: 1026 Nez Perce Dr Moscow ID 83843 Office: Office of the President U Ida Moscow ID 83843

GIBB, ROBIN, vocalist, songwriter; b. Manchester, Eng., Dec. 22, 1949; s. Hugh and Barbara G.; m. Molly Hullis, Dec. 10, 1968; children—Spencer, Melissa. Performed in: (with bros. Barry and Maurice as group) amateur shows The Blue Cats, Manchester, in 1950's; formed: (with bros.) The Bee Gees, 1958; disbanded, 1969; reunited, 1971; appeared in local clubs, Brisbane, Australia; released: 1st single record Three Kisses of Love, Australia, 1963; appeared on own weekly TV show, Australia, in 1960's; returned to, Eng., 1967; signed with, NEMS Enterprises; made: 1st U.S. TV appearance on Am. Bandstand, 1967; rec. group for, Robert Stigwood Orgn., 1973—; composer; music and lyrics for film Saturday Night Fever, 1977; for title song of film Grease, 1978; appeared in: movie Sgt Pepper's Lonely Hearts Club Band, 1978; albums include Bee Gees First, 1967, Horizontal, 1968, Idea, 1968, Rare, Precious and Beautiful, Volume I, 1968, Odessa, 1969, Best of the Bee Gees, 1969, Rare, Precious and Beautiful, Volume II, 1970, Cucumber Castle, 1970, Two Years On, 1971, To Whom It May Concern, 1972, Life In A Tin Can, 1973, Best of Bee Gees, Volume II, 1973, Mr. Natural, 1974, Main Course, 1976, Children of the World, 1976, Bee Gees Gold Volume I, 1976, Odessa, 1976, Here At Last. . .Bee Gees. . .Live, 1977, Saturday Night Fever, 1977, Sgt Pepper's Lonely Hearts Club Band, 1978, Spirits Having Flown, 1978, Bee Gees Greatest Hits, 1979. Named Pop Stars of Yr., Holland, 1967, Hon. Citizens of Man. (Can.) City of Winnipeg, 1975, State of Fla., 1978; recipient Nat. 2UE award, Australia, 1966, Golden Lion award Radio Luxemburg, 1967, Carl-Allan award, Eng., 1967, Valentine award, Eng., 1968, Ivor Novello award, 1968-69, 76-77, 77-78, Grammy award, 1971, 78, citation of achievement BMI, 1971, 75, 76, 77, Record of Yr. award Stereo Rev., 1973, Trendsetter award Billboard, 1977, Best Movie Soundtrack award Italian Record Reviewers, 1978, Ampex Golden Reel award, numerous Gold and Platinum albums and singles RIAA, numerous gold and platinum albums and singles, from various locations, including Can., South Africa, Germany, Belgium, Holland, Australia, N.Z., France, Hong Kong. Office: care Robert Stigwood Orgn Inc 1775 Broadway New York NY 10019 *

GIBBENS, ALFRED MORTON, univ. adminstr.; b. Tipton County, Ind., Aug. 18, 1935; s. Oren H. and Melva Madeline (Hershman) G.; m. Loretta Kellams, May 5, 1957; children—Thomas Oren, Ellen Lynne. B.A., Franklin (Ind.) Coll., 1958; M.A., Butler U., Indpls., 1968; Ph.D., U. Pitts., 1973; D.H.L., Yankton Coll., 1981. Dir. alumni relations Franklin Coll., 1960-64, instr. English, 1964-65; dir. financial devel. Butler U., 1965-67; dir. devel. Carnegie-Mellon U., Pitts., 1967-70, asst. to v.p. acad. affairs, 1970-73; pres. Yankton (S.D.) Coll., 1973-77, trustee, mem. exec. com., 1973-77; dir. univ. devel. Harvard U., 1977-79; v.p. devel. Pomona Coll., Claremont, Calif., 1979—. Mem. Blue Key, Phi Alpha Theta, Phi Delta Theta. Mem. United Ch. of Christ. Club: Los Angeles Athletic. Office: Pomona Coll Claremont CA 91711

GIBBON, RALPH HAILER, lawyer; b. Riverton, N.J., Nov. 4, 1916; s. Ralph Waldo and Anna (Hailer) G.; m. Harriet Joyce Hazen, Aug. 26, 1939; children: Peter, John, Frederick, Thomas, Christopher, Daniel. B.S., Harvard U., 1939, J.D., 1942. Bar: Ohio 1942. Assoc. Squire, Sanders & Dempsey, Cleve., 1942-55, ptnr., 1955—, coordinator pub. law practice, 1965—. Mem. exec. com., trustee Univ. Circle, Inc., Cleve., 1978. Served with USN, 1942-45. Clubs: Union, The Fifty, Cleve. Racquet.

GIBBONS, DON CARY, sociology educator, author; b. Newport, Wash., June 6, 1926; s. George and Mildred (Snow) G.; m. Carmen L. Baker, Sept. 1, 1951; children: Michael, Diane. B.A., U. Wash., 1950, M.A., 1953, Ph.D., 1956. Faculty U. B.C., 1956-57, San Francisco State Coll., 1957-69; prof. sociology Portland (Oreg.) State U., 1969—. Author: Changing the Lawbreaker, 1965, Society, Crime and Criminal Careers, 1968, Delinquent Behavior, 1970, Becoming Delinquent, 1970, The Study of Deviance, 1975, Criminal Justice Planning, 1977, The Criminological Enterprise, 1979. Served with USNR, 1944-46. Mem. Am. Sociol. Assn., Pacific Sociol. Soc. (pres. 1982-83), Nat. Council Crime and Delinquency. Home: 1100 SW Hillcroft Dr Portland OR 97225

GIBBONS, JAMES JOSEPH, engineering company executive, former army officer; b. Lawrence, Mass., Dec. 14, 1919; s. James

Joseph and Lillian (MacCormack) G.; m. Dorothy Cain, Sept. 18, 1943; children: Patricia, James, Robert, Susan. A.B. in chemistry, Harvard U., 1941; M.S. in Internat. Affiars, George Washington U., 1964. Comd. 2d lt. U.S. Army, 1941, advanced through grades to maj. gen., 1965, ret., 1973; with Bechtel Group, San Francisco, 1974—; mgr. office facilities Bechtel Power Corp., San Francisco, 1982—. Decorated D.S.M., Legion of Merit with oak leaf cluster. Home: 2085 9th Ave San Francisco CA 94116 Office: Bechtel Power Corp PO Box 3965 San Francisco CA 94119

GIBBONS, JERRY LEE, advt. exec.; b. Coalinga, Calif., Feb. 10, 1936; s. James A. and Hazel Bernice (Drummond) G.; m. Alba Valdez, Feb. 22, 1963; children—Jeffery Scott, Cristin Lyn, Trisha Leigh. B.A., U. Calif., San Jose, 1958. Trainee Young & Rubicam, San Francisco, 1957; account exec. McCann-Erickson, San Francisco, 1960-63; asst. to pres. Western Outdoor Markets, San Francisco, 1964; v.p., sales mgr. Naegele Outdoor Advt., Oakland, 1965-67; account exec. Blair Radio Co., San Francisco, 1968; Campbell-Ewald, San Francisco, 1969; v.p., account supr. Dailey & Assos., San Francisco, 1970-71; co-founder, pres. Pritikin & Gibbons Communications, San Francisco, 1971-73; pres. Ayer, Pritikin & Gibbons, San Francisco, 1973—; guest lectr. San Jose State U., 1965-70, San Francisco State U., 1970-73. Mem. adv. bd. Nat. Assn. Visually Handicapped, 1968-72; dir., mem. exec. com. Oakland Symphony Orch. Assn., 1979—; elder Montclair Presbyn. Ch., Oakland, 1974—. Served with U.S. Army, 1958-60. Mem. Am. Assn. Advt. Agys. (bd. govs. No. Calif. chpt.), Sales and Mktg. Assn. San Francisco (chmn. publicity com. 1975-76), San Francisco Soc. Communicating Arts (pres., dir. 1975-78), Alpha Delta Sigma (past pres., dir.). Clubs: San Francisco Advt., Montclair Swim and Raquet. Home: 1767 Woodhaven Way Oakland CA 94611 Office: 425 Bush St San Francisco CA 94108

GIBBONS, JOHN HOWARD, physicist, government official; b. Harrisonburg, Va., Jan. 15, 1929; s. Howard K. and Jessie C. G.; m. Mary Ann Hobart, May 21, 1955; children—Virginia Neil, Diana Conrad, Mary Marshall. B.S. in Math. and Chemistry, Randolph-Macon Coll., 1949, Sc.D., 1977; Ph.D. in Physics, Duke U., 1954. Group leader nuclear geophysics Oak Ridge Nat. Lab., 1954-69, dir. environ. program, 1969-73; dir. Office Energy Conservation, Fed. Energy Adminstrn., Washington, 1973-74; prof. physics, dir. Energy, Environ. and Resources Center, U. Tenn., Knoxville, 1974-79; dir. Office of Tech. Assessment, U.S. Congress, 1979—; chmn. panel on demand and conservation CONAES Study Nat. Acad. Sci., 1975-79; mem. adv. panel div. policy research and analysis NSF, 1978-79; chmn. adv. com. energy and environ. systems div. Argonne Nat. Lab., 1977-79; Mem. sr. adv. panel Energy Modeling Forum, 1980—; adv. bd. Land Pavilion EPCOT, 1980—; chmn. steering group Aspen Inst. Energy, 1981—; dir., Resources for the Future, 1983—; dir., mem. bd. sci. and tech. Internat. Devel., Nat. Acad. Scis., 1979—. Contbr. articles to profl. jours. Chmn. bd. assocs. Randolph-Macon Coll., 1980—. Recipient Disting. Service award Fed. Energy Adminstrn., 1974. Fellow Am. Phys. Soc., AAAS; mem. Sigma Xi, Pi Gamma Mu, Phi Beta Kappa, Omicron Delta Kappa, Pi Mu Epsilon. Episcopalian. Club: Cosmos. Home: 800 N Carolina Ave SE Washington DC 20003 also Sassafras Hill Farm Route 4 Concord TN 37720 Office: 600 Pennsylvania Ave SE Washington DC 20510 *My formal training in physics, backed by a liberal arts education, enabled me to drink deeply from the sweet spring of basic research for many years. When I took the opportunity to leave the shelter of my disciplinary research and become immersed in analysis of socio-technical issues, it was a most discomforting step. But having taken it, the new challenges are not only enlivening, but also surprisingly susceptible to the problem-solving approaches I had learned in science. The lessons? (1)Training in physics is an effective instrument to learn how to solve many kinds of problems; (2)A change in professional direction about every decade is a great tonic; (3)Attacking issues from fresh perspectives, including bringing seemingly orthogonal experiences to bear, is a natural ingredient of creativity.*

GIBBONS, JOHN JOSEPH, judge; b. Newark, Dec. 8, 1924; s. Daniel Lehane and Julia (Murray) G.; m. Mary Jeanne Boyle, Apr. 19, 1952; children—Daniel J., Mary E., Nora F., Richard G., Deirdre E., Maude A., David C. B.S., Holy Cross Coll., 1947, LL.D., 1970; LL.B. cum laude, Harvard U., 1950. Bar: N.J. bar 1950. Partner law firm Crummy, Gibbons & O'Neill, Newark, 1953-70; circuit judge U.S. Ct. of Appeals, 3d Circuit, 1970—; adj. prof. law Seton Hall U., Rutgers U., Suffolk U.; Mem. N.J. Bd. Bar Examiners, Trenton, 1959-64, chmn., 1963-64; mem. Gov.'s Select Commn. on Civil Disorders, N.J. Council Against Crime. Author articles in field. Trustee Practising Law Inst., 1973—, Holy Cross Coll., 1970—. Served to lt. (j.g.) USNR, 1943-46. Fellow Am. Bar Found.; mem. ABA (ho. of dels. 1968), N.J. Bar Assn. (pres. 1967-68), Essex County Bar Assn. (trustee 1961-64), Holy Cross Coll. Gen. Alumni Assn. (trustee, v.p. 1967-70). Home: 50 Grosvenor Rd Short Hills NJ 07078 Office: US Courthouse Newark NJ 07102

GIBBONS, JOSEPH JOHN, builders supply company controller; b. Wheatland, Wyo., Mar. 18, 1906; s. Michael and Edith (D'Arcy) G.; m. Hazel M. Bisson, Jan. 1, 1930; children: Betty Louise (Mrs. Donald G. Smith), Albert J., Robert J. Ph.B., U. Chgo., 1930; student, Northwestern U., 1931-33, DePaul U. Law Sch., 1933-35. C.P.A., Ill. Office mgr. George Hardin Constrn. Co., Chgo., 1927-35; exam. agt. IRS, 1935-40; sr. tax accountant Arthur Andersen and Co. (C.P.A.'s), Chgo., 1941; tax supr. U.S. Steel Corp., Duluth, Minn. and; Pitts., 1941-50; mgr. tax and ins. dept. Mine Safety Appliances Co., 1950-52; with Blaw-Knox Co., 1952-69, treas., 1967-68, v.p. finance, 1968-69; pres. Corde Co., 1967-69; treas. Blaw Knox Can. Ltd., 1967-69; controller Cleve. Builders Supply Co., 1969—. Mem. Am. Inst. C.P.A.'s, Tau Kappa Epsilon, Alpha Kappa Psi. Presbyn. (elder). Clubs: Crystal Lake Country., Deerfield Country. Home: Apt 303 1161 Ocean Blvd Hillsboro Beach FL 33062 *I do not think people are born equal, either in health or wealth; but I do think that in America, people have a greater opportunity of making the most of their potentials than in any other country in the world.*

GIBBONS, PETER JAMES, agribusiness company executive; b. Boston, May 24, 1937; s. Joseph Francis and Helene Gertrude (MacDonald) G.; m. Carole Anthony Miller, Feb. 23, 1962; children: Pamela, P.J., Christopher. A.B. in Econs., Providence Coll., 1959; M.B.A., Babson Inst., Wellesley Hills, Mass., 1962. With Raytheon Co., Lexington, Mass., 1962-70; fin. area dir. Borden Inc., Toronto, 1970-76; asst. v.p. fin. Gold Kist Inc., Atlanta, 1976-78, v.p. fin., 1978—; treas. AgriInternat., Atlanta, 1978—; chmn. Agvestments, Atlanta, 1980—; dir. ISC Leasing, Mpls., 1981—. Mgr. Sandy Springs (Ga.) Youth Sports, 1981-82. Served with Army NG, 1960-66. Mem. Fin. Exec. Inst. Club: Dunwood (Ga.) Country. Lodge: Kiwanis. Home: 7545 Ball Mill Rd Dunwood GA 30338 Office: Gold Kist Inc 244 Perimeter Pkwy NE Atlanta GA 30301

GIBBONS, ROBERT EBBERT, college president; b. Sharon, Pa., Nov. 15, 1940; s. Thomas Michael and Mary Jane (Ebbert) G.; m. Patricia Arlene Fox, Aug. 18, 1962; children: Patrick, Timothy, Roberta, Aaron. B.S., John Carroll U., 1962; M.A., Bowling Green State U., 1963, Ph.D., 1967. Asst. prof. English Our Lady of the Lake U., San Antonio, 1969-72, chmn. English dept., 1972-74, dir. humanities div., 1974-77, exec. asst. to pres., 1977-80; pres. Viterbo Coll., LaCrosse, Wis., 1980—. Bd. dirs. Wis. Found. of Ind. Colls., Milw., 1980—, Great River Festival of the Arts, LaCrosse, 1983—; mem. exec. council Gateway Area council Boy Scouts Am., LaCrosse, 1981—. Served to capt. U.S. Army, 1967-69. Mem. Am. Assn. Higher Edn., Nat. Assn. Ind. Colls. and Univs., Council Ind. Colls., AAUP, Wis. Assn. Ind. Colls. and Univs. (exec. com. 1983—), Assn. Cath. Colls. and Univs., Phi Kappa Phi. Roman Catholic. Club: LaCrosse. Home: 2812 Bliss Rd LaCrosse WI 54601 Office: Viterbo College 815 S 9th St LaCrosse WI 54601

GIBBONS, RONALD JOHN, microbiologist, educator; b. N.Y.C., Dec. 10, 1932; s. Ronald John and Martha Edith (Smith) G.; m. Marcia E. Day, Aug. 29, 1959; children: Sarah J., John A., David P. B.S., Wagner Coll., 1954; M.S., U. Md., 1956, Ph.D., 1958; Dr. Odontology (hon.), U. Goteborg, 1977, Dr. Medicine, U. Utrecht, 1981. Sr. staff mem., head dept. microbiology, asst. dir. Forsyth Dental Center, Boston, 1958—; clin. prof. oral biology Harvard U. Sch. Dental Medicine, Boston, 1958—. Contbr. articles to sci. jours. Recipient USPHS Career Devel. award, 1964-68. Mem. Internat. Assn. for Dental Research (award for basic research in oral sci. 1967), AAAS, Am. Soc. Microbiology, Sigma Xi. Home: 34 Priscilla Circle Wellesley MA 02181 Office: 140 Fenway St Boston MA 02115

GIBBONS, SAM MELVILLE, congressman; b. Tampa, Fla., Jan. 20, 1920; s. Gunby and Jessie Kirk (Cralle) G.; m. Martha Hanley, Sept. 14, 1946; children: Clifford, Mark, Timothy. J.D., U. Fla., 1947. Bar: Fla. bar 1947. Mem. Fla. Ho. of Reps. from, Hillsborough County, 1952-58, Fla. Senate, 1958-62, 88th-98th Congresses, 7th Dist. Fla., 1962—, mem. ways and means com. Founder, 1st pres. U.S. Fla. Found., 1958. Served to maj. AUS, 1941-45; ETO. Decorated Bronze Star; named Outstanding Young Man Tampa Jr. C. of C., 1954; recipient President's award Tampa C. of C., 1955. Mem. Tampa Bar Assn. (dir.), Hillsborough Bar Assn. (dir.), Greater Tampa C. of C. (dir.). Democrat. Presbyn. (deacon). Office: 2204 Rayburn House Office Bldg Washington DC 20515

GIBBONS, THOMAS MICHAEL, communications executive; b. Springfield, Mass., Nov. 11, 1925; s. Michael D. and Elizabeth A. (McCarthy) G.; m. Rita M. Nicholas, Jan. 14, 1950; children: Michael, Timothy, Gregory, Kathleen, Thomas, Mary Patricia, Brian, David. B.S., John Carroll U., 1949. With C&P Telephone Cos., 1956-73; dir. mktg. AT&T, N.Y.C., 1973-75; v.p. C&P Telephone Co. Md., Balt., 1975-79; exec. v.p., chief operating officer C&P Telephone Cos., Washington, 1979-82, pres., chief exec. officer, 1983—; dir. Arundel Corp., Towson, Md., Am. Security Bank, Washington. Washington trustee Fed. City Council; bd. dirs. Nat. Capital area council Boy Scouts Am., Bethesda, Md., Washington/Balt. Regional Assn. Served with USN, 1944-46. Roman Catholic. Office: C&P Telephone Cos 1710 H St NW Washington DC 20006

GIBBONS, WILLIAM REGINALD, JR., poet, editor; b. Houston, Jan. 7, 1947; s. William Reginald and Elizabeth (Lubowski) G.; m. Virginia Margaret Harris, June 8, 1968 (div. July 1982); m. Cornelia Maude Spelman, Aug. 8, 1983. A.B., Princeton U., 1969; M.A., Stanford U., 1971, Ph.D., 1974. Instr. Spanish Livingston Coll., Rutgers U., New Brunswick, N.J., 1975-76; lectr. creative writing Princeton U., 1976-80, Columbia U., N.Y.C., 1980-81; editor TriQuarterly, lectr. English (Northwestern U.), Evanston, Ill., 1981—. Author: Roofs Voices Roads, 1979 (Quar. Rev. prize), The Ruined Motel, 1981; translator: Selected Poems of Luis Gernuda, 1978, Guillen on Guillen, 1979; editor: The Poet's Work, 1979. Fulbright fellow, Spain, 1971-72; Woodrow Wilson fellow Stanford U., 1969-70; Guggenheim fellow, 1983-84; recipient Translation Prize Denver Quarterly, 1977. Mem. P.E.N. Am. Center, Poetry Soc. Am. Office: TriQuarterly Northwestern U. 1735 Benson Ave Evanston IL 60201

GIBBS, ALAN JOHN, govt. ofcl.; b. Chicago Heights, Ill., June 12, 1938; s. Irvin Willard and Rose Evelyn (Woodman) G.; m. Martha Ferguson, Jan. 1960; children—Philip, Cynthia. B.S. in Mgmt, U. Ill., 1960, M.A. in Labor and Indsl. Relations, 1963. Labor-mgmt. relations examiner NLRB, Balt., 1963-66; tech. assistance officer Equal Employment Opportunity Commn., Washington, 1966-68, area dir., Birmingham, Ala., 1968-70; asst. health services adminstr. N.Y.C. Health Services Adminstrn., 1970-72, first dep. commr. of health, 1972-74; dep. commr. N.J. Dept. Human Services, Trenton, 1974-77; asst. sec. army for installations, logistics and fin. mgmt. Dept. Army, Washington, 1977-81; sec. Wash. State Dept. Social and Health Services, Olympia, 1981—. Recipient Meritorious Service award EEOC, 1967; Disting. Civilian Service award Dept. Army, 1981. Mem. Indsl. Relations Research Assn., Am. Soc. Pub. Adminstrn. Democrat. Unitarian. Home: 1314 Eskridge Blvd Olympia WA 98501 Office: Mail Stop OB44 Olympia WA 98504

GIBBS, CLIFFORD EDGAR, architect; b. Jan. 11, 1926; s. John Harold and Doris Mary (Murray) G.; m. Ione Joyce Williams, Jan. 31, 1948; children—Steven, Stuart, Janice. Student, Tufts Coll., 1943-45; B.Arch., U. Mich., 1950. Archtl. draftsman MacKenzie, Knuth & Klein (architects), Flint, Mich., 1950-55; pvt. practice architecture, Flint, also Grand Blanc, Mich., 1956—. Prin. works include: Genesee Area Skill Center, 1968, Trade Tech. Bldg, 1967, Student Center, Genesee Community Coll., 1973, Grand Blanc Twp. Govt. Center, 1976. Mem. Grand Blanc Regional Planning Com., 1967-71. Served to lt. (j.g.) USNR, 1943-46. Recipient 1st Honor award for Kimbrough residence Flint area chpt. A.I.A., 1964; award for restaurant Progressive Architecture mag., 1957; Nat. award for Parkland Presbyn. Ch. Nat. Council Chs., 1958; cited for Grand Blanc Elementary Sch. Am. Assn. Sch. Adminstrs., 1967. Mem. AIA (charter pres. Flint area chpt. 1961), Mich. Soc. Architects (bd. dirs. 1962). Home: 7322 Porter Rd Grand Blanc MI 48439

GIBBS, DAVID GEORGE, food processing company executive; b. Vancouver, C., Can., May 5, 1925; s. Albert Edward and Florence (Bedford) G.; m. Lenore Joyce De Geer, Oct. 7, 1949; 1 dau., Susan Caroline. Grad. high sch.; M.B.A., Simon Fraser U., 1975. C.P.A., Can. Audit clk. Price Waterhouse (chartered accountants), 1943-46; with Kelly Douglas Co. Ltd., Vancouver, 1946—, controller, 1965—, v.p., 1975—. Named Ky. col., 1968. Mem. Fin. Execs. Inst. Clubs: Capilano Lions (charter pres. 1977), Masons.). Home: 956 Belgroave St North Vancouver BC Canada Office: PO Box 2039 Vancouver BC Canada

GIBBS, DELBRIDGE LINDLEY, lawyer; b. Jacksonville, Fla., Jan. 13, 1917; s. Elbridge Lindley and Myrtle Josephine (King) G.; m. Jane Phillips Reese, Nov. 23, 1947; children: Elizabeth (Mrs. Michael V. Milton), Joanne, Delbridge Lindley. B.S. in Bus. Adminstrn, U. Fla., 1939, LL.B., 1940. Bar: Fla. 1940. Practice in, Jacksonville, 1946—; partner firm Marks, Gray, Conroy & Gibbs, 1957—; mem. 1st Appellate dist. Nominating Commn. State of Fla., 1973-76; co-chmn. Nat. Conf. Reps. Am. Bar Assn.-AMA, 1973-75, mem., 1978—. Trustee U. Fla. Law Center Assn., 1973-80. Served with AUS, 1941-46; col. Res. ret. Fellow Am. Bar Found., Am. Coll. Trial Lawyers; mem. ABA (ho. dels. 1964-68), Fed. Bar Assn., Jacksonville Bar Assn. (pres. 1956), Fla. Bar (pres. 1963-64), Duval County Legal Aid Assn. (pres. 1952), Am. Judicature Soc., Judge Adv. Assn. Clubs: Rotarian., River, Timuquana Country (Jacksonville); Ponte Vedra (Ponte Vedra Beach, Fla.). Home: 4101 Venetia Blvd Jacksonville FL 32210 Office: PO Box 447 Jacksonville FL 32201

GIBBS, DONALD ROBERT, telecommunications executive; b. Keithley, Yorkshire, Eng., Dec. 13, 1945; s. Robert Lionel and Alice (Baker) G. B.Com., U. Ottawa, Ont., Can., 1969. Registered indsl. acct. Acct. M. Loeb Ltd., Ottawa, 1969-70, Leigh Instruments, 1970-72, Leigh Systems Ltd., Syracuse, N.Y., 1972-73; mgr. fin. Dylex Ltd., Toronto, 1973-75; comptroller Leigh Instruments, Ottawa, 1975-76; exec. v.p., chief ops. office Mitel Corp., Ottawa, 1976—. Office: Mitel Corp 350 Legget Dr Kanata ON Canada K2K 1X3

GIBBS, FREDERICK WINFIELD, communications company executive; b. Buffalo, Mar. 22, 1932; s. Walter L. M. and Elizabeth Mari (Georgi) G.; m. Josephine Janice Jarvis, Dec. 20, 1954; children: Michael, Mathew, Robyn. B.A. cum laude, Alfred U., 1954. With N.Y. Telephone Co., 1954-65; with ITT, 1965—; mng. dir. ITT Standard Electrica, S.A., 1971-75; chief exec. officer ITT Standard Electrica, Brazil, 1975-77, exec. dir. ops. ITT Communications Ops. Group, 1977; corp. v.p. ITT, 1977—; pres. U.S. Telephone and Telegraph Corp., 1977-79, exec. dir., sr. group exec., 1980—; dir. System 12, ITT, 1979-80; exec. v.p. ITT, 1980—, ITT Telecommunications Corp., 1983—. Trustee Alfred U., 1981—. Served with USMC, 1954-56. Home: 52 Stonefence Rd Allendale NJ 07401 Office: 320 Park Ave New York NY 10022

GIBBS, JOE JACKSON, professional football coach; b. Mocksville, N.C., Nov. 25, 1940. B.S., San Diego State U., 1964, M.S., 1966. Asst. coach San Diego State U., 1966, Fla. State U., 1967-68, U. So. Calif., 1969-70, U. Ark., 1971-72; asst. coach St. Louis Cardinals, NFL, 1973-77, Tampa Bay Buccaneers, 1978, San Diego Chargers, 1979-80; head coach Washington Redskins, 1981—; coached team to NFL Super Bowl championship, 1984. Office: Washington Redskins 13832 Redskin Dr PO Box 17247 Dulles Internat Airport Washington DC 20041 *

GIBBS, JUNE NESBITT, former Republican nat. committeewoman; b. Newton, Mass., June 13, 1922; s. Samuel Frederick and Lulu (Glazier) Nesbitt; m. Donald T. Gibbs, Dec. 8, 1945; 1 dau., Elizabeth. B.A. in Math, Wellesley Coll., 1943, M.A., Boston U., 1947. Mem. Republican Nat. Com. from, R.I., 1969-80; sec. Republican Nat. Com., 1977-80; mem. def. adv. com. Women in Services, 1970-72, vice chmn., 1972. Mem. Middletown Town Council, 1974-80, 82—, pres., 1978-80. Served to lt. (J.G.) USNR, 1942-46. Home: 163 Riverview Ave Middletown RI 02840 *To help restore faith in our government every elected official must constantly seek to do all he can for the people he serves and continually guard against doing anything which is self-serving or takes personal advantage of his office in any way.*

GIBBS, MARLA (MARGARET GIBBS), actress; b. Chgo., June 14, 1931; d. Douglas and Ophelia Birdie (Kemp) Bradley; children: Angela Elayne, Jordan Joseph, Dorian Demetrius. Student, Cortez Peters Bus. Sch., Chgo., 1950-52. Receptionist Service Bindery, Chgo., 1951-56; Addressograph machine operator Kelly Girls, 1956; switchboard operator Gotham Hotel, Chgo., 1957; info. operator Dept. Street Rwys., 1957; travel cons. United Airlines, Detroit, 1963-74; v.p. Hormar, Inc., Los Angeles, 1978—; pres. Marla Gibbs Enterprises, Los Angeles, 1978—. Actress Florence the Maid: The Jefferson's, 1974—. Recipient Image award NAACP, 1979, 80, 81, 82, 83; Appreciation award Los Angeles Sch. Dist., 1978; awards Nat. Acad. TV Arts and Scis., 1976, Miss Black Culture Pageant, 1977, United Negro Coll. Fund, 1977, Nat. Com. Household Employment, 1978, Women Involved, 1979, Paul Robeson Players, 1980, Watts Reportory Co., 1980, Calif. State Assembly, 1980; Community Service award Crenshaw High Sch., 1980; Emmy nominee, 1981, 82, 83. Mem. Sci. of Mind Ch. Office: 8461 S Vermont Ave Los Angeles CA 90044 *I thought I knew how to love but forgot to include myself. I learned my lesson and took my first real step in faith.*

GIBBS, MARTIN, educator, biologist; b. Phila., Nov. 11, 1922; s. Samuel and Rose (Sugarman) G.; m. Svanhild Karen Kvale, Oct. 11, 1950; children—Janet Helene, Laura Jean, Steven Joseph, Michael Seland, Robert Kvale. B.S., Phila. Coll. Pharmacy, 1943; Ph.D., U. Ill., 1947. Scientist Brookhaven Nat. Lab., 1947-56; prof. biochemistry Cornell U., 1957-64; prof. biology, chmn. dept. Brandeis U., Waltham, Mass., 1965—; Cons. NSF, 1961-64, 69-72, NIH, 1966-69; mem. corp. Marine Biol. Lab., Woods Hole, Mass., 1970—; RESA lectr., 1969; NATO cons. fellowship bd., 1968-70; mem. Council Internat. Exchange of Scholars, 1976—; chmn. adv. com. selection Fulbright scholars for Eastern Europe; adj. prof. Bot. Inst., U. Münster, W.Ger. Author: Structure and Function of Chloroplasts; Editor-in-chief: Plant Physiology, 1963—; asso. editor: Physiologie Vegetale, 1966—, Ann. Rev. Plant Physiology, 1966-71. Mem. AAUP, Am., Japanese socs. plant physiologists, Am. Acad. Arts and Scis., Am. Soc. Biol. Chemists, Council Biology Editors, Nat. Acad. Scis., Sigma Xi. Home: 32 Slocum Rd Lexington MA 02173 Office: Brandeis Univ Waltham MA 02154

GIBBS, MARVIN ERWIN, chemical company executive; b. St. Louis, Dec. 30, 1934; s. Marvin George and Irma Bertha (Martin) G.; m. Nancy Louise Robson, June 18, 1960; children: Jennifer, Deborah. B.S., Washington U., 1956, D.Sc., 1960. Research group leader Monsanto, St. Louis, 1971-77, mgr. research, 1977-78, dir. plan and control., 1978-80, dir. research-devel., 1980-82; dir. process tech. (Monsanto), 1983—. Mem. Am. Inst. Chem. Engrs. Home: 13445 Kings Glen Dr Saint Louis MO 63131 Office: Monsanto 800 N Lindbergh Blvd Saint Louis MO 63167

GIBBS, RAYMOND DOUGLAS, tenor, educator; b. Tucson, Dec. 3, 1942; s. Benjamin Franklin and Bernice June (Cletus) G. B.A. in Music, San Diego State U., 1966; M.M. in Opera Theater, Manhattan Sch. Music, 1968; student, Merola Tng. Program, San Francisco, 1965. Disting. prof. music Memphis State U., 1978-83; bd. dirs. Opera Memphis. Debut as Wagner in: Faust, San Diego Opera, 1966; mem. co., N.Y.C. Opera, 1968-74, Met. Opera, 1970—; leading tenor, 1973—; appeared as Tony in: N.Y. Premiere of Help, Help, The Globolinks, 1969; appeared in Met. Opera premier of: Lulu, 1976; leading tenor in revival and 1st English lang. performance of: Resurrection by Franco Alfano, 1983; repetoire includes: Don Jose in Carmen, Radames in Aida; Can. debut, Edmonton Opera Co., 1982. Regional winner San Francisco Opera Auditions, 1965; recipient award Music Makers, San Diego, 1964; Sullivan Found. grantee, 1967. Mem. Phi Mu Alpha. Changed from baritone to tenor while singing at Met. Opera.

GIBBS, RICHARD LESLIE, pub. relations firm exec.; b. Kewanee, Ill., Mar. 20, 1927; s. Harry Allen and Myrtle Mary (Haxton) G.; m. Joan Barbara Cornelius, Apr. 16, 1965; children—Elizabeth Haxton, Lesley Atherton, Jonathan Cornelius. B.S., U. Ill., 1949, M.S., 1950. Editor, pub. Adams County Rep., Brighton, Colo., 1950-51; asst. advt. and pub. relations mgr. Pub. Service Co. Colo., Denver, 1951-53; advt. and publicity mgr. Agrl. div. Shell Chem. Co., Denver and N.Y.C., 1953-55; account dir. Communications Counselors, Inc., McCann-Erickson, Inc., N.Y.C., 1955-56; pub. relations dir. Albert Sidney Noble, Advt., N.Y.C., 1956-69; group head dir. agrl. communications Burson-Marsteller, N.Y.C., 1969-71; pres. Gibbs & Soell, Inc., N.Y.C., 1971—. Served with AUS, 1945-46. Mem. Am. Agrl. Editors Assn., Sigma Delta Chi. Republican. Congregationalist. Office: 126 E 38th St New York NY 10016

GIBBS, SARAH PREBLE, biologist, educator; b. Boston, May 25, 1930; d. Winthrop Harold and Edith Dorothea (Hill) Bowker; m. Robert H. Gibbs, June 9, 1951 (div. 1962); 1 dau., Elizabeth Dorothea; m. Ronald J. Poole, Feb. 2, 1963 (div. 1980); 1 son, Christopher Harold. A.B., Cornell U., 1952, M.S., 1954; Ph.D., Harvard U., 1962. Research asso. Inst. Animal Genetics Edinburgh U., 1963-65; asst. prof. botany McGill U., Montreal, Que., Can., 1966-69, asso. prof. biology, 1969-74, prof., 1974—. Contbr. articles to profl. jours. Recipient Darbaker prize Bot. Soc. Am., 1965; NSF fellow, 1958-61; NIH fellow, 1961-63. Mem. Can. Soc. Cell Biology (pres. 1972-73), Am. Soc. Cell Biology, Am. Soc. Plant Physiologists, Phycol. Soc. Am., Soc. Evolutionary Protistology, AAAS, Can. Assn. Univ. Tchrs., Phi Beta Kappa, Sigma Xi, Phi Kappa Phi. Unitarian. Home: 70 Henley Ave Montreal PQ H3P 1V3 Canada Office: Dept Biology McGill U 1205 Avenue Docteur Penfield Montreal PQ H3A 1B1 Canada

GIBBS, WILLIAM EUGENE, chem. co. exec.; b. Akron, Ohio, Sept. 23, 1930; s. Marvin Hill and Mary (Frame) G.; m. Carol Ullrich, Oct. 3, 1948 (div. June 1968); children—Sheryl Gibbs McClary, Shelley Gibbs Infantino, Susan Gibbs Witt, Sharon Gibbs Gudorff, Scott; m. S. Janet Cottingim Sullender, Aug. 28, 1970; stepchildren—David Sullender, Leslie Sullender, Eric Sullender. B.S., U. Akron, 1954, M.S., 1954, Ph.D., 1959. Staff research chemist U. Akron Inst. Polymer Sci., 1953-55; research chemist Goodyear Tire & Rubber Co., Akron, 1955-58, Air Force Materials Lab., Wright Patterson AFB, Ohio, 1960-61, group leader, 1961-62, acting br. chief, 1962-64, br. chief, 1964-66, dir. polymer br., 1966-70; v.p., dir. research and devel. Foster Grant Co., Leominster, Mass., 1970-77; v.p., dir. research and devel., plastics div. Am. Hoechst Corp., Leominster, 1978—. Served to lt. USAF, 1958-60. Mem. Am. Chem. Soc. (chmn. div. polymer chemistry 1971), Nat. Acad. Sci. (com. macromolecules 1967—, com. fire toxicology 1976—), AAAS, Soc. Plastics Engrs., Faraday Soc., Soc. Chem. Industry, Ohio Acad. Sci., Alpha Chi Sigma. Home: 21 Pearl Brook Rd Lunenburg MA 01463 Office: 289 N Main St Leominster MA 01453

GIBIAN, GEORGE, educator; b. Prague, Czechoslovakia, Jan. 29, 1924; came to U.S., 1940, naturalized, 1944; s. Richard and Vera (Sindelarova) G.; m. J. Catherine Annis, Sept. 2, 1950 (div. Aug. 1967); children—Peter, Mark, Stephen, Gregory, Lauren. A.B., U. Pitts., 1943; M.A., Johns Hopkins U., 1947; Ph.D., Harvard U., 1951. Instr. to assoc. prof. Smith Coll., 1951-59; asst. prof. Amherst Coll., 1952-54; asso. prof. Russian lit. U. Calif., Berkeley, 1959-60; Goldwin Smith prof. Russian lit. Cornell U., Ithaca, N.Y., 1961—, chmn. dept. Russian lit., 1962-73, 78-82, chmn. Soviet Studies com., 1981-82; sr. assoc. Columbia U. Russian Inst., 1969; Exec. sec. Masaryk Publs. Trust, 1978—; chmn. bd. overseers com. to visit Ukrainian Research Inst., Harvard U. Author: Tolstoy and Shakespeare, 1957, Interval of Freedom: Soviet Literature During the Thaw, 1960, Russia's Lost Literature of the Absurd, 1971; Editor: Critical Editions of Crime and Punishment: War and Peace: Anna Karenina, 1964, 66, 69; co-editor: Russian Modernism: Culture and the Avant-Garde, 1976; Contbr. articles to profl. jours. Served with inf. AUS, 1943-46. Decorated Bronze Star medal with V, Combat Inf. badge.; Guggenheim fellow, 1959-60; Fulbright research fellow U. Paris, 1960; Nat. Endowment for Humanities sr. fellow, 1974; Internat. Research Exchanges Bd. grantee to visit USSR and Czechoslovakia, 1965-66. Mem. Am. Assn. Tchrs. Slavic and East European Langs., Comparative Lit. Assn. Am., Am. Assn. for Advancement Slavic Studies. Clubs: Adirondack 46'ers, Adirondack Mountain. Home: 311 Roat St Ithaca NY 14850 Office: Dept Russian Lit Cornell U Ithaca NY 14853

GIBIAN, THOMAS GEORGE, chemical executive; b. Prague, Czechoslovakia, Mar. 20, 1922; came to U.S., 1940, naturalized, 1951; s. Richard and Vera (Sindelar) G.; m. Laura Cynthia Sutherland, Feb. 19, 1949; children: Barbara Mary, Janet Cynthia, Thomas Richard, David George. B.S., U. N.C., 1942; Ph.D., Carnegie Mellon U., 1948. Research chemist Atlantic Refining Co., 1948-51; with W.R. Grace & Co., 1951-74; devel. engr. Dewey & Almy (Chem. div.); plant mgr., gen. mgr. battery separators, v.p., gen. mgr. organic chems. div., tech. group exec., corp. v.p.; pres. Chem. Constrn. Corp., N.Y.C., 1974-76; plant mgr., gen. mgr. battery separators, v.p., gen. mgr. organic chems. div., tech. group, corp. v.p.; pres. TGI Corp., Inc., 1976-80; dir., exec. v.p., chief operating officer Henkel of Am., Inc.; also pres., chief exec. officer dir. Henkel Corp. Bd. dirs. Sandy Spring Friends Sch., Montgomery Gen. Hosp.; trustee Carnegie-Mellon U., mem. vis. com. chemistry dept. Served with RAF, 1942-46. Recipient Merit award Carnegie-Mellon U., 1975, Internat. Palladium medal, 1983. Mem. Am. Chem. Soc., Am. Inst. Chem. Engrs., Indsl. Research Inst. Clubs: Cosmos (Washington); Union League (N.Y.C.); Univ. (Pitts.); RAF (London). Home: Box 219 Sandy Spring MD 20860 Office: 600 Madison Ave New York NY 10022

GIBLETT, ELOISE ROSALIE, hematology educator; b. Tacoma, Wash., Jan. 17, 1921; d. William Richard and Rose (Godfrey) G. B.S., U. Wash., 1942, M.S., 1947, M.D. with honors, 1951. Mem. faculty U. Wash. Sch. Medicine, 1957—, research prof., 1967—; asso. dir., head immunogenetics Puget Sound Blood Center, 1955-79, exec. dir., 1979—; former mem. several research coms. NIH. Author: Genetic Markers in Human Blood, 1969; Editorial bd.: Transfusion; Contbr. over 180 articles to profl. jours. Recipient fellowships, grants, Emily Cooley, Karl Landsteiner, Philip Levine and Alexander Wiener immunohematology awards. Fellow AAAS; Mem. Nat. Acad. Scis., Am. Soc. Human Genetics (pres. 1973), Am. Soc. Hematology, Am. Assn. Immunologists, Brit. Soc. Immunology, Internat. Soc. Hematologists, Am. Fedn. Clin. Research, Western Assn. Physicians, Assn. Am. Physicians, Sigma Xi, Alpha Omega Alpha. Home: 6533 53d St NE Seattle WA 98115 Office: Puget Sound Blood Center Terry and Madison Sts Seattle WA 98104

GIBLIN, EDWARD J., company director; b. 1917; married. B.S., Fordham U.; M.B.A., N.Y. U. With Peat, Marwick, Mitchell & Co. (C.P.A.s), prior to 1953; with Ex-Cell-O Corp., 1953—, v.p., treas., 1968-69, exec. v.p., 1969, pres., chief exec. officer, 1970-78, chmn. bd., 1978-82; ret., 1982; chief exec. officer Ex-Cell-O Corp., 1978-81, also dir.; dir. Detroit Bank and Trust Co., Tecumseh Products Co., Detroit Edison Co. Address: Ex-Cell-O Corp 2855 Coolidge Troy MI 48084

GIBLIN, PATRICK DAVID, banker; b. St. Louis, July 24, 1932; s. Patrick Joseph and Ann Jane (Gill) G.; children: Mary Clare, Christopher, Gregory. B.B.A., Manhattan Coll., 1954; M.B.A., St. John's U., Jamaica, N.Y., 1965. Staff auditor Peat, Marwick, Mitchell & Co., N.Y.C., 1956-59; chief plant acct. div. Am. Machine & Foundry, Bklyn., 1959-63; with CBS, N.Y.C., 1963-73, controller electronic video rec. div., 1968-73, dir. corp. acctg., 1967-68; exec. v.p. fin. United Va. Bankshares, Inc., Richmond, 1973—. Served with U.S. Army, 1954-56. Mem. Delta Mu Delta. Roman Catholic. Home: 13 Dahlgren Rd Richmond VA 23233 Office: 919 E Main St Richmond VA 23219

GIBNEY, FRANK BRAY, publisher, editor, writer, foundation executive; b. Scranton, Pa., Sept. 21, 1924; s. Joseph James and Edna May (Wetter) G.; m. Harriet Harvey, Dec. 10, 1948 (div. 1957); children: Alex, Margot; m. 2d Harriet C. Suydam, Dec. 14, 1957 (div. 1971); children: Frank, James, Thomas,; m. 3d Hiroko Doi, Oct. 5, 1972; children: Elise, Josephine. B.A., Yale U., 1945; D. Litt. hon., Kyung Hee U., Seoul, Korea, 1974. Corr., assoc. editor Time mag., N.Y.C., Tokyo and London, 1947-54; sr. editor Newsweek, N.Y.C., 1954-57; staff writer, editorial writer Life mag., N.Y.C., 1957-61; publisher, pres. SHOW mag., N.Y.C., 1961-64; pres. Ency. Brit. (Japan), Tokyo, 1965-69, TBS-Brit., 1969-75, vice chmn., 1976—; v.p. Ency. Brit., Inc., Chgo., 1975-79; vice chmn., bd. editors Ency. Brit., Chgo., 1978—; pres. Pacific Basin Inst., Santa Barbara, Calif., 1979—; mem. adv. com. Hubert H. Humphrey Inst., Mpls., 1981—; dir. Hudson Reports Internat., Paris, 1981—, Internat. Ednl. Devel. Co. Ltd., Tokyo; cons. Com. on Space and Aero Ho. of Reps., Washington, 1957-59. Author: Five Gentlemen of Japan, 1953, The Frozen Revolution, 1959, (with Peter Deriabin) The Secret World, 1960, The Operators, 1961, The Khrushchev Pattern, 1961, The Reluctant Space Farers, 1965, Japan: The Fragile Super-Power, 1975, Miracle by Design, 1983; editor: The Penkovskiy Papers, 1965; speech writer: Democratic Nat. Com., 1964. Served to lt. USNR, 1942-46. Decorated Order of the Rising Sun 3d Class, Japan. Fellow Ctr. for the Study of Democratic Instns.; mem. Council on Fgn. Relations, Tokyo Fgn. Corr. Club, Am. C.of C. (Tokyo), Japan-Am. Soc., Japan Soc. Roman Catholic. Clubs: Century Assn., Yale (N.Y.C.); Tokyo; Tavern, The Arts (Chgo.). Home: 1901 E Las Tunas Rd Santa Barbara CA 93103 Office: Ency Britannica Inc 310 S Michigan Ave Chicago IL 60604

GIBOR, AHARON, cell biologist; b. Jaffa, Israel, Sept. 15, 1925; came to U.S., 1948, naturalized, 1954; s. Gedaliao and Hasida (Rosenberg) G.; m. Lynn Stadtner, Jan. 29, 1950; children—Abigail, Sarah. B.A., U. Calif., Berkeley, 1950, M.A., 1952; Ph.D., Stanford U., 1955. Research scientist Alaska Dept. Fish and Game, 1957-59; asst. prof. biology Rockefeller U., 1960-66; prof. U. Calif., Santa Barbara, 1966—. Guggenheim fellow, 1978-79; NSF grantee, 1977-79; NASA grantee, 1978. Mem. Am. Soc. Cell Biology, Internat. Phycological Soc., Sigma Xi. Jewish. Research in cell physiology, eukaryotic flagella and algalpropogation. Office: Biology Dept U Calif Santa Barbara CA 93106

GIBRAN, KAHLIL, sculptor; b. Boston, Nov. 29, 1922; s. Nicholas and Rose (Gibran) G.; m. Jean English, July 1, 1957; children—Timothy; by previous marriage), Nicole. Student, Boston Mus. Sch., 1940-43. Exhibited widely as painter, 1949-52, life sized steel sculpture, 1953—, one-man show bronzes, Cambridge Art Assn., 1977; commd.: bronze plaque of Kahil Gibran, Copley Sq., Boston, 1977, Judge Francis Ford, Fed. Ct. House, Boston, 1977; rep. permanent collections, Pa. Acad., Tenn. Fine Arts Center, Norfolk (Va.) Mus., Chrysler Mus., William Rockhill Gallery, Swope Gallery, Brockton Fine Arts Center.; Author: Sculpture—Kahlil Gibran, 1970, (with wife Jean Gibran) Introduction to Lazarus and His Beloved, 1973, Kahlil Gibran His Life and World, 1974. Pres. Gibran Kahlil Gibran Scholarship Fund, Boston, 1974. Recipient George Widener award Pa. Acad., 1958; Guggenheim fellow, 1959-61; award Nat. Inst. Arts and Letters, 1961; Grand prize Boston Arts Festival, 1964; John Gregory award sculpture, 1965; Gold medal Internat. Sacred Art Show, Trieste, Italy, 1966. Address: 160 W Canton St Boston MA 02118

GIBSON, A.E., steamship lines company executive. Pres. DELTA Steamship Lines Lines, Inc., New Orleans. Office: Delta Steamship Lines Inc PO Box 52050 New Orleans LA 70150§

GIBSON, ALTHEA, tennis player, golfer, state official; b. Silver, S.C., Aug. 25, 1927; d. Daniel and Annie B. (Washington) G.; m. William A. Darben, Oct. 17, 1965; m. Sydney Llwellyn, Apr. 11, 1983. B.S., Fla. A&M. Coll., 1953; D. Pub. Service (hon.), Monmouth Coll., 1980. Amateur tennis player in, U.S., Europe and S.Am., 1941-58; asst. instr. dept. health and phys. edn. Lincoln U., Jefferson City, Mo., 1953-55; made profl. tennis tour with Harlem Globetrotters, 1959; community relations rep. Ward Baking Co., 1959; joined Ladies Profl. Golf Assn. as profl. golfer, 1963; apptd. to N.Y. State Recreation Council, 1964; staff mem. Essex County Park Commn., Newark, 1970, recreation supr., 1970-71; dir. tennis programs, profl. Valley View Racquet Club, Northvale, N.J., 1972; tennis pro Morven, 1973—, athletic commr., State of N.J., 1975—; recreation mgr., City of East Orange, N.J., 1980. Appeared in: movie in The Horse Soldiers, 1958; Author: I Always Wanted to Be Somebody, 1958. Named Woman Athlete of Yr. AP Poll, 1957-58; named to Lawn Tennis Hall of Fame and Tennis Mus., 1971; named to Black Athletes Hall of Fame, 1974; named to S.C. Hall of Fame, 1983; named to Fla. Sports Hall of Fame, 1984. Mem. Alpha Kappa Alpha. Won world profl. tennis championship, 1960. Home: PO Box 768 East Orange NJ 07019

GIBSON, ARRELL MORGAN, history educator; b. Pleasanton, Kans., Dec. 1, 1921; s. Arrell Morgan and Vina Lorene (Davis) G.; m. Dorothy Deitz, Dec. 24, 1942 (div. Apr. 1971); children: Patricia Gibson, Michael Morgan, Kathleen Camille. B.A., U. Okla., 1947, M.A., 1948, Ph.D., 1954. Prof. history Phillips U., Enid, 1949-57; prof. history U. Okla., Norman, 1957—, chmn. dept., 1964, 70—, George Lynn Cross Research prof., 1972—; curator history Stovall Mus., U. Okla., 1959—; vis. prof. Ariz. State U., Tempe, 1973, U. N.Mex., Albuquerque, 1975; Montgomery lectr. U. Nebr., Lincoln, 1978. Author: The Kickapoos, 1963, Life and Death of Colonel Albert Jennings Fountain, 1965, Oklahoma: A History of Five Centuries, 1965, Fort Smith: Little Gibraltar on the Arkansas, 1969, The Chickasaws, 1971, Wilderness Bonanza, 1972, Edward Everett Dale: Frontier Historian, 1975, The West in the Life of the Nation, 1976, The Oklahoma Story, 1978, The American Indian: Prehistory to the Present, 1979, Will Rogers: A Centennial Tribute, 1979, Santa Fe and Taos: Age of the Muses, 1900-1942, 1983. Mem. adv. bd. Mus. Gt. Plains, Lawton, Okla., 1962—. Served with USNR, 1942-45. Recipient Rockefeller Found. U. Okla. Press award, 1961; Am. Philos. Soc. Research grantee, 1963, 69; Duke Found. Research grantee, 1968, 69; U. Okla. Faculty Research grantee, 1957-71; named Okla. Writer of Yr., 1972; Outstanding Alumnus Mo. So. State Coll., 1972. Mem. Am. Hist. Assn., So., Western history assns., Orgn. Am. Historians, Southwestern Social Sci. Assn., Okla. Hist. Soc. (bd. dirs.), Phi Beta Kappa, Phi Alpha Theta. Home: 909 Birch Dr Norman OK 73069 Office: Faculty Exchange U Okla Norman OK 73069

GIBSON, BENJAMIN F., judge; b. Safford, Ala., July 13, 1931; s. Eddie and Pearl Ethel (Richardson) G.; m. Lucille Nelson, June 23, 1951; children: Charlotte, Linda, Gerald, Gail, Carol, Laura. B.S., Wayne State U., 1955; J.D. with distinction, Detroit Coll. Law, 1960. Bar: Mich. 1960. Acct., City of Detroit, 1955-56, Detroit Edison Co., 1956-61; asst. atty. gen., Mich., 1961-63, asst. pros. atty., Ingham County, Mich., 1963-64, pvt. practice law, Lansing, Mich., from 1964; judge U.S. Dist. Ct. Western Dist. Mich., Grand Rapids. Hearing officer, East Lansing; bd. dirs. Lansing Jr. Achievement, Greater Lansing Legal Aid Bur. Mem. Am. Trial Lawyers Assn., Am. Bar Assn., Ingham County Bar Assn., State Bar Mich. (grievance bd. hearing panel 1971), Sigma Pi Phi. Club: Rotary. Office: US Dist Ct 616 Federal Bldg 110 Michigan St NW Grand Rapids MI 49503 *

GIBSON, CHARLES COLMERY, rubber mfg. exec.; b. Edwards, Miss., Sept. 12, 1914; s. William Bayne and Anna (Colmery) G.; m. Margaret Eaton, Nov. 4, 1939; children—William Bayne II, John Clark. A.B., Harvard, 1937, grad. Advanced Mgmt. Program, 1953. With Goodyear Tire & Rubber Co., Akron, Ohio, 1937-73, v.p., 1956-73; mng. partner C.C. Gibson Co., Akron, 1970—. Trustee, pres. Knight Found., 1975—. Served from ensign to lt. comdr. USNR, World War II. Home: 3386 S Smith Rd Akron OH 44313 Office: Knight Foundation One Cascade Plaza Akron OH 44308

GIBSON, CHARLES DEWOLF, broadcast journalist; b. Evanston, Ill., Mar. 9, 1943; s. Burdett and Georgiana (Law) G.; m. Arlene Joy Gibson, July 20, 1976; children: Jessica Law, Katherine Burdett. A.B., Princeton Univ., 1965. Corr. RKO Radio, Washington, 1966; anchorman Sta.-WLVA-TV, Lynchburg, VA, 1967-69, Sta.-WMAL-TV (now WJLA-TV), Washington, 1970-73; corr. TVN, Inc., Washington, 1974-75, AB News, 1975-80, Capitol Hill corr., 1981—. Nat. journalism fellow Nat. Endowment for Humanities Univ. Mich., Ann Arbor, 1973-74. Home: 3511 Rittenhouse St NW Washington DC 20015 Office: ABC News 1717 DeSales St NW Washington DC 20036

GIBSON, COUNT DILLON, JR., physician, educator; b. Covington, Ga., July 10, 1921; s. Count Dillon and Julia (Thompson) G.; m. Katherine Vislocky, June 10, 1950; children—Gabriella, Thomas, Alexis, George. B.S., Emory U., 1942; M.D., 1944. Diplomate: Am. Bd. Internal Medicine. Intern Columbia-Presbyn. Med. Center, 1944-45, asst. resident medicine, 1947-50, med. resident, 1950-51; asst. prof., asso. prof. medicine Med. Coll. Va., 1951-57; prof. preventive medicine, chmn. dept. Tufts U. Sch. Medicine, Boston, 1958-69; physician-in-chief Home Med. Service; attending physician New Eng. Med. Center Hosps.; gen. dir. Tufts-Columbia Point Health Center; vis. physician Boston City Hosp., to 1969; prof., chmn. dept. family, community and preventive medicine Stanford (Calif.) U., 1969—; mem. Calif. Health Manpower Policy Commn., 1977—. Contbr. articles to profl. jours. Bd. dirs. Hayward (Calif.) Vesper Hosp., 1980—. Served from 1st lt. to capt., M.C. AUS, 1945-47. Mem. A.C.P. Roman Catholic. Home: 669 Cabrillo Ave Stanford CA 94305 Office: Stanford U Med Center Stanford CA 94305

GIBSON, DAVID ARGYLE, lawyer; b. Austin, Tex., Apr. 10, 1934; s. Benjamin Argyle and Virginia Claire (Ratlif) G.; m. Yahne Peto, 1981; children: Diane, Laura, Julie. B.S., U. Houston, 1955, J.D., 1957. Bar: Tex. 1957; Cert. in family, civil trial and criminal law Tex. Bd. Legal Specialization. Asst. dist. atty., Harris County, Tex., 1957-59, practiced law, Houston, 1959—; mem. firm Engel, Groom, Miglicco and Gibson, 1975—; Lectr. U. Houston Law Sch., 1975—; pres. Tex. Bill of Rights Found., 1974-75. Chmn. Democratic County Com., 1966-67; bd. dirs. Gulf Coast Legal Found., 1980—. Mem. Houston Bar Assn., Assn. Trial Lawyers Am., Cert. Civil Trial Lawyers Assn. (pres. 1981—), Am. Arbitration Soc. (arbitrator 1970—). Home: 111 W Cowen St Houston TX 77007 Office: 1818 Memorial Dr Houston TX 77007

GIBSON, DAVID MARK, educator, biochemist; b. Kokomo, Ind., Aug. 7, 1923; s. Carl Banta and Marie (Loop) G.; m. Margaret Lockhart, June 2, 1951; children—Carl L., John L., Shauna M., Heather R., Mark C. A.B., Wabash Coll., 1944; M.D., Harvard, 1948. Intern Northwestern U. Med. Sch., 1948-49; research asso. biochemistry U. Ill. at Urbana, 1950-53; research asso., asst. prof. Inst. Enzyme Research, U. Wis., 1953-55, 55-58; asso. prof. biochemistry Ind. U. Sch. Medicine, 1958-61, prof. biochemistry, 1961—, Grace M. Showalter prof., 1974—, chmn., 1967—; vis. prof. U. Padua, 1964-65, U. Utrecht, 1975; established investigator Am. Heart Assn., 1957-62. Recipient NIH career devel. award, 1962-67. Mem. AAAS, Am. Soc. Biol. Chemists, Am. Chem. Soc., Am. Diabetes Assn., Biochem. Soc. (Eng.), Sigma Xi. Research biochem. mechanisms and control fatty acid synthesis and cholesterol synthesis. Home: 3436 Brisbane Rd Indianapolis IN 46208

GIBSON, DON CORROLL, veterinarian; b. Downington, Ohio, Sept. 21, 1928; s. Frank and Lana Olive G.; m. Bertha Dolores Douglas, Mar. 17, 1952; children—Mark Douglas, Gay Lynne. Student, Ohio U., 1949-51; D.V.M., Ohio State U., 1957; M.P.H., U. Mich., 1967. Diplomate: Am. Coll. Vet. Preventive Medicine. Dep. health commr., Portsmouth, Ohio, 1957-64, health commr., 1964-68; biol. scientist Nat. Inst. Child Health and Human Devel., NIH, Bethesda, Md., 1968-69, health scientist adminstr., 1969-74; chief biophysiology and pathobiology program Nat. Inst. on Aging, 1975-79, asso. dir. planning and extramural affairs, 1979—; USPHS trainee, 1966-67. Co-editor: Menopause and Aging, 1973, Epidemiology of Aging, 1980. Fellow Gerontol. Soc.; mem. AAAS, AVMA, Am. Assn. Lab. Animal Sci., Ohio Vet. Assn., D.C. Vet. Med. Assn., Phi Zeta. Home: 9704 Aldersgate Rd Rockville MD 20850 Office: Nat Inst on Aging NIH 9000 Rockville Pike Bethesda MD 20205

GIBSON, EDWARD FERGUS, physicist, educator; b. Colorado Springs, Colo., Apr. 2, 1937; s. George Merrick and Elsie Ida (Schnurr) G.; m. Harriette Graham DuShane, June 1, 1963; children: Sascha, Graham, Clark, Eileen. B.A., U. Colo., 1959, M.A., 1964, Ph.D., 1966. Physicist Nat. Bur. Standards, Boulder, Colo., 1958-64; research asst., research assoc. U. Colo., Boulder, 1964-66; postdoctoral research assoc. U. Oreg., Eugene, 1966-68; scientist-in-residence Naval Radiol. Def. Lab., San Francisco, 1968-69; prof. physics Calif. State U., Sacramento, 1969—, chmn. dept., 1979—; cons. on alternative energy sources Calif. Energy Commn., 1977-78; cons. computer-assisted instrn. Control Data Corp., 1981. Assoc. Western Univs. fellow, 1971-72, 73. Mem. Am. Phys. Soc., Phi Beta Kappa, Sigma Xi, Sigma Pi Sigma. Home: 527 Blackwood St Sacramento CA 95815 Office: Dept Physics Calif State U Sacramwnto 6000 J St Sacramento CA 95819

GIBSON, EDWIN MARTIN, glassware company executive; b. Pitts., Apr. 10, 1938; s. Edwin M. and Dorothy (Hibbs) G.; m. Virginia E. Taylor, Aug. 27, 1960; children: Ann Taylor, Sallie Hibbs. B.S., Yale U., 1960; M.B.A., U. Pa., 1962. With Corning Glass Works, N.Y., 1962—, sales mgr., gen. mgr., 1967-73, corp. v.p., gen. mgr. med., N.Y., 1973-77, v.p. personnel, N.Y., 1977-80, sr. v.p. medicine and sci., 1980-83, pres. health and sci. group, 1983—; dir. Hardinge Bros., Inc., Elmira, N.Y., Foster Med. Corp., Dedham, Mass. Trustee Elmira Coll., 1978—, Robert Packer Hosp., Sayre, Pa., 1981—. Mem. Sci. Apparatus Makers Assn. (corp. rep.). Republican. Episcopalian. Club: Corning Country. Office: Corning Glass Works Houghton Park Corning NY 14831

GIBSON, ELEANOR JACK (MRS. JAMES J. GIBSON), psychology educator; b. Peoria, Ill., Dec. 7, 1910; d. William A. and Isabel (Grier) Jack; m. James J. Gibson, Sept. 17, 1932; children: James J., Jean Grier. B.A., Smith Coll., 1931, M.A., 1933, D.Sc., 1972; Ph.D., Yale U., 1938; D.Sc., Rutgers U., 1973, Trinity Coll., 1982. Asst., instr., asst. prof. Smith Coll., 1931-49; research asso. psychology Cornell U., Ithaca, N.Y., 1949-66, prof., 1972—, Susan Linm Sage prof. psychology, 1972—; fellow Inst. for Advanced Study, Princeton, 1959-60, Inst. for Advanced Study in Behavioral Scis., Stanford, Calif., 1963-64; vis. prof. Mass. Inst. Tech., 1973, Inst. Child Devel., U. Minn., 1980; vis. disting. prof. U. Calif., Davis, 1978; vis. scientist Salk Inst., La Jolla, Calif., 1979; vis. prof. U. Pa., 1984. Author: Principles of Perceptual Learning and Development, 1967 (Century award), (with H. Levin) The Psychology of Reading, 1975. Recipient Wilbur Cross medal Yale U., 1973; Howard Crosby Warren medal, 1977; medal for disting. service Tchrs. Coll., Columbia U., 1983; Guggenheim fellow, 1972-73. Fellow AAAS (div. chairperson 1983), Am. Psychol. Assn. (Distinguished Scientist award 1968, G. Stanley Hall award 1970, pres. div. 3 1977); mem. Eastern Psychol. Assn. (pres. 1968), Soc. Exptl. Psychologists, Nat. Acad. Edn., Psychonomic Soc., Soc. Research in Child Devel. (Disting. Sci. Contbn. award 1981), Nat. Acad. Sci., Am. Acad. Arts and Scis., Brit. Psychol. Soc. (hon.), N.Y Acad. Scis. (hon.), Italian Soc. Research in Child Devel. (hon.), Phi Beta Kappa, Sigma Xi. Home: 111 Oak Hill Rd Ithaca NY 14850

GIBSON, EVERETT KAY, JR., space scientist, geochemist; b. Seagraves, Tex., May 13, 1940; s. Everett Kay and Lillie Gertrude (Ivey) G.; m. Mary Morgan Shott, Oct. 13, 1973; 1 son, Bradford Pierce Gibson. B.S., Tex. Tech. U., Lubbock, 1963, M.S., 1965; Ph.D., Ariz. State U., 1969. Instr. Tex. Tech. U., 1963-65; research asst. Ariz. State U., Tempe, 1965-69; postdoctoral research asso. NASA Johnson Space Center, Houston, 1969-70, space scientist, geochemist, 1970—; vis. program mgr. NSF, Washington, 1979; mission sci. advisor Apollo 14; test dir. Lunar Receiving Lab., NASA, 1971; prin. investigator Lunar Sample Analysis Program, NASA, 1971—, mem., 1974-77, prin. investigator, 1978-79, 1979—; mem. U.S. Antarctic Meteorite Search Team, 1979-80; adj. prof. geology U. Houston, 1975—; lectr. Sch. Continuing Edn., 1976-79; cons. The Economist (London), BBC, London. Asso. editor, 5th, 6th, 7th, 8th, 9th and 12th Proc. Lunar and Planetary Sci. Conf., 1974-81; contbr. articles to sci. jours. Bd. dirs. Clear Creek Basin Authority, Harris County, Tex., 1974-75. Recipient outstanding performance rating NASA-Johnson Space Center, 1970-71, sustained performance award, 1971-72, group award for lunar sci. team participation, 1974, group award for preliminary exam. team for lunar samples, 1973, cert. of recognition, 1979, superior performance award, 1980; Disting. Achievement award Ariz. State U., 1980; named outstanding lectr. S.E. region Am. Astron. Soc., 1976; NASA-NRC postdoctoral fellow, 1969-70. Fellow Meteoritical Soc. (sec. 1974-80); mem. Am. Chem. Soc., Geochem. Soc., Internat. Assn. Geochemistry and Cosmochemistry, AAAS, Am. Geophys. Union, Mineral. Soc. Am., Am. Astron. Union, Sigma Xi, Phi Lambda Upsilon. Baptist. Home: 1015 Trowbridge Dr Houston TX 77062 Office: SN 4 Geochemistry NASA Johnson Space Center Houston TX 77058

GIBSON, FLOYD ROBERT, judge; b. Prescott, Ariz., Mar. 3, 1910; s. Van Robert and Katheryn Ida G.; m. Gertrude Lee Walker, Apr. 23, 1935; children: Charles R., John M., Catherine L. Gibson Jobst. A.B., U. Mo., 1931, LL.B., 1933. Bar: Mo. 1932. Practiced law, Independence, 1933-37, Kansas City, 1937-61; mem. firm Johnson, Lucas, Bush & Gibson (and predecessor), 1954-61; county counselor, Jackson County, 1943-44; judge U.S. Dist. Ct. Western Dist. Mo., 1961-65, chief judge, until 1965; judge U.S. Ct. Appeals 8th Circuit, Kansas City, Mo., 1965—, chief judge, 1974-80; former chmn. bd. Mfrs. & Mechanics Bank, Kansas City, Mo., Blue Valley Fed. Savs. & Loan Assn.; mem. Nat. Conf. Commrs. Uniform State Laws, 1957—, Jud. Conf. U.S., 1974-80; chmn. Chief Judges Conf., 1977-78; bd. mgrs. Council State Govts., 1960-61; pres. Nat. Legis. Conf., 1960-61. Mem. Mo. Gen. Assembly from 7th Dist., 1940-46; mem. Mo. Senate, 1946-61, majority floor leader, 1952-56, pres. pro tem, 1956-60; del. Nat. Democratic Conv., 1956, 60; Mem. Mo. N.G. Named 2d most valuable mem. Mo. Legislature Globe Democrat, 1958, most valuable, 1960; recipient Faculty-Alumni award U. Mo., 1968; citation of merit Mo. Law Sch. Alumni, 1975; Spurgeon Smithson award Mo. Bar Found., 1978. Fellow ABA (adv. bd. editors Jour.; chmn. jud. adminstrn. div. 1979-80, chmn. conf. sect. chairmen 1980-81, chmn. appellate judges conf. 1973-74); mem. Fed. Bar Assn., Mo. Bar, Kansas City Bar Assn. (Ann. Achievement award 1980), Lawyers Assn. Kansas City (past v.p.), Mo. Law Sch. Found. (life), Mo. Acad. Squires, Order of Coif, Phi Delta Phi, Phi Kappa Psi (Man of Year 1974). Clubs: University, Carriage, Mercury (Kansas City, Mo.). Home: 11521 Winner Rd Independence MO 64052 Office: US Ct House Kansas City MO 64106

GIBSON, GEORGE, artist; b. Edinburgh, Scotland, Oct. 16, 1904; came to U.S., 1930, naturalized, 1938; s. George and Elizabeth L. (Gilchrist) G.; m. Alice C. Milligan, June 4, 1937; 1 dau., Jean. Student, Edinburgh Sch. Art, Glasgow Sch. Art, Chouinard Art Inst., Los Angeles; pupil, William E. Glover, F. Tolles Chamberlain. Scenic art dir.; head scenic art dept., Metro-Goldwyn-Mayer Studios, 1934-69, One-man shows include, Chabot Galleries, Los Angeles, 1950, Chabot Galleries, Long Beach, Calif., Laguna Beach (Calif.). Art Assn., 1951, Santa Barbara Mus. Art, 1952, Santa Monica Library Art Gallery, 1958, St. Mary's Coll.; exhibited, Am. Watercolor Soc. anns., 1945-72, Calif. Watercolor Soc. anns. and travelling shows, also, galleries, museums in, U.S.; represented in permanent collections, San Diego Mus., Newport Union High Sch., Los Angeles County Mus., Santa Paula C. of C., Laguna Beach Art Gallery. Served with USMCR, World War II. Recipient 1st prize Santa Paula Ann., 1946, City Los Angeles Ann., 1947, 49, Santa Cruz Ann., 1948, 50, Ariz. State Fair, 1948, Montgomery (Ala.) Exhbn., 1949, Westwood Art Assn. Ann., 1951, Calif. Watercolor Soc. 32d Ann., 1953, Newport Beach 6th Ann., 1953; also numerous 2d and 3d prizes, hon. mentions. Asso. NAD; mem. Am. Watercolor Soc., Calif. Watercolor Soc. (pres.) (1950-51), Acad. Motion Picture Arts and Scis. Office: care Emerson Galleries 17230 Ventura Blvd Encino CA 91316

GIBSON, GEORGE DANDRIDGE, lawyer; b. Richmond, Va., May 8, 1904; s. George Armistead and Alice (McClung) G.; m. Edith Ludlow Sedgwick, Feb. 23, 1935 (div. 1966); children: Pamela (Mrs. John T. Farrar), Alice (Mrs. Malcolm W. Stothers); m. Roberta Pearson Grymes, Aug. 26, 1966. B.A., U. Va., 1924; A.M., Harvard, 1925, LL.B., 1928. Bar: Va. 1928. Practiced in, Richmond, 1928—; assoc. firm Hunton & Williams (and predecessors), 1931—, partner, 1934—; gen. counsel Va. Electric & Power Co., Richmond, 1958-75; mem. legal adv. com. N.Y. Stock Exchange, 1978-82; spl. counsel Va. Code Commn. on Corp. Law, 1955-56. Contbr. articles to legal jours. Mem. Va. Commn. Arts and Humanities, 1968-74; Trustee Va. Mus. Fine Arts, 1952-63. Fellow Am. Bar Found.; mem. Va. Bar Assn., Richmond Bar Assn. (chmn. com. portraits justices 1957-61), ABA (chmn. sect. pub. utility law 1940-41, chmn. sect. corp., banking and bus. law 1959-60, chmn. com. corporate laws 1962-65, chmn. com. sect. projects 1965-70, editor The Business Lawyer 1957-58), Am. Law Inst., Am. Judicature Soc., Assn. Bar City N.Y., Bar Assn. D.C., Edison Electric Inst. (chmn. legal com. 1965-67), Soc. Colonial Wars, S.R., Va. Hist. Soc. (trustee 1965—, chmn. nominating com. 1978—), English Speaking Union (nat. dir. 1964-71), Phi Beta Kappa (dir. assos. 1971-80, hon. dir. 1980—), Phi Kappa Sigma. Episcopalian. Clubs: Forum (past pres.), German, Commonwealth, Country, Downtown (Richmond); Met. (Washington); Knickerbocker, Brook (N.Y.C.). Home: 9 River Rd Richmond VA 23226 Office: 8th and Main Bldg PO Box 1535 Richmond VA 23212

GIBSON, HENRY, actor; b. Germantown, Pa., Sept. 21, 1935; s. Edmund Albert and Dorothy (Cassidy) Bateman; m. Lois Joan Geiger, Apr. 6, 1966; children: Jonathan David, Charles Alexander, James Bateman. B.A. in Drama cum laude, Cath. U. Am., 1957; observer, Royal Acad. Dramatic Arts, London, 1961. Appeared as child actor, Mae Desmond Theatre Co., Phila.; other East coast stock cos., 1943-57; made: Broadway debut in Lillian Hellman's My Mother, My Father and Me, 1962; appeared on stage, film and TV, 1962-68; co-star: TV show Laugh-In, 1968-72; film appearances include The Last Remake of Beau Geste, 1977, The Kentucky Fried Movie, 1977, A Perfect Couple, 1979, The Blues Brothers, Health, The Incredible Shrinking Woman, 1981, Tulips, 1981; appeared in: TV movie Every Man Needs One, 1972; (Recipient Best Supporting Actor award Am. Soc. Film Critics 1975-76); Author: A Flower Child's Garden of Verses, 1970, Carnival of the Animals, 1971, The Only Show on Earth, 1973; contbr.: articles to various mags., including Environ. Quality. Adviser Keep Am. Beautiful, 1967-69, Nat. Teach-In, 1970, Actors Fund, 1970—; mem. Citizens Com. on Population Growth and Am. Future, 1972-75. Served to 1st lt. USAF, 1957-60. Mem. Acad. Motion Picture Arts and Scis., Nat. Acad. TV Arts and Scis., UN Assn., Izaak Walton League (hon. pres. 1975—), Environ. Def. Fund. Address: care David Shapira & Assos 9100 Wilshire Blvd East Tower Suite 231 Beverly Hills CA 90210 *

GIBSON, HUGH FRANCIS, lawyer, former judge; b. Kingston, Ont., Can., Dec. 12, 1916; s. William and Kathleen Lillian (O'Reilly) G. B.A., Queens U., 1937, B.Comm., 1938. Bar: Called to Ont. bar 1942, apptd. Queen's Counsel 1960. Assoc. firm Gibson, Sands & Flanigan, Kingston, 1946-64; assoc. crown atty., County of Frontenac, 1946-52, solicitor, City of Kingston, 1950-64; judge Exchequer Ct. of Can., 1964-71; pres. Martial Appeal Ct. Can., 1964-81; judge Fed. Ct. Can., Ottawa, 1971-81; of counsel Gowling and Henderson, Toronto and Ottawa; commr. Ct. of Investigation of M.V. Ft. William loss in Montreal Harbour, 1965; chmn. Bd. Inquiry into accident of Douglas DC-8 aircraft at Toronto Internat. Airport, 1970, Airport Inquiry Commn., 1973, commn. inquiry into comml. practices of; Canadian Dairy Commn., 1980. Mem. Phi Delta Phi. Clubs: Ontario, University (Toronto); Cataraqui Golf and Country, Kingston Yacht (Kingston); Trident Yacht (Thousand Islands); Laurentian, Royal Ottawa Golf (Ottawa); St. James (Montreal). Address: 300 Queen Elizabeth Driveway Ottawa ON Canada K15 3M6

GIBSON, JAMES, lawyer, former state supreme court justice; b. Salem, N.Y., Jan. 21, 1902; s. James and Caroline H. (MacCartee) G.; m. Judith Angell, June 11, 1929 (dec. Mar. 1956); children: Caroline (Mrs. Paul Fordham Nugent, Jr.), Judith (Mrs. E.J. Conklin). A.B., Princeton U., 1923; LL.B., Albany Law Sch., 1926; LL.D., Union Coll., 1970. Bar: N.Y. 1926. Since practiced in, Hudson Falls; asso. firm Rogers & Sawyer, 1926-29; partner firm Sawyer & Gibson, 1929-36; pvt. practice, 1936-53, dist. atty., Washington County, N.Y., 1936-53; justice Supreme Ct., N.Y., 1953-69, designated appellate div., 1956, presiding justice appellate div., 1964-69; judge ct. appeals N.Y., Albany, 1969-72; justice Supreme Ct. N.Y., 1973-79; sole practice law, Glens Falls, N.Y., 1979—; Mem. adminstrv. bd. Jud. Conf. State of N.Y., 1964-69. Trustee Albany Law Sch., Union U. Served with AUS, 1943-45; ETO. Mem. ABA, N.Y. State Bar Assn. (chmn. jud. sect. 1970-71, mem. exec com 1970-71), Washington County Bar Assn. Clubs: Ft. Orange (Albany); Princeton (N.Y.C.). Home: PO Box 190 Hudson Falls NY 12839 Office: 288 Glen St Glens Falls NY 12801

GIBSON, JANICE THORNE, developmental psychology educator, author; b. Hartford, Conn., Feb. 26, 1934; d. Peter Arnold and Marjorie Ekeanor (Greenberg) Thorne; m. Robert Hahn Gibson, Feb. 13, 1957 (div. 1970); children: Robin Lynne, Mark Gregory; m. Eugene Dmitri Vinogradoff, Sept. 21, 1973. B.A., U. Conn., 1955; M.S., Brown U., 1957; Ed.D., U. Va., 1962. Asst. prof. psychology U. Pitts., 1962-70, assoc. prof., 1970-73; dir. Aegean Sch. Cultural Anthropology, Naxos, Greece, 1973; prof. devel. psychology U. Pitts., 1973—; del. U.S. Council Internat. Exchange to USSR, 1978. Author: Growing Up: A Study of Children, 1978, Psychology for the Classroom, 1976, Living: A Study of Human Development, 1983, Discipline is not a Dirty Word, 1983; mem. editorial bd.: Contemporary Ednl. Psychology, 1975—; editor (internat. issue), 1984; author: monthly column One Year Olds, Parents Mag., 1984—; contbr. articles on edn. and child devel. to profl. jours. Fulbright research prof., Greece, Yugoslavia, Bulgaria, Cyprus, Israel, 1971-72; research exchange scientist Nat. Acad. Scis., Moscow, 1977; vis. fellow Kennan Inst. Woodrow Wilson Internat. Ctr., 1978. Mem. Internat. Ednl. Research Assn., Am. Ednl. Research Assn., Am. Psychol. Assn., Northeastern Ednl. Research Assn. (pres. 1981-82). Office: U Pitts Forbes Quardrangle 5D24 Pittsburgh PA 15260

GIBSON, JERRY LEIGH, oil field drilling co. exec.; b. El Dorado, Ark., Jan. 24, 1930; s. Oscar Edward and Ruth (Coleman) G.; m. Alma Gail Peoples, Apr. 11, 1953; children—Sallie Gail, Gregory Leigh. B.B.A. with honors, N. Tex. State U., 1951; M.B.A., So. Meth. U, 1956. With Mobil Oil U.S.A., 1952-59, 60-62, asst. to asst. comptroller, 1961-62; mgmt. cons. Peat, Marwick, Mitchell and Co. (C.P.A.'s), 1959; with Exxon Corp., 1962-66, asst. controller, 1965-66; v.p., sec., treas. Riviana Foods Inc., Houston, 1966-69; pres., treas., chief exec. officer Intermedco Inc., Houston, 1969-73; pres., chief exec. officer Automated Fin. Services, Inc., Houston, 1973-75; v.p. finance A-Z Internat. Tool Co., Houston, 1975-80; v.p. fin., part owner JHJ Drilling Co., Houston, 1980—; tchr. acctg. So. Meth. U., 1956-57. Served with USAF, 1950-52. Mem. Am. Inst. C.P.A.'s. Home: 14223 Kellywood Lane Houston TX 77079

GIBSON, JOHN EGAN, university dean, educator; b. Providence, June 11, 1926; s. Arthur and Judith Agnes (Egan) G.; m. Nancy Gertrude McGuinness, Sept. 7, 1950; children: William Francis, John Egan, Robert Alan, Nancy Regina. B.S., U. R.I., 1950; M.E., Yale U., 1952, Ph.D., 1956. Asst. prof. elec. engring. Yale, 1956; asso. prof. elec. engring. Purdue U., 1957-60, prof., 1960-65; founding dean Sch. Engring., prof. Oakland U., 1965-73, John Dodge prof. engring., 1972-73; dean Sch. Engring. and Applied Sci., Commonwealth prof. engring. U. Va., Charlottesville, 1973—; leader U.S. team to U.S. Republic of China Conf. on Urban Systems, 1972; cons. on urban system design methodology Battelle Inst., 1971-73. Author: Control System Components, 1958 (transl. into Japanese, Polish), Nonlinear Automatic Control (transl. into Japanese, Polish, Romanian), 1963, Introduction to Engineering Design, 1968, Designing the New City, 1977. Served with AUS, 1944-46. Mem. IEEE, ASME, Am. Soc. Engring. Edn. (dir. nat. electronics conf. 1965-67), Soc. Automotive Engrs., Sigma Xi, Tau Beta Pi. Roman Catholic. Office: U Va Coll Engring and Applied Scis. Charlottesville VA 22903

GIBSON, JOHN ROBERT, judge; b. Springfield, Mo., Dec. 20, 1925; s. Harry B. and Edna (Kerr) G.; m. Mary Elizabeth Vaughn, Sept. 20, 1952; children: Jeanne, John Robert. A.B., U. Mo., 1949, J.D., 1952. Bar: Mo. 1952. Asso. firm Morrison, Hecker, Curtis, Kuder & Parrish, Kansas City, Mo., 1952-58, partner, 1958-81; judge U.S. Dist. Ct., Western Dist. of Mo., 1981-82, U.S. Ct. Appeals (8th cir.), 1982—; mem. Mo. Press-Bar Commn., 1979-81. Vice chmn. Jackson County Charter Transition Com., 1971-72; mem. Jackson County Charter Commn., 1970; v.p. Bd. Police Commrs., Kansas City, Mo., 1973-77. Served with AUS, 1944-46. Fellow Am. Bar Found.; mem. ABA, Kansas City Bar Assn. (pres. 1970-71), Mo. State Bar (gov. 1972-79, pres. 1977-78, Pres.'s award 1974), Lawyers Assn. of Kansas City (Charles Evan Whittaker award 1980), Phi Beta Kappa, Omicron Delta Kappa. Presbyterian. Home: 11921 Summit Kansas City MO 64145 Office: Rm 851 US Courthouse 811 Grand Ave Kansas City MO 64106

GIBSON, JOSEPH WHITTON, JR., chem. co. exec.; b. Norristown, Pa., Feb. 24, 1922; s. Joseph Whitton and Nellie (Dear) G.; m. Norma Jean Stewart, Sept. 21, 1946; children—Joseph Whitton, Winn S. Gobeil, Philip B. B.S., Worcester Poly. Inst., 1944; postgrad. in Electronics, Princeton U., 1944, M.I.T., 1945. With E. I. duPont de Nemours & Co., Wilmington, Del., 1946—, sr. research engr., 1961-79, sr. tech. specialist printing systems, photo products, 1979—. Contbr. articles to profl. jours. Treas. Mayfield Civic Assn.; v.p. Brandywine Babe Ruth; treas. Shellcrest Swim Club. Served to lt. USNR, 1944-46. Mem. Am. Assn. Textile Chemists and Colorists (Olney medal 1979), Am. Chem. Soc., Fiber Soc., Sigma Xi, Tau Beta Pi. Republican. Episcopalian. Inventor thermosol dyeing, sparkle hosiery, synthetic leather, fish swimway. Home: 1215 Hillside Blvd Wilmington DE 19803 Office: Photo Systems Lab Chestnut Run Wilmington DE 19898

GIBSON, KENNETH ALLEN, mayor of Newark; b. Enterprise, Ala., May 15, 1932; s. Willie Foy and Daisy (Lee) G.; m. Muriel Cook, June 1960; children—Joyce, Cheryl, JoAnne. B.S., Newark Coll. Engring., 1962,. Engr. N.J. Hwy. Dept., 1952-63; chief engr. Newark Housing Authority, 1963-67; chief structural engr., City of Newark, 1967-70, mayor of, Newark, 1970—; pres. U.S. Conf. Mayors, 1976-77; Co-chmn. Bus. and Indsl. Coordinating Council, 1964-65. Bd. dirs. Newark Urban Coalition, Newark YM-YWCA. Served with C.E. U.S. Army, 1956-58. Named Jaycees Man of Year, Newark, 1964, one of 200 outstanding young men in Am. and; one of 50 young world leaders by Time, Inc.; recipient Fiorello H. LaGuardia award. Mem. ASCE, Frontiers Internat. Democrat. Office: Office of Newark Studies 909 Broad St Suite 500 Newark NJ 07102 *When a philosophy cannot be altered to serve the honest needs of a living people, its pages should be placed in storage to collect dust and scholars, and its author cast in bronze to be viewed as an outmoded thing of the curious past.*

GIBSON, MELVIN ROY, pharmacognosy educator; b. St. Paul, Nebr., June 11, 1920; s. John and Jennie Irene (Harvey) G. B.S., U. Nebr., 1942, M.S., 1947; Ph.D., U. Ill., 1949. Asst. prof. pharmacognosy Wash. State U., Pullman, 1949-52, asso. prof., 1952-55, prof., 1955—. Editor: Am. Jour. Pharm. Edn, 1956-61; editorial bd., co-author: Remington's Pharm. Sci, 1970, 75, 80, 85; editor, co-author: Studies of a Pharm. Curriculum, 1967; author over 100 articles. Served as arty. officer AUS, 1942-46. Decorated Bronze star, Purple Heart; sr. vis. fellow Orgn. for Econ. Cooperation and Devel., Royal Pharm. Inst., Stockholm, Sweden and U. Leiden (Holland), 1962; recipient Nat. Kappa Psi citation for service, 1961, Rufus A. Lyman award, 1972, Washington State U. Faculty Library award, 1984. Founder, charter mem. Am. Diplomates in Pharmacy.; Fellow AAAS; asso. fellow Am. Coll. Apothecaries; mem. N.Y. Acad. Sci., Am. Pharm. Assn., Am. Soc. Pharmacognosy (pres. 1964-65), Am. Assn. Coll. Pharmacy (exec. com. 1961-63, bd. dirs. 1977-79, chmn. council of faculties 1975-76, pres. 1979-80, Disting. Educator award 1984), U.S. Pharmacopeia (revision com. 1970-75), Am. Found. Pharm. Edn. (life mem., bd. dirs. 1980—), Am. Found, Pharm. Edn. (exec. com. 1981—), Am. Found. Pharm. Edn. (vice chmn. bd. dirs. 1982-85), AAUP, Acad. Pharm. Sci., Am. Public Health Assn., Fedn. Internat. Pharm., Am. Inst. History of Pharmacy, Am. Acad. Polit. and Social Sci., Sigma Xi, Kappa Psi, Rho Chi, Phi Kappa Phi, Omicron Delta Kappa. Democrat. Presbyterian. Club: Spokane. Home: SE 625 Spring St Pullman WA 99163 Office: Coll Pharmacy Wash State U Pullman WA 99164

GIBSON, MOSES CARL, educator; b. St. Thomas, Nev., May 31, 1919; s. Robert Orson and Edith Alice (Hinton) G.; m. Irma Burdette, Dec. 6, 1944; children—Tanya, Randy, Marla, Steven, Brent. B.A., Brigham Young U., 1947, M.A., 1949; Ph.D., U. Oreg., 1960. Missionary Ch. of Jesus Christ of Latter Day Saints, Brazil, 1941-43; mem. faculty Brigham Young U., 1949-56, 58—, prof. langs., 1949—, dir. resident program, Madrid, 1961, Mexico City, 1962; mem. faculty U. Oreg., 1956-58. Contbr. articles to profl. jours. Served with USAAF, 1943-45. Mem. MLA, Am. Assn. Tchrs. Spanish and Portuguese, Rocky Mountain MLA. Mem. Ch. Jesus Christ of Latter-day Saints (bishop 1958-63, 73-76, pres. stake 1963-72, 78-81). Home: 410 S 1350 E Provo UT 84601

GIBSON, RALPH H(OLMES), photographer; b. Jan. 16, 1939. Student in photography, U.S. Navy, 1956-60, San Francisco Art Inst., 1960-61. Lectr. at numerous schs., museums. Exhibited photography in one-man shows, including, Castelli Graphics, N.Y.C., 1976, 80, Balt. Mus. Art, 1976, Swedish Mus. Photography, 1977, Mus. Modern Art, Oxford, Eng., Photographers Gallery, Melbourne, Australia, Robert Self Gallery, London, 1978, Mus. Modern Art, Brisbane, Australia, Canon Gallery, Geneva, 1979, Gradestake Gallery, San Francisco, Kunstmuseum, Dusseldorf, W. Ger., 1980, Night Gallery, London, others; exhibited in numerous group shows, including, Mus. Modern Art, N.Y.C., 1978, Hayden Gallery, M.I.T., Cambridge, Bologna (Italy) Art Fair, Walker Art Center, Liverpool, Eng., Cleve. Mus. Art, Musée Marseilles, 1980, others; represented in permanent collections, including, Nat. Gallery Ottawa, Ont., Can., Bibliotheque National de France, Paris, Mus. Modern Art, N.Y.C., Internat. Mus. Photography, George Eastman House, Rochester, N.Y., Fogg Art Mus., Boston, Met. Mus. Art, N.Y.C., Australian Nat. Gallery, Canberra, Nat. Gallery Victoria, Australia, Art Gallery South Australia, Victoria and Albert Mus., London, Mus. Modern Art, Brisbane, Fotografiska Museet, Moderna Museet, Stockholm, Sweden, Musee Reattu, Arles, France; Author, illustrator: The Strip, 1966, The Hawk, 1968, The American Civil Liberties Union Calendar, 1969, The Somnambulist, 1970, Deja-vu, 1973, Days at Sea, 1975. Nat. Endowment for Arts Fellowship grantee, 1973, 75; N.Y. State Council to Arts Creative Artists Public Service grantee, 1977. Address: 331 W Broadway New York NY 10013 *Photography is a way for measuring my perception—I trust my photographs and study them intensely. After working over twenty years, I realize that the years of struggle are over. Now begin the years of struggle.*

GIBSON, RANKIN MACDOUGAL, lawyer; b. Unionville, Mo., Oct. 9, 1916; s. Alexander R. and Murle L. (Fletcher) G.; m. Eloise M. Corns, Sept. 13, 1941; children: Phillip, Barbara. Student, N.E. Mo. State Tchrs. Coll., 1934-36; LL.B., U. Mo., 1939; B.S. in Law, St. Paul Coll. Law, 1948; LL.M., George Washington U., 1950. Bar: Mo. 1939, Ohio 1954, Supreme Ct. U.S 1951. Gen. practice law, Unionville, 1939-40; atty. T.H. Mastin & Co., St. Louis, 1940-42, VA, Des Moines, St. Paul, Washington, 1945-51; enforcement and litigation atty. Nat. Wage Stblzn. Bd., 1951; asso. prof. law U. Toledo Coll. Law, 1951-56; mem. firm DiSalle, Green, Haddad & Lynch, Toledo, 1956-59; asst. to gov., Ohio, 1959-61; dir. Ohio Dept. Commerce, 1961-62; mem. Pub. Utilities Commn., Ohio, 1962-63; judge Supreme Ct., Ohio, 1963-65; now partner firm Lucas, Prendergast, Albright, Gibson & Newman, Columbus, Ohio; tchr. adminstrv. law Franklin Sch. Law, 1960; tchr. labor law Franklin Law Sch., Capital U., 1967—; Mem. Nat. Enforcement Commn. Econ. Stblzn. Agy., 1952-53; chmn. labor law round table council Assn. Am. Law Schs., 1952-53; labor arbitrator panels Am. Arbitration Assn., Fed. Mediation and Conciliation Service, Toledo Labor-Mgmt. Citizens Com., 1952-53; rep. Ohio on interstate Coop. Com.; chmn. Gov. Ohio Com. Pub. Information, 1959-61; mem. Ohio Water Pollution Bd., Civil War Centennial Commn., Ohio Housing Bd.; Ohio rep. on Interstate Oil Compact Commn. and Nat. Rivers and Harbors Congress, 1961-62. Contbr. articles to profl. jours. Democratic nominee for rep. Mo. Gen. Assembly, 1940. Served to 2d lt. AUS, 1942-45. Mem. Fed. Bar Assn. (pres. Columbus chpt. 1967-68), Ohio Bar Assn., Columbus Bar Assn. (pres.), Indsl. Relations Research Assn. (pres. central Ohio chpt. 1966-68), Nat. Acad. Arbitrators (chmn. region 9 1975—), Am. Judicature Soc. Home: 7355 Feder Rd Galloway OH 43119 Office: 471 E Broad St Columbus OH 43215

GIBSON, RAYMOND EUGENE, clergyman; b. Shelbyville, Ky., Mar. 10, 1924; s. Wallace and Laura Belle (Lee) G.; m. Susan Cochran, June 29, 1945; children: Cyrus Noel, Mark Scott, Christopher Watt, Laurence Kristin, Jonathan Geoffrey. A.B. in Philosophy and History, Berea Coll., 1944; B.D., Union Theol. Sem., N.Y.C., 1947; Ph.D., Columbia, 1963. Ordained to ministry Congl. Ch., 1947; adminstrv. asst. Inst. Religious and Social Studies, N.Y.C., 1947-48; pastor in, New Lebanon, N.Y., 1948-49, Pittsfield, Mass., 1950-61, Central Congl. Ch., Providence, 1961—; prof. religious studies Providence Coll., 1971—; Mem. com. evangelism and devotional life R.I. Congl. Conf., 1962-65, dir., 1965—; exec. com. R.I. br. Acad. Religion and Mental Health, 1962; Danforth Found. Kenneth Underwood fellow, 1970-71. Author: God, Man and Time, 1966; Editor: Conversations with God: The Devotional Journals of Myrtie L. Elmer, 1962; asso. editor: Minister's Quar, 1958—. Chmn. R.I. adv. com. U.S. Commn. Civil Rights; mem. mayor's com. to end de facto segregation in Providence pub. schs.; Bd. dirs. R.I. Group Health Assn., Inc.; trustee Berea Coll., 1963—; vice chmn. Corp. for Hamilton House, 1972; founding mem., mem. exec. com. Hospice Care R.I., 1975—. Recipient Howard prize for citizenship Berea Acad., 1941; named Man of Year in Pittsfield Area, 1959; recipient Distinguished Service award Pittsfield Jr. C. of C., 1959; named one of four outstanding young men in state Mass. Jr. C. of C., 1959. Mem. Nat. Acad. Religion and Mental Health, Nat. Geog. Soc., R.I. State Council Churches (dir.). Home: 283 Wayland Ave Providence RI 02906 Office: Central Congl Church Angell and Diman Pl Providence RI 02906 *For me, a life lived fully requires something of the head, the heart, and the hands; thoughts, feelings, skills. Achievement is not what a person does, but what he or she is and becomes. It involves taking time for things that have meaning; contemplation, love, friendship, solitude, art, nature, dreams, doubts, poetry, philosophy, song, dance, worship, hills, plains, seas; time to live in time and time to dwell on eternity.*

GIBSON, REGINALD WALKER, federal judge; b. Lynchburg, Va., July 31, 1927; s. McCoy and Julia Ann (Butler) G.; m. Jeanette Roberts, Oct. 28, 1961 (div. May 1982); 1 son, Reginald S. B.S., Va. Union U., 1952; postgrad., Wharton Grad. Sch. Bus. Adminstrn., U. Pa., 1952-53; LL.B., Howard U., 1956. Bar: D.C. 1957, Ill. 1972. Agt. IRS, Washington, 1957-61; trial atty. tax div. U.S. Dept. Justice, Washington, 1961-71; sr. tax atty. Internat. Harvester Co., Chgo., 1971-76, gen. tax atty., 1976-82; judge U.S. Claims Ct., Washington, 1982—. Mem. bus. adbv. council Chgo. Urban League, 1974-82. Served with AUS, 1946-47. Recipient cert. award U.S. Dept. Justice Atty. Gen., 1969, spl. commendation U.S. Dept. Justice Atty. Gen., 1970. Mem. ABA, D.C. Bar Assn., Chgo. Bar Assn., Fed. Bar Assn., Nat. Bar Assn. Republican. Baptist. Club: Nat. Lawyers (Washington). Home: 4830 Ft Tottn Dr NE Apt 103 Washington DC 20011 Office: US Claims Ct 717 Madison Pl NW Washington DC 20005

GIBSON, ROBERT, baseball coach, former baseball player; b. Omaha, Nov. 9, 1935. Student, Creighton U. Player St. Louis Cardinals, 1959-75; coach N.Y. Mets, 1981-82, Atlanta Braves, 1982—. Recipient Cy Young award Nat. League, 1968-70; named Most Valuable Player Nat. League, 1968; named to Baseball Hall of Fame, 1981. Mem. Nat. League All Star team 8 times; player World Series, 1964, 67, 68. Office: care Atlanta Braves PO Box 4064 Atlanta GA 30302 *

GIBSON, ROBERT PAUL, publisher; b. Hamilton, Ont., Can., Oct. 2, 1941; s. Edgar Howlett and Dorothy Marie G.; m. Diana Brooke Barrett, May 16, 1964; children—Sarah, Beth, Peter. B.A., McGill U., Montreal, Que., Can., 1963. Sales mgr., then mgr. sch. dept. Holt Rinehart & Winston Can., Toronto, Ont., 1964-72; pres. Micromedia Ltd., Toronto, 1972—. Mem. Info. Industry Assn. Office: 144 Front St W Toronto ON M5J 2L7 Canada

GIBSON, ROBERT WALTER, newspaperman; b. Cin., July 21, 1928; s. Robert R. and Ethelyn (Johnson) G.; m. Carol Veronica Brazie, Sept. 25, 1954 (div. 1976); children: Christopher, Paula, Valerie; m. Esmeralda Treen, Oct. 25, 1980. B.A., Stanford U., 1950, M.A. (Melville Jacoby fellow Asian studies), 1956. Staff corr. UPI, 1950-53, AP, 1953-57; news editor McGraw-Hill, London, 1957-58, bur. chief, Moscow, 1958-60; asst. fgn. editor Bus. Week mag., 1960-63; sr. editorial writer Los Angeles Times, 1963-64, fgn. editor, 1964-83, internat. econs. corr., 1983—; sr. lectr. U. So. Calif., 1967—, bd. councilors Sch. Politics and Internat. Relations, 1970—. Trustee Monterey Inst. Internat. Studies, 1978—. Served with AUS, 1953-55. Mem. Los Angeles Com. Fgn. Relations, Phi Kappa Sigma. Club: Overseas Press (N.Y.C.).

GIBSON, SAM THOMPSON, physician, educator; b. Covington, Ga., Jan. 1, 1916; s. Count Dillon and Julia (Thompson) G.; m. Alice Chase, Oct. 31, 1942 (dec. Jan. 1971); children: Lena S. Gibson, Stephen C., Judith Gibson Hammer, Lucy F. B.S. in Chemistry, Ga. Inst. Tech., 1936; M.D., Emory U., 1940. Diplomate: Am. Bd. Internal Medicine. Med. house officer Peter Bent Brigham Hosp., Boston, 1940-41, asst. resident medicine, 1946-47, asst. medicine, 1947-49; research fellow medicine Harvard Med. Sch., 1941-42, spl. research asso., 1943, Milton fellow medicine, 1947-49; asso. medicine George Washington U. Med. Sch., also George Washington U. Hosp., 1949-63, asst. clin. prof. medicine, 1963—; clin. asst. prof. medicine Uniformed Services U. Health Scis., 1980—; asst. med. dir. ARC Blood Program, 1949-51, asso. med. dir., 1951-53, asso. dir., 1953-56, dir., 1956-66; sr. med. officer ARC, 1957-67; asst. dir. div. biologics standards; NIH, 1967-72; asst. dir. Nat. Ctr. Drugs and Biologics, Biologics, FDA, Bethesda, Md., 1972-74; asst. to dir. Bur. Biologics, FDA, 1974—, dir. div. biologics evaluation, 1977—; cons. blood Naval Med. Sch., Nat. Naval Med. Center, Bethesda, 1950-63; mem. med. adv. bd. CARE-Medico, 1962-70, cons., 1970—; chmn. U.S. com. for tranfusion equipment for med. use Am. Standards Assn., 1954-66, tech. adv. group transfusion equipment for med. use Nat. Commn. Clin. Lab. Standards/Am. Nat. Standards Inst., 1975—; adviser orgn. blood transfusion services League Red Cross Socs., 1955-66. Contbg. editor: Vox Sanguinis Jour. Blood Transfusion, 1956-65; mem. adv. bd., 1965-76. Served from lt. (j.g.) to comdr., M.C. USNR, 1941-46; capt. Res. ret. Mem. AMA, AAAS, Internat., Am. socs. hematology, Nat. Health Council (dir. 1957-60, 61-64), Internat. Soc. Blood Transfusion (regional counselor 1962-66), Am. Fedn. Clin. Research, N.Y. Acad. Scis., Delta Tau Delta, Alpha Kappa Kappa, Alpha Chi Sigma, Tau Beta Pi, Phi Kappa Phi, Omicron Delta Kappa, Alpha Omega Alpha. Home: 5801 Rossmore Dr Bethesda MD 20814 Office: Nat Ctr. Drugs and Biologics FDA Bethesda MD 20205

GIBSON, THOMAS JOSEPH, diversified holding company executive; b. Washington, Mar. 13 1935; s. Henry Justus and Margaret Mary (Biggins) G.; m. Shirley Ann Claus, June 9, 1956; children: Patricia Lynne Gibson Dixon, Glenn Thomas. B.E.E., Rensselaer Poly. Inst., 1956; J.D., George Washington U., 1962. Bar: Colo. 1963. Electronics engr. FCC, Washington, 1958-59; elec. engring. assoc. Nugent S. Sharp Engrs., Washington, 1959-60; elec. design engr. Datronics Engrs., Inc., Bethesda, Md., 1960-61; mgr. Honeywell, Inc., Denver, 1961-65; exec. v.p. fin. and legal, sec. Gates Rubber Co., Gates Corp., Denver, 1965—. Pres. Orchard Hills Homeowners Assn., Englewood, Colo., 1970-72. Served to lt. USNR, 1956-62. Mem. Colo. Assn. Commerce and Industry (dir. exec. com.), Denver C. of C. (dir, exec. com.). Republican. Office: Gates Corp 900 S Broadway PO Box 5887 Denver CO 80217

GIBSON, VERNA KAYE, retail company executive; b. Charleston, W.Va., June 22, 1942; d. Carl W. leMasters and Virginia E. (Meyers) LeMasters; m. James E. Gibson, Apr. 28, 1962; children: Kelly, Elizabeth. Grad. with honors in fashion mktg. and retailing, Marshall U., Huntington, W.Va., 1962. Buyer, merchandise mgr. Smart Shops, Huntington, W.Va., 1965-71; trainee to asst. buyer Limited Stores, Inc., Columbus, Ohio, 1971-72, assoc. buyer to buyer, 1972-77, div. merchandise mgr., 1977-79, v.p. sportswear, 1979-82, exec. v.p. gen., merchanise mgr., 1982—; dir. Midland Mutual Life Ins. Co., Columbus, J. Duffy's. Recipient Harry L. Wexner award Limited Stores, Inc., 1983. Office: Limited Stores Inc 1 Limited Pkwy Columbus OH 43213

GIBSON, WALTER SAMUEL, humanities educator; b. Columbus, Ohio, Mar. 31, 1932; s. Walter Samuel and Grace Buena (Wheeler) G.; m. Sarah Ann Scott, Dec. 16, 1972. B.F.A. cum laude, Ohio State U., 1957, M.A., 1960; Ph.D., Harvard U., 1969. Asst. prof. dept. art Case Western Res. U., 1966-71, asso. prof., 1971-78, acting chmn., 1970-71, chmn., 1971-79, Andrew W. Mellon prof. humanities, 1978—. Author: Hieronymus Bosch, 1973, The Paintings of Cornelis Engebrechtsz, 1977, Bruegel, 1977, Hieronymus Bosch: An Annotated Bibliography, 1983; Contbr. articles to profl. jours. Served with Fin. Corps U.S. Army, 1952-54. Fulbright scholar, 1960-61, 84; John Simon Guggenheim Found. fellow, 1978-79; NEH and Samuel H. Kress Found. grantee, 1970; Am. Council Learned Socs. grantee-in-aid, 1975. Mem. Coll. Art Assn. Am., Internat. Center Medieval Art, Renaissance Soc. Am., Midwest Art History Soc., Medieval Acad. Am. Club: Rowfant (Cleve.). Home: 3057 Washington Blvd Cleveland Heights OH 44118 Office: Dept Art Mather House Case Western Res U Cleveland OH 44106

GIBSON, WELDON BAILEY, research executive; b. Eldorado, Tex., Apr. 23, 1917; s. Oscar and Susie (Bailey) G.; m. Helen Mears, Mar. 1, 1941; children: Arthur (dec.), David Mears. A.B., Wash. State Coll., 1938; M.B.A., Stanford U., 1940, Ph.D., 1950. Staff asst. Standard Oil Co. Calif., San Francisco, 1939; salesman Burroughs Adding Machine Co., San Francisco, 1940; asst. dir. Air Force Inst. Tech., Dayton, Ohio, 1946-47; dir. economics research, chmn. internat. research Stanford Research Inst., Menlo Park, Calif., 1947-56, asso. dir., 1956-59, v.p., 1950-60, exec. v.p., 1960-77; sr. dir. SRI Internat., 1977—; lectr. Grad. Sch. Bus., Stanford U., 1948-53; Cons. Bur. Budget, Nat. Security Resources Bd., 1949-53; co-dir. Internat. Indsl. Conf., 1957, 61, 65, 69, 73, 77, 81; dir. Pacific Indsl. Conf., 1967, North Atlantic Indsl. Conf., 1967, others; exec. com. Pacific Basin Econ. Council, 1968—. Author: (with assocs.) Global Geography, 1944, (with Renner, Durand, White) Economic Geography, 1951; others. Chmn. Wash. State U. Found., 1979—. Mem. Soc. Internat. Devel., Am. Econ. Assn., Am. Geog. Assn., Beta Theta Pi, Alpha Kappa Psi. Clubs: Mason, Shriners. Home: 593 Gerona Rd Stanford CA 94305 Office: SRI Internat Menlo Park CA 94025

GIBSON, WILLIAM, author; b. N.Y.C., Nov. 13, 1914; s. George Irving and Florence (Doré) G.; m. Margaret Brenman, Sept. 6, 1940; children: Thomas, Daniel. Student, Coll. City N.Y. Author: play I Lay in Zion, 1947; poems Winter Crook, 1948; play Dinny and The Witches, 1950; novel The Cobweb, 1954; play Two for the Seesaw, 1958; theatre chronicle The Seesaw Log, 1958; play The Miracle Worker, 1960; musical Golden Boy, 1964; family chronicle A Mass for the Dead, 1968; play A Cry of Players, 1969, American Primitive, 1972; chronicle A Season in Heaven, 1974; play The Body & The Wheel, 1975, The Butterfingers Angel, Mary & Joseph, Herod The Nut, & The Slaughter of 12 Hit Carols In A Pear Tree, 1975, Golda, 1977; criticism Shakespeare's Game, 1978; play Monday after the Miracle, 1983. Address: Stockbridge MA 01262

GIBSON, WILLIAM CARLETON, physician, educator; b. Ottawa, Ont., Can., Sept. 4, 1913; s. John Wesley and Belle (Crawford) G.; m. Barbara Baird; children—David Baird Penfield, Ian Kenneth, Catherine Ann. B.A., U. B.C., 1933; M.S., McGill U., 1936, M.D., C.M., 1941; D.Phil., Oxford U., 1938. Diplomate: Am. Bd. Neurology. Demonstrator in physiology Oxford U., 1935-38; intern U. Tex. Hosp., Galveston, 1941; dir. research mental hosps., New South Wales, Australia; also lectr. neuropathology U. Sydney, Australia, 1948-49; dir. research mental hosps., B.C., Can., 1949-51; Kinsmen prof. neurol. research, lectr. dept. psychology U. B.C., Can., Vancouver, 1951-58, prof. history of medicine and sci., 1959-78; chmn. Univs. Council, Vancouver, Can., 1978—; research U. Marseille, France), U. London, 1958-59; mem. expert adv. panel on neuroscis. WHO; Rhoads lectr. Boston U.; Fitzpatrick lectr. Royal Coll. Physicians, London; Dunn lectr. U. Tex.; Grogan lectr. Acad. Medicine Toronto; others. Author: (with John Eccles) Sherrington—His Life and Thought; also numerous articles. Alderman, City of Vancouver, 1973-75, 77-78; commr. Vancouver Bd. Parks and Recreation, 1975-76; mem. council Rockefeller U., N.Y.C. Served with RCAF, 1941-45, 49-59. Fellow A.C.P., Royal Coll. Physicians (London); mem. muscular dystrophy assns. Can., Am. (chmn. sci. adv. com. 1973-75), Fairbridge Soc. (B.C. com.), Cedar Lodge Soc. (vice chmn.), Faculty Assn. U. B.C. (pres. 1957-58), Alumni Assn. U. B.C. (pres. 1961-62), Can. Neurol. Soc., Soc. Social History Medicine, EEG Soc. Gt. Britain, Am. EEG Soc., Vancouver Med. Assn., Physiol. Soc. London (asso.). Clubs: Univ. of Vancouver (pres.); Athenaeum (London)). Office: 500 805 W Broadway Vancouver BC V5Z 1K1 Canada

GIBSON, WILLIAM EDWARD, banker; b. Farragut, Idaho, Apr. 11, 1944; s. William E. and Lucille E. (Dickehut) G.; m. Judith Ten Brock, July 19, 1980; 1 son, William Edward. A.B., U. Chgo., 1964, M.A., 1965, Ph.D., 1967. Charted fin. analyst. Asst. prof. UCLA, 1967-70; sr. staff economist Pres.'s Council Econ. Advisers, Washington, 1971-74; v.p. Chase Manhattan Bank, N.Y.C., 1974-76; 1st v.p. Smith Barney, Harris Upham, N.Y.C., 1976-79; sr. v.p. McGraw-Hill, Ind., N.Y.C., 1979-81, Republic Bank Corp., Dallas, 1981—; chmn. bd. First Fed. Savs. and Loan Assn., Rochester, N.Y., 1981—; dir. V'Soske Carpets, Inc., Vega Baja, P.R., 1980—, First Fed. Savs. Bank, San Juan, P.R., 1983—. Author: Monetary Economics, 1972; contbr. articles to profl. jour. Trustee Howe Mil. Acad., (Ind.), 1983—. Named Disting. Alumnus Howe Mil. Acad., 1983. Mem. Am. Econs. Assn., Am. Fin. Assn. Methodist. Clubs: University (N.Y.C.); Tower, Dallas Economists (sec.); Cosmos (Washington)). Home: 3612 Harvard Ave Dallas TX 75205 Office: Republic Bank Corp PO Box 222105 Dallas TX 75222

GIBSON, WILLIAM MERRIAM, educator; b. Wilmette, Ill., Jan. 16, 1912; s. Thomas Benton and Mary Gertrude (Stanbery) G.; m. Barbara Chadwick Crane, Oct. 21, 1943; children: Julia Stanbery Gibson Kant, Thomas Crane. A.B. cum laude, Princeton U., 1933; M.A., U. Chgo., 1934, Ph.D., 1940. Mem. faculty dept. English U. Chgo., 1937-41, Williams Coll., 1941-42, 46-49; mem. faculty dept. English N.Y. U., 1949-73, prof., 1951-73; prof. English U. Wis.-Madison, 1973—; Fulbright lectr. U. Turin, Italy, 1960-61, U. Aix-Marseilles, summer 1961, U. Delhi, Mussoorie, India, 1963; Peking Lang. Inst./Com. on Scholarly Communication lectr., Peking, 1980. Author, editor: books in field, including Mark Twain-Howells Letters, 1960, (with Henry Nash Smith) The Art of Mark Twain, 1976, Three Humorists on Theodore Roosevelt, 1980. Served with AUS, 1942-46. Ford fellow, 1954-55; Guggenheim fellow, 1963-64, 76-77; NEH fellow, 1973. Mem. MLA (dir. Center for editions of Am. authors 1963-69), Am. Council Learned Socs. (mem. adv. com. in Am. studies 1966-69), Am. Studies Assn., AAUP, Internat. Assn. Univ. Profs. English. Home: 6309 Keelson Dr Madison WI 53705 Office: Dept English Univ of Wis Park St Madison WI 53706

GIBSON, WILLIAM SHEPARD, financial executive; b. Bklyn., Jan. 2, 1933; s. William S. and Mary (Keeney) G.; m. Charmaine Wallett, May 26, 1967; children: Susan, Joshua/1 stepdau., Tracy; children by previous marriage: William, Gregory. B.S. in Acctg., U. Ill., 1954, J.D., 1959. Counsel Am. Ins. Assn., Chgo., 1963-69; asst. dir. ins. State of Ill., Chgo., 1969-71; v.p. midwest Am. Ins. Assn., Chgo., 1971-77; v.p., gen. counsel Continental Ins., N.Y.C., 1977-82; v.p. govt. affairs Continental Corp., N.Y.C., 1982—; chmn. bd. N.J. Auto Ins. Assn., Newark, 1983—; chmn. Continental PAC, 1981—. Served with U.S. Army, 1954-56. Mem. ABA, Ill. State Bar Assn., N.Y. Bar Assn., Internat. Assn. Ins. Counsel;,e,/ N.Y. Med. Malpractice Ins. Assn.; mem. N.Y. Motor Vehicle Accident Indemnity Corp. Congregationalist. Home: 55 Southern Blvd Chatham NJ 07928 Office: 180 Maiden Ln New York NY 10038

GICOVATE, BERNARD, educator; b. Santos, Brazil, Apr. 21, 1922; came to U.S., 1944, naturalized, 1952; s. Jose and Clara G.; m. Alice Echeverz, July 4, 1944; 1 son, Henry S. Dr. en Filosofiá y Letras, U. Buenos Aires, 1943; B.A., Bowdoin Coll., 1945; M.A., U. N.C., 1946; Ph.D., Harvard, 1952. Asst. prof. Spanish U. Oreg., 1949-55; prof. Tulane U., 1955-65; prof. Spanish Stanford, 1965—, also chmn. dept. Spanish and Portuguese. Author: Julio Herrera y Reissig and the Symbolists, 1957, La poesía de Juan Ramón Jiménez, Asomante, 1959, Conceptos fundamentales de literatura comparada, Asomante, 1962, Ensayos sobre poesía hispánica, 1967, Saint John of the Cross, 1971, La poesía de Juan Ramón Jiménez, Obra en marcha, 1973, Garcilaso de la Vega, 1975. Mem. Modern Lang. Assn., Am. Assn. Tchrs. Spanish and Portuguese, Inst. Internat. Literatura Iberoamericana. Home: 1001 Pine St San Francisco CA 94109

GIDDINS, GARY MITCHELL, writer, critic, disc jockey; b. Bklyn., Mar. 21, 1948; s. Leo and Alice (Gelber) G.; m. Susan Rogers, Apr. 23, 1972 (div. 1979). B.A., Grinnell (Iowa) Coll., 1970. Film reviewer Hollywood (Calif.) Reporter, 1972; contbg. editor Down Beat, 1972-74; jazz columnist Village Voice, N.Y.C., 1973—; jazz critic N.Y. Mag., N.Y.C., 1975-80; jazz columnist Hifi-Stereo Buyer's Guide, N.Y.C., 1975-78; producer, disc jockey Sta. WBAI-FM, N.Y.C., 1975-80; freelance writer various publs., 1970—, freelance record producer, 1976—; instr. jazz tradition N.Y. U. Continuing Edn. program, 1977—; vis. prof. history of jazz U. Pa., 1982-83. Producer 2 concerts at, Kool Jazz Fest, N.Y.C., 1981, Concert tribute to Gil Evans, Lincoln Ctr., N.Y.C., 1983; Author: Riding on a Blue Note, 1981, (with Carol Friedman) A Moment's Notice, 1983; contbr. to: Vanity Fair, 1983—. Recipient Deems Taylor award ASCAP, 1976, 77; Smithsonian Instn. fellow in jazz studies, 1974. Jewish. Home: 145 E 15th St New York NY 10003 Office: Village Voice 842 Broadway New York NY 10003

GIDDON, DONALD B(ERNARD), dentistry educator; b. Newark, May 1, 1930; s. William and Ruth (Franklin) G.; m. Phoebe L. Rothman, Aug. 28, 1955; children: David, Kenneth, Joanna, James. A.B., Brown U., 1952; M.A., Boston U., 1953; D.M.D., Harvard U., 1959; Ph.D., Brandeis U., 1961. Lectr. psychology Brandeis U., 1954-71, 82-84; research dentist Harvard U., 1962-65, prof., chmn. dental ecology, 1972-75, vis. prof., 1976—, lectr. health services adminstrn., 1972-75, asst. dean adminstrn., 1973-75; asso. staff New Eng. Med. Center, 1973; asso. prof., chmn. dept. social dentistry Tufts U., Boston, 1964-67, prof., chmn. dept. social dentistry, 1967-72, asst. dean, 1967-69, asso. dean, 1969-71; prof. behavioral sci. and community health NYU Dental Center, N.Y.C., 1976—, dean, 1976-78; prof. psychology Grad. Sch. Arts and Scis., prof. anesthesiology NYU Med. Center, 1976-79; prof. Faculty of Medicine, U. Groningen, Netherlands, 1980-81; cons. Astra Pharm. Products, Inc., 1960—; cons. dept. medicine and surgery VA, 1966-69, Peter Bent Brigham Hosp., 1975-76, Meml. Sloan-Kettering Cancer Center, 1976-78, Brookdale Hosp. Med. Center, 1977—, Goldwater Meml. Hosp., 1977; cons. psychologist dept. anesthesiology Brigham and Women's Hosp., 1979—; vis. prof. U. Gothenburg, Sweden, 1971, Royal Dental Coll., Aarhus, Denmark, 1972, U. Pa., 1972, McGill U., 1981—; vis. lectr. Brown U., 1981-82; founding dir. Research Inst., Royal Victoria Hosp., Montreal, 1981-82. Contbr. articles to profl. jours. Bd. dirs. Mass. Health Council, 1965-70, pres., 1968-69; pres. Hamilton Sch. PTA, Newton Lower Falls, Mass., 1963-64. Fulbright scholar, 1971. Fellow Am. Pub. Health Assn., Am. Coll. Dentists, AAAS, Internat. Coll. Dentists; mem. Am. Statis. Assn., AAUP, Am. Psychol. Assn., Internat. Assn. Study Pain, Am. Psychosomatic Soc., ADA, Am. Dental Soc. Anesthesiology (asso. editor 1965-72, chmn. ethics com. 1979-81), Behavioral Sci. in Dental Research (pres. 1976-77), Internat. Assn. Dental Research (sec. pres. 1965-66), Am. Pain Soc. (dir. 1977-79), Korean Dental Assn., Sigma Xi. Office: New York Univ 421 1st Ave New York NY 10010

GIDEON, MIRIAM, composer; b. Greeley, Colo., Oct. 23, 1906; d. Abram and Henrietta (Shoninger) G.; m. Frederic Ewen, 1949. B.A., Boston U., 1926; M.A., Columbia, 1946; D.Sacred Music, Jewish Theol. Sem., 1970. Music faculty Bklyn. Coll., 1944-54, Coll. City N.Y., 1947-55, Cantors Inst., Jewish Theol. Sem., 1955—, Manhattan Sch. Music, N.Y.C., 1967—; vis. prof. music City Coll., CUNY, 1971-76, prof. emeritus, 1976—. Composer: opera Fortunato; for orch. Symphonia Brevis, Lyric Piece for Strings, 2 cantatas, 2 sacred services in Hebrew, 13 cycles for solo voice and instrumental ensemble; works for solo voice and piano, instrumental sonatas and suites; recs. orchestral and chamber works by, Westminster Records, CRI, New World Records, Desto Records, Serenus Records., works performed in, Europe, Far East, U.S. and, S.Am. by, Internat. Soc. Contemporary Music, League Composers, London, Tokyo, Zurich symphony orchs. Recipient Bloch prize for choral work, 1948; Nat. Fedn. Music Clubs and A.S.C.A.P. award for symphonic music, 1969; Nat. Endowment of Arts grantee, 1974; commd. Library of Congress, 1979. Mem. Am. Acad. Arts and Letters, Am. Composers Alliance (bd. govs.), Internat. Soc. Contemporary Music (gov.). Home: 410 Central Park W New York NY 10025

GIDWITZ, GERALD, business executive; b. Memphis, 1906; married; 5 children. Grad., U. Chgo., 1927. Chmn. bd., chmn. exec. com., chief exec. officer Helene Curtis Industries, Inc.; vice chmn. bd. Consol. Packaging Corp. Trustee Roosevelt U., Auditorium Theatre Council; bd. dirs. Chgo. Crime Commn., Nat. Hearing Assn. Mem. Ill. Mfg. Assn. (dir.). Office: 325 N Wells St Chicago IL 60610

GIDWITZ, JOHN DAVID, symphony orchestra executive; b. N.Y.C., June 25, 1941; s. Willard M. and Adele (Bretzfeld) G.; m. Patricia Lewy, Nov. 12, 1977. B.A., Wesleyan (Conn.) U., 1963; M.A., Columbia U., 1967. Asst. to mgr. Cin. Symphony, 1971-74; gen. mgr. Springfield (Mass.) Symphony, 1974-79; mgr. San Francisco Symphony, 1979—; Pres. Met. Orchs. Mgrs. Assn., 1978-79; bd. dirs. Springfield (Mass.) Central, 1977-79. Mem. Am. Symphony Orch. League (dir. 1978-79). Home: 16 5th Ave San Francisco CA 94118 Office: San Francisco Symphony Davies Symphony Hall San Francisco CA 94102

GIEDT, WARREN HARDING, mechanical engineer, educator; b. Leola, S.D., Nov. 1, 1920; s. William John Peter and Julia Emelia (Klauss) G.; m. Leta McCarty, June 24, 1950. Student, U. Chgo., 1938-40; B.S., U. Calif., Berkeley, 1944, M.S., 1946, Ph.D., 1950. Asst. prof. Air Force Inst. Tech., Wright Field, Ohio, 1946-47; instr. dept. mech. engring. U. Calif., Berkeley, 1947-50, asst. prof., 1950-56, assoc. prof., 1956-61, prof., 1961-65, Davis, 1965—83; prof. emeritus U. Calif, Davis, 1983—; chmn. dept. mech. engring. U. Calif., 1965-69, assoc. dean grad. studies, 1972-80; research engr. Detroit Controls div. Am. Standard, 1952-60, cons., 1961-65, Monolith Portland Midwest, 1962-

63, NASA, 1964-67, Boeing Co., 1962-66, Lawrence Livermore Lab., 1960—; Fulbright prof. U. Tokyo, 1963. Author: Principles of Engineering Heat Transfer, 1957, Thermophysics, 1971; editor: Jour. Heat Transfer, 1967-72, Procs. Heat Transfer and Fluid Mechanics Inst, 1964. Served with USAAF, 1943-47. Recipient Asso. Students Outstanding Tchrs. award U. Calif., 1966. Fellow ASME (Heat transfer meml. award 1976), Japan Soc. Promotion of Sci. (fellow 1980); mem. Am. Soc. Engring. Edn. (Western Electric award 1971, G. Edwin Burks award 1974), Am. Welding Soc. (Charles Jennings award 1971), Order of Golden Bear, Phi Beta Kappa, Sigma Xi, Tau Beta Pi, Pi Tau Sigma. Home: PO Box 3074 2945 Garden Ct El Macero CA 95618 Office: Dept Mech Engring Coll Engring U Calif Davis CA 95616

GIELEN, MICHAEL ANDREAS, conductor; b. Dresden, Germany, July 20, 1927; s. Josef and Rose (Steuermann) G.; m. Helga Augsten, May 20, 1957; children: Claudia, Lucas. Student, U. Dresden, 1936, U. Berlin, 1937, U. Vienna, 1940, Buenos Aires U., 1950. Coach, Teatro Colón, Buenos Aires, 1947-50; condr., Vienna State Opera, 1950-60, Stockholm Royal Opera, 1960-65; free lance condr., Cologne, Germany, 1965-68; mus. dir., Belgian Nat. Orch., Brussels, 1969-73; chief comdr., Netherlands Opera, 1973-75; music dir., gen. mgr., Frankfurt (Germany) Opera House, from 1977; music dir., Cin. Symphony Orch., 1980—; prin. guest condr., BBC Symphony Orch., London; guest condr., Washington Nat. Symphony, Chgo. Symphony, Pitts. Symphony, Minn. Orch., Detroit Symphony, others.; Composer: 4 Gedichte von Stefan George, 1958, Variations for 40 Instruments, 1959, Un dia Sobresale, 1963, die glocken sind auffalscher spur, 1969, Mitbestimmunes Modell, 1974. Office: Cin Symphony Orch 1241 Elm St Cincinnati OH 45210 *

GIELGUD, SIR ARTHUR JOHN, actor, dir.; b. London, Apr. 14, 1904; s. Frank and Kate (Terry-Lewis) G. Student, Hillside Godalming, 1913-18, Westminster Sch., 1918-20; with, Lady Benson, 1920-21, Royal Acad. Dramatic Art, 1922-23; LL.D. (hon.), U. St. Andrews, 1950, U. London, 1977, Litt.D., Oxford (Eng.) U., 1953. Established repretory theater in, London, 1938, Haymarket, 1943-44. Appeared in: Hamlet, 1929, 30, 34, 36, 37, 39, 44, Richard II, 1929, 38, Macbeth, 1929, 42; appeared as Mark Antony in: Julius Caesar, 1929; Hotspur in: Henry IV, 1930; achieved first London success as Lewis Dodd in: The Constant Nymph, 1926; Malvolio in: Twelfth Night, 1930, The Good Companions, 1930, movie of latter play, 1931, Musical Chairs, 1931, Richard of Bordeaux, 1932, School for Scandal, 1938; appeared as Shylock in: The Merchant of Venice, 1938, Queen's Theatre, Dear Octopus, 1939, The Importance of Being Earnest, 1930, 39-40, 43, The Duchess of Malfi, 1944; dir.: Lady Windermere's Fan, 1946; played in: movies including Diary for Timothy; documentary; appeared in: Love for Love, during war in England and again in Am., 1942-44, 47; in: Crime and Punishment, London, 1946, Medea, U.S.A., 1947-48; acted in: The Return of the Prodigal, 1948; London dir.: The Glass Menagerie starring Helen Hayes, 1948; dir.: Medea, 1948, The Heiress, 1949; actor, Stratford-on-Avon Festival, Measure for Measure, Julius Caesar, Much Ado About Nothing, King Lear, 1950, Winters Tale, 1951; dir., actor: Much Ado About Nothing, 1949, 52, 55; in: M.G.M. film Julius Caesar, 1952; dir., actor: A Day By the Sea, 1953, The Cherry Orchard, 1954; appeared in: King Lear, with Stratford-On-Avon Co., on tour and in London, 1955; dir., actor Sebastian: Nude with a Violin, 1956; Prospero in: The Tempest, 1957, 58; Cardinal Wolsey: Broaday recital Ages of Man, 1959; dir., actor: Much Ado About Nothing, N.Y.C., Boston, 1959; appeared as Julian in: Tiny Alice, N.Y.C., 1964-65; Producer, dir.: Berlioz's The Trojans, 1958, Britten's A Midsummer Nights Dream, Royal Opera House, Covent Garden, London, 1961; dir.: Big Fish, Little Fish, N.Y.C., 1961 (Tony award), Dazzling Prospect, 1961, The School for Scandal, Haymarket, 1962; played: Othello, Stratford-on-Avon, 1961; Gaev in: Cherry Orchard, Stratford-On-Avon, 1961, Aldwych, London, 1962; dir., played Joseph Surface in: School for Scandal, U.S., 1963, Ages of Man, Lyceum Theater, N.Y.C., 1963, Ages of Man, Australia and N.Z., 1963-64; dir.: Hamlet, Can., Boston, N.Y.C., 1974; film The Loved One, 1964, Chimes at Midnight, 1966, Mister Sebastian, 1967, The Charge of the Light Brigade, 1967, Ages of Man, Finland, Scandinavia, Poland, USSR, 1964, U.S.A., Eng., 1965-66; played in: Oedipus, Nat. Theatre, 1967-68; in: Julius Caesar; Sir Politick Woulbe in: Volpone, 1977; in: films Oh! What a Lovely War, 1967-68; dir.: Halfway Up a Tree; appeared in: Forty Years On, London, 1968, Home, London and N.Y.C., 1970-71, Veterans, London, 1972, No Man's Land, London and N.Y.C., 1977, Bingo, 1975, Half-Life, 1978; in: Secret Agent, 1935, Lost Horizon, 1972, QB VII, 1973, Murder on the Orient Express, 1974, Joseph Andrews, Providence, Portrait of a Young Man, Caligula, 1977, The Director, 1979, Chariots of Fire, Arthur, Sphinx, The Formula, The Conductor; appeared in: TV prodns. of Richard II, 1979, Brideshead Revisited, English Gardens, Neck, Parson's Pleasure, Why Didn't They Ask Evans?, Seven Dials Mystery; Author: autobiography Early Stages, 1938, Stage Directions, 1964, Distinguished Company, 1972, Gielgud: An Actor and His Time, 1980. Decorated knight Order Brit. Empire, Companion of Honor, chevalier Legion of Honor; recipient Antoinette Perry award Ages of Man, 1958, spl. award, 1959, directing award for Big Fish, Little Fish, 1961; named Brandeis University Companion, 1960; recipient Della Austrian medal for Tiny Alice Drama League of N.Y., 1965; named Best Actor for role in Providence N.Y. Film Critics, 1977. Mem. Shakespeare Reading Soc. (pres. 1958—), Royal Acad. Dramatic Art (pres. 1977—). Clubs: Garrick, Players (N.Y.C.). Home: South Pavilion Wotton Underwood Aylesbury Buckinghamshire England Office: care Internat Famous Agy 22 Grafron St London W1 England

GIERASCH, PETER JAY, educator; b. Washington, Dec. 19, 1940; s. Aiden Redmond and Marian Bell (Bookhout) G.; m. Maida Erika Wiesenthal, June 28, 1964; children—Adam Redmond, Amanda Farrar. B.A., Harvard U., 1962, Ph.D., 1968. Asst. prof. meteorology Fla. State U., Tallahassee, 1969-72; asst. prof. to prof. astronomy Cornell U., Ithaca, N.Y., 1972—. Contbr. articles to profl. jours. Sloan Found. research fellow, 1975-79. Mem. Am. Astron. Soc., Internat. Astron. Union, Am. Meteorol. Soc. Office: Dept Astronomy Cornell U Ithaca NY 14853

GIERTZ, J. FRED, economics educator; b. Wichita, Kans., Jan. 18, 1943; s. Joe L. and Frieda J. (Hamblin) G.; m. Donna Hyland, Sept. 13, 1969; children: Seth H., Gabrielle H. B.A., Wichita U., 1964; M.A., Northwestern U., 1966, Ph.D., 1970. Instr. econs. Miami U., Oxford, Ohio, 1968-70, asst. prof., 1970-73, asso. prof., 1973-78, prof., 1978-80; prof. econs. Inst. Govt. and Public Affairs, U. Ill., Urbana, 1980—; research dir. Ill. Tax Reform Commn., 1982-83; cons. in field. Mem. editorial bd.: Quarterly Rev. Econs. and Bus, 1979—; contbr. articles in field to profl. jours. Mem. Midwest Econs. Assn. (v.p. 1978-79), Am. Econ. Assn., Ill. Econs. Assn., Public Choice Soc., Nat. Tax Assn. Home: 601 Park Ln Champaign IL 61820 Office: 1201 W Nevada St Urbana IL 61801

GIES, THOMAS ANTHONY, publishing co. exec.; b. Chgo., Jan. 24, 1930; s. Charles P. and Marie S. (Simons) G.; m. Janet Seney, Oct. 23, 1955; children—John C., Kevin T., Elizabeth A. B.A., Northwestern U., 1955. Pres. Ency. Brit. Philippines, Manila, 1970-72, Ency. Brit. Japan, Tokyo, 1972-74; pres. Ency. Brit. Internat., Chgo., 1974—; chmn. Linguarama Britannica, Germany, 1980-81; dir. EB Pubs., Latin Am., Ency. Universalis, France. Served with U.S. Army, 1955-58. Mem. Japan/Am. Soc., Direct Selling Assn., Chgo. Book Clinic, Chgo. Council Fgn. Relations, Chgo. Com. Clubs: Tokyo Lawn Tennis, Manila Polo, Manila Overseas Press. Office: 425 N Michigan Ave Chicago IL 60611

GIES, THOMAS GEORGE, educator; b. Detroit, Jan. 12, 1921; s. Charles G. and Jane E. (Sturman) G.; m. Thelma Irene Young, Sept. 6, 1941; children: Laurie Hollis, Thomas Michael, Joseph Christopher. A.B., U. Mich., 1946, M.A., 1948, Ph.D., 1952. Instr. econs. U. Mich., 1948-51; fin. economist Fed. Res. Bank Kansas City, Mo., 1951-57; lectr. econs. U. Colo., 1955, 57, 70; lectr. fin. U. Mo., Kansas City, 1956-57; faculty U. Mich., Ann Arbor, 1957—, prof. fin., 1960—, chmn. fin. dept., 1977—; lectr. Netherlands Sch. Econs., 1964; cons. in field, 1957—; Chmn. Gov. Mich. Com. Revision Fin. Code, 1964-65; mem. Gov. Mich. Com. Econ. Growth, 1959-60, 61-62; vice chmn. Gov. Mich. Council Financial Advisers, 1965-69. Author: Consumer Installment Credit, 1957, Portfolio Policies and Regulations of Private Financial Institutions, 1962, Consumer Finance Companies in Michigan, 1960, Public Utility Regulations: New Directions in Theory and Policy, 1966, Legislating for Economic Expansion, 1970, Banking Markets and Financial Institutions, 1971, Investor Experience With Municipal Bond Ratings, 1974, Public Utility Regulation, 1975, Regulation in Further Perspective, 1974, Inflation in Wholesale Distribution, 1981, Deregulation-Appraisal Before the Fact, 1982; Contbr. articles to profl. jours. Served with AUS, USAAF, 1941-46. Mem. Am. Econ. Assn., Midwest Fin. Assn. (pres. 1971-72), Am. Fin. Assn., Phi Kappa Phi. Home: 502 Burson Pl Ann Arbor MI 48104

GIESE, LOUIS BERNHARDT, bank holding co. exec.; b. Milw., Nov. 7, 1927; s. Gustav Leopold and Eunice Dorothy (Muller) G.; m. Marcella Ruth Zolna, Sept. 10, 1949; children—Christopher, Thomas, Beth, Kay, Mark. B.A., Marquette U., 1950. C.P.A. Dep. comptroller First Wis. Nat. Bank at Milw., 1969; v.p., treas. First Wis. Bankshares Corp., 1971-73; exec. v.p. First Wis. Mortgage Co., 1973-81; 1st v.p. First Wis. Corp., 1981—; dir. J.W. Copps, Inc. Mem. Bank Adminstrn. Inst. (pres. Milw. 1974), Wis. Soc. C.P.A.'s, Am. Inst. C.P.A.'s. Home: 8949 N Greenvale Rd Bayside WI 53217 Office: 777 E Wisconsin Ave Milwaukee WI 53202

GIESECKE, G(USTAV) ERNST, educator; b. Marble Falls, Tex., Sept. 13, 1908; s. Walter C. and Ulrika (Matern) G.; m. Louise Helene Bittner, Sept. 17, 1943; children—Mark Ernst, Helene Louise Ebrill. A.B., Stanford U., 1931, A.M., 1934, Ph.D., 1938; LL.D., U. Toledo, 1962. Teaching asst. German Stanford U., 1932-37; instr. and asso. in German, counselor student personnel bur. U. Ill., 1937-42, supr. counseling in residence halls, 1946, asst. dean liberal arts sch., asst. prof. German, 1946, asst. dean, asst. prof. German, 1946-49; dean sch. applied arts and scis. N.D. State U., Fargo, 1949-53; v.p. Tex. Tech. U., Lubbock, 1953-59; prof. higher edn., asso. dean Grad. Sch. Edn., U. Chgo., 1959-65; univ. prof., provost U. Toledo, 1965-70; prof. humanities, acting v.p. acad. affairs Sangamon State U., Springfield, Ill., 1970-71, prof. higher edn., dir. ednl. relations, 1971-76, prof. emeritus, 1976—; planning cons. to alt. system of higher edn. in, Ill., 1976—; founder N.D. Inst. for Regional Studies, 1950, exec. sec., 1950-53, dir. summer session, 1950-53; Mem. SW adv. com. Inst. Internat. Edn., 1958-59; mem. visitation and appraisal com. Nat. Council Accreditation Tchr. Edn., 1963-66; cons., examiner N. Central Assn. Colls. and Secondary Schs., 1960-72; chmn., dir. Midwest Fulbright Terminal Conf., 1964; Chmn. Mayor's com. on the Young Citizen and the Ballot, 1956-58; mem. Tex. adv. com. conservation edn., 1956-59; chmn. Lubbock Internat. Affairs Com., 1954-59; mem. research adv. com. Tex. Commn. Higher Edn., 1956-59; chmn. Mental Health Week in Lubbock, 1958; co-dir. Ill. observance 75th anniversary of creation of first jr. coll., Joliet, 1974-77; mem. research adv. council Ill. Community Coll. Bd., 1972-81; mem. liaison com. Am. Assn. Community and Jr. Colls. Council Univs. and Colls. and Nat. Council State Dirs. Community and Jr. Colls., 1976-78. Author: N.D. Inst. for Regional Studies, Fargo, 1952, An Alternative System of Higher Education in Illinois, 1973; Contbr. articles to profl. publs.; Founder: Community Coll. Frontiers, Quar, 1972. Trustee Toledo Ednl. Television Found., 1967-70; pres. Springfield Local Devel. Corp., 1980—. Served as lt. USNR, 1942-46. Fellow Inst. Internat. Edn., Germany, 1931-32. Mem. Ill. Community Coll. Faculty Assn. (life), Am. Ednl. Research Assn. (mem. com. 1967-70), West Tex. C. of C. (dir. 1957-58). Made study tour, guest Fed. German Republic, 1958, Yugoslavia, 1974, USSR, 1976, People's Republic of China, Taiwan, 1981. Home: 1628 Dennison Dr Springfield IL 62704 *It has been deeply satisfying to me to devote a lifetime of work to the great idea embodied in the land-grant and the community college systems—to make man's best knowledge and wisdom available to the people of the world in the best position to make positive use of it.*

GIESEN, FRANK HARTMAN, consulting civil engineer; b. Superior, Wis., Oct. 5, 1932; s. Irving Walter and Tracy Josephine (O'Donnell) G.; m. Mary M. Girouard, Aug. 13, 1955; children: David, Stephen, Robert, Tracy, Mary Pat, Francis. B.C.E., Marquette U., Milw., 1955. Registered profl. engr., 32 states. With Consoer Townsend, 1955—, partner, pres., Chgo., 1966—; pres. Ky.-Tenn. Water Pollution Control Assn., 1976-78. Mem. Cons. Engrs. Tenn. (sec.-treas.), Water Pollution Control Assn., ASCE, Nat. Soc. Profl. Engrs., Am. Water Works Assn., Am. Public Works Assn. Roman Catholic. Clubs: Richland Country, Civitan (Nashville) (past pres.); Woodlands Country (Houston); Ill. Athletic, Mid-America (Chgo.); KC. Home: 3132 Walden Wilmette IL 60091

GIESEN, JOHN WILLIAM, advertising executive; b. St. Paul, Apr. 5, 1928; s. William J. and Salome Anna (Shopnitz) G.; m. Mary Lou Gilbertson, May 20, 1950; children: Cynthia, John, Lee Ann, Gregory, David, Laurie. Student, St. Thomas Coll., 1946-49, U. Minn., 1950-52, St. Paul Sch. Assoc. Arts, 1951-53. Advt. rep. St. Paul Dispatch-Pioneer Press, 1950-54; advt. mgr. Bruce Pub. Co., St. Paul, 1954-56; nat. advt. mgr. Duluth Herald News Tribune, 1956-60; account exec. N.W. Ayer & Son, Inc., Chgo., 1960-64, acct. supr., 1964-66; account exec. Leo Burnett, Inc., Chgo., 1966-68, v.p. account supr., 1968-74; exec. v.p. Barickman Advt., Denver, 1974-77, chmn. exec. com., 1977-82; pres. Doyle Dane Bernbach Advt., Denver, 1982—. Chmn. Sts. Faith-Hope Charity Elem. Sch. Bd., Winnetka, Ill., 1972-74. Served with U.S. Army, 1946-48. Mem. Denver Advt. Fedn. (dir. 1980-82). Republican. Roman Catholic. Club: Rotary. Home: 6186 E Princeton Ave Englewood CO 80111 Office: 7535 E Hampden Ave Suite 416 Denver CO 80231

GIESEN, RICHARD ALLYN, business executive; b. Evanston, Ill., Oct. 7, 1929; s. Elmer J. and Ethyl (Lillig) G.; m. Jeannine St. Bernard, Jan. 31, 1953; children: Richard Allyn, Laurie J., Mark S. B.S., Northwestern U., 1951. Research analyst new bus. and research depts. Glore, Forgan & Co., Chgo., 1951-57; asst. to pres. Gen. Dynamics Corp., N.Y.C., 1957-60, asst. treas., 1960-61, asst. v.p. ops. and contracts, 1961-63; fin. cons. IBM Corp., 1963, exec. asst. to sr. v.p., 1964-65; treas. subs. Sci. Research Assos., Inc., Chgo., 1965-66, v.p. finance and adminstrn., 1966-67, exec. v.p., chief operating officer, 1967-68, pres., chief exec. officer, 1968-80, Field Enterprises, Inc., Chgo., 1980-83, also dir., chmn. exec. com., until 1983; dir. JWT Group, Inc., N.Y.C.; dir. Stone Container Corp., GATX, Inc., Daubert Industries, Chgo. Mem. bus. adv. council Chgo. Urban League, 1968-83; prin. Chgo. United, 1980-83; mem. adv. council Technol. Inst., Northwestern U.; mem. pres.'s council Nat. Coll. Edn., Evanston, Ill.; bd. dirs. Am. Cancer Soc., Protestant Found. Greater Chgo.; chmn. Chgo. unit 1981 campaign Am. Cancer Soc.; mem. Midwest adv. bd. Inst. Internat. Edn., Chgo. Mem. Chgo. Pres. Orgn., Chief Execs. Orgn., Chgo. Assn. Commerce and Industry (dir.), Chgo. Council Fgn. Relations, Alpha Tau Omega, Beta Gamma Sigma. Clubs: Chicago; Glen View (Golf, Ill.); Shore acres (Lake Bluff, Ill). Office: 200 E Randolph Dr Chicago IL 60601

GIESEY, RALPH EDWIN, educator; b. Detroit, Jan. 7, 1923; s. William Carl and Mary Jane (Thomas) G. A.B., Wayne State U., 1944, M.A., 1947; Ph.D. (Fulbright scholar, Am. Council Learned Socs. fellow), U. Calif., 1954. Prof. history Vassar Coll., 1955-56, U. Wash., 1956-59, U. Minn., 1959-66, U. Iowa, Iowa City, 1966—; Vis. mem. Inst. for Advanced Study, 1964-66, 75-76. Author: Royal Funeral Ceremony in Renaissance France, 1960, The Juristic Basis of Dynastic Right to the French Throne, 1961, If Not, Not: The Oath of the Aragonese and the Legendary Laws of Sobrarbe, 1969, The Francogallia by Francois Hotman, 1972. Served to lt. (j.g.) USNR, 1943-45. Rockefeller Found. fellow, 1962; Guggenheim fellow, 1970; Nat. Endowment for Humanities sr. fellow, 1974. Mem. Am. Hist. Assn., Mediaeval Acad. Am., Renaissance Soc. Am., Am. Numis. Soc. Home: 601 S Governor St Iowa City IA 52240

GIFFEN, JAMES HENRY, financial company executive; b. Stockton, Calif., Mar. 22, 1941; s. Lloyd Henry and Lucille (Threlfall) G.; m. June Hopkins, Oct. 13, 1961; children: Allison Ann, David Lloyd. B.A., U. Calif.-Berkeley, 1962; J.D., UCLA, 1965. Bar: Calif., N.Y. Assoc. Baker, Ancel & Redmond, Los Angeles, 1966-67; pres. Satra Cons. Corp., N.Y.C., 1968-71; v.p. Satra Corp., N.Y.C., 1971-72; pres. Armco Internat. Inc., N.Y.C., 1973—; dir. corp. devel. Armco Inc., N.Y.C., 1977-81, corp. v.p., 1981—; dir. Am. Life Ins. Co. of N.Y., 1982-83, UNA of the USA, 1983; chmn. N.Y. Dist. Export Council, U.S. Dept. Commerce; mem. Nat. Com. Harvard-Columbia Russian Studies Fund; mem. East-West Adv. Com. U.S. Dept. Commerce; adj. prof. Grad. Sch. Bus.,Columbia U., Grad. Sch. Internat. Affairs, Columbia U. Author: The Legal and Practical Aspects of Trade with the Soviet Union, 1969; contbr. articles to profl. jours. Mem. Council Fgn. Relations, Bar State Calif., UNA-USA USSR Parrallel Studies Program. Clubs: Brook, Winged Foot. Office: 375 Park Ave New York NY 10152

GIFFIN, GLENN ORLANDO, II, music critic, writer; b. Denver, Feb. 27, 1943; s. Glenn Orlando and E. Louise (Mosler) G. B.Mus., U. Colo., 1965; M.A. in Librarianship, U. Denver, 1967. Scriptwriter, broadcaster radio sta. KRNW-FM, Boulder, 1965-67; asst. music critic San Francisco Chronicle, 1968; asst. music librarian Norlin libraries U. Colo., 1968-70; music critic, staff writer Denver Post, 1970-73, music editor, 1973—. Rockefeller Found. fellow, 1966-68; Corbett Found. fellow, 1969; Nat. Endowment for Arts grantee Dance Criticism Inst., Conn. Coll., summer 1971. Mem. Music Library Assn., Am. Musicol. Soc., Dance Critics Assn., Music Critics Assn., Sigma Delta Chi. Office: PO Box 1709 Denver CO 80201

GIFFORD, CHARLES LEVI, mining and chemical company executive; b. Cissna Park, Ill., Dec. 26, 1920; s. Jesse Junior and Lora Elizabeth (Smith) G.; m. Willie Claire Phillips, Mar. 8, 1947; children: Charles Robert, Pamela May, Margaret Elizabeth. Cert., Bryant & Stratton Coll., Chgo., 1939-40. Office mgr. Chgo. Switchboard Co., 1941-42; acctg. mgr. Edgar Bros. Co., Metuchen, N.J., 1946-54; asst. controller Minerals & Chems. Corp. Am., Menlo Park, N.J., 1954-60; controller Minerals & Chems. Phillipp Corp., Menlo Park, 1960-67; v.p., controller minerals and chems. div., asst. treas. Englehard Minerals & Chems. Corp., Menlo Park, Edison, N.J., 1967-74, sr. v.p. fin. minerals and chems. div., 1974-78, sr. v.p., asst. to pres., asst. treas. corp., 1978-81; sec.-treas. Englehard Corp., Menlo Park, Edison, 1981-82, v.p., sec., Menlo Park, N.J., 1982—; dir. Commonwealth Bank of Metuchen, N.J., Res. Net. Corp., Whippany, N.J. Trustee, exec. v.p. John F. Kennedy Med. Ctr., Edison, N.J., 1962—, bd. dirs., Edison, N.J., 1980—; sec., bd. dirs. Medishare Corp., Edison, N.J., 1982—; bd. dirs. JFK Found., Edison, N.J., 1980—. Served with USAAF, 1942-46; PTO. Mem. Nat. Assn. Accts. Clubs: Metuchen Golf and Country, River North Golf and Country. Home: 63 Beacon Hill Dr Metuchen NJ 08840 Office: Englehard Corp Menlo Park CN40 Edison NJ 08818

GIFFORD, FRANK NEWTON, broadcast journalist; b. Santa Monica, Calif., Aug. 16, 1930; s. Weldon Wayne and Lola (Hawkins) G.; m. Astrid Naess; children: Jeffery, Kyle, Victoria; m. Astrid Naess Lindley, Mar. 1978. Student, Bakersfield Jr. Coll., 1948-49; B.A., U. So. Calif., 1952. Mem. N.Y. Giants (profl. football team), 1952-65; sports reporter CBS Radio, N.Y.C., 1957-59; Nat. Football League pre-game show host CBS-TV Network, N.Y.C., 1959-62; sports reporter WCBS-TV, N.Y.C., 1962-71; reporter ABC Radio Info., N.Y.C., 1971-77; sports corr. ABC TV Network, N.Y.C., 1971-77; corr. Eyewitness News, N.Y.C., 1971—; host The Superstars Series.; Dir. sports writers and broadcasters Spl. Olympics, 1972-75. (Emmy award for outstanding sports personality 1977); Author: Frank Gifford's NFL-AFL Football Guide, 1968, rev. edits., 1969, 70, Frank Gifford's Football Guide Book, 1966, (with Charles Mangel) Gifford on Coverage, 1976. Bd. dirs. Nat. Soc. for Multiple Sclerosis, 1973-78. Named Sportsman of Yr. Cath. Youth Orgn., 1964; elected to Nat. Football Found. Hall of Fame, 1975; Pro Football Hall of Fame, 1977; recipient Gil Hodges Meml. sports award Cath. Med. Center, 1976, Adam award Men's Fashion Assn. Am., 1976. Office: ABC-TV 1330 Ave of Americas New York NY 10019 *

GIFFORD, HARRY CORTLAND FREY, health educator; b. N.Y.C., Sept. 21, 1919; s. Frank Dean and Hazel (Frey) G.; m. Catherine Huber, Sept. 14, 1946; children—Linda Gifford Reece, Frank Dean. Grad., Kent Sch., Conn., 1938; B.A. in History, Yale, 1942; M.S. in Hosp. Adminstrn, Columbia, 1947. Adminstrv. resident Greenwich (Conn.) Hosp., 1947; asst. supt. Hackensack (N.J.) Hosp., 1948-49; adminstr. Community Hosp., Glen Cove, N.Y., 1949-61; exec. dir. Springfield (Mass.) Hosp. Med. Center, 1961-67, exec. v.p., dir., 1967-74; pres. Baystate Med. Center, Springfield, 1974-81; lectr. U. Mass., Amherst, 1981—; vis. lectr. hosp. adminstrn. Columbia, 1961—, preceptor hosp. adminstrn. residency, 1953-60, Yale, 1973. Contbr. articles to profl. jours. Mem. Springfield Mental Health Bd., 1965-67; mem. gov.'s com. Health and Ednl. Facilities Authority, 1970-73; Corporator Springfield Tech. Community Coll. Served to 1st lt. Med. Services AUS, 1942-45. Decorated Bronze Star with palm. Fellow Am. Coll. Hosp. Adminstrs. (regents council 1970-71); mem. Am. Hosp. Assn. (trustee 1973-75, 77-80, del. at large 1971-73, del. 1967-70, 76—, chmn. regional adv. bd. 1969-70, 77-80), Mass. Hosp. Assn. (pres. 1967-68). Club: Rotarian (Glen Cove club) (pres. 1958-59). Home: 140 Chestnut St Springfield MA 01115 Office: Sch Pub Health U Mass Amherst MA 01003

GIFFORD, JOHN ARCHER, lawyer; b. Newark, Dec. 6, 1900; s. Charles Alling and Helen (Conyngham) G.; m. Barbara Prosser, June 20, 1928; 1 son, Prosser. Grad., Hill Sch., Pottstown, Pa., 1918; B.A., Yale, 1922; LL.B., Harvard, 1925. Bar: N.Y. 1926. Practiced in, N.Y.C., 1926—; partner firm White & Case, 1937-72, of counsel, 1973-77; hon. trustee N.Y. Bank Savs. Hon. dir. Commonwealth Fund; hon. trustee Presbyn. Hosp., N.Y.C. Served to lt. comdr. USNR, 1943-45. Mem. Am., N.Y. State bar assns., Bar Assn. City N.Y. Home: 117 E 72d St New York NY 10021

GIFFORD, NELSON SAGE, manufacturing company executive; b. Newton, Mass., May 3 1930; s. Gordon Babcock and Hariette Rose (Dooley) G.; m. Elizabeth B. Brow, Nov. 12, 1955; children: Susan Helen, Ian Christopher, Diane Brow. A.B., Tufts Coll., 1952. With Dennison Mfg. Co., Framingham and Waltham, Mass., 1954—, v.p., 1967-72, pres., 1972—; also dir.; dir. Dunn Paper Co., Port Huron, Mich., Nat. Blank Book Co., Holyoke, Mass., Establissments Doret s/a, Paris, Reed & Barton, John Hancock Mut. Life Ins. Co., Boston, Boston Edison Co., Bank of Boston, M/A Com, Burlington, Mass. Trustee New Eng. Colls. Fund, Boston, Tufts U., Medford, Mass. Served to lt. (j.g.) USNR, 1952-54. Mem. Silvanus Packard Soc., Mass. Bus. Roundtable (dir., vice-chmn.), Associated Industries Mass. (dir.). Clubs: Brae Burn Country (West Newton, Mass.); Beverley Yacht, Kittansett (Marion, Mass.). Home: 14 Windsor Rd Wellesley MA 02181 Office: 275 Wyman St Waltham MA 02154

GIFFORD, PORTER WILLIAM, construction materials manufacturing company executive; b. Dallas, Dec. 14, 1918; s. Porter William and Evelyn Victoria (Bonorden) G.; m. Elizabeth Butte, Jan. 19, 1946; children: Porter William, Sharon Elizabeth, Geoffrey Butte. B.S. in Mech. Engring, Cornell U., 1941. With Gifford-Hill & Co., Inc., Dallas, 1941—, pres., 1958-69, chmn. bd. dirs., 1969-71, now dir., mem. exec. and finance coms.; dir. Q-Dot Corp., Dallas; chmn. bd. Gen. Exploration Co., Dallas. Mem. Dallas Citizens Council; bd. dirs. Dallas County unit Am. Cancer Soc.; trustee Found. Econ. Edn., Internat. Linguistics Center, Dallas. Served to maj. AUS, 1941-45. Decorated Bronze Star. Mem. Dallas Salesmanship Club, Tau Beta Pi, Delta Kappa Epsilon. Clubs: Petroleum, Northwood Country (Dallas). Home: 9107 Devonshire Dr Dallas TX 75209 Office: Gifford-Hill & Co Inc PO Box 47127 Dallas TX 75247

GIFFORD, PROSSER, research institute administrator; b. N.Y.C., May 16, 1929; s. John Archer and Barbara (Prosser) G.; m. Shirley Mireille O'Sullivan, June 26, 1954; children: Barbara, Paula, Heidi. B.A., Yale, 1951; Ph.D., Yale U., 1964; B.A., Oxford (Eng.) U., 1953, M.A., 1958; LL.B., Harvard U., 1956; M.A., Amherst Coll., 1969, L.H.D., 1980; LL.D., Doshisha U., Kyoto, Japan, 1979. Bar: D.C. 1957. Asst. to pres. Swarthmore Coll., 1956-58; asst. prof. history Yale, 1964-66; dir. 5 yr. B.A. program, 1965-66; dean faculty Amherst Coll., 1967-79, asso. prof. history, 1967-69, prof. history, 1969-79; dep. dir. Woodrow Wilson Internat. Center for Scholars, Washington, 1975-76, 80—; Trustee Hotchkiss Sch., 1971-81, Concord Acad., 1972-78; chmn. bd. trustees Woods Hole Marine Biol. Lab. Co-editor, contbr.: Britain and Germany in Africa, 1967, France and Britain in Africa, 1971, Transfer of Power in Africa, 1982. Rhodes scholar, 1951-53; Fgn. Area fellow, No Rhodesia, 1963-64. Mem. Assn. Yale Alumni (gov. 1972-77), Woods Hole Oceanographic Inst. (mem. corp.). Clubs: Century, Cosmos; Elizabethan (Yale); Woods Hole (Mass.); Golf and Tennis.; Quisset Yacht (Mass.). Home: 560 N St SW N705 Washington DC 20024 Penzance Point Woods Hole MA 02543

GIFFORD, RAY WALLACE, JR., physician, educator; b. Westerville, Ohio, Aug. 13, 1923; s. Ray Wallace and Alma Marie (Wagoner) G.; m. Frances Anne Moore, Jan. 13, 1973; 1 son, Graydon; children by previous marriage: Peggy, Cynthia, Susan. B.S., Otterbein Coll., 1941; M.D., Ohio State U., 1947; M.Sc., U. Minn., 1952. Diplomate: Am. Bd. Internal Medicine. Intern Colo. Gen. Hosp., Denver, 1947-48; resident in internal medicine Mayo Clinic, Rochester, Minn., 1949-52; practice medicine specializing in hypertension and nephrology; asst. prof. medicine, cons. sect. medicine Mayo Clinic, Mayo Found., 1953-61; staff mem. dept. hypertension and nephrology Cleve. Clinic Found., 1961-67, head dept. hypertension and nephrology, 1967—, bd. govs., 1973-78, vice chmn., 1977-78, vice chmn. div. medicine, 1978—; mem. commn. on stroke Nat. Inst. Neurol. Disease and Stroke, 1972-74; chmn. Nat. Council on Drugs, 1976-78; chmn. hypertension task force Intersoc. Commn. on Heart Disease Resources, 1979-81; mem. nat. high blood pressure coordinating com. Nat. Heart, Lung and Blood Inst., 1978—; mem. 2d and 3d joint nat. coms. on detection, evaluation and treatment of high blood pressure, 1979-80, 83—; mem. Congl. Commn. on Drug Approval Process, 1981-82; mem. adv. com. to dir. NIH, 1983—. Author: (with William Manger) Pheochromocytoma, 1977; contbr. numerous papers to med. jours.; editorial bd.: Stroke Jour, 1971-74, Am. Jour. Cardiology, 1973-78, Geriatrics, 1974—. Mem. Rochester (Minn.) City Council, 1960-61; Republican precinct committeeman, Cleveland Heights, Ohio, 1966-70. Served as lt. comdr. MC USNR, 1954-56. Recipient Alumni Achievement award Ohio State U., 1962, Disting. Sci. Achievement award Otterbein Coll., 1970, Oscar B. Hunter Meml. award in therapeutics Am. Soc. for Clin. Pharmacology and Therapeutics, 1979. Fellow Am. Coll. Cardiology (bd. trustees 1969-70, gov. Ohio 1970-73), A.C.P., Am. Coll. Chest Physicians (chmn. com. on hypertension 1970-72, Simon Rodbard Meml. award 1982); mem. Am. Heart Assn. (bd. dirs. 1969-72, chmn. stroke council 1970-72), AMA (mem. council on sci. affairs 1976—, vice chmn. council on sci. affairs 1981-83, chmn. council on sci. affairs 1983—), Am. Soc. Clin. Pharmacology and Therapeutics (pres. 1976-77), Am. Soc. Nephrology, Central Soc. Clin. Research, Internat. Soc. Hypertension, Internat. Soc. Nephrology, Interstate Postgrad. Med. Assn. (pres. 1976-77). Methodist. Home: 3479 Glen Allen Dr Cleveland Heights OH 44121 Office: 9500 Euclid Ave Cleveland OH 44106

GIFFORD, WILLIAM LEO, utility company executive; b. Weston, Conn., Aug. 30, 1930; s. Rolland Wyckoff and Margaret Mary (Clifford) G.; m. Marion Frances Miletti, Oct. 27, 1956; children: Margaret Rose, William Leo, David W. A.B., Fordham U., 1952; postgrad., U. Conn. Sch. Law, 1952-55. Adminstrv. asst. to Rep. Charles E. Goodell, 1959-68, Rep. James F. Hastings, 1968-69; spl. asst. to sec. labor, Washington, 1969-70; spl. asst. to Pres. U.S., Washington, 1970-72; asst. to sec. treasury, Washington, 1972-73, dep. under sec. treasury, 1973-74; govt. affairs rep. Gen. Electric Co., Washington, 1974-75, mgr. exec. and legis. programs, 1975-80; v.p. GPU Nuclear Corp., Middletown, Pa., 1980—. Contbr. articles to profl. jours. Mem. Treasury Dept. Hist. Soc. Mem. Bull Elephants. Republican. Roman Catholic. Clubs: Georgetown, University, Capitol Hill. Office: PO Box 480 Middletown PA 17057

GIFFORD, WILLIAM WALLACE, English educator; b. Plainfield, N.J., Nov. 15, 1928; s. Ralph Staples and Jane (Wheelan) G.; m. Alice Heyroth, July 22, 1950; children: Caroline Jane, Daniel Wheelan. B.A., Swarthmore Coll., 1950; M.A., U. Calif.-Berkeley, 1952, Ph.D., 1955. Prof. English Vassar Coll., Poughkeepsie, N.Y., 1955—. Author Literary articles and short stories. Resident Yaddo Corp., 1967-70; Mellon grantee Vassar Coll., 1982. Mem. AAUP, Phi Beta Kappa. Home: 36 Vasser View Poughkeepsie NY 12603 Office: Dept English Vassar Coll Poughkeepsie NY 12601

GIFT, JESS REID, elctronics conpany executive; b. Mooreland, Okla., June 24, 1946; s. Elswick Ernest and Marjorie Joyce (Jameson) G.; m. Susan Lea Minnich, Oct. 25, 1980; 1 dau., Jessica Lea. B.S., U. Ill.-Chgo., 1969; M.B.A., DePaul U., 1971. Fin. and planning analyst Gould, Inc., Chgo., 1972-75, asst. to treas., 1975-76, asst. treas., 1976-77, v.p., treas., 1982—; v.p. fin. Gould Fla. Inc., West Palm Beach, 1977-81; pres. Adv. Mgmt. Services, Inc., West Palm Beach, 1981-82, Palm Beach Assocs., 1982—. Mem. U. Ill.-Chgo. Bus. Adv. Council, 1982. Served with USN, 1966-67. Mem. Nat. Assn. Corp. Treas., Nat. Tax. Assn. Clubs: Palm Beach Polo (West Palm Beach); Meadow (Rolling Meadows, Ill.). Home: 3155 Mallet Hill Ct West Palm Beach FL 33413 Office: Palm Beach Assocs 13198 Forest Hill Blvd West Palm Beach FL 33411

GIGANTE, ALEXANDER, publishing company executive; b. Bklyn., Aug. 3, 1946; s. Alexander and Yolanda (Giambalvo) G. B.A., Bklyn. Coll., 1967; J.D., NYU, 1970. Bar: N.Y. 1971, U.S. Supreme Ct. 1975, U.S. Ct. Appeals (2d cir.) 1973, U.S. Dist. Ct. (so. dist.) N.Y. 1973, U.S. Dist. Ct.(ea. dist.) N.Y. 1973. Asst. corp. counsel law dept. City of N.Y., 1970-76, div. chief, 1976-77; assoc. Porskauer Rose Goetz & Mendelsohn, N.Y.C., 1977-82; v.p., gen. counsel Simon & Schuster, Inc., N.Y.C., 1982—. Author: Timing Your Investments, 1976. Office: Simon & Schuster Inc 1230 Ave of The Americas New York NY 10020

GIGAX, LESTER EARL, retired rubber and plastics company executive; b. Pettibone, N.D., Aug. 30, 1918; s. George and Hazel (Hillstrom) G.; m. Cora Chaffee, Feb. 16, 1944; children: Leslie (Mrs. John McCoy), Larry W., Bruce A. B.S. in Mech. Engring, Purdue U., 1947; grad. Advanced Mgmt. Program, Harvard U., 1972; hon. doctorate, Baldwin-Wallace Coll., 1983. Quality control engr. Gen. Electric Co., Niles, Ohio, 1947-51; with Rubbermaid Inc., Wooster, Ohio, 1951-83, v.p., gen. mgr., 1965-71, exec. v.p. ops., 1971-74, pres., chief operating officer, 1974-81, vice-chmn. bd., dir., 1981-83; chmn., dir. Oxycon, Inc.; dir. People's Fed. Savs. & Loan Assn., Wooster, Huffy Corp., Dayton, Ohio, RPM, Inc., Medina, Ohio., Shaw Plastics Corp., Berkeley Heights, N.J., Prentke Romich Co., Shreve, Ohio, Medallion Plastics Inc., Middlebury, Ind., Gradall Co., New Philadelphia, Ohio, Fusion Kunststoffen b.v., Deventer, Netherlands. Mem. Wooster Planning Com., 1967, Wooster Airport Commn., 1959-67; mem. Bd. Hosp. Commrs., 1965-76; trustee YMCA, Wooster, 1968-74; chmn. bd. trustees Baldwin-Wallace Coll., Berea, Ohio; v.p. Wooster Interfaith Housing Corp., 1973-78; chmn. 175th Anniversary Con. of Wooster, 1982-83. Served to capt. USAAF, 1941-46. Mem. Soc. Plastics Industry (past pres.), Soc. Plastics Engrs. (past bd. dirs.), Wooster C. of C. (past chmn.). Methodist (lay leader). Club: Rotarian. Home: 151 Oakley Rd Wooster OH 44691

GIGLI, IRMA, physician, educator; b. Cordoba, Argentina, Dec. 22, 1931; d. Irineo and Esperanza Francisca (Pons de Gigli) G. B.A., Liceo Nacional Manuel Belgrano, Cordoba, 1950; M.D., Universidad Nacional de Cordoba, 1957. Intern Cook County Hosp., Chgo., 1957-58, resident in dermatology, 1958-60; fellow in dermatology NYU, 1960-61; mem. faculty Harvard Med. Sch., 1967-75, asso. prof. dermatology, 1972-75; chief dermatology service Peter Bent Brigham Hosp., Robert B. Brigham Hosp., 1971-75; prof. dermatology and exptl. medicine N.Y. U. Med. Center, N.Y.C., 1976-82, mem. Irvington Houst Inst., mem. faculty N.Y. Grad. Sch. Med. Scis., dir. Asthma and Allergic Disease Center for Immunodermatology Studies, 1980-82; prof. medicine, chief div. dermatology U. Calif.-San Diego, 1983—; chmn. study sect. Allergy and Immunology Inst., NIH. Contbr. articles to profl. jours. Recipient research award Am. Cancer Soc., 1970-72, NIH, 1972-76; Guggenheim Found. grantee, 1974-75. Mem. Am. Soc. Clin. Investigation, Am. Assn. Immunologists, Am. Acad. Dermatology, Soc. Investigative Dermatology, Am. Acad. Allergy, Assn. Am. Physicians. Office: Univ Hosp U Calif-San Diego 29 W Dickinson St San Diego CA 92103

GIGLIO, ANTHONY J., oil field products company executive; b. 1938; married. Grad., Bryant Coll. With Burndy Corp., 1957-64, Singer Corp., 1964-68; exec. v.p. Peabody Internat., 1969-74; pres., chief operating officer GEO Internat. Corp., Stamford, Conn., 1974—, dir. Office: GEO Internat Corp 1 Landmark Sq Stamford CT 06901 *

GIGNOUX, EDWARD THAXTER, federal judge; b. Portland, Maine, June 28, 1916; s. Frederick Evelyn and Katherine (Denison) G.; m. Hildegarde Schuyler Thaxter, June 30, 1938; children: Marie Andrée (Mrs. James F. Grisé), Edward Thaxter. A.B. cum laude, Harvard U., 1937, LL.B. magna cum laude, 1940; LL.D., Bowdoin Coll., 1962, U. Maine, 1966, Colby Coll., 1974, Nasson Coll., 1974, Bates Coll., 1977, Husson Coll., 1983, St. Joseph's Coll., 1984. Bar: D.C. bar 1941, Maine bar 1946. Asso. Slee, O'Brian, Hellings & Ulsh, Buffalo, 1940-41, Covington, Burling, Rublee, Acheson & Shorb, Washington, 1941-42; partner Verrill, Dana, Walker, Philbrick & Whitehouse, Portland, 1946-57; U.S. dist. judge, Portland, 1957—; judge U.S. Temp. Emergency Ct. Appeals, 1980—; former corporator Maine Savs. Bank; mem. adv. com. bankruptcy rules U.S. Supreme Ct.; mem. council and vis. com. Harvard Law Sch.; also chmn. vis. com.; past mem. adv. panel internat. law U.S. State Dept.; faculty Salzburg Seminar for Am. Studies, 1972; Asst. corp. counsel, City of Portland, 1947-48, mem. city council, 1949-55, chmn., 1952. Editor: Harvard Law Rev, 1939-40. Pres., bd. dirs. Greater Portland Community Chest, 1955-56, United Fund, 1956-57; former corporator, trustee Maine Med. Center; former trustee Maine Eye and Ear Infirmary, Portland Symphony Orch.; former bd. overseers Harvard Coll. Served as maj. AUS, 1942-46. Decorated Bronze Star, Legion of Merit. Mem. ABA (spl. com. on jud. conduct), Maine Bar Assn., Cumberland County Bar Assn., Inst. Jud. Adminstrn.; former mem. Jud. Conf. U.S. (chmn. standing com. on rules of practice and procedure 1980—, jud. ethics com.); mem. Am. Judicature Soc. (dir.), Am. Law Inst. (council, 2d v.p.). Episcopalian. Clubs: Harvard (Boston) (pres. Maine 1957); (N.Y.C.); Portland Country. Home: 25 Starboard Ln Cumberland Foreside ME 04110 Office: 156 Federal St Portland ME 04112

GIGUÈRE, PAUL ANTOINE, chemist; b. Quebec City, Can., Jan. 13, 1910; s. Joseph-Emile and Diana (Poitras) G.; m. Magdeleine Lippens, July 21, 1937. B.A., U. Laval, 1930, B.Sc., 1934; Ph.D., McGill U., 1937; D.Sc. (hon.), U. Sherbrooke, 1970. With Canadian Industries, Ltd., 1937-38; research fellow Calif. Inst. Tech., 1939-41; asst. prof. U. Laval, Que., 1941-43, asso. prof., 1943-47, prof., 1947-76, emeritus prof., 1978—, dir. chemistry dept., 1957-68, mem. exec. council, 1969-72. Contbr. numerous articles to profl. jours. Decorated Companion Order of Can.; Guggenheim Found. fellow, 1946-47. Mem. Royal Soc. Can., Chem. Inst. Can. (v.p., pres. 1965-67), N.Y. Acad. Sci., AAAS, Association Canadienne Française Avancement des Sciences (pres.). Patentee in field. Home: Le Louisbourg 500-380 Chemin St-Louis Quebec PQ G1S 4M1 Canada Office: Cité Universitaire Quebec PQ G1K 7P4 Canada

GIKAS, PAUL WILLIAM, medical educator; b. Lansing, Mich., July 23, 1928; s. John and Minnie (Neumann) G.; m. Lois Suzanne Haglund, Dec. 27, 1952; children—Sandra Jane, Sarah Elizabeth, Paula Suzanne. A.B., U. Mich., 1950, M.D., 1954. Diplomate: Am. Bd. Pathology. Chief lab. service VA Hosp., Ann Arbor, Mich., 1960-68; mem. faculty U. Mich. Med. Sch., Ann Arbor, 1963—, asso. prof. pathology, 1966-69, prof., 1969—; faculty rep. to Big Ten Intercollegiate Conf., 1982—; cons. Armed Forces Inst. Pathology, 1966-74. Author: The Accident Problem, 1976, Uropathology, 1976, Forensic Aspects of the Highway Crash, 1983; co-editor: The Prevention of Highway Injury, 1967. Mem. adv. com. traffic safety HEW, 1966-68; mem. Gov. Mich. Spl. Commn. Traffic Safety Mich., 1964; Bd. dirs. Pub. Citizen, Inc., 1971—; co-trustee Center Study Responsive Law, Washington, 1969-71. Served to capt. M.C. AUS, 1956-58. Recipient Auto Safety award Med. Tribune, 1966-67, Distinguished Service award U. Mich., 1965. Mem. Internat. Acad. Pathology, Alpha Omega Alpha, Nu Sigma Nu. Lutheran. Research with preservation of blood for transfusion by freezing. Home: 1900 Mershon St Ann Arbor MI 48103

GIL, FEDERICO GUILLERMO, educator; b. Havana, Cuba, Feb. 10, 1915; came to U.S., 1942, naturalized, 1951; s. Adolfo J. and Elena (Izquierdo) G. LL.D., U. Havana, 1940, Dr. Polit. and Social Sci., 1941, licentiate diplomatic and consular law, 1942. Instr. polit. sci. La. State U., 1942-43; instr. U. N.C., 1943-45, asst. prof., 1945-49, asso. prof., 1949-55, prof., 1955-66, Kenan prof. polit. sci., 1966—; vis. lectr. Duke, summer 1944; vis. prof. Middlebury Coll., summer 1947; dir. Inst. Latin Am. Studies. Author: Governments of Latin America, 1957, The Political System of Chile, 1966, Instituciones y desarrollo político de América Latina, 1966, El sistema político de Chile, 1969, Latin American-United States Relations, 1971, Chile, 1970-73, Lecciones de una experiencia, 1977, Chile at the Turning Point: Lessons of the Socialist Years, 1970-1973, 1979; contbg. author anthologies; contbr. articles to profl. jours. Trustee Latin Am. Scholarship program Am. Univs. Hon. prof. U. Chile; decorated Order Bernardo O'Higgins, Chile; recipient Nicolas Salgo Disting. Teaching award, 1978; Rockefeller Found. fellow, 1944-45, 55-57, 63; Ford Found. fellow, 1958. Mem. Nat. Acad. Law and Social Scis. Argentina, Mexican Inst. Culture, Am., So. polit. sci. assns., Latin Am. Studies Assn. (pres. 1971), Latin Am. Assn. Sociology, Southeastern Conf. Latin Am. Studies (pres. 1962), Order Golden Fleece, Delta Psi. Democrat. Roman Catholic. Home: 5 Mount Bolus Rd Chapel Hill NC 27514

GIL, PETER PAUL, management educator, consultant; b. Havana, Cuba, Dec. 7, 1922; came to U.S., 1923; s. Peter Paul and Julia Cancio (Heredia) Fumagalli; m. Anita Maxwell, June 20, 1949 (dec. Feb. 1976); Karen, Andrew, Geneve; m. 2d Karin Enebuske, Apr. 15, 1977; stepchildren: William, Mary and John Trelease. A.B. cum laude, Harvard U., 1949, M.B.A., 1951; Ph.D. magna cum laude, U. Geneva, Switzerland, 1963. Asst. dir. tng. and research Aluminum, Ltd., Montreal, Que., Can., 1951-56; asst. dir., prof. Internat. Mgmt. Inst., Geneva, 1956-62; assoc. dean, sr. lectr. Sloan Sch. Mgmt. MIT, Cambridge, 1962-82, hon. Alfred P. Sloan fellow, 1983—; dean, prof. mgmt. Clark U., Worchester, Mass., 1982—; hon. dir European Mgmt. Forum, Geneva, 1974—; dir. Standby Fund (Cowan), N.Y.C., Mechanics Bank (Multi-Fin. Bank Corp.). Incorporator Worchester Art Mus., 1983—; chmn. bd. trustees Cambridge City Hosp., 1980-82; mem. Cambridge Health Policy Bd., 1979-82; bd. dirs. Internat. Artists Series, Worchester, 1982—; mem. NCCJ; mem. adv. bd. U. Barcelona Faculty of Engring., Spain, 1972. Served to 2d lt. Q.M.C. U.S. Army, 1942-45; ETO. Mem. U.S. Council Fgn. Relations, Internat. Univ. Contact, Acad. Mgmt. Unitarian. Clubs: MIT Faculty (exec. com. 1963-65), Worchester, Hasty Pudding Inst.

GILBANE, JEAN ANN (MRS. THOMAS F. GILBANE), construction company executive; b. Providence, Aug. 22, 1923; d. Vincent Thaddeus and Edna (Leary) Murphy; m. Thomas F. Gilbane, Sept. 12, 1946; children: Thomas, Robert, Richard, Jean, John, James. Student, Elmhurst Acad., 1941, Coll. New Rochelle, 1945. Sec. Gilbane Bldg. Co., Providence, 1950-81, treas., 1982—. Active Women's R.I. Hosp. Guild; mem. corp. Sophia Little Home, Emma Bradley Hosp., Butler Hosp., Met. Nursing and Health Services R.I. Decorated lady Order Holy Sepulcher. Roman Catholic. Clubs: Dunes, Point Judith Country; Beach (Palm Beach); University (Providence). Home: 80 Don Ave Rumford RI 02916 Office: 7 Jackson Walkway Providence RI 02903

GILBERT, ALAN D., holding company executive; b. Jersey City, Jan. 7, 1929; s. Benjamin H. and Martha A. (Nessel) G.; (married); children—A. David, John H. B.S., Seton Hall U., 1951. Sec. Elizabethtown (N.J.) Gas Co., 1969-80; sec. NUI Corp., Elizabeth, N.J., 1969—; pres. Nat. Energy Leasing Co., Elizabeth, 1980—. Mem. Bd. Adjustment, Twp. of Bedminster (N.J.), 1976. Mem. Am. Soc. Corp. Secs. Republican. Presbyterian. Home: Box 147 Pluckemin NJ 07978 Office: 1 Elizabethtown Plaza Elizabeth NJ 07978

GILBERT, ALBERT FRANCIS, hospital administrator; b. Mansfield, Ohio, Apr. 25, 1937; s. Frank Howard and Ann (Eichof) G.; m. Jonne Elaine Bucher, Aug. 9, 1959; children: Sheryl Annette, Laura Lynn, Mary Ann. B.A., Heidelberg Coll., 1959; M.A., U. Mich., 1962; Ph.D., Ga. State U., 1973. Assoc. dir., asst. prof. Ga. State U., Atlanta, 1965-69; exec. v.p. Mercy Hosp., Inc., Balt., 1969-74; pres. Akron City Hosp., Ohio., 1974—. Chmn. Citizens Adv. Bd., Cuyahoga Falls, Ohio, 1974—; pres., mem. Akron Regional Hosp. Assn., 1974—; mem. NEOUCOM Council of Hosp. Assn. CEOs, Rootstown, Ohio, 1974—, Robert Wood Johnson Found. Community Programs for Affordable Healt Care, Chgo., 1981—. Mem. Ohio Hosp. Assn. (chmn. congl. action com. 1978-80, polit. action com. 1978—), Am. Hosp. Assn., Am. Coll. Hosp. Adminstrs., Robert Wood Johnson Found. Home: 106 N Revere Rd Akron OH 44333

GILBERT, ANNE WIELAND, journalist; b. Chgo., May 1, 1927; d. David and Joy (Arnold) Wiel; m. George Gale Gilbert III, Apr. 7, 1953; children—Douglas, Christopher. B.S., Northwestern U., 1949. Columnist Chgo. Daily News, 1973-78, United Features Syndicate, 1978-81; reporter NBC-TV Sunday in, Chgo., 1973; guest expert NBC-TV, N.Y.C. Today, 1974—. Producer: WSNS-TV spl. Collectors World, 1971; performer TV programs, KETC-TV, St. Louis; owner: syndicated radio spot The Antique Detective; Author: Antique Hunters Guide: For Freaks and Fanciers, 1974, Collecting the New Antiques, 1975, How to Be an Antiques Detective, 1978, Investing in the Antiques Market, 1980. Mem. Alpha Gamma Delta. Presbyterian. Club: Chgo. Press. Address: 4794 NE 17 Ave Fort Lauderdale FL 33334

GILBERT, ARTHUR JOSEPH, bishop; b. Hedley, C., Can., Oct. 26, 1915; s. George Miles and Ethel May (Carter) G. B.A., St. Francis Xavier U., N.S., Can., 1938; B.Th., Holy Heart Sem., Halifax, N.S., 1943. Ordained priest Roman Catholic Ch., 1943; curate St. Andrew's (N.B.) Parish; also sec. to bishop of St. John (N.B.), 1943-44; chancellor Diocese of St. John, 1944-49; dir. Cath. Orphanage, Saint John, 1949-55; pastor St. Pius X Parish, Saint John, 1955-69, St. Joseph's Parish, 1969-71, St. Joachim's Parish, 1971-74; bishop of, St. John, 1974—. Chancellor, chmn. bd. St. Thomas U., Fredericton, N.B., 1974—. Club: K.C. Address: 91 Waterloo St Saint John NB E2L 3P9 Canada

GILBERT, BENJAMIN FRANKLIN, historian; b. San Francisco, Feb. 3, 1918; s. Joseph Beverley and Cheltza Floa (Funk) G.; m. Donna Ann Bornman, Aug. 21, 1955; 1 dau., Charlene. A.B., U. Calif., Berkeley, 1939, M.A., 1940, Ph.D., 1951. Wire rope clk. Columbia Steel Co., div. U.S. Steel Corp., San Francisco, 1941-42; tchr. Bates High Sch., San Francisco, 1945-47, Oakland (Calif. Evening Schs.), 1945-48; instr. Naval Air Transport Service Coll., Oakland, 1945-46; teaching fellow in history U. Calif., Berkeley, 1948-50; asst. prof. history San Jose (Calif.) State U., 1950-55, asso. prof., 1955-58, prof., 1958—; cons. Calif. Office Atty. Gen., 1972-80; reviewer Nat. Endowment for Humanities, 1977—. Author: Scientific Discoveries and Inventions in the U.S. 1660-1913, 1964, State of California, 1974; co-editor: Ports in the West, 1982; mem. editorial adv. bd.: Jour. of West, 1962—. Hist. landmarks commr., City of San Jose, 1953-61, trustee, Sourisseau Acad., 1983—. Served with USNR, 1942-45. Recipient award of merit Soc. Tech. Communication, 1978; medal for distinguished public service City of San Jose, 1960; Sourisseau Acad. grantee, 1972, 73, 74-76. Mem. Calif. Hist. Soc. (award of Merit 1975), Friends of Sutro Library. Home: 736 Cambrian Dr Campbell CA

95008 Office: Dept History San Jose State U San Jose CA 95192 *During most of my life I have concentrated on the study of history in a pragmatic manner believing it may be useful in everyday living and also have aesthetic value. In particular I have enjoyed researching a variety of topics with a stress on local history that demonstrates its wider geographical importance. In teaching how to write history I have attempted to have students strive for a good style.*

GILBERT, BRUCE REGAN, motion picture producer; b. Los Angeles, Mar. 28, 1947; s. Ross and Laurie G.; m. Ellen Ruth Bernstein, Mar. 15, 1979; 1 son, Jordan Robert. Student, U. Calif., Berkeley, 1967-69, Boston U., 1965-67. Co-founder, producer IPC Films, Los Angeles, 1972—; pres. Am. Filmworks, Los Angeles, 1980—; assoc. producer Coming Home, 1978; exec. producer China Syndrome, 1979; producer 9 to 5, 1980, Rollover, 1980, On Golden Pond, 1981. Mem. Acad. Motion Picture Arts and Scis. Address: 3 Latimer Rd Santa Monica CA 90402

GILBERT, CHARLES EDWARD, political science educator; b. Albany, N.Y., May 29, 1927; s. Edward Strong and Genevieve (Hunt) G.; m. Annalee Schendorf, Nov. 27, 1954; children: Susan Elizabeth, Jonathan Hunt. B.A., Haverford Coll., 1950; student, London Sch. Econs., 1950-51; Ph.D., Northwestern U., 1955. Asst. to U.S. Senator Humphrey, 1954; instr. Oberlin Coll., 1955; mem. faculty Swarthmore (Pa.) Coll., 1955—, asso. prof. polit. sci., 1962-67, prof., 1967—, Richter prof., 1976—, chmn. commn. ednl. policy, 1967, provost, 1969-74; cons. Pa. Dept. Pub. Welfare, Com. Econ. Devel.; guest scholar Brookings Inst., 1964-65, 68-69, sr. fellow, 1968-69, 69-76. Author: (with W.H. Brown) Planning Municipal Investment, 1961, Governing the Suburbs, 1967; also articles. Past chmn. Delaware County (Pa.) Health and Welfare Council. Served with USNR, 1945-46. Research fellow Social Sci. Research Council, 1952-53, 59-60; fellow Rockefeller Found., 1964-65. Mem. Am. Polit. Sci. Assn. (council 1959-61, exec. com. 1959-60), Am. Soc. Pub. Adminstrn. Democrat. Home: 223 Kenyon Ave Swarthmore PA 19081

GILBERT, CHARLES RICHARD ALSOP, physician; b. Phila., May 26, 1916; s. Chauncey McLean and Frances Marguerite (Young) G.; m. Helene Scher, Dec. 24, 1973; children: Anita Ivonne, Charles Richard Alsop. M.D., U. Va., 1944. Diplomate: Am. Bd. Obstetrics and Gynecology., Am. Bd. Abdominal Surgeons. Rotating intern N.Y.C. Hosp., 1944-45, asst. resident in internal medicine, 1945-46; resident in surgery Nix Hosp., San Antonio, 1946; resident in gen. surgery, chief female abdominal surgery Ryder Meml. Hosp., Hunacao, P.R., 1952-55; house staff gynecology Johns Hopkins Hosp., Balt., 1948-49; asst. resident in obstetrics U. Md., 1949, chief resident in obstetrics, 1949-50, asst. resident in gynecology, 1950-51, chief resident in gynecology, 1951-52, asso. in gynecology, instr. gynecol. pathology, 1952; asst. clin. prof. obstetrics and gynecology U. P.R., 1952-55, George Washington U., 1972-74, asso. clin. prof. obstetrics and gynecology, 1974—; asso. chief gynecology Doctors Hosp., Washington, 1973, chief gynecology, 1973—; sr. attending in obstetrics and gynecology Washington Hosp. Center; instr. internal medicine Randolph Sch. Aviation, San Antonio, 1946. Author: Childbirth-The Modern Guide to Expectant Mothers, 1960, Better Health for Women, 1964; contbr. articles to profl. jours.; Mem. editorial staff: Jour. Abdominal Surgery, 1964-74. Served with M.C. USAF, as chief internal medicine, 1946-48; Selfridge AFB, Mt. Clemens, Mich. Fellow A.C.S., Am. Coll. Obstetrics and Gynecology, Am. Soc. Abdominal Surgeons (teaching faculty 1964-74, mem. exec. com. 1964-74, v.p. 1969-70, pres. 1971-72), Internat. Coll. Surgeons (regent, exec. com. U.S. sect. 1981—, sec. U.S. sect. 1982-83, membership chmn. U.S. sect. 1983, Regent of Yr. award 1981); mem. Pan Am. Med. Assn., Med. Soc. D.C., AMA, Med. and Surgery Soc. Johns Hopkins Hosp., Douglass Obstet. and Gynecol. Soc., Nat. Rifle Assn., African Safari Club Washington (v.p. 1974-77, pres. 1977), Am. Outdoors Council (dir.), Hunting Hall of Fame Found. (dir. 1978). Club: Boone and Crockett. Developer first audiovisual med. corr. teaching courses for continuing med. edn., 1973. Home: 705 E Franklin Ave Silver Spring MD 20901 Office: 1120 19th St NW Washington DC 20036 also 344 University Blvd W Silver Spring MD 20901

GILBERT, CREIGHTON EDDY, art historian; b. Durham, N.C., June 6, 1924; s. Allan H. and Katharine (Everett) G. B.A., N.Y. U., 1942, Ph.D., 1955. Jr. appts. Louisville U., Ind. U., Ringling Mus., 1946-61; assoc. prof. Brandeis U., 1961-65, Sidney and Ellen Wien prof. history of art, 1965-69, chmn. dept., 1963-66, 68-69; prof. Queens Coll. City U. N.Y., 1969-77, chmn. dept., 1969-72; Jacob Gould Schurman prof. history of art Cornell U., 1977-81; prof. Yale U., 1981—; Fulbright sr. lectr. U. Rome, 1951-52; Kress fellow Harvard Center for Italian Renaissance Studies, Florence, Italy, 1967-68; fellow Netherlands Inst. for Advanced Study, 1972-73; vis. prof. U. Leiden, 1974-75; Robert Sterling Clark vis. prof. Williams Coll., 1976. Author: Michelangelo, 1967, Change in Piero della Francesca, 1968, History of Renaissance Art, 1972; Editor: Renaissance Art: Contemporary Essays, 1970, Italian Art 1400-1500, Sources and Documents, 1979; editor-in-chief: The Art Bull, 1980—; Translator: Complete Poems and Selected Letters of Michelangelo, 1963, 3d edit., 1979; Contbr.: sect. 15th century Italian painting Propyläen Kunstgeschichte, Berlin, 1972. Recipient Mather award Coll. Art Assn., 1964. Fellow Am. Acad. Arts and Scis.; mem. Instituto per la Storia dell Arte (dir. 1983—). Office: Dept History of Art 56 High St Yale U New Haven CT 06520

GILBERT, DALE WINSTON, educator; b. Jefferson, Iowa, July 10, 1926; s. Vernie Merle and Jessie May (Gaer) G.; m. Lois May Talbot, Aug. 6, 1949; children: Jay Warren, Carol Ann. Mem. faculty dept. music U. Wis., Madison, 1955—, prof. music, 1965—, dir., 1974—; choral dir., profl. singer, 1950—. Bd. dirs. Madison Civic Symphony Orch., Wis. Youth Symphony Orch. Served with USNR, 1945-46. Mem. Nat. Assn. Tchrs. Singing, Chgo. Singing Tchrs. Guild, Nat. Assn. Schs. Music, Music Educators Nat. Conf., Nat. Assn. Music Execs. in State Univs., Assn. Wis. Coll. and Univ. Music Adminstrs., Phi Kappa Phi (hon.). Lodge: Rotary. Home: 5401 Lacy Rd Madison WI 53711 Office: 455 N Park St Madison WI 53706

GILBERT, DAVID ERWIN, university president, physicist; b. Fresno, Calif., June 23, 1939; s. Erwin Azel and Hester (Almond) G.; m. Carolyn Faye Parker, June 24, 1960; children: Ronald David, Joan Elaine. A.B., U. Calif.-Berkeley, 1962; M.A., U. Oreg., 1964, Ph.D., 1968. Prof. physics Eastern Oreg. State Coll., La Grande, 1968—, dean. acad. affairs, 1977-83, pres., 1983—; vis. researcher Obs. Paris, 1975—; commr. Northwest Assn. Schs. and Coll., 1982—; dir. Union Wallawa Baker Fed. Credit Union, La Grande. Contbr. articles on physics to profl. jours. Commr. La Grande Airport; v.p. Eastern Oreg. Regional Arts Council, 1979-80. Grantee NATO, Research Corp. U.S.A., U.S. Govt., pvt. founds. Mem. AAAS, Am. Assn. Physics Tchrs. (pres. Oreg. chpt. 1973-74), Pacific Assn. Coll. Physics (bd. dirs. 1970-74), Sigma Xi, Sigma Pi Sigma. Democrat. Home: 402 Washington St La Grand OR 97850 Office: Eastern Oreg State Coll La Grande OR 97850

GILBERT, DAVID HEGGIE, educational publisher; b. Healdsburg, Calif., Mar. 11, 1932; s. Lindley Dodge and Beatrice (Heggie) G.; m. Margaret Collins, Nov. 8, 1953; children: Stephen, Laura, Jennifer, Michael. Student, U. Calif. at Berkeley, 1949-51; B.A., U. of Pacific, 1956; M.A., U. Colo., 1957. Instr. English Oreg. State U., Corvallis, 1957-60, asst. prof. English, 1960-64; Oreg. coll. traveler Holt, Rinehart & Winston Inc., N.Y.C., 1964-65, N.Y. acquiring editor in speech, drama and English, 1965-66, mgr., Atlanta, 1966-67; asso. dir. U. Tex. Press, Austin, 1967-74; dir. U. Nebr. Press., Lincoln, 1975—; Instr. English on TV Oreg. Coll. of Air, 1961-62; moderator Face to Face Ednl. TV, Austin, 1970-72. Mem. Democratic Exec. Com., Benton County (Oreg.), 1959-61. Served with AUS, 1953-55. Mem. Assn. Am. Univ. Presses (dir. 1974-76, v.p. 1977-78, pres.-elect 1981-82, pres. 1982-83), Western Univ. Presses. Home: 3424 S 28th St Lincoln NE 68502 Office: U Nebr Press 901 N 17th St Lincoln NE 68588

GILBERT, ELMER GRANT, aerospace engineering educator, control theorist; b. Joliet, Ill., Mar. 29, 1930; s. Harry A. and Florence A. (Otterstrom) G.; m. Lois M. Verbrugge, Dec. 27, 1973. B.S. in Elec. Engring., U. Mich., 1952, M.S., 1953, Ph.D. in Instrumentation Engring., 1956. Instr. U. Mich., Ann Arbor, 1954-56, asst. prof., 1957-59, assoc. prof., 1959-63, prof. aerospace engring., 1963—; founder, dir., cons. Applied Dynamics Inc., Ann Arbor, 1957-69. Patentee computer devices, 1968-74. Fellow IEEE; mem. Soc. Indsl. and Applied Math. (editorial bd. jour. control 1965-73), AAAS. Office: Dept Aerospace Engring U Mich Ann Arbor MI 48109

GILBERT, FELIX, historian; b. Baden-Baden, Germany, May 21, 1905; came to U.S., 1936, naturalized, 1943; s. William Henry and Cecile Mendelssohn (Bartholdy) G.; m. Mary Raymond, Apr. 21, 1956. Ph.D., U. Berlin, 1931, Free U. Berlin, 1980, D.H.L., Middlebury Coll., 1981, D. Hist., U. Bologna, 1982. Research analyst OSS, 1943-45, State Dept., 1945-46; prof. history Bryn Mawr Coll., 1946-62; prof. Sch. Hist. Studies, Inst. Advanced Study, Princeton, N.J., 1962-75; Kennedy prof. Smith Coll., 1975-76; vis. prof. Harvard U., 1977, U. Calif. at San Diego, 1978; Bonsall prof. Stanford U., 1981. Author: To The Farewell Address, 1961 (Bancroft prize), Machiavelli and Guicciardini, 1965, The End of the European Era, 1970, History: Choice and Commitment, 1977, The Pope, His Banker and Venice, 1980; co-author: History, 1965; Editor: Hitler Directs His War, 1950, The Historical Essays of Otto Hintze, 1975, Bankiers, Künstler und Gelehrte: Briefe der Familie Mendelssohn, 1975; Co-editor: Makers of Modern Strategy, 1943, The Diplomats, 1953, Historical Studies Today, 1972. Fellow Am. Acad. Arts and Scis., Brit. Acad. (corr.); mem. Am. Philos. Soc., Soc. Italian Hist. Studies (pres. 1970), Am. Hist. Assn., Renaissance Soc. Am. (pres. 1978-79). Home: 266 Mercer St Princeton NJ 08540

GILBERT, GERALD FREDERICK, JR., diversified industry exec.; b. Reading, Pa., Apr. 28, 1926; s. Gerald Frederick and Florence Adella (Anderson) G.; m. Shirley Louise Douty, June 14, 1952; children—Heidi Jo, Gretchen Louise. B.S., Lehigh U., 1950. With Atlas Mineral Products Co., Mertztown, Pa., 1950-62; asst. sec. Harsco Co., Camp Hill, Pa., 1962-72, sec., 1972—, v.p., 1978—. Served to 1st lt. AUS, 1944-46. Mem. Internat. Brotherhood Magicians. Republican. Methodist. Home: 27 Meadow Dr Green Lane Farms Camp Hill PA 17011 Office: Harsco Corp Camp Hill PA 17011

GILBERT, HAROLD STANLEY, warehousing company executive; b. Ft. Worth, Jan. 22, 1924; s. Sydney Ralph and Reba Samuels (Lever) G.; m. Jeanne Schwarz, Apr. 6, 1950; children: Marsha Gilbert Kirstein, Mark S., John L. B.A., U. Tex., 1947, M.Ed., 1949; grad., Air Command and Staff Coll., 1961, Air War Coll., 1970, Indsl. Coll. Armed Forces, 1970. Sci. tchr., coach Houston Ind. Schs., 1949-51; asst. prin., head sci. dept., athletic dir., coach USAF Dependents Sch. System, Germany, 1953-55; v.p. Coastal Bag & Bagging Corp., Houston, 1968-71; exec. v.p., gen. mgr. Coastal Storehouse, Inc., Houston, 1968—; mem. def. strategy seminar Nat. War Coll., 1973. Parade marshal Bicentennial Armed Forces Week Parade, Houston, 1976; dir. gen. Armed Forces Week, 1977; bd. dirs. Houston council USO, 1977—, v.p., 1981. Served with AUS, 1943-45; Served with USAF, 1951-53; col. USAFR (ret.). Decorated Legion of Merit, Bronze Star, Meritorious Service medal, Purple Heart with oak leaf cluster; recipient USAFR Disting. Ednl. Achievement award, 1975. Mem. S.W. Warehouse and Transfer Assn., Houston Warehouse and Transfer Assn. (pres. 1980), Air Force Assn. (v.p. chpt. 1977-78, pres. 1978-79, Tex. conv. chmn. 1976), Res. Officers Assn. (pres. Eric Ellington chpt. 1974-75, chmn. rules com. 1975, mem. Tex. mil. affairs com. 1975-78), Nat. Fedn. Temple Brotherhoods (dir.), Jewish Chautauqua Soc. (chmn. S.W. region 1964-70), Houston C. of C. (mil. affairs com. 1969—, vice chmn. Air Force subcom. 1978-79), T Assn. U. Tex., Mil. Order World Wars, Nat. Hist. Soc., Houston Livestock Show and Rodeo Assn. (life), Phi Delta Kappa, Sigma Alpha Mu. Clubs: Elks, Rotary (pres. Rotary Activities Houston and Harris County 1969-70), Rotary (club sec. 1981). Home: 476 N Post Oak Ln Houston TX 77024 Office: PO Box 3207 Houston TX 77001

GILBERT, HARRY EPHRAIM, JR., hotel executive; b. Phila., Feb. 1, 1931; s. Harry Ephraim and Anna (Chilton) G.; children: Ronald C., Glen G.; m. Jacqueline J. Newton. B.S. in Hotel Adminstrn, Pa. State U., 1954. Resident mgr. Benjamin Franklin Hotel, Phila., 1954-71, gen. mgr., 1971-77, Cherry Hill Inns, N.J., 1977-78, Holiday Inn-City Line, Phila., 1978-80, Colony Inn, New Haven, 1980-81, Gideon Putnam Hotel and Conf. Center, Saratoga Springs, N.Y., 1981—; lectr. Hotel Sch., Pa. State U., 1956-58, Drexel U., Phila., 1962-63. Mem. Phila. Conv. and Tourist Bur., N.Y. Hotel/Motel Assn., Phila. Hotel and Motor Inn Assn. (sec. 1971-72, v.p. 1973-74, pres. 1975—), Pa. Hotel Restaurant Soc. (sec.-treas. 1973-74), Pa. Hotel Motor Inn Assn. (dir. 1975-76, treas. 1976-77), N.J. Hotel-Motel Assn. (dir. 1977-78), Conn. Hotel-Motel Assn., Assoc. Restaurants Conn., Hotel-Motel Greeter Internat., Pa. State Hotel Greeters (pres. 1952-54, 74—), Phila. Press Assn., Pa. State Alumni Club Phila., Hotel Sales Mgrs. Assn., Chestnut St. Assn. (dir. 1971-76). Clubs: Skal of North Am. (treas. 1979-80, sec. 1980-84), Bon Vivante). Home: 518 Foxwood Dr Clifton Park NY 12063 Office: Gideon Putnam Hotel Sarasota Springs NY 12866

GILBERT, JACKSON BEHR, banker; b. Houston, Sept. 13, 1932; s. C. Randolph and Elizabeth S. (Smith) G.; m. Maria Diez de Ponce de Leon, Sept. 6, 1961; children—Victoria Elizabeth, Marie Allegra. B.A. in Econs, U. Va., 1953, LL.B., 1956; postgrad., Oxford (Eng.) U. Bar: Va. bar 1956, N.Y. bar 1957. Asso. firm Sullivan & Cromwell, N.Y.C., 1960-65; v.p., counsel Adela Investment Co., Lima, Peru, 1965-67; rep. Morgan Bank, Madrid, Spain, 1968-71, head, 1971-73; mng. dir., gen. mgr. Banca Morgan Vonwiller, Milan, Italy, 1973-76, also dir., Milan; sr. v.p. in charge Latin-Am. area Morgan Guaranty Trust Co. N.Y., N.Y.C., 1976—; pres. Morgan Guaranty Fin. Corp., 1981-83; vice chmn. Riggs Nat. Bank, Washington, 1983—. Served to 1st lt. Judge Adv. Gen. Corps USAF, 1957-59. Decorated Commendative Order Republic of Italy). Mem. Va. State Bar Assn., N.Y. Bar Assn., Council Fgn. Relations. Clubs: River, Union (N.Y.C.); Piping Rock (Locust Valley, N.Y.); Met. (Washington); Norfolk (Va.) Yacht.; Farmington Country (Charlottesville, Va.). Office: 23 Wall St New York NY 10015

GILBERT, JAMES CAYCE, child care exec.; b. Nashville, Feb. 26, 1925; s. Gertis and Delia Mae (Snyder) G.; m. Freda Mae Mitchell, Sept. 3, 1949; children—Elizabeth, Suzanne, Kathryn, Rosalie. B.A., Bethel Coll., McKenzie, Tenn., 1945, D.D. (hon.), 1976; B.D., Cumberland Presbyn. Theol. Sem., McKenzie, 1947; M.A., Scarritt Coll., Nashville, 1948. Ordained to ministry Cumberland Presbyn. Ch., 1944; asso. pastor West Nashville Cumberland Presbyn. Ch., 1947-48; pastor River Oaks Cumberland Presbyn. Ch., Houston, 1948-55, Trinity Cumberland Presbyn. Ch., Ft. Worth, 1956-64; exec. dir. Cumberland Presbyn. Children's Home, Denton, Tex., 1964—; moderator gen. assembly Cumberland Presbyn. Ch., 1979-80. Mem. Nat. Assn. Homes Children, Southwestern Assn. Children's Home, Tex. Assn. Execs. Homes Children (past pres.), Denton C. of C. Democrat. Clubs: Lions, Masons, K.T. Office: 1304 Bernard St Denton TX 76201

GILBERT, JOHN BAPTISTE, pulp and paper consultant; b. San Rafael, Calif., Mar. 26, 1915; s. Louis Jules and Willa (Sale) G.; m. Lavinia Cresap, June 21, 1942; children: John Baptiste IV, Lavinia Grace, Joan Willa, Thomas Cresap. A.B., U. Calif., 1937; grad., Advanced Mgmt. Program, Harvard, 1956. Various positions Zellerbach Paper Co., 1937-41, exec. sales supr., gen. sales mgr., 1946-55, v.p., dir., 1955—, gen. mgr., 1959-61; v.p. marketing Crown Zellerbach Corp., 1961-63, sr. v.p., dir., 1963-74; pulp and paper cons., 1974—; dir. Xidex Corp. Served from 2d lt. to maj., inf. AUS, 1941-45. Episcopalian. Clubs: Orinda Country, Stock Exchange, Richmond Yacht. Address: 50 Hacienda Circle Orinda CA 94563

GILBERT, JOHN HUMPHREY VICTOR, educator; b. Bath, Somerset, U.K., Mar. 19, 1941; s. Daniel and Nancy (Johns) G.; (div.)children: Eliot Daniel, Oliver Gaius. Grad., U. London; Ph.D., Purdue U., 1966. Asst. prof. U. B.C., 1966-69, asso. prof., 1969-74, prof., 1974—, Med. Research Council postdoctoral scholar, 1969-74; now dir. Sch. Audiology and Speech Sci.; Cons. Prince George Sch. Dist., 1968-69; chmn. Interim Council for Sch. Audiology and Speech Scis., 1978-79; cons. Chilliwack Sch. Dist., 1980, Abbotsford Sch. Dist., 1980; mem. study sect. NIH, 1981. Mem. Med. Services Found. Grants Com., 1981. Mem. Canadian Linguistic Assn., Linguistics Soc. Am., Acoustical Soc. Am., B.C. Speech and Hearing Assn., Canadian Speech and Hearing Assn., AAAS, Internat. Assn. Child Lang. Clubs: Point Grey Golf and Country.; University (Vancouver). Home: 3350 W 37th St Vancouver BC Canada V6N 2V6 Office: Univ BC Sch Audiology and Speech Scis 5804 Fairview Crescent Vancouver BC Canada V6T 1M5

GILBERT, JOSEPH, association executive; b. Cleve., Dec. 18, 1920; s. Morris and Yetta (Schwedock) G.; m. Doris Chaiken, June 20, 1943; children: Jeffrey A., Karen Sue. B.C.E., CCNY, 1942; M.S. in Indsl. Engring, Columbia, 1950; Dr. Engring., Lawrence Inst. Tech., 1983. Mem. staff Soc. Automotive Engrs., 1946—, asst. gen. mgr., 1957-60, sec., gen. mgr., 1960—, exec. v.p., 1981—; group leader Man Mktg. Clinic, 1947-59. Served to 1st lt. USAAF, 1942-46. Sr. mem. Soc. Mfg. Engrs.; mem. Council Engring. and Sci. Soc. Secs. (sec. 1961-62, pres. 1963-64, award 1982), Soc. Automotive Engrs., ASME, AIAA, Engring. Soc. Detroit, Am. Rocket Soc., ASTM, Internat. Fedn. Automobile Engring. Socs. (pres. 1982-86), Am. Soc. Metals, Soc. Automotive Engrs. Australasia, Inst. Mech. Engrs. (Eng.), Société des Ingenieurs de l'Automobile (France), Associazione Tecnica Automobile (Italy), Soc. Automotive Engrs. (Japan), Am. Soc. Assn. Execs. (vice chmn., key award 1982). Home: 2185 Ben Franklin Dr Pittsburgh PA 15237 Office: 400 Commonwealth Dr Warrendale PA 15096 *There have been two key guidelines which shaped my career, both of which I assimilated from outstanding leaders under whom I served. From where I sit, it does not make sense to stop at the limit described by management. Rather one should go beyond. . ..in fact, stretch and tax his capabilities. For only in that way is there satisfaction from a job well done. A second principle which has guided me is the desire to make the world a better place than when I came on board. My feeling is that it took the collective output of countless millions to bring planet earth to this stage where it could provide me and my loved ones with all the good things of life. And so, as an expression of my appreciation to those who came before me, I feel that I must improve what I found when I came here to any small degree that I can, so that those who follow will enjoy a better world and, in turn, be inspired to make their contribution to the solution of man's continuing and changing problems.*

GILBERT, KATHIE SIMON, economist, educator; b. Akron, Ohio, Feb. 28, 1943; d. John Nicholas and Bernadine Mary (Ilg) Simon; m. John Randalph Gilbert, Jr., Jan. 28, 1964; children: Mark Ivan, Adam Stacy. B.A., U. Ala., 1964; M.A., La. State U., 1966, Ph.D., 1972. Asso. prof. econs. Miss. State U., Mississippi State, 1968-78, prof. econs., 1978—, prof. polit. sci., 1981—. Contbr. articles to profl. jours. Mem. Oktibbeha County Dem. Exec. Com., 1976-80, 84—; vice chmn. Miss. Internat. Women's Year Com., 1977. Am. Council on Edn. fellow, 1979-80; Miss. Com. for Humanities grantee, 1975, 83. Mem. Am. Econ. Assn., So. Econ. Assn., Miss. Econ. Council, Southwestern Social Scis. Assn. (v.p.), Nat. Women's Studies Assn., Southeastern Women's Studies Assn. (pres.), AAUW (pres. Starkville br. 1977-79, v.p. Miss. div. 1980-82, pres. 1982-84), LWV (treas. Starkville chpt. 1981—), Miss. State U. Faculty Women's Assn. (pres. 1981-82), Phi Kappa Phi, Omicron Delta Epsilon., Beta Gamma Sigma. Democrat. Roman Catholic. Office: Drawer JE Mississippi State MS 39762

GILBERT, KENNETH ALBERT, harpsichordist; b. Montreal, Can., Dec. 16, 1931; s. Albert George and Reta Mabel (Welch) G. Student, Conservatoire de Musique, Montreal, 1945-53, 1953-55; D.Mus. (hon.), McGill U., Montreal, 1981. Prof. Montreal Conservatoire de Musique, 1965-72; asso. prof. music Laval U., Que., Can., 1970-76; dir. early music dept. Conservatoire de Strasbourg (France), 1981—; instr. Haarlem Summer Sch., Holland, 1973-82, Antwerp Summer Internat. Course, Belgium, 1971-82, Giorgio Cini Found., Venice, 1977—, Accademia Chigiana, Siena, 1981—, Internat. Acad. Mozarteum, Salzburg, 1984—; prof. harpsichord Staatliche Hochschule für Musik und Darstellende Kunst, Stuttgart, 1981—. Recording artist, Archiv Produktion, Harmonia Mundi, Musical Heritage Records.; Author: Complete Harpischord Works of Couperin, 1969-72, Complete Harpischord Works of D. Scarlatti, 1972-84, Goldberg Variations, J.S. Bach, 1979, Complete Harpsichord Works of Rameau, 1979; concert tours major cities, Europe and U.S., numerous TV appearances. Can. Council fellow, 1968, 74; Calouste Gulbenkian fellow, 1971; Can. Cultural Inst. fellow, Rome, 1978-79; named Artist of Yr. Can. Music Council, 1979. Recording complete harpsichord works Couperin, Rameau; Well-tempered Clavier, Bach. Address: La Régie Château de Maintenon 28130 France

GILBERT, LAWRENCE IRWIN, biologist, educator; b. N.Y.C., Jan. 24, 1929; s. Charles and Matilda (Bronznick) G.; m. Doris Paule Millstein, Oct. 26, 1952; children—Scott David, Daniel Todd, Joanne Robin. B.S., L.I. U., 1950; M.S., N.Y. U., 1955; Ph.D., Cornell U., 1958. Mem. faculty Northwestern U., 1958-80, prof. biol. scis., chmn. dept., 1965-70, 78-80; also sec.-treas. div. comparative endocrinology, chmn. div. comparative endocrinology; William Rand Kenan, Jr. prof., chmn. dept. zoology U. N.C., Chapel Hill, 1980-82, chmn. dept. biology, 1982—; NSF sr. fellow U. Bern, Switzerland, 1964-65; mem. Presdl. Task Force on Pest Mgmt., 1971-72. Editor: Metamorphosis: A Problem in Developmental Biology, 1968, 2d edit., 1981, The Juvenile Hormones, 1976; Editorial bd.: Jour. Invertebrate Reprodn., Biochemistry, Experientia, Gen. Comparative Endocrinology; Contbr. others, articles to profl. jours. Mem. Soc. Developmental Biology, Soc. Exptl. Biology, Am. Soc. Zoologists, Am. Soc. Cell Biology, Entomol. Soc. Am., Soc. Gen. Physiologist, Phi Beta Kappa. Home: Rt 4 Box 535 Chapel Hill NC 27514 Office: U NC Chapel Hill NC 27514

GILBERT, LEONARD HAROLD, lawyer; b. Hutchinson, Minn., Apr. 3, 1936; s. Sidney and Clara (Franzblau) G.; m. Jean Buchman, Apr. 21, 1963; children—Jonathan Stuart, Suzanne Elaine. B.A., Emory U., 1958; LL.B., Harvard U., 1961. Bar: Fla. bar 1961. Mem. firm Carlton, Fields, Ward, Emmanuel, Smith & Cutler (P.A.), Tampa, Fla., 1961—. Bd. dirs. Gasparilla Sidewalk Art Festival, Tampa, 1970-74; chmn. Arts Council Tampa, 1973-74; mem. Hillsborough County (Fla.) Bicentennial Commn., 1973-76, Tampa Charter Revision Com., 1975; Bd. fellows U. Tampa. Served with USCGR, 1961-69. Fellow Am. Bar Found., Fla. Bar Found. (dir.); mem. Am. Bar Assn. (chmn. sect. gen. practice 1979-80), Fla. Bar (chmn. sect. corp. banking and bus. law 1970-71, chmn. sect. gen. practice 1972-73, bd. govs. 1975-79, pres.-elect 1979-80, pres. 1980-81), Bar Assn. Hillsborough County (pres. 1974-75), Am. Judicature Soc. (dir.), Am. Law Inst. Clubs: Harvard Law Sch Assn Fla (pres. 1982-83), Kiwanis (pres. club 1972), Ye Mystic Krewe of Gasparilla.). Office: PO Box 3239 Tampa FL 33601

GILBERT, PERRY WEBSTER, emeritus educator; b. North Branford, Conn., Dec. 1, 1912; s. Scott Warren and Hester (Weatherwax) G.; m. Claire Rachel Kelly, Sept. 3, 1938; children—Ann (Mrs. Bradley McDonald), David, Stephen, John, Mary (Mrs. Andrew Seyfried), Lois, Christopher, Philip. A.B., Dartmouth, 1934; Ph.D., Cornell U., 1940; L.H.D. (hon.), York Coll. of Pa., 1978. Asst. in zoology Cornell U., 1937-40, instr., 1940-43, asst. prof., 1943-46, assoc. prof., 1946-52, prof., 1952-78, prof. emeritus, 1978—, dir., 1967-78, dir. emeritus, 1978—; mem. panel biol. and med. scis. Polar Research Com., 1959-63; leader Tahiti-Tikehau Internat. Expdn., 1964; chief scientist Brit. Honduras Expdn. Shark, 1969; research assn. Lerner Marine Lab., 1964—. Editor: Sharks and Survival, 1963, Sharks, Skates and Rays, 1967; Contbr. numerous articles to sci. jours. Cramer fellow zoology Cornell U., 1936-37; Carnegie fellow embryology Carnegie Inst. Washington, Balt., 1949-50; Guggenheim fellow Lerner Marine Lab., Bimini, Bahamas, 1957, Scripps Instn. Oceanography, 1963. Fellow AAAS; mem. Am. Inst. Biol. Scis., Am. Soc. Zoology, Am. Assn. Anatomy, Inst. Internat. d'Embryologie, Marine Biol. Assn. India, Am. Soc. Icthyology and Herpetology, Am. Soc. Mammalogists, Am. Ornithologists Union, Am. Littoral Soc., Soc. Study Evolution, Animal Behavior Soc., Explorers Club, Sigma Xi. Club: Cosmos (Washington). Home: 852 Siesta Dr Sarasota FL 33581 Office: 1600 City Island Park Sarasota FL 33577 also Stimson Hall Cornell U Ithaca NY 14853 *As a scientist I have learned that there is no substitute for truth, however painful or disappointing it may be. As an administrator I have learned that listening to, and compassion for others fosters their loyalty and desire to do more than is asked of them.*

GILBERT, PHIL EDWARD, JR., lawyer; b. Chgo., Jan. 31, 1915; s. Phil Edward and Florence (Miller) G.; m. Nancy Thompson Merrick, June 24, 1939 (div. 1967); children: Mary Randolph, John Sale, Clinton Merrick; m. Joan Stulman, Oct. 6, 1968. A.B., Dartmouth Coll., 1936; LL.B., Harvard U., 1939. Bar: N.Y. 1941. Practiced in N.Y.C., 1941—; atty. Donovan, Leisure, Newton & Lumbard, 1939-41, Debevoise, Stevenson, Plimpton & Page, 1941; partner firm Gilbert, Segall & Young (and predecessor), 1946—; pres. Rolls-Royce, Inc., N.Y.C., 1957-71; dep. chmn. Magnesium Elektron, Inc.; dir. Rolls-Royce, Inc. Mem. council Salk Inst., 1976-83, trustee, 1983—. Served to maj. inf. AUS, 1941-46; ETO. Decorated Bronze Star, Croix de Guerre. Mem. Am., Fed., Westchester bar assns., Bar Assn. City N.Y., Phi Beta Kappa. Baptist. Home: The Croft Spring Valley Rd Ossining NY 10562 Office: 430 Park Ave New York NY 10022

GILBERT, ROBERT EMILE, political scientist, educator; b. N.Y.C., Oct. 20, 1939; s. EmilePaul and VeronicaFlorence (Noble) G. B.A. in Polit. Sci., Fordham U., 1961, M.A., 1963, Ph.D., U. Mass., 1967. Teaching asst. in polit. sci. U. Mass., Amherst, 1962-65; instr. polit. sci. Boston Coll., Chestnut Hill., Mass., 1965-67, asst. prof. polit. sci., 1967-73; assoc. prof. polit. sci. Northeastern U., Boston, 1973-82, chmn. dept. polit. sci., 1978—, prof., 1982—; vis. asst. prof. polit. sci. U. Wis.-Parkside, Racine, 1968; dir. Phabrica Corp., Stoughton, Mass., Spring Hill Corp., Easton Techs. Inc.; publ. cons. John Wiley and Sons, McGraw-Hill, Holbrook Press, Jour. Politics, Polity; publ. cons Am. Politics Quar. Contbr. articles, Presdl. Studies Quar., Jour. Social, Polit. And Econ. Studies, Ill. Politico, articles, U. Mo.-Kansas City Law Rev., Mass. Comml. Rev. Boston Coll. Faculty Research grantee, 1967; Northeastern U. research and devel. grantee, 1981-82. Mem. Ctr. Study Presidency, Am. Polit. Sci. Assn., New Eng. Polit. Sci. Assn., Presidency Research Group, Pi Sigma Alpha (pres. Delta Zeta chpt. 1960-61), Delta Tau Kappa. Democrat. Roman Catholic. Hoe: 1243 Beacon St Brookline MA 02146 Office: Northeastern University 360 Huntington Ave Boston MA 02115

GILBERT, ROBERT PERTSCH, mathematician, educator; b. N.Y.C., Jan. 8, 1932; s. Ralph H. and Ruth (Pertsch) G.; m. E. Eileen Manton, Oct. 28, 1955 (div. Jan. 1975); m. Ursula Murach, June 27, 1975 (div. Mar. 1979); m. Elizabeth Page Cogswell, Aug. 12, 1979. B.S., Bklyn. Coll., 1952; M.S. in Physics, Carnegie-Mellon U., 1955, Carnegie-Mellon U., 1955, Ph.D., 1958. Faculty U. Pitts., 1957-60, Mich. State U., 1960-63; research asst. prof. Inst. for Fluid Dynamics and Applied Math., U. Md., 1961-64, research asso. prof., 1964-65; prof. dept. math. Georgetown U., Washington, 1965-66; prof. math. Ind. U., Bloomington, 1966-75, dir., 1973-75; Unidel prof. math. U. Del., 1975—, also dir., 1975—; Cons. spl. coal research div. U.S. Bur. Mines, 1958-60, Naval Ordnance Lab., 1961-64; vis. Unidel prof. U. Del., 1972-73; guest prof. U. Glasgow, 1972, U. Dortmund, Germany, 1972, Hahn Meitner Inst. Nuclear Physics, Berlin, 1974, Free U. Berlin, 1974-75; vis. prof. Tech. U. Denmark, 1979, U. Karlsruhe, 1980, Oxford U., 1981-82. Author: Function Theoretic Methods in Partial Differential Equations, 1969, Constructive Methods for Elliptic Equations, 1973; co-author: Foundations of Applied Mathematics, First Order Elliptic Systems, 1983; Co-editor: Analytic Methods in Mathematical Physics, 1970; editor-in-chief: an internat. jour. Applicable Analysis; Complex Variables; assoc. editor: Jour. Nonlinear Analysis; adv. editor: Math. Method in Applied Scis; cons. editor, Pitman Press, London. Recipient von Humboldt Sr. Scientist award, 1975. Mem. Am. Math. Soc. (mem. council), Soc. for Indsl. and Applied Math. (asso. editor jour.), Washington Acad. Scis., Sigma Xi, Pi Mu Epsilon. Research and publs. on analysis, especially harmonic functions, boundary value problems, math. physics, partial differential equations, numerical analysis. Home: 112 Briar Ln Newark DE 19711

GILBERT, ROBERT RANDLE, III, banker; b. Dallas, May 17, 1938; s. Robert Randle and Yvonne (Welch) G.; m. Janet Ferrill, Feb. 4, 1961 (div. Mar. 1971); m. Mary Lynn Huntington, Mar. 18, 1972; children: Laura Ann, Kathryn, Mark, Sally, Susan. B.S. in Geol. Engring., U. Okla., 1961; M.B.A. in Fin., U. Tex., 1965. With 1st Nat. Bank & Trust Co. Tulsa, 1965-79, sr. v.p., 1971-74, exec. v.p., 1974-79, also dir.; exec. v.p. 1st Nat. Bank & Trust Co., Oklahoma City, 1979-83; dir. First City Bank, Dallas, 1983—; instr. fin. Tulsa Jr. Coll., 1972-73. Served with USNR, 1961-62. Mem. Ind. Petroleum Assn. Am., U. Okla. Alumni Assn., Okla. Bankers Assn., Am. Petroleum Inst., Soc. Petroleum Engrs., Sigma Alpha Epsilon. Club: So. Hills Country (Tulsa). Home: 3715 Wentwood Dallas TX 75225 Office: PO Box 50688 Dallas TX 75250

GILBERT, RONALD RHEA, lawyer, organization executive; b. Sandusky, Ohio, Dec. 29, 1942; s. Corvin and Mildred (Millikin) G.; m. Marilynn Davis, Aug. 26, 1966; children: Elizabeth, Lynne, Lisa. B.A., Wittenberg U., 1964; J.D., U. Mich., 1967, postgrad., 1967-68; postgrad., Wayne State U., 1973-74. Bar: Mich. Assoc. prosecutor Wayne County, Mich., 1969; assoc. Rouse, Selby, Dickinson, Shaw & Pike, Detroit, 1969-72; ptnr. Charfoos, Christensen, Gilbert & Archer, P.C., Detroit, 1972-84; founder, chmn. Aquatic Injury Safety Group, 1982—, speaker seminars, 1982-83; instr. Madonna Coll., Detroit, 1977-81; mem. faculty Inst. Continuing Legal Edn., 1977—; speaker symposium on social security law Detroit Coll. Law, 1984. Contbr. articles to legal jours. Patron Detroit Art Inst.; mem. Pres.'s Club U. Mich. Mem. Assn. Trail Lawyers Am., Mich. Trial Lawyers Assn., System Safety Soc., ABA, Mich Bar Assn., Detroit Bar Assn., Am. Judicature Soc. Clubs: Detroit Country, Renaissance, Detroit Athletic, U. Mich. Home: 290 McKinley St Grosse Pointe Farms MI 48236 Office: 4445 Penobscot Bldg Detroit MI 48226

GILBERT, ROY E., business executive; b. Chgo., Sept. 5, 1936; m. Jane M. Nisbet, Jan. 31, 1959; children: Jill N., Catherine D. B.S. with distinction in Engring., Purdue U., 1959, M.B.A., Harvard U., 1964. Dir. fin. Ford Mex., 1975-78; dir. acquisition Ford Motor Co., Dearborn, Mich., 1979-80, controller, 1980-81; v.p. planning and analysis Firestone Tire and Rubber Co., Akron, Ohio, 1981-82, v.p. strategic planning, 1983—. Bd. dirs. Red Cross Summit County, Akron, 1981, Stan Hywet Found., Red Cross Summit County, 1983. Served to lt. USN, 1959-62. Office: Firestone Tire and Rubber Co 1200 Firestone Pkwy Akron OH 44317

GILBERT, WALTER, molecular biologist, genetic engineering company executive; b. Boston, Mar. 21, 1932; s. Richard V. and Emma (Cohen) G.; m. Celia Stone, Dec. 29, 1953; children: John Richard, Kate. B.A., Harvard U., 1953, A.M., 1954; D.Phil., Cambridge U., 1957; D.Sc. hon., U. Chgo., 1978, Columbia U., 1978. NSF postdoctoral fellow Harvard U., 1957-58, lectr. physics, 1958-59, asst. prof. physics, 1959-64, assoc. prof. biophysics, 1964-68, prof. molecular biology, 1968-82, Am. Cancer Soc. prof. molecular biology, 1972-81, sr. assoc., 1982-84; co-chmn. Biogen, Inc., Cambridge, Mass., 1978-81, chmn. bd. advisors, 1978-83, co-chmn. supervisory bd., 1978-81, chmn. supervisory bd., prin. exec. officer, 1981—; v.p. Mattia lectr. Roche Inst. Molecular Biology, 1976. Recipient U.S. Steel Found. Nat. Acad. Sci., 1968, Ledhe prize Harvard U., 1969, Warren triennеal prize Mass. Gen. Hosp., 1977, Louis and Bert Freedman Found. N.Y. Acad. Scis., 1977, Prix Charles-Leopold Mayer Academie des Scis., Inst. de France, 1977, Nobel prize in chemistry, 1980; co-winner Louisa Gross Horwitz prize Columbia U., 1979, Gairdner prize, 1979, Albert Lasker Basic Sci, 1979; Guggenheim fellow, 1968-69. Mem. Am. Phys. Soc., Nat. Acad. Scis., Am. Soc. Biol. Chemists, Am. Acad. Arts and Scis. Office: Biogen Inc 14 Cambridge Center Cambridge MA 02142 *

GILBERT, WILLIAM JAMES, educator; b. Shelton, Wash., Feb. 10, 1916; s. Cyrus Lloyd and Bessie Mae (Carr) G.; m. Ruth Elizabeth Willoughby, June 27, 1942; children—Paul William, Bruce David, Mark Allen, Lee Ralph. B.S., U. Wash., 1938; M.S., U. Mich., 1939, Ph.D. in Botany, 1942. Research biologist Comml. Solvents Corp., Terre Haute, Ind., 1944-46; faculty Albion (Mich.) Coll., 1946—, prof. biology, 1957—, chmn. dept., 1957-71, asso. acad. dean, 1971-72, acting acad. dean, 1972-73, chmn. div. Sci. and Math., 1962-66; Faculty dir., sec. Mich. Intercollegiate Athletic Assn., 1947-57; coordinator Mich. Jr. Acad. Sci., Arts and Letters, 1949-51. Contbr. articles to profl. jours. Mem. Albion Bd. Edn., 1971-79. Mem. Mich. Acad. Sci., Arts and Letters (life, chmn. botany sect. 1950, exec. com. 1968-71), Am. Inst. for Biol. Scis., Phycological Soc. Am., Internat. Phycological Soc., Phi Beta Kappa, Sigma Xi, Phi Sigma. Presbyn. (elder). Home: 616 E Erie St Albion MI 49224

GILBOE, DAVID DOUGHERTY, physiology educator; b. Richland Center, Wis., July 13, 1929; s. Harvey Bernard and Margaret Lucille (Dougherty) G.; m. Myrtle Marie Kroll, Aug. 18, 1951; children—Andrew J., Sarah A. B.A., Miami U., 1951; M.S., U. Wis., 1955, Ph.D., 1958. Instr. surgery and physiol. chemistry U. Wis., Madison, 1959-61, asst. prof., 1961-67, asso. prof., 1967-73, prof. surgery and physiology, 1973—; ad hoc referee Am. Jur. Physiology; mem. Neurology B study sect. NIH. Contbr. articles to profl. jours. Served with USN, 1951-54. NIH grantee, 1965—; Wis. Alumni Research Found. fellow in surgery, 1958-59; Fulbright lectr. in med. sci. U. Chile, Santiago, 1970. Mem. Am. Physiol. Soc., Am. Soc. Biol. Chemists, Am. Soc. Neurochemistry, Internat. Soc. Neurochemistry, Soc. Neurosci., AAUP, Sigma Xi. Roman Catholic. Club: Rotary. Research in metabolism and physiology of isolated canine brain preparation. Home: 409 Blue Ridge Pkwy Madison WI 53705 Office: Dept Surgery Med Scis Center 1300 University Ave Madison WI 53706

GILBRETH, FRANK BUNKER, JR., writer, newspaper publisher; b. Plainfield, N.J., Mar. 17, 1911; s. Frank Bunker and Lillian Evelyn (Moller) G.; m. Elizabeth Cauthen, Sept. 29, 1934 (dec. 1954); 1 dau., Betsy; m. Mary Manigault, June 4, 1955; children: Edward, Rebecca Motte. Student, St. John's Coll., Md., 1928-29; B.A., U. Mich., 1933. Reporter N.Y. Herald Tribune, 1933-34; corr. A.P., Raleigh, N.C., 1938-42, cable editor, 1945-47; editorial writer News & Courier, Charleston, S.C., 1947-50, asso. editor, 1951-57; asst. pub., v.p. News & Courier and Charleston Evening Post, 1957—; sec. Aiken (S.C.) Communications, Inc., Cambridge (Md.) Banner, Waynesboro (Va.) News-Virginian, Portal Communications (KDBC-TV), El Paso, Tex., Sangre de Cristo Communication Inc. (KOAA-TV), Pueblo, Colo., Mardel Communications (AM-FM radio), Salisbury, Md., Sawtooth Communications, Inc. (KIVI-TV) Boise, Idaho; dir. Buenos Aires Herald, Aiken (S.C.) Cablevision. Author: (with Ernestine Gilbreth Carey) Cheaper by the Dozen, 1949, Belles on Their Toes, 1950, (with John Held, Jr.) Held's Angels, 1952, I'm a Lucky Guy, 1951, Innside Nantucket, 1955, Of Whales and Women, 1957, How to Be a Father, 1958, Loblolly, 1959, He's My Boy, 1962, Time Out for Happiness, 1971. Served from lt. (j.g.) to lt. comdr. USNR, 1942-45. Decorated Air medal, Bronze Star. Mem. Alpha Delta Phi. Home: 430 Maybank Hwy Charleston SC 29412 also The Shoe Hulbert Ave Nantucket MA 02554 Office: The News and Courier and The Charleston Evening Post Charleston SC 29402

GILBRIDE, JOHN THOMAS, shipyard executive; b. Bklyn., May 29, 1916; s. Francis Joseph and Mary (Figueira) G.; m. Rosemary Shelare, Sept. 7, 1940; children: Francis Joseph, John Thomas, Gary George. B.A., U. Pa., 1938; postgrad., Bklyn. Poly. Inst., Pratt Inst. With Bklyn. div. Todd Shipyards Corp., 1932-46, asst. gen. mgr. Los Angeles div., 1946, gen. mgr. Los Angeles div., 1946-58, pres., dir., 1958-75, chmn., 1975—; trustee Emigrant Savs. Bank, Atlantic Mut. Ins. Co.; dir. Centennial Ins. Co. Trustee United Seaman's Service; bd. dirs. Oceanic Ednl. Found.; mem. maritime policy adv. group Center Strategic and Internat. Studies; mem. maritime adv. com. U.S. Dept. Transp.; bd. mgrs. Seamen's Ch. Inst. N.Y. and N.J. Fellow Soc. Naval Architects and Marine Engrs. (hon. v.p.); mem. U.S. Naval Inst. (asso.), Am. Bur. Shipping (bd. mgrs., pension, mgmt. and nominating coms.), Lloyds Register of Shipping (Am. com., chmn. nominating com., exec. com.), Shipbuilders Council Am. (dir., exec. com.), Am. Soc. Naval Engrs., Maritime Assn. Port of N.Y., Am. Welding Soc., Nat. Def. Transp. Assn., Navy League U.S., N.E. Coast Instn. Engrs. and Shipbuilders (Eng.), Propeller Club U.S.A. (nat. exec. com.), Life Saving Benevolent Assn. N.Y., Newcomen Soc. N.Am., New Orleans C. of C., Marine Hist. Soc., Phi Sigma Kappa. Roman Catholic. Clubs: Whitehall Luncheon (past pres., bd. govs.), India House (bd. govs.), Chiselers, N.Y. Yacht (N.Y.C.); Capitol Hill (Washington); Nantucket Yacht, Oslo Golf. Lodge: Knights of Malta. Home: 180 Stanwich Rd Greenwich CT 06830 Office: 1 State St Plaza New York NY 10004

GILBRIDE, WILLIAM DONALD, lawyer; b. Detroit, July 31, 1924; s. William Andrew and Kathryne Agnes (Donnelly) G.; m. Helen A. Posselius, May 1, 1954; 1 son, William Donald. LL.B., U. Detroit, 1950. Bar: Mich. bar 1950. Assoc. firm Fildew, DeGree & Fleming, Detroit, 1951-53, ptnr., 1953-65; ptnr. firm Fildew, Gilbride, Miller & Todd (and predecessor firm), 1973-80, Fildew, Hinks, Gilbride, Miller & Todd, 1980—; mem. State Bd. Law Examiners., 1972-75. Pres. Friends of Detroit Public Library, 1968-70; pres. bd. trustees Liggett Sch., 1964-66. Served with AUS, 1943-46. Mem. Am. Legion, Detroit Bar Assn. (pres. 1972-73), Am. Bar Found., Am. Judicature Soc., Am. Bar Assn., Alpha Kappa Psi, Delta Theta Phi. Republican. Roman Catholic. Clubs: Detroit, Detroit Press, Detroit Racquet, University, Propeller, Grosse Pointe., Yondotega. Home: 18 Radnor Circle Grosse Pointe Farms MI 48236 Office: 3600 Penobscot Bldg Detroit MI 48226

GILCHREST, THRONTON CHARLES, association executive; b. Chgo., Sept. 1, 1931; s. Charles Jewett GilchresteC and Patricia (Thornton) Thornton; m. Barbara Dibbern, June 8, 1952; children: Margaret Mary, James Thornton. B.S., U. Ill., 1953. Cert. tchr., Ill. Tchr. pub. high sch., West Chicago, Ill., 1957; exec.l dir. Plumbing-Heating-Cooling Info. Bur., Chgo., 1958-64; asst. to pres. A.Y. McDonald Mfg. Co., Dubuque, Iowa, 1964-68; exec. dir. Am. Supply Assn., Chgo., 1968-77; exec. v.p. Am. Supply Assn.l, Chgo., 1977-82, Nat. Safety Council, 1982-83, pres., 1983—. Served with USN, 1953-55. Mem. Am. soc. Assn. Execs., Chgo. Soc. Assn. Execs. Methodist. Club: University (Chgo.). Office: Nat Safety Council 444 N Michigan Ave Chicago IL 60611

GILCHRIST, JAMES BEARDSLEE, banker; b. Cleve., Apr. 1, 1939; s. Hart D. and Alice (Beardslee) G.; m. Lewayne Dorman, Sept. 14, 1963; children: Hart D., Matthew J. A.B., Dartmouth Coll., 1961; LL.B., Stanford U., 1964; grad. with honors, Pacific Coast Banking Sch., U. Wash., 1970. Bar: Wash. 1964. Dep. pros. atty., King County, Wash., 1964-65; with Seattle First Nat. Bank, 1965—, v.p., 1973—, trust officer, 1970-77, corp. sec., 1977-82; sec. Seafirst Corp., 1977-82, mgr. instl. trust dept., 1982—; instr. Am. Inst. Banking, Seattle Community Coll., 1976-78. Mem. candidate evaluation team Seattle Mcpl. League, 1976-79, chmn., 1979; mem. adv. com. Mercer Island Sch. Bd., 1979-81; bd. dirs. Mercer Island Schs. Found., 1981—. Mem. ABA, Am. Soc. Corp. Secs. (chpt. pres. 1980-81, corp. practices com. 1981-83, dir. 1982—), Wash. Bar Assn., Colo. Bar Assn., Seattle-King County Bar Assn., Seattle Estate Planning Council (chmn. seminar 1975). Club: Wash. Athletic (Seattle). Office: Seattle First Nat Bank PO Box 3586 Seattle WA 98124

GILDEHAUS, THOMAS ARTHUR, manufacturing company executive; b. Little Rock, Sept. 29, 1940; s. Arthur Frederick and Susanna (Packham) G.; m. Barbara Lee Quimby, Oct. 29, 1960; children: Elizabeth, Thomas Arthur, Charles, Christopher, Allen. B.A. in History, Yale U., 1963; M.B.A. with distinction, Harvard U., 1970. With Citibank, N.Y.C. and P.R., 1963-70; v.p. Temple, Barker and Sloane, Inc., Lexington, Mass., 1970-80; exec. v.p., dir. Deere & Co., Moline, Ill., 1980—. Address: Deere & Co John Deere Rd Moline IL 61265

GILDENBERG, PHILIP LEON, neurosurgeron; b. Hazleton, Pa., Mar. 15, 1935; s. Samuel and Ida (Kline) G.; m. Sondra Burman, June 10, 1955; children—Susan, Steven, Ronald, Laura. A.B. in Zoology with honors (Edward Pendleton scholar 1952-55), U. Pa., 1955; M.D., M.S. in Exptl. Neurology (Pa. Senatorial scholar 1955-59), Temple U., 1959; Ph.D. in Neurophysiology (Nat. Inst. Neurol. Diseases and Blindness 1966-67, spl. fellow 1967, NIH grantee 1966), Temple U., 1970. Diplomate: Am. Bd. Neurol. Surgery. Intern Grace Hosp., Detroit, 1959-60; resident in surgery Temple U. Hosp., 1962, resident in neurosurgery, 1963-67, lectr. neurosurgery, 1963-67, Philippine Nurse Exchange Program Temple U. Health Scis. Center, 1965-67; research fellow neurophysiology Max Planck Inst. Brain Research, Frankfurt, W. Ger., 1968; staff neurosurgeon Cleve. Clinic Found., 1968-72, head clinician neurosurg. research, 1969-72; adj. asst. prof. Case Western Res. U., 1970-72; prof., chief div. neurosurgery U. Ariz. Med. Center, 1972-75; cons. Tucson VA Hosp., 1972-74; prof., chief div. neurosurgery U. Tex. Med. Sch., Houston, 1976-82, co-dir. pain clinic, 1975—; chief neurosurg. service Hermann Hosp., Houston, 1975-82; vis. prof. Temple U. Med. Sch., 1978, 80, Hahnemann Med. Sch., Phila., 1980, U. Fla. Med. Sch., 1981; mem. numerous nat. med. coms., study groups. Author numerous articles in field.; Editor: Applied Neurophysiology, Pain and Headache; mem. editorial bds. profl. jours. Served with USNR, 1960-62. Recipient Research award U. Ariz. Med. Sch., 1973, Fan Kane Research award, 1974; grantee NIH. Fellow A.C.S.; mem. World Soc. Stereotactic and Functional Surgery (sec.-treas.), Am. Soc. Stereotactic and Functional Surgery (sec.-treas.), Am. Assn. Neurol. Surgeons, Southwestern Surg. Congress, Congress Neurol. Surgeons, Soc. Neurol. Surgeons, Am. Physiol. Soc., Soc. U. Neurosurgeons, Research Soc. Neurol. Surgeons, Soc. Neurosci., Internat. Assn. Study Pain (a founder), Houston Neurol. Soc., Am. Trauma Soc. (a founder), Am. Acad. Neurology (assoc.), AAAS, Harris County Med. Soc., Rocky Mountain Neurosurg. Soc., So. Neurosurg. Soc., Neuroelectric Soc., AAUP, Neuroanesthesia Soc., N.Y. Acad. Scis., Council Biology Editors. Republican. Jewish. Address: 1530 Scurlock Tower 6560 Fannin St Houston TX 77030

GILDENHORN, JOSEPH BERNARD, lawyer; b. Washington, Sept. 17, 1929; s. Oscar and Celia (Koval) G.; m. Alma Lee Gross, June 28, 1953; children: Carol Ann, Michael Saul. B.S., U. Md., 1951; LL.B., Yale, 1954. Bar: D.C. 1954, Md. 1954. Counsel Office Gen. Counsel, SEC, 1956-58; individual practice, Washington, 1958—; partner firm Brown, Gildenhorn & Jacobs, 1958—; guest lectr. George Washington U., D.C. Bar Assn.; pres. JBG Properties, Inc., JBG Assos., Inc.; vice chmn. dir. D.C. Nat. Bank. Chmn. State of Israel Bonds, Washington, 1974—; past pres., bd. dirs. Hebrew Home Greater Washington, 1975-77; bd. dirs. Washington Jewish Community Found.; v.p., bd. dirs. United Jewish Appeal Fedn. Greater Washington. Served with AUS, 1954-56. Recipient David Ben Gurion award State of Israel, 1977, Hyman Goldman Humanitarian award, 1984. Mem. Apt. and Office Bldg. Assn. Washington. Clubs: Mason., Woodmont Country. Home: 7000 Loch Lomond Dr Bethesda MD 20034 Office: 1220 19th St NW Suite 800 Washington DC 20036

GILDER, ROSAMOND, writer, dramatic critic; b. Marion, Mass.; d. Richard Watson and Helena (deKay) G. Ed. pub. schs.; L.H.D., U. Denver, 1969. Editorial sec. Nat. Theatre Conf., 1932-35; dir. Playwrights' Bur., Fed. Theatre, 1935-36; dramatic critic, asso. editor, editor-in-chief Theatre Arts, 1938-48; bd. mem. ANTA, 1945-69; pres. Internat. Theatre Inst.; dir. U.S. Center, 1948—; lectr. Barnard Coll., 1948-55; Chmn. U.S. delegation 1st World Conf. on Theatre, Bombay, India, 1956, U.S. delegations Internat. Theatre Congresses, 1948—. Writer, 1916—; Author: books including Biography of Richard Watson Gilder, 1916, John Gielgud's Hamlet, 1937, Enter the Actress, 1960; Translator: My Life (Emma Calvé), 1922; Contbr. articles to profl. jours. Served with ARC, 1917-19; France; Served with Children's Bur., ARC, 1917-20. Decorated médaille d'Epidemie, médaille de Reconnaissance, France; officer l'Ordre des Arts et des Lettres, France; recipient Fulbright award, Paris, 1955-56. Club:

Cosmopolitan (N.Y.C.). Home: 24 Gramercy Park New York NY 10003

GILDERHUS, MARK THEODORE, historian, educator; b. Rochester, Minn., Nov. 15, 1941; s. M.R. and Thea L. (Enderson) G.; m. Nancy Loutzenheiser, June 24, 1967; children—Kirsten, Lesley. A.B., Gustavus Adolphus Coll., 1963; M.A. (NDEA Title IV fellow), U. Nebr., 1965, Ph.D., 1968. Asst. prof. Colo. State U., Fort Collins, 1968-72, asso. prof., 1972-77, prof. history, 1977—, chmn. dept., 1980—; editorial cons. jours. and pubs. Author: Diplomacy and Revolution: U.S.-Mexican Relations under Wilson and Carranza, 1977. Nat. Endowment for Humanities grantee, 1972. Mem. Orgn. Am. Historians, Am. Hist. Assn., Soc. Historians Am. Fgn. Relations, Conf. on Latin Am. History. Democrat. Unitarian. Home: 1033 Cypress Dr Fort Collins CO 80521 Office: Dept History Colorado State U Fort Collins CO 80523

GILEADI, AVIVA EVA, nuclear engineer; b. Budapest, Hungary, Nov. 26, 1917; came to U.S., 1959, naturalized, 1973; d. Samuel and Gisela (Kupferstein) Fischmann; m. Michael Gileadi, May 2, 1946; children: Amos, Noah, Ruth Hannah. Ph.D. in Physics, Peter Pazmany U., Budapest, 1941; M.Sc. in Nuclear Engring., U. Mich., 1960. Tchr., Israel, 1948-58; lectr., dir. lab. Technion-Israel Inst. Tech., Haifa, 1958-63; reactor physicist BONUS Nuclear Power Plant, P.R., 1963-65; dir. nuclear engring. dept. U. P.R., 1970-71; dir. div. nuclear engring. P.R. Nuclear Ctr., 1970-71, prof. nuclear engring., chief scientist ctr., 1965-75; prin. scientist KMS Fusion Inc., Ann Arbor, 1976-79; prin. engr. nuclear engring. div., generation engring. dept. Detroit Edison Co., 1979—; vis. scientist Brookhaven Nat. Lab., 1968. Contbr. articles to profl. jours.; co-author: Applied Nuclear Power Engineering for Practicing Engineers, 1972. Named Women Scientist of Yr. Am. Technion Soc., 1967. Mem. Am. Nuclear Soc., Health Physics Soc. Jewish. Home: 2711 Somerset Blvd Troy MI 48084 Office: 3331 W Big Beaver Rd Troy MI 48084

GILELS, EMIL, pianist; b. Odessa, Russia, Oct. 19, 1916; s. Grigory and Esphir (Zamoshina) G.; m. Farizet Hucistova, Jan. 19, 1947; 1 dau., Elena. Grad., Odessa Conservatory, 1935, Sch. of Mastership of Moscow Conservatory, 1938. Prof. Moscow Conservatory, 1954—. First concert, 1929, concerts through, USSR, 1933—, Europe, 1945—, U.S.A., 1955—, Mex., 1955, Japan, 1957, Can., 1958—; debut in N.Y. at, Carnegie Hall, 1969. Recipient 1st prize All Union Contest Musicians, Moscow, 1933, 2d prize Vienna Contest, 1936, 1st prize Internat. Contest Pianists, Brussels, 1938; State prize, 1946; Lenin prize, 1962; decorated Order Labor Red Banner, Order of Lenin, 1961, 2d Order of Lenin, 1966, Order de Commandeur Merite Culturel et Artisque de Paris, 1967; comdr. Order Leopold I, Brussels, 1964; Medaille de Vermeil de la Ville de Paris, 1967; Hero of Socialist Labor, 1976. Mem. Central Home Art WWirkers, Royal Acad. Music London (hon.). Address: care Columbia Artists Mgmt Inc 165 W 57th St New York NY 10019 *

GILES, ALEXANDER WETHERAL, JR., investment banker; b. Hackensack, N.J., Jan. 26, 1935; s. Alexander Wetheral and Mildred G.; m. Evelyn M. Exley, Dec. 12, 1959; children: Alexander G. III, Jennifer G. B.S., U.S. Mcht. Marine Acad., 1956; M.B.A., N.Y. U., 1963. Adminstrv. asst. Chubb Corp., N.Y.C., 1959-61, budget dir., 1966-68; asst. to zone controller Allstate Ins. Cos., White Plains, N.Y., 1961-63, regional controller, Hartford, Conn., 1963-66; v.p. fin., bond div. Gen. Host Corp., N.Y.C., 1968-70, asst. controller, 1970-73, controller, 1973-74, v.p. adminstrn., 1974; v.p. fin. Caron Internat., Inc., N.Y.C., 1974-76; sr. v.p. fin. Modular Computer Systems, Inc., Fort Lauderdale, Fla., 1976-79, pres., chief exec. officer, 1979-80, chmn. bd., chief exec. officer, 1980-81, dir., 1979-81; exec. v.p. Brean Murray, Foster Securities, N.Y.C., 1982-83, pres., 1983—; dir. Rexon Inc., Summit Software Systems Inc., Hetra Computer Systems, Infomark, Inc. Served to lt. USN, 1957-59. Republican. Episcopalian. Clubs: Met. (N.Y.C.); Knickerbocker (Tenafly, N.J.). Office: Brean Murray Foster Securities 67 Wall St New York NY 10005

GILES, EUGENE, anthropology educator; b. Salt Lake City, June 30, 1933; s. George Eugene and Eleanor (Clark) G.; m. Inga Valborg Wikman, Sept. 9, 1964; children: Eric George, Edward Eugene. A.B., Harvard U., 1955, A.M., 1960, Ph.D., 1966; M.A., U. Calif., Berkeley, 1956. Instr. in anthropology U. Ill., Urbana, 1964-66, assoc. prof., 1970-73, prof., 1973—, head dept. anthropology, 1975-80; asst. prof. Harvard U., 1966-70; vis. fellow Australian Nat. U., Canberra, 1967-68, 78. Editor: (with J.S. Friedlaender, jr. editor) The Measures of Man: Methodologies in Biological Anthropology, 1976. Served with U.S. Army, 1956-58. NSF postdoctoral fellow, 1967-68; NSF grantee, 1970-72; NIH grantee, 1965-68. Fellow Am. Anthrpol. Assn., AAAS, Am. Acad. Forensic Scis.; mem. Am. Assn. Phys. Anthropologists (exec. com. 1973-76, v.p. 1979-80, pres. 1981-83), Human Biology Council (exec. com. 1974-77), Am. Bd. Forensic Anthropology (diplomate), Phi Beta Kappa, Sigma Xi. Biol. anthropology research in Papua New Guinea and Australia. Home: 1106 S Lynn St Champaign IL 61820 Office: Dept Anthropology U Ill Urbana IL 61801

GILES, HOMER WAYNE, lawyer; b. Noble, Ohio, Nov. 9, 1919; s. Edwin Jay and Nola Blanche (Tillison) G.; m. Zola Ione Parke, Sept. 8, 1948; children: Jay, Janice, Keith, Tim, Gregory. A.B., Adelbert Coll., 1940; LL.B., Western Res. Law Sch., 1943, LL.M., 1959. Bar: Ohio bar 1943. Mem. firm Davis & Young, Cleve., 1942-43, William I. Moon, Port Clinton, Ohio, 1946-48; pres. Strabley Baking Co., Cleve., 1948-53; v.p. French Baking Co., Cleve., 1953-55; law clk. 8th Dist Ct. Appeals, Cleve., 1955-58; partner firm Kuth & Giles, Cleve., 1958-68, Walter, Haverfield, Buescher & Chockley, 1968—; pres. Clinton Franklin Realty Co., Cleve., 1958—, Concepts Devel., Inc., 1980—; sec. Holiday Designs, Inc., Sebring, Ohio, 1964—; trustee Teamster Local 52 Health and Welfare Fund, 1950-53; mem. Bakers Negotiating Exec. Com., 1951-53. Contbr. articles to profl. pubs.; editor: Banks Baldwin Ohio Legal Forms, 1962. Troop com. chmn. Skyline council Boy Scouts Am., 1961-63; adviser Am. Security Council; trustee Hiram House Camp, Florence Crittenton Home, 1965; chmn. bd. trustees Am. Econ. Found., N.Y.C., 1973-80, chmn. exec. com., 1973-80. Served with AUS, 1943-46; ETO. Mem. Am. Bar Assn., World Law Assn. (founding), Am. Arbitration Assn. (nat. panel), Com. on Econ. Reform and Edn. (life), Inst. Money and Inflation, Speakers Bur. Cleve. Sch. Levy, Citizens League, Pacific Inst., Phila. Soc., Aircraft Owners and Pilots Assn., Cleve. Hist. Soc., Mus. Modern Art, Mercantile Library, Delta Tau Delta, Delta Theta Phi. Unitarian. Clubs: Cleve. Skating, Harvard Bus. Home: 2588 S Green Rd University Heights OH 44122 Office: 1215 Terminal Tower Cleveland OH 44113

GILES, NORMAN HENRY, educator, geneticist; b. Atlanta, Aug. 6, 1915; s. Norman Henry and Alice (Guerard) G.; m. Dorothy Lunsford, Aug. 26, 1939 (dec. Jan. 1967); children—Annette Guerard, David Lunsford; m. Doris Vos Weaver, Aug. 1, 1969; stepchildren—Gayle Weaver (dec.), Alix Weaver. A.B., Emory U., 1937, Sc.D. (hon.), 1980; M.A., Harvard U., 1938, Ph.D., 1940; M.A. (hon.), Yale, 1951. Instr. botany Yale, 1941-45, asst. prof., 1945-46, asso. prof., 1946-51, prof., 1951-61, Eugene Higgins prof. genetics, 1961-72; Fuller E. Callaway prof. genetics U. Ga., 1972—; prin. biologist Oak Ridge Nat. Lab., 1947-50; cons. AEC, 1954-64; Mem. genetics study sect. NIH, 1960-64, mem. genetics tng. com., 1966-70; ednl. adv. bd. John Simon Guggenheim Meml. Found., 1977—. Editorial bd.: Radiation Research, 1953-58, Am. Naturalist, 1961-64, Devel. Genetics, 1979—. Bd. dirs. U. Ga. Research Found., 1979—. Parker fellow Harvard U., 1940-41; Fulbright and Guggenheim fellow U. Genetics Inst., Copenhagen, 1959-60; Guggenheim fellow Australian Nat. U., Canberra, 1966. Fellow Am. Acad. Arts and Scis., AAAS; mem. Nat. Acad. Scis. (chmn. genetics sect. 1976-79), Genetics Soc. Am. (treas. 1954-56, pres. 1970), Bot. Am., Am. Soc. Naturalists (pres. 1977), Am. Inst. Biol. Scis., Genetics Soc. Japan (hon.), Am. Ornithologists Union, Phi Beta Kappa, Sigma Xi. Home: 289 Hanover Dr Bogart GA 30622 Office: Dept Genetics U Ga Athens GA 30602

GILES, ROBERT HARTMANN, editor; b. Cleve., June 6, 1933; s. Robert Hamilton and Grace (Hartmann) G.; m. Nancy May Morgan, Feb. 6, 1960; children—David Morgan, Megan Elisabeth, Robert Hamilton II. B.A, DePauw U., 1955; M.S., Columbia, 1956. Reporter Newport News Daily Press, 1957-58; reporter Akron (Ohio) Beacon Jour., 1958-63, editorial writer, 1963-65, city editor, 1966-68, met. editor, 1968-69, mng. editor, 1969-73, exec. editor, 1973-76; spl. lectr. Sch. Journalism, U. Kans., 1976-77; exec. editor Gannett Newspapers, Rochester, N.Y., 1977-81, editor, 1981—. Trustee William Allen White Found., U. Kans., 1978—. Served with AUS, 1956-58. Nieman fellow Harvard, 1965-66; co-recipient Pulitzer prize for local reporting, 1971, Scripps-Howard 1st Amendment award, 1978. Mem. A.P. Mng. Editors Assn., Am. Soc. Newspaper Editors, Alpha Tau Omega, Sigma Delta Chi. Office: Gannett Rochester Newspapers 55 Exchange St Rochester NY 14614

GILES, WILLIAM BLISS, retired lawyer; b. Blissfield, Mich., May 7, 1903; s. John W. and Flora (Kurtz) G.; m. Margaret Lawson, May 17, 1930; 1 dau., Greta (Mrs. John E. Cunning). A.B., U. Mich., 1925, J.D., 1927; J.D. (hon.), Detroit Coll. Law, 1948. Bar: Mich. 1927. Practiced, Detroit; dir. Pelham Land Co., Detroit Airport Adv. Co.; prof. law Detroit Coll. Law, 1928-58. Trustee Crittenton Hosp. Named to U. Mich. Hall of Honor. Mem. Detroit, Mich., Am. bar assns. Clubs: Mason (K.T.), Detroit Golf, Detroit, Detroit Athletic. Home: 694 Rudgate Rd Bloomfield Hills MI 48013 Office: 24245 Northwestern Hwy Southfield MI 48075

GILES, WILLIAM CLEMENT, JR., ins. co. exec.; s. William Clement and Helen (Smith) G.; m. K. Louise Whittier, Sept. 30, 1944; children—Mary Louise, Margaret E. A.B., Brown U., 1942; J.D., Harvard, 1948. Bar: Mass. bar 1948. Practiced in, Springfield, 1948-66; atty. Monarch Life Ins. Co., Springfield, 1952-68, dir., 1964—, chmn. bd., 1968—; asso. gen. counsel Springfield Life Ins. Co., Inc., 1959-68, dir., 1965—, chmn. bd., 1968—; chmn. bd., dir. Monarch Capital Corp., Monarch Investment Mgmt. Corp.; dir. Valley Bank & Trust Co. Bd. dirs. Legal Aid Soc. Springfield, Mass. Council for Pub. Justice; chmn. bd. trustees Am. Internat. Coll.; trustee Springfield Central Bus. Dist., Basketball Hall of Fame. Served to 1st lt. USAAF, 1942-46. Mem. ABA, Mass. Bar Assn. (del. 1966-69), Hampden County Bar Assn., Assn. Life Ins. Counsel, Springfield C. of C. (trustee). Club: Colony (Springfield). Home: 237 Longmeadow St Longmeadow MA 01106 Office: 1250 State St Springfield MA 01101

GILES, WILLIAM ELMER, former newspaper editor, educator; b. Somerville, N.J., July 5, 1927; s. Elmer and Mary Jane (Reed) G.; m. Gloria Mastrangelo, June 4, 1949; children: William J., Michael E., Richard H. and Paul L. (twins), Joseph R. A.B. in Government, Columbia U., 1950, M.S. in Journalism, 1951. Reporter Plainfield (N.J.) Courier-News, 1946-47; copyreader, reporter Wall St. Jour., 1951- 58, mng. editor Southwest edit., Dallas, 1958-61, news editor Washington bur., 1961; an organizer nat. weekly newspaper Nat. Observer, 1961, editor, 1962-71; asst. gen. mgr. Dow Jones & Co., Inc., pub., 1971-76; dir. mgmt. programs, mem. Dow Jones mgmt. com., 1972-76; disting. editor in residence Baylor U., 1976; exec. editor Detroit News, 1976-77, editor, v.p., 1977-83; editor-in-residence, lectr. Mich. State U., East Lansing, 1983—. Mem. Sigma Delta Chi. Home: 509 Elizabeth St East Lansing MI

GILFILLEN, GEORGE C., JR., marketing company executive; b. Dayton, Ohio, Oct. 31, 1919; m. Betty Wright (dec.); children: George C. III, Mary Kimbrough (Mrs. Coughnour). Grad., Mercersburg (Pa.) Acad.; ed., Cornell U. Formerly assoc. with Standard Register Co., Inland Mfg. Div., Dictaphone Corp., Dayton; now chmn. bd. E.F. MacDonald Co., Dayton,, Dayton,,, all Dayton, San Francisco, Dayton, Cin. and Columbus, Ohio, also Richmond, Ind.; and Lexington, Ky.; dir. 3d Nat. Bank & Trust Co., Dayton; sustaining mem. Ohio Bankpac. Mem. adv. bd. Miami Valley council Boy Scouts Am.; bd. regents, devel. com. Mercersburg (Pa.) Acad.; trustee United Way, Dayton, Dayton Art Inst., Miami Valley Hosp., Dayton; trustee, mem. exec. com., v.p. charge news media and public relations Aviation Hall Fame, Dayton; mem. Ohio Found. Ind. Colls., Area Progress Council, Dayton; mem. new horizons fund steering com. U. Dayton; corp. mem. United Health Found., Dayton; mem. steering com. YMCA; mem. nat. bd. Boys' Club Am.; bd. dirs. Dayton Philharm. Assn., Dayton Devel. Council, Staff Assistance for Employers Com., Dayton. Mem. Newcomen Soc., Dayton Area C. of C. (dir., mem. solicitations rev. com.), Am. Def. Preparedness Assn. (dir. Wright Bros. chpt.), Montgomery County Hist. Soc. Clubs: Mason (32 deg.), Dayton Country, Bicycle, Dayton Y Athletic, Moraine Country, Dayton Racquet, Masons, Antioch Shrine, One Hundred (trustee), Miami Valley Skeet, Foreman's (Dayton); 8th Dist. Congl. (Ohio); N.Y. Athletic, Detroit Athletic; Burning Tree Country (Bethesda, Md.); Mission Hills Country (Rancho Mirage, Calif.); Vintage (Indian Wells, Calif.). Home: 2230 S Patterson Blvd Dayton OH 45409 Office: 111 N Main St Dayton OH 45401

GILFORD, JACK (JACK GELLMAN), actor, comedian; b. N.Y.C., July 25; s. Aaron and Sophie (Jackness) G.; m. Madeline Lee Letterman, Apr. 6, 1949; children—Joseph Edward, Lisa, Sam. Student public schs., Bklyn. Began career as vaudeville comedian, 1934; toured in vaudeville, 1934-39; with, Milton Berle Revue, 1935-39; Broadway debut in Meet the People, 1940; vaudeville and stage show comedian touring, U.S., 1941-50; with, USO, in Pacific, 1945; appeared on: TV shows The Defenders, Car 54, Lucy Show, Get Smart, Carol Burnett Show, Love Boat; with first film appearances in, 1944; in: Hey Rookie and Reckless Age; appeared as Frosch in: Fledermaus, Met. Opera, 1950, on tour, 1951-52; at, Met. Opera, 1958-59, 62-63, 66-67; appeared on: radio in Philip Morris Show, 1947; TV debut on Arrow Show, 1948, Gary Moore Show, 1950, Milton Berle Show, 1951, Jack Carson Show, 1951, Frank Sinatra Show, 1951; appeared on stage as Bontche Schweig in: The World of Sholom Aleichem, 1953, Passion of Gross, 1955, Once Over Lightly, 1955, Diary of Anne Frank, 1955, Romanoff and Juliet, 1957, Drink to Me Only, 1958, Once Upon a Mattress, 1959, The Tenth Man, 1959, The Policeman, 1961, A Funny Thing Happened On the Way to the Forum, 1962, Cabaret, 1966, Three Men on a Horse, 1969, No No Nanette, 1971, The Sunshine Boys, 1972, Sly Fox, 1976; appeared in: films including Main Street to Broadway, 1953, A Funny Thing Happened on the Way to the Forum, 1965, Enter Laughing, 1966, Who's Minding the Mint?, 1967, The Incident, 1967, Catch 22, 1969, Save the Tiger, 1972, Harvey and Walter Go to New York, 1976; Appeared on: TV shows The World of Sholom Aleichem, 1960, Cowboy and the Tiger, 1963, Once Upon a Mattress, 1964, Wholly Moses, 1979, Cheaper to Keep Her, 1979, Caveman, 1980; TV appearances on The Very Special Jack Gilford Special, CBS Cable; Broadway appearance The Supporting Cast, 1981; starred in: TV series Apple Pie, 1978, Soap. Office: care Internat Creative Mgmt 40 W 57th St New York NY 10019

GILINSKY, STANLEY ELLIS, department store executive; b. Trenton, N.J., Aug. 7, 1918; s. Charles Edgar and Rose (Kohn) G.; m. Gerry Braslove, Nov. 25, 1945; children: Michael, Ellen. B.S., Lehigh U., 1940; LL.B., J.D., U. Pa., 1944. Bar: Pa. 1944. Law sec. Justice Horace Stern Supreme Ct. Pa., Phila., 1944-45; assoc. firm Wolf, Block, Schorr & Solis-Cohen, Phila., 1944-46; asst. budget dir. L. Bamberger & Co., Newark, 1946-50; research, planning dir. Gimbels, Phila., 1950-58; dir. corp. expansion, devel. Gimbel Bros., Inc., N.Y.C., 1958-64, dir., 1964-68, corp. v.p., sec., 1968—; also v.p. charge expansion, planning, devel. for Gimbels and Saks Fifth Ave. subs., 1964-76; v.p. Saks & Co., 1968-76; sr. v.p. corp. devel. and real estate Saks Fifth Ave., 1975—, Gimbels, 1977-80, sr. v.p. Batus retail div., 1980—, dir., Saks & Co., Gimbel-Saks Retailing Corp. Mem. Teaneck (N.J.) Polit. Assembly, 1962—, Teaneck Redevel. Authority, 1970-74. Mem. Am. Mktg. Assn., Phi Beta Kappa, Pi Lambda Phi. Home: 32 Grayson Pl Teaneck NJ 07666 Office: 1270 Ave of Americas New York NY 10020

GILINSKY, VICTOR, physicist; b. Warsaw, Poland, May 28, 1934; came to U.S., 1941, naturalized, 1948; s. Shlome Faywysh and Luba (Kantorwicz) G.; m. Magdalena, June 13, 1964; children—David, Anessa. B.S. in Engring. Physics, Cornell U., 1956; Ph.D. in Physics, Calif. Inst. Tech., 1961. Physicist Rand Corp., Santa Monica, Calif., 1961-71, head dept. phys. sci., 1973-75; asst. dir. policy and program rev. AEC, Washington, 1971-73; mem. U.S. Nuclear Regulatory Commn., Washington, 1975—. Mem. Am. Phys. Soc., Internat. Inst. Strategic Studies. Office: 1717 H St Washington DC 20555

GILKERSON, YANCEY SHERARD, editor; b. Laurens, S.C., Mar. 5, 1919; s. Yancey S. and Harriet (Bentz) G.; m. Vashti Keys, July 29, 1941; 1 son, Richard B. Student, Furman U., 1936-38. City editor The Greenville (S.C.) Piedmont, 1946-48, San Diego Jour., 1949; asst. city editor New Orleans Item, 1950-54; bur. chief Fairchild Publs., Greenville, S.C., 1954-58; editor Women's Wear Daily, N.Y.C., 1958-61; exec. v.p. Textile Hall Corp., 1961-66, pres., treas., 1966-80, dir. emeritus, 1980—. Free-lance writer. Home: 112 Lanneau Dr Greenville SC 29605

GILKESON, MURRAY MACK, educator; b. Augusta, Kans., Feb. 8, 1922; s. Murray M. and LaVerna M. (Powell) G.; m. Janet Ada Todd, July 2, 1944; children: Jane Susan, Murray Mack III, Jo Anne, Todd Allen. B.E., U. So. Calif., 1944; M.S., Kans. State U., 1947; M.S.E., U. Mich., Ph.D., 1951; Ph.D., Claremont Grad. Sch., 1977. Research asst. Engring. Research Inst. U. Mich., 1948-51; asst., then assoc. prof. Tulane U., New Orleans, 1951-61; prof., chmn. faculty Harvey Mudd Coll., Claremont, Calif., 1961—; chief AID project, Brazil; program asso. NSF Internat. programs; dir. Claremont Colls. Program Public Policy Studies, 1973-76; Design engr. Papal Satinado S.A., Mexico City, 1956-57. Served with USN, 1944-46. NSF grantee. Mem. Am. Inst. Chem. Engrs., Am. Soc. Engring. Edn. Republican. Home: 402 E Blaisdell Dr Claremont CA 91711 Office: Harvey Mudd Coll Claremont CA 91711

GILKEY, GORDON WAVERLY, curator, artist; b. Albany, Oreg., Mar. 10, 1912; s. Leonard Ernest and Edna Isabel (Smith) G.; m. Vivian Malone, Oct. 17, 1938; 1 son, Gordon Spencer. B.S., Albany Coll., 1933; M.F.A., U. Oreg., 1936; Arts D. (hon.), Lewis and Clark Coll., 1957. Mem. art staff Stephens Coll., Mo., 1939-42; prof. art, head dept. Oreg. State U., 1947-64, dean, 1963-73, 1973-77; curator prints and drawings, printmaker-in-resident Portland (Oreg.) Art Mus. and Coll., 1978—; dir. Internat. Exchange Print Exhibits, 1956—; U.S. adviser IV Bordighera Biennale, Italy, 1957; Chmn. Gov.'s Planning Council for Arts and Humanities in, Oreg., 1965-67; mem. Gov.'s Commn. on Fgn. Lang. and Internat. Studies. Ofcl. etcher, New York World's Fair, 1939, 1937-39; etcher, Nat. Broadcasting Co., Radio City, N.Y.C., 1937-39; Artist-author: Etchings: New York World's Fair, 1939; Author articles on art.; major work in permanent collection, Met. Mus. Art, others. Bd. overseers Lewis and Clark Coll.; trustee Oreg. State U. Found.; chmn. exec. bd. Oreg. French Study Center, Oreg. German Study Center, Oreg. Japan Study Center, Oreg. Latin Am. Study Center, 1966-77. Entered U.S. Army; active duty, July 1942; combat intelligence officer, head of War Dept.; spl. staff art projects in Europe and chief of Joint-Chiefs-of-Staff Study in Europe of German Psychol. Warfare, 1946-47; collected War Dept. Hist. Properties collection of Nazi and German war art; discharged to Res. as maj. USAF, Oct. 1947; col. Res. ret. AIA-Carnegie Corp. fellow, summer 1930, 32; decorated officer with decoration Palmes Academiques French Acad.; officer's cross; comdr.'s cross Order of Merit, W. Ger.; Order Star of Solidarity, Italy; comdr. Order of Merit, Italy; officer Order Acad. Palms; chevalier Legion of Honor, France; King Carl XVI Gustaf's Gold Commemorative medal in art, Sweden). Mem. Portland Art Assn., Soc. Am. Graphic Artists, Calif. Soc. Printmakers, Coll. Art Assn., UN Assn. Oreg. (pres.), Oreg. Internat. Council (bd. dirs.), Phi Kappa Phi, Kappa Pi. Home: 6810 SE 31st Ave Portland OR 97202

GILKEY, KENNETH GEORGE, chemical company executive; b. New Kensington, Pa., Dec. 28, 1942; s. Kenneth Simpson and Betty Ida G.; m. Lisette Jacqueline Denis, Sept. 21, 1968. B.S., Pa. State U., 1964. C.P.A., N.Y. State. From staff acct. to mgr. Price Waterhouse & Co. (C.P.As), N.Y.C., 1967-72; asst. controller, then asst. v.p., dep. controller W.R. Grace & Co., N.Y.C., 1972-78, v.p., controller, 1978-81, v.p. fin. planning, 1981-83, sr. v.p. corp. adminstrn., 1983—. Served to 1st lt. U.S. Army, 1965-67. Mem. Am. Inst. C.P.A.s, N.Y. State Soc. C.P.A.s, Fin. Execs. Inst. Club: Union League. Home: 155 Ridge Rd Watchung NJ 07060 Office: Grace Plaza 1114 Ave of the Americas New York NY 10036

GILL, ARDIAN C., actuary; b. Griswold, Conn., Oct. 9, 1929; s. Lewis A. and Sarah (Geer) G.; m. Jill Freeman, May 29, 1954; children—Tracy, Claudia, John Freeman. B.A. with honors in Math, U. Conn., 1951. With Travelers Ins. Co., 1951-54; with Mut. Life Ins. Co., N.Y., 1954-77, 2d v.p., actuary, 1965-66, v.p., actuary, 1966-70, sr. v.p., chief actuary, 1970-77; mgmt. cons., N.Y.C., 1977-78; v.p., prin., dir. Tillinghast, Nelson & Warren, N.Y.C., 1978—. Trustee Village of Saltaire, 1970-72. Fellow Soc. Actuaries (v.p. 1978-80), Can. Inst. Actuaries; mem. Acad. Actuaries, N.Y. Actuaries Club (pres. 1971-72). Club: Union League (N.Y.C.). Home: 152 E 94th St New York NY 10028 Office: 405 Lexington Ave New York NY 10017

GILL, BERNARD IVES, librarian; b. Rockford, Ill., May 16, 1921; s. Richard Hackett and Floss Adeline (Campbell) G.; m. Dorothy Marie Hovde, Aug. 24, 1949; 1 son, Brian Hovde. Student, Beloit Coll., 1939, 42; B.A., U. Ill., 1943, M.S., 1949; grad. student, U. Minn., 1962, 63-64. Tchr., Bensenville, Ill., 1946-47; head librarian Moorhead (Minn.) State U., 1950-80. Served with USNR, 1943-46. Mem. NEA, ALA, AAUP. Methodist. Home: Box 325 Hillsboro ND 58045 *Success? Do what is best for the whole company, institution, or community. If you find yourself figuring out what is easiest or best for only you, stop right there. Connivers and manipulators go down the tube—usually sooner than later. The memory of age is surprisingly good; you live forever with all you have done. Insofar as possible, do what can be enjoyed in memory.*

GILL, BRENDAN, writer; b. Hartford, Conn., Oct. 4, 1914; s. Michael Henry Richard and Elizabeth (Duffy) G.; m. Anne Barnard, June 20, 1936; children: Brenda, Michael, Holly, Madelaine, Rosemary, Kate, Charles. A.B., Yale, 1936. Contbr. to New Yorker, 1936—, film critic, 1960-67, drama critic, 1968—. Author: The Trouble of One House, 1950, The Day The Money Stopped, (adapted play with Maxwell Anderson, 1958), 1957, Fat Girl, 1971, Tallulah, 1972, (with Robert Kimball) Cole, 1971, (with Jerome Zerbe) Happy Times, 1973, Ways of Loving, 1974, Here at the New Yorker, 1975, Lindbergh Alone, 1977, (with Dudley Witney) Summer Places, 1978, (with Derry Moore) The Dream Come True, 1980, Wooings, 1980. Chmn. bd. dirs. October Fund; chmn. bd. Film Soc. Lincoln Center; pres. Inst. for Art and Urban Resources, N.Y., Landmarks Conservancy of N.Y.; mem. N.Y.C. Commn. Cultural Affairs, Mayor's Com. in Pub. Interest, N.Y.C.; bd. dirs. Whitney Mus. Am. Art, Pratt Inst., MacDowell Colony, Mcpl. Art Soc. Mem. Irish Georgian Soc. (dir., Victorian Soc. Am., v.p.). Clubs: Coffee House, Century Assn. (N.Y.C.). Home: Bronxville NY 10708 also Norfolk CT 06058 Office: 25 W 43d St New York NY 10036

GILL, CLARK CYRUS, educator; b. Winona County, Minn., Feb. 19, 1915; s. John H. and Anna (Fluegel) G.; m. Ethel Spaller, Aug. 15, 1952. B.A., Hamline U., 1935; M.A., U. Minn., 1939, Ph.D., 1948. Tchr., high sch., Lake City, Minn., 1935-41, high sch. U. Minn., 1941-42; mem. faculty State Coll., Clarion, Pa., 1948-50; curriculum dir. U.S. Armed Forces Inst., Madison, Wis., 1950-52; coordinator, course writing project U. Wis., Madison, 1952-54; asso. prof. curriculum U. Tex., Austin, 1954-66, prof., 1966-81, prof. emeritus, 1981—. Author: Education and Social Change in Chile, 1966, Education in a Changing Mexico, 1969, The Educational System of Mexico, 1977, The Educational System of Costa Rica, 1980. Served with U.S. Navy, 1942-46. Fulbright prof. U. San Marcos, Lima, Peru, 1960. Mem. Nat. Council Social Studies, Tex. Council Social Studies, Phi Delta Kappa. Office: Coll Edn U Tex Austin TX 78712

GILL, DANIEL E., optical company executive; b. Ziegler, Ill., June 24, 1936; s. Herron E. G.; m. Dorothy Ann McBride, May 28, 1960. B.S. in Fin., Northwestern U., 1958. With Abbott Labs., Chgo., 1965-78, corp. v.p., pres. hosp. products div., 1976-78; group v.p. Soflens products div. Bausch & Lomb, Rochester, N.Y., 1978-80, pres. chief operating officer, 1980-81, pres. chief exec. officer, 1981-82, chmn. bd., pres., 1982—, also dir. Office: Bausch & Lomb 1 Lincoln First Sq Rochester NY 14601 *

GILL, DONALD GEORGE, state edn. ofcl.; b. O'Fallon, Ill., Dec. 3, 1927; s. Fred Kenneth and Anna (Mayer) G.; m. Betty Jo Brummal, Dec. 28, 1952; children—Donald Bruce, Ann Brummal, Gay Ellen. A.B., Ill. Coll., 1951; M.Ed., U. Ill., 1954, Ed.D., 1969; LL.D., Ill. Coll., 1981. Tchr. Waverly (Ill.) Public Schs., 1950-52; prin., elem. and jr. high schs., Taylorville, Ill., 1952-60; asst. dir., dir. Labs. Schs. Eastern Ill. U., Charleston, 1960-74; also prof. edn.; supt. schs. Volusia County, Deland Daytona Beach, Fla., 1974-80; supt. Ill. Dept. Edn., Springfield, 1980—; chmn. Ill. Tchr. Cert. Bd., 1980-81; pres. trustees Ill. Tchr. Retirement System, 1980-81; Ill. commr. Edn. Commn. U.S., 1980-81. Contbr. articles to profl. jours. Mem. Charleston (Ill.) Twp. Bd., 1964-74. Served with USN, 1945-46. Mem. Am. Assn. Sch. Adminstrs., Council Chief State Sch. Officers, Fedn. Urban Suburban Sch. Dists. (exec. com.), Phi Delta Kappa. Office: 100 N 1st St Springfield IL 62777 *From early in my youth onward I have had a deep commitment to the Democratic Ideal based upon the inherent dignity of man under the sovereignty of God.*

GILL, GEORGE NORMAN, newspaper pub. co. exec.; b. Indpls., Aug. 11, 1934; s. George E. and Urith (Dailey) G.; m. Kay Baldwin, Dec. 28, 1957; children—Norman A., George B. A.B., Ind. U., 1957. Reporter Richmond (Va.) News Leader, 1957-60; copy editor, reporter, acting Sunday editor, city editor, mng. editor Courier-Jour., Louisville, 1960-74; v.p., gen. mgr. Courier-Jour. and Louisville Times Co., 1974-79, sr. v.p. corp. affairs, 1979-80, pres., chief exec. officer, 1981—; chief exec. officer affiliates Standard Gravure Corp., WHAS Inc., 1981—. Served with USNR, 1954-56. Recipient Picture Editors award Nat. Press Photographers Assn., 1965. Mem. Am. Soc. Newspaper Editors, Asso. Press Mng. Editors, Louisville Com. on Fgn. Relations, Alpha Tau Omega, Sigma Delta Chi. Club: Mason. Home: 308 Rebel Dr Pewee Valley KY 40056 Office: 525 W Broadway Louisville KY 40202

GILL, HENRY HERR, photojournalist; b. Detroit, July 21, 1930; s. Henry Herr and Esther (King) G.; m. Mary Jane Brown, Aug. 26, 1957. Student, Vincennes (Ind.) U., 1948, Northwestern U., 1949, Ind. U., 1951, McNeese State U., La., 1952, U. Miami, 1962. Mem. publ. staff U. Miami, 1960; fgn. service photographer, then dir. photography Chgo. Daily News, 1976; dir. photography Chgo. Sun-Times, 1978—; lectr. in field, exhibitor of photographs, 1964—. Co-author: Mississippi Notebook, 1964; photographer: film A War of Many Faces, 1965, The Cocaine Express, 1982. Recipient photo reporting award on Vietnam Nat. Headliners Club, 1967, Overseas Press Club award, 1967, 81, Emmy award for documentary Nat. Acad. TV Arts and Scis., 1965, Best News Picture of Year award Inland Press Assn., 1968, 69, Faculty citation Vincennes U., 1979, Baker Meml. journalism award, 1980. Mem. Chgo. Press Photographers Assn., Sigma Delta Chi (Disting. Journalism award 1965). Clubs: Chgo. Press, Headliner (Chgo.). Office: 401 N Wabash Ave Chicago IL 60611

GILL, HOWARD READ, JR., publishing co. exec.; b. St. Louis, Nov. 18, 1922; s. Howard Read and Mary Belle (Palmer) G.; m. Renee Ann Walz, May 28, 1946; children—Howard Read, Deborah V., Scott A. B.E.E., Northwestern U., 1947. Salesman Pyle Nat. Co., Chgo., 1947-48; asst. pub. Chgo. Elec. News, 1949-51; pub. Golf Digest, Inc., Norwalk, Conn., 61951—, exec. v.p., 1972-78, pres., 1978—, Tennis Features, Inc.; pub. Tennis mag., Golf World mag., U.K.; bd. dirs. Nat. Golf Found., Tennis Found. N.Am., 1979—. Author: Fun in the Rough, 1954. Bd. dirs. New Canaan (Conn.) United Way, 1972-75. Served with USAAF, 1943-46. Club: Woodway Country. Home: 125 Frogtown Rd New Canaan CT 06840 Office: 495 Westport Ave Norwalk CT 06856 PO Box 5350 Norwalk CT 06856

GILL, JAMES JOSEPH, manufacturing company executive; b. Platteville, Wis., Aug. 18, 1931; s. Percy Edward and Esther LaSetta (Weist) G.; m. Virginia Karen Gotsche, Aug. 11, 1956; children: Susan, Grant, Gretchen. B.S.C.E., U. Wis., 1957; M.B.A., U. Toronto, 1971. Resident engr. Wis. Dept. Hwys., Waukesha, 1957-58; project mgr. Conco Constrn. Co., Kansas City, Mo., 1959-60; with J.I. Case Co., 1960—; v.p. div. constrn. equipment Conco Constrn. Co., Racine, Wis., 1977-79, exec. v.p., 1979—. Mem. adv. council S.E. Wis. dist. Boy Scouts Am. Served to 2d lt. USAF, 1951. Republican. Lodges: Masons; Kiwanis (local mem. chmn.). Office: J I Case Co. 700 State St Racine WI 53404

GILL, JOHN PATRICK, advertising agency executive; b. N.Y.C., Apr. 30, 1935; s. John J. and Katherine I. (McMahon) G.; m. June O'Hara, June 25, 1960; children: Mary Theresa, Maureen, Kathleen. B.B.A., Iona Coll., New Rochelle, N.Y., 1956; J.D., N.Y. U., 1959. Bar: N.Y. 1960; C.P.A., N.Y. Mem. audit staff Price Waterhouse & Co. (C.P.A.'s), N.Y.C., 1960-66; with Ogilvy & Mather Internat., Inc., N.Y.C., 1966—, controller, 1971—, sr. v.p., 1980—, sec., 1981—, treas., 1983—. Mem. Am. Inst. C.P.A.s, Fin. Execs. Inst., N.Y. State Bar Assn. Home: 230 Pennsylvania Ave Crestwood NY 10707 Office: Ogilvy & Mather Internat Inc 2 E 48th St New York NY 10017

GILL, JOHN WELCH, JR., U.S. attorney; b. Monterey, Tenn., Mar. 17, 1942; s. John Welch and Billie Gene (Mackey) G.; m. Kathleen Gay Broughan, Apr. 15, 1983; 1 son, Andrew Welch. B.A., Vanderbilt U., 1964, J.D., 1967. Bar: Tenn. 1967. Spl. agt. FBI, New Haven and N.Y.C., 1967-70; asst. dist. atty. Knox County Dist. Atty.'s Office, Knoxville, Tenn., 1970-81; atty. Harwell & Nichols, Knoxville, 1981; U.S. atty. Eastern Dist. Tenn. U.S. Atty.'s Office, Dept. Justice, Knoxville, 1981—; mem. adv. com. U.S. Atty. Gen., Washington, 1983—; mem. State of Tenn. Law Revision Commn., Nashville, 1973-76. Bd. dirs. Knoxville Ballet Co., 1983—; v.p. bd. dirs. Knoxville Jr. Achievement, 1981-82. Mem. ABA, Tenn. Bar Assn., Knoxville Bar Assn. (pres. young lawyer sect. 1975-76, bd. dirs. 1974-76). Republican. Baptist. Club: Knoxville Civitan (pres. 1982-83). Office: US Attys Office PO Box 872 Knoxville TN 37901 *The best thing about being a professional prosecutor is that the main factor in the job description is to treat people fairly and justly regardless of politics, wealth or social standing.*

GILL, RAYMOND JOSEPH, corp. exec.; b. Chgo., Aug. 3, 1930; s. Joseph and Anna V. (Pawlikowski) G.; m. Joan Marie Kolar, Aug. 11, 1951; children—Mark R., Pamela A. B.S., Ill. Inst. Tech., 1959, M.S., 1962. Sales adminstr. Johns-Manville, Chgo., 1949-51; contract adminstr. Webcor, Inc., Chgo., 1953-56; project mgr. Motorola Inc., Chgo., 1957-62; with ITT, Chgo., Boston, N.Y.C., 1962—, program mgr., dir. program mgmt., dir. ops., div. pres., from 1962, now group gen. mgr., corporate v.p., N.Y.C. Pres. Bd. Edn. Ill. Dist. 122, 1958-63. Served with USMC, 1951-53. Home: 79 Glenwood Road Upper Saddle River NJ 07458 Office: ITT Fluid Products Group-Worldwide Midland Park NJ 07432

GILL, RICHARD THOMAS, opera singer (bass); b. Long Branch, N.J., Nov. 30, 1927; s. Thomas Grant and Myrtle (Sickles) G.; m. Betty Bjornson, Jan. 6, 1950; children—Thomas Grandon, Peter Severin, Geoffrey Karl. A.B., Harvard U., 1948, Ph.D. in Econs, 1956; postgrad., Oxford (Eng.) U., 1948-49. Master, Leverett House, lectr. econs. Harvard U., 1963-71. Author: Economics and the Public Interest, 4th edit, 1980, Economics, 3d edit, 1978, others.; debuts, N.Y.C. Opera, 1971, Met. Opera, 1973, Houston Grand Opera, 1972, Chgo. Lyric Opera, 1976, N.Y. Philharm., 1977; appeared at, Edinburgh Festival, 1976; soloist with numerous opera cos. and symphonies in, U.S. and abroad. Served with inf. U.S. Army, 1946-47. Henry fellow, 1948-49; recipient Atlantic Monthly First Short Story prize, 1954. Mem. Am. Guild Mus. Artists (bd. govs.), Am. Econs. Assn. Home: 2800 NW 51st Pl Fort Lauderdale FL 33309 *I have been fortunate enough to pursue several careers, sometimes simultaneously: author, economist, college administrator, opera singer and, most recently, operatic stage director. In a time of increasing life expectancies, it may be that multiple careers may become the rule rather than the exception.*

GILL, SAMUEL LAFAYETTE, JR., banker; b. Alvarado, Tex., Feb. 15, 1936; s. Samuel Lafayette and Nora Lee (Farquhar) G.; m. Elizabeth Ann Seeton, July 17, 1965. B.B.A., U. Tex., Austin, 1957; postgrad., Southwestern Grad. Sch. Banking, So. Meth. U., 1966-68. With 1st Nat. Bank Fort Worth, 1957—, v.p. personnel, 1967-71, sr. v.p., 1971-80, exec. v.p., 1980—; instr. Southwestern Grad. Sch. Banking, So. Meth. U., 1969-73. Mem. bd. dirs. Tarrant County chpt. ARC, West Tex. chpt. NCCJ. Ft. Worth Personnel Indsl. Relations Assn. (pres. 1963), Am. Soc. Personnel Adminstrns. (bd. dirs. 1969-73), Tex. Mfrs. Assn. (chmn. indsl. relations com. 1972). Clubs: Longhorn, Ridglea Country, Ft. Worth (Ft. Worth). Home: 5020 Granite Shoals Fort Worth TX 76103 Office: 1 Burnett Plaza Fort Worth TX 76101

GILL, STANLEY JENSEN, chemist, educator; b. Salt Lake City, Aug. 21, 1929; s. Stanley Hewitt and Frances (Jensen) G.; m. Jane C. Pittenger, June 7, 1952; children—Elizabeth J., Stanley C. Student, Occidental Coll., 1947; A.B. magna cum laude, Harvard U., 1951; Ph.D. in Chemistry, U. Ill., 1954. Research and teaching asst. U. Ill., 1951-53; research asso. Cornell U., 1954; faculty U. Colo., Boulder, 1956—, prof. chemistry, 1964—; cons. NIH, 1966-69. Served with AUS, 1954-56. Mem. Am., Brit. chem. socs., Sigma Xi, Phi Lambda Upsilon, Alpha Chi Sigma. Research on properties of macromolecules biophys. chemistry, hemoglobin. Home: 495 College Ave Boulder CO 80302

GILL, STEPHEN PASCHALL, mathematician, physicist; b. Balt., Nov. 13, 1938; s. Robert Lee and Charlotte (Olmsted) G.; m. Margaret Ann Gaskins, Dec. 21, 1961; children: Elizabeth Olmsted, Richard Paschall. B.S., MIT, 1960; M.A., Harvard U., 1961, Ph.D., 1964. Cons. hypersonic aerodynamics Raytheon Corp., Bedford, Mass., 1963-64; research physicist Stanford Research Inst., Menlo Park, Calif., 1964-65, head high energy gasdynamics, 1965-68, Physics Internat. Co., San Leandro, Calif., 1968-70, mgr. shock dynamics dept., 1970-72; founder, pres. Artec Assocs., Inc., Hayward, Calif., 1972-77, chief scientist, 1977—; founder, pres. Votan Corp., Hayward, Calif., 1979—, chief scientist, chmn. bd., 1981—. Mem. San Francisco Symphony Assn., San Francisco Mus. Art. Mem. Am. Phys. Soc., AAAS, IEEE, AIAA, Am. Math. Soc., Soc. Indsl. and Applied Math., MIT Alumni Assn., Sigma Xi, Delta Kappa Epsilon. Republican. Episcopalian. Clubs: MIT; Harvard (San Francisco). Home: 32 Flood Circle Atherton CA 94025 Office: 26046 Eden Landing Rd Hayward CA 94545

GILL, THEODORE ALEXANDER, philosophy educator, writer; b. Eveleth, Minn., Jan. 7, 1920; s. Alexander Lawson G. and Lillian Louise Pfeiffer; m. Katherine Yonker, June 27, 1945; children: Theodore Alexander, Laurie Melissa. B.A., Univ. Wis., 1940; B.D., Princeton Theol. Sem., 1943; D.Theol., Union Theol. Sem., 1945, Univ. Zurich, Switzerland, 1948, Univ. Basel, Switzerland, 1948; D.D. hon., Occidental Coll., 1959, Grinnell Coll., 1964, L.H.D., Coll. Emporia, 1961, Litt.D., Coll. Idaho, 1964, Alma Coll., 1977. Ordained to ministry Presbyterian Ch. Pastor North Ave. Presbyn. Ch., New Rochelle, N.Y., 1943-46, West End Presbyn. Ch., N.Y.C., 1948-52; dean chapel Lindenwood Coll., St. Charles, Mo., 1952-55; mng. editor Christian Century, Chgo., 1955-57; pres. San Francisco Theol. Sem., San Anselmo, Calif., 1957-66; exec. dir. Study Commn. on Higher Edn., Geneva, 1966-68, Religious Studies Ctr., Detroit, 1968-71, Soc. for Art, Religion and Contemporary Culture, N.Y.C., 1970-79; prof. philosophy John Jay Coll. Criminal Justice, N.Y.C., 1971—, provost and dean faculty, 1975-82; Fondren lectr. So. Methodist U.; Verhuyst lectr. U. Wis., Madison; Green lectr. Andover-Newton; T.V. Moore lectr., San Francisco; bd. dirs. Affiliate Artists, N.Y.C., 1966—, Sears Found., Chgo., 1976—; del. UNESCO confs., 1966-68; moderator Permanent Jud. Commn., N.Y. Presbytery, 1980—; clk. Permanent Jud. Commn., Synod N.E., 1982—. Author: Recent Protestant Political Theory, 1953, The Sermons of John Donne, 1958; editor: Memo For a Movie, 1971, To God Be The Glory, 1973; maker: documentary films, including Mozart & Milnes, Omiros, Letter to Figaro, To Follow A Star, 1977. Fellow Soc. Arts, Religion, Contemporary Culture; mem. Acad. Arts and Scis. CUNY (bd. dirs. 1981—), Am. Acad. Religion, Karl Barth Soc., Bonhoeffer Soc., Interfilm (Hilversum, Netherlands), Philos. Assn. Clubs: Princeton, The Players (N.Y.C.). Home: 342 Dodds Ln Princeton NJ 08540 Office: John Jay Coll Criminal Justice 444 W 56 St New York NY 10019

GILL, THOMAS JAMES, III, physician, educator; b. Malden, Mass., July 2, 1932; s. Thomas James and Marguerite (Capobianco) G.; m. Faith Libbie Etoll, July 8, 1961; children: Elizabeth Ruth, Thomas James IV, Christopher Gregory. A.B. summa cum laude, Harvard U., 1953, M.A. in Chemistry, 1957, M.D., 1957. Asst. pathology Peter Bent Brigham Hosp., Boston, 1957-58; intern N.Y. Hosp.-Cornell Med. Center, 1958-59; jr. fellow Soc. Fellows Harvard U., 1959-62; mem. faculty Harvard Med. Sch., 1962-71, asso. prof. pathology, 1970-71; prof. pathology, chmn. dept. U. Pitts. Med. Sch., 1971—; pathologist-in-chief Univ. Health Center Pitts., 1971—; cons. to govt. and industry; mem. sci. adv. bd. St. Jude Children's Research Hosp., Memphis, 1969-77, chmn., 1974-76; mem. allergy and immunology research com. Nat. Inst. Allergy and Infectious Diseases, 1973-76; mem. med. research service merit rev. bd. in immunology VA, 1976-79, chmn., 1977-79; mem. sci. adv. com. Damon Runyon-Walter Winchell Cancer Fund, 1978-81; mem. com. on animal models and genetic stocks NRC, 1978—, chmn. com., 1983—, mem. com. on rabbit genetic resources, 1979-80; mem. surgery, anesthesiology and trauma study sect. NIH, 1983—; mem. Armed Forces Epidemiol. Bd., 1966-72. Editorial bds. several sci. and med. jours.; contbr. articles to profl. jours. Bd. dirs. Easter Seal Soc., Allegheny County, 1972-77, Univs. Asso. for Research and Edn. in Pathology, 1979—; trustee Am. Bd. Pathology, 1981—. Recipient Lederle med. faculty award, 1962-65, research career devel. award NIH, 1965-71; certificate appreciation for patriotic civilian service Dept. Army, 1973. Fellow Am. Soc. Clin. Pathologists, Am. Acad. Allergy, Assn. Pathology Chairmen (pres. 1978); mem. Am. Assn. Immunologists, Am. Assn. Pathologists, Am. Soc. Biol. Chemists, Internat. Acad. Pathology, Am. Soc. Human Genetics, Transplantation Soc. (v.p. 1982-84), Internat. Soc. Immunology Reprodn. (Sec.-gen. 1983—), Am. Chem. Soc., Am. Soc. Cell Biology, Genetics Soc. Am., AMA. Clubs: Harvard (Western Pa.); (Boston); Fox Chapel Racquet (Pitts.); Pitts. Athletic Assn., Harvard Varsity. Home: 117 Crofton Dr Pittsburgh PA 15238

GILL, WILLIAM ALBERT, JR., airlines union ofcl.; b. Charleston, W.Va., Oct. 26, 1924; s. William Albert and Lucille (Groves) G.; m. Bonita Gladys Ward, Jan. 20, 1944; children—William Ward, Robert Arthur. Student, U. Mo., 1942, U. Minn., 1948-49. Mechanic, insp. Capital Airlines, 1946-52; flight engr. Pan Am. World Airways, 1952—; mem. Flight Engrs. Internat. Assn., 1952—; v.p. Pan Am. World Airways chpt., 1957-63, master exec. bd. del., 1957-63, internat. pres., 1963-72, 74—; mem. gen. bd. AFL-CIO, 1963-72, 74—; chmn. civil aviation sect. Internat. Transport Workers Fedn., 1974—. Served with USAAF, 1942-46. Mem. Phi Gamma Delta. Home: 15975 Cove Ln Dumfries VA 22026

GILL, WILLIAM NELSON, chemical engineering educator; b. N.Y.C., Sept. 13, 1928; s. William Nelson and Frances (Murphy) G.; m. Chandlee Stevens, Aug. 13, 1982; children: Alison Louise, Christine Marie, Douglas Max, Max William. B.Chem. Engring., Syracuse U., 1951, M.A., 1955, Ph.D., 1960. Field engr. Am. Blower Corp., 1951-55; mem. faculty Syracuse U., 1957-65, asso. prof., 1963-65; prof. chem. engring., chmn. dept. Clarkson Coll. Tech., 1965-71; provost engring. and applied sci., State U. N.Y. at Buffalo, 1971-78, prof. chem. engring., 1982—; Glenn Murphy Disting. prof. engring. Iowa State U., Ames, 1980-82; Fulbright-Hays sr. research scholar Univ. Coll., London, 1977-78; cons. in field. Editor: Chem. Engring. Communications, 1979—; author numerous articles in field. Mem. Am. Inst. Chem. Engrs., AAAS, Am. Chem. Soc., Am. Soc. Engring. Edn., AAUP, N.Y. Acad. Sci., Sigma Xi. Office: 1014 Furnas Hall SUNY-Buffalo Amherst NY 14260

GILLAM, ISAAC THOMAS, IV, national space administration official; b. Little Rock, Feb. 23, 1932; s. Isaac Thomas and Ethel McNeal (Reynolds) G.; m. Norma Jean Hughes, Dec. 21, 1956; children: Michael, Teri, Traci, Kelli. A.B., Howard U., 1952. Joined U.S. Air Force, 1953, advanced through grades to capt., 1963; pilot, 1953-63, comdr. missile launch crew, 1961-63; various positions NASA, 1963-68, mgr. Delta program, 1968-71, program mgr. small launch vehicles, 1971-76, dir. shuttle ops., 1976-77, dep. dir. Dryden Flight Research Center, Edward, Calif., 1977-78, dir. Dryden Flight Research Center, 1978—, asst. assoc. adminstr., Washington, 1982—. Recipient distinguished service medal NASA, 1976, exceptional service medal NASA, 1981, 82. Fellow Am. Astronautical Soc., AIAA (assoc.); mem. Air Force Assn., Am. Mgmt. Assn., Alpha Phi Alpha. Democrat. Episcopalian. Office: NASA Hdqrs Washington DC 20546

GILLAM, MAX LEE, lawyer; b. Cleve., Apr. 28, 1926; s. Max Lee and Louise (Sellers) G.; m. Marcheta Condict, Mar. 3, 1951; children: Marcheta, Wade, Lynn, Anne, Mary; m. Carol McCully, Nov. 25, 1981; children: Re, Eric, Alex, Kate. B.S., U.S. Naval Acad., 1949; LL.B., Harvard U., 1956. Bar: Calif. 1957. With Latham, & Watkins, Los Angeles, 1956—, now sr. partner. Served with U.S. Navy, 1944-45; USAF, 1949-53. Mem. ABA, Assn. Bus. Trial Lawyers, Am. Coll. Trial Lawyers, Los Angeles Bar, Calif. Bar.

GILLAN, ANDREW STEELMAN, former computer company executive; b. Phila., June 3; s. Charles McDowell and Ethel (Steelman) G.; m. Helen Adelaide Hoover, Nov. 23, 1946; children: Rebecca Ann, Barbara Adelaide. Student, U. Md., 1935-39. With NCR Corp., 1935-80, pres., 1964-66, v.p. internat. adminstrn., 1967-74, v.p. Middle East-Africa region, 1974-80. Bd. dirs. Dayton Council World Affairs. Served to capt. U.S. Army, 1942-46. Decorated Bronze star. Mem. Ohio Dist. Export Council, Dayton Area C. of C., World Trade Council, S.A.R. Republican. Lutheran. Clubs: Masons, Scottish Rite, 99th Inf. Div. Assn. (past pres.), Moraine Country (Kettering, Ohio)). Home: 3524 Laurelwood Rd Kettering OH 45409

GILLARD, PETER MCCANN, librarian; b. Jamaica, N.Y., Sept. 13, 1941; s. William A. and Katherine (McCann) G.; m. Rose Marie Luchini, Sept. 12, 1964; children: Laura Katherine, Anne Christine, Marguetite, Peter Jerome. B.A., St. John's U., 1963, M.A. in Am. History, 1965, M.S.L.S., 1967. Librarian Queen's Borough Pub. Library, Jamaica, N.Y., 1965-68; br. librarian The Smithtown Library (N.Y.), 1968-79, dir., 1979—. Pres. Bellaire Civic Assn., N.Y., 1975-77. Mem. Suffolk County Library Assn. (pres. 1979), N.Y. Library Assn. (exhibits com. chmn. 1981—), ALA. Republican. Roman Catholic. Lodge: Rotary (pres. 1973-74). Home: 20 Sheryl Crescent Smithtown NY 11787 Office: The Smithtown Library 1 North Country Rd Smithtown NY 11787

GILLEECE, MARY ANN, government official; b. Effingham, Ill., Sept. 31, 1940. B.A., U. Conn., 1962; J.D., Suffolk U., 1972; LL.M., George Washington U., 1982. Bar: Mass. 1972. Assoc. Garguilo & Holian, Cambridge, Mass., 1972-77; asst. atty. gen. Commonwealth of Mass., 1972-74; counsel Com. on Armed Services, U.S. Ho. of Reps., Washington, 1977-83; dep. undersec. U.S. Dept. Def., Washington, 1983—. Mem. Fed. Bar Assn. (v.p. nat. circuit), ABA. Home: Watergate at Landmark 203 Yaokum Pkwy Unit 1425 Alexandria VA 22304 Office: Dept Defense The Pentagon Washington DC 20301

GILLELAND, BRADY BLACKFORD, educator; b. Wheeling, W.Va., July 12, 1922; s. Andrew J. and Catherine (Blackford) G.; m. Doris Warrick, June 4, 1945; children—Elizabeth Ann, Margaret Dale; m. Katharine Foster Marston, Mar. 1, 1975. A.B., Washington and Jefferson Coll., 1944; M.A., U. Okla., 1949; Ph.D., U. N.C., 1953. Instr. U. Tenn., 1953; asst. prof. Beloit (Wis.) Coll., 1954-57; mem.

faculty U. Vt., 1958—, prof. classics, 1960—, chmn. dept., 1968-74. Editor: (with Evan T. Sage) Petronius: The Satiricon, rev. edit, 1969; translator: Dolopathas: or the King and the Seven Wise Men (Johannes de Altasilva), 1981; also articles on Cicero and medieval folk tales. Holopathas: or the King and the Seven Wise Men. Served with USMCR, 1943-45. Mem. Classical Assn. New Eng., Vergilian Soc., Am. Philol. Assn., Modern Lang. Assn., Internat. Maledicta Soc. Home: 530 North St Burlington VT 05401

GILLEN, ALBERT J., communications executive; b. 1919. B.S., Syracuse U. Gen. sales mgr. Louisville Courier Jour., 1952-57; v.p. sales Newhouse Broadcasting Co., 1957-60; gen. sales mgr. Capital Cities Communications, Inc., 1960-64; pres. Poole Broadcasting Co., 1964-78; sr. v.p. Knight-Ridder Newspapers, Inc., 1978—; pres. Knight-Ridder Broadcasting, Inc., 1978—; sr. v.p. Viewdata Corp. Am., Inc., 1979—. Served with USCG, 1942-45. Address: Knight-Ridder Newspapers Inc 1 Herald Plaza Miami FL 33101 *

GILLEN, JAMES FREDERICK JOHN, educator; b. Winnipeg, Man., Can., May 6, 1935; s. Charles Frederick and Maud (Chisholm) G.; m. Sheila Cunningham Engert, Dec. 26, 1956; children—Isobel, Sara, Frederick. B.A., 1915, U. Wis., 1935, Oxford (Eng.) U., 1938, M.A., 1962, Harvard, 1938, Ph.D., 1942. Instr. Bowdoin Coll., 1946, Princeton, 1946-47; historian Army Dept., 1948-59, State Dept., 1950-53, cons., 1954-55, sr. research asso. human relations area files, 1955-58; asst. prof. Wabash Coll., 1958-60, asso. prof., 1960-62; prof., chmn. dept. history Cedar Crest Coll., 1962-68; prof. history State U. N.Y., Geneseo, 1968—. Author: Labor Problems in West Germany, 1952, State and Local Government in West Germany, 1953. Served to lt. comdr. USNR, 1942-46. Mem. Am. Hist. Assn., Am. Polit. Sci. Assn., Soc. for French Hist. Studies, Am. Assn. Rhodes Scholars, AAUP. Home: 19 Tuscarora Ave Geneseo NY 14454

GILLEN, JAMES ROBERT, insurance company executive; b. N.Y.C., Nov. 14, 1937; s. James Matthew and Katharine Isabel (Fritz) G.; m. Rita Marie Wahleithner, June 15, 1963; children: Jennifer Elaine, Nancy Louise, Paula Anne. A.B. magna cum laude, Harvard U., 1959, LL.B. cum laude, 1965. Bar: N.Y. 1966, N.J. 1975. Assoc. firm White & Case, N.Y.C., 1965-72; v.p., asso. gen. counsel Prudential Ins. Co. Am., Newark, 1972-77, sr. v.p., asso. gen. counsel, 1977-80, sr. v.p. public affairs, 1980-84, sr. v.p., gen. counsel, 1984—. Trustee United Way Essex and West Hudson Counties, 1981—; mem. Mendham Twp. (N.J.) Bd. Edn., 1981-82; trustee Mendham Twp. Library, 1979-82. Served to lt. (j.g.) USN, 1959-62. Mem. ABA, N.J. Bar Assn., Assn. Life Ins. Counsel. Club: Essex (Newark). Home: 12 Hamilton Dr Morristown NJ 07960 Office: Pruduential Plaza Broad St Newark NJ 07101

GILLEN, RALPH LEONARD, petroleum monitoring agency administrator; b. N.Y.C., May 3, 1928; s. Benjamin and Rose G.; m. Ruth Irene Sperling, Apr. 29, 1956; children: Gerald Roy, Jay Michael. B.A. magna cum laude, Queen's Coll., 1949; M.A., Fletcher Sch. Law and Diplomacy, Tufts and Harvard univs., 1950; postgrad. Fulbright fellow, U. Liverpool, Eng., 1950-51. Instr. econs. Tufts U., 1950-51; With Internat. Div. RCA, 1950; securities analyst E.F. Hutton, N.Y.C., 1951; mgmt. cons. McKinsey & Co., Washington, 1954-63, Cleve., 1963-68, ptnr., 1961-68; v.p. mktg. pulp and paper group MacMillan Bloedel Ltd., Vancouver, B.C., 1969-70, group v.p., 1970-71, v.p. strategic planning and devel., 1971-78; vice-chmn. bd. Ins. Corp. B.C., 1976-78, chmn., 1978-80; pres., chief exec. officer Can. Comml. Corp., Ottawa, Ont., 1978-82; chmn. Petroleum Monitoring Agy., 1982—; dir. Sunnyland Foods, Inc., Indsl. Am. Corp.; instr. econs. Tufts U., 1950-51; Mem. regional export expansion council Dept. Commerce, 1965-66; mem. exec. com. Nat. Mktg. Adv. Bd. to U.S. sec. commerce, 1967-68; sec.-treas., trustee Fed. Stats. Users Conf., 1957-64. Trustee, chmn. fin. com. Cleve. Inst. Music, 1965-69, mem. adv. council, 1969—; vice-chmn., trustee Vancouver Acad. Music, 1970-79; chmn. com. Univs. Council B.C., 1976-79; adv. council Multiple Sclerosis Soc. B.C., 1976-80; trustee Hudson Inst. Can., 1975—. Served with USN, 1951-53. Mem. Am. Mktg. Assn. (pres. Washington 1963). Clubs: Nat. Economists (Washington); Vancouver, University; St. James (Montreal); Vancouver, Montreal. Home: 28 Belvedere Crescent Ottawa ON K1M 2E4 Canada Office: 580 Booth St Ottawa Canada ON K1A 0E4 Office: 580 Booth St Ottawa ON K1A 0E4 Canada *

GILLEN, WILLIAM ALBERT, lawyer; b. Sanford, Fla., May 26, 1914; s. William D. and Marie Carolyn (Holt) G.; m. Lillian Thornton, Aug. 19, 1939; children: William Albert, Susan Marie. Student, U. Tampa, 1932-33; J.D., U. Fla., 1936. Bar: Fla. 1936. Since practiced in, Tampa; mem. firm Fowler, White, Gillen, Boggs, Villareal & Banker; dir. Freedom Savs. & Loan Assn., Tampa, 1972—, chmn. bd., 1978—; mem. Hillsborough County Home Rule Charter Com., 1969-70, 13th Circuit Jud. Nominating Com., 1972-76, Fla. Supreme Ct. Jud. Nominating Commn., 1979-83. Asso. editor: Am. Maritime Cases, 1948—. Bd. dirs. U. South Fla. Found., 1965-68, pres., 1967-68; pres. Gulf Ridge council Boy Scouts Am., 1959; bd. dirs. United Fund Tampa, 1956-64, Greater Tampa Citizens Safety Council, 1966-69. Served to maj., inf. AUS, 1942-46. Fellow Am. Coll. Trial Lawyers, Am. Bar Found., Fla. Bar Found.; mem. Bar Assn. Tampa and Hillsborough County (pres. 1953), Fla. Bar (gov. 1951-57), Fedn. Ins. Counsel (pres. 1960-61, chmn. bd. dirs. 1961-62), Internat. Assn. Ins. Counsel, Def. Research Inst. (v.p. 1961-62), Maritime Law Assn. U.S., Am. Bar Assn. (co-chmn. conf. lawyers, ins. cos. and adjusters 1975—), Nat. Assn. R.R. Trial Counsel, Com. of 100, Tampa C. of C. (pres. 1968-69), Am. Legion, Gasparilla Krewe (capt. 1968-70, King LVII 1970-71), Phi Delta Phi, Sigma Alpha Epsilon. Democrat. Episcopalian. Clubs: Rotary (pres. 1959-60), Tampa Yacht and Country (dir. 1962-64), Tower, University (dir. 1976-79), University (pres. 1978-79), Merrymakers, Palma Ceia Golf and Country, Masons (Tampa). Home: 3109 Sunset Dr Tampa FL 33609 Office: 501 E Kennedy Blvd Suite 1700 Tampa FL 33602

GILLENWATER, JAMES E., distbn. co. exec.; b. McComas, W.Va., Sept. 8, 1931; s. James Arthur and Elsie Irene (Sparks) G.; m. Elise C. Lott, Jan. 3, 1953; children—Linda Susan, Debora Diane, James Michael, Cheryl Beth. B.S., Concord Coll., 1957. Accountant EBASCO Internat., N.Y.C., 1957; staff accountant Arthur Young & Co., Bluefield, W.Va., 1958-63; with Bluefield Supply Co. (and subs.'s), W.Va., 1963—, comptroller, 1964—, v.p., 1970-74, exec. v.p., chief adminstrv. officer, 1974—, dir., 1980—; dir. 1st Fed. Savs. and Loan Assn., Bluefield. Treas., bd. dirs. United Way of Greater Bluefield. Served with USN, 1951-55. Mem. Am. Inst. C.P.A.'s, W.Va. Soc. C.P.A.'s, Bluefield C. of C. (v.p., dir.). Republican. Presbyterian. Clubs: Fincastle Country, Univ. Home: 611 Fairway Dr Bluefield VA 24605 Office: 100 Bluefield Ave Bluefield WV 24701

GILLENWATER, JAY YOUNG, physician; b. Kingsport, Tenn., July 27, 1933; s. Jay King and Anne (Young) G.; m. Shirley Brockman, June 22, 1955; children—Linda, Ann, Jay. Student, Furman U., 1951-53; B.S., U. Tenn., 1954, M.D., 1957. Diplomate: Am. Bd. Urology. Intern Grad. Hosp. U. Pa., 1958-59, med. resident, 1959-60, aurology resident, 1962-65; practice medicine specializing in urology, Charlottesville, Va., 1965—; asst. prof. dept. urology U. Va. Med. Sch., 1965-67, prof., chmn. dept. urology, 1967—; past chmn. council urology Nat. Kidney Found.; past chmn. sci. adv. bd., trustee Health Sci. Affairs Commn.; pres. Health Sci. Found., U. Va. Med. Sch. Editor: Investigative Urology, 1977—, Year Book of Urology, 1979, Urology; contbr. articles to profl. jours. Served to capt. AUS, Army, 1960-62. Fellow A.C.S.; mem. AMA, Am. Urol. Assn. (chmn. continuing edn. com. and resident essay contest), Clin. Soc. Genito-Urinary Surgeons, Soc. Univ. Surgeons, Univ. Urologists, Am. Assn. Genito-Urinary Surgery, Sigma Alpha Epsilon, Phi Rho Sigma. Home: Route 10 Box 58C Charlottesville VA 22901

GILLER, EDWARD BONFOY, govt. ofcl., ret. air force officer; b. Jacksonville, Ill., July 8, 1918; s. Edward Bonfoy and Ruth (Davis) G.; m. Mildred Florana Schmidt, July 2, 1943; children—Susan Ann, Carol Elaine, Bruce Carleton, Penny Marie, Paul Benjamin. B.S. in Chem. Engring, U. Ill., 1940, M.S., 1948, Ph.D., 1950. Chem. engr. Sinclair Oil Refining Co., 1940-41; commd. 2d lt. USAAF, 1942; advanced through grades to maj. gen. USAF, 1968; pilot, 1941-46, chief radiation br., Washington, 1950-54; dir. research directorate Air Force Spl. Weapons Center, Albuquerque, 1954-59; spl. asst. to comdr. (Office Aerospace Research), Washington, 1959-64; dir. sci. and tech. Hdqrs. USAF, 1964-67; asst. gen. mgr. for mil. application U.S. AEC, 1967-72; ret. from USAF, 1972; asst. gen. mgr. for nat. security AEC, 1972-75; dep. asst. adminstr. for nat. security U.S. ERDA, 1975-77; rep. of Joint Chiefs of Staff to Comprehensive Test Ban Negotiations, Geneva, Switzerland, 1977—. Decorated Silver Star, D.S.M., Legion of Merit with oak leaf cluster, D.F.C., Air medal with 17 oak leaf clusters, Purple Heart; Croix de Guerre, France). Fellow Am. Inst. Chemists; mem. AAAS, Am. Inst. Chem. Engrs., Sigma Xi, Alpha Tau Omega. Episcopalian. Home: 825 Mackall Ave McLean VA 22101 Office: Joint Chiefs of Staff Pentagon Dept of Def Washington DC 20301

GILLER, NORMAN MYER, architect, banker; b. Jacksonville, Fla., Feb. 14, 1918; s. Morris and Esther (Seltzer) G.; m. Frances Schwartz, June 30, 1946; children: Ira, Anita, Brian. B.Arch., U. Fla., 1945; student, Ga. Inst. Tech., 1943-44. Registered architect 15 states plus D.C., P.R., C.Z., Israel. Pvt. archtl. practice, Miami Beach, Fla., 1944—; pres., chmn. bd. dirs. InterAm. Nat. Bank, 1964-68; pres., vice chmn. bd. Jefferson Nat. Bank at Sunny Isles, 1968—; vice chmn., dir. Jefferson Bancorp.; dir. Jefferson Nat. Bank of Miami Beach; lectr. U. Fla., Ohio State U.; instr. U. Fla.; adj. prof. U. Miami; cons. U.S. Dept. State, govts. Panama, Brazil, Colombia, El Salvador, Nicaragua; Vice chmn. Interam. Authority; chmn. Fla. State Bd. Architecture, Miami Beach Housing Authority; mem. Met. Planning Adv. Bd., Bay Harbor Planning and Zoning Bd. Author: books latest being An Adventure in Architecture, 1977; archtl. works include USAF housing. Mem. nat. council, pres. S. Fla. council Boy Scouts Am.; chmn. architects div. United Fund; active United Jewish Appeal; bd. dirs. Parkinson Fund.; life dir. Douglas Gardens Home for Aged; pres. Concerned Citizens N.E. Dade County, 1974—. Served with USNR, 1942-46. Recipient award for best design Am. Assn. Sch. Adminstrs., 1969, for excellence in specifications Constrn. Specifications Inst., 1964, for Outstanding Concrete Bldg. Fla. Concrete Assn.; Norman Giller Bridge named in his honor, 1983. Mem. Archtl. Guild, Interama Area C. of C. (pres.), Greater Miami C. of C., AIA (pres. South Fla., dir. Fla. assn., Silver medal South Fla. chpt.), Gold Coast C. of C. (pres. 1973-74), Archtl. Soc. (pres.), Am., Fla., Dade County bankers assns., Bankers Adminstrn. Inst. Jewish. Clubs: Masons, Shriners, Elks, Exchange (dir.), Tiger Bay (Miami Beach.)). Office: 975 Arthur Godfrey Rd Miami Beach FL 33140

GILLESPIE, ALASTAIR WILLIAM, Canadian government official; b. Victoria, B.C., Can., May 1, 1922; s. Erroll Pilkington and Catherine (Oliver) G.; m. Diana Christie-Clark, June 17, 1947; children: Cynthia Gillespie Webb, Ian Alastair. Student, Brentwood Coll. Inst., 1941, U. B.C., 1941, McGill U., 1947; M.A. (Rhodes scholar), Oxford U., 1949; M.Comm., U. Toronto, 1958. Pres. Welmet Industries Ltd., Welland, 1962-68; pres. Can. Chromalox Co., Rexdale, 1966-68; v.p., dir. Can. Corp. Mgmt. Co. Ltd., Toronto, 1963-68; dir. Richardson, Bond & Wright, Ltd., Owen Sound, 1963-68, Internat. Equipment Co. Ltd., Montreal, 1963-68, Cashway Lumber Co. Ltd., 1963-68, Mechanics for Electronics Ltd., Cambridge, Mass., 1964-68; v.p. ops., dir. W.J. Gage Ltd., Toronto, 1949-70; M.P., Etobicoke, 1968—, vice chmn. finance, trade and econ. affairs com., 1968-70, Parliamentary sec. to pres. of treasury bd., 1970-71, minister of state for sci. and tech., 1971-72, minister of industry, trade and commerce, 1972-75, minister energy, mines and resources, 1975-79; chmn., dir. Carling O'Keefe Ltd.; chmn. Nat. Westminster Bank Can., Toronto; pres. Alastair Gillespie & Assocs. Ltd., Toronto; chmn. Scotia Coal Synfuels Project; dir. Uniroyal Ltd., Toronto, Rothman's Can., Rothman's Internat. P.L.C. Bd. dirs. Can. Paraplegic Assn., Toronto, Can. Opera Co., Toronto, Gage Research Inst., Toronto. Served to lt. Royal Canadian Navy, 1941-45. Clubs: Toronto, Badminton & Racquet, Toronto Golf, Osler Bluff Ski. Office: 175 Heath St West Toronto ON Canada M4V 1V1

GILLESPIE, ALEXANDER JOSEPH, JR., lawyer; b. N.Y.C., Sept. 2, 1923; s. Alexander Joseph and Catharine (Allen) G.; m. Elizabeth Margaret Roth, Dec. 4, 1944; children: Robert Daniel, James Edward, William Gerard, Patricia Elise, Anne Marie. A.B. magna cum laude, Dartmouth Coll., 1943; J.D., Fordham U., 1957. Credit mgr. cosmetic div. Vick Chem. Co., 1946-50; dist. sales mgr. Avco Mfg. Co., 1950-54; asso. atty. Breed Abbot & Morgan, 1957-60; asst. gen. counsel ASARCO Inc. (formerly Am. Smelting & Refining Co.), N.Y.C., 1960-68, sec., 1968-69, sec., gen. counsel, 1969—, v.p., 1972-77, sr. v.p., sec., gen. counsel, 1977—; dir. So. Peru Copper Corp., Mex. Desarollo Indsl. Minera, S.A., ASARCO Found., Lac D'Amiante du Quebec Ltee.; arbitrator Nat. Assn. Security Dealers, Am. Arbitration Assn. Mem. adv. bd. Southwest Legal Found.; bd. dirs. Silver Hill Found. Served to lt. (j.g.) USNR, 1943-46; PTO. Mem. ABA, N.Y. State Bar Assn., Assn. Bar City N.Y., Conn. Bar Assn., N.Y. County Lawyers Assn., N.Y. C. of C., Assn. Gen. Counsel, N.Y. Chamber Commerce and Industry, Council of Americas, Peruvian Am. Assn., Phi Beta Kappa, Delta Upsilon, Gamma Eta Gamma. Episcopalian. Clubs: Wall St., Dartmouth Coll., World Trade (N.Y.C.); Stanwich (Greenwich, Conn.). Home: 30 Will Merry Ln Greenwich CT 06830 Office: 120 Broadway New York NY 10271

GILLESPIE, DANIEL CURTIS, SR., chemical company executive; b. Shamokin, Pa., Sept. 22, 1922; s. John F. and Verna E. (Erdman) G.; m. Juliet Warren Yearns, Oct. 7, 1950; children: Julia W., Daniel Curtis, David R. B.S., Pa. State U., 1943; M.S. in Chem. Engring., U. Mich., 1948. Devel. engr. Tidewater Associated Oil Co., Bayonne, N.J., 1943-44; jr. scientist Manhattan Project, Los Alamos Sci. Lab., 1946; with Dorr-Oliver Inc., Stamford, Conn., 1948-82, v.p. mktg., 1973-75, exec. v.p., 1975-76, pres. and chief exec. officer, 1976-82, also dir.; v.p. bus. devel. Sohio Chems. & Indsl. Products Co., 1982—. Served with U.S. Army, 1944-46. Fellow Am. Inst. Chem. Engrs.; mem. Process Equipment Mfrs. Assn., Soc. Mining Engrs. of AIME, Stamford Area Commerce and Industry Assn. (dir.). Club: Greenwich (Conn.) Country. Home: 327 Stanwich Rd Greenwich CT 06830 Office: 77 Havemeyer Ln Stamford CT 06904

GILLESPIE, DAVID ELLIS, manufacturing company executive; b. Chgo., Dec. 18, 1933; s. David Ellis and Helen Leota (Andrews) G. B.A., Wayne State U., 1955; postgrad., U. Tex. Market research mgr. Gen. Steel Wares, London, Ont., Can., 1955-58; market research mgr. KLM Royal Dutch Airlines, Montreal, Que., 1958-60; media dir. Comcore Communications Ltd., Toronto, Ont., 1960-61, v.p., 1961-62, exec. v.p., 1963-65, pres., chief exec. officer, 1965-73; chmn. bd., chief exec. officer Glaser Bros., Los Angeles, 1974—, Core Mark Internat., Vancouver, Core Mark Distbrs. Ltd.; dir. Am. Merchandisers Inc., Los Angeles, Core Mark Import/Export Co., Bingo Cashs' Carry Inc., Core-Mark Distbrs., Inc., S. Bloom Inc., Chgo., Straus Keilson Cos., Cin., Western Smallacres Ltd., Winnipeg, Sandy's Fast & Fresh Inc., Los Angeles. Bd. dirs. Pritiken Research Found., Santa Barbara, Vancouver Symphony Orch. Mem. Nat. Assn. Tobacco Distbrs. (dir.), Calif. Assn. Tobacco and Candy Distbrs. (dir.). Republican. Episcopalian. Club: Ontario (Toronto). Home: 135 N Rossmore Los Angeles CA 90004 Home: Pym Island Sidney BC Canada V8L 3R9 Office: 3130 Leonis Blvd Los Angeles CA 90058 Office: 13951 Bridge Port Rd Richmond BC Canada V6V 1J6

GILLESPIE, DIZZY (JOHN BIRKS GILLESPIE), musician; b. Cheraw, S.C., Oct. 21, 1917; s. James and Lottie (Poe) G.; m. Lorraine Willis, May 9, 1940. Grad., Laurinburg (N.C.) Inst.; D.Mus. (hon.), Rutgers U., 1970. Jazz trumpet player, 1930—. Toured with Teddy Hill bank, 1937-39, Earl Hines, Billy Eckstine, others, 1939-44; led band, 1946-50, combo, 1950-56; rep., U.S. Dept. State on culture tour to, Iran, Pakistan, Lebanon. Syria, Turkey, Yugoslavia, Greece, S.A., 1956-58; leader quintet, 1958—; toured, Argentina, 1961; appeared at, Jazz Workshop, San Francisco, Monterey (Ca.) Jazz Festival, Juan-les-Pins (France) Festival, 1962; toured in: Giants of Jazz, Europe, Japan, U.S., 1971-72, Musical Life of Charlie Parker, Eastern and Western Europe, 1974; appeared in: concert Tribute to Dizzy Gillespie, Avery Fisher Hall, N.Y.C., 1975; many other tours, festivals, night club, TV appearances.; Author: To Be or Not. . .to Bop, 1979; Recent recs. include Trumpet Kings at Montreaux JF, 1975, Trumpet Kings Meet Joe Turner, Giants of Jazz, Something Old, Something New, Party, Bahiana, At Village Vanguard, 1969, My Way, 1969, Greatest Jazz Concert Ever, Oscar Peterson and Sizzy Gillespie, Carter, Gillespie, Inc, Havin' a Good Time in Paris, (with Lalo Schifrin) Free Ride. Recipient 1st prize for soundtrack Berlin Film Festival, 1962, award Downbeat Critics Poll, 1971-75, Handel medallion, 1972, Grammy awards, 1975, 80, Nat. Music award, 1976; named Musician of Yr. Inst. High Fidelity, 1975; honored by S.C. Legislature, 1976. Mem. Baha'i Faith. Office: care Assoc Booking Corp 1995 Broadway Suite 501 New York NY 10023 *

GILLESPIE, EDWARD MALCOLM, hospital administrator; b. Mpls., Oct. 19, 1935; s. Harold Livingston and Alice May (Thompson) G.; children: Karin, Timothy, Kenneth. B.S., U. Minn., 1957, M.P.A., 1959, M.H.A., 1962. Engaged in refugee adminstrn., Linz, Austria, 1958-60; asst. adminstr. Lutheran Med. Center, Denver, 1962-66; asst. gen. sec. Methodist Bd. Health and Welfare Ministries, Evanston, Ill., 1966-69; adminstr. Meth. Hosp., Rochester, Minn., 1969-74, Univ. Hosp., Augusta, Ga., 1974—; bd. dirs. Augusta Area Mental Health, Augusta Speech and Hearing Center, St. John's Towers, CSRA Blood Assurance; chmn. hosp. div. certification council Meth. Health and Welfare. Bd. dirs. local United Way, Boy Scouts Am. Fellow Am. Coll. Hosp. Adminstrs.; mem. Am., Ga. hosp. assns. Methodist. Club: Augusta Rotary (dir.). Home: 705 Gary St Augusta GA 30909 Office: 1350 Walton Way Augusta GA 30910

GILLESPIE, GEORGE JOSEPH, III, lawyer; b. N.Y.C., May 18, 1930; s. George Joseph Jr. and Dorothy Elizabeth (McKenna) G.; m. Eileen Tracy Dealy, July 27, 1955; children—Gail Gillespie Garcia, John D., Myles D., Eileen T. A.B. magna cum laude, Georgetown U., 1952, LL.B., Harvard U., 1955. Bar: N.Y. State bar 1957. Frederick Sheldon travelling fellow Harvard U., 1955-56; asso. firm Cravath, Swaine & Moore, N.Y.C., 1956-62, partner firm, 1963—; dir. Washington Post Co. Trustee, treas. John M. Olin Found.; sec. Mus. of Broadcasting; trustee Rye Country Day Sch., 1969-75, Practising Law Inst., 1968-78, Pinkerton Found., ARW Found.; v.p., bd. dirs. Madison Sq. Boys Club; bd. dirs., sec. Nat. Multiple Sclerosis Soc. Mem. Assn. Bar City N.Y., Am., N.Y. State bar assns. Republican. Roman Catholic. Clubs: Winged Foot Golf, Prouts Neck Country, Am. Yacht., Sailfish Point Golf. Office: Cravath Swaine & Moore 1 Chase Manhattan Plaza New York NY 10005

GILLESPIE, GERALD ERNEST PAUL, comparative literature educator, writer; b. Cleve., July 12, 1933; s. Francis and Nora Veronica (Quinn) G.; m. Adrienne Amalia Galante, Sept. 5, 1959. A.B., Harvard U., 1956; postgrad., U. Tubinger, Germany, 1956-57; M.A., Ohio State U., 1958, Ph.D., 1961; postgrad., U. Munich, W. Germany, 1960-61. Asst. prof. U. So. Calif., Los Angeles, 1961-65; assoc. prof., prof. suny-Binghamton, 1965-74; vis. prof. U. Pa., Phila., 1969, NYU, 1970; prof. Stanford U., Calif., 1974—; vis. prof. U. Minn., Mpls., 1978. Author: German Baroque Poetry, 1971; author, editor: Studien zum Werk D.C. von Lohenstein, 1983; translator, editor: Puss-in-Boots, 1974, Bohemian Lights, 1976; mem. editorial bd.: Comparative Lit., 1977—, Internationales Archiv, 1975—; assoc. mng. editor: Argenis, 1977-82. Andrew Mellon Found. fellow, 1966-67; John S. Guggenheim Found. fellow, 1967-68; NEH sr. fellow, 1973-74; vis. fellow Clare Hall, Cambridge U., Eng., 1979. Mem. Internat. Comparative Lit. Assn. (sec. 1979-85, editorial bd. bull. 1979—), Berliner Wissenschaftliche Gesellschaft (corr.), Modern Lang. Assn. (exec. com. comparative studies in romanticism and the 19th century 1982—), Comprative Lit. Assn., Renaissance Soc. Am. Office: Stanford U Stanford CA 94305

GILLESPIE, JAMES BENNETT, organization executive, physician; b. Traer, Iowa, Oct. 2, 1905; s. James Clay and Bertha Ella (Bennett) G.; m. Emily Jennie Johnson, Feb. 27, 1939; children—James Randall, Emilie (Mrs. William L. Henry). B.S., U. Iowa, 1929, M.D., 1929; M.S., U. Minn., 1933. Intern Robert Packer Hosp., Sayre, Pa., 1929-30; fellow Mayo Found., 1930-33; chief dept. pediatrics Carle Clinic and Carle Hosp., Urbana, Ill., 1933-65; dir. dept. chpts., treas. Am. Acad. Pediatrics, 1965-72, v.p., 1972—, pres., 1973-74; asst. clin. prof. Northwestern U. Med. Sch., 1966-72; clin. prof. pediatrics U. N.Mex. Med. Sch., 1972-75, spl. asst. to v.p. health scis., 1975-76. Contbr. articles to med. jours. Chmn. United Fund Champaign County, Ill., 1957; Pres. Carle Found., Urbana, 1946-51, 58-59; del. White House Conf. on Children and Youth, 1960. Served to maj. AUS, 1942-45. Mem. AMA, Ill. Med. Soc., Am. Acad. Pediatrics (pres. Ill. chpt. 1959-62), Chgo. Pediatric Soc., Sigma Xi, Nu Sigma Nu, Phi Kappa Sigma. Republican. Presbyn. Club: Rotarian (pres. Urbana club 1956). Address: 2019 Duncan Rd Champaign IL 61821

GILLESPIE, JOHN THOMAS, university dean; b. Thunder Bay, Ont., Can., Sept. 25, 1928; came to U.S., 1954, naturalized, 1961; s. William and Jeannie (Barr) G. B.A., U. B.C., 1948; M.A., Columbia U., 1957; Ph.D., N.Y. U., 1969. High sch. tchr., 1949-53, librarian, 1955-63; mem. faculty Palmer Grad. Library Sch., C.W. Post Center, L.I. U., 1963—, prof., 1975-80, dean, 1981-83; acad. v.p. C.W. Post Ctr., L.I. U., 1983—; vis. prof. Syracuse (N.Y.) U.; cons. in field. Author: Juniorplots, 1966, Introducing Books, 1970, Young Phenomenon, 1971, Creating the School Media Program, 1973, A Model School District Media Program, 1973, Paperback Books for Young People, 2d edit, 1977, More Juniorplots, 1977, Best Books for Children, 2d edit, 1981, Administering the School Library Media Center, 1983. Mem. ALA, Assn. Ednl. Communications and Tech., N.Y. Library Assn., L.I. Sch. Media Assn., Nassau County Library Assn., Phi Delta Kappa, Kappa Delta Pi. Home: 360 E 72d St New York NY 10021 Office: Greenvale NY 11548

GILLESPIE, KINGSLEY, publisher; b. Stamford, Conn., Aug. 15, 1895; s. Richard H. and Sarah E. (Scofield) G.; m. Doris Kenyon, June

2, 1928; children—Kenyon, Joan (dec.). S.B. in Chem. Engring, Mass. Inst. Tech., 1917. Registered chem. engr., Conn. Tech. mgr. and dir. research Stamford Rubber Supply Co., 1919-41; pub. Stamford Advocate, 1942-78; treas. Gillespie Bros., Inc., 1942-78, v.p., 1922-49, pres., 1949-78; pres., exec. dir. Western Conn. Broadcasting Co., 1946—; v.p. Stamford Rubber Supply Co., 1925-52, pres., 1952-67; v.p., dir. Fidelity Title & Trust Co.; pub. Greenwich Time, 1958-78; pres., treas. Fairview Enterprises, Inc., 1958-78; Greenwich Pub. Co., 1958-78. Sec. Ferguson Library, 1942-66; sec. Stamford Zoning Commn., 1937-49; mem. Conn. Aero. Commn., 1960-72. Mem. Am. Inst. Chem. Engrs., Am. Chem. Soc. Republican. Presbyterian. Clubs: Rotary, Stamford Yacht. Home: 91 Rogers Rd Stamford CT 06902 Office: Western Conn Broadcasting Co 117 Prospect St Stamford CT 06902

GILLESPIE, ROBERT JAMES, manufacturing company executive; b. Halifax, N.S., Can., July 16, 1942; s. Robert Leo and Pearl G.; m. Carol Anne Caliendo, Nov. 16, 1968; children—Erica Christine, Brooke Caroline. B.Sc., St. Mary's U., Can., 1962; B.Mech.Engring., Tech. U. N.S., 1964; M.S. in Indsl. Adminstrn, Purdue U., 1965. Group product mgr. indsl. div., then v.p. bus. mgmt. indsl. div. CPC Internat. Inc., 1970-76, pres., Englewood Cliffs, N.J., 1980, Can. Starch Co., Montreal, 1976-80; bd. dirs. Sch. Bus. Adminstrn., Dalhousie U., Halifax. Author: Selection of Engineering Materials and Their Use in a Marine Environment, 1966, Merger and Acquisiton Fact Book, 1970. Bd. dirs. Met. Montreal YMCA, 1980. Served with Can. Army, 1960-64. Mem. Corn Refiners Assn. (dir.). Clubs: Montreal Badminton and Squash, St. James (Montreal).

GILLESPIE, ROBERT WAYNE, banker; b. Cleve., Mar. 26, 1944; s. Robert Walton and Eleanore (Parsons) G.; m. Ann. L. Wible, June 17, 1967; children: Laura, Gwen. B.A., Ohio Wesleyan U., 1966; M.B.A., Case Western Res. U., 1968; postgrad., Harvard U., 1979. Credit analyst Soc. Nat. Bank, Cleve., 1968-70, v.p., 1970-76, sr. v.p., 1976-79; exec. v.p. Soc. Nat Bank, Cleve., 1979-81; vice-chmn., chief operating officer Soc. Nat. Bank, Cleve., 1981-83, pres., chief operating officer, 1983—. Chmn. comml. retail sect. United Way Services, Cleve.; trustee Univ. Hosps., Cleve., Fedn. Community Planning, Cleve. Office: Society Nat Bank 127 Public Square Cleveland OH 44114

GILLESPIE, THOMAS STUART, lawyer; b. Montreal, Que., Can., July 18, 1938; s. Alexander Robert and Lois Tully (O'Brien) G.; m. Caroline Pierce Doyle, June 28, 1963; children: Caroline Alexandra, Alexandra Olivia, Vanessa Margaret, Joshua William. B.A., McGill U., 1959, B.C.L., 1963. Assoc., Ogilvy, Renault, Montreal, 1964-72, ptnr., 1972—; tax cons. to Standing Senate Com. on Banking, Trade and Commerce; mem. tax adv. com. Montreal Bd. Trade; sec., dir. Providentia, Inc., Guerlain Can. Ltd., Bouverie Investments Ltd. Bd. dirs. Bishop's Coll. Sch.; bd. dirs. Montreal Transition Houses Inc., Study Endowment Fund; mem. tax adv. com. Comité de Promotion Economique de Montréal. Mem. Que. Bar Assn., Can. Bar Assn., Can. Tax Found., Internat. Fiscal Assn. Roman Catholic. Clubs: Mt. Bruno Country, Orleans Fish and Game; Tarrantine (Dark Harbour, Maine). Home: 48 Aberdeen Ave Westmount PQ H3Y 3A4 Canada Office: 1981 McGill College Ave Montreal PQ H3A 3C1 Canada

GILLESPIE, THOMAS WILLIAM, theological seminary administrator, religion educator; b. Los Angeles, July 18, 1928; s. William A. and Estella (Beers) G.; m. Barbara A. lungenbill, July 31, 1953; children: Robyn C., William T., Dayle E. B.A., George Pepperdine Coll., 1951; B.D., Princeton Theol. Seminary, 1954; Ph.D., Claremont Grad. Sch., 1971. Ordained to ministry Presbyterian Ch., 1954. Pastor 1st Presby. Ch., Garden Grove, Calif., 1954-66, Burlingame, Calif., 1966-83; pres., prof. N.T. Princeton Theol. Sem., N.J., 1983—; vis. lectr. N.T. San Francisco Theol. Sem., 1972-73; adj. prof. N.T. Fuller Theol. Sem., Pasadena, Calif., 1974-83, New Coll. Berkeley, Calif., 1979-83. Served to pfc. USMC, 1946-47. Recipient A.A. Hodge prize in systematic theology Princeton Theol. Sem., 1953. Mem. Soc. Bibl. Lit. Republican. Lodge: Rotary Internat. (Burlingame). Home: Springdale 86 Mercer St Princeton NJ 08540 Office: Princeton Theol Sem CN821 Princeton NJ 08542

GILLET, ANDRE, food processing company executive; b. Paris, 1926. Grad., U. Paris, 1944. Asst. mgr. Louis Dreyfus & Co., Ltd., Philippines, 1948-50; with Internat. Multifoods Corp., 1951—, gen. sales mgr., Venezuela, 1958-62, mng. dir., 1962-66, div. v.p., mng. dir. Overseas div., 1966-69, corp. v.p., gen. mgr. Internat. div., 1969-79, exec. v.p., 1979-83; pres., chief operating officer Internat. Multifood Corp., 1983—; also pres. Internat. Multifoods Corps. Office: Internat Multifoods Corp Box 2942 Minneapolis MN 55402 *

GILLETT, CHARLES, travel executive; b. Newport, Ky., Sept. 9, 1915; s. Louis B. and Sarah (Maller) G.; m. Virginia Margaret Littmann, June 11, 1949; children: Valerie, David, Brian Paul, Peter Guy. B.A., U. Cin., 1938. Pub. relations dir. Netherland Plaza Hotel, Cin., 1938-39; account exec. Swafford & Koehl Advt. Agy., N.Y.C., 1939-40; advt. and sales promotion dir. Hotel Gibson, Cin., 1940-41; promotion and pub. relations dir. N.Y. Conv. and Visitors Bur., N.Y.C., 1946-62, v.p., 1962-65, exec. v.p., 1966-74, pres., 1974—; Mem. travel adv. com. U.S. Dept. Commerce, 1963-65, 77—, nat. adv. com. on hwy. beautification, 1965-66; del. White House Conf. Natural Beauty, 1965; spl. adviser to Discover Am. Travel Orgns., 1967-68, dir., 1968—; mem. N.Y. State Bd. Tourist Commrs., 1977—; chmn. Nat. Urban Tourism Council, 1977—; mem. U.S. Congressional Travel and Tourism Caucus.; mem. adv. bd., exec. com. Travel and Tourism Govt. Affairs, Policy Council, 1982—. Editor: The Bridge, 1946; Writer, lectr. on travel bus. subjects. Mem. pub. affairs com. U.S. Air Force Acad., 1968-71. Served from pvt. to maj. AUS, 1941-46. Decorated Bronze Star.; Recipient Most Original Travel Idea award Midwest Travel Writers Assn., 1964; Golden Horseshoe award Discover Am. Travel Orgns., 1972; Golden Scroll award Broadway Assn., 1977; installed Order of Corte, 1972; medal of Amity, France, 1980; Am. Traditions award B'nai B'rith Youth Services, 1981; award of excellence U. Cin., 1981. Mem. Nat. Assn. Travel Orgns. (dir. 1960-62, pres. 1963-65, chmn. bd. 1965-67, award of merit 1966), Internat. Festivals Assn. (dir. 1957-59, sec. 1959-61, sec.-treas. 1966-67), Am. Soc. Travel Agts., Soc. Am. Travel Writers, N.Y. State Travel Council, Nat. Tour Brokers Assn., Hotel Sales Mgrs. Assn., Nat. Indsl. Recreation Assn., Pub. Relations Soc. Am., Sales Promotion Execs. Assn., Internat. Assn. Conv. Burs. (dir. 1968-71, v.p. 1971-72, pres. 1973-74), Travel Industry Assn. Am. (life dir., mem. exec. com., Nat. Travel Mktg. award 1981). Club: Overseas Press (N.Y.C.). Home: 8 Ridge Dr E Great Neck NY 11021 Office: Two Columbus Circle New York NY 10019

GILLETT, GEORGE NIELD, JR., business executive; b. Racine, Wis., Oct. 22, 1938; s. George Nield and Alyce (Herbert) G.; m. Rose Foster, Aug. 5, 1967; children: George Nield III, Alexander, Andrew, Foster. Student, Amherst Coll.; B.A., Dominican Coll., Racine, 1961. With McKinsey and Co., Inc. (mgmt. cons.), 1964-67; bus. mgr. Miami Dolphins, 1966-67; pres. Harlem Globetrotters, Inc., 1967-70, Globetrotter Communications, Inc., Chgo., 1970-76; vice-chmn. Globe Broadcasting Co., 1976-78; chmn. Lease Mgmt. Corp., Chgo., 1970—, Wausau Fin. Corp., Wis., 1970—; pres. Juneau Supply Co., Inc., 1976—, Wausau Energy Corp., 1976—; dir. Murray Machinery Co., Inc., 1976—; chmn. Gillett Group, Inc., 1977—, Gillett Broadcasting Co., 1978—, Gillett Greyhound Racing, Inc., 1981—, Packerland Packing Co., Inc., 1978—; v.p., dir. Walter's Foods; dir. Endata, Inc. Mem. Young Presidents Orgn.; mem. exec. com. Middle Tenn. council Boy Scouts Am.; bd. dirs. United Way. Mem. Am. Meat Assn., Am. Greyhound Track Operators Assn., Alexis de Tocqueville Soc., Chaine des Rotisseurs. Roman Catholic. Clubs: Racquet (Chgo.); Belle Meade Country, Onwentsia, Oneida. 5700 Knob Rd PO Box 4 Nashville TN 37202 F

GILLETT, JONATHAN NEWELL, publishing executive; b. Glen Ridge, N.J., Apr. 25, 1941; s. Ezra Kendall and Jean (Newell) G.; m. Ann Elizabeth Taylor, Oct. 2, 1965; children: Victoria Newell, Katherine Taylor. B.A., Washington and Lee U., 1963. Salesman McGraw-Hill Book Co., N.Y.C., 1965-67, mktg. supr., 1967-69, pub. jr. book div., dir. advt. and promotion, 1969-72, gen. mgr. gen. books, N.Y.C., 1972-81; pres. Franklin Watts, Inc. a Grolier Co., N.Y.C., 1981—. Served with USNR, 1963-65. Office: 387 Park Ave S New York NY 10016

GILLETT, LOWELL RENO, university president; b. Mpls., Feb. 23, 1925; s. Reno G. and Ethel I. (Smith) Gillett-P.; m. Ardis L. Keith, Aug. 14, 1948; children: Judy, Amy. B.A., Gustavus Adolphus Coll., 1947; M.A., U. Minn., 1954; Ed.D., U. N.D., 1965. Tchr., coach Amboy Pub. Schs., (Minn.), 1947-48, Sherburn Pub. Schs., 1949-51; tchr., asst. jr. high sch. prin. Austin Pub. Schs., (Minn.), 1951-62; grad. asst. U.N.D., Grand Forks, 1962-63; dean, prof., acting pres. St. Cloud State U., (Minn.), 1963-82; pres. Bemidji State U., (Minn.), 1982—, also ex-officio mem. alumni bd. Chmn. adv. com. libraries State Univ. System, 1977-78; chmn. Minn. Dept. Edn. Task Force Continuing Edn.; mem. adv. com. Minn. Environ. Quality Council; Austin community ambassador to Austria, 1956; mem. Minn. Bd. Teaching, 1973-78. Served with AC USN, 1943-45. Named St. Cloud State Coll. Tchr. of Yr., 1965. Mem. Am. Assn. State Colls. and Univs. (energy and environ. com.), Minn. Assn. Colls. Tchr. Edn. (exec. com., past pres., instl. rep.), Minn. Assn. Tchr. Educators (research com.), Phi Delta Kappa (exec. bd., past pres., nat. and regional conv. del.), Bemidji C. of C. Lodges: Rotary; Masons; Shriners. Home: 3400 Cedar Ln Bemidji MN 56601 Office: Bemidji State U 14th and Birchmont Bemidji MN 56601

GILLETT, MARGARET, educator; b. Wingham, Australia, Feb. 1, 1930; d. Leslie Frank and Janet (Vickers) G. B.A., U. Sydney, 1950, Dip. Ed., 1951; M.A., Russell Sage Coll., 1958; Ed.D., Columbia U., 1961. Tchr. English, Australia, Eng., 1950-54; edn. officer Colombo Plan Sect., Commonwealth Office Edn., Australia, 1954-57; asst. prof. edn. Dalhousie U., Halifax, N.S., Can., 1961-62; registrar Haile Sellassie I U., Addis Ababa, Ethiopia, 1962-64; asso. prof. edn. McGill U., Montreal, Que., Can., 1964-67, prof., 1967-82, MacDonald prof., 1982—; cons. social sci. and humanities div. Can. Council, 1965—; cons. Canadian Internat. Women's Secretariat bd.; internat. cons. Ednl. Futures Internat.; Mem. subcom. on women Can. Nat. Commn. for UNESCO. Author: A History of Education - Thought and Practice, 1966, (with Monika Kehoe) The Laurel and the Poppy, 1967, Educational Technology: Toward Demystification, 1973, We Walked Very Warily: A History of Women at McGill, 1981; Editor: Readings in the History of Education, 1969, (with John Laska) Foundation Studies in Education: Justifications and New Directions, 1973; founding editor: McGill Jour. Edn, 1966-77; cons. editor: Educational Studies, 1970—; Contbr. articles to profl. jours. Recipient Scholarship Altrusa Internat., 1957, grad. award Columbia, 1960. Mem. Comparative and Internat. Edn. Soc. Can. (v.p. 1968-71, pres. 1977-79), Am. Ednl. Studies Assn. (mem. exec. 1972-76). Home: 4800 DeMaisonneuve W Apt 610 Westmount PQ Canada H32 1M2 Office: Faculty Edn McGill U Montreal PQ Canada H3A 1Y2

GILLETTE, ANITA, actress; b. Balt., Aug. 16, 1938; d. J. Alfred and Juanita (Wayland) Luebben; m. Ronald William Gillette, Oct. 13, 1957 (div. 1967); children: Timothy Ronald, Chrisopher John; m. Armand Eugene Coullet, July 23, 1982. Actress: Broadway shows Carnival, All American, Mr. President, Kelly, Don't Drink the Water, Cabaret, Jimmy, Chapter Two, They're Playing Our Song; other theatres Pocohantas, London, Rich and Famous, N.Y.C., Tranvesites, The Importance of Being Earnest; TV shows Me and The Chimp, Bob and Carol and Ted and Alice, All That Glitters, The Baxters, Quincy. Recipient Los Angeles Drama Critics award for best actress Chapter Two, 1978. Office: care Francis Management 328 S Beverly Dr Beverly Hills CA 91604

GILLETTE, EDWARD SCRANTON, publisher; b. Phila., Feb. 3, 1898; s. Halbert Powers and Julia Washburn (Scranton) G.; m. Claribel Reed Thornton, July 14, 1921; 1 son, Halbert Scranton. Grad., Sheffield Sci. Sch., Yale, 1919; B.S. in Civil Engring, U. Pa., 1921. Bank clk., 1918; accountant in charge Municipal Water Works Co., S. Bellingham, Wash., 1921-22; bus. mgr. Gillette Pub. Co. (publs. Roads and Streets, Water and Sewerage Works, Caminos y Calles, Heavy Constrn., Cat, County and Township Roads, mag. Tech. books), 1924—, gen. mgr., v.p., sec., 1937—; gen. mgr., v.p. Gillette Co., pub., pres., 1952; pres. Scranton Pub. Co., Inc. (now merged into Scranton Gillette Communications); pub. Water Engring. and Mgmt., Indls. Wastes, Water and Wastes Digest, Rural and Urban Roads; chmn. bd. Scranton Gillette Communications (with additional publs. Seed World, The Diapason, Piano Trade), 1978—; past dir. Asso. Bus. Publs., Constrn. Industry. Chmn. bd. Cathedral Shelter.; Past pres. Chgo. Bus. Papers Assn.; Trustee Episcopal Charities. Mem. Constrn. Industry Mfrs. Assn., Am. Soc. C.E. (life mem.), Am. Legion, Delta Kappa Epsilon. Republican. Episcopalian. Clubs: Rotary, Lahaina Yacht, Maui Country; Villa Monterey (Scottsdale, Ariz.). Home: 681 S Beverly Pl Lake Forest IL 60045 Office: Scranton Gillette Communications Pub Co 380 Northwest Hwy Des Plaines IL 60016 *"Honesty is the best policy" and obeying the "Ten Commandments" are the best standards of conduct and the best principles.*

GILLETTE, HYDE, investment banker; b. Chgo., June 23, 1906; s. Edwin and Mabel (Hyde) G.; m. Marie Clarke Smith, Sept. 7, 1932; 1 dau., Marie Clarke Gerald. Grad., Exeter Acad., 1924; A.B. cum laude, Princeton, 1928; M.B.A. with distinction, Harvard, 1930. With Glore, Forgan & Co., 1930-53, partner, 1950-53; dep. and dep. under asst. sec. USAF, 1953-57; asst. postmaster gen., bur. finance U.S. Post Office, Washington, 1957-61; partner Auchincloss Parker & Redpath, 1961-70; regional v.p. Thomson & McKinnon Auchincloss, Inc., Washington, 1970-73; v.p. Thomson McKinnon Securities, 1973—. Exec. bd. Chgo. Area Project, 1936-53, chmn., 1948-53; bd. dirs., v.p. Nat. Capital area council Boy Scouts Am.; dir., vice chmn. budget com. Community Fund of Chgo., 1942; chmn. exec. com. Chgo. Opera Theatre, 1947; adv. bd. Dept. Public Welfare Ill., 1949-53; pres. Barrington Country Day Sch., 1941; v.p. Washington Heart Assn., 1961; bd. dirs. Am. Heart Assn., 1960-63. Served as lt. comdr. USNR, 1943-46. Recipient Exceptional Civilian Service award USAF, 1956; Distinguished Service award U.S. Post Office, 1960. Mem. Mayflower Descs., Soc. Colonial Wars, English Speaking Union (dir. 1977—), Barrington Countryside Assn. (pres. 1949-50), Chevalier Tastevin, Phi Beta Kappa. Presbyn. Clubs: Barrington Hills Country; Quadrangle (Princeton); Fox River Valley Hunt, Commonwealth (Chgo.); Chevy Chase, Metropolitan (Washington); India House (N.Y.C.); Beverly Yacht, Kittanset (Marion, Mass.). Home: 4100 Cathedral Ave NW Washington DC 20016 Home: 10 Holly Rd Marion MA 02738 Office: 1705 H St NW Washington DC 20016

GILLETTE, ROBERT STONE, business executive; b. Cortland, N.Y., July 7, 1913; s. Harold Ralph and Ada Fleming (Stone) G.; m. Janet French, Oct. 19, 1939; children—Deborah G. Law, Edward French. B.S., Mass. Inst. Tech., 1936. Chief planning engr. Jones & Lamson Machine Co., Springfield, Vt., 1936-44; prodn. mgr. Submarine Signal Co., Fall River, Mass., 1944-46; research United Shoe Machinery Corp., Boston, 1947-49; asst. gen. mgr. Rock of Ages Corp., 1949-52, exec. v.p., dir., 1952-54, pres., dir., 1954-72, chmn. bd., 1972-75, Nat. Life Ins. Co.; dir. Union Mut. Fire Ins. Co., Central Vt. Ry., Grand Trunk Corp., Amoskeag Co. Chmn. corp. Cardigan Mountain Sch., 1977—, pres., 1971-76; chmn. Vt. Gov.'s Cost Control Council, 1977; dir. Vt. Ednl. and Health Bldg. Financing Agy.; trustee Central Vt. Med. Center.; mem. Vt. State Bd. Edn. Clubs: Quissett (Mass.) Yacht; Algonquin (Boston); Woods Hole Golf. Home: Woodcrest Rd Montpelier VT 05602 Office: Nat Life Ins Co Montpelier VT 05602

GILLETTE, STANLEY C., apparel mfg. co. exec.; b. N.Y.C.; s. Charles and Ida G.; m. Joan Glickman, Apr. 3, 1959; children—Richard, Patty. Student, CCNY, Columbia U. Vice-pres. Van Heusen Co., N.Y.C., 1950-55, exec. v.p., 1955-63, pres., 1963-75; exec. v.p. Phillips-Van Heusen Corp., 1963-75; chmn. bd., pres. McGregor-Doniger, Inc., N.Y.C., 1975-79, Ship 'N Shore, Inc., 1979—; v.p. Gen. Mills, Inc., 1979—. Pres. Father's Day Council, 1973-74, chmn., 1975-77, chmn. exec. com., 1977—; chmn. exec. com. Mother's Day Council, 1978-80, pres., 1980—; industry chmn. N.Y. Heart Assn., Sister Kenney Found., Help for Retarded Children. Served to capt. U.S. Army, 1942-46; C.B.I. Recipient Man of Yr. award City of Hope Med. Center, 1972, Heart of Gold award N.Y. Heart Assn., 1974. Mem. Am. Apparel Mfrs. Assn. (pres.). Office: 1411 Broadway New York NY 10018

GILLETTE, WILLIAM, historian, educator; b. Bridgeport, Conn., Mar. 2, 1933; s. Samuel William and Lillian (Abeson) G.; m. Elisabeth L. Janes, May 23, 1971; children: Scott Douglas, Wendy Elisabeth. B.S., Georgetown U., 1955; M.A., Columbia U., 1956, postgrad., 1958-59; Ph.D., Princeton U., 1963. Instr. Ohio State U., 1962-64; acting asst. prof. U. Conn., Storrs, 1965-66; asst. prof. Bklyn. Coll. CUNY, 1966-67; asso. prof. Rutgers U., 1967-81, prof., 1981—; Fulbright prof. U. Salzburg (Austria), 1982-83; asso. prof. Rutgers U., 1967-81. Author: The Right to Vote: Politics and the Passage of the Fifteenth Amendment, 1965, 69, Retreat from Reconstruction, 1869-1879, 2d edit, 1981; contbr. articles to various books. Served with AUS, 1956-58. Social Sci. Research Council faculty fellow, 1970; recipient Landry award La. State U. Press, 1979; Chastain award So. Polit. Sci. Assn., 1980; Am. Philos. Soc. grantee. Mem. Am. Hist. Assn., Orgn. Am. Historians, So. Hist. Assn., Western Hist. Assn., AAUP. Democrat. Unitarian. Home: 43 South Dr East Brunswick NJ 08816 Office: Dept History Rutgers U New Brunswick NJ 08903

GILLEY, JAMES RAY, real estate company executive; b. Surry County, N.C., Apr. 25, 1934; s. William Hassel and Delsie May (Brinkley) G.; m. Sylvia Ray Messick, Mar. 28, 1954; children: William Michael, Elizabeth Dale, Nita Ann. B.A., Wake Forest U., 1957, M.B.A., 1972. Pres. 7-11 Food Store N.C., Inc., Winston-Salem, 1959-61; pres. Stop & Shop of N.C., Winston-Salem, 1957-66, Gilley Leasing Co., 1966-69, Convenient Systems, Inc., 1969-73; exec. v.p., chief fin. officer The Washington Group, Inc., Winston-Salem, 1973-75, pres., 1975-77; chmn. bd., pres., chief exec. officer Hungry Bull Assos., Spartanburg, S.C., 1978-80; pres. Southmark Communities, Inc., 1981—; v.p. Southmark Corp., 1981—; dir. Integon Corp., Northwestern Bank, Salem Carpet Co., Piedmont Fed. Savs. and Loan Assn., all Winston-Salem. Mem. Mayors Com. Recreation Parks, Forsyth County, N.C.; chmn. bd. dirs. Better Bus. Bur., Winston-Salem, 1974-76; trustee Wake Forest U., 1974—, Gardner Webb Coll., 1969-73; bd. visitors Babcock Sch. Mgmt., Wake Forest U., 1973—. Recipient Distinguished Alumni Service citation Wake Forest U., 1974. Mem. Winston-Salem C. of C., Fin. Execs. Inst., Newcomen Soc. Baptist (deacon). Clubs: Forsyth Country, Twin City (Winston-Salem). Home: 2712 Bartram Pl Winston-Salem NC 27106

GILLEY, MICKEY LEROY, musician; b. Natchez, Miss., Mar. 9, 1936; s. Arthur Philmore and Irene Frances (Lewis) G.; m. Vivian McDonald, Dec. 27, 1962; 1 son, Gregory Brent. Student pub. schs., Ferriday, La. Partner Gilley's Club, Pasadena, Tex., 1971—. Appeared in night clubs in, Houston, New Orleans, Biloxi, Miss., Mobile, Ala., Lake Charles, La., 1957-59; appeared at, Nesadel Club, Houston, 1960-70; (Named Most Promising Male Artist, Acad. Country Music 1974, 1 Most Promising Male Artist, Record World 1974, 1 Top New Country Singles Artist, Billboard 1974, Top New Male Vocalist in Album Category, Record World 1975, Most Promising Male Artist, Music City News 1976, Best Male Vocalist, Entertainer of Year, Acad. Country Music 1976). Mem. Country Music Assn., Acad. Country Music, AFTRA, Musicians Local 65. Club: Moose. Office: 4500 Spencer Hwy Pasadena TX 77504

GILLHAM, JOHN KINSEY, chemical engineering educator; b. London, Aug. 7, 1930; U.S., 1959, naturalized, 1968; s. Gerald Albert and Doris (Kinsey) G.; m. Helen Alyce Currier, Sept. 18, 1961; children: Matthew, Jane, Martha. B.A., Cambridge U., 1953, M.A., 1957; Ph.D. in Chemistry, McGill U., Montreal, 1959. Research chemist Am. Cynamid Co., Stamford, Conn., 1958-65; vis. research chemist Princeton U., 1964-65, mem. faculty, 1965—, prof. chem. engring., 1975—; cons. to chem. and polymer industries. Author papers in field. Vis. fellow Japan Soc. Promotion Sci. Mem. Am. Chem. Soc. (Borden award 1978, Doolittle award 1980), N. Am. Thermal Analysis Soc. (Mettler award 1978), Am. Inst. Chem. Engrs., Am. Phys. Soc., Soc. Plastics Engrs., N.Y. Acad. Scis., Plastics and Rubber Inst. London. Home: 11 Vernon Circle Princeton NJ 08540 Office: Dept Chem Engring Princeton U Princeton NJ 08544

GILLHAM, NICHOLAS WRIGHT, geneticist, educator; b. N.Y.C., May 14, 1932; s. Robert Marty and Elizabeth (Enright) G.; m. Carol Lenore Collins, June 2, 1956. A.B., Harvard, 1954, A.M., 1955, Ph.D. (USPHS fellow), 1962. From instr. to asst. prof. Harvard, 1963-68; asso. prof. zoology Duke, 1968-72, prof., 1973-82, James B. Duke prof. zoology, 1982—; Mem. biochemistry, molecular genetics and cell biology interdisciplinary cluster Pres.'s Biomed. Research Panel, 1975; mem. study sect. in genetics NIH, 1976-80. Author: (with R. Kreuger and J. Coggin) Introduction to Microbiology, 1973, Organelle Heredity, 1978; Mem. editorial bd.: Genetics, 1975-78, Jour. Cell Biology, 1977-79; sr. editor: Plasmid, 1977—. Served to 1st lt. Med. Service Corps USAF, 1955-58. Postdoctoral fellow, 1962-63; Spl. fellow, 1967-68; Research Career Devel. Award grantee, 1972-77; all USPHS). Mem. Am. Soc. Naturalists, Genetics Soc. Am., Soc. for Cell Biology, Sigma Xi. Home: 1211 Woodburn Rd Durham NC 27705 Office: Dept Zoology Duke U Durham NC 27706

GILLIAM, CARROLL LEWIS, lawyer; b. Union, S.C., Sept. 25, 1929; s. D. Few and Cynthia Carolyn (Stone) G.; m. Margaret Clark Eagan, May 7, 1960; 1 dau., Cynthia Clark. A.B. cum laude, U. S.C., 1949, M.A. magna cum laude, 1950; J.D. with highest honors, George Washington U., 1957. Bar: D.C. 1957. Practice law, Washington, 1957—; partner Grove, Jaskiewicz, Gilliam & Cobert, 1964—; mem. adv. com. on revision of rules Fed. Energy Regulatory Commn., 1978-81; mem. U.S. Dept. Edn. Appeal Bd., 1976-82. Served with USAF, 1950-53. Recipient Beaufort Watts Ball award U. S.C., 1949; John Bell

Larner award George Washington U., 1957. Mem. Fed. Power Bar Assn. (pres. 1975-76), Am. Bar Assn. (chmn. natural resources law sect. 1977-78, chmn. standing com. environ. law 1978-80, ho. of dels. 1980—, council adminstrv. law sect. 1974-75), D.C. Bar Assn., Blue Key, Phi Beta Kappa, Delta Theta Phi, Order of the Coif. Democrat. Episcopalian. Clubs: University (Washington); Beach and Racquet (Isles of Palms, S.C.). Home: 4101 Aspen St Chevy Chase MD 20015 Office: 1730 M St NW Washington DC 20036

GILLIAM, JACKSON EARLE, bishop; b. Heppner, Oreg., June 20, 1920; s. Edwin Earle and Mary (Perry) G.; m. Margaret Kathleen Hindley, Aug. 11, 1943; children—Anne Meredith, Margaret Carol, John Howard. A.B., Whitman Coll., 1942; B.D., Va. Theol. Sem., 1948, S.T.M., 1949, D.D., 1969. Ordained to ministry Episcopal Ch., 1948; rector in, Hermiston, Ore., 1949-53; canon St. Mark's Cathedral, Mpls., 1953-55; rector Ch. Incarnation, Great Falls, Mont., 1955-68; bishop Episc. Diocese Mont., 1968—; chmn. com. on pastoral devel., mem. council on ministry, mem. program, budget and fin. com. Episc. Ch., 1978, pres. Province VI. Served to 1st lt. AUS, World War II. Decorated companion Order of Cross of Nails, Coventry Cathedral, Eng., 1974. Club: Rotary. Home: 1100 LeGrande Cannon Blvd Helena MT 52601 Office: 515 N Park Helena MT 59601

GILLIAM, JAMES FRANKLIN, historian educator; b. Seattle, Mar. 14, 1915; s. Clinton Cailey G. and Hazel Elvira (Carr) Cailey; m. Elizabeth Holzworth, Sept. 6, 1941; children: Elizabeth, John Franklin, Anne. B.A., San Jose State Coll., 1935; M.A., Stanford U., 1936; Ph.D., Yale U., 1940. Instr. classics Yale U., 1940-41, 45-47; asst. prof. Wells Coll., 1947-49; from asst. prof. to prof. history and classics U. Iowa, 1949-61; prof. history U. Oreg., 1961-62; prof. Greek and Latin Columbia U., N.Y.C., 1962-65, curator Papyri, 1970-81, adj. prof., 1970—; vis. lectr. Princeton U., 1972-75; mem. Inst. Advanced Study, Princeton, 1958-59, 63-64, prof. Sch. Hist. Studies, 1965—. Co-author: The Excavations at Dura-Europos, V, The Parchments and Papyri, 1959. Served to capt. AUS, 1941-45. Decorated Bronze Star; Guggenheim fellow, 1955-56; Sather lectr. U. Calif.-Berkeley, 1979. Mem. Am. Philol. Assn., Archaeol. Inst. Am., Soc. Promotion Roman Studies, German Archaeology Inst. (corr.), Internat. Assn. Papyrologists, Am. Soc. Papyrologists (pres. 1971-73). Office: Inst. Advanced Study Princeton NJ 08540

GILLIAM, JOHN CHARLES, economist, educator; b. Boulder, Colo., Sept. 19, 1927; s. Arthur Woodson and Marguerite (Hubbard) G.; m. Katherine Frances Mihevc, July 16, 1947; children: Bruce, Charles, Carol Ann. B.A., Western State Coll., Colo., 1951; M.Bus.Ed., U. Colo., 1952; Ph.D., State U. Iowa, 1959. Instr. bus. Brush (Colo.) High Sch., 1952-55, State U. Iowa, 1955-57; asst. prof. commerce U. Wyo., 1957-62, asso. prof., 1962; asso. prof. bus. edn. Tex. Tech. U., 1962-66, prof., 1966—, asso. dean, 1968-73, prof. econs., 1973—; Program specialist Ford Found., Amman, Jordan, 1966-68, cons. in edn. for bus.; cons. to Govt. Saudi Arabia; vis. prof. several univs.; cons. bus. and econs. Contbr. articles to profl. jours. Served with USNR, 1945-47. Mem. Nat. Bus. Edn. Assn., Beta Gamma Sigma, Omicron Delta Epsilon, Alpha Kappa Psi, Delta Pi Epsilon, Pi Omega Pi. Episcopalian. Lodge: Elks. Home: 9311 Utica Dr Lubbock TX 79424

GILLIAM, SAM, artist; b. Tupelo, Miss., Nov. 30, 1933; s. Sam and Estery C. (Cousins) G.; m. Dorothy Butler, Sept. 1, 1962; children—Stephanie, Melissa, Leah. B.A., U. Louisville, 1955, M.A., 1961, L.H.D. (hon.), 1980. Instr. painting Corcoran Sch. Art, Corcoran Gallery, Washington, 1965-69; instr. painting Md. Inst. Art. Numerous one-man shows of paintings, latest being, Univ. Gallery, U. Mass., Amherst, 1978, Galerie Darthea Speyer, Paris, France, Dart Gallery, Chgo., 1979, Florence Dugl Gallery, N.Y.C., Nina Freudenheim Gallery, Buffalo, Hamilton Gallery of Contemporary Art, N.Y.C., 1979, U. Wis., Stevens Point, 1980, Hamilton Gallery Contemporary Art, 1981, numerous group shows, latest being, Galerie Darthea Speyer, Paris, 1978, Dade County Library, Miami, Fla., Grey Gallery, N.Y.C., 1979, Hamilton Gallery of Contemporary Art, N.Y.C., The Alternative Mus., Washington, 1980, SUNY, N.J. State Mus., Trenton; represented in numerous permanent collections including, Mus. Modern Art, N.Y.C., Rockefeller Collection, N.Y.C., Corcoran Gallery Art, Washington, Howard U., Washington, Phillips Collection, Washington, Gallery Modern Art, Washington, Mus. African Art, Washington, IBM Co., Washington, Carnegie Inst., Pitts., Balt. Mus. Art, Art Inst., Chgo., Tate Gallery, London, Eng., Musee d'art Moderne de la Ville de Paris, France, Boymans Mus., Rotterdam, Holland, and others. Recipient Disting. Alumnus award U. Louisville, 1975, Norman W. Harris prize award Art Inst. Chgo., 1969; Washington Gallery Modern Art fellow, 1968; Nat. Endowment for the Arts grantee, 1967; Guggenheim fellow, 1971. Home: 1752 Lamont St NW Washington DC 20010

GILLIAM, TERRY VANCE, animator, film director, actor, illustrator, writer; b. Mpls., Nov. 22, 1940; s. James Hall and Beatrice (Vance) G.; m. Margaret Weston; children: Amy Rainbow, Holly du Bois. B.A. in Arts, Occidental Coll., 1962. Asso. editor HELP! mag., 1962-64; free-lance illustrator, 1964-65, advt. copywriter/art dir., 1966-67; with Monty Python's Flying Circus, 1969-76. Animator: film And Now For Something Completely Different; co-dir., actor: Monty Python and the Holy Grail; dir.: Jabberwocky; designer, actor, animator: Monty Python's Life of Brian; co-author, producer, dir.: Time Bandits; actor: dir. Monty Python Live at the Hollywood Bowl, 1982; dir.: (film) Monty Python's Meaning of Life, 1983; author: film The Cocktail People, 1966, Monty Python's Big Red Book, Monty Python's Papperbook, 1977, Monty Python's Scrapbook, 1979, Animations of Mortality, 1979. Office: care Doubleday & Co Inc 245 Park Ave New York NY 10167 *

GILLIAND, MERLE ELLSWORTH, banker; b. Pitcairn, Pa., Dec. 21, 1921; s. Walter M. and Elsie N. (Dean) G.; m. Olive Lee Henry, June 11, 1954; 1 son, Mark. B.B.A. cum laude, Duquesne U., 1948. With Albert A. Logan (C.P.A.), 1948-53; instr. accounting Duquesne U., 1948-53; with Pitts. Nat. Bank, 1953—, exec. v.p., 1965-67, pres., 1967-70, chief exec. officer, 1970-84, chmn. bd., 1972-84, also dir., chmn. exec. com., 1984—; chmn., chief exec. offices, dir. PNC Fin. Corp., 1983—; dir. Kissell Co., Bell Telephone Co. Pa., Wean United, Inc., USAir, Inc., Cooper Tire & Rubber Co.; Mem. exec. council Allegheny Conf. Community Devel.; bd. dirs. Pa. Economy League, Duquesne U.; mem. policy com. Bus. Council Pa.; trustee U. Pitts.; bd. visitors Grad. Sch. Bus. Adminstrn., U. Pitts.; mem. exec., operating coms. Penn's S.W. Assn. Served with AUS, 1942-46. Mem. Bank Adminstrn. Inst. (past pres. Pitts. conf.), Pa. Inst. C.P.A.s, Fin. Execs. Inst., Assn. Res. City Bankers. Presbyterian (elder). Clubs: Duquesne, Allegheny, Fox Chapel Golf; Rolling Rock, Laurel Valley Golf (Ligonier, Pa.); Belleview Biltmore Country (Belleair, Fla.). Home: 300 Fox Chapel Rd 518 Pittsburgh PA 15238 Office: Pitts Nat Bldg Pittsburgh PA 15222

GILLIATT, NEAL, advertising executive; b. Plainville, Ind., Dec. 24, 1917; s. Oliver Breden and Katherine Ann (Henderson) G.; m. Mary Rees, Feb. 6, 1943; children: David Rees, John Neal. B.S., Ind. U., 1939; M.B.A., Northwestern U., 1940; postgrad. Advanced Mgmt. Program, Harvard U., 1960. Instr. Ind. U., 1940-42; with food price div. OPA, Chgo., 1942-45; with McCann-Erickson, Inc., Chgo., 1945-55, N.Y.C., 1955-66; dir. Interpublic Group of Cos., Inc., N.Y.C., 1966-70, vice chmn., 1970-80, chmn. exec. com., 1980—; dir. Chemed Corp., Omnicare, Inc. Bd. dirs. Epilepsy Found. Am.; chmn. bd. dirs. Insts. Religion and Health, Silverhill Found.; Bd. dirs. Boys' Clubs Am., N.Y. Philharmonic Soc., Religion in Am. Life, Ind. U. Found., Millikin U. Recipient Broadcasting and Advt. Industries Human Relations award Am. Jewish Com., 1969; Disting. Alumni Service award Ind. U., 1970. Mem. Beta Gamma Sigma (award 1963, 80), Sigma Alpha Epsilon. Congregationalist. Clubs: Greenwich Country (Conn.); Piedmont Driving (Atlanta); Links, Economic, University (N.Y.C.). Home: 266 Round Hill Rd Greenwich CT 06830 Office: 650 Fifth Ave 19th Floor New York NY 10019

GILLIATT, PENELOPE ANN DOUGLASS, author; b. London, Eng.; d. Cyril and Mary (Douglass) Conner; m. R.W. Gilliatt (div.); m. John Osborne (div.); 1 dau., Nolan. Student, Queen's Coll., London, Bennington Coll., Vt. Film critic: Observer, London, 1961-67; theatre critic, 1965; guest film critic: New Yorker, 1967; regular film critic, 1968—; writer feature film scripts and plays filmed for, BBC-TV; novelist; double play-bill at, Am. Pl. Theatre, N.Y.C., Property and Nobody's Business, 1980; Author: One by One, 1965, A State of Change, 1968, The Cutting Edge, 1979; short stories Come Back If It Doesn't Get Better, 1970, Nobody's Business, 1972, Splendid Lives, 1979, Sunday, Bloody Sunday (original film script) (Oscar nomination, 1971), 1971 (awards for 1971 best original screenplay Writers Guild Am., Writers Guild Eng., Nat. Soc. Film Critics, N.Y. Film Critics), Penguin Modern Stories, 1971; film and theatre essays Unholy Fools, 1973, Jean Renoir: Essays, Conversations, Reviews, 1975, Jacques Tati, 1976; short stories Splendid Lives, 1977, Three-Quarter Face, 1979; play But when all's said and done, 1981. Recipient award for creative work in lit. Am. Acad.-Nat. Inst. Arts and Letters, 1972. Fellow Royal Soc. Lit.; Mem. Brit. Labour Party. Office: New Yorker Mag 25 W 43d St New York NY 10036

GILLIES, CLARK, hockey player; b. Regina, Sask., Can., Apr. 7, 1954. With Regina Pats, World Cup Hockey League, 1971-74; with New York Islanders, 1974—; played with Clarence Campbell Conf. All-Star Team, 1977-79. Office: care New York Islanders Uniondale NY 11553 *

GILLIES, THOMAS DANIEL, librarian; b. South Bend, Wash., Oct. 18, 1920; s. Archibald Daniel and Emma (Clark) G. B.A., U. Mich., 1942; M.A., Cornell U., 1947; B.S. in L.S, Columbia U., 1948. Asst. librarian, instr. English, Willamette U., Salem, Oreg., 1948-50; reference librarian U. Kansas City (now U. Mo., Kansas City), 1950-52; with Linda Hall Library, Kansas City, 1953-82, dir., 1974-82; vis. asst. prof. U. Wash. Sch. Librarianship, Seattle, 1962, 63-64, 70. Served with AUS, 1942-46. Mem. ALA, AAAS, Pacific N.W. Library Assn. Club: University (Kansas City). Home: PO Box 366 South Bend WA 98586

GILLILAND, CHARLES HERBERT, SR., physician; b. Melrose, Iowa, Sept. 26, 1911; s. Herbert Roy and Maggie Jane (Clark) G.; m. Marion Charlotte Spjut, Mar. 6, 1942; children—Charles Herbert, Marion Charlotte, Patricia and Gilliland Zellner, Normal Paul, Cynthia Eileen. B.S., U. Fla., 1935, postgrad., 1936-37; M.D., U. Iowa, 1941. Diplomate: Am. Bd. Obstetrics and Gynecology. Sch. tchr., Appanoose County, Iowa, 1931-32, Monroe County, Iowa, 1932-33; salesman J. C. Penney Co., Albia, Iowa, 1928-33; pharmacist McCollum's Drug Store, Gainesville, Fla., 1935-37, Lockwood's Drug Store, Fernandina, Fla., 1936-37, Lewis Drug Store, Iowa City, Iowa, 1938-40; epidemiologist U. Iowa Hosps., Iowa City, 1940-41, intern, 1941-42; commd. lt. j.g. M.C. U.S. Navy, 1942, designated flight surgeon, 1943, resigned, 1954; resident obstetrics-gynecology U.S. Naval Hosp., 1948-51; practice medicine, specializing in obstetrics-gynecology, Gainesville, Fla., 1954—; clin. prof. dept. obstetrics and gynecology U. Fla., 1975—; mem. staff Alachua Gen., N. Fla. Regional hosps., both Gainesville; ret. Served to capt. USNR. Fellow A.C.S., Am. Coll. Obstetricians and Gynecologists (chmn. Fla. sect. 1975, dist. chmn. 1979-82); mem. South Atlantic Assn. Obstetricians and Gynecologists (v.p. 1976), Fla. Obstetric and Gynecologic Soc. (pres. 1972-73), AMA, So. Med. Assn., Fla. Med. Assn., Alachua County Med. Soc., Phi Kappa Phi, Alpha Kappa Kappa, Rho Chi, Phi Sigma. Clubs: Explorers of N.Y., Kiwanis (pres. 1979-80). Home: 3031 SW 70th Ln Gainesville FL 32601 Office: 1100 NW 8th Ave Gainesville FL 32601

GILLILAND, WILLIAM ELTON, lawyer; b. Hood County, Tex., May 8, 1919; s. Albert Floyd and Rosa Lee (Wood) G.; m. Frances Esmond; children: Chloe Ella (Mrs. Tipton Cole), John Marshall. Student, Tech. Tech. Coll., 1937-39, U. Tex., 1939-41, LL.B., 1947. Bar: Tex. 1947. County atty., Martin County, Tex., 1947-48, Howard County, Tex., 1948-49; dist. atty. 118th Jud. Dist., Tex., 1949-54; mem. firm Little & Gilliland, Big Spring, Tex., 1954-59; firm McDonald, Shafer & Gilliland, Odessa, Tex., 1959-62, Shafer, Gilliland, Davis, McCollum & Ashley, Odessa, 1962—. Served to capt. Signal Corps AUS, 1942-46. Mem. Am. Coll. Trial Lawyers, Am. Law Inst., Tex. Bar Found., State Bar Tex. (adminstrn. justice com.), Am. Bar Assn., Internat. Assn. Ins. Counsel, Am. Judicature Soc., Tex. Assn. Def. Counsel. Home: 11 Chimney Hollow Odessa TX 79762 Office: Shafer Gilliland Davis McCollum & Ashley 1st Nat Bank Bldg Drawer 1552 Odessa TX 79760

GILLILAND, WILLIAM NATHAN, geologist, educator; b. Portsmouth, O., May 23, 1919; s. Evan Russell and Elsie (Tipton) G.; m. Valarie; children—Sherrie Ann, William Kimberly (from previous marriage). B.A., Ohio State U., 1941, Ph.D., 1948. With TVA, 1941, U.S. Geol. Survey, 1948-49; mem. faculty U. Neb., 1949-65; chmn. dept. geology 1950-64; dean Coll. Arts and Scis.,Rutgers U., Newark, 1965-68; cons. to industry, 1950—; geol. cons. Nebr. Boundary Commn., 1964-70; register rep. Nat. Assn. Securities Dealers, 1969-72. Author: Geology of the Gunnison Quadrangle, Utah, 1951, also numerous articles, bulls. Served to 1st lt. USAAF, 1941-45. Mem. Am. Assn. Petroleum Geologists (certified), Assn. Profl. Geol. Scientists (certified), Geol. Soc. Am. Office: Dept Geology Rutgers Univ Newark NJ 07102

GILLILLAND, WHITNEY, lawyer; b. Glenwood, Iowa, Jan. 13, 1904; s. Shirley and Elsie (Moulton) G.; m. Virginia Wegmann, Feb. 19, 1926; children—William S., Thomas M. Student, Iowa State Coll., 1921-22, U. Nebr., 1923-26. Bar: Iowa and Wis. bars 1927. Practice in, Iowa, 1927-53, Washington, 1975—; judge 15th Jud. Dist., 1938-41; asst. to sec. agr., 1953; chmn. War Claims Commn., 1953-54, Fgn. Claims Settlement Commn. U.S., 1954-59; mem. CAB, 1959-75, chmn., 1960-61, vice chmn., 1969-75; mem. Administrv. Conf. U.S., 1961-62, 69-75; Chmn. Iowa Republican Com., 1947-50; chmn. exec. com. Nat. Rep. Strategy Com., 1949. Mem. ABA (ho. dels. 1962-63), Fed. Bar Assn. (pres. 1959-60), Iowa Bar Assn., Washington Fgn. Law Soc. (pres. 1965-66). Congregationalist. Home: 4150 N 41st St Arlington VA 22207 Office: Suite 1100 1660 L St NW Washington DC 20006

GILLIOM, JUDITH CARR, magazine editor; b. Indpls., May 19, 1943; d. Elbert Raymond and Marjorie Lucille (Carr) G. B.A., Northwestern U., 1964; M.A., U. Pa., 1966. Feature writer, asst. women's editor Indpls. News, summers 1961-63; research asst. cultural anthropology Northwestern U., 1963-64, asst. instr. freshman English, 1964; editorial asst. to dir. div. cardiology Phila. Gen. Hosp., 1965-67; asst. to ophthalmologist-in-chief Wills Eye Hosp., Phila., 1967-69; editor, writer Nat. Assn. Hearing and Speech Agencies, Washington, 1969-70; free-lance speech writer White House Conf. Children and Youth, 1969-70; free-lance editor, writer, abstractor, 1971-78; free-lance speechwriter President's Com. Mental Retardation, 1971-78; dir. pubbls. Nat. Assn. Hearing and Speech Action, Silver Spring, Md., 1972-74, dir. communications, 1975-77; editor Hearing & Speech Action mag., 1969-70, 72-77; program mgr. Interagy. Com. on Handicapped Employees, 1978, dep. exec. sec., 1979—; cons. U.S. Archtl. and Transp. Barriers Compliance Bd., 1976-77, Office Ind. Living for Disabled, HUD, 1977-78, Office for Handicapped Individuals, HEW, 1978. Mem. Nat. Spinal Cord Injury Found., 1971—, editor, pub. conv. jour., 1974-82; bd. dirs. D.C. chpt., 1975-81, nat. trustee, 1975-81, nat. bd. dirs., 1978-79; bd. dirs. Nat. Center for a Barrier-Free Environment, 1979—, v.p., 1980-81, pres., 1981-82; nat. bd. dirs., treas. League Disabled Voters, 1980—. Woodrow Wilson fellow, 1965. Mem. Phi Beta Kappa, Delta Delta Delta. Home: 901 Arcola Ave Wheaton MD 20902 Office: EEOC 2401 E St NW Washington DC 20506

GILLIS, BERNARD THOMAS, chemistry educator, university provost; b. Pierre, S.D., Mar. 7, 1931; s. Edward John and Evelyn (Lehrke) G.; m. Arlene F. Hamilton, Aug. 22, 1953; children: Gregory H., Gwendolyn K., Kathryn J., Theresa A. B.S., Loras Coll., 1952; Ph.D. (Ethyl Corp. summer fellow 1952), Wayne State U., 1956; postdoctoral fellow, MIT, 1956-57. Parke, Davis & Co. fellow Wayne State U., 1955-56, research asso., 1958; asst. prof. Duquesne U., Pitts., 1957-60, asso. prof., 1960-64, prof. chemistry, 1964, asso. chmn. chemistry dept., 1965-68, dean Grad. Sch., 1968-70; dean acad. affairs and faculty Indiana (Pa.) U., 1970-71, acad. v.p., provost, 1971-80; acad. v.p. Youngstown (Ohio) State U., 1980-82, provost, 1982—; chmn. Southwestern Pa. Higher Edn. Council, 1974-75; bd. regents Loras Coll., 1969—. Contbr. articles to profl. jours. Recipient Patriotic Civilian Service award Dept. Army, 1973, 80. Fellow AAAS, Am. Chem. Soc. (nat. councillor 1970-73), Pa. Inst. Chemists (pres. 1975-77); mem. Sigma Xi (research award 1955), Phi Lambda Upsilon, Phi Delta Kappa, Phi Kappa Phi. Home: 7280 Fairground Blvd Canfield OH 44406 *Avoid the extremes of egotism and despair; apply common sense, working hard to do the job well, and doing what you think is right.*

GILLIS, JOHN SIMON, psychologist, educator; b. Washington, Mar. 21, 1937; s. Simon John and Rita Veronica (Moran) G.; m. Mary Ann Wesolowski, Aug. 29, 1959; children: Holly Ann, Mark, Scott. B.A., Stanford U., 1959; M.S. (fellow), Cornell U., 1961; Ph.D. (NIMH fellow), U. Colo., 1965. Lectr. dept. psychology Australian Nat. U., Canberra, 1968-70; sr. psychologist Mendocino (Calif.) State Hosp., 1971-72; asso. prof. dept. psychology Tex. Tech U., Lubbock, 1972-76; prof., chmn. dept. psychology Oreg. State U., Corvallis, 1976—; cons. VA, Ciba-Geigy Pharms.; commentator Oreg. Ednl. and Pub. Broadcasting System, 1978-79; Bd. dirs. Oreg. Grad. Sch. Profl. Psychology, 1977-80; Fulbright lectr., India, 1982-83. Contbr. articles to profl. jours. Served with USAF, 1968-72. Ciba-Geigy Pharms. grantee, 1971-82. Mem. Am. Psychol. Assn., Western Psychol. Assn., Oreg. Psychol. Assn. Democrat. Roman Catholic. Home: 7520 Mountain View Dr Corvallis OR 97330 Office: Dept Psychology Oreg State U Corvallis OR 97331 *The real pleasures of life seem to come not from avoiding difficult tasks but rather from involving oneself with them - from working hard on those problems that need attention.*

GILLIS, MARVIN BOB, chemical and mining company executive; b. Treutlen County, Ga., Apr. 5, 1920; s. Bob Lee and Pearl (Gillis) G.; m. Helen Reed, Dec. 23, 1946; children: Margaret Susan, Marvin Reed, Kenneth Robert. B.S.A., U. Ga., 1940; Ph.D., Cornell U., 1947. Research asso. Cornell U., 1947-51; research chemist Internat. Minerals and Chem. Corp., from 1947, asst. dir. research, 1956-57, dir. research, 1957-64, dir. animal health and nutrition, 1964-66, div. v.p., 1966-70, corp. v.p., 1970-72, sr. v.p., 1972—; pres., dir. IMC Chems. Group, Inc., 1976-78; pres. Animal Products Group, 1978-82, cons. to exec. office, 1982—; pres. Micro-Pacific Ltd., 1982—; sec. Agrl. Research Inst., Nat. Acad. Scis.-NRC, 1958-69, v.p., 1960-62, 66-67, pres., 1962-63, 68-69, mem. agrl. bd., 1962-67; bd. dirs. Animal Health Inst., 1966-69. Author numerous papers in field. Served to 1st lt. USAAF, 1942-45. Decorated D.F.C. with oak leaf cluster, Air medal with 3 oak leaf clusters. Mem. Am. Chem. Soc., Mfg. Chemists Assn., Am. Inst. Nutrition, Poultry Sci. Assn. (Research prize 1948), Blue Key, Sigma Xi, Gamma Alpha, Alpha Zeta, Phi Kappa Phi. Baptist. Clubs: Lone Palm (Lakeland, Fla.); North Shore Country; Bent Tree (Jasper, Ga.). Patentee in field. Office: Internat Minerals & Chem Corp 2315 Sanders Rd Northbrook IL 60062

GILLIS, RICHARD SAMUEL, JR., mayor, association executive; b. Lawrenceville, Va., Sept. 10, 1915; s. Richard Samuel and Janie (Wilkins) G.; m. Margaret Crawford Shelton, July 10, 1948; 1 dau., Margaret Kimbrough. Student, U.S. Mil. Acad., 1935; B.A., Randolph Macon Coll., 1940. News editor Herald Progress, Ashland, Va., 1940-41; adminstrv. asst. Randolph Macon Coll., 1945-51; exec. v.p. Va. State C. of C., Richmond, 1951—; mayor, City of Ashland, 1966—. Past chmn. Mental Health and Mental Retardation Bd.; mem. Gov.'s Commn. on Mental Health and Mental Retardation, Ashland Town Council; trustee Jamestown Found.; mem. Hanover County (Va.) Community Services Bd. Served to capt. AUS, 1941-45. Recipient Disting. Service awards Randolph Macon Coll., 1960, Am. Cancer Soc., 1960. Mem. Richmond Public Relations Soc. (past pres.), Va. Assn. C. of C. Execs. (past pres., Disting. Service award), Am. Legion (past comdr.), Export Import Club (past pres.), Sigma Delta Chi. Baptist. Club: Kiwanis. Office: 611 E Franklin St Richmond VA 23219

GILLIS, ROBERT ELLIOT, food company executive; b. Lincoln, Maine, June 7, 1938; s. Hugh Allen and Helen (Bucknell) G.; m. Shirley Diane Smith, June 21, 1958; children: Jeffry Todd, Michael Darron, Lauren Ashley. B.A., Pacific U., 1961; postgrad., Grad. Sch. Internat. Relations and Law-U. Conn., 1961. Adminstrv. asst. United Fruit Co., Boston, 1961-62, mgr. export, 1962-63, mgr. sales adminstrn., 1963-65, dir. mktg., 1966-68; pres. Intermarket Internat. Inc., Boston, 1965-66, Concept Foods Corp., Chgo., 1968-70; mgmt. cons.-investor, Stowe, Vt., 1970-76, Dallas, 1970-76; gen. mgr. food service group Central Soya Co. Inc., Ft. Wayne, Ind., 1976-77, gen. mgr. food div., 1977, v.p., 1977-80, group v.p., 1980-83, exec. v.p., pres. food group, 1983—; chmn. bd. J.H. Filbert Inc. subs. Central Soya Co., 1979—, Butcher Boy Food Products Inc., subs., 1982—, Fred's Frozen Foods Inc., subs., 1982—. Bd. govs. Med. Ctr. Hosp., Burlington, Vt., 1974—; trustee Pacific U., Forest Grove, Oreg., 1978—. Mem. Internat. Food service Mfg. Assn. (dir. 1978—, chmn. bd. 1983), Nat. Restaurant Assn. (action com. 1973-75). Republican. Home: 5523 Sherington Rd Fort Wayne IN 46804 Office: Central Soya Co Inc 1300 Fort Wayne Nat Bank Bldg Fort Wayne IN 46802

GILLISPIE, CHARLES COULSTON, history of science educator; b. Harrisburg, Pa., Aug. 6, 1918; s. Raymond Livingston and Virginia Lambert (Coulston) G.; m. Emily Ramsdell Clapp, Jan. 29, 1949. A.B., Wesleyan U., Middletown, Conn., 1940, M.A., 1942, D.Sc., 1971; student, MIT, 1940-41; Ph.D., Harvard U., 1949. Teaching fellow, tutor history Harvard U., 1946-47; faculty Princeton U., 1947—, prof. history sci., 1959-67, Shelby Cullom Davis prof. European history, 1967-73, Dayton-Stockton prof. history, 1973—, chmn. dept. history, 1971-73, dir. program in history and philosophy of sci., 1960-66, 76-80;

AJ Balfour prof. history sci. Weizmann Inst., Israel, 1972; asso. dir. studies Ecole des Hautes Etudes en Sciences Sociales, Paris, 1980—. Author: Genesis and Geology, 1951, A Diderot Pictorial Encyclopedia of Trades and Industry, 2 vols, 1959, The Edge of Objectivity: An essay in the History of Scientific Ideas, 1960, Lazare Carnot, Savant, 1971, Science and Polity in France at the End of the Old Regime, 1980, The Montgolfier Brothers and the Invention of Aviation, 1783-1784, 1983; Editor-in-chief: Dictionary of Scientific Biography. Bd. mgrs. Bach Choir, Bethlehem, Pa., 1976-80. Served to capt. C.W.S. AUS, 1942- 45. Fellow Am. Council Learned Socs., 1951-52; Guggenheim fellow, 1954-55, 70-71; NSF fellow, 1958-59, 62-63; fellow Center for Advanced Study in Behavioral Scis., 1970-71; chaire d'histoire des Sciences, Fondation de France, 1980-82. Fellow AAAS; mem. History Sci. Soc. (council 1952-55, 59-60, pres. 1964-66), Am. Acad. Arts and Scis., Académie Internationale d' Histoire des Sciences (v.p. 1965-68), Am. Philos. Soc., Phi Beta Kappa, Sigma Xi. Clubs: Princeton (N.Y.C.); Nassau (Princeton, N.J.). Home: 3 Morgan Pl Princeton NJ 08540

GILLMAN, LEONARD, mathematician, educator; b. Cleve., Jan. 8, 1917; s. Joseph Moses and Etta Judith (Cohen) G.; m. Reba Parks Marcus, Dec. 24, 1938; children—Jonathan Webb, Michal Judith. Diploma (fellow in piano 1933-38), Juilliard Grad. Sch. Music, 1938; B.S., Columbia, 1941, M.A. (Carnegie fellow math. statistics 1942-43), 1945, Ph.D., 1953. Asst. math. Columbia, 1941-42; operations analyst Tufts Coll., also Mass. Inst. Tech., 1943-51; from instr. to asso. prof. math. Purdue U., 1952-60; prof. math., chmn. dept. U. Rochester, 1960-69; prof. math. U. Tex., Austin, 1969—, chmn. dept., 1969-73; mem. Inst. Advanced Study, Princeton, 1958-60; Cons. editor W.W. Norton Co., Inc., 1967-80. Author: (with Meyer Jerison) Rings of Continuous Functions, 1960, 76, (with Robert H. McDowell) Calculus, 1973, 78; editorial bd.: Topology and Its Applications, 1971—. Guggenheim fellow, 1958-59; NSF sr. post-doctoral fellow, 1959-60. Mem. AAAS, Am. Math. Soc. (asso. sec. 1969-71, mem. com. to monitor problems in communication 1972-77), Nat. Council Tchrs. Math., Math. Assn. Am. (treas. 1973—). Home: 1606 The High Rd Austin TX 78746 Office: Dept Math Univ Texas Austin TX 78712

GILLMAN, RICHARD, company executive; b. Newark, June 5, 1931; s. Julius and Betty (Prager) G.; m. Shaldine Henoch, Apr. 3, 1960; children: Scott, Marc. B.B.A., U. Miami(Fla.), 1954; postgrad., Seton Hall U., 1950-51. Gen. ptnr. Edwards & Hanley, N.Y.C., 1966-74; v.p., dir. Bally Mfg. Corp., N.Y.C., 1974-79; chmn. bd. Bally's Park Place Inc., Atlantic City, N.J., 1979—; dir. Waxman Industries, Cleve., 1975—. Bd. dirs. Atlantic City Casino Hotel Assn., 1983—, Atlantic City Conv. Bur., 1983—, Miss. Am. Pageant, 1982. Mem. N.Y. Stock Exchange. Lodges: Binai B'rith; Masons. Home: Claridge 1 Vernon NJ 07044 Office: Bally's Park Place Inc Park Place and Broadwalk Atlantic City NJ 08401

GILLMOR, CHARLES STEWART, history and science educator, researcher; b. Kansas City, Mo., Nov. 6, 1938; s. Charles Stewart and Evelyn (Noland) G.; m. Rogene Marie Godding, Nov. 28, 1964; Charles Stewart III, Alison Bogue. B.S.E.E., Stanford U., 1962; M.A., Princeton U., 1966, Ph.D., 1968; postgrad., U. Colo., 1963. Lic. 1st class radio telephone operator FCC. Ionospheric physicist Bur. Standards, Antarctica and Boulder, Colo., 1960-62; instr. history Wesleyan U., Middletown, Conn., 1967-68, asst. prof., 1968-72, assoc. prof., 1973-79, prof. history and sci., 1979—; cons. Office Sci. Edn., AAAS, 1973-75; adv. com. Council Internat. Exchange of Scholars, 1978-82; cons. NSF, 1983. Author: Coulomb and the Evolution of Physics and Engineering in 18th Century France, 1971; jour. editor: Transactions Am. Geophys. Union, 1983—; contbr. articles to profl. jours. Mem. troop com. Boy Scouts Am., Haddam, Conn., 1982—; deacon Higganum Congregational Ch., Conn., 1978—. Mt. Gillmor in Antarctica named in his honor, 1963; Social Sci. Research Council grantee, 1971; NSF research grantee, 1972-74, 75-77, 76-79; sr. Fulbright research scholar Cambridge U., Eng., 1976; NASA History scholar, 1980-81. Mem. History of Sci. Soc., AAAS, Am. Geophys. Union, Soc. History of Tech. (adv. council 1978-82), Am. Phys. Soc., Soc. Social Studies of Sci., Sigma Xi. Home: Spencer Rd Higganum CT 06441 Office: Dept of History Wesleyan University Middletown CT 06547

GILLMOR, JOHN EDWARD, lawyer; b. Phila., Oct. 26, 1937; s. John Edward and Louise Ann (Porter) G.; m. Allis Dale Brannon, Aug. 17, 1968; children: Sarah, Abigail, Susan, Eleanor, John, Matthew. B.A., Swarthmore Coll., 1959; LL.B., U. Pa., 1962. Bar: N.Y. 1963, Tenn. 1972, Pa. bar 1980. Asso. Dewey Ballantine Bushby Palmer & Wood, 1962-63, Dewey Ballantine et al, 1966-71; v.p., corp. counsel Hosp. Affiliates Internat., Nashville, 1971-78, sr. v.p., gen. counsel, 1978-79; staff v.p., asst. gen. counsel INA Corp., Phila., 1980; sr. v.p., gen. counsel INA Health Care Group, 1981; partner Gillmor, Mills & Gillmor, 1981—. Served with USMC, 1963-66. Mem. Am. Bar Assn., Bar Assn. City N.Y. Republican. Clubs: Union League (Phila.); World Trade (N.Y.C.). Home: 300 S Fairfield Rd Devon PA 19333 Office: 80 W Lancaster Ave Devon PA 19333

GILLON, JOHN WILLIAM, lawyer; b. Sherman, Tex., Apr. 24, 1900; s. John William and Lucie (Conner) G.; m. Itzselle L. Cook, July 8, 1930 (dec. Sept. 1977); children: John William, Allen C., Edward J., Paul K., Harvey E., David C.; m. Lillian Millar, Aug. 2, 1981. A.B., Miss. Coll.; LL.B. (Lafferty medal), U. Ky., 1925. Bar: Ky., Ala. 1925. Assoc. Coleman, Spain & Stewart, Birmingham, Ala., 1925-35; mem. firm Spain, Gillon & Young, Birmingham, 1935-66, Spain, Gillon, Riley, Tate & Ansley, 1966-72; of counsel Spain, Gillon, Riley, Tate & Etheredge, 1972—; mem. adv. com. on revision of probate code State Bar Ala.; dir., sec. Estes Lumber Co., 1939-64; Mem. Jefferson County Jud. Commn., 1953-58; Chmn. Med. Clinic Bd., City of Birmingham, 1966-74; bd. mem. Estate Planning Council, Birmingham, 1967-70. Served with SATC, 1918. Named Outstanding Lawyer, Birmingham Bar, 1983; cited Ala. Law Inst., 1982. Mem. Am., Ala. bar assns., Birmingham Bar (exec. com. 1955-57, pres. 1960, chmn. ednl. adv. com. 1966-67), Birmingham C. of C., Miss. Coll. Alumni Assn. (dir. 1973-74), Ala. Law Inst., Birmingham Real Estate Bd. (hon. life), Farrah Law Soc., Order of Coif, Blue Goose, Phi Alpha Delta. Club: Lions. Home: Rt 3 Box 444 Leeds AL 35094 Office: John A Hand Bldg Birmingham AL 35203

GILMAN, ALAN B., apparel manufacturing company executive; b. South Bend, Ind., Sept. 24, 1930; s. Sol M. and Lee R. (Rintzler) G.; m. Phyllis Schrager, Feb. 16, 1951; children: Bruce, Jeffrey, Lynn. A.B. with highest honors (Raymond Charles Stoltz scholar), Ind. U., 1952, M.B.A. (John H. Edwards fellow), 1954. With Lazarus Co. div. Federated Dept. Stores, Inc., Columbus, Ohio, 1954-64, div. mdse. mgr., 1961-64; with Sanger Harris div., 1965-74, chmn. bd., chief exec. officer, 1970-74, corp. v.p., 1974; with Abraham & Straus div., 1975-80, chmn. bd., chief exec. officer, 1978-80; pres. Murjani Internat. Ltd., N.Y.C., 1980—; bd. dirs. Ind. U. Found., Bklyn. Acad. Music, Ind. Soc. N.Y., N.Y. Conv. and Visitors Bur.; chmn. dean's adv. council Ind. U. Grad. Sch. Bus. Bd. dirs., pres.-elect, mem. exec. com. Greater N.Y. Fund-United Way; bd. dirs., mem. exec. com. United Way N.Y.C.; bd. govs. Bklyn. Museum. Recipient Humanitarian of Year award Juvenile Diabetes Found., 1979. Mem. Young Pres. Orgn. 49'er, Ind. U. Acad. Alumni Fellows, World Bus. Council, Phi Beta Kappa Assos., Phi Alpha Theta, Beta Gamma Sigma (charter mem. dirs. table). Home: 860 Park Ave New York NY 10021 Office: Murjani Internat Ltd 1411 Broadway New York NY 10018

GILMAN, BENJAMIN ARTHUR, congressman; b. Poughkeepsie, N.Y., Dec. 6, 1922; s. Harry and Esther (Gold) G.; m. Jane Prizant, Oct. 19, 1952 (div. 1978); children: Jonathan, Harrison, Susan, David, Ellen (dec.). B.S., U. Pa., 1946; LL.B., N.Y. Law Sch., 1950. Bar: N.Y. 1952. Dep. asst. atty. gen. N.Y. Dept. Law, 1952-54, asst. atty. gen., 1954-55; partner firm Gilman & Gilman, Middletown, N.Y., 1955-72; counsel N.Y. Assembly's Com. on Local Finance, 1956-64; N.Y. Assemblyman, 95th Dist., 1967-72; mem. 93d-97th Congresses from 26th Dist., N.Y., 1972-82, 98th Congress from 22d Dist. N.Y., 1982—, Fgn. Affairs, Post Office and Civil Service coms., select com. on narcotics; congl. rep. UN Law of Sea Conf., 1975-81, IMF Conf., 1975-78; del. U.S.-Mexican Interparliamentary Conf., 1976-83; mem. Presdl. Commn. on World Hunger, Ad-Hoc Com. on Irish Affairs, Republican Task Force on Handicapped and Task Force on Econ. Policy; chmn. House Task Force on Missing in Action; mem. U.S.-Mex. Consultative Mechanism Subcom. on Narcotics Trafficking; Congl. del. 11th spl. session UN.; chmn. House Task Force on Missing in Action; Mem. adv. com. N.Y. State Div. Youth's Start Center, 1962-67; mem. N.Y. State Southeastern Water Study Com., 1971-73, Lawyers' Com. for Civil Rights Under Law, 1963-75; mem. adv. com. Otisville Fed. Correctional Instn.; v.p., bd. dirs. Orange County Health Assn.; adv. council Lamont-Doherty Geol. Obs., Columbia U., 1979-82; mem. U.S. del. 36th session UN Gen. Assembly. Chmn. bd. dirs. Middletown Little League; bd. dirs. Goldenarea Hosp. Fund; bd. visitors U.S. Mil. Acad., 1973—; lt. col. CAP. Served with USAAF, 1943-45; served to col. USNG. Decorated D.F.C., Air medal. Mem. VFW (past county comdr.), Am. Legion, Masonic War Vets. (lt. comdr.), Jewish War Vets., Forty and Eight, Air Force Assn., Internat. Narcotics Enforcement Officers Assn., Middletown, Orange County, N.Y. State, Am. bar assns., Assn. Bar City N.Y., D.C. Bar, Am. Trial Lawyers Assn., N.Y. Soc. in Washington (pres.), Grange, La Société des 40 Hommes et 8 Chevaux. Republican. Jewish. Clubs: Masons, Capitol Hill Shriners (pres.), Elks.). Home: PO Box 358 Middletown NY 10940 Office: US House of Reps 2160 Rayburn House Office Bldg Washington DC 20515

GILMAN, COOPER LEE, manufacturing company finance executive; b. Tientsin, China, Oct. 3, 1928; s. Frank Shepard and Clare (Cooper) G.; m. Judith Matthews Partelow, July 29, 1961; children: Scott, Bradley. B.S., U.S. Naval Acad., 1951. Indsl. engr. Am. Viscose Corp., Front Royal, Va., 1955-56; fin., engring., mfg. staff and mgmt. positions Gen. Electric Co., Lynn, Mass., 1956-66; asst. controller ITT Semiconductors, West Palm Beach, Fla., 1966-67; controller ITT Gen. Controls, Glendale, Calif., 1967-70; v.p. fin. ITT Aetna, St. Louis, 1970-71; corp. mgr. fin. controls ITT, N.Y.C., 1971-72; v.p., controller Reed Tool Co., Houston, 1972-74; v.p. fin., dir. DeLaval Separator Co., Poughkeepsie, N.Y., 1974-78, Am. Biltrite Inc., Cambridge, Mass., 1978-79; v.p. fin. Caloric Corp., Topton, Pa., 1979-83; group audit mgr. Raytheon Co., Lexington, Mass., 1983—. Served to capt. USMC, 1951-55. Decorated D.F.C., Bronze Star, Air medal (8), Purple Heart. Mem. Am. Mgmt. Assn. Republican. Episcopalian. Home: 27 Lincoln Dr Acton MA 01720 Office: Raytheon Exec Offices Lexington MA 02173

GILMAN, DAVID ALAN, educator; b. Terre Haute, Ind., Sept. 26, 1933; s. Albert Maynard and Ruth Edna (Parsons) G.; m. Elizabeth Ann Barlow, Oct. 7, 1956; children—Ruth Ann, Thomas Alan, William Michael. B.S., Ind. State Tchrs. Coll., 1955; M.A., Mich. State U., 1962; Ph.D. (NSF fellow), Pa. State U., 1967. Tchr. Flint (Mich.) Public Schs., 1955-56, Utica (Mich.) Public Schs., 1957-62; prof. Shippensburg (Pa.) State Coll., 1963-65; prof. edn. Ind. State U., Terre Haute, 1967—; cons. Didactics Corp., 1968-73, NSF, 1974-75. Author: A Course-writer Guide for Teacher-Authors of Materials for Computer-Assisted Instruction, 1967, Alternatives to Tests, Marks and Class Ranks, 1974; contbr. articles to profl. jours. Served with CIC AUS, 1956-58. Recipient Caleb Mills Disting. Teaching award Ind. State U., 1973. Mem. Internat. Audiovisual Soc., Am. Ednl. Research Assn., Blue Key, Kappa Delta Pi, Phi Delta Kappa. Home: 500 Gardendale Rd Terre Haute IN 47803 Office: Ind State U Terre Haute IN 47809

GILMAN, DOROTHY (DOROTHY GILMAN BUTTERS), author; b. New Brunswick, N.J., June 25, 1923; d. J. Bruce and Essa M. (Starkweather) G.; children: Christopher Butters, Jonathan Butters. Student, Pa. Acad. Fine Arts, 1940-45, Art Students League, 1963-64. Instr. creative writing Cherry Lawn Sch., Darien, Conn., 1969-70. Author young people's novels as Dorothy Gilman Butters, 1949-62, including, Girl in Buckskin, 1956, Masquerade, 1961, Bells of Freedom, 1963; author: fiction as Dorothy Gilman Bells of Freedom, 1966—, including; film starring Rosalind Russell The Unexpected Mrs. Pollifax, 1966 (Reader's Digest Book Club selection); Uncertain Voyage, 1967, The Amazing Mrs. Pollifax, 1970 (Reader's Digest Book Club selection), The Elusive Mrs. Pollifax, 1971, A Palm for Mrs. Pollifax, 1973 (Reader's Digest Book Club selection), Nun in the Closet, 1975 (Religious Book award), The Clairvoyant Countess, 1975, Mrs. Pollifax on Safari, 1976 (Reader's Digest Book Club selection), A New Kind of Country, non-fiction, 1978; The Tightrope Walker, 1979 (Reader's Digest Book Club selection), The Maze in the Heart of the Castle, 1983, Mrs. Pollifax on the China Station (Readers Digest Book Club selection 1983); contbr.: short stories as Dorothy Gilman Butters to Redbook. Mem. Authors Guild, Mystery Writers Am. Home: 7 Fox Ct 410 Portland ME 04101 Office: care McIntosh & Otis 475 Fifth Ave New York NY 10017

GILMAN, GLENDELL WILLIAM (GLENN GILMAN), management educator, consultant; b. Waupaca County, Wis., Aug. 9, 1911; s. Francis Clarence and Izola Jane (Pray) G.; m. Elvira Katherine Czeskleba, June 10, 1938 (dec.); 1 dau., Katherine Annette Gilman Upshaw; m. Charlotte Anne Ripley, Jan. 17, 1974. B.S. in Am. History, Central State Coll., Stevens Point, Wis., 1940; M.S. in Mgmt., Ga. Inst. Tech., 1947; Ph.D. in Sociology, U. Chgo., 1955. Tchr. Antigo High Sch., Wis., 1940-41; prof. Coll. Mgmt., Ga. Inst. Tech., Atlanta, 1945-81, prof. emeritus, 1981—; Regents prof. Univ. System of Ga., Atlanta, 1968-81; personnel cons. Lockheed Aircraft, Marietta, Ga., 1955-60; cons. Ga. Cotton Mfg. Assn., Atlanta, 1960-63; dir., corp. sec. Scidata, Inc., Atlanta, 1965-69. Author: Human Relations in the Industrial Southeast, 1956, 78, Causes of Industrial Peace under Col. Bldg.: Case Studies, 1953. Mem. adv. council Ga. State Employment Security Agy., 1960-72; mem. legis. subcom. Ga. State Employment Security Agy., 1968-72. Served to capt. USMC, 1942-45; to col. USMCR, 1945-60. Mem. Am. Sociol. Assn. Episcopalian. Clubs: Commerce, Ansley Golf. Home: 275-A Lakemoore Dr NE Atlanta GA 30342

GILMAN, HERBERT, department store chain executive; b. Hartford, Conn., Dec. 25, 1924; s. Nathan and Pauline (Lapuk) G.; m. Evelyn S. Simon, June 20, 1948; children: Barbara R., Randy A. B.S.E.E., U. Conn., 1949. Project engr. Sperry Gyroscope Co., 1950-54; sales engr. Hewlett Packard Co., Palo Alto, Calif., 1954-58; exec. v.p. Ames Dept. Stores Inc., Rocky Hill, Conn., 1958-73; pres. Ames Dept. Stores Inc, Rocky Hills, Conn., 1973-82; chmn. bd. Ames Dept. Stores Inc., Rocky Hill, Conn., 1982—, dir. Trustee Mt. Sinai Hosp., Hartford; bd. dirs Hartford Jewish Fedn. Served with U.S. Army, 1943-45. Mem. Nat. Mass Retailers Inst. (bd. dirs. 1970—). Jewish. Office: Ames Dept Stores Inc 2418 Maine St Rocky Hill CT 06117

GILMAN, JOHN JOSEPH, oil company research director; b. St. Paul, Dec. 22, 1925; s. Alexander Falk and Florence Grace (Colby) G.; m. Pauline Marie Harms, June 17, 1950 (div. Dec. 1968); children: Pamela Ann, Gregory George, Cheryl Elizabeth; m. Gretchen Marie Sutter, June 12, 1976; 1 son, Brian Alexander. B.S., Ill. Inst. Tech., 1946, M.S., 1948; Ph.D., Columbia, 1952. Research metallurgist Gen. Electric Co., Schenectady, 1952-60; prof. engring. Brown U., Providence, 1960-63; prof. physics and metallurgy U. Ill., Urbana, 1963-68; dir. Materials Research Center Allied Chem. Corp., Morristown, N.J., 1968-78; dir. Corp. Devel. Center, 1978-80; mgr. corp. research Standard Oil Co. (Ind.), Naperville, Ill., 1980—; mem. solid state scis. com. Nat. Acad. Scis., 1979-82. Author: Micromechanics of Flow in Solids, 1969; Editor: The Art and Science of Growing Crystals, 1963, (with D.C. Drucker) Fracture of Solids, 1963, Atomic and Electronic Structures of Metals, 1967; editorial bd.: Jour. Applied Physics, 1969-72; Contbr. papers, articles to tech. jours. Served as ensign USNR, 1943-46. Recipient Mathewson gold medal Am. Inst. Mech. Engrs., 1959, Distinguished service award Alumni Assn. Ill. Inst. Tech., 1962. Fellow Am. Phys. Soc., Am. Soc. for Metals (Campbell lectr. 1966); mem. Nat. Acad. Engring., Phi Kappa Phi, Tau Beta Pi. Home: 1131 Franklin Ave River Forest IL 60305 Office: AMOCO Research Center Naperville IL 60540

GILMAN, LEONARD RAYMOND, U.S. attorney; b. Detroit, Jan. 7, 1942; s. Hyman Norman and Alice (Weiner) G.; m. Donna Marie Rachunok, Mar. 15, 1970; 1 dau., Kelly Ann. B.S., Wayne State U., 1963, J.D. with distinction, 1967. Bar: Mich. 1967, U.S. Dist. Ct. (ea. dist.) Mich. 1967, U.S. Ct. Appeals (6th cir.) 1978, U.S. Supreme Ct. 1980. Field att. NLRB, Detroit, 1966-68; asst. pros. atty. Wayne County Prosecutor's Office, Detroit, 1968-73; sr. trail lawyer Oakland County Prosecutor's Office, Pontiac, Mich., 1973-78; chief Criminal div. U.S. Atty.'s Office, Detroit, 1978-81, U.S. atty., 1981—; instr. Harvard Law Sch., 1973, U. Mich. Law Sch., Ann Arbor, 1978—. Recipient U.S. Dept. Justice Dir.'s award, 1980, Meritorious Service award Drug Enforcement Admistrn., 1981. Mem. State Bar Mich., Oakland County Bar Assn., Legal Aid Found. Detroit. Republican. Jewish. Office: U S Atty's Office 817 Federal Bldg Detroit MI 48226

GILMAN, RICHARD, author, educator; b. N.Y.C., Apr. 30, 1925; s. Jacob and Marion (Wolinsky) G.; 1 son, Nicholas; m. Lynn Nesbit; children: Priscilla, Claire. B.A., U. Wis., 1947; L.H.D., Grinnell Coll., 1967. Free-lance writer, 1950-54; assoc. editor Jubilee mag., 1954-57; drama critic, lit. editor Commonweal, 1961-64; assoc. editor, drama critic Newsweek mag., 1964-67; lit. editor New Republic, 1968-70; prof. drama Yale U., 1967-78, 79—; vis. lectr. English, Columbia U., 1964-65; vis. prof. drama Stanford U., summer 1967; vis. prof. theater arts CCNY, 1978-79; pres. PEN Am. Center, 1981-83, v.p., 1983—. Author: The Confusion of Realms, 1970, Common and Uncommon Masks, 1971, The Making of Modern Drama, 1974; Decadence, 1979; contbg. editor: Partisan Rev., 1972—. Served with USMCR, 1943-46. Recipient George Jean Nathan award for drama criticism, 1971; Morton Dauwen Zabel award Am. Acad. and Inst. Arts and Letters, 1979; fellow N.Y. Inst. for Humanities., 1977-80. Office: Yale Sch Drama New Haven CT 06520

GILMAN, RICHARD CARLETON, college president; b. Cambridge, Mass., July 28, 1923; s. George Phillips Brooks and Karen Elise (Theller) G.; m. Lucille Young, Aug. 28, 1948 (dec. June 1978); children: Marsha, Bradley Morris, Brian Potter, Blair Tucker. B.A., Dartmouth, 1944; student, New Coll., U. London, Eng., 1947-48; Ph.D. (Borden Parker Bowne fellow philosophy), Boston U., 1952, L.H.D., 1969; LL.D., Pomona Coll., 1966, U. So. Calif., 1968, Coll. Idaho, 1968. Teaching fellow religion Dartmouth, 1948; mem. faculty Colby Coll., 1950-56, asso. prof. philosophy, 1955-56; exec. dir. Nat. Council Religion Higher Edn., New Haven, 1956-60; dean coll., prof. philosophy Carleton Coll., 1960-65; pres. Occidental Coll., 1965—; Bd. dirs. Ind. Colls. So. Calif., pres., 1983-84; Bd. dirs. Assn. Ind. Calif. Colls. and Univs., Los Angeles World Affairs Council; mem. Intergovtl. Adv. Council on Edn., 1980-82; mem. council of pres.'s Assn. Gov. Bds.; mem. policy planning commn. Nat. Assn. Ind. Colls. and Univs. Served with USNR, 1944-46. Fellow Soc. Values in Higher Edn.; mem. Newcomen Soc., Calif. C. of C. (dir.), Phi Beta Kappa. Presbyterian. Clubs: Univ. (N.Y.C.); Calif. (Los Angeles). Home: 1852 Campus Rd Los Angeles CA 90041

GILMAN, SAMUEL VINCENT, JR., insurance company executive; b. Orange, N.J., Sept. 12, 1931; s. Samuel Vincent and Hellaine A. (Packard) G.; m. Cecilia Birdsall, June 16, 1962; children: Elizabeth, Samuel, Caroline. A.B., Harvard U., 1953, M.B.A., 1957. Sr. v.p. and dir. Chubb & Son, Warren, N.J., 1958—; dir. Summit and Elizabeth Trust Co., Summit, N.J., Bellmead Devel. Corp., Lyndhurst, N.J. Republican. Roman Catholic. Home: 129 Ridge Rd Rumson NJ 07760 Office: Chubb & Son Inc 15 Mountain View Rd Warren NJ 07061

GILMAN, SANDER LAWRENCE, German educator; b. Buffalo, Feb. 21, 1944; s. William and Rebecca (Helf) G.; m. Marina von Eckardt, Dec. 28, 1969; children: Daniel, Samuel. B.A., Tulane U., 1963, Ph.D., 1968; postgrad., univs. Berlin and Munich, Ger. Lectr. German St. Mary's Dominican Coll., New Orleans, 1963-64; instr. Dillard U., New Orleans, 1967-68; asst. prof. Case Western Res. U., 1968-69; mem. faculty Cornell U., 1969—, prof. German, 1976—; chmn. dept. German lit., 1974-81, 83-84; fellow dept. psychiatry Cornell U. Med. Coll., 1977-78, prof. history of psychiatry, 1978—; O'Connor prof. Colgate U., 1982. Author, editor: 10 books including Bertolt Brecht's Berlin, 1975; 15 books including Nietzschean Parody, 1976; 10 books including The Face of Madness, 1976, Klingers Werke, 1978, On Blackness without Blacks, 1982, Begegnungen mit Nietzsche, 1981, Seeing the Insane, 1981, Wahnsinn, Text und Kontext, 1981; also essays.; Editorial bd.: Diacritics, 1971-72, Lessing Yearbook, 1974—, German Quar, 1977—; asso. editor: Confinia psychiatrica, 1978-80. Guggenheim fellow, 1972-73; IREX exchange fellow German Democratic Republic, 1976; Soc. for Humanities faculty fellow Cornell U., 1981-82. Mem. Modern Lang Assn., Lessing Soc., Am. Assn. Tchrs. German, Soc. Internat. d'Études Littéraires et Psychiatres, Internat. Assn. Germanists. Democrat. Jewish. Home: 305 Cornell St Ithaca NY 14850 Office: Dept German Lit Goldwin Smith Hall Cornell Univ Ithaca NY 14853

GILMAN, SHIRLEY J., sports and recreational equipment manufacturing company executive. Pres., treas. Marty Gilman, Inc., Gilman, Conn. Office: Marty Gilman Inc Gilman CT 06336§

GILMAN, SID, neurologist; b. Los Angeles, Oct. 19, 1932; s. Morris and Sarah Rose (Cooper) G. B.A., UCLA, 1954; M.D., 1957. Intern UCLA Hosp., 1957-58; resident in neurology Boston City Hosp., 1960-63; from instr. to assoc. in neurology Harvard Med. Sch., 1965-68; from asst. prof. to prof. neurology Columbia U., N.Y.C., 1968-76; H. Houston Merritt prof. neurology, 1976-77; prof., chmn. dept. neurology U. Mich., Ann Arbor, 1977—; cons. VA Hosp., Ann Arbor; adj. attending neurologist Henry Ford Hosp., Detroit. Author: (with J.R. Bloedel and R. Lechtenberg) Disorders of the Cerebellum, 1981, (with Sarah S. Winans) Manter and Gatz's Essentials of Clinical Neuroanatomy and Neurophysiology, 1982; mem. editorial bd.: Jour. Neuropathology and Exptl. Neurology, (Neurology), (Annals of

Neurology), (Exptl. Neurology); contbr. articles to profl. jours. Mem. research adv. council United Cerebral Palsy Found.; mem. profl. adv. bd. Epilepsy Found. Am.; mem. sci. adv. council Nat. Amyotrophic Lateral Sclerosis Found. Served with USPHS, 1958-60. Recipient Weinstein Goldenson award United Cerebral Palsy Assn., 1981; Lucy G. Moses prize Columbia U., 1973. Mem. Am. Neurol. Assn., Am. Soc. Clin. Investigation, Am. Physiol. Soc., Am. Assn. Neuropathologists, Soc. Neurosci., Am. Acad. Neurology, Am. Epilepsy Soc., Assn. Research and Nervous and Mental Disease, AAAS. Home: 3411 Geddes Rd Ann Arbor MI 48105 Office: Dept Neurology U Mich Ann Arbor MI 48109

GILMAN, STANLEY FRANCIS, engineering educator; b. Portland, Maine, Mar. 31, 1921; s. Frank William and Elotia Ann (Noyes) G.; m. Jean Elizabeth Murphy, Feb. 4, 1943; children: Susan, Michael, Kathleen, Steven, Christine. B.S. in Mech. Engrng, U. Me., 1943; M.S., U. Ill., 1948, Ph.D., 1953. Registered profl. engr., N.Y., Pa. Co-owner Gilman Furnace Co., Portland, 1945-47; asst. prof. mech. engrng. U. Ill., 1949-53; research and engrng. mgmt. Carrier Corp., 1953-70; v.p. engrng. Climatrol Industries, Milw., 1970-71; mgr. mktg. internat. group Am. Air Filter Co., Louisville, 1971-73; prof. archtl. engrng. Pa. State U., University Park, 1973—. Contbr. articles to profl. jours. Served to lt. USNR, 1943-46. Mem. Am. Soc. Heating, Refrigrating and Air Conditioning Engrs. (dir., treas., v.p. 1964-72, pres. 1971-72), Nat. Soc. Prof. Engrs., Sigma Xi, Tau Beta Pi, Pi Tau Sigma, Sigma Alpha Epsilon. Republican. Roman Catholic. Patentee in field. Home: 505 Cricklewood Dr State College PA 16801 Office: Engring A Bldg University Park PA 16802

GILMER, B. VON HALLER, retired educator, industrial psychologist; b. Draper, Va., June 15, 1909; s. Beverly Tucker and Willie Sue (Graham) G.; m. Ellen Conduff, Aug. 23, 1934; 1 dau., Nancy Tucker. B.S., King Coll., 1930; M.S., U. Va., 1932, Ph.D., 1934. Instr. psychology King Coll., Bristol, Tenn., 1934-36; asst. prof. psychology Carnegie Inst. Tech. (now Carnegie-Mellon U.), 1936-42, prof. psychology, dept. head, 1947-76; prof. psychology Va. Poly. Inst. and State U., 1976—; asso. prof. psychology U. Va., 1946-47; vis. prof. U. Calif. at Berkeley, 1964-65; adviser U.S. Office Edn., 1949-51; cons. USAF, 1950-51. Author: 18 books on psychology, including Industrial and Organizational Psychology, 4th edit, 1977, Applied Psychology, 1975; also numerous research publs. Bd. dirs. Pitts. Child Guidance Center, Inc., 1952—, Mental Health Soc. Allegheny County, 1954—; bd. visitors King Coll., 1970-76. Served from 1st lt. to maj. USAAF, 1942-46. Recipient Nat. Author award Am. Soc. Tng. and Devel., 1966. Fellow Am. (mem. edn. and tng. bd. 1955-57), Eastern psychol. assns.; mem. So. Soc. Philosophy and Psychology (pres. 1948), Pa. Psychol. Assn. (dir. 1953-54), Pitts. Psychol. Assn. (dir. 1950-51), Sigma Xi, Phi Kappa Phi, Phi Sigma Pi. Presbyn. Home: RD Box 134 Draper VA 24324 *The behavioral sciences will provide no easy solutions in the near future to our many human problems, but they are a good bet in the long run.*

GILMER, ROBERT, mathematics educator; b. Pontotoc, Miss., July 3, 1938; s. Robert William and Lucy Marie (Jernigan) G.; m. Rachel Grace Colson, Aug. 24, 1963; children: David Patrick, Stephen Douglas. Student, Itawamba Jr. Coll., 1955-56; B.S., Miss. State U., 1958; M.S., La. State U., 1960, Ph.D., 1961. Instr., Miss. State U., Starkville, 1958, vis. prof., 1962; research instr. La. State U., Baton Rouge, 1961-62; vis. lectr. U. Wis., Madison, 1962-63; mem. faculty Fla. State U., Tallahassee, 1963—, prof. math., 1968—, Robert O. Lawton disting. prof., 1981—; vis. prof. Latrobe U., Bundoora, Victoria, Australia, 1974, U. Tex., Austin, 1976-77; vis. research prof. U. Conn., Storrs, 1982. Author: Multiplicative Ideal Theory, 1967, 72; also articles.; assoc. editor: Am. Math. Monthly, 1971-73; editorial bd.: Jour. Communications in Algebra, 1974—. Office Naval Research fellow, 1962-63; Alfred P. Sloan Found. fellow, 1965-67; NSF grantee, 1965—; Fulbright sr. scholar to Australia, 1974. Mem. Am. Math. Soc., Math. Assn. Am. Baptist. Home: 2414 Perez Tallahassee FL 32304

GILMONT, ERNEST RICH, chemist; b. Boston, July 1, 1929; s. Bernard I. and Ethel (Rich) Goldberg; m. Joy L. Pasternack, Oct. 23, 1965. A.B., Middlebury Coll., 1951, M.S., 1952; Ph.D. (Bristol Overseas fellow), MIT, 1956. Research chemist FMC Corp., 1956-58, group leader, 1958-61; dir. research and devel. U.S. Peroxygen Corp., 1961-62; sr. scientist Millmaster Chem. Corp., Berkeley Heights, N.J., 1962-66; dir. research and devel. A. Gross & Co., Newark, 1966-70, tech. dir., 1970-78; gen. mgr. Copygraphics, Fairfield, N.J., 1978-82; dir. tech. M&T Chems. Inc., Woodbridge, N.J., 1982—; v.p. Sci. Manpower Commn., 1976, 77; Robert A. Welch Found.; lectr., 1975. Contbr. articles to profl. jours. Recipient Disting. Service award Assn. Cons. Chemists Chem. Engrs., 1977. Fellow AAAS; mem. Am. Chem. Soc., Am. Inst. Chem. Engrs., Am. Inst. Chemists (pres. 1973-75, chmn. bd. 1976), Assn. Research Dirs., Council Sci. Soc. Presidents (chmn. 1975, 76, 77-78), Soc. Chem. Industry, N.J. Inst. Chemists (pres. 1970-71, Honor Scroll 1974), Sigma Xi. Club: Chemists (trustee 1977-79). Patentee organic peroxides. Home: 146 Central Park W New York NY 10023 Office: M&T Chems One Woodbridge Ctr Woodbridge NJ 07095

GILMORE, ART, TV performer; b. Tacoma, Mar. 18, 1912; s. Oscar Borden and Ada Louise (Wells) G.; m. Grace Elsie Weller, May 18, 1938; children—Marilyn Grace, Barbara Jo. Student, Coll. Puget Sound, 1930-31, 34, Wash. State Coll., 1934-35. V.p. Hollywood Radio Pubs., Chalo Pines Corp. Singer, commentator radio stas., Tacoma, 1934; staff announcer, KWSC, Pullman, Wash., 1934, KOL, Seattle, 1935, CBS-KNX, Hollywood, Calif., 1936-41; free lance, 1941—, TV, 1950—; narrator: children's albums Am. Bapt. Conv. Laymen's Hour, Capitol Records, short subjects, Warner Bros., Universal, Dudley Pictures, tng. films, Armed Forces; show announcer: Red Skelton Hour, 1954-71; Author: (with G.Y. Middleton) Television and Radio Announcing, 1946. Bd. dirs. Rec. for the Blind. Served to lt. USNR, 1943-45. Mem. Pacific Pioneer Broadcasters (founding pres.), Episcopal Theater Guild Los Angeles (founding pres.), AFTRA (nat. pres. 1961-63, past pres. permanent charities com. of entertainment industry). Clubs: Rotarian (Sherman Oaks) (past pres.); Icarian Flying.). Home: 14115 Greenleaf St Sherman Oaks CA 91423

GILMORE, ARTIS, profl. basketball player; b. Chipley, Fla., Sept. 21, 1949. Grad., Jacksonville U., 1971. Center Ky. Cols., Louisville, 1971-76; with Chgo. Bulls, 1976—; mem. Am. Basketball Assn. All-Star team, 1972-76, Nat. Basketball Assn. All-Star Team, 1978. Named Rookie of the Year Am. Basketball Assn., 1972, Player of the Year, 1972. Address: C/O San Antonio Spurs PO Box 530 San Antonio TX 78292

GILMORE, CLARENCE PERCY, writer, editor; b. Baton Rouge, Feb. 8, 1926; s. Clarence Percy and Clara (Cobb) G.; m. Noel Dillard, Mar. 17, 1956; children—Robert Dillard, Patricia Anne. Student, La. State U., 1942-44, 46-48. Reporter various radio, TV stas., 1948-56, free-lance mag. writer, 1956—; sci. editor Metromedia TV, 1967—; editor-in-chief Times Mirror Mags., N.Y.C., 1971—; Cons. in field. Served with USNR, 1944-46. Recipient Claude Bernard sci. journalism award Nat. Soc. Med. Research, 1969; Albert and Mary Lasker Found. award, 1969; Howard W. Blakeslee award Am. Heart Assn., 1969; Spl. commendation med. journalism A.M.A., 61969, 70; Sci. Writing award physics and astronomy Am. Inst. Physics, 1970, AAAS, 1980. Mem. Nat. Assn. Sci. Writers, AAAS. Home: 201 W 70th St New York NY 10023 Office: 380 Madison Ave New York NY 10017

GILMORE, HORACE WELDON, U.S. dist. judge; b. Columbus, Ohio, Apr. 4, 1918; s. Charles Thomas and Lucille (Weldon) G.; m. Mary Hays, June 20, 1942; children—Lindsay Gilmore Lasser, Frances Gilmore Hayward. A.B., U. Mich., 1939, J.D., 1942. Bar: Mich. bar 1946. Law clk. U.S. Ct. Appeals, 1946-47; practiced in, Detroit, 1947-51; spl. asst. U.S. atty., Detroit, 1951-52; mem. Mich. Bd. Tax Appeals, 1954; dep. atty. gen. State of Mich., 1955-56; circuit judge 3d Jud. Circuit, Detroit, 1956-80; judge U.S. Dist. Ct., 1980—; adj. prof. law Wayne State U. Law Sch., 1966—; lectr. law U. Mich. Law Sch., 1969—; faculty Nat. Coll. State Judiciary, 1966—; mem. Mich. Jud. Tenure Commn., 1969-76; chmn. Mich. Com. To Revise Criminal Code, 1965—, Mich. Com. To Revise Criminal Procedure, 1971-79; trustee Inst. for Ct. Mgmt. Author: Michigan Civil Procedure Before Trial, 2d edit, 1975; contbr. numerous articles to legal jours. Served with USNR, 1942-46. Mem. Am. Bar Assn., State Bar Mich., Am. Judicature Soc., Am. Law Inst., Nat. Conf. State Trial Judges. Office: 802 US Courthouse Detroit MI 48226

GILMORE, JAMES STANLEY, JR., broadcasting company executive; b. Kalamazoo, June 14, 1926; s. James Stanley and Ruth (McNair) G.; m. Diana Holdenreide Fell, May 21, 1949 (dec.); children: Bethany, Sydney, James Stanley III, Elizabeth, Ruth; m. Susan Chitty Maggio, Sept. 13, 1980. Student, Culver Mil. Acad., Western Mich. U., Kalamazoo Coll., 1945; Litt.D. (hon.), Nazareth Coll. Owner, pres. Jim Gilmore Enterprises, Kalamazoo, 1960—; pres. Gilmore Broadcasting Corp.; chmn. bd., pres. Gilmore Advt., Inc.; pres. Jim Gilmore Cadillac-Pontiac Datsun Inc., Gilmore Racing Team, Inc. (A.J. Foyt, driver); v.p., dir. Holiday Inn-Continental Corp. Mich.; asst. sec., dir. Fabri-Kal Plastics Corp., Kalamazoo; partner Hotel Investment Realty Corp., Greater Kalamazoo Sports, Inc. (hockey franchise), Kalamazoo Stadium Co.; dir., mem. trust com. First Nat. Bank & Trust Co., Kalamazoo; dir. First Nat. Bank Financial Corp., Mich. Carton div. St. Regis Paper Co., So. Mich. Inn Corp., Sturgis, Continental Lanes, Kalamazoo; presdl. advisor Republic Airlines.; Mem. Pres.' Citizens Adv. Com. on Environmental Quality; dir. Fed. Home Loan Bank Bd., Indpls.; mem., past chmn. Mich. Water Resources Commn.; mem. Mich. Gov.'s Forum; mem. nat. adv. cancer council HEW; mem. Nat. Assn. Broadcasters' adv. com. to Corp. for Pub. Broadcasting.; Pres. Kalamazoo County Young Rep. Club, 1947-49; mayor Kalamazoo, 1959-61; past mem. Kalamazoo County Bd. Suprs.; past chmn. Kalamazoo County Rep. Exec. Com.; del. Rep. Nat. Conv. Asso. bd. dirs. Boys Clubs Am.; bd. dirs., past chmn. Kalamazoo County chpt. A.R.C.; former chmn. bd. trustees Nazareth Coll.; trustee, mem. finance com. Greater Mich. Devel. Found.; mem., chmn. bldg. com. fund dr. Constance Brown Speech and Hearing Center; past trustee Kalamazoo Coll.; mem. adv. group Center Urban Studies and Community Services; trustee past vice chmn. Kalamazoo Nature Center; mem. bldg. and exec. coms. Bronson Hosp., also chmn. ad hoc legis. com.; past trustee, past v.p. Mich. Found. for Arts, Detroit; founder bd. dirs. Martin Luther King Meml. Fund; life dir. Family Service Center Kalamazoo; mem. Mich. bd. dirs. Radio Free Europe; nat. sponsor Ducks Unlimited; life mem. March Dimes; chmn. spl. reorganizational com. United Fund; mem. fund raising com. Pres. Ford Library/Mus.; hon. trustee Mich. Alvin Bentley Charitable Found. Served with USAAF, 1943-46. Named Kalamazoo Young Man of 1960, One of Mich.'s 5 Young Men of 1960, hon. citizen of Houston and Indpls.; recipient Ann. Service to Mankind award Sertoma Club; Man of Yr. award Mich. Auto Racing Fan Club, Auto Racing Found. Frat.; honors Hoosier Racing Assn., Auto Racing Frat. Found., Inc., Milw. Mem. Kalamazoo County C. of C. (past pres., past dir., mem. exec. com. of indsl. devel. com.), Mich. C. of C. (mem. law and order com.), N.A.M., Mich. Acad. Sci., Arts and Letters. Episcopalian (mem. bd. diocese Western Mich., chmn. cathedral drive, mem. com. Bishop Whittemore Found.). Clubs: Capitol Hill (Washington); Park (Richland, Mich.) (past dir.); Mid-America (Chgo.); Otsego Ski (Gaylord, Mich.); Ocean Reef (Key Largo, Fla.). Home: 1550 Long Rd Kalamazoo MI 49008 also 5040 Woodlawn Beach Gull Lake Hickory Corners MI 49060 25 Card Sound Ocean Reef Club Key Largo FL Office: Jim Gilmore Enterprises 202 Mich Bldg Kalamazoo MI 49006

GILMORE, JERRY CARL, lawyer; b. Memphis, Dec. 29, 1933; s. Hugh Bailey and Gladys Herd (Jones) G.; m. Martha Niendorff, Dec. 1, 1956; children: Daniel, Susan, Charles. B.A., U. Tex., 1955, J.D., 1957. Bar: Tex. 1957. Since practiced in Dallas; Pres. North Central Tex. Council Govts., 1974-75, also exec. bd.; chmn. steering com. transp. Nat. League of Cities, 1974; mem. Dallas City Council, 1971-75. Mem. City of Dallas Transit Bd., 1979-80; Former bd. dirs., pres. Suicide Prevention of Dallas; former chmn. bd. trustees Dallas County Mental Health-Mental Retardation Center; trustee Dallas County Community Coll. Dist., 1979—, chmn., 1981-82; dir. home mission bd. So. Bapt. Conv., 1979—, chmn., 1983—. Named Outstanding Young Lawyer, Dallas Jr. Bar Assn., 1971; recipient Outstanding Community Service award Oak Cliff Civitan Club, 1972. Mem. Dallas, Am. bar assns., State Bar Tex., High Noon Club of Dallas (pres. 1967-68), Dallas Assembly, Oak Cliff C. of C., Delta Theta Phi. Baptist (deacon). Clubs: Masons, Shriners, Lions. Home: 1608 W Colorado St Dallas TX 75208 Office: 1800 N Market St Dallas TX 75202

GILMORE, JESSE LEE, educator; b. Grants Pass, Oreg., Jan. 22, 1920; s. Rufus Alva and Eda Augusta (Haberman) G.; m. Chloe Eleanor Anderson, Dec. 21, 1946; children—Cherie Elaine, Eric Franklin. B.A., Willamette U., 1942; M.A., U. Calif. at, Berkeley, 1948; Ph.D., U. Calif.-, Berkeley, 1952. Mem. faculty Portland (Oreg.) State U., 1953—, prof. history, 1967—; chmn. dept., 1965-75. Served with AUS, 1942-45; ETO, CBI. Mem. Am. Hist. Assn., Orgn. Am. Historians., AAUP. Home: 11720 SW Blakeney St Beaverton OR 97005 Office: PO Box 751 Portland OR 97207

GILMORE, JOSEPH PATRICK, educator; b. N.Y.C., Sept. 30, 1928; s. Thomas E. and Veronica (Burns) G.; m. Harriet E. Kuhlmann, Sept. 4, 1950; children—Cathleen, JoAnne, Dennis, Gerard. B.S.; St. John's Coll., Bklyn., 1950; M.S., St. John's U., Bklyn., 1952; Ph.D., George Washington U., 1963. Head dept. physiology Navy Med. Research Lab., Camp Lejeune, N.C., 1952-58; with lab. cardio-physiology NIH, Bethesda, Md., 1958-66; prof. physiology U. Va., Charlottesville, 1966-70; prof., chmn. dept. physiology U. Neb., Omaha, 1970—; Cons. Nat. Heart and Lung Inst.; Mem. med. adv. bd. Council for High Blood Pressure, Am. Heart Assn., 1974—. Mem. editorial bd.: Am. Jour. Physiology, 1966-72, Jour. Applied Physiology, 1966-72, Circulation Research, 1972-77, 80—, Basic Research in Cardiology, 1973—; Contbr. articles to profl. jours. Recipient NIH Career Devel. award, 1967. Fellow Am. Coll. Cardiology; mem. Am. Physiol. Soc., Am. Soc. for Pharmacology and Exptl. Therapeutics, Am. Soc. Nephrology, Am. Heart Assn., Soc. for Exptl. Biology and Medicine (council 1978—). Home: 208 S 119th St Omaha NE 68154

GILMORE, MAURICE EUGENE, mathematics educator; b. N.Y.C., Jan. 2, 1938; s. Mauirce Eugene and Mary Wells (Barnes) G.; m. Julie Anne Rogers, June 20, 1964; children: Peter Barnes, Christopher Alan, Jessica Lynne. B.A., Georgetown U., 1959; M.S., Syracuse U., 1961; Ph.D., U. Calif., Bereley, 1966. Instr. Northeastern U., Boston, 1966-68, asst. prof., 1968-72, assoc. prof., 1972-78, prof., 1978-83, chmn. math. dept., 1975—; vis. prof. U. Tecnica Del Estado, Santiago, Chile, 1968. NSF grantee, 1979. Mem. Math. Assn. Am., Am. Math. Soc. Democrat. Roman Catholic. Office: Northeastern U 360 Huntington Ave Boston MA 02115

GILMORE, ROBERT CURRIE, rail company executive; b. Vancouver, B.C., Can., Aug. 22, 1926; s. Robert H. and Isabel M. (Currie) G.; m. Shelagh M. Rowlette, Mar. 9, 1957; children: Katherine, Claudia, Robin, Jennifer. B. Comm., U. B.C., 1954. With Can. Pacific Rail, 1961—, asst. to gen. mgr. and mgr. mktg., Montreal, Que., Can., 1961-66, systems mgr. market planning, 1966-70, regional mgr. mktg. and sales, Toronto, Ont., Can., 1970-71, gen. mgr. mktg. and sales, 1972-74, asst. v.p. mktg. and sales, Montreal, Que., Can., 1974-75, 77, v.p. mktg. and sales, 1977—; dir. Aroostook River R.R. Co., Can. Pacific Steamships Ltd., CanPac Terminals Ltd., Houlton Br. R.R. Co., Incan Ships Ltd., Incan Superior Ltd., Internat. R.R. Co. of Maine, Soo Line R.R. Co., Thunder Bay Terminals Ltd.; apptd to coal industry adv. bd. Internat. Energy Agy., Paris, 1980. Mem. Nat. Freight Transp. Assn., Montreal Bd. Trade. Clubs: Whitlock Golf (Hudson, Que.); Can. Ry., Traffic of Montreal. Home: 630 Main Rd Hudson Heights PQ Canada J0P 1J0 Office: CP Rail 910 Peel St Room 321 Montreal PQ Canada H3C 3E4

GILMORE, ROBERT EUGENE, earthmoving machinery manufacturing executive; b. nr. Peoria, Ill., May 4, 1920; s. Myron E. and Lillian G. (Mallm) G.; m. Marguerite A. Best, May 1, 1948; children: Christine Ann, Scott Eugene. Grad. high sch. With Caterpillar Tractor Co., Peoria, 1938—; pres. Caterpillar France, Grenoble, 1963-68, gen. mgr. worldwide mfg. and facilities planning, 1968, gen. mgr. U.S. mfg. plants, 1968-69, v.p. U.S. mfg. plants, 1969-73, exec. v.p., 1973-77, pres., chief operating officer, 1977—, also dir.; dir. Santa Fe So. Pacific Corp., Security Savs. & Loan Assn., Peoria.; bd. dirs. SME Mfg. Engring. Edn. Found. Chmn., Peoria Area Hosp. Council; bd. dirs. Peoria Econ. Devel. Council. Served to 1st lt. USAAF, 1943-45; ETO. Decorated Air medal with 4 oak leaf clusters. Mem. Soc. Automotive Engrs., Nat. Exec. Service Corps. (mem. council). Republican. Lutheran. Clubs: Peoria Country; Union League (Chgo.). Lodge: Masons. Office: 100 NE Adams St Peoria IL 61629

GILMORE, ROBERT KARL, univ. adminstr.; b. Springfield, Mo., June 6, 1927; s. Herbert F. and Beulah M. (Whitehead) G.; m. Martha M. Lyons, Aug. 7, 1950; children—Julie, Tom, Michael. B.S., S.W. Mo. State Coll., 1950; M.A., St. Louis U., 1954; Ph.D., U. Minn., 1961. Tchr. public schs., St. Louis County, Mo., 1949-57; instr. U. Minn., 1957-59; asst. prof. speech and theatre S.W. Mo. State U., 1959-61, asso. prof., 1961-65, prof., 1965—, head dept. speech and theatre, 1965-67, dean, 1967-71, provost, dean faculties, 1971—. Served with USN, 1945-46. Mem. North Central Assn. Acad. Deans, Speech Communication Assn., Central States Speech Assn. Lutheran. Club: Rotary. Office: 901 S National St Springfield MO 65802

GILMORE, ROGER, educational administrator; b. Phila., Oct. 11, 1932; s. Wheeler and Edith Seal (Thompson) G.; m. Beatrice Reynolds, Sept. 17, 1952; children: Christopher, Jennifer E., Lesley Margaret. A.B., Dartmouth Coll., 1954; postgrad., U. Chgo. Div. Sch., 1958-63. Social worker N.H. Dept. Pub. Welfare, Woodsville, 1954-55; adminstrv. asst. Furn Corp. Lisbon (N.H.), 1955-56; office mgr., asst. to pres. Cole's Mill Inc., Littleton, N.H., 1956-58; accountant, office supr. U. Chgo., 1958-61, asst. dir. fin. aid, 1961-63; asst. to dean Sch. Art Inst. Chgo., 1963-65, acting dean, 1965-68, dean, 1968—; Dir. commn. accreditation and membership Nat. Assn. Schs. Art, 1976-79; chmn. deans com. Union Ind. Colls. Art, 1975-78; mem. Joint Commn. on Dance and Theatre Accreditation, 1979-82. Mem. Soc. Archtl. Historians, Nat. Trust for Historic Preservation, Advs. for Arts, Am. Assn. Higher Edn., Internat. Council Fine Arts Deans; mem. Coll. Art Assn., Landmarks Preservation Council, Nat. Art Edn. Assn. Democrat. Episcopalian. Home: 4371 Central Ave Western Springs IL 60558 Office: Sch of Art Inst Chgo Columbus Dr and Jackson Blvd Chicago IL 60603

GILMORE, STUART IRBY, speech and lang. pathologist; b. N.Y.C., July 24, 1930; s. Charles Theodore and Henrietta (Kohn) Goldman; m. Jewel Louise Pollak, June 19, 1950 (dec.); children—Harmony Gilmore Miller, Barry, Christopher, Megan, Eric, Ford. B.A., SUNY, Albany, 1950, M.A., 1951; Ph.D., U. Wis., 1962. Instr. Talladega (Ala.) Coll., 1951-53; dir. Jr. League Speech and Hearing Clinic, Columbia, S.C., 1954-60; dir. speech pathology Bill Wilkerson Hearing and Speech Center, Nashville, also; asst. prof. Vanderbilt U., 1960-62; asst. prof. speech U. Wis., 1962-65; mem. faculty La. State U., Baton Rouge, 1965—, prof. speech, 1971—, dir. speech and hearing clinic, 1965-80; pres. Wis. Speech and Hearing Assn., 1964-65; cons. in field. Author articles in field. Mem. exec. bd. Baton Rouge Assn. Retarded Citizens; exec. council La.-El Salvador div. Partner of Americas. Recipient Alumni Disting. Faculty award La. State U., 1974; disting. lectr. U. Miss., 1980. Fellow Am. Speech, Lang. and Hearing Assn.; mem. Am. Cleft Palate Assn., Am. Assn. Mental Deficiency (v.p. 1977-79), La. Speech and Hearing Assn. (pres. 1971-72), Sigma Xi. Quaker. Office: Speech and Hearing Clinic La State U Baton Rouge LA 70803 *Success is individually defined and not synonymous with recognition. Seek to know yourself and what brings you excitement, joy and fulfillment. Cherish life and nurture love.*

GILMORE, VOIT, travel executive; b. Winston-Salem, N.C., Oct. 13, 1918; s. John Merriman and Helen (Hensel) G.; m. Kathryn Kendrick, Jan. 21, 1945 (div. 1975); children: Kathryn, Geraldine, Susan, Peter, David.; m. Tatiana Dominick, July 4, 1982. B.J., U. N.C., 1939; grad., Nat. Inst. Pub. Affairs, Washington, 1940. Asst. to div. mgr. Pan Am. Airways, Miami, Fla., 1940-41; personnel mgr. Pan Am. Airways-Africa Ltd., Accra, Gold Coast, 1942-43; pub. relations dir. Pan Am. Airways, San Francisco, 1946-48; pres. Storey Corp. and affiliated cos., 1948-61, 64—; pres; Four Seasons Travel Service, Inc., 1971—; dir. U.S. Travel Service, Washington, 1961-64, So. Nat. Bank of N.C.; news corr. to, Arctic, 1958, Antarctic, 1958, 60, 61, 63. Contbr. articles on polar exploration to newspapers, mags. Mem. town council, mayor, Southern Pines, N.C., 1953-57; mem. N.C. Senate, 1965-69, N.C. Bd. Conservation and Devel., 1957-61; bd. dirs. N.C. Symphony; trustee U. N.C., Fayetteville.; mem. Gov.'s Adv. Com. on Travel and Tourism, 1982, N.C. Forestry Adv. Com., 1983; candidate for U.S. Congress from 8th Dist. N.C., 1968. Mem. Explorers Club, Am. Soc. Travel Agts. (dir., nat. legis. com.), Am. Forestry Assn. (pres. 1973-75), N.C. Forestry Assn. (dir., gov.'s travel adv. com. 1980—, N.C. Inst. Outdoor Drama.). Clubs: Bohemian (San Francisco); Cosmos (Washington); Country of N.C. (Pinehurst). Home: PO Box 289 Southern Pines NC 28387 Office: PO Box 289 Southern Pines NC 28387

GILMOUR, ALLAN DANA, automotive company executive; b. Burke, Vt., June 17, 1934; s. Albert Davis and Marjorie Bessie (Fyler) G. A.B. cum laude; Harvard Coll., 1956; M.B.A.; U. Mich., 1959. Financial analyst, sect. supr., dept. mgr., asst. to exec. v.p. Ford Motor Co., Dearborn, Mich., 1960-72; exec. v.p. adminstrn. Ford Motor Credit Co., Dearborn, 1972-73, exec. v.p. adminstrn. and spl. financing ops., 1973-75, pres., 1975-77; exec. dir. Ford Motor Co., 1977-79, v.p., controller, 1979—; Mem. citizens adv. com. U. Mich., Dearborn, 1974-82; mem. devel. fund U. Mich. Grad. Sch. Bus. Adminstrn. Mem. Phi Kappa Phi, Beta Gamma Sigma. Clubs: Fairlane (Dearborn); Econ. (Detroit). Home: 36 Blair Ln Dearborn MI 48120 Office: The American Rd Dearborn MI 48121

GILPATRIC, ROSWELL LEAVITT, lawyer; b. Bklyn., Nov. 4, 1906; s. Walter Hodges and Charlotte (Leavitt) G.; m. Margaret Fulton Kurtz, June 18, 1932 (div. Sept. 1945); children—Joan Bradshaw, John Fulton, Elizabeth Leavitt; m. Harriet Heywood, Oct. 25, 1946 (div. Apr. 1958); m. Madelin Thayer Kudner, Sept. 18, 1958 (div. Feb. 1970); m. Paula Melhado Washburn, May 12, 1970. A.B. prima academica honoris, Yale, 1928, LL.B., 1931; LL.D., Franklin and Marshall Coll., 1962, Bowdoin Coll., 1963. Bar: N.Y. bar 1932, U.S. Supreme Ct. bar 1935, Fed. Ct 1936. Partner Cravath, Swaine & Moore (and predecessor firm), N.Y.C., 1931-51, 53-61, 64-77, counsel, 1977—; chmn. bd. trustees Aerospace Corp., 1960-61; Sterling vis. lectr. law sch. Yale, 1945-46; asst. sec. materiel Air Force, 1951, undersec., 1951-53; dep. sec. Dept. Def., 1961-64; dir. CBS, Eastern Air Lines; chmn. bd. Fairchild Camera & Instrument Corp., 1975-77, Fed. Res. Bank N.Y., 1973-75; dir. emeritus Corning Glass Co. Mem. Rockefeller Bros. Spl. Studies Project, 1956-57; mem. council Yale, 1957-63; Trustee, vice chmn. Met. Mus. Art; trustee N.Y. Pub. Library, 1963-76. Named Hotchkiss Man of Year, 1962; recipient citation of merit Yale Law Sch., 1963. Mem. Assn. Bar City N.Y., N.Y. State Bar Assn., Council on Fgn. Relations, Phi Beta Kappa, Chi Psi. Conglist. Clubs: River, Century Assn. (N.Y.C.); Yacht (Nantucket, Mass.). Home: 3 E 77th St New York NY 10021 Office: 1 Chase Manhattan Plaza New York NY 10005

GILPIN, LARRY VINCENT, retail executive; b. Benton, Ill., Sept. 8, 1943; s. Otis Edgar and Beulah May (Stalcup) G.; m. Daryl Elana Scott, Aug. 21, 1965; children: Valory, Lana, Scott, Lorra. B.S., Western Ky. U., 1965; M.B.A., U. Ky., 1971; postgrad., La. State U. Sr. staff cons. IBM Corp.; mgr. orgn. devel. Unijax, Kaiser Aluminium Co.; dir. personnel planning and employment Target Stores div. Dayton Hudson Corp., Mpls., to, 1981, sr. v.p., 1981—. Coach, bd. dirs. Wayzata Soccer Team. Office: Target Stores 33 S 6th St PO Box 1392 Minneapolis MN 55440

GILPIN, ROBERT GEORGE, JR., political science educator; b. Burlington, Vt., July 2, 1930; s. Robert George and Beatrice (Sandspra) G.; m. Jean Millis, Aug. 13, 1955; children—Linda, Elizabeth, Robert. B.A., U. Vt., 1952; M.S., Cornell U., 1954; Ph.D., U. Calif. at, Berkeley, 1960. Postdoctoral fellow Harvard, 1960-61; lectr. Columbia, 1961-62; mem. faculty Princeton, 1962—, prof. polit. sci., 1970—, Eisenhower prof. internat. affairs, 1978—; mem. Pres.'s Advisory Group Tech. and the Economy, 1975-76. Author: American Scientists and Nuclear Weapons Policy, 1962, France in the Age of the Scientific State, 1968, U.S. Power and the Multinational Corporation, 1975, War and Change in World Politics, 1981; co-author, co-editor: Scientists and National Policy Making, 1964. Served with USNR, 1954-57. Congl. fellow, 1959-60; Guggenheim fellow, 1969; Rockefeller fellow, 1967-68, 76-77. Home: 134 Moore St Princeton NJ 08540

GILREATH, WARREN DEAN, packaging company executive; b. Ames, Iowa, Jan. 16, 1920; s. John MacMillan and Bertha (Holmdahl) G.; m. Jane Sheaff, Dec. 19, 1942; children: John Mac, David S., Peter H. B.S. in Engring., Iowa State U., 1941; M.B.A., U. Chgo., 1959. Engr. Aluminum Co. Am., New Kensington, Pa., 1941-44; v.p. engring. Chgo. Carton Co., 1947-62; gen. mgr. Inland Container Corp, Indpls., 1962-69, div. v.p., 1969-70, group v.p., 1971-77, sr. v.p., Indpls., 1978—; pres., dir. Inland Paper co., Vega Alta, P.R., 1978—, El Morro Corrugated Box Co., 1978—; chmn., dir. Eastex Packaging, Inc., Indpls., 1982—; pres. Inland Internat. Inc., Indpls., 1977-83. Mem. sch. bd., Palos Park, Ill., 1957-61; elder Orchard Park Presbyn. Ch., Carmel, Ind., 1975-78; mem. bus. adv. council Miami U. Sch. Bus. Served to lt. USN, 1944-46. Republican. Presbyterian. Office: Inland Container Corp 151 N Delaware St Indianapolis IN 46206

GILROY, FRANK DANIEL, playwright; b. N.Y.C., Oct. 13, 1925; s. Frank B. and Bettina (Vasti) G.; m. Ruth Dorothy Gaydos, Feb. 13, 1954; children: Anthony, John and Daniel (twins). B.A. magna cum laude, Dartmouth Coll., 1950; postgrad., Yale Sch. Drama. Became TV writer, 1952; TV writer: scripts produced on programs including Playhouse 90, U.S. Steel Hour, Omnibus, Kraft Theatre, LuxVideo Theatre, Studio One; author play: Who'll Save the Plowboy?, 1957; presented off-Broadway, 1962; completed play: The Subject Was Roses, 1962; presented on Broadway, 1964; plays presented on Broadway That Summer-That Fall, 1967, The Only Game in Town, 1968, Last Licks, 1979; producer, writer, dir.: film Desperate Characters, 1970 (best screenplay award Berlin Film Festival); writer, dir.: From Noon Till Three, 1977; producer, writer, dir.: Once in Paris (original screenplay), 1978; author: Present Tense, produced off-Broadway, 1972; Author: novels Private, 1970, (with Ruth Gilroy) Little Ego, 1970, From Noon till Three, 1973; screenplays Desperate Characters, 1971; Screenplays The Subject was Roses; screen plays The Only Game in Town, From Noon till Three, Once in Paris. Served with AUS, 1943-46; ETO. Recipient Obie award for best Am. play, 1962; Outer Circle award, 1964; Drama Critics Circle award, 1964; N.Y. Theatre Club award, 1964-65; Antoinette Perry award, 1965; Pulitzer prize for drama, 1965. Mem. Writers Guild Am., Dramatists Guild (pres. 1969-71), Dirs. Guild Am.

GILRUTH, ROBERT ROWE, aerospace consultant; b. Nashwauk, Minn., Oct. 8, 1913; s. Henry Augustus and Frances Marion (Rowe) G.; m. E. Jean Barnhill, Apr. 24, 1937 (dec. 1972); 1 dau., Barbara Jean (Mrs. John Wyatt); m. Georgene Hubbard Evans, July 14, 1973. B.S. in Aero. Engring, U. Minn., 1935, M.S., 1936, D.Sc., 1962; D.Sc., George Washington U., 1962, Ind. Inst. Tech., 1962; D.Eng., Mich. Tech. U., 1963; LL.D., N.Mex. State U., 1970. Flight research engr. Langley Aero. Lab., NACA, Langley Field, Va., 1937-45, chief pilotless aircraft research div., 1945-50, asst. dir., 1950-58; dir. NASA Project Mercury, 1958-61, NASA Manned Spacecraft Center, Houston, 1961-72, dir. key personnel devel., 1972-73, ret., 1973; cons. to adminstr. NASA, 1974—; dir. Bunker Ramo Corp. Ind. experimenter and cons. hydrofoil craft, 1938-58; advisor on guided missiles, aeros. and structures, high temperature facilities U.S. Dept. Def., 1947-58; mem. com. space systems NASA Space Adv. Council, 1972—; chmn. mgmt. devel. edn. panel NASA, 1972-73; mem. ad hoc com. fire safety aspects of polymeric materials Nat. Materials Adv. Bd., 1973-74. Recipient Outstanding Achievement award U. Minn., 1954, Great Living Am. award U.S. C. of C., 1962, Distinguished Fed. Civilian Service award Pres. U.S., 1962, Americanism award CBI Vets. Assn., 1965, Spirit of St. Louis medal, 1965, Internat. Astronautics award Daniel and Florence Guggenheim, 1966, Distinguished Service medal NASA, spring 1969, fall 1969, Pub. Service at Large award Rockefeller Found., 1969, ASME medal, 1970, James Watt Internat. medal, 1971; Achievement award Nat. Aviation Club, 1971; Robert J. Collier trophy with Nat Aero. Assn., 1972; Space Transp. award Louis W. Hill; Distinguished Service medal NASA; medal of honor N.Y.C.; Robert H. Goddard Meml. trophy Nat. Rocket Club; named to Nat. Space Hall of Fame, 1969, Internat. Space Hall of Fame, 1976. Mem. Nat. Acad. Engring. (aeros. and space bd. 1974—), Nat. Acad. Scis. Home: Route 1 Box 1486 Kilmarnock VA 22482

GILSON, EDITH MARIE, market researcher; b. Essen, Germany, Sept. 18, 1938; came to U.S., 1963, naturalized, 1983; d. Josef and Edith Roos; m. Gary J. Gilson, June 21, 1965 (div. 1975). B.A., U. Cologne, W. Ger., 1962. Research sr. analyst Cunningham & Walsh, N.Y.C., 1966-68; research analyst D'Arcy, N.Y.C., 1968-69; research assoc. dir. Grey, N.Y.C., 1969-72; sr. v.p. in charge of research and planning J. Walter Thompson Co., N.Y.C., 1972—; lectr. Hofstra U., 1978—, NYU, 1978—, Kent U., 1978—, NOW og N.Y., 1982. Contbr. articles on market research to profl. jours. Mem. Research Dir. Council (pres. N.Y. 1983), Am. Assn. Advt. Agys. (research com. N.Y. 1983), Am. Mktg. Assn. (research com. N.Y. 1979), Advt. Research Found. (copy testing council N.Y. 1982). Roman Catholic. Home: 15 W 72d St New York NY 10023 Office: J Walter Thompson 466 Lexington Ave New York NY 10017 *The most important goal or principle that governs much of my decision at work as well as outside of work is to create an environment in which talent can flourish.*

GILTNER, THOMAS A., railroad executive; b. Cleve., Apr. 16, 1931; s. Kenneth E. and Catherine M. (Wenneman) G.; children—Teresa L., Karen J., Thomas A., Robert H. B.S., Central Mo. State U., 1957. Audit mgr. Price Waterhouse & Co., Kansas City, Mo., 1957-70; v.p., comptroller Kansas City So. Ind., Inc., Mo., 1970—. Coach Boys Football, Kansas City, 1969-72, 78, 79. Served with USAF, 1951-54. Mem. Am. Inst., C.P.A.'s, Mo. Soc. C.P.A.'s, Nat. Assn. Accountants, Fin. Execs. Inst., Phi Kappa Phi. Office: 114 W 11th St Kansas City MO 64105

GIMBEL, NORMAN, lyricist, music publisher; b. Bklyn., Nov. 16; s. Morris and Lottie (Nass) G.; m. Elinor Rowley, Jan. 29, 1961; children: Anthony Seth, Nelly Ransom. B.B.A. cum laude, Baruch Coll., N.Y.C., 1950; M.A., Columbia U., 1952. Lyricist: stage prodns. (Broadway) Whoop Up, 1959, The Conquering Hero, 1962, Los Angeles Shakespeare Festival prodn., A Midsummer Night's Dream, 1978; songs include I Will Wait for You (Acad. award nomination 1971), Richard's Window, (Acad. award nomination 1976), Killing Me Softly With His Song, (Grammy award 1973), Ready to Take a Chance Again, (Acad. award nomination 1978), It Goes Like It Goes, (Acad. award 1980), also), Canadian Sunset, The Girl From Ipanema, Meditation, How Insensitive, Summer Samba, Watch What Happens, Live for Life, I Got a Name, Bluesette, Suzy., (Young N.Y. Film Critics award 1973); song scores for films The Phantom Tollbooth, 1968, Pufnstuf, 1969, Where's Poppa?, 1970; TV theme songs Happy Days, Laverne and Shirley, Wonder Woman, Paper Chase, Angee Blansky's Beauties; pub. song scores for films, Butterfield Music Corp., N.Y.C., 1960—. Served with AUS, 1946-47. Named to Songwriters Hall of Fame, 1984. Mem. Authors League Am., Dramatists Guild, Composers and Lyricists Guild Am., Acad. Motion Picture Arts and Scis. (exec. com. 1974—), Broadcast Music, Inc. Office: PO Box 1138 Beverly Hills CA 90213

GIMBEL, PETER ROBIN, film producer-director; b. N.Y.C., Feb. 14, 1928; s. Bernard Feustman and Alva Belle (Bernheimer) G.; children—Peter Bailey, Leslie Laird. B.A., Yale U., 1951. Exec. trainee Gimbel Bros., Inc., N.Y.C., 1951; research analyst White, Weld & Co. (investment bankers), N.Y.C., 1952-60; pres. Blue Gander, Inc. Producer, dir.: film Blue Water, White Death, 1971, The Mystery of the Andrea Doria; TV spl., 1976, Andrea Doria: The Final Chapter, 1983. Trustee N.Y. Zool. Soc., 1957-78. Served to 2d lt. inf. AUS, 1946-47. Mem. Dirs. Guild Am. Address: 10 E 63d St New York NY 10021

GIMBUTAS, MARIJA, archaeologist, educator; b. Vilnius, Lithuania, Jan. 23, 1921; came to U.S., 1949, naturalized, 1955; d. Daniel and Veronica (Janulaitis) Alseika; m. Jurgis Gimbutas, 1942; children: Danute, Zivile, Rasa. M.A., U. Vilnius, 1942; Ph.D., U. Tubingen, Germany, 1946; postgrad., U. Heidelberg and Munich., Germany, 1947-49. Research fellow Peabody Mus., Harvard U., Boston, 1955-63, lectr. dept. anthropology, 1962-63; fellow Center for Advanced Study in Behavioral Scis., Stanford, Calif., 1961-62; prof. European archaeology and Indo-European studies UCLA, 1963—; fellow Netherlands Inst. for Advanced Studies, 1973-74; project dir. excavations of Neolithic S.E. Europe, Obre, Bosnia, 1967-68, excavations at Sitagroi, N.E. Greece, 1968-69; excavations at Anza, Central Macedonia, 1969-70, at Achilleion, Thessaly, Greece, 1973-74, (at Scaloria, nr. Manfredonia, Italy), 1976-79. Author: Die Bestattung in Litauen in de vorgeschichtlichen Zeit, 1946, Prehistory of Eastern Europe, 1956, Ancient Symbolism in Lithuanian Folk Art, 1958, The Balts, 1963, The Bronze Age Cultures of Central and Eastern Europe, 1965, The Slavs, 1971, The Gods and Goddesses of Old Europe, 1974, Neolithic Macedonia, 1976, The Goddesses and Gods of Old Europe, 1982, Die Balten, 1983; editor: Jour. Indo-European Studies, 1973—, Monumenta Archaeologica, 1976—. Recipient Woman of Yr. award Los Angeles Times, 1968; NSF fellow, 1959-60, 68-69, 73-76; Smithsonian fellow, 1967-71; Nat. Endowment for Humanities grantee, 1967; Kress Found. fellow, 1967-72. Mem. Assn. Field Archaeologists, Assn. for Advancement Baltic Studies (pres. 1980-82), Council for Old World Archaeology, Am. Anthrop. Assn., Internat. Assn. for Promotion of Studies of Southeastern Europe, Inst. of Lithuanistics, Internat. Assn. Proto-and Prehistoric Religion. Home: 21434 W Entrada Rd Topanga CA 90290 Office: 115 Kinsey Hall UCLA 405 Hilgard Ave Los Angeles CA 90024

GIMÉNEZ-MUÑOŹ, MIGUEL ANGEL, atty. gen. P.R.; b. San Juan, P.R., Oct. 7, 1929; s. Miguel G. and Ana (Muñoź); m. Bessie Cruz, July 17, 1959; children: Lizzette, Benilith, Alberto, Miguel, Bessie. B.A. in Social Scis., Niagara U., 1952; LL.B., Walter F. George Sch. Law, Mercer U., 1957; grad. spl. course on wage and hour law, U. P.R., 1968, U. Nev. Nat. Coll. State Judiciary, 1974. Bar: P.R. bar 1957. Law clk. Supreme Ct., P.R., 1957; atty. Dept. Justice, San Juan, 1957-60; asso. firm Geigel & Silva, 1963-69; judge Superior Ct., San Juan, 1969-76; presiding judge; partner firm Gonzalez & Gimenez-Munoz, Hato Rey, P.R., 1976-77; atty. gen. P.R., San Juan, 1977—; judge Intermediate Ct. Appeals; pres. Spl. Bd. on Unjust Comml. Practice of Commonwealth PR., State Planning Bd., Law Enforcement Adminstrn. P.R. Mem. Am. Bar Assn., Bar Assn. P.R., Bar Assn. Guayama (past pres.), Fed. Bar Assn., Phi Alpha Delta. Roman Catholic. Office: Office Atty Gen La Fortaleza San Juan PR 00901 *

GIMLETT, JAMES IRWIN, geophysicist; b. Salt Lake City, Dec. 10, 1929; s. Irwin Grodal and Mildred Joy (Tomkins) G.; m. Luna VanEaton Brite, Aug. 21, 1954; children—James, Leslie, Lisa, Daniel, Michael. Student, U. Puget Sound, 1946-48; B.S., Stanford U., 1950, M.S., 1952, 61, Ph.D., 1965. Geophysicist Hycon Aerial Surveys, Pasadena, Calif., 1955-58; asst. prof. U. Nev., Reno, 1958-63; chief scientist Actron, Monrovia, Calif., 1963-79; staff mgr. McDonnell Douglas Astronautics Co., Huntington Beach, Calif., 1979. Contbr. articles to profl. jours. Mem. AAAS, Soc. Exploration Geophysicists, European Assn. Exploration Geophysicists, Am. Soc. Photogrammetry. Home: 1324 Sierra Madre Villa Pasadena CA 91107 Office: 5301 Bolsa Ave Huntington Beach CA 92647

GIMLIN, ROBERT CHARLES, forest products company executive; b. Chgo., Jan. 11, 1921; s. Guy M. and Corinne M. G.; m. Jane Elizabeth Haltom, Apr. 19, 1942; children: Gail, Hal. B.S.Me., Purdue U., 1942. With U.S. Gypsum Co., Chgo., 1945-66; v.p. Abitibi Paper Co. Ltd. (name changed to Abitibi-Price Inc. 1979), Toronto, Ont., Can., 1966-68, group v.p., 1974-76, pres., chief operating officer, 1978-79, pres., chief exec., 1979-83, chmn., chief exec., 1983—; pres. Abitibi Corp., Birmingham, Mich., 1968-74; chmn. Abitibi-Price Sales Corp., N.Y.C., 1976-78; dir. Fishery Products Internat. Ltd., St. John's, Nfld., Can. Served as officer USN, 1942-45. Clubs: Toronto, York, Toronto Hunt (Toronto); Mt. Royal (Montreal, Que.); Pinehurst Golf and Country (N.C.). Home: 31 McKenzie Ave Toronto ON M4W 1K1 Canada Office: Box 21 Toronto-Dominion Centre Toronto ON M5K 1B3 Canada

GIMMA, JOSEPH A., financial company executive; b. Bari, Italy, 1907. Sr. v.p. Shearson/Am. Express Inc.; former chmn. N.Y. State Racing Commn.; dir. Lionel Corp.; Mem. Commn. on Rev. Nat. Policy Toward Gambling, Washington; dir. Joint Legis. Task Force to Study and Evaluate Pari-mutuel Racing and Breeding Industry. Past chmn. N.Y. Republican County Com.; mem. adv. bd. Marymount Coll.; trustee Marymount Manhattan Coll., N.Y.C., Saratoga Mus. Racing, Bagby Found. for Musical Arts; bd. regents St. Peter's Coll.; trustee, pres. Puccini Found., N.Y.C.; econ. devel. liaison to Mayor Edward Koch and City of N.Y., 1981—. Decorated knight of Malta, knight grand cross Order Holy Sepulchre. Mem. Met. Opera Club. Home: 800 Park Ave New York NY 10021 Office: 2 World Trade Center 104th Floor New York NY 10048

GINADER, GEORGE HALL, business executive; b. Buffalo, Apr. 5, 1933; s. George Edward and Meredith (Hall) G. B.A., Allegheny Coll., 1955; M.S. in Library Sci, Drexel U., 1964. Asst. Buyer Lord & Taylor, N.Y.C., 1957-59; job analyst Ins. Co. N.Am., Phila., 1959-60; asst. buyer John Wanamaker, Phila., 61960-61; acting curator Automobile Reference Collection, Free Library Phila., 1961-63; librarian N.Y. C. of C., N.Y.C., 1964-66; chief librarian N.Y. Stock Exchange, N.Y.C., 1966-67; exec. dir. Spl. Libraries Assn., N.Y.C., 1967-70, chmn. bus. and fin. div., 1974-75, pres., 1981-82; mgr. research library Morgan Stanley & Co., N.Y.C., 1970-79; cons. to spl. libraries and info. centers, 1979-82; dir. ops. Internat. Creative Mgmt., N.Y.C., 1982—. Mem. N.Y. Geneal. and Biog. Soc., Internat. Platform Assn., Am. Records Mgmt. Assn. (treas. N.Y. chpt. 1975-76), Adminstrv. Mgmt. Soc., Nat. Microfilm Assn., Nat. Trust for Historic Preservation, N.Y. C. of C., S.A.R., Phi Delta Theta (asst. sec. chpt. 1967-68, pres. N.Y. alumni club 1970—). Republican. Episcopalian. Home: 45 S Main St Cranbury NJ 08512 Office: 40 W 57th St New York NY 10019

GINDER, WILLIAM M., petroleum corporation executive; b. 1922; married. B.S., Johns Hopkins U., 1954. With Crown Central Petroleum Corp., contractor, asst. treas., 1967-69, treas., contractor, 1969-72, v.p., treas., contractor, 1972-73, v.p. fin., chief fin. officer, 1973-74, group v.p., chief fin. officer, 1974-82, exec. v.p., chief fin. officer, 1982—. Served with USAAF, 1942-46. Office: Crown Central Petroleum Corp 1 Charles Blaustein Bldg PO Box 1168 Baltimore MD 21203 *

GINGER, LEONARD GEORGE, mgmt. cons.; b. Chgo., 1918; m. Mary Blasius, Dec. 18, 1943; children—Edward, Marilyn, Deborah, Lawrence, Gregory, Elizabeth. B.S., Northwestern U., 1939; M.S., U. Chgo., 1941; Ph.D., Yale, 1943. With Merck & Co., 1940; with atomic research Manhattan Project, U. Chgo., 1944-45; faculty Northwestern U., 1946-49; with Baxter Travenol Labs. Inc., Deerfield, Ill., 1949-81, v.p. research and devel., 1960-69, sr. v.p., 1969-81; cons., 1981—; pres. L. G. Ginger & Assos., Glenview, Ill., 1981—; dir. 1st Nat. Bank Morton Grove, Alto Automotive, Inc. Bd. dirs. Crusade of Mercy, Suburban Community Chest Council, Jr. Achievement. Mem. Am. Chem. Soc., N.Y. Acad. Scis., AAAS, Am. Inst. Chemists, Research Dirs. Assn., Am. Pharm. Assn. Home: 2100 Burr Oak Dr Glenview IL 60025

GINGERICH, OWEN JAY, astronomer, educator; b. Washington, Iowa, Mar. 24, 1930;, 1954; 3 children. B.A., Goshen Coll., 1951; M.A., Harvard U., 1953, Ph.D. in Astronomy, 1962. Dir. obs. Am. U., Beirut, 1955-58, instr., 1955-57, asst. prof., 1957-58; lectr. astronomy Wellesley Coll., 1958-59; astrophysicist Smithsonian Astrophys. Obs., 1961—; lectr. Harvard, 1960-68, asso. prof. astronomy and history of sci., 1968-69, prof., 1969—; Sigma Xi nat. lectr., 1971; George Darwin lectr. Royal Astron. Soc., 1971; councilor Am. Astron. Soc., 1973-76; Mem. Harvard Obs. eclipse expdn. to Ceylon, 1955; mem. Harvard expdn. to observe occultation of Regulus by Venus, Beirut, 1959; astronomy cons. Harvard Project Physics, 1964-69; dir., central telegram bur. Internat. Astronomical Union, 1965-67, asso. dir., 1967-79, pres. commn. history astronomy, 1970-76, chmn. U.S. nat. com., 1982-84. Asso. editor: Jour. History Astronomy, 1975—; mem. editorial bd.: Am. Scholar, 1975-80; dir.: Harvard mag, 1978—. Corp. mem. Boston Mus. Sci., 1979—. Decorated Order of Merit comdr. class People's Republic of Poland, 1981. Mem. AAAS (chmn. sect. D 1981), Academie Internationale d'Histoire des Sciences (corr.), Am. Philos. Soc. (v.p. 1982—, John F. Lewis prize 1976), Am. Acad. Arts and Scis., Am. Astron. Soc. (councilor 1973-76, chmn. hist. astronomy div. 1983—), Phi Beta Kappa. Clubs: Odd Volumes, Examiner. Research and publs. on model stellar atmospheres and in history of astronomy. Office: Center for Astrophysics Cambridge MA 02138 *Our most earnest ambitions are in effect unspoken prayers-they define our deepest views on the meaning of life far more precisely than any outward profession of religion or ethics.*

GINGERICH, RICHARD ALLAN, labor union exec.; b. Kitcherner, Ont., Can., Apr. 20, 1929; s. George Henry and Elsie Price (White) G.; m. Jean Emma Cater, July 3, 1948; children—Mark, Peter, John, Wendy, Matthew. Student acctg., LaSalle Extension U. With Ahrens Shoe Ltd., Kitchener, 1948-50, Can. Nat. Rwys., 1950-62; rep. edn. dept. Can. Brotherhood Ry., Transp. and Gen. Workers, 1963-70, nat. sec.-treas., 1970—; Mem. Duke of Edinburgh Commonwealth Conf., Australia, 1968; mem. exec. com. Fed. New Democratic Party, 1970—. Mem. Can. Com. Polit. Edn., Sec.-Treas. Assn., Can. Rwy. Labour Assn. Lutheran. Home: 65 Beaumaris Dr Ottawa ON K2H 7K6 Canada Office: 2300 Carling Ave Ottawa ON K2B 7G1 Canada

GINGERICH, VERNON JASON, educator; b. Kalona, Iowa, Nov. 3, 1914; s. Jess and Lydia Marie (Plank) G.; m. Dorothy Burroughs, June 12, 1942 (dec. Jan. 1964). B.A., U. Iowa, 1935, M.A., 1936, Ph.D., 1950. Instr. French and German, Burlington (Iowa) Jr. Coll., 1937-42, 46-51; asso. prof., chmn. lang. dept. Mich. Coll. Mining and Tech., Sault br., 1951-59; asso. prof. French and German, Mankato (Minn.) State Coll., 1959-62; prof. French, chmn. dept. fgn. langs. U. Wis., Eau Claire, 1962-80; chmn. bd. Carnegie Library, Sault Ste. Marie, Chmn. bd., Mich., 1957-59. Served with USAAF, 1942-46. Mem. MLA, Am. Assn. Tchrs. French, Am. Assn. Tchrs. German. Home: 1615 Iowa St Mission TX 78572

GINGISS, BENJAMIN JACK, formal clothing stores executive; b. St. Paul, Feb. 27, 1911; s. Samuel and Betty (Illiewitz) G.; m. Rosalie Eisenschiml, Apr. 20, 1940; children: Peter J., Joel D., Randall J. Student, U. Ill., 1929-32, Northwestern U., 1934, Ill. Inst. Tech., 1941. Co-founder Gingiss Bros., Inc., Chgo., 1936; (named later changed to Gingiss Formalwear, Inc.); now chmn. Gingiss Formalwear, Inc.; chmn. Gingiss Internat., Inc. Chmn. Fedn. for an Open Lakefront, Chgo., 1967; pres. USO of, Chgo., 1969, 73-74; v.p. Welfare Council Met. Chgo., 1968; commr. Lake Mich. and Adjoining Lands Study, 1969—; mem. Urban Action Commn. YMCA, 1969; city commr. Commn. on Youth Welfare, 1966; chmn. men's clothing div. Combined Jewish Appeal, 1959; bd. dirs. Center Sports Medicine, Goodwill Industries, Lyric Opera Chgo., Union Am. Hebrew Congregations; sr. v.p. bd. dirs. USO, Chgo.; bd. dirs., pres. Ill. Humane Soc.; former trustee Rosary Coll.; bd. assos. DePaul U.; former vice-chmn. pres.'s adv. bd. Mus. Sci. and Industry. Recipient Phoenix award DePaul U., 1969, Prime Ministers medal State of Israel, 1968, Navy Certificate Merit, 1969, awards U. Dept. Def., U.S. Air Corps, U.S.C.G., U.S. Army, 9th Naval Dist., U.S.O., Chgo., 1977.

Mem. C. of C. Clubs: City (past pres., dir.), Tavern, Executives (Chgo.). Home: 175 E Delaware St Chicago IL 60611 Office: 180 N LaSalle St Chicago IL 60601

GINGOLD, HERMIONE FERDINANDA, actress; b. London, Eng.; d. Jame and Kate (Walter) G.; m. Michael Joseph; children: Leslie, Stephen. Student pvt. schs., London, governesses, Paris. Actress: Shakespeare at Stratford on Avon, also Paris; film appearances include: Gigi; mem. cast Broadway shows: Side by Side by Sondheim, A Little Night Music; TV appearances on The Girl from U.N.C.L.E; author: Sirens Should be Seen and Not Heard, 1963; recordings Peter and the Wolf (Grammy award), Carnival of Animals, Chitty Chitty Bang Bang, Lysistrata. Recipient Donaldson award; decorated dame Knights of Malta. Home: 405 E 54th St New York NY 10022

GINGOLD, JOSEF, musician, educator; b. Brest-Litovsk, Russia, 1909; came to U.S., 1920. Pupil, Vladimir Graffman, Eugene Ysayë; D.Music hon., Ind. U., Kent State U., Baldwin-Wallace Coll., Cleve. Inst. Music, New Eng. Conservatory Music. Prof. music, now Disting. prof. Ind. U.; now distin. prof.; tchr. Conservatoir National Superior de Musique; Mischa Elman prof. Manhattan Sch. Music; vis. prof. Conservatoire Nationale Superiore, Toho Sch., Tokyo, also others; jury numerous internat. violin competitions, including hon. chmn. Internat. Violin Competition of Indpls. Charter mem., NBC Symphony; concertmaster; soloist, Detroit Symphony Orch., Cleve. Orch.; recs., Columbia, RCA Victor, Fidelio Records. Address: Dept Music Ind U Bloomington IN 47401

GINGRAS, BERNARD ARTHUR, research assn. exec., chemist; b. Montreal, Que., Can., Jan. 23, 1927; s. Charles E. and Eva (Caron) G.; m. Denise Rivest, Sept. 6, 1952; children—Bernard L., Marie, Jean-Francois, Isabelle. B.Sc., U. Montreal, 1948, M.Sc. (Province Que. scholar), 1949, Ph.D., 1952; D.Phil.; NRC Can. fellow; Merck postdoctoral overseas fellow, Oxford (Eng.) U., 1954; D.Sc. (hon.), York U., Toronto, 1979. Can.-French Assn. Advancement Sci. scholar Harvard U. Med. Sch., 1952; mem. staff Nat. Research Council Can., 1954—, asst. v.p., then v.p. univ. research, 1972-78, v.p. external relations, 1978—. Author papers in field. Fellow Chem. Inst. Can. (chmn. bd. qualification examiners 1971—); mem. Order Chemists Que., Can. Com. on Financing Univ. Research, Soc., Research Adminstrs., Assn. canadienne française pour l'avancement des scis. (pres.). Office: Nat Research Council Can Montreal Rd Ottawa ON K1A 0R6 Canada

GINGRAS, GUSTAVE, physician; b. Outremont, Que., Can., Jan. 18, 1918; s. Gustave and Augusta (Descaries) G.; m. Rena MacLean, July 13, 1948. B.A., Bourget Coll., Rigaud, Que., 1936; M.D., U. Montreal, 1943; LL.D. (hon.), U. Winnipeg, 1970, U. Western Ont., 1971, McMaster U., 1982, D.M., U. Sherbrooke, 1973, D.C.L., Bishop's U., 1974. Diplomate: Am. Bd. Phys. Medicine and Rehab. Founding exec. dir. Rehab. Inst. Montreal, 1949-76; chief of service, phys. medicine and rehab. Queen Mary Vets. Hosp. and D.V.A. Montreal Dist., Can., 1945-76; chancellor U. P.E.I. (Can.), Charlottetown, 1974-82; dir. rehab. services, med. dir. Rehab. Centre, P.E.I. Dept. Health, 1977-81; mem. Can. Forces Med. Council, 1973—; life gov. Cerebral Palsy Assn. Que.; hon. v.p. Can. Nat. Inst. for Blind, 1975—; mem. Can. Social Scis. and Humanities Research Council, 1978—, mem. exec. bd., 1983—; mem. sci. and tech. com. CBC, 1979-81; cons. med. rehab. WHO, 1955—; prof. phys. medicine and rehab. Faculty of Medicine, U. Montreal, 1954-76, emeritus prof. medicine, 1977—; past mem. numerous adv. coms. in field; dir. Abbott Labs. Ltd.; pres. St. John Ambulance Council P.E.I., 1980. Contbr. numerous articles to profl. publs. Served with M.C., Royal Can. Army, 1941-45. Decorated companion Order of Can., Can. Centennial medal; knight of justice Order St. John of Jerusalem; cavaliere Order St. Agatha, Republic of San Marino; Order Cedar of Lebanon; recipient Silver medal of Internat. Coop., 1965; Humanitarian award B'nai B'rith, 1966; Albert Lasker award Internat. Soc. Rehab. of Disabled, 1969; Outstanding Citizen award Montreal Citizenship Council, 1970; Royal Bank of Can. award, 1972; medal of Honour, Pharm. Mfrs. Assn. Can., 1973; F.N.G. Starr award Can. Med. Assn., 1978; Province Que. Hosp. Assn. award, 1980. Fellow Royal Coll. Physicians Can., Am. Acad. Phys. Medicine and Rehab., Internat. Coll. Surgeons, Am. Geriatric Soc.; mem. Can. Med. Assn. (pres. 1972-73), Can. Assn. Phys. Medicine and Rehab. (past pres.), Can. Coll. Health Service Execs., L'Association des medecins de langue française du Canada, Federation des medecins specialistes de Que., Med. Council P.E.I., P.E.I. Hosp. Assn. (pres. 1980), Med. Soc. P.E.I., Royal Soc. Medicine, Internat. Med. Soc. Paraplegia, Internat. Rehab. Medicine Assn., Internat. Soc. Prosthetics and Orthotics, Sociedad Colombiana de Medicina Fisica y Rehabilitacion (corr.), Heraldry Soc. Can., Can. R.R. Hist. Assn.; hon. mem. AMA, Can. Red Cross Soc., phys. medicine and rehab. socs. of Italy, Venezuela, Uruguay, Mex., Argentina, France, Belgium, and Brazil. Office: Glen Green Monticello PE C0A 2B0 Canada

GINGRICH, GREGG AUSTIN, lawyer; b. Tulsa, Oct. 11, 1954; s. Jerry G. and Shirley M. G.; m. Katherine Kennedy, May 2, 1976; children: Margaret, Claire. B.B.A., U. Okla., 1976; J.D., So. Meth. U., 1979, M.B.A., 1983. Bar: Tex. 1979. Atty. Campbell Taggart, Inc., Dallas, 1979-82, corp. sec., 1982—. Mem. State Bar Tex., ABA. Republican. Roman Catholic. Office: Campbell Taggart Inc 6211 Lemmon Ave Dallas TX 75222

GINGRICH, NEWELL SHIFFER, physicist, educator; b. Orwigsburg, Pa., Jan. 29, 1906; s. Felix Moyer and Minnie (Shiffer) G.; m. Fern Priscilla Riedel, June 5, 1928; children—Phillip Riedel, Katherine Ann (Mrs. Thomas Allan Brady). A.B., N. Central Coll., Naperville, Ill., 1926; M.A., Lafayette Coll., 1927; Ph.D., U. Chgo., 1930. Mem. faculty physics Lafayette Coll., Easton, Pa., 1927-28, Mt. Allison U., Sackville, N.B., Can., 1930-31, Mass. Inst. Tech., 1931-36; faculty U. Mo., Columbia, 1936—, prof. physics, 1943-73, emeritus prof. physics, 1973—; Physicist Oak Ridge Nat. Lab., 1952, summer 1953, Argonne Nat. Lab., Ill., summers 1956-58. Reviser: Physics-A Textbook for Colleges, 1950, 57; Cons. editor: McGraw-Hill Ency. Sci. & Tech, 1960-73; Contbr. articles to sci. jours. Recipient citation of Merit OSRD, 1945; named Distinguished Prof. U. Mo., 1962; NSF fellow Mass. Inst. Tech., 1959-60. Fellow Am. Phys. Soc., AAAS; mem. Am. Assn. Physics Tchrs., Am. Crystallographic Assn., AAUP, Phi Beta Kappa (hon.), Sigma Xi. Home: 313 E Brandon Rd Columbia MO 65201

GINGRICH, NEWTON LEROY, congressman; b. Harrisburg, Pa., June 17, 1943; s. Robert Bruce and Kathleen (Daugherty) G.; m. Jacqueline Battley, June 19, 1962 (div. 1981); children: Linda Kathleen, Jacqueline Sue.; m. Marianne Ginther, Aug. 1981. B.A., Emory U., 1965; M.A., Tulane U., 1968, Ph.D., 1971. Faculty W. Ga. Coll., Carrollton, 1970-78, prof. history, to 1978; mem. U.S. Ho. of Reps. from 6th Dist. Ga., Washington, 1979—. Mem. AAAS, World Futurist Soc., Ga. Conservancy. Republican. Baptist. Clubs: Kiwanis, Moose. Office: 417 Cannon House Office Bldg Washington DC 20515

GINIGER, KENNETH SEEMAN, publisher; b. N.Y.C., Feb. 18, 1919; s. Maurice Aaron and Pearl (Triester) G.; m. Carol Virginia Wilkins, Sept. 27, 1952. Student, U. Va., 1935-39, N.Y. Law Sch., 1940-41. Ptnr. Signet Press, 1939-40; asso. editor Arts and Decoration and The Spur, 1940-41; dir. pub. relations Prentice-Hall, Inc., 1946-49, editor-in-chief trade book div., 1949-52; v.p., gen. mgr. Hawthorn Books div., 1952-61; pres. Hawthorn Books, Inc., N.Y.C., 1961-65, K.S. Giniger Co., Inc., 1965—, Consol. Book Pubs. div. Processing & Books, Inc., Chgo., 1969-74, Tradewinds Group div. IPC Ltd., Sydney, Australia, 1974-76; lectr. New Sch. Social Research, 1948-49, NYU, 1979-81, adj. asst. prof., 1981-83, adj. assoc. prof., 1983—. Author: The Compact Treasury of Inspiration, 1955 (NCCJ Brotherhood Week citation), America, America, America, 1957, A Treasury of Golden Memories, 1958, What Is Protestantism?, 1965, A Little Treasury of Hope, A Little Treasury of Comfort, A Little Treasury of Healing, A Little Treasury of Christmas, The Sayings of Jesus, all 1968, Heroes for Our Times, 1969, The Family Advent Book, 1979; editor: Internat. Pub. Newsletter, 1983—; editorial bd.: RAM Reports, 1977-83, Communications and the Law, 1978—. Sec. Com. Collective Security, 1952-65; nat. adv. bd. Found. Religious Action, 1956—; dir. Laymen's Nat. Bible Com., 1957—, pres., 1963-71. Served from pvt. to capt. AUS, 1941-45; asst. to dir. CIA, 1951-52. Decorated chevalier French Legion of Honor. Mem. P.E.N., Phi Delta Phi. Republican. Episcopalian. Clubs: Garrick, Authors (London); Nat. Press, Army and Navy (Washington); Overseas Press, Players, Dutch Treat (N.Y.C.). Home: 1045 Park Ave New York NY 10028 Office: 235 Park Ave S New York NY 10003

GINN, JOHN CHARLES, newspaper publisher, communications company executive; b. Longview, Tex., Jan. 1, 1937; s. Paul S. and Bernice Louise (Coomer) G.; m. Diane Kelly, Jan. 2, 1976; children—John Paul, Mark Charles, William Stanfield. B.J., U. Mo., 1959; M.B.A., Harvard U., 1972. Successively reporter, copy editor, chief copy desk Charlotte (N.C.) Observer, 1959-62; editor Kingsport (Tenn.) Times-News, 1962-63; city editor Charlotte News, 1963-69; dir. corp. devel. Des Moines Register & Tribune, 1972-73; editor, pub. Jackson (Tenn.) Sun, 1973-74; pres., pub. Anderson (S.C.) Ind. and Daily Mail, 1972—; v.p. Harte-Hanks Communications, Inc., 1978—; pres. Century Group of Harte-Hanks Communications, Inc., 1977—; mem. Pulitzer Prize jury, 1977-79; frequent lectr. Am. Press Inst. Pres. Anderson Area C. of C., 1977, Anderson YMCA, 1975-76; mem. adv. council Anderson Coll. Served with USAFR, 1959-61. R.H. Macy Retail fellow Harvard U., 1972; recipient award for best editorial of year Tenn. Press Assn., 1964, 73,74. Mem. Am. Newspaper Pubs. Assn., So. Newspaper Pubs. Assn. (dir.), S.C. Press Assn. (exec. com.), Sigma Delta Chi. Home: Route 14 Box 54 Anderson SC 29621 Office: 1000 Williamston Rd Anderson SC 29621

GINN, ROBERT MARTIN, utility company executive; b. Detroit, Jan. 13, 1924; s. Lloyd T. and Edna S. (Martin) G.; m. Barbara R. Force, 1948; children: Anne, Martha, Thomas. B.S. in Elec. Engring., U. Mich., 1948, M.S., 1948. With Cleve. Electric Illuminating Co., 1948—, controller, 1959-62, v.p. gen. services, 1963-70, exec. v.p., 1970-77, pres., 1977-83, chmn., 1983—, chief exec. officer, 1979—, dir.; dir. Soc. Corp., Soc. Nat. Bank Cleve., Ferro Corp. Mem. Shaker Heights Bd. Edn., (Ohio), 1968-75, pres., 1973-74; pres. Welfare Fedn. Cleve., 1968-69; chmn. Cleve. Commn. on Higher Edn., 1983—; trustee John Carroll U., Martha Holden Jennings Found., 1983—. Served with USAAF, 1943-46. Office: Cleve Electric Illuminating Co 55 Public Sq PO Box 5000 Cleveland OH 44101

GINN, RONALD (BO GINN), congressman; b. Morgan, Ga., May 31, 1934; m. Gloria Averitt, 1956; children—Kacy, Julie, Bryan. Student, Abraham Baldwin Agrl. Coll., 1951-53, Ga. So. Coll., 1953-56. Tchr.; businessman; farmer; adminstrv. asst. to Rep. G. Elliott Hagan, 1961-66, Sen. Herman E. Talmadge, 1967-71; mem. 93d-97th Congresses from 1st Dist. Ga. Democrat. Baptist.

GINN, RONN, architect, urban planner, general contractor; b. Jacksonville, Fla., Apr. 17, 1933; s. Angus Theodore and Joan Adelaide (Bailey) G.; m. Valerie Jeanne Broderson, Mar. 15, 1969; children: Sharon Lee, John Norman. A.A., U. Fla., 1957, B.Arch., 1960, B.Landscape Architecture, 1961. Urban design specialist Model Cities Adminstrn., HUD, Washington, 1967-68; practice architecture, constrn., urban planning, landscape architecture, St. Petersburg, Fla., 1968—; pres. ARG Constrn. Corp., 1975-76, ARG/Corp., 1977—, Ginn Corp., 1967-70, Atrium Corp., 1965-72; urban design lectr. U. N.Mex., 1967; planning cons. State Dept., 1967-68; design cons. Am. Revolution Bicentennial Commn., 1967-69; vis. design critic Rice U., 1974; mem. Pinellas County (Fla.) Bd. Adjustments and Appeals, 1981—; Mem. Albuquerque Fine Arts Commn., 1965-67, St. Petersburg Design Goals Com., 1971-73; moderator radio program Design in Our Community WPKM, Tampa, Fla., 1971-72; founder, bd. dirs. Pinellas County Red Flag Charrette, 1972—, Catalyst, St. Petersburg; bd. dirs. Fla. Council Clean Air, Fla. Red Flag Charrette; mem. Pinellas County Planning Council, 1972-73. Supervising architect, urban designer: Roswell (N.Mex.) central bus. dist. redesign, 1964, Tucumcari (N.Mex.) central bus. dist. redesign, 1967, Treasure Island (Fla.) civic center design, 1971; architect, urban designer, prin., Atrium One, Albuquerque, 1965-67; Contbg. editor: Urban Affairs Symposia, 1965-73; guest columnist: St. Petersburg Evening Independent, 1974; Important works include Albuquerque central bus. dist. redesign (nat. AIA award 1966), new town Fla. Center (nat. Am. Soc. Landscape Architects award 1970), Brown residence (AIA Merit award 1975), Penguin Restaurant, Treasure Island, Fla., 1973, Cross residence, 1974, Sheridan Gallery, 1974, Madeira Beach C. of C, 1975, Greenpepper Restaurant, 1975, Mixon Bldg, Ruskin, Fla., 1976, Congregation Beth Chai Synagogue, Seminole, Fla., 1979, Villa Dos Santos Master Plan, St. Petersburg Beach, Fla., 1979, Congregation Kol Ami Synagogue, Tampa, Fla., 1981, Markham residence, St. Petersburg, 1981, The Moorings, Tierra Verde, Fla., 1981, Ginn Residence, St. Petersburg, 1981, Congregation B'nai Israel Synagogue, Clearwater, Fla., 1981, Lilly Residence, Treasure Island, Fla., 1983, Anchor Bank Office Bldg., St. Petersburg, 1984. Mayoral candidate City of Treasure Island, Fla., 1973; bldg. dir. City of Seminole, 1975-78; mem. Leadership St. Petersburg, 1978—. Recipient numerous archtl., landscape architecture, urban design awards, Addy awards, 1981, 82. Mem. AIA (mem. nat. com. on regional devel. 1969-76, vice chmn., commr. pub. affairs Fla. chpt.), Am. Inst. Planners, Constrn. Specifications Inst., Am. Inst. Landscape Architects, So. Bldg. Code Congress, Fla. Planning and Zoning Assn. Republican. Presbyterian. Office: Floor 14 One Plaza Pl Saint Petersburg FL 33701 *As a child, I was fascinated by the size and shape of buildings. In my teens, I became interested in the arrangement and construction of buildings. When in my twenties, I learned to guide my hand in transferring logic and feeling from my mind's eye to the art of expression. My thirties were spent in the study of pure design as an art form. Now, it is in my forties and beyond that I wish to help shape the future world of men and women. This, the remainder of my life, I owe to my profession — to fulfill the role it has given me.*

GINN, SAM L., telephone company executive; b. St. Clair, Ala., Apr. 3, 1937; s. James Harold and Myra Ruby (Smith) G.; m. Meriann Lanford Vance, Feb. 2, 1963; children: Matthew, Michael, Samantha. B.S., Auburn U., 1959; postgrad., Stanford U. Grad. Sch. Bus., 1968. Various positions AT&T, 1960-78; with Pacific Telephone & Telegraph Co., 1978—, exec. v.p. network, San Francisco, 1979-81, exec. v.p. services, 1981-82, exec. v.p. network services, 1982, exec. v.p., strategic planning and adminstrn., 1983—, vice chmn. bd., strategic planning and adminstrn., 1983—, dir., San Francisco; mem. adv. bd. Sloan program Stanford U. Grad. Sch. Bus., 1978—. Trustee Mills Coll., 1982—. Served to capt. U.S. Army, 1959-60. Sloan fellow, 1968. Republican. Clubs: Blackhawk Country (Dabville, Calif.); San Francisco Comml. Office: Pacific Tel & Tel Co 140 New Montgomery St San Francisco CA 94105

GINSBERG, ALLEN, poet; b. Newark, June 3, 1926; s. Louis and Naomi (Levy) G. A.B., Columbia U., 1948. With various cargo ships, 1945-56; addressed conf. Group Advancement Psychiatry, 1961; dir. Com. on Poetry Found., 1971—, Kerouac Sch. Poetics, Naropa Inst., Boulder, Colo. Assoc. with early Beat Generation prose-poets, 1945—; poetry readings, Columbia U., Harvard U., Yale U.,, numerous other univs. and assembly halls in, Chile, Peru, Eng., India, Havana, Warsaw, Prague, London, Moscow, Rome; also, Corcoran Art Gallery, Washington, 1971; actor: motion picture Pull My Daisy, 1961, Guns of the Trees, 1962, Wholly Communion, 1965, Chappaqua, 1966, Renaldo and Clara, 1978; narrator: film Kaddish, NET, 1977; Author: Howl and Other Poems, 1955, Empty Mirror, 1960, Kaddish and Other Poems, 1960, Reality Sandwiches, 1963, Planet News, Poems, 1961-67, 1968, Indian Journals, 1970, The Fall of America: Poems of these States, 1973 (Nat. Book award 1974), The Gates of Wrath: Early Rhymed Poems 1948-51, 1973, Allen Verbatim, 1974, First Blues, 1975, Journals Early 50's Early 60's, 1977, Contest of Bards, 1977, Mind Breaths, Poems 1972-1977, 1978, As Ever: Correspondence A.G. and Neal Cassady 1948-68, 1978, Poems All Over the Place, 1978, Mostly Sitting Haiku, 1978, Composed on the Tongue, Literary Conversations, 1967-77, 1980, Straight Hearts Delight: Love Poems and Selected Letters, 1980; author: Plutonium Ode, Poems 1977-1980, 1982, Collected Poems, 1947-80, 1984; recs. include: Songs of Innocence and of Experience by William Blake Tuned by Allen Ginsberg, 1970, Two Evenings with Allen Ginsberg, 1980, First Blues: Songs, 1982, Birdbrain, 1981, Allen Ginsberg First Blues, 1981. Guggenheim fellow in poetry, 1965-66. Mem. Am. Inst. Arts and Letters. Buddhist. Collaborated with Timothy Leary anti-war new consciousness activism, 1961. Home: PO Box 582 Stuyvesant Sta New York NY 10009 Office: care City Lights 261 Columbus Ave San Francisco CA 94133

GINSBERG, DAVID LAWRENCE, architect; b. N.Y.C., Sept. 21, 1932; s. Harry Seaman and Zena (Sagal) G.; m. Emily Boor, Dec. 29, 1969; children: Stuart Samuel, Daniel Paul, Laura Ruth. B.Arch., Cornell U., 1955. Pntr. charge N.Y. offices Perkins & Will, 1957-78, exec. v.p., Chgo., 1978-79; dir. Office of Planning, Presbyn. Hosp., N.Y.C., 1979—; mem. faculty Sch. Public Health, Columbia U., N.Y.C., 1979—. Prin. works include Primary Children's Med. Center, Salt Lake City, Scripps Meml. Hosp, La Jolla, Calif.; U. Utah Med. Center, Salt Lake City, Meth. Hosp, N.Y.C., L.I.-Jewish Hillside Med. Center. Served with AUS, 1955-57. Recipient medal N.Y. Soc. Architects, 1955. Fellow AIA; mem. Am. Hosp. Assn., Assn. Am. Med. Colls., Soc. Hosp. Planning, Am. Public Health Assn., Regional Planning Assn., Gargoyle Soc. Club: Town (Scarsdale). Home: 18 Autenrieth Rd Scarsdale NY 10583 Office: Presbyn Hosp Office Planning 161 Ft Washington Ave New York NY 10032

GINSBERG, DONALD MAURICE, educator, physicist; b. Chgo., Nov. 19, 1933; s. Maurice J. and Zelda (Robbins) G.; m. Joli D. Lasker, June 10, 1957; children: Mark D., Dana L. B.A., U. Chgo., 1952, B.S., 1955, M.S. (NSF fellow), 1956, Ph.D., U. Calif. at Berkeley, 1960. Mem. faculty U. Ill. at Urbana, 1959—, prof. physics, 1966—; vis. scientist in physics Am. Assn. Physics Tchrs.-Am. Inst. Physics, 1965-71; vis. scientist IBM, 1976; Mem. materials research adv. com., mem. evaluation com. for Nat. Magnet Lab., NSF, 1977-79; mem. rev. com. for solid state sci. div. Argonne Nat. Lab., 1977-83, chmn., 1980; mem. rev. panel for basic energy scis. div. Dept. Energy, 1981. Alfred P. Sloan research fellow, 1960-64; NSF fellow, 1966-67. Fellow Am. Phys. Soc.; mem. AAAS, Phi Beta Kappa, Sigma Xi. Research and publs. on low temperature physics, super conductivity, cryogenic instrumentation. Home: 1707 Parkhaven Dr Champaign IL 61820

GINSBERG, EDWARD, lawyer; b. N.Y.C., May 30, 1917; s. Charles and Rose G.; m. Rosalie Sinek, Aug. 11, 1941; children—William, Robert. B.A. with honors, U. Mich., 1938; J.D., Harvard, 1941; D.H.L., Hebrew Union Coll., 1972. Bar: Ohio bar 1941. Former sr. partner law firm Ginsberg, Guren & Merritt; former exec. v.p. and trustee U.S. Realty Investments; past partner N.Y. Yankees Am. League baseball club; past dir. El Al Israel Air Lines, Chgo. Bulls Nat. Basketball Assn., First Israel Bank & Trust Co. N.Y. Pres., mem. exec. com., nat. campaign cabinet United Jewish Appeal, formerly gen. chmn; v.p. Jewish Telegraphic Agy.; former chmn. Am. Jewish Joint Distbn. Com., now hon. pres.; v.p. Hebrew Sheltering and Immigrant Aid Soc.; Trustee United Israel Appeal, Jewish Community Fedn. Cleve. (life), Mt. Sinai Hosp., Jewish Convalescent Home Cleve. Served with USAAF. Hon. fellow Hebrew U., Jerusalem. Mem. Cleve., Ohio State bar assns., Phi Kappa Phi, Phi Sigma Delta. Jewish religion (pres. temple). Home: 2112 Acacia Park Dr Lyndhurst OH 44124 Office: 900 Illuminating Bldg Cleveland OH 44113

GINSBERG, ERNEST, lawyer, banker; b. Syracuse, N.Y., Feb. 14, 1931; s. Morris Henry and Mildred Florence (Slive) G.; m. Harriet Gay Scharf, Dec. 20, 1959; children: Alan Justin, Robert Daniel. B.A., Syracuse U., 1953, J.D., 1955; LL.M., Georgetown U., 1963. Bar: N.Y. State bar 1955, U.S. Supreme Ct. bar 1964. Pvt. practice law, Syracuse, 1957-61; mem. staff, office chief counsel IRS, 1961-63; tax counsel Comptroller of Currency, Washington, 1964-65, asso. chief counsel, 1965-68; v.p. legal affairs, sec. Republic Nat. Bank N.Y., U.S.A., N.Y.C., 1968-75, sr. v.p. legal affairs, sec., 1975-81; sr. v.p., sec. legal affairs Republic New York Corp., N.Y.C., 1974—; dir. SafraBank, Miami., Safra Bank II, Pompano Beach, Fla., Colonial Savs. and Loan, Ocala, Fla. Served with AUS, 1955-57. Mem. Am. Bar Assn., N.Y. State Bar Assn., Phi Sigma Delta, Phi Delta Phi. Office: 452 Fifth Ave Republic Nat Bank New York NY 10018

GINSBERG, FRANK CHARLES, advertising executive; b. N.Y.C., Mar. 8, 1944; s. Robert G. and Frances (Ginsberg) Porcell; m. Joan Barbara Cocoziello; 1 child, Alison. B.F.A., Boston U., 1965; M.F.A., NYU, 1968. Art dir. Grey Advt., N.Y.C., 1966-69; exec. art dir. Marshalk Co., N.Y.C., 1969-71, PGI, 1971-74; creative dir. Avrett Free & Ginsberg, N.Y.C., 1974-82, sr. exec. v.p., creative dir., 1982—. Chmn. annual fund Riverdale Country Sch., 1983. Recipient Clio award, 1974, 79, Bronze Lion Cannes Film Festival, 1978, 24 certs. or merit, 1971-83, 14 Andy awards, 1971-83. Mem. One Club, Art Dirs. Club (Silver One Club award (5) 1971-83). Home: 737 Park Ave New York NY 10021 Office: Avrett Free & Ginsberg 800 Third Ave New York NY 10019

GINSBERG, HAROLD LOUIS, educator; b. Montreal, Que., Can., Dec. 6, 1903; came to U.S., 1936, naturalized, 1942; s. Mendel and Golda Anna (Levinson) G.; m. Anne Gelrud, Nov. 7, 1937 (dec.). B.A., U. London, Eng., 1927, Ph.D., 1930. Auditor Hebrew U., Jerusalem, 1928-29; Instr. Bible Jewish Theol. Sem. Am., N.Y.C., 1936-40, Sabato Morais prof. Bibl. history and lit., 1941—; Vis. prof. Hebrew U., Jerusalem, 1957, 62, U. Pa., 1957-58, 68-69, Yale, spring 1967, Dropsie U., 1971-72, Columbia, 1972-73, Inst. for Advanced Studies, Hebrew U. Jerusalem, 1979-80; co-editor Jewish Publ. Soc. Bible Transl., 1956-62, editor-in-chief, 1962-77, mem. publ. com., 1958—; hon resident mem. Acad. Hebrew Lang., Jerusalem; mem. council World Union of Jewish Studies. Author: The Ugarit Texts, 1936, The Legend of King Keret, 1946, Studies in Daniel, 1948, Studies in Koheleth, 1950, Commentary on Koheleth, 1961, 2d edit., 1977, The Israelian Heritage of Judaism, 1982; contbg. author: Ancient Near Eastern Texts relating to The Old Testament, 1950, 55, 69, Handbook of Aramaic, 1967; Editor: The Five Megilloth and the Book of Jonah, 1969, 2d edit., 1974, Texts and Studies of American Academy for Jewish Research, vol. I, 1941, The Book of Isaiah, 1973, The Prophets, 1978; divisional editor for: Bible, Ency. Judaica, 1971. Fellow Am. Acad. Jewish Research (v.p.); mem. Soc. Bibl. Lit. and Exegesis (hon. pres.), Am. Oriental Soc., Israel Exploration Soc., Am. Schs. Oriental Research (asso.). Home: 280 Riverside Dr New York NY 10025

GINSBERG, HAROLD SAMUEL, virologist, educator; b. Daytona Beach, Fla., May 27, 1917; s. Jacob and Anne (Kalb) G.; m. Marion Reibstein, Aug. 4, 1949; children: Benjamin Langer, Peter Robert, Ann Meredith, Jane Elizabeth. A.B., Duke, 1937; M.D., Tulane U., 1941. Resident Mallory Inst. Pathology, Boston, 1941-42; intern, asst. resident Boston City Hosp., 4th Med. Service, 1942-43; resident physician, asso. Rockefeller Inst., 1946-51; asso. prof. preventive medicine Western Res. U. Sch. Medicine, 1951-60; prof. microbiology, chmn. dept. U. Pa. Sch. Medicine, 1960-73, Coll. Phys. and Surg. Columbia, 1973—; Mem. commn. acute respiratory diseases Armed Forces Epidemiological Bd., 1959-73; cons. NIH, 1959-72, 75—, Army Chem. Corps, 1962-64, NASA, 1969—, Am. Cancer Soc., 1969-73, mem. council on research and personnel, 1976-80; v.p. Internat. Com. on Nomenclature of Viruses, 1966-75; mem. space sci. bd., chmn. panel microbiology Nat. Acad. Sci., 1973-74; chmn. microbiology exam. com. Nat. Bd. Med. Examiners, 1974-79; mem. microbiology and infectious disease com. Nat. Inst. Allergy and Infectious Disease, NIH, 1976-81, chmn., 1979-81. Contbr. textbooks.; Co-author: Microbiology, 1967, 3d edit., 1980; mem. editorial bd.: Jour. Infectious Diseases, Jour. Immunology, Jour. Exptl. Medicine, Jour. Virology and Bacteriological Revs.; editor: Jour. Virology, 1979—, Cancer Research, 1978—. Served to maj. M.C. AUS, 1943-46. Decorated Legion of Merit. Mem. Nat. Acad. Scis.; Mem. Inst. Medicine of Nat. Acad. Scis., Assn. Am. Physicians, Am. Acad. Microbiologists (chmn. bd. govs. 1971-72), Am. Soc. Clin. Investigation (councillor 1958-60), Am. Assn. Immunologists, Am. Soc. Microbiology (chmn. virology div. 1961-62, councilor div. 1977—), Soc. Exptl. Biology and Medicine, Assn. Med. Sch. Microbiology Chairmen (pres. 1972-73), Harvey Soc. (pres.-elect 1983), Central Soc. Clin. Research, Am. Soc. Biol. Chemists, Am. Soc. Virology (pres. 1983), Alpha Omega Alpha. Home: 450 Riverside Dr New York NY 10027 Office: Dept Microbiology Columbia U Coll Physicians and Surgeons 701 W 168th St New York NY 10032

GINSBERG, LEON HERMAN, state educational administrator; b. San Antonio, Jan. 15, 1936; s. Sam and Lillian (Gindler) G.; m. Elaine Myrna Kaner, July 29, 1956 (div. 1983); children: Robert, Michael, Meryl Sue.; m. Connie Mooney, June 2, 1983; stepchildren: Gretchen, Kathleen Mooney. B.A., Trinity U., 1957; M.S.W., Tulane U., 1959; Ph.D., U. Okla., 1966. Dist. dir. B'nai B'rith Youth Orgn., New Orleans, 1958-61; dir. community activities Jewish Community Council, Tulsa, 1961-63; assoc. prof. Sch. Social Work U. Okla., Norman, 1963-68; prof., dir. Sch. Social Work W.Va. U., Morgantown, 1968-71, prof., dean, 1971-77; commr. welfare State of W.Va., Charleston, 1977-84; chancellor W.Va. Bd. Regents for Higher Edn., 1984—; Fulbright prof. U. Pontificia Bolivariana, Medellin, Colombia, fall 1974; Cons. tng. programs Peace Corps, Head Start, Community Action, Bur. Indian Affairs, pub. welfare depts. Okla., Pa., Wis., W.Va. Co-author: Human Services for Older Adults, 1979; author: Social Work Practice in Public Welfare, 1983; Editor: Social Work in Rural Communities, 1976; co-editor: Life-Span Developmental Psychology, 1975; contbr. articles to profl. jours. Served to lt. AUS, 1957-58. Recipient Disting. Service award W.Va. Welfare Conf., 1970; named W.Va. Social Worker of Yr., 1978. Mem. Council Social Work Edn., Nat. Assn. Social Workers, Am. Public Welfare Assn. (pres.), Internat. Conf. on Social Welfare, B'nai B'rith., Child Welfare League of Am. Home: 2106 Kanawha Blvd E Apt 201 Charleston WV 25311 Office: WVa Bd Regents 950 Kanauha Blvd East Charleston WV 25301

GINSBERG, LEWIS ROBBINS, Lawyer; b. Chgo., May 7, 1932; s. Maurice Jesse and Zelda (Robbins) G.; m. Linda Cox, June 16, 1973; children: Aaron, Brenda, Stephen. A.B., U. Chgo., 1953, J.D., 1956.. Assoc. firm Lederer, Livingston, Kahn & Adsit, Chgo., 1956, 60-63; corp. atty. Maremont Corp., Chgo., 1963-66; assoc. firm McDermott, Will & Emery, Chgo., 1966-69, ptnr., 1969—. Bd. dirs. Ravenswood Hosp. Med. Ctr., Chgo., 1981—. Served to capt. U.S. Army, 1957-60. Mem. Chgo. Bar Assn., Order of Coif. Democrat. Jewish. Club: University (Chgo.). Home: 2800 Lake Shore Dr Chicago IL 60657 Office: McDermott Will & Emery 111 W Monroe St Chicago IL 60603

GINSBERG, MITCHELL I., social worker, educator; b. Boston, Oct. 20, 1915; s. Harry J. and Rose (Harris) G.; m. Ida Robbins, Aug. 22, 1948. B.A., Tufts Coll., 1937, postgrad., 1938, L.H.D., 1975; M.S.W., Columbia U., 1941; L.H.D., Adelphi U., 1974; LL.D., U. Md., 1974. Project dir. Peace Corps tng. project in urban community action, Columbia, Venezuela; asso. prof. Columbia U. Sch. Social Work, 1954-56, prof., 1956, asst. to acting dean, 1958-60, assoc. dean, 1960-66, dean, spl. adv. to pres. on community affairs, 1970-81, prof., dean emeritus, 1981—; co-dir. Center for Study Human Rights, 1978—, mem. com. on gen. edn., 1977—; commr. N.Y.C. Dept. Social Services, 1966-67; adminstr. N.Y.C. Human Resources Adminstrn., 1967-70; cons. community action program Office Econ. Opportunity, welfare policy, N.Y.C., 1965-68; mem. select panel for promotion child health Office Asst. Sec. for Health, HEW, 1979-81; cons. HEW, Ford Found., 1978—; Mem. tech. com. Com. for Nat. Health Ins.; adv. panel nat. ins. subcom. on health Ways and Means Com., 1975; chmn. Nat. Conf. on Social Welfare Task Force on Title XX Issues, 1976; Bd. dirs. Health Security Action Council, 1971—, HIP, 1971-78, Whitney M. Young Meml. Found., 1971—, Health Care Inst.; mem. com. nat. legis. Council on Social Work Edn., 1973-76; trustee Community Service Soc., 1974—; mem. nat. adv. council Hospice, Inc.; mem. task force on cost and financing mental health President's Commn. on Mental Health, 1977; mem. com. on evaluation assistance Greater N.Y. Fund, 1977; mem. N.Y.C. Task Force on Human Services; mem. adv. com. on services to children and families Edna McConnell Clark Found. Editorial adv. bd.: Man and Medicine; adv. bd.: Jour. Inst. Socioeconomic Studies. Served with AUS, 1942-46. Fellow social work Adelphi U., 1967; recipient Michael Schwerner Meml. award civil rights work N.Y.C., 1966, Blanche Ittleson award, 1967; William J. Schieffelin award Citizens Union N.Y.C., 1968. Mem. Nat. Assn. Social Workers (exec. com. N.Y.C. chpt., chmn. social policy and action 1966—, nat. pres. 1971-73, mem. welfare reform task force 1977), AAUP, Nat. Conf. Social Welfare (Distinguished Service award 1975, pres. 1979—), Nat. Acad. Public Adminstrn. (trustee 1978, co-chmn. nat. panel on coordination of services to children and elderly), Nat. Assn. Jewish Center Workers, Am. Pub. Welfare Assn. (chmn. com. social service policy 1975-76, 77, dir. 1974-77), Conf. Deans and Dirs. Schs. Social Work (chmn. 1975-79), Nat. Conf. on Social Welfare, Phi Beta Kappa. Home: 372 Central Park W Apt 9-D New York NY 10025

GINSBERG, REUBEN M., lawyer; b. Dallas, Aug. 16, 1922; s. Jacob B. and Hinda (Bernstein) G.; m. Regine Silven, Aug. 17, 1947; children—Michael D., Debra S., Jacqueline B., Lisa A. A.B., Am. U., 1943; summer student, U. Mexico, 1942; LL.B., Columbia, 1949; grad. student taxation, So. Methodist U., 1951-53. Bar: Tex. bar 1949, Okla. bar 1949. Pvt. practice in, Okla., 1949-50, practice in, Dallas, 1950—; partner firm Ginsberg & Farman, 1965—; lectr., tax counselor. Chmn. speakers bur. NCCJ, 1956—; mem. adv. council Community Chest Trust, 1960—. Bd. dirs. Am. Jewish Com.; chpt. chmn. Dallas chpt., 1972—, Dallas chpt. ACLU; trustee Hexter Found.-Crippled Children's Endowment Fund. Served with AUS, 1942-46. Recipient citation Tex. Soc. Crippled Children. Mem. Home Builders Assn. Dallas County (chmn. legislative com.), Am., Tex., Dallas County bar assns. Jewish religion (dir. religious sch. com. 1961-64). Club: Mason (32 deg.). Home: 7239 S Jan Mar St Dallas TX 75230 Office: 820 Hartford Bldg 400 N St Paul Dallas TX 75211

GINSBURG, CHARLES DAVID, lawyer; b. N.Y.C., Apr. 20, 1912; s. Nathan and Rae (Lewis) G.; m. Marianne Laïs; children by previous marriage: Jonathan, Susan, Mark. A.B., W.Va. U., 1932; LL.B., Harvard U., 1935. Atty. for public utilities div. and office of gen. counsel SEC, 1935-39; law sec. to Justice William O. Douglas, 1939; asst. to commr. SEC, 1939-40; legal adviser Price Stblzn. Div., Nat. Def. Adv. Com., 1940-41; gen. counsel Office Price Adminstrn. and Civilian Supply, 1941-42, OPA, 1942-43; pvt. practice law, Washington, 1946—; partner firm Ginsburg, Feldman, Weil & Bress; adminstrv. asst. to Senator M.M. Neely, W.Va., 1950; adj. prof. internat. law Georgetown U. (Grad. Sch. Law), 1959-67; Dep. commr. U.S. del. Austrian Treaty Commn., Vienna, 1947; adviser U.S. del. Council Fgn. Ministers, London, 1947; Mem. Presdl. Emergency Bd. 166 (Airlines), 1966; mem. Pres.'s Commn. on Postal Orgn., 1967; chmn. Presdl. Emergency Bd. 169 (Railroads), 1969; exec. dir. Nat. Adv. Commn. Civil Disorders, 1967. Author: The Future of German Reparations; Contbr. to legal jours. Bd. mem., chmn. exec. com. Nat. Symphony Orch. Assn., 1960-69; bd. govs. Weizmann Inst., 1965 (hon. fellow 1972); mem. vis. com. Harvard-Mass. Inst. Tech. Joint Center on Urban Studies, 1969; trustee St. John's Coll., 1969-75, chmn. bd., 1974-76; overseers com. Kennedy Sch. Govt. Harvard, 1971—; mem. council Nat. Harvard Law Sch. Assn., 1972—. Served from pvt. to capt. AUS, 1943-46; dep. dir. econs. div. Office Mil. Govt., 1945-46; Germany. Decorated Bronze Star medal, Legion of Merit; recipient Presdl. Certificate of Merit. Mem. Am. Law Inst., Council on Fgn. Relations, Phi Beta Kappa. Democrat. Clubs: F Street, Federal City, Army and Navy. Home: 619 S Lee St Alexandria VA 22314 Office: 1700 Pennsylvania Ave NW Washington DC 20006

GINSBURG, GERALD J., lawyer, business executive; b. Poughkeepsie, N.Y., Aug. 29, 1930; s. Abraham and Anna (Murkoff) G.; m. Vera Evelyn Curtis, Feb. 2, 1963; children: Jason Andrew, Stephanie Carla. B.S., Syracuse U., 1952; J.D., Bklyn. Law Sch., 1958. Bar: N.Y. 1959. Pub. acct., 1954-59; v.p. fin. and ops., dir. Sheffield Watch Corp., N.Y.C., 1959-70, dir., 1967-70; exec. v.p., dir. Kurt Orban Co., Wayne, N.J., 1971-83; pres. Pacific Marine Holdings Corp., 1983—; dir. Ramapo Fin. Corp., Pilgrim State Bank. Served with USNR, 1952-53. Mem. ABA, N.Y. Bar Assn. Office: Pacific Marine Holdings Corp 4 Embarcadero Ctr San Francisco CA 94111

GINSBURG, MARCUS, lawyer; b. Marietta, Ohio, Feb. 16, 1915; s. Louis and Dora (Brachman) G.; m. Martine Heilbron, Feb. 23, 1949; children: Harold Heilbron, Robert L. Student, Marietta Coll., 1932-33; A.B., U. Mich., 1936; J.D., Harvard U., 1939. Bar: Md. 1939, Tex. 1940. Since practiced in, Ft. Worth; partner firm McDonald, Sanders, Ginsburg, Phillips, Maddox & Newkirk, 1951—; dir., exec. com. Continental Nat. Bank, Ft. Worth; sec. Ryan Mortgage Investors; dir. Originala Petroleum Corp. Pres. United Fund and Community Services, Ft. Worth, 1962, Tarrant Council Community Council, 1966-67, Traveller's Aid Soc., Ft. Worth, 1953-54; vice chmn. city solicitations commn., Ft. Worth, 1963-67; past nat. v.p. Am. Jewish Congress; past v.p. Nat. Community Relations Adv. Council; mem. U.S. nat. commn. UNESCO, 1959-64, exec. com., 1963-64, steering com., 1964, chmn. pub. information com., 1962-64; past v.p., treas. Children's Mus. Ft. Worth; mem. Nat. Budget and Consultation Com., 1966—; trustee Retina Research Found.; bd. dirs. Ft. Worth Art Assn. Served to 2d lt. USAAF, 1942-45. Decorated Army Commendation medal; recipient award excellency United Fund Ft. Worth; award Ft. Worth Traveller's Aid Soc. Ft. Worth Community Council. Mem. Harvard Law Sch. Assn. (life mem., pres. Tex. 1955-56, nat. v.p. 1956-57, dir. 1978), Assn. Life Ins. Council, Nat. Assn. Coll. and Univ. Attys., Newcomen Soc. N.Am., Confrerie des Chevaliers du Tastevin (commandeur N.Tex. chpt.), Pi Lambda Phi. Jewish (v.p. temple). Clubs: Ft. Worth, Petroleum, Shady Oaks Country, Ridglea Country (Ft. Worth). Home: 3860 Bellaire Circle Fort Worth TX 76109 Office: Continental Nat Bank Bldg Fort Worth TX 76102

GINSBURG, MARTIN D., lawyer, educator; b. N.Y.C., June 10, 1932; s. Morris and Evelyn (Bayer) G.; m. Ruth Bader, June 23, 1954; children: Jane, James. A.B., Cornell U., 1953; J.D., Harvard U., 1958. Bar: N.Y. 1959, D.C. 1980. Practiced in N.Y.C., 1959-79; mem. firm Weil, Gotshal & Manges, N.Y.C., 1963-79; of counsel firm Fried, Frank, Harris, Shriver and Kampelman, Washington, 1980—; Charles Keller Beekman prof. law Columbia U. Law Sch., N.Y.C., 1979-80; adj. prof. law N.Y. U. Law Sch., N.Y.C., 1967-79; prof. law Georgetown U. Law Center, Washington, 1980—; vis. prof. law Stanford (Calif.) U., 1978; lectr. Salzburg Seminar, Austria, 1984; mem. tax div. adv. group Dept. Justice, 1980-81; mem. adv. group to Commr. Internal Revenue, 1978-80; mem. adv. bd. U. Calif. Securities Regulation Inst., 1973—; lectr. various tax insts., 1963—. Contbr. articles to legal jours.; co-author; editor: Tax Consequences of Investments, 1969. Served to 1st lt., arty. U.S. Army, 1954-56. Fellow Am. Coll. Tax Counsel; mem. Am. Law Inst. (cons. Fed. Income Tax Project 1974—), N.Y. State Bar Assn. (mem. tax sect. exec. com. 1969—, chmn. tax sect. 1975), Assn. Bar City N.Y. (chmn. com. taxation 1977-79, mem. audit com. 1980-81), ABA (mem. com. corp.-stockholder relations tax sect. 1973—, chmn. com. simplification 1979-81, mem. tax sect. council 1984-86). Office: 600 New Hampshire Ave NW Washington DC 20037

GINSBURG, NORTON SYDNEY, geography educator; b. Chgo., Aug. 24, 1921; s. Morris and Sarah (Ginsberg) G.; m. Diana Roselle Peterson, Aug. 12, 1973; children: Jeremy, Alexander. B.A., U. Chgo., 1941, M.A., 1947, Ph.D., 1949. Geographer, U.S. Army Map Service, 1941-42; prof. geography U. Chgo., 1947—, chmn. dept., 1978—, assoc. dean Coll., 1963-66, assoc. dean social scis., 1967-69; dean academic program, sr. fellow Center for Study Democratic Instns., Santa Barbara, 1971-74; cons. Social Sci. Research Council, Ency. Brit., Ford Found. (East-West Center), Nat. Acad. Sci., NRC, SCOPE, UN, UNESCO. Co-author, editor: Pattern of Asia, 1958, Malaya, 1958, China: The 80's Era, 1984; author: Atlas of Economic Development, 1961; co-editor: The Ocean Yearbooks, 1978, 80, 82, 83. Served to lt. USNR, 1942-46. Guggenheim fellow, 1983. Mem. Assn. Am. Geographers (pres. 1970-71), Phi Beta Kappa, Sigma Xi. Clubs: Quadrangle, Cosmos. Home: 1320 E Madison Park Chicago IL 60615

GINSBURG, RUTH BADER, federal judge; b. Bklyn., Mar. 15, 1933; d. Nathan and Celia (Amster) Bader; m. Martin David Ginsburg, June 23, 1954; children: Jane Carol, James Steven. A.B., Cornell U., 1954; postgrad., Harvard Law Sch., 1956-58; LL.B., Columbia Law Sch., 1959; LL.D., Lund (Sweden) U., 1969, Am. U., 1981, Vt. Law Sch., 1984. Bar: N.Y. 1954, D.C. 1975, U.S. Supreme Ct. 1967. Law sec. to judge U.S. Dist. Ct. (So. Dist. N.Y.), 1959-61; research assoc. Columbia Law Sch., N.Y.C., 1961-62, assoc. dir. project internat. procedure, 1962-63; asst. prof. Rutgers U. Sch. Law, Newark, 1963-66, assoc. prof., 1966-69, prof., 1969-72, Columbia U. Sch. Law, N.Y.C., 1972-80; U.S. Circuit judge U.S. Ct. Appeals, D.C. Circuit, Washington, 1980—; Phi Beta Kappa vis. scholar, 1973-74; fellow Center for Advanced Study in Behavioral Scis., Stanford, Calif., 1977-78; lectr. Salzburg Seminar, Austria, 1984; Bd. dirs. Am. Bar Found., 1979—, exec. com., 1981—. Author: (with Anders Bruzelius) Civil Procedure in Sweden, 1965, Swedish Code of Judicial Procedure, 1968, (with Herma Hill Kay and Kenneth M. Davidson) Sex-Based Discrimination, 1974, supplement, 1978; contbr. numerous articles to legal jours.; vol. editor: Business Regulation in the Common Market Nations, vol. 1, 1969. Mem. ABA, Am. Law Inst. (council mem. 1978—), Council on Fgn. Relations., Am. Acad. Arts and Scis. Office: US Court of Appeals for DC Circuit US Courthouse Washington DC 20001

GINSBURG, SEYMOUR, educator; b. Bklyn., Dec. 12, 1927; s. William and Bessie (Setomer) G.; children—Diane, David. B.S., CCNY, 1948; Ph.D., U. Mich., 1952, M.S., 1949. Asst. prof. math. U. Miami, Coral Gables, Fla., 1951-55; engr. Northrop Corp., Hawthorne, Calif., 1955-56, sr. research engr., 1956-59; sect. head Hughes Aircraft, Los Angeles, 1959-60; sr. mathematician System Devel. Corp., Santa Monica, Calif, 1960-71; Fletcher Jones prof. computer sci. U. So. Calif., Los Angeles, 1966—. Author: An Introduction to Mathematical Machine Theory, 1962, The Mathematical Theory of Context-Free Languages, 1966, Algebraic and Automata-Theoretic Properties of Formal Languages, 1975; Contbr. articles to various publs. Served with U.S. Army, 1946-47. Guggenheim fellow, 1974-75. Fellow IEEE; mem. Am. Math. Soc., Assn. Computing Machinery, Soc. Indsl. and Applied Math., Math. Assn. Am. Jewish. Office: Computer Sci Dept Univ of Southern California Los Angeles CA 90089

GINSBURG, SIGMUND G., university administrator; b. N.Y.C., Oct. 12, 1937; s. Saul and Rose (Rich) G.; m. Judith Ann Jacobson, July 4, 1965; children: Beth Alison, David Grant. B.A. magna cum laude, Dartmouth Coll., 1959; postgrad., London Sch. Econs., 1959-60; M.P.A., Harvard U., 1961. Mgmt. intern Office of Sec. of Def., Washington, 1961-62; asst. to pres. Hudson Inst., 1964; asst. mgr. personnel adminstrv. services, mgmt. analyst Port Authority of N.Y. and N.J., 1964-66; sr. mgmt. cons. and spl. asst. to dep. mayor Office of the Mayor, City of N.Y., 1966-67, asst. city adminstr., 1967-72; v.p. for adminstrn. and planning, treas. Adelphi U., Garden City, N.Y., 1972-78; assoc. dir. CICCO and Assocs., Inc., 1977—; v.p. for fin., treas. U. Cin., 1978—, adj. prof. higher edn. adminstrn., bus. adminstrn., 1980—; adj. assoc. prof. mgmt. Adelphi U., 1972-78;; adj. asst. prof. City U. N.Y., 1966-72; lectr. profl. meetings; mgmt. commentator Sta. WGUC, Cin., 1980; Mem. City Mgr.'s Working Rev. Com. Cin. 2000 Plan, 1979-82; mem. citizen's adv. com. Wyo. Bd. Edn., 1980. Co-author: Managing the Higher Education Enterprise, 1980; author: Management: An Executive Perspective, 1982, Ropes for Management Success: Climb Higher, Faster, 1984; contbr. articles to profl. jours., chpts. to books. Served as lt. U.S. Army, 1962-64. Recipient Colby prize in govt. Dartmouth Coll., 1959, Merit award City of N.Y., 1969; Daniel Webster nat. scholar Dartmouth Coll., 1955-59; James B. Reynolds Scholar London Sch. Econs., 1959-60; Littauer fellow Harvard U., 1961. Mem. Phi Beta Kappa. Office: 300C Administration Bldg Univ of Cin Cincinnati OH 45221

GINSBURGH, ROBERT NEVILLE, financial consultant, retired air force officer; b. Ft. Sill, Okla., Nov. 19, 1923; s. A. Robert and Elsie (Pinney) G.; m. Nancy Brand, Dec. 28, 1948 (div. Feb. 1958); children: Robert Brand, Charles Lee; m. Gail H. Whitehead Winslow, Apr. 4, 1959; children: Carolyn, Anne; stepchildren: Alan F. Winslow III, William C. Winslow. Grad., Phillips Acad., Andover, 1940; B.S., U.S. Mil. Acad., 1944; M.P.A., Harvard, 1947, M.A., 1948; Ph.D., 1949; postgrad., Field Arty. Sch., 1944, Air Tactical Sch., 1950, Air Command and Staff Coll., 1953, Indsl. Coll., 1960, Air War Coll., 1961, Nat. War Coll., 1963. Commd. 2d lt. F.A., 1944; advanced through grades to maj. gen USAF, 1971; asst. prof. social scis. U.S. Mil. Acad., 1948-51; with Air Force Legis. Liaison, 1951-55, Allied Air Forces So. Europe, Naples, 1955-58, Air Proving Ground Center, 1958; pub. affairs Dept. Def., 1959; asst. exec. air force chief of staff, 1959-62; research fellow Council Fgn. Relations, 1963-64; with Policy Planning Council, State Dept., 1964-66; staff group Office of Chmn. JCS; sr. staff mem. Nat. Security Council, 1966-69; comdr. Aerospace Studies Inst., Air U., Maxwell AFB, Ala., 1969-71; chief Air Force History, 1971-72; dir. Air Force Info., 1972-74; dep. dir. joint staff Orgn. Joint Chiefs Staff, 1974-75; editor in chief Strategic Rev., 1975-76, Neville Assos., 1977—; dir. Sterling Drilling & Prodn., Inc.; Bd. dirs. Air Force Hist. Found. Author: US Military Strategy in the Sixties, 1965, US Military Strategy in the Seventies, 1970, The Nixon Doctrine and Military Strategy, 1971; Editor: Principles of Insurance, 1949-50; Contbr. to: Economics of National Security, 1950, also articles in profl. jours. Decorated D.S.M., Silver Star, Legion of Merit with oak leaf cluster, Purple Heart Joint Services, Air Force, Army commendation medals. Mem. Council on Fgn. Relations. Clubs: Kenwood; Internat. (Washington); Rehoboth Bay Sailing Assn. Home: 5319 Oakland Rd Chevy Chase MD 20815

GINZBERG, ELI, economist, educator, govt. cons.; b. N.Y.C., Apr. 30, 1911; s. Louis and Adele (Katzenstein) G.; m. Ruth Szold, July 14, 1946; children—Abigail, Jeremy, Rachel. Student, U. Heidelberg, U. Grenoble, 1928-29; A.B., Columbia U., 1931, A.M., 1932, Ph.D., 1934, Litt. D., 1982; Litt.D., Jewish Theol. Sem., 1966; LL.D., Loyola U., Chgo., 1969. Dir. research econs., group behavior Columbia U., 1939-42, 48-49, faculty, 1935—; A. Barton Hepburn prof. econs. Columbia (Grad. Sch. Bus.), 1967-79; emeritus Columbia U. (Grad. Sch. Bus.), 1979—, spl. lectr., 1979—, dir. conservation human resources project, 1950—, dir. Revson fellows program on future, City N.Y., 1979—; spl. lectr. health and society Barnard Coll., 1980—; Hon. faculty mem. Indsl. Coll. Armed Forces, 1971—; chmn. bd. Manpower Demonstration Research Corp., 1974-82, chmn. bd. emeritus, 1982—; Spl. asst. to chief statistician U.S. War Dept., 1942-44, spl. asst. to dir. hosp. div., 1944, dir. resources analysis div., 1944-46; cons. Dept. Army, 1946-70, Dept. State, 1953, 56, 65-69, Dept. Labor, 1954-82, Dept. Def., 1964-71, Dept. Commerce, 1965-66, 79-80, GAO, 1973—, Exec. Office Pres., 1942; mem. med. adv. bd. to Sec. War, 1946-48; U.S. rep. 5 power Conf. Reparations for Non-Repatriable Refugees, 1946; dir. N.Y. State Hosp. Study, 1948-49; mem. Com. on Wartime Requirement for Sci. and Specialized Personnel, 1942; med. cons. Hoover Commn., 1952; adviser Commn. Chronic Illness, 1950-53; mem. adv. council NIMH, 1959-63; chmn. com. on studies White House Conf. on Children and Youth, 1960; dir. staff studies Nat. Manpower Council, 1951-61; chmn. Nat. Manpower Adv. Com., 1962-74, Nat. Commn. for Manpower Policy, 1974-79, Nat. Commn. for Employment Policy, 1979-82; mem. Nat. Adv. Allied Health Council, 1968-72; mem. sci. adv. bd. USAF, 1969-73; chmn. taskforce manpower research Dept. Def., 1970-71; mem. Inst. Medicine, Nat. Acad. Scis., 1972—; cons. to various bus. and nonprofit orgns. Author: The House of Adam Smith, 1934, The Illusion of Economic Stability, 1939, Grass on the Slag Heaps: The Story of the Welsh Miners, 1942, The Unemployed, 1943, The Labor Leader, 1948, A Pattern for Hospital Care, 1949, Agenda for American Jews, 1950; Occupational Choice, 1951, The Uneducated, 1953, Psychiatry and Military Manpower Policy, 1953, What Makes an Executive, 1955, The Negro Potential, 1956, Effecting Change in Large Organizations, 1957, Human Resources, 1958, The Ineffective Soldier, 3 vols, 1959, The Nation's Children, 3 vols, 1960, Planning for Better Hospital Care, 1961, The Optimistic Tradition and American Youth, 1962, The

American Worker in the Twentieth Century, 1963, The Troublesome Presence, 1964, Talent and Performance, 1964, The Negro Challenge to the Business Community, 1964, The Pluralistic Economy, 1965, Keeper of the Law: Louis Ginzberg, 1966, Life Styles of Educated Women, Educated American Women-Self-Portraits, 1966, Manpower Strategy for Developing Countries, 1967, The Middle Class Negro in the White Man's World, 1967, Manpower Strategy for the Metropolis, 1968, Business Leadership and the Negro Crisis, 1968, Men, Money and Medicine, 1969, Urban Health Services-The Case of New York, 1971, Career Guidance, 1971, Manpower for Development, 1971, Manpower Advice for Government, 1972, New York Is Very Much Alive, 1973, Corporate Lib: Women's Challenge to Management; editor, 1973, Federal Manpower in Transition, 1974, The Great Society: Lessons for the Future, 1974, The University Medical Center and the Metropolis, 1974, The Future of the Metropolis, 1974, The Manpower Connection: Education and Work, 1975, Jobs for Americans, 1976, The Human Economy, 1976, Regionalization and Health Policy, 1977, The Limits of Health Reform, 1977; The, House of Adam Smith Revisited, 1977, Health Manpower and Health Policy, 1978, Good Jobs, Bad Jobs, No Jobs, 1979, American Jews: The Building of a Voluntary Community (in Hebrew), 1980, Employing the Unemployed, 1980, The School/Work Nexus, 1981; Editor: The Delivery of Health Care: What Lies Ahead, 1982, The Coming Physician Surplus: In Search of a Public Policy, 1983, Home Health Care: Its Role in the Changing Health Services Market, 1983, Health Dollars and Health Services: The New York City Experience, 1983. Dir. research United Jewish Appeal, 1941; gov. Hebrew U., Jerusalem, 1953-59. Fellow AAAS, Am. Acad. Arts and Scis.; mem. Am. Econ. Assn., Acad. Polit. Sci., Indsl. Relations Research Assn., A.A.U.P., Soc. Med. Consultants to Armed Forces (asso.), Allen O. Whipple Surg. Soc., Phi Beta Kappa, Beta Gamma Sigma. Home: 845 West End Ave New York NY 10025

GINZBURG, RALPH, editor, publisher; b. Bklyn., Oct. 28, 1929; s. Raymond and Rachel G. (Lipkin) G.; m. Shoshana Brown, Dec. 16, 1958; children—Bonnie, Shepherd, Lark. B.B.A., Coll. City N.Y., 1949; postgrad., Bklyn. Coll., 1950; diploma, Henry George Sch. Econs., 1951. Copyboy N.Y. Daily Compass, 1949-50; re-write man Washington Times-Herald, 1950-51. Freelance writer, photographer for: mags. including Parade; others, 1951-53; staff writer, NBC, 1954-55; mng. bd.: Look mag, 1955-56; articles editor Esquire, 1956-58; editor: Eros, 1962-63, Fact, 1964-68, Avant-Garde, 1969—, Moneysworth, 1971—, Am. Business, 1976—, EXTRA!, 1977—, Better Living, 1980—, Uncle Sam, 1981—; Author: 100 Years of Lynching, 1961, An Unhurried View of Erotica, 1956, Eros on Trial, 1964, Castrated: My Eight Months in Prison, 1973. Served with AUS, 1950-51. Mem. ACLU, Sierra Club, Wilderness Soc., Friends of Earth, Urban Coalition, Fellowship of Reconciliation, War Resisters League, N.Y. Ramblers, Adirondack Mountain Club, Common Cause, Quaker Action Group, Scenic Hudson Preservation Soc., Audubon Soc., Green Mountain Club, Am. Youth Hostels. Office: 251 W 57th St New York NY 10019 *My life is dedicated to the greater liberation of man's healthier instincts.*

GINZTON, EDWARD LEONARD, engineering corporation executive; b. Dnepropetrovsk, Ukraine, Dec. 27, 1915; came to U.S., 1929; s. Leonard Louis and Natalie P. (Philipova) G.; m. Artemas A. McCann; children: Anne, Leonard, Nancy, David. B.S., U. Calif., 1936, M.S., 1937; E.E., Stanford U., 1938, Ph.D., 1940. Research engr. Sperry Gyroscope Co., N.Y.C., 1940-46; asst. prof. applied physics and elec. engring. Stanford U., 1946-47, assoc. prof., 1947-50, prof., 1951-68; dir. Microwave Lab., 1949-59, Varian Assocs., 1948—, chmn. bd., 1959-84, chmn. exec. com., 1984—, chief exec. officer, 1959-72, pres., 1964-68; dir. Stanford Bank, 1967-71, Stanford Project M, Stanford Linear Accelerator Center, 1957-60; Mem. commn. 1 U.S. nat. com. Internat. Sci. Radio Union, 1958-68; mem. Lawrence Berkeley Lab. Sci. and Adv. Com., 1972-79; chmn. adv. bd. Sch. Engring., Stanford, 1968-70; bd. dirs., mem. exec. com. co-chmn. Stanford Mid-Peninsula Urban Coalition, 1968-72; bd. dirs. Nat. Bur. Econ. Research, 1981—. Author: Microwave Measurements, 1957; Contbr. articles to tech. jours. Bd. dirs. Mid-Peninsula Housing Devel. Corp., 1970—, Stanford Hosp., 1975-80; trustee Stanford U., 1977—. Recipient Morris Liebmann Meml. prize I.R.E., 1958, Calif. Manufacturer of Yr. award, 1974. Fellow IEEE (bd. dirs. 1971-72, chmn. awards bd. 1971-72, medal of honor 1969); mem. Nat. Acad. Scis. (chmn. com. on motor vehicle emissions 1971-74, co-chmn. com. nuclear energy study 1975-80), Am. Acad. Arts and Scis., Nat. Acad. Engring. (mem. council 1974-80), Sigma Xi, Eta Kappa Nu, Tau Beta Pi. Patentee in field. Home: 28014 Natoma Rd Los Altos Hills CA 94022 Office: 611 Hansen Way Palo Alto CA 94303

GIOBBI, EDWARD GIACCHINO, artist; b. Waterbury, Conn., July 18, 1926; s. Achille and Teresa (Gasparetti) G.; m. Elinor E. Turner, Feb. 14, 1959; children—Eugenia, Elizabeth, Chambless Martino. Student, Whitney Sch. Art, New Haven, 1946-47, Vesper George Sch. Art, Boston, 1947-50, Cape Sch. Art, Provincetown, Mass., summer, 1949-50, Art Students League, N.Y.C., 1950-51, 55-56, Acad. Fine Arts, Florence, Italy, 1951-54. One man shows include, Ward Eggleston Gallery, N.Y.C., 1951, Matatuck Mus., Conn., 1955, Artists Gallery, N.Y.C., 1956, Contempories Gallery, N.Y.C., 1956, 60-61, 63, Heller Gallery, N.Y.C., 1957, 58, Brooks Meml. Art Gallery, Memphis, 1961, 72, 80, New Arts Center, London, Eng., 1964, 67, Bear Lane Gallery, Oxford, Eng., 1964, Queen Sq. Gallery, Leeds Gallery, Tirca Karlis Gallery, Provincetown, 1964-66, 67, Michelson Gallery, Washington, 1966, Alan Gallery, N.Y.C., Ark. Art Centre, Little Rock, Waddell Gallery, N.Y.C., 1967, Obelisk Gallery, Boston, 1968, Gertrude Kasle Gallery, Detroit, Hopkins Center, Dartmouth, 1972, Galleria del Obelisco, Rome, 1974, Crane Kalman Gallery, London, 1975, Neuberger Mus., Purchase, N.Y., 1977, Gruenebaum Gallery, N.Y.C., Katonah (N.Y.) Gallery, 1978, Alice Ringham Gallery, Memphis, 1980, two-man shows include, Galeries an der Reuss, Lucerne, Switzerland, 1953, Nexus Gallery, Boston, 1956; group exhbns. include Recent Drawings U.S.A, Mus. Modern Art, 1956, Am. Fedn. Arts Travelling Show, 1956, 58, 61, 63, Whitney Mus. Ann., 1957-61, 66, Corcoran Gallery, 1958, Pa. Acad. Fine Arts, 1961, Young Am, Whitney Mus., 1961, 40 painters under 40, Whitney Mus., 1962, Figure USA, Mus. Modern Art, 1962, Art in Progress, Finch Coll., N.Y.C., 1967, rep. permanent collections, Tate Gallery, London, Eng., Magdalen Coll., Cambridge, Eng., St. Edmund Hall, Oxford, Eng., Poole Tech. Coll., Dorset, Eng., Whitney Mus., Balt. Mus. Art Inst. Chgo., Brooks Meml. Art Gallery, Marion Koogler McNay Art Inst., San Antonio, Boston Mus. Fine Arts, Spellman Coll., Atlanta, Allentown (Pa.) Mus., Wesleyan Coll., Macon, Ga., Syracuse U., Academia di Belle Arti, Florence, Memphis Acad. Arts, U. Mich., Albright Knox Gallery, Leeds (Eng.) City Art Gallery, Bklyn. Mus., Finch Coll.; artist in residence, Memphis Acad., 1960-61, Ford Found., Ark. Arts Centre, 1966, Ford Found., Ark. Arts Centre, Dartmouth, 1972. Served with inf. AUS, 1944-46; ETO. Recipient Emily Lowe award, 1951-52; Guggenheim fellow, 1972; Decorated Combat Inf. Badge. Mem. adv. bd. Westchester Council Arts, Katonah Gallery. Address: 161 Croton Lake Rd Katonah NY 10536

GIORDANO, ANDREW ANTHONY, naval officer; b. Passaic, N.J., May 17, 1932; s. Samuel and Sarah (Pollara) G.; m. Felice Rochman, Mar. 3, 1957; children: Andrew Anthony, II, Dean James, Catherine Lisa. B.B.A. cum laude, CCNY, 1953; M.B.A. with distinction, Harvard U., 1962; student, Naval War Coll., 1965; L.H.D. (hon.), Nat. U., San Diego, 1965. Commd. ensign U.S. Navy, 1953, advanced through grades to rear adm., 1978; supply officer U.S.S. Kitty Hawk, Vietnam, 1968-70; ops. officer Aviation Supply Office, Phila., 1970-72; dir. material div. Office of Chief of Naval Ops., Washington, 1977—; comdr. Naval Supply Systems Command, Chief Supply Corps, 1981—; asso. prof. acctg. George Washington U., 1966-67, Nat. U., 1970-72; hon. pres. Naval Supply Corps Assn.; bd. dirs. Navy Mut. Aid Assn., Navy Fed. Credit Union. Decorated Legion of Merit. Mem. Inst. Internal Auditors, Nat. Soc. Mil. Comptrollers, Nat. Def. Transp. Assn. Roman Catholic. Club: Army-Navy Country (dir.). Home: 1506 20th St S Arlington VA 22202 Office: Comdr Naval Supply System Command Dept Navy Washington DC 20376

GIORDANO, ANTHONY BRUNO, college dean; b. N.Y.C., Feb. 1, 1915; s. Sabino and Natalina (Amato) G.; m. Peggy Cozzi, Dec. 23, 1939; 1 son, Clyde Anton. B.E.E., Poly. Inst. Bklyn., 1937, M.Elec. Engring., 1939, D.Elec. Engring., 1946. Faculty Poly. Inst. N.Y., 1939—, prof. elec. engring., 1953—, dean, 1960—, acting dean engring., 1978-79; scientist OSRD, 1942-45; research supr. Microwave Research Inst., Bklyn., 1945-65; dir. Northeast Radio Astronomy Council, 1970—; Chmn. engring. adv. com. Bd. Edn. City N.Y., 1958-60. Co-author: Network Theory, 1964; Author: also articles in field. Network Theory; Asso. editor: Jour. Radio Sci, 1967-73. Recipient Meritorious award IEEE Communications Soc., 1976. Fellow I.R.E. (chmn. N.Y. sect. 1954-55, regional dir. 1960-62, nat. dir. 1960-62), IEEE (chmn. basic scis. com. 1967-71, chmn. 1967, internat. conv., mem. awards bd. 1972—, rep., achievement award edn. soc. 1982, Centennial medal 1984), Engring Found. of United Engring. (Trustees 1968—, chmn. projects com. 1973-76, chmn. bd. 1979-80, sec. communications soc. 1963-75, chmn. external awards com. 1975-77, chmn. Edison medal awards com. 1978, chmn. Edn. medal awards com. 1981-83), AAAS, Am. Inst. E.E. (chmn. basic sci. div. 1955-56, rep. Hoover medal awards com. 1976—); mem. Am. Soc. Engring. Edn. (chmn. meetings com. Middle Atlantic States sect. 1969-71, chmn. sect. 1971-72, chmn. sr. research award com. 1979-81, dir. zone 1 1973-75, v.p. at large 1974-75, chmn. grad. studies div. 1979-80, Western Electric Fund award 1981, Charter Fellow award 1983), Internat. Sci. Radio Union, Sigma Xi, Tau Beta Pi, Eta Kappa Nu. Spl. research microwave waveguide attenuators. Home: 35-46 74th St Jackson Heights NY 11372 Office: 333 Jay St Brooklyn NY 11201

GIORDANO, AUGUST T. (GUS GIORDANO), choreographer, dancer; b. St. Louis, July 10, 1923; s. Paul and Rose (Tedesco) G.; m. Peggy Ann Thoelke, Oct. 14, 1950; children: Patrick Nelson, Marc August, Nan Elizabeth, Amy Paul. Student, Buckman Dancing Sch., St. Louis, 1932-40; B.A., U. Mo., 1950. Proprietor, dir. Gus Giordano Dancer Center, Evanston, Ill. Dancer, Roxy Theatre, N.Y.C., summers 1948, 49; choreographer, dancer: play On the Town, 1953; dancer, choreographer: Perry Como Show, 1954, Ed Sullivan Show, 1954, Colgate Comedy Hour, 1955; film conv. coordinator, Film Council, 1953-56; dir., choreographer, Gus Giordano Jazz Dance Chgo. Co., 1968—; choreographer, Goodman Theatre, 1978—, Sta. WTTW-TV, 1968—, ABC-TV, 1972-74, NBC, 1969—; concert tours in, U.S. and Europe, 1975—; producer numerous stage and indsl. shows, 1955-; Editor: Anthology of American Jazz Dance, 1976. Served with USMC, 1944-46. Recipient Emmy award, 1968, 75, 78, 81; Outstanding Dancer award Boston Dance Masters, 1970; Dance Masters of Am. award, 1978; Ill. Gov.'s award, 1971; Chgo. Nat. Assn. Dancer Tchrs. award, 1974; Dance Educators of Am. award for outstanding contbn. to world jazz dance, 1984. Mem. Lambda Chi Alpha. Roman Catholic. Office: 614 Davis St Evanston IL 60201

GIORDANO, JOHN READ, conductor; b. Dunkirk, N.Y., Dec. 31, 1937; s. John C. and Mildred G.; m. Sept. 3, 1960; children: Anne, Ellen, John. B.M., Tex. Christian U., 1960, M.M., 1962; grad.; Fulbright scholar, Royal Conservatory, Brussels, 1965. Mem. music faculty North Tex. State U., 1965-72; mem. faculty, condr. univ. symphony Tex. Christian U., 1972—; chmn. jury Van Cliburn Internat. Piano Competition, 1973, permanent jury chmn., 1974—; founder, condr. Tex. Little Symphony, 1976—. Appeared as saxophone soloist and with orchs., throughout Europe and U.S., 1965-72; music dir. youth Orch., Greater Ft. Worth, 1969—; guest condr., Ft. Worth Symphony, 1971; music dir. and condr., 1972—; guest condr. with various orchs., including, Nat. Symphony of Belgium, Nat. Symphony of El Salvador, Amsterdam Philharm., Brazilian Nat. Symphony, Belgian Nat. Radio Orch., Nat. Symphony of Portugal, English Chamber Orch.; Composer: Composition for Jazz Ensemble and Symphony Orchestra, 1974; subject of: feature film Symphony, 1978. Served with USAR, 1960-68. Recipient Premiere Prix with distinction Royal Conservatory, Brussels, 1965. Mem. Phi Mu Alpha Sinfonia, Phi Kappa Lambda, Kappa Kappa Psi. *

GIORDANO, JOSEPH FRANCIS, advertising executive; b. Glen Cove, N.Y., Oct. 28, 1932; s. Frank Charles and Loretta (Pinto) G. B.A., Columbia Coll., 1949. Creative dir. Hockaday Assocs., N.Y.C., 1950-55, Hockaday Giordano, 1955-63, Brandwynne Giordano, 1963-70; sr. writer Young & Rubicam, N.Y.C., 1970-75; sr. v.p. Benton & Bowles, N.Y.C., 1975—. Mem. ASCAP. Republican. Roman Catholic. Home: 420 E 72d St New York NY 10021 Office: Benton & Bowles Advt 909 3d Ave New York NY 10020

GIORDANO, NICHOLAS ANTHONY, stock exchange executive; b. Phila., Mar. 7, 1943; s. Nicola and Aida (Gioiso) G.; m. Joanne M. Pizzuto, Oct. 21, 1967; children: Jeannine, Colette and Nicholas (triplets). B.S., LaSalle Coll., 1965. C.P.A., Pa. Mem. staff Price Waterhouse & Co., Phila., 1965-68; with various brokerage cos., Phila., 1968-71; controller stock exchange and stock clearing corp PBW (later Phila.) Stock Exchange, Inc., 1971-72, v.p. ops., 1972-75, sr. v.p., 1975-76, exec. v.p., 1976-81, pres., 1981—; chmn. bd. Stock Clearing Corp. Phila., Phila. Depository Trust Co., Fin. Automation Corp. Phila.; dir. Options Clearing Corp. Trustee LaSalle Coll.; Bd. dirs. World Affairs Council Phila., Urban Affairs Partnership. Served with Pa. Air N.G., 1965-70. Mem. Pa. Inst. C.P.A.s. Club: Variety. Home: 501 Kurt Dr Blue Bell PA 19422 Office: 1900 Market St Philadelphia PA 19103

GIORDANO, RICHARD VINCENT, chemical executive; b. N.Y.C., Mar. 24, 1934; s. Vincent and Cynthia (Cardetta) G.; m. Barbara Claire Beckett, June 16, 1956; children: Susan, Anita, Richard. B.A., Harvard U., 1956; LL.B., Columbia U., 1959; D.Comml. Sci., St. John's U., 1975. Bar: N.Y. 1961. Asso. Shearman & Sterling, N.Y.C., 1960-63; asst. sec. Air Reduction Co. Inc., N.Y.C., 1963-64, v.p. distbr. products div., 1964-65, exec. v.p., 1965-67; group v.p. Airco, Inc., 1967-71, pres., chief operating officer, 1971—, chief exec. officer, 1977—, vice chmn., 1979—; mng. dir., chief exec. officer BOC Internat. Ltd., 1979—. Mem. Assn. Bar City N.Y., Am. Iron and Steel Inst. Club: The Links (N.Y.C.). Office: BOC Group Hammersmith House London W6 England

GIORDANO, SAVERIO PAUL (SAM), association executive; b. Kansas City, Mo., Feb. 26, 1943; s. Paul Joseph and Ann (Cervello) G.; children: Paul, Lisa. B.A., Park Coll., Parkville, Mo., 1981; postgrad., Grad. Sch. Mgmt., U. Dallas, 1981-83. Registered respiratory therapist Nat. Bd. Respiratory Care. Chief respiratory therapist St. Mary's Hosp., Kansas City, Mo., 1963-67; tech. dir. respiratory services Barnes Hosp., St. Louis, 1967-69, Cook County Hosp., Chgo., 1969-73; dir. respiratory biomed. services St. Luke's Hosp., Kansas City, Mo., 1973-81; exec. dir. Am. Assn. Respiratory Therapy, Dallas, 1981—. Mem. Am. Assn. Respiratory Therapy (v.p. Eastern Kans.-Western Mo. chpt. 1964, pres. 1965, pres. Greater St. Louis chpt. 1967, dir. 1973-75, treas. 1976, v.p. 1977, pres. 1980), Mo. Soc. Respiratory Therapy, Ill. Soc. Respiratory Therapy, Nat. Bd. for Respiratory Care (Assoc. examiner 1968-78). Office: Am Assn Respiratory Therapy 1720 Regal Row Dallas TX 75235

GIORDANO, TONY, director; b. Bklyn., Jan. 25, 1939; s. Vincent and Evelyn G. B.A. in English Lit., Fairfield U., 1960; M.A. in Drama, Catholic U. Am., 1962. Dir. Eugene O'Neill Playwrights Conf., Waterford, Conn., 1973-83; assoc. artistic dir. Circle Repertory Co., N.Y.C., 1980-81; radio dir. Earplay Prodns., 1978, 79; adj. prof. grad. directing Yale Sch. Drama, 1982-83. Dir.: over 100 plays throughout U.S., including Snow Orchid, The Chekhov Sketchbook, Ladyhouse Blues, G. R. Point; Hello and Goodbye, The Curse of the Starving Class; over 100 plays; network TV dir.: Another World, NBC, The Doctors, NBC. Mem. Dirs. Guild Am., Soc. Stage Dirs. and Choreographers (v.p. 1983-85).

GIORDMAINE, JOSEPH ANTHONY, physicist; b. Toronto, Ont., Can., Apr. 10, 1933; came to U.S., 1955; s. John Nichol and Anna Kathleen (Cain) G.; m. Mary Auxilda Mills, Sept. 13, 1958; children: Paul Raymond, Anne Augusta, Claire Ellen. B.A., U. Toronto, 1955; M.A., Columbia U., 1957, Ph.D., 1960. Instr. physics Columbia U., N.Y.C., 1959-61; mem. tech. staff Bell Labs., Murray Hill, N.J., 1961—, head solid state spectroscopy research, 1967-71, dir. chem. physics research, 1971-74, dir. solid state electronics research, 1974-81, dir. electronic and photonic tech., 1981—; extension lectr. UCLA, 1964-68; vis. prof. physics Tech. U., Munich, W.Ger., 1966; mem. NRC-NAS Com. Basic Research adv. to Army Research Office, 1967-72; com. Atomic Molecular Physics, 1971-74; mem. vis. com. M.I.T. Nat. Magnet Lab., 1971-73; nat. lectr. IEEE Microwave Theory and Techniques Soc., 1982-83; chmn. Joint Council on Quantum Electronics; mem. com. on employment of fgn. scientists in U.S. NRC, 1979-80; mem. quantum electronics commn. Internat. Union Pure and Applied Physics, 1981-84. Adv. editor: Optics Communications, 1970-75, Jour. Nonmetals Semiconductors, 1972—; asso. editor: Optics Letters, 1977-79; editorial com.: Ann. Revs. of Materials Sci., 1979—; contbr. numerous articles to books and tech. jours. Fellow IEEE, Am. Phys. Soc., Optical Soc. Am., N.Y. Acad. Scis., AAAS; mem. European Phys. Soc., Am. Astron. Soc., Sigma Xi. Roman Catholic. Holder 17 patents. Home: 38 Laurel Ave Summit NJ 07901 Office: 600 Mountain Ave Murray Hill NJ 07974

GIOVACCHINI, PETER LOUIS, psychoanalyst; b. N.Y.C., Apr. 12, 1922; s. Alex and Therese (Chicca) G.; m. Louise Post, Sept. 29, 1945; children: Philip, Sandra, Daniel. B.S., U. Chgo., 1941, M.D., 1944; student, Columbia, 1939. Diplomate: Am. Bd. Psychiatry and Neurology.; cert. Chgo. Inst. Psychoanalysis. Intern Fordham Hosp., N.Y.C., 1944-45; resident U. Chgo. Clinics, 1945-46, resident and research fellow, 1948-50; candidate Chgo. Inst. Psychoanalysis, 1949-54, clin. asso., 1957—; clin. prof. U. Ill. Coll. Medicine, 1961—; pvt. practice, Chgo., 1950—; chief cons. psychodynamic unit Barclay Hosp., Chgo., 1979-81; cons. Wilmette (Ill.) Family Service Bur. and United Charities. Author: (with L.B. Boyer) Psychoanalytic Treatment of Schizophrenia and Characterological Disorders, 1967, Psychoanalytic Treatment, 1971, also several books on character structure, primitive mental states, psychopathology and psychoanalytic technique, also articles.; Co-editor: Annals of Adolescent Psychiatry, 1972-80. Served to capt. M.C. AUS, 1946-48. Fellow Am. Psychiat. Assn., Am. Orthopsychiat. Assn. (bd. dirs. 1979-83); mem. Soc. Adolescent Psychiatry, Chgo. Psychoanalytic Soc., Am. Psychoanalytic Assn., Chgo. Soc. Adolescent Psychiatry (pres. 1966-67). Home: 270 Locust Rd Winnetka IL 60093 Office: 505 N Lake Shore Dr Chicago IL 60602 *As a scientist and a clinician, I would say that the two most basic ingredients are curiosity and enthusiasm. Find everything interesting, even ugliness! Boredom is the disease of an inactive mind. Humor will make it fun, so I advocate an attitude of playful dedication—not frivolous but intense and still not grim.*

GIOVANNI, NIKKI, poet; b. Knoxville, Tenn., June 7, 1943; d. Jones and Yolande Cornelia (Watson) G.; 1 son, Thomas Watson. B.A. with honors in history, Fisk U., 1967; postgrad., U. Pa. Sch. Social Work, 1967; student; Nat. Found Arts grantee, Columbia Sch. Fine Arts, 1968; L.H.D. (hon.), Wilberforce U., 1972, Worcester U., 1972, D.Litt., Ripon U., 1974, Smith Coll., 1975. Founder pub. firm TomNik Ltd., 1970. Poet, writer, lectr.; Author: Black Feeling, Black Talk, 1968, Black Judgement, 1969, Re-Creation, 1970, Broadside Poem of Angela Yvonne Davis, 1970, Night Comes Softly, 1970, Spin a Soft Black Song, 1971, Gemini, 1971, My House, 1972, A Dialogue: James Baldwin and Nikki Giovanni, 1973, Ego Tripping and Other Poems for Young Readers, 1973, A Poetic Equation: Conversations Between Nikki Giovanni and Margaret Walker, 1974, The Women and the Men, 1975; also recorded album Truth Is On Its Way, 1972; TV appearances Soul!, Nat. Ednl. TV network; also numerous talk shows, including the Tonight Show; participant Soul at the Center, Lincoln Center Performing Arts, N.Y.C., 1972. Vol. worker Nat. Council Negro Women, now life mem. Recipient Mademoiselle mag. award outstanding achievement, 1971, Omega Psi Phi award, others; Ford Found. grantee, 1967. Address: care Eugene Winick 5 W 45th St New York NY 10022 *

GIOVANNITTI, LEN, writer; b. N.Y.C., Apr. 16, 1920; s. Arturo and Carrie (Zaikaner) G.; m. Sara Steinberg, Aug. 28, 1943 (div. May 1977); children: David, Nina. B.S., St. John's U., 1942. Labor journalist, 1946-58; asst. prof. Inst. Film and TV, Sch. Arts, N.Y. U., 1978. Free-lance writer, 1959- 61; tv documentary writer, 1961-62; writer, dir., producer: NBC News, 1962-70; producer, writer, dir.: The Decision of Japan to Surrender, 1965; producer, writer: NBC TV documentaries Lyndon Johnson's Texas, 1966, The Am. Alcoholic, 1968; assoc. producer, NBC, White Paper programs The Death of Stalin, 1963, The Rise of Khrushchev, 1963; asso. producer: Cuba: The Bay of Pigs, 1964, Cuba: The Missile Crisis, 1964; assoc. producer: The Decision to Drop the Bomb, 1965; writer: ABC TV documentaries Winston Churchill: The Valiant Years, 1961, Walking Hard, 1962; producer, writer: Black Business in White America, ABC News, 1972; The Energy Crisis (NBC White Paper), 1973, And Who Shall Feed This World? (NBC White Paper), NBC News, 1974; Author: Sidney Hillman: Labor Statesman, 1948; novel The Prisoners of Combine D, 1957 (ALA liberty and justice award 1958); history The Decision to Drop the Bomb, 1965; novel The Man Who Won The Medal of Honor, 1973, The Nature of the Beast, 1977. Served with USAAF, 1942-45. Recipient Lasker Med. Journalism award, 1969, Ohio State U. award, 1969, Peabody award, 1975. Mem. Authors Guild, Writers Guild Am. East. Home: 265 Riverside Dr New York NY 10025

GIOVENCO, JOHN VINCENT, hotel executive; b. Chgo., Apr. 2, 1936; s. Vincent and Nicasia (Cardella) G.; m. Kathleen Giovenco; children—Catherine, Lori, Marianne, Daniel, Julie, Holly. B.S.C., Loyola U., Chgo., 1958; postgrad., U. Chgo., 1961-63. C.P.A., Ill., Calif. Partner Pannell Kerr Forster (C.P.A.'s), Chgo., 1958-72; treas. Hilton Casinos, Inc., Las Vegas, Nev., 1972-74; exec. v.p. fin. Hilton Hotels Corp., Beverly Hills, Calif., 1974—; dir. United Geophys. Corp.; lectr. in field. Co-editor: Uniform Systems of Accounts for

Hotels, 7th edit, 1976. Bd. dirs. Big Bros. Los Angeles, Ind. Colls. of So. Calif., Jeannine Schultz Sch. for Handicapped. Mem. Am. Inst. C.P.A.s, Ill. Soc. C.P.A.s, Fin. Execs. Inst., Am. Hotel and Motel Assn. Clubs: Saddle and Sirlion, West Hills Hunt. Home: 449 22d St Santa Monica CA 90402 Office: 9880 Wilshire Blvd Beverly Hills CA 90210

GIPFEL, HOWARD, SR., food wholesale distribution company executive. Chmn. Associated Grocers Co. St. Louis. Mo. Office: Associated Grocers Co St Louis Mo 5030 Berthold Ave St Louis MO 63110§

GIPS, EDWARD U., association executive; b. N.Y.C., Dec. 21, 1922; s. Harry L. G. and Margaret T. (Unger) Greenwald. Student, CCNY, 1946-48. Dir. membership services Nat. Soc. Interior Designers, N.Y.C., 1967-75, exec. dir. services, 1975—. Mem. editorial quality bd.: Successful Meetings Mag., 1972. Served with U.S. Army, 1942-45. Named Hon. Citizen City of Houston, 1982. Mem. Nat. Assn. Exposition Mgrs., Am. Soc. Assn. Execs., N.Y. Soc. Assn. Execs. Lodge: Masons. Home: 7 Park Ave New York NY 10016 Office: Am Soc Interior Designers 1430 Broadway St New York NY 10018 *Any success I may have achieved in life is due not only to hard work and dedication, but to my strong belief that by doing for others you do more for yourself. This is particularly true of my conviction that one can receive no greater benefit in life than in watching the success of a young person you helped get started, who achieves the goals you envisioned for that person.*

GIPS, WALTER FULD, JR., mfg. co. exec.; b. N.Y.C., May 24, 1920; s. Walter Fuld and Louise (Klee) G.; m. Ann Arenberg, June 19, 1948; children—Walter Fuld, Robert L., Donald H., Ellen C. B.A., Yale U., 1941; M.B.A., Harvard U., 1943. Asst. to v.p. U.S. Plywood, 1947-50; chmn. bd. Luminator Inc., 1950-69; chmn., pres., chief exec. officer, dir. Gulton Industries, Inc., Princeton, N.J., 1969—; chmn. Electro-Voice, Inc., So. States, Inc.; dir. Metex Corp. Gulton Europe, Inc., N.J. Nat. Bank, Cirfico, Inc. Served to capt. U.S. Army, 1943-46. Clubs: Harvard Bus. Sch. (past pres. chpt.), Mid America (Chgo.); Yale (N.Y.C.); Metropolitan (Washington). Home: 92 Brookstone Dr Princeton NJ 08540 Office: PO Box CN-63 101 College Rd E Princeton NJ 08540

GIPSON, GORDON, publishing co. exec.; b. Caldwell, Idaho, Oct. 26, 1914; s. James Herrick and Esther (Sterling) G.; m. Tryntje Heeling, Dec. 27, 1961; children—Craig, Amy. Student, Coll. Idaho. With The Caxton Printers, Ltd., Caldwell, 1935—, treas., 1945—, v.p., 1964—, pub., 1965—. Served with USAAF, 1942-45. Club: Elk. Home: 2211 S 10th St Caldwell ID 83605 Office: 312 Main St Caldwell ID 83605

GIPSON, JAMES HERRICK, printing and publishing co. exec.; b. Caldwell, Idaho, Sept. 3, 1912; s. James H. and Esther (Sterling) G.; m. Glyde June Pease, Oct. 3, 1941; children—James Herrick III, David G. Student, Coll. Idaho, 1934. With Caxton Printers, Ltd., Caldwell, 1935—, pres., 1964—. Mem. Republican State Central Com., 1968-77. Served with USNR, 1941-45. Mem. V.F.W. Club: Elks. Home: 1912 S Montana St Caldwell ID 83605 Office: 312 Main St Caldwell ID 83605

GIRALDI, ROBERT NICHOLAS, production company executive; b. Paterson, N.J., Jan. 17, 1939; s. Armand and Minnie (DeLuccia) G.; m. Marian Arline McCarthy, May 28, 1961; children: Theresa, Robert Nicholas, Maria. B.F.A., Pratt Inst., 1960. Assoc. creative dir. Young & Rubicam, N.Y.C., 1960-71; v.p., head creative dept., assoc. creative dir. Della Femina, Travisano, N.Y.C., 1971-73; ptnr. Ampersand Prodns., N.Y.C., 1973-74, dir.; pres. Bob Giraldi Prodns., N.Y.C., 1974—; instr. head advt. and design, asst. dir. Sch. Visual Arts, N.Y.C., 1969-73; lect., instr. New Sch. Social Research, N.Y.C., 1973-74. Writer, dir.: promotional film Burnt Umber, 1980; dir.: stage play Laughing on the Outside, 1982; writer, dir.: short film Beat It, 1983. Bd. dirs. Catholic Big Bros., N.Y.C., 1982—, Greeley Street Theater, Chappaqua, N.Y., 1982—. Recipient Gold award Art Dirs. Club N.Y., N.Y.C., 1974—, Andy award Advt. Club N.Y., N.Y.C., 1974—, Clio award, 1974—, One Show award Copy Club N.Y., N.Y.C., 1974—, Gold award Cannes Film Festival, 1974, 76, 79, 81, 82. Mem. Dirs. Guild Am. Roman Catholic. Office: Bob Giraldi Prodns 581 6th Ave New York NY 10011 *If you do quality you will always do quantity, but it never works the other way around.*

GIRAND, CHARLES ANDREW, lawyer; b. San Antonio, Tex., June 10, 1937; s. Charles Francis and Violet (McGuiness) G.; m. Camelia L. Dethloff, Aug. 17, 1963; children—Mark A., Christopher C., Todd A. B.B.A., So. Methodist U., 1959, LL.B., 1962. Bar: Tex. bar 1962. Since practiced in, Dallas; partner firm De Hay & Blanchard, 1981—. Served as capt. USAF, 1962-65. Mem. Dallas Bar Assn. Address: 2300 South Tower Plaza of Americas Dallas TX 75201

GIRARD, ALEXANDER HAYDEN, architect; b. N.Y.C., May 24, 1907; s. Carlo Matteo and Lezlie (Cutler) C.; m. Susan Needham, Mar., 1936; children: Sansi, Marshall. Grad., Royal Inst. Brit. Architects, 1929, Royal Sch. Architecture, Rome, Italy, 1931, N.Y.U., 1935. Registered architect,, N.Y., Mich., Conn., N.M. Worked archtl. offices, Florence, Rome, London, Paris, N.Y.C., practice of architecture, Florence, 1930-32, N.Y.C., 1932-37, Detroit, 1937; now dir. fabric div. Herman Miller Furniture Co. Designer: Design for Use traveling show, Mus. Modern Arts, 1950, Herman Miller Furniture Co. exhibit, Furniture Mus., Grand Rapids, Mich., 1951; spl. fabric catalog, 1952, Good Design exhbn, Mdse. Mart, Chgo., 1952, 53, Herman Miller Showroom, San Francisco, 1958, La Fonda del Sol Restaurant, N.Y.C., 1959-60, Herman Miller Textile and Objects Shop, N.Y.C., other exhbns. in home furnishings, textile and ornamental arts, Mus. Modern Art, 1954, 55; contbr. fabric designs to, Am. Fabrics Exhbn., 1956; exhbn. table settings, Georg Jensen, Inc., N.Y.C., 1955, 56; design and color project Main St. Rehab, Columbus, Ind., 1963; interiors, Cummins Engine Co., offices, Columbus, Ind., 1964, 3-dimensional historic mural, John Deere & Co. Adminstry. Center, Moline, Ill., 1964; redesign visual aspects entire airport, Braniff Airlines, Dallas, 1965; cons., Internat. Exec. Service Corps, Mexico City, 1969, Juror Good Design exhibit, Merchandise Mart, Chgo., 1950, Internat. Fabric Competition, Greensboro, N.C., 1952, Craftsman of N.M., 1962, Craft Guild, San Antonio, Own Your Own Exhibit, Denver Art Mus., 1963, The Magic of a People Exhbn., Hemisfair, 1968; Author: The Magic of a People, 1968; Contbr. articles trade publs.; works exhibited, Barcelona, Florence, London, N.Y.C., Detroit, Walker Art Center, Rochester Mus., Cranbrook Acad., Mus. Modern Art, Cooper Union, Mus. Internat. Folk Art, Santa Fe, Nelson Gallery, Atkins Mus., Kansas City, Mo., exhbns. include, Mus. Internat. Folk Art, Santa Fe, 1974, 77, Mus. Contemporary Art, Chgo., 1975, Santa Fe Festival of the Arts, 1978, inaugural exhbn., Girard Found. Collection, Mus. Internat. Folk Art, 1982, outstanding works include part of Italian exhibit, Internat. Exhbn., Barcelona, 1929, offices Ford Motor Co., Dearborn, Mich., 1943, cafeteria Lincoln Motor Co., Detroit, 1946, pvt. residences, Mich., 1962, L'Etoile Restaurant, N.Y.C. for, Brody Corp.; color cons., San Francisco Civic Auditorium Rehab., 1963-64, Golden Gateway Redevel. Project, San Francisco, interiors and furnishings for, St. John's College, Santa Fe, N.M., 1963, El Encanto de un Pueblo, Hemisphere '68, San Antonio; established, Girard Found., 1961; dir. Modern Living exhbn., Detroit Inst. Arts, 1949; color cons., Gen. Motors Research Center, Detroit, 1951-52. Founder Girard Found., 1961; Girard Found. Collection donated to State of N.Mex., 1978; Girard wing added to Mus. Internat. Folk Art, Santa Fe. Received Florence traveling scholarship Royal Inst. Br. Architects, Eng., 1929, Gold medal Barcelona Exhibition, 1929, fabric competition Mus. Modern Art, N.Y.C, Trail Blazer award for Herman Miller Fabric Coll. Home Fashion League N.Y., 1952; Collaborative medal honor Archtl. League N.Y., 1965; Allied Professions medal A.I.A., 1966; Elsie de Wolfe award Am. Inst. Interior Designers, 1966; Hon. Distinction of Royal Designer for Industry diploma Royal Soc. Arts, London, Eng., 1966; Gold medal Tau Sigma Delta, 1980; Gov's award for outstanding contbn. to fine arts in N.Mex., 1981; others. Benjamin Franklin fellow Royal Soc. Arts London; mem. AIA, Archtl. Assn. London (Eng.). Club: Archtl. League (silver medal for design La Fonda del Sol Restaurant 1962) (N.Y.C.). Address: PO Box 2168 Santa Fe NM 87501

GIRARD, LOUIS JOSEPH, ophthalmologist; b. Spokane, Mar. 29, 1919; s. Harry and Agnes (Cain) G.; m. Bonita Crossnay, Mar. 31, 1945; children—Hilaire Michelle (Mrs. Cliff Richey), Bryan Suzanne, Christina Ann (Mrs. E.J. Hudson, Jr.), Michael Sanford (dec.), Hugh Ashley, Gabrielle Inez; m. Loraine McMurrey, June 30, 1967; m. Louise Bell, June 14, 1975; 1 son, Louis McMurrey. B.A., Rice U., 1941; M.D., U. Tex., 1944; postgrad., N.Y. U.; Postgrad., Med. Sch., 1947-48. Diplomate: Am. Bd. Ophthalmology. Intern Jersey City Med. Center, 1944-45; asso. to Dr. Conrad Berens, N.Y.C., 1947-49, 51-53; resident ophthalmology N.Y. Eye and Ear Infirmary, 1949-51; asst. surgeon, 1951-53, dir. chronic infection project, 1949-52, asso. dir. dept. research, 1951-53; asst. attending St. Clare's Hosp., 1948-53, Willard Parker Hosp., 1949-53, N. Country Community Hosp., 1951-53, Nassau Hosp., 1951-53; cons. ophthalmologist Southside Hosp., 1951-53; attending ophthalmologist Jefferson Davis Hosp., 1953-59, VA Hosp., Houston, 1954-58, Tex. Children's Hosp., 1954-57, St. Luke's Episcopal Hosp., 1954-61, Meth. Hosp., 1955—; cons. Montgomery County Hosp., 1955—, Tex. Children's Hosp., 1957—, VA Hosp., Houston, 1958—, St. Luke's Episcopal Hosp., 1961—, St. Joseph's Hosp., 1965—; sr. attending Ben Taub Gen. Hosp., 1959—, Meth. Hosp., 1959—; chief ophthalmology, co-chief surgery Center Pavilion Hosp., 1970-76; coordinator grad. course ophthalmology N.Y. U. Postgrad. Med. Sch., 1948-49, instr., 1951- 53; clin. asst. prof. U. Tex. Postgrad. Sch. Medicine, 1953-57, lectr., 1957—; assoc. prof., assoc. chmn. Baylor U. Coll. Medicine, 1953-58, prof. ophthalmology, chmn. dept., 1958-71, clin. prof., 1971—; Assoc. mng. dir. Ophthal. Found., 1951-55, cons., 1957; founder Tex. Med. Center-Lions Eye Bank, 1953; cons. Meth. Hosp., St. Luke's Hosp.; exec. dir. Inst. Ophthalmology, Tex. Med. Center, 1960-80; mem. Am. Orthoptic Council, 1962-72; pres. Internat. Eye Film Library, 1967-71; mem. med. adv. bd. Internat. Eye Bank, 1965-70; Pres. IX Pan Am. Congress Ophthalmology, 1972. Author: Advanced Techniques in Ophthalmic Microsurgery, Vol. I: Untrasonic Fragmentation for Intraocular Surgery, 1979, Vol. II: Corneal Surgery, 1978; contbr. 244 articles to profl. jours.; producer 28 films.; Editor: Corneal Contact Lenses, 1964, 2d edit., 1971, Corneal Scleral Contact Lenses, 1967; Mem. editorial bd.: Ophthalmologia, 1965-72, Annals of Ophthalmology, 1968-74; Cons.: Highlights Ophthalmology, 1972. Recipient Alfred H. Bond award for research in ophthalmology, 1950; Prof. Ignacio Barraquer Meml. award Smith, 1965; 2d prize Internat. Eye Film Festival, 1966; 1st prize, 1970, 1972; Golden Eagle award Internat. Film Festival NANTES, France, 1970, 71. Fellow A.C.S. (bd. govs. 1966-72); mem. Am. Acad. Ophthalmology and Otolaryngology (2d pl. award sci. exhibits 1960), Pan Am. Assn. Ophthalmology (1st pl. award sci. exhibits 1960, 62, vis. prof. 1967, v.p. 1972), Assn. Research Ophthalmology, N.Y. Acad. Medicine, N.Y. Acad. Sci., Nassau, Houston ophthal. socs., French Soc. Ophthalmology, Houston Neurol. Soc., Jules Gonin Club, Tex. Opthal. Assn., Alumni Assn. N.Y. Eye and Ear Infirmary, Am. (certificate of merit sci. exhibit 1961), So. med. assns., Nat. Med. Found. Eye Care, Assn. Am. Physicians and Surgeons, Am. Assn. Ophthalomologists, Nat. Med. Found. Eye Care, Tex. Rehab. Assn., Harris County Med. Soc., Am. U. Profs. Ophthalmologists, Med. Research Found. Tex., Contact Lens Soc. Ophthalmologists (Exceptional Merit award 1968), Inst. Horacio Ferrer (corr.). Inventor several instruments; originator numerous surg. techniques. Home: 59 Tiel Way Houston TX 77019

GIRARD, RENÉ NOEL, educator, writer; b. Avignon, France, Dec. 25, 1923; came to U.S., 1947; s. Joseph and Thérèse (Fabre) G.; m. Martha McCullough, June 18, 1951; children—Martin, Daniel, Mary. Archiviste-paléographe, Ecole des chartes, Paris, 1947; Ph.D., Ind. U., 1950. Tchr. Romance langs. Ind. U., 1947-52, Duke U., 1952-53, Bryn Mawr Coll., 1953-57; faculty Johns Hopkins U., 1957-68, prof. French lit., 1961-68, chmn. dept. Romance langs., 1966-68, James M. Beall prof. French and humanities, 1977-80; Andrew B. Hammond prof. French lang., lit. and civilization Stanford U., 1981—; disting. faculty prof. arts and letters SUNY at Buffalo, 1971-77; sr. fellow Sch. Criticism and Theory, U. Calif., Irvine, 1975—. Author: Mensonge romantique et vérité romanesque, 1961, 78, Marcel Proust: A Collection of Critical Essays, 1962, 77, Deceit, Desire and the Novel, 1967, 76, La Violence et le Sacrè, 1972, English trans., 1977, Critique dans un souterrain, 1976, Des Choses cachées depuis la fondation du monde, 1978, To Double Business Bound, 1978, Le Bouc emissaire, 1982; gen. editor: M.L.N, 1962-68, 77-81; Contbr. articles to profl. jours. Guggenheim fellow, 1960, 67. Mem. Modern Lang. Assn. (exec. council 1969-72), Acad. Arts and Scis. Office: Stanford U Bldg 260 Stanford CA 94305

GIRARD, STEPHEN A., steel company executive; b. Hoquiam, Wash., Sept. 18, 1913; s. Stephen A. and Lena L. (Rogers) G.; m. Laurina Banks; children: Julie Girard Miller, Caron Girard Cox, Stephanie Girard LeBoutillier, Stephen A. Student, U. Wash., 1932-35. Pres. Kaiser Jeep Corp., Oakland, Calif., 1959-70, dir.; sr. v.p. Kaiser Industries Corp., Oakland, 1971, pres., dir. group ops., 1973-78, pres., 1978-80, dir.; pres. Kaiser Resources Ltd., Vancouver, B.C., Can., 1972-73, dir., Vancouver, B.C; vice chmn. Kaiser Steel Corp., Oakland, 1980-81, chmn., chief exec. officer, 1981—; dir. Am. Motors Corp., Southfield, Mich., 1974—. Chmn. United Bay Area Crusade, San Francisco, 1970; mem. Spl. Adv. Com. Indsl. Devel., Washington, Spl. Alliance for Progress, Washington, Nat. Export Expansion Council, Washington. Recipient Vasco Nunez de Balboa Pres. Republic Panama, 1966. Office: Kaiser Steel Corp 300 Lakeside Dr Oakland CA 94604

GIRARDEAU, MARVIN DENHAM, educator; b. Lakewood, Ohio, Oct. 3, 1930; s. Marvin Denham and Maude Irene (Miller) G.; m. Susan Jessica Brown, June 30, 1956; children—Ellen, Catherine, Laura. B.S., Case Inst. Tech., 1952; M.S., U. Ill., 1954; Ph.D., Syracuse U., 1958. NSF postdoctoral fellow Inst. Advanced Study, Princeton, 1958-59; research asso. Brandeis U., 1959-60; staff mem. Boeing Sci. Research Labs., 1960-61; research asso. Enrico Fermi Inst. Nuclear Studies, U. Chgo., 1961-63; asso. prof. physics, research asso. Inst. Theoretical Sci., U. Oreg., Eugene, 1963-67, prof. physics, research asso., 1967—, dir., 1967-69, chmn. dept. physics, 1974-76. Contbr. articles to profl. jours. NSF research grantee, 1965-79; ONR research grantee, 1981—. Fellow Am. Phys. Soc.; mem. AAUP. Research on quantum-mech. many-body problems, statis. mechanics. Home: 2398 Douglas Dr Eugene OR 97405 Office: Dept Physics U Oreg Eugene OR 97403

GIRAUD, RAYMOND DORNER, educator; b. N.Y.C., Aug. 26, 1920; s. Gabriel and Mabel (Dorner) G.; m. Lise Kurzmann, Feb. 1, 1948. B.A., Coll. City N.Y., 1941; M.A., U. Chgo., 1949; Ph.D., Yale, 1954. Instr. English and French Ill. Inst. Tech., 1946-49; instr., then asst. prof. French Yale, 1952-58; mem. faculty Stanford, 1958—, prof. French, 1962—, chmn. dept. French and Italian, 1968-72. Author: The Unheroic Hero, 1957, Flaubert, A Collection of Critical Essays, 1964. Served with AUS, 1942-45. Mem. Am. Assn. U. Profs., Modern Lang. Assn. Home: 2200 Byron St Palo Alto CA 94301 Office: Dept French and Italian Stanford Univ Stanford CA 94305

GIRDANY, BERTRAM RONALD, radiologist; b. N.Y.C., May 27, 1919; s. Morris L. and Gertrude (Friedlander) G.; m. Gertrude Ula Ninomiya, Jan. 26, 1944; children: Martha, David, Paul. A.B., Columbia Coll., 1939; M.D., Johns Hopkins U., 1943. Diplomate: Am. Bd. Radiology, Am. Bd. Pediatrics. Intern. Bellevue Hosp., N.Y.C., 1944; resident Babies Hosp., N.Y.C., 1946-47, 1948-50, Johns Hopkins U., Balt., 1947-48; dir. dept. radiology Children's Hosp., Pitts., 1950-79; assoc. prof. radiology U. Pitts., 1950-56, prof., 1956—, assoc. prof. pediatrics, 1950-68, prof., 1968—; chmn. Dept. radiology U. Pitts. Med. Sch., 1979—. Contbr. artices to med. jours. Served to lt. USNR, 1944-46; PTO. Fellow Am. Coll. Radiology, Acad. Pediatrics; mem. John Caffey Soc. (pres. 1966—), Am. Pediatric Soc., Soc. Pediatric Radiology (pres. 1970), Pitts. Roentgen Soc. (pres. 1978), Pitts. Pediatrics Soc. (pres. 1965). Office: Dept Radiology Univ M272 Scaife Hall Pittsburgh PA 15261

GIRDEN, EUGENE LAWRENCE, lawyer; b. N.Y.C., Oct. 17, 1930; s. Jules and Freda (Mannes) G.; m. Charlene Margot Tobin, July 4, 1958; children: Lisa Jan, Steven Scott. B.A., U. Md., 1951, LL.B., 1953. Bar: Md. 1953, N.Y. 1957, U.S. Supreme Ct. 1963, U.S. Ct. Mil. Appeals 1954, U.S. Customs Ct., U.S. Ct. Customs and Patent Appeal 1958. Atty. Barnes, Richardson & Colburn, N.Y.C., 1957-58; ptnr. Coudert Bros., N.Y.C., 1959-82, Patterson Belknap Webb & Tyler, 1982—; guest lectr. NYU Law Sch., 1965—, Columbia Law Sch., 1975—, Cornell Law Sch., 1973—, Practicing Law Inst., 1965—. State v.p. Conn. Young Dems., Hartford, 1959. Served to lt. USN, 1953-57. Mem. Copyright Soc. U.S.A. (trustee, exec. com. 1967-70, 81-83), Assn. Bar City N.Y., ABA, N.Y. Bar Assn. Democrat. Clubs: Rockrimmon Country (gov. 1978—, ct. sec. 1978—. Home: Brookdale Dr Stamford CT 06903 Office: 30 Rockefeller Plaza New York NY 10112

GIRGUS, JOAN STERN, psychologist, university dean; b. Albany, N.Y., Mar. 21, 1942; d. William Barnet and Louise (Mayer) Stern; m. Alan Chimacoff, Jan. 2, 1981. B.A., Sarah Lawrence Coll., 1963; M.A., The Grad. Faculty New Sch. for Social Research, 1965, Ph.D.; NSF fellow, NIH fellow, 1969. Asst. prof. dept. psychology CCNY, N.Y.C., 1969-72, asso. prof., 1972-77, asso. dean div. social sci., 1972-75, dean, 1975-77; now prof. psychology, dean coll. Princeton U. Contbr. articles and chpts. to profl. jours. and books. Research grantee CUNY, 1971-74; Nat.Inst. Child Health and Human Devel. research grantee, 1972-74; NSF grantee, 1975-79. Fellow Am. Psychol. Assn.; mem. Eastern Psychol. Assn., Psychonomic Soc., Soc. Research in Child Devel., Sigma Xi. Home: 109 Broadmead Princeton NJ 08540 Office: 401 W College Princeton Univ Princeton NJ 08540

GIRODO, ALBERT ANTHONY, financial company executive; b. Reading, Pa., May 5, 1928; s. Celestine and Louise (Tosetti) G.; m. Eleanor Marie Melcher, May 24, 1952; children: Michael, Christine, Mary Katherine, Mark, Anthony, Felicia, Francis X., Teresa. B.A., Kutztown (Pa.) State Coll. Adjuster Gen. Acceptance Corp., Allentown, Pa., 1952-56, mgr., 1956-59; auditor Gen. Accpt. Corp., Allentown, Pa., 1959-60; supr. Gen. Accpt. Corp, Allentown, Pa., 1960-70; v.p. Gen. Accpt. Corp., Allentown, Pa., 1970-80; sr. v.p. Fin. Am. Corp., Birmingham, Ala., 1980—. Bd. dirs. Greater Birmingham Ministries, 1982-83. Served with USAF, 1947-50. Roman Catholic. Home: 1517 Saulter View Rd Birmingham AL 35209 Office: Finance America Corp suite 126 400 Century Park South Birmingham AL 35226

GIRONE, VITO ANTHONY, architect, city planner, artist; b. Orange, N.J., Feb. 12, 1910; s. Joseph and Rose (Pastore) G.; m. Nancy Katherine Tenore, Sept. 6, 1945; children: Donald William, David Paul (dec.). Diploma, Newark sch. Fine and Indsl. Arts, 1931; student (scholar), NYU, 1932-35; scholar, Harvard Grad. Sch. Design, 1935-36; diploma, Fontainbleau Sch. Architecture, 1937; student, New Sch. Social Research, 1937; diploma, Nat. Inst. Archtl. Edn., 1937; pupil Eliel Saarinen (fellow), Cranbrook Acad. Art, 1939-40; diploma, Famous Artists Sch., 1981. Individual practice architecture, 1940—, design cons., Ind., Ky.; prof. architecture U. Notre Dame, 1945-64, U. Ky., 1965-75. Contbr. articles to profl. jours.; several one-man shows. Mem. Lake Michigan Region Planning Council. Served with C.E., AUS, World War II. Recipient medals for design as student, numerous design awards, awards for art exhbns. Fellow Internat. Inst. Arts and Letters (Pres.'s medal 1964); mem. Am. Soc. Planning Ofcls., AIA (pres. elect. chpt.), Tau Sigma Delta. Presbyterian (deacon). Home: 535 Woodbine Rd Lexington KY 40503

GIROUX, JACQUES CARTIER, neurosurgeon; b. Montreal, Que., Can., Nov. 2, 1926; s. Camille and Therese (Cartier) G.; children: Michel, Pierre, Eric, Stephane, Natalie. B.A., U. Montreal, 1947, M.D., 1952; M.Sc., Tufts U., 1954. Intern Notre-Dame Hosp., Montreal, 1947-52, resident, 1952-56, Nat. Hosp., London, 1956-57; dir. neurosurgery tng. program U. Montreal, 1969-78; chief neurosurgery dept. Notre Dame Hosp., Montreal, 1971—; cons. neurosurgeon Honore-Mercier Hosp., St. Hyacinthe, 1963—, Bellechasse Hosp., Montreal, 1980—, Neurol. Inst., 1980—, Charles LeMoyne, Greenfield Park, 1981—. Co-author: Nursing en Neurologie et Neuro-Chirurgie, 1978. McLaughlin Found. grantee, 1956-57. Fellow ACS, College Royal Medecins et Chirurgiens; mem. Assn. Neurosurgeons Que. (pres. 1961-65, 72-80), Federation des Medecins Specialistes du Que (dir. 1969-71), Societe Neurologique Montreal (pres. 1972-73), Am. Assn. Neurol. Surgeons, Congress Neurol. Surgeons, Can. Neurol. Soc. (pres. 1976-77), Royal Coll. Surgeons. Roman Catholic. Home: 2065 Rockland St Montreal PQ Canada H3P 2Y9 Office: Notre Dame Hosp 1560 Sherbrooke St E Montreal PQ Canada H2L 4M1

GIROUX, ROBERT, publishing company executive; b. N.J., Apr. 8, 1914; S. Arthur J. and Katharine (Lyons) G.; m. Carmen de Arango, Aug. 30, 1952 (div. 1969). A.B. with honors, Columbia U., 1936. Editor-in-chief Harcourt Brace & Co., 1948-55; v.p., editor-in-chief, dir. Farrar, Straus & Giroux, Inc., 1955-73, chmn. bd., 1973—; Pres. Nat. Bd. Rev. Motion Pictures, from 1975. Served as lt. comdr. USNR, 1942-45. Mem. Phi Beta Kappa, Phi Beta Kappa Assos. Clubs: Century, Players. Home: RD 1 Pittstown NJ 08867 Office: 19 Union Sq W New York NY 10003 *

GIRTH, MARJORIE LOUISA, lawyer, educator; b. Trenton, N.J., Apr. 21, 1939; d. Harold Brookman and Marjorie Mathilda (Simonson) G. A.B., Mt. Holyoke Coll., 1959; LL.B., Harvard U., 1962. Bar: N.J. 1963, N.Y. 1976, U.S. Supreme Ct. 1969. Pvt. practice, Trenton, 1963-65; research assoc. Brookings Instn., 1965-70; assoc. prof. law SUNY Law Sch., Buffalo, 1971-79, prof., 1979—; vis. prof. U. Va. Law Sch., 1979-80. Author: Poor People's Lawyers, 1976, Bankruptcy Options for the Consumer Debtor, 1981, (co-author) Bankruptcy: Problem, Process, Reform, 1971. Bd. dirs. Buffalo and

Erie County YWCA, 1972-76, Buffalo Unitarian-Universalist Ch., 1981-84; mem. commn. on peace, justice and human rights Internat. Assn. Religious Freedom, 1976-79. Mem. ABA (mem. com. to study fed. law enforcement agencies 1977-78, consumer bankruptcy com. 1978—, chmn. consumer bankruptcy com. 1983—), N.Y. Bar Assn. (mem. exec. com. bus. law sect. 1980—, mem. bankruptcy law com. 1980—, chmn. bankruptcy law com. 1980-82), Erie County Bar Assn., Law and Soc. Assn. (trustee 1976-77), Mt. Holyoke Alumnae Assn. (Centennial award 1972). Office: O'Brian Hall SUNY North Campus Buffalo NY 14260

GIRVIGIAN, RAYMOND, architect; b. Detroit, Nov. 27, 1926; s. Manoug and Margaret G.; m. Beverly Rae Bennett, Sept. 23, 1967; 1 son, Michael Raymond. A.A., UCLA, 1947; B.A. with honors, U. Calif.-Berkeley, 1950; M.A. in Architecture, U. Calif.-Berkeley, 1951. With Hutchason Architects, Los Angeles, 1952-57; owner, prin. Raymond Girvigian (Architect), Los Angeles, 1957-68, South Pasadena, Calif., 1968—; co-founder, Advisor Los Angeles Cultural Heritage Bd., 1961—; vice chmn. Historic Am. Bldgs. Survey, Nat. Park Service, Washington, 1966-70; mem. Calif. Hist. Resources Commn., 1970-78; chmn. adv. bd. Calif. Hist. Bldgs. Code, 1976—; bd. dirs. Calif. Heritage Council, 1979—. Co-editor, producer: film Architecture of Southern California for Los Angeles City Schs, 1965; historical monographs of HABS Landmarks, Los Angeles, 1958-80; historical monographs of Califs. State Capitol, 1974, Pan Pacific Auditorium, 1980; designed: city halls for Pico Rivera, 1963, LaPuente, 1966, Rosemead, 1968, Lawndale, 1970 (all Calif.); architect for restoration of Calif. State Capitol, 1975-82; Workman/Temple Hist. Complex, City of Industry, Calif., 1974-81. Mem. St. James Episc. Ch., South Pasadena, Calif. Served with AUS, 1945-46. Recipient Archtl. Design medal U. Calif., Berkeley, 1947, Outstanding Achievement in Architecture award City of Pico Rivera, Calif., 1968, Neasham award Calif. Hist. Soc., 1982. Fellow AIA (Calif. state preservation chmn. 1970-75, state preservation coordinator 1975—, co-recipient nat. honor award for restoration Calif. State Capitol 1983); mem. Soc. Archtl. Historians, Assn. for Preservation Tech., Nat. Trust for Historic Preservation, Archtl. Guild, U. So. Calif., S.W. Mus., Los Angeles. Independent Democrat. Home: 203 Oaklawn Ave South Pasadena CA 91030 Office: 1401 Fair Oaks Ave South Pasadena CA 91030 *I believe that we must all serve society in whatever way that we are best able; and if a worthy cause I have undertaken appears to have failed, I should ignore that possibility and press on with even greater determination and vigor to succeed. I would hope by that example to encourage others to join the cause and thereby further the likelihood of a successful effort for the good of all.*

GIRVIN, EB CARL, educator; b. Georgetown, Tex., Dec. 27, 1917; s. Fitzhugh Bryson and Meta (Perlitz) G.; m. Virginia Lessor, Aug. 29, 1944; chilren: John Lessor, Eric Reed, Stacey Virginia. B.A., U. Tex., 1940, M.A., 1941, Ph.D., 1948. Prof. biology Millsaps Coll., 1948-53; prof. biology, head dept. Southwestern U., Georgetown, 1953—; Mem. Tex. Bd. Examiners Basic Sci., 1960-79; Mem. div. coll. work Episcopal Diocese Tex., 1962-65. Contbr. articles to profl. jours. Mem. Georgetown City Council, 1981—. Served to lt. comdr. USNR, 1941-45. Mem. Tex. Acad. Sci. (bd. dirs.), AAAS, Sigma Xi. Home: 1256 Main St Georgetown TX 78626

GISH, LILLIAN, actress; b. Springfield, Ohio; d. James Lee and Mary (Robinson) G. A.F.D., Rollins Coll.; H.H.D., Mt. Holyoke Coll.; D.F.A. (hon.), Bowling Green State U., 1976, Middlebury Coll. Debut on stage at 5; appeared in motion pictures, 1913—; films include Birth of a Nation, Hearts of the World, Broken Blossoms, Way Down East, Orphans of the Storm, Scarlet Letter, Annie Laurie, The Wind, The Enemy, Night of the Hunter, Duel in the Sun, Portrait of Jennie, The Unforgiven, 1960, Follow Me Boys, 1966, The Comedians, 1967, La Boheme, A Wedding, 1978, Thin Ice (TV), 1980, Hambone and Hillie, 1984; movies made in Italy include The White Sister, Romola; appeared in the theatre, 1930—; plays include Crime and Punishment, 1948, Miss Mabel (title role), 1950, The Curious Savage, 1950, The Trip to Bountiful, Portrait of a Madonna, The Wreck of the 5:25, The Family Reunion (Pulitzer Prize play), All the Way Home, 1960-61, Romeo and Juliet (role of nurse), 1965, Anya, 1966, I Never Sang for My Father, 1967, 68, Too True To Be Good, 1963, A Passage to India, 1963, Uncle Vanya, 1973, A Musical Jubilee, 1975; many TV plays including Twin Detectives, 1976, Sparrow, 1977, Hobson's Choice, 1983; TV series Love Boat; Toured Europe, Russia, U.S. as lectr. on art films, 1969, 71-73; Royal Command appearance, Queen Elizabeth the Queen Mother, 1980; Author: The Movies, Mr. Griffith and Me, 1969, Dorothy and Lillian Gish, 1973. Recipient hon. Acad. Award, 1971, Handel medallion City of N.Y., 1973, Kennedy Center honors, 1982, Life Achievement award Am. Film Inst., 1984. Address: 430 E 57th St New York NY 10022

GISH, NORMAN RICHARD, business executive; b. Eckville, Alta., Can., Oct. 13, 1935; s. Robert Bruce and Lillian (Foster) G.; m. Joan Ann Thompson, Sept. 5, 1959; children—David Cole, Carolyn Nancy, Graeme Christopher. B.A., U. Alta., 1957; LL.B., U. B.C., 1960. Asst. trade commr. Fgn. Trade Service of Canadian Govt., Ottawa, 1961-62, Hong Kong, 1962-65; asst. to v.p. and sec. B.C. Forest Products, Ltd., Vancouver, 1965-67, sec., 1967-72, gen. counsel, sec., 1972-74, v.p., 1974-76; chmn. B.C. Energy Commn., 1977-80; v.p. Turbo Resources Ltd., 1980-83, pres., chief executive officer, 1983—. Mem. Law Soc. B.C., Canadian Bar Assn. Clubs: Canadian, Lawn Tennis (Vancouver); Glenmore Racquet (Calgary). Home: 8940 Bayridge Dr Calgary AB T2V 3M8 Canada Office: 1035 7th Ave SW Calgary AB T2P 3E9 Canada

GISLASON, SIDNEY PAYSON, lawyer; b. Minnesota, Minn., May 22, 1908; s. Bjorn B. and Joan (Peterson) G.; m. Marjorie L. Fleck, Sept. 17, 1938; children: James H., Daniel A., Marion F. LL.B., U. Minn., 1935. Bar: Minn. 1935. Asst. county atty., Brown County, 1936-42, county atty., 1942, city atty., New Ulm, Minn., 1946-50; dist. judge 9th Minn. Dist., 1950-51; lectr. legal trial techniques. Govt. appeal agt. SSS, 1941-67; chmn. 85th Dist. War Finance, 1946—; mem. faculty Law Sci. Inst.; chancellor Law-Sci. Found., 1957-58. Chmn. Little Crow dist. Boy Scouts Am., 1950-54; mem. Minn. Coll. Bd., 1967-73, Minn. Higher Edn. Coordinating Com., 1969-73; Bd. dirs. Courage Found., 1973—. Fellow Am. Bar Found.; mem. ABA (ho. dels. 1954-57), Minn. Bar Assn. (chmn. ct. rules com., bd. govs. 1951-72, v.p. 1953, pres. 1954-55), Am. Coll. Trial Lawyers, Internat. Acad. Trial Lawyers (dir. 1956—, pres. 1959). Lodges: Masons; Shriners. Home: 600 Summit Ave New Ulm MN 56073 Office: State and Center Sts New Ulm MN 56073

GIST, HOWARD BATTLE, JR., lawyer; b. Alexandria, La., Sept. 17, 1919; s. Howard Battle and Marcie (Luckett) G.; m. Rosemary Flynn, Sept. 30, 1950; children—Howard Battle III, Marcie, Stephanie, Robert C., Ellen K., William M. Student, Washington and Lee U., 1936-38; B.A., Tulane U., 1941, LL.B., J.D., 1943. Bar: La. bar 1943. Mem. firm Gist, Methvin, Hughes & Munsterman (and predecessors), Alexandria, 1946—; dir. Security 1st Nat. Bank.; Bd. dirs. St. Frances Cabrini Hosp., Inc., Alexandria. Mem. La. State Bar Assn. (pres. 1977-78), Alexandria Bar Assn. (pres. 1967), La. City Attys. Assn. (past pres.), La. Def. Attys. (pres. 1972-73), Am. Coll. Trial Lawyers, La. State Law Inst. (council). Home: 2009 Polk St Alexandria LA 71301 Office: 803 Johnston St Alexandria LA 71301

GITELMAN, ZVI, political scientist, educator; b. Bronx, N.Y., Nov. 4, 1940; s. Louis and Bella (Margolies) G.; m. Marlene J. Cern, June 12, 1969; children: Yitzhak, Miriam. B.A., Columbia U., 1962, M.A., 1965, Ph.D., 1968; B.H.L., Jewish Theol. Sem., 1962. Assoc. in govt. Columbia U., N.Y.C., 1966-68; jr. fellow Research Inst. Communism Affairs, N.Y.C., 1966-68; asst. prof. polit. sci. U. Mich., Ann Arbor, 1968-73, assoc. prof., 1974-80, prof., 1980—; dir. Ctr. for Russian and Eastern European Studies, U. Mich., Ann Arbor, 1980-83; cons. Meml. Found. for Jewish Culture, N.Y.C., 1977-83. Author: Jewish Nationality and Soviet Politics, 1972, Becoming Israelis, 1982, (with others) Public Opinion in European Socialist Systems, 1977, East-West Relations and the Future of Eastern Europe, 1981. Fellow John Simon Gugenheim Meml. Found., 1983; grantee Ford Found., 1980, Rockefeller Found., 1979. Mem. Am. Polit. Sci. Assn., Am. Assn. for Advancement Slavic Studies, Phi Beta Kappa. Office: Dept. Polit. Sci Univ Mich Haven Hall Ann Arbor MI 48109

GITHENS, JOHN HORACE, JR., physician, educator; b. b Woodbury, N.J., Jan. 2, 1922; s. John Horace and Gladys (Jones) G.; m. Virginia R. Freeman, Mar. 29, 1945; children—James S., Wendy M. B.A., Swarthmore Coll., 1944; M.D., Temple U., 1945. Diplomate: Am. Bd. Pediatrics, Am. Bd. Pediatric Hematology/Oncology. Intern Abington (Pa.) Meml. Hosp., 1945-46; resident in pediatrics, fellow in hematology Phila. Children's Hosp., 1948-50, U. Colo. Med. Center, 1950-51; from instr. to asso. prof. pediatrics U. Colo., 1951-60; asso. dir. gen. med. clinic Denver Gen. Hosp., 1952-57; asst. dir. Rheumatic Fever Diagnostic Clinic, Denver, 1951-53; prof. pediatrics, chmn. dept. U. Ky. Med. Center, 1960-63; prof. pediatrics U. Colo. Med. Center, Denver, 1963—; asso. dean U. Colo. Sch. Medicine, 1964-73, vice chmn. dept. pediatrics, 1973-74; dir. Colo. Sickle Cell Center, 1974—. Co-author: Teaching Comprehensive Medical Care: a Psychological Study of a Change in Medical Education, 1959; Contbr. articles to profl. jours. Served to lt. (j.g.) USNR, 1946-48. Recipient Disting. Alumnus award Temple U., 1964. Fellow Am. Acad. Pediatrics; mem. Soc. Pediatric Research, Western Soc. Pediatric Research (1st Ross award 1957), Transplantation Soc., Am. Pediatric Soc. Office: 4200 E 9th Ave Denver CO 80262

GITLOW, ABRAHAM LEO, university dean; b. N.Y.C., Oct. 10, 1918; s. Samuel and Esther (Boolhack) G.; m. Beatrice Alpert, Dec. 12, 1940; children: Allan Michael, Howard Seth. B.A., U. Pa., 1939; M.A., Columbia U., 1940, Ph.D., 1947. Substitute instr. Bklyn. Coll., 1946-47; instr. N.Y.U., N.Y.C., 1947-50, asst. prof., 1950-54, asso. prof., 1954-59, prof. econs., 1959—, acting dean, 1965-66, dean, 1966—; v.p. Servi-Clean Industries, Inc., Youngstown, Ohio, 1970—; dir. Macmillan, Inc., Bank Leumi Trust Co. N.Y.; Pres. bd. edn. Ramapo Central Sch. Dist. 2, 1963-66; v.p., sec. Samuel and Esther Gitlow Found., N.Y.C. Author: Economics, 1962, Labor and Manpower Economics, 1971; Co-editor: General Economics: A Book of Readings, 1963; Contbr. articles to profl. jours. Served to 1st lt. USAAF, 1943-46; PTO. Recipient Univ. medal Luigi Bocconi U., 1983. Mem. Am. Arbitration Assn. (mem. nat. panel 1948—), Am. Econ. Assn., Royal Econ. Soc., Indsl. Relations Research Assn. Home: PO Box 167 Spring Valley NY 10977 Office: NY U Washington Sq Coll Bus and Pub Adminstrn New York NY 10003

GITNER, GERALD L., airline executive; b. Boston, Apr. 10, 1945; s. Samuel and Sylvia (Berkovitz) G.; m. Deanne Gebell, June 24, 1968; children: Daniel Mark, Seth Michael. B.A., Boston U., 1966. Staff v.p. TransWorld Airlines, N.Y.C., 1972-74; sr. v.p. mktg. and planning Tex. Internat. Airlines, Houston, 1974-80; pres., founder People Express Airlines, Newark, 1980-82; chmn. Pan Am. World Services Inc., N.Y.C., 1982—, exec. v.p., chief fin. officer, 1982—, vice chmn., 1984—; dir. Pan Am. World Airways Inc., Pan Am. World Services Inc. Named to Collegium of Disting. Alumni Boston U., 1982. Mem. Am. Econ. Assn., Phi Alpha Theta. Clubs: Sky; Wings (N.Y.C.). Office: Pan Am World Airways Inc 200 Park Ave New York NY 10166

GITTELSON, BERNARD, public relations consultant, author, lecturer; b. N.Y.C., June 13, 1918; s. Sam and Gussie (Lef) G.; m. Rosalind Weinstein, Mar. 1, 1945; children—Louise Barbara, Steven Henry. B.A., St. John's U., 1939. Cons. on race relations N.Y. State War Council, 1939-41, N.Y. Com. on Industry and Labor Relations, 1941-42; dir. N.Y. State Legis. Com. on Discrimination, 1943-45; asso. coordinator Com. on Community Inter-relations, 1945-46; pres. Roy Bernard Co., Inc., 1946-65; chmn. Roy Bernard Co. Ltd., London, 1955-65; pres. Biorhythm Computers, Inc.; chmn. bd. Time Pattern Research Inst., N.Y.C.; pres. Med. News Service; cons. to govts., corps., instns. Author: Gittelson Biorhythm Code Book, Biorhythm, A Personal Science, How to Make Your Own Luck; Syndicated writer column on biorhythm, 1978—; pub.: Med. Hot Line. Mem. Am. Journalists and Authors, Authors Guild. Home: 96 Division Ave Summit NJ 07901

GITTELSON, NATALIE LEAVY, editor, writer; b. N.Y.C., Jan. 22, 1929; d. Abraham Harris and Celia (Siegel) Leavy; m. Mark R. Gittelson (div.); children: Celia, Eve, Anthony. B.A., N.Y. U. Formerly editor and/or writer with, Vogue mag., Glamour mag., Seventeen mag., Harper's Bazaar mag.; editor, N.Y. Times Sunday Mag.; now exec. editor, McCall's mag., N.Y.C.; Author: Dominus: A Woman Looks at Men's Lives, 1978. Home: 1 Lincoln Plaza New York NY 10023 Office: 230 Park Ave New York NY 10169

GITTERMAN, ALEX, social work educator; b. Kolomea, Poland, Mar. 21, 1938; came to U.S., 1948; s. Paul and Fay (Hirsch) G.; m. Naomi Janet Pines, Sept. 1963; children: Daniel Paul, Sharon Lynn. B.A., Rutgers U., 1960; M.S.W., Hunter Coll., 1962; Ed.D., Columbia U., 1972. Div. dir. Bronx River Settlement, 1962-65; dir. East Side House Millbrook Ctr., Bronx, 1965-66; faculty Columbia U., N.Y.C., 1956—, prof., 1972—, assoc. dean, 1981—; cons. Manhattan VA, N.Y.C., 1974-80, Family Service of Westchester (White Plains), 1978-80, Bur. Child Welfare, 1977-80, Jewish Welfare Bd, 1973-76. Contbr. articles to profl. jours.; author: (with L. Shulman) Mut. Aid Groups & The Life Cycle, 1985, (with C.B. Germain) The Life Model of Social Work Practice, 1980. Mem. adv. com. Westchester YM-YWHA, New Rochelle, 1982—. Recipient Hexter award Hunter Coll., 1981. Mem. Am. Orthopsychiat. Assn., Am. Pub. Health Assn., Soc. Hosp. Social Work Dirs., Com. on Social Work Edn., Nat. Assn. Social Workers. Democrat. Jewish. Office: Columbia U Sch Social Work 622 W 113 St New York NY 10025

GITTES, RUBEN FOSTER, urological surgeon; b. Mallorca, Spain, Aug. 4, 1934; s. Archie and and Cicely Mary (Foster) G.; m. K.S. Zipf, June 10, 1955; m. Rita R. Drum, Feb. 21, 1976; children: Julia S., Frederick T., George K., Melissa S., Robert F. Grad., Phillips Acad., Andover, Mass., 1952; A.B., Harvard U., 1956, M.D., 1960. Intern, then resident in surgery and urology Mass. Gen. Hosp., Boston, 1960-67; asst. prof. UCLA Med. Sch., 1968-69; assoc. prof., then prof., chief urology U. Calif. at San Diego Med. Sch., 1969-75; prof. urol. surgery Harvard U. Med. Sch., chmn. Harvard program urology Longwood area, 1975—; mem. study sects., task forces NIH, 1973—. Author, editor publs. in field. Served with USPHS, 1963-65. NIH grantee, 1969—. Mem. Endocrine Soc., Soc. Univ. Surgeons, Soc. Univ. Urologists, Am. Assn. Genito-Urinary Surgeons, Clin. Soc. Genito-Urinary Surgeons, A.C.S., Am. Urol. Assn., AAAS, Soc. Ancient Numismatics, Am. Soc. Bone and Mineral Research, Phi Beta Kappa, Alpha Omega Alpha. Home: 88 Rockport Rd Weston MA 02193 Office: Brigham and Women's Hosp Boston MA 02115

GITTINS, ARTHUR RICHARD, school administrator; b. Edmonton, Alta., Can., May 26, 1926; came to U.S., 1953; s. David Richard and Jessie Irene (Sharp) G.; m. Eleanor Jeanne Hoffman, Sept. 9, 1949; children: David Allan, Richard Arthur. B.Sc., U. Alta., 1952; M.S., U. Idaho, 1955; Ph.D., Mont. State U., 1962. Dept. head entomolgy U. Idaho, Moscow, 1967-77, dean grad. sch., 1978—, dir. univ. research office, 1978—; prin. entomolgist U.S. Dept. Agr., Washington, 1976-77; mng. dir. Idaho Reserch Found., Moscow, 1978-83; acting dir. Water and Energy Resource Research Inst., Moscow, 1980-82. Contbr. articles to profl. jours. Fellow Royal Entomol. Soc., Entomol. Soc. Am. (pres. Pacific br. 1979-80), Entomol. Soc. Can., Soc. Systematic Zoology, Idaho Acad. Sci. Home: 624 N Lincoln Moscow ID 83843 Office: U Idaho Grad Sch 111 Morrill Hall Moscow ID 83843

GITTLEMAN, SOL, foreign language educator, university official; b. Hoboken, N.J., June 5, 1934; s. Frank and Edna (Schlanger) G.; m. Robyn Singer, Sept. 9, 1956; children: Julia, Peter Thomas. B.A., Drew U., 1955; M.A., Columbia U., 1956; Ph.D., U. Mich., 1961. Asst. prof., German Mt. Holyoke Coll., South Hadley, Mass., 1962-64; asst. prof. Tufts U., Medford, Mass., 1964-70, prof. German, 1971—, chmn. dept. German and Russian, 1966-81, McCollester prof. religious studies, 1978—, provost, acad. v.p., 1981—; dir. summer seminars NEH. Author: Frank Wedekind, 1969, Sholem Aleichem, 1974, From Shtetl to Suburbia, 1978. Recipient Harbison award Danforth Found., 1970. Mem. MLA, Am. Assn. Tchrs. Yiddish, Am. Assn. Tchrs. German. Home: 48 Professors Row Medford MA 02155 Office: Office of the Provost Ballou Hall Tufts U. Medford MA 02155

GITTLER, JOSEPH BERTRAM, sociology educator; b. N.Y.C., Sept. 21, 1912; s. Morris and Toby (Rosenblatt) G.; m. Lami Shapiro, June 28, 1934 (dec. 1966); 1 dau., Josephine; m. Susan Wolters, Sept. 15, 1968. B.S., U. Ga., 1934, M.A., 1936; Ph.D., U. Chgo., 1941. From instr. to assoc. prof. sociology U. Ga., 1936-43; research assoc. Va. Planning Bd., 1942-43, U. Chgo., 1944; prof. sociology Iowa State U., 1945-54; prof. sociology, chmn. dept., dir. Center Study Group Operations, U. Rochester, 1954-61; dean faculty, prof. social scis. Queensborough Coll., CUNY, 1961-66; prof. sociology, dean Ferkauf Grad. Sch. Humanities and Social Scis., Yeshiva U., N.Y.C., 1966-78; disting. vis. prof. sociology George Mason U. of State U. Va., Fairfax, 1978-79, disting. prof., 1980—; vis. prof. Hiroshima (Japan) U., 1979-80; lectr. various univs., U.S., Japan, Spain, Eng., Israel, Finland, Taiwan, cons. in field, 1940—; Mem. Rochester council N.Y. State Commn. Against Discrimination, 1955-60; chmn. regional selection com. Woodrow Wilson Fellowship Found., 1955-58; co-chmn. Brotherhood Week edn. com. NCCJ, 1950; council fellows Upland Inst., 1965-72. Author: Social Thought Among the Early Greeks, 1941, Virginia's People, 1944, Social Dynamics, 1952, Review of Sociology, 1957, Understanding Minority Groups, 1964, Ethnic Minorities in the U.S.: Perspectives from the Social Sciences, 1977, Conflict and Conflict Resolution: Philosophical and Sociological Foundations, 1983; author, editor: Jewish Life in the United States: Perspectives from the Social Sciences, 1981; contbr. numerous articles to profl. jours. Recipient Walter B. Hill prize philosophy U. Ga., 1934; poetry award; best tchr. award. Fellow Am. Sociol. Assn., N.Y. Acad. Scis.; mem. P.E.N., Internat. Sociol. Soc., Eastern Sociol. Soc., Assn. for Higher Edn., Am. Assn. Acad. Deans, Phi Beta Kappa. Home: 4301 Beaumont Ct Fairfax VA 22030 Office: Dept Sociology George Mason U Fairfax VA 22030

GITTLIN, A. SAM, industrialist, banker; b. Newark, Nov. 21, 1914; s. Benjamin and Ethel (Bernstein) G.; m. Fay Lerner, Sept. 18, 1938; children: Carol (Mrs. Alan H. Franklin), Regina (Mrs. Peter Gross), Bruce David, Steven Robert. B.C.S., Rutgers U., 1938. Partner Gittlin Bag Co. name now changed to Gittlin Cos. Inc., Fairfield, N.J., 1935-40; v.p., dir. Gittlin Bag Co., 1954—, chmn. bd., 1963—; v.p., dir. Abbey Record Mfg. Co., Newark, 1958-60; chmn., treas. Packaging Products & Design Co. (now PPD Corp.), Newark and Glendale, Calif., 1959-71, chmn. exec. com., treas., 1972—; chmn. Pines Shirt & Pajama Co., N.Y.C., 1960—, Pottsville Shirt & Pajama Co. (Pa.), 1960—, Barrington Industries, N.Y.C., 1963-72, First Peninsula Calif. Corp., 1964-68, Wall-co Imperial, Miami, Fla., 1965—, Levin & Hecht, Inc., N.Y.C., 1966-72, Wallco of San Juan (P.R.), Brunswick Shirt Co., N.Y.C., 1966-72, Fleetline Industries, Garland, N.C., 1966-72, All State Auto Leasing & Rental Corp., Beverly Hills, Calif., 1968-72, Packaging Ltd., Newark, 1970-76, Kans. Plastics, Inc., Garden City, 1970—, Bob Cushman Distbrs., Inc., Phoenix, 1972—, Wallpaper Supermarkets, 1976-80, Wallco Internat. Inc.,, Miami, 1976, Overwrap Equipment Corp., Fairfield, 1978—, GCI Ala. Inc., Birmingham, 1981—, Wallpapers Inc., Oakland, Calif., 1982—, Portland, Oreg., 1982—, Honolulu and Denver, 1982—; pres. Covington Funding Co., N.Y.C., 1963—; vice chmn. bd. Peninsula Savs. and Loan Assn., San Mateo and San Francisco, 1964-67, chmn., 1967-68; chmn. bd., treas. Bob Cushman Painting & Decorating Co. (now Wallco West), Phoenix, 1972—; treas., dir. Flex Pak Industries, Inc., Atlanta, 1973-76, Ploy Plax Films, Inc., Santa Ana, Calif., 1973-76; sec., chmn. exec. com. Zins Wallcoverings, Newark; ptnr. Benjamin Co., N.Y.C., Laurel Assocs. (Md.), Seaboard Realty Assocs., Miami, 1980—, GHG Realty Assocs., N.Y.C., 1980; ptnr., investors cons. Mission Pack, Inc., Los Angeles; vice chmn., dir., chmn. exec. com. Falmouth Supply, Ltd., Montreal, Que., Can., Ascher Trading Corp., Newark, Aptex, Inc.; dir. Harris Paint & Wall Covering Super Marts, Miami, Morgan Hill Mfg. Co., Reading, Pa.; dir., fin. cos. Ramada Inns, Phoenix; dir., fin. cons. Ramada Inns Realty Equities Corp. N.Y., N.Y.C. Chmn. N.C. com. B'nai B'rith, 1940; treas. N.C. Fedn. B'nai B'rith Lodges, 1941-43, v.p., 1943-44, pres., 1944-47; mem. com. to rev. dept. banking and ins. N.J. Commn. on Efficiency and Economy in State Govt., 1967—; Trustee Benjamin Gittlin Charity Found., Newark, BAMA Master Retirement Program, Hillel Found. at Rutgers U.; bd. visitors Franklin & Marshall U., Allentown, Pa. Jewish (pres., trustee, Onai Abraham, Livingston N.J.). Club: Greenbrook Country (Caldwell, N.J.). Home: 59 Glenview Rd South Orange NJ 07079 Office: 60 E 42d St St New York NY 10165

GIUDICE, SAL JOHN, container co. exec.; b. N.Y.C., Oct. 23, 1923; s. John and Rose (Intoci) G.; m. Elizabeth Ann Poland, Feb. 16, 1950; children—John, William, Philip, Barbara. B.S., Bowling Green State U., 1949; postgrad., Harvard Bus. Sch., 1969. With Am. Can Co., Greenwich, Conn., 1950—, v.p. beverage packaging, 967-70, v.p. mktg. and packaging, 1970-73, v.p. and gen. mgr. food packaging, 1973-75, sr. v.p. human resources, 1975-81, exec. v.p., 1981—; dir. Reads Ltd., Liverpool, Eng., 1968-77; Trustee Fairfield U. Served with AUS, 1943-45. Mem. Nat. Assn. Mfrs., Can Mfrs. Inst., Am. Paper Inst. Club: Greenwich Country. Home: 163 Stanwich Rd Greenwich CT 06830 Office: Am Can Co American Ln Greenwich CT 06830

GIUFFRIDA, JOSEPH GILBERT, anesthesiologist, educator; b. Bklyn., Oct. 24, 1916; s. Anthony and Anna (Giustolisi) G.; m. Mildred T. Lotierzo, Aug. 15, 1943; children: Nina Giuffrida Dorsett, Anthony, Elaine Giuffrida Sevush, Regina, Jo Ann. B.A., N.Y. U., 1938, M.D., 1942. Diplomate: Am. Bd. Anesthesiology. Intern Met. Hosp., N.Y.C., 1942-43, resident, 1946-48; practice medicine specializing in anesthesiology, N.Y.C., 1948—; chief anesthesia services Met. Hosp. Center, N.Y.C., 1973—, Bird S. Coler Hosp., 1973—; attending staff Westchester County Med. Center, Valhalla,

N.Y., Lincoln Med. and Mental Health Center; instr. dept. anesthesiology N.Y. Med. Coll., N.Y.C., 1949-63, asst. prof., 1963-67, asso. prof., 1967-73, prof. anesthesiology, 1973—, asso. chmn., 1979—. Contbr. articles to med. jours. Served to capt. M.C. U.S. Army, 1943-46. Fellow Am. Coll. Anesthesiologists, Internat. Coll. Surgeons; mem. Bay Ridge Med. Soc. (pres. 1964-65). Home: 47 Saddle Ridge Rd Millwood NY 10546 Office: 1901 1st Ave New York NY 10029

GIUFFRIDA, LOUIS ONORATO, former military officer, government official; b. Middletown, Conn., Oct. 2, 1920; s. Innocenzio and Rosa (LaBella) G.; m. Genevieve Theresa Chapowicki, Aug. 29, 1959; children: Luisa Alexandra, John Christopher, Bruno, Matthew Alexander, Elena Lauren Arnett. B.A., U. Conn., 1947; M.A., Boston U., 1966. Commd. lt. U.S. Marine Corps., 1943, advanced through ranks to maj. gen., 1981, served in PTO, 1943-46; served in N.G. State Calif., 1948-81 (ret.); dir. Fed. Emergency Mgmt. Agy, Washington, 1981—; pres. Universal Cons., San Luis Obispo, Calif., 1971-77, Specialized Mgmt. Services Co., 1977-81; dist. lectr. Calif. State U-Los Angeles, 1981; founder, dir. Calif. Specialized Tng. Inst., 1971-81; sr. U.S. rep. to NATO Sr. Civil Emergency Planning Com.; dist. lectr. NATO Civil Def. Com.; U.S. chmn. U.S./Can. Civil Emergency Planning Consultative Group, U.S./Mex. Consultative Com. on Natural Disasters; co-chmn. nat. security com. Fowler McCracken Commn. Editor: textbook Help Me —I'm Hurt, 1980. Commr. Human Relations Commn., San Luis Obispo, 1973-80; mem. regional council Boy Scouts Am., San Luis Obispo, 1973-74; bd. govs. (Presdl. appointment) ARC, Washington, 1981-83. Named Man of Yr., Middletown, Conn., 1983. Fellow Acad. Criminal Justice Scis.; mem. Internat. Assn. Chiefs Police, Am. Soc. Indsl. Security, Omicron Delta Kappa, Alpha Psi Omega, Alpha Gamma Rho. Republican. Methodist. Home: 1931 Relda Ct Falls Church VA 22043 Office: Fed. Emergency Mgmt Agy 500 C Street SW Washington DC 20472

GIUGGIO, JOHN PETER, newspaper executive; b. Boston, July 5, 1930; s. John Peter and Theresa H. (Gagliard) G.; m. Barbara Savage, May 9, 1953; children: Barbara, John, Patricia, Stephen. B.S. in Bus. Adminstrn, Boston Coll., 1951. With Boston Globe Newspaper, 1945—, pres., 1978—, Affiliated Publs.; dir. Affiliated Broadcasting Co.; Trustee Boston Coll. High Sch.; bd. dirs. North Conway (Mass.) Inst. Trustee Carney Hosp. Mem. Boston Coll. Alumni Assn. (pres. 1981-82), Boston C. of C. (dir.), Boston Better Bus. Bur. (assoc. chmn.). Club: Univ. (Boston) (pres.). Home: 46 Jerusalem Rd Cohasset MA 02025 Office: 135 Morrissey Blvd Boston MA 02107

GIULIANI, RUDOLPH W., lawyer, government official; b. N.Y.C., May 28, 1944. A.B. magna cum laude, Manhattan Coll., J.D., N.Y. U. Law clk. U.S. Dist. Ct. Judge, N.Y.C., 1968-70; asst. U.S. atty. So. Dist. N.Y.; exec. asst. U.S. atty., chief narcotics sect., and chief spl. prosecutions sect. Dept. Justice; assoc. dep. atty. gen., 1975-77, asso. atty. gen., 1981-83, U.S. atty., N.Y., 1983—; mem. firm Patterson, Belknap, Webb and Taylor, N.Y.C., 1977-81; lectr. in field. Mem. Order of Coif. Address: US Atty's Office 1 St Andrews Plaza New York NY 10007

GIULINI, CARLO MARIA, conductor; b. Barletta, Italy, May 9, 1914; (married); 3 sons. Ed., Accademia Santa Cecilia, Rome, Chigiana Acad., Siena.. Played viola, Santa Cecilia Orch., Augusteo Orch., Rome; debut as orchestral conductor, Rome, 1944; asst. condr., Rome Radio Orch., 1944-46; prin. condr., 1946-50; founder, prin. condr., Orch. of Radio Milan, 1950-54; debut as opera condr., Bergamo Festival, 1951; prin. conductor, La Scala, Milan, 1954-58; condr. symphony orchs. in, Boston, Phila., N.Y.C., Los Angeles, Israel, Berlin, London, Vienna, Paris, symphony orch., Chgo.; prin. guest condr., 1969-72; condr. for music festivals in, Edinburgh, London, Venice, Florence, Strasbourg, Prague, Aix-en-Provence; condr.: opera Covent Garden, Prague Nat., Zurich, Prague Nat., Amsterdam, Prague Nat., Tel Aviv, Florence Maggio, Turin, Venice; prin. condr., Rome Opera; music dir., Los Angeles Philharmonic Orch., 1978— (Recipient Grammy award for best classical rec. 1971), Recs. for, Deutsche Grammophon, RCA, Angel, London, EMI. Recipient Columbus award, 1983. Home: Los Angeles CA Office: Los Angeles Philharmonic 135 N Grand Ave Los Angeles CA 90012

GIURGOLA, ROMALDO, architect, educator; b. Rome, Italy, Sept. 2, 1920; s. Vincenzo and Maria Luigia (Petrin) G.; m. Adelaide F. Bencivenga, Dec. 20, 1952; 1 dau., Paola F. Laurea summa cum laude, Scuola Di Architettura Universita' Di Roma, 1948; M.S. in Architecture, Columbia, 1951. Partner firm Mitchell/Giurgola Architects, Phila. and N.Y.C., 1958—; chmn. dept. architecture Columbia, 1968-71, Ware prof. architecture, 1971—. Fellow AIA (gold medal 1982); mem. Am. Acad. and Inst. Arts and Letters (inst. mem.), Academia Nazionale di San Luca (corr.). Home: 50 E 89th St New York NY 10028 Office: 170 W 97th St New York NY 10025

GIUS, JULIUS, newspaper editor; b. Fairbanks, Alaska, Dec. 31, 1911; s. Julius and Mary (Sarja) G.; m. Elizabeth Gail Alexander, Aug. 24, 1940; children—Gary Alexander, Barbara Gail. Student, U. Puget Sound, 1930-33. Reporter Tacoma (Wash.) Times, 1929-35; founding editor Bremerton (Wash.) Sun, 1935-60; editor Ventura (Calif.) Star-Free Press; also editorial dir. John P. Scripps Newspapers, 1961—. Mem. Am. Soc. Newspaper Editors, Sigma Delta Chi. Clubs: Elk, K.C., Rotarian. Home: 4675 Clubhouse Dr Camarillo CA 93010 Office: 5250 Ralston St Ventura CA 93003

GIUSTI, GEORGE, artist, designer, sculptor; b. Milano, Italy; came to U.S., 1938, naturalized, 1946; s. Emil and Edmeda (Giusti) Wuermli; m. Margot Louise Reiche Joachimsthal, July 11, 1936. Student, Reale Accademia Di Belle Arti Di Brera, Milano, 1923-27. Free-lance artist, cons. to industry, editorial and advt. designer, 1931—, exhibited at maj. capitals of world.; Author: The Human Heart, 1961. Recipient Golden medals art dirs. clubs, Chgo., 1951, 56, Phila., 1954, 58, N.Y.C., 1955, Milw., 1959, others; Golden T. Square award; named Art Dir. of Year, 1958, named to Hall of Fame, 1979. Mem. Am. Inst. Graphic Arts, Alliance Graphique Internationale, Internat. Center for Typog. Arts, Art Dirs. Club (N.Y.C.). Home and Studio: 20 Chalburn Rd West Redding CT 06896 *I believe that every true artist is a discoverer, forever seeking new horizons to explore. His is a continual search for clues that help him envision the world of tomorrow. He looks upon accepted forms and conventions, not as immutable laws but as forerunners of new concepts and solutions. He is a free man, and is not ruled by false notions of what must be and what must not be. It is impossible to be creative without this interchange between fantasy and the real. Thus, the true artist molds vague ideas into an art and reality that is far above and beyond the easy alternatives of the past or present.*

GIUSTI, GINO PAUL, natural resources company executive; b. New Kensington, Pa., May 31, 1927; s. Peter Paul and Rose (Bonadio) G.; m. Ruth Marie Greblunas, May 4, 1957; children: Paul, Susan, Patricia, John, Christopher. B.S. in Chem. Engring, U. Pitts., 1949, M.S., 1953, Ph.D. in Bus. and Econs, 1959. Registered profl. engr., Pa. Texasgulf research fellow Mellon Inst. Indsl. Research, Pitts., 1948-57; asst. to pres. Texasgulf Inc., Stamford, Conn., 1958-61, mgr. market research, 1962-64, corp. personnel mgr., 1965-71, v.p. employee relations and adminstr., 1972-77, v.p. agrl. chems. div., 1978-79, sr. v.p., 1979, pres., chief operating officer, 1979-82, pres., chief exec. officer, 1982—, also dir.; pres. Texasgulf Chems. Co., 1979; vice chmn., dir. Elf Aquitaine Inc., 1983—; dir. M & T Chems. Inc., Union Trust Co., Northeast Bancorp, Inc.; Mem. metals and minerals unit Nat. Def. Exec. Res., Dept. Interior, 1962—; bd. dirs. Potash and Phosphate Inst., Sulphur Inst. Bd. dirs. Found. Agronomic Research; trustee Fairfield U., Stamford Hosp. Served with USAAF, 1945-46. Mem. Am. Chem. Soc., Am. Econs. Assn., Am. Inst. Chem. Engrs., Chem. Market Research Assn., Soc. Mining Engrs., AIME. Roman Catholic. Clubs: Woodway Country, Landmark, Sky. Home: 236 W Haviland Ln Stamford CT 06903 Office: Texasgulf Inc High Ridge Park Stamford CT 06904

GIUSTI, JOSEPH PAUL, university chancellor; b. Harrisburg, Pa., Mar. 4, 1935; s. Joseph and Ellen C. (Carletti) G.; m. Marie D. Mazza, Jan. 30, 1960; children: Jeannine Carolyn, Lynn Christine, Susan Marie. B.A. in English Lit., Villanova U., 1957; M.S. in Bus. Adminstrn., Pa. State U., 1959, Ed.D., 1962; D.Litt. (hon.), St. Vincent Coll., 1976. Instr. dept. commerce and fin. Pa. State U., 1958-60, grad. asst., 1961-62, asst. to v.p., 1963-65, mem. grad. faculty, 1963-79, asso. prof. higher edn., 1965-79; campus dir. Beaver campus, 1965-79; chancellor univ., profl. higher edn. Ind. U.-Purdue U., Fort Wayne, 1979—; cons. hemolytic disease study group div. blood diseases and resources Nat. Heart, Lung, and Blood Inst., NIH, 1975—; mem. adv. com. Edn. Mgmt. Info. System, Commonwealth of Pa., 1971-79; Chmn. exec. com. Allen County (Ind.) United Way, 1979-80; mem. joint adv. council Fort Wayne Med. Edn. Program, 1979—; mem. exec. com. Fort Wayne Future, Inc., 1979—, Fort Wayne Ednl. Found., 1979—; sec. Beaver Campus Adv. Bd., 1966-79, dir. emeritus, 1979—; bd. dirs. Med. Center of Beaver County, Pa., 1966-79, pres., 1972-75, dir. emeritus, 1979—; bd. dirs. Fort Wayne Public TV, 1980—; mem. Corp. Council, Fort Wayne, 1981; bd. dirs. Parkview Meml. Hosp. Contbr. articles on fin. mgmt. and ednl. adminstrn. to profl. publs.; contbr. chpts. to books on fin. mgmt. Recipient Beaver Campus Disting. Service award, 1974; Trustee award Community Coll. of Beaver County, 1972; Civic Improvement League award, 1972; Benjamin Rush award Med. Soc. of Beaver County, 1976. Mem. Greater Fort Wayne C. of C. (dir. 1981—), Ind. U. Ft. Wayne Alumni Assn. (life dir. 1982—), Purdue U. Ft. Wayne Alumni Assn. (life dir. 1982—), Phi Delta Kappa, Alpha Kappa Psi, Pi Gamma Mu. Roman Catholic. Beaver Campus Amphitheater named in his honor. Office: 2101 Coliseum Blvd East Fort Wayne IN 46805

GIVAN, RICHARD MARTIN, chief justice state supreme court; b. Indpls., June 7, 1921; s. Clinton Hodell and Glee (Bowen) G.; m. Pauline Marie Haggart, Feb. 28, 1945; children: Madalyn (Mrs. Larry R. Hesson), Sandra (Mrs. Michael O. Chenoweth), Patricia (Mrs. Thomas Siwek), Elizabeth. LL.B., Ind. U., 1951. Bar: Ind. bar 1952. Partner firm Bowen, Myers, Northam & Givan, 1960-69; dep. pub. defender, Ind., 1952-53, dep. atty. gen., 1953-64, dep. pros. atty., Marion County, 1965-66; justice Ind. Supreme Ct., 1969—, now chief justice.; Mem. Ind. Ho. Reps., 1967-68. Served to 2d lt. USAAF, 1942-45. Mem. Ind., Indpls. bar assns., Ind. Soc. Chicago, Newcomen Soc. N.Am., Internat. Arabian Horse Assn. (dir., chmn. ethical practices rev. bd.), Ind. Arabian Horse Club (pres. 1971-72), Sigma Delta Kappa., Soc. of Friends (clk.). Club: Lion. Office: Supreme Ct Ind 324 State House Indianapolis IN 46204

GIVENCHY *See* **DE GIVENCHY, HUBERT**

GIVENS, AUSTIN LAWRENCE, magazine editor; b. Pitts., May 7, 1937; s. Frank Joseph and Ruth Wilson (Logan) G.; (married); children: Adam Lawrence, Mark Patrick. B.A. in English Lit, U. Pitts., 1961, M.A. in Musicology, 1963. Mfr. player piano music rolls, 1959-74; with Automotive Engring. mag., Warrendale, Pa., 1974—, editor-in-chief, 1976—. Author: Rebuilding The Player Piano, 1963, Re-Enacting the Artist, 1970. Mem. Soc. Automotive Engrs., Soc. Automotive Historians. Republican. Home: 10415 Grubbs Rd Wexford PA 15090 Office: 400 Commonwealth Dr Warrendale PA 15096

GIVENS, HARRISON, JR., insurance company executive; b. Ft. Lauderdale, Fla., Nov. 3, 1926; s. Harrison and Gladys (Golladay) G.; m. Marion Thomas, Oct. 12, 1953; children—Harrison, III, Anne Benton. B.S., Yale U., 1946. With Equitable Life Assurance Soc. U.S., 1947—, sr. v.p., N.Y.C., 1980—; bd. dirs. ERISA Industry Com.; bd. actuaries Civil Service Retirement System; bd. pensions Presbyn. Ch.; mem. pension research council U. Pa. Fellow Soc. Actuaries; mem. Am. Acad. Actuaries (charter). Republican. Club: N.Y. Athletic. Home: 116 E 68th St New York NY 10021 Office: Equitable Life Assurance Soc US 1285 Ave Americas New York NY 10019

GIVENS, JOHN KENNETH, roofing material manufacturing company executive; b. Highland Park, Mich., Aug. 21, 1940; s. John Hamilton and Marion Florence (Harris) G.; m. Bonnie L. Turner Higgens; children: Kevin John, Kirk David; m. Patricia Ann Bowlby, May 23, 1980. B.A., Mich. State U., 1963. Sales promotion mgr. Lincoln-Mercury div. Ford Motor Co., Dearborn, 1975-77; sr. v.p. Wells. Rich, Greene Advt., Los Angeles, 1977-79; v.p. mktg. Chrysler Corp., Highland Park, Mich., 1979-82; pres. Seal-Dry USA, Inc., Pontiac, Mich., 1982—. Mem. Assn. Nat. Advertisers (dir. 1980-82). Office: Seal-Dry USA Inc. PO Box 719 Pontiac MI 48056

GIVENS, PAUL RONALD, univ. chancellor; b. Wellsburg, W.Va., Nov. 16, 1923; s. George D. and Anna (Peters) G.; m. Leona Janssen, Dec. 20, 1945; children—Gregg, Stann, Rodney, Deborah. Student, Graceland Coll., 1941-43; B.A., George Peabody Coll., 1948, M.A., 1949; postgrad., U. Iowa, 1949-50; Ph.D., Vanderbilt U., 1953. Instr. Lawrence Coll., Appleton, Wis., 1949-51; counselor Vanderbilt U., Nashville, 1951-53; chmn. psychology dept. Birmingham So. Coll., Birmingham, Ala., 1953-60, U. So. Fla., Tampa, 1960-67; dean arts and scis. Ithaca (N.Y.) Coll., 1967-72; v.p. acad. affairs Millikin U., Decatur, Ill., 1972-79; chancellor Pembroke (N.C.) State U., 1979—. Author: (with others) Human Behavior, 1966. Served with USNR, 1943-46. Home: Chancellor's Residence Box 815 Pembroke NC 28372

GKONOS, JAMES WILLIAM, chemist; b. Owosso, Mich., Jan. 26, 1924; s. George S. and Wilma (Pierow) G.; m. Dorothy Jean Hart, June 25, 1949; children—Peter J., James S., Susan J. B.S. in Chem. Engring, U. Mich., 1947, 1948, M.S., 1949. With E.I. DuPont de Nemours & Co., Inc., 1949—, plant mgr., Toledo, 1968-69, mgr. mfg., Wilmington, Del., 1969-74, mgr. research and devel., 1974—. Served with USNR, 944-46. Republican. Office: F & F Dept Brandywine Bldg Wilmington DE 19898

GLAAB, CHARLES NELSON, educator, historian; b. b Williston, N.D., Dec. 19, 1927; s. Reuben and Betty (Nelson) G.; m. Mary Ellen Anderson, Nov. 5, 1949; children—Martha Ann, John Reuben. B.Ph., U. N.D., 1951, M.A., 1952; Ph.D., U. Mo., 1958. Research asso. history Kansas City project U. Chgo., 1956-58; instr., asst. prof. history Kans. State U., 1958-60; asso. prof., prof. history U. Wis. at Milw., 1960-68; dir. urban history sect. Wis. Hist. Soc., 1960-63; prof. history U. Toledo, 1968—; Dir. Fox Valley research project Wis. Hist. Soc., 1963-64; mem. Milw. Landmarks Commn., 1965-68, Toledo Landmark Com., 1968-70, Ohio Hist. Site Preservation Bd., 1979-81. Author: Kansas City and the Railroads, 1962, The American City: A Documentary History, 1963, (with A.T. Brown) A History of Urban America, 1967, (with L.H. Larsen) Factories in the Valley, 1969, (with Morgan A. Barclay) Toledo: Gateway to the Great Lakes, 1983; Editor: Urban History Group Newsletter, 1962-68; co-editor, 1968-70; bd. editors: Urban Affairs Quar, 1966-74, Soc. Press Wis, 1966-78, Jour. Urban History, 1973—, Urban Affairs Ann. Rev, 1978—. Served with AUS, 1946-48. Mem. Orgn. Am. Historians, Phi Beta Kappa. Home: 3021 Hopewell Pl Toledo OH 43606

GLAD, EDWARD NEWMAN, lawyer; b. Polk, Nebr., June 30, 1919; s. Lewis Olaf and Esther Ruth (Newman) G.; m. Suzanne Watson Lockley, Nov. 7, 1953; children: Amy Lockley, Lisanne Watson Lantz, William Edward. Student, U. Omaha, 1938-41; J.D., U. Mich., 1948. Bar: N.Y. 1949, Calif. 1959, D.C. 1964. Assoc. Barnes, Richardson & Colburn, N.Y.C., 1948-59; sr. ptnr. Glad & Tuttle, Los Angeles, San Francisco, 1959-71, Glad, Tuttle & White, 1971-79, Glad & White, 1979-81, Glad, White & Ferguson, 1981—; lectr. customs law seminars ABA, IIT Conf., Tex. A & I, Laredo.; pres. Fgn. Trade Assn. So. Calif., 1965; v.p. Japan Am. Soc., 1969-73; pres. British-Am. C. of C., 1963-64, 70-72, Spain-U.S. C. of C., 1977-81; dir. Swedish-Am. C. of C., 1976-78, 82—; chmn. adv. council Calif. State World Trade Commn., 1983—. Author articles on U.S. customs law. Trustee St. George's Episcopal Nursery and Ungraded Sch., 1968-72. Served to lt. comdr. USNR, 1941-46; ETO. Decorated Order Brit. Empire. Mem. State Bar Calif., Bar Assn. D.C., N.Y. State Bar. Home: 519 Meadow Grove St Flintridge CA 91011 Office: 350 S Figueroa St Los Angeles CA 90071 also 625 Market St 13th Floor San Francisco CA 94105

GLADE, WILLIAM PATTON, JR., university administrator; b. Wichita Falls, Tex., July 29, 1929; s. William Patton and Billie (Hatcher) G.; m. Marlene Louise Joseph, July 10, 1954; children: Anita, Mary, William, John. B.B.A., U. Tex., 1950, M.A., 1951, Ph.D., 1955. Instr., asst. prof. econs. U. Md., 1957-60; faculty U. Wis., Madison, 1960-71, prof. Sch. Bus. and dept. econs., 1966-71; prof. econs. U. Tex.; dir. Inst. Latin Am. Studies, Austin, 1971—; Bd. dirs. Fund for Multinat. Mgmt. Edn. Author: Las empresas gubernamentales descentralizadas, 1959, The Political Economy of Mexico, 1963, The Latin American Economies, 1969, Marketing in a Developing Economy—the Case of Peru, 1970. Mem. Am. Econ. Assn., Midwest Council Latin Am. Studies (pres. 1963), Latin Am. Studies Assn. (v.p. 1978, pres. 1979), S.W. Council Latin Am. Studies, Assn. Evolutionary Econs. Club: Cosmos. Office: Dept of Economics U Tex Austin TX 78712

GLADIEUX, BERNARD LOUIS, management consultant; b. Toledo, Apr. 12, 1907; s. Victor Modest and Anna (Cook) G.; m. Persis Skilliter, June 19, 1930; children: Bernard Louis, Russell Victor, Lawrence Edward, Jay Arthur. A.B., Oberlin Coll., 1930; student, Zimmern Sch. Internat. Studies, Geneva, Switzerland, summer 1929; A.M. in Pub. Adminstrn, Syracuse U., 1943. Tchr., prin. Am. Sch. in, Japan, Tokyo, 1930-34; exec. sec. City Mgr. League, Toledo, 1935; adminstrv. cons. Pub. Adminstrn. Service, Chgo., 61936-39; mgmt. cons., chief war orgn. staff U.S. Bur. Budget; exec. Office of Pres., 1939-42; adminstrv. asst. to chmn. and chief adminstrv. officer WPB, 1943-44; dep. chief operations and adminstrn. UNRRA, 1944; exec. asst. sec. U.S. Dept. Commerce, 1945-50; asst. to pres. The Ford Found., 1950-54; fiscal policy cons. Philippine Govt., 1955-56; cons. Com. Govt. Reorgn., 1952; lectr. dept. pub. law and govt., Columbia, 1953; pub. adminstrn. cons. Pakistan Govt., 1955; partner, v.p. Booz, Allen & Hamilton, Inc., 1957- 66; partner, dir. Knight & Gladieux, 1967-69; dir. Knight, Gladieux & Smith, 1969-74; spl. cons. Dept. State, 1968, ICA, 1978—, Dept. Def., 1980, World Bank, 1981; cons. Pres.'s Adv. Council Exec. Orgn., 1970-71; adviser on adminstrn. Govt. of Iran, 1975—; pub. mgmt. adviser Govt. of Kuwait, 1977—; Mem. nat. adv. council Hampshire Coll.; mem. com. govt. Com. Econ. Devel., 1963-71; mem. Com. Pub. Service, 1961-68; corp. mem. Nat. Assembly Social Policy and Devel. Author articles in field. Past v.p., bd. dirs., chmn. adv. council YMCA Greater N.Y.; past mem. nat. student com. Nat. Council of YMCA's; bd. mgrs. YMCA Schs., N.Y., 1951-55; adv. council dept. politics Princeton U., 1954-57; trustee Oberlin Coll., 1955-67, hon. trustee, 1981—; incorporator, bd. dirs. Tng. Resources for Youth, Inc., 1965-68; advisor Edna McConnell Clark Found., 1973-77; mem. adv. council Sch. Internat. Affairs Columbia U., 1976—; chmn. vis. com. grad. program in public affairs Columbia U., 1978—. Hon. fellow Harry S. Truman Library Inst. Mem. Govtl. Research Assn., Wilderness Soc., Sierra Club, Acad. Polit. Sci., Am. Soc. Pub. Adminstrn., Oberlin Alumni Bd. (treas. 1945-48, Alumni citation 1953), Nat. Civil Service League (chmn. bd. dirs. 1961-74), Nat. Social Welfare Assembly (exec. com. 1961-67), Group Health Assn. (past dir. Washington), UN Assn. (vice chmn. policy panel U.S. fgn. policy adminstrn. 1972-73), Nat. Municipal League, Nat. Planning Assn., Nat. Acad. Pub. Adminstrn. (chmn. mgmt. panel NASA 1973-74, co-chmn. com. on fin. devel.), Regional Plan Assn., Nat. Recreation and Park Assn., Inst. Mgmt. Cons. (a founder), Japan Soc., Phi Beta Kappa. Presbyn. (past mem. exec. devel. bd.). Clubs: University, Town, Scarsdale (N.Y.), Golf; Army and Navy (Manila, Philippines); Potomac Appalachian Trail (Washington); Red Carpet. Home: 821 Emerald Dr Alexandria VA 22308 Office: 1700K St NW Suite 700 Washington DC 20006

GLADMAN, MAURICE, association executive; b. Winnipeg, Man., Can., Mar. 19, 1919; came to U.S., 1934, naturalized, 1943; s. Jack Gladman; m. Rosabelle St. Clair, Oct. 22, 1943; children: Dennis, Patricia Ann. Gen. mgr. Roger S. Marshall Tire Co., Santa Monica, Calif., 1939-54; co-owner, then pres. Gladman & Wallace Tire Co., Santa Ana, Fullerton and Garden Grove, Calif., 1954-73; exec. dir. So. Calif. Tire Dealers and Retreaders Assn., Anaheim, 1973—; chmn. bd. Am. State Bank, Newport Beach, Calif., 1973-79; internat. pres. Kiwanis, 1977-78. Pres. Santa Ana C. of C., 1963; chmn. bd. Salvation Army, Santa Ana, 1969-71; pres. Santa Ana-Tustin YMCA, 1961-62, Children's Hosp. Padrinos, 1981, Kiwanis Internat. Found., 1983-84; chmn. bd. St. Joseph Hosp. Found., Orange, Calif., 1974-75; vice chmn. Goodwill Industries Orange County, 1981, chmn., 1982; bd. dirs. Goodwill Industries Am., 1983—. Served to col. AUS, 1942-46, 50-52; Korea. Decorated Bronze Star, Legion of Merit; Disting. Order Aux. Service Salvation Army; recipient Spirit of Life award City of Hope. Mem. Nat. Tire Dealers and Retreaders Assn. (past pres.), Am. Soc. Assn. Execs. Republican. Presbyterian. Address: 12331 Alray Pl Tustin CA 92680

GLADSTEIN, ROBERT DAVID, dancer, choreographer; b. Berkeley, Calif., Jan. 16, 1943; s. Morris and Wilda (Hetke) G.; m. Nancy Sharon Robinson, May 9, 1964; 1 son, Marcus Joseph. Student, San Francisco State Coll., 1960-62; dance tng., San Francisco Ballet Sch. Trustee Archives for Performing Arts, San Francisco. Mem., San Francisco Ballet Co., 1960-67, 70-75; ballet master, San Francisco Ballet Co., 1975—; asst. dir., San Francisco Ballet Co., 1981—; asst. dir., ballet master, choreographer, San Francisco Ballet Co., 1981; mem., Am. Ballet Theatre, 1967-70; soloist, San Francisco Opera, 1962, 63, 64, Dallas Opera Co., 1968; danced for, Pres. Nixon, White House, 1969, TV credits include, Ed Sullivan, 1965; Beauty and the Beast film, ABC-TV, 1968, Macy's Thanksgiving Parade, 1969; choreographer 29 ballets for, San Francisco Ballet Co., 23 ballets for, Am. Ballet Theatre, Ballet West, Sacramento Civic Ballet, Pacific N.W. Ballet; asst. to choreographer: Romeo and Juliet; Dance in Am. series, Sta. WNET-TV; The Tempest, WNET-KQED-TV; also Life of Virgil Thomson, 1978; choreographer: Symphony in 3 Movements, for KQED-TV, 1982 (nominated 2 Emmy awards), San Francisco Opera, 1983,84; mem. dance panel, Nat. Endowment Arts, 1983. Office: 455 Franklin St San Francisco CA 94102

GLADSTONE, HERBERT JACK, mfg. co. exec.; b. N.Y.C., May 12, 1924; s. Joseph D. and Ella (Shabman) G.; m. Sylvia Rosenberg, Dec. 28, 1946; children—Alan, Linda, Karen. Student, Hamilton Coll., 1944, Harvard, 1945; B.B.A., Coll. City N.Y., 1947. Mem. staff Gershon & Strell (C.P.A.'s), N.Y.C., 1947-51; budget dir. F.M.C., N.Y.C., 1951-55; v.p., treas. Condec Corp., Old Greenwich, Conn., 1955—; lectr. M.B.A. Program, U. Conn.; dir. Consol. Controls Corp., Hammond Valve Corp. Pres. P.T.A., 1956-57; asst. scoutmaster Toquam council Boy Scouts Am., 1960-63. Served with USAAF, 1943-46. Mem. Fin. Execs. Inst. (dir.), Am. Inst. C.P.A.'s, N.Y. State Soc. C.P.A.'s. Clubs: Roxbury Country (dir.), Roxbury Tennis and Swim (trustee). Home: 284 West Hill Rd Stamford CT 06902 Office: 1500 Post Rd Old Greenwich CT 06870

GLADSTONE, RICHARD BENNETT, publishing company executive; b. Orwell, N.Y., June 29, 1924; s. Irving Rea and Dorothy Bennett (Shufelt) G.; m. Kathleen L. Dandy, June 12, 1953; children: Sarah Martin, Margaret Ellen, Emily Bennett, William Dandy. A.B., Harvard U., 1948. With Houghton Mifflin Co., Boston, 1948—, editorial dir., 1973, v.p., dir. ednl. div., 1973-74, sr. v.p., 1974—; dir. Houghton Mifflin Can. Ltd., 1974—. Mem. adv. com. Ctr. for the Book, Library of Congress. Served with AUS, 1943-46. Mem. Am. Ednl. Pubs. Inst. (past dir.), Assn. Am. Pubs. (dir.). Clubs: St. Botolph; Union (Boston). Home: 50 Elm St Wellesley Hills MA 02181 Office: 1 Beacon St Boston MA 02107

GLADSTONE, WILLIAM LOUIS, accountant; b. Bklyn., May 23, 1931; s. Archie C. and Bernice T. (Turk) G.; m. Mildred R. Rosenberg, June 21, 1953; children: Susan, Douglas. B.S., Lehigh U., 1951; LL.B., Bklyn. Law Sch., 1955. C.P.A., N.Y., other states, N.Y. 1956. Staff acct. Arthur Young & Co., N.Y.C., from 1951, ptnr., 1963, mng. ptnr., 1981—; lect. acctg. Columbia U., N.Y.C., 1960-63. Contbr. articles to profl. jours. Served to lt. USAF, 1952-53. Mem. Am. Inst. C.P.A.s, N.Y. State Soc. C.P.A.s, Lehigh Alumni Assn. (award 1976), Bklyn. Law Sch. Alumni Assn., Beta Gamma Sigma (dir. table 1982—), Board Room (bd. govs. 1983—). Home: 5 Knollwood Dr Larchmont NY 10538 Office: Arthur Young & Co 277 Park Ave New York NY 10172

GLADWELL, GRAHAM MAURICE LESLIE, civil engineering educator; b. Oxford, Kent, Eng., Feb. 21, 1934; emigrated to Can., 1969; s. Basil Maurice Edwin and Doris Alexander (New) G.; m. Joyce Eugenie Nation, Mar. 29, 1958; children: Graham Hugh, Geoffrey Norman, Malcom Timothy. B.Sc., U. London, 1954, Ph.D., 1957, D.Sc., 1969. Lectr. U. London, 1956-60, U. W. Indies, Jamaica, 1960-62; sr. lectr. U. Southampton, Eng., 1962-69; prof. dept. civil engring. U. Waterloo, Ont., Can., 1969—; prof. dept. applied math., Ont., Can., 1979—. Author: Matrix Analysis of Vibration, 1965, Contact Problems in the Classical Theory of Elasticity, 1980; editor: Computed Aided Engineering, 1971. Fellow Am. Acad. Mechanics (dir. 1979-82), Inst. Math. and Its Applications, Royal Soc. Arts. Presbyterian. Office: Univ Waterloo Waterloo ON Canada N2L 3G1

GLAGOV, SEYMOUR, physician, educator, research scientist; b. N.Y.C., Aug. 8, 1925; s. Benjamin and Gussie (Sternberg) G.; m. Sylvia Held, May 18, 1946; 1 son, Hersh Monroe. B.A. in Physics, Bklyn. Coll., 1946; M.D., U. Geneva, Switzerland, 1953. Diplomate: Am. Bd. Pathology. Intern Kings County Hosp., Bklyn., 1953-54; resident Beth-El Hosp., Bklyn., 1954-56; jr. pathologist Cook County Hosp., Chgo., 1956-57; resident Pathology U. Chgo. Clinics, 1957-58, mem. faculty, 1957—, prof. pathology, 1970—; mem. staff and faculty U. Chgo. Hosps. and Clinics (Pritzker Sch. Medicine and the Coll.), U. Chgo., also dir. autopsy service, coordinator undergrad. pathology teaching; practice medicine, specializing in pathology, Chgo., 1956—; Research fellow Am. Heart Assn., 1959-61, advanced research fellow, 1961-62, established investigator, 1962-67; vis. research asso. Nuffield Inst. Med. Research, Oxford (Eng.) U., 1963-64; mem. cardiovascular study sect., research grant div. Nat. Heart and Lung Inst., 1970-74; mem. research grant com. Am. Heart Assn., 1977-80; asso. editor translation supplement Fedn. Am. Socs. Exptl. Biology, 1962-66. Asso. editor: (Cardiovascular Disease) of Human Pathology. Served with AUS, 1946-47. NIH grantee, 1960—. Mem. Am. Soc. Pathologists and Bacteriologists, Am. Soc. Exptl. Pathology, Chgo. Pathol. Soc. (pres. 1976-77), Biophys. Soc., Am. Assn. Study Liver Disease, Am. Heart Assn. (council on arteriosclerosis, chmn. com. on lesions and myocardial infarctions), Sigma Xi. Home: 5233 S University Ave Chicago IL 60615

GLAID, ANDREW JOSEPH, III, chemist, educator; b. Pitts., July 14, 1923; s. Andrew J. and Barbara E. (Sommer) G.; m. Mary L. Brown, June 27, 1953; children—Andrew IV, Elaine, Karen, Amy, Mark. B.S., Duquesne U., 1949, M.S., 1950; Ph.D.; NIH fellow, Duke U., 1955. Asst. prof. chemistry Duquesne U., Pitts., 1954-57, asso. prof., 1957-61, prof., 1961—, chmn. dept. chemistry, 1975—. Contbr. research publs. to sci. jours. Mem. Am. Chem. Soc., AAUP. Office: Dept Chemistry Duquesne U Pittsburgh PA 15282

GLANCEY, THOMAS FRANCIS, investment company executive; b. Phila., Aug. 31, 1919; s. John T. and Catherine (Hannigan) G.; m. Maryhelen Flynn, Sept. 5, 1942; children: Gerald, Thomas Francis, Maryhelen, Michael, Christopher. B.S., U. Pa., 1942. C.P.A., Pa. Accountant Main & Co., 1945-48; v.p., treas. Wellington Fund, Inc., Phila., 1948-63; v.p. Windsor Fund, Inc. (formerly Wellington Equity Fund, Inc.), 1963-69; exec. v.p. Del. Mgmt. Co., Mo., 1969—, Del. Fund, Inc., 1969—, Decatur Income Fund, Inc., 1969—, Delta Trend Fund, Inc., 1969—, Delchester Mut. Fund, Inc., 1969—, D.M.C. Tax Free Income Fund, Pa., 1975—, Del. Cash Res. Fund, 1978—, Del. Treasury Res., 1982—, Del. Tax-Free Income Fund, 1981—. Home: 107 Orchard Way Rosemont PA 19010 Office: 10 Penn Center Plaza Philadelphia PA

GLANCY, WALTER JOHN, lawyer; b. Los Angeles, Mar. 8, 1942; s. Walter Perry and Elva Thomasin (Douglass) G.; m. Sharon Marie Owens, Nov. 24, 1973; children: Jill Marie, Gregory Owens. A.B., Princeton U., 1964; B.A. (prize for best work in econs.), Oxford (Eng.) U., 1966; LL.B. (note and comment editor Law Jour. 1968-69), Yale U., 1969. Bar: Tex. 1971. Law clk. to U.S. Supreme Ct. Justice Byron R. White, 1969-70; staff asst. Nat. Security Council, 1970-71; staff asst. to Peter M. Flanigan, The White House, 1971; asso., then partner firm Jackson, Walker, Winstead, Cantwell & Miller, Dallas, 1972-76; partner firm Hughes & Hill (and predecessor), Dallas, 1976—; dir. Holly Corp., sec., 1975-80. Mem. bd. mgmt. Dallas YMCA Urban Services, 1975-84; bd. dirs. Dallas Family Guidance Ctr. Nat. Merit scholar, 1960-64; Marshall scholar, 1964-66. Mem. ABA, Dallas Bar Assn. (chmn. legal ethics com. 1980-81), Am. Law Inst., State Bar Tex. (profl. ethics com. 1982—, sec. tax. sect. 1983-84), Order of Coif, Phi Beta Kappa. Republican. Home: 4515 Kelsey Rd Dallas TX 75229 Office: 1000 Mercantile Dallas Bldg Dallas TX 75201

GLANVILLE-HICKS, PEGGY, composer, music critic; b. Melbourne, Australia, Dec. 29, 1912; emigrated to U.S., 1940, naturalized, 1948; d. Ernest and Myrtle (Bailey) Glanville-H.; m. Stanley Bate, 1938. Scholarship, Royal Coll. Music, London, 1932-36, Ecole Normale, Paris; pvt. study with, Egon Wellesz, Nadia Boulanger. With Dr. Carleton Sprague Smith, founded Internat. Music Fund to assist European artists; music critic N.Y. Herald Tribune, 1948-58. Dir. Composers Forum, prod. concert series for young composers, Donnell Library Auditorium and Columbia U., 1950-60; with, Chandler Cowles; prod.: own opera Transposed Heads, 1958, Lou Harrison's opera Rapunzel, under name of The Artists Co., N.Y.C., 1959; with, Yehudi Menuhin, master of ceremonies for concerts of Indian music Mus. Modern Art, 1955; commd. to compose: ballet score Masque of the Wild Man for, first Spoletto Festival, Italy, 1958; ballet Saul for, CBS-TV, 1959; full-length opera Nausicaa, Athens Festival, 1961; Composer: operas Transposed Heads, 1st Louisville Commn. Opera, 1954, The Glittering Gate, 1959, Navsikaa, Athens Festival, Greece, 1961, Sappho (commd. by Ford grant, San Francisco); ballet scores for, CBS-TV, film scores for, UN.; Contbr. articles popular mags., profl. periodicals. Recipient award Am. Acad. Arts and Letters, 1953; Guggenheim fellow, 1956-57, 57-58; Rockefeller travel grant for research Middle East, 1960; Fulbright research grant for comparative study folk music of Greek Islands, 1961. Mem. League Composers, Contemporary Music Soc., Jr. Council of Mus. Modern Art. Address: care BMI 40 W 57th St New York NY 10019 Address: care Australia Music Centre 2d Floor 80 George St The Rocks Sydney NSW Australia 2000

GLANZER, SEYMOUR, lawyer; b. N.Y.C., May 22, 1926; s. Max and Norma (Reichenthal) G.; m. Rita Preisman, May 30, 1957; children—Judith Elaine, Steven Lee. B.S., Juilliard Sch. Music, 1955; LL.B. (bd. law rev.), N.Y. Law Sch., 1960. Bar: N.Y. bar 1961, D.C. bar 1965. Enforcement atty. SEC, 1961-65; asst. U.S. atty., Washington, 1966-74; chief fraud sect. U.S. Atty.'s Office, Washington, 1966-74; partner firm Dickstein, Shapiro & Morin, Washington, 1974—; adj. prof. Georgetown U. Law Sch., 1974-75, Columbus Law Sch., Cath. U. Am., 1978; lectr. Am. U. Law Sch., 1973, Criminal Practice Inst., 1973-77, FBI Acad., 1974-75, Advocacy Inst., 1975; mem. Jud. Conf. D.C. Circuit, 1974-81. Served with AUS, 1944-46. Recipient spl. commendation Dept. Justice, 1971, 73. Mem. Am. Bar Assn., D.C. Bar. Jewish. Home: 3519 Albemarle St NW Washington DC 20008 Office: 2101 L St NW Washington DC 20037

GLASAUER, FRANZ ERNST, neurosurgeon; b. Khoau, Czechoslovakia, Feb. 19, 1930; s. Rudolf and Marie (Eckert) G.; m. Elizabeth A. Garofalo. M.D. magna cum laude, U. Heidelberg, Germany, 1955. Diplomate: Am. Bd. Neurosurgery. Intern St. Mark's Hosp., Salt Lake City, 1955-56; resident in surgery, neurosurgery New Eng. Med. Center, Boston, 1957-61; asst. in neurosurgery Tufts U. Sch. Medicine, Boston, 1960-61; asst. prof. neurosurgery SUNY, Buffalo, 1965-69, asso. prof., 1969-72, prof., 1972—, acting chmn. dept. neurosurgery; clin. dir. neurosurgery Erie County Med. Ctr., Buffalo, 1983; attending neurosurgeon numerous hosps., Buffalo; cons. Meml. Hosp., Mt. St. Mary's Hosp., Niagara Falls, N.Y.; Trustee Found. for Internat. Edn. in Neurol. Surgery Inc., 1981—. Author: (with Louis Bakay) Head Injury, 1980; contbr. articles to med. jours. Served with USNR, 1961-63. Mem. ACS, Congress Neurol. Surgeons, Am. Assn. Neurol. Surgeons, N.Y. Acad. Scis., Am. Spinal Injury Assn., Found. Internat. Edn. Neurol. Surgery, N.Y. State Neurosurg. Soc. (dir. 1971-73), Internat. Soc. Pediatric Neurosurgery. Office: 462 Grider St Buffalo NY 14215

GLASBERG, PAULA DRILLMAN, advertising executive; b. Dusseldorf, Germany, Nov. 22, 1939; came to U.S., 1940, naturalized, 1942; d. Solomon and Regina (Rubin) Drillman; m. H. Mark Glasberg, June 19, 1960; children: Scot Bradley, Hilary Jennifer. B.A., Bklyn. Coll., 1957; M.A., New Sch. Social Research, 1959, Ph.D., 1962. Research asst. McCann Erickson, N.Y.C., 1962-64; v.p. Marplan, Inc., N.Y.C., 1964-70, Tinker/Pritchard Wood, Inc., 1970-72; exec. v.p., chmn. exec. com. Rosenfeld, Sirowitz & Lawson, Inc., N.Y.C., 1972-78; exec. v.p., chmn. exec. com., dir. Marschalk Co. div. Interpublic Group of Cos., N.Y.C., 1978-1982; exec. v.p., dir., dir. strategic planning McCann-Erickson World Wide, Inc., 1983—. Mem. Am. Assn. Advt. Agys., Am. Mktg. Assn., Advt. Research Found., AAAS, Am. Psychol. Assn. Home: 43 E 63d St New York NY 10021 Office: 485 Lexington Ave New York NY 10017

GLASCO, JOSEPH MILTON, artist; b. Pauls Valley, Okla., Jan. 19, 1925; s. Lowell Marion and Pauline Elizabeth (Suddath) G. Student, U. Tex., 1946, Art Students League, N.Y.C., 1948. One-man exhbns. include, Perls Gallery, N.Y.C., 1950, Catherine Viviano Gallery, N.Y.C., 1951, 52, 53, 54, 58, 61, 63, 65, 70; represented in permanent collections, Bklyn. Mus., Albright Mus., Buffalo Mus., Mus. Modern Art, Met. Mus., Newark Mus., Whitney, Mus., Hirshhorn Mus., Princeton Mus. Served with U.S. Army, 1943-46. Mem. Nat. Soc. Lit. and the Arts. Roman Catholic. Address: 2116½ The Strand Galveston TX 77550

GLASER, CLAUDE EDWARD, JR., insurance company executive; b. N.Y.C., Mar. 14, 1919; s. Claude Edward and Hermine (Wolf) G.; m. Alice E. Sommer, Oct. 30, 1948; children: Cathy, Gail, Dianne. LL.B., Fordham U., 1940. Bar: N.Y. 1941. Staff atty. Hartford A&I, N.Y.C., 1946-49, claims mgr., White Plains, N.Y., 1949-52, N.Y.C., 1952-56, dir., 1981—; claims mgr. Hartford Ins. Group, N.Y.C., 1956-68, v.p., Hartford, Conn., 1968-75, sr. v.p., 1975—; dir. N.Y. Underwriters, N.Y.C., Hartford Casualty Co., 1979—, Twin City Fire Co., Mpls., Hartford Splty. Co., Hartford, Hartford Ins. Midwest, Netmet Ins., Hartford; chmn. bd. govs. Ins. Crime Prevention Inst., Westport, Conn., 1976-77. Trustee, chmn. Bd. Edn. Eastchester (N.Y.), 1954-63. Served to capt. U.S. Army, 1941-46; served to lt. col. Res., ret. Mem. ABA, N.Y. State Bar Assn., Def. Research Inst., Internat. Assn. Ins. Counsel. Lutheran. Office: Hartford Ins Group Hartford Plaza Hartford CT 06115

GLASER, DANIEL, sociologist; b. N.Y.C., Dec. 23, 1918; s. Samuel Jacob and Lena (Solway) G.; m. Pearl Bennett, Oct. 11, 1946; 1 dau., Lenore Meryl. A.B., U. Chgo., 1939, A.M., 1947, Ph.D., 1954. Prisons officer U.S. Mil. Govt., Germany, 1946-49; sociologist-actuary Ill. Parole and Pardon Bd., Pontiac Prison, 1950-52, Joliet Prison, 1952-54; faculty U. Ill., 1954-68, prof. sociology, 1964-68, head dept., 1964-68; prof. Rutgers U., 1968-70, U. So. Calif., 1970—; vis. asso. prof. U. Calif. at Los Angeles, summer 1961; vis. prof. Ariz. State U., 1963-64; cons. in field, 1956—; Mem. research council Nat. Council Crime and Delinquency; asso. commr. charge research div. N.Y. State Narcotic Control Commn., 1968-1970. Author: The Effectiveness of a Prison and Parole System, 1964, rev., 1969, Crime in the City, 1969, Adult Crime and Social Policy, 1971, Social Deviance, 1971, Routinizing Evaluation, 1973, Strategic Criminal Justice Planning, 1975, Crime in Our Changing Society, 1978; also numerous articles, pamphlets, chpts. in books.; Editor: Handbook of Criminology, 1974; Assoc. editor: Am. Jour. Sociology, 1965-70, Social Problems, 1965-68, Jour. Research on Crime and Delinquency, 1968—, Federal Probation, 1968—, Law and Society Rev, 1975-79, Am. Sociol. Rev., 1978—, Ency. of Crime and Justice, 1983; editor: Sociology and Social Research, 1973-76; Contbr. to: Ency. of Social Scis. Served with AUS, 1942-46. Mem. Ill. Acad. Criminology (pres. 1964-65), Am. Sociol. Assn. (chmn. criminology sect. 1965-66), Am. Soc. Criminology (E.H. Sutherland award 1976, pres. 1979-80), Assn. Criminal Justice Research (pres. 1980-81), Soc. Study Social Problems (chmn. crime and delinquency div. 1978—), Pacific Sociol. Assn. (v.p. 1981-82), Law and Soc. Assn. Home: 901 S Ogden Dr Los Angeles CA 90036 *To expand practical knowledge that can alleviate mankind's problems, seek not just precision, but the grounding of facts in abstract explanatory principles. This, I hope, is the main theme conveyed by my teaching, research and writing.*

GLASER, DONALD A(RTHUR), physicist; b. Cleve., Sept. 21, 1926; s. William Joseph Glaser. B.S., Case Inst. Tech., 1946, Sc.D., 1959; Ph.D., Cal. Inst. Tech., 1949. Prof. physics U. Mich., 1949-59; prof. physics U. Calif. at Berkeley, 1959—, prof. physics and molecular biology, 1964—. Recipient Henry Russel award U. Mich., 1955; Charles V. Boys prize Phys. Soc., London, 1958; Nobel prize in physics, 1960; NSF fellow, 1961; Guggenheim fellow, 1961-62. Fellow Am. Physics Soc. (prize 1959); mem. Nat. Acad. Scis., Sigma Xi, Tau Kappa Alpha, Theta Tau. Office: Molecular Biology Dept U Calif Berkeley CA 94720 *

GLASER, EDWARD LEWIS, electrical engineer; b. Evanston, Ill., 1929; s. James and Margaret (Barnes) G.; m. Anne Sims MacIntyre, Nov., 1950; children: Eliot, Cheryl Anne. A.B. in Physics, Dartmouth Coll., 1951; D.Sc. (hon.), Heriot-Watt U., 1980. Mem. planning group on large size computers IBM, 1951-55; extension instr. computer architecture UCLA, 1958-59; cons. to dir. engring. ElectroData Corp. (div. Burroughs Corp.), 1958-60; mgr. systems research dept. Burroughs Corp., 1960-63; asso. prof. elec. engring. M.I.T., 1963-67; dir. Andrew R. Jennings Computer Center, Case Western Res. U., 1967-75; mgr. product engring. and devel. dept. System Devel. Corp., Santa Monica, Calif., 1975-78, chief tech. officer, v.p. products group, 1978-79; dir. advanced computer systems tech. Memory Products div. Ampex Corp., El Segundo, Calif., 1979—; chmn. bd. IRI, Inc., 1982-84; chmn. bd., chief tech. officer Marcus Info. Systems, 1984—. Contbr. articles to profl. jours. Trustee Seeing Eye, Morristown, N.J., 1964. Named Computer Man of Yr. Data Processing Assn., 1976. Fellow IEEE; mem. Nat. Acad. Engring. Christian Scientist.

GLASER, GILBERT HERBERT, educator, physician, neuroscientist; b. N.Y.C., Nov. 10, 1920; s. Burnard Richard and Sidelle (Rogers) G.; m. Morfydd Mai Pugh, Mar. 17, 1946; children—Gareth Evan, Sara Elizabeth. A.B., Columbia, 1940, M.D., 1943, Med. Sc.D., 1951; M.A. (hon.), Yale, 1963. Diplomate: Am. Bd. Psychiatry and Neurology. Intern Mt. Sinai Hosp., N.Y.C., 1943-44; resident neurology N.Y. Neurol. Inst., 1944-46; from research asst. to asso. neurology Columbia Coll. Physicians and Surgeons, 1948-52; research scientist N.Y. Psychiat. Inst., 1948-50; head. sect. neurology Yale Sch. Medicine, 1952-71, chmn. dept. neurology, 1971—, asst. prof. neurology, 1952-55, asso. prof., 1955-63, prof. neurology, 1963—; Commonwealth Fund vis. prof. neurology U. London, Eng., 1965-66; cons. West Haven (Conn.) VA Hosp., 1955—; vis. prof. neurology Nat. Hosp., London, 1972, Park Hosp., Oxford, 1973—; Fulbright disting. prof., 1981; mem. neurology research adv. com. USPHS, 1956-60, 68-72, spl. cons., 1973, epilepsy adv. com., 1974-77, chmn. basic sci. subcom., 1977—; mem. neurobiology rev. com. VA, 1975—, chmn., 1977-78. Author: EEG and Behavior, 1963; Editor: Epilepsia, 1958-76; adv. editor, 1976—; editor: Recent Advances in Clinical Neurology, 1978, 81, 84, Antiepileptic Drugs: Mechanisms of Action, 1980; mem. editorial bd.: Jour. Nervous and Mental Diseases; Contbr. articles to profl. jours. Served as capt. M.C. AUS, 1946-48. Recipient Janeway prize Columbia U., 1943, Bicentennial medal award, 1968, Book award Commonwealth Fund, 1975. Fellow Royal Soc. Medicine, A.C.P.; mem. Am. Neurol. Assn. (1st v.p. 1977-78), Am. Acad. Neurology (pres. 1973-75), Am. Epilepsy Soc. (pres. 1963), Am. Electroencephalographic Soc. (council 1958-61, bd. qualifications), Eastern Assn. Electroencephalographers (pres. 1958), EEG Soc. (Gt. Britain), Assn. Brit. Neurologists, Soc. for Neurosci., Epilepsy Found. Am. (med. adv. bd.), Myasthenia Gravis Foundation (med. adv. bd. chmn. 1964-65), Multiple Sclerosis Soc. (chmn. research programs com. 1973-74, med. adv. bd.). Club: Athenaeum (London). Home: 205 Millbrook Rd Hamden CT 06518 Office: 333 Cedar St New Haven CT 06510

GLASER, HAROLD, physicist, university administrator; b. Kurseni, Lithuania, Aug. 28, 1924; s. Joseph and Emma G.; m. Margaret Stoney, Dec. 29, 1945; children: Roberta L., Miriam L., Ruth H. M.S., Northwestern U., 1949, Ph.D., 1953. Sr. staff physicist Applied Physics Lab., Johns Hopkins U., 1952-54; head theoret. analysis sect. Applications Research div. Naval Research Lab., Washington, 1954-57, physicist Electronics br., 1957-59, physicist Physics br., 1959-62; spl. asst. div. math., phys. and engring. scis. NSF, Washington, 1962; physicist Physics br. Office of Naval Research, Washington, 1962-65, head Nuclear Physics br., 1964-66; acting chief solar physics NASA, Washington, 1966-68, chief, 1968-70; chief long-range planning Nat. Bur. Standards, Washington, 1970-71; (detailed Office of Sci. and Tech.); Exec. Office of President, Washington, 1971-72; acting dir., dep. dir. Exptl. Tech. Incentives Program Nat. Bur. Standards, Washington, 1972; dep. dir. sci. and tech. office nat. research and devel. assessment NSF, Washington, 1972-75; dir. solar terrestrial div. NASA, Washington, 1975-80; asst. to pres. U. Calif., Berkeley; cons. Office of Mgmt. and Budget, U. Colo. Served with AUS, 1943-46. Fellow Washington Acad. Sci.; Mem. Am. Phys. Soc., Am. Geophys. Union, Am. Astronom. Soc., Internat. Astronom. Union, N.Y. Acad. Scis., Washington Acad. Sci., Sigma Xi. Address: 1346 Bonita Berkeley CA 94709 *My professional career has been to serve the public interest, without regard to self-promotion, and to do so with dedication, doing the best I could professionally.*

GLASER, HERBERT OTTO, retail executive; b. Chgo., Jan. 21, 1927; s. Otto and Regina (Heiden) G.; m. Eleonore Weise, June 15, 1949 (div. Aug. 1967); children: John, Judy, Janet; m. Beverly A. Burns, Feb. 10, 1968. B.A. summa cum laude, Lake Forest Coll., (Ill.), 1949. Buyer Cohen Bros., Jacksonville, Fla., 1949-55; divisional mdse. mgr. Rich's, Inc., Atlanta, 1955-68; gen. mdse. mgr. May Co., Los Angeles, 1968-72; exec. v.p. J.L. Hudson Co., Detroit, 1972-78; pres., chief exec. officer P.A. Bergner & Co., Peoria, Ill., 1978—. Trustee, mem. exec. com. Methodist Hosp., Peoria. Republican. Baptist. Club: Peoria Country. Home: 2300 N Main St East Peoria IL 61611 Office: P A Bergner & Co 200 SW Adams St Peoria IL 61626

GLASER, JOSEPH BERNARD, association executive; b. Boston, May 1, 1925; s. Louis James and Dena Sophie (Harris) G.; m. Agathe Maier, Sept. 23, 1951; children: Simeon, Meyer, Sara, John. A.B., UCLA, 1948; J.D., U. San Francisco, 1951; B.H.L., Hebrew Union Coll., 1954, M.H.L., 1956, D.Div., 1980; postgrad. (Merrill Trust grantee), Law Faculty Hebrew U., Jerusalem, 1969-70. Rabbi, 1956; rabbi Temple Beth Torah, Ventura, Calif., 1956-59; regional dir. Union Am. Hebrew Congregations, San Francisco, 1959-71; exec. v.p. Central Conf. Am. Rabbis, N.Y.C., 1971—; Registrar Hebrew Union Coll., Los Angeles, 1956-59, instr. homiletics, 1956-59; instr. Bible, Hebrew Union Coll., Cin., 1954-56; Vice chmn. San Francisco Conf. Religion and Peace, 1964-71, San Francisco Conf. Religion and Race, 1963-68; chmn. Clergy Com. Farm Labor Negotiation, 1967-68; chmn. bd. Religion in Am. Life, 1977-82; v.p. Am. Friends of Oxford Centre for Postgrad. Hebrew Studies.; trustee Howard Thurman Ednl. Trust. Served with inf. AUS, 1943-46. Decorated Purple heart with oak leaf cluster. Mem. Central Conf. Am. Rabbis, Synagogue Council Am., Conf. of Presidents of Maj. Jewish Orgns. Office: 21 E 40th St New York NY 10016

GLASER, JULIUS SIMSON, book publishing company executive; b. Boston, June 13, 1916; s. William and Esther (Berkowitz) G.; m. Jane C. Schmidt, June 21, 1939 (dec. 1966); children: Daniel L., Sue Ann, Debora Jane; m. Chawa Rome, Dec. 22, 1968 (dec. 1982). B.A., Williams Coll., 1937; postgrad., Harvard U., 1937-38. Treas., Gen. mgr. Best Mfg. Co. Inc., Irvington, N.J., 1939-50; pres., chmn. bd.

Glaser-Steers Corp., Newark, 1950-63; v.p. planning Ametek Inc., N.Y.C., 1963-69; pres., chmn. bd. Schocken Books Inc., N.Y.C., 1973—; chmn. bd. Labor Zionist Letters Inc., 1972—. Trustee Village of South Orange, N.J., 1959-63. Mem. Phi Beta Kappa. Clubs: Williams (N.Y.C.); Cranberry Isles (Maine); Tennis (pres. 1982-83). Office: Schocken Books Inc 200 Madison Ave New York NY 10016

GLASER, KURT, educator; b. Ann Arbor, Mich., Aug. 19, 1914; s. Otto Charles and Dorothy Gibbs (Merrylees) G.; m. Florence W. Riddle, Aug. 11, 1939 (div. Aug. 1948); children: Jeffrey, Kristin; m. Ingeburg Elfriede Halle, Mar. 8, 1950 (div. Mar. 1976); children: Robin, Angela.; m. Dorothy Myrl Conyers, June 27, 1983. A.B., Harvard U., 1935, A.M., 1938, Ph.D., 1941. With Social Security Bd., U.S. Dept. Agr., Washington, 1938-46; prof. emeritus Southern Ill. U., 1983—; with Mil. Govt., Germany, 1946-49; govt. affairs officer Office U.S. High Commn., Frankfurt, Germany, 1949-50; curriculum cons. and journalist, Munich, Germany, 1950-52; exchange officer, project dir. Govt. Affairs Inst., Washington, 1952-54; office and mgmt. analyst Records Engring., Inc., Wash., 1954-55; asst. prof. U. Md., Germany, 1956-59; lectr. Southern Ill. U., Edwardsville, 1959-60, asso. prof., 1960-65, prof. govt., 1965-83; dir. spl. projects Found. Fgn. Affairs, Chgo., 1973—; vis. prof. Tamkang U., Taipei, Taiwan, 1983—; Fulbright lectr. U. Kiel, Ger., 1966-67; lectr. Freedoms Found., Valley Forge, Pa., 1978—. Author: Czecho-Slovakia: A Critical History, 1961, Der zweite Weltkrieg und die Kriegsschuldfrage, 1964, (with S.T. Possony) Victims of Politics: The State of Human Rights, 1979; editor: (with David S. Collier) Found. for Fgn. Affairs series on East-West relations, 1962-69, (with J. Barratt, S. Brand and D.S. Collier) Accelerated Devel. in South Africa, 1974, (with J. Barratt, D.S. Collier and Herman Mönnig Strategy for Development), 1976; asso. editor: (with J. Barratt) Modern Age, 1973—, Plural Societies, 1975—. Coordinator Dynamic Citizenship Forum, St. Louis, 1961-63; Bd. dirs. Found. for Study Plural Socs., 1974-80. Hoover Inst. grantee, 1968-69. Mem. Univ. Profs. for Acad. Order (dir. 1975-80). Office: Tamkang U Kinhua St Taipei Taiwan *If I have achieved any originality as a scholar, it has been by examining the assumptions built into the wording of questions, rather than simply trying to answer the questions as posed.*

GLASER, LUIS, biochemistry educator; b. Vienna, Austria, Mar. 30, 1932; came to U.S., 1953, naturalized, 1961; s. Hermann and Gisela (Kohn) G.; m. Ruth Walliser, May 18, 1961; children—Miriam, Nichole. B.A., U. Toronto, Ont., Can., 1953; Ph.D., Washington U., St. Louis, 1956. Asst. prof. biol. chemistry Washington U., 1959-62, asso. prof., 1962-67, prof., 1967-75, chmn. dept. biol. chemistry, 1975—; dir. Div. Biology and Biomed. Scis. Contbr. numerous articles on bacterial and mammalian metabolism to profl. jours.; editor: Jour. Biol. Chemistry, 9-74, 81—, Jour. Supramolecular Structures, 1969-79, Jour. Cell Biology, 1981—. Helen Hay Whitney fellow, 1956-59; NIH grantee; NSF grantee. Mem. Am. Soc. Biol. Chemists, Am. Chem. Soc., Am. Soc. Microbiology, Am. Soc. Neurochemists, AAAS. Democrat. Jewish. Home: 26 Chaminade Dr Saint Louis MO 63141 Office: 660 S Euclid St Saint Louis MO 63110

GLASER, MICHAEL LANCE, lawyer; b. Washington, June 9, 1939; s. Theodore Allen and Margaret Esther (Bielaski) G.; m. Catherine Mary Connor, June 16, 1962; children: Michael Lance, Casey Lynn, Shannon Michele, Timothy Edwin, Regan Marie. B.A. in Econs, George Washington U., 1961, J.D. with honors, 1965. Law clk. asso. Judge Frank Meyers, D.C. Ct. Appeals, Washington, 1965-66; asso. firm Smith & Pepper, Washington, 1966-68; partner firm Bilger & Glaser, Washington, 1968-70, Glaser, Fletcher & Johnson (P.C.), 1971-81, Gardner, Carton & Douglas, 1981—; Mem. atomic safety and licensing bd. U.S. Nuclear Regulatory Commn., AEC, Washington, 1972-81. Mem. Am., Fed., Fed. Communications bar assns., Bar Assn. D.C., D.C. Bar. Roman Catholic. Home: 7753 S Waco St Aurora CO 80016 Office: 1875 Eye St NW Washington DC 20006 Office: PO Box 27437 Denver CO 80227

GLASER, MILTON, graphic artist; b. N.Y.C., June 26, 1929; s. Eugene and Eleanor (Bergman) G.; m. Shirley Girton, Aug. 13, 1957. Student, Cooper Union Art Sch., 1948-51; Fulbright scholar, Acad. Fine Arts, Bologna, Italy, 1952-53; D.F.A. (hon.), Mpls. Inst. Arts, 1971, Moore Coll., Phila., 1975, Phila. Coll. and Sch. Visual Arts, 1979. Co-founder, pres. Push Pin Studios, N.Y.C., 1954-74; co-founder, pres., chmn. bd., design dir. N.Y. mag., 1968-77; v.p., design dir. Village Voice, N.Y.C., 1975-77; founder, 1977; since pres. Milton Glaser, Inc., N.Y.C.; bd. dirs. Internat. Design Conf., Aspen, Colo., 1972—, co-chmn., 1973; instr. Cooper Union. Author: Milton Glaser: Graphic Design, 1973, The Milton Glaser Poster Book, 1977; co-author: If Apples Had Teeth, 1960, The Underground Gourmet, 1974. Recipient St. Gauden's medal Cooper Union, 1972; hon. fellow Royal Soc. Arts, 1979. Mem. Am. Inst. Graphic Arts (Gold medal 1972), ArtDirs. Club (named to Hall of Fame 1979), Alliance Graphique Internat. Jewish. Executed 600 foot mural New Fed. Office Bldg., Indpls.; designed observation deck World Trade Center Twin Towers, N.Y.C., 1975; graphic and interior designer Sesame Pl., Bucks County, Pa., 1980. Office: 207 E 32d St New York NY 10016

GLASER, ROBERT JOY, physician, foundation executive; b. St. Louis, Sept. 11, 1918; s. Joseph and Regina G.; m. Helen Louise Hofsommer, Apr. 1, 1949; children: Sally Louise, Joseph II, Robert Joy. S.B., Harvard U., 1940, M.D. magna cum laude, 1943; D.Sc. (hon.), U. Health Scis.-Chgo. Med. Sch., 1972, Temple U., 1973, U. N.H., 1979, U. Colo., 1979; L.H.D., Rush Med. Coll., 1973. Med. intern Barnes Hosp., St. Louis, 1944, asst. resident physician, 1945-46, resident physician, 1946-47, asst. physician, 1949-57; asst. resident physician Peter Bent Brigham Hosp., Boston, 1944-45; NRC fellow med. scis. Wash. U. Med. Sch., 1947-49, instr. medicine, 1949-50, asst. prof., 1950-56, assoc. prof., 1956-57, asst. dean, 1947, 53-55, assoc. dean, 1955-57; dean, prof. medicine Med. Sch. U. Colo., 1957-63, v.p. for med. affairs, 1959-63; vis. physician Washington U. Med. Service, St. Louis City Hosp., 1950, chief service, 1950-53, cons., 1953-57; attending physician Colo. Gen. Hosp., Denver, 1957-63; cons. medicine VA Hosp., Denver, 1957-63, Fitzsimons Army Hosp., Aurora, Colo., 1957-63; cons. Lowry AFB, Denver, 1957-63; prof. social medicine Harvard, Boston, 1963-65; pres. Affiliated Hosps. Center, Inc., 1963-65; v.p. med. affairs, dean Sch. Medicine, prof. medicine Stanford, 1965-70, cons. prof., 1972—, acting pres., 1968; Mem. Harvard Fund Council, 1953-56, Harvard Med. Alumni Council, 1956-59; bd. visitors Charles Drew Postgrad. Med. Sch., 1973-79; mem. com. on med. affairs Yale U., 1969, advisory bd., 1976—; vis. com. Tufts Med. Sch., 1975—; bd. regents Georgetown U., 1976-78; bd. dirs. Kaiser Found. Hosps., Kaiser Found. Health Plan, 1967-79, Council on Founds., 1974-79, Henry J. Kaiser Family Found., 1970-83, pres., chief exec. officer, 1972-83; dir. for med. sci. Lucille P. Markey Charitable Trust, 1984—; attending physician Columbia-Presbyn. Med. Center, N.Y.C., 1971-72, clin. prof. medicine, 1971-72; mem. nat. adv. council NIMH, 1970-72; asso. mem. streptococal commn. Armed Forces Epidemiologic Bd., 1958-61; chmn. com. study nat. needs biomed. and behavioral research personnel Nat. Acad. Scis.-NRC, 1974-77; dir. Hewlett-Packard Co., First Boston Inc., Equitable Life Assurance Soc. U.S., Calif. Water Service Co.; trustee Commonwealth Fund, 1969—, David and Lucille Packard Found., 1984—; v.p. Commonwealth Fund, 1970-72; mem. vis. com. Med. Sch. Harvard U., 1968-74, Sch. Pub. Health, 1971-77; trustee Pacific Sch. Religion, 1972-77, Washington U., St. Louis, 1979—; mem. Sloan Commn. on Govt. in Higher Edn., 1977-79. Editor: Pharos, 1962—; Contbr. articles to sci. jours., chpts. to books. Fellow AAAS, Am. Acad. Arts and Scis. (exec. bd., v.p. 1972-76); mem. Am. Clin. and Climatological Assn. (pres. 1982-83), Am. Fedn. Clin. Research (chmn. midwestern sect. 1954-55), Central Soc. Clin. Research (councillor 1955-58), Am. Soc. Clin. Investigation, Assn. Am. Med. Colls. (asst. sec. 1956-59, chmn. com. edn. and research 1958-62, mem. exec. council 1959-62, 76-79, v.p. 1962-63, chmn. exec. council and assembly 1968-69), Assn. Am. Physicians, Western Assn. Physicians (councillor 1960-63), Am. Soc. Exptl. Pathology, Nat. Inst. Allergy and Infectious Disease (tng. grant com. 1957-60), Inst. Medicine, Nat. Acad. Scis. (mem. exec. com. 1970-73, chmn. membership com. 1970-72, acting pres. 1971-72), Sigma Xi, Alpha Omega Alpha (dir. 1963-77). Clubs: Harvard, Century (N.Y.C.). Office: 525 Middlefield Rd Suite 130 Menlo Park CA 94025

GLASER, ROBERT LEONARD, TV executive; b. Chgo., Jan. 9, 1929; s. Maurice L. and Sara (Ziegler) G.; m. Nancy Lehman Field, Jan. 4, 1959; children: Robert Leonard, Jr., Geoffrey L., Douglas L. B.A., U. Miami, 1950. Midwest mgr. Metromedia, 1960-64; Midwest sales mgr. ABC, 1964-66; v.p., gen. mgr. WOR-TV, N.Y.C., 1967-70, 1971; corporate v.p. RKO Gen., Inc., N.Y.C., 1971—; pres. RKO Gen. TV Inc., N.Y.C., 1973—; chmn. bd. RKO Gen. TV Reps., 1974—; pres. VIACOM Internat., 1982—. Bd. dirs. Learning to Read Through the Arts, Guggenheim Mus., United Cerebral Palsy Assn. Served to 1st lt. AUS, 1950-53. Mem. Internat. Radio and TV Soc. (gov.), Nat. Acad. TV Arts and Scis. (treas.), Acad. Motion Picture Arts and Scis., Ind. TV Assn. Clubs: Patterson Country (Fairfield, Conn.); Union League (N.Y.C.). Home: 88 Morningside Dr S Greens Farms CT 06436 Office: 1440 Broadway New York NY 10018

GLASER, RONALD, microbiology educator; b. N.Y.C., Feb. 27, 1939; s. Irving and Pauline G.; m. Janice Kiecolt, Jan. 17, 1980; children: Andrew, Eric. B.A., U. Bridgeport, 1962; M.S., U. R.I., 1964; Ph.D., U. Conn., 1968; postgrad., Baylor Coll. Medicine, 1968-69. Instr. biology Eastern Conn. State Coll., Willimantic, 1966-67, asst. prof., 1967-68; asst. prof. virology Ind. State U., Terre Haute, 1969-70; asst. prof. microbiology Pa. State U., Hershey, 1970-73, asso. prof., 1973-77, prof., 1977-78; prof. chmn. dept. med. microbiology and immunology Ohio State U., Columbus, 1978—; ad hoc reviewer NIH study sects. Author: (with T. Gottleib-Stematsky) Human Herpes Virus Infections: Clinical Aspects, 1982. NIH fellow, 1968-69; Franco-Am. exchange Program; Fogarty Internat. Center; NIH and INSRM fellow, 1975, 77; Leukemia Soc. Am. scholar, 1974-79. Mem. Electron Microscopy Soc. Am., Am. Soc. Microbiology, AAAS, Am. Assn. Cancer Research, Soc. Exptl. Biology and Medicine. Office: 333 W 10th Ave Columbus OH 43210

GLASER, VERA ROMANS, journalist; b. St. Louis; d. Aaron L. and Mollie (Romans); m. Herbert R. Glaser, Apr. 16, 1939; 1 dau., Carol Jane Barriger. Student, Washington U., St. Louis, George Washington U., Am. U., 1937-40. Reporter-writer Nat. Aero. mag., 1943-44; reporter Washington Times Herald, 1944-46; pub. relations specialist Great Lakes-St. Lawrence Assn., 1950-51; promotion specialist, writer Congl. Quar. News Features, 1951-54; writer-commentator radio sta. WGMS, Washington, 1954-55; mem. Washington bur. N.Y. Herald Tribune, 1955-56; press officer U.S. Senator Charles E. Potter, 1956-59; dir. pub. relations, women's div. Rep. Nat. Com., 1959-62; press officer U.S. Senator Kenneth B. Keating, 1962-63; Washington corr. N.Am. Newspaper Alliance, 1963-69, bur. chief, 1965-69; contbg. editor Washingtonian mag., 1966-69; columnist, nat. corr. Knight-Ridder Newspapers, Inc., 1969-81; assoc. editor The Washingtonian Mag., 1981—; Mem. Pres.'s Commn. on White House Fellows, Pres.'s Task Force on Women's Rights and Responsibilities; judge 1981 Robert Kennedy Journalism Awards. Free-lance writer nat. publs. Mem. White House Corrs. Assn. Unitarian. Clubs: Washington Press (pres. 1971-72); Overseas Press (N.Y.C.); Nat. Press, Sigma Delta Chi. Home: 5000 Cathedral Ave NW Washington DC 20016 Office: 1828 L St NW Washington DC 20036

GLASGOW, HAROLD G., marine corps officer; b. Heflin, Ala., Feb. 4, 1929; s. Ralph S. and Vera Floretta (Johnson) G.; m. Jean Carol Cunningham, Sept. 4, 1954; children: John Stephen, Jeffrey Glyn, Jennifer leigh. B.S. in Phys. Edn., U. Ala.-Tuscaloosa, 1951; M.A. in Internat. Affairs, George Washington U., 1972. Commd. U.S. Marine Corps, advanced through grades to maj. gen.; exec. asst. to ACMC, HQMC, Washington, 1972-75; comdg. officer 6th Marines, Camp Lejeune, N.C., 1976-77; comdg. gen. 7th Marine Amphibian Bn., The Combat Ctr., 29 Palms, Calif., 1978-81; dir. devel. ctr. Marine Corps Devel. and Edn. Command, Quantico, Va., 1981-82; dir. ops. Hdqrs., U.S. Marine Corps, Washington, 1982—. Mem. Marine Corps Assn. (v.p. 1982—), Marine Corps Found., Nat. War Coll. Assn., Armed Forces Assn. (bd. dirs.). Club: Optimist. Home: 2317 9th St S Arlington VA 22204 Office: Hdqrs USMC Washington DC 20380

GLASGOW, JAMES HERSMAN, retired university dean; b. Woodson, Ill., June 6, 1906; s. Samuel Arthur and Carrie (Hersman) G.; m. Ruth Ora Adams, July 27, 1929. B.Ed., Ill. State Normal U., 1928; M.A., Clark U., 1929; Ph.D., U. Chgo., 1939. Cartographer McKnight Geog. Pub. Co., 1929-31; head dept. geography and geology Roosevelt Coll., 1932-36; asst. prof. geography Western Mich. U., 1936-39; prof. geography, head dept. U. Hawaii, 1952-53; prof., head dept. geography and geology Eastern Mich. U., Ypsilanti, 1939-57, dean Grad. Sch., 1950-70; Summer lectr. Eastern Ill. U., 1939, 48, Northwestern U., 1949; cons. Ill. Housing Bd., 1935-36, Chgo. Met. Housing Council, 1935-36. Author: Shawneetown, Illinois: A Survey of Factors Relating to the Shawneetown Removal Project, 1936, Muskegon, Michigan: The Evolution of a Lake Port, 1939, Trends in the Population of the United States as Indicated by the Census of 1940, a series of seven maps, 1941, Geography of Michigan, 1947, The North American Midwest. A Regional Geography, 1952. Mem. Am. Geog. Soc., Assn. Am. Geographers. Home: PO Box 1105 Orange City FL 32763

GLASGOW, JESSE EDWARD, newspaper editor; b. Monroe, N.C., Mar. 28, 1923; s. Jesse Edwin and Alma (Brown) G.; m. Beth BonDurant, June 25, 1949; children—Jeffrey David, Charles Christopher. B.S., Wake Forest U., 1948. Reporter Kannapolis (N.C.) Ind., 1947, Durham (N.C.) Sun, 1948, Norfolk Virginian-Pilot, 1949-52; reporter Balt. Sun, 1953-59, financial editor, 1960—. Served with AUS, 1943-45. Democrat. Methodist. Home: 4904 Wilmslow Rd Baltimore MD 21210 Office: Balt Sun Calvert and Centre Sts Baltimore MD 21203

GLASGOW, VAUGHN LESLIE, museum official; b. Portland, Ind., Apr. 23, 1944; s. Leslie Lloyd and Garnet Lucile (Confer) G. B.A., La. State U., 1967; M.A., Pa. State U., 1970, Ph.D. Research asst., asst. to curator Anglo-Am. Art Mus., La. State U., 1965-67; instr. art history, adminstrv. asst. dept. art history Pa. State U., 1970-71; asst. prof. art history Middle Tenn. State U., 1972-73; arts mgr. La. Council for Music and Performing Arts, 1973-75; chief curator La. State Mus., New Orleans, 1975-83, assoc. dir. for spl. programs, 1983—; lectr. dept. art Newcomb Coll., Tulane U., New Orleans, 1975-79; Am. commr. Sun King: Louis XIV and the New World, 1982—; Mem. adv. panel youth and student programs NEH, 1970-73; cons. Madewood Arts Festival; bd. dirs. La. Alliance for Arts Edn., 1978-79; bd. dirs., treas. Photography Council La.; cons. Hermann-Grima Historic House Mus., New Orleans; art adv. bd. St. Mary's-Dominican Coll. Contbr. articles to profl. jours. Mem. La. State Folklife Commn., 1982—. Mem. Inst. La. Music and Folklore (dir.). Office: PO Box 2458 751 Chartres New Orleans LA 70176

GLASHOW, SHELDON LEE, physicist, educator; b. N.Y.C., Dec. 5, 1932; s. Lewis and Bella (Rubin) G.; m. Joan Glashow; children: Jason David, Jordan, Brian Lewis, Rebecca Lee. A.B., Cornell U., 1954; A.M., Harvard U., 1955, Ph.D., 1958; D.Sc. (hon.), Yeshiva U., 1978, U. Marseille, 1982. NSF fellow U. Copenhagen, Denmark, 1958-60; research fellow Calif. Inst. Tech., 1960-61; asst. prof. Stanford U., 1961-62; asst. prof., asso. prof. U. Calif. at Berkeley, 1962-66; faculty Harvard U., 1966—, prof. physics, 1967—, Higgins prof. physics, 1979—; cons. Brookhaven Nat. Lab., 1966-73, 75—; mem. sci. policy com. CERN, 1979—; vis. prof. U. Marseille, 1971, MIT, 1974, 80, Boston U., 1983; affiliated sr. scientist U. Houston, 1983—; univ. scholar Tex. A & M U., 1983—. Contbr. articles to profl. jours. and popular mags. Pres. Andrei Sakharov Inst., 1980—. Recipient J.R. Oppenheimer Meml. prize, 1977; George Ledlie prize, 1978; Nobel prize in physics, 1979; Castiglione di Sicilia prize, 1983; NSF fellow, 1955-60; Sloan fellow, 1962-66; CERN vis. fellow, 1968. Fellow Am. Phys. Soc., AAAS; mem. Am. Acad. Arts and Scis., Nat. Acad. Scis., Sigma Xi. Home: 30 Prescott St Brookline MA 02146

GLASS, ALEXANDER JACOB, business executive; b. Pittsfield Twp., N.Y., Jan. 4, 1933; s. Lawrence Louis and Anna Constance (Kaufman) G.; m. Joanna McClelland, Dec. 18, 1959 (div. 1976); children: Jennifer, Mavis, Lawrence; m. 2d Judith Anderson, Aug. 7, 1977. B.S. in Physics, Rensselaer Poly. Inst., 1954, M.S., Yale U., 1955, Ph.D., Rensselaer Poly. Inst., 1963; D.Sc. hon., Eastern Mich. U., 1983. Prof. elec. engring. Wayne State U., Detroit, 1968-70, chmn. elec. engring., 1970-73; lectr. applied sci. U. Calif.-Davis, 1973-81; head laser design group Lawrence Livermore Nat. Lab., Calif., 1973-78, asst. assoc. dir. lasers, 1978-81; pres. KMS Fusion Inc., Ann Arbor, 1981—; dir. KMS Industries, Ann Arbor, 1983—; chmn. and pres. Covalent Tech., Ann Arbor, 1983—; staff scientist Dept. Energy, Washington, 1978; cons. LaJolla Inst., Calif., 1976-80. Co-editor ann. procs. profl. conf., 1969-80; contbr. articles to profl. publs. Served as capt. U.S. Army, 1955-57. Sterling fellow Yale U., 1960; recipient Outstanding Tchr. award Wayne State U., 1969. Fellow Optical Soc. Am. (dir. 1980-82), IEEE; mem. Am. Phys. Soc. (sec. treas. Joint Council on Quantum Electronics 1972—). Democrat. Home: 2025 Hill St Ann Arbor MI 48104 Office: KMS Fusion Inc PO Box 1567 Ann Arbor MI 48106

GLASS, BRYAN PETTIGREW, educator; b. Mandeville, La., Aug. 21, 1919; s. Wiley Blount and Jessie Ligon (Pettigrew) G.; m. Carolyn Elizabeth Smith, Aug. 24, 1946; children—Janis Elizabeth, Peggy Lee. A.B., Baylor U., 1940; M.S., Tex. A. and M. Coll., 1946; Ph.D., Okla. State U., 1952. Grad. asst. biology Tex. A. and M. Coll., 1940-42, 45-46; faculty Okla. State U., Stillwater, 1946—, prof. zoology, 1961—; dir. Okla. State U. Mus., 1966—. Author: Key to the Skulls of North American Mammals, 1951, 2d edit., 1973. Bd. dirs. Introgene Found. Served with USAAF, 1942-45; Pacific, CBI. Research grantee for research on pub. health importance of bats in Okla. NIH, 1955-59; NSF grantee, 1962; NIH grantee, 1962—; Brazilian Govt. contract for mammal survey of Serra da Canastra Nat. Park, 1978—. Fellow Okla. Acad. Sci.; mem. Am. Soc. Mammalogists (life, exec. sec.-treas. 1957-77), Am. Soc. Ichthyologists and Herpetologists (life), Southwestern Assn. Naturalists, Sigma Xi. Home: 517 S Willis St Stillwater OK 74074

GLASS, CARSON MCELYEA, lawyer; b. Farmersville, Tex., Oct. 8, 1915; s. Emery Carson and Chassie Victoria (McElyea) G.; m. Miriam Celeste Mollberg, Oct. 8, 1938 (div.); 1 son, Christopher C.; m. Lois Adair Felder, Dec. 29, 1960 (dec. 1973); m. Rhoda Swegles Price, Feb. 2, 1979. B.A., U. Tex., 1941, LL.B., 1938. Bar: Tex. 1937. Atty. Justice Dept., 1938-39, Dept. Labor, 1939; spl. atty. antitrust div. Justice Dept., 1939-47; spl. asst. to atty. gen., U.S., 1947-48; partner firm Fischer, Wood, Burney & Glass, Corpus Christi, Tex., 1949-50; mem. firm Clifford & Miller, Washington, 1950-68; partner firm Clifford, Warnke, Glass, McIlwain & Finney, Washington, 1968-77, Clifford, Glass, McIlwain & Finney, from 1977; partner Clifford & Warnke, to 1980; lectr. econs. U. Corpus Christi, 1948-50. Contbr. articles to profl. jours. Served to lt. (j.g.) USNR, 1943-46. Mem. ABA, Fed. Bar Assn. (nat. council 1961-69), Bar Assn. D.C., State Bar Tex., White House Hist. Assn. (atty.-adviser 1961—, dir. 1975—), Sat. Morning Coffee Soc. (Corpus Christi); founding mem. Nat. Lawyers Club, U.S. Supreme Ct. Hist. Soc. Presbyterian. Home: 3518 37th St Lubbock TX 79413 Office: 815 Connecticut Ave NW Washington DC 20006

GLASS, CHARLES LEE, airline financial executive; b. Jacksonville, Fla., Dec. 15, 1939; s. Charles E. and Martha S. (Peters) G.; m. Wanda Kay Galbreath, June 24, 1961; children: Martha, Stephen, Deborah. A.B. with honors (Outstanding Student in Acctg. 1961), Duke U., 1961. C.P.A., N.C. Staff auditor Price Waterhouse & Co. (C.P.A.s), Miami, Fla., 1961-64; with Eastern Air Lines Inc., 1964-81, asst. treas., Miami, 1976-77, v.p., treas., 1977-81; v.p., controller Trans World Air Lines, N.Y.C., 1981—. Mem. Am. Inst. C.P.A.s, Fin. Execs. Inst., Phi Beta Kappa. Baptist. Home: 57 Willowbrook Ln New Canaan CT 06840 Office: Trans World Air Lines Inc 605 3d Ave New York NY 10158

GLASS, DENNIS ROBERT, financial company executor; b. Milw., Oct. 4, 1949; s. Robert Josep and Carmella (Bellart) G. B.B.A., M.B.A., U. Wis.-Milw. Investment analyst Northwestern Mut. Life Ins. Co., Milw., 1973-77, v.p., treas., 1977-82, mgr. treasury ops., 1983; with Portman Cos., Atlanta, 1983—; mem. acad. staff U. Wis., Milw., 1973-83. Organizer United Way, Milw. Mem. Fin. Execs. Inst. Office: Portmand Cos 225 Peachtree St Atlanta GA 30303

GLASS, DOROTHEA DANIELS, physician, educator; b. N.Y.C.; d. Maurice B. and Anna S. (Kleegman) Daniels; m. Robert E. Glass, June 23, 1940; children: Anne Glass Roth, Deborah, Catherine Glass Barrett, Eugene. B.A., Cornell U., 1940; M.D., Woman's Med. Coll. Pa., 1954; postgrad., U. Pa., 1960-61. Diplomate: Am. Bd. Phys. Medicine and Rehab. (guest bd. examiner 1978). Intern Albert Einstein Med. Center, Phila., 1954-55, clin. asst. dept. medicine, 1956-59, attending phys. medicine and rehab., 1968-70, chmn. dept. phys. medicine and rehab., sr. attending, 1971—; Lois Mattox Miller fellow preventive medicine Woman's Med. Coll. Pa., 1955-56, instr. preventive medicine, 1956-59, instr. medicine, 1960-62; resident phys. medicine and rehab. VA Hosp., Phila., 1959-62, chief phys. medicine and rehab., 1966-68, cons., 1968—; asst. clin. dir. Jefferson Med. Coll. Hosp., Phila., 1963-66, Camden County Stroke Program, Cooper Hosp., Camden, N.J., 1963-66; gen. practice medicine, Phila., 1956-59; asst. med. dir., chief rehab. medicine and rehab. Moss Rehab. Hosp., Phila., 1968-70, med. dir., 1971-82, sr. cons., 1982—; mem. active staff Temple U., Phila., 1968—, asso. prof. rehab. medicine, 1968-73, prof., 1973—, dir. residency tng. rehab. medicine, 1968-82; program dir. Rehab. Research and Tng. Center, 1977-80, chmn. dept. rehab. medicine, 1977—; staff physician Hosp. Med. Coll. Pa., Phila., 1955-59, vis. asso. prof. neurology, 1973-79, clin. prof., 1977—; mem. cons. staff Frankford Hosp., Phila., 1968—, Phila. Geriatric Center, 1975—; mem. active staff Willowcrest-Bamberger Hosp., Phila., 1980—; asso. phys. medicine and rehab. U. Pa. Sch. Medicine, Phila., 1962-66; asst. prof. clin. phys. medicine and rehab., 1966-68; asst. clin. dir. dept. phys. medicine and rehab. Jefferson Med. Coll., Phila., 1963-66.

Contbr. articles to profl. jours. Mem. profl. adv. com. Easter Seal Soc. Crippled Children and Adults Pa., 1975-82; active Goodwill Industries Phila., 1973—, Community Home Health Services Phila., 1974-82, Eastern Pa. chpt. Arthritis Found., 1968—. Recipient Humanitarian Service Cert. Gov's. Com. on Employment Handicapped, 1974; Outstanding Alumnae award Commonwealth Pa. Bd., Hosp. Med. Coll. Pa., 1975; Humanitarian award Pa. Easter Seal Soc., 1981. Mem. Am. Acad. Med. Dirs., Am. Acad. Phys. Medicine and Rehab., Am. Assn. Electromyography and Electrodiagnosis (asso.), Am. Assn. Sex Educators, Counselors and Therapists, Am. Burn Assn., Am. Coll. Angiology, Am. Coll. Utilization Rev., Am. Congress Rehab. Medicine (bd. govs., 2d v.p.), Am. Heart Assn. (council on cerebrovascular disease), Am. Lung Assn. Phila. and Montgomery County (bd. dirs. 1977-79), AMA, Am. Med. Women's Assn., Assn. Acad. Physiatrists, Assn. Med. Rehab. Dirs. and Coordinators, Coll. Physicians Phila., Emergency Care Research Inst., Gerontol. Soc., Internat. Assn. Rehab. Facilities, Internat. Rehab. Medicine Assn., Pan Am. Med. Assn., Pa. Acad. Phys. Medicine and Rehab. (pres. 1975-77), Pa. Med. Soc. (phys. medicine and rehab. adv. com. 1975—), Pa. Thoracic Soc., Delaware Valley Hosp. Council Forum, Philadelphia County Med. Soc., Phila. PSRO (bd. dirs. 1975-82), Phila. Soc. Phys. Medicine and Rehab. (pres. 1968-69), Laennec Soc. Phila., Royal Soc. Health, Alpha Omega Alpha. Home: 1512 Spruce St Apt 2301 Philadelphia PA 19102 Office: Moss Rehab Hosp 12th and Tabor Rds Philadelphia PA 19141

GLASS, HENRY PETER, industrial designer, interiror architect, educator; b. Vienna, Austria, Sept. 24, 1911; came to U.S., 1939; s. Ernst and Berta (Zaitschek) G.; m. Eleanor C. Knoop, Mar. 4, 1937; children: Ann Karin, Peter. Diploma architect, Wiener Tech. Hochschule, Vienna, 1933; M.Arch., Meisterschule Prof. Theiss, Vienna, 1935; Indsl. Design, Sch. Design, Chgo., 1953. Prin. architect Studio H. Glass, Vienna, 1935-38; designer Office Gilbert Romde, N.Y.C., 1939-40, Morris Sanders, 1940; head design dept. W.L. Stensgaard Assocs., Chgo., 1941-45; prin. Henry P. Glass, Assocs., Northfield, Ill., 1946—; prof. indsl. design Chgo. Art Inst., 1946-69. Designs include, Swingline, Children's Furniture; patentee in field; author: Design & Consumer, 1981. Trustee Bd. of Northfield, 1966-67. Recipient Ann. award Fine Hardwoods Assn., 1955, 56, Best Booth award Ski Show Expo Ctr., Chgo., 1972, Excellence in Design award Indsl. Design Mag., 1978. Fellow Indsl. Design Soc. Am. (chmn. Chgo. chpt. 1959-60, nat. vice chmn. 1960-62). Roman Catholic. Clubs: Am. Friends of Austria (v.p. 1976—); Austro Am. Council for the Mid-West (Chgo.) (pres. 1983—). Home: 245 Dickens Rd Northfield IL 60093 Office: Henry P Glass Assocs PO Box 53 Northfield IL 60093

GLASS, HERBERT, magazine editor; b. Frankfurt aM, Germany, Apr. 17, 1934; came to U.S., 1941, naturalized, 1946; s. Leon and Rose (Langmann) G.; m. Susanne Joan Pleibel, July 9, 1965; 1 son, Alexander David. B.A. in English, Brandeis U., 1955. Asst. press dir. N.Y. Philharm., 1962-65; public relations dir. San Francisco Opera, 1965-67; editor-in-chief Performing Arts mag., Beverly Hills, Calif., 1967—, Playbill mag. (Los Angeles, San Francisco and San Diego edits.), 1981—; editorial dir. Performing Arts Network, 1978—; music critic (under name Fred Pleibel) Los Angeles Times, 1970—; programming dir. Los Angeles Chamber Orch., 1969-74; cons. for program devel. Sta. KUSC-FM (Nat. Public Radio), 1978—. Office: 9025 Wilshire Blvd Beverly Hills CA 90211

GLASS, IRVINE ISRAEL, aerospace scientist, engineer, educator; b. Slupia Nowa, Poland, Feb. 23, 1918; s. Samuel Solomon and Gitel (Helf) G.; m. Anne Medres, Aug. 30, 1942; children: Vivian (Mrs. Shimon Felsen), Ruth (Mrs. Robert Moses), Susan. B.A.Sc. with Honours in Aero. Engring, U. Toronto, 1947, M.A.Sc., 1948, Ph.D. in Aerophysics, 1950. Stress analyst, aerodynamicist Canadair, Ltd., Montreal, 1946, Can. Car and Foundry, 1947, A.V. Roe, Toronto, 1948—, Canadian Armament Research and Devel. Establishment, Valcartier, Que., 1953; mem. faculty Inst. for Aerospace Studies, U. Toronto, 1950—, prof., 1960—, Univ. prof., 1981—, asst. dir. inst., 1968-74, chmn. dept. aerospace studies, 1961-66; Mem. asso. com. space research NRC, 1962-65; basic research adv. subcom. fluid mechanics NASA, 1965-70; mem. sci. adv. com. Ont. Sci. Centre, Toronto; pres. Aerospace Engring. & Cons. Ltd., 1978-79; chmn. Internat. Shock Tube Symposium, 1969—; mem. adv. com. Internat. Colloquia on Gasdynamics of Explosives and Reactive Systems, 1969—; vis. prof. phys. and chem. engring. depts. Imperial Coll. Sci. and Tech., London, 1957-58; vis. prof. aeros. dept. Kyoto (Japan) U., Technion, Israel, 1975; holder several named lectureships. Author: Shock Waves and Man, 1974 (Russian edit. 1977, Polish edit. 1980, Chinese edit. 1983); assoc. editor: Jour. Physics of Fluids, 1967-70, Progress in Aerospace Sci. series, 1974—; Contbr. numerous articles on gasdynamics, shock-wave phenomena, aerophysics to sci. jours. and books. Served to capt. RCAF, 1942-45. Recipient Sesquicentennial award U. Toronto, 1977; named Disting. univ. prof. U. Toronto, 1981. Fellow Am. Phys. Soc., AAAS, AIAA, Canadian Aeros. and Space Inst., Royal Soc. Can. Jewish. Home: 31 Heathdale Rd Toronto ON Canada M6C 1M7

GLASS, JAMES RICHARD, tire and rubber manufacturing company executive; b. Springfield, Ohio, Jan. 10, 1923; s. Stewart Burdette and Mary Catherine (Brunner) G.; m. Frieda Berta Hess, June 12, 1946; children: Michael Andrew, Timothy Joseph, James Thomas, John Edward. B.S. in Bus. Adminstrn., Ohio State U., 1948. Diplomate: C.P.A., Ohio, N.Y. Pres. Companhia Goodyear do Brasil, 1975-79, Motor Wheel Corp., Lansing, Mich., 1979-81; asst. to group exec. v.p. fin. Goodyear Tire & Rubber Co., Akron, 1982, v.p., comptroller, 1982, group exec. v.p., 1982, dir. group exec. v.p. fin. and planning, 1983—. Bd. dirs. YMCA, Akron, 1982—, Akron Priority Corp., 1983—, Greater Akron Mus. Assn., 1983—. Served with U.S. Army, 1943-45. Mem. Officer Conf. group, Fin. Exec. Inst., Nat. Assn. Accts., Am. Inst. C.P.A.s, Ohio Soc. C.P.A.s, Soc. Automotive Engrs. Roman Catholic. Clubs: Firestone Country, Fairlawn Country; Cascade (Akron). Lodge: K.C. Home: 1019 Bunker Dr Akron OH 44313 Office: Goodyear Tire & Rubber Co 1144 E Market St Akron OH 44316

GLASS, LAUREL, developmental biologist, physician, educator; b. Selma, Calif., Oct. 1, 1923; d. Sydney L. and Marie (Damron) G. B.A., U. Calif.-Berkeley, 1951; Ph.D., Duke U., 1958; M.D., U. Calif., 1974. Teaching asst. zoology Duke U., 1953-56; research assoc. Pathology Research Lab., Med. Research Div., VA Hosp., Durham, N.C., 1957-58; part-time instr. anatomy Duke U. Med. Sch., 1958; instr. dept. anatomy U. Calif. Med. Sch., San Francisco, 1958-61, asst. prof., 1961-66, assoc. prof., 1968-72, prof., 1972—, adj. prof. psychiatry, 1983—, dir. Center on Deafness, 1983—; adj. prof. family and community medicine U. Calif. Med. Affiliate, Aging and Health Policy Center, U. Calif. Sch. Nursing, 1983—; mem. San Francisco adv. com. Child Health and Disability Prevention Program, 1974—; mem. exec. com., bd. dirs. Mission Neighborhood Health Center, 1974-77; mem. med. adv. com. Coalition for Med. Rights of Women, 1974—; mem. adv. bd. P.R. Orgn. Women Health Edn. Project, 1976—; v.p. Developmental Disabilities Programs, Inc., 1976—. Mem. edn. commn. cons. NAACP, Ocean View-Merced Heights Community Stblzn. and Improvement Project; exec. com. Ocean View-Ingleside Dist. Council; mem. Bay Area Social Planning Council, 1969-73; Bd. dirs. Service Com. on Pub. Edn., 1963-66, Constl. Rights Found., 1965-73; trustee Glide Found., 1966-75; bd. govs. Pub. Advs. Inc., 1975-79; mem. San Francisco Bd. Edn., 1967-71, pres., 1969; regent Lone Mountain Coll., 1973-76. Mem. Am. Assn. Anatomists, Developmental Biology Soc., Gerontol. Soc. Am., Western Gerontol. Soc., NOW, Phi Beta Kappa, Sigma Xi. Democrat. Methodist. (adminstrv. bd.). Office: Center on Deafness U Calif Medical Sch 1474 5th Ave San Francisco CA 94143

GLASS, M. MILTON, architect; b. N.Y.C., Jan. 30, 1906; s. Louis and Sarah B. (Hertzoff) G.; m. Rose T. Schlamowitz, June 12, 1983; children: Joan Dorothy Cantor, Elliott Michael. Student, CCNY, 1925-28, 30-32, Columbia U., 1925-30, N.Y.U., 1930-31, Beaux-Arts Inst. Design, 1925-31. Draftsman various archtl. offices, 1925-40; chief draftsman Mayer & Whittlesey (architects and town planners), 1940-45; partner Mayer, Whittlesey & Glass, 1945-60; sr. partner Glass & Glass, N.Y.C., 1960-67, 70—; instr. site planning Sch. Architecture, Cooper Union, 1961-62. Important works include Master Plan City of Kitimat, B.C., Can.; cons.: Master Plan City of Ashdod, Israel; apt. houses Butterfield House and The Premier, N.Y.C., Forest Park Crescent, Queens, N.Y. Bd. dirs. Citizens Housing and Planning Council N.Y., 1940—, chmn. com. on community renewal and planning criteria, 1963; mem. com. on city planning Citizens Union N.Y., 1962—; mem. Municipal Arts Soc. N.Y.; mem. architects adv. com. N.Y.C. Housing and Redevel. Bd., 1966-67; mem. adv. com. N.Y. State Commr. Housing and Community Renewal, 1962-63; chmn. Bd. Standards and Appeals, City N.Y., 1967-70; mem. architects' liaison com. N.Y.C. Housing and Devel. Adminstrn., 1973—; mem. N.Y.C. Master Plumbers License Bd., 1973-82; mem. adv. com. Grad. div. Columbia U. Sch. Architecture, 1950; panel mem. of seminars Real Estate Inst., Sch. Continuing Edn., N.Y. U., 1978. Recipient medal of honor N.Y. chpt. AIA, 1952, Apt. House medal N.Y. chpt. AIA, 1952, 1st Design award Progressive Architecture, 1959, 60, certificate of merit Municipal Arts Soc. N.Y., 1961, 63, Bard award City Club N.Y., 1963, 1st Honor award for residential design FHA, 1963, award Merit Queens C. of C., 1965. Fellow AIA (sec., chmn. com. on admissions N.Y. chpt. 1949-50, chmn. civic design com. 1961-62, mem. urban design com. 1970-75); mem. N.Y. Soc. Architects (dir. 1950-62, 71—, v.p. 1973, pres. 1973-75), Nat. Inst. Archtl. Edn. (trustee; del. to N.Y.C. Fine Arts Fedn. 1974, v.p. Fine Arts Fedn. 1982—, chmn. com. on nominations to N.Y.C. Art Commn. 1974), Architects Council N.Y.C. (pres. 1973-75, mem. jury to select Mayor's panel architects for pub. works 1973), N.Y. State Assn. Architects (jury on awards 1971-75, pres. Architects Council N.Y. 1973-75, dir. 1975-76), K.P. Office: 200 Park Ave S New York NY 10003

GLASS, MILTON LOUIS, manufacturing company executive; b. Burlington, Vt., Mar. 7, 1929; s. Joseph and Mary Lena (Smith) G.; m. Renee Peritz, Feb. 5, 1950; children: Jill Sharlene, Mikel Lewis. Grad., Bentley Coll., 1948; B.B.A. with high honors, Northeastern U., 1954, M.B.A., 1956; postgrad., Harvard Grad. Sch. Bus., 1962. With Gillette Co., Boston, 1952—, now v.p. and treas.; vice chmn. Blue Shield Mass., Inc., 1968—. Chmn. Sch. Com., Mashpee, Mass., 1970—; treas. Mashpee Wampanoag Indian Mus.; officer Exec. Res. Corps, U.S. Govt.; Mem. regional bd. B'nai B'rith Anti Defamation League; bd. dirs. Concerts in Black and White; chmn. investment com. Hillel Founds. of Greater Boston; bd. dirs. Boston Opera Assn. Served with AUS, 1948-51. Mem. Nat. Assn. Corporate Treas.' (dir.), Harvard, Bentley, Northeastern alumni assns., Sigma Epsilon Rho. Clubs: Boston Treasurers, University. Office: Prudential Tower Bldg Boston MA 02199

GLASS, PHILIP, composer, musician; b. Balt., Jan. 31, 1937; s. Benjamin C. and Ida (Gouline) G.; (div.)children: Juliet, Zachary. A.B., U. Chgo., 1956; M.S. in Composition, Julliard Sch. Music, 1964. Composer in residence Pitts. Pub. Schs., 1962-64; composition student with Nadia Boulanger, Paris, 1964-66. Founder, performer with, Philip Glass Ensemble, 1968—; various U.S. and European concert tours, 1968—; founder record co., Chatham Sq. Prodns., N.Y.C., 1972; recs. include North Star, Glassworks, Facades, The Photographer, others; composer: (with Robert Wilson) opera Einstein on the Beach, which toured Europe, Akhnaten, 1984; played at, Met. Opera, Nov. 1976; composer: opera Satyagraha, Akhnaton. Recipient Broadcast Music Industry award, 1960, Lado prize, 1961, Benjamin award, 1961, 62, Young Composer's award Ford Found., 1964-66; composition grantee Fulbright, 1966-67, Found. for Contemporary Performance Arts, 1970-71, Changes, Inc., 1971-72, Nat. Endowment for the Arts, 1974, 75, Menil Found., 1974. Mem. ASCAP, SACEM (France). Office: care Internat Prodn Assocs 853 Broadway Room 2120 New York NY 10003

GLASS, RON, actor; b. Evansville, Ind., July 10; s. Crump and Lethia G. B.A., U. Evansville. Acting debut with, Guthrie Theatre., Mpls.; stage appearances include Slow Dance on the Killing Ground, 1972, House of Ptreus, Misalliance, The Taming of the Shrew; TV debut in Sanford and Son, 1972; appeared in: Good Times, 1972-74; TV series Barney Miller, 1975-82, The New Odd Couple, 1982-83; TV movies include Shirts and Skins, 1973; TV appearance on Streets of San Francisco. Recipient Medal of Honor U. Evansville. Office: care Lawrence Kubik 8278 Sunset Blvd Los Angeles CA 90046 *

GLASS, THOMAS FRANKLIN, JR., construction company executive; b. Uniontown, Ala., Aug. 22, 1918; s. Thomas Franklin and Gertrude (Arnold) G.; m. Frances Louise Chapman, Aug. 23, 1943; children—Thomas Franklin III, Edwin Chapman, Kay Glass Easton, Judith Glass Mabrito. A.A., Marion Inst., 1937; B.A., Rice U., 1939, M.A., 1941. Prof. math. Marion Inst., 1941-44; physicist Tex. Devel. Corp., Bellaire, Tex., 1944-45; estimator, purchasing agt., v.p. Farnsworth & Chambers, Houston, 1945-52; co-founder Spaw-Glass Inc., Houston, 1953, pres., 1953-70, chmn. bd., chief exec. officer, 1970—; pres. Medix Inc., 1969-75, chmn. bd., 1975—, Cahaba Constrn. Co., 1979—; dir. Interfirst Bank Fannin, Houston, Paisan Constrn. Co., Cahaba Constrn. Co.; bd. dirs. Constrn. Scis. Research Found., Washington. Bd. dirs. Houston Heritage Soc.; bd. dirs., v.p. bd. Houston Pub. Library; mem. ofcl. bd. First Methodist Ch. of Houston. Paul Harris fellow, 1976—. Mem. Constrn. Specifications Inst., Presidents Assn., Conf. Bd., Sigma Xi. Democrat. Clubs: Rotary (past pres.), Warwick., Heritage of Houston. Home: 143 Stoney Creek St Houston TX 77024 Office: Spaw-Glass Inc 2727 Kirby Dr Houston TX 77098 *Life becomes exciting when one applies energy and talent to the continuing challenge of it. One finds excitement in study, work, business or profession when such structures permit a freeing of spirit for highest development of those engaged with him. Successful people usually have learned to know something about who they are and where they are in their societies, and have chosen their services well.*

GLASS, WILLIAM EVERETT, physician; b. Amarillo, Tex., May 14, 1906; s. William P. and Gertrude (Compton) G.; m. Margaret H. Quam, Nov. 21, 1931; children—William Lewis, Cynthia Anne Paige. B.S., U. Ill., 1928, M.D., 1931. Diplomate: Am. Bd. Psychiatry and Neurology. Staff physician Worcester (Mass.) State Hosp., 1931-36; city physician, Marlboro, Mass., 1936-37; asst. supt. Grafton (Mass.) State Hosp., 1938-47; hosp. insp. Boston Dept. Mental Health, 1947-48; supt. Taunton (Mass.) State Hosp., 1948-73; instr. psychiatry Tufts U. Med. Sch., 1939-48; dir. clinics Bristol County Mental Health Inst., 1949-65; cons. psychiatry Sturdy Meml. Hosp., Attleboro, Mass., 1960—, Union, Truesdale hosps., Fall River, Mass., 1960—, Morton Hosp., Taunton, 1967—. Fellow AMA, Am. Psychiat. Assn.; mem. Mass. Med. Soc., Mass. Soc. Research Psychiatry, New Eng. Soc. Psychiatry (past pres.), Am. Soc. Clin. Hypnosis. Club: Rotarian. Home and office: 66 Whitehill St Taunton MA 02780

GLASSE, JOHN HOWELL, philosophy theology educator; b. Buffalo, June 1, 1922; s. John Alfred and Jessie Elizabeth (Howell) G.; m. Wanda Lou Howard, June 16, 1950; children: Jeffrey Howell, Paulding Howard. B.A., Williamette U., 1945; B.D., Yale U., 1948, Ph.D., 1961. Ordained to ministry Presbyterian Ch. U.S.A., 1948; dir. field work Christian Activities Council, Hartford, Conn., 1948-50, exec. dir., 1950-52; dir. Danish program Scandinavian Seminar, Inc., 1952-53; mem. faculty Vassar Coll., Poughkeepsie, N.Y., 1956—, prof. religion, 1969—, Frederick Weyerhaeuser chair, 1971—, chmn. dept. religion, 1965-67, 77-83; vis. prof. Harvard Div. Sch., 1970, vis. scholar, 1962, 69, Columbia U., Union Theol. Sem., 1980-81. Contbr. articles to profl. jours. Trustee Scandinavian Seminar, 1950—. Hon. fellow Am. Scandinavian Found., 1952; grantee Am. Philos. Soc., 1964, Am. Council Learned Socs., 1965, 67. Mem. Am. Acad. Religion, Am. Philos. Assn., Metaphys. Soc. Am., Soc. Values in Higher Edn., AAUP. Address: Vassar Coll Poughkeepsie NY 12601

GLASSELL, ALFRED CURRY, JR., investor; b. Cuba Plantation, La., Mar. 31, 1914; s. Alfred Curry and Frances (Lee) G.; m. Clare Attwell; children: Jean Curry, Alfred Curry III. B.A., La. State U., 1934. Ind. oil and gas investor, 1936—; cons. Glassell Producing Co., Inc., 1938—; dir. First City Bancorp. Bd. dirs. Houston Symphony Soc.; trustee Houston Mus. Natural Sci., Internat. Oceanographic Found., Houston Fine Arts Mus., Kinkaid Sch., Tex. Children's Hosp.; asso. trustee Smithsonian Instn. Assos. Recipient Marine Sci. ann. award Internat. Oceanographic Found., 1971. Mem. Am. Geog. Soc., Am. Mus. Natural History, Tex. Angus Assn., Canadian Chianini Assn., Houston Horse Show Assn., Tex. Cattle Feeders Assn., Am. Nat. Cattlemen's Assn., Mil. and Hospitaller Order St. Lazarus of Jerusalem. Clubs: Atlantic Tuna (Providence); Boston (New Orleans); Cabo Blanco Fishing (Peru); Tex. Game Fishing (Dallas); Texas Corinthian Yacht (Kemah); Bay of Islands Swordfish and Mako Shark (N.Z.); Long Island (N.Y.); Anglers of N.Y.; Houston, Petroleum, Ramada, Bayou, River Oaks Country, Houston Country (Houston); Coronado, Explorers. Holder record of world's largest fish, former holder numerous world record salt water game fish. Office: 2300 First City Nat Bank Bldg 1021 Main St Houston TX 77002

GLASSER, FRANCES PAUL, publisher; b. N.Y.C., Sept. 20, 1919; d. Albert and Lillian (Lublin) Paul; m. Joseph Glasser, June 17, 1941; children: Richard P., Jane H. B.A., N.Y. U., 1940. Sec.-treas., dir. Delphan Co. Inc., N.Y.C., 1957—; pres. Duaal Pub. Corp., N.Y.C., 1962—; partner Basic Research Assos., N.Y.C., 1965—. Home: 12 Beekman Pl New York NY 10022 Office: 515 Madison Ave New York NY 10022

GLASSER, ISRAEL LEO, judge; b. N.Y.C., Apr. 6, 1924; s. David and Sadie (Krupp) G.; m. Grace Gribetz, Aug. 24, 1952; children—Dorothy, David, James, Marjorie. LL.B., Bklyn. Law Sch., 1948; B.A., CUNY, 1976. Bar: N.Y. 1948. Fellow Bklyn. Law Sch., 1948-49, instr., 1950-52, asst. prof. law, 1952-53, asso. prof., 1953-55, prof., 1955-74, adj. prof., 1974, dean, 1977-82; judge U.S. Dist. Ct. N.Y., 1982—; judge N.Y. State Family Ct., N.Y.C., 1969-77. Mem. Am. Bar Assn. Office: US District Court 225 Cadman Plaza East Brooklyn NY 11201

GLASSER, JAMES J., leasing company executive; b. Chgo., June 5, 1934; s. Daniel D. and Sylvia G. G.; m. Louise D. Rosenthal, Apr. 19, 1964; children: Mary, Emily, Daniel. A.B., Yale U., 1955; J.D., Harvard U., 1958. Bar: Ill. 1958. Asst. states atty., Cook County, Ill., 1958-61; mem. exec. staff GATX Corp., Chgo., 1961-69, pres., 1974—, chmn. bd., chief exec. officer, 1978—, also dir.; gen. mgr. Infilco Products Co., 1969-70; v.p. GATX Leasing Corp., San Francisco, 1970-71, pres., 1971-74; dir. Harris Bankcorp, Inc., Harris Trust & Savs. Bank, Mut. Trust Life Ins. Co., Oak Brook, Ill. Bd. dirs. Northwestern Meml. Hosp., Chgo., Michael Reese Hosp. and Med. Center.; trustee Chgo. Zool. Soc. Mem. Econ. Club Chgo., Chi Psi. Clubs: Casino, Chicago, Racquet, Tavern, Commercial (Chgo.); Onwentsia, Winter (Lake Forest, Ill.); Lake Shore Country (Glencoe, Ill.). Home: 644 E Spruce Ave Lake Forest IL 60045 Office: 120 S Riverside Plaza Chicago IL 60606

GLASSER, JOSEPH, business executive; b. Phila., May 17, 1925. B.S. in Econs., U. Pa., 1947, M.B.A., 1948, postgrad., 1948-51. With NLRB, 1948-51; internal mgmt. cons., 1954-55; mem. faculty Sch. Bus. Adminstrn., U. Conn., 1955-81, prof. emeritus, 1981—; pres. Ewen Devel. Corp., 1971—; arbitrator Fed. Mediation and Conciliation Service; Arbitrator Nat. Mediation Bd.; fact finder Conn. Bd. Mediation and Arbitration; mediator Conn. Bd. Edn.; rev. officer FAA; mem. Nat. Def. Exec. Res.-Fed. Emergency Mgmt. Agy.; speaker seminars, also mgmt. groups in Eng., Austria and Hungary Am. Mgmt. Assn. Author: Fundamentals of Applied Industrial Management; contbr. articles to profl. jours. Served to lt. col. USAAF; ETO. Decorated Air medal with four oak leaf clusters, Air Force commendation medal. Mem. Am. Arbitration Assn. (arbitrator), Soc. Profls. in Dispute Resolution, Indsl. Relations Research Assn., Nat. Assn. Industry-Edn. Cooperation, Nat. Assn. Mgmt. Educators (Innovative Mid-Mgmt. Edn. award 1976), Nat. Assn. Suggestion Systems (winner internat. papers competition 1975), Res. Officers Assn., Air Force Assn. Home: 15 Westwood Rd Storrs CT 06268 Office: 383 S Main St Windsor Locks CT 06096

GLASSER, LEO GEORGE, scientist; b. Wilkes-Barre, Pa., July 20, 1916; s. Leo George and Lillian Reynolds (Cave) G.; m. Helen Sharpe Morgan, June 26, 1941; children: Frederick Morgan, Ellen Lee Glasser Hamilton, Robert Scott. B.A., Cornell U., 1938, M.A., 1940. Registered profl. engr., Del. Physicist, Bur. Ordnance, Dept. Navy, 1940-44; Physicist Tenn. Eastman Corp., Oak Ridge, 1944-45; with E.I. du Pont de Nemours & Co., Inc., Wilmington, Del., 1945-80, mgr. engring. research and devel., 1956-63; dir. Engring. Physics Lab., 1963-80; obs. dir. Mt. Cuba Astron. Obs., 1963—, chmn. bd. dirs., 1973—; dir. Lambert L. Jackson Meml. Library, 1961—; mem. U. Del. Research Found.; cons. instrument engring. and applied physics. Bd. dirs. Trinity Found., Torch Found., 1978—. Mem. AAAS, Am. Astron. Soc., Astron. Soc. Pacific, Del. Astron. Soc., Optical Soc. Am., Internat. Assn. Torch (dir. 1971-76, pres. 1974-75), U. Del. Marine Assn., Sigma Xi. Episcopalian. Clubs: Greenville Country, DuPont Country, New Castle Cotillion (pres. 1961-62). Patentee in field. Home: 112 Somerset Rd Wilmington DE 19803

GLASSER, OTTO JOHN, bus. exec., former air force officer; b. Wilkes-Barre, Pa., Oct. 2, 1918; s. Leo George and Lillian (Cave) G.; m. Norma Mayo, Sept. 11, 1943; children—Charlene Lee, Carole Jeanne. E.E., Cornell U., 1940; M.S. in Elec. Engring, Ohio State U., 1947. Test engr. Gen. Electric Co., 1940-41; commd. 2d lt. U.S. Army, 1941; advanced through grades to lt. gen. USAF, 1969; program dir. (Atlas and Minuteman programs), 1954-59; asst. dep. chief staff research and devel. Hdqrs. USAF, Washington, 1966-69, dep. chief staff research and devel., 1969-73; v.p. internat. Gen. Dynamics Corp., St. Louis, 1973-76, Washington, 1976—. Decorated D.S.M. Legion of Merit, Air Force Commendation medal, Legion d'Honneur, France). Home: 7723 Crossover Dr McLean VA 22102

GLASSER, PAUL HAROLD, sociologist, social worker; b. N.Y.C., Aug. 21, 1929; s. David and Rae (Startz) G.; m. Lois Hannah Naefach,

Nov. 25, 1954; children: Heather Denys, Frederick Naefach. B.S., CCNY, 1949; M.S., Columbia U., 1951; Ph.D., U. N.C., 1961. Chief psychiat. social work sect. Mental Hygiene Clinic, Camp Chaffee Army Hosp., Ark., 1952-53; asst. dir. residence Child Guidance Home, Inc.; instr. psychiat. group work, dept. psychiatry U. Cin., Med. Sch., 1953-55; asst. prof. U. Mich., Ann Arbor, 1958-63, asso. prof., 1963-65, prof., 1965-78; dean Grad. Sch. Social Work, U. Tex., Arlington, 1978—. Author: Small Groups in Hospital Community, 1967, Families in Crisis, 1970, Social Work Education for Family and Population Planning, 1973, Individual Change Through Small Groups, 1974, Social Work Roles and Function in Family and Population Planning, 1974, Child Abuse and Neglect: A Challenge to the Caring Community, 1977; Sr. editor: Ency. Social Work, 1971, LaRicerca Valutative, 1972; editor: Jour. Health and Social Behavior, 1970-73, Jour. Social Work, 1965-67, 68-69, Jour. Marriage and Family Counseling, 1974-82, Social Work with Groups. Bd. dirs. Washtenau County Family Service, 1964-66, 69-70. Served to 1st lt. AUS, 1952-53. Fulbright Hays lectr., Italy, 1971, U. Philippines, 1966-67, Australia, 1973-74. Mem. Nat. Assn. Social Workers (chpt. chmn. 1962-63), Am. Sociol. Soc. Club: Masons. Home: 1515 Waltham Ct Arlington TX 76012 Office: 301D Bldg A Cooper Center U Tex Arlington TX 76019 *The generation and the dispersal of knowledge are the two primary ways in which the academician contributes to the society. He is an agent of change as he studies what is, in order to suggest what might be, and communicates this to his students. My career has been devoted to these principles and to stimulating others to follow them.*

GLASSER, ROBERT GENE, physics educator; b. Chgo., Apr. 14, 1929; s. Morris and Beatrice (Drues) G.; children by previous marriage: Matthew David, Lawrence Alan, Nancy Sarah Richter, Martin George. A.B., U. Chgo., also; B.S., M.S., Ph.D. Research assoc. U. Chgo., 1954-55; physicist U.S. Naval Research Lab., 1955-65; mem. faculty U. Md., 1965—, prof. physics and computer sci., 1968-75, prof. physics and astronomy, 1975—; vis. scientist Deutsches Elektronen Synchrotron, 1978. NSF sr. fellow, 1962-63; recipient Meritorious Civilian Service medal U.S. Navy, 1965. Mem. Am. Phys. Soc., Fedn. Am. Scientists, Assn. Computing Machinery. Office: Dept Physics Univ of Md College Park MD 20742

GLASSGOLD, ALFRED EMANUEL, physicist, educator; b. Phila., July 20, 1929; s. Solomon S. and Anna (Blaukopf) G.; m. Irene Mihaly, Jan. 25, 1953; children—Judith, Eric. B.A., U. Pa., 1950; Ph.D., Mass. Inst. Tech., 1954. Research and teaching physics Oak Ridge Nat. Lab., 1954-55, U. Minn., 1955-57, U. Calif., 1957-63; mem. faculty N.Y.U., 1963—, prof., 1969—, head dept. physics, 1969-73. Fellow Am. Phys. Soc.; mem. AAAS, Am. Astron. Soc., Internat. Astron. Union, Phi Beta Kappa, Sigma Xi. Research on theoretical physics, astrophysics. Home: 3035 Palisade Ave Bronx NY 10463 Office: 4 Washington Pl New York City NY 10003

GLASSICK, CHARLES ETZWEILER, college president; b. Wrightsville, Pa., Apr. 6, 1931; s. Gordon J. and Melva G. (Etzweiler) G.; m. Mary Williams, Feb. 27, 1952; children: Bruce, Judith, Jeffrey, Robert, Jonathan. B.S. with honors, Franklin and Marshall Coll., 1953; M.A., Ph.D., Princeton U., 1957; D.Sc., U. Richmond, 1977. Research chemist Rohm & Haas Co., Phila., 1957-62; instr. gen. chemistry Temple U., Phila., 1957-62; prof. chemistry Adrian (Mich.) Coll., 1962-68; v.p. Great Lakes Colls. Assn., Ann Arbor, Mich., 1968-69; asso. dean for acad. affairs Albion (Mich.) Coll., 1969-71, v.p. for acad. affairs, 1971-72; pres. Va. Inst. Scientific Research, Richmond, 1972-77; provost, v.p. for acad. affairs U. Richmond, Va., 1972-77; pres. Gettysburg (Pa.) Coll., 1977—; cons. Nat. Endowment for Humanities, 1971-72, NSF, 1963-67, Va. Council High Edn., 1972-76; mem. program policy com. Luth. Ednl. Conf. of N.Am.; mem. exec. com. Found. Ind. Colls.; mem. exec. com., chmn. instl. research com. Council Ind. Colls. and Univs. of Pa.; mem. com. to choose Fred Ness book award Am. Assn. Colls. Mem. editorial bd. Liberal Edn., 1978, 81-82; contbr. articles to jours. Mem. Mental Health and Mental Retardation Task Force Manpower Devel., Richmond, 1975-77; bd. dirs. Am. Cancer Soc., Adrian, Mich., 1964-67, Methodist Conf. Homes for Aging, York-Adams Area council Boy Scouts Am., 1979—, Eisenhower Soc., Hist. Gettysburg/Adams County, 1979—. Harvard fellow, 1955-56; Gen. Electric fellow, 1956-57; NSF grantee, 1962-67; Am. Council Edn. fellow in acad. adminstrn. Fresno State Coll., 1967-68; Lincoln fellow, 1983. Mem. Inst. Mediterranean Studies, Am. Chem Soc., N.Y. Acad. Scis., AAUP, Danforth Assocs., AAAS, Am. Chem. Soc., Phi Beta Kappa, Beta Gamma Sigma, Omicron Delta Kappa, Alpha Chi Omega. Methodist. Home: 243 W Broadway Gettysburg PA 17325 Office: Gettysburg Coll Office of Pres Gettysburg PA 17325

GLASSMAN, ARMAND BARRY, physician, scientist; b. Paterson, N.J., Sept. 9, 1938; s. Paul and Rosa (Ackerman) G.; m. Alberta C. Macri, Aug. 30, 1958; children: Armand P., Steven B., Brian A. B.A., Rutgers U., 1960; M.D. magna cum laude (Johnson and Avalon Found. scholar), Georgetown U., 1964. Diplomate: Am. Bd. Pathology, Am. Bd. Nuclear Medicine. Intern Georgetown U. Hosp., Washington, 1964-65; resident Yale-New Haven Hosp., West Haven VA Hosp., 1965-69; asst. prof. pathology U. Fla. Coll. Medicine; chief radioimmunoassary lab. Gainesville VA Hosp.; practice lab. and nuclear medicine, 1969-71; dir. clin. labs. Med. Coll. Ga., Augusta, 1971-76; cons. physician in pathology VA Hosp., Augusta, 1973-76; cons. physician in nuclear medicine U. Hosp., Augusta, 1973-76; med. dir. clin. labs. Med. U. Hosp., Med. U. S.C., Charleston, 1976—, attending physician in lab. and nuclear medicine, 1976—, assoc. med. dir., 1982—; med. dir. clin. labs. Charleston County (S.C.) Hosp., 1976—; cons. VA Hosp., Charleston, 1976—; prof., chmn. dept. lab. medicine Med. U. S.C., 1976—, med. dir. MT and MLT programs, 1976—, asso. dean, 1979—. Contbr. articles on lab. medicine to profl. jours. Adv. council Trident Tech. Coll., 1976—; bd. dirs. Fetter Family Health Center, 1976-79; trustee Coll. Prep. Sch., 1979—, chmn. bd., 1983—. Served with USMC, 1956-64. Fellow Coll. Am. Pathologists (edn. adv. com. 1973-80, chmn. 1982—), A.C.P., Assn. Clin. Scientists, Am. Soc. Clin. Pathology (bd. registry 1972-76, rep. to Am. Bd. Pathology test com. on blood banking 1984—), Am. Coll. Nuclear Medicine; mem. Internat. Acad. Pathology, Am. Assn. Pathologists, Soc. Nuclear Medicine (chmn. membership com. S.E. chpt. 1972-74, chmn. edn. com. 1973-77, acad. council 1979—), Ga. Radiol. Soc., AMA (Physician's Recognition award, instl. rep. to sect. on med. schs.), So. Med. Assn., Am. Geriatric Soc. (founding fellow So. div.), Am. Soc. Microbiology, Ga. Heart Assn., Am. Assn. Blood Banks (chmn. cryobiology com. 1974—, mem. com. on edn. 1978—, Sci. program com. 1981—, mem. com. on autologous transfusion 1979—), Assn. Schs. Allied Health Professions (bd. editors jour.), Soc. Cryobiology, AAAS, N.Y. Acad. Scis., Acad. Clin. Lab. Physicians and Scientists (exec. council 1978—, pres. 1982-83), S.E. Area Blood Bankers (pres. 1979-81, exec. council 1980—), Sigma Xi (program chmn., pres.-elect Med. Coll. Ga. chpt. 1975-76), Alpha Eta, Alpha Omega Alpha. Club: Charleston Tennis. Home: 167 Broad St Charleston SC 29401 Office: 171 Ashley Ave Charleston SC 29425 *Striving to do a good job of attaining reasonable goals through practical assessment of opportunities and resources while dealing with people under the Golden Rule have guided my career development. My wife, children, parents and grandparents have tremendously influenced my attitudes. Be a pragmatic optimist, confident in your abilities, respectful, listening and charitable in personal interactions.*

GLASSMAN, CAROLINE DUBY, state justice; b. Baker, Oreg., Sept. 13, 1924; d. Charles Ferdinand and Caroline Marie (Colton) Duby; m. Harry Paul Glassman, May 21, 1953; 1 son, Max Avon. LL.B. summa cum laude, Williamette U., 1944. Bar: Oreg. 1944, Calif. 1952, Maine 1969. Title ins. atty. Title Ins. & Trust Co., Salem, Oreg., 1944-46; assoc. mem. firm Belli, Aske & Pinney, San Francisco, 1952-58; ptnr. firm Glassman, Beagle & Ridge, Portland, Maine, 1978—; judge Maine Supreme Ct., Portland; lectr. Sch. Law, U. Maine, 1967-68, 80. Author: Legal Status of Homemakers in State of Maine, 1977. Mem. ABA, Oreg. Bar Assn., Calif. Bar Assn., Maine Bar Assn., Maine Trial Law Assn. Roman Catholic. Home: 56 Thomas St Portland ME 04102 Office: Maine Supreme Ct 142 Federal St Portland ME 04112

GLASSMAN, EDWARD, biochemistry educator; b. N.Y.C., Mar. 18, 1929; s. Jacob S. and Riesa (Bronfman) F.; children—Lyn Judith, Susan Fiona, Ellen Ruth, Marjorie Riesa. A.B., N.Y. U., 1949, M.S., 1951; Ph.D., Johns Hopkins U., 1955. Mem. staff City of Hope Med. Center, Duarte, Calif., 1959-60; faculty biochemistry dept. U. N.C. Med. Sch., Chapel Hill, 1960—, prof., 1967—; mem. grants rev. study sect. NIMH, 1966-69; vis. prof. Stanford U. Med. Sch., 1968-69, U. Calif., Irvine, 1978; vis. fellow Ctr. Creative Leadership, Greensboro, N.C., 1983. Author: Molecular Approaches to Neurobiology, 1967; Mem. editorial bd.: Behavior Genetics, 1970-71; mem. editorial adv. bd.: Behavioral Biology, 1971-78, Pharmacology, Biochemistry and Behavior, 1973-78; mem. bd. advs.: Neurochem. Research, 1975-78; contbr.: 80 articles to profl. jours. Adam T. Bruce fellow, 1954-55; Am. Cancer Soc. fellow, 1955-57; NIH fellow, 1958-59; NIH Career Devel. award, 1961-71; Guggenheim fellow, 1968-69. Fellow AAAS, Royal Soc. Edinburgh; mem. N.C. Soc. Neurosci. (pres. chpt. 1974-75), Elisha Mitchell Sci. Soc. (v.p. 1965-66). Democrat. Home: 112 Kenan St Chapel Hill NC 27514 Office: Dept Biochemistry U NC Med Sch Chapel Hill NC 27514

GLASSMAN, HERBERT HASKEL, architect; b. Boston, Mar. 29, 1919; s. Jacob and Jennie Rose (Levine) G.; m. Anne Shirley Resnick, June 20, 1948; children—Elsa Jan, Karin Melvey, Jack Ian. Student, Ga. Inst. Tech., 1937-38; certificate in architecture (Spl. Student scholar), Mass. Inst. Tech., 1942, Boston Archtl. Center, 1941; student in structures, Cath. U. Am., 1942-43, George Washington U., 1942-43. With Perley F. Gilbert Assos., Inc., Lowell, Mass., 1946—, partner in charge archtl. div., 1949-59, v.p., 1950-59, pres., 1959—; critic in archtl. design devel. Boston Archtl. Center Sch., 1947-59; v.p. Sch. Architecture, Boston Archtl. Center, 1973-77, pres., 1977—; vis. lectr. U. Mass. State Coll., Framingham, 1959—. Important works include schs. in, East Jaffrey, N.H., Springfield, Vt., Ayer, Mass., Attleboro, Mass., Portsmouth, N.H., Sterling (Mass.) High Sch, Brockton (Mass.) High Sch, Ayer (Mass.) Ednl. Park, Acton (Mass.) Ednl. Park; student Union, high rise dormitory Temple Isaiah, Lexington, Mass., Little Harbour Sch, Portsmouth, N.Y. Bd. dirs., exec. com. Human Services Corp., Lowell, Mass.; bd. dirs., steering com. Soc. for Energy Conservation in Architecture. Served with U.S. Coast and Geodetic Survey, 1942-43; Served with USAAF, 1943-44. Fellow Internat. Inst. Arts and Letters, Kreuzlingen, Switzerland, 1960. Mem. Boston, Mass. State assns. architects, AIA, Constrn. Specifications Inst., Internat. Inst. Fine Arts and Letters, Soc. Archtl. Historians, Architects-Engrs. Lodge. Jewish (v.p. temple 1966-68). Club: B'nai B'rith. Office: Perley F Gilbert Assos Inc Sun Bldg Lowell MA 01852 Home: 19 Hancock St Lexington MA 02173

GLASSMAN, IRVIN, engineering educator, consultant; b. Balt., Sept. 19, 1923; s. Abraham and Bessie (Snyder) G.; m. Beverly Wolfe, June 17, 1951; children: Shari Powell, Diane Geinger, Barbara Ann. B.E., Johns Hopkins U., 1943, D.Eng., 1950. Research asst. Manhattan Project, Columbia U., N.Y.C., 1943-46; mem. faculty Princeton (N.J.) U., 1950—, prof. mech. and aero. engring., 1964—; cons. to industry. Author: (with R.F. Sawyer) Performance of Chemical Propellants, 1971, Combustion, 1977; editor: 3 books Combustion; contbr.: articles to tech. jours. Combustion. Served with U.S. Army, 1944-46. NSF fellow, 1966-67. Mem. Combustion Inst. (Sir Alfred Edgerton Gold medal 1982), Am. Chem. Soc., AAUP, Tau Beta Pi. Patentee rocket propellants (2). Home: PO Box 14 Princeton NJ 08540 Office: Princeton U Princeton NJ 08544

GLASSMAN, JAMES KENNETH, magazine publisher; b. Washington, Jan. 1, 1947; s. Stanley and Elaine Ruth (Schiff) G.; m. Mary Claire Hanby, Aug. 16, 1969; children: Zoe Ann, Kate Julia. B.A., Harvard, 1969. Editor, pub. Provincetown (Mass.) Advocate, 1971-72; editor-in-chief, exec. pub. Figaro, New Orleans, 1972-78; exec. editor Washingtonian Mag., 1979-81; pub. New Republic, Washington, 1981—. Office: 1220 19th St NW Suite 200 Washington DC 20036 *

GLASSMEYER, EDWARD, investment banker; b. Jersey City, Sept. 14, 1915; s. Edward and Claire (Stuckert) G.; m. Elizabeth Fellows, Jan. 5, 1939 (dec. Sept. 1982); children: Marion Glassmeyer Treynor, Edward, Mary Glassmeyer Maloney, Edith Glassmeyer Mathews. B.A., Princeton U., 1936. Statistician, Blyth & Co., Inc., N.Y.C., 1936-47, syndicate mgr., 1947-50, v.p., 1950-62, dir., 1950-70, exec. com., 1960-70, sr. v.p., 1962-70; pres. Athens (Greece) Coll., 1970-73; chmn. bd. Inter-Am. Life Ins. Co. (subs. INA), Athens, 1973-76; ptnr. Grubb & Co., Atlanta; dir. By-Word Corp., Heizer Corp., Chgo., Genzyme Corp., Boston; mem. adv. council dept. classics Princeton U.; guest lectr. other colls. Trustee, v.p., past chmn. exec. com. Beekman Downtown Hosp., N.Y.C.; trustee Athens Coll., Near East Coll. Assn.; mem. Alumni Council, Princeton. Served with OSS, AUS, 1945-46; Ger. Fellow Am. Numis. Soc. (council); mem. Investment Bankers Assn. Am. (v.p., gov. 1958-60, chmn. N.Y. group 1959-60), Archeol. Inst. Am. (trustee, treas.). Republican. Presbyterian. Clubs: Bond (pres. 1966-67), Wee Burn Country, Princeton, Links (N.Y.C.); Reading Room (York Harbor, Maine); Royal Yacht of Greece, Propellor of United States in Greece (pres. 1974-75). Home: 6 Coves End Rd Darien CT 06820 Office: 310 Lexington Ave New York NY 10016

GLASSOCK, RICHARD JAMES, nephrologist; b. San Bernardino, Calif., Feb. 4, 1934; s. Richard James and Merne Rosaline (Wickham) G.; m. Jo-Anne Theresa Bourke, May 21, 1977; children by previous marriage—Ellen Virginia, Scott Laurence, Sharon Elde. B.S. in Pharmacy, U. Ariz., 1956; postgrad., Duke U., 1956-57; M.D., UCLA, 1960. Diplomate: Am. Bd. Internal Medicine. Intern UCLA Center for Health Scis., 1960-61, resident in internal medicine, 1961-63; jr. asso. medicine, coordinator USPHS transplantation and immunology Peter Bent Brigham Hosp., 1966-67; instr. medicine Harvard U., 1966-67; chief div. nephrology Harbor-UCLA Med. Center, 1967-80, chmn. dept. medicine, 1980—; asst. prof. medicine UCLA, 1967-71, asso. prof., 1971-75, prof., 1975—; cons. NIH, 1980—; chmn. sci. adv. bd. Nat. Kidney Found., 1977-78; cons. career devel. program VA; NIH mem. Pathology Study Sect. A; cardiovascular faculty Merck, Sharp & Dohme; lic. pharmacist, Calif. Author: (with S. Massry) Textbook of Nephrology, 1981, The Kidney, (edited by B. Brenner and F. Rector); contbr. numerous articles to profl. jours., chpts. in books. Served with USNR, 1951-61. USPHS fellow, 1963-65; NIH grantee, 1967-80; Am Heart Assn. grantee, 1967-69. Fellow A.C.P.; mem. AAAS, Am. Fedn. Clin. Research, Western Assn. Physicians, Australasian Soc. Nephrology (hon.), Soc. Clin. Trials, Inc., Am. Lupus Soc. (adv. bd.), Am. Soc. Artificial Internal Organs, Am. Assn. Pathology, Am. Soc. Nephrology (council), Internat. Soc. Nephrology (council, pres.-elect 1984), Transplant Soc., Western Soc. Clin. Investigation, Western Dialysis and Transplant Soc., West Coast Micro-circulatory Club, Los Angeles Soc. Internal Medicine, Los Angeles Transplant Soc., N.Y. Acad. Scis., Kidney Found. So. Calif., Alpha Omega Alpha, Rho Chi. Office: Harbor UCLA Medical Center 1000 W Carson St Torrance CA 90509

GLASSON, LLOYD, sculptor, educator; b. Chgo., Jan. 31, 1931; s. Albert and Fay (Bass) G.; m. Cathleen Rita Naso, May 13, 1968. Student, So. Ill. U., 1950-52; B.F.A., Sch. Art Inst. Chgo., 1957; M.F.A., Tulane U., 1959. Maniken sulptor Greneker Corp., N.Y.C., 1959-60; exhibits designer Neward Museum, 1961-62; prof. sculpture and drawing U. Hartford, (Conn.), 1964—; jewelry designer; co-founder, temporary chmn. Artists Tenants Assn., 1960—. Exhibited one-man shows, Trinity Coll., Hartford, 1977, Dorsky Gallery, N.Y.C., 1966, 74, group shows, U. N.H., Durham, 1976, John Slade Ely House, New Haven, 1975; represented in permanent collections, U. N.H., Karen Horney Inst., N.Y.C., Yale U., New Haven, Forma Viva, Kostanjevica, Yugoslavia, others. Served with U.S. Army, 1952-54. Recipient First prize Regional Exhbn. Delgado Mus., New Orleans, 1959, others. Mem. Nat. Acad. Design (assoc.), Sculptors Guild (v.p.). Home: Wilcox Hill Rd Portland CT 06480 Office: 200 Bloomfield Ave West Hartford CT 06117 Studio: 229 Grand St New York NY 10013

GLATFELTER, CHARLES HENRY, history educator; b. Glen Rock, Pa., May 11, 1924; m. Miriam G. Krebs, June 21, 1947; children: Christina E., Philip H. B.A., Gettysburg Coll., 1946; Ph.D., Johns Hopkins, 1952. Mem. faculty Gettysburg Coll., 1949—, dean coll., 1960-66, prof. history, 1963—, chmn. dept. history, 1969-74. Mem. Am., Pa. hist. assns., Adams County Hist. Soc. (pres. 1962-64, dir. 1964—), Phi Beta Kappa (sec. local chpt. 1955-73, pres. 1975-77), Phi Alpha Theta. Lutheran. Home: 36 Apple Ave Gettysburg PA 17325

GLATFELTER, PHILIP HENRY, III, pulp and paper executive; b. Spring Grove, Pa., Mar. 17, 1916; s. Philip H. and Cassandra (McClellan) G.; m. Anne C. Manifold, Nov. 15, 1940; children: Patricia Anne Glatfelter McQuaid, Elizabeth M. Glatfelter Kegler. A.B., Brown U., 1938; L.H.D. (hon.), York Coll., 1977. With P.H. Glatfelter Co., Spring Grove, 1938—, pres., 1954-80, chmn., 1980—; staff asst. W.P.B., 1941-42. Bd. dirs. York Welfare Fedn., 1952-54; past trustee U. Maine Pulp and Paper Found. Served with USNR, 1942-46. Mem. Inst. Paper Chemistry (trustee 1976-83), Printing Paper Mfrs. Assn. (chmn. 1961-62), Am. Paper Inst. (past dir.), Am. Forest Inst. (dir.), Nat. Council Air and Stream Improvement (dir.), Mfg. Assn. York (pres. 1954). Home: Hickory Hill Spring Grove PA 17362 Office: 228 S Main St Spring Grove PA 17362

GLAUBER, MICHAEL A., manufacturing company executive; b. East St. Louis, Ill., Mar. 10, 1943; s. Wilfred B. and Mary (Wakefield) G.; m. Mary Louse Barry, Aug. 28, 1964; children: Christine, Marcella. B.A. in acctg., St. Mary's U., San Antonio, 1965. C.P.A., Tex., 1967. Staff acct. Alexander Grant & Co., Dallas, 1966-69; controller Leggett & Platt, Carthage, Mo., 1969-76, treas., 1976-78, v.p. fin., treas., 1978—. Mem. Am. Inst. C.P.A.'s. Republican. Roman Catholic. Office: Leggett & Platt 1 Leggett Rd Carthage MO 64836

GLAUBMAN, MICHAEL JUDA, educator; b. Balt., Dec. 21, 1924; s. Mordecai Gimple and Rachel (Katz) G.; m. Hilda Marjorie Dunn, May 30, 1961; children—David Jacob, Judith Anne, Jane Marjorie, Sarah Susanna. M.S., Hebrew U., 1947; postgrad., U. Chgo., 1948; Ph.D., U. Ill., 1953. Research asst. Princeton, 1953-55, Columbia, 1955-56; sr. physicist Atomics Internat., Canoga Park, Calif., 1956-59; asst. prof. physics Northeastern U., Boston, 1959-61, asso. prof., 1961-69, prof., 1969—, chmn. dept., 1969-73. Mem. Am. Phys. Soc., AAAS. Home: 9 Blueberry Ln Lexington MA 02173 Office: Northeastern University Boston MA 02115

GLAVES, DONALD WILLIAM, lawyer; b. Chgo., Mar. 1, 1935. B.A., Ill. Coll., 1956; J.D., U. Chgo., 1962. Bar: Ill. bar 1962. Assoc. firm Ross & Hardies, O'Keefe, Babcock & Parsons, Chgo., 1962—; clk. to judge U.S. Ct. Appeals D.C. Circuit, 1963. Mem. Am. Law Inst., ABA. Office: One IBM Plaza Suite 3100 330 N Wabash Ave Chicago IL 60611

GLAVIANO, VINCENT VALENTINO, educator, physiologist; b. Frankford, N.Y., July 19, 1920; s. Salvatore and Josephine (Manzo) G.; m. Eleanor Spargimino, July 18, 1943; children: Joan J., Vincent S. B.S., CCNY, 1950; Ph.D., Columbia U., 1954; M.D., Chgo. Med. Sch., 1982. Faculty Columbia U., 1951-53; fellow Columbia, 1954-56; instr. Hunter Coll., N.Y.C., 1952-54; asst. prof. physiology U. Ill. Coll. Medicine, Chgo., 1956-60; asso. prof. physiology Loyola U. Sch. Medicine, Chgo., 1960-64, prof., 1964-70; prof., chmn. Chgo. Med. Sch., 1970—; cons. Cook County Hosp. Cardiopulmonary Lab., Abbot Labs.; cons./physicist in therapeutic radiobiology Hines (Ill.) VA Hosp. Editorial bd.: Circulatory Shock. Postdoctoral research fellow N.Y. Heart Assn., 1954-56; travel awards Nat. Acad. Scis., 1962, 65, 67, 77. Fellow AAAS, N.Y. Acad. Scis.; mem. Am. Physiol. Soc., Soc. Exptl. Biology and Medicine, Am., Chgo. heart assns., Harvey Soc., Am. Soc. Pharmacology and Exptl. therapeutics, Internat. Soc. Heart Research, Sigma Xi, Alpha Omega Alpha. Research and publs. on heart function in hypotension, role of cardiac neuro-hormones in states of stress, mechanism of tranquilizer drugs on central nervous system, metabolism of heart. Home: 517 Carlisle Ct Glen Ellyn IL 60137 Office: Chicago Med Sch U Health Scis 3333 Green Bay Rd North Chicago IL 60064 *The desire to explore the unknown becomes a successful adventure only when honesty, love of fellow human beings and country are used as ingredients.*

GLAVICKAS, JOSEPH ALBERT, financial services corporation executive; b. Worcester, Mass., Feb. 21, 1939; s. Joseph George and Anna Audrey (Stelmok) G. B.S. in Mgmt., Northeastern U., 1962, M.S. in Acctg., 1966. Acct. McGraw Hill Book Co., Hightstown, N.J., 1965-66; sr. asst. acct. Deloitte Haskins & Sells, Boston, 1967-69; dir., fund adminstr. Nel Equity Services Corp., Boston, 1969-72, v.p. ops., 1972—; treas. Nel & Loomis-Sayles Funds, Boston, 1972—; 2d v.p. New Eng. Mut. Life ins. Co., Boston, 1982—. Served to capt. U.S. Army, 1962-65. Office: Nel Equity Services Corp 500 Boylston St Boston MA 02117

GLAVIN, DENIS JOSEPH, union ofcl.; b. Dec. 25, 1926. Pipefitter Westinghouse Electric Corp., 1943-78; bus. rep. United Elec. Radio and Machine Workers of Am., 1967-78, pres., 1978—. Served with USN, 1944-46; PTO. Office: United Elec Radio and Machine Workers of Am 11 E 51st St New York NY 10022 *

GLAVIN, JAMES EDWARD, landscape architect; b. Syracuse, N.Y., Aug. 18, 1923; s. James Edward and Florence Ellen (Nelson) G.; m. Helen Catherine Hartnett, Aug. 24, 1946; children—Kathleen Glavin Kopitsky, Timothy, David, Matthew, Martin, Maureen. B.S. in Landscape Architecture, SUNY Coll. Environ. Sci. and Forestry, Syracuse, 1948. City planner Syracuse Planning Commn., 1948-49; chief land planning dept. Sargent Webster Crenshaw & Folley, Syracuse, 1951-56; partner Hueber Hares Glavin (architects, landscape architects, and engr., and predecessor), Syracuse, 1956—, James E. Glavin & Assos. (landscape architects), 1956—, Syracuse Scale Models, 1968—; vis. juror, lectr. State U. Coll. Environ. Sci. and Forestry, 1959, 65, 69, State U. Coll. Agr., Cornell U., 1970—; cons.

N.Y. State Council Arts, 1971. Contbr. articles to profl. publs.; contbg.; editor: Empire State Architect, 1957-60. Mem. Citizens Found., Syracuse, 1967—, St. Thomas More Found., 1965—. Served with AUS, 1942-46. Recipient Design award Am. Assn. Nurserymen, 1969, 71. Fellow Am. Soc. Landscape Architects (past co-chmn. pvt. practice com., Design award 1968, 71); mem. ASCE (past v.p. Syracuse chpt.). Home: 229 Robineau Rd Syracuse NY 13207 Office: 726 W Onondaga St Syracuse NY 13204

GLAZE, ROBERT PINCKNEY, university administrator; b. Birmingham, Ala., Apr 14, 1933; s. Andrew Lewis and Mildred (Ezell) G.; m. Barbara Catherine Malloy, Aug. 23, 1958; children: David, Jennifer. B.S., U. South, 1955; Ph.D., U. Rochester, N.Y., 1961; postgrad. fellow, Johns Hopkins U. Med. Sch., 1961-64. Asst. prof. biochemistry U. Ala., Birmingham, 1964-72, mem. adminstrv. staff, 1967—, dean adminstrn., 1976-77, v.p. research and grad. studies, 1977-81, acting v.p. instl. advancement, 1980-81, v.p. research and instl. advancement, 1981—; asst. dean Med. Coll. Ala. and Sch. Dentistry, 1967-69. Trustee Gorgas Scholarship Found., 1968; Bd. dirs. Camp Fire Inc., Birmingham, 1978-81, Children's Aid Soc., Birmingham, 1976-81, 83—; bd. dirs., v.p., mem. exec. com. Operation New Birmingham, 1981-83. Trainee USPHS, 1955-58; fellow, 1958-61, 62, 63-64; grantee NSF, 1966-68. Mem. AAAS, Am. Chem. Soc., Nat. Council U. Research Adminstrs., Soc. Research Adminstrs., Am. Inst. Chemists, So. Assn. Colls. and Schs. (cons. 1971—), Ala. Acad. Sci., N.Y. Acad. Scis., Birmingham Com. Fgn. Relations, Sigma Xi, Omega Delta Kappa. Home: 906 Sheridan Dr Birmingham AL 35213 Office: University Station Birmingham AL 35294

GLAZER, DAVID, clarinet soloist; b. Milw., May 7, 1913; s. Benjamin and Clara (Glass) G.; m. Mia Helen Deutsch, Feb. 16, 1959. B.E., Milw. State Tchrs. Coll., 1935; student, Berkshire Music Center, summers 1940-42. Bandleader, Plymouth (Wis.) High Sch., 1935-37; faculty Longy Music Sch., Cambridge, Mass., 1937-42; faculty Mannes Coll. Music, N.Y., N.Y. Coll. Music, 1967; faculty music dept. NYU, SUNY-Stony Brook; tchr. summer sessions U. Wis., Milw.; master class sessions Inst. for Advanced Mus. Studies, Montreux, Switzerland, 1974, music conservatories Peking and Shanghai, summer 1982; mem. jury Internat. Clarinet Competition, Munich, Germany, 1967, 73, 82, Que. Conservatory of Music, 1984. Chamber music concerts, mem., WPA Symphony; mem., Cleve. Symphony Orch., 1946-51, N.Y. Woodwind Quintet, 1951—; tour of S.Am. for, U.S. State Dept., 1956, 69; tour of Far East, U.S. State Dept., 1962; solo and chamber music concerts; appeared, Casals Festival, Prades, France, 1953, ann. European tours, 1953—; on tour with, Fine Arts String Quartet for Dept State, E. Asia, 1967; mem. jury clarinet competition, Eindhoven, Holland, 1978, Coleman chamber music competition, Pasadena, Calif., 1983; recordings, Vox Records including, Stamitz Concerto in B Flat, Brahms Sonatas, Brahms Clarinet Quintet with Hungarian Quartet (EMI), Beethoven and Brahms Trios, with Frank Glazer, David Soyer, other recordings, N.Y. Woodwind Quintet, Fine Arts Quartet. Served with AUS, 1942-46; with AAF Band, 1944-46; Bolling Field, Washington. Home: 25 Central Park W New York NY 10023

GLAZER, ESTHER, violinist; b. Chgo.; d. Louis and Sarah (Zeidman) G.; m. Irwin Hoffman, Feb. 20, 1946; children—Joel, Gary, Toby, Deborah. Grad. (fellow 1944-48), Juilliard Sch. Music, 1948. Mem. music faculty U. B.C., 1961-64; artist-in-residence U. Tampa, Fla., 1971—; vis. prof. violin U. Wis., Madison, 1980. Performed world premiers of new compositions, including 1st Chgo. performance of Schoenberg Violin Concerto.; concerts, U.S., Can., Europe, Israel, S. Am.; appeared with various orchs. including, Chgo. Symphony, Royal Philharmonic Orch., BBC Symphony. Recipient Naumburg music competition award, 1950. Debut as concert violinist at age 9, Chgo. Home: 1901 Brightwaters Blvd St Petersburg FL 33704

GLAZER, FREDERIC JAY, librarian; b. Portsmouth, Va., Feb. 20, 1937; s. Moses Herman and Charlotte Esther (Blachman) G.; m. Sylvia Katherine Lerner, Aug. 18, 1963; children—Hoyt Eric, Hilary Alison. B.A., Columbia U., 1954, M.S., 1964. Librarian Kirn Meml. Library, Norfolk, Va., 1964-67; dir. Chesapeake (Va.) Pub. Library, 1967-72; exec. sec.-dir. W.Va. Library Commn., Charleston, 1972—; cons. in field. Creator library six pack, library book bucks, instant carousel library, outpost library; contbr. articles to profl. jours.; commd. by ALA to write, produce and dir. media presentation commemorating 25th anniversary of fed. library services and constrn. act legislation. Vice pres. Tidwater Lit. Council, 1970-71; exec. dir. Va. Nat. Library Week, 1970, 71. Served with AUS, 1960-62. Recipient Presdl. certificate appreciation, 1968; spl. recognition Grolier Nat. Library Week, 1970; Gold award 15th Internat. TV and Film Festival, 1972; Region III Outstanding Citizen's award HEW, 1977; Dora R. Parks award W.Va. Library Assn., 1979. Mem. ALA (gen. chmn. membership com. 1974-77, councilor 1975-80). Home: 114 Sheridan Circle Charleston WV 25314 Office: Library Commn Science and Cultural Center Charleston WV 25305

GLAZER, LARRY SYLVESTER, financial executive; b. Ft. Worth, Sept. 30, 1939; s. Yale and Ida (Gilden) G.; m. Barbara Lynne Bomash, Oct. 7, 1961; children—Tracy Marie, William Frank, Courtney Suzanne. B.A. in History, U. Tex., 1961; M.B.A., Harvard, 1964. C.P.A., Tex. With Touche, Ross & Co., Houston, 1964-66; mgmt. cons. Booz, Allen and Hamilton, Dallas, 1966-69; pres. Nat. Pride Equipment, Inc., Livonia, Mich., 1969-70; v.p., treas., dir. DuPont-Glore Forgan, Inc., N.Y.C., 1971-76; chief fin. officer Glazer's Wholesale Drug Co., Dallas, 1976-79; pres. Fin. Cons.'s, Inc., Dallas, 1979—; ptnr. Railhead Energy, Dallas, 1981—. Served to 2d lt. AUS, 1961-62. Mem. Am. Inst. C.P.A.'s, Tex. Soc. C.P.A.'s, Sigma Alpha Mu. Jewish. Home: 6725 Caulfield Dr Dallas TX 75248 Office: PO Box 400845 Dallas TX 75240

GLAZER, NATHAN, educator, sociologist; b. N.Y.C., Feb. 25, 1923; s. Louis and Tillie (Zacharevich) G.; m. Ruth Slotkin, Sept. 26, 1943 (div. 1958); children: Sarah, Sophie, Elizabeth; m. Sulochana Raghavan, Oct. 4, 1962. B.S.S., CCNY, 1944; M.A., U. Pa., 1944; Ph.D., Columbia U., 1962; LL.D., Franklin and Marshall Coll., 1971, Colby Coll., 1972; D.H.L. (hon.); L.I. U., 1978. Mem. editorial staff Commentary mag., 1945-53, Doubleday-Anchor Books, 1954-55; Walgreen lectr. U. Chgo., 1955; mem. staff Communism in Am. Life project Fund for Republic, 1956-57; vis. lectr U. Calif.-Berkeley, 1957-58; instr. Bennington Coll., 1958-59; vis. assoc. prof. Smith Coll., 1959-60; fellow Joint Center Urban Studies, Harvard-Mass. Inst. Tech., 1960-61; study and travel in, Japan, 1961-62; urban sociologist HHFA, Washington, 1962-63; prof. sociology U. Calif.-Berkeley, 1963-69; vis. prof. Grad. Sch. Edn., Harvard U., 1968-69, prof. edn. and social structure, 1969—. Author: (with D. Riesman and R. Denney) The Lonely Crowd, 1950, (with D. Riesman) Faces in the Crowd, 1952, American Judaism, 1957, 2d edit., 1972, The Social Basis of American Communism, 1961, (with D. P. Moynihan) Beyond the Melting Pot, 1963, 2d edit., 1970 (Anisfield-Wolf award Sat. Rev. 1964), Remembering the Answers, 1970, Affirmative Discrimination, 1976, Ethnic Dilemmas, 1983; Co-editor: The Public Interest mag, 1973—. Guggenheim fellow, 1954, 66. Mem. Am. Acad. Arts and Scis., Nat. Acad. Edn., U.S. Bd. Fgn. Scholarships. Office: Grad Sch Edn Harvard U Cambridge MA 02138

GLAZIER, LOUIS, business executive; b. Detroit, Aug. 2, 1949; s. Maurice G. and Bessie (Faxstein) Galzier; m. Paula Sharon Lazarus, Oct. 16, 1971; children: Ilana, Mindy. B.S., Wayne State U., 1972; J.D., U. Detroit, 1977. Bar: Mich. 1973; C.P.A., Mich. Acct. Southfield, Mich., 1972-75; v.p. fin. Frederick & Herrud, Inc., Southfield, 1975—. Mem. ABA, State Bar Mich., Mich. Assn. C.P.A.'s (William A. Paton award 1972). Office: Frederick & Herrad Inc 18700 W 10 Mile Rd Southfield MI 48075

GLAZIER, ROBERT CARL, publishing executive; b. Brandsville, Mo., Mar. 26, 1927; s. Vernie A. and Mildred F. (Beu) G.; m. Harriette Hubbard, June 5, 1949; children: Gregory Kent, Jeffrey Robert. Student, Drury Coll., 1944-46; B.A., U. Wichita, 1949. Reporter Springfield (Mo.) Daily News, 1944-46; asst. city editor Wichita Eagle, 1946-49; journalism instr. U. Wichita, 1949-53; dir. pub. relations Springfield (Mo.) Pub. Schs., 1953-59; asso. dir. dept. radio and TV The Methodist Ch., Nashville, 1959-61; gen. mgr. WDCN-TV (Channel 2), Nashville, 1961-65, KETC (Channel 9), St. Louis, 1965-76; also exec. dir. St. Louis Ednl. TV Commn.; pres. So. Ednl. Communications Assn., 1976-80, Springfield Communications, Inc., Mo., 1980—. Bd. dirs. Adult Edn. Council Greater St. Louis, 1965-76. Served with AUS, 1945-46. Mem. Nat. Sch. Public Relations Assn. (past regional dir.), Nat. Acad. TV Arts and Scis. (gov.), Mo. Instructional TV Council, Ill. Instructional TV Commn., Nat. Assn. Ednl. Broadcasters. Methodist. Club: Rotary Internat. Home: 2305 E Meadow St Springfield MO 65804 Office: 1350 S Glenstone Springfield MO 65804

GLEASON, ANDREW MATTEI, educator; b. Fresno, Calif., Nov. 4, 1921; s. Henry Allan and Eleanor Theodalinda (Mattei) G.; m. Jean Berko, Jan. 26, 1959; children—Katherine Anne, Pamela, Cynthia. B.S., Yale, 1942; jr. fellow, Soc. Fellows, Harvard, 1946-50, M.A. (hon.), 1953. Asst. prof. math. Harvard, 1950-53, asso. prof., 1953-57, prof., 1957—, Hollis prof. math. and natural philosophy, 1969—. Author: Fundamentals of Abstract Analysis, 1966. Served from ensign to lt. (s.g.) USNR, 1942-46; lt. comdr., 1950-52. Recipient Newcomb Cleveland prize AAAS, 1952. Mem. Am. Math. Soc. (pres. 1981-82), Math. Assn. Am., Am. Philos. Soc., Societe Mathematique de France, Am. Acad. Arts and Scis., Nat. Acad. Scis. Club: Cosmos (Washington). Home: 110 Larchwood Dr Cambridge MA 02138

GLEASON, ELIZA ATKINS, librarian, educator; b. Winston Salem, N.C., Dec. 15, 1909; d. Simon Green and Oleona (Pegram) Atkins; m. Maurice F. Gleason, Nov. 5, 1937; 1 dau., Joy Patricia. A.B., Fisk U., 1930; B.S., U. Ill., 1931; M.A., U. Calif. at Berkeley, 1936; Ph.D., U. Chgo., 1940. Asst. librarian Louisville Municipal Coll., 1931-32, librarian, 1932-36; head reference dept., asst. prof. Fisk U. Library, 1936-37; dir. libraries Talladega Coll., 1940-46; prof., dean Sch. Library Service Atlanta U., 1941-46; guest lectr. Grad. Library Sch., U. Chgo., 1953; head reference dept. Wilson Jr. Coll. Library, Chgo., 1953-54; asso. prof., head reference dept. Chgo. Tchrs. Coll. Library, 1954-63; asso. prof. library sci. Ill. Tchrs. Coll. Chgo. South, 1964-67; asst. librarian John Crerar Library; prof. library sci. Ill. Inst. Tech., 1967-70; asst. chief librarian charge regional centers Chgo. Pub. Library, 1970-73; prof. library sci. No. Ill. U., DeKalb, 1974-75. Author: History of the Fisk University Library, 1936, The Southern Negro and the Public Library, 1941, also articles. Exec. dir. Chgo. Black United Fund, 1978-79; Mem. Hyde Park Kenwood Community Conf., 1950—, S.E. Chgo. Commn., 1952—, Ind. Voters Ill., 1952—; exec. com. Fisk U. Alumni Assn., 1969—; co-chmn. Fisk U. Centennial campaign, 1963-65; bd. dirs. Chgo. Public Library, 1978-79; mem. women's aux. Cook County Physicians Assn., 1940—; women's aux. Meharry Med. Coll. Alumni Assn., 1940—, Internat. Coll. Surgeons. Recipient Alumni award Fisk U., 1964. Mem. A.L.A. (council 1942-46, fellow 1938-40), A.A.U.P., Phi Beta Kappa. Home: 5000 East End Apt 25D Chicago IL 60615

GLEASON, FRANCIS JOSEPH, pharmaceutical company executive; b. Bklyn., Jan. 15, 1921; s. Benedict and Mary (Skelly) G.; m. Patricia Ann Hooks, Apr. 26, 1947; children: Owen, Mary, Mark, Hugh, Angela, Nora. B.S., Fordham U., 1943; M.B.A, Harvard, 1947. With Schering-Plough Corp., 1947—, v.p. internat. ops., 1965, sr. v.p. charge, 1970—; pres. Schering Corp., 1973—; exec. v.p. Schering-Plough Corp., 1975—, also dir. Bd. dirs. Am. Found. Pharm. Edn., Caldwell Coll., Montclair Art Mus.; trustee Schering Found., N.J. Coll. Fund Assn.; mem. council Fordham U. Served to lt. USNR, 1943-46. Clubs: University, Montclair Golf. Home: 25 Ramsay Rd Montclair NJ 07042 Office: Schering-Plough Corp Galloping Hill Rd Kenilworth NJ 07033

GLEASON, JACKIE, actor; b. Bklyn., Feb. 26, 1916; m. Genevieve Halford, 1936 (div. 1971); children: Geraldine, Linda; m. Beverly McKittrick, July 4, 1971 (div. 1974); m. Marylin Taylor. Appeared in: Follow the Girls on Broadway, 1945; TV series Life of Riley, 1949-50, Cavalcade of Stars, 1950-52, The Honeymooners, 1955-56; then in: Jackie Gleason Show, 1952-55, 57-59, 66-70, star, writer; condr. mus. score The Million Dollar Incident; 38 recorded albums with, Jackie Gleason Orch.; motion pictures include Navy Blues, 1941, Springtime in the Rockies, 1942, The Desert Hawk, 1950, The Hustler, 1961, Gigot, 1962, Requiem for a Heavyweight, 1962, Soldier in the Rain, 1963, The Time of Your Life, Papa's Delicate Condition, 1963, Skidoo, 1968, How to Commit a Marriage, 1969, Don't Drink the Water, 1969, How Do I Love Thee?, 1970, Smokey and the Bandit, 1977, Smokey and the Bandit II, 1980, The Toy, 1982, Sting II, 1983; appeared on stage in Sly Fox, 1978 (Recipient Antoinette Perry award best Broadway actor in Take Me Along 1959). Office: care Publicity Universal Pictures 445 Park Ave New York NY 10022 *

GLEASON, JAMES ARTHUR, lawyer; b. Cleve., Feb. 20, 1905; s. M. James and Mary A. (O'Hare) G.; m. Helen Mary Nightingale, Feb. 8, 1936 (dec. Apr. 1957); 1 son, Michael Robert; m. Elinor Ferguson, June 6, 1959 (dec. Nov. 1975); stepchildren: Sandra (Mrs. Ed Harris), Barbara (Mrs. Lawrence C. Phillips), Jeannie E. (Mrs. Jeffrey Hutzler); m. Anita Wilker, Apr. 9, 1977. A.B., Georgetown U., 1928; J.D., Case-Western Res. U., 1931. Bar: Ohio 1932. Practiced in Cleve., specializing in probate, tax, corp. real estate, and ins. law, 1932-41, 46—; dir. Automatic Auto-Park, Inc., N.Y.C.; Bd. govs. Georgetown U., Washington, 1950—, mem. senate, 1953—; Pres. and comdg. brig. gen. emeritus Cleveland Grays, 1960-70; adv. bd. Marycrest Sch., Independence, Ohio, 1950—. Entered USAAF, 1941; assigned Judge Adv.'s Dept. Hdqrs. 2d Air Force, 1943; Colorado Springs, Colo.; in charge Kornberg jewel cases; trial judge adv. Watson Q.M.C. case, 1946; col. JAG Corps Res. Decorated Bronze Star. Mem. ABA (state chmn. jr. bar conf. 1937-38, council mem. 6th dist. 1939-40, ho. dels. 1943—, mem. standing com. on lawyers in armed forces 1974—, chmn. 1974-76), Bar Assn. Greater Cleve. (Golden Card mem.), Ohio State Bar Assn. (del. Internat. Bar Conf., Madrid 1952, gen. chmn. 86th ann. conv. com. 1966, council of dels. 1980-84), Internat. Bar Assn. (del. conv. 1966), Inter-Am. Bar Assn., Fed. Bar Assn. (pres. Cleve. chpt. 1961-62), Judge Advs. Assn. (dir. 1972-82), Am. Soc. Internat. Law, Mil. Order World Wars (comdr. Cleve. 1961-62, dir. 1970—), Am. Legion (comdr. Shaker Heights post 1963-64), VFW (judge adv. post 937 1975—), Res. Officers Assn., Assn. U.S. Army. Roman Catholic. Clubs: University (Washington); Grays, University, Georgetown, Cleve. Skating, Union (Cleve.); Shaker Heights Country. Home: 13605 Shaker Blvd Apt 2A Cleveland OH 44120 also Suite 5 172 N County Rd PO Box 564 Palm Beach FL 33480 Office: 505 Park Bldg 140 Public Sq Cleveland OH 44114

GLEASON, JAMES S., machinery parts manufacturing company executive; b. 1934. A.B., Princeton U., 1955; M.B.A., U. Rochester, 1973. With The Gleason Works, Rochester, N.Y., 1959—, mfg. specialist, 1962-64, supr. systems and procedures, 1964-67, asst. sec., asst. treas., 1967-73, v.p., treas., 1973-79, v.p. fin., treas., Rochester, N.Y., 1979-80, pres., 1980—, chief operating officer, 1980-81, chief exec. officer, 1981—, dir. Served with U.S. Army, 1956-59. Office: The Gleason Works 1000-1044 University Ave Box 22970 Rochester NY 14692 *

GLEASON, JEAN BERKO, psychology educator, linguistics researcher; b. Cleve., Dec. 19, 1931; d. Arthur E. and Alice (Gelbberger) Berko; m. Andrew Mattei Gleason, Jan. 26, 1959; children: Katherine, Pamela, Cynthia. A.B., Radcliffe Coll., 1953, A.M., 1955, Ph.D., 1958. USPHS fellow Mass. Inst. Tech., 1958-59; research asso. VA Hosp., Boston, 1961—; research asso. edn. Harvard, 1968-70; prin. research assoc. psychiatry Harvard U., 1970-72; vis. asst. prof. psychology Boston U., 1972-73, assoc. prof., 1973-76, dir. grad. program developmental psychology, 1975-78, 82—, prof., 1976—; research scholar in residence Inst. Linguistics, Hungarian Acad. Scis., 1981; Mem. mental retardation research com. Nat. Inst. Child Health and Human Devel., 1981—. Mem. editorial bd.: Child Devel, 1971-77; asso. editor Jour. Speech and Hearing Research, 1972-73; contbr. articles to profl. jours. Recipient Editors award Jour. Speech and Hearing Research, 1970; NSF grantee; 956-80. Fellow Am. Psychol. Assn., AAAS; mem. New Eng. Psychol. Assn., Linguistic Soc. Am. (chmn. program com. 1980-81), Radcliffe Grad. Soc. (past pres.), Radcliffe Alumni Assn. (dir. 1969-72), Acad. Aphasia, Soc. for Research in Child Devel., Internat. Neuropsychol. Soc., New Eng. Child Lang. Assn., Gypsy Lore Soc. (exec. bd. 1983—), ACLU, Phi Beta Kappa (pres. Radcliffe chpt. 1965-68). Home: 110 Larchwood Dr Cambridge MA 02138 Office: Dept Psychology Boston University 64 Cummington St Boston MA 02215

GLEASON, JOHN JAMES, theatrical lighting designer; b. Bklyn., Apr. 10, 1941; s. John James and Sue (Manzolillo) G. B.A., Hunter Coll., 1963. Theatre design cons. Mummer Theatre, Oklahoma City, 1968-71, NTID, Rochester, N.Y., 1968-72, Repertory Theatre of Lincoln Ctr., N.Y.C., 1972, NYU, 1983; master tchr. design Tisch Sch. of the Arts NYU, 1972. Lighting designer: The Great White Hope, 1968, Over Here, 1974, My Fair Lady, 1976, The Royal Family, 1976, Der Rosenkavalier, Dallas Opera, 1982; Black Angel Off Broadway, 1982; The Survivor, Broadway, 1981, The Philadelphia Story, Lincoln Ctr. Theatre Co., Madame Butterfly, Dallas Opera. Recipient Annual Theatre Design award Maharam Found., N.Y.C., 1972-73, Drama Critics Circle award Los Angeles, 1975. Home: 170 W 73rd St NY 10023 Office: Dept Design NYU Tisch Sch of Arts 725 Broadway New York NY 10003

GLEASON, JOHN MARTIN, community development consultant; b. N.Y.C., May 10, 1907; s. James S. and Letitia (Haydock) G.; m. Margaret Nicholson, Oct. 15, 1929; children: Nancy (Mrs. Nancy G. Scrantom), John Martin. Student, Columbia, 1927, N.E. Traffic Officers Tng. Sch., Harvard U., 1936, Northwestern Traffic Safety Inst., 1936, Northwestern Exec. Officers Tng. Sch., 1938-41, Rutgers U., 1940, Yale, 1941, 43; grad., FBI Nat. Acad., 1944. Cadet engr. Conn. Light & Power Co., 1927-30; with Greenwich (Conn.) Police Dept., 1930-56, beginning as patrolman, successively detective, sgt., lt., capt., chief of police, 1930-54, town chief adminstrv. officer, 1954-56; nat. dir. Boys' Clubs of Am., 1956-69, now mem. bd. dirs.; coordinator community devel., Greenwich, 1969-71; instr. FBI Acad., Washington, 1945-55; guest lectr. Northeastern U., Northwestern U., Yale, Columbia; mem. adv. com. N.Y. U. Grad. Sch. Pub. Adminstrn.; Chmn. state and local ofcls. Nat. Hwy. Safety Commn.; pub. safety specialist U.S. Army in, Germany, 1949, Office U.S. High Commr. for, Office Polit. Affairs, 1951; mem. Atty. Gen.'s Conf. Organized Crime, Washington; staff Pres.'s Hwy. Safety Conf.; gen. chmn. traffic sect., mem. exec. com. Nat. Safety Council, Chgo.; police cons. U.S. Office Civil Def.; nat. com. Uniform Traffic Laws and Ordnances, 1947—. Mem. Citizens Adv. Com. on Fitness Am. Youth.; rep. non-govtl. orgn. UN, for Boys' Clubs of Am.; bd. dirs. ARC, Conn. Assn. Mental Health, Community Chest; pres. Greenwich Safety Council, 1965-70; mem. Pres.'s Task Force on Crime and Law Enforcement, 1969—. Recipient spl. honor diploma Cuban Soc. Police Sci. and Criminalistics, 1949; diploma of honor Bd. Traffic Control, Fed. Republic Germany, 1952. Mem. Internat. Assn. Chiefs Police (pres. 1950, life mem. exec. com.), N.E. Chiefs Police Assn. (dir.), Internat. Assn. Identification, Conn. Police Assn. (life mem.), Nat. Safety Council, Greenwich Safety Council (pres.), Detective Endowment Assn., Nat. Law Enforcement Assns., Greenwich Taxpayers Assn., Jr. C. of C., Nat. Inst. Social Sci. N.Y.C., Nat. Assn. Realtors, Conn. Assn. Realtors, Greenwich bds. realtors. Clubs: K.C., Kiwanis, Boat and Yacht, Rotary (hon.), Kiwanis (Greenwich) (hon.); Union League (N.Y.C.); Harpoon, The 13 (pres.). Home: 2 Putnam Hill Greenwich CT 06830

GLEASON, RALPH NEWTON, econ. devel. cons.; b. Townville, S.C., Jan. 5, 1922; s. Arthur Bryan and Clara Belle (McAdams) G.; m. Marjorie Nelle Little, Apr. 4, 1942; children—Ralph Newton Jr., Delno Rex, Charles Stanley, Edward Dean, Cindy Ann. B.S. with honors, Clemson Coll., 1942; certificate, Internat. Corr. Schs., 1957, U.S. Dept. Agr. Grad. Sch., 1957; M.S., Ohio State U., 1963. Statis. adviser to South Korean interim govt., 1947-48; food and econ. adviser ECA, Seoul, Korea, 1949-50; chief food and fertilizer div. Sino-Am. Joint Commn. Rural Reconstrn., Taipei, Taiwan, 1950-56; agrl. programs officer Near East South Asia FOA, Washington, 1957-58; dep. chief agriculturist Tech. Cooperation Mission to India, New Delhi, 1958-62; chief food and agr. div. Econ. Mission to Turkey, 1963-68; dep. dir. Agr. and Rural Devel. Service Office War on Hunger, Washington, 1968-70; dep. asso. dir. food and agr. AID, South Vietnam, 1970-75; econ. devel. cons., 1975—. Mem. dels. UN Food and Agr. Agy. Confs.; Bd. dirs., treas. Taipei Am. Sch., 1950-56; bd. dirs. Ponderosa Parks-Lake Hartwell, 1974—; v.p. Tranpac Enterprises, Inc., 1975—. Served to maj. AUS, 1942-47; ETO, Korea. Decorated Silver Star, Bronze Star. Mem. Am. Fgn. Service Assn., Farm Bur. Fedn., Blue Ridge Rural Electric Co-op, Phi Kappa Phi, Alpha Zeta. Clubs: Elk, Mason. Home: 504 Blvd Anderson SC 29621 Office: 17481 Newhope Fountain Valley CA 92708

GLEASON, ROBERT REILLY, JR., government official; b. Jersey City, N.J., Mar. 26, 1947; s. Robert R. and Anne Elizabeth (Paul) G.; m. Barbara Chiasson, July 1, 1977; 1 dau., Kathleen Clinton. B.S., Tri-State Coll., 1969. Internal auditor Kay Jewelry Stores, Inc., Washington, 1970-71; asst. to exec. dir. Nat. Assn. Trade and Tech. Schs., Washington, 1971-76; exec. asst. to co-chmn. Republican Nat. Com., Washington, 1976-77; polit. cons., 1977-81; spl. asst. for internat. affairs Pres. of U.S., White House, 1981—; dir. transp. 1980 Republican Nat. Conv., Detroit; event corrdinator Election Night Watch, Republican Nat. Com., 1980; dir. concert com. 1981 Inaugural Com. Co-chmn. D.C. Young Republicans, 1973-74; mem. D.C. Republican Central Com., 1974—, sec., 1976-78; alt. del. 1976 Republican Nat. Conv.; alt. Republican nat. committeman for D.C., 1980—. Named Best Editorial Writer Ind. Collegiate Press Assn., 1969. Mem. Washington Soc. Assn. Execs. Roman Catholic. Club: The Capitol Hill. Home: 18 14th St SE Washington DC 20003 Office: The White House Washington DC 20500

GLEASON, THOMAS, labor union official; b. N.Y.C., Nov. 8, 1900. LL.D. (hon.), Molloy Coll., Rockville Centre, N.Y., 1980. Dockworker, longshoreman, N.Y.C., from 1915; later dock supt.; bus. agt., pres. Local 1, Internat. Longshoremen's Assn., organizer, 1947-51, exec. v.p., chief negotiator with waterfront employees, 1951-63; pres. Internat. Longshoremen's Assn., 1963—; v.p. Maritime Trades Dept., AFL-CIO, 1965—; v.p., mem. gen. council Internat. Trade Workers Fedn., 1965—; v.p. AFL-CIO, 1969—, chmn. internat. affairs com., 1983; Mem. N.Y.C. Council on Port Devel. and Promotion. V.p. Irish Inst. N.Y.; pres. Pres. Reagan's Maritime Adv. Com.; also del. numerous confs. Recipient citations Am. Legion, VFW, 52 Assn., Cath. War Vets., Jewish War Vets. Mem. Friendly Sons St. Patrick, Ancient Order Hibernians, Irish-Am. Hist. Soc. Office: Internat Longshoremen's Assn AFL-CIO 17 Battery Pl New York NY 10004 *

GLEASON, THOMAS DAUES, shoe company executive; b. St. Louis, Jan. 24, 1936; s. Thomas J. and Hermine (Daues) G.; m. Sarah M. Santen, Feb. 6, 1960; children: Margaret E., Thomas Daues, J. Andrew, Anthony L. A.B., Holy Cross Coll., 1957; M.B.A., Harvard U., 1959. Co-founder, pres. Talent Assistance Program, Chgo., 1968-70; v.p. Wolverine World Wide, Inc., Rockford, Mich., 1970-72, pres., 1972—, chief exec. officer, 1972—, chmn., 1980—. Bd. dirs. Grand Rapids Symphony Soc., 1974—. Mem. Am. Footwear Industries Assn. (dir. 1973—), Harvard Bus. Sch. Assn. Chgo. (past v.p.). Clubs: Kent Country (Grand Rapids); Univ. (Chgo.). Office: Wolverine World Wide Inc 9341 Courtland Dr Rockford MI 49351 *

GLEAZER, EDMUND JOHN, JR., educator; b. Phila., Aug. 24, 1916; s. Edmund John and Jane Hunter (Laurie) G.; m. Charlene A. Allen, Apr. 14, 1940; children—Allen, Sandra Jo, John, Susan. A.A., Graceland Coll., 1936; A.B., U. Cal. at Los Angeles, 1938; Ed.M., Temple U., 1943; Ed.D., Harvard, 1953. Minister Reorganized Ch. of Jesus Christ of Latter Day Saints, Phila., 1938-43, pres., 1943-46, Graceland Coll., Lamoni, Ia., 1946- 57; exec. dir. Am. Assn. Jr. Colls., Washington, 1958-81; vis. prof. George Washington U., Washington, 1981—; Mem. U.S. Tech. Edn. Del. to USSR, 1961, 76; edn. survey team AID, Kenya, 1962; chmn. Def. Adv. Com. on Edn. in Armed Forces, 1962; mem. vis. com. Stanford U., Sch. Edn., 1962; mem. Pres.'s Commn. on Fgn. Lang. and Internat. Studies, 1979; v.p. for N. Am., Internat. Council for Adult Edn., 1979. Author: This is The Community College, 1968, Project Focus: A Forecast Study of Community Colleges, 1974, The Community College: Values, Vision and Vitality, 1980; Editor: American Junior Colleges, 1960, 63, 67, 71. Mem. North Central Jr. Colls. (pres. council 1954), Am. Assn. Jr. Colls. (pres. 1957), Am. Council on Edn. (sec., award for outstanding lifetime contbns. to Am. higher edn. 1980), Phi Delta Kappa. Clubs: Harvard, Rotary, Cosmos (Washington). Home: 8208 Woodhaven Blvd Bethesda MD 20817 Office: Dept Edn George Washington U Washington DC 20052

GLECKNER, ROBERT FRANCIS, educator; b. Rahway, N.J., Mar. 2, 1925; s. Adam F. and Frieda A. (Froehlich) G.; m. Glenda J. Karr, Feb. 7, 1946; children—Jeffrey M., Susan F. Jr. B.A., Williams Coll., 1948; Ph.D., Johns Hopkins, 1954. Instr. English Johns Hopkins, 1949-51; editor Research Studies Inst., Maxwell AFB, Ala., 1951-52; instr. English U. Cin., 1952-54, U. Wis., 1954-57; asst., then asso. prof. Wayne State U., Detroit, 1957-62; prof. English U. Calif. at Riverside, 1962-78, chmn. dept., 1962-66, lectr. extension div., 1962-64, 74, divisional dean humanities, 1968-70; dean Coll. Humanities, 1970-75, faculty research lectr., 1973; prof. English Duke U., Durham, N.C., 1978—; main speaker U. Calif. at Los Angeles; extension conf. humanities, Lake Arrowhead, Calif., 1964, U. Calif., Berkeley, 1976; lectr. Am. Blake Found., 1981, U. Tulsa, U. Tex., U. Wash., U. Calif., Berkeley, U. Pa., U. N.Mex., Memphis State U., La. State U., Skidmore Coll.; manuscript reader jours., univ. presses; del. Am. Assn. Higher Edn. meeting, 1963, 69, 72; cons. Nat. Endowment for Humanities, 1975-77. Author: The Piper and the Bard: A Study of William Blake, 1959, Byron and the Ruins of Paradise, 2d edit, 1980; Editor: (with G.E. Enscoe) Romanticism: Points of View, 1962, rev. edit. (sole editor), 1970, 75, Selected Writings of William Blake, 1967, rev. edit., 1971, The Complete Poetical Works of Lord Byron, 1975; Contbr.: A James Joyce Miscellany, 3d Series, 1962, A Blake Bibliography, 1964; also contbr.: Twelve and a Tilly: Essays on the 25th Anniversary of Finnegans Wake, 1966, William Blake: Essays for S. Foster Damon, 1969, A Concordance to the Writings of William Blake, 1967, Earl R. Wasserman Memorial Volume of ELH, 1975, Blake and the Moderns, 1981; mem. editorial bd., Wayne State U. Press, 1960-62; asso. editor: Criticism: A Jour. for Lit. and the Arts, 1960-62; adv. bd., 1962-76; adv. editor: Blake Studies, 1968—; mem. adv. bd.: Studies in Romanticism, 1977—; mem. editorial bd.: Romanticism Past and Present, 1979—; contbr. articles to profl. jours., chpts. to books. Mem. adv. bd. dirs. Am. Blake Found., 1970—. Served to 1st lt. USAAF, 1943-45. Recipient Poetry Soc. Am. award, 1959; Faculty Research Lectr. award U. Calif., at Riverside, 1973; Nat. Endowment for Humanities summer grantee, 1978; Am. Council Learned Socs. grantee, 1978-79; Nat. Endowment for Humanities sr. research fellow, 1980-81. Mem. Am. Com. Byron Soc. (charter), MLA, Phi Beta Kappa, Beta Theta Pi. Episcopalian. Home: Hickory Grove Rd Route 6 Box 353 Raleigh NC 27612 Office: English Dept Duke Univ Durham NC 27706

GLEESON, MARTIN A., mayor; b. London, Ont., Can., Oct. 3, 1932; s. Patrick J. and Elizabeth M. (Ryan) G.; m., Dec. 27, 1958; children: Paul, Michael, Brian. B.A., U. Western Ont., 1957; M.B.A., McMaster U., 1971. Tchr., London, Ont., 1965-69; instr. Fanshawe Coll., london, 1969-79; mayor City of London, 1979—. Roman Catholic. Home: 3 Novello Ct London ON Canada N6J 3B1 Office: City of London 300 Dufferin Ave London ON Canada N6A 4L9

GLEICH, GERALD JOSEPH, medical scientist; b. Escanaba, Mich., May 14, 1931; s. Gordon Joseph and Agnes (Ederer) G.; m. Elizabeth Louise Hearn, Aug. 16, 1955 (div. 1976); children: Elizabeth Genevieve, Martin Christopher, Julia Katherine; m. Kristin Marie Leiferman, Sept. 26, 1976; children: Steven Joseph, David Francis. B.A., U. Mich., 1953, M.D., 1956. Diplomate: Am. Bd. Internal Medicine. Intern Phila. Gen. Hosp., 1956-57; resident Jackson Meml. Hosp., Miami, Fla., 1959-61; instr. in medicine and microbiology U. Rochester, N.Y., 1961-65; cons. in medicine, prof. immunology and medicine Mayo Clinic-Med. Sch., Rochester, Minn., 1965—; chmn. dept. immunology Mayo Clinic, Rochester, Minn., 1982—; mem. bd. sci. counselors Nat. Inst. Allergy and Infectious Disease, 1981-83; chmn. subcom. on standardization allergens WHO, Geneva, 1974-75; lectr. Am. Acad. Allergy, 1976, 82. Contbr. articles to profl. jours. Served to capt. USAF, 1957-59. Grantee Nat. Inst. Allergy and Infectious Disease, 1970-83. Fellow ACP, Am. Acad. Allergy and Immunology; mem. Am. Soc. Clin. Investigation, Am. Assn. Immunologists, Assn. Am. Physicians, Phi Beta Kappa, Phi Kappa Phi, Alpha Omega Alpha. Roman Catholic. Home: 799 SW 3d St Rochester MN 55902 Office: Mayo Clinic Mayo Found 200 1st St SW Rochester MN 55905

GLEISSER, MARCUS DAVID, author, lawyer, journalist; b. Buenos Aires, Argentina, Feb. 14, 1923; s. Ben and Riva (Kogan) G.; m. Helga Marianne Rothschild, Oct. 23, 1955; children: Brian Saul, Julia Lynne, Hannah Tanya, Ellyn Ruth. B.A. in Journalism, Case Western Res. U., 1945, M.A. in Econs., 1949; J.D., Cleve. State U., 1958. Bar: Ohio 1958, U.S. Supreme Ct. 1962. Police reporter Cleve. Press, 1942-44, copy editor, 1944-47; advt. copy writer McDonough-Lewy, Inc., 1947-50; copy editor Cleve. Plain Dealer, 1950-52, gen. assignment reporter, 1952-57, courthouse reporter, 1957-63, real estate editor, 1963-81, fin. writer, 1981—. Author: The World of Cyrus Eaton, 1965, Juries and Justice, 1968; also articles.; editor-in-chief: Cleve.-Marshall Law Rev., 1956, 57. Trustee Cleve. Coll. Alumni Assn., 1968, Euclid Mayor's Exec. Council, 1973-76, Euclid Charter Commn., 1975-76. Recipient Nat. Bronze medal Am. Newspapers Pubs. Assn., 1944; Nat. Silver Gavel award ABA, 1958; Bronze medal Nat. Legal Aid and Defender Assn., 1963; Loeb award for disting. bus. and fin. writing U. Conn., 1966; cert. of recognition NCCJ, 1967; Silver Medal award consistently outstanding spl. feature columns Nat. Headliners Club, 1969; award Ohio Bar Assn., 1957, 58, 59, 60, 61, 62; award pub. service Cleve. Newspaper Guild, 1959; award for best column Cleve. Newspaper Guild, 1976, Nat. Assn. Real Estate Editors, 1965, 71, 72, 73, 80, 81, Nat. Assn. Real Estate Bds., 1966, 67, 68, 69, 70, 71, 73, Nat. Assn. Home Builders, 1970; 1st prize Nat. Assn. Realtors, 1980; Bus.-Fin. Writing award Press Club Cleve., 1969; Disting. merit award Cleve. Assn. Real Estate Brokers, 1976. Mem. Am. Newspaper Guild, Nat. Assn. Real Estate Editors, Sigma Delta Chi. Club: City of Cleve. Home: 575 Hemlock Dr Euclid OH 44132 Office: 1801 Superior Ave Cleveland OH 44114 *Honest and honorable communication with my fellow man is of the utmost importance... to inform, debate, educate, understand, persuade, listen, be open to new thoughts-never to ignore.*

GLEKEL, NEWTON, meat products corporation executive; b. 1914. B.A., Bklyn. Coll., 1935; LL.B., Columbia U., 1938. With Glekel & Drummer, N.Y.C., until 1956; pres. Wayne Works Inc. (acquired by Divco-Wayne Corp.), until 1956; pres., chief exec. officer parent co. Wayne Works Inc., 1956-57; chmn. exec. com., dir. Beck Industries, Inc., 1968-70; chmn. bd., chmn. exec. com., dir. Hygrade Food Products Corp., Southfield, Mich., 1969—, also chief exec. office. Office: Hygrade Food Products Corp 26300 Northwestern Hwy Southfield MI 48075 *

GLEN, ROBERT STORY, psychiatrist; b. Tokyo, Nov. 21, 1920; came to U.S., 1948, naturalized, 1953; s. Robert Roger and Jane (Story) G.; children—Robert, Douglas, Alan. B.S., Stanford U., 1949, M.D., 1953. Intern Jackson Meml. Hosp., Miami, Fla., 1953-54, resident, 1954-56; resident in psychiatry Lafayette Clinic, Detroit, 1956-58, mem. staff, 1957-58; asst. prof. psychiatry U. Fla., 1958-62; asso. prof. U. Tex., Dallas, 1962-72, prof., 1972-73; mem. staff VA Hosp., Dallas, 1973-77; practice medicine, specializing in psychiatry, Rusk, Tex., 1977—; med. dir. Davis Mountain Achievement Center, Ft. Davis, Tex., 1977-78; supt. Rusk State Hosp., 1979—; adj. prof. law So. Meth. U., 1962-74; adj. prof. pastoral counseling Brite Div. Sch., Ft. Worth, 1970-78; adj. prof. occupational therapy Tex. Women's U., 1978; cons. in field. Served to capt. Brit. Army, 1940-47. Fellow Am. Psychiat. Assn. Clubs: Chaparral, Kiwanis. Home and Office: PO Box 318 Rusk TX 75785

GLENDENING, EVERETT AUSTIN, architect; b. White Plains, N.Y., May 20, 1929; s. Gilbert Leslie and Elsie Jane (Fanjoy) G.; m. Wilhelmina Louise Hanley, Nov. 26, 1949; children: Nancy, James, Thomas, Terry, Susan. B.Arch., U. Cin., 1953; M.Arch., M.I.T., 1954. With Duffy Constrn. Co., Cleve., 1951-55, SIS Architects, Cin., 1956-58, T.J. Moore (architect), Denver, 1959; prof. architecture U. Cin., 1960-67; pvt. practice architecture, Cin., 1959—. Prin. works include: Queen's Towers, Cin., 1964, Summit Chase, Columbus, Ohio, 1966, Norwood High Sch, Cin., 1972, St. Bernard-Elmwood Place High Sch, 1976, W.Va. Mus, Moundsville, 1978, Douglass Elem. Sch, Cin., 1979, Christie Lane Workshop, Norwalk, Ohio, 1980, Coll. Law, U. Cin., 1981, Elks Lodge, Columbus, Ind., 1981, Geology/Physics Sci. Ctr., U. Cin., 1983. Served as 1st lt. USAF, 1954-56. Fellow AIA (Honor award Ohio chpt. 1967-71, 71, Cin. chpt. 1966-68, 70, 76, Bronze medal 1969); mem. Architect's Soc. Ohio, Scarab. Methodist. Club: Masons. Home: 5425 Drake Rd Cincinnati OH 45243 Office: 8050 Montgomery Rd Cincinnati OH 45236 *A consistently positive point of view has perhaps been the single, most important factor in making possible what has been accomplished in my lifetime. I have always felt that anything was possible as long as I was willing to make the effort and, in fact, I can recall telling myself as a new college freshman that "while I may not be the most intelligent man in the class, there was no reason why I should not be the hardest working member of that class."*

GLENDINNING, RALPH ORTON, marketing and promotion consultant; b. Rahway, N.J., Nov. 19, 1923; s. John Edmund and Mildred Potter (Rowe) G.; m. Mary Rhodes, June 27, 1975; children: Randall, Scott, Janet; stepchildren: Richard, Charles, Robert. B.A. summa cum laude, Princeton U., 1948. Mgr. promotion dept. Procter & Gamble Co., 1948-60; chmn. bd. Glendinning Cos. Inc., Westport, Conn., 1960—, MBI Co., Norwalk, Conn., 1970—, P&G Mining Co., Silverton, Colo., 1980—; dir. Kellwood Co. Author: novel Ultimate Game. Mem. alumni council Princeton U., 1978; nat. adv. bd. Salvation Army, 1981—. Service to capt. USMC, 1941-45. Decorated D.F.C. (2), Air medal (7); named to Mktg. and Promotion Hall of Fame, 1979. Republican. Congregationalist. Clubs: Princeton (N.Y.C.); Gt. Harbour (Bahamas); Aspetuck Valley Country, Lost Tree, Jupiter Hills Golf, Tamarron Golf. Home: 11935 Lost Tree Way Lost Tree Village North Palm Beach FL 33408 Office: 1 Glendinning Pl Westport CT 06880

GLENDON, WILLIAM RICHARD, lawyer; b. Medford, Mass., May 1, 1919; s. Henry Richard and Ellen L. (Harrigan) G.; m. Susan Webb, Apr. 1, 1945; children: W. Richard, John B. Lisa A. A.B., Holy Cross Coll., 1941; postgrad., Harvard Bus. Sch., 1941; LL.B., Georgetown U., 1948. Bar: D.C. 1948, N.Y. 1958. Law clk. to judge U.S. Dist. Ct. D.C., 1948-49; asst. U.S. atty., Washington, 1950-53; from assoc. to sr. ptnr. Rogers & Wells and predecessors, N.Y.C. and Washington, 1953—; mem. 2d Circuit Jud. Nominating Panel, 1980-81. Trustee Village of Scarsdale, N.Y., 1982—; bd. regents Georgetown U., 1982—. Served to lt. (s.g.) USN, 1942-46. Recipient John Carroll medal of Honor Georgetown U., 1973. Mem. ABA, Assn. Bar City N.Y., D.C. Bar, Fed. Bar Council. Democrat. Roman Catholic. Clubs: Fishers Island Yacht (N.Y.) (commodore 1977-79); Scarsdale Town (pres. 1979-80), Scarsdale Golf). Office: Robers & Wells 200 Park Ave New York NY 10166

GLENISTER, BRIAN FREDERICK, geologist, educator; b. Albany, Western Australia, Sept. 28, 1928; came to U.S., 1959, naturalized, 1967; s. Frederick and Mabel (Frusher) G.; m. Anne Marie Treloar, Feb. 16, 1956; children: Alan Edward, Linda Marie, Kathryn Grace. B.Sc., U. Western Australia, 1949; M.Sc., U. Melbourne, 1953; Ph.D., U. Iowa, 1956. Lectr., sr. lectr. geology U. Western Australia, Perth, 1956-59; asst. prof. U. Iowa, Iowa City, 1959-62, asso. prof., 1962-66, prof., 1966-68, prof., chmn. geology dept., 1968-74, A.K. Miller prof. geology, 1974—. Mem. Paleontol. Soc., Palaeontol. Assn., Paläontologischen Gesellschaft, Soc. Econ. Paleontologists and Mineralogists, Geol. Soc. Am., AAAS, Paleontol. Research Instn., Internat. Palaeontol. Union, Sigma Xi. Home: Box 148 B RR2 North Liberty IA 52317

GLENN, CHARLES MELANCTHON, JR., insurance company executive; b. Richmond, Va., Nov. 2, 1916; s. Charles Melancthon and Hazel (Cole) G.; children—Nancy Scott, Cynthia McLean; children by previous marriage—Martha Cole, Virginia. Student, Va. Mil. Inst., 1935-36, U. Richmond, 1937-38. With Home Beneficial Life Ins. Co., Richmond, 1938—, asst.treas., 1947-60, corp. sec., 1960—, v.p., 1972—, treas., 1979—. Served with Va. State Guard, 1943-45. Mem. Nat. Rifle Assn. (life), Co. Mil. Historians, Va. Hist. Soc. Clubs: Commonwealth, Country of Va. (Richmond). Home: 33 Countryside Ln Richmond VA 23229 Office: 3901 W Broad St PO Box 27572 Richmond VA 23230

GLENN, DAVID WRIGHT, federal savings and loan official; b. Brigham City, Utah, Nov. 22, 1943; s. Alma Wray and Lois (Wright) G.; m. Cherie Jean Tilleman, June 9, 1967; children: David Wray, Shannon, Chelece, Daniel William. B.S., Weber State Coll., 1968; M.B.A., Stanford U., 1971, Ph.D., 1974. Asst. prof. U. N.C., Chapel Hill, 1973-74; vis. asst. prof. Stanford U., (Calif.), 1974-75; asst. prof. U. Utah, Salt Lake City, 1975-78; vis. asst. prof. Harvard U., 1977; assoc. prof. U. Utah, 1978-83; dir. Fed. Savs. & Loan Ins. Corp., Washington, 1983—. Author numerous articles in bus. and fin. Mem. Am. Fin. Assn., Western Fin. Assn., Fin. Mgmt. Assn. Republican. Home: 6811 Tennyson Dr McLean VA 22010 Office: Fed Savs & Loan Ins Corp 1700 G St NW Washington DC 20552

GLENN, JAMES FRANCIS, physician, educator; b. Lexington, Ky., May 10, 1928; s. Cambridge Francis and Martha (Morrow) G.; m. Gale Brooke Morrison, Dec. 29, 1948; children: Cambridge Francis II, Sara Brooke, Nancy Carrick, James Morrison Woodworth. Student (Yale Regional scholar), Univ. Sch., Lexington, 1946; B.A. in Gen. Sci. (Bausch and Lomb Nat. Sci. scholar), U. Rochester, 1949; M.D., Duke U., 1952. Diplomate: Am. Bd. Urology (mem.), Nat. Bd. Med. Examiners. Intern Peter Bent Brigham Hosp., Boston, 1952-54; asst. resident urology Duke U. Med. Center, 1956-58, resident, 1958-59; instr. urology Duke U., 1958-59; prof., chief div. urology, Duke U., 1963-80; prof. Yale U., 1959-61; asso. prof. Bowman Gray Sch. Medicine, Wake Forest Coll., 1961-63; practice medicine specializing in urology, New Haven, 1959-61, Winston-Salem, N.C., 1961-63, Durham, N.C., 1963-80; prof. surgery, dean Med. Sch., Emory U., 1980-83; pres. Mt. Sinai Med. Center, 1983—; nat. cons. USAF Med. Service, 1971-80. Contbg. author: Renal Neoplasia, 1967, Urodynamics, 1971, Textbook of Surgery, 1972, Plastic and Reconstructive Surgery of The Genital Area, 1973, Current Operative Urology, 1975, Campbell's Urology, 1977; author, editor: Diagnostic Urology, 1964, Ureteral Reflux in Children, 1966, Urologic Surgery, 1969, rev. edit., 1975; contbr. numerous articles to profl. jours. Served to capt. M.C., USAF, 1954-56. Mem. Am. Assn. Genitourinary Surgeons, Am. Surg. Assn., ACS, AMA (sec. sect. urology 1972-73, chmn. 1975-77), Assn. Am. Med. Colls., Internat. Urol Soc., Clin. Soc. Genito-Urinary Surgeons, N.Y. Acad. Scis., Soc. Pediatric Urology, Soc. Pelvic Surgeons, Soc. Univ. Surgeons, Soc. Univ. Urologists (pres. 1971-72), Am. Acad. Pediatrics, German Urol. Assn. (hon.), Royal Soc. Medicine, Am. Assn. Clin. Urologists, Australasian Urologic Soc. (hon.), Brit. Assn. Urologic Surgeons (corres.). Home: 1120 Park Ave New York NY 10128 Office: Mount Sinai Med Center Fifth Ave at 100th St New York NY 10029

GLENN, JERRY HOSMER, JR., foreign language educator; b. Little Rock, Sept. 5, 1938; s. Jerry Hosmer and Anne (Matthews) G.; m. Renate Drexl, July 29, 1978. B.A., Yale U., 1960; postgrad., Free U. Berlin, 1962-63; M.A., U. Tex., 1962, Ph.D., 1964. Asst. prof. German U. Wis., Milw., 1964-67; asst. prof. German U. Cin., 1967-69, asso. prof., 1969-72, prof., 1972—, head dept., 1980-83, dir. honors program, 1977-79. Author: Deutsches Schrifttum der Gegenwart (ab 1945), 1971, Paul Celan, 1973; Mng. editor: Lessing Yearbook, 1969-74. Mem. Lessing Soc. (sec. treas. 1968-74), MLA, Mideast Honors Assn. (exec. sec. 1977-78, pres. 1979-80), Am. Assn. Tchrs. German. Republican. Home: 854 Rue de la Paix B-5 Cincinnati OH 45220

GLENN, JOHN HERSCHEL, JR., U.S. senator; b. Cambridge, Ohio, July 18, 1921; s. John Herschel and Clara (Sproat) G.; m. Anna Margaret Castor, Apr. 1943; children: Carolyn Ann, John David. Student, Muskingum Coll., 1939, D.Sc., 1961; naval aviation cadet, U. Iowa, 1942; grad. flight sch., Naval Air Tng. Center, Corpus Christi, Tex., 1943, Navy Test Pilot Tng. Sch., Patuxent River, Md., 1954. Commd. 2d lt. USMC, 1943, advanced through grades to col.; assigned 4th Marine Aircraft Wing, Marshall Islands campaign, 1944, advanced through grades to col.; assigned 9th Marine Aircraft Wing, 1945-46; with 1st marine Aircraft Wing, North China Patrol, also Guam, 1947-48; flight instr. advanced flight tng., Corpus Christi, 1949-51; asst. G-2/G-3 Amphibious Warfare Sch., Quantico, Va., 1951; with Marine Fighter Squadron 311, exchange pilot 25th Fighter Squadron USAF, Korea, 1953; project officer fighter design br. Navy Bur. Aero., Washington, 1956-69; astronaut Project Mercury, Manned Spacecraft Center NASA, 1959-64; pilot Mercury-Atlas 6 orbital space flight launched from Cape Canaveral, Fla., Feb., 1962; v.p. corp. devel. and dir. Royal Crown Cola Co., 1962-74; U.S. Senator from, Ohio, 1975—. Co-author: We Seven, 1962; Author: P.S., I Listened to Your Heart Beat. Trustee Muskingum Coll. Decorated D.F.C. (five), Air medal (18), Astronaut medal USMC, Navy unit commendation; Korean Presidential unit citation; Distinguished Merit award Muskingum Coll.; Medal of Honor N.Y.C.; Congl. Space Medal of Honor, 1978. Mem. Soc. Exptl. Test Pilots, Internat. Acad. of Astronautics (hon.). Democrat. Presbyn. Nonstop supersonic transcontinental Flight, July 16, 1957. Office: 503 Hart Office Bldg Washington DC 20510

GLENN, JOSEPH CHRISTOPHER, broadcast journalist; b. N.Y.C., Mar. 23, 1938; s. Jack and Althea (Hill) G.; m. Dianne West, Mar. 26, 1960; children: Rebecca, Lindsay. B.A., U. Colo., 1959. Reporter, producer, anchor WICC Radio News, Bridgeport, Conn., 1963-64; reporter, producer, anchor WNEW Radio News, N.Y.C., 1964-70; mng. editor Metromedia Radio News, Washington, 1970-71; producer, reporter, corr. CBS News, N.Y.C., 1971—. Corr., anchor: series. In the News and 30 Minutes. Served with U.S. Army, 1960-63. Recipient George F. Peabody award; TV Acad. Emmy; AP award; Action for Children's TV award; Am. Bar Assn. award; others. Mem. Am. Fedn. TV and Radio Artists, Writers Guild Am., Mensa, Sigma Delta Chi. Office: 524 W 57th St New York NY 10019 *

GLENN, JOSEPH LEONARD, biochemist; b. Albany, N.Y., Jan. 20, 1925; s. Francis Jerome and Josephine Marie (White) G.; m. Barbara Schlegel, Sept. 23, 1950; children: Kevin, Steven, Michael, Kathleen. B.S., St. Lawrence U., 1950; M.S., Syracuse U., 1952, Ph.D., 1954. NIH fellow U. Wis., 1954-56; asst. prof. biochemistry Albany Med. Coll., 1956-59, asso. prof., 1959-65, prof., 1965-83, chmn. dept. biochemistry, 1974-79; prof. med. tech. Coll. St. Rose, 1983—. Served with USN, 1943-46; PTO. Recipient Lederle award Am. Cyanamid, 1959-62; Research Career award NIH, 1962-72. Mem. Am. Soc. Biol. Chemistry. Roman Catholic. Research, publs. in field. Home: 24 David Ave Troy NY 12180

GLENN, MICHAEL DOUGLAS, lawyer; b. Greenville, S.C., Sept. 18, 1940; s. Harland Douglas and Mildred Elizabeth (Carpenter) G.; m. Sue Ann Flint, Dec. 26, 1962; children: Michael Douglas, Caroline Flint, Elizabeth Ilene. Student, Clemson Coll., 1958-60; B.A., Furman U., 1962; LL.B., U. S.C., 1965. Bar: S.C. 1965. Asso. Robert N. Daniel, Jr., 1965, Watkins, Vandiver, Kirven, Long & Gable, 1965-69; partner Fant, Doyle, Glenn & Vaughan, 1970-72; county judge, Anderson County, S.C., 1972-78; ptnr. firm McIntosh, Threlkeld, Glenn & Sherard, 1978-83; city recorder, Anderson, 1969-72. Mem. Gov.'s Com. on Criminal Justice, Crime and Delinquency, 1979-81;

chmn. Gov.'s Juvenile Justice Adv. Council, 1979-81; Chmn. bd. Head Start, 1971-72, Family Counseling Center, 1971-72; bd. dirs. YMCA, 1970, 76-79, S.C. Dept. Youth Services, 1981—; pres. Sch. of Theology, 1971; mem. Anderson-Oconee Alcohol and Drug Commn., 1980—. Mem. Anderson County Bar Assn. (pres. 1981—), Anderson County Young Lawyers Club (pres. 1970), Anderson Area C. of C. (dir. 1979—). Presbyterian. Club: Cobb's Glen Golf and Racquet. Home: 412 Shannon Way Anderson SC 29621 Office: 213 E Calhoun St Anderson SC 29621

GLENN, NORVAL DWIGHT, sociologist, educator; b. Roswell, N.Mex., Aug. 13, 1933; s. William N. and Mary E. (Cochrain) G.; m. Graciela Edna Gonzalez, Sept. 18, 1978. B.A., N.Mex. State U., 1954; Ph.D., U. Tex., 1962. Instr. Miami U., Oxford, Ohio, 1960-61; instr. U. Ill., 1961-63, asst. prof., 1963-64, U. Tex., Austin, 1964-65, assoc. prof. sociology, 1965-70, prof. sociology, 1970-84, Asbel Smith prof. sociology, 1984—. Author: (with Leonard Broom) Transformation of the Negro American, 1965, Cohort Analysis, 1977; editor: (with Charles Bonjean) Blacks in the United States, 1969, Contemporary Sociology, 1977-80, Jour. Family Issues, 1984—; compiler: (with Jon Alston and David Weiner) Social Stratification: A Research Bibliography, 1969; contbr. articles to profl. jours. Mem. council Inter-Univ. Consortium for Polit. and Social Research, 1980-84, assoc. dir., 1984—. Served to 1st lt AUS, 1954-56. Mem. Am. Sociol. Assn., Am. Assn. Public Opinion Research, Nat. Council on Family Relations, Population Assn. Am., World Assn. Pub. Opinion Research. Home: 3019 Honey Tree Ln Austin TX 78746

GLENN, WILLIAM WALLACE LUMPKIN, surgeon; b. Asheville, N.C., Aug. 12, 1914; s. Eugene Byron and Elizabeth Elliot (Lumpkin) G.; m. Amory Potter, May 15, 1943; children: William Amory Lumpkin, Elizabeth Glenn Covert. B.S., U. S.C., 1934; M.D., Jefferson Med. Coll., 1938; M.A. (hon.), Yale U., 1962, M.D., U. Cadiz, 1981. Diplomate: Am. Bd. Surgery, Am. Bd. Thoracic Surgery. Intern Pa. Hosp., Phila., 1938-40; surg. resident Mass. Gen. Hosp., Boston, 1940-42, 45-46; asst. physiology Harvard Sch. Pub. Health, 1941-43; asso. surgery Jefferson Med. Coll., Phila., 1946-48; mem. faculty Yale Med. Sch., 1948—, prof. surgery, 1962-74, Charles W. Ohse prof. surgery, 1974—, chief cardiothoracic surgery, 1948-75; attending surgeon Yale-New Haven Hosp.; cons. VA Hosp.; Cons. Surgeon Gen. Com. Environ. Medicine, 1962-64. Co-author: Thoracic and Cardiovascular Surgery, 1962, 75; editor, 1983; Co-author: Complex Surgical Problems, 1981; editorial bd. numerous jours.; cons. editor: Cardiac Pacemakers, 1964; contbr. articles to profl. jours. Mem. com. cardiovascular systems NRC, 1955-56; Bd. dirs. Charles E. Culpepper Found. Served to maj., M.C. AUS, World War II; ETO. Mem. Am. Heart Assn. (chmn. council cardiovascular surgery 1960-62, v.p. 1962-65, pres. 1970-71, award of merit 1966, Gold Heart award 1973), Internat. Soc. Surgery (treas. 1968-74, v.p. 1974-77), Internat. Surg. Group (pres. 1964), Am. Surg. Assn., ACS (chmn. Conn. adv. com. 1963-66, gov. 1967-72), Soc. Univ. Surgeons, New Eng. Surg. Soc. (v.p. 1977-78, pres.-elect 1982-83), So. Surg. Assn., New Eng. Soc. Vascular Surgeons (pres. 1979-80), Am. Assn. Thoracic Surgery, Vascular Surg. Soc., Halstead Soc., Alpha Omega Alpha, Sigma Xi. Episcopalian. Club: Morys' Assos. (New Haven). Home: 685 Forest Rd New Haven CT 06515

GLENNON, HARRISON RANDOLPH, JR., shipping company executive; b. Port Gibson, Miss., Nov. 4, 1914; s. Harrison Randolph and May (Redus) G.; m. Dickie Glen Bailey, Oct. 27, 1944; children: Harrison Randolph, Francis Whaley (dec.), Blair Bailey. B.S., U.S. Naval Acad., 1937. Supr. ship repair and operation, engring. dept. Moore-McCormack Lines, Inc., N.Y.C., 1937-41, 46-53, supt. engr., 1953-57, v.p., head engring. div., 1959-62, exec. v.p. ops., dir., 1962-68; chmn. vessel replacement com. Am. S.S. Lines, 1962-64; pres. Comml. S.S. Co., Inc., 1968-71, Gt. Republics Transport, Inc., 1971—, Zapata Bulk Transport, Inc., 1971-77, Titan Nav., Inc., N.Y.C., 1977—; founder Equity Carriers, Inc., 1978; dir. Portsmouth Terminals, Inc.; cons. Falcon Carriers, Inc., 1977-78, Ernst & Ernst, 1978, IHI-George Sharp, Inc., 1978; mem. N.Y. Shipping Labor Policy Com., 1962—; v.p., dir. N.Y. Shipping Assn., 1967-69. Served from ensign to comdr. USNR, 1941-46. Mem. Soc. Naval Architects and Marine Engrs. (v.p., mem. exec. com. and council), Am. Bur. Shipping (mem. classification and engring. com.), Am. Marine Inst. (tng. and upgrading com.), Am. Inst. Mcht. Shipping (chmn. standard ship com.), Maritime Service Com. (sec. 1966-67). Episcopalian. Clubs: Riverside Yacht, Kollegwidgwok Yacht, N.Y. Yacht. Office: Titan Navigation Inc Suite 2900 1000 Louisiana St Houston TX 77002

GLENNY, LYMAN ALBERT, educator; b. Trent, S.D., Jan. 26, 1918; s. Walter and Ann (Henning) G.; m. Carolyn Joy Ballou, Dec. 19, 1942 (div. Mar. 1977); children—Terence Alan, Celia Joy, Colleen Marie; m. Helen S. Thompson, June 24, 1978. B.S., U. Minn., 1947; M.A., U. Colo., 1948; Ph.D., State U. Iowa, 1950. Instr. U. Iowa, 1948-50; asst. prof., assoc. prof., then. prof. Sacramento State Coll., 1950-62; assoc. dir. Ill. Bd. Higher Edn., 1962-65, exec. dir., Springfield, 1965-69; prof. higher edn. U. Calif.-, Berkeley, 1969-83; dir. Center for Research and Devel. in Higher Edn. U. Calif.-, Berkeley, 1969-76; dir. Nebr. Study Adminstrn. Higher Edn., 1960. Author: Autonomy of Public Colleges, 1959, Coordinating Higher Education for the 70's, 1971, State Budgeting for Higher Education: Interagency Conflict and Consensus, 1976, Issues in Higher Education: A Six Nation Analysis, 1980, (with J. R. Kidder) State Tax Support of Higher Education: Revenue Appropriation Trends and Patterns, 1963-73, 1973, (with T. K. Dalglish) Public Universities, State Agencies, and the Law: Constitutional Autonomy in Decline, 1973, (with others) Presidents confront reality: From edifice complex to university without walls, 1975, (with Janet Ruyle) Trends in State Revenue Appropriations for Higher Education, 1968-78, (with F.M. Bowen) Uncertainty in Public Higher Education, 1980, Signals for Change: Stress Indicators, 1980, Quality and Accountability, 1981, also other publs. on state budgeting for higher edn.; editor: Statewide Planning for Post-Secondary Education, 1971; contbr. articles, chpts. to profl. publs.; bd. editors: Western Polit. Quar, 1959-62. Served to capt. U.S. Army, 1941-46, 51-52. Mem. AAUP, Am. Assn. Higher Edn., Am. Soc. Public Adminstrn., Am. Inst. Research, State Higher Edn. Exec. Officers Assn. (Oho) (hon.), Western Polit. Sci. Assn. Research series Assn. Instl. Research, 1976. Home: 3123 Lippizaner Ln Walnut Creek CA 94598 Office: Tolman Hall U Calif Berkeley CA 94720

GLENVILLE, PETER, performing arts director, producer, actor; b. London, Eng., Oct. 28, 1913; s. Shaun and Dorothy (Ward) G. Studied at, Stonyhurst Coll., Christ Ch. at Oxford (Eng.) U. Appeared in: plays in Eng. including The Swan, 1934, On the Spot, The Maitlands, Candida, Rosetti, Twelfth Night, Man and Superman, The Hangman, The Royal Family, Romeo and Juliet, The Taming of the Shrew, Julius Caesar, Behind the Scenes; plays in Eng. include Down Our Street, The Infernal Machine, All's Well That Ends Well, Henry IV, Part 1, The Light of Heart, The Doctor's Dilemma, John Gabriel Borkman, Point Valaine; plays in Eng. including School for Scandal, The Alchemist, Hamlet, Duet for Two Hands, The Assassin, A Bequest to the Nation, 1970; dir.: plays in Eng., including Lisa, 1944, Separate Tables, 1954, The Time of Your Life, Point Valaine, Major Barbara, The Giaconda Smile, Crime Passionnel, The Browning Version, A Harlequinade, The Return of the Prodigal, Adventure Story, The Power of Darkness, Summer and Smoke, The Prisoner, Hotel Paradiso; plays in N.Y., including The Browning Version, 1949, A Harlequinade, Separate Tables, 1956, Hotel Paradiso, Rashamon, Take Me Along, Tovarich, Out Cry, Silent Night Lonely Night, Tchin Tchin, Dylan, Everything in the Garden, 1967, A Patriot for Me, 1969; motion pictures The Prisoner, 1955, Me and the Colonel, Summer and Smoke, Term of Trail, Becket, Hotel Paradiso. Office: care Elliott Lefkowitz 641 Lexington Ave New York NY 10022

GLEYSTEEN, WILLIAM HENRY, JR., assn. exec., former ambassador; b. Peking, China, May 8, 1926; s. William Henry and Theodora (Culver) G.; m. Zoe Marianna Clubb, Dec. 27, 1952; children—Thea, Guy, Michael. B.A., Yale, 1949, M.A., 1951; fellow, Harvard Center Internat. Affairs, 1965-66. With Exec. Secretariat, Dept. of State, 1951-55; with Am. Embassy, Taipei, Taiwan, 1956-58, Tokyo, Japan, 1958-62; Am. consulate gen., Hong Kong, 1962-65; with Office UN Polit. Affairs, State Dept., 1966-69; dir. Office Research and Analysis for East Asia, 1969-71; dep. chief mission Am. Embassy, Taipei, 1971-74; dep. asst. sec. state for East Asian affairs, 1974-76, 77-78; sr. staff mem. Nat. Security Council, 1976-77; ambassador to, Korea, 1978-81; dir. Washington Center, Asia Soc., Inc., 1981—. Served with USNR, 1944-46. Recipient Superior Honor award Dept. State, 1971, 79. Home: 5010 Worthington Dr Washington DC 20816 Office: Asia Soc 1785 Massachusetts Ave Washington DC 20036

GLEZOS, MATTHEWS, manufacturing company executive; b. Montreal, Aug. 27, 1927; s. George and Katerina (Bakalos) G.; m. Sophia Protonotarios, Sept. 23, 1953; children: George, Mary. B. in commerce, McGill U., 1952. Tax assessor taxation div. Govt. of Can., Montreal, 1953-55; tax mgr., treas. Imasco Ltd., Montreal, 1955-78, v.p., treas., 1978—. Clubs: St. James, Royal Montreal Golf. Home: 366 Kindersley St Mount Royal PQ Canada H3R IR9 Office: Imasco Ltd 4 Westmount Sq Westmount PQ Canada H3R 2S8

GLICK, ALAN H., financial executive; b. N.Y.C., Nov. 15, 1938; s. Henry Bernard and Rose (Brensilver) G.; m. Marilyn Edythe Rubin, Aug. 21, 1960; children: Madeleine, Cherise. A.B., Dartmouth Coll., 1960, M.B.A., 1961. C.P.A., N.Y. Acct. S.D. Leidersdorf & Co., N.Y.C., 1961-66, Henry Brout & Co., 1966-68; gen. ptnr. First Manhattan Co., N.Y.C., 1968—. Mem. Am. Inst. C.P.A.'s, N.Y. Soc. C.P.A.'s, Fin. Analyst Fedn. Club: Dartmouth (pres. 1973-76). Office: First Manhattan Co 437 Madison Ave New York NY 10017

GLICK, DAVID, histochemist, educator; b. Homestead, Pa., May 3, 1908; s. Max and Anne (Lasday) G.; m. Ruth Mueller, Sept. 16, 1929; children: David, Peter; m. Annette Zelzer, Aug. 9, 1941; m. Irene Ross, Sept. 2, 1945; children: Jonathon Michael, Jeffrey Alan.; m. Dorothy von Redlich, Nov. 18, 1981. B.S., U. Pitts., 1929; Ph.D., 1932; LL.D. (hon.), U. Glasgow, 1980. Cert. Am. Bd. Clin. Chemistry. Fellow Mt. Sinai Hosp., N.Y.C., 1932-34, OSRD war research, 1942-43; chief chem. lab. Mt. Zion Hosp., San Francisco, 1934-36; Rockefeller Found. fellow Carlsberg Lab., Copenhagen, 1936-37; head chem. lab. Beth Israel Hosp., Newark, 1937-42; head vitamin-enzyme research Russell Miller Milling Co., Mpls., 1943-46; cons. toxicity lab. U. Chgo., 1945-46; asso. prof. physiol. chemistry U. Minn., 1946-50, prof., 1950-61; prof. pathology, head div. histochemistry Stanford Med. Sch., 1961-73, prof. emeritus, 1973—; staff Cancer Biology Research Lab., 1978—; dir. center for histochem. research Stanford Research Inst., 1973-78, staff scientist, 1978—; Macfarlane prof. exptl. medicine U. Glasgow, 1970-71; Evans lectr. U. Minn., 1981; cons. VA Hosp., Mpls., 1946-47, Palo Alto, Calif., 1961—; advanced med. fellow Commonwealth Fund, Carlsberg Lab., Copenhagen, 1958, Stazione Zoologica, Naples, 1959, Karolinska Inst., Stockholm, 1949, 59. Author: Black and White and other Poems, 1946, Techniques of Histo- and Cytochemistry, 1949, Quantitative Chemical Techniques of Histo- and Cytochemistry, Vol. 1, 1961, II, 63; Editor: Methods of Biochemical Analysis, 1953—; co-editor: Techniques of Biochemical and Biophys. Morphology, 1972-77; mem. editorial bd.: Jour. Histo- and Cytochemistry, 1953-56, 65—, Procs. Soc. Exptl. Biol. Medicine, 1957-58, Jour. Investigative Dermatology, 1968-72, Basic and Applied Histochemistry (Italian), 1977—, Histochem. Jour. (Gt. Brit.), 1981; Contbr. articles to sci. publs. Recipient Career award USPH, 1962-73; Donald D. Van Slyke award in clin. chemistry, 1977; Ames award Am. Assn. Clin. Chemists, 1980. Fellow AAS; Mem. Internat., Am. socs. cell biology, Royal Danish Acad. Sci. and Letters (hon. mem.), Histochem. Soc. Finland (hon.), Histochem. Soc. U.S.A. (pres. 1951-52, 69-70, hon. mem.), Nat. Acad. Clin. Biochemistry (charter 1976), Am. Assn. Clin. Chemistry, Am. Soc. Biol. Chemists, Am. Chem. Soc., AAAS, Internat. Fedn. Histochemistry and Cytochemistry (pres. 1972-76), Soc Exptl. Biology and Medicine, AAUP, Sigma Xi, Phi Lambda Upsilon. Home: 680 Junipero Serra Blvd Stanford CA 94305

GLICK, GARLAND WAYNE, theol. sem. pres.; b. Bridgewater, Va., Jan. 27, 1921; s. John T. and Effie (Evers) G.; m. Barbara Roller Zigler, Jan. 1, 1943; children—Martha (Mrs. Howard Berthold), John, Mary. B.D., Bethany Bibl. Sem., Chgo., 1946; M.A. in N.T, U. Chgo., 1949; Ph.D. in Ch. History, U. Chgo., 1957; LL.D., Bridgewater Coll., 1969. Ordained to ministry Ch. of Brethren, 1942; pastor, Lombard, Ill., 1945-48; instr., then asst. prof. Bibl. studies Juniata Coll., Huntingdon, Pa., 1948-53; mem. faculty Franklin and Marshall Coll., 1955-65, asso. prof. religion, 1958-65, prof., 1965, v.p., 1962-65, dir. research and long-range planning, 1960, asst. to dean, 1960-61, dean coll., 1961-65; pres. Keuka Coll., Keuka Park, N.Y., 1966-74; dir. Moton Center Ind. Studies, Gloucester, Va., 1975-78; pres. Bangor (Maine) Theol. Sem., 1978—; vis. prof. Lancaster (Pa.) Theol. Sem., 1958-60, 64; coordinator of cons. Knox Seminars Ednl. Mgmt., 1963-65; seminar dir. Nat. Cath. Edn. Assn. Long-Range Planning Seminars, 1968; Bd. dirs. Empire State Found. Ind. Liberal Arts Colls. Author: Maker of Modern Theology: Adolf von Harnack, 1967; Contbr. to Ency. Brit. Mem. Nat. Assn. Bibl. Instrs., Am. Soc. Ch. History, Am. Conf. Acad. Deans (treas. 1965-66), Societas Orphea, Pi Gamma Mu, Tau Kappa Alpha. Home: 15 5th St Bangor ME 04401 Office: 300 Union St Bangor ME 04401

GLICK, J. LESLIE, biotechnology company executive; b. N.Y.C., Mar. 2, 1940; s. Arthur Harvey and Hilda Lillian (Lichtenfeld) G.; Judith Sumiye Mihara; children: Geoffrey Michael, Jessica Michele. A.B., Columbia U., 1961, Ph.D., 1964. Nat. Cancer Inst. postdoctoral fellow Princeton U., 1964-65; sr., then asso. cancer research scientist Roswell Park Meml. Inst., Buffalo, 1965-69; assoc. research prof. physiology, physiology chmn. Roswell Park div. SUNY, Buffalo, 1968-70; from exec. v.p. to chmn. bd. Asso. Biomedic Systems, Inc., Buffalo, 1969-77; pres. Inst. Sci. and Social Accountability, Washington, 1975-79; from pres. to chmn. bd. Genex Corp., Rockville, Md., 1977—; chmn. HTI Corp., Buffalo, 1972-75; dir. Nat. Assn. Life Sci. Industries, 1975-77; research prof. biology Niagara (N.Y.) U., Canisius Coll., Buffalo, 1968-70; exec. com. SUNY Grad. Sch., Buffalo, 1968-70; vis. lectr. NATO Advanced Study Inst., Brussels, 1970. Author: Fundamentals of Human Lymphoid Cell Culture, 1980; also articles. Mem. Am. Assn. Cancer Research, Am. Physiol. Soc., Tissue Culture Assn., N.Y. Acad. Scis., Sigma Xi. Office: Genex Corp 6110 Executive Blvd Rockville MD 20852

GLICK, JACOB EZRA, marine corps officer; b. Burlington, Iowa, Feb. 12, 1920; s. Russell C. and Clara A. (Deputy) G.; m. Marjorie L. Gardner, Dec. 7, 1951; children—Jeffrey Alan, Susan Goff, Thomas Bryan. B.S., U.S. Naval Acad., 1941; M.S. in Elec. Engring, Naval Postgrad. Sch., 1949; M.B.A., George Washington U., 1965; student, Nat. War Coll., 1964-65. Registered profl. engr., D.C. Commd. 2d lt. USMC, 1942, advanced through grades to brig. gen., 1967; combat duty, World War II, Korea, asst. div. comdr., Vietnam; dep. chief research and devel. USMC, 1962-64; chief ops. directorate Joint Staff, Washington, 1968-71; exec. sec. Ret. Officers Assn., Washington, 1971; instr., head dept. Marine Corps Schs., 1956-59; guest lectr. Nat. War Coll., 1963-70. Decorated D.S.M., Legion of Merit (3), Bronze Star, Navy Commendation Medal, Vietnamese Cross Gallantry with palm, Vietnamese Honor medal. Mem. Marine Corps Assn., First Marine Div. Assn., U.S. Naval Acad. Alumni Assn., U.S. Naval Inst., 12th Def. Bn. Assn., Ret. Officers Assn. Home: 407 Skyhill Rd Alexandria VA 22314 Office: 201 N Washington St Alexandria VA 22314

GLICK, PHILIP MILTON, lawyer; b. Kiev, Russia, Dec. 9, 1905; naturalized, 1924; s. David and Rebecca (Sussman) G.; m. Rose Deborah Rosenfield, May 13, 1933. Student, Crane Jr. Coll., 1924-26; Ph.B. cum laude, U. Chgo., 1928, J. D., 1930. Gen. counsel fed. subsistence homesteads corp. U.S. Dept. Interior, 1933-34; chief land policy div., asst. solicitor, office of solicitor USDA, 1934-42; solicitor War Relocation Authority, 1942-44, dep. dir., 1945-46; gen. counsel Fed. Pub. Housing Authority, 1946-48, The Inst. Inter-Am. Affairs, 1948-53; legal counsel Tech. Cooperation Adminstrn., Dept. State, 1951-53; vis. prof. econ. devel. and cultural change U. Chgo., 1953-55; mem. law firm Dorfman & Glick, 1955-67; asst. dir., legal adviser Fed. Water Resources Council, 1967-69; legal counsel Nat. Water Commn., 1969-73; individual practice law, Chevy Chase, Md., 1973—. Author: The Administration of Technical Assistance, 1957; Contbr. to profl. publs. Served with USNR, 1944-45. Mem. Am. Bar Assn., Am. Polit. Sci. Assn., Soc. for Internat. Devel., Am. Soc. for Pub. Adminstrn., Internat. Inst. Adminstrv. Scis., Order of Coif, Phi Beta Kappa. Club: Cosmos (Washington). Home and office: 116 E Melrose St Chevy Chase MD 20815

GLICK, RICHARD EDWIN, chemistry educator; b. Chgo., Apr. 7, 1927; s. Samuel Edward and Gertrude Beatrice (Amsterdam) G.; m. Roberta Coale, May 20, 1947 (div. Dec. 1980); children: D'Ann, Randolph, Deborah, Dan. B.S., U. Ill., 1951; Ph.D., UCLA, 1954. Research fellow Brookhaven Nat. Lab., Upton, L.I., N.Y., 1954-55; research fellow Harvard, 1955-56; mem. faculty Pa. State U., University Park, 1956-59, Fla. State U., Tallahassee, 1959—, prof. chemistry, 1966—, dir. Inst. for Future Resources, 1982—; research fellow Lab. for High Energy Molecular Physics, Peymeinade, France, 1970-71. Served with USNR, 1945-46. Mem. Am. Soc. for Mass Spectrometry., Sigma Xi. Home: 1909 Chowkeebin Ct Tallahassee FL 32301

GLICK, WARREN W., lawyer, banker; b. Balt., July 14, 1927; s. Louis B. and Sadye L. G.; m. Judith Dessen, Oct. 18, 1953; children—Francie, Mark. A.B., Johns Hopkins U., 1949; J.D., Harvard U., 1952; postgrad., Johns Hopkins Sch. Advanced Internat. Studies. Individual practice law, Balt., until 1955; with Export-Import Bank, Washington, 1955, asst. gen. counsel, 1963-69, v.p., 1969-70, sr. v.p. for financing, 1970-73, acting exec. v.p., 1973-75, gen. counsel, 1975—. Served with USCG. Mem. Phi Beta Kappa. Home: 10905 Fiesta Rd Silver Spring MD 20901 Office: 811 Vermont Ave NW Rm 947 Washington DC 20571

GLICKMAN, ALBERT SEYMOUR, psychologist, educator; b. Bklyn., Feb. 7, 1923; s. Irving and Molly G.; m. Blanche Buller, June 14, 1945; children: Ralph, Marc, Judith, Debra. B.A. summa cum laude, Ohio State U., 1943, M.A., 1947, Ph.D., 1952. Asst. prof. psychology Ga. Inst. Tech., Atlanta, 1947-52; project dir. Am. Insts. for Research, Newport, R.I., Pitts., 1952-55; dir. psychol. research dept. U.S. Naval Personnel Research Activity, Washington, 1955-62; chief personnel research staff U.S. Dept. Agr., Washington, 1962-67; dir. Inst. for Research in Organizational Behavior; dep. dir. Washington office Am. Insts. for Research, 1967-76; v.p. Advanced Research Resources Orgn., Washington, 1976-78; eminent prof. psychology Old Dominion U., Norfolk, Va., 1979—; pres. Orgn. Research Group of Tidewater, Inc., 1979—. Cons. editor: Jour. Applied Psychology, 1971-81; co-author: Top Management Development and Succession, 1968, Police-community Action: A Program for Change in Police-community Behavior Patterns, 1973, Changing Schedules of Work: Patterns and Implications, 1974; editor: Changing Composition of the Workforce: Implications for Future Research and Its Applications. Active Common Cause. Served to lt. (j.g.) USN, 1943-46. Recipient Louis Brownlow Meml. Fund prize Internat. Pub. Personnel Assn., 1965, author award Tng. and Devel. Jour., Am. Soc. Tng. and Devel., 1967. Fellow Am. Psychol. Assn., Internat. Assn. Applied Psychology, Soc. Indsl. and Organizational Psychology, AAAS; mem. Soc. Psychol. Study Social Issues, Southeastern Psychol. Assn., Tidewater Human Factor Soc., Phi Beta Kappa. Jewish. Home: 141 S Ridgeley Rd Norfolk VA 23505 Office: Dept Psychology Old Dominion U Norfolk VA 23508

GLICKMAN, CARL DAVIS, banker; b. Cleve., July 29, 1926; s. Jack I. and Dora R. (Rubinowitz) G.; m. Barbara H. Schulman, Oct. 16, 1960; children: Lindsay Dale, David Craig, Robert Todd. Student, Miami U., Oxford, Ohio, 1943, U. Minn., 1944, Inst. Fin. Mgmt., Harvard U., 1970. Pres. Glickman Orgn., Cleve., 1953—; chmn. bd., chief exec. officer Computer Research, Inc., Pitts., 1964-67, Am. Steel & Pump Corp., N.Y.C., 1968-71, Shelter Resources Corp., Cleve., 1971-75; pres. Leader Bldg., Inc., Cleve., 1959—, Capital Bancorp., 1971-75, Real Property Corp., 1975—; spl. ltd. ptnr. Bear Stearns & Co., 1978—; chmn. Univ. Nat. Bank, Chgo., 1968-70; chmn. exec. com., dir. Capital Nat. Bank Cleve., 1970-75, dir., 1975—, Nat. Kinney Corp., Royal Petroleum Properties Corp., Progressive Systems Inc. Mem. Mayor's Com. Urban Renewal, 1965-67; mem. Mayors Task Force on Higher Edn.; trustee Cleve. Growth Assn.; co-chmn. Herzog Loan Fund Cleve. State U.; chmn. Med. Arts Hosp., Houston, 1976—; bd. visitors Case Western Res. Sch. Law; trustee Montifiore Home Aged, Mt. Sinai Hosp.; mem. grievance com. Cleve. Bar Assn., 1982—. Served with USAAF, 1944-46. Mem. Am. Bankers Assn., Am. Arbitration Assn. (arbitrator), Cleve. Growth Bd., Phi Sigma Delta, Phi Eta Sigma. Clubs: Beechmont Country, City, Mid-Day, Commerce, Univ., Pine Lake Trout, Masons (Cleve.); Standard (Chgo.); Harmonie, Town (N.Y.C.); La Coquille (Palm Beach). Office: 1140 Leader Bldg Cleveland OH 44114

GLICKMAN, CARL KENNETH, business executive; b. Wilkes-Barre, Pa., June 25, 1933; s. Jack;; s. Gertrude and (Yudkovitz) G.; m. Eileen L. Morris, May. 18, 1961; children: Rachel, Susan, Janet. B.S., Columbia U., 1958; M.B.A. (V. Kolodny thesis award), N.Y. U., 1965. With Gen. Foods Corp., White Plains, N.Y., 1960-70; v.p., gen. mgr. Custom Chef Inc., Cleve., 1968-70; pres. Ovaltine Products, Villa Park, Ill., 1970-77; chmn., pres Cott Corp., New Haven, 1977-78; pres., chief exec. officer D & S Inc., Greenwich, Conn., AGP/Gentech Inc., Linden, N.J.; acquisition and investment cons. Served with U.S. Army, 1952-54. Mem. Am. Mgmt. Assn., Young Pres.'s Orgn.

GLICKMAN, DAN, congressman; b. Wichita, Kans., Nov. 24, 1944; s. Milton and Gladys Anne (Kopelman) G.; m. Rhoda Joyce Yura, Aug. 21, 1966; children: Jonathan, Amy. B.A., U. Mich., Ann Arbor, 1966; J.D., George Washington U., Washington, 1969. Bar: Kans. 1969, Mich. 1970. Trial atty. SEC, 1969-70; assoc., then ptnr. Sargent, Klenda & Glickman, Wichita, 1971-76; mem. 95th-98th Congresses from 4th Kans. Dist. Mem. Wichita Bd. Edn., 1973-76, pres., 1975-76.

Mem. Order of Coif, Phi Delta Phi, Sigma Alpha Mu. Democrat. Jewish. Office: 2435 Rayburn Bldg Washington DC 20515

GLICKMAN, FRANKLIN SHELDON, dermatologist, educator; b. Bklyn., Dec. 14, 1929; s. Arthur Zachary and Hilda (Kurtz) G.; m. Leatrice Sallie Alter, Mar. 29, 1953; children: Todd Scott, Jeff Bret. B.A. cum laude, Hofstra Coll., 1950; M.D., SUNY-Bklyn., 1954. Diplomate: Am. Bd. Dermatology. Intern Flushing (N.Y.) Hosp., 1954-55; resident in dermatology Kings County Hosp., Bklyn., 1957-58, Bronx VA Hosp., 1958-60; practice medicine specializing in dermatology, Bklyn., 1960—; mem. faculty dermatology dept. SUNY-Bklyn., 1960—, clin. prof., 1982—. Author: General Dermatology; contbr. articles to profl. jours. Served to capt. M.C. USAF, 1955-57. Fellow N.Y. Acad. Medicine, ACP; mem. Bklyn. Dermatol. Soc. (pres. 1970-72), N.Y. State Med. Soc., Kings County Med. Soc., AMA, N.Y. State Soc. Dermatology (pres. 1983—), N.Y. Acad. Scis. Homeq: 33 Farm Ln Roslyn Heights NY 11577 Office: 122 A St Nicholas Ave Brooklyn NY 11237

GLICKMAN, HARRY, athletics executive; b. Portland, Oreg., May 13, 1924; s. Sam and Bessie (Karp) G.; m. Joanne Carol Matin, Sept. 28, 1958; children: Lynn Carol, Marshall Jordan, Jennifer Ann. B.A., U. Oreg., 1948. Press agt., 1948-52; pres. Oreg. Sports Attractions, 1952—, Portland Hockey Club, 1960-73; exec. v.p. Portland Trail Blazers, 1970—. Trustee B'nai B'rith Jr. Camp, 1965; bd. dirs. U. Oreg. Devel. Fund. Served with AUS, 1943-46. Mem. Portland C. of C. (dir. 1968-72), Sigma Delta Chi, Sigma Alpha Mu. Jewish. Office: Lloyd Bldg Suite 950 700 NE Multnomah St Portland OR 97232 *

GLICKMAN, LOUIS, tractor manufacturing company executive; b. Chgo., June 7, 1933; s. Michael C. and Florence (Leibov) G.; m. Donna B. Horwitz, Mar. 18, 1962; children: Steven L., Daniel B. B.S., U. Ill., 1955; LL.B., John Marshall Law Sch., 1961. Bar: Ill. 1962. Acct. Inland Steel Co., Chgo., 1955-63; tax mgr. Helene Curtis Industries, Inc., Chgo., 1963-67; treas. J.I. Case Co., Racine, Wis., 1967—; dir. First Am. Nat. Bank, Wausaw, Wis. Mem. adv. com. Pub. Expenditure Survey of Wis., 1977—. Mem. Ill., Chgo. bar assns., Nat. Assn. Corp. Treas. Home: 310 Sumac Rd Highland Park IL 60035 Office: 700 State St Racine WI 53404

GLICKMAN, ROBERT MORRIS, physician, educator; b. Bklyn., June 23, 1939; s. David B. and Sally G.; m. Mary Holahan, June 20, 1961; children: Jonathan, Michael. B.A. magna cum laude, Amherst Coll., 1960; M.D. cum laude, Harvard U., 1964. Diplomate: Am. Bd. Internal Medicine. Intern Harvard Med. Services, Boston City Hosp., 1964-65, asst. resident in medicine, 1965-66; research fellow in medicine Harvard Med. Sch., Boston, 1966-68; clin. and research fellow in medicine Mass. Gen. Hosp., Boston, 1966-68, asst. in medicine, 1970-74, asst. physician, 1974-75; instr. medicine Harvard Med. Sch., 1970-72, asst. prof., 1972-77, assoc. prof., 1977; chief div. gastroenterology, asst. physician Beth Israel Hosp., Boston, 1975-77; chief div. gastroenterology Columbia Presbyn. Med. Center, N.Y.C., 1977—; asso. prof. medicine Columbia U. Coll. Physicians and Surgeons, N.Y.C., 1977-81, prof. medicine, 1981-83, chmn., Samuel Bard prof. medicine, 1983—; chmn. gastrointestinal sect. abnormal human biology, 1978—; dir. Med. Service Presbyn. Hosp., 1983—. Mem. editorial bd.: Jour. Lipid Research, 1978-79, Jour. Clin. Investigation, 1979-84, Am. Jour. Medicine, 1981—; contbr. articles to med. jours. Served to maj. M.C. U.S. Army, 1968-70. Mem. Am. Fedn. Clin. Research (councillor Eastern sect. 1975-79, sec.-treas. 1976-79), Am. Gastroent. Assn., Harvey Soc., Nat. Found. Ileitis and Colitis (mem. sci. adv. bd. 1978), Am. Soc. Clin. Investigation (councillor 1981—, pres. elect 1983, pres. 1984-85), Phi Beta Kappa, Sigma Xi, Alpha Omega Alpha. Office: 630 W 168th St New York NY 10032

GLICKSMAN, ARVIN S(IGMUND), physician; b. Bklyn., Mar. 14, 1924; s. Charles and Myrtle (Fetner) G.; m. Bernice R. Grobstein, Jan. 30, 1956; children: Jonathan, Jane Ellen, Merrylee, Caroline, Jeanette. M.B., M.D., Chgo. Med. Sch., 1949. Intern Kings County Hosp., Bklyn., 1948-50; AEC postdoctoral research fellow Duke U., 1950-51; postgrad. research fellow Brookhaven Nat. Labs., Upton, N.Y., 1951-52; resident in medicine Meml. Hosp., N.Y.C., 1952-54, clin. asst. physician in medicine, 1955-64, asst. attending radiation therapist, 1964-65; research fellow Sloan-Kettering Inst., N.Y.C., 1954-60, asso., 1960-65; mem. med. research inst. Michael Reese Hosp., Chgo., 1964-65, asso. chmn. dept. radiation therapy, 1965-67; dep. dir. radiotherapy Mount Sinai Hosp., N.Y.C., 1967-73; prof. radiotherapy Mount Sinai Sch. Medicine, 1971-73; dir. radiation oncology R.I. Hosp., Providence, 1973—; prof. med. scis., chmn. radiation medicine Brown U., 1973—; practice medicine specializing in radiation oncology; hon. med. cons. NIH, Royal Marsden Hosp.; mem. cancer clin., investigation rev. com. Nat. Cancer Inst., 1975-79, mem. radiation oncology com., 1976—. Editor: (with others) Computers in Radiotherapy, 1970, 73; contbr.: numerous articles to profl. jours. Mem. exec. com. R.I., Am. Cancer Soc.; chmn. radiotherapy com. Cancer and Acute Leukemia Group B; chmn. task force info. systems R.I. Cancer Control Bd., also mem. exec. com. Dillon fellow Royal Marsden Hosp., Surrey, Eng., 1961-62; Research Career Devel. awardee NIH, 1962-64. Fellow Am. Coll. Radiology; mem. New Eng. Soc. Radiation Oncologists (pres. 1975-76), N.Y. Roentgen Ray Soc. (chmn. sect. therapeutic radiology 1972-73), Am. Soc. Clin. Oncology, Am. Assn. Cancer Edn., Am. Assn. Cancer Research, Am. Radium Soc., Am. Soc. Therapeutic Radiologists, Brit. Inst. Radiology. Home: Old Blackstone Rd Uxbridge MA 01569 Office: Rhode Island Hosp Providence RI 02902

GLICKSMAN, MAURICE, engineering educator, university dean and provost; b. Toronto, Ont., Can., Oct. 16, 1928; came to U.S., 1949, naturalized, 1961; s. Robert Maxwell and Fanny Bella (Lachowitz) G.; m. Yetta Leich, Dec. 18, 1949; children: Howard David, Roslynn Sue, Marcie Ann. Student, Queen's U., 1946-49; M.Sc., U. Chgo., 1952, Ph.D., 1954. Research asso. Inst. Nuclear Studies, U. Chgo., 1954; mem. tech. staff RCA Labs., Princeton, N.J., 1954-61, head Plasma Physics Group, 1961-63; dir. research RCA Research Labs., Tokyo, 1963-67; head Gen. Research Group, Princeton, 1967-69; Univ. prof., prof. engring. Brown U., 1969—, dean Grad. Sch., 1974-76, dean faculty and acad. affairs, 1976-78, provost, dean faculty, 1978—; cons. RCA Corp., 1969-77; vis. scientist MIT, 1983-84; chmn. com. materials for radiation detection devices Nat. Acad. Scis., 1971-74; chmn. vis. com. U. Pa., 1977-83, Vanderbilt U., 1977-81; mem. vis. com. Emory U., 1981—. Contbr. research articles to profl. jours. Pres., Jewish Center, Princeton, 1962-63; v.p. cultural and ednl. Jewish Community Center, Tokyo, 1965-67; mem. Bur. Jewish Edn., R.I., 1974—, v.p., 1975-80; v.p. Jewish Fedn., R.I., 1980-83; trustee Miriam Hosp., 1979—, chmn. bd., 1983-84; bd. dirs. Ctr. Research Libraries, 1983-84. Recipient Outstanding Achievement award RCA, 1956, 62. Fellow Am. Phys. Soc., IEEE; mem. N.Y. Acad. Scis., Phys. Soc. Japan, Am. Soc. Engring. Edn., AAAS, Phi Beta Kappa, Sigma Xi. Jewish (trustee 1972—). Patentee frequency multipliers, hall-effect devices, semiconductor devices and circuits. Home: 10 Westwood Ln Barrington RI 02806 Office: Univ Hall Brown U Providence RI 02912

GLIDDEN, ALLAN HARTWELL, insurance company executive; b. Waltham, Mass., Apr. 19, 1920; s. George H. and Irene G.; m. Mary C. Ward, Apr. 20, 1941; children: Bruce, Kenneth, Irene. Student, Bryant and Stratton Bus. Sch., 1939-40; student seminars, Harvard Bus. Sch., Princeton U. With Home Owners Loan Corp., Boston, 1940-41; with Bethlehem Steel Corp., 1941-44, Prudential Ins. Co. Am., 1946-71, gen. mgr. real estate investments, 1969-71; v.p. real estate and mortgage investments Mut. Life Ins. Co. N.Y., N.Y.C., 1971—; vice chmn., trustee MONY Mortgage Investors, 1971-82; dir. A & A Investment Corp., Pub. Storage N.V., Greerco Co.; mem. loan screening com. Lincoln First Real Estate Credit Corp.; mem. real estate adv. bd. Investment Mgmt. Group Citibank.; mem. mortgage adv. com. N.Y. State Employees Pension Fund, 1972-81. Served with AUS, 1944-46. Mem. Soc. Indsl. Realtors, N.Y. Real Estate Bd., Internat. Council Shopping Centers, Urban Land Inst., West Side Assn. Commerce. Republican. Home: 36 Crosby Ln Brewster MA 02631 Office: Mut of NY 1740 Broadway New York NY 10019

GLIDDEN, LLOYD SUMNER, JR., insurance executive, investment executive; b. Wakefield, Mass., Aug. 11, 1922; s. Lloyd Sumner and Ida Emma (Dow) G. Student, Bentley Sch. Acctg., 1947. With Liberty Mut. Ins. Co., Boston, 1939—; sr. v.p., treas., 1983—; treas. Liberty Mut. Fire Ins. Co., 1958—, Liberty Life Assurance Co., 1963—; v.p., treas. Liberty Ins. Corp., 1983—; treas., asst. sec. Liberty N.W. Ins. Corp., Portland, Oreg., 1983—. Trustee Northwestern U., Boston. Served with USCG, 1942-46. Mem. Boston Security Analysts Soc., Boston Econ. Club, Treas. Club Boston. Home: 4 Cooks Farm Ln Lynnfield MA 01940 Office: Liberty Mutual Ins Co 175 Berkeley St Boston MA 02117

GLIDDEN, ROBERT BURR, musician, educator; b. Rippey, Iowa, Nov. 29, 1936; s. Burr Harold and Lora Elsie (Groves) G.; m. Rene Colete Siefken, Apr. 26, 1964; children: Melissa, Michele, Briana. B.A., U. Iowa, 1958, M.A., 1960, Ph.D., 1966. Tchr. instrumental music Morrison (Ill.) Community High Sch., 1958-63, Univ. Schs., Iowa City, 1963-66; asst. prof. music Wright State U., Dayton, Ohio, 1966-67, Ind. U., Bloomington, 1967-69; also asst. dir. bands; asso. prof. music U. Okla., 1969-72, Norman; also dir. grad. studies in music; exec. dir. Nat. Assn. Schs. Music, Washington, 1972-75, treas., 1977-82, v.p., 1982—; dean Coll. Musical Arts, Bowling Green (Ohio) State U., 1975-79, Sch. Music, Fla. State U., Tallahassee, 1979—; cons. music curricula and adminstrn., condr., clinician; chmn. Council Specialized Accrediting Agys., 1976-77. Bd. dirs. Council on Postsecondary Accreditation, 1977-84, exec. com., 1979-84, chmn., 1981-83; bd. dirs. Arts, Edn. and Ams., Inc., 1978-81; chmn. advanced placement music com. Coll. Bd., 1977-79; mem. Nat. Council on Arts Task Force on Edn., Tng. and Devel. of Profl. Artists and Arts Educators, 1977-78; mem. adv. council on accreditation Nat. League for Nursing, 1977-81. Mem. Coll. Music Soc. (chmn. govt. relations com. 1976-78), Music Educators Nat. Conf., Music Tchrs. Nat. Assn., Phi Beta Kappa, Pi Kappa Lambda (nat. v.p. 1979-81, pres. 1981—). Episcopalian. Home: 6759 Circle J Rd Tallahassee FL 32312 Office: Sch Music Fla State U Tallahassee FL 32306

GLIEDMAN, MARVIN L., surgeon, educator; b. N.Y.C., Aug. 3, 1929; m. Natalie Gliedman, 1954; children: Charles H., Joanna. B.A., Syracuse U., 1950; M.D., State U. N.Y., 1954. Asst. instr. surgery State U. N.Y. Downstate Med. Center, Bklyn., 1959-60, asst. prof., 1960-64, asso. prof., 1964-66; prof. Albert Einstein Coll. Medicine, 1967—, chmn. dept. surgery, 1972—, Montefiore Hosp. and Med. Center, Bronx, N.Y., 1967-72; Surgeon-in-chief Combined Depts. Surgery, Albert Einstein Coll. of Medicine and Montefiore Hosp. and Med. Center, 1976—; asst. attending surgeon Kings County Hosp., Bklyn., 1960—. Served to lt. M.C. USNR, 1956-58. Recipient Dudley Meml. medal, 1954, Linder Surg. prize, 1954, Alumni Achievement medallion for disting. service to Am. medicine SUNY; Markle scholar Acad. Medicine, 1964-69. Mem. Am. Soc. Nephrology, Am. Surg. Assn., N.Y. Acad. Sci., ACS (chpt. pres. 1974, gov. 1974), Internat. Cardiovascular Soc., European Soc. for Exptl. Surgery, Internat. Biliary Assn., Transplantation Soc., Soc. Vascular Surgery, Surgery Alimentary Tract, Soc. Surg. Chairmen, Internat. Soc. Surgery, Am. Gastroenterological Soc., Univ. Surgeons Soc., Acad. Surgery, Halsted Soc., Alpha Omega Alpha. Address: Montefiore Hosp and Med Center 111 E 210th St Bronx NY 10467

GLIER, INGEBORG JOHANNA, educator; b. Dresden, Germany, June 22, 1934; came to U.S., 1972; d. Erich Oskar and Gertrud Johanne (Niese) G. Student, Mt. Holyoke Coll., 1955-56; Dr. phil. (studienstiftung des deutschen Volkes), U. Munich, Germany, 1958, Habilitation, 1969; M.A. (hon.), Yale U., 1973. Asst., lectr. U. Munich, 1958-69, universitätsdozentin, 1969-72; vis. prof. Yale U., 1972-73, prof. German, 1973—, chmn. dept., 1979-81, sr. faculty fellow, 1974-75; vis. prof. U. Cologne, Germany, 1970-71, U. Colo., Boulder, spring 1983. Author: Struktur und Gestaltungsprinzipien in den Dramen John Websters, 1958, Deutsche Metrik, 1961, Artes amandi, Untersuchung zu Geschichte, Überlieferung und Typologie der deutschen Minnereden, 1971; Contbr. articles, book reviews to profl. jours. Mem. Internationaler Germanisten-Verband, Modern Lang. Assn., Mediaeval Acad. Am., Internat. Courtly Lit. Soc., Wolfram von Eschenbach Gesellschaft. Home: 111 Park St Apt 12-T New Haven CT 06511 Office: Dept Germanic Langs Yale Univ PO Box 18-A New Haven CT 06520

GLIKES, ERWIN ARNO, publishing company executive; b. Heide, Belgium, June 30, 1937; came to U.S., 1942, naturalized, 1947; s. Morris I. and Gella (Lubowski) G.; m. Toni Marlene Brown, June 24, 1959; children: Michael Joseph, Lela Maeve. A.B., Columbia U., 1959, postgrad., 1960-62; postgrad., U. Tübingen, Germany, 1962-63. Lectr. English and comparative lit. Columbia, 1960-62, asst. dean coll., 1965-69; with Basic Books Inc., N.Y.C., 1969-72, exec. v.p., 1971-72, pres., pub., 1972—; also v.p. Harper & Row, Pubs., Inc., 1975-76, pub., group v.p. for adult trade books, 1976-80; sr. v.p. Simon and Schuster, N.Y.C.; pres. Touchstone Books div., 1980-83; pres., pub. Free Press div. Macmillan Pub. Co., 1983—; v.p. Macmillan Pub. Co., 1983—; dir. Harper & Row, Ltd., London; cons. Nat. Endowment for Humanities, Washington, 1971-76; mem. nat. adv. council Center for the Book, Library of Congress, from 1978; mem. ALA Commn. Freedom and Equality of Access to Info., 1983—. Author: Of Poetry and Power, 1964. Woodrow Wilson fellow, 1962-63; German Acad. Austanschdienst fellow, 1962-63. Mem. Assn. Am. Pubs. (vice-chmn. gen. pub. div. 1974-75, chmn. 1975-76), Phi Beta Kappa. Office: The Free Press 866 3d Ave New York NY 10022

GLIMCHER, ARNOLD BRUCE, art executive; b. Duluth, Minn., Mar. 12, 1938; s. Paul and Eva (Fishman) G.; m. Mildred Louise Cooper, Dec. 20, 1959; children: Paul William, Marc Cooper. B.A., Mass. Coll. Art., 1969; postgrad., NYU Sch. Psychology, Boston U. Founder, owner Pace Gallery, Boston, 1961-63, founder, pres., N.Y.C., 1963—; founder Pace Editions, 1968—. Author: Louise Nevelson, 1972, paperback edit., 1976; (with Paul Vitz) Modern Art and Modern Science: The Parallel Analysis of Vision, 1983; contbr. articles to art jours. Fellow Israel Mus. (chmn. devel. com. 1976-77); mem. Am. Acad. Arts and Letters, Art Dealers Assn. Am. (bd. dirs.). Editor, cataloger, text writer for various art vols. selector, installer various mus. exhibits and retrospectives. Office: Pace Gallery 32 E 57th St New York NY 10022

GLIMCHER, MELVIN JACOB, orthopedic surgeon; b. Brookline, Mass., June 2, 1925; s. Aaron and Clara (Fink) G.; m. Geraldine Lee Bogolub, June 22, 1946; children: Susan Deborah, Laurie Hollis, Nancy Blair. Student, Duke, 1943-44; B.S. in Mech. Engring. with highest distinction, Purdue U., 1946; M.D. magna cum laude, Harvard, 1950; postgrad., Mass. Inst. Tech., 1956-59. Intern surgery Strong Meml. Hosp., Rochester, N.Y., 1950-51; 3d asst. resident surgery Mass. Gen. Hosp., Boston, 1951-52, 2d asst. resident, 1952-53, asst. resident orthopedic surgery, 1954-55, chief resident, 1956, chief orthopedic service, 1965-71, chmn. dept. orthopedic surgery, 1968-71; asst. resident orthopedic surgery Children's Med. Center, Boston, 1953-54, jr. resident, 1955-56; mem. faculty Harvard Med. Sch., 1956—, Edith M. Ashley prof. orphopedic surgery, 1965-71, Harriet M. Peabody prof., 1971—; also chmn. dept.; orthopedic surgeon-in-chief Children's Hosp. Med. Center, Boston, 1971—. Trustee Forsyth Dental Infirmary. Served with USMCR, World War II. Recipient Soma Weiss award Harvard Med. Sch., 1950, Borden Research award, 1950; Kappa Delta award, 1959; Internat. Assn. Dental Research award, 1964; Ralph Pemberton award Am. Rheumatism Soc., 1969. Fellow Am. Acad. Arts and Scis., Am. Acad. Orthopaedic Surgeons (Silver anniversary Kappa Delta prize 1974), Am. Orthopedic Assn.; mem. Orthopedic Research Soc. (past pres.), Assn. Bone and Joint Surgeons (Nicholas Andry award 1978), Internat. Soc. for Study Lumbar Spine (Volvo award 1983), Societe Internationale de Chirurgie Orthopedique et de Traumatologie. Home: 14 Channing Rd Brookline MA 02146 Office: 300 Longwood Ave Boston MA 02115

GLIMM, JAMES GILBERT, mathematician; b. Peoria, Ill., Mar. 24, 1934; s. William Frederick and Barbara Gilbert (Hooper) G.; m. Adele Strauss, June 30, 1957; 1 dau., Alison. A.B., Columbia U., 1956, A.M., 1957, Ph.D., 1959. From asst. prof. to prof. math. MIT, 1960-69; prof. Courant Inst., NYU, 1969-74; prof. math. Rockefeller U., N.Y.C., 1974-82; prof. Courant Inst., NYU, N.Y.C., 1982—. Co-author: Quantum Physics, 1981; mem. editorial bds. profl. jours.; contbr. articles to sci. publs. Recipient Dannie Heineman prize in math. physics, 1980; Guggenheim fellow, 1963, 65. Mem. Internat. Assn. Math. Physicists, Am. Math. Soc., Nat. Acad. Scis., Soc. Indsl. and Applied Math., Am. Acad. Arts and Scis., Soc. Petroleum Engrs., N.Y. Acad. Scis. (award in phys. and math. scis. 1979). Office: Courant Inst 251 Mercer St New York NY 10012

GLIMP, FRED LEE, univ. adminstr.; b. Boise, Idaho, Feb. 15, 1926; s. Fred Lee and Emily Massie (Turner) G.; m. Eleanor Croxon Foley, Dec. 22, 1951; children—Emily Ellen, Frederick Lee, Sarah Susan, Rebecca Jane. Student, George Washington U., 1943-44; A.B., Harvard, 1950, postgrad., 1950-54, Ph.D., 1964; postgrad., Queens Coll., Cambridge, 1952-53. Asst. to the dean admission and financial aids Harvard, 1954-58, dir. freshman scholarships, 1958-60, teaching fellow econs., 1956-59, dean admissions and financial aids, 1960-67; dean Harvard Coll., 1967-69; exec. dir. Com. Permanent Charity Fund, Boston, 1969-79; v.p. alumni and devel. Harvard U., 1979—. Dir. Charlestown Savs. Bank, Northeast Investors Trust.; Mem. Belmont Sch. Com., 1968-73; Trustee Belmont Hill Sch., 1973—, Browne and Nichols Sch., 1969-75, Coll. Entrance Exam. Bd., 1965-69; chmn. Coll. Scholarship Service, 1965-66, St. Sebastian's Sch., 1973—, Pub.-Pvt. Forum on Higher Edn. in Mass., 1974-76. Served to s/sgt. USAAF, 1944-46. Mem. Assn. Coll. Admissions Counselors (exec. bd. 1963-65), Phi Beta Kappa. Clubs: Commercial, Harvard (Boston and N.Y.); Mill Reef, Tavern. Home: 613 Pleasant St Belmont MA 02178

GLINDEMAN, HENRY PETER, JR., real estate developer; b. Coeur d'Alene, Idaho, Sept. 26, 1924; s. Henry Peter and Laura Mae (Buchanan) G.; m. Stormy W. Smith, Mar. 22, 1977; children: Pamela, Henry Peter, III, John. B.S., U.S. Naval Acad., 1945; postgrad., U.S. Naval War Coll., 1959-60. Commd. ensign U.S. Navy, 1945, advanced through grades to rear adm., 1973; exec. officer, comdg. officer Fighter Squadron 154, 1962-63, comdr. Attack Carrier Air Wing 15, 1964-65, tng. officer attack carrier air wing, staff, comdr. U.S. Naval Forces, U.S. Pacific Fleet, 1965-66, readiness officer, staff comdr. U.S. First Fleet, 1966-68, comdg. officer U.S.S. Passumpsic, 1968-69, head Attack Carrier Weapons Requirements br. Office Chief Naval Ops., 1970-71, comdg. officer U.S.S. Ranger, 1971-73, chief Fleet Coordinating Group, Nakhon Phanom, Thailand, 1973-74, dir. Office Program Appraisal, Office Sec. Navy, 1974-75, comdr. Carrier Group 7, 1975-76, comdr. Carrier Group 3, 1976, comdr. Carrier Group 5, Carrier Strike Force, 7th Fleet, 1976-77, comdr. Naval Safety Center, 1977-78; pres. Mr. Quick Lube Inc., Clearwater, Fla., 1978-81; v.p. Fla. Light and Save Inc., 1981-83; real estate developer, 1983—. Pres. Edgar Allan Poe Jr. High Sch. PTA, Annandale, Va., 1960-61, Annandale Am. Little League, 1961-62; sec. exec. com. Troop 674, Boy Scouts Am., Annandale, 1961-62. Decorated Legion of Merit with 4 gold stars, D.F.C., Air medal with gold star, Navy Commendation medal with Combat V. Mem. U.S. Naval Acad. Alumni Assn., Navy League, Mil. Order World Wars, Assn. Naval Aviation. Episcopalian. Club: Golden Gate Breakfast (San Francisco). Home: 2725 Northridge Dr Clearwater FL 33519

GLINES, CARROLL VANE, JR., editor; b. Balt., Dec. 2, 1920; s. Carroll Vane and Elizabeth Marion (Cross) G.; m. Mary Ellen Edwards, Oct. 1, 1943; children: Karen Ann (Mrs. Claude K. Hudson), David Edwards, Valerie Jean. Student, Drexel Inst. Tech., 1938-40, Canal Zone Jr. Coll., 1946-48, U. Munich, 1948; B.B.A., U. Okla., 1952, M.B.A., 1954; M.A., Am. U., 1969. Commd. 2d lt. USAF, 1942, advanced through grades to col., 1965; military service, 1941-68; mgr. publs. Nat. Bus. Aircraft Assn., Washington, 1968; assoc. editor Armed Forces Mgmt. mag., Washington, 1969-70; editor Air Cargo mag., Washington, 1970-71, Air Line Pilot mag., 1971—; sr. editor Aviation Space mag.; mgr. publs. Air Line Pilots Assn.; lectr. U. Dayton, U. Alaska, Am. U. Author 24 books; contbr. articles to mags.; Gen. editor: Air Force Acad. series, 1970-74; editorial cons.: Van Nostrand Reinhold, 1980—; contbg. editor: Nation's Bus, 1981—; mem. adv. bd.: Aviation Hist. Collection, U. Tex., Dallas, 1981—. Recipient numerous awards from press assns. Freedoms Found. Mem. Aviation-Space Writers Assn. (Lauren D. Lyman award), Air Force Assn., Air Force Hist. Found., Quiet Birdmen, Explorers Club, Soc. Profl. Journalists-Sigma Delta Chi. Clubs: International Aviation, National Aviation., Army-Navy. Home: 7212 Warbler Ln McLean VA 22101 Office: 1625 Massachusetts Ave NW Washington DC 20036

GLISSON, FLOYD WRIGHT, food company executive; b. Akron, Ohio, Aug. 13, 1947; s. Floyd Wright G. and Audrey Mae (Hill) Pardee; m. Janice Talbert, Aug. 22, 1970; children: Tenley, Evan. B.S., U. Akron, 1969; M.B.A., U. Pitts., 1970. C.P.A., Colo. Staff auditor Arthur Andersen & Co., Denver, 1970-72; controller More, Combs & Burch, Denver, 1972-74; v.p. controller Armour-Dial co., Phoenix, 1974-80; v.p. corp. devel. Hunt-Wesson Foods, Inc., Fullerton, Calif., 1980—. Mem. bus. adv. council Calif. State U.-Fullerton, 1982-83. D.G. Sisterson fellow U. Pitts., 1970. Home: 23851 Inverness Pl Laguna Niguel CA 92677 Office: Hunt-Wesson Foods Inc 1645 W Valencia Dr Fullerton CA 92634

GLITMAN, MAYNARD WAYNE, foreign service officer; b. Chgo., Dec. 8, 1933; s. Ben and Reada (Kutok Klass) G.; m. G. Christine Amundsen, Dec. 22, 1956; children: Russell M., Erik W., Karen C., Matthew M., Rebecca S. B.A. with highest honors, U. Ill., 1955; M.A., Fletcher Sch. Law and Diplomacy, 1956; postgrad., U. Calif., Berkeley, 1965-66. Joined fgn. service Dept. State, 1956, economist, 1956-59; vice consul, Nassau, Bahamas, 1959-61; econ. officer Am. Embassy, Ottawa, Ont., Can., 1961-65, Dept. State, 1966-67; mem. U.S. Del. to UN Gen. Assembly, 1967, Nat. Security Council staff, 1968; polit. officer, 1st sec. Am. Embassy, Paris, 1968-73; dir. Office of Internat. Trade, Dept. State, Washington, 1973-74, dep. asst. sec. of state for internat. trade policy, 1974-76, dep. asst. sec. def. for Europe and NATO affairs, 1976-77; dep. U.S. permanent rep. to NATO, Brussels, Belgium, 1977-81; ambassador, dep. chief U.S. del. Intermediate Nuclear Forces Negotiations, ACDA, Geneva, Switzerland, 1981—. Served with U.S. Army, 1957. Recipient Public Service medal U.S. Dept. Def., 1981. Mem. Phi Beta Kappa. Home: Fletcher Vt Gen Delivery Jeffersonville VT 05464 Office: ACDA 1-3 Ave de la Poix Geneva Switzerland

GLIXON, DAVID M(ORRIS), editor; b. Bklyn., Sept. 23, 1908; s. Montague and Bertha Helen (Simons) G.; m. Helen Bertha Marx, Feb. 5, 1938; children: Jonathan E., Judith Glixon Kutt. B.A. magna cum laude, Washington Sq. Coll., NYU, 1934. Editor Book Prodn. Mag., 1934-43; with various pubs., N.Y.C., 1945-47; mgr. Story Classics, Emmaus, Pa., 1948-53; asst. editor, asst. art dir. Ltd. Editions Club and Heritage Club, N.Y.C., 1954-58, editor, art dir., 1958-76; editor Lit. I.Q.; reference book reviewer Saturday Rev., 1962-72; editor Tchrs. Quiz, Lit. Cavalcade, Scholastic Mags., 1973—; book reviewer Hartford Courant, 1981—; editorial cons. Heritage Club, Easton Press, Norwalk, Conn., 1977—, Ltd. Edits. Club, N.Y.C., 1979—, Lawrence Urdang, Inc., 1982—. Translator: La Fontaine's Adonis, 1954, Hugo's The Sea and the Wind, 1961; Contbr. articles to lit. and profl. publs. Chmn. Trade Book Clinic, Am. Inst. Graphic Arts, 1941; Mem. Ardsley (N.Y.) Area Fair Housing Com., 1964-67. Home and office: 108 Montclair Dr West Hartford CT 06107

GLOBETTI, GERALD, sociologist, educator; b. Birmingham, Ala., Feb. 22, 1934; s. Joseph and Nella (Roda) G.; m. Rose Elaine Cockrell, Aug. 13, 1966; children: Rosemary, Suzanne. B.A., La. Coll., 1959; M.A., Miss. State U., 1961, Ph.D., 1963. Asst. prof. Miss. State U., State University, 1963-66, assoc. prof., 1966-70, Murray State U., Ky., 1970-72; prof. U. Ala., University, 1973—, chmn. dept. sociology, 1978—; dir. Ctr. Alcohol and Drug Edn. Editor Jour. Alcohol and Drug Edn., 1972. Office: U Ala Box 6109 University AL 35486

GLOCK, CHARLES YOUNG, sociologist; b. N.Y.C., Oct. 17, 1919; s. Charles and Philippine (Young) G.; m. Margaret Schleef, Sept. 12, 1950; children: Susan Young, James William. B.S., N.Y. U., 1940; M.B.A., Boston U., 1941; Ph.D., Columbia U., 1952. Research asst. Bur. Applied Social Research, Columbia U., 1946-51, dir., 1951-58, lectr., then prof. sociology, 1954-58; prof. sociology U. Calif. at Berkeley, 1958-79, prof. emeritus, 1979—, chmn., 1967-68, 69-71; dir. Survey Research Center, 1958-67; adj. prof. Grad. Theol. Union, 1971-79; Luther Weigle vis. lectr. Yale U., 1968. Co-author: Wayward Shepherds, The Anatomy of Racial Attitudes; sr. author: Adolescent Prejudice, To Comfort and To Challenge, Religion and Society in Tension, Christian Beliefs and Anti-Semitism, The Apathetic Majority; contbg. editor: Am. Jour. Sociology; editor: The New Religious Consciousness, Survey Research in the Social Sciences, Beyond the Classics?, Religion in Sociological Perspective, Prejudice U.S.A.; contbr.: numerous articles on social scis. Mem. bd. parish edn. Luth. Ch. Am., 1970-72; mem. mgmt. com. Office Research and Planning, 1973-80; bd. dirs. Inst. Research in Social Behavior, Cornerhouse Fund, Center for Ethics and Social Policy. Served from pvt. to capt. USAAF, 1942-46. Decorated Bronze Star, Legion of Merit; recipient Roots of Freedom award Pacific bd. Anti-Defamation League, 1977; Berkeley citation U. Calif., Berkeley, 1979; Rockefeller fellow, 1941-42; fellow Center Advanced Study Behavioral Scis., 1957-58, Soc. for Religion in Higher Edn., 1968-69. Mem. Am. Assn. Pub. Opinion Research (v.p., pres. 1962-64, pres. Pacific chpt. 1959-60), Soc. Sci. Study Religion (Western rep., pres. 1968-69), Am. Sociol. Assn. (v.p. 1978-79), Religious Research Assn., Sociol. Research Assn. Home: Star Route Coeur d'Alene ID 83814

GLOCK, MARVIN DAVID, educator; b. San Jose, Ill., Nov. 19, 1912; s. David William and Lydia (Gruensfelder) G.; m. Elva Ruth Snell, Apr. 13, 1941; children—Carol Sue, Sandra Kay. Student, Blackburn Coll., 1930-32; A.B., U. Nebr., 1934; M.S., U. Ill., 1935-38; Ph.D., State U. Iowa, 1947. Tchr. Edison (Neb.) High Sch., 1934-36; prin. Mason City (Ill.) Community High Sch., 1936-41; asst. prof. edn. Mich. State U., 1947-49; prof. ednl. psychology Cornell U., Ithaca, N.Y., 1949-83, prof. emeritus, 1983—. Author: (with J.S. Ahmann and Helen Wardeberg) Evaluating Elementary School Pupils, 1960, (with J.S. Ahmann) Evaluating Pupil Growth: Principles of Tests and Measurements, 6th edit, 1980, Readings in Educational Psychology, 1971, Measuring and Evaluating Educational Achievement, 2d edit, 1975, PROBE: An Audiotutorial College Reading Program, 2d edit, 1980, PROBE II: An Audio tutorial Reading Program, 1978; author: numerous sci. papers. PROBE II: An Audio tutorial Reading Program. Served to lt. USNR, 1942-45. Fulbright fellow Ceylon, 1962-63; recipient numerous research grants. Fellow Am. Psychol. Assn.; mem. Sigma Xi, Phi Kappa Phi. Presbyn. Home: 101 Homestead Terr Ithaca NY 14850

GLOCKER, THEODORE WESLEY, JR., lawyer; b. Knoxville, Tenn., Aug. 10, 1925; s. Theodore W. and Julia (McClarty) G.; m. Eleanor Julia, Nov. 30, 1950; children: Theodore William, Margaret McClarty, Eleanor Julia, David Hansen. Student, U. of South, 1943-44, U. Tex., 1944-45; B.S., U. Tenn., 1947; LL.B., Harvard U., 1950. Bar: N.Mex. 1951, D.C. 1953, Fla. 1956. Practiced in, Albuquerque, 1950-51, Jacksonville, Fla., 1956—; trial atty. lands div. Dept. Justice, Washington, 1952-53; atty. Tax Ct. U.S., 1953-56; mem. firm Buck, Drew & Glocker (and predecessor), 1956-75, Glocker & Lanahan (and predecessor), 1975—; mem. Spl. Liaison Tax Com. Southeastern Region, Jacksonville, 1956-57, 59-60, 65—. Chmn. bd. Duval County (Fla.) Beaches Hosp., 1959-63; pres. Ch. Alliance Greater Jacksonville, 1970-71; v.p. Kairos Prison Ministry. Served with USNR, 1943-46. Mem. Am., N.Mex., Jacksonville bar assns., Bar Assn. D.C., Fla. Bar (chmn. tax sect. 1963-64), Sigma Chi, Tau Beta Pi, Beta Gamma Sigma, Phi Kappa Phi. Presbyterian. Home: 949 Elder Ln Jacksonville FL 32207 Office: 1000 Atlantic Bank Bldg Jacksonville FL 32202

GLOCKNER, PETER G., engineering educator; b. Moragy, Hungary, Jan. 26, 1929; emigrated to Can., 1946. B.Sc. in Civil Engring., McGill U., Montreal, 1955, M.Sc., MIT, 1956, Ph.D., U. Mich., 1964. Asst. prof. applied mechanics U. Alta., 1958-60; asst. prof. dept. civil engring. U. Calgary, Alta., Can., 1960-62, assoc. prof., 1962-68, prof., 1968—, chmn. dept. mech. engring., 1976—. Contbr. articles on shell theory, stability and non-linear behavior of thinwalled structures, dielectrics and non-linear constitutive theory to profl. jours. Whitney fellow, 1955-56; Ford Found. fellow, 1962-64; recipient Gzowski Gold Medal Engring. Inst. Can., 1971. Mem. Can. Soc. Mech. Engring., Can. Soc. Civil Engring., Engring. Inst. Can., Assn. Profl. Engrs., Geologists and Geophysicists Alta. (bd. examiners 1978—), Am. Acad. Mechanics, ASCE, U. Calgary Faculty Assn., Can. Assn. Univ. Tchrs., Am. Hungarian Lit. Guild. Home: 2536 Charlebois Dr Calgary AB Canada T2L OT6 Office: U Calgary Dept Mech Engring Calgary AB Canada T2N 1N4

GLOMSET, DANIEL ANDERS, physician; b. Des Moines, Aug. 28, 1913; s. Daniel Johnson and Anna (Glerum) G.; m. Frances R. Morehouse, June 14, 1937; children: Martha Ann, Carol Anitra, Leif Morehouse. B.S., U. Chgo., 1935, M.D., 1938; M.S., Mayo Clinic, U. Minn., 1943. Intern Barnes Hosp., St. Louis, 1938-40; fellow, 1st asst. Mayo Found., 1940-43; practice internal medicine, Des Moines, 1946—; treas. Internal Med. Clinic, 1947—; mem. staff Broadlawns Gen. Hosp., 1946-67, Iowa Meth. Hosp.; clin. lectr. U. Iowa; cons. Div-Med Internat.; also diving physician. Served to capt. M.C. AUS, 1943-46. Mem. AMA, ACP, Am. Soc. Internal Medicine, Iowa Soc. Internal Medicine (past pres.), Des Moines Med. Library Club (past pres.), Iowa Clin. Med. Soc. (past pres.), Iowa Med. Soc., Am. Gastroenterol. Assn., Am. Soc. Gastrointestinal Endoscopy. Club: Des Moines Prairie (past pres.). Address: 3100 Grand Ave 6A Des Moines IA 50312

GLOS, MARGARET BEACH, mgmt. co. exec.; b. N.Y.C., Jan. 20, 1936; d. Stewart Taft and Josephine (Cushman) Beach; m. Stanley Glos, June 1, 1961; children—Alexander Beach, Maya Cushman, Andrew Bishop. B.A. summa cum laude, Smith Coll., 1958; postgrad., Columbia U., 1959-61, M.I.T., 1978. Editor McGraw-Hill Book Co., N.Y.C., 1958-61; editor Nucleonics mag., 1961-68; exec. dir. Soc. Nuclear Medicine, Am. Bd. Nuclear Medicine, 1968-79; pres. G & T Mgmt. Inc., N.Y.C., 1979—. Author numerous children's books, also profl. articles. Bd. dirs. Brit. Am. Ednl. Found. Mem. Am. Soc. Assn. Execs. (dir.), Profl. Conv. Mgmt. Assn., Meeting Planners Internat., Soc. Nuclear Medicine, Phi Beta Kappa, Sigma Xi. Club: Cosmopolitan. Office: 211 E 43d St New York NY 10017 *

GLOSSER, ALVIN, business executive; b. Johnstown, Pa., 1923. Pres., chief operating officer Glosser Bros., Inc., Johnstown, Pa. Office: Glosser Bros Inc Franklin & Locust Sts Johnstown PA 15901

GLOSTER, HUGH MORRIS, coll. pres.; b. Brownsville, Tenn., May 11, 1911; s. John and Dora (Morris) G.; m. Louise Elizabeth Torrence, June 1, 1935 (div.); children—Alice Louise, Evelyn Elaine; m. Beulah Victoria Harold, Sept. 9, 1957; 1 son, Hugh Morris. Student, LeMoyne Coll., 1927-29; B.A., Morehouse Coll., 1931; M.A. (Univ. fellow), Atlanta U., 1933; Ph.D. (Gen. Edn. Bd. fellow), N.Y. U., 1943; hon. doctorate, U. Haiti, 1968, N.Y. U., 1971, Wayne State U., 1976, Washington U., St. Louis, 1977. Instr., asso. prof. English LeMoyne Coll., 1933-41; prof. English Morehouse Coll., 1941-43; program dir. USO, Ft. Huachuca, Ariz., 1943-44, asso. regional exec., Atlanta, 1944-46; prof. English, chmn. dept. lang. and lit. Hampton Inst., 1946-67, dir. summer session, 1952-62, dean faculty, 1963-67; pres. Morehouse Coll., Atlanta, 1967—; prof. English Atlanta U., summers 1942, 43; guest prof. English N.Y. U., summers 1949, 62; Fulbright prof. English Hiroshima U., Japan, 1953-55; lectr. Orientation Center Fgn. Grad. Students, Coll. William and Mary, summer 1955; vis. prof. Am. lit. U. Warsaw, Poland, 1961-62; lectr. tours, 1933-55, 56, 59, 72, 73, 75, 77, mem. summer faculty various univs. and colls. Author: Negro Voices in American Fiction, 1948; Co-editor: The Brown Thrush: An Anthology of Verse by Negro College Students, 1935, My Life-My Country-My World: College Readings for Modern Living, 1952; Contbg. editor: Phylon: The Atlanta U. Review of Race and Culture, 1948-53; adv. editor: Coll. Lang. Assn. Jour, 1957—. Vice chmn. Ga. Postsecondary Edn. Commn.; mem. pres.'s council Am. Forum for Internat. Studies and Inst. European Studies; past v.p., now mem. exec. com. Assn. Pvt. Colls. and Univs. in Ga.; mem. bd. nominators Am. Inst. for Pub. Service; mem. exec. com. Coll. Entrance Exam. Bd., 1967-71; mem., chmn. exec. com. Ednl. Testing Service, 1971-75; Bd. dirs. United Bd. for Coll. Devel., Com. on Econ. Devel., Inst. European Studies, Martin Luther King Jr. Center for Social Change, So. Christian Leadership Conf.; bd. dirs., trustee United Negro Coll. Fund; trustee Atlanta U., Morehouse Coll., Interdenominational Theol. Center. Recipient research grant Alpha Phi Alpha, summer 1940, Carnegie Found., 1950-51; distinguished contbns. award Coll. Lang. Assn., 1958; Centennial medallion Hampton Inst., 1968; Alumnus of Year award LeMoyne Coll., 1967. Mem. Coll. Lang. Assn. (founder, pres. 1937-38, 48-50), Am. Assn. Higher Edn. (exec. com. 1967-69), Am. Assn. U. Adminstrs. (trustee), Phi Beta Kappa, Sigma Pi Phi Boule, Alpha Phi Alpha. Office: Office of Pres Morehouse College Atlanta GA 30314 *

GLOTH, ALEC ROBERT, retail executive; b. Spokane, Wash., Mar. 26, 1927; s. Erick Carl and Ella L. (Felsch) G.; m. Catharine E. Seabloom, May 26, 1954; children: A. Stephen, Rebecca J. S.E.P., Stanford U., 1973. With Albertson's, 1951—, v.p. mktg., Boise, Idaho, 1970-75, v.p. store planning, 1975-77, v.p., div. mgr., Spokane, Wash., 1977-79, sr. v.p. retail ops., Boise, 1979-81, sr. v.p. store planning, 1981—. Active Boy Scouts Am., Eagle Scout. Served with U.S. Army, 1954-56. Republican. Methodist. Home: 1193 Kingfisher Boise ID 83709 Office: Albertson's Inc 250 Parkcenter Boise ID 83726

GLOVER, CLIFFORD CLARKE, construction company executive; b. Newnan, Ga., May 15, 1913; s. Howard Clarke and Fannie Virginia (Jones) G.; m. Louise Liles, Jan. 16, 1937; children—Edmund Cook, Nancy Liles Glover Kennedy, Virginia Johnston Glover Lee, Laura Clarke. B.C.E., U. N.C., 1934. With Batson-Cook Co., West Point, Ga., 1934—; now chmn.; chief engrs. Contractors, Jacksonville, Fla., 1940-43; dir. First Nat. Bank West Point, Ga.-Ala. Supply Co. Mem. West Point Sch. Bd., 1951-69, chmn., 1964-68; chmn. West Point Planning Bd., 1964—; trustee LaGrange Coll.; pres. George H. Lanier council Boy Scouts Am., 1977-78. Served with USNR, 1945-46. Recipient Silver Beaver award Boy Scouts Am. Mem. Assoc. Gen. Contractors (pres. Ga. br.). Methodist (ofcl. bd.). Clubs: Rotary; Commerce, Capital City (Atlanta); Riverside (West Point). Home: 103 Hillcrest Rd West Point GA 31833 Office: Box 151 West Point GA 31833

GLOVER, JIMMIE THOMPSON, oil company executive; b. Dallas, Oct. 13, 1946; s. Louis Edward and Henrietta (Thompson) G.; m. Diann Carroll Williams, Dec. 28, 1968; children: Jimmie T., Jason O., Jade T. B.A., Prairie View A&M U., 1969. Acct. Shell Oil Co., Tulsa, 1969-74, acctg. supr., 1974-77, Aminoil Inc., Houston, 1977-79, planning and ecol. mgr., Huntington Beach, Calif., 1979-80, v.p., treas., Houston, 1981—. Democrat. Baptist. Home: 13510 Tara Oak Dr Houston TX 77065 Office: Aminoil Inc 2800 N Loop W Houston TX 77292

GLOVER, WILLIAM, theatre critic; b. N.Y.C., May 6, 1911; s. William Harper and Lily P. (Freir) G.; m. Isobel M. Cole, Oct. 26, 1936 (div. 1973). Litt.B., Rutgers U., 1932. City editor Asbury Park (N.J.) Press, 1935-39; news editor AP newsfeatures, 1941-53, theatre writer, 1953—; drama critic for AP, 1960-78. Contbr. to periodicals. Served to lt. (j.g.) U.S. Maritime Service, 1943-45. Mem. N.Y. Drama Critics Circle (pres.), New Drama Forum, N.Y. Press Club, N.Y. Acad. Scis., Phi Beta Kappa, Sigma Delta Chi. Clubs: The Players, Overseas Press (N.Y.C.). Home: 4 E 88th St New York NY 10028

GLOVER, WILLIAM WAYNE, banker; b. Bedford, Ind., Dec. 31, 1901; s. Isaac Newton and Cornelia Jane (Ikerd) G.; m. Gladys Gardner, Aug. 11, 1921; children—Jeanne Clair (Mrs. Joseph Othman Kilian, Jr.), Gladys Elaine (Mrs. Charles E. Kelly). Student, U. So. Calif., 1918-21. With Citizens Nat. Trust & Savs. Bank, Los Angeles, 1921-23; asst. cashier Euclid Savs. Bank, Ontario, Calif., 1923-24; regional dir. Pacific Coast offices C.F. Childs & Co., 1924-30; municipal bond buyer Nat. City Co. of N.Y., San Francisco, 1930-34; v.p., dir. Shaw, Glover & Co., Los Angeles and San Francisco, 1935-37; Pacific Coast rep. N.Y. Stock Exchange firm Salomon Bros. & Hutzler, 1937-38; with Calif. Bank, Los Angeles, 1938—, v.p. charge investments, 1938-59, sr. v.p., 1959—; v.p. Western Bancorp., 1959-64, exec. v.p., 1965—, investment adviser, 1967—; exec. v.p. United Calif. Bank, 1964—; owner orange groves. Mem. Central Calif. Citrus Exchange.; Mem. USCG Aux., U.S. Power Squadron, State Assn. County Treas., Calif., Los Angeles chambers commerce. Clubs: Stock Exchange, Bond (Los Angeles); Shark Island Yacht. Home: 2027 Circle Way Hanford CA 93230

GLOWER, DONALD DUANE, university dean, mechanical engineer; b. Shelby, Ohio, July 29, 1926; s. Raymond W.W. and Irva (Scheerer) G.; m. Betty Stahl, June 18, 1953; children: Donald, Michel, Leilani, Jacob. B.S., U.S. Mcht. Marine Acad., 1946, Antioch Coll., 1953; M.S., Iowa State U., 1958; Ph.D. (NSF fellow), Iowa State U., 1960. Engring. officer Grace Lines, Inc., San Francisco, 1947-49; research engr. Battelle Meml. Inst., Columbus, Ohio, 1953-54; asst. prof. Coll. Engring., Iowa State U., 1954-58, 60-61; mem. research staff Sandia Corp., Albuquerque, 1961-63; head radiation effects dept. Gen. Motors Corp., Milw., 1963-64; prof., chmn. dept. mech. and nuclear engring. Ohio State U., 1964-76, dean, 1976—; also dir. Engring. Expt. Sta.; cons. to industry, 1964—. Author: Graphical Theory and Application, 1957, Basic Drawing and Projection, 1957, Working Drawings and Applied Graphics, 1957, Experimental Reactor Analysis and Radiation Measurements, 1965. Bd. dirs. Ohio Transp. Research Center; bd. dirs. Indsl. Tech. Enterprise Bd. Ohio; Bd. dirs. Orton Found., OSU Devel. Fund, Nat. Regulatory Research Inst. Recipient Outstanding Bus. Achievement award U.S. Mcht. Marine Acad., 1961; Outstanding Profl. Achievement award Iowa State U., 1979. Fellow Am. Nuclear Soc.; fellow ASME; mem. Am. Soc. Engring. Edn., Ohio Acad. Sci., Argonne Univs. Assn., Ohio Energy Task Force, Sigma Xi, Tau Beta Pi, Texnikoi. Home: 2338 Kensington Dr Columbus OH 43221 Office: Hitchcock Hall 2070 Neil Ave Columbus OH 43210

GLOYNA, EARNEST FREDERICK, environmental engineer, educator, dean; b. Vernon, Tex., June 30, 1921; s. Herman Ernst and Johanna Bertha (Reithmayer) G.; m. Agnes Mary Lehman, Feb. 17, 1946; children: David Frederick, Lisa Anna (Mrs. Jack Grosskopf). B.S. in Civil Engring, Tex. Technol. U., 1946, M.S., U. Tex., 1949; Dr. Engring., Johns Hopkins U., 1952. Registered profl. engr. Engr. Tex. Hwy. Dept., 1945-46; office engr. Magnolia Petroleum Co., 1946-47; instr. civil engring. U. Tex., Austin, 1947-49, asst. prof., 1949-53, asso. prof., 1953-59, prof., 1959—, Joe J. King prof. engring., 1970-82, Bettie Margaret Smith prof. environ. engring., 1982—, dir. Environ. Health Engring. Labs., 1953-70, dir. Center for Research in Water Resources, 1963-76, dean Coll. Engring., 1970—, dir. Bur. Engring. Research, 1970—; Cons. on water and wastewater treatment and water resources, 1947—; dir. Parker Drilling Co.; cons. numerous industries WHO, World Bank, U.S. Air Force, U.S. Army, U.S. Senate, fgn. cities and govts., UN, 1952—; past chmn. sci. adv. bd. EPA. Author: Waste Stabilization Ponds, 1971 (also French and Spanish edits), (with Joe O. Ledbetter) Principles of Radiological Health, 1969; Editor: (with W. Wesley Eckenfelder, Jr.) Advances in Water Quality Improvement, 1968, Water Quality Improvement by Physical and Chemical Processes, 1970, (with William S. Butcher) Conflicts in Water Resources Planning, 1972, (with Woodson and Drew) Water Management by Electric Power Industry, 1975, (with Malina and Davis) Ponds as a Wastewater Treatment Alternative, 1976; Contbr. numerous articles to profl. jours. Served with Corps Engrs. AUS, 1942-46; ETO. Recipient Harrison Prescott Eddy medal Water Pollution Control Fedn., 1959, Gordon Maskew Fair medal, 1979, Hon. Mem. award, 1980; Water Resources Div. award Am. Water Works Assn., 1959; named Distinguished Engr. Grad. Tex. Tech. U., 1971, Distinguished Alumnus, 1973, Disting. Engring. Grad. U. Tex., Austin, 1982; recipient Joe J. King award U. Tex., Austin, 1982, EPA regional environ. educator award, 1977, Nat. Environ. Devel. award, 1983, Order of Henri Pittier, Nat. Conservation medal Venezuela, 1983. Fellow ASCE (Meritorious Paper award Tex. sect. 1968); mem. Nat. Acad. Engring. (council mem.), Am. Inst. Chem. Engrs., Assn. Environ. Engring. Profs. (past pres.), Am. Soc. for Engring. Edn., Am. Water Works Assn., Am. Acad. Environ. Engrs. (diplomate, past pres., Gorden Maskew Fair award 1981), Water Pollution Control Fedn. (pres.), Tex. Soc. Profl. Engrs. (Engr. of Year award Travis chpt. 1972), Southwestern Soc. Nuclear Medicine (hon.), Nat. Acad. Engring. Mex. (fgn. corr. mem.), Nat. Acad. Scis. Venezuela (fgn. corr.), Sociedad Mexicana de Aguas (Jack Huppert award), Sigma Xi, Tau Beta Pi, Chi Epsilon, Phi Kappa Phi, Pi Epsilon Tau (hon.), Omicron Delta Kappa. Clubs: Cosmos (Washington); Headliners, Faculty Center (Austin). Lodge: Rotary (Washington). Home: 3317 River Rd Austin TX 78703

GLUCK, HERMAN RANDOLPH, mathematician, educator; b. N.Y.C., Nov. 8, 1937; s. Harold and Jeannette Ruth (Copeland) G.; m. Doris Lee Heffer, June 8, 1958; children: Mark, Roberta. A.B., NYU, 1958; M.A., Princeton U., 1960, Ph.D., 1961. Postdoctoral fellow U. Calif., 1961, Inst. Advanced Study at Princeton, 1962; asst. prof. math. Harvard U., 1962-66; asso. prof. math. U. Pa., 1966-69, prof., 1969—, vice chmn. dept., 1971-72, 78-83. Contbr. articles to profl. jours. Woodrow Wilson fellow, 1958-59; Bell Telephone Labs. fellow, 1959-60; NSF predoctoral fellow, 1960-61; Nat. Acad. Sci. postdoctoral fellow, 1961-62; Sloan Found. fellow, 1963-65; NATO sr. fellow, 1971; Guggenheim fellow, 1972-73. Mem. Am. Math. Soc., AAUP, Math. Assn. Am., Phi Beta Kappa. Research in topology, differential geometry and dynamical systems. Home: 1117 Penshurst Ln Narberth PA 19072 Office: U Pa Philadelphia PA 19174

GLUCK, LOUISE ELISABETH, poet; b. N.Y.C., Apr. 22, 1943; d. Daniel and Beatrice (Grosby) G.; m. Charles Hertz (div.); 1 son, Noah Benjamin; m. John Dranow, 1977. Student, Sarah Lawrence Coll., 1962, Columbia U., 1963-65. Vis. poet Goddard Coll., U. N.C., U. Va.; vis. poet U. Iowa; Elliston prof. U. Cin., 1978; vis. faculty Columbia U., 1979; faculty M.F.A. program Goddard Coll., also Warren Wilson Coll., Swannanoa, N.C.; Holloway lectr. U. Calif., Berkeley, 1982, vis. prof., Davis, 1983; Scott prof. poetry Williams Coll., 1983. Author: Firstborn, 1968, The House On Marshland, 1975, Descending Figure, 1980. Rockefeller Found. grantee; NEA grantee, 1979-80; Guggenheim Found. grantee. Address: Creamery Rd Plainfield VT 05667

GLUCKSBERG, SAM, psychology educator; b. Montreal, Que., Can., Feb. 6, 1933; came to U.S., 1946, naturalized, 1954; s. Murray and Sonia (Afrin) G.; m. Trudy Hoenigswald, June 5, 1955; children—Matthew, Kenneth, Nadia. B.S., CCNY, 1956; Ph.D., NYU, 1960. Mem. faculty Princeton, 1963—, prof. psychology, 1970—, chmn. dept., 1974-80. Author: (with others) Experimental Psycholinguistics, 1975, Psychology: An Introduction, 1981; Assoc. editor: Am. Scientist, 1965-70; Editorial bd.: Cognitive Psychology, 1972-79, Child Devel, 1972-78, Jour. Exptl. Psychology, 1981-83; gen. editor, 1984—; Contbr. to (with others) profl. jours. Served to capt. AUS, 1958-63. Home: 14 Aiken Ave Princeton NJ 08540

GLUCKSON, ALBERT, lawyer; b. N.Y.C., Mar. 16, 1924; s. Jacob and Hattie (Berkowitz) G.; m. Gerene Hendricks, Apr. 27, 1967. B.S. in Bus. Adminstrn., NYU, 1952, LL.B., 1954. Bar: NY 1954, Calif. 1963. Vice pres., sec. Computer Scis. Corp., El Segundo, Calif., 1980—. Editorial bd., NYU Law Rev., 1953. Served with USAAF, 1943-46. Home: 6650 Halm Ave Los Angeles CA 90056 Office: Computer Scis Corp 650 N Sepulveda Blvd El Segundo CA 90245

GLUCKSTERN, ROBERT LEONARD, physics educator; b. Atlantic City, N.J., July 31, 1924; s. Louis and Frieda (Dworkin) G.; m. Norma Block, Jan. 24, 1948; children: Steven, Barbara, Amy. B.E.E., CCNY, 1944; Ph.D., MIT, 1948. Asst. prof. physics Yale, New Haven, Conn., 1950-57, asso. prof., 1957-64; prof. physics U. Mass., Amherst, 1964-

75, head dept., 1964-69, asso. provost, 1969-70, provost, vice chancellor for acad. affairs, 1970-75; prof. physics, chancellor U. Md., College Park, 1975—, chancellor, 1975-82; vis. prof. U. Tokyo, Japan, 1969; Cons. on theory of high energy particle accelerators Brookhaven Nat. Lab., Nat. Accelerator Lab., Los Alamos Sci. Lab. Served with USNR, 1944-46. AEC fellow U. Cal. at Berkeley, 1948-49, Cornell U., Ithaca, N.Y., 1949-50; Yale fellow, 1961-62. Fellow Am. Phys. Soc.; mem. AAAS, Fedn. Am. Scientists, Am. Assn. Physics Tchrs. Home: 6100 Westchester Park Dr College Park MD 20740 Office: Physics Dept U Md College Park MD 20740

GLUSHIEN, MORRIS P., arbitrator, lawyer; b. Bklyn., Oct. 15, 1909; s. Isaac and Minnie (Hoffman) G.; m. Anne Williams, Nov. 18, 1945; children: Minna Taylor, Ruth Wedgwood. A.B. with honors, Cornell U., 1929, J.D., 1931. Bar: N.Y. 1932, U.S. Supreme Ct. bar 1940. Pvt. practice, Bklyn., 1932-38; mem. faculty Cornell Law Sch., 1938-39, New Sch. for Social Research, 1977-78; chief U.S. Supreme Ct. sect., asso. gen. counsel NLRB, 1939-47; gen. counsel Internat. Ladies Garment Workers Union, A.F.L.-C.I.O., 1947-72, arbitrator, 1972—; spl. master fed. ct., 1976-78; mem. Nat. Acad. Arbitrators; mem. arbitration panels Am. Arbitration Assn., Fed. Mediation and Conciliation Service, various state and city agys. Editorial bd.: Cornell Law Quar, 1930-31; Contbr. legal periodicals. Bd. dirs. Nat. Legal Aid and Defender Assn., 1954-72. Served with AUS, as cryptanalyst, 1942-45. Mem. ABA (past chmn. labor law sect.), N.Y. State Bar Assn. (labor relations com.), Assn. Bar City N.Y. (past chmn. com. labor and social security legislation), Indsl. Relations Research Assn., Practicing Law Inst., Am. Jewish Congress (com. law and social action), Ams. for Democratic Action, ACLU (com. free speech and assn.), N.Y. U. Conf. on Labor, Phi Beta Kappa, Phi Kappa Phi, Curia. Home: 11 Station Rd Great Neck NY 11023 Office: 21 E 73d St New York NY 10021

GLYNN, ARTHUR LAWRENCE, educator; b. Boston, Jan. 1, 1916; s. John Francis and Mary Ann (Johnson) G.; m. Fern Matthews, May 22, 1945; children—Kristin, Arthur Lawrence, John, Katharine, Steven, Karen. Student, Boston Coll., 1934-36, LL.B., 1939; M.B.A., Boston U., 1941. Bar: Mass. bar 1939. Spl. agt. FBI, 1939-45; practice law, Boston, 1946—; with tax dept. Peat Marwick & Mitchell (C.P.A.'s), Boston, 1945-46; faculty Coll. Bus. Adminstrn., Boston Coll., 1946—, chmn. accounting dept., 1953—, prof. accounting, 1954—. Trustee 128 Trust, Yewelltide Trust; treas. Instrument Leasing Corp.; dir. Yewell Assos., Inc. Mem. Natick (Mass.) Indsl. Devel. Commn. C.P.A., Mass., Mass. Bar Assn., Am. Inst. C.P.A.'s, Financial Execs. Inst., Mass. Soc. C.P.A.'s, Nat. Assn. Accountants, Am. Accounting Assn., Soc. Former Agts. FBI, Beta Gamma Sigma (faculty adviser). Roman Catholic. Home: 31 Robinhood Rd Natick MA 01762 Office: Boston College Chestnut Hill MA 02167

GLYNN, CARLIN (CARLIN MASTERSON), actress; b. Cleve., Feb. 19, 1940; d. Guilford Cresse and Lois Carlin (Wilks) G.; m. Peter Masterson, Dec. 29, 1960; children: Carlin Alexandra, Mary Stuart, Peter C.B. Student, Sophie Newcomb Coll., 1957-58. Resource person Sundance Film Inst. Actress, Alley Theatre, Houston; Off-Broadway appearances include The Match Maker; TV appearances include Today's Health (hostess 1972); appears on most talk shows; appeared in N.Y. as Miss Mona in: The Best Little Whorehouse in Texas, 1978-80; in London, 1981; lead role in: play Winterplay, N.Y.C., 1983, Alterations, Montclair, N.J., 1984; films include Three Days of the Condor, 1974, Resurrection, 1978, Continental Divide, 1981, Sixteen Candles, 1984. Bd. dirs., trustee Consumer Action Now, N.Y.C. Recipient Theatre World award, 1978, Antoinette Perry award, 1979, best actress award in musical Soc. West End Theatres, London, 1981. Mem. Actor's Studio, Actors' Equity Assn., Screen Actors Guild, AFTRA. Episcopalian. Office: 1165 Fifth Ave New York NY 10029

GLYNN, THOMAS JOSEPH, advt. agy. exec.; b. Queens, N.Y., Jan. 18, 1927; s. Thomas A.J. and Irene M. (Shaw) G.; m. Fairlie E. Fraser, Sept. 15, 1951; children—Barbara, Thomas, Nancy, Martha. Student, Bklyn. Coll., 1947; B.B.A., St. John's U., 1950. In prodn. and research J. Walter Thompson Co., N.Y.C., 1950-53, media buyer, 1953-59, asso. media dir., 1959-67, media dir., Chgo., 1967-74; sr. v.p., dir. U.S. Media Resources, N.Y.C., 1974-76; v.p., media dir. N.W. Ayer, A.B.H. Internat., N.Y.C., 1976-77; exec. v.p., mem. exec. com., dir. media services, dir. Campbell Ewald Co., Detroit, 1977—. Bd. dirs. Nat. Outdoor Advt. Bur., 1977-78, Traffic Audit Bur., 1977. Served with USAAF, 1945-46. Mem. Am. Assn. Advt. Agys. (media policy com. 1977), Internat. Radio and TV Execs. Soc., Detroit Advt. Assn., Broadcast Advt. Club: Alpha Kappa Psi. Home: 480 Thetford Ln Bloomfield Hills MI 48013 Office: Campbell Ewald Co Detroit MI

GLYNN, WILLIAM EDWARD, lawyer; b. Schenectady, July 7, 1923; s. William Albert and Marie Veronica (Fitzgerald) G.; m. Jacquelyn Mullaney, June 8, 1957; children: J. Garrett Tilton, William E., Sarah M., Mary Elizabeth, Molly Ann. B.S., U.S. Mil. Acad., 1945; LL.B., Harvard U., 1953. Bar: Conn. 1954. Mem. firm Day, Berry & Howard, Hartford, Conn., 1953—, ptnr., 1959—. Commr. Hartford Housing Authority, 1958-61; mayor City of Hartford, 1961-63, 63-65; mem., chmn. Hartford Found. Pub. Giving, 1968-83. Served to 1st lt. Signal Corps U.S. Army, 1945-50. Mem. ABA, Conn. Bar Assn., Hartford County Bar Assn. Democrat. Roman Catholic. Office: Day Berry and Howard Cityplace Hartford CT 06103

GNANADESIKAN, RAMANATHAN, statistician, researcher; b. Madras, India, Nov. 2, 1932; d. Ambalavanan and Jegathambal (Singaram) Ramanathan; m. Mrudulla R. Gnanadesikan, Feb. 18, 1965; children; Anand, Mukund. B.Sc. with honors, U. Madras, 1952, M.A., 1953; Ph.D., U. N.C., 1957. Sr. research statistician Procter & Gamble Co., Cin., 1957-59; mem. tech. staff Bell Labs., Murray Hill, N.J., 1959—, dept. head, 1968—; vis. prof. U. Cin., 1958-59, Courant Inst. Math. Scis., NYU, 1960-62, Imperial Coll. Sci. and Tech., London, 1968-69, Princeton U., 1971; mem. U.S. Census Adv. Com., 1965-68; mem. com. applied and theoretical stats. Nat. Acad. Sci./NRC, 1978—; cons. Author 2 books, numerous articles. Co-chmn. Asian Indians in Am., Inc., 1970-71. Fellow AAAS, Am. Statis. Assn., Inst. Math. Stats., Royal Statis. Soc.; mem. Internat. Statis. Inst., Biometric Soc., Math. Assn. Am., Internat. Assn. Statis. Computing, Bernoulli Soc., Order Golden Fleece.

GNAT, RAYMOND EARL, librarian; b. Milw., Jan. 15, 1932; s. John and Emily (Syperko) G.; m. Jean Helen Monday, June 19, 1954; children—Cynthia, Barbara, Richard. B.B.A., U. Wis., 1954, postgrad., 1959; M.S., U. Ill., 1958; M.P.A., Ind. U., Indpls., 1981. Page Milw. Pub. Library, 1950-53, jr. librarian, 1954, librarian, 1958-63; circulation asst. U. Ill., 1956-57, serials cataloger, 1957-58; asst. dir. Indpls.-Marion County Pub. Library, 1963-71, dir., 1972—; Exec. dir. Ind. Nat. Library Week, 1965. Served with AUS, 1954-56. Mem. ALA, Ind. Library Assn. (pres. 1980), Bibliog. Soc. Am., Greater Indpls. Info. Inc., Indpls. Adult Edn. Council. Club: Literary. Home: 8246 Shadow Circle Indianapolis IN 46260 Office: 40 E St Clair St Indianapolis IN 46204

GNIEWEK, RAYMOND, violinist; b. East Meadow, N.Y., Nov. 13, 1931; s. Jacenty and Leona (Kurowski) G.; m. Judith Blegen, May 12, 1977; children by previous marriage: Davi Gniewek Loren, Susan Gniewek Law. Mus.B., Eastman Sch. Music, 1953. Mem. Rochester (N.Y.) Philharmonic Orch., 1949-53, concertmaster, 1953-57, Met. Opera Orch., N.Y.C., 1957—, Santa Fe Opera, 1958. Soloist with symphony orchs. in, Chgo., Detroit, San Diego, Miami, Fla., Newport (R.I.), Romantic Music Festivals, Tanglewood Recital Series, (with wife, soprano Judith Blegen.). Recipient Distinguished Alumni award Eastman Sch. Music, 1977. Office: Metropolitan Opera Lincoln Center New York NY 10023

GO, MATEO LIAN POA, educator; b. Amoy, Fukien, China, Sept. 17, 1918; came to U.S., 1956, naturalized, 1961; s. Ramon Occo and Luy (Tan) G.; m. Jean Cheng, May 18, 1946; children—Genevieve, Mateo Jr., Marilyn. B.C.E. (Chi Epsilon, C.E., MacMillan scholar), Cornell U., 1942, Ph.D. in Structural Engrng. (McGraw fellow), 1946; S.M.C.E. (M.I.T. scholar), Mass Inst. Tech., 1943. Constrn. engr. Mahony-Troast Constrn. Co., Passaic, N.J., 1942, 1946- 47; pres. Mateo L.P. Go Constrn. Co., Hamilton Furniture Co., Philippines, 1947-53; mgr. Go Occo & Co., Manila, 1954-56, tech. cons., 1949-54; structural designer R.C. Reese & Assos., Toledo, 1956; asst. prof. Syracuse U., 1957-59; asso. prof. U. Hawaii, 1959-63, prof. engrng., 1963—, chmn. dept. civil engrng., 1969-72, 81—, dir. nuclear defense design summer inst. for engrng., archtl. faculty, 1965, 66, 68; tech. cons. archtl. and engrng. devel. div. Office of Civil Defense, Washington, 1966-67. Dirs. Cebu Chinese High Sch., Philippines, 1951-53, Profl. Adv. Service Center, 1967-71. Mem. Engrng. Assos. (treas. 1969, pres. 1971, 79), Hawaii Acad. Sci., ASCE Am. Soc. Engrng. Edn., Am. Concrete Inst., Sigma Xi, Chi Epsilon, Tau Beta Pi, Phi Kappa Phi, Rho Psi. Home: 2415 Ferdinand Ave Honolulu HI 96822

GOADE, WILLIAM RICHARD, banker, ret. air force officer; b. St. Louis, Mar. 23, 1922; s. Jesse Louis and Edna Rachel (Robertson) G.; m. Margaret Marian Motley, July 3, 1943; children—Christine Goade Orth, Thomas, Deborah Goade Feuring, William, Jonathan. Student, Sacramento Coll., 1951, U. Omaha, 1958, Nat. War Coll., 1966. Commd. 2d lt. USAAF, 1942; advanced through grades to brig. gen. USAF, 1969; pilot with 62 missions over, Europe, 1942-45, flying tng. positions in, 1945-50, pilot, staff officer, 1951-61, duty, Madrid, 1961-63, Hdqrs. USAF, Washington, 1963-66; comdr., Laughlin AFB, Tex., 1967-69; air force mem. Joint U.S. Mil. Mission for AID to Turkey, Ankara, 1969-71; dir. Air Force Tech. Applications Center, Patrick AFB, Fla., 1971-73; ret., 1973; v.p., cashier Del Rio Bank & Trust Co., Tex., 1974-78, Alamo Nat. Bank, San Antonio, 1978—. Decorated D.S.M., Legion of Merit with oak leaf cluster, D.F.C., Air medal with 2 silver, 1 bronze oak leaf cluster. Mem. Air Force Assn., Order of Daedalians. Methodist. Home: 9207 Standing Creek San Antonio TX 78230

GOALD, HAROLD JEROME, neurosurgeon; b. Phila., Apr. 28, 1929; s. Isadore and Anna (Balen) G. A.B., Temple U., 1950, M.D., 1954. Intern Temple U. Hosp., Phila., 1954-55; resident in neurosurgery U. Ala., 1960-62; fellow in neurosurgery Mayo Clinic, Rochester, Minn., 1955; practice medicine specializing in micro neurosurgery of spine No. Va., 1962—; asst. clin. prof. Georgetown U. Sch. Medicine, Washington, 1972—; chief div. neurosurgery Jefferson Meml. Hosp., Alexandria, Va., 1977—; vis. prof. neurosurgery Am. U. of Caribbean Sch. Medicine. Served with USPHS, 1957-60. Fellow A.C.S.; mem. Am. Assn. Neurologic Surgeons, Congress Neurologic Surgeons, Washington Acad. Neurosurgery. Office: 4600 King St Alexandria VA 22302

GOBEIL, H. PAUL, food company executive; b. St.-Remi de Tingwick, Que., Can., Mar. 1, 1942; s. Jean Marie and Marie Reine (Potvin) G. B.A., Laval U., Quebec, Que., Can., 1961; Baccalaureat en commerce, Sherbrooke (Que.) U., 1963; Advanced Mgmt. Program, Harvard U., 1981. Chartered acct. Maitrise en sciences comptables Sherbrooke (Que.) U., 1965; Partner Larochelle, Savard, Gosselin, Gobeil & Assocs. (C.A.), 1966-70, Samson Belair, Cote, Lacroix & Assocs. (C.A.), 1970-73; advisor Larochelle, Savard & Assos. (C.A.), Sherbrooke, 1973-75; mgmt. cons., Montreal, Que., 1974-75; asst. to v.p. fin. and adminstrn. Provigo Inc., Montreal, 1974-76, dir. fin., 1975-76, v.p. fin. and adminstrn., treas., 1976-81, v.p. fin., 1981—, also dir., 1981—; pres., chief operating officer M. Loeb, Ltd., 1981—; vice chmn., dir. IGA Can. Ltd., 1981—; pres. Mobigesco; v.p. Ltee Placement Jaguar Inc., Le Domaine Hippique de l'Estrie Inc.; treas., asst. sec. Les Placements Denault Inc., Provigo (Retail) Inc., Provigo (Distbn.) Inc.; v.p., treas., asst. sec. Provi-Soir Inc.; treas. Les Promenades Montarville Inc. Mem. Montreal Bd. Trade, Order Chartered Accts. Can., Ont. Inst. Chartered Accts., Que. C. of C. Home: PO Box 60 Russell Rd Carlsbad Springs Gloucester ON K0A 1K0 Canada Office: 400 Industrial Ave Ottawa ON K1G 3K8 Canada

GOBEL, JOHN HENRY, railroad company executive; b. Oak Park, Ill., Oct. 21, 1926; s. Henry Andrew and Mary Ann (Coughlan) G.; m. Carol Zvara, Mar. 8, 1969; children: Kristina, Gregory. B.A. cum laude, DePaul U., 1950, J.D., 1952. Bar: Ill. 1951, Md. 1975, Ohio 1976. Various positions law dept. Chgo. and North Western R.R. Co., Chgo., 1952-60, Balt. and Ohio R.R. Co., Balt., 1960-75; asst. gen. counsel Chesapeake and Ohio Ry. Co., Cleve., 1975-77, gen. solicitor, 1977-80, gen. counsel, 1980-82; v.p. govt. relations CSX Corp., Cleve., 1982—. Served with U.S. Army; 1945-46. Fellow Internat. Soc. Barristers; mem. ABA (spl. com. on rules 1967-71), Ill. Bar Assn. (chmn. profl. ethics com., mem. assembly 1973-74), Nat. Assn. R.R. Trial Counsel (nat. sec. 1971-75), Soc. Trial Lawyers Ill. (dir. 1968-70), Ohio R.R. Assn. (chmn.), W.Va. R.R. Assn. (chmn.). Clubs: Union League, Law (Chgo.). Office: Chessie Systems Railroads PO Box 6419 Cleveland OH 44101

GOBELMAN, ROBERT CARL, lawyer; b. East St. Louis, Ill., July 7, 1927; s. Carl John and Daisy Emmaline (Baylor) G.; (div.)1 son, David Leslie. B.A. cum laude, Wittenberg U., 1955; J.D. Nat. Honor scholar, U. Chgo., 1958. Bar: Fla. 1958. Practice, Jacksonville, Fla., 1958—; ptnr. Mathews, Osborne, McNatt, Gobelman & Cobb, Jacksonville, 1963—; chmn. bd., chief exec. officer Gobelman Enterprises, Inc., Jacksonville, 1971—. Mem. Zoning Bd., City of Jacksonville, 1968-72, chmn., 1968-70; pres. Duval County Legal Aid Assn., 1972-73. Served with USNR, 1945-49; served with U.S. Army, 1950-52. Mem. ABA, Am. Judicature Soc., Am. Arbitration Assn. (Nat. panel), Fla. Bar Assn., Fla. Def. Lawyers Assn. (dir. 1972-73, 77-78, sec.-treas. 1981, pres. elect 1982, pres. 1983), Jacksonville Bar Assn., Jacksonville Assn. Def. Counsel (pres. 1971-72), Phi Delta Phi. Clubs: San Jose Country, Ponte Vedra, Timuquana Country, Sawgrass River. Home: 6A Broadview Towers 1596 Lancaster Terr Jacksonville FL 32204 Office: 1500 American Heritage Bldg Jacksonville FL 32202

GOBIN, LEO CALVIN, pub. co. exec.; b. Charlestown, Ind., Mar. 3, 1917; s. Estal Calvin and Alma (Spencer) G.; m. Mildred L. Schuch, Nov. 4, 1939; children—Ronald, Daniel Joseph. Student, Ind. U., 1935-40. Accountant Citizens Gas & Coke Utility, Indpls., 1935-42; auditor War Dept. Contract Audit, 1942-43; asst. controller Consol. Vultee Aircraft, 1943-44; v.p., gen. mgr. Bobbs-Merill Co., Indpls., 1946-62, exec. v.p., 1963-65, pres., 1965—; dir. Implement & Tractor, Inc. Served to staff sgt. AUS, 1944-46. Mem. Indpls. C. of C., Am. Mgmt. Assn., Am. Legion. Home: 4258 Westbourne Dr Indianapolis IN 46205 Office: 4300 W 62d St Indianapolis IN 46268

GOBLE, GEORGE G., educator; b. Eagle, Idaho, Sept.11, 1929; s. William W. and Beatrice (Kolander) G.; m. Sabine Marianne Weber, Apr. 16, 1953; children—Tanya Bettina, Gregory George. B.S., U. Idaho, 1951; M.S., U. Wash., 1957, Ph.D., 1961; postgrad., Stuttgart Technische Hochschule, 1957-58. Structural insp. Oreg. Dept. Hwys., Roseburg, 1953-55; structural designer Marshall, Barr & Assos., Seattle, 1956-61; asst. prof. to prof. civil engrng. Case-Western Res. U., 1961-76, chmn. dept. civil engrng., 1975-76; prof. civil engrng., chmn. dept. civil, environ. and archtl. engrng U. Colo., Boulder, 1977—; vis. prof. U. Calif., 1968-69; cons. structural design and analysis; founder Pile Dynamics, Inc., Cleve., 1972, Goble & Assos., 1976, Bridge Weighing Systems, Inc., 1980. Served to capt. USAF, 1951-53. Recipient Collingwood prize ASCE, 1965, profl. structural design award Lincoln Found., 1966. Mem. ASCE, Am. Concrete Inst., Prestressed Concrete Inst., Soc. Exptl. Stress Analysis, Am. Soc. for Engrng. Edn., Deep Founds. Inst. (trustee), Kappa Sigma. Home: 370 Inca Pkwy Boulder CO 80303

GOBLE, PAUL, author, illustrator, artist; b. Haslemere, Eng., Sept. 27, 1933; s. Robert John and Elizabeth Marian (Brown) G.; m. Janet A. Tiller, June 2, 1978; 1 son, Robert George; children by previous marriage: Richard, Julia. Diploma in Design with distinction, Central Sch. Art and Design, London, 1959. Vis. lectr. indsl. design Central Sch. Art and Design, London, 1960-68; sr. lectr. indsl. design Ravensbourne Coll. Art and Design, London, 1968-77; artist in residence Gallery of Indian and Western Arts, Mt. Rushmore Nat. Meml., 1977. Author, illustrator numerous children's books including: The Fetterman Fight, 1972; author, illustrator: numerous children's books including Custer's Last Battle, 1969, Lone Bull's Horse Raid, 1973, The Friendly Wolf, 1974, The Girl Who Loved Wild Horses, 1978 (Caldecott medal), The Gift of the Sacred Dog, 1980, Star Boy, 1983. Fellow Royal Soc. Arts, Soc. Indsl. Artists and Designers. Address: Nemo Route 1749 Deadwood SD 57732 *I have felt the pull of the Native American tradition as long as I can remember, probably since the time my mother read to me stories of Grey Owl and Ernest Thompson Seton. As I grew up in England, I read everything I could lay my hands on about Indians. It was the books concerning the wisdom of Black Elk which finally determined my life's orientation.*

GOCHMAN, STANLEY I., psychologist; b. N.Y.C., Sept. 12, 1936; s. Jack G. and Lillian (Gochman); m. Eva R. Grubler, Jan. 15, 1956; children: David Edgar, Julie-Anne. B.S., Queens Coll., 1950; M.A., Columbia U., 1951; Ph.D., NYU, 1956; cert. psychoanalysis, Adler Inst., 1956. Intern in psychology Hosp. for Chronic Diseases, Bklyn., 1950-51, resident psychologist, 1951-52, sr. psychologist, co-dir. Parents' Inst., 1952-53; cons. staff psychologist Alfred Adler Mental Hygiene Clinic, N.Y.C., 1953-56; sr. psychologist Topeka State Hosp.-Menninger Found., 1956-57; mem. faculty U. Md. Overseas Program, Paris, 1957-58; chief psychologist Hunterdon Med. Center, N.J., 1958-59; asst. prof. psychology, supr. clin. psychology and sch. psychology grad. tng. programs Rutgers U., 1959-62; dir. Bergen Ctr. Psychol. Services, N.J., 1959-67; dir. tng. Inst. Analytic Psychotherapy, Englewood, N.J., 1962-67; field assessment officer Peace Corps, St. Annde de la Pocatiere, Que., 1966, P.R., C.Am., 1967-68; prof. psychology U. P.R., 1968-79; clin. adminstr. NIMH, 1974-76; prof. Howard U., 1979—, dir. grad. doctoral program clin.-community, 1979-80; lectr. Bklyn. Coll., 1952-54; pvt. practice, 1959—; mem. primary prevention research team NIMH, 1976—; cons. sch. psychologist Flemington Raritan Schs., N.J., 1960-62; pres. pro-tem Nat. Consortium on Psychol. Aspects of Social Change and Community Devel., 1979-81; media guest expert. Author: A Psychological Profile of the Puerto Rican University Student, 1977; contbr. articlesto profl. jours. Served with U.S. Maritime Service and Mcht. Marines, 1945-48. Recipient award Psychol. Reports, 1961, research paper award 2d Ann. Conf. on Research Topics in Psychiatry, 1981; Rutgers U. Research Council grantee, 1960-62. Mem. Am. Psychol. Assn. (Washington chpt. rep. to nat. bd. dirs. 1980—, chmn. chpt. tng. com. 1980—), Am Psychol. Assn. (chpt. dir. planned postdoctoral insts. 1980—, v.p. chpt. 1981-82, chmn. com. social issues and public policy div. psychoanalysis 1980—), Eastern Psychol. Assn., Bklyn. Psychol. Assn. (founder, officer 1953-56), Nat. Council Psychol. Aspects Disability (exec. com. div. 1951-53). Home: 8519 Wilkesboro Ln Potomac MD 20854

GOCKE, DAVID JOSEPH, physician, med. scientist; b. Fairmont, W.Va., June 10, 1933; s. Charles and Josephine G.; m. Barbara Donohoe, Apr. 12, 1958; children: Christopher, Susan, John, Gregory, Patricia, Robert, Mary Anne, Meghan. Ed., St. Vincent's Coll., Latrobe, Pa., 1954; M.D., U. Pa., 1958. Diplomate: Am. Bd. Internal Medicine. Intern Columbia-Presbyn. Hosp., N.Y.C., 1958-59, asst. resident, 1959-60, program dir. clin. research center, 1971-73; fellow in microbiology Johns Hopkins Sch. Medicine, Balt., 1960-63; asst. prof. to asso. prof. medicine Columbia U. Coll. Physicians and Surgeons, N.Y.C., 1963-73; prof. medicine and microbiology, chief div. immunology and infectious disease Rutgers Med. Sch., Piscataway, N.J., 1973-77, 78—, dean med. sch., 1977-78; spl. cons. Nat. Research Council on Hepatitis. Co-author: Viral Hepatitis, 1978; contbr. articles on infectious diseases and immunology to profl. jours. Mem. Am. Soc. Clin. Investigation, Infectious Diseases Soc. Am., Am. Assn. Immunologists, Am. Assn. Study of Liver Disease, Am. Fedn. Clin. Research, AAAS, Alpha Omega Alpha. Roman Catholic. Office: Rutgers Med Sch CN 19 New Brunswick NJ 08903

GOCKENBACH, HAROLD CONRAD, savings and loan executive; b. Columbus, Ohio, Feb. 11, 1923; s. Harold Conrad and Dorothy L. (Curran) B.; m. Mary Jo Smith, May 31, 1944; children: Philip, JoAnn, Theresa, Michelle. B.S., Ohio State U., 1944. Teller Dollar Fed. Savs. & Loan Assn., Columbus, 1946-47, asst. treas., 1947-48, bd. dirs., 1948—, sec., 1948-50, exec. v.p., 1950-56, pres., chmn. bd., 1956—. Chmn. Franklin County Boys and Girls Fund, 1957, Christmas in Capitol Square, 1961-62, Downtown Area Com., 1961—, Geman Village Com., 1963-69, St. Agatha's Building Fund, 1953; Bd. dirs. Diocesan Child Guidance Center, Convent of Good Shepard, Franklin County Soc. Crippled Children, Franklin County Chpt. Nat. Found., Pontifical Coll. Josephium; bd. dirs., pres. Citizen's Research Inc. Served to lt. (j.g.) USNR, 1944-46. Recipient two George Washington medals Freedom Found., 1964-66; named Hon. Citizen Korea Navy League Columbus, 1964. Mem. Columbus Bd. Realtors, Am. Savs. and Loan Inst. (past pres.), Columbus Savs. and Loan League (past pres.), Navy League Columbus, Phi Gamma Delta, Beta Alpha. Republican. Roman Catholic. Clubs: Lion., Executive, Columbus Country, Columbus Maennerchor, Columbus Athletic, University. Home: 5694 Notre Dame Columbus OH 43213 Office: 1 E Gay St Columbus OH 43215

GOCKLEY, DAVID WOODROW, ecumenical exec.; b. Ephrata, Pa., Oct. 9, 1918; s. David and Elizabeth (Donner) G.; m. Olive Porter; children—Pamela, Charles, David, Sally, Stephanie, Brian. A.B., Lebanon Valley Coll., 1942, D.D., 1978; M.Div., United Theol. Sem., Dayton, Ohio, 1945; M.A., Temple U., 1955. Ordained to ministry United Methodist Ch., 1945; youth pastor Westminster Presbyn. Ch., Dayton, Ohio, 1943-45; dir. public relations and chaplain Lebanon Valley Coll., 1945-51; pastor United Meth. Ch., Phila., 1951-56; exec. sec. dept. public relations Greater Phila. Council Chs., 1956-61; dir. public relations Religion in Am. Life, N.Y.C., 1961-69, dir., exec. v.p., 1969—, now pres.; mem. TV Commn. Pa. Council Chs., 1959-61; bd. mgrs. broadcasting and film commn. Nat. Council Chs., 1959-62. Mem. Phila. Youth Services Bd., 1958-61; chmn. Alcoholism Council Mid-Fairfield County, Conn., 1971-77. Mem. Religious Public Relations Council (pres. Phila. chpt. 1960-61, nat. pres. 1964-66),

Lebanon Valley Alumni Assn. (citation 1975). Home: 8 Pond Edge Rd Westport CT 06880 Office: 815 2d Ave New York NY 10017

GODARD, JAMES MCFATE, educational organization executive; b. Kankakee, Ill., Aug. 3, 1907; s. Gerald Darlington and Sarah (McFate) G.; m. Aura Holton, Dec. 21, 1930; children: Mary Grace, Gerald Holton, Elizabeth Holland. A.B., Park Coll., 1929; A.M., Duke U., 1930; LL.D., Tex. Christian U., 1952; Litt.D., Midwestern U., Tex., 1952; L.H.D., Lander Coll., 1957, St. Ambrose Coll., 1968; Pd.D., Belmont Abbey Coll., 1959; LL.D., Hobart and William Smith Colls., 1963, St. Ambrose Coll., 1969. Instr. Park Coll., 1931-32, Duke, 1933-36; prof. edn., dean coll. Queen's Coll., N.C., 1936-49; exec. sec. commn. colls. and univs. So. Assn. Colls. and Secondary Schs., Atlanta, 1949-54; v.p., dean adminstrn. U. Miami, Fla., 1954-56, exec. v.p., 1956-60; exec. dir. Council Protestant Colls. and Univs., 1960-66; cons. Inst. Higher Ednl. Opportunity, So. Regional Edn. Bd., Atlanta, 1966—; cons. Charlotte (N.C.) Mental Hygiene Clinic, 1937-47. Author: Understanding Marriage and Family Relations, 1948, The Blue Light, 1964; co- author: Christian Bases of World Order. Mem. So. Assn. Colls. Women, Am. Arbitration Assn., N.C. Mental Hygiene Soc. (bd. 1948-49), Charlotte Mental Hygiene Soc. (pres. 1949), Kappa Delta Pi, Phi Kappa Pni. Presbyn. Clubs: Kiwanis, Executives (Charlotte). Home: 729 Lindbergh Dr NE Atlanta GA 30324 Office: 130 6th St NW Atlanta GA 30324 *To realize that the past is not gone, that it is simply somewhere else, provides a basis for understanding the present and for anticipating the future.*

GODARD, JEAN LUC, motion picture director; b. Paris, Dec. 3, 1930; m. Anna Karina, Mar. 2, 1961 (div.); m. Anne Wiasemsky, 1967. Ed., Lycee Buffon, Paris. Journalist, film critic Cahiers du Cinema. Producer: motion pictures including Operation Beton, 1954, Une Femme Coquette, 1955, Tous les garcons s'appelent Patrick, 1957, Charlotte et son Jules, 1958, A Bout de Souffle, 1959 (prix Jean Vigo), Le sept peches captiaux, 1961, The Little Soldier, The Carabiniers, 1963, Une Femme est une Femme, 1961, Vivre et sa Vie, 1962, Weekend, 1967 (diploma of merit Edinburgh Film Festival 1968), La Chinoise, 1967 1968, Les puls belles escroqueries du Monde, 1963 1968, Une femme mariee, 1964 1968, Alphaville, 1965 1968, Pierrot le fou, 1965 1968, Sympathy for the Devil 1968, Lion du Vietnam, 1967 1968, Le plus vieux metier du monde, 1967 1968, Vangelo '70, 1967 1968, Un film comme les autres, 1968 1968, British Sounds, 1969 1968, Made in U.S.A., 1966 1968, Masculine-Feminine, 1966 1968, One Plus One, 1968 1968, One American Movie—1 A.M., 1969 1968, Le Vent d'est, 1969 1968, Lotte in Italia, 1970 1968, Vladmir et Rosa, 1971 1968, Tout va bien, 1972 1968, Numero deux, 1975 1968, Ici et ailleurs, 1976 1968, Bugsy, 1979 1968, Sauve quipeut, 1980 1968, Every Man for Himself, 1980 1968, Passion, 1982 1968. Recipient spl. prize Festival of Venice, 1962, Prix Pasinetti, 1962, Best Picture Berlin Film Festival. Office: Zoetrope Studios 1040 N Las Palmas Los Angeles CA 90038 *

GODBOLD, JAKE MAURICE, mayor; b. Jacksonville, Fla., Mar. 14, 1934; s. Charles B. and Irene Noegel (Whitfield) G.; m. Jean Jenkins, Feb. 16, 1957; 1 son, Ben. Student public schs., Jacksonville. Agt., then supt. nat. hdqrs. Ind. Life Ins. Co., until 1969; founder, owner, operator Gateway Chem. Co.; mem. Jacksonville City Council, 1967-79, pres., 1971, 78; mayor, City of Jacksonville, 1979—. Bd. dirs. Gator Bowl Assn., Boys Club of Jacksonville, Muscular Dystrophy Assn.; pres. bd. dirs. Big Bros., Jacksonville. Served with U.S. Army, 1951-53; Korea. Recipient Disting. Service award Jacksonville Area C. of C., 1968. Mem. Fla. League of Cities, Nat. League of Cities, U.S. Conf. Mayors. Democrat. Methodist. Clubs: Rotary, Northside Businessmen's, Springfield Businessmen's. Office: Office of Mayor 220 E Bay St Jacksonville FL 32202 *

GODBOLD, JOHN COOPER, judge; b. Coy, Ala., Mar. 24, 1920; s. Edwin Condie and Elsie (Williamson) G.; m. Elizabeth Showalter, July 18, 1942; children: Susan, Richard, John C., Cornelia, Sally. B.S., Auburn U., 1940; J.D., Harvard U., 1948; LL.D. (hon.), Samford U., 1981. Bar: Ala. 1948. With firm Richard T. Rives, Montgomery, 1948-49; partner firm Godbold, Hobbs & Copeland (and predecessors), 1949-66; U.S. circuit judge Ct. Appeals 5th Circuit, 1966-81, chief judge, 1981, U.S. Ct. Appeals 11th Circuit, 1981—. Bd. dirs. Fed. Jud. Center, 1976-81. Served with F.A. AUS, 1941-46. Mem. Am., Fed., Ala., Montgomery County bar assns., Alpha Tau Omega, Omicron Delta Kappa, Phi Kappa Phi. Episcopalian. Club: Montgomery Country. Home: 3590 Thomas Ave Montgomery AL 36111 Office: Federal Courthouse Montgomery AL 36102 also US Ct of Appeals Courthouse Atlanta GA 30303

GODCHAUX, FRANK AREA, III, food company executive; b. Nashville, Feb. 5, 1927; s. Frank Area, Jr. and Mary Lawrence (Ragl) G.; m. Agnes Kirkpatrick, May 23, 1953; children: Katherine Area, Mary Lawrence, Leslie Kirkpatrick, Frank Kirkpatrick. B.B.A., Vanderbilt U., 1949. Pres. Lastarmco Inc., Abbeville, La., 1964-78, chmn. bd., 1978—, Riviana Foods Inc., Houston, 1965—, chief exec. officer, 1980—; v.p. Colgate-Palmolive Co., N.Y.C., 1976—; dir. New Orleans br. Fed. Res. Bank Atlanta, 1958-63, Chart House, Inc., Lafayette, La., First Nat. Bank Lafayette, Coastal Chem. Co. Inc., Abbeville; mem. nat. rice adv. com. Dept. Agr., 1964-66, 71-73, 76. Mem. Evangeline area council Boy Scouts Am.; trustee Vanderbilt U., 1967—; mem. U. Southwestern La. Found., 1955—. Served with USNR, 1945-46. Mem. Phi Delta Theta. Episcopalian. Home: 600 5th St Abbeville LA 70510 Office: PO Box 278 Abbeville LA 70510

GODDARD, DAVID ROCKWELL, educator; b. Carmel, Calif., Jan. 3, 1908; s. Pliny Earle and Alice (Rockwell) G.; m. Doris Martin, Aug. 21, 1933 (dec.); children—Alison G. Elliott; Robert Martin; m. Katharine Evans, Feb. 2, 1952. A.B., U. Calif., 1929, A.M., 1930, Ph.D., 1933. NRC fellow Rockefeller Inst. Med. Research, 1933-35; instr. to prof. U. Rochester, 1935-46, chmn. dept., 1938-46; prof. botany U. Pa., 1946-58, chmn. dept., 1952-57, dir. div. biology, 1957-61, provost, 1961-70, emeritus provost, 1973—, Gustave C. Kuemmerle prof. botany, 1958-64, prof. biology, 1964-71, univ. prof. biology, 1972-75, emeritus, 1975—; univ. prof. sci. and pub. policy, 1971-72; home sec. Nat. Acad. Scis., Washington, 1975-79; Walker-Ames prof. U. Wash., 1955; vis. prof. Rockefeller U., 1956-64; Guggenheim fellow U. Chgo., 1942-43, U. Cambridge, 1950. Author: (with Höber) Physical Chemistry of Cells and Tissues, 1945; also articles sci. periodicals.; Contbg. author: Treatise of Plant Physiology (Steward), Vol. 1A, 1960; Mem. editorial bd.: Ann. Rev. Plant Physiology, 1948-54; asso. editor: Quar. Rev. of Biology, 1950-75; editor-in-chief: Plant Physiology, 1953-57; asso. editor, 1958-63; bd. trustees: Biol. Abstracts, 1950-56; pres., 1955-56. Mem. nat. adv. council health research facilities NIH, 1962-67, mem. health scis. advancement award rev. com., 1965-66, 67-70; cons. to President's spl. asst. for sci. and tech., cons. President's Sci. Adv. Com., 1961-63; chmn. ad hoc panel on drug abuse White House, 1962; Trustee Wistar Inst. Anatomy and Biology, 1971—. Recipient Stephen Hales award Am. Soc. Plant Physiology, 1948. Fellow Am. Acad. Arts and Scis.; mem. Am. Philos. Soc., Nat. Acad. Sci. (chmn. com. on USSR and Eastern Europe 1964-68), AAAS (bd. dirs. 1963-68), Bot. Soc. Am., Am. Soc. Plant Physiology (pres. 1958), Soc. Study Growth and Devel. (pres. 1953), Soc. Gen. Physiologists (pres. 1948). Club: Franklin Inn (Phila.). Home: 738-A 1 Wolcott Dr Philadelphia PA 19118

GODDARD, JOE DEAN, chemical engineering educator, researcher; b. Buncombe, Ill., July 13, 1936; s. Bon Andrew and Helen May (Hudgens) G.; m. Shirley May Keltner, Sept. 1, 1957; children: Paul, Suzanne, Anna P., Andrew, Jessica. B.S. in Chem. Engring., U. Ill., 1957, Ph.D., U. Calif.-Berkeley, 1962. NATO postdoctoral fellow, Paris, 1961-63; asst. prof. to prof. chem. engring. U. Mich., Ann Arbor, 1963-76; prof., chmn. dept. chem. engring. U. So. Calif., Los Angeles, 1976—; cons. Dow Chem. Co., Midland, Mich., 1964, Hercules, Inc., Parlin, N.J., 1964-66, Jet Propulsion Lab., Pasadena, Calif., 1979. Contbr. articles to profl. jours. NSF postdoctoral fellow, Cambridge, Eng., 1971; D.L. Katz lectr. U. Mich., Ann Arbor, 1983. Mem. Am. Inst. Chem. Engrs., Brit. Soc. Rheology, Am. Chem. Soc., Am. Phys. Soc. Office: Dept Chem Engring U Southern Calif Los Angeles CA 90089

GODDARD, JOSEPH PAUL, educator; b. Harriman, Tenn., Feb. 6, 1920; s. Frank Louis and Julia (Evans) G.; m. Martha Essex Duke, Aug. 24, 1946; children—Mary Ann (Mrs. A. Joseph Dent), Joseph Timberlake, Frank Moss. B.S., U. Tenn., 1947, M.S., 1950, Ed.D., 1959; hon. degree in Human Engring., Ga. Inst. Tech., 1960. Adminstrv. asst. to dean Coll. Bus., U. Tenn., Knoxville, 1947-51, asst. dean students, 1951-55; dir. Univ. Evening Sch., 1960-67, asst. dean div. univ. extension, 1967-70, dean continuing edn., 1970—; personnel dir. Rich's, Knoxville, 1955-56; tech. personnel rep. Union Carbide Nuclear Co., Oak Ridge, 1956-60. Sec. Tenn. Indsl. Personnel Conf., 1967-81; mem. Knox County Personnel Commn., Knox County Gen. Govt. Merit Bd., 1979-80, E. Tenn. Bapt. Hosp. outreach bd.; dep. comdr. Tenn. Wing, Civil Air Patrol, 1960-69; Bd. dirs. Florence Crittenton Agy., Knoxville, 1969-81, pres., 1976. Served to capt. Q.M.C. AUS, 1942-45; PTO. Mem. Assn. Continuing Higher Edn. (pres., v.p. dir., program chmn.), Nat. U. Continuing Edn. Assn. (chmn., vice chmn. long-term ednl. council 1970-73, chmn. Region III 1976-78, nat. dir. 1976-78, sec. 1979-80, pres.-elect 1980-81, pres. 1981-82, Leadership award 1982), Nat. Aerospace Edn. Council, Tenn. Adult Edn. Assn. (Outstanding Adult Educator 1973), Tenn. Edn. Assn., Tenn. Valley Personnel Assn. (past pres.), Nat. Assn. State Univs. and Land-Grant Colls. (legis. liaison, council on extension and continuing edn. 1975—, dir. 1980-81), Scarabbean, Phi Kappa Phi (pres., sec.), Beta Gamma Sigma, Phi Delta Kappa, Omicron Delta Kappa. Baptist (deacon). Home: 7000 Wellington Dr NW Knoxville TN 37919

GODDARD, PAULETTE, actress; b. Whitestone, N.Y., June 3, 1915; m. Edgar James; m. Charles Chaplin; m. Burgess Meredith, June 21, 1944 (div.); m. Erich Maria Remarque, Feb. 25, 1958 (dec. 1971). Ed. at pub. schs. Began on New York stage; went to Hollywood for: small part in Kid from Spain; played in: Modern Times, 1936, Duffy's Tavern, 1945, Kitty, 1945, Standing Room Only, 1944, Diary of a Chambermaid, 1946, Proudly We Hail, 1943, Unconquered, 1947, An Ideal Husband, 1947, Hazard, 1948, On Our Merry Way, 1948, Anna Lucasta, 1949, Woman of Vengeance, 1948, The Torch, 1949, Time of Indifference, 1966; TV movies include the Snoop Sisters, 1972 *

GODDARD, ROBERT HALE IVES, investment manager; b. Providence, Dec. 9, 1909; s. Robert Hale Ives and Margaret (Hazard) G.; m. Hope Linton Drury, June 18, 1937; children—Margaret H. (Mrs. Robert Leeson, Jr.), Robert Hale Ives III, William Holland Drury, Thomas Poynton Ives, Moses Brown Ives. B.A., Yale U., 1932; M.B.A., Harvard U., 1934; Dr. Humanitarian Service (hon.), Providence Coll., 1968, D. Laws, Brown U., 1982. Mng. partner Lonsdale Co., Providence, 1940-43; mgr. machinery export dept. Anderson, Clayton & Co., 1946-50; trustee Providence Instn. for Savs., 1939-66; dir. Mchts. Cold Storage & Warehouse Co., Inc., Providence Washington Ins. Co., 1942-74, New Eng. Tel.&Tel. Co., 1962-78, Providence Investors Co., 1952-78; treas., dir. Warwick Land Co., 1932-74, pres., 1960-74, chmn. bd., 1974—. Author: articles sailing vessels Am. Neptune mag. Bd. dirs. R.I. Hosp. Trust Co., 1938—, exec. com., 1959-82, trust com., 1960-82, hon. dir., 1982; Chmn. R.I. United Fund campaign, 1959; pres. Providence Athenaeum, 1966-70, Butler Hosp., 1972-78, Slater Mill Historic Site, 1981-83; trustee Brown & Ives, 1946—; pres. United Fund, 1964-67, Greater Providence YMCA, 1967-69; vestry St. Stephen's Episcopal Ch., 1973-82, jr. warden, 1982. Served to 1st lt. Transp. Corps AUS, 1944-46. Episcopalian. Clubs: Agawam Hunt, Hope (Providence). Home: 64 Angell St Providence RI 02906 Office: 50 S Main St Providence RI 02903

GODDARD, SAMUEL PEARSON, JR., lawyer, former gov. Ariz.; b. Clayton, Mo., Aug. 8, 1919; s. Samuel Pearson and Florence Hilton (Denham) G.; m. Julia Hatch, July 1, 1944; children: Samuel Pearson III, Pascal Hatch, William Denham. A.B., Harvard, 1941; LL.B., U. Ariz., 1949. Bar: Ariz. 1949. Practiced in, Tucson, 1949-64, Phoenix, 1964—; sr. partner Goddard & Goddard (and predecessor firms), 1960—; gov. of, Ariz., 1965-67. Co-chmn. Tucson Civic and Conv. Center Study Com., 1958-59; chmn. Tucson Youth Study Com., 1959; mem. White House Conf. Com. Children and Youth, 1959; Campaign chmn. United Fund, 1959; pres. Leffingwell Forest Preserve, 1960-61; Chmn. Democratic Party of Ariz., 1960-62, 78—; Bd. dirs. Ariz. Acad., 1963-64, Catalina council Boy Scouts of Am., 1963-64; pres. United Fund, 1960-62, Western Conf. Community Chests, United Funds and Councils Am., 1961-63; mem. exec. com. United Community Funds and Councils Am., 1966-69; task force chmn. United Way Am., bd. govs., 1972-78; bd. dirs., chmn. nominating com. overseers and dirs. Associated Harvard Alumni, 1970-71, v.p., 1971-74; mem. Tucson Hosp. Co-ordinating Com., 1964; Dem. nat. committeeman for Ariz., mem. exec. sect. charter commn., 1972-76; chmn. Nat. Acad. Volunteerism, 1973-75; chmn. blue ribbon study com. on U.S.O.s, 1974-75; an organizer Tucson Civic Chorus, Tucson Festival Soc., Tucson Watercolor Guild; Bd. dirs. Phoenix Symphony Assn., Govt. Relations Com., Transition Zone Horticultural Zone; trustee Nat. Rowing Found., Nat. Council on Philanthropy, 1979—. Served to maj. USAAF, 1941-46. Named Tucson Man of Yr., 1959. Mem. Am., Ariz., Pima County, Maricopa County bar assns., Res. Officers Assn., VFW, Air Force Assn., Am. Legion, Phi Alpha Delta. Unitarian. Clubs: Harvard Varsity, Old Pueblo. Home: 4724 E Camelback Canyon Dr Phoenix AZ 85018 Office: Ariz Bank Bldg Phoenix AZ 85003 also SAB Financial Center Tucson AZ 85011

GODDARD, WESLEY RAWDON, educator; b. St. Louis, July 29, 1915; s. Charles Baldwin and Beatrice (Montgomery) G.; m. Shirley Beryl Tolin, Sept. 3, 1946; children—David Shandy, Christopher, Ghislaine. B.A., Swarthmore Coll., 1937; M.A., U. Calif. at Berkeley, 1939; Doctorat, U. Paris, France, 1950. Mem. faculty San Jose State U., 1939-77, prof. French, 1956—, chmn. dept. fgn. langs., 1958-69, 75-77; resident dir. Calif. State Internat. Programs for, France, 1964-65, for, Italy, 1969-71. Author: (with Paul Roberts) Preface to Composition, rev. edit, 1955; Translator, editor: (Racine) Phedre, 1961. Pres. Santa Clara Valley (Calif.) Verdi Festival. Home: 19140 Panorama Dr Saratoga CA 95070

GODDARD, WILLIAM ANDREW, III, chemist, applied physicist, educator; b. El Centro, Calif., Mar. 29, 1937; s. William Andrew and Barbara Worth (Bright) G.; m. Yvonne Amelia Correy, Oct. 27, 1957; children: William Andrew, Susan Yvonne, Cecelia Moniqué, Lisa Sharéll. B.S. in Engring. with highest honors, UCLA, 1960; Ph.D. in Engring. Sci, Calif. Inst. Tech., 1964. Mem. faculty Calif. Inst. Tech., Pasadena, 1964—, asso. prof. theoretical chemistry, 1971-75, prof. theoretical chemistry, 1975-78, prof. chemistry and applied physics, 1978—; vis. staff mem. Los Alamos Sci. Lab., 1973—; cons. Gen. Motors Research Labs., 1978—, Argonne Nat. Lab., 1978—, Sandia Labs., 1979—, Bell Labs., 1979—, Gen. Electric Research and Devel. Labs., 1982—, Shell Devel., 1982—. Mem. adv. editorial bd.: Chem. Physics, 1972—, Jour. Phys. Chemistry, 1976-80. Recipient Buck-Whitney medal for major contbns. in chemistry, 1978; NSF fellow, 1960-61, 62-64; Shell Found. fellow, 1961-62; Alfred P. Sloan Found. fellow, 1967-69. Fellow Am. Phys. Soc.; Mem. Am. Chem. Soc., Am. Vacuum Soc., Calif. Catalysis Soc., Combustion Inst., Sigma Xi, Tau Beta Pi. Home: 2700 Oak Knoll Ave San Marino CA 91108 Office: Calif Inst Tech Pasadena CA 91125

GODDING, GEORGE ARTHUR, corporation executive, former army officer; b. Lawrence, Kans., July 12, 1920; s. Frank Eugene and Leota (House) G.; m. Mae Elizabeth Evans, June 20, 1945; children: Elizabeth Katherine Godding Lytle, George Arthur, Ruth Alta. Student, U. Kans., 1938-40; B.S., Md. U., 1951; grad., Command and Gen. Staff Coll., 1952, Army War Coll., 1961; M.A., George Washington U., 1961. Commd. 2d lt. U.S. Army, 1942, advanced through grades to maj. gen., 1971; dep. chief staff for intelligence, Pacific, 1969-72, dir., Vietnam, 1972, comdr., Arlington, Va., 1973-75; dir. intelligence tech. BDM Corp., Columbia, Md., 1975—. Contbr. to govt. publs. on electronic warfare. Active Boy Scouts Am. Decorated D.S.M. with two oak leaf clusters, Silver Star, Legion of Merit with 2 oak leaf clusters, Bronze Star with oak leaf cluster and V device, Air medal, Purple Heart; Medal Cloud and Banner, Republic China; 2d class knight comdr. Most Exalted Order White Elephant, Thailand; 5th class Nat. Order Vietnam, Republic Vietnam; named to Honor Roll Inf. Officer Candidate Hall of Fame. Mem. Assn. U.S. Army, Kappa Sigma. Club: Masons (32 deg.). Home & Office: 10164 Clover Glen Dr Vienna VA 22180

GODENNE, GHISLAINE DUDLEY, physician, psychoanalyst; b. Brussels, Belgium; came to U.S., 1951; d. Pierre and Olive Dudley (Short) G. B.S., Universite Catholique de Louvain, Belgium, 1948, M.D., 1952. Intern Providence Hosp., Washington, 1951-52, resident in pediatrics, 1952-54; fellow in pediatrics Mayo Clinic, Rochester, Minn., 1954-57; fellow in pediatric research Johns Hopkins U., 1957-58, asso. prof. mental hygiene, 1966-74, asso. prof. psychiatry and pediatrics, 1966-82, psychoanalyst, 1972—, prof. psychology, 1973—, prof. psychiatry, pediatrics, and mental hygiene, 1982—; resident in psychiatry Johns Hopkins Hosp., Balt., 1958-62, chief adolescent psychiat. service, 1964-73, dir. counseling and psychiat. services, 1973—, dir. health services, 1978—; mem. staff various hosps., Balt.; cons. psychiatrist Clyburn Children's Home, Balt., 1960—, Catonsville (Md.) Community Coll., 1968-75. Mem. editorial bd.: Adolescent Psychiatry, 1978—, Clinical Update Adolescent Psychiatry, 1982—; Contbr. articles to profl. jours. Bd. dirs. Balt. Girl Scouts Assn., 1958-60, 81—, Met. Balt. Assn. Mental Health, 1965-69, Florence Crittendon Home, 1966-68; trustee McDonough Sch., 1975-83; pres. bd. Trustees Richmond Fellowship Md., 1975-77. Decorated Knight Order of Leopold, Belgium).; Grantee Fulbright Found., 1951-52, Parke & Davis Co., 1957, NIMH, 1961-63; recipient Career Teaching award NIMH, 1963-65. Fellow A.C.P., Am. Psychiat. Assn., Am. Public Health Assn., Am. Orthopsychiat. Assn., Am. Soc. Adolescent Psychiatry (pres. 1981-82); mem. Md. Soc. Adolescent Psychiatry (pres. 1968-69), Md. Psychiat. Soc. (past chmn. program com), Md. State Conf. Social Welfare (past mem. child welfare com.), Am. Soc. Adolescent Medicine (charter), Am. Psychoanalytic Assn., Internat. Psychoanalytic Assn., Am. Med. Women's Assn., Balt.-Washington Soc. Psychoanalysis, AAUP, others. Home: 15 Edgevale Rd Baltimore MD 21210 Office: Johns Hopkins U Baltimore MD 21218

GODFREY, EDWARD FARLEY, real estate trust co. exec.; b. Springfield, Mass., May 13, 1949; s. Edward Henry and Jane (Elmer) G.; m. Judith Carl, May 17, 1975; children—Spencer, Grant. B.A., Southampton (N.Y.) Coll., 1971. With Equitable Life Mortgage & Realty Investors Co., Boston, 1975—, sr. v.p., chief fin. officer, 1978-80, pres., chief operating officer, trustee, 1980—. Mem. Nat. Assn. Real Estate Investment Trusts (bd. govs., treas.)

GODFREY, EDWARD SETTLE, III, judge; b. Phoenix, July 21, 1913; s. Edward Settle and Alma (McDonald) G. A.B., Harvard, 1934; LL.B., Columbia, 1939. Bar: N.Y. bar 1939. Instr. English Albany Acad., 1935-36; asst. atty. Fed. Home Loan Bank Bd., 1939-40; practiced law in, Albany, 1946-48; prof. law Union U. Albany Law Sch., 1948-61; dean U. Maine Sch. Law, 1962-73, prof. law, 1973-76, provost univ., 1970; asso. justice Supreme Jud. Ct. Maine, 1976—; Cons. N.Y. Law Revision Commn., 1953-55, 59-60; exec. sec. bar exam. service com. Nat. Conf. Bar Examiners, 1953-61. Contbr. articles to legal jours. Chmn. Senatorial Reapportionment Commn. Maine, 1966-67; commr. Portland Renewal Authority, 1966-70. Served to maj. AUS, 1941-46. Decorated Bronze Star medal. Mem. Am. Law Inst., Am., Maine, N.Y. State bar assns., Am. Soc. Internat. Law, Am. Judicature Soc., Acad. Polit. Sci. Home: 69 Falmouth St Portland ME 04102

GODFREY, GEORGE DENTON, business executive; b. New Rochelle, N.Y., Nov. 6, 1922; s. A. Merwin and Georgia (Denton) G.; m. Elizabeth Vognild, Jan. 3, 1951; children: Leslee, Cheryl, Alan, Carolyn Sue. A.B. in Bus. Adminstrn, Colby Coll., 1943. Textile broker, 1946-47; prodn. mgr. Southbridge Finishing Co., Mass., 1947-49; with W.J. Voit Rubber Corp., Santa Ana, Calif., 1949-70, asst. to pres., 1949-57, v.p. mktg., 1957-60, pres., 1960-70; also dir.; pres., dir. Whitely, Inc., Maywood, N.J., 1960-70; v.p., dir. internat. bus. devel. Sports Products AMF, Inc., 1970-73; partner Sports and Leisure Internat. Mgmt. Services, Irvine, Calif., 1973—; chmn., chief fin officer Sports and Leisure Internat., Inc., Irvine. Served to lt. (j.g.) USNR, 1943-46. Decorated Silver Star, Purple Heart, Presdl. Letter of Commendation. Mem. Sporting Goods Mfrs. Assn. (v.p.), Athletic Inst. (dir.), Adventure Unltd. (nat. devel. com.). Club: Balboa Bay. Home: 191 Emerald Bay Laguna Beach CA 92651 Office: 16641 Hale Ave Irvine CA 92714

GODFREY, JAMES BROWN, lawyer; b. Everett, Mass., Sept. 19, 1909; s. Frederick E. and Ruth (Brown) G.; m. Barbara Leach, Oct. 6, 1934; children: James Brown, Anne K. Godfrey Feichtinger, Eugene L. A.B., Dartmouth Coll., 1931; J.D., Harvard U., 1934. Bar: N.H. 1934. Since practiced in Concord; of counsel Ransmeier & Soden; dir. Concord Nat. Bank, First N.H. Banks, Inc. Trustee Holderness Sch. Fellow Am. Coll. Probate Counsel; mem. Am., N.H. bar assns., Phi Beta Kappa. Episcopalian. Club: Harvard (Boston). Home: 37 Ridge Rd Concord NH 03301 Office: 110 N Main St Concord NH 03301

GODFREY, JOHN A., food company executive; b. Laurium, Mich., 1914; married. With Godfrey Co., Waukesha, Wis., 1937—, buyer frozen food dept., 1937-50, treas., 1950-54, v.p., treas., 1954-56, v.p., sec., dir. merchandising, advt. and sales, 1956-63, exec. v.p., 1963-69, pres., treas., chief exec. officer, 1969-74, pres., 1974-79, chmn. bd., chief exec. officer, 1979—, dir.; dir. Sentry Markets Inc., Crestwood Bakery, Store Equipment Inc., Artesian Farms Inc., Ball Motor Service, Sentry Drugs, Jim Handy Hardware. Office: Godfrey Co Inc 1200 W Sunset Dr Box 298 Waukesha WI 53187 *

GODFREY, JOHN MORROW, Canadian senator; b. Port Credit, Ont., Can., June 28, 1912; s. Justice John Milton and Lily (Connon) G.; m. Mary Buwell Ferguson, Sept. 10, 1940; children: John, Sally Godfrey Forrest, Anne, Stephen. Student, U. Toronto, 1922-29, Royal Mil. Coll. Can., 1929-31; LL.B., Osgoode Hall Law Sch., 1939. Bar:

Ont. 1939. Ptnr. Campbell, Godfrey and Lewtas, Toronto, Ont., Can., 1945-77; mem. Senate of Can., Ottawa, Ont., 1973—; chmn. fin. and treas. coms. Liberal Party of Can., Ottawa, 1968-74; dir. Dover Industries Ltd., Toronto. Pres. Nat. Ballet of Can., Toronto, 1967-69; founding dir. Can. Opera Co., Toronto, 1949-53. Served as wing comdr. RCAF, 1940-45. Unitarian. Clubs: Toronto, Toronto Golf; Osler Bluff Ski (Collingwood, Ont.). Office: Senate of Can Ottawa ON Canada K1A OA4

GODFREY, SAMUEL ADDISON, telephone company executive; b. Seattle, Sept. 9, 1922; s. Roland Addison and Imogen Frances (Hamer) G.; m. Florence Olive Lee, Dec. 9, 1945; children: Eric, Bret, Kim, Tye. Student, Willamette U., 1943, Harvard Bus. Sch., 1945; B.A., U. Wash., 1947. Various accounting positions with Pacific Tel. & Tel. Co. and Am. Tel. & Tel. Co., 1947-73; v.p., comptroller Pacific Tel. & Tel. Co., San Francisco, from 1973, now ret.; v.p., comptroller, dir. Bell Telephone Co. of Nev. Served with USNR, 1942-46. Club: Los Altos Golf and Country. Home: 1965 Deodara Dr Los Altos CA 94022

GODIN, EDGAR, bishop; b. Negauc, N.B., Can., May 31, 1911; s. Joseph Albanie and Marguerite (Breau) G. B.A., Bethurst Coll., 1935; License in Canon Law, Laval U., 1947, Gregorian U., Rome, Italy, 1948; Ph.D., U. Moncton; LL.D., St. Thomas U., 1970. Ordained priest Roman Catholic Ch., 1941; dir. Retreat House, Bathurst, N.B., Can., 1942-46; vice-chancellor Diocese of Bathurst, 1948-51, chancellor, 1951-69; bishop of, Bathurst, 1969—. Author: Hospital Ethics, 1959. Mem. Can. Assn. Cath. Hosp. (pres. 1967-69). Address: PO Box 460 Bathurst NB E2A 3Z4 Canada *

GODINE, DAVID RICHARD, pub. co. exec.; b. Cambridge, Mass., Sept. 4, 1944; s. Morton Robert and Bernice (Beckwith) G. B.A. (Sr. fellow), Dartmouth Coll., 1966; Ed.M., Harvard U., 1968. Founder David R. Godine, Pub., Inc., Boston, 1969, pres., 1969—, pub., editor, 1969—. Author: Renaissance Books of Science, 1970. Served with AUS, 1967. Fellow Mass. Hist. Soc., Am. Antiquarian Soc., Pierpont Morgan Library; mem. Soc. Printers. Clubs: Grolier (N.Y.C.); St. Botolph (Boston). Office: 306 Dartmouth St Boston MA 02116

GODINEZ FLORES, RAMON, auxiliary bishop; b. Jamay, Jalisco, Mexico, Apr. 18, 1936; s. Ortega J. Cleofas G. and Maria del Refugio (Flores). Lic. in Philosophy, Sem. Guadalajara, (Jalisco, Mexico); theology degree, U. Gregoriana, Rome, postgrad. in canon law. Ordained priest Roman Catholic Ch., 1959, aux. bishop, 1980. Prof., superior Diocesan Sem., Guadalajara; chaplain religious communities, Templo de San Jorge, Vallarta-San Jorge, Guadalajara; pastor Parroco de Nuestra Senora de la Luz, Guadalajara; sec. Archdiocese of Guadalajara, 1972-80, aux. bishop, 1980—. Contbr. articles to religious jours. Home: Garibaldi n 770 Guadalajara Jalisco Mexico 44290 Office: Obisop Auxiliar de Guadalajara Liceo 17 Guadalajara Jalisco Mexico 44100

GODLEY, GENE EDWIN, lawyer, former asst. sec. treasury; b. Houston, Oct. 6, 1939; s. Thomas Edwin and Dannie Jewell (Drain) G.; m. Lisbeth N. Kamborian, Sept. 19, 1964; children—Amanda Joan, Meredith Pamela Elizabeth. B.A., So. Methodist U., 1960; J.D., U. Chgo., 1963. Bar: D.C. bar 1970, Tex. bar 1963. Counsel U.S. Senate Labor and Pub. Welfare Com., 1964, Labor Subcom., 1967, gen. counsel, 1970; press asst. to U.S. Sen. Ralph Yarborough, 1965, legis. asst., 1968, adminstrv. asst., 1969; cons. Booz, Allen & Hamilton, 1966-67; gen. counsel Senate Com. on D.C., 1971-72; adminstrv. asst. to U.S. Sen. Thomas Eagleton, 1973-76; mem. staff Carter-Mondale Compaign, 1976; v.p.-elect Mondale, 1976-77; asst. sec. Treasury for legis. affairs, Washington, 1977-80; partner firm Bracewell & Patterson, Washington, 1981—; adj. prof. law Cath. U. Law Sch., 1971. Served with USAR, 1964-65. Mem. Am., D.C., Tex. bar assns., Phi Delta Phi. Home: 3008 45th St NW Washington DC 20016 Office: 1850 K St NW Washington DC 20006

GODOSFSKY, STANLEY, lawyer; b. N.Y.C., May 24, 1928; s. Eli Godofsky and Lily (Deutsch) Godosfsky; m. Elaine Gloria Weiss, Dec. 15, 1951; children: Janice, David. A.B., Columbia U., 1949, J.D., 1951. Bar: N.Y. 1951, U.S. Supreme Ct. 1961. Assoc. Rogers & Wells, and predecessors, N.Y.C., 1951-64, ptnr., 1965—; spl. asst. counsel N.Y. State Crime Commn., 1952. Mem. bd. editors: Columbia U. Law Rev., 1950; revising editor, 1951. Mem. Am. Law Inst., ABA, N.Y. State Bar Assn., Assn. Bar City N.Y., Fed. Bar Council, Am. Judicature Soc., Internat. Bar Assn., Union Internationale des Avocats, World Assn. Lawyers, Internat. Assn. Jewish Lawyers and Jurists. Home: 22 Holbrooke Rd White Plains NY 10605 Office: Rogers & Wells Pan Am Bldg 200 Park Ave New York NY 10166

GODSCHALK, DAVID ROBINSON, educator; b. Enid, Okla., May 14, 1931; s. Harold J. and Helen Faye (Robinson) G.; m. Lallie Moore Kain, June 27, 1959; 1 son, David Kennedy. B.A., Dartmouth Coll., 1953; B.Arch., U. Fla., 1959; M.Regional Planning, U. N.C., 1964, Ph.D., 1971. Vice pres. Milo Smith Assos., Tampa, Fla., 1959-61; planning dir., City of Gainesville, Fla., 1964-65; asst. prof. Fla. State U., Tallahassee, 1965-67; editor AIP Jour., Chapel Hill, N.C., 1968-71; asso. prof. Univ. N.C., Chapel Hill, 1972-77, prof., 1977—, chmn. dept. city and regional planning, 1978-83; cons., State of Fla., 1967, 83, State of N.C., 1971-72, HUD, 1977, City of West Palm Beach, Fla., 1979-80. Author: (with others) Constitutional Issues of Growth Management, 1979; Editor: Planning in America: Learning from Turbulence, 1974, Am. Inst. Planners Jour, 1968-71; Editorial bd.: Jour. Planning Edn. and Research, 1983—. Served with USNR, 1953-56, 1961-62; comdr. Res.; ret. Recipient Service medal Am. Inst. Planners, 1971, Profl. Achievement award Am. Planning Assn., 1983. Mem. Am. Planning Assn. (bd. govs. 1978-79), Am. Soc. Planning Ofcls. (bd. dirs. 1974-77), Am. Inst. Cert. Planners. Office: Dept of City and Regional Planning Univ of North Carolina Chapel Hill NC 27514

GODSEY, JOHN DREW, clergyman, educator; b. Bristol, Tenn., Oct. 10, 1922; s. William Clinton and Mary Lynn (Corns) G.; m. Emalee Caldwell, June 26, 1943; children: Emalee Lynn Godsey Murphy, John Drew, Suzanne Godsey Douglas, Gretchen Godsey Brownley. B.S., Va. Poly. Inst. and State U., 1947; B.D., Drew U., 1953; D.Theol., U. Basel, Switzerland, 1960. Ordained to ministry United Methodist Ch., 1952. Instr. systematic theology, asst. dean Drew U., Madison, N.J., 1956-59, asst. prof., 1959-64, assoc. prof., 1964-66, prof., 1966-68; prof., assoc. dean Wesley Theol. Sem., Washington, 1968-71, prof. systematic theology, 1971—; Fulbright scholar U. Goettingen, W. Germany, 1964-65. Author: The Theology of Dietrich Bonhoeffer, 1960, Karl Barth's Table Talk, 1963, Preface to Bonhoeffer, 1965, Introduction and Epilogue to Karl Barth's How I Changed My Mind, 1966, The Promise of H. Richard Niebuhr, 1970; co-author: Ethical Responsibility: Bohnoeffer's Legacy to the Churches, 1981. Mem. Montgomery County Fair Housing Assn., Md. Served with AUS, 1943-46. Am. Assn. Theol. Schs. faculty fellow, 1964-65. Mem. Am. Acad. Religion, Am. Theol. Soc., Bibl. Theologians, Internat. Bonhoeffer Soc., Karl Barth Soc. N. Am., New Haven Theol. Discussion Group, Common Cause, Omicron Delta Kappa, Phi Kappa Phi, Alpha Zeta. Democrat. Home: 8306 Bryant Dr Bethesda MD 20817 Office: Wesley Theol Seminary 4500 Massachusetts Ave NW Washington DC 20016 *Z My goal has been to serve others with integrity, to do every job to the best of my ability, and to respect and further the rights and welfare of my fellow creatures on planet earth. Thus should my life be a testimony to my faith.*

GODSON, GODFREY NIGEL, molecular geneticist, educator; b. London, June 20, 1936; s. Godfrey Edward and Elsie Louise (Harrington) G.; m. Barbara Cohne, Aug. 9, 1969; children: Rebecca Charlotte, Vanessa Alexandra. B.S., London U., 1957, Ph.D., 1961. Research fellow Calif. Inst. Tech., 1964-67; staff scientist Nat. Insts. Med. Research, Med. Research Council, Mill Hill, London, 1968-69; asst. prof., assoc. prof. radiobiology Yale Med. Sch., New Haven, 1969-74, 1974-80; prof./chmn. dept. biochemistry NYU Med. Sch., N.Y.C., 1980—. Contbr. chpts. to books, articles to popular and profl. jours. Mem. Am. Chem. Soc., N.Y. Acad. Scis. Office: NYU Med Sch 550 1st Ave New York NY 10016

GODSON, JOSEPH, fgn. service officer; b. Poland, Jan. 15, 1913; s. Aaron and Clara (Drach) G.; m. Ruth Perlmann, Jan. 10, 1958; children—Roy, Carla. B.S.S., CCNY, 1937; LL.B., N.Y. U., 1940. Dean. Pub. relations dir. labor, charity orgns., 1940-50; joined U.S. fgn. service; attache Am. embassy, Ottawa, 1950-52, labor attache, London, 1953-59, 1st sec., Belgrade, Yugoslavia, 1959-61; Am. consul. gen., Zagreb, Yugoslavia, 1962-64; labor, UN adviser European Bur., Dept State, 1964-68; Am. consul gen., Edinburgh, Scotland, 1968-71; coordinator Europe-Am. Conf., 1971-73; sec. Labour Com. for Transatlantic Understanding, 1974—; European cons. Bd. for Internat. Broadcasting of U.S., 1976—; European coordinator Center for Strategic and Internat. Studies, Georgetown U., 1976—; cons. Adv. Com. European Democracy and Security, 1982—. European editor: The Washington Quar., A Rev. of Strategic and Internat. Issues, 1977—; Author, editor: Transatlantic Crisis: Europe and America in the '70s; author, co-editor: The Soviet Worker—Illusions and Realities, 1981; co-editor: Labour and Trade Union Press Service, 1975—. Clubs: Hurlingham, Reform (London). Home: 8 Campden Hill Ct London W8 England

GODSON, WARREN LEHMAN, meteorologist; b. Victoria, B.C., Can., May 4, 1920; s. Walter Ernest Henry and Mary Edna (Lehman) G.; m. Harriet Burke, Dec. 28, 1977; children: Elliott, Marilyn, Murray, Ralph, Ellen; stepchildren—Alan, Alison, Stephen Bloom. B.A., U. B.C., Vancouver, 1939, M.A., 1941; M.A., U. Toronto, Ont., 1944, Ph.D., 1948. Lab. demonstrator U. B.C., 1939-41; lab. demonstrator U. Toronto, 1941-42, spl. lectr. physics dept., 1948-61, hon. prof., 1975; meteorologist Can. Meteorol. Service (name changed to Atmospheric Environ. Service 1971), Toronto, 1942-51, supt. atmospheric research sect., 1951-72, dir. atmospheric processes research br., 1972-73; dir. gen. Atmospheric Research Directorate, 1973-84, sr. sci. adviser, 1984—. Author: (with J.V. Iribarne) Atmospheric Thermodynamics, 1974, 81; Contbr. (over 100) articles to profl. jours. Recipient Gov.-Gen.'s medal, 1935, Lefevre Gold medal, 1939, Patterson medal, 1968, IMO prize, 1975. Fellow Am. Meteorol. Soc. (councillor 1967-70, asso. editor Jour. Atmospheric Scis. 1962-70), Royal Soc. Can.; mem. World Meteorol. Orgn. (v.p. Commn. for Atmospheric Scis. 1957-61, pres. 1973-77, alt. permanent rep. of Can. 1977—, chmn. six working groups), Internat. Assn. Meteorology and Atmospheric Physics (sec., bur. dir. 1960-75, v.p. 1975-79, pres. 1979-83, convenor com. on meteorol. data for research 1960-64), Can. Meteorol. Soc. (exec. com. 1955-61, pres. 1957-59, Pres.'s prize), Can. Assn. Physicists (councillor 1955-57, chmn. earth physics div. 1967-68), Royal Meteorol. Soc. (v.p. Can. 1959-61, Can. Darton prize, Buchan prize 1964). Pioneer Arctic stratospheric jet stream and final warming process in polar winter stratosphere, Curtis-Godson approximation technique, Ozonagram diagram used for ozone representation. Office: 4905 Dufferin St North York Downsview ON M3H 5T4 Canada

GODUNOV, ALEXANDER BORIS, ballet dancer; b. Sakhalin Island, Russia, Nov. 28, 1949; s. Boris Ilaryion and Lydia Nicolaivna (Studensova) G.; m. Ludmilla Vlasova, Oct. 1971. Student, Riga Music Sch., 1958-67, Riga Choreography Sch., 1967, Stella Adler Acting Sch., after 1981. Mem., Bolshoi Dance Co., 1967-79; mem., Am. Ballet Theater, N.Y.C., 1979-82; premier dancer, 1980-82; TV appearance: Gudunov: The World to Dance In, 1983-84; free lance guest artist numerous world tours. Recipient Gold medal Moscow Internat. Compeition, 1973. Office: care Evelyn Shriver 501 Madison Ave New York NY 10022

GODWIN, DONALD FULTON, health program administrator; b. Wade, N.C., Aug. 15, 1933; s. Morris Fulton and Mary Magdalene (Royal) G.; m. Sarah Vivian Fryar, Sept. 1, 1957; children: Donna Elaine Baker, Kelly Fulton, Gwendolyn Denise Dunford. A.A., Campbell U., 1957; B.S. in Public Health, U. N.C., 1959, M.Ed., 1960. Head dept. sci. Titusville High Sch., (Fla.), 1960-65, track coach, 1961-65; regional program advisor W.Va. Dept. Mental Health, Elkins, 1965-68; exec. dir. Balt. Area Council on Alcoholism, 1968-71; asst. br. chief Nat. Inst. Alcohol Abuse and Alcoholism, Rockville, Md., 1971-73, chief occupational program br., 1973-80, dir. occupational programs div., 1980-82; assoc. dir. occupational programs Alcohol, Drug Abuse and Mental Health, Rockville, 1982—; bd. dirs. Hidden Brook, Belaire, Md., Mainstream, Balt., Nat. Occupational Tng. Inst., Bethesda, Md.; mem. adv. bd. White House Task force on Drug Abuse, Appalachian Community Mental Health Ctr., Elkins, W.Va.; mem. drug and alcohol adv. com. U.S. Dept. Army; mem. health promotion in worksite com. HHS. Mem. Md. Horseman's Benevolent Protective Assn., Balt., 1983. Served with USMC, 1953-56. Dupont scholar U. N.C., 1959; recipient Occupational award P.R. Dept. Addictions, 1984. Mem. Brevard County Sci. Tchrs. Assn. (founding pres.), Assn. Labor Mgmt. Cons. and Adminstrs. on Alcoholism, Occupational Programs Cons. Assn. (Nat. Leadership award 1980), Am. Rocket Soc., Am. Council on Alcoholism, Nat. Council on Alcoholism, Elkins Jaycees (v.p.). Lodge: Elks. Pioneered in devel. nat. movement focusing on early identification of employee problems adversely affecting job performance. Home: 6806 E Ridge Rd Baltimore MD 21207 Office: Nat Inst on Alcohol Abuse and Alcoholism 5600 Fishers Ln Rockville MD 20857 *It is the deep reaching within yourself for decisions when no other single soul, of which you are aware, can be counted on for understanding, guidance, support or appreciation. Alone and unsure, you decide believing in its rightness and your own vision and judgment for affecting change in the desired direction.*

GODWIN, GAIL KATHLEEN, author; b. Birmingham, Ala., June 18, 1937; d. Mose Winston and Kathleen (Krahenbuhl) G. Student, Peace Jr. Coll., Raleigh, N.C., 1955-57; B.A. in Journalism, U. N.C., 1959; M.A. in English, U. Iowa, 1968, Ph.D., 1971. News reporter Miami Herald, 1959-60; rep., cons. U.S. Travel Service, London, 1961-65; editorial asst. Saturday Evening Post, 1966; lectr. Iowa Writers Workshop, 1972-73, Vassar Coll., 1977, Columbia U. Writing Program, 1978, 81. Author: novels including The Perfectionists, 1970, Glass People, 1972, The Odd Woman, 1974, Violet Clay, 1978, A Mother and Two Daughters, 1982; short stories Dream Children, 1976, Mr. Bedford and The Muses, 1983; (with Robert Starer) librettos The Last Lover, 1975, Apollonia, 1979, Anna Margarita's Will, 1981. Fellow Center for Advanced Study, U. Ill., Urbana, 1971-72; Am. specialist USIS, 1976; Nat. Endowment Arts grantee, 1974-75; Guggenheim fellow, 1975-76; recipient award in lit. Am. Acad. and Inst. of Arts and Letters, 1981. Mem. P.E.N., Authors Guild, Authors League, Nat. Book Critics Circle, ASCAP. Home: RD 1 Box 248 Woodstock NY 12498

GODWIN, MILLS EDWIN, JR., former governor of Virginia; b. Chuckatuck, Va., Nov. 19, 1914; s. Mills Edwin and Otelia (Darden) G.; m. Katherine Beale, Oct. 26, 1940; 1 dau., Becky (dec.). LL.B., U. Va., 1938, Elon (N.C.) Coll., Coll. William and Mary, Roanoke Coll., Washington and Lee U., Elmira Coll., Hampden-Sydney Coll., U. Richmond, Bridgewater Coll. Bar: Va. 1937. Practiced in, Suffolk, 1938-60; spl. agt. FBI, 1942-46; mem. Va. Ho. Dels. from Suffolk-Nansemond County, 1947-52, senate, 1952-61; lt. gov., Va., 1962-66, gov., 1966-70, 74-78; dir. Sovran Bankshares, Inc., Nabisco Brands, Inc., Union Camp Corp., Am. Electric Power Co., Dan River, Inc.; Chmn. So. Regional Edn. Bd., 1968-69, 76-77; chmn. Appalachian Govs. Council, 1968-69, So. Govs. Conf., 1975-76; mem. exec. com. Nat. Govs. Conf., Republican Gov.'s Conf., Council State Govts. Bd. dirs. Beazley Found., Camp Found. Recipient Disting. Service award Va. State C. of C., 1970, Thomas Jefferson citation for pub. service, 1971. Mem. Raven Soc., Omicron Delta Kappa, Phi Delta Phi, Sigma Phi Epsilon. Republican. Mem. Christian Ch. Clubs: K.P., Mason (33 deg., Shriner), Rotarian, Moose, Ruritan (nat. pres. 1952).

GODWIN, WILLIAM COLIN, dentist, educator; b. Welland,.Ont., Can., Jan. 28, 1922; came to U.S., 1924, naturalized, 1942; s. Lloyd Stafford and Effie (Milloy) G.; m. Lois Elizabeth Walker, Feb. 14, 1944; children—David, Robert, Carl, Christopher. Student, Wayne State U., 1940-42; D.D.S., U. Mich., 1951, M.S., 1954. Practice dentistry, Ann Arbor, Mich., 1951—; clin. instr. U. Mich., Ann Arbor, 1951-55, asso. prof., 1955-63, 63-71, prof., 1971—. Cons. editor: Jour. ADA, 1965—. Chmn. athletic dentistry, 1962—; mem. Am. Med. Com. on Athletic Medicine for Washtenaw County, Mich., 1970—; Mem. curriculum com. Washtenaw Community Coll., Ann Arbor, 1970—; bd. dirs. Ann Arbor Amateur Hockey Assn., 1967-69. Served to 1st lt. USAAC, 1942-45. Decorated Purple Heart, Air medal; recipient Mich. Gov.'s trophy for Med. Scis., 1962. Mem. ADA, Mich. Dental Assn., Washtenaw Dist. Dental Soc., Richard H. Kingery Prosthetic Group, Omicron Kappa Upsilon. Home: 1205 Country Club Rd Ann Arbor MI 48105 Office: 1110 Henry St Ann Arbor MI 48104

GOEBEL, CHARLES H., commercial banker; b. Garber, Okla., Oct. 16, 1924; m. Jeannine J. Bedford, June 24, 1950; children: Mark, Karen. B.B.A., U. Mich., 1950, M.B.A., 1954. Chmn., chief exec. officer Wayne Oakland Bank, Royal Oak, Mich., 1978—. Trustee Downtown Devel. Authority, Royal Oak, Hosp. authority, Southeastern Oakland County. Mem. Mich. Bankers Assn., Delta Sigma Pi. Club: Red Run Golf. Home: 3280 Greentree Rd Bloomfield Hills MI 48013

GOEBEL, EDWARD LEE, business educator, university dean, consultant; b. Washington, Ind., Jan. 15, 1936; s. Cyril J. and Nancy J. (Hahn) G.; m. Ima Sue Zehring, Nov. 24, 1956 (div. July 1981); 1 dau., Jacklyn Sue; m. Christine A. Dodds, Mar. 5, 1982. B.S., Ind. U., 1959, M.B.A., 1960; Ph.D., U. Ga., 1968. Adminstrv. asst. to dean U. Ga., Athens, 1960-67; dir. M.B.A. program Ind. State U., Terre Haute, 1969-74, interim dean, Terrre Haute, 1974, dean Sch. Bus., Terre Haute, 1975—; dir. Valley Fed. Savs. & Loan Assn., Wabash Services Corp., Terrehaute, 1980—; mem. region V SBA Adv. Council, State of Ind., 1975—. Bd. dirs. Nat. Coll., Rapid City, S.D., 1979—, Leadership Terre Haute, 1977-82; pres. Jr. Achievement, 1979-80. Named Small Bus. Advocate of Yr. Region V, SBA, 1976. Mem. Acad. Mgmt., Am. Assembly Collegiate Schs. Bus. (dir. Mid-Continent East div. 1983), Am. Mktg. Assn., Terre Haute Area C. of C. (dir. 1976-79), Phi Kappa Phi, Beta Gamma Sigma, Omicron Delta Epsilon. Republican. Methodist. Club: Country (Terra Haute). Home: 1365 Winterberry Ct Terre Haute IN 47802 Office: Ind State U Sch Bus East Tower Terre Haute IN 47809

GOEBEL, WALTHER FREDERICK, biochemist; b. Palo Alto, Calif., Dec. 24, 1899; s. Julius and Kathryn (Vreel) G.; m. Cornelia Van Rensselaer Robb, Oct. 23, 1930 (dec. Oct. 1974); children—Cornelia Van Rensselaer Bronson, Anne Kathryn Barkman; m. Alice Lawrence Behn, Nov. 12, 1976. A.B., U. Ill., 1920, A.M., 1921, Ph.D., 1923, scholar in chemistry, 1920-21, fellow, 1921-23; postgrad., U. Munich, Germany, 1923-24; D.Sc. (hon.), Middlebury (Vt.) Coll., 1959, Rockefeller U., 1978. Research asst. Rockefeller U., 1924-27, asso., 1927-34, asso. mem., 1934-44, mem., 1944-57, prof., 1957-70, prof. emeritus, 1970—. Contbr. monographs, reports and articles on chem. and immunological subjects sci. jours. Mem. Nat. Acad. Scis., Am. Chem. Soc., Am. Soc. Biol. Chemists, Harvey Soc., Am. Assn. Immunologists, Am. Soc. Microbiology, Conn. Acad. Sci. and Engring., Gesellschaft für Immunologie (Avery-Landsteiner award 1973), Phi Beta Kappa, Sigma Xi, Phi Lambda Upsilon, Phi Eta. Home: 15 Lyon Farm Dr E Greenwich CT 06830 Office: Rockefeller U New York City NY 10021

GOEBEL, WILLIAM MATHERS, lawyer; b. Jacksonville, Ill., Nov. 5, 1922; s. William George and Elizabeth (Mathers) G.; m. Barbara Leeper, Mar. 10, 1944; children: William Mathers, Helen Elizabeth. A.B., Ill. Coll., 1946; J.D., U. Mich., 1949. Bar: Ill. bar 1949. Practice in, Carmi, 1949-59, Bloomington, 1961—; partner Conger, Elliott, Goebel & Elliott, 1949-59; asst. gen. counsel Ill. Agrl. Assn. (and affiliated cos.), 1959-64; partner Dunn, Goebel, Ulbrich, Morel & Hundman, 1964—; lectr. dept. ednl. adminstrn. Ill. State U.; instr. Ill. Wesleyan U. Contbr. to: U. Ill. Law Forum, 1962. Mem. Ill. Citizens Com. for Uniform Comml. Code; mem. Ill. Sch. Problems Commn., 1965-69; Bd. dirs Bloomington-Normal Symphony Soc., 1967-73; trustee Brokaw Hosp., Normal, Ill., 1964-69; sec. bd. trustees, mem. exec. com. Ill. Wesleyan U., Bloomington. Served with AUS, World War II. Mem. Am. Judicature Soc., ABA, Ill. Bar Assn. (past council chmn. comml. banking and bankruptcy law sect., mem. fed. judiciary appointments com. 1976-80), McLean County Bar Assn. (pres. 1983-84). Democrat. Presbyn. Club: Bloomington Country. Lodge: Rotary. Home: 1311 E Washington St Bloomington IL 61701 Office: Peoples Bank Bldg Bloomington IL 61701

GOEDICKE, HANS, educator; b. Vienna, Austria, Aug. 7, 1926; s. Erich and Alice V. (Schuller-Götzburg) G.; m. Lucy McLaughlin, Mar. 1969. Ph.D., U. Vienna, 1949. With Egyptian sect. Mus. Fine Arts, Vienna, 1949-51; research asso. Brown U., 1952-56; with UNESCO, 1956-58, U. Göttingen, 1958-60; faculty Johns Hopkins, Balt., 1960—, prof. dept. Near Eastern studies, 1968—, chmn. dept., 1969-73, 79—, field dir. archaeol. expdn., Giza, Egypt, 1972, 74, condr. epigraphic survey, Aswan area, 1964, 67; dir. survey Wadi Tumilat, 1977, 78; chmn. symposium on ancient Near East Am. Council Learned Socs., 1973; dir. summer seminar on ancient Egypt Nat. Endowment Humanities, 1977; guest prof. U. Vienna, 1978-79; Bd. govs. Am. Research Center in Egypt; adv. Nat. Humanities Center. Author: The Report About the Dispute of a Man with his BA, 1970, Near Eastern Studies in Honor of William Foxwell Albright, 1971, Queen Nofretari, The Documentation of her Tomb, 1970, Reused Blocks from the Pyramid of Amenemhet I at Lisht, 1971, Die Geschichte des Schiffbrüchigen, 1974, The Report of Wenamun, 1975, The Protocol of Neferyt, 1977, Die Darstellung des Horus, 1982, Egypt and Early Israel, 1984; editor-in-chief: Near Eastern Studies; rev. editor: Jour. Am. Research Center in Egypt. Bd. dirs. Ecumenical Inst., Balt. John Simon Guggenheim fellow, 1966; George A. and Eliza Gardner Howard Found. fellow, 1956-57. Mem. Egypt Exploration Soc., Am.

Research Center in Egypt, Fondation Egyptologique Reine Elisabeth, Société D'Archeologie Copte. Home: 3959 Cloverhill Rd Baltimore MD 21218

GOEGLEIN, RICHARD JOHN, casino/hotel exec.; b. Los Angeles, Aug. 23, 1934; s. Myrwil Louis and Pauline Yvette (Rizer) G.; children—Eric John, William Scott. B.S., U. Wyo., 1957; M.B.A., Stanford U., 1960. Dist. sales rep. Continental Oil Co., Houston, 1960-63; div. v.p. Interstate United Corp., Mountain View, Calif., 1963-70; pres., chief exec. officer Uniworld Foods, Inc., Culver City, Calif., 1970-72; chmn., pres., chief exec. officer Hungry Tiger, Inc., Van Nuys, Calif., 1972-74; v.p. W.R. Grace & Co., N.Y.C., 1974-78; exec. v.p., dir. Holiday Inns, Memphis, 1978—; also pres., chief exec. officer, dir. Harrah's, Inc., Reno. Trustee Culinary Inst. Am. Served with USN, 1957. Mem. Stanford Bus. Sch. Assn., Stanford Alumni Assn., Reno-Sparks C. of C. (dir.). Republican. Home: 3353 Skyline Blvd Reno NV 89509 Office: Harrah's PO Box 10 Reno NV 89504

GOEHRING, KENNETH, artist; b. Evansville, Wis., Jan. 8, 1919; s. Walter A. and Ruth I. (Rossman) G.; m. Margretta M. Macnicol, Dec. 1, 1945. Student, Cass Tech. Inst., 1933-35, Meinzinger Sch. Applied Art, 1945-46, Colorado Springs Fine Arts Ctr., 1947-50. Works have appeared in over 100 exhibitions in 17 states and 20 museums; works have appeared in over 100 exhibitions in 17 sttes and 20 museums: 17 one-man shows; exhibitor, Terry Inst., Miami, Symphony Hall, Boston, de Cordova Mus., Fitchburg Mus., Mass., Farnsworth Mus., Maine, Corcoran, Washington, Joslyn Meml. Mus., Nebr., Detroit Inst. Arts U, U. Nebr. Galleries, Stanford U. Galleries, Calif, De Young Mus., San Francisco; represented in permanent collections, Sheldon Art Ctr., Lincoln, Nebr., in many pvt. collections throughout U.S. Purchase awards include Colorado Springs Fine Arts Ctr., 1958; Washburn U., 1957, Am. Acad. Design, 1977. Address: 2017 W Platte Ave Colorado Springs CO 80904

GOEKE, LEO FRANCIS, tenor; b. Kirksville, Mo.; s. Edward Jerome and Rosella (Aeschliman) G.; m. Margery Ryan, July 6, 1963; 1 son, Matthew. B.S., Mo. State Coll., 1957; Mus. M., La. State U., 1960; M.F.A., Iowa State U., 1961. Leading tenor, Met. Opera, N.Y.C., 1970—, N.Y. State Opera, 1972—; guest performer leading tenor roles various opera cos., including, Glyndebourne (Eng.) Opera Festival, Netherlands Opera, Amsterdam, Netherlands Opera, Utrecht and Rotterdam, Teheran (Iran) Opera, Capetown (S. Africa) Opera, Seattle Opera, Portland (Oreg.) Opera, Santa Fe Opera Co., Stravinsky L'Autome Festival, Paris, Ky. Opera Assn., Miami Opera Assn., Can. Opera Assn., debuts in, Covent Garden, London, Maggio Musicale, Florence, Italy, La Fenice, Venice, Italy, Greek Nat. Opera, Athens, Phila. Orch., Saratoga Performing Arts Ctr., La Scala Opera, Milan, Italy, Wuttembergische Staatstheater, Stuttgart, W. Ger., recs. for, So. TV, I.T.V., Eng. Roman Catholic. Home: Box 47 Route 203 Chatham NY 12037

GOELDNER, CHARLES RAYMOND, educator; b. Fort Dodge, Iowa, Mar. 21, 1932; s. Leslie Raymond and Beulah (Bohrer) G.; m. Jacquelyn Rae Anderson, Dec. 31, 1954; children: JoLynn, Bradley Allen, Deborah Kay. B.A., State U. Iowa, 1954, M.A., 1958, Ph.D., 1961. Asst. prof. Calif. State U., Northridge, 1959-63; asso. prof., dir. Bur. Bus. Research and Services, 1963-67; prof., dir. bus. research div. U. Colo., Boulder, 1967—, head mktg. div., 1976-79; Mem. faculty UCLA, summer 1963, 65; lectr. Grad. Sch. Bus., U. So. Calif., Los Angeles, 1963-66. Editor: Jour. Travel Research, 1967—; author: Bibliography of Tourism and Travel Research Studies, Reports and Articles, 9 vols, 1980; Author: Travel Trends in the United States and Canada, 1981, 2d edit., 1984, Automatic Merchandising, A Selected and Annotated Bibliography, 1964, Business Facts: Where to Find Them, 1976, Economic Analysis of North American Ski Areas, 1982, 2d edit., 1983, (with Robert McIntosh) Tourism: Principles, Practices, Philosophies, 1984; editor: Colo. Bus. Rev., 1972—. Trustee U.S. Travel Data Center, 1972—. Served with AUS, 1954-56. L.R. Fairall scholar; Ford Found. Mktg. Research Workshop fellow. Mem. Western Council Travel Research (1st vice chmn. 1970-71), Travel Research Assn. (pres. 1974), Assn. Univ. Bus. and Econ. Research (sec.-treas. 1970-73), Assn. U. Bus. and Econ. Research (v.p. 1973-74, pres. 1974-75), Am. Econ. Assn., Am. Acad. Advt., Inst. Cert. Travel Agts. (acad. council 1974—), Am. Mktg. Assn. (reprints editor 1970-73), Phi Beta Kappa. Home: 3147 Westwood Ct Boulder CO 80302

GOELET, ROBERT G., business executive; b. Sandricourt, France, Sept. 28, 1923; s. Robert Walton and Anne Marie (Guestier) G.; m. Alexandra Gardiner Creel, Sept. 9, 1976. A.B., Harvard U., 1945. Chmn. R.I. Corp.; pres. Goelet Realty Co.; v.p. Goelet Estate Co.; dir. Chem. Bank, Chem. N.Y. Corp., N. Central Oil Corp. Trustee Am. Mus. Natural History, 1958—, pres., 1975—; dir. Boscobel Restoration Inc., 1976—; trustee French Inst./Alliance Française de N.Y., 1951—, pres., 1967—; trustee N.Y. Hist. Soc., 1961—, pres., 1971—; trustee N.Y. Zool. Soc., 1951—, pres., 1971-75; trustee Phipps Houses, 1959—, Carnegie Instn., Washington, 1980—, St. Catherine's Island Found., 1981, Edward John Noble Found., 1981, Mus. Comparative Zoology, 1980—; bd. dirs. Nat. Audubon Soc., 1956-67, 69-75, treas., 1959-69. Served as naval aviator USNR, 1943-45. Office: 425 Park Ave New York NY 10022

GOELL, JAMES EMANUEL, electronics company executive; b. N.Y.C., Oct. 13, 1939; s. Milton Jacob and Amy (Jacob) G.; m. Tamara Greenberg, Sept. 11, 1960; children: Lisa Sue, Fredric Scott. B.E.E., Cornell U., 1962, M.S., 1963, Ph.D., 1965. Mem. tech. staff Bell Labs., Holmdel, N.J., 1965-74; v.p., dir. engring., dir. fiber optics lab. Electro-Optical Products div. ITT, Roanoke, Va., 1974-81; pres. Lightwave Technologies, Inc., Van Nuys, Calif., 1981—. Vice pres. Middletown Twp. (N.J.) Bd. Edn. Fellow IEEE; mem. Optical Soc. Am., Am. Phys. Soc., Sigma Xi, Eta Kappa Nu, Tau Beta Pi, Phi Kappa Phi. Home: 4052 Bon Homme Rd Woodland Hills CA 91364 Office: LTI 6737 Valjean Ave Van Nuys CA 91406

GOELLNER, JACK GORDON, publishing executive; b. Cleve., Aug. 16, 1930; s. Fred William and Ella (Rohde) G.; m. Sarah Frances Williams, Aug. 16, 1952 (div. Sept. 28, 1982); children: Katherine, Ellen, Michael, Kirsten.; m. Barbara B. Lamb, Apr. 14, 1984. B.A., Allegheny Coll., 1952, Litt.D., 1979; M.A., U. Wis., 1953. Reporter Springfield (Ohio) Sun, 1955-57; sr. writer, pub. information Cleve. Electric Illuminating Co., 1957-61; mgr. sales and advt. Johns Hopkins U. Press, Balt., 1961-65, editorial dir., 1965-73, asso. dir., 1973-74, dir., 1974—, Am. Univ. Press Services, 1963-66, treas., 1972-74, chmn. bd., 1979-80; dir. York Press; chmn. bd. Internat. Book Export Group Ltd., Johns Hopkins Press Ltd., 1974—; mem. nat. adv. bd. and exec. com. Center for the Book, Library of Congress, 1979—; mem. U.S. Govt. Adv. Com. on Internat. Book and Library Programs, 1975-78; head pubs. mission to Eastern Europe Dept. State, 1977; cons. Nat. Endowment for Humanities, 1977—. Contbr. articles to profl. and popular jours.; Mem. editorial bd.: Scholarly Pub, 1980—; mem. adv. bd.: Lit. Classics of U.S, 1980—. Bd. dirs. Southland Hills Community Assn., 1965-68, 76-79. Served with AUS, 1953-55. Am. Council Learned Socs. fellow, 1952-53; Danforth fellow, 1952-53. Mem. Assn. Am. Univ. Presses (dir. 1972-74, 78-81, treas. 1972-74, pres. 1979-80), Soc. Scholarly Pub. (dir. 1978—), Assn. Am. Pubs. (mem. exec. council profl. and scholarly pub. div. 1981—), Md. Fly Anglers (sec. 1970-72), Trout Unltd., Phi Beta Kappa. Democrat. Episcopalian. Clubs: Tudor and Stuart, Hamilton St. Home: 215 Ridgemede Rd Baltimore MD 21210 Office: Johns Hopkins U Press Baltimore MD 21218

GOELTZ, RICHARD KARL, distilled spirits and wine co. exec.; b. Chgo., Sept. 11, 1942; s. Karl George and Adeline Caroline (Hoffeins) G. A.B., Brown U., 1964; M.B.A., Columbia, 1966; student, London (Eng.) Sch. Econs., 1962-63. Financial analyst Office Treas. Exxon Corp., N.Y.C., 1966-70; asst. treas. Joseph E. Seagram & Sons, Inc., N.Y.C., 1970-73, fin. v.p., 1976—, also dir. Mem. Beta Gamma Sigma. Clubs: Sleepy Hollow Country, Metropolitan Opera, Racquet & Tennis. Home: 953 Fifth Ave New York NY 10021 Office: 375 Park Ave New York NY 10022

GOELZ, PAUL CORNELIUS, university dean; b. Bartelso, Ill., Oct. 7, 1914; s. Peter Paul and Clara (Bross) G. Cert., St. Louis U., 1939; B.B.A., U. Dayton, 1943, M.A., 1946; M.B.A., Northwestern U., 1951, Ph.D., 1954. Credit mgr. Adjustable Shoe Co., St. Louis, 1937-39; asst. comptroller Key Refinery Equipment Co., St. Louis, 1939-40; auditor Gen. Motors Acceptance Corp., St. Louis, 1940-41; instr. Southside High Sch., St. Louis, 1943-46; chmn. dept. mktg. St. Mary's U., San Antonio, 1946-62; dean Sch. Bus. Adminstrn., 1962—, Myra Stafford Pryor prof. free enterprise, 1978—; vis. lectr. staff Army Mgmt. Engring. Tng. Agy., U.S. Dept. Def., Rock Island Arsenal; lectr. Exec. Devel. Insts. in, U.S. and Mexico; cons. to bus. and govt. Chmn. spl. series of sessions at Internat. Conf. Am. Inst. Indsl. Engrs., 1963. Contbr. articles to profl. publs. Recipient award Freedoms Found. at Valley Forge, 1979, Liberty Bell award Young Lawyers Assn., 1982. Mem. Acad. Mgmt., Am. Mktg. Assn., Sales and Mktg. Execs. Internat., Am. Inst. Indsl. Engrs., San Antonio C. of C., Nat. Assn. Bus. Economists, Southwestern Assn. Bus. Sch. Deans (pres. 1968-69), Fin. Execs. Inst., Assn. Pvt. Enterprise Edn. (pres. 1982-83), Am. Assembly Collegiate Schs. Bus. (bd. dirs.), Delta Epsilon Sigma, Alpha Sigma Tau, Pi Sigma Epsilon. Home: One Camino Santa Maria San Antonio TX 78284

GOERING, GORDON DAVID, petroleum company executive; b. Pretty Prairie, Kans., May 3, 1922; s. Gerhardt Gustav and Helen Ella (Unruh) G.; m. Margaret Joyce Nickerson, June 3, 1944; children: Susan Gail, Nancy Jean, Anita Marlyse. B.S. in Chem. Engring, Kans. State U., 1945. Registered profl. engr., Tex. With Phillips Petroleum Co., 1946—, v.p., Bartlesville, Okla., 1978-80, sr. v.p., 1980—; dir. Phillips Imperial Petroleum U.K., Cochrin Refineries, Ltd., India, Phillips R.R. Core Inc., San Juan. Served with USNR, 1943-46. Mem. Am. Inst. Chem. Engrs., Nat. Soc. Profl. Engrs., Nat. Petroleum Refiners Assn., Am. Petroleum Inst., Okla. Soc. Profl. Engrs., Bartlesville C. of C. Methodist. Club: Hillcrest Country (Bartlesville). Home: 3433 Hawthorne Ct Bartlesville OK 74003 Office: 17 Phillips Bldg Bartlesville OK 74006

GOERING, KENNETH JUSTIN, coll. adminstr.; b. San Francisco, Dec. 26, 1913; s. George Hans and Elsa (Toepper) G.; m. Marjory Gieseker, Aug. 14, 1936; children—Patricia DeBedout, John D., Kenneth Don. B.S., Mont. State Coll., 1936; M.S., Calif. Inst. Tech., 1939; Ph.D., Iowa State U., 1941. Research chemist Anheuser Busch Co., St. Louis, 1941-42; instr. Iowa State U., 1942-43; research chemist WPB, Lincoln, Nebr., 1943-44; asst. chief chemist Omaha Alcohol Plant, 1944-45; v.p., gen. mgr. Mold Bran Co. and Enzymes, Inc., Eagle Grove, Iowa, 1945-49; mem. faculty Mont. State U., Bozeman, 1949—, prof. biochemistry, 1960—, grad. dean, 1967-75; cons. Kurth Malting Co., Sunburst Biochem. Co., Farm Bur., Idaho Potato Foods. Asso. editor: Cereal Chemistry. Recipient Blue and Gold award Mont. State U., 1978, Charles and Nora Wiley Career Research award, 1980. Mem. Am. Chem. Soc., Am. Assn. Cereal Chemists, Sigma Xi (Mont. chpt. award 1961), Phi Kappa Phi. Patentee in field. Home: 8383 Saddle Mountain Rd Bozeman MT 59715

GOERKE, GLENN ALLEN, university administrator; b. Lincoln Park, Mich., May 15, 1931; s. Albert W. Goerka and Cecile P. (Crowl) G.; m. Joyce Leslie Walker, Mar. 3, 1973; children: Lynn, Jill, Kurt. A.B., Eastern Mich. U., 1952, M.A., 1955; Ph.D., Mich. State U., 1964. Dean univ. services Fla. Internat. U., Miami, 1970-71, assoc. dean faculty, 1971-72, assoc. v.p. acad. affairs, provost North campus, 1972-73; v.p. community affairs Fla. Internat U., Miami, 1973-78; dean coll. continuing edn. U. R.I., 1978-81; chancellor Ind. U. East, Richmond, 1981—; adminstr. first VISTA tng. program and Operation Head Start, 1964; cons. adult higher edn., Bahamas, 1975-79, Jamaica, El Salvador, Colombia, Bahamas. Bd. dirs. Reid Meml. Hosp. Found., Richmond Symphony Orch.; chmn. edn. adv. panel Ind. Arts Commn. Recipient Outstanding Service award Adult Educators Assn. U.S., 1975, Eastern Mich. U. Disting. Alumni award, 1982. Mem. Nat. Univ. Continuing Edn. Assn. (pres. 1973-74), Nat. Assn. State Univs. and Land Grant Colls. (dell. 1980-81), Am. Assn. State Colls. and Univs., Phi Delta Kappa. Democrat. Methodist. Office: Ind U East 2325 Chester Blvd Richmond IN 47374

GOERLITZ, HARVEY THEODORE, insurance company executive; b. Oakland, Calif., Oct. 5, 1922; s. Harvey F. and Alma M. (Hoffman) G.; m. Frances Virginia McNevin, May 3, 1946; children: Barbara Ann, Robert Harvey. A.A., San Diego Jr. Coll., 1948; B.A. in Bus, San Diego State Coll., 1950; postgrad., Wharton Sch. U. Pa., 1977. With Farmers Ins. Group, 1950—, exec. and adminstrn. positions in claims, mut. funds and life ops.; dir. life sales Farmers New World Life; pres. Investors Guaranty Life Ins. Co., Mercer Island, Wash.; now pres. Ohio State Life. Bd. dirs. Griffith Found. Served with USN, 1942-46. Republican. Clubs: E Clampus Vitus, Masons, Rotary; Athletic (Columbus). Office: 2500 Farmers Dr Columbus OH 43085

GOERNER, JOSEPH KOFAHL, chemical company executive; b. Houston, Mar. 20, 1925; s. Joseph August and Mae Bess (Kofahl) G.; m. Elsie Virginia Barton, July 10, 1946; children: Deborah, Carol, Patricia, Pamela, Gary. B.S. in Chem. Engring., Rice U., 1945. Registered profl. engr., Tex. Research chem. engr. Jefferson chem. Co., Houston, 1946-56, v.p. research and devel., 1974-80, Texaco Chem. Co. div. Texaco Inc., 1980-82, v.p. mktg., 1982—. Inventor, patentee ethanolamines process, oxo process. Served with USN, 1945-46. Mem. Am. Chem. Soc., Am. Inst. Chem. Engrs., Soap and Detergent Assn. (dir. 1981-83). Republican. Episcopalian. Office: Texaco Chem Co Div Texaco Inc 4800 Fournace Bellaire TX 77401

GOERS, MELVIN ARMAND, retired army officer; b. Sadorus, Ill., Aug. 29, 1918; s. Arthur Daniel and Marie (Schwerdtfeger) G.; m. Kathryn Louise Lindsay, Nov. 20, 1941; children: Nancy Kay (Mrs. William Edwin Banta), Susan Jane (Mrs. Donald Ray Briggs), Gayle Ann (Mrs. Thomas Scott Hofmann), Julie Lindsay (Mrs. Stephen Jeffrey White). B.S., U. Ill., 1940; grad., Cavalry Sch., 1941, Army Command and Gen. Staff Coll., 1946, Armed Forces Staff Coll., 1956, Indsl. Coll. Armed Forces, 1959. Commd. 2d lt. U.S. Army, 1940, advanced through grades to brig. gen., 1967, officer Cavalry Div. and Armored Div., U.S. and Europe, 1940-45, comptroller Exchange Service, Europe, 1946-47; staff officer (Hdqrs. Far East and UN Command), 1950-53, comdr. 81st RCN Bn., personnel dir. 1st Armored Div., 1953-55, exec. officer, comdr. sch. regt. Armor Sch., 1956-58, officer Gen. Staff and Orgn. Joint Chiefs of Staff, Washington, 1959-62, chief joint staff MAAG Rep. of China, Taiwan, 1962-64, dir. operations Hdqrs. 5th Army, Ft. Sheridan, Ill., 1964-67, sr. mil. adviser 1st ROK Army, Korea, 1967-68, dir. R.O.T.C. Hdqrs. CONARC, Ft. Monroe, Va., 1969-72; ret.; dir. Va. Peninsula Office Manpower Programs, Hampton, 1972-77; Mem. Va. Gov.'s Employment and Tng. Council, 1974-81, chmn., 1979-81; mem. Va. Adv. Council for Vocat. Edn., 1976-79, chmn., 1978-79. Mem. planning div. Peninsula United Way, 1974-81; Pres. bd. govs. Taiwan Am. Sch., 1963-64; bd. dirs. Va. Peninsula chpt. ARC, 1978-83. Decorated D.S.M., Legion of Merit with 2 oak leaf clusters, Joint Service Commendation Medal, B.S.M. with oak leaf cluster, U.S., Presdl. Medal of Merit, Czechoslovakia). Mem. Assn. U.S. Army, Armor Assn. Lutheran. Club: Hampton Kiwanis (pres. 1978). Home: 305 Gaines Mill Ln Hampton VA 23669

GOERTZ, AUGUSTUS FREDERICK, III, artist; b. N.Y.C., Aug. 15, 1948; s. Augustus Frederick and Esther (Meyer) G.; m. Dione Christensen, Sept. 2, 1978. B.F.A. with honors, San Francisco Art Inst., 1971. Cons. League Internat. Artists, Ground Zero Prodn. Co., N.Y.C. Exhbns. include, San Francisco Art Inst., 1971, New Britain (Conn.) Mus., 1974, Soho Center for Visual Artists, N.Y.C., 1975, Am. Fedn. Arts, 1977, Aldrich Mus. Contemporary Art, 1973-78, Sarah Y. Rentschler Gallery, N.Y.C., 1978-79, Art Fiera, Bologna, Italy, 1978, Parke-Bernet Gallery, N.Y.C., 1979; represented in permanent collections, Aldrich Mus. Contemporary Art, Chgo. Art Inst., San Francisco Art Inst., N.Y. Law Sch., Harmonious Arts Found. N.Y., others. Mem. Orgn. Ind. Artists, San Francisco Art Inst. Alumni Assn., Works Project Assn., Inc. Democrat. Address: 319 Greenwich St New York NY 10013 *Every person has a responsibility to evolve away from materialistic environmental destruction, and towards linking, intellect, spirit, body, and expanding universe.*

GOESCHEL, ARTHUR L., manufacturing company executive; b. 1922; (married). B.S., Coll. City N.Y., 1943; M.B.A., N.Y. U., 1951. Plant mgr. Stauffer Chem. Co., Nat. Research Corp., Dixon Chem. Co., 1947-59; dist. mgr. Air Products & Chems., Inc., 1959-60; pres. Metalsalts Corp., 1960-66; mgr. metasol products Merck Chem. div. Merck & Co., Inc., 1966-67, asst. gen. mgr., 1967-68, gen. mgr. indsl. and fine chems., 1968-69, v.p. indsl. and fine chems., 1969-72; pres. Calgon Corp., Pitts., 1972—, also dir. *

GOESSEL, WILLIAM W., corporate executive. Pres., chief operating officer Harnischfeger Corp. Office: PO Box 554 Milwaukee WI 53201§

GOETCHIUS, EUGENE VAN NESS, clergyman; b. Augusta, Ga., Mar. 26, 1921; s. Eugene Foster and Agnes Louise (Stelling) G.; m. Ann Oliver Kirkpatrick, Dec. 17, 1955; children—Charles L.T., Nathaniel K., Edward V.N., John M. B.A., U. Va., 1941, M.S., 1947, M.A., 1948, Ph.D., 1949; B.D., Episcopal Theol. Sch., Cambridge, Mass., 1952; Th.D., Union Theol. Sem., N.Y.C., 1963; postgrad., U. Zurich, Switzerland, 1964, Mansfield Coll., Oxford, Eng., 1970-71. Master Woodberry Forest Sch., 1947-49; instr. math. Tufts U., 1950-52; instr. religion Trinity Coll., Hartford, Conn., 1952-54; fellow, tutor Gen. Theol. Sem., N.Y.C., 1954-56; ordained to ministry Episcopal Ch., 1952; asst. Grace Ch., N.Y.C., 1954-55; asst. chaplain Columbia, 1955-56; head dept. math. Am. Acad. in Athens, Greece, 1957; asst. prof. N.T. Episcopal Theol. Sch., 1957-60, asso. prof., 1960-63, prof. Bibl. langs., 1963—, Edmund Swett Rousmaniere prof. lit. and interpretation N.T., 1978—; lectr. Hellenistic Greek Harvard, 1957-58, 77—; dir. Inst. Bibl. Langs. and Linguistics, Vanderbilt U., summer 1968; vis. prof. Greek Andover Newton Theol. Sch., 1968; vis. prof. Hebrew Boston U., 1969; mem. heraldry com. Episcopal Ch. Author: The Language of the New Testament, 1965; co-author: Teaching the Biblical Languages, 1967; Translator: Exegetical Method (by O. Kaiser and W. K ummel). Trustee Boston Theol. Inst. Mem. Studiorum Novi Testamenti Societas, Schweizerische Heraldische Gesellschaft, New Eng. Historic-Geneal. Soc. (mem. council, chmn. com. heraldry), Phi Beta Kappa, Phi Epsilon Pi (asso.). Clubs: Odd Volumes, Barnstable Yacht. Home: 6 St John's Rd Cambridge MA 02138 *Belief in the importance of one's work is the basic ingredient of any kind of success.*

GOETHERT, BERNHARD HERMANN, aerospace en, educator; b. Hannover, Germany, Oct. 20, 1907; came to U.S., 1945, naturalized, 1954; s. Bernhard August and Elise (Rickmeyer) G.; m. Hertha Tod, Mar. 29, 1935; children—Hella (Mrs. D.A. Lacy), Winfried, Wolfhart, Reinhard. B.S., Tech. U. Hannover, 1930; M.S., Tech. U. Danzig, Germany, 1934; Ph.D. cum laude, Tech. U. Berlin, Germany, 1938. Research engr. DVL German Research Inst. Aeros., Berlin, 1934-36, sci. staff engr., 1936-39, chief dept. high speed aerodynamics, 1939-45; cons. USAF Center Wright Field, Dayton, O., 1945-52; chief propulsion wind tunnel facility ARO, Inc., Tullahoma, Tenn., 1952-56, chief engine test facility, 1956-59, dir. engring., 1959-63, research v.p., chief scientist, 1963-64, dir., 1959-64; chief scientist USAF Systems Command, Andrews AFB, Washington, 1964-66; PRof., dir. U. Tenn. Space Inst., Tullahoma, 1964-71, prof. aerospace engring. dean, 1971—; prof. Tech. U., Aachen, Germany, 1961—; NASA research adv. com. fluid mechanics, 1963-65; cons. Nat. Acad. of Sci., 1966-69, FAA, 1969—; mem. panel fluid dynamics, adv. com. aeros. NATO, 1960-68. Author: Transonic Testing, 1961; contbr. numerous articles in field. Recipient Spl. Appreciation plaque USAF Chief Staff, 1959; Meritorious Civilian Service award USAF, 1966; plaque of honor Tech. U. Aachen, Germany, 1972; Humboldt award Humboldt Found., 1976; plaque of tribute Aerospace Industry, 1978. Fellow Am. Inst. Aeros. and Astronautics (chmn. tech. com. for ground testing 1960-62, mem. tech. activity com. 1967-69, Simulation and Ground Testing award 1976), N.Y. Acad. Sci.; mem. German Assn. Aeros. and Astronautics (hon.). Lutheran. Home: 1703 Sycamore Circle Manchester TN 37355 Office: U Tenn Space Inst Tullahoma TN 37388

GOETTEL, GERARD LOUIS, federal judge; b. N.Y.C., Aug. 5, 1928; s. Louis and Agnes Beatrice (White) G.; m. Elinor Praeger, June 4, 1951; children: Sheryl, Glenn, James. Student, The Citadel, 1946-48; B.A., Duke U., 1950; J.D. (Harlan Fiske Stone scholar), Columbia U., 1955. Bar: N.Y. 1955. Asst. U.S. atty. So. Dist. N.Y., N.Y.C., 1955-58; dep. chief atty. gen.'s spl. group on organized crime Dept. Justice, N.Y.C., 1958-59; asso. firm Lowenstein, Pitcher, Hotchkiss, Amann & Parr, N.Y.C., 1959-62; counsel N.Y. Life Ins. Co., N.Y.C., 1962-68; with Natanson & Reich, N.Y.C., 1968-69; asso. gen. counsel Overmyer Co., N.Y.C., 1969-71; asst. counsel N.Y. Ct. on the Judiciary, 1971; U.S. magistrate U.S. Dist. Ct., So. Dist. N.Y., 1971-76, U.S. dist. judge, 1976—; adj. prof. law Fordham U. Law Sch., 1978—; mem. com. on criminal justice act U.S. Jud. Conf., 1981—. Mem. council Fresh Air Fund, N.Y.C., 1961-64; bd. dirs. Community Action Program, Yonkers, N.Y., 1964-66. Served to lt. (j.g.) USCG, 1951-53. Mem. Am. Bar Assn., Am. Judicature Soc., Nat. Conf. Fed. Ct. Judges, Columbia Law Sch. Alumni Assn. Club: Greenwoods Country (Winsted, Conn.). Home: 2 Peter Cooper Rd New York City NY also 232 Lakeridge Torrington CT 06790 Office: US Dist Ct Foley Sq New York NY 10007

GOETZ, JOHN BULLOCK, editor, designer; b. Natchez, Miss., July 8, 1920; s. Charles Clifton and Katie G. (Meath) G.; m. Lorette Graves McClatchy, Feb. 17, 1945 (div. May 1980); children—Charles, Christopher, Karen, Stephen. A.B., Spring Hill (Ala.) Coll., 1941; postgrad., Pratt Inst., 1946-48. Reporter Mobile (Ala.) Press-Register, 1941-42; prodn. editor Henry Holt & Co., N.Y.C., 1946-48; book designer Am. Book Co., N.Y.C., 1948-49; mgr. prodn. and design U. Calif. Press, Berkeley, 1950-58; mgr. prodn. U. Chgo. Press, 1958-62, asst. dir., 1963-65; mng. editor Am. Dental Assn., Chgo., 1966—; lectr.

publ. design U. Chgo. Downtown Center, 1959-60; lectr. dental editors seminar Ohio State U., 1967-73, Mich. State U., 1974—. Contbr. articles to profl. jours. Served to lt. USNR, 1942-46; PTO. Decorated Bronze Star; recipient Bronze medal for book design Leipzig (Germany) Book Fair, 1963; Gold medal for book design Sao Paulo (Brazil) Biennial, 1964; Distinguished Service award for journalism Am. Coll. Dentists, 1974; Disting. Service award Am. Assn. Dental Editors, 1978. Mem. Am. Inst. Graphic Arts, Chgo. Book Clinic (pres. 1965). Roman Catholic. Club: Caxton. Home: 33 E Cedar St Chicago IL 60611 Office: Am Dental Assn 211 E Chicago Ave Chicago IL 60611

GOETZ, PHILIP, editor. Editor-in-chief Ency. Brit., Inc. Office: Ency Brit Inc 310 S Michigan Ave Chicago IL 60604§

GOEWEY, GORDON IRA, university administrator; b. Troy, N.Y., June 25, 1924; s. Ira A. and Flossie (Warger) G.; m. Marie Matteson Huening, May 30, 1968; children by previous marriage—Lynne Dee, Todd Ira. B.Mus., Boston U., 1948, Mus.A.D., 1969; M.A. in Teaching, Harvard, 1953. Mem. faculty SUNY Coll. Arts and Sci., Geneseo, 1949-72, prof. music, 1963-72, chmn. dept., 1952-69, dean grad. studies, 1969-72, dir. summer session, 1969-72, chmn. faculty, 1963-64; v.p. acad. affairs Trenton (N.J.) State Coll., 1972-78, provost, 1978—; Mem. State Negotiating Team, 1973-75; mem. N.J. Licensure and Approval Adv. Bd., 1975-82, chmn., 1975-79, State Acad. Vice Presidents, 1975-77, 82-83; bd. dirs. N.J. Edn. Consortium, 1975-78; resource asso. Am. Assn. State Colls. and Univs. Author: (with John Kucaba) Understanding Musical Form, 1962. Bd. dirs., v.p. George Washington council Boy Scouts Am., 1978—. Served with AUS, 1943-44. Mem. Music Educators Nat. Conf., N.J. Jazz Soc., Faculty Assn. State U. N.Y. (exec. com. 1964-67), Am. Assn. for Higher Edn., Am. Assn. U. Adminstrs. (dir. 1976—), Am. Coll. Personnel Assn. (N.E. regional conf. acad. affairs adminstrs., N.E. regional dir. 1976—), Phi Mu Alpha. Clubs: Rotary (dir. Trenton 1976-79, v.p. Trenton 1983), Torch, of Trenton (dir. 1977—). Home: 20 Crown Rd Trenton NJ 08638

GOFF, ABE MCGREGOR, lawyer; b. Colfax, Wash., Dec. 21, 1899; s. Herbert William and Mary (Dorsey) G.; m. Florence Richardson, Aug. 24, 1927; children—Timothy R. (dec.), Annie McGregor. LLB., U. Idaho, 1924. Bar: Idaho bar 1924. Since practiced in that state; pros. atty., Latah County, Idaho, 1926-34; solicitor, later gen. counsel Post Office Dept., 1954-58; mem. ICC, Washington, 1958-67, chmn., 1964; mem. Idaho Bar Commn., 1938-41, Idaho Senate, 1940-42, 80th U.S. Congress from 1st Dist. Idaho; Republican candidate U.S. Senator, 1950; mem. Rep. steering com. Bd. dirs. Fed. Bar Found. Served as pvt. U.S. Army, World War I; from maj. to col., JAGC AUS, 1941-46. Recipient award of legal merit Coll. Law, U. Idaho; named to Idaho State Athletic Hall of Fame.; Decorated Legion of Merit. Mem. Fed. Bar Assn., Idaho Bar Assn. (pres. 1940-41), ABA (ho. dels. 1941), Am. Soc. Internat. Law, Mil. Order Carabao, Beta Theta Pi, Scabbard and Blade. Episcopalian. Club: Mason. Address: 503 E C St Moscow ID 83843

GOFF, JAMES MATTHEW, transportation corporation executive; b. Memphis, June 20, 1927; s. Volney Barlow and Marguerite (Moreland) G.; m. Jennifer Joan Anderson, Aug. 25, 1973. B.A., Yale U., 1950; LL.B., U. Mich., 1953. Bar: Ill. 1953. Assoc. firm Sonnenschein, Carlin, Nath & Rosenthal, Chgo., 1953-59, partner, 1959-77; sr. v.p. GATX Corp., Chgo., 1977-79; pres., chief exec. officer Gen. Am. Transp. Corp., Chgo., 1979—; dir. 1st Nat. Bank of East Chicago (Ind.). Served with USN, 1945-46. Mem. Chgo. Bar Assn., Ill. State Bar Assn., ABA, Am. Coll. Trial Lawyers, Am. Bar Found. Clubs: Chgo., Glen View, Casino. Home: 1441 N Dearborn St Chicago IL 60610 Office: 120 S Riverside Plaza Chicago IL 60606

GOFF, KENNETH WADE, elec. engr.; b. Salem, Va., June 14, 1928; s. Wetzel and Alma (Beeghley) G.; m. Hazel Lucille Sullivan, July 1, 1950; children—Jerry Kenneth, Deborah Lucille, Brian Lee. B.S., W.Va. U., 1950; M.S., M.I.T., 1952, Sc.D., 1954. Cons. engr. Bolt Beranek & Newman, Inc., Cambridge, Mass., 1954-56; project mgr. Gruen Precision Labs., Cin., 1956-57; mgr. systems analysis Leeds & Northrup Co., North Wales, Pa., 1957-69, mgr. systems devel., 1969—; vis. lectr. Franklin Inst., 1962, 63. Contbr. articles to profl. jours. M.I.T. acoustical materials fellow, 1954. Fellow Instrument Soc. Am., IEEE; mem. Sigma Xi, Tau Beta Pi, Eta Kappa Nu. Baptist. Patentee in field. Home: 2143 Horace Ave Abington PA 19001 Office: Leeds and Northrup Tech Center North Wales PA 19454

GOFF, REGINA MARY, educator; b. St. Louis; d. Ward Wellington and Annabelle (Young) G.; m. Josiah F. Henry, Jr., Sept. 23, 1960. B.A. in Edn, Northwestern U., 1934; M.A., Columbia, 1940, Ph.D., 1948. Dir. nursery sch., St. Louis, 1935, tchr. kindergarten, Kansas City, Kan., 1936-39; instr. Lincoln U., Jefferson City, Mo., 1940-46; dir. student teaching Stowe Tchrs. Coll., St. Louis, 1947-48; prof. child devel. Fla. A. and M. Coll., Tallahassee; also supr. Fla. Dept. Edn., 1949-50; faculty Morgan State Coll., Balt., 1950-65, chmn. dept. edn., 1963-65; asst. commr. Office Programs for Disadvantaged, U.S. Office Edn., Washington, 1965-71; prof. U. Md. Coll. Edn., College Park, 1971-76, Union Grad. Sch., Coppin Coll., Balt., 1976—; cons. Ministry Edn. Iran, 1955-56. Contbr. articles to profl. jours. Bd. dirs. Urban League Md., 1959-64, pres., 1961-63; bd. dirs. UN Assn. Md., Children's Guild Md., Md. Commn. UNICEF. Recipient Pub. Service in Edn. awards Urban League Balt., 1963, St. Louis Assn. Negro Women's Clubs, 1965, Nat. Bus. and Profl. Women's Clubs, 1966, Alpha Kappa Alpha, 1966; Rockefeller Found. fellow, 1945-46. Mem. Am. Psychol. Assn., Md. Assn. Tchr. Edn. (pres.), N.E.A., Pi Lambda Theta, Kappa Delta Pi, Psi Chi, Alpha Kappa Alpha, Phi Delta Kappa. Democrat. Roman Catholic. Home: 2306 Montebello Terr Baltimore MD 21214 *My life has been shaped by the constant setting of goals, and persistence in pursuit of them. Having a sense of direction prevented emotional dangling. The development of a personal philosophy based on ethical and spiritual values provided support for endeavors as well as a basis for independence in decision making. A major factor was parental warmth and encouragement.*

GOFF, ROBERT BURNSIDE, food co. exec.; b. Arcadia, La., Aug. 8, 1924; s. Carl and Ruth (Capers) G.; m. Mary Jane Ellis, June 14, 1947; children—Gayle M., Robert B. B.S., Rice U., 1947. Engr. Tex. Pipe Line Co., Tulsa, 1947-48; v.p., dir. Comet Rice Mills, Inc., Houston, 1948-58; sr. v.p., dir. Riviana Foods, Inc., Houston, 1958-75; pres., dir. Food Corp. Internat., Houston, 1975—. Served to lt. (j.g.) USNR, 1942-46. Mem. Exec. Assos. Presbyn. Clubs: Houston Met. Racquet, River Oaks Country (Houston). Home: 2710 Essex Terr Houston TX 77027 Office: 2001 Kirby Dr Suite 1313 Houston TX 77019

GOFFART, WALTER ANDRÉ, history educator; b. Berlin, Germany, Feb. 22, 1934; emigrated to U.S., 1943, naturalized, 1959; s. Francis Leo and Andree Juliette (Steinberg) G.; m. Ellen Horvath, May 19, 1961; children: Vivian, Andrea Judith; m. Roberta Frank, Dec. 31, 1977. A.B., Harvard U., 1955, A.M., 1956, Ph.D., 1961; postgrad., Ecole pratique des Hautes-Etudes, Paris, France, 1957-58. Lectr. history U. Toronto, Ont., Can., 1961-63, asst. prof., 1963-66, asso. prof., 1966-71, prof., 1971—, acting dir. Ctr. for Medieval Studies, 1971-72; Vis. asst. prof. U. Calif. at Berkeley, 1965-66; vis. fellow Inst. Advanced Study, Princeton, N.J., 1967-68, Dumbarton Oaks Center Byzantine Studies, Washington, 1973-74. Author: The Le Mans Forgeries, 1966, Caput and Colonate, 1974, Barbarians and Romans, A.D. 418-584, 1981; translator: The Origin of the Idea of Crusade (C. Erdmann), 1978. Can. Council fellow, 1967-68; Am. Council Learned Socs. fellow, 1973-74; Guggenheim fellow, 1979-80; Connaught sr. fellow in humanities, U. Toronto, 1983-84. Fellow Mediaeval Acad. Am. (councillor 1977-80); Mem. Am. Hist. Assn., Phi Beta Kappa. Office: Dept of History U of Toronto Toronto ON M5S 1A1 Canada

GOFFMAN, WILLIAM, mathematician, educator; b. Cleve., Jan. 28, 1924; s. Sam and Mollie (Stein) G.; m. Patricia McLoughlin, Feb. 7, 1964. B.S., U. Mich., 1950, Ph.D., 1954. Math. cons., 1954-59; research asso. prof. Case Western Res. U., Cleve., 1959-71, dean, 1971-77, dir., 1972-75. Contbr. numerous publs. to sci. jours. Served with USAAF, 1943-46. Recipient research grants NSF, NIH, USAF, others. Fellow AAAS. Home: 12023 Lakeshore Bratenahl OH 44108 Office: Case Western Reserve University Cleveland OH 44106

GOFRANK, FRANK LOUIS, machine tool co. exec.; b. Detroit, Dec. 23, 1918; s. Louis and Katherine E. (Schweninger) G.; m. Helen J. Rzeznik, Dec. 27, 1945; children: Shirley, Catherine, Ronald. B.A., Walsh Coll., 1950, LL.B. (hon.), 1982. C.P.A., Mich. Staff acct. Parker & Elsholz (C.P.A.s), 1947-48; staff acct. Lyons & Teetzel (C.P.A.s), 1949-50, partner, 1951-58, Coopers & Lybrand (C.P.A.s), Detroit, 1959-67; pres. Wilson Automation Co., Warren, Mich., 1967-73; chmn. bd., chief exec. officer Newcor, Inc., Warren, 1973—. Mem. Detroit met. adv. bd. Salvation Army, 1971-73; trustee Walsh Coll., 1968—. Served with U.S. Army, 1941-46. Mem. Mich. Assn. C.P.A.s, Am. Inst. C.P.A.s, Mich. Assn. of the Professions. Clubs: Country of Detroit, Renaissance; Otsego Ski (Gaylord, Mich.); Royal Palm Yacht and Country (Boca Raton, Fla.). Office: 3270 W Big Beaver Troy MI 48084

GOGGIN, JOSEPH ROBERT, ins. co. exec.; b. Chgo., Apr. 24, 1926; s. William Nobel and Loretta Ann (Davis) G.; m. Barbara Jean Laibach, Sept. 21, 1957; children—Tracy Jean, Sandra Lynn. With Mut. Trust Life Ins. Co., Chgo., exec. v.p., 1968—, dir., 1970—. Served with USMCR, 1942-46. Mem. Investment Analysts Soc. Chgo., Financial Execs. Inst. Clubs: Chgo., Met. (Chgo.). Home: 101 E 29th St LaGrange Park IL 60525 Office: 1200 Jorie Blvd Oak Brook IL 60521

GOGGIN, MARGARET KNOX, librarian, educator; b. Nyack, N.Y., Feb. 24, 1919; d. Henry Julian and Eleanor (Green) Knox; m. John Mann Goggin, Nov. 22, 1962. A.B., Maryville Coll., 1940; B.S., Peabody Coll., 1942; M.S., U. Ill., 1948, Ph.D., 1957. Tchr., librarian Flintville (Tenn.) High Sch., 1940-42; reference asst. Joint U. Library, Nashville, 1942-43, acting reference librarian, 1943-45; vis. instr. Peabody Library Sch., Nashville, 1943-45; readers adviser Youngstown (Ohio) Pub. Library, 1945-46; bibliographer, reference librarian Office Tech. Services Dept. Commerce, Washington, 1946-47; reference asst. U. Ill., 1948-49; asst. to dir. U. Fla. Libraries, asst. prof. library sci., 1949-50, head dept. reference and bibliography, asso. prof. library sci., 1950-62, asst. dir., asso. prof. library sci., 1965-66, asst. dir. libraries, prof. library sci., 1966, acting dir. libraries, 1967-68; dean Grad. Sch. Librarianship, U. Denver, 1968-79, prof., 1979—; vis. lectr. U. Okla. Library Sch., summer 1959, Emory U. Sch. Librarianship, 1965; dir. Satellite Library Info. Network, 1974-76; prin. investigator Telefax Library Info. Network, 1978-79; cons. U.S. Office Edn. div. Library Programs, 1968-69, Aims Community Coll., Greeley, Colo., 1973, Wash. State Library, 1978-79, Loretto Heights Coll., Denver, 1981. Haitian research, Haiti and Paris on Rockefeller Found. grants, 1958, 61-62; Fulbright grantee, 1972; OAS grantee for multi-nat. library edn. program, 1974-75. Mem. ALA (past div. pres.), Colo. Library Assn. (dir. 1978-79), Mountain Plains Library Assn. (dir. 1978-79), Assn. Am. Library Schs. (pres. 1977), Nat. League Am. Pen Women, Delta Kappa Gamma, Beta Phi Mu (past dir.). Clubs: Altrusa (bd. dirs. Denver 1974-76, 80-82, pres. 1983-84. Home: 6151 S Kearney St Englewood CO 80111 Office: U Denver Grad Sch Librarianship Denver CO 80208

GOGGINS, JOHN FRANCIS, dentist, research institute executive; b. Flint, Mich., Oct. 26, 1933; s. King Pierre and Genevieve Adeline (Bouchard) G.; m. Madeleine Alice Murray, Sept. 17, 1960; children: Patrick, Colleen, William. Student, U. Notre Dame, 1951-54; D.D.S., Marquette U., 1958, M.S., 1965. Gen. practice dentistry, Flint, 1960-63; instr. Marquette U. Dental Sch., Milw., 1963-65; mem. staff Nat. Inst. Dental Research, NIH, 1966—, assoc. dir. collaborative research, 1974-81, dep. dir. inst., 1981-83, acting dir., 1982-83, dep. dir., assoc. dir. extramural programs, 1983—; chmn. fluoridation com. Genesee County Dental Soc., 1961-63. Author articles in field. Served to capt. Dental Corps USAF, 1958-60. Postdoctoral fellow USPHS, 1965-66; Recipient Commendation medal USPHS, 1977, Meritorious Service medal USPHS, 1983. Fellow AAAS; Mem. Internat. Assn. Dental Research, Am. Assn. Dental Research, ADA, Histochem. Soc., Commd. Officers Assn. USPHS. Roman Catholic. Office: NIH 5333 Westbard Ave Rm 503 Bethesda MD 20205

GOGICK, KATHLEEN CHRISTINE, magazine editor; b. N.J., Aug. 3, 1945; d. Joseph John and Emeline (Radwin) Wadowski; m. Robert Joseph Gogick, Feb. 24, 1968; 1 son, Jonathan. B.S., Fairleigh Dickinson U., Rutherford, N.J., 1967. Asst. beauty and fiction editor Cosmopolitan mag., N.Y.C., 1967-68; mdsg. and publicity coordinator Co-ed mag., N.Y.C., 1968-69; creative services coordinator Estee Lauder, Inc., N.Y.C., 1969-71; asso. beauty and health editor Town and Country mag., N.Y.C., 1971-75; editor-in-chief Co-ed mag., 1976-80; editorial dir. home econs. div. Scholastic Inc., 1981—. Mem. Women's Econ. Roundtable, Advt. Women N.Y., Women in Communications, Am. Soc. Mag. Editors. Home: 41 E Hartshorn Dr Short Hills NJ 07078 Office: 730 Broadway New York NY 10003

GOGLIA, GENNARO LOUIS, mechanical engineering educator; b. Hoboken, N.J., Jan. 15, 1921; s. Fred Goglia and Rose (Coppola) G.; m. Lieselotte Pause, Oct. 4, 1942; children: Diann, Linda. B.S., U. Ill., 1942, M.S., Ohio State U., 1950; Ph.D., U. Mich., 1959. Registered profl. engr., Ohio, Mich. Jr. engr. Rochester (N.Y.) Ordnance Dist., 1942- 44; devel. engr. Gen. Electric Co., 1945-47; tech. writer Detroit Edison Co., 1951-54; engring. cons. Overhead Heaters Co., Detroit, 1957-58; instr. Ohio State U., 1947-51; asst. prof. U. Detroit, 1951-59; asso. prof., acting head mech. engring. dept. N.C. State Coll., 1961-62; prof., head dept. mech. engring. U. Maine, Orono, 1962-64; prof., head power and energy conversion Old Dominion Coll., Norfolk, Va., 1964, prof., chmn. dept. thermal engring., 1965-71, 72-73, asst. dean engring., 1971—, prof., chmn. mech. engring., 1973-79, Eminent prof. and chmn. mech. engring., 1979—; co-dir. Am. Soc. Engring. Edn.-NASA Langley Research Center Summer Faculty Insts., 1967-79; cons. NASA, 1966-79; dir. research projects NSF. Contbr. articles to profl. jours. Recipient Disting. Faculty award Old Dominion U., 1983; DuPont research grantee, 1960; Am. Soc. Engring. Edn.-NASA post doctorate fellow, summers 1965-66. Fellow ASME (cert. award 1963, chmn. Norfolk group 1966-67); mem. Am. Soc. Engring. Edn., Sigma Xi (chpt. pres. 1966-67), Tau Beta Pi, Pi Tau Sigma, Phi Kappa Phi. Home: 7416 Gardner Dr Norfolk VA 23518

GOH, CHOO SAN, choreographer; b. Singapore, Sept. 14, 1948; s. Kim Tak and Siew Han (Ch'ng) G. B.S., U. Singapore, 1970. Tchr. Boston Sch. Ballet, Joffrey Ballet Sch., Jacob's Pillow, Mass. Dancer, Dutch Nat. Ballet, 1971-76; resident choreographer, Washington Ballet, 1976-79; asst. artistic dir., 1979—; ballets created include Helena, 1980, Birds of Paradise, Fives, 1978, Variaciones Concertantes, 1979, Leitmotiv, 1980, Celestial Images, 1980, Configurations, 1981, Due Pezzi Sacri, 1981, In the Glow of the Night, 1982, Scenic Invitations, 1983. Grantee Nat. Endowments Arts, 1978. Office: care H Robert Magee 395 Bleecker St New York NY 10014

GOHEEN, HARRY EARL, mathematics educator; b. Bellingham, Wash., July 19, 1915; s. Frank and Minnie (Clement) G.; m. Malchen Pearl, Jan. 20, 1940; children: David Clement, Miriam (Mrs. Goheen-Fjelleman), Mark Stewart. Student, Western Wash. Coll., 1932-35; B.A., Stanford U., 1936, M.A., 1938, Ph.D., 1940. Teaching fellow Reed Coll., Portland, Oreg., 1939-40; instr. U. Wis., Madison, 1940-42; mathematician Office Naval Research, 1946-47; asst. prof. U. Del., Newark, 1947-48, Syracuse (N.Y.) U., 1948-50, U. Pa., Phila., 1950-51; asso. prof. Iowa State U., Ames, 1951-55, Oreg. State U., Corvallis, 1955-58, prof. math., 1958-81, prof. emeritus, 1981—; vis. mem. Inst. Advanced Studies, Dublin, Ireland, 1967; vis. prof. Cork Coll., U. Ireland, 1975-76. Served with USNR, 1942-46. Mem. Assn. for Computing Machinery (founding mem.). Home: 1300 NW Grant St Corvallis OR 97330

GOHEEN, ROBERT FRANCIS, classicist, educator, former ambassador; b. Vengurla, India, Aug. 15, 1919; s. Robert H.H. and Anne (Ewing) G.; m. Margaret M. Skelly, June 21, 1941; children: Anne Goheen Crane, Gertrude Goheen Swain, Stephen, Margaret Goheen Lower, Elizabeth Goheen Klevans, Charles. B.A., Princeton U., 1940, M.A. (Woodrow Wilson fellow), 1947, Ph.D. (Procter fellow), 1948; hon. degrees from 26 univs. and colls. Instr. classics Princeton U., 1948-50, asst. prof., 1950-57, prof., 1957, pres., 1957-72, emeritus, 1972—; chmn. Council on Founds., 1972-77; pres. Edna McConnell Clark Found., 1977; ambassador to, India, 1977-80; sr. fellow Woodrow Wilson Sch., 1981—; dir. Mellon Fellowships in the Humanities, Princeton, 1981—, Thompson Newspapers, Inc., Midlantic Banking Corp.; internat. adv. bd. Chem. Bank; mem. adv. com. oceans and internat. sci. and environ. affairs/U.S. Dept. State. Author: The Imagery of Sophocles' Antigone, 1951, The Human Nature of a University, 1969. Trustee Inst. Info. Edn., Am. U. Beirut, Fund for N.J., Bharatiya Vidya Bhavan (USA), Carnegie Endowment for Internat. Peace, Inst. Internat. Edn.; trustee United Bd. Christian Higher Edn. in Asia. Served from pvt. to lt. col. AUS, 1941-45. Decorated Legion of Merit, Bronze Star. Mem. Am. Philol. Soc., Council Fgn. Relations, Am. Acad. Arts and Scis., Asia Soc. (trustee), Phi Beta Kappa. Clubs: Princeton, Century Assn., Univ. (N.Y.C.); Cosmos (Washington); Nassau, Pretty Brook, Springdale (Princeton); Eastward Ho (Mass.); Gymkhana and Delhi Golf (India). Address: 1 Orchard Circle Princeton NJ 08540

GOHLKE, FRANK WILLIAM, photographer; b. Wichita Falls, Tex., Apr. 3, 1942; s. Robert Lee and Nellie May (Ross) G.; m. Madelone Marie Sprengnether, June 17, 1966 (div. June 1981); 1 dau., Jessica Lee. B.A. in English Lit., U. Tex., 1964; M.A., Yale U., 1966. Photographer, 1967—; vis. prof. Yale U. Grad. Sch., New Haven, 1981. Photographer: series include Grain Elevators, 1977, Aftermath: The Wichita Falls Tornado, 1981; murals, Tulsa Airport, 1981. Guggenheim fellow, 1975; NEA fellow, 1977; Bush Found. Artist's fellow, 1979; McKnight fellow, 1983. Home: 1322 Adams NE Minneapolis MN 55413

GOIN, JOHN MOREHEAD, plastic surgeon; b. Los Angeles, Mar. 29, 1929; s. Lowell Sidney and Margaret Catherine (Morehead) G.; m. Marcia Stewart Kraft, Mar. 5, 1960; children: Suzanne Jennifer, Jessica Michele. B.A. in Zoology, UCLA, 1951; M.D., St. Louis U., 1955. Diplomate: Am. Bd. Plastic Surgery (dir. 1980—). Intern U. Calif. Med. Center, San Francisco, 1955-56, asst. resident in surgery, 1956-59, asst. resident to chief resident in plastic surgery, Los Angeles, 1959-62; fellow in plastic surgery Queen Victoria Hosp., East Grinstead, Sussex, Eng., 1961; pvt. practice specializing in plastic and reconstructive surgery, Los Angeles, 1962—; clin. prof. surgery U. So. Calif.; chief plastic surgery Los Angeles County/U. So. Calif. Med. Center, 1971-80; head div. plastic surgery Children's Hosp. of Los Angeles, 1976-79. Author: (with Marcia Kraft Goin) Changing the Body: Psychological Effects of Plastic Surgery, 1980; Contbr. articles to profl. jours. Fellow A.C.S. (gov. 1983—); mem. AMA, Calif. Soc. Plastic Surgeons (past pres.), Am. Soc. Plastic and Reconstructive Surgeons (sec. 1979-82, v.p. 1982-83, pres.-elect 1983-84), Am. Soc. Aesthetic Plastic Surgery, Am. Assn. Plastic Surgeons, Pacific Coast Surg. Assn. Republican. Episcopalian. Home: 2500 Park Oak Dr Los Angeles CA 90068 Office: 1245 Wilshire Blvd Los Angeles CA 90017

GOIN, LAUREN JACKSON, public safety company executive; b. Mt. Vernon, Wash., Jan. 8, 1922; s. Irel Lauren and Ina Lorraine (Tittle) G.; m. Evelyn Winn, July 12, 1947; children: Susan Loreen, Thomas Richard, Peter Jackson. B.A. in Tech. Criminology, U. Calif. at Berkeley, 1943, M.Criminology, 1948; grad., Fed. Execs. Inst. Chief microanalysis sect. Wis. Crime Lab., 1948-53; dir. Pitts. and Allegheny County Crime Lab., 1953-55; pub. safety adviser criminalistics, Indonesia, 1955-57, Turkey, 1958-60, Brazil, 1960-62; chief tech. services div. Office Pub. Safety, AID, Washington, 1963-64, chief operations div., 1964-72, dep. dir., 1972-73, dir., 1973-75; pres. Public Safety Services, Inc., Washington, 1975—. Fellow Am. Acad. Forensic Scis. (past chmn. criminalistics sect.); mem. Am. Soc. Ind. Sec. (cert.), Internat. Assn. Chiefs Police. Home: 3054 N Oxford St Arlington VA 22207 Office: 1250 Connecticut Ave Washington DC 20036

GOING, WILLIAM THORNBURY, educator; b. Birmingham, Ala., June 3, 1915; s. Clarence Johnston and Louise (Thornbury) G.; m. Margaret Moorer, Dec. 15, 1951. A.B. with honors, U. Ala., 1936; M.A. (scholar, fellow English), Duke U., 1938; Ed.D., U. Mich., 1954. Tchr. English West End High Sch., Birmingham, 1938-39; asst. prof. edn. Samford U., Birmingham, summer 1939; instr. to asso. prof. English U. Ala., 1939-57; teaching fellow U. Mich., 1952-53; prof. English So. Ill. U., Edwardsville, 1957-80, prof. emeritus, 1980—, dean instruction, 1958-63, dean academic affairs, 1963-65; mem. faculty com. Ill. Bd. Higher Edn.; mem. Ill. Fulbright com. Author: Wilfrid Scawen Blunt and the Tradition of the English Sonnet Sequence in the 19th Century, 1953; editor: 99 Fables by William March, 1960, Regional Perspective: Essays on Alabama Literature, 1975, Scanty Plot of Ground: Studies in the Victorian Sonnet, 1976; Contbr.: articles on lang. and lit. to profl. jours. including Victorian Poetry, Ga. Rev., Jour. Modern Lit. Mem. adv. bd. Alton Meml. Hosp. Nursing Sch. Rhodes scholar-elect from Ala., 1938. Mem. Midwest Modern Lang. Assn., Nat. Council Tchrs. English, NEA, Modern Lang. Assn. Am., Ill. Edn. Assn., Phi Beta Kappa, Phi Delta Kappa, Phi Kappa Phi, Phi Eta Sigma, Sigma Alpha Epsilon. Democrat. Presbyterian. Home: 1 Hickory Knoll Edwardsville IL 62025

GOINGS, RALPH, artist; b. Corning, Calif., 1928. Student, Calif. Coll. Arts and Crafts, Sacramento State Coll. One-man shows, Artists Coop. Gallery, Sacramento, 1960, 62, Artists Contemporary Gallery, Sacramento, 1968, O.K. Harris Works of Art, N.Y.C., 1970, 73, 77, 80, 83, group shows include, U. Oshkosh, Wis., 1983, Contemporary Art Ctr., New Orleans, 1982, Pa. Acad. Fine Arts European tour, 1982-83, Brainerd Art Gallery, SUNY-Potsdam, 1982, Stockholm Internat. Art Expo., Sweden, O.K. Harris West, Scottsdale, Ariz., Butler Inst. Am. Art, Youngstown, Ohio; represented in permanent collections, Mus. Modern Art, Guggenheim Mus., N.Y.C.; contbg. author chpts. in books; contbr. numerous articles in field. Office: OK Harris Works of Art 383 W Broadway New York NY 10012

GOIZUETA, ROBERTO CRISPULO, food company executive; b. Havana, Cuba, Nov. 18, 1931; s. Crispulo D. and Aida (Cantera) G.; m. Olga Casteleiro, June 14, 1953; children: Roberto S., Olga M. Goizueta Rawls, Javier C. B.S., B.Engring. in Chem. Engring., Yale U., 1953. Process engr. Indsl. Corp. of Tropics, Havana, 1953-54; with tech. dept. The Coca-Cola Co., Havana, 1954-60, asst. to sr. v.p., Nassau, Bahamas, 1960-64, asst. to v.p. for research and devel., Atlanta, 1964-66, v.p. engring., 1966-74, sr. v.p., 1974-75, exec. v.p., 1975-79, vice chmn., 1979-80, pres., chief operating officer, dir., 1980, chmn. bd., chief exec. officer, 1981—; dir. Trust Co. of Ga., Trust Co. Bank, Atlanta, Sonat, Inc., Birmingham, Ala., Ford Motor Co.; mem. U.S.-USSR Trade Council, Conf. Bd., Bus. Roundtable. Trustee Emory U., Atlanta Arts Alliance, Atlanta Symphony Orch. League, Am. Assembly, Atlanta U. Ctr., Boys Club Am.; bd. dirs. Central Atlanta Progress; mem. nat. bd. govs. United Way Am.; hon. trustee U.S.-Asia Inst. Mem. Soc. Soft Drink Technologists, Inst. Food Technologists, Am. Soc. Corp. Execs., U.S. C. of C. (dir.), Council on Fgn. Relations, Japan Soc. (mem. bd.), Am. Film Inst. Clubs: Commerce (dir.), Piedmont Driving, Capital City, Peachtree Golf (Atlanta); International (Washington); Variety Internat. Office: The Coca-Cola Co 310 North Ave NW Atlanta GA 30313

GOLAND, MARTIN, research institute executive; b. N.Y.C., July 12, 1919; s. Herman and Josephine (Bloch) G.; m. Charlotte Nelson, Oct. 16, 1948; children—Claudia, Lawrence, Nelson. M.E., Cornell U., 1940; LL.D. (hon.), St. Mary's U., San Antonio. Instr. mech. engring. Cornell U., 1940-42; sect. head structures dept. research lab., airplane div. Curtiss-Wright Corp., Buffalo, 1942-46; chmn. div. engring. Midwest Research Inst., Kansas City, Mo., 1946-50, dir. for engring. scis., 1950-55; v.p. Southwest Research Inst., San Antonio, 1955-57, dir., 1957-59, pres., 1959—, S.W. Found. Research and Edn., San Antonio, 1972-82; dir. Nat. Bancshares Corp. Tex.; Chmn. subcom. vibration and flutter NACA, 1952-60; chmn. research adv. com. on aircraft structures NASA, 1960-68, chmn. materials and structures group, aeros. adv. com., 1979-82; sci. adv. com. Harry Diamond Labs., U.S. Amry Materiel Command, 1955-75; adv. panel com. sci. and astronautics Ho. of Reps., 1960-73; mem. high speed ground transp. panel Dept. Commerce, 1966-67, nat. inventors council, 1966-67, mem. state tech. services evaluation com., 1967-69; mem. adv. bd. on undersea warfare Dept. Navy, 1968-70, chmn., 1970-73; mem. spl. aviation fire reduction com. FAA, 1979-80; sci. adv. panel Dept. Army, 1966-77; chmn. U.S. Army Weapons Command Adv. Group, 1966-72; mem. materiels adv. bd. NRC, 1969-74; vice-chmn. Naval Research Adv. Com., 1974-77, chmn., 1977, mem., 1978—; dir. Nat. Bank Commerce, San Antonio.; Dir. Engrs. Joint Council, 1966-69; mem. adv. group U.S. Armament Command, 1972-76; mem. sci. adv. com. Gen. Motors, 1971-81; mem. Nat. Commn. on Libraries and Info. Scis., 1971-78, Nat. Bd. on Grad. Edn., 1972-75; mem. adv. bd. on mil. personnel supplies Nat. Acad. Sci., 1973-76; chmn. NRC Bd. Army Sci. and Tech., 1982—, Army Missile Command ROLAND Blue Ribbon Panel, 1983—. Editor: Applied Mechanics Review, 1952-59; editorial adviser, 1959—. Bd. govs. St. Mary's U., San Antonio, 1970-76; research adv. com. coordinating bd. Tex. Coll. and Univ. System, 1966-68; pres. San Antonio Symphony, 1968-70, chmn. bd., 1970-71; bd. dirs. So. Meth. U. Found. Sci. and Engring., Dallas, 1979—; trustee Univs. Research Assos., Inc., 1979—. Recipient Spirit of St. Louis jr. award ASME, 1945, jr. award, 1946, Alfred E. Nobel prize ASCE, 1947. Fellow A.A.A.S., Am. Inst. Aeros. and Astronautics (pres. 1971); hon. mem. ASME (dir., mem. bd. tech., mem. tech. devel. com., v.p. communications); mem. C. of C. (dir.), Nat. Acad. Engring., Research Soc. Am., Sigma Xi, Tau Beta Pi. Home: 306 Country Ln San Antonio TX 78209 Office: 6220 Culebra Rd San Antonio TX 78284

GOLANY, GIDEON S., urban and regional planner; b. Jan. 23, 1928; U.S., 1967, naturalized, 1975; s. Jacob and Rajena G.; m. Esther Klein, Jan. 10, 1956; children: Ofer, Amir. B.A., Hebrew U., Jerusalem, 1956, M.A. in Urban Geography, 1962, Ph.D., 1966; M.Sc. in Environ. Studies, Technion-Israel Inst. Tech., Haifa, 1965; diploma comprehensive planning, Inst. Social Studies, The Hague, Netherlands, 1965. Lectr. architecture and town planning Technion-Israel Inst. Tech., 1963-67; lectr. city and regional planning Cornell U., 1967-68, research planner, 1968; asso. prof. urban and regional planning Coll. Architecture, Va. Poly. Inst. and State U., Blacksburg, 1968-70; vis. prof. urban and regional planning Inst. Desert Research, Ben-Gurion U. of the Negev, Beer Sheva, Israel, 1975-76; prof. urban and regional planning Pa. State U., 1970—, chmn. grad. program, 1971-76; propr. Gideon Golany Assos., 1970—; cons. in field. Author, editor: Geography of Israel, 1962, New Town Planning and Development—A Worldwide Bibliography, 1973, Strategy for New Community Development in the United States, 1975, Innovations for Future Cities, 1976, New-Town Planning: Principles and Practice, 1976, Urban Planning for Arid Zones: American Direction and Experience, 1978; co-author: New Geographic Dictionary, 2 vols, 1966; co-editor: The Contemporary New Communities Movement in the United States, 1974, International Urban Growth Policies, 1978, Arid Zone Settlement Planning: Israeli Experience, 1979, Housing in Arid Lands: Design and Planning, 1980, Desert Planning: International Lessons, 1982, Design for Arid Regions, 1983, Earth-Sheltered Habitat: History, Architecture and Urban Design, 1983; also articles, monographs. Mem., founder Kibbuts Baeri, communal settlement, Negev, 1946-52. Served with Hagana, 1946-48; Served with Israeli Army, 1948-50, 56, 67. Grantee Govt. Netherlands, 1965, NSF, 1972-74; recipient prize Com. Encouragement Towards Research and Higher Studies, Histadrut, Tel-Aviv, 1963. Mem. Am. Inst. Planners, Am. Soc. Planning Ofcls., Assn. Engrs. and Architects Israel. Home: 292 Douglas Dr State College PA 16803 Office: Pa State Univ 210 Engring C Bldg University Park PA 16802

GOLAY, FRANK HINDMAN, economist; b. Windsor, Mo., July 2, 1915; s. Frank Leslie and Alice (Hindman) G.; m. Clara Ruth Wood, Oct. 23, 1945; children: Frank Hindman, John Wood, David Clark, Jane White. B.S. in Edn, Central Mo. State Coll., Warrensburg, 1936; M.A. in Econs, U. Chgo., 1948, Ph.D., 1951; LL.D., Ateneo de Manila U., 1966. Economist internat. div. Fed. Res. System, 1950-52; mem. faculty Cornell U., Ithaca, N.Y., 1953—, prof. econs., 1962—, chmn. dept., 1963-67, assoc. dir. Cornell Southeast Asia program, 1961-70, dir., 1970-76; vis. lectr. U. London Sch. Oriental and African Studies, 1965-66; dir. London-Cornell Project, 1968-70, Cornell Philippines Project, 1967-74; vis. prof. sch. econs. U. Philippines, 1973-74. Author: The Philippines: Public Policy and National Economic Development, 1961; editor: The Santo Tomas Story (A.V.H. Hartendorp), 1964; editor, contbr.: American Assembly, The U.S. and The Philippines, 1966; co-author: Land and People in 1990: Philippine Rice Needs, Output and Input Requirements, 1967, Underdevelopment and Economic Nationalism in Southeast Asia, 1969, 1980's Project, Diversity and Development in Southeast Asia, 1977. Served to lt. comdr. USNR, 1941-45. Decorated Silver Star medal with gold star, Bronze Star; Fulbright fellow, 1955-56; Guggenheim and Social Sci. Research Council fellow, 1960-61; Nat. Endowment for Humanities fellow, 1977-78. Mem. Philippines-Am. Soc. (bd. dirs. 1966—), Assn. Asian Studies, Asia Soc. (chmn. Philippines council 1964-67), Nat. Acad. Scis. (Pacific sci. bd. Philippines com.). Home: 109 N Sunset Dr Ithaca NY 14850

GOLD, ALBERT, artist; b. Phila., Oct. 31, 1916; s. Rubin and Dora (Sklar) G.; m. Aurora Mary Vanelli, Mar. 3, 1953; children: Madelaine, Robert. Grad., Pa. Mus. Sch. Indsl. Art, 1938. Tchr. pictoral expression Pa. Mus. Sch., Phila., 1945-48; dir. dept. illustration Phila. Mus. Coll. Arts; prof. emeritus Phila. Coll. Art; tchr. art centers, pvt. classes. Exhibited at maj. ann. shows including, Pa. Acad. Fine Arts, Corcoran Gallery, Met. Mus., Art Inst., Chgo., Carnegie Inst., World's Fair, N.Y.C., 1939, Nat. Gallery, London, 1943, Musee Galliera, Paris, La Tausca exhbn., Burlington Acad. Galleries, 1962, Phila. (Alumni grant) Coll. Art, 1968, one-man shows at, Pa. Acad. Fine Arts; Phila. Art Alliance; represented in collections, Library of Congress, Soc. Illustrators, N.Y.C., N.Y. Pub. Library, Phila. Mus. Art, War Dept., Pentagon Bldg., U. Pa., Phila., U. Del., Newark, U. Minn., Smithsonian Instn., Atwater-Kent Mus., Phila., New Britain (Conn.) Mus. Am. Art, Forbes Collection, Ford Collection, Pa. Acad. Fine Arts, Soc. Illustrators, N.Y.C., Fogg Mus., U. Pa., Harvard U., Gimbel Pa. collection; numerous pvt. collections; commd. to paint various documentary series; illustrator various mags.; (book) The Commodore (Robert L. Abrahams), 1954; Illus.: book This Was Our War (Frank Brookhouser), 1961, The Court Factor, 1964, The Captive Rabbi (Lillian S. Freehof). Decorated Order Brit. Empire; recipient John Gribbel Meml. prize Phila. Print Club, 1939; Prix de Rome, Am. Acad. in Rome, 1942; Geizel award Phila. Sketch Club, 1982, 83; Tiffany Found. grant, 1947-48; Jennie Sesnan Gold medal, 1950; Dorothy Kohl prize Phila. Art Alliance, 1953; Am. Artist citation Am. Water Color Soc., 1954; Am. Artists Guild award Am. Water Color Soc., 1955; Regional Water Color prize Phila. Art Alliance, 1955; Wm. W. Esty prize Am. Water Color Soc. Ann., 1961; award for series of illustrations Brandywine Ohio State U. Sch. Journalism; prize Phila. Watercolor Club, 1977; Silver Star award Phila. Coll. Art, 1979; Woodmere Endowment Fund grantee, 1968. Mem. Artists Equity (dir.), AAUP. Selected by War Dept. as one of 12 men in U.S. Army to make pictorial record of war, 1943, spent 3 yrs. in Eng., France and Germany on project. Home: 6814 McCallum St Philadelphia PA 19119 *I have endeavored to "be myself" in my behavior and in my work as an artist. I've always felt that the surest way to oblivion was to "follow the herd". "Style" in art should be as personal as one's handwriting.*

GOLD, ARNOLD HENRY, lawyer; b. Santa Monica, Calif., Apr. 12, 1932; s. Louis and Rose (Shalat) G.; children: Jeffrey Alan, Kenneth Clarke, Susan Elizabeth. A.B. with distinction, Stanford, 1953, J.D., 1955. Bar: Calif. bar 1955, U.S. Supreme Ct. bar 1955, U.S. Ct. Appeals for Ninth Circuit bar 1955, U.S. dist. cts. for So., Central, No. dists. Calif 1955. Law clk. to Justice John W. Shenk of Calif. Supreme Ct., San Francisco, 1955-56; asso. atty. firm Loeb & Loeb, Los Angeles, 1956-61; practice law, Beverly Hills, Calif., 1961-70; partner firm Pachter, Gold & Schaffer (and predecessor firms), Los Angeles, 1970—; Judge pro tempore Beverly Hills Municipal Ct., 1967-74, Los Angeles Municipal Ct., 1974—, Los Angeles Superior Ct., 1980—; chmn. com. attys. Los Angeles Council Nat. Voluntary Health Agys., 1969—; lectr. Calif. Continuing Edn. of Bar, 1969, 76, 77, 79, 80, 81, 82, 84; mem. Calif. Atty. Gen's Com. on Charitable Reporting Standards, 1970-71, Calif. Atty. Gen.'s Task Force on Charitable Solicitation Legis., 1975-78; mem. exec. com. Stanford Law Soc. So. Calif., 1973-77. Contbg. author: California Family Law Handbook, California Nonprofit Corporations Handbook; Mng. editor, bd. editors: Stanford Law Rev, 1954-55. Mem. State Bar Calif., Los Angeles County Bar Assn. (trustee 1981-83), Beverly Hills Bar Assn., ABA., Phi Beta Kappa, Alpha Epsilon Pi, Phi Alpha Delta, Delta Sigma Rho. Club: Mulholland Tennis. Office: 5757 Wilshire Blvd Los Angeles CA 90036

GOLD, BELA, educator, economist; b. Kolozsvar, Hungary, Jan. 30, 1915; came to U.S., 1920, naturalized, 1927; s. Leo and Esther (Ludwig) G.; m. Sonia Steinman, July 5, 1938; 1 son, Robert. B.S. in Mech. Engring, NYU, 1934; Ph.D. (Univ. fellow 1936-37), Columbia U., 1948. Research cons. Life Ins. Sales Research Bur., Hartford, Conn., 1938-39; asst. head div. program surveys Bur. Agr. Econs., 1939-42; econ. cons. subcom. war mblzn. U.S. Senate, 1943-44; econ. adviser FEA and Dept. Commerce, 1944-46; prof. indsl. econs. U. Pitts. Grad. Sch. Bus., 1947-66; Timken prof. and William E. Umstattd prof. indsl. econs., dir. research program indsl. econs. Case Western Res. U., 1966-83, chmn. dept. econs., 1967-73; Fletcher Jones prof. tech. and mgmt. Claremont Grad. Sch. (Calif.), 1983—; pres. Indsl. Econs. and Mgmt. Assocs., Inc., 1980—; vis. professorial fellow Nuffield Coll., Oxford (Eng.) U., 1964; vis. prof. Imperial Coll. Scis. and Tech., London, Eng., 1967, 73; cons. to industry and ednl. instns., 1950—; Mem. com. on steel industry Nat. Acad. Scis.-Nat. Materials Adv. Bd., 1977-78; mem. assembly of engring. com. on computer-aided mfg. NRC, 1978-82, mem. mfg. studies bd., 1982—, mem. com. on machine tool industry, 1982-84; mem. Interdepartmental Adv. Com. on Fed. Policy on Indsl. Innovation, 1978-79; mem. ferrous metals panel Nat. Acad. Engring., 1980-84. Author: Wartime Economic Planning in Agriculture, 2d edit, 1969, How is Higher Education Financed?, 1959, Foundations of Productivity Analysis, 1955, Explorations in Managerial Economics, 1971, Japanese edit., 1977, Technological Change: Economics, Management and Environment, 1975, 80, Applied Productivity Analysis for Industry, 1976, Russian edit., 1981, Chinese edit., 1982, Research, Technological Change and Economic Analysis, 1977, Productivity, Technology and Capital, 1979, 2d edit., 1982, Evaluating the Effects of Technological Innovations, 1980, Technological Progress and Industrial Leadership, 1984, Appraising and Stimulating Technological Advances in Industry, 1980; Editorial bd.: Acad. Mgmt. Jour, 1962-73, Omega: Internat. Jour. Mgmt. Scis, 1972—, Jour. Product Innovations Mgmt., 1983—; corr. mem. editorial bd.: Revue d'Économie Industrielle, 1978—; contbr. numerous articles to profl. jours., chpts. in books. Social Sci. Research Council fellow, 1937-38, 77, 83; Ford Found. fellow, 1961-62, 66-67, 72. Mem. Am. Econ. Assn., Inst. Mgmt. Scis. (chmn. Coll. on Mgmt. of Technol. Change 1970—), Soc. Mfg. Engrs., Nat. Assn. Accountants (subcom. on productivity measurement 1977-79), Acad. Mgmt. (bd. editors 1962-73), AAUP, AAAS. Home: 641 Hood Dr Claremont CA 91711

GOLD, BILL (WILLIAM EMIL GOLD), newspaper reporter; b. Bklyn., Aug. 9, 1912; s. Mayer and Miriam (Feldman) G.; m. Bernice Radine Ellman, 1933; 1 son, Walter Leslie. B.S. in Journalism, Ohio State U., 1933. Reporter, condr. Dist. Line column The Washington Post, 1947-81; Bd. dirs. Nat. Press Found. Mem. White House Corrs. Assn., Sigma Delta Chi. Club: Nat. Press. Home: 7036 Wilson Ln Bethesda MD 20817

GOLD, CAROL SAPIN, management consultant; b. N.Y.C., June 28; d. Cerf Saul and Muriel Louise (Fudin) Rosenberg; m. Joseph Bernard Weinstein, Dec. 26, 1976; children from previous marriage: Kevin Bart Sapin, Craig Paul Sapin, Courtney Byrens Sapin. B.A., U. Calif., Berkeley, 1955. Asst. credit mgr. Union Oil Co., 1956; with U.S. Dept. State, 1964-66; mem. pub. relations dept. Braun & Co., Los Angeles, 1966-68; corporate dir. personnel tng. Gt. Western Fin. Corp., Los Angeles, 1968-71; pres. Carol Sapin Gold & Assocs., Los Angeles, 1971—; dir. Cortex, Inc.; cons., Can., Mex., India. Author: Solid Gold Customer Relations; producer: tng. films Power of Words; Author: Customer Relations. Mem. Sales and Mktg. Execs., Am. Soc. Tng. and Devel., World Affairs Council, Internat. Soc. Tng. and Devel., Women in Business, Nat. Platform Assn. Club: Music Ctr. 100. Office: 701 Washington St Suite 5 Marina del Rey CA 90291

GOLD, DELAYNE DEDRICK, investment company executive, management consultant; b. N.Y.C., July 15, 1938; d. Gilman Teal and Helen Anne (Smullen) Dedrick; m. Laurence James Gold, Mar. 20, 1968. B.A., Manhattanville Coll., 1960. Exec. v.p. Irving L. Straus Public Relations Agy., N.Y.C., 1969-76; v.p. public relations Prudential-Bache Securities, N.Y.C., 1977-79; 1st v.p. public relations and investor relations, 1979-80; sr. v.p., dir. Bache Halsey Stuart Shields, Inc., 1980-83; chmn., dir. Prudential Bache Securities Tax Managed Utility Fund, Govt. Securities Fund, High Yield Fund, Cash Fund, Quality Income Fund, Equity Fund, Option Growth Fund, Chancellor Tax-Free Fund, Chancellor High Yield Muni Fund; Chancellor New Decade Fund; dir. Money Mart Assets, Command Funds. Mem. Securities Industry Assn. (ednl. com.). Democrat. Roman Catholic. Home: Belgo Rd Lakeville CT 06039

GOLD, GERALD SEYMOUR, lawyer; b. Cleve., Feb. 2, 1931; s. David N. and Geraldine (Bloch) G.; m. Suzanne Kravitz, July 10, 1954; 1 dau., Anne. A.B., Case-Western Res. U., 1951, LL.B., 1954. Bar: Ohio 1954, U.S. Supreme Ct. 1961. Practiced in, Cleve., 1954-60; chief asst. legal aid defender Cuyahoga County, Cleve., 1960-61, chief legal aid defender, 1961-65; asso. firm Ulmer, Byrne, Laronge, Glickman & Curtis, Cleve., 1965-66; partner firm Gold, Rotatori, Messerman & Schwartz, Cleve., 1966—; instr. in law Case-Western Res. U., 1965-66, Cleve. State Law Sch., 1968-69, Case-Western Res. Law-Medicine Center, 1961-77; lectr. to bar assns. commr. Cuyahoga County Pub. Defender, 1977—. Contbg. author: American Jurisprudence Trials, 1966; Contbr. articles to law revs. Fellow Am. Coll. Trial Lawyers; mem. Case-Western Res. U. Law Alumni (pres. 1974-75), Cuyahoga County Criminal Ct. Bar Assn. (chmn.), Am. Bar Assn. (criminal justice council), Ohio State Bar Assn. (Merit award 1975), Greater Cleve. Bar Assn. (Merit award 1974, trustee 1978—, pres. 1982-83), Nat. Assn. Criminal Def. Lawyers (Merit award 1975, pres. 1977), Ohio Acad. Trial Lawyers (Merit award 1969-77). Clubs: Court of Nisi Prius, Cleve. Skating. Home: 2750 Claythorne Rd Shaker Heights OH 44122 Office: 1100 Ohio Savings Plaza Cleveland OH 44114

GOLD, HERBERT, author; b. Cleve., Mar. 9, 1924; s. Samuel and Frieda (Frankel) G.; m. Edith Zubrin, Apr. 1, 1948 (div. 1956); children: Ann, Judy; m. Melissa Dilworth, Jan. 26, 1968 (div. 1975); children—Nina, Ari, Ethan. B.A., Columbia, 1948, M.A., 1949; postgrad., U. Paris, France, 1949-51. Vis. prof. Cornell U., 1958, U. Calif. at Berkeley, 1963, Harvard, summer 1964, Stanford, 1967, U. Calif. at Davis, 1973-79. Author: novels Birth of a Hero, 1951, The Prospect Before Us, 1954, The Man Who Was Not With It, 1956, The Optimist, 1958, Therefore Be Bold, 1961, Salt, 1963, Fathers, 1967, The Great American Jackpot, 1970, Swiftie the Magician, 1974, Waiting for Cordelia, 1977, Slave Trade, 1978, He/She, 1980, Family, 1981, True Love, 1982; short stories Love and Like, 1960, The Magic Will, 1971; essays The Age of Happy Problems, 1962, My Last Two Thousand Years, 1973, A Walk on the West Side: California on the Brink, 1981. Recipient award for best novel Commonwealth Club, 1982; Fulbright fellow, 1950-51; Hudson Rev. fellow, 1956; Guggenheim fellow, 1957; Ford Found. grantee, 1960, award Am. Inst. Arts and Letters, 1957; Longview award, 1959. Address: 1051-A Broadway San Francisco CA 94133 *As a writer, I try to express a contradictory truth—that life is both tragic and a festival. To combine these two ideas is the highest intention of story.*

GOLD, HERBERT FRANK, insurance executive; b. Boston, Jan. 2, 1939; s. Harry and Sophie E. (Levine) G.; m. Paula Wagner, June 27, 1962 (div. 1982); children: Scott, Lesley. B.S., Boston U., 1961. C.L.U., 1970. Ins. agt. John Hancock Life Ins. Co., Danvers, Mass., 1961-63, supr., Wakefield, Mass., 1963-67; gen. agt. Wakefield, Brookline, Mass., 1967-80, sr. v.p., Boston, 1980—; chmn. bd. Profesco Corp., N.Y.C., 1981—; dir. Hanesco, Boston, John Hancock Distbrs., N.E. Inst.; chmn. bd., dir. Commonwealth Bank-Norfolk, Brookline, 1973-82. Bd. dirs. Fisher Hill Neighborhood Assn., Brookline, Hebrew home for Aged, 1976. Mem. Boston Life Underwriters Assn. (dir. 1973-77), Gen. Agts. and Mgrs. Assn. (dir. 1978). Jewish. Home: 1501 Beacon St Apt 1905 Brookline MA 02146 Office: John Hancock Mut life Ins Co John Hancock Pl Boston MA 02117

GOLD, JEFFREY MARK, publishing company executive; b. Bronx, N.Y., Jan. 7, 1945; s. Samuel L. and Sylvia E. G.; m. Lenore N. Gold, May 29, 1966; children: Brian, Steven, Samuel. B.B.A. in Acctg, Pace U., 1967. Sr. acct. Main Hurdman, internat. C.P.A.s, N.Y.C., 1967-71; v.p., corp. controller Nat. Patent Devel. Corp., N.Y.C., 1971-78; exec. v.p. fin. and adminstrn., chief fin. officer Esquire, Inc., N.Y.C., 1978-84; exec. v.p. Simon & Schuster, N.Y.C., 1984—. Mem. transp. task force Chappaqua Sch. Bd. Mem. Fin. Execs. Inst. Club: Willowbrook Swim and Tennis. Home: 48 North Way Chappaqua NY 10514 Office: 1630 Ave of Americas New York NY 10020

GOLD, JOSEPH, cancer researcher; b. Binghamton, N.Y., Jan. 17, 1930; s. Leon and Gertrude J. G.; m. Judith Barbara Taylor, June 12, 1955; children: Shannon Gabriel, Skye Raphael. A.B., Cornell U., 1952; M.D., SUNY Upstate Med. Center, Syracuse, 1956. Fellow dept. pharmacology SUNY Upstate Med. Center, 1961-62, research asst. prof., 1962-64, asst. prof. pathology, 1964-65; dir. Syracuse Cancer Research Inst., 1965—, trustee, 1965—. Served with USAF, 1958-61. Recipient Presdl. citation for work in Mercury Astronaut Selection Program, 1960; USPHS postdoctoral research fellow U. Calif. Sch. Medicine, Berkeley, 1956-58. Mem. Am. Assn. Cancer Research, Onondaga County (N.Y.) Med. Soc., Med. Soc. State N.Y. Pioneer in proposing gluconeogenesis as means of cancer cachexia, 1968; developer hydrazine sulfate, 1st specific anti-cachexia drug to be used in human cancer; patentee in field. Home: 127 Edgemont Dr Syracuse NY 13214 Office: 600 E Genesee St Syracuse NY 13202

GOLD, JUDITH HAMMERLING, psychiatrist; b. N.Y.C., June 24, 1941; d. James S. and Anne (Linder) Hammerling; m. Edgar Gold, June 27, 1965. M.D., Dalhousie U., 1965. Intern Victoria Gen. Hosp., Halifax, N.S., Can., 1964-65; resident Dalhousie U., Halifax, 1967-71; practice medicine specializing in psychiatry, Halifax, 1971—; staff psychiatrist Dalhousie U. Student Health Clinic, 1971-73; vis. colleague U. Wales Med. Sch., 1973-75; asst. prof. dept. psychiatry Dalhousie U., Halifax, 1975-78, assoc. prof., 1978-80, part-time, 1980—. Contbr. articles to profl. jours. Bd. govs. Mt. St. Vincent U. Med. Research Council Can. fellow, 1973-75; Health and Welfare Bd. Can. grantee, 1976-78. Mem. Can. Psychiat. Assn. (pres. 1981-82), Am. Psychiat. Assn., Am. Coll. Psychiatrists, Alpha Omega Alpha. Office: 5991 Spring Garden Rd #1020 Halifax NS Canada B3H 1Y6

GOLD, LEONARD SINGER, librarian, translator; b. Bklyn., July 3, 1934; s. Hyman B. and Gertrude (Singer) G.; m. Stella Schmidt, June 5, 1960; children: Yael, Dalia. B.A., McGill U., Montreal, Que., Can., 1956; M.S. in Library Service, Columbia U., 1966; M.A., NYU, 1967, Ph.D., 1975. Cert. profl. librarian, N.Y. Tchr. high sch., Kiryat Hayim, Israel, 1960-61; tchr. Hugim High Sch., Haifa, Israel, 1961-63; tech. asst. N.Y. Pub. Library, N.Y.C., 1963-66, chief Jewish div., 1971—, asst. dir. Jewish, Oriental and Slavonic studies, 1980—. Translator: (Nathan Shaham) 3 novellas The Other side of the Wall, 1983; contbr. to bibliog. publs. Mem. Assn. Jewish Libraries (pres. 1974-76), Council Archives and Research Libraries in Jewish Studies (pres. 1978-80), Jewish Book Council (v.p. 1980—), Assn. Jewish Studies. Office: NY

Pub Library Jewish Div Room 84 Fifth Ave and 42d St New York NY 10018

GOLD, LORNE W., Canadian government official; b. Saskatoon, Sask., Can., June 7, 1928; s. Alexander Stewart and Grace Dora (Davis) G.; m. Elizabeth Joan L'Ami, Sept. 8, 1951; children: Catherine Anne, Patricia Ellen, Judith Sharon, Kenneth Robert. B.Sc., U. Sask., 1950; M.Sc. in Physics, McGill U., 1952, Ph.D., 1970. Research officer div. bldg. research NRC Can., Ottawa, Ont., 1950-52, head snow and ice sect., 1953-69, head geotech. sect., 1969-74, asst. dir. div., 1974-79, asso. dir. div., 1979—, chmn., asso. com. geotech. research, 1976-83. Fellow Royal Soc. Can.; mem. Internat. Glaciol. Soc. (pres. 1978-81), Asso. Profl. Engrs. Ont., Engring. Inst., Can., Can. Geotech. Soc., Can. Soc. Civil Engrs., Arctic Inst. N.Am., Can. Assn. Physicists (affiliate), Council Internat. du Batement (bd. dirs. 1983—). Mem. United Ch. of Canada. Home: 1903 Illinois Ave Ottawa ON K1H 6W5 Canada Office: Div Bldg Research Nat Research Council of Can Ottawa ON K1A 0R6 Canada

GOLD, NORMAN MYRON, lawyer; b. Chgo., May 21, 1930; s. Harry and Irene (Alpern) G.; m. Barbara George, Sept. 8, 1962; children: Judith Ann, Walter Robert. B.B.A., U. Mich., 1951; J.D., Harvard U., 1954. Bar: Ill. 1954; C.P.A., Ill. Since practiced in, Chgo.; assoc. Abbell & Abbell, 1954-58; assoc., partner Altheimer & Gray, 1957—; dir. Ford City Bank, Intercraft Industries Corp., Rentar Industries, Inc. Mem. Am., Ill., Chgo. bar assns., Beta Gamma Sigma, Phi Kappa Phi, Alpha Kappa Psi. Club: Standard (Chgo.). Home: 1300 Lakeshore Dr Chicago IL 60610 Office: 333 W Wacker Dr Chicago IL 60606

GOLD, RAYMOND L., sociologist, educator; b. Chgo., Nov. 15, 1921; s. Samuel and Shirley (Katz) G.; m. Marjorie Doris McClelland, Dec. 23, 1948; 1 dau., Karen Joan. Student, Wilson Jr. Coll., Chgo., 1946-47; M.A., U. Chgo., 1950, Ph.D., 1954. Asst. prof. sociology U. Ala., 1953-57; from asst. prof. to prof. sociology U. Mont., 1957—; dir. Social Research and Applications, Missoula; sociol. cons. bus. and govt. Contbr. articles to profl. jours. and books. Served with AUS, 1942-46. Fellow Am. Sociol. Assn. Unitarian-Universalist (pres. Missoula fellowship 1970-71, 82-83). Home: 413 King St Missoula MT 59801

GOLD, THOMAS, educator, astronomer; b. Vienna, Austria, May 22, 1920; s. Max and Josefine (Martin) G.; m. Merle Eleanor Tuberg, June 21, 1947; children—Linda, Lucy, Tanya; m. Carvel Lee Beyer, Dec. 27, 1972; 1 dau., Lauren. B.A., Cambridge (Eng.) U., 1942, M.A., 1945, Sc.D., 1969; fellow, Trinity Coll., Cambridge, 1947; M.A. (hon.), Harvard, 1957. Lectr. physics Cambridge (Eng.) U., 1948-52; chief asst. to Astronomer Royal, Gt. Britain, 1952-56; prof. astronomy Harvard, 1958, Robert Wheeler Willson prof., 1958-59; prof. astronomy, dir. Center Radiophysics and Space Research Cornell U., 1959-81, chmn. dept., 1959-68, asst. v.p. for research, 1970-71, John L. Wetherill prof., 1971—. Contbr. articles to profl. jours. Fellow Royal Soc. London; mem. U.S. Nat. Acad. Sci., Am. Philos. Soc., Am. Acad. Arts and Scis., Royal Astron. Soc. (past councillor), Am. Astron. Soc., Am. Geophys. Union. Address: Space Scis Bldg Cornell U Ithaca NY 14853

GOLDBERG, ALICE SUSAN, advertising agency executive; b. New Britain, Conn., Mar. 5, 1932; d. Zundie A. and Sally (Hoffman) Finkelstein; m. Irwin Ulysses Goldberg, June 3, 1956. B.A., Barnard Coll., 1953. Research analyst Biow Co., N.Y.C., 1953-56; project dir. Benton & Bowles, Inc., N.Y.C., 1956-60, market research supr., 1960-68, v.p., assoc. research dir., 1968-74, sr. v.p., research mgr., 1974-83, sr. v.p., research dir., 1983—, chmn. profit-sharing com., 1976—. Mem. ARF TV Copy Research Council (vice chmn.), Am. Mktg. Assn. (dir), Market Research Council, Copy Research Council. Home: 450 E 63d St New York NY 10021 Office: 909 3d Ave New York NY 10022

GOLDBERG, ALVIN, hospital adminsitrator; b. Jersey City, May 12, 1919; s. David and Sadie (Markel) G.; m. Shirley Lipshitz, May 20, 1943; children: Howard, Ellen. B.S. in Pharmacy, Rutgers U., 1940; cert. in hosp. administrn., Ga. State Coll., 1958; postgrad. in personnel mgmt., U. So. Fla., 1966; grad. exec. devel. program, Cornell U., 1965. Asst. adminstr. So. Fla. Baptist Hosp., Plant City, 1954-61; dir. Polk County Div. Hosps. and Welfare, (Fla.), 1961-66; asst. dir. Grady Meml. Hosp., Atlanta, 1966-68; exec. dir. Mt. Sinai Med. Ctr., Miami Beach, Fla., 1968-80, exec. v.p., 1980—; mem. pharmacology and chemistry faculty Grady Hosp. Sch. Nursing, 1957-58; mem. psychology faculty Polk Coll., 1964-65; adj. prof. dept. epidemiology U. Miami; preceptor schs., hosp. adminstrn. U. Fla., George Washington U., Yale U. Mem. Fla. Task Force on Competition and Consumer Choices in Health. Recipient citation Fla. Rehab. State Assn., Fla. C. of C., Acad. Carsbie Adams award Ga. State Coll., 1958; named Man of Yr. Temple Emanuel, Lakeland, Fla., 1956. Fellow Am. Coll. Hosp. Adminstrs.; mem. Fla. Hosp. Assn. (chmn. 1981), South Fla. Hosp. Assn. Home: 9520 SW 93d St Miami FL 33176 Office: Mt Sinai Med Ctr 4300 Alton Rd Miami Beach FL 33140

GOLDBERG, ARTHUR H., financial services company executive; b. N.Y.C., May 13, 1942; s. Irving and Pearl (Ruben) G.; m. Hedy S. Krauss; children: Jill Marla, Mia Joy. B.S., NYU, 1963, J.D., 1966. Atty. Javits & Javits, N.Y.C., 1966-69; exec. Integrated Resources, Inc., N.Y.C., 1969-73, pres., 1973—; chmn. bd. Resources Life Ins. Co.; Providence Life Ins. Co. Trustee Jerusalem Inst. Mgmt, Boston, Children's Med. Fund of N.Y., N.Y.C. Named Man of Yr. Boys Town Jerusalem, 1982. Mem. N.Y. State Bar Assn., Young Presidents Orgn., Order of Coif. Office: Integrated Resources Inc 666 3d Ave New York NY 10017

GOLDBERG, ARTHUR JOSEPH, lawyer; b. Chgo., Aug. 8, 1908; s. Joseph and Rebecca (Perlstein) G.; m. Dorothy Kurgans, July 18, 1931; children—Barbara L. Goldberg Cramer, Robert M. B.S.L., Northwestern U., 1929, J.D. summa cum laude, 1930. Bar: Ill. bar 1929, U.S. Supreme Ct. bar 1937. Practiced in, Chgo., 1929-48; sr. partner firm Goldberg, Devoe, Shadur & Mikva, Chgo., 1945-61, Goldberg, Feller & Bredhoff, Washington, 1952-61; gen. counsel CIO, 1948-55, United Steelworkers Am., 1948-61; spl. counsel indsl. union dept. AFL-CIO, 1955-61, also numerous other internat. unions; sec. labor, 1961-62; asso. justice U.S. Supreme Ct., Washington, 1962-65; U.S. rep. to UN, 1965-68, ambassador-at-large, 1977-78; sr. partner Paul, Weiss, Goldberg, Rifkind, Wharton & Garrison, N.Y.C., 1968-71; practice law, Washington, 1971—; Charles Evans Hughes prof. Princeton U., 1968-69; distinguished prof. Columbia, 1969-70; prof. law and diplomacy Am. U., Washington, 1972-73; distinguished prof. Hastings Coll. Law, San Francisco, 1974—; chmn. Center for Law and Social Policy, 1968-78, hon. chmn., 1978—; disting. vis. prof. Santa Clara U., 1980, Nova Law Center, 1980; Former chmn. Pres.'s Com. on Migratory Labor, Pres.'s Missile Sites Labor Commn., Pres.'s Com. on Youth Employment, Pres.'s Temporary Com. on Implementation of Fed. Employee-Mgmt. Relations Program, Workers' Adv. Com. on U.S., Pres.'s Adv. Com. on Labor-Mgmt. Policy, Pres.'s Com. on Equal Employment Opportunity; former mem. numerous other Presdl. and federal coms. and councils; former ex-officio mem. and ad hoc participant Nat. Security Council; former pres. Internat. Edn. Assn.; U.S. rep., chmn. U.S. del. Conf. on Security and Cooperation in Europe with rank amb.-at-large; spl. asst. to dir. OSS. Author: AFL-CIO; Labor United, 1956, Defenses of Freedom, 1966, Equal Justice: the Warren Era of the Supreme Court, 1972; editor-in-chief: Ill. Law Rev, 1929-30; contbr. articles to profl. jours. and jours. of opinion. Past pres., now hon. chmn. Am. Jewish Com. Served from capt. to maj.; OSS; Served from capt. to maj. U.S. Army, 1942-44; ETO; col. USAF Res. ret. Recipient numerous awards and hon. degrees; Medal of Freedom Pres. Carter, 1978. Mem. Am., Ill., Chgo., D.C. bar assns., Assn. Bar City N.Y., UN Assn. (hon. chmn.), Order of Coif. Address: 2801 New Mexico Ave NW Washington DC 20007

GOLDBERG, ARTHUR LEWIS, manufacturing company executive; b. N.Y.C., Feb. 23, 1939; s. George and Rachel (Ablon) G.; m. Bernice Guller, May 31, 1964; 1 dau., Deborah Ruth. B.B.A., CCNY, 1959; LL.B., NYU, 1962, LL.M., 1967; M.B.A., U. Chgo., 1982. Bar: N.Y. State 1962, Ohio 1978, Ill. 1982; C.P.A., Ohio, N.Y., Ill. Tax asst. Arthur Andersen & Co., N.Y.C., 1962-63; asso. firm Gordon, Brady, Keller & Ballen, N.Y.C., 1963-67, Langer & Sternfield, 1967-68; sr. tax atty. CBS, Inc., N.Y.C., 1968-69; asst. to chief fin. officer, corporate counsel, sec. Condec Corp., Old Greenwich, Conn., 1969-77; asst. to pres. NRM Corp., Akron, Ohio, 1977-78, dir. fin., Columbiana, Ohio, 1978-79; v.p. Conval Internat., Ltd., Chgo., 1979-80; dir. adminstrn. and ops. analysis Flow Control Group, Condec Corp., Chgo., 1980-81; v.p. fin., treas. Hexco, Inc., Addison, Ill., 1981-82; sr. v.p., chief fin. officer, treas., sec. Xonics, Inc., Des Plaines, Ill., 1982—; instr. Grad. Sch. Bus., U. Conn., 1971-72. Served with AUS, 1962-63. Mem. ABA. Home: 2731 Orchard Ln Wilmette IL 60091 Office: 515 E Touhy Ave Des Plaines IL 60018

GOLDBERG, ARTHUR SAMUEL, lawyer; b. St. Joseph, Mo., Nov. 20, 1916; s. Benjamin and Dora (Wilk) G.; m. Ruth Miriam Friedman, Oct. 19, 1947; children: Donna Raye, David Victor. A.A., St. Joseph Jr. Coll., 1935; A.B., Washburn U., 1939; J.D., So. Methodist U., 1939. Bar: Tex. 1939, Okla. 1942, U.S. Supreme Ct. 1942. Practiced in, Dallas, 1946—; partner firm Goldberg & Alexander; sec. Liberty Steel Co., Friedman Investment Co., M&W Realty Co.; Lectr. S.W. Legal Found. Pres. I Zesmer dist. Zionist Orgn. Am., 1950-51, mem. nat. exec. com., bd. dirs. S.W. Region, 1968—; bd. dirs. Jewish Family Service, Jewish Welfare Fedn., Dallas, Schepps Community Center. Served to 1st lt. AUS, 1942-46. Mem. Am., Dallas bar assns., State Bar Tex., Am. Judicature Soc., Comml. Law League Am.; mem. B'nai B'rith. Jewish (dir., past co-treas. congregation). Club: Mason (Shriner). Office: Goldberg & Alexander 5924 Royal Ln Suite 250B Dallas TX 75230 *

GOLDBERG, AVRAM JACOB, retailing company executive; b. Boston, Jan. 26, 1930; s. Lewis and Mildred (Levine) G.; m. Carol Rabb, June 18, 1950; children: Deborah Beth, Joshua Rabb. A.B. magna cum laude, Harvard U., 1951, J.D. cum laude, 1954. Bar: Mass. 1954, U.S. Supreme Ct 1954. Asso. firm Hill, Barlow, Goodale & Wiswall, Boston, 1954-55; with The Stop & Shop Cos., Inc., 1958—, exec. v.p., 1968-71, pres., 1971—, chief exec. officer, 1979—; dir. The Boston Co., Boston Safe Deposits' Trust Co. Mem. class com. Harvard Class of 1951; exec. com. Mass. Com. Catholics, Protestants and Jews; trustee Mass. Eye and Ear Infirmary; past trustee Boston Coll.; hon. life trustee Beth Israel Hosp.; v.p., hon. trustee, mem. exec. bd. Combined Jewish Philanthropies Greater Boston; former mem. bd. dirs. Mass. Bus. Devel. Corp.; former chmn. Brookline Redevel. Authority; mem. corp. Boston Mus. Sci.; bd. overseers Boston Symphony Orch.; bd. dirs. New Eng. region Am. Friends Hebrew U.; bd. dirs. Food Mktg. Inst., Harvard Bus. Sch. Assocs. Served with USNR, 1955-58. Fellow Am. Acad. Arts and Scis.; mem. Nat. Retail Mchts. Assn. (dir., v.p.), Boston C. of C. (v.p. dir.), Confrerie des Chevaliers du Tastevin (Chevalier, bailli honoraire). Jewish (trustee temple). Office: Box 369 Boston MA 02101

GOLDBERG, BARRY BENSON, physician; b. Phila., July 26, 1937; s. Emanuel and Anne (Malkin) G.; m. Phyllis Renee Newman, June 2, 1963; children: Marla Ruth, Mitchell Craig. B.A. in Chemistry, U. Pa., 1959, M.D., 1963. Diplomate: Diplimate Am. Bd. Radiology. Sr. instr. radiology Hahnemann Med. Coll. and Hosp., Phila., 1968; from asst. prof. to prof. radiology Temple U. Health Scis. Center, Phila., 1968-77; prof. radiology, dir. diagnostic ultrasound Thomas Jefferson U. Med. Sch., Phila., 1977—. Editor 5 books; contbr. articles to med. jours. Fellow Am. Coll. Radiology; mem. Am. Inst. Ultrasound Medicine (pres. 1980-82), World Fedn. Ultrasound in Medicine (treas. 1982—), AMA, Radiol. Soc. N.Am., Nat. Council Radiation Protection and Measurements, Pa. Med. Soc., Phila. County Med. Soc. Office: 1015 Walnut St Philadelphia PA 19107

GOLDBERG, BERTRAND, architect; b. Chgo., July 17, 1913; s. Benjamin R. and Sadie (Getzhof) G.; m. Nancy S. Florsheim, Dec. 4, 1946; children: Nan, Lisa, Geoffrey. Student, Harvard, 1930-32, Bauhaus, Berlin, Germany, 1932-33, Armour Inst. Tech., 1934. Propr. archtl. and engring. office Bertrand Goldberg Assos., Chgo., 1937—, Richmond, Va., 1940-45; archtl. engr. for plastic freight car, 1950; lectr. throughout, U.S. and Can., 1958—. Prin. works include Marina City, Chgo., 1963, Astor Tower Hotel, Chgo., 1963, Joseph Brennemann Pub. Sch, Chgo., 1962, Elgin (Ill.) State Hosp, 1964, Affiliated Hosps. Center, Boston, 1964, Raymond Hilliard Housing Center, Chgo., 1966, Health Scis. Center SUNY-Stony Brook, Stanford Med. Center, Palo Alto, Calif., 1967, Chgo. Women's Hosp, 1968, St. Joseph's Hosp, Tacoma, Wash., 1968, Charles Dana Center, Boston, 1973, Affiliated Hosps. Center, Boston, 1975, Prentice Hosp., Northwestern U., Chgo., 1975, Good Samaritan Center, Phoenix, 1978, Research Bldg., Brigham Women's Hosp., Boston, 1983, Providence Hosp., Mobile, Ala. Bd. dirs. Chgo. Maternity Center, Inst. Psychiatry, Northwestern U.; bd. dirs. Soc. Contemporary Music; Bd. dirs. City Venture Corp.; trustee St. Xavier Coll., Coll. Recipient award Archtl. Forum, 1945, 52, Progressive Architecture, 1954, Hardware Assn., 1956, AIA-C. of C., 1959, Chgo. Leading Architect award, 1961; citation Assn. Sch. Adminstrs., 1962; Silver medal Archtl. League N.Y., 1965; Man of Yr. (field arch.), Chgo., 1965; Am. Registered Architects award, 1979; ORT Centennial award, 1979; Ariz. Rock Products Assn. merit award, 1982. Fellow AIA, Am. Concrete Inst.; mem. Nat. Soc. Profl. Engrs., Ill. Soc. Architects, Am. Assn. Engrs., Soc. Am. Mil. Engrs., Bldg. Research Inst., Chgo. Sch. Architecture Found. Clubs: Cliff Dwellers, Tavern, Arts (Chgo.); Harvard (Chgo. and Boston). Office: Bertrand Goldberg Assos 300 N State St Chicago IL 60610 *New technology and engineering now give us unique power to shape buildings to our needs. To shape the world's communities might now be an architect's philosophy. For the first time we can build whatever we can think; what shall we think to build for man?*

GOLDBERG, CAROL RABB, retail chain executive; b. Newton, Mass., Mar. 25, 1931; d. Sidney Rabinovitz and Rabb (Esther Vera (Cohn) Rabb; m. Avram J. Goldberg, June 18, 1950; children: Deborah, Joshua. B.A. magna cum laude in Sociology, Jackson Coll. Tufts U., 1955; postgrad., Harvard U. Bus. Sch., 1969. Fashion model Hart Agy.; free-lance fashion coordinator; trousseau coordinator Joseph Magnin, San Francisco, until 1958; with Stop & Shop Cos., Inc., 1958—, market mgr. North New Eng. Region, Bradlees div., 1971, v.p., gen. mgr. Boston Supermarket div., 1972-77; pres. Stop & Shop Mfg. Co., 1977-79; sr. v.p. Stop & Shop Cos., Inc., Boston, 1979, now exec. v.p. chief operating officer, also dir.; dir. Fed. Res. Bank Boston; trustee, dir. Putnam Fund Groups. Mem. Task Force on Future Planning, U.S. Office Edn.; mem. bd. visitors Sch. Mgmt., Boston U.; bd. dirs. Permanent Charity Fund, Inc., Arts and Humanities Found.; mem. vis. com. Harvard U. Bus. Sch.; mem. retail adv. com. Simmons Coll. Recipient Pride award Simmons Coll., 1977; named Advt. Woman of Yr., Boston, 1967. Office: Stop & Shop Cos Inc 393 E St Boston MA 02110

GOLDBERG, DAVID ALAN, investment banker, lawyer; b. N.Y.C., Oct. 31, 1933; s. Joseph R. and Rose (Trutt) G.; m. Victoria Liebson, July 7, 1957 (div. Mar. 1976); children: Eric S., Jeremy P. A.B. magna cum laude, Harvard U., 1954, J.D., 1957, postgrad. in bus. adminstrn, 1956-57. Bar: N.Y. 1958. Counsel firm R.W. Pressprich & Co., N.Y.C., 1958-64, gen. partner, 1965-68; exec. v.p. R.W. Pressprich & Co., Inc., 1968-78, also chmn. exec. com.; dir. Alexander's Inc., S&S Corrugated Paper Machinery Co. Inc. Trustee Beth Israel Med. Center, N.Y.C. Served with AUS, 1957-58. Mem. Phi Beta Kappa. Club: Harvard (N.Y.C.) (chmn. univ. relations com.). Home: 750 Park Ave New York NY 10021 Office: 1350 Ave of Americas New York NY 10019

GOLDBERG, DAVID MEYER, biochemistry educator; b. Glasgow, Scotland, Aug. 30, 1933; emigrated to Can., 1975; s. Samuel Simon and Ethel (Elyan) G.; m. Pearl Gertrude Goldberg; children: Susan Simone, Tanya Marion. B.Sc. with honors in Biochemistry, U. Glasgow, 1959, M.B., Ch.B., 1959, Ph.D., 1967, M.D., 1974. Intern Stobhill Hosp., Glasgow, 1960, So. Gen. Hosp., 1961; resident Western Infirmary, Glasgow, 1962-66; prof., chmn. dept. clin. biochemistry U. Toronto, 1977—; biochemist-in-chief dept. biochemistry Hosp. for Sick Children, Toronto, 1975—; cons. chem. pathology and hon. lectr. United Sheffield Hosp., U. Sheffield, Eng., 1967-75. Joint editor-in-chief: Clin. Biochemistry, 1975—; editorial bd.: Enzyme, 1978—; editorial: Clin. Chemica Acta, 1981—. Recipient Van Slyke award Am. Assn. Clin. Chemistry, 1982, Roman award Australian Assn. Clin. Chemists, 1983. Mem. Am. Assn. Clin. Chemistry, Can. Soc. Clin. Chemists, Can. Assn. med. Biochemists, Internat. Soc. Clin. Enzymology, Can. Soc. Clin. Investigation, Biochem. Soc., Can. Biochem. Soc., Internat. Soc. Clin. Enzymology (v.p.). Jewish. Home: 9 Harrison Rd Willowdale ON Canada M2L 1V3 Office: Dept Clin Biochemistry Univ Toronto 100 College St Toronto ON Canada M5G 1L5

GOLDBERG, EDWARD DAVID, geochemist, educator; b. Sacramento, Aug. 2, 1921; s. Edward Davidow and Lillian (Rothholz) G.; m. Kathe Bertine, Dec. 26, 1973; children—David Wilkes, Wendy Jean, Kathi Kiri, Beck Bertine. B.S., U. Calif. at Berkeley, 1942; Ph.D., U. Chgo., 1949. Mem. faculty Scripps Instn. Oceanography, La Jolla, Calif., 1949—, prof. chemistry, 1960—; provost Revelle Coll., U. Calif. at San Diego, 1965-66. Author: (with J. Geiss) Earth Sciences and Meteorites, 1964, Guide to Marine Pollution, 1972, North Sea Science, 1973, The Sea: Marine Chemistry, Vol. V, 1974, The Health of the Oceans, 1976; Contbr. numerous articles to profl. jours. Guggenheim fellow, 1961; NATO fellow, 1970. Mem. Am. Geophys. Union, AAAS, Geochem. Soc., U.S. Acad. Scis., Sigma Xi. Research, publs. primarily on marine pollution, chem. composition sea water, sediments, marine organisms, environmental mgmt.; radioactive dating techniques in marine environment and glaciers. Home: 750 Val Sereno Dr Encinitas CA 92024

GOLDBERG, E(LLIOTT) MARSHALL, physician; b. North Adams, Mass., Dec. 18, 1930; s. Jack and Ida (Lenhoff) G.; m. Barbara Young; children: Brett, Carey, Sandra, Jeff, Dara. A.B. with high honors, U. Rochester, N.Y., 1952; M.D., Tufts U., 1956. Intern D.C. Gen. Hosp., Washington, 1956-57; resident in medicine Meml. Hosp., Worcester, Mass., 1960-61, Univ. Hosps., Madison, Wis., 1962-63; asst. prof. Wayne State U. Med. Sch., Detroit, 1964-65; mem. faculty Mich. State U. Coll. Human Medicine, East Lansing, 1966—, prof. medicine, 1973—; chief medicine Hurley Med. Center, Flint, Mich., 1968-78, chief endocrinology, 1978—; chief med. corr. ABC World News, 1979—. Author: novels The Karamonov Equations, 1972, The Anatomy Lesson, 1974, Critical List, 1978, Skeletons, 1979, (with Kenneth Kay) Disposable People, 1980, Nerve, 1981; also med. articles. Bd. dirs. Medgar Evers Found., 1972. Served to capt. M.C., AUS, 1957-59. Recipient Outstanding Tchr. award Mich. State U. Coll. Human Medicine, 1973, Humanitarian award NAACP, 1974; Endocrine fellow U. Wis. Med. Sch., 1961-62, NIH, 1963-64. Fellow ACP; mem. Endocrine Soc., Am. Diabetes Assn., Mich. Med. Soc., Mich. Assn. Med. Edn. (pres. 1972-75), Genesee County Med. Soc., Royal Coll. Physicians (asso.). Home: 2151 Crestline Dr Burton MI 48509 Office: Hurley Med Center 1 Hurley Plaza Flint MI 48502

GOLDBERG, GARY DAVID, writer, producer; b. Bklyn., June 25, 1944; s. George and Anne (Prossman) G.; m. Diana Meehan; children: Shana Goldberg-Meehan, Cailin Elizabeth Goldberg-Meehan. Student, Brandeis U., 1962-64; B.A., San Diego State U., 1975. Writer: Bob Newhart Show, CBS-TV, 1976; story editor: Tony Randall Show, 1976-77, producer, 1977-78; producer: Lou Grant, 1978-79; creator, producer: The Last Resort, CBS, 1979; creator: Making the Grade, CBS, 1982; creator, exec. producer: Family Ties, NBC, 1982—. Recipient Peabody award U. Ga., 1979, Emmy award, 1979. Mem. Writers Guild Am. (Best Episodic Comedy TV Script award 1978), Actors Equity, AFTRA. Office: Paramount Pictures 555 Marathon Hollywood CA 90038

GOLDBERG, HAROLD SEYMOUR, electrical engineer; b. Bklyn., Jan. 22, 1925; s. David and Rose (Maslow) G.; m. Florence Meyerson, May 29, 1949; children: Lawrence, Irene. B.E.E. (Schweinberg scholar), Cooper Union, 1944; M.E.E., Poly. Inst. Bklyn., 1949; student, Columbia U. Engring. draftsman Cole Electric Products Co., 1944-45; radio engr. Press Wireless, Inc., 1945-47; asst. project engr. Radio Receptor Co., 1947-48; project engr. No. Radio Co., 1948-50; mgr. prodn. test, test equipment design sects. Allen B. DuMont Labs., Inc., 1950-56; mgr. engring. fabrication dept. Emerson Radio & Phonograph Corp., 1956-57; chief devel. engr. Consol. Avionics Corp., Westbury, N.Y., 1957-59; engring. mgr. data systems EPSCO, Inc., Cambridge, Mass., 1959-62; v.p. research Lexington Instruments Corp., Waltham, Mass., 1962-66; prin. research engr. AVCO-Research div., Everett, Mass., 1966-68; ops. mgr. Orion Research Inc., 1968-70; v.p. applications Analogic Corp., Wakefield, Mass., 1970-71; ops. mgr. Data Precision Corp., Danvers, Mass., 1971-72, pres., 1972—; v.p. Analogic Corp., 1979—. Served with AUS, 1945-47. N.Y. State Vets, scholar, 1957; recipient award of distinction Poly. Inst. N.Y., 1980. Sr. mem. IEEE (chmn. Boston group on medicine and biology 1965-66, mem. exec. com. Boston sect. 1967-69, vice chmn. Boston 1969-70, chmn. Boston 1970-71, internat. bd. dirs. 1971-75, v.p. 1975, dir. Electro 1975—, fellow, citation of honor U.S. Activities Bd. 1978); mem. Instrumentation and Measurement Soc. of IEEE (sec./treas. 1983), Tau Beta Pi. Home: 10 Alcott Rd Lexington MA 02173 Office: Danvers Indsl Park Danvers MA 01923 *The highest achievement to which a person can aspire is that the world be a better place after he leaves it than before and that this be partly the result of his contributions to it.*

GOLDBERG, HERMAN RAPHAEL, ednl. adminstr.; b. Bklyn., Nov. 20, 1915; s. Isidore Baruch and Rose (Saltser) G.; m. Harriette Balacaier, Jan. 23, 1943; children—Robert, Arnold. B.S., Bklyn. Coll., 1935; M.A., Columbia Tchrs. Coll., 1944; postgrad., N.Y.U., 1941-42, U. Rochester, 1956-57, LL.D., 1965. Tchr. spl. edn., English, social studies N.Y.C. pub. schs., 1939-48; cons. spl. edn. City Sch. Dist., Rochester, N.Y., 1948-49, dir. spl. edn., 1949-58, coordinator instructional services, 1958-63, supt. schs., 1963-71; U.S. asso. commr. elementary and secondary edn. U.S. Office Edn., HEW, 1971—; U.S.

asso. commr. Bur. Equal Edn. Opportunity, 1972—, State and Local Ednl. Programs, 1978—; dep. asst. sec. U.S. Dept. Edn., 1980—; asst. sec. Office of Spl. Edn. and Rehab. Services, 1981—; lectr. edn. U. Rochester, 1949—, N.Y.U., 1943-48; Fulbright prof. U. Bologna, Italy, 1960-61; cons. Ministry Edn., Italy, Israel, 1960-61; N.Y. del. Edn. Commn. of States, 1966—. Contbg. author: Otolaryngology, 1960, Education for the Exceptional, 1956, Educating for Tomorrow: The Role of Media, Career Development and Society, 1970; Editor: Rochester Occupational Reading Series, 1953-63, The Job Ahead, 1963, Getting It Together, 1973, Career Reading Series, 1977. Mem. N.Y. State Council for Exceptional Children (charter pres.); chmn. Nat. Adv. Council Edn. Disadvantaged, 1969-70. Inventor linguistics teaching machine. Home: 5101 River Rd Washington DC 20816 Office: 400 Maryland Ave Washington DC 20202

GOLDBERG, IRVING HYMAN, physician, pharmacology educator; b. Hartford, Conn., Sept. 2, 1926; s. Morris Wolfe and Rose (Krechevsky) G.; m. Margaret Field Ziskin, Apr. 15, 1956; children: Daniel Eliot, Nancy Elizabeth. B.S., Trinity Coll., 1949; M.D., Yale U., 1953; Ph.D., Rockefeller U., 1960; A.M. (hon.), Harvard U., 1964. Intern Columbia-Presbyn. Med. Center, N.Y.C., 1953-54, asst. resident, chief resident, instr. medicine, 1954-57; practice medicine, specializing in endocrinology and metabolism, Chgo., 1960-64, Boston, 1964—; asst. prof. medicine, biochemistry U. Chgo., 1960-64, assoc. prof., 1964; assoc. prof. medicine Med. Sch. Harvard, 1964-68; prof. medicine Med. Sch. Harvard U., 1968—, chmn. div. med. scis. Faculty Arts and Scis., 1968-70, Gustavus Adolphus Pfeiffer prof. pharmacology, chmn. dept. pharmacology, 1972-83, Otto Krayer prof. pharmacology, 1983; Chief endocrinology-metabolism unit Beth Israel Hosp., 1964-68, physician, 1964-72, mem. bd. consultation in medicine, 1972—; physician div. med. oncology Sidney Farber Cancer Inst., Boston, 1980—; cons. in medicine (pharmacology) Peter Bent Brigham Hosp., Boston, 1972—; cons. in clin. pharmacology Children's Hosp. Med. Center, Boston, 1972—; Mem. research com. Med. Found. Boston, 1968-77; mem. exptl. therapeutics study sect. NIH, 1974-77; mem. com. proposed legislation to restructure FDA Assembly Life Scis., Nat. Acad. Scis.-NRC, Inst. Medicine, 1976. Editorial bd.: Endocrinology, 1964-68; hon. editorial adv. bd.: Jour. Biochem. Pharmacology, 1973—; editorial bd.: Antimicrobial Agents and Chemotherapy, 1974—. Served with USNR, 1945-46. Recipient Faculty Research award Am. Cancer Soc., 1960-71; Guggenheim fellow dept. genetics Oxford (Eng.) U., 1970-71; sr. fellow Trinity Coll., 1974-76. Mem. Am. Soc. Biol. Chemists, Am. Soc. Clin. Investigation, Endocrine Soc., Am. Acad. Arts and Scis., Assn. of Am. Physicians, Am. Chem. Soc., AAUP, Am. Soc. Pharmacology and Exptl. Therapeutics, Am. Soc. Microbiology, Brit. Pharm. Soc., Phi Beta Kappa, Sigma Xi, Alpha Omega Alpha. Home: 61 Blake Rd Brookline MA 02146 Office: 25 Shattuck St Boston MA 02115

GOLDBERG, IRVING LOEB, judge; b. Port Arthur, Tex., June 29, 1906; s. Abraham and Elsa (Loeb) G.; m. Marian Jessel Melasky, Dec. 30, 1928; children—Nancy Paula (Mrs. Jay L. Todes), Julie Elsa (Mrs. Michael Lowenberg). B.A., U. Tex., 1926; LL.B., Harvard, 1929; L.H.D., Hebrew Union Coll.-Jewish Inst. Religion, 1974; LL.D., So. Methodist U., 1975. Bar: Tex. bar 1929. Partner Goldberg, Akin, Gump, Strauss & Hauer, Dallas, 1950-66; judge U.S. Ct. Appeals 5th Circuit, 1966—. Past vice chmn. Tex. adv. com. U.S. Commn. Civil Rights; past pres. Jewish Welfare Fedn. Dallas, Dallas Home and Hosp. for Jewish Aged; past nat. v.p. Am. Jewish Com.; Past bd. dirs. Dallas UN Assn., Dallas Council Social Agys., Nat. Conf. Christians and Jews, United HIAS Service, Council Jewish Fedns. and Welfare Funds. Served to lt. USNR, 1942-46. Recipient Brotherhood citation Nat. Conf. Christians and Jews, 1968. Mem. Am., Dallas bar assns. Clubs: Dallas, Columbian (Dallas). Home: 6148 Averill Way Apt 107-E Dallas TX 75225 Office: US Courthouse 1100 Commerce St Dallas TX 75242

GOLDBERG, JOEL, department store executive; b. Worcester, Mass., Feb. 19, 1925; s. Max I. and Rebecca Anne (Goldberg) G.; m. Carole Brockey, June 17, 1956; children: Jeffrey, James, Debra. A.B., Dartmouth Coll., 1946. Buyer William Filene Sons, Worcester, 1947-53; asso. Merchandising Corp., N.Y.C., 1953-54; with Rich's, Inc., Atlanta, 1954—, sr. v.p., gen. merchandise mgr., 1969-72, pres., 1972-78, chmn., 1978-80, now chmn. exec. com.; dir. First Nat. Bank, Atlanta, Nat. Service Industries, Inc. Trustee Temple Sinai, Atlanta, pres., 1972-73; bd. dirs. Central Atlanta Progress; bd. dirs., past chmn. Atlanta chpt. ARC; v.p. Rich Found., Inc.; chmn. Atlanta Bus. Coalition; chmn., mem. fin. com., bd. dirs. Met. Atlanta Rapid Transit Authority; bd. dirs., chmn. Ga. Heart Assn.; chmn. Atlanta Regional Panel for Selection of White House Fellows, 1977-81; trustee Oglethorpe U., Atlanta Arts Alliance, St. Joseph's Infirmary, Wesley Homes, Inc. Served to lt. USNR, 1942-46. Recipient Human Relations award Atlanta Anti-Defamation League of B'nai B'rith; Gov.'s Community Service award, 1980. Mem. Atlanta C. of C. (dir., past pres.), Assn. U.S. Army (pres. Greater Atlanta chpt. 1977—). Clubs: Masons; Rotary (Atlanta) (Arminmaier award 1980). Home: 3888 Randall Ridge Rd NW Atlanta GA 30327 Office: PO Box 4539 Atlanta GA 30302

GOLDBERG, JOSEPH, food company executive. Chmn. Cert. Grocers Calif. Ltd. Office: Cert Grocers Calif Ltd 2601 S Eastern Ave Los Angeles CA 90040§

GOLDBERG, JOSEPH B., supermarket chain executive; b. N.Y.C., Sept. 25, 1915; s. Jacob and Rose (Kremen) G.; m. Helen Smith, May 4, 1968; children from previous marriage: Jan B., Betty L. B.A., UCLA, 1937; student, Southwestern Sch. of Law, 1937-39; grad. Mgmt. Exec. program, UCLA, 1960. Pub. accountant, 1937-42; dir. produce operations King Cole Markets, Inc., 1946-52, exec. v.p., gen. mgr., 1952-61, pres., chief exec. officer, Los Angeles, 1961—; chmn. bd. dirs. Certified Grocers of Calif.; dir. Grocer's Splty. Co., Springfield Ins. Co., Grocers Equipment Co., Golden Creme Farms, Inc. Mem. founders circle City of Hope, 1974—. Served with U.S. Army, 1942-46. Mem. U. Calif. Los Angeles Alumni Assn., Am. Friends of Hebrew Univ. of Jerusalem (bd. dirs.). Clubs: Beverly Hills Tennis, Friars. Home: 979 Bel Air Rd Bel Air CA 90024 Office: 11203 E Washington Blvd Whittier CA 90606

GOLDBERG, LAWRENCE IRWIN, financial planner; b. Chgo., Sept. 23, 1940; s. Joseph and Mollie (Distelheim) G.; m. Janice Kay Kiser, Jan. 30, 1972; children: Barbara, Barrie. B.S.C., DePaul U., 1963; M.B.A., U. Chgo., 1980. Treas. Aldine Pub. Co., Chgo., 1963-69, exec. v.p., gen. mgr., 1971-73, pres., 1974—; treas. Henry Regnery Co. (book pub.), Chgo., 1969-71; dir. Media Features, Inc., Cowles Book Co. Home: 1005 Independence Ave Saint Charles IL 60174 Office: 527 James St Geneva IL 60134

GOLDBERG, LEON ISADORE, clinical pharmacologist; b. Charleston, S.C., Sept. 26, 1926; s. Harry and Goldy (Cohen) G.; m. Faye Joan Girsh, Feb. 2, 1958 (div.); children—Mark, Claudia. B.S. Pharmacy, Med. U. S.C., 1946, M.S., 1951, Ph.D., 1952; D.H.L.; M.D. cum laude, Harvard U., 1956. Intern Mass. Gen. Hosp., Boston, 1956-57, intern, asst. resident in medicine, 1957-58, research fellow anesthesia, 1954-56; research asst. in pharmacology Med. Coll. S.C., 1949-52, research asso., 1952-54; clin. asso. Exptl. Therapeutics Br., NIH, 1958-61; prof. medicine, pharmacology, dir. clin. pharmacology program Emory U., Atlanta, 1961-74; prof. medicine, pharmacology, chmn. com. on clin. pharmacology U. Chgo., 1974—; cons. NIH, VA, FDA, Nat. Acad. Scis. Editor: Jour. Cardiovascular Pharmacology; mem. editorial bds. several pharmacology jours., 1961—; contbr. chpts. to books, numerous articles on clin. pharmacology, cardiovascular pharmacology to profl. jours. Served as surgeon USPHS, 1958-61. Burroughs Welcome Fund scholar in clin. pharmacology, 1961-66. Fellow Am. Coll. Cardiology; mem. Am. Soc. Clin. Investigation, Am. Soc. for Pharmacology and Exptl. Therapeutics, Soc. for Exptl. Biology and Medicine, Am. Soc. for Clin. Pharmacology and Therapeutics, Am. Heart Assn., Council for High Blood Pressure Research, Assn. Am. Physicians. Home: 5000 S Cornell Apt 21B Chicago IL 60615 Office: Dept Pharmacology Sch Medicine U Chgo 947 E 58th St Chicago IL 60637

GOLDBERG, LEONARD, television and movie producer; b. N.Y.C., Jan. 24, 1934; s. William and Jean (Smith) G.; m. Wendy Howard, Nov. 26, 1972; 1 dau., Amanda Erin. B.S. in Econs, U. Pa., 1955. With research dept. ABC, 1956; supr. spl. projects NBC-TV Research, 1957-61; charge daytime television programs, overall broadcasting coordinator Batten, Barton, Durstine & Osborne, 1961-63; mgr. program devel. ABC-TV, N.Y.C., 1963-64, dir. program devel., v.p. charge daytime programming, 1964-66, v.p. network programming, 1966-69; v.p. in charge of prodn. Screen Gems (name now Columbia Television), Los Angeles, 1969-72; co-owner, operator Spelling-Goldberg Prodns., Los Angeles, 1972—; owner, operator Leonard Goldberg Prodns. (now Leonard Goldberg Co.), 1972—, Mandy Films. Bd. dirs. Cedars Sinai Hosp. Mem. Producers Assn., Hollywood Acad. Television Arts and Scis., Hollywood Radio and TV Soc. Club: Malibu Racket. Office: MGM Studios Culver City CA

GOLDBERG, MARTIN, physician, educator; b. Phila., Sept. 15, 1930; s. Samuel and Esther (Schreibman) G.; m. Lynn Taksey, June 17, 1951 (dec. Aug. 31, 1976); children: Meryl I., Karen L., Dara S.; m. Marion Lindblad, May 26, 1978; 1 son, David S. B.A., Temple U., 1951, M.D., 1955; M.A. (hon.), U. Pa., 1971. Diplomate: Am. Bd. Internal Medicine (chmn. nephrology com. 1976—, bd. govs. 1976—), Nat. Bd. Med. Examiners. Intern Phila. Gen. Hosp., 1955-56, resident, 1957-59, sr. attending physician, 1970-76; resident Cleve. Clinic, 1956-57; fellow nephrology Hosp. U. Pa., Phila., 1959-61, sr. attending physician, 1962-79, mem. faculty, 1960-79, prof. medicine, 1970-79, chief renal electrolyte sect., 1966-79, acting chmn. dept. medicine, 1975-76; sr. attending physician Phila. VA Hosp., 1968-79; Gordon and Helen Hughes Taylor prof. medicine U. Cin., 1979—; dir. internal medicine U. Cin. Coll. Med. and Hosp., 1979—; mem. sci. adv. bd. Nat. Kidney Found., 1970-76; chmn. kidney council Am. Heart Assn., 1973-74; study cons. NIH, 1968-72, 82—. Mem. editorial com.: Jour. Clin. Investigation, 1969-70, Kidney Internat, 1972-74, Jour. Mineral and Electrolyte Metabolism, 1977—. Recipient Alumni prize Temple U. Sch. Medicine, 1955, Lindback award for distinguished teaching U. Pa., 1972, Research Career Devel. award NIH, 1963-70; research grantee NIH, 1962—, John Hartford Found., 1970-73. Fellow A.C.P. (nat. sci. program com. 1976-81), Am. Coll. Clin. Pharmacology; mem. Assn. Am. Physicians, Am. Soc. Clin. Investigation, Am. Physiol. Soc., Am. Fedn. Clin. Research (chmn. eastern sect. 1967), Am. Soc. Nephrology (sec.-treas. 1975-78), Interurban Clin. Club, Internat. Soc. Nephrology (council 1975—), Alpha Omega Alpha. Research and publs. in renal physiology and disease; electrolyte and acid-base metabolism. Office: Dept Internal Medicine 6065 MSB 231 Bethesda Ave Cincinnati OH 45267

GOLDBERG, MELVIN ARTHUR, communications executive; b. N.Y.C., Feb. 5, 1923; s. Louis and Anna (Bergman) G.; m. Norma N. Nertz, Oct. 18, 1956; children: Ronald, Richard, Joan Sandra. B.S., CCNY, 1942; A.M., Columbia U., 1950. Staff Bur. Applied Social Research, Columbia, 1946-47; news editor, research dir. TV mag., 1947-49; dir. sales planning and research DuMont TV Network, 1949-52; dep. dir. Office Research and Evaluation, U.S. Information Agy., 1952-53; exec. sec. Ultra-High Frequency TV Assn., 1953-54; cons., head research M-G Research, 1954-56; dir. research Westinghouse Broadcasting Co., 1956-62; v.p., dir. research Nat. Assn. Broadcasters, 1962-64; v.p. planning and research John Blair & Co., 1964-69; pres. Melvin A. Goldberg, Inc., N.Y.C., 1969-77; v.p. primary and social research ABC-TV, 1977-80, v.p. news, social and tech. research, 1980—; v.p. market planning, technology and social research ABC, Inc.; mem. ABA Commn. on Pub. Understanding About the Law. Mem. editorial bd. TV Quar.; Contbr. articles to profl. publs. Served as capt. USAAF, 1943-45. Decorated D.F.C., Air medal with clusters. Mem. Nat. Assn. Broadcasters, TV Bur. Advt. (chmn. research com.), Am. Assn. Pub. Opinion Research, Am. Mktg. Assn., Radio-TV Research Council, Nat. Acad. TV Arts and Scis., Am. Sociol. Soc. Home: 17 North Dr Kensington Great Neck NY 11021 Office: 1330 Ave of Americas New York NY 10019

GOLDBERG, MICHAEL, painter; b. N.Y.C., Dec. 24, 1924; s. Nathan and Henriette (Goldstein) G.; stepchildren: Lucas Matthiessen, Sarah Carey Matthiessen. Student, Art Students League, N.Y.C., 1938-42, 46; pupil of, Jose de Creeft, City Coll. N.Y., 1940-42, 46-47; student, Hofmann Sch., 1941-42, 48-50. Tchr. U. Cal. at Berkeley, 1961-62, Yale, 1967, U. Minn., 1968. One-man exhbns. include, Tibor de Nagy Gallery, N.Y.C., 1953, Poindexter Gallery, N.Y.C., 1956, 58, Martha Jackson Gallery, N.Y.C., 1960, 62, 64, 66, Paul Kantor Gallery, Los Angeles, 1960, B.C. Holland Gallery, Chgo., 1961, Galerie Anderson-Mayer, Paris, 1963, Holland-Goldowsky Gallery, Chgo., two-man, 1960, Bob Keene Gallery, 1963, Paley & Lowe Gallery, N.Y.C., 1971, 72, 73, Cunningham Ward, N.Y.C., 1975, 76, Galerie Hecate, Paris, Clock tower, N.Y.C., 1976, 77, Galerie Denise Réné, N.Y.C., 1977, Galerie Sonnabend, Paris, 1978, Galerie December, Dusseldorf, W. Ger., Young-Hoffman Gallery, Chgo., Loyse Oppenheim Gallery, Geneva, Dan Weinberg Gallery, San Francisco, Sonnabend, N.Y.C., Thomas Segal Gallery, Boston, group exhbns. include, 9th St. Exhbn., N.Y.C., 1951, Stable Gallery anns., N.Y.C., 1952-57, Four Younger Americans, Sidney Janis Gallery, N.Y.C., 1956, Martha Jackson Gallery, 1958, 60, 61, 63, 64, 65, 67, Carnegie Mus., 1958, Whitney Mus., 1958, 65, 67, 73, Gutai 9, Osaka, Japan, 1958, Turin (Italy) Art Festival, 1959, V Sao Paula (Brazil) Biennial, Documenta II, Kassel, Germany, Walker Gallery, Mpls., 1960, Am. Painters, 1960, Columbus (O.) Comtemporary Am. Painting, 1960, Hans Hofmann and His Students, Mus. Modern Art, 1963-64, Musee Cantonal des Beaux Arts, Lausanne, Switzerland, 1963, I Salon Internat. des Galeries Pilotes, Gallery Modern Art, N.Y.C., 1964, Am. Fedn. Arts, 1965, Am. Art Gallery, Copenhagen, Smithsonian Instn., 1966, Mus. Modern Art, N.Y.C., 1968, Corcoran Bienale, 1969, Rykert Gallery, N.Y.C., 1969, 70, Paula Cooper Gallery, N.Y.C., 1970, 71, Whitney Ann., 1973, Corcoran Biennial, 1977; represented in permanent collections, Mus. Modern Art, Chgo. Art Inst., Dayton Art Inst., Corcoran Gallery Art, Nat. Gallery, Walker Art Center, Balt. Mus. Art, Albright-Knox Gallery, Buffalo, Cornell U., De Cordova Mus., Whitney Mus., N.Y.C., Provincetown Chrysler Art Gallery, Guggenheim Mus., Smithsonian Instn., Mus. Modern Art, Israel, Mus. Modern Western Art, Tokyo. Served with AUS, World War II. Address: 222 Bowery Pl New York NY 10012

GOLDBERG, MICHAEL ARTHUR, land policy and planning educator; b. Bklyn., Aug. 30, 1941; s. Harold and Ruth (Abelson) G.; m. Rhoda Lynne Zacker, Dec. 22, 1963; children: Betsy Anne, Jennifer Heli. B.A. cum laude, Bklyn. Coll., 1962; M.A., U. Calif., Berkeley, 1965, Ph.D., 1968. Acting instr. Sch. Bus. Adminstrn., U. Calif., Berkeley, 1967-68; asst. prof. Faculty of Commerce and Bus. Adminstrn., U. B.C., Vancouver, 1968-71, asso. prof., 1971-76, prof., 1976—, asso. dean, 1980—, Herbert R. Fullerton prof. urban land policy, 1981—; mem. Vancouver Econ. Adv. Commn., 1980—. Author: (with P. Horwood) Zoning: Its Costs and Relevance for 1980's, 1980, The Housing Problem: A Real Crisis?, 1983; editor: Recent Perspectives in Urban Land Economics, 1976, (with P. Horwood) North American Housing Markets into the Twenty-first century, 1983. Trustee Temple Sholom, 1980—. Can. Council fellow, 1974-75; Social Scis. and Humanities Research Council fellow, 1979-80; Inst. Land Policy fellow, 1979-80. Mem. Am. Planning Assn., Am. Econ. Assn., Western Regional Sci. Assn., Regional Sci. Assn., Canadian Regional Sci. Assn., Canadian Econs. Assn., Am. Real Estate and Urban Econs. Assn. (dir. 1978—, pres. 1984), Urban Land Inst. Home: 5587 Olympic St Vancouver BC V6N 1Z4 Canada Office: Faculty of Commerce Univ British Columbia Vancouver BC V6T 1Y8 Canada *On reflection, notions of social justice have been as important as any of the guides that I have looked to in working with others and in doing my own work. Operationally, this has meant that I have attempted to deal with students, colleagues and staff in like ways treating people with a basic respect for the inherent human dignity and abhorring those of my colleagues who have treated people in a less respectful way. It has meant that I answer my mail, respond to phone calls and remain available. The cost in the short run to my work has been high at times, but all in all well worth it.*

GOLDBERG, MORTON EDWARD, pharmacologist; b. Phila., July 11, 1932; s. Herman and Ethel (Shill) G.; m. Janet Louise Werlin, Aug. 15, 1954; children—Shellie, Ellen, David. B.S., Phila. Coll. Pharmacy and Sci., 1954, M.S. in Pharmacology, 1955, D.Sc., 1958. Sr. pharmacologist Abbott Labs., North Chicago, Ill., 1958-60; asst. dir. pharmacology Union Carbide Corp., Tuxedo, N.Y., 1960-69; dir. pharmacodynamics Warner Lambert Research Inst., Morris Plains, N.J., 1969-73; dir. pharmacology Squibb Inst. Med. Research, Princeton, N.J., 1973-77; v.p. biomed. research Stuart Pharms. div. ICI Americas, Wilmington, Del., 1977—; vis. prof. toxicology Phila. Coll. Pharmacy and Sci.; vis. asso. prof. Med. Coll. Pa., Phila. Editor-in-chief: series Pharmacological and Biochemical Properties of Drug Substances; contbr. articles to profl. jours. Asst. scoutmaster Boy Scouts Am., Glenrock, N.J., 1968-72. NIH grantee, 1961-64. Fellow Acad. Pharm. Sci., AAAS; mem. Am. Soc. Pharmacology and Exptl. Therapeutics, Behavioral Pharmacology Soc., Internat. Soc. Biochem. Pharmacology, N.Y. Acad. Sci., Soc. Toxicology (charter), Sigma Xi, Rho Chi. Office: Stuart Pharms Wilmington DE 19897 *

GOLDBERG, RAY ALLAN, agribusiness educator; b. Fargo, N.D., Oct. 19, 1926; s. Max and Anne G.; m. Thelma R. Englander, May 20, 1956; children: Marc E., Jennifer E., Jeffrey L. A.B., Harvard U., 1948, M.B.A., 1950; Ph.D., U. Minn., 1952. Officer, dir. Moorhead Seed & Grain Co., Minn., 1952-62; dir. Experience, Inc., Mpls., 1963-78; chmn. bd. Agribus. Assocs., 1978—; dir. Internat. Basic Economy Corp., N.Y.C., H.K. Webster Co.; mem. faculty Harvard U. Grad. Bus. Sch., 1955—, Moffett prof. agr. and bus., 1970—, also dir. continuing edn. programs, participant seminars; dir. Pioneer Hi-Bred Internat., Inc., Sporto, All-Flow, Inc.; vis. prof. U. Minn. Grad. Sch., summer 1960; adv. council Foods Multinat., Inc., 1972-77; mem. agrl. investment com. John Hancock Ins. Co., 1971—; cons. in field, 1955—; adviser Instituto Centroamericano de Administracion de Empresa, Managua, Nicaragua, 1973—, Instituto Panamericano de Alta Direccion de Empressa, Mexico City, 1973—, U.S. Comptroller of Currency, 1975—, Food and Agr. Policy Project, Ctr. Nat. Policy, 1984—; mem. study team, subgroup chmn. world food and nutrition study NRC-Nat. Acad. Scis., 1975—; mem. com. tech. factor contbg. to nation's fgn. trade positions Nat. Acad. Engring., 1976—; chmn. agribus. adv. com. on Caribbean Basin U.S. Dept. Agr., 1982—; mem. com. on indsl. policy for developing countries Commn. on Engring. and Tech. Systems, NRC, 1982—; mem. task force on agr. Fowler-McCracken Commn., 1984—. Author numerous books, 1948—; Agribusiness Management for Developing Countries-Latin America, 1974, (with Lee F. Schrader) Farmers' Cooperatives and Federal Income Taxes, 1974, (with John T. Dunlop et. al.) The Lessons of Wage and Price Controls—The Food Sector, 1977, (with Richard C. McGinity et. al.) Agribusiness Management for Developing Countries—Southeast Asian Corn Study, 1979; editor: Research in Domestic and International Agribusiness Management, Vol. 1, 1980, Vol. 2, 1981, Vol. 3, 1982, Vol. 4, 1983; also numerous articles.; chmn. editorial adv. bd.: Jour. Agribus., 1983—. Bd. govs. Internat. Devel. Research Center, Govt. of Can., 1978—; trustee Roxbury Latin Sch., Boston, 1973-76, Beth Israel Hosp., Boston, 1978—; mem. com. on patents and tech. transfer Beth Israel Hosp., Boston, 1982—; mem. adv. com. to prep. sch. New Eng. Conservatory Music, 1974—, assoc. trustee, 1978—. Mem. Am. Agrl. Econs. Assn. (editorial council 1974-78, agribus. com. 1982—), Am. Mktg. Assn., Am. Dairy Sci. Assn., Food Distbn. Research Soc. Club: Harvard (Boston and N.Y.C.). Address: 5 Rangeley Rd Chestnut Hill MA 02167

GOLDBERG, RICHARD LEFTWICH, assn. exec.; b. Nashville, July 2, 1922; s. Albert Lewis and Gerladine (Leftwich) G.; m. Frederica Puckhaber, Mar. 18, 1947; children—Geraldine Mae, Richard Leftwich, Joan. B. Engring., Vanderbilt U., 1943. Naval architect U.S. Navy, Charleston, S.C., 1943-45; partner A.L. Goldberg & Son (bldg. materials), Nashville, 1946-52; engr. Barge, Waggoner, Sumner & Cannon, Nashville, 1952-63; asst. exec. sec. Am. Contract Bridge League, Memphis, 1963-71, exec. sec., gen. mgr., 1971—. Bd. dirs. Tam council Girl Scouts U.S.A., 1977-80. Served with USN, 1945-46. Republican. Jewish. Club: Whitehaven Rotary (pres. 1978-79). Home: 2618 Crimmins Cove Memphis TN 38119 Office: 2200 Democrat Rd Memphis TN 38116

GOLDBERG, RICHARD W., government official; b. Fargo, N.D., Sept. 23, 1927; s. Jacob H. and Frances (Gilles) G.; m. Mary Borland, Apr. 26, 1964; children: Julie, John. B.B.A., U. Miami, Fla., 1950, J.D., 1952. Bar: Fla. 1952, N.D. 1952, D.C. 1957. Pres., chief exec. officer Goldberg Feed & Grain Co.; now under sec. of Internat. Affairs and Commodity Program Dept. Agr., Washington. Served to capt. USAF, 1953-56. Office: Dept Agr 14th and Independence Ave SW Washington DC 20250 *

GOLDBERG, RITA MARIA, foreign language educator; b. N.Y.C., Oct. 1, 1933; d. Abraham Morris and Hilda (Weinman) G. B.A. (N.Y. State Regents scholar), Queens Coll., 1954; M.A., Middlebury Coll., 1955; Ph.D., Brown U., 1968. Mem. faculty Queens Coll., N.Y.C., 1956, Oberlin (Ohio) Coll., 1957; mem. faculty St. Lawrence U., Canton, N.Y., 1957—, Dana prof. modern langs., 1975—, chmn. dept., 1972-75, 83—; chmn. Regional Conf. Am. Programs in Spain, 1979-81. Author: Tonos a lo divino y a lo humano, 1981; translator: A Priest Confesses (Jose Luis Martin Descalzo), 1960; Contbr. articles to profl. jours. Spanish Ministry of Fgn. Affairs scholar, 1954-56; Danforth grantee, 1960-62, 63-64; Brown U. scholar, 1960-62. Mem. Am. Assn. Tchrs. Spanish and Portuguese, AAUP, MLA, Am. Council Teaching of Fgn. Langs., Phi Beta Kappa, Sigma Delta Pi. Roman Catholic. Home: 47 State St Canton NY 13617 Office: Dept Modern Langs and Lits St Lawrence U Canton NY 13617

GOLDBERG, SAMUEL, mathematician; b. N.Y.C., Mar. 14, 1925; s. Gedalia and Fannie (Lieberman) G.; m. Marcia Chinitz, June 21, 1953; 1 son, David. B.S., CCNY, 1944; Ph.D., Cornell U., 1950. Instr., then asst. prof. math. Lehigh U., Bethlehem, Pa., 1950-53; mem. faculty Oberlin (Ohio) Coll., 1953—, prof. math., 1961—; vis. assoc. prof. Harvard U. Grad. Sch. Bus. Adminstrn., 1959-60; vis. prof. U. W.Australia, 1976; mem. com. math. in social scis. Social Sci. Research Council, 1979; participant African Math. Project, Mombasa, Kenya, 1965, 68. Author: Probability: An Introduction, 1960 (translated into Greek, German and Spanish), Introduction to Difference Equations, 1958 (translated into Spanish, German and Japanese), Some Illustrative Examples of the Use of Undergradute Mathematics in the Social Sciences, 1977; author: Probability in Social Science, 1983. Bd. dirs. Allen Meml. Hosp., Oberlin, 1980—. Served with AUS, 1944-46. NSF sci. faculty fellow, 1960-61, 67-68. Mem. Math. Assn. Am., Am. Statis. Assn., Ops. Research Soc. Am., Soc. for Med. Decision Making, Phi Beta Kappa, Sigma Xi. Office: King Bldg Dept Math Oberlin Coll Oberlin OH 44074

GOLDBERG, SAMUEL IRVING, mathematics educator; b. Toronto, Ont., Can., Aug. 15, 1923; s. Jacob L. and Rachel (Berkovitz) G.; m. Sheila Richmond, Nov. 11, 1951; children: Julia Anna, Barry Howard, Jay Michael. Student, Cambridge (Eng.) U., 1945-46; B.A., U. Toronto, 1948, M.A., 1949, Ph.D., 1951. Sci. officer Def. Research Bd., Valcartier, Que., Can., 1951-52; asst. prof. math Lehigh U., Bethlehem, Pa., 1952-55; asso. prof. Wayne State U., Detroit, 1955-61; Harvard research fellow, 1959-60; asso. prof. U. Ill., Urbana, 1960-65, prof., 1965—; vis. prof. U. Toronto, 1968, Cambridge U., 1979, Coll. de France, 1979; Sci. Research Council vis. fgn. scientist U. Liverpool, Eng., 1973; Lady Davis fellow Technion, Israel, 1979; Queen's Quest prof. Queen's U., Can., 1980-81. Author: Curvature and Homology, 1962, (with R.L. Bishop) Tensor Analysis on Manifolds, 1968, (with W.C. Weber) Conformal Deformations of Riemannian Manifolds, 1969. Served with Can. Army, 1943-46. Recipient medal Coll. de France, 1979. Mem. Am. Math. Soc. Home: 24 Greencroft Dr Champaign IL 61820 Office: Dept Math U Ill Urbana IL 61801

GOLDBERG, SEYMOUR, mathematics educator; b. Bklyn., Mar. 24, 1928; s. Benjamin and Florence (Cohen) G.; m. Lillian E. Slominsky, Mar. 29, 1952; children: Florence Gail, Benjamin Frederick. A.B., Hunter Coll., 1950; M.A., Ohio State U., 1952; Ph.D., UCLA, 1958. Math. analyst Lockheed Aircraft Co., 1952-54; asst. prof. N.Mex. State U., 1959-62; faculty U. Md., College Park, 1962—, prof. math., 1966—; Cons. to industry. Author: Unbounded Linear Operators, 1966, (with I. Gohberg) Basic Operator Theory, 1981; contbr. papers to profl. lit. Served with AUS, 1945-47. Charles Brown fellow Hebrew U. Jerusalem, 1958. Mem. Am. Math. Soc., Math. Assn. Am., Phi Beta Kappa. Home: 1612 Peacock Ln Silver Spring MD 20904 Office: Math Dept Univ Md College Park MD 20742

GOLDBERG, SID, editor; b. N.Y.C., Mar. 1, 1931; s. Emanuel and Florence (Fischbein) G.; m. Lucianne S. Cummings, April 10, 1966; children: Joshua John, Jonah Jacob. B.A., U. Mich., 1950, M.A., 1952; student, N.Y. U., 1952-53. Editorial asst. Washington Post & Times Herald, 1955-56; fgn. affairs editor World Week mag., N.Y.C., 1955-57; asst. editor North Am. Newspaper Alliance, 1957-58, news editor, 1958-60, editor, 1960—, gen. mgr., v.p., 1964—; editor Women's News Service, 1964-81; pres. N.Am. Newspaper Alliance, Inc., Bell-McClure Syndicate, 1972, exec. editor, 1973-81; gen. exec. United Feature Syndicate, 1973, mng. editor, 1974-78, v.p., exec. editor, 1978—, Newspaper Enterprise Assn., 1979—; exec. editor Ind. News Alliance, 1980—. Served with AUS, 1953-55. Mem. Nat. Cartoonists Soc., Soc. of Silurians, Sigma Delta Chi. Clubs: Overseas Press Am., Dutch Treat, Hudson Harbor Yacht (N.Y.C.). Home: 255 W 84th St New York NY 10024 Office: 200 Park Ave New York NY 10166

GOLDBERG, STANLEY ROBERT, bus. exec.; b. N.Y.C., Apr. 12, 1931; s. Max M. and Rae (Getansky) G.; m. Harriet B. Motzkin, Aug. 3, 1958; children—Donald Jay, Peter Daniel. B.S., N.Y. U., 1956. Sr. acct. Coopers & Lybrand, N.Y.C., 1956-60; asst. comptroller Ancorp Nat. Services, Inc., N.Y.C., 1960-63; controller Pancake Kitchens, Inc., N.Y.C., 1963-64; corporate controller J.R. McMullen Co., Inc., N.Y.C., 1964-66; treas. Seagrave Corp., N.Y.C., 1966-72; pres., dir. Allegri-Tech, Inc., Nutley, N.J., 1972-74; partner, exec. dir. Hampshire Assos., 1975—, Hampshire Agy., 1975—, X-Mate Planning Co., 1977—, Execuplan Co., 1977—; guest lectr. Grad. Sch., Poly. Inst. Bklyn., Am. Mgmt. Assn.; dir. Gen. Glass Imports, Ltd., Vista Chem. & Fiber Products, Inc., SVE Corp., Collagen Internat. Products Corp., Fabricated Equipment Corp. Treas. Voice of Community Affairs League, Great Neck, N.Y., 1968-69; dir. Nassau County Grand Jurors Assn., pres., 1974-77; mem. adv. council Nassau County Bd. Coop. Edn. Services, 1979—. Served with AUS, 1952-54. Mem. Nat. Assn. Accountants (dir. N.Y. chpt. 1956-68, past v.p.), Financial Execs. Inst., Am. Mgmt. Assn., N.Y. Credit and Fin. Mgmt. Assn., Fedn. Grand Juror Assns. N.Y. State (v.p. 1979-81, pres. 1981—, dir. 1978—), Beta Alpha Psi. Clubs: K.P., New York Univ. (founder). Home: 56 Piccadilly Rd Great Neck NY 11023 Office: 33 Great Neck Rd Great Neck NY 11021

GOLDBERG, VICTOR JOEL, data processing co. exec.; b. Chgo., Oct. 19, 1933; s. Albert J. and Ruth R. (Rosenberg) G.; m. Harriet A. David, June 1, 1958; children—Susan A., Alan J. B.S., Northwestern U., 1955, M.B.A., 1956. With IBM Corp., 1959—, corp. dir. bus. plans, 1977-78, v.p. communications, Armonk, N.Y., 1979-81, corp. v.p., pres. communication products div., 1981—. Bd. govs. Westchester chpt. Am. Jewish Com., 1976—; trustee Inst. Internat. Edn., 1979—. Served with U.S. Army, 1956-59. Mem. Beta Gamma Sigma. Office: IBM Corp Old Orchard Rd Armonk NY 10504

GOLDBERGER, ARTHUR STANLEY, economics educator; b. N.Y.C., Nov. 20, 1930; s. David M. and Martha (Greenwald) G.; m. Iefke Engelsman, Aug. 19, 1957; children: Nina Judith, Nicholas Bernard. B.S., N.Y.U., 1951; M.A., U. Mich., 1952, Ph.D., 1958. Acting asst. prof. econs. Stanford U., 1956-59; assoc. prof. econs. U. Wis., 1960- 63, prof., 1963-70, H.M. Groves prof., 1970-79, Vilas research prof., 1979—; vis. prof. Center Planning and Econ. Research, Athens, Greece, 1964-65; Keynes vis. prof. U. Essex, 1968- 69. Author: (with L.R. Klein) An Econometric Model of the United States, 1929-52, 1955, Impact Multipliers and Dynamic Properties, 1959, Econometric Theory, 1964, Topics in Regression Analysis, 1968; Editor: (with O.D. Duncan) Structural Equation Models in the Social Sciences, 1973, (with D.J. Aigner) Latent Variables in Socioeconomic Models, 1976; Assoc. editor: Jour. Econometrics, 1973-77; bd. editors: Am. Econ. Rev, 1964-66, Jour. Econ. Lit, 1975-77. Fulbright fellow Netherlands Sch. Econs., 1955-56, 59-60; vis. prof. U. Hawaii, 1969, 71; fellow Center for Advanced Study in Behavioral Scis., Stanford, 1976-77, 80-81; Guggenheim fellow Stanford U., 1972-73. Fellow Am. Statis. Assn., Econometric Soc. (council 1975-80), Am. Acad. Arts and Scis., AAAS; mem. Am. Econ. Assn. Home: 2828 Sylvan Ave Madison WI 53705 Office: U Wis Dept Econs Madison WI 53706

GOLDBERGER, EDWARD, bus. exec.; b. Providence, Nov. 15, 1905; s. Samuel and Bertha (Steiner) G.; m. Marjorie A. Lowenstein, Dec. 19, 1935; children—Ann G. Jurdem, Susan G. Jacoby. A.B., Brown U., 1927; J.D., Harvard U., 1931. Bar: R.I. bar 1931, N.Y. bar 1938. Practiced with McGovern & Slattery, Providence, 1931-36; with M. Lowenstein Corp., Inc., N.Y.C., 1936—, sec., 1936-70, treas., 1945-74, vice chmn., 1970—; Mem. exec. com, textile sect. N.Y. Bd. Trade, 1949-72, chmn., 1951; mem. fgn. trade com. Am. Cotton Mfrs. Inst., 1969-72; dir. Textile Distbrs. Assn., 1962-65, Am. Textile Mfrs. Inst., 1961-64, 70-72. Mem. nat. commn., N.Y. exec. Anti-Defamation League, B'nai B'rith. Clubs: Metropolis Country (White Plains, N.Y.); City Athletic, Brown U.; Fairview Country (Greenwich, Conn.). Home: 30 E 71st St New York NY 10021 also 1367 Flagler Dr Mamaroneck NY 10543 also 2730 S Ocean Blvd Palm Beach FL 33480 Office: 1430 Broadway New York NY 10018

GOLDBERGER, MARVIN L., educator, physicist, institute technology president; b. Chgo., Oct. 22, 1922; s. Joseph and Mildred (Sedwitz) G.; m. Mildred Ginsburg, Nov. 25, 1945; children: Samuel M., Joel S. B.S., Carnegie Inst. Tech., 1943; Ph.D., U. Chgo., 1948. Research asso. Radiation Lab., U. Calif., 1948-49; research asso. Mass. Inst. Tech., 1949-50; asst.-asso. prof. U. Chgo., 1950-55, prof., 1955-57; Higgins prof. physics Princeton U., 1953-54, 57-78, chmn. dept., 1970-76, Joseph Henry prof. physics, 1977-78; pres. Calif. Inst. Tech., Pasadena, 1978—; Mem. President's Sci. Adv. Com., 1965-69; Chmn. Fedn. Am. Scientists, 1971-73; dir. Gen. Motors Corp., Haskel, Inc., Interactive Systems Corp. Fellow Am. Phys. Soc., Am. Acad. Arts and Scis.; mem. Nat. Acad. Scis., Am. Philos. Soc., Council on Fgn. Relations. Club: Princeton (N.Y.C.). Home: 415 S Hill Ave Pasadena CA 91106

GOLDBLATT, MARVIN ELIJAH, diversified manufacturing corporation executive; b. Hamilton, Ont., Canada, 1922. Grad., Western U., 1943. Pres. Intermetco Ltd., Hamilton. Office: Intermetco Ltd 1 James St North Hamilton ON Canada L8R 2K3 *

GOLDBLATT, STANFORD JAY, lawyer; b. Chgo., Feb. 25, 1939; s. Maurice and Bernice (Mendelson) G.; m. Ann Dudley Cronkhite, June 17, 1968; children: Alexandra, Nathaniel, Jeremy. B.A. magna cum laude, Harvard U., 1960, LL.B. (magna cum laude), 1963. Bar: Ill. 1963. Law clk. U.S. Ct. Appeals, 5th Jud. Circuit, New Orleans, 1963-64; mem. firm Winston & Strawn, Chgo., 1964-67; v.p. Goldblatt Bros., Inc., Chgo., 1967-76, pres., chief exec. officer, 1976-77, chmn. exec. com., 1977-78; ptnr. Hopkins & Sutter, 1978—. Trustee U. Chgo., U. Chgo. Cancer Research Found., Newberry Library. Clubs: Economic, Standard. Office: Suite 4300 Three First Nat Plaza Chicago IL 60602 *

GOLDBLITH, SAMUEL ABRAHAM, food science educator; b. Lawrence, Mass., May 5, 1919; s. Abraham and Fannie (Rubin) G.; m. Diana Greenberg, Apr. 27, 1941; children: Errol (dec.), Judith Ann, Jonathan Mark. S.B., Mass. Inst. Tech., 1940, S.M., 1947, Ph.D., 1949. Research Arthur D. Little Co., Cambridge, Mass., 1940-41; faculty Mass. Inst. Tech., 1949—, prof. food tech., 1959-74, Underwood Prescott prof. food sci., 1974-78, acting head dept., 1959-61, exec. officer dept., 1961-66, dep. dept. head, 1967-72, asso. dept. head, 1972-74, dir. indsl. liaison, 1974-78, prof. food sci., v.p., 1978—; Mem. coms. radiation preservation and radionuclides in foods, chmn. com. radiation preservation of foods NRC-Nat. Acad. Scis.; Dir. Mchts. Cold Storage and Warehouse Co., Providence, Florasynth Co., Ionics, Inc., High Voltage Engrng. Corp. Author: An Introduction to Thermal Processing of Foods, 1961, Milestones in Nutrition, 1964—, Annotated Bibliography on Microwaves In Food Preservations, Freeze Drying and Advanced Food Technology, 1975; also numerous sci. papers. Vice chmn., pub. trustee Nutrition Found. Served to capt. AUS, 1941-46; PTO. Decorated Silver Star medal, Bronze Star with oak leaf cluster, Order of Sacred Treasure 2d class (Japan); named One of Ten Outstanding Young Men of Greater Boston, 1953; recipient Babcock-Hart award, 1969; Nicholas Appert medal, 1970. Fellow Inst. Food Technologists (chmn. N.E. sect. 1958, Monsanto Presentation award 1953, Distinguished Food Scientist award N.Y. sect. 1969, Phila. sect. 1976), Inst. Food Sci. and Tech. (U.K.), AAAS; mem. Am. Chem. Soc., Am. Inst. Nutrition, Sigma Xi, Phi Tau Sigma (pres. 1958). Clubs: Cosmos (Washington); Univ. (N.Y.C.); St. Botolph, New Century (Boston) (pres. 1962-63). Lodge: Masons. Home: 6 Meadowview Rd Melrose MA 02176 Office: Mass Inst Tech 77 Massachusetts Ave Cambridge MA 02139 *My participation in the defense of the Philippines and survival of the "Bataan Death March" and subsequent events led me to my choice of graduate study and further research and teaching at M.I.T. in food science and technology. The results of this professional career have led me into close relationship and friendship with a number of Japanese and postdoctoral students and have helped build bridges of friendship among us.*

GOLDBLOOM, RICHARD BALLON, pediatrics educator; b. Montreal, Que., Can., Dec. 16, 1924; s. Alton and Annie Esther (Ballon) G.; m. Ruth Miriam Schwartz, June 25, 1946; children—Alan L., Barbara Issenman, David S. B.Sc., McGill U., 1945, M.D., C.M., 1949, diploma in pediatrics, 1953, cert., Royal Coll. Physicians and Surgeons, Can., 1954. Intern Royal Victoria Hosp., Montreal, 1949-50, Montreal Children's Hosp., 1950-51; resident Children's Hosp., Boston, 1951-52; teaching fellow dept. pediatrics Harvard U., 1951-52; chief resident Montreal Children's Hosp., 1952-53, asst. physician dept. medicine, 1957, physician, 1964-67, asso. dept. metabolism, 1964-67; Hosmer teaching fellow dept. pediatrics McGill U., 1953-56, demonstrator, 1957, asso. prof., 1964-67; prof., head dept. pediatrics Dalhousie U., Halifax, N.S., Can., 1967—; physician in chief, dir. research Izaak Walton Killam Hosp. for Children, Halifax, 1967—; cons. staff St. John Regional Hosp., N.S. Rehab. Centre; lectr. in field. Contbr. numerous articles to profl. jours. Bd. dirs. Atlantic Symphony Orch., 1969-73, hon. dir., 1973-75, v.p., 1975-76, pres., 1976-79; chmn. med. adv. com. Can. Cystic Fibrosis Found., 1969-72; dir. Atlantic Research Centre for Mental Retardation, 1967-75, 75—; bd. dirs. Opera East, 1974, Bonny Lea Farm, N.S. Festival of Arts; trustee Queen Elizabeth II Fund for Research in Diseases of Children; bd. dirs. Muscular Dystrophy Assn. Can. Recipient Queen's Jubilee medal, 1978. Mem. Soc. Pediatric Research, Can. Soc. Clin. Investigation, Am. Pediatric Soc., Assn. Med. Sch. Pediatric Dept. Chmn., Can. Pediatric Soc. (v. p. 1983—), Am. Acad. Pediatrics, Can. Assn. Pediatric Hosps., Can. Med. Assn., Halifax Med. Soc., Alpha Omega Alpha. Jewish. Clubs: Royal N.S. Yacht Squadron, Saraguay. Office: 5850 University Ave Halifax NS B3J 3G9 Canada

GOLDE, DAVID WILLIAM, physician, educator; b. N.Y.C., Oct. 23, 1940. B.S. in Chemistry, Fairleigh Dickinson U., 1962; M.D., McGill U., 1966. Diplomate: Am Bd. Internal Medicine, Am. Bd. Med. Oncology, Nat. Bd. Med. Examiners. Asst. research chemist Gen. Foods Corp., 1962; research and clin. fellow in cardiology San Juan de Dios Hosp. (San Jose, Costa Rica, summer 1963, 64, 65); intern. U. Calif. Hosps., San Francisco, 1966-67, resident in medicine, 1970-71, fellow Cancer Research Inst., 1971-72; staff cons. continuing edn. and tng. br. div. regional med. program (NIH), 1967-68; hematology fellow, resident in clin. pathology NIH, 1969-70; instr. medicine U. Calif., San Francisco, 1972-73, asst. prof., 1973-74; asst. prof. medicine UCLA, 1974-75, assoc. prof., 1975-79, prof., 1979—; co-dir. Clin. Research Ctr. (UCLA), 1974—; chief div. hematology-oncology UCLA, 1981—. Mem. editorial bd.: Leukemia Research, 1977, Blood, 1978, Peptides, 1979-83, Stem Cells, 1980, Leukemia Revs., 1981; contbr. numerous articles to profl. jours. Served with USPHS, 1967-70. N.J. Coll. Surgeons Med. scholar, 1963-65. Mem. Am. Assn. Cancer Research, AAAS, ACP; MEM. Am. Fedn. Clin. Research; mem. Am. Soc. Clin. Investigation, Am. Soc. Clin. Oncology, Am. Soc. Hematology, Internat. Assn. Comparative Research on Leukemia and Related Diseases, Internat. Soc. Exptl. Hematology, Reticuloendothelial Soc., Soc. Exptl. Biology and Medicine, Western Soc. Clin. Research, Phi Omega Epsilon, Alpha Omega Alpha. Home: 251 Beloit Ave Los Angeles CA 90049

GOLDEN, ALFRED LOWELL, writer, marketing consultant; b. Pitts., May 28, 1909; s. Benjamin and Rose (Kendall) G.; m. Dorothy Maret, May 26, 1934; children: Harvey Paul, Vickie Ann. B.A. in Psychology, U. Pitts., 1931, M.A., 1935. Psychol. researcher Western State Penitentiary, Pitts., 1930-31, criminologist, 1934-43; head dept. criminology Allegheny County Prison, Pa., 1934-35; spl. investigtor Allegheny County Quar.Sessions Ct., Pitts., 1935-36; screenwriter, playwrwight, freelance writer, N.Y.C., 1934—, dir., 1934-47; assoc. prof. speech and drama Duquesne U., 1938-41; tchr. pub. relations CCNY, 1945-46, New Sch. Social Research, 1947-49; prof. playwriting, lectr. UCLA, 1967-68; founder, dir. Blue Cross and Blue Shield, 1933-57; v.p. pub. relations Beneficial Standard Life Ins. co.; pres. Mass. Mktg. Council, Inc., Los Angeles, 1976-78, chmn., 1978—; founder, pres. Direct Mktg. Corp. Am., 1968-76, Direct Mktg. Internat., 1975-79; chmn. Super Market Media, Inc., 1976—. Author: plays The Female of the Species, 1935, A Young Man's Fancy, 1947, Mimie Scheller, 1936, Lady Behave!, 1943, Collectors Item, 1951; screenplays One Mile From Heaven, 1936, Born Reckless, 1937, The Hughes Mystery, 1977. Dir. nat. exec. bd. Boy Scouts Am. Mem. Dramatists Guild, Pub. Relations Soc. Am., Money Mgmt. Council (founder). Home: 3541 E Oaks Dr Salt Lake City UT 84117

GOLDEN, CHARLES FRANKLIN, bishop; b. Holly Springs, Miss., Aug. 24, 1912; s. J.W. and Mary P. (Tyson) G.; m. Ida Elizabeth Smith, May 24, 1937. A.B., Clark Coll., Atlanta, 1936; B.D., Gammon Theol. Sem., 1937, D.D., 1958; S.T.M., Boston U., 1938, postgrad., 1946-47; LL.D., W.Va., Wesleyan Coll., 1964; D.D., Rust Coll., 1974. Ordained to deacon Meth. Ch., 1934, elder, 1938; asst. pastor, Birmingham, Ala., Atlanta, Cooksville, Tenn., Clarkdale, Miss., 1935-41; dir. field service, dept. Negro work Meth. Bd. Missions, 1947-52; asso. sec. nat. div. Bd. Missions, 1952-56, dir. nat. div., 1956-60; bishop, Nashville-Birmingham area, Nashville-Carolina area, 1960-68, San Francisco area, 1968-72, Los Angeles area, 1972—; ofcl. rep. World Div. Bd. Missions to India Centennial, Lucknow, India, 1956; mem. gen. bd. missions Meth. Ch.; sec. Central Jurisdiction Coll. Bishops, pres., 1967, Bd. Christian Social Concerns, United Meth. Ch., 1968-72; vice chmn. Commn. on Religion and Race, 1968-72, mem. program council, 1968-72; chmn. div. peace and world order Bd. Christian Concerns of Meth. Ch., 1964-68; chmn. joint com. on missionary personnel Bd. Missions of Meth. Ch., 1964-68; Meth. rep. to central com. World Council of Chs., Enugo, Nigeria, West Africa, 1965; Council Bishops rep. Iglesia Evangelica Metodisto de Costa Rica, 1973; chmn. dept. renewal, life and mission div. Nat. Council of Chs. of U.S.A., 1967-68; Mem. Bd. Higher Edn., and Ordained Ministry, 1972—; mem. governing bd. Nat. Council Chs., 1972—; pres. Council Bishops United Meth. Ch., 1973-74. Contbr. articles to religious publs. Pres. bd. trustees Gammon Theol. Sem., 1968—; mem. Bennett Coll., 1964-70, Scarrit Coll., 1964-70, Morristown Coll., 1962-68, Pacific Sch. Religion, 1969-72; regent U. of Pacific, 1969—; bd. mgrs. Bd. of Missions, 1960-72; Sec. Little Rock Interdenominational Ministers Alliance, 1939-42. Served to capt., Chaplians Corps AUS, 1942-46. Mem. Meth. Rural Fellowship (sec. 1952-56), Omega Psi Phi, Sigma Pi Phi. *

GOLDEN, CHRISTOPHER ANTHONY, lawyer; b. N.Y.C., Sept. 24, 1937; s. Christopher A. and Helen (Foley) G.; m. Maureen A. Fitzpatrick, May 30, 1964; children: Colleen, Laureen. B.A., St. John's Coll., 1955; LL.B., St. John's U., 1967, M.B.A., 1977. Bar: N.Y. 1967, U.S. Dist. Ct. (so. and ea. dist.) N.Y. 1969, U.S. Ct. Appeals (2d cir.) 1969, U.S. Supreme Ct. 1974. Mem. firm Food, Conway, Walsh, Stahl & Farrell, N.Y.C., 1964-77; asst. gen. counsel Dry Dock Savs. Bank, N.Y.C., 1977-82, counsel, 1982—; ptnr. Golden & Upton, P.C., Lynbrook, N.Y., 1982. Served with U.S. Army, 1960-61. Mem. ABA, N.Y. Bar Assn. Office: 300 Merrick Rd 4th Floor Lynbrook NY 11563

GOLDEN, DAVID AARON, communications company executive; b. Sinclair, Man., Can., Feb. 22, 1920; s. Solomon Wilfred and Rose (Pearlman) G.; m. Molly Berger, Sept. 9, 1946; children: Mark, Peter, Sari (dec.). LL.B., U. Man., 1941, Oxford U., 1941; LL.D. (hon.), Carleton U., Ottawa, Can., 1975. Dep. minister def. prodn. Govt. of Can., 1954-62, dep. minister industry, 1963-64; pres. Air Industries Assn. Can., 1962-63; 64-69; pres., chief exec. officer Telesat Can., Ottawa, 1969-80, chmn. bd., 1980—; dir. Atomic Energy Can., Ltd., Pratt and Whitney Can. Inc., Provigo Inc., D.S. Fraser Equipment Inc. Chmn. bd. Parliamentary Center Fgn. Affairs and Fgn. Trade; mem. Ottawa adv. bd. Royal Trust Co.; former chmn. bd. govs. Carleton U.; former pres. Canadian Inst. Internat. Affairs.; bd. dirs. Conf. Bd. Can., Conf. Bd. Inc. Served to capt. Canadian Army, 1941-45. Decorated officer Order of Can. Mem. Canadian Aeros. and Space Inst. Jewish. Clubs: Rideau, Le Cercle Universitaire d'Ottawa. Office: Telesat Canada 333 River Rd Ottawa ON Canada K1L 8B9

GOLDEN, HAWKINS, lawyer; b. Morton, Miss., June 24, 1905; s. John J. and Mary Elizabeth (Hawkins) G.; m. Margaret Jackson, Feb. 25, 1939; children—Margaret, Hawkins. B.A., Vanderbilt U., 1926; M.A., Harvard, 1927; J.D., So. Methodist, U., 1930. Bar: Aditted to Tex. bar 1930. Practiced in, Dallas, 1930—; mem. firm Leake, Henry, Young & Golden, 1932-47; sr. partner Leake, Henry, Golden & Burrow, 1947-59, Leake, Henry, Golden, Burrow & Potts, 1959-66, Golden, Potts, Boeckman & Wilson, 1966—. Mem. Dallas Hosp. Found.; research fellow Southwestern Legal Found.; Organizing dir. Dallas Crime Commn.; bd. rev. Judge Adv. Gen. Dept., World War II; Bd. devel. So. Meth. U. Mem. SAR, ABA, Tex. Bar Assn., Dallas Bar Assn. (pres. 1950, chmn. 1952), Phi Beta Kappa, Sigma Chi, Delta Theta Phi. Methodist (chmn. ofcl. bd. 1955). Clubs: Mason (Shriner, Jester, 32), Dallas Country, Salesmanship, Idlewild, Terpsichorean, Calyx, Rotary (pres. 1955-56), Knife and Fork (pres. 1958-60), Press (Dallas)). Home: 8931 Preston Rd Dallas TX 75225 Office: Republic Nat Bank Tower Dallas TX 75201

GOLDEN, JEROME BENJAMIN, lawyer, corp. exec.; b. N.Y.C., Nov. 26, 1917; s. Morris and Ida (Burke) G.; m. Rosamond Lukin, Sept. 7, 1947 (dec. Feb. 1965); children—Mark D., Dean P. Student, Coll. City N.Y., 1938; LL.B., St. Lawrence U., Canton, N.Y., 1942. Bar: N.Y. bar 1942. Mem. legal dept. Paramount Pictures, Inc., 1942-50, United Paramount Theatres, Inc., 1950-53; with Am. Broadcasting-Paramount Theatres, Inc. (now Am. Broadcasting Cos., Inc.), N.Y.C., 1953—, sec., 1958—, v.p., 1959—. Home: 400 E 56th St New York City NY 10022 Office: 1330 Ave of the Americas New York City NY 10019

GOLDEN, LEON, classics educator; b. Jersey City, Dec. 25, 1930; s. Nathan and Regina (Okun) G. B.A., U. Chgo., 1950, M.A., 1953, Ph.D., 1958. Instr. ancient langs. Coll. William and Mary, 1958-60, asst. prof. ancient langs., 1960- 65; assoc. prof. classical langs. Fla. State U., 1965-68, prof., 1968—, dir. program in humanities, 1976—; bd. dirs. Fla. Endowment for Humanities, 1983—. Author: In Praise of Prometheus: Humanism and Rationalism in Aeschylean Thought, 1966, (with O.B. Hardison Jr.) Aristotle's Poetics, 1968. Served with AUS, 1953-55. Fellow coop. program humanities U.N.C. and Duke, 1964-65, Soc. for Religion in Higher Edn., 1971-72. Mem. Am. Philol. Assn., Archeol. Inst. Am., Classical Assn. Middle West and South (pres. So. sect. 1972-74), Am. Soc. Aesthetics, Phi Beta Kappa. Office: Dept of Classics Florida State U Tallahassee FL 32306

GOLDEN, MAX, lawyer, manufacturing company executive; b. Passaic, N.J., Feb. 18, 1913; s. Jacob and Pauline (Kitaeff) G.; m. Hannah G. Gleicher, Sept. 14, 1940; children: David, Jeffrey, Paul. Student, N.Y.U., 1931, Dana Coll., 1932; LL.B. magna cum laude, Rutgers U., 1935. Bar: N.J. bar 1936. Practice of law, 1936-41; atty. legal div. office chief ordnance Dept. Army, 1941-48; asst., then asso. gen. counsel procurement office sec. USAF, 1948-51, dep. for procurement and material programs under sec., 1952, dep. to asst. sec. materiel, 1953-57, dep. asst. sec. materiel, 1957-58; gen. counsel Dept. Air Force, 1958-62; asst. to pres. Gen. Dynamics Corp., 1963-64, v.p., 1964-78; partner McKenna, Conner & Cuneo, Washington, 1979-80, of counsel, 1980—. Recipient exceptional civilian service award Dept. Air Force; Nat. Civil Service League award, 1961; Disting. Civilian Service award Dept. Def., 1963. Mem. Am. Bar Assn., Fed. Bar Assn. Home: 1515 S Jefferson Davis Arlington VA 22202 Office: 1575 I St NW Washington DC 20005

GOLDEN, MILTON M., paint company executive; b. Chgo., Apr. 24, 1915; s. Elias and Lena (Shapiro) G.; m. Sylvia M. Persin, June 6, 1937; children: Sharlene (Mrs. Sy Lauretz), Beverly (Mrs. Mark Fienberg), Jeffry. B.S., Roosevelt U., Chgo., 1939. Chemist, tech. dir., supt., mgr. sales mfg. Capitol Chem. Co., Chgo., 1941-57; mgr. Maj. Paint div. Standard Brands Paint Co., Torrance, Calif., 1957-61, corp. v.p. mfg., 1961-81, sr. v.p., 1981—; dir. Britt Electronic Corp., 1972-73. Sec. Intra-Sci. Research Found., 1973-74, chmn., 1974-76, chmn. exec. com., dir., 1977—, also trustee; chmn. paint, plastic and chem. div. Los Angeles United Jewish Welfare Fund, 1970, 74, 75, mem. paints, plastics and petroleum cabinet, 1976-77, co-chmn. paints, plastics and petroleum div., 1978, co-chmn. paints, plastics, petroleum, and chems. div., 1979. Recipient Louis Pasteur Humanitarian award, 1975; Recipient Ike Sinaiko Humanitarian award, 1981. Mem. Am. Chem. Soc., Nat. Paint and Coatings Assn. (dir. 1980—), Calif. Paint and Coatings Assn. (exec. com., sec.-treas. 1981, v.p. 1982-83, pres. 1983-84), AAAS. Home: 1531 Camden Ave Los Angeles CA 90025 Office: 4300 W 190th St Torrance CA 90509

GOLDEN, MORLEY ROBERT, contractor; b. San Diego, May 18, 1942; s. Robert Morley and Dorothy Isabel (Cubberley) G.; children: Brian Morley, Jill Suzanne. Student, Stanford U., San Diego State U. Project mgr. M.H. Golden Co., San Diego, 1962-72, v.p., 1972-74, exec. v.p., 1974-76, pres., 1976—; dir. First Nat. Bank, San Diego. Chmn. San Diego Children's Hosp; chmn. adv. bd. KPBS, San Diego. Mem. Associated Gen. Contractors (dir. 1978-84), Young Pres. Orgn., San Diego C. of C. (dir.). Home: 1161 Pacific Beach Dr San Diego CA 92109 Office: MH Golden Co 123 Camino de la Reina San Diego CA 92108

GOLDEN, ROBERT MORLEY, business executive; b. Salt Lake City, Sept. 18, 1920; s. Morley Hiref and Agnes (Hughes) G.; m. Dorothy Cubberley, Sept. 13, 1941 (div.); children: Morley R., Marilyn Golden Kelly; m. Consuelo Marie Kintop, June 16, 1974. A.B., Stanford U., 1941. Pres. M.H. Golden Co., San Diego, 1954-76, chmn., 1976-82, Silvergate Corp., 1982—. Served with U.S. Army, 1944-46. Club: San Diego Yacht. Office: Silvergate Corp PO Box 84688 San Diego CA 92138

GOLDEN, SIDNEY, educator, chemist; b. Boston, June 23, 1917; s. Harry and Fannie (Sher) G.; m. Muriel Nirenberg, Aug. 24, 1941; children: Harriet Rachel, Nancy Sue. B.S., Coll. City N.Y., 1938; student, Purdue U., 1940-42; Ph.D., Harvard U., 1948. Research supr. sect. H div. 3 Nat. Def. Research Com., George Washington U., 1942-46; phys. chemist Hydrocarbon Research, Inc., N.Y.C., 1948-51; adj. instr. Poly. Inst. Bklyn., 1949-50; mem. faculty Brandeis U., Waltham, Mass., 1951—, prof. chemistry, 1959-81, emeritus prof., 1981—; vis. prof. U. Calif., Berkeley, 1963, Hebrew U., Jerusalem, 1967-68, 74-75; exchange prof. Université de Paris-Sud at Orsay, 1975; cons. Nat. Bur. Standards, 1957-61. Author: Introduction to Theoretical Physical Chemistry, 1961, Elements of Theory of Gases, 1964, Quantum Statistical Foundations of Chemical Kinetics, 1969, General University Chemistry: A Developmental Approach, 1975; also articles. NRC predoctoral fellow, 1946-48; recipient Presdl. Certificate of Merit, 1948; Fulbright sr. scholar Cambridge (Eng.) U., 1959-60; Guggenheim fellow, 1959-60; Weizmann sr. fellow, 1974-75. Fellow Am. Acad. Arts and Scis. (emeritus), Am. Phys. Soc. (emeritus); mem. Am. Chem. Soc. (emeritus;, vis. scientist 1963-68)

GOLDEN, SOMA SUZANNE, journalist; b. Washington, Aug. 27, 1939; d. Benjamin Earl and Dita Edith (Seiden) G.; m. William Alexander Behr, Nov. 28, 1974; children: Ariel, Zachary. B.A., Radcliffe Coll., 1961; M.S., Columbia U., 1962. Asst. econs. editor Bus. Week mag., N.Y.C., 1962-69; econ. and writing cons. Tahal, Inc., Tel Aviv, 1969-70; assoc. in journalism Columbia U. Grad. Sch. Journalism, 1970—, lectr. journalism, 1976-77, dir. Walter F. Bagehot fellowship program for econs. and bus. journalism, 1976-77; asst. to pres. Nat. Bur. Econ. Research, N.Y.C., 1970-71; econs. corr. McGraw-Hill World News Bur., Washington, 1971-73; econs. reporter New York Times, 1973-77, mem. editorial bd., 1977-82; Sunday fin. editor, 1982—. Recipient Stanford Profl. Journalism fellowship, 1966-67; Pub.'s award N.Y. Times, 1974. Office: NY Times 229 W 43d St New York NY 10036

GOLDEN, WILLIAM LEE, singer, member vocal group; b. Brewton, Ala., Jan. 12, 1939; s. Luke and Ruth Mae (Morgan) G.; children: William Lee, Craig, Christopher. Mgr. The Boys Band (soft rock group.). Singer, mem. several gospel groups, until 1964; chmn. bd., baritone, partner, Oak Ridge Boys, 1964—. Recipient 4 Grammy awards; 12 Dove awards Gospel Music Assn.; named Vocal Group of Year, Country Music Assn.; Gold record for American Made, 1983. Mem. Country Music Assn., Gospel Music Assn., AFTRA, Nat. Acad. Rec. Arts and Scis., Acad. Country Music. Office: care Jim Halsey Co Inc 3225 S Norwood Tulsa OK 74135 *

GOLDEN, WILLIAM THEODORE, corporate director and trustee; b. N.Y.C., Oct. 25, 1909; s. S. Herbert and Rebecca (Harris) G.; m. Sibyl Levy, May 2, 1938; children: Sibyl Rebecca, Pamela Prudence. A.B., U. Pa., 1930, LL.D. (hon.), 1979; postgrad., Harvard Grad. Sch. Bus. Adminstrn., 1930-31; D.Sc. (hon.), Poly. Inst. N.Y., 1975; M.A., Columbia U., 1979. Bar: Lic. amateur radio operator. Asst. to pres. Cornell, Linder & Co. (indsl. and fin. mgmt.), N.Y.C., 1931-34; with Carl M. Loeb & Co. and Carl M. Loeb, Rhoades & Co. (investment brokers and bankers), 1934-41; asst. to commr. AEC, 1946-50, cons., 1950-58; spl. cons. to Pres. Truman to rev. govt. sci. activities, 1950-51; (led to creation Pres.'s Sci. Adv. Com.); adviser to dir. Bur. Budget on orgn. NSF, 1950-51; mem. mil. procurement task force Commn. on Orgn. Exec. Br. Govt. (Hoover Commn.), 1954-55; mem. State Dept.'s Adv. Com. on Pvt. Enterprise in Fgn. Aid, 1964-65, Nat. Acad. Pub. Adminstrn. adv. panel on space transp. ops. to NASA, 1976-77; chmn. bd. Nat. U.S. Radiator Co. (and successor cos.), 1952-74; dir. Crowell, Collier & Macmillan, Inc., 1964-71, Verde Exploration, Ltd., 1946—, Gen. Am. Investors Co., Inc., 1961—, Block Drug Co., Inc., 1970—; chmn. trustees City Univ. Constrn. Fund, 1967-71; trustee Mitre Corp., 1958-72, 76—, System Devel. Corp., 1957-66, chmn., 1961-66; mem. Mayor's Commn. on Delivery Personal Health Services (Piel Commn.), 1966-68; mem. council Rockefeller U., 1978—; mem. adv. panel U.S. Postal Service, 1981-83; adv. council Sch. Gen. Studies, Columbia U., 1966—; vice chmn. governing council Courant Inst. Math. Scis. (NYU), 1962—; mem. exec. com. Health Research Council, City N.Y., 1968-75; bd. overseers Sch. Arts and Scis., U. Pa., 1976—; chmn. vis. com. astronomy Princeton U., 1969—; mem. vis. com. on astronomy Harvard U., 1976—, on engring. and applied physics, 1969-77, on medicine and dental medicine, 1969-77; bd. visitors CUNY Grad. Sch. and Univ. Center, 1979—; vice-chmn. Mayor's Commn. Sci. and Tech., 1984—; vis. com. Assn. Univs. for Research in Astronomy, 1973-76; trustee United Neighborhood Houses, 1952-61, Mt. Sinai Hosp., 1955—, Mt. Sinai Med. Sch., 1963—, vice-chmn., 1977—; mem. vis. com. Space Telescope Sci. Inst., 1982—; trustee N.Y. Found., 1963-84, treas., 1974-78; mem. Carnegie Corp. Commn. Coll. Retirement, 1984—; trustee Asso. Hosp. Service N.Y. (Blue Cross), 1959-74, Hebrew Free Loan Soc., 1935—, Am. Mus. Natural History, 1968—, v.p., 1971—; trustee Nat. Humanities Center, 1978—, Marine Biol. Lab., Woods Hole, Mass., 1968-77, 79—, Riverside Research Inst., 1967-76, Carnegie Instn. Washington (sec. 1971—),, 1969—, The Population Council, 1979—, Am. Trust for the Brit. Library, 1980—, Center Advanced Study Behavioral Scis., 1970-76, Univ. Corp. for Atmospheric Research, 1965-74, N.Y.C.-Rand Inst., 1969-75, Bennington Coll., 1971-76, Haskins Labs., 1971—, SIAM Inst. Math. and Soc., 1973—, treas., 1984—; trustee Barnard Coll., 1973—, vice chmn., 1975—, treas., 1980-83; trustee Columbia U. Press, 1974-77, N.Y. Council for Humanities, 1975-78 (chmn. 1976-78), John Simon Guggenheim Meml. Found., 1976-81, Catskill Center for Conservation and Devel., Inc., 1981—; chmn. Neurosci. Research Found., 1981—; pub. mem. Hudson Inst., 1964—. Editor, co-author: Science Advice to the President, 1980; author papers on govt. and sci. Served to lt. comdr. USNR, 1941-45. Recipient Letters of Commendation with ribbon from sec. of navy and from chief Bur. Ordnance for invention naval gunfire device used in World War II, award Mus. City of N.Y., 1981, Disting. Pub. Service award NSF, 1982. Benjamin Franklin fellow Royal Soc. Arts (London); fellow N.Y. Acad. Scis. (bd. govs.), AAAS (treas., dir. 1969—); mem. Council Fgn. Relations, NYU Soc. Fellows, Soc. Protozoologists, Am. Acad. Arts and Scis., Nat. Acad. Public Adminstrn., Am. Philos. Soc., Assn. Computing Machinery. Clubs: Army and Navy, Cosmos (Washington); Century Assn., City Midday (N.Y.C.). Home: 730 Park Ave New York NY 10021 also Olive Bridge NY 12461 Office: 40 Wall St New York NY 10005

GOLDENBERG, GERALD JOSEPH, physician, educator; b. Brandon, Man., Can., Nov. 27, 1933; s. Jacob and Fanny (Walker) G.; m. Sheila Claire Melmed, Jan. 4, 1959; children: Lesley Peace, Jacob Alan, Suzanne Elise, Ellen Rachel. M.D., U. Man., 1957; Ph.D., U. Minn., 1965. Intern Winnipeg Gen. Hosp., 1957-58; resident U. Minn. Hosps., Mpls., 1958-62; lectr. dept. medicine U. Man., Winnipeg, 1964-66, asst. prof., 1966-70, assoc. prof., 1970-75, prof., 1975—; clin. research assoc. Nat. Cancer Inst. Can., 1967-73; research dir. Man. Inst. Cell Biology, 1973-74, dir., 1974—; cons. oncology Winnipeg Children's Hosp. Recipient Gold medal U. Man., 1957. Fellow Royal Coll. Physicians (Can.); mem. Am. Soc. Exptl. Pathology, Am. Assn. Cancer Research, Canadian Soc. Clin. Investigation, Can. Oncology Soc. Lodge: Masons. Office: 100 Olivia St Winnipeg MB Canada R3E 0V9

GOLDENBERG, ROBERT ARLIN, ear surgeon; b. Dayton, Ohio, July 5, 1941; s. Theodore Ezra and Judith Lois (Raffel) G.; m. Deborah Sue Dorsey, June 7, 1968; 1 son, Theodore. A.B., Stanford U., 1963; M.D., U. Louisville, 1968; M.S., U. Ill., 1973. Diplomate: Am. Bd. Otolaryngology. Intern Rush-Presbyn. (St. Luke's Med. Ctr.), Chgo., 1968-69, resident in gen. surgery, 1969-70; resident in otolaryngology U. Ill. Eye and Ear Infirmary, Chgo., 1970-73; practice medicine, specializing in otology, Dayton, 1976—; chmn. dept. otolaryngology Wright State U. Sch. Medicine, Dayton, 1976—; dir. Am. Sales Inc., Dayton, 1976—; dir., pres. N. Soifer & Assocs., Dayton, 1982—; lectr. in field. Contbr. articles to profl. jours. Pres. assoc. bd. Dayton Performing Arts Fund, 1983—. Served to lt. comdr. USN, 1974-76. Recipient 1st prize sci. exhibit Diagnostic and mgmt. of acoustic neuroma, Ohio Med. Assn., 1978. Mem. ACS, Am. Acad. Otolaryngology Head and Neck Surgery (bd. govs. 1982-83), Assn. Acad. Dept. Otolaryngology (adminstrv. com.), Soc. Univ. Otolarlyngologists, Am. Neurotology Soc. Jewish. Home: 246 W Thruston Blvd Dayton OH 45419 Office: 2345 Philadelphia Dr Dayton OH 45406

GOLDENBERG, RONALD EDWIN, educational administrator; b. Hammond, Ind., Aug. 14, 1931; s. James Abraham and Edna Sarah (Hirsch) G.; m. Carolyn Sachs, Dec. 25, 1955; children: Mark Robert, Cheryl Goldenberg. B.S., Washington U., 1956, M.S., 1956; Ed.D., Okla. State U., 1971. Tchr. pub. schs., Normandy, Mo., 1956-59; prin. elem. sch. University City, Mo., 1963-68; asst. prof. elem. edn. U. Ga., 1970-73, assoc. prof., coordinator student teaching, 1973-78; prof., dean Sch. Edn. U. Evansville, Ind., 1978-80, prof., dean Sch. Grad. Studies, 1980—. Editor: Children and Youth, 1978—; mem. adv. bd.: Jour. Alternative Higher Edn., 1977—; adv. editor: Hacourt-Brace Pub. Co.; contbr. chpts. to books, articles to profl. jours. Bd. dirs. Raintree council Girl Scouts Am. Served with USN, 1951-55. Mem. Assn. Tchr. Educators, Council Grad. Sch., Assn. Supervision and Curriculum Devel., Am. Assn. Colls. Techr. Edn., Phi Kappa Phi. Lodge: Rotary. Office: PO Box 329 U Evansville Evansville IN 47702

GOLDENHERSH, JOSEPH HERMAN, justice state supreme court; b. East St. Louis, Ill., Nov. 2, 1914; s. Benjamin and Bertha (Goldenberg) G.; m. Maxyne Zelenka, June 18, 1939; children: Richard, Jerold. LL.B., Washington U., St. Louis, 1935. Bar: Ill. 1936. Pvt. practice law, East St. Louis, 1936-64; judge Appellate Ct. Ill., 1964-70; justice Supreme Ct. Ill., 1970-78, 82—, chief justice, 1979-82. Chmn. Initial Gifts United Fund East St. Louis, 1952-53; dir. Mississippi Valley council Boy Scouts Am., 1952-58; pres. Jewish Fedn. So. Ill., 1949-51; Trustee emeritus Christian Welfare Hosp., East St. Louis. Mem. Appellate Judges Conf. (exec. com. 1969-70), East St. Louis Bar Assn. (pres. 1962-63), ABA, Ill. Bar Assn. Clubs: Mason (33 deg., Shriner), Missouri Athletic (St. Louis)). Home: 7510 Claymont Ct Belleville IL 62223 Office: 6464 W Main St Suite 3A Belleville IL 62223

GOLDENSON, LEONARD HARRY, corp. exec.; b. Scottdale, Pa., Dec. 7, 1905; s. Lee and Esther (Broude) G.; m. Isabelle Weinstein, Oct. 10, 1939; children—Loreen Arbus, Maxine. Grad., Harvard Coll., 1927, Harvard Law Sch., 1930; LL.D.,-Emerson Coll., 1981. Bar: N.Y. bar, Pa. bar 1930. Practice in, N.Y.C., 1930-33; with Paramount Pictures, N.Y.C., from 1933, v.p. charge theatre ops., 1938, v.p., N.Y.C., 1942-50; dir. Paramount Pictures, Inc., 1944-50; chmn., pres. and dir. United Paramount Theatres, Inc., 1950-52; pres., dir. Am. Broadcasting-Paramount Theatres, Inc (name changed to ABC, Inc. 1965), from 1953, chief exec. officer, now chmn. and chief exec. officer; dir. Allied Stores Corp. Co-founder, past pres., dir. United Cerebral Palsy Assn., Inc., 1949-53, chmn. bd., 1954—; vice chmn. bd. dirs. United Cerebral Palsy Research and Ednl. Found.; trustee Children's Cancer Research Found. of Children's Med. Center, Boston, Will Rogers Meml. Hosp., Saranac Lake, N.Y., Temple Emanu-El, N.Y.C.; bd. dirs. Daus. of Jacob Geriatric Center, N.Y.C., World Rehab. Fund; founding mem. Hollywood Mus.; mem. Nat. Citizen's Adv. Com. on Vocat. Rehab.; adv. council White House Conf. on Handicapped Individuals. Mem. Motion Picture Pioneers, Nat. Acad. TV Arts and Scis., Internat. Radio and TV Soc. Club: Harvard (N.Y.C.). Office: 1330 Ave Americas New York NY 10019

GOLDENSON, ROBERT MYAR, psychologist; b. Albany, N.Y., Feb. 2, 1908; s. Dr. Samuel Harry and Claudia (Myar) G.; m. Irene Herz, June 25, 1940; children: Ronald, Daniel. B.A. magna cum laude, Princeton U., 1930; M.A., U. Pitts., 1932; Ph.D., Harvard U., 1940. Teaching fellow philosophy U. Pitts., 1931-32; instr. Black Mountain Coll., 1934-37; instr., asst. prof. psychology Hunter Coll., 1940-59; prof. Internat. Grad. U., 1975—; ednl. dir. Book-of-the-Month Club, 1960-68; panel mem. It's a Problem, NBC-TV, 1951-52; mem. children's program rev. com., 1955; mem. edn. commn. Internat. Congress Mental Health, 1949; del. U.S. Commn. UNESCO Conf., 1951. Writer, condr.: vet. readjustment series When He Comes Home, radio sta. WMCA, N.Y.C., also, Armed Forces Network, 1945-46; writer: (with Dr. Luther Woodward) radio series Inquiring Parent, 1946-50; condr.: TV series Keep Up to Date, NBC, later, ABC, 1953-54; Author: (with R. E. Hartley, L. K. Frank) Understanding Children's Play, 1952, Helping Your Child to Read Better, 1957, (with R.E. Hartley) The Complete Book of Children's Play, 1957, rev. edit., 1963, All About the Human Mind, 1963, Encyclopedia of Human Behavior, 1970, Mysteries of the Mind, 1973; editor-in-chief: The Disability and Rehabilitation Handbook, 1978, Longman Dictionary of Psychology and Psychiatry, 1984; contbr. articles to family periodicals. Mem. Tri-State Council Family Relations (pres. 1953), Am. Psychol. Assn., Phi Beta Kappa. Address: 551-A Sheldon Way Jamesburg NJ 08831

GOLDENSTEIN, ERWIN HARMON, educator; b. Sterling, Nebr., Jan. 11, 1921; s. Frank and Grace (Wehmer) G.; m. Valda Marie Panko, May 25, 1942 (div. dec. Feb. 3, 1960); children: Diana, Ronald; m. Pearl Rosa Schaaf, Aug. 26, 1961; 1 son, Jeffrey. B.S., U. Nebr., 1942, M.A., 1949, Ph.D., 1951. Tchr. secondary schs., supt., Nebr., 1946-48; part-time instr. U. Nebr., Lincoln, 1948-50, asst. prof. secondary edn., 1954-56, asso. prof. history and philosophy edn., 1956-59, prof., 1959—, chmn. dept., 1959-70, coordinator, 1970-73, coordinator doctoral studies in edn., 1974-81; supr. secondary edn. Nebr. Dept. Pub. Instrn., 1950-51, 52-54; Instr. field arty. gunnery and math. U.S. Army F.A. Sch., Fort Sill, Okla., 1951-52. Contbr. ednl. monographs, articles to periodicals. Del. 4th Assembly World Council Chs., Sweden, 1968; pres. Luth. Student Found., Lincoln.; Trustee Martin Luther Home and Sch., Beatrice, Nebr.; regent Dana Coll., Blair, Nebr.; mem. bd. coll. and univ. services Am. Luth. Ch. Served to capt. F.A. AUS, 1942-46. Mem. AAUP, Am. Ednl. Studies Assn., History of Edn. Soc., NEA, Soc. Profs. Edn. (sec.-treas. 1964-68, v.p. 1968, pres. 1969), Phi Delta Kappa. Home: 2201 N 61st St Lincoln NE 68505

GOLDEY, JAMES MEARNS, physicist; b. Wilmington, Del., July 3, 1926; s. Robert Perkins and Ellen (Mearns) G.; m. Jeanne Calvert Potts, June 29, 1951; children: James P., Kristina. B.S. with honors, U. Del., 1950; Ph.D. in Physics, M.I.T., 1955. Mem. tech. staff Bell Labs., Murray Hill, N.J., 1954-56, supr., 1956-59, head integrated circuit and silicon transistor dept., 1959-60, dir. integrated circuit customer service lab., Allentown, Pa., 1981—. Contbr. articles in field to profl. jours. Served with U.S. Army, 1944-46. Fellow IEEE. Republican. Presbyterian. Patentee in field. Home: 3930 Azalea Rd Allentown PA 18103 Office: 1255 S Cedar Crest Blvd Allentown PA 18103

GOLDFARB, BERNARD SANFORD, lawyer; b. Cleve., Apr. 15, 1917; s. Harry and Esther (Lenson) G.; m. Barbara Brofman, Jan. 4, 1966; children—Meredith Stacey, Lauren Beth. A.B., Case Western Res. U., 1938, J.D., 1940. Bar: Ohio bar 1940. Since practiced in, Cleve.; sr. partner firm Goldfarb & Reznick, 1967—; spl. counsel to atty. gen. Ohio, 1950, 71-74; mem. Ohio Commn. Uniform Traffic Rules, 1973—. Contbr. legal jours. Served with USAAF, 1942-45. Mem. Am., Ohio, Greater Cleve. bar assns. Home: 39 Pepper Creek Dr Pepper Pike OH 44124 Office: 1800 Illuminating Bldg Cleveland OH 44113

GOLDFARB, DONALD, engineering educator; b. N.Y.C., Aug. 14, 1941; s. Leon and Hannah (Marcus) G.; m. Ranny Lichtman, June 29, 1968; children: Benjamin, Cora. B.Chem. Engring., cornell U., 1963; M.A., Princeton U., 1965, Ph.D., 1966. Asst. research scientist Courant Inst. Math. Sci., N.Y.C., 1966-68; mem. faculty CCNY, 1968-83, prof. computer sci., 1977-83; prof. indsl. engring. and ops. research columbial U., N.Y.C., 1982—; cons.to industry Office Emergency Preparedness, Washington; mem. com. recommendations U.S. Army Basic Sci. Research of Nat. Research Council; summer research faculty mem. T.J. Watson Research lab. IBM, Yorktown Heights, N.Y., summers 1972-76; research assoc. Atomic Energy Research Establishment, Harwell, Eng., 1974-75; vis. prof. Cornell U., Ithaca, N.Y., 1979-80. Editor: SIAM Jour. Numerical Analysis, 1982—; assoc. editor: Math. of Computation, 1969—, Ops. Research, 1983—, Math. Programming, 1983—. NSF fellow, 1963-66; NSF grantee, 1973-75, 80—; ARO grantee, 1977-80,7 82—. Mem. Am. Math. Soc., Soc. Indsl. and Applied Math., Ops. Research Soc. Am., Math. Programming Soc. (mem. council). Home: 6 Peter Cooper Rd Apt 8C New York NY 10010 Office: Dept of Indsl Engring and oprations Research Columbia Univ 316 S W Mudd Bldg New York NY 10027

GOLDFARB, ROBERT STANLEY, economics educator; b. Bronx, Feb. 7, 1943; s. Walter A. and Rose H. (Ginsberg) G.; m. Marsha Geier, Nov. 27, 1969; 1 son, Steven Gerald. B.A., Columbia U., 1964; M.A., Yale U., 1965, M.Phil., 1967, Ph.D., 1968. Asst. prof. Yale U., New Haven, 1968-73; assoc. prof. econs. George Washington U., Washington, 1973-80, prof., 1980—; sr. economist U.S. Council on Wage and Price Stability, Washington, 1980; cons. Nat. Commn. on Employment and Unemployment Stats., 1977-78. Contbr. articles to profl. jours. Woodrow Wilson fellow, 1964-65, 67-68; Ford Found. fellow, 1966-67. Mem. Am. Econ. Assn., Western Econ. Assn., Atlantic Econ. Assn., Indsl. Relations Research Assn. Office: Dept Econs George Washington Univ Washington DC 20052

GOLDFARB, RONALD LAWRENCE, lawyer; b. Jersey City, N.J., Oct. 16, 1933; s. Robert S. and Aida J. (Weintraub) G.; m. Joanne Jacob, June 9, 1957; children: Jody, Nicholas, Maximilian Goldfarb. A.B., Syracuse U., 1954, LL.B., 1956; LL.M., Yale, 1960, J.S.D., 1962. Bar: N.Y. 1956, Calif. 1959, D.C. 1965, U.S. Supreme Ct 1965. Practice law, Washington, 1966—; spl. asst. to U.S. atty. gen. (organized crime sect.), 1961-64; partner Goldfarb, Singer and Austern, 1966—; Dir. Brookings Instn. program on cts. and adminstrn. Justice, 1966-67; mem. staff counsel com. on law and social action Am. Jewish Congress, 1960-61; cons. Pres.'s Poverty Program, 1964, Riots Commn., 1967-68. (Recipient Fed. Bar Assn. award for book Ransom 1966); Author: The Contempt Power, 1963, Ransom: A Critique of the American Bail System, 1965, (with Alfred Friendly) Crime and Publicity, 1967, (with Linda Singer) After Conviction—A Review of the American Correction System, 1973, Jails: The Ultimate Ghetto, 1975, Migrant Farm Workers: A Caste of Despair, 1981, (with James Raymond) Clear Understandings: A Guide to Legal Writing, 1983; contbr. articles to profl. jours., popular mags., also syndicated newspaper column. Served to capt. JAG Corps USAF, 1957-60. Arthur Garfield Hays fellow N.Y.U., 1960-61; Woodrow Wilson fellow. Mem. Am., Fed., D.C., N.Y., Calif. bar assns., ACLU, Sigma Alpha Mu, Phi Delta Phi. Home: 7312 Rippon Rd Alexandria VA 22307 Office: 918 16th St NW Washington DC 20006

GOLDFARB, WARREN D(AVID), philosophy educator; b. N.Y.C., Aug. 25, 1949; s. Norman J. and Ella (Kaback) G. A.B., Harvard U.,

1969, A.M., 1971, Ph.D., 1975. Asst. prof. philosophy Harvard U., Cambridge, Mass., 1975-80, assoc. prof., 1980-82, prof., 1982—; vis. prof. U. Calif.-Berkeley, 1984. Author: (with Burton Dreben) The Decision Problem, 1979; editor: Jacques Herbrand, Logical Writings, 1971. Mem. Am. Philos. Assn., Assn. Symbolic Logic (exec. com. 1982-84). Office: Harvard U Dept Philosophy Cambridge MA 02138

GOLDFEDER, HOWARD, retail executive; b. N.Y.C., Apr. 28, 1926; s. Herman and Betty (Epstein) G.; m. Helen Wiggs; children: Carole, Joan. B.A., Tufts U., 1947. With Bloomingdale's, N.Y.C., 1947-67; exec. v.p. Famous-Barr, St. Louis, 1967-69; pres. May Co., Los Angeles, 1969-71; pres., then chmn. Bullock's, Los Angeles, 1971-77; with Federated Dept. Stores, Inc., Cin., 1977—, pres., 1980—, chief exec. officer, 1981—, chmn., 1982—, also dir.; dir. Champion Internat. Corp., Conn. Mut. Life Ins. Co. Recipient Nat. Brotherhood award NCCJ, 1981. Mem. Nat. Retail Mchts. Assn. (dir., exec. com.), Bus. Roundtable, Bus. Council. Clubs: Commercial, Queen City, Losantiville Country (Cin.). Office: 7 W 7th St Cincinnati OH 45202

GOLDFELD, STEPHEN MICHAEL, educator; b. Bronx, N.Y., Aug. 9, 1940; s. Julius Morris and Ethel (Hammer) G.; m. Laura Heend, July 1, 1962; children—Melanie, Keith. A.B., Harvard, 1960; Ph.D., Mass. Inst. Tech., 1963. Asst. prof. Princeton, 1963-66; sr. economist Council Econ. Advisers, 1966-67, asso. prof., 1966-69, prof. econs., 1969—; vis. prof. Universite Catholique de Louvain, 1970-71, U. Calif. at Berkeley, 1975-76, Israel Inst. Tech., 1980; mem. Council Econ. Advisers, 1980-81; cons. Nat. Indsl. Conf. Bd., Mathematica, Fed. Res. Bd.; Mem. Brookings Panel on Econ. Activity. Author: Commercial Bank Behavior and Economic Activity, 1966, Precursors in Mathematical Economics, 1968, Nonlinear Methods In Econometrics, 1972, Studies in Nonlinear Econometrics, 1976, the Economics of Money and Banking, 1981; Asso. editor: Internat. Econ. Rev, 1971—, Jour. Econometrics, 1972—, Rev. Econs. and Statistics, 1973—, Jour. Money, Credit and Banking, 1980—; contbr. articles to profl. jours. Democratic campaign finance chmn., Princeton, 1969; Bd. dirs. N.J. Ednl. Computing Center, 1969-70. NSF sr. postdoctoral fellow, 1970-71. Fellow Econometric Soc.; mem. Am. Econ. Assn., Am. Statis. Assn., Am. Finance Assn. Home: 40 Leabrook Ln Princeton NJ 08540 Office: Dept Econs Princeton U Princeton NJ 08544

GOLDFIELD, EDWIN DAVID, statistician; b. N.Y.C., Oct. 26, 1918; s. Maurice and Sarah (Spears) G. B.S., City U. N.Y., 1939; M.A., Columbia U., 1940; postgrad., Am. U., 1940-46. Research assoc. dept. investigation, N.Y.C., 1938-39; statis. adviser Ct. Spl. Sessions, N.Y.C., 1939; with Bur. Census, Washington, 1940-75, asst. dir., 1967-71, chief internat. programs, 1971-75; with Nat. Acad. Scis., Washington, 1975—, exec. dir. com. on nat. statistics, 1978—; cons. in field, 1951—; staff dir. subcom. census and statistics Ho. of Reps., 1959-60, 67. Contbr. articles.; Editor: Papers on Labor Force Statistics in the United States, 1952. Recipient Meritorious Service award Dept. Commerce, 1954. Fellow Am. Statis. Assn.; mem. Washington Statis. Soc. (past pres.), Am. Econ. Assn., Population Assn. Am., Conf. Research Income and Wealth, Inter-Am. Statis. Inst., Internat. Assn. Survey Statisticians, Internat. Statis. Inst., Phi Beta Kappa. Home: 4311 23d Pkwy Temple Hills MD 20748 Office: Nat Academy of Sciences Washington DC 20418

GOLDFRANK, ESTHER S., anthropologist; b. N.Y.C., May 5, 1896; d. Herman J. and Matilda (Metzger) Schiff; m. Walter S. Goldfrank, Dec. 8, 1922 (dec. 1935); 1 dau., Susan G. Lennhoff; stepchildren—Max, Alexander, Thomas; m. Karl August Wittfogel, Mar. 8, 1940. Grad., Ethical Culture Sch., N.Y.C., 1914; A.B., Barnard Coll., 1918. Field work on Am. Indian Pueblos in, N.M., 1920-22, 24, among Blackfoot Indians of, Alta., Can., 1939; staff anthropologist Chinese History project, N.Y.C., 1943—. Author: The Artist of Isleta Paintings in Pueblo Society, 1967; monograph The Social and Ceremonial Organization of Cochiti, 1927, Changing Configurations in the Social Organization of a Blackfoot Tribe during the Reserve Period, 1945, Notes on an Undirected Life: As One Anthropologist Tells It, 1978; editor: Isleta Paintings with Notes and Commentary by Elsie Clews Parsons, 1962. Fellow N.Y. Acad. Scis., Am. Anthrop. Assn.; mem. Am. Ethnol. Soc. (sec.-treas. 1945-47, pres. 1948, editor 1952-56). Home: 420 Riverside Dr New York NY 10025

GOLDGAR, BERTRAND ALVIN, educator; b. Macon, Ga., Nov. 17, 1927; s. Benjamin Meyer and Annie (Shapiro) G.; m. Corinne Cohn Hartman, Apr. 6, 1950; children: Arnold Benjamin, Anne Hartman. B.A., Vanderbilt U., 1948, M.A., 1949; M.A., Princeton U., 1957, Ph.D., 1958. Instr., Clemson (S.C.) U., 1948-50, asst. prof., 1951-52; instr. Lawrence U., Appleton, Wis., 1957-61, asst. prof. English, 1961-65, asso. prof., 1965-71, prof., 1971—, John N. Bergstrom prof. humanities, 1980—; mem. fellowship panel NEH, 1979. Author: The Curse of Party: Swift's Relations with Addison and Steele, 1961, Walpole and the Wits: The Relation of Politics to Literature, 1722-1742, 1976; editor: The Literary Criticism of Alexander Pope, 1965; adv. editor: 18th Century Studies, 1977—. Served with AUS, 1952-54. Recipient Teaching Excellence award Lawrence U., 1976; Am. Council Learned Socs. fellow, 1973-74; NEH fellow, 1980-81. Mem. Am. Soc. 18th Century Studies, MLA, Johnson Soc. of Central Region. Home: 914 E Eldorado St Appleton WI 54911 Office: Dept English Lawrence U Appleton WI 54912

GOLDHABER, GERALD MARTIN, communication educator, author, consultant; b. Brookline, Mass., Jan. 23, 1944; s. Robert and Ruth Irene G.; m. Marylynn Blaustein, Aug. 17, 1969; children—Michelle, Marc. B.A., U. Mass., 1965; M.A., U. Md., 1967; Ph.D., Purdue U., 1970. Asst. prof. communication U. N.Mex., 1970-74; asso. prof., asso. chmn. dept. communication SUNY, Buffalo, 1974-78, chmn. dept., 1979—; pres. Goldhaber Research Assos., Buffalo, London, Las Vegas, 1975—; polit. analyst N.Y. Post, CKO-Radio Can., WEBR Radio, Buffalo, WKBW-TV; cons. polit. candidates, pollster. Author: Organizational Communication, 1974, 3d edit., 1983, (with B. Peterson and R.W. Pace) Communication Probes, 1974, 3d edit., 1982, (with L. Rosenfeld and V. Smith) Experiments in Human Communication, 1975, (with M.B. Goldhaber) Transactional Analysis, 1976, (with E. Zannes) Stand Up and Speak Out, 1978, 2d edit., 1982, (with M. Dennis, H. Richetto and O. Wilo) Information Strategies: New Pathways to Corporate Power, 1979, 2d edit., 1983, (with D. Rogers) Auditing Organizational Communication Systems: The ICA Communication Audit, 1979; contbg. author numerous books; rev. editor: Orgnl. Communication Abstracts; contbr. articles to profl. jours. Bd. dirs. Temple Beth El, Buffalo, 1980-83; polit. pollster, Republican County polit. pollster, Erie County, N.Y. Recipient Disting. Alumnus award U. Mass., 1983, numerous teaching awards and grants. Fellow Inst. Internat. Sociol. Research (life); mem. Internat. Communication Assn. (v.p., dir. 1974-76), Am. Mktg. Assn., Mktg. Research Assn., Indsl. Communication Council, Am. Assn. Public Opinion Research, Internat. Soc. Social Network Analysis. Home: 48 Jamestead Ct Williamsville NY 14221 Office: Dept Communication SUNY-Buffalo Buffalo NY 14260 *I have always believed that the search for excellence should govern the lives of all people. There is virtually nothing that a human being cannot achieve if he or she lives in accordance with this standard and possesses a strong sense of morality and a good sense of humor. I have lived my entire life according to these precepts and owe much to those who have stood with me for excellence.*

GOLDHABER, GERTRUDE SCHARFF, physicist; b. Mannheim, Germany, July 14, 1911; came to U.S., 1939, naturalized, 1944; d. Otto and Nelly (Steinharter) Scharff; m. Maurice Goldhaber, May 24, 1939; children: Alfred Scharff, Michael Henry. Student, univs. Freiburg, Zurich, Berlin; Ph.D., U. Munich, 1935. Research assoc. Imperial Coll., London, Eng., 1935-39; research physicist U. Ill., 1939-48, asst. prof., 1948-50; assoc. physicist Brookhaven Nat. Lab., Upton, N.Y., 1950-58, physicist, 1958-62, sr. physicist, 1962—; cons. nuclear data group NRC, Nat. Acad. Scis., AEC Labs. ACDA, 1974-77; adj. prof. Cornell U., 1980-82, Johns Hopkins U., 1983—; mem. Phi Beta Kappa vis. scholar program, 1984-85. Mem. editorial com.: Ann. Rev. Nuclear Sci, 1973-77; N. Am. rep. bd. editors: Jour. Physics G (Europhysics Jour.), 1978-80. Trustee-at-large Univ. Research Assn. governing Fermi Nat. Accelerator Lab., 1972-77. Fellow Am. Phys. Soc. (council 1979-82, chmn. panel on improvement pre-coll. physics literacy 1979-82, chmn. audit com. 1980, mem. com. on profl. opportunities 1979-81, com. on history of physics, exec. com. 1983-84), AAAS; mem. Nat. Acad. Scis. (mem. report rev. com. 1973-81, mem. acad. forum adv. com. 1974-81, mem. com. on edn. and employment of women in sci. and engring. 1978-83, commn. on human rights 1984—), Sigma Xi. Home: 91 S Gillette Ave Bayport NY 11705 Office: Brookhaven Nat Lab Upton NY 11973

GOLDHABER, JACOB KOPEL, mathematician, educator; b. Bklyn., Apr. 12, 1924; s. Joseph and Shirley (Heller) G.; m. Ruth Last, Dec. 25, 1951; children—Doreet, David, Aviva. B.A., Bklyn. Coll., 1944; M.A., Harvard, 1945; Ph.D., U. Wis., 1950. Instr. U. Conn., Storrs, 1950-53; instr. Cornell U., Ithaca, N.Y., 1953- 54; asst. prof. Washington U., St. Louis, 1954-59, asso. prof., 1959- 61, U. Md., College Park, 1961-62, prof., 1962—, chmn. math. dept., 1968-77; exec. sec. Office Math. Scis., NRC, 1975—; Vis. research assoc. (NSF Sci. Faculty fellow) U. London (Eng.), 1966-67. Author: (with Gertrude Ehrlich) Algebra, 1970; Contbr. papers to profl. jours. Mem. AAAS, Am. Math. Soc., Math. Assn. Am., Sigma Xi. Home: 5517 39th St NW Washington DC 20015 Office: Dept Math U Md College Park MD 20742

GOLDHABER, MAURICE, physicist; b. Lemberg, Austria, Apr. 18, 1911; came to U.S., 1938, naturalized, 1944; s. Charles and Ethel (Frisch) G.; m. Gertrude Scharff, May 24, 1939; children: Alfred S., Michael H. Ph.D., Cambridge U., Eng., 1936, Tel-Aviv U., Israel, 1974, Dr., U. Louvain-La-Neuve, Belgium, 1982, D.Sc., SUNY, Stony Brook, 1983. Bye fellow Magdalene Coll., Cambridge, 1936-38; asst. prof. physics U. Ill., 1938-43, assoc. prof., 1943-45, prof., 1945-50; sr. sci. Brookhaven Nat. Lab., 1950-60, chmn. dept. physics, 1960-61, dir., 1961-73, AUI distinguished Scientist, 1973—; cons. labs. AEC; Morris Loeb lectr Harvard U., 1955; adj. prof. physics SUNY, Stony Brook, 1965—; Mem. nuclear sci. com. NRC. Assoc. editor: Phys. Rev, 1951-53; Contbr. articles on nuclear physics to sci. jours. Mem. bd. govs. Weizmann Inst. Sci., Rehovoth, Israel, Tel Aviv U.; trustee Univs. Research Assn. Recipient citation for meritorious contbns. U.S. AEC, 1973, J. Robert Oppenheimer meml. prize, 1982. Fellow Am. Phys. Soc. (pres. 1982), Am. Acad. Arts and Scis., AAAS; mem. Nat. Acad. Sci., Am. Philos. Soc. (Tom W. Bonner prize in nuclear physics 1971). Home: 91 S Gillette Ave Bayport NY 11705 Office: Brookhaven Nat Laboratory Upton NY 11973

GOLDHAMMER, ROBERT FREDERICK, investment banking executive; b. N.Y.C., Feb. 9, 1931; s. Frederick and Helen (Thompson) G.; m. Joan Patricia Ditmars, Jan. 31, 1953; children: Susan Goldhammer Davis, Robert Kent, Richard Frederick. B.S. in Econs., Boston U. Registered rep. Kidder, Peabody & Co., Boston, 1956-63, v.p., dir., mgr. New England, 1964-79; v.p., dir. nat. sales Charles River Breeding, N.Y.C., Boston, 1980—; dir. Charles River Breeding, Wilmington, Mass., 1968—, EG&G, Wellesley, Mass., 1981—, Esterline Corp., Darien, Conn., 1974—, Northland Investment, Wellesley, 1973—. Treas. Gov.'s Mgmt. Task Force; treas. and dir. Mass. Commn. Devel. Fin. Corp.; trustee Belmont Hill Sch., Boston U.; mem. presdl. adv. com. on arts. Served to lt. (j.g.) USN, 1952-56. Mem. Boston Stock Exchange (chmn. 1969-72), New Eng. Group Investent Bankers Assn. (chmn. 1966-67), Investment Bankers Assn. (bd. govs. 1967). Clubs: Winchester Country (Mass.); Union of Boston; Comml. (Boston). Home: 1 Taft Dr Winchester MA 01890 Office: Kidder Peabody & co Inc 10 Hanover Sq New York NY 10005

GOLDHAR, JOEL D., educational administrator; b. 1942. B.S., Rensselaer Polytech. Inst., 1963; M.B.A., Harvard U., 1965; D.B.A., George Washington U., 1970. With Nat. Acad. Scis.-RC, 1978-82; dean Coll. Bus. Adminstrn. Ill. Inst. Tech., Chgo., 1983—. Office: Bus Adminstrn Ill Inst Tech 3300 S Federal St Chicago IL 60616 *

GOLDHOR, HERBERT, librarian, educator; b. Newark, Feb. 8, 1917; s. Adolph and Dora (Balshan) G.; m. Eleanor Payne Cheydleur, May 29, 1948; children: Jonathan Dana, Richard Scott, Elizabeth Payne, Barbara Ashley. B.A., Dana Coll., 1935; B.S. in L.S., Columbia U., 1938; Ph.D., U. Chgo., 1942. Jr. asst. Newark Pub. Library, 1933-35, 36-37; asst. to librarian Iowa State Coll., Ames, 1938-39; asst. prof., asso. prof. U. Ill. Library Sch., Urbana, 1946-52, asso. dir. Grad. Sch. Library Sci., 1962-63, dir. Grad. Sch. Library Sci., 1963-78, dir. Library Research Center, 1975—; chief librarian Evansville (Ind.) Pub. Library, 1952-61. Author: (with Joseph L. Wheeler) Practical Administration of Public Libraries; contbr. articles to profl. jours. Served to 2d lt. AUS, 1944-46. Mem. Am., Ind., Ill. library assns., Phi Beta Kappa, Beta Phi Mu. Mem. Soc. Friends. Home: 39 Maple Ct Lake Park Champaign IL 61820 Office: 410 David Kinley Hall U of Illinois Urbana IL 61801

GOLDHURST, WILLIAM, author, humanities and English educator; b. N.Y.C., Aug. 8, 1929; s. Harry Golden and Genevieve (Gallagher) G.; m. Ellen Eiseman.; children: Barney, Rex. B.A., Kenyon Coll., 1953; M.A., Columbia, 1956; Ph.D., Tulane U., 1962. Asst. instr. English Ohio State U., 1955-56; teaching fellow Tulane U. and Newcomb Coll., 1956-59; asso. prof. English U. P.R., 1960-63; prof. humanities and English U. Fla., 1964—; Fulbright prof. Am. lit. univs. Buenos Aires, and La Plata, Argentina, fall 1969; lectr. Am. lit. to Peace Corps U. P.R., 1963; Edgar Allan Poe Meml. lectr., Richmond, Va., 1973; lectr. Santa Fe Community Coll. Author: F. Scott Fitzgerald and His Contemporaries, 1963, Our Own Confidence Man, 1979, also articles, photo—stories in mags.; book reviewer l it. jours.; Editor: Contours of Experience, 1967. Recipient Broome Lit. Agt. award for short fiction, 1979; So. fellow, 1959-60; grantee Humanities Council and Faculty Devel., Grad. Sch. Research U. Fla., 1970-71, 72; Presdl. scholar U. Fla., 1975-76. Mem. South Atlantic Modern Lang. Assn., Poe Soc. (Balt.), Poe Soc. (Richmond). Home: 3927 NW 21st St Gainesville FL 32605

GOLDIAMOND, ISRAEL, experimental psychologist, educator; b. Ukraine, Nov. 1, 1919; s. Samuel and Clara (Rothenburg) G.; m. Betty Ann Johnson, Feb. 28, 1946; children: Lisa Catherine Plymate, Joe David, Shana Aucsmith. B.A., Bklyn. Coll., 1942; Ph.D., U. Chgo., 1955. Adminstrv. asst. Inst. Design, Chgo., 1947-48; from research asst. to asso. U. Chgo., 1948-55; from asst. to asso. prof. psychology So. Ill. U., 1955-60; prof. psychology Ariz. State U., 1960-63; asso. to exec. dir. Inst. Behavioral Research, 1963-68; from asso. prof. to prof. psychiatry and behavioral sci. Johns Hopkins Med. Sch., 1965-68; prof. psychiatry and psychology U. Chgo., 1968—; clin. fellow Behavior Therapy Research Soc.; staff cons. div. neuropsychiatry Walter Reed Army Inst. Research, 1963-68. Contbr. profl. jours.; Editorial bds.: Jour. Exptl. Analysis Behavior, 1963-68, Jour. Applied Behavior Analysis, 1968—, Jour. Abnormal Psychology, 1966-74, Communications in Behavior Biology, 1968-71, Behaviorism, 1971—, Behavior Modification, 1976—. Bd. dirs. Schwab Rehab. Hosp., Chgo. Served with AUS, 1942-45. Recipient Research Career Devel. award NIMH, 1963-67. Fellow AAAS, Assn. Advancement Behavior Therapy, Am. Psychol. Assn. (v.p. div. exptl. analysis behavior 1967-70); mem. Am. Ecol. Soc., AAUP, Psychonomic Soc., Assn. Behavior Analysis (pres. 1977-78), Sigma Xi. Home: 5555 S Everett Ave Chicago IL 60637

GOLDIN, ALAN GARY, advertising executive; b. N.Y.C., Aug. 5, 1942; s. Harvey and Nita Conde and Goldin; m. Harriet Doreen Brandler, June 28, 1969; children: Stacy Erica, Allison Sarah. B.S., CCNY, 1964; M.B.A., CUNY, 1968. Poject dir. Grey Advt., N.Y.C., 1965-67; mgr. media research Ogilvy & Mather, N.Y.C., 1967-76; v.p., dir. media research BBDO, N.Y.C., 1976-79, sr. v.p., media dir., 1979-82, Kenyon & Eckhardt, N.Y.C., 1982—; instr. Am. Mktg. Assn., N.Y.C., 1978-81. Served with U.S. Army Res., 1965-71. Mem. Agy. Media Research Council (chmn. 1977-80), Consumer Mag. Com., Radio-TV Research Council. Club: Whippoorwill (Armonk, N.Y.). Office: Kenyon & Eckhardt Inc 200 Park Ave New York NY 10166

GOLDIN, JUDAH, Hebrew literature educator; b. N.Y.C., Sept. 14, 1914; s. Gerson David and Rachel (Robkin) G.; m. Grace Avis Aaronson, June 21, 1938; children: Robin Elinor (dec.), David Lionel. B.S., Coll. City N.Y., 1934; diploma, Sem. Coll., 1934; M.A., Columbia, 1938; M.H.L., Jewish Theol. Sem., 1938, D.H.L., 1943, H.L.D., 1968; M.A., Yale, 1958; D.D., Colgate U., 1973. Lectr., vis. asso. prof. Jewish lit. and history Duke, 1943-45; asso. prof. religion U. Iowa, 1946-52; dean, asso. prof. Agada Sem. Coll., Jewish Theol. Sem., 1952-58; adj. prof. religion Columbia, 1955-58; prof. Jewish studies Yale, 1958-62, prof. classical Judaica, 1962-73; prof. postbibl. Hebrew lit. U. Pa., Phila., 1973—. Author: The Two Versions of Abot de Rabbi Nathan, 1945, Hillel the Elder, 1946, The Period of the Talmud, 1949, The Fathers, 1955, The Living Talmud, 1957, The Three Pillars of Simeon the Righteous, 1958, A Philosophical Session in a Tannaite Academy, 1965, The End of Ecclesiastes, 1966, The Song at the Sea, 1971, Profile of Aqiba ben Joseph, 1976, The First Pair, 1980; editor: The Jewish Expression, 1970, The Munich Mekilta, 1980. Am. Philos. Soc. grantee, 1957, 71; Guggenheim fellow, 1958; Fulbright fellow, 1958, 64-65; Am. Council Learned Socs., 1978. Fellow Am. Acad. Jewish Research, Am. Acad. Arts and Scis.; mem. Archeol. Inst. Am., Am. Schs. Oriental Research, Soc. Bibl. Lit., Conn. Acad. Arts and Scis., Phi Beta Kappa. Home: 405 Thayer Rd Swarthmore PA 19081 Office: Oriental Studies Dept U Pa Philadelphia PA 19194

GOLDIN, LEON, artist, educator; b. Chgo., Jan. 16, 1923; s. Joseph P. and Bertha (Metz) G.; m. Meta Solotaroff, July 30, 1949; children—Joshua, Daniel. B.F.A., Art Inst. Chgo., 1948; M.F.A., U. Iowa, 1950. From Instr. to assoc. prof. Columbia U., 1964-82, prof., 1982—, chmn. dept. painting and sculpture, 1973-75, 77-80; former tchr. Calif. Coll. Arts and Crafts, Phila. Coll. Art, Queen's Coll., Cooper Union; vis. prof. painting Stanford, summer 1973. Exhibited one man shows, Oakland Art Mus., 1955, Felix Landau Gallery, Los Angeles, 1956, 57, 59, Galleria L'Attico, Rome, 1958, Kraushaar Galleries, N.Y.C., 1960, 64, 68, 72, U. Houston, 1981; rep. permanent collections, Bklyn. Mus., City Mus. St. Louis, Worcester Mus., Addison Gallery Am. Art, Pa. Acad. Fine Arts, Los Angeles County Mus., Santa Barbara Mus., Oakland Art Mus., Munson Proctor Inst., Va. Mus. Fine Arts, Portland (Maine) Mus., Everson Mus., Syracuse, N.Y., U. Ark., Okla. Art Center. Served with AUS, 1943-46; ETO. Recipient Prix de Rome Am. Acad. Rome, 91955-58, Jennie Sesnan gold medal Pa. Acad. Fine Arts, 1966; Tiffany grantee, 1951; Fulbright scholar to, France, 1952; Guggenheim fellow, 1959; Nat. Endowment for Arts grantee, 1967, 80; Nat. Inst. Arts and Letters grantee, 1968; N.Y. Caps grantee, 1981. Home: 438 W 116th St New York NY 10027

GOLDIN, MILTON, fund raising cons.; b. Cleve., Jan. 8, 1927; s. Hyman and Ida (Felsher) G.; m. Aranka Nemcek, June 17, 1950; children—Karen, David. B.A., N.Y. U., 1953, M.A., 1955. Adminstrv. dir. Am. Choral Found., 1955-61; asso. dir. devel. Brookdale Hosp. Center, 1963-66; fund raising campaign dir. Washington Sq. Coll. and Grad. Sch. Arts and Sci., N.Y. U., 1966-67; v.p. Oram Assos., Inc., 1967-72, exec. v.p., 1972-75; fund raising cons., 1975—; mgr. Amor Artis Chorale and Orch., 1961-78. Mem., N.Y.C. Symphony, 1944-45, Denver Symphony Orch., 1949-51; Author: The Music Merchants, 1969, Why They Give, 1976; Contbr. articles to periodicals. Served with AUS, 1945-46. Recipient Deems Taylor award ASCAP, 1970. Mem. Orgn. Am. Historians, Authors Guild, Phi Beta Kappa, Psi Chi, Mu Sigma. Home: 266 Crest Dr Tarrytown NY 10591 *Knowledge is not understanding, but the ability to present facts so as to permit people to realize their own deepest and most unique capabilities is perhaps the most important tool an executive can possess.*

GOLDIN, SOL, mktg. cons.; b. N.Y.C., Mar. 5, 1909; s. Isaac and Fanny (Barr) G.; m. Doris Margaret Curley, Nov. 26, 1930; children—Richard Thomas, Barbara (Mrs. James MacDonald), Kenneth Lee, Arlene (Mrs. Paul Cavaness), Steven Edward. B.B.A., Bryant Coll., 1928. With Sears Roebuck & Co., Chgo., 1933-49; buyer appliances Goldblatt Bros., Chgo., 1949-51; sales mgr. Henry N. Clark Co., Boston, 1951-52; buyer, mgr. appliances and TV Strawbridge & Clothier, Phila., 1952-55; with Whirlpool Corp., Benton Harbor, Mich., 1955-74; pres. Mktg. Affiliates Corp., Benton Harbor, 1974—; Lectr. in, U.S., France, Belgium, Australia.; Chmn. bd., chmn. exec. com. Brand Names Found., N.Y.C., 1971—. Writer: column Home Appliance Builder mag, 1961-67; Contbr. articles to profl. jours. Recipient Appreciation certificate Am. U., 1964, Nat. Alumni Council award Bryant Coll., 1964; Torch of Truth award Indpls. Advt. Club, 1972. Mem. Home Furnishings Industry Inst. (chmn. trustees 1971—), Nat. Appliance-Radio-TV Dealers Assn. (Man of Year award 1963), Nat. Account Mktg. Assn. (co-founder, bd. dirs. 1962-66), Inst. Appliance Mfrs. (Statesmanship award 1963, pres. 1965-67), Sales Execs. Club N.Y.C., Whirlpool Mgmt. Club (pres. 1966). Home and Office: 2045 Colfax Ave Benton Harbor MI 49022

GOLDING, BRAGE, former university president; b. Chgo., Apr. 28, 1920; s. Leon M. and Viola B. (Brage) G.; m. Hinda F. Wolf, Dec. 21, 1941; children: Brage, Susan, Julie. B.S., Purdue U., 1941, Ph.D., 1948; LL.D., Wright State U., 1975. Assoc. dir. research Lilly Varnish Co., Indpls.; also research assoc. Purdue U., 1948-57; vis. prof. engring. Purdue U., dir. research Lilly Varnish Co., 1957-59; head Sch. Chem. Engring. Purdue U., 1959-66; v.p. Ohio State U. and; Miami U., 1966-67; pres. Wright State U., Dayton, Ohio, 1967-72, San Diego State U., 1972-77, Kent State U., 1977-82; cons. to industry. Author: Polymers and Resins, 1959; Contbr. articles to profl. jours. Fellow AAAS; mem. Am. Chem. Soc., Phi Beta Kappa (hon.). Address: RFD 1 Box 202 Stonington CT 06378

GOLDING, ELIZABETH BASS, judge; b. N.Y.C., Apr. 12, 1902; d. William and Dora (Binkow) Bass; m. Samuel Golding, Nov. 26, 1931. LL.B. (scholar), N.Y. U.; postgrad., Wellesley Coll., Adelphi Coll. Bar: N.Y. 1923. Practiced in, N.Y.C., 1923-40, in, Hempstead, N.Y., 1940—; specialist in real estate law; dir. corps.; lectr. and community cons.; regional chmn. Office Civilian Def., 1942-45; vice chmn. USO, Nassau County, 1943-46; chmn. Serviceman's Legal Aid Com. for

Mitchel Field., N.Y., 1942-46; legal adviser Wayside Home of Salvation Army, 1949-50; commr. of correction State of N.Y., 1961-63; family ct. judge for, Nassau County, 1963—. Author: The Health of the Nation, 1940, Don't Underestimate Woman Power; also pamphlets. Organized Nat. Woman's Forum, Inc. (founder 1946), Woman's Forum of Nassau County (founder-organizer 1944), Woman's Forum of Worcester County, Mass. (founder-organizer); pioneered in inter-group edn. of women's orgns. on community level; organized Human Relations Workshop, 1948-50; pres. Hope for Youth, Inc., agy. establishing group homes for homeless children, 1970—, founder-pres. emeritus, 1979—. Recipient Nassau County award for leadership and valuable contbn. in field of human relations and intergroup community activity, 1950; award for outstanding and dedicated service to youth of county Nassau-Suffolk council Jewish War Vets., 1972; award for meritorious service to children of Am. Nat. Council Juvenile and Family Ct. Judges, 1980. Mem. Nat. Council Jewish Women (dir. nat. bd. and exec. com., nat. chmn. social legis. 1938-44), Nat. Woman's Forum, Inc. (pres. 1952), Internat. Assn. Women Lawyers (del. to UN Commn. on Human Rights 1959), United Hias Service, Inc. (exec. com., nat. bd.), Nat. Assn. Women Lawyers (chmn. labor relations, regional dir. 1959-61), Nassau County Bar Assn. (chmn. community relations com.), Woman's Bar Assn. Nassau County (pres. 1943-45), Zonta (hon. mem. L.I.). Home: 312 East Shore Dr Massapequa NY 11758

GOLDING, MARTIN PHILIP, philosopher; b. N.Y.C., Mar. 30, 1930; s. Sidney Israel and Mildred (Lewis) G.; m. Naomi Holtzman, Apr. 8, 1951; children—Shulamith, Belinda, Joshua. B.A., UCLA, 1949, M.A., 1952; Ph.D., Columbia U., 1959. Asso. prof. philosophy Columbia U., 1957-70, adj. prof., 1971—; prof. philosophy John Jay Coll. Criminal Justice, City U. N.Y., 1970-76; vis. prof. jurisprudence Faculty Law, Bar-Ilan U., Israel, 1971-72; prof. philosophy and law, chmn. dept. Duke U., 1976—. Author: The Nature of Law, 1966, Philosophy of Law, 1975, also articles. Mem. Am. Soc. Polit. and Legal Philosophy, Internat. Soc. Legal and Social Philosophy, Am. Philos. Assn. Jewish. Office: Philosophy Dept Duke Univ Durham NC 27708

GOLDING, STUART SAMUEL, constrn. co. exec.; b. Boston, Apr. 1, 1917; s. Harry and Pauline (Simon) G.; m. Roberta Marks, June 13, 1943; children—Paul R., Kenneth A., Harriet S. B.A., Brown U., 1939; M.B.A., Harvard, 1947. Asst. to pres. R.H. White Corp., Boston, 1947-50; mdse. mgr. Raymonds, Inc., Boston, 1950-52; pres. Stuart S. Golding, Inc. (shopping center developers), Tampa, Fla., 1952-71; sr. v.p. U.S. Home Corp., Clearwater, Fla., 1971-73, pres., chief ops. officer, dir., 1973-76; chmn. Stuart S. Golding Co.; dir. Community Banks of Fla.; adv. bd. New Eng. Life Ins. Co.; Trustee Internat. Council Shopping Centers.; mem. Tampa Bay Regional Planning Council, Tampa Bay Area Com. Fgn. Relations; mem. pres.'s council Brandeis U.; developer historic Willard Hotel restoration, Washington, 1980; Redeveloper historic Willard Hotel, Washington, 1979. Served to lt. comdr. USNR, 1941-45. Recipient hon. award Brown U., 1979. Clubs: Rotarian., Brown of West Coast Fla. (pres. 1964-66), West Coast Fla. Harvard (v.p. 1970-71), Boston Yacht.). Home: 5010 Bayshore Blvd Tampa FL 33611 Office: 842 Countryside Mall Clearwater FL 33515

GOLDING, WILLIAM GERALD, author; b. St. Colum Minor, Cornwall, Eng., Sept. 19, 1911; s. Alec A. nd and Mildred A. G.; m. Ann Brookfield, 1939; children: David, Judith. B.A., Brasenose Coll., Oxford, Eng., 1935, 1966; D. Litt. (hon.), U. Sussex, 1970, U. Kent, 1974, U. Warwick, 1981, Sorbonne, 1981, Oxford U., 1982. Tchr. Bishop Wordsworth's Sch., Wiltshire, Eng., 1939, 45-61. Settlement house work, dir., actor, writer, 1935-39; writer-in-residence, Hollins Coll., 1961-62; author: Poems, 1934, Lord of the Flies, 1954, The Inheritors, 1955, Pincher Martin, 1950, Free Fall, 1959, The Spire, 1964, The Hot Gates, 1965, The Pyramid, 1967, The Scorpion God, 1971, Darkness Visible, 1979 (James Tait Black Meml. prize), Rites of Passage, 1980 (Booker McConnel prize, Nobel prize for lit. 1983), A Moving Target, 1982; play Brass Butterfly, 1958. Served to lt. Royal Navy, 1940-45. Fellow Royal Soc. Lit., 1955. Office: Ebble Thatch Bowerchalke Wiltshire England

GOLDIS, SY, advertising agency executive; b. N.Y.C., Oct. 14, 1928; s. Abraham and Mollie (Roth) G.; m. Lenore Gloria Wertheim, May 21, 1955; 1 dau., Ellen Tracy. B.S., N.Y. U., 1951. Market research analyst Lennen & Newell, N.Y.C., 1951-54; broadcast buyer J. Walter Thompson, N.Y.C., 1954-56, McCann-Erickson, 1956-57, broadcast supr., 1957-59, media supr., 1960-63; media group supr. Doyle Dane Bernbach, Inc., N.Y.C., 1963-64, asso. media dir., 1964-65, media dir., 1966-69, v.p., dir. media planning, 1970-74, sr. v.p., dir. media services, including data and word processing, telecommunications, 1975—; guest lectr. N.Y. U., Folio Mag. seminars. Columnist: Marketing and Media Decisions, 1980—. A founder, 1st v.p. Tourette Syndrome Assn., N.Y.C., 1970-73, pres., 1974-76, 2d v.p., 1977-78. Served with U.S. Army, 1946-48. Mem. Internat. Radio and TV Soc. Jewish. Office: 437 Madison Ave New York NY 10022

GOLDMAN, ALAN IRA, computer company executive; b. N.Y.C., July 29, 1937; s. Julius and Florence (Blum) G. A.B., Cornell U., 1958; M.B.A., N.Y. U., 1962; grad., Stonier Grad. Sch. Banking, 1967. Methods analyst, personnel-researcher Fed. Res. Bank of N.Y., N.Y.C., 1958-62; platform asst. Bankers Trust Co., N.Y.C., 1962-63, asst. mgr., 1963-64, mgr., 1964-65, asst. treas., 1965-66, asst. v.p., 1967-69; asso. investment banking dept. Lehman Bros., N.Y.C., 1969-70; v.p. fin., chief fin. officer, treas. Interway Corp., N.Y.C., 1970-74; mgmt. cons., Montclair, N.J., 1974-75; v.p. fin. Mgmt. Assistance Inc., N.Y.C., 1975-80, sr. v.p. fin., 1980—; lectr., adv., examiner Stonier Grad. Sch. Banking, 1968-71; lectr. Am. Inst. Banking, 1968-69. Co-chmn. Montclair chpt. campaign ARC, 1970-73; chmn. Cornell Funds' N.Y. Area Phonathons, 1972-74, UN Week, Montclair, 1973. Mem. Fin. Execs. Inst., Am. Platform Tennis Assn., Phi Beta Kappa, Phi Kappa Phi, Zeta Beta Tau. Clubs: Bradford Bath and Tennis, Montclair Racquets (Montclair); Cornell of N.Y.; Economic, University (N.Y.C.). Office: 560 Lexington Ave New York NY 10022

GOLDMAN, ALFRED EMMANUEL, survey research company executive; b. Bklyn., Dec. 19, 1925; s. Samuel and Julia (Schwartz) G.; m. Adele Lieb, Mar. 30, 1952; children: Julia Madelaine, Marshall Scott. B.S., CCNY, 1949, M.A., cert. in clin. sch. psychology, 1950; Ph.D. in Clin. Psychology, Clark U., 1955. Research clin. psychologist Boston State Hosp., 1953-54; asst. prof. Northeastern U., Boston, 1954-55; research assoc. Sch. Public Health, Harvard U., 1955-56; asst. dir. psychol. services Norristown (Pa.) State Hosp., 1956-60; dir. research devel. Nat. Analysts div. Booz-Allen & Hamilton Inc., Phila., 1960-64; exec. v.p., dir. research Nat. Analysis div. Booz-Allen & Hamilton Inc., 1964-70, pres., 1970-82, sr. v.p., 1982—; founding chmn., bd. dirs. Council Am. Survey Research Orgns., 1975-77, bd. dirs., 1977-80. Contbr. articles in field to various publs. Served with USAAF, 1944-46. Fellow Am. Psychol. Assn.; mem. Am. Assn. for Public Opinion Research, Am. Mktg. Assn., Product Devel. and Mgmt. Assn. (bd. dirs. 1983—), Phi Beta Kappa. Home: 324 Marvin Rd Elkins Park PA 19117 Office: National Analysts Div of Booz Allen & Hamilton Inc 400 Market St Philadelphia PA 19106 *

GOLDMAN, BERNARD, leasing company executive; b. Boston, Apr. 16, 1928; s. Samuel and Edith E. (Feister) G.; children: Adria Lee Frenzel, Risa Joy, Gerald Scott, Jami Sue. A.S., Cambridge Jr. Coll., 1946; student, E.C.C., Boston U., 1947-54. With Bankers Leasing and Fin. Corp. subs. Sante Fe So. Pacific Corp., Chgo., 1955—, v.p., 1955-64, sr. v.p., controller, 1964-68, pres., dir., chief operating officer, 1969—, chief exec. officer, 1975—. Past trustee Temple Beth Shalom, Needham, Mass.; treas., trustee Peninsula Temple Beth El, San Mateo; bd. dirs. Peninsula YMCA, San Mateo, Calif.; vice chmn. Calif. Draft Appeal Bd. Mem. Am. Assn. Equipment Lessors (acctg. com.), Western Assn. Equipment Lessors (tax com.), Am. Automotive Leasing Assn. (bd. dirs.), World Affairs Council. Republican. Clubs: Peninsula Golf and Country (San Mateo); Bombay Bicycle Riding (Burlingame, Calif.); Masons. Home: 2303 Armada Way San Mateo CA 94404 Office: 2655 Campus Dr Suite 200 San Mateo CA 94403

GOLDMAN, BERNARD MARVIN, art history educator; b. Toronto, Ont., Can., May 30, 1922; came to U.S., 1925, naturalized, 1943; m. Norma Wynick, Aug. 1, 1944; 1 son, Mark. Ph.D., U. Mich., 1959. Prof. art history Wayne State U., Detroit, 1966—; dir. Wayne State U. Press, 1974—. Author: Sacred Portal, 1966, Reading and Writing in the Arts, 1972, rev. edit., 1978; editor: Hopkins, Discovery of Dura-Europos. Served with USAAF, 1943-45. Fellow Am. Council Learned Socs. Home: 6239 Eastmoor St Birmingham MI 48010 Office: Wayne State U Detroit MI 48202

GOLDMAN, BERT ARTHUR, psychologist, educator; b. N.Y.C., Apr. 4, 1929; s. Jack W. and Clara R. G.; m. Phyllis Barkas, June 10, 1956; children: Lisa, Linda. B.A., U. Md., 1951; M.Ed., U. N.C., 1956; Ed.D., U. Va., 1960. Mem. faculty U. N.C., Greensboro, 1965—, prof. ednl. psychology, 1971—, dean, 1970—. Served with U.S. Army, 1951-53. Mem. Am. Psychol. Assn., Am. Council Measurement Edn., Nat. Soc. Study Edn. Office: U NC Greensboro NC 27412

GOLDMAN, BO, screen writer; b. N.Y.C., Sept. 10, 1932; s. Julian and Lillian (Levy) G.; m. Mab Ashforth, Jan. 2, 1954; children—Mia, Amy, Diana, Jesse, Serena, Justin. A.B., Princeton U., 1953. Lyricist: Broadway musical First Impressions, 1959; asso. producer: Playhouse 90, CBS-TV, 1958-60; writer-producer: Theater in Am, 1972-74, NET Playhouse, 1970-71; screenwriter: One Flew Over the Cuckoo's Nest, 1976, The Rose, 1978, Melvin and Howard, 1980, Shoot the Moon, 1981; screen writer, dir., Beverly Hills, Calif., 1981—; (Recipient Academy award for screenplay One Flew Over the Cuckoo's Nest, 1976, for screenplay Melvin and Howard 1981). Served with U.S. Army, 1954-56. Mem. Writers Guild W., Acad. Motion Picture Arts and Scis., Dramatists Guild, ASCAP. Address: care William Morris Agy 151 El Camino Beverly Hills CA 90212

GOLDMAN, CHARLES NORTON, lawyer, corporation executive; b. N.Y.C., Feb. 15, 1932; s. Morris and Mary Celia (Tames) G.; m. Jane Barbara Webbink, July 21, 1968; children: Alexander Daniel, Jeffrey David. A.B. with honors, Columbia U., 1953, LL.B., 1955. Bar: N.Y. 1956. Practiced in, N.Y.C., 1955-60; atty.-advisor AID, Washington, 1960-62; regional legal advisor for India, Nepal and Ceylon AID mission to India, New Delhi, 1962-64, asst. gen. counsel for Latin Am., 1965-68, dep. gen. counsel, 1968; staff counsel for Latin Am. ITT, N.Y.C., 1969-72, sr. counsel, asst. to gen. counsel, 1972-74, sr. counsel for Latin Am., 1974-75; v.p., gen. counsel ITT Europe Inc., Brussels, 1975-81; v.p. ITT, 1976—, assoc. gen. counsel, 1981—; bd. dirs. Nat. Fgn. Trade Council Inc. Recipient Younger Fed. Lawyer award Fed. Bar Assn., 1966. Mem. Phi Beta Kappa. Club: Mid-Atlantic of N.Y. Inc. (mem. exec. com.). Office: 320 Park Ave New York NY 10022

GOLDMAN, CHARLES REMINGTON, scientist, educator; b. Urbana, Ill., Nov. 9, 1930; s. Marcus Selden and Olive (Remington) G.; m. Shirley Ann Aldous, Apr. 4, 1953 (div. June 1975); children: Christopher Selden (dec.), Margaret Blanche, Olivia Remington, Ann Aldous; m. Evelyne de Amezaga, May 12, 1977. B.A., U. Ill., 1952, M.S., 1955; Ph.D., U. Mich., 1958. Asst. aquatic biologist Ill. Natural History Survey, 1954-55; teaching fellow fisheries U. Mich., 1955-58; fishery research biologist U.S. Fish and Wildlife Service, Alaska, 1957-58; mem. faculty U. Calif.-Davis, 1958—, prof. zoology, 1966-71, dir., 1966-69, prof. limnology, div. environ. studies, 1971—; cons. hydroelectric and water pollution to govt. and industry, U.S., Africa, S. Am., Australia and N.Z., 1959—; cons. UN Purari River Dam project, Pupua New Guinea, 1974, Niger River Dam Project, 1977—, Parana River Flood Control, Argentina, 1979; mem. Calif. Assembly Sci. and Tech. Adv. Council, 1970-73, Calif. Solid Waste Mgmt. Bd., 1973-77; U. Calif. rep. Orgn. Tropical Studies, 1977—; NSF and Nat. Acad. Scis. on coastal pollutions problems, Taiwan, 1974; mem. Sci. Com. on Problems of Environ. Editor: Primary Productivity in Aquatic Environments, 1966; Co-editor: Environmental Quality and Water Development, 1973. Served to capt. USAF, 1952-54. Guggenheim fellow, 1965; NSF sr. fellow, 1964; Goldman Glacier named in Antarctica, 1967; recipient Antartic Service medal, 1968. Fellow AAAS, Calif. Acad. Scis. (fed. del. to USSR on water pollution 1973); mem. Am. Soc. Limnology and Oceanography (editorial bd. 1964-67, nat. pres. 1967-68, pres. Western sect. 1966-67), Ecol. Soc. Am. (editorial bd. 1966-68, mem.-at-large 1972-73, v.p. 1973-74), Internat. Soc. Theoretical and Applied Limnology; hon. mem. Culver chpt. Cum Laude Soc. Club: Explorers. Discoverer trace element limiting factors in N.Am. and N.Z. lakes.

GOLDMAN, DONALD HOWARD, lawyer; b. N.Y.C., July 18, 1942; s. Leon and Jean (Burke) G.; m. Madeleine Blane, July 23, 1967; children: Diane, David. B.B.A., City U. N.Y., 1964; J.D., Bklyn. Law Sch., 1967. Bar: N.Y. 1968. Fla. 1977. Atty. firm Fleishaker & Shulman, N.Y.C., 1968-69; atty. CBS Inc., N.Y.C., 1969-73, Teleprompter Corp., 1973-74; partner firm Anderson & Goldman, N.Y.C., 1974-78, Kliegman, Israel and Goldman, 1978-79; individual practice law, N.Y.C., 1979—; adj. prof. real estate Pace U.; lectr. communications. Mem. N.Y. State, N.Y. County, Nassau County bar assns., Bklyn. Law Sch., City Coll. alumni assns., Nat. Acad. TV Arts and Scis. Home: 115 Soundview Dr Port Washington NY 11050 *In order to succeed one must be prepared to risk.*

GOLDMAN, ELLIOT, communications executive; b. N.Y.C., Apr. 15, 1935; s. Benjamin and Ethel (Littmann) G.; m. Jill Montag, Dec. 11, 1966; children: Benjamin, Elizabeth, Catherine. B.A., Cornell U., 1957; LL.B., Columbia U., 1961. Bar: N.Y. 1962. With Goldman's Yarn Stores, N.Y.C., 1961-64; campaign co-dir. Senator Robert F. Kennedy, 1964; legis. counsel to N.Y. state senator, 1964; exec. asst. N.Y.C. Rent Adminstrn., 1965-67; dir. bus. affairs CBS Records, N.Y.C., 1967-70, v.p. bus. affairs, 1970-71, adminstrv. v.p., 1971-74; exec. v.p., gen. mgr. Arista Records, N.Y.C., 1974-82; v.p. U.S. and Canadian ops. Ariola Internat. Group, 1979-82; sr. v.p. Warner Communications, Inc., 1982—. Mem. exec. com. N.Y. Young Democrats, 1965-67; mem. exec. com. Lenox Hill Democratic Club, 1965-72; mem. Rye City Bd. Appeals, 1976-78. Jewish. Office: Warner Communications, Inc 75 Rockfeller Plaza New York NY 10019

GOLDMAN, GERALD HILLIS, consumer products distribution company executive; b. Omaha, July 26, 1947; s. Lester Jack and Lilyan Haykin (Weiskopf) G.; m. Cathy Evelyn Brightman, Dec. 15, 1973; children: Lori, Jeffrey. B.S.B.A., U. Nebr., 1969; M.B.A., U. So. Calif., 1975. C.P.A., Calif.; C.P.A., Nebr. Sr. acct. Arthur Andersen & Co., Los Angeles, 1969-72; exec. v.p., chief fin. officer CORE-MARK Internat., Inc., Richmond, B.C., Can., 1972—. Mem. Am. Inst. A.P.A.s, Calif. Soc. C.P.A.s. Home: 5550 Somerset Crescent Vancouver BC Canada V6M 1S6 Office: CORE-MARK Internat Inc 13951 Bridgeport Rd Richmond BC Canada V6V 1J6

GOLDMAN, HENRY MAURICE, peridontology educator; b. Boston, Dec. 9, 1911; s. Joseph and Rebecca (Levy) G.; m. Dorothy Alter, June 7, 1936; children: Richard, Gerald. Student, Brown U., 1929-31, D.Sc. (hon.), 1978; D.M.D., Harvard U., 1935; D.Sc. (hon.), Boston U., 1976, N.J. Coll. Medicine and Dentistry, 1977, U. Pa., 1978, Central U., Venezuela. Diplomate: Am. Bd. Periodontology (dir. 1952-58), Am. Bd. Oral Pathology (pres. 1955-56, dir. 1948-55), Am. Bd. Oral Medicine. Research fellow oral pathology Harvard, 1935-37, instr. oral pathology, 1938-46; chief stomatology and dental research, dir. Riesman Dental Clinic, Beth Israel Hosp., 1948; prof. peridontology, chmn. dept. Grad. Sch. Medicine U. Pa., 1955-64; prof., chmn. dept. stomatology Sch. Medicine, Boston U., 1958-64, mem. exec. com., 1963—, prof., chmn. dept. oral pathology, 1964-77, dean, 1963-77, now dean emeritus, also chief stomalogical service, bd. incorporators, trustee; asso. dir. Boston U. Med. Center, 1972-78; Cons. dental and oral registry Army Inst. Pathology, Washington; sub-com. periodontia, com. dentistry NRC, 1948-51; cons. to NIH, 1969; surgeon gen. U.S. Army, 1965—; mem. vis. com. Boston U. Sch. Medicine, 1983—. Author: Periodontia, 4th rev. edit, 1959, Atlas of Dental and Oral Pathology, 3 rev. edit, 1944; co-author: Periodontal Therapy, 6th edit, 1979, Introduction to Periodontia, 6th edit, 1977, Treatment Planning in Practice of Dentistry, 1959, Thoma's Oral Pathology, 1970, 6th edit, Current Therapy in Dentistry, 6th edit, 1977, Oral Pathology Atlas, 1973, 2d edit., 1979, Biologic Basis of Orthodontics, 1971, Periodontal Pathology, Oral Pathology, Surgical Management of Periodontal Disease, 1981; editor: Jour. Periodontology, 1968-80; editor emeritus, 1980—; contbr. numerous articles to profl. jours. Served as capt., chief dental pathologic sect. AUS, 1943-45; pathologist dental registry Army Inst. Pathology. Recipient Thomas P. Hinman award, 1952, 67; Gold medal Am. Acad. Periodontolgoy, 1968; Gies award, 1970; 70th Year Celebration award, Sao Paulo, Brazil; Alpha Omega award; Orban prize, 1976; Internat. award Friends of U. Conn., 1977; Fones medal and award, 1978; Henry M. Goldman Sch. Grad. Dentistry, Boston U., named in his honor. Fellow Am. Acad. Oral Pathology (pres. 1952-53), Am. Acad. Periodontology, Am. Coll. Dentists, Royal Soc. Medicine, Internat. Coll. Dentists; mem. Am. Pub. Health Assn., AAAS (mem. Ivory Cross expdn. 1948), Am. Soc. Perodontists (pres. 1963-64, editor jour.), M. Dental Assn. (council on dental research 1952-54, 58—), Acad. Periodontology, New Eng. Pathologic Soc., Internat. Assn. Dental Research, Nat. Inst. Dental Research (ad hoc com. periodontology 1972-75, cons. to dir. 1971-75), Harvard Odontological Soc., Sr. Soc. Harvard Sch. Dental Medicine, Brit. Periodontology Soc. (hon. mem.), Italian Periodontology Soc. (hon.), Sigma Xi, Pi Lambda Phi, Omicron Kappa Upsilon. Clubs: Harvard (Boston); Belmont (Mass.) Country. Home: 176 Grant Ave Newton Center MA 02159 Office: 1443 Beacon St Brookline MA 02146 *It is my belief that it is the obligation of every individual to fulfill his or her fullest potential. Integrity and reliability are important. Each task should be assumed with full responsibility towards its completion. Judgment should be made on the basis of values and not whim and fancy.*

GOLDMAN, IRVING, anthropology educator; b. N.Y.C., Sept. 2, 1911; s. Louis and Golda (Levine) G.; m. Hannah Stern, June 13, 1934. B.S., Bklyn. Coll., 1933; Ph.D., Columbia, 1941. Asst. in anthropology Columbia, 1936-37, lectr., 1938; tutor Bklyn. Coll., 1940-42; research analyst Office Coordinator Inter-Am. Affairs, Washington, 1942-44; chief br. Latin Am. div. Office Research and Analysis, U.S. Dept. State, 1945-47; prof. anthropology Sarah Lawrence Coll., Bronxville, N.Y., 1947-81, prof. emeritus, 1981; sr. research asso. in anthropology Grad. Faculty, New Sch. for Social Research, N.Y.C., 1981—, vis. prof. anthropology, 1982—. Author: The Cubeo: Indians of the Northwest Amazon, 1963, Ancient Polynesian Society, 1970, The Mouth of Heaven, An Introduction to Kwakiutl Religious Thought, 1975; Contbr. articles and essays to profl. jours. Served to 2d lt. OSS AUS, 1944-45. Bollingen Found. fellow, 1960-62; Social Sci. Research Council fellow, 1969-70. Mem. AAAS, Am. Anthrop. Assn., Am. Ethnol. Soc., N.Y. Acad. Scis. Research in Carrier Indians B.C., 1935-36, Cubeo Indians Vaupes, Colombia, 1939-40, 68, 69-70. *As a cultural anthropologist my highest aim has always been to represent authentically the native societies that I study so that they can be understood, insofar as that is possible, as they are; and to contribute thereby to the awareness of human diversity in unity.*

GOLDMAN, JAMES, playwright, screenwriter, novelist; b. Chgo., June 30, 1927; s. M. Clarence and Marian (Weil) G.; 1962 (div. 1974); children: Julia, Matthew; m. Barbara Deren, Oct. 25, 1975. Ph.B., U. Chgo., 1947, M.A., 1950; postgrad., Columbia, 1950-52. Writer screenplays, drama, novels, N.Y.C., 1954—; Author: (with William Goldman) plays Blood, Sweat and Stanley Poole, 1964, (with William Goldman and John Kander) Family Affair, 1964; They Might Be Giants, 1961; play The Lion in Winter, 1966, screenplay (Am. Screenwriters award, Acad. award, Brit. Screenwriters award); novels Waldorf, 1965, The Man from Greek and Roman, 1974; screenplays They Might Be Giants, 1970, Nicholas and Alexandra, 1971, Follies, 1971 (Drama Critics award for best musical), Robin and Marian, 1975; TV musical Evening Primrose, 1967; novel Myself as Witness, 1980; Adaptation Oliver Twist, CBS-TV, 1982. Served with AUS, 1952-54. Mem. Dramatists Guild (council 1966—), Authors League Am. (council 1967—), Acad. Motion Picture Arts and Scis. Address: care Sam Cohn ICM 40 W 57th St New York NY 10021

GOLDMAN, JAMES M., financial executive; b. Bklyn., June 23, 1936; s. Henry and Tess (Goldstein) G.; m. Frances M. Lisson, June 21, 1960; children: Amy M., Alicia S. B.A., Brandeis U., 1958; M.B.A., Cornell U., 1960. Securities analyst Merrill Lynch Pierce Fenner Smith, N.Y.C., 1962-65; v.p. Wall St. Cons., Inc., N.Y.C., 1965-71; pres. Goldman, Auletta & Co., Inc., N.Y.C., 1971-78; dir. mktg. services Savin Corp., Valhalla, N.Y., 1978-80; ptnr. The Fin. Relations Bd., Inc., N.Y.C., 1981—. Served with U.S. Army, 1960-61. Home: 851 Club Rd Teaneck NJ 07666 Office: 655 3d Ave New York NY 10017

GOLDMAN, JOSEPH BERNARD, lawyer; b. Washington, Jan. 29, 1917; s. Jacob and Sophie (Sures) G.; m. Loretta Irma Martone, July 20, 1948; children—Alan Richard, Bettie Ellen. A.B. with distinction, George Washington U., 1937; LL.B. cum laude, Harvard, 1940. Bar: D.C. bar 1940. Atty. Bituminous Coal Consumers' Counsel, Washington, 1940-41; with OPA, 1941-44, Dept. Justice, 1944-47; spl. asst. to atty. gen., 1947-49; with CAB, 1947-70, gen. counsel, 1966-70; partner Baker & Hostetler; adj. prof. law Georgetown U. Law Sch., 1967-71; guest lectr. Am. U., Harvard, U. Mich.; U.S. del. numerous internat. confs. Home: 5250 Linnean Ave NW Washington DC 20015 Office: 818 Connecticut Ave NW Washington DC 20006

GOLDMAN, LEO, psychologist, educator; b. Kingston, N.Y., June 13, 1920; s. Morris and Tillie (Kushner) G.; m. Elsie Kamber, June 25, 1950 (div. 1982); children—Deborah Maxine, Amy Beth. B.S., Coll. City N.Y., 1940; M.A., Tchrs. Coll. Columbia, 1947, Ph.D. in Counseling Psychology, 1950. Diplomate: Am. Bd. Profl. Psychology (trustee 1966-71, v.p. 1969-71). Psychometrist Stevens Inst. Tech., 1947-48; vocat. counselor VA, N.Y.C., 1948-49; asst. prof. to assoc. prof. psychology and edn. U. Buffalo, 1950-58; assoc. prof. Bklyn. Coll., 1958-64; prof. CUNY Grad. Sch., 1964-82, Fordham U. Grad.

Sch. Edn., 1982—; cons. Lorge Sch., 1982—; Fulbright lectr. U. Amsterdam, Netherlands, 1965-66; vis. prof. Syracuse U., U. Wis., U. Pa., Rutgers U., Columbia U., Hebrew U. of Jerusalem, Israel; mem. coms. Ednl. Testing Service, Coll. Entrance Examination Bd.; adv. editor John Wiley & Sons Inc., 1975-78. Author: Using Tests in Counseling, 1961, 2d edit., 1971, Research Methods for Counselors, 1978; Editor: Personnel & Guidance Jour, 1969-75; Contbr. articles to profl. jours. Served to staff sgt. USAAF, 1942-46. Fellow Am. Psychol. Assn. (sec. div. 1966-69, council 1984—); mem. Assn. Measurement and Evaluation in Guidance (pres. 1967-68), Am. Personnel and Guidance Assn. (Research award 1962, exec. council 1966-68), Nat. Vocat. Guidance Assn. Home: 321 West 29 St Apt 5B New York NY 10001 Office: 113 W 60th St New York NY 10023

GOLDMAN, LEONARD MANUEL, physicist, engineering educator; b. N.Y.C., Mar. 22, 1925; s. Robert and Edith G.; m. Dovie Lee McSwain, June 15, 1952; children: Douglas Alan, Ellen Rebecca, Judith Andrea. Student, CCNY, 1941-44; A.B., Cornell U., 1945; M.Sc., McGill U., Can., 1948; Ph.D., U. Rochester, 1952. Research asso. Princeton U., 1952-56; research physicist Gen. Electric Co. Research and Devel. Center, Schenectady, 1956-75; prof. mech. and aerospace sci. U. Rochester, 1975—, asso. dir. lab. for laser energetics, 1977—; vis. fellow Culham (Eng.) Lab., U.K. Atomic Energy Assn., 1965-66; cons. in field. Contbr. articles to physics jours. Mem. Schenectady Sch. Bd., 1968-72. Served with USNR, 1944-46. Fellow Am. Phys. Soc.; Mem. Am. Nuclear Soc., AAAS. Home: 2 Sheridan Ct Pittsford NY 14534 Office: Mech Engring Dept Coll Engring and Applied Sci U Rochester Rochester NY 14627

GOLDMAN, MARSHALL IRWIN, economist, educator; b. Elgin, Ill., July 26, 1930; s. Sam and Bella (Silvian) G.; m. Merle Rosenblatt, June 14, 1953; children—Ethan Harris, Avra Lea, Karla Ann, Seth Abraham. B.S., Wharton Sch. of U. Pa., 1952; M.A., Harvard, 1956, Ph.D., 1961. Mem. faculty Wellesley Coll., 1958—, prof. econs., 1967-75, Class of 1919 prof. econs., 1975—, chmn. dept., 1971-77; asso. dir. Russian Research Center, Harvard, 1975—; vis. asst. prof. Brandeis U., 1961-62; Fulbright vis. lectr. Moscow State U., 1977; cons. in field. Dir. Century Bank and Trust Co., Somerville, Mass. Author: Soviet Marketing: Distribution in a Controlled Economy, 1963, Comparative Economic Systems: A Reader, rev. edit, 1971, Soviet Foreign Aid, 1967, Controlling Pollution: The Economics of a Cleaner America, 1967, The Soviet Economy: Myth and Reality, 1968, The Spoils of Progress: Environmental Pollution in The USSR, 1972, Ecology and Economics: Controlling Pollution in the 70's, 1972, Detente and Dollars: Doing Business with the Soviets, 1975, The Enigma of Soviet Petroleum: Half Empty or Half Full, 1980, U.S.S.R. in Crisis: The Failure of an Economic System, 1983. Mem. Wellesley Clean Air Com., 1969-71, Wellesley Conservation Commn., 1971-74, Wellesley Town Meeting, 1969-77; mem. Wellesley Town Democratic Com., 1964—, sec., 1969; trustee Noble & Greenough Sch., 1983—. Served with AUS, 1953-55. Huber Found. study grantee, 1959; Brookings Instn. research prof., 1964. Mem. Council Fgn. Relations, Boston Com. Fgn. Relations, Boston Econ. Club, Am. Econ. Assn., Assn. Comparative Econs. (exec. com. 1968-70). Club: Cosmos (Washington). Home: 17 Midland Rd Wellesley MA 02181

GOLDMAN, MARTIN RAYMOND RUBIN, editor; b. N.Y.C., Oct. 3, 1920; s. David and Rose (Arkin) Rubin; m. Marian Beatrice Gordon, Mar. 30, 1947; 1 dau., Susanna Linda. A.B. summa cum laude, N.Y. U., 1942; M.A., Harvard U., 1947; postgrad., St. Antony's Coll., Oxford, 1954-56. Research historian Research Studies Inst., Air U., Montgomery, Ala., 1949-57; Social Sci. Research Council grantee, 1958-60; lectr. history N.Y. U., 1960-61; asso. editor Ency. Internat., N.Y.C., 1961-62; sr. copy editor Look mag., N.Y.C., 1962-67, asst. mng. editor, 1967-68, mng. editor, 1968-71; editor Intellectual Digest, N.Y.C., 1971-74; sr. editor Time mag., 1974-77; editor, pub. New Harvest mag., 1977—; contbg. editor Working Woman mag., 1982—; cons. editor Am. Health mag., 1971—; vis. lectr. Yale U., asso. fellow Branford Coll.; Cons. Modern Lang. Assn.-Nat. Endowment for Humanities.; Mem. adv. bd. Johns Hopkins Mag., N.Y. U. Alumni News. Contbg. author: The Army Air Forces in World War II, 1958. Trustee Temple Israel, N.Y.C. Served with USAAF, 1942-45. Decorated Air medal with oak leaf cluster, Purple Heart. Mem. Am. Hist. Assn., Am. Soc. Mag. Editors, Phi Beta Kappa. Democrat. Jewish. Club: Harvard (N.Y.C.). Home and office: 1 Captains Walk The Springs East Hampton NY 11937

GOLDMAN, NORMAN LEWIS, chemist, educator; b. Bklyn., Aug. 11, 1933; s. Sam and Rose (Schrager) G. B.S., CCNY, 1954; A.M., Harvard U., 1956; Ph.D., Columbia U., 1959; Postdoctoral NSF fellow, Imperial Coll. Sci. and Tech. U. London, 1959-60; NIH postdoctoral fellow, Columbia U., N.Y.C., 1960-61. Mem. faculty Queens Coll. CUNY, 1961—, prof. chemistry, 1976—, chmn. dept., 1972-77, acting asso. dean faculty, 1977-78, acting dean faculty, div. math. and natural scis., 1977-79, dean faculty, div. math. and natural scis., 1979—. Contbr. articles to profl. jours. Mem. Am. Chem. Soc., Royal Soc. Chemistry (London), Sigma Xi, Phi Beta Kappa. Home: 75-10 Grand Central Pkwy Forest Hills NY 11375 Office: 125 Remsen Hall Queens Coll CUNY Flushing NY 11367

GOLDMAN, OSCAR, mathematics educator; b. Bklyn., Feb. 2, 1925; s. Isaac and Esther (Schwartz) G.; m. Madge Rosenbaum, Aug. 8, 1949. B.S., CCNY, 1944; A.M., Princeton U., 1946, Ph.D., 1948. Benjamin Peirce instr. Harvard U., 1948-51; mem. faculty Brandeis U., 1951-61, prof. math., 1961- 62, chmn. dept., 1956-61; prof. math. U. Pa., Phila., 1962-80, chmn. dept., 1962-67, mem., 1960-62; ret., 1981; Vis. scholar U. Calif. at Berkeley, 1967-68, 73-74. Author research papers algebra, theory numbers.; Asso. editor: Jour. Franklin Inst, 1963-67; mem. editorial com.: Mathmatical Revs, 1969-73. Sci. faculty fellow NSF, 1960-61. Mem. Am. Math. Soc., Math. Assn. Am., Assn. for Computing Machinery. Office: Math Dept U Pa Philadelphia PA 19104

GOLDMAN, RALPH, physician, educator; b. N.Y.C., June 11, 1919; s. Henry and May (Hoffman) G.; m. Helen C. Wolfson, Jan. 15, 1941; children—Paul, Richard, Elizabeth. A.B., U. Calif. at Berkeley, 1939; M.D., U. Calif. at San Francisco, 1942. Intern Los Angeles County Gen. Hosp., 1942-43, resident internal medicine, 1943-44, VA Center Los Angeles, 1946-48, chief metabolic and renal disease sect., 1948-55; chief med. service VA Hosp., Sepulveda, Calif., 1955-58; prof. medicine U. Calif. at Los Angeles Med. Sch., 1958-77, asst. dean allied health Professions, 1971-75; chief intermediate care and geriatric med. sect. VA Center Los Angeles, 1975-77; asst. chief med. dir. for extended care VA Central Office, Washington, 1977-80; asso. chief staff for edn. VA Wadsworth Med. Center, Los Angeles, 1980—. Contbr. articles to profl. jours. Served to lt., M.C. USNR, 1944-46. Fellow A.C.P., Gerontol. Soc., Geriatrics Soc.; mem. Internat. Assn. Gerontology, Am. Geriatric Soc. (Willard O. Thompson award 1970), Internat., Am. socs. nephrology. Home: 10501 Wilshire Blvd Los Angeles CA 90024

GOLDMAN, ROBERT HURON, lawyer; b. Boston, Nov. 24, 1918; s. Frank and Rose (Sydeman) G.; m. Charlotte R. Rubens, July 5, 1945; children: Wendy Eve, Randolph Rubens. A.B., Harvard U., 1939, LL.B., 1943. Bar: N.Y. State 1945, Mass. 1951. Practiced in, N.Y.C., 1945-50, Lowell, Mass., 1951—; law clk. Judge Learned Hand, U.S. Ct. Appeals, 1943-44; partner firm Goldman and Curtis (and predecessor firms), 1951—; columnist Lowell Sunday Sun Daily, 1954-78; v.p., asso. pub. Malden (Mass.) Evening News, Medford (Mass.) Daily Mercury, Melrose (Mass.) Evening News; mem. adv. bd. Baybank Middlesex.; Radio commentator on internat. affairs, 1954—. Author: A Newspaperman's Handbook of the Libel Law of Massachusetts, 1966, rev., 1974, The Law of Libel—Present and Future, 1969; Editor: Harvard Law Review, 1943. Chmn. Greater Lowell Civic Com., 1952-55, Lowell Hist. Soc., 1957-60, Lowell Devel. and Indsl. Commn., 1959-60; Del. Republican State Conv., 1960-62; Bd. dirs. Boston World Affairs Council, 1960-82. Named Citizen of Year Greater Lowell Civic Com., 1956. Mem. ABA (mem. nat. com. on consumer protection 1972-73, Sherman Act com. 1973—), Mass. Bar Assn. (chmn. bar-press com. 1973-76), Middlesex County Bar Assn., Lowell Bar Assn., Phi Beta Kappa. Club: Harvard (dir. Lowell 1968—). Home: 8 Rolling Ridge Rd Andover MA 01810 Office: 4th Floor 144 Merrimack St Lowell MA 01852

GOLDMAN, ROBERT IRVING, financial services company executive; b. Bklyn., Sept. 24, 1932; s. Maurice E. and Agnes (Wilson) G.; m. Vira Hladun, Dec. 31, 1963; 1 child, Oleksa; children by previous marriage: William D., Peter L. A.B. magna cum laude, Harvard U., 1954; LL.B., Yale U., 1957. With Congress Fin. Corp., N.Y.C., 1957—, sec.-treas., 1957-62, exec. v.p., 1962-67, pres., dir., 1967—. Mem. vis. com. Harvard Ukrainian Research Inst.; bd. dirs. Hebrew Immigrant Aid Soc., Am. Acad. Dramatic Arts. Mem. Nat. Comml. Finance Assn., Am. Jewish Com., Phi Beta Kappa, Young Pres.'s Orgn. Jewish. Home: 1021 Park Ave New York NY 10028 Office: 1133 Ave Americas New York NY 10036

GOLDMAN, SHELDON, educator; b. Bronx, N.Y., Sept. 18, 1939; s. Yehuda and Anne (Slochower) G.; m. Marcia Liebeskind, June 16, 1963; children—Ellen, Jeremy, Sara. B.A. summa cum laude, N.Y. U., 1961; Ph.D. (Woodrow Wilson Dissertation fellow), Harvard, 1965. Teaching fellow in govt. Harvard, 1963-64; asst. prof. govt. U. Mass., Amherst, 1965-69, asso. prof., 1970-73, prof. polit. sci., 1974—. Author: Roll Call Behavior in the Massachusetts House of Representatives, 1968, The Federal Judicial System, 1968, The Federal Courts as a Political System, 2d edit, 1976, American Court Systems, 1978, Constitutional Law and Supreme Court Decision-Making, 1981; Contbr. articles to profl. jours. Woodrow Wilson fellow, 1961-62; NSF grantee, 1966; Social Sci. Research Council grantee, 1967. Mem. Am., Northeastern, Midwestern, So. polit. sci. assns., Law and Society Assn., NEA, Phi Beta Kappa, Phi Sigma Alpha. Office: Dept Polit Sci U Mass Amherst MA 01003

GOLDMAN, SIMON, broadcasting executive; b. Carthage, N.Y., Jan. 18, 1913; s. Isaac and Ida G.; m. Meurice H. Finer, Jan. 4, 1948 (dec. Aug. 1972); children: Richard Michael, Gail Meurice, Paul Simon; m. Marilyn Gross Fink, Feb. 7, 1976. B.S. magna cum laude, Syracuse U., 1931. In various sales positions, 1931-36; with Sta. WJTN and WWSE, Jamestown, N.Y., 1936—, v.p., gen. mgr., 1940-55, pres., 1955—; v.p., dir. James Broadcasting Co., Inc., Jamestown, 1940—, chief owner, gen. mgr., pres., 1955—; pres. Sta. WDOE, Dunkirk, N.Y., 1957-78, Sta. WVMT, Burlington, Vt., 1964—, Sta. WLKK and WLVU, Erie, Pa., 1961—, Sta. WTOO, Bellefontaine, Ohio, 1968-72, Sta. WSYB and WRUT, Rutland, Vt., 1970—; owner Goldman Group, Jamestown, 1955—; charter mem. bd. govs. ABC; mem. adv. bd. Erie County Savs. Bank; mem. Broadcast Rating Council, 1964-72. Mem. adv. bd. St. Bonventure U. Sch. Journalism, 1966—; mem. exec. bd. Jamestown chpt. NCCJ, 1960-68; mem. nat. council, Jamestown Areas rep. USO, 1959—; active United Fund, United Negro Coll. Fund, YMCA, Better Jamestown Com.; pres. Ops. Jobs, Jamestown, 1964—; trustee Fredonia Coll. Found., 1977-81; mem. Blue Cross-Blue Shield Task Force, Mayor's Com. Indsl. Expansion; bd. dirs. Western N.Y. Anti-Defamation League, Chautauqua council Boy Scouts Am.; trustee Jamestown Community Coll., 1964-79, chmn. bd., 1968-72; pres. congregation Temple Hesed Abraham, Jamestown, 1951-56. Served with AUS, 1943-45; ETO. Recipient Brotherhood award NCCJ, 1974. Mem. Radio Advt. Bur. (a founder, dir., officer 1951-58), Nat. Assn. Broadcasters (chmn. com. on small market stas. 1947-49, dir. 1956-62, 68-72, mem. copyright com. 1983), Am. Info. Network Affiliates Assn. (treas.), Community Broadcasters Assn. (dir. 1970—), Fenton Hist. Soc. (trustee), Am. Legion. Clubs: Univ., Chautauqua Lake Yacht, Moon Brook Country, Masons, Shriners. Home: Winch Rd Lakewood NY 14750 Office: Orchard Rd WE PO Box 1139 Jamestown NY 14701 *If you are going to be a garbage collector, be the best; if you are going to be a broadcaster, teacher, whatever you strive to do, do your best and it will lead to your goal.*

GOLDMAN, STEVEN LOUIS, humanities educator, consultant; b. N.Y.C., Apr. 12, 1941; s. Saul and Dorothy (Sperling) G.; m. Risa Ebert, Oct. 29, 1968; children: Nechama, Dov, Miryam, Yedidah. B.S. in Physics, Poly. Inst. Bklyn., 1962; M.A., Boston U., 1966, Ph.D. in Philosophy, 1970. Prof. philosophy Baruch Coll., CUNY, 1968-69, Pa. State U., University Park, 1969-77; Andrew W. Mellon disting. prof. humanities Lehigh U., Bethlehem, Pa., 1977—, dir. sci., tech. and society program, 1977—; cons. NEH, Washington, 1980—; bd. dirs. Com. for Understanding of Tech. in Human Affairs, Cambridge, Mass., 1982—. Author: Science, Philosophy and Religion, 1982; contbr. articles to profl. jours. Mem. pub. adv. council Pa. Power and Light Co., Allentown, 1982. Mem. Internat. Soc. for Study of Time (dir.), Am. Phys. Soc., Philosophy of Sci. Assn., Soc. for History of Tech., Am. Philos. Assn., AAAS. Home: 127 Maple Ave Bala Cynwyd PA 19004 Office: Maginnes Hall 9 Lehigh U Bethlehem PA 18015

GOLDMAN, WILLIAM, writer; b. Chgo., Aug. 12, 1931; s. M. Clarence and Marion (Weil) G.; m. Ilene Jones, Apr. 15, 1961; children: Jenny, Susanna. B.A., Oberlin Coll., 1952; M.A., Columbia U., 1956. Author: (novels) The Temple of Gold, 1957; novels Your Turn to Curtsy, My Turn to Bow, 1958, Soldier in the Rain, 1960, Boys and Girls Together, 1964, The Thing of It Is, 1967; (pseudonyn Harry Longbaugh) No Way to Treat a Lady; (with James Goldman) (play) Blood Sweat and Stanley Poole, 1961; (with James Goldman and John Kander) (mus. comedy) A Family Affair, 1962; (film) Harper, 1966; The Season: A Candid Look at Broadway, 1969; (film) Butch Cassidy and The Sundance Kid, 1969; novels Father's Day, 1971; The Princess Bride, 1973, Marathon Man, 1974, Wigger, 1974, Magic, 1976, Tinsel, 1979, Control, 1982, The Silent Gondoliers, 1983, The Color of Light, 1984; non-fiction Adventures in the Screen Trade, 1983; (film) Marathon Man, 1976, All the President's Men, 1976, A Bridge Too Far, 1977, Magic, 1978. Recipient Acad. award best original screenplay Butch Cassidy and the Sundance Kid, 1970, Acad. award best screenplay adaptation, 1977.

GOLDNER, HERMAN WILSON, lawyer; b. Detroit, Nov. 12, 1916; s. Michael and Ethel (Wilson) G.; m. Winifred Herlan Munyan, Nov. 3, 1938; children—Brian Early, Michael Herlan. B.S., Miami U., Oxford, Ohio, 1939; LL.B., Western Res. U., 1942; M.B.A., Harvard U., 1948. Bar: Ohio bar 1942, Mass. bar 1947, Fla. bar 1948, U.S. Supreme Ct. bar 1952. Of counsel firm Goldner, Reams, Marger, Davis, Piper and Kiernan (and predecessors), St. Petersburg, Fla., 1948—; dir. Central Plaza Bank & Trust Co., Home TV, Inc.; prof. mcpl. law Stetson Law Sch., 1973-75. Mayor City of St. Petersburg, 1961-67, 71-73; founder, past chmn. Tampa Bay Regional Planning Council; founder Allied Arts Council, St. Petersburg; bd. dirs. Bayfront Med. Center, 1970, Sci. Center of St. Petersburg Inc., 1970; mem. Pres.'s Advisory Commn. on Intergovtl. Relations, Pres.'s Nat. Citizens Com. for Community Relations; mem. exec. bd. U.S. Conf. Mayors, chmn. community relations com.; chmn. Mayors' Council of Fair Apportionment. Served to lt. USN, 1942-46. Recipient Good Govt. award St. Petersburg Jr. C. of C., 1967. Mem. ABA, St. Petersburg Bar Assn. (bd. govs. 1970-71), Am. Trial Lawyers Assn., DAV, Am. Legion, Mil. Order World War II. Republican. Jewish. Clubs: Treasure Island Tennis, St. Petersburg Yacht, Commerce of Pinellas County (St. Petersburg). Office: 5665 Central Ave Saint Petersburg FL 33710

GOLDNER, JOSEPH LEONARD, surgeon, educator; b. Omaha, 1918. M.D., U. Nebr., 1943. Diplomate: Am. Bd. Orthopedic Surgery. Intern, then asst. resident U. Nebr. Hosp., 1942-44; asst. resident orthopedics, then resident Duke U. Hosp., Durham, N.C., 1946-49; orthopedic resident, then staff orthopedic surgery Ga. Warms Springs Found., 1947-48; mem. faculty Duke U. Med. Sch., 1950—, prof. orthopedic surgery, 1957—, James B. Duke prof. orthopaedic surgery, 1978—, chmn. div., 1967—; Research cons. physiology NIH, VA Hosp., Ft. Bragg (N.C.) Army Hosp.; surgeon N.C. Crippled Children's Program and Vocational Rehab.; mem. faculty Internat. Fedn. Socs. for Surgery of Hand. Chmn. managerial bd.: Jour. Foot and Ankle; mem. managerial bd.: Jour. Hand Surgery; Contbr. articles to med. jours. Served to lt. (j.g.), M.C. USNR, 1944-46. Fellow Royal Australasian Coll. Surgeons (hon.); mem. AMA, So. Med. Assn. (v.p. 1968, pres.-elect 1969, pres. 1970), Am. Acad. Orthopedic Surgeons (chmn. program com. 1974), Am. Soc. Surgery Hand (pres. 1969-70), Am. Orthopedic Assn., Am. Acad. Cerebral Palsy (chmn. ednl. council 1976-77), Am. Orthopaedic Foot Soc. (v.p. 1977, pres. 1979), Internat. Soc. for Study of Lumbar Spine, Piedmont Orthopaedic Soc. (exec. sec. 1951—), Sigma Xi. Presbyn. (deacon 1965-67). Home: 602 E Forest Hills Blvd Durham NC 27707 Office: Duke Univ Med Center Durham NC 27710

GOLDNER, SHELDON HERBERT, export-import company executive; b. Bklyn., Aug. 3, 1928; s. David and Esther (Maskowsky) G.; m. Lila Diane Silber, Aug.14, 1954. B.S. in acctg., L.I. U., 1950. C.P.A., N.Y. Acct. S.H. Goldner & Co., N.Y.C., 1950-59; v.p. fin. Connell Rice & Sugar Co., Inc., Westfield, N.J., 1959—. Served with U.S. Army, 1946-47; PTO. Mem. Am. Inst. C.P.A.s, N.Y. State Soc. C.P.A.s. Jewish. Club: Halloween Yacht (Stamford, Conn.). Home: 999 chimney Ridge Dr Mountainside NJ 07092 Office: Connell Rice & Sugar Co Inc 45 Cardinal Dr Westfield NJ 07092

GOLDOVSKY, BORIS, musician; b. Moscow, Russia, June 7, 1908; came to U.S., 1930, naturalized, 1937; s. Onesim and Lea (Luboshutz) G.; m. Margaret Codd, 1933; children—Michael, Marina. Student, Conservatory Music, Moscow, 1918-21, Acad. Music, Berlin, 1921-23; grad., Liszt Acad. Music, Budapest, 1930, Curtis Inst. Music, Phila., 1932; Mus.D., Bates Coll., 1956, Cleve. Inst., 1969, Southeastern Mass. U., 1981; D.F.A., Northwestern U., 1972. Dir. opera dept. N.E. Conservatory Music, 1942—; head opera dept. Music Center, Berkshire Festival, Lenox, Mass., 1946-61; artistic dir. Goldovsky Opera Inst., Boston, 1963—; head opera dept. Curtis Inst. Music, Phila., 1977. Debut as pianist, Berlin Philharmonic, 1921, extensive tours in, U.S.; intermission commentator, Met. Opera Co. broadcasts, 1946—; pianist, condr., lectr.; Author: Accents on Opera, 1953, Bringing Opera To Life, 1968, (with Arthur Schoep) Bringing Soprano Arias to Life, 1973, (with Thomas Wolf) Manual of Operatic Touring, 1975, (with Curtis Cate) My Road to Opera, 1979. Fellow Am. Acad. Arts and Scis. Home: 183 Clinton Rd Brookline MA 02146

GOLDREICH, PETER MARTIN, educator, astrophysicist; b. N.Y.C., July 14, 1939; s. Paul and Edith (Rosenfield) G.; m. Susan Kroll, June 14, 1960; children—Eric, Daniel. B.Engring. Physics, Cornell U., 1960, Ph.D. in Physics, 1963. Instr. Cornell U., 1963; postdoctoral fellow Cambridge (Eng.) U., 1963-64; asst. prof. astronomy and geophysics U. Calif. at Los Angeles, 1964-66; asso. prof. astronomy and planetary sci. Calif. Inst. Tech., 1966-69, prof., 1969—, Lee A. Dubridge prof. astrophysics and planetary physics, 1981—. Mem. Nat. Acad. Sci., Am. Acad. Arts and Scis. Home: 999 San Pasqual Apt 7 Pasadena CA 91106 Office: 1201 E California Blvd Pasadena CA 91109

GOLDRING, NORMAN MAX, advertising executive; b. Chgo., June 22, 1937; s. Jack and Carolyn (Wolf) G.; m. Cynthia Lois Garland, Dec. 20, 1959; children: Jay Marshall, Diane. B.S. in Bus., Miami (Ohio) U., 1959; M.B.A., U. Chgo., 1963. Advt. account mgr. Edward H. Weiss & Co., Chgo., 1959-61; sr. v.p., dir. mktg. services Stern, Walters & Simmons, Inc., Chgo., 1961-68; chmn. Goldring & Co., Inc. (mktg. research), Chgo., 1968—; pres. CPM, Inc. (advt.), 1969—; instr. mktg. and advt. mgmt. Roosevelt U., 1965-68. Commr. Ridgeville Park Dist., Evanston, Ill., 1971-75; bd. dirs., treas. Mus. Broadcast Communications, 1983—; pres. Ridgeville Park Dist., 1974-75. Mem. Am. Mktg. Assn. (speaker), Advt. Council Inc. (Midwest adv. bd. 1983—), Am. Mgmt. Assn. Home: 1212 Austin St Evanston IL 60202 Office: 919 N Michigan Ave Chicago IL 60611

GOLDRING, PAT MAYER, orgn. exec.; b. Seattle, June 5, 1923; d. Siegfried and Pearl (Oberleder) Mayer; m. David M. Goldring, Dec. 5, 1942; children—Susan Lynne, Peter Ronald. Student, Barnard Coll., 1940-42. Pres. North central region N.J. Women's Am. ORT, East Orange, 1958-60, mem. nat. exec. com., 1960—, nat. exec. com., 1967-71, pres., 1971—; v.p. World ORT Union, 1970—, Am. ORT Fedn., 1970—; chmn. editorial bd. Women's Am. ORT Reporter, 1966-71; now Morris County dir. State of Israel Bonds, Livingston, N.J.; Pres. GG Lighting Corp., 1961—. Home: 22-4B Olde Forge W Morristown NJ 07960 Office: 2 W Northfield Rd West Orange NJ 07039

GOLDSBORO, BOBBY, singer, songwriter; b. Marianna, Fla., Jan. 11, 1941; m. Mary Alice Goldsboro; 3 children. Attended, Auburn U. Singer, songwriter, 1963—; songs written include Summer; songs recorded include The Straight Life; star: syndicated TV show The Bobby Goldsboro Show (Recipient Song of Year award for Honey, Country Music Assn. 1968). Office: care Internat Creative Mgmt 8899 Beverly Blvd Los Angeles CA 90048 *

GOLDSBOROUGH, JOHN (JACK) BYRON, security service company executive; b. N.Y.C., Oct. 23, 1943; s. John Brice and Joan (Borough) G.; m. Maureen Anna Brandon, May 10, 1969; children: John Brice, Brandon Scott. B.A. in English, St. Bonaventure U., 1965. Adminstrv. asst. Burns Internat. Security Services, Inc., Briarcliff Manor, N.Y., 1965-68, dir. adminstrv. services, 1968-71; asst. to sr. officers Burns Internat. Security Services, Inc.l, Briarcliff Manor, N.Y., 1971-72; asst. mgr. Detroit office Burns Internat. Security Services, Inc., Briarcliff Manor, N.Y., 1972-73, asst. mgr. Houston office, Briarcliff Manors, N.Y., 1972-74, mgr. Houston office, 1974-76, corp. dir. ops. services, Briarcliff Manor, 1977-78, exec. v.p. planning and adminstrn., 1978—. Mem. Am. Soc. Indsl. Security. Republican. Roman Catholic. Office: Burns Internat Security Services Inc 320 Old Briarcliff Rd Briarcliff Manor NY 10510

GOLDSBOROUGH, ROBERT GERALD, journalist; b. Chgo., Oct. 3, 1937; s. Robert Vincent and Wilma (Janak) G.; m. Janet Elizabeth Moore, Jan. 15, 1966; children: Suzanne Joy, Robert Michael, Colleen Marie, Bonnie Laura. B.S., Northwestern U., 1959, M.S. (McCormick scholar), 1960. Reporter A.P., 1959, City News Bur., Chgo., 1959; with Chgo. Tribune, 1960-82, reporter neighborhood news sect., asst. TV editor, asst. editor Sunday mag., 1963-66, editor TV Week mag., 1966-

67, asst. to features editor, 1967-71, asst. to editor, 1971-72, Sunday editor, 1972-75, editor Sunday mag., 1975-82; exec. editor Advt. Age Mag., 1982—. Author: Great Railroad Paintings, 1976. Served with AUS, 1961. Mem. Am. Assn. Sunday and Feature Editors (past pres.). Presbyterian. Clubs: Chgo. Press, Arts. Office: 740 Rush St Chicago IL 60611

GOLDSCHMID, HARVEY JEROME, legal educator; b. N.Y.C., May 6, 1940; s. Bernard and Rose (Braiker) G.; m. Mary Tait Seibert, Dec. 22, 1973; children: Charles Maxwell, Paul MacNeil. A.B., Columbia U., 1962, J.D., 1965. Bar: N.Y. 1965, U.S. Supreme Ct. 1970. Law clk. to judge 2d Circuit Ct. Appeals, N.Y.C., 1965-66; assoc. firm Debevoise & Plimpton, N.Y.C., 1966-70; asst. prof. law Columbia U., 1970-71, assoc. prof., 1971-73, prof., 1973—, dir. Center for Law and Econ. Studies, 1975-78; cons. in field to public and pvt. orgns.; bd. dirs., mem. exec. com. Am. Assn. Internat. Commn. Jurists.; mem. planning and program com. 2d Cir. Jud. Conf. Author: (with others) Cases and Materials on Trade Regulation, 1975, 2d edit., 1983; editor: Industrial Concentration: The New Learning, 1974, Business Disclosure: Government's Need to Know, 1979. Mem. Am. Law Inst. (dep. chief reporter corp. governance project), Am. Bar Assn., N.Y. State Bar Assn., Assn. Bar City N.Y. (mem. exec. com., chmn. com. on trade regulation 1971-74), Assn. Am. Law Schs. (chmn. sect. antitrust and econ. regulation 1977-78), Phi Beta Kappa. Clubs: Century Assn., Riverdale Yacht. Office: 435 W 116th St New York NY 10027

GOLDSCHMIDT, NEIL EDWARD, business executive, former secretary U.S. Dept. Transportation; b. Eugene, Oreg., June 16, 1940; s. Lester H. and Annette (Levin) G.; m. Margaret Wood; children: Joshua, Rebecca. A.B. in Polit. Sci., U. Oreg., 1963; LL.B., U. Calif., 1967. Atty. Legal Aid Oreg., 1967-70; city commr., Portland, 1971-72, mayor, 1973-79, sec. transp., Washington, 1979-81; v.p. internat. mktg. NIKE/BRS, Inc., Beaverton, Oreg., 1981—; dir. Nat. Semi-Condr. Corp., Gelco Corp. Civil rights worker, Miss., 1964; Former chmn. transp. com. U.S. Conf. Mayors, also chmn. housing and community devel. com.; former co-chmn. energy task force Nat. League Cities; bd. dirs. Kaiser Permanente Found. Health Plan, 1981—. Named Outstanding Young Man Am., 1972. Address: 3900 SW Murray Blvd Beaverton OR 97005

GOLDSCHMIDT, WALTER R., educator, anthropologist; b. San Antonio, Feb. 24, 1913; s. Hermann and Gretchen (Rochs) G.; m. Beatrice Lucia Gale, May 27, 1937; children: Karl Gale, Mark Stefan. B.A., U. Tex., 1933, M.A., 1935; Ph.D., U. Calif. at Berkeley, 1942. Social scientist Bur. Agrl. Econs., 1940-46; mem. faculty UCLA, 1946—, prof. anthropology, 1956—, chmn. dept., 1964-69, prof. anthropology and psychiatry, 1970-83, prof. emeritus, 1983—; Vis. lectr. Stanford, summer 1945, U. Calif. at Berkeley, 1949, Harvard, 1950. Dir.: radio program Ways of Mankind, 1951- 53, Culture and Ecology in E. Africa, 1960-68; spl. editor, Aldine Pub. Co., 1966-75; Author: Small Business and the Community, 1946, As You Sow, 1947, 2d edit., 1978, Nomlaki Ethnography, 1951, Ways to Justice, 1953, Man's Way, 1959, Exploring the Ways of Mankind, 1960, 3d edit., 1977, Comparative Functionalism, 1966, Sebei Law, 1967, Kambuya's Cattle, The Legacy of an African Herdsman, 1968, On Being an Anthropologist, 1970, Culture and Behavior of the Sebei, 1976; Editor: The U.S. and Africa, rev, 1963, French edit., 1965, The Anthropology of Franz Boas, 1959, (with H. Hoijer) The Social Anthropology of Latin America, 1970, The Uses of Anthropology, 1979, Am. Anthropologist, 1956-59; founding editor: Ethos, 1972-79. Fulbright scholar, U.K., 1953; grantee Social Sci. Research Council, 1953, Wenner-Gren Found., 1953; NSF postdoctoral fellow, 1964-65; fellow Center Advanced Study Behavioral Scis., 1964-65; sr. sci. fellow NIMH, 1970-75. Fellow Am. Anthrop. Assn. (pres. 1975-76), African Studies Assn. (founding, bd. dirs. 1957-60); mem. AAAS, Soc Applied Anthropology, Southwestern Anthrop. Assn. (pres. 1950-51), Am. Ethnol. Soc. (pres. 1969-70), Phi Beta Kappa, Sigma Xi. Home: 978 Norman Pl Los Angeles CA 90049

GOLDSMITH, ARTHUR AUSTIN, editor; b. Merrimac, Mass., July 7, 1926; s. Arthur Austin and Daisy (Bishop) G.; m. Carolyn Milford, Sept. 2, 1948; children: Arthur, James, Susan, Amy. Student, U. N.H., 1946-47; B.S. in Journalism, Northwestern U., 1951, M.S., 1951. Asst. editor to exec. editor Popular Photography, N.Y.C., 1951-60; picture editor This Week, N.Y.C., 1960-62; editor, head of instrn. Famous Photographers Sch., Westport, Conn., 1962-69, pres., dir., 1969-72; ediotrial dir. Popular Photography, N.Y.C., 1972—; lectr., moderator Internat. Ctr. Photography, N.Y.C., 1974-75; mem. faculty Focus 82, 83, New Sch. Social Research, 1982—. Contbr.: photography Ency. Brit. Yearbook, 1974—; columnist: PTN Newsletter, 1981—; author: How To Take Better Pictures, 1956, The Photography Game, 1971, The Nude in Photography, 1975, The Camera and Its Images, 1979, (with Alfred Eisenstadt) The Eye of Eisenstaedt, 1969; editor: Photojournalism: The World Gallery of Photography, 1983. Photography chmn. Wilton (Conn.) Arts Council, 1982—. Served with USN, 1944-46. Recipient Harrington award Medill Sch. Journalism, Northwestern U., 1951, Photokina Eye award City of Colgne, Germany, 1980, Photokina Obelisk, 1982, Editor of Yr. award United Jewish Appeal, 1982. Mem. Am. Soc. Mag. Photographers, German Photog. Soc., Chinese Photographers Assn., Photog. Adminstrs. Inc., Kappa Tau Alpha. Office: Popular Photography 1 Park Ave New York NY 10016

GOLDSMITH, BARBARA, author, journalist; b. N.Y.C., May 18, 1931; d. Joseph J. and Evelyn (Cronson) Lubin; m. Frank Perry; children: Andrew, Alice and John Goldsmith. B.A., Wellesley Coll., 1953; D.Litt. (hon.), Syracuse U., L.H.D., Pace U., 1980. Entertainment editor Woman's Home Companion, N.Y.C., 1954-57; contbr. N.Y. Herald Tribune, Esquire Mag., New Yorker, 1957-64; founder, contbg. editor N.Y. Mag., 1968-73; sr. editor Harpers Bazaar Mag., N.Y.C., 1970-74; lectr. N.Y. U., 1969, 75. Spl. writer TV documentaries and entertainments; author: (novel) The Straw Man, 1975; (non-fiction) Little Gloria... Happy at Last, 1980. Mem. jr. council Mus. Modern Art, N.Y.C., 1951-73; dir. Parks Council N.Y.C., 1965—; mem. acquisitions com. Friends of Whitney Mus. Art, 1964-69; mem. pres.'s council Mus. City N.Y., 1970—; dir. Nat. Dance Inst., 1979; founder Center for Learning Disabilities, Albert Einstein Coll. Medicine. Recipient Brandeis U. Library Trust award, 1980, 81. Address: care Lynn Nesbit Internat Creative Mgmt 40 W 57th St New York NY 10019

GOLDSMITH, BRAM, banker; b. Chgo., Feb. 22, 1923; s. Max L. and Bertha (Gittelsohn) G.; m. Elaine Maltz, Nov. 10, 1942; children: Bruce, Russell. Student, Herzl Jr. Coll., 1940, U. Ill., 1941-42. Asst. v.p. Pioneer-Atlas Liquor Co., Chgo., 1945-47; pres. Winston Lumber and Supply Co., East Chicago, Ind., 1947-50; v.p. Medal Distilled Products, Inc., Beverly Hills, Calif., 1950-52; pres. Buckeye Realty and Mgmt. Corp., Beverly Hills, 1952-75; exec. v.p. Buckeye Constrn. Co., Inc., Beverly Hills, 1952-75; chmn. bd., chief exec. officer City Nat. Corp., Beverly Hills, 1975—; dir. City Nat. Bank, Beverly Hills, 1964—, chmn. bd., chief exec. officer, 1975—; dir. Los Angeles br. San Francisco Fed. Res. Bank. Pres. Jewish Fedn. Council of Greater Los Angeles, 1969-70; nat. chmn. United Jewish Appeal, 1970-74; regional chmn. United Crusade, 1976; co-chmn. bd. dirs. NCCJ. Served with Signal Corps U.S. Army, 1942-45. Jewish. Clubs: Hillcrest Country, Masons (Los Angeles). Office: 400 N Roxbury Dr Beverly Hills CA 90210

GOLDSMITH, CLAUDE ORVILLE, petroleum co. exec.; b. Robinson, Ill., Aug. 10, 1932; s. Alonzo Fremont and Ona Cleo (Bean) G.; m. Shirley Ann Moore, Aug. 29, 1954; children—Christopher Kent, Gretchen Claudette. B.S. in Bus. Adminstrn, Ohio State U., 1954, J.D., 1956. Bar: Ohio bar 1956. Accountant Marathon Oil Co., Findlay, Ohio, also Tripoli, Libya, 1956-58, auditor, 1958-59, supr. accounting, 1960-61, chief accountant, 1961-62, tax specialist, 1962-65; with Atlantic Richfield Co., 1965—, mgr. fin. reporting, Phila., 1965, controller internat. div., Los Angeles, 1966-68, asst. treas. finance, N.Y.C., 1969-71, treas., 1971-75, v.p. financing and tax, 1975-80, sr. v.p., chief fin. officer, 1980—; dir. Mitsui Bank Calif. Bd. dirs. Big Bros. Greater Los Angeles. Mem. Am. Petroleum Inst., Fin. Execs. Inst. (pres., dir.), Beta Gamma Sigma, Delta Theta Phi, Sigma Pi. Republican. Mem. Disciples of Christ Ch. Club: Jonathan (Los Angeles). Office: Atlantic Richfield Co 515 S Flower St Los Angeles CA 90071

GOLDSMITH, CLIFFORD HENRY, tobacco company executive; b. Leipzig, Germany, Sept. 6, 1919; came to U.S., 1940, naturalized, 1943; s. Conrad and Elise (Stahl) G.; m. Katherine W. Kaynis; children: Corinne Elizabeth Goldsmith Dickinson, Audrey Jane Goldsmith Kubie, Alexandra Eve. Grad., Bradford (Eng.) U., 1939. Technologist, Glenside Mills Corp., Skaneateles, N.Y., 1940-41; supt. Falls Yarn Mills, Woonsocket, R.I., 1941-42, Aldon Spinning Mills, Talcotville, Conn., 1942-43; with Benson & Hedges Co., 1943-53, plant mgr., 1945-53; with Philip Morris, Inc., 1954—, now dir., vice chmn.; dir. Central Fidelity Banks, Inc. Bd. dirs., dep. chmn. Nat. Multiple Sclerosis Soc.; trustee Mt. Sinai Med. Center, Poly. Inst. N.Y., Inner-City Scholarship Fund; bd. dirs. Work in Am. Inst. Served with inf. AUS, 1943-45. Asso. mem. Textile Inst. (Manchester, Eng.). Clubs: Commonwealth, Downtown (Richmond). Office: 120 Park Ave New York NY 10017

GOLDSMITH, EDWARD IRA, surgeon; b. Far Rockaway, N.Y., Nov. 13, 1927; s. Abraham J. and Gertrude (Epstein) G.; m. Gene Louise French, Aug. 29, 1952; children: Joel Andrew (dec.), Jeremy Adam, William Glenn, Daniel French. A.B., Cornell U., 1947, M.D., 1950. Diplomate: Am. Bd. Surgery. Intern N.Y. Hosp., 1950-51, resident, 1954-57, attending surgeon, 1972—; resident Boston Childrens Hosp., 1952, U. Colo. Med. Center, Denver, 1957-58; practice medicine specializing in gen. and cardiovascular surgery, N.Y.C., 1958—; faculty dept. surgery Cornell U. Med. Coll., N.Y.C., 1954—, clin. asso. prof., 1966-72, prof., 1972—; mem. adv. com. Joint Legis. Com. Mental Retardation, Physically Handicapped, N.Y. Legislature, 1960—; chmn. Com. Scientists for Use Primates in Med. Research, 1966—; mem. com. on primates NRC.; mem. N.Y. State Mental Hygiene Med. Rev. Bd. Editor: Medical Primatology, 1970, 72, Jour. Med. Primatology, 1972; Contbr. articles to profl. jours. Bd. dirs. Nassau Center for Emotionally Disturbed Children, Woodbury, N.Y.; bd. visitors Rockland Childrens Psychiat. Center; mem. adv. council to N.Y. State Commn. on Quality of Care of Mentally Disabled. Served to 1st lt. M.C. AUS, 1952-54. Recipient Presdl. Merit medal, Philippines, 1968, Trumpeldor medal State Israel, 1971. Fellow A.C.S.; mem. Med. Soc. County N.Y., AMA, Am. Heart Assn., N.Y. Soc. Cardiovascular Surgery, N.Y. Surg. Soc., AAAS, N.Y. Acad. Scis., N.Y. Acad. Medicine, Am. Soc. Artificial Internal Organs, Transplantation soc., Internat. Primatological Soc., Am. soc. Tropical Medicine and Hygiene, Royal Soc. Tropical Medicine and Hygiene, N.Y. Cardiol. Soc., N.Y. Soc. Nephrology, Harvey Soc., N.Y. Gastroenterology Assn., N.Y. State Soc. Med. research (v.p.), Explorers Club, Phi Sigma Delta, Phi Delta Epsilon.; Mem. B'nai B'rith. Home: Ridge Rd Katonah NY 10536 Office: 525 E 68th St New York NY 10021

GOLDSMITH, HARRY SAWYER, surgeon; b. Newton, Mass., Sept. 30, 1929; s. Leo and Dorothy Amy (Appleton) G.; m. Linda Perry, Dec. 8, 1961; children: John, Robert, Lynne. A.B., Dartmouth, 1952; M.D., Boston U., 1956. Intern Boston City Hosp., 1956-57, resident in surgery, 1957-61, Meml. Sloan Kettering Inst., N.Y.C., 1963-65, chief gastric and mixed tumor service, 1965-70; practice medicine specializing in surgery, Phila., 1970-77; cons. staff Meml. Sloan Kettering Center, N.Y.C.; cons. Boston VA Hosp.; staff Univ. Hosp., Boston, Boston City Hosp.; Samuel D. Gross prof. surgery, chmn. dept. Jefferson Med. Coll., Phila., 1970-77, distinguished prof. surgery, 1977—, adj. prof. neurosurgery, 1983—; prof. surgery Dartmouth Coll. Med. Sch., Hanover, N.H., 1977-83; surgeon-in-chief Jefferson U. Hosp., 1970-77. Editor-in-chief: Goldsmith's Practice of Surgery, 1976; Contbr. articles to profl. jours. Served as capt. U.S. Army, 1961-63. Mem. A.C.S., Soc. Vascular Surgery, British Assn. Surg. Oncology, Soc. for Surgery of Alimentary Tract, Soc. Internat. de Chirugie. Home: 157 Beacon St Boston MA 02116 Office: Boston U Sch Medicine 75 E Newton St Boston MA 02118

GOLDSMITH, JACK LANDMAN, former retail co. exec.; b. Memphis, Apr. 10, 1910; s. Fred and Aimee (Landman) G.; m. Dorothy Metzger, Feb. 9, 1960; children—Joan Goldsmith Marks, Jack Landman; stepchildren—Larry, Melvin. Grad., Memphis Law Sch.; student, Washington U., St. Louis, N.Y. U. With Federated Dept. Stores, Inc., 1959—, v.p., 1961—; ret. chmn. bd., chmn. exec. com. Goldsmith's Dept. Store; past dir. world trade adv. com. Dept. Commerce; mem. U.S. Trade Mission to, Greece, 1957, to Austria, 1958. Former trustee Brooks Art Gallery, Memphis; pres. Goldsmith Found.; past bd. dirs. Bapt. Hosp., Memphis; del. to Tenn. Constnl. Conv., 1953. Mem. Nat. Retail Mchts. Council (past pres.), Tenn. Retail Mchts. Council, Downtown Assn. (v.p.). Clubs: Rotary (past dir.), One Hundred (Memphis)). Home: 601 Putting Green Ln Longboat Key FL 33548 Office: Goldsmiths 123 S Main St Memphis TN 38103

GOLDSMITH, JERRY, composer; b. Los Angeles, 1930. Student, Los Angeles City Coll.; piano student, Jacob Gimpel; composition student, Mario Castelnuovo Tedesco. Music tchr. Host: show Romance, then Suspense, CBS Radio; composer: scores TV shows Gunsmoke, Climax, Playhouse 90, Studio One; film scores include Freud, 1962, Lilies of the Field, 1963, Black Patch, 1963, The Stripper, 1963, The Prize, 1963, Seven Days in May, 1964, In Harm's Way, 1965, Von Ryan's Express, 1965, A Patch of Blue, 1966, Our Man Flint, 1966, Stagecoach, 1966, The Blue Max, 1966, Seconds, 1966, The Sand Pebbles, 1966, In Like Flint, 1967, Patton, 1970, Papillon, 1973, The Reincarnation of Peter Proud, 1975, Breakheart Pass, 1976, High Velocity, 1976, Logan's Run, 1976, The Omen, 1976, The Cassandra Crossing, 1977, Islands in the Stream, 1977, Twilight's Last Gleaming, 1977, MacArthur, 1977, Damnation Alley, 1977, Coma, 1978, The Boys from Brazil, 1978, Capricorn One, 1978, Damien-Omen II, 1978, Magic, 1978, The Swarm, 1978, The Great Train Robbery, 1979, Star Trek: The Motion Picture, 1979; TV spl. QB VII, 1974 (Emmy award). Office: care ASCAP ASCAP Bldg One Lincoln Plaza New York NY 10023 *

GOLDSMITH, JOHN ALAN, government official; b. Cin., Oct. 13, 1920; s. Alan G. and Mary (Boyd) G.; m. Rosemarie Mullany, Sept. 11, 1948; children: Alan, Gregory. Grad., Choate Sch., 1938; A.B. cum laude, Kenyon Coll., 1942. Mem. staff Troy (N.Y.) Record, 1946-47; reporter U.P.I., 1947-68; profl. staff mem. U.S. Senate Armed Services Com., 1971-77; spl. asst. to asst. sec. of def. for pub. affairs Dept. Def., 1977-81; staff dir. legis. and public affairs Def. Logistics Agy., 1981—. Writer (with Robert S. Allen); syndicated column Inside Washington, 1968-71. Mem. Fairfax County (Va.) Sch. Bd., 1964-72, vice chmn., 1966-69, 71-72, chmn., 1969-70; Bd. dirs. Mellett Fund Free and Responsible Press, 1966-72, v.p., 1967. Served to lt. USNR, 1943-46. Mem. Wire Service Guild (charter mem., pres. 1960). Home: 4605 Franconia Rd Alexandria VA 22310 Office: Room 3D243 Cameron Station Alexandria VA 22314

GOLDSMITH, JUDITH BECKER, feminist leader, association executive; b. Manitowoc, Wis., Nov. 26, 1938; m. Dick Goldsmith; 1 dau., Rachel. B.A., U. Wis.; M.A., SUNY-Buffalo. Faculty mem. English lit. SUNY-Buffalo, U. Wis. System; worker civil rights and peace causes, participant various polit. campaigns; joined NOW, 1974—, pres. Two Rivers-Manitowoc chpt., became pres. Wis. chpt., 1975, mem. nat. bd., 1977—, v.p. nat. orgn., 1978-82, nat. pres., 1982—. Office: Nat Orgn for Women Suite 723 425 13th St NW Washington DC 20004 *

GOLDSMITH, JULIAN ROYCE, geochemist, educator; b. Chgo., Feb. 26, 1918; s. Mitchel and Cecelia (Kallis) G.; m. Ethel J. Frank, Sept. 4, 1940; children—Richard, Susan (Mrs. Kent Wooldridge), John. S.B., U. Chgo., 1940, Ph.D., 1947. Research chemist Corning Glass Works, N.Y., 1942-46; mem. faculty U. Chgo., 1946 —, prof. geochemistry, 1958—, asso. dean div. phys. scis., 1960-72, chmn. dept. geophys. scis., 1963-71, Charles E. Merriam Distinguished Service prof., 1969—; Mem. earth-sci.-panel NSF, 1958-60, chmn., 1960, mem. nat. sci. bd., 1964-70; mem. U.S. Nat. Com. on Geology, 1972—; cons. Lawrence Radiation Lab., U.S. Geol. Survey. Author articles in field.; Co-editor: Jour. Geology, 1957-62; cons. editor: Ency. Sci. and Tech. Chmn. of gov. bd. Lab. Schs. U. Chgo., 1959-60. Fellow A.A.A.S., Mineral. Soc. Am. (counsellor 1960-62, award 1955, v.p. 1968-69, pres. 1970-71), Geol. Soc. Am. (counsellor 1968-71, v.p. 1973-74, pres. 1974-75), Am. Geophys. Union, Am. Acad. Arts and Scis.; mem. Geochem. Soc. (charter v.p. 1955, pres. 1965-66), Renaissance Soc. (pres. 1966-68), Am. Chem. Soc., Am. Crystallographic Assn., Am. Ceramic Soc., Mineral. Soc. Gt. Brit., Phi Beta Kappa, Sigma Xi. Clubs: Quadrangle (v.p. 1973, pres. 1974. Home: 5631 Blackstone Ave Chicago IL 60637 Office: Dept Geophys Scis U Chgo 5734 S Ellis Ave Chicago IL 60637

GOLDSMITH, LEE SELIG, lawyer, physician; b. N.Y.C., Nov. 18, 1939; s. Isidore L. and Elsie (Friedman) G.; m. Arlene F. Applebaum, June 10, 1962; children: Ian Lance, Helena Ayn, Jordan Seth. B.S. with honors, N.Y. U., 1960, M.D., 1964, LL.B., 1967. Bar: N.Y. 1968, N.J. 1974. Asso. clk. Speiser, Shumate, Geoghan Krause & Rheingold, 1965-70; individual practice law, 1970-72; mem. firm Lea, Goldberg, Goldsmith & Spellen, N.Y.C., 1972-74; individual practice law, Newark, 1974—, counsel, 1974-77; mem. firm Goldsmith, Cohen & Simon, 1976-77, Goldsmith & Cohen, 1977-80, Greenstone, Greenstone, Naishuler & Goldsmith, Newark, 1981, Goldsmith & Tabak, P.C., N.Y.C., 1981—, Goldsmith & Tabak, P.A., Englewood, N.J., 1981—; adj. prof. law Fordham U., 1976—; spl. counsel N.Y. State Senate health com., 1971; chmn. com. legis. rev. Am. Coll. Legal Medicine; lectr. Practicing Law Inst. Author: Malpractice Made Easy, 1976, Hospital Liability Law, 1972; editor: Jour. Legal Medicine, 1978-81, Legal Aspects of Med. Practice, 1981—; contbr. articles to various publs. Fellow Am. Coll. Legal Medicine (bd. govs. 1982), N.Y. Acad. Medicine; mem. AMA, N.Y., N.Y. Country med. socs., Assn. Bar City N.Y., N.Y. Trial Lawyers Assn., Am., N.Y., N.J. bar assns. Home: 1 Boulder Brook Rd Scarsdale NY 10583 Office: 747 3d Ave New York NY 10017 also 185 Engle St Englewood NJ

GOLDSMITH, MYRON, architect, structural engineer; b. Chgo., Sept. 15, 1918; s. Martin and Fannie (Fetman) G.; m. Robin W. Squier, July 29, 1962; children: Marc, Chandra. B.S. in Architecture, Armour Inst. Tech., Chgo., 1939; M.S., Ill. Inst. Tech., 1953. Architect, structural engr. firm Ludwig Mies van der Rohe, Chgo., 1946-53; with Skidmore, Owings & Merrill, Chgo., 1955—, chief structural engr., San Francisco, 1955-58, asso. partner, sr. designer, Chgo., 1958-67, gen. partner, 1967—, cons. partner, 1980—; prof. architecture Ill. Inst. Tech. Grad. Sch. Chgo., 1961—. Bldgs. include Norton Office Bldg, Seattle, 1959, United Air Lines hangers, San Francisco, 1959, Assn. Univs. for Research in Astronomy solar telescope, Kitt Peak, Ariz., 1962, Oakland-Alameda County (Calif.) Coliseum, 1966, United Air Lines Exec. Office Bldg. and Edn. and Tng. Center, Chgo., 1962, Home News Enterprises Daily Jour. Bldg, Franklin, Ind., 1963, The Brunswick Bldg, Chgo., 1965, Met. Structures, Dewitt-Chestnut Apts. Chgo, 1965, Spectrum Arena, Phila., 1967, Inland Steel Co. research labs, East Chicago, Ind., 1969, Ill. Inst. Tech. Life Scis. Bldg, 1967; gymnasium, 1969, engring. bldg., 1968, rapid transit stas. on Kennedy and Dan Ryan Expressways, 1970, Central Bus. Dist. Plan, Columbus, Ind., 1969, The Republic newspaper plant, Columbus, Ind., 1971; engring. bldg. Ill. Inst. Tech. Mgmt. Bldg, Chgo., 1972, Diamond Shamrock Bldg, Cleve., 1974, St. Joseph Valley Bank, Elkhart, Ind., 1974; Europoint II Office Bldg, Rotterdam, Holland, 1974, Royal Gazette Ltd, Hamilton, Bermuda, 1974, Percy L. Julian High Sch, Chgo., 1975, George Henry Corliss High Sch, Chgo., 1975, Equibank Bldg, Pitts., 1975, Europoint III Office Bldg. and Parking Garage, Rotterdam, 1976, Ft. Dearborn Sta. Post Office, Chgo., 1978, Europoint IV Office Bldg, Rotterdam, 1978, Ruck-A-Chucky Bridge Consultation, Auburn, Calif., 1978, Nat. City Bank Bldg, Cleve., 1979, Ten Penn Ctr. Office Bldg., Phila., 1981, Lincoln Park Zoo Large Mammal Complex, Chgo., 1982, Harlem Sta. Complex, Chgo. Transit Authority, 1982. Served with C.E. AUS, 1945-46. Fellow AIA; mem. ASCE. Office: 33 W Monroe St Chicago IL 60603

GOLDSMITH, ROBERT HILLIS, educator; b. East Lansing, Mich., Sept. 3, 1911; s. Robert and Edith (Darrow) G.; m. Mary Alice Glass, June 1, 1942; children—Alice Darrow, Robert Glass. B.A., Pa. State U., 1936; M.A., Columbia, 1943, Ph.D., 1952. Instr. dept. English Temple U., Phila., 1946-52, U. Md., College Park, 1952-55; asso. prof. Emory and Henry Coll., Emory, Va., 1955-60, prof., 1960—, chmn. dept., 1971—, Henry Carter Stuart prof. English, 1974—; Reader Folger Library, Washington, 1959; intern Southeast Renaissance Inst., U. N.C., Chapel Hill, 1965; humanities fellow Duke, 1966-67. (Recipient 1st prize playwriting Cal. Western U., San Diego 1963); Author: Wise Fools in Shakespeare, 1955, Survey of English Literature, vol. I, 1976; Contbr. articles to profl. jours. Served with USAAF, 1942-46. Mem. A.A.U.P. (pres. chpt. 1964-65), Modern Lang. Assn., Shakespeare Assn. Am., Southeastern Renaissance Conf. (pres.), Phi Kappa Phi. Home: 1829 Graybark Ave Charlotte NC 28205 *As I look back upon my teaching career—where I taught, whom I taught, and what I taught—I find that it was good. The writings of Shakespeare, Chaucer and other English poets provided the material of my teaching. Over the years, I have enjoyed the friendship of bright, eager, and enthusiastic students. Part of my pleasure in teaching comes from following the successful careers of former students.*

GOLDSMITH, ROBERT LEWIS, youth association magazine executive; b. N.Y.C., Jan. 9, 1928; s. Arthur and Elizabeth (Kohn) G.; m. Joan M. Hartman, 1976. B.S., NYU, 1950. Advt. promotion mgr. Esquire, Inc., N.Y.C., 1952-53; advt. dir. Schine Hotels, N.Y.C., 1953; promotion dir. Dell Pub. Co., N.Y.C., 1953-58, Outdoor Life Mag., 1958-65; assoc. dir. mag. div. Boy Scouts Am., N.Y.C., 1965—. Bd. dirs. Inst. Asian Studies, N.Y.C., 1981—. Mem. N.Y. Sales Execs. Club, Mktg. Communications Execs. Assn., Am. Mktg. Assn., Asia Soc., China Inst. Am., N.Y. Zool. Soc. Club: NYU (bd. govs., v.p. exec. com.). Office: Boy Scouts Am 271 Madison Ave New York NY 10016 *The general purpose I have had in mind is to leave the world no* *worse a place than I found it, and to try in my own way to make improvements whereverpossible. To help people, to teach them to help themselves, to combat ignorance, to give material and emotional support to those who need, to the extent that is possible. . . are all factors of great importance. I have tried to learn about a wide variety of subjects and to use that knowledge to make both my business life and my personal life more satisfying and more productive.*

GOLDSMITH, SAMUEL LUNT, JR., assn. exec.; b. N.Y.C., Sept. 25, 1916; s. Samuel Lunt and Margaret (Thurston) G.; m. Sybil Graham, Oct. 12, 1939 (div. 1966); children—Peter Lunt, John Graham; m. Beatrice A. Brennan, Dec. 1967 (div. 1979); m. Kay M. Stevens, Feb. 1981. B.A., Amherst Coll., 1939; postgrad., Columbia U., N.Y. U. With John H. Graham & Co. Inc., 1939-42, 1945-59, treas., 1952-59; dir. econ. problems dept. NAM, 1959-64; exec. dir. Sales and Mktg. Exec.-Internat., 1964-74; pres. The Aluminum Assn., 1974—. Served as lt. USNR, 1942-45; liaison officer Brit. Royal Navy. Mem. Am. Soc. Assn. Execs. (chmn.). Clubs: Met. (Washington); Union League (N.Y.C.). Office: 818 Connecticut Ave NW Washington DC 20006

GOLDSMITH, SIDNEY, physician, scientist, inventor; b. N.Y.C., Dec. 21, 1930; s. Max and Annie (Schneider) G.; m. Nancy Carrol Stinich, Apr. 2, 1966. B.Sc. cum laude, CCNY, 1950; M.Sc., U. Geneva, Switzerland, 1952, M.D., 1956. Diplomate: Am. Bd. Internal Medicine. Intern Hosp. for Joint Diseases, N.Y.C., 1957-58; resident internal medicine Bronx VA Hosp. and Columbia-Presbyn. Hosp., N.Y.C., 1958-61; fellow gastroenterology Temple U., 1961-62, instr. medicine, 1962-64, assoc. prof., 1964; research assoc. Fels Research Inst., Temple U. Hosp., Phila., 1962-65; practice medicine specializing in internal medicine and gastroenterology, Phila., 1963—; prof. medicine, chmn. dept. St. George's U. Sch. Medicine, Grenada, W.I., 1981—; cons. Hahnemann Med. Coll. and Hosp., Phila.; cons. medicine Merck & Co., Rahway, N.J.; chief cons. internal medicine City of Phila. Police and Fireman's Med. Clinic; chief med. cons. Quick Test Inc., Phila.; cons. gastroenterolgy Oxford Hosp.; med. cons., advisor Lyndon B. Johnson, 1967-69, med. cons., advisor Richard M. Nixon, 1969-74. Book reviewer: Am. Jour. Med. Scis. Served as capt. M.C. AUS, 1959-64. Recipient prize in immunology Pasteur Inst., Paris, France, 1956, meritorious achievement award Inventors Mfrs. Exchange, 1969; Author's certificate in medicine and sci. Govt. USSR; Legion of Honor award Chapel of Four Chaplains, 1978. Fellow A.C.P.; mem. Am. Gastroenterol. Assn., Phila. Gastrointestinal Research Forum, N.Y. Acad. Scis., French Nat. Acad. Medicine, Internat. Platform Assn., AAAS, Assn. Advancement Med. Instrumentation. Inventor human tetanus antitoxin serum, multipurpose med. biopsy needle; discoverer new method of diagnosing silicosis; holder Russian patent on biopsy needle. Home and office: 6912 Loretto Ave Philadelphia PA 19111

GOLDSMITH, ULRICH KARL, German language educator; b. Freiburg, Germany, Jan. 19, 1910; came to U.S., 1946, naturalized, 1955; s. Hans Julius and Sophie Clara (Bickel) G.; m. Helen Hart, 1951 (div. 1956); 1 dau., Sheila H.; m. Bobra Ballin, Dec. 19, 1966. Juristischer Referendar, Hamburg U., 1931; scholar, London (Eng.) Sch. Econs., 1932-34; B.A., U. Toronto, 1942, M.A., 1946; Ph. D., U. Calif. at Berkeley, 1960. Tchr., Wimbledon, Eng., 1934-40; tchr. German lang., German and comparative lit. U. Sask., Can., 1944-46, Princeton, 1947-50, U. Man., Can., 1950-51, U. Mass., 1951-55, Yale, 1955-57; mem. faculty U. Colo., Boulder, 1957—, chmn. dept. Germanic langs. and lit., 1961-65, prof. German, 1962—, chmn. comparative lit., 1965-71; Vis. prof. dept. German U. Calif., Berkeley, 1970. Author: Stefan George: A Study of His Early Work, 1959, Stefan George (Columbia Essays on Modern Writers), 1970; Editor: corr. of Arthur Schnitzler and F.v. Unruh in Modern Austrian Literature, 1977; editor: corr. of Verse Concordance of the Total Lyrical Poetry of Rainer Maria Rilke, 1980; contbr. numerous articles and revs. Mem. Am. Comparative Lit. Assn., Internat. Comparative Lit. Assn., Am. Assn. Tchrs. German, MLA, Internat. Brecht Soc., ACLU, Internat. Arthur Schnitzler Research Assn., Modern Humanities Research Assn. Home: 865 7th St Boulder CO 80302

GOLDSMITH, WILLIAM M., industrial designer; b. Rochester, N.Y., Feb. 20, 1917; s. William M. and Florence (Hirsch) G.; m. Jean Ann Rosenbaum, June 30, 1943; children: Jan Ellen, Ted Grant; m. Ruth Epstein Saichek, Oct. 17, 1969; stepchildren: Daniel, Lisa, Gerald, Richard. B.A. in Indsl. Design, Carnegie Inst. Tech., 1939. With Dave Chapman, Goldsmith & Yamasaki, Inc. (formerly Dave Chapman, Inc.), indsl. design), Chgo., 1939-70, partner, v.p., 1951-55, exec. v.p., 1955-66, pres., 1966—; v.p. Design Research, Inc., 1955—; founder, pres., chmn. bd. Goldsmith Yamasaki Specht Inc. (and predecessor firm), Chgo., 1970—; Head U.S. tech. assistance team in, Pakistan and Afghanistan, 1955-57; co-chmn. Am. Design Bicentennial, Inc., 1976—; pres. Congregation Solel, 1979-81. Served with AUS, 1942-46. Fellow Indsl. Designers Soc. Am. (pres. 1971-72, chmn. 1973-74); fellow Soc. Typographic Arts (sec. 1981-82, v.p. 1983-84); mem. Package Designers Council (past dir.), Chgo. Council Fgn. Relations, Am. Inst. Graphic Arts. Home: 233 E Wacker Dr Suite 1507 Chicago IL 60601 Office: 840 N Michigan Ave Chicago IL 60611

GOLDSTEIN, ABRAHAM S., lawyer, educator; b. N.Y.C., July 27, 1925; s. Isidore and Yetta (Crystal) G.; m. Ruth Tessler, Aug. 31, 1947; children: William Ira, Marianne Susan. B.B.A., CCNY, 1946; LL.B., Yale U., 1949, M.A. (hon.), 1961, Cambridge (Eng.) U., 1964, LL.D., N.Y. Law Sch., 1979. Bar: D.C. bar 1949. Law clk. to judge U.S. Ct. Appeals, 1949-51; partner firm Donohue & Kaufmann, Washington, 1951-56; mem. faculty Yale Law Sch., 1956—, prof. law, 1961—, dean, 1970-75, Sterling prof. law, 1975—; vis. prof. law Stanford Law Sch., summer 1963; vis. fellow Inst. Criminology, fellow Christ's Coll. Cambridge U., 1964- 65; faculty Salzburg Seminar in Am. Studies, 1969, Inst. on Social Sci. Methods in Legal Edn., U. Denver, 1970-72; vis. prof. Hebrew U., Jerusalem, 1976, UN Asia and Far East Inst. for Prevention Crime, Tokyo, 1983; Cons. Pres.'s Com. Law Enforcement; mem. Conn. Bd. of Parole, 1967-69, Conn. Commn. Revise Criminal Code, 1966-70; mem. of the Conn. Planning Com. on Criminal Adminstrn., 1967-71; sr. v.p. Am. Jewish Congress, 1977—. Author: The Insanity Defense, 1967, The Passive Judiciary, 1982, (with L. Orland) Criminal Procedure, 1974, (with J. Goldstein) Crime, Law and Society, 1971; contbr. numerous articles and revs to profl. jours. Served with AUS, 1943- 46. Guggenheim fellow, 1964-65, 75-76. Office: Yale Law Sch New Haven CT 06520

GOLDSTEIN, ALFRED GEORGE, consumer products company executive; b. N.Y.C., Sept. 22, 1932; s. Milton and Pauline M. G.; m. Hope D. Perry, July 5, 1959; children: Mark, Robert. A.B., CCNY, 1953; M.S., Columbia U., 1954. With Sears, Roebuck & Co., Chgo., 1956-79, v.p. mdse., 1976-79; sr. v.p. consumer businesses Am. Can. Co., Greenwich, Conn., 1979—, exec. v.p., sector exec. distbn. splty. retailing, 1983—, also mem. corp. ops. com., mgmt. exec. com.; chmn. bd., dir. Fingerhut Corp.; dir. Pinewing Internat. Exec. editor: Internat. Jour. Addictions, 1975-80. Trustee Archeus Found.; bd. dirs. Inst. Study Drug Misuse. Served with AUS, 1954-56. Mem. Am. Arbitration Assn. (arbitrator), Columbia U. Grad. Bus. Assos. Office: Am Can Co American Ln Greenwich CT 06830

GOLDSTEIN, ALLAN LEONARD, biochemist, educator; b. Bronx, N.Y., Nov. 8, 1937; s. Morris and Miriam (Siegel) G.; m. Linda Jo Tish, Dec. 23, 1975; children: Jennifer Joy, Dawn Eden, Adam Lee. B.S., Wagner Coll., 1959; M.S., Rutgers U., 1961, Ph.D., 1964. Teaching asst. Rutgers U., New Brunswick, N.J., 1959-61; asst. instr. biology, 1961-63, instr. physiology, 1963-64; research fellow Albert Einstein Coll. Medicine, 1964-66, instr. biochemistry, 1966-67, asst. prof., 1967-71, asso. prof., 1971-72; prof., dir. div. biochemistry U. Tex. Med. Br., Galveston, 1972-78, acting dir. multidisciplinary research program in mental health, 1973-78; prof., chmn. dept. biochemistry George Washington U. Sch. Medicine, Washington, 1978—; chmn. bd. Alpha 1 Biomeds.; cons. Syntex Research, 1972-74, Hoffmann-LaRoche, 1974-82; spl. cons. bd. sci. counselors Nat. Inst. Allergy and Infectious Diseases, 1975—; mem. med. research service rev. bd. in oncology VA, 1977—; cons. mem. decisive network com. Biol. Response Modifiers Program, Div. Cancer Treatment, Nat. Cancer Inst., 1982—; mem. sci. adv. com. to pres. Papanicolaou Cancer Research Inst. Miami, Inc., 1981—; mem. AIDS task force adv. com. Nat. Cancer Inst., 1983—. Recipient Career Scientist award Health Research Council, City of N.Y., 1967; Alumni Achievement award Wagner Coll., 1974; Gordon Wilson medal Am. Clin. and Climatol. Soc., 1976; Distinguished Faculty Research award U. Tex. Sch. Biomed. Scis., 1976; Van Dyke award in pharmacology Columbia Coll. Phys. and Surgs., 1984. Mem. Internat. Soc. Exptl. Hematology, AAAS, Endocrine Soc., Am. Soc. Biol. Chemists, Am. Assn. Immunologists, N.Y. Acad. Scis., Reticuloendothelial Soc., Transplantation Soc., Assn. Med. Sch. Chmn. of Depts. Biochemistry, AAUP, Sigma Xi. Club: Toastmasters Internat. (pres. N.Y. chpt. 1971). Discoverer (with Abraham White) Thymosins, hormones of thymus gland. Home: 2795 28th St NW Washington DC 20008

GOLDSTEIN, ALVIN, lawyer; b. N.Y.C., Nov. 21, 1929; s. Abraham and Florence (Bruckner) G.; m. Eleanor Kronish, Dec. 27, 1959; children—Eric, Michael, Eileen. B.S.S., Coll. City N.Y., 1950; LL.B., Bklyn. Law Sch., 1953, S.J.D. magna cum laude, 1960. Bar: N.Y. State bar 1953. Asso. firm Levine & Berman, N.Y.C., 1955-59, partner, 1963; practiced in, N.Y.C., 1960-62; partner firm Berman, Paley, Goldstein & Berman, N.Y.C., 1964—. Contbr. articles to profl. publs. Served with AUS, 1953-55. Mem. N.Y. State Bar Assn., Assn. Bar City of N.Y., N.Y. Fencers Club (dir.). Home: 1 Chester Terr Hastings-on-Hudson NY 10706 also Barnegat Light NJ Office: Berman Paley Goldstein & Berman 500 Fifth Ave New York NY 10110

GOLDSTEIN, AVRAM SHALOM, educator; b. N.Y.C., July 3, 1919; s. Israel and Bertha (Markowitz) G.; m. Dora Benedict, Aug. 29, 1947; children—Margaret, Daniel, Joshua, Michael. A.B., Harvard, 1940, M.D., 1943. Intern Mt. Sinai Hosp., N.Y.C., 1944; successively instr., asso., asst. prof. pharmacology Harvard, 1947-55; prof. dept. pharmacology Stanford, 1955—, exec. head dept., 1955-70; dir. Addiction Research Found., Palo Alto, Calif., 1973—. Author: Principles of Drug Action. Served from 1st lt. to capt., M.C. AUS, 1944-46. Mem. Nat. Acad. Scis., Am. Soc. Pharmacolology and Exptl. Therapeutics, AAAS, Am. Soc. Biol. Chemists. Home: 735 Dolores St Stanford CA 94305 Office: Dept Pharmacology Stanford U Stanford CA 94305

GOLDSTEIN, BERNARD, transportation company executive; b. Rock Island, Ill., Feb. 5, 1929; s. Morris and Fannie (Borenstein) G.; m. Irene Alter, Dec. 18, 1949; children: Jeffrey, Robert, Kathy, Richard. B.A., U. Ill., 1949, LL.B., 1951. Bar: Iowa bar 1951. With Alter Co., Davenport, Iowa, 1951—, pres., dir., 1973—; owner, mgr. A.G.S. Chartering Co., Davenport, 1963—; dir. Alter Trucking & Terminal Corp., Quad City Devel. Group. Pres. Quad City Jewish Fedn., 1975. Mem. Water Resources Assn., Bur. Industriale de Recuperation, Inst. Scrap Iron and Steel, Nat. Assn. Recycling Industries Inst., Davenport C. of C. Jewish. Lodge: Rotary. Home: 4001 N Ocean Blvd 707-B Boca Raton FL 33431 Office: 2333 Rockingham Rd Davenport IA 52808

GOLDSTEIN, BERNARD HERBERT, lawyer; b. N.Y.C., June 7, 1907; s. Joseph D. and Gesela (Jerchower) G.; m. Edith I. Spivack, Dec. 22, 1933; children—Rita (Mrs. Robert Christopher), Amy (Mrs. Geoffrey Bass). B.S.S., CCNY, 1927; LL.B., Columbia U., 1930. Bar: N.Y. bar 1932, U.S. Supreme Ct. bar 1964. Asso. gen. counsel Liggett Drug Co., Inc., N.Y.C., 1933-44; partner Roy M. Sterne & Bernard H. Goldstein, N.Y.C., 1944-48, Gettner, Simon & Asher, 1948-59, Tenzer, Greenblatt, Fallon & Kaplan, 1959—; Lectr. joint com. Am. Law Inst.-Am. Bar Assn., 1969—. Contbr. articles to profl. jours. Mem. World Peace Through Law Center, Washington, 1969—; mem. Citizens Adv. Com. to Dept. Housing Preservation and Devel., N.Y.C., 1969—; Bd. dirs. Conf. Jewish Social Studies, N.Y.C., 1948—. Mem. Assn. Bar City N.Y. (com. chmn. 1971-82), N.Y. County Lawyers Assn. (dir. 1971-78), ABA. Club: Princeton. Home: 21 Colonial Rd Port Washington NY 11050 Office: Chrysler Bldg 405 Lexington Ave New York NY 10174

GOLDSTEIN, BURTON JACK, physician; b. Balt., Sept. 23, 1930; s. Maurice and Roz (Levin) G.; m. Amber Ellen Bischoff, Dec. 3, 1966; children—Howard, Herbert, Brian. B.S. in Pharmacy, U. Md., 1953, M.D., 1960. Diplomate: Am. Bd. Psychiatry and Neurology (bd. examiner). Intern Jackson Meml. Hosp., Miami, Fla., 1960-61, NIMH fellow in psychiatry, 1961-63, chief resident, 1963-64; dir. div. addiction sci. and clin. psychopharmacology, dept. psychiatry U. Miami, 1964—, chief div. research, 1964-71, acting chmn. dept. psychiatry, 1971-83, prof. pharmacology, 1973—, prof. psychiatry, 1973—; cons. in psychiat. research S. Fla. State Hosp., West Hollywood; cons. indsl. security program Dept. Def.; cons. VA Psychiatry Service, Miami; mem. com. on neuropharmacologic drugs U.S. Pharmacopeial Conv., Inc. Mem. editorial bd.: Jour. Hosp. and Community Psychiatry; contbr. chpts. to books, articles to profl. publs. Served to capt. AUS, 1953-55. Fellow Am. Psychiat. Assn., Am. Coll. Psychiatrists; mem. Fla., Dade County med. assns., Am. Coll. Neuropsychopharmacology, Royal Soc. Health, Am. Assn. Clin. Pharmacology and Chemotherapy, Collegium Internationale Neuropsychopharmacologium, Fla. Psychoanalytic Soc. (adj.), South Fla. Psychiat. Soc. Office: U Miami Sch Medicine Dept Psychiatry (D29 Box 016960). Miami FL 33101

GOLDSTEIN, CARL LIPTNER, retail dept. store chain exec.; b. Mattoon, Ill., Apr. 1, 1915; s. Samuel and Ida (Palan) G.; m. Selma A. Kuhn, Aug. 28, 1940; children—Helaine, Barbara, Joan, Patrice. B.S. in Commerce and Law, U. Ill., 1937, J.D., 1939. Bar: Ill. bar 1939. Asso. firm. H.F. Simonson, Champaign, Ill., 1939-40; mgmt. trainee, store mgr., dist. mgr. Kuhn's-Big K Stores Corp., Nashville, 1940-46, office mgr., 1946-50, treas., 1950—, also dir. Jewish. Club: Woodmont Country. Home: 415 Ellendale Dr Nashville TN 37205

GOLDSTEIN, CHARLES H., lawyer; b. Newark, Oct. 17, 1939; s. Joseph Carl and Ann (Cohen) G.; m. Francine Blau, July 30, 1972; children—Joseph A., Jonathan A., Gennifer A.; children by previous marriage—Sandra R., Michael B. A.B., Case Western Res. U., 1961; J.D. with honors, George Washington U., 1964. Bar: Va. bar 1964, Calif. bar 1965. Field atty. NLRB, Los Angeles, 1964-66; asso. firm Camil & Ross, Santa Fe Springs, Calif., 1966-67; practiced in, Santa Monica, Calif., 1967-70; partner firm Nelson, Kirshman, Goldstein & Rexon, Los Angeles, 1970-77; sr. partner firm Goldstein, Freedman, Ownbey and Klepetar, Los Angeles, 1977-79, Goldstein, Freedman and Klepetar, 1979—; lectr. spl. mgmt. programs Mchts. and Mfrs. Assn. of Los Angeles, 1971—; lectr. U. Calif. Extension at Los Angeles, 1975—. Contbr. articles to profl. jours. Mem. United Democratic Finance Com., Los Angeles, 1973-74; Bd. dirs. Child Guidance Center, Whittier, Calif., 1966-68, N.E. Los Angeles unit Am. Cancer Soc. Mem. Am., Los Angeles bar assns., Lawyers' Club of Los Angeles, So. Calif. Moving and Storage Assn. (chmn. 1973-79), Phi Delta Phi, Omicron Delta Kappa, Phi Sigma Alpha, Phi Alpha Theta, Delta Sigma Rho. Office: 1900 Ave of Stars Suite 1500 E Los Angeles CA 90067

GOLDSTEIN, DORA BENEDICT, pharmacologist, educator; b. Milton, Mass., Apr. 25, 1922; d. George Wheeler and Marjory (Pierce) Benedict; m. Avram Goldstein, Aug. 29, 1947; children: Margaret E. Wallace, Daniel P., Joshua S., Michael B. Student, Bryn Mawr Coll., 1940-42, Stanford U., 1945; M.D., Harvard U., 1949. Research assoc. Stanford U., 1955-70, sr. research assoc., 1970-74, adj. prof., 1974-78, prof., 1978—. Author: Pharmacology of Alcohol, 1983; mem. editorial bd.: Jour. Pharmacology and Exptl. Therapeutics, Psychopharmacology; contbr. articles to sci. jours. Research grantee Nat. Inst. Drug Abuse; research scientist Nat. Inst. Drug Abuse; research grantee Nat. Inst. Alcohol Abuse and Alcoholism. Mem. Research Soc. Alcoholism (pres. 1979-81, award for excellence 1980), Am. Soc. Pharmacology and Exptl. Therapeutics, Am. Soc. Biol. Chemists, Internat. Soc. Biomed. Research on Alcoholism. Office: Stanford U Sch Medicine Stanford CA 94305

GOLDSTEIN, E. ERNEST, lawyer; b. Pitts., May 9, 1918; s. Nathan E. and Annie (Ginsberg) G.; m. Peggy Janet Rosenfeld, June 22, 1941; children: Susan M. Goldstein Lipsitch, Daniel F. A.B. cum laude, Amherst Coll., 1939; student, U. Chgo. Law Sch., 1940-42; LL.B., Georgetown U., 1947; S.J.D., U. Wis., 1956. Bar: D.C. 1947, Tex. 1958, U.S. Supreme Ct., conseil juridique, France 1973-79. Pvt. practice, Washington, 1947; with Dept. Justice, also War Claims Commn., 1947-50; asso. counsel crime com. U.S. Senate, 1950-51; gen. counsel antitrust subcom. for com. jud. Ho. of Reps., 1951-52; restrictive trade practices specialist Office U.S. Spl. Rep., Paris; also U.S. rep. productivity and applied research com. OEEC, 1952-53; prof. law U. Tex., 1955-65; counsel Coudert Freres, Paris, 1966-67, partner, 1969-79; cons. CBS, Inc., 1980—; spl. asst. to Pres. U.S., 1967-69; lectr. Inst. Advanced European Studies, U. Nice, France, 1967, Free U. Brussels, 1967, Europa Inst., Amsterdam, 1970; vis. prof. U. P.R. Law Sch., 1962; prof. Am. seminar, Salzburg, Austria, 1963, 79; internat. law cons. Naval War Coll., 1963; chmn. Internat. Lawyers Ann. Conf. Mgmt. Center Europe, 1971-79. Author: Trademark and Copyright Law, 1959, American Enterprise and Scandinavian Antitrust Law, 1962. Chmn. S.W. regional adv. bd. Anti Defamation League, 1964-65; bd. dirs. Am. C. of C. in France, 1970-79, Centre Internat. de Formation Européenne, 1971—; bd. govs., sec. Am. Hosp. Paris, 1972-79, sec., 1974-79; chmn. fund raising Democratic Party Com. in, France, 1973-77; mem. nat. com. Lyndon B. Johnson Meml. Grove, 1972-74; mem. nat. finance council Democratic Nat. Com., 1975-77. Served with AUS, 1942-46. Decorated Legion of Merit; chevalier Légion d'Honneur, 1971; chevalier Ordre des Arts et des Lettres, 1981; recipient Carl Fulda Internat. Law award U. Tex., 1978; Ford Found. Internat. Studies fellow, 1959-60. Mem. Internat. Bar Assn., Am. Soc. Internat. Law, Internat. Co. Lawyers Conf. (chmn. 1972-77), Order of Coif, Phi Delta Phi. Clubs: Cercle Interallie, Travellers (Paris); Am. of Paris (pres. 1976-78). Home: Armorial II-2 La Residence CH 1884 Villars-s-Ollon Switzerland

GOLDSTEIN, EDWARD DAVID, glass company executive; b. N.Y.C., July 12, 1927; s. Michael and Leah (Kirsh) G.; m. Rhoda Gordon, Apr. 18, 1950; children: Linda, Ellen, Ruth, Michael. A.B., U. Mich., 1950, J.D., 1952. Bar: Calif. 1952. Asso. Orrick, Dahlquist, Herrington & Sutcliffe, San Francisco, 1952-54, Johnston & Johnston, 1954-56; with legal dept. Ohio Match Co., Hunt Foods & Industries, 1956-58; asst. gen. mgr., sales mgr. Glass Containers Corp., Fullerton, Calif., 1958-62, v.p., gen. mgr., 1962-65, pres. West Coast, 1965-68, pres., chief exec. officer, 1968—; chmn. bd. Knox Glass Co., Fairmount Glass Cos., 1967-68; dir. Pioneer Bank, Fullerton. Past chmn. adv. bd. St. Jude Hosp., Fullerton., trustee. Served with USNR, 1945-46. Mem. ABA, State Bar Calif., Orange County Bar Assn., Young Pres.'s Orgn. Home: 2230 Yucca St Fullerton CA 92635 Office: 535 N Gilbert Ave Fullerton CA 92634

GOLDSTEIN, ELLIOTT, lawyer; b. Atlanta, Oct. 23, 1915; s. Max Fullmore and Sarah Ray (London) G.; m. Harriet Weinberg, Oct. 24, 1942; children: Lillian, Ellen. Student, Ga. Sch. Tech., 1932-33; B.S., U. Ga., 1936; LL.B., Yale U., 1939. Bar: Ga. 1938, D.C. 1977. Asso. firm Little, Powell, Reid & Goldstein, Atlanta, 1939-40; partner firm Powell, Goldstein, Frazer & Murphy, Atlanta, 1946-77, 80—, Washington, 1977—; spl. counsel com. on standards ofcl. conduct U.S. Ho. of Reps., 1978; dir. SCI Systems, Inc., Ellman's, Inc., other corps. Former chmn. Atlanta Lawyers' Com. for Civil Rights Under Law; exec. com. Nat. Lawyers' Com. for Civil Rights Under Law.; Bd. dirs. United Way of Met. Atlanta, Econ. Opportunity Atlanta, Central Atlanta Progress; regional chmn. Yale Law Sch. Fund. Served to lt. col., F.A. U.S. Army, 1941-46; ETO. Decorated Bronze Star. Mem. ABA (chmn. corp. laws, mem. council sect. corp., banking and bus. law 1983—), Ga. Bar Assn., Atlanta Bar Assn., Am. Law Inst., Lawyers Club Atlanta. Democrat. Jewish. Clubs: Commerce, Standard, World Trade (Atlanta); Metropolitan, Burning Tree (Washington). Home: 336 Valley Rd NW Atlanta GA 30305 Office: 11th Floor C&S Bank Bldg Atlanta GA 30335 also Suite 1050 1110 Vermont Ave NW Washington DC 20005

GOLDSTEIN, GEORGE, real estate appraiser, cons.; b. N.Y.C., Dec. 17, 1901; s. Morris and Elizabeth (Rothman) G.; m. Stella Levi, July 13, 1933. A.B., Columbia, 1922. Estimator The Stein Co., N.Y.C., 1923-25; broker Goldstein & Goldstein, Englewood, N.J., 1925-28; owner George Goldstein (real estate appraiser, cons.), Newark, 1928—; dir. First Nat. State Bank of N.J., First Nat. State Bancorp.; Mem. adv. council zone I War Assets Corp., 1947; rev. appraiser, cons. Navy Dept., 1941-47. Contbr., lectr. on valuation of real estate. Trustee, pres. Hosp. Center of Oranges; chmn. bd. Hosp. Service Plan N.J. (Blue Cross); trustee Griffith Music Found., Cancer Inst. N.J. Recipient Meritorious Civilian Service award Bur. of Yards and Docks, 1945; Distinguished Civilian Service award Navy Dept., 1945; N.J. honoree NCCJ, 1965. Mem. Am. Soc. Real Estate Counselors (bd. govs.), Am. Inst. Real Estate Appraisers (pres. 1950, regional v.p. 1947-49), Am. Arbitration Assn. (dir.). Clubs: Mountain Ridge Country (West Caldwell, N.J.) (pres.); Downtown (Newark); Economic (N.Y.C.). Home: Eagle Ridge Way West Orange NJ 07052 Office: 810 Broad St Newark NJ 07102

GOLDSTEIN, HAROLD, university dean, librarian; b. Norfolk, Va., Oct. 3, 1917; s. Samuel and Jennie (Michelson) G.; m. Julia S. Deutsch, Nov. 4, 1943; children: William M., Richard H. B.S., U. Md., 1942; B.L.S., Columbia U., 1947, M.A., 1948, Ed.D., 1949. Asst. librarian Enoch Pratt Free Library, Balt., 1938-42; asst. prof. U. Minn., 1949-51; dir. library services USIS, Ceylon, 1951- 53; dir. Davenport (Iowa) Pub. Library, 1955-59; prof. U. Ill., 1959-67; dean Sch. Library and Info. Studies, Fla. State U., Tallahassee, 1967—; cons. N.Y. State LIbrary, Md. State Library, Pa. State Library, N.J. State Library, various community libraries. Author: (with others) State Library Policy, 1971; editor: Milestones to the Present: Library History Seminar V, 1976. Served with USAAF, 1942-46. Mem. AAUP, Am., Fla., S.E. library assns., NEA, Nat. Conf. Audiovisual Uses in

Library Edn. (editor 1963), Conf. Evaluation of Library Edn. (editor 1967). Home: 1911 Angels Hollow Tallahassee FL 32308

GOLDSTEIN, IRVING, communications company executive; b. Catskill, N.Y., Mar. 27, 1938; s. Hyman and Leah (Koletsky) G.; m. Susan Wallack, Dec. 21, 1962; children: Elizabeth Jane, Jill Audrey. Student, U. Buffalo, 1955-57; B.A., Queens Coll., CUNY, 1960; J.D., N.Y. U., 1963. Bar: N.Y. 1964, D.C. 1967, U.S. Supreme Ct 1964. Gen. atty. internat. communications FCC, Washington, 1963-66; with Communications Satellite Corp., 1966—; gen. atty. office gen. counsel, Washington, 1966-71, dir. European office, Geneva, 1971-74, dir. internat. affairs, Washington, 1974-77, asst. gen. mgr. external relations and bus. devel., internat. communications, 1977-79, v.p. internat. ops., 1979-80, sr. v.p. internat. communications services, 1980-81; pres., dir. Satellite Television Corp., Washington, 1981-82; exec. v.p. Communications Satellite Corp., Washington, 1982-83, pres., dir., 1983—; mem. ptnrs.' com. Satellite Bus. Systems, 1982—; bd. govs. Internat. Telecommunications Satellite Orgn., 1974-81, chmn., 1980-81; dir. ASB Capital Mgmt., Inc. Contbr. articles to profl. jours. Mem. telecommunications studies adv. council George Washington U., 1980—; bd. dirs. Wolf Trap Found., 1984—. Mem. D.C. Bar Assn., FCC Bar Assn. Club: Internat. (Washington). Home: 3201 Cummings Ln Chevy Chase MD 20815 Office: Communications Satellite Corp 950 L'Enfant Plaza SW Washington DC 20024

GOLDSTEIN, JACK STANLEY, astrophysics educator; b. N.Y.C., May 10, 1925; s. Samuel S. and Lillian (Glantz) G.; m. Nita Thorner, Sept. 5, 1948; children: Philip, Sara, Naomi. B.S., Coll. City N.Y., 1947; M.S., U. Okla., 1948; Ph.D., Cornell U., Ithaca, N.Y., 1953. With Cornell Aero. Lab., 1948-50, Inst. for Advanced Study, 1952- 53, Mass. Inst. Tech., 1953-54, Baird-Atomic, Inc., 1954-57; asst. prof. Brandeis U., Waltham, Mass., 1957-60, asso. prof., 1960-66, prof. astrophysics, 1966—, dir. Astrophysics Inst., 1963-72, chmn. physics dept., 1967-69, 83—, dean Grad. Sch. Arts Scis., 1972-74, dean faculty, 1974-81; spl. cons. UNESCO, 1971-74; Chmn. steering com. African Primary Sci. Program, 1965-72; vis. scholar Kyoto U. (Japan), 1982. Served to lt. (j.g.) USNR; PTO. Fulbright research scholar, Israel, 1960-61, Italy, 1966-67; Guggenheim fellow, 1966-67. Mem. Am. Phys. Soc., Am. Astron. Soc., AAAS, N.Y. Acad. Scis., Sigma Xi. Home: 75 Kingswood Rd Auburndale MA 02166 Office: Physics Dept Brandeis U Waltham MA 02154

GOLDSTEIN, JACOB HERMAN, phys. chemist; b. Atlanta, Dec. 18, 1915; s. David and Jennie (Levine) G.; m. Audrey Jones, Dec. 26, 1952. A.B., Emory U., 1942, M.S., 1944; M.A., Harvard U., 1947, Ph.D., 1949. Phys. chemist Manhattan Project, 1944-46; asst. prof. Emory U., Atlanta, 1949-51, asso. prof., 1951-57, prof., 1958-60, Candler prof. chemistry, 1960—; cons. industry and govt. Contbr. 200 articles to profl. jours. NRC fellow, 1946-49; recipient Charles Herty medal, 1981. Fellow Am. Phys. Soc.; mem. Am. Chem. Soc., Biophys. Soc., N.Y. Acad. Scis., Phi Beta Kappa, Sigma Xi. Jewish. Office: Emory U Atlanta GA 30322

GOLDSTEIN, JEROME S., banker; b. St. Louis, Nov. 22, 1940; s. Hyman H. and Ida M. (Feldman) G.; m. Linda Hall Barnes, Aug. 23, 1970; children—Jacob, Sarah, Rachel. B.S., U. Ill., 1963. With RCA, 1967-71, Citicorp, Boston and N.Y.C., 1971-75; with Mercantile Bancorp. Inc., St. Louis, 1975—, sr. v.p., 1979—; pres. N.D.C. User Group, 1980, Mid-Am. Payment Exchange, 1981-83. Served with U.S. Army, 1963. Mem. Nat. Automated Clearinghouse Assn. (dir. 1981-83). Jewish. Clubs: Media, Benchrest (St. Louis). Home: 137 Meadowlark Dr Creve Coeur MO 63146 Office: Mercantile Tower St Louis MO 63166

GOLDSTEIN, JOSEPH, legal educator; b. Springfield, Mass., May 7, 1923; s. Nathan E. and Anna (Ginsberg) G.; m. Sonja Lambek, Aug. 3, 1947; children: Joshua, Anne, Jeremiah, Daniel. A.B., Dartmouth Coll., 1943; Ph.D., London (Eng.) Sch. Econs., 1950; LL.B., Yale U., 1952; grad., Western New Eng. Inst Psychoanalysis, 1968. Bar: Va. 1953. Law clk. to judge U.S. Ct. Appeals D.C., 1952-53; acting asst. prof. Stanford Law Sch., 1954-56; Russell Sage resident, vis. scholar Harvard Law Sch., 1955-56; asso. prof. Yale Law Sch., 1956-59, prof., 1959—, Justus S. Hotchkiss prof. law, 1968, Walton Hale Hamilton prof. law, sci. and social policy, 1970, prof., 1976—, Sterling prof. law, 1978—; Exec. sec., research dir. Gov. Conn. Prison Study Com., 1956-57; cons. devel. neighborhood legal service Community Progress, Inc., New Haven, 1963-64; mem. U.S. atty. gen. com. poverty and adminstrn. criminal justice, 1962-63; cons. Legal Assistance Assos., Inc., New Haven, 1964-73; pres., bd. dirs. Friends of Legal Services South Central Conn., 1981—; bd. dirs. Vera Inst. Justice, 1966—, Sigmund Freud Archives, 1968; mem. life scis. and social policy com. NRC, 1968; on legal services Office Econ. Opportunity, 1965, Council on Biology in Human Affairs, Salk Inst., 1969. Author: The Government of a British Trade Union, 2d edit, 1953, (with others) Criminal Law, 1962, The Family and the Law, 1965, Psychoanalysis, Psychiatry, and Law, 1967, Crime, Law and Society, 1971, (with Anna Freud and Albert J. Solnit) Beyond the Best Interests of the Child, 1973, 2d edit., 1979, Before the Best Interests of the Child, 1979; with: Criminal Law-Theory and Process, 1974, (with Burke Marshall and Jack Schwartz) The My Lai Massacre and Its Coverup: Beyond the Reach of Law, 1976. Served with AUS, 1943-46. Fulbright scholar, 1949-50; law fellow U. Wis., 1958; Fulbright sr. lectr., 1973; Guggenheim fellow, 1982. Fellow Am. Acad. Arts and Scis.; mem. New Haven Legal Assistance Assn. Office: Yale U Law Sch New Haven CT 06520

GOLDSTEIN, JOSEPH LEONARD, physician, genetics educator; b. Sumter, S.C., Apr. 18, 1940; s. Isadore E. and Fannie A. G. B.S., Washington and Lee U., Lexington, Va., 1962; M.D., U. Tex., Dallas, 1966; D.Sc. (hon.), U. Chgo., 1982, Rensselaer Poly. Inst., 1982. Intern, then resident in medicine Mass. Gen. Hosp., Boston, 1966-68; clin. assoc. NIH, 1968-70; postdoctoral fellow U. Wash., Seattle, 1970-72; mem. faculty U. Tex. Health Scis. Center, Dallas, 1972—, Paul J. Thomas prof. medicine, chmn. dept. molecular genetics, 1977—; Harvey Soc. lectr., 1977; mem. sci. rev. bd. Howard Hughes Med. Inst., 1978—; non-resident fellow The Salk Inst., 1983—. Co-author: The Metabolic Basis of Inherited Disease, 5th edit., 1983; editorial bd.: Jour. Biol. Chemistry, 1980—, Cell, 1983—, Jour. Clin. Investigation, 1977-82, Ann. Rev. Genetics, 1980—, Arteriosclerosis, 1981—. Recipient Heinrich-Wieland prize, 1974, Pfizer award in enzyme chemistry Am. Chem. Soc., 1976; Passano award Johns Hopkins U., 1978; Gairdner Found. award, 1981; award in biol. and med. scis. N.Y. Acad. Scis., 1981; Lita Annenberg Hazen award, 1982. Mem. Nat. Acad. Scis. (Lounsbery award 1979), Assn. Am. Physicians, Am. Soc. Clin. Investigation (pres. 1985-86), Am. Soc. Human Genetics, Am. Soc. Biol. Chemists, A.C.P., Am. Fedn. Clin. Research, Phi Beta Kappa, Alpha Omega Alpha. Home: 3730 Holland Ave Apt H Dallas TX 75219 Office: 5323 Harry Hines Blvd Dallas TX 75235

GOLDSTEIN, LOUIS LAZARUS, state official; b. Prince Frederick, Md., Mar. 14, 1913; s. Goodman and Belle G.; m. Hazel Horton, Nov. 22, 1947; children: Philip, Louisa, Margaret Senate. B.S., Washington Coll., 1935; J.D., U. Md., 1938; hon. degrees, Morgan State U., Western Md. Coll., 1973, Washington Coll., U. Balt., 1977. Mem. Md. Ho. of Dels., 1938-42; mem. Md. Senate, 1946-59, former majority floor leader, former pres. senate; comptroller State of Md., 1958—; chmn. trustees Md. State Employees Retirement System; trustee State Police System, State Tchrs. System; mem. Md. State Banking Commn., Md. Hall of Records Commn. Chmn. bd. visitors Washington Coll.; bd. dirs. Balt. Symphony Orch., Md. Hist. Soc. Served with USMC, 1942-46. Recipient Calvert prize for historic preservation, 1978. Mem. Nat. Assn. State Auditors, Comptrollers and Treas., Md. Public Fin. Officers Assn., Mcpl. Fin. Officers Assn. U.S. and Can., Md.-Del., D.C. Press Assn., ABA, Md. Bar Assn., D.C. Bar Assn., Sigma Delta Chi, Phi Delta Phi. Democrat. Jewish. Home: Oakland Hall Prince Frederick MD 20678 Office: PO Box 466 State Treasury Bldg Annapolis MD 21404 *

GOLDSTEIN, MARC STEVEN, advertising agency executive; b. Bklyn., Apr. 29, 1945; s. Louis B. and Martha (Dobkin) G.; m. Linda Ruth Goldstein, Apr. 9, 1972; children: Julie, Janna. B.S., NYU, 1970. Assoc. dir. research Columbia Pictures TV, N.Y.C., 1970-73; sr. v.p. broadcast programming Benton & Bowles, N.Y.C., 1973-83; sr. v.p. network and programming Ogilvy & Mather, N.Y.C., 1983—. Office: Ogilvy and Mather Inc 2 E 48th St New York NY 10017

GOLDSTEIN, MARTIN, chemistry educator; b. N.Y.C., Nov. 18, 1919; s. Charles Zalman and Susan (Garman) G.; m. Inge Futter, Mar. 17, 1954; children: Eric, Michael, Aviva. B.S., CCNY, 1940; Ph.D., Columbia U., 1950. Research fellow Bklyn. Poly. Inst., 1950-51, Harvard U., 1951-53; fellow Mellon Inst., 1953-58; vis. scientist Nat. Phys. Lab., Israel, 1958-59; staff scientist Ford Motor Co. Sci. Lab., Dearborn, Mich., 1960-64; vis. prof. ceramics MIT, 1964-65; prof. chemistry Yeshiva U., 1965—; vis. prof. ceramic engring. U. Ill., 1967-68; vis. prof. mechanics Technion, Haifa, 1972; vis. prof. chemistry U. Bristol, summer 1972, 73; vis. prof. phys. chemistry U. Paris Sud, Orsay, France, 1980; Sci. Research Council vis. fellow, U.K., 1980; Chmn. Gordon Glass Conf., Tilton, N.H., 1965; co-chmn. workshop Conf. on Glass Transition and Nature Glassy State, N.Y. Acad. Scis., 1975; co-chmn. Conf. on Structure and Mobility in Molecular and Atomic Glasses, 1980. Author: (with Inge F. Goldstein) How We Know—An Exploration of The Scientific Process, 1978; author sci. papers. Served with AUS, 1942-45. Recipient Forrest and Meyer award Am. Ceramic Soc., 1965. Fellow Am. Phys. Soc.; mem. Am. Chem. Soc., AAUP, AAAS, Sigma Xi. Home: 1222 Kensington Rd Teaneck NJ 07666 Office: Div Nat Sci Math Yeshiva Univ New York NY 10033

GOLDSTEIN, MELVYN C., anthropologist, educator; b. N.Y.C., Feb. 8, 1938; s. Harold and Rae (Binen) G.; 1 son, Andre. B.A., U. Mich., 1959, M.A., 1960; Ph.D., U. Wash., 1968. Asst. prof. Case Western Res. U., Cleve., 1968-71, asso. prof., 1971-76, prof., chmn. dept. anthropology, 1976—. Author: Modern Spoken Tibetan, 1970, Modern Literary Tibetan: A grammar and reader, 1973, Tibetan English Dictionary of Modern Tibetan, 1975; contbr. articles to profl. jours. Am. Council Learned Socs. grantee, 1973-74; NIH grantee, 1976-77, 80-82; Nat. Endowment for Humanities grantee, 1980-82; Dept. of Edn. grantee, 1980-82; Smithsonian Instn. grantee, 1981-83; Nat. Geographic Soc. grantee, 1980-81. Mem. Nepal Studies Assn. (treas. 1980-83), Am. Anthropol. Assn., Internat. Mountain Soc., Soc. Applied Anthropology, Soc. Med. Anthropology, Assn. for Anthropology and Gerontology. Home: 2258 Grandview Ave Cleveland Heights OH 44106 Office: 436 Yost Hall Case Western Res Univ Cleveland OH 44106

GOLDSTEIN, MICHAEL HENRY, association executive; b. N.Y.C., July 14, 1938; s. Leon and Mary Elizabeth (Cohen) G.; m. Jo-anne Green, Sept. 17, 1963; children: Beth Anne, Mara, Lee Barry. B.A., Brandeis U., 1960. Nat. sales exec. Sta. WMMM, Westport, Conn., 1960-61; account exec. Continental Broadcasting, N.Y.C., 1961-62; supr. N.Y.C. Dept. Welfare, 1962-65; account exec. Cherenson/ Carroll & Assos., Livington, N.J., 1965-66; acct. exec. Howard J. Rubenstein Assos., N.Y.C., 1966-67; owner, mgr. Goldstein Stone Assos., N.Y.C., 1967-69; sr. account exec. Harshe-Rotman & Druck, N.Y.C., 1969-75; exec. dir. Nat. Assn. Catalog Showroom Merchandisers, N.Y.C., 1975—; occasional lectr. to profl. seminars. Contbr. articles to profl. jours. Pres., chmn. bd. Link Center for Drug Information, Lynbrook, N.Y. Served with U.S. Army, 1957. Recipient Link Service award, 1981, Link Champion of Youth award, 1982, Pub. Service Citation Town of Hempstead, 1982. Mem. Am. Mgmt. Assn., Am. Soc. Assn. Execs. Club: Men's at Lido (bd. govs.). Office: 276 Fifth Ave New York NY 10001

GOLDSTEIN, MORRIS, publishing company executive; b. Pitts., Feb. 2, 1945; s. Irving and Clara (Caplan) G.; m. Diane Donna Davis, Aug. 21, 1966; children: Jonathan, Julie. B.S., Carnegie Inst. Tech., 1967; M.B.A., Wharton Sch., U. Pa., 1979. Sales rep. computer div. RCA, Cherry Hill, N.J., 1968-70; sales mgr. Sedgwick Printout Systems, Princeton, N.J., 1970-76, pres., 1976-80; v.p. Courier-Jour. Louisville Times, 1980-81; mgr. bus. devel. Ziff-Davis Pub., N.Y.C., 1981-82, pres. Information Access Corp. div., Belmont, Calif., 1982—. Dep mayor Mt. Laurel Twp., N.J., 1974-78. Mem. Info. Industry Assn., Am. Soc. Info. Scientists. Club: Wharton (San Francisco). Home: 955 Hayman Pl Los Altos CA 94022 Office: Info Access Corp div Ziff-Davis Pub 11 Davis Dr Belmont CA 94002

GOLDSTEIN, MURRAY, osteopathic physician, government official; b. N.Y.C., Oct. 13, 1925; s. Israel and Yetta (Zeigen) G.; m. Mary Susan Michael, June 13, 1957; children—Patricia Sue, Barbara Jean. A.B. in Biology, N.Y. U., 1947; D.O., Des Moines Still Coll. Osteo Medicine, 1950; M.P.H. in Epidemiology, U. Calif., 1959; D.Sc. (hon.), Kirksville Coll. Osteo. Medicine, 1966, D.D.L., N.Y. Inst. Tech., 1982. Intern Des Moines Still Coll. Osteo Medicine Hosp., 1950-51, resident in internal medicine, 1951-53; commd. sr. asst. surgeon USPHS, 1953, advanced through ranks to asst. surgeon gen., 1980; asst. chief grants and tng. br. Nat. Heart Inst., NIH, Bethesda, Md., 1953-58; asst. chief research grants rev. br., dir. epidemiology and biometry tng. grant program div. research grants NIH, Bethesda, 1956-60; acting sect. chief Bur. Acute Communicable Disease, Calif. Dept. Public Health, Berkeley, 1958; chief spl. projects br. Nat. Inst. Neurol. Diseases and Blindness NIH, Bethesda, 1960-61; dir. extramural programs Nat. Inst. Neurol. and Communicative Disorders and Stroke, NIH, Bethesda, 1961-76, dir. stroke and trauma program, 1976-78; dep. dir. NINCDS-NIH, 1978-82, dir., 1982—; vis. scientist Mayo Clinic and Grad. Sch., Rochester, Minn., 1967-68; v.p. Eisenhower Inst. for Stroke Research; cons. WHO; clin. prof. medicine N.Y. Coll. Osteo Medicine, N.Y. Inst. Tech.; trustee Am. Osteo. Coll. Public Health and Preventive Medicine; mem. med. adv. bd. Am. Parkinson's Disease Assn.; bd. dirs. United Cerebral Palsy Research and Edn. Found. Editorial bd.: Osteo. Annals, 1973—, Internat. Jour. Neurology, 1980—, Jour. Neuroepidemiology. Served with U.S. Army, 1943-45. Decorated Silver Star, Purple Heart.; Recipient Meritorious Service medal USPHS, 1971, Disting. Service medal USPHS, 1983. Fellow Am. Public Health Assn., Am. Heart Assn. (liaison mem. exec. com. Council on Stroke, asso. editor Stroke, Jour. Cerebral Circulation 1976—), Am. Coll. Osteo. Internists (hon.), Am. Acad. Neurology; mem. Am. Neurol. Assn. (2d v.p., cert. merit), Am. Osteo. Assn., AAAS, Assn. Research in Nervous and Mental Disease, Soc. Neurosci., Am. Osteo. Coll. Public Health and Preventive Medicine, World Fedn. Neurology. Office: 9000 Rockville Pike Bethesda MD 20205

GOLDSTEIN, NORMAN PHILIP, neurologist; b. Bklyn., Mar. 31, 1921; s. Charles and Sadie (Fink) G.; m. Gloria Silver, Nov. 14, 1943; children: Bette Karen, Carol Sue, Ellen Marie. B.A. magna cum laude, N.Y. U., 1941; M.A., George Washington U., 1942, M.D. with distinction, 1946. Diplomate: Am. Bd. Psychiatry and Neurology. Intern Mt. Sinai Hosp., N.Y.C., 1946-47; instr. biochemistry George Washington U., 1947-49; fellow Mayo Clinic, 1949-53; commd. officer USPHS, 1953-55; mem. staff Mayo Clinic, 1955-83, head sect. neurology, 1966-77, vice chmn. dept. neurology, 1977-81; prof. neurology Mayo Grad. Sch. Medicine, U. Minn., 1967-73, Mayo Med. Sch., 1973-83, prof. emeritus, 1983—; professorial lectr. George Washington U., 1967-83. Author articles in field. Fellow Am. Acad. Neurology; mem. Central Soc. Neurol. Research (pres. 1968-69), Am., Minn. med. assns., Am. Neurol. Assn., Assn. Research Nervous and Mental Diseases, Phi Beta Kappa, Sigma Xi, Alpha Omega Alpha. Home: 866 16th Ave N Saint Petersburg FL 33704

GOLDSTEIN, RICHARD JAY, engineer, educator; b. N.Y.C., Mar. 27, 1928; s. Henry and Rose (Steierman) G.; m. Anita Nancy Klein, Sept. 5, 1963; children: Arthur Sander, Jonathan Jacob, Benjamin Samuel, Naomi Sarith. B.M.E., Cornell U., 1948; M.S.M.E., U. Minn., 1950, 1951, Ph.D., 1959. Instr. U. Minn., 1948-51, instr., research fellow, 1956-58, mem. faculty, 1961—, prof. mech. engring., 1965—, head dept., 1977—; research engr. Oak Ridge Nat. Lab., 1951-54; asst. prof. Brown U., 1959-61; cons. in field, 1956—; NSF sr. postdoctoral fellow, vis. prof. Cambridge (Eng.) U., 1971-72. Served to 1st lt. AUS, 1954-55. NATO fellow, Paris, 1960-61; Lady Davis fellow Technion, Israel, 1976. Fellow ASME (Heat Transfer Meml. award 1978, Centennial medallion 1980); mem. AAAS, Am. Phys. Soc., Sigma Xi, Tau Beta Pi, Pi Tau Sigma. Research, publs. in thermodynamics, fluid mechanics, heat transfer, optical measuring techniques. Home: 520 Janalyn Circle Golden Valley MN 55416 Office: Dept Mech Engring U Minn Minneapolis MN 55455

GOLDSTEIN, ROBERT, educator; b. Plymouth, Pa., Sept. 7, 1924; s. Reuben and Celia (Halpin) G.; m. Gay Letta Swartz, Dec. 23, 1948; children: Mark Harold, Neal Stewart. B.S., Pa. State U., 1948; Ph.D., Washington U., St. Louis, 1952. Physicist sound sect. Nat. Bur. Standards, Washington, 1948; research asso., clin. audiologist Central Inst. for Deaf, St. Louis, 1950-67; asso. prof. audiology Washington U., 1964-67; research asso. dept. otolaryngology, dir. div. audiology and speech pathology Jewish Hosp., St. Louis, 1958-67; prof. communicative disorders dept. communicative disorders Coll. Letters and Sci. and dept. rehab. medicine Sch. Medicine, U. Wis.-Madison, 1967—. Contbr. chpts. to books, articles profl. jours. Served with AUS, 1943-46. Decorated Purple Heart; recipient Research Career Devel. award Nat. Inst. Neurol. Diseases and Blindness, 1965. Fellow Am. Speech and Hearing Assn. (pres. 1971-72); mem. Alexander Graham Bell Assn. Deaf, Acoustical Soc. Am., AAAS, Am. EEG Soc., Wis. Speech and Hearing Assn., Madison Assn. Edn. Deaf, Sigma Xi. Home: 6502 Gettysburg Dr Madison WI 53705

GOLDSTEIN, ROBERT ARNOLD, physician; b. Bklyn., Dec. 1, 1941; s. Hyman and Irene G.; m. Bunnie Hoffman; children—Joshua, Mark David, Julie, Debbi. A.B., Brandeis U., 1962; M.D., Jefferson Med. Coll., 1966; Ph.D., George Washington U., 1976. Diplomate: Am. Bd. Allergy and Immunology. Mixed med. intern Phila. Gen. Hosp., 1966-67; resident in internal medicine VA Hosp., Washington, 1967-69, fellow in pulmonary disease, 1969-70, asso. chief pulmonary immunology research lab., 1972-74, chief lab., 1974-78, asso. chief sect. pulmonary disease, 1977-78; staff physician pulmonary disease sect. George Washington U. Med. Center, 1972-74, 76-78, acting dir. pulmonary disease div., 1974-76, asst. prof. medicine, 1972-78, asso. prof., 1978—; chief allergy and clin. immunology br. NIH Nat. Inst. Allergy and Infectious Diseases, Bethesda, Md., 1978—; cons. in field; vis. prof. Tripler Army Med. Center, Honolulu, 1976, U. Ark. Med. Center, Little Rock, 1978. Served to maj. M.C. U.S. Army, 1970-72. Decorated Army Commendation medal. Fellow Am. Coll. Chest Physicians (chmn. sect. on allergy and immunology 1981), A.C.P., Am. Acad. Allergy; mem. AAAS, Am. Assn. Immunologists, Am. Fedn. Clin. Research, Am. Thoracic Soc. (chmn. program com. 1976-77, Presdl. commendation 1977), D.C. Lung Assn., N.Y. Acad. Scis., Sigma Xi. Research, publs. on Tb, sarcoidosis. Office: NIH Nat Inst Allergy and Infectious Diseases Westwood 755 Bethesda MD 20205

GOLDSTEIN, ROBERT V(ERNON), advertising executive; b. Omaha, Apr. 1, 1937; s. Arthur Harold and Ruth Marie (Cohen) G.; m. Nancy Sue Barron, June 29, 1958; children: Lawrence, Blaine, Jeffrey. B.A., Harvard Coll., 1959; M.B.A., U. Chgo., 1961. With Procter & Gamble Co., Cin., 1961—, brand asst., 1961-62, asst. brand mgr., 1962-64, brand mgr., 1964-69, assoc. advt. mgr., 1969-73, advt. mgr. toilet goods, 1973-75, advt. mgr. packaged soap and detergent div., 1975-77, project mgr. spl. products, 1977-79, gen. advt. mgr., 1979, v.p. advt., 1979—; bd. dirs. Advt. Council, N.Y.C., 1979—; mem. council of judges Advt. Hall of Fame, Washington, 1983—; mem. Nat. Advt. Rev. Bd., N.Y.C., 1981-83; mem. com. on advt. edn. Advt. Ednl. Found. Vice pres. Jewish Fedn. Cin., chmn. pub. relations com., strategy planning bd.; past pres. No. Hills Synagogue; bd. dirs. Cin. Jewish Community Relations Council; mem. nat. pub. relations com. United Jewish Appeal. Recipient Silver medal Cin. Advt. club, 1982. Mem. Assn. Nat. Advertisers (chmn. 1983-84, dir. 1979—), Harvard Alumni Assn., U. Chgo. Alumni Assn. Republican. Club: Queen City (Cin.). Office: Procter & Gamble Co 301 E 6th St Cincinnati OH 45202

GOLDSTEIN, SETPHEN BARRY, hospital administrator; b. Bklyn., Apr. 23, 1947; s. Isidore and Ida (Weitzman) G.; m. Mona Susan Kurtz, Jan. 24, 1970; children: Ross, Seth. B.S., SUNY-Albany, 1969; M.H.A., Washington U., 1972. Osp. adminstrn. intern N.Y. State Dept. Mental Hygiene, Albany, 1969-72; asst. bus. officer Utica (N.Y.) Psychiat. Ctr., 1972-73, Kings Park (N.Y.) Psychiat. Ctr., 1974-75, dep. dir. adminstrn., 1975-81, exec. dir., 1981—; corp. mem. Nassau-Suffolk Health Systems Agy., Plainview, N.Y., 1978—. Trustee North Shore Jewish Ctr., Port Jefferson Station N.Y., 1979—. Mem. Am. Coll. Hosp. Adminstrs., Assn. Mental Health Adminstrs., N.Y. Assn. Mental Health Adminstr. (trustee 1978—). Office: Kings Park Psychiat Ctr Kings Park NY 11754

GOLDSTEIN, SIDNEY, sociologist, demographer, educator; b. New London, Conn., Aug. 4, 1927; s. Max and Bella (Hoffman) G.; m. Alice Dreifuss, June 21, 1953; children: Beth Leah, David Louis, Brenda Ruth. B.A., U. Conn., 1949, M.A., 1951; Ph.D. (Harrison fellow), U. Pa., 1953. Instr. sociology U. Pa., 1953-55; mem. faculty Brown U., Providence, 1955—, prof. sociology, 1960—, George Hazard Crooker Univ. prof., 1977—, chmn. dept. sociology and anthropology, 1963-70, dir. population studies and tng. center, 1965—; Demographic adviser Chulalongkorn U., Bangkok, Thailand, 1968-69; research fellow Inst. Contemporary Jewry, Hebrew U., Jerusalem, 1969—; sr. fellow East-West Population Inst., Honolulu, 1976, 82; vis. fellow Australian Nat. U., Canberra, 1977; cons. UN Econ. Social Commn. for Asia and Pacific, 1971-72, 77-82, Nat. Center for Health Statistics, 1970-77, Internat. Program Population Analysis Smithsonian Instn., 1971-76; mem. U.S. Bur. Census Adv. Com. Population Statistics, 1965-71, Rand Corp., 1975—; mem. population research study sect. NIH, 1973-78; disting. scholar com. on scholarly communication with China, Nat. Acad. Sci., 1981; mem. nat. com. for research on 1980 census Social Sci. Research Council, 1981—; mem. governing bur. Com. on Internat. Cooperation in National Research in Demograpy, 1981—. Author: Patterns of Mobility, 1910-1950, 1958,

Consumption Patterns of the Aged, 1960, The Norristown Study: An Experiment in Interdisciplinary Research Training, 1961, (with Kurt B. Mayer) The First Two Years: Problems of Small Business Growth and Survival, 1961, Migration and Economic Development in Rhode Island, 1958, (with Calvin Goldscheider) Jewish Americans, 1968, Urbanization in Thailand, 1947-60, 1970, The Demography of Bangkok, 1972, (with Visid Prachuabmoh and Alice Goldstein) Urban-Rural Migration Differentials in Thailand, 1974, (with Alden Speare and William Frey) Residential Mobility, Migration and Metropolitan Change, 1975, Circulation in the Context of Total Mobility in Southeast Asia, 1978; Editor: (with David F. Sly) Basic Data Needed for the Study of Urbanization, 1975, The Measurement of Urbanization and the Projection of Urban Population, 1975, Patterns of Urbanization: Comparative Country Studies, 1977, (with wife) A Test of the Potential Use of Multiplicity in Research on Population Movement, 1979, Differentials in Repeat and Return Migration in Thailand, 1965-1970, 1980, Surveys of Migration in Developing Countries: A Methodological Review, 1981, Migration and Fertility in Peninsular Malaysia, 1983. Bd. dirs. Jewish Fedn. R.I., 1964-68, 78—, Bur. Jewish Edn., Providence, 1959-82. Guggenheim fellow, 1961-62; Social Sci. Research Council fellow, 1961-62; Fulbright research scholar, Denmark, 1961-62; Recipient Disting. Service medal Chulalongkorn U., 1969; sr. research awardee Nat. Acad. Scis., 1983. Mem. Am. Sociol. Assn., Population Assn. Am. (pres. 1975-76), Assn. Jewish Demography and Statistics (dir.), Am. Statis. Assn., Internat. Union Sci. Study Population (chmn. com. on urbanization and population distbn. 1971-76), Assn. for Asian Studies, European Center Population Studies, Assn. Sociol. Study of Jewry, Phi Beta Kappa. Home: 95 Kiwanee Rd Warwick RI 02888 Office: Brown U Providence RI 02912

GOLDSTEIN, SIDNEY, lawyer; b. Bklyn., Oct. 13, 1906; s. Joseph and Esther (Mutchnick) G.; m. Olga Stein, Jan. 7, 1945 (dec.); 1 dau., Helena (Mrs. Peter Leslie). LL.B., St. John's Coll., 1930; M.A. in Polit. Sci, Columbia U., 1977. Bar: N.Y. 1931. Since practiced in, N.Y.C.; atty. Port of N.Y. Authority, 1934-72, asst. gen. counsel, 1942-52, gen. counsel, 1952-72, cons. port and airport matters, 1972—; Dir. 1172 Corp.; Panel mem. on noise abatement, commerce tech. adv. bd. Office Asst. Sec. Commerce, 1968—. Contbr. articles to profl. jours. Served with Signal Corps AUS, World War II. Recipient Distinguished Pub. Service award Nat. Inst. Municipal Law Officers, 1956, Distinguished Service medal Port of N.Y. Authority, 1959, Distinguished Contbns. to Am. Aerospace Power award Met. Squadron Air Force Assn., 1961. Mem. ABA (com. chmn.), N.Y. State Bar Assn., Assn. Bar City N.Y., N.Y. County Lawyers Assn. Airport Operators Council Internat. (gen. counsel), Am. Arbitration Assn. Address: 1172 Park Ave New York NY 10128

GOLDSTEIN, STANLEY PHILIP, educator; b. Bklyn., Feb. 3, 1923; s. Max and Rose (Ahrenstein) G.; m. Wanda Rouse, June 6, 1949; children—Bruce, Richard. B.S., U. Okla., 1949; M.S., N.Y. U., 1956; Ph.D. in Astronautics, Poly. Inst. Bklyn., 1969. Engr. Vapor Recovery Systems Corp., Compton, Calif., 1950-52; project engr. Alderson Research Labs., N.Y.C., 1952-54; mem. faculty Hofstra U., Hempstead, N.Y., 1954—, prof. engring., 1957—, chmn. engring. sci. dept., 1956-68, 70-72, 80—, dir. acad. computer center, 1970-72, asso. dean, 1973-74, 77, asso. provost for planning, budgeting and instl. research, 1974-76; cons. Alcorn Combustion Co., N.Y.C. Transit Authority. Served to 1st lt. USAAF, 1942-45. Decorated D.F.C., Air medal with 4 oak leaf clusters. Mem. Am. Soc. Engring. Edn., Sigma Xi, Pi Sigma Pi. Home: 21 Harvard St Westbury NY 11590 Office: Hofstra U Hempstead NY 11550

GOLDSTEIN, WILLIAM MARKS, lawyer; b. Phila., Aug. 28, 1935; s. David and Estelle (Marks) G.; m. Lilia E. Demchuk; children by previous marriage: Adam, Benjamin, Daniel. A.B., Princeton U., 1957; J.D. magna cum laude, Harvard U., 1960. Bar: Pa. 1961, D.C. 1977. Law clk. to judge U.S. Ct. Appeals, Phila., 1960-61; asso. firm Morgan Lewis & Bockius, Phila., 1961-66, partner, 1967-75, 77-82, Drinker, Biddle & Reath, Phila., 1982—; dep. asst. sec. for tax policy Dept. Treasury, Washington, 1975-76; dir. Dominion Holdings, Inc., Rehab. Hosp. Services Corp. Contbr. numerous articles on fed. taxation to law publs. Mem. Democratic Party Com. Lower Merion, Pa., 1965-68; candidate for Sch. Bd. Lower Merion, 1965, for state legis., 1966. Mem. Am. Bar Assn., Pa. Bar Assn., Phila. Bar Assn., D.C., Bar Assn., Am. Law Inst., NAM (tax com.). Jewish. Home: 787 Trephanny Ln Strafford PA 19087 Office: 1100 PNB Bldg Philadelphia PA 19107

GOLDSTICK, THOMAS KARL, chemical engineering educator; b. Toronto, Ont., Can., Aug. 21, 1934; came to U.S., 1955; s. David and Ira Sarah (Kaplan) G.; m. Marcia Adrienne Jenkins, July 4, 1982. B.S., MIT, 1957, M.S., 1959; Ph.D., U. Calif.-Berkeley, 1966, postgrad., 1966-67; postgrad., U. Calif.-San Francisco, 1966-67. Asst. prof. Northwestern U., Evanston, Ill., 1967-71, assoc. prof. chem. engring. and biol. sci., 1971-81, prof. chem. engring., biomed. engring. neurobiology and physiology, 1981—; spl. research fellow U. Calif.-San Diego, LaJolla, 1971-73; adj. prof. ophthalmology U. Ill., Chgo., 1981—, research cons. dept. ophthalmology, 1981—. Editor: Oxygen Transplant Tissue V, 1983. Research grantee NIH, 1968—. Mem. Internat. Soc. Oxygen Transport to Tissue (sec. 1980—), Biomed. Engring. Soc. (chmn. membership com. 1982—, bd. dirs. 1983—). Home: 729 Emerson St Evanston IL 60201 Office: Chem Engring Dept Northwestern U Evanston IL 60201

GOLDSTINE, ABNER DON, investment company executive; b. Chgo., Dec. 26, 1929; s. Samuel J. and Minnie N. (Meyers) G.; m. Roslyn Gewarter, Sept. 2, 1963; 1 son, Ethan Samuel. B.S., Northwestern U., 1950; postgrad., M.I.T. Fin. economist Fed. Res. Bank Chgo., 1952-59; v.p., economist Union Bank, Los Angeles, 1959-65; chief dep. savs. and loan commnr. State of Calif., 1965-67; sr. v.p. Capital Research and Mgmt. Co., Los Angeles, 1967—; pres., dir. Bond Fund Am., 1967—; pres., trustee Cash Mgmt. Trust Am., 1967—, Tax Exempt Bond Fund Am., 1967—; pres., dir. Continental Ill. Realty Co., 1970-79; lectr. UCLA, 1960-63, U. So. Calif. Pres. Jewish Vocat. Service Los Angeles, 1976-79; bd. dirs. Jewish Fedn. Council Greater Los Angeles, 1977—; v.p., dir. Sinai Temple, Los Angeles, 1974—. Mem. Am. Econ. Assn., Am. Fin. Assn., Nat. Assn. Bus. Economists. Home: 305 S Almont Dr Beverly Hills CA 90211 Office: 333 S Hope St Los Angeles CA 90071

GOLDSTINE, STEPHEN JOSEPH, college president; b. San Francisco, Nov. 16, 1937; s. Edgar Nathan and Regina Thelma (Benno) G.; m. Emily Raechel Miller Keeler, Apr. 12, 1981; children: Rachel, Bettina. Student, Calif. Sch. Fine Arts, 1951, 58; B.A., U. Calif., Berkeley, 1961, postgrad. in philosophy, 1962-67. Teaching asst. rhetoric dept. U. Calif., Berkeley, 1963-66; asst. prof. St. Mary's Coll., Moraga, Calif., 1964-70, chmn. art dept., 1969-70; cons. Freeman & Gossage, San Francisco, 1967-69; dir. neighborhood arts program Art Commn. City and County San Francisco, 1970-77; exec. sec. Mayor's Interagency Com. for Arts, San Francisco, 1971-75; founding dir. Performing Arts for the Third Age, San Francisco, 1973; co-dir. Rockefeller Tng. Fellowships in Mus. Edn., San Francisco, 1975; pres. San Francisco Art Inst., 1977—; Mem. chancellor's adv. bd. Univ. Art Mus., U. Calif., Berkeley, 1979—; mem. prominent orgns. panel Calif. Arts Council, 1981, vice chmn., 1983; lectr. UCLA, 1976, Stanford U., 1966, Harvard U., 1976, 78. Democrat. Jewish. Home: 1331 Green St San Francisco CA 94109 Office: 800 Chestnut St San Francisco CA 94133

GOLDSTONE, HARMON HENDRICKS, architect; b. N.Y.C., May 4, 1911; s. Lafayette A. and Aline (Lewis) G. S.B. cum laude, Harvard U., 1932, postgrad Sch. Architecture, 1933-35; M.Arch., Columbia U., 1936. Designer firm Harrison & Fouilhoux (later Harrison & Abramovitz), N.Y.C., 1936-41, 46-52; with Office Coordinator Inter-Am. Affairs, Washington, 1941-42; individual practice, N.Y.C., 1953-55; partner Goldstone & Dearborn, N.Y.C., 1955-70, Goldstone, Dearborn & Hinz, 1970-73, Goldstone & Hinz, 1973—. Prin. works include Dorado Beach Hotel, P.R., Aquatic Bird House, Bronx Zoo, Osborn Labs. of Marine Scis, Bklyn., Rockefeller Archive Center, Pocantico Hills, N.Y.; Author: (with Martha Dalrymple) History Preserved—New York City Landmarks and Historic Districts, 1974. Mem. Planning Commn. N.Y.C., 1962-68; chmn. Landmarks Preservation Commn. N.Y.C., 1968-73; pres. Municipal Art Soc., N.Y.C., 1960-61; Trustee N.Y. Hist. Soc., 1969—, N.Y. Society Library, 1978—, Am. Scenic and Historic Preservation Soc., 1981—; vice chmn. jr. council Mus. Modern Art, N.Y.C., 1953-59; mem. adv. council Cooper-Hewitt Mus. of Smithsonian Instn., 1978—. Served with USAAF, 1942-46. Fellow A.I.A. (sec. N.Y. 1952, 54-56); asso. N.A.D. Clubs: Harvard; Century Assn. (N.Y.C.). Home: 1172 Park Ave New York NY 10128 Office: 104 E 40th St New York NY 10016

GOLDSTONE, SANFORD, educator; b. N.Y.C., July 17, 1926; s. Albert and Anna (Steckel) G.; children—Susan Beth, Arthur Craig, Nancy Lynn; m. Lois Adams. B.S., Coll. City N.Y., 1947; Ph.D., Duke, 1953. Lic. psychologist, N.Y. State, Maine. Intern Duke Sch. Medicine, 1949-51, chief clin. psychologist, 1951-54, lectr. psychology, 1953-54, asso. dept. psychiatry, 1953-54; asst. prof. to prof. psychiatry, chief psychologist, program dir. Baylor U. Coll. Medicine, 1955-67; prof., head div. psychology dept. psychiatry Cornell U. Med. Coll., 1967-79, prof. psychology field neurobiology, 1969-79; prof., dir. clin. tng., dept. psychology U. Maine, Orono, 1979—; Cons. VA Hosps., Durham, N.C., 1953-54, Houston, 1959-67, Temple, Tex., 1964-67, Montrose, N.Y., 1968-79, Togus, Maine, 1979—; mem. profl. staff Eastern Maine Med. Center and; Bangor Mental Health Inst., 1980—; cons. criminal law sect. Am. Bar Assn., 1967-69, Westchester County Probation Dept., 1968-71, Community Service Bur., N.Y. State Tng. Schs., 1969-75; head div. psychology Houston State Psychiat. Inst., 1958-67, acting bus. mgr., 1959-60, head div. crime and delinquency, 1966-67; clin. asso. prof. to clin. prof. U. Houston, 1958-67; dir. mental health services Harris County Probation Dept., Houston, 1963-67; cons. Silver Hill Found., 1974-81; psychologist-in-chief Payne Whitney Psychiat. Clinic, 1967-74, Westchester div. N.Y. Hosp., 1967-74; attending psychologist N.Y. Hosp., 1967-79; head, community cons. services outpatient dept. Payne Whitney Psychiat. Clinic, 1970-73; head community cons. services Westchester div. N.Y. Hosp.-Cornell Med. Center, 1973-75. Contbr. numerous articles to profl. jours. Served with USAAF, 1945. USPHS grantee, 1955-65, 79—. Fellow AAAS, N.Y. Acad. Scis., Am. Psychol. Assn.; mem. Am. Psychopath. Assn., Sigma Xi. Home: 136 Broadway Bangor ME 04401 Office: Psychology 301B Little Hall U Maine Orono ME 04469

GOLDTHROPE, JOHN CLIFFORD, hospital administrator; b. Chgo., Feb. 21, 1931; s. Clifford Victor and May Adeline (Fisher) G.; m. Marilee Joan Benedict, Aug. 22, 1957; children: Jeffrey, Micki, Clifford. B.S.E., Western Ill. U., 1956; M.P.A., U. So. Calif., 1970. Asst. adminstr. Nebr. Meth. Hosp., Omaha, 1963-66; materials mgr. Cedars-Sinai Med. Center, Los Angeles, 1966-68; assoc. adminstr. St. Joseph Med. Center, Burbank, Calif., 1968-76; exec. v.p. St. Joseph Hosp., Orange, Calif., 1976-83; pres., chief exec. officer Hillcrest Med. Center, Tulsa, 1983—; advisor U. So. Calif. program in health adminstrn., Los Angeles, 1983; dir. Orange County Health Planning Council, Tustin, Calif., 1978-82. Served to cpl. U.S. Army, 1953-54. Recipient Outstanding Achievement award Health Care Execs. S.C., 1978. Mem. Am. Coll. Hosp. Adminstrs., Calif. Assn. Cath. Hosps. (dir. 1978-83). Republican. Methodist. Office: Hillcrest Med Center Utica on the Park Tulsa OK 74104

GOLDTHWAIT, JOHN TURNER, educator; b. Duluth, Minn., Mar. 31, 1921; s. Charles Francis and Isabel (Thatcher) G.; m. Elizabeth Virginia Benefield, Nov. 26, 1946; 1 son, Christopher Edgar. B.A., M.A., Oglethorpe U., 1944; Ph.D., Northwestern U., 1957. Faculty Oglethorpe U., 1941-43, 46-50, Sacramento State Coll., 1952-55, U. Calif. at Davis, 1956-64; prof. philosophy State U. N.Y. at Plattsburgh, 1964—, chmn. div. humanities, 1964-67, dean faculty humanities, 1967-69; faculty Pacific Philosophy Inst., U. Pacific, summer 1962; coordinator ednl. program for Diagnostic and Treatment Center, Clinton Correctional Facility, Dannemora, N.Y., 1966-73. Translator, editor: Observations on the Feeling of the Beautiful and Sublime (Kant), 1960, 2d edit., 1981; contbr. articles to profl. jours. Mem. Lake Champlain Com., 1969—. Served to lt. USNR, 1943-46. Faculty summer research fellow U. Calif., Davis, 1958; SUNY faculty grantee, summer 1981. Mem. Am. Philos. Assn., Am. Soc. Aesthetics, Am. Soc. Value Inquiry, Council on Religion in Internat. Affairs, Berkeley Aesthetics Seminar, Central Calif. Philos. Assn. (pres. 1959), Speech Assn. Am., Nat. Council Tchrs. English, Am. Translators Assn., AAUP. Home: 16 Wood Cliff Dr Plattsburgh NY 12901

GOLDWASSER, EDWIN LEO, physicist, educator; b. N.Y.C., Mar. 9, 1919; s. Israel Edwin and Edith (Goldstein) G.; m. Elizabeth Weiss, Oct. 27, 1940; children—Michael, John, Katherine, David, Richard. B.A., Harvard U., 1940; student, Columbia U., 1941; Ph.D., U. Calif.-Berkeley, 1950. Physicist U.S. Navy Bur. Ordnance, 1941-45; sr. physicist 12th Naval Dist., also U.S. Navy Yard, Mare Is., Caland., 1943-45; teaching asst., research asst. U. Calif. at Berkeley, 1948-50, research asso., 1950-51; mem. faculty U. Ill., 1951—, prof. physics, 1959—, mem. phys. scis. study com., 1956-61; dep. dir. Fermi Nat. Accelerator Lab., 1967-78; vice chancellor for research, dean Grad. Coll., U. Ill., Urbana, 1978-80, vice chancellor for acad. affairs, 1979—; Mem. physics survey com. NRC, 1964-66, vice chmn. div. phys. scis., 1961-66, chmn., 1966-69; gen. adv. com. AEC, 1966-72; mem. panel high energy accelerator physics gen. adv. com. AEC and Pres.'s Sci. Adv. Com., 1962-63; sec. Commn. Particles and Fields Internat. Union Pure and Applied Physics, 1975-81, chmn., 1978-81. Author: Optics, Waves, Atoms and Nuclei, 1965; also numerous articles; contbr. to books. Westinghouse fellow, 1949-50; Fulbright fellow to, Italy, 1957-58; Guggenheim fellow, 1957-58. Fellow Am. Phys. Society; mem. Fedn. Am. Scientists, Phi Beta Kappa, Sigma Xi, Phi Kappa Phi. Spl. research primary cosmic radiation, energy loss charged particles, photoprodn. of pi mesons, interactions of strange particles. Home: 612 Delaware Ave Urbana IL 61801 Office: U Ill 601 E John St Champaign IL 61820

GOLDWASSER, EUGENE, biochemist, educator; b. N.Y.C., Oct. 14, 1922; s. Herman and Anna (Ackerman) G.; m. Florence Cohen, Dec. 22, 1949; children—Thomas Alan, Matthew Laurence, James Herman. B.S., U. Chgo., 1943, Ph.D., 1950. Am. Cancer Soc. fellow U. Copenhagen, Denmark, 1950-52; research asso. U. Chgo., 1952-61, mem. faculty, 1962—, prof. biochemistry, 1963—, chmn. com. on developmental biology. Served with AUS, 1944-46. Guggenheim fellow U. Oxford (Eng.), 1966-67. Mem. Am. Soc. Biol. Chemists, Biochem. Soc., AAAS, Internat. Soc. Developmental Biologists, Internat. Soc. Exptl. Hematology, Endocrine Soc., Sigma Xi. Research biochemistry red blood cell formation. Home: 5727 Dorchester Ave Chicago IL 60637 Office: Dept Biochemistry U Chgo Chicago IL 60637

GOLDWATER, BARRY MORRIS, U.S. senator; b. Phoenix, Jan. 1, 1909; s. Baron and Josephine (Williams) G.; m. Margaret Johnson, Sept. 22, 1934; children: Joanne Goldwater (Mrs. Eugene Butler), Barry, Michael, Margaret (Mrs. Bob Clay). Student, Staunton Mil. Acad., U. Ariz., 1928. With Goldwater's, Inc., 1929—, pres., 1937-53, U.S. senator from, Ariz., 1953-65, 69—; mem. Armed Services Com., Commerce Com.; chmn. Select Com. on Intelligence.; mem. Select Com. Indian Affairs; Councilman, Phoenix, 1949-52; mem. adv. com. Indian affairs Dept. Interior, 1948-50. Author: Arizona Portraits (2 vols.), 1940, Journey Down the River of Canyons, 1940, Speeches of Henry Ashurst, The Conscience of a Conservative, 1960, Why Not Victory?, 1962, Where I Stand, 1964, The Face of Arizona, 1964, People and Places, 1967, The Conscience of the Majority, 1970, Delightful Journey, 1971, The Coming Breakpoint, 1976, Barry Goldwater and the Southwest, 1976, With No Apologies, 1979. Bd. dirs. Heard Mus., Mus. No. Ariz., St. Joseph's Hosp. Served as pilot USAAF, 1941-45; col., chief staff Ariz. NG, 1945-52; maj. gen. Res. Recipient award U.S. Jr. C. of C., 1937; named Man of year, Phoenix, 1949. Mem. Royal Photog. Soc., Am. Assn. Indian Affairs (dir.), Am. Legion, V.F.W., Municipal League (v.p.), Am. Inst. Fgn. Trade (dir.), Eta Mu Pi, Sigma Chi. Clubs: Mason (Shriner), Elk.). Republican candidate for President of the U.S., 1964. Office: 363 Russell Bldg Washington DC 20510 *

GOLDWATER, BARRY MORRIS, JR., Congressman; b. Los Angeles, July 15, 1938; s. Barry Morris and Margaret (Johnson) G.; (div.)1 son, Barry Morris III. Student, U. Colo., 1958-60; B.A., Ariz. State U., 1962. Partner Noble-Cooke div. Gregory & Sons., Los Angeles, 1962-68; mem. 91st-93d Congresses from 27th Calif. Dist., 94th-96th Congresses from 20th Calif. Dist.; Mem. (Sci. and Tech. Com.), 1969—, pub. works and transp. com., 1975—,; Mem. Calif. Republican State Central Com., 1968—. Recipient Watchdog of the Treasury award Nat. Assn. Businessmen. Mem. San Fernando Valley Bus. and Profl. Assn., SAR. Episcopalian.

GOLDWATER, JOHN L., writer, publisher; b. N.Y.C., Feb. 14, 1916; s. Daniel and Edna (Bogart) G.; (m), Nov. 27, 1956; children—Richard, Jonathan, Jared. Litt.D. (hon.), William Penn Coll., Oscaloosa, Iowa, 1981. Pub. Archie Comic Publs., Inc., N.Y.C., 1947—, pres., 1947—; dir. Mus. of Cartoon Art. Nat. Creator: syndicated comic character Archie; Collaborator: Best of Archie, 1980, animated TV series, 1969-77; author: Americana in Four Colors, 1973. Commr., nat. exec. com. Anti-Defamation League; pres. N.Y. Soc. for the Deaf, 1974-77. Mem. Comics Mag. Assn. Am. (pres. 1954—, award 1979). Republican. Jewish. Clubs: Old Oaks Country, Friars, Masons. Office: 325 Fayette Ave Mamaroneck NY 10543

GOLDWATER, LEONARD JOHN, emeritus medical educator; b. N.Y.C., Jan. 15, 1903; s. Abraham Lincoln and Belle (Delmar) G.; m. Margaret F. Jones, 1978. A.B., U. Mich., 1924; M.D., NYU, 1928, D.M.S., 1936; M.S. in Pub. Health, Columbia U., 1941. Diplomate: Am. Bd. Internal Medicine, Am. Bd. Preventative Medicine. Intern and resident physician Bellevue Hosp., N.Y.C., 1929-32; instr. medicine N.Y. U. Coll. Medicine, 1932-36; sr. indsl. hygiene physicians N.Y. Dept. Labor, N.Y.C., 1936-38; instr. and asst. prof. preventive medicine N.Y. U. Coll. Medicine, 1938-41, asso. prof., 1946; prof. indsl. hygiene Columbia U. Sch. Pub. Health, 1946-52, prof. occupational medicine, 1952-68, emeritus, 1969—, spl. lectr., from 1969; cons. Office Vocational Rehab., Dept. Health, Edn. and Welfare, 1952-60; social and occupational health WHO, 1951-77, AEC, 1947-48; Harben lectr. Royal Inst. Pub. Health and Hygiene, London, 1964; dir. Interuniversity Consortium for Environmental Studies, 1971—; cons. indsl. hygiene physician N.Y. Dept. Labor, 1954-68; corr. com. on occupational health and safety ILO; vis. scholar Duke U. Med. Center, 1967-69, prof., 1970-72, cons., 1973—; vis. prof. U. N.C. Sch. Pub. Health, 1970-72, adj. prof., 1973—; Praelector St. Andrews U., Scotland, 1966; Mem. N.C. State Water Quality Council, 1975-78. Author: Mercury: A History of Quicksilver, 1972; Contbr. articles indsl. medicine profl. jours. Trustee Village of Irvington, N.Y., 1958 -60, 61-63. Served with M.C. USN, 1941-46; PTO. Fellow Am. Occupational Med. Assn. (William S. Knudsen award 1980), N.Y. Acad. Medicine, Am. Pub. Health Assn., Am. Acad. Occupational Medicine (pres. 1959, Robert A. Kehoe award of merit 1975), Royal Inst. Pub. Health and Hygiene (hon.); mem. Am. Indsl. Hygiene Assn., Sigma Xi, Nu Sigma Nu, Alpha Omega Alpha. Home: Route 3 Box 197 Chapel Hill NC 27514 Office: Box 2914 Duke U Med Center Durham NC 27710 *I believe in prejudice and intolerance if they are directed toward such things as dishonesty and hypocrisy.*

GOLDWATER, RICHARD, credit card company executive; b. Bronx, N.Y., Jan. 24, 1946; s. David A. and Shirley (Gardner) G.; m. Roberta Seidman, June 14, 1969; children: Deena Sara, Darren Matthew. B.B.A., CCNY, 1968. Account exec. Ted Bates, Inc., N.Y.C., 1967-72; product mgr. T.J. Lipton Co., Englewood Cliffs, N.J., 1972-74; v.p. strategic planning card products div. Citicorp., 1974-78; sr. v.p., gen. mgr. Citicorp. Fin. Inc., Balt., 1978-80; sr. v.p. mktg. Carte Blanche Corp., Los Angeles, 1980-82; pres. Prevention Inc., subs. Credit Card Service Corp., Alexandria, Va., 1982—. Bd. dirs. United Way Central Md. Served with USMCR, 1967-72. Office: 510 King St Alexandria VA 22314

GOLDWHITE, HAROLD, educator; b. London, Eng., Dec. 25, 1931; came to U.S., 1962, naturalized, 1967; s. Morris and Hannah (Van Gelder) G.; m. Marie Louise Hyman, June 29, 1958; children—Julian, Paul, Lisa, Philip. B.A., Cambridge (Eng.) U., 1953, M.A., Ph.D., 1956. Research asso. Cornell U., Ithaca, N.Y., 1956-58; lectr. U. Manchester (Eng.), Inst. Sci. and Tech., 1958-62; prof. chemistry Calif. State U. at Los Angeles, 1962—; vis. prof. U. Strasbourg, France, 1968-69, U. Sussex, Eng., 1975-76. Author: Introduction to Phosphorus Chemistry, 1981; contbr. articles to profl. jours. Named Outstanding Prof. Calif. State U. and Coll. System, 1978. Mem. Am. Chem. Soc., Chem. Soc. (London), Sigma Xi, Phi Kappa Phi. Research in phosphorus and fluorine chemistry. Home: 1704 Oak St South Pasadena CA 91030

GOLDWYN, SAMUEL JOHN, JR., motion picture producer; b. Los Angeles, Sept. 7, 1926; s. Samuel John and Frances (Howard) G.; m. Peggy Elliott, Aug. 23, 1969; children: Catherine, Francis, John, Anthony, Elizabeth, Peter. Student, U. Va. Owner, chief exec. Samuel Goldwyn Co., Los Angeles, 1978—. Producer, dir.: films including CBS Adventure. Pres. Samuel Goldwyn Found.; Pres. trustees Fountain Valley Sch. Colo. Served with AUS, 1944-46, 50-52. Mem. Am. Film Inst. (dir.), Centre Theater Group Los Angeles (dir.). Office: Samuel Goldwyn Co 10203 Santa Monica Blvd Los Angeles CA 90067

GOLEMBESKI, JEROME JOHN, wire and cable co. exec.; b. Nanticoke, Pa., Mar. 16, 1931; s. Edward and Mary Ellen (Grozio) G.; m. June Beverly Chadwick, Aug. 9, 1958; children—Dale, Gary, Gregg, Cheryl, Kim. B.S., U. Conn., 1957. Auditor Price Waterhouse & Co., Hartford, Conn., 1957-59; mem. controller's staff Insilco Corp., Meriden, Conn., 1959-68; controller, treas. Times Wire & Cable Co., Wallingford, Conn., 1969—. Served with USNR, 1949-53. Mem. Nat. Assn. Accountants (Cost Accounting award Hartford chpt.). Home: 76 Alexander Dr Meriden CT 06450 Office: 358 Hall Ave Wallingford CT 06492

GOLEMBIEWSKI, ROBERT THOMAS, business administration educator, consultant; b. Lawrenceville, N.J., July 2, 1932; s. John and Pauline (Pelka) G.; m. Margaret M. Hughes, Sept. 1, 1956; children—Alice, Hope, Geoffrey. A.B., Princeton U., 1954; M.A., Yale U., 1956, Ph.D., 1958. Instr. politics Princeton U., 1958-60; asst. prof. mgmt. U. Ill., 1960-63; lectr. indsl. adminstrn. Yale U., 1963-64; research prof. pub. mgmt. U. Ga., Athens, 1964—; cons. UNIDO, AT&T Co., Smith Kline Corp., others; Killam vis. scholar, fall 1980; disting. vis. scholar U. Calgary (Alta., Can.), fall 1981-83. Author: The Small Group, 1962, Men, Management and Morality, 1965, Public Administration, 1967, Renewing Organizations, 1972, Learning and Change in Groups, 1976, Public Administration As A Developing Discipline, Parts 1 and 2, 1977, Approaches To Planned Change, Vols. 1 and 2, 1979; 35 other books; contbr. numerous articles to profl. publs. Recipient Douglas McGregor Meml. award for excellence in application behavioral scis., 1975; Chester I Barnard Meml. award, 1980; Hosp. Adminstr.'s Book of Yr. award, 1966; award Am. Soc. Tng. Dirs., 1969; Ford fellow, 1961; Lilly Found. grantee, 1962-64; NIMH grantee. Mem. Internat. Assn. Applied Social Scientists, Acad. Mgmt., Am. Soc. Pub. Adminstrn., Am. Soc. for Tng. and Devel., Am. Polit. Sci. Assn., So. Polit. Sci. Assn. Roman Catholic. Home: 145 Highland Dr Athens GA 30606

GOLEMON, ALBERT SIDNEY, architect; b. Whistler, Ala., Sept. 19, 1904; s. James Oliver and Anna Ruth (Abbott) G.; m. Frances Elizabeth Perkins, May 4, 1930; 1 dau., Anabeth (Mrs. George M. Boedeker, Jr.). B.S., Auburn U., 1924, H.H.D. (hon.), 1978; M.Arch., Mass. Inst. Tech., 1925; diploma, Ecole des Beaux Arts, Fontainebleau, France, 1927. Partner Steinman & Golemon, 1931-42, Golemon & Rolfe, Houston, 1946—; Pres. Nat. Archtl. Accrediting Bd., 1962. Outstanding works include F.B.I. Acad, Quantico, Va., Houston Intercontinental Airport, VA Hosp, San Antonio, Golemon & Rolfe Office Bldg, Houston, 1951, Med. Towers Office Bldg, Houston, 1955, Dominican Coll. Bldgs, Houston, 1954-60, Galveston-Houston Diocese Chancery, 1963, U. Houston Engring. Bldg, 1966, Union Carbide Corp. Bldg, Houston, St. Joseph's Hosp, Houston, (with others) FAA Air Route Traffic Control Center, Houston, 1965, River Oaks Country Club, Houston, One Woodway Office Complex, Houston, 1976, Meth. Neurosensory Hosp, Houston; cons. architect: Humble Oil Co. office bldg, Houston. Pres. Tex. Archtl. Found., 1956; mem. City Houston Appeals Bd., 1963—; participant Pres.'s White Conf. Natural Beauty, 1965; mem. Gen. Services Adminstrn. Archtl. Adv. Panel, 1966. Served as lt. col. C.E. AUS, 1943-45. Fellow AIA (nat. dir. 1954-57, chancellor coll. fellows 1973-74); mem. Tex. Soc. Architects (pres. 1953), Phi Kappa Theta. Clubs: Petroleum, Houston, M.I.T. Alumni of South Tex., Auburn Alumni, River Oaks Country, Fontainebleau Alumni; Eldorado Country (Calif.). Office: 2941 Exxon Bldg Houston TX 77002

GOLENBOCK, JUSTIN MERTON, lawyer; b. N.Y.C., May 31, 1919; s. Philip Leo and Lillian (Barnett) G.; m. Hazel Bernice Taylor, Feb. 11, 1945; children: Susan Ann, Jeffrey Taylor, Douglas. A.B. cum laude, Univ. Heights Coll., N.Y. U., 1940, LL.B., Yale, 1946. Bar: N.Y. 1947. Assoc. firm Milbank, Tweed, Hope, Hadley & McCloy, N.Y.C., 1946-48; ptnr. Lans, Goldstein, Golenbock & Abrams, N.Y.C., 1948-49, Goldstein & Golenbock, 1949-51, Goldstein, Golenbock & Barell, 1951-60, Golenbock & Barell, 1960—; Dir. Fab Industries, Inc., Williams Electronics, Inc., Xcor Internat. Inc., Movielab Inc., Internat. Citrus Corp.; Vis. lectr. Yale Law Sch., 1973, 78, 79, 83—. Editor: Yale Law Jour, 1942; comment editor, 1946. Mem. Scarsdale (N.Y.) Non-Partisan Nominating Coms., 1967-73, Scarsdale Planning Bd., 1976—; chmn. Scarsdale Planning Bd., 1981-83; bd. govs. Yale Law Sch. Fund, 1974-80, 81—, Com. for Modern Cts., 1978—, N.Y. chpt. Multiple Sclerosis Soc., 1978—, N.Y. Fedn. Jewish Philanthropies. Served to capt. USAAF, 1941-46. Mem. Am. Bar Found., Am. Judicature Soc., Assn. Bar City N.Y. (mem. corp. law sect. 1968-71, com. profl. responsibility 1972-78, chmn. com. 1978-81, com. on sports and entertainment 1981—), Am. Bar Assn., N.Y. State Bar Assn. (spl. com. on pre-paid legal services plan 1981—), Order of Coif, Phi Beta Kappa. Clubs: Yale (N.Y.C.); Beach Point (Mamaroneck, N.Y.) (bd. govs.); Quaker Ridge (Scarsdale) (gov. 1981—); Scarsdale Town (bd. govs. 1975-78). Home: 19 Griffen Ave Scarsdale NY 10583 Office: Golenbock & Barell 645 Fifth Ave New York NY 10022

GOLER, PATRICIA ANNE, coll. dean; b. Boston, Apr. 28, 1929; d. Clarence H. and Getrude V. (Thomas) G. A.B., Regis Coll., 1950, LL.D. (hon.), 1969; M.A., Boston Coll., 1951, Ph.D., 1957; D.H.L. (hon.), Emmanuel Coll., 1974. Instr. history Xavier U., New Orleans, 1951-53, Boston Coll., 1955-57; prof. history Lowell (Mass.) State Coll., 1957-74; dean Coll. Liberal Arts U. Lowell, 1975—. Trustee Ednl. Devel. Center, Boston Coll., 1974—. Mem. Boston Archdiocesan Bd. Edn., Freedom House Inst. Edn. Democrat. Roman Catholic. Club: Women in Politics. Home: 33 Webb St Lexington MA 02173 Office: South Campus University of Lowell MA 01854 *

GOLIBERSUCH, DAVID CLARENCE, physicist; b. Buffalo, Jan. 20, 1942; s. Clarence August and Ann Marie G. B.S. in Physics, Rensselaer Poly. Inst., 1963; M.S. in Physics (NASA grad. fellow 1964-66), U. Pa., 1965, Ph.D., 1969. NSF postdoctoral fellow Imperial Coll. Sci. and Tech., London, 1969-70; with Gen. Electric Co., Schenectady, 1970—, mgr. tech. relations—phys. sci. and engring., 1974-75, mgr. energy scis. br., 1975-77, mgr. signal electronics lab., 1977-83, cons. research and devel. strategic analysis, 1983—. Author. Mem. Am. Phys. Soc., AAAS, IEEE. Patentee in field. Home: 828 Londonderry Rd Schenectady NY 12309 Office: Gen Electric Co Corp Research and Devel PO Box 8 Schenectady NY 12301

GOLIGHTLY, LENA MILLS, radio producer, composer; b. Horse Cave, Ky.; d. Julius C. and Lee (White) Mills. Student, Ky. State Coll., 1936. Producer, interviewer radio programs, WBEH, Edgewater Beach Hotel, Chgo., 1966-68, WXFM-Radio, Chgo., 1966—, WBEE-Radio, Chgo., 1967—; Composer: I Don't Worry, 1955, Sugarpie, Tears, Easy Now, 1955, Jack is Back, 1957, Mis Bronzeville, 1961, Eternal Flame, 1964, Resurrection City, U.S.A, 1968, Do Your Thing and I'll Do Mine, 1969, King Drive, 1969, I Had Too Much to Dream Last Night, 1970, others.; Author: Premonition of Last Christmas, 1947, Top of the Mountain, 1967, The Seventh Child, 1967; poems Golden Chain of Friendship, 1967, America You're Dying, 1969. Active pub. relations Ada S. McKinley Community Service, 1967. Recipient Am. Friendship Club award, 1962-65, awards Chgo. No. Dist., Assn. Federated Clubs, 1966; award of merit WVON, 1965, 69; awards WXFM, 1966, Carey Temple, 1966, Chgo. Music Assn., 1965, WGRT, Chgo., 1970, Nat. Acad. Best Dressed Churchwomen, 1972, 73; Humanitarian award Bapt. Fgn. Mission Bur., 1973; Dr. Martin Luther King Jr. Humanitarian award Love Meml. Missionary Bapt. Ch., 1974. Mem. Chgo. Music Assn., N.A.A.C.P., Urban League, Nat. Assn. Media Women, Civic Liberty League of Ill. (dir.). Democrat. Mem. A.M.E. Ch. Club: American Friendship (dir.). Address: 5333 S Michigan Ave Chicago IL 60615

GOLIGHTLY, TRUEMAN HARLAN, banker; b. Metropolis, Ill., Feb. 25, 1897; s. Leander H. and May (Hanna) G.; m. Gertrude MacDonald, Mar. 11, 1918 (dec. June 1955); 1 dau., Katherine Hanna Golightly Burks; m. Hazel Bullock, Nov. 22, 1956. Grad., Sch. Commerce, Northwestern U., 1936. Gen. acct., clk. Chgo. Savs. Bank & Trust Co., 1918-23; successively auditor, asst. v.p., v.p Chgo. Trust Co., 1924-29; v.p. Nat. Bank of the Rep., Chgo., 1929-32; asst. gen. receiver Ill. state banks in liquidation, 1933-35; pres., chmn. bd. Nat. Bank of Commerce, Chgo., 1936-64; merged with Central Nat. Bank, 1964, vice chmn. bd., 1964—, mem. dirs. adv. com., 1966—. Mem. nat. council Boy Scouts Am., 1946—; Pres., chmn. finance com. Trustees of Endowment Fund of Episcopal Diocese of Chgo., 1968-76. Served with USN; World War I. Recipient citation Chgo. Financial Advertisers, 1967, Silver Beaver award Boy Scouts Am. Mem. Ill. Bankers Assn. (past pres. bd. govs.), Chgo. Fin. Advertisers (pres. 1942), Robert Morris Assos. (life), Financial Pub. Relations Assn., Am. Legion, Tau Delta Kappa. Clubs: Mason (Shriner), Economic, University (Chgo.); Oak Park Country. Home: 376 Parkview St Elmhurst IL 60126 *The old saying still holds true: "The mind is everything; what you think, you become."*

GOLIN, ALVIN, public relations company executive; b. chgo., June 19, 1929; s. Charles and Jeanette G.; m. June Kerns, Aug. 25, 1961; children: Barry, Karen, Ellen. B.J., Roosevelt U., 1950. Publicity rep. MGM Pictures, N.Y.C., 1951-54; chmn. Golin Harris Communications Inc., Chgo., 1975—; lectr. to numerous univs. Advisor Chgo. council Boy Scouts Am., Nat. Multiple Sclerosis Soc., U. Tenn. Mem. Pub. Relations Soc. Am., Publicity Club of Chgo. Office: Golin Harris Communications Inc 500 N Michigan Ave Chicago IL 60611

GOLINO, CARLO LUIGI, educator; b. Pescara, Italy, June 6, 1913; s. Vittore and Elisabetta (Petrucciani) G.; m. Anna Jean Martin, Dec. 14, 1940; children—Carlo M., Elizabeth, Bruce, Jean, Susan, Robert, Michael, Laura, John. B.A., Coll. City N.Y., 1936; M.A., Columbia, 1937; student, U. Florence, Italy, 1937-39; Ph.D., U. Calif. at Berkeley, 1948. Teaching asst. Italian U. Calif. at Berkeley, 1939-42, 46-47; mem. faculty U. Calif. at Los Angeles, 1947-65, prof. Italian, 1960-65, chmn. dept. Italian, 1956-62, dean humanities, 1961-65; prof. Italian and dean Coll. Letters and Sci., U. Calif. at Riverside, 1965-69, vice chancellor univ., 1969-73; chancellor U. Mass., Boston, 1973-78, Commonwealth prof., 1978—. Author: Contemporary Italian Poetry, 1962, Galileo Reappraised, 1966, also 2 vols. Italian Baroque lit., text books.; Editor: Italian Quar, 1957—. Served to lt. (j.g.) USNR, 1942-46. Fulbright research scholar, Italy, 1960-61; decorated Star of Solidarieta, Italy; recipient Commenda Pres. of Italian Republic, 1978. Mem. Modern Lang. Assn. Am., Am. Assn. Tchrs. Italian, Dante Soc. Am. Home: 2825 Rumsey Dr Riverside CA 92506

GOLINO, FRANK R., government official; b. Erie, Pa., Oct. 26, 1936; s. Dominic F. and Mary (Dober) G.; m. Christine J. Harrison, jan. 31, 1981; children by previous marriage: Fabrizio R., Louis R. A.B. cum laude, Gfannon U., 1957; M.A., Fordham U., 1960; Cert., Bologna Center, Sch. for Advanced Internat. Studies, Italy, 1959. Chmn. Middle East and North Africa area studies Fgn. Service Inst., Dept. State, Washington, 1968-70; internat. relations officer Dept. State, 1970-72; 2d sec. Am. Embassy, Valletta, Malta, 1972-74, Amk. Embassy, Rome, 1974-76; consul Am. Consulate, Jahannesburg, Africa, 1976-81; prin. officer Amk. Consulate, Trieste, Italy, 1981—; lectr. Loyola U., Rome, 1975-76, St. Mary's-Notre Dame, rome, 1976. Editor Middle East sect. Colliers Ency., 1960-61; contbr. articles to profl. jours. Recipient Superior Honor award Dept. State, 1980; Italian Fgn. Ministry fellow, 1958. Mem. Am. Fgn. Service Assn., Am. Polit. Sci. Assn., Internat. Polit. Sci. Assn., Middle East Inst., Middle East Studies Assn. Roman Catholic. Lodge: Rotary. Home: Via Marchesetti 25 Trieste Italy 34142 Office: Am Consulate Via Roma 9 Triest Italy 34121

GOLLATTSCHECK, JAMES FRANKLIN, community college president; b. West Palm Beach, Fla., Nov. 22, 1928; s. Emil Frank and Anna (Bell) G.; m. Alice Frances Fernandez, June 2, 1951; children—Andrea, Nicholas. B.A., U. Fla., 1949, M.Ed., 1952; Ph.D., Fla. State U., 1961. Classroom tchr. Pinellas County (Fla.) schs., 1954-56, sch. adminstr., then acting supt. public instrn., 1968-66; exec. v.p. Valencia Jr. Coll., Orlando, Fla., 1967-70; pres. Valencia Community Coll., Orlando, 1970—. Co-author: College Leadership for Community Renewal, 1976; co-editor: Implementing Community-Based Education, 1978. Bd. dir. Sta. WMFA, Public TV, 1971-76, pres., 1973-74; bd. dirs. United Way Orlando, 1974—, Orlando Opera Co., 1978—; trustee John Young Museum and Planetarium, 1979—. Served with USN, 1952-54. Named Man of Yr. Nat. Council Community Services and Continuing Edn., 1975. Mem. Am. Assn. Community and Jr. Colls. (bd. dirs.), Am. Assn. Higher Edn., Coop. Advancement Community-Based Post Secondary Edn., Am. Council Edn., Coalition Adult Edn. Orgns. (pres.-elect), Phi Delta Kappa. Club: Kiwanis: University (Orlando). Home: 1005 E Ridgewood St Orlando FL 32803 Office: PO Box 3028 Orlando FL 32802

GOLLIN, RICHARD M., film educator, researcher; b. Chgo., Aug. 19, 1927; s. Morris and Ida (Copper-Smith) G.; m. Rita Kaplan, Jan. 1, 1950; children: Kathryn, Michael, James. B.A., Queens Coll., 1949; M.A., U. Minn., 1951, Ph.D., 1959; postgrad, Oxford U., 1953-54. Teaching asst. U. Minn., Mpls., 1950-53; instr. Colgate U., Hamilton, N.Y., 1954-55; asst. prof. English and film studies U. Rochester (N.Y.), 1955-64, prof., 1964-78, 1978—, dir. Film Studies program, 1974—; program chmn. Rochester Internat. Film Festival, 1970, 1972; cons. Univ. Presses. Author: Arthur Hugh Clough, 1967; co-author: New CBEL, 1969. Served USAF, 1946-47. Ford Found. fellow, 1954; Fulbright grantee, 1953; Am. Council Learned Socs. grantee, 1974; NEH grantee, 1976-79. Mem. AAUP (pres. U. Rochester chpt. 1971-73), MLA (bibliog. com. 1982—), Soc. Cinema Studies, Univ. Film and Video Assn.

GÖLLNER, MARIE LOUISE, musicologist, educator; b. Fort Collins, Colo., June 27, 1932; d. Francis Gilbert and Gertrude Valentine (Steele) Martinez; m. Theodor W. Göllner, Sept. 30, 1959; children: Katharina, Philipp. B.A., Vassar Coll., 1953; postgrad., Eastman Sch. Music, 1953-54, U. Heidelberg, Germany, 1954-56; Ph.D. summa cum laude, U. Munich, 1962, Dr. phil. habil., 1975. Research asst. Bavarian State Library, Munich, 1964-67; lectr. Coll. Creative Studies, U. Calif., Santa Barbara, 1968; asst. prof. UCLA, 1970-74, asso. prof., 1974-78, prof. musicology, 1978—, chmn. dept. music, 1976-80. Author: Die Musik des fruhen Trecento, 1963, Katalog der Musikhandschriften der Bayerischen Staatsbibliothek Munchen 2, 1979, Joseph Haydn, Symphonie 94, 1979, Orlando di Lasso: Samtliche Werke, Neue Reihe, Das Hymnarium, 1580-81), 1980, Eine neve Quelle zur italienischen Orgelmusik des Cinquecento, 1982. Mem. Internat. Assn. Music Libraries, Am. Musicol. Soc., Internat. Musicol. Soc., Medieval Acad. Am. Episcopalian. Home: 817 Knapp Dr Santa Barbara CA 93108 Office: Dept Music U Calif Los Angeles CA 90024

GOLLOB, HERMAN COHEN, publishing company executive, editor; b. Waco, Tex., July 7, 1930; s. Abe and Ruybe (Cohen) G.; m. Barbara Kowal, Apr. 9, 1961; children: Emily, Jared. B.A., Tex. A & M U., 1951. Lit. agt. MCA, Beverly Hills, Calif., 1956-58, William Morris, N.Y.C., 1958-59; editor Little, Brown & Co., Boston, 1959-64, Atheneum Pubs., N.Y.C., 1964-68, v.p., editor-in-chief, 1971—; editor-in-chief Harper's Mag. Press, N.Y.C., 1968-71; v.p., editorial dir. The Literary Guild, N.Y.C., 1979-81; v.p., sr. editor Simon & Schuster, N.Y.C., 1981—. Served to lt. USAF, 1951-53. Home: 40 Frederick St Montclair NJ 07042 Office: 1230 Avenue of the Americas New York NY 10020

GOLLONG, PAUL BERNHARD WERNER, consulting engineer; b. Berlin, Germany, May 24, 1916; came to U.S., 1925, naturalized, 1938; s. Richard Julius and Margaret (Hietzig) G.; m. Mildred Brannan, May 13, 1944 (dec. 1978); m. Marianna Jennings Wofford, Nov. 2, 1978. I.E., B.S., U. Cin., 1941. Registered profl. engr., Wash., Ohio, Pa., Ill. Signaling systems engr. Holtzer-Cabot Co., Ill., 1941-42; research engr. Celotex Corp., Chgo., 1942-43; project engr. Armstrong Cork Co., Lancaster, Pa., 1943-46; cons. engr. Griffenhagen & Assos., Chgo., 1947-50, prin. asso., 1950-51; research engr. IIT Research Inst. (formerly Armour Research Found.), Chgo., 1951-52, chief Asia and Far East ops., 1952-54, mgr. internat. dept., 1954-58, dir. internat. div., 1958-62; internat. adminstr. Boeing Asso. Products, The Boeing Co., 1961-63; spl. indsl. devel. adviser to UN, 1963-66; UN project mgr. Center Indsl. Research, Haifa, Israel, 1966-69, sr. sci. affairs officer, 1970-77; internat. research and devel. cons., 1977—; cons. on research and devel. to govts., Syria, Turkey, Portugal, Cyprus, Trinidad & Tobago; dir. Applied Tech., Ltd., U.K.; Mem. Internat. Exec. adv. Council. Author papers, lectr. on tech. devel. Asian, African and Latin Am. countries. Mem. AAAS, Am. Inst. Indsl. Engrs., Am. Mgmt. Assn., U.S. C. of C., Nat., N.Y., Ill. socs. profl. engrs., Chgo. Hist. Soc., Asia Soc., Soc. Internat. Devel., Library Internat. Relations. Home: 244 Stanwich Rd Greenwich CT 06830

GOLODNER, JACK, labor union official, government relations consultant, cons.; b. N.Y.C., Nov. 2, 1931; s. Maurice S. and Regina (Gaber) G.; m. Linda Louise Fowler, June 14, 1964; children: Dean Dovid, Daniel Dimmick, Jonathan Wilmot. B.S., Cornell U., 1953; J.D., Yale U., 1958. Labor arbitrator, Washington, 1958-60; exec. asst. to U.S. Congressman Giaimo, 1960-62; cons. pub. affairs, 1962—; exec. sec. Council AFL-CIO Unions for Profl. Employees, 1967-77; dir. dept. for profl. employees AFL-CIO, 1977—; pres. J. Golodner Assocs., 1969—; mem. com. specialized personnel Dept. Labor, 1968. Vice pres. bd. trustees Ford's Theater, Washington, 1973-79; bd. dirs. Nat. Theatre, Washington, 1978—, Am. Council for the Arts, 1981—; chmn. pub. policy com., adv. council nat. orgns. Corp. Pub. Broadcasting, 1976-77; mem. Labor Adv. Com. for Multilateral Trade Negotiations of Dept. of Labor, Edn./Manpower Council Manpower Inst., Washington; mem. arts and humanities com. Pres.'s Commn. on Internat. Women's Year, 1975-76; mem. U.S. del. UNESCO govtl. experts meeting, Paris, 1980; U.S. del. to adv. com. on salaried and profl. workers Internat. Labor Orgn., 1981. Served to capt. USAF, 1953-55. Recipient William B. Groat award Cornell U., 1979. Mem. Indsl. Relations Assn. (bd. dirs. D.C. chpt. 1970), Vol. Lawyers for Arts (adv. bd. 1974—), Phi Kappa Phi. Home: 8800 Mansion Farm Pl Alexandria VA 22309 Office: 1140 Connecticut Ave NW Washington DC 20036

GOLOMB, FREDERICK MARTIN, surgeon, educator; b. N.Y.C., Dec. 18, 1924; s. Jacob J. and Hannah (Loewy) G.; m. Joan E. Schneider, Nov. 28, 1954; children: James Bradley, Susan Lynn. B.S., Yale U., 1945; M.D., U. Rochester, 1949. Diplomate: Am. Bd. Surgery. Intern Johns Hopkins Hosp., 1949-50; resident NYU Hosp., 1950-56; practice medicine specializing in surgery, N.Y.C.; mem. staff N.Y. U. Med. Center, 1950—, dir. chemoimmunotherapy div. tumor service dept. surgery, 1967—; dep. div. dir., chief patient research unit div. II, clin. research div., chief chemotherapy unit div. IV N.Y. U. Cancer Center, 1975-79; attending surgeon Univ., Drs. hosps.; cons. in gen. surgery Manhattan VA Hosp.; cons. surgeon Cabrini Health Care Center; vis. surgeon Bellevue Hosp.; mem. faculty N.Y. U. Sch. Medicine, 1956—, prof., clin. surgery, 1977—; cons. N.Y.C. div. Am. Cancer Soc., 1968—; mem. clin. trials rev. com. Nat. Cancer Inst., 1976-79; chmn. melanoma com. Eastern Coop. Oncology Group, 1978-81; prin. investigator Central Oncology Group, 1969-77, exec. com., 1976-77; bd. dirs. N.Y. State Cancer Programs Assos.; mem. met. med. com. Chemotherapy Found. Contbr. articles to profl. jours. Served with M.C. AUS, 1953-54; Korea. Fellow A.C.S.; mem. Soc. Head and Neck Surgeons, Soc. Surgery Alimentary Tract, Am. Assn. Cancer Research, Am. Soc. Clin. Oncology (a founder), AMA, N.Y. Cancer Soc. (pres. 1974-75), N.Y. Surg. Soc., N.Y. State, N.Y. County med. socs., Soc. Surg. Oncology, George Hoyt Whipple Soc., Brit. Assn. Surg. Oncology (editorial adv. panel), Pan Am. Med. Soc., Sigma Xi. Clubs: Am. Alpine, Explorers. Office: NY U Sch Medicine 530 First Ave New York NY 10016

GOLOMB, SOLOMON WOLF, mathematician, electrical engineer, educator; b. Balt., May 31, 1932; s. Elhanan Hirsh and Minna (Nadel) G. A.B., Johns Hopkins U., 1951; M.A., Harvard U., 1953, Ph.D., 1957; postgrad., U. Oslo, 1955-56. Mem. faculty Boston U., 1954-55, Harvard U., 1954-55, UCLA, 1957-61, Calif. Inst. Tech., 1960-62; sr. research engr. Jet Propulsion Lab., Pasadena, Calif., 1956-58, research group supr., 1958-60, asst. chief telecommunications research sect., 1960-63; assoc. prof. U. So. Calif., Los Angeles, 1963-64, prof. elec. engring. and math., 1964—; dir. TSC Incorp., Cyclotomics Inc.; cons. to govt. and industry. Author: Digital Communications with Space Applications, 1964, Polyominoes, 1965, Shift Register Sequences, 1967, 82; contbr. articles to profl. jours. Recipient Rogers prize in math. Harvard U., 1953-54, Univ. Assocs. Research award U. So. Calif., 1968-69, Archimedes Circle award, 1978; Fulbright fellow, 1955-56. Fellow IEEE; mem. Nat. Acad. Engring., Internat. Sci. Radio Union, Am. Math. Soc., Math. Assn. Am., Soc. Indsl. and Applied Math., AAAS, AAUP, Phi Beta Kappa, Sigma Xi, Pi Delta Epsilon, Eta Kappa Nu, Phi Kappa Phi. Office: PHE 506 U So Calif Los Angeles CA 90089

GOLOMSKI, WILLIAM ARTHUR, consulting company executive; s. John Frank and Margaret Sophia (Glisczinski) G.; m. Joan Ellen Hagen, June 18, 1960; children: Gretchen, William. Prin. W.A. Golomski & Assocs., Chgo., 1949—, pres., 1971—. Recipient award for excellence, quality and reliability Am. Inst. Indsl. Engrs., 1981. Fellow Am. Soc. Quality Control (Edwards Medalist), AAAS, N.Y. Acad. Sci., Royal Soc. Health; fellow Am. Statis. Assn.; mem. Nat. Assn. Accts., Am. Inst. Indsl. Engrs. Office: 59 E Van Buren St Chicago IL 60605

GOLSON, GEORGE BARRY, editor; b. Lynn, Mass., Dec. 12, 1944; s. George Albert and Beverly Margaret G.; m. Thia Anne MacKenzie, Aug. 24, 1968. B.A., Yale U., 1967; postgrad., Stanford U., 1967-68. Columnist, mng. editor Atlas World Press Rev., 1969-71; asst. articles editor Playboy mag., N.Y.C., 1972-74, sr. editor, 1974-76, exec. editor, 1976—. Free-lance writer, 1971-72; Editor: The Playboy Interview, 1981; contbr. articles on politics, satire and travel to various publs. Recipient 1st Pl Writer's award Playboy Mag., 1972; Ford fellow, 1968. Mem. Am. Soc. Mag. Editors, Am. Soc. Journalists and Authors, PEN. Office: care Playboy Mag 747 3d Ave New York NY 10017

GOLTZ, ROBERT WILLIAM, physician, educator; b. St. Paul, Sept. 21, 1923; s. Edward Victor and Clare (O'Neill) G.; m. Patricia Ann Sweeney, Sept. 27, 1945; children: Leni, Paul Robert. B.S., U. Minn., 1943, M.D., 1945. Diplomate: Am. Bd. Dermatology (pres. 1975-76). Intern Ancker Hosp., St. Paul, 1944-45; resident in dermatology Mpls. Gen. Hosp., 1945-46, 48-49, U. Minn. Hosp., 1949-50; practice medicine specializing in dermatology, Mpls., 1950-65; clin. instr. U. Minn. Grad. Sch., 1950-58, clin. asst. prof., 1958-60, clin. asso. prof., 1960-65, prof., head dept. dermatology, 1971—; prof. dermatology, head div. dermatology U. Colo. Med. Sch., Denver, 1965-71. Editorial bd.: Archives of Dermatology; editor: Dermatology Digest. Served from 1st lt. to capt., M.C. U.S. Army, 1946-48. Mem. Am. Dermatol.

Assn. (dir. 1976—), Am. Soc. Dermatopathologists (pres. 1981), Am. Dermatology Soc. Allergy and Immunology (pres. 1981), AMA (chmn. sect. on dermatology 1973-75), Dermatology Found. (past dir.), Minn. Dermatol. Soc., Soc. Investigative Dermatology (pres. 1972-73), Histochem. Soc., Am. Acad. Dermatology (pres. 1978-79, past dir.), Colombian Dermatol. Soc. (corr. mem.), Can. Dermatol. Soc. (hon. mem.), Pacific Dermatol. Soc. (hon.-mem.), S. African Dermatol. Soc. (hon. mem.), Rocky Mountain Dermatol. Soc., Chgo. Dermatol. Soc., Assn. Profs. Dermatology (sec.-treas. 1970-72, pres. 1973-74). Home: 2234 Lee Ave N Minneapolis MN 55422 Office: U Minn Med Sch Dept Dermatology Minneapolis MN 55455

GOLUB, GENE HOWARD, computer science educator, academic administrator, researcher; b. Chgo., Feb. 29, 1932; s. Nathan and Bernice (Gelman) G. B.S. in Math., U. Ill., 1953, M.A. in Math.-Stats., 1954, Ph.D, 1959. NSF postdoctoral fellow Cambridge U., Eng., 1959-60; mem. tech. staff Space Tech. Labs., Inc., 1961-62; vis. asst. prof. computer sci. Stanford U., 1962-64, assoc. prof., 1966-70, prof., 1970—, chmn. dept. computer sci., 1980—; adj. asst. prof. Courant Inst. Math. Scis. NYU, N.Y.C., 1965-66; Forsythe lectr. Assn. Computing Machinery, 1978; mem. adv. com. on computer sci. NSF, 1982-84; cons. in field. Author: (with Gerard Meurant) Resolution Numerique des Grandes Systems Lineaires, 1983, (with Charles Van Loan) Advanced Matrix Computations, 1984; contbr. articles to profl. jours.; assoc. editor various jours., 1967-79; editor: Numerische Mathematik, 1978. Recipient Alumni Honor award U. Ill., Urbana, 1984; hon. fellow St. Catherine's Coll., Oxford U., Eng., 1983. Fellow AAAS; mem. Soc. for Indsl. and Applied Math. (mem. council 1975-77, trustee 1982—, pres. 1985—, vis. lectr. 1976-77, founder, editor Jour. Sci. and Statis. Computing 1980—), Spl. Interest Group in Numerical Analysis (bd. dirs. 1976-78), Gesellschaft fuer angewandte Mathematik und Mechanik (governing council 1982—), U.S. Nat. Com. for Math. Home: 576 Constanzo Stanford CA 94305 Office: Dept Computer Sci Stanford U Bldg 460 Stanford CA 94305

GOLUB, LEON ALBERT, artist; b. Chgo., Jan. 23, 1922; s. Samuel and Sara (Sussman) G.; m. Nancy Spero, Dec. 15, 1951; children: Stephen S., Philip S., Paul S. B.A., U. Chgo., 1942; B.F.A., Sch. Art Inst. Chgo., 1949, M.F.A., 1950. Chmn. Exhbn. Momentum, Chgo., 1950; tchr. grad. painting Ind. U., 1957-59; resided in, Italy, 1956-57, Paris, 1959-64; now prof. art Mason Gross Sch. Arts, Rutgers U. One-man shows include, Hanover Gallery, London, 1962, Galerie Iris Clert, Paris, 1962, 64, Am. Cultural Center, Paris, 1960, Inst. Contemporary Arts, London, 1957, 82, Pasadena (Calif.) Mus. Art, 1956, Pomona (Calif.) Coll., Ind. U., 1958, Purdue U., 1951, Gallery A, Melbourne, Australia, 1963, Temple U., 1964, U. Chgo., 1966, LoGiudice Gallery, Chgo., 1968, Mass. Inst. Tech., 1970, Nat. Gallery of Victoria, Melbourne, 1970-71, Herbert Lehman Coll., N.Y.C., 1972, Mus. Contemporary Art, Chgo., 1974, N.Y. Cultural Center, 1975, N.J. State Mus., San Francisco Art Inst., 1976, SUNY at Stony Brook, 1978, Colgate U., Sch. Visual Arts, N.Y.C., 1979, Susan Caldwell Gallery, N.Y.C., 1982, Young-Hoffman Gallery, Chgo.; group shows include Internat. Exhbn. Modern Graphics, Austria, Germany, 1952, Exhbn. Momentum, Chgo., 1948-58, Carnegie Internat., 1955, 64, 67; anns. Am. Art at, Whitney Mus., 1955, 56, Expressionism, 1900-1950 at, Walker Art Center, 1956, Surrealist and Dadaist sculpture, Chgo. Arts Club, 1958, Mus. Dirs. Choice at, Balt. Mus., 1959, Young Am. Painters exhbn, Guggenheim Mus., 1954, also traveling exhbn., 1956; ann. U. Ill, 1957, 61, 63, New Images of Man at, Mus. Modern Art, 1959, 2d interam. biennial, Acad. Fine Arts, Mex., 1961 (hon. mention), San Paolo Biennale, 1962, 61st Am. Exhbn. at, Chgo. Art Inst. (Florsheim Meml. prize 1961, Watson F. Blair purchase prize 1962), Ann. Am. Art exhbn., Corcoran Mus., 1963, Realities Nouvelles, Paris, Forum Exhbn. Contemporary Art, Ghent, Belgium, Prix Marzotto, 1964-65, 67-68, Documenta III, Kassel, Germany, 1964, Dunn International Tate Gallery, Va. Mus., 1966, 70, Musée d'Art Moderne, Paris, 1967, Inst. Contemporary Art, London, 1968, II Bienial Internacional del Deporte en las Bellas Artes, Madrid, 1969, N.Y. Cultural Center, 1971, 72, Mus. Contemporary Art, Chgo., 1972, Woburn Abbey, Eng., Musée de l'Abbaye Sainte Croix, Sables d'Olonne, France, 1973, Pratt Graphic Center, N.Y.C., 1974, U. Tex., 1966-76, 150th ann., NAD, N.Y.C., 1976, 41st Internat. Eucharistic Congress, Phila., 1976, Paris/N.Y., Centre Beaubourg, Paris, 1977, Centennial exhbn., Art Inst. Chgo., 1979, Rose Art Mus., Brandeis U., 1980, Wright State U., Chrysler Mus., Norfolk, Va., 1981, Indpls. Mus. Art, 1982, Whitney Mus. Am. Art., N.Y.C., 1983, also others; represented in permanent collections, Mus. Modern Art, Art Inst. Chgo., La Jolla (Calif.) Art Center, Mus. Tel Aviv, Smithsonian Instn., Kansas City Mus., others. Served with AUS, 1943-46. Ford Found. grantee, 1960; Cassandra Found. grantee, 1967; Guggenheim Found. grantee, 1968; Am. Acad. Arts and Letters; Nat. Inst. Arts and Letters grantee, 1973. Home and office: 530 LaGuardia Pl New York NY 10012

GOLUB, LEWIS, supermarket company executive. Chmn., chief exec. officer Golub Corp., Schenectady. Office: Golub Corp 501 Duanesburg Rd Schenectady NY 12306§

GOLUB, WILLIAM, food chain executive; b. Schenectady, June 30, 1904; s. Lewis and Matilda (Gurkin) G.; m. Estelle Dolores Ginsberg, Apr. 6, 1930; children: Paul David, Neil Mark, Meta Jill. Student, Union Coll., 1922-24; B.A., U. Mich., 1926. With Lewis Golub, wholesale grocer, 1926-30; v.p. Grosberg-Golub Co., Inc., 1930-43, Central Markets, Inc., 1933-43; dir., v.p. Central Market Operating Co., Inc., 1937-43, pres., 1943-72; v.p. Golub Corp., Schenectady, 1943-68, pres., 1968-76, chmn. bd., 1972-82, hon. chmn., 1982—, dir., officer, various subs. cos.; pres. Price Chopper Supermarkets, 1972-76, chmn., 1976-82, hon. chmn., 1982—; lectr. in field. Contbr. articles in profl. jours. Bd. dirs., trustee Jewish Community Ctr.; past bd. dirs. Capital Dist. Daus. of Sarah Jewish Home for Aged; mem. adv. bd. Schenectady Community Coll., Jr. Achievement; vice chmn. Schenectady Traffice Safety Commn.; chmn. bd. Schenectady City Hosp. Found.; bd. dirs. Schenectady Found., Sunnyview Hosp., Schenectady Kiwanis Found. Named hon. patron City of Schenectady, 1957; recipient Man of Yr. B'nai B'rith, 1962, 78, Seal of Israel, 1967, award Prime Ministers Club State of Israel, 1977, N.Y. State Gov.'s egg industry, 1969, N.Y. State Sammy, 1975, awards Kiwanis, other nat. and state. Mem. Food Mktg. Inst., C. of C., Nat. Rehab. Soc., Food Distbn. Research Soc., Am. Mktg. Assn., Internat. Platform Assn., Super Market Inst. (bd. dirs.), Nat. Assn. Food Chains (bd. dirs., past v.p.), Tau Epsilon Rho Legal Soc. Republican. Lodges: B'nai B'rith; Kiwanis. Office: 501 Duanesburg Rd Schenectady NY 12306

GOLUB, WILLIAM WELDON, lawyer; b. Bklyn, Oct. 7, 1914; s. Joseph and Sarah (Resnek) G.; m. Barbara Lewis, July 3, 1942; 1 dau., Joan L. A.B., Columbia U., 1934, J.D., 1937. Bar: N.Y. 1937. Practice law, N.Y.C., 1937-39, 40—; mem. staff atty. gen.'s com. on adminstrv. procedure State of N.Y., 1939-40; spl. counsel N.Y. State Moreland Commn. on Alcoholic Beverage Control Law, 1966; mem. firm Rosenman Colin Freund Lewis & Cohen (and predecessor), 1969—; mem. Council Adminstrv. Conf. U.S. Trustee Columbia U., 1981-82. Recipient Alumni medal Columbia, 1972. Mem. Am. Law Inst., Am. Bar Assn., Assn. Bar City N.Y., Fed. Bar Council, Phi Beta Kappa. Democrat. Clubs: Friars, Bohemians (N.Y.C.); Nat. Lawyers (Washington). Home: 1148 Fifth Ave New York NY 10128 Office: 575 Madison Ave New York NY 10022

GOLUSKIN, NORMAN LEWIS, advt. agy. exec.; b. N.Y.C., Sept. 25, 1938; s. Harry and Sylvia (Eisenstadt) G.; m. Judith M. Collier, Nov. 7, 1965 (div. Mar. 1973); 1 dau., Lisa; m. Susan B. Scher, Mar. 5, 1977. B.B.A., CUNY, 1963; Postgrad., Harvard U. Advanced Mgmt. Program, 1973. Media buyer, planner J. Walter Thompson, N.Y.C., 1959-63; account exec. Ogilvy & Mather, N.Y.C., 1963-67; account dir. Ted Bates, N.Y.C., 1967-71; exec. v.p. Smith/Greenland Inc., N.Y.C., 1971-73, pres., 1973—. Dir. U.S. com. Sports for Israel; pres. Central Park Track Club., 1172 Corp. Served with USMCR, 1957-59. Mem. Young Pres.'s Orgn. Home: 1172 Park Ave New York NY 10028 Office: 1414 Ave of Americas New York NY 10019 *Set goals which are realistic but beyond what one can do comfortably. We are all capable of more than we think—we need a challenge. Every experience, whether you win or lose, is worthwhile—learn something from it.*

GOMBERG, ABBOTT, dept. store exec.; b. Fall River, Mass., May 8, 1921; s. Alexander and Gertrude (Covitz) G.; m. Miriam Kayle Krasow, Oct. 4, 1945; children—Lisa Gomberg Szeman, Peter. Student, Mass. Coll. Art, 1942. Vice pres. sales promotion and public relations Lasalle & Koch, Toledo, 1960-68; sr. v.p., dir. sales promotion and public relations Shillito's, Cin., 1968-73; sr. v.p. Bambergers, Newark, 1973—. Exhibited etchings, Addison Gallery, Andover, Mass., Nat. Gallery Design, N.Y.C. Trustee Newark Art Museum, 1976—. Served with U.S. Army, 1942-45. Mem. Nat. Retail Mchts. Assn., Laurel Hill Conservation Assn., Trout Unlimited, Internat. Center Photography. Home: Fort Lee NJ also Box 764 Stockbridge MA 01262 Office: 131 Market St Newark NJ 07102

GOMBERG, EDITH LISANSKY, psychologist; b. N.Y.C., Jan. 14, 1920; d. Barnet and Dorothy (Resnick) Silverglied; m. Henry Jacob Gomberg, June 24, 1967; children: Stephen, Judith, Eugene, Richard, Robert. M.A., Columbia U., 1940; Ph.D., Yale U., 1949. Lectr., research asst., research asso. Center Alcohol Studies, Yale U., New Haven, 1949-67; assoc. prof. dept. psychology U. P.R., 1968-71; prof. Sch. Social Work and research scientist Inst. Gerontology, U. Mich., Ann Arbor, 1974—; vis. prof. psychology Center Alcohol Studies, Rutgers U., New Brunswick, N.J., 1972—. Author: Gender and Disordered Behavior, 1979, Alcohol, Science and Society Revisited, 1982; contbr. chpts. to books, articles to profl. jours. Mem. Rep. Town Meeting, Hamden, Conn., 1964-65; mem. Blue Ribbon Study Commn. on Alcoholism and Aging, Nat. Council on Alcoholism, 1979—; chmn. panel on prevention, participant study to assess sci. opportunities of alcohol-related research Inst. Medicine, Nat. Acad. Sci.; mem. alcohol psychosocial research rev. com. Nat. Inst. Alcohol Abuse and Alcoholism, 1981-82. Mary E. Ives fellow, 1944; AAUW Elizabeth Avery Colten fellow, 1955. Mem. Am. Psychol. Assn., Psychonomic Soc., Sociedad Interamericana de Psicologia, Sigma Xi. Jewish. Home: 430 Hillspur Rd Ann Arbor MI 48105 Office: 1065 Frieze Bldg U Mich Ann Arbor MI 48109

GOMBERG, HENRY JACOB, nuclear engr.; b. N.Y.C., Apr. 16, 1918; s. Alexander and Marie (Shuloff) G.; m. Edna M. Cohen, Dec. 28, 1940 (dec. Nov. 1965); children—Richard, Robert; m. Edith Silverglied, June 24, 1967; stepchildren—Stephen, Judith, Eugene Lisansky. B.S.E., U. Mich., 1941, M.S.E., 1943, Ph.D. in Elec. Engring, 1951; Sc.D. (hon.), Albion Coll., 1968. Dir. Mich. Meml.-Phoenix Project, 1959-61; chmn. com. nuclear engring. U. Mich., 1955-58, chmn. dept. nuclear engring., 1958-61, prof. nuclear engring., 1955-61; dep. dir. P.R. Nuclear Center, Mayaquez, 1961-66, dir., 1966-71; pres., chief operating officer KMS Fusion, Inc., Ann Arbor, Mich., 1971, chmn., 1976-80; pres., chief exec. officer KMS Industries, Inc., 1976-78, pres., 1978-80; pres., chmn. Ann Arbor Nuclear Inc., 1981—; Carnegie vis. prof. U. Hawaii, 1961; cons. Hawaiian Electric Co., Atomic Power Devel. Assos., Inc., Gen. Motors Corp., Lockheed Aircraft Co., Nuclear Products Co., Cook Research Labs., ICA, AEC, Nat. Acad. Scis. Chmn. com. research reactors NRC; del. Internat. Conf. Peaceful Uses Atomic Energy, 1955; U.S. rep. Nat. Acad. Sci. to, USSR, 1957. Recipient Henry Russel award U. Mich., 1952. Fellow Am. Nuclear Soc., AAAS, Radiation Research Soc.; mem. Am. Phys. Soc. (com. on fusion Atomic Indsl. Forum), Am. Soc. Engring. Edn., Sigma Xi, Tau Beta Pi, Eta Kappa Nu, Phi Kappa Phi. Home: 430 Hillspur Rd Ann Arbor MI 48105 Office: 3300 Plymouth Rd PO Box 8618 Ann Arbor MI 48107

GOMENA, JOHN EDWARD, corporation executive; b. 1927; married. B.S., U. R.I., 1951; postgrad., Carnegie-Mellon U., 1972. Indsl. engr. U.S. Rubber Co., 1951-52, Bostitch, Inc., 1954; area mfg. and engring. mgr. Birds Eye div. Gen. Foods Corp., 1964-66; with Amfac Inc., Honolulu, 1966—, v.p. ops. Lamb-Weston, 1966-73, pres., 1973-80, vice chmn. Amfac Foods Group, 1980-81, chmn., 1981; pres. Amfac Foods, Inc., Portland, Oreg., 1981—; also exec. v.p. Amfac Inc., 1981—. Served with USNR, 1945-46. Mem. Am. Frozen Food Assn. (past chmn.), Frozen Food Assn. (past v.p.). Office: Amfac Inc 700 Bishop St Box 3230 Honolulu HI 96801 *

GOMER, ROBERT, scientist; b. Vienna, Austria, Mar. 24, 1924; m. Anne Olah, 1955; children: Richard, Maria. B.A., Pomona Coll., 1944; Ph.D. in Chemistry, U. Rochester, 1949; AEC fellow chemistry, Harvard, 1949-50. Instr. dept. chemistry and James Franck Inst. U. Chgo., 1950-51, asst. prof., 1951-54, asso. prof., 1954-58, prof., 1958—; dir. James Franck Inst. U. Chgo., 1977-83. Bd. dirs.: Bull. Atomic Scientists. Served with AUS, 1944-46. Recipient Kendall award in surface chemistry Am. Chem. Soc., 1975; Davisson-Germer prize Am. Phys. Soc., 1981; Sloan fellow, 1958-62; Guggenheim fellow, 1969-70; Bourke lectr., Eng., 1959. Mem. Leopoldina Acad. Scis., Nat. Acad. Scis., Am. Acad. Arts and Sci. Home: 4824 Kimbark Ave Chicago IL 60615 Office: 5640 Ellis Ave Chicago IL 60637

GOMERSALL, EARL RAYMOND, consultant; b. Mpls., Dec. 4, 1930; s. John Raymond and Florence Judith (Olson) G.; m. Patricia Jean Burfield, Aug 14, 1971; children: Earl Raymond, Lea Diane. B.S. in Bus. Adminstrn., Northwestern U., 1952, M.B.A., 1957. Project engr. Elgin Watch Co., Ill., 1952-57; ops. mgr. Texas Instruments, Dallas, 1957-71; corp. v.p. Motorola, Inc., Schaumburg, Ill., 1971-1983; cons. Research Components, Inverness, Ill., 1983—; dir. Sweeney-Todd, London, 1975—, On Tyme Products, Morton Grove, Ill., 1983—, ICOM Software, Inc., Wheeling, Ill., 1983—, Apache AX Omigraphics, Oak Brook, Ill., 1983—, LICRON, Santa Clara, 1983—. Contbg. author: Manufacturing Man and His Job; inventor on-line real-time pricing; patentee method for operating mfg. line. Serrved as spl. agt. U.S. Army, 1952-54. Recipient Best Methods Improvement of Yr. awards Indsl. Mgmt. Soc., 1952, 58, 59. Mem. Am. Mgmt. Assn. (planning council 1978—), John Evans Club (Northwestern U.), Delta Sigma Pi (life), Delta Mu Delta, Am. Legion, Nat. Rifle Assn. Republican. Episcopalian. Home: 1934 Cheviot Dr Inverness IL 60010 Office: Research Components 1945 Cheviot Dr Inverness IL 60010

GOMES, PETER JOHN, clergyman; b. Boston, May 22, 1942; s. Peter L. and Orissa Josephine (White) G. A.B., Bates Coll., Lewiston, Maine, 1965; S.T.B. (Rockefeller fellow 1967-68), Harvard U., 1968; D.D. (hon.), New Eng. Coll., 1974, L.H.D., Waynesburg Coll., 1978. Ordained to ministry Am. Baptist Ch., 1968; instr. history, dir. freshmen exptl. program Tuskegee (Ala.) Inst., 1968-70; asst. minister, then acting minister Meml. Ch., Harvard U., 1970-74, minister, 1974—; Plummer prof. Christian morals Harvard U., 1974—; nat. chaplain Am. Guild Organists, 1978-82. Co-author: Books of the Pilgrims; editor: Parnassus, 1970, History of the Pilgrim Society, 1970. Pres., trustee Internat. Fund Def. and Aid in S. Africa, 1977—; trustee Bates Coll., 1973-78, 80—, Pilgrim Soc., 1970—, Charity of Edward Hopkins, 1974—, Donation to Liberia, 1973—, Plimoth Plantation, 1977—, Boston Freedom Trail, 1976—, Roxbury Latin Sch., 1982—, Ella Lyman Cabot Trust, 1975—. Fellow Royal Soc. Arts; mem. Royal Soc. Ch. Music, Colonial Soc. Mass., Mass. Hist. Soc., Farmington Inst. Christian Studies, Am. Bapt. Hist. Soc., Unitarian Hist. Soc., Signet Soc. (pres.), Harvard Musical Assn., English-Speaking Union (dir.), Phi Beta Kappa. Clubs: Tavern, St. Botolph, Odd Volumes, Examiner, Shop, Harvard. Home: Sparks House 21 Kirkland St Cambridge MA 02138 Office: Memorial Ch Harvard Univ Cambridge MA 02138

GOMEZ, FRANCIS DEAN, public affairs consultant former foreign service officer; b. Belle Fourche, S.D., July 24, 1941; s. Frank Garcia and Mae Elizabeth (Larive) G.; m. Esperanza Narino, Sept. 30, 1966; children: Frank T., Laura E. B.A., U. Wash., 1964; M.S. in Adminstrn., George Washington U., 1982. Mid-career fellow Woodrow Wilson Sch. Pub. and Internat. Affairs, Princeton, N.J., 1973-74; pub. affairs Am. Embassy, Bamako, Mali, 1974-76, Haiti, 1976-78; chief fgn. service personnel USIA, Washington, 1978-80; dep. asst. sec. pub. affairs Dept. State, Washington, 1980-82; dir. fgn. press centers USIA, Washington, 1982-84; v.p. Internat. Bus. Communications, Washington, 1984—. Founder, pres. Hispanic Employees Council, Dept. State, 1979-81. Recipient USIA awards, Superior Honor award USIA, 1967, Meritorious Honor awards, 1976, 78, Annual Agy. EEO award, 1980. Mem. Am. Fgn. Service Assn., Nat. Assn. Hispanic Journalists, Nat. Press Club, Pi Alpha Alpha. Home: 6564 Williamsburg Blvd Arlington VA 22213 Office: Internat Bus Communicators 1607 New Hampshire Ave NW Suite 300 Washington DC 20009

GOMEZ, MANUEL RODRIGUEZ, physician; b. Minaya, Spain, July 4, 1928; came to U.S., 1952, naturalized, 1961; s. Argimiro Rodriguez Herguedas and Isabel Gomez Torrente; m. Joan A. Stormer, Sept. 25, 1954; children: Christopher, Gregory, Douglas, Timothy. M.D., U. Havana, Cuba, 1952; M.S. in Anatomy, U. Mich., 1956. Intern Michael Reese Hosp., 1952-53, asst. resident in pediatrics, 1953-54; resident in neurology U. Mich., 1954-56; fellow in pediatric neurology U. Chgo. Med. Sch., 1956-57; instr. neurology U. Buffalo Med. Sch., 1957-58, 59-60; clin. clk. neurology Inst. Neurology, U. London, 1958-59; asst. prof., then assoc. prof. neurology Wayne State U. Med. Sch., 1960-64; mem. faculty Mayo Med. Sch., Rochester, Minn., 1964—, prof. pediatric neurology, 1975—; cons. pediatric neurology, head sect. Mayo Clinic, 1964—. Author: Tuberous Sclerosis, 1979; adv. bd.: Bull. Orton Soc., Brain and Devel. Mem. Am. Acad. Neurology, Am. Neurol. Assn., Child Neurology Soc., Central Soc. Neurol. Research, Assn. Research Nervous and Mental Disease, Orton Soc. Home: 4225 Meadow Ridge Dr SW Rochester MN 55901 Office: Mayo Clinic 200 1st St SW Rochester MN 55901

GOMEZ, RUDOLPH, univ. ofcl.; b. Rawlins, Wyo., July 17, 1930; s. Jesus Jose and Guadalupe (Navarro) G.; m. Polly Katherine Petty, Nov. 11, 1956; children—Robert Moorman, Clay Petty. B.S., Utah State U., Logan, 1959; M.S., Stanford U., 1960; Ph.D., U. Colo., Boulder, 1963. Instr., then asst. prof. polit. sci. Colo. Coll., Colorado Springs, 1962-68; asso. prof. U. Denver, 1968-70, Memphis State U., 1970-72; prof. polit. sci. U. Tex., El Paso, 1972-80, chmn. dept., 1973-74, grad. dean, 1974-80, v.p. for adminstrn., San Antonio, 1980—, prof. polit. sci., 1980—; Fulbright Hays sr. prof. Catholic U., Lima, Peru, 1967. Author: The Peruvian Administrative System, 1969; co-author: Colorado Government and Politics, rev. edit, 1972; Gen. editor: The Social Reality of Ethnic America, 1974; Contbr. to profl. jours., books. Mem. Mayor El Paso Adminstrv. Rev. Bd., 1972-74; mem. rev. com. crime and delinquency NIMH, 1977-79. Served with USAF, 1950-54. Woodrow Wilson fellow, 1959-60. Mem. Am. Polit. Sci. Assn., Am. Soc. Pub. Adminstrs., Nat. Council U. Research Adminstrs. Democrat. Roman Catholic. Home: 12506 King Elm St San Antonio TX 78230 Office: U Tex San Antonio TX 78285

GOMEZPLATA, ALBERT, chemical engineering educator; b. Bucaramanga, Colombia, July 2, 1930; came to U.S., 1939, naturalized, 1948; s. Roberto and Carmencita (Cespedes) GomezPlata; m. Eva Maria Wolf, June 11, 1960; children: Elizabeth Ann, Theresa Maria, Catherine Eve. B.Chem.Engring., Bklyn. Poly. Inst., 1952; M.Chem.Engring., Rensselaer Poly. Inst., 1954, Ph.D., 1958. Registered profl. engr., Md. Process engr. Gen. Chem., Del. Works, Claymont, 1952-53; faculty U. Md., College Park, 1959—, prof. chem. engring., 1968—, chmn. dept., 1975-78, assoc. dean engring., 1982—; Year-in-industry prof. engring. dept. E.I. DuPont de Nemours & Co., Inc., Wilmington, Del., 1965-66; vis. prof. U. P.R., Mayaguez, 1970-71; cons. Am. Machine & Foundry Co., 1962-64, Melpar Inc., 1967-68, Md. Div. Air Quality Control, 1970-75, Ensci Inc., 1978, EPA Sci. Adv. Bd., 1980-82, Energy Concepts, 1983—. Served with USAF, 1954-56. Fellow Am. Inst. Chemists; mem. Am. Chem. Soc., Am. Soc. Engring. Edn., N.Y. Acad. Scis., Am. Inst. Chem. Engrs. (chmn. Md. sect. 1969), Sigma Xi, Tau Beta Pi, Phi Lambda Upsilon. Home: 513 Powell Dr Annapolis MD 21401

GOMEZ-QUIROZ, JUAN, painter, printmaker, educator; b. Santiago, Chile, Feb. 20, 1939; naturalized, 1975; s. Juan Gomez and Maria Quiroz (Tapia) Bravo. Student, Sch. Fine Art U. Chile; Fulbright fellow, R.I. Sch. Design; certificate (Fulbright fellow), Yale. Asst. prof. Sch. Fine Art U. Chile, 1961-62; Pan Am. Union fellow Pratt Graphic Art Center, 1964-66; lectr. U. Calif. at Santa Barbara, 1967, N.Y. Community Coll., 1969-70, Summit (N.J.) Art Center, 1972—; represented by Sutton Gallery, N.Y.C.; adj. prof. art N.Y. U., 1969—; dir. N.Y. U. Photo-Etching Workshop, 1972-73. Rep. by, Sutton Gallery, N.Y.C. (1st prize Salon de Alumnos U. Chile 1960), Sutton Gallery, N.Y.C. (2d prize in painting Salon de Primavera, Santiago 1961), Sutton Gallery, N.Y.C. (Guggenheim fellow in painting 1966-67), Sutton Gallery, N.Y.C. (Nat. Endowment for Arts grantee 1974-75), Sutton Gallery, N.Y.C. (Fulbright grantee 1975), Sutton Gallery, N.Y.C. (prize 4th Biennale, San Juan, P.R. 1979); Author: Printmaking; one-man shows, Sala Decor, Santiago, 1961, Kie Kor Gallery, New Haven, 1964, Ledesma Gallery, N.Y.C., Alonzo Gallery, N.Y.C., 1968, 70, 72, Summit Art Center, 1972, Ars Concentra Gallery, Lima, Peru, 1975, Pecanins Gallery, Mexico City, Balcon Les Images, Montreal, Gloria Cortella Gallery, N.Y.C., San Sebastian Gallery, P.R., 1980, Sutton Gallery, N.Y.C., 1981, 83; exhibited in numerous group shows, the latest being, Montreal (Que., Can.) Mus. Fine Art, 1971, 10 Downtown group show, N.Y.C., Second Bienal de San Juan (P.R.) of Printmaking, 1972, Third Ann. Nat. Print Exhbn., Atlanta, Loeb Student Center N.Y. U., Hudson River Mus., N.Y., 1973, O. K. Harris Gallery, N.Y.C., (1974), Levitan Gallery, Soho, N.Y., 1974, N.Y. Printmakers, Lima, Bienal of Drawing, Riejka, Yugoslavia, Latin Am. Prints from, Mus. Modern Art, traveling exhbn., N.Y.C., 1974; represented in permanent collections, De Menil Collection, Houston, Boston Mus. Fine Art, Bklyn. Mus. Art, Cin. Art Mus., Center Inter Am. Relations, Chase Manhattan Bank, Everson Mus. Art, Library of Congress, M.I.T., Solomon Guggenheim Mus., N.Y.C., Met. Mus. Art, N.Y.C., Mus. Modern Art, N.Y.C., N.Y. Pub. Library, N.Y. U., U. Mass. Recipient Mention of Honor Salon de Alumnos U. Chile, 1958; 3rd prize Salon Oficial de Chile, 1960; 1st prize Salon de Alumnos U. Chile, 1960; 2d prize in painting Salon de Primavera, Santiago, 1961; Guggenheime fellow in painting, 1966-67; Nat. Endowment for Arts grantee, 1974-75; Fulbright grantee, 1975;

prize 4th Biennale, San Juan, P.R., 1979. Home: 44 Grand St New York NY 10013 Studio: 365 Canal St New York NY 10013

GOMEZ-RODRIGUEZ, MANUEL, physicist, college dean; b. Ponce, P.R., Oct. 15, 1940; s. Manuel Gomez-Acevedo and Lucila Rodriguez; m. Adele M. Mousakad, June 12, 1965; children: Marisol, Beatriz Cristina. B.Sc., U. P.R., 1962; Ph.D., Cornell U., 1968. NRC postdoctoral fellow Naval Research Lab., Washington, 1967-69; asst. prof. physics U. P.R., Mayaguez, 1969-71, assoc. prof., Rio Piedras, 1971-75, prof., 1979—, chmn. dept. physics, 1971-75, dean Coll. Natural Scis., 1975—, dir. NSF-sponsored Resource Center for Sci. and Engring., 1980—. Editor: Jour. Ferroelectrics, 1977; contbr. articles to profl. jours. Grantee Internat. Union Pure and Applied Physics, 1975, NSF, 1974, 76, 77, 80, Office Naval Research, 1974, Dept. Energy, 1976-78, Army Research Office, 1981. Mem. Am. Phys. Soc., Sci. Tchrs. Assn. P.R. (hon. pres. 1973), Sigma Xi. Office: U PR Rio Piedras PR 00931

GOMEZ-SICRE, JOSE ROMUALDO, art critic and historian, art consultant and evaluator; b. Matanzas, Cuba, July 6, 1916; came to U.S., 1945, naturalized, 1983; s. Clemente Gomez Guillermina and Sicre. Licenciado en Dere Internacional, Havana U., 1939, Dr. in Polit., Social and Econ. Scis., 1941. Art specialist OAS (formerly Pan Am Union), Washington, 1946-73; chief div. visual arts (OAS (formerly Pan Am Union), Washington, 1973-82; dir. Mus. Modern Latin Am. Art, 1982-83; ret., 1983; lectr. Latin Am. art in (all Latin Am. nations, W. Ger., Spain, Sweden, Italy, Japan And others). Author: Cuban Printing Today, 1944, Leonardo Mierman, 1978, Jose Luis Cuevas, 1983. Home: 1756 Lanier Pl NW Washington DC 20009

GOMORY, RALPH EDWARD, mathematician, business machines manufacturing company executive; b. Brooklyn Heights, N.Y., May 7, 1929; s. Andrew L. and Marian (Schellenberg) G.; m. Laura Dumper, 1954 (div. 1968); children: Andrew C., Susan S., Stephen H. B.A., Williams Coll., 1950, Sc.D. (hon.), 1973; student, Kings Coll., Cambridge (Eng.) U., 1950-51; Ph.D., Princeton U., 1954. Research assoc. Princeton U., 1951-54, asst. prof. math., Higgins lectr., 1957-59; with IBM, Yorktown Heights, N.Y., 1959—, dir. math. scis., research div., 1968-70, mem. corp. tech. com., 1970, dir. research, 1970—, v.p., 1973—, also mem. corp. mgmt. bd.; Andrew D. White prof.-at-large Cornell U., 1970-76; dir. IBM World Trade Ams./Far East Corp., Bank of N.Y.; Mem. vis. com. Sloan Sch. Mgmt., M.I.T., 1971-77; chmn. council Grad. Sch. Bus., U. Chgo., 1971-80; mem. adv. council dept. math. Princeton, 1974—; mem. adv. council Sch. Engring., Stanford U., 1978—. Trustee Hampshire Coll., 1977—; mem. governing bd. Nat. Research Council., 1980-83. Served with USN, 1954-57. Recipient Lanchester prize Ops. Research Soc. Am., 1963; IBM fellow. Fellow Econometric Soc., Am. Acad. Arts and Scis.; mem. Nat. Acad. Scis. (council 1977-78, 80-83), Nat. Acad. Engring. Research integer and linear programming, non-linear differential equations. Home: 260 Douglas Rd Chappaqua NY 10514 Office: IBM Thomas J Watson Research Center Box 218 Yorktown Heights NY 10598

GONDA, THOMAS ANDREW, physician, educator; b. Vienna, Austria, Aug. 24, 1921; came to U.S., 1924, naturalized, 1929; s. Victor E. and Ossy (Kopp) G.; m. Elizabeth Marie Chandler, July 3, 1944; children—Paul Chandler, William Stuart, Lynn. Student, U. Chgo., 1939-40; A.B., Stanford, 1942, M.D., 1945. Intern San Francisco Hosp., 1944-45; resident Langley Porter Clinic, San Francisco, 1948-51; clin. dir. psychiatry San Francisco Hosp., 1949-51; chief neurology and psychiatry VA Hosp., San Francisco, 1951-53; instr. psychiatry Stanford U. Sch. Medicine, 1954-55, asst. prof., 1955-58, asso. prof., 1958-65, prof., 1965—, acting exec., 1955-56, 58-61, asso. dean, 1967-75; dir. Stanford U. Hosp., 1968-74; med. dir. Stanford U. Med. Center, 1974-75; chmn. dept. psychiatry and behavioral scis. Stanford U., 1975—; vis. prof. Inst. Exptl. Psychology and spl. NIMH research fellow Oxford U., Eng., 1961-62; cons. VA, Calif. Dept. Mental Hygiene, 1956—; chmn. Nat. Psychiat. Residency Adv. Bd., 1968. Mem. profl. adv. bd. Found. Thanatology, 1968—. Served to capt., M.C. AUS, 1946-48. Fellow Am. Psychiat. Assn., Am. Coll. Psychiatrists; mem. Am., Calif. med. assns., AAAS. Home: 586 Foothill Rd Stanford CA 94305

GONEDES, NICHOLAS JAMES, accountant, educator; b. Bklyn., Feb. 6, 1946; s. Thomas and Daspin (Cokas) G. S.B. in Econs, U. Pa., 1967; Ph.D. in Acctg. and Fin, U. Tex., 1969. Asst. prof. acctg. Grad. Sch. Bus., U. Chgo., 1969-74, asso. prof., 1974-76, prof., 1976-79; prof. acctg. and fin. Wharton Sch., U. Pa., Phila., 1979—; vis. prof. Grad. Sch. Indsl. Adminstrn., Carnegie-Mellon U., 1971-72. Contbr. articles on fin. and acctg. research to profl. jours.; editorial bd.: Jour. Acctg. Research, 1970—. Recipient Notable Contribution to Acctg. Lit. award Am. Inst. C.P.A.'s, 1974; Humble Oil and Refining Co. fellow, 1968-69. Mem. Am. Acctg. Assn. (research bd. 1976-77), Am. Econ. Assn., Ops. Research Soc. Am., Am. Statis. Assn., Econometric Soc., Inst. Mgmt. Scis., AAAS, Beta Gamma Sigma, Beta Alpha Psi. Office: Wharton Sch-Dietrich U Pa Philadelphia PA 19104

GONG, EDMOND JOSEPH, lawyer; b. Miami, Fla., Oct. 7, 1930; s. Joe Fred and Fayline G.; m. Sophie Vlachos, July 25, 1957 (dec.); children: Frances Fayline, Peter Joseph (dec.), Madeleine, Joseph Fred, II, Edmond Joseph. A.B. cum laude, Harvard U., 1952, postgrad. in law, 1954-55; J.D., U. Miami, 1960. Bar: Fla. bar 1960. Spl. writer Hong Kong Tiger Standard, 1955-56; staff writer Miami Herald, 1958-59; asso. firm Helliwell, Melrose and DeWolf, 1960-61; practice law, Miami, 1962—; asst. U.S. atty. So. Dist. Fla., 1961-62; mem. Fla. Ho. of Reps., 1963-66, Fla. Senate, 1966-72; trustee Fla. Gulf Realty Trust, 1974-80; pres. Inflahedge Resources Fund, Edmond Gong and Co., Inc., 1979—; dir., sec. Security Atlantic Corp., 1980-81; former dir. Good Taco Corp.; chmn. Fla. Land Sales Advisory Council, 1974-76; vice chmn. Bd. Bus. Regulation, State of Fla., 1976-77; dir. Dadeland Bank, Dadeland Bancshares, Inc.; Fellow Inst. Politics John Fitzgerald Kennedy Sch. Govt., Harvard U., 1969-70, asso. dir., 1971-72. Mem. Am., Dade County, Fed. bar assns., Harvard U. Alumni Assn. (dir.-at-large). Methodist. Clubs: Miami, Standard; Harvard (Miami); Ocean Reef (Key Largo, Fla.). Home: 7751 SW 78th Ct Miami FL 33143 Office: 8585 Sunset Dr Suite 190 Miami FL 33143

GONICK, ELY, paper company executive; b. 1925. A.B., Drew U., 1948; Ph.D., Pa. State U., 1951. Dir. research and devel. fabrics and finishes dept. E. duPont de Nemours & Co., 1951-81; exec. v.p. Internat. Paper Co., N.Y.C., 1981, sr. v.p. tech., 1981—. Served with USNR, 1943-46. Office: Internat Paper Co 77 W 45th St New York NY 10036 *

GONICK, PAUL, urologist; b. Bklyn., July 5, 1930; s. Benjamin and Yetta (Shedrofsky) G.; m. Angela M. Furlong, Mar. 24, 1963; children—Brian Michael, Peter Benjamin, Julia Nancy. B.A., N.Y. U., 1951; M.D., Yale U., 1955. Diplomate: Nat. Bd. Med. Examiners. Intern Albany (N.Y.) Hosp., 1955-56; resident VA Hosp. and U. Minn., Mpls., 1958-62; instr. urology Wayne State U., Detroit, 1964-65, asst. prof. urology, 1965; asst. clin. prof. urology Columbia U., N.Y.C., 1966-69; asso. prof. urology Hahnemann Med. Coll. and Hosp., Phila., 1969-74, prof. urology, 1974—, dir. div. urology, 1969-80; practice medicine specializing in urology, Phila., 1969—; chief urology sect. VA Hosp., Dearborn, Mich., 1963-66, acting asso. chief staff for research and edn., 1964-65; jr. attending physician Detroit Receiving Hosp., 1964-65; chief urology sect. VA Hosp., Bronx, 1966-69; asst. urologist Presbyn. Hosp., N.Y.C., 1966-69; cons. urology Harlem Hosp., 1967-69; cons. numerous hosps. Contbr. numerous articles to med jours. Served to capt. USAF, 1956-58. James Hudson Brown fellow, 1953. Fellow A.C.S.; mem. AMA, Yale Med. Soc., Am. Urol. Assn., Detroit Urol. Soc., Vets. Urol. Assn. (treas. 1969—), Soc. Univ. Urologists, Phila. Urol. Soc., Pa. Med. Soc., Philadelphia County Med. Soc., Phila. Acad. Surgery, Caducean Soc., Phi Beta Kappa, Mu Chi Sigma, Beta Lambda Sigma. Home: 70 Fairview Rd Narberth PA 19072 Office: 227 N Broad St Philadelphia PA 19107

GONSER, THOMAS HOWARD, lawyer, bar association executive; b. Berkeley, Calif., May 8, 1938; s. William Adam and Alice Gertrude (Lease) G.; m. Stephanie Jane Griffiths, Nov. 27, 1960; children: Thomas Howard, Catherine Ruth. A.A., U. Calif., Berkeley, 1958, B.A. in Polit. Sci., 1960, J.D., 1965. Bar: Calif. 1965, Idaho 1970. Atty. S.P. Co., San Francisco, 1965-68; asst. gen. counsel Boise Cascade Corp., Idaho, 1969-72, assoc. gen. counsel, 1972-81, asst. sec., 1972-81; exec. dir. Am. Bar Assn., Chgo., 1981—. Author: The Bar Foundation, 1979. Served with U.S. Army, 1960-62. Fellow Am. Bar Found.; mem. Idaho Law Found. (pres. 1977-80), Calif. Bar Assn., Idaho State Bar, Nat. Conf. Bar Founds. (pres. 1980-81), Internat. Bar Assn. (dep. sec. gen. 1982—, asst. sec. gen. 1983—). Methodist. Office: 1155 E 60th St Chicago IL 60637

GONYEA, EDWARD FRANCIS, neurologist, educator; b. Plattsburgh, N.Y., Jan. 14, 1932; s. George Herbert and Eleanor (Rausch) G.; m. Patricia Louise Olson, Sept. 22, 1966; children: Gregory Joseph, Bruce Chandler, Larisa Marie, Carol Nadine. B.S. cum laude, Georgetown U., 1953, M.D., 1957. Diplomate: Am. Bd. Neurology (jr. examiner 1970-72). Intern D.C. Gen. Hosp., Washington, 1957-58; resident in internal medicine Emory U. Hosp.-VA Hosp., Atlanta, 1958-59, 60-61; resident in neurology Jefferson Hosp., Phila., 1959-60, 63-65; chief neurol. service VA Hosp., Indpls., 1965-67, Gainesville, Fla., 1967-74, Memphis, 1974—; asst. prof. neurology Ind. U. Med. Center, 1965-67; asst. prof. medicine and neurology U. Fla. Med. Sch., 1967-74; asso. prof. neurology U. Tenn. Center Health Scis., Memphis, 1974-78, prof., 1978—. Author articles in field, chpts. in books. Served as officer M.C. USAR, 1961-63. Fellow Nat. Inst. Neurol. Diseases and Blindness, 1959-60, 63-65. Fellow Am. Acad. Neurology; mem. AMA, Silver Stick Soc., Ind. Neurol. Soc., Memphis Acad. Neurology (pres. 1981). Democrat. Roman Catholic. Club: Germantown Kiwanis (dir. 1980—). Home: 2445 Dogwood Trail Dr Germantown TN 38138 Office: VA Hosp 1030 Jefferson Ave Memphis TN 38104 *Every patient presents a new challenge.*

GONZALES, JOHN EDMOND, history educator; b. New Orleans, Sept. 17, 1924; s. Joseph Edmond and Sadie Julia (Albritton) G. B.S., La. State U., 1943, M.A., 1945; Ph.D., U. N.C., 1957. Mem. faculty U. So. Miss., Hattiesburg, 1945—, William D. McCain prof. history, 1968—, distinguished univ. prof., 1973—. Editor: Jour. of Miss. History, 1963—, A Mississippi Reader, Hattiesburg: A Pictorial History; asso. editor: A History of Mississippi, 1973; contbr. to: Readers Ency. of the Am. West; contbr. articles to profl. jours. Bd. dirs. Univ. Press of Miss. Mem. So., La. hist. assns., Miss. Hist. Soc. (pres. 1975-76), Omicron Delta Kappa, Phi Kappa Phi (pres. chpt.), Kappa Phi Kappa, Kappa Delta Pi, Pi Gamma Mu, Phi Alpha Theta, Mu Phi Epsilon, Alpha Psi Omega, Kappa Sigma (Outstanding Faculty Mem. award 1968). Democrat. Baptist. Home: 111 S 29th Ave Hattiesburg MS 39401

GONZALES, PANCHO *See* **GONZALES, RICHARD A.**

GONZALES, RICHARD A. (PANCHO GONZALES), professional tennis player; b. Los Angeles, May 9, 1928; s. Manuel A. and Carmen (Alire) G.; (div.)children: Richard, Michael, Danny, Christina, Andrea; m. Betty Steward, Dec. 31, 1972; 1 dau., Jeanna Lynn.; m. Rita Agassi, Mar. 31, 1984. Profl. tennis player, participant profl. tennis championships, 1953-60; now tennis profl. Caesar's Palace, Las Vegas, Nev.; Tournament chmn., 1971, participant sr. grand master tournaments. Served with USNR, 1945-47. U.S. champion,1948, 49; winner Davis Cup, 1949. Office: Caesar's Palace Tennis Shop 3570 Las Vegas Blvd Las Vegas NV 89109

GONZALEZ, EFREN WILLIAM, science information services administrator; b. N.Y.C., June 16, 1929; s. Efren and Grace (Dorety) G.; m. Rita Ciliotta, June 14, 1952; children: Efren T., Janet M., Barbara A., Lisa M., Lara E. B.A. in Philosophy, Iona Coll., 1951; M.S. in Library Sci, Columbia, 1952. Part-time librarian Carroll Club, N.Y.C., 1951-53; librarian Mil. Sea Transp. Service, Atlantic Area, Bklyn., 1952-53; asst. librarian Material Lab., N.Y. Naval Shipyard, Bklyn., 1953-55; librarian Nepera Chem. Co., Yonkers, N.Y., 1955-56; tech. librarian Grove Labs., St. Louis, 1956-57, dir. tech. communications, adminstrv. asst. to v.p. research and devel., 1957-67; mgr. tech. communications Bristol-Myers Products, Hillside, N.J., 1967-69, mgr. sci. info. services, 1969-76, mgr. research quality compliance, 1977-83, dir. research and devel. administrn., 1983—; mem. council on library edn. N.J. Dept. Edn., 1976-80; adv. com. library photocopying U.S. Copyright Office, 1978-83. Mem. Spl. Libraries Assn. (pres. Greater St. Louis chpt. 1959-60, assn. dir. 1967-73, assn. pres. 1971-72, chmn. awards com. 1973-74, nominating com. 1979, mem. seminar on second draft of Nat. Commn. Libraries and Info. Sci. nat. program for library and info. services 1974, chmn. copyright spl. com. 1975-76, chmn. copyright law implementation com. 1978-83, N.J. chpt. rep. to N.J. planning com. White House Conf. on Libraries and Info. Services 1975-76), Pharm. Mfrs. Assn. (mem. sci. info. subsect. 1973—, mem. steering com. 1974-79), Council Nat. Library Assns. (rep. from Spl. Libraries Assn. 1971-73, dir. 1973-76, chmn. 1974-75, rep. to Conf. on Resolution of Copyright Issues 1974-75, rep. to conf. on Nat. Commn. Libraries and Info. Sci. continuing library and information sci. edn. project 1974-75), Universal Serials and Book Exchange (chmn. nominating com. 1973-74, mem. rev. com. 1974-75, chmn. copyright law practices and implementation com. 1979-83), Assn. Research Libraries (mem. adv. com. to study centralized and regionalized inter-library loan centers 1973-74). Home: 167 Watchung Ave Chatham NJ 07928 Office: 1350 Liberty Ave Hillside NJ 07207

GONZALEZ, EMILIO, educator, author; b. La Coruna, Spain, Nov. 13, 1903; came to U.S., 1939, naturalized, 1950; s. Antonio and Carmen (Lopez) G.; m. Maria Nunez, June 2, 1931. B.A., Inst. Gen. y Tecnico, La Coruna, 1920; M. Social Scis. and Law summa cum laude, U. Madrid, 1926, Ph.D., 1928; U. Madrid scholarum, U. Munich, Germany, 1927-28. Adj. prof. U. Madrid, 1929-30; prof. U. La Laguna, Canary Islands, 1931-32; dean (Law and Social Scis. Sch.), La Laguna, 1931-32; prof. U. Salamanca, Spain, 1932-36, U. Oviedo, 1936-37, U. Valencia, 1937, U. Barcelona, 1938; mem. faculty Hunter Coll., N.Y.C., 1940—, prof. Spainsh, 1959—, chmn. dept. Romance langs., 1964-67; exec. officer doctoral program in Spanish City U. N.Y., 1967-74, emeritus prof., 1974—; vis. lectr. Middlebury (Vt.) Coll., 1947-63, dir., 1963-70; lectr. history Spain Columbia Grad. Sch., 1956-63; vis. prof. N.Y. U. Grad. Sch., 1958-59, 61, Bklyn. Coll. Grad. Sch., 1960. Author: The Spirit of the University, 1930, The Principles of Justice, 1930, The Theory of Crime, 1931, Emilia Pardo Bazan, novelista de Galicia, 1944, Galicia, su alma y su cultura, 1954, Spanish Review Grammar, 2d edit, 1964, Historia de la civilizacion espanola, 3d edit, 1970, Grandeza y decadencia del reino de Galicia, 1957, La insumision gallega: martires y rebeldes, 1963, The Argentine Penal Code, 1963, Historia de la Literatura Espanola, La Edad Media y el Siglo de Oro, 1962, 2d edit., 1972, Historia de la Literatura española: la Edad Moderna, 1965, El arte dramatico de Valle-Inclan: Del decadentismo al expresionismo, 1967, Los políticos gallegos en la Corte de España y la convivencia europea, Galicia en los reinados de Felipe III y Felipe IV, 1969, Bajo la doble águila: Galicia en al reinado de Carlos V, 1970, Spanish Cultural Reader, 1970, El arte narrative de Pio Baroja: las trilogias, 1971, Siempre de negro: La Contrareforma en Galicia, Galicia en el reinado de Felipe II, 1970, El águila cáida: Galicia en los reinados de Felipe IV y Carlos II, 1973, La Poesía de Valle-Inclán: del simbolismo al expresionismo, 1973, El águila gala y el bubo gallego: la insurrección gallega contra los franceses-Galicia en la Guerra de la Independencia, 1974, El teatro infantil de Benavente, 1975, John Adams and John Quincy Adams in Spain, 1976, Bajo las luces de la Ilustracion: Galicia en los reinados de Carlos III y Carlos IV, 1977, Grandeza e decadencia do Reino de Galicia, 1978, El alba flor de lis: Galicia en los reinados de Felipe V. Luis I y Fernando VI, 1978, El aguila desplumada: de Sampayo a San Marcial, 1977, Canonistas del Noroeste de Espana: su influencia en el desarrollo del Derecho Canonico y en la formación de las Universidades españolas, 1978, Historia de Galicia, 1980, Entre el antiguo y el nuevo regimen: el reinado de Fernando VII en Galicia, 1981, others, also numerous articles, revs. Recipient Extraordinary prize for licenoisture U. Madrid, 1926, Extraordinary prize for doctorate, 1928. Mem. Royal Galician Acad. (corr.), La Coruna (corr.), Eucilides da Cunha Soc. (hon.) (Para, Brazil). Home: 425 W 57th St New York NY 10019

GONZALEZ, EUGENE ROBERT, investment banker; s. Eugenio Tomas and Alice Marie (Macdonald) Gonzalez-M. B.A. in Internat. Relations, Yale U., 1952; postgrad. in advanced mgmt, L'Institut pour l'Etude des Methodes de Direction de l'Enterprise, Lausanne, Switzerland, 1967. Civil engr. Dept. Pub. Works Commonwealth Mass., Boston, 1952; econ. officer Dept. Defense, Washington, 1954-57; project fin. officer Devel. Loan Fund (now AID), Washington, 1957-58; fin. mgr. RCA Internat., N.Y.C., 1958-61; fin. instns. specialist Interam. Devel. Bank, Washington, 1961-62, fin. officer, 1962-63, dep. regional rep. for Europe, Paris, 1964; exec. v.p. Adela Investment Co., Luxembourg, 1969-74, mng. dir., 1974-75, pres., chief exec. officer, 1975-76; adviser, regional coordinator for Ibero Am. Morgan Stanley Internat., N.Y.C., 1977—. Author: International Sources of Financing, 1961. Served with U.S. Army, 1952-54. Fellow Internat. Bankers Assn. (disting.); mem. Am. Enterprise Inst. (nat. com. on Am. fgn. policy), Accion Internat. (dir.), Internat. Assn. Fin. Planners, Pan Am. Soc. U.S. (dir.), Am. Soc. Profl. Cons., Presidents Assn., Center for Interam. Relations, Spanish Inst., Club de Banqueros de Mex., Club de Industriales de Mex. (Mexico City). Clubs: Met., City Tavern (Washington); Brook, River, Racquet and Tennis (N.Y.C.); Meadow (Southampton, N.Y.); Union (Santiago, Chile); Pacific Union (San Francisco). Home: 137 E 66th St New York NY 10021 Office: 1251 Ave Americas New York NY 10020

GONZALEZ, HENRY B., congressman; b. San Antonio, May 3, 1916; s. Leonides and Genevieve (Barbosa) G.; m. Bertha Cuellar, 1940; children: Henry B., Rosemary, Charles, Bertha, Stephen, Genevieve, Francis, Anna Marie. Grad., San Antonio Jr. Coll., St. Mary's U. Sch. Law; student, U. Tex. Formerly with father's translating co., pub. relations counselor for ins. co., San Antonio, chief probation officer, Bexar County, 1946; exec. sec. Jr. Deps. of Am. (predecessor Pan Am. Progressive Assn.); mem. San Antonio City Council, 1953-56, mayor pro-tem, 1955-56; state senator, 1956-61; mem. 87-98th Congresses from 20th Dist. Tex.; chmn. subcom. housing and community devel. 87-96th Congresses from 20th Dist. Tex., 1981—; mem. banking, fin. and urban affairs com., small bus. com., zone whip Tex. Democratic house del., majority whip orgn., 1973—. Civilian cable and radio censor Mil. and Naval Intelligence, World War II. Democrat. Office: 2413 Rayburn House Office Bldg Washington DC 20515 *

GONZALEZ, JOSE ALEJANDRO, JR., judge; b. Tampa, Fla., Nov. 26, 1931; s. Jose A. and Luisa Secundina (Collia) G.; m. Frances Frierson, Aug. 22, 1956 (dec. Aug. 1981); children—Margaret Ann, Mary Frances. B.A., U. Fla., 1952, J.D., 1957. Bar: Fla. bar 1958. Practice in, Ft. Lauderdale, 1958-64; claim rep. State Farm Mutual, Lakeland, Fla., 1957-58; asso. firm Watson, Hubert and Sousley (attys.), 1958-61, partner, 1961-64; asst. state atty. 15th Circuit Fla., 1961-64; circuit judge 17th Circuit Ft. Lauderdale, 1964-78, presiding judge, 1970-71; asso. judge 4th Dist. Ct. Appeals, W. Palm Beach; U.S. dist. judge So. Dist. Fla., 1978—. Bd. dirs. Arthritis Found., 1962-72; bd. dirs. Henderson Clinic Broward County, 1964-68, v.p., 1967-68. Served to 1st lt. AUS, 1952-54. Named Broward County Outstanding Young Man, 1967; one of Fla.'s Five Outstanding Young Men Fla. Jaycees, 1967; Broward Legal Exec. of Yr., 1978. Mem. Fla. Bar, Am. Bar Assn., Broward County Bar, Ft. Lauderdale Jaycees (dir. 1960-61), Fla. Blue Key, Sigma Chi, Phi Alpha Delta. Democrat. Club: Kiwanian (pres. 1971-72). Home: 4820 NE 15th Way Oakland Park FL 33334 Office: 205D US Courthouse 299 E Broward Blvd Fort Lauderdale FL 33301

GONZALEZ, MICHAEL IBS, lawyer; b. San Diego, Calif., Oct. 4, 1915; s. Miguel and Ella (Ibs) G.; m. Elizabeth Sibley, May 31, 1941 (dec. Aug. 1974); children: Elizabeth Farr, Victoria Harding, Georgiana Sibley (Mrs. James C. McShane), Michael Ibs, Cynthia Ella (Mrs. M. Boone Hellmann); m. Anne Bushnell Snyder, Sept. 3, 1976. A.B., Stanford U., 1937; LL.B., Harvard U., 1940. Bar: Calif. bar 1940. Since practiced in, San Diego; partner Luce, Forward, Hamilton & Scripps. Pres. Fine Arts Soc. of San Diego, 1957-59; former mem. bd. dirs. Natural History Soc. of San Diego, YMCA, San Diego Opera Assn.; pres. Symphony Assn., 1967-68; chmn. Episcopal Community Services, 1969-71; pres. Combined Arts and Edn. Council San Diego County, 1973-75; Bd. dirs., sec., chancellor, lay dep. Episcopal Diocese San Diego; trustee Ch. Div. Sch. of Pacific; bd. govs., pres. San Diego Community Found. Served to lt. USNR, 1942-45. Mem. ABA. Episcopalian (sr. warden). Home: 2174 Guy St San Diego CA 92103 Office: Suite 1700 110 W A St San Diego CA 92101

GONZALEZ, NANCIE LOUDON, anthropologist; b. Chgo., Dec. 9, 1929; d. Archibald Niven and Dorothy Helen (Ayers) Loudon; children: Ian, Kevin, Tania. B.A., U. N.D., 1951; M.A., U. Mich., 1955, Ph.D., 1959. Instr. Jamestown Coll., 1952-53; prof. anthropology U. San Carlos, Guatemala, summers 1957, 61-63; vis. lectr. U. Calif., 1958-60; research anthropologist INCAP, 1961-63; asst. prof. to asso. prof. U. N.Mex., 1965-69; prof., chairwoman dept. anthropology U. Iowa, 1969-72, Boston U., 1972-75; program dir. for anthropology NSF, Washington, 1975-77; vice chancellor acad. affairs U. Md., 1977-81, prof. dept. anthropology, 1981—; Mem. joint com. on agrl. devel. U.S. Dept. State. Author: A Heritage of Pride: the Spanish Americans of New Mexico, 1969, Black Carib Household Structure: a Study of Migration and Modernization, 1969, The Saga of Santiago: Dependency and Development in the Dominican Republic, 1977; Editor: Social and Technological Management in Dry Lands, 1979. Mem. Soc. for Applied Anthropology (exec. bd. 1970-73, pres. 1974), Am. Ethnol. Soc. (exec. bd. 1970-73), Am. Anthrop. Assn., AAAS (exec. bd. 1980—), Caribbean Studies Assn. (exec. bd. 1981-83), Anthrop. Soc. Washington, Soc. Med. Anthropology, Phi Beta Kappa, Sigma Xi, Phi Kappa Phi. Home: 228 12th St SE Washington DC 20003

GONZALEZ, ORLANDO GERONIMO, mfg. co. exec.; b. Havana, Cuba, July 4, 1927; came to U.S., 1961, naturalized, 1966; s. Ignacio and Manuela (Lamelas) G.; m. Irma Aguirrechu, Oct. 18, 1951; children—Orlando, Jorge, Irma, Patricio, Ada E., Maria A. B.S. in Acctg. and Fin, U. Havana, 1950. Auditor, internal audit Phelps Dodge Corp., N.Y.C., 1961-63; v.p., gen. mgr. PHELDOCA, El Salvador, 1964-68; asst. v.p., gen. mgr. PHELDOBRAS, Brazil, 1969-70; exec. v.p. Phelps Dodge Internat. Corp., N.Y.C., 1970, pres., 1971-78, Coral Gables, Fla., 1978—. Mem. Am. Mgmt. Assn., Cuban Public Accts. Assn. Office: 2122 Ponce de Leon Blvd Coral Gables FL 33134

GONZALEZ, RAYMOND EMMANUEL, foreign service officer; b. Pasadena, Calif., Dec. 24, 1924; s. Raymond Mercado and Maria (Agreda) G.; m. Ernestine Dora Fraide, Jan. 29, 1949; children: Carlos, Paul, Gregory, Richard, Christopher, Philip. B.A., U. So. Calif., 1949; M.A., Fletcher Sch. Law and Diplomacy, Tufts U., 1950; cert., Sorbonne, U. Paris, 1946; grad., Nat. War Coll., 1966. Commd. fgn. service officer Dept. State, 1951; vice consul Am. consulate, Guayaquil, Ecuador, 1951-54; 2d sec. Am. embassy, Rome, 1954-58, attache U.S. mission to, European Communities, Luxembourg and Brussels, 1958-62; served at Dept. State, Washington, 1962-66; adv. to U.S. del. Council of OAS, 1963-65; first sec. Am. embassy, San Jose, Costa Rica, 1966-70; polit. counselor, Lima, Peru, 1970-74, minister, counselor, Panama, 1974-78, AEP to Ecuador, Quito, 1978-82; diplomat-in-residence Monterey Inst. Internat. Studies, 1982-83; sr. insp. Fgn. Service, Washington, 1983—. Served with U.S. Army, 1943-46. Decorated Purple Heart; recipient Meritorious Service award Dept. State, 1970. Mem. Am. Fgn. Service Assn., Phi Beta Kappa, Phi Kappa Phi, Delta Phi Epsilon. Roman Catholic. Club: Rotary (Quito). Home: 8503 Crown Pl Alexandria VA 22308 Office: Dept State Washington DC 20520

GONZALEZ, RICHARD FLORENTZ, management scientist, educator; b. Sioux City, Iowa, June 30, 1927; s. Florentino Vasquez and Soledad (Rodriguez) G.; m. Ellen T. Kepros, Feb. 4, 1956; children: Alexis, Aimee, Hilary, Timothy, Richard, Matthew. Student, Iowa State U., 1945, 47; B.S., U. Iowa, 1950, M.A., 1953, Ph.D., 1957. Instr. Mich. State U., East Lansing, 1956-57, asst. prof., 1957-63, asso. prof., 1963-65, prof. mgmt. sci., 1965—, chmn. dept. mgmt., 1971-78; vis. prof. Escola de Administracaõ de Empressas, Saõ Paulo, Brazil, 1958-60, U. Tex., Austin, 1978-79, 80. Author: (with others) International Enterprise in a Developing Economy, 1964, The American Overseas Executive, 1966, Machine Computation, 1971, Systems Analysis, 3d edit., 1977, The Operations Manager, 1981; editorial bd.: Acad. Mgmt. Rev. Served with AUS, 1945-47. Ford Found. fellow, 1962, 64. Fellow Am. Inst. Decision Scis. (v.p. 1976-78); mem. Inst. Mgmt. Scis., Ops. Mgmt. Assn. (v.p. 1982—), Acad. Mgmt., Purchasing Mgmt. Assn. Central Mich., Am. Inst. Indsl. Engrs., Nat. Assn. Purchasing Mgmt., Am. Prodn. and Inventory Control Soc. (cert. prodn. inventory mgr.), Univ. Club Mich. State U., Delta Sigma Pi, Omicron Delta Gamma, Sigma Iota Epsilon. Home: 1505 Abbott Rd East Lansing MI 48823

GONZALEZ, RICHARD JOSEPH, consulting economist; b. San Antonio, Aug. 17, 1912; s. Rafael and Catarina (Trello) G.; m. Eugenie S. Kamrath, Apr. 10, 1976. A.B., U. Tex., 1931, M.A., 1932, Ph.D., 1934. Instr. econs. U. Tex., Austin, 1932-35, asst. prof., 1936-37, U. N. Mex., Albuquerque, 1935-36; econ. adviser Humbole Oil & Refining Co., Houston, 1937-51, dir., 1951-65; cons. economist, Houston, 1965-83; sr. research fellow Inst. Constructive Capitalism, Austin, Tex., 1983—; vis. prof. Stanford U., Palo Alto, Calif., 1974; former dir. Western Co. N.Am., Ft. Worth, River Oaks Bank & Trust Co., Houston. Mem. Nat. Petroleum Council, Am. Econ. Assn., Am. Petroleum Inst., Phi Beta Kappa. Office: Inst Constructive Capitalism 2815 San Gabriel St Austin TX 78705

GONZALEZ, WILLIAM G., hospital administrator, educator; b. Hackensack, N.J., Mar. 28, 1940; s. William G. and Blanche (Saffery) G.; m. Shirley Ann Mos, Aug. 15, 1964; children: Dana Lynn,Liane Renee. B.A., Rutgers U., 1964; M.B.A., Cornell U., 1966; cert., Sloan Inst. Hosp. Adminstrn., 1966; M.P.A., N.Y. U., 1980. Bus. adminstr. U. Calif.-San Francisco Med. Ctr., 1966-68, asst. dir., various positions, 1968-74; dep. dir. Capital Dist. Psychol. Ctr., Albany, N.Y., 1974-79; dir. U. Calif.-Irvine Med. Ctr., Orange, 1979—; instr. Albany Med. Coll., 1974-79, adj. asst. prof., 1978-79; sr. lectr. U. Calif.-Irvine Grad. Sch. Mgmt., 1980—; bd. dirs. Hosp. Council So. Calif., Orange, 1983—. Active Health Professions Council, San Francisco, 1971-74, Planned Parenthood-World Population, Alameda,Calif. and San Francisco, 1972-74. Served with M.C. U.S. Army, 1961-64; ETO. William Stout scholar, 1964; Alfred P. Sloan scholar, 1964-65; N.Y. State Regents scholar, 1964-65; Rotary exchange fellow in hosp. adminstrn., Australia, summer 1982. Mem. Am. Coll. Hosp. Adminstrs., Health Care Execs. No. Calif. (pres. 1973-74).

GONZÁLEZ ALVAREZ, JUVENCIO, bishop; b. Matehuala, Mex., Feb. 28, 1917. Ordained priest Roman Cath. Ch., 1942; elevated to bishop, 1980, now bishop of, Ciudad Valles, Mex. Address: Apartado 170 Cuidad Valles San Luis Potosi Mexico *

GONZALEZ-BUNSTER, ROLANDO, corporate executive; b. Buenos Aires, Argentina, Oct. 24, 1947; came to U.S., 1975; s. Luis and Cora Gonzalez-B.; m. Monica Martinez-Thedy, Jan. 12, 1974; children: Luis Andres, Adriana, Carolina. B.S. in Econs, Georgetown U., 1968. Pres. Sistol S.A. (trading co.), Buenos Aires, 1973-75; with Gulf & Western Industries Inc., 1975—, v.p., N.Y.C., 1979—; mem. Caribbean-Central Am. Task Force. Roman Catholic. Clubs: N.Y. Athletic, Fairfield County Hunt, Westchester Country. Office: 1 Gulf & Western Plaza New York NY 10023

GOOCH, FORREST WENDELL, banker; b. Wright City, Mo., Dec. 3, 1932; s. Lyndell F. and Lois I. (Morris) G.; m. Helen, June 6, 1955; children—Lyndell, Debbie, Kriston, Wendell. B.S. in Gen. Bus, U. Mo., Columbia, 1955. With Harris Trust and Savs. Bank, Chgo., 1955—, sr. v.p., group exec., 1976-78, sr. v.p., dept. exec., 1978, exec. v.p., trust dept. exec., 1978—. Mem. investment com. Methodist Found.; chmn. trustees United Meth. Homes and Services, Chgo.; mem. com. Young Life, Hinsdale, Ill.; bd. dirs. Christian Counseling Found. Mem. Ill. Corp. Fiduciaries Assn. (v.p.) *

GOOCH, JAMES THOMAS, lawyer; b. Vanndale, Ark., Dec. 10, 1913; s. Samuel Amos and Augustus (Halk) G.; children—Edris Johanna Gooch Quinn, Marilyn Kay Gooch Peterson. Student, Ark. State U., 1937, Ark. Law Sch., 1940. Bar: Ark. bar 1940. Practiced in, Wynne, 1940-46, Arkadelphia, 1954—; mem. firm Gooch & Gooch, 1940-46; U.S. atty. Eastern Dist. Ark., 1946-54; partner firm Lookadoo, Gooch & Lookadoo, 1954-75, Lookadoo, Gooch & Ashby, 1975—; Vice pres., dir. Elk Horn Bank & Trust Co.; Pres., U.S. Atty.'s Conf., 1948-50; Pres. Ark. Trial Lawyers Assn., 1971-73. Mem. War Meml. Stadium, Little Rock, 1946-67, Ark. Senate, 1940-44; chmn. Clark County Democratic Com., 1960-72. Served to lt. USNR, 1942-45. Mem. Am. Judicature Soc., Am., Ark., S.W. Ark., Clark County bar assns., Am. Trial Lawyers Assn., Ark. Trial Lawyers Assn. (pres. 1971-73). Home: Route 5 Box 294 Lake Hamilton AR 71901 Office: Lookadoo Bldg PO Box 357 Arkadelphia AR 71923

GOOD, CHARLES E., distributing company executive; b. Red Oak, Iowa, Feb. 19, 1921; s. Lou and Mable (Brown) G.; m. Joyce Rodda, Jan. 1, 1950; children: Deborah, Susan. Student, Van Sant Sch. Bus., Omaha, Red Oak Jr. Coll., Iowa, Sawyers Sch. Bus., Los Angeles. With Buena Vista Distbg. Co., 1957—, asst. domestic sales mgr., v.p., gen. sales mgr., 1972-80, pres., gen. sales mgr., 1980—; v.p. Walt Disney Telecommunications and Theatrical Co. Bd. dirs. Will Rogers Meml. Fund. Served with U.S. Army, World War II. Mem. Acad. Motion Picture Arts Scis., Internat. Variety Club, Found. Motion Picture Pioneers (dir.). Presbyterian. Club: Chevy Chase Country. Office: Buena Vista Distribution Co Inc 350 Buena Vista Burbank CA 91521

GOOD, CLARENCE ALLEN, physician, radiologist; b. St. Joseph, Mo., Sept. 20, 1907; s. Clarence Allen and Sophie Love (Evans) G.; m. Virginia McClure, Sept. 6, 1930; children—Clarence Allen III, John McClure, Andrew Evans, Stephen Conrad. A.B., Williams Coll., 1929; M.D., Washington U., 1933; M.S. in Radiology, U. Minn., 1938. Diplomate: Am. Bd. Radiology (asst. sec., asst. treas.). Asst. radiology Mallinkrodt Inst. Radiology, Washington U., 1933; intern medicine Barnes Hosp., St. Louis, 1934-35; fellow radiology Grad. Sch. Mayo Found., U. Minn., 1935-38; successively instr., asst. prof., asso. prof., prof. radiology, head sect. diagnostic roentgenology Mayo Clinic, sr. cons. diagnostic roentgenology, 1967-73, emeritus, 1973—. Fellow Am. Coll. Radiology (emeritus); mem. AMA, Am. Roentgen Ray Soc., Radiol. Soc. N.Am., Minn. Radiol. Soc., Phi Beta Kappa, Sigma Xi, Alpha Omega Alpha, Theta Delta Chi, Nu Sigma Nu. Home: 1211 7th St SW Rochester MN 55902

GOOD, CYNTHIA ANNETTE, publishing company executive; b. Toronto, Ont., Canada, Apr. 11, 1951; d. Philip and Charlotte (Dawson) G.; m. Alan James Pratt, June 27, 1975. B.A., U. Toronto, 1973, M.A., 1974. Editor Dorset Pub. Inc., Toronto, 1978-80; mktg. mgr. Doubleday Can. Ltd., Toronto, 1980-82; editorial dir. Penguin Books Can. Ltd., Toronto, 1982—; owner, mgr. Menagerie Players Acting Co., Toronto, 1973-77; teaching fellow U. Toronto, 1974-77. Woodhouse scholar, 1972; recipient Reuben Wells Leonard University Coll., U. Toronto, Toronto, 1973; Can. Council grantee, 1975-77. Office: Penguin Books Can Ltd 2801 John St Markham ON Canada L3R 1B4

GOOD, DANIEL JAMES, investment banker; b. Chgo., Apr. 4, 1940; s. Lillian (Senft) G.; m. Marlene Emma Good, Oct. 14, 1961; children: Julie, Laura. B.A., DePaul U., 1961; postgrad., U. Chgo., 1963. Assoc. Warburg Paribas Becker, Chgo., 1964-71, mgr. corp. fin., 1971-78, v.p., 1968, mng. dir., 1976-78, gen. mgr. investment banking, 1978-80, sr. vice chmn., 1980-82, co-chmn. mgmt. com., 1982-83; pres., chief operating officer A.G. Becker Paribas Inc., Chgo., 1983—. Bd. dirs. Lincoln Park Zool. Soc., Chgo. Republican. Episcopalian. Clubs: Chicago, Mid-Am., Winter. Office: A G Becker Paribas Inc 2 First Nat Plaza Chicago IL 60603

GOOD, GERALD LEROY, retail executive; b. Reading, Pa., Jan. 31, 1943; s. William Dennis and Grace Lillian G. A.B., U. N.C., 1964; M.B.A. (Baker fellow 1971), Harvard U., 1971. Asso. McKinsey & Co. Inc. (mgmt. cons.), N.Y.C., 1971-76; dir. AO Labs., Am. Optical Corp., Southbridge, Mass., 1976-78; sr. v.p. mktg. and planning Gt. Atlantic & Pacific Tea Co., Inc., Montvale, N.J., from 1978, now pres. Super Fresh Food Markets subs., Florence, N.J. Bd. dirs. Univ. Settlement House, N.Y.C., 1980—. Served with USN, 1964-69. Decorated Navy Commendation medal with combat V. Clubs: Harvard Bus. Sch. N.Y. (bd. dirs. 1980-83, pres. 1981. Office: PO Box 68 Florence NJ 08518

GOOD, LAURANCE FREDERIC, insurance underwriter; b. Wheeling, W.Va., Sept. 26, 1932; s. Sidney Samuel and Jeannette (Berg) G.; m. Barbara S. Mayer, Oct. 18, 1959; children—Jay, Paul, Jenny, Heidi, Philip (dec.). B.A., Brown U., 1954; postgrad., U. Va., 1955. Vice pres. Goodbro Enterprises Inc., Wheeling, 1956-80; v.p., gen. mdse. mgr. L.S. Good & Co., Wheeling, 1961-69, exec. v.p., 1969-80, vice chmn., sec. bd., 1961-80; vice chmn. bd. William F. Gable Co., Altoona, Pa., 1968-80, The Hub of Steubenville Inc., Ohio, 1969-80, J. W. Knapp Co., Lansing, Mich., 1970-80, Smith-Bridgman & Co., Flint, Mich., 1970-80, L. W. Robinson Co., Battle Creek, Mich., 1970-80, D.M. Christian Co., Owosso, Mich., 1970-80; pres. Good's Dept. Stores, Inc., 1980, Personal History Systems, Inc.; life underwriter Equitable Life Assurance Soc. Am., 1983—; dir. Wheeling Dollar Savs. and Trust Co., 1968-80. Producer: Wheeling Rediscovered; Author: My Lifetime Book. Mem. Wheeling Symphony Soc., 1964-67, 68-73; mem. exec. com. Ohio Valley Indsl. & Bus. Devel. Corp., Wheeling, 1971; area chmn. Brown U. Alumni Program, 1954-80; Christmas seals chmn. Tb Assn. Ohio Valley, 1973; co-chmn. United Jewish Appeal, 1971-73; co-founder Good Zoo; also pres. Good Zoo Friends, 1974-78; chmn. establishment com. Wheeling Devel. Conf.; bd. found. W. Liberty State Coll., 1971; bd. dirs. Wheeling Hosp., 1972-77, R. and J. Kennedy Inst. Bioethics, Georgetown U., 1977-79; bd. visitors Bethany Coll., 1972-77; trustee Oglebay Inst., 1972-80. Served with USN, 1955-57. Recipient Distinguished West Virginian award, 1976. Mem. Nat. Retail Merchants Assn. (dir. merchandising div. 1966-71, del. conf. 1969), Am. Technion Soc. (trustee Pa. chpt.). Home: 112 Warden's Run Rd Wheeling WV 26003 Office: 1134 Market St Wheeling WV 26003

GOOD, LEONARD PHELPS, artist; b. Chickasha, Okla., June 25, 1907; s. Jacob Calvin and Belle (Leonard) G.; m. Nancye Dooley, July 15, 1932 (dec. May 1969); 1 son, Leonard Jacob; m. Yoshie Tobe, Nov. 26, 1970. B.F.A., U. Okla., 1927; student, Art Students' League, N.Y.C., 1930, Clarence White Sch. Photography, N.Y.C., 1937, State U. Iowa, 1940. Tchr. pub. sch. art depts., Tex. and Okla., 1927-30; mem. faculty U. Okla. Sch. Art, 1930-50, U. Wis., 1950-52; prof., head dept. art Drake U., 1952-77, emeritus prof., 1977—; curator paintings Mus. Art, U. Okla., 1935-50; vis. artist-in residence Iowa State U., Ames, 1966, Shenandoah (Iowa) Community High Sch. for Nat. Endowment for Arts, 1970-71, Central Coll., Pella, Iowa, 1984. Exhibited: paintings nat. exhbns. Am. Art, 1936, 37, Am. Painters in Paris, France, 1975-76, traveling exhbns., Am. Fedn. Art, 1940-41; rep. permanent collections, Okla. Art Center, Okla. Art Mus., Okla. Hist. Mus., Philbook Art Center, Tulsa, Kans. Fedn. Arts, Brunnier Mus., Iowa State U., Ames, Iowa, Milw. Art Center, Des Moines Art Center, Mabee-Gerrer Mus. Art, Shawnee, Okla., Iowa Hist. Mus., Springville (Utah) Mus. Art; juror nat. exhbns. Mem. Omicron Delta Kappa (hon.), Delta Phi Delta (nat. pres. 1958-60). Home: 1320 Oregon Ave Chickasha OK 73018

GOOD, MARY LOWE (MRS. BILLY JEWEL GOOD), business executive, chemist; b. Grapevine, Tex., June 20, 1931; d. John W. and Winnie (Mercer) Lowe; m. Billy Jewel Good, May 17, 1952; children: Billy, James. B.S., Ark. State Tchrs. Coll., 1950; M.S., U. Ark., 1953, Ph.D., 1955, LL.D. (hon.), 1979, D.Sc., U. Ill., Chgo., 1983. Instr. Ark. State Tchrs. Coll., Conway, summer 1949; instr. La. State U., Baton Rouge, 1954-56, asst. prof., 1956-58, asso. prof., New Orleans, 1958-63, prof., 1963-80, Boyd prof. materials sci., div. engrng. research, Baton Rouge, 1979-80; v.p., dir. research UOP, Inc., Des Plaines, Ill., 1980—; chmn. Pres.'s Com. for Nat. Medal Sci., 1979-82; mem. Nat. Sci. Bd., 1980-86. Contbr. articles to profl. jours. Bd. dirs. Oak Ridge Asso. Univs. Recipient Agnes Faye Morgan research award, 1969; Distinguished Alumni citation U. Ark., 1973; Scientist of Yr. award Indsl. R & D Mag., 1982; AEC tng. grantee, 1967; NSF internat. travel grantee, 1968; NSF research grantee, 1969-80. Fellow Am. Inst. Chemistry (Gold medal 1983), Chem. Soc. London; mem. Am. Chem. Soc. (1st woman dir. 1971-74, regional dir. 1972-80, chmn. bd. 1978, 80, Garvan medal 1973, Herty medal 1975, award Fla. sect. 1979), Phi Beta Kappa, Sigma Xi, Iota Sigma Pi (regional dir. 1967—), hon. mem. 1983). Clubs: Zonta (past pres. New Orleans club, chmn. dist. status of women com. and nominating com., chmn. internat. Amelia Earhart scholarship com. Home: 295 Park Dr Palatine IL 60067 Office: Corp Research Center UOP Inc Ten UOP Plaza Des Plaines IL 60016

GOOD, RAYMOND F., clothing manufacuturing corporation executive; b. Torrington, Conn., 1928. B.B.A., U. Conn.; M.B.A., Harvard U. With Standard Oil Co., Ohio, 1953-60, McKinsey & Co., Inc., 1960-66; pres. Heinz U.S., H.J. Heinz Co., 1967-76; exec. v.p. Pillsbury Co., 1976-79; pres. Munsingwear Inc., Mpls., 1979—, chief exec. officer, 1980—, also dir. Office: Munsingwear Inc 718 Glenwood Ave Minneapolis MN 55405

GOOD, ROBERT ALAN, physician, educator; b. Crosby, Minn., May 21, 1922; s. Roy Homer and Ethel Gay (Whitcomb) G.; children: Robert Michael, Mark Thomas, Alan Maclyn, Margaret Eugenia, Mary Elizabeth. B.A., U. Minn., 1944, M.B., 1946, Ph.D., 1947, M.D., 1947; M.D. (hon.), U. Uppsala, Sweden, 1966, D.Sc., N.Y. Med. Coll., 1973, Med. Coll. Ohio, 1973, Coll. Medicine and Dentistry N.J., 1974, Hahnemann Med. Coll., 1974, U. Chgo., 1974, St. John's U., 1977, U. Health Scis., Chgo. Med. Sch., 1978. Teaching asst. dept. anatomy U. Minn., Mpls., 1944-45, instr. pediatrics, 1950-51, asst. prof., 1951-53, asso. prof., 1953-54, Am. Legion Meml. research prof. pediatrics, 1954-73, prof. microbiology, 1962-72, Regents prof. pediatrics and microbiology, 1969-73, prof., head dept. pathology, 1970-72; intern U. Minn. Hosps., 1947, asst. resident pediatrics, 1948-49; pres., dir. Sloan-Kettering Inst. for Cancer Research, 1973-80, mem., 1973-81; prof. pathology Sloan-Kettering div. Grad. Sch. Med. Scis. Cornell U., 1973-81, dir., 1973-80; adj. prof., vis. physician Rockefeller U., 1973-81; prof. medicine and pediatrics Cornell U. Med. Coll., 1973-81; dir. research Meml. Sloan-Kettering Cancer Ctr., v.p., 1980-81; dir. research Meml. Hosp. for Cancer and Allied Diseases, 1973-80, also attending physician depts. medicine and pediatrics; attending pediatrician N.Y. Hosp., 1973-81; mem., head cancer research program Okla. Med. Research Found., 1982—; prof. pediatrics, research prof. medicine, OMRF prof. microbiology and immunology U. Okla. Health Scis. Ctr., 1982—; attending physician, head div. immunology Okla. Children's Meml. Hosp., 1982—; attending physician in internal medicine Okla. Meml. Hosp., 1983—; vis. investigator Rockefeller Inst. for Med. Research, N.Y.C., 1949-50, asst. physician to Hosp., 1949-50; attending pediatrician Hennepin County Gen. Hosp., 1950-73, cons., 1960-73; Mem. Unitarian Service Commn. Med. Exchange Team to, France, Germany, Switzerland and Czechoslovakia, 1958; cons. VA Hosp., Mpls., 1959-60; cons., sci. adviser Nat. Jewish Hosp., Denver and Childrens Asthma Research Inst. and Hosp., Denver, 1964-69; mem. study sects. USPHS, 1952-69; mem. expert adv. panel on immunology WHO, 1967—; cons. Merck & Co., N.J., 1968—, Nat. Cancer Inst., 1973-74; mem. ad hoc com. President's Sci. Adv. Council on Biol. and Med. Sci., 1970, Pres.'s Cancer Panel, 1972; mem. Lyndon B. Johnson Found. awards com., 1972; mem. adv. com. Bone Marrow Transplant Registry, 1973—; fgn. adv. Acad. Med. Scis., People's Republic of China, 1980—. Author, editor numerous books.; Contbr. articles to profl. jours. Mem. adv. council Childrens Hosp. Research Found., Cin., 1954-58; bd. dirs. Allergy Found. Am., 1973; bd. sci. advisers Jane Coffin Childs Meml. Fund Med. Research, 1972-74, Merck Inst. Therapeutic Research, 1972-76; chmn. Internat. Bone Marrow Registry, 1977-79. Recipient Borden Undergrad. Research award U. Minn. Med. Sch., 1946; E. Mead Johnson First award, 1955; Theobald Smith award, 1955; Parke-Davis 6th Ann. award, 1962; Rectors medal U. Helsinki, 1963-64; Pemberton Lectureship award, 1966; Gordon Wilson Gold medal, 1967; R.E. Dyer Lectureship award, 1967; Clemens Von Pirquet Gold medal 9th Ann. Forum on Allergy, 1968; Presidents medal U. Padua, Italy, 1968; Robert A. Cooke Gold medal Am. Acad. Allergy, 1968; John Stewart Meml. award Dalhousie U., 1969; Borden award Assn. Am. Med. Colls., 1970; Howard Taylor Ricketts award U. Chgo., 1970; Gairdner Found. award, 1970; City of Hope award, 1970; Am. Acad. Achievement golden plate award, 1970; Albert Lasker award for clin. and med. research, 1970; A.C.P. award, 1972; Am. Coll. Chest Physicians award, 1974; Lila Gruber award Am. Acad. Dermatology, 1974; award in cancer immunology Cancer Research Inst. N.Y., 1975; Outstanding Achievement award U. Minn., 1978; award Am. Dermatological Soc. Allergy and Immunology, 1978; 1st Sarasota Med. award, 1979; sect. on mil. pediatrics award Am. Acad. Pediatrics, 1980; recipient Univ. medal Hacettepe U., Ankara, Turkey, 1982; numerous others.; Fellow Nat. Found. for Infantile Paralysis, 1947; Helen Hay Whitney Found. fellow, 1948-50; Markle Found. scholar, 1950-55. Fellow Acad. Multidisciplinary Research, AAAS, N.Y. Acad. Sci., Am. Acad. Arts and Scis.; mem. Am. Assn. History of Medicine, Am. Fedn. Clin. Research, Am. Assn. Anatomists, Am. Assn. Immunologists (past pres.), AAUP, Am., Mpls., Northwestern pediatric socs., Am. Rheumatism Assn., Am. Soc. Clin. Investigation (past pres.), Am. Soc. Exptl. Pathology (past pres.), Am. Soc. Microbiology, Assn. Am. Physicians, Central Soc. Clin. Research (past pres.), Harvey Soc., Infectious Disease Soc. Am. (Squibb award 1968), Internat. Soc. Nephrology, Internat. Acad. Pathology, Internat. Soc. for Transplantation Biology, Minn. State Med. Assn., Nat. Acad. Sci., Nat. Acad. Sci. Inst. Medicine (charter), Reticuloendothelial Soc. (past pres.), Soc. for Exptl. Biology and Medicine, Soc. for Pediatric Research, Am. Clin. and Climatol. Assn. (Gordon Wilson Gold medal 1967), Detroit Surg. Assn. (McGraw medal 1969), Internat. Soc. Blood, Transfusion, Practitioners' Soc., Am. Assn. Pathologists, Internat. Soc. Exptl. Hematology, Transplant Soc., Western Assn. Immunologists, Internat. Soc. Immunopharmacology (founding mem.), Phi Beta Kappa, Sigma Xi, Alpha Omega Alpha. Office: Oklahoma Medical Research Foundation 825 NE 13th St Oklahoma City OK 73104

GOOD, ROBERT CROCKER, college president; b. Mt. Vernon, N.Y., Apr. 7, 1924; s. Alfred and Josephine (Crocker) G.; m. Nancy Louise Cunningham, Aug. 21, 1946; children: Stephen L., Karen L., Kathleen J. B.A., Haverford (Pa.) Coll., 1945; B.D., Yale U., 1951, Ph.D. in Internat. Relations, 1956. Instr., then asst. prof. internat. relations Social Sci. Found., U. Denver, 1953-58; research asso. Washington Center Fgn. Policy Research, 1958-61; dir. Carnegie Endowment Seminars Diplomacy, Washington, 1960-61, President-Elect Kennedy's Task Force Africa, 1960, Office Research and Analysis Africa, Bur. Intelligence and Research, Dept. State, 1961; U.S. ambassador to, Zambia, 1965-69; dean Grad. Sch. Internat. Studies, U. Denver, 1970-76; pres. Denison U., Granville, Ohio, 1976—; cons. and/or mem. bd. Center Global Perspectives, 1974—, Global Perspectives in Edn., 1975—, Council Religion in Internat. Affairs, 1975-81, Patterson Sch. Internat. Diplomacy and Commerce, U. Ky., 1975-77; external bd. govs. Nat. U. Lesotho, Roma, 1977—. Author: Congo Crisis: The Role of the New States, 1961, U.D.I.: The International Politics of the Rhodesian Rebellion, 1973; co-author: Alliance Policy in the Cold War, 1959, Neutralism and Non-alignment: The New States in World Affairs, 1962, Foreign Policy in the Sixties: Issues and Instrumentalities, 1965, South Africa: Time Running Out, 1981; Co-editor: Reinhold Niebuhr on Politics, 1960. Pres. Neighbors, Inc., Washington, 1961-65; mem. Study Commn. on U.S. Policy toward So. Africa, 1979—. Kent fellow, 1951; recipient Superior Honor award Dept. State, 1964. Mem. Am. Polit. Sci. Assn.,

Ohio Coll. Assn. (pres. 1983-84), Internat., African studies assns., Soc. Values in Higher Edn., Phi Beta Kappa. Democrat. Unitarian. Office: Denison Univ PO Box B Granville OH 43023

GOOD, ROLAND HAMILTON, JR., educator, theoretical physicist; b. Toronto, Ont., Can., Oct. 22, 1923; came to U.S., 1948, naturalized, 1950; s. Roland Hamilton and Marie (Smith) G.; m. Ferol Hendrickson, May 7, 1944; children—Roland Hamilton III, Patricia Gail, Sue Marie. B.M.E., Lawrence Inst. Tech., 1944; M.A.E., Chrysler Inst. Engring., 1946; M.S., U. Mich., 1948, Ph.D., 1951. Engr. Chrysler Corp., Windsor, Ont. and Highland Park, Mich., 1942-47; instr. U. Calif., Berkeley, 1951-53; asst. prof., asso. prof. Pa. State U., 1953-56, prof., 1972—, head physics dept., 1972-81; asso. prof., prof. physics Iowa State U., Ames, 1956-72, distinguished prof. scis. and humanities, 1970—; physicist, sr. physicist Ames Lab. of U.S. AEC, 1956-72; vis. lectr. U. Colo., summer 1958; NSF sr. postdoctoral fellow Inst. Advanced Study, Princeton, 1960-61; vis. prof. Inst. Math. Sci., Madras, India, 1968, Seoul Nat. U., 1979; guest Stanford Linear Accelerator Center, 1968-69. Author: (with T.J. Nelson) Classical Theory of Electric and Magnetic Fields, 1971. Fellow Am. Phys. Soc. Research, publs. theoretical physics, especially relativistic wave equations, polarization of elementary particles, metallic binding, electron emission from metals and spectroscopy of rare earths. Home: 24 S Barkway Ln State College PA 16803

GOOD, WALTER RAYMOND, business executive; b. Oak Park, Ill., Sept. 9, 1924; s. Walter William and Elsie Sophia (Lussow) G.; m. Jean S. Stockman, Feb. 5, 1949; children: Elizabeth, Deborah, William. Ph.B., U. Chgo., 1947, M.B.A., 1949. Buyer fats and oil Procter and Gamble, Cin., 1949-52; dir. research Brown Bros. Harriman, N.Y.C., 1952-70; exec. v.p., dir. Lionel D. Edie, N.Y.C., 1970-80; v.p. Continental Group Inc., Stamford, Conn., 1980—; mem. investment adv. panel Pension Benefit Guaranty Corp., Washington, 1980—. Assoc. editor: Fin. Analysts Jour., 1972—. Served with USAAF, 1943-46. Recipient Graham and Dodd award Fin. Analysts Fedn., 1979. Mem. Inst. Cert. Fin. Analysts (council examiners 1980—), N.Y. Soc. Security Analysts, Pension Execs. Conf. (chmn. 1983). Republican. Presbyterian. Club: Landmark (Stamford). Office: Continental Group Inc 1 Harbor Plaza Stamford CT 06904

GOODALE, FAIRFIELD, physician, college dean; b. Framingham, Mass., May 4, 1923; s. Fairfield and Anna (Perkins) G.; m. Mary Margaret Lyman, Aug. 19, 1945; children: Fairfield, Anna P. Goodale Witt, John B., Susan C., Timothy P. Student, Harvard U., 1941-42; M.D., Western Res. U., 1950. Diplomate: Am. Bd. Pathology, Nat. Bd. Med. Examiners (mem. pathology test com. 1975-78, chmn. 1978-81. Intern Mt. Auburn Hosp., Cambridge, Mass., 1950-51; resident in pathology Mass. Gen. Hosp., Boston, 1951-54, chief resident in pathology, 1954-55, USPHS research fellow, asst. in pathology, 1957-58; teaching fellow Harvard Med. Sch., Cambridge, 1954-55, asst. in pathology, 1957-58; USPHS research fellow St. Mary's Hosp., London, 1955-56; research fellow U.S. Pub. Health Dept., Oxford, Eng., 1956-57; asst. prof. pathology Darmouth U. Med. Sch.; also asso. dir. labs. Mary Hitchcock Meml. Hosp. and Clinic, Hanover, N.H., 1958-60; asso. prof. pathology Albany (N.Y.) Med. Coll., 1960-63; prof., chmn. dept. pathology Med. Coll. Va., Richmond, 1963-76, asst. dean curriculum, 1972-76; dean Sch. Medicine Med. Coll. Ga., Augusta, 1976—. Contbg. author: Etiology of Myocardial Infarction, 1963; contbr. articles in field to med. jours. Served with USAAF, 1942-45. Fellow Coll. Am. Pathologists; mem. Internat. Acad. Pathologists (exec. council), AMA, Am. Soc. Clin. Pathologists (councillor), Am. Assn. Pathologists, Am. Soc. Exptl. Pathology, Assn. Pathology Chairmen (advisory bd.), New Eng., Va., Ga. socs. pathologists, Soc. Exptl. Biology and Medicine, Inter-soc. Pathology Council (past pres.), Assn. Am. Med. Colls. (chmn. So. Council Deans 1981-82, exec. council 1982-85, adminstrv. bd. council of deans 1982-85), Alpha Omega Alpha. Researcher causes of fever, atherosclerosis; isolated protein released from white blood cells which produces fever. Home: 914 Milledge Rd Augusta GA 30904 Office: Med College Ga Augusta GA 30912

GOODALE, JAMES CAMPBELL, lawyer; b. Cambridge, Mass., July 27, 1933; s. Robert Leonard and Eunice (Campbell) G.; m. Toni Krissel, May 3, 1964; children: Timothy Fuller, Ashley Krissel. Grad., Pomfret Sch., 1951; B.A., Yale U., 1955; J.D., U. Chgo., 1958. Bar: N.Y. 1960. Assoc. Lord, Day & Lord, N.Y.C., 1959-63; gen. atty. N.Y. Times Co., 1963-67, gen. counsel, 1967-72, v.p., 1969-72, sr. v.p., 1972-73, exec. v.p., 1973-79, vice-chmn., 1979-80; mem. Debevoise & Plimpton, 1980—; dir. Gaspesia Pulp & Paper Co. Ltd., N.Y. Times Broadcasting Inc., Malbaie Paper Co. Ltd., Family Circle Inc.; with Community Law Office, East Harlem, 1968-70; vis. lectr. Yale U. Law Sch., 1977-80; adj. prof. NYU Sch. Law, 1983—; mem. N.Y. State Privacy and Security Com., 1976-79. Compilor, editor: The New York Times Company vs. U.S, 1971; co-founder, bd. editors: Media Law Reporter; bd. editors Nat. Law Jour., 1983—; columnist nat. and N.Y. law jours.; Contbr. articles on communications law to profl. jours. Past bd. dirs. N.Y. Times Neediest Cases Fund; Bd. dirs. N.Y. Times Found.; trustee Pomfret Sch., Gunnery Sch., St. Bernard's Sch., Boys' Club N.Y., Salzburg Seminar, Fed. Bar Council; mem. vis. com. U. Chgo. Law Sch., 1977-80; chmn. bd. Cable TV Law and Fin., 1983—. Served with AUS, 1959. Named one of 200 Rising Leaders in U.S. Time mag., 1974; William Brinckerhoff Jackson scholar, 1954-55; Nat. Honor scholar U. Chgo. Law Sch. Mem. N.Y.C. Bar Assn. (chmn. communications law com. 1978-83, mem. corp. law com. 1977-81), N.Y. State Bar Assn. (chmn. spl. com. on access), ABA (governing bd. communications law forum), Ctr. on Info. on Am. Media and Soc. Seminar. Clubs: Yale (gov. 1964-67), Century Assn., Economic, St. Elmo, Elihu (gov. 1966-70), Washington Conn. (gov. 1972-78). Home: 1050 Park Ave New York NY 10028 Office: 875 Third Ave New York NY 10171

GOODALL, JACKSON WALLACE, JR., restaurant company executive; b. San Diego, Oct. 29, 1938; s. Jackson Wallace and Evelyn Violet (Koski) G.; m. Mary Esther Buckley, June 22, 1958; children—Kathleen, Jeffery, Suzanne, Minette. B.S., San Diego State U., 1960. With Foodmaker, Inc., San Diego, 1965—, pres., 1970—, chief exec. officer, 1979—; v.p. Ralston Purina Co.; founder, dir. Grossmont Bank, La Mesa, Calif. Bd. dirs. San Diego Met. YMCA; assoc. dir. Faith Chapel, Patriot Found., Laymen's Bible Week; chmn. advancement council Point Loma Coll. Recipient Disting. Alumni of Year award San Diego State U., 1974, Golden Chain award, 1982. Mem. Am. Restaurant Assn., San Diego State U. Alumni Assn. (bd. dirs.). Republican. Club: Fairbanks Ranch Country (founder). Office: 9330 Balboa San Diego CA 92112

GOODALL, LEON STEELE, insurance company executive; b. Lebanon, Tenn., Aug. 24, 1925; s. William Thomas and Effie (Steele) G.; m. Billie Rice, Sept. 9, 1949; children: David Christian, Katherine Stuart. Student, U. Tenn., 1943; B.S., U. S.C., 1947, LL.B., 1950. Bar: S.C. 1950. Spl. agt. FBI, 1950-52; sr. auditor S.C. Tax Commn., Columbia, 1952-53; sales devel. mgr. Allstate Ins. Co., Charlotte, N.C., 1953-59; agency v.p. Colonial Life & Accident Ins. Co., Columbia, S.C., 1959-70, pres., 1970-79, dir., 1964-79; pres., chmn. bd. Carolina Continental Ins. Co., 1979—, Continental Am., Inc., 1982—; chmn. bd. LifeCo Systems, Inc., 1981—. Former chmn. bd. trustees Columbia Coll. Served with USN, 1943-47. Mem. S.C. State Bar Assn., Am. Bar Assn., S.C. Found. Ind. Colls., Soc. Former FBI Agts. Methodist. Clubs: Sertoma, Sales Mktg. Execs. Home: 6328 Eastshore Rd Columbia SC 29206 Office: Carolina Continental Ins Co PO Box 427 Columbia SC 29202

GOODALL, LEONARD EDWIN, university chancellor; b. Warrensburg, Mo., Mar. 16, 1937; s. Leonard Burton and Eula (Johnson) G.; m. Lois Marie Stubblefield, Aug. 16, 1959; children: Karla, Karen, Greg. B.A., Central Mo. State U., 1958; M.A., U. Mo., 1960; Ph.D. (Kendrick C. Babcock fellow), U. Ill., 1962; A.A. (hon), Schoolcraft Coll., 1977. Asst. prof. polit. sci., asst. dir. Bur. Govt. Research, Ariz. State U., Tempe, 1962-65, dir. Bur., 1965-67; asso. prof. polit. sci., asso. dean faculties U. Ill. at Chgo. Circle, 1968-69, vice chancellor, 1969-71; chancellor U. Mich., Dearborn, 1971-79; pres. U. Nev., Las Vegas, 1979—; cons. Ariz. Acad., Phoenix, 1964-67; dir. Peace Corps tng. program for Chile, 1965. Author: The American Metropolis: Its Governments and Politics, 1968, rev. edit., 1975, Gearing Arizona's Communities to Orderly Growth, 1965, State Politics and Higher Education, 1976; Editor: Urban Politics in the Southwest, 1967. Mem. univ. exec. com. United Fund, 1966-67; v.p. Met. Fund, Inc.; mem. Mich. Gov.'s Commn. Long Range Planning, 1973-75; Mem. Tempe Planning and Zoning Commn., 1965-67, New Detroit Com., 1972—; mem. Wayne County (Mich.) Planning Commn., 1973—, vice chmn., 1976-79; mem. exec. bd. Clark County chpt. NCCJ, 1979—; bd. dirs. Nev. Devel. Authority, 1980—, Boulder Dam council Boy Scouts Am., 1980—. Served with AUS, 1959. Mem. Am. Polit. Sci. Assn., Am. Soc. Pub. Adminstrn., Western Govtl. Research Assn. (exec. council 1966-68), Dearborn C. of C. (dir. 1974-79), Phi Sigma Epsilon, Phi Kappa Phi. Club: Las Vegas Country. Home: 6565 Banbridge Las Vegas NV 89103 Office: U Nev Las Vegas NV 89154

GOODBODY, JOHN COLLETT, consultant, church official; b. Omaha, May 15, 1915; s. Maurice Fitzgerald and Nellie Jane (Collett) G.; m. Harriet Tuthill Linen, Aug. 5, 1939; children: Margaretta Goodbody Niles, David Lister, Joan Tuthill. A.B., Williams Coll., 1937; postgrad., Harvard U., 1939-41, 46. Corr. UP, 1937; reporter Toledo News-Bee, 1938; asso. editor School Exec. mag., 1938; asst. sec. to pres. Williams Coll., 1939; teaching fellow Harvard U., 1945-46; staff Colonial Williamsburg, 1946-61; spl. asst. to John D. Rockefeller III, 1949-50, v.p., 1957-61, cons., 1961—; pres. Seabury Press, N.Y.C., 1961-72, trustee, 1972—; exec. for communication Episcopal Ch., 1971-80; cons. Trinity Parish, N.Y.C., 1980—; communications officer Episc. Diocese of S.C., 1980—; mem. bd. The Episcopalian; mem. adv. bd. The Forward Movement, 1981—. Served to lt. comdr. USNR, 1941-45. Mem. Gargoyle Assn., Chi Psi. Club: Seabrook Island (S.C.). Home: 3212 Seabrook Island Rd John's Island SC 29455

GOODBY, JAMES EUGENE, foreign service officer; b. Providence, Dec. 20, 1929; s. Frank William and Florence Merle (Bixby) G.; m. Priscilla Dean Staples, June 30, 1956; children: James Laurence, Sarah Walcott. A.B., Harvard U., 1951, postgrad., 1953-54; postgrad., U. Mich., 1951-52. Geologist U.S. Army C.E., Boston, 1951-52; fgn. affairs specialist AEC, Washington, 1954-59; fgn. affairs officer Office Spl. Asst. to Sec. State for Atomic Energy, Washington, 1960-61; officer-in-charge nuclear test ban treaty negotiations U.S. ACDA, 1961-63; mem. policy planning council State Dept., 1963-67; 1st sec. U.S. Mission to European Communities, Brussels, Belgium, 1967-69; officer in charge def. policy affairs Office NATO Affairs, Dept. State, 1969-71; counselor for polit. affairs U.S. Mission to NATO, Brussels, 1971-74; dep. dir. Bur. Politico-Mil. Affairs, State Dept., Washington, 1974-77, dep. asst. sec. state for European affairs, 1977-80; ambassador to Finland, 1980-81; vice chmn., Dept. State rep. to SALT with Soviet Union Dept. State, 1981—. Served to 2d lt. USAF, 1952-53. Recipient Superior Honor award State Dept., 1970. Mem. Council on Fgn. Relations. Office: Dept State Washington DC

GOODCHILD, ANTHONY ALBERT, business exec.; b. London, Eng., May 11, 1928; came to U.S., 1956, naturalized, 1967; s. Albert William and Florence (Greebe) G.; m. Anne Elizabeth Larson, Aug. 13, 1960; children—Christian Elizabeth, Peter Anthony Clay, Matthew Edward. Student, Emanuel Sch., London, 1939-46. Vice pres. operations Elliott Bus. Machines, Inc., Randolph, Mass., 1961-67; group v.p. Transitron Electronic Corp., Wakefield, Mass., 1967-69; pres. Smithcraft Lighting, Inc., Wilmington, Mass., 1969-70; group v.p. IU Internat., Phila., 1970-75; group exec. W.R. Grace, 1975-78; pres., chief exec. officer Armatron Internat. Inc., 1978—; chmn., pres., chief exec. officer Walworth Co., Bala Cynwyd, Pa.; pres. chmn. bd. IU Energy Systems, Inc., Phila.; chmn., dir. Frick Co., Waynesboro, Pa., Southwest Fabricating Co., Houston, Delta So. Co., Baton Rouge, Frick (India) Ltd., Delhi; dir. Hills-McCanna Co., Carpentersville, Ill., Hills McCanna Ltd., London, Eng., Valve Castings Co., Columbus, Ohio, Ledeen Co., Los Angeles, Seatrain Lines, Inc., N.Y.C., Walworth-Aloyco S.P.A., Rome, Italy, Internat. Utilities Indsls. of U.S., Chem. Corp., Cin. Served with Brit. Army, 1946-48. Clubs: Metropolitan, Princeton (N.Y.C.). Home: 214 Westover Rd Stamford CT 06902 Office: 2 Main St Melrose MA 02176

GOODE, CLEMENT TYSON, English educator; b. Richmond, Va., July 10, 1929; s. Clement Tyson and Bessie Mae (Trimble) G.; m. Jane Anderson, Aug. 19, 1952; children: Sara Elizabeth, Robert Clement. A.B., Hendrix Coll., 1951; M.A., Vanderbilt U., 1953, Ph.D., 1959. Instr. English Vanderbilt U., Nashville, 1954-56; instr. English, Baylor U., Waco, Tex., 1957-58; asst. prof., 1958-60, asso. prof., 1960-63, prof., 1963—, Exchange prof. Seinan Gakuin U., Fukuoka, Japan, 1972-73. Author: (with Oscar Santucho) A Comprehensive Bibliography of Secondary Materials in English: George Gordon, Lord Byron with a Review of Research, 1976; contbr. articles to profl. jours. Mem. adv. bd. Salvation Army, Waco, 1968-69; deacon First Bapt. Ch., Waco, 1970—. So. Fellowship Fund grantee, 1956-57; named Outstanding Tchr. Baylor U., 1971. Mem. MLA, South Central MLA, Coll. Conf. Tchrs. English, Byron Soc., Keats Shelley Assn., Nat. Council Tchrs. English. Democrat. Home: 2720 Braemar St Waco TX 76710 Office: Dept English Baylor U Waco TX 76798

GOODE, JOHN MARTIN, financial executive; b. Chgo., Sept. 24, 1934; s. Robert C. and Alyce (Belz) G.; children: John Martin, Sue Ellen, James Edward, Leslie Maureen. B. Commerce, DePaul U., 1960; M.B.A., U. Chgo., 1966; postgrad., No. Ill. U. C.P.A. Ill.; cert. mgmt. acct. Ill. Controller farm equity div. Allis Chalmers, Milw., 1966-69; v.p., controller Maremont Corp., Chgo., 1969-73; sr. v.p. Whittakers Corp., Chgo.,, 1973-75; assoc. dean DePaul U., Chgo., 1976-78, asst. prof., 1975-80; sr. v.p. fin. and corp. planning J.I. Case Co., Racine, Wis., 1980—; chmn. bd. Intertractor Viehmann GmbH & Co., W. Germany, 1982—; dir. Datronic Rental Corp., Chgo., Marine First Nat. Bank, Racine. Mem. Fin. Execs. Inst. Clubs: Econs.; Columbia Yacht (Chgo.); Racine Country. Home: 300 N State St Chicago IL 60610 Office: 700 State St Racine WI 53404

GOODE, LEWIS BOULDIN, JR., banker; b. Lynchburg, Va., May 13, 1929; s. Lewis Bouldin and Annie (Osborne) G.; m. Martha Wallace, Oct. 6, 1951; children: Ellen Goode Hill, Robert Lewis, Ann Lee. Ed., Hampden-Sydney Coll., Bank Mgmt. Sch., U. Va. With Peoples Bank & Trust Co., Chase City, Va., chmn. bd., 1964-69; with Central Fidelity Bank, Lynchburg, 1969—, sr. v.p., then exec. v.p., 1971—, pres., 1973—, also dir.; exec. v.p., dir. Central Fidelity Banks Inc.; dir. Central Fidelity Computer Services, Inc., C.F.B. Adv. Corp., Craddock-Terry Shoe Corp. Trustee Patrick Henry Meml. Found., Randolph Macon Women's Coll., Va. Episcopal Sch.; pres. Williams Home. Served with USAF. Mem. Am. Inst. Banking, Ducks Unlimited (sponsor), Jamestowne Soc., Soc. Cincinnati, Omicron Delta Kappa. Episcopalian. Clubs: Piedmont, Boonsboro Country, Oakwood Country. Home: 1936 Parkland Dr Lynchburg VA 24503 Office: 828 Main St Lynchburg VA 24505

GOODE, RICHARD BENJAMIN, economist; b. Ft. Worth, July 31, 1916; s. Flavius M. and Laura Nell (Carson) G.; m. Liesel Gottscho, June 23, 1943. A.B., Baylor U., 1937; M.A., U. Ky., 1939; Ph.D., U. Wis., 1947. Economist U.S. Bur. Budget, 1941-45, Treasury Dept., 1945-47; asst. prof. econs. U. Chgo., 1947-51; with IMF, Washington, 1951-59, 65-81, dir. fiscal affairs dept., 1965-81; mem. staff Brookings Instn., Washington, 1959-65, guest scholar, 1981—; professorial lectr. Sch. Advanced Internat. Studies, Johns Hopkins U., 1981—; cons. Treasury Dept., 1947-51, World Bank, 1964. Author: The Corporation Income Tax, 1951, The Individual Income Tax, 1964, rev. edit., 1976; Editor: Nat. Tax Jour, 1948-51. Mem. Am. Econ. Assn., Royal Econ. Soc., Nat. Tax Assn. Home: 4301 Massachusetts Ave NW Washington DC 20016 Office: Brookings Instn 1775 Massachusetts Ave NW Washington DC 20036

GOODE, STEPHEN HOGUE, publishing company executive; b. Charlotte, N.C., Dec. 25, 1924; s. Henry Grady and Marie Louella (Creamer) G.; m. Jean Cameron Advena, Oct. 16, 1953; children: Elizabeth Whitston Joane Downe, Polly Turpin Dulcinea Hogue. B.A., U. Md., 1948; M.A., U. Pa., 1954, Ph.D., 1958. Asst. prof. English Rensselaer Poly. Inst., 1958-59; asst. prof. Fairleigh Dickinson U., 1960-65; dir. libraries, asso. prof. English Russell Sage Coll., 1965-78; pres., chmn. bd. Whitston Pub. Co., Troy, N.Y., 1968-81, Turpin Book Corp., Troy, 1973-80; pres. Penkevill Pub. Co., Greenwood, Fla., 1982—; dir. Trenowyth Pub. Co., Penkivil Book Co. Author: Index to Little Magazines, 1943-47, 1965, Index to Little Magazines, 1940-42, 1967, Index to Commonwealth Little Magazines, 1966-67, 68, plus biennial, Index to American Little Magazines, 1920-39, 1969, 1900-1919, 1974; editor: Studies in 20th Century, 1968-75; mng. editor: Holocaust Studies Ann., Studies in Black Am. Lit., Graham Greene Rev. Ann., Modern Lits. Ann. Served with AUS, 1943-46, 49-52. Decorated Purple Heart, Bronze Star with oak leaf cluster. Mem. Bibliog. Soc. (London), Bibliog. Soc. Am., Bibliog. Soc. U. Va., Index Soc. (London). Club: Grolier (N.Y.C.). Office: Route 2 Box 40 Greenwood FL 32443

GOODE, WILLIAM JOSIAH, sociology educator; b. Houston, Aug. 30, 1917; s. William J. and Lillian Rosalie (Bare) G.; m. Josephine Mary Cannizzo, Dec. 22, 1938 (div. 1946); children: Brian, Erich, Rachel (dec.), Barbara Nan; m. Ruth Siegel, Oct. 20, 1950 (div. 1971); 1 son, Andrew Josiah. B.A., U. Tex., 1938, M.A., 1939; Ph.D., Pa. State U., 1946; D.Sc. (hon.), Upsala U., 1970. Instr. sociology Pa. State U., 1941-43; social sci. analyst Inter-Am. Statis. Inst., 1943-44; asst. prof. Wayne State U., 1946-50; asso. research dir. Columbia U., 1950-52, asso. prof. sociology, 1952-56, prof., 1956-74; Giddings prof. sociology Stanford U., 1975-77, prof., 1977—; prof. Free U. Berlin, 1954; vis. fellow Wolfson Coll., Oxford U., 1980; U.S. del. UN Conf. Aid to Tech. Undeveloped Nations, 1963; bd. dirs., sec. Social Sci. Research Council; gov., asso. dir. Bur. Applied Social Research; mem. behavioral scis. tng. com. Nat. Inst. Gen. Med. Scis., NIMH, 1966-67. Author: Religion Among the Primitives, 1961, Methods in Social Research, 1952, After Divorce, 1956, Struktur Der Familie, World Revolution and Family Patterns, 1963, The Family, 1964, 82, Family and Society, 1965, Dynamics of Modern Society, 1966, (with L. Mitchell and F. Furstenberg) Willard Waller: On the Family, Education and War, 1970, Principles of Sociology, 1977, The Celebration of Heroes: Prestige as a Social Control Process, 1979; co-author: The Other Half, 1971, Explorations in Social Theory, 1973, Social Systems and Family Patterns, 1971; editor: series Sociol, 1953; asso. editor: Marriage and Family Living, 1956; contbr. articles to profl. jours. Served with USNR, 1944-45. Guggenheim fellow, 1965-66, 83-84; sr. scientist career grantee NIMH, 1969-74; recipient MacIver award Am. Sociol. Soc., 1965, Burgess award Nat. Council Family Relations, 1969. Fellow Am. Acad. Arts and Scis.; mem. Am. Sociol. Soc. (exec. com., council 1959-62, pres. 1971-72), Eastern Sociol. Soc. (pres. 1959-60, exec. com. 1959-61), ACLU (dir.), Sociol. Research Assn. (exec. council, pres. 1967—). Office: Dept Sociology Stanford U Stanford CA 94305

GOODELL, CHARLES ELLSWORTH, lawyer, former U.S. Senator; b. Jamestown, N.Y., Mar. 16, 1926; s. Charles Ellsworth and Francesca (Bartlett) G.; m. Jean Rice, Aug. 28, 1954 (div. 1978); children: William Rice, Timothy Bartlett, Roger Stokoe, Michael Charles Ellsworth, Jeffrey Harris; m. Patricia Goldman. A.B., Williams Coll., 1948; LL.B., Yale U., 1951, M.A. (Ford Found. faculty fellow), 1952; hon. degree, Houghton (N.Y.) Coll., Alfred U., N.Y., St. Bonaventure U., N.Y. Bar: N.Y. 1954, Conn. 1951. Instr., Quinnipiac Coll., New Haven, 1950-51; congressional liaison asst. Dept. Justice, 1954-55; partner Van Vlack, Goodell & McKee, Jamestown, N.Y., 1955-59, Roth, Carlson, Kwit, Spengler & Goodell, N.Y.C., 1971-72; mem. 86th-87th Congresses from 43d Dist. N.Y., 88th-90th Congresses from 38th Dist. N.Y., chmn. Planning and Research Com.; mem. U.S. Senate from N.Y., 1968-71; now of counsel King & Spalding, Washington; chmn. bd. DGA Internat., Inc., Washington. Author: Political Prisoners in America, 1973. Chmn. Republican Com. Chautauqua County, 1958-59; chmn. Presdl. Clemency Bd., 1974-75. Served as seaman USNR, World War II; 1st lt. USAAF, Korea. Mem. Jamestown Jaycees, Jamestown C. of C. (chmn. govtl. affairs com. 1956-58), ABA, Jamestown Bar Assn., Phi Beta Kappa, Gamma Sigma Chi. Episcopalian. Clubs: Capitol Hill, 86th Congress (Washington); Yale, New Yorker. Home: 5022 V St NW Washington DC 20007 Office: 1915 I St NW Washington DC 20006

GOODELL, FORREST ALBERT, banker; b. Ada., Okla., Jan. 10. 1942; s. Leonard Lee and Doris Marian (King) G.; m. Nancy Kay Platt, June 5, 1965; children: Amy, Lori. B.B.S., East Central State U., Ada, 1964, B.S.Ed., 1964; grad., S.W. Grad. Sch. Banking So. Meth. U., 1978. Ops. officer investments Malon S. Andrus, Inc., N.Y.C., 1965-66; investment underwriter First Nat. Bank, Dallas, 1966-69; commodity broker Barnes Brokerage, Dallas, 1969-70; stockbroker Bache & Co., Dallas, 1970-71; exec. v.p. investments First City Nat. Bank, Houston, 1971—; mem. fin. com. Spring Br. Christian Ch., Houston, 1978-83, Shadow Oaks Recreation Assn., 1983. Dir. fin. com. Houston Pops Orch., 1982-83, Avondale House for Autistic Children, Houston, 1982-83; mem. allocations panel United Way, Houston, 1982-83; mem. asset mgmt. com. Tex. Treas. Office, Austin. Served with USN, 1964. Republican. Club: Govt. Bond of Houston (pres. 1977-78). Office: First City Nat Bank 1111 Fannin St Houston TX 77002

GOODELL, GEORGE SIDNEY, finance educator; b. Sheboygan, Wis., Nov. 29, 1921; s. George Sidney and Emma (Kreuter) G.; m. Anna Stubenrauch, June 16, 1951; children: Margaret Anne, John Winfield. B.A., Carroll Coll., 1943; M.B.A., U. Chgo., 1947; J.D., Marquette U., 1949; Ph.D., Northwestern U., 1959. Bar: Wis. 1949; chartered fin. analyst. Assoc. prof. fin. Ohio State U., Columbus, 1957-66; prof. fin. Kent State U., Ohio, 1966-71; dean Coll. Bus. Roosevelt U., Chgo., 1971-75; prof., chmn. dept. fin. Loyola U., Chgo., 1975-80, Miami U., Oxford, Ohio, 1980—; sole practice law, Sheboygan, Wis.,

1949-51. Served to lt. (j.g.) USN, 1943-46; PTO. Mem. Inst. Chartered Fin. Analysts, Fin. Mgmt. Assn., Am. Fin. Assn., Midwest Fin. Assn., Wis. Bar Assn. Methodist. Home: 909 Arrowhead Dr Apt 31-F Oxford OH 45056 Office: Miami U Sch Bus Oxford OH 45056

GOODELL, SOL, retired lawyer; b. St. Louis, Aug. 24, 1906; s. Abram and Jennie (Silverberg) G.; m. Beatrice Cholden, Feb. 24, 1946; children: Thomas C., Susan Jean. LL.B., U. Tex., 1929. Bar: Tex. 1929. Asso. prof. law U. Tex. Law Sch., 1929-30; asso., then mem. firm Thompson & Knight (and predecessors), Dallas, 1930-76. Former chmn. bd. Greenhill Sch., Dallas; trustee bd. devel. U. Tex. at Dallas; trustee, v.p. Excellence in Edn. Found.; former sec., trustee Goals for Dallas; trustee Dallas Grand Opera Assn., Dallas Symphony Found., Found. for Callier Center and Communication Disorders. Served to capt. AUS, 1942-46. Mem. ABA, Dallas Bar Assn., State Bar Tex. Jewish (past pres. temple). Clubs: Dallas, Columbian Country (Dallas). Home: 5927 Joyce Way Dallas TX 75225 Office: 3300 First City Center Dallas TX 75201

GOODELL, WARREN FRANKLIN, university administrator; b. Champaign, Ill., May 10, 1924; s. Warren Franklin and Dorothy Newell (Talbot) G.; m. Suzanne Vassamillet, Aug. 25, 1946; children—Warren Emile, Kenneth Franklin. B.S. in Engring. Physics, U. Ill., 1944; M.A. in Physics, Columbia, 1947, Ph.D., 1951. Mem. staff Radiation Lab., MIT, 1944-46; assoc. dir. Nevis Cyclotron Lab., Columbia U., N.Y.C., 1951-64, assoc. dir. Office Projects and Grants, 1964-67, v.p. adminstrn., 1967-72; v.p., dean Pleasantville Campus Pace U. (N.Y.), 1972-77; dir. planning Mercy Coll., 1977—; trustee Columbia U. Press, 1967-72; dir. Yale-Columbia So. Obs., Inc. Mem. Bd. Edn., Irvington, N.Y., 1957-67. Mem. Nat. Assn. Coll. and U. Bus. Officers (com. govt. relations 1968-72), Sigma Xi, Phi Kappa Phi, Tau Beta Pi, Beta Theta Pi. Republican. Presbyn. Home: Riverview Rd Irvington NY 10533

GOODEN, REGINALD HEBER, bishop; b. Long Beach, Calif., Mar. 22, 1910; s. Robert Burton and Alice Leonard (Moore) G.; m. Victoria Elena F. de Mendia y Miranda; children: Reginald Heber, Hiram Richard. A.B., Stanford U., 1931; S.T.B., Berkeley Div. Sch., New Haven, 1934, S.T.D., 1946; student, U. Madrid, 1934-35, Centro de Estudios Historicos, Madrid (Spain), 1934-35; D.D., Trinity Coll., Hartford, 1963. Ordained to ministry Protestant Episcopal Ch., 1934; hon. asst. chaplain Brit. Embassy Ch., Madrid, 1934-35; priest in charge St. Paul's Ch. and Sch., Camaguey, Cuba, 1935-39; dean Holy Trinity Cathedral, Havana, Cuba, 1939-45; bishop of missionary dist. P.E. Ch. in, Panama C.Z., 1945-72, also bishop in charge, Ecuador, 1956-64; bishop in charge, Central Central-Am., 1956-57; asst. bishop Diocese La., Shreveport, 1972-75, acting bishop, 1975-76, ret., 1976; bishop-in-residence Ch. of Holy Cross, Shreveport, 1976—. Decorated Gran Cruz Order Vasco Nunez de Balboa, Panama; recipient Distinguished Community Service award Govt. C.Z., 1972; John Henry Watson fellow Berkeley Div. Sch. Clubs: Mason., The Breakers (Stanford U.). Home: 109 E Southfield Rd #72 Shreveport LA 71105 Office: 875 Cotton St Shreveport LA 71101

GOODENOUGH, WARD HUNT, anthropologist, educator; b. Cambridge, Mass., May 30, 1919; s. Erwin Ramsdell and Helen Miriam (Lewis) G.; m. Ruth Gallagher, Feb. 8, 1941; children: Hester G. (Mrs. Steven M. Gelber), Deborah L. (Mrs. Paul Gordon), Oliver R., Garrick G. Grad., Groton (Mass.) Sch., 1937; A.B., Cornell U., 1940; Ph.D., Yale, 1949. Instr. anthropology U. Wis., 1948-49; mem. faculty U. Pa., 1949—, prof., 1962-80, univ. prof., 1980—, chmn. dept., 1976-82; vis. prof. Cornell U., 1961-62, vis. lectr., summer 1950, Swarthmore Coll., spring 1955, Bryn Mawr Coll., fall 1955, U. Hawaii, summer 1959, 75, 76, 77; vis. prof. U. Wis., Milw., summer 1967, Yale U., spring 1969, Colo. Coll., spring 1979, U. Hawaii, 1982-83; anthrop. studies in, Truk, 1947, 64-65, Gilbert Islands, 1951, New Guinea, 1951, 54; Pacific Sci. bd. Nat. Acad. Scis.-NRC, 1962-66; standing com. anthropology and social scis. Pacific Sci. Assn., 1962-66; cons. Office Sci. and Tech., 1961-62. Author: Property, Kin and Community on Truk, 1951, Cooperation in Change, 1963, Explorations in Cultural Anthropology, 1964, Description and Comparison in Cultural Anthropology, 1970, Culture, Language and Society, 1971, Trukese-English Dictionary, 1980. Mem. health com. Phila. Dist. Health and Welfare Council, 1963-64; Bd. dirs. Human Relations Area Files, Inc., 1964—, chmn., 1971-81. Served with AUS, 1941-45. Fellow Center Advanced Study Behavioral Scis., 1957-58; Guggenheim fellow, 1979-80. Mem. Nat. Acad. Scis.; fellow Am. Philos. Soc., Am. Acad. Arts and Scis.; mem. Royal Anthrop. Inst., Am. Anthrop. Assn. (editor 1966-70), A.A.A.S. (v.p., chmn. sect. H 1971, dir. 1972-75), Am. Ethnol. Soc. (pres. 1962), Soc. Applied Anthropology (pres. 1963), Linguistics Soc. Am., Polynesian Soc., Assn. Social Anthropology in Oceania, Phi Beta Kappa, Sigma Xi, Phi Kappa Phi. Home: 204 Fox Ln Wallingford PA 19086 Office: Univ Museum Philadelphia PA 19104

GOODFRIEND, ARTHUR, educator; b. N.Y.C., June 21, 1907; s. Samuel and Fannie G.; m. Edith Del Mar; children: Jill Goodfriend Johnstone, Arthur, Bret Meredith. Student, NAD, 1924; B.Sc., Coll. City N.Y., 1928; postgrad., Harvard U., 1978-79; postgrad., Hughes Hall, Cambridge U., 1981-82. Merchandising dir. Amos Parrish & Co., N.Y.C., 1928-35; around-the-world rep. Esquire mag., Herald Tribune, 1936-37; advt. dir. Goodall Corp., Sanford, Maine, 1938-41; corr. N.Y. Times, Holiday, Life mags., other publs., Latin Am., 1948-49; mem. Joint Commn. on Rural Reconstrn., Canton, China, also Taipei, Formosa, 1949-50; fellow Council on Econ. and Cultural Affairs, Indonesia, 1954-55; fgn. service officer, New Delhi, 1958-60; Fed. Exec. fellow Brookings Instn., 1961-62; cons. for W. Africa USIA, 1963-65; spl. asst. to chancellor East-West Center, Honolulu, 1966-69; asst. to pres. People to People Health Found. (Project HOPE), 1969-70; prof. Am. Studies New Coll. U. Hawaii, 1970-75; prof. U. Bohol, Tagbilaran, Philippines, 1979-81; resident scholar Cambridge U., 1981-83. Author: If You Were Born in Russia, 1952, The Only War We Seek, 1953, What Can a Man Believe?, 1954, What Can a Man Do?, 1955, Something is Missing, 1956, Two Sides of One World, 1956, What is America?, 1957, Rice Roots, 1958, Stand Fast in Liberty, 1959, Indonesia; A Case Study in Intercultural Communication, 1962, The Twisted Image, 1963, India: A Case Study in Intercultural Communication, 1962, They Wanted Freedom, 1963, The Cognoscenti Abroad, 1969, The Life and Death of New College, 1975, The Adventures of Superboy Lito, 1979; others; contbr. articles to govt. publs. Sr. del. U.S. del. to SEATO Conf., Manila, 1967; protocol officer univ. campus Round-the-World Cruise, 1977; Peace Corps vol., Philippines, 1979-80. Served to lt. col. AUS, 1941-46; editor-in-chief Stars and Stripes, 1944-45; Europe; editor-in-chief Stars and Stripes, 1946; China. Decorated Legion of Merit, Bronze Star; Army Commendation medal; Combat Infantryman's badge, U.S.; Croix de Guerre, France). Mem. N.H. Council World Affairs (dir.), Soc. Illustrators, Pacific and Asian Affairs Council (gov.), Fgn. Service Assn. Clubs: Cannon, Press, Outrigger Canoe, Cosmos, Ragged Mountain Fish and Game, Harvard Faculty, Diplomatic and Consular. Home: Outrigger Canoe Club 2909 Kalakaua Ave Honolulu HI 96815 *I live my life as though it were a book, each chapter dealing with separate and significant experiences, partly accidental but mainly so contrived that at the end it may be written: Little of life's feast remained uneaten.*

GOODFRIEND, JAMES HERMAN, lawyer; b. N.Y.C., Dec. 8, 1933; s. Arthur and Phyllis (LeVine) G.; m. Phyllis Poresky, Jan. 3, 1960 (div.); children—Lisa Ruth, David Peter. A.B., U. Chgo., 1953; J.D., Columbia U., 1956. Bar: N.Y. bar 1956, Fla. bar 1975, U.S. Supreme Ct. bar 1967. Partner firm Tenzer, Greenblatt, Fallon & Kaplan, N.Y.C., 1959—. Served with AUS, 1957-59. Mem. N.Y. County Lawyers Assn. Club: K.P. Home: 82 25 Surrey Pl Jamaica NY 11432 Office: 405 Lexington Ave New York NY 10017

GOODGAME, RONALD EDWARD, lawyer, business executive; b. Los Angeles, Nov. 14, 1938; s. Robert Edward G. and Virginia Louise (Tyner) Braverman; m. June Elizabeth Colyear, Dec., 1961 (div. 1975); children: Robert Edward, Randolph Colyear; m. Marilyn G. McDowell, Aug. 15, 1981. B.A., U. So. Calif., 1961, LL.B., 1964. Bar: Calif. 1965. Atty. Carnation Co., Los Angeles, 1969-80, asst. gen. counsel, 1980-81, v.p., gen. counsel, 1981—. Contbr. articles to legal jours. Mem. ABA, Calif. State Bar Assn., Los Angeles County Bar Assn., State Bar Calif. (exec. com. antitrust and trade regulation law sect.). Club: Los Angeles Country. Office: Carnation Co 5045 Wilshire Blvd Los Angeles CA 90036

GOODGER, JOHN VERNE, specialty materials co. exec.; b. Milton, Wis., Mar. 25, 1936; s. Harry E. and Elsie (Wachlin) G.; m. Priscilla C. Arnold, Oct. 18, 1958; children—Steven J., Karin. Student, Whitewater State Coll., 1954-56; B.B.A., U. Wis., Milw., 1958. C.P.A., Wis. M. Staff auditor Price, Waterhouse & Co., Milw., 1958-63; with Bucyrus-Erie Co., Milw., 1963-66, mgr. corp. data processing, 1965-66; mgr. internal auditing Koehring Co., Milw., 1966-69, mgr. corp. accounting, 1969-71, asst. treas., 1971-74; treas. Ferro Corp., Cleve., 1974—. Served with U.S. Army, 1959-62. Mem. Fin. Execs. Inst., Am., Wis., Ohio insts. C.P.A.'s, Cleve. Treas's. Clubs: Greater Cleve. Growth Assn., Tax Council, Nat. Investor Relations Inst. Home: 2996 Falmouth Rd Shaker Heights OH 44122 Office: One Erieview Plaza Cleveland OH 44114

GOODGOLD, JOSEPH, physician, educator; b. N.Y.C., Mar. 21, 1920; s. Ben and Celia (Berr) G.; m. Mildred Simons, May 2, 1942; children: Ellen (Mrs. Daniel Frohwirth), Shelley. B.S., Bklyn. Coll., 1942; M.D., Middlesex U., 1945. Diplomate: Am. Bd. Phys. Medicine and Rehab. Intern Beth-El Hosp., Brookdale, Bklyn., 1945-46, asst. resident in medicine, 1946-47; fellow Inst. Rehab. Medicine, NYU, Bellevue Med. Center, 1953-54, Howard A. Rusk prof. rehab. research, 1975—; chmn. dept. rehab. medicine NYU Sch. Medicine; cons.-lectr. postgrad. div. N.Y. U. Sch. Medicine (Sch. of Edn.), 1956—; dir. Electrodiagnostic Service, N.Y. U. Med. Center, 1957, dir. rehab. med. services, 1981—; attending physician dept. rehab. medicine (Univ. Hosp.), 1960; cons. Brookdale Hosp. Center, Manhattan VA Hosp., Morristown Meml. Hosp., St. Barnabas Hosp. for Chronic Diseases, Bronx. Contbr. articles to med. jours. Mem. med. adv. bd. Muscular Dystrophy Assn.; cons. HEW, Social Security Adminstrn., N.Y. State Dept. Vocat. Rehab. Served with M.C. AUS, 1951-53. Fellow Am. Coll. Cardiology, A.C.P., Am. Acad. Compensation Medicine, N.Y. Acad. Medicine, N.Y. Acad. Sci.; mem. Am. Assn. Electromyography and Electrodiagnosis (pres. 1966-67), A.M.A., Am. Congress Rehab. Medicine, Am. Rheumatism Assn., Am. Acad. Phys. Medicine and Rehab., Am. Assn. Acad. Physiatrists (pres. 1973-74), Med. Soc. Kings County. Clubs: Lords Valley Country; University (N.Y.C.). Home: 300 E 40th St New York NY 10016 Office: 400 E 34th St New York NY 10016

GOODHEART, CLYDE RAYMOND, virologist; b. Erie, Pa., June 9, 1931; s. Edmund James and Helen (Husted) G.; m. Barbara Jean Peterson, Dec. 26, 1953; children—Kenneth James, Karen Jean, Diane Louise. B.S., Northwestern U., 1953, M.S., 1957, M.D., 1957. Research fellow Cal. Inst. Tech., 1958-61; asst. prof. pediatrics, then asso. prof. Childrens Hosp., Los Angeles, 1961-65; asso. mem., then mem. Inst. Biomed. Research, Edn. and Research Found., AMA, 1965-70; sr. microbiologist Rush-Presbyn.-St. Luke's Med. Center, Chgo., 1970-71; prof. microbiology Rush Med. Coll., 1971—; pres. BioLabs, Inc., Northbrook, Ill., 1971—; tchr. microbiology U. Calif. at Los Angeles, 1961-64. Author: An Introduction to Virology, 1969; co-author: Fundamentals of Microbiology, 1974; Contbr. papers in field. Mem. Am. Soc. for Microbiology, Ill. Soc. for Microbiology (pres. 1974), AAAS, Biophys. Soc., Am. Soc. for Cell Biology, Phi Beta Kappa, Sigma Xi, Phi Rho Sigma. Home: 15 Sheffield Ct Lincolnshire Deerfield IL 60015 Office: BioLabs Inc 2910 MacArthur Blvd Northbrook IL 60062

GOODHEART, EUGENE, educator; b. Bklyn., June 26, 1931; s. Samuel and Miriam G.; m. Patricia Somer, Aug. 13, 1960 (div. July 1973); children: Eric, Jessica; m. Joan Bamberger, July 8, 1977. B.A., Columbia U., 1953, Ph.D. in English and Comparative Lit, 1961, M.A., U. Va., 1954; postgrad. (Fulbright fellow), Sorbonne, U. Paris, 1956-57. Instr., then asst. prof. English, Bard Coll., 1958-62; asst. prof. U. Chgo., 1962-66; asso. prof. Mt. Holyoke Coll., 1966-67; asso. prof., then prof. MIT, 1967-74; prof., chmn. dept. English, Boston U., 1974-83; Edythe Macy Gross prof. humanities Brandeis U., 1983—; vis. prof. Wesleyan U. Summer Sch., 1963, 64, 66, 69; Gauss seminarist Princeton U., 1972. Author: The Utopian Vision of D. H. Lawrence, 1963, The Cult of the Ego, 1968, Culture and The Radical Conscience, 1973, The Failure of Criticism, 1978. Am. Council Learned Socs. fellow, 1965-66; Guggenheim fellow, 1970-71; Nat. Endowment for Humanities fellow, 1980-81. Mem. MLA, AAUP. Home: 25 Barnard Ave Watertown MA 02172

GOODHUE, FRANCIS ABBOT, JR., lawyer; b. Needham, Mass., June 11, 1916; s. Francis Abbot and Nora Forbes (Thayer) G.; m. Mary Elizabeth Brier, May 15, 1948; 1 son, Francis Abbot. A.B., Harvard U., 1937, LL.B., 1940. Bar: N.Y. 1941. Since practiced in, N.Y.C.; mem. firm Dewey, Ballantine, Bushby, Palmer & Wood (and predecessor firms), 1939—, partner, 1952—, chmn. mgmt. com., 1980-82. Served to lt. comdr. USNR, 1941-46. Mem. Am. Bar Assn., N.Y. State Bar Assn., Assn. Bar City N.Y., N.Y. County Lawyers Assn. Republican. Home: McLain St Mount Kisco NY 10549 Office: 140 Broadway Rm 4500 New York NY 10005

GOODIN, VERNON LEE, lawyer; b. Heraldsburg, Calif., Apr. 6, 1915; s. Robert Lee and Margaret Regina (Mooney) G.; m. Marion E. Sproul, Nov. 4, 1945; children—Robert Allan, Douglas Sproul, Sarah Elizabeth. B.A., U. Calif., Berkeley, 1937, J.D., 1940. Bar: Calif. bar 1940, diplomate: Am. Bd. Trial Advocates. Spl. agt. FBI, 1940-45; dep. dist. atty., Alameda County, Calif., 1946-51; partner Bronson, Brownson & McKinnon, San Francisco, 1951—. Fellow Am. Bar Found.; mem. Am. Coll. Trial Lawyers, Assn. Def. Counsel No. Calif. (pres. 1963), Am. Bar Assn., Calif. Bar Assn., San Francisco Bar Assn., Lawyer Pilots Bar Assn. Democrat. Clubs: Pacific Union, Bankers, Commonwealth of California (bd. govs., pres. 1974). Home: 97 Tamalpais Rd Berkeley CA 94708 Office: 555 California St San Francisco CA 94104

GOODIN, WILLIAM CHARLES, trade publications company executive; b. Louisville, Sept. 18, 1917; s. Edward C. and Bertha (Vorhies) G.; m. Emily Ellen Percefull, Sept. 8, 1946; children: Sue Ellen Goodin Bach, Charles W. B.A. in Econs., U. Colo., 1941. Owner, operator Petroleum Info. Corp., Denver, 1946-68; ptnr., v.p. Petroleum Info. Corp., subs. A.C. Nielson Co., Denver, 1968-75; pres. Petroleum Info. Corp., subs. A.C. Nielsen Co., Denver, 1975-79, chmn. bd., chief exec. officer, Littleton, Colo., 1979-83, chmn. bd., 1983—; dir. A.C. Nielsen Co., Northbrook, Ill.; mem. Colo. Oil and Gas Commn., 1972-76, Interstate Oil Compact Commn. Bd. dirs. Swedish Med. Ctr. Found., Englewood, Colo., 1979—, U. Colo. Found., Inc., Boulder, 1983—. Served to lt. CIC, AUS, 1942-46; Philippines, Korea. Recipient Betty McWhorter award Denver chpt. Desk & Derrick, 1979. Mem. Rocky Mountain Oil and Gas Assn. (dir. 1982—), Denver Landmen's Assn., Soc. Petroleum Engrs., Am. Assn. Petroleum Geologists, Rocky Mountain Petroleum Pioneers, Assn. Petroleum Writers, Ind. Petroleum Assn. Mountain States; hon. life mem. Rocky Mountain Assn. Petroleum Geologists. Republican. Presbyterian. Clubs: Denver Petroleum (bd. dirs. 1958-62, v.p. 1961), mem. (pres. 1962), Denver Athletic; Cherry Hills Country, Met. (Englewood, Colo.); Garden of God's (Colorado Springs, Colo.); 25 Yr. Club of Petroleum Industry (Solvang, Calif.). Home: 11 Parkway Dr Englewood CO 80110 Office: Petroleum Info Corp 4100 E Dry Creek Rd Littleton CO 80122

GOODING, CHARLES ARTHUR, physician; b. Cleve., Feb. 28, 1936; s. Joseph J. and Florence G. (Pitt) G.; m. Gretchen Wagner, June 19, 1961; children: Gunnar, Justin, Britta. B.A., Western Res. U., 1957; M.D., Ohio State U., 1961. Intern Ohio State U. Hosp., 1961-62; resident in radiology Peter Bent Brigham Hosp., Children's Hosp. Med. Center, both Boston, 1963-65; research fellow radiology Harvard Med. Sch., Boston, 1962, teaching fellow, 1965-66; Harvard Med. Sch. fellow Hosp. for Sick Children, London, Karolinska Hosp., Stockholm, 1966; mem. faculty U. Calif. Med. Center, San Francisco, 1967—, prof. radiology and pediatrics, 1976—, exec. vice chmn. dept. radiology, 1974—; pres. Radiology Research and Edn. Found., 1973—. Author articles in field; contbr. chpts. to books.; Editor: Pediatric Radiology, 1973; editor: Diagnostic Radiology, 1972—. Served to capt. M.C. USAR, 1967-68. Fellow Am. Coll. Radiology; mem. Am. Roentgen Ray Soc., Assn. Univ. Radiologists, European Soc. Pediatric Radiologists, Pacific Coast Pediatric Radiologists Assn., Radiol. Soc. N. Am., San Francisco Med. Soc., Soc. Pediatric Radiology, Rocky Mountain Radiol. Soc. (hon.). Home: 8 Overhill Rd Mill Valley CA 94941 Office: Dept Radiology U Calif Med Center M-380 San Francisco CA 94143

GOODING, CHARLES THOMAS, psychology educator, college dean; b. Tampa, Fla., Nov. 18, 1931; s. Charles T. and Gladys (Bingman) G.; m. Shirley Ann Puckett, June 7, 1953; children: Steven Thomas, Carol Ann, David Lee, Mark Charles. B.A., U. Fla., 1954, M.Ed., 1962, Ed.D., 1964; postgrad., U. Tampa, 1956-58. Tchr. Meml. Sch., Tampa, 1956-58; asst. prin. to prin. St. Mary's Sch., Tampa, 1958-62; grad. fellow U. Fla., Gainesville, 1962-63, instr., 1963-64; assoc. prof. to prof. SUNY, Oswego, 1964-79, prof. psychology, 1980—, dean grad. studies, 1982—; vis. prof. U. Liverpool, Eng., 1979-80; mem. SUNY Chancellor's Task Force on Tchr. Edn., 1984; grad. fellow U. Fla., Gainesville, 1962-63. Author: Learning Theories in Educational Practice, 1971; contbr. articles to profl. jours. Bd. dirs. Oswego County unit Am. Cancer Soc., N.Y., 1972-74, 82-84; mem. commn. on ordination Episcopal Diocese Central N.Y., 1980-84. Served to 1st lt. USAR, 1954-56. SUNY Research Found. grantee, 1966, 69, 70; N.Y. State Dept. Edn. grantee, 1971-72; NSF grantee, 1980-81. Mem. Eastern Ednl. Research Assn. (v.p. 1979-81, treas., dir. 1983-85), Am. Psychol. Assn., Brit. Ednl. Research Assn., Am. Ednl. Research Assn., AAAS, Nat. Conf. Computers in Psychology, Classic Jaguar Assn., Pathfinder Antique Auto Club (pres. 1980-82). Home: 4169 W River Rd-PO Box 231 Minetto NY 13115 Office: Grad Office Culkin Hall SUNY Oswego NY 13126 *Z As an educator, the opportunities for service to my fellow men and women and for explorations on the frontiers of knowledge provide for a rich professional life. On a personal level, my family, friends, church, and community continue to be significant sources of inspiration for growth in faith, hope, and love.*

GOODING, DAVID EUGENE, insurance company executive; b. Alexandria, Ind., July 21, 1941; s. Herbert Francis and Jeanne Marie (Beatham) G.; m. Ann Reed, July 9, 1962; children: David J., Karen, Jennifer, James. B.S. in Math., Oreg. State U., 1962. Actuarial student State Farm Life, Bloomington, Ill., 1962-64; actuary Cal-Western Life, Sacramento, 1964-74; sr. v.p., chief actuary Nat. Life & Accident Co., Nashville, 1974-82; sr. v.p., corp. mktg. and planning Transamerica Occidental Life Ins. Co., Los Angeles, 1983—. Fellow Soc. of Actuaries; mem. Am. Acad. of Actuaries (enrolled actuary), Southeastern Actuaries Club. Episcopalian. Home: 1725 Hillcrest Ave Glendale CA 91202 Office: Transamerica Occidental Life Ins Co 1150 S Olive St Los Angeles CA 90015

GOODING, JUDSON, writer; b. Rochester, Minn., Oct. 12, 1926; s. Arthur Faitoute and Frances (Judson) G.; m. Francoise Ridoux, June 21, 1952; children: Anthony, Amelie, Timothy. Grad. with honors, Yale U., 1948; diplome d'Etudes Francaises, U. Paris, 1950. Staff writer Dept. Army, Hdqrs. EUCOM, Germany, 1950-52; script writer Affiliated Film Producers, N.Y.C., 1952-53; news writer WCCO-CBS, Mpls., 1953; reporter Mpls. Tribune, 1953-57, Life mag., N.Y.C., 1957-60, fgn. corr., Paris, 1960-62, Time mag., 1962-65; chief of bur. Time-Life News Service, San Francisco, 1966-68; edn. editor Time mag., N.Y.C., 1968-69; asso. editor Fortune mag., 1969-73; v.p. Urban Research Corp.; also editor Trend Report, Chgo., 1973-75; mng. partner Trend Analysis Assos., 1975—; exec. editor Next Mag., N.Y.C., 1979-81, contbg. editor, 1981-82; counselor for pub. affairs U.S. Permanent Del. to UNESCO, 1982-84; writing cons. UN, Ford Found., Am. Assembly, also corps. Author: The Job Revolution, 1972; contbr. to: American Dreams, The Environment, The Hippies, The Survival Equation, The Failure of Success; Contbr. articles to popular mags. and profl. jours. Bd. patrons Wilson Ctr., Faribault, Minn.; mem. program com. Internat. Found. for Cultural Cooperation, Courchevel, France. Served with USNR, 1944-46. Recipient 1st place award U. Mo. Sch. Journalism Penney-Mo., 1980, hon. certificate Program Mgmt. Devel. Harvard U. Grad. Sch. Mem. Common Cause, World Future Soc., Nat. Trust Hist. Preservation, Am. Soc. Journalists and Authors, Mensa. Clubs: Business; Elizabethan (New Haven); Century Assn., Yale (N.Y.C.); Bedford Bicycle Polo (founder, co-capt.). Office: PO Box 542 Bedford NY 10506

GOODINGS, ALLEN, bishop; b. Barrow-in-Furness, Lancashire, Eng., May 7, 1925; s. Thomas Jackson and Ada (Tate) G.; m. Joanne Talbot, Oct. 26, 1959; children—Suzanne, Thomas. B.A., Sir George Williams U., Montreal, Que., Can., 1959; B.D., McGill U., Montreal, 1959; L.Th., Montreal Diocesan Theol. Coll., 1959, D.D. (hon.), 1978. Engr., draftsman in industry, 1941-54; ordained to ministry Anglican Ch., 1959; curate, then priest chs. in, Montreal, 1959-65; rector Ch. of Ascension, Montreal, 1965-69; dean Cathedral of Holy Trinity, Quebec, 1969-77; bishop Anglican Diocese of Que., 1977—; chaplain Can. Grenadier Guards, Montreal, 1966-69. Clubs: Cercle universitaire, Officer Mess Royal 22d Regt., Garrison (Quebec) (hon.). Office: 36 rue des Jardins Quebec PQ G1R 4L5 Canada

GOODKIN, MICHAEL JON, publishing company executive; b. N.Y.C., June 10, 1941; s. Harold and Rose (Mostkoff) G.; m. Helen Graham Fairbank, Oct. 1, 1971; children: Graham Laird, Nathalie Fairbank. B.A., Harvard U., 1963; postgrad., U. Chgo. Bus. Sch., 1964. Trainee Random House, N.Y.C., 1964-65; asst. dir. Simulmatics, N.Y.C., 1966-67; account exec. World Book Ency., Inc., Chgo., 1967-70, research dir., 1970-73, v.p. mktg., 1973-76, v.p., gen. mgr. mail order div., 1976-78, pres., 1978—, chmn., chief exec. officer, dir., 1983—; v.p. World Book Internat., 1978-79, sr. v.p., 1979-80, exec. v.p., corp. dir. mktg., dir., 1980—; pres. World Book Life Ins. Co., 1983, World Book Ins. Group Inc., 1983—; dir. World Book Pty. Ltd. (Australian subs.), 1983—. Bd. dirs. Chgo. Area Project; pres. aux. bd. Art Inst. Chgo., 1975-77, trustee, 1975—, also chmn. mktg. com.; trustee Modern Poetry Assn., Latin Sch. Chgo., 1983—, DMA Edn. Found., 1983—. Served with Army N.G., 1963-69. Mem. Direct Mktg. Assn. (internat. council steering com. 1983), Direct Selling Assn. (instl. com.). Clubs: Racquet, Harvard (N.Y.C.); Harvard (Boston); Mcht. and Mfrs., Casino. Office: 510 Merchandise Mart Plaza Chicago IL 60654

GOODKIND, LOUIS WILLIAM, lawyer; b. St. Paul, Aug. 29, 1914; s. Leo and Grace (Goldsmith) G.; m. Jean Wald Morgenthau, Apr. 8, 1942 (dec. July 1975); children: Barbara (Mrs. Jeffrey G. Pepper), Mary (Mrs. C. Lindley Garner), Kathryn (Mrs. Robert J. Boyle); m. Carol Eaton Bourquin, Oct. 30, 1976; stepchildren: Philip F. Eaton, Dorothee R. Eaton. B.A., Yale, 1936, J.D., 1939. Bar: N.Y. 1939, D.C. 1951. Pvt. practice, N.Y.C., 1939-40; asst. U.S. atty. So. Dist. N.Y., 1940-43; with CAB, Washington, 1943-52, sr. atty., 1943-46; asso. dir. Bur. Econ. Regulation, 1946-51; dep. dir. Bur. Air Operations, 1951-52; chief econ. def. div. Dept. State, Washington, 1952-56; partner Zimet, Haines, Moss & Friedman (and predecessor firms), 1956-78, of counsel, 1979—; guest lectr. air transp. Am. U., 1946-51; acting village justice, Irvington, N.Y., 1971-72; Mem. U.S. delegations 3d Session Facilitation div. Internat. Civil Aviation Orgn., Buenos Aires, 1951, Consultative Group, Paris, 1954, Four Power Fgn. Ministers Meeting, Geneva, 1955. Mem. Village Democratic Com., Irvington, N.Y., Town Dem. Com., Greenburgh, N.Y., County Dem. Com., Westchester, N.Y., 1964-71; Past pres., trustee Green Acres Sch., Bethesda, Md.; corp. sec., bd. dirs., sec. Neighborhood Playhouse Inc., N.Y.C.; sec. Yale Law Sch. Class of 1939; class agt. Yale Law Sch. Fund; mem. exec. com. Yale Law Sch. Assn. Mem. Assn. Bar City N.Y., Phi Beta Kappa, Phi Delta Phi. Clubs: Yale (N.Y.C.); Nat. Aviation (Washington). Home: Harriman Rd Irvington NY 10533 Office: 460 Park Ave New York NY 10022

GOODLAD, JOHN INKSTER, educator; b. North Vancouver, B.C., Can., Aug. 19, 1920; s. William James and Mary (Inkster) G.; m. Evalene M. Pearson, Aug. 23, 1945; children: Stephen John, Mary Paula. Teaching certificate, Vancouver Normal Sch., 1939; B.A., U. B.C., 1945, M.A., 1946; Ph.D., U. Chgo., 1949; L.H.D., Nat. Coll. Edn., 1967, U. Louisville, 1968, So. Ill. U., 1982, Bank Street Coll. Edn., 1984; LL.D., Kent State U., 1974, Pepperdine U., 1976, Simon Fraser U., 1983; D.Ed., Eastern Mich. U., 1982. Tchr. Surrey Schs., B.C., 1939-41, prin., 1941-42; dir. edn. Provincial Sch. For Boys, B.C., 1942-46; cons. curriculum Atlanta Area Tchr. Edn. Service, 1947-49; asso. prof. Emory U., 1949-50; prof., dir. div. tchr. edn. Agnes Scott Coll. and Emory U., 1950-56; prof., dir. U. Chgo. Center Tchr. Edn., 1956-60, Univ. Elem. Sch., UCLA, 1960—; dean Grad. Sch. Edn., UCLA, 1967-83; chmn. Council on Coop. Tchr. Edn., Am. Council Edn., 1959-62; dir. research Inst. for Devel. of Ednl. Activities, 1966-82; mem. governing bd. UNESCO Inst. for Edn., 1971-79, vice chmn., 1974-75. Author: (with others) The Elementary School, 1956, Educational Leadership and the Elementary School Principal, 1956, (with Robert H. Anderson) The Nongraded Elementary School, 1959, rev. edit., 1963, (with others) Computers and Information Systems in Education, 1966, Looking Behind the Classroom Door, 1970, rev. edit., 1974, Toward a Mankind School, 1974, The Conventional and the Alternative in Education, 1975, Curriculum Inquiry: The Study of Curriculum Practice, 1979, Planning and Organizing for Teaching, 1963, School Curriculum Reform, 1964, The Changing School Curriculum, 1966, School, Curriculum and the Individual, 1966, The Dynamics of Educational Change, 1975, Facing the Future, 1976, What Schools Are For, 1979, A Place Called School, 1983; author, editor: The Changing American School, 1966, (with Robert H. Anderson) The Elementary School in the United States, 1973, (with M. Frances Klein and Jerrold M. Novotney) Early Schooling in the United States, 1973, (with Norma Feshback and Alvima Lombard) Early Schooling in England and Israel, 1973, (with Gary Fenstermacher) Individual Differences and the Common Curriculum, 1983; bd. editors: (with Norma Feshback and Alvima Lombard) Sch. Rev, 1956-58, Jour. Tchr. Edn, 1958-60; contbg. editor: Progressive Edn, 1955-58; mem. editorial adv. bd.: Child's World, 1952—; chmn. editorial adv. bd.: New Standard Ency, 1953—; chmn. ednl. adv. bd.: Ency. Brit. Ednl. Corp, 1966-69; contbr. chpts. to books, articles to profl. jours. Fellow Internat. Inst. Arts and Letters; mem. Nat. Acad. Edn. (sec.-treas.; charter mem.), Am. Ednl. Research Assn. (past pres.), AAAS, Nat. Soc. Coll. Tchrs. Edn. (past pres.), Nat. Soc. Study of Edn. (dir.). Office: Lab Sch and Community Edn Grad Sch Edn U Calif Los Angeles CA 90024

GOODLING, WILLIAM F., congressman; b. Loganville, Pa.; m. Hilda Wright; children: Todd, Jennifer. B.S., U. Md.; M.S., Western Md. Coll.; doctoral studies, Pa. State U. Various teaching positions including prin. West York Area High Sch.; supt. Spring Grove Area Schs.; supr. student tchrs. Pa. State U.; mem. 94th-98th congresses from 19th Pa. Dist.; mem. select com. on intelligence, edn. and labor coms. 94th-98th Congresses from 19th Pa. Dist. Served with Armed Forces, 1946-48. Republican. Methodist. Club: Lions. Office: 2263 Rayburn House Office Bldg Washington DC 20515

GOODMAN, ALFRED (GRANT GOODMAN), composer; b. Berlin, Mar. 1, 1920; emigrated to U.S., 1940, naturalized, 1943; s. Oskar and Paula Guttmann. Grad., Gymnasium in Berlin, 1937; student, Stern's Conservatory, Berlin, 1938-39; B.S., Columbia U., 1952, M.A., 1953; Ph.D., Tech. U. Berlin, 1972. Instr. Henry St. Settlement, N.Y.C., 1956-60; occasional music critic N.Y. weekly Aufbau; editor Westminster Records, N.Y.C., 1955; free lance music editor Bavarian Broadcasting Service, Munich, 1961, music editor, 1971—; instr. State Coll. Music, Munich, 1976—. Composer, accompanist theatre group in London, occasional scoring for, BBC, 1939-40; several tours with, Jimmie Lunceford and Charlie Barnet, 1944-46; arranger for, Buddy Rich, Noro Morales, Benny Goodman, and several other dance bands, N.Y.C., 1946-50; composer, arranger for: Movie Tone, 1957-60; incidental music for: Broadway play Bride in the Morning, 1960; Composer: 5 Inventions for Strings & Piano, 1946, String Quartet in C, 1947, Uptown-Downtown for Symphony Orchestra, 1947, The Audition; opera, 1948; Psalm XII for Baritone Solo, Women's Chorus and Organ, 1949, Divertimento for 3 Saxophones, 1949, Symphony No. 1, 1949, 7 Sketches for Piano, 1950, Cycle of 10 Songs for Tenor and Piano, 1950, Prelude 51 for Symphony Orchestra, 1950, Sinfonietta for Orchestra, 1951, Piano Pieces for Young People, 1951, Sonata for Trumpet and Piano, 1954, 5 Songs from the Bronx for Soprano, Woodwind Ensemble and Harpsichord, 1954, Sonata for Violin and Piano, 1955, 3 Madrigals Without Words for Mixed Chorus, 1956, 3 Sonatinas for Harpsichord, 1956, 4 Songs for Soprano Voice and Piano, 1956, 3 Odes for Mixed Chorus, 1956, String Quartet No. 2, 1959, Mayfair Overture for Symphony Orchestra, 1960, Prelude and Fugue for Organ, 1960, 4 Pieces for Organ, 1961, 7 Essays on Poems by Dylan Thomas for Alto, Tenor and Guitar, 1961, 3 Bagatelles for Piano, 1961, 3 Pictures for Tenor Voice and Big Band, 1961, Concerto for Clarinet and Orchestra, 1961, 3 Chants for Voice, Saxophone and Cembalo, 1962, Suite for Soprano-Alto Saxophone, Double Bass, Cembalo, 1963, Brass Quintet in Seven Rounds, 1963, 3 Meditations on Israel for Piano, 1965, 3 Monologues for Violoncello, 1965, Chamber Concerto for Violoncello, Doublebass and Keyboard Instrument, 1965, Little Suite for Flute, Oboe and Clarinet, 1966, Symphony No. 2, 1966, Quintet for Woodwind Ensemble, 1966, Seven Studies for String Trio, 1967, The Runner, 1972, Pro Memoria, 1973, Duo for Alto Saxophono and Harpsichord, 1972, 3 Ornaments for Voice, Flute and Piano, 1971, Individuation for Vocal and Orchestra, 3 Chants for Soprano and 8 Instruments, Aphorism for 2 Woodwind Quartets, 3 Meditations for Mixed Chorus, 1975-77, 2 Soliloquies for Double Bass, Across the Board for Brass Ensemble, 1977-78, 3 1/2 Moments for Flute, Viola, Guitar, 1980, Models for Big Band, 1980, Checking In for Voice and Piano, 1980, Ad Absurdum for Voice and Piano, 1980; others; arranger for: Olympic Hymn, 1972; also other music for Olympics.; Author: Musik in Blut, 1968, Music from A-Z, 1970, Die Amerikanischen Schueler Franz Liszt's, 1972, Dictionary of Musical Terms, 1982. Served with AUS, 1942-44. Address: Clemens Krauss St 22 8 Munich 60 Federal Republic of Germany *Music as a universal language has served and is obligated in serving for any understanding between peoples around the globe without discrimination of race or creed. Music has the task to contribute peaceful co-existence between mankind. There is no more glorious interpretation than the musical sound to be absorbed by the living.*

GOODMAN, ANDREW, business executive; b. N.Y.C., Feb. 13, 1907; s. Edwin and Belle Dorothy (Lowenstein) G.; m. Consuelo Man ach, Sept. 29, 1935; children: Vivien Malloy, Mary Ann Quinson, Edwin Andrew, Pamela Lichty. Student, U. Mich., 1924-26. With Bergdorf Goodman, 1926—, pres., 1951—, chmn., 1975—; gen. partner 754 Fifth Ave. Assos. (L.P.), N.Y.C., 1979—; dir. Guardian Life Ins. Co., H.M. Rayne, Ltd. of Eng.; hon. dir. Carter Hawley Hale Stores, Inc.; Bd. dirs. Fifth Ave. Assn.; trustee Fashion Inst. Tech. Life trustee Fedn. Jewish Philanthropies; bd. dirs., trustee United Jewish Appeal; v.p. Am. Jewish Com.; bd. dirs. Better Bus. Bur., N.Y.C.; hon. chmn. bd. Nat. Jewish Hosp., Denver. Served as lt. USN, 1944-46. Recipient Tobe award, 1960; decorated Star of Solidarity, Italy). Club: Westchester Country (Rye). Home: Hilltop Pl Rye NY 10580 Office: 754 Fifth Ave New York NY 10019

GOODMAN, BENJAMIN, lawyer; b. Memphis, Jan. 18, 1904; s. Ben and Leah A. (Hirsch) G. A.B., Princeton U., 1924; LL.B. (J.D.), Harvard U., 1927. Bar: Tenn. bar 1926. Since practiced in, Memphis; mem. Armstrong, Allen, Braden, Goodman, McBride and Prewitt, 1932—. Gov. A.R.C., 1955-61, chmn. com. resolutions, 1954; pres. Memphis Acad. of Arts, 1955-59; mem. Tenn. Law Revision Commn., 1963-69; chmn. Memphis Arts and Sci. Commn., 1970-77. Served from capt. to lt. col. USAAF, 1942-46. Mem. Am., Tenn., Memphis, Shelby County bar assns., Phi Beta Kappa. Home: 115 S Rose Rd Memphis TN 38117 Office: Commerce Sq Tower Memphis TN 38103

GOODMAN, BENNY, orch. condr., clarinetist; b. Chgo., May 30, 1909; m. Alice Hammond Duckworth, Mar. 1942; children—Rachel, Benjie. Student, Lewis Inst., Chgo.; studied clarinet with, Franz Schoepp of Chgo. Symphony Orch.; LL.D., Ill. Inst. Tech., 1968. Began in orch. Lake Mich. excursion boats; played in theatre orchs. in, N.Y.C.; organized own orch., 1933; began popular: radio program Let's Dance, 1934; conducted swing concerts at, Carnegie Hall, N.Y.C., Symphony Hall, Boston, Ravinia (Ill.) Park, Hollywood Bowl; clarinet soloist with, Budapest String Quartet, N.Y. Philharmonic Symphony, Phila. Symphony, Rochester Symphony, others, also concerts with various artists; radio programs including Camel Caravan, 1937-40, Old Gold, 1941, Victor Borge-Benny Goodman Show, 1946-47; appeared in: motion pictures A Song is Born; others; commentator on serious music, WNEW; TV show Star Time; recorded for, Columbia, Capitol, Chess, Command, Decca, Philips, RCA Victor records; life story filmed The Benny Goodman Story, 1956; re-formed big band, 1955 for engagements, U.S. and abroad; organized new band, 1958, Brussels World's Fair; toured, Europe, 1959; appeared with, London Philharmonic, 1961, State Dept. Cultural Exchange Program, tour of, Russia, 1962; toured, Europe with Brit. musicians, 1970-71 (Winner Internat. Jazz Critics Poll (clarinet), Europe with Brit. musicians (Apollo award 1956), Europe with Brit. musicians (named to Playboy Hall of Fame), Europe with Brit. musicians (Downbeat Hall of Fame.); Commissioned works by, Bartok, k4Copland, Hindemith.; Author: (with Irving Kolodin) Kingdom of Swing. Mus. good-will ambassador on tour Far East, under auspices of Dept. State and ANTA exchange program. Known as the King of Swing. Address: 200 E 66th St New York NY 10021

GOODMAN, BERNARD, engineering and construction firm executive. Chmn. Heyward-Robinson Co., Inc., N.Y.C. Office: Heyward-Robinson Co Inc. One World Trade Ctr New York NY 10048§

GOODMAN, BERTRAM, painter; b. N.Y.C., Sept. 21, 1904; s. Saul and Rose (Cohen) G.; m. Marie Caputa, Aug. 18, 1928. Student, Sch. Am. Sculpture, 1923-24, Art Students League, 1925. Has served on juries of Tiffany Awards, Bklyn. Soc. Artists (pres.), Nat. Assn. Women Artists. (Recipient First Prize in watercolor Screen Publicists Guild 1946, Purchase Prize, Abraham Lincoln Gallery 1947, Jo and Emily Lowe prize (oil painting) 1956, awarded one man show, Emily Lowe Award Gallery, N.Y.C. 1956), Exhbns. include, Am. Watercolor Soc., Pa., Acad. Fine Arts, Bklyn. Mus., Art Inst. Chgo., Mus. Modern Art, Whitney Mus. Am. Art, Balt. Mus. Art, Okla. Art Center, Carnegie Art Inst., Fine Arts Gallery San Diego, Met. Mus. Art, Albany Inst. History and Art, Nat. Acad. Fine Arts, Phila. Art Alliance, Soc. Graphic Arts, Am. Soc. Etchers, N.A.D., Art Inst. and Sch. of Design, Kansas City, Mo., City Art Mus., St. Louis, Mus. N.Mex., one man exhbns. include, Butler Art Inst., Youngstown, Ohio, Hudson Park Library, N.Y.C., The Research Studio, Maitland, Fla., Delgado Mus.; work in permanent collections of, Bklyn. Mus., Library of Congress, Abbott Labs., Chgo., Butler (Ohio) Art Inst., Tenn. Wesleyan Coll., Norfolk (Va.) Mus., N.Y. Pub. Library Print Collection, Abraham Lincoln High Sch. Collection, N.Y.C., Mus. City N.Y., lithography in, Met. Museum, also, pvt. collections., Dir. Village Art Center, N.Y.C. Mem. Artists Equity Assn. (dir. 1955-56), Bklyn. Soc. Artists, Am. Soc. Graphic Artists (governing council). Club: Print (Phila.). Home and studio: 299 W 12th St New York City NY 10014 *Although humanity has been reproduced by artists endlessly throughout the ages, I have always felt that it is possible to find in the mores of our contemporary life, the essence of image making with a new vitality.*

GOODMAN, CHARLES SCHAFFNER, educator; b. Detroit, Apr. 5, 1916; s. Lawrence Manche and Carolyn Jeanette (Schaffner) G.; m. Dorothy Ruth Irvin, Dec. 4, 1943; children: Carol Suzanne, Charles Schaffner. B.S., UCLA, 1938, M.A., 1940; Ph.D., U. Mich., 1948. Lectr. mktg. Wharton Sch., U. Pa., Phila., 1946-48, asst. prof., 1948-53, asso. prof., 1953-57, prof., 1957—, chmn. dept. mktg., 1974-78; dir. Auerbach Corp. for Sci. and Tech. Author: (with Reavis Cox) Distribution in a High-Level Economy, 1965, Management of the Personal Selling Function, 1971, La Force de Vente, 1973; contbr. articles to profl. jours. Served to lt. USNR, 1942-46. Recipient Alpha Kappa Psi award for best article in Jour. Mktg., 1968. Mem. Am. Mktg. Assn. (proc. mng. editor 1960-68), Beta Gamma Sigma, Pi Gamma Mu. Home: 393 Gen Washington Rd Wayne PA 19087 Office: Dietrich Hall Wharton Sch Philadelphia PA 19104

GOODMAN, DEWITT STETTEN, physician, scientist, educator; b. N.Y.C., July 18, 1930; s. Max and Jennie (Katz) G.; m. Ann Bregstein, July 7, 1957; children: Daniel W., Elizabeth. A.B., Harvard U., 1951, M.D., 1955. Intern Presbyn. Hosp., N.Y.C., 1955-56, asst. resident, 1958-59; investigator Nat. Heart Inst., 1956-58, 60-62; vis. fellow Hammersmith Hosp., London, Eng., 1959-60; mem. faculty, Columbia Coll. Phys. and Surg., 1962—, prof. medicine, 1969—, Tilden-Weger-Bieler prof., 1971—, dir. div. metabolism and nutrition, dept. medicine, 1971—; dir. Arteriosclerosis Research Center, 1976—; mem. staff Presbyn. Hosp., 1962—, attending physician, 1971—; vis. fellow Clare Hall, Cambridge (Eng.) U., 1972-73; adj. prof. Rockefeller U., N.Y.C., 1974-77; vis. prof. Hebrew U.-Hadassah Med. Sch., Jerusalem, 1981-82; Mem. metabolism study sect. NIH, 1966-70; mem. arteriosclerosis, hypertension and lipid metabolism adv. com. Nat. Heart, Lung and Blood Inst., 1978—; chmn. Gordon Research Confs. on Lipid Metabolism, 1968, chmn. on Arteriosclerosis, 1981. Co-editor, asso. editor: Jour. Clin. Investigation, 1967-71; editor, 1971-72; editorial bd.: Jour. Lipid Research, 1965-70; adv. bd., 1974—; editorial bd.: Jour. Biol. Chemistry, 1979—, Arteriosclerosis, 1981—. Career scientist Health Research Council, N.Y.C., 1964-74. Recipient Meltzer award Soc. Exptl. Biology and Medicine, 1963, Stevens Triennial award Columbia, 1971, Macy Faculty Scholar award, 1981-82; Guggenheim fellow, 1972-73. Mem. Am. Soc. Clin. Investigation (councillor 1973-76), Assn. Am. Physicians, Am. Soc. Biol. Chemists, Council Arteriosclerosis (chmn. 1979-81), Council Arteriosclerosis Am. Heart Assn. (exec. com. 1969-72, 78—), Endocrine Soc., Am. Inst. Nutrition (Osborne and Mendel award 1974), Harvey Soc. (councillor 1978-81, v.p. 1981-82, pres. 1982-83), Am. Oil Chemists Soc., AAAS, Phi Beta Kappa, Alpha Omega Alpha. Research, publs. on metabolism of cholesterol and cholesterol esters; turnover of cholesterol in man; atherosclerosis research; platelets and platelet-derived growth factor; metabolism of B-Carotene and Vitamin A; biosynthesis of Vitamin A from B-Carotene; retinol-binding protein and vitamin A transp.; transp. of blood lipids in blood plasma and interaction of lipids with proteins. Home: 7 Ernst Pl Tenafly NJ 07670 Office: Dept Medicine Columbia Coll Phys and Surg New York NY 10032

GOODMAN, DODY (DOLORES GOODMAN), actress, comedienne; b. Columbus, Ohio, Oct. 28; d. Dexter and Leona G. Student, Sch. Am. Ballet, Met. Opera Ballet Sch., N.Y.C. Stage debut as dancer with corps de ballet, Radio City Music Hall, N.Y.C., 1940; Broadway debut as dancer: High Button Shoes, 1947; in chorus: Miss Liberty, 1949; appeared: stage shows Call Me Madam, 1950, Wonderful Town, 1953, Shoestring '57, 1956, Parade, 1960, Fiorello!, 1962, A Rainy Day in Newark, 1963, A Thurber Carnival, 1965, Ben Bagley's Cole Porter Revue, 1965, My Daughter, Your Son, 1969, The Front Page, 1969, The Matchmaker, 1971-72, Lorelei, 1974, George Washington Slept Here, Kindling, Side by Side by Sondheim; toured in: Once Upon a Mattress, 1960-61; author: play Mourning in a Funny Hat; film script Women, Women, Women!; regular on: TV series Mary Hartman, Mary Hartman, 1976-77, Fernwood Forever, 1977, The Mary Tyler Moore Hour, 1979; other TV appearances include Love Boat; appeared in: film Bedtime Story, 1964, Grease, 1978, Valentine Day on Love Island, Grease II, 1982. Mem. AFTRA. Care Robert G Hussong Agy Inc 721 N La Brea Ave Suite 201 Los Angeles CA 90038 *

GOODMAN, DONALD C., university administrator; b. Chgo., Nov. 24, 1927; s. Alexander Goodman and Freda (Mermelstein) G.; m. Martha Huggins, July 3, 1968; children—Brian and Eric (twins), Michael and Susan (twins), Elaine Alison; stepchildren—Bruce, Adam, Mitchell. B.S., U. Ill., 1949, M.S., 1950, Ph.D., 1954. Instr. U. Pa., 1954-56; mem. faculty U. Fla., 1956-68, prof., 1963-68, chmn. dept. anatomical scis., 1965-68; co-dir. Center Neurol. Sci., 1964-68; prof. anatomy, chmn. dept. SUNY Med. Center, Syracuse, 1968-82, dean, 1973-82, interim dean med. scis., 1975-76, v.p. acad. affairs, 1975-78, v.p. research and acad. affairs, 1978—; v.p. acad. affairs East Tenn. State U., 1982, v.p. center, 1983—, v.p. health related professions, 1983—. Author books and articles.; Editor: Brain, Behavior and Evolution. Mem. study sect. NIH. Served with AUS, 1946-48. Recipient Annual Research award Fla. chpt. Sigma Xi. Mem. Am. Assn. Anatomists (exec. com. 1978—), Nat. Council Univ. Research Adminstrs., Soc. Neurosci., Am. Assn. Higher Edn., Sigma Xi. Home: Old Erie View Dr Fayetteville NY 13066

GOODMAN, ELLEN HOLTZ, journalist; b. Newton, Mass., Apr. 11, 1941; d. Jackson Jacob and Edith (Weinstein) Holtz; 1 dau., Katherine Anne. B.A. cum laude, Radcliffe Coll., 1963; hon. degrees, Mt. Holyoke Coll., Amherst Coll., U. Pa. Researcher, reporter Newsweek Mag., 1963-65; feature writer Detroit Free Press, 1965-67; feature writer columnist Boston Globe, 1967—; syndicated columnist Washington Post Writers Group, 1976—; radio commentator Spectrum, CBS, 1978—; commentator NBC Today Show, 1979—. Author: Close to Home, 1979, Turning Points, 1979, At Large, 1981. Named New Eng. Newspaper Woman of Year New Eng. Press Assn., 1968; recipient Catherine O'Brien award Stanley Home Products, 1971, Media award Mass. Commn. Status Women, 1974, Columnist of Year award New Eng. Women's Press Assn., 1975, Pulitzer prize for commentary, 1980, prize for column writing Am. Soc. Newspaper Editors, 1980; Nieman fellow Harvard U., 1974. Office: Boston Globe Boston MA 02102

GOODMAN, ELLIOT RAYMOND, polit. scientist, educator; b. Indpls., Sept. 3, 1923; s. Lazure L. and Esther (Miller) G.; m. Norma B., Mar. 1, 1947; children—Laura Goodman Humphrey, Jordan, Roger. A.B., Dartmouth Coll., 1948; M.A. and cert. Russian Inst., Columbia U., 1951, Ph.D., 1957; M.A. (hon.), Brown U., 1960. Ford teaching intern Brown U., Providence, 1955-56, instr., 1956-58, asst. prof., 1958-60, asso. prof., 1960-70, prof. polit. sci., 1970—. Author: The Soviet Design for a World State, 1960, The Fate of the Atlantic Community, 1975; contbr. numerous articles to profl. jours. Served with U.S. Army, 1943-46. Guggenheim fellow, 1962-63; NATO research fellow, 1962-63. Mem. Internat. Inst. Strategic Studies (London), Atlantic Council U.S. (politico-mil. com. 1971-74), New Eng. Polit. Sci. Assn., Am. Polit. Sci. Assn., Am. Assn. Advancement of Slavic Studies, Com. Atlantic Studies (N. Am. sect.). Home: 45 Amherst Rd Cranston RI 02920 Office: Dept Polit Sci Brown U Providence RI 02912

GOODMAN, ERIKA, dancer, actress; b. Phila., Oct. 9; d. A. Allan and Laura (Baylin) G. Student, Sch. of Am. Ballet, 1961-63. Mem. faculty Actors and Dirs. Lab., N.Y.C., 1979—. Dancer, N.Y.C. Ballet Co., 1964-65; dancer, Joffrey Ballet, N.Y.C., 1966—; prin. dancer, 1975. Office: American Ballet Center 434 Ave of the Americas New York NY 10011 *In my life as with my art, I have strived to achieve purity, truth and beauty—to preserve my integrity when it was challenged, and never to compromise the dictates of my heart.*

GOODMAN, GEORGE JEROME WALDO (ADAM SMITH), author, editor, investment executive; b. St. Louis, Aug. 10, 1930; s. Alexander Mark and Viola (Cremer) G.; m. Sallie Cullen Brophy, Oct. 6, 1961; children: Alexander Mark, Susannah Blake. A.B. magna cum laude, Harvard U., 1952, Oxford (Eng.) U., 1952-54. Reporter N.Y. Herald Tribune, 1952, Collier's mag., 1956, Barron's, 1957; contbg. editor, asso. editor Time and Fortune mags., 1958-60; portfolio mgr., v.p. Lincoln Fund, 1960-62; co-founder New York mag., 1967, contbg. editor, v.p., 1967-77; mem. editorial bd. N.Y. Times, 1977; exec. editor Esquire, 1978—; 1st editor Instl. Investor and Corporate Financing (formerly Investment Banking) mags.), 1967-72; chmn. Continental

Fidelity Group, 1980—, also dir.; exec. v.p., dir. Instl. Investor Systems, 1969-72; dir. USAIR, Inc., Hyatt Hotels, Gas Chem, Inc., Westengrand Fund; occasional lectr. Harvard Bus. Sch., Princeton; occasional columnist Newsweek, 1973; commentator NBC News, 1974, PBS, 1981—; editorial chmn. N.J. Monthly, 1976-79; adv. com. publs. U.S. Tennis Assn., 1978-83. Screenwriter, Los Angeles, 1962-65; Author: novel The Bubble Makers, 1955, A Time for Paris, 1957, Bascombe, The Fastest Hound Alive, 1958, A Killing in the Market, 1958, The Wheeler Dealers, 1959; pseudonym Adam Smith: The Money Game, 1968, Supermoney, 1972, Powers of Mind, 1975, Paper Money, 1980, also articles. Trustee Glassboro (N.J.) State Coll., 1967-71, co-chmn. presdl. selection com., 1968; trustee C.G. Jung Found.; mem. adv. council econs. dept. Princeton U., 1970—, chmn., 1975—; rep. com. on shareholder responsibility Harvard U., 1971-74, mem. vis. com. psychology and social relations dept., 1974—, mem. vis. com. Middle East Inst.; mem. adv. council Sloan Fellowships, Princeton U., 1976-79. Served with AUS, 1954-56. Recipient G.M. Loeb award for distinguished achievement in writing about bus. and fin. U. Conn., 1969, Media award for econ. understanding for TV documentary The Forty-Five Billion Dollar Connection Amos Tuck Sch., Dartmouth Coll., 1978. Mem. Writers Guild Am. (West), Asso. Harvard Alumni (dir. 1972-75), Authors Guild (dir. 1975—). Clubs: Harvard, Century (N.Y.C.). Home: 141 Fairway Dr Princeton NJ 08540 Office: care Internat Creative Mgmt 40 W 57th St New York NY 10019

GOODMAN, HAROLD S., lawyer; b. St. Louis, Aug. 17, 1937; s. David and Eva Katherine (Wasserman) G.; m. Karen K. Mauldin, Aug. 5, 1979; 1 son, James Richardson. A.B., U. Mo., 1960; LL.B., J.D., Washington U., St. Louis, 1963. Bar: Mo. 1963. Asso. firm Bishop & Goodman, St. Louis, 1963-70; v.p., gen. counsel, sec. World Color Press, Inc., St. Louis, 1970-75; individual practice law, St. Louis, 1975-81; partner firm Gallop, Johnson & Neuman, St. Louis, 1981—; dir. Warren Communications Corp., Spartan Printing Corp., Mango & Co., Chem. Color Plate Corp., Engravers Supply Corp., Mac-Fab Products, Inc. Mem. St. Louis County CSC, 1976-80; bd. dirs. World Color Press Charitable Found.; trustee Cystic Fibrosis Found., 1971—, pres., 1975; mem. Mo.-St. Louis Met. Airport Authority, 1980—. Mem. ABA, Mo. Bar Assn., Bar Assn. St. Louis, Washington U. Law Alumni Assn. (pres. 1976-77), Zeta Beta Tau (pres. trustee corp. 1964-69), Phi Delta Phi. Home: 466 Meadow Green Pl Creve Coeur MO 63141 Office: 7733 Forsyth Blvd Suite 1800 Saint Louis MO 63105

GOODMAN, HENRY MAURICE, educator, physiologist; b. Glen Cove, N.Y., May 4, 1934; s. Ely Barney and Mary (London) G.; m. Sandra Jacobson, June 25, 1961; children—Michelle Zeva, Julie Myra, Cara Beverly. A.B., Brandeis U., 1956; A.M., Harvard, 1957, Ph.D., 1960. Jr. fellow Harvard, 1960-62; instr. physiology Harvard Med. Sch., 1962, asso. physiology, 1962-65, asst. prof., 1965-69, asso. prof., 1969-70; prof. physiology, chmn. dept. U. Mass. Med. Sch., 1970—. Mem. Endocrine Soc., Am. Physiol. Soc. Research and publs. on growth hormone and physiology of adipose tissue. Home: 10 Dennison Rd Worcester MA 01609 Office: 55 Lake Ave N Worcester MA 01605

GOODMAN, HERBERT IRWIN, petroleum company executive; b. Pitts., Mar. 11, 1923; s. Meyer Irwin and Bessie (Crossof) G.; m. Mary Katherine Schilken, Aug. 12, 1978; children: Michael Christopher, Annekathryn, Nancy Hjortshoj, Sara Elizabeth, Mary Ellen. B.S., U. Pitts., 1943; cert., U. Besancon, 1945; M.B.A., Harvard U., 1949, A.M., 1950. Univ. fellow Harvard U., 1950-51; commd. officer U.S. Fgn. Service, 1951-57; 3d sec. Am. embassy, Copenhagen, 1951-53, Saigon, Vietnam, 1953-54, charge d'affaires, Phnom Penh, Cambodia, 1954-55; intelligence research officer Dept. State, 1956-57; with Gulf Oil Corp., 1957—, dir. fgn. crude oil sales, 1957-58, coordinator European sales, London, 1958-59; gen. mgr. Pacific Gulf Oil, Tokyo, 1960-64, coordinator crude oil dept., Pitts., 1964-66, coordinator for, Asia and Pacific, 1966-70; pres. Gulf Oil Co. South Asia, Singapore, 1970-72, Gulf Oil Trading Co., Pitts., 1972-75, Gulf Trading and Transp. Co., 1975—. Mem. adv. council Fletcher Sch. Law and Diplomacy; dir. U.S.-Korea Econ. Council.; mem. adv. council Energy and Environ. Ctr. Harvard U.; bd. govs. Middle East Inst.; trustee Caribbean Central Am. Action; mem. N.E. Asia Council for Strategic and Internat. Studies, Georgetown U.; bd. dirs. Mental Health Assn. Houston and Harris County; mem. scholarship com. Houston Livestock Show and Rodeo. Served to 1st lt. U.S. Army, 1943-46. Decorated Bronze Star; médaille de la Réconnaissance, France).; Aspen Inst. fellow, 1975—. Mem. Am. Petroleum Inst., Am. Chem. Soc., Am. Inst. Mgmt. (exec. council), Am. Mgmt. Assn., Council on Fgn. Relations, Assn. Asian Studies, Middle East Inst., Asia Soc., Japan Soc. Roman Catholic. Clubs: Duquesne (Pitts.); Aspen (Colo.); Harvard (N.Y.C.); Am. (London); Racquet, University, Petroleum, Woodlands Country (Houston). Office: PO Box 3726 Houston TX 77001

GOODMAN, HOWARD M., biochemistry educator; b. Bklyn., Nov. 29, 1938; s. Samuel G.; children: Sylena, William. Ed., Williams Coll., Mass. Inst. Tech., Cambridge (Eng.) U. Asst. prof. biochemistry U. Geneva, 1969-70; asst. prof. U. Calif., San Francisco, 1970-71, assoc. prof., 1971-76, prof., 1976-81; investigator Howard Hughes Med. Inst., 1978-81; chief dept. molecular biology Mass. Gen. Hosp., Boston, 1981—; prof. genetics Harvard Med. Sch., 1981—. Contbr. articles to profl. jours. Helen Hay Whitney Found. fellow; Am. Cancer Soc. fellow; Josiah Macy Faculty scholar. Mem. Am. Soc. Biol. Chemists. Office: Dept Molecular Biology Mass Gen Hosp Boston MA 02114

GOODMAN, JOSEPH WILFRED, electrical engineering educator; b. Boston, Feb. 8, 1936; s. Joseph and Doris (Ryan) G.; m. Hon Mai Lam, Dec. 5, 1962; 1 dau., Michele Ann. B.A., Harvard, 1958; M.S. in E.E., Stanford U., 1960, Ph.D., 1963. Postdoctoral fellow Norwegian Def. Research Establishment, Oslo, 1962-63; research asso. Stanford U., 1963-67, asst. prof., 1967-69, asso. prof., 1969-72, prof. elec. engring., 1972—; vis. prof. Univ. Paris XI, Orsay, France, 1973-74; dir. Info. Systems lab., dept. elec. engring., Stanford U., 1981—; cons. to govt. and industry, 1965—. Author: Introduction to Fourier Optics, 1968; contbr. articles to profl. jours. Recipient F.E. Terman award Am. Soc. Engring. Edn., 1971; research grants NSF; Air Force Office Sci. Research Office Naval Research. Fellow Optical Soc. Am. (dir. 1977—, Max Born award 1983), IEEE, Soc. Photo-optical Instrumentation Engrs. (bd. govs. 1979—); mem. AAAS, Sigma Xi. Home: 570 University Terrace Los Altos CA 94022 Office: Dept Elec Engring Durand 127 Stanford U Stanford CA 94305

GOODMAN, JULIAN, broadcasting executive; b. Glasgow, Ky., May 1, 1922; s. Charles Austin and Clara (Franklin) G.; m. Betty Davis, Oct. 13, 1946; children: Julie, John, Jeffrey, Gregory. A.B., Western Ky. U., 1943; A.B. in Econs., George Washington U., 1948; LL.D., William Jewell Coll., 1967; L.H.D., U. Fla., Gainesville, 1973. News reporter in, Ky.; news writer NBC, 1945-50, mgr. news, Washington, 1950-59; dir. news and pub. affairs NBC Network, 1959-61; v.p. NBC News, 1961-65, exec. v.p., 1965; sr. exec. v.p. NBC, Inc., 1965, pres., 1966-74, chief exec. officer, 1970-77, chmn. bd., 1974-78; dir. Gannett, Inc., Gulf Oil Inc.; past dir. NBC, RCA Corp., A.P.; Past chmn. radio and TV corrs. exec. com. U.S. Capitol. Trustee Mus. of Broadcasting. Recipient Robert E. Sherwood Meml. award, 1959; Gold medal Internat. Radio and Television Soc., 1972; Distinguished Communications medal Radio and Television Commn. So. Bapt. Conv., 1973; Paul White Meml. award Radio and Television News Dirs. Assn., 1973; George Foster Peabody award, 1975. Mem. Radio-TV Corrs. Assn. (past pres.), Radio-TV News Dirs. Assn., Broadcast Pioneers, Internat. Radio and TV Soc., Sigma Delta Chi (Hall of Fame N.Y. chpt.). Clubs: The Players, Federal City (Washington); Winged Foot (Mamaroneck, N.Y.). Office: NBC 30 Rockefeller Plaza New York NY 10020

GOODMAN, LAWRENCE BARON, retail exec.; b. N.Y.C., Nov. 10, 1926; s. Arthur Hirsch and Jeanette (Baron) G.; m. Claire Garber, Mar. 3, 1957 (dec. Apr. 1979); children—Laura Rose, Frank Garber, Emily Jean. B.A., Dartmouth Coll., 1947. Trainee Triumph Hosiery Mills, Inc., N.Y.C., 1948; asst. treas. Ormond Hosiery Shops, Inc., N.Y.C., 1949, partner, 1950-52; treas. The Ormond Shops, Inc., N.Y.C., 1953-69, pres., North Bergen, N.J., 1970—. Served with U.S. Navy, 1944-46. Jewish. Home: Premium Point New Rochelle NY 10801 Office: 7300 West Side Ave North Bergen NJ 07047

GOODMAN, LEO MAGILL, foreign service officer, judge; b. Dec. 7, 1909; s. Tobias and Emma (Magill) G. B.S.S., CCNY, 1931; student, Columbia U., 1931, J.D., 1934; postgrad., Hunter Coll., 1942, Practising Law Inst., N.Y.C., 1952, Indsl. Coll. Armed Forces, 1958-59, George Washington U., 1959; LL.D., U. Munich, 1972. Bar: N.Y. bar 1934. Practiced in, N.Y.C., until 1941; atty., examiner Dept. Justice, 1941-42; chief trial div. U.S. War Crimes Group, Germany, 1946-47; chief adminstrn. German justice div. Office Mil. Govt. Bavaria, 1948-48; chief presiding judge for Bavaria. U.S. cts. of Allied High Commn. for Germany, 1948-54; justice Ct. of Appeals, 1954-55; legal adviser Am. Embassy, Vienna, Austria, 1955-57, 1st sec., consul, 1956-57; assigned Dept. State, 1957-62; attended Nat. War Coll., 1962; consul gen. Am. Consulate Gen., Bremen, Germany, 1962-70; spl. adviser for Europe to Tobacco Assos., Washington, 1970-72, Bavaria to Am. C. of C. in, Germany, 1970—; U.S. justice Supreme Restitution Ct. in, Germany, 1977—; judge U.S. Ct. for Berlin, 1978—; mem. U.S. Adoption Rev. Bd. for Bavaria, 1948; U.S. mem. 4 power reparations, deliveries and restitution directorate Allied Council for, Austria, 1955-56, Joint Property Control and Restitution Commn. for, Vienna, 1955-56, Fulbright Scholarship Selection Com. for, Bavaria, 1953-54. Author: Selected Opinions of Leo M. Goodman, 3 vols, 1954, Bavarian Digest of Current Legal Opinions, 1949; contbr. to: Erwartungen, 1980. Founder, hon. pres. Leo Goodman Internat. Law Library, U. Munich, Germany, 1954; introduced Am. system of probation in, Germany, 1950; Mem. adv. bd. Munich Internat. Sch., also; European law internship program McGeorge Sch. Law, U. Pacific, also, Max-Planck Inst. for Internat. Patent and Copyright Laws, Munich. Served with AUS, 1942-46; ETO; col. USAF Res. Decorated Bronze Star, U.S.; Grand Cross with star Order Merit; Order Merit Bavaria, Fed. Republic Germany; recipient award City of Aachen, Germany, 1953. Mem. ABA, Am. Soc. Internat. Law, Am. Judicature Soc., Am. Assn. Comparative Study Law, Am. Fgn. Service Assn., Air Force Assn., Res. Officers Assn., German Am. Lawyers Assn. (adv. bd.), Alumni Fedn. Columbia U., Diplomat and Consular Officers Ret., Am. C. of C. in Germany (hon.), Fed. Bar Assn., Verein von Freunde des Fockemuseums Bremen, Carl Schurz Gesellschaft e.V., Ostasiatischer Verein Bremen, Fedn. German-Am. Clubs (v.p., bd. mem. 1970-72), Columbus Soc. Munich (curatorium), Gesellschaft für Auslandskunde (Munich), Peutinger Kollegium Munich, Smithsonian Assos. Clubs: zu Bremen, zur Vahr, Munich Herrenklub; Columbia Univ. (N.Y.C.); Internat., Nat. Lawyers, Dacor House (Washington); Kiwanis (hon.). Address: care American Consulate General APO New York NY 09108

GOODMAN, LEON, chemist; b. Livingston, Mont., Dec. 16, 1920; s. Sam and Sadie Clara (Kopald) G.; m. Marilyn Gene Shear, Feb. 1, 1956; children—Laura Elizabeth, Andrew Bentley. Student, Fresno State Coll., 1937-40; B.S. in Chemistry, U. Calif. at Berkeley, 1941; Ph.D., U. Calif. at Los Angeles, 1950. Chemist Los Alamos Sci. Lab., 1950-53; research asso., instr. U. So. Calif., 1953-54; chemist Stanford Research Inst., 1955-70, chmn. dept. bio-organic chemistry, 1961-70; prof., chmn. dept. chemistry U. R.I. at Kingston, 1970-76. Mem. Am. Chem. Soc., Chem. Soc. (London), N.Y. Acad. Scis., Sigma Xi. Spl. research chemotherapy cancer. Home: 118 Woodruff Ave Wakefield RI 02879 Office: Univ Rhode Island Kingston RI 02881

GOODMAN, LESLIE EUGENE, banker; b. Jersey City, June 1, 1943; s. Julius Victor and Sylvia (Miller) G.; m. Joyce Fischler, June 13, 1965; children: Deborah, Daniel. B.A., Rutgers U., 1965, M.B.A., 1970, J.D., 1980. Bar: N.J. 1981, Pa. 1981. Asst. v.p. First Nat. State Bank of N.J., Newark, 1966-73; sr. v.p. First Nat. State Bank of Central Jersey, Trenton, 1973-74, exec. v.p., chief operating officer, 1974-79, pres., chief exec. officer, 1979-80, First Nt. State Bank-County, Tenafly, N.J., 1980—; dir. FNSBancorp., Newark, FNSB-County, Hill Internat., Inc. Trustee, bd. govs. Hackensack Med. Center, 1982; trustee Greenwood House Home for Jewish Aged, 1977. Mem. ABA, N.J. Bar Assn., Pa. Bar Assn., Commerce and Industry Assn. No. N.J. (dir. 1980—), Phi Beta Kappa. Club: Greenacres Country. Office: 239 Main St Box 545 Hackensack NJ 07602

GOODMAN, MAX A., lawyer; b. Chgo., May 24, 1924; s. Sam and Nettie (Abramomitz) G.; m. Marlyene Monkarsh, June 2, 1946; children—Jan, Lauren, Melanie. A.A., Herzl Jr. Coll., 1943; postgrad., Northwestern U., 1946-47; J.D., Loyola U., 1948. Bar: Calif. bar 1948; Cert. family law specialist. Prof. Southwestern U. Law Sch., Los Angeles, 1966—. Contbr. articles to profl. jours. Served with AUS, 1943-45. Mem. State Bar Calif. (del. conf. dels. 1972, 80, 81), ABA, Los Angeles County Bar Assn. (chmn. family law sect. 1971-72). Home: 9466 Rembert Ln Beverly Hills CA 90210 Office: 675 S Westmoreland Ave Los Angeles CA 90005

GOODMAN, MICHAEL A., architect, educator; b. Lithuania, Jan. 7, 1903; came to U.S., 1921, naturalized, 1927; s. Agran and Yacha (Barger) Gutman; m. Mildred Jacobs, Mar. 9, 1935; children: Michael A., Jr., Louise M. A.B., U. Calif. at Berkeley, 1925, M.A., 1927. Faculty U. Calif. at Berkeley, 1927—, prof. architecture, 1945-70, emeritus, 1970—; research architect for Inst. Transp. and Traffic Engring., U. Calif., 1971-74; propr. firm Michael A. Goodman, architect, Berkeley, 1934—; mgmt. cons.; speaker on housing and bus. planning insts., Calif.; chmn. Berkeley City Planning Commn., 1954; pres. Bay Area Fedn. Planning Councils, 1964; chmn. Berkeley Housing Authority, Redevel. Agy. City of Berkeley. (Recipient Gold medal San Francisco Art Assn. 1925, award Fifty Prints of Year, Am. Graphic Artists Soc. 1930, 4 prizes state-wide exhbn. Calif. artists 1929-34, Berkeley Citation for distinguished achievement and notable service to U. Calif. 1970); Contbr. to archtl. publs.; prin. works include Bio-Chemistry and Virus Lab, all U. Calif. at Berkeley, County of San Mateo Hall of Justice and Records, Jail, East Bay Municipal Utility Dist. Adminstrn. Bldg, Berkeley Pub. Health Adminstrn. Bldg, First Savs. & Loan Office Bldg, Research Facility of Decombinant DNA Particles, Berkeley; one man exhbn., de Young Mus. and War Meml. Mus., San Francisco, 1934; participant annual shows, throughout U.S., 1929—; rep. museums, pvt. collections.; Sr. tech. def. planner, Fed. Office Civilian Def. for 8 Western States, 1941-43; contbr. to: OWI and Inter-Am. programs, 1942-46. Fellow Coll. of A.I.A.; mem. Am. Inst. Planners, Am. Pub. Works Assn., Am. Planning and Civic Assn., San Francisco Art Assn., San Francisco, Berkeley chambers commerce, San Francisco Mus. Art. Democrat. Clubs: Commonwealth (San Francisco); U. Calif. (Berkeley). Home: 29 Northgate Ave Berkeley CA 94708

GOODMAN, MURRAY, chemistry educator; b. N.Y.C., July 6, 1928; s. Louis and Frieda (Bercun) G.; m. Zelda Silverman, Aug. 26, 1951; children: Andrew, Joshua, David. B.S., Bklyn. Coll., 1949; Ph.D., U. Calif. at Berkeley, 1952. Postdoctoral fellow MIT, 1952-55; research fellow U. Cambridge (Eng.), 1955-56; mem. faculty Poly. Inst. Bklyn., 1956-71, prof. chemistry, 1964-71; dir. Polymer Research Inst., 1967-71; prof. chemistry U. Calif. at San Diego, 1971—, chmn. chemistry dept., 1976-81; Provost Revelle Coll., 1972-74; mem. steering com. human reprodn. unit WHO, 1974-79; mem. U.S. nat. com. Internat. Union Pure and Applied Chemistry, 1980—; Lady Davis vis. prof. Hebrew U., 1982. Author: (with F. Morehouse) Organic Molecules in Action, 1973. Editor: Biopolymers Jour, 1963—. Recipient Distinguished Alumnus medal Bklyn. Coll., 1965; Scoffone medal U Padova, Biopolymer Research Center, 1980. Mem. Am., Brit. chem. socs., Am. Soc. Biol. Chemistry, Biophys. Soc. Research, publs. on model systems of biopolymers, conformations, biologically active peptides, biospectroscopy, carrier drug conjugates, structure of macromolecules. Home: 9760 Blackgold Rd La Jolla CA 92037

GOODMAN, OSCAR R., economist, educator; b. Chgo., July 25, 1922; s. Benjamin and Anna (Faber) G. B.S., Northwestern U., 1943; M.S., U. Wis., 1948, Ph.D., 1952, J.D., 1960. C.L.U.; chartered fin. analyst. Mdse. control mgr. Alden's, Inc., Chgo., 1943-45; sr. market analyst Spiegel's, Inc., Chgo., 1945-46; instr. U. Wis., 1948-52; asso. prof. fin. State U. Wash., 1953-56, U. Calif. at Berkeley, 1956-58; vis. prof. U. Geneva, 1963, U. Mich., 1966; asso. prof. fin. Northwestern U., 1958-65; prof. fin. and econs. Roosevelt U., Chgo., 1966—, chmn. fin. dept., 1968-76, trustee, 1972-78; econ. cons. U.S. Dept. Justice Antitrust Div., U.S. House Banking and Currency Com.; expert witness U.S. Senate Com. on Antitrust and Monopoly; econ. cons. to fin. instns. and industry; lectr. Nat. Trust Sch., Am. Bankers Assn. Mortgage Banking Sch., Conf. State Bank Suprs. Sch. Author: Sales Forecasting, 1953; contbr.: articles to profl. jours. Ency. Brit. Mem. Am. Econ. Assn., Nat. Assn. Bus. Economists, Royal Econ. Soc., Am. Fin. Assn., Midwest Fin. Assn. (editor jour. 1977—, pres. 1978-79), Fin. Mgmt. Assn., Am. Risk and Ins. Assn., Inst. Chartered Fin. Analysts, Am., Ill. bar assns., AAUP, Acad. Internat. Bus., Beta Gamma Sigma, Phi Delta Kappa, Phi Delta Phi. Office: 430 S Michigan Ave Chicago IL 60605

GOODMAN, PERCIVAL, architect, planner; b. N.Y.C., Jan. 13, 1904; s. Barnet and Augusta (Goodman) G.; m. Naomi Ascher, Sept. 28, 1944; children—Rachel, Joel. Student, Beaux Arts Inst. Design, Ecole Nat. des Beaux Arts, Am. Sch. Fine Arts, all France. Pvt. practice architecture, N.Y.C., 1936—; faculty N.Y. U., 1931, Columbia U., 1946-71, prof. emeritus, 1972—; lectr. numerous colls. and univs. Painter, sculptor, book illustrator.; Author: (with Paul Goodman) Communitas, 1947, rev. edit., 1960, Double E, 1977; Contbr.: articles on art, architecture and city planning to encys. and mags. Double E; works include over 50 religious and community bldgs. throughout U.S. for Jewish orgns., numerous bldgs. for city and state of N.Y., planning studies especially for riverfront improvements, N.Y.C. Fellow AIA. Jewish. Home: 40 W 77th St New York NY 10024

GOODMAN, RICHARD EUGENE, advertising agency executive; b. Bklyn., Jan. 17, 1928; s. Carl Babe and Ruth E. (Glaubinger) G.; m. Susan Leach, Mar. 7, 1959; children—Todd, Lee. B.A., B.Letters, Rutgers U., 1949. Jr. copywriter Hicks & Greist Advt., N.Y.C., 1953-56; copywriter, then copy group head Grey Advt., N.Y.C., 1956-66; asso. creative dir. D'Arcy Advt., N.Y.C; creative dir. Dancer, Fitzgerald, Sample, Inc., N.Y.C., 1966—. Mem. Rutgers U. Alumni Assn. Unitarian. Clubs: Colony Beach and Tennis (Longboat Key, Fla.); Fairmount Country (Chatham). Home: 15 Huron Dr Chatham NJ 07928 Office: 405 Lexington Ave New York NY 10017

GOODMAN, ROBERT NORMAN, plant pathologist, educator; b. Yonkers, N.Y., Dec. 15, 1921; s. Sidney William and Margaret (Fried) G.; m. Phoebe Newman, Sept. 4, 1949; children: Joyce Beth, Rachael Lea, Janet Faith. B.S., U. N.H., 1948, M.S., 1950; Ph.D., U. Mo., 1952. Grad. asst. U. N.H., 1948-50; grad. asst. U. Mo., 1950-52, asst. prof., 1952-55, asso. prof., 1955-61, prof., 1961—, chmn. dept. plant pathology, 1968-79; postdoctoral fellow Swiss Fed. Inst. Tech., 1958-59, U. Leeds, Eng., 1965-66; vis. research prof. Hebrew U., Rehovot, Israel, also; vis. scientist Volcani Research Center, Bet Dagan, Israel, 1972-73; vis. scientist in residence dept. biophysics Weizmann Inst. for Sci., Rehovot, 1979-80. Author: (with H.S. Goldberg) Antibiotics: Their Chemistry and Non-Medical Uses, 1959, Advances in Pest Control Research, 1961, Antibiotics in Agriculture, 1963, Biochemistry of Physiology of Infectious Plant Disease, 1967; Contbr. articles profl. jours. Guggenheim Found. fellow, 1958-59; Lalor Found. fellow, 1958-59; NIH spl. fellow, 1965-66; Recipient U. Mo. Jr. Faculty Research award of merit, 1955, Sr. Faculty Research award, 1978. Fellow Am. Phytopath. Soc.; mem. Am. Soc. Microbiology, Sigma Xi, Gamma Sigma Delta. Home: 605 Crestland St Columbia MO 65201

GOODMAN, ROY MATZ, state senator, business executive; b. N.Y.C., Mar. 5, 1930; s. Bernard A. and Alice (Matz) G.; m. Barbara Christine Furrer, June 28, 1955; children: Claire Barbara, Leslie Alice, Randolph Bernard. A.B. cum laude, Harvard, 1951, M.B.A. with distinction, 1953; grad., Naval Officer Candidate Sch., 1953, Naval Supply Corps Sch., 1954. Dir. Ex-Lax, Inc., 1955-75, pres., 1962-71, chmn. bd., 1971-75, Ex-Lax Distbg. Co., Inc., 1975-80, also dir.; asso. buying and new bus. dept. Kuhn, Loeb & Co., investment bankers, 1956-60; pres., dir. Roycemore, Inc., 1968-70; dir. Manhattan Industries, Inc.; mem. Bklyn. adv. bd. Chem. Bank N.Y. Trust Co., 1963-65; commr. finance, finance adminstr. City of N.Y., 1966-68, mem. mayor's cabinet and supercabinet, 1966-68; mem. N.Y. State Senate, 1968—, chmn. housing and urban devel. com., 1968-76, chmn. investigations, taxation and govt. ops. com., vice chmn. spl. com. on culture industry; mem. finance, cities, edn., crime and correction, banks, aging coms., mem. spl. com. on moral obligation financing vice chmn. spl. com. on culture industry, 1976—; chmn. State Charter Revision Commn. for N.Y.C., 1972-76; adj. prof. pub. adminstrn. Baruch Coll. City U. N.Y., 1975. Mem. N.Y.C. Banking Commn., 1966-67; past trustee N.Y.C. Police Pension Fund, N.Y.C. Fire Dept. Pension Fund.; Chmn. Parents Com., Dalton Schs. Devel. Program; trustee, mem. Brotherhood-In-Action; trustee Heart Research Found.; mem. adv. council Inst. Philosophy and Politics of Edn. of Tchrs. Coll., Columbia; bd. advisors Council on Municipal Performance; exec. asst. to chmn. N.Y. State Assembly Jud. Com., 1963-64; asst. to atty. gen. State N.Y., 1960; pres. 9th A.D. Republican Club, 1963-64; del. N.Y. State Rep. Convs., 1966, 68, 70, Rep. Nat. Conv., 1972, 76, 80; mem. exec. com. N.Y. State Rep. Com., 1974—; treas. N.Y. County Rep. Com., 1965, now chmn.; Rep. candidate for Mayor of N.Y.C., 1977; past trustee Barnard Coll.; trustee Carnegie Hall Soc., Inc., Carnegie Hall Corp., Columbia Coll. Pharm. Scis., L.I. Coll. Hosp., N.Y. Com. Young Audiences, United Jewish Appeal, Tel Aviv U.; past bd. dirs. Freedom House, Dalton Sch.; mem. council advisors N.Y. Com. for Young Audiences. Served to lt. USNR, 1953-56. Recipient Distinguished Service award (Young Man of Year) Jr. C. of C., 1966, Mt. Scopus citation Hebrew U., Jerusalem, 1968; Scroll of Honor United Jewish Appeal, 1970; N.Y. State Republican of Year Ripon Soc., 1972; Medal of Merit City U., 1972; Man of Yr. award Brotherhood-in-Action, 1972; Humanitarian award Bronx County Soc. for Prevention Cruelty to Children, 1976; citation for community service Odyssey House, 1976; Our Town newspaper award for leadership in City Charter revision, 1976; Fiorella H. LaGuardia

Meml. award, 1979-80; citation Rep. Law Students Assn. of N.Y., 1981; citation for outstanding service N.Y. Young Rep. Club, 1982; named to honor scroll Columbia Assn. of N.Y.C. Police Dept., 1979. Mem. Anti-Defamation League (bd. govs. N.Y.), Am. Young Pres'. Orgn., Fin. Analysts Fedn., N.Y. Soc. Security Analysts, Council on Fgn. Relations, Am. Arbitration Assn. (panel arbitrators), Assoc. Harvard Alumni (past dir.), Omicron Delta Epsilon (hon.). Clubs: City, Wall Street (N.Y.C.); Senate of N.Y. State; Harvard (gov.), Harvard Business School (N.Y.C.); Century Country (Purchase, N.Y.); Fort Orange (Albany, N.Y.). Home: 1035 Fifth Ave New York NY 10028 Office: Suite 2400 270 Broadway New York NY 10007

GOODMAN, SAM RICHARD, consumer co. exec.; b. N.Y.C., May 23, 1930; s. Morris and Virginia (Gross) G.; m. Beatrice Bettencourt, Sept. 15, 1957; children—Mark Stuart, Stephen Manuel, Christopher Bettencourt. B.B.A., Coll. City N.Y., 1951; M.B.A., N.Y.U., 1957, Ph.D., 1968. Chief accountant John C. Valentine Co., N.Y.C., 1957-60; supr. budgets and analysis Gen. Foods Corp., White Plains, N.Y., 1960-63; budget dir. Crowell Collier Pub. Co., N.Y.C., 1963-64; v.p., controller Nestle Co., Inc., White Plains, 1964; chief fin. officer Aileen, Inc., N.Y.C., 1973-74, Ampex Corp., 1974-76; exec. v.p. fin. and adminstrn. Baker & Taylor Co. div. W.R. Grace Co., N.Y.C., 1976-79, Magnusen Computer Systems, Inc., San Jose, Calif., 1979-81; v.p., chief fin. officer Datamac Computer Systems, Sunnyvale, Calif., 1981—; lectr. N.Y. U. Inst. Mgmt., 1965-67; asst. prof. mktg. Iona Coll. Grad. Sch. Bus. Adminstrn., 1967—; prof. Golden Gate U., 1974—; prof. finance and mktg. Pace U. Grad. Sch. Bus. Adminstrn., 1969—. Author: also articles. Controller's Handbook. Served to lt. (j.g.) USNR, 1951-55. Mem. Fin. Execs. Inst., Nat. Assn. Accountants, Am. Statis. Assn., Am. Econs. Assn., Planning Execs. Inst. Home: 11566 Arroyo Oaks Los Altos CA 94022 Office: 680 Almanor Ave Sunnyvale CA 94086

GOODMAN, SHELDON LAWRENCE, investment banking company executive; b. N.Y.C., July 9, 1940; s. Elliott and Florence (Kleiderman) G.; m. Valerie Alice Jacobson, June 19, 1965; children: Jonathan, Alexandra. B.A. in Econs., CCNY, 1962, M.A., CUNY, 1967. Govt. bond trader Fed. Res. Bank of N.Y., N.Y.C., 1964-67; convertible bond trader Goldman Sachs, N.Y.C., 1967-70; gen. ptnr. Bear Stearns & Co., Chicago, 1970—. Home: 2121 Old Briar Rd Highland Park IL 60034

GOODMAN, STANLEY, lawyer; b. Cin., June 16, 1931; s. Sol and Ethel (Barsman) G.; m. Diane Elaine Kassel, Apr. 15, 1956; children—Julie Susan, Jeffrey Stephen, Richard Paul. B.A., U. Cin., 1953, J.D., 1955. Bar: Ohio, Ky. Partner firm Goodman & Goodman, Cin., 1955—; dir. Cin. Butchers' Supply Co., Winbco Tank Co., Ottumwa, Iowa, Bec, Inc., Trussville, Ala., Omeco-Boss Co., Omaha, Mi-Lo Health & Beauty Aids, Inc.; lectr. Ohio Bar Continuing Legal Edn. Series. Mem. ABA, Ohio Bar, Ky. Bar, Cin. Bar. Republican. Jewish. Clubs: Bankers, Losantiville Country. Office: 36 E 4th St Cincinnati OH 45202

GOODMAN, STANLEY JOSHUA, department store executive; b. Montreal, Que., Can., Mar. 23, 1910; came to U.S., 1932, naturalized, 1940; s. Issac and Jenny (Edinsweig) G.; m. Alice Theresa Hahn, June 16, 1936; children: Ellen, John Edgar. B.A., McGill U., 1931, M.A., 1932; M.B.A., Harvard U., 1934. With Arco Co., Cleve., 1934-36, C.I.T. Fin. Corp., 1936-42, Interstate Dept. Stores, 1942-48, May Dept. Stores Co., St. Louis, 1948-76, v.p., 1958-67, pres., 1967-76, chief exec. officer, 1969-76, chmn. bd., 1969-76; chmn. exec. com., dir. May Dept. Stopres Co., St. Louis; pres. Famous-Barr Co., St. Louis, 1959-67; owner Top Mgmt. Services, St. Louis, 1976—. Author: How to Manage a Turnaround, 1982; contbr. articles to popular mags. and profl. jours. Pres. Grand Ctr. Assn.; v.p. St. Louis Symphony Soc.; dir. Japan-Am. Soc., St. Louis; mem. bd. overseers, music vis. com. Harvard U.; mem. emeritus Civic Progress Inc. Fellow Royal Soc. Arts (London); mem. Nat. Retail Mchts. Assn. Clubs: Harvard (St. Louis, N.Y.C.); Noonday, University, Frontenac Racquet; Rowfant (Cleve.); Whittemore House (Washington U.). Home: 35 Briarcliff Saint Louis MO 63124 Office: Stanley J Goodman Top Mgmt Services 611 Olive St Suite 1914 Saint Louis MO 63101

GOODMAN, STANLEY LEONARD, advt. exec.; b. N.Y.C., Jan. 21, 1920; s. Abraham and Leah (Fellman) G.; m. Anita Davis, Aug. 30, 1960; children—Patricia, Laurence; stepchildren—Marilyn Rice, Stuart Rice. B.S. in Econs, Wharton Sch. U. Pa., 1941; certificate electronics, U. Richmond, 1943. Asst. to pres. Decca Records, Inc., N.Y.C., 1941-56; v.p., mktg. dir. Grayson Robinson Stores, N.Y.C., 1956-61; club plan creative dir. Popular Mdse. Co., Inc., Passaic, N.J., 1961-62, dir. mktg., 1962-64; pres. Elliot, Goodman & Russell, Inc., advt., N.Y.C., 1964, EGR Travel Promotion, Inc., 1969—, EGR Mktg., Inc., 1968—, EGR Communications, Inc., Detroit, 1969—; pres., dir. EGR Communications, Inc., N.Y.C., 1968—; dir. Pub. Service Mut. Ins. Co., N.Y.C.; Lectr. Am. Mgmt. Assn., 1964—; instr. mktg. dept. Pace Coll. Contbr. articles to sales mags. Mem. Sales Promotion Execs. Assn. (Sales Promotion Man of Year N.Y. 1959, internat. pres. 1960-62, honored Stanley Goodman grant 1954—), Direct Mail Advt. Assn., Council Sales Promotion Agys. (pres. 1969-71), Am. Mktg. Assn., Hundred Million Club, Westchester Alumni Assn. U. Pa. (v.p. 1966—). Home: 46 Crosshill Rd Hartsdale NY 10530 Office: 275 Madison Ave New York City NY 10017

GOODMAN, STEVEN BENJAMIN, singer, guitarist; b. Chgo.; s. Joseph Bayer and Minnette (Erenburg) G.; m. Nancy Pruter, Feb. 6, 1970; children—Jessie, Sarah, Rosanna. Student, U. Ill., Lake Forest Coll. Singer, guitarist clubs and concert halls, throughout U.S., 1967—; producer phonograph records.; Composer: City of New Orleans. Office: 4121 Wilshire Blvd Los Angeles CA 90010

GOODMAN, THOMAS J., ednl. adminstr.; b. Jersey City, May 5, 1931; s. Herbert Joseph and Elizabeth Agnes (Kelly) G.; m. Joan L. Blankenhorn, Sept. 13, 1958; children—Eileen Mary, Michael Thomas, Joan Theresa, Timothy James. B.S., Monmouth Coll., 1959; M.Ed., U. Hawaii, 1966; Ed.D., Syracuse U., 1976. Tchr. Woodbridge (N.J.) High Sch., 1957-58, Deal (N.J.) public schs., 1959-61, Lakewood (N.J.) public schs., 1961-66; dir. Nat. Tchr. Corps Program, 1966-67; tchr. seriously emotionally disturbed Syracuse (N.Y.) City Schs., 1967-70; dir. edn. Elmcrest Children's Center, Syracuse, 1970-76, asso. exec. dir., 1976-77; dir. child find N.Y. State Edn. Dept., 1977-78; supt. Columbus (Ohio) Devel. Center, 1978-81; commr. Div. of Programs and Services, Dept. Mental Retardation/Developmental Disabilities, State of Ohio, 1981—; bd. dirs. accreditation council; cons. in field. Guest editor: Forum of Profl. Jour. Council Exceptional Children, N.Y. State, 1976; editor: Jour. Am. Assn. Mental Deficiency, State of Ohio, 1980—. Served with USCG, 1952-56. Mem. N.Y. State Council Orgns. for Handicapped, NEA, N.Y. State Tchrs. Assn., Internat. Council Exceptional Children, Internat. Council Adminstrs. Spl. Edn., Nat. Assn. State Dirs. Spl. Edn., Am. Assn. Mental Deficiency, Nat. Assn. Supts. Public Residential Facilities for Mentally Retarded, Ohio Assn. Spl. Edn. Adminstrs., Phi Delta Kappa. Roman Catholic. Home: 5446 Taylor Ln Hilliard OH 43220 Office: 30 E Broad St Columbus OH 43215

GOODMAN, THOMAS LEO, superintendant of schools; b. Corvallis, Oreg., Oct. 14, 1929; s. Leo and Beatrice A. (Sasse) G.; children: Laurie Kay, Melissa C., Timothy T., Lindsay Susan, Amy Elizabeth. B.S., Oreg. State U., 1951, M.Ed., 1958; Ph.D., Ohio State U., 1965. Adminstrv. asst. to supt. San Diego Unified Sch. Dist., 1966-70, supt. schs., 1971-82, South Bay Union Sch. Dist., 1983—, Torrance Unified Sch. Dist., 1970-71, San Diego Community Coll. Dist., 1971-74. Mem. Gov.'s Commn. on Tchr. Preparation and Licensing, 1971-73; mem. exec. bd. San Diego Manpower Area Planning Council, 1973; mem. regional bd. NCCJ, 1971—. Recipient Distinguished Service award Miami U., Oxford, Ohio, 1972. Mem. Music Educators Nat. Conf. (hon. life). Presbyterian (elder). Home: 3410 Hawk St San Diego CA 92103 Office: 4100 Normal St San Diego CA 92103

GOODMAN, WALTER, author, editor; b. N.Y.C., Aug. 22, 1927; s. Hyman and Sadie (Rybakof) G.; m. Elaine Egan, Feb. 10, 1951; children: Hal, Bennet. B.A. magna cum laude, Syracuse U., 1949; M.A., Reading (Eng.) U., 1953. Editor, N.Y. Times, N.Y.C., 1974—, mem. editorial bd., 1977—, critic, 1983—; exec. editor WNET, 1979—, dir. humanities programming, 1980—; lectr. Salzburg Seminar in Am. Studies, Breadloaf Writers Conf., Columbia U. Sch. Journalism. Author: The Committee, 1968, All Honorable Men, 1963, The Clowns of Commerce, 1957, Black Bondage, 1969, A Percentage of the Take, 1971; also numerous articles. Guggenheim fellow, 1974. Mem. ACLU, P.E.N. Home: 4 Crest Dr White Plains NY 10607

GOODMAN, WILLIAM BEEHLER, editor; b. Bklyn, July 1, 1923; s. Philip Howard and Anne Louise (Landersman) G.; m. Lorraine Rappaport, Nov. 24, 1948; children: Jonas Robert, Sara Emily. B.A., Washington Sq. Coll., NYU, 1948; M.A., U. Mich., 1952. Editor coll. and trade Harcourt Brace Jovanovich Inc., N.Y.C., 1956-76; gen. editor Harvard Univ. Press, Cambridge, Mass., 1976-79; editorial dir. David R. Godine Pub. Inc., Boston, 1979—; tutor history and lit. Harvard U., 1953-54, lectr. in English, 1982-83, 84—. Contbr.: essay Reading in the 1980's, 1983. Trustee Warner Library, Tarrytown, N.Y., 1973-75. Served with U.S. Army, 1943-44. Mem. PEN Am. Ctr. Club: Harvard (N.Y.C.). Home: 240 Brattle St Cambridge MA 02138 Office: David R Godine Pub Inc 306 Dartmouth St Boston MA 02116

GOODMAN, WILLIAM I., urban planner, educator; b. Detroit, June 24, 1919; s. Morris and Bella (Kecner) G.; m. Pearl Meisner, Dec. 28, 1946; children—Ann, Deborah. A.B., Wayne State U., 1942, M.Pub. Adminstrn., 1950; M.City Planning, Mass. Inst. Tech., 1952. Planner Detroit City Planning Commn., 1943-50; resident planner Adams, Howard & Greeley, Hartford, Conn., 1952-53; dir. rezoning study Boston City Planning Bd., 1953-54; asst. prof. city planning Harvard, 1953-56; asso. prof. urban planning U. Ill., Urbana, 1956-60, prof., 1960-65, 71—, chmn. dept. urban planning, 1965-71, dir., 1976-79; planning cons., 1955—; dir. Office Urban Transp. Systems, U.S. Dept. Transp., 1971-73, now cons.; cons. ICA, Govt. Costa Rica, U.S. Office Regional Econ. Devel. in, Mass., Ill., Wis., S.D. Author: Principles and Practice of Urban Planning, 1968; Contbr. articles to profl. jours. Mem. Wabash Valley Interstate Commn., 1966—. Served with AUS, 1945. Recipient Merit award Am. Inst. Planners, 1969; Fulbright scholar to U.K., 1962-63; Am. Soc. Pub. Adminstrn. fellow, 1971-72. Mem. Internat. Fedn. for Housing and Planning, Am. Planning Assn., Am. Soc. Planning Ofcls. (edn. council), Am. Inst. Cert. Planners, Am. Inst. Planners (v.p., past mem. bd. govs., adv. bd. Jour.), Assn. Collegiate Schs. of Planning (pres. 1970-71). Home: 310 W Michigan St Urbana IL 61801

GOODNER, DWIGHT BENJAMIN, mathematician, emeritus educator; b. What Cheer, Iowa, Aug. 15, 1913; s. William Clifford and Myrtle Elizabeth (Harbour) G.; m. Mildred E. Wilson, June 29, 1936. B.A. with honors, William Penn Coll., 1934; M.A. (T. Wistar Brown fellow), Haverford Coll., 1935; Ph.D., U. Ill., 1949. Faculty S.D. State Coll., Brookings, 1937-42, 46; faculty Fla. State U., Tallahassee, 1949-78, prof. math., 1954-78, prof. emeritus math., 1978—, asso. dean, 1953-58; Cons. Com. on Accreditation of Armed Services Ednl. Experiences, 1950-59, Ednl. Testing Service, Princeton, N.J., 1965-70; mem. Com. on Undergrad. Program in Math., 1966-70, mem. cons. bur., 1963-71; cons., lectr. AID Summer Insts. for Coll. Tchrs., India, 1966, 67; visitor Inst. for Advanced Study, Princeton, 1971. Math. editor: Jour. Communication, 1959-61; Contbr. articles to tech. jours. Served with USNR, 1942-46. Mem. Math. Assn. Am. (cons. com. on ednl. media 1964, gov. 1967-71, cons. bur. 1971—), Am., London, Edinburgh, Indian math. socs., Phi Beta Kappa, Sigma Xi, Phi Kappa Phi, Pi Mu Epsilon, Phi Delta Kappa, Chi Gamma Iota, Lambda Chi Alpha. Presbyn. (elder). Home: 1317 Lemond St Tallahassee FL 32312

GOODNER, JAMES ERNEST, banker; b. Etowah, Tenn., Aug. 6, 1926; s. Miles Ernest and Callie Elizabeth (Howard) G. B.S., U. Tenn., 1948; postgrad., Rutgers U., 1963. With Am. Nat. Bank & Trust Co. of Chattanooga, 1949—, exec. v.p., 1973—; dir. N.E. Ala. Data Services, Inc.; State dir. Bank Adminstrn. Inst., 1974-75. Bd. dirs. Greater Chattanooga Area Heart Assn., 1968—; nat. bd. dirs. Children's Charities of Am., 1970—. Mem. Chattanooga C. of C., Sigma Alpha Epsilon. Episcopalian (treas.). Clubs: Lookout Mountain Fairyland; Ponte Vedra (Fla.). Home: 20 Stonedge Lookout Mountain TN 37350 Office: Am Nat Bank & Trust Co Chattanooga TN 37401

GOODNER, JOHN ROSS, JR., magazine editor; b. Beaver, Okla., Apr. 13, 1927; s. John Ross and Vesta (Carter) G.; m. Charlotte Gustafson, Aug. 19, 1950; 1 son, Charles; m. Sue Lummus, Feb. 11, 1962; 1 dau., Mary. Student, Panhandle A&M Coll., Goodwell, Okla., 1947-49; B.A., U. Okla., 1954. Sports writer Daily Oklahoman, Oklahoma City, 1953-62, N. Y. Times, 1962-66; mng. editor Golf mag., N.Y.C., 1966-67, editor, 1967-71, exec. editor, 1974-77; asso. editor Golf Digest mag., Norwalk, Conn., 1977—; sr. writer Grand Bahama Devel. Co., Freeport, Bahamas, 1971-72; mgr. N. Y. News Bur., Bermuda Dept. Tourism, 1973. Author: Golf's Greatest, 1978; Editor: Tips From the Teaching Pros, 1969, America's Golf Book, 1970; Contbr. to: Ency. of Golf, 1975. Bd. dirs. World Golf Hall of Fame. Served with AUS, 1945-46. Mem. Golf Writers Assn. Am. (Best mag. Story of Year award 1974). Office: 495 Westport Ave Norwalk CT 06856

GOODNIGHT, CLARENCE JAMES, educator; b. Gillespie, Ill., May 30, 1914; s. Charles A. and Phoebe (Personeus) G.; m. Marie Louise Ostendorf, Aug. 25, 1940; children—Ann Marie, Charles James. Student, Ill. Coll., 1932-33; A.A., Blackburn Coll., 1934; A.B., U. Ill., 1936, M.A., 1937, Ph.D., 1939. Instr. zoology U. Ill., 1936-39, 42-44, research asso., 1939-40; instr. biology Bklyn. Coll., 1940-42, N.J. State Tchrs. Coll., 1944-46; asst. prof. biology Purdue U., 1946-49, asso. prof., 1949-55, prof., 1955-65; prof. biology Western Mich. U., 1965—, head dept., 1965-75; cons. Sch. Sci. Curriculum Project U. Ill.; mem. com. Grad. Record Exam. Biology, Ednl. Testing Service, Princeton, N.J. Author: (with M. L. Goodnight) Zoology, 1954, (with M.L. Goodnight and R.R. Armacost) Biology: An Introduction to the Science of Life, 1962, (with M. L. Goodnight and P. Gray) General Zoology, 1964; also articles. Fellow A.A.A.S. (council); mem. A.A.U.P., Ecol. Soc. Am., Am. Micros. Soc. (pres. 1971), Am. Soc. Limnologists and Oceanographers, Soc. Systematic Zoology, N. Am. Benthological Soc. (sec.), Am. Inst. Biol. Scis. (governing bd.), Am. Soc. Zoologists (sec. 1973-76), Am. Arachnological Soc., Nature Conservancy, Am. Mus. Natural History (research asso.), Phi Beta Kappa, Sigma Xi. Democrat. Unitarian. Home: 1633 Chevy Chase Blvd Kalamazoo MI 49008

GOODNOUGH, ROBERT ARTHUR, artist; b. Cortland, N.Y., Oct. 23, 1917; s. Leo J. and Hariett (Summers) G. B.F.A., Syracuse U., 1940; M.A., NYU, 1950; student, New Sch. for Social Research, 1949, Ozenfant Sch. Art, 1950-51, Hoffman Sch. Art, 1951. Instr. painting NYU, 1953, Fieldston Sch., Riverdale, N.Y., 1953-60, Cornell U., 1960. Contbr. articles to nat. mags.; one-man shows, Tibor de Nagy Gallery, N.Y.C.; work exhibited in permanent collections, Albright Art Gallery, Buffalo, Art Inst. Chgo., Mus. Modern Art, N.Y.C., Whitney Mus., N.Y.C., NYU Mus., R.I. Sch. Design Mus., N.C. Mus. Art, also pvt. collections. Served with U.S. Army, 1941-45. Recipient award Art Inst. Chgo., 1962; Guggenheim fellow, 1972. Studio: 38 W 9th St New York NY 10011

GOODPASTER, ANDREW JACKSON, retired army officer; b. Granite City, Ill., Feb. 12, 1915; s. Andrew Jackson and Teresa Mary (Mrovka) G.; m. Dorothy Dulaney Anderson, Aug. 28, 1939; children: Susan Dulaney, Anne Morgan. Student, McKendree Coll., 1931-33; B.S., U.S. Mil. Acad., 1939; M.S.E., Princeton U., 1949, M.A., 1949, Ph.D. in Internat. Relations, 1950. Commd. 2d lt., C.E. U.S. Army, 1939, advanced through grades to gen., 1968; comdg. officer 48th Engr. Combat Bn., World War II, strategic and policy staff duty War Dept. Gen. Staff, 1944-47, mem. Joint Adv. Study Com., 1950, spl. staff asst. SHAPE, 1950-54, dist. engr. C.E., San Francisco, 1954, def. liaison officer and staff sec. to Pres. U.S., 1954-61, asst. div. comdr. 3d Inf. Div., 1961, div. comdr. 8th Inf. Div., 1961-62, asst. to chmn. Joint Chiefs Staff, 1962-66, dir. Joint Staff, 1966-67; dir. spl. studies Office Chief of Staff U.S. Army, 1967; sr. U.S. Army mem. mil. staff com. UN; comdt. Nat. War Coll., 1967-68; mem. U.S. Del. Paris negotiations with N.Vietnam, 1968, dep. comdr. U.S. forces, Vietnam, 1968-69, comdr.-in-chief U.S. forces, supreme allied comdr., Europe, 1969-74, ret., 1974, recalled, 1977-81, supt. U.S. Mil. Acad., 1977-81, ret., 1981; pres. Inst. Def. Analyses, 1983—; sr. fellow security and strategic studies Woodrow Wilson Internat. Center for Scholars, 1975-76; prof. govt. and internat. studies The Citadel, Charleston, S.C., 1976-77; chmn. Eisenhower World Affairs Inst.; spl. cons. to Vice Pres. U.S., Commn. Orgn. Govt. for Conduct Fgn. Policy, 1975; dir. New York Life Ins. Co., Bullock Funds. Author: For the Common Defense, 1977. Trustee Inst. for Def. Analyses, George C. Marshall Found.; v.p. Atlantic Council U.S., Internat. Inst. for Strategic Studies; mem. numerous adv. groups on strategy, security, internat. affairs, mgmt. and orgn. Decorated D.S.C., Def. D.S.M. with oak leaf cluster, Army D.S.M. with 3 oak leaf clusters, Navy D.S.M., Air Force D.S.M., Silver Star, Legion of Merit with oak leaf cluster, Purple Heart with oak leaf cluster, U.S. Medal of Freedom; numerous fgn. decorations including; Italian Mil. Cross of Valor; Korean Order Mil. Merit; Vietnamese Cross Valor; grand cross Mil. Order Aviz, Portugal; grand cordon Order Leopold, Belgium; grand cross with swords Order Orange-Nassau, Netherlands; grand cross 1st class Order of Merit, Fed. Republic Germany; Distinguished Service medal Turkish Armed Forces. Mem. Nat. Acad. Pub. Adminstrn., Council Fgn. Relations, Soc. Am. Mil. Engrs., Sigma Xi, Phi Kappa Phi. Club: University (N.Y.C.). Home: 409 N Fairfax St Alexandria VA 22314 Office: care Dept Army Washington DC 20310

GOODPASTURE, JAMES DALE, lawyer, fin. co. exec.; b. Frederick, Okla., Nov. 8, 1942; s. Robert James and Maenette (Taylor) G. B.B.A., U. Okla., 1964, LL.B., 1966. Bar: Okla. bar 1966, N.Y. bar 1967. Atty. Morgan Guaranty Trust Co., N.Y.C., 1966-68, asst. resident counsel, 1968-72, asst. resident counsel, asst. sec., 1972-77, sec., 1977—, J.P. Morgan & Co., 1977—. Mem. Am. Bar Assn., N.Y. State Bar Assn., Assn. Bar City N.Y., Okla. Bar Assn., Am. Soc. Corp. Secs. Methodist. Home: 80 Lakewood Rd Staten Island NY 10301 Office: 23 Wall St New York NY 10015

GOODREDS, JOHN STANTON, newspaper publisher; b. Buffalo, July 7, 1934; s. V. Spencer and Pansy (Nisbet) G.; m. Helen Walter, Aug. 11, 1962; children—John, Cynthia. B.A. in Econs. with honors, Colgate U., 1956; M.B.A. in Fin, Syracuse (N.Y.) U., 1970. Mgmt. trainee Gen. Electric Co., Syracuse, 1956-60; with Bristol Labs., Syracuse, 1960-70, budget mgr., 1968-70; exec. v.p. Ottaway Newspapers, Inc., Campbell Hall, N.Y., 1970—. Bd. dirs. Arden Hill Hosp., Goshen, N.Y., 1978—, Hudson-Delaware council Boy Scouts Am. Served with AUS, 1957-58. Mem. Inst. Newspaper Cotrollers and Fin. Officers, N.Y. State Pubs. Assn. Episcopalian. Club: Orange County Golf (pres. 1979). Home: 43 Gregory Dr Goshen NY 10924 Office: PO Box 401 Campbell Hall NY 10916

GOODRICH, GEORGE HERBERT, judge; b. Charleston, W.Va., June 19, 1925; s. Edgar Jennings and Beulah Etta (Lenfest) G.; m. Nancy Ann Needham, Sept. 3, 1949; children: George Herbert, Craig N., Thomas A. B.A., Williams Coll., 1949; LL.B., U. Va., 1952. Bar: D.C. bar 1953, Md. bar 1958. Gen. practice law, Washington, also, Md., 1953-69; asso. judge D.C. Superior Ct., 1969—; lectr. law Am. U., 1969-74. Pres. Homemakers Service, 1962-63; v.p. Hillcrest Children's Center, 1963-69; mem. community adv. com. Jr. League D.C., 1969-73; bd. dirs. ARC. Served with USNR, 1943-46. Mem. D.C. Bar Assn., Am. Law Inst., Delta Psi. Republican. Episcopalian. Club: Chevy Chase. Home: 6003 Corbin Rd NW Washington DC 20816 Office: DC Superior Ct 500 Indiana Ave NW Washington DC 20001

GOODRICH, HENRY CALVIN, natural resource and energy company executive; b. Fayetteville, Tenn., Apr. 24, 1920; s. Charles Landess and Maude (Baxter) G.; m. Billie Grace Walker, Sept. 10, 1943; children: Thomas Michael, William Walker, Sydney Lee Goodrich Green. Student, Erskine Coll., 1938-39; B.S. U. Tenn, 1943; LL.D. (hon.), Butler U., 1976, D.B.A., Marion Coll., 1978. Engr., project engr., project mgr. to sr. v.p., dir. Rust Engring. Co., Birmingham, Ala. and; Pitts., 1946-67; exec. v.p., dir. Inland Container Corp., Indpls., 1968-69, chmn., pres., chief exec. officer, 1970-79; chmn. Ga. Kraft Co., Rome, Ga., 1974-79; pres., chief operating officer So. Natural Resources, Inc., Birmingham, Ala., 1980, chmn., pres., chief exec. officer, 1980—; dir. Time, Inc., Protective Life Ins. Co., Ball Corp., Muncie, Ind., Offshore Co., Sonat Exploration Co., Houston, So. Natural Gas Co., Birmingham, Ala. Bd. dirs. St. Vincents Hosp. Found., Birmingham, 1980—; trustee Inst. Paper Chemistry; mem. adv. council U. Ala., Birmingham. Served to lt., C.E. USNR, 1943-46. Fellow ASCE; mem. Am. Paper Inst. (dir.), TAPPI, Newcomen Soc., Kappa Alpha, Tau Beta Pi, Omicron Delta Kappa, Beta Gamma Sigma. Presbyterian. Clubs: Rotary; Blind Brook (N.Y.); Mountain Brook, Shoal Creek (Birmingham); Lyford Cay (Bahamas); Ramada (Houston). Home: 2608 Caldwell Mill Ln Birmingham AL 35243 Office: 3000 First Nat-So Natural Bldg Birmingham AL 35203

GOODRICH, JOHN BERNARD, lawyer, ry. exec.; b. Spokane, Wash., Jan. 4, 1928; s. John Casey and Dorothy (Koll) G.; m. Therese H. Vollmer, June 14, 1952; children—Joseph B., Bernadette M., Andrew J., Philip M., Thomas A., Mary Elizabeth, Jennifer H., Rosanne M. J.D., Gonzaga U., 1954. Bar: Ill. bar 1955, Wash. bar 1954. Indsl. traffic mgr. Pacific N.W. Alloys, Spokane, 1950-54; asst. to gen. counsel Cromium Mining & Smelting Corp., Chgo., 1954-56; with Monon R.R., 1956-69, atty., gen. solicitor, 1956-66, sec., 1957-69, treas., 1959-66, v.p. law, 1966-69; also dir.; sec.-treas. I.C.G.R.R., Chgo., 1970-79, sec., gen. atty., 1979—; sec. G.M. & O. Land Co., Gulf Transport Co., Chgo. Intermodal Co., all Chgo.; dir. Peoria & Pekin Union R.R., Terminal R.R. Assn. St. Louis, St. Louis, Kansas City Terminal Ry. Co., Miss. Export R.R., Moss Point, Trailer Train Co.,

Chgo., Railbox Co. Mem. Park Forest, Traffic and Safety Commn., 1963-66; mem. Park Forest Recreation Bd., 1966-77, chmn., 1969-70; trustee Village of Park Forest, 1977-80. Served with AUS, 1946-48. Mem. Wash. Bar Assn., Newcomen Soc. Republican. Roman Catholic. Clubs: K.C. (4 deg.), Elk., University, Economic (Chgo.); Olympia Fields Country. Home: 47 Apple Ln Park Forest IL 60466 Office: 233 N Michigan Ave Chicago IL 60601

GOODRICH, KENNETH PAUL, univ. dean; b. Elkhorn, Wis., 1933; s. Kenneth Potter and Helene (Keller) G.; m. Elaine L. Ashby, June 12, 1954; children—Laurel Lynn, David Kenneth, Paul Ashby, Karen Elaine. A.B. Oberlin Coll, 1955; M.A., U. Ia., 1958, Ph.D., 1959. Mem. faculty U. Pa. Phila., 1959-63; lectr., project asso. U. Wis., Madison, 1963-65; mem. faculty psychology Macalester Coll., St. Paul, 1965-73, chmn. dept. psychology, 1965-67, dean coll., 1967-69, dean and dir. ednl. resources, 1969-71, v.p. for acad. affairs and provost, 1971-73; dean Coll. Arts and Scis., prof. psychology Syracuse (N.Y.) U., 1973-78; provost, prof. psychology Ohio Wesleyan U., Delaware, 1978—. Dir. Group Health Plan, Inc., St. Paul, 1970-73. Mem. AAUP, Am. Assn. Higher Edn., Am. Conf. Acad. Deans. Home: 213 W Lincoln Ave Delaware OH 43015 office: linfield college mcminville oregon 97128

GOODRICH, LELAND MATTHEW, international relations educator; b. Lewiston, Maine, Sept. 1, 1899; s. Fred Bartlett and Alice Mae (Tibbetts) G.; m. Eleanor Allen, June 30, 1928; children: Richard Allen, John Bradbury. A.B., Bowdoin Coll., 1920, Sc.D., 1952; A.M., Harvard, 1921, Ph.D., 1925; LL.D., Columbia, 1972. Instr. polit. sci. Brown U., 1922-23, asst. prof. polit. sci., 1926-31, asso. prof., 1931-46, prof., 1946-50; instr. govt. and law Lafayette Coll., 1925-26; prof. internat. orgn. and administrn. Columbia, 1950-67, acting chmn. dept. pub. law and govt., 1965-66, James T. Shotwell prof. internat. relations, 1967-68, emeritus, 1968—; vis. lectr. in govt. Harvard, 1949-50; prof. internat. orgn. and adminstrn. Fletcher Sch. of Law and Diplomacy, 1944—; vis. prof. Sch. Internat. Affairs, Columbia, 1948-49, U. Toronto, 1969-71; dir. World Peace Found., 1942-46, Belgian-Am. Ednl. Found., 1953—; Mem. Sec. Gen.'s com. to review orgn. and activities UN Secretariat, 1961. Author: (with Edvard Hambro) Charter of the United Nations: Commentary and Documents, rev, 1949, 69, (with Anne Simons) The United Nations and the Maintenance of International Peace and Security, 1955, Korea: A Study of United States Policy in the United Nations, 1956, The United Nations, 1959, The United Nations in a Changing World, 1974; Editor: (with S. Shepard Jones and Denys Myers) Documents on Am. Foreign Relations, Vol. IV, 1942, (with Marie J. Carroll), Volumes V-VII, 1945, 46, 47; co-editor: The United Nations in the Balance, 1965; Author articles. Mem. Internat. Secretariat, UN Conf. on Internat. Orgn., 1945; chmn. bd. editors Internat. Orgn., 1947-54, mem., 1947-75; Trustee World Peace Found.; trustee overseer Bowdoin Coll. Mem. Fgn. Policy Assn. (chmn. R.I. 1928-35), Council on Fgn. Relations (sec. Providence com. fgn. relations 1942-48), Am. Soc. Internat. Law (exec. council 1940-43), Am. Polit. Sci. Assn., Acad. Polit. Sci (dir. 1973—), Phi Beta Kappa, Psi Upsilon. Conglist. Home: 460 Riverside Dr New York NY 10027

GOODRICH, LLOYD, museum officer, author; b. Nutley, N.J., July 10, 1897; s. Henry Wickes and Madeleine (Lloyd) G.; m. Edith Havens, Jan. 12, 1924; children: David Lloyd, Madeleine Goodrich Noble. Ed., Nutley High Sch., Art Students League and Nat. Acad. of Design, N.Y.C.; D.F.A., Cornell Coll., Iowa, 1963, Colby Coll., 1964, R.I. Sch. Design, 1977. With Macmillan Co. (pubs.), 1923-25; asso. editor The Arts, 1925-27, 1928-29, European editor, 1927-28, contbg. editor, 1929-31; asst. art critic N.Y. Times, 1929; writer, researcher Whitney Mus. Am. Art, 1931-35, research curator, 1935-47, asso. curator, 1947-48, asso. dir., 1948-58, dir., 1958-68, adv. dir., 1968-71, dir. emeritus, 1971—; mem. N.Y. Regional Com., Pub. Works Art Project, 1933-34; founder, dir. Am. Art Research Council, 1942-49; chmn. editorial bd. Mag. of Art, 1942-50; former mem. editorial bd. Art Bull., Art in Am.; mem. editorial bd. Am. Art Jour.; mem. adv. bd. Carnegie Study Am. Art; adv. com. Archives of Am. Art; chmn. Com. on Govt. and Art, 1948-54; mem. Nat. Council on Arts and Govt., 1954-74, vice-chmn., 1962-74; v.p. Sara Roby Found., 1956—; trustee Am. Fedn. Arts, 1942—, v.p., 1957-62, hon. v.p., 1962—; mem. Nat. Mus. Am. Art Commn.; adv. bd. Swann Found. for Caricature and Cartoons; co-chmn. Joint Artists-Mus. Com., 1950-58; mem. Counseil Scientifique Internat., Enciclopedia Universale dell'Arte; asso. seminar Am. Civilization, Columbia; trustee Whitney Mus. Am. Art, 1961-75, hon. trustee, 1975—; mem. Adv. Com. Art for the White House, 1960-63; bd. dirs. Edward MacDowell Assn., 1965-72; mem. adv. com. Friends of Am. Art in Religion. Lectr. and writer on art, especially Am. art; author: books and exhbn. catalogs including Thomas Eakins, 1933, Winslow Homer, 1944, Yasuo Kuniyoshi, 1948, Max Weber, 1949, John Sloan, 1952, Albert P. Ryder, 1959, Pioneers of Modern Art in America, 1963, Three Centuries of American Art, 1966, Graphic Art of Winslow Homer, 1968, Winslow Homer's America, 1969, Georgia O'Keeffe, 1970, Edward Hopper, 1971, Reginald Marsh, 1972, Raphael Soyer, 1972, Thomas Eakins, 2 vols., 1982; co-author: Am. Art of Our Century, 1961; editor: Research in American Art, 1945, Mus. and the Artist, 1958; Contbr. to: New Art in America, 1957. Recipient Art in Am. award, 1959, art award Nat. Art Materials Trade Assn., 1964, award of merit Phila. Mus. Coll. Art, 1964; Creative Arts award Brandeis U., 1970; award for excellence in art history Art Dealers Assn. Am., 1977, for disting. service to arts Am. Acad. and Inst. Arts and Letters, 1979, for disting. contbn. to Am. art history Archives Am. Art, 1979; Gov.'s award Skowhegan Sch. Painting and Sculpture, 1981. Fellow Am. Acad. Arts and Scis.; hon. mem. Art Students League N.Y., Assn. Art Mus. Dirs.; mem. Internat. Art Critics Assn., Drawing Soc., Am. Inst. Interior Designers (hon.). Office: Whitney Mus Am Art 945 Madison Ave at 75th St New York NY 10021

GOODRICH, NORMA LORRE (MRS. JOHN H. HOWARD), educator; b. Huntington, Vt., May 10, 1917; d. Charles Edmund and Edyth (Riggs) Falby; m. J.M.A. Lorre, Dec. 10, 1943 (div. June 1946); 1 son, Jean-Joseph; m. John Hereford Howard, Jan. 20, 1964. B.S. cum laude, U. Vt., 1938; postgrad. (U. Vt. fellow), U. Grenoble, France, 1938-39; Ph.D. (Ellis fellow), Columbia, 1965. Tchr. high schs. in Vt., 1939-43, Bentley Sch., N.Y.C., 1943-47; owner dir. Am. Villa in Normandy, Trouville, France, 1947-53; tchr. Fieldston Sch., N.Y.C., 1954-63; asst. prof. French U. So. Calif., 1964-66, asso. prof., 1966-71; dean faculty Scripps Coll., Claremont, Calif., 1971-72; prof. French and comparative lit. Claremont Colls., 1972; vis. scholar Calif. Luth. Coll., 1975. Author: Ancient Myths, 1959, rev. edit., 1977, Medieval Myths, 1960, rev. edit., 1977, Doctor and Maria Theresa, 1961, Myths of the Hero, 1961, Ways of Love, 1963, Charles of Orleans: A Study of Themes in His French and English Poetry, 1967, Giono: Master of Fictional Modes, 1973; contbr. articles to internat. profl. jours. Mem. pub. relations staff Worthington Corp., N.Y.C., 1953-54; Bd. dirs., patron West End Opera Assn., 1973-74, program dir., 1975-76. Mem. Assn. Study of Dada and Surrealism (sec. 1970-72), Philol. Assn. Pacific Coast (nominating com. 1971-72), Modern Lang. Assn. Am. (mem. del. assembly's election com. 1975), Phi Kappa Phi. Home: 620 Diablo Dr Claremont CA 91711 *I believe in the creative power of certain individuals who, because of this power or gift, must be allowed by society to be alone, work alone, and alone to perfect their work. Our education must be more lenient to these individuals and more understanding of that individual who does not conform to the average.*

GOODRICH, ROBERT EDWARD, JR., clergyman; b. Cleburne, Tex., June 9, 1909; s. Robert Edward and Moye (Wilson) G.; m. Thelma Quillian, June 5, 1939; children—Thelma Jean, Lucy Goodrich Gadol, Robert Edward III, Paul Quillian. B.A., Birmingham-So. U., 1931; M.A., Perkins Theol. Sch., 1940; D.D., Centenary Coll., 1950; LL.D., Central Coll., 1973. Ordained to ministry Methodist Ch., 1933; pastor in, Port Arthur, Tex., 1935-37, Houston, 1937-44, El Paso, Tex., 1944-46, First Meth. Ch., Dallas, from 1946; bishop United Meth. Ch., 1972—; formerly presiding over Mo. area, now bishop-in-residence St. Luke's Meth. Ch., Houston.; Past chmn. jurisdictional council So. Central Jurisdiction Meth. Ch., also; past chmn. jurisdictional TV, radio and film commn.; del. World Meth. Conf., 1966, 76; Gen. Conf., 1952, 66, 60, 64, 68, 70, 72. Author: What's It All About, 1955, Reach for the Sky, 1960, Lift Up Your Heart, 1961, On the Other Side of Sorrow, 1962, 70, Dear God Where Are You?, 1969; Created 1st dramatic religious TV show, 1949; preacher on radio. Chmn. bd. trustees St. Paul Sch. Theology, Kansas City, Mo., 1972—; trustee Southwestern U., So. Meth. U., Meth. Home for Children. Mem. Kappa Alpha. Address: St Luke's United Meth Ch PO Box 22013 Houston TX 77227

GOODRUM, DANIEL SHEPARD, banker; b. Leslie, Ga., July 11, 1926; s. John Warren and Inez (Culp) G.; m. Margaret Emily Swanson, June 8, 1949; children: John Daniel, William James. B.S.B.A., U. Fla., 1949. Trainee to store supt. B.F. Goodrich Co., Jacksonville, Fla., 1949-57; v.p. Fla. Nat. Bank, Jacksonville, 1957-62; sr. v.p. 1st Nat. Bank, Ft. Lauderdale, Fla., 1962-66; v.p. 1st Marine Banks Inc., Riviera Beach, Fla., 1966-73; pres., chief exec. officer Century Banks Inc., Ft. Lauderdale, 1973-82; sr. exec., v.p. Sun Banks of Fla., Ft. Lauderdale, 1982—; dir. Fed. Res. Bank, Miami br., 1981—. Bd. dirs. Broward Community Coll. Found. Trustees, Ft. Lauderdale, 1975—. Served to sgt. USAF, 1950-51. Mem. Fla. Bankers Assn. (pres. 1972-73), Am. Bankers Assn. (exec. council 1977-79). Republican. Episcopalian. Clubs: Sail Fish (Palm Beach, Fla.); Coral Ridge Country (Ft. Lauderdale). Home: 900 Virginia Dr Winter Park FL 32789 Office: Sun Banks of Florida Inc 200 Orange Ave Orlando FL 32802

GOODSON, CARL EDWARD, religion educator; b. St. Louis, July 31, 1917; s. Harry Edward and Clara (Cummins) G.; m. Rozelle Wordingham, May 31, 1944; children: Mary (Mrs. Lynn Clark), Nancy Lea (Mrs. Dennis Mills), Margery (Mrs. Daniel Lumpkin), Charlotte Rose (Mrs. Howard Jones), Timothy Carl. A.B., William Jewell Coll., 1939; Th.M., So. Baptist Theol. Sem., 1944; Th.D., Central Bapt. Theol. Sem., 1951. Ordained to ministry Baptist Ch., 1940; pastor Baptist Ch. Smiths Grove, Ky., 1944-45, Columbia, Mo., 1945-46; mem. faculty Southwest Bapt. Coll., Bolivar, Mo., 1946-61; prof. Ouachita Bapt. U., Arkadelphia, Ark., 1961-68, 82—, v.p. for acad. affairs, 1970-82; dean Mo. Bapt. Coll., St. Louis, 1968-70. Mem. edn. commn. So. Bapt. Conv., 1950-56; mem. hist. commn. Mo. Bapt. Conv., 1969-70; Mem. Nat. Collegiate Honors Council. Recipient Disting. Alumni award S.W. Bapt. Coll., 1977. Mem. Soc. Bibl. Lit., Am. Acad. Religion, Kiwanis. Club: Rotary. Home: 144 Evonshire Dr Arkadelphia AR 71923 *I have faced few adversities, or "hard times" in my life, but those that have come my way have invariably presented a challenge, when I was willing to take the dare. I've observed that those who don't rise to such occasions are left with little. When difficulties are faced and overcome, the risks proved to be worth the try. Fortunately, human beings are made so that the bad memories fade and the good take on a glow. The ones who refused to take the dare are left bad memories.*

GOODSON, JAMES BUTLER, life insurance company executive; b. Waco, Tex., Aug. 15, 1923; s. William Lloyd and Susie (Butler) G.; m. Molly Barnes, Mar. 20, 1949; children: Laurie, Liza, James Butler, Thomas Barnes. B.B.A., U. Tex., 1948. Analyst Rauscher, Pierce & Co., Dallas, 1948-52; with Southland Life Ins. Co., Dallas, 1952—, pres., chief exec. officer, 1969-80, chmn., chief exec. officer, 1980—; also dir., mem. exec. com.; exec. v.p., dir. Southland Fin. Corp.; dir. Sabine Corp., Tex. Commerce Bank, Dallas. Past pres., bd. dirs. Children's Devel. Center, Dallas, 1967; past mem. exec. com. Dallas Council Chs.; mem. Dallas Assembly, 1962, Cotton Bowl Council, after 1962; active United Fund, YMCA.; Bd. dirs. Goodwill Industries Dallas, Hope Cottage, Dallas, Jr. Achievement Dallas. Served with AUS, World War II. Mem. Salesmanship Club Dallas (bd. dirs. 1965-66), Sigma Alpha Epsilon. Presbyterian (chmn. deacons 1961, elder 1962-65, deacon 1961). Office: Southland Life Ins Co PO Box 2220 Dallas TX 75221

GOODSON, LOUIE AUBREY, JR., textile company executive; b. N.C., Dec. 20, 1922; s. Louie Aubrey and Lenna Sue (Neal) G.; m. Bernice Carroll, July 23, 1945; children—Louie Aubrey, III, Gayle, Mark, Mary Ellen. B.S. in Chemistry, N.C. State U., 1943; J.D., Georgetown U., 1951. Bar: D.C. bar 1951. With Dan River, Inc., Danville, Va., 1946-48, house patent lawyer, asst. dir. research, 1951-52, sr. v.p., 1959—; patent searcher firm Fisher & Christen, Washington, 1948-51; partner firm Fisher, Christen & Goodson, 1953-62; chmn. First Fed. Savs. & Loan Assn. Danville. Trustee Averett Coll., Danville, 1963-75; bd. dirs. Danville Mus. Fine Arts and History, 1980—. Served with AUS, 1943-46. Decorated Silver Star, Bronze Star, Purple Heart; hon. fellow Textile Research Inst., 1980. Mem. Am. Textile Mfrs. Inst., Am. Assn. Textile Chemists and Colorists, Am. Chem. Soc., Am. Assn. Textile Tech., Am. Bar Assn., Am. Patent Law Assn. Republican. Baptist. Clubs: Rotary, Danville Golf. Home: 174 Fairmont Circle Danville VA 24541 Office: 2291 Memorial Dr Danville VA 24541

GOODSON, MARK, TV producer; b. Sacramento, Jan. 24, 1915; s. Abraham Ellis and Fannie (Gross) G.; children (by previous marriages): Jill, Jonathan, Marjorie. A.B., U. Calif., 1937. Announcer, newscaster, dir. Radio Sta. KFRC, San Francisco, 1938-41; radio announcer, dir., N.Y.C., 1941-43; radio dir. U.S. Treasury War Bond Drive, 1944-45; 1st v.p. Mid-Atlantic Newspapers, Inc.; chmn. bd. Central States Pub. Co.; 1st v.p. Capitol City Pub. Co.; v.p. New Eng. Newspapers, Inc.; dir. Am. Film Inst. Formed, Goodson-Todman Prodns., 1946; originated: radio shows Winner Take All, 1946, Stop the Music, 1947, Hit the Jackpot, 1947-49; creator: TV game programs What's My Line, It's News to Me, The Name's the Same, I've Got a Secret, Two for the Money, The Price is Right, Password, Match Game, What's My Line, To Tell the Truth, Password, Price is Right, Family Feud, others, Child's Play; others; TV film series The Web, The Rebel, Richard Boone Theater, Branded. Recipient nat. television award Great Britain, 1951; Emmy award Acad. TV Arts and Scis., 1951, 52; Sylvania award. Mem. Acad. TV Arts and Sci. (pres. N.Y.C. 1957-58), Phi Beta Kappa. Office: 375 Park Ave New York NY 10152 also 6340 Sunset Blvd Hollywood CA 90028

GOODSON, R. EUGENE, automotive supply executive; b. Canton, N.C., Apr. 22, 1935; s. Lon R. G. and Ruby M. (Goodson); m. Susie Elisabeth Tweed, Aug. 10, 1957; children: Kathryn, Kenneth. A.B., Duke U., 1957, B.S.M.E., 1959; M.S.M.E., Purdue U., 1961, Ph.D., 1963. Registered profl. engr., Ind. Mem. faculty Purdue U., West Lafayette, Ind., 1963-81; chief scientist U.S. Dept. Transp., Washington, 1973-75; dir. Interdisciplinary Inst., Purdue U., 1975-80, assoc. dean research, 1980-81; pres., chief exec. officer GLN, Lafayette, Ind., 1971-81; group v.p. Hoover Universal, Inc., Ann Arbor, Mich., 1981—. Patentee in field; contbr (articles to tech. jours.). Mem. Soc. Automotive Engrs., ASME (chmn. exec. com. 1965-70). Republican. Presbyterian. Office: 135 E Bennett St Saline MI 48176

GOODSON, WALTER KENNETH, retired clergyman; b. Salisbury, N.C., Sept. 25, 1912; s. Daniel Washington and Sarah (Peeler) G.; m. Martha Ann Ogburn, July 12, 1937; children: Sara Ann (Mrs. Larry M. Faust), Walter Kenneth, Nancy Craven (Mrs. Thomas S. Johnson). A.B., Catawba Coll., 1934; also; L.H.D.; student, Duke Div. Sch., 1934-37, D.D., 1960; D.D., High Point (N.C.) Coll., 1951, Birmingham-So. Coll., Athens Coll., Shenandoah Coll.; L.H.D., St. Bernard Coll.; LL.D., U. Ala. Ordained to ministry Methodist Ch., 1939; pastor in Western N.C. Conf., 1935-64; bishop, Birmingham area, 1964-72, Richmond area, 1972-80, ret., 1980; now bishop-in-residence Duke U. Divinity Sch., Durham, N.C.; Del. World Conf. Meth. Ch., Oxford, Eng., 1951, Lake Junaluska, N.C., 1956, London, 1966, Denver, 1971, Dublin, 1977; mem. Meth. World Council; bd. dirs. Meth. Com. Overseas Relief, 1964-72; mem. (Mission Team to Gt. Britain), 1962, study team to, France and Berlin, 1962; chmn. finance com. bd. missions United Meth. Ch., 1968-72, pres. commn. on religion and race, 1968-72, pres. gen. bd. discipleship, 1972-80, also pres. council on ministries, 1972-76. Pres. J.B. Cornelius Found., 1946-64; Trustee Duke Endowment, Brevard Coll., Duke U., Shenandoah Coll. Clubs: Rotarian., Mason (32 deg.). Home: 2116 Front St Apt D-2 Durham NC 27705 Office: Duke U Divinity Sch Durham NC 27706

GOODSPEED, STEPHEN SPENCER, univ. adminstr.; b. Berkeley, Calif., Nov. 15, 1915; s. Thomas Harper and Florence (Beman) G.; m. Grace Frances Halloran, May 12, 1938; 1 son, Roger Halloran. A.B., U. Calif. at Berkeley, 1937, Ph.D., 1947. Instr. U. Calif. at Santa Barbara, 1946-49, asst. prof., 1949-55, asso. prof., 1955-60, prof., 1960—, asst. to chancellor, 1958-60, vice-chancellor, 1960-78, emeritus, 1979—; summer faculty U. Calif. at Berkeley, 1942, 1950, 59; cons. 4th Army and Western Def. Command, 1942, Civil Disturbance Orientation Seminar, Ft. Gordon, Ga., 1970, Calif. Specialized Tng. Inst., San Luis Obispo, 1972, 77, Nat. Security Seminar, Carlisle Barracks, Pa., 1974; radio commentator, 1946-49. Author: Nature and Function of International Organization, 1967; Contbr. articles to profl. jours. Mem. Standard Oil Co. Calif. Faculty Seminar, 1954, U.S. Army War Coll. Strategy Seminar, 1965; Vice pres., trustee Laguna Blanca Sch.; bd. dirs. Nat. Council on Alcoholism, Montecito Water Dist., UN Assn. Santa Barbara County, Calif., United Way, Center for Law Related Edn. Served from ensign to lt. USNR, 1942-46. Recipient Distinguished Service award Alpha Delta Phi, 1966. Mem. Am., Western polit. sci. assns., Pan-Am. Inst. History and Geography, Pacific Coast Athletic Assn. (1st pres.), C. of C. (bd. dirs.), Alpha Delta Phi, Pi Sigma Alpha. Clubs: Valley (v.p., dir.), Santa Barbara.). Home: 1225 E Mountain Dr Santa Barbara CA 93108 *Any man who is successful in life will be envied by those less successful. I have always thought that an excerpt from Parkenham Beatty's Self Reliance contained a good philosophy for anyone: "By your own soul learn to live/ And if men thwart you, take no heed/ If men hate you, have no care/ Sing your song, dream your dream, hope your hope and pray your prayer." I am sure that if a person will follow this philosophy of life, he will be successful. To sit and worry about criticism, which too often comes from the misinformed or from those incapable of passing judgement on an individual or a problem, is a waste of time.*

GOODSTEIN, BARNETT MAURICE, lawyer; b. Dallas, Oct. 1, 1921; s. Arthur Louis and Viola Esther (Levy) G.; m. Mira Brodsky, Jan. 26, 1947; children—Pamela Renee, Heather Ann, Robin Leslie. Student, Rice Inst., 1938-40; B.A., U. Tex., Austin, 1942, M.A., 1942; postgrad., U. Wis., 1949-51; J.D., So. Meth. U., 1957. Bar: Tex. bar 1957. Acting dir. case analysis Wage Stblzn. Bd., Dallas, 1951-53; since practiced in, Dallas; partner Goodstein and Starr, 1957—; lectr. econs. So. Meth. U., Dallas, 1946-48, 51-60; lectr. Massey Realty Coll., Real Estate Inst., Dallas; labor arbitrator, 1953—. Hearing officer work suspensions appeals bd., City of Dallas, 1971-83; mem. Dallas County Sch. Bd., 1980—. Served with USAAF, 1942-46. Mem. ABA, Tex. Bar Assn., Dallas Bar Assn., Nat. Acad. Arbitrators, Am. Arbitration Assn. Home: 5022 DeLoache Ave Dallas TX 75220 Office: 5925 Forest Ln Dallas TX 75230

GOODSTEIN, DAVID LOUIS, physics educator; b. Bklyn., Apr. 5, 1939; s. Sam and Claire (Axel) G.; m. Judith R. Koral, June 30, 1960; children: Marcia, Mark. B.S. cum laude, Bklyn. Coll., 1960; Ph.D., U. Wash., 1965. Research instr. U. Wash., Seattle, 1965-66; research fellow Calif. Inst. Tech., Pasadena, 1966-67, asst. prof., 1968-71, asso. prof., 1971-76, prof., 1976—; vis. scientist Frascati Nat. Lab., Italy, 1971—; mem. adv. council Jet Propulsion Lab., 1979-81. Author: States of Matter, 1975; mem. editorial bd.: Resource Letters Am. Assn. Physics Tchr, 1980-82; contbr. articles to profl. jours.; project dir., host: physics TV course The Mechanical Universe. NSF postdoctoral fellow, 1967-68; Sloan Found. fellow, 1969-71. Mem. AAAS, Am. Phys. Soc., Am. Inst. Physics. Home: 430 S Parkwood St Pasadena CA 91107 Office: Dept Physics Calif Inst Tech Pasadena CA 91125

GOODSTONE, EDWARD HAROLD, insurance company executive; b. N.Y.C., July 19, 1934; s. Abraham and Gladys (Lande) G.; m. Harriet Jill Pearle, Oct. 16, 1955; children: Marjorie Faith, Michael Stuart. B.A., CUNY, 1956; C.L.U., Coll. Life Underwriters, 1973. Agt. Penn. Mut. Ins. Co., N.Y.C., 1957-67, assoc. gen. agt., 1971-72; agy. mgr. Lincoln Nat. Life of N.Y., N.Y.C., 1967-71, 2d v.p., dir. advanced markets, Pearl River, N.Y., 1972-75; v.p. U.S. Life Ins. Co., N.Y.C., 1975-78; sr. v.p. USLIFE Corp., N.Y.C., 1978—. Mem. Am. Soc. C.L.U.'s, Nat. Assn. Life Underwriters, Life Underwriters Assn. N.Y. Jewish. Home: 211 Beach 145 St Neponsit NY 11694 Office: USLIFE Corp 125 Maiden Ln New York NY 10038

GOODWILLIE, JOHN MORLEY, advertising agency executive; b. Wausau, Wis., May 26, 1910; s. Clarence James and Rhoda Ann (Day) G.; m. Mary Louise Rhodes, May 12, 1939 (div. Feb. 1961); 1 dau., Susan Rhodes; m. Lee Marko, Dec. 31, 1961 (div. July 1976); 1 dau., Kate; m. Muriel Stiefel Rosenbluth, Nov. 28, 1976. Grad., Phillips Exeter Acad., 1929; B.A., Williams Coll., 1933. Asst. publicity dir. R.H. Macy Co., N.Y.C., 1935-41; copy writer, account exec. Benton & Bowles, 1945-47; dir. advt. and pub. relations Alexander Smith & Sons Carpet Co., 1948-51, v.p. charge advt. and pub. relations, 1951; account exec. Young & Rubicam (advt. agy.), 1952-55, C.J. LaRoche & Co., Inc., N.Y.C., 1955-58, v.p., 1958-60, exec. v.p., vice chmn. plans bd., 1960-65; sr. v.p. Norman, Craig & Kummel, Inc., 1965-68; pres. John Goodwillie Inc., N.Y.C., 1968—. Bd. dirs. United Fund, North Westchester, 1959-61, Irvington House, 1950—; v.p. Irvington House Inst. for Med. Research, 1976-82. Served to maj. USAAF, 1942-45. Mem. Am. Iris Soc., Zeta Psi. Home and office: 1185 Park Ave New York NY 10028 *The older I get, the sounder Henry David Thoreau's advice becomes: "Simplify...simplify".*

GOODWIN, ALFRED THEODORE, judge; b. Bellingham, Wash., June 29, 1923; s. Alonzo Theodore and Miriam Hazel (Williams) G.; m. Marjorie Elizabeth Major, Dec. 23, 1943 (div. 1948); 1 son, Michael Theodore; m. Mary Ellin Handelin, Dec. 23, 1949; children—Karl Alfred, Margaret Ellen, Sara Jane, James Paul. B.A., U. Oreg., 1947; J.D., 1951. Bar: Oreg. bar 1951. Newspaper reporter Eugene (Oreg.) Register-Guard, 1947-50; practiced in Eugene until, 1955; circuit judge Oreg. 2d. Jud. Dist., 1955-60; assoc. justice Oreg. Supreme Ct., 1960-69; U.S. dist. judge Dist. Oreg., 1969-71; judge U.S. Ct. Appeals 9th

Circuit, 1971—. Contbr.: articles to Oreg. Law Rev, 1949-51; student editor, 1950-51. Bd. dirs. Central Lane YMCA, Eugene, 1956-60, Salem (Oreg.) Art Assn., 1960—; adv. bd. Eugene Salvation Army, 1956-60, chmn., 1959. Served to capt., inf. AUS, 1942-46; ETO. Mem. Am. Judicature Soc., Am. Law Inst., ABA, Order of Coif, Phi Delta Phi, Sigma Delta Chi, Alpha Tau Omega. Republican. Presbyn. Club: Multnomah Athletic (Portland, (Oreg.). Home: 311 E Glenarm St #6 Pasadena CA 91106 US Court of Appeals PO Box 547 San Francisco CA 94101

GOODWIN, ANDREW JACKSON, investment banker; b. Anniston, Ala., Oct. 18, 1911; s. Andrew Jackson and Viola (Farley) G.; m. Charlotte Barton Head, Dec. 20, 1939 (div. Sept. 1963); children: Andrew Jackson, James Barton, Charlotte. Grad., Hill Sch., Pottstown, Pa., 1930; A.B., Princeton U., 1934; M.B.A., Harvard U., 1936, Command and Gen. Staff Sch., 1943. With Dillon, Read & Co., N.Y.C., 1936-39; with First Nat. Bank, Anniston, 1939-40; v.p., dir. Anniston Nat. Bank, 1946-52; dir. Fed. Res. Bank of Atlanta (Birmingham br.), 1952-53, Life Ins. Co. of Ala., Gadsden, 1952-53; commr. SEC, Washington, 1953-56; v.p., dir. Lee Higginson Corp. (investment bankers), Chgo., 1956-64; mgr. Washington office Burton, Dana & Co., 1964-70; pres. Goodwin Investments, Inc., Anniston, 1970—. Commr. water bd., Anniston, 1952-53; chmn. Downtown Devel. Commn., Anniston, 1974—, Anniston Parking Authority, 1975—; bd. dirs. Gov.'s Adv. Bd. Ala. Indsl. Devel., Montgomery. Served as lt. col. F.A. AUS, 1940-46; asst., aide to undersec. war Robert Patterson, 1943-44; served; PTO; served; ETO. Mem. Nat. Assn. Securities Dealers (bd. govs. 1961-64), Newcomen Soc., V.F.W., Am. Legion. Democrat. Episcopalian. Clubs: Anniston Country; Mountain Brook Country (Birmingham, Ala.); Capital City (Atlanta); Nassau (Princeton, N.J.); Chevy Chase Country (Washington); Chicago, Attic (Chgo.); Shoreacres Country, Onewentsia Country (Lake Forest, Ill.); Princeton (N.Y.C. and Birmingham). Home and office: 1230 Woodstock Ave Anniston AL 36201

GOODWIN, BERNARD, lawyer, executive, educator; b. N.Y.C., Dec. 19, 1907; s. Mayer and Hannah (Wald) G.; children: Charles Stewart, Wendy Melinda, Nadine Antonia. Sc.B. cum laude, N.Y.U., 1928, J.D., Harvard U., 1931. Lawyer, Seattle, 1931-34, N.Y.C., 1935—; lawyer, exec. Paramount Pictures Corp., 1934-57; sec., dir. Allen B. Dumont Labs., Inc., Clifton, N.J., 1938-55; pres., dir. Metro Media, Inc., N.Y.C., 1955-59; chmn. bd. Sunrise Broadcasting Corp., Ft. Lauderdale, Fla., 1965-77; guest lectr. U. Mich. Law Sch., 1965-68, U. Bologna, Italy, 1971-80; prof. ospite U. Padua, Italy, 1970; adj. prof. N.Y. Law Sch., N.Y.C., 1981—; Trustee emeritus U. Detroit, 1966—. Author books and articles on legal and govtl. subjects. Mem. Am., Wash. State bar assns., Assn. Bar City N.Y., A.S.C.A.P. (dir.), Acad. Motion Picture Arts and Scis., Am. Soc. Internat. Law, Am. Fgn. Law Assn., Broadcast Pioneers, Copyright Soc. U.S.A., Am. Arbitration Assn. (nat. labor panel), Union Internationale des Avocats, Phi Beta Kappa. Club: Harvard (N.Y.C.). Home and Office: 225 E 49th St New York NY 10017 *The most significant factor in my life has been the motivation of an ethic for work and achievements that would create sufficient financial success to obtain the opportunity to concentrate on enterprises for the commonweal; not to accumulate money for the sake of wealth or power alone.*

GOODWIN, CLAUDE ELBERT, lawyer, former gas utility executive; b. Ripley, W.Va., Aug. 9, 1910; s. Claude Earl and Marie (Vail) G.; m. Ireta Joy Watson, Aug. 15, 1931; 1 dau., Judith. A.B., W.Va. Wesleyan Coll., 1931; LL.B., W.Va. U., 1940; grad. student speech, Northwestern U., 1932. Bar: W.Va. 1940. Mem. firm Goodwin & Goodwin, Ripley, 1941-47, 73—; prof. W.Va. U. Coll. Law, 1947-48; sec., counsel United Fuel Gas Co., 1963-67; v.p., gen. counsel, dir. Charleston group companies Columbia Gas System, Inc., 1967-73; dir. First Nat. Bank Ripley, 1949—, Vail Furniture, Inc. Editor-in-chief: W.Va. Law Rev, 1939-40; Contbr. legal articles to publs. Past pres., mem. alumni exec. council W.Va. U.; bd. dirs. Charleston (W.Va.) Area Med. Center Found., 1977—. Served with USNR, 1943-46. Decorated Commendation medal. Mem. Am., W.Va. bar assns., Am. Judicature Soc., Order of Coif. Episcopalian. Home: Evans Rd Ripley WV 25271 Office: Goodwin & Goodwin Charleston Nat Plaza Charleston WV 25301

GOODWIN, CRAUFURD DAVID, economics educator; b. Montreal, Que., Can., May 23, 1934; came to U.S., 1962; s. George G. and Roma (Stewart) G.; m. Nancy Virginia Sanders, June 7, 1958. B.A., McGill U., 1955; Ph.D., Duke, 1958. Econ. research asst. Courtauld's Can., Ltd., 1955; lectr. econs. U. Windsor, Ont., 1958-59; exec. sec. Commonwealth Studies Center, Duke, also; vis. asst. prof., 1959-60; hon. research fellow Australian Nat. U., 1960-61; asst. prof. econs. York U., Toronto, 1961-62; asst. prof. econs., asst. to provost Duke U., 1962-63, assoc. prof. econs., sec. to Univ., asst. to provost, 1963-64, asso. prof. econs., sec. Univ., asst. provost, 1964- 66, assoc. prof. econs., asst. provost, dir. internat. studies, 1966-68, prof. econs., vice provost for internat. studies, 1968-69, prof. econs., vice provost, dir. internat., 1969-71, prof. econs., 1971-74, James B. Duke prof. econs., 1974—, dean Grad. Sch., vice provost for research, 1980—; officer in charge European and internat. affairs Ford Found., 1971-77. Author: Canadian Economic Thought: The Political Economy of a Developing Nation 1814-1914, 1961, Economic Enquiry in Australia, 1966, The Image of Australia, 1974, (with M. Nacht) Absence of Decision; Editor: (with W.B. Hamilton and Kenneth Robinson) A Decade of the Commonwealth 1955-64, 1966, (with I.B. Holley) The Transfer of Ideas, 1968, (with R.D.C. Black and A.W. Coats) The Marginal Revolution in Economics, 1973, Exhortation and Controls, 1975, Energy Policy Perspective, 1981; Editor jour.: History of Political Economy, 1969—. Smuts vis. fellow Cambridge U., 1967-68; Guggenheim fellow, 1967-68. Home: PO Box 957 St Mary's Rd Hillsborough NC 27278

GOODWIN, DONALD WILLIAM, psychiatrist; b. Parsons, Kans., Sept. 25, 1931; s. William G. and Georgia M. (Coed) G.; m. Sarah Hovorka, Jan. 5, 1957; children—Caitlin, Mary, Sarah, William. B.A., Baker U., Baldwin, Kans., 1953; M.D., Kans. U., 1964. Intern St. Luke's Hosp., 1964-65; resident in psychiatry Washington U., St. Louis, 1965-68; prof. psychiatry Washington U. Med. Sch., St. Louis, 1974-76; prof. psychiatry, chmn. dept. Kans. U. Med. Sch., 1976—. Author: Is Alcoholism Hereditary?, 1976, Alcoholism: The Facts, 1981; co-author: Psychiatric Diagnosis, 1980; Contbr. articles med. jours. Served with AUS, 1953-55. Recipient Jellinek Meml. award Addiction Research Found., 1975. Mem. Am. Psychiat. Assn. (Hoffheimer award 1974), AMA, Royal Coll. Psychiatrists, Psychiat. Research Soc., Am. Psychpath. Assn., Soc. Biol. Psychiatrists, Am. Acad. Clin. Psychiatrists. Home: 6130 Morningside Dr Kansas City MO 64113 Office: Kans U Med Sch 39th and Rainbow Sts Kansas City KS 66103

GOODWIN, FREDERICK KING, psychiatrist; b. Cin., Apr. 21, 1936; s. Robert Clifford and Marion Cronin (Schmadel) G.; m. Rosemary Powers, Oct. 19, 1963; children: Kathleen Kelly, Frederick King, Daniel Clifford. B.S., Georgetown U., 1958; philosophy fellow, St. Louis U., 1958-59, M.D., 1963. Intern medicine and psychiatry SUNY, Syracuse, 1963-64; resident psychiatry U. N.C., Chapel Hill, 1964-65; commd. med. officer USPHS, 1965; clin. assoc. adult psychiatry br. NIMH, 1965-67; research fellow Lab. Biochemistry, Nat. Heart Inst., NIH, Bethesda, Md., 1967-68; chief sect. on psychiatry Lab. Clin. Sci., NIMH, Bethesda, 1970-77; chief clin. psychobiology br. Lab. Clin. Sci., NIMH, 1970-81, sci. dir., 1981—; pvt. practice medicine, specializing in psychiatry, Bethesda, 1967—; faculty George Washington U. Sch. Medicine, Washington Sch. Psychiatry, Uniformed U. Sch. Health Scis.; vis. prof. U. Calif., Irvine, U. Wis., Boston U., U. So. Calif., Duke U.; cons. AMA Council on Drugs; participant pub. edn. programs on local and network television and radio. Editor-in-chief: Psychiatry Research, 1979—; mem. editorial bd.: Archives of Gen. Psychiatry, 1977—, Psychopharmacology, 1976-79; Contbr. articles to med. jours. Mem. adv. bd. Max Planck Inst., Munich, W. Ger. NIMH spl. fellow, 1967-68; Recipient Psychopharmacology Research prize Am. Psychol. Assn., 1971; Internat. Anna Monica prize for research in depression, 1971; Taylor Manor award, 1976; Adminstrs. award HEW, 1977; Superior Service award USPHS, 1980; Strecker award, 1983. Fellow Am. Psychiat. Assn. (chmn. com. on protection of human subjects, task force on research tng., Hofheimer prize for research 1971), Am. Coll. Neuropsychopharmacology (chmn. com. on problems of public concern); mem. AAAS, Am. Psychosomatic Soc., Soc. Biol. Psychiatry (A.E. Bennett award 1970), Am. Acad. Psychoanalysis, Soc. for Neuroscience, Psychiat. Research Soc., Washington Psychiat. Soc. (peer rev. com.). Club: Cosmos (Washington). Home: 5712 Warwick Pl Chevy Chase MD 20015 Office: NIH Bldg 10 Room 4S-239 Bethesda MD 20014 *Many aspects of one's innerself contribute to shaping a career, most, I suspect, evolving and changing along the way. For me, one characteristic stands out as unchanging - the capacity to derive genuine pleasure and a special sense of satisfaction from the successes and the growth of those whose careers you have helped - in a sense, your professional "children."*

GOODWIN, GEORGE EVANS, public relations executive; b. Atlanta, June 20, 1917; s. George and Carrie (Clark) G.; m. Lois Milstead, Nov. 2, 1940; children: Clark, Allen. A.B. with cert. in journalism, Washington and Lee U., 1939. Reporter, Atlanta Georgian, 1939, Charleston (S.C.) News and Courier, 1940, Washington Times-Herald, 1940-41, Miami Daily News, 1941-42; staff writer Atlanta Jour., 1945-52; exec. dir. Central Atlanta Improvement Assn., 1952-54; v.p. First Nat. Bank of Atlanta, 1954-64; exec. v.p. Bell & Stanton, Inc., 1965-76; pres. Manning, Selvage & Lee, Atlanta, 1976—; exec. sec. Ga. Senatorial Transit Study Com., 1954. Chmn. Atlanta Bicentennial Commn., 1974-76; trustee emeritus Oglethorpe U.; trustee Annandale at Suwanee, Literary Action, Inc. Served as lt., motor torpedo boat squadrons, 1942-45; Attu, New Guinea and Philippines. Decorated Navy Unit Commendation; Purple Heart; Philippines Liberation ribbon with one star; Asiatic-Pacific theater ribbon with three stars.; recipient Pultizer Prize for local reporting, 1948; Sigma Delta Chi award for gen. reporting (vote fraud), 1948; award for Reporting (vote fraud) AP Ga., 1948; Pall Mall Big Story award, 1949. Mem. Public Relations Soc. Am., Delta Tau Delta, Sigma Delta Chi, Omicron Delta Kappa. Democrat. Presbyterian (elder). Home: 3302 Ivanhoe Dr NW Atlanta GA 30327 Office: 1600 Peachtree Cain Tower 229 Peachtree St NE Atlanta GA 30303

GOODWIN, HARRY EUGENE, journalist, educator; b. Council Bluffs, Iowa, Dec. 19, 1922; s. Harry Lars and Mary Ellen (James) G.; m. Frances Jean Prudhon, July 3, 1943; children: Geri, Gibson Eugene, Susan, Michael Jay. B.A., U. Iowa, 1946, M.A., 1947. Editor The Daily Iowan, Iowa City, 1946-47; copy editor Balt. Sun, 1947-48; writer Asso. Press, Balt., 1948-50; columnist, reporter Washington Star, 1950-57; dir., prof. Sch. Journalism, Pa. State U., 1957-69, prof., 1969—. Author: Groping for Ethics in Journalism, 1983; Editorial adv. bd.: Mass Com Rev, 1978—. Bd. dirs. Mellet Fund for a Free and Responsible Press, 1967—, pres., 1976—; mem. admissions com. Washington Journalism Center, 1968—. Served as 1st lt., 8th Air Force USAAF, World War II. Recipient Outstanding Tchr. award Amoco Found., 1980. Mem. Pa. Soc. Newspaper Editors, Am. Assn. Schs. and Depts. Journalism (v.p. 1960-61), Assn. Edn. Journalism (chmn. div. mass communications and soc. 1966-67), Am. Council on Edn. for Journalism, Pa. Council for Mass Communications Studies (pres. 1969-71), Soc. Profl. Journalists, Omicron Delta Kappa. Home: 119 Bathgate Dr State College PA 16801 Office: School of Journalism Pennsylvania State University University Park PA 16802

GOODWIN, JOHN MITCHELL, lawyer; b. St. Louis, Mar. 5, 1921; s. John Mitchell and Theresa (Longinotti) G.; m. Mary Susan Farris, Feb. 15, 1947; children: Mary Ellen (Mrs. Lewis), John Mitchell III. Student, St. Louis U., 1942; J.D., Washington U., St. Louis, 1946. Bar: Mo. 1946. Since practiced in, St. Louis; ptnr. Hocker, Goodwin, Koenig, Gibbons & Fehlig (and predecessors), 1953-73, Thomas, Busse, Goodwin, Cullen, Clooney & Gibbons, 1973—. Mem. City of Clayton (Mo.) Plan Commn., 1971-76. Fellow Am. Coll. Trial Lawyers; mem. Bar Assn. St. Louis (pres. 1965-66), Lawyers Assn. St. Louis (pres. 1952-53, Annual Award of Honor 1978), Mo. Bar (bd. govs. 1966—, mem. exec. com. 1968—, pres. 1972-73), ABA (Ho. of Dels.), Mo. Hist. Soc., Civil War Round Table (pres. 1962), Navy League U.S., Sigma Chi, Delta Theta Phi. Home: 460 Edgewood Dr Clayton MO 63105 Office: 8631 Delmar Blvd Saint Louis County MO 63124 515 Olive St Saint Louis MO 63101

GOODWIN, NANCY LEE, college president; b. Peoria, Ill., Aug. 11, 1940; d. Raymond Darrell and Mildred Louise (Brown) G. B.A. (Nat. Meth. scholar, Nat. Merit scholar), MacMurray Coll., 1961; M.A., U. Colo., 1963; Ph.D., U. Ill., 1971. Tchr. Roosevelt Jr. High Sch., Peoria, 1961-62; counselor U. Ill., Urbana, 1963-66, staff asso., asst. prof. edn. measurement, Chgo., 1967-71; asst. v.p., asso. prof. stats. Fla. Internat. U., Miami, 1971-78; pres. Greenfield (Mass.) Community Coll., 1978-82, Arapahoe Community Coll., Colo., 1982—; dir. Cons. Mid-Am. Computer Corp., First Chance Network U.S. Office Edn., 1972-78. Mem. Com. on Ill. Govt., Higher Edn. Task Force; mem. Vol. Action Center, Miami, 1972-78; active Girl Scouts U.S.A.; mem. Franklin/Hampshire Area Service Planning Team, 1978; incorporator Franklin County (Mass.) United Way, Farren Meml. Hosp.; adv. Franklin County Public Hosp.; bd. dirs. Women's Inst. Fla., Franklin County Arts Council, Franklin County Devel. Corp., Western Welcome Week, Inc.; bd. dirs., mem. fin. monitoring com. New Eng. Soy Dairy, 1980. Recipient Merit award Chgo. Tchrs. Assn., 1969; citation Girl Scouts U.S.A., 1973. Mem. NEA, Am. Assn. Higher Edn., Am. Ednl. Research Assn., Assn. Instl. Research, Centennial C. of C. (dir. 1983). Home: 6318 S Gallup Court Littleton CO 80120 Office: Arapahoe Community Coll Littleton CO 80120

GOODWIN, PAUL RICHARD, transportation company executive; b. N.Y.C., Feb. 6, 1943; s. Paul Richard Fetyko and Ellen Mary (Goodwin) Estherson; m. Nina Presant, Oct. 10, 1965; children: Elizabeth, Ross. B.C.E., Cornell U., 1965; M.B.A., George Washington U., 1970. Mgmt. trainee Chessie System, Balt., 1965-66, in various mgmt. positions fin. dept., 1966-76, asst. to v.p.-fin., Cleve., 1977-78, asst. v.p.-fin., 1978-80, v.p.-fin., 1980-81, sr. v.p.-fin., 1982—; dir. Chesapeake & Ohio Ry. Co., Balt. & Ohio R.R. Co., Fruit Growers Express Co. Mem. Greater Cleve. Growth Assn. Mem. Fin. Execs. Inst., Cleve. Treas. Club. Office: Chessie System RR 3305 Terminal Tower PO Box 6419 Cleveland OH 44101

GOODWIN, ROBERT DELMEGE, association executive; b. Des Moines, Sept. 14, 1920; s. Charles Otis and Lorraine Lee (Delmege) G.; m. June Schuyler Patterson, Feb. 15, 1946; 1 dau., Meredith Lee. B.S., Northwestern U., 1941, M.S. in Journalism, 1942. Chief historian SAC, Washington, 1946-47; pub. relations exec. N.W. Ayer & Son, Inc., N.Y.C., 1948-49; dir. community program devel. N.A.M., 1949-53; dir. pub. relations Carpet Inst., N.Y.C., 1954; dir. press relations Pan Am. Coffee Bur., N.Y.C., 1955-58; dir. advt. and pub. relations Sugar Info. Bur., N.Y.C., 1958-60; dir. Hat Council, N.Y.C., 1960-62; dir. pub. relations Grocery Mfrs. Am., N.Y.C., 1963-70; exec. v.p. Nat. Assn. Credit Mgmt., N.Y.C., 1970—; v.p. Credit Research Found., Lake Success, N.Y., 1972—. Editorial bd.: Credit Manual of Comml. Laws, 1971—. Served with USAAF, 1942-46. Mem. Am. Soc. Assn. Execs., Pub. Relations Soc. Am., Sales Execs. Club N.Y.C., Comml. Law League Am. Club: Army and Navy. Home: 151 Frog Town Rd New Canaan CT 06840 Office: 475 Park Ave S New York NY 10016

GOODWIN, RODNEY KEITH GROVE, international trade company executive; b. Emsworth, Hants., Eng., Nov. 9, 1944; s. Richard John Grove and Joan Avril (Gamon) G.; m. Linda Elaine Brown, May 19, 1967; children—Keith Randal Grove, Kathryn Julie, Kara Dawn. Student, Eastbourne Coll., Sussex, Eng., NYU, Abilene Christian U.; B.A., SW Mo. State U.; M.A., U. Mo., 1972. Passenger rep. Grace Line Inc., N.Y.C., 1963-66; univ. youth coordinator L'Englise du Christ, Lausanne, Switzerland, 1966-68; asst. instr. French U. Mo., 1971-72; internat. sales rep. Mueller Internat. Sales Corp. subs. Paul Mueller Co., Springfield, Mo., 1973-76; v.p. internat. Peabody Tec Tank, Parsons, Kans., 1976-78; group dir. exports water/fluids group Peabody Internat. Corp., 1976-80, dir. exports, 1980—; v.p. exports/trading, 1980—; pres. Peabody World Trade. Mem. Greater Ozarks World Trade Club. Club: Southeast Kans. World Trade (pres.). Home: 5 Rouleau Ln Huntington CT 06484 Office: 4 Landmark Sq Stamford CT 06901

GOODWIN, WILLARD E., urologist; b. Los Angeles, July 24, 1915; s. Willard and Olive (Belt) G.; m. Mary Pearson Josephs, Feb. 21, 1942; children—Mary Devereux (Mrs. E.B. Cabot), Peter Colt (dec.), Willard II. A.B., U. Calif. at Berkeley, 1937; M.D., Johns Hopkins U., 1941, Frei Universitat Berlin, 1978. Diplomate: Am. Bd. Urology. Mem. faculty Johns Hopkins Med. Sch., 1948-51; asso. prof. urology U. Calif. at Los Angeles, 1951—, prof., 1953—; cons. urology Wadsworth VA Hosp., Los Angeles. Fellow A.C.S., Am. Acad. Pediatrics; mem. A.M.A., Am. Urol. Assn., Pacific Coast Surg. Assn., Am. Surg. Assn., Am. Assn. Genito-urinary Surgeons, Clin. Soc. Genito-urinary Surgeons, Assn. Univ. Surgeons. Research and numerous publs. on urol. surgery, kidney transplantation, pediatric urology. Home: 254 Bronwood Ave Los Angeles CA 90049

GOODWIN, WILLIAM RICHARD, business executive; b. Pendleton, Oreg., June 21, 1924; s. Carl W. and Pearl (Taylor) G.; m. Patricia Earnest, Mar. 3, 1956; children: Douglas Richard, Barbara. B.A., Reed Coll., 1949, M.A., 1950; Ph.D., Stanford U., 1955. With RAND Corp., Santa Monica, Calif., 1955; with System Devel. Corp., Paramus, N.J., 1957-65, asst. div. mgr., 1958; mgr. SAC system design div., 1959-65; owner W.R. Goodwin & Co., Fort Lee, N.J., 1965-69; v.p. corp. planning Johns-Manville Corp., N.Y.C., 1969-70, pres., chief exec. officer, 1970-76; past pres., dir. several Johns-Manville subsidiaries; pres., chief exec. officer Goodwin Cos., Inc., Littleton, Colo., 1977-80, Hughes Capital Corp., Denver, 1980—, Vidtor Communications, Inc.; dir. Rand Corp.; Trustee Reed Coll., Inst. Civil Justice, Santa Monica, Calif. Office: 2121 S Oneida St Denver CO 80224

GOODWYN, ULYSSES VINCENT, investment executive; b. Cullman, Ala., Sept. 27, 1923; s. Andrew Sylvester and Thella (Quattlebaum) G.; m. Mary Mozelle Anderson, July 15, 1944; children: Janet Leigh, William Vincent, Robert Andrew. B.S., U. Ala., 1947; LL.B., Birmingham (Ala.) Sch. Law, 1958. Bar: Ala. 1959. With So. Natural Resources, Birmingham, 1947-80, treas., 1964, v.p., treas., 1967-71, exec. v.p., 1971-80; also dir.; sole propr. Goodwyn Investment Co., Birmingham, 1980—; dir. So. Natural Gas Co.; chmn. bd., chief exec. officer, dir. Offshore Co., after 1966, Sonat Exploration Co.; dir. Fed. Res. Bank Atlanta; instr. U. Ala., 1946-47. Trustee Bapt. Med. Centers, Birmingham. Served to capt., Q.M.C. AUS, 1943-46. Mem. Ala. Bar Assn., Beta Gamma Sigma, Pi Mu Epsilon, Delta Sigma Kappa. Clubs: Shoal Creek Country, Vestavia Country (Birmingham). Home: 2740 Altadena Rd Birmingham AL 35243 Office: 1236 First National-Southern Natural Bldg Birmingham AL 35203

GOODY, RICHARD MEAD, geophysicist; b. Welwyn-Garden-City, Eng., June 19, 1921; came to U.S., 1958, naturalized, 1966; s. Harold Earnest and Lilian (Rankine) G.; m. Elfriede Koch, Sept. 11, 1946; 1 dau., Brigid. Ph.D., Cambridge U., 1949; M.A. (hon.), Harvard U., 1958. With Brit. Civil Service, 1942-46; fellow St. John's Coll., Cambridge, 1950-53; reader London U., 1953-58; prof. div. applied scis. Harvard U., 1958—; dir. Blue Hill Obs., 1958-70, Center for Earth and Planetary Physics, 1970-71. Author: Physics of the Stratosphere, 1947, Atmospheric Radiation, 1964, Atmospheres, 1974. Mem. Royal Meteorol. Soc. (Buchan prize 1955), Am. Meteorol. Soc. (50th Anniversary medal 1970, Cleveland Abbé award 1977), Am. Acad. Arts and Scis., Nat. Acad. Scis. Club: Cosmos (Washington). Home: Box 430 Falmouth MA 02541 Office: Pierce Hall 29 Oxford St Cambridge MA 02138

GOODYEAR, FRANK HENRY, JR., curator; b. N.Y.C., Jan. 5, 1944; s. Frank Henry and Alison (Harrison) G.; m. Elizabeth Wanton Balis, July 6, 1944; children: Frank Henry III, Alison H., Grace Wanton. B.A., Yale, 1966; M.A., Winterthur Program, Early Am. Culture, U. Del., 1969. Curator R.I. Hist. Soc., Providence, 1969-72; curator Pa. Acad. Fine Arts, Phila., 1972-83, pres., 1983—; Mem. mus. rev. com. Henry Francis dePont Winterthur (Del.) Mus. Contbr. articles profl. jours. Bd. dirs. Fairmont Park Art Assn., Pa. Arts Council, 1980—. Home: 7308 Elbow Ln Philadelphia PA 19119 Office: Pa Acad Fine Arts Broad and Cherry Sts Philadelphia PA 19102

GOODYEAR, JAMES HAROLD, investment company executive; b. Bklyn., July 11, 1936; s. Ambrose Edward and Cecelia (McGrath) G. B.A., Pace U., 1957. With corp. trust div. Irving Trust Co., N.Y.C., 1957-59, trust div. Citibank N.A., 1960-70; dir., shareholder dealer relations Calvin Bullock Ltd., N.Y.C., 1970—, corp. sec. numerous investment cos. managed; dir. Frankli United Life Ins. Co., Inc. div. Am. Brands, Inc. Republican. Roman Catholic. Clubs: Pilgrims of U.S.; St. George's Soc. (N.Y.C.). Office: Calvi Bullock Ltd 1 Wall St New York NY 10005

GOODYEAR, JOHN LAKE, artist, educator; b. Los Angeles, Oct. 22, 1930; s. Ronald Ralph and Lillian Katherine (Lake) G.; m. Anne Marie Dixon, July 14, 1953; children: Sarah, Amy. B.Design, U. Mich., 1952, M.Design, 1954. Mem. faculty dept. art U. Mich., Grand Rapids, 1956-62, U. Mass., 1962-64; mem. faculty visual arts dept. M.G.S.A., Rutgers U., New Brunswick, N.J., 1964—; prof. art Douglass Coll., Rutgers U., 1976—. Exhbns. include, N.J. State Mus., 1981, III Bienal de Arte, Medellin, Colombia, 1972, The Jewish Mus., N.Y.C., 1970, Mus. Modern Art, N.Y.C., 1965, Martha Jackson Gallery, N.Y.C., 1960; represented in permanent collections, Mus. Modern Art, N.Y.C., Newark Mus., N.J. State Mus., Princeton U. Art Mus., Whitney Mus. Am. Art, N.Y.C., Guggenheim Mus., N.Y.C., Milw. Art Center, Corcoran Gallery Art, Washington, Nat. Mus. Am. Art, Washington. Served with U.S. Army, 1954-56. Graham Found. for Advanced Studies in Fine Arts fellow, 1962, 70; Center for

Advanced Visual Studies, M.I.T. fellow, 1970-71. Office: Visual Art Dept MGSA Rutgers U New Brunswick NJ 08903

GOODYEAR, RICHARD, auto company executive, lawyer; b. New Haven, Dec. 9, 1941; s. John and Julia (Owsley) G.; m. Clelia Pinza, Dec. 18, 1962 (div. 1967); 1 dau., Sarah; m. Constance Martin, June 6, 1970; children: Charles, James, Bradley. B.A., Yale U., 1964, LL.B., 1967. Bar: N.Y. 1968, Calif. 1976, Mich. 1981. Assoc. firm Debevoise, Plimpton, Lyons & Gates, N.Y.C., 1967-71, 1972-75; asst. gen. counsel Ford Found., N.Y.C., 1971-72, Occidental Petroleum, Los Angeles, 1975-79; pres. Occidental Resource Recovery Systems, Inc., N.Y.C., 1979-81; assoc. gen. counsel Chrysler Corp., Detroit, 1981, v.p., gen. counsel, sec., 1981—. Trustee Univ. Liggett Sch., Grosse Pointe, Mich. Mem. ABA, Am. Corp. Counsel Assn. Club: Country of Detroit. Home: 61 Moran Rd Grosse Pointe Farms MI 48236 Office: Chrysler Corp PO Box 1919 Detroit MI 48288

GOODYKOONTZ, CHARLES ALFRED, newspaper editor; b. Radford, Va., Dec. 29, 1928; s. Charles A. and Claudine (Noell) G.; m. Jean Shirley Beasley, Sept. 17, 1955; 1 son, Charles Alfred. Student, Emory and Henry Coll., 1946-48. Sports editor Radford News Jour., 1948-50; mem. staff Richmond (Va.) Times-Dispatch, 1952-81, mng. editor, 1969-81; v.p., exec. editor Richmond (Va.) Times-Dispatch and The Richmond News Leader, 1982—; Chmn. Va. UPI. Served with AUS, 1950-52. Recipient George Mason award for service to Va. journalism, 1973. Mem. Soc. Profl. Journalists, Sigma Delta Chi (regional dir. 1971-74, nat. officer 1975-79, pres. 1978, Wells Key award 1982). Home: 8207 Shannon Hill Rd Richmond VA 23229 Office: 333 E Grace St Richmond VA 23219

GOOKIN, RALPH BURTON, food company executive; b. Chariton, Iowa, June 23, 1914; s. Albert Burton and Maude Mary (McFarl) G.; m. Mary Louise Carroll, Dec. 11, 1948; children—Cristy Carroll, David Burton. B.S., Northwestern U., 1935; M.B.A., Harvard, 1940. With H. J. Heinz Co., Pitts., 1945-79, comptroller, 1951-59, v.p. finance, 1959-64; exec. v.p. U.S. ops., 1964-66, pres., chief exec. officer, 1966-73, vice chmn. bd., chief exec. officer, 1973-79, chmn. exec. com., 1966-79, also; dir.; dir. Westinghouse Electric, BankAm. Corp., PPG Industries, Inc., Pitts. br. Fed. Res. Bank of Cleve.; past chmn. Grocery Mfrs. Am. Inc.; Past pres., dir. Pa. Golf Assn.; past pres. Western Pa. Golf Assn.; past mem. exec. com. Pa. Economy League. Bd. dirs. Allegheny Health, Edn. and Research Corp.; past mem. bd. dirs. Regional Indsl. Devel. Corp., Southwestern Pa., 1974—; former bd. dirs. United Way Allegheny County; bd. govs. Uniform Grocery Product Code Council, 1975—; bd. visitors Grad. Sch. Bus., U. Pitts.; past pres. Financial Execs. Research Found.; mem. bus. adv. council Grad. Sch. Indsl. Adminstrn., Carnegie-Mellon U., 1978—. Mem. Financial Execs. Inst., Harvard Bus. Sch. Assn. (exec. council 1973-76). Clubs: University, Duquesne, Fox Chapel (Pitts.); Laurel Valley Golf, Rolling Rock (Ligonier, Pa.) (bd. govs.); Augusta (Ga.); Nat. Golf. Home: 106 Foxtop Dr Pittsburgh PA 15238 Office: 1062 Progress St Pittsburgh PA 15212

GOOLSBEE, CHARLES THOMAS, lawyer; b. Houston, Jan. 13, 1935; s. Charles Culberson and Mary Pearl (Gipson) G.; m. Carol Anne Brindley, Apr. 3, 1961; children: Catherine Anne, Charles Thomas, Mary Patricia. B.A., Baylor U., 1956, LL.B., 1958. Bar: Tex. 1958, Ill. 1964. Individual practice law, Houston, 1958-59; atty. SEC, Washington, 1959-63; sr. atty. Allstate Ins. Co., Northbrook, Ill., 1963-68, asst. counsel, 1968-71, asso. counsel, 1971-72; asst. gen. counsel CNA Fin. Corp., Chgo., 1972-73, asso. gen. counsel, 1973-75; asso. counsel Am. Gen. Ins. Co., Houston, 1975-76, v.p., gen. counsel, 1976-80; sr. v.p., gen. counsel, sec. Tex. Air Corp., Houston, 1980—. Mem. Am. Bar Assn. Club: Houston Racquet. Home: 9027 Briar Forest Houston TX 77024 Office: Capital Bank Plaza Suite 4040 333 Clay St Allen Pkwy Houston TX 77002

GOORWITZ, ALLEN, actor; b. Newark, Nov. 22, 1939; s. Philip and Alice (Lavroff) G. Grad., Anthony Mannino Studio, N.Y.C., 1965. Star in: motion picture The Candidate, 1973, The Conversation, 1974, The Front Page, 1974, Nashville, 1975, Gable and Lombard, 1976, Skateboard, 1978, The Stunt Man, 1979, The Brink's Job, 1979, One Trick Pony, 1980. Life mem. Actors Studio. Office: care William Morris Agy 151 El Camino Beverly Hills CA 90212 *

GOOS, ROGER DELMON, mycologist; b. Beaman, Iowa, Oct. 29, 1924; s. Gus and Georgiana Bertha (Witt) G.; m. Mary Lee Engel, Sept. 21, 1946; children: Marinda Lee, Suzanne Maurine. B.A., U. Iowa, 1950, Ph.D., 1958. Mycologist United Fruit Co., Norwood, Mass., 1958-62; scientist USPHS, NIH, Bethesda, Md., 1962-64; curator of fungi Am. Type Culture Collection, Rockville, Md., 1964-68; assoc. researcher, vis. assoc. prof. botany U. Hawaii, Honolulu, 1968-70; assoc. prof. botany U. R.I., Kingston, 1970-72, prof. botany, 1972—, prof., chmn. dept. botany, 1981—; Trustee Am. Type Culture Collection, Rockville, Md., 1977-83. Served with U.S. Army, 1944-46, 50-51. Decorated Bronze Star, Purple Heart. Mem. AAAS, Mycol. Soc. Am. (sec.-treas. 1980-83, v.p. 1983-84, pres.-elect 1984-85), Bot. Soc. Am., Am. Soc. Microbiology, Am. Phytopath. Soc., Mycol. Soc. Japan, Brit. Mycol. Soc., Mycol. Soc. India. Home: 4 Tanglewood Trail Narragansett RI 02882 Office: Dept Botany U RI Kingston RI 02881

GOOSTREE, ROBERT EDWARD, educator; b. nr. Clarksville, Tenn., Sept. 23, 1923; s. William Lee and Lucy (Frech) G.; m. Jane Rogers, July 16, 1955; children—Laura, Frederic, Samuel. A.B., Southwestern at Memphis, 1943; M.A., State U. Ia., 1948, Ph.D., 1950; J.D., Am. U., 1962. Instr. polit. sci. U. Ia., 1946-50, U. Md., 1951-53; asst. prof. Am. U., 1953-56, asso. prof., 1956-60, prof., 1960-71, asst. dean, 1958-62, acting dean, 1962-63, prof. law and govt., 1963-71, acting dean law sch., 1970-71; prof. Capital U. Law Sch., Columbus, Ohio, 1971—, dean, 1971-79; cons. John F. Kennedy Center for Performing Arts, Washington, 1964-71. Contbr. articles to legal jours. Mem. Reynoldsburg (Ohio) City Charter Commn., 1978-79. Served with AUS, 1943-46. Mem. D.C., Supreme Ct. bars, Am., Fed. bar assns., Am. Polit. Sci. Assn., Am. Trial Lawyers Assn. Club: Nat. Lawyers (Washington). Home: 999 Matterhorn Dr Reynoldsburg OH 43068

GOOTT, DANIEL, government official; b. N.Y.C., Apr. 23, 1919; s. Hyman and Min (Novak) G.; m. Sylvia Blousman, Aug. 29, 1940; children—Alan F., Eugene M. B.S.S., City Coll. N.Y., 1940; postgrad., Columbia, 1940-41; grad., Sch. Internat. Studies, Geneva, Switzerland, 1946. Asso. chief labor relations br. WPB, 1942-43; spl. asst. internat. labor affairs to under sec. state Dept. State, Washington, 1955-61; dep. coordinator internat. labor affairs Office Sec. State, 1961-62; 1st sec., labor attache Am. embassy, Paris, France, 1962-65; became chief spl. profl. affairs Office of Dep. Undersec. of State for Adminstrn., Washington, 1965; labor and UN adviser Bur. European Affairs; mem. U.S. del. 7th spl. and 30th regular sessions UN Gen. Assembly, 1975; now pvt. cons. on internat. labor and bus. affairs. Served with AUS, 1943-46. Mem. Am. Econ. Assn., Indsl. Relations Research Assn., Am. Fgn. Service Assn., Am. Acad. Polit. and Social Sci. Club: American (Paris). Home: 10904 Oakwood St Silver Spring MD 20901

GOPPERS, VELTA MANEKS, chemist; b. Gostini, Latvia, Feb. 28, 1915; came to U.S., 1949, naturalized, 1954; d. Karlis G. and Milda (Udris) Maneks; m. Sergejs Goppers, 1941 (div. 1947); 1 dau., Ilze Goppers Oredson. B.S., U. Riga, 1942, M.S., 1944. Asst. U. Riga, 1940-44; analytical chemist Farben Industries, Germany, 1945-47; mgr. Pharmacy and Chem. Preparation Lab., Esslingen, Germany, 1947-49; analytical chemist Twin City Testing & Engring. Lab., St. Paul, 1949-52; technologist sci. dept. U. Minn., 1952-53, jr. scientist dept. physiology, 1953-59, sr. scientist environ. health, 1959-68; sr. scientist Space Sci. Ctr., U. Minn., 1968-70, Environ. Health and Research Ctr., U. Minn., 1970—; tchr. microchemistry and chromatography dept. environ. health Grad. Sch., U. Minn. Contbr. research articles to profl. publs. Recipient Recognition award planetary quarantine dept. NASA, 1974; Recipient U. Minn. Sch. Pub. Health award, 1983. Fellow Am. Inst. Chemists, AAAS; mem. Am. Chem. Soc., Am. Indsl. Hygiene Assn. (treas. 1966-68), Sigma Xi, Iota Sigma Pi (pres. Mercury chpt. 1973-74, research award in chemistry 1976), Sigma Delta Epsilon (treas. 1966-69). Lutheran. Home: 5164 Abercrombie Dr Minneapolis MN 55435 Office: Dept Environ Health U Minn Minneapolis MN 55455

GORALSKI, ROBERT, writer, lecturer; b. Chgo., Jan. 2, 1928; s. Stanley and Caroline (Bielas) G.; m. Margaret Anne Walton, Aug. 22, 1948; children: Douglas, Dorothy, Katherine. B.S., U. Ill., 1949; student, Sch. Advanced Internat. Studies, Johns Hopkins, 1960-61; Litt.D., William Jewell Coll., 1969. News announcer WDWS, Champaign, Ill., 1948-51; combat corr. U.S. Navy, Korea, 1951-53; prodn. supr. Radio Free Asia, Tokyo, Japan, 1953-54; asst. rep. Asia Found., Karachi and Dacca, Pakistan, 1954-56; editor, desk supr. Voice of Am., Washington, 1956-61; White House and State Dept. and Pentagon corr. NBC News, 1961-75; dir. pub. info. Gulf Oil Corp., Washington, 1975-83; now writer/lectr.; Nat. Security fellow Hoover Inst., 1972-73. Author: World War II Almanac, 1981. Trustee The Media Inst. Served with USNR, 1945-46; PTO; Served with USNR, 1951-53; PTO; Served with USNR; Korea. Mass media fellow Ford Found. Fund Adult Edn., 1960-61. Mem. Sigma Alpha Epsilon. Home: 1399 Wendy Ln McLean VA 22101

GORAN, MICHAEL J., acctg. firm exec. psychiatrist; b. Alexandria, La., Aug. 27, 1941; s. Joseph R. and Margaret M. (Finley) G. A.B., U. Chgo., 1963; M.D., U. Ill., 1967. Diplomate Am. Bd. Psychiatry Neurology. Intern Michael Reese Med. Center, Chgo., 1967-68; resident and fellow in psychiatry N.Y. State Psychiat. Inst. and Columbia U., N.Y.C., 1970-73; cons. on med. care adminstrn. NIMH, HEW, Bethesda, Md., 1968-70; project leader panel on effectiveness Sec.'s task force on Medicaid and related programs, Arlington, Va., 1969-70; dep. dir. Community Health Service, Health Services and Mental Health Adminstrn., Rockville, Md., 1972-73; dir. bur. quality assurance Health Services Adminstrn., Rockville, 1973-77; acting dir. health standards and qualit bur. Health Care Financing Adminstrn., 1977-78; dir. office of profl. standards Review Orgns., Health Care Financing Adminstrn., 1978; med. dir. Rockridge Health Care Plan, Oakland, Calif., 1978-79, exec. dir., 1979-80; prin. Ernst & Whinney, San Francisco, 1980—; cons. in field. Contbr. articles in field to med. and profl. jours. Served with USPHS, 1968-70. Recipient Superior Service award Health Services Adminstrn., 1974; Meritorious Service award USPHS, 1979. Mem. Alpha Omega Alpha. Democrat. Home: 5940 Miles Ave Oakland CA 94618 Office: 555 California St Suite 3000 San Francisco CA 94104

GORAN, MORRIS, science educator; b. Chgo., Sept. 4, 1916; s. David and Sara (Klein) G.; m. Cymia Walen, June 3, 1951; children: Marjorie, Ruth. B.S., U. Chgo., 1936, M.S., 1939, Ph.D., 1957. Chemist Dearborn Chem. Co., 1941-42; asst. prof. physics Ind. U., 1942-43; scientist Manhattan Dist. Corps of Engrs., Oak Ridge, 1943-45; prof., chmn. dept. phys. sci. Roosevelt U., 1945—; cons. Plastofilm, Croft Ednl. Services; lectr. George Williams Coll., Elmhurst Coll.; Pres. Lincolnwood Bd. Edn., 1959-68. Author: Story of Fritz Haber, 1967, The Future of Science, 1971, Science and Anti-Science, 1974, The Modern Myth: Ancient Astronauts and UFOs, 1978, Fact, Fraud and Fantasy: The Occult and Pseudosciences, 1979, Ten Lessons of the Energy Crisis, 1980, Conquest of Pollution, 1981, Can Science Be Saved?, 1981, (with Marjorie Goran) The Myth of Longevity, 1984; contbr. articles to profl. jours. Fellow Am. Inst. Chemists; mem. Am. Chem. Soc., Am. Phys. Soc., AAAS, AAUP, History of Sci. Soc. Home: 7330 N Kilbourn St Lincolnwood IL 60646 Office: 430 S Michigan Ave Chicago IL 60605

GORANS, GERALD ELMER, accountant; b. Benson, Minn., Sept. 17, 1922; s. George W. and Gladys (Schneider) G.; m. Mildred Louise Stallard, July 19, 1944; 1 dau., Gretchen. B.A., U. Wash., Seattle, 1947. C.P.A., Wash. With Touche, Ross & Co., C.P.A.s (and predecessor), Seattle, 1947—; partner Touche, Ross & Co., 1957—, in charge, 1962-82, mem. policy group, adminstrv. com., bd. dirs., 1974—, sr. partner, 1979—, chmn. mgmt. group, 1982—. Vice pres. budget and fin. Seattle Worlds Fair, 1962; chmn. budget and fin. com. Century 21 Center, Inc., 1963-64; mem. citizens adv. com. Seattle License and Consumer Protection Com., 1965; head profl. div. United Good Neighbor Fund campaign, Seattle, 1963-64, head advanced gifts div., 1965, exec. v.p., 1966, pres., 1967; adv. bd. Seattle Salvation Army, 1965-80, treas., 1974-80; fin. com. Bellevue Christian Sch., 1970-77; citizens adv. bd. public affairs sta. KIRO-TV, 1970-71; treas., bd. dirs., exec. com. Scandinavia Today in Seattle, 1981-83; treas., bd. dirs. Seattle Citizens Council Against Crime, 1972-80, pres., 1976, 77; bd. dirs. U. Wash Alumni Fund, 1967-71, chmn., 1971; trustee U. Wash. Pres.'s Club, 1980—; bd. dirs., chmn. devel. com. Northwest Hosp. Found., 1977—, trustee hosp., 1980—, treas. bd., 1981—; chmn. fin. com. Com. for Balanced Regional Transp., 1981—. Served to lt. (j.g.) USNR, 1943-45. Mem. Am. Inst. C.P.A.'s (chmn. nat. def. com. 1969-75), Nat. Office Mgmt. Assn. (past pres.), Wash. Soc. C.P.A.'s, Seattle C. of C. (chmn. taxation com. 1970-71, bd. dirs. 1971-74, 76-79, 80-81, mem. exec. com. 1980-83, v.p. 1981—, vice chmn. facilities fund drive), Nat. Def. Exec. Res. Clubs: Harbor., Seattle Golf, Wash. Athletic (pres. 1975—), Rainier (treas. 1976-77), Quarterback, 101; Family (San Francisco). Home: 9013 NE 37th Pl Bellevue WA 98004 Office: 1111 3d Ave Seattle WA 98101

GORBMAN, AUBREY, biologist, educator; b. Detroit, Dec. 13, 1914; s. David and Esther (Korenblit) G.; m. Genevieve D. Tapperman, Dec. 25, 1938; children—Beryl Ann, Leila Harriet, Claudia Louise, Eric Jay. A.B., Wayne State U., 1935, M.S., 1936; Ph.D., U. Calif., 1940. Research asso. U. Calif., 1940-41; instr. zoology Wayne U., 1941-44; Jane Coffin Childs fellow in anatomy Yale, 1944-46; asst. prof. zoology Barnard Coll., Columbia, 1946-49, asso. prof., 1949-53, prof., 1953-63, exec. officer dept. zoology, 1952-55; prof. zoology U. Wash., Seattle, 1963—, chmn. zoology dept., 1963-66; biologist Brookhaven Nat. Lab., 1952-58; Fulbright scholar College de France, Paris, 1951-52; Guggenheim fellow U. Hawaii, 1955-56; vis. prof. biochemistry Nagoya U. Japan, 1956, Tokyo U., 1960. Editor: Comparative Endocrinology; editorial bd.: Endocrinology, 1957-61; editor-in-chief: Gen. and Comparative Endocrinology. Fellow A.A.A.S., N.Y. Zool. Soc., N.Y. Acad. Sci.; mem. Endocrine Soc., Am. Inst. Biol. Scis. (governing bd. 1969-75), Am. Soc. Zoologists (pres. 1976), Soc. Exptl. Biology and Medicine, Phi Beta Kappa. Home: 4218 55th Ave NE Seattle WA 98105

GORCHELS, CLARENCE CLIFFORD, librarian; b. Oshkosh, Wis., Aug. 26, 1916; s. Arthur Frederick and Mary Elizabeth (Korsch) G.; m. Eugenia Hayes, June 16, 1945; children: Catherine Marilee, Christopher Michael, Melissa Jean, Gregory Francis. B.S., Wis. State Coll., Oshkosh, 1940; B.L.S. (Wis. Library Assn. fellow 1944-45), U. Wis., 1945; M.S., Columbia, 1952, D.L.S., 1971. With Wash. State U., 1945-58, chief tech. services div., 1947-50, chief readers service div., 1950-56, acting asst. dir. of libraries, 1956-58; vis. asst. prof. U. Wash. Sch. Librarianship, 1958-59; asso. library service Columbia Sch. Library Service, 1959-60; dir. libraries, chmn. dept. library sci. Central Wash. State Coll., Ellensburg, 1960-63; librarian Calif. State Coll. at, Palos Verdes, 1963-66; dir. library Western Oreg. State Coll., 1966—; dir. World Affairs Inst., Wash. State U., 1978; mem. adv. bd. Sch. Library Service, U. So. Calif., 1966—; cons. for univ. libraries King Faisal U., Saudi Arabia, 1983. Editor: Foreshadow, Bull. Regional Hist. Research, 1957—; asst. to editor: Coll. and Research Libraries, 1959-62; books appraisal staff Library Jour, 1947—; abstractor: Historical Abstracts, 1956—; Author articles. Mem. Am. (council 1956-57, chmn. statistics com. 1952-54, 56-57, chmn. budgeting, costs and accounting com. 1965—), Pacific N.W. (vice chmn. 1956), Wash. State (exec. bd.), Wash. State Sch. library assns., Assn. Coll. and Reference Librarians, AAUP, Calif. State Coll. Librarians (sec. 1963-65), Phi Alpha Theta, Kappa Delta Pi. Roman Catholic. Club: Kiwanian. Home: 342 Stadium Dr S Monmouth OR 97361

GORDAN, GILBERT SAUL, physician, educator; b. San Francisco, July 8, 1916; s. Gilbert Saul and Sadie (Joseph) G.; m. Cynthia Vaughan, Feb. 2, 1978. A.B., U. Calif., 1937, M.D., 1941, Ph.D., 1947. Intern U. Calif. Hosp., San Francisco, 1940-41, resident, 1941-42; mem. faculty U. Calif., San Francisco, 1946—, prof. medicine, 1962—; Lady Davis vis. prof. Hebrew U., Jerusalem, 1978; cons. in field. Author: Endocrinology in Clinical Practice, 1953, The Parathyroids, 1971, Clinical Management of the Osteoporoses, 1976; editor: Yearbook of Endocrinology, 1951-63; contbr. numerous articles to profl. jours. Served with M.C. AUS, 1942-45. Decorated Bronze Star.; Commonwealth fellow, 1947-48, 62-63; Guggenheim fellow, 1967-68. Mem. Assn. Am. Physicians, Am. Soc. Clin. Investigation, Endocrine Soc., Royal Soc. Medicine (hon.), Israel Med. Assn. Democrat. Jewish. Office: University of California San Francisco CA 94143

GORDENKER, LEON, educator; b. Detroit, Oct. 7, 1923; s. Samuel and Anna (Posalsky) G.; m. Belia Emilie Strootman, Aug. 16, 1956; children—Robert Jan Mario, Hendrik Willem Paul, Emilie Elise Saskia. A.B., U. Mich., 1943; student, Inst. d'Etudes Politiques, Paris, France, 1951-52; M.A., Columbia U., 1954, Ph.D., 1958. Acad. Internat. Law, The Hague, Netherlands, 1958. Journalist A.P., 1943, Detroit Free Press, 1944-45; information officer NWLB, 1945; pub. infor. officer UN, 1945-53; instr. Dartmouth, 1956-58; mem. faculty Princeton U., 1958—, prof. politics, 1966—; faculty assoc. Center Internat. Studies, 1963—; vis. prof. Columbia, 1961, 67, Makerere U., Uganda, 1969-70, U. Pa., 1971, 74, U. Witwatersrand, South Africa, 1976, Institut Universitaire de Hautes Etudes Internationales, Geneva, 1979-80; cons. UN, 1961—; Fellow Netherlands Inst. Advanced Study, 1972-73. Author: The United Nations and the Peaceful Unification of Korea, 1959, The UN Secretary-General and the Maintenance of Peace, 1967, The United Nations in the International System, 1971, International Aid and National Decisions, 1976, The International Executive, 1978, (with W.P. Davison) Resolving Nationality Conflicts, 1980; Editor: World Politics. Mem. Am. Polit. Sci. Assn., Internat. Studies Assn. Address: Dept Politics Princeton U Princeton NJ 08544

GORDIN, SIDNEY, artist, educator; b. Chelybinsk, Russia, Oct. 24, 1918; came to U.S., 1923; s. Michael Naum and Bertha G.; m. Victoria Sierra, 1945 (div. 1960). Grad., Cooper Union, N.Y.C., 1941. Mem. art faculty Pratt Inst., Bklyn., 1953-58, Bklyn. Coll., 1955-58, Sara Lawrence Coll., Bronxville, N.Y, 1957-58, U. Calif.-Berkeley, 1958—. Home: 903 Camelia St Berkeley CA 94710

GORDIS, LEON, physician; b. N.Y.C., July 19, 1934; s. Robert and Fannie (Jacobson) G.; m. Hadassah Cohen, June 14, 1955; children: Daniel, Elihu, Jonathan. B.A., Columbia, 1954; B.H.L., Jewish Theol. Sem., 1954; M.D., SUNY, 1958; M.P.H., Johns Hopkins U., 1966, D.P.H., 1968. Intern, then resident in pediatrics Jewish Hosp., Bklyn., 1958-61; fellow in pediatrics Sch. Medicine Johns Hopkins U., 1962-66, instr. Sch. Medicine, 1966-68, assoc. prof. epidemiology, Sch. Hygiene and Pub. Health, 1971-73; asst. med. dir. ambulatory care Sinai Hosp., Balt., 1966-68, chief dept. community medicine, 1968-69; prof. Sinai Hosp.-Johns Hopkins, 1973—, chmn. dept. epidemiology, 1975—; vis. prof. med. ecology Hebrew U., Jerusalem, 1969-71. Served with USPHS, 1961-65. Fellow Am. Acad. Pediatrics; mem. Soc. Epidemiologic Research (pres. 1979-80), Am. Epidemiol. Soc. (pres. 1983-84), Am. Pediatric Soc., Soc. Pediatric Research, Am. Public Health Assn., Am. Heart Assn., Assn. Tchrs. Preventive Medicine. Home: 2408 Sugarcone Rd Baltimore MD 21209 Office: 615 N Wolfe St Baltimore MD 21205

GORDIS, ROBERT, Biblical scholar, clergyman, educator, author, editor; b. Bklyn., Feb. 6, 1908; s. Hyman and Lizzie (Engel) G.; m. Fannie Jacobson, Feb. 5, 1928; children: Enoch, Leon, David. A.B. cum laude, Coll. City N.Y., 1926; Ph.D., Dropsie Coll., 1929; rabbi (with distinction), Jewish Theol. Sem. Am., 1932, D.D., 1950; D.H.L. (hon.), Spertus Coll., Chgo., 1981. Teacher Hebrew Tchrs. Tng. Sch. for Girls, 1926-28, Yeshiva Coll., 1929-30, Sem. Coll. of Jewish Studies, 1931; lectr. Rabbinical Sch. Sem., 1937-40; prof. Bibl. exegesis, 1940-60; rabbi Rockaway Park (N.Y.) Hebrew Congregation, 1931-69, rabbi emeritus, 1969—; Adj. prof. religion Columbia, 1948-57; cons. and asso. Center for Study Dem. Instns., Santa Barbara, Calif., 1960-79; vis. prof. O.T. Union Theol. Sem., 1953-54; Sem. prof. Bible Jewish Theol. Sem., 1961-69, prof. Bible, also Rapaport prof. philosophies of religion, 1974-81, prof. emeritus, 1981—; vis. prof. religion Temple U., 1967-68, prof., 1968-74; vis. prof. Bible Hebrew U., Jerusalem, 1970; Chmn. soc. justice com. Rabbinical Assembly Am., 1935-37, mem. exec. council, 1935; del. Synagogue Council of Am., 1937-40, pres., 1940-41, Rabbinical Assembly, 1944-46; founder Beth-El (now Robert Gordis) Day Sch., Belle Harbor, L.I., N.Y., 1950; mem. council on religious freedom Nat. Conf. Christians and Jews; bd. dirs. Inst. Ch. and State, Villanova U.; Lectr. radio and TV, pub. forums speaker. Asso. editor dept. of Bible: Universal Jewish Ency; Contbg. editor: Medical Aspects of Human Sexuality; bd. editors: Judaism (jour.), 1942-68; editor, 1969—; Contbr. to jours. and mags.; Author: books including Wisdom of Ecclesiastes, 1945, Conservative Judaism-An American Philosophy, 1945, Koheleth, The Man and His World, 1951, The Song of Songs, 1954, Judaism for the Modern Age, 1955, A Faith for Moderns, 1960, The Root and The Branch-Judaism and the Free Society, 1962, The Book of God and Man, A Study of Job, 1965, Judaism in A Christian World, 1966, Leave a Little to God, 1967, Sex and the Family in Jewish Tradtion, 1967, Poets, Prophets and Sages, Essays in Biblical Interpretation, 1970, The Biblical Text in the Making, augmented edit, 1971; Editor: Rabbinical Assembly and United Synagogue Sabbath and Festival Prayer Book, 1946, Song of Songs-Lamentations, 1973, The Book of Esther, 1974, The Word and the Book: Studies in Biblical Language and Literature, 1976, The Book of Job: Commentary, New Translation and Special Studies, 1978, Love and Sex—A Modern Jewish Perspective, 1978, Understanding Conservative Judaism, 1978. Overseas mission War-Navy depts., investigating religious condition armed forces, Pacific, Asiatic theatres, 1946; Mem. exec. com. Nat. Hillel Commn., 1960-80; nat. adminstrv. council United Synagogue Am.; bd. govs. Nat. Acad. Adult Jewish Studies; mem. Nat. Com. on Scouting; pres. Synagogue Council of Am., 1948-49, Jewish Book Council Am., 1980-83; trustee Ch. Peace Union; cons. on religion Fund for Republic, 1957-60; asso. trustee

Am. Sch. Oriental Research, 1971-73. Recipient Nat. Jewish Book award, 1979. Fellow Am. Acad. Jewish Research. Home: 150 West End Ave New York NY 10023 Office: 15 E 84th St New York NY 10028

GORDON, ALBERT HAMILTON, investment banker; b. Scituate, Mass., July 21, 1901; s. Albert Franklin and Sarah V. (Flanagan) G.; m. Mary F. Rousmaniere, Oct. 5, 1935; children: Albert F., Mary Gordon Roberts, Sarah F. Gordon Bickler, John R., Daniel F. A.B., Harvard U., 1923, M.B.A., 1925, LL.D., 1977; LL.D., St. Anselm Coll., 1974; grad. hon., Winchester Coll., Eng. Statistician Goldman Sachs & Co., 1925-31; ptnr. Kiddler, Peabody & Co., Inc., N.Y.C., 1931—; now also chmn. Kidder, Peabody & Co., Inc.; dir. Allen Group, Inc., Carnation Co., Deltec Panamerica S.A. Bd. dirs. Ctr. Inter-Am. Relations; trustee, chmn. Roxbury Latin Sch., Chapin Sch.; bd. overseers, bd. mgrs. Meml. Sloan-Kettering Cancer Ctr., 1957—; bd. dirs. Assocs. Harvard Bus. Sch. Mem. Council Fgn. Relations. Republican. Clubs: Links, Harvard (N.Y.C.); Somerset (Boston); Piping Rock (Locust Valley, N.Y.). Home: 10 Gracie Sq New York NY 10028 Office: Kidder Peabody & Co Inc 10 Hanover Sq New York NY 10005

GORDON, AMBROSE, educator; b. Savannah, Ga., May 23, 1920; s. Ambrose and Leonore (Hunter) G.; m. Mary Spainhour, Sept. 1, 1960; children—Marion Robertson, Ambrose. B.A., Yale U., 1942, M.A., 1951, Ph.D., 1952. Lectr. Hunter Coll., 1946-48; instr. Yale U., 1951-54; mem. faculty Sarah Lawrence Coll., 1954-58, U. Tex., Austin, 1958—, prof. English, 1972—; Fulbright lectr., 1966, 69. Author: The Invisible Tent: The War Novels of Ford Madox Ford, 1964; mem. editorial bd.: Furioso, 1946-50; contbr. poems, essays and revs. to various publs. Served with USNR, 1942-46. Mem. AAUP, MLA, Chi Delta Theta. Club: Elizabethan of Yale U. Office: Department of English University of Texas Austin TX 78712

GORDON, ANGUS NEAL, JR., utilities executive, retired electric company executive; b. Henderson, Ky., Jan. 23, 1919; s. Angus Neal and Judith (Lyle) G.; m. Louise Patterson Stites, Nov. 21, 1942. Grad., Phillips Acad., Andover, Mass., 1937; B.A., Yale, 1941, LL.B., 1948. Bar: Conn. bar 1948. With firm Wiggin & Dana, New Haven, 1948-64, partner, 1953-64; pres. United Illuminating Co., New Haven, 1964-74, chmn. bd., 1974-76, chief exec. officer, 1970-76, dir., 1964—; chmn. N.E. Power Coordinating Council, N.Y.C., 1976-82; dir. New Haven Savs. Bank. Trustee N.Am. Electric Reliability Council, Princeton, N.J., 1976-82. Served to lt. col. USAAF, 1941-46. Mem. Order of Coif, Phi Beta Kappa, Sigma Xi (asso.), Alpha Sigma Phi, Phi Delta Phi. Home: 206 Armory St New Haven CT 06511 Office: 1250 Broadway New York NY 10001

GORDON, ARNOLD LEWIS, physical oceanographer, educator; b. N.Y.C., Feb. 4, 1940; s. Abraham and Blanche (Hornstein) G.; m. Susan Ellen Greenberg, Apr. 5, 1970; children: Abigail, Rebecca, Benjamin. B.A., Hunter Coll., 1961; Ph.D., Columbia U., 1965. Asst. prof. Columbia U., N.Y.C., 1966-72, assoc. prof., 1972-76, prof. dept. geol. scis., 1976—; sr. staff Lamont-Doherty Geol. Obs., Palisades, N.Y., 1972—. Contbr. (articles to profl. jours.). NSF grantee, 1965—; ONR grantee, 1982—; Dept. Energy grantee, 1970—. Mem. Am. Geophys. Union, AAAS, Am. Meteorol. Soc., Sigma Xi. Jewish.

GORDON, ARNOLD MARK, lawyer; b. Norwich, Conn., Oct. 2, 1937; s. Barney and Rose (Bilsky) G.; m. Carolyn; children—Lori, Adam, Jennifer. B.Sc. in Bus. Adminstrn, Wayne State U., Detroit, 1959, J.D., 1962. Bar: Mich. bar 1962. Since practiced as prin. partner firm Weinstein, Kroll & Gordon; arbitrator Am. Arbitration Assn., 1969—; lectr. in field. Mem. State Bar Mich. (chmn. med.-legal com. 1976—, negligence sect. 1977-78, pub. negligence sect. bull.), Detroit Bar Assn. (co-chmn. trial advocacy program continguing legal edn. 1972—), Assn. Trial Lawyers Am. (exec. bd. Mich. 1967—), Mich., Detroit trial lawyers assns., Tau Epsilon Rho. Club: Masons. Home: 3874 Wabeek Lake Dr W Bloomfield Hills WI 48013 Office: 701 Travelers Tower Southfield MI 48076

GORDON, ARTHUR ERNEST, Latin epigraphist; b. Marlborough, Mass., Oct. 7, 1902; s. Arthur Ernest and Susan Esther (Porter) G.; m. Maddalena Belloni, Sept. 15, 1924; 1 dau., Paola (Mrs. Paola Zinnecker); m. Joyce A. Stiefbold, June 11, 1937. A.B., Dartmouth Coll., 1923; student, Am. Acad. in Rome, 1923-25; Ph.D. in Latin (Johnston scholar), Johns Hopkins, 1929. Instr. Latin Dartmouth, 1925-27; student asst. Johns Hopkins, 1927-28; instr. Latin Western Res. U., summer 1928; asso. prof. Latin, ancient history U. Vt., 1929-30; asst. prof. to prof. Latin U. Calif. at Berkeley, 1930-70, prof. emeritus, 1970—, chmn. dept. classics, 1953-59; prof. classical langs. Ashland (Ohio) Coll., 1970; prof. classics Ohio State U., 1971; sr. research fellow classical studies Am. Acad., Rome, 1948-49. Author: Epigraphics I-II, 1935-36, Supralineate Abbreviations in Latin Inscriptions, 1948, reprinted 1977, A New Fragment of the Laudatio Turiae, 1950, Q. Veranius, Consul A.D. 49, 1952, Potitus Valerius Messalla, 1954, Notes on the Res Gestae of Augustus, 1968, On the Origins of the Latin Alphabet, Modern Views, 1969, The Letter Names of the Latin Alphabet, 1973, The Fibula Praenestina, Problems of Authenticity, 1975, Notes on the Duenos-Vase Inscription in Berlin, 1976, Illustrated Introduction to Latin Epigraphy, 1983, (with Joyce S. Gordon) Contributions to the Palaeography of Latin Inscriptions, 1957, reprinted, 1977, Album of Dated Latin Inscriptions, Parts I-IV, 1958-65; also monographs, articles and revs. in field. Mem. 2d Internat. Congress Greek and Latin Epigraphy, Paris, 1952. Guggenheim fellow and Fulbright research scholar, 1955-56; Nat. Endowment for Humanities sr. fellow, 1972-73. Mem. Am. Philol. Assn., Philol. Assn. Pacific Coast (pres. 1952), Calif. Classical Assn., Internat. Assn. for Greek and Latin Epigraphy, Fondation Hardt pour L'étude de L'antiquité classique, Vandoeuvres/Geneva. Clubs: Faculty (Berkeley); Inverness Yacht. Home: 401 Santa Clara Ave Apt 514 Oakland CA 94610

GORDON, BASIL, educator; b. Balt., Dec. 23, 1932; s. Basil and Helen (Williams) G. M.A., Johns Hopkins, 1953; Ph.D., Calif. Inst. Tech., 1956. Instr. Calif. Inst. Tech., 1956-57; asst. prof. math. U. Calif. at Los Angeles, 1959-63, asso. prof., 1963-67, prof., 1967—. Editor: Pacific Jour. Mathematics, 1969-70, 72-73, Jour. Combinatorial Theory, 1970—; Contbr. articles to profl. jours. Served with AUS, 1957-59. Alfred P. Sloan fellow, 1962-64. Mem. Math. Assn. Am., Pi Mu Epsilon. Research on number theory, combinatorics, group theory, and function theory. Home: 526 Palisades Ave Santa Monica CA 90402 Office: 405 Hilgard Ave Los Angeles CA 90024

GORDON, BERNARD, management and communications cons.; b. N.Y.C., Apr. 24, 1922; m. Margaret V. Cohn, June 20, 1948; children—Anne J., Jonathan M., Alan D. B.S., Coll. City N.Y., 1943; M.B.A., Harvard U., 1948. With William Filene's Sons Co., Boston, 1948-50; comptroller, chief bus. officer Brandeis U., Waltham, Mass., 1950-58; adminstrv. v.p., dir. foreign operations Wasco Chem. Co., Cambridge, Mass., 1958-60; pres. Chgo. div. Cahners Pub. Co., 1960-68; pres., chief exec. officer Denoyer-Geppert Co., Chgo., 1968-72; gen. mgr. Dun-Donnelley Pub. Co., Chgo., 1972-77; pres. Bernard Gordon and Assocs., Mgmt. and Communications Cons., Glencoe, Ill., 1977—; ptnr. Gordon's Hand, Inc., Chgo., 1982—; vis. lectr. Medill Sch. Journalism, Northwestern U., 1977—. Pres. Fine Arts Music Found. Chgo., 1978-79. Served with AUS, 1943-46. Mem. Chgo. Bus. Publications Assn. (pres. 1976-77). Home: 1030 Forest Ave Glencoe IL 60022 Office: 655 Fifteenth St Suite 320 NW Washington DC 20005

GORDON, CHARLES, lawyer; b. N.Y.C., Oct. 12, 1905; s. Louis and Sarah (Tannenbaum) G.; m. Anne Chachanowsky, Mar. 17, 1940; children: Michael, Ellen. Student, CCNY, 1923-26; LL.B., NYU, 1927. Bar: N.Y. 1929, D.C. 1974, U.S. Supreme Ct. 1949. Atty. N.Y.C., 1929-39; with U.S. Immigration and Naturalization Service, 1939-74, dep. gen. counsel, 1962-66, gen. counsel, 1966-74; practice law, Washington, 1974—; Adj. prof. law Georgetown U., 1963—, U. San Diego, 1974—; lectr. immigration law symposiums Practicing Law Inst., also various bar assns. and law schs. Author: (with Rosenfield) Immigration Law and Procedure, rev. edit, 1966, also; (with Ellen Gordon) ann. supplements and revisions Immigration and Nationality Law, student edit, 1979, Immigration Law and Procedure, desk edit, 1980. Active local civic orgns. and P.T.A. Recipient Annual Authorship award Fed. Bar Assn., 1965. Mem. ABA (vice chmn. com. immigration and nationality 1967-73, chmn. 1973—), Am. Immigration Lawyers Assn. (Outstanding Contbns. award 1983). Home: 11810 Seven Locks Rd Rockville MD 20854 Office: 1511 K St NW Washington DC 20005 *I am fortunate to have been born to immigrant parents in this land of freedom and opportunity. As a lawyer, government official, teacher, and writer I have tried to contribute to the development of the law and the assurance of fair and humane government policies.*

GORDON, CYRUS HERZL, orientalist, educator; b. Phila., June 29, 1908; s. Benjamin Lee and Dorothy (Cohen) G.; m. Joan Elizabeth Kendall, Sept. 22, 1946; children: Deborah J. Gordon Friedrich, Sarah Y. Gordon Krakauer, Rachel K. Gordon Bernstein, Noah D., Dan K. A.B., U. Pa., 1927, M.A., 1928, Ph.D., 1930; D.H.L. (hon.), Balt. Hebrew Coll., 1981. Instr. semitics U. Pa., 1930-31; field archaeologist, fellow Am. Schs. Oriental Research, Near East, 1931-35; teaching fellow Oriental Sem., Johns Hopkins U., 1935-38; lectr. Bible, Smith Coll., 1938-39, 40-41; mem. Inst. Advanced Study, Princeton, N.J., 1939-40, 41-42; prof. Assyriology and Egyptology, Dropsie U., Phila., 1946-56; prof. Near Eastern studies Brandeis U., Waltham, Mass., 1956-73, emeritus, 1973—, also chmn. dept. Mediterranean studies, 1958-73; dir. Grad. Sch. (Brandeis U.), asso. dean faculty, 1957-58; Gottesman prof. Hebrew studies NYU, 1973—; vis. fellow humanities U. Colo., 1967; Gay lectr. Simmons Coll., 1970; vis. prof. NYU, 1970-73; vis. fellow Japan Found., 1974; vis. prof. history and anthropology U. N.Mex., 1976; vis. prof. humanities S.W. Mo. State U., 1977, 79; disting. vis. prof. N.Mex. State U., Las Cruces, 1979-80; vis. prof. Judaic studies SUNY, Albany, 1981-82; archeol. expdns. East Mediterranean lands, 1957-58, 59, 61, 67-79. Author: Ugaritic Grammar, 1940, Ugaritic Handbook, 1947, Ugaritic Manual, 1955, The Living Past, 1941, Adventures in the Nearest East, 1957, Ugaritic Literature, 1949, Smith College Tablets, 1952, Introduction to Old Testament Times, 1953, Hammurapi's Code, 1957, The World of the Old Testament, 1958, rev. as The Ancient Near East 1965, Before the Bible, 1963, rev. as The Common Background of Greek and Hebrew Civilization, 1965, Ugaritic Textbook, 1965, rev. with supplement, 1967, Ugarit and Minoan Crete, 1966, Evidence for the Minoan Language, 1966, Forgotten Scripts, 1968, rev. edit., 1971, rev. and enlarged, 1982; also numerous articles.; contbg. editor: Am. Jour. Archaeology, 1938-45; editorial council: Encounter, 1956; internat. adv. com.: Jewish Quar. Rev., 1979-82. Trustee, Boston Hebrew Coll.; corr. mem. Inst. Antiquity and Christianity Claremont Grad. Sch. and Univ. Center; trustee Internat. Council Etruscan Studies of Order of Holy Cross; mem. mng. com. Am. Sch. Classical Studies, Athens, 1958-73. Served as officer U.S. Army, 1942-46; col. USAF Res., ret.; flight comdr. Boston Air Res. Center, 1958-61; moblzn. assignee Hdqrs. USAF, 1961-67. Harrison scholar U. Pa., 1928-29; Harrison fellow, 1929-30; Am. Council Learned Socs. fellow, 1932-33; Am. Scandinavian Found. fellow, 1939; recipient Alumni award Gratz Coll., Phila., 1961; honored 2 Festschriften: Orient and Occident: Essays presented to Cyrus H. Gordon on the Occasion of his 65th Birthday, 1973, The Bible World: Essays in Honor of Cyrus H. Gordon, 1980. Fellow Am. Acad. Arts and Scis., Royal Asiatic Soc. (hon.), Explorers Club, Am. Acad. Jewish Research; mem. Am. Hist. Assn., Am. Oriental Soc. (exec. com. 1964-67), Am. Philol. Assn., Archaeol. Inst. Am., Soc. Bibl. Lit. and Exegesis. Home: 130 Dean Rd Brookline MA 02146 Office: 637 East Bldg NY U Washington Sq New York NY 10003 *Transmitting the growing humanistic tradition along with the spirit of scientific enlightenment, motivates my life as a parent, teacher, scholar and author.*

GORDON, DAVID J., construction company executive; b. Monroe, N.C., June 10, 1920; s. Craven N. and Judith (Laney) G.; m. Frances Mott, Feb. 3, 1944; children: Susane, David J., Michael Mott. Roller operator R.B. Tyler Co., Louisville, 1938-39, timekeeper, 1939-40, asst. supt., 1940-48; supt. Dickerson Inc., Monroe, N.C., 1948-53, gen. supt., 1953—, v.p., dir., 1956—, pres., dir. contractors and materials, Rockingham, N.C., 1980—.

GORDON, DAVID JAMIESON, tenor; b. Phila., Dec. 7, 1947; s. David William and Lois Irene (Lukens) G.; m. Barbara Jean Bixby, June 14, 1969. Student, Coll. of Wooster, 1965-68, McGill U., 1968-70; student of Dale Moore, 1965—. Debut with, Lyric Opera Chgo., 1973; leading tenor, Landestheater Linz (Austria), 1975-79; prin. roles with, San Francisco Opera, Houston Grand Opera, Washington Opera, Tulsa Opera, Mostly Mozart Festival, Wolf Trap Farm Park, Salzburg Festival; artist-mem., 20th Century Ensemble; concert soloist with, Handel and Hayden Soc., Musica Sacra, Bach Festivals, Carmel, Calif. and Bethlehem, Pa. Y Chamber Symphony, Boston Symphony, Vienna Symphony,, St. Louis Symphony, Seattle Symphony, Phila. Orch., Nat. Symphony, Washington, Mozarteum Orch., Emerson String Quartet; appears in opera, concerts, chamber music, throughout U.S. and Europe; recs. for, Delos Records, Telarc Records, Smithsonian Collection of Recs. Address: 251 W 97th St Apt 6C New York NY 10025

GORDON, DEXTER KEITH, jazz musician; b. Los Angeles, Feb. 27, 1923. Played saxaphone with, Lionel Hampton, Louis Armstrong, Billy Eckstine, Charlie Parker, Wardell Gray; now soloist. (Winner Downbeat Readers Poll 1977). Office: care Ms Mgmt 130 E 31st St New York NY 10016 *

GORDON, DIANA RUSSELL, non-profit organization executive; b. North Adams, Mass., July 18, 1938; d. Hallett Darius and Mary Elizabeth (Earl) Smith; m. James D. Lorenz, Aug. 20, 1960 (div. 1966); m. David M. Gordon, Sept. 7, 1967. B.A., Mills Coll., 1958; M.A., Radliffe Coll., 1959; J.D., Harvard U., 1964. Law clk. Beardsley, Hufstedler & Kemble, Los Angeles, 1964-65; program analyst OEO, Washington, 1965-66; legis. asst. Budget Bur., N.Y.C., 1967-70; research fellow Inst. Politics, Harvard U., 1970-71; dir. Citizens Inquiry on Parole, N.Y.C., 1973-78; v.p. Nat. Council Crime and Delinquency, Hackensack, N.J., 1978-81, pres., Newark, 1982—; cons. various urban affairs orgns., N.Y.C., 1971-78. Author: City Limits: Barriers to Change in Urban Government, 1973. Bd. dirs. Green Hope Residence for Women, 1975—, Legal Action Ctr., 1979—, Prisoner's Legal Services, 1982—. Democrat. Office: Nat Council on Crime and Delinquency 15 Washington St Newark NJ 07102

GORDON, EDWARD, music association executive; b. 1930. D.F.A., North Central Coll., Naperville, Ill., 1980. Asso. mgr. Grant Park summer concerts, Chgo. Park Dist., 1958-65, mgr., 1965-68; gen. mgr. Ravinia Festival Assn., Chgo., 1968-70, exec. dir., 1970—, chief operating officer, 1982—; Mem. music adv. panel U.S. Dept. State; mem. recommendation bd. Avery Fisher Artist Award program; judge, mem. adv. bd. Naumburg Award; mem. adv. bd. Van Cliburn Internat. Piano Competition, Internat. Piano Competition, Sydney, Australia; mem. festivals panel Nat. Endowment for Arts.; mem. Music panel Arts Club of Chgo. Former concert pianist. Performed age 9 with Chgo. Symphony under Frederick Stock. Office: Ravinia Festival Assn 22 W Monroe St Chicago IL 60603

GORDON, ELLEN (PATRICIA RUBIN), candy company executive; d. William B. and Cele H. (Travis) Rubin; m. Melvin J. Gordon, June 25, 1950; children: Virginia, Karen, Wendy, Lisa. Student, Vassar Coll., 1948-50; B.A., Brandeis U., 1965; postgrad., Harvard U., 1968. With Tootsie Roll Industries, Chgo., 1968—, corp. sec., 1974-78, v.p. product devel., 1974-77, sr. v.p., 1977-78, pres., 1978—; also dir.; dir. HDI Investment Corp. Pres. Cele H. and William B. Family Fund Inc. Office: 7401 S Cicero Ave Chicago IL 60629

GORDON, ERNEST, clergyman; b. Greenock, Scotland, May 31, 1916; naturalized, 1960; s. James and Sarah Rae (Macmillan) G.; m. Helen McIntosh Robertson, Dec. 17, 1945; children: Gillian Margaret, Alastair James. B.D., Hartford Theol. Sem., 1948, S.T.M., 1949; postgrad., U. Glasgow, 1950-51; LL.D., Bloomfield Coll., 1957; D.C.L. (hon.), Bishop's U. of Can., 1966; L.H.D., Marshall U., 1973; D.D., St. Andrews U., Scotland, 1976. Ordained to ministry Ch. of Scotland, 1950; dep. minister Paisley Abbey, 1950-52; supply minister Amagansett and Montauk chs., 1953-54; Presbyn. chaplain Princeton U., 1954-55, dean univ. chapel, 1955-81; now pres. Christian Rescue Effort for Emancipation of Dissidents; Danforth lectr. Davis and Elkins Coll., 1968; Turnbull preacher, Melbourne, Australia, 1969, Staley distinguished scholar, 1972—; tchr. in residence Presbyn. Ch., Houston, 1983. Author: A Living Faith for Today, 1956, Through the Valley of the Kwai, 1962, Miracle on the River Kwai, 1963, Meet Me at the Door, 1969, A Guidebook for the New Christian, 1972, Solan, 1973, Islands Apart, 1977, Me, Myself & Who?, 1980; Contbr. articles to periodicals. Chmn. N.J. Mental Health Research and Devel. Fund. Served as capt. 93d Highlanders, 1939-46; PTO. Fellow Victoria Inst. London; mem. Royal Inst. Philosophy (London), Am. Soc. Ch. History, Ch. Service Soc. Am. (founder). Clubs: Princeton (N.Y.C.); Highland Brigade (London); Burma Star, Brit. Officers. Prisoner of war, 1942-45. Home: 117 Prince St Alexandria VA 22314 also Bendigo Rd Amagansett NY 11850

GORDON, EUGENE ANDREW, federal judge; b. Guilford County, N.C., July 10, 1917; s. Charles Robert and Carrie (Scott) G.; m. Virginia Stoner, Jan. 1, 1943; children: Eugene Andrew, Rosemary Anne. A.B., Elon Coll., 1938, LL.D. (hon.), 1982; LL.B., Duke U., 1941. Bar: N.C. 1941. Practiced law, 1946-64; mem. firm Young, Young & Gordon, Burlington, 1947-64; solicitor Alamance Gen. County Ct., 1947-54; county atty., Alamance County, 1954-64; U.S. judge Middle Dist. N.C., 1964—, chief judge, now sr. judge. Former chmn. adv. bd. Salvation Army.; Former nat. committeeman N.C. Young Democrats; former pres. Alamance County Young Democrats; chmn. Alamance County Dem. Exec. Com., 1954-64. Served to capt. AUS, 1942-46; comdg. officer N.G., 1946-47; Burlington. Mem. Alamance County Bar Assn. (past pres.), Burlington-Alamance County C. of C. (past pres.), Burlington Jr. C. of C., Phi Delta Phi. Clubs: Rotary (past pres.), American Business (Burlington) (past pres.). Office: PO Box 3285 Greensboro NC 27402

GORDON, EUGENE IRVING, telecommunications company executive; b. N.Y.C., Sept. 14, 1930; s. Sol and Gertrude (Lassen) G.; m. Barbara Young, Aug. 19, 1956; children—Laurence Mark, Peter Eliot. B.S., CCNY, 1952; Ph.D., Mass. Inst. Tech., 1957. Research asso. Mass. Inst. Tech., Cambridge, 1957; mem. tech. staff Bell Labs., Murray Hill, N.J., 1957-59, supr., 1959-63, dept. head, 1963-68, dir., 1968-83; cons., 1983—. Patentee in field.; Editor: EDS Trans, 1963-64, Jour. Quantum Electronics, 1964-76; Contbr. articles to profl. jours. Fellow IEEE (Zworykin award 1975); mem. Nat. Acad. Engring., Am. Phys. Soc. Democrat. Jewish. Club: B'nai Brith. Home: 14 Braidburn Way Convent NJ 07961 Office: Bell Laboratories 600 Mountain Ave Murray Hill NJ 07974 *The philosophy underlying my approach to life has been "Better light a candle than curse the dark". As a physicist I know that it is virtually impossible to produce light without some heat, but it always has come as a surprise to me how little heat human beings will tolerate even in the presence of abundant illumination.*

GORDON, EZRA, architect, educator; b. Detroit, Apr. 5, 1921; s. Abraham and Rebecca (Reimer) G.; m. Jeanette Greenberg, Oct. 8, 1942; children: Cheryl P. Gordon Van Ausdal, Rana Gordon Oremland, Judith Gordon. Student, Roosevelt Coll., 1946-48; B.S. inArchitecture, U. Ill., 1951. Draftsman Pace Assos. Architects, 1951-53; sr. planner Chgo. Plan Commn., 1953-54; project architect Harry Weese & Assos., 1954-61; ptnr. Gordon-Levin & Assocs., Chgo., 1961—; cons. Dept. Urban Renewal City Chgo.; Prof. U. Ill.-Chgo., Chgo.; mem. Mayor's Adv. Council on Bldg. Code Ammendments. Works include South Commons, Chgo., 1968, IBM Office bldgs, Kalamazoo, 1969, Omaha, 1971, Wexler Pavilion and Siegel Inst., Michael Reese Hosp., Chgo., 1971, Newberry Plaza, Chgo., 1973, River Plaza, Chgo., 1976, Elm St. Plaza, Chgo., 1976, Dearborn Park, Chgo., 1979, Huron Plaza, Chgo., 1981, 400 Streeterville, Chgo., 1983, East Bank Club, Chgo., 1983. Bd. dirs. Hyde Park-Kenwood Community Conf.; v.p. Harper Ct. Found. Served with AUS, 1942-45. Decorated Croix de Guerre with palm; recipient Honor award Dept. Housing and Urban Devel., 1967, AIA-Chgo. C. of C., 1967, award AIA-House & Home Mag., 1967, Distinguished Bldg. award, 1957, 63, 69, 71, 73, 75, award City of Chgo. Beautification, 1969, 75, award of excellence Post Fensioning Inst. Fellow AIA (dir. Chgo. chpt.); mem. Labor Zionist Alliance, Am. Profs. for Peace in Middle East, Am. Jewish Congress, Lambda Alpha. Jewish. Club: Cliff Dwellers. Home: 1300 Lake Shore Dr Chicago IL 60610 Office: 101 E Ontario St Chicago IL 60611

GORDON, FRANK X., JR., judge; b. Chgo., Jan. 9, 1929; s. Frank X. and Lucille (Gburek) G.; m. Joan C. Gipe, Sept. 17, 1950; children—Frank X., Candace Gordon Lander. B.A., Stanford U., 1951; LL.B., U. Ariz., 1954. Bar: Ariz. bar 1954. Asso. firm Gordon & Gordon, Kingman, Ariz., 1954-62; atty. City of Kingman, 1955-57; judge Superior Ct. Mohave County (Ariz.), Kingman, 1962-75; justice Ariz. Supreme Ct., Phoenix, 1975—; mem. various coms. State Bar Ariz.; Ariz. rep. to Council fo State Ct. Reps. for Nat. Center State Cts.; bd. visitors U. Ariz. Law Sch., 1972-75. Bd. trustees Chester H. Smith Meml. Scholarship Fund; past dir. and pres. Mohave County Mental Health Clinic, Inc.; past mem. Gov.'s Commn. Mental Health; state bd. dirs. Ariz. Heart Assn.; active Boulder Dam Area council Boy Scouts Am. Mem. Am., Ariz., Maricopa County bar assns., Am. Judicature Soc., Mohave County C. of C. (past pres.). Democrat. Methodist. Clubs: Rotary, Elks. Office: Ariz Supreme Ct State Capitol Bldg Phoenix AZ 85007

GORDON, GEORGE STANLEY, advertising executive; b. N.Y.C., Nov. 19, 1931; s. George and Emily (Miller) G.; m. Janet Morgen, June 17, 1969; children: George Stanley, Troy, Kim, Dana. B.A., Brown U., 1949; M.B.A., Wharton Sch. U. Pa., 1950; postgrad., advanced mgmt. program Harvard U., 1968. Copy writer Benton &

Bowles, 1955-58; dir. mktg. Massey-Ferguson LTD, Toronto, Ont., Can., 1958-63; v.p. mktg. Eastern Airlines, N.Y.C., 1963-68; sr. v.p., creative dir. Foote, Cone & Belding, N.Y.C., 1968-73; founder, pres., chmn. bd. Gordon & Shortt, N.Y.C., 1974—; chmn. bd. Wells, Rich, Greene, Gordon, Dallas, 1979—, Gordon, Shortt and Burton Advt. Inc., Detroit; dir. Craven Industries, Greensboro, N.C., Alladin Industries, Trenton, Meriden, Conn., Bemiss Equipment Inc., Richmond, Va. Author of designs for jet aircraft based on painting by Alexander Calder; producer: play Jeweler's Shop (author Pope John Paul II), 1982. Served with USNR, 1950-52. Mem. Young Presidents Orgn. Clubs: N.Y. Athletic, Scarsdale Golf, Wings. Home: 40 Morris Ln Scarsdale NY 10583 1 Water St White Plains NY

GORDON, GILBERT, chemist, educator; b. Chgo., Nov. 11, 1933; s. Walter and Catherine Gilbert; m. Joyce Elaine Masura; children: Thomas, Susan. B.S., Bradley U., 1955; Ph.D., Mich. State U., 1959. Postdoctoral research asso. U. Chgo., 1959-60; asst. prof. U. Md., College Park, 1960-64, asso. prof., 1964-67, prof., 1967; prof. chemistry U. Iowa, Iowa City, 1967-73; prof., chmn. dept. Miami U., Oxford, Ohio, 1973—, Volweiler Disting. Research prof., 1984—; vis. prof. Japanese Soc. Promotion Sci., 1969; cons. Nat. Bur. Standards, Am. Cyanamid Corp., John Langdon Enterprises, Olin Corp. Editor: catalysis kinetics sect. Chem. Abstracts, 1970—; editorial bd. synthesis inorganic metalorganicchemistry: Ohio Jour. Sci, 1971—; contbr. articles to chem. jours. Named Cin. Chemist of Yr., 1981. Mem. Am. Chem. Soc., Chgo. Soc. London, Faraday Soc., Sigma Xi, Phi Kappa Phi. Home: 190 Shadowy Hills Dr Oxford OH 45056 Office: Dept Chemistry Miami U Oxford OH 45056 *My objectives have been to investigate meaningful areas of chemistry in an attempt to better understand chemical phenomena affecting our everyday lives (such as better and less expensive ways to purify drinking water), and to work diligently with students while helping to educate them to be better citizens and aware of the tremendous potential of science.*

GORDON, HAROLD, book publishing company executive; b. Bklyn., Oct. 24, 1926; s. Herman and Beatrice (Posner) G.; m. Madeline R. Tragerman, Apr. 1, 1958; 1 son, Scott Jay. B.B.A. cum laude, CUNY, 1956, M.B.A., 1964. Mgr. accounts receivable Pocket Books, Inc., N.Y.C., 1956-60, credit mgr., 1960-65; v.p. Affiliated Pubs., Inc., N.Y.C., 1966-67; divisional v.p. Simon & Schuster, Inc., N.Y.C., 1967-71, corp. v.p., 1971—, also. dir.; pres., dir. Total Warehouse Services Corp., Bristol, Pa., 1976—. Served with USAAF, 1945-46. Mem. Beta Gamma Sigma. Home: 35 Seacoast Terr Brooklyn NY 11235 Office: 1230 Ave of Americas New York NY 10020

GORDON, HARRY HASKIN, physician, educator; b. Bklyn., Aug. 4, 1906; s. Samuel and Ida (Haskin) G.; m. Lois Chasins (dec. 1943); m. Fayga Halpern, June 8, 1948; children: Charles, Deborah. B.A., Cornell U., 1926, M.D., 1929; D.Sc., Yeshiva U., 1969. Intern Montefiore Hosp., N.Y.C., then; New Haven Hosp., 1929-31; resident New Haven Hosp., then N.Y. Hosp., 1931-33; asso. attending pediatrician N.Y. Hosp., 1932-46; pediatrician-in-chief Colo. and Denver Gen. hosps., 1946- 52, Sinai Hosp., Balt., 1952-62; attending pediatrician Johns Hopkins Hosp., 1952-62, Bronx Municipal Hosp. Center, 1962—, med. cons., 1976—; cons. pediatrician Montefiore Hosp. and Med. Center, 1964—; dir. Rose Fitzgerald Kennedy Center for Research in Mental Retardation and Human Devel., 1965-72, dir. emeritus, 1972—; asst. prof. Cornell U. Med. Coll., 1933-46; prof. pediatrics U. Colo., 1946-52; asso. prof. pediatrics Johns Hopkins U., 1952-62; prof. pediatrics Albert Einstein Coll. Medicine, 1962-77, prof. emeritus, 1977—, asso. dean, 1966-67, dean, 1967-70; cons. in pediatrics Surgeon Gen. U.S. Army, 1947-62, U.S. Childrens Bur. for Maternal and Child Health and Crippled Childrens Services, 1948-51; cons. Surgeon Gen. USPHS, 1949-78; mem. food and nutrition bd. NRC, 1955-59, mem. adv. com. on child devel., 1971-73, mem. bd. on maternal, child and family health research, 1975-77; mem. Health Task Force, N.Y. Urban Coalition, 1970-73; cons. Kennedy Center for Bioethics, Georgetown U., 1974—; Career scientist Health Research Council City N.Y., 1962-67. Contbr. articles to profl. jours. Served from capt. to lt. col. M.C., AUS, 1942-46. Recipient Borden award for nutritional research Am. Acad. Pediatrics, 1944; Grover F. Powers Disting. prof. Nat. Assn. for Retarded Children, 1963—. Fellow AAAS; mem. Am. Pediatric Soc. (John Howland award 1975, past pres.), Soc. Pediatric Research (past pres.), Am. Acad. Pediatrics (C. Anderson Aldrich award 1976), Am. Soc. Clin. Investigation, Am. Assn. Mental Deficiency (Disting. Service award 1973), Sigma Xi, Alpha Omega Alpha. Home: 720 Milton Rd Apt 4NF Rye NY 10580 Office: 1410 Pelham Pkwy S Bronx NY 10461

GORDON, HORACE EARL, surgeon; b. Arbuckle, Calif., July 21, 1924; s. Horace Curby and Matilda (Richter) G. A.B., U. Calif.-Berkeley, 1944, M.D., 1947. Diplomate: Am. Bd. Surgery. Intern San Francisco Gen. Hosp., 1947-48; resident in surgery Wadsworth Hosp. VA Center, Los Angeles, 1954-58, asst. chief surgery, 1960-63, chief surgery, 1963-77, chief staff, 1977—; asso. prof. surgery UCLA Med. Center, 1973-77, prof., 1977—, vice chmn. dept. surgery, 1973-77, asst. dean, 1977—. Contbr. articles to sci. jours. Bd. dirs. Coastal Cities unit Am. Cancer Soc., 1974—, pres., 1982. Served with USNR, 1943-46, 50-53. Fellow A.C.S. (gov. 1981—); mem. Assn. VA Surgeons (pres. 1974), Western Surg. Assn., So. Calif. Soc. Gastroenterology, Pacific Coast Surg. Assn., Los Angeles Surg. Soc. (pres. 1974), Bay Surg. Soc. (pres. 1970), Soc. Surgery Alimentary Tract. Office: VA Wadsworth Hosp Center Los Angeles CA 90073

GORDON, HOWARD FREDERICK, supermarket chain exec.; b. Phila., Jan. 15, 1941; s. Myer Michael and Sylvia Sonya (Robinson) G.; m. Sheila P. Berman, June 20, 1963; 2 daus. B.S. in Indsl. Relations, U. N.C., 1963; J.D., Temple U., 1966. Bar: Pa. bar 1967. Asst. personnel mgr. Food Fair, Inc. (name changed to Pantry Pride, Inc. 1981), Balt., 1966-70, resident counsel, Phila., 1972-74, corporate counsel, 1974-75, sec., corporate counsel, 1975-79, sec., asst. gen. counsel, 1979-81, v.p., gen. counsel, sec., 1981—; asso. firm Stein & Rosen, N.Y.C., 1970-72. Mem. Am., Phila. bar assns., Tau Epsilon Rho. Clubs: Locust, Woodmont Country. Home: 10422 NW 2d St Coral Springs FL 33065 Office: 6500 N Andrews Ave Fort Lauderdale FL 33309

GORDON, HOWARD SCOTT, economics educator; b. Halifax, N.S., Can., Aug. 14, 1924; came to U.S., 1966; s. Ely and Dora (Shabbes) G.; m. Barbara Rowe, Aug. 27, 1945; children: Geoffrey William, Paul Maxwell Ivan, James Marshall. B.A., Dalhousie U., 1944; M.A., Columbia U., 1947; Ph.D., McGill U., 1964. Asst. prof. Carleton U., 1948-53, asso. prof., 1953-57, prof., 1957-66; prof. econs. Ind. U., 1966-81, disting. prof. econs., 1981—; prof. econs. Queen's U., Can., 1969—. Home: 314 Arbutus Ave Bloomington IN 47401 Office: Econs Dept Indiana U Bloomington IN 47405

GORDON, HUGH W., JR., construction company executive; b. Houston, 1926; married. B.S.I.E., U. Tex., 1948. With Tex. Automatic Sprinkler Co., 1950-51, Mid-Continental Supply, 1951; engr. Brown & Root, Inc., Houston, 1951-65, v.p., 1965-68, sr. v.p., 1968-70, group v.p., 1970, now exec. v.p., dir.; pres. Taylor Diving & Salvage Co., Inc.; pres., dir. Arctic Constructors, Inc.; v.p., dir. Jackson Marine Corp., Ocean Optics, Inc., Oil Field Service, Inc.; dir. various subs. Brown & Root. Office: Brown & Root Inc 4100 Clinton St Box 3 Houston TX 77020 *

GORDON, IRVING, physician, educator; b. Cleveland, June 20, 1914; s. N. Beryl and Minna (Singer) G.; m. Toini Lefren, June 16, 1939 (dec. May 1967); children—James Norrby, Elizabeth Britt (Mrs. Michael Ascher), Thomas Rolf; m. Francis Maxwell Hawkes, Oct. 18, 1968. M.D., U. Mich., 1937. Diplomate: Am. Bd. Pathology, Am. Bd. Microbiology, Nat. Bd. Med. Examiners. Intern L.I. Coll. Med. Sch. Hosp., 1937-38, resident, 1938-39; fellow Rockefeller Found., 1941; profl. asso. commn. acute respiratory disease Army Epidemiological Bd., Ft. Bragg, N.C., 1943-46; staff mem. div. labs. and research N.Y. State Health Dept., 1946-55, asst. dir., 1952-55; asso. prof. medicine and bacteriology Albany (N.Y.) Med. Coll.; also asso. attending physician Albany Hosp., 1949-55; prof. dept. microbiology U. So. Calif. Med. Sch., 1955—, chmn., 1955-81, asso. dean, 1963-65; sr. attending physician U. So. Calif. Med. Center, 1956—; Mem. coms. NIH, Armed Forces Epidemiological Bd., WHO. Author research contributions to virology and infectious deseases.; Contbr. to med. microbiol. textbooks.; Editorial bd. sci. jours. Mem. Am. Cancer Nat. Tb Assn. Home: 375 S San Rafael Ave Pasadena CA 90033 Office: U Southern Calif Med Sch Los Angeles CA 90033

GORDON, JACK DAVID, financial consultant, state senator, real estate developer; b. Detroit, June 3, 1922; s. A. Louis and Henrietta (Rodgers) G.; children: Andrew Louis, Deborah Mary, Jonathan Henry. B.A., U. Mich., 1942. Engaged in real estate and ins. businesses, Miami Beach, Fla., 1946-52; founding dir., pres., chief mng. officer Washington Savs. & Loan Assn., Miami Beach, 1952-80, vice chmn. bd., 1980-81; founding dir. Jefferson Nat. Bank of Miami Beach, 1962-77, past chmn. exec. com.; mem. Fla. Senate, 1972—; housing fin. cons. Dept. State and; expert cons. UN Tech. Assistance Program in, Costa Rica, Nicaragua, Panama, Ethiopia, Somali Republic, Nigeria, 1959-63; cons. to ROCAP, 1962-64, Eastern Nigerian Housing Corp., 1963; contract supr. AID Housing Guaranty Program in, Latin Am., 1966-69; Chmn. Miami Beach Housing Authority, 1947-56. Author: (with others) A Survey of New Home Financing Institutions in Latin America, 1969. Mem. Dade County Bd. Public Instrn., 1961-68. Served with AUS, 1943-46. Mem. Am. Jewish Congress, Am. Friends of Hebrew U., ACLU. Democrat. Home: 48 Palm Island Miami Beach FL 33139 Office: 1701 Meridian Ave Miami Beach FL 33139

GORDON, JACK LEONARD, construction company executive; b. Cedar Rapids, Iowa, Aug. 17, 1928; s. W. Ward and Agnes (Knox) G.; m. Zahave; children—Gaile A. Leukhardt, Scott W., Timothy R., Asae, Anat. Student, U. Calif. at Berkeley; grad., Advanced Mgmt. Program, Harvard, 1975. Adjuster Comml. Credit Corp., Stockton, Calif., 1949-50; salesman U.S. Gypsum Co., Sacramento, 1950-54, Calaveras Cement Co. div. Flintkote Co., San Francisco, 1954-64, asst. sales mgr., 1957-59, mgr. sales, 1959-64; gen. mgr. Standard Materials Co. subsidiary Flintkote Co., Modesto, Calif., 1964, pres., 1964-68; group mgr. Western Aggregate Products div. Flintkote Co., Los Angeles, 1968-70; group corporate v.p. stone products The Flintkote Co., White Plains, N.Y., 1970-74, sr. v.p., 1974-76; also dir.; pres. Centex Homes Corp. subs. Centex Corp., 1976-79; pres., chief exec. officer Atlantic Cement Co., Inc. subs. Newmont Mining Corp., Stamford, Conn., 1979—. Served with U.S. Army, 1945-48. Clubs: Jonathan (Los Angeles); Winged Foot Golf (Mamaroneck, N.Y.); Harvard Bus. Sch.; Landmark (Stamford). Home: 128 W Hills New Canaan CT 06840 Office: PO Box 30 25 Crescent St Stamford CT 06904

GORDON, JAMES BRAUND, management consultant; b. Battle Creek, Mich., July 30, 1911; s. James Howard and Emma (Braund) G.; m. Evelyn H. Riley, Aug. 10, 1940; children: Constance, Douglas, Martha. B.A., Williams Coll., 1932; LL.B., Harvard U., 1935. Bar: N.Y. 1936, Mich. 1944. Practice in, N.Y.C., 1936-44; gen. atty. Bendix Corp., 1944-67, sec., 1960-69, Washington counsel, 1969-71; mgmt. cons., 1971—. Mem. Unitarian-Universalist Laymens League (regional v.p. 1962-70), Greater Detroit Meml. Soc. (pres. 1964-69). Unitarian. Home: 15401 Bassett Ln 3D Silver Spring MD 20906 Office: 1001 Connecticut Ave NW Washington DC 20036

GORDON, JAMES FLEMING, judge; b. Madisonville, Ky., May 18, 1918; s. John F. and Ruby (James) G.; m. Iola Young, Sept. 1, 1942; children: Maurice K. II, James Fleming, Marianna. LL.B., U. Ky., 1941. Bar: Ky. 1941. Practice in, Madisonville, 1941-65; judge U.S. Dist. Ct., Western Dist. Ky., Owensboro, 1965—, chief judge, 1968-75, sr. judge, 1975—; Chmn. Ky. Pub. Service Commn., 1955-59; Speakers chmn. Ky. Democratic Party, 1955, campaign chmn., 1962. Bd. dirs. Clinic Found., Madisonville. Served to 1st lt., Judge Adv. Gen. Dept. AUS, 1941-46; PTO. Mem. Am. Coll. Trial Lawyers, Am. Legion, VFW, Phi Delta Phi. Office: Fed Bldg Owensboro KY 42301

GORDON, JOHN EDWARD, chemist; b. Columbus, Ohio, Aug. 5, 1931; s. Edward Lambert and Marie Belle (McGough) G.; m. Peggy Jean Kwong, July 21, 1956; children—Alison A.K., Douglas C. B.Sc., Ohio State U., 1953; Ph.D. (NSF fellow), U. Calif., Berkeley, 1956. Instr. Brown U., Providence, 1956-58; fellow Mellon Inst., Pitts., 1958-65; asso. scientist Woods Hole (Mass.) Oceanographic Instn., 1965-68; prof. dept. chemistry Kent State U., Ohio, 1968—; vis. research scientist Chem. Abstracts Service, Columbus, Ohio, 1980-81. NSF grantee, 1965, 67, 80-83; Petroleum Research Fund grantee, 1969-73. Mem. Royal Soc. Chemistry (London), N.Y. Acad. Scis., Phi Beta Kappa, Sigma Xi. Office: Dept Chemistry Kent State U Kent OH 44242

GORDON, JOHN LEO, anesthesiologist; b. Cedar Rapids, Nebr., May 24, 1933; s. Harold E. and Catherine M. (McCurdy) G.; m. Margaret J. McAleer, Oct. 17, 1959; Kathleen M., David W., Michael J., Mary E. B.S., Creighton U., Omaha, 1959, M.D., 1959. Diplomate: Am. Bd. Anesthesiology. Intern St. Elizabeth Hosp., Lincoln, Nebr., 1959-60; gen. practice medicine, Valentine, Nebr., 1960-64; resident in anesthesiology U. Nebr., Omaha, 1965-66, instr., 1967-68; staff anesthesiologist Bergan Mercy Hosp., Omaha, 1968-77, chief, 1972-77; staff anesthesiologist St. Joseph Hosp., Omaha, 1968—, chief, 1977—; chmn. dept. anesthesiology Creighton U., 1977—. Fellow Am. Coll. Anesthesiologists; mem. Nebr. Soc. Anesthesiologists (pres. 1972-75, Outstanding Service award 1976), Am. Soc. Anesthesiologists, Am. Soc. Regional Anesthesia, Soc. Acad. Anesthesia Chairmen, AMA, Nebr. Med. Assn., Metro-Omaha Med. Soc. Roman Catholic. Lodge: K.C. (grand knight 1964). Office: Creighton Univ 601 N 30th St Omaha NE 68131

GORDON, JOHN LUTZ, utility exec.; b. Lincoln, Ill., Oct. 10, 1899; s. Frank B. and Marian C. (Lutz) G.; m. Ruth Coddington, Apr. 30, 1928; 1 dau., Marian (Mrs. Jack A. McCann). B.S. in Elec. Engring, Milw. Sch. Engring., 1920, E.E., 1953. Cons. engr. Vaughan & Meyer, Milw., 1920-23; engr. C.A. Shaler Co., Waupun, Wis., 1923-26; with Central Ill. Electric & Gas Co. (now div. of Commonwealth Edison Co.), Rockford, 1926—, chmn. bd., 1963—. Trustee Rockford Coll.; bd. regents Milw. Sch. Engring.; trustee Rockford Meml. Hosp. Served with AUS, World War I. Mem. Ill. C. of C. (past v.p., chmn. econ. devel. com., dir.), Rockford C. of C. (chmn. indsl. devel. com.), Ill. SAR. Episcopalian. Clubs: Green Valley Country, Old Pueblo, Tucson, Masons (Shriner). Home: 36 Los Pinos Green Valley AZ 85614

GORDON, JOHN PETER GEORGE, steel company executive; b. Toronto, Ont., Can., Nov. 14, 1920; m. Joan Muriel MacPherson; 2 children. B.Sc. in Mech. Engring, U. Toronto, 1943; grad., Harvard Advanced Mgmt. Program, 1966; LL.D., York U., 1980. With Stelco Inc. (formerly Steel Co. Can., Ltd.), 1946—, supt. cold mill, tin mill and galvanizing depts., 1963, gen. supt. flat rolled div., 1964, v.p. mfg. tubular and finishing plants, 1964, v.p. operating div., 1966, sr. v.p., 1970, pres., 1971-76, chief exec. officer, after 1973, chmn., 1976—; dir. Bank of Montreal, Gulf Oil Corp., Pitts., Molson Cos., Sun Life Assurance Co. Can.; mem. N. Am. adv. bd. Swissair; also dir. Mem. fin. adminstrn. com. Nat. council Can. YMCA; mem. hon. adv. bd. Greater Hamilton YMCA; trustee Schenley Football Awards; pres. Hamilton chpt. Ont. Heart Found.; dir., vice-chmn. Bus. Council on Nat. Issues; mem. fin. com., nat. adv. council, past bd. dirs. Boys' and Girls Clubs Can.; bd. dirs. Jr. Achievement Can., Wellesley Hosp., Toronto, Canadian Council Christians and Jews; bd. govs. Olympic Trust Can., McMaster U., Hamilton. Served to capt. RCEME, 1942-46. Recipient Benjamin F. Fairless award AIME, 1980. Mem. Assn. Profl. Engrs. Ont., Iron and Steel Inst. (Eng.), Am. Iron and Steel Insts. (dir.), Internat. Iron and Steel Insts. (dir.), Can. Mfrs. Assn., Conf. Bd., Delta Upsilon. Presbyterian. Clubs: Toronto, York (Toronto); Mississauga Golf and Country; Union (Cleve.); Mount Royal (Montreal); Rideau (Ottawa); Tamahaac (Ancaster); Hamilton, Hamilton Golf and Country. Home: Stonecrest 1343 Blythe Rd Mississauga ON L5H 2C2 Canada Office: PO Box 205 Toronto Dominion Centre Toronto ON M5K 1J4 Canada

GORDON, JOSEPH ELWELL, univ. dean; b. Deatsville, Ala., July 2, 1921; s. Joseph Elwell and Martha (Berry) G.; m. Doris Elizabeth Smith, June 5, 1948; children—Cecile Lizabeth, Joseph Elwell, Melissa Innes. A.B., Birmingham-So. Coll., 1942; M.S., Auburn U., 1949; Ph.D., U. Chgo., 1951. Tchr. math., Montgomery, Ala., 1946-48; instr. math. Auburn U., 1948-49; research asst. N. Central Assn. Colls. and Secondary Schs., Chgo., 1949-51; program analyst Air U., Maxwell AFB, 1951-54; mem. faculty Tulane U., 1954—, asst. prof. edn., 1958—, asso. dean admissions, 1957-63, dean, 1964—. Served to lt. USNR, 1942-46. Mem. Omicron Delta Kappa, Phi Delta Kappa, Pi Kappa Alpha. Democrat. Presbyn. Home: 1108 Lowerline St New Orleans LA 70118

GORDON, JOSEPH HAROLD, lawyer; b. Tacoma, Mar. 31, 1909; s. Joseph H. and Mary (Obermiller) G.; m. Jane Wilson, Sept. 12, 1936 (dec.); children—Joseph H., Nancy Jane; m. Eileen Rylander, Jan. 7, 1967. B.A., Stanford, 1931; LL.B., U. Wash., 1935. Bar: Wash. bar 1935. Since practiced in, Tacoma; partner Gordon, Thomas, Honeywell, Malanca, Peterson & O'Hern.; Personnel dir. Todd Pacific Shipyards, 1942-44. Mem. ABA (ho. dels., bd. govs. 1962-72, treas. 1965-72), Wash. State Bar Assn., Tacoma Bar Assn. (past pres.). Presbyn. (elder). Clubs: Rotary, Tacoma, Tacoma Golf and Country. Home: 2819 N Junett St Tacoma WA 98407 Office: 2200 One Washington Plaza Tacoma WA 98402

GORDON, LEONARD, sociology educator; b. Detroit, Dec. 6, 1935; s. Abraham and Sarah (Rosen) G.; m. Rena Joyce Feigelman, Dec. 25, 1955; children: Susan Melinda, Matthew Seth, Melissa Gail. B.A., Wayne State U., 1957; M.A., U. Mich., 1958; Ph.D., Wayne State U., 1966. Instr. Wayne State U., Detroit, 1960-62; research dir. Jewish Community Council, Detroit, 1962-64; dir. Mich. area Am. Jewish Com., N.Y.C., 1964-67; asst. prof. Ariz. State U., Tempe, 1967-83, prof., 1983—, chmn. dept. sociology, 1981—; cons. OEO, Maricopa County, Ariz., 1968. Author: A City in Racial Crisis, 1971, Sociology and American Social Issues, 1978; co-author: (with W. Mayer) Urban Life and the Struggle to Be Human, 1979. Sec. Cong. Religion and Race, Detroit, 1962-67; mem. exec. bd. dirs. Am. Jewish Com., Phoenix chpt., 1969-70. Grantee NSF, 1962, Rockefeller found., 1970. Fellow Am. Sociol. Assn.; mem. Pacific Sociol. Assn. (v.p. 1978-79, pres. 1980-81), AAUP, Ariz. State U. Alumni Assn. (faculty dir. 1981-82). Democrat. Jewish. Home: 52652 N Woodmere Fairway Scottsdale AZ 85253 Office: Ariz State U Dept Sociology Tempe AZ 85287

GORDON, LEONARD VICTOR, educational psychology educator; b. Montreal, Que., Aug. 15, 1917; U.S., 1936, naturalized, 1938; s. Peter Z. and Bessie Victoria (Kirsch) G.; m. Katharine Ann Burton, Nov. 30, 1946; children: John Christopher, Jeffrey Burton. Instr. Ohio State U., Columbus, 1947-49, research assoc., 1949-50; assoc. dir. Office Research Services Boston U., 1950-51; vis. asst. prof. U. N.Mex., Albuquerque, 1951-52; div. dir. Naval Personnel Research Activity, San Diego, 1952-62; lab chief U.S. Army Personnel Research Office, Washington, 1962-66; prof. ednl. psychology and state SUNY, Albany, 1966—; Disting. vis. prof. Wilford Hall U.S. Air Force Med. Ctr., Lackland AFB, Tex., 1977-79. Author: (with Ross L. Mooney) Mooney Problems Check Lists, 1950, Gordon Personal Profile, 1953, (rev. edit.) Gordon Personal Profile, 1978, Gordon Personal Inventory, 1956, (rev. edit.) Gordon Personal Inventory, 1978, Survey of Interpersonal Values, 1960, (rev. edit.) Survey of Interpersonal Values, 1976, Gordon Occupational Check List, 1963, (rev. edit.) Gordon Occupational Check List, 1981, Work Environment Preference Schedule, 1973, Measurement of Interpersonal Values, 1975, (with Akio Kikuchi) Social Psychology of Values, 1975, (rev. edit. with Akio Kikuchi) Social Psychology of Values, 1981, Survey of Personal Values, 1967, (rev. edit.) Survey of Personal Values, 1984, School Environment Preference Survey, 1978; contbr. articles to profl. jours. Served with USAAC, 1941-44. Fellow Am. Psychol. Assn., AAAS; mem. Internat. Assn. Applied Psychology, Am. Ednl. Research Assn., Nat. Council Measurement in Edn. Home: 385 Highland Dr Schenectady NY 12303 Office: SUNY Edn Bldg 230 Albany NY 12222

GORDON, LINCOLN, political economist; b. N.Y.C., Sept. 10, 1913; s. Bernard and Dorothy (Lerned) G.; m. Allison Wright, June 25, 1937; children: Anne, Robert W., Hugh, Amy. A.B., Harvard, 1933; D. Phil. (Rhodes scholar), Oxford (Eng.) U., 1936; LL.D., Fairleigh Dickinson U., 1965, Columbia, 1967, Rutgers U., 1967, U. Md., 1968, Wash. Coll., 1968, U. Del., 1969; L.H.D., Loyola Coll., Balt., 1968. Instr., faculty instr. govt. Harvard, 1936-41, William Ziegler prof. internat. econ. relations, 1955-61; research technician water, energy resources U.S. Nat. Resources Planning Bd., Washington, 1939-1940; sr. econ. analyst adv. commn. Council Nat. Def., Washington, 1940; mem. staff requirements com. W.P.B., 1942-45, dep. vice chmn. program, 1944-45, program vice chmn., 1945; dir. bur. reconversion priorities Civilian Prodn. Adminstrn., 1945-46; asso. prof. bus. Harvard, 1946-47, prof. govt. and adminstrn., 1947-50; cons. U.S. Rep. UN AEC, 1946, Army and Navy Munitions Bd., Dept. of State, 1947, ECA, 1948; North Atlantic Council Com. of Three on non-mil. aspects of NATO, 1956; dir. program div. Office ECA spl. rep. in, Europe, 1949-50; econ. adviser to spl. asst. to President, 1950-51; asst. dir. for Mut. Security Agy., 1951-52, chief mission to, U.K., 1952-55; minister econ. affairs in Am. embassy, London, 1952-55; U.S. ambassador to, Brazil, 1961-66, asst. sec. state for inter-Am. affairs, 1966-67; pres. Johns Hopkins, Balt., 1967-71; vis. prof. polit. economy Sch. Advanced Internat. Studies, Washington, 1971-72; fellow Woodrow Wilson Internat. Center for Scholars, 1972-75; sr. fellow Resources for Future, Washington, 1975-80; mem. sr. rev. panel CIA, 1980-82, nat. intelligence officer-at-large, 1982-83; guest scholar Brookings Instn., 1984—; Dir. Equitable Life Assurance Soc. U.S., Fayette Mfg. Corp. Author: The Public Corporation in Great Britain, 1938, Government and the American Economy, (with M. Fainsod), 1941, rev. edit., 1948,

59, Fuel and Power in Industrial Location and National Policy, Nat. Resources Planning Bd, 1942, Representation of the U.S. Abroad (in part), 1956, rev. edit. 1964, (with Engelbert L. Grommers) United States Manufacturing Investment in Brazil, 1961, A New Deal for Latin America, 1963, Growth Policies and the International Order, 1979, (with Joy Dunkerley and others) Energy Strategies for Developing Nations, 1981; editor: International Stability and Progress; U.S. Interests and Instruments, 1957, From Marshall Plan to Global Interdependence, 1978. Bd. dirs. Atlantic Council U.S.; hon. trustee Com. for Econ. Devel. Decorated Grand Cross Order Quetzal, Guatemala; Grand Cross Order Cruzeiro do Sul, Brazil). Fellow Am. Acad. Arts and Scis.; mem. Am. Polit. Sci. Assn., AAAS, Am. Econ. Assn., Council on Fgn. Relations, Royal Econ. Soc., Phi Beta Kappa, others. Club: Cosmos (Washington). Home: 3069 University Terr NW Washington DC 20016 Office: Brookings Instn Washington DC 20036

GORDON, LOIS GOLDFEIN, English language educator; b. Englewood, N.J., Nov. 13, 1938; d. Irving David and Betty (Davis) Goldfein; m. Alan Lee Gordon, Nov. 13, 1961; 1 son, Robert Michael. B.A. (Nat. Merit supplementary scholar, Barbour scholar), U. Mich., 1960; postgrad., Columbia U., 1960-61; M.A., U. Wis., 1962, Ph.D. (Dissertation Completion fellow), 1966. Teaching asst. U. Wis., 1962-64; lectr. CCNY, 1964-66; asst. prof. U. Mo., Kansas City, 1966-68; asst. prof. English Fairleigh Dickinson U., Teaneck, N.J., 1968-71, assoc. prof., 1971-75, prof., 1975—, chmn. dept. English and comparative lit., 1982—; cons. U. Mo. Press, 1968-69, Doubleday Inc., 1974, Kennikat Press, 1974—, Prentice Hall, 1977—. Author: Stratagems to Uncover Nakedness: The Dramas of Harold Pinter, 1969, Donald Barthelme, 1981, Robert Coover: The Universal Fiction-Making Process, American Yearbook, 1985; asst. editor: Lit. and Psychology, 1968-71; contbr. articles to profl. jours. Research grantee U. Mo., 1968. Mem. Internat. Bach Soc., MLA, Nat. Assn. Psychoanalytic Criticism (exec. com.). Jewish. Home: 300 Central Park W New York NY 10024 Office: Dept of English Fairleigh Dickinson University Teaneck NY 07666

GORDON, LYLE JOSEPH, paper company executive; b. Rupert, Idaho, Aug. 19, 1926; s. John Arthur and Mary Nilla (Campbell) G.; m. Gloria Ercell Moser, Sept. 7, 1946; children: Robert Steven, Gail Ann, John Gregory. B.S. in Chem. Engring, U. Wash., 1948, M.S., 1950, Ph.D. (Engring. Expt. Sta. fellow), 1963. Registered profl. engr., Wash. Teaching fellow U. Wash., Seattle, 1948-51; project engr. Scott Paper Co., Everett, Wash., 1953-57, process engr., 1957-59, mgr. pulp research and devel., West Coast, 1959-69, corporate mgr. pulping research and devel., 1969-76, dir. pulping research and devel., 1976—. Mem. exec. bd. Evergreen council Boy Scouts Am., 1969-70; active YMCA, PTA, United Good Neighbors.; Bd. dirs. Snohomish County (Wash.) Sci. Fair, 1962-66, pres., 1965-66; trustee Snohomish County Family Counseling Service, 1966-69, pres., 1969. Served with USNR, 1944-46. Fellow TAPPI (chmn. Pacific sect. 1962-63, exec. com. 1960-64, Shibley award 1956, nat. bd. dirs. 1966-69, exec. com. 1968-72, pres. 1971-72, chmn. fellows com. 1973-74, nominating com. 1981, joint textbook com. 1981—, chmn. joint textbook com. 1982—); mem. Am. Nat. Standards Inst. (chmn. com. P-3 1976-82), Am. Paper Inst. (Olmsted award com. 1975-78), Empire State Paper Research Assocs. (bd. dirs. 1977-83, exec. com. 1980-83), Am. Inst. Chem. Engrs. (chmn. Puget Sound sect. 1960), Sigma Xi, Phi Lambda Upsilon. Baptist (ch. sch. supt. 1955-60, ch. pres. 1962-63, chmn. pastoral relations com. Am. Baptist Chs. Pacific N.W. 1968, chmn. bd. deacons. 1981-82, ch. sch. supt. 1983—, bd. mgrs. Am. Bapt. Chs. of Pa. and Del. 1983—. Patentee pulping process. Home: 1027 Putnam Blvd Wallingford PA 19086 Office: Scott Plaza 3 Philadelphia PA 19113

GORDON, MALCOLM STEPHEN, biology educator; b. Bklyn., Nov. 13, 1933; s. Abraham and Rose (Walters) G.; m. Diane M. Kestin, Apr. 16, 1959 (div. Sept. 1973); 1 son, Dana Malcolm; m. Marjorie J. Weinzweig, Jan. 28, 1976. B.A. with high honors, Cornell U., 1954; Ph.D. (NSF fellow), Yale, 1958. Instr. U. Calif. at Los Angeles, 1958-60, asst. prof., 1960-65, asso. prof., 1965-68, prof. biology, 1968—, dir. Inst. Evolutionary and Environ. Biology, 1971-76; asst. dir. research Nat. Fisheries Center and Aquarium, U.S. Dept. of Interior, Washington, 1968-69; vis. prof. zoology Chinese U. Hong Kong, 1971-72; Mem. panel on marine biology, panel on oceanography Pres.'s Sci. Adv. Com., 1965-66; mem. nat. adv. com. R/V Alpha Helix, Scripps Inst. Oceanography, 1969-73; mem. com. on Latimeria Nat. Acad. Scis., 1969-72. Author coll. textbooks.; Contbr. articles to sci. jours. Officer So. Calif. chpt. ACLU, Los Angeles; v.p. Friends Santa Monica Mountains and Seashore. Fulbright fellow, U.K., 1957-58; Guggenheim fellow, Italy and Denmark, 1961-62; Sr. Queen's fellow in marine sci., Australia, 1976. Fellow AAAS; mem. Am. Physiol. Soc., Am. Soc. Ichthyologists and Herpetologists, Am. Soc. Zoologists (chmn. div. ecology 1979-80), Soc. for Exptl. Biology. Home: 2801 Glendower Ave Los Angeles CA 90027 Office: Dept Biology UCLA Los Angeles CA 90024

GORDON, MARGARET SHAUGHNESSY, economist; b. Wabasha, Minn., Sept. 4, 1910; d. Michael James and Mary (O'Brien) Shaughnessy; m. Robert Aaron Gordon, Aug. 15, 1936 (dec. 1978); children: Robert James, David Michael. B.A., Bryn Mawr Coll., 1931; M.A., Radcliffe Coll., 1933, Ph.D., 1935; student, London Sch. Econs., 1933-34. Instr. Wellesley Coll., 1935-36; research fellow Harvard-Radcliffe Bur. Internat. Research, 1936-39; head research unit Export-Import office OPA, Washington, 1942-43; asst. research economist Inst. Indsl. Relations, U. Calif. at Berkeley, 1950-54, asso. dir., 1954-77, lectr. econs., 1965—; Mem. Calif. Gov.'s Commn. on Employment and Retirement of Older Workers, 1959-60; mem. Personnel Bd., City of Berkeley, 1961-65, 70-75; asso. dir. Carnegie Commn. on Higher Edn. (name later changed to Carnegie Council on Higher Edn.), 1969-79; mem. Pres.'s Commn. on Income Maintenance Programs, 1968-69; cons. unemployment ins. U.S. Bur. Employment Security, 1962-66; adv. com. research devel. U.S. Social Security Adminstrn., 1965-68, chmn., 1966-67. Author: Employment Expansion and Population Growth, 1954, The Economics of Welfare Policies, 1963, Youth Education and Unemployment Problems: An International Perspective, 1979; editor: Poverty in America, 1965, (with E.F. Cheit) Occupational Disability and Public Policy, 1963, Higher Education and the Labor Market, 1974; Mng. editor: Indsl. Relations, 1961-63, 65-66. Mem. council, City of Berkeley, 1965-69. Mem. Am. Econ. Assn., Indsl. Relations Research Assn., Western Gerontological Soc. (pres. 1961-62). Home: 1515 Oxford St. Berkeley CA 94709

GORDON, MARJORIE, opera director, coloratura soprano, educator; b. N.Y.C.; d. Theodore and Minnie (Glantz) Fishberg; m. Nathan Gordon; children: Maxine, Peter Jon. B.A. cum laude, Hunter Coll. Prof. voice Duquesne U., 1957-59, Wayne State U., 1961—, Nat. Music Camp, Interlochen, 1963-65, Meadowbrook Sch. Music, 1966-71, U. Mich., 1970, Mich. State U., 1971; soloist, tchr. Am. U.-Wolf Trap Program, Washington, 1973; spl. edn. cons. Detroit Grand Opera Assn. Solo debut, N.Y. Philharmonic Symphony, 1950; soprano soloist, N.Y.C. Opera, 1955-57, Chautauqua Opera Co., 1949-61; dir., Detroit Opera Theatre, 1960-72, Piccolo Opera Co., Detroit, 1961—; soloist with orchs., opera cos., on radio and TV; recitals, U.S., Europe, Can., Israel; Editor: Opera Study Guide, 1968—. Mem. music adv. panel Mich. Arts Council. Mem. Mich. Music Tchrs. Assn. (voice chmn. 1970-76), Detroit Musicians League, Tues. Musicale, Music Study Group, AFTRA, Am. Guild Mus. Artists, Music Tchrs. Nat. Assn., Nat. Opera Assn., Nat. Assn. Tchrs. Singing, Central Opera Service, Mich. Orch. Assn., Mu Phi Epsilon. Office: 18662 Fairfield Ave Detroit MI 48221

GORDON, MARSHALL, university president; b. La Center, Ky., Sept. 1, 1937; m. Annette Waters, Mar. 17, 1962; 1 dau., Mary Ann. B.A., Murray State U., 1959; Ph.D., Vanderbilt U., 1963. Teaching asst. dept. chemistry Vanderbilt U., Nashville, 1959-63; assoc. prof. chemistry Vanderbilt, Nashville, summer 1965; research chemist E. I. duPont de Nemours Co., Chattanooga, summer 1961; asst. prof. Murray State U. (Ky.), 1963-65, assoc. prof., 1965-68, prof., 1968-75, dean Coll. Environ. Scis., 1975-77, trustee found., 1977-83, v.p. univ. services, 1977-83; pres. S.W. Mo. State U., Springfield, 1983—; mem. adv. council NSF, Washington, 1978-82; bd. dirs. Purchase Tng. Ctr., Mayfield, Ky., 1981-83, Environ. research, 1981, 82. Bd. dirs. Murray Calloway County Indsl. Found., 1981-82; mem. regional adv. bd. Hammons Heart Inst., Springfield, 1983—. Mem. Am. Chem. Soc. (sec.-treas. Ky. Lake sect. 1968-70), AAAS, Ky. Acad. Sci. (assoc. editor Transactions 1968-73), Internat. Assn. Water Pollution Research, Am. Assn. State Colls. and Univs. (com. on sci. and tech. 1983—), Springfield C. of C. (dir. 1983—), Sigma Xi. Lodge: Rotary (Murray and Springfield). Home: 1515 S Fairway Springfield MO 65804 Office: SW Mo State U 901 S National Springfield MO 65804

GORDON, MARTIN, publisher, print dealer; b. N.Y.C., Aug. 15, 1939; s. Alexander and Ruth G.; m. Gatle Gunderman, Mar. 13, 1966; children: Kelly, Jeffrey. Assoc. in Applied Sci., Rochester Inst. Tech., 1960, B.S., 1961. Pres. Martin Gordon Inc, N.Y.C., 1964—; gen. ptnr. Sigma Art Fund, N.Y.C., 1971-82. Auhtor, publisher: Gordon's Print Price annuals. Served with AUS, 1952-57. Mem. Art Dealers Assn. Am., Print Dealers Assn. Am. Jewish. Home: 1000 Park Ave New York NY 10028 Office: Martin Gordon Inc 25 E 83d St New York NY 10028

GORDON, MARY CATHERINE, author; b. L.I., N.Y., Dec. 8, 1949; d. David and Anna (Gagliano) G.; m. Arthur Cash, 1979; 1 dau., Anna Gordon. B.A., Barnard Coll., 1971; M.A., Syracuse U., 1973. Tchr. English Dutchess Community Coll., Poughkeepsie, N.Y., 1974-78, Amherst (Mass.) Coll. Novels include Final Payments, 1978; The Company of Women, 1981; also short stories. Recipient Kafka prize, 1980. Roman Catholic. Address: care Random House Inc Publicity Dept 201 E 50th St New York NY 10022 *

GORDON, MAX, night club executive; b. Lithuania, Mar. 12, 1903; came to U.S., 1908, naturalized, 1908; s. Reuben and Sarah G.; m. Lorraine, Apr. 20, 1946; children: Rebecca, Deborah. B.A., Reed Coll., 1924. Owner, operator Blue Angel night club, N.Y.C., 1943-64, Le Directoire, 1948-49, Village Vanguard, 1934—. Author: Live At The Village Vanguard, 1980. Democrat. Jewish. Office: Village Vanguard 178 7th St S New York NY 10014 *I am still operating the Village Vanguard. It is open every night. And I am there every night. The New Yorker magazine calls it "the greatest jazz club in the world."* *

GORDON, MELVIN JAY, manufacturing company executive; b. Boston, Nov. 26, 1919; s. Jacob S. and Sadye Z. (Lewis) G.; m. Ellen Rubin, June 25, 1950; children: Virginia Lynn, Karen Dale, Wendy Jean, Lisa Jo. B.A., Harvard, 1941, M.B.A., 1943. Vice pres. Clear Weave Hosiery Stores, Inc., Boston, 1945-50; v.p. Tenn. Knitting Mills, Inc., Columbia, 1945-56; pres. P.R. Hosiery Mills, Inc., Arecibo, 1956-61; chmn. bd. Tootsie Roll Industries, Chgo., 1962—, pres., 1968-69, 75-78; ptnr. Manchester Hosiery Mills, N.H., 1946-69; pres. Hampshire Designers Inc., 1969-77, HDI Investment Corp., 1977—; adv. com. Mfrs. Hanover Bank, N.Y.C., 1967—. Author: Better Than Communism, 1958. Mem. Pres.'s Citizens Adv. Com. Fitness Am. Youth, 1957-60, mem. exec. com., 1959-60; del. White House Conf. Econ. Issues, 1962, White House Conf. Youth Fitness, 1962; co-chmn. Com. Support Psychol. Offensive, 1961-63; dir., mem. exec. com. Council World Tensions, N.Y.C., 1960-65; chmn. Mass. Gov.'s Com. Youth Fitness, 1958-64; bd. dirs. New Eng. Econ. Edn. Council, 1960-63, N.H. Council on World Affairs, 1962-65; bd. dirs., chmn. exec. com. Citizen Exchange Corps, N.Y.C., 1964-66, hon. chmn. adv. council, 1966-67; del. Prime-Minister's Econ. Conf. Israel, 1968, 73; Bd. overseers Harvard Coll., mem. vis. com. behavioral scis., 1967-71, vis. com. psychology, 1972; vis. com. Russian Research Center, 1972—; dir. Inst. Man and Sci., 1966—; chmn. N.E. region Am. Com. for Weizmann Inst. Sci., Rehovot, Israel, 1972-73; dir. Am. com., 1973-75. Recipient Dean's award Nat. Candy Wholesalers Assn., 1978. Mem. Young Presidents Orgn., Chief Execs. Forum, World Bus. Council, World Affairs Council Boston (treas., dir. 1966-67, v.p., dir. 1968-74), New Eng. Soc. N.Y.C. Clubs: Harvard (Boston); Varsity (Harvard). Office: Tootsie Roll Industries 7401 S Cicero Ave Chicago IL 60629

GORDON, MICHAEL, stage and film director, educator; b. Balt., Sept. 6, 1909; s. Paul and Eva (Kunen) G.; m. Elizabeth Cane, Nov. 27, 1939; children: Jonathan Evan, Jane Ellen, Susannah Ruth. B.A., Johns Hopkins U., 1929; M.F.A., Yale U., 1932. Prof., then prof. emeritus theater arts UCLA, 1971—. Actor, stage mgr., dir. plays Broadway; mem., Group Theater, N.Y.C., 1935-40; dir., Columbia Pictures, Hollywood, Calif., 1940-43; dir. prodns. Broadway, 1943-46; dir. films for, Universal-Internat., Stanley Kramer, 20th Century Fox, Hollywood, 1946-51, various cos., N.Y.C., 1951-59; film and TV dir., various cos., Hollywood, 1959-70; films include Underground Agent, 1942, Another Part of the Forest, 1946, An Act of Murder, 1947, I Can Get It for You Wholesale, 1950, Cyrano de Bergerac, 1950, The Secret of Convict Lake, 1951, Pillow Talk, 1959, Boys' Night Out, 1961, Move Over Darling, 1963, Texas Across the River, 1965, The Impossible Years, 1968; plays directed include Home of the Brave. Mem. Dirs. Guild Am., Screen Writers Guild, Acad. Motion Picture Arts and Scis. Office: Macgowan Hall U Calif 405 Hilgard Ave Los Angeles CA 90024

GORDON, MILTON A., mfg. co. exec.; b. Chgo., Jan. 9, 1912; s. Julius H. and Diana (Edison) G.; m. Elinor Loeff, Oct. 20, 1941; children—Stephen, Leslie Susan. Ph.B., U. Chgo., 1933, J.D., 1935. Bar: Ill. bar 1935. Practice in, Chgo., 1935-43; pres. Morris, Mann & Reilly, Inc., Chgo., 1943-45; v.p., dir. Walter E. Heller & Co., Chgo., 1945-53; founder, 1953, TV Programs Am., Inc., N.Y.C., pres., 1953-58; founder, 1958; pres., now chmn. bd. M.A. Gordon and Co., Inc., N.Y.C.; sr. partner Halle & Stieglitz, N.Y.C., 1969-71; chmn. bd. Halle & Stieglitz, Inc., N.Y.C., 1971—, Cable Funding Corp., 1972-73, Halle Industries, Inc., 1975—, Vincennes Steel Corp., 1979—; chmn. exec. com. Irvin Industries Inc., 1979—. Mem. fiscal commn., N.Y.C., 1964-66; mem. Presdl. del. to independence celebration of Kenya, 1963. Office: 630 Fifth Ave New York NY 10111

GORDON, MILTON G., consultant, real estate counselor; b. Detroit, June 1, 1922; s. Abe and Anna (Pragg) G.; m. Sandra Louise Driver, Apr. 2, 1966; children: Jonathan, Shoshana Meira. A.B., Wayne State U., 1944; A.M., UCLA, 1947. Pres. Milton Gordon Co. (realtors), Los Angeles, 1951-62, Village Realty-Milton Gordon Co., 1962-63; Calif. real estate commr., 1963, mem. Gov.'s cabinet as sec. bus. and commerce, State of Calif., 1964-67; v.p. finance and devel., treas. HDC Corp., San Diego, 1969—; pres. Milton G. Gordon Corp. (mgmt. cons.'s and real estate counselors), 1976—; Mem. Gov.'s Emergency Resources Planning Commn., 1966, Calif. Council on Criminal Justice, 1979—; mem. adv. com. to Real Estate Commr.; mem. exec. com. Community Relations Conf. So. Calif.; commr. Los Angeles County Efficiency and Economy Commn.; mem. Calif. Pub. Works Bd., 1963-65; mem. assessment practices adv. com. Los Angeles Assessor. Vice chmn. bd. dirs., exec. com. U. Judaism, 1972—. Served with AUS, 1942-44. Recipient Outstanding Alumnus award Wayne State U., 1964. Mem. Nat. Assn. Real Estate License Ofcls. (v.p. 1965), Calif. Home Loan Mortgage Assn. (bd. dirs.), D.A.V., Am. Legion. Democrat. Jewish. Address: 10504 Cheviot Dr Los Angeles CA 90064 *I have always strived for a standard of excellence in my business career and also during my service in government. I have structured my daily life to permit my involvement in community action and philanthropic programs. The latter has more than matched in personal satisfaction whatever I may have given in time, talent, and money to the community.*

GORDON, MILTON PAUL, educator; b. St. Paul, Feb. 8, 1930; s. Abraham and Rebecca (Ryan) G.; m. Elaine Travis, Jan. 1, 1955; children—David, Karen, Nancy, Peter. B.A. summa cum laude, U. Minn., 1950; Ph.D., U. Ill., 1953. Upjohn Co. fellow U. Ill., 1950-51; Am. Cancer Inst. fellow Sloan-Kettering Inst. for Cancer Research, N.Y.C., 1953-55, research asst., 1955-57; lectr. Bklyn. Coll., 1955-57; asst. research biochemist Virus Lab., U. Calif. at Berkeley, 1957-59; mem. faculty U. Wash., Seattle, 1959—, prof., 1966—; Sec., treas. Pacific Slope Biochem. Conf., 1964-68, pres., 1968; vis. scholar Max Planck Inst., Tübingen, W. Ger., 1975. Assoc. editor: Biochemistry. Mem. Am. Chem. Soc., AAAS, Am. Soc. Biol. Chemists. Research and publs. on plant tumorogenesis. Home: 8255 45th Ave NE Seattle WA 98115

GORDON, MYRON LEE, fed. judge; b. Kenosha, Wis., Feb. 11, 1918; s. Samuel and Janet (Ruppa) G.; m. Peggy Siesel, Aug. 16, 1942; children—Wendy, John, Polly. B.A., U. Wis., 1939, M.A., 1939; LL.B., Harvard, 1942. Bar: Wis. bar 1942. Practiced in, Milw., 1942-50, civil judge, 1950-54, circuit judge, 1954-61; asso. justice Supreme Ct. Wis., 1962-67; U.S. dist. judge Eastern Wis., 1967—; Pres. Milw. Hearing Soc., 1951-53. Served with USNR, World War II. Mem. DAV (comdr. Wis. 1959), Phi Beta Kappa. Office: Chambers US Dist Ct US Ct House 517 E Wisconsin Ave Room 271 Milwaukee WI 53202 *

GORDON, NICHOLAS, broadcasting executive; b. Chgo., Apr. 12, 1928; s. Jacques and Ruth (Janeway) G.; m. Gladys Sack, Apr. 10, 1950 (div. 1976); children: Catherine, Christopher, Susan; m. Julie E. Miles, Aug. 12, 1977. Ph.B., U. Chgo., 1946. Reporter City News Bur., Chgo., 1948; radio-TV analyst William Weintraub Agy., N.Y.C., 1949-50; dir. research and sales planning Keystone Broadcasting System, N.Y.C., 1951-52; with NBC, 1953-74, mgr. rates and program evaluation, 1956-58, mgr. sales devel. NBC-TV Sales, 1959-60, dir. sales devel. NBC-TV Sales, 1960-63, account exec. TV sales, 1964-68, v.p. Eastern sales, 1968-70, v.p. radio network sales, N.Y.C., 1970-74; pres. Keystone Broadcasting System, N.Y.C., 1974—. Vice chmn. Riverdale Community Council, 1968-71; mem. N.Y.C. Planning Bd., Riverdale, 1969-75, vice chmn., 1972-74; pres. Riverdale Community Planning Assn., 1972-76; mem. vol. corps N.Y.C. Dept. Commerce, 1968-70; bd. dirs. Wave Hill Center Environ. Studies, 1969-80, exec. v.p., 1970-80; mem. Bronx Democratic County Com., 1968; bd. dirs. Music Mountain, Inc., Falls Village, Conn., 1970—, pres., 1974—; bd. dirs. Riverdale Neighborhood House, Bronx, N.Y., 1970-74, Bronx Council Arts, 1970-72; trustee St. Hilda's and St. Hugh's Sch. Clubs: Tavern, Cliff Dwellers (Chgo.); University, Explorers (N.Y.C.). Office: Keystone Broadcasting System 527 Madison Ave New York NY 10022

GORDON, NORMAN BOTNICK, psychology educator; b. N.Y.C., Feb. 12, 1921; s. Moses and Molvine (Botnick) G.; m. Diana Jean Drews, July 27, 1974; children: Jane Ellen, Judith Ann, Marc Daniel, Aaron Drew. B.A., Bklyn. Coll., 1942; M.A., New Sch. Social Research, 1951; Ph.D., NYU, 1957. Research psychologist U.S. Naval Tng. Device Ctr., Port Washington, N.Y., 1951-58; assoc. prof. psychology Yeshiva U., N.Y.C., 1959-68, prof., 1968-74; guest investigator Rokefeller U., N.Y.C., 1964-77; prof., chmn. dept. SUNY-Oswego, 1977—. Served with U.S. Army, 1942-46. Grantee USPHS, 1966-74, 64-67. Mem. Am. Psychol. Assn., AAAS, Eastern Psychol. Assn., Sigma Psi. Home: RD 3 Box 332 Oswego NY 13126 Office: Dept Psychology SUNY Coll Oswego NY 13126

GORDON, PAUL, educator; b. Hartford, Conn., Jan. 1, 1918; s. Charles Dana and Anne Mabel (Hirshberg) G.; m. Evelyn Rubin, Oct. 16, 1941; children—Dana Charles, Jane Ellen. Student, Wesleyan U., Middletown, Conn., 1935-37; B.S. in Metallurgy, Mass. Inst. Tech., 1939, M.S., 1940, Sc.D., 1949. Research asso. metallurgy Mass. Inst. Tech., 1941-42; group leader Manhattan Project, 1942-47; mem. faculty Ill. Inst. Tech., 1949-50, 54—, prof. metall. engring., 1957—, chmn. dept., 1966-76; asst. prof. Inst. Study Metals, U. Chgo., 1951-54. Author: Principles of Phase Diagrams in Materials Systems, 1968; Contbr. articles to profl. jours., chpts. to books. Fellow Am. Soc. for Metals; mem. Am. Inst. Mining and Metall. Engrs. (Mathewson gold medal 1957), Inst. Metals, AAAS, Am. Soc. Engring. Edn., Engrs. Council Profl. Devel., Am. Soc. for Testing and Materials, Sigma Xi. Home: 1220 Park Ave W Highland Park IL 60035

GORDON, PAUL CURTIS, electronics and communications service company executive; b. Balt., Apr. 8, 1927; s. Paul C. and Viola V. (Primrose) G.; m. Maureen Angela Cadogan, Apr. 23, 1955; children: Jeanne, Paul, Maureen, Thomas, Timothy. B.S. in Bus. Adminstrn. cum laude, U. Notre Dame, 1949; M.B.A., N.Y. U., 1955. Profl. basketball player for Balt. Bullets, 1949-50; spl. agt. FBI, 1950-57; with ITT Corp., 1957—; now pres. ITT Fed. Electric Corp., Paramus, N.J.; and corp. v.p. ITT; asso. dir. United Jersey Bank. Pres. Found. for Free Enterprise.; bd. govs. Ramapo Coll. N.J. Served with USNR, 1945-46. Mem. Commerce and Industry Assn. No. N.J. (vice chmn.). Office: ITT Fed Electric Corp 621 Industrial Ave Paramus NJ 07652

GORDON, PAUL JOHN, educator; b. N.Y.C., Oct. 14, 1921; s. Arthur L. and Georgiana (McDonough) G.; m. Mary Brigid Keany, Jan. 28, 1950; children: Brian Joseph, Peter Christopher, Martha Ann, Hugh John, Paul John. B.B.A., CCNY, 1945; M.B.A., Cornell U., 1949; Ph.D., Syracuse U., 1958. With Brooks Bros., N.Y.C., 1941-43; with Lago Oil & Transp. Co., Ltd., Netherlands W. Indies, also Bayway Refinery, Linden, N.J. and Standard Oil Co. N.J., 1943-48; asst. prof. Cornell U., 1949-54; prof., chmn. dept. mgmt. Sch. Bus., Duquesne U., 1954-55; research cons. Sloan-Kettering Meml. Center for Cancer, 1955-56; asso. prof., planning dir. grad. program hosp. adminstrn. Sch. Bus. Adminstrn., Emory U., 1956-59; asso. prof. Grad. Sch. Bus., Ind. U., 1959-63, prof., chmn. dept. mgmt. adminstrv. studies, 1963-67, prof. mgmt., 1963—, chmn. adminstrv. and behavioral studies, 1980—; chief U.S. Dept. State-Ford Found. party Ljubljana U., Yugoslavia, 1967; vis. prof. Trinity Coll., Dublin, 1967; vis. prof., Fulbright lectr. Istituto Post-Universitario Per Lo Studio Dell Organizzazione Aziendale, Turin, Italy, 1963; Fulbright lectr., cons. Nat. U. Republic Uruguay, 1970; Disting. guest Systems Research Inst., Polish Acad. Scis., 1980; mem. U.S. AID Mgmt. Edn. Reconnaissance Survey, India, also Pakistan, 1971; cons. Internal Revenue Service, 1956—, Am. Coll. Hosp. Adminstrs., 1957—; with Inst. Higher Studies of Adminstrn., Caracas, Venezuela, 1973—. Editor: Acad. Mgmt. Jour, 1964-66; editorial cons.; editorial cons. adv. bd.: Bus. Horizons, Hosp. Adminstrn, W.B. Saunders Co.; Contbr. articles to profl. jours. Mem. Catholic Commn. on Intellectual and Cultural Affairs, 1973—, chmn., 1980—; chmn. UNESCO multi-nat. bus. conf. Ind. U., 1972; chmn. adv. screening com. in bus. mgmt. Council for Internat. Exchange of Scholars, Fulbright-Hays Program,

1979—; Bd. dirs. Ind. Newman Found., 1971-82. Ford Found. grantee, 1963, 70; IBM fellow, 1965. Fellow Acad. Mgmt. (v.p. program 1967, pres. 1969), Internat. Acad. Mgmt., Am. Acad. Med. Adminstrs. (hon.). Home: 1422 Winfield Rd Bloomington IN 47401

GORDON, RICHARD EDWARDS, psychiatrist; b. N.Y.C., July 15, 1922; s. Richard and Virginia (Ryan) G.; m. Katherine Lowman Kline, Nov. 12, 1949; children: Richard Edwards, Katherine Lowman Gordon Reed, Virginia Lamborn Gordon Ford, Laurie Lloyd Gordon Hardy. B.S., Yale U., 1943; M.D., U. Mich., 1945; M.A., Columbia U., 1956, Ph.D., 1961. Diplomate: Am. Bd. Psychiatry and Neurology. Intern City Hosp., N.Y.C., 1945-46; resident in neurology N.Y. Postgrad Hosp., N.Y.C., 1946-47; resident in psychiatry N.Y. Psychiat. Inst., N.Y.C., 1947-48, Manhattan (N.Y.) State Hosp., 1948-49; fellow in psychosomatic medicine and child psychiatry Mt. Sinai Hosp., N.Y.C., 1949-51; practice medicine specializing in psychiatry, N.Y.C., 1950-51, Englewood, N.J., 1953-67; mem. staffs Univ. Settlement House, 1950-51, Englewood Hosp., 1953-67, Shands Teaching Hosp., Gainesville, Fla., 1967—, Gainesville VA Hosp., 1967-76; sr. research psychiatrist, EEG cons. Rockland State Hosp., Orangeburg, N.Y., 1953-54; founder Englewood Hosp. EEG Clinic, 1953; also dir.; dir. research unit Englewood Hosp., 1954-60; prof. psychology, cons. psychiatrist Wagner Coll., S.I., N.Y., 1960-67; asso. prof. psychiatry and psychology, research dir. multiphasic health testing center U. Fla., Gainesville, 1967—; dir. Fla. Mental Health Inst., Tampa, 1975-79; adj. prof. clin. psychology U. South Fla., Tampa, 1977—; founder Mental Health Consultation Center, Hackensack, N.Y., 1956, trustee, 1956-57; founder Community Multiphasic Health Testing Center, Gainesville; mem. N.J. Mental Health Commn., 1957-61; dir. Biosystems, Inc., Protel, Inc. Author: Prevention of Postpartum Emotional Difficulties, 1961, (with K.K. Gordon, M. Gunther) The Split-Level Trap, 1961, (with K.K. Gordon) The Blight on the Ivy, 1963, Systems of Treatment for the Mentally Ill: Filling the Gaps, 1981, (with B. Franklin et al) Towards Better Mental Health in New Jersey, 1961; contbr. numerous articles to profl. jours.; editor: Bull. So. Psychiatry. Pres. Kirkwood Environ. Improvement Assn., Gainesville, 1970-75; cons./surveyor Joint Commn. on Accreditation of Hosps., 1980—. Served to capt. AUS, 1943-45, 51-53. Grantee in field. Fellow Am. Psychiat. Assn. (del. to assembly), Soc. Advanced Med. Systems; mem. AAAS, Fla. Psychiat. Soc. (pres. 1978-79), Sigma Xi. Club: Yale of Gainesville.

GORDON, RICHARD LEWIS, mineral economics educator; b. Portland, Maine, June 19, 1934; s. Benjamin M. and Sara G. G.; m. Nancy Ellen Helfand, June 8, 1958; children: David William, Benjamin Mark. A.B., Dartmouth Coll., 1956; Ph.D., MIT, 1960. Econ. analyst Union Carbide Corp., 1960-64; asst. economist First Nat. City Bank, N.Y.C., 1964; mem. faculty Pa. State U., State College, 1964—, prof. mineral econs., 1970—; Shell lectr. on energy econs. Surrey (Eng.) U., 1981. Author: The Evolution of Energy Policy in Western Europe, 1970, U.S. Coal and the Electric Power Industry, 1975, Coal in the U.S. Energy Market, 1978, An Economic Analysis of World Energy Problems, 1981, Reforming the Regulation of Electric Utilities, 1982. Mem. AIME (chmn. council econs. 1973, Mineral Econs. award 1981), Internat. Assn. Energy Economists, Am. Econ. Assn., Econometric Soc., Royal Econ. Soc., AAAS. Jewish. Home: 429 Kemmerer Rd State College PA 16801 Office: Pa State U 204 Walker Bldg University Park PA 16802

GORDON, ROBERT BOYD, geophysics educator; b. East Orange, N.J., Dec. 25, 1929; s. Myron Boyd and Catherine (Rote) G.; m. Joan Parke Ruttiger, Sept. 13, 1952; children: Penelope, Margaret. B.S., Yale U., 1952, D.Eng., 1955. Asst. prof. Sch. Mines, Columbia U., 1955-57; mem. faculty Yale U., 1957—, assoc. prof. applied sci., 1960-68, prof. geophysics and applied mechanics, 1968—, chmn. dept. geology and geophysics, 1979-82. Author: Physics of the Earth, 1972, (with R.M. Brick and A.W. Pense) Structure and Properties of Engineering Materials, 1977; Contbr. articles to profl. jours. Mem. Am. Phys. Soc., Am. Geophys. Union, Am. Inst. Mining and Metall. Engrs., Phi Beta Kappa, Sigma Xi. Home: 239 Everit New Haven CT 06511 Office: Kline Geol Lab Box 6666 New Haven CT 06511

GORDON, ROBERT EDWARD, university administrator; b. N.Y.C., June 20, 1925; s. Lewis Francis and Claire (McEvoy) G.; m. Catherine Tigner, Sept. 16, 1948; children—Claire Catherine, Martha Lee. A.B., Emory U., 1949; M.S., U. Ga., 1950; Ph.D., Tulane, U., 1956. Curator Highlands (N.C.) Museum Biol. Sta., 1949-50; mem. faculty N.E. La. State Coll., 1954-58, U. Notre Dame, South Bend, Ind., 1958—, prof. biology, 1966—, chmn. dept., 1964-67, asso. dean, 1967-71, v.p. for advanced studies, 1971—; Mem. working party sci. publs. UNESCO, Phila., 1963, Paris, France, 1964; mem. panel primary publs. U.S.-Japan Coop. Sci. Program, Tokyo, 1965, 67; mem. sci. info. council NSF, 1969-72, chmn., 1971-72; biomed. communications study sect. NIH, 1967-71; mem. U.S. Nat. com. for F.I.D., 1969-71, U.S. Nat. Com. for Internat. Union Biol. Socs., 1969-75; chmn. bd. council biol. scis. information Nat. Acad. Scis.-NRC, 1967-68. Editor: Am. Midland Naturalist, 1958-64; sect. editor: Biol. Abstracts, 1963-69; Contbr. articles to profl. jours. Trustee Biol. Abstracts, pres., 1978; trustee Argonne Univs. Assn., 1973-83, v.p., 1979; bd. dirs. Assn. Cath. Colls. and Univs., 1980—; pres. Council Grad. Schs., 1982—; trustee Grad. Record Exam., 1982—. Served with M.C. AUS, 1944-46. Fellow AAAS (council 1964-70), Herpetologists League; mem. Am. Inst. Biol. Sci. (nat. lectr. 1960-65, mem. at large bd. govs. 1968—, v.p. 1975, pres. 1976), Am. Soc. Icthyologists and Herpetologists, Am. Soc. Naturalists, Council Biology Editors (sec. 1963-69), Ecol. Soc. Am., Herpetological Soc. Japan, Soc. Study Amphibians and Reptiles (chmn. 1971), Sigma Xi. Club: Explorers. Home: 19551 Oakdale Ave South Bend IN 46637

GORDON, ROBERT JAMES, economics educator; b. Boston, Sept. 3, 1940; s. Robert Aaron and Margaret (Shaughnessy) G.; m. Julie S. Peyton, June 22, 1963. A.B., Harvard U., 1962; M.A., Oxford U., Eng., 1969; Ph.D., MIT, 1967. Asst. prof. econs. Harvard U., 1967-68; asst. prof. U. Chgo., 1968-73; prof. econs. Northwestern U., Evanston, Ill., 1973—; research assoc. Nat. Bur. Econ. Research, 1968—; mem. Brookings Panel Econ. Activity, 1970—; co-chmn. Internat. Seminar Macroecons., 1978—; mem. exec. com. Conf. Research, Income and Wealth, 1978—; mem. panel rev. productivity measures Nat. Acad. Scis., 1977-79; cons. bd. govs. Fed. Res. System, 1973—, U.S. Dept. Treasury, 1967-80. Editor: Jour. Polit. Economy 1970-73; author Macroeconomics, 1978, 3d edit., 1984; auhtor Milton Friedman's Monetary Framework, 1974; Challenges to Interdependent Economies, 1979. Marshall fellow, 1962-64; fellow Ford Found., 1966-67; grantee NSF, 1971—; fellow Guggenheim Meml. Found., 1980-81. Fellow Econometric Soc. (treas. 1975—); mem. Am. Econ. Assn. (bd. editors 1975-77, mem. exec. com. 1981-83), Phi Beta Kappa. Office: Econs Dept Northwestern U Evanston IL 60201

GORDON, ROBERT SIRKOSKY, JR., physician; b. N.Y.C., Mar. 26, 1926; s. Robert Sirkosky and Dorothy (Dodson) G.; m. Elizabeth Wilkins Brown, June 30, 1951; children: Hilary Ruth, Andrew Sirkosky, Peter Taylor, Dana Elizabeth. A.B., M.D., Harvard U., 1949; M.H.S., Johns Hopkins U., 1976. Intern, then resident Presbyn. Hosp., N.Y.C., 1949-53; investigator Nat. Heart Inst., 1953-64; chief clin. research Pakistan-SEATO Cholera Lab., 1961-64, tech. cons., 1964-69; clin. dir. Nat. Inst. Arthritis, Metabolism and Digestive Diseases, NIH, Bethesda, Md., 1964-73, dir. Clin. Center, 1974-75; vis. prof. U. Md. Med. Sch., 1975-76; spl. asst. to dir. NIH, Bethesda, Md., 1976—. Editorial bd.: Jour. Lipid Research, 1965-68, Controlled Clin. Trials, 1980—. Mem. Am. Physiol. Soc., Am. Soc. Clin. Investigation, Am. Fedn. Clin. Research, Assn. Am. Physicians, Am. Gastroenterol. Assn., Soc. Epidemiol. Research, Am. Geriatrics Soc., Soc. Clin. Trials (v.p. 1979-81, pres. 1981-83). Republican. Episcopalian. Spl. clin. investigation physiol. chemistry. Home: 3915 Prospect St Kensington MD 20895 Office: Bldg 1 Room 238 NIH Bethesda MD 20205

GORDON, ROY GERALD, educator; b. Akron, Ohio, Jan. 11, 1940; s. Nathan Gold and Frances (Teitel) G.; m. Myra Shela Miller, Dec. 24, 1961; children—Avra Karen, Emily Francine, Steven Eric. A.B. summa cum laude, Harvard, 1961, A.M. in Physics, 1962, Ph.D. in Chem. Physics, 1964. Jr. fellow Soc. of Fellows, Harvard, 1964-66, mem. faculty, 1966—, prof., 1969—. Sloan Found. fellow, 1966-69. Fellow Am. Phys. Soc.; mem. Am. Chem. Soc. (award in pure chemistry 1972, Baekeland award 1979), Faraday Soc., Union of Concerned Scientists, Nat. Acad. Scis., Am. Acad. Arts and Scis., Phi Beta Kappa, Sigma Xi. Theoretical research discovering forms of forces between molecules, the way molecules collide with each other, motion of molecules in liquids and solids. Inventions in energy conservation and solar energy. Office: Harvard U Cambridge MA 02138

GORDON, ROY H., engineering design firm executive. Pres., chief exec. officer Gibbs & Hill, Inc., N.Y.C. Office: Gibbs & Hill Inc 393 Seventh Ave New York NY 10001§

GORDON, RUTH, actress; b. Quincy, Mass., Oct. 30, 1896; d. Clinton and Annie Tapley (Ziegler) Jones; m. Gregory Kelly, 1918; 1 son, Jones Harris; m. Garson Kanin, Dec. 4, 1942. Ed. Quincy Schs. Made first appearance, Empire Theatre, N.Y.C., 1915; as Nibs in: (with Maude Adams) Peter Pan; other appearances include Seventeen, 1917-19, Saturday's Children, 1928, Serena Blandish, 1929, Hotel Universe, 1930, The Church Mouse, 1930-31, Ethan Frome, 1935, The Country Wife, 1936-37; Nora in: A Doll's House, 1938; Natasha in: The Three Sisters, 1942-43, Over Twenty-One, 1943-45, The Leading Lady, 1948, The Smile of the World, 1949, The Matchmaker, London and Berlin, 1954, N.Y.C., 1955, The Good Soup, 1960, A Time to Laugh, in London, 1962, My Mother, My Father and Me, 1963, The Loves of Cass McGuire, 1966; Dreyfus in: Rehearsal, 1974, Mrs. Warren's Profession, 1976, films; Mary Todd in: Abe Lincoln in Illinois, 1939; Mrs. Ehrlich in: Dr. Ehrlich's Magic Bullet, 1939, Two Faced Woman, Action in the North Atlantic, Edge of Darkness, Inside Daisy Clover, 1965, Lord Love a Duck, 1966, Rosemary's Baby, 1968 (Acad. award Best Supporting Actress), Whatever Happened to Aunt Alice?, 1969, Where's Poppa?, 1970, Harold and Maude, 1971, The Big Bus, 1976, Every Which Way But Loose, 1978, Brighton Beach, 1979, Any Which Way You Can, 1980; TV films Isn't It Shocking, 1973, Prince of Central Park, 1975, Rosemary's Baby II, 1976, The Great Houdini, 1976, Perfect Gentlemen, 1978, Scavenger Hunt, 1979; guest appearance: TV shows Kojak, 1975, Rhoda, 1975, Medical Story, 1975; playwright, star: A Very Rich Woman, 1965, Ho! Ho! Ho!, 1976; TV Mommy in The American Dream, 1963, Madame Arcati in Blithe Spirit; Author: plays The Leading Lady; (with Garson Kanin) screenplays Pat and Mike; Myself Among Others, 1971; autobiography My Side, 1976, An Open Book, 1980, Shady Lady, 1981; Contbr. to: N.Y. Times (Winner Emmy award for appearance on Taxi 1979). Gold medal Holland Soc., 1980. Address: PO Box 585 Edgartown MA 02539 Office: 200 W 57th St Suite 1203 New York NY 10019

GORDON, SAMUEL, food company executive; b. Jacksonville, Fla., Apr. 6, 1934; s. Robert Joseph and Lillian (Hecht) G.; m. Norma Susan Goldberg, Aug. 26, 1956; children: Lynn Ellen, Debra Ann, Roberta Joy, Alisa Beth. B.S., Wharton Sch. Bus., U. Pa., 1955. Pres. Del Monte Banana Co., Miami, Fla., 1972—; pres. worldwide fresh fruit Del Monte Corp., San Francisco, 1978—. Mem. Produce Mktg. Assn. (dir. 1982—), Nat. Banana Assn. (pres. 1975—). Democrat. Jewish. Home: 3014 Brickell Ave Miami FL 33129 Office: Del Monte Banana Co 1201 Brickell Ave Miami FL 33131

GORDON, SANFORD DANIEL, economics educator; b. Newark, June 23, 1924; s. Harry Louis and Beatrice (Safris) G.; m. Alice Lillian Pressman, May 27, 1948; children—Ellen Ann, Eric Alan. Student, Tulane U., 1942; B.S. magna cum laude, N.Y. U., 1947, M.A., 1948, Ph.D., 1953. Instr. econ. N.Y. U., 1948-50; mem. faculty State U. Coll., Oneonta, N.Y., 1950—, prof. econs., 1957—, chmn. dept., 1960—; asst. vice chancellor for policy and planning State U. N.Y. Central Adminstrn., 1972-76, provost for policy analysis, 1976-79; exec. dir. N.Y. State Council on Econ. Edn., 1979—; prof. econs. Russell Sage Coll., 1979—; econ. editor Kennikat Press., Inc., Port Washington, N.Y., 1970—; cons. govt., industry, banks, pub. schs., 1954—; Vis. prof. State U. N.Y., Buffalo, 1965, U. Miami, 1967. Author: (with J. Witchel) An Introduction to the American Economy, 1967, A Visual Analysis of the American Economy, 1968, (with G. Dawson) The American Economy, 1969, Introductory Economics, 1972, 4th edit., 1980; Lectr., writer: pub. TV series The American Economy, Conversations on Economic Issues, 1970—. Mem. Parks Commn., also Charter Revision Com., Oneonta, 1957—; v.p. Oneonta Brotherhood, 1958. Served to sgt. USAAF, 1942-44. Recipient Kazajian Found. award, 1967. Mem. N.Y. Econ. Assn. (past pres.), AAUP (past pres. N.Y. conf.). Home: 1 Tudor Rd Albany NY 12203 *Success has less to do with innate ability than with self-confidence, motivation, and perhaps most important, resiliancy.*

GORDON, SHIRLEY BLOM, college president; b. Bremerton, Wash., Feb. 26, 1922; d. Waldemer and Edith Mary (Sterns) Blom; m. Thomas I. Gordon, Aug. 18, 1944. B.S., Wash. State U., 1944, M.A., 1947, Ph.D., 1957; postgrad., U. Calif., 1959, Seattle U., 1960, Reed Coll., 1961. Instr. in chemistry Wash. State U., 1946-49; instr. in chemistry and math. Grays Harbor Coll., 1950-57; tchr., math./sci. coordinator Highline Sch. Dist., Seattle, 1957-61; dean instrn. Highline Community Coll., 1961-72, v.p., 1972-76, pres., 1976—; mem. Nat. Commn. on Excellence in Edn.; co-chmn. Wash. Commn. on Ednl. Excellence. Mem. various community coms. and adv. groups.; Active United Way of King County. Mem. Am. Assn. Community and Jr. Colls. (dir.), N.W. Assn. Schs. and Colls. (dir., mem. Commn. on Colls.), Wash. Assn. Community Coll. Pres. (pres.), Delta Delta Delta, Iota Sigma Pi, Pi Lambda Theta. Episcopalian. Home: PO Box 98318 Seattle WA 98188 Office: Highline Community Coll Midway WA 98031

GORDON, STEPHEN MAURICE, manufacturing company executive; b. Chgo., Aug. 20, 1942; s. Milton A. and Elinor (Loeff) G.; m. Helene Lindow, Feb. 11, 1978; 2 daus., Hallie Lindow, Lacey Edison. Student, Middlebury Coll., 1960-61; B.A., U. Chgo., 1964; J.D., N.Y. U., 1967; D.I.L., Cambridge (Eng.) U., 1968. Bar: N.Y. State 1968. Aide to Vice Pres. Hubert Humphrey, Democratic Nat. Com., Washington, 1968; asso. firm Marshall, Bratter, Greene, Allison & Tucker, N.Y.C., 1968-70; sr. research asso. Halle & Stieglitz, Inc., N.Y.C., 1970-72, v.p., 1972-75, pres., 1975-79; pres., chief exec. officer Irvin Industries Inc., N.Y.C., 1979—; dir. Halle & Stieglitz, Inc., Vincennes Steel Corp., Irvin Industries Inc., Irvin Gt. Brit. Ltd., Sheffield Steel Products, Inc.; Irvin Manifatture Industriali S.p.A. Mem. Am. Soc. Internat. Law, Am. Seat Belt Council, Am. Mgmt. Assn., Young Pres.'s Orgn., Beta Gamma Sigma, Psi Upsilon. Club: Gipsey Trail. Home: 1120 Park Ave New York NY 10028 Office: 630 Fifth Ave New York NY 10111

GORDON, STEVEN STANLEY, automotive parts company executive; b. Detroit, Aug. 29, 1919; s. Andrew C. and Mary V. (Matlak) G.; m. Eleanore Clare Pazgrat, Apr. 27, 1946; 1 dau., Kathleen Gordon Putnam. B.B.A., Detroit Inst. Tech., 1954. Asst. to pres. Republic Parts, Inc., St. Clair Shores, Mich., 1946-49, v.p. adminstrn., 1949-54, v.p. sales, 1954-58, pres., dir., 1958-71, chmn., chief exec. officer, 1971—; also dir.; with Republic Automotive Parts, Inc., East Detroit, Mich., 1969—, pres., chief exec. officer, dir., 1969—, chmn., chief exec. officer, 1982; dir. Hayes-Albion Corp., Hayden, Inc., Parts Warehouse-Alaska, Republic Parts, Inc.; Chmn. joint operating com. Internat. Automotive Service Industries Show, 1977-82; chmn. Eastern Automotive Show, 1978-81. Served to capt. U.S. Army, 1942-46. Recipient Automotive Replacement Edn. award Northwood Inst., 1975. Mem. Motor and Equipment Mfrs. Assn. (pres. 1963-64, dir. 1959-70, treas. 1971-75, adv. bd. 1975-79, Triangle award 1983), Automotive Presidents Council (pres. 1972-73), Automotive Sales Council (pres. 1966-67, dir. 1963-67), Automotive Acad., Newcomen Soc. Roman Catholic. Clubs: Detroit Athletic, Renaissance (Detroit); Lochmoor Country (Grosse Pointe, Mich.); Wings (N.Y.C.); Merion Golf (Ardmore, Pa.). Home: 818 Sunningdale Dr Grosse Pointe MI 48236 Office: Republic Automotive Parts Inc 22777 Kelly Rd East Detroit MI 48021

GORDON, STEWART GEORGE, manufacturing company executive; b. Searcy, Ark., Mar. 21, 1937; s. Oliver and Freida (Stewart) G.; m. Sandra Elaine Russell, Sept. 5, 1959; children: Leslie, Adam, Ian. B.A., U. Mich., 1959. Dir. mkg. Boise Cascade Corp., Portland, Oreg., 1966-72; v.p. mktg. Williamhouse-Regency, N.Y.C., 1972-73; group v.p. paper and pulp Reed Paper Ltd., Toronto, Ont., Can., 1973-74, exec. v.p., 1978-79; exec. v.p. ops. ITT Rayonier, Stamford, Conn., 1979—; v.p. Rayonier Environ. Properties, Stamford, 1981—; dir. Grays Harbor Paper Co., Seattle, Rayland Corp., Fernandina Beach, Fla., So. Wood Piedmont, Spartanburg, S.C. Treas. Windrose Way Assn., Greenwich, Conn., 1980—; bd. dirs. ITT Rayonier Found., 1982—. Office: 1177 Summer St Stamford CT 06904

GORDON, STUART, theater producer and director, playwright; b. Chgo., Aug. 11, 1947; s. Bernard Leo and Rosalie (Sabbath) G.; m. Carolyn Purdy, Dec. 20, 1968; 1 dau., Suzanna Katherine. Student, U. Wis. Founder, producing dir. Organic Theater Co., Chgo., 1969—, dir. nat. TV show Bleacher Bums; dir. Broadway, off-Broadway, throughout U.S. and Europe. Former mem. bd dirs. Ill. Arts Council. Recipient Emmy award for Bleacher Bums, Golden Hugo award for Bleacher Bums Chgo. Internat. Film Festival, Joseph Jefferson awards for writing and directing. Mem. League Chgo. Theaters (dir.), Theater Communications Group (past dir.). Jewish. Office: Organic Theater Co 3319 N Clark St Chicago IL 60657

GORDON, THOMAS CHRISTIAN, JR., former justice; b. Richmond, Va., July 14, 1915; s. Thomas Christian and Ruth Nelson (Robins) G. B.S., U. Va., 1936, LL.B., 1938. Bar: Va. bar 1937. Assoc. Parrish, Butcher & Parrish, Richmond, 1938-40; assoc., then partner McGuire, Woods & Battle (and predecessors), Richmond, 1940-65, 72-83; justice Supreme Ct. Va., 1965-72; lectr. Law Sch., U. Va., 1970-72, Marshall-Wythe Sch. Law, 1979—. Bd. editors: Va. Law Rev, 1937-38. Trustee, past pres. Crippled Childrens Hosp., Richmond. Served to maj. AUS, 1941-45. Fellow Am. Bar Found.; mem. Am. Bar Assn., Va. Bar Assn. (pres. 1963-64). Episcopalian (vestry, sr. warden). Home: 1435 Floyd Ave Richmond VA 23220 Office: PO Box 1315 Richmond VA 23210

GORDON, WALTER, architect; b. Buffalo, Sept. 8, 1907; s. Walter William and Florence (Green) G.; m. Margaret Murray, July 4, 1936. B.S., Princeton U., 1930, M.F.A. in Architecture, 1932; spl. student, Yale U., 1936-37, U. Paris, France, 1934. Curator San Francisco Mus. Art, 1937-39; asst. dir. Portland (Oreg.) Art Mus., 1939-41; practicing architect, Portland, 1946-58; dean Sch. Architecture, U. Oreg., 1958-62; faculty mem. Reed Coll., 1962-65; sr. partner Gordon & Hinchliff, architects, 1962-72; prin. Walter Gordon, architect, 1972—; Design cons. Portland Devel. Commn., 1962-76, Eugene Renewal Agy., 1972—, Salem (Oreg.) Renewal Agy., 1973—; mem. Gov.'s Adv. Com. for Preservation Yaquina Head, 1977—, Oreg. Bd. Architect Examiners, 1956-58, Portland Art Commn., 1955-57, Oreg. Capitol Planning Commn., 1959-68. Prin. works include Southwest Hills Library, Portland, Alpha Phi sorority house, Corvallis, Oreg.; numerous residences, Pacific N.W.; coll. dormitories, faculty residence, library Marylhurst Coll., Portland; visitor's lodge, infirmary, Trappist Abbey, Lafayette, Oreg., parish hall, chapel, Sacred Heart Ch., Newport, Oreg. Trustee Portland Art Mus., 1947-51. Fellow A.I.A. (mem. nat. edn. com. 1960-62); mem. Phi Beta Kappa. Clubs: City of Portland (v.p. 1971-72), University.). Home and office: 105 Wade Way Newport OR 97365

GORDON, WALTER KELLY, provost, educator; b. Bklyn., Jan. 15, 1930; s. William Benjamin and Grace Adele (Kelly) G.; m. Lydia Caroline Fruchtman, Aug. 29, 1959; 1 dau., Karyn Gay. A.B., Clark U., 1950; M.A., U. Pa., 1956, Ph.D., 1961. Instr. Cedar Crest Coll., 1959-61; faculty Rutgers-State U. N.J., Camden, 1961—, prof., dean coll., 1974-81, acad. dean, provost Camden campus, 1981—; cons. Campbells Soup Co., 1976—. Author: (with J.L. Sanderson) Exposition and the English Language, 1963, 2d edit., 1968, Literature in Critical Perspectives, 1969. Bd. dirs. Walt Whitman Internat. Poetry Center, 1974-77. Served to lt. USNR, 1951-56. Recipient Lindback award for disting. teaching, 1970. Home: 2803 Salem Dr Cinnaminson NJ 08077 Office: Office of Dean Camden Coll Arts and Scis Rutgers-State U NJ 379 Armitage Hall Camden NJ 08102

GORDON, WALTER LOCKHART, Canadian govt. ofcl; b. Toronto, Ont., Can., Jan. 27, 1906; s. Harry D.L. and Kathaleen H. (Cassels) G.; m. Elizabeth Marjorie Leith Counsell, 1932; children—Kyra (Mrs. Jean Montagu), Jane (Mrs. William Glassco), John Counsell Lockhart. Ed., Upper Can. Coll., also. With firm Clarkson, Gordon & Co. (chartered accountants), 1927-63, partner, 1935-63, Woods & Gordon (mgmt. cons.), 1940-63; minister finance Govt. Can., Ottawa, 1963-65, mem., 1967—, pres., 1967-68; chmn. bd., past pres. Canadian Corporate Mgmt. Co., Ltd., 1968—; Assisted with orgn. Fgn. Exchange Control Bd., 1939; spl. asst. to dep. minister finance, 1940-42; pres. Toronto Bd. Trade, 1947; chmn. nat. exec. com. Canadian Inst. Internat. Affairs, 1951-56; chmn. Royal Commn. Adminstrv. Classification in Pub. Service, 1946, Royal Commn. Can.'s Econ. Prospects, 1955, Com. Orgn. Govt. Ont., 1958; Mem. Ho. of Commons for Toronto-Davenport, 1962-63; chmn. nat. campaign Liberal Party, 1962, 63. Author: Troubled Canada-The Need for New Domestic Policies, 1961, A Choice for Canada-Independence or Colonial Status, 1966. Bd. govs. U. Toronto, 1945-63. Office: Parliament Bldgs Ottawa ON Canada *

GORDON, WENDELL CHAFFEE, economics educator; b. Birmingham, Ala., Oct. 9, 1916; s. Dugald and Gertrude (Mills) G. B.A., Rice Inst., 1937; M.A., Am. U., 1938; Ph.D., NYU, 1940. With dept. econs. U. Tex., Austin, 1940-58, prof. econs., 1958—; pres. Assn. Evolutionary Econs., 1983. Author: Expropriation of Foreign-Owned Property in Mexico, 1941, International Trade, 1958, Political Economy of Latin America, 1965, Institutional Economics, 1980.

Served with U.S. Army, 1942-45. Mem. Phi Beta Kappa. Democrat. Presbyterian. Home: 6630 Belmont Houston TX 77005 Office: Dept Econs U Tex Austin TX 78712

GORDON, WILLIAM EDWIN, physicist, educator, university official; b. Paterson, N.J., Jan. 8, 1918; s. William and Mary (Scott) G.; m. Elva Freile, June 22, 1941; children:Larry Scott, Nancy Lynn. B.A., Montclair (N.J.) State Coll., 1939, M.A., 1942; M.S., N.Y. U., 1946; Ph.D., Cornell U., Ithaca, N.Y., 1953. Registered profl. engr., Tex. Asso. prof. Cornell U., 1953-59, prof., 1959-65; dir. Arecibo Ionospheric Obs., P.R., 1960-65, Walter R. Read prof. engring., 1965; prof. elec. engring. and space physics and astronomy Rice U., Houston, 1966—, dean engring. and sci., 1966-75, dean, 1975-80, provost, v.p., 1980—; mem. com. solar terrestrial research Nat. Acad. Scis., 1966-74; mem. NSF panel on atmospheric sci., 1967-74; panel on Jicamarca Radio Obs., 1969-74; mem. research adv. com. NSF, 1973-76; chmn. bd. trustees Upper Atmosphere Research Corp., 1971, 73-78, Univ. Corp. for Atmospheric Research, 1979-81; trustee Cornell U., 1976-80; mem. Arecibo Obs. Adv. Bd., 1977-80; mem. com. on solar power systems NRC. Served to capt. USAAF, 1942-46. Recipient Balth. Vander Pol award for distinguished research in radio sci., 1966; 50th Anniversary medal Am. Meteorol. Soc., 1969; Guggenheim fellow, 1972-73. Fellow IEEE (chmn. profl. group on antennas and propagation 1964-65), Am. Geophys. Union; mem. Nat. Acad. Sci., Nat. Acad. Engring., Internat. Sci. Radio Union (commns. F, G, H, past chmn. USNC/URSI, v.p. 1975-81, pres. 1981—), Am. Meterology Soc., AAAS, Philos. Soc. Tex., Sigma Xi, Tau Beta Pi, Kappa Delta Pi, Sigma Kappa Nu, Phi Kappa Phi. Club: Cosmos. Spl. research radio scattering. Conceived, directed constrn. world's largest antenna reflector. Office: Office of Provost and Vice Pres Rice U Box 1892 Houston TX 77251

GORDON, WILLIAM LIVINGSTON, physicist, educator; b. Tanta, Egypt, Jan. 17, 1927; (parents Am. citizens); m. Jean Crea, June 18, 1949; children—David W., Amy J., Timothy L. B.S., Muskingum Coll., 1948; M.S., Ohio State U., 1950, Ph.D., 1954. Instr. physics Ohio State U., 1954-55; mem. faculty Case Western Res. U., 1955—, prof. physics, 1968—, chmn. dept., 1979—. Mem. Am. Phys. Soc. Address: Dept of Physics Case Western Reserve University University Circle Cleveland OH 44106

GORDON, WILLIAM RICHARD, university finance official; b. Phila., Nov. 17, 1913; s. William Murray and Lucille Kerzie (Tribble) G.; m. Mary Alice Wagner, May 20, 1950; children: Anne Morrison, William Murray, Robert Duff, Douglas Andrew. B.S., U. Pa., 1936. Investment officer U. Pa., Phila., 1936-42, asst. treas., 1942-55, treas., 1955-75, sec. investment bd., 1975—, asst. instr. accounting, corp. finance, investment banking, 1937-57; pres. Franklin Investment Co., 1975-82; dir. Transp. Mut. Ins. Co., Finance Co. Pa., Sigma Spl. Fund, Drexel Burnham Fund, Quaker City Ins. Co. Curator arms Valley Forge Hist. Soc. Museum; former commr. Valley Forge State Park.; Bd. dirs. Presbyn. Ministers' Fund; trustee Moore Sch. Elec. Engring. Served with 2d Regt., Arty. U.S. Army, 1942-46; capt. Gen. Staff Corps Dept. Army, The Pentagon, 1951-52. Mem. S.R., Soc. Colonial Wars Pa., Soc. War of 1812, St. Andrews Soc. of Phila., Mil. Order Fgn. Wars U.S., Res. Officers Assn. U.S., Hist. Soc. Pa. (dir.), Valley Forge Hist. Soc., State Soc. Cin. Pa., Phila. Soc. Promoting Agr., Delta Psi. Presbyn. Clubs: Rittenhouse, St. Anthony (Phila.); Penn. Home: 109 Arlington Rd Paoli PA 19301 Office: 1500 Walnut St Philadelphia PA 19102

GORDON, WILLIAM TALBOTT, ret. banker; b. Richmond, Va., Sept. 4, 1914; s. Robert Latimer and Anne (Talbott) G.; m. Eleanor Stuart Holladay, Aug. 23, 1943; children—Ellen S. (Mrs. Jesse Frank Williams), William Talbott, Anne M. (Mrs. John F. Carson), James H. Student, U. Va., 1934-36. With Bank of Va., Richmond, 1936-78, former pres., chief exec. officer, chmn. exec. com., dir., chmn. bd. dirs., until 1978; ret., 1978; chmn. bd., exec. com. Bank of Va.-Petersburg; dir. Bank of Va. Co., Bank of Va. Internat., Bank Va. Service Co., Bank Va. Credit Card Co., BVA Ins. Agy., Inc. Bd. dirs., mem. exec. com. Va. Indsl. Devel. Corp.; bd. dirs. Va. Thanksgiving Festival, Inc.; adv. bd., bd. dirs., chmn. fin. com., treas. Salvation Army Va.; trustee United Way of Greater Richmond; mem. capital funds bd. United Givers Fund. Served to lt. USNR, 1942-45. Mem. Am. Inst. Banking, Va., Richmond chambers commerce, Assn. Reserve City Bankers, Clearing House Assn. of Richmond (pres.), Navy League of U.S. Clubs: Commonwealth, Downtown (Richmond). Home: 9912 Drouin Dr Richmond VA 23233

GORDONE, CHARLES, playwright; b. Cleve., Oct. 12, 1927; s. William Lee and Camille (Morgan) G.; m. Jeanne Warner; 1 dau. Ed., Los Angeles City and State Coll., N.Y. U., Columbia U. Actor: off Broadway prodn. The Blacks; appeared in: No Place to Be Somebody, Of Mice and Men, Mrs. Patterson, The Climate of Eden, Gordone is a Mutha; author: No Place to Be Somebody (Pulitzer prize for drama 1970), The Last Chord, 1976, also, Gordone is a Muthah; dir.: plays Fortunato, Tobacco Road, Detective Story, Hell Bent for Heaven, Faust; asso. producer: film Nothing But a Man, 1964; Co-founder (with Godfrey Cambridge), Com. for Employment of Negro Performers, 1962 (Recipient award Nat. Inst. Arts and Letters 1971), Com. for Employment of Negro Performers (also Drama Desk award), Com. for Employment of Negro Performers (Critic's Circle award), Com. for Employment of Negro Performers (1970), Com. for Employment of Negro Performers (Vernon Rice award 1970), Com. for Employment of Negro Performers (Obie award for acting 1964). Office: care William Morris Agy 1350 Ave of Americas New York NY 10019 *

GORDONSMITH, JOHN ARTHUR HAROLD, collection agency executive; b. Montreal, Que., Can., Dec. 7, 1942; s. Erith Orman and Alexes (Fraser) G.; m. Lorrenne Surprenant, Sept. 9, 1967. B.Sc., Bishop's U., Can., 1964; chartered accountant, McGill U., Montreal, 1968. Auditor Coopers & Lybrand, Montreal, 1964-71; data processing mgr. Ronprint Data Ltd., Montreal, 1971-72; treas. Ronalds-Federated Ltd., Montreal, 1972-74; v.p. fin., sec., dir. FCA Internat. Ltd., Montreal, 1974—, also dir., officer subsidiary cos. Mem. Can. Inst. Chartered Accountants, Que. Inst. Chartered Accountants, Am. Mgmt. Assn. Mem. United Ch. Can. Club: Royal Montreal Golf. Home: 3477 Drummond St Montreal PQ H3G 1X6 Canada Office: 376 Victoria Ave Westmont PQ H32 1C3 Canada

GORDY, BERRY, record company and motion picture executive; children—Berry IV, Hazel Joy, Terry James, Kerry A., Kennedy W., Stefan K. Founder Motown Record Corp.; chmn. Motown Industries (entertainment complex); exec. producer motion pictures. Dir.: motion picture Mahagony, 1975; (2d Ann. Am. Music award for outstanding contbn. to industry 1975); Exec. producer: film Lady Sings the Blues, 1972, Bingo Long Traveling All-Stars and Motor Kings, 1975, The Last Dragon, 1984. Recipient Bus. Achievement award Interracial Council for Bus. Opportunity, 1967, Whitney M. Young Jr. award Los Angeles Urban League, 1980; named One of Five Leading Entrepreneurs of Nation Babson Coll., 1978. Mem. Dirs. Guild Am. Office: 6255 Sunset Blvd Hollywood CA 90028

GORDY, WALTER, emeritus physics educator; b. Miss., Apr. 20, 1909; s. Walter Kalin and Gertrude (Jones) G.; m. Vida Brown Miller, June 19, 1935; children: Eileen, Walter Terrell. A.B., Miss. Coll., 1932, LL.D., 1959; M.A., U. N.C., 1933, Ph.D., 1935; Dr. honoris causa, U. Lille, France, 1955; D.Sc. hon., Emory U., 1983. Assoc. prof. math. and physics Mary Hardin-Baylor Coll., 1935-41; NRC fellow Calif. Inst. Tech., 1941-42; staff radiation lab. Mass. Inst. Tech., 1942-46; assoc. prof. physics Duke, Durham, N.C., 1946-48, prof., 1948-79, James B. Duke prof., 1958-79, James B. Duke prof. emeritus, 1979—; Vis. prof. U. Tex., 1958; Mem. NRC, 1954-57, 68-74. Author: (with W.V. Smith, R.F. Trambarulo) Microwave Spectroscopy, 1953, (with Robert L. Cook) Microwave Molecular Spectra, 1970, Theory and Applications of Electron Spin Resonance, 1980; Assoc. editor: Jour. Chem. Physics, 1954-58, Spectrochimia Acta, 1957-60; editorial bd.: Radiation Research, 1969-72. Recipient Sci. research award Oak Ridge Inst. Nuclear Studies, 1949, Disting. Alumnus award U. N.C., 1976, N.C. award for sci., 1979; 50th Anniversary award Miss. Acad. Scis., 1980. Fellow Am. Phys. Soc. (chmn. S.E. sect. 1953-54, mem. council 1967-71, 73-77, recipient Jessie W. Beams award Southeastern sect. 1974, Earle K. Plyler prize 1980), AAAS (council 1955); mem. Radiation Research Soc. (mem. council 1961-64), Nat. Acad. Scis., Sigma Xi. Home: 2521 Perkins Rd Durham NC 27706

GORE, ALBERT, JR., congressman; b. Mar. 31, 1948; s. Albert and Pauline (LaFon) G.; m. Mary Elizabeth Aitcheson, May 19, 1970; children: Karenna, Kristin, Sarah, Albert III. B.A. cum laude (Univ. scholar), Harvard U., 1969; postgrad., Grad. Sch. of Religion, Vanderbilt U., 1971-72, Law Sch., 1974-76. Investigative reporter, editorial writer The Tennessean, 1971-76; mem. 95th Congress from Tenn.; homebuilder and land developer Tanglewood Home Builders Co., 1971-76; livestock and tobacco farmer, 1973—. Served with U.S. Army, 1969-71; Vietnam. Mem. Farm Bur., Tenn. Jaycees. Democrat. Baptist. Clubs: Am. Legion, VFW. Home: Route 2 Carthage TN 37030 Office: 1131 Longworth House Office Bldg Washington DC 20515

GORE, CHESTER A., advt. agy. exec.; b. N.Y.C., Aug. 14, 1918; s. Benjamin and Rosalind Beatrice (Sachs) G.; m. Gerie Shank, Sept. 27, 1942; 1 dau., Eloise. B.B.A., N.Y. U., 1938. Copywriter Lord & Thomas (advt. agy.), N.Y.C., 1938, Gimbels Dept. Store, 1938-40, Macy's Dept. Store, N.Y.C., 1940-42; v.p. Norman Waters Advt., N.Y.C., 1946-55; pres., creative dir. Chester Gore Co., Inc., 1955—; Mem. Nat. Advt. Rev. Bd. Served with USAAF, 1942-46. Mem. Am. Assn. Advt. Agencies, N.Y. U. Club, Whippoorwill Club, Friars Club. Home: 425 E 58th St New York City NY 10022 Office: 515 Madison Ave New York City NY 10022

GORE, WILLIAM JAY, political science educator; b. Medford, Oreg., Feb. 23, 1924; s. Jay Ish and Gertrude (Moore) G.; m. Dorothy Elaine Mathson, Sept. 24, 1947; children: Edmond J., Kathleen J., Brian J. B.A., U. Wash., 1948; M.Pub. Adminstrn., U. So. Calif., 1950, D.P.A., 1952. Instr. U. Wash., Seattle, 1951-56, prof. polit. sci., 1966—; asst. prof. polit. sci. Kans. U., Lawrence, 1956-57, 58-61, Cornell U., Ithaca, N.Y., 1957-58; assoc. prof. polit. sci. Ind. U., Bloomington, 1961-66; asst. dir. Govt. Research Ctr., Kans. U., 1958-61; cons. U. So. Calif. (NASA Project), 1967-69, Nat. Safety Council, Chgo., Il., 1962-66, USPHS, 1980-81. Author: Administrative Decision-Making, 1964, (with Wiley) The Making of Decision, 1964, Change in the Small Community, 1967. Ford Career Devel. grantee, 1959-61; HEW grantee, 1956-58; Washington Com. for Humanities grantee, 1979-81. Mem. Am. Soc. Pub. Adminstrn. (jour. editor 1967-70), Western Polit. Sci. Assn. (dir. 1953-56). Methodist. Home: 4310 43d St Seattle WA 98105 Office: Dept Polit Sci U Wash Seattle WA 98195 *The force of the creative intellect in fully unpacked only as we come to appreciate the frustration with what we were unable to accomplish in the past is one of the most legitimate motives for what we undertake in the present. The determination to lay bare the dilemmas and contradictions that once dogged us, and seek thereby to transcend them, is one of the proper expressions of the open mind.*

GORECKI, JAN, sociologist, educator; b. Warsaw, Poland, Apr. 10, 1926; came to U.S., 1969, naturalized, 1974; s. Jozef Hilary and Jadwiga Barbara (Frendzel) G.; m. Danuta M. Wojnar, Dec. 26, 1954; children: Piotr S., Marie J. Magister Juris, Cracow (Poland) U., 1947, Dr.Jur., 1949, Dr.Sc.Jur., 1958. Asst. to assoc. prof. law Cracow U., 1947-68; fellow Center for Advanced Study in Behavioral Scis., Stanford, Calif., 1969-70; research assoc. Stanford Law Sch., 1970; prof. sociology U. Ill., Urbana, 1970—, exec. com. Russian and East European Center, 1971—, assoc. Center for Advanced Study, 1976-77, 83-84; fgn. univs. Exchange Scheme visitor U. London, 1963; Brit. Council scholar London Sch. Econs., 1959-60; Rockefeller fellow in humanities, 1976-77. Author: Divorce in Poland, A Contribution to Sociology of Law, 1970, A Theory of Criminal Justice, 1979, Capital Punishment, 1983; editor, contbr.: Sociology and Jurisprudence of Leon Petrazycki, 1975; contbr. articles to profl. jours. Mem. Am., Internat. sociol. assns., Internat. Soc. Family Law, Law and Society Assn., Am. Assn. Advancement of Slavic Studies, AAUP. Home: 510 W Washington St Urbana IL 61801

GOREN, ARNOLD LOUIS, university official; b. Bklyn., Oct. 26; s. Harry A. and Anna (Spector) G.; m. Rhoda G. Goldberg, Dec. 23, 1948; children: Shelley and Susan (twins). Student, Bklyn. Coll., 1942, Cornell U., 1943; B.S., N.Y. U., 1947, M.A., 1948; L.H.D. (hon.), Canisius Coll., 1977, Litt.D., Mercy Coll., 1980, D.Sc., N.Y. Inst. Tech., 1983. Instr. N.Y. U. Sch. Edn., 1948-55, asst. prof., 1955-59, asso. prof., 1959-64, prof., 1964—, asst. dean, 1962-65, dean, 1965-68, asst. chancellor, 1968-73, vice chancellor, 1973—; Cons. banks, labor unions, TV stas.; bd. dirs. Knickerbocker Fed. Savs. Loan Assn.; Adviser N.Y. Com., other fed. and state agys. Former v.p., gen. campaign mgr. 6th dist. N.Y.C. Democratic Com.; Past trustee, mem. exec. bd. Coll. Entrance Exam. Bd. Served with AUS, 1943-46. Mem. AAUP, Am. Assn. Univs. (council on fed. relations 1976—), Anti-Defamation League (exec. com.). Club: City (pres. 1979-81). Home: 505 La Guardia Pl New York NY 10012 *There is a classical saying by Hillel which begins, "If I am not for myself, who will be for me? If I am for myself alone, what am I?" This statement indicates the way I hope that I behave and it contains a standard of conduct which I try to use as a guide.*

GOREN, CHARLES HENRY, contract bridge expert, columnist; b. Phila., Mar. 4, 1901; s. Jacob and Rebecca G. LL.B., McGill U., Can., 1922, LL.M., 1923, LL.D., 1973. Bar: Pa. bar 1923. Since practiced in, Phila. Author: various books including Contract Bridge in a Nutshell, 1946, Point Count Bidding, 1950, Contract Bridge Complete, 1951, The Italian Bridge System, 1958, New Contract Bridge in a Nutshell, 1959, An Evening of Bridge with Charles Goren, 1959, Goren's Hoyle, 1961, Goren's Bridge Complete, 1963, Bridge is My Game, 1965, Go With the Odds, 1969, Charles Goren Presents the Precision System, 1971, Goren on Play and Defense, 1974, Goren's Modern Backgammon Complete, 1974, Goren Settles the Bridge Arguments, 1974, Charles H. Goren's One Hundred Challenging Bridge Hands, 1976, Goren on Bridge; daily column syndicated by numerous newspapers including, Chgo. Tribune; weekly column Sports Illus. mag; master ceremonies, commentator: TV program Championship Bridge, 1965. Office: Chgo Tribune-NY Times Syndicate Inc 220 E 42d St New York NY 10017 *

GORENSTEIN, SHIRLEY SLOTKIN, anthropologist, educator; b. N.Y.C., Mar. 4, 1928; d. Harry and Mary (Pfeffer) Slotkin; m. Samuel Gorenstein, July 3, 1948; children: Ethan Ezra, Gabriel William. B.A., Queen's Coll., 1949; M.A., Columbia U., 1953, Ph.D., 1963. Lectr. anthropology Columbia U., N.Y.C., 1963-71, asst. prof., 1971-74, asso. prof., 1974-75; prof. anthropology Rensselaer Poly. Inst., Troy, N.Y., 1975—, chmn. dept. sci. tech. studies, assoc. dean Sch. Humanities and Social Scis. Author works in field. Mem. N.Y. State Bd. for Hist. Preservation, 1976. Mem. Am. Anthropol. Assn. (exec. bd. 1976-79), Soc. Am. Archaeology., Soc. Profl. Archaeologists (bd. standards 1983—). Office: Rensselaer Poly Inst 5506 Sage Lab Troy NY 12181

GORES, JOSEPH NICHOLAS, scriptwriter; b. Rochester, Minn., Dec. 25, 1931; s. Joseph Mathias and Mildred Dorothy (Duncanson) G.; m. Dori Jane Corfitzen, May 21, 1976; children: Timothy, Gillian. B.A., U. Notre Dame, 1953; M.A., Stanford, 1961. Investigator L.A. Walker Co., San Francisco, 1955-57, 59; pvt. investigator David Kikkert & Assos., San Francisco, 1960-61, 65-66; tchr. Kakamega Boys Secondary Sch., Kenya, E. Africa, 1963-64; mgr./auctioneer Automobile Auction Co., San Francisco, 1968-76. (Recipient Edgar Allan Poe award for A Time of Predators as best first novel Mystery Writers Am., 1969, for Goodbye, Pops as best short story in Am. mags., 1969, for best teleplay in a dramatic series (Kojak) 1976); Author: A Time of Predators, 1969, Marine Salvage, 1971, Dead Skip, 1972, Final Notice, 1973, Interface, 1974, Hammett, 1975, Gone, No Forwarding, 1978; screenplays Hammett, 1977, Deadfall, 1977, Paper Crimes, 1978, Paradise Road, 1978, A Wayward Angel, 1981; teleplays Kojak, 1975-77, Golden Gate Memorial, 1978, Eischied, 1979, Kate Columbo, 1979, The Gangster Chronicles, 1981, Magnum, P.I., 1983; Editor: Honolulu: Port of Call, 1974; (with Bill Pronzini) teleplays Tricks and Treats, 1976; Contbr. articles to profl. jours. Served with AUS, 1958-59. Mem. Mystery Writers Am. (regional v.p. 1967, 69-70), Crime Writers Assn., Writers Guild Am. Republican. Roman Catholic. Address: 401 Oak Crest Rd San Anselmo CA 94960 *The great challenge of writing is striving for a perfection you can never achieve; no book is ever as good as it could be, as good as you thought it would be. You are always trying to beat yourself, not other writers.*

GORES, LANDIS, architect; b. Cin., Aug. 31, 1919; s. Guido and Paula Margaret (Landis) G.; m. Pamela Whitmarsh, Dec. 12, 1942; children: Catherine Gores Keefe, Ainslie Gores Gilligan, Valerie, Karl, Elizabeth Anne. A.B., S.C.L., Princeton U., 1939; B.Arch., Harvard U., 1942. Assoc. with Philip C. Johnson, N.Y.C., 1945-51; individual archtl. practice, New Canaan, Conn., 1951—; lectr. Pratt Inst., 1947-48, 52-53. Contbg. bd.: Jour. AIA, 1958-62; prin. works include custom residences in, Conn., N.Y., Va., middle sch. and sci. bldgs, Van Doren Hosp, Fairfield, Strathmoor Village, Stamford, York Research Corp. Offices and Labs, Stamford. Served to maj. AUS, 1942-46. Decorated Legion of Merit, Order Brit. Empire.; Recipient Sch. medal AIA, 1942, nat. honor award AIA, 1955, Sao Paulo Bieniale award, 1955, Award Merit Boston Arts Festival, 1956, New Haven Festival Arts, 1959, First Honor Awards Program Conn. AIA, 1964. Fellow AIA; mem. Phi Beta Kappa. Republican. Episcopalian. Address: 192 Cross Ridge Rd New Canaan CT 06840

GOREY, EDWARD ST. JOHN, author, artist; b. Chgo., Feb. 22, 1925; s. Edward Leo and Helen Dunham (Garvey) G. B.A., Harvard U., 1950. Author: The Unstrung Harp, 1953, The Doubtful Guest, 1957, The Hapless Child, 1961, The Willowdale Handcar, 1962, The Wuggly Ump, 1963, The Remembered Visit, 1965, The Gilded Bat, 1966, The Blue Aspic, 1968, The Other Statue, 1968, The Epiplectic Bicycle, 1969, The Awdrey-Gore Legacy, 1972, Amphigorey, 1972, Category, 1973, Amphigorey Too, 1975, The Broken Spoke, 1976, The Loathsome Couple, 1977, The Doubtful Guest, 1978, The Gilded Bat, 1979, Gorey Endings, 1979; numerous other works. Served with AUS, 1943-46. Address: care Congdon & Weed Inc 298 Fifth Ave New York NY 10001 *

GORHAM, DONALD R., clinical psychologist; b. Kalamazoo, May 23, 1903; s. Adelbert Leroy and Emma Louise (Rogers) G.; m. Elizabeth Ann Young, June 23, 1926; children: Ann Emily, Janet Susan. B.Th., Colgate U., 1926, M.A., 1927; scholar, U. Pa., 1929-30, Ph.D., 1934. Prof., dir. Sch. Edn., Eastern Bapt. Theol. Sem., 1931-43; prof. edn. and psychology Keuka Coll., 1943-50; clin. psychologist VA Neuro-psychiat. Hosp., Waco, Tex., 1950-59; prof. clin. psychology (part time) Baylor U., 1950-59; cons. The Hogg Found., 1957-58; research psychologist VA Hosp., Perry Point, 1959-69; chief psychol. service VA Center, Bath, N.Y., 1969-70; cons. and ltd. pvt. practice, 1970—; Mem. Md. Bd. Examiners in Profl. Psychology. Author: books including Understanding Adults, 1948, Proverbs Test, 1954, (with J.E. Overall) Brief Psychiatric Rating Scale, 1961; Contbr. articles to profl. jours. Fellow Internat. Council Psychology, Am. Psychol. Assn.; mem. Md. Psychol. Assn. Interam. Soc. Psychology. Home: Hill Acres Bluff Point NY 14417

GORHAM, EVILLE, scientist, educator; b. Halifax, N.S., Can., Oct. 15, 1925; s. Ralph Arthur and Shirley Agatha (Eville) G.; m. Ada Verne MacLeod, Sept. 29, 1948; children: Kerstin, Vivien, Jocelyn, James. B.Sc. in Biology with distinction, Dalhousie U., 1945, M.Sc. in Zoology, 1947; Ph.D. in Botany, U. London, Eng., 1951. Lectr. botany U. Coll., London, Eng., 1951-54; sr. sci. officer Freshwater Biol. Assn., Ambleside, Eng., 1954-58; lectr., asst. prof. botany U. Toronto, 1958-62; assoc. prof. botany U. Minn., Mpls., 1962-65, prof., 1966—, head dept., 1967-71, prof. ecology, 1975—; prof., head dept. biology U. Calgary, Alta., Can., 1965-66; Mem. for Can. Internat. Commn. on Atmospheric Chemistry and Radioactivity, 1959-62; mem. Scientists Inst. for Pub. Info., 1971—, fellow, 1972—; mem. vis. panel to review toxicology programs Nat. Acad. Scis.-NRC, 1974-75; mem. coordinating com. for sci. and tech. assessment of environ. pollutants Environ. Studies Bd., 1975-78; mem. com. on med. and biologic effects of environ. pollutants Assembly Life Scis., 1976-77; mem. com. on atmosphere and biosphere Bd. Agr. and Renewable Resources, 1979-81; mem. panel on environ. impact Diesel Impact Study Com., Nat. Acad. Engring.-NRC, 1980-81; mem. U.S./Can./Mex. Joint Sci. Com. on acid precipitation Environ. Studies Bd., Nat. Acad. Scis.-NRC-Royal Soc. Can.-Mex. Acad. Scis., 1981—. Editorial bd.: Ecology, 1965-67, Limnology and Oceanography, 1970-72; Contbr. articles on limnology, ecology and biogeochemistry to profl. jours. Royal Soc. Can. fellow State Forest Research Inst., Stockholm, Sweden, 1950-51; NSF, AEC, NIH, ERDA, NRC Can. grantee; grantee Office Water Resources Research, Dept. Interior. Mem. Am. Soc. Limnology and Oceanography, Ecol. Soc. Am., Internat. Assn. Pure and Applied Limnology., Internat. Peut. Soc.; hon. mem. Swedish Phytogeographical Soc. Home: 1933 E River Terr Minneapolis MN 55414

GORHAM, FRANK DEVORE, JR., petroleum co. exec.; b. St. Louis, June 4, 1921; s. Frank DeVore and Lillian (Hawley) G.; m. Marie Ellis Kelly, Sept. 1, 1947; children—Frank DeVore III, Daniel Kelly, Timothy Walker, Robert Hawley, Mark Linton. A.B., U. Mo., 1943. Petroleum geologist Creole Petroleum Co., Venezuela, 1946-49; dist. geologist Pure Oil Co., Denver, 1949-50; chief geologist Pubco Petroleum Corp., Albuquerque, 1950-60, exec. v.p., 1960-65, pres., 1965-73, Questa Petroleum Inc., 1973—; dir. Bank of N.Mex. Served to capt. AUS, 1943-46; MTO. Decorated Silver Star. Fellow Geol. Soc. Am., Am. Assn. Petroleum Geologists (pres. Rocky Mountain sect. 1959). Home: 218 16th St SW Albuquerque NM 87104 Office: Suite 800 Sandia Savs Bldg Albuquerque NM 87103

GORHAM, WILLIAM, orgn. exec.; b. N.Y.C., Dec. 14, 1930; s. Jack and Fay (Blank) G.; m. Gail Wiley Finsterbusch, 1973; children from previous marriage—Sarah, Nancy, Kim, Jennifer, Becky. Student, Mass. Inst. Tech., 1949-50; B.A., Stanford, 1952. Mem. research staff RAND Corp., 1953-62; dep. asst. sec. def. U.S., 1962-65, asst. sec. health, edn. and welfare, 1965-68; co-chmn. Pres.'s Panel Social Indicators, 1967-68; chmn. Pres.'s Task Force on Child Devel., 1966; pres. Urban Inst., Washington, 1968—; Mem. U.S. adv. com. Internat. Inst. for Applied Systems Analysis, 1974—; Dir.-at-large Social Sci. Research Council, 1970-71. Editor: (with Nathan Glazer) The Urban Predicament, 1976; bd. editors: Policy Scis, 1969—, Jour. Public Policy, 1980—. Recipient Disting. Civilian Service award Dept. Def., 1965. Mem. Nat. Acad. Pub. Adminstrn., Assn. for Public Policy Analysis and Mgmt. (policy council 1979—). Office: 2100 M St NW Washington DC 20037

GORIGIN, EUGENE BORIS, pharmaceutical consultant; b. St. Petersburg, Russia, Sept. 28, 1919; came to U.S., 1941, naturalized, 1946; s. Joseph and Olga (Aronstams) G.; m. Helena Vazquez, Aug. 4, 1950. Student, U. Basle, Switzerland, 1938-41. With Hoffmann La Roche Inc., Nutley, N.J., 1941-47, SAPAC Corp., Montevideo, Uruguay, 1947-52, Parke, Davis & Co., Detroit, 1952-55, Geigy Chem. Corp., Ardsley, N.Y., 1955-63; with Richardson-Merrell Inc., Wilton, Conn., 1963—, exec. v.p., 1970-81, ret., 1981; cons. to pharm. industry, 1981—. Home: 515 Middlesex Rd Darien CT 06820

GORIN, GEORGE, educator; b. Como, Italy, Aug. 19, 1925; came to U.S., 1939, naturalized, 1946; s. Victor and Piera (Jahn) G.; m. Helen S. Surber, June 16, 1952; children—Sarah A., Victor W. A.B., Bklyn. Coll., 1944; M.S., Princeton, 1947, Ph.D., 1949. Chemist Heyden Chem. Corp., Garfield, N.J., 1945; instr. Rutgers U., New Brunswick, N.J., 1948-50; postdoctoral fellow Purdue U., Lafayette, Ind., 1950-51; asst. prof. U. Ore., Eugene, 1952-55, Okla. State U., Stillwater, 1955-58, asso. prof., 1958-61, prof., 1962—. Contbr. sci. papers on sulfur compounds, proteins, radiation damage to profl. jours. Recipient NIH Career Devel. award, 1963-73. Mem. Am. Chem. Soc. (chmn. Okla. sect. 1968), Am. Soc. Biol. Chemists, Radiation Research Soc. Home: 1302 S Western St Stillwater OK 74074

GORIN, WILLIAM, retail co. exec.; b. Woburn, Mass., Feb. 8, 1908; s. Nehemias and Rebecca (Caban) G.; m. Helaine M. Falkson, May 14, 1945 (dec. Aug. 1971); children—Howard F., Ralph E. LL.B., Boston U., 1928. Bar: Mass. bar 1929. With Almy Stores Inc., Boston, 1928—, now chmn. bd. Trustee Nehemias Gorin Charitable Found. Home: 101 Monmouth St Brookline MA 02146 Office: 1330 Beacon St Brookline MA 02146

GORING, ROBERT THOMAS, hockey player; b. St. Boniface, Man., Can., Oct. 22, 1949. Player Los Angeles Kings, 1969-79, N.Y. Islanders, 1979—, asst. coach, 1981—. Recipient Lady Byng Meml. Trophy for Sportsmanship, 1977-78; Masterson Meml. trophy for Dedication to Hockey, 1977-78. Office: New York Islanders Uniondale NY 11553 *

GORKIN, JESS, editor; b. Rochester, N.Y., Oct. 23, 1913; s. Barnett and Bessie (Berk) G.; m. Dorothy Kleinberg, June 23, 1940; children: Michael, Brett, Scott. B.A., U. Iowa, 1936. Editor-in-chief Daily Iowan, Iowa City, 1936-37; assoc. editor Look Mag., N.Y.C., 1937-41; originated and edited picture mag. for distbn. in friendly and occupied countries Photo Review, OWI, 1942-46; mng. editor Parade, N.Y.C., 1947-49, editor, 1949-79, cons. editor, 1983—; editor 50 Plus, N.Y.C., 1979—. Recipient Christopher Award, 1956, citation Overseas Press Club, 1955, editorial award Nat. Comdr. Am. Legion. Mem. Overseas Press Club, Sigma Delta Chi. Club: Dutch Treat. Home: 4320 Falmouth Dr Longboat Key FL 33548 Office: 750 3d Ave New York NY 10017

GORLIN, RICHARD, physician, educator; b. Jersey City, June 30, 1926; s. Sol George and Henrietta (Bernfeld) G.; m. Winifred Leifer, Feb. 18, 1970; children from previous marriage: Wendy, William, Douglas; 1 stepdau., Jill Cabitt. M.D., Harvard U., 1948. Diplomate: Am. Bd. Internal Medicine, Nat. Bd. Med. Examiners. Intern Peter Bent Brigham Hosp., Boston, 1948-49, resident, 1948-52, mem. staff, 1953-74, sr. asso. medicine, 1960-66, physician, dir. cardiovascular unit, 1967-74, chief cardiovascular div., 1969-74; cons. physician VA Hosp., Bronx, N.Y., 1974—; faculty Harvard Med. Sch., 1949-74, asst. prof. medicine, 1961-67, asso. prof., 1968-74; physician-in-chief Mt. Sinai Hosp. and Med. Center, N.Y.C., 1974—; prof., chmn. dept. medicine Mt. Sinai Med. Sch., 1974—; hon. asst. St. Thomas Hosp., London, 1952-53; lectr. internal medicine Chelsea (Mass.) Naval Hosp., 1957-74; vis. lectr. numerous internat. colls. including Rogers lectr. U. Wis.-Madison; McArthur lectr. U. Edinburgh, Scotland, R.T. Hall Trust lectr., Australia; Centennial lectr. U. Ill. Med. Sch., Chgo.; Lewis Meml. lectr. Stanford Sch. Medicine; Merck, Sharpe & Dohme vis. lectr. Yale U., 1971; prin. lectr., vis. prof. U. Cin. Med. Sch.; Sir James Wattie prof., New Zealand, 1972; George Fahr lectr. U. Minn., 1974; Fried Meml. lectr., 1976, Avila Berger lectr., 1981, George Cecil Clarke Meml. lectr., 1981; Laurence B. Ellis Meml. lectr. Harvard U. Med. Sch., 1982; vis. prof. St. Vincent's Hosp., Worcester, Mass., 1983; James V. Warren lectr. Ohio State U. Sch. Medicine, 1983; F. Mason Sones lectr. Cleve. Clinic Fedn., 1983; Macklin lectr. Portsmouth Naval Hosp. (Va.), 1983; mem. cardiovascular program study sect. NIH, 1964-68, tng. grant com., 1969-72, task force coronary artery disease, 1972—, Internat. Study Group Research in Cardiac Metabolism; spl. cons. U. Ill. Med. Sch., 1968; cons. in field; mem. steering com. coop. study in cardiac catheterization Nat. Heart Inst., 1963—; research allocations com. Mass. Heart Assn., 1965-70; exec. com. thrombosis council Am. Heart Assn., 1972—. Editorial bd.: Am. Jour. Cardiology, 1964-70, Am. Jour. Med. Scis, 1967, Circulation, 1970, Am. Jour. Medicine, 1973, Catheterization and Cardiovascular Diagnosis; Contbr. articles to profl. jours. Pres. Freedom, Inc., 1957. Served to lt. comdr. USNR, 1954-56. Recipient Cummings Humanitarian award, 1963; Moseley travelling fellow, 1952-53; Bower traveling scholar A.C.P., 1960; Nat. Heart and Lung Inst. grantee, 1969. Fellow Am. Coll. Cardiology (v.p.); mem. Am. Fedn. Clin. Research (nat. councillor 1960-64), New Eng. Cardiovascular Soc. (pres. 1967-68), Mass. Heart Assn. (pres. elect 1973-74), Brit. Cardiac Soc. (corr. mem.), Argentine Cardiac Soc., Assn. Am. Physicians, Am. Soc. Clin. Investigation, Am. Physiol. Soc., Royal Soc. Medicine (U.K.), Assn. Univ. Cardiologists, Am. Clin. and Climatol. Assn., Cardiac Muscle Soc. Clubs: Harvard, Badminton and Tennis (Boston); Appalachian Mountain. Home: Buxton Rd Bedford Hills NY 10507 Office: Fifth Ave and 100th St: New York NY 10029

GORMAN, BURTON WILLIAM, educator; b. Mitchell, Ind., Mar. 29, 1907; s. William James and Minnie Rose (Burton) G.; m. Rebecca Evelyn Tolle, Dec. 29, 1931; children: Benjamin Lee, Joseph Tolle, John Burton. A.B., Ind. U., 1930; M.S., 1936; Ph.D., George Peabody Coll. Tchrs. (Knudson F.), 1953; student, U. Chgo., summers 1943, 45. Tchr. history and music, Bardstown, Ky., 1930-36, supt. schs., Ohio County, Ind., 1936-37, prin. high sch., Lawrenceburg, Ind., 1937-39, counselor boys high schs., Connersville, Ind., 1939-42, high sch. prin., 1942-46, supt. schs., 1946-49; prin. Emmerich Manual Tng. High Sch., Indpls., 1949-51; prof., head edn. dept. De Pauw U., 1953-54; prof., head dept. secondary edn. Kent (Ohio) State U., 1954-72; prof. edn. George Peabody Coll. for Tchrs., 1972-74, Stetson U., DeLand, Fla., 1974—; Vis. prof. Butler U., 1946, George Peabody Coll., 1948, 49, 51, 52, 53, 61, Ind. U., 1954, also U. N.C., U. Vt. Author: Education for Learning To Live Together, 1969, The High School America Needs, 1971. Recipient Distinguished Alumnus award George Peabody Coll. for Tchrs., 1972. Mem. NEA, Am. Assn. Sch. Adminstrs., AAUP, Phi Delta Kappa, Kappa Delta Pi, Acacia. Methodist. Lodges: Masons; Kiwanis (pres. Connersville 1946, lt. gov. 9th Ind. div., Internat. 1947). Home: 1330 Lemon St DeLand FL 32720

GORMAN, CLIFF, actor; b. N.Y.C., Oct. 13, 1936; s. Samuel and Ethel (Kaplan) G.; m. Gayle Stevens, May 31, 1963. Student, U. N.Mex., 1954-55; B.S. in Edn, N.Y.U., 1959. Mem. Jerome Robbins' Am. Theatre Lab., 1966-67. N.Y.C. appearances include Hogan's Goat, 1965, Ergo, 1968, The Boys in the Band, 1968, Lenny, 1971, Chapter Two, 1977; film appearances in Justine, 1969, The Boys in the Band, 1970, Cops and Robbers, 1973, An Unmarried Woman, 1978, Night of the Juggler, 1979, All That Jazz, 1979; TV appearances in The Trial of The Chicago Seven, 1970, Class of 63, 1973, The Bunker, 1981 (Recipient Obie award 1968, La Guardia Meml. award 1972, Show Bus. award 1972, Drama Desk award 1972, Tony award 1972). Mem. Honor Legion N.Y.C. Police Dept., Friends George Spelvin (life). Office: care William Morris Agy 1350 6th Ave New York NY 10019

GORMAN, CORNELIUS EUGENE, physician; b. Lynchburg, Va., Dec. 8, 1906; s. James and Ellizabeth Jane (Magri) G.; m. Mary Elizabeth Skender, Oct. 17, 1944; children—Cornelius, Joan, Thomas. Student, U. Va., 1924-26; B.A., Mt. St. Mary's Coll., 1928; M.D., Med. Coll. Va., 1932; M.A., Loyola U. of South, 1934. Rotating internship St. Vincents Hosp., Norfolk, Va.; resident Hotel Dieu, New Orleans, Charity Hosp. of La.; pvt. practice, New Orleans, 1934-40, 46-79; established Gorman Med. Center, 1949; clin. instr. gynecology and obstetrics La. State U. Med. Center; prof. mico-anatomy Loyola U. of South; mem. vis. staff Hotel Dieu Hosp., Charity Hosp. of La., Methodist Hosp.; dir. Med. Center; vis. surgeon Metarie Hosp.; terminal surgeon 7515 ARTU, New Orleans. Served from maj. to col. M.C. AUS, 1940-45. Decorated Legion of Merit. Mem. AMA, La., So., La. State U. med. socs., Am. Bd. Abdominal Surgery, New Orleans, U.S. power squadrons, Nat. Rifle Assn., Phi Beta Pi, Pi, Sigma Zeta, Theta Beta. Democrat. Roman Catholic. Clubs: Rotary (pres. Carrollton; dist. gov. 1967-68), Army-Navy.). Developed and compiled phys. standards for selection of inductees and phys. profiling of enlisted men. Invented Gorman solid blade low (outlet) obstet. forcep; performed successful open-heart surgery, 1932. Home: 546 Lakeshore Pkwy New Orleans LA 70124 Office: 1626 S Carrollton Ave New Orleans LA 70118

GORMAN, JOHN LEONARD, newspaper executive; b. Palmyra, N.Y., May 8, 1906; s. Walter J. and Margaret E. (Hickey) G.; m. Mary Elizabeth Edwards, Aug. 23, 1934 (dec. Dec. 1955); children: Jane (dec.), John, Ann (Mrs. Timothy T. Schenck); m. Mary Lighthall Verbeck, Dec. 30, 1957 (dec. Aug. 1977); stepsons: K. Channing, Pieter L.; m. Iva A. Holzwarth, June 10, 1983; stepchildren: Bruce Holzwarth, Paul F. Holzwarth, Anne E. Holzwarth Hutchins. Grad., Syracuse U., 1929. Reporter Syracuse (N.Y.) Herald, 1929; pub. relations Syracuse U., 1930-32; copy reader Syracuse Post-Standard, 1933-41, editorial writer, 1941-47, city editor, 1947-53, mng. editor, 1953-59, exec. editor, 1959-60, 66-83, editor, 1960-66, exec. editor emeritus, 1983—. Mem. N.Y. State Fair Adv. Com.; Bd. dirs. Syracuse Cerebral Palsy Clinic, N.Y. State div. Am. Cancer Soc., Onondaga chpt. A.R.C.; trustee Syracuse and Onondaga County Pub. Library. Mem. Syracuse C. of C. (dir.), Asso. Press Mng. Editors Assn., N.Y. Asso. Press Assn. (pres. 1956), Am. Soc. Newspaper Editors, N.Y. Soc. Newspaper Editors (pres. 1960-61), Syracuse U. Library Assos., Pi Delta Epsilon, Sigma Delta Chi, Phi Kappa. Republican. Roman Catholic. Clubs: Rotary, Syracuse Press, University (Syracuse). Home: 122 Kensington Rd Syracuse NY 13210 Office: The Post-Standard Syracuse NY 13221

GORMAN, JOHN WILLIAM, public opinion research company executive; b. Rockford, Ill., May 6, 1950; s. Donald Edward and Mary Virginia (Doyle) G. A.B., Harvard U., 1972. Co-founder Cambridge Survey Research Inc., Mass., 1971, sec.-treas., 1971—; co-founder Cambridge Reports Inc., 1974; owner, pres. Brattle Theater Corp.; pres. CBL, Inc., Club Casablanca, Inc., R.I. Club: Harvard (Boston, Chgo.). Office: 675 Massachusetts Ave Cambridge MA 02138

GORMAN, JUDY A., life insurance company executive; b. Dayton, Ohio, Feb. 9, 1939; d. Mark and Bernice Adele Goldman. B.F.A., Boston U., 1961. Account exec. Staff Builders, Inc., 1961-66; sr. account exec. Uniforce, Inc., 1966-68; consumer affairs officer Chase Manhattan Bank, N.Y.C., 1968-74; dir. consumer and community services Am. Council Life Ins. Cos., N.Y.C., 1974-76; 2d v.p. office corp. responsibility N.Y. Life Ins. Co., N.Y.C., 1976-78, v.p., 1978-82, v.p. mktg., 1982—. Actress: TV shows The Patty Duke Show, 1961-65. Mem. Soc. Consumer Affairs Profls. in Bus. (dir. 1975-78, pres. 1978-79), Council Better Bus. Burs. (dir. 1978—). Office: NY Life Ins Co 51 Madison Ave New York NY 10010

GORMAN, MEL, educator; b. San Francisco, Nov. 18, 1910; s. Daniel Joseph and Mary Ellen (Haugh) G.; m. Ann Marguerite Ingoglia, July 27, 1937; children—Geraldine Ann, Daniel Paul. B.S., U. San Francisco, 1931; M.S., U. Calif. at Berkeley, 1939; Ph.D., Stanford, 1946. Mem. chemistry faculty U. San Francisco, 1931—, prof., 1952—, Ford Found. faculty fellow, 1954-55, NSF faculty fellow, 1959-60; postdoctoral fellow Harvard-Mass. Inst. Tech., 1954-55. Mem. Am. Chem. Soc., AAAS, AAUP, Calif. Hist. Soc., History Sci. Soc., Western History Assn., Sigma Xi. Club: Olympic (San Francisco). Research and publs. on chemistry, chem. edn., history of sci. Home: 756 Arguello Blvd San Francisco CA 94118

GORMAN, WILLIAM DAVID, painter, graphic artist; b. Jersey City, June 27, 1925; s. William Daniel and Margaret (Johnson) G.; m. Janice Echols Gary, Feb. 9, 1957. Grad., Newark Sch. Fine and Indsl. Arts, 1949. Art evaluator N.J. Council of Arts, 1975. Contbr. articles to art mags.; One-man shows, Jersey City Mus., 1962, Revel Gallery, N.Y.C., 1963, East Side Gallery, N.Y.C., 1970, Madison (N.J.) Library, 1975, Caldwell (N.J.) Coll., 1976, SUNY, Alfred, 1977, Martin (Tenn.) Arts Commn., 1978, Old Bank Gallery, Port Washington, N.Y., 1981, group shows include, Davenport (Iowa) Mcpl. Art Gallery, 1975, Canton (Ohio) Art Inst., 1971, NAD, 1971-81, Am. Acad. and Inst. Arts and Letters, N.Y.C., 1979, 80; represented in permanent collections, U.S. State Dept., NAD, N.Y.C., Newark Mus., Montclair (N.J.) Art Mus., Springfield (Mo.) Art Mus., Colorado Springs Fine Arts Center, Syracuse (N.Y.) U., Butler Inst. Am. Art, Ohio. Served with U.S. Army, 1943-44; ETO. Recipient De Maree award, 1981, FitzGerald Meml. award, 1982. Mem. Allied Artists Am. (Gold medal of honor 1973, v.p. 1975-78, pres. 1978-81, hon. life pres. 1983, dir. watercolor 1981—), Am. Watercolor Soc. (1st v.p. 1981—, Emily Lowe meml. award 1984), Audubon Artists (exhbn. chmn. 1974-77, dir. 1977-80), Nat. Soc. Painters in Casein and Acrylic, N.J. Water Color Soc. (pres. 1957-59, Grumbacher Silver medal 1982, Warga award 1983), Artists Fellowship, Am. Vets. Soc. Artists, Associated Artists N.J., Hudson Artists (founder 1955), Jersey City Mus. Assn. (dir. 1953-60), Painters and Sculptors Soc. (dir. 1960-70), NAD (asso., Henry Ward Ranger Fund purchase awards 1965, 71), Old Bergen Art Guild (pres. and dir. 1962—). Home and Studio: 43 W 33d St Bayonne NJ 07002

GORME, EYDIE, singer; b. N.Y.C., Aug. 16; m. Steve Lawrence, Dec. 29, 1957; children: David, Michael. Various night club engagements; mem. Steve Allen's TV troupe Tonight Show, 1954; Broadway debut (with husband) in Golden Rainbow, 1967; numerous theater appearances throughout U.S. Emmy award winning TV spls. include Steve and Eydie honoring Gershwin, Porter and Berlin. Chairwoman entertainment com. Cerebral Palsy. Recipient Grammy award as best female vocalist of yr. for If He Walked into My Life, 1967. Ofice: care Lee Solters 9255 Sunset Blvd Los Angeles CA 90069

GORMLEY, ROBERT JOHN, book publisher; b. Lynn, Mass., Oct. 14, 1939; s. Ernest Raymond and Catherine Louise (Maitl) G.; m. Beatrice LeCount, Sept. 4, 1966; children: Catherine, Jennifer. B.A., Williams Coll., 1961; M.A., U. Calif. at Berkeley, 1964. With Wadsworth Inc., 1964—; pres. pub. PWS Pubs. (encompassing various divs. Wadsworth, Inc.), Boston, 1971—, asst. corp. v.p., 1973-81, corp. v.p., 1981—. Chmn. Washington affairs com., coll. div. Assn. Am. Pubs. Served with AUS, 1962-69. Mem. Williams Coll. Alumni Assn. (exec. com. Boston), Assn. Am. Pubs. (chmn. Washington affairs com. coll. div., exec. com. higher edn. div.). Democrat. Roman Catholic. Club: Duxbury Yacht. Home: 37 Western Way Duxbury MA 02332 Office: 20 Park Plaza Boston MA 02116

GORMLEY, WILLIAM CLARKE, business executive; b. Lexington, Ky., Apr. 9, 1939; s. James Joseph and Alma (Kreitz) G. B.S. in Commerce, U. Ky., 1961, J.D., 1963. With Texaco Inc., New Orleans, 1964-69, Forest Oil Corp., Houston, 1969-73; corp. sec., counsel Zapata Corp., Houston, 1973-82, Well Tech, Inc., 1982—. Served to capt. JAGC U.S. Army. Mem. ABA; Mem. Ky. Bar Assn.; mem. Tex. Bar Assn. Home: 808 Hyde Park Blvd Houston TX 77006 Office: Well Tech Inc 700 Rusk Ave Houston TX 77002

GORNICK, ALAN LEWIS, lawyer; b. Leadville, Colo., Sept. 23, 1908; s. Mark and Anne (Grayhack) G.; m. Ruth L. Willcockson, 1940 (dec. May 1959); children: Alan Lewis, Diana Willcockson (Mrs. Lawrence J. Richard, Jr.), Keith Hardin; m. Pauline Martoi, 1972. A.B., Columbia, 1935, LL.B., 1937. Bar: N.Y. bar 1937, Mich. bar 1948. Practiced with Baldwin, Todd & Young, N.Y.C., 1937-41, Milbank, Tweed, Hope & Hadley, 1941-47; asso. counsel charge tax matters Ford Motor Co., Dearborn, Mich., 1947-49, dir. tax affairs, tax counsel, 1949-64; pres. Ostego Ski Club, Hidden Valley, Inc., Perry-Davis, Inc., Meadow Brook Park Devel. Co.; v.p., dir. Bloomfield Center, Inc.; v.p. Seagate Hotel, Inc., Delray Beach, Fla.; pres. Bloomfield Center, Inc.; Lectr. tax matters N.Y. U., Inst. Fed. Taxation, 1947-49, Am. Bar Assn. and Practicing Law Inst. (courses on fundamentals in fed. taxation), 1946-55, Am. Law Inst. (courses in continuing legal edn.), 1950; spl. lectr. sch. bus. adminstrn. U. Mich., 1949, 53; adv. editor Nat. Tax Jour., 1952-55. Author: Estate Tax Handbook, 1952, Arrangements for Separation or Divorce, Handbook of Tax Techniques, 1952, Taxation of Partnerships, Estates and Trusts, rev. edit, 1952; Contbr. articles tax matters to profl. jours. Exec. bd. Detroit area council Boy Scouts Am., chmn. fin. com., 1960; pres. Mich. Assn. Emotionally Disturbed Children, 1962-65; v.p. Archives of Am. Art; mem. Mich. Heart Assn.; mem. Columbia Coll. council Columbia U., N.Y.C.; Trustee Council on World Affairs, Detroit.; pres. Detroit Hist. Soc.; mem. Bd. Zoning Appeals City Bloomfield Hills, 1980—. Recipient Gov.'s Spl. award State Colo., 1952. Mem. ABA (council tax sect. 1957-58), Detroit Bar Assn., N.Y. City Bar Assn. (chmn. subcom. estate and gift taxes 1943-47), Am. Law Inst., Tax Inst. Inc. (pres. 1954-55), U.S. C. of C., Empire State C. of C., Council on Fgn. Relations, Nat. Tax Assn. (exec. com.), Internat. Fiscal Assn. (council, nat. reporter 6th Internat. Congress Fiscal Law, Brussels 1952), Internat. Law Assn., Assn. Ex-Mems. Squadron A, Nat. Fgn. Trade Council (mem. com. taxes 1950), Automobile Mfrs. Assn. (chmn. com. on taxation 1960-62), Tax Execs. Inst. (pres. 1956-57), Fedn. Alumni Columbia (dir. 1946), Class 1935 Columbia Coll. (permanent pres.), N.Y. Adult Edn. Council (dir. 1939-45), Detroit Hist. Soc. (v.p. and trustee), Phi Delta Phi. Clubs: Bloomfield Hills (Mich.) Country, Detroit, Detroit Athletic; University, Nat. Lawyers (Washington); Columbia University, Church (N.Y.C.); Lawyers of University of Michigan, Columbia University Alumni of Mich. (pres. 1950—). Home: 150 Lowell Ct Bloomfield Hills MI 48013 Office: 1565 Woodward Ave Suite 8 Bloomfield Hills MI 48013

GORODETZKY, CHARLES WILLIAM, physician; b. Boston, May 31, 1937; s. Saul and Rose (Leavit) G.; m. Barbara Labovich, June 18, 1961; children: Amy Lynne, Mark Steven, David Barry, Theodore Alan. B.S., MIT, 1958; M.D., Boston U., 1962; Ph.D., U. Ky., 1975. Intern Boston City Hosp., 1962-63; commd. sr. asst. surgeon USPHS, 1963, advanced through grades to med. dir., 1976; med. officer Addiction Research Center, Nat. Inst. Drug Abuse, Lexington, Ky., 1963-65, 68, chief sect. on drug metabolism and kinetics, 1969-80, dep. dir., 1977-80, sci. dir., 1981—; mem. adj. vol. faculty dept. pharmacology U. Ky. Sch. Medicine, 1966-71, 75—, U. Louisville Sch. Medicine, 1977—; cons. on drug abuse Fayette County (Ky.) PUblic Schs., 1971-75; mem. adv. com. on proficiency testing Drug Abuse, CDC, Atlanta, 1972—; mem. drug abuse adv. com. FDA, 1978-83; mem. Com. on Problems of Drug Dependence, 1978-83, mem. exec. com., 1979-83. Author: (with S. T. Christian) What You Should Know About Drugs, 1970; contbr. articles to profl. jours. Chmn. Central Ky. United Jewish Appeal, 1976; bd. dirs. Jewish Community Assn., Central Ky., 1969-73, pres., 1971-73; bd. dirs. Midwest council Union Am. Hebrew Congregations, 1978-82, nat. bd. dirs., 1982—. Mem. AAAS, AMA, Am. Soc. Pharmacology and Exptl. Therapeutics, Am. Soc. Clin. Pharmacology and Therapeutics, N.Y. Acad. Scis., Soc. Neurosci., Central Ky. Jewish Assn. (pres. 1977-78), Sigma Xi. Republican. Jewish (trustee 1971—, sec. 1973-75, treas. 1975-77, 2d v.p. 1977-79, pres. 1981—). Home: 2084 Harmony Ct Lexington KY 40502 Office: PO Box 12390 Lexington KY 40583

GORODEZKY, ELI, lawyer; b. Kansas City, Kans., Mar. 15, 1909; s. Aaron Louis and Celia (Spector) G.; m. Helen Gertrude Evans, Oct. 15, 1947 (dec. Nov. 1976); m. Margaret W. Kerley. J.D., U. Ariz., 1933. Bar: Ariz. 1933. Since practiced in, Phoenix, asst. city atty., 1938-40; partner firm Gorodezky Law Offices, 1955—; Chmn. Charter Rev. Com. Phoenix, 1967-70; v.p. Neurol. Scis. Found.; pres. Barrow Neurol-Found., 1968-69, now mem. adv. com. Field dir. A.R.C., World War II; mem. Nat. Adv. Council Vocational Rehab., 1956-59; v.p. Nat. Soc. Crippled Children and Adults, 1954-56; pres. Ariz. Soc., 1950-53; co-chmn. City of Phoenix Charter Rev. Com., 1975; Bd. dirs. Maricopa County Better Bus. Bur.; v.p. S.W. Biomed. Research Inst., 1978—. Named Citizen of Year Phoenix Realty Bd., 1956, Man of Year Phoenix Advt. Club, 1955. Mem. Am., Ariz., Maricopa County bar assns., Phoenix C. of C., Newcomen Soc., Phi Alpha Delta, Pi Delta Epsilon. Republican. Clubs: Arizona (life mem.), Phoenix Executive (pres. 1960-61), Downtown Phoenix Lions (Phoenix)). Home: 3701 E Pierson St Phoenix AZ 85018 Office: 3020 E Camelback Rd Phoenix AZ 85016 *Being handicapped from birth, I owe my achievements, if any I have earned, to my dear parents, grandmother and classmates in treating me as a normal person, and conducting myself to the best of my ability as a self-sufficient individual, asking no mercy or pity and accepting assistance in mobility only where necessary. Above all, at all times, I feel that there is a Supreme Being who guides our destiny, and for years I have worn a flower in my lapel as a symbol of His handiwork.*

GOROG, WILLIAM FRANCIS, association executive; b. Warren, Ohio, Sept. 2, 1925; s. Frank and Margaret R. G.; m. Gretchen Elizabeth Meister, June 11, 1949; children: Robin, Jonathan, William Christopher, Lesley Anne, Jennifer, Peter. B.S., U.S. Mil. Acad, 1949; M.S., Ohio State U., 1951. Mktg. mgr. Bulova Watch Co., N.Y.C., 1954-55; exec. v.p. Data Corp., Dayton, Ohio, 1956-63, chmn., chief exec. officer, 1963-75; dep. asst. to pres. The White House, Washington, 1975; exec. dir. White House Council on Internat. Econ. Policy, 1976; pres. Arbor Internat., McLean, Va., 1977-82; pres., chief exec. officer Mag. Pubs. Assn., N.Y.C., 1982—; dir. Commerce Union Corp., Nashville, Chief Execs. Orgn., Palm Beach, Fla., Kurz Kasch Inc., Dayton, Ohio, The Ad Council, N.Y.C. Mem. adv. bd. Georgetown U. Grad. Sch. Bus., 1982. Served to capt. USAF, 1949-53. Republican. Roman Catholic. Club: Moraine Country (Dayton). Home: 60 Sutton Pl S New York NY 10022 Office: Mag Pubs Assn 575 Lexington Ave New York NY 10022

GOROVSKY, MARTIN A., cell biologist, educator; b. Chgo., Apr. 26, 1941; s. Meyer and Dorothy (Marcus) G.; m. Diane Joyce Kohn, July 16, 1967; children: Marcia Ellen, Nicole Elizabeth. A.B., U. Chgo., 1963, Ph.D., 1968. NSF postdoctoral fellow Yale U., 1968-70; asst. prof. biology U. Rochester (N.Y.), 1970-75, assoc. prof., 1975-80, prof., 1980—, chmn. dept. biology, 1981—; mem. biol. devel. panel NSF, Am. Cancer Soc. Recipient numerous research grants NSF, NIH. Mem. Am. Soc. Cell Biology, AAAS. Office: University of Rochester Dept Biology Rochester NY 14627

GORR, LOUIS FREDERICK, museum director; b. North Platte, Nebr., Aug. 1, 1941; s. Ernest Frederick and Eileen Bethel (Green) G.; m. Madeleine Zangla, Dec. 12, 1967; 1 dau., Michaela. B.A., U. Nebr., 1963, M.A., 1967; Ph.D., U. Md., 1972; M.B.A., U. Dallas, 1981; mgmt. and real estate courses, So. Meth. U. Spl. asst. to dir. Nat. Mus. History and Tech., Smithsonian Instn., Washington, 1969-73; dir. div. museums and historic preservation Fairfax (Va.) County Govt., 1973-77; dir. Dallas County (Tex.) Heritage Soc., 1977-79, Dallas Mus. Natural History, 1979—, Dallas Aquarium; ptnr. East End Devel. Corp.; cons., lectr. in field, 1970—; adj. prof. mus. studies U. Okla.; mem. bd. commerce Dallas Nat. Bank, 1980—; chmn. bd. commerce Republic Bank Dallas East. Author numerous articles, revs. in field. Pres. Fairfax Symphony Orch., 1976-77; bd. dirs. Met. Washington Cultural Alliance, 1976, Prince George's County (Md.) Arts Council, 1973, Fairfax County Assn. Civic Orgns., 1976-77; mem. arts and culture adv. com. Dallas Ind. Sch. Dist.; leadership devel. trainer United Way. Served with USAF, 1963-64. Research fellow Smithsonian Instn., 1971, Naval Inst. Mem. Am. Assn. Museums (dir.), Tex. Assn. Museums (pres. 1981-83, dir.), Am. Mgmt. Assn., Nat. Recreation and Parks Assn., Internat. Council Museums, Assn. Sci. Mus. Dirs. (v.p.), Dallas Bus. League, Am. Soc. Pub. Adminstrn., Council Advancement and Support of Edn., Dallas C. of C., East Dallas C. of C., Leadership Dallas Alumni Assn., Sigma Iota Epsilon., Lambda Chi Alpha. Republican. Clubs: Dallas Commerce, Dallas Lancers, Rotary, Dallas County Rep. Men's, Masons (32 deg.). Home: 1606 Yale Blvd Richardson TX 75081 Office: PO Box 26193 Fair Park Dallas TX 75226

GORRELL, FRANK CHEATHAM, lawyer; b. Russellville, Ky., June 20, 1927; s. Lilburn D. and Vandalia Van Dyke (Strudwick) G.; m. Bette Jamison, June 14, 1947; children: Frank C. III, Jamison R. B.S., Vanderbilt U., 1949, LL.B., 1952. Bar: Tenn. 1952. Partner firm Bass, Berry & Sims, Nashville, 1952—; dir. Jamison Bedding Co., Franklin, Tenn., Downs, Inc., Nashville.; Mem. Tenn. Senate, 1963-70, speaker and lt. gov. Tenn., 1966-70; chmn. Tenn. Appellate Ct. Nominating Com., 1982—. Trustee Acquinas Jr. Coll., Mills Sch. Mem. Am., Tenn., Nashville bar assns., Am., Tenn. trial lawyers assns., Am. Judicature Soc., Am. Coll. Trial Lawyers, Beta Theta Pi, Omicron Delta Kappa. Club: Elk. Home: Route 2 Columbia Park Thompson Station TN 37179 Office: 2700 First Am Center Nashville TN 37238

GORRELL, ROBERT MARK, former educator; b. Bremen, Ind., Aug. 9, 1914; s. James Kenneth and Edna Pearl (Stock) G.; m. Johnnie Belle Thomas, Aug. 9, 1939 (dec. 1978); children: Mark, Sara Gorrell Peterson; m. Mary Gojack, Dec. 19, 1979. Student, Ind. U., 1931-33; A.B., Cornell U., 1936, Ph.D., 1939; D.H.L. (hon.), U. Nev., 1980. Mem. faculty Deep Springs (Calif.) Coll., 1939-42, Ind. U., 1942-45; prof. English U. Nev., Reno, 1945-80, prof. emeritus, 1980—, grad. dean, 1967-68, dean extension, 1967-69, dean arts and sci., 1972-76, v.p. acad. affairs, 1976-80; vis. prof. U. Calif. at Los Angeles, 1952, U. Sydney, Australia, 1954-55, U. Helsinki, Finland, 1961-62. Author: Practice in English Communication, 1947, Modern English Handbook, 6th edit, 1976, English as Language, 1961, Reading About Language, 1971, Writing and Language, 1972, Writing Modern English, 1973, Modern English Reader, 1976. Chmn. bd. dirs. Reno Little Theatre, 1959-63. Mem. Modern Lang. Assn., Nat. Council Tchrs. English (chmn. coll. sect. 1965-67), Conf. Coll. Composition and Communication (chmn. 1963-64), Renaissance Soc., Rhetoric Soc. Am., Phi Beta Kappa, Kappa Sigma, Phi Kappa Phi. Home: 3855 Skyline Blvd Reno NV 89509

GORSHIN, FRANK, impressionist, singer, comedian, actor; b. Pitts., Apr. 5, 1934; s. Frank and Fanny G.; m. Christina Gorshin; 1 son, Mitchell. Attended, Carnegie Inst. Tech. Sch. Drama, (now Carnegie-Mellon Inst. Tech.), 2 years. Profl. debut as winner of talent contest The Carousel, Pitts., 1951; motion picture debut in The Proud and The Profane; other motion pictures appearances include Where the Boys Are, Bells are Ringing; starring role in: film The Upper Crust; Hollywood night club debut at, The Purple Onion, 1958, Las Vegas debut at, The Flamingo, other Las Vegas appearances, The Aladdin Hotel's Bagdad Theater, The Sands; Atlantic City appearances at, Caesars Boardwalk, The Playboy, The Claridge; other night club appearances include, The Empire Room, N.Y.C., Carribe-Hilton, P.R., Queen Mary Suite, London.; appeared as The Riddler: TV series Batman; also appeared: Hennessey, Kopy Kats, Edge of Night; guest appearances on Stories from the Bible; numerous other TV variety and drama shows and spls., CBS-TV; appeared in: TV film Death Car on the Freeway, 1979, Goliath Awaits; concert engagements include Frank Gorshin at Westchester Premier Theater; Broadway debut as star of Jimmy, 1969; star: Broadway prodn. Whodunnit, 1983; appeared in: touring cos. of What Makes Sammy Run? (Outstanding Stage Performer, Burns Mantle Yearbook), Promises, Promises, Prisoner of Second Avenue; starred in: The Man With The Plastic Sandwich, Drury Lane Theatre, Chgo., 1981, Windmill Theater, Houston, Same Time Next Year, Deathtrap. Served with U.S. Army, 1953-55. Office: care Shefrin Co PO Box 48559 Los Angeles CA 90048

GORSKE, ROBERT HERMAN, lawyer; b. Milw., June 8, 1932; s. Herman Albert and Lorraine (McDermott) G.; m. Antonette Dujick, Aug. 28, 1954; 1 dau., Judith Mary (Mrs. Charles H. McMullen). Student, Milw. State Tchrs. Coll., 1949-50; B.A. cum laude, Marquette U., 1953; J.D. magna cum laude, Marquette U., 1955; LL.M. (W.W. Cook fellow), U. Mich., 1959. Bar: Wis. bar 1955, D.C. bar 1968, U.S. Supreme Ct. bar 1970. Asso. firm Quarles, Spence & Quarles, Milw., 1955-56; atty. Allis-Chalmers Mfg. Co., West Allis, Wis., 1956-62; instr. law U. Mich. Law Sch., Ann Arbor, 1958-59; lectr. law Marquette U. Law Sch., 1963; asso. firm Quarles, Herriott & Clemons, Milw., 1962-64; atty. Wis. Electric Power Co., Milw., 1964-67, gen. counsel, 1967—, v.p., 1970-72, 76—; mem. firm Quarles & Brady, Milw., 1972-76; dir. Wis. Natural Gas Co., Racine, Wis., Wis. Mich. Power Co., Appleton. Contbr. articles to profl. jours.; Editor-in-chief: Marquette Law Rev, 1954-55. Bd. dirs. Guadalupe Children's Med. Dental Clinic, Inc., Milw., 1976—. Mem. State Bar Wis., Am. Bar Assn., Edison Electric Inst. (vice chmn. legal com. 1975-77, chmn. 1977-79). Home: 12700 Stephen Pl Elm Grove WI 53122 Office: 231 W Michigan St Milwaukee WI 53203

GORSKI, JACK, biochemistry educator; b. Green Bay, Wis., Mar. 14, 1931; s. John R. and Martha (Kenney) G.; m. Harriet M. Fischer, Sept. 9, 1955; children: Michael, Jo Anne. Student, Calif. Poly. Coll., 1949-50; B.S., U. Wis., 1953; postgrad., U. Utah, 1957; M.S., Wash. State U., 1956, Ph.D., 1958. NIH postdoctoral fellow U. Wis., 1958-61; asst. prof., asso. prof. physiology U. Ill., Urbana, 1961-66, prof. physiology, 1967—, prof. biochemistry, 1969—; prof. biochemistry and animal scis. U. Wis., Madison, 1973—; NSF research fellow Princeton, 1966-67; mem. endocrinology study sect. NIH, 1966-70, molecular biology study sect., 1977-81; mem. biochemistry adv. com. Am. Cancer Soc., 1973-76, mem. personnel for research com., 1983—. Contbr. articles to profl. jours. Mem. Am. Soc. Biol. Chemists, Am. Physiol. Soc., Endocrine Soc., Am. Soc. Cell Biology. Democrat. Unitarian. Address: Dept Biochemistry 420 Henry Mall Madison WI 53706

GORSKI, ROGER ANTHONY, neuroendocrinologist, educator; b. Chgo., Dec. 30, 1935; s. Casimir Michael and Mary (Wajrowski) G.; m. Judith Ann Bentley, Sept. 6, 1959; children—Denise May, Kevin Bentley, Brian Michael. B.S., U. Ill., 1957, M.S., 1959; Ph.D., U. Calif. at Los Angeles, 1962. Asst. prof. dept. anatomy Sch. Medicine, U. Calif. at Los Angeles, 1962-66, asso. prof., 1966-70, prof., 1970—, vice chmn. grad. affairs, 1967-74, chmn., 1980—; Vis. prof. dept. animal sci. Cornell U., 1968. Editorial bd.: Neuroendocrinology, 1967-75, Anatomical Record, 1968-77, Endocrinology, 1973-77, Biology of Reprodn, 1974-78; Contbr. articles profl. jours. Recipient Lederle Med. Faculty award, 1966. Mem. Am. Assn. Anatomists, AAAS, Am. Physiol. Soc., Endocrine Soc. (Ernst Oppenheimer award 1976), Internat. Soc. Neuroendocrinology, Soc. Exptl. Biology Medicine, Soc. Neurosci., Internat. Brain Research Orgn., Soc. for Study Reprodn. (sec. 1973-77, pres. 1978, Research award 1983), Phi Beta Kappa., Sigma Xi. Home: 3832 Minerva Ave Los Angeles CA 90066 *There is one almost certain route to success: Always do your absolute best*

GORSLINE, GEORGE WILLIAM, computer science educator; b. Battle Creek, Mich., Dec. 19, 1923; s. James M. and Lora (Gates) G.; m. Anne Bonner, Aug. 9, 1947; children: George William, Gary B., Cynthia S. Student, Mich. Coll. Mining and Tech., 1942-43; B.S. in Agronomy, Va. Poly. Inst., 1948; M.S., Pa. State U., 1957, Ph.D., 1959. Asst. prof. agronomy Pa. State U., 1956-63; dir. consultation, applied programming, customer relations Computer Center, Inst. Sci. and Engring., 1963-65; dir. computer center Ohio U., 1965-67; also lectr. math.; prof. computer sci. dept. Va. Poly. Inst. and State U., 1967—. Author: Computer Organization: Hardware/Software, 1980, Modern Microcomputers: The INTEL 18086 Family, 1984; contbr. articles to profl. jours. Served with AUS, 1943-45. Fellow AAAS; mem. AAUP, Assn. Computing Machinery (lectr., chmn. ACM/Sigsmall conf. and symposium), Sigma Xi, Phi Epsilon Phi, Gamma Sigma Delta, Upsilon Pi Epsilon. Home: 624 Watson Ln NW Blacksburg VA 24060

GORSUCH, JOHN ELLIOTT, lawyer; b. Denver, Sept. 2, 1899; s. John C. and Nancy (Johnson) G.; m. Freda H. Munz, Aug. 21, 1930; children: John Philip, Diane B. Kepner, David Ronald, Keith Edward. A.B., U. Denver, 1921, LL.B., 1925. Bar: Colo. 1925. Since practiced in, Denver; of counsel firm Gorsuch, Kirgis, Campbell, Walker and Grover.; Lectr. U. Denver, U. Colo. Law Sch., Southwestern Legal Found. Life trustee Legal Aid Soc. Denver; vice chmn. Non-Ferrous Metals Commn., Nat. War Labor Bd.; Mem. adv. bd. Denver YWCA.; Bd. dirs. Denver Community Chest; life trustee U. Denver, Florence Crittendon Home; bd. govs. Presbyn. Hosp.; mem. adv. bd. Mt. Airy Hosp. Recipient Distinguished Law Alumni award U. Denver, 1962, Evans award, 1973, award Grad. Sch. Social Work, 1980; Distinguished Service award Denver Jaycees. Mem. Assn. Life Ins. Counsel, ABA (mem. labor law com.), Denver Bar Assn. (past pres., Award of Merit 1971), Colo. Bar Assn. (mem. bd. govs. 1947-48), Denver Symphony Soc. (past trustee), Colo. Conf. Social Workers (past pres.), Am. Arbitration Assn. (labor law com.), Nat. Acad. Arbitrators (past mem. bd. govs.), Phi Beta Kappa, Beta Theta Pi, Phi Delta Phi. Clubs: Mason., Mile High, Denver Athletic, Press, Denver Country, Kiwanis (past internat. v.p.). Home: 900 Pennsylvania Apt 4 Denver CO 80203 Office: 1401 17th St Suite 1100 Denver CO 80202 *Time is well spent that is spent with a friend.*

GORSUCH, JOHN WILBERT, publisher; b. Bloomingdale, Ohio, Apr. 6, 1930; s. John Simpson and Suzanna Mae (Poe) G.; m. Georgia Anne Batting, Sept. 26, 1953; children—Neil Justin, Greta Jean. B.A., U. N.M., 1956. Field rep., acquisitions editor John Wiley & Sons, N.Y.C., 1957-60; regional sales mgr. coll. dept. Macmillan Co., 1960-64, market mgr., 1965-67; v.p., dir. coll. dept. William C. Brown Co., Dubuque, Iowa, 1967-76; pres. Gorsuch Scarisbrick, pubs., Dubuque, 1976—; Bd. dirs. Dubuque Indsl. Bur., 1971—. Served with AUS, 1952-54. Mem. Dubuque C. of C. (dir.). Clubs: Rotarian., Dubuque Golf and Country. Home: 495 W 5th St Dubuque IA 52001 Office: 576 Central Ave Dubuque IA 52001

GORTER, JAMES POLK, investment banker; b. Balt., Dec. 10, 1929; s. T. Poultney and Swan (Deford) G.; m. Audrey Fentress; children: James Jr., David F., Mary H., Kevin D. A.B., Princeton U., 1951; postgrad., London Sch. Econ., 1951-52. Ptnr. Goldman, Sachs & Co., 1956—; dir. Baker, Fentress & Co., Sears Investment Mgmt. Co. Vice chmn. Lake Forest Coll.; mem. adv. Northwestern U. Kellogg Sch. Mgmt. Served with USN, 1952-55. Clubs: Chicago Commonwealth, Chicago, Economic, Commercial; Metropolitan (Chgo.). Office: Goldman Sachs & Co 4900 Sears Tower Chicago IL 60606

GORTH, WILLIAM PHILLIP, computer software company executive; b. Bklyn., Nov. 1, 1943; s. Philip William and Lena (Desena) G.; m. Janet Ismond, Nov. 30, 1980; Philip, Pamela. B.S., SUNY-Buffalo, 1964; Ph.D., Stanford U., 1971. Mem. faculty U. Mass., Amherst, 1969-75, dir. Ctr. for Ednl. Research, 1973-75; pres. Nat. Evaluation Systems, Inc., Amherst, 1972—. Author: Comprehensive Achievement Monitoring, 1975. Mem. Am. Ednl. Research Assn., Am. Psychol. Assn. Club: Rotary. Home: 1081 S East St Amherst MA 01002 Office: Nat Evulation Systems 30 Gatehouse Rd Box 226 Amherst MA 01004

GORTIKOV, STANLEY MERRILL, association executive; b. Los Angeles, May 14, 1919; s. Joseph and Goldie (Harris) G.; children: Jane, James, Scott. A.B., U. So. Calif., 1941. Prodn. mgr. L.K. Shapiro Co., 1949-60; dir. corp. devel. Capitol Records, Inc., 1960, sr. v.p., 1966-68, pres., 1968-69; v.p., then pres. Capitol Records Distbg. Corp., Hollywood, Calif., 1960-68; exec. v.p. Capitol Industries, Inc., 1969, pres., chief exec. officer, 1969-71; pres. Rec. Industry Assn. Am., 1972—. Served to lt. col. AUS, 1941-45. Decorated Bronze Star. Home: 90 Riverside Dr Apt 8-G New York NY 10024 Office: Recording Industry Assn Am 888 7th Ave 9th Floor New York NY 10106

GORTNER, ROSS AIKEN, JR., biochemist, educator; b. Cold Spring Harbor, L.I., N.Y., June 2, 1912; s. Ross Aiken and Catherine (Willis) G.; m. Mary Priscilla Cahill, Dec. 20, 1938; children: Katherine Gortner Hood, Douglas Ross. Student (Alumni scholar), Oberlin Coll., 1929-30; A.B. magna cum laude, U. Minn., 1933, M.S., 1934; Ph.D., U. Mich., 1937; M.A. (hon.), Wesleyan U., Middletown, Conn., 1948. Faculty fellow, grad. teaching asst. U. Mich., 1934-37; faculty Wesleyan U., Middletown, Conn., 1937-80, prof. biochemistry, 1948-80, prof. emeritus, 1980—; dir. Sci. Center, 1967-80; Fulbright lectr., Copenhagen, Denmark, 1954-55; vis. research prof. U. Giessen, Max Planck Inst. Biochemistry, Munich, Germany, 1961-62; assoc. exec. sec. food and nutrition bd. NAS/NRC, 1943-44; dir. coll. sci. curriculum improvement program NSF, 1966-67; mem. bd. control Conn. Agrl. Expt. Sta., 1963-79, sec., 1967-79. Author: (with W. A. Gortner) Outlines of Biochemistry, 1949, (with P. E. Marsh) Federal Aid to Science Education: Two Programs, 1963; also articles. Mem. council Middlesex Meml. Hosp. Sch. Nursing, 1948-54; corporator Middlesex Meml. Hosp., 1967-75, corporator emeritus, 1975—. Served to lt. USNR, 1944-46. Fellow AAAS; mem. Am. Chem. Soc., Am. Inst. Nutrition, Conn. Acad. Sci. and Engring., Conn. Nutrition Council (chmn. 1952-54), Phi Beta Kappa, Sigma Xi, Phi Lambda Upsilon, Gamma Alpha, Alpha Chi Sigma. Club: Faculty (Middletown). Home: 84 Bretton Rd Middletown CT 06457

GORTNER, WILLIS ALWAY, nutritional biochemist, author; b. Cold Spring Harbor, N.Y., Dec. 20, 1913; s. Ross Aiken and Catherine (Willis) G.; m. Susan Leet Reichert, Aug. 25, 1960; children—Willis Alway II, David Allen, Catherine Willis, Frederick Aiken. B.A. magna cum laude, U. Minn., 1934; Ph.D., U. Rochester, 1940. Research chemist Gen. Mills, Inc., Mpls., 1934-37, 40-42; teaching asst. biochemistry U. Rochester Med. Sch., 1937-40; asst. prof. biochemistry and chem. engring. Cornell U., 1943-45, asso. prof. biochemistry, 1945-48; head chemistry dept. Pineapple Research Inst., Hawaii, Honolulu, 1948-64; dir. human nutrition research div. Agrl. Research Service, USDA, Beltsville, Md., 1964-72, mem. nat. program staff coordinating human nutrition and family living, 1972-76; exec. officer Am. Inst. Nutrition, Bethesda, Md., 1976-78; Hoffman LaRoche lectr. Canadian Nutrition Soc., 1971; with Bikini Sci. Resurvey Team, 1947, Bjorksten Research Found., Madison, Wis., 1953, NRC-Nat. Acad. Sci., 1957, Nat. Canners Assn. Research Lab., 1960-61; dept. nutritional scis. U. Calif. at Berkeley, 1963; affiliate grad. faculty U. Hawaii, 1956-64; chmn. Nat. Acad. Scis. com. Internat. Union Nutritional Scis., 1973-76; secretariat Internat. Congress Food Sci. and Tech., 1970; adv. com. Honolulu County Air Pollution Control, 1957-64, State Hawaii Radiol. Health, 1958-64, Nutrition Found., 1968-79, Cornell U. Inst. Food Sci., 1971-76, Am. Health Found., 1973-76, Fedn. Am. Socs. Exptl. Biology Life Scis. Research Office, 1974-77, Diet, Nutrition and Cancer Program, Nat. Cancer Inst., 1975-77, Office Biochem. Nomenclature, NRC, 1976-77; bd. dirs. Nat. Nutrition Consortium, 1973-78. Author Ancient Rock Carvings of the Central Sierras: The North Fork Indian Petroglyphs, 1983; Co-author: Principles of Food Freezing, 1948, The Food Additives Book, 1982; co-editor, author: Outlines of Biochemistry, rev. edit, 1949; Contbr. articles to profl. jours. Recipient Thomas Andrews award for undergrad. research U. Minn., 1934. Fellow AAAS, Inst. Food Technologists (mem. com. on constn. 1947, councilor 1955-57, editorial bd. 1965-70); mem. Am. Soc. Biol. Chemists, Am. Soc. for Clin. Nutrition, Am. Chem. Soc. (Cornell exec. com. 1946-47, Hawaii exec. com. 1948-53, 56-59, Hawaii chmn. 1949-50, councilor 1950-53, 56-59), Am. Inst. Nutrition (exec. officer 1976-78), Sigma Xi (Hawaii pres. 1955-56), Phi Lambda Upsilon, Alpha Chi Sigma. Club: Cosmos (Washington). Patentee in field. Home: 470 Cervantes Rd Portola Valley CA 94025

GORTON, ARLENE ELIZABETH, physical education educator; b. Providence, Mar. 16, 1931; d. Kingdon D. and Eveline (Wright) G. A.B., Brown U., 1952; M.Ed., U. N.C., 1954. Asst. prof. phys. edn. Conn. Coll., New London, 1954-60; assoc. prof. phys. edn. Brown U., Providence, 1960-71, prof., 1971—, assoc. dir. athletics, 1973—; dir. phys. edn. Pembroke Coll., Providence, 1954-60; cons. Providence Sch. Dept., Curriculum Guide in Phys. Edn., 1964-66; chmn. ethics and eligibility com. Assn. Intercollegiate Athlectics for Women, 1981-82. Recipient Outstanding Woman of Yr. award YMCA, 1978. Mem. AAHPER (Presdl. medallion), Nat. Assn. Phys. Edn. Coll. Women, ACLU, R.I. Assn. Health, Phys. Edn. and Recreation (honor award 1971), Brown Alumni Assn. Club: Rotary. Office: Dept Athletics and Phys Edn Brown U Providence RI 02912

GORTON, SLADE, Senator; b. Chgo., Jan. 8, 1928; s. Thomas Slade and Ruth (Israel) G.; m. Sally Jean Clark, June 28, 1958; children—Tod, Sarah Jane, Rebecca Lynn. A.B., Dartmouth Coll., 1950; LL.B. with honors, Columbia U., 1953. Bar: Wash. bar 1953. Practiced in, Seattle, 1953-69, partner law firm, 1965-69, atty. gen. Wash., Olympia, 1968-80, U.S. Senator from, Wash., 1980—; Mem. Wash. Ho. of Reps., 1959-69, majority leader, 1967-69. Trustee Pacific Sci. Center, Seattle, found. mem., 1977-78; mem. Pres.'s Consumer Adv. Council, 1975-77, Wash. State Law and Justice Commn., 1969-80; chmn. Wash. State Law and Justice Commn., 1969-70; mem. State Criminal Justice Tng. Commn., 1969-80, chmn., 1969-76. Served with AUS, 1945-46; to 1st lt. USAF, 1953-56; col. Res. Mem. Am., Wash. bar assns., Nat. Assn. Attys. Gen. (pres. 1976-77, Wyman award 1980), Phi Delta Phi, Phi Beta Kappa. Clubs: Seattle Tennis, Wash. Athletic (Seattle). Office: United States Senate 513 Hart Office Bldg Washington DC 20510

GORTON, THOMAS ARTHUR, composer, pianist, educator; b. Oneida, N.Y., Mar. 12, 1910; s. Thomas Joel and May Lovica (Kelley) G.; m. Catherine Geib Urlass, Nov. 11, 1933; 1 dau., Judith Louise (Mrs. Leonard F. Parkinson). Mus.B., Eastman Sch. Music, Rochester, N.Y., 1932, Mus.M., 1935, Ph.D., 1948. Teaching fellow Eastman Sch. Music, Rochester, N.Y., 1933-35; instr. David Hochstein Music Sch., Rochester, 1933-35; instr. music Riverside (Calif.) Jr. Coll., 1935-37; condr. Riverside Community Opera Assn., 1935-37; head piano dept. Memphis Coll. Music, 1937-38, U. Tex., 1938-44; dir. Sch. Music, Ohio U., 1947-50; dean Sch. Fine Arts, U. Kans., Lawrence, 1950-75, dean emeritus, prof. music history, 1975-77; condr. Univ. Little Symphony, 1950-75; pianist St. Louis Symphony, 1943, Houston Symphony, 1939, Rochester Civic Orch., 1932-35; Mem. acad. music com. Cultural Presentations Program, Dept. State, 1958-77, chmn., 1973-74. Author: The Puffett Family, 1979, Samuel Gorton of Rhode Island and His Descendants, 1982; Composer: music including Symphony No. 1, 1947; Variations on a Welsh Folk-Tune for symphonic band, 1949, also piano pieces and songs. Served to lt. USNR, 1944-46. Mem. Nat. Assn. Schs. Music (pres. 1958-62, chmn. devel. council 1962-65, chmn. commn. on curricula 1965-70, cons. commn. on undergrad. studies 1970-77), Kans. Music Tchrs. Assn., Nat. Assn. Music Execs. State Univs., Internat. Council Fine Arts Deans, Phi Mu Alpha, Kappa Kappa Psi, Pi Kappa Lambda. Home: 831 Illinois St Lawrence KS 66044

GOSCHI, NICHOLAS PETER, lawyer; b. Chgo., Nov. 2, 1925; s. Nick and Katherine (Kesselring) G.; m. Barbara V. Deere, Oct. 23, 1954; children—Deborah J., Nicholas J., Peter E., Paul R., Margaret E., Michelle M. B.S.C., Loyola U., Chgo., 1949, J.D., 1953. Bar: Ill. bar 1953. Since practiced in, Chgo.; asso. George D. Crowley, 1953-60; partner firm Crowley & Goschi, 1960-79; individual practice law, Chgo., 1979—; sec., treas., dir. Janler Corp.; dir. Computer Supplies, Inc. Served with OSS AUS, 1943-46. Mem. Am., Ill. bar assns. Home: 3642 N Harding Ave Chicago IL 60618 Office: 135 S LaSalle St Chicago IL 60603

GOSE, ELLIOTT BICKLEY, JR., English language educator; b. Nogales, Ariz., May 3, 1926; emigrated to Can., 1956, naturalized, 1969; s. Elliott Bickley and Eleanor (Paulding) G.; m. Kathleen Kavanaugh Brittain, Oct. 14, 1950; children—Peter Christoph, Sarah Elliott. B.A. cum laude, Cornell U., 1949, M.A., 1950, Ph.D., 1954. Instr. English La. State U. at, Baton Rouge, 1954-56; mem. faculty U. B.C. (Can.) at, Vancouver, 1956—, prof. English, 1967—. Author: Imagination Indulged, 1972, The Transformation Process in Joyce's Ulysses, 1980, The World of the Irish Wonder Tale. Pres. The New Sch., Vancouver, 1965-66; trustee Vancouver Sch. Bd., 1973-76. Served with CIC AUS, 1946-47. Can. Council sr. fellow, 1971-72. Mem. Phi Beta Kappa. Home: 2956 Blanca St Vancouver BC V6R 4G1 Canada

GOSE, WULF ACHIM, geophysicist, educator; b. Recklinghausen, Germany, Apr. 8, 1938; came to U.S., 1965, naturalized, 1976; s. Karl and Margaretha (Schreier) G.; m. Susan Frances Malone, Nov. 26, 1969; children: Karlin, Robin. B.S., U. Gottingen, 1960, M.S., 1964; postgrad., U. Bonn, 1960, Case Western Res. U., 1965-66; Ph.D., So. Methodist U., 1970. Grad. research asst. Case Western Res. U., 1965-66, S.W. Center for Advanced Studies, Dallas, 1966-70; vis. scientist Lunar Sci. Inst., Houston, 1970-72, staff scientist, 1972-74; lectr. geology U. Houston, 1974; asst. prof. U. Tex. Marine Sci. Inst., Galveston, 1974-81; research scientist, sr. lectr. dept. geol. sci. U. Tex., Austin, 1981—, vis. scientist Inst. for Geophysics, 1981—; prin. investigator Lunar Sample Program, 1975-80; mng. editor Proc. 4th and 5th Lunar Sci. Confs., 1973-74. Contbr. sci. articles to profl. jours. Recipient Shuler prize for best student publ. So. Meth. U., 1970, spl. recognition NASA, 1979. Mem. Am. Geophys. Union, Deutsche Geophysikalische Gesellschaft. Home: 6706 Cypress Point N Austin TX 78746 Office: Univ of Texas PO Box 7909 Austin TX 78712

GOSLIN, FRANCIS GEORGE, financial corporation executive; b. Manchester, Iowa, Mar. 21, 1926; s. Francis George and Edna Mary (Dorman) G.; m. Colleen Cos, June 12, 1946; children; Franics George III, Stephen Alan, Susan Lynne. B.S., U.S. Mil. Acad., 1946; M.S. in Civil Engring., Calif. Inst. Tech., 1954. Commd. 2d lt. U.S. Army, 1946, advanced through grades to col., 1967; policy and planning officer Mils Assistance Command, Vietnam, 1967-68; brigade comdr., chief of staff U.S. Army Tng. Ctr., Ft. Knox, Ky., 1968-70; exec. to sec. Army Dept. Army, Washington, 1971-73; ret. U.S. Army, 1973; v.p. adminstrn. Fed. Nat. Mortgage Assn., Washington, 1973-82, sr. v.p. adminstrn., 1982—. Decorated D.S.M. Presbyterian. Office: Fed Nat Mortgage Assn 3900 Wisconsin Ave Washington DC 20016

GOSLINE, ROBERT BRADLEY, lawyer; b. Toledo, Jan. 9, 1913; s. Robert Gates and Ella Irene (Bradley) G.; m. D. Martha Long, Nov. 29, 1941; children: Robert Bradley, William H., Mary R. A.B. cum laude, U. Toledo, 1933; J.D., Ohio State U., 1936. Bar: Ohio 1936, Mich. 1979. Practiced in, Toledo, 1936—; assoc., partner firm Shumaker, Loop & Kendrick (and predecessor firms), 1936—, head litigation dept., 1964-73; Chmn. bd. bar examiners Ohio Supreme Ct., 1960-61, mem. bd. commrs. for grievances and discipline of bar, 1982—. Chmn. March of Dimes Lucas County, 1951; mem. City Charter Commn., Maumee, Ohio, 1951; Mem. City Council, Maumee, 1952-54; Sec., trustee Boys Club Toledo, 1955-78, sec., 1964-75. Served to maj. AUS, 1942-46. Recipient Bronze Keystone Boys Clubs Am., 1972, medallion, 1976. Fellow Am. Coll. Trial Lawyers; mem. ABA, Ohio Bar Assn., Mich. Bar Assn., Toledo Bar Assn. (past pres.), Phi Delta Phi. Presbyterian (trustee, elder). Home: 232 E Wayne St Maumee OH 43537 Office: 1000 Jackson Blvd Toledo OH 43624

GOSMAN, ALBERT LOUIS, educator; b. Detroit, May 27, 1923; s. Saul and Eva (Cohen) G.; m. Marguerite Emilie Lemieux, Mar. 9, 1946; children—Erica Jan, Stephanie Frances. B.S., U. Mich., 1950; M.S., U. Colo., 1955; Ph.D., U. Ia., 1965. Asst. prof. Colo. Sch. Mines, 1950-55, 58-62; research engr. Northrop Aircraft, Inc., Los Angeles, 1956-58; asso. prof. Wayne State U., Detroit, 1965-67; prof., chmn. mech. engring. dept. Wichita (Kans.) State U., 1967-71, asso. dean engring., 1971-80, prof. mech. engring., 1980—, also asso. dir. engring. research.; Research engring. cons. cryogenics Nat. Bur. Standards. Author monograph; contbr.: chpt. to Tech. Navair Manual of Oxygen/Nitrogen Cryogenic Systems, 1971. Served with C.E. AUS, 1943-45. Recipient Outstanding Tchr. awards Colo. Sch. Mines, 1952, 53, Best Tchr. award Wayne State U., 1967; Ford Found. fellow, 1964-65. Mem. ASME (dir. Midwest sect.), Am. Soc. Engring. Edn. (research adminstrn. council, publs. com. of engring. research com., bd. dirs. research council), Blue Key, Sigma Xi, Phi Kappa Phi, Pi Tau Sigma, Alpha Tau Omega. Home: 244 Bonnie Brae Wichita KS 67207

GOSNELL, CHARLES FRANCIS, librarian, publicist; b. Rochester, N.Y., July 7, 1909; s. James Francis and Alameda (Whipple) G.; m. Patria Aran-Soler, Mar. 31, 1934; children: Alice, Rita; m. Helen Louise Kuhlman, Dec. 29, 1951; children—Marsh Kuhlman, Deborah, Susan, Catherine. A.B., U. Rochester, 1930; B.S., Columbia, 1932, M.S., 1937; Ph.D., N.Y. U., 1943; certificate, Centro de Estudios Históricos, Madrid, Spain, 1934. Asst. U. Rochester Library, 1927-31; corr. Rochester Democrat and Chronicle, 1928-30; reference asst. N.Y. Pub. Library, 1931-37; librarian, asso. prof. Queens Coll., 1937-45; asso. Sch. Library Service, Columbia, 1943-47; asst. commr. edn., N.Y., 1949-62; state librarian N.Y. State, 1945-62; dir. libraries, prof. library adminstrn. N.Y. U., 1962-74, emeritus, 1974—; adviser to U.S. Gen. Services Adminstrn. on archives and records centers, 1974—; chmn. Pub. Affairs Info. Service, 1976—; spl. cons., library orgns., and assns., library mus. and historic bldgs. for fire protection, library lighting. U.S. del. to UNESCO Conf. on Libraries, Sao Paulo, Brazil, 1951; head UNESCO survey pub. library services in, Colombia, S.Am., 1959; cons. to Ford Found. and U. Brasilia, Brazil, 1963—; cons. Inter-Am. Devel. Bank, 1966-67. Author: several books latest being New York State's Freedom Train, 1948; Copyright: Grab-bag, 1968, Spanish Personal Names, 1971, Obsolescence of Books, 1978; Contbr. articles to profl. jours. Sec. N.Y. State Freedom Train Commn., N.Y. Cultural Heritage Found.; trustee Center for Study Presidency, Mohawk-Caughnawaga Mus., Fonda, N.Y., Skidmore Coll., Saratoga Springs, N.Y.; chmn. Council Nat. Library Assns., 1956-57; past pres. Nat. Assn. State Libraries. Recipient Grand Cross Eloy Alfaro Internat. Found., 1968; comdr. Order Jacques Ignace Fresnel, Haiti; Good Citizenship gold medal S.A.R.; Lafayette medal Merit, 1977; Benjamin Franklin fellow Royal Soc. Arts, London. Mem. A.L.A. (mem. exec. bd. 1953-57, pres. library adminstrn. div. 1966-67), N.Y. Library Assn. (pres. 1968-69, Moore award 1978), Middle Atlantic Regional Library Council (bd. dirs.), various spl. library assns., nat., state and local bibliog. and library assns., and also assns. in related fields, such as statis., archivist and hist. socs. Clubs: Mason (N.Y.C.) (33 deg., grand historian, grand master N.Y., chmn. Empire State Mason mag., chmn. conf. grand masters N.Am. 1968-69, hon. grand master Guanabara, Rio de Janeiro, hon. mem. supreme council Brazil, hon. past grand master York grand lodge Mexico, Henry Price medalist grand lodge Mass., hon. grand warden grand lodge nat. France); Grolier, Masonic, N.Y. University (N.Y.C.); Rotary (Bklyn.); University (Albany). Home: 11 Orchard Circle Suffern NY 10901 Office: 71 W 23d St Room 1700 New York NY 10010 also 11 W 40th St Room 225 New York NY 10018

GOSS, DONALD CARPENTER, advertising executive; b. White Plains, N.Y., Oct. 22, 1930; s. Clarence Edward and Priscilla (Carpenter) G.; m. Lillian Prakelt, Sept. 11, 1954; children: Diane Catherine Goss Farrell, Jonathan Carpenter, Thomas Carpenter, Holly Elizabeth. A.B., Dartmouth Coll., 1953. Product mgr. Vick Chem. Co., Conn., 1953-57; account supr. N.W. Ayer & Son, Inc., N.Y.C., 1957-65; v.p. Ketchum, MacLeod & Grove, Inc., N.Y.C., 1965-67; exec. v.p., dir., mem. ops. com. McCaffrey & McCall, Inc., N.Y.C., 1967—. Author: The First 25 Years, 1978; contbr. articles to mags. Trustee Greens Farms Congl. Ch., 1968-69; chmn. Westport Ecumenical Council, 1961-63; dist. officer U.S. Power Squadron, 1965-69; bd. dirs. United Fund, 1965-67; mem. Dartmouth Alumni Council; editorial rev. bd. Dartmouth Alumni Mag.; trustee Westport Masonic Scholarship Fund, 1967—. Mem. N.Y. Sales Execs. Club, Am. Assn. Advt. Agys. (client services com.), New Eng. Soc. City N.Y. (life), Soc. Descs. Mayflower, Theta Delta Chi (founders corp.), Phi Beta Chi. Republican. Clubs: Masons, K.T. (life), Block Island Yacht (past pres., gov.). Home: 30 N Maple Ave Westport CT 06880 also Westside Rd Block Island RI 02807 65 E Wheelock St Hanover NH 03755

GOSS, DONALD E., accountant; b. Chgo., Feb. 6, 1931; s. Anton J. and Pansy M. (Sanders) G.; m. Kay A. Hesson, Aug. 21, 1954; children—William, Donna, Thomas, Robert, Marilee, Donald E. B.S. in Accountancy, U. Ill., 1953; grad., Advanced Mgmt. Program, Harvard U., 1973. C.P.A., Ill. With Arthur Young & Co. (C.P.A.'s), Chgo., 1953—, prin., 1961-62, partner, 1962—, Midwest regional mng. partner, 1976—; adv. council U. Ill. Coll. Commerce, 1977—. Mem. Chgo. Crime Commn., 1970, U. Ill. Found., 1972. Served with AUS, 1953-54. Mem. Am. Inst. C.P.A.'s, Ill. Soc. C.P.A.'s. Clubs: Ill. Athletic (Chgo.); Edgewood Valley Country. Home: 4807 Johnson Ave Western Springs IL 60558 Office: Arthur Young & Co 1 IBM Plaza Chicago IL 60611

GOSS, FREDERICK DANIEL, association executive; b. Phila., Nov. 26, 1941; s. Frederick Daniel and Wilma Dorothy (Craver) G.; m. Melinda Mary Mohan, Aug. 1, 1970; 1 dau., Meredith. B.A., George Washington U., 1964. With Nat. Telephone Coop. Assn., Washington, 1968-79, legis. dir., 1972-76, asst. exec. v.p., 1976-79; exec. dir. The Newsletter Assn. Am., Washington, 1979—; lectr. George Washington U. Author: Success in Newsletter Publishing-A Practical Guide, 1982. State del. Va. Easter Seal Soc., 1978; bd. dirs. Resurrection Pre-School, 1977-80. Served to lt. (j.g.) USN, 1964-68; Vietnam. Mem. Am. Soc. Assn. Execs., Nat. Press Club. Democrat. Episcopalian. Home: 307 Kentucky Ave Alexandria VA 22305 Office: The Newsletter Assn 1341 G St NW Suite 603 Washington DC 20045

GOSS, HARRY THAYER, outdoor advertising company executive; b. Phoenix, Mar. 29, 1929; s. Harry Leslie and Grace (Jenkins) G.; m. Ann Marie Pitman, Mar. 28, 1951; children: Michael Leslie, Mark Pitman, Melinda Goss Longwell. LL.B., U. Ariz., 1953. Bar: Ariz. 1953. Ptnr. Mariscal & Goss, Phoenix, 1953-69; v.p. Combined Communications, Phoenix, 1969-79; pres. Gannett Outdoor Group, Phoenix, 1979—. Mem. Outdoro Advt. Assn. Am. (vice chmn. 1974-75, vice chmn. 1976-77). Home: 5829 Calle Del Norte Pheonix AZ 85018 Office: Gannett Outdoor Group 1111 N Central Ave Pheonix AZ 85004

GOSS, KENNETH GEORGE, physician, educator; b. N.Y.C., Dec. 6, 1922; s. Charles Henry and Ruth Colina (Mackenzie) G.; m. Dorothy Jean Burdick, Sept. 22, 1946; children: Kenneth MacKenzie, Jeffrey Dean, David Victor, John Charles, Patricia Jean. B.A., Alfred U., 1948; M.D., U. Rochester, 1952. Diplomate: Am. Bd. Family Practice. Intern Strong Meml. Hosp., Rochester, N.Y., 1952-53; practice family medicine, Rochester, 1953-60; mem. staff med. dept. Eaton Labs., 1960-61; med. dir. Dean L. Burdick Assos., N.Y.C., 1961-72; practice family medicine, New Canaan, Conn., 1961-73; asst. prof. family practice Med. U. S.C., Charleston, 1974-77; asso. prof. family and community medicine U. Ark. Med. Coll., Little Rock, 1977-78, prof., chmn., 1978—. Mem. exec. council Ark. Episc. Diocese. Served with AUS, 1942-45. Fellow Am. Acad. Family Physicians; mem. Soc. Tchrs. Family Medicine, Am. Acad. Family Physicians, N. Am. Primary Care Research Group, Pulaski County Med. Soc., Ark. Med. Soc. Home: 1521 Spring St Little Rock AR 72202 Office: 1700 W 13th St Little Rock AR 72202

GOSS, MARY E. WEBER, sociology educator; b. Chgo., May 8, 1926; m. Albert E. Goss, 1945; 1 son, Charles. B.A. in Sociology with distinction (Univ. Merit scholar 1946-47, Chi Omega Sociology prize 1947), State U. Iowa, 1947, M.A., 1948; Ph.D. (Gilder fellow 1951-52), Columbia U., 1959. Research asst. State U. Iowa, 1947-48, Amherst Coll., 1949; instr. Smith Coll., 1949-50, U. Mass., 1950-51, 55-56, adj. mem. grad. faculty, 1961-66; research asso. Bur. Applied Social Research, Columbia U., 1952-53; cons. sociology, research staff mem., then research coordinator comprehensive care and teaching program N.Y. Hosp.-Cornell U. Med. Center, 1957-66; mem. faculty Dept. Medicine Cornell U. Med. Coll., 1959-72, prof. sociology in public health, 1973—; mem. grad. faculty sociology Cornell U., 1973—. Author: Physicians in Bureaucracy, 1980; also numerous articles; editor: Jour. Health and Social Behavior, 1976-78; co-editor: Comprehensive Medical Care and Teaching: A Report on the N.Y. Hospital-Cornell Medical Center Program, 1967; mem. editorial bd. profl. jours. Fellow Am. Public Health Assn.; mem. Am. Acad. Polit. and Social Sci., Am. Sociol. Assn., Soc. Study Social Problems, AAAS, AAUP, Assn. Tchrs. Preventive Medicine, Soc. Public Health Edn., N.Y. Acad. Medicine (asso. fellow), Eastern Sociol. Soc., Phi Beta Kappa, Sigma Xi. Address: Dept Public Health Cornell U Med Coll 1300 York Ave New York NY 10021

GOSS, RICHARD JOHNSON, biologist, educator; b. Marblehead, Mass., July 19, 1925; s. Donald Chapin and Ruth (Johnson) G.; m. Marcella Hyde, June 2, 1951; children: Stephen Harley, Elizabeth Alden. A.B., Harvard U., 1948, Ph.D., 1952. Instr. biol. and med. scis. Brown U., 1952-54, asst. prof., 1954-58, asso. prof., 1958-64, prof., 1964—, chmn. sect. developmental biology, 1972-77, dean biol. scis., 1977—. Author: Adaptive Growth, 1964, Principles of Regeneration, 1969, The Physiology of Growth, 1978, Deer Antlers: Regeneration, Function and Evolution, 1983; Editor: (with W.W. Nowinski) Compensatory Renal Hypertrophy, 1969, Regulation of Organ and Tissue Growth, 1972. Trustee Mt. Desert Island Biol. Lab., 1960-64; bd. dirs. Roger Williams Park Zoo, Providence, 1963-74. Served with inf. AUS, 1943-45. Fellow dept. embryology Carnegie Instn. of Washington, 1960-61. Mem. R.I. Zool. Soc. (pres., dir.), Am. Soc. Zoologists (chmn. div. developmental biology, 1969), AAAS (sec. sect. biol. scis.). Research on regeneration of animal appendages and on regulation of organ and tissue growth. Home: 44 S Meadow Ln Barrington RI 02806 Office: Brown Univ Providence RI 02912

GOSS, ROBERT FRANCIS, union executive; b. Escanaba, Mich., Nov. 10, 1921; s. John Arthur and Grace (Dean) G.; m. Frances King, July 21, 1946; children: Gary, Nancy, Bradley. Student public schs. With Union Oil Co., Los Angeles refinery, 1940-42, from 1946; mem. Oil, Chem. and Atomic Workers Internat. Union, adminstrv. asst. to pres., then internat. v.p., 1967-79, internat. pres., Denver, 1979—; mem. exec. council AFL-CIO. Served with USNR, 1942-46. Democrat. Methodist. Office: 1636 Champa St Box 2812 Denver CO 80201 *

GOSS, WESLEY PERRY, mining company executive; b. Garland, Kans., Nov. 4, 1899; s. Frank Bailey and Lola May (Perry) G.; m. Nellie F. McIntosh, Apr. 5, 1923; children: John Wesley, Patricia Caroline. B.S., U. Calif., 1922. Asst. supt. United Verde Copper Co., Jerome, Ariz., 1933-34; gen. supt. Park City (Utah) Consol. Mines Co., 1934-37; mine supt. O'Kiep Copper Co., Namagualand, South Africa, 1937-41; asst. gen. mgr. Gray Eagle Copper Co., Happay Camp, Calif., 1942-44; v.p., gen. mgr., dir. Magma Copper Co., 1944-53, pres., gen. mgr., dir., 1954-71, chmn. bd., dir., 1972-82, chmn. emeritus, dir., 1983—; v.p., gen. mgr. Magma Ariz. R.R., 1944-71, dir., 1944—; Mem. Ariz. Copper Tariff Bd., Ariz. Bd. Regents, 1963-70. Mem. AIME, Am. Mining Congress, Mining and Metall. Soc. Am., Am. Legion. Home: Box 676 San Manuel AZ 85631 Office: Box M San Manuel AZ 85631

GOSSAGE, JOHN RALPH, photographer; b. S.I., Mar. 15, 1946; s. John and Edith (Geifer) G.; m. L. Denise Sines, Mar. 18, 1975. Student, Walden Sch., 1965-67. Rep. by Leo Castelli Castelli Graphics, N.Y.C., Lunn Gallery, Washington; instr. photography Grad. Sch., Dept. Art U. Md., College Park. Exhibited one-man shows in photography, Camera Infinity Gallery, N.Y.C., 1963, Hinckley Grohel Gallery, Washington, 1968, Ohio. U., 1971, Pyramid Gallery, Washington, 1972, one-show in photopgraphy, Jefferson Place Gallery, Washington, 1974, one-man shows in photography, Castelli Graphics, N.Y.C., 1976, 78, 80, Werkstaat fur Photographie der VHS Kreuzberg, Berlin, 1982, Forum Stadtpart, Graz, Austria, Gallerie Lange-Irschl, Munich, Mus. of Hart, Hannover, Castelli Gallery, 1983, group shows, N.Y. Coliseum Photo Expo, 1975, Lever House, Washington Gallery Modern Art, Corcoran Gallery, 1975, San Francisco Art Inst., Pasadena Mus. Art, Balt. Mus. Art, Newport Harbor Mus., LaJolla Mus. Contemporary Art, 1972, Walker Art Center, 1975, Ft. Worth Art Mus., groups shows, Phila. Print Club, 1976, group shows, Broxton Gallery, 1976, U. N.M. Art Gallery, Castelli Uptown, Houston Mus. Fine Art, Internat. Photography, Mus. Modern Art, City of Paris, Nd. Art Gallery, Mus. Nice (France), MIT, 1977, Chgo. Ctr. Contemporary Photography, Mus. Modern Art Strasbourg (France., U. Mass. Gallery, 1978, groups shows, Addison Gallery Am. Art, group shows, Santa Barbara Mus. Art, Corcoran Gallery Art, Cranbrook Acad., Mus. Contemporary Art, Chgo., Corcoran Gallery, 1979, Internat. Center Photography, Washington Art Consortium, Hoffer Meml. Photography Collection, Colgate U., Seattle Art Mus., 1980, George Eastman House, Inst. Contemporary Art, U. Pa, Castelli Photography, Oakland Mus., Arlington Arts Crt., 1981, Impressions Gallery, Boston, 1982, permanent collections, Smithsonian Instn., Mus. Modern Art, N.Y.C., Pasadena Mus., Nat. Endowment for Arts, Library of Congress, permanent collection, Princeton U., permanent collections, Pan Am. Union, group collections, Houston Mus. Fine Art, permanent collections, Cororan Gallery Art, Phila. Mus. Art, Walker Art Ctr.; represented, Bibliotheque Nationale, Paris, Addison Gallery Am. Art, Australian Nat. Gallery, Canberra, Oakland Mus. Art, San Francisco Mus. Art, others; lectr. (in field); contbr. articles to profl. jours. Washington Gallery Modern Art Fund fellow, 1969, 70; Nat. Endowment Arts grantee, 1973m 74, 78; Stern Family Found. grantee, 1974. Address: 1875 Mintwood Pl NW Apt 30 Washington DC 20009

GOSSAGE, RICHARD MICHAEL, professional baseball player; b. Colorado Springs, Colo., July 5, 1951; s. Jack Andrew and Susanne (Radich) G.; m. Cornelia Lukaszewicz, Oct. 28, 1972; children: Jeffrey Carlton, Keith Michael. With Chgo. White Sox, 1972-77, Pitts. Pirates, 1977-78; pitcher N.Y. Yankees, 1978-83, San Diego Padres, 1984—. Named Midwest Player of Yr., 1971, Fireman of Yr., 1975, 78. Mem. Assn. Profl. Ballplayers Am.

GOSSAGE, THOMAS LAYTON, chemical company executive; b. Nashville, May 7, 1934; s. Walker E. and Mildred (Davis) G.; m. Virginia Eastman, July 27, 1957; children: Laura Eastman, Virginia Lowry. B.S., Ga. Inst. Tech., 1956, M.S., 1957. Process engr. Humble Oil Co., 1957; asst. dir. govt. relations Monsanto Research Corp., Dayton, Ohio, 1961-66, dir. research and devel. mktg., Dayton, 1966-68; group mktg. dir. Monsanto Co. New Enterprises div., St. Louis, 1968-70; mktg. dir. Monsanto Co. Specialty Products, St. Louis, 1970-75; dir. results mgmt. Monsanto Indsl. Chems. Co., St. Louis, 1975-77, asst. gen. mgr. plasticizers div., 1977, gen. mgr. plasticizers div., 1977-79, gen. mgr. detergents and phosphates, 1979-80, asst. mng. dir., 1980-81, v.p., mng. dir., 1981-83; group v.p., mng. dir. Monsanto Internat., St. Louis, 1983—. 1st lt. USAF, 1957-60. Home: 53 Portland Pl Saint Louis MO 63108 Office: Monsanto Co 800 N Lindbergh Blvd Saint Louis MO 63167

GOSSARD, ARTHUR CHARLES, physicist; b. Ottawa, Ill., June 18, 1935; s. Arthur Paul and Mary Catherine (Lineberger) G.; m. Marsha Jean Palmer, Jan. 8, 1965; children: Girard Christopher, Elinore Suzanne. B.A., Harvard U., 1956; Ph.D., U. Calif., Berkeley, 1960. Solid state physicist, mem. tech. staff Bell Telephone Labs., Murray Hill, N.J., 1960—. Author tech. papers magnetic resonance, magnetism, transition metals, molecular beam epitaxy, semiconductors. Environ. commnr., Warren, N.J., 1973—. NSF postdoctoral fellow, 1962-63. Fellow Am. Phys. Soc. Address: Bell Telephone Labs Murray Hill NJ 07974

GOSSELIN, CLAUDE A(LPHONSE) R(ENÉ), curator; b. Valleyfield, Que., Can., June 5, 1944; s. Sauveur and Georgette (Belair) G. D.E.S., U. Montreal, Que., 1969; Bacc. Spec., U. Que., 1969-71, postgrad. in history art, 1971. Tchr., Burundi, 1966-68; coordinator Que. Profl. Artists Soc., 1972-74; art critic Le Devoir newspaper, Montreal, 1974-75; visual arts officer Can. Council, Ottawa, Ont., 1975-79; curator, head exhbns. Musee d'Art Contemporain, Montreal, 1979—. Mem. Societe Des Musees Quebecois. Office: Musee d'Art Contemporain Montreal PQ Canada H3C 3R4 *

GOSSELIN, JOHN WILLIAM, lawyer; b. Aurora, Ill., Feb. 20, 1934; s. John Stephen and Betty (Willoughby) G.; m. Judith Ann Wheeler, Sept. 14, 1956; children—Kathleen, Gabrielle, John Wheeler, Thomas Willoughby. Student, Wabash Coll., 1952-53; B.A., Beloit Coll., 1953-56; LL.D., U. Chgo., 1959. Bar: Ill. bar 1959. Practice in, Aurora, 1959-66, Batavia, 1966—; asso. Thomas P. O'Malley, 1959-61; pvt. practice, 1961-66; partner Benson, Mair & Gosselin, 1966—; City atty., Batavia, 1964-77. Mem. Am., Ill., Kane County bar assns. Home: Lockwood Hall Batavia IL 60510 Office: 133 S Batavia Ave Batavia IL 60510

GOSSELIN, RICHARD PETTENGILL, educator; b. Springfield, Mass., June 29, 1921; s. A. Edmond and Grace Lillian (Pettengill) G.; m. Mary A. Doyle, Jan. 30, 1971; children from previous marriage—Philip W., Janet R. B.S., U. Chgo., 1944, Ph.D., 1951; M.A., U. Rochester, 1948. Prof. math. Youngstown (Ohio) U., 1952-55; faculty U. Conn., Storrs, 1955—, prof. math., 1961—. Served with USAAF, 1942-46. Research grantee U.S. Air Force, NSF, 1956—. Mem. Am. Math. Soc., Math. Assn Am. Office: Dept Math U Conn Storrs CT 06268

GOSSELIN, ROBERT EDMOND, educator; b. Springfield, Mass., Sept. 2, 1919; s. A. Edmond and Grace (Pettengill) G.; m. Ruth L. Smith, June 26, 1948 (dec. Dec. 1977); children—Peter Gordon, Andrea Lee; m. Patricia S. Whitaker, July 25, 1981. A.B., Brown U., 1941; Ph.D., U. Rochester, 1945, M.D., 1947. Med. intern Yale service Grace-New Haven Hosp., 1947-48; instr. pharmacology U. Rochester, 1948-52, asst. prof. pharmacology, scientist atomic energy project, 1954-56; prof. dept. pharmacology and toxicology Dartmouth Med. Sch., 1956—, chmn. dept., 1956-75; dir. poison info. center Hitchcock Hosp., 1957-82; cons. USPHS, 1959-63, U.S. Army Chem. Corps, 1954-59; mem. toxicology study sect. USPHS, 1964-68; mem.

toxicology adv. bd. U.S. Consumer Product Safety Commn., 1978—. Contbr. articles to profl. jours. Pres. Norwich Devel. Assn., 1965. Served with AUS, 1944-46; to capt., M.C. AUS, 1952-54. Mem. Am. Physiol. Soc., Am. Soc. Exptl. Pharmacology and Therapeutics, AAAS, Toxicology Soc., Phi Beta Kappa, Sigma Xi. Home: The Holm Meriden NH 03770 Office: Dartmouth Med Sch Hanover NH 03756

GOSSETT, LOUIS, JR., actor; b. Bklyn., May 27, 1936; s. Louis and Helen (Wray) G. B.A., N.Y. U., 1959; studied with, Frank Silvera, Nola Chilton, Eli Rill, Lloyd Richards. Made Broadway debut in Take a Giant Step, 1953; other stage performance include The Charlatan; appeared: motion pictures including A Raisin in the Sun, 1961, The Landlord, 1970, The Bushbaby, 1970, Skin Game, 1971, The Laughing Policeman, 1973, The White Dawn, 1974, The River Niger, 1976, J.D.'s Revenge, 1976, The Deep, 1977, The Choirboys, 1977, Pvt. Benjamin, An Officer and a Gentleman, 1982 (Acad. award for Best Supporting Actor); TV film Delancey Street: The Crisis Within, 1975, Roots, part 1, 1977, Backstairs at the White House, Don't Look Back, 1981; Benny's Place, 1982, Sadat, 1983; also various TV series, including The Lazarus Syndrome, 1979, The Powers of Matthew Star; singer in nightclubs, 1960's (Recipient Emmy award for Roots, Nat. Acad. TV Arts and Scis. 1977). Mem. Acad. Motion Picture Arts and Scis., Actors Equity, Screen Actors Guild, AFTRA, Am. Guild Variety Artists, Am. Fed. Musicians, Negro Actors Guild Am., Alpha Phi Alpha. *

GOSSETT, OSCAR MILTON, advertising executive; b. N.Y.C., May 27, 1925; s. Oscar Percival and Helen (Deutsch) G.; m. Anna C. Scheid, May 29, 1949; children: Susanne, Michael, Thomas, Lorraine, James M. Student, Stevens Inst. Tech., 1943-44, 46-47, Columbia, 1947-48, Northwestern U. With Compton Advt., Inc., 1949—, pres., 1968—, chmn. bd. and chief exec. officer, 1971-83; chmn. bd., chief exec. officer Compton Communications Holding Co., 1982—, Saatchi & Saatchi Compton Worldwide, 1982—. Adv. bd. Religion in Am. Life; trustee Methodist Hosp.; bd. dirs. Eye Bank for Sight Restoration. Served as officer USNR, 1944-46. Mem. Am. Assn. Advt. Agys. (bd. govs.), Advt. Women of N.Y. (1st hon. male mem.). Methodist. Inventor mobile of solar system. Office: 625 Madison Ave New York NY 10022 *

GOSSETT, PHILIP, musicologist; b. N.Y.C., Sept. 27, 1941; s. Harold and Pearl (Lenkowsky) G.; m. Suzanne Solomon, Aug. 4, 1963; children—David, Jeffrey. B.A. summa cum laude, Amherst Coll., 1963; student, Columbia U., 1961-62; M.F.A., Princeton U., 1965, Ph.D., 1970. Asst. prof. music and humanities U. Chgo., 1968-73, asso. prof., 1973-77, prof., 1977—; vis. asso. prof. Columbia U., 1975; cons. in field. Coordinating editor: The Works of Giuseppe Verdi; gen. editor: Opera Omnia di Giochino Rossini; editorial bd.: Jour. Am. Musicol. Soc, 1972-78; cons. editor: Critical Inquiry, 1974—, Nineteenth-century Music, 1976—; Translator: (with Charles Rosen) Early Romantic Opera; transl. also numerous critical edits. Panelist Ill. Arts Council, 1977—. Woodrow Wilson fellow, 1963-64, 66-67; Fulbright scholar, Paris, 1965-66; Martha Baird Rockefeller fellow, 1967-68; Guggenheim fellow, 1971-72; NEH sr. scholar, 1982-83. Mem. Am. Musicol. Soc. (council 1972-74, dir. 1974-76, Alfred Einstein award 1969), Internat. Musicol. Soc., Am. Inst. Verdi Studies (dir.), Societa Italiana di Musicologia. Home: 5509 S Kenwood Ave Chicago IL 60637 Office: Dept Music U Chgo Chicago IL 60637

GOSSETT, WILLIAM THOMAS, lawyer; b. Gainesville, Tex., Sept. 9, 1904; s. James Tillman and Orrie B. (Laverty) G.; m. Elizabeth Evans Hughes, Dec. 19, 1930; children: Antoinette Gossett Denning, William T., Elizabeth Evans Karaman. A.B., U. Utah, 1925, LL.D., 1961; LL.B., Columbia, 1928, LL.D., 1978; LL.D., Coe Coll., 1947, Bethany Coll., 1962, Kalamazoo Coll., 1965, Tuskegee Inst., 1966, Detroit Coll. Law, 1967, Oakland U., 1967, Duke, 1968, U. Mich., 1968, Drury Coll., 1969, Brown U., 1969, U. Dallas, 1969, Atlanta U., 1978, Morehouse Coll., 1978; H.H.D., Wayne U., 1957, U. Detroit, 1980. Bar: N.Y. bar 1929. Practiced in, N.Y., 1929-47; gen. counsel Bendix Aviation Corp., 1943-47, dir., 1946-47; mem. firm Hughes, Schurman & Dwight, 1935-37, Hughes, Hubbard & Ewing (and predecessor firm), 1937-47; v.p., gen. counsel, dir., mem. exec. and adminstrn. coms. Ford Motor Co., 1947-62; served as dep. spl. rep. for trade negotiations, Washington, 1962-63; counsel Dykema, Wheat, Spencer, Goodnow & Trigg, Detroit, 1964-70; partner Dykema, Gossett, Spencer, Goodnow & Trigg, 1970-77, counsel, 1977—; dir. emeritus One William St. Fund, Inc.; dir. Dart & Kraft Inc.; chmn. emeritus exec. com. Twentieth Century Fox Film Corp. Chmn. bd. United Negro Coll. Fund., 1961-67; trustee emeritus Columbia U.; trustee Riverside Ch., N.Y.C., 1935-47, pres., 1947; trustee Cranbrook Found., Bloomfield Hills, Mich., 1954-73, Atlanta U., Morehouse Coll., Harper-Grace Hosps., Detroit; bd. dirs. Detroit Symphony Orch. Recipient Amity award Women's div. Am. Jewish Congress, 1955, ann. Brotherhood award Detroit Round Table, Nat. Conf. Christians and Jews, 1958, Layman of Year award Detroit Council Chs., 1960; Medal for Excellence Columbia Law Sch., 1974. Fellow Am. Bar Found. (chmn. fellows 1960-62, pres. 1964-66, dir.); mem. ABA (pres. 1968-69), N.Y. Bar Assn., Detroit Bar Assn., Nat. Legal Aid and Defender Assn. (pres. 1961-64, dir.), Assn. Bar City of N.Y., State Bar Mich., Order of Coif, Beta Theta Pi, Delta Theta Phi. Republican. Baptist. Clubs: Detroit, Bloomfield Hills Country (Detroit); Ocean of Fla. (Ocean Ridge); Little (Delray Beach, Fla.). Home: 1276 Covington Rd Birmingham MI 48010 Office: 35th Floor 400 Renaissance Detroit MI 48243

GOSSICK, LEE VAN, corporate executive, retired air force officer; b. Meadville, Mo., Jan. 23, 1920; s. Clark and Myrtle (Staats) G.; m. Ruth Matter, Apr. 29, 1942; children: Roger V., Cynthia L. B.S. in Aero. Engring, Ohio State U., 1951, M.S., 1951; grad., Air War Coll., 1959, Advanced Mgmt. Program, Harvard, 1961. Aviation cadet, 1941-42; commd. 2d lt. USAAF, 1942; advanced through grades to maj. gen. USAF, 1968; fighter pilot (87th Fighter Squadron), North Africa, 1942- 43, various research and devel. posts, 1951-64; comdr. Arnold Engring. Devel. Center, 1964-67; dep. for F-111 Aero. Systems div., Wright-Patterson AFB, Ohio, 1967-68; vice comdr. div. Aero. Systems Div., 1968-69; comdr. Aero. Systems div., 1969-70; dep. chief staff systems Hdqrs. Air Force Systems Command, Andrews AFB, Md., 1970-71, chief of staff, 1971-73, ret., 1973; asst. dir. regulation AEC, Washington, 1973-74; exec. dir. ops. Nuclear Regulatory Commn., Washington, 1975-79; v.p., dep. gen. mgr. SVERDRUP Tech. Inc., Tullahoma, Tenn., 1980—. Decorated D.S.M. with oak leaf cluster; Legion of Merit with oak leaf cluster; D.F.C.; Air medal with 9 oak leaf clusters; named Distinguished Alumnus Ohio State U., 1960, Centennial Achievement award, 1970; recipient Vandenberg trophy Arnold Air Soc., 1967, Distinguished Service award AEC, 1974. Fellow Am. Inst. Aeros. and Astronautics. Home: 909 Country Club Dr Tullahoma TN 37388 Office: SVERDRUP Tech Inc Arnold AFB TN 37389

GOSSMAN, FRANCIS JOSEPH, bishop; b. Balt., Apr. 1, 1930; s. Frank M. and Mary Genevieve (Steadman) G. B.A., St. Mary Sem., Balt., 1952; S.T.L., N. Am. Coll., in Rome, 1955; J.C.D., Cath. U. of Am., 1959. Ordained priest Roman Cath. Ch., 1955; asst. pastor Basilica of the Assumption, Balt., 1959-68; asst. chancellor Archdiocese of Balt., 1959-65, vice chancellor, 1965-68; pro-synodal judge Balt. Tribunal, 1961; vice officialis Tribunal of Archdiocese of Balt., 1962-65, officialis, 1965-68; made papal chamberlain with title Very Rev. Monsignor, 1965; elected to Senate of Priests of Archdiocese, 1967-68; adminstr. Cathedral of Mary Our Queen, 1968-70; named aux. bishop of Balt. and titular bishop of Aguntum, 1968, apptd. vicar gen., 1968; apptd. to Bd. Consultors, 1969; urban vicar Archdiocese of Balt., 1970-75; bishop of, Raleigh, N.C., 1975—; Mem. Balt. Community Relations Commn., 1969-75; mem. exec. com. Md. Food Com., Inc., 1969-75. Bd. dirs. United Fund Central Md., 1974-75. Mem. Canon Law Soc. Am., Nat. Conf. Cath. Bishops, U.S. Cath. Conf. Office: 300 Cardinal Gibbons Dr Raleigh NC 27606 *

GOSSMAN, LIONEL, literature educator; b. Glasgow, Scotland, May 31, 1929; came to U.S., 1958; s. Norman and Sarah (Gold) G.; m. Eva R. Reinitz, Mar. 7, 1963; 1 dau., Janice Naomi. M.A., Glasgow U., 1951; D. Phil., Oxford U., 1958. Asst. lectr. U. Glasgow, 1957-58; asst. prof. Johns Hopkins U., Balt., 1958-62, assoc. prof., 1962-66, prof., 1966-76, Princeton U., N.J., 1976—; cons. Ford, Found., 1966-68, Social Sci. Research Council, 1977-82. Author: Men and Masks: A Study of Moliere, 1963, Medievalism and the Ideologies of Enlightenment, 1968, French Society and Culture, 1972, Augustin Thierry and Liberal Historiography, 1976, The Empire Unpossessed: An Essay on Gibbon, 1981, Orpheis Philologus: Bachofen Versus Mommsen, 1983; editorial bd.: MLN, 1959-76, Comparative Lit., Eighteenth Century Studies, French Forum. Nat. Endowmnet Humanities fellow, 1978-79; Pro Helvetia Found. fellow, 1983; Am. Council Learned Soc. fellow, 1969-70. Mem. Acad. Lit. Home: 54 Maclean Circle Princeton NJ 08540 Office: Princeton U Princeton NJ 08544

GOTFRYD, ALEXANDER, art dir., photographer; b. Warsaw, Poland, Apr. 26, 1931; came to U.S., 1946, naturalized, 1951; s. Bernard and Regina (Lurie) G. B.A., Queens Coll., Sorbonne, L'Ecole des Beaux Arts, 1954; postgrad., Yale, 1954-55. Free lance comml. artist, 1955-60; art dir., v.p. Doubleday & Co., N.Y.C., 1960—, v.p., 1981—; freelance photographer. Exhibited at, Bodley Gallery, N.Y.C., 1959; Co-author: plays The Blasphemy of Arthur Rimbaud's Sister, 1973, An Absence of Heroes, 1974; (text by Allen Drury) book of color photographs entitled Egypt-The Eternal Smile, 1980. Home: 444 E 57th St New York NY 10022 Office: 245 Park Ave New York NY 10017

GOTH, JOHN WILLIAM, mining and metals company executive; b. Ree Heights, S.D., Apr. 22, 1927; s. Perry E. and Alma L. (Wooley) G.; m. Ree Moulton, Dec. 12, 1952; children: Jay, Patrick, William. B.S. in Metallurgy, S.D. Sch. Mines, 1950, D.B.A. (hon.), 1981; M.Engring. in Metallurgy (Rotary Found. fellow), McGill U., Montreal, Que., Can., 1951; grad., advanced mgmt. program Harvard U., 1973. With AMAX Inc., 1954—, v.p. sales, Greenwich, Conn., 1972-75, v.p., 1975-81, exec. v.p., 1981-82, sr. exec. v.p., 1982—; pres. Climax Molybdenum Co. div., Greenwich, 1975-78, group exec., molybdenum, nickel, tungsten and specialty metals group, 1978—. Served with USN, 1945-46. Fellow Am. Soc. for Metals (past chmn. govt. and public affairs com.); mem. AIME, Am. Iron and Steel Inst. Home: 41 Sawmill Ln Greenwich CT 06830 Office: AMAX Inc Amax Ctr Po Box 1700 Greenwich CT 06836

GOTHERMAN, JOHN E., lawyer; b. Port William, Ohio, Mar. 21, 1933; s. John Elmer and Margaretta (Devoe) G.; m. Colleen Woods, Oct. 26, 1975; children: John E., Clara Ann Gotherman Smith, JoAnn. B.S. in Bus. Adminstrn, Ohio State U., 1954, postgrad., 1958-60; J.D., Capital U., 1960. Bar: Ohio bar 1961, U.S. Supreme Ct. bar 1978. Research asso. Ohio Mcpl. League, 1957-59, research dir., 1960-65, chief counsel, 1965-77, counsel, 1977—; individual practice law, Reynoldsburg, Ohio, 1962-75; resident partner firm Columbus office Peck, Shaffer and Williams, 1977-80; partner firm Calfee, Halter & Griswold, Cleve., 1980—; cons. to mcpl. corps. Author: Gotherman and Babbit Ohio Municipal Law, 1962, rev. edit., 1981, Gotherman's Ohio Municipal Service, 1975-79, Municipal Government in Ohio, 1968-80, Gotherman's Guide - A Handbook for Municipal Councilmen, 1973; prin. editor: Desk Book for Ohio Municipal Attorneys, 1979. Safety dir. City of Reynoldsburg, 1962; mem. City Council, 1963. Served to 1st lt. USAF, 1955-56. Mem. Nat. Assn. Bond Lawyers, Ohio Mcpl. Attys. Assn. (asst. sec.-treas.), Cuyahoga County Law Dirs. Assn., Am. Bar Assn., Ohio Bar Assn., Columbus Bar Assn., Greater Cleve. Bar Assn. Republican. Club: Athletic (Columbus). Home: 19101 Van Aken Blvd Apt 501 Shaker Heights OH 44122 Office: Calfee Halter & Griswold 1800 Central Nat Bank Bldg Cleveland OH 44114 *Quality, sensitivity and dedication are the only acceptable standards for a lawyer who represents public entities.*

GOTLIB, LORRAINE, lawyer; b. Toronto, Ont., Can., May 13, 1931; m. Christopher B. Paterson. B.A., U. Toronto, 1952; grad., Osgoode Hall. Bar: Ont. 1959, Named Queen's Counsel 1973. Partner firm Kingsmill, Jennings, Toronto; also mem. Bd. Trade Met., Toronto, mem. house com., 1977-79, mem. council, 1979-83; group seminar instr. Bar Admission Course, 1968-72; Mem. council Ont. Coll. Art, 1976-79. Recipient Jubilee medal, 1977. Mem. Canadian Bar Assn. (nat. exec. com. 1976-78, pres. Ont. br. 1983-84), County of York Law Assn., Women's Law Assn. Ont., Med.-Legal Soc. Toronto, Univ. Coll. Alumnae Assn., Kappa Beta Pi (nat. dir. 1968-72). Clubs: Royal Can. Yacht, Lawyers of Toronto, Empire of Can. (dir.). Address: Suite 4700 PO Box 124 1 First Canadian Pl Toronto ON Canada M5X 1G1

GOTLIEB, ALLAN E., Canadian ambassador; b. Winnipeg, Man., Can., Feb. 28, 1928; s. David Phillip and Sarah (Schiller) G.; m. Sondra Kaufman, Dec. 20, 1955; children: Rebecca, Marcus, Rachel. B.A., U. Calif., 1949; LL.B., Harvard U., 1954; M.A., B.C.L. (Vinerian Law scholar), Oxford U.; LL.D., U. Windsor, 1982. Bar: Eng. 1956. Fellow Wadham Coll. and univ. lectr. in law Oxford U., 1954-56; joined Can. Dept. External Affairs, 1957; 2d sec. Can. mission to UN, Geneva, 1960-62; 1st sec. Can. del. 18 Nation Disarmament Conf., 1962-64; head legal div. Dept. External Affairs, 1965-66; asst. under sec. for external affairs and legal adviser Can. Dept. State, 1967-68, dep. minister communications, 1968-73, dep. minister manpower and immigration, 1973-76; chmn. Can. Employment and Immigration Commn., 1976-77; under sec. Dept. External Affairs, 1977-81; Can. ambassador to U.S., Washington, 1981—; spl. lectr. Queen's U., 1965-66; vis. prof. polit. sci. Carleton U., 1966-71; adj. prof. internat. relations, 1975-78; vis. fellow All Souls Coll., Oxford, 1975-76; dir. Export Devel. Corp. Author: Disarmament and International Law, 1965, Canadian Treaty-Making, 1968; contbr. articles to profl. jours.; editor: Harvard Law Rev., 1950-51. Bd. govs. Internat. Devel. Research Centre; mem. Nat. Film Bd.; Can. mem. Permanent Ct. of Arbitration. Decorated officer Order of Can., 1983. Office: Embassy of Can 1746 Massachusetts Ave NW Washington DC 20036 *

GOTLIEB, CALVIN CARL, computer scientist, educator; b. Toronto, Ont., Can., Mar. 27, 1921; s. Israel and Jennie (Sherman) G.; m. Phyllis Fay Bloom, June 12, 1949; children: Leo, Margaret, Jane. B.A., U. Toronto, 1942, M.A., 1944, Ph.D., 1947; Dr. Math. (hon.), U. Waterloo, Can., 1968. Faculty U. Toronto, 1949—; dir. Inst. Computer Sci., 1962-70, chmn. dept. computer sci., 1964-67, prof. computer sci., 1962—; dir. York-Ryerson Computer Centre, Toronto, 1973-79, Data Use and Access Labs., Arlington, Va., 1972—; pres. C.C. Gotlieb Cons. Ltd., 1978—; cons. info. scis. to various govts., internat. orgns., indsl. cos., 1969—; McKay vis. prof. U. Calif., Berkeley, 1981; chmn. tech. com. 9 on relationship between computers and soc. Internat. Fedn. for Info. Processing, 1975-81. Author: (with J.N.P. Hume) High-Speed Data Processing, 1958, (with A. Borodin) Social Issues in Computing, 1973, (with L.R. Gotlieb) Data Types and Structures, 1978; editor, editor-in-chief, contbr. various Can., Netherlands, U.S. sci. jours. Recipient Silver Core award, 1974; NRC Can. research grantee, 1955—. Fellow Royal Soc. Can.; mem. Assn. Computing Machinery, Can. Info. Processing Soc., Brit. Computer Soc., Data for Devel. (Marseille, France). Jewish. Clubs: Faculty (U. Toronto); Nat. Yacht (Toronto). Home: 29 Ridgevale Dr Toronto ON M6A 1K9 Canada Office: Dept Computer Sci U Toronto Toronto ON M5S 1A7 Canada

GOTLIEB, PHYLLIS FAY BLOOM, author; b. Toronto, Ont., Can., May 25, 1926; d. Leo and Mary (Kates) Bloom; m. Calvin Gotlieb, June 12, 1949; children—Leo, Margaret, Jane. B.A., U. Toronto, 1948, M.A., 1950. Author: poetry Within The Zodiac, 1964, Ordinary, Moving, 1969, Doctor Umlaut's Earthly Kingdom, 1974, The Works, 1978; novels Sunburst, 1964; Why Should I Have All The Grief?, 1969, O Master Caliban!, 1976, A Judgement of Dragons, 1980, Emperor, Swords, Pentacles, 1982. Mem. Sci. Fiction Writers Am. Home: 29 Ridgevale Dr Toronto ON M6A 1K9 Canada

GOTO, SHIGERU, trading company executive; b. Kyoto, Japan, May 6, 1931; came to U.S., 1981; s. Kosaburo and Ieko (Adachi) G.; m. Yukiko Sugiyama, Oct. 23, 1954; children: Shigeyuki, Yasuyuki. B.A. in Econs., Keio U., Tokyo, 1954. Gen. mgr. electronics, elec. machinery div. C. Itho & Co., Ltd., Tokyo, 1954-69; exec. v.p. C. Itoh & Co. (Am.), Inc., N.Y.C., 1981-82, pres., 1983—; dir. C. Itoh & Co., Ltd., Tokyo. Clubs: Nippon; Board Room (N.Y.C.). Home: 425 E 58th St New York NY 10022 Office: C Itoh & Co (America) Inc 270 Park Ave New York NY 10017

GOTOFF, SAMUEL PETER, pediatrician; b. N.Y.C., Mar. 22, 1933; s. Arnold Isaac and Ruth (Harris) G.; m. Myra Lowenthal, July 1, 1956; children: Elizabeth, Robert, David. B.A., Amherst Coll., 1954; M.D., U. Rochester, 1958. Intern, resident in pediatrics Yale-New Haven Hosp., 1958-61; asst. prof. pediatrics U. Ill., Chgo., 1965-68, asso. prof., 1968-71, prof., 1971-73, acting chmn. dept. pediatrics, 1972-73; prof. pediatrics Pritzker Sch. Medicine, U. Chgo., 1973—, assoc. chmn. dept. pediatrics, 1981—; chmn. dept. pediatrics Michael Reese Hosp. and Med. Center, 1973—. Contbr. numerous articles to profl. jours. Served with USPHS, 1961-63. NIH grantee. Mem. Am. Acad. Pediatrics, Am. Pediatric Soc., Am. Assn. Immunologists, Central Soc. Clin. Investigation, AAAS, N.Y. Acad. Sci., Am. Soc. Microbiology. Home: 323 W Eugenie St Chicago IL 60614 Office: 2901 Ellis Ave Chicago IL 60616

GOTSCHLICH, EMIL CLAUS, physician, educator; b. Bangkok, Thailand, Jan. 17, 1935; came to U.S., 1950, naturalized, 1955; s. Emil Clemens and Magdalene (Holst) G.; m. Kathleen-Ann Haines, May 24, 1975; children—Emil Christofer, Hilda Christina, Emil Chandler. B.A., N.Y. U., 1955, M.D., 1959. Intern Bellevue Hosp., N.Y.C., 1959-60; mem. faculty Rockefeller U., N.Y.C., 1960—, prof. microbiology, 1978—, sr. physician, 1978—. Served as capt. M.C. U.S. Army, 1966-68. Decorated Army Commendation medal; recipient Squibb award Am. Soc. Infectious Disease, 1974; Lasker award Albert and Mary Lasker Found., 1978. Mem. Am. Assn. Immunologists, Assn. Am. Physicians, Am. Soc. for Clin. Investigation, Sigma Xi, Alpha Omega Alpha. Club: Peripatetic. Office: Rockefeller U 1230 York Ave New York NY 10021

GOTT, EDWIN HAYS, steel company executive; b. Pitts., Feb. 22, 1908; s. Leonard Hays and Isabel (Dalzell) G.; m. Mary Louise Carr, Oct. 6, 1934; children: Elizabeth C. Gott Byerly, Edwin H., Barbara D. Gott Martha. B.S. in Indsl. Engring., Lehigh U., 1929. With U.S. Steel Corp., 1937—, successively indsl. engr. Ohio Works, indsl. engr. Clairton Works, indsl. engr. Gary Steel Works, asst. div. supt. maintenance Gary Steel Works, asst. div. supt. Central Mills, asst. gen. supt. service depts., asst. gen. supt. South Works, Chgo., gen. supt. Youngstown Dist. Works, gen. mgr. operations-steel Youngstown Dist. Works, 1937-56, v.p. ops.-steel, 1956-58, v.p. prodn., steel producing divs., 1958-59, adminstrv. v.p. central operations, 1959, exec. v.p. prodn., 1959-67, pres., chief adminstrv. officer, 1967-68, chmn., chief exec. officer, 1969-73, dir., mem. exec., orgn. coms., 1973-80; dir. Internat. Husky, Inc.; past dir. Pitts. Baseball Club. Trustee Children's Hosp. Pitts., Lehigh U., Carnegie-Mellon U.; mem. adv. bd. Nat. Boy Scouts Am.; mem. exec. bd. Allegheny Trails council; chmn. Nat. Flag Founc.; past bd. dirs. Internat. Wilderness Leadership Found. Mem. Am. Iron and Steel Inst., Assn. Iron and Steel Engrs., Pa. Soc., Eastern States Blast Furnace and Coke Oven Assn., Western Pa. Engrs. Soc., Business Council. Clubs: Fox Chapel Golf, Duquesne (Pitts.); Longue Vue Country (Verona, Pa.); Royal Poinciana Golf (Fla.); Ottawa Gun, Rolling Rock, Pine Valley Golf, Naples Yacht. Home: 213 Hampton Rd Fox Chapel Pittsburgh PA 15215 Office: 600 Grant St Pittsburgh PA 15230

GOTT, VINCENT LYNN, physician; b. Wichita, Kans., Apr. 14, 1927; s. Henry Vivian and Helen (Lynn) G.; m. Iveagh Foreman, Sept. 4, 1954; children—Deborah Lynn, Kevin Douglas, Cameron Bradley. B.A., Wichita U., 1951; M.D., Yale, 1953. Intern U. Minn. Hosp., 1953-54; resident surgery U. Minn. Hosps., 1954-60; asst. prof. surgery U. Wis., 1960-65; asso. prof. surgery Johns Hopkins, 1965-68, prof., 1968—; cardiac surgeon in charge Johns Hopkins, Hosp., 1965—. Contbr. articles to profl. jours. Served with USNR, 1945-46. Recipient Hektoen gold medal A.M.A., 1957; John and Mary R. Markle scholar, 1962. Fellow A.C.S.; mem. Am. Surg. Assn., Soc. Univ. Surgeons, Am. Assn. Thoracic Surgery, Soc. Thoracic Surgeons, Soc. Vascular Surgeons, Am. Heart Assn. Co-developer Gott-Daggett artificial heart valve, 1963; developer graphite-benzalkonium-heparin coating for plastic surfaces. Home: 203 Kemble Rd Baltimore MD 21218

GOTTESMAN, CALLMAN, lawyer; b. N.Y.C., Mar. 27, 1909; s. Morris Louis and Bertha (Kurz) G.; m. Eleanor Gluckman, Aug. 2, 1964; children: Carol Siegel, Erika Bell, Barbara Bell. B.S., NYU, 1929; LL.B. cum laude, Harvard U., 1932. Bar: N.Y. 1933. Mem. firm Greenbaum, Wolff & Ernst, N.Y. C., 1933-41; asst. gen. counsel OPA, Washington, 1942-44; chief enforcement atty. (N.Y. Met. Office), 1945-46; mem. Shapiro & Gottesman, N.Y.C., 1948-53; partner Kugel, Berkeley & Gottesman, N.Y.C., 1953-68, Blumberg, Singer, Ross, Gottesman & Gordon, 1968—; dir., sec. Fairfield-Noble Corp., Roundabout Theatre Co., Presdl. Life Ins. Co. Pres., South Shore Jewish Community Council, 1948-52, Five Towns Am. Jewish Congress, 1949-53, South Shore chpt. ADA, 195-52; mem. exec. com. Am. Jewish Congress, 1968—; chmn. bd. Life Scis. Found. Mem. Assn. Bar City N.Y., Washington Sq. Coll. Alumni Assn. (pres. 1977-79). Democrat. Clubs: Woodmere (L.I.); City Athletic (N.Y.C.). Office: 245 Park Ave New York NY 10017

GOTTESMAN, DAVID SANFORD, company executive; b. N.Y.C. Apr. 16, 1926; s. Benjamin and Esther (Garfunkel) G.; m. Ruth Levy, Aug. 17, 1950; children: Robert, Alice, William. B.A., Trinity Coll., 1948; M.B.A., Harvard U., 1950. Ptnr. Hallgarten & Co., N.Y.C., 1950-64; mng. ptnr. First Manhattan Co., N.Y.C., 1964—; dir. Sun Chem. Corp., Eagle Star Ins. Co. Am. Trustee, chmn., fin. com. Community Service Soc., N.Y.; trustee Yeshiva U.; v.p., trustee Fedn. Jewish Philanthropies; mem. adv. council Columbia U. Sch. Gen. Studies. Served with AUS, 1943-46. Mem. N.Y. Soc. Security Analysts.

Clubs: Harmonie; Board Room (N.Y.C.). Office: First Manhattan Co 437 Madison Ave New York NY 10022

GOTTESMAN, FREDERICK IRVING, retired trade magazine editor, free-lance editor and writer; b. Boston, June 3, 1920; s. Joseph J. and Elizabeth (Goldblatt) G.; m. Charlotte Levine, June 20, 1943; children: Roberta Lynn, Alan Richard, Jon Stephen. Student, U. Chgo., 1943-45. Dir. publs. U. Chgo., 1945-47; asst. editor Berwyn (Ill.) Beacon, 1947-49; editor Levittown (N.Y.) Eagle, 1950-52; editor, pub. Suburban Herald, Huntington, N.Y., 1953-54; from copy editor to dir. copy desk Women's Wear Daily, N.Y.C., 1952-65, mng. editor, 1965-67; dir. corrs., then asst. dir. news service Fairchild Publs., N.Y.C., 1965-72; exec. editor, assoc. pub. Merchandising mag., N.Y.C., 1973-80, ret., 1980; free-lance editor, writer, 1980—. Democrat. Jewish. Home: 2020 Waltoffer Ave North Bellmore NY 11710

GOTTFREDSON, DON MARTIN, criminal justice educator, university dean; b. Sacramento, Sept. 25, 1926; s. Don Angus and Marion Dorothy (Williams) G.; m. Betty Jane Hunt, Oct. 9, 1946; children: Gary Don, Stephen David, Michael Ryan, Eric Bert, Ronald Lee. B.A., U. Calif.-Berkeley, 1951; M.A., Claremont Grad. Sch., 1955, Ph.D., 1959. Project dir. Inst. for Study Crime and Delinquency, Sacramento, 1962-66; dir. Nat. Council on Crime and Delinquency Research Ctr., Davis, Calif., 1965-73; prof. Sch. Criminal Justice, Rutgers U.-Newark, 1973—, dean, 1973—. Author: (with Wilkins and Hoffman) Guidelines for Parole and Sentencing, 1978, (with Gottfredson) Decisionmaking in Criminal Justice, 1980; exec. editor: Jour. Research in Crime and Delinquency, 1965-73; editor: Criminal Justice and Behavior, Newark, 1981—. Mem. bd. fellows Nat. Ctr. Juvenile Justice, Pitts., 1973—; mem. adv. bd. Nat. Inst. Justice, Washington, 1980; trustee N.J. Assn. on Corrections, Trenton, 1983. Served with U.S. Army, 1944-46. Recipient Outstanding Nat. Contbns. to Criminal Justice Adminstrn. award Am. Soc. Pub. Adminstrn., 1978. Mem. Am. Soc. Criminology (v.p. 1976-78, August Vollmer award 1982), Acad. Criminal Justice Scis. Democrat. Home: 12 Yorktown Ct Princeton Junction NJ 08550 Office: Sch Criminal Justice Rutgers U 15 Washington St Newark NJ 07102

GOTTFRIED, BRIAN EDWARD, tennis player; b. Balt., Jan. 27, 1952; m. Windy.; 1 son, Kevin. Student, Trinity U., San Antonio. Profl. tennis player, 1972—; formed doubles team with Raul Ramirez, 1974. Named All-Am. at Trinity U., 1971, 72. Mem. Davis Cup Team, 1976, 78; winner U.S. Men's Pro Doubles, 1975, Pro Indoor Doubles, 1973, 75, Clay Ct. Doubles, 1976, Italian Doubles, 1974, 75, 76, 77, French Doubles, 1975, 77, Japanese Doubles, 1975, Australian Indoor Doubles, 1975, Wimbledon Doubles, 1976, Spanish Doubles, 1976, S.African Doubles (with Sherwood Stewart), 1976; winner in singles Alan King Classic, 1973, Johannesburg, 1973, Portland, Oreg., 1974, Balt., 1974, 77, Dayton, 1974, Paris, 1976, 80, Vienna, 1977, 80, Basle Swiss Indoors, 1979, Surbitton, Eng., 1980, others, ranked among top 10 U.S. male tennis players by U.S. Tennis Assn. for 10th yr. Office: US Tennis Assn 51 E 42d St New York NY 10017 *

GOTTFRIED, BYRON STUART, educator; b. Detroit, May 24, 1934; s. Sidney and Faye (Fradkin) G.; m. Marcia Faye Singer, June 21, 1959; children—Sharon, Gail, Susan. B.S., Purdue U., 1956; M.S., U. Mich., 1958; Ph.D., Case-Western Res. U., 1962. Asso. engr. Westinghouse Electric Corp., Pitts., 1958-59, Lewis Research Center, NASA, Cleve., 1959-62; research engr. Gulf Research & Devel. Co., Pitts., 1962-65, supr., 1968-70; asst. prof. dept. mech. engring. Carnegie-Mellon U., Pitts., 1965-68; assoc. prof. dept. indsl. engring. U. Pitts., 1970-75, prof., dir. energy resources program, 1975-76, prof. indsl. engring., 1975—; cons. U.S. Dept. Interior Bur. Mines, Dept. Energy. Author: Programming with Fortran IV, 1972, 82, 84, (with Joel Weisman) Introduction to Optimization Theory, 1973, Data Processing, 1974, Programming with Basic, 1975, Introduction to Engineering Calculations, 1979, Elements of Stochastic Process Simulation, 1984, Programming with Pascal, 1984; contbr. articles to profl. jours. Served with Signal Corps AUS, 1958. Mem. Am. Inst. Indsl. Engrs., IEEE Computer Soc. Home: 129 Old Suffolk Dr Monroeville PA 15146 Office: U Pitts Pittsburgh PA 15261 *Technology, if used intelligently, can enhance our lives, but it cannot provide a substitute for basic human values.*

GOTTFRIED, KURT, physicist, educator; b. Vienna, Austria, May 17, 1929; came to U.S., 1952, naturalized, 1965; s. Salomon and Augusta (Werner) G.; m. Sorel B. Dickstein, June 26, 1955; children: David M., Laura S. B.Eng., McGill U., 1951, M.S., 1952; Ph.D., MIT, 1955. Jr. fellow Soc. Fellows, Harvard, 1955-58; research fellow Inst. Theoretical Physics, Copenhagen, 1958-59, Harvard, 1959-60, asst. prof. physics, 1960-64; asso. prof. physics Cornell U., Ithaca, N.Y., 1964-68, prof. physics, 1968—; Staff mem. European Orgn. for Nuclear Research, Geneva, Switzerland, 1970-73. Author: Quantum Mechanics, 1966. Fellow Am. Acad. Arts and Scis., Am. Phys. Soc. (chmn. div. particles and fields 1981); mem. Union Concerned Scientists (dir. 1978—). Address: Lab Nuclear Studies Cornell U Ithaca NY 14853

GOTTFRIED, LEON ALBERT, English language educator; b. Ames, Iowa, Nov. 6, 1925; s. Samuel and Louise G.; children: Laura, Ann. A.B., U. Ill., 1948, M.A., 1951, Ph.D. (Univ. fellow), 1958. Teaching asst. U. Ill., 1948-50; instr. English U. Conn., 1953-54, Washington U., St. Louis, 1954-58, asst. prof., 1958-63, asso. prof., 1963-69, prof., 1969-81, chmn. dept. art and archaeology, 1972-76, dean, 1976-78; prof., chmn. dept. English Purdue U., 1981—; Fulbright prof. U. Malaya, 1970-71. Author: Matthew Arnold and the Romantics, 1963; Contbr. articles to profl. jours. Trustee Mary Inst., 1977-80. Served with USNR, 1944-46; PTO. Am. Philos. Soc. grantee, 1966, 71. Mem. MLA, AAUP. Office: Dept English Purdue U West Lafayette IN 47907

GOTTIER, RICHARD CHALMERS, computer company executive; b. Columbus, O., Oct. 12, 1918; s. Chalmers M. and Grace (Eisnaugle) G.; m. Mary S. Hiatt, Nov. 13, 1965; children: Barbara, Diane, Richard Chalmers, Penny. B.S. in Bus. Adminstrn, Ohio State U., 1939; postgrad., Northwestern U. Grad. Sch. Bus., 1969. Spl. agt. FBI, Washington, 1940-51; with dept. materials mgmt. RCA, Indpls., 1951-59; dir. mfg. Magnavox Co., Ft. Wayne, Ind., 1959-70; sr. v.p. Control Data Corp., Mpls., 1970; chmn. Standard Komputen, Frankfort, Germany; pres. MSCF Inc., Mpls. Home: 4735 Sparrow Rd Minnetonka MN 55343 Office: 1660 S Hwy 100 Suite 146 Minneapolis MN 55416

GOTTLICH, ROBERT PHILIP, fast food executive; b. Panama City, C.Z., Apr. 2, 1926; s. Samuel and Ruth (Terwilliger) G.; m. Carole Ann Jones, Nov. 20, 1953; children: Rob, Peggy, Matt, Todd. B.S., Tex. A&M U. Sales rep. S.W. Drug Corp., San Antonio, 1961-67; sr. v.p., regional mgr. Church's Inc., San Antonio, 1967—. Served to col. USMC, 1943-63. Mem. Ch. fo Christ. Club: Rotary (fellow, dir. 1963-65). Home: 3010 Farmington Rd Vinings GA 30339 Office: 2036 Carroll Ave Chamblee GA 30341

GOTTLIEB, A(BRAHAM) ARTHUR, physician, immunologist; b. N.Y.C., Dec. 14, 1937; s. Jacob and Minnie (Pierson) G.; m. Marise Suss, June 8, 1958; children: Mindy Cheryl, Joanne Meredith. A.B., Columbia U., 1957; M.D., NYU, 1961. Intern Peter Bent Brigham Hosp., Boston, 1961, resident, 1962; clin. asso. NIH, 1963-65; spl. fellow in chemistry Harvard U., 1965-68, asst. prof. medicine, Boston, 1968-69; asso. prof. Waksman Inst. Microbiology, Rutgers U., New Brunswick, N.J., 1970-72, prof., 1973-75; prof. microbiology and immunology, chmn. dept. microbiology and immunology, prof. medicine Tulane U. Med. Sch., 1975—; mem. adv. panel Am. Bd. Med. Lab. Immunology; mem. breast cancer task force Nat. Cancer Inst., 1976-80; mem. sci. adv. bd. Cancer Assn. Greater New Orleans, 1979—; vis. prof. Walter and Eliza Hall Inst. Med. Research, Melbourne, Australia, 1979. Editorial bd.: Immunol. Communications, 19—, Internat. Research Communications Service Jour. Med. Sci, 1978—. Served with USPHS, 1963-65. Recipient Research Career Devel. award NIH, 1968-69, Frances Stone Burns award Am. Cancer Soc., 1968; Royal Soc. Medicine traveling fellow, 1974-77; NIH grantee, 1968-81; NSF grantee, 1970-72, 79; Research Corp. grantee, 1973-74. Fellow A.C.P., Am. Acad. Microbiology; mem. Am. Assn. Immunologists, Am. Soc. Clin. Investigation, Am. Soc. Biol. Chemists, Am. Assn. Cancer Research, Am. Chem. Soc., Am. Soc. Cell Biology, Reticuloendothelial Soc. (jour. editorial adv. bd. 1978-80), Soc. Exptl. Biology and Medicine, AAAS, Sigma Xi, Alpha Omega Alpha. Office: 1430 Tulane Ave New Orleans LA 70112

GOTTLIEB, ABRAHAM MITCHELL, physician, hosp. cons.; b. Chgo., Feb. 22, 1909; s. Michael and Frieda (Mantus) G.; m. Florence Handelman, May 23, 1934 (dec.); children—Joel David (dec.), Judith Ann; m. Mary Ashley, Mar. 22, 1975. B.S., U. Ill., 1930, M.D., 1934. Diplomate: Am. Bd. Internal Medicine. Mem. house staff Cook County Hosp., Chgo., 1933-35; staff physician Hines (Ill.) VA Hosp., 1937-38; internist VA Hosp., Tuscaloosa, Ala., 1938-39, chief cardiologist, Wood, Wis., 1939-42, chief cardiology, dir. profl. services, cons. internal medicine, Dearborn, Mich., 1946- 59, hosp. dir., Madison, Wis., 1959-68, Palo Alto, Calif., 1968-75, cons. internal medicine, 1975—; from instr. to asso. prof. medicine Wayne State U. Med. Sch., 1946-59; from asso. prof. to prof. medicine U. Wis. Med. Sch., 1959-68; prof. medicine Stanford Med. Sch., 1968—. Contbr. articles to profl. jours. Served as med. officer U.S. Army, 1935-37; served to col. USAAF, 1942-46. Decorated Bronze Star; D.S.M. Fellow A.C.P.; mem. AMA, Assn. Mil. Surgeons U.S., Am. Physicians Art Assn. (pres. 1971-72), Omicron Alpha Tau (nat. v.p. 1935), Phi Delta Epsilon. Home and Office: 101 Alma St Palo Alto CA 94301

GOTTLIEB, BERTRAM, indsl. engr., labor arbitrator; b. N.Y.C., Feb. 9, 1921; s. Samuel and Bessie (Halpern) G.; m. Phyllis Virginia Jacobson, Mar. 24, 1940; children—Richard Allan, Deborah Ann, Lisa Susan. B.S., Ill. Inst. Tech., 1949, M.S., 1950; postgrad., U. Wis., 1950-54. Registered profl. engr. Instr. econs. Ill. Inst. Tech., 1948-50; instr. indsl. engring. and labor relations U. Wis., 1950-54, 56-57; research prof. assigned to U. Philippines, U. Conn., 1954-56; indsl. engr. AFL-CIO, 1957-66, asst. dir. research, 1967-68; prof. bus. adminstrn. U. Iowa, 1966-67; dir. research Transp. Inst., Washington, 1968-74; Indsl. engring. cons., 1950-54, 56-57, 68—; Labor arbitrator Fed. Mediation and Conciliation Service and Am. Arbitration Assn.; mem. tech. adv. bd. U.S. Dept. Commerce, 1957-68; mem. prodn., tech. and growth com., wages and indsl. relations com. Dept. Labor, 1957-74; mem. central com. to standardize indsl. engring. terminology Am. Nat. Standards Inst., 1964—; investigator sex and race discrimination complaints in pvt. and govt. employment; expert witness fed. and state cts. and agys.; speaker, lectr. various univs., profl. socs., radio, TV. Contbr. articles to profl. jours., textbooks. Served with USAAF, 1943-46. Fellow Am. Inst. Indsl. Engrs. (editorial bd. 1960-72, nat. dir. div. indsl. and labor relations 1968-70, chpt. dir., mem. various coms.), Nat. Acad. Sci., Indsl. Relations Research Assn. (gov. 1966-68), Sigma Iota Epsilon. Address: 703 Hillsboro Dr Silver Spring MD 20902

GOTTLIEB, EDWARD, public relations and communications consultant; b. N.Y.C., June 24, 1910; s. Max B. and Sarah G.; m. Janet Laib, Apr. 30, 1983; children: Richard, Elizabeth Ann. B.S., L.I. U., 1932; postgrad., U. Goettingen (Ger.), 1932-33; postgrad. (Switzerland), U. Basel, 1934; M.S., U. Basel (Switzerland), 1934. Writer, reporter, editor INS, 1934-40; public relations account exec. Carl Byoir & Assos., 1940-42, 45-48; chmn., chief exec. officer Edward Gottlieb & Assos., Ltd., N.Y.C., 1948-76; chmn. subs. Hill & Knowlton, N.Y.C., 1976-78; partner Chester Burger & Co., Inc., N.Y.C., 1978-83; pres. Edward Gottlieb, Inc., 1983—; dir. Mpls. Moline Corp., 1957-62; pres. E.G.A. Internat., Inc., 1956—; cons. NASA, 1957-64; adj. prof. journalism NYU, 1979-81; public relations cons. New Rochelle (N.Y.) Bd. Edn., 1956-59; cons. Fedn. Jewish Philanthropies, 1964-72. Author: (with others) Ladies Day, 1939, Successful Publicity, 1966; contbr. articles to mags. Trustee Hosp. for Joint Diseases, Orthopedic Inst., 1968—; bd. dirs. N.Y. chpt. Am. Cancer Soc., 1974—; cons. Office of Mayor N.Y.C., 1974-75. Served with Office War Info. and U.S. Army, 1942-45; ETO. Decorated chevalier Merite Agricole, Economie Nationale, France; recipient citations SHAEF, 12th U.S. Army Group. Mem. Public Relations Soc. Am. (v.p. 1969-71), Internat. Public Relations Assn. Clubs: Lotos, Overseas Press.

GOTTLIEB, GIDON ALAIN GUY, legal educator; b. Paris, Dec. 9, 1932. LL.B. with honors, London Sch. Econs., 1954, Trinity Coll., Cambridge (Eng.) U., 1956; diploma in comparative law, Cambridge (Eng.) U., 1958; LL.M., Harvard U., 1957, J.S.D., 1962. Bar: Called to bar Lincoln Inn 1958. Lectr. govt. Dartmouth Coll., 1960-61; assoc. firm Shearman & Sterling, N.Y.C., 1962-65; mem. faculty N.Y. U. Law Sch., 1965-76; Leo Spitz prof. internat. law U. Chgo. Law Sch., 1976—; UN rep. Amnesty Internat., 1966-72; mem. founding com. World Assembly Human Rights, 1968; adv. bd. Internat. League Rights of Man; cons. in field. Author: The Logic of Choice: An Investigation of the Concepts of Rule and Rationality, 1968. Mem. U.S. Inst. Human Rights, Internat. Law Assn. (chmn. com. humanitarian law Am. chpt.), Am. Soc. Internat. Law., Council on Fgn. Relations. Club: Century Assn. (N.Y.C.). Office: U Chgo Law Sch 1111 E 60th St Chicago IL 60637 *

GOTTLIEB, JEROME, television production company executive; b. Bklyn., Sept. 4, 1942; s. Saul and Sylvia (Friedman) G.; m. Deborah Ann Capogrosso, Jan. 21, 1978; Benjamin, Jonathan. B.A., Hamilton Coll., 1964; J.D., NYU, 1970. Bar: N.Y. 1971. Atty. Screen Gems, N.Y.C., 1971-74; dir. bus. affairs Columbia Pictures TV, Burbank, Calif., 1974-76; bus. affairs exec. William Morris Agy., Beverly Hills, Calif., 1976-78; v.p. bus. affairs Viacom Prodns., Studio City, Calif., 1978-80, Universal TV, Universal City, Calif., 1980-81; exec. v.p. MGM/UA TV, Culver City, Calif., 1982—. Contbr. articles to profl. jours. Mem. Acad. TV Arts and Scis., Hollywood Radio and TV Soc. Democrat. Jewish. Office: MGM/UA Television 10202 W Washington Blvd Culver City CA 90230

GOTTLIEB, JERROLD HOWARD, advertising executive; b. N.Y.C., Aug. 25, 1946; s. Saul and Sylvia (Siegel) G.; m. June L. Brownstein, June 18, 1978; 1 son, Steven Andrew. B.A., Mich. State U., 1968; M.B.A., Am. U., 1969. Sales rep. Gen. Foods Corp., White Plains, N.Y., 1969-71; v.p., account mgr. J. Walter Thompson, N.Y.C., 1971-75, sr. v.p., 1980—; sr. product mgr. Gen. Foods Corp., White Plains, 1976-78; v.p., account mgr. Batten, Barton, Durstein & Osborn, N.Y.C., 1978-80. Founder Washington Saturday Coll., 1969; chmn. Am. U. campus, Washington, 1969. Jewish. Clubs: Anti Defamation League B'nai B'rith; Longshore (Westport, Conn.); Doral Squash. Home: 225 E 70th St New York NY 10021 Office: 466 Lexington Ave New York NY 10016

GOTTLIEB, JOSEPH AARON, investment banker; b. N.Y.C., June 16, 1928; s. Arthur A. and Beatrice (Sipkin) G.; m. Lois Joan Glass, June 17, 1956; children: Alison B., Jonathan A. B.S., NYU, 1950; LL.B.l, Bklyn. Law Sch., 1955. Bar: N.Y. Mng. dir. Lehman Bros. & Co. Inc., N.Y.C., 1975; mgr. div. margin N.Y. Stock Exchange Inc., N.Y.C., 1955-63; with Abraham & Co., N.Y.C., 1963-75, gen. ptnr., 1969-75, sr. v.p., sec., 1972-75; exec. v.p. Lewco Securities Inc., N.Y.C., 1975; with Bear, Stearns & Co., N.Y.C., 1975—, gen. ptnr., 1981—; dir. Options Clearing Corp., Chgo.; mem. N.Y. Stock Exchange Arbitration Bd., 1983, N.Y. Stock Exchange Credit Rev. Com., 1983; mem. hearing panel N.Y. Stock Exchange Inc., N.Y.C., 1977—. Com. chmn. Cub Scouts, Ardsley, N.Y., 1974-75; mgr. Little League, Ardsley, 1974-80. Served with U.S. Army, 1950-52. Mem. Nat. Assn. Security Dealers (arbitration panel 1974—), Nat. Assn. Security Dealers (capital and margin com. 1981), Securities Industry Assn. (corr. sec. legal and compliance div. 1964-65, exec. com. credit div. 1979-82). Republican. Lodge: Masons (master 1961-62). Home: 28 Sherbrooke Rd Hartsdale NY 10530 Office: Bear Stearns & Co 55 Water St New York NY 10041

GOTTLIEB, LEONARD SOLOMON, pathology educator; b. Boston, May 26, 1927; s. Julius and Jeanette (Miller) G.; m. Dorothy Helen Apt, Mar. 23, 1952; children: Julie Ann Gottlieb Texeira, William Apt, Andrew Richard. A.B., Bowdoin Coll., 1946; M.D., Tufts U., 1950; M.P.H., Harvard U., 1969. Diplomate: Am. Bd. Anatomic Pathology. Intern and resident in pathology Boston City Hosp., 1950-55; asst. chief pathology U.S. Naval Hosp., Chelsea, Mass., 1955-57; assoc. pathologist Mallory Inst. Pathology, Boston, 1957-66, assoc. dir., 1966-72, dir., 1972—; prof. pathology Boston U. Sch. Medicine, 1970—, chmn. dept., 1980—; dir. Mallory Inst. Pathology Found., 1980—; lectr. Harvard U., 1963—. Contbr. over 100 articles on exptl. and human gastrointestinal and liver diseases. Served to lt. M.C. USNR, 1955-57; to lt. comdr., 1960-63. James Bowdoin scholar, 1945. Mem. Am. Soc. Exptl. Pathology, Am. Assn. Study of Liver Disease, Internat. Acad. Pathology, Am. Soc. Cell Biology, Am. Gastroent. Assn., New Eng. Soc. Pathologists, Am. Soc. Clin. Pathology, Mass. Soc. Pathology, Coll. Am. Pathologists, Am. Inst. Nutrition. Home: 120 Willard Rd Brookline MA 02146 Office: 784 Massachusetts Ave Boston MA 02118

GOTTLIEB, MORTON EDGAR, theatrical and film producer; b. Bklyn., May 2, 1921; s. Joseph William and Hilda (Newman) G. B.A., Yale U., 1941. Asst. press rep. Theatre Inc., N.Y.C., 1945, bus. mgr., 1946; gen. mgr. Cape Playhouse, Dennis, Mass., 1947-48, New Stages, N.Y.C., 1947-48; mgr. to Robert Morley during Australian prodn., Theatre Royal, Sydney, 1949; gen. mgr. Gilbert Miller Prodns. and Henry Miller's Theatre, N.Y.C., 1948-53; guest lectr. Emerson Coll., Yale U., Columbia U., Northwestern U., Queens Coll., Harvard U., Wesleyan U.; treas. Friends of Theatre and Music Collection, Mus. City N.Y., 1966—. Singer: charity show Go Home and Tell Your Mother, Bklyn. Acad. Music, 1928; producer, Broadway, London shows, 1954-62; gen. mgr.: Sail Away, 1961, The Affair, 1962, The Hollow Crown, 1963; co-producer: (with Helen Bonfils) Enter Laughing, 1963, Chips With Everything, 1963, The White House, 1964, The Killing of Sister George, 1966, The Promise, 1967, Lovers, 1968, We Bombed in New Haven, 1968, The Mundy Scheme, 1969, Sleuth, 1970; producer: films Sleuth, 1972, Same Time Next Year, 1978; plays Veronica's Room, 1973, Same Time Next Year, 1975, Tribute, 1978, Faith Healer, 1979, Romantic Comedy, 1979; contbr. articles to popular mags. Mem. League N.Y. Theatres (treas.). Clubs: Yale; Players. (N.Y.C.). Home: Warren CT 06754 Office: 165 W 46th St New York NY 10036 *My early life was spent dreaming about some day working in the Broadway Theatre, and the rest of my life has been spent living out my youthful fantasies on Broadway. Whether the times have been Ups or Downs, they've all been worth while — and the only way I want to live.*

GOTTLIEB, PAUL, publishing company executive; b. N.Y.C., Jan. 16, 1935; s. Vitaly Matthew and Liza (Rabinowitz) G.; m. Linda Ellen Salzman, June 19, 1960; children: Nicholas, Andrew. B.A., Swarthmore Coll., 1956. Lit. agt. William Morris Agy., N.Y.C., 1956-57, 59-60; asst. to pres. Omni Products Corp., N.Y.C., 1960-62; with Am. Heritage Pub. Co. Inc., N.Y.C., 1962-75, pres., 1970-75; chmn. bd. Fulfillment Corp. Am.; pres. Paul Gottlieb Assos., Inc., 1975—, Thames and Hudson Inc., 1977-79; pres., pub., editor-in-chief Harry N. Abrams, Inc., N.Y.C., 1980—; dir. Tanya Corp.; pub. cons., 1967. Guide U.S. exhbns., Moscow, 1959, 61; Vice chmn. E. Harlem Coll. and Career Counseling Program, 1971-74; Trustee Museum Modern Art, Dalton Sch. Mem. Assn. Am. Pubs., Am. Inst. Graphic Arts (dir.). Clubs: Coffee House, Century Assn. (N.Y.C.). Home: 211 Central Park W New York NY 10024 Office: 100 Fifth Ave New York NY 10011

GOTTLIEB, ROBERT ADAMS, publisher; b. N.Y.C., Apr. 29, 1931; s. Charles and Martha (Keen) G.; m. Maria Tucci, Apr. 26, 1969; children—Roger, Elizabeth, Nicholas. B.A., Columbia, 1952; postgrad., Cambridge (Eng.) U., 1952-54. Editor-in-chief, v.p. Simon & Schuster, 1955-68; editor-in-chief Alfred A Knopf, Inc., N.Y.C., 1968—, exec. v.p., 1968-73, pres., 1973—. Bd. dirs. N.Y.C. Ballet. Mem. Phi Beta Kappa. Office: 201 E 50th St New York NY 10022

GOTTLIEB, SHELDON FRED, biologist, educator; b. Bronx, N.Y., Dec. 22, 1932; s. Elias and Dorothy (Gerstenfeld) G.; m. Eda Judith Robin Held, Aug. 25, 1956; children: Stephen Eric, Pamela Lynn, Glenn Ira, William Scott. B.A., Bklyn. Coll., 1953; M.S., U. Mass., 1956; Ph.D. (teaching fellow), U. Tex. Med. Br., 1959. Research physiologist Linde div. Union Carbide Corp., Tonawanda, N.Y., 1959-64; asst. prof. physiology and anesthesiology Jefferson Med. Coll., Phila., 1964-68; prof. biol. scis. Ind. U.-Purdue U., Fort Wayne, Ind., 1968-80; dean (Grad. Sch.); dir. reserach U.S. Ala., Mobile, 1980—; cons. Edn. Devel. Center, Inc., 1976—, hyperbaric unit, Brooks AFB, San Antonio, 1975—, Gorsuch Scarisbrick publishers, 1978-80; mem. Council Grad. Deans, Ala. Commn. Higher Edn., 1980—, exec. bd., 1981—; guest speaker various radio and TV programs, 1969—, guest lectr. various civic, ednl., religious and profl. orgns., 1968—. Contbr. articles to sci. jours. Chmn. com. troop 491 Boy Scouts Am., 1969-70; judge Sci. Fair, Fort Wayne Community Schs., 1969-75, 77-79; mem. Ind. State Bd. advs., Anti-Defamation League B'nai B'rith, 1968-80, Jewish Community Relations Council Fort Wayne, 1969-80; pres. B'nai Jacob Synagogue, 1972, Tamarack Homeowners Assn., 1970-71; mem. Coalition for Environment, Fort Wayne, 1970-80, pres., 1970-71; mem. NE area adv. council No. Ind. Health Systems Agy., 1976-80; bd. dirs. Miss.-Ala. Sea Grant Consortium, 1980—, vice chmn., 1981-82, chmn., 1982-83; co-chmn. Mobile Anti-Defamation League, 1981-82, v.p., 1982-83. Served with U.S. Army, 1954-56. Eli Lilly Found. grantee, 1968; NIH grantee, 1968; Hoffman La Roche grantee, 1977. Mem. Am. Inst. Biol. Scis., Am. Physiol. Soc., Am. Soc. Microbiology, Soc. Gen. Physiologists, Fedn. Am. Socs. for Explt. Biology (nat. corr. 1976—), Undersea Med. Soc. (pres. elect Gulf Coast chpt. 1983-84), AAAS, Aerospace Med. Assn., N.Y. Acad. Scis., Izaak Walton League Am., Am. Heart Assn. (dir. Allen County br. 1969-80, pres. N.E. Ind. chpt. 1971-79, pres. 1974, dir. Ind. affiliate 1974-80, dir. Mobile County 1980—), Sigma Xi. (pres. elect chpt. 1983-84). Home: 8213 Tahoe Dr Mobile AL 36609 Office: 211 Instructional Lab Bldg U

South Alabama Mobile AL 36688 *I learned that only repayment in kind is proper recompense for the assistance extended to me when I was pursuing my education; i.e., do for other young struggling and promising students what someone did for me. Further, strive for excellence and do not permit nonsense, ignorance, and solecism to prevail.*

GOTTMANN, JEAN, geographer, educator; b. Kharkov, Russia, Oct. 10, 1915; s. Elie and Sonia (Ettinger) G.; m. Bernice Adelson, Aug. 11, 1957. Bacc. Lettres, U. Paris, 1932, D. Et. Sup. in History and Geography, 1934, Docteur es Lettres, 1970; LL.D., U. Wis., 1968; M.A, Oxford U., 1968; D.Sc., So. Ill. U., 1969. Asst. dept. geography Sorbonne, Paris, 1937-40; several times mem. Inst. Advanced Study, Princeton, N.J., 1942-65; cons. Bd. Econ. Warfare, FEA, 1942-44; instr. Princeton U., 1943; lectr., assoc., then assoc. prof. Johns Hopkins U., 1943-48; adviser French Ministry Nat. Economy, Paris, 1945-46; dir. studies and research, dept. social affairs UN, N.Y.C., 1946-47; research assoc. Conseil National de la Rêcherche Scientifique, Paris, 1948-51; prof. Institut d'Etudes Politiques, U. Paris, 1948-60, Ecole des Hautes Etudes, Paris, 1960-83; prof. geography Oxford (Eng.) U., 1968—; research dir. study of megalopolis Twentieth Century Fund, N.Y.C., 1956-61; vis. prof. Columbia U., 1949, 56, U. Geneva, 1950, U. Durham, Eng., 1951, Hebrew U., Jerusalem, 1956, 79, 83, U. Pitts., 1962, So. Ill. U., 1964, Laval U., 1964, U. Calif., Berkeley, 1966, 79, U. Wis.-Milw., 1968, 79, U. Va., 1971, U. Hong Kong, 1973, Brandeis U., 1977, U. B.C., 1981, U. Rome, 1981, U. Tsukuba, Japan, 1982; first Elkins prof. U. Md., 1982; fellow Hertford Coll., Oxford, 1968—. Author: A Geography of Europe, 1950, Virginia at Midcentury, 1955, Megalopolis, 1961, The Significance of Territory, 1973; editor: Centre and Periphery, 1980. Chmn. commn. on regional planning Internat. Geog. Union, 1949-52; Trustee Research Group European Migration Problems, The Hague, Netherlands; bd. govs. U. Haifa (Israel), Institut d'Etudes Americaines, Paris, 1966-80; bd. mgmt. Town Planning Rev., Liverpool, Vaughan Cornish Bequest, Oxford, 1970-82. Recipient Charles P. Daly medal Am. Geog. Soc., 1964; Bonaparte-Wyse award Paris Geog. Soc., 1962; Keys to City of Yokohama, Japan; decorated chevalier Légion d'Honneur Palmes Académiques France. Fellow Royal Geog. Soc. (London) (recipient Victoria medal 1980, v.p. 1981—), Brit. Acad.; mem. World Soc. for Ekistics (pres. 1971-73), Am. Geog. Soc. (hon.), Assn. Am. Geographers, Inst. Brit. Geographers, Assn. de Géographes Français, Assn. Française de Science Politique, Royal Netherlands Geog. Soc. (hon.), Am. Acad. Arts and Scis. (fgn. hon.), Societa Geografica Italiana (hon.). Home: 19 Belsyre Ct Oxford England

GOTTO, ANTONIO MARION, JR., physician, educator; b. Nashville, Oct. 10, 1935; s. Antonio M. and Reather (Gray) G.; m. Anita Louise Safford, July 21, 1959; children: Jennifer, Gillian, Teresa. B.A. magna cum laude, Vanderbilt U., 1957, M.D., 1965; D. Phil., Oxford (Eng.) U., 1961; LL.D. (hon.), Abilene Christian U., 1979. Diplomate: Am. Bd. Internal Medicine. Intern Mass. Gen. Hosp., Boston, 1965-66, resident, 1966-67; practice medicine specializing in internal medicine, 1967—; head molecular disease br. Nat. Heart and Lung Inst. NIH, Bethesda, Md., 1969-71; dir. and prin. investigator Lipid Research Clinic, Houston, 1971—; prof. medicine, chief div. artherosclerosis and lipoprotein research Baylor Coll. Medicine, Houston, Tex., 1971—, J.S. Abercrombie prof., 1976—; sci. dir. Meth. Hosp. and Baylor Nat. Research and Demonstration Center, 1974—, Bob and Vivian Smith prof., physician in chief internal medicine ser., 1977—; research scholar Am. Cancer Soc., 1963-65; hon. guest lectr. various med. socs., schs. and hosps., 1972—; mem. nat. diabetes adv. bd. HEW (now HHS), 1977—; mem. steering com. Italian-Am. com. on cardiovascular disease NIH, 1977—. Author: (with Michael E. DeBakey) The Living Heart, 1977, The Living Heart Diet, 1984; contbr. articles on biochem. and cardiovascular research to profl. publs.; editorial bd.: Jour. Biol. Chemistry, 1976-81, Advances in Lipid Research, 1974-79, Am. Heart Jour, 1980—, Arteriosclerosis, 1981—, Circulation Research, 1974-79, Cardiovascular Research Center Bull, 1972—; editor: Atherosclerosis Revs. Series, 1975—. Mem. sci. adv. bd. Fondation Cardiologue Princesse Lillian, Brussels, Belgium, 1974—. Served with USPHS, 1967-69. Recipient Albert Weinstein award, 1965, Laurea ad Honorem U. Bologna; John A. Hartford Found. grantee, 1971-75. Fellow Am. Coll. Cardiology; mem. Am., So. socs. clin. investigation, Internat. Soc. of Atherosclerosis (Disting. Service award), Am. Soc. Biol. Chemists, Am. Diabetes Assn., Am. Heart Assn. (pres. 1983-84), Am. Assn. of Rhodes Scholars, Am. Longevity Assn., Alpha Omega Alpha. Mem. Ch. of Christ. Club: River Oaks Country. Home: 3439 Piping Rock Rd Houston TX 77027 Office: Dept Medicine Baylor Coll of Medicine and Methodist Hosp Mail Sta A-601 6565 Fannin St Houston TX 77030

GOTTSCHALK, ALEXANDER, radiologist, diagnostic radiology educator; b. Chgo., Mar. 23, 1932; s. LouisR. and Fruma (Kasden) G.; m. Jane Rosenbloom, Aug. 13, 1960; children: Rand, Karen, Amy. B.A. magna cum laude, Harvard U., 1954; M.D., Washington U., St. Louis, 1958. Diplomate: Am. Bd. Radiology, Am. Bd. Nuclear Medicine. Intern U. Ill. Research and Edn. Hosps., Chgo., 1958-59; resident U. Chgo., 1959-62, asst. prof., 1964-66, assoc. prof., 1966-68, prof. radiology, 1968-74, chmn. dept. radiology, 1971-72; research assoc. Donner Lab., Lawrence Radiol. Lab., Calif.; dir. Frnklin McLean Meml. Research Hosp., 1962-64; prof. and dir. nuclear medicine Sch. Medicine Yale U., New Haven, 1974-77, acting chmn. radiology, 1980-81; vice-chmn. radiology Sch. Medicine Yfale U., New Haven, 1977—. Contbr. chpts. to books, articles to publs. in field. Fleischner lectr., 1983. Fellow Am. Coll. Radiology; mem. Radiol. Soc. N.Am. (ed v.p. 1977), Assn. Univ. Radiologists (pres. 1971), Soc. Nuclear Medicine (pres. 1974-75), Am. Roentgen Ray Soc., Fleischner Soc. (treas. 1978-83). Home: 230 Six Rod Hwy Hamden CT 06518 Office: yale-New haven Med Center 333 Cedar St New Haven CT 06510

GOTTSCHALK, ALFRED, college president; b. Oberwesel, Germany, Mar. 7, 1930; came to U.S., 1939, naturalized, 1945; s. Max and Erna (Trum-Gerson) G.; m. Deanna Zeff Frank, 1978; children by previous marriage: Marc Hillel, Rachel Lisa. A.B., Bklyn. Coll., 1952; B.H.Lit., Hebrew Union Coll.-Jewish Inst. Religion, 1957, M.A. with honors, 1957, LL.D., 1976; Ph.D., U. So. Calif., 1965, S.T.D. (hon.), 1968, D.H.L., 1971; LL.D. (hon.), U. Judaism, 1976, D.Litt., Dropsie U., 1974, D.H.L., U. Cin., D.Religious Edn., Loyola-Marymount U., 1977, LL.D., Xavier U., 1981, Litt.D., St. Thomas Inst.; hon. fellow, Hebrew U. Jerusalem. Rabbi, 1957; mem. faculty, adminstr. Hebrew Union Coll.-Jewish Inst. Religion, Los Angeles, 1957—, prof. Bible and Jewish religious thought, 1965—, pres. coll., 1971—; Mem. interreligious inst. Loyola U., Los Angeles, 1965—. Author: Your Future as a Rabbi-A Calling that Counts, 1967, The Future of Human Community, 1967, The Man Must be the Message, 1968, Jewish Ecumenism and Jewish Survival, 1968, Ahad Ha-Am, Maimonides and Spinoza, 1969, Ahad Ha-Am as Bible Critic, 1971, A Jubilee of the Spirit, 1972, Israel and the Diaspora: A New Look, 1974, Limits of Ecumenicity, 1979, Israel and Reform Judaism: A Zionist Perspective, 1979, Ahad Ha-Am and Leopold Zinz: Two Perspectives on the Wissenschaft Des Judentums, 1980, Hebrew Union College and Its Impact on World Progressive Judaism, 1980, Diaspora Zionism: Achievements and Problems, 1980, 1980, What Ecumenism Means to a Jew, 1981, A Laudatio for Gershom G. Scholem, 1981, Introduction: Religion in a Post-Holocaust World, 1982, Tribute to Judaism, 1982, Some Jewish Perspectives on Ecumenism, 1982, Problematics in the Future of American Jewish Community, 1982, Introduction to The American Synagogue in the Nineteenth Century, 1982, A Strategy for Non-Orthodox Judaism in Israel, Our Problems and Our Future: Jews and America, 1983; translator: From the Kingdom of Night to the Kingdom of God: Jewish Christian Relations and the Search for Religious Authenticity after the Holocaust, 1983, Hesed in the Bible, 1967; Contbr. to: Studies in Jewish Bibliography, History, and Literature, 1971, The Yom Kippur War: Israel and the Jewish People, 1974, The Image of Man in Genesis and the Ancient Near East, 1976, The Public Function of the Jewish Scholar, 1978, The Reform Movement and Israel: A New Perspective, 1978, also numerous articles to profl. publs. Mem. Mayor's Community Devel. Adv. Com., Los Angeles, 1965—, Pres.'s Com. on Equal Employment Opportunity, 1964—, Gov.'s Poverty Support Corps Program, 1964-66, Community Redevel. Agy. Adv. Bd., 1965—, Pres.'s Commn. on Holocaust, 1979, U.S. Holocaust Meml. Council, 1980, Pres.'s Seminar; co-chmn. exec. com. U.S. Holocaust Meml. Council, 1980; chmn. N.Am. adv. com. Internat. Center Univ. Teaching of Jewish Civilization, 1982; trustee Cin. United Appeal, 1982, Am. Sch. Oriental Research, 1982; mem. Pres.'s Council Near Eastern Studies N.Y.U., 1983. Bet Ha-Nasi State Dept. research grantee, 1963; Guggenheim fellow, 1967, 69; recipient award for contbns. to edn. Los Angeles City Council, 1968, 71; Myrtle Wreath award Hadassah, 1977; Brandeis award, 1977; Nat. Brotherhood award NCCJ, 1979; Alfred Gottschalk Chair in Jewish Communal Service Hebrew Union Coll.; Gottschalk Dept. Judaica named in his honor; Kfar Silver, Israel, 1979. Mem. Albright Inst. Jerusalem (exec. com.), Union Am. Hebrew Congregations and Central Conf. Am-Rabbis (exec. com.), AAUP, NEA, Soc. Study Religion, Am. Acad. Religion, Soc-Bibl. Lit and Exegesis, Internat. Conf. Jewish Communal Service, Israel Exploration Soc., So. Calif. Assn. Liberal Rabbis (past pres.), So. Calif. Jewish Hist. Soc. (hon. pres.), World Union Jewish Studies, Synagogue Council Am. (inst. research and planning), Am. Jewish Com. (exec. com.), World Union Progressive Judaism (v.p.). Home: 17 Belsaw Pl Cincinnati OH 45220 *I value the need for the individual to feel unique and for the collective to remain hospitable to diversity. I believe in unity without uniformity and in man's capacity to redeem himself.*

GOTTSCHALK, CARL WILLIAM, physician, educator; b. Salem, Va., Apr. 28, 1922; s. Carl and Lula (Helbig) G.; m. Helen Marie Scott, Nov. 22, 1947; children—Carl S., Walter P., Karen E. B.S., Roanoke Coll., 1942, Sc.D., 1966; M.D., U. Va., 1945. Intern, asst. resident, resident in medicine Mass. Gen. Hosp., Boston, 1945-52; research fellow physiology Harvard, 1948-50; fellow U. N.C. Med. Sch., Chapel Hill, 1952-53, faculty, 1953—, Kenan prof. medicine and physiology, 1969—; established investigator Am. Heart Assn., 1957-61, career investigator, 1961; Bowditch lectr., 1960, Harvey lectr., 1962; Mem. physiology study sect. NIH, 1961-65; mem. research career award com. Nat. Inst. Gen. Med. Scis., 1965-69, mem. physiology tng. com., 1970-73, mem. med. scientist tng. com., 1973; chmn. com. chronic kidney disease Bur. Budget, 1966-67; adv. com. biol. and med. scis. NSF, 1967-69, vice chmn., 1968, chmn., 1969; mem. Inst. Medicine of Nat. Acad. Scis., Nat. Adv. Gen. Med. Scis. Council, 1977-80, Nat. Arthritis, Diabetes and Digestive and Kidney Diseases Adv. Council, 1982—. Author books and papers on physiology of kidney. Mem. adv. com. Burroughs Wellcome Fund for Clin. Pharmacology, 1980—; Pres. Children's Theatre N.C., 1967-68. Served to capt., M.C. AUS, 1946-48. Recipient N.C. award, 1967, Modern Medicine Distinguished Achievement award, 1966, Horsley Meml. prize U. Va., 1956, Homer W. Smith award N.Y. Heart Assn., 1970, David Hume award Nat. Kidney Found., 1976, O. Max Gardner award U. N.C., 1978. Mem. Assn. Am. Physicians, Am. Physiol. Soc., Am. Soc. Clin. Investigation, Am. Clin. and Climatol. Assn., Soc. Exptl. Biology and Medicine, A.C.P., AAUP (council 1970-73), Nat. Acad. Scis., Am. Soc. Nephrology (council 1971-77, pres. 1975-76), Am. Acad. Arts and Scis., Phi Beta Kappa, Sigma Xi. Home: 1300 Mason Farm Rd Chapel Hill NC 27514

GOTTSCHALK, CHARLES MAX, United Nations administrator; b. Bochum, Germany, Feb. 2, 1928; emigrated to U.S., 1941, naturalized, 1949; s. Josef and Elsbeth (Ermeler) G.; m. Marianne Ida Besser, Dec. 24, 1948; children: Diane Linda, Leslie Anne. B.E.S. in Physics, Cleve. State U., 1950; M.A., Pa. State U., 1951; M.S. in L.S, Catholic U., 1966. Research analyst Library of Congress, 1951-54, phys. sci. adminstr., head reference sect., sci. and tech. div., 1956-62, chief stack and reader div., 1962, head systems identification and analysis sect., 1962-63; instrumentation physicist Nat. Bur. Standards, 1954-56; information systems specialist AEC, 1963-66, dir. libraries, 1966-69; sr. officer Internat. Atomic Energy Agy., Vienna, Austria, 1969-73, Energy Research and Devel. Adminstrn., Washington, 1973-77, Dept. Energy, 1977-79; sr. ofcl. UNESCO, Paris, 1979—; Lectr. Dept. Agr. Grad. Sch., 1964—; cons. Arctic Inst. N.Am., 1954-59; research asst. Ohio State U., 1958-59; exec. sec. operating com. Fed. Council Sci. and Tech. Com. on Sci. and Tech. Information, 1965, exec. sec. panel edn. and tng., 1965-66, mem. panel information scis. and tech., 1966—, mem. nuclear cross sect. adv. group, 1965—. Author articles, monographs. Served with AUS, 1946-47; Served with USMCR, 1947-49. NSF grantee, 1961-62. Mem. Am. Nuclear Soc., Am. Phys. Soc., A.A.A.S., Am. Soc. Metals, Mensa, Beta Phi Mu. Office: UNESCO SC/TER Paris F-75700 France

GOTTSCHALK, JOHN SIMISON, assn. exec.; b. Berne, Ind., Sept. 27, 1912; s. Thurman Arthur and Nellie Louise (Simison) G.; m. Edith E. Liechty, Apr. 17, 1937; children—Sara Nell (Mrs. George W. Davis VI), Thomas Andrew. A.B. in Biology, Earlham Coll., 1934, LL.D., 1966; M.A. in Zoology, Ind. U., 1943. With Ind. Dept. Conservation, 1930-41, supt. fisheries, 1937-41; with U.S. Fish and Wildlife Service, 1945—; chief div. fisheries Bur. Sport Fisheries and Wildlife, 1957-59; dir. N.E. region, Boston, 1959-64, Washington, 1964-70; asst. to dir. Nat. Marine Fisheries Service, Dept. Commerce, 1970-73; exec. v.p. Internat. Assn. Fish and Wildlife Agys., 1973-79, legis. counsel, 1979-81, counsel, 1981—. Recipient Nash Conservation award Am. Motor Co., 1955; Distinguished Service award U.S. Dept. Interior, 1971; Seth Gordon award Internat. Assn. Fish and Wildlife Agys., 1975. Mem. Am. Fisheries Soc. (v.p. 1941, 62-63, pres. 1963-64), Wildlife Soc. (past v.p., Leopold medal 1976), Sigma Xi. Home: 4664 34th St N Arlington VA 22207 Office: 1412 16th St NW Washington DC 20036

GOTTSCHALK, LOUIS AUGUST, psychiatrist, psychoanalyst; b. St. Louis, Aug. 26, 1916; s. Max W. and Kelmie (Mutrux);; s. Max W. and Kelmie (Gottschalk); m. Helen Reller, July 24, 1944; children—Guy H., Claire A., Louise H., Susan E. A.B., Washington U., St. Louis, 1940, M.D., 1943. Asst. in neuropsychiatry Washington U. Sch. Medicine, 1944-46; commd. asst. surgeon USPHS, 1946, advanced through grades to med. dir., 1979; instr. psychiatry S.W. Med. Coll., Dallas, 1947-48; research psychiatrist NIMH, Bethesda, Md., 1950-53; coordinator research, research prof. psychiatry U. Cin. Coll. Medicine, 1953-67; attending psychiatrist Cin. Gen. Hosp., 1953-67; faculty Inst. Psychoanalysis, Chgo., 1957-67, So. Calif. Psychiat. Inst., Los Angeles, 1970—; chmn. research com. Hamilton County (Ohio) Diagnostic Center, 1958-67; prof. psychiatry, social sci. and social ecology, dept. psychiatry and human behavior U. Calif. - Irvine Coll. Medicine, 1967—, chmn. dept., 1967-78; also program dir. psychiat. residency tng.; dir. psychiat. services U. Calif. - Irvine Med. Center, 1967-78, dir. cons. and liaison program, 1978—, sci. co-dir., 1978—; Mem. clin. psychopharmacology study sect. NIMH, 1968-71; mem. research rev. com. Nat. Inst. Drug Abuse, 1973-77, Mental Health Study Center, 1978—. Author: (with G. C. Gleser) The Measurement of Psychological States through the Content Analysis of Verbal Behavior, 1969, How to Understand and Analyze Your Own Dreams, 1975, Greek edit., 1978, Spanish edit., 1981; Editor: Comparative Psycholinguistic Analysis of Two Psychotherapeutic Interviews, 1961, (with A. H. Auerbach) Methods of Research in Psychotherapy, 1966, (with S. Merlis) Pharmacokinetics of Psychoactive Drugs: Blood Levels and Clinical Responses, 1976, Pharmacokinetics of Psychoactive Drugs: Further Studies, 1979, The Content Analysis of Verbal Behavior: Further Studies, 1979, (with F.L. McGuire and others) Drug Abuse Deaths in Nine Cities: A Survey Report, 1980, (with R. Craveny) Toxicological and Pathalogical Studies on Psychoactive Drug-Involved Deaths, 1980; Editorial bd.: Psychosomatic Medicine, 1960-70, Psychiatry, 1967—, Am. Jour. Psychotherapy, 1975; others.; Contbr. numerous articles to tech. lit. Recipient Franz Alexander Essay prize So. Calif. Psychoanalytic Inst., Los Angeles, 1973; Disting. Research award U. Calif. Irvine Alumni Assn., 1974. Fellow AAAS, Am. Psychiat. Assn. (Found. Fund prize research 1978), Am. Coll. Neuropsychopharmacology, Am. Coll. Psychiatrists; mem. Assn. for Research Nervous and Mental Diseases, Am. Psychosomatic Soc., Cin. Soc. Neurology and Psychiatry (past pres.), Am. Psychoanalytic Assn., AMA, Orange County Med. Assn., So. Calif. Psychiat. Soc., Am. Assn. Child Psychoanalysts, So. Calif. Psychoanalytic Soc., Phi Beta Kappa, Sigma Xi, Alpha Omega Alpha., Omicron Delta Kappa. Club: Cosmos. Home: 4607 Perham Rd Corona Del Mar CA 92625 Office: Dept Psychiatry and Human Behavior Coll Medicine U Calif Irvine CA 92717

GOTTSCHALK, WALTER HELBIG, mathematician, educator; b. Lynchburg, Va., Nov. 3, 1918; s. Carl and Lula (Helbig) G.; m. Margaret Hemsworth, Aug. 27, 1952; children: Heather, Steven. B.S., U. Va., 1939, M.A., 1942, Ph.D. in Math, 1944; M.A. (hon.), Wesleyan U., Middletown, Conn., 1964. From instr. to prof. math. U. Pa., 1944-63, chmn. dept., 1955-58; prof. math. Wesleyan U., 1963-82, chmn. dept., 1964-69, 70-71; Mem. Inst. Advanced Study, Princeton, 1947-48; research asso. Yale U., 1960-61. Author: (with G.A. Hedlund) Topological Dynamics, 1955; Mem. editorial bd.: Math. Systems Theory, 1967-75; Contbr. articles to profl. jours. Mem. Am. Math. Soc. (asso. editor proc. 1954-56, asso. sec. for East 1971-76), Math. Assn. Am., Soc. Indsl. and Applied Math., AAUP, Phi Beta Kappa, Sigma Xi. Democrat. Unitarian. Home: 38 S Angell St Apt 2 Providence RI 02906

GOTTSCHALL, EDWARD MAURICE, graphic arts company executive; b. N.Y.C., Dec. 28, 1915; s. Myer and Stephanie (Kraus) G.; m. Lee Beatrice Natale, Feb. 6, 1943; 1 son, Robert J. B.S., CCNY, 1937; M.S., Columbia U., 1938. Mng. editor Graphic Arts Prodn. Yearbook, Colton Press, 1937-51; editor Art Direction, 1952-69; sr. editor Popular Merchandising Co., Passaic, N.J., 1964-67; co-pub., editorial dir. Advt. Trade Publs., Inc., 1967-69; exec. dir. Am. Inst. Graphic Arts, N.Y.C., 1969-75; exec. v.p. Internat. Typeface Corp., N.Y.C., 1975—; editor U & lc, 1981—; v.p. Design Processing Internat., Inc., 1977—; U.S. rep. Assn. Typographique Internat., 1978—; lectr. Pratt Inst. Evening Art Sch., 1947-64, N.Y. U., 1955-64. Author: (with F.C. Rodewald) Commercial Art as a Business, 3d edit, 1972, Vision '80s, 1980, Graphic Communication '80s, 1981; Co-editor: Advertising Directions, vols. 1-4, 1960-64, Editor Typographic i, 1969-79; cons. editor: Graphic Arts Manual, 1973—. Served with USAAF, 1942-45; ETO. Mem. Type Dirs. Club (past pres., Spl. award 1963), Phi Delta Pi. Club: Masons. Home: 281 Garth Rd Scarsdale NY 10583 Office: 2 Hammarskjold Plaza New York NY 10017 *Knowledge is never enough. One must be able to evaluate, to judge, and to have taste.*

GOTTSEGEN, GLORIA, psychologist, educator; b. N.Y.C., Nov. 15, 1930; d. Marco and Flora (Salti) Behar; m. Paul D. Park, Jan. 10, 1981; children: Abby Jean, Paul Richard. B.A., N.Y. U., 1950; M.A., CCNY, 1951; Ph.D., N.Y. U., 1967. Diplomate: Lic. psychologist, N.Y. State. Postgrad. fellow N.Y. Med. Coll., N.Y.C., 1957-58; remedial psychologist Jewish Child Care Assn., N.Y.C., 1958-61; psychologist Bronx (N.Y.) Consultation Center, 1961-64, supervising psychologist, 1964-68; asst. prof. psychology Hebert H. Lehman Coll., City U. N.Y., Bronx, 1968-75, asso. prof., 1975-79, prof., 1979—, chmn. dept. specialized services edn., 1976-81; pres. Sch. Psychology Educators Council N.Y. State, 1977-78. Editor: Professional School Psychology, Vols. I-III, 1960, 63, 69, Confrontation: Encounters in Self and Interpersonal Awareness, 1971, Group Behavior: A Guide to Information Sources, 1979, Humanistic Psychology: A Guide to Information Sources, 1980; assoc. editor: Psychotherapy: Theory, Research and Practice, 1976-82. Fellow Am. Psychol. Assn. (pres. div. humanistic psychology 1976-77, sec. div. psychotherapy 1975-78, rep. to council 1978—, chmn. bd. conv. affairs 1983-84); mem. N.Y. Psychol. Assn. (pres. div. sch. psychology 1975-76), Eastern Psychol. Assn., Fla. Psychol. Assn., Southeastern Psychol. Assn. Office: Herbert H Lehman Coll City U NY Bronx NY 10468

GOTTWALD, BRUCE COBB, chemical company executive; b. Richmond, Va., Sept. 28, 1933; s. Floyd Dewey and Anne Ruth (Cobb) G.; m. Nancy Hays, Dec. 22, 1956; children—Bruce Cobb, Mark Hays, Thomas Edward. B.S., Va. Mil. Inst., 1954; postgrad., U. Va., Inst. Paper Chemistry, Appleton, Wis. With Albemarle Paper Mfg. Co., 1956—; v.p., sec. parent co. Ethyl Corp., 1962-64; exec. v.p., sec. Albemarle Paper Mfg. Co. (Ethyl Corp.), 1964-69, pres., dir., 1969—; dir. Reco Industries, Inc., Va. Electric & Power Co., James River Corp. Pres. Va. Mus.; bd. visitors Va. Mil. Inst.; bd. govs. Va. Council Econ. Edn. Mem. Va. Mfrs. Assn. (bd. dirs.). Home: 4203 Sulgrave Rd Richmond VA 23221 Office: 330 S 4th St Richmond VA 23219

GOTTWALD, FLOYD DEWEY, JR., business executive; b. Richmond, Va., July 29, 1922; s. Floyd Dewey and Ann (Cobb) G.; m. Elisabeth Morris Shelton, Mar. 22, 1947; children: William M., James T., John D. B.S., Va. Mil. Inst., 1943; M.S., U. Richmond, 1951. With Albemarle Paper Co., Richmond, 1943—, sec., 1956-57, v.p., sec., 1957-62, pres., 1962-64, also dir.; exec. v.p. Ethyl Corp., Richmond, 1962-64, vice chmn., 1964-68, chmn., 1968—, chief exec. officer, chmn. exec. com., 1970—; dir. CSX Corp., Reid-Provident Labs., Inc. Trustee V.M.I. Found., Inc., U. Richmond. Served to 1st lt. USAR, 1943-46. Decorated Bronze Star, Purple Heart. Mem. Va. Inst. Sci. Researh (trustee), Am. Petroleum Inst. (dir.), NAM (dir.), Chem. Mfgr. Assn. (dir.). Home: 300 Herndon Rd Richmond VA 23229 Office: 330 S 4th St Richmond VA 23219

GOTTWALD, GEORGE J., bishop; b. St. Louis, May 12, 1914. Student, Kenrich Sem., Mo. Ordained priest Roman Catholic Ch., 1940. Ordained titular Cedamusa and aux. bishop, St. Louis, 1961—. Office: 1264 Arch Terr Richmond Heights MO 63117 *

GOTWALS, CHARLES PLACE, JR., lawyer; b. Muskogee, Okla., May 19, 1917; s. Charles Place and Anna M. (Koehler) G.; m. Mary Frances Brownlee, Jan. 31, 1948; children: Charles William, James Robert, Frances Ann, Virginia Hunt. A.B., U. Okla., 1938, J.D., 1940. Bar: Okla. 1940. Since practiced in Tulsa; partner Gable & Gotwals; gen. counsel, dir. 4th Nat. Bank Tulsa, 1958—. Served to maj. AUS, 1942-46; ETO. Decorated Bronze Star. Mem. ABA, Tulsa County Bar Assn. (sec. 1949), Okla. Bar Assn., Am. Judicature Soc., Order of Coif,

Phi Beta Kappa, Phi Delta Phi, Beta Theta Pi. Episcopalian (vestryman, jr. warden 1956-60). Clubs: Kiwanian (pres. 1961), Tulsa, Summit. Home: 1108 Woodward Blvd Tulsa OK 74114 Office: 4th Nat Bldg Tulsa OK 74119

GOTWALS, VERNON DETWILER, JR., musician, educator; b. Conshohocken, Pa., Nov. 12, 1924; s. Vernon Detwiler and Helen (Jones) G.; m. Carol Joyce, June 13, 1953; children—Frank, Thomas, Philip. Student, Drew U., 1941-43; A.B., Amherst Coll., 1947; M.F.A., Princeton, 1951. Instr. music Princeton, 1951-52; faculty Smith Coll., Northampton, Mass., 1952—, prof. music, 1966—, chmn. dept., 1962-68, 71-75. Author: (with Philip Keppler) La Sfera armoniosa of Paolo Quagliati, 1957, Brahms's Folk Songs for Women's Voices, 1968, Joseph Haydn, 18th Century Gentleman and Genius, 1963. Served with AUS, 1943-45. Mem. AAUP, Music Library Assn., Am. Musicol. Soc., Am. Guild Organists, Phi Beta Kappa. Home: RFD Box 971 Stonington Me 04681

GOTZ, IGNACIO LEOPOLDO, economist, educator; b. Caracas, Benezuela, Aug. 10, 1933; came to U.S., 1964; s. Rederico and Ilsa (Romer) G.; m. Katheine Reeder, Aug. 21, 1965; children: Christine, Mariella, Sonya. B.A., Pontificial Athenaeum, poona, India, 1956; B.D., St. Mary's Coll., 1963; M.A., Columbia U., 1965; Ph.D., NYU, 1968. Tchr. English St. Xavier's Schs., Rosary Schs., Baroda, India, 1957-59; instr. English St. Cavier's Coll., Ahmedabad, India, 1963; instr. Bibl. exegesis St. Stanislaus Coll., Haxaribagh, India, 1964; mem. faculty Hofstra U., Hempstead, N.Y., 1966—, prof. philosophy, 1975—, dir. Div. Spl. Studies, 1972—. Author: Pavitra Gulabmala, 1961, No Schools, 1971, The Psychedelic Teacher, 1972, Creativity, 1978. Named Hofstra Tchr. of Yr., 1971. Mem. AAUP, Philosophy of Edn. Soc., Kappa Delta Pi. Home: 386 California Ave Uniondale NY 11553 Office: Hofstra Univ Hempstead NY 11550

GOTZES, HUBERT RICHARD, manufacturing company executive; b. Chgo., May 29, 1926; s. Hubert and Werra C. (Von Puttkamer) G.; m. Jane Marie Lawson, Nov. 16, 1957; children: Teresa Ann, Jane Marie. B.S.C., Loyola U., Chgo. Bonus estimator R.R. Donnelley & Sons Co., Chgo., 1947-48, head timekeeper, 1948-49, gen. salesman, 1949-54, dir. forward planning, 1954-58, exec. salesman, 1958-59, v.p. exec. sales, 1959-67, v.p. Warsaw (Ind.) mfg. div., 1967-68, pres. staff, 1968-69, group v.p., 1969—. Served with USNR, 1944-46. Mem. Graphic Arts Tech. Found. (dir., regional v.p. 1980-81, pres. 1981-82). Clubs: Chgo. Yacht, Economics, North Shore Country, Caxton. Office: 2223 S King Dr Chicago IL 60616 *

GOUGH, WILLIAM ALBERT GORDON, food company executive; b. Vancouver, B.C., Can., Nov. 15, 1938. B.Sc., U. B.C. Devel. engr. Cyanamid of Can., 1962-65; tech. supt. Electric Reduction Co., 1965-70; plant engr. Sun Rype Products, 1970-76; mgr., ptnr. Plants Plus, 1976-79; pres. Empress Foods Ltd., Vancouver. Mem. Assn. Profl. Engrs. B.C. Office: Empress foods Ltd 7280 Fraser St Vancouver BC Canada V5X 2V9

GOUGHLIN, MAGDALEN, college president; b. Wenatchee, Wash., Apr. 16, 1930; d. William J. and Cecelia (Diffley) G. B.A. in History and Social Scis, Coll. St. Catherine, St. Paul, 1952; M.A. in Medieval History, Mt. St. Mary's Coll., Los Angeles, 1962; Ph.D. in Am. History (Haynes dessertation fellow), U. So. Calif., 1970; L.H.D. (hon.), Loyola Marymount U., Los Angeles, 1983. Joined Sisters of St. Joseph Carondelet, Roman Cath. Ch., 1957; tchr. history schs. in, Calif., 1960-63; asst. prof. history, then dean acad. devel. Mt. St. Mary's Coll., Los Angeles, 1970-74, pres., 1976—; provincial councilor/regional superior Los Angeles province Sisters St. Joseph Carondelet, 1974-76. Contbr. articles and revs. to hist. publs. Fulbright scholar U. Nijmegen, Netherlands, 1952-53. Mem. Nat. Fedn. Carondelet Colls. (pres. 1980), Assn. Cath. Colls. and Univs. (dir. 1979), Assn. Ind. Cath. Colls. and Univs. (exec. bd. 1979—), Am. Hist. Soc., Calif. Hist. Soc., Phi Alpha Theta, Pi Gamma Mu, Kappa Gamma Pi, Lambda Iota Tau. *It seems to me that a key to achievement is not to aim toward the achievement at all. Rather, an attitude of seeing all tasks and interactions as important, often discreetly, but always as a part of something of significance. For a scholar there is little that is insignificant, for a teacher the development of each mind is of infinite importance. When each person and each task in one's path is given one's best, achievement is the inevitable end.*

GOUKE, CECIL GRANVILLE, economist, educator; b. Bklyn., Dec. 5, 1928; s. Joseph and Etheline (Grant) G.; m. Mary Noel, June 19, 1964; 1 son, Cecil Granville. B.A., CCNY, 1956; M.A., N.Y. U., 1958, Ph.D., 1967. Instr. econs. Fisk U., 1958-60; asst. prof. Grambling Coll., 1962-64, asso. prof., 1964-67; prof., chmn. Hampton (Va.) Inst., 1967-73; prof. Ohio State U., 1973—; cons. U.S. Treasury Dept., 1973. Author: Amalgamated Clothing Workers of America, 1940-66, 1972; asso. editor: Jour. Behavioral and Social Scis, 1974—. Served with U.S. Army, 1947-49, 50-51. Recipient Founders Day award N.Y. U., 1967; sr. Fulbright scholar, 1979-80. Mem. Am. Econ. Assn., Am. Fin. Assn., Am. Statis. Assn., Indsl. Relations Research Assn., Western Econ. Assn., Nat. Econ. Assn., Hampton NAACP (exec. bd. 1968-70), Phi Beta Sigma. Democrat. Episcopalian. Home: 1788 Kenwick Rd Columbus OH 43209 Office: Dept Econs Ohio State U Columbus OH 43210

GOULARD, EVERETT MAURICE, lawyer; b. Bayonne, N.J., Aug. 23, 1913; s. Thomas and Eva Adele (Fitzgerald) G.; m. Marion Reed Ganzenmuller, June 12, 1935; children—James Everett, Sarah Reed. A.B., Cornell U., 1934; LL.B., Harvard, 1937. Bar: N.Y. State bar, D.C. bar. V.p. Pan Am. World Airways, Inc., N.Y.C., 1954-71; partner firm Poletti, Freidin, Prashker, Feldman & Gartner, N.Y.C., 1971, 75-78, counsel, 1979—; exec. v.p. Airline Indsl. Relations Conf., Washington, 1972-74. Served to lt. col. AUS. Mem. Delta Tau Delta. Clubs: Wee Burn Country (Darien, Conn.); Harvard (N.Y.C.). Home: 18 Overbrook Ln Darien CT 06820 Office: 1185 6th Ave New York NY 10036

GOULART, RONALD JOSEPH, writer; b. Berkeley, Calif., Jan. 13, 1933; s. Joseph Silveira and Josephine (Macri) G.; m. Frances Ann Sheridan, June 13, 1964; children: Sean, Steffan. B.A., U. Calif., Berkeley, 1955. Copywriter Guild, Bascom & Bonfigli, San Francisco, 1955-57, 58-60, Alan Alch, Inc., Los Angeles, 1960-63, Hoefer, Dietrich & Brown, San Francisco, 1966-68, freelance writer, 1968—. Author: sci. fiction Brinkman; sci. fiction story collections Odd Job 101; mystery novels Ghosting; novel The Tremendous Adventures of Bernie Wine; sci. fiction The Robot in the Closet, The Cyborg King, Big Bang; non-fiction from TV An American Family; from films Capricorn One; from comics Snakegod; editor: The Great British Detective. Recipient Edgar Allan Poe award Mystery Writers Am., 1971. Mem. Sci. Fiction Writers Am. (past v.p.), Mystery Writers Am. (dir. 1979-83). Democrat. Address: 232 Georgetown Rd Weston CT 06883

GOULAZIAN, PETER ROBERT, broadcasting executive; b. N.Y.C., Apr. 17, 1940; s. G.B. and Alice Goulazian; m. Mary C. Holland, Dec. 19, 1965; children: Cindy Ann, Peter Robert. B.A., Columbia U., 1962. With media and programming dept. Dancer-Fitzgerald-Sample, Inc., N.Y.C., 1963-67; v.p., mktg. dir. Katz Communications, Inc., N.Y.C., 1967-79, v.p. broadcasting, 1980-81; pres. Continental TV div., 1981—; corp. sec., 1979—. Mem. bus. adv. bd. U.S. Senate, 1981—. Episcopalian. Clubs: Amelia Island Plantation, Varsity C. Home: 4 Concord Ct Montvale NJ 07645 Office: Katz Agy 1 Dag Hammarskjold Plaza New York NY 10017

GOULD, ALVIN R., international business executive; b. Seattle, May 16, 1922; s. Charlie I. and Laura (Klos) G.; m. Ruth Nelson, May 25, 1946; children: Stephen Charles, Jon Patrick. Grad. pub. schs. Mem. engrng. dept. Pacific Car & Foundry Co., Renton, Wash., 1943-45, asst. mgr. indsl. sales, 1945-48, mgr. indsl. sales, 1948-55, gen. sales mgr., 1956-60, Peterbilt Motors Co., Newark, Calif., 1961-64; v.p., dir., gen. sales mgr. Honolulu Iron Works Co., 1964-66, exec. v.p., dir., chief operating officer, 1966, pres., dir., chief exec. officer, 1966-71; group pres. Food Equipment Group Ward Foods Inc., N.Y.C., 1970-71; v.p. merchandising Dillingham Corp., Honolulu, 1972-75, v.p. mining and merchandising, 1973-74, group v.p. mining and merchandising, mem. exec. mgmt. com., 1975-76; pres. T.C.C. Corp., Seattle, 1978—; dir. Haleakala Storage & Transfer Inc., Kahului, Maui, Hawaii, Canmore Mines Ltd., Alta., Can., Honiron Philippines, Inc. (Manila), J&L Engrng. Co., Inc., Jeanerette, La., Tweedy Holdings Ltd., Burnley, Eng., Holsum Hawaii Baking, Inc., Honolulu. Mem. nat. export expansion Council Dept. Commerce, 1969-74, chmn. regional export expansion council, 1969-74; mem. Western Regional Export Council; chmn. Honolulu Export Council, 1975-77; Chmn. bd. trustees Hawaii Pacific Coll., 1973-77; bd. dirs. Center for Internat. Bus. Mem. Hawaii C. of C. (chmn. trade com. 1968-69), Hawaii World Trade Assn. (mem. exec. com. 1968-69), Hawaii Assn. Industries (v.p., dir. 1975-76), Navy League (dir.). Clubs: Rotarian., Walalae Country, Honolulu 200, Outrigger Canoe, Rainier. Home: 8464 W Mercer Way Mercer Island WA 98040

GOULD, ARTHUR IRWIN, lawyer; b. Chgo., July 31, 1929; s. Gerson M. and Molly (Sitron) G.; m. Barbara Young, Jan. 7, 1961; Jonathan, Thomas, David. B.S., U. Ill., 1951; J.D., Northwestern U., 1956. Bar: Ill. 1956, U.S. Supreme Ct. 1961, numerous cts. of appeals, U.S. Dist. Ct. (no dist.) Ill. 1963, U.S. Tax Ct. 1963. Trial atty. Tax Div., Dept. Justice, Washington, 1956-63; assoc. Winston & Strawn, Chgo., 1963-68, ptnr., 1968—; lectr. tax insts. and seminars. Contbr. articles to legal jours. Mem. Winnetka Design Rev. Bd., Ill.; chmn. pub. affairs com. Winnetka Caucus, 1976-77. Served to 1st lt. USAF, 1951-53. Participant Program for Honor Law Grads. Dept. of Justice, 1956. Fellow Am. Coll. Tax Counsel; mem. ABA, Chgo. Bar Assn., Ill. Bar Assn., Internat. Fiscal Assn. (exec. com.), Chgo. Fed. Tax Forum (vice chmn.). Clubs: Mid-Day (Chgo.); Old Willow (Northfield, Ill.) (dir.). Home: 470 Willow Rd Winnetka IL 60093 Office: Winston & Strawn One First National Plaza Chicago IL 60603

GOULD, BENJAMIN Z., lawyer; b. Chgo., July 27, 1913; s. Samuel and Fanny (Tendrich) G.; m. Shirley Handleman, Nov. 22, 1942; children: Fredrick G. (dec.), Edward S., Barbara F. (Mrs. James Vincunas). A.B., U. Chgo., 1935, J.D. cum laude, 1937. Bar: Ill. 1937. Since practiced in, Chgo.; asso. firm Gould & Ratner (and predecessors), 1937-49, sr. partner, 1949—; sec., gen. counsel, dir. Henry Crown and Co., Univ. Exchange Corp., San Francisco, Century-Am. Corp., CHF Industries, Producers Supply Co., Stickney Terminal Corp., Monticello Realty Corp., Froning's Towing, Inc., Crown Point Envelope Co., Kratex of Troy, Inc., Kratex Products, SCNO Terminal, Inc., SCNO Barge Lines, Inc., Henderson Comp Products; sec., gen. counsel Material Service Corp. (subs. Gen. Dynamics Corp.), Marblehead Lime Co., Utah Marblehead Lime Co., Freeman United Coal Mining Co-div. Material Service Corp., Arie and Ida Crown Meml., Aberdeen Mfg. Corp., Finkel Outdoor Products, Inc., Werner-Finkel, Inc., Univ. Village Golf Course div. Univ. Exchange Corp., Thomas B. Bishop Co. div., Univ. Village Plaza div. Univ. Exchange Corp., Mills-Am. Envelope Co., Lemont Shipbldg. & Repair Co. div., Powell & Minnock Brick Works, Inc., Nat. Aircraft Inc., Nu-Art, Inc., Exchange Bldg. Corp., J.S. Lock Co., Jefferson Lock Co., El Paso Sand Products, Inc., El Paso Rock Quarries, Inc., Valley Concrete Co., MLRT, Inc., Vowell Constrn. Co., Inc.; v.p., gen. counsel Standard Forgings Corp. Bd. dirs. Hebrew Theol. Coll. Chgo., Columbia Coll., North Light Repertory, Chgo. Loop Synagogue. Served with USCGR, World War II. Mem. Am. Arbitration Assn. (mem. nat. panel), Chgo. Council Fgn. Relations, Am. Soc. Corporate Secs., AIM (asso.), Internat., Am., Ill., Chgo. bar assns., Am. Soc. Internat. Law, Navy League U.S., Am. Judicature Soc., Phi Beta Kappa. Jewish (dir. Chgo. congregations). Clubs: Executive, Standard, One Hundred of Cook County (Chgo.). Home: 1170 Michigan Ave Wilmette IL 60091 Office: 300 W Washington St Chicago IL 60606

GOULD, BERNARD ALBERT, consultant; b. Chelsea, Mass., Jan. 30, 1912; s. Harry and Rebecca (LeVine) G.; m. Edith Solomon, June 16, 1936; children: Susan Deborah, John Richard. B.C.S., NYU, 1936, J.D., 1941; postgrad., George Washington U., 1937-38. Bar: N.Y. 1942, D.C. 1979, U.S. Supreme Ct. 1960. With r.r. industry, N.Y.C., 1929-36; various positions in govt. service, 1936—; dir. Bur. Enforcement, ICC, Washington, 1967-76, cons., 1976—; instr. interstate commerce law and procedure NYU; lectr. transp. law to industry and legal groups and seminars. Pres. J.F.K. Bldg. Fund for Retarded; pres. Montgomery County Assn. for Retarded Citizens; bd. dirs., legis. chmn. Md. Assn. Retarded Citizens. Recipient Disting. Service citation for war transp. activities, 1945. Mem. Fed. Bar Assn., D.C. Bar Assn., Am. Judicature Soc., Nat. Lawyers Club, Alpha Epsilon Pi. Home: 9205 Sligo Creek Pkwy Silver Spring MD 20901 Office: ICC 12th and Constitution Ave Washington DC 20423

GOULD, CHARLES LESSINGTON, found. exec.; b. Youngstown, Ohio, Aug. 17, 1909; s. Fred Jay and Kathleen Helen (Murphy) G.; m. Peggy Ann Shannon, Mar. 30, 1951; children—Charles Lessington, Michael Edward. Spl. student, Northwestern U.; LL.D. (hon.), Golden Gate U., 1963, Western States U., 1975. Machinist Steel & Tubes, Inc., Cleve., 1927-28; engr. Am. Tel. & Tel., Cleve., 1928-29; reporter, writer, promotion mgr. Cleve. News, 1930-34; sales promotion mgr. Universal Match Corp., Chgo., 1934-35; writer, radio announcer, promotion dir. Chgo. American, 1935-42; plans dir. N.Y. Jour.-American, 1946-50, asst. pub., 1951-61; pub. San Francisco Examiner, 1961-75; San Francisco News Call Bull., 1962-65; v.p. William Randolph Hearst Found. and Hearst Found., 1975—. Bd. govs. San Francisco Bay Area Council, United Bay Area Crusade, San Francisco Symphony Assn.; bd. dirs. San Francisco Boys' Club, Fine Arts Mus., San Francisco Conv. and Visitors Bur., Bay Area U.S.O., Ft. Point Museum Assn., Calif. Jockey Club Found., Louis R. Lurie Found.; bd. regents St. Mary's Coll., St. Ignatius Coll. Prep.; trustee Golden Gate U., U. San Francisco. Served from lt. (j.g.) to capt. USNR, 1942-46; dir. combat photography U.S. Navy, 1950-51; Korea; capt. Res. ret. Decorated D.S.M., Bronze Star, Air medal; recipient gold medal award Freedoms Found., 1964, 65, 70, 71, 72, 73. Mem. Navy League (nat. dir.), Knights Malta. Clubs: Commonwealth, Bohemian (San Francisco); N.Y. Athletic. Home: 336 Poett Rd Hillsborough CA 94010 Office: 690 Market St San Francisco CA 94104

GOULD, CHARLES PERRY, lawyer; b. Los Angeles, Mar. 11, 1909; s. Thomas Charles and Viola Frank (Keeney) G.; m. Mary Dalrymple, Sept. 1, 1932; children—Thomas Charles, Mary (Mrs. Robert Lancefield), Anne (Mrs. Thomason). Student, Pomona Coll., 1926-28; Ph.B., U. Chgo., 1930; LL.B., U. So. Calif., 1932. Bar: Calif. bar 1932. Asso. firm Frankley & Spray, Los Angeles, 1932- 35; mem. firm Spray, Gould & Bowers, 1935—; dir. Gould Music Co. Served to lt. comdr. USNR, 1942-45. Mem. Am. Bar Assn., Internat. Assn. Ins. Counsel, Am. Judicature Soc. (dir. 1979), Nat. Club Assn. (pres. 1962, dir.), World Affairs Council, Navy League U.S., Legion Lex, Delta Theta Phi. Republican. Episcopalian. Clubs: Elk., Jonathan, Town Hall, Los Angeles (Los Angeles); Balboa Bay (Balboa, Calif.); Calif. Book (San Francisco). Home: 1200 Old Mill Rd San Marino CA 91108 Office: 3550 Wilshire Blvd Los Angeles CA 90010

GOULD, CHESTER, cartoonist; b. Pawnee, Okla., Nov. 20, 1900; s. Gilbert R. and Alice M. (Miller) G.; m. Edna Gauger, Nov. 6, 1926; 1 dau., Jean. Student, Okla. A. & M. U., 1919-21; grad., Northwestern U., 1923. Cartoonist Hearst Publs., 1924-29, Chgo. Tribune, 1931-77; ind. cartoonist, 1977—. Creator: cartoon Dick Tracy, 1931; appearing in, Chgo. Tribune-N.Y. News Syndicate, Inc., and syndicated newspapers. Mem. Nat. Cartoonists Soc., Lambda Chi Alpha. Clubs: Tavern, Lake Zurich Golf, Woodstock Country. Home: Woodstock IL 60098

GOULD, DIRK SAMUEL, lawyer; b. N.Y.C., Jan. 18, 1933; s. Joseph and Helen (Garey) G.; m. Libby Tombacher, Aug. 20, 1959; children: Michael, Peter. B.A., Queens Coll., N.Y.C., 1955; J.D., NYU, 1960, LL.M., 1964. Bar: N.Y. 1960. Asso. Sereni, Herzfeld & Rubin, N.Y.C., 1960-61, Squadron, Alter & Weinrib, 1962-65; mem. Pross, Halpern, Lefevre, Raphael & Alter (now Alter, Lefevre, Raphael, Lowry & Gould), N.Y.C., 1966-74, sec., 1974-78; mem. Arnow, Brodsky Bohlinger Einhorn & Alter, N.Y.C., 1979-83; sr. v.p., gen. counsel Van Wagner Advt. Corp., N.Y.C., 1983—; lectr. constl. law, pub. opinion, and propaganda Queens Coll., N.Y.C., 1961-64. Served as pilot USAF, 1955-58. Mem. ABA (labor law sect.), N.Y. County Lawyers Assn. (law of space com. 1966-73, mem. aero. law com. 1966-74), Am. Arbitration Assn. (nat. panel labor arbitration). Office: 420 Lexington Ave New York NY 10017

GOULD, EDWARD PENROSE, banker; b. Chattanooga, Jan. 14, 1931; s. Edward P. and Frances (Powell) G. B.B.A., Emory U., 1953. Asst. v.p. Trust Co. Bank, Atlanta, 1961-64, v.p., 1965-67, group v.p., 1968-69, sr. v.p., 1970-73, exec. v.p., 1974-76, pres., 1977—, dir., Trust Co. of Ga., Trust Co. Mortgage; chmn. Munich Am. Reassurance Co., Atlanta, 1980—. Trustee Agnes Scott Coll., Decatur Ga., 1979—, Baylor Sch., Chattanooga, 1978—, Jesse Parker William Hosp., Atlanta, 1976—; bd. dirs. Atlanta U., 1978—. Served to 1st lt. USMC, 1953-55. Mem. Assn. Res. City Bankers, Am. Textile Mfrs. Inst. Republican. Presbyterian. Clubs: Capital City (bd. dirs. 1983—); Piedmont Driving (Atlanta).

GOULD, EDWIN SHELDON, educator, chemist; b. Los Angeles, Aug. 19, 1926; s. Ben and Margaret (Mandel) G.; m. Marjorie McFarlin, Jan. 25, 1952; children: Richard Forrest, Kirk Benson. B.S., Calif. Inst. Tech., 1946; Ph.D., UCLA, 1950. Instr. Poly. Inst. Bklyn., 1950-52, asst. prof., 1952-56; asso. prof. chemistry Polytech. Inst. Bklyn., 1956-59; sr. inorganic chemist Stanford Research Inst., 1959-66; prof. San Francisco State U., 1966-67, Kent State U., 1967-82, Univ. Prof., 1982—. Author: Inorganic Reactions and Structure, 1962, Mechanism and Structure in Organic Chemistry, 1959. Mem. London, Am. chem. socs., U.S. Volleyball Assn., Amateur Chamber Music Players Assn. Research inorganic chemistry. Home: 1583 Morris Rd Kent OH 44240

GOULD, ELLIOTT, actor; b. Bklyn., Aug. 29, 1938; s. Bernard and Lucille (Raver) Goldstein; m. Barbra Streisand, Mar. 21, 1963 (div.); 1 son, Jason; m. Jennifer Bogart; children—Jennifer, Sam. Student, Profl. Children's Sch., N.Y.C., 1955; pupil of, Jerome Swinford, Sonya Box, Bill Quinn, Colin Romoff, Charles Lowe, Eugene Lewis, Matt Mattox. Theatrical appearances include Rumple, 1957, Say, Darling, 1958, Irma La Douce, 1960, I Can Get It For You Wholesale, 1962, On The Town, 1963; also The Fantastiks; TV appearances in Once Upon A Mattress, 1964; appeared in: film Bob & Carol & Ted & Alice, 1969, M.A.S.H, 1970, I Love My Wife, 1970, Little Murders, 1971, The Long Goodbye, 1973, Spys, 1974, Busting, 1974, California Split, 1974, Nashville, 1975, Whiffs, 1975, I Will, I Will... For Now, 1976, Harry & Walter Go to N.Y, 1976, Mean Johnny Barrows, 1976, A Bridge Too Far, 1977, Capricorn One, 1978, Matilda, 1978, The Silent Partner, 1979, Escape to Athena, 1979, The Lady Vanishes, 1979, The Muppet Movie, 1979, Falling in Love Again, 1980, The Devil and Max Devlin, 1981. Mem. Artists Equity Assn., AFTRA. Address: care William Morris Agy 151 El Camino Beverly Hills CA 90212 *

GOULD, FLOYD JEROME, mathematics educator, commodities trader, author; b. Cleve., Feb. 15, 1936; s. Jack Ernest and Rose (Levin) G.; m. Susan Schaeffer, 1962; children: Lawrence, Jonathan; m. Katharine McCarthy, Dec. 23, 1972; stepchildren: Emile and Matteo Levisetti. Student, Yale U., 1953-55; B.S. in Biochemistry, U. Chgo., 1958; postgrad. in Physics, U. Chgo., 1959; Ph.D. in Ops. Research, U. Chgo., 1967; M.S. in Math, Ill. Inst. Tech., 1962. Ops. analyst, mathematician Labs. Applied Scis. U. Chgo., 1958-62, head computer services, 1963-68; vis. prof. Ford Found., 1972-73; prof. mgmt. sci., dir. doctoral programs Grad. Sch. Bus., 1973-75, prof. applied math. and mgmt. sci., 1976-78, Hobart W. Williams prof., 1978—; asso. prof. U. N.C., Chapel Hill, 1968-70, asso. prof., chmn. curriculum in ops. research and systems analysis, 1970-72; vis. prof. U. Paris, 1978-79; prin. investigator Office Naval Research, NSF, 1969-82; gen. partner Gould Trading Co., 1976—. Author: (with G. Eppen) Quantitative Concepts for Management-Decision Making Without Algorithms, 1979, Introductory Management Science, 1983; author: numerous works of fiction including An Explanation, 1967; asso. editor: Ops. Research, 1970-78, Mgmt. Sci, 1970-75, Math. Rev, 1970-75; referee numerous profl. jours.; contbr. numerous articles to profl. jours. Mem. Soc. Indsl. and Applied Math., Ops. Research Soc. Am., Inst. Mgmt. Scis., Math. Programming Soc. Club: Univ. (Chgo.). Home: 5827 S Blackstone Ave Chicago IL 60637 Office: 1101 E 58th St Chicago IL 60637

GOULD, FRANK NELSON, JR., banker; b. Mpls., May 19, 1926; s. Frank Nelson and Ella (Exe) G.; m. June Marilyn Beach, Sept. 1, 1948; children—Howard Nelson, Gregory Jay, Tracy Dee. B.A., Mont. State U., 1950. Asst. v.p. Metal Bank & Trust Co., Butte, Mont., 1950-60; with First Interstate Bank, Los Angeles, 1960—, now sr. v.p. Served with USNR, 1944-46. Clubs: Athenian-Nile, Orinda Country. Home: 409 Birchwood Dr Moraga CA 94556 Office: 1330 Broadway Oakland CA 94612

GOULD, GEORGE D., investment company executive; b. Boston, 1927. B.A., Yale U., 1951; M.B.A., Harvard U., 1955. Supr.-acct. Brundage, Story & Ross, 1951-53; with treas. dept. F.W. Dodge, 1954; assoc. Jeremiah Milbank, 1955-61; chmn. bd. D-L-J Securities Corp., 1961-76; pres., chief exec. officer Madison Fund Inc., Wilmington, Del., 1976-82, also dir., chmn., 1980, chmn., chief exec. officer, 1982—; dir. Appalachian Co., Wenonah Devel. Co. Served to 2d lt. U.S. Army, 1945-47. Office: Madison Fund Inc 919 Market St Wilmington DE 19801 *

GOULD, GORDON, physicist, optical communications executive; b. N.Y.C., July 17, 1920; s. Kenneth Miller and Helen Vaughn (Rue) G. B.S. in Physics, Union Coll., 1941, D.Sc., 1978; M.S. in Physics, Yale U., 1943, Columbia U., 1952. Physicist Western Electric Co., Kearny, N.J., 1941; instr. Yale U., 1941-43; physicist Manhattan Project, 1943-45; engr. Semon Bache Co., N.Y.C., 1945-50; instr. CCNY, 1947-54; research asst. Columbia U., 1954-57; research dir. TRG, Inc./Control

Data Corp., Melville, N.Y., 1958-67; prof. electrophysics Bklyn. Poly. Inst., 1967-74; v.p. engring./mktg., dir. Optelecom, Inc., Gaithersburg, Md., 1974—. Contbr. sci. articles to profl. jours. Recipient 63 research grants and contracts, 1958—; named Inventor of Year for laser amplifier Patent Office Soc., 1978. Mem. Am. Inst. Physics, Optical Soc. Am., IEEE, AAAS, Fiber Optic Communications Soc., Laser Inst. Am. (pres. 1971-73, dir. 1971—). Patentee in field. Home: 9101 Deer Park Rd Great Falls VA 22066

GOULD, HAROLD, actor; b. Schenectady, N.Y., Dec. 10, 1923. M.A., Ph.D., Cornell U. Films include Two for the Seesaw, Harper, Inside Daisy Clover, Marnie, The Arrangement, The Lawyer, Where Does It Hurt?, The Sting, The Big Bus, Love and Death, The Front Page, Silent Movie, The One and Only, Seems Like Old Times; TV appearances include The Long Road Home, Washington—Behind Closed Doors, Soap, Love Boat, Feather and Father, Rhoda, Gunsmoke, Petrocelli, Double Solitaire, Streets of San Francisco, Mary Tyler Moore Show, The 11th Victim, Aunt Mary, Man in the Santa Claus Suit, Insight/Holy Moses, The Gambler, Moviola, King Crab; appeared in plays Seidman and Son, Once in a Lifetime, The Miser, The Devils, The Birthday Party, House of Blue Leaves, The Price, The World of Ray Bradbury, Rhinocerous *

GOULD, HAROLD ALTON, anthropologist, educator; b. Boston, Feb. 18, 1926; s. Harold A. and Mabel (LeBlanc) G.; m. Ketayun H. Gould, Nov. 24, 1955; children: Sheru, Armeen; 1 dau. by previous marriage, Bethanne. B.A., U. R.I., 1951; M.A., Ohio State U., 1954; postgrad., Lucknow U., India, 1954-55; Ph.D., Washington U., St. Louis, 1959. Instr. U. Kans., 1957-59; NSF fellow to, India, 1959-60, NIMH fellow to, 1960-62; Andrew W. Mellon fellow U. Pitts., 1962-63, asso. prof., 1965-69; prof. anthropology U. Ill., Urbana, 1969—, dir. Center for Asian Studies, 1976-79; faculty research fellow Am. Inst. Indian Studies, 1967-68, 81-82, v.p., 1976-79. Author: Caste and Class: A Comparative View, 1971, Lucknow and Kanpur: Contrasting Cities on the North Indian Plain, 1974, The Emergence of Modern Politics: Political Development in Faizabad, 1974, The Second Coming: The 1980 Elections in the Hindi Belt, 1980; Contbr. numerous articles to profl. jours. Served with USN, 1943-46. Recipient short term grants to, India, 1969, 70, 74, 77, 80. Mem. Am. Anthrop. Assn., Assn. for Asian Studies (chairperson S.Asia Council 1974-77), Royal Anthrop. Inst. Gt. Britain and Ireland. Home: 1807 Shadowlawn Dr Champaign IL 61820 Office: Dept Anthropology Davenport Hall U Ill Urbana IL 61801 *In all aspects of my career, I have endeavored to deepen American sensitivity to the nature and aspirations of the peoples of the Third World because upon such understanding depends both their survival and our own.*

GOULD, HARRY EDWARD, JR., industrialist; b. N.Y.C., Sept. 24, 1938; s. Harry E. and Lucille (Quartucy) G.; m. Barbara Clement, Apr. 26, 1975; children: Harry Edward, III, Katharine Elizabeth. Student, Oxford U., 1958; B.A. cum laude, Colgate U., 1960; postgrad., Harvard Bus. Sch., 1960-61; M.B.A., Columbia U., 1964. Asso. in corporate fin. dept. Goldman, Sachs & Co., N.Y.C., 1961-62; exec. asst. to sr. v.p. ops. Universal Am., N.Y.C., 1964-65; sec., treas. Young Spring & Wire Corp., Detroit, 1965-67, exec. v.p., chief operating officer, 1967-69; also dir.; v.p. adminstrn. and fin. Universal Am. Corp., 1968-69; mem. exec. com., v.p., sec.-treas. Daybrook-Ottawa Corp., Bowling Green, Ohio, 1967-69; dir., mem. exec. com. Am. Med. Ins. Co., N.Y.C., 1966-74; pres., chmn., chief exec. officer, dir. Gould Paper Corp., N.Y.C., 1969—; chmn. bd., dir. Samuel Porritt & Co., East Peoria, Ill., 1969—, Computer Copies Corp., N.Y.C., 1970-73, Ingalls Mfg., Inc., Ceres, Calif., 1971—, McNair Mfg., Inc., Chico, Calif., 1972—, Hawthorne Paper Co., Kalamazoo, 1974—, Weiss Mfg., Inc., Chico, 1974—, Vrisimo Mfg., Inc., Ceres, 1974—; chmn. bd. Lewis & Gould Paper Co., Inc., Northfield, Ill., 1975-78; pres., dir. Carlyle Internat. Sales Corp., N.Y.C., 1975—; dir. Reinhold-Gould GmbH, Hamburg, Germany; ltd. partner Hardy & Co. (mem. N.Y. Stock Exchange), N.Y.C., 1973-78. Co-chmn. Pacesetter's com. Boy Scouts Am., 1966-69; participant as U.S. Pres.'s rep. UN E-W Trade Devel. Commn., 1967; mem. N.Y. Gov.'s Task Force on N.Y. State Cultural Life and Arts, 1975—; Pres. Harry E. Gould Found., N.Y.C., 1971—; bd. dirs. Ophthalmol. Found. Am., Inc., 1973—; mem. nat. council Colgate U., 1973-76, trustee, mem. budget, devel., fin. and student affairs coms., 1976—; mem. adv. bd. Columbia U. Grad. Sch. Bus., 1980—; bd. dirs. United Cerebral Palsy Research and Ednl. Found., 1976—, Nat. Multiple Sclerosis Soc., 1977—, N.Y.C. Housing Devel. Corp., 1977—, USO of Met. N.Y., 1981—,; bd. dirs., chmn. exec. com. Cinema Group, Inc., Los Angeles, 1979—, chmn., pres., Los Angeles, 1982—; mem. Democratic Nat. Fin. Council, 1974—, also vice chmn. exec. com., chmn. budget and audit coms.; treas. N.Y. State Dem. Com., 1976-77; mem. mayor's citizens com. Dem. Nat. Conv., 1976; mem. U.S. Pres.'s Export Council (exec. com., chmn. export expansion subcom., mem. export promotion subcom.), 1979-82; nat. trustee, mem. exec. com. Nat. Symphony Orch., Washington, 1978—. Mem. Nat. Paper Trade Assn. (dir., mem. printing paper com. 1973—), Paper Mchts. Assn. N.Y. (dir. 1972—), Young Pres. Orgn., Paper Club N.Y., Fin. Execs. Inst., Columbia U. Grad. Sch. Bus. Alumni Assn. (dir. 1980—), Phi Kappa Tau. Clubs: Pres.'s N.Y. (co-chmn. assos. div. 1964-68), City Athletic, Harvard, Harvard Business, Friars, Marco Polo (N.Y.C.); Les Ambassadeurs (London); Rockrimmon Country (Stamford, Conn.). Home: 25 Sutton Pl S New York NY 10022 also Cherry Hill Farm 429 Taconic Rd Greenwich CT 06830 Office: 315 Park Ave S New York NY 10010 *In business the most difficult problem to resolve is blending the profit goals with the dignity of human relations. In the long run, it is probably best to forego some of the profits in order to successfully meld the economic and human sides of business.*

GOULD, JAMES SPENCER, manufacturing company executive; b. Albany, N.Y., Oct. 18, 1922; s. James Spencer and Elsie May (Spielgel) G.; m. Shirley Joan Burrett, June 12, 1948; children: Deborah Ann, Jeffrey George, Douglas Spencer. B.S. cum laude, Syracuse U., 1944; A.M.P., Harvard U., 1958. C.P.A., N.Y.; C.P.A., Calif. Ptnr. Arthur Young & Co., Buffalo and Los Angeles, 1949-65, N.Y.C., 1966-82; chief fin. officer, v.p. fin. Stanley Works, New Britain, Conn., 1982—; task force on segments Fin. Acctg. Standards Bd., Stamford, Conn., 1973-76. Served to 1st lt. inf. U.S. Army, 1943-46; ETO; served to 1st lt. inf. Fin. Corps, 1951-52; Korea. Recipient Disting. Merit award Syracuse U. Sch. Mgmt., 1982. Mem. Am. Inst. C.P.A.'s, Fin. Execs. Inst. Republican. Episcopalian. Clubs: Union League N.Y.C. (gov.) (1981-82); Greenwich (Conn.) Country, Shuttle Meadow Country. Home: 38 Cheltenham Way Avon CT 06001 Office: Stanley Works 195 Lake St New Britain CT 06050

GOULD, JAY MARTIN, economist, consultant; b. Chgo., Aug. 19, 1915; s. Max and Ida (Dolger) G.; m. Paula Halpern, Nov. 10, 1942 (div.); children: Diana, Emily; m. 2d Jane S. Auerbach, Nov. 17, 1970. B.A., Bklyn. Coll., 1936; M.A., Columbia U., 1938, Ph.D., 1946. Economist McGraw-Gill, N.Y.C., 1946-48; mng. dir. Market Statistics, N.Y.C., 1948-66; pres. Econ. Info. Systems, N.Y.C., 1966-81; cons. economist Winston and Strawn, Chgo., 1960-80; cons. Dept. Justice, Washington, 1954-55; exec. cons. Control Data Corp., Mpls., 1981—; dir. Ctr. Internat. Mgmt. Studies, Chgo., 1978—, Feminist Press, Woodbury, N.Y., 1980—, Inst. Policy Studies, Washington, 1982—. Author: Productivity Trends in U.S. Public Utilities, 1946, The Technical Elite, 1966, Input-Output Databases, 1979, Structure of U.S. Business, 1980. Home: PO Box 822 Westbrook CT 06498 Office: Econ Info Systems 310 Madison Ave New York NY 10017

GOULD, JEAN ROSALIND, writer; b. Greenville, Ohio, May 25, 1919; d. Aaron J. and Elsie E. (Elgutter) G. A.B., U. Toledo, 1939. Free-lance writer, 1941—. Author: Miss Emily, 1946, Robert Frost, The Aim Was Song, 1964, The Poet and Her Book: A Biography of Edna St. Vincent Millay, 1969, Amy-The World of Amy Lowell and the Imagist Movement, 1975, American Women Poets, Pioneers of Modern Poetry, 1980; numerous others; works include short stories, biographies; editorial re-writer, radio-script writer. Committeewoman dist. Democratic party, N.Y.C., 1961-62. Fellow Va. Center Creative Arts (adv. bd.), MacDowell Colony, Huntington Hartford Found., Wurlitzer Found.; Mem. PEN Club, Authors League Am., Phi Kappa Phi. Address: care Dodd Mead & Co 79 Madison Ave New York NY 10016

GOULD, JOHN ALEXANDER, oil exploration company executive; b. Antler, Sask., Can., Aug. 2, 1921; s. George Thomas and Lillian Christena (Campbell) G.; m. Jane B. D. McCurdy, Sept. 14, 1946; 1 son, David George. Grad., Mount Royal Coll., 1951. Acct. Robinson Machine & Supply Co., Calgary, Alta., Can., 1948-52; chief acct. Can. Bishop Oil Co., Calgary, 1952-61; v.p., treas. Murphy Oil Co. Ltd., Calgary, Alta., 1961—. Served with Can. Army, 1939-45; ETO. Mem. Fin. Execs. Inst., Registered Indsl. Acctg. Soc., Calgary Petroleum Club. Clubs: 400, Inglewood Golf and Curling (Calgary) (dir. 1980—). Office: 17th Floor 800 6th Ave SW Calgary AB Canada T2P 2M7 *

GOULD, JOHN PHILIP, JR., economist, educator, university dean; b. Chgo., Jan. 19, 1939; s. John Philip and Lillian (Jicka) G.; m. Kathleen J. Hayes, Sept. 14, 1963; children: John Philip III, Jeffrey Hayes. B.S. with highest distinction, Northwestern U., 1960; Ph.D. (Earhart Found. fellow), U. Chgo., 1966. Faculty U. Chgo., 1965—, prof. econs., 1974—, Disting. Service prof., 1984—, dean Grad. Sch. Bus., 1983—; vis. prof. Nat. Taiwan U., 1978; spl. asst. econ. affairs to sec. labor, 1969-70; spl. asst. to dir. Office Mgmt. and Budget, 1970; past chmn. econ. policy adv. com. Dept. Labor. Author: (with C.E. Ferguson) Microeconomic Theory, 5th edit, 1980; contbg. author: Microeconomic Foundations of Employment and Inflation Theory, 1970, Editor Jour. of Bus, 1976—, Jour. Fin. Econs, 1976, Jour. Accounting and Econs, 1978; Contbr. articles to profl. jours. Recipient Wall St. Jour. award, 1960; Am. Marketing Assn. award, 1960. Mem. Am. Econ. Assn., Western Econ. Assn., Econometric Soc. (chmn. local arrangements 1968). Home: 5514 S Kenwood Ave Chicago IL 60637

GOULD, KENNETH LANCE, physician, educator; b. Wilsonville, Ala., Oct. 28, 1938; s. Kenneth Newton and Elizabeth May (Barrett) G.; m. Helene Freiin von Eckardstein, Sept. 28, 1970; 1 son, Stefan Anton. B.A. in Physics, Oberlin Coll., 1960; M.D., Western Res. U., 1964. Intern U. Wash. Hosps., Seattle, 1964-65, resident, 1965-67; instr. medicine U. Wash., Seattle, 1970-72, asst. prof., 1972-76, asso. prof., 1976-79; prof. dept. internal medicine and cardiology U. Tex., Houston, 1979—, dir. div. cardiology, 1979—, vice chmn. clin. affairs dept. medicine, 1980—; dir. Positron Diagnostic and Research Center, 1979—. Contbr. articles to profl. jours. Recipient George von Hevesy prize, 1978, ACC Young Investigators award, 1983. Fellow Am. Coll. Cardiology, Am. Heart Assn. (council on circulation); mem. Am. Soc. Clin. Investigation, Soc. Nuclear Medicine, N.Am. Soc. Cardiac Radiology, Am. Physiologic Soc., Assn. Am. Physicians, Houston Cardiol. Soc. (pres.). Democrat. Office: PO Box 20708 Houston TX 77025

GOULD, KENNETH LAWRENCE, newspaper executive; b. Miami, Fla., Jan. 31, 1925; s. Kenneth Leroy and Mary (Wilson) G.; m. Helen Marilynn Brand, Aug. 12, 1950; children—Alison DeLong, Lawrence Brand, Meredith Wanner. B.A., Coll. William and Mary, 1947. Reporter Richmond (Va.) News Leader, 1947-50, 52-54, asst. city editor, 1954-58; city editor Roanoke (Va.) Times, 1958-59; asst. city editor Richmond News Leader, 1959-63, city editor, 1963-69, mng. editor, 1969-72; v.p., gen. mgr. Media Gen. Financial Services, Inc., 1972—; exec. editor M/G Financial Weekly, 1970—; pres. M/G Fin. Services, 1979—. Served with USNR, 1943-46, 50-52. Mem. Va. Press Assn., A.P. Mng. Editors Assn., Sigma Delta Chi. Episcopalian. Club: Fishing Bay Yacht. Home: 10409 Medina Rd Richmond VA 23235 Office: 119 N 3d St Richmond VA 23219

GOULD, LEWIS LUDLOW, historian; b. N.Y.C., Sept. 21, 1939; s. John Ludlow and Carmen L. (Lewis) G.; m. Karen D. Keel, Oct. 24, 1970. A.B., Brown U., 1961; M.A., Yale U., 1962, Ph.D., 1966. Instr., then asst. prof. history Yale U., 1965-67; mem. faculty U. Tex., Austin, 1967—, prof. history, 1976—, Eugene C. Barker centennial prof. Am. History, 1983—, chmn. dept., 1980-84. Author: Wyoming: A Political History, 1868-1896, 1968, Progressives and Prohibitionists: Texas Democrats in the Wilson Era, 1973, Reform and Regulation: American Politics, 1900-1916, 1978, The Presidency of William McKinley, 1980, The Spanish-American War and President McKinley, 1982; co-author: Photojournalist: The Career of Jimmy Hare, 1977; editor: The Progressive Era, 1974; co-editor: The Black Experience in America, 1970. Recipient Carr P. Collins award Tex. Inst. Letters, 1973; Younger Humanist fellow NEH, 1974-75. Mem. Am. Hist. Assn., So. Hist. Assn., Tex. Hist. Assn., Phi Beta Kappa. Democrat. Address: 2602 La Ronde St Austin TX 78731

GOULD, LOIS, author; m. Philip Benjamin, 1959 (dec.); children: Anthony, Roger; m. Robert E. Gould. B.A., Wellesley Coll. Former police reporter, feature writer L.I. Star Jour.; former exec. editor Ladies Home Jour. Contbr.: articles to N.Y. Times, McCalls, Ms.; columnist: N.Y. Times, 1977; author: novels Such Good Friends, 1970, Necessary Objects, 1972, Final Analysis, 1974, A Sea-Change, 1976, La Presidenta, 1981; essays Not Responsible for Personal Articles, 1978; story X: A Fabulous Child's Story, 1978. Address: care Brandt & Brandt Lit Agy 1501 Broadway New York NY 10036 *

GOULD, MILTON SAMUEL, lawyer, business executive; b. N.Y.C., Oct. 8, 1909; s. David H. and Ida (Berman) G.; m. Eleanor Greenburg, 1937; children: Patricia, Judson, Jonathan. B.A., Cornell U., 1930, LL.B., 1933. Bar: N.Y. 1933. Assoc. of fed. judge Samuel H. Kaufman, 1933-48; spl. atty. investigation and prosecutions violations immigration and naturalization laws Dept. Justice, 1935-37; ptnr. Kaufman & Cronan and successors, N.Y.C., 1938-48, Gallop Climenko & Gould, 1948-64; sr. ptnr. Shea & Gould, N.Y.C., 1964—; chmn. bd. Elgin Nat. Industries, Inc., Chgo., 1971—, dir.; dir., gen. counsel Citizens Utilities Co., 1945-70; dir., mem. exec. com. Tex. Oil & Gas Corp., Dallas; lectr. in field; lectr. in law Cornell U., Ithaca, N.Y., 1969-70, vis. prof., Stevens Meml. lectr., 1971, adj. prof., 1974-77, N.Y. Law Sch., 1977. Author: The Witness Who Spoke with God, 1979, A Cast of Hawks, 1984; bd. editors: N.Y. Law Jour., 1969. Mem. N.Y.C. Mayor's Com. on Judiciary; chmn. lawyers div. Anti-Defamation League, N.Y.C., 1972; mem. law council, chmn. law fund Cornell U. Recipient lawyers div. award United Jewish Appeal, 1972, Joseph M. Proskauer award, 1977, Dean's medal N.Y. Law Sch., 1978, Torch of Learning award Am. Friends of Hebrew U., 1978. Mem. N.Y. County Lawyers Assn., Assn. Bar City N.Y., Cornell Law Assn. (pres. 1978-80). Clubs: Statler; Tower (Ithaca); Lake Waramaug Golf (New Preston, Conn.); Cornell; Sky (N.Y.C.). Home: 35 E 75th St New York NY 10021 Home: Warren CT 06754 Office: 330 Madison Ave New York NY 10017 Office: Elgin Nat Industries Inc 120 S Riverside Plaza Chicago IL 60606

GOULD, MORLEY DAVID, advertising agency executive; b. Los Angeles, Feb. 24, 1936; s. Joseph Morley and Ruth Merrill (Goldstein) G.; m. Myrna R. Weintraub, Dec. 6, 1959 (div. Dec. 1973); children: Jeffrey Bennett, Jennifer Ann. B.S. in Advt, U. So. Cal., 1958. Pres. Publicity Promotions, Los Angeles, 1959-63; pres., sec. Asher/Gould Advt. Inc., Beverly Hills, Cal., 1963—; dir. Media Buyers Inc., Creative Prodns. Inc. Bd. Dirs. Jewish Home for Aged, Los Angeles, 1970—; bd. dirs., founding mem. Founders Club of City of Hope, Duarte, Calif., 1968. Served with AUS, 1958. Mem. Western States Advt. Agy. Assn., YMCA, Guardians, Alpha Delta Sigma. Democrat. Jewish. Office: 8383 Wilshire Blvd Beverly Hills CA 90211

GOULD, MORTON, composer, conductor; b. Richmond Hill, L.I., N.Y., Dec. 10, 1913; s. James and Frances (Arkin) G.; (married); four children. Student pub. schs., Richmond Hill. Later, NBC staff; at age 21 conducted and arranged series of programs over, WOR Mutual, Columbia networks; guest condr. major symphony orchs., concert and radio appearances, Europe, 1966, Australia, 1977, Japan, 1979, major compositions played by Toscanini, Mitropolous, Monteux, Stokowski, Rodzinski, Reiner, Golschmann, etc., Works include: 3 symphonies, Foster Gallery, Concerto for Orchestra, Latin Am. Symphonette, Spirituals, Cowboy Rhapsody, Lincoln Legend, Interplay, American Salute, etc; Wrote music and appeared film: Delightfully Dangerous; wrote: music for stage show Billion Dollar Baby; commd. by Ballet Theatre to write: music for ballet Fall River Legend; wrote: mus. score Windjammer; wrote and conducted symphony for, Band for West Point sesquicentennial celebration, 1952; wrote: CBS-TV documentary series entitled World War I; musical host: Nat. Ednl. TV series The World of Music Morton Gould; composer, condr.: score NBC-TV miniseries Holocaust, 1978; score recorded, RCA Records, world premiere of commd. work, Burchfield Gallery, (with Lorin Maazel and), Cleve. Orch., 1981; Composer: Inventions, 1953, Dance Variations, 1953, Showpiece for Orchestra, 1954, Cinerama Holiday, 1954, Declaration; symphonic narrative for orchestra, 1957, Jekyll and Hyde Variations; for orchestra, 1957, St. Lawrence Suite, 1958; Dialogues for Piano and Orchestra Venice for Double Orchestra, Vivaldi Gallery, Columbia, Troubador Music, Soundings, Symphony of Spirituals; commd. by, Nat. Endowment for Arts, American Ballads, N.Y. State Council for Arts, Something To Do; musical, lyrics by Carolyn Leigh, commd. by, U.S. Dept. Labor, also shorter works, numerous recs., RCA, Columbia, others; made first digital and direct disc recs. with, London Symphony and London Philharm., 1978 (Recipient Grammy award for best classical record 1966). Mem. ASCAP (dir.), Nat. Assn. Composers and Condrs., Am. Symphony Orch. League (dir.). Played piano and composed at age of four; concertized extensively as composer pianist during early years; vaudeville and stage work, radio; on staff of Music Hall at age 17. Address: 327 Melbourne Rd Great Neck NY 11021 *I have tried to make music as well as I possibly can, and through my craft to communicate to listeners.*

GOULD, RICHARD ALLAN, anthropologist, archaeologist, educator; b. Newton, Mass., Oct. 22, 1939; s. Samuel Brookner and Laura Johanna (Ohman) G.; m. Elizabeth Barber, Dec. 22, 1962. B.A. cum laude, Harvard, 1961; Ph.D., U. Calif., Berkeley, 1965. Asst. curator N. Am. archaeology Am. Mus. Natural History, N.Y.C., 1965-71, research asso., 1971—; asso. prof. anthropology U. Hawaii, Honolulu, 1971-76, prof., 1976-80, Brown U., Providence, R.I., 1980—; cons. in charge of planning exhibits Wattis Hall of Man, Calif. Acad. Scis., San Francisco, 1975-76. Author: The Archaeology of the Point St. George Site and Tolowa Prehistory, 1966, Yiwara, Foragers of the Australian Desert, 1969, Man's Many Ways, 1973, Puntutjarpa Rockshelter and the Australian Desert Culture, 1977, Explorations in Ethnoarchaeology, 1978, Living Archaeology, 1980, Modern Material Culture: The Archaeology of Us, 1981, Shipwreck Anthropology, 1983. Served with U.S. Army, 1972. Australian Nat. U. vis. fellow, 1977; Social Sci. Research Council research grantee, 1966-67; F.G. Voss research grantee Am. Mus. Natural History, 1969-70; NSF research grantee, 1973-77, 80, 81. Fellow Am. Anthrop. Assn.; mem. Soc. Am. Archaeology, Australian Inst. Aboriginal Studies (corr. mem.), AAAS (Chmn. sect. H-anthropology). Club: N.Y. Explorers. Office: Dept Anthropology Brown Univ Providence RI 02912

GOULD, ROY WALTER, engineer, physicist, educator; b. Los Angeles, Apr. 25, 1927; s. Roy Walter and Rosamonde (Stokes) G.; m. Ethel Savage Stratton, Aug. 23, 1952; children: Diana Stratton, Robert Clarke. B.S., Calif. Inst. Tech., 1949, Ph.D., 1956; M.S., Stanford, 1950. Mem. faculty Calif. Inst. Tech., Pasadena, 1955—, exec. officer for applied physics, 1973-79, chmn. div. engring. and applied sci., 1979—, Simon Ramo prof. engring., 1980—; dir. div. controlled thermonuclear research AEC, 1970-72. Served with USNR, 1945-46. Fellow Am. Phys. Soc., IEEE; mem. Nat. Acad. Scis., Nat. Acad. Arts and Scis., Nat. Acad. Engring. Home: 808 Linda Vista Ave Pasadena CA 91103

GOULD, STEPHEN JAY, paleontologist, educator; b. N.Y.C., Sept. 10, 1941; s. Leonard and Eleanor (Rosenberg) G.; m. Deborah Ann Lee, Oct. 3, 1965; children: Jesse, Ethan. A.B., Antioch Coll., Yellow Springs, Ohio, 1963; Ph.D., Columbia U., 1967. Mem. faculty Harvard U., 1967—, prof. geology, 1973—. Author: Ontogeny and Phylogeny, 1977, Ever Since Darwin, 1977, The Panda's Thumb, 1980, A View of Life, 1981, The Mismeasure of Man, 1981, Hen's Teeth and Horse's Toes, 1983; also numerous articles, monthly column This View of Life in Natural History mag. Recipient Nat. Mag. award for essays and criticism, 1980; Nat. Book award in sci., 1981; award for gen. non-fiction Nat. Book Critics Circle, 1982; McArthur Found. prize fellow, 1981—; grantee NSF. Fellow AAAS; mem. Paleontological Soc. (Schuchert award 51975), Soc. Study Evolution, Soc. Systematic Zoology, Am. Soc. Naturalists, Sigma Xi. Address: Museum Comparative Zoology Harvard Univ Cambridge MA 02138

GOULD, WESLEY LARSON, political science, educator; b. Cleve., May 15, 1917; s. Francis E. and Helen M. (Larson) G.; m. Jean Sarah Barnard, Jan. 24, 1946; children: Francis Barnard, Sarra Marie, Margaret Elizabeth Gould Guldan, Leona Larson. A.B., Baldwin-Wallace Coll., 1939; M.A., Ohio State U., 1941; postgrad. U. Calif., Berkeley, 1941-42; Ph.D., Harvard U., 1949. Instr. Northeastern U., Boston, 1946-49; asst. prof. Purdue U., Lafayette, Ind., 1949-58, asso. prof., 1958-61, prof., 1961-67; vis. prof. Northwestern U., 1963-64; prof. polit. sci. Wayne State U., Detroit, 1967-83, prof. emeritus, 1984—; cons. internat. law study U.S. Naval War Coll., summer 1960; Ph.D. examiner Patna U., India, 1963-64; vis. scholar U. Winnipeg, summer 1979; cons. Detroit City Charter Revision, 1972-73, Can. Rev. of Studies in Nationalism, 1973-74. Author: An Introduction to International Law, 1957, (with L. Erades) International and Municipal Law in the Netherlands and the U.S, 1961, (with M. Barkun) International Law and Social Sciences, 1970; contbr. articles to profl. jours. Mem. adv. council on community service of continuing edn. programs Mich. Dept. Edn., 1971-72; Mem. regional structure, transp. and communications coms. Regional Citizens Project, Met. Fund, Inc., 1973-74; del. Mich. Democratic Conv., 1971, 72; bd. dirs. Citizens Council for Land Use Research and Edn., 1974-79. Served with U.S. Army, 1942-45; PTO. Recipient Alumni Merit award Baldwin-Wallace Coll., 1984; Fellow, U. Liverpool, 1974-75; Am. Soc. Internat. Law grantee, 1964; Wayne U. research grantee, 1970; Earhart Found. grantee, 1974; Social Sci. Research Council grantee, 1957. Mem. Am. Polit. Sci. Assn., Internat. Polit. Sci. Assn., Midwest Polit. Sci. Assn., Acad. Polit. Sci., Am. Soc. Legal and Polit. Philosophy, Internat. Assn. Philosophy of Law and Social Philosophy, Am. Soc. Internat. Law (exec. council 1959-62), Ind. Acad. Social Scis. (dir. 1958-60), Am. Assn. Higher Edn., Soc. Gen. Systems, Law and Society Assn., Detroit Econ. Club, Detroit Council World Affairs, Internat. Studies Assn. (exec. com.), AAUP, Am. Soc. Public Adminstrn., Assn. Can. Studies U.S., Sigma Pi Alpha. Democrat. Episcopalian. Club: Harvard of Eastern Mich. Home: 21611 Whitmore St Oak Park MI 48237 Office: Dept Polit Sci Wayne State U Detroit MI 48202 *A scholar's life should be a search for the unknown either through finding hard-to-get information, or by seeking new techniques for extracting the deeper meanings of data. Even if one discovers that a seemingly effective path toward better use of knowledge is a dead end, that in itself is worth discovering so that others will not attempt what does not work.*

GOULD, WILLIAM EBEN, mathematics educator; b. Orange, N.J., May 7, 1934; s. Eben Cassius and Margaret (Purple) G. B.A., Rutgers U., 1956, M.S., 1958; M.A., Princeton U., 1964, Ph.D., 1966. Instr. Rutgers U., New Brunswick, N.J., 1961-62, Washington Coll., Chestertown, Md., 1962-66; assoc. prof. Bradley U., Peoria, Ill., 1966-69; assoc. prof. math. Calif. State U. -Dominguez Hills, Carson, 1969-74, prof., 1974—. Mem. Math. Assn. Am., AAUP, Sigma Xi. Home: 12529 Sleepyhollow Ln Cerritos CA 90701 Office: Dept math Calif State U -Dominguez Hills Carson CA 90747

GOULD, WILLIAM RICHARD, utility executive, engineer; b. Provo, Utah, Oct. 31, 1919; s. William Gilbert and Pauline Eva (Faser) G.; m. Erlyn Arvilla Johnson, Mar. 20, 1942; children: Erlyn Sharon, William Richard, Gilbert John, Wayne Raymond. B.S. in Mech. Engring, U. Utah, 1942; postgrad., MIT, UCLA, U. Idaho. Registered profl. engr., Utah, Calif. With So. Calif. Edison Co., 1948—, mgr. engring., 1962-63, v.p. engring., constrn., planning, 1963-67, sr. v.p., 1967-73, exec. v.p., 1973-78, pres., 1978—, chmn. bd., chief exec. officer, 1980—, also dir.; dir. Union Bank, Aerospace Corp., Kaiser Steel Corp., Energy Services, Inc., Mono Power Co., Electric Systems Co., Project Mgmt. Corp., Breeder Reactor Corp., Associated So. Investment Co., Beckman Instruments.; Chmn. Calif. Tech. Services Adv. Council. Pres. U.S. nat. com. Internat. Congress Large Electric Systems; past chmn. bd. Atomic Indsl. Forum.; Mem. sci. and engring. com. U. Redlands; bd. councilors Sch. Engring., U. So. Calif.; mem. energy adv. bd., trustee Calif. Inst. Tech.; mem. nat. regulatory commn., exec. com. Assembly Engring.; mem. nat. adv. bd. U. Utah; mem. adv. com. electric certificate program U. Calif. at Los Angeles.; Trustee Long Beach Community Hosp.; bd. dirs. Nat. Energy Found., Electric Power Research Inst., Eyring Research Inst., Los Angeles World Affairs Council, Los Angeles Philharm. Assn. Served to lt. USN, 1942-47. Recipient George Westinghouse Gold Medal award Assn. Mech. Engrs., 1979, Disting. Alumni award U. Utah, 1981, Disting. Contbn. award Inst. Advancement Engrs., 1982, Engring. award for Disting. Mgmt. U. So. Calif., 1983; named Electric Industry Man of Yr. Electric Light and Power Mag., 1983. Fellow ASME (Centennial award for service 1980), Inst. Advanced Engring. (chmn. bd., Engr. of Year 1970); mem. Nat. Acad. Engring., Newcomen Soc. N.Am., Edison Electric Inst. (dir., chmn. exec. adv. bd. policy com. on nuclear power, mem. policy com. on research), Los Angeles Council Engrs. and Scientists (adv. com.), Pacific Coast Elec. Assn. (dir.), Los Angeles C. of C. Mem. Ch. of Jesus Christ of Latter-day Saints. Club: California. Home: 6441 Shire Way Long Beach CA 90815 Office: 2244 Walnut Grove Ave Rosemead CA 91770

GOULDEN, JOSEPH CHESLEY, author; b. Marshall, Tex., May 23, 1934; s. Joe C. and Lecta M. (Everitt) G.; m. Leslie Cantrell Smith, 1979; children by previous marriage: Joseph C., Jim Craig. Student, U. Tex., 1952-56. Reporter Marshall News Messenger, 1956, Dallas News, 1958-61, Phila. Inquirer, 1961-68. Books include The Curtis Caper, 1965, Monopoly, 1968, Truth is the First Casualty, 1969, The Money Givers, 1971, Meany, 1972, The Superlawyers, 1972, The Benchwarmers, 1974, The Best Years, 1976, The Million Dollar Lawyers, 1978, Korea: The Untold Story of the War, 1982, Jerry Wurf: Labor's Last Angry Man, 1982; co-author: (with Paul Dickson) There Are Alligators in Our Sewers, 1983; editor: books include Mencken's Last Campaign, 1976. Served with U.S. Army, 1956-58. Mem. Tex. Inst. Letters, Washington Ind. Writers, H.L. Mencken, Phi Kappa Tau. Home: 2500 Q St NW Washington DC 20007 Office: Brandt & Brandt 1501 Broadway New York NY 10036

GOULDING, ALAN C., supermarket executive; 1930; married. B.A., Rutgers U., 1956. Corp. exec. v.p., pres. Colonial Store div. Grand Union Co., 1953-79; exec. v.p. mktg. and purchasing Great Atlantic & Pacific Tea Co., Inc., Montvale, N.J., 1980-82, sr. exec. v.p., 1982—. Served to 1st lt. U.S. Army, 1951-53. Office: Great Atlantic & Pacific Tea Co Inc 2 Paragon Dr Montvale NJ 07645 *

GOULDING, RAYMOND WALTER, actor; b. Lowell, Mass., Mar. 20, 1922; s. Thomas M. and Mary (Philbin) G.; m. Elizabeth Leader, May 18, 1945; children: Raymond, Thomas, Barbara, Bryant, Mark, Melissa. Pres. Goulding, Elliot, Greybar Prodns. Inc., N.Y.C., 1954—. Actor numerous network radio and TV prodns., motion pictures; co-star: Bob and Ray Show, NBC, CBS, ABC, from 1951; appeared: in movie Cold Turkey, 1969, Author! Author!, 1982; Broadway play The Two and Only, 1970-71; author: (with Bob Elliot) book From Approximately Coast to Coast. . .It's the Bob and Ray Show, 1983. Served to 1st lt. AUS, 1942-46. Screen Actors Guild, AFTRA, Am. Guild Variety Artists. Office: Goulding-Elliot-Greybar Prodns 420 Lexington Ave New York NY 10017 *

GOULDNER, HELEN, university dean, political science educator; b. Seattle, Dec. 26, 1923; d. John W. and Nell B. (Saltgaver) Beem; 1 son, Andrew W. B.A., U. Puget Sound, 1945; M.Ed., U. Wash., 1950; Ph.D., UCLA, 1959. Asso. prof., chmn. dept. sociology Lindenwood Coll., St Charles, Mo., 1959-62; asso. prof. dept. sociology, coordinator undergrad. program Washington U., St. Louis, 1963-67, prof. dept. sociology, 1968-72, prof., chmn. dept., 1972-73; prof. sociology U. Del., Newark, 1973—, chmn. dept., 1973-74; dean Coll. Arts and Sci., 1974—; bd. dirs. council Coll. Arts and Scis., 1976—; cons. U. Md., 1978, St. Francis Coll., 1979, Va. Commonwealth U., 1980, U. Ala., 1980. Author: Teachers' Pets, Troublemakers and Nobodies: Black Children in Elementary School, 1978; co-author: Modern Sociology. Asso. editor Sociol. Quar., Sociology of Edn. Bd. dirs. Wilmington World Affairs Council, 1976—; trustee Wilmington Med. Center, 1983—. Recipient Educator's award Delta Kappa Gamma, 1979; Social Sci. Research Council research tng. fellow; U.S. Office of Edn. grantee. Mem. Internat. Sociol. Assn., Am. Sociol. Assn., Eastern Sociol. Assn. (exec. council 1975-78), Nat. Assn. State Univs. and Land Grant Colls. (commn. on arts and scis. 1975-77), Mo. Soc. Sociology and Anthropology (pres. 1971). Home: 4 Kent Way Newark DE 19711 Office: Dean's Office Coll Arts and Science U Del Newark DE 19716

GOULET, CHARLES RYAN, insurance company executive; b. Fond du Lac, Wis., Oct. 13, 1927; s. Charles N. and Irene (Ryan) G.; m. Jeanne Comfort, Aug. 18, 1951; 1 son, Christopher Robert. B.A., Beloit Coll., 1951; M.B.A., U. Chgo., 1953. Adminstrv. resident Jefferson-Hillman Hosp., Birmingham, Ala., 1952-53; adminstrv. asst., asst. supt. Cleve. City Hosp., 1953-55; asst. prof. U. Pitts., 1955-58; asso. dir. Johns Hopkins Hosp., 1958-62; dir. U. Chgo. Hosps. and Clinics, 1962-69; prof. hosp. adminstrn. U. Chgo., 1962-69, asso. dir. program in hosp. adminstrn., 1962-69; prin. Cresap, McCormick and Paget, Inc., mgmt. cons., Chgo., 1969-71; v.p. Blue Cross-Blue Shield, Chgo., 1971-75, exec. v.p., 1975—; exec. sec. Assn. U. Programs in Hosp. Adminstrn., 962-65; pres. Chgo. Hosp. Council, 1968; pres. HMO Ill., Inc., 1976-82, vice chmn., 1982—; treas. Ill. Hosp. Assn., 1969; mem. exec. com. Council Teaching Hosps., Assn. Am. Med. Colls., 1966-69. Mem. adv. council Kellogg Found., 1965-67; Bd. dirs. Hyde Park Dept. YMCA, 1966-68, Coop. Blood Replacement Plan, Home for Destitute Crippled Children, 1965-69, Chgo. Home for Incurables, 1966-69, Harvard-St. George Sch. Chgo., 1968-72, Hosp. Planning Council Met. Chgo., 1968-69, Comprehensive Health Planning, Chgo., 1968-71, Ill. Regional Med. Program, 1967-69; bd. dirs. Am. Blood Commn., 1976—, v.p., 1978-83; mem. governing commn. Cook County Hosp., 1969-70; mem. Ill. Health Fin. Authority, 1979-82. Served to 2d lt. Med. Adminstrn. Corps AUS, 1946-47. Recipient Bachmeyer award U. Chgo., 1953; Disting. Service award Beloit Coll., 1976. Fellow Am. Coll. Hosp. Adminstrs.; mem. Am., Ill. hosp. assns., Assn. Tchrs. Preventive Medicine, Phi Kappa Psi. Clubs: Skyline, Quadrangle, Mid America (Chgo.); St. Charles (Ill.) Country; Big Foot Country (Fontana, Wis.). Home: 1001 S Batavia Ave Geneva IL 60134 Office: 233 N Michigan Ave Chicago IL 60601

GOULET, LEO D., diversified company executive; b. 1926. A.A., Canal Zone Jr. Coll., 1948; B.S., U. Denver, 1949. Gen. mgr. C.O. Mason, Panama, S.Am., 1949-52; procurement officer Panama Canal Co., 1952-55; gen. mgr. Gerber Products Co., Panana (subs.), 1960, Gerber Products Co., Venezuela (subs.), 1955—; with Gerber Products Co., 1955—, asst. export mgr., 1955-59, export sales mgr., 1959-68, gen. mgr., Central and S.Am., 1968-70, Latin Am., 1970-73, v.p., 1973-81, v.p., gen. mgr. gen. merchandising div., Fremont, Mich., 1981-82, exec. v.p., gen. mgr. merchandising div., 1982-83, chief operating officer, dir., 1983—. Served with USN, 1944-46. Office: Gerber Products Co 445 State St Fremont MI 49412 *

GOULET, ROBERT GERARD, singer, actor; b. Lawrence, Mass., Nov. 26, 1933; s. Joseph and Jeanette (Gauthier) G.; m. Louise Longmore, 1956 (div.); 1 dau., Nicolette; m. Carol Lawrence, Aug. 1963; children: Christopher, Michael. Student, Royal Conservatory Music, Toronto, Ont., Can. Made: Broadway debut in Camelot, 1960; star: ABC-TV series Blue Light, 1966, numerous guest TV appearances; star films Honeymoon Hotel, 1964, I'd Rather Be Rich, 1964, I Deal in Danger, 1966, Underground, 1970, Atlantic City, 1981. Recipient Grammy award for best new artist of, 1962; Gold medal award, 1964; Tony award for performance in play The Happy Time, 1968. Office: care Internat Creative Mgmt 8899 Beverly Blvd Los Angeles CA 90048

GOULETAS-CAREY, EVANGELINE, wife of gov. of N.Y.; m. Hugh Carey, 1981. M.A. in Math, Northeastern Ill. State Coll. Mem. faculty dept. math. Northeastern Ill. State Coll.; with Chgo. Bd. Edn.; prin. Am. Invesco Corp., Chgo., from 1969; ptnr. IMB (internat. mcht. banking), Chgo., from 1969. Trustee DePaul U.; chairperson bd. trustees Com. for Thalassemia Concern; chairperson Combined Cardiac Research Women's Found., U. Chgo.; mem. exec. bd. Chgo. City Ballet. Recipient Businesswoman of Year award Soc. of the Little Flower, 1979; Great Am. award B'nai B'rith, 1977. Mem. Nat. Assn. Realtors, Inst. Real Estate Mgmt., Chgo. Real Estate Bd., Women in Real Estate, Women's Council Realtors, Chgo. Network, Am. Mgmt. Assn., Pres.'s Assn. of Am. Mgmt. Assn. Greek Orthodox. Address: 870 UN Plaza New York NY 10017

GOULIAN, MEHRAN, physician, biochemist, hematologist, educator; b. Weehawken, N.J., Dec. 31, 1929; s. Dicran and Shamiram (Mzrakjian) G.; m. Susan Hook, Aug. 5, 1961; children—Eric, Mark, Jonathan. A.B., Columbia, 1950, M.D., 1954. Intern Barnes Hosp., St. Louis, 1954-55; resident Mass. Gen. Hosp., Boston, 1958-59, 61; fellow hematology Harvard, 1960, 62-63, Yale-New Haven Hosp., 1959-60; fellow biochemistry Stanford, 1965-67; instr. medicine Harvard Med. Sch., 1963-65; asso. prof. medicine, research asso. biochemistry U. Chgo.-Argonne Cancer Research Hosp., 1967-69, asso. prof. and biochemistry, 1969-70; prof. medicine U. Calif. at San Diego, 1970—. Served with USPHS, 1955-57. Home: 8433 Prestwick Dr La Jolla CA 92037 Office: Dept Medicine M-013 U Calif at San Diego La Jolla CA 92093

GOUNARIS, ANNE DEMETRA, biochemistry educator, researcher; b. Boston, Oct. 27, 1924; d. Demetrios Themistocles and Kalio (Gouvalaris). R.N. Mass. Gen. Hosp., 1946; A.B., Boston U., 1955; Ph.D., Harvard U., 1960. Research assoc. Brookhaven Nat. Lab., Upton, N.Y., 1960-62, Carlsberg Lab., Copenhagen, 1962-64, Rockefeller U., N.Y.C., 1964-66; prof. Vassar Coll., Oughkeepsie, N.Y., 1966—; vis. fellow Mass. Gen. Hosp., Boston, 1978-83.; vis. scientist Strangeways Research Lab., Cambridge, Eng., 1980-81. Contbr. (articles to profl. jours.). NIH grantee, 1968-71, 1972-76; Ann Horton Fellow, 1980-81; named Collegium Disting. Alumnae, Boston U., 1974. Mem. Am. Chem. Soc., Am. Soc. Biol. Chemists, AAUP, AAAS, N.Y. Acad. Scis., Phi Beta Kappa, Sigma Xi. Office: Vassar Coll. Raymond Ave Poughkeepsie NY 12601

GOURD, ROBERT, member Canadian Parliment, businessman; b. Amos, Que., Can., 1933. Student, Academie Roussin, Montreal. Mfr. and dir. electric cable co. and four wheel drive firm; dir. Liberal Party of Can., Que., 1974-78; elected to House of Commons, Que., 1979—, mem. caucus policy group for resources and small bus. and culture and recreation, 1979-80, chmn. standing com. on communications and culture. Office: 10991 rang St Etienne St Benoit Mirabel PQ Canada J0N 1K0 *

GOURDEAU, ROBERT, pediatrician, hematologist, association executive; b. Quebec, Que., Can., July 2, 1920; s. Raoul G. and Marie-Ange (Gosselin) G.; m. Pauline Hebert, July 4, 1947; 1 dau., Diane. B.A., Laval U., Quebec, 1940, M.D., 1944. Gen. practice medicine St. Quentin, N.B., Can., 1947-53; resident in pediatrics and hematology Montreal Children's Hosp., 1953-60; practice medicine specializing in pediatrics and hematology Montreal Children's Hosp. and Royal Victoria Hosp.; also mem. faculty McGill U. Med. Sch., 1960-69; dir. pediatrics Laval U. Hosp., 1969-74, med. dir., 1974-76; prof. pediatrics Laval U. Med. Sch., 1969—, dir. continuing med. edn., 1975-80, asst. dean, 1975-80; dir. fellowship affairs Royal Coll. Physicians and Surgeons of Can., Ottawa, Ont., 1980—. Author; editor publs. in field; pres., editor-in-chief: La Vie Medicale au Canada Francais, 1976-80; editor-in-chief: Royal Coll. Annals, 1980—. Bd. govs. Laval U. Found. Served with M.C. Canadian Army, 1942-46. Mem. Canadian Med. Assn. (bd. adminstrn., pres.), Que. Med. Assn. (bd. adminstrn), Canadian Pediatric Soc., Royal Coll. Physicians and Surgeons Can., Am., Internat. hematology socs., Council Biology Editors, World Fedn. Hemophilia, French Soc. Pediatrics (corr.). Roman Catholic. Home: 525 St Laurent Blvd Unit 7 Ottawa ON K1K 2Z9 Canada Office: RCPSC 74 Stanley Ave Ottawa ON K1N 1P4 Canada

GOURDINE, SIMON PETER, foundation executive; b. Jersey City, July 30, 1940; s. Simon Samuel and Laura Emily (Rembert) G.; m. Patricia Campbell, Aug. 1, 1964; children: David Laurence, Peter Christopher, Laura Allison. B.A., City Coll. N.Y., 1962; J.D., Fordham U., 1965; P.M.D., Harvard Bus. Sch., 1979. Bar: N.Y. 1966, U.S. Dist. Ct. (so. dist.) N.Y. 1967, U.S. Supreme Ct. 1976. Asst. U.S. atty. So. Dist. N.Y., 1967-69; atty. Celanese Corp., 1969-70; asst. to commr. Nat. Basketball Assn., N.Y.C., 1970-72, v.p. adminstrn., 1973-74, dep. commr., 1974-81; commr. N.Y.C. Dept. Consumer Affairs, 1982-84; sec. The Rockefeller Found., 1984—; mem. N.Y. State Banking Bd., 1979—. Bd. dirs. 100 Black Men, Inc., 1974—, Police Athletic League, 1974—; mem. N.Y.C. Civil Service Commn., 1981-82, Gov.'s Exec. Adv. Commn. on Adminstrn. Justice, 1981-82, Mayor's Com. on Taxi Regulatory Issues., 1981-82. Served to capt. U.S. Army, 1965-67. Decorated Army Commendation medal. Home: 5251 Fieldston Rd Bronx NY 10471 Office: The Rockefeller Found 1133 Ave of the Americas New York NY 10036

GOUREVITCH, PETER ALEXIS, educator; b. N.Y.C., June 25, 1943; s. Alexander and Sylvia (Garvy) G.; m. Lisa N. Hirschman, Oct. 23, 1976; children: Alexander, Nicholas. B.A., Oberlin Coll., 1963; Ph.D., Harvard U., 1969. Asst. prof. Harvard U., Cambridge, 1969-73, assoc. prof., 1973-74, dir. Ctr. European Studies, 1971-72, 1975-76; assoc. prof. McGill U., Montreal, Que., Can., 1974-79; prof. polit. sci. U. Calif.-San Diego, 1979—, chmn. dept. polit. sci., 1980-83. Author: Paris and the Provinces, 1980; co-editor: Industrial Relations in Comparative Perspective, 1981, France in be Troubled World and Economy, 1982; editor: Public Policy, 1971; mem. editorial bd. Internat. Orgn., 1981—. Mem. Council European Studies (exec. com. 1980-82), Socila Sci. Research Council (W. European com. 1981—), Am. Polit. Sci. Assn. Home: 2270 Middleton Way San Diego CA 92109

GOURLEY, DESMOND ROBERT HUGH, pharmacologist, educator; b. Thunder Bay, Can., Nov. 2, 1922; s. Hugh and Ida (Wilson) G.; m. Marjorie Edith Curl, Sept. 6, 1946; children—Robin C., David W., Alan W.H., Bruce D., Donald R. B.A., U. Toronto, 1945, Ph.D., 1949; postgrad., U. Freiburg, 1968-69. Demonstrator in zoology U. Toronto, 1945-49; research asst. U. Va., Charlottesville, 1949-51, asst. prof., 1951-53, asso. prof., 1953-62, prof. pharmacology, 1962-73, acting chmn. dept. pharmacology, 1965, chmn., 1967-68; adj. instr. Sch. Continuing Edn., 1970—; mem. Senate, 1966-73; prof., chmn. pharmacology Eastern Va. Med. Sch., Norfolk, 1973—; adj. prof. dept. chem. scis. Old Dominion U., Norfolk, 1975—; mem. U.S. Pharmacopeial Conv., 1960, 80. Author: Interactions of Drugs with Cells, 1971, Problems in Pharmacology, 4th edit, 1981; Contbr. articles to profl. jours. Fellow A. Von Humboldt Found., Germany, 1968. Mem. Am. Physiol. Soc., Am. Soc. Pharmacology and Exptl. Therapeutics, Pharmacology Soc. Can., Soc. for Exptl. Biology and Medicine. Home: 7425 Dehlman Ave Norfolk VA 23505

GOURLEY, RONALD ROBERT, college dean, architect; b. St. Paul, Oct. 5, 1919; s. Robert Thomas and Eva Irene (Cardle) G.; m. Phyllis Mary McDonald, Apr. 10, 1950; children: Robert McDonald, Karen Ellen, Geoffrey James. B.Arch., U. Minn., 1943; M.Arch., Harvard U., 1948. Instr. architecture MIT, 1948-53; vis. prof. Royal Acad., Copenhagen, 1952; prof. architecture Harvard U., 1953-70; partner, co-founder firm Sert, Jackson & Gourley, Cambridge, Mass., 1958-64; co-founder, partner Integrated Design Services Group, Cambridge, 1966-72; partner Gourley/Richmond (architects), 1972-76, Gourley, Richmond and Mitchell (Architects), 1976-82; tech. coordinator Boston Archtl. Center, 1976-77; dean Coll. Architecture, U. Ariz., Tucson, 1977—; pvt. practice, Cambridge, 1954-58, 64-66. Prin. works include Wheaton Coll. Library. Served with AUS, 1944-46. Fellow AIA; mem. Boston Soc. Architects, Ariz. Soc. Architects, Boston Archtl. Center. Home: 2522 E 3d St Tucson AZ also Middle Rd Martha's Vineyard Chilmark MA Office: Coll Arch U Ariz Tucson AZ 85721

GOUSE, S. WILLIAM, JR., scientist; b. Utica, N.Y., Dec. 15, 1931; s. S. William and Charlotte Virginia (Parzych) G.; m. Jacqueline Ann McLaughlin, Aug. 6, 1955; children: Linda Ellen, S. William III. S.B., S.M., Mass. Inst. Tech., 1954, Sc.D., 1958. Instr. mech. engring. Mass. Inst. Tech., 1956-57, asst. prof., 1957-61, 62-65, assoc. prof., 1965-67, lectr., 1967-68; prof. mech. engring., prin. research engr. Transportation Research Inst. of Carnegie-Mellon U., 1967-69; staff mem. Office Sci. and Tech. of Exec. Office of the Pres., Washington, 1969-70; asso. dean Carnegie Inst. Tech. and Sch. Urban and Pub. Affairs of Carnegie-Mellon U., 1971-73; dir. Office Research and Devel. U.S. Dept. Interior, 1973-75; acting dir. Office Coal Research, 1974-75; dep. asst. adminstr. fossil energy ERDA, 1974-77; chief scientist Mitre Corp., 1977-79, v.p., 1979-80, v.p., gen. mgr., 1980—; cons. to industry. Contbr. articles to profl. jours. Served with ordnance AUS, 1961-62. Visking Corp. fellow, 1954-55; Gen. Electric Co. W. Rice Jr. fellow, 1955-56; recipient Ralph Teetor award Soc. Automotive Engrs., 1966. Clubs: Cosmos, Explorers. Home: 8410 Martingale Dr McLean VA 22102

GOUSHA, RICHARD PAUL, educator; b. Balt., Sept. 3, 1923; s. Paul T. and Emma (Cartwright) G.; m. Catherine Morris, Aug. 20, 1949; children—Catherine Anne, Michael Richard. A.B., Heidelberg (Ohio) Coll., 1947; M.A., Western Res. U., 1949; Ed.D., Ind. U., 1960. Tchr., Bettsville, Ohio, 1947-48, local sch. exec., Putnam County, Ohio, 1949, McCutchenville, Ohio, 1950-53, Woodville, Ohio, 1954-56, supt. schs., Amherst, Ohio, 1956-59; asst. to dir. research and field service Ind. U. Sch. Edn., 1959; supt. pub. schs., Cuyahoga Falls, Ohio, 1960-64, supt. pub. instruction Del., 1964-67, supt. pub. schs., Milw., 1967-74; dean Sch. Edn., Ind. U., Bloomington, 1974-80; mem. interim steering com. Edn. Commn. of States, 1965-67; ex officio mem. sec.; Higher Edn. Adv. Com. Del., 1964-67; chmn. Nat. Schs. Com. Econ. Edn.; vis. prof. U. Wis.-Milw. Sch. Edn., summer 1970; mem. policy council Tchr. Corps, 1974-80. Mem. Mental Health Planning Com. Milwaukee County; mem. adv. com. Milw. Children's Ct.; mem. Wis. regional bd. NCCJ; pres. Wis. council Econ. Edn., 1972-74; pres., exec. com. Council Great City Schs., 1973-74; bd. dirs. Milwaukee County chpt. ARC, Milw. Symphony Orch., Milw. Tech. Coll., 1967-74; trustee Jt. Council on Econ. Edn.; bd. govs. Jr. Achievement Southeastern Wis. Served with inf. AUS, World War II; ETO. Decorated Bronze Star. Mem. Am. Edn. Research Assn., Am. Assn. Sch. Adminstrs., Am. Assn. for Higher Edn., Ind. Assn. Pub. Sch. Supts. (asso.), Council Econ. Edn., Nat. Tchr. Exam. Council, Ohio PTA (hon. life), Phi Delta Kappa, Pi Lambda Theta. Presbyn. Clubs: Schoolmasters of Wis., Masons, Rotary. Home: 707 Christopher Dr Bloomington IN 47401 Office: Education Bldg Indiana U Bloomington IN 47405

GOUSSELAND, PIERRE LEOPOLD, mining company executive; b. Tonnay-Charente, France, Jan. 14, 1922; s. Edmond and Marthe (Lemarre) G.; m. Mireille Bonnet, Apr. 3, 1948; children: Marie Christine, Dominique, Philippe. Ingenieur Civil des Mines, Ecole Nationale Superieure des Mines, Paris, 1947; LL.B., U. Paris, 1947; postgrad., Mass. Inst. Tech., 1947-48. With AMAX Inc., 1948—; pres. Climax div., 1970-75, exec. v.p., 1975, pres., 1975-77, chmn. bd., chief exec. officer, Greenwich, Conn., 1977—, also dir.; dir. Am. Internat. Group, Inc., French Am. Banking Corp., Compagnie Francaise d'Entreprises Mineres, Metallurgiques et d'Investissements., IBM, Degussa A.G., Frankfurt, W. Ger.; mem. internat. adv. bd. Chase Manhattan Bank, N.Y.C., Credit Anstalt Bank verein, Wien, Austria. Mem. Brit. Iron, Steel Inst., Societe Francaise de Metallurgie, Verein Deutscher Eisenhuttenleute, Soc. Automotive Engrs., French-Am. C. of C. in U.S., Am. Soc. Metals, Am. Mining Congress (dir.), Copper

Devel. Assn. (dir.), Soc. Promotion de Mines (dir.), Council on Fgn. Relations, Metall. Soc.; mem. Asia Soc., Conf. Bd. Clubs: Economic (N.Y.C.); Copper. Home: 21 Deer Park Dr Greenwich CT 06830 Office: AMAX Center Greenwich CT 06830

GOUTERMAN, MARTIN PAUL, educator; b. Phila., Dec. 26, 1931; s. Bernard and Melba (Buxbaum) G. B.A., Central High Sch., Phila., 1949, U. Chgo., 1951, M.Sc., 1955, Ph.D. in Physics (NSF Predoctoral fellow), 1958. Faculty Harvard U., Cambridge, Mass., 1958-66; successively postdoctoral fellow, instr., asst. prof. chemistry dept.; faculty U. Wash., Seattle, 1966—, prof. chemistry, 1968—. Fellow Am. Inst. Physics; mem. Am. Chem. Soc., Sigma Xi. Research and publs. in spectroscopy, quantum chemistry, and solid state electronic properties of porphyrins. Office: Dept Chemistry U Wash Seattle WA 98195

GOVAN, JAMES FAUNTLEROY, librarian; b. Chattanooga, May 9, 1926; s. Gilbert Eaton and Christine (Noble) G.; m. Ann Henegar Bright, June 6, 1952; children: James Gardner, Andrew Eaton, Christine Noble, David Bright. B.A., U. of South, 1948; postgrad., Inst. Hist. Research, U. London, 1951-52; M.A., Emory U., 1955; Ph.D., Johns Hopkins U., 1960. Asst. prof. history U. of South, 1949; readers services librarian U. Ala., 1955-60; head librarian, prof. history Trinity U., 1961-65; head librarian Swarthmore (Pa.) Coll., 1965-73, lectr., 1969-73; univ. librarian, prof. library sci. U. N.C.-Chapel Hill, 1973—; coll. and univ. div. Tex. Library Assn., 1963-64, chmn. com. coll. library standards, 1964, mem. library devel. com., 1964-65; cons. Hampshire Coll. Library Conf., 1967. Author: The Pat Ireland Nixon Collection, 1965. Bd. dirs. Pa. Union Catalogue, 1966-73, treas., 1968-71, pres., 1971-73; bd. dirs. Swarthmore Pub. Library, 1971-73, Southeastern Library Network, 1974-77; chmn. Southeastern Library Network, 1976-77; mem. bibliog. services devel. program com. Council Library Resources, 1979—. Served with USNR, 1944-46; Served with U.S. Army, 1953-55. Council Library Resources fellow, 1970. Mem. ALA (com. on accreditation 1972-75, mem. council 1969-70, 75-76), N.C. Library Assn. (network com. 1979—), ARL (dir. 1980—, pres. 1982-83), Phi Beta Kappa, Beta Phi Mu. Home: 420 Whitehead Circle Chapel Hill NC 27514

GOVE, HARRY EDMUND, nuclear physicist, educator; b. Niagara Falls, Can., May 22, 1922; came to U.S., 1963, naturalized, 1969; s. Harry Golden and Lucia (Olmsted) G.; m. Elizabeth Alice dePencier, Aug. 20, 1945; children: Pauline Lucia, Diana Elizabeth. B.Sc., Queen's U., Kingston, Ont., 1944; Ph.D., MIT, 1950. Research asst. Nat. Research Council, Chalk River, Can., 1945-46, Mass. Inst. Tech., 1946-50, research asso., 1950-52; asso. research officer Atomic Energy of Can., Ltd., Chalk River, 1952-59, br. head nuclear physics, 1956-63, sr. research officer, 1959-63; on leave with Niels Bohr Inst., Copenhagen, 1961-62; prof. physics, dir. nuclear structure research lab. U. Rochester, 1963—, chmn. dept. physics and astronomy, 1977-80; on leave with Lab. de Physique Nucléaire et d'Instrumentation Nucléaire, C.R.N., Strasbourg, 1971-72; Mem. vis. com. Mass. Inst. Tech. Lab. Nuclear Research, 1966-68, Argonne Nat. Lab. physics div., 1966-69, Queen's U. Coll. Engring., 1968-70; mem. adv. com. physics div. NSF, 1969-71; mem. grant selection com. nuclear physics Nat. Sci. and Engring. Research Council Can., 1979-81; mem. ad hoc panel on meson factories Office Sci. and Tech., 1963; mem. selection panel NSF Postdoctoral Fellows, 1967, 69, 70; mem. vis. com. physics and accelerator depts. Brookhaven Nat. Lab., 1979—; mem. nat. heavy-ion lab. policy com. Oak Ridge Nat. Lab., 1975-76; chmn. panel on basic nuclear data compilations, NRC-Nat. Acad. Scis, 1975-80, mem. panel on future of nuclear sci., 1975-77; chmn. vis. com. Cyclotron Lab., U. Md., 1977-79. Divisional asso. editor: Phys. Rev. Letters, 1975-79; asso. editor: Ann. Rev. Nuclear Sci; Contbr. articles to profl. jours. Pres. Metro Act of Rochester, Inc., 1970-71; trustee Associated Univs., Inc., 1978-83. Served from sublt. to lt. Royal Canadian Navy, 1944-45. Recipient Pergamon Press Jari award, 1980. Fellow Am. Phys. Soc.; mem. Canadian Assn. Physicists. Democrat. Episcopalian. Club: Cosmos (Washington). Home: 113 Burrows Hill Dr Rochester NY 14625

GOVE, ROGER MADDEN, physician; b. Mechanicsburg, Ohio, Nov. 30, 1914; s. Thurman Harrison and Leah Marie (Madden) G.; m. Eleaner Jane Rooney, June 15, 1938; children—Jon Duane, Janet Marie (Mrs. David Dye), Joann Leah (Mrs. Jerry Webb) and Judith Lynn (twins). B.A., Ohio State U., 1937, M.D., 1941. Intern White Cross Hosp., Columbus, Ohio, 1941-42; resident psychiatry Columbus State Hosp., 1942, 45-46; Commonwealth Fund fellow child psychiatry Children's Service Center Wyoming Valley, Wilkes Barre, Pa., 1946-47; dir. Upper Miami Valley Guidance Center, Piqua, Ohio, 1947-50; supt. Columbus State Sch., 1950-54, 58-66; asst. commr. Ohio Div. Mental Hygiene, 1966-70, commr., 1970-74; chief Bur. Mental Retardation, 1954, 66—; med. dir. mental retardation unit Athens Mental Health and Mental Retardation Center, Athens, Ohio, 1977-78; practice medicine specializing in psychiatry, 1978—; supt. Juvenile Diagnostic Center, Columbus, 1954-58; clin. asst. prof. psychiatry and prof. pediatrics Ohio State U. Coll. Medicine, 1951—; Chmn. Task Force Mental Retardation Planning Ohio, 1963-65; mem. com. long term care United Cerebral Palsy Assn., 1963—. Trustee Urbana (Ohio) Coll., 1964-71. Served to capt. M.C. USAAF, 1942-45. Fellow Am. Assn. Mental Retardation (chmn. exam. bd. 1963-67); mem. Am. Psychiat. Assn., Ohio Psychiat. Assn. (pres. 1961), Epilepsy Assn. Ohio (v.p. 1979). Home and Office: 235 Old Village Rd Columbus OH 43228

GOVE, SAMUEL KIMBALL, political science educator; b. Walpole, Mass., Dec. 27, 1923. Student, Mass. State Coll., 1941-43; B.S. in Econs, U. Mass., 1947; M.A. in Polit. Sci, Syracuse U., 1951. Research asst. govt. and pub affairs U. Ill., 1950-51, research asso., 1951-54, mem. faculty, 1954—, prof. polit. sci., 1966—; dir. Inst. Govt. and Pub. Affairs, 1967—; Staff asst. Nat. Assn. Assessing Officers, 1949; mem. research staff Ill. Commn. Study State Govt., 1950-51; staff fellow Nat. Municipal League, 1955-56; exec. asst. Ill. Auditor Pub. Accounts, 1957; program coordinator Ill. Legis. Staff Intern Program, 1962-70; mem. com. financing higher edn. Ill. Master Plan Higher Edn., 1963; mem. Ill. Commn. Orgn. Gen. Assembly, 1965-69, 70-73, Ill. Commn. State Govt., 1965-67; cons. elections ABC, 1964, 66, 68; chmn. Champaign (Ill.) County Econ. Opportunity Council, 1966-67; state legis. research fellow Am. Polit. Sci. Assn., 1966-68; cons. Am. Council Edn., 1966-67; sec. Local Govts. Commn., 1967-69; staff dir. Ill. Constn. Study Commn., 1968-69; exec. sec. Gov. Ill. Constn. Research Group, 1969-70; mem. Ill. Constn. Study Commn., 1969-70; chmn. Citizens Task Force on Constl. Implementation, 1970-71; mem. Gov. Elect's Task Force on Transition, 1972; adv. council Ill. Dept. Local Govt. Affairs, 1969-79. Author numerous books, monographs and articles. Chmn. Champaign-Urbana Study Commn. on Intergovtl. Coop., 1976-78. Served to lt. (j.g.) USNR, 1943-46. Mem. AAUP (past chpt. pres., mem. nat. com. R 1969-75, 78—, nat. council 1978-80), Am. Polit Sci. Assn., Am. Soc. Pub. Adminstrn. (past chpt. chmn.; chmn. univs. govtl. research conf. 1969-71), Govtl. Research Assn. (dir. 1969-71), Ill. Hist. Soc., Midwest Polit. Sci. Assn. (v.p. 1978-80), Nat. Municipal League (council 1972-80, 81—), Nat. Acad. Public Adminstrn. Club: Cosmos. Home: 2006 Bruce Dr Urbana IL 61801 Office: Inst Govt and Pub Affairs Urbana-Champaign Campus Urbana IL

GOVIER, GEORGE WHEELER, chemical engineering educator; b. Nanton, Alta., Can., June 15, 1917; s. George Arthur and Gertrude (Wheeler) G.; m. Doris Eda Kemp, Feb. 23, 1940; children: Gertrude Rose, Katherine Mary, Susan Elizabeth. B.A.Sc. in Chem. Engring, U. B.C., 1939; M.Sc. in Phys. Chem, U. Alta., 1945; Sc.D. in Chem. Engring, U. Mich., 1949; LL.D., U. Calgary, 1976. Registered profl. engr., Province Alta. Faculty U. Alta., 1940—, prof. chem. engring., 1948—, head dept. chem. and petroleum engring., 1948-49, dean faculty engring., 1959-63; part-time prof. engring. U. Calgary, 1963-75; pres. Govier Cons. Services Ltd., 1978—; chmn. bd. Alta. Helium Ltd.; mem. Energy Resources Conservation Bd. Alta., 1948-78, dep. chmn. bd., 1959-62, chmn. bd., 1962-78; chmn. sci. program com. World Petroleum Congress, 1975-83; bd. dirs., v.p. Petroleum Recovery Inst., 1966—; bd. dirs. Sulphur Devel. Inst. Can., 1973-78; v.p. Coal Mining Research Centre, 1978-79; dir. Can. Foremost Ltd., Can. Mont. Gas Co. Ltd., Roan Resources Ltd., Texaco Can., Inc., Stone & Webster Can. Ltd., Coop. Energy Devel. Corp., Bow Valley Resource Services Ltd., others. Author: (with K. Aziz) The Flow of Complex Mixtures in Pipes, 1972; Contbr. numerous tech. papers to tech. lit. Decorated officer Order of Can.; recipient merit award Canadian Natural Gas Processing Assn., 1964; Sesquicentennial award U. Mich., 1967; Centennial medal, Can., 1967; gold medal Canadian Council Profl. Engrs., 1976; Achievement award Govt. Alta., 1976. Fellow Chem. Inst. Can. (chmn. chem. engring. div. 1948-49, vice chmn. 1959-60, councillor 1951-52, recipient R.S. Jane Meml. award 1964), Engring. Inst. Can. (chmn. chem. engring. div. com. tech. operations 1961-63), Am. Inst. Chem. Engrs.; mem. Can. Inst. Mining and Metallurgy (chmn. petroleum and natural gas div. 1950-51, pres. 1966-67, Selwyn G. Blaylock medal 1971), Assn. Profl. Engrs. Alta. (pres. 1957-58, mem. council 1959-60, Centennial award 1970, life). Clubs: Calgary Petroleum, Ranchmen's. Home: 1507 Cavanaugh Pl NW Calgary AB T2L 0M8 Canada Office: 335-8th Ave SW: Calgary AB Canada

GOVINDJEE, biophysics educator; b. Allahabad, India, Oct. 24, 1933; came to U.S., 1956, naturalized, 1972; s. Visheshwar Prasad and Savitri (Asthana) Asthana; m. Rajni Varma, Oct. 24, 1957; children: Anita Govindjee, Sanjay Govindjee. B.Sc., U. Allahabad, 1952, M.Sc., 1954; Ph.D., U. Ill., 1960. Lectr. botany U. Allahabad, 1954-56; grad. fellow U. Ill., Urbana, 1956-58, research asst., 1958-60, USPHS postdoctoral trainee biophysics, 1960-61, mem. faculty, 1961—, asso. prof. botany and biophysics, 1965-69, prof., 1969—, disting. lectr. Sch. Life Scis., 1978. Author: Photosynthesis, 1969; Editor: Bioenergetics of Photosynthesis, 1975, Photosynthesis: Carbon Assimilation and Plant Productivity; Energy Conversion by Plants and Bacteria, 2 vols, 1982; guest editor spl. issue: Biophys. Jour., 1972; spl. issue: Photochemistry and Photobiology, 1978; contbr. articles to profl. jours. Fellow AAAS, Nat. Acad. Scis. (India); mem. Am. Soc. Plant Physiologists, Biophys. Soc. Am., Am. Soc. Photobiology (council 1976, pres. 1981), AAUP, Sigma Xi. Home: 2401 Boudreau Dr Urbana IL 61801

GOWAN, ARTHUR MITCHELL, univ. dean; b. Cleghorn, Iowa, Dec. 1, 1910; s. William and Annie (Mitchell) G.; m. Marjorie Mace, June 19, 1940; children—Barbara (Mrs. Donald K. Watkins), Sandra (Mrs. Gary R. Kirk). B.A., U. No. Iowa, 1932; M.A., U. Ia., 1939; Ph.D., Iowa State U., 1947. Adminstr. secondary sch., Nevada, Iowa, 1932-42; supr. math. U.S. Naval Tng. Sch., Iowa State U., 1942-44; asst. to dean of engring. Iowa State U. at Ames, 1944-46, asst. registrar, 1946-51, registrar, 1951-65, dean admissions and records, 1965—; Ford Found. cons. Nat. Engring. U., Lima, Peru, 1965. Mem. Ames City Planning Commn., 1970—. Mem. Am. Assn. Collegiate Registrars and Admissions Officers, Am. Assn. Higher Edn., Phi Kappa Phi, Phi Mu Epsilon. Club: Kiwanian (lt. gov. Nebr.-Iowa dist. 1965). Home: 2532 Eisenhower St Ames IA 50010

GOWDY, CURTIS, sportscaster; b. Green River, Wyo., 1919; m. Jerre Dawkins, June 1949; children: Cheryl Ann, Curtis, Trevor. B.S., U. Wyo., 1942, LL.D., 1972. Formerly broadcaster for radio stas. in, Cheyenne, Wyo., and Oklahoma City; with Mel Allen broadcast N.Y. Yankees Baseball Team games, 1949-51; announcer for Boston Red Sox Baseball Team games, 1951-66; broadcaster Am. Football League games, 1961—; sports broadcaster NBC-TV, Major League Baseball Game of Week, World Series, Profl. Game of Week, Rose Bowl, Super Bowl, 1961-79; sports broadcaster NFL Football, Sports Spectacular CBS-TV, 1979—; host Am. Sportsman Outdoor Series for ABC-TV; owner radio stas. KOWB, Laramie, Wyo., WCCM-AM, WCGY-FM, Lawrence, Mass., WEAT AM-FM, West Palm Beach, Fla.; Pres. Basketball Hall Fame; chmn. Am. League Anglers. Served with USAAF, 1942-43. Named Sportscaster of Year, Nat. Assn. Sportwriters and Sport Broadcasters, 1965, 67; named to Sports Broadcasters Hall of Fame, 1981, Baseball Hall of Fame, 1984; recipient George Foster Peabody award, 1970, 4 Emmy awards as host and co-producer American Sportsman. Address: Curt Gowdy Broadcasting Inc 33 Franklin St Lawrence MA 01840

GOWEN, RICHARD JOSEPH, educational administrator; b. New Brunswick, N.J., July 6, 1935; s. Charles David and Esther Ann (Hughes) G.; m. Nancy A. Applegate, Dec. 28, 1955; children: Jeff, Cindy, Betsy, Susan, Kerry. B.S. in Elec. Engring., Rutgers U., 1957; M.S., Iowa State U., 1961, Ph.D., 1962. Registered profl. engr., Colo. Research engr. RCA Labs., Princeton, N.J., 1957; commd. USAF; ground electronics officer Yaak AFB, Mont., 1957-59; instr. USAF Acad., 1962-63, research assoc., 1963-64, asst. prof., 1964-65, assoc. prof., 1965-66, tenure assoc.prof. elec. engring., 1966-70, tenure prof. elec. engring, 1973-73, dir., prin. investigator NASA instrumentation group for cardiovascular studies, 1968-77; mem. NASA launch and recovery med. team Johnson Space Center, 1971-77; v.p., dean engring., profl. elec. engring. S.D. Sch. Mines and Tehc., Rapid City, 1977—; dir., prin. investigator NASA Program in support space cardiovascular studies, 1977—; co-chmn. Joint Industry; Nuclear Regulatory IEEE; Am. Nuclear Soc. Probabilistic Risk Assessment Gudelines for Nuclear Power Plants Project, 1980-83; mem. Dept. Def. Software Engring. Inst. Panel, 1983. Contbr. aritcles tp profl. jours.; patentee in field. Bd. dirs. St. Martins Acad., Rapid City, S.D. Named Outstanding Young Man of Colorado Springs Jaycees, 1967; reicpient Marrs Arnold Air Soc., 1967; recipient Outstanding Achievement in Field of Engring. Rutgers U., 1977, Profl. Achievement Citation in Engring. Iowa State U., 1983. Fellow IEEE; mem. Sigma Xi, Phi Kappa Phi, Tau Beta Phi, Eta Kappa Nu, Pi Mu Epsilon. Roman Catholic. Club: Rotary (Rapid City, S.D.). Home: 1609 Palo Verde Rapid City SD 57701 Office: SD Sch Mines and Tech 500 E St Joseph St Rapid City SD 57701

GOWETZ, IRENE, lawyer; b. Worcester, Mass., Aug. 28, 1907; d. Arthur E. and Alice (Hemenway) G.; m. Carl A. Remington, June 18, 1959. LL.B. cum laude, Northeastern U., 1929. Bar: Mass. 1929. Became partner firm Bowditch, Gowetz and Lane, Worcester, 1950, now ret.; Chmn. Mass. Ballot Law Commn., 1955-58. Bd. dirs. Girls Clubs Am., 1955-81. Republican. Home: Bunker Hill Apt 5C 1051 S Highland Ave Mount Dora FL 32757

GOY, ROBERT WILLIAM, psychologist, research administrator; b. Detroit, Jan. 25, 1924; s. George Frederick and Charlotte Elizabeth (McDowell) G.; m. Barbara Elaine Perry, Nov. 13, 1948; children: Michael Frederick, Peter William, Elizabeth Ruth. B.S., U. Mich., 1947; Ph.D., U. Chgo., 1953. Assoc. prof. anatomy U. Kans. Med. Sch., 1954-63; prof. med. psychology U. Oreg. Med. Sch.; chmn. dept. reproductive physiology and behavior Oreg. Regional Primate Research Center, 1963-71; prof. psychology U. Wis.; dir. Wis. Regional Primate Research Center, 1971—. Author: (with B.S. McEwen) Sexual Differentiation of the Brain, 1980; assoc. editor: Archives of Sexual Behavior, 1968—; editor: Hormones and Behavior, 1976—. Served with U.S. Army, 1943-46. USPHS postdoctoral fellow, 1954-56; USPHS grantee, 1954-56; NIMH grantee, 1963—. Mem. Am. Assn. Anatomists, Am. Psychol. Assn., Soc. Study Fertility, Soc. Study Reprodn., Endocrine Soc., Internat. Acad. Sex Research. Home: 1845 Summit Madison WI 53705 Office: 1220 Capitol Ct Madison WI 53706

GOYAN, JERE EDWIN, university dean, former government official; b. Oakland, Calif., Aug. 3, 1930; s. Gerald H. and Lucille (Johnson) G.; m. Patricia B. Mesirow, Aug. 24, 1952; children: Pamela, Terrence H., Andrea. B.S., U. Calif. Sch. Pharmacy, 1952, Ph.D., 1957. Asst. prof. pharmacy U. Mich., 1956-61, assoc. prof., 1961-63; assoc. prof. pharmacy and pharm. chemistry U. Calif. at San Francisco, 1963-65, prof., 1965-79, 81—; assoc. dean Sch. Pharmacy, 1966-67, dean, 1967-79, 80—; commr. FDA, 1979-81. Fellow AAAS; mem. Inst. Medicine, Nat. Acad. Scis., N.Y. Acad. Scis., AAUP, Am. Pharm. Assn., Acad. Pharm. Scis., Calif. Pharm. Assn., Am. Pub. Health Assn., Am. Assn. Colls. Pharmacy (pres. 1978-79), Sigma Xi, Rho Chi, Kappa Psi, Phi Lambda Upsilon. Office: U Calif Sch Pharmacy San Francisco CA 94143 *

GOYAN, MICHAEL DONOVAN, stockbroker; b. Eureka, Calif., Sept. 18, 1938; s. Gerald Hazen and Lucille (Johnson) G.; m. Marylee Grant, Nov. 24, 1961; children: Michael Donovan, Kevin Lee. A.B., Occidental Coll., 1960. Stockbroker, allied mem. William R. Staats, Los Angeles, 1961-74; ptnr., stockbroker Crowell, Weedon & Co., Los Angeles, 1974—; mem. hearing bd. N.Y. Stock Exchange, 1970—. Bd. dirs. Inst. Internat. Edn., Los Angeles and N.Y.C., 1972-78, West Coast nat. trustee. Mem. Newcomen Soc. Clubs: Annandale Golf (Pasadena); Long Beach Yacht; Alamitos Bay Yacht (Long Beach); Los Angeles Bond (dir. 1970—, pres. 1983-84. Office: Crowell Weedon & Co 1 Wilshire Blvd Los Angeles CA 90017

GOYER, JEAN-PIERRE, lawyer, former Canadian govt. ofcl.; b. St. Laurent, Que., Can., Jan. 17, 1932; s. Gilbert and Marie-Ange G.; children: Christine, Sophie, Julie. B.A., U. Montreal, LL.B., 1957. Bar: Called to Que. bar, Ont. bar, created queen's counsel 1976. Practiced in, Montreal; mem. Canadian Ho. of Commons for Montreal-Dollard, 1965-78; parliamentary sec. to sec. state for external affairs, 1968-70, solicitor gen., Can., 1970-72; minister of supply and services, receiver gen. for Can. Govt. of Can., Ottawa, 1972-78; ptnr. firm Clarkson, & Tétrault, Montreal, 1979—; chmn. bd., dir. Can. Lands Co. (Mirabel) Ltd.; vice chmn. Canadair Ltd.; dir. Lavalin Internat. Inc., Bombardier, Inc. Pres. Arts Council of Montreal Urban Community; trustee Heritage Montreal Found. Mem. Canadian, Ont., Que. bar assns., Cercle Universitaire (Ottawa). Liberal. Club: Forest and Stream (Dorval). Home: Habitat '67 Suite 518 Cité du Havre Montréal PQ Canada H3C 3R6 Office: 22d Floor 630 Dorchester Blvd W Montreal PQ Canada H3B 1V7

GOYER, ROBERT ANDREW, physician, health research adminstr.; b. Hartford, Conn., June 2, 1927; s. Andrew R. and Cecelia P. (Castonquay) G.; m. Mary Ellen Wilke, Feb. 4, 1955; children—Barbara, John, Peter, Ellen. B.S., Holy Cross Coll., 1950; M.D., St. Louis U., 1955. Diplomate: Am. Bd. Pathology. Intern St. Francis Hosp., Hartford, 1955-56; resident in pathology St. Louis U. Hosps., 1956-60; practice medicine specializing in pathology, St. Louis, 1956-65; instr. pathology St. Louis U., 1960-62, asst. prof., 1962-65, Sch. Medicine, U. N.C., Chapel Hill, 1965-68, asso. prof., 1968-71, prof. pathology, 1971-74, adj. prof. pathology, 1979—; clin. pathologist Cardinal Glennon Meml. Hosp. for Children, St. Louis, 1961-62, dir. labs., 1962-64; staff pathologist N.C. Meml. Hosp., Chapel Hill, 1965-74; chief pathology U. Hosp., London, Ont., Can., 1974-79; prof. pathology Health Scis. Centre, U. Western Ont., Can., 1974-79; dept. dir. Nat. Inst. Environ. Health Scis., Research Triangle Park, N.C., 1979—. Contbr. articles to profl. jours.; editorial bd.: Yearbook Pathology, 1979—, AMA Archives of Pathology, 1973—. Served with USN, 1945-47. Nat. Found. fellow, 1959-60. Mem. Coll. Am. Pathology, Am. Assn. Pathologists, Internat. Acad. Pathology, Am. Soc. Clin. Pathology, Soc. Exptl. Biology and Medicine, Royal Coll. Physicians and Surgeons of Can. Roman Catholic. Research in exptl. pathology and metal toxicology. Home: 1079 Burning Tree Dr Chapel Hill NC 27514 Office: Nat Inst Environ Health Scis PO Box 12233 Research Triange Park NC 27709

GOYETTE, PIERRE, banker; b. Montreal, Nov. 7, 1930; s. Wilfrid and Albina (Larose) G.; m. Lyse Viziau, Mar. 6, 1954; children: Jean-Pierre, Jocelyne, Marie, Hélène, Stéphane. M. Comml. Sci., Ecole des Hautes Etudes Commerciales, Montreal, 1952. Sec., treas., dir. Société de Placements Inc., Montreal, 1954-64; v.p. Zodiac Inc., Montreal, 1964-66; asst. dep. minister fin. Govt. of Que., 1966-72, dep. minister fin., 1972-77; v.p. fin. Consol. Bathurst Inc., Montreal, 1977-81; exec. v.p., gen. mgr. Montreal City and Dist. Savs. Bank, 1981-82, pres., chief operating officer, 1982—; dir. Hydro-Que., Les Rôtisseries St-Hubert, Crédit Foncier., Sceptre Resources. Mem. adminstrn. adv. bd. Dalhousie Sch. Bus. Mem. Montreal C. of C. (pres.), Canadian Inst. Chartered Accts (acctg. research adv. bd.). Clubs: St-Denis, Cercle de la Place d'Armes. Home: 376 Wiseman Ave Outremont PQ Canada H2V 3J6 Office: 266 St Jacques St Montreal PQ Canada H2Y 1N1

GRABAR, OLEG, educator; b. Strasbourg, France, Nov. 3, 1929; U.S., 1948, naturalized, 1960; s. Andre and Julie (Ivanova) G.; m. Terry Ann Harris, June 9, 1951; children—Nicolas Howard, Anne Louise. B.A. magna cum laude, Harvard, 1950; licence d'Histoire, U. Paris, 1950; Ph.D., Princeton, 1955. Instr. U. Mich., 1954-55, asst. prof., 1955-59, asso. prof., 1959-64, prof., 1964-69; dir. Am. Sch. of Oriental Research, Jerusalem, Jordan, 1960-61, v.p., 1968—; prof. fine arts, Harvard, 1969—. Author: Coinage of Tulunids, 1957, Islamic Architecture and its Decoration, 1967, Sasanian Silver, 1967, The Formation of Islamic Art, 1973, The Alhambra, 1978, City in the Desert, 1978; editor: Ars Orientalis, 1957-71; contbr. articles to profl. jours. Mem. Coll. Art Assn. (dir. 1968-72), Archeol. Inst. Am., Mediaeval Acad. Am., German Archeol. Inst., Middle Eastern Studies Assn., Am. Acad. Arts and Scis. Dir. Mich.-Harvard excavations in Syria, 1964-71. Home: 37 Wolf Pine Way Concord MA 01742 Office: Fogg Museum Cambridge MA 02138

GRABEMANN, KARL WERNER, lawyer; b. Chgo., Apr. 27, 1929; s. Karl H. and Trude (Stockram) G.; m. Mary Darr, Dec. 6, 1958; children: Robert S., Lisa D. B.S., Northwestern U., 1951, J.D., 1956. Bar: Ill. 1957, U.S. Supreme Ct. 1960, U.S. Ct. Appeals for D.C. 1957, U.S. Ct. Appeals for 7th Circuit 1957, U.S. Ct. Appeals for 5th Circuit 1967, U.S. Ct. for D.C. 1957, U.S. Dist. Ct. for No. Dist. Ill. 1957. Atty. NLRB, Chgo., 1956-60; ptnr. firm Turner, Hunt & Woolley, Chgo., 1960-69, Keck, Mehin & Cate, 1969-79, McDermott, Will & Emery, 1979—. Mem. ABA, Ill. Bar Assn., Chgo. Bar Assn. Republican. Club: Metropolitan (Chgo.). Office: McDermott Will & Emery 111 W Monroe St Chicago IL 60603

GRABER, DORIS APPEL, political scientist, editor, author; b. St. Louis, Nov. 11, 1923; d. Ernest and Martha (Insel) Appel; m. Thomas M. Graber, June 15, 1941; children: Lee Winston, Thomas Woodrow, Jack Douglas, Jim Murray, Susan Doris. A.B., Washington U., St.

Louis, 1941, M.A., 1942; Ph.D., Columbia U., 1947. Feature writer St. Louis County Observer, Univ. City Tribune, St. Louis, 1939-41; civilian dir. U.S. Army Ednl. Reconditioning Program, Camp Maxey, Tex., 1943-45; editor legal mags. Commerce Clearing House, Chgo., 1945-46; lectr. polit. sci. Northwestern U., 1948-49, U. Chgo., 1950-51, North Park Coll., 1952; research asso. Center for Study Am. Fgn. and Mil. Policy, U. Chgo., 1952-71; mem. faculty U. Ill.-Chgo.; editor textbooks Harper & Row, Evanston, 1956-63; asso. prof. polit. sci. U. Ill., Chgo., 1964-69, prof., 1970—. Author: The Development of the Law of Belligerent Occupation, 1949, 68, Crisis Diplomacy: A History of U.S. Intervention Policies and Practices, 1959, Public Opinion, The President, and Foreign Policy, 1968, Verbal Behavior and Politics, 1976, The Mass Media and Politics, 1980, Crime News and the Public, 1980, (with others) Media Agenda Setting in a Presidential Election, 1981, Processing the News: How People Tame the Information Tide, 1984; editor, contbr.: The President and the Public, 1982; editor: Media Power in Politics, 1984; contbr. articles to profl. jours. Mem. Am. Assn. Pub. Opinion Research, Midwest Assn. Pub. Opinion Research (program chmn. 1978-79, pres. 1980-81), Midwest Polit. Sci. Assn. (past pres.), Am. Polit. Sci. Assn. (council 1978-79, v.p. 1980-81, program chmn. 1984), Internat. Polit. Sci. Assn., Internat. Communication Assn. (div. program chmn. 1978-80, div. chmn. 1980-82), Assn. Edn. Journalism, Acad. Polit. Sci., Am. Soc. Internat. Law, Am. Acad. Polit. and Social Sci., League Women Voters, Pi Sigma Alpha, Phi Beta Kappa. Home: 2895 Sheridan Pl Evanston IL 60201 Office: U Ill at Chgo Circle Box 4348 Chicago IL 60680

GRABER, EDWARD ALEX, obstetrician, gynecologist, educator; b. Chgo., July 24, 1914; s. Irving D. and Grace (Davis) G.; m. Sylvia H. Hess, Nov. 24, 1938; 1 son, Fredric Jay. M.D., Emory U., 1936. Diplomate: Am. Bd. Gyn. Assoc. dir. ob-gyn Lenox Hill Hosp., N.Y.C., 1972-75; prof. ob-gyn Cornell U. Med. Sch., N.Y.C., 1975—; attending physician N.Y. Hosp.-Cornell Med. Ctr., N.Y.C., 1971—. Author: Gynecologic Endocrinology, 1961, (with Barber) Are The Pills Safe?, Obstetric and Gynecology Procedures, 1969, Gynecological Oncology, 1970, Surgical Disease in Pregnancy, 1974, (with G. Schaefer) Complications of Gynecological Surgery, 1982; contbr. articles to profl. jours. Fellow Am. Coll. Ob-Gyn, ACS, N.Y. Acad. Medicine (pres. ob-gyn sect. 1971-72), N.Y. Gynecol. Soc. (pres. 1972-73); mem. AMA. Home: 130 E 75th St New York NY 10021 Offcie: Cornell U Med Sch 525 E 68th St New York Ny 10021 *Three words have had a marked influence on my life. They are excellence, responsibility, and love. If followed they bring fulfillment, satisfaction, and happiness.*

GRABER, THOMAS M., dentist; b. St. Louis, May 27, 1917; s. Joseph Jay and Adeline Maud (Nathan) G.; m. Doris Appel, June 15, 1941; children: Lee, Thomas, Jack, Jim, Susan. D.M.D., Washington U., St. Louis, 1940; M.S. in Dentistry, Northwestern U., 1946; Ph.D. in Anatomy, Northwestern U., 1950. Mem. faculty Northwestern U. Dental Sch., 1946-58, asso. prof. orthodontics, 1954-58, dir. research, 1947-58; asso. attending orthodontist Children's Meml. Hosp., Chgo., 1951-58; vis. lectr. U. Mich. Dental Sch., 1958-67; dir. Kenilworth (Ill.) Research Found., 1967—; prof. Zoller Dental Clinic; pediatrics research asso. (prof.) anthropology and anatomy U. Chgo., 1969-80, plastic and reconstructive surgery, 1980-82; research scientist ADA Research Inst., Chgo., 1980—; dir. G.V. Black Inst. for Continuing Edn., 1982—; cons. in field. Author textbooks, articles. Served as capt. Dental Corps AUS, 1941-44. Named Disting. Alumnus Washington U., 1980; NIH grantee, 1954, 56-60, 76, 77, 79, 80. Mem. Am., Ill. dental socs., Am. Assn. Orthodontists (gen. chmn. 1960, 77, 80, founding mem., chmn. council on orthodontic edn. and audio visual com. 1962, 67, gen. chmn. jour. 1977, Grieve Meml. award 1964, 84, Disting. Service award 1970, Ketcham award 1975), Internat. Assn. Research (chmn. Chgo. sect. 1973-74), Chgo. Orthodontists Assn. (pres. 1961-62), European Orthodontists Soc., Ill. Orthodontists Soc. (pres. 1969-70), Am. Soc. Phys. Anthropology, Angle Soc. (pres. 1968), Internat. Soc. Cranio-Facial Biology, SAR. Republican. Presbyterian. Home: 2895 Sheridan Pl Evanston IL 60201 Office: 450 Green Bay Rd Kenilworth IL 60043

GRABNER, GEORGE JOHN, mfg. co. exec.; b. Muskogee, Okla., Aug. 25, 1918; s. George and Helen (Leitch) G.; m. Monica Meyer, June 24, 1950; children—George John, Jan, Heidi, John, Thomas. B.A., Western Res. U., 1939; postgrad., Harvard Grad. Sch. Bus. Adminstrn., 1940. C.P.A., Ohio. Asst. mgr. Ernst & Ernst (C.P.A.'s), Cleve., 1946-57; v.p., dir. Cyrus Eaton Interests, 1957-58; fin. v.p., treas., Weatherhead Co., Cleve., 1958-63, exec. v.p., 1963-65, pres., dir., 1965-70, Weatherhead Co. Can., Ltd., 1966-70, LPG Leasing Corp., Cleve., 1958-70; pres., chief exec. officer, dir. Lamson & Sessions Co., 1970—, chmn. bd., 1978—; dir. Fisher Food Co., Nat. City Bank Cleve.; trustee 1st Union Realty. Chmn. bd. Greater Cleve. Growth Assn., 1966-69; chmn. Cleve. Devel. Found., 1966-69, Fin. Supervisory Commn. of City of Cleve., 1980—; trustee S.A. Horvitz Testamentary Trust. Served to 1st lt. USAAF, 1942-45. Mem. Ohio Soc. C.P.A.'s, Am. Ordnance Assn. (past pres., dir.). Clubs: Union (Cleve.); Pepper Pike (Ohio) Country, Kirtland Country. Home: Oxgate Lane Daisy Hill Hunting Valley OH 44022 Office: 1300 E 9 St Cleveland OH 44114

GRABO, NORMAN STANLEY, literary historian; b. Chgo., Apr. 21, 1930; s. Stanley Valentine and Effie Louise (Nelson) G.; children: Carolyn Deane, Scott David. B.A., Elmhurst Coll., 1952; M.A., UCLA, 1955, Ph.D., 1958. Instr., then asst. prof. English, Mich. State U., 1958-63; from asso. prof. to prof. English, U. Calif., Berkeley, 1963-77; tutor St. John's Coll., Santa Fe, 1972-74; Disting. prof. English, Tex. A&M U., College Station, 1977-83; Univ. prof. U. Tulsa, 1983—. Author: Edward Taylor, 1961, American Thought and Writing, 1965, American Poetry and Prose, 1970, The Coincidental Art of Charles Brockden Brown, 1981; editor: Arthur Mervyn, 1980. Folger Shakespeare Library fellow, 1959; Guggenheim fellow, 1970-71; Nat. Endowment Humanities fellow, 1980; Soc. Religion in Higher Edn. fellow, 1966-67. Mem. MLA, Mich. Acad. Sci., Arts and Letters, Internat. Assn. Univ. Profs. of English, South Central MLA. Office: English Dept U Tulsa Tulsa OK 74104

GRABOIS, NEIL ROBERT, mathematics educator, college official; b. N.Y.C., Dec. 11, 1935; s. Lazarus Lawrence and Florence (Graber) G.; m. Miriam Blau, Aug. 19, 1956; children: Adam, Daniel. B.A., Swarthmore (Pa.) Coll., 1957; M.A., U. Pa., 1959, Ph.D., 1963. Instr. math. Lafayette Coll., Easton, Pa., 1961-63; mem. faculty Williams Coll., Williamstown, Mass., 1963—, prof. math., 1972—, dean coll., dean faculty, then provost, 1970-80, chmn. dept. math. scis., 1981-83, provost, 1983—; bd. dirs. Roper Center. Co-author: Linear Algebra and Multivariable Calculus, 1970. Mem. Am. Math. Soc., Math. Assn. Am., AAAS, N.Y. Acad. Scis. Home: 176 Southworth St Williamstown MA 01267 Office: Williams Coll Williamstown MA 01267 *Without the support of our fellows, there can be no success; without understanding, and compassion, ideas have shape but may lead only into darkness; without honesty and clarity, and a willingness to hear the other side, tactics may succeed but the right path will be lost; no person sees the whole truth but the leader can help us find our way*

GRABOW, STEPHEN HARRIS, architecture educator; b. Bklyn., Jan. 15, 1943; s. Philip and Ida (England) G.; m. Wileen Williams, Aug. 21, 1969; 1 dau., Nicole Elizabeth. B. Arch., U. Mich., 1965; M. Arch., Pratt Inst., 1966; postgrad., U. Calif.-Berkeley, 1966-67; Ph.D., U. Wash., 1972. Architect-planner U.S. Peace Corps, Tunisia, 1967-69; regional planning cons. Teheran, Iran, 1969; asst. prof. architecture U. Ariz., 1969-70; teaching assoc. U. Wash., 1970-72; lectr. town and regional planning Duncan of Jordanstone Coll. Art, U. Dundee, Scotland, 1972-73; asst. prof. architecture and urban design U. Kans.-Lawrence, 1973-76, assoc. prof., 1976-82, prof., 1982—, dir. architecture, 1979-82, 83—; vis. fellow U. Calif.-Berkeley, 1977; research and design cons. Design Build Architects, Lawrence; bd. dirs. Assn. Collegiate Schs. Architecture, 1982—. Author: Christopher Alexander and the Search for a New Paradign in Architecture, 1983; mem. editorial bd.: Jour. Archtl. Edn., 1982—. Recipient award Nat. Endowment for Arts, 1974, citation for excellence in design research Nat. Endowment for Arts, 1980; NEH fellow, 1976-77. Home: 1616 Louisiana St Lawrence KS 66044 Office: Sch Architecture and Urban Design U Kans Lawrence KS 66045

GRABOYS, GEORGE, banker; b. Fall River, Mass., Sept. 26, 1932; s. Lewis M. G. and Rebecca S. (Graboys); m. Lois Ann Wolpert, June 1, 1958; children: Angela, Kenneth, James. B.A., Dartmouth Coll., 1954; J.D., U. Pa., 1957. Bar: R.I. 1958. V.p. legal counsel U.S. Fin. Corp., 1958-69; v.p. Citizens Bank, Providence, 1969-72, exec. v.p., 1973-75, pres., 1975-81, pres., chief exec. officer, 1981—; pres., treas. Mut. Savs. Banks R.I., Providence, 1983—; chmn. com. on comml. loans (Nat. Assn. Mut. Savs. Banks), 1981—. Bd. dirs. R.I. Urban Project, Providence, 1982, R.I. Pub. Expenditure Council, 1976; trustee Miriam Hosp., Providence, 1982; mem. bd. govs. Bd. Govs. for Highter Edn. Mem. Robert Morris Assocs. (sr. assoc.), R.I. Bar Assn., Greater Providence C. of C. (dir. 1979). Clubs: Hope; University (Providence). Home: 2 Terrace Dr Barrington RI 02806

GRABURN, NELSON HAYES HENRY, anthropologist, educator; b. London, Nov. 25, 1936; s. Henry Long Kingsforth and Cecily Marion (Finch) G.; m. Katherine Kazuko Yaguchi, June 25, 1966; children: Eva Mariko, Cecily Atsuko Ring. B.A., Cambridge (Eng.) U., 1958; M.A., McGill U., 1960; Ph.D., U. Chgo., 1963. Research anthropologist Govt. of Can., 1959-60; research asso. Northwestern U., Evanston, Ill., 1963-64; mem. faculty dept. anthropology U. Calif., Berkeley, 1964—, prof., 1974—, chmn. dept., 1981—; curator N. Am. ethnology Lowie Mus., 1975—; cons. NSF, NIMH, Can. Council. Author: Lake Harbour N.W.T, 1963, Taqagmiut Eskimo Kinship Terminology, 1964, Eskimos Without Igloos, 1969, Readings in Kinship and Social Structure, 1971, Circumpolar Peoples, 1973, Ethnic and Tourist Arts, 1976, To Pray, Pay and Play: The Cultural Structure of Japanese Domestic Tourism, 1983; Co-editor: Working Papers in Traditional Arts, 1976—, Annals of Tourism Research, 1977—. Served with Brit. Army, 1953-55. NSF grantee, 1967-69, 79-80; recipient Nat. Mus. Can. award, 1976. Mem. Royal Anthropol. Inst., Am. Anthropol. Assn., Can. Ethnology Soc. Office: Dept Anthropology Univ of Calif Berkeley CA 94720

GRACE, J. PETER, business executive; b. Manhasset, N.Y., May 25, 1913; s. Joseph and Janet (Macdonald) G.; m. Margaret Fennelly, May 24, 1941. Student, St. Paul's Sch., Concord, N.H., 1927-32; B.A., Yale U., 1936; LL.D., Mt. St. Mary's Coll., Manhattan Coll., Fordham U., Boston Coll., U. Notre Dame, Belmont Abbey, Stonehill Coll., Christian Bros. Coll., Adelphi U.; Dr. Latin Am. Relations, St. Joseph's Coll.; D.C.S., St. John's U. With W.R. Grace & Co., 1936—, sec., 1942, dir., 1943—, v.p., 1945, pres., chief exec. officer, 1945-81, chmn., chief exec. officer, 1981—; chmn. Chemed Corp.; dir. Brascan Ltd., Citicorp, Citibank (N.A.), Ingersoll-Rand Co., Stone & Webster, Inc., Milliken & Co.; trustee Atlantic Mut. Ins. Co. Bd. dirs., pres. Cath. Youth Orgn. of Archdiocese of N.Y.; bd. dirs. Boys Clubs Am.; chmn. RFE/RL Fund, Inc.; pres., trustee Grace Inst.; mem. bd. lay trustees, investment com. Notre Dame U.; treas. Nat. Jewish Hosp. and Research Center/Nat. Asthma Center, Denver. Decorated knight grand cross Equestrian Order Holy Sepulchre of Jerusalem; decorated by govts. of Colombia, Chile, Ecuador, Panama, Peru. Mem. Newcomen Soc., Council on Fgn. Relations. Roman Catholic. Clubs: Knights of Malta (pres. Am. chpt., bd. founders), Racquet and Tennis, Madison Square Garden (gov.), Links, India House (N.Y.C.); Links Golf, Meadow Brook, Pacific Union (San Francisco); Everglades. Office: Grace Plaza 1114 Ave of Americas New York NY 10036 *

GRACE, JASON ROY, advertising agency executive; b. N.Y.C., Dec. 5, 1936; s. Jack and Mitzi (Goldstick) G.; m. Marcia Jean Bell, May 16, 1966; children: Jessica Bell, Nicholas Bell. Student, Cooper Union, 1955-56, 58-62. Art dir. Benton & Bowles Inc., N.Y.C., 1962-63, Grey Advt., 1963-64; sr. v.p., creative mgmt. supr. Doyle Dane Bernbach Inc., N.Y.C., 1964-72, creative dir., exec. v.p., 1975-79, exec. v.p., exec. creative dir., 1979—, vice chmn., 1981-82, chmn. bd. U.S., exec. creative dir., 1982—; creative dir., exec. v.p. Gilbert, Grace & Stark, N.Y.C., 1972-74; film dir., 1970—. Served with U.S. Army, 1956-58. Recipient 8 Andy awards Advt. Club N.Y., 20 Clio awards Am. Film Festival, 5 Gold Lion awards, 3 Silver Lion awards Cannes Film Festival, 9 Gold medals Art Dirs. Club, Best TV Comml. of Last 20 Years award; recipient Internat. Broadcasting award, 1980; St. Gaudens medal Cooper Union Alumni Assn.; named to Clio Hall of Fame; 4 commls. placed in permanent collection Mus. Modern Art. Mem. Dirs. Guild Am. Home: Clark Hill Rd Old Lyme CT 06371 Office: 437 Madison Ave New York NY 10022

GRACE, JOHN EUGENE, business forms company executive; b. Dundee, Ill., Nov. 22, 1931; s. Arnold Victor and Louise Joan (Boncosky) G.; m. Janice Rae Fohey, June 30, 1956; children: Gregory Alan, Michael Brian, Michele Marie. B.S. in Bus. Adminstrn. with high honors in Acctg., U. Ill., 1958; M.S.B.A. in Fin., No. Ill. U., 1976. Gen. acctg. mgr. Elgin Watch Co., Ill., 1958-60; corp. controller Newell Cos., Freeport, Ill., 1960-68; controller jewelry div. Josten's, Inc., Owatonna, Minn., 1968-71; v.p. fin., chief fin. officer, asst. sec. Duplex Products Inc., Sycamore, Ill., 1971—. Active local United Fund, Little League, YMCA. Served with USAF, 1951-53. Mem. Fin. Execs. Inst. (past pres., dir. Fox-Rock chpt.), Nat. Assn. Accts. (past dir.), Adminstrv. Mgmt. Soc. (past dir.), Jaycees, C. of C., Beta Alpha Psi. Republican. Methodist. Clubs: Toastmasters, Germania, Quadrille, Owatonna Country, Elks. Home: 189 Nichols Dr Sycamore IL 60178 Office: 1947 Bethany Rd Sycamore IL 60178

GRACE, JOHN ROSS, chem. engr.; b. London, Ont., Can., June 8, 1943; s. Archibald John and Mark Kathleen (Disney) G.; m. Sherrill Elizabeth Perley, Dec. 20, 1964; children—Elizabeth, Malcolm. B.E.Sc., U. Western Ont., 1965; Ph.D., Cambridge (Eng.) U., 1968. From asst. prof. to prof. chem. engring. McGill U., Montreal, Que., 1968-79; sr. research engr., surveyor Nenniger & Chenevert Inc., 1974-75; prof. chem. engring., head dept. U. B.C., Vancouver, 1975—; cons. NRC Can. Co-author: Bubbles, Drops and Particles, 1978, Fluidization, 1980; Contbr. articles to profl. jours. Sr. indsl. fellow; Athlone fellow. Mem. Can. Soc. Chem. Engring., Assn. Profl. Engrs. B.C., Instn. Chem. Engrs., Chem. Inst. Can. Office: 2216 Main Mall Vancouver BC V6T 1W5 Canada *

GRACE, OLIVER RUSSELL, business executive; b. Great Neck, N.Y., Dec. 2, 1909; s. Morgan H. and Ruth (Eden) G.; m. Anne Chilton McDonnell, Nov. 29, 1934 (div. 1944); children: Helen Miller (Mrs. Ralph McDermid, Jr.), Ann Chilton (Mrs. Ratus Lee Kelly), Ruth Elizabeth (Mrs. Wayne Jervis); m. Lorraine Graves, Oct. 23, 1949; children: Lorraine (Mrs. David Grace-Charry), Gwendolyn Grace, Oliver Russell, John Sheffield. Ph.B., Yale, 1930. Statistician Grace Nat. Bank, N.Y.C., 1930-36; ptnr. Sterling, Grace & Co., 1936—, chmn., 1969—, Andersen Group, Bloomfield, Conn., 1959—; dir., chmn. exec. com. Grace Geothermal Corp.; dir. Alpha Portland Industries. Pres. Cancer Research Inst., Inc., 1953-58, 66-73, chmn., 1974—; bd. dirs. Theodore Roosevelt Assn.; trustee Cold Spring Harbor Lab. Mem. Nat. Inst. Social Scis. (treas.), Newcomen Soc., N.Y. C. of C. Episcopalian. Clubs: Regency Whist, Down Town Assn., India House (N.Y.C.); Piping Rock, Seawanaka Corinthian Yacht; Bath and Tennis. (Palm Beach, Fla.); Portland (London). Home: 306 Cove Neck Rd Oyster Bay NY 11771 Office: 111 Broadway New York NY 10006

GRACE, RICHARD EDWARD, engineering educator; b. Chgo., June 26, 1930; s. Richard Edward and Louise (Koko) G.; m. Consuela Cummings Fotos, Jan. 29, 1955; children: Virginia Louise, Richard Cummings (dec.). B.S. in Metall. Engring., Purdue U., 1951; Ph.D., Carnegie Inst. Tech., 1954. Registered profl. engr., N.J. Asst. prof. Purdue U., West Lafayette, Ind., 1954-58, asso. prof., 1958-62, prof., 1962—, head sch. materials sci. and metall. engring., 1965-72, head div. interdisciplinary engring. studies, 1969-82, head freshman engring. dept., asst. dean engring., 1981—; cons. to Midwest industries. Contbr. articles to profl. jours. Past dir. and officer engring. edn. and accreditation com. Engrs. Council for Profl. Devel. Mem. Am. Soc. Metals (tchr. award 1962, fellow award 1974), AIME, Am. Soc. Engring. Edn., AAUP, Sigma Xi, Tau Beta Pi, Omicron Delta Kappa, Phi Gamma Delta. Clubs: Rotary, Elks, Lafayette Country. Home: 2175 Tecumseh Park Ln West Lafayette IN 47906

GRACE, WALTER LAW, insurance company executive; b. Albany, N.Y., July 4, 1924; s. Charles J. and Lucile C. (Walter) G.; m. Janet C. Fletcher, Mar. 3, 1945; children: John F., Susan W. Grace Holt, Ellen L. Grace Sordillo. Student, Johns Hopkins U., 1942-43; B.S., U. Mich., 1948, M.A., 1949. C.L.U. With Mass. Mut. Life Ins. Co., Springfield, 1949—, successively asst. group actuary, asst. actuary, asso. group actuary, asso. actuary, 1951-62, head pension dept., 1960-66, 2d v.p., 1962-66, 2d v.p., actuary, 1966-74, v.p., actuary, 1974—; v.p. MML Bay State Life Ins. Co., MML Pension Ins. Co., MML Life Ins. Co.; v.p., dir. MML Equity Investment Co., Inc., MML Managed Bond Investment Co., Inc., MML Money Market Investment Co., Inc. Served to 1st lt. USAAF, 1942-47. Fellow Soc. Actuaries (treas. 1960-62, sec. 1962-65, gov. 1965-68, 70-73, 76-79), Am. Acad. Actuaries (dir. 1974-77, pres.-elect 1979, pres. 1980-81). Home: 8 Wilbraview Dr Wilbraham MA 01095 Office: 1295 State St Springfield MA 01111

GRACE, WILLIAM PORTER, real estate co. exec.; b. Dardanelle, Ark., Oct. 14, 1908; s. William Porter and Bertha (Cox) G.; m. Eleanor Curry, Nov. 16, 1936; children—William Porter III, Perry Rutledge. B.S., B.A., U. Ark., 1931; LL.B., So. Law U., 1940. With HOLC, 1936-38, Memphis C. of C., 1938-50; with Union Planters Nat. Bank, Memphis, 1950-70, exec. v.p., 1963-68, pres., 1968-69, vice chmn., 1970; pres., dir., vice chmn., dir. Cooper Communities, Inc., Bella Vista, Ark., 1971—; dir. Grace Devel. Co. Bd. dirs. Am. Indsl. Devel. Council, 1956; pres. So. Indsl. Devel. Council, 1952, bd. dirs., 1948; chmn. Memphis Community Chest, 1955, Nat. Alliance Businessmen, Memphis & Shelby County Port Com.; bd. dirs. Memphis chpt. A.R.C., 1960—; exec. com. Shelby United Neighbors, 1964-70, Meth. Hosp., Memphis, 1964-70; pres. U. Ark. Endowment and Trust Fund, 1970. Served with U.S. Army, 1933-36, 41-45. Decorated Legion of Merit Order Brit. Empire; Croix de Guerre, France). Mem. Am., Tenn. bankers assns., U. Ark. Found. (dir.). Clubs: Mason., Memphis Country, Bella Vista Country. Home: 1 Lakeside Dr Bella Vista AR 72712 Office: Cooper Communities Inc PO Box 60 Bentonville AR 72712

GRACEY, JAMES STEELE, coast guard officer; b. Newton, Mass., Aug. 24, 1927; s. Ernest James and Edna Alicia (Steele) G.; m. Dorcas Randall Neal, June 15, 1949; children: Kevin S., Cheryl A., Pamela R. B.S., U.S. Coast Guard Acad., 1949; M.B.A., Harvard U., 1956. Commd. ensign U.S. Coast Guard, 1949, advanced through grades to adm.; comptroller 2d Coast Guard Dist., St. Louis, 1962-65; asst. project officer 3d Coast Guard Dist., N.Y., 1965-66; exec. officer Coast Guard Base, Governors Island, N.Y., 1966-69; chief programs div. Chief of Staff's Office, Washington, 1969-74; chief of staff 5th Coast Guard Dist., Portsmouth, Va., 1974-77, U.S. Coast Guard, Washington, 1977-78; comdr. Coast Guard Pacific Area and 12th Coast Guard Dist., San Francisco, 1978-81, Coast Guard Atlantic Area and 3d Coast Guard Dist., Governors Island, 1981-82; commandant of Coast Guard, Washington, 1982—. Decorated Legion of Merit with gold star, D.S.M. Mem. Nat. Def. Transp. Assn., Propeller Club U.S., Coast Guard Acad. Alumni Assn., Coast Guard Acad. Found. Home: 6601 Kennedy Dr Chevy Chase MD 20815 Office: Coast Guard Hdqrs Washington DC 20593

GRACIA, JORGE JESUS EMILIANO, philosopher, educator; b. Camaguey, Cuba, July 18, 1942; s. Ignacia Jesue Loreto and Leonila (Otero) G.; m. Norma Elida Silva, Sept. 3, 1966; children: Leticia Isabel, Clarisa Raquel. B.A., Wheaton Coll., Ill., 1965; M.A., U. Chgo., 1966; M.S.L., Pontifical Inst. Mediaeval Studies, Toronto, 1970; Ph.D., U. Toronto, 1971. Asst. prof. SUNY-Buffalo, Amerherst, 1971-76, assoc. prof., 1976-80, prof., 1980—, assoc. chmn. dept. philosophy, 1974-76, chmn. dept., Amerherst, 1980—. Author: Suarez on Individuation, 1982, Introduction to the Problem of Individuation, 1983; editor: Man and His Conduct, 1980, (with others) El Hombre y los valores, 1975. NEH grantee, 1981-82. Mem. Am. Philos. Assn. (mem. com. internat. cooperation 1981), Am. Cath. Philos. Assn. (mem. exec. com. 1983—). Home: 420 Berryman Dr Amherst NY 14226 Office: SUNY-Buffalo Amherst NY 14260

GRACIDA, RENE HENRY, bishop; b. New Orleans, June 9, 1923; s. Henry J. and Mathilde (Derbes) G. Student, Rice U., 1942-43; B.S. in Architecture, U. Houston, 1950; postgrad., U. Fribourg, Switzerland, 1950, St. Vincent Coll., Latrobe, Pa., 1951-53, St. Vincent Maj. Sem., 1953-60. Faculty U. Houston Sch. Architecture, 1948-51; practice architecture with Donald Bartheline & Assos., Houston, 1949-51; ordained deacon Roman Catholic Ch., 1958, priest, 1959, bishop, 1971; asst. pastor Holy Family Parish, North Miami, Fla., 1961-62, St. Coleman Parish, Pompano Beach, Fla., 1962-63, St. Matthew Parish, Hallandale, Fla., 1963-64; adminstr. St. Ambrose Parish, Deerfield Beach, Fla., 1964; asst. pastor Visitation Parish, North Dade, Fla., 1964-65; adminstr. St. Ann Parish, Naples, Fla., 1966-67; pastor Nativity Parish, Hollywood, Fla., 1967-69; rector St. Mary Cathedral, Miami, Fla., 1969-71, St. Patrick Parish, Miami Beach, Fla., 1971-72; pastor St. Kiernan Parish, Miami, 1973-75; 1st bishop Diocese of Pensacola-Tallahassee, 1975-83; apptd. 5th bishop Diocese of Corpus Christi (Tex.), 1983—; mem. Archdiocesan Bldg. Commn., Archdiocese of Miami, 1961-75, sec., 1962-65, chmn., 1967-73, West Coast Deanery, Human Relations Bd., 1966-67; senator Priests Senate, 1967-69, archdiocesan consultor, 1967-75; chmn. Broward Deanery, Human Relations Bd., 1967-69, chancellor, 1968-72, treas., 1969-72, vicar gen., 1969-75; steering com. Biennial Congress Worship, 1966-72; aux. bishop Archdiocese Miami, 1971-75, supt. edn., 1973-75; chmn. com. on migration and tourism Nat. Conf. Cath. Bishops, 1975-81; nat. episcopal promoter of Apostleship of the Sea in U.S., 1975—. Important archtl. works include: remodelling St. Vincent Archabbey Basilica, Latrobe, Ch. of the Nativity, Hollywood, St. Ambrose Ch, Deerfield Beach. Pres. Community Action Fund; bd. dirs. Community Act Fund, 1966-72; mem. bishop's com. liturgy Nat. Conf. Cath.

Bishops, 1972-77, chmn., 1977-78, mem. policy and rev. com., 1973-77. Served with USAAF, 1943-45. Decorated Air medal. Mem. Guild for Religious Architecture, Phi Kappa Phi. Address: 4109 Ocean Dr Corpus Christi TX 78411

GRAD, FRANK PAUL, law lawyer; b. Vienna, Austria, May 2, 1924; came to U.S., 1939, naturalized, 1943; s. Morris and Clara Sophie (Scher) G.; m. Lisa Szilagyi, Dec. 6, 1946; children: David Anthony, Catharine Ann. B.A. magna cum laude, Bklyn. Coll., 1947; LL.B., Columbia U., 1949. Bar: N.Y. 1949. Asso. in law Columbia U. Law Sch., 1949-50, asst. dir. Legis. Drafting Research Fund, 1953-55, dir. Legis. Drafting Research Fund, 1969—, mem. faculty Legis. Drafting Research Fund, 1954—; prof. law, 1969—; Joseph P. Chamberlain prof. legis. Columbia U. Law Sch., 1982—; asso. firm House, Grossman, Vorhaus & Hemley, N.Y.C., 1950-53; mem. legal adv. com. U.S. Council Environ. Quality, 1970-73; mem. N.Y. Deptl. Com. Ct. Adminstrn., Appellate Div., 1st Dept., 1970-74; counsel N.Y. State Spl. Adv. Panel Med. Malpractice, 1975; legal counsel Nat. Mcpl. League, 1967—; cons. in field, 1955—; reporter U.S. Super fund Study group, 1981-82; dir. research N.Y.C. Charter Revision Commn., 1982-83. Author: Public Health Law Manual, 7th edit, 1981, The Drafting of State Constitutions, 1963, Environmental Law: Sources and Problems, 2d edit, 1978, Treatise on Environmental Law, 5 vols, 1973-83; co-author other legal reports; contbr. legal jours.; draftsman mcpl. codes and state legislation. Served with AUS, 1943-46. Mem. Am. Bar Assn., Am. Public Health Assn., Assn. Bar City N.Y., Am. Law Inst. Office: 435 W 116th St New York NY 10027

GRAD, HAROLD, applied mathematician; b. N.Y.C., Jan. 14, 1923; s. Herman and Helen (Selinger) G.; m. Betty Jane Miller, Jan. 23, 1949; children: Hilary Lynn Grad Goldberg, Michael Jonathan. B.E.E., Cooper Union, 1943; M.S., N.Y. U., 1945, Ph.D., 1948. Research asst. N.Y. U., 1944-48, mem. faculty, 1948—; prof. math. Courant Inst., 1957—, founder, 1956, dir. magneto-fluid dynamics div., 1956-80; adv. com. fusion energy Oak Ridge Nat. Lab., 1964-67, 73-76; dir. Space Scis., Inc., 1966-71; vis. disting. prof. Faculty Sci., Nagoya U. (Japan), 1981; cons. to industry and U.S. govt. Author papers, monograph on kinetic theory gases, statis. mechanics, magneto-fluid dynamics, plasma physics, fusion energy; editorial bd.: Physics of Fluids, 1968-71, Jour. Statis. Physics, 1969-75, Internat. Jour. Engring. Sci, 1963—. Recipient Eringem medal Soc. Engring. Scis., 1982; Guggenheim fellow, 1981-82. Fellow AAAS, Am. Phys. Soc. (chmn. fluid dynamics div. 1963, chmn. plasma physics div. 1968); mem. Nat. Acad. Scis., Soc. Engring. Scis. (dir. 1963-74), N.Y. Acad. Scis. (Pregel award 1970, bd. govs. 1979—), Am. Math. Soc., Soc. Indsl. and Applied Math., Soc. Natural Philosophy. Home: 248 Overlook Rd New Rochelle NY 10804 Office: 251 Mercer St New York NY 10012

GRADDICK, CHARLES ALLEN, attorney general Alabama; b. Mobile, Ala., Dec. 10, 1944; s. Julian and Elvera (Smith) G.; m. Corinne Whiting, Aug. 19, 1966; children: Charles Allen, Herndon Whiting, Corinne. J.D., U. Ala. 1970. Bar: Ala. 1970. Clk. Ala. Supreme Ct., 1970; asst. dist. atty. Mobile County, Ala., 1971-75, dist. atty., 1975-79; atty. gen. State of Ala., Montgomery, 1979—. Served with U.S. N.G., 1969-75. Named Outstanding Young Man of Mobile Mobile Jaycees, 1976; recipient cert. appreciation Ala. Peace Officers, 1978, Appreciation award Optimists, 1978. Mem. Nat. Assn. Attys. Gen., Am. Trial Lawyers Assn., Am. Bar Assn., Ala. Bar Assn., Ala. Dist. Attys. Assn., Nat. Dist. Attys. Assn. Democrat. Episcopalian. Office: Office of Atty Gen 64 N Union St Montgomery AL 36130

GRADE, LEW, entertainment corporation executive; b. Dec. 25, 1906; s. Isaac and Olga Winogradsky; m. Kathleen Sheila Moody; 1 son. Joint mng. dir. Lew and Leslie Grade Ltd., until, 1955; dep. mng. dir. Associated Television Ltd., 1958—; chmn. Stoll Theatres Corp., 1973—, Moss Empires, 1973—; chmn., chief exec. Embassy Communications Internat., London, 1982—; dir. Bermans (Holdings) Ltd., Bentray Investments, Ltd., Associated Television Corp. (Internat.) Ltd., Switzerland, Ind. Television Corp., U.S.A., Pye Records Ltd., ATV Licensing Ltd.; chmn., chief exec. Associated Communications Corp. Ltd.; pres. ATV Network Ltd., 1977—; mng. dir. ITC Entertainment Ltd. Office: Embassy House 3 Audley Square London W1Y 5DR England *

GRADE, MICHAEL IAN, television producer; b. London, Mar. 8, 1943; U.S., 1982; s. Leslie and Winifred (Smith) G.; m. Penelope Jane Levinson, Mar. 20, 1967 (div. Mar. 1981); children: Alison Jane, Jonathan James; m. Sarah Jane Lawson, Sept. 11, 1982. Student, pvt. schs., Eng. Sports columnist Daily Mirror newspaper, London, 1960-66; joint mng. dir. London Mgmt. Ltd., 1967-73; dep. controller programs London Weekend TV, 1974-76, dir. programs, 1976-81; pres. Embassy TV, Los Angeles, 1981-82; chief exec. officer Grade Co., Los Angeles, 1983—. Sr. creative exec. for numerous prize-winning TV programs. Mem. council Royal Coll. Art, London, 1980-81; com. mem. Queen's Silver Jubilee London Com., 1976-77. Mem. Brit. Acad. Film and TV Arts (council 1980-81), Royal TV Soc., Acad. TV Arts and Sci. Jewish. Office: Grade Co 100 Universal City Plaza Bldg 426-2 Universal City CA 91068

GRADEN, JOSEPH CONWAY, manufacturing company executive; b. Florence, Ala., Feb. 2, 1928; s. Joseph Conway and Margaret (Zorn) G.; m. Almelia Wilson, Mar. 24, 1951; children: Joseph Conway, Lee W. B.S.M.E., U. Ala.-Tuscaloosa, 1950; postgrad., Harvard U., 1969. Dir. internat. prodn. Goodyear Internat., Akron, Ohio, 1969-72, v.p. mfg., Akron, 1975—; dir. gen. products Goodyear-G.B., Wolverhampton, Eng., 1972-75; v.p. Goodyear Tire & Rubber Co., Akron, 1975—.

GRADISON, HEATHER JANE, federal commissioner; b. Houston, Sept. 6, 1952; d. David Lowe Stirton and Dorothy Johanne (Flatt) Cox; m. Willis D. Gradison Jr., Nov. 29, 1980; children: Maile Jo, Benjamin David. B.A., Radford Coll., 1975; postgrad., George Washington U., 1976, 78. Summer intern So. Ry. System, Washington, 1974, mgmt. trainee, research asst., asst. rate officer, 1975-82, rate officer, 1975-82; commr. ICC, Washington, 1982—. Mem. Rebublican Congl. Wives Club. Office: ICC 12th & Constitution NW Washington DC 20423

GRADISON, WILLIS DAVID, JR., congressman, investment broker; b. Cin., Dec. 28, 1928; s. Willis David and Dorothy (Benas) G.; m. Helen Ann Martin, June 25, 1950 (div. 1974); children: Ellen, Anne, Margaret, Robin, Beth; m. Heather Jane Stirton, Nov. 29, 1980; children: Maile Jo, Benjamin David. A.B., Yale, 1948; M.B.A., Harvard, 1951, D.C.S., 1954. With W.D. Gradison & Co., Cin., 1949; research asst., also research asso. Harvard Bus. Sch., 1951-53; asst. to undersec. Dept. Treasury, 1953-55; asst. to sec. HEW, 1955-57; gen. partner W.D. Gradison & Co., 1958—; mem. Cin. City Council, 1961-74, mayor, 1971; mem. 94th-98th Congresses. Home: 2027 Calvin Cliff Ln Cincinnati OH 45206 Office: Federal Bldg Cincinnati OH 45202

GRADO, ANGELO JOHN, artist, painter; b. N.Y.C., Feb. 17, 1922; s. Pasquale and Rose (Valenti) G.; m. Justine Barbara Johnson, June 26, 1943; children: Barbara, Paul, John,Frank, Richard. Student, Art Students League. Comml. artist N.Y. Jour.-Am., N.Y.C., 1946-52; art dir. Harrison Publs., N.Y.C., 1952-55; art dir., owner advy. agy., N.Y.C., 1955-70, artist oils and pastels, 1970—. Served with USAAF, 1943-46. Recipient 35 nat. awards, 1957—, Best in Show-Newington award, 1980. Mem. Am. Artists Profl. League (pres. N.Y. 1977—), Hudson Valley Art Assn., Pastel Soc. Am., Am. Watercolor Soc., Salmagundi Club. Home: 641 46th St Brooklyn NY 11220 Office: American Artists Profl League 47 Fifth Ave New York NY 10003

GRADWELL, JOHN DAVID, utilities executive; b. Meriden, Conn., June 22, 1920; s. James Edward and Charlotte (Schneider) G.; m. Elenore Marie Swenson, Oct. 3, 1942; children: David Lee, Peter James. Grad., Bentley Coll., 1941. Acct., Brideport Brass Co., Conn., 1941-46; comptroller, v.p. So. New Eng. Telephone Co., New Haven, 1946—, chief fin. officer, 1983—, also mem. audit com.; dir. Meriden Trust Co., Colonial Bank. Pres. Meriden Council Chs., 1965-68; mem. Mayor's Community Devel. Action Plan, Meriden, 1968—; mem. audit com., bd. dirs. Meriden-Wallingford Hosp.; treas., past pres. bd. dirs. Curtis Home Meriden. Served with USAAF, 1943-46. Mem. Fin. Execs. Inst. (pres., dir. Hartford chpt.), Conn. Bus. and Industry Assn. (tax com.), Nat. Tax Assn. Protestant Episcopalian (sr. warden ch. 1965-67, pres. Ch. Club Diocese Conn. 1967-69). Clubs: Home of Meriden, Wallingford Country. Home: 59 Live Oak Ln Meriden CT 06450 Office: 227 Church St New Haven CT 06506

GRADWOHL, BERNARD SAM, lawyer; b. St. Joseph, Mo., Apr. 5, 1905; s. Ben W. and Hattie (Hilpp) G.; m. Elaine Mayer, June 21, 1928; children: John Mayer, David Mayer. A.B., U. Nebr., 1923; J.D. cum laude, 1924; LL.M., Columbia U., 1925. Bar: Nebr. 1926. Since practiced in Lincoln; nat. exec. sec. Am. Interprofl. Inst.; editor Quar., 1942-66, pres., 1966-67, pres. Lincoln chpt., 1948-49. Nat. adv. bd. Am. Council Judaism, 1944-68, co-chmn. nat. com. religious programs, 1949-58, mem. exec. com., 1954-58; mem. bd. Lincoln Social Welfare Soc., 1944-45; exec. council Nebr. Welfare assn., 1947-49; past pres. Open Forum Club; past chmn. Lincoln bd., NCCJ; chmn. Nebraskans Say America is Beautiful Com., 1970—. Mem. ABA, Nebr. Bar Assn., Lincoln Bar Assn. (past treas.), Nebr. Assn. Fire Fighters (hon.), Lincoln C. of C., Izaak Walton League, Phi Beta Kappa, Order of Coif, Delta Sigma Rho. Jewish. Clubs: Open Forum (Lincoln); Hillcrest Country (past pres.). Lodges: Masons; Shriners. Home: 1633 Crestline Dr Lincoln NE 68506 Office: 914 Lincoln Benefit Life Bldg Lincoln NE 68508

GRADY, JAMES WALTER, JR., lawyer, fin. services co. exec.; b. New Haven, July 24, 1924; s. James Walter and Marion Agnes (Flanagan) G.; m. Joan Caryl O'Neill, May 15, 1954; children—Debra, Barbara, Susan, Jeffrey, Bruce. B.A., Yale U., 1947; LL.B., Harvard U., 1952. Bar: Conn. bar 1952, N.Y. bar 1958, D.C. bar 1962. Asst. gen. counsel CIT Fin. Corp., 1966-68; sr. v.p., gen. counsel Assos. Corp. N. Am., 1968-74; asso. gen. counsel J.P. Stevens & Co., Inc., N.Y.C., 1974-76, gen. counsel, 1976-81; v.p., gen. counsel Merrill Lynch & Co. Inc., 1981—. Trustee Stanley Clark Sch., South Bend, Ind., 1969-74; mem. lawyers steering com. Bus., Roundtable, 1980—. Served as ensign USN, 1943-46. Mem. Am. Bar Assn. (past chmn., past sec. com. corp. law depts. 1977-81), N.Y. State Bar Assn., Bar Assn. City N.Y. Roman Catholic. Clubs: Harvard (N.Y.C.); Darien Boat. Home: 2 Haskell Ln Darien CT 06820 Office: 165 Broadway New York NY 10080

GRADY, JOHN F., federal judge; b. Chgo., May 23, 1929; s. John F. and Lucille F. (Shroder) G.; m. Patsy Grady, Aug. 10, 1968; 1 son, John F. B.S., Northwestern U., 1952, J.D., 1954. Bar: Ill. 1955. Practice law Chgo., 1955; asst. U.S. atty. for no. dist. Ill., 1956-61; practice law, Waukegan, Ill., 1967-76; judge U.S. Dist. Ct. (no. dist.) Ill., Chgo., 1976—. Assoc. editor: Northwestern U. Law Rev. Mem. Phi Beta Kappa. Office: US Courthouse 219 S Dearborn St Chicago IL 60604

GRADY, JOHN FRANCIS, conductor, organist; b. Great Neck, L.I., N.Y., May 19, 1934; s. John Francis and Florence Annette (Blake) G. B.A., Fordham U., 1957; postgrad., Columbia U., 1958, Juilliard Sch. Music, 1958-60; Doctorate h.c., State of Michoagan (Mex.), 1974. Ofcl. organist Met. Opera Assn., 1964—; dir. music St. Patrick's Cathedral, N.Y.C., 1970—; head organ dept. Manhattan Sch. Music, 1970-71; Am. judge exams. Conservatory of Nice, France, 1976; Am. judge Internat. Organ Competition Chartres Cathedral, France, 1978; organist Internat. Eucharistic Congress, Phila., 1976; tchr. organ workshops Gregorian Inst. Am., 1968-72, Cathedral Sts. Peter and Paul, 1977-78, 79; prof. music history Archdiocesan Sch. Liturgical Music, N.Y.C., 1979-80. Composer: Gloria for Chorus and Orch, 1979; Editor, annotator: Acts of the Pagan Martyrs by Herbert Musurillo, 1956; editor: oratorio Nisi Dominus (G. F. Handel), 1978; concert tour, France, March and July 1979. Chevalier dans l'Ordre des Arts et Lettres (France). Mem. Nat. Assn. Cathedral Organists (founder, past pres.), Am. Guild Organists, Broadcast Music Inc. Club: Century, Bohemians. Condr., organist Papal Visit to N.Y.C., St. Patrick's Cathedral and Yankee Stadium, 1979. Home: 177 E 77th St New York NY 10021 Office: St Patrick's Cathedral Parish House 14 E 51st St New York NY 10022 *The most important aspect of the life of the creative artist is the ability to share one's art. I have been indeed fortunate in my present positions to have the opportunity of sharing whatever creativity I possess with large masses of people.*

GRADY, JOHN HENRY, computer company executive; b. San Mateo, Calif., Jan. 10, 1928; s. John H. and Monica (Klatt) G.; m. Alexandra Diepenbrock, Dec. 29, 1956; children—Kathleen, John Henry, Carolyn, James. A.A., Coll. San Mateo, 1949; B.S., U. Calif. at Berkeley, 1951. With Am. President Lines, 1951-52; with IBM, 1952—, dir. stockholder relations, Armonk, N.Y., 1963-65, asst. sec., 1965-70, sec., 1970—. Served with AUS, 1945-47. Mem. Am. Soc. Corp. Secs., Stockholder Relations Soc. N.Y. Office: old orchard rd armonk new york 10504

GRADY, STAFFORD R., banker; b. Grand Rapids, Mich., Apr. 9, 1921; s. Stafford R. and Josephine (Cusick) G.; m. Roberta Patterson, Aug. 26, 1950; children: Stafford R., Maureen H., Shaun P. A.B., George Washington U., 1943, LL.B., 1945. Bar: Mich. 1945, D.C. 1945, Calif. 1952. Law clk. to judge U.S. Ct. Appeals, 1945-47; asst. U.S. atty., Washington, 1947-51; spl. atty. IRS, 1951-52; partner firm Mackay, McGregor and Bennion, Los Angeles, 1952-63; ins. commr., Calif., 1963-66; pres. Lloyds Bank Calif., Los Angeles, 1966-74, chmn. bd., 1968—; dir. Lloyds Bank Internat., Cigna Corp.; mem. adv. com. 8 Coldwell Banker Funds. Bd. dirs. Community TV So. Calif.; bd. dirs. House Ear Research Inst.; chmn. bd. trustees Occidental Coll.; bd. visitors UCLA Sch. Medicine, Loyola Law Sch.; chmn. Los Angeles County United Way Campaign, 1981-82, dep. chmn., 1983-84. Mem. Am., Calif., Mich., D.C., Los Angeles County bar assns., Calif. Bankers Assn., Assn. Res. City Bankers, Phi Delta Phi, Sigma Nu. Office: 612 Flower St Los Angeles CA 90017

GRADY, THOMAS J., bishop; b. Chgo., Oct. 9, 1914; s. Michael and Rose (Buckley) G. S.T.L., St. Mary of Lake Sem., Mundelein, Ill., 1938; student, Gregorian U., Rome, 1938-39; M.A. in English, Loyola U., Chgo., 1944. Ordained priest Roman Catholic Ch., 1938; prof. Quigley Prep. Sem., Chgo., 1939-45; procurator St. Mary of Lake Sem., 1945-56; dir. Nat. Shrine Immaculate Conception, Washington, 1956-67; titular bishop Vamalla, aux. bishop Chgo., 1967-74; pastor St. Hilary Ch., Chgo., 1968-74, St. Joseph Ch., Libertyville, Ill., 1974; bishop of, Orlando, Fla., 1974—; Chgo. Archdiocesan dir. seminaries and post-ordination priestly tng., 1967-74; chmn. Chgo. Archdiocesan Liturg. Commn., 1968-74; dir. program Permanent Diaconate, Chgo., 1969-74; cons. Bishops' Com. on Priestly Formation, 1967—, chmn., 1969-72; mem. Ad Hoc Com. on Priestly Life and Ministry, 1971-73; chmn. Bishops' Com. on Priestly Life and Ministry, 1973—. Home: PO Box 1800 Orlando FL 32802

GRAEBEL, WILLIAM PAUL, engineering educator; b. Manitowoc, Wis., July 15, 1932; s. Adolph Fred and Erna Violet (Huhn) G.; m. June Erna Ness, June 12, 1954; children: Jeffrey Paul, Susan Kay. B.S., U. Wis.-Madison, 1954, M.S., 1955; Ph.D., U. Mich., 1959. Registered profl. engr., Mich. Mem. tech. staff Bell Telephone Labs., Whippany, N.J., 1955-56; instr. engring. U. Mich., 1956-59, asst. prof., 1959-62, asso. prof., 1962-67, prof., 1967—; design specialist Douglas Aircraft Co., Santa Monica, Calif., 1962; summer visitor Nat. Center Atmospheric Research, Boulder, Colo., 1963; research collaborator Centre d'Etudes Nucléaires de Grenoble, France, 1979; research scientist Netherlands Ophthalmic Research Inst., Amsterdam, 1979; sr. design analyst Westinghouse Marine Div.; cons. in field. Contbr. numerous articles to profl. jours. Mem. Am. Phys. Soc., ASME, U. Mich. Research Club, Am. Theatre Organ Soc., Detroit Theater Organ Club, Sigma Xi. Unitarian Universalist. Home: 1318 Fountain St Ann Arbor MI 48103

GRAEBNER, HERBERT CONRAD, educator; b. Bay City, Mich., Jan. 3, 1908; s. M.G. and Emma (Umbach) C.; m. Mildred Fessel, Aug. 24, 1933; children—James, Jane. B.S., Valparaiso (Ind.) U., 1930; postgrad., Northwestern U., 1930-31; M.B.A., U. Pa., 1948. Supt. A.J. Rehmus Constrn. Co., Bay City, Mich., 1931-32; instr. econs. Valparaiso U., 1932-35, asst. bus. mgr., 1935-39; prof. econs. Westminster Coll., 1939-46; v.p. Econ. Found Pa., 1942-46; prof. econs., dean coll. bus. adminstrn. Butler U., 1948-55; dean, trustee Am. Coll. of Bryn Mawr, 1955-70, v.p. and dean, 1964-67, exec. v.p., treas., 1967-70; pres. Bldg. Owners and Mgrs. Inst. Internat., 1970-75, dir., 1970—; chmn. bd. Certified Med. Reps. Inst., 1967—. Contbr. articles to profl. jours. Contbg. and/or cons.; editor several bus. handbooks. Mem. Am. Acad. Polit. and Social Sci., Adult Edn. Assn., Am. Risk and Ins. Assn., AAUP, Phi Kappa Phi, Sigma Iota Epsilon. Lutheran. Home: 149 Clemson Rd Bryn Mawr PA 19010 *Concern for one another and learning to cope with inevitable changes are important for the preservation of civilization.*

GRAEBNER, JAMES HERBERT, county transportation executive; b. New Castle, Pa., Aug. 5, 1940; s. Herbert Conrad and Mildred Elizabeth (Fessel) G.; m. Harriet Brooks, 1982; 1 son, James Conrad. B.A., Valparaiso U., 1962; M.B.A., Case Western Res. U., 1970. Asso. W.C. Gilman & Co., Inc. (transit cons.), Cleve., 1967-71; transp. engr. Regional Transp. Dist., Denver, 1971-74, mgr. bus. ops. support, 1974-75; gen. mgr. R.I. Public Transit Authority, Providence, 1975-78; dir. Santa Clara County (Calif.) Transp. Agy., 1978—; v.p. San Jose Historic Trolley Corp.; vis. prof. Northeastern U., 1979; guest. lectr. at numerous univs. Mem. Am. Public Transit Assn. (pres. 1983-84), Calif. Assn. Publically Owned Transit Systems (exec. com.), Regional Transit Assn. Bay Area (past pres.). Lutheran. Office: 1555 Berger Dr San Jose CA 95112

GRAEBNER, NORMAN ARTHUR, history educator; b. Kingman, Kans., Oct. 19, 1915; s. Rudolph William and Helen (Brauer) G.; m. Laura Edna Baum, Aug. 30, 1941. B.S., Milw. State Tchrs. Coll., 1939; M.A., U. Okla., 1940; Ph.D., U. Chgo., 1949; Litt.D., Albright Coll., 1976; M.A., Oxford (Eng.) U., 1978; D.H.L., U. Pitts., 1981, Valparaiso U., 1981. Asst. prof. Okla. Coll. for Women, 1942-43, 46-47; from asst. prof. to prof. Iowa State Coll., 1948-56; prof. history U. Ill., Urbana, 1956-67, chmn. dept. history, 1961-63; Edward R. Stettinius prof. modern Am. history U. Va., 1967-82, Randolph P. Compton prof. pub. affairs, 1982—; vis. prof. Stanford U., 1952-53, summers 1959, 72, U. Colo., summer 1968, Concordia Tchrs. Coll., summer 1971, U.S. Mil. Acad., West Point, N.Y., 1981-82; Commonwealth Fund lectr. U. Coll., London, 1958; Fulbright lectr. U. Queensland, Brisbane, Australia, 1963, U. Sydney (Australia), 1983; disting. vis. prof. history Pa. State U., 1978-79; Harmsworth prof. Am. history Oxford U., 1978-79; Phi Beta Kappa vis. scholar, 1981-82. Author: Empire on the Pacific, 1955, The New Isolationism, 1956, Cold War Diplomacy, 1962, rev. edit., 1977, The Age of Global Power, 1979; co-author: A History of the United States, 2 vols, 1970, A Hstory of the American People, 1970, 2d edit., 1975, Recent United States History, 1972; Editor: The Enduring Lincoln, 1959, Politics and the Crisis of 1860, 1961, An Uncertain Tradition: American Secretaries of State in the Twentieth Century, 1961, The Cold War: A Conflict of Ideology and Power, 1963, rev. edit., 1976, Ideas and Diplomacy, 1964, Manifest Destiny, 1968, Nationalism and Communism in Asia: The American Response, 1977, Freedom in America: A 200-Year Perspective, 1977, American Diplomatic History before 1900, 1978; Contbr. articles to hist. jours. Dir. bicentennial program Pa. State U., 1975-76. Served to 1st lt. U.S. Army, 1943-46. Mem. Am., So. hist. assns., Orgn. Am. Historians, Soc. Am. Historians, Soc. Historians Am., Mass. Hist. Soc., Fgn. Relations (pres. 1972), Phi Beta Kappa. Lutheran. Home: 106 Falcon Dr Charlottesville VA 22901 *One should never demand more of society than society can grant to all without suffering chaos or disintegration.*

GRAEFE, JAMES ARTHUR, clergyman; b. Rajamundry, India, Mar. 20, 1924; U.S., 1937; s. John E. and Wilhelmina (Beyer) G.; m. Eleanor M. Stroehmann, June 9, 1946; children: John, David, Thomas, Stephen. B.A., Gettysburg Coll., Pa., 1947; M.Div., Lutheran Theol. Sem., Phila., 1950; D.D. hon., Upsala Coll., East Orange, N.J., 1974. Ordained to ministry Luth. Ch. Am., 1950; pastor Ascension Luth. Ch., Lancaster, Pa., 1950-53, Salem Luth. Ch., Phila., 1953-59, Resurrection Luth. Ch., Mt. Kisco, N.Y., 1959-69; bishop Met. N.Y. Synod Luth. Ch. Am., N.Y.C., 1969—; mem. council Theol. Edn. in the Northeast Bd., 1969—. Bd. dirs. Wagner Coll., S.I., N.Y., 1969—, Phila. Sem., 1969—. Served with U.S. Army, 1943-46. Named Man of Yr. Mt. Kisco Village Bd., 1969. Lodge: Lions (Mt. Kisco). Home: 43 Roundhill Rd Dobbs Ferry NY 10522 Office: Met NY Synod Luth Ch Am 360 Park Ave S New York NY 10010

GRAESE, CLIFFORD ERNEST, accountant; b. Canova, S.D., Jan. 5, 1927; s. Arthur Edward and Alma M. (Neugebauer) G.; m. LaVonne Marie Bohn, May 3, 1953; children: Diane, Sally Jo Graese Daugherty, Susan Graese Alfirevic, Larry. B.S., U. S.D., 1949, LL.D., 1980. C.P.A. With Peat, Marwick, Mitchell & Co., Mpls., N.Y.C., 1949—, audit partner, 1958-63, partner in charge mgmt. cons., 1963-75, partner in charge accounting and auditing, N.Y.C., 1975-77, vice chmn. accounting and auditing, 1977—. Mem. Bd. Edn., Saddle River, N.J., 1972-78; trustee U. S.D. Found., 1979—, Shrine to Music Mus., 1981—; mem. Planning Bd., Saddle River, 1981—. Served with USNR, 1945-46. Mem. Am. Inst. C.P.A.'s (past chmn. div. profl. ethics), N.Y. Soc. C.P.A.'s, Am. Accounting Assn. Republican. Lutheran. Clubs: Ridgewood Country, Board Room. Home: 7 Ridge Crest Rd Saddle River NJ 07458 Office: 345 Park Ave New York NY 10022

GRAESSLEY, WILLIAM WALTER, industrial research scientist; b. Muskegon, Mich., Sept. 10, 1933; s. William Walter and Mary Iva (Isler) G.; m. Helen Lorraine Carlsen, June 13, 1953; children: Kathryn Lorraine, William W., Laurie Jo. B.S., U. Mich., 1956, 1956, M.S., 1957, Ph.D., 1960. With Air Reduction Co., 1959-63, group leader, 1962-63; mem. faculty Northwestern U., Evanston, Ill., 1963-82, assoc. prof. chem. engring. and materials sci., 1966-70, prof., 1970-

81, Walter P. Murphy prof., 1981-82, asst. dir. Materials Research Center, 1968-69; sr. sci. advisor Exxon Research and Engring. Co., 1982—; sr. vis. fellow Cambridge U., 1979-80. Contbr. articles to profl. jours.; Asst. editor trans.: Soc. Rheology, 1969-75; editorial adv. bd.: Jour. Polymer Sci, 1979—, Rubber Revs, 1981—, Macromolecules, 1983—. NSF fellow, 1956-59; Bingham medalist Soc. Rheology. Fellow Am. Phys. Soc. (exec. com., div. high polymer physics 1975-78); mem. Soc. Rheology (exec. com. 1971-73), Am. Inst. Chem. Engrs. Research in synthetic polymers. Home: 51 Madonna Ln Annandale NJ 08801

GRAETTINGER, JOHN SELLS, physician, educator; b. Ontario, Calif., June 24, 1921; s. Rupert Frederick and Alice (Sells) G.; m. Elizabeth Dun Shorey, June 29, 1946; children—John Sells, William Frederick, Alan Mitchell, Robert Shorey, George Douglass. Candidate A.B., Harvard, 1943, M.D., 1945. Diplomate: Am. Bd. Internal Medicine. Intern Harvard Med. Service, Boston City Hosp., 1945-46, asst. resident, 1946, 48-49; research asst. cardiology and internal medicine U.S. Naval Sch. Aviation Medicine, Pensacola, Fla., 1949-53; dir. sect. cardio-respiratory diseases, dept. medicine Presbyn. Hosp., also Presbyn.-St. Luke's Hosp., Chgo., 1953-68; chmn. div. medicine Presbyn.-St. Luke's Hosp., Chgo., 1966-70; asst. prof. U. Ill. Coll. Medicine, 1953-58, asso. prof., 1958-64, prof. medicine, 1964-70, Rush Presbyn.-St. Luke's Med. Center, Rush Med. Coll., also dean student and faculty affairs at coll., 1970-72; dean Rush U., 1972—; exec. v.p. Nat. Intern and Resident Matching Program, 1975—. Publs., monographs on the heart and circulation. Pres. Bishop Anderson Found., 1960-62, bd. dirs., 1954-70; bd. dirs. Chgo. Heart Assn. Served to lt. U.S. Navy, 1946-53. Fellow A.C.P.; mem. Am. Soc. Clin. Investigation, Central Soc. Clin. Research, Assn. U. Cardiologists (councillor 1964-69, pres. 1969-70), Chgo. Soc. Internal Medicine (v.p. 1970-71, pres. 1971-72), Inst. Medicine Chgo., N.Y. Acad. Sci. Clubs: Harvard (Chgo.) (chmn. scholarship com. 1962-64, dir. 1968—); University, Yacht (Chgo.); Cosmos (Washington). Home: 999 N Lake Shore Dr Chicago IL 60611 Office: 1753 W Congress Pkwy Chicago IL 60612

GRAF, CARL N., indsl. corp. exec.; b. 1926. B.A., Mass. Inst. Tech., 1951; M.B.A., Harvard, 1953. With W.R. Grace & Co., 1953—, pres., 1964, corporate v.p., group exec. indsl. chem. group, 1967, exec. v.p., group exec., 1972-78, exec. v.p., sector exec., 1978-81, pres., chief operating officer, 1981—, also dir. Address: W R Grace & Co Grance Plaza 1114 Ave of Americas New York NY 10036

GRAF, EDWARD LOUIS, JR., lawyer; b. Pitts., Sept. 24, 1938; s. Edward Louis and Laura Mae (Flaherty) G.; m. Mary Ann Johnston, July 8, 1961; children—John, Stephen, Timothy. B.B.A., U. Pitts., 1960; J.D., Duquesne U., 1967. Bar: Pa. bar 1967; C.P.A., Pa. Auditor, tax accountant Main Lafrentz & Co., Pitts., 1960-65; treas. G.E. Smith Inc., Pitts., 1965-67; controller Cecast Group, Combustion Engring. Inc., Pitts., 1967-70; sec., legal counsel Ketchum, MacLeod & Grove, Inc., Pitts., 1970-71, exec. v.p. finance and law, 1977—. Editor, pub.: Law Quar, 1972—. Treas. Pi Sigma Ednl. Found. Clubs: Univ., Ad (Pitts.) (chmn. legal/ethics com.); Duquesne.). Home: 6933 Church Ave Pittsburgh PA 15202 Office: Four Gateway Center Pittsburgh PA 15222

GRAF, PAUL EDWARD, electronics company executive; b. Hempstead, N.Y., Feb. 12, 1944; s. F. Edward and Dorothy (David) G.; m. Sandra Ann Oakley, Apr. 16, 1966; 1 dau., Alexa Elbereth. B.E.E., Rensselaer Poly. Inst., 1965; M.B.A., Boston U., 1971. With Tex. Instruments, Attleboro, Mass., 1965-74; mng. dir. TI Brazil, Sao Paulo, 1974-79; group v.p. Conrac Corp., Stamford, Conn., 1979-81, exec. v.p., 1981—. Home: 645 Hulls Farm Rd Southport CT 06490 Office: 3 Landmark Sq Stamford CT 06901

GRAF, RUDOLF F., electronic engineer, author; b. Vienna, Austria, Aug. 17, 1926; came to U.S., 1941; s. Oskar and Berta (Witler) G.; m. Bettina Knisbacher, Apr. 20, 1952; children: Jeffrey Howard, Debra Helene. Gen. tech. degree, RCA Insts., 1947; B.S. in Elec. Engring, Poly. Inst. Bklyn., 1951; M.B.A., N.Y. U., 1954. Test engr. Hudson Am. Corp., Bklyn., 1943-45; sr. design, devel. engr. Radio City Products Co., Inc., N.Y.C., 1945-48; asst. to v.p. French-van Breems, Inc., N.Y.C., 1948-49; chief instr. Gotham Radio Inst., Bronx, N.Y., 1949-52; dir. engring., dir. sales Camburn, Inc., Woodside, N.Y., 1952-54; asst. dist. mgr. Sprague Electric Co., N.Y.C., 1954; Tech., editorial cons. electronic projects. Author: Using and Understanding Probes, 1960, Modern Dictionary of Electronics, 1962, 5th rev. edit., 1977, The Safe and Simple Book of Electricity, 1964, ABC's of Electronic Test Probes, 1966, Practical Electricity and Magnetism, 1967, Electronic Design Data Book, 1971, Automotive Electronics, 1971, 25 Solid State Projects, 1971, Manual of Car Electronics, 1972, Safe and Simple Electricity Experiments, 1973, How It Works, Illustrated, 1974, Electronic Databook, 1974, 3d edit., 1983, Solid State Ignitions Systems, 1974, Electronics Quizbook, 1975, Build It Book of Fun and Games, 1975, Build-it-Book of Car Electronics, 1975, Build-it Book of Safety Electronics, 1976, Build-it Book of Home Electronics, 1976, Ency. of Biomedical Engineering Terms, 1977, Van Nostrand's Guide to Power Tools, 1978, Directory of Toll-Free Numbers, 1983; Contbr. to: Popular Sci. Homeowners Ency., 1975; Contbr. articles, charts to tech. publs.; Eastern editor: Radio-TV Maintenance, 1949-52. Served with USNR, 1944-45. Sr. Mem. IEEE. Home: 111 Van Etten Blvd New Rochelle NY 10804

GRAF, TRUMAN FREDERICK, agricultural economist, educator; b. New Holstein, Wis., Sept. 18, 1922; s. Herbert and Rose (Sell) G.; m. Sylvia Ann Thompson, Sept. 6, 1947; children: Eric Kindley, Siri Lynne, Peter Truman. B.S., U. Wis., 1947, M.S., 1949, Ph.D., 1953. Mktg. specialist, coop. agt. U.S. Dept. Agr. and U. Wis., 1948-50; instr. agrl. econs. U. Wis., Madison, 1951-53, asst. prof., 1953-56, asso. prof., 1956-61, prof., 1961—; mem. Gov.'s Com. on Wis. Dairy Mktg.; mem. 3-man team to make mktg. analysis in Nigeria U.S. Dept. Agrl., 1962; made mktg. analyses in 13 Carribbean countries, 1964; made mktg. analysis U. Wis., Max., 1965; made mktg. analyses U.S. Ednl. Found., Finland, 1970, Rumanian Ministry Edn., U.S. Dept. State, Rumania, 1976; made U.S. milk mktg. study U.S. Dept. Agrl., 1971; researcher for internat. agrl. mktg. agys., 1963—. Contbr. articles to profl. jours. Active Cub Scouts; bd. dirs. Univ. Houses Assn., 1955-56, Univ. Hill Farm Assn., 1958-59, Univ. Hill. Farm Swim Club, 1959-60. Served with USNR, 1942-45; comdr. Res. Recipient Uhlman award Chgo. Bd. Trade, 1952, Man of Yr. award World Dairy Expn., 1976, Disting. Service award U. Wis. Extension, 1981, Cooperative Builder award Fedn. Coops., 1982. Mem. Am. Agrl. Econs. Assn (Published Research 1974), Am. Mktg. Assn., Madison Naval Res. Assn. (pres. 1968—), Am. Econ. Assn., Hist. Soc., Civil War Club. Lutheran. Lodge: Kiwanis (chmn. internat. relations com.). Applied research study for dairy firms, orgns. state ed. regulatory agys. and agrl. bus. firms. Home: 5022 LaCrosse Ln Madison WI 57305 Office: Dept of Agr U Wis Madison WI 53706 Z *My goal in life has been to make a contribution to society which will long outlast my stay on earth. I have attempted to do this through teaching, research, and public service work in my professional field, agricultural economics, and also as a "good citizen" in non-professional related volunteer work. My philosohy of life is that we all owe society far more than it owes us, and I hope to make at least a partial payment on my share of the debt.*

GRAF, UTA, soprano, educator; b. Karlsruhe/Baden, Germany, Jan. 5, 1915; came to U.S., 1948, naturalized, 1954; s. Lukas and Martha (Weiss) G.; 1 dau., Angèle Aimée Georgette Breyer. Abiturienten reife, Humanistisches Gymnasium Bruchsal/Baden, 1933; teaching diploma in voice, Dr. Hoch's Konservatorium, Frankfurt/Main, 1937. Tchr. voice Vassar Coll., 1949, Pa. Coll. Women, 1953, New Eng. Conservatory Music, Boston, 1958-66, Manhattan Sch. of Music, N.Y.C., 1964—, Phila. Mus. Acad., 1968-69, Queens Coll., N.Y.C., 1975-78; pvt. tchr. vocal technique and interpretation, N.Y.C., 1960-. Artist in residence, Aspen, Colo., 1950; Made debut under composer, Wolfgang Fortner, 1938, debut, Düsseldorf Opera House, 1940-41; leading soprano, Stadttheater Aachen, 1941-43, Koeln Opera, 1943-44, San Francisco Opera Co., 1949-51, Royal Opera, Covent Garden, London, 1950- 51, Nederlandsche Opera, Amsterdam, 1955-58, operatic, recital, concert appearances under numerous noted condrs. in, U.S., Can., Europe, S.Am. Address: Dept Voice Manhattan Sch Music New York City NY 10027 *Pursuit of perfection, artistic honesty.*

GRAFF, DONALD FREDERICK, editor, columnist; b. Billings, Mont., Jan. 31, 1928; s. Fred William and Ina (MacMillan) G.; m. Margaret Eleanor Huffman, Nov. 6, 1961; children: David Andrew, Donald Huffman. B.A., U. Mont., 1951, M.A., 1952. Newsman UP, Los Angeles, Pitts. and Newark, 1954-57; editor Radio Free Europe, Munich, W. Ger., 1957-60, bur. chief, Stockholm, 1960-61, Vienna, Austria, 1961-63; public affairs asso. Western Electric Corp., N.Y.C., 1964-65; mng. editor Newspaper Enterprise Assn., Cleve., 1965-71, N.Y.C., 1971-83, chief editorial writer, 1977-82, columnist, 1982—; mng. editor United Feature Syndicate, N.Y.C., 1979-83. Served with AUS, 1952-54. Mem. Sigma Delta Chi, Sigma Alpha Epsilon. Home: 25 Eastview Ave Pleasantville NY 10570 Office: 200 Park Ave New York NY 10166

GRAFF, GEORGE STEPHEN, aerospace company executive; b. N.Y.C., Mar. 16, 1917; s. George Russell and Marjory Eleanor (Dolan) G.; m. Mary Rita Shaughnessy, Oct. 3, 1942; children: Mary Ann, George Stephen, James Russell, Thomas Gerald, Maureen Rita. A.B. cum laude, DeSales Coll., Toledo, 1939; B.Aero. Engring., U. Detroit, 1942. Draftsman Continental Aviation & Engring. Corp., Detroit, 1940-42; with McDonnell Aircraft Co., 1942—, dir. system tech., 1961-64, v.p. engring. tech., 1964-68, v.p. engring., 1968-70, exec. v.p., 1970-71, pres., 1971-82; also dir.; v.p. McDonnell Douglas Corp., 1971—, mem. exec. com., 1974—, also dir.; Mem. subcom. stability and control NACA, 1951-56; mem. subcom. aerodynamic stability and control NASA, 1956-58, com. missile and spacecraft aerodynamics, 1959-61, com. aircraft aerodynamics, 1964-65, chmn. aircraft aerodynamics com., 1965-67, mem. research and tech. adv. com. on aeros., 1967-71. Mem. industry com. Parks Coll., St. Louis, 1950-58; Chmn. bd. trustees Fontbonne Coll., St. Louis, 1977; bd. dirs. Jr. Achievement of Mississippi Valley, Inc. Recipient trophy for design excellence Continental Aviation and Engring. Corp., 1942; Outstanding Engring. Alumnus of Yr. award U. Detroit, 1973. Fellow AIAA (regional dir., chmn. com. aircraft design 1964-67, fellow grade com. 1975-76); mem. Nat. Acad. Engring., Tau Beta Pi. Home: 1249 Kings Glen Ct Saint Louis MO 63131 Office: PO Box 516 Saint Louis MO 63166

GRAFF, HAROLD, psychiatrist, psychoanalyst; b. Phila., Apr. 11, 1932; s. Joseph and Blanche (Katz) G.; m. Diane Goldblum; children: David, Caron, Robert. B.S., U. Pa., 1954, M.D., 1958. Intern Phila. Gen. Hosp., 1958-59; resident Inst. Pa. Hosp., Phila., 1959-62; postdoctoral fellow Inst. Neurol. Sci., U. Pa., 1959-62; psychoanalytic trainee Inst. of Phila. Assn. for Psychoanalysis, Bala Cynwyd, Pa., 1962-67; research scientist, dept. clin. sci. Eastern Pa. Psychiat. Inst., Phila., 1963-74, dir. div. psychoanalytic studies, dept. clin. research and tng., 1974-79; dir. adolescent psychiatry Pa. Dept. Pub. Welfare, 1977-79; chmn. research and publs. com. Inst. of the Pa. Hosp., Phila., 1968-78; chmn. psychoanalytic research group, 1968-78; clin. assoc. prof. psychiatry Health Scis. Center Temple U., 1974-77; research asst. prof. psychiatry Hahnemann Med. Coll., Phila., 1963-70, assoc. prof., 1970-74; vis. prof., psychiat. cons. Inst. for Human Resource Devel., 1974-76; clin. prof. psychiatry and human behavior Jefferson Med. Coll., 1977—; vis. faculty Inst. of Phila. Assn. for Psychoanalysis, 1971—; pres., research dir. Psychiat. Services, Inc., Wynnewood, Pa., 1969-81; chief of psychiatry St. Francis Hosp., 1980—; staff Inst. of Pa. Hosp., Wilmington Med. Center, Phila. Psychiat. Center, Rockford Center; spl. cons. Spl. Action Office for Drug Abuse Prevention, Washington, 1973-74; cons. psychiatry Republic of Panama, 1980. Contbr. articles to profl. jours. Fellow Am., Pa. psychiat. assns., Phila. Coll. Physicians; mem. Del. Psychiat. Soc. (counsellor 1981—, treas. 1983), Am. Soc. Adolescent Psychiatry (chmn. Eastern States liaison com. 1977-78, cluster chmn. internal affairs 1979-81), Phila. Soc. Adolescent Psychiatry (pres. 1978-79), AMA, Del., New Castle County med. assns., Internat., Am., Phila. psychoanalytic assns., AAUP, Med. Club Phila., Phila. Coll. Physicians, N.Y. Acad. Sci., AAAS, Mensa, Phi Beta Kappa. Clubs: Rodney Square, University and Whist. Home: 9 Woodbrook Circle Wilmington DE 19810 Trolley Sq Suite 22B Wilmington DE 19806

GRAFF, HENRY FRANKLIN, educator, historian; b. N.Y.C., Aug. 11, 1921; s. Samuel F. and Florence Babette (Morris) G.; m. Edith Krantz, June 16, 1946; children: Iris Joan (Mrs. Andrew R. Morse), Ellen Toby. B.S.S., Coll. City N.Y., 1941; M.A., Columbia, 1942, Ph.D., 1949. Fellow history Coll. City N.Y., 1941-42, tutor history, 1946; lectr. history, Columbia, 1946-47, instr. to asso. prof., 1946-61, prof. history, 1961—, chmn. dept. history, 1961-64; lectr. Vassar Coll., 1953; Chmn. advanced placement com. Am. history Coll. Entrance Exam. Bd., 1959-63; mem. Nat. Hist. Publs. Commn., 1965-71; mem. hist. adv. com. to sec. Air Force, 1972-80; acad. cons. Gen. Learning Corp., Time-Life Books; cons. editor Alfred A. Knopf, Inc.; hist. adviser to CBS for Bicentennial TV series The American Parade, 1973-76; dir. Rand McNally & Co. Author: Bluejackets with Perry in Japan, 1952, (with Jacques Barzun) The Modern Researcher, 1962, rev. edit., 1970, 3d edit., 1977, (with Clifford Lord) American Themes, 1963, (with John A. Krout) The Adventure of the American People, 3d edit, 1973, The Free and the Brave, 4th edit, 1980, Thomas Jefferson, 1968, American Imperialism and the Philippine Insurrection, 1969, The Tuesday Cabinet, 1970, (with Paul J. Bohannan) The Call of Freedom, 1978, The Promise of Democracy, 1978, This Great Nation, 1983; Cons. editor: Life's History of the United States, 1963-64; Contbr. articles to profl. jours. Served to 1st lt. AUS, 1942-46. Recipient citation War Dept.; Am. Council Learned Socs. fellow, 1942; Townsend Harris medal CCNY, 1966; Mark Van Doren award Columbia U., 1981; Gt. Tchr. award Columbia U., 1982. Mem. Orgn. Am. Historians, Am. Hist. Assn., Author's Guild, P.E.N., Nat. Council Social Studies, Soc. Am. Historians, Soc. Historians Am. Fgn. Relations, Phi Beta Kappa. Club: Century Assn. (N.Y.C.). Home: 47 Andrea Ln Scarsdale NY 10583 Office: Fayerweather Hall Columbia U New York NY 10027

GRAFFMAN, GARY, pianist; b. N.Y.C., Oct. 14, 1928; s. Vladimir and Nadia (Margolin) G.; m. Naomi Helfman, Dec. 5, 1952. Student, Curtis Inst. Music, 1936-46, Columbia U., 1947-48. Soloist debut, Phila. Orch., 1947, first U.S. tour, 1951, S.Am. tour, 1955, European tour, 1956, Asian-Australian tour, 1958, South African tour, 1961; solo appearances with, N.Y. Philharmonic, Boston, Chgo., Cleve., San Francisco, Los Angeles symphony orchs., Philharmonia London, London Symphony, Halle Orch. of Manchester, Royal Liverpool Philharmonic, Berlin, Lisbon, Oslo, Warsaw philharmonics, Johannesburg, Sydney, Melbourne orchs., Cape Town Symphony, others; rec. artist with, N.Y., Phila., Boston, Cleve., Chgo., San Francisco orchs., also solo recs.; Author: I Really Should Be Practicing, 1981. Recipient Rachmaninoff Fund spl. award, 1948, Leventritt award, 1949; Fulbright scholar, 1950; Ford Found. fellow, 1962. Address: C/O Beall Mgt 119 W 57th St New York NY 10019 *

GRAFTON, SAMUEL, publishing co. exec.; b. N.Y.C., Sept. 4, 1907; m. Edith Kingstone, June 28, 1931; children—Abigail Alice, John William, Anthony Thomas. A.B., U. Pa., 1929. Editorial writer Phila. Record, 1929-34; asso. editor N.Y. Post, 1934-49; editor Lithopinion, 1966-69; pres. Grafton Publs., Inc., N.Y.C., 1969—. Writer: daily column I'd Rather Be Right, N.Y. Post, Chgo. Sun-Times, St. Louis Star-Times, Los Angeles Daily News, Phila. Inquirer, other newspapers, 1939-49; editor: Addiction and Substance Abuse Report; Author: All Out, 1940, An American Diary, 1943, A Most Contagious Game, 1955; Contbr. to mags. Decorated chevalier Legion of Honor, France). Address: 667 Madison Ave New York NY 10021

GRAFTON, THURMAN STANFORD, medical research consultant; b. Chgo., Dec. 20, 1923; s. Thurman Stump and Ethel (Anderson) G.; m. Jean Marie Robinson, Dec. 21, 1946; children: T. Scott, Michael W., Donald A., Glynis M. D.V.M., Mich. State U., 1947, postgrad., 1947-48; postgrad., U. Md., 1950, U. N.Mex., 1963-64, U. London, Eng., 1972-73. Diplomate: Am. Coll. Lab. Animal Medicine. Commd. 2d lt. U.S. Army, 1948; advanced through grades to lt. col. USAF, 1953; sr. scientist Aeromed. Research Lab., Holloman AFB, N.Mex.; exec. officer Med. Clin. Lab., London; with Dept. Virus and Rickettsial Diseases, 406th Med. Gen. Lab., Tokyo, Walter Reed Army Inst. Research; ret., 1966; prof., chmn. dept. lab. animal sci. SUNY-Buffalo, 1966-76; exec. dir. Nat. Soc. Med. Research, Washington, 1977-80; cons. hosps., colls., univs. Decorated Air Force Commendation medal; recipient Disting. Faculty award SUNY-Buffalo, 1977; Vet. Alumni award Mich. State U., 1978. Mem. AVMA, Am. Assn. Lab. Animal Sci., Assn. Schs. Allied Health Professions (charter), Am. Soc. Lab. Animal Practitioners (charter; pres. 1971-72), Am. Assn. Zoo Veterinarians, Internat. Assn. Aquatic Animal Medicine (charter). Office: 907 Sea Castle New Port Richey FL 33552

GRAGG, GENE BALFORD, linguistics educator; b. Amsterdam, N.Y., Aug. 24, 1938; s. Clarence Balford and Pearl (Cross) G.; m. Michele Rochat, Sept. 18, 1969; children: Theo, Laura. B.A., Loyola U., Chgo., 160; Ph.D., U. Chgo., 1966. Research assoc. U. Amsterdam, Holland, 1967-69; asst. prof. U. Chgo., 1969-73, assoc. prof., 1973-80, prof. depts. linguistics and ancient near eastern lang. and civilization, 1979—. Author: Sumerian Dimensional Infixes, 1973, Ormo Dictionary, 1982. Research grantee to Ethiopia NSF, 1974-75. Mem. Am. Oriental Soc., Linguistic Soc. Am. Office: Oriental Inst U Chgo 1155 E 58th St Chicago Il 60637

GRAHAM, ALBERT BRUCE, audiologist, speech and lang. pathologist; b. Oil City, Pa., Aug. 8, 1919; s. Albert Vanderlin and Octavia (Kellogg) G.; m. Mary Margaret Zeller, June 4, 1943; children—Janice, Michael. A.B., Colo. State Coll. Edn., 1940; A.M., U. Denver, 1949; Ph.D., Northwestern U., 1953. Tchr. high sch. drama, Coolidge, Kans., 1940-42; prin. Schofield High Sch., Schofield Barracks, Hawaii, 1946-48; dir. Speech and Hearing Clinic, also Cerebral Palsy Center Bowling Green State U., 1951-52; chief div. audiology, speech and lang. pathology Henry Ford Hosp., Detroit, 1952-78; audiology cons. Blue Cross/Blue Shield Mich.; clin. asso. prof. audiology Wayne State U. Sch. Medicine, 1979—. Editor: Sensorineural Hearing Processes and Disorders, 1967. Bd. dirs. Detroit Hearing and Speech Center, 1956-70, pres., 1961-62, 66-67; bd. dirs. Mich. Assn. Better Hearing and Speech, 1967—, pres., 1976-77; mem. profl. adv. council United Cerebral Palsy Assn. Mich., 1960—, chmn., 1968-69; bd. dirs. Nat. Assn. Hearing and Speech Agys., 1960-72, 79—, 1st v.p., 1968-69; mem. speakers bur. United Found., Detroit; survey cons. Commn. on Accreditation Rehab. Facilities, 1970-72. Served with USAAF, 1942-46. Fellow Am. Speech and Hearing Assn. (legis. council 1969-75, 78—); asso. fellow Am. Acad. Ophthalmology and Otolaryngology; mem. Acad. Rehab. Audiology, Assn. Research in Otolaryngology, Am. Audiological Soc. (exec. com. 1974—), Soc. Med. Audiologists, Mich. Speech and Hearing Assn. (pres. 1957), Council Exceptional Children, asso. mem., Mich. Otol. Soc. Home: 3236 Lincoln St Dearborn MI 48124 Office: Henry Ford Hospital 2799 W Grand Blvd Detroit MI 48202

GRAHAM, ALEXANDER JOHN, classics educator; b. Lowestoft, Eng., Mar. 9, 1930; s. Godfrey Michael and Edith Mary (Meek) G.; m. Jenny Elizabeth Fitter, July 6, 1963; children: William Richard, Oliver James. B.A., Cambridge (Eng.) U., 1952, M.A., 1956, Ph.D., 1957. Asst. lectr. classics U. London, 1955-57; asst. lectr. ancient history U. Manchester, Eng., 1957-59, lectr., 1959-70, sr. lectr., 1970-77; prof. classical studies U. Pa., Phila., 1977—; chmn. Grad. Group Ancient History, 1978-81, chmn. dept. classical studies, 1982—; external examiner ancient history U. Leeds, Cambridge U., U. Liverpool, 1970-77. Author: Colony and Mother City in Ancient Greece, 1964, An Attic Country House Below the Cave of Pan at Vari, 1974; Contbr. articles to profl. jours. Served with Brit. Army., 1948-49. Recipient Cromer Greek prize Brit. Acad., 1956; Hare prize U. Cambridge, 1960; Nat. Endowment Humanities fellow, 1981-82. Mem. Archaeol. Inst. Am., Am. Philol. Assn., Soc. Hellenic Studies, Brit. Sch. Athens, Cambridge Philol. Soc., Assn. Internationale d'Epigraphie Grecque et Latine. Office: Dept Classical Studies 720 Williams Hall CU U Pa Philadelphia PA 19104

GRAHAM, ALEXANDER STEEL, cartoonist; b. Glasgow, Scotland, Mar. 2, 1917; m. Winnifred Margaret Bird, Nov. 9, 1944; children: Neil Graham, Arran Graham. D iploma in Drawing and Painting, Glasgow Sch. Art, 1939. Free lance cartoonist, 1945—; syndicated cartoonist: Fred Basset strip, 1964—, cartoon collections published in over 10 books. Office: care News America Syndicate 1703 Kaiser Ave Irvine CA 92714 *

GRAHAM, ANGUS FREDERICK, educator, microbiologist; b. Toronto, Ont., Can., Mar. 28, 1916; emigrated to U.S., 1958, naturalized, 1963; s. Frederick J. and Mary (Ball) G.; m. Jacqueline Francoise Poirier, July 3, 1953; children—Robert J., Andrew D., Paul F. B.A.Sc., U. Toronto, 1938, M.A.Sc., 1939; Ph.D., U. Edinburgh, Scotland, 1942, D.Sc., 1952. Lectr. biochemistry Carnegie Teaching fellow U. Edinburgh, 1942-47; research asso. Connaught Med. Research Labs., U. Toronto, 1947-58, asso. prof. microbiology, 1953-58; mem. Wistar Inst. Anatomy and Biology; Wistar prof. microbiology U. Pa., Phila., 1958-70; Gilman Cheyney prof. McGill U., Montreal, Que., 1970—, chmn. dept. biochemistry, 1970-80. Editor-in-chief: Jour. Cellular Physiology, 1965-70; editorial bd.: Jour. Virology, 1964-79, Nucleic Acids Research, 1972-78, Intervirology, 1972-78. Eleanor Roosevelt Internat. Cancer fellow Institut du Radium, Paris, France, 1964-65; Recipient Josiah Macy Faculty Scholar award, 1977-78. Fellow Royal Soc. Can.; mem. Am. Soc. Microbiologists, AAAS. Research and publs. on chemistry of enzymes and viruses, especially mechanism of multiplication of viruses in living cells. Home: 447 Strathcona Ave Westmount PQ Canada Office: Dept Biochemistry McGill U Montreal 2 PQ Canada

GRAHAM, ANNE, government official; b. Annapolis, Md., Dec. 28, 1949. Grad., Bradford Coll.; postgrad., Columbia U. Spl. asst. to dep. dir. for communications Republican Nat. Com., Washington, 1971; with White House News Summary Office, Washington, 1973, Office of Sec. of Treasury, 1974-75; press sec. to Senator Harrison Schmitt, Washington, 1976-79; asst. press sec. Reagan-Bush Campaign, 1980-81; dep. spl. asst. to Pres. for communications, Washington, 1981; asst. sec for legislation and pub. affairs Dept. Edn., Washington, 1981—. Office: Office Legislation and Pub Affairs Dept Edn 400 Maryland Ave SW Washington DC 20202 *

GRAHAM, ARNOLD HAROLD, law school official, legal educator; b. N.Y.C., Dec. 29, 1917; s. Julius E. and Rose Goldstein; m. Roselle Lesser, Dec. 23, 1939; children: Stuart R., Joel M., Jul E. B.S. with honors, N.Y. U., 1945, LL.B., J.D., N.Y. Law Sch., 1952. Bar: N.Y. 1952, U.S. Supreme Ct. 1959, also U.S. Internat. Trade 1959, U.S. Tax Ct. 1959, U.S. Ct. Appeals for 2d Circuit 1959, U.S. Dist. Ct. for Hawaii 1959; C.P.A., N.Y. Practice public acctg., N.Y.C., 1945-52, individual practice law, 1952-76, dep. atty. gen., N.Y., 1952-54; cons. N.Y. Law Sch., N.Y.C., 1952-76, asst. dean, prof., treas., 1976-77, vice dean, prof., treas., 1977—; cons., arbitrator Am. Arbitration Assn., 1952—; examiner of attys., N.Y.C.; law cons. exam. div. Am. Inst. C.P.A.s, 1976—; bd. visitors Appellate div., 1st dept. Supreme Ct. N.Y.; mem. jud. screening panel bankruptcy div. U.S. Dist. Ct. for So. Dist. N.Y., 1983-84; numerous guardianship appointments N.Y. State Supreme Ct., Surrogate's Ct. Trustee Ave R Temple, Kings Hwy. Bd. Trade; bd. advisers United Jewish Appeal; mem. exec. com. trusts and estates div. United Jewish Appeal-Fedn. Jewish Philanthropies. Recipient Ira Stone award for prof. of yr. N.Y. Law Sch., 1981. Fellow Am. Bar Found.; Mem. Am. Assn. Attys.-C.P.A.s (founder), Am., N.Y. State trial lawyers assns., Consular Law Soc., Fed. Bar Assn., Am. Bar Assn., Inst. Jud. Adminstrn., N.Y. State C.P.A. Soc., Fed. Bar Council, N.Y. County Lawyers Assn., Am. Arbitration Assn., Jewish Lawyers' Guild, Phi Delta Phi (hon., Disting. Alumnus award Dwight Inn 1984). Jewish. Club: Merchants. Home: 2223 Ave T Brooklyn NY 11229 Office: New York Law Sch 57 Worth St New York NY 10013

GRAHAM, BILL, producer; b. Berlin, Germany, Jan. 8, 1931; came to U.S., 1941, naturalized, 1953; s. Jacob and Frieda (Zess) Grajonca; m. Bonnie McLean, June 1967 (div. 1969); 1 son, David. B.A. in Bus. Adminstrn, City Coll. N.Y., 1955. Statistician Pace Motor Trucking Co., from 1955; paymaster Guy F. Atkinson Constructors; office mgr. Allis-Chalmers Mfg. Co., to 1965. Concert promoter producer/mgr. maj. rock music artists, Santana, Ronnie Montrose, Eddie Money, Van Morrison; creator, Fillmore Auditoriums East, N.Y.C., 1968-71, and West, San Francisco, 1965-71; pres., FM Prodns., San Francisco, 1966—, Bill Graham Presents, San Francisco, 1976—, Bill Graham Mgmt., Wolfgang Records, San Francisco; producer outdoor musical events including, Watkins Glen, N.Y., 1974, country-wide tours, Bob Dylan, Crosby, Stills, Nash and Young and George Harrison, 1975, 30 maj. outdoor concerts at, Oakland (Calif.) Stadium, 1974-79; originator: Bill Graham's World of Plants, 1976, 77; actor, producer: concert for film A Star Is Born, 1976; actor: Apocalypse Now, 1976-77; concert prodn. cons. Organizer, producer maj. benefit concerts for causes including, Center for Self-Determination, 1975, Save Our Cities, 1976, Save the Whales, San Francisco Sch. Dist.; (commendation of excellence Broadcast Music Inc. 1975, St. Francis of Assisi award City of San Francisco 1975, Billboard Conv. award as promoter of the Year 1975, 76, 77, others.). Served with U.S. Army, 1951-53. Decorated Bronze Star medal, Purple Heart.; Recipient B'nai B'rith Lodge award, 1973. Office: 201 11th St San Francisco CA 94103

GRAHAM, BRUCE DOUGLAS, pediatrician; b. Roberts, Wis., Dec. 15, 1915; s. Francis J. and Mary (Turner) G.; m. Louise Alice Rowekamp, Jan. 21, 1946; children: John Gardiner, Mary Augusta, Anne Louise. A.B., U. Ala., 1939; M.D., Vanderbilt U., 1942. Diplomate: Am. Bd. Pediatrics. Intern U. Mich. Hosp., 1942-43, resident dept. pediatrics, 1946-48, dir. pediatric labs., 1949-59; faculty pediatric dept. U. Mich., 1948-59, asso. prof., 1954-59, prof., 1959; prof., head dept. pediatrics U. B.C., 1959-63; pediatrician-in-chief Vancouver (B.C., Can.) Gen. Hosp., 1959-63; chief pediatrics Children's Hosp., Vancouver, 1961-63; prof. pediatrics Ohio State U. Coll. Medicine, 1964—, chmn. dept., 1964-76; chief staff Children's Hosp., Columbus, Ohio, 1964-70, chief pediatrics, 1964-76, med. dir., 1970-74; chief pediatric div. U. Hosp., Ohio State U., 1964-76; med. dir. Children's Hosp. Research Found., Columbus, 1966-76; dir. Ambulatory Services Children's Hosp., 1976—; mem. areawide project rev. com. Mid-Ohio Health Plan Fedn.; mem. Nat. Joint Practice Commn.; med. advisory bd. Crippled Childrens Services. Mem. Greater Dublin Community Council. Served to maj., M.C. AUS, 1943-46. Mem. Soc. Pediatric Research, Am. Pediatric Soc., AMA, Am. Acad. Pediatrics (dist. V chmn., pres. 1979—), Assn. Am. Med. Colls., Midwest Soc. Pediatric Research, Ohio State Med. Assn., Central Ohio Pediatric Soc., Acad. Medicine Columbus and Franklin County, Am. Assn. Maternal and Child Health, Alpha Omega Alpha. Home: 4915 Brand Rd Dublin OH 43017 Office: 700 Children's Dr Columbus OH 43205

GRAHAM, CHARLES ESTON, oil pipeline executive; b. Atlanta, Jan. 10, 1928; s. James David and Callie (Rice) G.; m. Mary Lou Harne, June 26, 1954; children: Charles Alan, Karan Marie, Sharon Ann. B.C.S., Ga. State U., 1953; J.D., Emory U., 1960. Bar: Ga. 1960. Legal. adminstr. Plantation Pipe Line Co., Atlanta, 1948-62; v.p., gen. counsel Colonial Pipeline Co., Atlanta, 1962—. Chmn. div. United Way, Atlanta, 1982. Served with U.S. Army, 1946-48. Mem. Atlanta Tax Club (pres. 1969-70), Risk and Ins. Mgrs. Soc. (pres. Atlanta chpt. 1970-71), Atlanta Lawyers Club, Assn. Oil Pipe Lines (chmn. judiciary 1982-84). Republican. Club: Atlanta Atheltic. Office: Colonial Pipeline Co 3390 Peachtree Rd NE Atlanta GA 30326

GRAHAM, CHARLES JOHN, university president; b. Peru, Ill., May 29, 1929; s. John William and Pauline (Powell) G.; m. Florence Yvonne Ure, Sept. 2, 1951; children: John Charles, James Spencer, David Powell. A.B., U. Ill., 1950, M.A., 1951, Ph.D., 1955. Mgmt. intern Navy Dept., 1953-54; contract negotiator Bur. Ships, 1954; from instr. to prof. polit. sci. Wis. State U., River Falls, 1954-63, chmn. dept. social scis., 1962-63; vis. lectr. U. Wis., summer 1957, U. Ill., summer 1959; legislative asst. to Senator Proxmire, 1960-61; dean Coll. Art and Scis., Wis. State U., Whitewater, 1963-70, asst. to pres. for fed. programs, 1965-68, acting chmn. dept. polit. sci., 1970-71; pres. St. Cloud (Minn.) State U., 1971-81, Hamline U., St. Paul, 1981—. James W. Garner fellow polit. sci., 1951-52, 52-53. Mem. Phi Beta Kappa, Phi Kappa Phi. Methodist. Home: 830 Simpson St Saint Paul MN 55104 Office: Office of Pres Hamline U Saint Paul MN 55104 *I have come to believe that my life has a purpose beyond any created by my own designs. My objective is to live a life of service, although that objective is periodically eclipsed by the shadow of self-interest and materialism. A basic principle is to deal with each person as a specially created child of God, worthy of my respect and concern. While life is not ultimately perfectible by our own efforts, each of us can help to make it better for some other people. A liberal arts education is one of the ways to make life better.*

GRAHAM, CHARLES PASSMORE, army officer; b. Seward, Alaska, Dec. 19, 1927; s. Thomas Phillip and Lynnie Ethel (Passmore) G.; m. Alice Ann Chandler, Nov. 20, 1954; children: Susan Kay, Edwin C., Richard. B.S., U.S. Mil. Acad., 1950; M.S. in Engring, U. Mich., 1957. C. Commd. 2d lt. U.S. Army, 1950, advanced through grades to lt. gen., 1977; dir. force programs and structure, office of dep. chief of staff for ops. Hdqrs. Dept. Army, Washington, 1975-77, comdg. gen. 2d Armored Div., Ft. Hood, Tex., 1977-80, dep. chief of staff for ops. Hdqrs. U.S. Army Forces Command, Ft. McPherson, Ga., 1980-81, chief of staff Hdqrs. U.S. Army Forces Command, 1981-83, comdg. gen. 2d U.S. Army, Ft. Gillem, Ga., 1983—. Decorated Legion of Merit, Bronze Star. Mem. Assn. U.S. Army (chpt. exec. bd.), Armor Assn., Field Arty. Assn., Assn. Grads. U.S. Mil. Acad., 2d Armored Div. Assn. Presbyterian. Office: Hdqrs 2d US Army Fort Gillem GA 30050 *Guided by the principle of "Duty, Honor, Country" learned as a cadet at West Point, my goal was to do my very best in every assignment I was given, remembering that what was best for the United States, best for the U.S. Army, and best for the American soldier was the proper solution to each problem. With that goal, success would come naturally.*

GRAHAM, C(LYDE) BENJAMIN, JR., physician; b. Hannibal, Mo., Jan. 15, 1931; s. Clyde Benjamin and Eileen (Legan) G.; m. Pearl Louise Relling, Sept. 7, 1956; 1 dau., Leslie Eileen. Student, Wash. State U., 1948-49; B.A. with highest honors, U. Ill., 1954; M.D., U. Wash., 1958. Diplomate: Am. Bd. Radiology. Intern Children's Orthopedic Hosp. and Med. Center, Seattle, 1958-59; resident in radiology U. Wash. Affiliated Hosps., 1959-62; faculty radiology and pediatrics U. Wash. Sch. Medicine, Seattle, 1963—, prof., 1974—; dir. pediatric radiology U. Wash. Hosp., 1964—; dir. radiology Children's Med. Center; cons. pediatric radiology Madigan Gen. Hosp., others; vis. radiologist Pediatric Clinic, Karolinska Inst., Stockholm, 1964. Contbr. articles to profl. publs. Named to Hall of Fame Nat. Wheelchair Basketball Assn., 1979; James Picker Found. fellow, 1962-64; scholar, 1964-66. Fellow Am. Coll. Radiology; mem. Soc. Pediatric Radiology (past dir.), Am. Roentgen Ray Soc., Radiological Soc. N.Am., Pacific Coast Pediatric Radiologists Assn. (past pres.), Alpha Omega Alpha. Home: 5116 Kenilworth Pl NE Seattle WA 98105 Office: Children's Orthopedic Hosp and Med Center Dept Radiology PO Box C-5371 Seattle WA 98105

GRAHAM, COLIN, stage director; b. Hove, Sussex, Eng.; s. Frederick Eaton and Diana Alexandra (Finlay) G. Diploma, Royal Acad. Dramatic Art, 1953. Dir. prodns., English Opera Group, 1963-75; artistic dir., founding dir., English Music Theatre, 1975—; artistic dir., Aldeburgh Festival, 1969—; dir. prodns., English Nat. Opera, London, 1978-83; asso. artistic dir., dir. prodns., Opera Theater of St. Louis, 1978—, also prodns. for, Met. Opera, N.Y.C., N.Y.C. Opera, Santa Fe Opera, Glyndebourne Opera, Royal Opera Covent Garden, others; lighting and set designer: Penny for a Song (Bennett), 1967, Golden Vanity (Britten), 1967, Postman Always Rings Twice, 1982, Joruri (Miki), 1982, others. Recipient Orpheus award for War and Peace, 1973; Churchill fellow, 1974. Mem. Brit. Actors Equity, Can. Actors Equity, Am. Guild Mus. Artists. Club: Garrick (London). Office: PO Box 13148 Saint Louis MO 63119

GRAHAM, D. ROBERT (BOB), governor of Florida; b. Coral Gables, Fla., Nov. 9, 1936; m. Adele Khoury; children: Gwendolyn Patricia, Glynn Adele, Arva Suzanne, Kendall Elizabeth. B.A., U. Fla., 1959; LL.B., Harvard U., 1962. Atty.; cattle and dairy farmer; real estate developer; mem. Fla. Ho. of Reps., 1966-70; mem. Fla. Senate, 1971-78; gov. State of Fla., Tallahassee, 1979—; chmn. Edn. Commn. of the States, Caribbean/C. Am. Action, U.S. intergovtl. adv. council on edn., So. Growth Policies Bd.; chmn. elect So. Govs.' Assn.; chmn. com. trade and fgn. affairs Nat. Govs.' Assn. Active 4-H Youth Found., Nat. Commn. on Reform Secondary Edn., Nat. Found. Improvement Edn., Nat. Com. for Citizens in Edn., Sr. Centers of Dade County, Fla.; chmn. So. Regional Edn. Bd. Named one of 5 Most Outstanding Young Men in Fla. Fla. Jaycees, 1971; recipient Allen Morris award for outstanding 1st term mem. senate, 1972, Allen Morris award for most valuable mem. senate, 1973, Allen Morris award for 2d most effective senator, 1976. Mem. Fla. Bar. Democrat. Mem. United Ch. of Christ. Office: Office Of Gov The Capitol Tallahassee FL 32301

GRAHAM, DANIEL ARTHUR, economist; b. Amarillo, Tex., Jan. 17, 1944; s. William T. and Ava Kate (Tipps) G.; m. Ellen Rust Peirce, June 10, 1978. B.S., W. Tex. State U., 1967; Ph.D. (NDEA fellow), Duke U., 1969. Research asst. Econometrics Systems Simulation Program, Duke U., Durham, N.C., 1968-69, asst. prof., 1969-74, asso. prof., 1974-77, prof. econs., 1977—; vis. faculty research fellow Nat. Bur. Econ. Research, N.Y.C., 1976-77. Contbr. revs., articles in field to profl. jours. Mem. Phi Beta Kappa. Office: Dept Econs Duke U Durham NC 27706

GRAHAM, DAVID ANTHONY, golfer; b. Windsor, Australia, May 23, 1946; came to U.S., 1971; s. Albert George and Patricia Hanna (Quirk) G.; m. Maureen Burdett, Nov. 30, 1968; children: Andrew, Michael. Student, Australian schs. Golf club designer MacGregor Co., 1973-77. Designer: 1977 model Jack Nicklaus V.I.P. golf clubs. Named Australian sportsman of year, 1976. Mem. Tournament Players Assn. Am., Australian, Fla. profl. golfers assns. Club: Hamlet Golf and Tennis. Winner French Open, 1970, Thailand Open, 1970, World Cup, 1970, Caracas Open, 1971, Cleve. Open, 1972, Japan Open, 1975, Wills Masters, 1975, Am. Golf Classic, 1976, Chunichi Crowns Invitational, 1976, Picadilly World Match Play, 1976, Westchester Open, 1976, Australian Open, 1977, South African PGA, 1977, Mex. Cup, 1978, U.S. PGA, 1979, Air N.Z. Open, 1979, Phoenix Open, 1981, U.S. Open, 1981, Houston Open, 1983. Office: Box 12458 Palm Beach Gardens FL 33410 *

GRAHAM, DAVID TREDWAY, medical educator, physician; b. Mason City, Iowa, June 20, 1917; s. Evarts Ambrose and Helen (Tredway) G.; m. Frances Jeanette Keesler, June 14, 1941; children: Norma VanSurdam, Andrew Tredway, Polly Brewster. B.A., Princeton U., 1938; M.A., Yale U., 1941; M.D., Washington U., St. Louis, 1943. Intern Barnes Hosp., St. Louis, 1944, asst. resident medicine, 1944-45, 47-48; research fellow medicine Cornell U. Med. Coll., 1948-51; asst. prof. medicine Washington U. Med. Sch., 1951-57, asst. prof. psychiatry, 1956-57; assoc. prof. medicine U. Wis. Med. Sch., 1957-63, prof. medicine, 1963—, assoc. chmn. dept., 1969-71, chmn., 1971-80, asst. dean and/or chmn. med. sch. admissions, 1964-69; vis. prof. psychiatry U. Va. Sch. Medicine, 1960. Research editor: Clin. Research Proc, 1954-59. Alt. del. Democratic Nat. Conv., 1968. Served to capt., M.C. AUS, 1945-47. Mem. State Med. Soc. Wis., Am. Fedn. Clin. Research, Am. Psychosomatic Soc. (council 1952-55, 64-67, pres. 1978-79), Soc. Psychophysiol. Research (bd. dirs. 1964-67, pres. 1969-70), Central Soc. Clin. Research. Home: 2927 Harvard Dr Madison WI 53705

GRAHAM, DEE MCDONALD, food company executive; b. Dixon, Miss., Oct. 11, 1927; s. Homer Yancy and Pearl (Nicholson) G.; m. Marjory May Cox, Jan. 4, 1948; children: Dee McDonald, Kenneth L., Thomas R., Timothy A., Robert D., Marjory F., Michael A. B.Sc., Miss. State U., 1950; M.S., Iowa State U., 1951; Ph.D., 1954. Asso. prof. Clemson U., 1953-58; asso. dir. research Pet Inc., 1958-66, tech. dir., 1967-69; prof. food sci. and nutrition, chmn. dept. U. Mo., Columbia, 1969-75; asst. dir. sci. research Del Monte Corp., 1975-80, dir. central research, 1980—; cons., speaker in field; mem. food protection com. Nat. Acad. Sci., 1972-75, food additive com., 1969—; mem. Adv. Bd. Mil. Personnel Supplies, 1979-82. Served with AUS, 1946-48. Mem. Evaporated Milk Assn. (chmn. research and devel. council 1956-66), Inst. Food Technologists, Am. Dairy Sci. Assn., Am. Acad. Pediatrics, AAAS, Sigma Xi. Presbyterian (elder 1964, 79-83). Club: Marriage Encounter. Lodges: Masons (32 deg.); Kiwanis. Patentee in field. Home: 1290 Mountbatten Ct Concord CA 94518 *The future of life on this planet depends on individual excellence blended into group achievement. Each of us must add more than we subtract from the balance of assets in the world community.*

GRAHAM, DONALD ANDREW, computer company executive; b. Chism, Okla., Mar. 17, 1924; s. William Andrew and Levera (Cooke) G.; m. Marion L. Runyon, Mar. 16, 1946; children: Gary Vance, Lisa Anne. B.A. in Acctg. with distinction, San Jose (Calif.) State U., 1953. Vice pres. Sperry Remington Co., Ohio, 1969-72, pres., Pa., 1972-74; v.p. Sperry Univac Co., Pa., 1974-78; pres., dir. Microdata Corp., Irvine, Calif., 1978-81; chmn., chief exec. officer Pacific Regency Bancorp.; dir. Nippon Univac Kaisha Ltd., Oki Univac Kaisha Ltd. Served with AUS, 1942-45. Decorated Purple Heart. Mem. Fin. Execs. Inst. Republican. Roman Catholic. Club: Mission Viejo Country. Home: 24805 Argus Dr Mission Viejo CA 92691

GRAHAM, DONALD EDWARD, publisher; b. Balt., Apr. 22, 1945; s. Philip L. and Katharine (Meyer) G.; m. Mary L. Wissler, Jan. 7, 1967; children: Liza, Laura, William. B.A., Harvard U., 1966. With The Washington Post, 1971—, asst. mng. editor sports, 1974-75, asst. gen. mgr., 1975-76, exec. v.p., gen. mgr., 1976-79, pub., 1979—; dir. Washington Post Co., Bowaters Mersey Paper Co. Ltd. Trustee Fed. City Council, 1976; bd. dirs. Am. Press Inst. Served with U.S. Army, 1966-68. Mem. Am. Antiquarian Soc. Office: 1150 15th St NW Washington DC 20071 *

GRAHAM, ELMER ALBERT, petroleum executive; b. Evansville, Ind., Oct. 6, 1926; s. William J. and Mary (Grimwood) G.; m. Jean; children: William Earl, Terri Ellen; stepchildren: Eric Matthew, Leanne Elizabeth Toler. B.S., Evansville Coll., 1949; grad. Advanced Mgmt. Program, Harvard U., 1966; J.D. (hon.), Findlay Coll., 1978, Kenyon Coll., 1982. With Marathon Oil Co., Findlay, Ohio, 1955—, asst. treas., 1961-62; treas. Marathon Internat. Oil Co., 1962-67, treas. parent co., 1967-68, v.p., treas., 1969-73, v.p. finance, 1973-77, sr. v.p. fin. and adminstrn., 1977—, dir., 1973—; dir. First Nat. Bank Findlay, Internat. Steel Co., SeaGate Capital Mgmt. Co., Libbey-Owens-Ford Co. Past pres. Blanchard Valley Hosp. Assn.; past mem. Findlay Bd. Edn.; past mem. bd. Hancock County Joint Vocat. Sch.; trustee, vice chmn. bd. Kenyon Coll.; trustee Toledo Mus. Art.; bd. dirs. Exec. Council Fgn. Diplomats. Served with USNR, 1943-46. Mem. Am. Petroleum Inst. (past v.p. fin. and accounting, dir.), Fin. Execs. Inst., Findlay Area C. of C. Presbyterian. Clubs: Elks, Rotary, Catawba Island Yacht, Findlay Country, Ocean Reef, Board Room. Home: 2033 Old Mill Rd Findlay OH 45840 Office: 539 S Main St Findlay OH 45840

GRAHAM, ERWIN HERMAN, ret. automobile co. exec.; b. Detroit, Jan. 28, 1921; s. Jacob and Marie Pauline (Schulz) G.; m. Ellen Marie Eliasen, Sept. 12, 1944; children—Leigh Ellen, Michael Randall. Grad. in accounting, Bus. Inst., 1943. C.P.A., Mich. Cost accountant Parke, Davis & Co., 1939-43; pub. accountant Ernest & Ernst, 1945-51; comptroller's staff Chrysler Corp., 1951-54; comptroller DeSoto div., Detroit, 1954-58, comptroller corp., 1958-67, corp. v.p., 1964-80. Bd. dirs. YMCA Met. Detroit; trustee Detroit Inst. Tech., 1970-80. Served to 1st lt. USAAF, 1943-45. Mem. Am. Inst. C.P.A.'s, Mich. Assn. C.P.A.'s (life), Fin. Execs. Inst. Clubs: Detroit Athletic, Detroit Golf. Home: 529 Lake Shore Rd Grosse Pointe Shores MI 48236

GRAHAM, EVARTS AMBROSE, JR., newspaper editor; b. St. Louis, Feb. 4, 1921; s. Evarts A. and Helen (Tredway) G.; m. Perugina Adler, June 30, 1951; children: Helen, Sarah. B.S., Harvard, 1941. With St. Louis Post-Dispatch, 1941, mng. editor, 1968-79, contbg. editor, 1979—. Bd. dirs. Community Sch., St. Louis, Asso. Harvard Alumni. Served with AUS, 1942-46. Office: 1701 Pennsylvania Ave NW Suite 550 Washington DC 20006

GRAHAM, FORD MULFORD, oil company executive; b. Sumner, Mich., May 29, 1911; s. Frederick Joseph and Anna (Mulford) G.; m. Maxine Ingold, July 22, 1933; children: Shirley (Mrs. Louis Wiginton), John J. A.B., Alma Coll., 1932; J.D., U. Mich., 1938. Div. landman Humble Oil & Refining Co., 1938-46; La. mgr. mineral div. Gaylord Container Corp., 1946-54; independent oil operator, 1954-58; pres. Citizens Nat. Bank in Hammond, La., 1954-57, chmn. bd., 1957-61; v.p. Monterey Oil Co., 1958-60; v.p., dir. Monterey Pipe Line Co., 1960; v.p. La. Land & Exploration Co., New Orleans, 1960, pres., 1961-67, chief exec., 1962-67, chief exec. officer, 1967-72, chmn. bd., 1967-74, chmn. exec. com., 1971—, also dir.; chmn. bd. Graham Resources Inc.; Mem. Nat. Petroleum Council, 1963-75. State crusade chmn. Am. Cancer Soc., 1964-65. Club: Boston. Home: 2 Mockingbird Dr Covington LA 70433 Office: 3510 N Causeway Blvd Suite 200 Metairie LA 70002

GRAHAM, FRANCES KEESLER (MRS. DAVID TREDWAY GRAHAM), psychologist, educator; b. Canastota, N.Y., Aug. 1, 1918; d. Clyde C. and Norma (Van Surdam) Keesler; m. David Tredway Graham, June 14, 1941; children: Norma, Andrew, Polly. B.A., Pa. State U., 1938; Ph.D., Yale U., 1942. Acting dir. St. Louis Psychiat. Clinic, 1942-44; instr. Barnard Coll., 1948-51, Sch. Medicine, Washington U., St. Louis, 1942-48, 53-55, research asso., 1953-57, U. Wis., Madison, 1957-64, asso. prof., 1964-68, prof. pediatrics and psychology, 1968—, Hilldale research prof., 1980—; Cons. Nat. Inst. Neurol. Diseases and Blindness perinatal research br.; mem. exptl. psychology research review com. NIMH, 1970-74, NRC, 1971-74; mem. bd. sci. counselors NIMH, 1977-81, chmn., 1979-81; mem. Pres.'s Commn. for Study of Ethical Problems in Medicine and Biomed. and Behavioral Research, 1980—. Mem. editorial bd.: Jour. Exptl. Child Psychology, 1964-67, Child Devel., 1966-68, Jour. Exptl. Psychology, 1968-73, Psychophysiology, 1968-73; Contbr. articles to profl. jours. Recipient Research Scientist award NIMH, 1964—, Disting. Alumna award Pa. State U., 1983. Mem. Am. Psychol. Assn. (council 1975-77, pres. div. physiol. and comparative psychology 1978-79, A. Stanley Hall award 1982), Soc. Research Child Devel. (council 1965-71, pres. 1975-77), Soc. Psychophysiol. Research (dir. 1968-71, 72-75, pres. 1973-74, Disting. Contbns. award 1981), Soc. Exptl. Psychologists, Soc. Neurosci., Psychonomic Soc., Acoustical Soc. Am., Internat. Soc. Developmental Psychobiology, AAAS (chmn. sect. psychology 1979), Phi Beta Kappa, Sigma Xi. Home: 2927 Harvard Dr Madison WI 53705

GRAHAM, FRANCIS WILLIAM, consumer products company executive; b. Urbana, Ill., Aug. 2, 1937; s. Francis William and Mary G. (Gleason) G.; m. Helen T. Grady, Dec. 31, 1960; children—Francis William, III, J. Brian, Mary Helen, Katherine G., David M. B.S., U. Notre Dame, 1959; M.B.A., Harvard U., 1964. With Gen. Mills, Inc., Mpls., 1964-77, div. gen. mgr., 1969-71, v.p., gen. mgr., 1971-73, group v.p., 1973-77; corp. v.p., pres. consumer products group Dart Industries, Inc., Los Angeles, 1977-81; corp. group v.p., pres. Home and Comml. Products Group, Dart & Kraft, Inc., 1981-82; sr. exec. v.p., chief operating officer Cambridge Plan Internat., Monterey, Calif., 1982—. Bd. dirs. Holy Family Adoption Services, Los Angeles; trustee Harvard Sch., Los Angeles. Served with USN, 1959-62. Mem. Am. Mgmt. Assn., Am. Apparel Mfrs. Assn. (dir. 1977). Home: 340 N

Saltair Ave Los Angeles CA 90049 Office: PO Box 3157 Terminal Annex Los Angeles CA 90051

GRAHAM, GEORGE ADAMS, political scientist, educator; b. Cambridge, N.Y., Dec. 23, 1904; s. Andrew Allen and Anna Katherine (Adams) G.; m. Rosanna Grace Webster, Aug. 20, 1930; children—Andrew Allen, Lora Katherine (Mrs. C. R. K. Lunt), Mary Margaret (Mrs. Kurt J. Jenne). A.B., Monmouth Coll., 1926, LL.D., 1959; A.M., U. Ill., 1927, Ph.D., 1930. Instr. Monmouth Coll., 1927-28; asst. U. Ill., 1929-30; faculty Princeton, 1930-58, instr., 1930-31, asst. prof., 1931-39, asso. prof., 1939-45, prof., 1945-58, chmn. dept. politics, 1946-49, 52-55; dir. govtl. studies Brookings Inst., 1958-67; exec. dir. Nat. Acad. Pub. Adminstrn., 1967-72, sr. social scientist, 1972-73; prof. pub. adminstrn. Nova U., Ft. Lauderdale, Fla., 1974—; Mem. staff Detroit Bur. Govt. Research, 1929-30; with U.S. Bur. Budget, 1942-46, as adminstrn. cons., 1942-43, chief war supply sect., 1943-45; sec. Com. on Records War Adminstrn., 1944-45; chief Govt. Orgn. Br. and asst. chief Div. Adminstrv. mgmt., 1945; cons., 1945-46; chmn. com. on Indian Affairs, Hoover Commn. on Orgn. Exec. Br. Govt., 1948, staff dir., task force on personnel and civil service, 1953-54; cons. Senate subcom. Ethics in Govt., 1951; dir. pub. affairs program Ford Found., 1956-57. Author: books including Education for Public Administration, 1941, (with Henry Reining) Regulatory Administration, 1943; Morality in American Politics, 1952, America's Capacity to Govern, 1960. Mem. Am. Polit. Sci. Assn., Am. Soc. Pub. Adminstrn., Theta Chi. Presbyn. Clubs: Kenwood, Cosmos. Home: 8509 Old Country Manor Apt 305 Fort Lauderdale FL 33328 Office: Nova U 3301 College Ave Fort Lauderdale FL 33314

GRAHAM, GEORGE GORDON, physician; b. Hackensack, N.J., Oct. 4, 1923; s. Charles Stewart and Angelica (Gomez de la Torre) G.; m. Simone H. Custer, Mar. 3, 1949; children—Marianne, Alexander, Monica, Carol. A.B., U. Pa., 1941, M.D., 1945. Diplomate: Am. Bd. Pediatrics, Am. Bd. Nutrition. Intern, resident Brit. Am. Hosp., Lima, Peru, 1946-48, staff pediatrics, 1948-50, 52-55, dir. research, 1960-71, Instituto de Investigacion Nutricional, Lima, Peru, 1971—; research resident U. Pa. Hosp., 1951; resident pediatrics Balt. City Hosp., 1955-56, asso. chief pediatrician, 1965-68; asso. prof. pediatrics Johns Hopkins U., 1965—, prof. human nutrition, 1968—, dir. nutrition program, 1976—; staff pediatrician Cleve. Clinic, 1957-59; lectr. nutrition Mass. Inst. Tech., 1962-65; vis. prof. nutrition Agrarian U. Peru, 1962-65; Mem. com. amino acids Food and Nutrition Bd. of NRC, 1966-71, com. internat. nutrition programs, 1978-79; mem. Food and Nutrition Bd., 1981—; cons. nutrition AID, GAO, NIH; mem. nutrition study sect. NIH, USPHS, 1971-75, chmn., 1973-75. Mem. editorial bd.: Jour. Nutrition, 1968-73, Jour. Clin. Nutrition, 1969-74. Recipient Orden al Merito Agricola, Peru, 1964; Joseph Goldberger award AMA, 1972; Borden award Am. Acad. Pediatrics, 1977. Mem. Am. Inst. Nutrition, Am. Soc. Clin. Nutrition (council 1980—), Soc. Pediatric Research, Am. Pediatric Soc. Research on infantile malnutrition, its long-term effects, its prevention by new protein sources. Home: 3126 Golf Course Rd W Owings Mills MD 21117 Office: 615 N Wolfe St Baltimore MD 21205

GRAHAM, GEORGE GRIMSLEY, surgeon; b. Goldsboro, N.C., Dec. 1, 1921; s. William Howard and Lillian (Austin) G.; m. Barbara Holt, Aug. 22, 1972; children by previous marriage: George Grimsley, Lawrence Lain, Louis Austin. Student, Hendrix Coll., 1938-41, Cornell U., 1943-44; B.S., U. Ark., 1946, M.D., 1947; postgrad. (Mayo Clinic fellow), U. Minn., 1948-52. Diplomate: Am. Bd. Surgery. Intern Ancken Hosp. (St. Paul-Ramsay County Hosp.), St. Paul, 1947-48; resident Mayo Clinic, Rochester, Minn., 1948-52; practice medicine specializing in gen. and thoracic surgery, Little Rock, 1955—; chief staff Ark. Children's Hosp., Little Rock, 1958, Bapt. Med. Center, 1962—, chief surgery, 1974-76, Meml. Hosp., Little Rock, 1963; med. dir. Union Life Ins. Co., 1963—. Contbr. articles to profl. jours. Active United Way, Little Rock, 1957-60. Served with U.S. Army, 1943-46; Served with USN, 1952-54. Recipient Am. Cancer Soc. award, 1963. Fellow A.C.S., Am. Coll. Chest physicians; mem. Alpha Omega Alpha. Presbyterian. Club: Country of Little Rock. Home: 18 Sunset Dr Little Rock AR 72207 Office: 990 Med Towers Lile Dr Little Rock AR 72205

GRAHAM, GORDON MARION, business executive, retired air force officer; b. Ouray, Colo., Feb. 16, 1918; s. Alexander and Margaret (Wilson) G.; children—Eloise L., Helen H., G. Alexander E.; m. Vivian Fox, Dec. 4, 1967. B.S., U. Calif. at Berkeley, 1940; M.S., U. Pitts., 1948. Grad. Flying Sch., 1941; commd. 2d lt. USAAF, 1941; advanced through grades to lt. gen. USAF, 1968; comdr. 354th Fighter Squadron, 1944-45, 361st Fighter Group, 1945; asst. chief staff operations 8th Fighter Command, 1945-46; dep. asst. chief staff operations 10th Air Force, Brooks AFB, Tex., 1946; comdr. 182d Base Unit Res. Tng. Detachment, Carswell AFB, Tex., 1946-47, 178th Base Unit Res. Tng., Brooks AFB, 1947; chief target analysis div. Office Dir. Intelligence Hdqrs. USAF, 1949-53; dir. targets, directorate intelligence Hdqrs. Far East Air Force, 1953-55; dep. comdr. 31st Strategic Fighter Wing, Turner AFB, Ga., 1955, comdr., 1955-59; chief tactical div., directorate operations Hdqrs. USAF, 1959-60, dep. dir. operational forces, 1961-62; comdr. 4th Tactical Fighter Wing, Seymour Johnson AFB, N.C., 1962-63; vice comdr. Hdqrs. 19th Air Force, 1963-64; dep. operations Hdqrs. Tactical Air Command, Langley AFB, Va., 1964-66; vice comdr. 7th Air Force, Pacific Air Forces, 1966-67; comdr. 9th Air Force, Shaw AFB, S.C., 1967-68; vice comdr. Tactical Air Command, Langley AFB, Va., 1968-70; comdr. U.S. Forces Japan, 5th Air Force, 1970-72, 6th Allied Tactical Air Force, 1972-73; corporate v.p. Far East, McDonnell Douglas Corp.; also pres. McDonnell Douglas Japan, Ltd., Tokyo, 1973-77, corp. v.p., Washington, 1977—. Decorated D.S.M., Silver Star, Legion of Merit, D.F.C. with oak leaf cluster, Air medal with 28 oak leaf clusters, Joint Service Commendation medal, Air Force Commendation ribbon. Mem. Am. Inst. Mining, Metall. and Petroleum Engrs., Am. Fighter Aces Assn., Air Force Assn., Order Daedalians, Nat. Rifle Assn. (life), Tau Beta Pi. Office: McDonnell Douglas Corp 1225 Jefferson Davis Hwy Suite 800 Arlington VA 22202

GRAHAM, HOWARD BARRET, publishing company executive; b. Boston, Dec. 7, 1929; s. Robert M. and Belle (Brown) G.; m. Rita Joyce Mahony; children: Ronni M., Erica. B.A., Syracuse U., 1951. Gen. mgr. sch. supply div., sales mgr. ednl. div. Milton Bradley Co., Springfield, Mass., 1954-63; gen. mgr. jr. book div. McGraw-Hill Co., 1964-69; pres., dir. Franklin Watts Inc., N.Y.C., 1970—; chmn. bd. Franklin Watts Ltd.; sr. v.p. mktg./product devel., pub., dir. Grolier, Inc., 1983—. Served with USAF, 1951-53. Mem. Mensa. Home: 25 E 83d St New York NY 10028 Office: 387 Park Ave S New York NY 10016

GRAHAM, HUGH DAVIS, educator; b. Little Rock, Sept. 2, 1936; s. Otis L. and Lois (Patterson) G.; m. Ann Clary, June 11, 1966; children: Hugh Patterson (dec.), Holter Ford. B.A. magna cum laude, Yale, 1958; M.A. (Woodrow Wilson fellow 1960-61, 63-64), Stanford, 1961, Ph.D., 1964. History instr. Foothill Coll., Los Altos, Calif., 1962-64; asst. prof. San Jose (Calif.) State Coll., 1964-65; tng. officer, regional dir. Peace Corps, Washington, 1965-66; vis. asst. prof. history Stanford U., 1966-67; assoc. prof. history Johns Hopkins U., Balt., 1967-71; prof. U. Md.-Balt. County, 1972—, acting dir. Inst. So. History, 1969-70, dean div. social scis., 1971-77, dean grad. studies and research, 1982—. Author: Crisis in Print, 1967, Since 1954: Desegregation, 1972, (with Numan V. Bartley) Southern Politics and The Second Reconstruction, 1975, The Uncertain Triumph, 1984; Co-editor: Violence in America, 1969, rev. edit., 1979, Southern Elections, 1978; editor: Huey Long, 1970, Violence, 1971, American Politics and Government, 1975. Co-dir. history task force Nat. Com. on Causes and Prevention of Violence, 1968-69. Served to 1st lt., arty. USMCR, 1958-60. Recipient Merit award Am. Assn. State and Local History, 1968; Chastain award for best book on So. politics So. Polit. Sci. Assn., 1975; Guggenheim fellow, 1970-71. Mem. Am. Hist. Assn., So. Hist. Assn., Orgn. Am. Historians. Office: 5401 Wilkens Ave Baltimore MD 21228

GRAHAM, IRWIN PATTON, air force officer; b. Charlotte, N.C., May 20, 1927; s. Irwin Patton and Theo Lulu (Terrell) G.; m. Mali Soong Liang, Feb. 5, 1982. B.S.C.E., The Citadel, 1949; postgrad., Carnegie Inst. Tech., 1950; M.S. in Aero. Engring, Air Force Inst. Tech., 1958; grad., Air Command and Staff Coll., 1963, Indsl. Coll. Armed Forces, 1968; M.B.A., George Washington U., 1968. Registered profl. engr., Md. Served as enlisted man U.S. Army, 1945-46; structure engr. Am. Bridge Co., Ambridge, Pa. and J.E. Sirrine Co., Greenville, S.C., 1949-50; commd. 2d lt. U.S. Air Force, 1950, advanced through grades to maj. gen., 1979; B-36 navigator, Tex., 1953-57, instr. in engring., sr. USAF rep., 1958-62, B-57 navigator, Japan, Korea, 1963-64, planner/programmer, Hickam AFB, Hawaii, 1964-67, 69-73; chief war plans div. Hdqrs. 7th Air Force, Tan Son Nhut Air Base, Vietnam, 1968-69; dep. chief, chief eastern regional div., asst. dep. dir. for plans and policy Directorate of Plans, Hdqrs USAF, Washington, 1973-75; exec. asst. to chmn Joint Chiefs of Staff, Pentagon, Washington, 1976-77; staff group mem. Office of Chmn., 1975-77; dir. politico-mil. affairs Plans and Policy Directorate, Joint Chiefs of Staff, Washington, 1977-79; dep. chief of staff for plans Pacific Air Forces, Hickam AFB, 1979—; ret., 1982. Decorated Def. Superior Service medal, Legion of Merit with oak leaf cluster, Bronze Star medal, Air medal, Air Force Commendation medal. Mem. AIAA, Air Force Assn. Presbyterian. Home: 11801 Becket St Potomac MD 20854

GRAHAM, JAMES BERNARD, state govt. ofcl.; b. Fairfield, Ky., Dec. 24, 1923; s. Bruce Alexander and Bessie (Caldwell) G.; m. Lorena Pauley, June 7, 1952; children—Diana Gail, Janet Marie. A.B., William Jewell Coll., 1945; M.A., U. Kans., 1947; Ph.D., U. Ky., 1956. Supt. schs. Nelson County, Bardstown, Ky., 1954-68, Ashland, Ky., 1968-70, Bowling Green, Ky., 1970-75; supt. pub. instruction, Commonwealth Ky., Frankfort, 1976-79, auditor public accounts, State of Ky., 1979—; vice chmn. Study of Minimum Found. Program of Ky., 1966; mem. Ky. Crime Commn., Council Pub. Higher Edn., Ky. Authority Ednl. TV. Trustee Ky. Tchrs. Retirement System, Oneida (Ky.) Inst.; sec. Ky. Textbook Commn.; Pres. trustees Stephen Foster Drama Assn., 1957-65. Kellogg Found. grantee, 1956. Mem. Am. Assn. Sch. Adminsrrs., Ky. Assn. Sch. Adminsrrs. (past pres.), NEA, Ky. Sch. Bds. Assn., Order Ky. Cols., Kappa Delta Pi, Phi Delta Kappa. Democrat. Baptist. Clubs: Century, Masons, Kiwanis (Bardstown) (past pres.). Home: 639 Cottonwood Dr Bowling Green KY 42101 Office: 1718 Capital Plaza Tower Frankfort KY 40601

GRAHAM, JAMES EDMONT, service management executive; b. Coboconk, Ont., Can., Dec. 24, 1933; s. Henry Roy and Etta Isobel (Jackson) G.; m. Lorna Margaret Christian, 1951; children: Deobrah, Catherine, Jeffrey, Stephanie, Meredit. Sr. matriculation, Lindsay Collegiate Inst., 1951. With VS Services Ltd., Toronto, Ont., 1977—, pres., chief exec. officer, 1980—, dir., 1980—; vice chmn., chief exec. officer, dir. Maj Foods Ltd., Halifax, N.S., 1982—; v.p., dir. Versabec Inc., Montreal, 1980—; pres., chief exec. officer, dir. Vancouver Enterprise, 1981—. Treas., dir. 2nd Mil Club of Tronto, 1983—; founding mem. Advanced Mgmt. Program for Hospitality Industry, Guelph,Ont., 1981—; mem. Ont. Bus. Adv. Council, 1982—. Home: 275 Oakhill Rd Mississauga L5G ONCanada y Office: VS Services Ltd PO Box 950 Station U Toronto ONCanada M8Z 5Y7

GRAHAM, JAMES HERBERT, physician; b. Calexico, Calif., Apr. 25, 1921; s. August K. and Esther (Choudoin) G.; m. Anna Kathryn Luiken, June 30, 1950; children: James Herbert, John A., Angela Joann. Student, Brawley Jr. Coll., 1941-42; A.B., Emory U., 1945; M.D., Med. Coll. Ala., 1949. Diplomate: Am. Bd. Dermatology (dir. 1977—); diplomate in dermatopathology Am. Bd. Dermatology and Am. Bd. Pathology. Intern Jefferson-Hillman Hosp., Birmingham, Ala., 1949-50; resident in dermatology VA Center and UCLA Med. Center, 1953-56; clin. asso. in medicine UCLA, 1954-56; Osborne fellow and NRC fellow in dermal pathology Armed Forces Inst. Pathology, Washington, 1956-58, vis. scientist, 1958-69, chmn. dept. dermatopathology, 1980—; registrar Registry of Dermatopathology, Armed Forces Inst. Pathology, 1980—, also program dir. dernatopathology; program dir. dermatopathology Walter Reed Army Med. Center, Washington, 1979—; asst. prof. dermatology and pathology Temple U., 1958-61, asso. prof., 1961-65, prof. dermatology, 1965-69, asso. prof. pathology, 1965-67, prof. pathology, 1967-69; prof. medicine, chief div. dermatology, prof. pathology, dir. sect. dermal pathology and histochemistry Coll. Medicine, U. Calif., Irvine, 1969-78, chief dermatology, 1977-78, prof. emeritus, 1978—; head sect. dermatology Orange County (Calif.) Med. Center, 1969-73; cons. dermatology VA Hosp., Long Beach, Calif., 1969-73, chief dermatology sect., 1973-78, acting chief med. service, 1976-77; cons. dermatology, dermal pathology Regional Naval Med. Center, San Diego, 1969-82, Long Beach, 1969-78, Camp Pendleton, Calif., 1972-78, Meml. Hosp. Med. Center, Long Beach, 1972—, Fairview State Hosp., Costa Mesa, Calif., 1969-78; cons. for career devel. for rev. clin. investigator applications VA Central Office, Washington, 1973-78; Disting. Eminent physician VA physician and dentist-in-residence program, 1980—; mem. organizational com. Am. Registry Pathology, Armed Forces Inst. Pathology, Washington, 1976-77, mem. exec. com., 1977-78; prof. dermatology, clin. prof. pathology Uniformed Services U. of Health Scis., Bethesda, Md., 1979—. Sr. author: Dermal Pathology, 1972; contbr. articles to profl. publs. Served with M.C. USNR, 1949-53. Mem. AMA (residency rev. subcom. for dermatopathology 1974—, mem. residency rev. com. dermatology 1977—, cert. of merit 1960), Assn. Profs. Dermatology, Soc. Investigative Dermatology, Internat. Acad. Pathology, Am. Assn. Pathologists, Am. Dermatol. Assn. (essay award 1958), Am. Soc. Dermatopathology (pres. 1975-76), Dermatopathology Club (pres. 1980-81), Assn. Mil. Dermatologists, Am. Acad. Dermatology (dir. 1974-77, 82, v.p. 1980-81, rep. to bd. mems. Am. Registry Pathology 1977-78), Pa. Acad. Dermatology, Pacific Dermatologic Assn. (dir. 1972-75), Dermatology Found., Phila. Dermatol. Soc., Alpha Omega Alpha. Club: Cosmos (Washington). Home: 4928 Sentinel Dr 303 Summer Village Bethesda MD 20816 Office: Armed Forces Inst Pathology Washington DC 20306 *I have achieved far more than dreamed possible but it could only happen in America. Being generally optimistic, enthusiastic and persistent has resulted in my serving society in a positive way.*

GRAHAM, JARLATH JOHN, publishing executive; b. Chgo., Dec. 18, 1919; s. Jarlath John and Isabelle Marie (Corboy) G.; m. Elizabeth Grace Carlson, Aug. 23, 1958; children: Carol, Karen. B.A., U. Chgo., 1949. With Advt. Age, Chgo., 1950—, editor, 1969-75; v.p. Crain Communications Inc., Chgo., 1963—, dir. editorial devel., 1975-77, v.p. communications/editorial devel., 1977-83, v.p., dir. external relations, 1983—; dir. Crain Books. Contbr. to: Ency. Brit, 1966—. Served to capt. AUS, World War II. Mem. Sigma Delta Chi. Home: 415 Aldine Ave Chicago IL 60657 Office: Advertising Age Magazine 740 N Rush St Chicago IL 60611

GRAHAM, JOHN B., bishop; b. Phila., Sept. 11, 1913. Student, St. Charles Borromeo Sem., Pa., Pontifical Roman Sem., Rome. Ordained priest Roman Catholic Ch., 1938. Ordained titular bishop Sebrate and aux. bishop, Phila., 1964—. Office: St Helena Ch 6161 N 5th St Philadelphia PA 19120 *

GRAHAM, JOHN BORDEN, medical educator; b. Goldsboro, N.C., Jan. 26, 1918; s. Ernest Heap and Mary (Borden) G.; m. Ruby Barrett, Mar. 23, 1943; children: Charles Barrett, Virginia Borden, Thomas Wentworth. B.S., Davidson Coll., 1938, D.Sc. (hon.), 1984; M.D., Cornell U., 1942. Asst. Cornell U., 1943-44; mem. faculty U. N.C., Chapel Hill, 1946—, Alumni Disting. prof. pathology, 1966—, chmn. genetics curriculum, 1963—, asso. dean medicine for basic scis., 1968-70, coordinator interdisciplinary grad. programs in biology, 1968—, dir. hemostasis program, 1974—; vis. prof. haematology St. Thomas's Hosp. Med. Sch., London, 1972; vis. prof. Teikyo U. Med. Sch., Tokyo, 1976; mem. selection com. NIH research career awards, 1959-62; genetics tng. com. USPHS, 1962-66, chmn., 1967-71; mem. genetic basis of disease com. Nat. Inst. Gen. Med. Scis., 1977-80; mem. pathology test com. Nat. Bd. Med. Examiners, 1963-67; mem. research adv. com. U. Colo. Inst. Behavioral Genetics, 1967-71; mem. Internat. Com. Haemostasis and Thrombosis, 1963-67; chmn. bd. U. N.C. Population Program, 1964-67; sec. policy bd. Carolina Population Center, 1972-78; cons. Environ. Health Center, USPHS, WHO, Bolt, Beranek & Newman, Inc.; mem. med. and sci. adv. council Nat. Hemophilia Found., 1972-76; hon. cons. in genetics Margaret Pyke Centre, London, 1972—. Mem. editorial bd.: N.C. Med. Jour., 1949-66, Am. Jour. Human Genetics, 1958-61, Soc. Exptl. Biology and Medicine, 1959-62, Human Genetics Abstracts, 1962-72, Haemostasis, 1975-80, Christian Scholar, 1958-60. Markle scholar in med. sci., 1949-54; Recipient O. Max Gardner award U. N.C., 1968. Mem. AMA, AAAS, Elisha Mitchell Sci. Soc. (pres. 1963), AAUP, Soc. Exptl. Biology and Medicine, Am. Soc. Exptl. Pathology, Assn. Univ. Pathologists, Am. Assn. Pathologists and Bacteriologists, Am. Soc. Human Genetics (sec. 1964-67, pres. 1972), Genetics Soc. Am., Internat. Soc. Hematology, Am. Inst. Biol. Sci., Royal Soc. Medicine (London), Med. Soc. N.C., Mayflower Soc., Sigma Xi. Democrat. Presbyterian. Club: Cosmos (Washington). Publs. on blood clotting, inherited diseases in humans, human population dynamics; co-discoverer blood coagulant Factor X (Stuart factor). Home: 108 Glendale Dr Chapel Hill NC 27514

GRAHAM, JOHN DALBY, public relations executive; b. Maryville, Mo., Aug. 24, 1937; s. Kyle T. and Irma Irene (Dalby) G.; m. Jean Elizabeth Landon, Aug. 30, 1958; children—Katherine Elizabeth, David Landon. B.J., U. Mo., 1959. Editor Hallmark Cards, Inc., Kansas City, Mo., 1959-62; dir. pub. relations St. Louis Met. YMCA, 1962-66; pres. Fleishman-Hillard, Inc., St. Louis, 1966—. Bd. dirs. Met. YMCA, Loretto-Hilton Repertory Theatre, St. Louis, Bus. Resource Center, St. Louis, Webster U.; mem. downtown adv. bd. U. Mo.-St. Louis. Served to capt. U.S. Army, 1959-66. Mem. Pub. Relations Soc. Am., Nat. Investor Relations Inst. Clubs: University, Noonday (St. Louis); Bermuda Bath and Tennis. Home: 83 Bellerive Acres Saint Louis MO 63121 Office: 1 Memorial Dr Saint Louis MO 63102

GRAHAM, JOHN DARLINGTON, financial company executive; b. Harrisburg, Pa., Aug. 10, 1934; s. Arch and Margaret G.; m. Patricia Miller, Oct. 18, 1958; children: John, Kathleen, Patrick, Christine, Michael. B.S. in Econs, Mt. St. Mary's Coll., 1957. With Penn Mut. Life Ins. Co., 1957-81, gen. agt., San Francisco, 1970-74, v.p. agys., Phila., 1974-76, sr. v.p. mktg., 1976-81; chmn., chief exec. officer Keystone Fin. Group Inc., 1982—. Mem. campaign leadership com. United Way of Southeastern Pa., 1979-80; bd. dirs. Walnut St. Theatre., Mount St. Mary's Coll. Named Disting. Alumni Mt. St. Mary's Coll., 1979. Mem. Life Ins. Mktg. and Research Assn. Clubs: Overbrook Golf; Union League (Phila.). Office: 101 Bryn Mawr Ave Bryn Mawr PA 19010

GRAHAM, JOHN EDGAR, JR., symphony orchestra executive; b. Jacksonville, Fla., June 18, 1941; s. John E. G. and Nadine (McCullough) Dibblee; m. Judy Wells, Jan. 12, 1964 (div. Jan. 1973). B.A. in History, U. Va., 1963; M.P.A., U. Wash., 1971. Dir. devel. Seattle Symphony Orch., 1971-78; gen. mgr. Oreg. Symphony Assn., Portland, 1978—. Served to lt. USN, 1963-39. Mem. Am. Symphony Orch. League (dir. 1980-81), Am. Arts Alliance (dir. 1982—). Club: University (Portland). Office: Oregon Symphony Assn 813 SW Alder St Portland OR 97205

GRAHAM, JOHN FINLAYSON, economics educator; b. Calgary, Alta., Can., May 31, 1924; s. William and Hazel Marie (Lund) G.; m. Hermioni Sederis, Apr. 30, 1956; children: Andrew, James, Johanna, Nicholas. B.A. with honours in econs, U. B.C., 1947; A.M. in Econs, Columbia U., 1948, Ph.D., 1959. Mem. faculty dept. econs. Dalhousie U., Halifax, N.S., 1949—, prof., 1960—, head dept., 1960-69; Skelton-Clark vis. research fellow Queen's U., 1963-64; vis. prof. Inst. for Advanced Studies, Vienna, 1964; chmn. N.S. Royal Commn. on Edn., Pub. Services and Provincial-Municipal Relations, 1971-74; mem. econ. adv. panel of minister of fin., 1982. Author: Fiscal Adjustment and Economic Development, 1963; gen. editor: Atlantic Provinces Studies, 1959—; contbr. articles to profl. jours. Past chmn. Pub. Accts. Bd. N.S. Served to 2d lt., arty. and inf. corps Canadian Army, 1943-45. Fellow Royal Soc. Can. Can. Council fellow, 1968-69; Social Sciences and Humanities Research Council sr. fellow, 1979-80. Fellow Royal Soc. Can. (v.p. 1977-78); mem. Can. Econs. Assn. (pres. 1970-71), Acad. Humanities and Social Scis. of Royal Soc. Can. (pres. 1977-78), Canadian Tax Found., Can. Inst. Internat. Affairs (past chmn. Halifax br.). Home: 6606 South St Halifax NS Canada B3H 1V2 Office: Dept Econs Dalhousie U Halifax NS Canada B3H 3J5

GRAHAM, JOHN GOURLAY, utility company executive; b. Orange, N.J., JULy 25, 1938; s. Robert and Marie (Finkler) G.; m. Irene M. Graham, June 23, 1962; children: Thomas, Michael, Christopher. A.B. with honors, Upsala Coll., East Orange, N.J., 1960; J.D. with high honors, Rutgers U., 1963. Bar: N.J. 1963. Asst. prosecutor Essex county, N.J., 1964-65; assoc. prof. law Rutgers U., 1968-71, asst. dean, 1968-71; ptnr. Ruprecht & Graham, Newark, 1970-76; v.p. law Jersey Central Power & Light, Morristown, N.J., 1976-78; treas. Gen. Pub. Utilities Corp., Parsippany, N.J., 1978—; v.p. fin. planning, treas. GPU Sevice Corp., Parsippany, N.J., 1978—; treas. GPU Nuclear Corp., Parsippany, N.J., 1978—; dir. Utilities Mut. Ins. Co., N.Y.C., Nuclear Mutual Ltd. (Hamilton and Bermuda), Nuclear Electric Ins. Ltd.; adj. prof. Seton Hall Law Sch., Newark, 1972-80. Sec. N.J. Criminal Law Revision Commn., 1968-72; trustee Bonme Brae Sch., Millington, N.J., 1978—. Mem. N.J. State Bar Assn. Democrat. Home: 21 Candace Ln Chatham Township NJ 07928 Office: Gen Pub Utilities Corp 100 Interpace Pkwy Parsippany NJ 07054

GRAHAM, JOHN WEBB, lawyer; b. Toronto, Ont., Can., Sept. 10, 1912; s. George Wilbur and Rosaline (Webb) G.; m. Velma Melissa Taylor, June 19, 1941 (dec. Nov. 1971); children: Edward Samuel Rogers (stepson), Ann Taylor; m. Natalia Nikolaevna Popowa, July 15, 1976. Student, Upper Can. Coll., 1920-30; B.A., Trinity Coll., U.

Toronto, 1933, D.S. Litt., 1981; Barrister-at-law, Osgoode Hall Law Sch., Can., 1936. Bar: Queen's counsel 1956. Corp. trust officer Toronto Gen. Trusts Corp., 1936-39; solicitor Daly, Thistle, Judson & McTaggart, Toronto, 1946-48; gen. counsel Imperial Life Assurance Co. Can., Toronto, 1949-58; partner firm Payton, Biggs & Graham, Toronto, 1958-77, Cassels Brock, 1977—; chmn. bd. Rogers Telecommunications Ltd., Rogers Cablesystems Inc., Rogers Cable TV Ltd., Rogers Radio Broadcasting Ltd.; vice chmn. bd. Rogers UA Cablesystems, Inc.; dir. numerous cos., including Natomas of Can. Ltd., Victoria & Grey Trustco Ltd., Victoria & Grey Trust Co. Mem. exec. com. Trinity Coll., Toronto, 1960-71, also chmn., 1966-69; Pres. St. Paul's Progressive Conservative Assn., 1957-61. Served with Royal Canadian Armoured Corps, 1939-46; ETO. Decorated Efficiency Decoration, 1944; hon. lt. col. Gov. Gen's Horse Guards, 1970-75. Mem. Canadian Bar Assn., County of York Law Assn., Lawyers Club Toronto, Assn. Life Ins. Counsel, Canadian Tax Found., Estate Planning Council Toronto, Progressive Bus. Men's Club Met. Toronto (v.p. 1968-70), Sigma Chi (internat. pres. 1971-73). Mem. Conservative party. Mem. Anglican Ch. Can. Clubs: Albany, Toronto Hunt, York, Royal Canadian Mil. Inst. (Toronto); Empire of Can. Home: 2 Wood Ave Toronto ON Canada M4N 1P4 Office: 130 Adelaide St W Toronto ON Canada M5H 3C2

GRAHAM, KATHARINE, newspaper co. exec.; b. N.Y.C., June 16, 1917; d. Eugene and Agnes (Ernst) Meyer; m. Philip L. Graham, June 5, 1940 (dec. 1963); children—Elizabeth Morris (Mrs. Elizabeth Weymouth), Donald Edward, William Welsh, Stephen Meyer. Student, Vassar Coll., 1934-36; A.B., U. Chgo., 1938. Reporter San Francisco News, 1938-39; mem. editorial staff Washington Post, 1939-45, also Sunday, circulation and editorial depts., pub., 1969—; pres. Washington Post Co., 1963-73, chmn. bd., 1973—; dir. Bowaters Mersey Paper Co., Ltd., Newspaper Advt. Bur. Inc.; Mem. adv. com. Inst. Politics, John Fitzgerald Kennedy Sch. Govt., Harvard.; Bd. dirs. Overseas Devel. Council, A.P.; bd. dirs. Am. Newspaper Pubs. Assn., chmn. and pres., 1980. Trustee George Washington U., U. Chgo., Urban Inst., Fed. City Council, Conf. Bd. Mem. Am. Soc. Newspaper Editors (dir.), Sigma Delta Chi. Clubs: Cosmopolitan (N.Y.C.); 1925 F Street, Nat. Press, Washington Press (Washington). Home: 2920 R St NW Washington DC 20007 Office: 1150 15th St NW Washington DC 20071

GRAHAM, KATHLEEN MARGARET (K. M. GRAHAM), artist; b. Hamilton, Ont., Can., Sept. 13, 1913; d. Charles and G. Blanche (Leitch) Howitt; m. J. Wallace, Dec. 17, 1938; children: John Wallace, Janet Howitt. B.A., U. Toronto, Ont., 1936. Solo exhbns. include, Carmen Lamanna Gallery, Toronto, 1967, Trinity Coll., U. Toronto, 1968, Founders Coll., York U., Toronto, 1970, Pollock Gallery, Toronto, 1971, 73, 75, Art Gallery Cobourg, Ont., 1973, City Hall, Toronto, 1974, David Mirvish Gallery, Toronto, 1976, Klonaridis, Inc., Toronto, 1978, Watson-Willour Gallery, Houston, 1980, Downstairs Gallery, Edmonton, Alta., 1980, 82, Lillian Heidelberg Gallery, N.Y.C., 1981, Klonaridis, Inc., Toronto, 1981, 82, London Gallery, Montreal, Que., Can., 1983, Stewart Art Centre, Guelph, Ont., 1984, numerous group shows, including, Montreal Mus. Fine Arts, 1976, Hirshhorn Mus., Washington, 1977, Edmonton (Alta., Can.) Art Gallery, Norman MacKenzie Art Gallery, Regina, Sask., Can., David Mirvish Gallery, Toronto, Watson De Nagy Gallery, Houston, Galerie Wentzel, Hamburg, W. Ger., Beaverbrook Gallery, Fredericton, N.B.; also travelling shows Certain Traditions, 1976; represented in permanent collections, Art Gallery of Ont., Toronto, Edmonton Art Gallery, Ont. Govt. Bldg., Hamilton, Ont., Toronto City Hall, also numerous corp. collections. Office: care Klonaridis Inc 144 Front St W Toronto ON M5J 2L7 Canada

GRAHAM, KENNETH L., educator; b. Coffeyville, Kans., Apr. 25, 1915; s. Ethan L. and Maud (Huff) G.; m. Barbara Louise Fowler, Dec. 15, 1945 (dec. July 1969); children—Greg Fowler, Sherry Lynn Graham Nelson. B.A., State U. Iowa, 1936; M.A., Northwestern U., 1939; Ph.D., U. Utah, 1947. Speech, drama tchr. Watertown (S.D.) High Sch., also; North Kansas City (Mo.) High Sch.; dir. Sch. of Theatre, Cain Park Theatre, Cleveland Heights, Ohio, summers 1941, 42, 46, 47; faculty speech, communication, theatre arts dept. U. Minn., asst. prof., 1948-51, asso. prof., 1952-56, prof., 1957-80, prof. emeritus, 1980—, chmn. dept., 1963-71, chmn. dept. theatre arts, 1971-77; dir. Univ. theatre, 1971-77. Served with USNR, 1942-45. Fellow Am. Theatre Assn. (exec. sec.-treas. 1946-58, 2d v.p. 1962, 1st v.p. 1963, pres. 1964); mem. Actors Equity Assn., Screen Actors Guild, AFTRA, Nat. Theatre Conf., Citizens League Mpls., Beta Theta Pi. Universalist. Address: 2007 W 49th St Minneapolis MN 55409

GRAHAM, LOIS, mechanical engineering educator; b. Troy, N.Y., Apr. 4, 1925; d. Paul Seabrook and Marion (Cooley) G.; m. Sanford A. Weil, Apr. 28, 1967. B.M.E., Rensselaer Poly. Inst., 1945; M.S.M.E., Ill. Inst. Tech., 1949, Ph.D., 1959. Test engr. Carrier Corp., Syracuse, N.Y., 1945-46; instr. Ill. Inst. Tech., Chgo., 1949-53, asst. prof., 1953-59, asso. prof., 1959-75, prof. mech. engring., 1975—, asst. chmn. mechanics, mech. and aerospace engring. dept., 1950-70, also dir. minorities in engring., dir. women's engring. program. Recipient Ralph R. Teetor award Ill. Inst. Tech., 1980; Alumni Profl. Achievement award, 1980; Alumni Key award Rensselaer Poly. Inst., 1980; Outstanding Women's award in Edn. YWCA Met. Chgo., 1981. Fellow Soc. Women Engrs. (sr. trustee), AAAS; mem. ASME, ASHRAE. Office: Illinois Inst Tech Ill Inst Tech Center Chicago IL 60616

GRAHAM, LOREN RAYMOND, historian, educator; b. Hymera, Ind., June 29, 1933; s. Ross Raymond and Hazel Mae (McClanahan) G.; m. Patricia Parks Albjerg, Sept. 6, 1955; 1 dau., Marguerite Elizabeth. B.S., Purdue U., 1955; M.A., Columbia U., 1960, Ph.D., 1964; postgrad., Moscow U., 1960-61. Gandy-dancer Pa. R.R., 1950-51; research chem. engr. Dow Chem. Co., 1955; lectr. dept. history Ind. U., 1963-64, asst. prof., 1965-66; vis. asst. prof. dept. public law and govt. Columbia U., 1965-66, asso. prof., dept. history, 1967-72, prof., 1972-78, adj. prof., 1978—; mem. Russian Inst., 1966-78; asso., mem. exec. com. Russian Research Center Harvard U., 1980—; prof. M.I.T., 1978—. Author: the Soviet Academy of Sciences and the Communist Party, 1967, Science and Philosophy in the Soviet Union, 1972, Between Science and Values, 1981; contbr. numerous articles to profl. jours. Served with USN, 1955-58. Woodrow Wilson fellow, 1958-59; Danforth fellow, 1958-63; Fulbright Hayes fellow, 1966; Guggenheim fellow, 1969-70; Rockefeller fellow, 1976-77; Smithsonian Instn. fellow, 1981-82. Fellow Am. Acad. Arts and Scis.; Mem. Am. Hist. Assn., Am. Assn. Advancement of Slavic Studies, AAAS, History of Sci. Soc., Soc. History of Technology. Soc. Social Study of Sci. Home: 7 Francis Ave Cambridge MA 02138 Office: Bldg E-51 70 Memorial Dr Cambridge MA 02139

GRAHAM, LOUIS ATKINS, textile company executive, association executive; b. Kenbridge, Va., Mar. 27, 1925; s. Samuel Lyle and Natalie Cathleen (Hardy) G.; m. Jean Nelson, June 18, 1955; 1 dau., Natalie Jean. Student, Hampden-Sydney Coll., 1942-43; B.S. in Chem. Engring, U. Va., 1949, M.S., U. Louisville, 1950. Chem. engr. Am. Viscose Corp., Parkersburg, W.Va., 1950-56, quality control supr., 1954-56, plant color engr., 1953-56, color engr., corp. tech. dept., Marcus Hook, Pa., 1956-62, color specialist, sales dept., 1962-63, Am. Viscose div. FMC Corp., Marcus Hook, 1963-66, leader synthetic fiber research sect., 1967; sr. color engr., mgr. color lab., 1967-70; mgr. color and dyeing labs., corp. research and devel. Burlington Industries, Greensboro, N.C., 1970-79, sr. research and devel. mgr., chem. analysis, color and dyeing, corp. research and devel., 1979—; asso. adj. prof. Sch. Textiles, N.C. State U., 1969-79; nat. pres. Inter-Society Color Council, 1982-84. Served with USNR, 1942-45. Mem. Color Mktg. Group (past nat pres., F.L. Dimmick award 1981, chairholder, hon. mem.), Am. Assn. Textile Chemists and Colorists, Soc. Dyers and Colorists, Alpha Chi Sigma. Republican. Presbyterian. Clubs: Kiwanis (Greensboro); Bur-Mil Country. Office: PO Box 21327 Greensboro NC 27420

GRAHAM, MARTHA, dancer, choreographer; b. Pitts., May 11, 1894. Studied with, Ruth St. Denis; LL.D., Mills Coll., Brandeis U., Smith Coll., Harvard, 1966, also numerous others. Faculty Eastman Sch., 1925. Soloist, Denishawn Co., 1920, Greenwich Village Follies, (1923); debut as choreographer-dancer, 48th St. Theatre, N.Y.C., 1926; founder, artistic dir., Martha Graham Dance Co., Martha Graham Sch. Contemporary Dance; choreographer: 150 works including Witch of Endor, 1965, Cortege of Eagles, 1967, A Time of Snow, 1968, Plain of Prayer, 1968, Lady of the House of Sleep, 1968, Archaic Hours, 1969, Mendicants of Evening, 1973, Myth of a Voyage, 1973, Holy Jungle, 1974, Dream, 1974, Chronique, 1974, Lucifer, 1975, Scarlet Letter, 1975, Adorations, 1975, Point of Crossing, 1975; with music composed by Aaron Copland, Paul Hindemith, Carlos Chavez, Samuel Barber, Gian-Carlo Menotti, William Schuman, others; guest soloist leading, U.S. orchs. in solos Judith, Triumph of St. Joan; fgn. tours with, Martha Graham Dance Co., 1950, 54, 55-56, 60, 62-63, 67, 68; some under auspices, U.S. Dept State, U.S. tours, 1966, 70; sponsored by, Nat. Endowment for Arts. (Recipient Aspen award 1965), Nat. Endowment for Arts. (Creative Arts award Brandeis U. 1968), Nat. Endowment for Arts. (Distinguished Service to Arts award Nat. Inst. Arts and Letters 1970), Nat. Endowment for Arts. (Handel medallion City of N.Y. 1970), Nat. Endowment for Arts. (N.Y. State Council on Arts award 1973), Nat. Endowment for Arts. (Presdl. Medal of Freedom 1976), Nat. Endowment for Arts. (Kennedy Center Achievement Honor 1979), Nat. Endowment for Arts. (others.); Author: Notebooks of Martha Graham, 1973. Decorated knight Legion of Honor (France); recipient Alger H. Meadows award, 1984; Guggenheim fellow, 1932. Office: 316 E 63d St New York NY 10021 *

GRAHAM, OTTO EVERETT, JR., athletic dir.; b. Waukegan, Ill., Dec. 6, 1921; s. Otto Everett and Cordonna (Hayes) G.; m. Beverly Jean Collinge, Oct. 7, 1945; childrenDuey, Sandy, David. B.A., Northwestern U., 1944. Quarterback with Cleve. Browns, 1946-55; coach Coll. All-Stars vs. Nat. Football League champions, 1958-65, 69-70; athletic dir., head football coach USCG Acad., New London, Conn., 1959-66, athletic dir., 1970—; gen. mgr., head coach Washington Redskins, 1966-68. Pres. Fellowship Christian Athletes, 1956-57; Bd. dirs. Washington YMCA, 1967—. Served with USNR, 1944-45; now capt. USCG. Named All Am. in Football and Bakeball, 1943; All Pro Quarterback, 1951, 52, 54, 55; named to Coll. Football Hall of Fame, 1955; Pro Football Hall of Fame, 1965. Home: Heritage Rd East Lyme CT 06333 Office: Athletic Dept USCG Academy New London CT 06320

GRAHAM, PATRICIA ALBJERG, educator; b. Lafayette, Ind., Feb. 9, 1935; d. Victor L. and Marguerite (Hall) Albjerg; m. Loren R. Graham, Sept. 6, 1955; 1 dau., Marguerite Elizabeth. B.S., Purdue U., 1955, M.S., 1957, D.Lett. (hon.), 1980; Ph.D., Columbia U., 1964; M.A. (hon.), Harvard U., 1974; D.H.L., Manhattanville Coll., 1976; LL.D., Beloit Coll., 1977, Clark U., 1978; D.P.A., Suffolk U., 1978; LL.D., Ind. U., 1980; D.Litt., St. Norbert Coll., 1980; D.H., Emmanuel Coll., 1983. Tchr. high sch., Norfolk, Va., 1955-56, 57-58, N.Y.C., 1958-60; lectr., asst. prof. Ind. U., 1964-66; asst. prof. history of edn. Barnard Coll. and Columbia Tchrs. Coll., N.Y.C., 1965-68, asso. prof., 1968-72, prof., 1972-74; dean Radcliffe Inst.; also v.p. Radcliffe Coll., Cambridge, Mass., prof., Harvard U., 1974-79, Warren prof., 1979—, dean, 1982—; dir. Nat. Inst. Edn., Washington, 1977-79, Northwestern Mut. Life., trustee, 1980—. Author: Progressive Education: From Arcady to Academe, 1967, Community and Class in American Education: 1865-1918, 1974. Am. Council on Edn. fellow Princeton, 1969-70; Bd. dirs. Dalton Sch., 1973-76, Josiah Macy, Jr. Found., 1976-77, 79—; trustee Beloit Coll., 1976-77, 79-82, Found. for Teaching Econs., 1980—. Mem. Sci. Research Assn. (dir. 1980—), Phi Beta Kappa. Episcopalian. Office: Grad Sch Edn Harvard U Cambridge MA 02138

GRAHAM, RAMONA *See* **COOK, RAMONA GRAHAM**

GRAHAM, RICHARD HARPER, lawyer, broadcasting co. exec.; b. San Diego, May 8, 1911; s. John A. and Edith (Harper) G.; m. Ethel Stevens, June 3, 1937; children—Hollis Ann (Mrs. Terry Harmon), Alan S. Student, N.Y. U., 1929-30; J.D., Loyola U., Los Angeles, 1936. Bar: Calif. bar 1937. Atty. RCA, Hollywood, Calif., 1937-41, Pacific coast counsel, 1941-43, 46-57; v.p. law Pacific div. NBC, Burbank, Calif., 1957-76. Served from lt. (j.g.) to lt. USNR, 1943-46; lt. comdr. Res., 1946-53. Recipient citation Navy Dept., 1945. Mem. Am. Bar Assn., So. Calif., Pasadena symphony assns. Home: 1036 San Marino Ave San Marino CA 91108 also 175 Lake View Dr Palmdale CA 93550 Office: 3808 Riverside Dr Burbank CA 91505

GRAHAM, ROBERT C., manufacturing company executive; b. Mpls., June 7, 1925; s. Samuel A. and Sybil F. (Fleming) G.; m. Elizabeth Needham, Nov. 26, 1946; children: Christopher, Peter.; m. Janice Tellefsen, Aug. 1983. B.S. in Engring., U. Mich., 1945, M.S., 1948. Aero. research scientist Cleve. Flight Propulsion Lab., NASA, 1948-52; with Ford Motor Co., 1954—; pres., dir. Ford Brasil (S.A.), Sao Paulo, 1977-80; v.p. Latin Am. automotive ops. parent co., Dearborn, Mich., 1980—; v.p. diversified products Ford Motor Co.; instr. U. Mich. Coll. Engring. Served with USNR, 1942-46. Mem. Soc. Automotive Engrs. Home: 19 Timberlane Ct Dearborn MI 48126 Office: Ford Motor Co World Hdqrs Dearborn MI 48123

GRAHAM, ROBERT G., petroleum products manufacturing company executive. Pres. Can. Hydrocarbons, Ltd., Winnipeg, Man. Office: Can Hydrocarbons Ltd 444 St Mary Ave Winnipeg MB Canada R3C 3T7§

GRAHAM, ROBERT WILLIAM, research engineer; b. Cleve., Oct. 10, 1922; s. William and Annie Stitt (Inglis) G.; m. Katherine Helen Irwin, Aug. 4, 1951; children: William, George, James. B.S.M.E., Case Inst. Tech., 1948; M.S.M.E., Purdue U., 1950, Ph.D., 1952. Instr. Purdue U., 1948-52; aero. research scientist NASA Lewis Research Center, Cleve., 1953—; now sr. scientist; adj. prof. N.C. State U., 1965-72. Co-author: Transport Processes in Boiling and Two-Phase Flow, 1976; contbr. articles to profl. jours. Pres. chpt. Am. Field Service, 1974; active Boy Scouts Am. Served with U.S. Army, 1943-46. Fellow ASME; asso. fellow AIAA; mem. Sigma Xi. Methodist. Home: 22895 Haber Dr Cleveland OH 44126 Office: 21000 Brookpark Rd Cleveland OH 44135 *The term "success" is one I try to avoid as a measure of fulfillment in life because the word has connotations of self-aggrandizement. My experience in life continually reminds me of my indebtedness to many people, living and dead, who have enriched my life by their contributions. Family members, teachers, colleagues, and many others whom I knew only through their writings, have contributed more than I can repay. Perhaps the greatest challenge for living is in the obligation of contributing something worthy that others can enjoy and appreciate. Any awareness of such repayment will be accompanied by feelings of real achievement.*

GRAHAM, RONALD LEWIS, mathematician; b. Taft, Calif., Oct. 31, 1935; s. Leo Lewis and Margaret Jane (Anderson) G.; children: Cheryl, Marc. Student, U. Chgo., 1951-54; B.S. (Ford Found. scholar), U. Alaska, 1958; M.A. (NSF fellow), U. Calif., Berkeley, 1961; Ph.D. (Woodrow Wilson fellow), U. Calif., Berkeley, 1962. Mem. tech. staff Bell Labs., Murray Hill, N.J., 1962—, head discrete math. dept., 1968—, dir. Math. Scis. Research Ctr., 1983—; Regents' prof. UCLA, 1975; vis. prof. computer sci. Stanford U., 1979, 81; Fairchild disting. scholar Calif. Inst. Tech., 1983. Author: Ramsey Theory, 1980. Served with USAF, 1955-59. Recipient Polya prize, 1975; named Scientist of Yr. World Book Encyclopedia, 1981. Mem. Am. Math. Soc., Math. Assn. Am., Soc. Indsl. and Applied Math., Ops. Research Soc. Am., Assn. Computing Machinery, Math. Program Soc. Club: Internat. Jugglers Assn. (past pres.). Office: Bell Labs Murray Hill NJ 07974

GRAHAM, STEVE HOWARD, zoo director; b. Waynesboro, Pa., Feb. 25, 1945; s. Donald Albert and Virginia Louise (Steck) G.; m. Pamela Caras, May 5, 1980 (div. May 1982). B.S., Mt. St. Mary's Coll., 1971. Dir. Salisbury Zoo, (Md.), 1972-77, Detroit Zoo, Royal Oak, Mich., 1982—; assoc. dir. Balt. Zoo, 1977-78, dir., 1978-82; adj. asst. prof. comparative pathology Wayne State U., Detroit, 1982—. Author: (with Roger Caras) Amiable Little Beasts, 1980. Recipient Disting. Alumni award Mt. St. Mary's Coll., 1979. Fellow Am. Assn. Zool. Parks and Aquariums (chmn. animal welfare com. 1980—, vice chmn. bd. regents Mgmt. Sch.); mem. Ariz. Primate Found. (mem. adv. bd.), Ward Wildfowl Found. (mem. adv. bd.). Home: 8450 W 10 Mile Rd Royal Oak MI 48068 Office: Detroit Zool Parks Dept PO Box 39 Royal Oak MI 48068

GRAHAM, THOMAS CARLISLE, steel company executive; b. Greensburg, Pa., Jan. 26, 1927; s. Arch R. and Clara (Beatty) G.; m. Irene Wallace, Apr. 24, 1948; children: Susan Lee (Mrs. John R. Scheessele), Thomas C., John D., Sara Ann. B.C.E., U. Louisville, 1947. With Jones & Laughlin Steel, Pitts. and Star Lake, N.Y., 1947-52; with Jones & Laughlin Steel Corp., Pitts., 1954-83, pres., chief operating officer, 1974-75, pres., chief exec. officer, 1975-83; vice chmn., chief operating officer U.S. Steel Corp., 1983—; group v.p., dir. LTV Corp., 1975—. Bd. dirs. Pa. Economy League, Regional Indsl. Devel. Corp. Southwestern Pa., United Way Allegheny County, Allegheny Gen. Hosp.; trustee Commn. for Econ. Devel.; mem. corp. North Hills Passavant Hosp.; adv. council Jr. Achievement. Served with USNR, 1952-54. Mem. Am. Iron and Steel Inst., Pa. Soc. Presbyn. Clubs: Duquesne, Allegheny, Laurel Valley Country, Carlton, Rolling Rock, Fox Chapel Golf. Office: US Steel Corp 600 Grant St Pittsburgh PA 15230

GRAHAM, THOMAS PEGRAM, JR., pediatric cardiologist; b. Charlotte, N.C., Mar. 1, 1937; s. Thomas P. and Margaret (Martin) G.; m. Carol Ann Noggle, June 1, 1960; children: Bethany, Brent, Brooke. A.B., Duke U., 1959, M.D., 1963. Diplomate: Am. Bd. Pediatrics. Resident in pediatrics Children's Hosp., Boston, 1963-65; research assoc. Nat. Heart Inst., Bethesda, Md., 1965-67; fellow in pediatric cardilolgy Duke U., Durham, N.C., 1967-69, asst. prof. pediatrics, 1969-71; dir. pediatric cardiology, prof. pediatrics Vanderbilt U., Nashville, 1971—. Contbr. articles to profl. jours. Fellow Am. Acad. Pediatrics (exec. com. 1972-74), Am. Coll. Cardiology (chmn. pediatric cardiology subcom. 1979-83), Am. Heart Assn. (dir. 1973—). Presbyterian. Office: Banderbilt Univ West End Ave Nashville TN 37232

GRAHAM, VICTOR ERNEST, French educator; b. Calgary, Alta., Can., May 31, 1920; s. William John and Mary Ethel (Wark) G.; m. Mary Helena Faunt, Aug. 1, 1946; children: Ian Robert, Gordon Keith, Miriam Elizabeth, Ross William. B.A., U. Alta., 1946, Oxford U., 1948, M.A., 1952, D.Litt., 1968; Ph.D., Columbia U., 1953. Asst. prof. French and English U. Alta., 1948-52, asso. prof. French, 1952-57, prof., 1957-58, asst. to dir., 1952-58; asso. prof. French U. Toronto, Ont., 1958-60, prof., 1960—, chmn. grad. dept. French, 1965-67, asso. dean, 1967-69; vice prin. Univ. Coll., 1969-70; vis. prof. U. Mich., 1954-55, U. Victoria, 1980-81; mem. governing council U. Toronto, 1973-76. Author: Critical Edition of the Poetry of Philippe Desportes, 7 vols, 1958-63, The Imagery of Proust, 1966, Rymes, Pernette du Guillet, 1968, (with W. McAllister Johnson) Le Recueil des Inscriptions 1558, 1972, The Paris Entries of Charles IX and Elisabeth of Austria 1571, 1974, The Royal Tour of France by Charles IX and Catherine de' Medici (1564-1566), 1979, Bibliographie des etudes sur Marcel Proust et son oeuvre, 1976; others. Columbia U. open fellow, 1948; Can. Council sr. fellow, 1963; Guggenheim fellow, 1970; Connaught sr. research fellow in humanities, 1978. Fellow Royal Soc. Can. Home: 100 Glenview Ave Toronto ON Canada M4R 1P8 Office: 150 Univ Coll U Toronto Toronto ON Canada M5S 1A1

GRAHAM, VIRGINIA, radio, television, and thatrical performer, lecturer, charity worker; b. Chgo., July 4, 1912; d. David Stanley and Bessie (Feiges) Komiss; m. Harry W. Guttenburg, May 2, 1935; 1 dau., Lynn Guttenburg Boffrer. Radio writer, 1936-38; emcee: Internat. Beauty Show, 1947-51; performer: TV shows including Dave Garroway Show, Where Was I, 1950, Food for Thought, N.Y.C., 1951-57, This is Your Life, 1956; co-hostess: radio program Week Day, 1956; emcee: TV program Girl Talk, 1962-69, 80—; author: autobiography There Goes What's Her Name, 1967; Don't Blame the Mirror, 1967, Tonight or Never Cook Book, 1968, If I Made It So Can You, 1979. Goodwill ambassador Clairol Co., 1961; nat. crusade chmn. Am. Cancer Soc.; active March of Dimes, Kidney Found., ARC, mental health and cerebral palsy orgns., others; appeared on numerous fund-raising telethons. Named Woman of Yr. K.P., 1957, Am. Cancer Soc., 1961, Internat. Woman of Yr. Women's Clubs Am., 1959; recipient numerous citations for civic and charitable work. Office: care Pinnacle Books 175 Madison Ave New York NY 10016

GRAHAM, WALTER WILLIAM, JR., cons. engr.; b. DeQueen, Ark., Mar. 13, 1925; s. Walter William and Grace Abigail (Chapman) G.; m. Bobbie Bradley, Sept. 2, 1949; children—Gail Leslie Graham Rader, Walter William III, Robert Bradley. B.S. in Civil Engring, U. Ark., 1949; M.S., 1974. Pres. W. William Graham, Jr., Inc. (Cons. Engrs.), Little Rock, 1964—; engr.-in-tng. U.S. Corp. Engrs., Little Rock, 1949; design engr. Mehlburger Engrs., Little Rock, 1949-64. Served with USN, 1943-46. Fellow Am. Cons. Engrs. Council (v.p. 1975-77); mem. Associated Gen. Contractors Ark. (Engr. of Yr. award 1980), ASCE, Am. Water Works Assn., Water Pollution Control Fedn., Am. Arbitration Assn. Presbyterian. Club: Rotary. Office: 100 N Rodney Parham Rd Little Rock AR 72205

GRAHAM, WILLIAM B., pharmaceutical executive; b. Chgo., July 14, 1911; s. William and Elizabeth (Burden) G.; m. Edna Kanaley, June 15, 1940; children: William J., Elizabeth Anne, Margaret, Robert B. S.B. cum laude, U. Chgo., 1932, J.D., 1936; LL.D., Carthage Coll., 1974, Lake Forest Coll., 1983; L.H.D., St. Xavier Coll. and Nat. Coll. Edn., 1983. Bar: Ill. bar 1936. Patent lawyer Dyrenforth, Lee, Chritton & Wiles, 1936-40; mem. Dawson & Ooms, 1940-45; v.p., mgr. Baxter Travenol Labs., Inc., Deerfield, Ill., 1945-53, pres., chief exec. officer, 1953-71, chmn. bd., chief exec. officer, 1971-80, chmn. bd., 1980—, also dir.; dir., mem. exec. com. 1st Nat. Bank, Chgo., N.W. Industries; dir. Deere & Co.; prof. Weizmann Inst., 1978. Bd. dirs., pres. Lyric

Opera Chgo.; Bd. dirs. Chgo. Hort. Soc., Nat. Park Fedn.; trustee Orchestral Assn., U. Chgo., Evanston Hosp. Recipient V.I.P. award Lewis Found., 1963; Disting. Citizen award Ill. St. Andrew Soc., 1974; Decision Maker of Yr. award Am. Statis. Assn., 1974; Marketer of Yr. award AMA, 1976; Bus. Statesman of Yr. award Harvard Bus. Sch. Club Chgo., 1983. Mem. Am. Pharm. Mfrs. Assn. (past pres.), Ill. Mfrs. Assn. (dir., past pres.), Pharm. Mfrs. Assn. (dir., past chmn.), Phi Beta Kappa, Sigma Xi, Phi Delta Phi. Clubs: Chicago (past pres.), Commonwealth, Mid-Am., Commercial, Indian Hill, Casino, Old Elm (Chgo.); Seminole, Everglades, Bath & Tennis (Fla.); University, Links (N.Y.C.). Home: 40 Devonshire Ln Kenilworth IL 60043 Office: One Baxter Pkwy Deerfield IL 60015

GRAHAM, WILLIAM EDGAR, JR., lawyer, utility company executive; b. Jackson Springs, N.C., Dec. 31, 1929; s. William Edgar and Minnie Blanch (Autry) G.; m. Jean Dixon McLaurin, Nov. 24, 1962; children: William McLaurin, John McMillan, Sally Faircloth. A.B., U. N.C., 1952, J.D. with honors, 1956. Bar: N.C. bar. Law clk. U.S. Ct. Appeals 4th Circuit, 1956-57; individual practice law, Charlotte, N.C., 1957-69; judge N.C. Ct. Appeals, 1969-73; sr. v.p., gen. counsel Carolina Power & Light Co., Raleigh, N.C., 1973-81, exec. v.p., 1981—. Served with USAF, 1952-54. Mem. Am. Bar Assn., N.C. Bar Assn., Wake County Bar Assn., Edison Electric Inst. (legal com.). Presbyterian. Home: 409 Hillandale Dr Raleigh NC 27609 office Carolina Power & Light Co PO Box 1551 Raleigh NC 27602

GRAHAM, WILLIAM FRANKLIN, evangelist; b. Charlotte, N.C., Nov. 7, 1918; s. William Franklin and Morrow (Coffey) G.; m. Ruth McCue Bell, Aug. 13, 1943; children: Virginia Leftwich, Anne Morrow, Ruth Bell, William Franklin, Nelson Edman. A.B., Wheaton Coll. (Ill.), 1943; Th.B., Fla. Bible Sem., Tampa, 1940, Houghton (N.Y.) Coll., Baylor U., The Citadel, William Jewell Coll. Ordained to ministry So. Baptist Conv.; minister First Bapt. Ch., Western Springs, Ill., 1943-45; 1st v.p. Youth for Christ, Internat., 1945-48; pres. Northwestern Coll., Mpls., 1947-52; founder World Wide Pictures, Inc., Burbank, Calif.; worldwide evangelistic campaigns, 1949—; speaker weekly Hour of Decision radio program, 1950—; also periodic Crusade Telecasts; founder Billy Graham Evangelistic Assn.; Hon. chmn. Lausanne Congress World Evangelization, 1974. Author: Peace with God, 1953, World Aflame, 1965, The Jesus Generation, 1971, Angels: God's Secret Agents, 1975, How to Be Born Again, 1977, The Holy Spirit, 1978, Till Armageddon, 1981; also writer of daily newspaper column. Recipient numerous awards, including; Bernard Baruch award, 1955; Humane Order of African Redemption, 1960; gold award George Washington Carver Meml. Inst., 1963; Horatio Alger award, 1965; Internat. Brotherhood award NCCJ, 1971; Sylvanus Thayer award Assn. Grads. U.S. Mil. Acad., 1972; Franciscan Internat. award, 1972; Man of South award, 1974; Liberty Bell award, 1975; Templeton prize for Progress in Religion, 1982. Home: Montreat NC 28757 Office: 1300 Harmon Pl: Minneapolis MN 55403

GRAHAM, WILLIAM JAMES, packaging company executive; b. Johnstown, Pa., Sept. 20, 1923; s. John Ellis and Margaret (Euwer) G.; m. Natalie Joan Stolk, Feb. 17, 1951; children: Susan, Margaret, John, Elizabeth, Joan, Catherine. B.A. cum laude, Amherst Coll., 1948. Salesman, Owens-Ill., Inc., 1953-60, closure sales mgr., 1960-66, v.p. sales Pacific region, 1966-69, v.p., gen. mgr. Pacific region, 1969-72, v.p. sales and mktg., 1972-75, v.p., gen. mgr. plastic products div., Toledo, 1975—, group v.p. plastics and closures, 1982—; dir. Nat. Petro Chems. Corp. Served to 1st lt. U.S. Army, 1943-46, 50-51. Mem. Soc. Plastics Industry (dir.-at-large, exec. com.), Plastic Bottle Inst. (chmn. 1983—), Mgmt. Policy Council (exec. com.). Republican. Presbyterian. Clubs: Belmont Country, Muirfield Golf, Shadow Valley, Toledo Tennis. Home: 5223 Cambrian Rd Toledo OH 43623 Office: Owens-Ill Inc One SeaGate Toledo OH 43666

GRAHAM, WILLIAM PATTON, III, plastic surgeon, educator; b. Plainfield, N.J., Apr. 30, 1934; s. William Patton and Mary Alice (Bucher) G.; m. Susan Ames Fox, Nov. 27, 1968; children: Susan Patton, Elizabeth Ames. A.B., Princeton U., 1955; M.D., U. Pa., 1959. Diplomate: Am. Bd. Surgery, Am. Bd. Plastic Surgery. Intern U. Colo. Med. Ctr., Denver, 1959-60; resident in surgery U. Calif., San Francisco, 1961-64, chief resident in surgery, 1964-65; instr. plastic surgery U. Pa., Phila., 1965-67, asst. prof. surgey, 1967-70; assoc. prof. surgery Pa. State U., Hershey, 1971-74, prof. surgery, 1974—; chmn. Plastic Surgery Research Council, Hershey, 1979-80. Co-author: The Hand-Surgical and Non-Surgical Management, 1977, Practical Points in Plastic Surgery, 1980. Trustee Harrisburg Acad. Maj. USAR, 1960-73. USPHS research grantee, 1974-76; advanced clin. fellow Am. Cancer Soc., Phila., 1969-70. Fellow ACS; mem. Am. Surg. Assn., Am. Assn. Plastic Surgeons (trustee 1983), Am. Soc. Surgery of Hand, Am. Soc. Head and Neck Surgeons, Robert H. Ivy Soc. (pres. Hershey 1974-75). Republican. Office: Pa State U 500 University Dr Box 850 Hershey PA 17033

GRAHAME, ORVILLE FRANCIS, lawyer, business executive; b. Palo, Iowa, Apr. 2, 1904; s. Samuel G. and Dawn (Booth) G.; m. Paula Patton, Nov. 3, 1923; 1 dau., Sarah Jane (Cairns). B.A., U. Iowa, 1925; J.D., 1929. Bar: Iowa 1929, N.Y. 1932, Mass. 1940, U.S. Supreme Ct. 1954. Asso. Guardian Life Ins. Co., 1929-39, asst. sec., 1936-39; cons., former v.p., dir. gen. counsel Paul Revere Life Ins. Co., Worcester, Mass., Paul Revere Variable Annuity Ins. Co., Paul Revere Corp., Avco Corp. and several affiliated cos.; dir. Thompson Steel Co., Inc.; corporator Worcester Devel. Corp., Worcester County Instn. for Savs.; Mem. nat. adv. com. White House Conf. Aging, 1959-61, tech. com. on income, 1971-72; Exec. com. Health and Accident Underwriters Conf., 1954-55; author, sponsor concept of guaranteed renewable adjustable premium accident and sickness ins., 1948; mem. Mass. Pension Study Commn., 1953-55, Mass. Variable Annuity Study Commn., 1956-60, Zoning Appeals Bd., Worcester, 1958-63; mem. com. on employment and retirement Nat. Council Aging; mem. U.S. Bus. Com. for Tax Reduction, 1963-64; lectr. N.Y. Coll. Ins., 1938-39. Author: (with others) The Life Insurance Contract, 1953; also legal articles.; Mem. editorial bd.: Insurance Decisions, 1933-37. Bd. dirs. Worcester Red Cross, 1957-63, 66-74, U. Iowa Found., 1969-74, Iowa Law Sch. Found., 1970-73; Mem. N.Y. County Republican Com., 1934-36; organizer Thomas E. Dewey for Pres. Club, 1940; asst. mgr. campaign Lt. Gov. S.G. Whittier, 1952, 56; coordinator campaign Lt. Gov. E.L. Richardson, 1964. Served with inf. U.S. Army Res., 1925-39. Recipient Distinguished Service award U. Iowa, 1964. Fellow Ins. Inst. Am.; mem. ABA, Mass., Worcester County bar assns., Assn. Bar City N.Y., N.Y. County Lawyers Assn., Acad. Polit. Sci., Am.-Scottish Found., Nat. Hist. Soc., Nat. Trust Historic Preservation, Assn. Nat. Archives, Assn. Life Counsel, Ins. Econs. Soc. Am. (pres. 1954-55), Worcester Hist. Soc., Am. Bar Found., Mass. Bar Found., Worcester Music Festival Assn., Am. Arbitration Assn. (arbitrator), Sierra Club, Newcomen Soc., Phi Alpha Delta, Order of Coif. Republican. Unitarian. Clubs: Mason, Shriner, Rotary, Worcester. Home: 6 Bancroft Tower Rd Worcester MA 01609

GRAHMANN, CHARLES V., bishop; b. Halletsville, Tex., July 15, 1931. Student, Assumption-St. John's Sem., Tex. Ordained priest Roman Catholic Ch., 1956. Ordained titular bishop Equilium and aux., San Antonio, 1981—, 1st bishop, Victoria, Tex., 1982—. Office: PO Box 4708 Victoria TX 77903 *

GRAINGER, DAVID WILLIAM, electrical distribution company executive; b. Chgo., Oct. 23, 1927; s. William Wallace and Hally (Ward) G. B.S.E.E., U. Wis., 1950. With W.W. Grainger, Inc., Chgo., 1952—, v.p., sec., dir., 1958-68, chmn. bd., 1968—, pres., 1974—. Pres. Grainger Found. Office: 5500 Howard St Skokie IL 60077

GRALEN, DONALD JOHN, lawyer; b. Oak Park, Ill., Mar. 18, 1933; s. Oliver Edwin and Rosalie Marie (Buskens) G.; m. Jane Walsh, Dec. 29, 1956; children: Alana, Mark, Paul, Ann, Sarah. B.S., Loyola U., Chgo., 1956, J.D. with honors, 1957. Bar: Ill. 1958. Assoc. Sidley & Austin, Chgo., 1959-66, ptnr., 1967—. Co-author (chpt. in book). Trustee Village LaGrange, Ill., 1973-77; chmn. LaGrange Zoning Bd., 1971-73, LaGrange Econ. Devel. Com., 1982; bd. dirs. Carson Pirie Scott Found., Chgo., 1980—, Jr. Achievement, Chgo., 1978—, Met. Housing and Planning Council, 1982—, Community Family Service and Mental Health Assn., 1983—. Served to 1st lt. U.S. Army, 1957-59. Mem. Chgo. Bar Assn., Ill. State Bar Assn., ABA. Clubs: Univ., Law; Legal (Chgo.); LaGrange Country. Home: 338 S Waiola LaGrange IL 60525 Office: Sidley & Austin 1 First Nat Plaza Chicago IL 60603

GRALLA, EUGENE, natural gas company executive; b. N.Y.C., May 3, 1924; s. Jacob and Anna Ruth (Kleiman) G.; m. Beverly Dorman, Apr. 7, 1946; children: Rhona Gralla Spilka, Steven Stuart. B.S., U.S. Naval Acad., 1945; M.B.A., Harvard U., 1947. Commd. ensign USN, 1945, advanced through grades to comdr., 1961; served sea duty, 1947-49, 54-56, control officer, Cuba, 1959-61, with, 1961-64, ret., 1966; dir. data systems planning Trans World Airlines, N.Y.C., 1966-68; corp. dir. mgmt. info. systems Internat. Paper Co., N.Y.C., 1968; v.p. electronic data processing Columbia Gas System Service Corp., Wilmington, Del., 1969-73; sr. v.p. Columbia Gas Distbn. Cos., Columbus, Ohio, 1973—. Trustee Ohio Pub. Expenditure Council. Mem. U.S. Naval Inst., Navy League Columbus, Harvard Bus. Sch., Club Columbus, Agonis Club Columbus. Club: Mason. Home: 5850 Forestview Dr Columbus OH 43213 Office: Columbia Gas Distbn Cos 200 Civic Center Dr Columbus OH 43215

GRALLA, LAWRENCE, pub. co. exec.; b. Bronx, N.Y., June 24, 1930; s. Meyer and Julia (Barnett) G.; m. Yvette Glickenstein, Dec. 24, 1952; children—Adele, Heidi. B.S., CCNY, 1951. Vice pres. Nationwide Trade News Service, N.Y.C., 1951-55; pres. Gralla Publs., N.Y.C., 1955—; founding pub. Kitchen Bus., 1955, Bank Systems & Equipment, 1964, Multi-Housing News, 1966, Meeting News, 1977; twice ann. lectr. Face-to-Face Nat. Pub. Conf., 1976—. Pres. Woodlands Community Temple, White Plains, N.Y., 1979-81; active fund raising United Jewish Appeal, 1978, State of Israel Bonds, 1977. Recipient Govt. Israel Spl. Trade award to Nat. Jeweler, 1980. Jewish. Office: Gralla Publs 1515 Broadway New York NY 10036

GRALLEY, ROBERT EMORY, insurance company executive; b. Balt., Jan. 10, 1926; s. George Charles and Margaret (Scherer) G.; m. Elizabeth Jean Giese, June 18, 1949; children—Jean Margaret, Kevin George, Craig Robert. B.S., U. Md., 1949; grad., Advanced Mgmt. Sch., Columbia U., 1975. C.L.U. With Mut. of N.Y., 1949—, v.p., sec., 1975—. Trustee United Meth. Ch., Westport, Conn.; bd. dirs. Alcoholism Council Mid-Fairfield County., Religion in Am. Life. Served to comdr. USNR, 1944-46, 51-53. Mem. Soc. C.L.U.'s, Res. Officers Assn., Am. Soc. Corp. Secs., Sigma Chi. Republican. Home: 15 St George Pl Westport CT 06880 Office: 1740 Broadway New York NY 10019

GRALNICK, JEFF, broadcasting company executive; b. N.Y.C., Apr. 3, 1939; s. Abraham and Mildred (Feinstein) G.; m. Elizabeth Baumgart, Aug. 15, 1969; children: Robert Howard, Kate. B.S. in Mktg, N.Y. U., 1961. With CBS News, 1959-70; press sec. Senator George McGovern, 1971; producer ABC News, N.Y.C., 1972-77, exec. producer spl. events programming, 1977—, v.p., 1978—, exec. producer World News Tonight, 1979—, exec. producer polit. programming, 1983—. Served with USAR, 1968. Office: 7 W 66th St New York NY 10023

GRALTON, RICHARD T., diversified company executive; b. 1930. B.A., Holy Cross Coll., 1954; M.B.A., Harvard U., 1956. Pres., chief operating officer, dir. Lenox Inc., 1974-75; gen. mgr. audio elec. products dept. Gen. Electric Co., 1971-74, gen. mgr. home laundry product dept., 1975-77, v.p., gen. mgr. major appliance product mgmt. div., 1977-78, v.p., gen. mgr. major appliance sales and distbn. ops., 1978-79, v.p., gen. mgr. major appliance mktg. ops., 1979-82; pres., dir. Savin Corp., Valhalla, N.Y., 1982—. Office: Savin Corp Columbus Ave Valhalla NY 10595 *

GRAM, HARVEY B., JR., investment banker; b. Washington, Aug. 31, 1903; s. Harvey B. and Virginia Lee (Jones) G.; m. Mary Worthington Dunbar, June 18, 1936; children: Harvey B. III, W. Dunbar, John Worthington (dec.). Ph.B., Wesleyan U., Middletown, Conn., 1927, L.H.D., 1983. With Spencer Trask & Co., N.Y.C., 1927-30, J.G. White & Co., 1930-32; with Johnston, Lemon & Co., Washington, 1932—, gen. partner, 1936-69, mng. partner, 1969—, vice chmn. bd., chmn. exec. com., 1973-77, chmn. bd., 1977—; chmn. bd. emeritus Washington Mut. Investors Fund; hon. dir. GEICO Corp., Govt. Employees Ins. Co.; Govt. Employees Financial Corp., Denver; dir. Internat. Gen. Industries, Inc.; pres., dir. St. Mary's Devel. Corp., Washington. Trustee emeritus Fed. City Council, Washington; chmn. bd. James M. Johnston Charitable & Ednl. Trust, Washington. Served to lt. col. USAAF, 1942-45. Mem. Alpha Delta Phi. Clubs: University (Washington) (pres. 1960-62); Columbia Country (Chevy Chase, Md.) (bd. govs. 1961-64); Burning Tree (Bethesda, Md.)). Home: 3514 Overlook Ln NW Washington DC 20016 Office: 1101 Vermont Ave NW Washington DC 20005

GRAMATGES, DANIEL ALBERTO, banker; b. Santiago, Cuba, 1939; came to U.S., 1957. B.B.A., Tex. A & M U., 1962; Grad., Southwestern Grad. Sch. Banking, 1971, Nat. Comml. Lending Sch., 1983. Exec. trainee Tex. Commerce Bank, Houston, 1962-64, asst. cashier, 1966-68, asst. v.p., 1968-71, v.p. in charge of Latin Am., Houston, 1971-76, sr. v.p. Western Hemisphere, 1976-77; with Southwest Bancshares Inc., 1977—, sr. v.p., 1983—; sr. v.p. affiliate bank Continental Nat. Bank. of Fort Worth, founder internat. dept., 1977-80, exec. v.p., 1980-83; apptd. mem. Dist. Export Council, 1981—. Active Dallas-Ft. Worth Airport Assistance Bd., various civic orgns. Office: Southwest Bancshares Inc PO Box 910 Fort Worth TX 76101

GRAMBSCH, PAUL VICTOR, business management educator; b. Dayton, Ohio, Mar. 14, 1919; s. Rinold Herman and Victoria Catherine (Danecker) G.; m. Ada Elizabeth Branch, June 20, 1945; children: E. Donald, Paul Victor, Kathryn, Nancy, Richard, William, Anne, Mary. B.A., North Central Coll., 1941; M.A., U. Miss., 1947; D.B.A., Ind. U., 1955. Instr. Equality (Ill.) Twp. High Sch., 1940-42; asst. prof., acting chmn. dept. economics U. Miss., 1948-50; asso. prof. mgmt. Tulane U. Sch. Bus. Adminstrn., 1952-60, dean, 1956-60, Sch. Bus. Adminstrn., U. Minn., 1960-70, prof. mgmt., 1970—; mgmt. cons. Educator cons. U.S. GAO; dir. research project on univ. goals Ford Found., 1970-71; Pub. interest dir. Fed. Home Loan Bank, Des Moines, 1971-78, chmn., 1972-78; dir. DTL-Tech. Inc.; Midwest Fed. Savs. & Loan, Mpls., McQuay-Perfex, Inc. Author: (with E. Gross) University Goals and Academic Power, Changes in University Organization, 1964-71. Mem. Gov.'s Adv. Commn. to Dept. Bus. Devel., 1961-63, Upper Midwest Regional Export Expansion Council; chmn. Gov's Tax Study Com., 1962; trustee Seabury Press. Served as lt. USNR, 1942-46. Fellow Acad. Mgmt.; mem. Inst. Mgmt. Scis., Financial Execs. Inst., Strategic Mgmt. Soc., Mpls. C. of C., Beta Gamma Sigma, Delta Sigma Pi. Episcopalian. Clubs: Rotary, Campus (Mpls.). Home: 15 S 1st St Minneapolis MN 55401

GRAMLEY, LYLE ELDEN, govt. ofcl.; b. Aurora, Ill., Jan. 14, 1927;, 1951. B.A., Beloit (Wis.) Coll., 1951; M.A., Ind. U., 1952, Ph.D., 1956. Fin. economist Fed. Res. Bank of Kansas City, 1955-62; asso. prof. monetary econs. U. Md., 1962-64; fin. economist Fed. Res. Bd., 1964-66, asso. adviser, 1966-67, adviser, 1968-77; mem. Council Econ. Advisers, Exec. Office of Pres., Washington, 1977-80; bd. govs. FRS, Washington, 1980—. Author: Scale Economics in Banking, 1962; co-author: Essays in Commercial Banking, 1962. Served in USN, 1944-47. Mem. Am. Econ. Assn., Am. Fin. Assn. Office: Fed Res System Washington DC 20551

GRAMM, WILLIAM PHILIP, congressman, economist; b. Fort Benning, Ga., July 8, 1942; s. Kenneth Marsh and Florence (Scroggins) G.; m. Wendy Lee, Nov. 2, 1970; children: Marshall Kenneth, Jefferson Philip. B.A., U. Ga., 1964, Ph.D., 1967. Mem. faculty dept. econs. Tex. A. and M. U., College Station, 1967-78, prof., 1973-78; ptnr. Gramm & Assocs., 1971-78; mem. 96th-98th Congresses from 6th Tex. Dist.; cons. NSF, U.S. Bur. Mines, USPHS, Arms Control and Disarmament Agy. Contbr. articles to profl. jours., periodicals. Recipient Freedom Found. award, 1975. Mem. Am. Econs. Assn. Democrat. Episcopalian. Office: 1721 Longworth House Office Bldg Washington DC 20515 *Of all the attributes that I have observed in myself and others, as factors contributing to the success of an individual's enterprise, hard work is clearly the most important. Without hard work, talent and intellect are wasted.*

GRAMPP, WILLIAM DYER, economics educator; b. Columbus, Ohio, Aug. 22, 1914; children: Wendy P., Heather M., Christopher W. A.B., U. Akron, 1936; A.M., U. Chgo., 1942, Ph.D., 1944; student, Columbia U., 1941. Mem. editorial staff Akron Times-Press, 1937-38, Press Wireless, Paris, 1938, Chgo. Tribune, London, 1939; instr. Adelphi Coll., 1942; vice consul econ. sect. Am. embassy, Rome, 1944-45; asst. prof. econs. Elmhurst Coll., 1942-44; asst. prof., then prof. econs. Coll. Commerce, DePaul U., 1945-46; mem. faculty Coll. Bus. Adminstrn., U. Ill., 1947—, prof. econs., 1957-80, prof. emeritus, 1980—; vis. prof. Lake Forest (Ill.) Coll., UCLA, Ind. U., CCNY, U. Wis., U. Chgo., Wake Forest U.; vis. scholar Hoover Instn. Author: The Manchester School of Economics, 1960, Economic Liberalism, 1965, Editor, (with E.T. Weiler) Economic Policy, 3d edit, 1961. Mem. Am. Econ. Assn., Midwest Econs. Assn. (pres. 1972-73), History of Econs. Soc. (pres. 1980-81). Home: 5426 Ridgewood Ct Chicago IL 60615

GRANATSTEIN, JACK LAWRENCE, history educator; b. Toronto, Ont., Can., May 21, 1939; s. S. Benjamin Cranatstein and Shirley (Geller) G.; m. Mary Elaine Hitchcock, 1961; children: Carole, Michael. B.A., Royal Mil. Coll., Kingston, Ont., 1961; M.A., U. Toronto, 1962; Ph.D., Duke U., 1966. Historian Dept. Nat. Def., Ottawa, Ont., 1965-66; prof. history York U., 1966—. Author: Politics of Survival, 1967, Canada's War, 1975, Broken Promises, 1977, A Man of Influence, 1981, The Ottawa Men, 1982. Served to lt. Can. Army, 1956-66. Killam research fellow Canada Council, 1982-84; Dept. External Affiars Can. research grantee, 1978-80; SSHRCC research grantee, 1978-79, 82-84. Fellow Royal Soc. Can.; mem. Can. Hist. Assn., Can. Inst. Internat. Affairs. Home: 53 Marlborough Ave Toronto ON Canada M5R 1X5 Office: York Univ 47 Keele St Downsview ON Canada M3J 1PS

GRAND, RICHARD D., lawyer; b. Danzig, Feb. 20, 1930; U.S., 1939, naturalized, 1944; s. Morris and Rena G.; m. Marcia Kosta, Jan. 27, 1952; 1 dau., Cindy. B.A., N.Y. U., 1951; J.D., U. Ariz., 1958. Bar: Ariz. bar 1958, Calif. bar 1973, U.S. Supreme Ct. bar 1973. Dep. atty., Pima County, Ariz., 1958-59, pvt. practice trial law, Tucson, 1959—; founder, 1st pres. Inner Circle Advocates, 1972-75; founder, 1966; now chmn. Richard Grand Found. Legal Research and Edn. Contbr. articles to legal publs. Mem. bd. visitors Ariz. State U. Law Sch.; mem. nat. adv. bd. Touro Law Sch. Recipient citation of honor Lawyers Coop. Pub. Co., 1964. Fellow Am. Acad. Forensic Scis., Internat. Soc. Barristers; asso. mem. Internat. Med. Soc. Paraplegia, Am. Coll. Legal Medicine; mem. Assn. Trial Lawyers Am. (gov. 1964-66), Am., Pima County bar assns., N.Y. State, Calif., San Francisco, Los Angeles trial lawyers assns., Am. Bd. Trial Advs., Brit. Acad. Forensic Scis., Lawyers Club San Francisco, President's Club of U. Ariz. Address: 127 W Franklin St Tucson AZ 85701 *His thinking is his passport. Dream—there is no charge for alterations. The Jury grows a communal nose with which it smells out the strengths and weaknesses of a case.*

GRANDMAISON, J. JOSEPH, political consultant; b. Nashua, N.H., May 19, 1943; s. Oscar N. and Irene P. (Bouchard) G. B.A., Burdett Coll., 1963. Campaign dir. Dukakis for Gov., Boston, 1973-74; adminstrv. asst. Sen. John A. Durkin, N.H., 1975; dir. fed. state relations Commonwealth of Mass., Washington, 1975—; Democratic candidate U.S. Ho. of Reps., 1976; polit. analyst Sta. WBZ-TV, Boston, 1976; fellow John F. Kennedy Inst. Politics Harvard U., 1976—; fed. co-chmn. New Eng. Regional Commn., Washington, 1977-81; econ. devel. and polit. cons., 1981-82, nat. polit. dir. John Glenn for Pres., 1983—. Mem. Bd. of Aldermen, Nashua, N.H., 1970-71; bd. visitors Boston U. Sch. Econs. Democrat. Roman Catholic. Home: 92 Allds St Nashua NH 03060 Office: 1627 Ocean Blvd Rye NH 03870

GRANDY, FRED, actor; b. Sioux City, Iowa, June 29; s. William Frederick and Bonnie G. B.A. in English, Harvard U., 1970. Founder improvisational group The Proposition, Harvard U. Appeared: in play Green Julia, N.Y.C.; collaborator rev.: Pretzels; appeared in: Joe Papp's In the Boom Boom Room, until, 1974; film appearances include Close Encounters of the Third Kind; television films include Love Boat III; television series The Love Boat, 1977—; other television appearances include Welcome Back Kotter. Office: care William Morris Agy 151 El Camino Beverly Hills CA 90212 *

GRANDY, JAMES FREDERICK, business executive, consultant; b. Fort William, Ont., Can., Nov. 24, 1919; s. Clarence Wood and Anne Minetta (Adams) G.; m. Alexandria Irene Shaw, Aug. 18, 1945; children: David, John, Kathleen. B.A., U. Western Ont., 1941; M.Phil., Oxford U., 1948. Fgn. service officer External Affairs Dept., Ottawa, Ont., 1948-57; with Dept. Fin., Ottawa, 1957-67, dep. minister consumer and corp. affairs, 1967-71; dept. minister Dept. Industry and Trade Can. Govt., Ottawa, 1971-75; pres. Reisman & Grandy Ltd., Ottawa, 1975—; chmn. Can. Marconi Co., Montreal, Que., 1981—; dir. Brascan Ltd., Toronto, Ont., Monsanto Can., Toronto. Trustee Royal Ottawa Hosp., 1979—; chmn. Royal Ottawa Hosp. Found., 1983. Served to maj. Royal Can. Arty., 1941-46. Mem. United Ch. Can. Office: Reisman and Grandy Ltd. 401-275 Slater St Ottawa ONCanada K1P 5H9

GRANDY, LEONARD A., educator; b. N.J., June 1, 1916; m. Marjorie; children: Michael, Russell, James, Leslyn. M.A., Tchrs. Coll., Columbia U., 1949; Ed.D., U. So. Calif., 1959. Tchr., dept.

chmn. public schs., N.J., 1941-42, 46-49; tchr. math. and drafting, dir. child welfare and attendance Whittier (Calif.) Union High Sch. Dist., 1949-51, asst. supt. bus., 1951-63, asst. supt., 1962-63; asst. supt., v.p. Rio Hondo Coll., 1963-76; supt., pres. Rio Hondo Community Coll. Dist., Whittier, 1976-82; adj. prof. Whittier Coll., 1982—; mem. pres.'s adv. com. Calif. State U., Pepperdine U. Contbr.: articles to Calif. Sch. Bds. Jour., Coll. Mgmt. Bd. dirs. YMCA Women's Center, Whittier. Served to lt. USN, 1942-46. Mem. Chief Exec. Officers Assn. of Calif. Community Colls., founders com., Assn. Chief Bus. Ofcls. (pres. 1974-75), dir. (1973-74), Assn. Calif. Community Coll. Adminstrs. (founders com., dir.). Republican. Episcopalian. Office: 3600 Workman Mill Rd Whittier CA 90608

GRANDY, WALTER THOMAS, JR., physicist; b. Phila., June 1, 1933; s. Walter Thomas and Margaret Mary (Hayes) G.; m. Patricia Josephine Langan, Dec. 27, 1955; children—Christopher, Neal, Mary, Jeanne. B.S., U. Colo., 1960, Ph.D., 1964. Physicist Nat. Bur. Standards, Boulder, Colo., 1958-63; mem. faculty U. Wyo., Laramie, 1963—, prof. physics, 1969—, head dept., 1971-78; Fulbright lectr. U. Sao Paulo, Brazil, 1966-67, vis. prof., 1982, U. Tubingen, W. Germany, 1978-79. Author: Introduction to Electrodynamics and Radiation, 1970. Served with USNR, 1953-57. Fellow AAAS; mem. Am. Phys. Soc., Brasilian Phys. Soc., Am. Assn. Physics Tchrs., Sigma Xi, Sigma Pi Sigma. Research on statis. mechanics, electrodynamics, quantum theory. Home: 604 S 18th St Laramie WY 82070

GRANGAARD, DONALD R., banker; b. 1918; (married). B.S. in Commerce, U. N.D., 1939; J.D., William Mitchell Coll. Law, 1948. With 1st Bank System, Inc., Mpls., 1939—; formerly v.p. 1st Nat. Bank of Fairmont; v.p., dir. 1st Nat. Bank of Austin, v.p., liaison officer Eastern div. parent co., 1959-68, sr. v.p. adminstrn., 1968-69, pres., chief exec. officer, 1969-77, chmn. bd., 1977—, chief exec. officer, 1977-81, also dir. Served with AUS, 1942-46. Office: 1200 First Bank Pl E Minneapolis MN 55402

GRANGER, BILL, writer; b. Chgo., June 1, 1941; s. William Cecil and Ruth Elizabeth (Griffith) G.; m. Lori Meschke, June 27, 1967; 1 son, Alec. Student, DePaul U., 1959-63. Reporter UPI, Chgo., 1963, Chgo. Tribune, 1966-69, freelance columnist, 1980—; reporter, columnist Chgo. Sun-Times, 1969-78. Author: The Novermber Man, 1979, Sweeps, 1980, Public Murders, 1980, Schism, 1981, Queen's Crossing, 1981, Time for Frankie Coolin, 1981, The Shattered Eye, 1982, The British Cross, 1983, (with Lori Granger) Fighting Jane, 1980, Chicago Pieces, 1983. Served with U.S. Army, 1963-65. Roman Catholic. Home: 244 Hillside Ave Hillside IL 60162

GRANGER, DAVID, investment banker; b. N.Y.C., June 26, 1903; s. David and Felicia (Newton) G.; m. Lee Mason, May 5, 1950; 1 son, Mason. Student, Phillips Exeter Acad., 1917-19; Ph.B., Yale, 1924, Christ's Coll., Cambridge (Eng.) U., 1924-25, U. Caen, 1926. Partner Granger & Co., N.Y.C., 1926—, sr. partner, 1946-81; vice chmn. Granger div. Seligman Securities, 1981—; Mem. N.Y. Stock Exchange, 1926—. Bd. dirs., v.p. Southampton Hosp.; adv. council Episcopal Ch. Found., N.Y.C.; trustee St. Luke's Hosp., N.Y.C., Cathedral Ch. of St. John the Divine; v.p. Museum City N.Y.; adv. council Victoria Home for Aged, Ossining, N.Y.; bd. dirs., treas. Musicians Emergency Fund; bd. govs. Order St. John; bd. dirs. Hort. Soc. N.Y., Barker Welfare Found., Planned Parenthood, N.Y.C. Served from 1st lt. to maj. USAAF, 1942-45. Decorated officer Order Brit. Empire. Mem. English-Speaking Union (nat. v.p.), St. George's Soc. (past v.p.), World Affairs Council L.I. (dir.), Pilgrims U.S. Episcopalian (past mem. vestry). Clubs: Union, Knickerbocker, Down Town Assn., Southampton, Church (past trustee, v.p.), Yale, Metropolitan Opera (N.Y.C.); Bucks (London); Nat. Golf Links Am.; Meadow (Southampton, N.Y.); Travellers (Paris). Home: 640 Park Ave New York NY 10021 Office: 111 Broadway New York NY 10006

GRANGER, LUC ANDRE, university dean, psychologist; b. St. Jean, Que., Can., Apr. 8, 1944; s. Andrew and Georgette (Lacasse) G. B.A., U. Montreal, 1962, B.Sc., 1964, L.P.S., 1966, Ph.D., 1969. Asst. prof. psychology U. Montreal, 1969-73, assoc. prof., 1973-79, prof., 1979—, head dept., 1979-83, assoc. dean, 1983—. Author: Apprentissage et Therapie, 1972, La Therapie Behaviorale, 1976, La Communication dans le Couple, 1979. Postdoctoral fellow U. Lille, France, 1969. Mem. Can. Psychol. Assn. (sec.-treas. 1982—), Corp. des Psychologues (treas. 1974-78). Home: 822 Stuart Co Outremont PQ Canada H3V 3H6 Office: Faculte des arts et des scis 3150 Jean Brillant Montreal PQ Canada H3C 3J7

GRANGER, WILLIAM WOODARD, JR., food company executive; b. Norfolk, Va., Mar. 10, 1919; s. William Woodard and Grace (Williams) G.; m. Norma White, Sept. 7, 1946; children: Shirley W., Gail P., William Woodard III. Student, Coll. William and Mary, 1938-40. With Norfolk Shipbldg. & Dry Dock Corp., 1940; with Beatrice Foods Co. (and subsidiaries), 1946—; mgr. Meadow Gold Dairies, Inc., Pitts., 1963-66, regional v.p. Eastern region, 1966-76; pres. Internat. Foods div., Chgo., 1976—, sr. v.p., 1977, exec. v.p., 1977—, vice chmn., 1982—, also dir.; dir. La Salle Nat. Bank, Towle Mfg. Co. Served with AUS, 1942-45. Office: 2 N La Salle St Chicago IL 60602

GRANICK, DAVID, economist, educator; b. N.Y.C., Jan. 13, 1926; s. Harry and Ray (Weiss) G.; m. Kaete Loette Boenheim, Sept. 12, 1950; children: Steve, Barbara Liza, Jim Timothy. B.S.S., CCNY, 1944; M.A., Columbia U., 1948, Ph.D., 1951; certificate, Russian Inst., 1949. Asso. prof. econs. Fisk U., 1951-57; asst. prof. econs. Carnegie Inst. Tech., 1957-59; asso. prof. U. Wis., Madison, 1959-62, prof. econs., 1962—, chmn. Russian area program, 1965-66; chmn. Western European area program, 1972-74; Econ. affairs officer UN Secretariat, summers 1951, 52; research asso. U. N.C., 1953-54, Russian Research Center, Harvard, 1956-57; sr. research scholar U. Glasgow, Scotland, 1959-60; dir. d'etudes Associe, Ecole Pratique des Hautes Etudes, U. Paris, 1963-64; vis. prof. U. Manchester, Eng., 1964, Ecole des Hautes Etudes Commerciales, U. Montreal, 1975; mem. exec. com. Council for European Studies, 1972-74; mem. acad. council Kennan Inst. Advanced Russian Studies Woodrow Wilson Internat. Ctr. for Scholars. Author: Management of Industrial Firm in the USSR, 1954, The Red Executive, 1960, The European Executive, 1962, Soviet Metalfabricating and Economic Development, 1967, Managerial Comparisons of Four Developed Countries: France, Britain, United States, and Russia, 1972, Enterprise Guidance in Eastern Europe, 1976; Contbr. articles to profl. jours. Served with AUS, 1944-46. Social Sci. Research Council fellow, 1949-50; Guggenheim fellow, 1956-57; Fulbright fellow, 1959-60; sr. research fellow European Inst. Columbia, 1966-67; Internat. Research and Exchanges Bd. fellow Rumania, Hungary, Poland, 1970-71; fellow Netherlands Inst. for Advanced Study, 1974-75, Kennan Inst. Advanced Russian Study, Woodrow Wilson Center, 1978-79. Mem. Am. Econ. Assn., Assn. for Comparative Econ. Studies, Phi Beta Kappa. Club: Rotarian. Home: 4249 Manitou Way Madison WI 53711

GRANING, HARALD MARTIN, physician; b. Mpls., Feb. 14, 1912; s. Martin Kristian and Laura Elise (Kaaberg) G.; m. Thelma Dagmar Forus, July 5, 1938; children—Harald Martin, Karen Ann (Mrs. Robert Gardner), George Edward. B.S., U. Minn., 1934, B.M., 1937, M.D., 1938; M.P.H., Johns Hopkins, 1940. Diplomate: Am. Bd. Preventive Medicine. Commd. USPHS, 1938, asst. surgeon gen., 1963; assigned hosp. service and quarantine, 1940, Pedro, Calif., 1938-39, plague lab., San Francisco, 1940, field epidemiology and exec. officer, 1942-43; dir. Kitsap County Health Dept., Bremerton, Wash., 1941; med. officer civil affairs U.S. Navy, 1944-45; dir. div. local health services Ga. Dept. Health, 1945-47; cancer control cons., New Orleans, 1947-48, chief state and local health services, Washington, 1948-50, regional med. dir., 1951-58, 1958-63, asst. surgeon gen., 1963-75, chief div. hosp. and med. facilities, Washington, 1963-68, dir. health facility planning and constrn. service, 1968-75, hosp. and health care cons., 1975-81. Recipient Meritorious Service medal USPHS, 1963, Distinguished Service medal, 1973; Health Care Achievement award Health Industries Assn., 1972. Fellow Am. Pub. Health Assn. (sec. joint com. study edn. pub. health 1959—, chmn. health officers sect. 1962-63), Am. Coll. Hosp. Adminstrs. (hon.); mem. A.M.A., Am. Assn. Hosp. Cons. (hon.), Am. Hosp. Assn. (ho. of dels.), Am. Assn. Hosp. Planning (treas. 1976—, v.p. 1977, pres. 1979), Am. Dietetic Assn. (hon.). Home and Office: 744 Oak Grove Circle Severna Park MD 21146

GRANIRER, EDMOND ERNEST, mathematician, educator; b. Constanza, Romania, Feb. 19, 1935; s. Jacob G. M.Sc., Hebrew U., Jerusalem, 1959, Ph.D., 1962. Mem. faculty dept. math. U. Ill., 1962-64, Cornell U., 1964-65; mem. faculty dept. math. U. B.C., Vancouver, 1965-66, 67—, prof. math., 1970—; faculty U. Montreal, 1966-67. Contbr. articles to profl. jours. Fellow Royal Soc. Can.; mem. Can. Math. Soc., Am. Math. Soc. Office: Dept Math U BC Vancouver BC Canada

GRANIT, RAGNAR ARTHUR, neurophysiologist; b. Finland, Oct. 30, 1900; m. Baroness Marguerite (Daisy) Bruun; 1 son, Michael. Grad., Swedish Normallyceum, Helsinki, Finland, 1919; Mag. phil., Helsinki U., 1923, M.D., 1927; D.Sc. (hon.), U. Oslo, U. Oxford, Loyola U., U. Pisa, U. Helsinki. Docent Helsinki U., 1932-37, prof. physiology, 1937-40; fellow med. physics Eldridge Reeves Johnson Research Found., U. Pa., 1929-31; mem. staff Royal Caroline Inst., Stockholm, 1940-67, emeritus mem., 1967—, prof. neurophysiology, 1946-67; Thomas Young orator Phys. Soc. London, Eng., 1945; Silliman lectr. Yale U., 1954; Sherrington lectr., London, 1967, Liverpool, 1970, Murlin lectr., Rochester, N.Y., 1973; Jackson lectr. McGill U., 1975; vis. prof. Rockefeller U., N.Y.C., 1956-66, St. Catherine's Coll., Oxford, 1967, Smith-Kettlewell Inst. Med. Sci., San Francisco, 1969, Fogarty Internat. Center, NIH, Bethesda, Md., 1971-72, 75, Düsseldorf U., 1974, Max-Planck Inst., Bad Nauheim, W.Ger., 1976. Author: Ung Mans Väg till Minerva, 1941, Sensory Mechanisms of the Retina, 1947, Receptors and Sensory Perception, 1955, Charles Scott Sherrington, An Appraisal, 1966, Basis of Motor Control, 1970, Regulation of the Discharge of Motoneurons, 1971, The Purposive Brain, 1977, Hur Det Kom Sig (autobiography), 1983. Co-recipient Nobel prize in medicine, 1967; recipient Donders, Retzius, Sherrington, Purkinje medals; 3d Internat. St. Vincent prize, 1961; Jahre prize Oslo U., 1961. Mem. Royal Swedish Acad. Sci. (pres. 1963-65, v.p. 1965-69), Royal Soc. London (fgn. mem.), Nat. Acad. Sci. (U.S.), Am. Philos. Soc., Indian Acad. Sci. (hon.), Acad. di Med. (hon.) (Turin), Acad. Nat. d. Lincei (Rome), Physiol. Soc. Eng., Physiol. Soc. U.S., Am. Acad. Arts and Scis. (hon.), Societas Scientiarum Fennicae (hon.), Royal Danish Acad. Sci. Address: 14 Eriksbergsgatan 11430 Stockholm Ö Sweden

GRANN, PHYLLIS, publisher, editor; b. London, Sept. 2, 1937; d. Solomon and Louisa (Bois-Smith) Eitingon; m. Victor Grann, Sept. 26, 1962; children: Alison, David, Edward. B.A. cum laude, Barnard Coll., 1958. Sec. Doubleday Pubs., N.Y.C., 1958-60; editor William Morrow Inc., N.Y.C., 1960-62, David McKay Co., 1962-70, Simon & Schuster Inc., 1970, v.p., 1976; pres., pub. G. P. Putnam's & Sons., N.Y.C., 1976—. Office: G P Putnam's Sons 200 Madison Ave New York NY 10016 *

GRANNON, CHARLES LEE, investment banking official; b. Lafayette, Ind., Dec. 2, 1915; s. Charles Dale and Verena Ruth (Benedict) G.; m. Alice Fay Conard, Nov. 8, 1951; children: Michael L., Craig C., Charles P., Mark W. B.S., Purdue U., 1939; M.A., U. Iowa, 1941. With Goldman, Sachs & Co., N.Y.C., 1945—, ptnr., 1959-82, ltd. ptnr., 1982—; dir. Fed.-Mogul Corp., Detroit, 1968—. Trustee DePauw U., 1981, Ridgewood YMCA, 1970, Valley Hosp. Found., Ridgewood, N.J., 1981. Served to lt. comdr. USN, 1942-45, 50-51. Republican. Presbyterian. Clubs: Ridgewood Country; Recess (N.Y.C.); Broken Sound Golf (Boca Raton, Fla.); Ocean Reef (Key Largo, Fla.). Home: 307 Heights Rd Ridgewood NJ 07450 Office: Goldman Sachs & Co 85 Broad St New York NY 10004

GRANSTROM, MARVIN LEROY, educator; b. Anaconda, Mont., Sept. 25, 1920; s. Carl August and Alida Sophia (Eckstrom) G.; m. Ruth Maybelle Olsen, Jan. 1, 1944; children—David Marvin, Kay Ruth, Chris Carl. B.S., Morningside Coll., 1942, Iowa State Coll., 1943; M.S. in San. Engring, Harvard, 1947, Ph.D., 1955. Engring. aide Soil Conservation Service, Whiting, Iowa, 1939; cons. engr., Sioux Falls, S.D., 1946; instr. civil and san. engring. Case Inst. Tech., 1947-49; asso. prof. san. engring. U. N.C., 1949-58; prof. civil engring. Rutgers U., New Brunswick, N.J., 1958—; research participant Oak Ridge Nat. Labs., 1954; cons. Nat. Engring. Sch., Lima, Peru, 1955-57, WHO, 1966—; cons. in hydrology, 1970—. Author articles in field. Served with USMCR, 1943-46. Research grantee N.C., 1953, NIH, 1954-58, NSF, 1954-63, Army Chem. Center, 1961-64, surgeon gen. U.S. Army, 1962, Office Water Resources Research, Dept. Interior, 1965-76, N.J. Dept. Environ. Protection, 1957—; fellow Nat. Found., 1946-47, USPHS, 1952-53. Mem. Am. Chem. Soc., ASCE, Am. Water Works Assn., Am. Water Resources Assn., Am. Acad. Environ. Engrs., Tau Beta Pi, Sigma Xi, Delta Omega, Chi Epsilon. Home: 931 Oakwood Pl Plainfield NJ 07060 Office: Rutgers Univ New Brunswick NJ 08903

GRANT, ALAN J., business executive; b. Chgo., Dec. 18, 1925; s. Hugo Bernard and May (Gardner) G.; m. Margaret Stewart, Dec. 21, 1946; children: Pamela Rose, Deborah May, Bruce David. B.S., Ill. Inst. Tech., 1946, M.S., 1948; grad., Inst. Mgmt., Northwestern U., 1961. Instr. elec. engring. Ill. Inst. Tech., Chgo., 1946-49; with N.Am. Aviation, Inc. (Autonetics), Anaheim, Calif., 1949-64, v.p., gen. mgr. computer and data systems div., 1962-64; pres. Lockheed Electronics Co. div. Lockheed Aircraft Corp., Plainfield, N.J., 1965-69; also v.p. parent co.; exec. v.p. Aerojet-Gen. Corp., El Monte, Calif., 1970-74; chmn., pres. Wavecom Industries, Sunnyvale, Calif., 1974-78, Primark Corp., San Mateo, Calif., 1975-80; chmn., chief exec. officer Internat. Rotex, Inc., Reno, Nev., 1980—; dir. UNC Resources Inc, Falls Church, Va., 1974-81; chmn. Atasi Corp., San Jose, Calif., 1982—; gen. ptnr. Enterprise Mgmt. Co. II, La Jolla, Calif., 1984—; adj. prof. managerial scis. U. Nev., Reno, 1976—. Bd. trustees Sierra Arts Found., Reno., 1981—. Served with USNR, 1944-46. Mem. Am. Electronics Assn. (chmn. 1973, dir. 1970-74), Sigma Xi, Tau Beta Pi, Eta Kappa Nu, Pi Delta Epsilon. Home: 1835 Solari Dr Reno NV 89509 Office: 8950 Villa La Jolla Dr Suite 2132 La Jolla CA 92037

GRANT, ALEXANDER MARSHALL, ballet director; b. Wellington, N.Z., Feb. 22, 1928; emigrated to Can., 1976; s. Alexander Gibb and Eleather May (Marshall) G. Ed., Wellington Coll.; scholarship student, Sadler's Wells Sch., London, 1946-46. Mem., Sadler's Wells Ballet (now Royal Ballet), 1946-76; prin. dancer, 1950-76; co-dir., Ballet for All, touring co., 1970-71; dir., 1971-76; artistic dir., Nat. Ballet Can., 1976-83; dancer: numerous leading roles on stage, also in film Tales of Beatrice Potter; others. Decorated comdr. Order Brit. Empire, 1965.

GRANT, BARRY M(ARVIN), judge; b. Detroit, Jan. 16, 1936; s. Daniel and Pauline (Dantzig) G.; m. Lisa Geffen, Jan. 31, 1960; children: James D., Nanci J., L. Scott. B.A., Mich. State U., 1957; J.D., Wayne State U., 1960; postgrad., Northwestern U., 1964, Harvard U. Bar: Mich. 1961, U.S. Supreme Ct. 1961, U.S. Ct. Appeals. Probate clk., Oakland County, Mich., 1960, legal investigator, asst. pros. atty., Oakland County, 1961-64, probate ct. referee, 1962-63, 71, 74; chmn. Oakland County Condemnation Commn., 1964, 73; trial atty., Oakland County, from 1961; presiding judge Oakland County Probate Ct.; Traffic safety commr., 1964; sec., state jud. coordinator Spl. Com. on Ct. Reorgn.; weekly columnist Judge Grant column Detroit News. Mem. Parent-Youth Guidance Commn., 1963-64; chmn. Oakland County Lawyers United Found. Torch Drive, 1968, 71; exec. sec. Southfield Beautification Com., 1963; trustee Wm. Beaumont Hosp.; treas. Southfield Bd. Edn., Oakland County Sch. Bd. Assn., 1968, also trustee; mem. exec. com., bd. dirs. Camp Oakland; Bd. dirs. Mich. Soc. Mental Health, Oakland County Hist. Soc., Mich. Cancer Found., March of Dimes, Boy Scouts Am. Mem. Nat. Council Juvenile Ct. Judges, Mich. Probate-Juvenile Judges Assn. (bd. dirs.), ABA, Mich. Bar Assn. (mem. rep. assembly), Oakland County Bar Assn., Am. Trial Lawyers Assn., Oakland County Law Enforcement Assn. Clubs: Mich. State U., Oakland County. Address: 1200 N Telegraph Rd Pontiac MI 48053

GRANT, BROOKE, financial executive, real estate holding company executive; b. Pitts., Aug. 27, 1935; s. Van Hatch and Mildred Larkin (Blood) G.; m. Sara Jane Moyle Creer, Dec. 30, 1957; children: Preston, Elizabeth, Gregory, Allison, Pamela. Student, UCLA, 1953-55, U. Utah, 1956, 57; B.A., Stanford U., 1958, J.D., 1960. Mgr. Van Grant & Co., 1955-57; auditor, tax accountant Touche Ross & Co., San Francisco, 1960-62, mgr. mgmt. services, 1968-69; asst. corp. counsel, mgr. mktg. Varian Assos., Palo Alto, Calif., 1962-68; pres., chmn. bd. Tracy Bancorp., Salt Lake City, 1969-71, 78—; asst. prof. Brigham Young U., Provo, Utah, 1971-73; owner, operator Hanover, Ltd., Salt Lake City, 1971—; mng. partner Lantrust Cos.; chmn. bd., chief exec. officer Intermountain Pipe & Welding Co., Inc., 1971—; chmn., chief exec. officer Talcott Nat. Corp., James Talcott, Inc., N.Y.C., 1976-77; chmn. Uintah Nat. Corp., 1975-79. Bd. dirs. Utah Symphony. Mormon. Clubs: Alta, Fort Douglas (Salt Lake City). Office: 40 E South Temple Suite 300 Salt Lake City UT 84111

GRANT, CARL N., communications executive; b. Sharon, Pa., July 10, 1939; s. Carl and Hedwig Theressa N.; m. Carol Ann Pasacic, June 12, 1965; children: Carl, Kevin, Heather Lee. B.A., Kent State U., 1963; M.A., 1966; Ph.D., Ohio State U., 1972. Program dir. Sta. WKNT-FM, Kent, Ohio, 1962-64; news anchorman WJIM-TV, Gross Telecasting Co., Lansing, Mich., 1963-65, WFMJ-TV, Vindicator Co., Youngstown, Ohio, 1965-67; asst. news dir. WLWC-TV, Avco Broadcasting, Columbus, Ohio, 1967-69; news and public affairs dir. WKBS-TV, Kaiser Broadcasting Co., Phila., 1969-72; exec. staff dir. Nat. Com. Employer Support Guard and Res., Dept. Def., 1972-73; dir. Pres.'s Commn. White House Fellows, 1973-74; news and public affairs dir. Kaiser Broadcasting Co., Washington, 1974; assoc. dir., editor Def. Manpower Commn., Washington, 1974-76; dir. public affairs GSA, 1976-77; group v.p. communications C. of C. U.S., 1977—. (Emmy nominee 1968). Served with U.S. Army, 1958-60; now Res. Recipient Ohio AP Best TV Investigative Reporting award, 1968, 69, others. Office: 1615 H St NW Washington DC 20062 *

GRANT, CARY, actor; b. Bristol, Eng., Jan. 18, 1904; came to U.S., 1921, naturalized, 1942; s. Elias and Elsie (Kingdom) Leach; m. Virginia Cherill, Feb. 1934 (div. Sept. 1934); m. Barbara Hutton, July 8, 1942 (div. Aug. 1945); m. Betsy Drake; m. Dyan Cannon, July 22, 1965 (div.); 1 dau., Jennifer; m. Barbara Harris, 1981. Student, Fairfield Acad., Somerset, Eng., 1914-19. Dir. Faberge, Inc., Hollywood Park, Inc., Metro-Goldwyn-Mayer, Inc.; dir. emeritus Western Airlines. Began as actor in, New York, 1921; Played in: Street Singer, Nikki, Golden Dawn, Polly Boom Boom, Wonderful Night; starred in: motion pictures Walk, Don't Run, Mr. Lucky, Arsenic and Old Lace, Destination Tokyo, None But the Lonely Heart, The Bishop's Wife, I Was a Male War Bride, The Bachelor and the Bobby Soxer, Every Girl Should Be Married, Crisis, People Will Talk, Room for One More, Monkey Business, Dream Wife, To Catch a Thief, An Affair to Remember, Indiscreet, Houseboat, North By Northwest, Operation Petticoat, That Touch of Mink, Charade, Father Goose. Bd. govs. USO. Recipient Spl. Academy award for contbns. to film industry Acad. Motion Picture Arts and Scis., 1969, Kennedy Center honors medal, 1981. Mem. Ch. of Eng. Address: care Faberge 1345 Ave of the Americas New York NY 10019 *

GRANT, DANIEL ROSS, university president; b. Little Rock, Aug. 18, 1923; s. James Richard and Gracie (Sowers) G.; m. Betty Jo Oliver, June 17, 1947; children: Carolyn, Shirley, Ross. B.A., Ouachita Bapt. U., 1945; M.A., U. Ala., 1946; Ph.D., Northwestern U., 1948. Asst. prof. polit. sci. Vanderbilt U., 1948-54, asso. prof., 1954-63, prof., 1963-70; pres. Ouachita Bapt. U., 1970—; vis. prof. mcpl. govt. and planning Thammasat U., Bangkok, 1958-59; cons. U.S. Adv. Commn. Intergovtl. Relations, 1962-67; asso. dir. Harris County Home Rule Commn., Houston, 1957; mem. adv. com. federalism and met. govt. Nat. Com. Econ. Devel., 1969—. Author: The Christian and Politics, 1968, (H.C. Nixon) State and Local Government in America, 4th edit., 1982, (with others) The States and the Metropolis, 1968, Metropolitan Surveys: a Digest, 1958, Government and Politics: an Introduction to Political Science, rev. edit., 1971, Plan of Metropolitan Government for Nashville and Davidson County, 1956. Dir. Urban and Regional Devel. Center of Vanderbilt U., 1969-70; mem. So. Bapt. Found., 1959-60; mem. commn. on religious liberty and human rights Bapt. World Alliance, 1971—; mem. edn. commn. So. Bapt. Conv., 1973—, chmn., 1978-80; mem. Ark. Postsecondary Edn. Planning Commn., 1980—. Mem. Am., So. polit. sci. assns., Am. Soc. Pub. Adminstrn., AAUP. Club: Rotary. Home: 904 N 26th St Arkadelphia AR 71923

GRANT, DAVID RUSSELL, manufacturing company executive; b. Pitts., Dec. 22, 1939; s. Edward Joseph and Helen Margaret (Matz) G.; m. Suzanne Stevens, Sept. 12, 1964; children: Kevin, Geoff. B.A., Lawrence U., Appleton, Wis., 1961; M.B.A., Columbia U., 1969. From salesman to gen. mgr. S.C. Johnson Co., Eng. and Greece, 1961-67; sr. product mgr. Clairol Co., N.Y.C., 1969-72; dir. sales and mktg. Repco Inc., Orlando, Fla., 1972-77; pres. Penn Athletic Products Co., Monroeville, Pa., 1977—. Founder U.S. Tennis Assn./Penn Circuit, 1973. Mem. Phi Delta Theta. Republican. Roman Catholic. Home: 3591 Windover Rd E Murrysville PA 15668 Office: 4220 William Penn Hwy Parkvale Bldg Monroeville PA 15146

GRANT, EDWARD, educator; b. Canton, Ohio, Apr. 6, 1926; s. Rudolph and Rose (Spitz) G.; m. Sydelle Rhoda Chapnick, Jan. 28, 1951; children: Robyn Joan, Marshall Leslie, Jonathan Alan. B.S.S., CCNY, 1951; M.A., U. Wis., 1953, Ph.D., 1957. Instr. history U. Maine, 1957-58; instr. history of sci. Harvard U., 1958-59; asst. prof. history Ind. U., 1959-60, asst. prof. history, also history and philosophy of sci., 1960-63, assoc. prof., 1963-64, prof., 1964-83, disting. prof., 1983—; vis. asst. prof. history of sci. U. Wis., spring, 1962; mem. Inst. for Advanced Study, Princeton U., 1965-66, U.S. nat. com. Internat. Union for History and Philosophy of Sci., 1963-69, chmn., 1968-69. Author: Nicole Oresme: De Proportionibus Proportionum and Ad Pauca Respicientes, 1966, Nicole Oresme and the Kinematics of Circular Motion, 1971, Physical Science in the Middle Ages, 1971, A Source Book in Medieval Science, 1974, Much Ado About Nothing: Theories of Space and Vacuum from the Middle Ages to the Scientific Revolution, 1981; Adv. editor: Isis, 1981—. Served with USNR, 1943-46. Guggenheim fellow, 1965-66; NSF research grantee, 1959-70, 71-74, 80—; Am. Council Learned Socs. fellow, 1975-76. Fellow AAAS, Medieval Acad. Am. (editorial bd. Speculum 1972—, council 1979-82); Mem. Internat. Acad. History Sci., History of Sci. Soc. (gov. council 1963-66, v.p. 1983-84). Home: 2124 Woodstock Pl Bloomington IN 47401

GRANT, EDWARD DONALD, chem. mfg. exec.; b. Glascow, Scotland, June 18, 1897; came to U.S., 1909, naturalized, 1922; s. Charles and Jemina (McDonald) G.; m. Georgia Voyles, July 14, 1921; 1 son, Edward Donald. A.B., Austin Coll., Sherman, Tex., 1920, Litt. D., 1933; postgrad., YMCA Grad Sch., 1924- 25; M.A., George Peabody Coll. for Tchrs., 1929; L.H.D., Southwestern U. at Memphis, 1954. Profl. fund raiser, 1920-21; sec. edn. and promotion Fgn. Mission Bd., Presbyn. Ch. in U.S., 1921-34; also acting sec. Com. on Stewardship and Finance, 1931-35; exec. sec. Bd. Edn., Richmond, Va., 1934-52; mem. personnel bd., City of Richmond, 1950-52, dir. instns., State of La., 1952-58; pres. Grant Chem. Co., 1958-69; chmn. bd. Grant-Lehr Corp., 1962-65; sec.-treas. Gramor Chems., Inc., 1965-68; chmn. bd., pres. Roadways Internat. Corp.; treas. Plasticos Y Estabalizadores (S.A.), Mexico. Author: The Ambassador Supreme, 1933. Pres. Baton Rouge YMCA, 1969,70; past pres. Am. Leprosy Missions, Inc.; moderator Presbyn. Ch. in U.S., 1962-63, dir. bd. ch. extension, 1959-67; Del. to Internat. Missionary Council, Madras, India, 1938, to World Council of Christian Edn., Birmingham, Eng., 1947. Served as 2d lt. U.S. Army, 1918. Recipient Pub. Service award La. Coll., 1954; La. Mental Health award, 1955; La. Brotherhood medal, 1976; Kiwanis Dist. Laymans award, 1976; Austin Coll. Founders award, 1976, Americanism award DAR, 1978; Golden Deeds award, 1978; named La. Outstanding Naturalized Citizen for, 1978. Mem. Phi Delta Kappa. Democrat. Presbyn. Club: Mason. Home: 5837 Boone Dr Baton Rouge LA 70808 Office: 1911 N 4th St Baton Rouge LA 70802

GRANT, GERARD GRAY, priest, philosophy educator; b. Chgo., Aug. 27, 1908; s. Samuel Thomas and Elizabeth Gray G. Student, Loyola U., Chgo., 1926-28; A.B., St. Louis U., 1934, M.A., 1934, Ph.L., 1937, S.T.L., 1941. Joined S.J., Roman Catholic Ch., 1928, ordained priest, 1940; exec. dir. Loyola U. Alumni Assn., 1942-51; assoc. prof. philosophy Loyola U., Chgo., 1951-78, prof. emeritus, 1978—; pres. World Federalists in Chgo., 1060-62; exec. v.p. Chgo. World Federalists, 1962—; mem. Nat. Council World Federalists, 1958—; v.p. World Federalists U.S.A., 1968-75; mem. Federalist World Council, 1963—; chmn. exec. com. World Assn. World Federalists, 1975-77, chmn. council, 1977—, 1st v.p., 1983—; chmn. Inter-Univ. Survey on World Law, 1969—. Author: Elevation of the Host, 1942. Chmn. Chgo. Com. to Save Lives in Chile, 1974, Com. for Freedom in India, 1975-77. Mem. AAUP, Clergy and Laity Concerned, Chgo. Com. to Defend Bill of Rights, Am. Cath. Philos. Assn. Democrat. Home: 6525 N Sheridan Rd Chicago IL 60626 *I have always lived with the purpose of helping my fellowman. The great crisis of our time is the anarchy in the world which leads inevitably to war and more war. Long ago I concluded that the principles which enabled 13 independent American governments to give us their sovereignty and adopt the Constitution are precisely those which alone will make it possible to establish a secure and lasting peace. I have been inspired by the confidence that what our founding fathers achieved in 1787 we should be able to do also today.*

GRANT, IRVING MAXWELL, lawyer; b. Bay City, Mich., Feb. 22, 1931; s. Morris W. and Ida (Levinson) G.; m. Barbara Schostak, June 23, 1952; children: Kathy, Michael, Jacqueline. B.B.A., U. Mich., 1952; J.D., UCLA, 1955. Bar: Calif. 1955. Since practiced in, Los Angeles; partner firm Willis, Butler, Scheifly, Leydorf & Grant, 1959-81, Pepper, Hamilton & Scheetz, 1981-83, Hufstedler, Miller, Carlson & Beardsley, 1984—; instr. masters in taxation program U. So. Calif. Sch. Bus. Adminstrn., 1976-79; lectr. U. So. Calif. Tax Inst., 1960, 62, 63, 69, 79, 84, N.Y. U. Tax Inst., 1974, Hawaii Tax Inst., 1970. Author: Subchapter S Taxation, 1974, 2d edit., 1980; also articles on taxation. Mem. Am., Los Angeles County bar assns., State Bar Calif., Order of Coif. Clubs: Univ. (Los Angeles); Porter Valley Country (Northridge, Calif.). Home: 19133 Merion Dr Northridge CA 91326 Office: 700 S Flower St Los Angeles CA 90017

GRANT, JAMES COLIN, banker; b. N.S., Can., Jan. 24, 1937; s. Jack Danial and Isabel G.; m. Sonia Chicorli, July 3, 1965; 1 dau., Allison Lee. Student, St. Francis Xavier U., 1954-57, Tech. U. N.S., 1957-59. Engr. Dept. Transport, Fed. Govt., 1959-65; mgr. tech. support Gulf Oil Ltd., Toronto and Montreal, 1965-69; mgr. tech. design Royal Bank of Can., Montreal, 1969-72, dir. ops., 1972-75, asst. gen. mgr. systems, 1975-79, v.p. systems, 1979-81, v.p. strategic planning, retail banking, 1981-84, sr. v.p. ops. and systems, 1984—; Can. rep. bus. industry adv. com. OECD; chmn. bd. Syscor Corp.; mem. transnat. data report Adv. Panel on Info. Policy and Regulation. Mem. editorial bd.: Info. and Mgmt. Bd. dirs. Tech. U. N.S., 1974-78. Mem. Order Profl. Engrs. Que., Can. Info. Processing Soc. (bd. dirs. Montreal 1970-72), Internat. C. of C. (Can. del., commn. on computing, telecommunications and info. policies). Office: Royal Bank Canada 1 Place Ville Marie Montreal PQ Canada H3C 3A9

GRANT, JAMES DENEALE, food company executive; b. Washington, July 9, 1932; s. Deneale and Frances (Hoskins) G.; m. Bonnie Carol Johnson, June 14, 1955; children: Glenn James, Bruce William, Scott Stockman. B.S., William and Mary Coll., 1954; M.B.A., Wharton Sch. U. Pa., 1956; postgrad. (Pub. Affairs fellow), Stanford U., 1963-64. Mem. staff AEC, Washington, 1956-64; v.p. Nat. Inst. Pub. Affairs, Washington, 1964-69; dep. dir. White House Conf. Food, Nutrition and Health, 1969-70; dep. commr. FDA, Washington, 1970-72; asst. to chmn. CPC Internat. Inc., Englewood Cliffs, N.J., 1972-73, v.p., 1973—; dir. Best Foods N. Am. div. CPC, Ketchum Co.; cons. U.S. Bur. Budget, 1965-69, CSC, 1965-69. Chmn. Bergen County United Fund, 1974-75; trustee Nutrition Found., 1973-78; chmn. adv. group to sec.-gen. UNCSTD, 1979. Recipient U.S. Govt. Career Edn. award, 1963. Mem. Am. Chem. Soc., AAAS, Omicron Delta Kappa. Club: Univ. (N.Y.C.). Home: 860 Fifth Ave New York NY 10021 Office: CPC International Inc Box 8000 Englewood Cliffs NJ 07632

GRANT, JAMES PINEO, official UNICEF; b. Peking, China, May 12, 1922; s. John Black and Charlotte (Hill) G.; m. Ethel Henck, Dec. 30, 1943; children: John Putnam, James Dickinson, William Joseph. A.B., U. Calif., 1943; LL.B., J.D., Harvard U., 1951; hon. degrees, Notre Dame U., 1980, Hacetteppe U., 1980, Maryville Coll., 1981; H.H.D., Denison U., 1983, Tufts U., 1983. Rep., UNRRA in North China, 1946-47; cons., spl. asst. to dir. U.S. Econ. Aid Mission to China, 1948-49, 50; asso. Covington & Burling, Washington, 1951-54; regional legal counsel U.S. Econ. Aid Missions in South Asia, 1954-56; dir. U.S. Econ. Aid Mission to Ceylon, 1956-58; spl. asst. to dir. Internat. Cooperation Adminstrn., 1958; dep. dir. ICA, Washington, 1958-61; dep. asst. sec. state for Near Eastern and South Asian affairs, 1962-64; dir. U.S. Econ. Aid Mission to Turkey, 1964-67; asst. adminstr. AID, Washington, 1967-69; pres. Overseas Devel. Council, 1969-79; exec. dir. UNICEF, 1980—. Bd. dirs., trustee Rockefeller Found.; bd. dirs. Internat. Vol. Services, New Directions, Johns Hopkins U., Overseas Devel. Council. Served as capt. AUS, 1943-45; CBI. Decorated Bronze Star with cluster; Breast Order of Yun Hui, China; recipient Disting. Public Service award AID, 1961; Rockefeller Public Service award, 1980. Mem. Soc. Internat. Devel. (pres. 1978—), Council Fgn. Relations, Bar Assn. D.C., North-South Round Table. Clubs: Met., Cosmos (Washington); U.S. of Rome. Office: UNICEF 866 UN Plaza New York NY 10017

GRANT, JOHN BENJAMIN, lawyer; b. Willimantic, Conn., May 1, 1908; s. Frederick Benjamin and Ida (Lincoln) G.; m. Eleanor Quin, July 14, 1934; children: John Benjamin, Frances Grant Moore, Judith Grant McMeekin, Eleanor Grant Grave. B.A., Yale U., 1930, LL.B., 1932. Bar: Conn. 1933, R.I. 1975. Practiced in New Haven, 1933—; mem. firm Tyler, Cooper, Grant, Bowerman & Keefe, 1944-81; of counsel Tyler, Cooper & Alcorn; instr. law New Haven Coll., 1942-46; dir. F.D. Grave & Son Inc.; sec., dir. Conn. Radio Found. Inc., 1944-67. U.S. concilliation commr. in farm bankruptcies, 1942-46; judge Orange Town Ct., 1939-43; mem. bd., sec. Orange Zoning Commn., 1941-51. Mem. Am., Conn., R.I., New Haven bar assns., Newcomen Soc. N.Am., Phi Alpha Delta. Episcopalian (past vestry). Clubs: Point Judith Country (Narragansett, R.I.); Quinnipiack (New Haven); Port Malabar Country (Palm Bay, Fla.). Home: Arnolda Charlestown RI 02813 Office: 205 Church St New Haven CT 06509

GRANT, JOHN HERBERT, steel construction company executive; b. Akron, Ohio, Dec. 19, 1928; s. Jesse Herbert and Hazel Rose (Enborg) G.; m. Marilyn Ann Mayer, Sept. 16, 1950; children: John Jeffrey, Herbert Campbell, Elizabeth Beryl, Douglas Holden. B.S. in Civil Engring., U. Pa., 1950, M.S., 1955. Engr. G & H Steel Service, Inc., Broomall, Pa., 1950-55, treas.-v.p., 1955-75, pres., 1975—; dir. Winlink Ltd. Airlines, Castries, St. Lucia, 1982—. Nat. Constrn. Employees Council, Washington, 1981—, Contech Group Services, Broomall, 1981—. Pres., dir. Marple Newtown Sch. Bd., Newtown Square, Fla., 1971-83; dir.-treas. Radnor Hist. Soc., (Pa.), 1970-81; adminstrv. bd. Wayne Methodist Ch., (Pa.), 1980-83. Mem. Am. Concrete Inst. (mem. bldg. code com. 1983), Concrete Reinforcing Steel Inst., ASCE, Nat. Assn. Reinforcing Steel (pres.-dir. 1976—), Ironworkers Industry Inst. (dir. 1981—). Republican. Clubs: Rotary (Newtown Square) (pres. 1978-79); Union League Phila., Edgemont Country. Home: 35 Dunminning Rd Newtown Square PA 19073 Office: G & H Steel Service Inc 390 Reed Rd Broomall PA 19008

GRANT, JOHN L., business executive; b. Los Angeles, Oct. 26, 1922; m. Carolyn Jane Hubbell, Dec. 9, 1960. B.A., Union Coll., 1945; M.B.A., Harvard U., 1949. Vice-pres. First Pa. Banking & Trust Co., Phila., 1949-60; v.p. fin. Sinclair Oil Corp., 1960-68; v.p. Atlantic Richfield Co., 1968-69; exec. v.p. fin. and adminstrn. Am. Standard, Inc., N.Y.C., 1970—, dir., N.Y.C.; DIR. Air Products & Chems., Inc.; dir. Transway Internat., Inc. Home: 641 Fifth Ave Apt. 49B New York NY 10022 Office: Am Standard Inc 40 W 40th St New York NY 10018

GRANT, JOSEPH MOORMAN, banker; b. San Antonio, Oct. 30, 1938; s. George William and Mary Christian (Moorman) G.; m. Sheila Ann Peterson, Aug. 26, 1961; children: Mary Elizabeth, Steven Clay. B.B.A., So. Methodist U., 1960; M.B.A., U. Tex., Austin, 1961, Ph.D., 1970. Asst. cashier Citibank, N.Y.C., 1961-65; sr. v.p., economist Tex. Commerce Bank (N.A.); also Tex. Commerce Bancshares, Houston, 1970-73; pres., dir. Capital Nat. Bank, Austin, 1974-75, Tex. Am. Bank/Ft. Worth, 1975—; dir. Tex. Am. Bancshares, Inc., 1976—; chmn. comml. banking major Southwestern Sch. Banking. Author: (with Lawrence L. Crum) The Development of State-Chartered Banking in Texas, 1978. Past chmn. North Tex. Commn.; trustee So. Meth. U.; chmn. bd. Tex. Christian U. Research Found. Mem. Ft. Worth C. of C. (chmn.), Young Pres. Orgn. (dir., area v.p., sr. v.p. fin. and adminstrn., exec. com.), Nat. Assn. Bus. Economists, Am. Bankers Assn., Assn. Res. City Bankers, Blue Key, Sigma Alpha Epsilon. Episcopalian. Clubs: Ft. Worth, Exchange. Home: 1408 Shady Oaks Ln Fort Worth TX 76107 Office: 500 Throckmorton St Box 2050 Fort Worth TX 76113

GRANT, LEE (LYOVA HASKELL ROSENTHAL), actress, director; b. N.Y.C., Oct. 31, 1931; d. A.W. and Witia (Haskell) Rosenthal; m. Arnold Manoff (dec.); 1 dau., Dinah; m. Joseph Feury; 1 dau., Belinda. Student, Julliard Sch. Music, Neighborhood Playhouse Sch. Theatre, Met. Opera Ballet Sch. Stage debut as child in: L'arocolo, Met. Opera House, N.Y.C., 1934; Broadway appearances include Prisoner of Second Avenue, 1972, Detective Story, Two for the See-Saw; off-Broadways appearances include The Maids (Obie award), Electra, N.Y. Shakespeare Festival; motion pictures include Detective Story, 1952 (best actress Cannes Film Festival), The Balcony, 1963, Divorce American Style, 1967, Heat of the Night, 1968, Marooned, 1970, There Was a Crooked Man, 1970, The Landlord, 1970, Plaza Suite, 1971, Shampoo, 1975 (Acad. award for best supporting actress), Voyage of the Damned, 1976, Airport '77, 1977, The Swarm, 1978, The Mafu Cage, 1978, Damien-Omen II, 1978, When You Comin' Back, Red Ryder, 1979, Little Miss Marker, 1980, Charlie Chan and the Curse of the Dragon Queen, 1981, Visiting Hours, 1982; TV appearances include Peyton Place (Emmy award for best supporting actress 1966), Neon Ceiling, Ransom for a Dead Man, Robert Young and Family; guest star: Lieutenant Shuster's Wife, 1972, Partners in Crime, 1973; dir.: TV spl. Shape of Things, 1973; appeared in: TV series Fay, 1975; dir.: play Private View, 1983. Address: care William Morris Agy 151 El Camino Beverly Hills CA 90212 *The prescription for success is the same as for failure. When one is conflicted between fear and desire, choose desire.* *

GRANT, LEONARD TYDINGS, college president; b. Lakewood, N.J., May 8, 1930; s. Allaire Harrison and Edith Dorothy (MacEntee) G.; m. Nancy Elisabeth MacKerell, June 21, 1958; children: Scott Alexander, Elisabeth Tydings, Constance Allaire. B.A., Rutgers U., 1952; B.D., Princeton Theol. Sem., 1955; S.T.M., Temple U., 1958; Ph.D., U. Edinburgh, 1961. Ordained to ministry Presbyn. Ch. U.S.A., 1955; pastor 4th Presbyn. Ch., Camden, N.J., 1955-58, Meml. Presbyn. Ch., Wenonah, N.J., 1961-65; instr. Rutgers U., 1956-58; lectr. Conwell Sch. Theology, Phila., 1961-65; prof. history Ind. Central U., 1965-76, dean grad. studies, acad. dean, 1966-76; pres. Elmira (N.Y.) Coll., 1976—; trustee Elmira Savs. Bank; pres. Ind. Coll. Fund of N.Y. Author: Prayers and Devotions of Richard Baxter, 1965; Contbr. articles to jours. Bd. dirs. Arnot-Ogden Hosp., Council Ind. Colls. and Univs. of N.Y.; mem. council Boy Scouts Am. Mem. Am. Soc. Ch. History, Internat. Assn. Univ. Presidents, Alpha Sigma Lambda, Phi Alpha Theta, Phi Delta Kappa. Clubs: Rotary, Torch. Office: Elmira Coll Park Pl Elmira NY 14901

GRANT, MERRILL THEODORE, TV producer; b. N.Y.C., July 9, 1932; s. Samuel and Rae (Renko) G.; m. Barbara Rosner, May 24, 1961; children: Andrea, Jonathan Samuel. B.B.A., CCNY, 1953; M.S., Columbia U., 1954. Vice pres., dir. programming Benton & Bowles, 1957-70; sr. v.p., dir. radio and TV, Grey Advt., N.Y.C., 1970-72; v.p. Viacom Internat., N.Y.C., 1972-74; pres. Don Kirshner Prodns., N.Y.C., 1974-78, Grant Case McGrath, 1978-79, Grant-Reeves Entertainment, N.Y.C., 1979—. Served with AUS, 1954-56. Home: 6 Cayuga Rd Scarsdale NY 10583 Office: 605 Third Ave New York NY 10158

GRANT, MICHAEL PETER, electrical engineer; b. Oshkosh, Wis., Feb. 26, 1936; s. Robert J. and Ione (Michelson) G.; m. Mary Susan Corcoran, Sept. 2, 1961; children: James, Steven, Laura. B.S., Purdue U., 1957, M.S., 1958, Ph.D., 1964. With Westinghouse Research Labs., Pitts., summers 1953-57; mem. tech. staff Aerospace Corp., El Segundo, Calif., 1961; instr. elec. engring. Purdue U., 1958-64; sr. engr. Indsl. Nucleonics Corp., Columbus, Ohio, 1964-67, mgr. advanced devel. and control systems, 1967-72, mgr. control and info. scis. div., 1972-74, asst. gen. mgr. indsl. systems div., 1974-76, mgr. system design, 1976—. Contbr. articles to profl. jours.; patentee in field of automation. Mem. IEEE, Sigma Xi, Eta Kappa Nu, Pi Mu Epsilon, Tau Beta Pi. Home: 4461 Sussex Dr Columbus OH 43220 Office: AccuRay Corp 650 Ackerman Rd Columbus OH 43202

GRANT, MURRAY, physician, govt. ofcl.; b. London, Eng., June 24, 1926; s. Abrahm and Jenny (Harbour) G.; m. Trudy Shein, Nov. 25, 1951; children—Bradley, Schuyler, Stephanie, Darryl, Valerie. Student, U. London, 1944-46; M.D., St. George's Hosp. Med. Sch., U. London, 1949; D.P.H., U. Toronto, 1950. Intern Toronto East Gen. Hosp., 1949; asst. health officer Balt. Co. Health Dept., Towson, Md., 1950-51; commr. health Cattaraugus Co. Health Dept., Olean, N.Y., 1951-55; dir. health Clay Co. Health Dept., Liberty, Mo., 1955-57; asst. health officer Prince George Co. Health Dept., Cheverly, Md., 1957-59, health officer, 1959-62; dir. pub. health D.C. Dept. Pub. Health, 1962-69; exec. v.p. Miamonides Med. Center, 1969-71; asst. dir. Touro Infirmary, 1971-73; chief med. advisor U.S. GAO, Washington, 1973—; clin. prof. George Washington U., Georgetown U., Howard U. Author: Handbook on Preventive Medicine and Public Health; Contbr. articles profl. jours. Fellow Am. Pub. Health Assn.; mem. D.C. Med. Soc., Assn. State and Territorial Health Officers, U.S. Conf. City Health Officers, Am. Assn. Pub. Health Physicians, Met. Health Officers Assn. (pres. 1964-66). Address: 6200 Starwood Way Rockville MD 20852

GRANT, NICHOLAS JOHN, metallurgy educator; b. South River, N.J., Oct. 21, 1915; s. John and Mary (Sudnik) G.; m. Anne T. Phillips, Sept. 12, 1942 (dec. Apr. 1957); children—Anne P., William D., Nicholas P.; m. Susan Mary Cooper, Aug. 1963; children—Johnathan, Katharine. S.B., Carnegie Inst. Tech., 1938; Sc.D., MIT, 1944. Metallurgist Bethlehem Steel Co., 1938-40; mem. faculty Mass. Inst. Tech., 1942—, prof. metallurgy, 1955—; dir. Center Materials Sci. and Engring., 1968-77, ABEX prof. advanced materials, 1975—; pres., dir. N.E. Materials Lab., Inc., 1954-66; tech. dir. Investment Castings Inst., 1954—; cons. industry, 1947—; Dir. Loomis-Sayles Mut. Fund, Capital Devel. Fund, Interpace Corp., Kimball Physics Corp., Inc., Instron Corp., Indsl. Materials Tech., Inc., Electronic Instrument & Splty. Corp.; mem. materials com. NASA, 1958-67, research com., 1970-76; chmn. working group electrometallurgy and materials U.S.-USSR Joint Sci. and Tech. Agreement. Contbr. articles profl. jours., chpts. in books. Recipient distinguished service award Investment Castings Inst., 1956; Merit award Carnegie Mellon U.; J. Wallenberg award Royal Acad. Engring. Scis., Sweden, 1978. Fellow Am. Soc. Metals, Am. Inst. Mining, Metall. and Petroluem Engrs.; mem. Nat. Acad. Engring., Inst. Metals (London), ASTM, Am. Acad. Arts and Scis., Sigma Xi, Tau Beta Pi, Theta Tau, Alpha Xi Epsilon. Home: 10 Leslie Rd Winchester MA 01890 Office: Massachusetts Inst Technology Cambridge MA 02139

GRANT, PERRY JAMES, television writer, producer; b. San Diego, Jan. 26, 1924; s. Perry Morris and Mary Hannah (Ericson) G.; m. Edith Barbara Walter, July 14, 1946; children—Cheryl Lynn, Richard Craig. B.A., UCLA, 1946. Staff writer: Ozzie and Harriet television show, 1953-67; television writer: numerous shows including One Day at a Time; producer, 1976-77; exec. producer, 1977—. Served as officer USNR, 1942-45. Recipient Christopher award, 1956. Mem. Writers Guild Am. West, Am. Acad. TV Arts and Scis. Republican. Roman Catholic. Club: Riviera Tennis. Inventor of 26 children's games, 1960-83. Office: 100 Universal City Plaza University City CA 91608

GRANT, ROBERT ALLEN, judge; b. Marshall County, Ind., July 31, 1905; s. Everett F. and Margaret E. (Hatfield) G.; m. Margaret Anne McLaren, Sept. 17, 1933; children—Robert A., Margaret Ann. A.B., U. Notre Dame, 1928, J.D., 1930. Bar: Ind. bar 1930, U.S. Supreme Ct. bar 1940. Practiced in, South Bend, Ind., dep. pros. atty., St. Joseph County, 1935-36; mem. 76th-80th congresses from 3d Ind. Dist.; U.S. dist. judge No. Dist. Ind., 1957—, chief judge, 1961-72, sr. judge, 1972—; apptd. to Temp. Emergency Ct. Appeals U.S., 1976. Trustee Ind. Central U., 1976—; mem. nat. council representing No. Indian, Boy Scouts Am., 1967. Mem. Am., Ind. bar assns. SAR. Republican. Methodist. Clubs: Mason (33 deg., K.T., Shriner), Rotarian, Elk, Eagle; Order DeMolay (internat. supreme council, past grand master), Columbia (Indpls.); Summit (South Bend); Union Leaque (Chgo.). Home: 98 Schellinger Sq Mishawaka IN 46544 Office: Federal Bldg South Bend IN 46601

GRANT, ROBERT WALLACE, assn. exec.; b. Washington, Mar. 10, 1936; s. William Eskew and Virginia (O'Hara) G.; m. Wanda Smith, July 21, 1962; children—Robert Wallace, William, Susan. B.S. in Botany, U. Md., 1957, postgrad., 1957-60. Capt. College Park (Md.) Fire Dept., 1960; fire marshal, Guilford County, N.C., 1961-67; fire service specialist Nat. Fire Protection Assn., Boston, 1967-70, asst. gen. mgr., 1970-72, v.p., 1972-78, exec. v.p., 1978-80, pres., 1980—; chmn. Internat. Conf. Fire Protection Assns., 1980—; dir. Kirby Lithographic Co., Washington, 1980—. Author: Public Fire Safety Inspections, 1967, Handbook of Civil War Patriotic Envelopes and Post History, 1976, The George Walcott Collection of Used Civil War Patriotic Covers, 1975; contbr. articles to profl. jours. Sec.-treas. Joint Council of Nat. Fire Service Orgns., 1970-79; mem. nominating com. Fed. Awards Program, Govt. Employees Ins. Co., 1980—. Mem. Fire Marshals Assn. of N.Am. (exec. sec. 1967-74), Cardinal Spellman Philatelic Library, Am. Soc. Assn. Execs., Internat. Assn. Fire Chiefs, Am. Nat. Standards Inst., Futurists Soc., Am. Philatelic Soc., Soc. Philatelic Writers, Assn. History of Printing. Office: Batterymarch Park Quincy MA 02269

GRANT, ROBERT YEARINGTON, former govt. ofcl.; b. Seattle, 1913; s. Charles Ernst and Amy Jane (Mahon) G.; m. Eleanor May Lewis, May 24, 1941. B.S., U. Wash., 1938, postgrad., 1939-40. Chief geologist Cornucopia Gold Mines, Oreg., 1940-41; chief mining and geology div. Gen. Hdqrs. Supreme Comdr. Allied Powers, Japan, 1946-51; asst. dir. for industry Mut. Security Agy., Dept. State, Taiwan, 1952-58; industry-transp. officer Fgn. Operations Adminstrn., Indonesia, 1958-62; industry officer AID, Ceylon-Guatemala, 1962-63, dep. provincial dir., Dacca, East Pakistan, 1964-68, spl. asst. to dir., Islamabad, Pakistan, 1968-70, asst. dir. population and health, Islamabad, 1970-73; chief Asia/Near East-N. Africa div. Office Population, AID, Washington, 1974-76, asst. dir. field services, 1976-77, ret.; cons. population/family planning Am. Pub. Health Assn., Egypt, Bangladesh, Thailand, Indonesia and Nepal, 1978-80. Contbr. articles profl. jours. Served from lt. to lt. col. AUS, 1941-45. Recipient Dept. Army commendation for meritorious civilian service, 1951, Dept. State Meritorious Honor award, 1971, 73, Superior Honor award, 1977. Fellow Geol. Soc. Am., AAAS; mem. Am. Geophys. Union, Am. Geol. Inst., Am. Pub. Health Assn., World Population Soc., Diplomatic and Consular Officers Ret. Club: Wash. Athletic (Seattle). Home: PO Box H Greenbank WA 98253

GRANT, STANLEY CAMERON, geologist; b. Cedar Rapids, Iowa, Apr. 21, 1931; s. Hobart McKinley and Elizabeth (Cameron) G.; children: Laura Lynn, Stuart Cameron, Douglas Stevens. Student, Cornell Coll., Iowa, 1949-51; B.A., Coe Coll., 1953; M.A., U. Wyo., 1954; Ph.D., U. Idaho, 1971. Petroleum geologist Calif. Co., Casper, Wyo., 1955; chief geologist Gas Hills Uranium, Am. Nuclear, Riverton, Wyo., 1955-56; prof. geology U. No. Iowa, Cedar Falls, 1970-75; state geologist, dir. Iowa Geol. Survey, Iowa City, 1975-80; v.p. for ops. Bishop Oil & Refining Co., 1980-81; partner Geo-Horizons Unltd., 1981—; cons. oil and gas mgmt. Served to maj. USAF, 1956-69. Danforth fellow, 1953-71. Fellow Iowa Acad. Sci.; mem. Am. Inst. Mining, Metall. and Petroleum Engrs., Geol. Soc. Am., Am. Inst. Profl. Geologists, Am. Assn. Petroleum Geologists, Sigma Xi. Episcopalian. Club: Rotary. Office: 220 Overlook Rd Elizabeth CO 80107 *I have tried to pattern my life to serve humankind and to contribute to the quality of our environment. To paraphrase Stephen Grillet sums it up best for me. Any good that I can do, any service I can perform, any kindness that I can show to any human being, let me do it now, for I shall not pass this way again.*

GRANT, THOM, advertising agency executive; b. Englewood, N.J., July 29, 1936; s. Thomas and Lucia Guerra (Sacchi) Gramaglia; m. Susan Middleton, July 29, 1978; children—John Christopher, Nicholas Middleton. B.A. in English, Wagner Coll., 1958; postgrad., N.Y. U., 1958. With CIA, Washington, 1958-59; sports editor Union (N.J.) Register, 1959; dir. pub. relations Luther Coll., Wahoo, Nebr., 1960-61; editor Bus. Automation mag., N.Y.C., 1961-62; pub. relations account exec. Ellington & Co., N.Y.C., 1962-63; advt. account exec. West, Weir & Bartel, N.Y.C., 1963-65; gen. mgr. Cadwell Davis Co., N.Y.C., 1965-67; v.p., account supr. McCann-Erickson, Inc., N.Y.C., 1967-76, sr. v.p., mgmt. supr., 1976-79, exec. v.p., gen. mgr., Los Angeles, 1979—; dir. McCann-Erickson U.S.A. Contbr. data processing articles to profl. jours. Mem. Bank Mktg. Assn., Am. Soc. Travel Agts., Western States Advt. Agys. (dir.), Western States Tourism Assn. Club: Bel Air Country (Los Angeles). Home: 3658 Mandeville Canyon Rd Los Angeles CA 90049 Office: McCann-Erickson Inc 6420 Wilshire Blvd Los Angeles CA 90048

GRANT, VERNE EDWIN, biology educator; b. San Francisco, Oct. 17, 1917; S. Edwin and Bessie (Swallow) G.; m. Alva Day, June 12, 1946 (div. Aug. 1959); children: Joyce Grant Mixon, Brian, Brenda Grant Aley; m. Karen Alt, Nov. 3, 1960. A.B., U. Calif.-Berkeley, 1940, Ph.D., 1949. Teaching asst. botany U. Calif.-Berkeley, 1946-49; NRC fellow Carnegie Inst., Stanford, Calif., 1949-50; geneticist Rancho Santa Ana Bot. Garden, Claremont, Calif., 1950-67; asst. prof. Claremont Grad. Sch., 1951-53, asso. prof., 1953-57, prof., 1957-67; prof. biology Inst. Life Sci., Tex. A&M U., College Station, 1967-68; prof., dir. Boyce Thompson Southwestern Arboretum, U. Ariz.-Superior, 1968-70; prof. botany U. Tex.-Austin, 1970—. Author: Natural History of the Phlox Family, 1959, The Origin of Adaptations, 1963, The Architecture of the Germplasm, 1964, (with Karen Grant) Flower Pollination in the Phlox Family, 1965, Hummingbirds and Their Flowers, 1968, Plant Speciation, 1971, 2d edit., 1981, Genetics of Flowering Plants, 1975, Organismic Evolution, 1977; editorial bd.: Ency. Americana, 1955-64, Brittonia, 1957-62, Evolution, 1960-62, Am. Naturalist, 1964-67, Biologisches Zentralblatt, 1974—; contbr. numerous articles to profl. jours. Recipient Sci. award Phi Beta Kappa, 1964. Fellow Am. Acad. Arts and Scis.; mem. Nat. Acad. Scis., Am. Soc. Naturalists, Soc. for Study of Evolution (pres. 1968), Bot. Soc. Am. (cert. of merit 1971), Internat. Soc. Plant Taxonomists, Am. Soc. Plant Taxonomists, Southwestern Assn. Naturalists, Soc. Systematic Zoology. Home: 2811 Fresco St Austin TX 78731 Office: Dept Botany U Tex Austin TX 78712

GRANT, WILLIAM, lawyer; b. Estes Park, Colo., Aug. 29, 1910; s. William West and Gertrude (Hendrie) G.; m. Katherine Mullen O'Connor, 1931 (div. 1934); m. Helen Prindle, June 6, 1938; children—William West, Melanie, Mary Grant Smith, Gertrude, Charles Hendrie. A.B. magna cum laude, Dartmouth Coll., 1931; LL.B. cum laude, Harvard U., 1938. Bar: Colo. bar. Partner Boettcher-Newton & Co. (stockbrokers), N.Y.C., 1933-34; mem. N.Y. Stock Exchange, 1934-35; mem. firm Grant, Shafroth, Toll & McHendrie, Denver, 1940-75; firm Grant, McHendrie, Haines & Crouse, Denver, 1975—; pres. Met. TV Co. (KOA radio-TV), 1952-63, chmn. bd., 1963-68; pres. Sangre de Cristo Broadcasting Co. (KOAA-TV and KCSJ radio), Pueblo, 1968-73; dir. Colo. Nat. Bank, Hendrie Investment Co., Denver. Chmn. Democratic State Central Com., 1965-69; Bd. dirs. Kaiser Found. Health and Hosp. Plans, 1971-80. Served from lt. (j.g.) to lt. comdr. USNR, 1942-46. Decorated Bronze Star. Mem. Casque and Gauntlet, Phi Beta Kappa, Psi Upsilon. Clubs: Denver, Denver Country. Home: 101 S Humboldt St Denver CO 80209 Office: 1700 Western Fed Bldg Denver CO 80202

GRANT, WILLIAM DOWNING, insurance executive; b. Kansas City, Mo., Feb. 10, 1917; s. William Thomas and Frances (Downing) G.; m. Mary Noel, June 24, 1941; children: Laura Noel Grant Myers, William Thomas II. A.B., U. Kans., 1939; grad., Wharton Sch. Fin., U. Pa., 1940. C.L.U. With Bus. Men's Assurance Co., Kansas City, Mo., 1941—, v.p. charge reins., 1951-56, exec. v.p., 1956-60, pres., chief exec. officer, 1960-69, chmn. bd., chief exec. officer, 1969—; dir. Union Pacific Corp., 1st Nat. Bank, Kansas City Power & Light Co.; mem. Lloyd's of London; past chmn. Am. Life Conv. Mem. U.S. Pres.'s Commn. on Fin. Structure, 1970-71; Past pres., past chmn. bd. Kansas City Area council Scouts Am.; gen. chmn. Kansas City United Campaign, 1964; past nat. trustee, past bd. dirs. Am. Field Service; bd. govs. Nelson Gallery; mem. exec. com. Am. Council Life Ins.; past chmn. bd. trustees Conservatory Music of U. Mo. at Kansas City; past trustee U. Kansas City. Served as lt. comdr., naval aviator USNR, World War II. Mem. Am. Coll. Life Underwriters (past vice chmn. bd. trustees, mem. exec. com.). Clubs: Kansas City Country, River, Links (N.Y.C.). Office: BMA Tower Kansas City MO 64141

GRANT, WILLIAM FREDERICK, geneticist, educator; b. Hamilton, Ont., Can., Oct. 20, 1924; s. William Aitken and Myrtle Irene (Taylor) G.; m. Phyllis Kemp Harshaw, July 23, 1949; 1 son, William Taylor. B.A., McMaster U., Hamilton, 1947, M.A., 1949; Ph.D., U. Va., Charlottesville, 1953. Botanist, geneticist under Colombo Plan to Dept. Agr., Malaysia, 1953-55; asst. prof. McGill U., Montreal, Que., 1955-61, asso. prof., 1961-66, prof. depts. plant sci. and biology, 1967—, in charge genetics lab.; cons. Internat. Register of Potentially Toxic Chems. of UN Environ. Program; environ. contaminants adv. com. Ministers of Environ. and Nat. Health and Welfare, Ottawa, Ont. Editor: Lotus Newsletter, 1970—, Can. Jour. Genetics and Cytology, 1974-82; mem. editorial bd.: Mutation Research, 1978—. Recipient Andrew Fleming award, 1953, Gov. Gen. Silver medal commemorating 25th Ann. of Accession of H.M. Queen Elizabeth to Throne, 1977; Blandy research fellow, 1950-53. Fellow AAAS, Linnean Soc. London; mem. Internat. Orgn. Plant Biosystematists (pres. 1981—), Genetics Soc. Can. (pres. 1975, life), Genetics Soc. Am., Environ. Mutagen Soc., Am. Soc. Naturalists, Can. Bot. Assn., Am. Soc. Plant Taxonomists, Soc. for Study Evolution (v.p. 1972), Biol. Council Can. (treas. 1974-78), Sigma Xi (chpt. pres. 1975). Home: 43 St Andrews Rd Baie d'Urfe PQ H9X 2T9 Canada Office: Genetics Lab Box 282 McGill U Macdonald Campus Ste Anne de Bellevue PQ H9X 1C0 Canada

GRANT, WILLIAM ROBERT, investment counselor; b. N.Y.C., Jan. 9, 1925; s. William Vincent and Adelaide (Marshall) G.; m. Dorothy Annetta Corbin, June 29, 1951; children: Deborah, Byron, Gregory, Melissa, Elise. B.S. in Chemistry, Union Coll., Schenectady, 1949. Trainee Gen. Electric Co., 1949-50; with Smith, Barney, Harris Upham & Co., Inc., 1950-77, vice chmn., 1976-77; also dir.; vice chmn. Endowment Mgmt. Corp., 1977-78; chmn. MacKay Shields Co., 1979—; dir. Witco Chem. Co., Fluor Corp., Smith Kline Beckman Corp.; mem. N.Y. State Banking Bd. Trustee Union Coll., Elfun Trust, Conf. Bd., Econ. Forum, N.Y. Bot. Garden, Fin. Analysts Research Found. Mem. Fin. Analysts Fedn., Nat. Assn. Bus. Economists, Delta Upsilon. Roman Catholic. Clubs: University, Madison Square Garden, Knickerbocker (N.Y.C.); Nat. Golf, Creek, Maidstone (L.I.); Links (N.Y.C.). Home: M R 25 Oyster Bay NY 11771 Office: 551 Fifth Ave New York NY 10176

GRANT, WILLIAM WEST, III, banker; b. N.Y.C., May 9, 1932; s. William West and Katherine O'Connor (Neelands) G.; m. Rhondda Lowery, Dec. 3, 1955. B.A., Yale U., 1954; postgrad., Columbia U. Grad. Sch. Bus., 1968, Harvard U. Grad. Sch. Bus., 1971, N.Y. U. Grad. Sch. Bus., 1958. With Bankers Trust Co., N.Y.C., 1954-58, br. credit adminstr., 1957-58; with Colo. Nat. Bank, Denver, 1958—, pres., 1975—; dir. Midlands Energy Co. Trustee Denver Mus. Natural History; trustee Gates Found. Denver, Presbyn. St. Luke's Med. Center, Denver, Midwest Research Inst., Kansas City. Mem. Assn. Res. City Bankers, Colo. Bankers Assn. Episcopalian. Clubs: Denver Country, Denver. Office: Colo Nat Bank 17th and Champa St Denver CO 80202

GRANTHAM, DEWEY WESLEY, historian, educator; b. Manassas, Ga., Mar. 16, 1921; s. Dewey W. and Ellen (Holl) G.; m. Virginia Burleson, Dec. 26, 1942; children: Wesley, Clinton, Lauren. B.A., U. Ga., 1942; M.A., U. N.C., 1947, Ph.D., 1949. Asst. prof. history North Tex. State Coll., 1949-50; asst. prof. history Womans Coll., U. N.C., 1950-52, Vanderbilt U., Nashville, 1952-55, assoc. prof., 1955-61, prof., 1961—, Harvie Branscomb Disting. prof., 1971-72, Holland N. McTyeire prof. history, 1977—; dir. Nat. Endowment Humanities Seminar Tchrs., summer 1975, 1976-77; vis. prof. Coe Inst. SUNY, Stony Brook, summer 1970. Author: Hoke Smith and the Politics of the New South, 1958, The Democratic South, 1963, Contemporary American History: The United States since 1945, 1975, The United States since 1945: The Ordeal of Power, 1976, The Regional Imagination: The South and Recent American History, 1979, Southern Progressivism: The Reconciliation of Progress and Tradition, 1983; Editor: Following the Color Line: American Negro Citizenship in the Progressive Era, 1964, The South and the Sectional Image: The Sectional Theme since Reconstruction, 1967, Theodore Roosevelt, 1970, The Political Status of the Negro in the Age of FDR, 1973; gen. editor: Twentieth-Century America series, 1975—. Chmn. regional selection com. Woodrow Wilson Nat. Fellowship Program, 1957-59; mem. advanced placement exam com. in Am. history Coll. Entrance Exam. Bd., 1966-67. Served with USCG, 1942-46. Recipient Sydnor award for best book in So. history, 1959; Ford Found. fellow, 1955-56; Social Sci. Research Council faculty fellow, 1959; John Simon Guggenheim Meml. fellow, 1960; Huntington Library research fellow, 1968-69; Fulbright-Hays vis. lectr. U. Provence, 1978-79; Nat. Humanities Ctr. fellow, 1982-83. Mem. Am. Hist. Assn. (council 1969-71, bd. editors 1975-77, chmn. com. on program 1977), Orgn. Am. Historians (exec. bd. 1965-68, chmn. com. on program 1973), Am. Studies Assn., AAUP, So. Hist. Assn. (exec. council 1960-62, chmn. com. on program 1959, pres. 1966), Phi Beta Kappa. Democrat. Unitarian. Home: 3510 Echo Hill Rd Nashville TN 37215 Office: Dept History Vanderbilt U Nashville TN 37235

GRANTHAM, GEORGE LEIGHTON, lawyer, banker, utility co. exec.; b. Robeson County, N.C., Nov. 24, 1920; s. George Leighton and Mary Belle (Ricks) G.; m. Dorothy Folger Hagood, June 20, 1942; children—George Leighton, III, Dorothy Grantham Reid, James H. B.S., Davidson Coll., 1941; J.D. with honors, U. N.C., 1948. Bar: S.C. Supreme Ct. bar 1948, U.S. Supreme Ct. bar 1960. Pvt. practice law, 1948—; chief exec. officer Ft. Hill Natural Gas Authority, Easley, S.C., 1952—; pres., chmn. bd. First Nat. Bank, Easley, 1955—. Trustee Thornwell Home for Children, Clinton, S.C.; mem. S.C. Senate, 1951-55. Served with USNR, 1942-46. Fellow Am. Bar Found.; mem. Pickens County (S.C.) Bar Assn. (pres. 1974-76), S.C. Bar Assn., Am. Bar Assn (ho. of dels. 1965-70), Am. Law Inst., Am. Judicature Soc., S.C. Bankers Assn. (pres. 1978-79, dir. 1976—). Democrat. Presbyterian. Clubs: Poinsett (Greenville, S.C.); Palmetto (Columbia, S.C.); Carolina Yacht (Charleston, S.C.). Home: 417 N Bee St Easley SC 29640 Office: W First Ave Easley SC 29640

GRANTHAM, RICHARD ROBERT, trust company executive; b. Ogden, Utah, July 25, 1927; s. Arthur and Dorothy (Taylor) G.; m. Charlotte Blackwood, Aug. 10, 1951; children: Robert Arthur, Scott Ford, Ann Margaret, Susan Marie. B.S. magna cum laude, Claremont Men's Coll., 1950. C.P.A., Calif. Acct., Price Waterhouse & Co., Los Angeles, 1950-57; asst. controller Cyprus Mines Corp., Los Angeles, 1957-64, div. controller, 1964-65, budget dir., 1965-72, v.p., treas., 1972-74, sr. v.p., treas., 1975-79, sr. v.p., controller, 1979-81; controller Amoco Minerals Co., 1980-81; with Trust Co. of the West, Los Angeles, 1982—; Lectr. in field. Trustee Claremont Men's Coll., 1965-68, 74—, vice chmn., 1976—. Served with USNR, 1945-46. Mem. San Marino Men's Republic Club (pres. 1967), Calif. Soc. C.P.A.s, Am. Inst. C.P.A.s, Claremont Men's Coll. Alumni Assn. (pres. 1956), Republican Assos., Fin. Execs. Inst. Clubs: California, Alamitos Bay Yacht. Home: 1660 Oak Grove Ave San Marino CA 91108 Office: 800 W 6th St Los Angeles CA 90017

GRANVILLE, ELIZABETH ELSTER, lawyer, performing rights licensing organization executive; b. N.Y.C.; d. David Aaron and Jeanne (Flichtenfeld) Elster; m. Irwin Earle Granville; children: Alexandra Madeleine, Claudia Louise. A.B., Adelphi U., 1961; LL.B., NYU, 1964. Bar: N.Y., U.S. Supreme Ct. Atty.-in-charge Juvenile Rights div. Legal Aid Soc. Bronx County; atty. Broadcast Music, Inc., N.Y.C., exec. dir. public adminstrn., asst. v.p. publisher relations; guest lectr. Cardozo Sch. Law, New Sch. for Social Research, N.Y. Law Sch.; bd. dirs. Com. on Modern Cts., Inc., MFY Legal Services, Inc. Mem. Citizens Com. for Children; nat. commr. Juvenile Justice Standards Project; mem. standards and goals adv. panel State N.Y. Div. Criminal Justice Services; mem. adv. com. on internat. intellectual property Dept. State; mem. adv. bd. N.Y. U. Sch. Edn., Health, Nursing and Arts Professions. Woodrow Wilson fellow. Mem. Am. Law Inst., Practising Law Inst. (panelist), Am. Bar Assn. (forum com. on entertainment industries of music, motion picture, TV and radio, chmn. subcom. on legislation), N.Y. State Bar Assn. (ho. of dels. 1977—), Assn. Bar City N.Y. (chmn. com. on family ct. and family law, chmn. com. copyright and lit. property, com. profl. responsibility, com. child abuse and delinquent children, nominating com. of exec. com., com. immigration and nationality law, mem. judiciary com., com. on communications law), New York County Lawyers Assn. (chmn. com. on communications and entertainment law), Confedn. Internationale des Sociétés d'Auteurs et Compositeurs (juridical and legis. com.), Internationale Gesellschaft für Urheberrecht, Phi Beta Kappa. Jewish. Home: 320 W 76 St New York NY 10023 Office: 320 W 57 St New York NY 10019

GRANZ, NORMAN, record producer; b. Los Angeles, Aug. 6, 1918. Student, UCLA. Former film editor, MGM Studios; began series of jazz concerts at, Music Town, Los Angeles, and at Los Angeles Philharmonic Auditorium, 1944; supervised: short film Jammin' The Blues; produced own records, released them on, Philo and Asch labels 1944-45, on Mercury, 1948-51; and then on own labels Clef, 1951-57, Norgran, 1954-57, Verve, 1957-61, Pablo, 1973—; concert promoter in, U.S., Europe, Japan, Australia, including tours by, Jazz at Philharmonic, Ray Charles, Count Basie, Duke Ellington, Ella Fitzgerald, Oscar Peterson. Served with U.S. Army, 1941-44. First took group of musicians on tour of western states and Can. under banner of Jazz at the Philharmonic, 1945. Office: care Pablo Records 451 N Canon Dr Beverly Hills CA 90210 *

GRASS, ALEXANDER, retail company executive; b. Scranton, Pa., Aug. 3, 1927; s. Louis and Rose (Breman) G.; m. Lois Lehrman, July 30, 1950; children: Linda Jane, Martin L., Roger L., Elizabeth Ann; m. Louise B. Gurkoff, Apr. 26, 1974. LL.B., U. Fla., 1949. Bar: Fla. 1949, Pa. 1953. Individual practice law, Miami Beach, Fla., 1949-51; v.p. Rite Aid Corp., Shiremanstown, Pa., 1952-66, pres., 1966-69, 77—, chmn., chief exec. officer, 1969—; dir. Hasbro Industries. Mem. nat. exec. com. United Jewish Appeal, 1968, Nat. vice chmn., 1970-79, gen. chmn., 1984; pres. Harrisburg (Pa.) Jewish Fedn., 1970-72; chmn. Israel Edn. Fund, 1975—; bd. dirs. Pa. Right to Work Found., 1972-74, Harrisburg Hosp., 1977—; Mem. Pa. Council Arts, 1982; Bd. dirs. Keystone State Games, 1982; Trustee Friends of Jerusalem, 1983; Bd. govs. Friends of Israel Center Social and Econ. Studies, 1983. Served with USNR, 1945-46. Mem. Nat. Am. Wholesale Grocers Assn. (dir. 1971-73), Nat. Assn. Chain Drug Stores (dir. 1972—). Jewish (dir. temple). Home: 4025 Crooked Hill Rd Harrisburg PA 17110 Office: Trindle Rd and Railroad Ave Shiremanstown PA 17013

GRASSHOF, ALEX, writer, producer, director. Writer, producer, dir.: TV series Rockford Files, CHiPs, Nightstalker. Recipient Acad. award nomination for Really Big Family, 1966, Acad. award nomination for Journey to the Outer Limits, 1974, Acad. award for documentary Young Americans, 1968, Emmy award for Journey to the Outer Limits, 1974, Emmy award for The Wave, 1982. Office: Talent Mgmt Internat Los Angeles CA 90048 *

GRASSI, JOSEPH GERALD, philosophy educator; b. Rochester, N.Y., July 16, 1919; s. Andrew and Phyllis (DeFelice) G. A.B., St. Bernard's Coll., Rochester, 1942; M.A., Cath. U. Am., 1949; postgrad. (Italian Govt. fellow), U. Florence, Italy, 1953-55; Ph.D., U. Buffalo, 1960. Lectr. Howard U., 1947; instr. La Salle Coll., Phila., 1948-53; asst. prof. Rochester Inst. Tech., 1955-61; prof. Fairfield (Conn.) U., 1961—; also chmn. philosophy dept., dir. Humanities Summer Inst. Author: The Political Philosophy of B. Croce, 1960, The Need for Dissent, 1969, Toward a Philosophy of Credit, 1970, Croce's Attitude toward Present Day Political Ideologies, 1971, (with King J. Dyheman) A Critique of a Symposium on Benedetto Croce, 1972, Science, Technology and Man in the Philosophy of Spirit, 1973, International Unity and Religion, 1974, Moral Vacuum, 1975, The Philosophy and Problem of Peaceful Coexistence, 1976, The Moral Ramifications of Global Population Problems, 1975, Social Progress: Its Problems and Necessity, 1976, The Continuing Revolution: A Call for a Humanistic Society, 1979, Can the Scientific-Technological Revolution Be Humanized?, 1979, The Social, Political and Moral Goals of a Humanistic Society, 1979, Can a Morality System Be Justified?, 1980, Is Gun Control Legislation a Solution for Protecting Victims?, 1981, What's Wrong with Intercollegiate Sports, 1982, The Role of Labor in Our Day, 1983. Served with USNR, 1941-43. Mem. Am. Philos. Assn., Metaphys. Soc. Am., Phenomenological and Existential Soc., Soc. for Advancement Am. Philosophy (exec. sec.). Home: 167 Ruane St Fairfield CT 06430

GRASSIE, JOSEPH ROBERTS, real estate developer; b. Buenos Aires, Argentina, Oct. 3, 1933; s. Joseph Flagg and Vida Clarissa (Roberts) G.; m. Josette Krespi, Mar. 23, 1958; children: Yvonne Gail, Scott Roberts. Student, U. Chgo., 1953-54, 57-58, B.A. in Polit. Sci., 1958, M.A., 1960. Mgmt. cons. state and local govt. Pub. Adminstrn. Service, Chgo., 1959-64; chief tech. assistance group AID, State Dept., 1965-68; dep. mgr., City of Grand Rapids, Mich., 1968-70, city mgr., City of Grand Rapids, 1970-76, City of Miami, Fla., 1976-80; pres. Gamma Investments, Miami, Fla., 1981, Worsham Bros. Co., Inc., 1981—. Mem. univ. adv. bd. Western Mich. U., Ferris State Coll., Grand Valley State Coll., U. Miami; trustee Grand Valley Found., Public Adminstrn. Service, Govtl. Affairs Inst. Served with USMCR, 1955-56. Mem. Internat. City Mgmt. Assn., Am. Soc. Pub. Adminstrn. Home: 2880 SW 33d Ct Miami FL 33133 Office: 100 N Biscayne Blvd Miami Beach FL 33132

GRASSL, THEODORE PETER, newspaper exec.; b. Stratford, Wis., Nov. 12, 1931; s. Ferdinand V. and Rebecca M. (Fandre) G.; m. Marlene Joan Palmer, Aug. 25, 1962; 1 dau., Melody Karen. B.B.A., U. Wis., Madison, 1959. Advt. and sales promotion acctg. supr., sr. computer analyst, acctg. and control mgr. Comml. Devel. (div. Pillsbury Co.), Mpls., 1959-67; systems supr. Control Data Corp., Mpls., 1967-69; bus. systems mgr., EDP mgr., dir. acctg. Mpls. Star & Tribune Co., 1969-75; bus. mgr., gen. mgr. Trenton Times Corp., 1975-78; gen. mgr. Los Angeles Herald Examiner, 1978—; instr. in field. Author articles in field. Bd. dirs. New Trenton Corp., 1977, George Washington council Boy Scouts Am., 1976-77, Mercer County C. of C., 1976-77; pres. Minn. chpt. Nat. Campers and Hikers Assn., 1973-75. Served with USN, 1951-55. Mem. Inst. Newspaper Controllers and Fin. Officers, Town Hall Calif., Beta Alpha Psi. Republican. Roman Catholic. Clubs: Los Angeles Athletic, Malibu (Calif.) Riding and Tennis, Lions. Home: 12401 Littler Pl Granada Hills CA 91344 Office: 1111 S Broadway Los Angeles CA 90015

GRASSLE, KAREN, actress; b. Berkeley, Calif.; d. Gene F. and Frae Ella (Berry) G.; m. J. Allen Radford, June 1982. B.A., U. Calif., Berkeley, 1964; postgrad., London Acad. Music and Dramatic Art, 1965. Appeared in: Broadway play The Gingham Dog, 1968, Butterflies are Free, 1969-70; appeared in: Cymbeline, Shakespeare in the Park, N.Y.C., 1970; appeared as Caroline in: TV series Little House on the Prairie, 1973—; appears in: TV films include Battered, 1978; appeared in: Cocaine: One Man's Poison, 1982; repertory and stock theatres throughout U.S.; Co-author (with Cynthia Sears); television screenplay Battered, 1979. Fulbright fellow, 1965; Recipient Public service award Women's Transitional Living Center, Orange County (Calif.), 1979, Pub. Service award Riverside County Coalition Against Domestic Violence, 1983, award Am. Women in Radio and TV, 1979. Mem. AFTRA, Screen Actors Guild, NOW, Writer's Guild Am., Actors Equity Assn. Office: care Francis Mgmt 328 S Beverly Dr Beverly Hills CA

GRASSLEY, CHARLES E., U.S. Senator; b. New Hartford, Iowa, Sept. 17, 1933; m. Barbara Ann Speicher; children—Lee, Wendy, Robin Lynn., Michele Marie, Jay Charles. B.A., U. No. Iowa, 1955, M.A., 1956; postgrad., U. Iowa, 1957-58. Farmer; instr. polit. sci. Drake U., 1962, Charles City Community Coll., 1967-68; mem. Iowa Ho. of Reps., 1959-75, 94th-96th Congresses from 3d Iowa Dist., U.S. Senate from Iowa, 1980—. Mem. Am. Farm Bur., Iowa Hist. Soc., Pi Gamma Mu, Kappa Delta Pi. Baptist. Clubs: Masons, Order of Eastern Star. Home: Rural Route 1 New Hartford IA 50660 Office: Senate Office Bldg Washington DC 20510

GRASSMUCK, GEORGE LUDWIG, political science educator; b. Nebraska City, Nebr., Sept. 17, 1919; s. Ralph O. and Katherine (Ballard) G.; m. Barbara Lois Lamb, Sept. 6, 1953; children: Janice Ballard Grassmuck Lilja, Karen Elizabeth, Terri Ellen Grassmuck Millson. A.B., UCLA, 1941, M.A., 1943; Ph.D., Johns Hopkins U., 1949. Instr. polit. sci. Boston U., 1949-50; vis. asst. prof. U. Cal. at Los Angeles, 1951-53; asso. prof. Am. U., Beirut, Lebanon, 1953-57, dept. chmn., 1955-57; mem. faculty U. Mich., Ann Arbor, 1957—, prof. polit. sci., 1964—, asst. v.p. internat. programs, 1967-69; Cons. internat. div. Ford Found., 1968-69. Author: Sectional Biases in Congress on Foreign Policy, 1951, Reformed Administration in Lebanon, 1964, also articles.; Editor: (with L.W. Adamec and F.H. Irwin) Afghanistan: Some New Approaches, 1969; others. Spl. cons. to Vice Pres. of U.S., 1959-61; spl. asst. internat. affairs to sec., also dir. Office of Internat. Affairs, Dept. Health, Edn. and Welfare, 1969-70; exec. asst. White House staff, 1970-72; chmn. adv. com. on accreditation and instnl. eligibility U.S. Commr. Edn., 1973-76; cons. examiner North Central Assn., Colls. and Secondary Schs., 1966-79; chmn. dedication Gerald R. Ford Library, 1981; bd. dirs., sec. Gerald R. Ford Found., 1982—; Chmn. Blue Ribbon Com. Fiscal Reform, Ann Arbor, 1967-68; dir. research Republican presdl. campaign, 1960; cons. critical issues council, Rep. Citizens Com., 1963. Served to lt. (j.g.) USNR, 1943-46. Fulbright research grantee, 1965-66; guest scholar Brookings Instn., 1975. Mem. Am. Polit. Sci. Assn., Am. Assn. Middle Eastern Studies (charter), others. Home: 2403 Geddes Ave Ann Arbor MI 48104

GRATCH, SERGE, engineer; b. Monte San Pietro, Italy, May 2, 1921; s. Isaak F. and Tatiana (Dermaner) G.; m. Rosemary Delay, June 30, 1951; children: Susan, Mary, Lucia, Karen, Elizabeth, Ann, Barbara, Amy, Ellen, Thomas Charles. B.S.Ch.E., U. Pa., 1943, M.S., 1945, Ph.D., 1950. Instr., U. Pa., 1943-45, asst. prof., 1945-50, asso. prof., 1950-51; research scientist Rohm & Haas Co., Phila., 1951-59; asso. prof. mech. engring. Northwestern U., Evanston, Ill., 1959-61; supr. processes and devices Ford Motor Co., Dearborn, Mich., 1961-62, mgr. chem. processes and devices, 1963-69, asst. dir. engring. sci., 1969-72, dir. chem. sci. lab., 1972—; mem. adv. bd. Coll. Engring. U. Iowa, 1969-73, Coll. Engring. U. Detroit, 1971—; adv. bd. dept. mech. engring. U. Pa., 1973—; chmn. air pollution research adv. com. Coord. Research Council; mem. Nat. Alcohol Fuels Commn., 1979-81. Regional editor: Internat. Jour. Fracture, 1965—; Contbr. articles to profl. jours. Mem. ASME (hon.; past v.p. research, past pres.), Nat. Acad. Engring., Am. Soc. Engring. Edn., Am. Chem. Soc., Engring. Soc. Detroit (dir.), Soc. Automotive Engrs. (chmn. lubricant rev. bd.), AAAS, Sigma Xi, Tau Beta Pi, Sigma Tau. Roman Catholic. Home: 32475 Bingham Rd Birmingham MI 48010 Office: PO Box 2053 Dearborn MI 48121

GRATTON, JEAN, clergyman; b. Hendover, Ont., Can., Dec. 4, 1924. Ordained priest Roman Catholic Ch., 1952; bishop of Mont-Laurier, Que., Can., 1978—. Address: 435 rue de la Madonne Mont-Laurier PQ Canada J9L 151 *

GRATTON, ROBERT, trust company executive; b. Montreal, Que., Can., Oct. 23, 1943; s. Bernard and Judith (Dufour) G.; m. Nicole Marcil, Aug. 27, 1966; children: Marie-Sophie, Francois, Elisabeth. LL.L., U. Montreal, Que., Can., 1966; LL.M., London Sch. Econs. and Polit. Sci., 1969; M.B.A., Harvard U., 1971. Exec. asst. Minister Edn., Que., Can., 1966-68, Credot Foncier, Montreal, Que., Can., 1971-75; exec. v.p. Credit Foncier, Montreal, Que., Can., 1975-79, pres., chief exec. officer, 1979-82; chmn., chief exec. officer Montreal Trust Co., Que., Can., 1982—; dir. societe general de financement, Montreal, Que., Can., 1980—, Marathon Realty Co. Ltd., Toronto, Ont., Can., 1982—, Pratt & Whitney Can., Longueil, Que., 1983—; A BGR Precious Metals Inc., Toronto, Ont., Can., 1983—. Bd. dirs. Can. Council Christians and Jews, Montreal, Que., 1981—, can. Indsl. Renewal Bd., Ottawa, Can., 1982—, Arthritis Soc., Montreal, Que., Can., 1982—, Conf. Bd. Can., Ottawa, Ont., 1983—. Clubs: Mt. Royal (Montreal, Que., Can); St. James's (Montreal, Que., Can.). Office: Montreal Trust Co 1 Place Ville Marie PQ Canada H3B 4A8

GRATWICK, JOHN, university center administrator, educator; b. Langley, Eng., Mar. 2, 1923; emigrated to Can., 1956, naturalized, 1973; s. Ernest Frank and Doris Hilda (Shepherd) G.; m. Dorothy Shirley Vincent, Aug., 1945 (div. 1957); children: Jane Mary, Paul Vincent; m. Gwendoline Johnston, Mar. 23, 1957; 1 son, Afrian. Cert. in Physics, London U., 1942, B.Sc., 1948. Chmn. Transp. Devel. Agy., Montreal, 1970-72; v.p. research and devel. Canadian Nat., Montreal, 1972-76, corp. v.p., 1980-82; pres. CN Marine, Montreal, 1976-80; dir. Canadian Marine Transp. Centre-Dalhousie U., Halifax, N.S., 1983—; prof. Sch. Bus. Adminstrn. Dalhousie U., Halifax, NS, 1983—; chmn. Halifax Industries Ltd., 1978—; dir. Focal Marine Ltd., Dartmouth; ptnr. J.W. Hickling Consultants, Ottawa. Served with RAF, 1942-46. Fellow Royal Statis. Soc.; mem. Canadian Operational Research Soc. (pres. 1969-70), Canadian Tranps. Research Forum (pres. 1971-72), Internat. Fedn. Operational Research Soc. (v.p. 1977-79), Sigma Xi. Clubs: University (Montreal); Halifax. Home: 984 Bellevue Ave Halifax NS Canada B3H 3L7 Office: Canadian Marine Transportation Centre 1321 Edward St-Dalhousie U Halifax NS Canada B3H 3H5

GRATZ, PAULINE, educator; b. N.Y.C., Mar. 30, 1924; d. John and Rose (Berman) G.; m. Sidney Aaronson, July 25, 1969. B.A., Hunter Coll., 1945; M.A., Columbia U., 1948, Ed.D., 1961. Jr. bacteriologist Queens Gen. Hosp., 1945-47; research technician Jewish Hosp. Bklyn., 1947-48; instr. biology and phys. sci. Bayonne (N.J.) Hosp. Sch. Nursing, 1948-51; sci. coordinator N.Y. Med. Coll. Sch. Nursing, 1951-56, New Rochelle (N.Y.) Hosp. Sch. Nursing, 1956-61; instr. nursing edn. Columbia U., 1961-62, asst. prof. natural scis. and nursing edn., 1963-65, asst. prof. natural scis., 1965-67, asso. prof., 1967-69; prof. human ecology Duke U., Durham, N.C., 1969—; vis. prof. physiology N.C. Health Manpower Project, summer 1973; cons. in field. Author: Integrated Science, 1966, (with others) Human Physiology, 1982, Experiments in Physiology, 1982, Teachers Edition in Human Physiology, 1982; contbg. author chpts. to books. NSF fellow, 1965; Shell fellow, 1969. Fellow AAAS; mem. Am. Assn. Higher Edn., AAUP, New Hope Audubon Soc., Nat. Geog. Soc., Nat Sci. Tchrs. Assn., Nat. Assn. Research in Sci. Teaching, Nat. Wildlife Fedn., Durham Mental Health Assn., Kappa Delta Pi, Pi Lambda Theta, Iota Sigma Pi, Sigma Theta Tau (hon.). Home: 102 Montrose Dr Durham NC 27707 Office: 132 Hanes House Duke U Sch Nursing Durham NC 27710

GRATZER, GEORGE ANDREW, mathematics educator; b. Budapest, Hungary, Aug. 2, 1936; emigrated to U.S., 1963; emigrated to Can., 1966, naturalized, 1971; s. Jozsef and Maria (Herzog) G.; m. Catherine M. Zahony, Jan. 25, 1961; children—Thomas G., David G. Dipl. Applied Math, L. Eötvös Univ., Budapest, 1959, Dr. Rer. Nat., 1960; Ph.D., Hungarian Acad. Sci., 1960. Researcher Math. Research Inst. Hungarian Acad. Sci., 1959-63; asst. prof. to prof. Pa. State U., 1963-66; prof. U. Man., Winnipeg, 1966—. Author: Elmesport Egy Esztendöre, 1959, Universal Algebra, 1968, 2d edit., 1979, Lattice Theory, 1971, General Lattice Theory, 1977, expanded and rev. edit. in Russian, 1981, Fast Basic: Beyond TRS-80 Basic, 1982; contbr. numerous articles to profl. jours. Recipient W.R. Steacie award Nat. Research Council Can., 1971. Fellow Royal Soc. Can.; mem. Can. Math. Congress, Am. Math. Soc. Home: 416 Lamont Blvd Winnipeg MB Canada R3P 0G3

GRAU, ALBERT A., educator; b. Switzerland, 1918; came to U.S., 1926, naturalized, 1938; s. Albert G. and Martha (Koehler) G.; m. Doris Teague, June 15, 1965; 1 dau. B.S. with distinction and honors in Math, U. Mich., 1940, M.S., 1941, Ph.D. in Math, 1944. Doris Anne. Univ. fellow U. Mich., 1941-44, instr., 1944-45, Horce H. Rackham postdoctoral fellow, 1944-45; mem. Inst. Advanced Study, 1944-45; instr. Drake U., 1945-46; asst. prof. U. Ky., 1946-47; asso. prof. U. Ala., 1947-48; U. Okla., 1948-56; sr. mathematician Oak Ridge Nat. Lab., 1956-63; prof. Northwestern U., 1963—; cons. Argonne Nat. Lab., 1966—; lectr. George Washington U., 1947, U. Tenn., 1957-60. Author: (with others) Translation of Algol 60, 1967; also articles. Bd. dirs. Grace Inst. Bible, Oklahoma City, 1951-52, Swiss Benevolent Soc. Chgo., 1973—. Mem. Am. Math. Soc., Math. Assn. Am., Assn. Computing Machinery, Soc. Indsl. and Applied Math., Phi Beta Kappa, Sigma Xi, Phi Kappa Phi. Mem. Gospel Ch. Home: 826 Milburn St Evanston IL 60201

GRAU, SHIRLEY ANN (MRS. JAMES KERN FEIBLEMAN), writer; b. New Orleans, July 8, 1929; d. Adolph and Katherine (Onions) G.; m. James Kern Feibleman, Aug. 4, 1955; children—Ian, James, Nora Miranda, William, Katherine. B.A., Tulane U., 1950. Writer for, Holiday, New Yorker, New World Writing, Mademoiselle, Sat. Eve. Post, Atlantic, The Reporter, 1954—; Author: The Black Prince and Other Stories, 1955, The Hard Blue Sky, 1958, The House on Coliseum Street, 1961, The Keepers of the House, 1964 (Pulitzer prize for fiction 1965), The Condor Passes, 1971, The Wind Shifting West and Other Stories, 1973, Evidence of Love, 1977. Mem. Phi Beta Kappa. Office: care Brandt and Brandt 1501 Broadway New York NY 10036

GRAUBARD, SEYMOUR, lawyer; b. N.Y.C., Mar. 8, 1911; s. John and Edna (Kiesler) G.; m. Blanche Kazon, Aug. 24, 1941; 1 dau., Katherine (Mrs. William Calvin). A.B., Columbia, 1931, LL.B., 1933. Bar: N.Y. bar 1933. Legislative asst. to bd. aldermen, N.Y.C., 1934-35; partner Joseph D. McGoldrick, N.Y.C., 1936-37; law sec. to comptroller, N.Y.C., 1937-41; sec. to justice Supreme Ct. N.Y. County, 1942, 45-46; practice in, N.Y.C., 1949—; mem. firm Graubard, Moskovitz, McGoldrick, Dannett & Horowitz, 1969—; lectr. municipal govt. N.Y. U., New Sch. Social Research, 1938-40. Co-author: Building Regulation in New York City, 1944. Mem. N.Y.C. Commn. Govtl. Operations, 1959-61, Coordinating Council Criminal Justice, 1967—; Nat. chmn. Anti-Defamation League, B'nai B'rith, 1970-76; pres. ADL Found., 1976—; chmn. bd. dirs. Fund for N.Y.C., to, 1978. Served to maj. U.S. Army, 1942-45. Mem. Assn. Bar City N.Y. (past chmn. com. city cts.), N.Y. State Bar Assn., N.Y. County Lawyers Assn. Clubs: City (trustee past pres.), Harmonie (N.Y.C.)). Home: 993 Park Ave New York NY 10028 Office: 345 Park Ave New York NY 10154

GRAUBARD, STEPHEN RICHARDS, history educator, editor; b. N.Y.C., Dec. 5, 1924; s. Harry and Rose (Polk) G.; m. Margaret Cavendish-Bentinck Georgiades, Aug. 5, 1978. A.B., George Washington U., 1945; A.M., Harvard U., 1946, Ph.D., 1951; D.H.L., Providence Coll., 1971. Instr. history and gen. edn. Harvard U., 1952-55, asst. prof., 1955-60, lectr., 1960-63, exec. sec. com. on gen. edn., 1952-59, research asso. in internat. affairs, 1963-65; vis. prof. history Brown U., 1965-66, prof. history, 1966—; mng. editor Daedalus, 1960-61, editor, 1961—; asst. editor Confluence, 1952-55; dir. studies Assembly on Univ. Goals and Governance, 1969-75. Author: British Labour and the Russian Revolution, 1956, Burke, Disraeli and Churchill: The Politics of Perseverance, 1961, Kissinger: Portrait of a Mind, 1973; editor: (with G. Holton) Excellence and Leadership in a Democracy, 1962, A New Europe?, 1964, (with G. Ballotti) The Embattled University, 1970, (with F. Gilbert) Historical Studies Today, 1972, (with S.N. Eisenstadt) Intellectuals and Tradition, 1973, (with F. Cavazza) Il Caso Italiano, 1974, A New America?, 1979, Generations, 1979, The State, 1980, Reading in the 1980s, 1983. Trustee Alfred U., N.Y.; mem. adv. com. Giovanni Agnelli Found., Italy. Served with AUS, 1943. Social Sci. Research Council fellow, 1948-50. Fellow Am. Acad. Arts and Scis. (editor 1963—), Council on Fgn. Relations, Mass. Hist. Soc. Clubs: Century, Signet. Home: 83 Whits End Rd Concord MA 01742 Office: Norton's Woods 136 Irving St Cambridge MA 02138

GRAUE, FREMONT DAVID, cartoonist; b. Oak Park, Ill., Sept. 6, 1926; s. Fremont Derek and Helen Amerilla (Williams) G.; m. Eliza Fusz Brownrigg, Oct. 11, 1955; children—Karen Elizabeth Graue Dowdy, Jefferson David, Daniel Williams. Grad., Art Inst. Pitts., 1948. Staff artist Pitts. Post-Gazette, 1949; asst. to V.T. Hamlin (Alley Oop comic strip), 1950-71; producer continuity and art for daily and Sunday Alley Oop comic strip, NEA Inc., N.Y.C., 1971—; occasional chalk-talks at schs. and before civic groups. Served with USAAF, 1945-46. Route 1 Box 79-E Brevard NC 28712

GRAUER, ALLAN L., telephone company executive; b. Marcus, Iowa, Apr. 8, 1930; s. Albert J. and Esther (C.) G.; m. Julie M. Fargo, June 15, 1952; children—Gregory F., Valerie J. B.S. in Econs, Iowa State U., 1952; LL.B., U. S.D., 1956. Bar: Nebr. bar 1956, N.Y. bar 1962, Minn. bar 1967, S.D. bar 1956. Atty. Northwestern Bell Telephone Co., Omaha, 1956-61, AT&T Co., N.Y.C., 1961-66; gen. atty. Northwestern Bell Telephone Co., 1966-75, gen. solicitor legal dept., corp. sec., 1975—. Served with USAF, 1952-54. Mem. ABA, N.Y. Bar Assn., Minn. Bar Assn., S.D. Bar Assn., Nebr. Bar Assn. Republican. Lutheran. Office: 1314 Douglas St Omaha NE 68102

GRAULTY, WILLIAM WILLARD, lawyer; b. Troy, N.Y., Dec. 30, 1923; s. William and Grace (Colton) G.; m. Dorothy Burke Yeomans, Oct. 4, 1968; children (by previous marriage): William Willard, Colton D., Susan, Martha, Henry H., Roger D. B.A., Dartmouth Coll., 1946; LL.B., Harvard U., 1951. Bar: Conn. 1951. With firm Robinson, Robinson & Cole, Hartford, 1951-56; with Conn. Bank & Trust Co., Hartford, 1956-76, exec. v.p., 1967—; chmn. Criterion Capital Mgmt. Corp., 1971-76; pvt. practice law, West Hartford, Conn., 1977—; dir. Nat. Fire Ins. Co., Hartford. Served with USNR, 1943-46. Mem. Conn. Bankers Assn. (chmn. trust div. 1966-68), Am. Bankers Assn. (v.p. trust div. 1973-74, pres. div. 1974-75). Episcopalian (vestryman 1955-58, 60-63, 66-69). Home: 35 Ironwood Rd West Hartford CT 06117 Office: 65 La Salle Rd West Hartford CT 06107

GRAUSMAN, PHILIP, sculptor; b. N.Y.C., July 16, 1935; s. Roland and Elizabeth (Block) G.; 1 son, David. Student, Skowhegan Sch. Painting & Sculpture, Maine, 1956, 1957; B.A. cum aldue, Syracuse U., 1957; M.F.A., Cranbrook Acad. Art, 1959; student, Jose de Creeft Art Students League, 1959. One man shows Borgenicht Gallery, N.Y.C., 1966, 1974, 1979, Dartmouth Coll., 1972, Alpha Gallery, Boston, 1975, U. Conn., 1976, Pa. State U., 1977, Image Gallery, Stockbridge, Mass., 1978, Robert Schoelkopf Gallery, 1983; group shows include Jersy City Mus. Painting and Schulpture exhbn., 1958, Nat. Inst. Arts and Letters, 1961, Am. Acad., Rome, 1963, 1964, 1965, Art in the Embassies Program U.S. Dept. State, 1966, U. Nebr., 1969, Borgenicht Gallery, N.Y.C., 1969, Yale U. Art Gallery, 1970-73, Hartford Arts Festival, Wadsworth Atheneaum, 1974, Mus. Modern Art, N.Y.C., 1976, St. Paul Art Ctr., 1978, Rockland Ctr. for Arts, N.Y.C., 1979, Robert Schoelkopf Gallery, 1983; represented in permanent collections Akron Art Inst., Ohio, 1983, Balt. Mus. Art, Jewish Mus., N.Y.C., Nat. Portrait Gallery, Washington, U. Conn., Storrs, Wadsworth Atheneum, Hartford, Worcester Art Mus., Yale U. Art Gallery; instr. design Cooper Union, 1965-67; instr. design and drawing Pratt Inst., 1965-69; artist in residence Dartmouth Coll., 1972; instr. sculpture and drawing Skowheagan Sch. Painting & Sculpture, 1973; vis. asst. prof. art Yale U., 1974-76; vis. critic archtl. drawing Grad. Sch. Architecture, 1976—. Recipient Purchase award Ford. Found., 1962; Am. Acad. in Rome fellowship awardee sculpture, 1962-65. Fellow Am. Acad. in Rome; mem. NAD (Dessie Greer prize 1981). Gallery: Robert Schoelkopf Gallery 825 Madison Ave New York NY 10021

GRAVEN, PAUL HELMER, architect; b. Madison, Wis., July 31, 1921; s. Paul Helmer and Emily Jean (Ingram) G.; m. Patricia Martin, Sept. 14, 1956; children: Krista Kay, Peder Martin, Eric Paul. B.Arch., U. Ill., 1948. Registered architect, Wis., Minn. Designer, Graham, Anderson, Probst & White, Chgo., 1948; instr. in archtl. design Okla. State U., Stillwater, 1948-50; designer Law, Law, Potter & Nystrom (Architects), Madison, 1950-60, asso., 1958-60; founding partner Graven, Kenney & Iverson (Architects-Engrs.), Madison, 1960-74; owner, architect Graven/Assos. (Architects/Planners), Madison, Wis., 1974—; dir. First Capitol Investment Corp., 1st Fed. Savs. & Loan, Madison; examiner Wis. Registration Bd. Architects and Engrs., 1965-71; panelist Am. Arbitration Assn., 1973—; pres. Interprofl. Council on Registration, 1978-79; mem. Nat. Archtl. Accrediting Bd., 1979—, sec.-treas., 1983-84. Archtl. works include James Madison Meml. High Sch., Madison, 1965, Baraboo-Sauk County Center Coll., 1967, U. Wis. at Platteville Indsl. Edn.-Agr. Tech. Bldg., 1969 (Wis. chpt. AIA Merit award 1971), U. Wis. at River Falls Fine Arts Bldg., 1970, Madison Gen. Hosp. Lab. Bldg., 1970 (Wis. chpt. AIA Disting. Bldg. award 1971), U. Wis. at Madison Geology-Geophysics Bldg., 1972. Served to 1st lt. inf. U.S. Army, World War II; ETO, Nuremberg. Recipient Scarab medal in design U. Ill., 1941. Fellow AIA (pres. Western sect. 1963, chmn. Wis. chpt. fellowship com. 1979); mem. Wis. Soc. Architects (nat. bd. dirs. 1971-79, exec. com. 1973-79, chmn. exec. com. 1977, pres. 1977—), VFW, Phi Gamma Delta. Clubs: Blackhawk Country, Madison. Home: 5018 Bayfield Trail Madison WI 53705 Office: 817 Forward Dr Madison WI 53711

GRAVENSTEIN, JOACHIM STEFAN, educator, anesthesiologist; b. Berlin, Germany, Jan. 25, 1925; came to U.S., 1952, naturalized, 1959; m. Alix Trutschler, Aug. 27, 1949; children—Nikolaus, Alix, Frederike, Stefan, Ruprecht, Dietrich, Constanze, Katharina. Dr. med., U. Bonn, Germany, 1951; M.D., Harvard, 1958. Resident and staff appointments anesthesia Mass. Gen. Hosp., 1952-58; fellow, tchr. Harvard Med. Sch., 1952-58; chief anesthesiology Coll. Medicine, U. Fla., 1958-69; prof. anesthesiology, chmn. dept. Case Western Res. Med. Sch., 1969-79; grad. research prof. Coll. Medicine, U. Fla., Gainesville, 1979—. Mem. Am. Soc. Anesthesiology, Am. Soc. Pharmacology and Exptl. Therapeutics. Home: 7424 NW 18th Ave Gainesville FL 32605 Office: U Fla Coll Medicine Gainesville FL 32610

GRAVER, LAWRENCE STANLEY, educator; b. N.Y.C., Dec. 6, 1931; s. Louis and Rose (Pearlstein) G.; m. Suzanne Levy, Jan. 28, 1960; children—Ruth, Elizabeth. B.A., CCNY, 1954; M.A., U. Calif., Berkeley, 1959, Ph.D., 1961. Asst. prof. English UCLA, 1961-64; asst. prof. English, Williams Coll., Williamstown, Mass., 1964-67, asso. prof., 1967-72, prof., 1972—, William R. Kenan, Jr. prof., 1977-81, John H. Roberts prof., 1981—. Author: Conrad's Short Fiction, 1969, Carson McCullers, 1969; Editor: Mastering the Film, 1977, Samuel Beckett, 1979. Served with U.S. Army, 1954-56. Nat. Endowment for Humanities fellow, 1980-81. Mem. MLA, AAUP. Democrat. Home: 117 Forest Rd Williamstown MA 01267 Office: Dept English Williams Coll Williamstown MA 01267

GRAVES, ALLEN WILLIS, clergyman, educator; b. Rector, Ark., Jan. 20, 1915; s. James Henry and Anna Joyce (Keaster) G.; m. Helen Elizabeth Cannan, June 1, 1937; children: Joyce (Mrs. Carl Olney), John Raymond, Dorothy (Mrs. William Dinwiddie), David, Virginia (Mrs. John Weisz), Thomas. B.Ed., So. Ill. U., 1935; Th.M., So. Bapt. Theol. Sem., 1939, Ph.D., 1942. Pub. sch. tchr., Herrin, Ill., 1935-36; ordained to ministry Bapt. Ch., 1935; pastor in, Ill. and Ky., 1935-41; dir. young peoples work Bapt. Tng. Union Dept., Bapt. Sunday Sch. Bd., Nashville, 1941-43; pastor in, Fla., 1943-45, Va., 1945-50, Okla., 1950-55; dean Sch. Religious Edn., So. Bapt. Theol. Sem., 1955-69, 76-80, sr. prof., 1980—, adminstrv. dean, 1969-72; exec. dir. Ministry Tng. Center, also Boyce Bible Sch., Louisville, 1972-76; vis. prof. Nigerian Bapt. Theol. Sem., 1980-81. Author: Christ in My Career, 1958, Church Committee Manual, 1958, (with B.B. McKinney) Let Us Sing, 1943, Using and Maintaining Church Property, 1965, The Church at Work: A Handbook of Church Polity, 1972, How Southern Baptists Do Their Work, 1977, Principles of Administration for a Baptist Association, 1978. Mem. So. Bapt. Religious Edn. Assn. (pres. 1962-63). Home: 307 Godfrey Ave Louisville KY 40206

GRAVES, BENJAMIN BARNES, educator; b. Jones County, Miss., Nov. 5, 1920; s. Thomas Cannon and Velma (Barnes) G.; m. Hazeline Wood, May 25, 1946; children—Benjamin Barnes, Janis Elizabeth, Cynthia Wood. B.A., U. Miss., 1942; M.B.A., Harvard, 1947; Ph.D., La. State U., 1961; LL.D., U. Ala., 1970. Staff and supervisory positions Exxon Co., 1947-60; spl. lectr. Coll. Bus. Adminstrn., La. State U., 1959-60, asst. prof., 1960-62; asso. prof. U. Va., 1962-64; Milner prof. indsl. econs. U. Miss., 1964-65; pres. Millsaps Coll., Jackson, Miss., 1965-70; prof. bus. adminstrn. U. Ala. in Huntsville, 1970—, pres., 1970-79; Guest lectr. Mid-South Exec. Devel. Program, La. State U., 1962-68, also asso. dir. program, 1961-62; guest lectr. mgmt. program Natural Resources Mgrs., Pa. State U., 1962-72, Va.-Md. Sch. Banking, U. Va., 1962-73; vis. prof. bus. adminstrn. U. N.C. at Charlotte, 1976-77. Author articles in field. Pres. Miss. Found. Ind. Colls., 1967-68; mem. com. human investigation U. Miss. Sch. Medicine, 1964-70; v.p. Miss. Jr.-Sr. Coll. Conf., 1968-69; pres. Miss. Assn. Colls., 1969-70; mem. exec. com. Ind. Coll. Funds Am.; mem. adv. com. Am. Council on Edn.'s Inst. for Coll. and U. Adminstrs.; mem. Am. Assn. Schs. and Colls. univ. pres.'s del. to People's Republic of China, 1975, Republic of China, 1976; Pres. Huntsville Research Park Adv. Bd., 1973; Mem. exec. bd. Andrew Jackson council Boy Scouts Am., 1966—; bd. dirs. Jackson Symphony Assn., 1965-70. Served to lt. (s.g.) USNR, 1942-46. Mem. Acad. Mgmt., Am. Mktg. Assn., Southwestern Social Sci. Assn., So. Econ. Assn., A.I.M. (pres.'s council), Jackson C. of C., Pi Kappa Alpha (mem. centennial com. 100), Phi Kappa Phi, Omicron Delta Kappa. Methodist. Club: Rotarian (dir. Huntsville 1973). Home: 1808 Mountain Brook SE Huntsville AL 35801

GRAVES, CHARLES EDWARD, lawyer; b. S.I., N.Y., Mar. 22, 1931; s. Charles Edward and Helen Joyce (Rundlett) G.; children: Elizabeth Leigh, Janet Kimberly, Anne Kristen. B.A., Duke U., 1953; LL.B., U. Colo., 1959. Bar: Wyo., Colo., U.S. Supreme Ct. Partner firm Roncalio, Graves and Smyth, Cheyenne, Wyo., 1960-70, Graves and Hacker, Cheyenne, 1972-77; U.S. atty. for Dist. of Wyo., Cheyenne, 1977-81; partner firm Graves, Hacker & Phelan, 1981-83; sole practice, 1983—; faculty Western Trial Advocacy Seminar, 1981; instr. seminars Laramie County Community Coll., Eastern Wyo. Coll.; lectr. U. Wyo.; gen. counsel Wyo. Edn. Assn., 1964-77. Pres. Laramie County Young Democrats, 1963; exec. sec. Wyo. Youth Council, 1961-63; state treas. Wyo. Easter Seal Soc., 1966-68; chmn. bd. Community Action of Laramie County, 1967-69; bd. dirs. vice chmn., chmn. Cheyenne-Laramie County Joint Planning Commn., 1974-82; trustee

Laramie County Community Coll., 1982—; mem. Wyo. Dem. State Com., 1983—. Served with CIC U.S. Army, 1954-56. Mem. Am., Wyo., Colo., Laramie County bar assns., Arabian Horse Assn. Democrat. Unitarian. Club: Cheyenne Lions. Home: 307A Western Hills Blvd Cheyenne WY 82001 Office: Tower Suite Rocky Mt Plaza 2020 Carey Ave Cheyenne WY 82001

GRAVES, EARL GILBERT, publisher; b. Bklyn., 1935; s. Earl Godwin and Winifred (Sealy) G.; m. Barbara Kydd, July 2, 1960; children: Earl Gilbert, John, Michael. B.A. in Econs., Morgan State Coll., Balt., 1958, LL.D., 1973; LL.D., Rust Coll., 1974, Wesleyan U., 1982, Dowling Coll., 1980, Va. Union Coll., 1976, Fla. Meml. Coll., 1978. Adminstrv. asst. to Senator Robert F. Kennedy, 1965-68; owner mgmt. cons. firm, 1968-70; editor, pub. Black Enterprise mag., N.Y.C., 1970—; pres. Earl G. Graves Pub. Co., Inc., Earl G. Graves Mktg. and Research Co., Earl G. Graves Devel. Co., EGG Dallas Broadcasting Co. Mem. nat. bd., exec. com. Interracial Council for Bus. Opportunity; Mem. nat. bd., exec. com. Center Civil Rights U. Notre Dame, mem. adv. council; mem. Commn. Reform Relationship between Govt. and Pvt. Philanthropy; mem. exec. com. Greater New York council Boy Scouts Am.; chmn. communications com. nat. Boy Scouts Am.; trustee Tuskegee Inst.; bd. dirs. Coalition N.Y.; bd. govs. Corporate Fund Performing Arts at Kennedy Center; mem. vis. com. Harvard U. John F. Kennedy Sch. Govt.; mem. Pres.'s Com. Small and Minority Bus.; mem. pres. council for bus. adminstrn. U. Vt.; bd. selectors Am. Inst. Pub. Service; trustee Am. Mus. Natural History and Planetarium Authority. Served to capt. U.S. Army, 1958-60. Recipient Scroll of Honor, Nat. Med. Assn., 1971, Nat. award of excellence U.S. Dept. Commerce, 1972, Silver Beaver award Boy Scouts Am., 1969, Publisher for Freedom award Operation PUSH; listed as one of 100 influential Blacks in Am. Ebony mag.; recipient Black Achiever award Talk mag., 1972; Key award Nat. Assn. Black Mfrs., 1972; Chgo. Econ. Devel. Corp. award, 1974; Nat. Alliance Black Sch. Educators award, 1974; named One of Ten Most Outstanding Minority Businessmen in Country by Pres. U.S., 1973, Outstanding Citizen of Year, Omega Psi Phi, 1974, also one of 200 Future Leaders of Country, Time mag., Outstanding Black Businessman, Nat. Bus. League; Poynter fellow Yale U., 1978. Mem. NAACP, SCLC, Interracial Council Bus. Opportunity (award), Young Pres. Orgn., Mag. Pubs. Assn. (dir.), Advt. Council, Bus. Mktg. Corp. N.Y.C., Sigma Pi Phi, Omega Psi Phi. Democrat. Episcopalian. Club: N.Y. Econ. (trustee). Office: 130 Fifth Ave New York NY 10011

GRAVES, ERNEST, JR., retired army officer, engineer; b. N.Y.C., July 6, 1924; s. Ernest and Lucy (Birnie) G.; m. Nancy Herbert Barclay, May 12, 1951; children: Ralph Henry, Robert Barclay, William Hooper, Emily Birnie. B.S., U.S. Mil. Acad., 1944; Ph.D., M.I.T., 1951; postgrad., Engr. Sch., Ft. Belvoir, Va., 1954-55, Command and Gen. Staff Coll., Ft. Leavenworth, Kans., 1957-58, Army War Coll., Carlisle Barracks, Pa., 1964-65, Harvard Bus. Sch., 1968. Commd. 2d lt. U.S. Army, 1944, advanced through grades to lt. gen., 1978, ret., 1981; with (SHAPE), Paris, 1951-54, Ft. Belvoir, 1955-57, comdr., Korea, 1958-59, dir., Livermore, Cal., 1962-64, exec. to sec. army, Washington, 1967-68, comdr., Vietnam, 1968-69, div. engr., Chgo., 1970-73; asst. gen. mgr. for mil. application U.S. AEC, Washington, 1973-75; dir. civil works Office Chief Engrs., Washington, 1975-77, dep. chief engr., 1977-78; dir. Def. Security Assistance Agy., Washington, 1978-81; fellow Georgetown U. Center for Strategic and Internat. Studies, Washington, 1982—. Contbr. articles profl. jours. Decorated D.S.M., Legion of Merit, Bronze Star, Air medal. Mem. Soc. Am. Mil. Engrs. Home: 2328 S Nash St Arlington VA 22202 Office: 1800 K St NW Washington DC 20006

GRAVES, FRED HILL, librarian; b. Rockdale, Tex., Feb. 11, 1914; s. Fred Hill and Etta Sherman (Loper) G. B.A., Southwest Tex. State Coll., San Marcos, 1935; postgrad., U. Tex., 1938, 41, U. Chgo., 1943-46; M.S., Columbia U., 1954; advanced cert. in librarianship, Columbia U., 1973. Successively tchr. English, librarian, prin. Rockdale (Tex.) High Sch., 1935-43; asst. librarian Bemidji (Minn.) State Coll., 1943-44; acting librarian Hardin-Simmons U., 1944-45; librarian Tex. A. and I. U., Kingsville, 1945-51; asst. to dean Sch. Library Service, Columbia U., 1952-54, vis. lectr., spring terms 1968, 69, 70, 71, 72, 73, 76, Sch. Library Service, Columbia, summer terms 1979, 80, 81, 82; asst. prof. Grad. Sch. Library Service, Rutgers U., 1954-60; vis. instr. So. Conn. State Coll., New Haven, fall 1960; head librarian Cooper Union, N.Y.C., 1960-78. Editor: Tex. Library Jour, 1948-49. Mem. Jamestowne Soc., ALA, N.Y. Library Assn., N.Y. Tech. Services Librarians (exec. bd. 1960-66, pres. 1965-66). Home: 360 E 55th St New York NY 10022

GRAVES, GEORGE, insurance company executive; b. Santa Barbara, Calif., Oct. 14, 1921; s. Thomas William and Mary (Lang) G.; m. Barbara E. Hampton, Dec. 26, 1942; children: Thomas N., Cheri A., Vicki S. B.A., U. Calif.-Santa Barbara, 1948. Agt., asst. mgr., br. mgr. Conn. Gen. Life Ins. Co., Los Angeles and St. Louis, 1953-64; pres. Great Heritage Life Ins. Co. (merged into Equity Educators Life Ins. Co.), St. Louis, 1964-70; v.p. Florist Mut. Life Ins. Co., St. Louis, 1972; 2d v.p., v.p. sr. v.p United Services Life Ins. Co., Washington, 1972-81; pres. Bankers Secutity Life Ins. Co., Washington, 1981—; dir. Banker Security Life Ins. Soc., Gen. Services Life Ins. Co., Washington. Served to 2d lt. USAAF, 1943-46. Mem. C.L.U. Group, Nat. Assn. Life Underwriters. Republican. Club: Country of Fairfax (Va.). Home: 4221 Willow Woods Annandale VA 22003 Office: Bankers Security Life Ins Soc. 1701 Pennsylvania Ave NW Washington DC 20006

GRAVES, JAMES B(URYLE), corporation executive; b. Uvalde, Tex., July 22, 1927; s. Lee Wilson and Clara Agnes (Studer) G.; m. Billie Bert Tucker, Mar. 22, 1958; children: Tucker, Sally, Christi. B.B.A., U. Tex.-Austin, 1948. C.P.A. Tax acct. Magnet Cove Barium (wholly-owned subs. Dresser Industries, later Magcobar Div.), 1951-56, controller Magcobar Div., 1956-66, controller Petroleum & Menerals Group, 1966-68; controller of ops., Dallas Hdqrs. Dresser Industries, Inc., 1968-71, dir. planning, office of pres., 1971-75, staff v.p.-planning, 1975-76, v.p.-corp. planning, 1976-80, sr. v.p.-corp. planning, 1980—; chmn. N. Tex. and Okla. chpt. Dist. Export Council, 1979, 80. Mem. Nat. Assn. Accts., Tex. Soc. C.P.A.s, Nat. Soc. C.P.A.s, Fin. Execs. Inst., Assn. for Corp. Growth (pres. Dallas-Ft. Worth chpt.), Chi Phi. Republican. Methodist. Office: Dresser Industries Inc 1505 Elm St Dallas TX 75201

GRAVES, LAWRENCE LESTER, university dean; b. Perry, N.Y., Nov. 17, 1917; s. Leonard Stanley and Anna Maud (Lalor) G.; m. Mary Rita Ralph, June 21, 1948 (dec. 1965); m. Opal Louise Oden, Nov. 23, 1966. B.A., U. Mo., 1942; M.A., U. Rochester, N.Y., 1947; Ph.D., U. Wis., 1954. Instr. history Woman's Coll., U. N.C., 1950-51, 52-55; mem. faculty Tex. Tech. U., Lubbock, 1955—, assoc. dean Grad Sch., 1967-68, interim dean, 1968-70, prof. history, dean arts and scis., 1970—; pres. Nat. Acad. Deans Summer Conf., 1976-77, interim pres., 1979-80; mem. commn. arts and scis. Nat. Assn. State Univs. and Land Grant Colls., 1977-80. Author articles, revs.; Editor, contbr.: A History of Lubbock, 1962. Served with AUS, 1942-46, 51-52. Mem. AAUP (chpt. pres. 1953-54, 64-66), Am. Hist. Assn., Council Colls. Arts and Scis. (pres. 1976-77), Orgn. Am. Historians, So., Western history assns., Southwestern Social Sci. Assn. (pres. 1981-82), Tex. Hist. Assn. (sr. assoc. editor 1982—), West Tex. Museum Assn., Phi Kappa Phi. Club: Masons. Home: 4514 8th St Lubbock TX 79416 Office: PO Box 4379 Tex Tech Univ Lubbock TX 79409 *I believe that teachers through their training of the minds and shaping of the character of their students perform one of the most valuable services to society and deserve our highest recognition.*

GRAVES, MARIE LEONTINE *See* **BULLOCK, MRS. HUGH**

GRAVES, MICHAEL, architect; b. Indpls., July 9, 1934; s. Thomas Browning and Erma Sanderson (Lowe) G.; children by previous marriage: Sarah Browning, Adam Daimhin; stepchildren: Anne Ashby Gilbert, Elizabeth Eastman Gilbert. B.S.Arch., U. Cin., 1958, hon. doctorate, 1982; M.Arch., Harvard U., 1959; postgrad. (Acad. fellow), Am. Acad. in Rome, 1960-62. Lectr. architecture Princeton U., 1962-67, asso. prof., 1967-72, prof., 1972—, now Schirmer prof. architecture, 1972—; prin. Michael Graves (Architect), Princeton, N.J., 1964—; architect in residence Am. Acad. in Rome, 1979; Mem. N.J. Commn. Historic Sites. Exhibited in group shows, Museum Modern Art, N.Y.C., 1967, 68, 75, 78, 79, 80, 81, Cooper-Hewitt Mus., N.Y.C., 1976, 78, 79, Roma Interrotta, Rome, 1978, XV Triennale, Milan, Italy, 1973, Venice Biennale, 1980; Designer: Newark Mus, 1968, Rockefeller House, 1969 (Progressive Architecture Design award 1970), Hanselmann House, 1967 (AIA Nat. Honor award 1975), Snyderman House, 1972 (Progressive Architecture Design award 1976), Crooks House, 1976 (Progressive Architecture Design award 1977), Moorhead (Minn.) Cultural Center, 1977-79 (Progressive Architecture Design award 1979), Chem-Fleur Inc, 1977 (Progressive Architecture Design award 1978), Graves House, 1977 (Progressive Architecture Design award 1978), Plocek House, 1978 (Progressive Architecture Design award 1979), Sunar Showrooms, N.Y.C., 1979, Chgo., 1979, Houston, 1980, Los Angeles, 1980, N.Y.C., 1981 (Interiors award 1981), Portland Bldg, 1980, Whitney Mus. Am. Art addition, 1981, Pub. Library, San Juan Capistrans, Calif, Newark Mus. Master Plan and Renovation, 1982, Humana Bldg, Louisville, 1982, Cin. Symphony Summer Pavilion, 1983; designer furniture and textiles: Sunar, 1980-82; Author: Michael Graves, Architectural Monographs, 1979, Michael Graves, Buildings and Projects, 1966-181. Trustee Am. Acad. Rome. Recipient Prix de Rome Am. Acad. in Rome, 1960-62; Arnold W. Brunner Meml. prize in architecture, 1981; Designer of Yr. Interiors, 1981; Euster award, 1984. Fellow Soc. Arts, Religion and Culture, AIA (nat. honor awards 1975, 79, 82, 83); mem. Conf. Architects for Study of Environment, Soc. Fellows Am. Acad. in Rome (trustee, pres.), Inst. Architecture and Urban Studies (trustee). Office: 341 Nassau St Princeton NJ 08540

GRAVES, MORRIS COLE, artist; b. Fox Valley, Oreg., Aug. 28, 1910; s. Edwin Lyman and Helen (Malson) G. Works exhibited, Seattle Art Mus., 1936-56, Mus. Modern Art, 1942, Arts Club Chgo., 1943, Calif. Palace Legion of Honor, 1948, Whitney Mus. Am. Art, 1956; retrospective exhbns., in 1956, in Mus. Fine Arts, Boston, Whitney Mus., N.Y.C., De Young Meml. Mus., San Francisco, retrospective show at, Brussels Fair, 1958 (Recipient 1st purchase prize Seattle Art Mus. 1933); also the, Brussels Fair (Harris medal Art Inst. Chgo. 1947); Brussels Fair (Blair prize 1948), Brussels Fair (purchase prize U. Ill. 1955), U.S. State Dept. travelling show, Europe, Asia, 1957, Pavilion Gallery, Balboa, Calif., 1963, retrospective exhbns., Sch. Visual Arts, N.Y.C., 1978, others, one man shows, Willard Gallery, N.Y.C., 1942, 44, 45, 48, 53, 54, 55, 59, 71, 73, 76, 78, 81, 82, Univ. Gallery, Mpls., 1943, Detroit Inst. Art, Phillips Gallery, Washington, 1943, 54, Santa Barbara Mus. Art, 1948, Los Angeles County Mus., Art Inst Chgo., Beaumont (Tex.) Art Mus., 1952, Oslo (Norway) Kunstforening, 1955, Bridgestone Gallery, Tokyo, 1957, Charles Campbell Gallery, San Francisco, 1982, annual exhibitions, Philadelphia Art Alliance, 1946, N.Y. World's Fair, 1939, Art Inst. Chgo., 1947, Tate Gallery, London, 1946, 56, Solomon R. Guggenheim Mus., N.Y.C., 1956, others; works represented in permanent collections, Art Inst. Chgo., Balt., Cleve., San Francisco museums of art, Detroit, Milw. art insts., Mus. Modern Art, Phillips Gallery, Museum of Contemporary Art, Dublin, Ireland; also the, Whitney Mus. Am. Art; Tate Gallery London, and others. Guggenheim fellow, 1946; Windsor award, 1957; grantee Nat. Inst. Arts and Letters, 1956. Mem. Nat. Inst. Arts and Letters. Address: Willard Gallery 29 E 72d St New York NY 10021

GRAVES, NANCY STEVENSON, artist; b. Pittsfield, Mass., Dec. 23. B.A., Vassar Coll., 1961; B.F.A., Yale U., 1961, M.F.A., 1964. Numerous one-man shows, including, Whitney Mus. Am. Art, N.Y.C., 1969, Nat. Gallery Can., Ottawa, 1971, Neue Galerie der Stadt Aachen, Ger., Mus. Modern Art, N.Y.C., Inst. Contemporary Art, U. Pa., Phila., 1972, La Jolla (Calif.) Mus. Art, 1973, Art Mus. S. Tex., Corpus Christi, André Emmerich Gallery, Inc., N.Y.C., 1974, 77, Janie E. Lee Gallery, Houston, 1977, 78, M. Knoedler & Co., 1979, 80, 81, retrospective show travelled to, Albright Knox Gallery, Buffalo, Akron (Ohio) Art Inst., Contemporary Arts Mus., Houston, 1980, Brooks Art Gallery, Memphis, Neuberger Mus., Purchase, N.Y., Des Moines Art Center, Walker Art Center, Mpls., 1981, numerous group shows, including, Whitney Mus. Am. Art, N.Y.C., 1970, 76, Corcoran Gallery Art, Washington, 1971, 76, Parc Floral, Paris, 1971, Neue Galerie, Kassel, Ger., 1972, Serpentine Gallery, London, 1973, Project 74, Cologne, Ger., 1974, Berlin Nat. Galerie, 1976, Vancouver (B.C.) Art Gallery; represented in permanent collections, Mus. Modern Art, N.Y.C., Whitney Mus. Am. Art, N.Y.C., Ludwig Mus., Cologne, Nat. Gallery Can., Ottawa, Des Moines (Iowa) Art Center, La Jolla Mus. Contemporary Art, Art Mus. S. Tex., Corpus Christi, Berkeley (Calif.) Mus. Art, Albright-Knox Art Gallery, Buffalo, N.Y., Chgo. Art Inst. Vassar Coll. fellow, 1971-72; Fulbright-Hayes grantee, 1965-66; Paris Biennale grantee, 1971; Nat. Endowment for Arts grantee, 1972-73; Creative Artist Pub. Service grantee, 1974-75. Subject of numerous profl. publs., films. Office: care Knoedler Gallery 19 E 70th St New York NY 10021

GRAVES, PETER, actor; b. Mpls., Mar. 18, 1926; s. Rolf C. and Ruth E. (Duesler) Aurness; m. Joan E. Endress, Dec. 16, 1950; children: Kelly Jean, Claudia King, Amanda Lee. Ed., U. Minn., 1949. Engaged in motion pictures and TV, 1951—; star: TV series Mission Impossible, 1967—; (Recipient Outstanding Achievement award U. Minn. 1968, honoree Am. Acad. Achievement 1972). Hon. Calif. chmn. Am. Cancer Soc., 1968, hon. nat. crusade chmn., 1974. Served with USAAF. Mem. Phi Kappa Psi. Address: care Barman Mgmt Co 415 N Crescent Dr Suite 210 Beverly Hills CA 90210

GRAVES, RALPH A., editorial director; b. Washington, Oct. 17, 1924; s. Ralph and Elizabeth (Evans) G.; m. Patricia Monser, Oct. 14, 1950 (div.); children: William, Katherine; m. Eleanor Mackenzie, Oct. 27, 1958; children: Sara, Andrew. B.A., Harvard U., 1948. Reporter, writer Life mag., 1948-58, articles editor, 1958-61, asst. mng. editor, 1961-67, mng. editor, 1969-72; sr. staff editor Time, Inc., 1968, editor for film and cable, 1974; assoc. pub. Time, 1975, corp. editor, 1976-78; editorial dir. publs. Time, Inc., N.Y.C., 1978-84. Author: Thanks for the Ride, 1949, The Lost Eagles, 1955. Chmn. Citizen Crime Commn., N.Y.C. Home: 1158 5th Ave New York NY 10029 Office: Time Mag Inc Time & Life Bldg 1271 Ave of the Americas New York NY 10020

GRAVES, RAY, lawyer; b. Seattle, Feb. 23, 1924; s. Ralph Raymond and Naomi (Capron) G.; m. Joan Catherine Kikkert, May 19, 1946; children—Valerie Ann, Jon Carlton. B.A., Wash. State Coll., 1950; J.D., Duke U., 1952. Bar: Wash. bar 1952. Since practiced in, Tacoma, pvt. practice, 1952-60; partner McGavick, Graves, Beale, McNerthney & Gagliardi (and predecessor), 1960—; mem. Wash. Bd. Bar Examiners, 1968-76; pres., dir. Western Land Mgmt., Inc.; sec., dir. Tacoma Boatbuilding Co., First Security Bank. Contbr. articles to profl. jours. Served with USMCR, 1943-46. Mem. Am., Wash. bar assns., Order of Coif. Republican. Presbyterian. Club: Tacoma Country and Golf. Home: 12101 Clover Creek Dr Tacoma WA 98499 Office: One Washington Plaza Tacoma WA 98402

GRAVES, RICHARD GORDON, army officer; b. Tangier, Ind., Oct. 30, 1933; s. William Dallas and Mary Catherine (Marks) G.; m. Beverly Sue Fewell, Feb. 7, 1959; children—William Walter, Thomas Christopher, Myra Ellen. Student, Purdue U., 1951-54; B.S., U.S. Mil. Acad., 1958; M.A. in Polit. Sci, Ind. U., 1972; postgrad., Armed Forces Staff Coll., 1967, U.S. Army War Coll., 1973-74. Commd. 2d lt. U.S. Army, 1958, advanced through grades to brig. gen.; mem. staff, Ft. Leavenworth, Kans., 1962-64; advisor (Mil. Assistance Command), Vietnam, 1965-66, assignments officer, Washington, 1967-69, brigade officer, Vietnam, 1969, comdr., staff officer, 1972-74, dep. brigade comdr., Ger., 1974,, assigned, Washington, 1979, chief of staff, Ft. Hood, Tex., 1979-80, 1980-81, asst. div. comdr., 1981—. Decorated Silver Star, Legion of Merit with oak leaf cluster, D.F.C. with oak leaf cluster, Bronze Star, Air medal. Mem. Assn. Army U.S., Assn. Grads. U.S. Mil. Acad., Kappa Delta Rho. Club: Masons. Office: Office Asst Div Comdr 1st Cavalry Fort Hood TX 76545 *

GRAVES, RICHARD LAYTON, educator; b. Houston, Jan. 14, 1931; s. A.J. and Lucille (Martin) G.; m. Eloise Davis, June 10, 1955; children: Rebecca, Jeffrey, Kathryn. B.A., Baylor U., 1956; M.Ed., U. Fla., 1960; Ph.D., Fla. State U., 1965. Tchr. Tampa pub. schs., 1957-63; research asst. Fla. State U., Tallahasse, 1963-65; prof. English edn. Auburn U., Ala., 1965—. Author: Rhetoric and Composition: A Sourcebook for Teachers, 1976. Served with USAF, 1951-54. Mem. Nat. Council Tchrs. English, Conf. Coll. Composition and Communications, Rhetoric Soc. Am. Baptist. Home: 415 Blake St Auburn AL 36830 Office: Dept Curriculum and Instrn Arburn U Auburn AL 36849

GRAVES, ROBERT LAWRENCE, educator, mathematician; b. Chgo., Sept. 1, 1926; s. Lawrence Murray and Josephine (Wells) G.; m. Barbara Junette Sward, Oct. 20, 1951; children—Susan Johanna, Julia Lowell, Christine Craig, Virginia Anne. B.A., Oberlin Coll., 1947; M.A., Harvard, 1948, Ph.D., 1952. Teaching fellow Harvard, 1949-51; supervisory and research positions Standard Oil Co., Ind., 1951-58; mem. faculty Grad. Sch. Bus., U. Chgo., 1958—, prof. applied math., 1965—, asso. dean, 1972-73, 75-81, dep. dean, 1981—; on leave as dir. European Inst. Advanced Studies in Mgmt., Brussels, Belgium, 1973-75. Author: (with H.B. Thorelli) INTOP, The International Operations Simulation, 1964, (with L.G. Telser) Functional Analysis in Economics, 1972; Editor: (with Philip Wolfe) Recent Advances in Mathematical Programming, 1963. Served to ensign USNR, 1944-46. Mem. Am. Math. Soc., Math. Assn. Am., Operations Research Soc., Inst. Mgmt. Sci. (mem. council 1971-73), Assn. Computing Machinery (co-chmn. spl. interest group for math. programming 1961-63). Episcopalian. Club: Quadrangle (U. Chgo.). Home: 830 Park Dr Flossmoor IL 60422 Office: Grad Sch Business Univ Chicago Chicago IL 60637

GRAVES, ROBERT ROY, oil company executive, geologist; b. Winnipeg, Man., Can., July 13, 1930; came to U.S., 1964. B.S., U. Alta. Registered profl. geologist. Geologist Mobil Oil of Can., Calgary, Alta., 1953-64; various lication U.S.A. and Fgn. Mobil Oil Corp., 1964-78, v.p. exploration, N.Y.C., 1978—. Office: Mobil Oil Corp 150 E 42d St New York NY 10017

GRAVES, THOMAS ASHLEY, JR., college president; b. Buffalo, July 3, 1924; s. Thomas Ashley and Esther (Brittain) G.; m. Zoe Ann Wasson, June 12, 1962; children: Thomas, Stephen, Mary, Andrew, Elizabeth. B.A., Yale U., 1947; M.B.A., Harvard U., 1949, D.B.A. (Ford Found. fellow), 1958; LL.D., U. Pa., 1975; Litt.D., Coll. of Charleston, 1976. Asst. dean, asso. dir. doctoral program Harvard. Grad. Sch. Bus. Adminstrn., 1950-60; dir. IMEDE, Internat. Mgmt. Devel. Inst., Lausanne, Switzerland, 1960-64; asso. dean, dir. Internat. Center for Advancement of Mgmt. Edn., Stanford Grad. Sch. Bus., 1964-67; asso. dean. Harvard Grad. Sch., 1967-71; pres. Coll. William and Mary, Williamsburg, Va., 1971—; dir. United Va. Bank, Williamsburg, Lawyers Title Ins. Co., Life Ins. Co. Va., Western Employers, Reynolds Metals Co., Investors Mortgage Ins. Co. Served with USNR, 1943-46. Hon. mem. Phi Beta Kappa, Phi Sigma, Beta Gamma Sigma. Clubs: Forum, Commonwealth (Richmond, Va.); Univ. (Washington); Rotary (Williamsburg, Va.). Home: President's House Coll William and Mary Williamsburg VA 23185

GRAVES, THOMAS WILLIAMS, JR., textile company executive; b. Wilson, N.C., June 7, 1940; s. Thomas Williams and Mary Virginia (Thompson) G.; m. Sara Kathryn Thomasson, Aug. 28, 1965; children: Kathryn Thomasson, Sara Virginia. A.B., Duke U., 1962, J.D., 1965. Bar: N.C. 1965. Assoc. firm Carr & Gibbons, Wilson, 1965-68; solicitor Recorder's Ct., City of Wilson, 1966-68; instr. Atlantic Christian Coll., also Am. Inst. Banking, Wilson, 1966-67; with Fiedcrest Mills, Eden, N.C., 1968—, counsel, 1972-75, sec., 1973—, gen. counsel, 1975—, v.p., 1977—, chmn. co. polit. action com., 1980—. Bd. dirs. Fieldcrest Found., 1982—; Chmn. N.C. Job. Tng. Coordinating Council, 1983—; Mem. Gov.'s Council on Arts and Humanities, 1983—, N.C. Com. for Math./Sci. Edn.; pres. bd. dirs. Eden YMCA, 1982-83; adv. bd. Eden City Schs., 1979—; bd. dirs. Eden United Fund, 1974—, N.C. Natural Resources and Community Devel.; chmn. dist. council ministries United Meth. Ch., 1980-84, mem. conf. bd. pensions, 1980—; bd. dirs. N.C. Citizens Bus. and Industry, 1976—, mem. exec. com., 1984—. Recipient Disting. Service award Eden Jaycees, 1972, President's plaque Eden YMCA, 1971. Mem. Am. Bar Assn., N.C. Bar Assn., 17th Jud. Bar Assn., Rockingham County Bar Assn. Club: Rotary. Home: 343 Maplewood Dr Eden NC 27288 Office: 326 E Stadium Dr Eden NC 27288

GRAVES, WALLACE BILLINGSLEY, univ. pres.; b. Ft. Worth, Feb. 10, 1922; s. Ellery George and Edith (Billingsley) G.; m. Barbara Jeanne Abey, Nov. 20, 1943; children—David W., Emily B. (Hay), John R., Julia A. B.A., U. Okla., 1943; M.A., Tex. Christian U., 1947; Ph.D., U. Tex., 1953; LL.D., Ind. State U., 1970, Valparaiso U., 1972; L.H.D., Morningside Coll., 1971. Teaching fellow Tex. Christian U., 1946-47, U. Tex., 1947-50; prof. polit. sci. DePauw U., 1950-58; vis. prof. Butler U., summer 1956; Armstrong prof. govt., dean men Tex. Wesleyan Coll., 1958-63, asst. to pres., 1963-65; acad. v.p. U. Pacific, 1965-67; pres. U. Evansville, Ind., 1967—; Dir. Citizens Nat. Bank Evansville.; Pres. Asso. Colls. Ind., 1972; mem. commn. on instns. higher edn. N. Central Assn. Colls. and Secondary Schs., 1971—; mem. exec. com. Ind. Conf. Higher Edn., 1972—. Contbr. articles to profl. jours. Mem. univ. senate United Methodist Ch., 1972—; mem. Ind. State Scholarship Commn., 1969—; Mem. adv. bd. St. Mary's Hosp.; mem. exec. com. Evansville's Future, 1968—; mem. exec. bd., chmn. home service com. Tarrant County chpt. A.R.C., 1960-65; exec. bd. Buffalo Trace council Boy Scouts Am., 1968—; Trustee Evansville Day Sch., 1967—; bd. dirs. Ft. Worth Assn. Retarded Children, 1963-65, World Affairs Council, Stockton, Cal., 1965-67; adv. bd. Carl Duisberg Soc., 1960—. Served with AUS, 1943-45. Ford fellow, summer 1951, 55. Mem. Am. Assn. Ind. Coll. and Univ. Presidents (bd. dirs.), AAUP, Evansville Met. C. of C. (exec. com. 1969—), Phi

Kappa Phi, Gold Key, Blue Key, Sigma Nu, Phi Mu Alpha, Pi Sigma Alpha. Methodist (ofcl. bd. temple). Clubs: Rotarian., Commonwealth (San Francisco); Columbia (Indpls.); Petroleum, Evansville Country, Kennel (Evansville)

GRAVES, WALTER ALBERT, ret. assn. exec., editor; b. Elmira, N.Y., Jan. 28, 1920; s. Fritz Karl and Bernice Julia (Miller) G.; m. Joanne Hutton Gardner, Mar. 3, 1950; 1 son, Randall Walter. Certificate in journalism, Northwestern U., 1936; A.B., Syracuse U., 1941, A.M., 1942; Ed.D., George Washington U., 1966. Reporter Elmira (N.Y.) Star-Gazette, 1940; tchr. English Syracuse (N.Y.) Pub. Schs., 1941, Marcellus (N.Y.) Pub. Schs., 1941; asst. editor NEA, Washington, 1946-65, asso. editor, 1965-68, mng. editor, 1968-75, editor, 1975-80; tchr. journalism workshops.; Tutor D.C. pub. schs., 1970-71. Contbr. numerous articles to profl. jours. Served with U.S. Naval Intelligence, 1942-46. Recipient Community Action Vol. Service awards United Planning Orgn., 1970-71. Mem. Am. Soc. Assn. Execs., Am. Soc. Bus. Press Editors, Ednl. Press Assn., Fed. Schoolmen's Club, Horace Mann League, NEA, Soc. Nat. Assn. Publs. Democrat. Congregationalist. Home: 1411 Harrison St Hollywood FL 33020

GRAY, ALLEN GIBBS, metallurgist, materials engineer, editor; b. Birmingham, Ala., July 28, 1915; s. Crawford H. and Marie (Gibbs) G.; m. Jean Breckenridge, Apr. 5, 1948; children: Alice, James. M.S., Vanderbilt U., 1938; Ph.D., U. Wis., 1940. Chemist, metallurgist E.I. du Pont de Nemours & Co., 1940-52; tech. work Manhattan Atomic Bomb Project, 1943-45; tech. editor Steel mag., 1952-58; editor Metal Progress mag., Am. Soc. Metals, 1958-72, pub., 1972-81; dir. periodical publs. Am. Soc. Metals, 1963-81, tech. dir., 1974—; adj. prof. metallurgy and mgmt. of tech. Vanderbilt U., Nashville, 1983—; Adv. com. on indsl. info. AEC, 1952—; chmn. spl. com. tech. aspects critical and strategic materials nat. materials bd. Nat. Acad. Scis., 1969—; Disting. Fishel lectr. Vanderbilt U., 1976; gave Congl. testimony on nat. materials policy and substitution, 1979; adv., speaker on materials substitution, raw materials planning and resources mgmt. Mem. Ohio Gov.'s Council on Atomic Energy, 1956-58; gen. chmn. Nat. Conf. on Materials Availability and Utilization, 1975, 7th Biennial Conf. on Nat. Materials Policy, 1982; mem. adv. bd. Fedn. Materials Socs., 1975—, Welding Research Council, 1970—; mem. tech. adv. com. Metal Properties Council, 1975—. Author: Modern Electroplating, 1953; Contbr.: sect. steel tech. Ency. Americana; sect. alloy steels Ency. Brit. Fellow Am. Soc. Metals, Am. Inst. Chemists; mem. Inst. Metals, Brit., Am. socs. testing materials, Assn. Technique de Traitement Thermique (hon.), Sigma Xi, Sigma Delta Chi. Issued patents. Home: 4301 Esteswood Dr Nashville TN 37215 Office: Metals Park Novelty OH 44072 also Office: Engring Sch Vanderbilt U Nashville TN 37235 *If our work and productivity are to grow, a continuing program of self-renewal is essential. Setting up and carrying out a program of self-development poses a formidable task. But the course of action is up to the individual. The rapid technological change in the industrial scene offers the greatest challenges ever to an individual's development as a professional in his field and to his ability to take advantage of the many opportunities which exist.*

GRAY, ANN MAYNARD, broadcasting co. exec.; b. Boston, Aug. 22, 1945; m. Richard R. Gray, Jr. B.A., U. Mich., 1967; M.B.A., N.Y. U., 1971. With Chase Manhattan Bank, N.Y.C., 1967-68; with Chem. Bank, N.Y.C., 1968-73, asst. sec., 1971-73; asst. to treas., then asst. treas. ABC, Inc., 1974-76, treas., 1976—, v.p. corp. planning, 1979—. Address: 1330 Ave of Americas New York NY 10019

GRAY, ARTHUR, JR., investment counselor; b. N.Y.C., Dec. 21, 1922; s. Arthur and Beatriz (Lerner) G.; m. Adele Hall, Dec. 1944 (div. 1954); children—Michael H., Kathleen W., John M., Wendy L.; m. Betty Johnson; children—Lydia B., Elisabeth C. Asso. Student, Lawrenceville (N.J.) School, 1937-40, Mass. Inst. Tech., 1941-42. With Kuhn, Loeb & Co., 1945-53; pres. Michael Myerberg Prodns., 1953-57; exec. v.p., dir. A.M. Kidder & Co., Inc., 1957-59; sr. partner Gray & Co.; mems. N.Y. Stock Exchange, 1959-74; 1st v.p. Mitchell, Hutchins; mems. N.Y. Stock Exchange, 1974-75; chmn. Tallasi Mgmt. Co., N.Y.C., 1975-80; mng. dir. Dreman Gray & Embry, 1981—; chmn. Christine Valmy, Inc., Ingrip Fasteners, Inc.; dir. Prudential Lines, Inc. Pres. bd. Boys Athletic League, 1960-64, Speech and Hearing Inst., 1970-74; Chmn. spl. events Citizens for Eisenhower-Nixon, 1952; Trustee Am. Mus. Natural History; pres. Lerner-Gray Found.; bd. dirs. ICD Internat. Center for Disabled. Served to 1st lt. USAAF, 1942-45. Decorated D.F.C., Air medal with 4 oak leaf clusters. Mem. Am. Arbitration Assn. (dir.), Sigma Alpha Epsilon. Presbyn. (trustee). Clubs: Wall Street, Lambs (N.Y.C.). Home: Bliss Tavern Haverhill NH 03765 Office: Dreman Gray & Embry 605 Madison Ave New York NY 10022

GRAY, BARRY SHERMAN, radio commentator; b. Red Lion, N.J., July 2, 1916; s. Manuis Joseph and Dora (Horowitz) Yaroslaw; children: Melodie, Michael N. Grad. high sch. Commentator-interviewer, WKAT, Miami Beach, Fla., 1947-50, WMCA, N.Y.C., 1950—; Author: My Night People, 1975; contbr. travel articles to: New York Times; contbg. editor: Diversion mag.; weekly columnist: Our Town newspaper. Served to lt. col. AUS. Recipient Legion of Honor, N.Y. Police Dept., 1953, Michael award, 1953, award English Speaking Union, 1956. Mem. AFTRA, Screen Actors Guild, Nat. Rifle Assn. (life), Commanderie de Bordeaux, Sigma Delta Chi. Home: 425 E 58th St New York NY 10022 Office: 888 7th Ave New York NY 10019

GRAY, BOWMAN, III, investment banker; b. Winston-Salem, N.C., Mar. 31, 1938; s. Bowman, Jr. and Elizabeth Palmer (Christian) C.; (div.)children: Elizabeth, Alice, Bowman, IV. Student, U. Va., U. N.C. Salesman, then mktg. mgr. R.J.R. Archer Co. (div. R.J. Reynolds Industries), Winston-Salem, 1965-70; dir. internat. affairs Gen. Occidentale, Paris, 1971-72; pres. Gen. Occidental, Inc., N.Y.C., 1972—, Cavenham Holdings, Inc., 1980—; chmn. bd. Grand Union Co., 1980-81, Cavenham U.S.A., Inc., 1980—; dir. Diamond Internat. Corp. Trustee Woodberry Forest (Va.) Sch., Pasquaney Trust, Bristol, N.H. Served with AUS, 1957-60. Republican. Episcopalian. Clubs: Brook, Links (N.Y.C.); Metropolitan (Washington); Capital City (Atlanta). Office: Gen Occidental Inc 650 Fifth Ave New York NY 10019

GRAY, BRUCE WILLIAM, publisher; b. Los Angeles, June 13, 1944; s. William Price and Fredrika Amalia (Ryl) G.; m. Donna Sherman, Oct. 26, 1980; children: Bruce William, Jesse Bennett. B.A., Jamestown Coll., 1967. N.Y. advt. sales mgr. World Tennis Mag., N.Y.C., 1976-77; advt. dir. Sea Mag., Newport Beach, Calif., 1978; publisher World Tennis Mag. and Tennis Bus., Tennis USA, N.Y.C., 1979-81; pres., publisher Atlantic Monthly, Boston, 1981-82; v.p., pub. Mag. div. R.R. Bowker Co., including Pub. Weekly, Library Jour., Sch. Library Jour., Small Press, 1982-83; pres. R.R. Bowker, 1983—. Served with mil. intelligence U.S. Army, 1968-71. Republican. Clubs: Norwalk (Conn.) Yacht; Overseas Press (N.Y.C.). Home: 394 Brookside Rd Darien CT 06820 Office: RR Bowker Co 205 E 42d St New York City NY 10017

GRAY, CHARLES ELMER, lawyer; b. Elvins, Mo., July 23, 1919; s. Grover P. and Martha Elizabeth (Sullivan) G.; m. Beulah Henrich Gray, July 4, 1942; children—Karen Lee, Cecilia Jean, Bette Sue, Marsha Dawn. Student, Flat River Jr. Coll., 1937-38, U. Hawaii, 1940-41; LL.B., Washington U., St. Louis, 1947. Bar: Mo. bar 1947. Since practiced in, St. Louis; partner firm Gray and Ritter; sec., gen. counsel Don V. Davis Co.; pres. Don-Ite Corp.; gen. counsel, dir. United Mo. Bank, St Louis; mem. Mo. Appellate Jud. Commn.; mem. rules com. Supreme Ct. Mo., 1970-81. Served to capt. USAF, 1939-45. Fellow Internat. Acad. Trial Lawyers (dir.), Am. Coll. Trial Lawyers, Internat. Soc. Barristers (state chmn., dir.); mem. Am., Mo. St. Louis bar assns., Lawyers Assn. St. Louis (v.p. 1954, bd. govs., Honor award 1977), Phi Delta Phi. Home: Apt 1003 625 S Skinker St St Louis MO 63105 also Apt 290 950 Beach Rd Johns Island Vero Beach FL 32960 Office: 900 Locust Bldg 1015 Locust St St Louis MO 63101

GRAY, CLAYLAND BOYDEN, lawyer; b. Winston-Salem, N.C., Feb. 6, 1943; s. Gordon and Jane (Craige) G. J.D. with high honors, U. N.C., 1968; B.A. in History magna cum laude, Harvard U., 1964. Bar: D.C., N.C. Law clk. to chief justice Earl Warren, 1968; asso. Wilmer, Cutler & Pickering, 1969, partner, 1976—; now counsel and dep. chief of staff to Vice Pres. George Bush, Washington; chmn. Summit Communications, Inc., Winston-Salem. Mem. Com. on Univ. Devel., Harvard U.; trustee St. Mark's Sch., Southboro, Mass. Served with USMC, 1964-70. Mem. ABA, D.C. Bar Assn., N.C. Bar Assn., Fed. Bar Assn. Republican. Episcopalian. Clubs: Met., Chevy Chase., Alibi. Home: 2720 Dumbarton St NW Washington DC 20007 Office: Room 280 Old Executive Office Bldg Washington DC 20501

GRAY, CLEVE, artist; b. N.Y.C., Sept. 22, 1918; s. Jacob and Sylvia (Fields) G.; m. Francine du Plessix, Apr. 23, 1957; children: Thaddeus Ives, Luke Alexander. B.A. summa cum laude, Princeton U., 1940. Author, editor: David Smith by David Smith, 1968, John Marin by John Marin, 1970, Hans Richter by Hans Richter, 1971; contbg. editor: Art in America, 1960-70; One-man shows, J. Seligmann Gallery, 1947-50, 52, 54, 57, 59, Staempfli Gallery, 1960, 62, 64, Saidenberg Gallery, 1965, 67, Betty Parson Gallery, 1969, 72, 73, 76, 78, 79, 80, 81, 82, 83, Addison Gallery Am. Art, 1969, Mus. Art, Princeton U., Honolulu Acad. Fine Arts, 1970, Albright-Knox Gallery, Columbus Gallery Fine Art, 1977, also shows in, Can., France, Italy; exhibited in group shows, 1946—; including Whitney Mus. annuals; including, U. Ill. annuals, Guggenheim Mus., 1961, 65, Chgo. Art Inst., 1946, 61, U. Nebr. annuals, Corcoran Mus. annuals; represented in permanent collections, Whitney Mus., Met. Mus., Guggenheim Mus., R.I. Sch. Design Mus., Wadsworth Atheneum, Columbus Mus., Krannert Art Mus., Honolulu Acad. Fine Arts, NYU Mus., U. Calif.-Berkeley, U. Ill. Mus., Vanderbilt U. Mus., Columbia U., Nat. Collection, Sheldon Meml. Gallery; others. Trustee R.I. Sch. Design, 1969-72, 76—, Wadsworth Atheneum, 1976-78, Conn. Commn. for Arts, 1977-82, N.Y. Sch. Drawing, Painting and Sculpture, 1970-75. Served with AUS, 1943-46. Club: Century Assn. (N.Y.C.). Address: Graystones Cornwall Bridge CT 06754

GRAY, DAVID EUGENE, business executive, former recreation administration educator; b. Hollywood, Calif., June 21, 1918; s. King David and Myrtle G. (Nichols) G.; m. Frances Lenore Tulleys, Nov. 8, 1941; children: Cathleen Gray Burns, Christopher David, Jonathan David. B.A., Los Angeles State Coll., 1950; M.S., UCLA, 1953; D.P.A., U. So. Calif., 1961. Recreation dir., City of Los Angeles, 1937-41; civilian chief spl. services USAF, London, 1958-59; mem. faculty Calif. State U., Long Beach, from 1954, prof. recreation adminstrn., from 1960, chmn. dept. recreation, 1964-67, assoc. dean, 1967-69, v.p. adminstrn. Sch. Applied Arts and Scis., 1969-83; pres. David Gray & Assocs., Orange, Calif., 1983—; research assoc. U. So. Calif., 1960-64; sec.-treas. Calif. State U. Long Beach Found., 1970-83; pres. Long Beach Recreation Commn., 1975-76; vis. prof. U. Hawaii, Oreg. State U., U. So. Calif., U. Mass., U. N.C., Chapel Hill; cons. in field. Co-author: Motivation and Modern Management, 1970, Reflections on the Recreation and Park Movement - A Book of Readings, 1973; cons. editor, William C. Brown Pubs.; contbr. articles to profl. jours. Served with AUS, 1942-46. Decorated Bronze Star. Mem. Nat. Recreation and Park Assn. (Lit. award 1980, mem. accreditation council 1975—), Calif. Park and Recreation Soc., SCAPA, Praetors, Blue Key, Phi Kappa Phi. Office: David Gray & Assocs 4731 E Blue Jay Orange CA 92669

GRAY, DUNCAN MONTGOMERY, JR., bishop; b. Canton, Miss., Sept. 21, 1926; s. Duncan Montgomery and Isabel (McCrady) G.; m. Ruth Miller Spivey, Feb. 9, 1948; children: Duncan Montgomery, Anne Gray Finley, Lloyd Spivey, Catherine Gilmer. B.E.E., Tulane U., 1948; M.Div., U. South, 1953, D.D. (hon.), 1972. Ordained priest Episcopal Ch., 1953, bishop, 1974; priest-in-charge Calvary Ch., Cleveland, Miss. and Grace Ch., Rosedale, Miss., 1953-57, Holy Innocents Ch., Como, Miss., 1957-60; rector St. Peter's Ch., Oxford, Miss., 1957-65, St. Paul's Ch., Meridian, Miss., 1965-74; bishop coadjutor Diocese of Miss., Jackson, 1974, bishop, 1974—; chmn. Standing Commn. on Constn. and Canons of Gen. Conv. of Episc. Ch., 1977-83, House of Bishops' Com. Canons, 1975—. Contbr. articles in field to religious publs. Chmn. bd. trustees All Saints Episc. Sch., Vicksburg, 1975-77; trustee U. South, Sewanee, Tenn., 1974—, regent, 1981—; chmn. Miss. Religious Leadership Conf., 1977-79, So. Regional Council, 1967-73; mem. Miss. Mental Health Assn., 1968-73; bd. dirs. Miss. Council on Human Relations, 1962—, pres., 1963-67; mem. Miss. Adv. Com. to U.S. Commn. on Civil Rights, 1975—. Recipient Nat. Speaker of Year award Tau Kappa Alpha, 1962. Home: 3775 Old Canton Rd Jackson MS 39216 Office: PO Box 1636 Jackson MS 39205

GRAY, D'WAYNE, marine corps officer; b. Corsicana, Tex., Apr. 9, 1931; s. Henry Oliver and Myrtle Daisy (Lee) G.; m. Mary Joan Sobieck, Oct. 11, 1955; children—Stephen D'Wayne, Elizabeth Joan, Theresa Mary. Student, N. Tex. Agrl. Coll., 1948-49; B.A., U. Tex., 1952; M.S. in Internat. Affairs, George Washington U., 1971; postgrad., Naval War Coll., 1970-71, Harvard U., 1980. Commd. 2d lt. U.S. Marine Corps, 1952, advanced through grades to lt. gen., 1983; asst. div. comdr. 1st Marine Div., Camp Pendleton, Calif., 1977-79, dir. plans Hdqrs., Washington, 1979-80, dir. ops. Hdqrs., 1980-81, dir. personnel mgmt. div. Hdqrs., 1981-83, chief of staff, 1983—; del. Inter-Am. Def. Bd., 1980; dir. U.S. Naval Inst., 1979—. Chmn. editorial bd., U.S. Naval Inst. Press, 1980—. Mem. maritime policy study group Ctr. for Strategic and Internat. Studies, Georgetown U., 1981—. Decorated Legion of Merit with gold star and V, Bronze Star medal with V, Meritorious Service medal with gold star. Mem. Marine Corps Assn., Uniformed Services Benefit Assn. (gov. Kansas City, Mo. 1982-83), U.S. Naval Inst. Roman Catholic. Home: Quarters E Washington Navy Yard Washington DC 20374 Office: Hdqrs US Marine Corps Code CS Washington DC 20380

GRAY, EDWARD, publisher; b. Bucharest, Romania, 1915; came to U.S., 1961, naturalized, 1965; m. Carol Nader, 1955. M.A., U. Lille, France, 1934; D. Econs., U. Nancy, France, 1936. Vice pres. Maxwell Sci. Internat., Inc., N.Y.C. and Elmsford, N.Y., 1966-68, pres., dir., 1968—, Microforms Internat. Mktg. Corp., Elmsford, 1971—; dir. micropublishing Pergamon Press, Inc., Elmsford, 1974—, pres., 1975-77, sr. v.p. and micropub. dir., 1978—; pres. Brit. Book Centre, N.Y.C. and Elmsford, 1972—. Author papers microfiche alternative for current subscriptions and microfilm pub.; Editor: Micropub. of Current Periodicals, 1977-82; editor: Internat. Jour. Micrographics and Video Technology, 1982—; Editor: Malthus Library Catalogue, 1983. Recipient Best Thesis award U. Nancy, 1936. Mem. N.Y. Acad. Scis., Soc. for Scholarly Pub., Nat. Micrographics Assn., Internat. Micrographics Congress, Antique Booksellers Assn. Office: Pergamon Press Inc Fairview Park Elmsford NY 10523

GRAY, EDWIN JOHN, government official; b. Modesto, Calif., Aug. 22, 1935. B.A., Calif. State U., Fresno, 1957. News reporter KMJ Radio, Fresno, 1957-60; staff writer, day news editor UPI Bur., Madrid, Spain, 1961-63; press staffer to Gov. Reagan, Sacramento, 1967-72, press sec., 1972-73; sr. v.p. San Diego Fed. Savs. & Loan Assn., 1973-80; campaign press sec., dep. chief staff, dir. policy communications Reagan-Bush Com., 1980; asso. dir. policy coordination human services Office of Pres.-Elect, 1980-81; dep. asst. to Pres. for policy devel., dir. White House Office Policy Devel., Washington, 1981-83; chmn. Fed. Home Loan Bank Bd., Washington, 1983—; Bd. dirs., mem. exec. com. Calif. Taxpayers Assn., 1979-81; pres., bd. dirs. San Diego Taxpayers Assn., 1974-81. Office: 1700 G St NW Washington DC 20552 *

GRAY, FRANCES M., lectr., ret. coll. pres.; b. Little Rock, Jan. 6, 1910; d. Daniel L. and Nancy (Miller) G. B.A., Southwestern at Memphis, 1930, D.Hum., 1977; M.A., U. Chgo., 1939; M.S., Columbia., 1954; LL.D., Whitworth Coll., 1959. Field dir. A.R.C., 1944-46; exec. sec. Presbyn. Ch. U.S.A., 1946-50, rep. for overseas mission in Africa and Middle East, 1950-56; prof. religion and social studies Beirut (Lebanon) Coll. for Women, 1956-59, pres., 1959-65, Damavand Coll., Teheran, Iran, 1965-75; ret., 1975. Decorated Taj medal, Iran, 1974; recipient gold medal in edn., Lebanon, 1965. Home: 2095 Jackson St Apt 302 San Francisco CA 94109

GRAY, FRANCINE DU PLESSIX, author; b. Warsaw, Poland, Sept. 25, 1930; came to U.S., 1941, naturalized, 1952; d. Bertrand Jochaud and Tatiana Liberman (Iacovleff) du Plessix; m. Cleve Gray, Apr. 23, 1957; children: Thaddeus Ives, Luke Alexander. B.A., Barnard Coll., 1952; Litt.D. (hon.), City U. N.Y., 1981. Reporter UP, 1952-54; book editor Art in Am., 1964-66; disting. vis. prof. CCNY, 1975, part-time prof. English, 1976-77; vis. lectr. Yale U., New Haven, 1981-82. Writer, The New Yorker mag., 1968—; author: Divine Disobedience: Profiles in Catholic Radicalism, 1970 (Nat. Cath. Book award), Hawaii: The Sugar-Coated Fortress, 1972 (Newswomen's Club N.Y.C. award), Lovers and Tyrants, 1976, World Without End, 1981. Mem. Am. P.E.N., Authors Guild, Nat. Book Critics Circle. Democrat. Roman Catholic. *

GRAY, FRANK GEORGE, insurance company executive; b. Dunshalt, Scotland, May 16, 1942; came to U.S., 1971; s. Robert McNaughton and Agnes Helen G.; m. June Langdon, Aug. 19, 1977; children: Scott Nathan, Kevin Franklin. B.Commerce, McGill U., Montreal, Que., Can., 1965. Chartered accountant, Can. Sr. auditor Coopers & Lybrand (chartered accountants), Montreal, 1959-67, audit mgr., Toronto, 1970-71; asst. treas. Am. Internat. Reins. Co. Inc., Hamilton, Bermuda, 1967-70; v.p., comptroller N.H. Ins. Co., Manchester, 1971-79; chief internal auditor Am. Internat. Group, N.Y.C., 1979-82, v.p., dep. comptroller, 1982—. Mem. Soc. Ins. Accountants, Can. Inst. Chartered Accountants. Republican. Club: Elks. Office: 70 Pine St New York NY 10005

GRAY, FRANK TRUAN, lawyer; b. Prince Frederick, Md., Oct. 22, 1920; s. John B. and Aimée Atlee (Truan) G.; m. Sally A. Jackson, Dec. 31, 1976; children—John W., Edward A., Philip L., Theodora R. A.B., Princeton U., 1942; student, Cambridge (Eng.) U., 1945; LL.B., Harvard U., 1948. Bar: Md. bar 1949. Asso. firm Piper & Marbury, Balt., 1948-56, partner, 1957—; asst. atty. gen., State of Md., 1955-56; pres. Balt. Estate Planning Council, 1975-76. Editor: Harvard Law Rev, 1947-48. Pres. Citizen's Planning and Housing Assn., Balt., 1958-60; bd. dirs. Balt. Neighborhoods, Inc., 1959—; trustee Provident Hosp., Inc., Balt., 1961-74. Fellow Am. Bar Found., Md. Bar Found.; mem. Am., Md., Balt. City bar assns., Am. Law Inst.

GRAY, FRANKLIN DINGWALL, lawyer; b. Mpls., July 19, 1904; s. William Irving and Isabelle Wenonah (Welles) G.; m. Laura Erf, June 18, 1932; 1 dau., Ellen Gray Horton. B.A. magna cum laude, U. Minn., 1925, Oxford (Eng.) U., 1927, B.C.L., 1928, M.A., 1953. Bar: Minn. 1929. Ptnr. firm Gray, Plant, Mooty, Mooty & Bennett, and predecessors, Mpls., 1942—; lectr. bus. law Sch. Bus. Adminstrn., U. Minn., 1937-45. Fellow Am. Coll. Trial Lawyers; mem. ABA, Minn. Bar Assn., Am. Arbitration Assn. (Twin Cities council), U. Minn. Alumni Assn. (pres. 1963-64), Phi Beta Kappa, Theta Delta Chi, Phi Delta Phi. Club: Rotary (pres. Mpls. 1965-66). Home: 5253 Richwood Dr Minneapolis MN 55436 Office: City Ctr Minneapolis MN 55402

GRAY, FREDERICK THOMAS, JR., educator; b. Hopewell, Va., Mar. 22, 1951; s. Frederick Thomas and Evelyn Helms (Johnson) G. B.A. with distinction, U. Va., 1972, J.D., 1975; postgrad., U. Richmond, 1981—. Bar: Va. 1976. Law clk. Williams, Mullen & Christian, Richmond, Va., 1975-76, assoc., 1976-78; sec. Commonwealth of Va., Richmond, 1978-81; now high sch. tchr. Mem. Chesterfield County Democratic Com. Mem. Chesterfield Jaycees (pres. 1980-81), Chesterfield Edn. Assn. Club: Chesterfield Kiwanis. Home: 11721 S Briarpatch Dr Midlothian VA 23113

GRAY, GEORGE, mural painter; b. Harrisburg, Pa., Dec. 23, 1907; s. George Zacharias and Anna Margaret (Barger) G. Ed., Harrisburg Tech. High Sch., Sch. Indsl. Art, Phila., 1927-30, Acad. Fine Arts, Wilmington, Del., 1931-33, Art Students League, N.Y.C., Howard Pyle Sch. Illustration, Wilmington. Designer stage scenery, N.Y.C., 1926; invited to sketch scenes of army life in various forts and camps; tchr. anatomy and figure constrn. while attending art classes, Phila., Wilmington; later staff artist, U.S. Inf. Jour., U.S. Cav. Jour., Washington, N.Y. Nat. Guardsmen, Pa. N.G. Mag.; mural painter patron, Gen. J. Leslie Kincaid; pres., Am. Hotels Corp., N.Y.C., 1934—; murals exhibited in hotels throughout U.S., including MacArthur of Battan, Hotel Jefferson-Clinton, Syracuse, N.Y.; Gen. George Rogers Clark, Louisville; 3 murals Hist. L.I, Suffolk County Savs. and Loan Bank, Babylon, L.I.; mural painting Brooklyn Bridge, Seamen's Ch. Inst., N.Y.C.; hist. picture map, Hotel Huntington, L.I., portraits and paintings in pvt. collections, U.S. and abroad; mil. artist, Engring. Bd., Ft. Belvoir, Va.; combat artist, U.S. Coast Guard Hdqrs., Washington; originator, chmn., Navy Art Cooperation and Liaison Com. of Salmagundi Club. Recipient Meritorious Pub. Service citation Dept. Navy, 1964; Louis E. Seley NACAL award, 1970; medal of honor Salmagundi Club, 1973; George Gray award U.S. Coast Guard, 1983. Life fellow Royal Soc. Arts (London); mem. Soc. Illustrators, Am. Mil. Inst., Co. Mil. Collectors and Historians, Nat. Soc. Mural Painters, Am. Vets. Soc. Artists, Am. Artists Profl. League, Nat. Hist. Soc. (founding mem.), Assn. Mil. Surgeons U.S., Navy League U.S., U.S. Naval Inst., Armed Forces Mgmt. Inst., Artists Fellowship. Clubs: Arts (Washington); Salmagundi (N.Y.C.). Address: Salmagundi Club 47 Fifth Ave New York NY 10003

GRAY, GORDON L., communications educator; b. Hampton, Iowa, May 18, 1924; s. Leroy Ernest and Arianna (Oldham) G.; m. Barbara Ann Smith, Feb. 5, 1949; children: David Gordon, Jonathan William. B.A., Cornell Coll., 1948; M.A., Northwestern U., 1951, Ph.D., 1957. Radio announcer and newsman, 1948-50; broadcast coordinator NBC-TV, Chgo, 1951; instr. to asso. prof. television and radio Mich. State U., 1953-67; prof. communications Temple U., Phila., 1967—, chmn. dept. radio, TV and film, 1967-74, 78-82; Program assoc. Ednl. TV and

Radio Center, Ann Arbor, Mich., 1956-57. Served to staff sgt. AUS, 1943-46. Fulbright scholar Inst. Edn. U. Leeds, U.K., 1965-66.

GRAY, HANNA HOLBORN, university pres.; b. Heidelberg, Germany, Oct. 25, 1930; d. Hajo and Annemarie (Bettmann) Holborn; m. Charles Montgomery Gray, June 19, 1954. A.B., Bryn Mawr Coll., 1950; Fulbright scholar, Oxford U., 1950-52, D.Litt., 1979; Ph.D., Harvard U., 1957,; M.A., Yale U., 1971, LL.D., 1978; L.H.D., Grinnell Coll., Lawrence U., Denison U., 1974, Wheaton Coll., 1976, Marlboro Coll., 1979, Rikkyo U., 1979, Roosevelt U., 1980, Knox Coll., 1980, Coe Coll., 1981, Duke U., 1982, New Sch. for Social Research, 1982, Clark U., 1982, Brandeis U., 1983, Colgate U., 1983, Thomas Jefferson U., 1981, Wayne State U., 1984, Miami U., 1984; Litt.D., St. Lawrence U., 1974; H.H.D., St. Mary's Coll., 1974; LL.D., Union Coll., 1975, Regis Coll., 1976, Dartmouth Coll., 1978, Trinity Coll., 1978, U. Bridgeport, 1978, Dickinson Coll., 1979, Brown U., 1979, Wittenberg U., 1979, U. Rochester, 1980, U. Notre Dame, 1980, U. So. Calif., 1980, U. Mich., 1981, Princeton U., 1982, Georgetown U., 1983, Marguette U., 1984. Instr. Bryn Mawr (Pa.) Coll., 1953-54; teaching fellow Harvard, 1955-57, instr., 1957-59, asst. prof., 1959-60, vis. lectr., 1963-64; asst. prof. U. Chgo., 1961-64, asso. prof., 1964-72; dean, prof. Northwestern U., Evanston, Ill., 1972-74; provost, prof. history Yale U., 1974-78, acting pres., 1977-78; pres., prof. history, U. Chgo., 1978—; dir. Cummins Engine Co., J.P. Morgan & Co., Morgan Guaranty Trust Co., Atlantic Richfield Co.; fellow Center for Advanced Study in Behavioral Scis., 1966-67, vis. scholar, 1970-71. Editor: (with Charles Gray) Jour. Modern History, 1965-70; Contbr. articles to profl. jours. Mem. Nat. Council on Humanities, 1972-78; trustee Yale Corp., 1971-74; bd. dirs. Council Fin. Aid to Edn., Chgo. Council Fgn. Relations, Andrew W. Mellon Found.; mem. Pulitzer Prize Bd.; trustee Mus. Sci. and Industry, Bryn Mawr Coll., Field Found. Ill., Mayo Found., Brookings Instn., Howard Hughes Med. Inst. U. Chgo. Newberry Library fellow, 1960-61; Phi Beta Kappa vis. scholar, 1971-72; hon. fellow St. Anne's Coll., Oxford U., 1978—. Fellow Am. Acad. Arts and Scis.; mem. Renaissance Soc. Am., Am. Philos. Soc., Phi Beta Kappa (senate).

GRAY, HARRY BARKUS, chemistry educator; b. Woodburn, Ky., Nov. 14, 1935; s. Barkus and Ruby (Hopper) G.; m. Shirley Barnes, June 2, 1957; children: Victoria Lynn, Andrew Thomas, Noah Harry Barkus. B.S., Western Ky. U., 1957; Ph.D., Northwestern U., 1960. Postdoctoral fellow U. Copenhagen, 1960-61; faculty Columbia U., 1961-66, prof., 1965-66; prof. chemistry Calif. Inst. Tech., Pasadena, 1966—, now Arnold O. Beckman prof. chemistry, chmn. div.; vis. prof. Rockefeller U., Harvard U., U. Iowa, Pa. State U., Yeshiva U., U. Copenhagen, U. Witwatersrand, Johannesburg, South Africa, U. Canterbury, Christchurch, New Zealand; cons. govt., industry. Author: Electrons and Chemical Bonding, 1965, Molecular Orbital Theory, 1965, Ligand Substitution Processes, 1966, Basic Principles of Chemistry, 1967, Chemical Dynamics, 1968, Chemical Principles, 1970, Models in Chemical Science, 1971, Chemical Bonds, 1973, Chemical Structure and Bonding, 1980, Molecular Electronic Structures, 1980. Recipient Franklin Meml. award, 1967; Fresenius award, 1970; Shoemaker award, 1970; Harrison Howe award, 1972; award for excellence in teaching Mfg. Chemists Assn., 1972; Remsen Meml. award, 1979; Tolman medal, 1979; Guggenheim fellow, 1972-73; Phi Beta Kappa scholar, 1973-74. Mem. Nat. Acad. Scis., Am. Chem. Soc. (award pure chemistry 1970, award inorganic chemistry 1978, award for disting. service in advancement of inorganic chemistry 1984), Royal Danish Acad. Scis. and Letters, Alpha Chi Sigma, Phi Lambda Upsilon. Home: 1415 E California Blvd Pasadena CA 91106

GRAY, HARRY JACK, business executive; b. Milledgeville Crossroads, Ga., Nov. 18, 1919; m. Helen Buckley; children: Pam, Vicky Lynn. B.S. with honors, U. Ill., 1941, M.S., 1947; LL.D., Trinity Coll., Conn., 1976, U. Hartford, 1978, U. Conn., 1982; D.Sc. (hon.), Fla. Inst. Tech., 1980, D.Engring., Worcester Poly. Inst., 1983. Instr. U. Ill., 1946-47; sales mgr. truck div. Esserman Motor Sales, Chgo., 1947-50; exec. salesman Platt, Inc., Chgo., 1950-51; exec. v.p., gen. mgr. Greyvan Lines, div. Greyhound Corp., Chgo., 1951-54; pres. U.S. Engring. div. Litton Industries, Van Nuys, Calif., 1956; v.p. Litton Industries, Beverly Hills, Calif., 1958-61; group v.p., 1961-64, sr. v.p. components, 1964-65, sr. v.p. for finance and adminstrn., 1965-67, exec. v.p., 1967-69, sr. exec. v.p., 1969-71; also dir.; pres. United Technologies Corp. (formerly United Aircraft), Hartford, Conn., 1971—, chief exec. officer, 1972—, chmn., pres., 1974-81, chmn., pres., chief operating officer, 1981—, also dir.; dir. Citicorp, Citibank (N.A.), Union Carbide, Greater Hartford Corp. Corporator Hartford Hosp., Inst. of Living, Hartford; mem. Pres.'s Nat. Security Telecommunications Adv. Com.; bd. dirs. Old State House Assn., Hartford.; chmn. bd. dirs. Nat. Sci. Center for Communications and Electronics Found. Served to capt. AUS, 1941-46. Decorated Silver Star, Bronze Star. Mem. Bus. Council Washington (bd. dirs.), Conf. Bd. N.Y.C., IEEE, Club, Navy League U.S. Club: Econs. of N.Y. Office: United Technologies Corp Hartford CT 06101

GRAY, HARRY JOSHUA, electrical engineer, educator; b. St. Louis, June 24, 1924; s. Harry Joshua and Mary Margaret (Davis) G.; m. Cecilia M. McNulty, Apr. 23, 1949; children— Margaret, Cecilia, Kathleen (dec.), Mary. Student, Lehigh U., 1941-43; B.S.E.E., U. Pa., 1944, Ph.D., 1953. Registered profl. engr., Pa. Instr. The Moore Sch. Elec. Engring., U. Pa., Phila., 1947-51, asso., 1951-53, asst. prof., 1953-54, asso. prof., 1957-64, prof. elec. engring. and computer and info. sci., 1964—; with Remington Rand Univac, Phila., 1954-57; cons. in field; bd. dirs. Pa. Research Assocs., Inc., 1963. Contbr. articles to profl. jours.; author: Digital Computer Engineering, 1963, High Speed Digital Circuits and Memories, 1976. Served with USN, 1943-46. Grantee U.S. Atomic Energy Com., 1966-69, NSF, 1966-68, NIMH, 1971-73, Burroughs Corp., 1973-75. Mem. IEEE, Am. Soc. Engring. Edn., IEEE Profl. Groups, Sigma Xi, Tau Beta Pi, Eta Kappa Nu, Pi Mu Epsilon, Phi Eta Sigma. Patentee in field. Office: Moore Sch Elec Engring 200 S 33d St Philadelphia PA 19104

GRAY, HELEN THERESA GOTT, editor; b. Jersey City, July 2, 1942; d. William E. and Cynthia (Williams) Gott; m. David L. Gray, Aug. 15, 1976; 1 son, David Lee. B.A. cum laude, Syracuse U., 1963; M. Internat. Affairs (John Hay Whitney Found. fellow), Columbia U., 1965. Summer intern Washington Post, 1964; reporter Kansas City (Mo.) Star, 1965-71, religion editor, 1971—; editor The New Birth. Bd. advisers Sch. of Discovery. Mem. United Prayer Movement, Theta Sigma Phi. Baptist. Participant, Experiment in Internat. Living, 1962. Home: PO Box 12250 Kansas City KS 66117 Office: 1729 Grand Ave Kansas City MO 64108

GRAY, HERBERT WALTER, banker; b. North Andover, Mass., Jan. 25, 1921; s. Herbert Walter and Grace (Woodcock) G.; m. Janet Haigh, June 14, 1952; children: David, Stephen, Cynthia, Timothy. Student, Boston U., 1946-50; grad. with honors, Grad. Sch. Savs. Banking, Brown U., 1963; grad. mgmt. devel. program, Dartmouth Coll., 1966. Youth worker, camp dir. YMCA, Lawrence, Mass., 1953-56; with Suffolk Franklin Savs. Bank of Boston, 1956—, exec. v.p., 1969-72, chief adminstrv. officer, 1969—, pres., 1972—, chief exec. officer, 1976—; chmn. bd., chief exec. officer Mut. Bank (formed by merger of Suffolk Franklin Savs. Bank of Boston and Mut. Bank of Newton, Mass.), 1981—; dir. Investors Bank & Trust Co., Boston. Trustee, treas. Gen. Ins. Guarantee Fund Commonwealth of Mass.; v.p. Greater Lawrence YMCA; bd. dirs. Boston Municipal Research Bur.; chmn. bd. trustees Center Fin. Studies, Fairfield, Conn.; trustee Lawrence Gen. Hosp., Mass. Eye and Ear Infirmary, Pike Sch.; corporator Merrimack Valley Textile Mus.; dir. Mass. Taxpayers Found.; lay reader St. Paul's Ch., North Andover, Mass. Served with Canadian Armoured Forces, 1939-41; Served with USAAF, 1941-45. Decorated Air medal. Mem. Nat. Assn. Mut. Savs. Banks (past chmn.), Savs. Banks Assn. Mass. (past pres.). Episcopalian. Club: Union (Boston). Home: 14 Stacy Dr North Andover MA 01845 Office: 45 Franklin St Boston MA 02110

GRAY, JAMES, English literature educator; b. Montrose, Scotland, May. 11, 1923; s. James and Matilda (Smythe) G.; m. Pamela Doris Knight, July 26, 1947. M.A., U. Aberdeen, 1946; B.A. with honours, U. Oxford, Eng., 1948, M.A., 1951; Ph.D., U. Montreal, 1970. Prof. English Bishops U., Lennoxville, Que., Can., 1948-72, chmn. humanities div., 1971-72; prof., chmn. dept. English Dalhousie U., Halifax, N.S., 1972-75, dean Faculty Arts and Sci., 1975-80, Thomas McCulloch prof. English, 1980—; mem. Humanities Research Council of Can. Author: The Sermons of Samuel Johnson: A Study, 1972; co-editor: The Religious Writings of Samuel Johnson, 1978; mem. editorial bd.: Yale U. Press edit. Works of Samuel Johnson; contbr. articles to profl. jours. Served with Brit. and Indian Armies, 1942-46. Recipient Queen Elizabeth II Coronation medal, Jubilee medal. Fellow Royal Soc. Arts, Royal Soc. Can.; mem. Can. Inst. Internat. Affairs (br. pres.), MLA, English Inst., Am. Assn. for Eighteenth Century Studies, Can. Assn. for Eighteenth Century Studies, Internat. Assn. for Eighteenth Century Studies, Assn. Can. Univ. Tchrs. English (pres. 1982—), Humanities Assn. Can. (past pres.). Mem. Liberal Party. Presbyterian. Club: Univ. Faculty. Home: 42 Laurentide Dr Halifax NS B3M 2N1 Canada Office: Dept English Dalhousie U Halifax NS B3H 3J5 Canada

GRAY, JAMES ALEXANDER, historic preservation official; b. Winston-Salem, N.C., Dec. 12, 1920; s. James Alexander and Pauline Lisette (Bahnson) G.; m. Yvonne Winifred Jackson, Aug. 12, 1944; children: Susan Winifred, James Alexander, David Bahnson; m. Evelyn Mashburn Cuddy, Nov. 28, 1970. A.B., U. N.C., 1941; M.B.A., Harvard, 1943. Mfrss. rep., 1946-49; with Jour. and Sentinel newspapers, Winston-Salem, 1949-61, gen. mgr., 1957- 59, pub., 1959-61; exec. dir. Winston-Salem Found., 1961-62, Mobile (Ala.) Historic Devel. Commn., 1970-71, 75-76; dir. devel. Salem Coll., Winston-Salem, 1971, v.p., 1972-75; exec. dir. Historic Preservation Fund N.C., 1976—. Mem. N.C. Hwy. Commn., 1953-57; chmn. Winston-Salem United Fund campaign, 1958; Bd. visitors Bowman Gray Sch. Medicine, 1959-70; pres. Old Salem, Inc., 1950-53, 63-70. Served to lt. USNR, 1943-46. Named Young Man of Year Winston-Salem Jr. C. of C., 1949. Mem. Moravian Ch. Club: Rotary. Home: 311 Muirfield Dr Winston-Salem NC 27104

GRAY, JAMES LORNE, consultant; b. Brandon, Man., Can., Mar. 2, 1913; s. James Bruce and Sarah Edna (Elder) G.; m. Anne Evelyn Lawrence, June 1, 1940; 1 son, James Michael. B.Eng., U. Sask., 1935, M.Sc. in Mech. Engring, 1938; LL.D., 1961; D.Sc., U. B.C., 1961, Carleton U., 1975. Canadian Gen. Electric Co. Test Course, 1938-39; lectr. U. Sask., 1939; asst. dir. gen. Dept. Reconstrn. & Supply, Ottawa, 1945-46; asst. to pres. Montreal Armature Works Ltd., Montreal, 1946-47; sci. asst. to pres. Nat. Research Council, Ottawa, 1947-49; chief adminstrn. NRC, Chalk River, 1949-52; gen. mgr. Atomic Energy of Can., Ltd., Chalk River, 1952-53, v.p. adminstrn., operation, 1954-58, pres., 1958-74; pvt. cons., 1975—. Served to wing comdr. RCAF, 1939-45. Decorated Companion Order of Can.; recipient Profl. Engrs. Gold medal Assn. Profl. Engrs. Province Ont., 1973. Clubs: Deep River Golf, Pinawa Golf, Royal Ottawa Golf, Rideau Club, Deep River Curling (Ottawa); St. George's Hill Golf (London, Eng.). Home: 25 Beach Ave Deep River ON K0J 1J0 Canada Office: 25 Beach Ave Deep River ON K0J 1J0 Canada

GRAY, JEROME BETHEL, advt. exec.; b. Harrisburg, Pa., July 18, 1899; s. Norman D. and Alice (Hoopes) G.; m. Miriam Fertig, Nov. 13, 1920; children—Alice, Jane; m. Thelma Packman, July, 1961. Student, Hill Sch., 1916-19. Staff mem. Barta Press, Cambridge, Mass., 1921-23; service mgr. Franklin Printing Co., Phila., 1923-27; partner Gray & Rogers (advt. agy.), Phila., 1927-64; pres. Gray & Rogers, Inc. (advt. agy.), Phila., 1964-67, chmn. bd., chief exec. officer, 1967-73; chmn. creative com. T. Gray Assos., Inc., 1973—; creative chmn. Thelma Gray/Compton Pub. Relations, Phila. Republican. Episcopalian. Clubs: Racquet, Merion Golf. Home: The Dower House West Chester PA 19380 Office: 1819 John F Kennedy Blvd Philadelphia PA 19103

GRAY, JOHN DELTON, manufacturing company executive; b. Ontario, Oreg., July 29, 1919; s. Elmer R. and Mabel (Ridgley) G.; m. Elizabeth Neuner, Jan. 4, 1946; children—Anne, Joan, Janet, John Richard, Laurie. B.Secretarial Sci., Oreg. State Coll., 1940; M.B.A., Harvard, 1947; LL.D., Lewis and Clark Coll., 1967. Asst. to pres. Pointer-Willamette Co., Portland, 1947; asst. gen. mgr. Oreg. Saw Chain Corp. (now Omark Industries, Inc.), Portland, 1948-50, gen. mgr., 1950-53, pres., gen. mgr., 1953-67, chmn. bd., 1961-83, vice chmn. bd., 1983—; dir. Castle & Cooke, Inc., Precision Castparts Corp., First Nat. Bank Oreg., Standard Ins. Co., Tektronix, Inc. Past pres. Portland area council Boy Scouts Am., 1959-61; past mem. exec. bd., also past pres. Columbia-Pacific council.; Trustee Com. Econ. Devel., 1967-81; mem. Chief Execs. Orgn., 1969—; Trustee Reed Coll., Portland, 1961—, chmn., 1968-82, chmn. steering com. capital campaign, 1983—; trustee Oreg. Grad. Center. Served from 2d lt. to lt. col. AUS, 1941-46. Decorated Bronze Star medal; recipient Silver Beaver award Portland Area council Boy Scouts Am. Republican. Episcopalian. Club: Rotarian. Home: 6134 SW Riverpoint Ln Portland OR 97201 Office: 5550 SW Macadam Ave Portland OR 97201

GRAY, JOHN EDMUND, chemical engineer; b. Woonsocket, R.I., Apr. 13, 1922; s. John Joseph and Alice (Naylor) G.; m. Mary Lightbody, Dec. 3, 1944 (div. Mar. 1980); children: Jane Elizabeth Gray Redmond, John Carlton, Jeffrey Naylor. B.S. in Chem. Engring, U. R.I., 1943. Research engr. Westinghouse Electric Corp., Bloomfield, N.J., 1943-46; sr. design engr. engring. div. Gen. Electric Co., Hanford, Wash., 1946-47; head materials sect. atomic power dept. Gen. Engring. and Cons. Lab., Schenectady, 1948-49; materials adminstr. Naval Reactors br. AEC, U.S. Navy, 1949-50; dir. tech. and prodn. div. U.S. AEC (Savannah River Plant), S.C., 1950-54; project mgr. Shippingport Atomic Power Sta., Duquesne Light Co., Pitts., 1954-60; pres., chmn., chief exec. officer NUS Corp., Rockville, Md., 1960-72; energy cons. Ford Found. Energy Policy Project, 1972-73, Mass. Inst. Tech. Center for Policy Alternatives, 1973, Edison Electric Inst., 1974-77; chmn., chief exec. officer Internat. Energy Assocs. Ltd., Washington, 1976—; chmn. IEA of Japan Co., Ltd., Tokyo, 1982—; pres., dir. Insulation Research Corp.; dir. IEAL (Australia) Pty. Ltd., Materials Tech. Corp., TECOP-3H (Paris), Abacus Controls, Inc., Evaluation Research Corp. Author: Energy Policy: Industry Perspectives, 1975, (with others) Energy Research and Development, 1975, Nuclear Fuels Policy, 1976, International Cooperation on Breeder Reactors, 1978, Nuclear Power and Nuclear Weapons Proliferation, 1978, U.S. Energy Policy and U.S. Foreign Policy in the 1980s, 1981. Bd. dirs. Atlantic Council U.S., chmn. energy policy com., 1979—; chmn. nuclear fuels working group, 1975-79; mem. non-proliferation group Council on Fgn. Relations, 1977; dir. U.S. nat. com. World Energy Conf., 1983—; trustee U. R.I. Found., 1983—. Served with U.S. Army, 1945-46. Mem. AAAS, Am. Inst. Chem. Engrs., Am. Nuclear Soc., Atomic Indsl. Forum. Club: Univ. (Washington). Home: 502 Cameron St Alexandria VA 22314 Office: 2600 Virginia Ave NW Washington DC 20037

GRAY, JOHN HUBERT, clergyman, university official, English educator; b. Cupertino, Calif., Jan. 27, 1924; s. Clyde Peter and Margaret (Oddie) G. B.A. in Philosophy, Gonzaga U., 1948; M.A. in English, Loyola U. at Los Angeles, 1952; Ph.D., U. London, Eng., 1961. Ordained priest Roman Catholic Ch., 1955; mem. faculty U. Santa Clara, Calif., 1949-79, instr. English, 1949-51, asst. prof., 1961-67, asso. prof., 1967-79, chmn. English dept., 1963-68, dean, 1968-79; asso. prof. English St. Louis U., 1979—, acad. v.p., 1979—. Trustee Mexican-Am. Cultural Found., v.p., 1968-70; bd. dirs. Family Service Assn., Santa Clara County, treas., 1973, 1st v.p., 1974, pres., 1975-77; trustee Seattle U., 1974—; bd. dirs. Creighton U., 1982—. Mem. Renaissance Soc. Am., Shakespeare Soc. Am., MLA. Home: 3601 Lindell Blvd Saint Louis MO 63108

GRAY, JOHN JUSTIN, coll. dean; b. New Concord, Ohio, Nov. 21, 1919; s. Charles Irving and Faith (McCall) G.; m. Patricia May Brunton, Dec. 28, 1947; children—Stephen, Christine, Cynthia. Mus.B., U. Mich., 1942; Mus.M., Eastman Sch. Music, U. Rochester, 1945; D.Mus. Arts, U. So. Calif., 1960. Supr. music Charlevoix (Mich.) pub. schs., 1944-45; asst. prof. Ohio State U., 1945-46; asso. prof. U. Mont., 1946-58; prof. music Calif. State U., Fullerton, 1961—, asso. dean, 1965-68, dean, 1968-76. Contbr. articles to profl. jours. Mem. Am. Musicol. Soc., Music Educators Nat. Conf. (life), Coll. Band Dirs. Nat. Assn., A.A.U.P., Phi Mu Alpha Sinfonia, Kappa Kappa Psi, Pi Kappa Lambda. Home: 33622 Dana Vista Dr Dana Point CA 92629

GRAY, JOHN LATHROP, III, advertising agency executive; b. N.Y.C., Apr. 9, 1931; s. John L. and Eleanor R. (Snow) G.; m. Cynthia Hunt, June 13, 1953; children: Lisa L., Phyllis H.; m. Frances W. Pratt, Sept. 22, 1967; stepchildren: Robert T., Duncan P., Theodore P. Hennes. B.S., Yale U., 1953. Media planner J. Walter Thompson, N.Y.C., 1956-60, media supr., 1961-66, v.p., assoc. media dir., 1966-77, v.p., group media dir., 1978-80, sr. v.p., dir. media planning, 1980—. Served with U.S. Army, 1953-56. Mem. Am. Assn. Advt. Agencies. Republican. Episcopalian. Club: Apawamis (Rye, N.Y.). Office: J Walter Thompson USA Inc 466 Lexington Ave New York NY 10017

GRAY, JOHN STEPHENS, physiologist; b. Chgo., Aug. 11, 1910; s. Joseph William and Carrie (Weston) G.; m. Elma Nash, June 15, 1935; children—Ann R., Virginia B. B.S., Knox Coll., Galesburg, Ill., 1932; M.S., Northwestern U., 1934, Ph.D., 1936, M.D., 1946. Instr. in physiology Northwestern U., 1936-40, asst. prof., 1940-45, asso. prof., 1946, Nathan Smith Davis prof., 1946-70, prof. emeritus, 1974—; research physiologist A.A.F. Sch. of Aviation Medicine, Randolph Field, Tex., 1942-45. Author: The Sioux War of 1876, 1976, Cavalry and Coaches: The Story of Camp and Fort Collins, 1978; contbr. research articles in physiology and in Am. frontier history to various publs. Mem. A.A.A.S., Am. Physiol. Soc., Soc. Exptl. Biology and Medicine, Chgo. Westerners, Sigma Xi, Phi Gamma Delta. Home: 1408 W Lake St Fort Collins CO 80521

GRAY, JOHN WALKER, mathematician, educator; b. St. Paul, Oct. 3, 1931; s. Clarence Walker and Helen (Ewald) G.; m. Eva Maria Wirth, Dec. 30, 1957; children—Stephen, Theodore, Elisabeth. B.A., Swarthmore Coll., 1953; Ph.D., Stanford U., 1957. Temp. mem. Inst. for Advanced Study, Princeton, N.J., 1957-59; Ritt instr. Columbia U., 1959-62; asst. prof. math. U. Ill., Urbana, 1962-64, asso. prof., 1964-66, prof., 1966—; organizer Category Theory Session, Oberwolfach, Germany, 1971, 72, 73, 75, 77, 79. Contbr. to: Springer Lecture Notes in Mathematics, 1974. NSF sr. fellow, 1966-67; Fulbright-Hays sr. lectr., 1975-76. Mem. Am. Math. Soc., AAAS. Home: 303 W Michigan St Urbana IL 61801 Office: Dept Math U Ill Urbana IL 61801

GRAY, KENNETH EUGENE, petroleum engineering educator; b. Herrin, Ill., Jan. 11, 1930; m., 1955; 3 children. B.S., U. Tulsa, 1956, M.S., 1957; Ph.D., U. Tex., 1963. Drilling engr. Calif. Co., 1957-59; reservoir engr. Sohio Petroleum Co., 1959-60; faculty mem. U. Tex., Austin, 1962—, chmn. dept., 1966-74, Halliburton prof. petroleum engring., dir. Ctr. Earth Sci., 1968—; cons. research dept. Continental Oil Co., 1963—; mem. U.S. Nat. Com. on Rock Mechanics. Research grantee Petroleum Research Fund, Am. Chem. Soc., Tex. Petroleum Research Com., 1963—, Am. Petroleum Inst., Gulf Research & Devel. Co., 1964—. Fellow Am. Inst. Chemists, N.Y. Acad. Scis., Am. Acad. Mechanics. Office: Dept Petroleum Engring U Tex Austin TX 78712 *

GRAY, KENNETH JOHN, civil engineer; b. Australia, Apr. 6, 1919; s. Andrew Arthur and Muriel Jean (Wilkie) G.; m. Eileen McInteer, Mar. 3, 1944; 1 son, Ian Charles. B.Eng. in C.E. (with honors), U. Sydney, 1949; diploma, Imperial Coll., London, 1951. Cert. engr. Order Engrs. Que., Assn. Profl. Engrs., Geologists and Geophysicists of Alta. Engr. Hydro-Elec. Commn. Tasmania, 1949-50, design engr., team leader, 1952-57; engr. design dept. Shawinigan Engring. Co., Ltd., Montreal, 1957, chief resident engr., Bombay, 1958-64, v.p., 1964-70, pres., dir., 1970-77; chmn., chief exec. officer Shawinigan Consultants Internat., Ltd., Montreal, 1977-80, chmn. bd., 1980—; vice chmn. Shawinigan Lavalin Inc., 1982—, Lavalin Inc., 1982—. Served with Royal Australian Air Force, 1940-46. Decorated D.F.C. Fellow ASCE; mem. Assn. Cons. Engrs. Can., Corp. Engrs. Que., Corp. Engrs. Ont., Internat. Fedn. Cons. Engrs. (v.p.), Engring. Inst. Can. Clubs: National, Lambton Golf and Country (Toronto); Masons. Home: 21 Dale Ave Toronto ON Canada M4W 1K3 Office: 33 Yonge St Toronto ON Canada M5E 1E7

GRAY, LAMAN A., JR., thoracic and cardiovascular surgeon; b. Louisville, May 28, 1940; s. Laman A. and Alice (Crothers) G.; m. Juliet Cooper, June 1967; children: Juliet, Alice, Virginia. B.A., Wesleyan U., Middletown, Conn., 1963; M.D., Johns Hopkins U., 1963. Diplomate: Am. Bd. Surgery, Am. Bd. Thoracic Surgery. Asst. prof. surgery U. Louisville, 1974-78, assoc. prof., 1978-84, prof., 1984—, acting dir. thoracic and cardiovascular surgery, 1975-76, dir., 1976—. Contbr. chpts. to books, articles to profl. jours. Program chmn. Louisville Heart Assn., 1981-82; pres. Greater Louisville div. Am. Heart Assn., 1983-84. Humana Inc. grantee, 1984. Fellow Am. Coll. Cardiology; mem. ACS; fellow Am. Coll. Chest Physicians; mem. Am. Assn. Throacic Surgery; mme. So. Thoracic Surg. Assn. (chmn. membership com. 1983-84); mem. Soc. Thoracic Surgeons, Societe Internationale de Chirurgie. Home: 428 Lightfoot Rd Louisville KY 40202 Office: Dept Surgery Univ Louisville Louisville KY 40292

GRAY, LINDA, actress; b. Santa Monica, Calif., Sept. 12; m. Ed Thrasher (div. 1983); children: Jeff, Kelly. Studied with, Charles Conrad. Worked as model appeared in over 400 television commls.; film appearances include Dogs; television films include The Two Worlds of Jenny Logan, Haywire, Chimps, Not in Front of the Children; appeared in: television series All That Glitters, 1977, Dallas, 1978—; other television appearances include Marcus Welby, M.D; host CBS documentary: The Body Human: The Loving Process, 1981; co-host: Golden Globe awards, 1981. Emmy nominee for Dallas, 1981; recipient Bambi award for best actress Germany, 1982, Il Gato award for best actress Italy, 1983, 84; named Woman of Yr. Hollywood Radio and TV Soc., 1982. Office: care Richard Grant Lippin & Grant 8124 W 3d St Los Angeles CA 90048

GRAY, MILTON HEFTER, lawyer; b. Chgo., Dec. 2, 1910; s. Jacob S. and Fannie (Hefter) G.; m. Florence Adele Subin, Apr. 12, 1937; children: Roberta (Mrs. Paul L. Katz), James. A.B., Northwestern U., 1931, J.D., 1934. Bar: Ill. 1934. Assoc., then partner Gardner, Carton & Douglas, 1934-43; pvt. practice, Chgo., 1943-60; sr. partner Altheimer & Gray, Chgo., 1960—; spl. master for City Savs. Assn. U.S. Dist. Ct., 1973-78, for; (Milw. R.R. reorgn.), 1979—; commr. Supreme Ct. Ill., 1957-62, 66-68, 70-73; corp. officer and dir.; lectr. Inst. Banking, 1943-45, U. Ill. Law Sch., 1953, Northwestern U. Law Sch., 1956, Harvard Law Sch., 1967. Editorial bd.: Ill. Bus. Corp. Act Annotated, 1947; Contbr. articles to legal publs. Pres. N.E. Ill. council Boy Scouts Am., 1957-59, hon. pres., 1977—, exec. bd. region VII, 1959-73, vice chmn., 1966-68, chmn., 1968-70, mem. nat. exec. bd., 1968-70, mem. nat. adv. council, 1970—. Recipient Silver Beaver, Silver Antelope, Silver Buffalo, Disting. Eagle Scout Citizens awards Boy Scouts Am.; merit award Northwestern U., 1973; Baden Powell fellow World Scout Orgn. Mem. Internat., World assns. lawyers, ABA (com. state regulation securities 1961—, com. fed. regulation securities 1963—, com. corp. law and accounting 1973—), Ill. Bar Assn. (past chmn. corp. and securities laws sect.), Chgo. Bar Assn. (past chmn. corp. law com., past chmn. securities law com., bd. mgrs. 1966-68, 1st v.p. 1970-71, pres. 1971-72), Am. Judicature Soc., Order of Coif. Clubs: Standard, Tavern, Northmoor Country. Co-drafter: Ill. Not for Profit Corporation Act, 1945; Ill. Securities Law, 1953. Home: 420 Lakeside Pl Highland Park IL 60035 Office: 333 W Wacker Dr Chicago IL 60606

GRAY, MYLES MCCLURE, insurance company executive; b. Lansing, Mich., Aug. 28, 1932; s. Carlyle Avery and Lucile (Meitz) G.; m. Marilyn Ida Osberg, Feb. 14, 1953; children: Kathleen Gray Abraham, David, Patricia. B.B.A. with distinction, U. Mich., 1954. Div. mgr. Nat. Life & Accident Ins. Co., Nashville, 1954-58; from asst. actuary to exec. v.p., actuary United Benefit Life Ins. Co., Omaha, 1958-67; v.p., actuary Gen. Reins. Life Corp., N.Y.C., 1967-69, Cal. Western States Life Ins. Co., Sacramento, 1969-74; v.p. Alexander & Alexander, N.Y.C., 1974-75, Nat. Life & Accident Ins. Co., Nashville, 1975-81, NLT Corp., 1981-83; v.p., chief actuary Life Investors, Inc., Cedar Rapids, Iowa, 1983—. Fellow Soc. Actuaries (sec., mem. exec. com. 1977-80, bd. govs. 1977-83); mem. Am. Acad. Actuaries, Southeastern Actuaries Club, Alpha Kappa Psi, Phi Kappa Phi, Beta Gamma Sigma. Republican. Presbyn. (elder). Home: 2508 White Eagle Trail Cedar Rapids IA 52403 Office: 4333 Edgewood Rd NE Cedar Rapids IA 52499

GRAY, PAUL EDWARD, university president; b. Newark, Feb. 7, 1932; s. Kenneth Frank and Florence (Gilleo) G.; m. Priscilla Wilson King, June 18, 1955; children: Virginia Wilson, Amy Brewer, Andrew King, Louise Meyer. S.B., Mass. Inst. Tech., 1954, S.M, 1955, Sc.D., 1960. Mem. faculty Mass. Inst. Tech., 1960-71, Class of 1922 prof. elec. engring., 1968-71, dean, 1970-71, chancellor, mem. corp., 1971-80, pres., 1980—; dir. Shawmut Bank, Boston, New Eng. Mut. Life Ins. Co., A.D. Little Inc., Cambridge, Cabot Corp., Boston. Trustee, mem. corp. Mus. of Sci., Boston, Woods Hole Oceanographic Inst.; chmn. bd. trustees Wheaton Coll., Mass., 1976—; mem. White House Sci. Council, 1982—. Served to 1st lt. AUS, 1955-57. Recipient C.E. Tucker award teaching Mass. Inst. Tech. Fellow Am. Acad. Arts and Scis., IEEE (publs. bd. 1969-70); mem. Nat. Acad. Engring., Mex. Nat. Acad. Engring., AAAS, Sigma Xi, Eta Kappa Nu, Tau Beta Pi, Phi Sigma Kappa. Mem. United Ch. Christ (deacon 1969-72, moderator 1973-77). Home: 111 Memorial Dr Cambridge MA 02142 Office: 77 Massachusetts Ave Cambridge MA 02139

GRAY, PHILIP HOWARD, psychologist, educator; b. Cape Rosier, Maine, July 4, 1926; s. Asa and Bernice (Lawrence) G.; m. Iris McKinney, Dec. 31, 1954; children: Cindelyn, Howard. M.A., U. Chgo., 1958; Ph.D., U. Wash., 1960. Asst. prof. dept. psychology Mont. State U., Bozeman, 1960-65, assoc. prof., 1965-75, prof., 1975—; vis. prof. U. Man., Winnipeg, Can., 1968-70; pres. Mont. Psychol. Assn., 1968-70; chmn. Mont. Bd. Psychologist Examiners, 1972-74; speaker sci. and geneal. meetings on ancestry of U.S. presidents. Organized exhbns. folk art in Mont. and Maine, 1972-79; Author: The Comparative Analysis of Behavior, 1966, (with F.L. Ruch and N. Warren) Working with Psychology, 1963, A Directory of Eskimo Artists in Sculpture and Prints, 1974; contbr. numerous articles on behavior to psychol. jours., poetry to lit. jours. Served with U.S. Army, 1944-46. Recipient Am. and Can. research grants. Fellow Am. Psychol. Assn., AAAS, Internat. Soc. Research on Aggression; mem. History of Sci. Soc., Nat. Geneal. Soc., New Eng. Hist. Geneal. Soc., Deer Isle-Stonington Hist. Soc., Psychonomic Soc., Internat. Soc. for Human Ethology, Descs. of Illegitimate Sons and Daus. of Kings of Britain, Piscataqua Pioneers, Animal Behavior Soc., Flagon and Trencher, SAR, Sigma Xi. Home: 1207 S Black Ave Bozeman MT 59715 Office: Dept Psychology Montana State U Bozeman MT 59717
We are human to the extent that we have bondings and the more bondings we have the more human we are. These attachments include familial bonding (imprinting), friendship bonding, marital bonding, ethnic-religious bonding, possession and goal bondings, and bonding to the land and ocean. My life's work is the study of these bondings and I am thereby more firmly connected to the human race.

GRAY, PHYLLIS ANNE, librarian; b. Boston, Jan. 2, 1926; d. George Joseph and Eleanor (Morrison) G. Ph.B., Barry Coll., 1947, M.B.A., 1979; M.S., Cath. U. Am., 1950. Librarian U.S. Air Force Base, Miami, Fla., 1952-53; asst. librarian Brockway Meml. Library, Miami Shores, Fla., 1953-55; head librarian N. Miami Public Library, 1955-59; supervising librarian Santa Clara County Library, San Jose, Calif., 1959-61; library dir. City of Commerce (Calif.) Public Library, 1961-68; adminstrv. librarian Miami Dade Public Library, 1969-76; library dir. Miami Beach (Fla.) Public Library, 1978—. Councilwoman Bal Harbour Village, 1979-83; treas. Women in Govt. Service, 1981—. Mem. ALA, Am. Soc. Public Adminstrn., Fla. Library Assn., Southeastern Library Assn., Dade County Library Assn., Barry Coll. Alumni Assn. Democrat. Roman Catholic. Clubs: Pilot (rec. sec. 1981-82, pres. 1982-83. Home: 54 Park Dr Apt 6 Bal Harbour FL 33154 Office: Miami Beach Public Library 2100 Collins Ave Miami Beach FL 33139

GRAY, RICHARD ALEXANDER, JR., chemical company executive; b. Pitts., Apr. 28, 1927; s. Richard Alexander and Margaret Katherine (Imler) G.; m. Lucia I. Long, Sept. 8, 1956; children: Richard Alexander III, James W. Student, U.S. Mcht. Marine Acad., 1945-47; B.A., Princeton U., 1950; LL.B., Harvard U., 1954; postgrad., Univ. Coll., Southampton, Eng., 1949. Bar: Pa. bar 1955, U.S. Supreme Ct. bar 1975. Asso. firm Reed Smith Shaw & McClay, Pitts., 1954-62; with Air Products and Chems., Inc., Allentown, Pa., 1962—, asst. gen. counsel, 1976-78, corp. sec., 1978—, asso. gen. counsel, 1980—; Mem. bd. regents Mercersburg (Pa.) Acad., 1968-82; bd. dirs. Kirkland Village, Inc., Bethlehem, Pa., 1980-82. Trustee First Presbyn. Ch. of Allentown. Served to lt. (j.g.) USN, 1950-51. Mem. Am. Soc. Corp. Secs., Am. Arbitration Assn., Am. Bar Assn. Office: PO Box 538 Allentown PA 18105

GRAY, RICHARD G., investment company fund executive. Pres., chief exec. officer Investors Mut. Inc., Mpls., IDS New Dimensions Fund, Inc. Office: IDS New Dimensions Fund Inc 1000 Roanoke Bldg Minneapolis MN 55402

GRAY, ROBERT HUGH, college dean; b. Dallas, Sept. 22, 1931; s. Harold K. and Margaret L. G.; m. Constance Montmenny, Dec. 26, 1957; 1 son, Richard Bailey. B.F.A., Yale U., 1959, M.F.A., 1961. Instr. art Cooper Union, N.Y.C., 1960-66; dean Silvermine Coll. Art, New Canaan, Conn., 1966-71; head dept. art Pa. State U., University Park, 1972-76; dean div. visual arts SUNY, Purchase, 1976-80; dean Coll. Fine Arts, UCLA, 1980—; cons. in art edn., 1968—. Mem. exec. com. Neuberger Mus. Art, Purchase, N.Y., 1978-80; bd. dirs. Empire Studio Sch., N.Y.C., 1979-80, Clayworks, N.Y.C., 1978-79, Crafts and Folk Arts Mus., Los Angeles, Young Musician Found.; trustee Bruce Mus. Art, Greenwich, Conn., 1978-80. Mem. Nat. Council Arts Adminstrs., Greenwich Arts Council, 1978-80; mem. com. Nat. Crafts Apprenticeship Programs, Internat. Council Fine Arts Deans, Nat. Planning and Implementation Bd. for Crafts. Office: College of Fine Arts UCLA Los Angeles CA 90024

GRAY, ROBERT LEE, clergyman, ch. ofcl.; b. Wilkinsburg, Pa., Dec. 3, 1927; s. Harry C. and Margaret Jane (McCreight) G.; m. Ruth Lois McCarrell, Apr. 7, 1951; 1 dau., Margaret Ruth (Mrs. Melvin Dean Stewart). B.S., Wheaton (Ill.) Coll., 1949; postgrad., Moody Bible Inst., 1953-56. Ordained to ministry Independent Fundamental Chs. Am., 1958; founding pastor Westchester (Ill.) Bible Ch., 1953—; pres. Ind. Fundamental Chs. Am., 1972-74, 79-81. Trustee Pacific Broadcasting Assn., Citadel Bible Coll., Ozark, Ark., Berean Mission Bd., 1981—; mem. exec. com. Ill. Bible Ch. Mission, Light Bearers Assn. and Open Air Campaigners. Served with M.I. AUS, 1950-52. Address: 2105 Sunnyside Westchester IL 60153

GRAY, ROBERT STEELE, publisher, editor; b. Beaumont, Tex., Oct. 6, 1923; s. Fred and Ruth Louise (Lewelling) G.; m. Nellie Frances McGuinness, July 3, 1945; children: Robert Steele, Laura, Ruth Ellen (Mrs. Paul Lindholm). B.S., U. Houston, 1954. Founder Cordovan Corp., Houston, 1960, pub., editor, 1960—, chmn. bd., 1982—; pub. Cordovan Bus. Jours.; co-founder Golfer mag., 1984—. Newscaster, KPRC-AM, Houston, 1947; news dir., KNUZ, Houston, 1948-49; reporter, Citizens Papers, Houston, 1950; newsfilm dir., KPRC-TV, Houston, 1951-56; writer, Houston Post, 1956-60; Author or co-author 5 books on horses and horse tng. Served to 2d lt. USMCR, 1942-46; PTO; to 1st lt., 1951-52; Korea. Mem. Am. Hist. Assn., Sigma Delta Chi. Home: 8441 Winningham Houston TX 77055 Office: 5715 NW Central Dr Suite 111 Houston TX 77092

GRAY, ROBIN BRYANT, aerospace engineer, educator; b. Statesville, N.C., Dec. 4, 1925; s. James Perry and Annie (Hartsell) G.; m. F. R. Thompson, Apr. 30, 1949; children: Robin, William Carl. B. Aero. Engring., Rensselaer Poly. Inst., 1946; M.S. in Aero. Engring, Ga. Inst. Tech., 1947; Ph.D., Princeton U., 1957. Research engr. Ga. Inst. Tech., Atlanta, 1947-49; research asst. then research asso. Princeton U., 1949-56; asso. prof. Ga. Inst. Tech., Atlanta; then Regents prof., asso. dir. Sch. Aerospace Engring., 1956—. Contbr. tech. articles and reports on aerospace engring. to profl. jours. Councilman, North Atlanta, Ga., 1963-64, councilman, vice-mayor, 1964-65. Served to ensign USNR, 1943-46. Mem. Am. Helicopter Soc., AIAA, Sigma Xi, Tau Beta Pi. Presbyterian (deacon 1961-63, 66-68, treas. trustee 1965—). Home: 1077 Spring Mill Ln NE Atlanta GA 30319

GRAY, WILLIAM BARTON, lawyer; b. Brattleboro, Vt., Feb. 14, 1942; s. Edwin William and Mabel Louise (Hawkes) G.; m. Sarah Kerlin, June 19, 1965; children: Joshua Barton, Sarah Hawkes. A.B., Harvard U., 1964; LL.B., U. Pa., 1967. Bar: N.Y., Vt., D.C. Asso. firm Paul, Weiss, Rifkind, Wharton & Garrison, N.Y.C., 1967; law clk. to judge U.S. Ct. Appeals 2d Circuit, N.Y.C., 1968; asst. U.S. atty. So. Dist. N.Y., 1968-72; asst. U.S. atty. Dist. Vt., 1972-75, U.S. atty., 1977-81; mem. firm Sheehey, Brue & Gray, Burlington, Vt., 1981—; dir. exec. office for U.S. attys. Dept. Justice, Washington, 1976-77; adj. prof. Vt. Law Sch., 1975-76; adj. asso. prof. St. Johns U., Jamaica, N.Y., 1972-73. Mem. Am., Vt., D.C. bar assns., Assn. Bar City N.Y., Fed. Bar Council. Home: Old Pump Rd Jericho VT 05465 Office: Box 66 Burlington VT 05402

GRAY, WILLIAM H., III, congressman; b. Baton Rouge, Aug. 20, 1941; m. Andrea Dash, Apr. 17, 1971; children—William H. IV, Justin Yates, Andrew Dash. B.A., Franklin and Marshall Coll., 1963; M.Div., Drew Theol. Sem., Madison, N.J., 1966; M.Th., Princeton Theol. Sem., 1970; postgrad., U. Pa., 1965, Temple U., 1966, Oxford U., 1967. Ordained to ministry Baptist Ch.; asst. minister Bright Hope Baptist Ch., Phila., 1963-64; dir. 1st Baptist Ch., Montclair, N.J., 1964-65; co-pastor Union Baptist Ch., Montclair, 1966-72; asst. prof., dir. St. Peter's Coll., Jersey City, 1970-74; sr. minister Bright Hope Baptist Ch., 1972—; lectr. Jersey City State Coll., 1968, Rutgers U., 1971, Montclair State Coll., 1970-72; mem. 96th and 98th Congresses from Pa. 2d Dist. Trexler Found. scholar, 1962; Rockefeller Protestant fellow, 1965. Mem. Phila. Pastor's Conf., Phila. Baptist Assn., Progressive Nat. Baptist Assn., Am. Baptist Conv., Alpha Phi Alpha. Democrat. Clubs: Masons, Elks, Frontier Internat. Office: Room 204 Cannon House Office Bldg Washington DC 20515

GRAY, WILLIAM PERCIVAL, judge; b. Los Angeles, Mar. 26, 1912; s. Jacob L. and Catherine (Percival) G.; m. Elizabeth Polin, Nov. 8, 1941; children—Robin Marie, James Polin. A.B., U. Calif. at Los Angeles, 1934; LL.B. cum laude, Harvard, 1939. Bar: Calif. bar 1941. Legal sec. to judge U.S. Ct. Appeals, Washington, 1939-40; with firm O'Melveny & Myers (lawyers), Los Angeles, 1940-41; pvt. practice, Los Angeles, 1945-49; partner Gray, Pfaelzer & Robertson, Los Angeles, 1950-66; U.S. dist. judge Central Dist. Calif., 1966—; spl. asst. to atty. gen. U.S., 1958-64; chmn. Calif. Conf. State Bar Dels., 1952. Trustee Ch. of Lighted Window, La Canada. Served from 1st lt. to lt. col. AUS, 1941-45. Fellow Am. Bar Found.; mem. Am. Law Inst., Am. Bar Assn., Los Angeles County Bar Assn. (pres. 1956), State Bar Calif. (bd. govs. 1960-63, pres. 1962-63). Home: 5495 Burning Tree La Canada CA 91011 Office: US Court House Los Angeles CA 90012

GRAYBEAL, SIDNEY NORMAN, system planning company executive; b. Butler, Tenn., May 20, 1924; s. Lyman B. and Mary Dove (Hazelwood) G.; m. Josephine Graybeal, May 7, 1948; children: Douglas Lee, Joan Louise. Student, Cortland State Tchrs. Coll. (N.Y.), 1940-42; B.S. in Transp, U. Md., 1949; M.B.A. in Air Transp, U. Md., 1950. Div. chief fgn. missile and space activities CIA, 1950-64; dep. asst. dir. bur. sci. and tech. ACDA, 1964-76; mem. strategic weapons panel Dept. Def., 1961-64; mem. U.S. delegation to Strategic Arms Limitations Talks (SALT), 1969-73; U.S. commr. U.S.-USSR Standing Consultative Commn. for Implementing SALT, 1973-77; dir. Office Strategic Research, CIA, 1977-79; v.p. System Planning Corp., Arlington, Va., 1979—. Served as pilot USAAF, World War II; PTO. Decorated D.F.C., Air medal with 3 oak leaf clusters. Mem. Am. Inst. Aeros. and Astronautics, Air Force Assn., Sigma Chi, Phi Kappa Phi, Beta Gamma Sigma. Presbyn. Home: 10101 Langhorne Court Bethesda MD 20817 Office: System Planning Corp 1500 Wilson Blvd Arlington VA 22209

GRAYBIEL, ASHTON, physician; b. Port Huron, Mich., July 24, 1902; s. William and Lucy Ann (Young) G.; m. Moira Barkley Martin, Mar. 23, 1934; children: Ashton L., Ann M. Moseley. A.B., U. So. Calif., 1924, A.M., 1925; M.D., Harvard U., 1930. Diplomate: Am. Bd. Preventive Medicine (aviation med.). Traveling fellow, 1932-33, Dalton fellow, 1933-34; Intern Mass. Gen. Hosp., Boston, 1930-32; (cardiac clinic), 1934-42; asso. Harvard Fatigue Lab., 1936-42; instr. medicine and grad. courses Harvard, 1940-42, research staff, 1942-45; dir. research Naval Aerospace Med. Inst., Pensacola, Fla., 1945-70; spl. asst. sci. programs, head biol. scis. dept. Naval Aerospace Med. Research Lab., Pensacola, 1970-80; chief sci. advisor, 1980—; adj. prof. psychology Brandeis U., Waltham, Mass., 1981—. Author: Clinical Electrocardiography, 1950, (with P.D. White, L. Wheeler, C. Williams) Electrocardiography in Practice, 3d edit., 1952. Recipient Theodore C. Lyster award for researches in aviation medicine, 1950; Legion of Merit, 1952, with gold star, 1967; Adm. William S. Parsons award for sci. and technical progress Navy League, 1960; The Eric J. Liljencrantz award for contbns. aviation and space medicine, 1961; John J. Jeffries Award, 1962; Melbourne W. Boynton award for space medicine, 1962; Groedel Meml. award Am. Coll. Cardiology, 1962; Hubertus Strughold award for space medicine, 1963; Arnold J. Tuttle award aviation medicine, 1965; Capt. Robert Dexter Conrad award for tech. and sci. achievement in research and devel. for Navy, 1965; Exceptional Sci. Achievement medal NASA, 1974; Disting. Service medal NASA, 1982; Ashton Graybiel Spatial Orientation Lab. at Brandeis U. named in his honor, 1982. Fellow Aerospace Med. Assn. (pres., Louis H. Bauer Founders award 1963), AAAS; mem. Am. Coll. Cardiology (past pres.), Assn. Mil. Surgeons, Am. Coll. Sports Medicine, Internat. Acad. Aviation Medicine, Space Medicine Assn., Am. Physiol. Soc., Am. Heart Assn., Am. Inst. Aeros. and Astronautics, Fla. Acad. Scis., Internat. Acad. Astronautics (trustee). Club: Cosmos (Washington). Home: PO Box 4063 Warrington FL 32507 Office: Naval Aerospace Med Research Lab Pensacola FL 32508

GRAYBILL, WILMER BERNARD, chemical engineer; b. Council Bluffs, Iowa, Dec. 27, 1928; s. Amos Dewey and Ada Viola (Larsen) G.; m. Mary Ann Turk, June 18, 1950; children: Clark Steven, Marta Sue, Craig Allen, Janet Marie. Student, Graceland Coll., Lamoni, Iowa, 1948-49; B.S., Iowa State U., 1952; grad., Advanced Mgmt. Program, Harvard Bus. Sch., 1977. With PPG Industries, Inc. (various locations), 1952—, prodn. supt., Lake Charles, La., 1966-71, tech. mgr., 1971-73, bus. mgr. organic chems., Pitts., 1974-76, dir. research and devel., 1977-82, dir. environ. affairs chems., 1982—. Mem. Am. Inst. Chem. Engring., Am. Chem. Soc., Tau Beta Pi. Republican. Club: Rolling Hills Country (Pitts.). Patentee in field. Office: One PPG Pl Pittsburgh PA 15272

GRAYCK, MARCUS DANIEL, lawyer; b. N.Y.C., Aug. 28, 1927; s. Jack and Gertrude (Seeman) G.; children from previous marriage—Howard Alexander, Amelia Beth, Joshua Avram, David Louis. A.B., Bklyn. Coll., 1948; LL.B., Harvard U., 1951; LL.M., N.Y. U., 1958. Bar: N.Y. bar, Ill. bar, U.S. Supreme Ct. Partner firm Baker & McKenzie, Chgo., 1974—; mem. adj. faculty, grad. tax program N.Y. U. Law Sch., 1959-75; adj. prof. law Loyola U. Law Sch., 1976—. Editor: Compensation and fringe benefits column Jour. Corp. Taxation; contbr. articles to profl. jours. Served with USN, 1945-46. Mem. Am. Bar Assn., Chgo. Bar Assn. Jewish. Club: Mid-America. Office: Baker and McKenzie 2800 Prudential Plaza Chicago IL 60601
I was blessed by parents who cared and taught—two essentials for a youth in his formative years. I also had the good fortune of being born in a country where, and at a time when, freedom and opportunity were available. I was able to learn early on from others that effort unstinted was to be my contribution to life. Having learned this, I still marvel at Browning's statement in Andrea del Sarto that ". . .man's reach should exceed his grasp, or what's a heaven for?"

GRAYHACK, JOHN THOMAS, urologist, educator; b. Kankakee, Ill., Aug. 21, 1923; s. John and Marie (Keckich) G.; m. Elizabeth Houlehin, June 3, 1950; children: Elizabeth, Anne Marie, Linda Jean, John, William. B.S., U. Chgo., 1945, M.D., 1947. Diplomate Am. Bd. Urology. Intern medicine Billings Hosp., Chgo., 1947; intern gen. surgery Johns Hopkins Hosp., 1947-48, asst. resident, 1948-49, fellow urology, 1949-50, asst. resident, 1950-52; resident urology, 1952-53; dir. Kretschmer Lab., Northwestern U. Med. Sch., 1956—, prof. urology, 1963—, chmn. dept.; Cons. VA Research Hosp. Editor: Year Book of Urology, 1963-78; mem. editorial bd.: Surgery, Gynecology and Obstetrics; assoc. editor: Jour. Urology. Served to capt. USAF, 1954-56. Recipient Outstanding Achievement award USAF.; Fellow Am. Cancer Soc., 1949-50, Damon Runyon Fund, 1953-54. Mem. AMA, Ill., Chgo. med. socs., Am. Assn. Genitourinary Surgeons (Barringer medal), Am. Urology Assn. (Hugh H. Young award), Chgo. Urology Soc., Endocrine Soc., Clin. Soc. Genitourinary Surgeons, Am. Surg. Assn., Soc. Univ. Urologists, Nephrology Soc., Phi Beta Kappa, Alpha Omega Alpha. Home: 95 N Park Rd LaGrange IL 60525 Office: 303 E Chicago Ave Chicago IL 60611

GRAYSMITH, ROBERT, polit. cartoonist; b. Pensacola, Fla., Sept. 17, 1942; s. Robert Gray and Frances Jane (Scott) Smith; m. Melanie Krakower, Oct. 15, 1975; children—David Martin, Aaron Vincent, Margot Alexandra. B.A., Calif. Coll. Arts and Crafts, 1965. Polit. cartoonist: Oakland (Calif.) Tribune, 1964-65, Stockton (Calif.) Record, 1965-68, San Francisco Chronicle, 1968— (Recipient 2d place awards Fgn. Press Awards 1973, World Population Contest 1976). Democrat. Presbyterian. Office: San Francisco Chronicle 901 Mission St San Francisco CA 94103

GRAYSON, ALBERT KIRK, near Eastern studies educator; b. Windsor, Ont., Can., Apr. 1, 1935; s. Albert Kirk and Helen (Smith) G.; m. Eunice Marie Service, Aug. 3, 1956; children: Vera lorraine, Sally Frances. B.A., U. Toronto, Ont., 1955, M.A., 1958; postgrad., U. Vienna, Austria, 1959-60; Ph.D., Johns Hopkins U., 1962. Research asst. Chgo. Assyrian Dictionary Oriental Inst., Chgo., 1962-63; asst. prof. history Temple U., Phila., 1963-64; asst. prof. Near Eastern studies U. Toronto, 1964-67, assoc. prof., 1967-72, prof., 1972—; dir. Royal Inscriptions of Mesopotamia project, 1981—; vis. lectr. U. Pa., Phila., 1963-64; spl. asst. dept. Western Asiatic Antiquities Brit. Mus., London, intermittently, 1967-76; invited lectr. various univs., mus., U.S., Germany, Iraq, Eng., Austria, Italy. Author: Assyrian Royal Inscriptions vol. I, 1972, Assyrian Royal Inscriptions vol. II, 1976, Assyrian and Babylonian Chronicles, 1975, Babylonian Historical-Literary Texts, 1975; contbr. chpts. to books. Can. Council fellow, 1959-61; Samuel S. Fels Fund fellow, 1961-62; Social Scis. and Humanities Research Council Can. editorial grantee, 1981—. Fellow Royal Soc. Can.; mem. Soc. Mesopotamian Studies (pres. 1980—), Fondation Assyriologique Georges Dossin (Belgium), Oriental Club Toronto (sec. 1969-70, pres. 1970-80), Rencontre Assyriologique Internationale (sessional chmn. Berlin 1978, sessional chmn. Vienna 1980, sessional chmn. Leiden, Netherlands 1983), Am. Oriental Soc. (sec. Midwest br. 1965-68). Mem. Anglican Ch. of Canada. Office: U Toronto Dept Near Eastern Studies 280 Huron St Toronto ON Canada M5S 1A1

GRAYSON, CHARLES JACKSON, JR., productivity center executive; b. Ft. Necessity, La., Oct. 8, 1923; s. Charles Jackson and Daphne (DeGraffenreid) G.; m. Carla O'Dell, Dec. 11, 1982; children: Christopher Jackson, Michael Wiley, Randall Charles, Daniel Jackson. B.B.A., Tulane U., 1944; M.B.A., U. Pa., 1947; D.B.A., Harvard, 1959. C.P.A., La. Instr., then asst. prof. Sch. Bus. Adminstrn., Tulane U., 1947-55, asso. prof., 1959-63, asso. dean, 1961-63, dean, prof., 1963-68; dean Sch. Bus. Adminstrn., So. Meth. U., 1968-75, prof., 1968-75; chmn. Am. Productivity Center, 1975—; chmn. Price Commn., Washington, 1971-73; vis. prof. Grad. Sch. Bus., Stanford, spring

1967; prof. IMEDE (Mgmt. Devel. Program), Switzerland, 1963-64; spl. agt. FBI, Washington, 1950-52; partner James E. O'Neill & Assos., New Orleans, 1952-53. Reporter: New Orleans Item, 1949-50; Author: Decisions Under Uncertainty: Drilling Decisions by Oil and Gas Operators, 1960, Confessions of a Price Controller, 1974; Contbr.: chpt. to Financial Research and Management Decisions, 1967; also articles to profl. publs. Served with USNR, 1943-46. Mem. Operations Research Soc. Am., Inst. Mgmt. Scis., Am. Finance Assn., Beta Gamma Sigma, Delta Tau Delta. Home: 123 N Post Oak Ln Houston TX 77024

GRAYSON, EDWARD DAVIS, manufacturing company executive; b. Davenport, Iowa, June 20, 1938; s. Charles E. and Isabelle (Davis) G.; m. Alice Ann McLaughlin, Oct. 8, 1966; children: Alice Ann, Maureen Isabelle, Edward Davis, Charles Timothy. B.A., U. Iowa, 1964, J.D., 1967. Bar: Mass. 1967. Atty. Goodwin, Procter & Hoar, Boston, 1967-74; v.p., gen. counsel Wang Labs., Inc., Lowell, Mass., 1974-83, sr. v.p., 1983—, corp. sec., clk., 1976—; sec. Wang Inst. Grad. Studies, Tyngsboro, Mass., 1979—; trustee Wang Ctr. for Performing Arts, Boston, 1982—. Trustee U. Lowell, (Mass.), 1981—, chmn. bd. tustees, (Mass.), 1982—; trustee Pregnancy Help of Greater Boston, 1973—; advisor Weston Sch. Theology, 1984—. Served to capt. USAF, 1964-67. Mem. Mass. Bar Assn. (bd. dels. 1977-80), Boston Bar Assn., ABA (com. on corp. law depts.). Democrat. Roman Catholic. Club: The Skating of Boston. Home: 33 Audubon Ln Belmon MA 02178 Office: Wang Labs Inc One Industrial Ave Lowell MA 01851

GRAYSON, GERALD HERBERT, educator, publisher; b. Bklyn., June 23, 1940; s. Frank and Sylvia (Cohen) G.; m. Florence M. Herbstman, Dec. 24, 1964; children—Todd Zachary, Douglas Philip. B.A., Bklyn. Coll., 1961; M.A., U. Ill., 1963; Ph.D., N.Y. U., 1973. With Dept. Labor, Washington, 1963; labor economist N.Y.C. Bd. Edn., 1963-66; prof., chmn. social sci. dept. N.Y.C. Tech. Coll., 1966—; pub., editor Senior Publs. Ltd., N.Y.C., 1971—; adj. prof. Adelphi U., Garden City, N.Y., 1974—. Served with USAR, 1962-63. Mem. Indsl. Relations Research Assn. Jewish. Home: 43 Northcote Dr Melville NY 11747 Office: 300 Jay St Brooklyn NY 11201

GRAYSON, KATHRYN, singer; b. Winston-Salem, N.C., Feb. 9, 1929. Student, Minnaletha White, M.-G.-M. Studio Schoolhouse. Stage appearances in musicals include The Merry Widow, 1961, Naughty Marietta, 1961, Rosalina, 1962, Camelot, 1962-64, Something's Afoot, 1983; also S. Am. tour in Show Boat; motion picture appearances include Now I Lay Me Down to Sleep, Kiss Me Kate, Show Boat, The Vagabond King, numerous others; TV appearances Die Fledermaus, 1966; hostess: Italian Music Festival, San Francisco, 1983; numerous appearances on concert stage, TV and radio, also numerous recs. Address: care Ruth Webb Enterprises 7500 Devista Dr Los Angeles CA 90046 *

GRAYSON, LAWRENCE PETER, educational administrator; b. Bklyn., May 16, 1937; s. Walter Henry and Lottie Dorothy (Bronikowski) G.; m. Mary Susan Phelan, June 6, 1964; children: Mary Louise, Catherine Anne, Lawrence Peter, Elizabeth Therese, Maureen Anne, Therese Marie. B.E.E., Poly. Inst. Bklyn., 1958, M.E.E., 1959, Ph.D. in Elec. Engring., 1962. Asst. prof. elec. engring. Johns Hopkins U., Balt., 1962-67; faculty resident IBM, Yorktown Heights, N.Y., 1967-68; asso. prof. elec. engring. Manhattan Coll., Bronx, N.Y., 1968-69; computer specialist Office Edn., Washington, 1968-70, dep. dir. div. ednl. tech., 1970-73, dir. div. tech. devel., 1972-73; mem. task force on productivity and tech. Nat. Inst. Edn., HEW, Washington, 1973-75, dir. div. tech. devel., 1975-78, head info. tech., media and public communications, 1978-81; asst. dir. for regional programs Nat. Inst. Edn., Dept. Edn., Washington, 1981-82, inst. adv. math., sci. and tech., 1982—; cons. Frankford Arsenal, 1963-66, Johns Hopkins Hosp., 1967, UNESCO, 1973-82, Gen. Electric Co., Lawrence Livermore Nat. Labs.; adj. prof. library and info. sci. Cath. U. Am., Washington, 1980—. Author: (with others) Man-Made Moons: Satellite Communications for Schools, 1972, U.S. Office of Education Support of Computer Projects, 1965-71, 1972, The Design of Engineering Curricula, 1977; contbg. author: Adaptive Control Systems, 1961; editor: Individualized Instruction in Engineering Education, 1974, Teaching Aids in the College Classroom, 1975; co-editor: Proc. 3d Ann. Frontiers in Edn. Conf, 1973, 5th-14 ann. edits., 1975-84, Procs. 1st Ann. Coll. Industry Edn. Conf, 1976, 2d-9th edits., 1977-84, Proc. of Ann. Conf. of Am. Soc. Engring. Edn, 1979-84, Procs. First World Conf. Continuing Engring. Edn., 1979. Mem. U.S. Nat. Commn. for UNESCO, 1977-82. Served to 1st lt. AUS, 1961-62. Recipient Disting. Service award HEW, 1976; spl. award in social justice Nat. Assn. for Public Continuing and Adult Edn., 1975; 2d Century award Poly. Inst. N.Y., 1980; citation outstanding achievement The Learning Channel, 1984; Ford Found. faculty resident in engring., 1967-68; Microwave Research Inst. fellow, 1958-61. Fellow IEEE (achievement award 1979, Centennial award 1984), AAAS; fellow Am. Soc. Engring. Edn. (v.p. 1972-74, dir. 1971-74, William Elgin Wickenden award 1979, Disting. Service award 1977, 81); mem. World Fedn. Engring. Orgns. (edn. com. 1976-81), Research Soc. Am., Sigma Xi, Tau Beta Pi, Eta Kappa Nu. Patentee in field optical laser configuration. Office: Nat Inst Education Washington DC 20208

GRAYSON, MERRILL, medical educator, ophthalmologist; b. N.Y.C., Apr. 19, 1919. B.A., NYU, 1938, M.D., 1941. Diplomate: Am. Bd. Ophthalmology. Intern Harlem Hosp., 1941-42; fellow otolaryngology N.Y. Med. Coll., 1942-43; researcher, intern, N.Y.C, New London; asst. prof. Ind. U. Med. Ctr., Indpls., 1957-60, assoc. prof., 1961-68, prof. ophthalmology, 1968—, now Disting. prof.; assoc. prof., chmn. dept. U. Ark. Sch. Medicine, 1960-61; surg. dir. Lions Eye Bank of Ind., 1961—. Served to maj. M.C. USAF, 1953-55. Fellow ACS; mem. AMA, Am. Acad. Ophthalmology and Otolaryngology (Merit 1971). Office: Dept Ophthalmolgy Ind Univ Med Ctr Indianapolis IN 46202 *

GRAYSON, RICHARD CARL, transportation executive; b. Cuba, Mo., Dec. 16, 1920; s. William James and Lenna (James) G.; m. Evelyn Honey, Sept. 24, 1939; children: Susanne, Shari, Richard Carl. With St. Louis-San Francisco Ry. Co., 1941-80, v.p. ops., Springfield, Mo., 1964-68, pres., 1969-73, chmn. bd., 1973-80; vice-chmn., pres. transp. div., dir. Burlington No. Inc., St. Paul, 1980—, chief exec. officer Transp. Group, 1982—, vice chmn., 1983—; pres., chief exec. officer, dir. Burlington No. R.R., 1981—, chmn., 1982—; dir. N.Mex. & Ariz. Land Co., Centerre Bancorp., Centerre Bank, St. Louis, El Paso Co., Laclede Gas Co., Gen. Am. Life Ins. Co. Mem. exec. com. St. Louis Area council Boy Scouts Am.; bd. dirs. Barnes Hosp., St. Louis; trustee Drury Coll., Springfield, Mo. Clubs: Noonday, Bogey, St. Louis, Old Warson Country. Office: One Centerre Plaza Saint Louis MO 63101

GRAYSON, RICHARD STEVEN, international legal and political management consultant; b. Harlingen, Tex., June 21, 1944; s. Bernard Lewis and Lucille Ruth (Kliston) G.; m. Katherine Lilian Hunston, June 4, 1971; children: Karyn Elizabeth, Lindsey Anne. B.S., Bucknell U., 1966; M.A., Sch. Internat. Service Am. U., 1968; Ph.D., Cambridge (Eng.) U., 1974. Research and lectr. in internat. law and politics Oxford (Eng.) U., 1970-74; adviser, negotiator 2d Diplomatic Conf., Geneva; mem. secretariat and sec. Round Table Diplomatic Conf., Italy; also research fellow, writer and editor Inst. Henry Dunant, Geneva, 1974; internat. legal and polit. adviser, Geneva, 1974; asso. dir. Inst. World Affairs, 1975, exec. dir., 1976-77; internat. legal and polit. mgmt. cons., N.Y.C., and Washington, 1975, internat. legal and polit. cons.. univ. lectr., speaker in field and adviser various internat. and nat. orgns., TV and radio programs on fgn. policy, 1976—; pres. Grayson Assos. Internat., Inc., 1978—; Bd. dirs. UNESCO Assn. USA, Center for Farm and Food Research, Am. Ibsen Theatre; bd. dirs. Ibsen Soc. Am.; bd. dirs., corp. mem. Assn. for World Univ.; trustee InterFuture; del. Fed. Trust Edn. and Research Conf., Eng., 1969. Author: Basic Background Study of Southeast Asia, 3 vols, 1968, Political and International Legal Implications of the Problems of Civil War, 1986. Avalon fellow, 1966-68; grantee Inst. Henry Dunant, 1971-73. Mem. Internat. Inst. Strategic Studies, Inst. Hist. Research, Inst. Advanced Legal Studies, Inst. U.S. Studies, Mensa, Am. Soc. Internat. Law, Am. Polit. Sci. Assn., Internat. Law Assn., Internat. Polit. Sci. Assn., Am. Acad. Polit. and Social Sci., Oxford Soc., Brit. and Commonwealth Inst. (charter), Brit. Inst. Internat. and Comparative Law, Internat. Inst. Humanitarian Law, Cambridge U. Grad. Soc. (pres. 1969-70), U.S. Polo Assn., Oxford and Cambridge Soc.; mem. English-Speaking Union; Mem. Westchester Council for the Arts, Am. Film Inst., Pi Sigma Alpha, Pi Gamma Mu. Clubs: University (N.Y.C.); United Oxford and Cambridge Univ. (London); Pilgrims (N.Y.C. and London). Home: 255 Chatterton Pkwy White Plains NY 10606

GRAYSON, ROBERT ALLEN, marketing executive, educator; b. N.Y.C., Oct. 8, 1927; s. Julius and Lillian (Davidson) G.; m. Suzanne B. Bomse, June 18, 1960; children: Peter, Jocelyn, Andrea. B.S., U. Ill., 1948; M.B.A., NYU, 1962, Ph.D., 1968. Vice pres. Henry S. Harris Assos. (mgmt. cons.), 1952-58; v.p. mktg. I. Rokeach & Sons, 1958-62; new products mgr. Lever Bros., 1962-68; sr. v.p., mem. exec. com. Daniel & Charles, Inc., N.Y.C., 1968-71; chmn. Grayson Assos., Inc. (mgmt. cons. and trade show producers), Ft. Lee, N.J., 1971—; prof. bus. adminstrn. NYU Grad. Sch., 1966—; prof. bus. policy Fordham U., 1972—; dir. Am. Commonwealth Ins. Co., FM Guide, Cosmo Expo. Author: Introduction to Marketing, 1971, Resumes that Get Interviews, Interviews that Get Jobs, 1973; editor: Marketing and the Computer, 1967; pub.: Jour. Consumer Mktg. Mem. Am. Marketing Assn. (pres. 1969-70), Inst. Mgmt. Sci., AAUP, Acad. Mgmt. Home: 269 Fountain Rd Englewood NJ 07631 Office: 210 E Route 4 Paramus NJ 07652

GRAYSON, WALTON GEORGE, III, lawyer, business executive; b. Shreveport, La., Aug. 18, 1928; s. Walton George and Mary Alice (Lowrey) G.; m. Bennetta McEwen Purse, May 20, 1955; children: Walton Grayson IV, Mark C., Bennett P., Dwight P. A.B., Princeton U., 1949; LL.B., Harvard U., 1952. Bar: Tex. 1952. Since practiced in, Dallas; asst. counsel Gt. Nat. Life Ins. Co., Dallas, 1954-69; v.p., gen. counsel Southland Corp., Dallas, 1965-72, exec. v.p., 1972—, also dir.; ptnr. Atwell, Grayson & Atwell, 1961-69, Grayson & Simon, 1969-73; of counsel Simon & Twombly, 1973—. Served with USN, 1952-54. Mem. Tex. Bar Assn., Dallas Bar Assn., ABA. Mem. Christian Ch. (Disciples of Christ). Club: Masons. Home: 10525 Strait Ln Dallas TX 75229 Office: 2828 N Haskell Ave Dallas TX 75204

GRAYSTON, J. THOMAS, medical educator; b. Wichita, Kans., Sept. 6, 1924; s. Jesse T. and Luzia B. (Thomas) G.; children: Susan, Jesse, David; m. M. Nan Bryant, June 7, 1980. Student, Carleton Coll., 1942-43; B.S., U. Chgo., 1947, M.D., 1948, M.S., 1952. Diplomate: Am. Bd. Internal Medicine, Am. Bd. Preventive Medicine. Intern Albany (N.Y.) Med. Sch., 1948-49; Seymour Coman fellow preventive medicine U. Chgo., 1949-50, asst. resident medicine, 1950-51; epidemiologist epidemic intelligence service USPHS, U. Kans. Med. Center, 1951-53; chief resident medicine U. Chgo., 1953-54, instr. medicine, 1953-55; fellow Nat. Found. Infantile Paralysis, 1954-56; asst. prof. medicine U. Chgo., 1955-60, asso. prof., 1960; chief div. microbiology and epidemiology U.S. Naval Med. Research Unit 2, Taipei, Taiwan, 1957-60, cons., 1960-79; prof. preventive medicine, chmn. dept. Sch. Medicine, U. Wash., 1960-70, dean Sch. Pub. Health and Community Medicine, 1970-71, v.p. for health scis., 1971-83, prof. dept. epidemiology, 1970—, adj. prof. pathobiology, 1982—; mem. exec. com. Regional Primate Research Center, 1964-70, research affiliate, 1967-70; attending physician medicine Univ. Hosp., Seattle, 1960-70; asso. mem. commn. acute respiratory diseases Armed Forces Epidemiol. Bd., 1962-65, mem., 1965-73; mem. research and engring. adv. panel biology and medicine Dept. Def., 1963-67; sci. group trachoma research WHO, 1963; virology and rickettsiology study sect. NIH, 1963-67; mem. internat. centers com. Nat. Inst. Allergy and Infectious Diseases, 1967-71; mem. expert adv. panel on Trachoma, WHO, 1970—; chmn. exec. com., mem. nat. adv. council on health professions edn. NIH, 1972-75. Contbr. numerous articles to profl. jours. Fellow Am. Coll. Preventive Medicine (v.p. gen. preventive medicine 1970-71, regent 1971-74), Am. Pub. Health Assn. (governing bd. 1978-80); mem. Am. Assn. Immunologists, Am. Assn. Physicians, Am. Epidemiol. Soc. (pres. 1982-83), Am. Fedn. Clin. Research, Am. Soc. Clin. Investigation, Am. Soc. Tropical Medicine and Hygiene, Assn. Acad. Health Centers (dir. 1975-80, pres. 1978-79), Assn. Tchrs. Preventive Medicine, Infectious Diseases Soc., Internat. Epidemiol. Assn., Soc. Exptl. Biology and Medicine, Inst. Medicine of Nat. Acad. Scis., Western Assn. Physicians, Western Soc. Clin. Research, Sigma Xi. Office: Dept Epidemiology SC-36 U Wash Seattle WA 98195

GRAZIANI, LEONARD JOSEPH, pediatric neurologist; b. Phila., Nov. 17, 1929; s. Annibale and Norina G.; m. Amelia Honeyford, June 29, 1956; children—Paul, Amy, Virginia, David. B.A., LaSalle Coll., 1951; M.D., Jefferson Med. Coll., 1955. Diplomate: Am. Bd. Psychiatry and Neurology, Am. Bd. Pediatrics. Intern Valley Forge (Pa.) Army Hosp., 1955-56; resident in pediatrics Brooke Army Hosp., San Antonio, 1957-59; asst. chief pediatrics Ireland Army Hosp., Ft. Knox, Ky., 1959-60, chief pediatrics, 1960-61; resident in neurology Bronx Municipal Hosp. Center, N.Y.C., 1961-63; asso. attending physician pediatrics and neurology, 1964-68; asst. prof. neurology and pediatrics Albert Einstein Coll. Medicine, Bronx, N.Y., 1964-68; prof. neurology and pediatrics, chief div. child neurology and devel. Jefferson Med. Coll. of Thomas Jefferson U., Phila., 1968—; pediatrician, neurologist Thomas Jefferson U. Hosp.; cons. pediatrician Wills Eye Hosp., Phila.; cons. neurologist Woods Sch., Langhorne, Pa., Children's Heart Hosp., Phila. Served with AUS, 1955-61. Mem. Am. Acad. Neurology, Am. Acad. Pediatrics, Soc. Pediatric Research, Am. Pediatric Assn., Child Neurology Soc., Sigma Xi, Alpha Omega Alpha. Research on brain growth and function in newborn infants, learning disabilities and lang. devel. in children. Home: 1257 Lenox Rd Jenkintown PA 19046 Office: Jefferson Medical College 1025 Walnut St Philadelphia PA 19107

GRAZIANI, SANTE, artist, art educator; b. Cleve., Mar. 11, 1920; s. Giovanni and Cleonice (Riccardi) G.; m. Jacquelee McMurry, Apr. 22, 1944; children: Michael, Alexandra, Gregory Philip. Student, Cleve. Sch. Art, 1938-41; B.F.A., Yale U., 1943, M.F.A., 1948. Instr. drawing and painting Sch. Fine Arts, Yale U., 1946-51; dean Whitney Sch. Art, 1950-51; head Sch. Worcester (Mass.) Art Mus., 1951-81, dean emeritus, 1981—; acad. dean Paier Coll. Art, Hamden, Conn., 1982—. Executed murals for, Bluffton (Ohio) Post Office, 1941, Columbus Post Office, 1942, Springfield (Mass.) Mus. Fine Arts, 1947, Holyoke (Mass.) Pub. Library, 1949-51, Burncoat Sch., Worcester, 1954, Am. Battle Monument, Henri-Chapelle, Belgium, 1957, Creativity, Mayo Clinic, 1969, Worcester Sci. Mus., 1978; designed: overseas airmail stamp Philip Mazzei, 1980; executed prep. drawings, color sketches Springfield murals; exhibited, various museums, schs., galleries, throughout U.S., 1947-50, one-man exhbns. at, Babcock Galleries, N.Y.C., 1962, 63, 65, 67, 69, 71, 73, 74, 76, Kanegis Gallery, Boston, 1964, 65, 66, 67, 68, 69, 70, 72, U. Conn., Storrs, 1970, Fairweather-Hardin Gallery, Chgo., 1970, 72, 73, 76, Allentown (Pa.) Art Mus., 1970, Manchester (N.H.) Inst. for Arts and Scis., 1981, Jersey City State Coll., retrospective exhbn., Springfield (Mass.) Mus., 1977; (Recipient Pulitzer prize 1942, won internat. competition for mural Springfield Mus. Fine Arts 1943, Edwin Austin Abbey prize 1948, Gold medal award Archtl. League N.Y., 1951, Boston Art Dirs. Club 1954, spl. drawing award Norfolk (Va.) Mus. 1961). Served with AUS, 1943-46; conducted army arts contest; PTO; with culmininating exhbn. Imperial Household Mus., 1946; Tokyo. Mem. Nat. Soc. Mural Painters. Home: 6 Bowden Ave Barrington RI 02806 Office: Paier Coll Art 6 Prospect Ct Hamden CT 06511

GRAZIANO, ANTHONY WALTER, JR., lawyer; b. N.Y.C., Sept. 29, 1941; s. Anthony Walter and Muriel Dorathea (MacPeck) G.; m. Robin Lee Ryckman, Aug. 27, 1966; children—Anthony Walter, Robin Virginia. A.B., Coll. Holy Cross, 1963; LL.B., U. Va., 1966. Bar: N.Y. State bar 1967, N.J. bar 1980. Lectr. U. Va. Sch. of Law, 1966-67; asso. firm Cahill, Gordon and Reindel, N.Y.C., 1967-70, 72-76, Paris, France, 1970-72; v.p., gen. counsel Purolator, Inc., Piscataway, N.J., 1977—. Office: Purolator Inc 255 Old New Brunswick Rd Piscataway NJ 08854

GRAZIANO, FRANK JOSEPH, corporation executive; b. Jersey City, Feb. 25, 1918; s. Samuel and Catherine (Lacava) G.; m. Jo Anne Divisek, Apr. 22, 1946 (div.); children: Gayle, James, Joseph, David; m. 2d Anne Dysart, Jan. 30, 1982. B.E.E., U.S. Naval Acad., 1940; M.S. in Mech. Engring., MIT, 1945; postgrad. in advanced mgmt., NYU, 1947. Commd. ensign U.S. Navy, 1940, advanced through grades to comdr.; assigned Pacific and Atlantic World War II; engring. duty officer, serving various engring. and mfg. mgt. positions, 1945-55, resigned, 1955; v.p. mfg., dir., sec. Monarch Machine Tool Co., 1955-61; dir. ops. Continental Copper & Steel Industries, Inc., 1961-63; with Am. Can Co., 1963-69, group v.p., gen. mgr. Canco, Glass and Plastic Products Group, 1964-67, v.p., gen. mgr. mfg., 1967-68, sr. v.p. adminstrn., 1968-69; pres., chief exec. officer Crompton & Knowles Corp., N.Y.C., 1969—; dir. Chemplex Corp. Mem. Community Citizens Adv. Bd., 1960—, County Com. on Edn.; chmn. bd. trustees United Fund, Shelby Country, Ohio, 1959, Webb Inst., Glen Cove/ L.I. Clubs: Sky (N.Y.C.); Baltusrol Golf (Springfield, N.J.). Home: 30 Westview Rd Short Hills NJ 07078 Office: Crompton & Knowles Corp 345 Park Ave New York NY 10154

GRAZIANO, JOHN VICTOR, govt. ofcl.; b. Bklyn., July 3, 1927; s. John B. and Anna (Attivissimo) G.; m. Carol Louise Frantz, May 6, 1966; children—David, Mitchell, Angela. B.S., St. John's U., Bklyn., 1951. Investigator CSC, 1952-63; asst. chief investigations and security FAA, 1963-65, chief investigations and security Okla. region, 1965-70, chief investigation, Washington, 1970-71; chief cargo security div. Office Sec., Dept. Transp., 1971-74; dir. Office of Investigation, Dept. Agr., 1974-78, spl. coordinator for grain elevator safety and security, 1978-79; asst. insp. gen. for investigations Dept. Commerce, Washington, 1979-81; insp. gen. Dept. Agr., Washington, 1981—. Served with AUS, 1945-47. Recipient Outstanding Performance award Dept. Transp., 1973. Mem. Internat. Assn. Chiefs Police, Am. Soc. Indsl. Security, Internat. Assn. Narcotic Enforcement Officers, Assn. Fed. Investigators, Fed. Criminal Investigators Assn. Office: Office of Insp Gen 14th St and Independence Ave SW Washington DC 20250 *

GREACEN, NAN, artist, educator; b. Giverny, France; came to U.S., 1912; d. Edmund William and Ethol (Booth) G.; m. Rene Bard Faure, Dec. 7, 1936; children: Nancy Faure Waesche, Renee. Student, Grand Central Sch. Art, N.Y.C., 1928-32. Tchr. Grand Central Sch. Art, 1932—; tchr. pvt. art classes. Exhibited one-man shows, Grand Central Art Gallery, 1967, Daytona Beach Art Gallery(Fla.), 1969, Fla. Gulf Coast Art Ctr., 1972, 74, Gateway Gallery, Palm Beach, Fla., group shows, NAD, N.Y.C., one-man shows, Audubon Artist, N.Y.C., Hudson Valley Art Assn., N.Y., Fla. Watercolor Soc., Jacksonville Watercolor Soc.; represented permanent collections, Old Lyme Mus. (Conn.); author: The Magic of Flower Painting, 1970, Still-Life is Exciting, 1965. Mem. NAD (medal 1937), Allied Artists of N.Y.C. (medal 1951), Hudson Valley Art Assn. (medal 1966), Audubon Artists, Fla. Watercolor soc. (numerous awards), St. Augustine Art Assn., Montclair Art Mus. (medal). Clubs: Ponte Vedra; Sawgrass (Ponte Vedra Beach, Fla.). Home: 184 San Juan Dr Ponte Vedra Beach FL 32082

GREACEN, THOMAS EDMUND, II, architect; b. Bklyn., Sept. 12, 1907; s. Walter James and Bertha (Semple) G.; m. Wynfred Vultee Fox, Aug. 28, 1941; children: John Morley, Thomas Edmund, Edward Semple, Amelia. A.B., Princeton U., 1928; student, Am. Sch. Fine Arts, Fontainebleau, France, 1931. Draftsman Delano & Aldrich, N.Y.C., 1929-31; partner firm Amon & Greacen, N.Y.C., 1932-36; prin. Thomas E. Greacen, II, N.Y.C., 1937-40, Houston, 1946-52; partner firm Greacen, Houston & Rogers (and predecessors), Houston, 1953-80; vis. critic archtl. design U. Houston, 1950-52. Prin. works include First Unitarian Ch, Houston, 1953, Sylvan Beach Pavilion, La Porte, Tex., 1956, Gibraltar Savs. Bldg, Houston, 1959, First Congl. Ch, Houston, 1961, M.D. Anderson-Magnolia Park br. YWCA, Houston, 1963, Courtland Sq. bldgs, Houston, 1968-75, St. Cyprians Episcopal Ch. and Sch, Lufkin, Tex., 1972. Mem. alumni council Princeton U., 1968-70; mem. Am. Friends Service Com., 1948—. Served with USAAF, 1940-45. Recipient citation Houston Municipal Art Commn., 1973, Comdg. Gen. USAF. Fellow AIA (dir. Houston chpt. 1955-57, medal of honor Houston chpt. 1960); mem. Princeton U. Alumni Assn. (pres. Houston 1967), Tex. Soc. Architects (chmn. edn. com. 1950, award merit 1953, 59). Club: Forest (Houston). Developer type of windrose used universally to determine optimum directions for alignment of runways on airfields. Home: 66 Saddlebrook Ln Houston TX 77024 Office: 1729 Sunset Blvd Houston TX 77005

GREASER, MAYLIN H., dredging company executive; b. North Wales, Pa., Jan. 15, 1909; s. John B. and Katie (B) G.; m. Ruth N. Philipp, Mar. 13, 1943. B.S. in Civil Engring., Pa. State U., 1930. Engaged in constrn. and dredging bus., 1930-79; with Am. Dredging Co., Ft. Washington, Pa., 1949-79, successively gen. supt., dir., 1951-79, v.p., 1953, pres., 1954-79; ret., 1979; exec. pres., bd. mgrs. Ivy Hill Cemetery Co., Phila. Mem. Delaware River Ports' Council for Emergency Ops. Served as lt. col. C.E., AUS, 1942-45. Fellow Soc. Am. Mil. Engrs. (past pres., dir. Phila. post); mem. Port of Phila. Maritime Soc. (past pres.), ASCE (life), Delaware Valley Council (past pres.), Mil. Order World Wars, Am. Legion, Seamens Church Inst. (bd. mgrs.), Pa. Soc., Permanent Internat. Assn., Nav. Congress. Presbyterian. Clubs: Phila. Cricket, Union League (Phila.); Skytop (Pa.). Home: 6003 Cricket Rd Flourtown PA 19031

GREASON, ARTHUR LEROY, JR., educator; b. Newport, R.I., Sept. 13, 1922; s. Arthur LeRoy and Pauline (Brown) G.; m. Pauline Schaaf, Dec. 29, 1945; children—Randall Mark, Katherine, Douglas Bradford. B.A., Wesleyan U., Middletown, Conn., 1945; M.A., Harvard, 1947, Ph.D., 1954. Asst. to dean Wesleyan U., 1945-46; teaching fellow English Harvard, 1948-52; mem. faculty Bowdoin

Coll., 1952—, asso. prof. English, 1961-66, prof., 1966—, dean students, 1962-66, dean of coll., 1966-75, acting pres., 1981, pres., 1981—. Kent fellow Soc. Religion Higher Edn., 1946. Mem. Phi Beta Kappa. Conglist. Home: 34 McKeen St Brunswick ME 04011

GREATHOUSE, IDA KAY, museum administrator; b. Bellingham, Wash., Dec. 26, 1905; d. Samuel J. and Bessie A. (McClelland) Myers. Student, U. Wash., 1934. Exec. and dir. Frye Mus., Seattle, 1966—. Office: Frye Art Mus 704 Terry Ave Seattle WA 98104

GREAVER, HARRY, artist; b. Los Angeles, Oct. 30, 1929; s. Harry Jones and Lucy Catherine (Coons) G.; m. Hanne Synnestvedt Nielsen, Nov. 30, 1955; children—Peter, Paul, Lotte. B.F.A., U. Kans., 1951, M.F.A., 1952. Asso. prof. art U. Maine, Orono, 1955-66; exec. dir. Kalamazoo Inst. Arts, 1966-78; dir. Greaver Gallery, Cannon Beach, Oreg., 1978—; mem. visual com. Mich. Council Arts, 1976-78. One-man exhbns. include, Baker U., Baldwin, Kans., 1955, U. Maine, Orono, 1958, 59, group exhbns. include, U. Utah Mus. Fine Arts, 1972-73, Purdue U., 1977, Drawings/U.S.A, St. Paul, 1963, San Diego Mus., 1971. Served with AUS, 1952-54. Recipient Purchase award Nat. Endowment Arts, 1971; grantee U. Maine, 1962-64. Address: Box 120 Cannon Beach OR 97110

GREAVES, CLIVE WALTER, distilled spirits company executive; b. London, June 21, 1936; U.S., 1967; s. Walter Henry and Kate Winifred (Rogers) G.; m. Jennifer Moore, Mar. 19, 1960; children: Karen Julie, Robert Clive. Student, Preston Manor, Wembley, Middlesex, Eng., 1947-53. Accountant Arthur Young, London, 1953-60, Reed Internat., 1960-62; sec. various subs. Distillers Co. Ltd., London, also dir., 1962-67, N.Y.C., 1967—. Mem. Inst. Chartered Accountants Scotland. Clubs: Wee Burn, Shinnecock Hills Golf, Union, Hon. Co. Edinburgh Golfers. Home: 5 Rabbit Ln Darien CT 06820 Office: Distillers Co Ltd 41 Harbor Plaza Dr PO Box 10175 Stamford CT 06904

GREAVES, THOMAS GUY, JR., lawyer; b. Lynchburg, Va., Apr. 19, 1918; s. Thomas Guy and Ellen duVal (Radford) G.; m. Annie Jean Bell, Feb. 28, 1942; children: Thomas Guy III, Mac Bell. B.S. in Econs, Wharton Sch. U. Pa., 1939; LL.B., U. Ala., 1947. Bar: Ala. 1948. Since practiced in, Mobile; partner firm Hand, Arendall, Bedsole, Greaves & Johnston, 1952—. Pres. Mobile County chpt. ARC, 1966-68; pres. Episcopal Churchmens Assn. Ala., 1960-61; legal adv. bd. South Eastern Legal Found., 1977—. Served to capt., inf. AUS, 1941-45. Fellow Am. Bar Found., Ala. Bar Found.; mem. ABA (ho. dels. 1959-74, ho. dels. 75-76, bd. govs. 1966-69, chmn. rules and calendar com. ho. of dels. 1970-72, mem. exec. council young lawyers sect. 1953-55, mem. adv. bd. jour. 1961-63), Ala. Bar Assn. (pres. 1975-76, pres., young lawyers sect. 1950-51), Mobile Bar Assn. (pres. 1968), Am. Judicature Soc. (dir. 1959-63), Fedn. Ins. Counsel (dir. 1963-65), Internat. Assn. Ins. Counsel, Conf. Bar Pres.'s, U. Ala. Law Sch. Alumni Assn. (pres. 1963-64), Am., Ala. law insts., English Speaking Union (pres. 1970), Farrah Order of Jurisprudence, NOW, Order of Coif, Phi Eta Sigma, Phi Delta Phi, Delta Kappa Epsilon. Home: 77 Clarise Circle Mobile AL 36608 Office: First Nat Bank Bldg: Mobile AL 36602

GREAVES, WILLIAM, film director and producer; b. N.Y.C.; s. Garfield G. and Phillis (Muir) G. Student, Film Inst., CCNY, 1949-51. Mem. prodn. staff Nat. Film Bd. Can., 1952-60; founder, dir. Canadian Drama Studio, Montreal, Toronto and Ottawa, 1952-63; founder Nat. Assn. Black Media Producers, 1970. Featured actor on Broadway, screen, radio and TV, 1946-52; producer-dir., UN TV, 1963-64; ind. documentary film producer, 1964—; exec. producer: Black Jour, 1968-70; feature film dir. and producer, 1967—; (Recipient Emmy award Nat. Acad. TV Arts and Scis. 1970, Russwurm award Nat. Newspaper Pubs. Assn. Am. 1970, over 60 Internat. Film Festival awards, named to Black Filmmakers Hall of Fame, spl. hommage and retrospective Black Am. Filmmakers, Paris 1980, N.Y. Actors Studio Dusa award.). *Success is largely dependent on an individual's capacity to convert the most negative experience or circumstance into something constructive and productive.*

GREB, GORDON BARRY, educator, writer; b. Irvington, Calif., Aug. 7, 1921; s. Walter H. and Irene A. (Benbow) G.; m. Darlene Alcock, Dec. 28, 1950; children: Gary Benbow, Darla Jean. A.A., U. Calif.-Berkeley, 1942, B.A., 1947; student, Ohio State U., 1943-44; M.A., U. Minn., 1951; postgrad., U. So. Calif., 1951, Stanford U., 1951-54. With San Leandro News-Obs., 1939-43, San Rafael Ind., 1947; teaching asst. journalism U. Minn., 1948-49; instr., asst. to pres. for pub. relations San Bernardino (Calif.) Valley Coll., 1949-50; instr. journalism U. Oreg., Eugene, 1950-51; news editor Radio Sta. KNX, CBS, Hollywood, Calif., 1951; teaching asst. polit. sci. Stanford U., 1952-54; news dir. Radio Sta. KSJO, San Jose, Calif., 1954-57; newscaster TV Sta. KNTV, San Jose, 1961; newsman KABC-TV, Hollywood, summer 1966; moderator TV discussion series KNTV, KTEH, San Jose; also producer TV documentary KQED, San Francisco, 1967; dir. Radio-TV News Center, San Jose State U., 1956-78, prof. journalism, 1956—, coordinator grad. studies in mass communications, 1978-83, dir. internat. program, 1980—; vis. prof. Sch. Journalism, U. Wis., summers 1968-70; vis. prof. journalism Centre for Arts and Related Studies, City U., London, 1980-81; judge Emmy awards for news and documentary programs Nat. Acad. TV Arts and Scis., 1974; curator Charles David Herrold Pioneer Radio Collection. Editor: Contemporary Issues in American Society, 1967; writer, editor, Newsmakers Syndicate, 1971—; narrator ednl. films. Mem. Calif. Democratic Central Com., 1954-56. Served with AUS, 1943-46. Recipient Commendation by Spl. Resolution, Calif. State Senate, 1959, Research award Sta. KCBS, San Francisco, 1959. Mem. Radio-TV News Dirs. Assn., Assn. Edn. in Journalism (chmn. research com. radio-TV div. 1968-70), Calif. A.P. TV and Radio Assn. (chmn. com. 1967-70), World Affairs Council No. Calif., Kappa Tau Alpha, Sigma Delta Chi. Home: 2646 Hill Park Dr San Jose CA 95124 *Life is like hiking in the mountains. There is no permanent up. There is no permanent down. Views are different from wherever you are. Some people are content with the spot in which they find themselves. Others struggle to higher ground. What's most important along the way, though, is to learn how to look. That takes time. So don't go rushing pell-mell up and down, over and across, higher and yon, else you'll miss the whole thing.*

GREBANIER, MICHAEL PETER, musician, educator; b. Bklyn., Apr. 27, 1937; s. Joseph Phillip and Lillian (Greenberg) G.; m. Patricia Parr, Mar. 7, 1959; children: Loren, Steven; m. Lynn Beckstrom, Aug. 2, 1974; m. Sharon Wood, Aug. 30, 1983. Diploma, Curtis Inst. Music, 1958. Mem. faculty San Francisco Conservatory of Music, 1977—; tchr. Duquesne U., 1963-70, Temple U., 1970-74, Carnegie-Mellon U., 1975-77. Violoncellist, Cleve. Orch., 1959-63; solo violoncellist, Pitts. Symphony, 1963-77, San Francisco Symphony, 1977—; ann. solo appearances with, Pitts. Symphony Orch., Pitts. Chamber Orch., solo recitals; mem., Carnegie Mellon Trio. Recipient Naumberg award, 1957. Home: 677 43d Ave San Francisco CA 94121 Office: San Francisco Symphony Davies Symphony Hall San Francisco CA 94102

GREBEN, STANLEY EDWARD, psychiatrist; b. Toronto, Ont., Can., Aug. 6, 1927; s. Abraham and Kitty (Goodman) G.; m. Marilyn Elma Scher, Dec. 3, 1929; children—Daniel Howard, Jan Elizabeth. B.A., U. Toronto, 1949, M.D., 1953. Diplomate: Am. Bd. Psychiatry and Neurology, also examiner. Intern Kings County Hosp., Bklyn., 1953-54; resident Johns Hopkins, Balt., 1954-56, 57-58; sr. house officer Maudsley Hosp., London, 1956-57; practice medicine, specializing in psychiatry, Toronto, Ont., Can., 1958—; psychiatrist-in-chief Mt. Sinai Hosp., Toronto, 1964—, Baycrest Centre for Geriatric Care, 1964-82, sr. cons., 1983—; prof. psychiatry U. Toronto, 1973—; vis. prof. U. Calif., San Francisco, 1981-82; Hebrew U., Jerusalem, 1982; cons. Clarke Inst. Psychiatry, Women's Coll. Hosp.; mem. profl. adv. bd. C.K. Clarke Psychiat. Research Found.; psychiat. cons. Nat. Ballet Sch. Can., Toronto Western Hosp. Author: Love's Labor: Twenty-Five Years in the Practice of Psychotherapy, 1984; editor, contbr.: A Method of Psychiatry, 1980; Contbr. articles to psychiat. jours. Fellow Laidlaw Found., 1979. Fellow Am. Psychiat. Assn., Royal Coll. Physicians Can. (examiner), Royal Coll. Psychiatry, Am. Coll. Psychiatrists, Am. Assn. Social Psychiatry; mem. Can. Med. Assn., Canadian Psychoanalytic Soc. (pres. Toronto br. 1975-77), Internat. Psycho-Analytical Assn., Canadian Psychoanalytic Inst. (tng. and supervising analyst), Canadian Psychiat. Assn. (chmn. bd. dirs. 1975—). Home: 148 Dunvegan Rd Toronto ON M5P 2N9 Canada Office: 600 University Ave Toronto ON M5G 1X5 Canada

GREBENE, ALAN BEKIR, electronics company executive; b. Istanbul, Turkey, Mar. 13, 1939; came to U.S., 1961, naturalized, 1970; s. Muzaffer N. G.; m. Karen Gale, June 11, 1967; 1 son. M.Sc. in Elec. Engring, U. Calif., Berkeley, 1963; Ph.D., Rensselaer Polytechnic Inst., Troy, 1968. Sr. engr. Sprague Electric Co., North Adams, Mass., 1964-65; mgr. circuit research Signetics Corp., Sunnyvale, Calif., 1968-71; founder, sr. v.p. Exar Integrated Systems, Inc., Sunnyvale, 1971-82; founder, pres. Pace Microsystems Inc., Saratoga, Calif., 1983—. Author: Analog Integrated Circuit Design, 1972, Analog Integrated Circuits, 1978, Bipolar and MOS Analog Integrated Circuit Design, 1983; contbr. articles in field. Fellow IEEE. Patentee semiconductor devices and integrated circuits.

GREBER, ROBERT MARTIN, entertainment company executive; b. Phila., Mar. 15, 1938; s. Joseph and Golda (Rubin) G.; m. Judith Ann Pearlstein, Dec. 23, 1962; children: Matthew, Jonathan. B.S. in Fin., Temple U., 1962. Account exec. Merrill Lynch, Phila., 1962-68; portfolio mgr. v.p. Afuture Funds Inc., Lima, Pa., 1968-70; instl. account exec. Merrill Lynch, Phila., 1970-75, officer, mgr.-v.p., Los Angeles, 1975-79; chief fin. officer Lucasfilm Ltd., Los Angeles, 1979-80, pres., chief exec. officer, San Rafael, Calif., 1980—; mem. Western Behavior Scis. Inst., La Jolla, 1982—. Bd. dirs. KQED Pub. Broadcasting System, San Francisco, 1983, Film Inst. No. Calif., Marin Symphony Orch., 1981—. Served with Army N.G., 1959-60. Office: Lucasfilm Ltd 3270 Kerner Blvd San Rafael CA 94901

GREBEY, CLARENCE RAYMOND, profl. sports adminstr.; b. Chgo., Mar. 10, 1928; s. Clarence R. and Inez (Fuller) G.; m. Marilyn Irene Isett, Nov. 24, 1951; children—Nancy Virginia, Christine E., Clarence Raymond. B.A., Kenyon Coll., 1949; M.B.A., U. Chgo., 1956. With Inland Steel Co., 1949-56, sr. wage and salary analyst, 1956; with Gen. Electric Co., 1956-78, mgr. wage and salary, 1963-67, mgr. employee relations, 1967-69, cons. corp. employee relations, mgr. union relations, 1969-74, mgr. corp. planning and strategy, 1974-75, mgr. union relations planning and strategy, 1975-78, chief negotiator corp. employee relations, 1978; dir., sec.-treas. player relations com. Major League Baseball, N.Y.C., 1978—. Chmn. Personnel Bd. Appeals, City of Stamford, Conn.; bd. advisors Indsl. and Labor Relations Sch., Cornell U. Served with U.S. Army, 1951-52; Korea. Roman Catholic. Club: Stanwich (Greenwich, Conn.). Office: 1270 Ave of Americas New York NY 10020

GREBIN, BURTON, physician; b. Bklyn., Mar. 7, 1941; s. Herman and Mary G.; m. Marilyn Trapani, July 30, 1976; children: Perry and Jason (twins). B.A. in Biology, Adelphi U., Hempstead, N.Y., 1962; M.D., N.Y. Med. Coll., 1966. Asst. attending pediatrician Harlem Hosp. Center and Columbia-Presbyn. Med. Center, N.Y.C., 1971—; asso. dir. div. pediatric ambulatory care Columbia-Presbyn. Med. Center, 1975, dir. pediatric clinic, 1975; asso. attending pediatrician Roosevelt Hosp.; mem. faculty Columbia U. Coll. Phys. and Surg., 1971—, asst. prof. clin. pediatrics, 1975—; med. dir. St. Mary's Hosp. Children, Bayside, N.Y., 1975-82, exec. dir., 1982—; med. adviser, pres. Leonia (N.J.) Bd. Health; cons. PAHO/WHO. Served to lt. comdr. USNR. Norman Jolliffe fellow, 1970; recipient Lawrence J. Slobody award N.Y. Med. Coll., 1966; Gerard B. Lambert award, 1975. Mem. Am. Pediatrics Assn., Am. Pub. Health Assn., Am. Acad. Pediatrics, N.Y. State Med. Soc., Metroplex Amateur Comm. Assn. (pres.). Home: PO Box 237 Leonia NJ 07605 Office: 29-01 216th St Bayside NY 11360

GREBOW, EDWARD, banker; b. Lakewood, N.J., July 17, 1949; s. Benjamin and Ruth (Blume) G. B.B.A., George Washington U., 1971, M.B.A., 1972. Asst. treas. Morgan Guaranty Trust Co., N.Y.C., 1973-76, asst. v.p., N.Y.C., 1976-78, v.p., 1978—, J.P. Morgan & Co., Inc., 1980—; pres. J.P. Morgan Leasefunding Corp., N.Y.C., 1982—; mgn. dir. J.P. Morgan Internat. Fin. N.V., Curaco, Netherlands, 1982—; chmn. bd. Morgan Data Services Inc., Wilmington, Del., 1982—. Chmn. Republican Municipal Com., Lakewood, N.J., 1973-74; pres. Waterside Tenants Assn., N.Y.C., 1979-81. Mem. Nfat. Assn. Bank Cost Analysis (dir. 1980-83). Republican. Home: 1 Clubhouse Rd Bricktown NJ 08723 Office: J P Morgan & Co Inc 23 Wall St New York NY 10015

GREBSTEIN, SHELDON NORMAN, university president; b. Providence, Feb. 1, 1928; s. Sigmund and Sylvia (Skotkin) G.; m. Phyllis Strumar, Sept. 6, 1953; children: Jason Lyle, Gary Wade. B.A. cum laude, U. So. Calif., 1949; M.A., Columbia U., 1950; Ph.D., Mich. State U., 1954. Instr., then asst. prof. English U. Ky., 1953-62; asst. prof. U. South Fla., 1962-63; mem. faculty SUNY, Binghamton, 1963-81, prof. English, 1968-81, asst. to pres., 1974-75; dean arts and scis. Harpur Coll., 1975-81; pres. SUNY, Purchase, 1981—; Fulbright-Hays lectr. U. Rouen, France, 1968-69; vis. lectr. Caen, Hull and Edinburgh univs., 1969. Author: Sinclair Lewis, 1962, John O'Hara, 1966, Hemingway's Craft, 1973; Editor: Monkey Trial, 1960, Perspectives in Contemporary Criticism, 1968, Studies in For Whom The Bell Tolls, 1971; editorial cons. univ. presses, publishers.; Contbr. articles to profl. jours. Mem. Am. Assn. Higher Edn. Home: Beechwood Purchase St Purchase NY 10577 Office: SUNY Purchase NY 10577

GRECH, ANTHONY PAUL, law librarian; b. N.Y.C., July 16, 1930; s. Annibale H. and Anna Jane (Cassar) G. B.B.A., Manhattan Coll., 1952; M.L.S., Columbia U., 1961. Asst. reference librarian Assn. Bar City N.Y., 1958-65, reference librarian, 1965-67, librarian, 1967-84, curator, 1984—; mem. library com. of Eastman Arbitration Library, Am. Arbitration Assn., 1984—. Mem. Am. Assn. Law Libraries (Joseph L. Andrews Bibliog. award 1967, chmn. micro fascimiles com. 1965-67, chmn. publs. com. 1975-76, exec. bd. 1980-83), Assn. Law Libraries Upstate N.Y. (treas. 1976-77), Bibliog. Soc. Am., Spl. Libraries Assn., Law Library Assn. Greater N.Y. (pres. 1967-68), ALA, Bibliog. Soc. U. Va., Internat. Assn. Law Libraries, Am. Printing History Assn., Nat. Micrographics Assn., Supreme Ct. Hist. Soc., Beta Phi Mu. Home: 15 W 72d St New York NY 10023 Office: 42 W 44th St New York NY 10036

GRECO, JOSE, choreographer; b. Montorio nei Frentani, Italy, Dec. 23, 1918; came to U.S., 1928, naturalized, 1928; s. Paolo Emilio and Carmela (Bucci) G.; m. Nila Amparo. Student, Leonardo da Vinci Art Sch., N.Y.C.; studied dancing with, Helene Veola. Tchr. dancing, hotels and resorts, 1936-45; founder Jose Greco Found. for Hispanic Dance, Inc., N.Y.C., 1971. First profl. appearance as dancer in: Carmen, N.Y. Hippodrome Opera Co., 1937; joined Gloria Belmonte in engagement at La Conga, N.Y.C. (profl. name Ramon Serrano), 1938; appeared with, Argentinita, 1943; toured, U.S., 1943-45, guest appearances, Ballet Theater at Met. Opera House; dancer: ballets including Carmen; Spanish debut with, Ballet Espanol, Madrid, 1946; choreographer: Pictures of Goya, 1950; composer: (with Roger Machado) La Molinera Caprichosa and Other Works; dancer: motion picture Manolete, 1948; organized ballet co., Ballets y Bailes de Espana, 1948; appeared, Barcelona, Paris, also Norway, Sweden, Denmark, other European countries; toured, Argentina, Uruguay, Chile, Peru, 1950; appeared, Sadler's Wells Theater, London, 1951, North Am. debut with, Spanish Ballet, Shubert Theater, N.Y.C., 1951; appeared in role of Count Dracula in: Passion of Dracula, U.S. tour, 1979; role of Jonathan in: Arsenic and Old Lace, 1981; Author: (with Harvey Ardman) Gypsy in My Soul, 1978. Comdr. Calvellero of La Cruz del Merito Civil, Spain; recipient Silver Bowl award Internat. Platform Assn., 1971, hon. doctorates Fairfield U., Northwood Inst., Midland Inst., 1971. Office: 866 United Nations Plaza New York NY 10017

GRECO, PHILIP ANTHONY, business executive; b. St. Louis, Oct. 22, 1932; s. Anthony Thomas and Annetta V. (Salia) G.; m. Janet Ann Schaus, Apr. 12, 1954 (div. 1978); children: Christopher, Anthony, Philip,; m. Brenda K. Woodlock, Dec. 15, 1978. B.S., Western Mich. U., 1958. Mgmt. sci. coordinator Kellogg Co., Battle Creek, Mich., 1958-66; mgr. data processing Nat. Water Lift Co., Kalamazoo, 1966-68; mktg. rep. IBM Corp., Kalamazoo, 1968-70; v.p., gen mgr. Pneumo Services Corp., Syracuse, N.Y., 1970-78; v.p. adminstrn. and fin. Cleve. Pneumatic Co., 1978-79, exec. v.p., 1979-82, pres., gen. mgr., 1982—; dir. Machine Trades Inst., Cleve., 1978-80. Bd. dirs. Planned Parenthood, Boston, 1977-78. Served with USAF, 1952-56. Mem. Data Processing Mgmt. Assn. (v.p. 1965), Assn. Computing Machinery, Kappa Rho Sigma. Club: Cleve. Athletic. Home: 615 Falls Rd Chagrin Falls OH 44022

GREEHEY, WILLIAM EUGENE, b. Forest Dodge, Iowa, 1936. B.B.A., St. Mary's U., 1960. Auditor Price Waterhouse & Co., 1961-63; sr. v.p. fin. Coastal Corp. (and predecessor), 1963-74; with Valero Energy Corp. (formerly Coastal States Gas Producing Co.), 1947—; chief exec officer LoVaca Gathering Co. (named changed to Valro Transmission Co. subs. 1980), 1974—; chief exec. officer, dir. LoVaca Gathering Co. (named changed to Valero Transmission Co. subs. 1980), 1980-83, chmn. bd., 1983—, chief exec. officer, exec., 1983. Office: Valero Energy Corp 530 McCullough San Antonio TX 78292 *

GREEK, DAROLD I., lawyer; b. Kunkle, Ohio, Mar. 30, 1909; s. Albert F. and Iva (Shaffer) G.; m. Catherine Johnson, Oct. 12, 1935 (dec. 1962); 1 son, Darold I (dec.); m. Elizabeth Tracy Ridgley, Sept. 18, 1970 (dec. May 1972); stepsons—Thomas B., David Ridgley; m. Nadine Berry Weisheimer Bivens, Dec. 23, 1976; stepchildren—Richard A. Weisheimer, Jon B. Weisheimer. Student, Bowling Green State U., 1926-28; LL.B., Ohio State U., 1932. Bar: Ohio bar 1932. Treas., Williams County, Ohio, 1932-33; atty. Ohio Dept. Taxation, 1934-36; practiced in, Columbus, 1937—; partner firm George, Greek, King, McMahon & McConnaughey (and predecessors), 1937-79; of counsel Baker & Hostetler, 1979—. Mem. ABA, Ohio Bar Assn., Columbus Bar Assn. (pres. 1966-67). Presbyn. Clubs: Rotarian., Univ.; Columbus Country (Columbus); The Golf. Home: 6635 Lake of the Woods Point Galena OH 43021 Office: 100 E Broad St Columbus OH 43215

GREELEY, ANDREW MORAN, sociologist, author; b. Oak Park, Ill., Feb. 5, 1928; s. Andrew T. and Grace (McNichols) G. A.B., St. Mary of Lake Sem., 1950, S.T.L., 1954; M.A., U. Chgo., 1961, Ph.D., 1961. Ordained priest Roman Catholic Ch., 1954; asst. pastor Ch. of Christ the King, Chgo., 1954-64; program dir. Nat. Opinion Research Center, Chgo., 1961-68; dir. Center for Study Am. Pluralism, 1973—; lectr. sociology U. Chgo., 1963-72; prof. sociology U. Ariz., Tucson, 1978—; cons. Hazen Found. Commn. Syndicated columnist: People and Values; Author: The Church and the Suburbs, 1959, Strangers in the House, 1961, Religion and Career, 1963, (with Peter H. Rossi) Education of Catholic Americans, 1966, Come Blow Your Mind With Me, 1971, Friendship Game, 1971, Life for a Wanderer: A New Look at Christian Spirituality, 1971, The Denominational Society: A Sociological Approach to Religion in America, 1972, Priests in the United States: Reflections on A Survey, 1972, The Sinai Myth, 1972, That Most Distressful Nation, 1972, New Agenda, 1973, Jesus Myth, 1971, The Denominational Society: A Sociological Approach to Religion in America, 1973, Unsecular Man, 1974, Ethnicity in the United States: A Preliminary Reconnaissance, 1974, Ecstasy: A Way of Knowing, 1974, The Devil, You Say!, 1974, Building Coalitions: American Politics in the 1970's, 1974, Sexual Intimacy, 1975, The Great Mysteries: An Essential Catechism, 1976, The Communal Catholic: A Personal Manifesto, 1976, Death and Beyond, 1976, The American Catholic: A Social Portrait, 1977, The Mary Myth: On the Femininity of God, 1977, The Making of the Popes, 1978, 79, The Magic Cup: An Irish Legend, 1979, Women I've Met, 1979, The Cardinal Sins, 1981, Thy Brother's Wife, 1982, Ascent Into Hell, 1983; contbr. articles to profl. jours. Recipient Cath. Press Assn. award for best book for young people, 1965, Thomas Alva Edison award for radio broadcast, 1963, C. Albert Kobb award Nat. Cath. Edn. Assn., 1977. Mem. Am. Sociol. Assn., Soc. for Sci. Study Religion, Religious Research Assn. Office: 6030 S Ellis Ave Chicago IL 60637

GREELEY, JOHN BERNARD, III, clothing brokerage executive, management consultant; b. Columbus, Ohio, June 12, 1935; s. John Bernard and Blanche Hall (Armstrong) G.; m. Lana M. McNabb, Oct. 3, 1970; children—Kimberly J., Sean M. Student, Washington U., St. Louis. Sr. engring. cons. Unified Mgmt. Cons., St. Louis, 1960-64; exec. v.p. Coronet Mfg. Co., Kansas City, Mo., 1967-71; v.p. mfg. apparel div. W.R. Grace & Co., Norwich, Conn., 1971-74; v.p. Hart, Schaffner & Marx, Chgo., 1974-76; founder Kimean Industries Corp., Reynoldsburg, Ohio, 1976—; v.p. Bobbie Brooks, Cleve., 1977—; founder, pres. Assoc. Precision Grinding Co., Plano, Tex., 1979—; founder Greeley & Assocs. Inc., cons., Dallas, 1982—; founder also subs. J.J. of Dallas Mktg. div., 1982—; rep., adv. Clothing Mfrs. Assn. U.S.A., 1974—. Patentee in field. Address: 3913 Matterhorn Plano TX 75075

GREELEY, JOSEPH MAY, advt. cons.; b. Winnetka, Ill., Sept. 13, 1902; s. Morris Larned and Anne (Foote) G.; m. Margery Gerould, Dec. 18, 1928 (div. June 1958); children—Margery (Mrs. Forrest I. Watson), Samuel Joseph May; m. Elizabeth Knode Conrad, Apr. 8, 1961. Student, Phillips Exeter Acad.; B.S., Harvard, 1925, M.B.A., 1927. Advt. mgr. Quaker Oats, Ltd., London, Eng., 1930-39; asst. gen. mgr. Hecker Products Corp., N.Y.C., 1939-41; account exec. Pedlar & Ryan, N.Y.C., 1941-42; v.p. Dancer, Fitzgerald, Sample, Chgo., 1942-48, Leo Burnett, 1948-55, v.p. charge marketing, 1955-58, exec. v.p. marketing services, 1958-70, cons., 1971—, also former dir., mem. exec. com. Mem. Asso. Harvard Alumni (regional dir. 1972-75). Clubs: University (Chgo.); Harvard of Chicago (pres., dir.), Mid-America, Indian Hill; Port Royal, Royal Poinciana, Golf, Hole-In-The-Wall

Golf (Naples). Home: 966 Fisher Ln Winnetka IL 60093 also 600 Galleon Dr Naples FL 33940

GREELEY, PAUL WEBB, plastic surgeon; b. Waterman, Ill., July 10, 1902; s. Paul Eber Norman and Maud Nancy (Webb) G.; m. Eunice Cooksy Goebel, June 12, 1927 (dec. 1978); 1 son, Paul Julius Goebel; m. Vivian Anderson, Aug. 1, 1981. A.B., U. Ill., 1923; M.D., Northwestern U., 1928. Diplomate: Am. Bd. Plastic Surgery (bd. govs. 1951-58). Rotating intern Evanston (Ill.) Hosp., 1927-28; gen. surgery tng. under Dr. Frederick Christopher, 1928-31; pvt. practice medicine specializing in gen. surgery, Chgo., 1931-34, plastic surgery, 1936—; clin. asst. gen. surgery Northwestern U. Med. Sch. Chgo., 1930-34; vol. asst. plastic surgery to Sir Harold Gillies and Sir Archibald McIndoe, London, additional tng. in plastic surgery in, Freiburg, Munich, Vienna, 1934-35; clin. prof. surgery, head dept. plastic surgery U. Ill. Coll. Medicine, Chgo., 1937-70; prof. plastic surgery Rush Presbyn.-St. Lukes Med. Center, Chgo., 1971—; attending plastic surgeon, chief plastic surgery service U. Ill. Hosp., Presbyn.-St. Lukes Hosp.; cons. plastic surgeon West Side VA Hosp., Municipal Tb Sanitarium, Chgo., U.S. Naval hosps., Great Lakes, Ill. and; San Diego. Contbr. numerous monographs to profl. lit., chpts. to textbooks. Served with M.C. USNR, 1943-46; now rear adm. Res., res. cons. plastic surgery Bur. Medicine and Surgery, Dept. Navy, 1947—. Mem. Am. Soc. Plastic and Reconstructive Surgery (pres. 1950-51), Am. Assn. Surgery Trauma, Am. Assn. Plastic Surgeons, A.C.S., AMA, Am., Western, Central surg. assns., Internat. Fedn. Plastic Surgeons, Am. Assn. Ry. Surgeons, Ill. Med. Soc., Inst. Medicine Chgo., Chgo. Surg. Soc. (v.p. 1960), Argentine Soc. Plastic Surgeons (hon.), Internat. Soc. Surgeons, Warren H. Cole Surg. Soc., Kappa Delta Rho, Omega Beta Pi, Nu Sigma Nu. Clubs: University (Chgo.); Indian Hill (Winnetka, Ill.). Home: 7474 Hillside Dr LaJolla CA 92037 also Castle Park MI 49422 Office: 310 S Michigan Ave Chicago IL 60604

GREELEY, SAMUEL SEWALL, lawyer; b. Winnetka, Ill., Sept. 14, 1914; s. Samuel Arnold and Dorothy (Coffin) G.; m. Irene E. Mares, Oct. 28, 1945; children: Sara S., Samuel Sewall. A.B., Harvard U., 1936, LL.B., 1939. Bar: Ill. 1939. Practice in, Chgo., 1939-42, 46-51; gen. counsel Masonite Corp., Chgo., 1951-69, sec., 1958-69, treas., 1961-64, fin. v.p., 1964-66, exec. v.p., 1966-69, pres., 1969-76, chief exec. officer, 1971-77, chmn., 1976—, also dir.; dir. Tyler Corp. Served to lt. comdr. USNR, 1942-46. Mem. Ill. Bar Assn., Legal Club. Clubs: Tower, Economic (Chgo.); Indian Hill (Winnetka). Home: 800 Tower Rd Winnetka IL 60093 Office: 29 N Wacker Dr Chicago IL 60606

GREELY, MICHAEL TRUMAN, attorney general of Montana; b. Great Falls, Mont., Feb. 28, 1940; s. Myril Jay and Laura Harriet (Haugh) G.; m. Marilyn Jean Myhre, Dec. 1, 1972; children: Winston Truman, Morgen. B.A., Yale U., 1962; J.D., U. Mont., 1967. Bar: Mont. 1967. Tchr. pub. schs., Oklahoma City, 1962-63, asst. atty. gen., Mont., 1968-70, atty. gen., 1977—; chmn. Mont. Justice Project, 1975; dep. county atty. Cascade County, Mont., 1970-74. Mem. Mont. Ho. of Reps., 1971-74, Mont. Senate, 1975-77; Pres. 8th Dist. Youth Guidance Home, Great Falls, 1971-72. Mem. Nat. Assn. Attys. Gen. (pres. 1983-84), Mont., Cascade County bar assns. Democrat. Office: Justice Bldg 215 N Sanders St Helena MT 59620

GREEN, ADOLPH, playwright, lyricist; b. N.Y.C., Dec. 2, 1915; s. Daniel and Helen (Weiss) G.; m. Phyllis Newman, Jan. 31, 1960; children—Adam, Amanda. Student pub. schs., N.Y.C. Writer, author: (with Betty Comden) On the Town, 1944-45, Billion Dollar Baby, Two on the Aisle, Wonderful Town, Take Me Out to the Ball Game, Good News, Barkleys of Broadway, Band Wagon, Singing in the Rain, Bells are Ringing, 1960, Do Re Mi, 1960, Subways are for Sleeping, 1962, Fade Out-Fade In, 1964, (with Betty Comden and Jules Styne) Say Darling, 1959, The Cockeyed Tiger; songs, 1977, Wonderful Town; lyrics, 1977, On the Twentieth Century; book and lyrics, 1978; (with Betty Comden) screenplays What a Way to Go, Aunt Mame; co-author: Applause; writer-dir.: By Bernstein, 1975, Lorelei; TV prodns. include Peter Pan, Wonderful Town; appeared as actor in: film Simon, 1979 (Co-recipient Donaldson award for Wonderful Town 1953, Tony award for co-writer music and lyrics for Hallelujah Baby and co-writer best score 1967-68, for Applause as best mus. 1970, Tony awards for best book of musical (with Comden) and for best score (with Comden and Coleman) for On the Twentieth Century 1978, named to Songwriters Hall of Fame 1980) *

GREEN, AL, singer, clergyman; b. Forest City, Ark., Apr. 13, 1946; s. Robert and Cora G. Ordained minister Full Gospel Tabernacle, Memphis, 1976—. Formerly rec. artist with, Bell, then with, Hi-Records (earning 4 gold albums and 7 gold singles); songs recorded include Rhymes, 1975, Lets Stay Together, Tired of Being Alone, How do You Mend a Broken Heart, Back up Train, Love and Happiness; appeared in Broadway prodn.: Your Arms Too Short to Box with God, 1982. Recipient Grammy awards for best soul gospel performance, 1981, 83, 84. Office: care Network Talent Internat PO Box 82 98 Cuttermill Rd Suite 343A Great Neck NY 11021 *

GREEN, ALAN, JR., government official; b. Portland, Oreg., May 1, 1925; s. Alan and Helen Ladd (Corbett) G.; m. Joan Irwin, Dec. 2, 1949; children: Carter Green Peterson, Kelsey Green Grout, Helen Ladd Green. B.A., Stanford U., 1949. Chmn. bd. Tom Benson Co., Inc., Portland, Comprehensive Care, Inc., Newport Beach, Calif.; pres. Port of Portland Commn., 1974, 81; chmn. Fed. Maritime Commn., Washington. Mem. exec. bd. Columbia Pacific council Boy Scouts Am. Served with AUS, 1941-45. Mem. Portland Execs. Assn. (pres. 1977). Republican. Episcopalian. Clubs: Arlington (2d v.p. 1974), Waverly Country, Racquet, University (Portland) (pres. 1967); Thunderbird Country (Palm Springs, Calif.); City Tavern, Metropolitan, Chevy Chase Country (Washington). Home: 2719 Poplar St NW Washington DC 20007 Office: 1100 L St NW Washington DC 20573

GREEN, ALEX EDWARD SAMUEL, physicist, university administrator; b. N.Y.C., June 7, 1919; s. Joseph Marvin and Celia (Kahn) G.; m. Freda Kaplow, June 2, 1946; children: Bruce, Deborah, Marcia, Linda, Tamara. B.S. in physics, CCNY, 1940; M.S. in Physics, Calif. Inst. Tech., 1941, Ph.D., U. Cin., 1948. Exptl. physicist Calif. Inst. Tech., Pasadena, 1940-44; assoc. prof. U. Cin., 1946-53; sci. dir. Fla. State U., Tallahassee, 1953-59; mgr. space sci. lab. Gen. Dynamics, San Diego, 1959-63; dir. Interdisciplinary Ctr. for aeronomy and (other) Atmospheric Scis. U. Fla., 1970—; cons. in field. Author: Nuclear Physics, 1955, Atomic and Space Physics, 1965, Nuclear Shell and Optical Moedl, 1968; editor contbg. author: Middle Ultraviolet, 1966. Served with USAF, 1944-45; Asia. Decorated Medal of Freedom; recipient citation for outstanding overseas service War Dept., 1945; named Outstanding Scientist of Fla. Fla. Acad. Scis., 1975. Fellow Am. Phys. Soc., Optical Soc. Am.; mem. Am. Geophys. Union, Phi Beta Kappa, Sigma Xi (pres. Fla. chpt. 1973). Democrat. Office: Interdisciplinary Ctr for Aeronomy and (other) Atmospheric Scis U Fla 311 SSRB Gainesville FL 32611

GREEN, ALVIN, shipping co. exec.; b. Elgin, Ill., Mar. 13, 1931; s. Samuel and Rose (Brustein) G.; m. Miriam E. Blau, June 13, 1954; children—Andrew, Marie, Jennifer. B.A., U. Mich., 1953, M.A., 1954; LL.B., Harvard U., 1957. Bar: N.Y. bar, Ill. bar. Atty. Eastern Air Lines, Inc., N.Y.C., 1957-65; asst. to gen. counsel C.I.T. Corp., N.Y.C., 1965-70, gen. counsel, 1970-72; v.p. Condren, Walker & Co., N.Y.C., 1972-75; v.p., gen. counsel, sec. Seatrain Lines, Inc., N.Y.C., 1975-81, exec. v.p., gen. counsel, 1981—. Woodrow Wilson fellow, 1953-54. Mem. Am. Bar Assn., Assn. Bar City N.Y., Phi Beta Kappa, Phi Kappa Phi. Club: Harvard (N.Y.C.). Home: 22 Arleigh Rd Great Neck NY 11021 Office: 1 Chase Manhattan Plaza New York NY 10005

GREEN, ANDREW WILSON, economist, lawyer, educator; b. Harrisburgh, Pa., May 17, 1923; s. M. Edwin and Gladys (Wilson) G.; m. Betty M. Wilson, Nov. 23, 1977. Student, Princeton U., 1940-43; B.S., NYU, 1944; J.D., Dickinson Law Sch., 1948; M.B.A., U. Pa., 1963, Ph.D., 1968; diploma, U. Amsterdam, 1967. Bar: Pa. 1950. Legal asst. Pa. Utility Commn., 1949-51; sole practice, Harrisburg, 1951-61; asst. atty. gen. State of Pa., 1965-66; research assoc. Inst. Strategic and Internat. Studies, Belguim, 1968-70; mem. faculty West Chester U., Pa., 1970—, prof. bus. adminstrn., 1974—; prof. Del. Law Sch., Wilmington, 1973-76, adj. prof., 1976—; mem. Reagan Transition Team, 1980-81. Author: Political Integration by Jurisprudence, 1969. Served to capt. USAAF, 1943-46. Pennfield fellow, 1966-67. Clubs: Cercle Gaulois, Chateau Ste. Anne (Brussels); Gremio Literario (Lisbon). Home: Etienne Arbordeau Apts Berwyn Baptist Rd Devon PA 19333 Office: Dept Bus Adminstrn West Chester Univ West Chester PA 19383

GREEN, ARTHUR GEORGE, elec. utility exec.; b. Columbus, Ohio, Dec. 14, 1911; s. George Jacob and Clara Pauline (Moeffert) G.; m. Josephine Virginia Courtright, Sept. 24, 1938; children—George Frederick, Sarajo Courtright. B.S. in Bus. Adminstrn, Ohio State U., 1933. With Columbus & So. Ohio Electric Co., 1934-76, pres., 1971-76, chmn. bd., 1973-76, now dir. Former pres. Jr. Achievemnt of Columbus; pres. Central Ohio Council Boy Scouts Am., 1973—; Bd. dirs. Met. YMCA, Columbus, 1972—, Childrens Hosp., 1974—, Center of Sci. and Industry, 1974—. Mem. Nat. Assn. Accountants (past pres. Columbus), Fin. Execs. Inst. (past pres. Columbus), Columbus C. of C. (dir. 1972-76). Presbyterian (elder, treas., past commr.). Clubs: Controllers, Columbus Country, Masons. Home: 1149 Kingslea Rd Columbus OH 43209 *Be factual, honest, trustworthy and helpful to other people.*

GREEN, ARTHUR NELSON, artist, educator; b. Frankfort, Ind., May 13, 1941; emigrated to Can., 1969; m. Natalie Jean Novotny, July 5, 1969; children: Catherine Marie, Nicholas David. B.F.A., Sch. of Art Inst. Chgo., 1965. Lectr. Wright Jr. Coll., Chgo., 1967-68; head dept. art Kendall Coll., Evanston, Ill., 1968-69; asst. prof. N.S. (Can.) Coll. Art, Halifax, 1969-71; lectr. U. B.C., Vancouver, 1975-76; asst. prof. fine arts U. Waterloo, Ont., Can., 1977—; dir., chmn. acquisition com. Gallery Stratford, Ont., 1980—. Artist one-man shows, Phillis Kind Gallery, N.Y.C. and Chgo., 1978, 79, 81, 83, Ban-Xi Gallery, Toronto, 1979, 83. Recipient Cassandra award for painting Cassandra Found., Chgo., 1969; grantee Can. Council Arts, 1971-73, 76-77. Mem. United Ch. of Can. Home: 5 Elizabeth St Stratford ON Canada N5A 4Z1 Office: U Waterloo Waterloo ON Canada N2L 3G1

GREEN, ASA NORMAN, university president; b. Mars Hill, Maine, July 22, 1929; s. Clayton John and Annie Glenna (Shaw) G.; m. Elizabeth Jean Zirkelbach Ross, May 27, 1965; 1 son, Stephen Richard Ross. A.B. cum laude, Bates Coll., Lewiston, Maine, 1951; M.A., U. Ala., 1955; LL.D., Jacksonville (Ala.) U., 1975. Research dir. Ala. League Municipalities, Montgomery, 1955-57; city mgr., Mountain Brook, Ala., 1957-65; exec. sec. Ala. Assn. Ins. Agts., 1965-66; dir. devel. Birmingham-So. Coll., 1966-71; dir. devel. and communications Dickinson Coll., Carlisle, Pa., 1971-72; pres. Livingston (Ala.) U., 1972—; instr. polit. sci. U. Ala. Extension Center, Montgomery and Birmingham, 1955-57, 58-60. Author: Revenue for Alabama Cities, 1956. Served with CIC U.S. Army, 1952-54. Grad. fellow So. Regional Tng. Program in Pub. Adminstrn., 1951. Mem. Newcomen Soc. N. Am., Phi Beta Kappa. Democrat. Methodist. Clubs: Capitol City (Montgomery); Livingston Country. Home: President's House Livingston Univ Livingston AL 35470

GREEN, ASHBEL, editor; b. N.Y.C., Mar. 15, 1928; s. Ashbel and Katherine McKenzie (Murchison) G.; m. Anna Welsh McCagg, June 17, 1960; children—Ashbel Stockton, Alison McKenzie. Grad., Kent (Conn.) Sch., 1945; B.A., Columbia, 1950, M.A. in History, 1952. With U.S. Govt., 1951-53, Music Corp. Am., 1954-56, Monroe B. Scharff & Co., 1957-60; sr. editor Prentice-Hall, Inc., 1960-64; mng. editor Alfred A. Knopf, Inc., N.Y.C., 1964-73, v.p., sr. editor, 1973—. Co-author: Get the Most From Your Money in New York, 1970. Pres. St. Anthony Ednl. Found., 1970-76. Served with USNR, 1946-48. Mem. Delta Psi. Democrat. Presbyn. Club: University (N.Y.C.). Home: 70 E 96th St New York City NY 10028 Office: 201 E 50th St New York City NY 10022

GREEN, BARRY L., petroleum company executive. Exec. v.p. Charter Oil Co. Office: Charter Oil Co 21 Church St Jacksonville FL 32202§

GREEN, BERT FRANKLIN, JR., psychologist; b. Honesdale, Pa., Nov. 5, 1927; s. Bert Franklin and Emily May (Brown) G.; m. Hasseltine Beck Robinson, Apr. 29, 1961 (div. 1974); children—Malcolm Edward. A.B., Yale, 1949; M.A., Princeton, 1950, Ph.D., 1951. Mem. psychology group Lincoln Lab., Mass. Inst. Tech., 1951-62, leader, 1958-62; cons. RAND Corp., 1961; prof. psychology Carnegie Inst. Tech., Pitts., 1962-69, head psychology dept., 1962-67; prof. psychology Johns Hopkins, Balt., 1969—. Author: Digital Computers in Research, 1963. Mem. Am. Psychol. Assn., Am. Statis. Assn., Psychometric Soc., Psychonomic Soc., AAAS. Home: 311 Eastway Ct Baltimore MD 21212

GREEN, BILL, Congressman; b. N.Y.C., Oct. 16, 1929; m. Patricia Freiberg; children: Catherine, Louis. A.B. magna cum laude, Harvard U., 1950, J.D., 1953. Bar: D.C. 1953, N.Y. 1954. Law sec. to presiding judge U.S. Ct. Appeals for D.C. Cir., 1955-56; practice law, N.Y.C., 1956-70; counsel N.Y. State Joint Legis. Com. on Housing and Urban Devel., 1961-64; mem. N.Y. State Assembly, 1965-68; regional adminstr. HUD, 1970-77; mem. 96th-98th congresses from 15th N.Y. Dist., 1978—; ranking Republican on HUD and Ind. agys. subcom.; mem. Appropriations Com., Congl. Arts Caucus, Arms Control and Fgn. Policy Caucus, Mil. Reform Caucus, House Wednesday Group. Founding trustee Jewish Assn. for Services to Aged; trustee Montefiore Med. Ctr.; bd. overseers Albert Einstein Coll. Medicine; sec. F.D. Roosevelt Meml. Commn.; mem. U.S. Holocaust Meml. Council; bd. overseers Grad. Sch. Mgmt. and Urban Professions-New Sch. for Social Research; mem. adv. com. NYU Sch. Pub. Adminstrn.; alt. trustee Fedn. Jewish Philanthropies N.Y. Served as lt. J.A.G. U.S. Army, 1953-55. Office: 1110 Longworth House Office Bldg Washington DC 20515 Office: 5th Floor Grand Central PO Bldg 110 E 45th St New York NY 10017

GREEN, CECIL HOWARD, consulting geophysicist, educator; b. Manchester, Eng., Aug. 6, 1900; s. Charles Henry and Maggie (Howard) G.; m. Ida M. Flansburgh, Feb. 6, 1926. Student, U. B.C.; S.B. in Elec. Engring, MIT, 1923, S.M., 1924; D.Eng., Colo. Sch. Mines, 1953; D.Sc., U. Tulsa, 1961, U. Sydney, Australia, 1961, U. B.C., 1964, So. Meth. U., 1967, U. Mass., 1974, Tex. Christian U., 1974; LL.D., Austin Coll., 1966; D.Civil Jurisprudence, U. Dallas, 1976; D. Comml. Sci. (hon.), Suffolk U., 1978. Research engr. A.C. engring. dept. Gen. Electric Co., Schenectady, 1924-26; research engring. Raytheon Mfg. Co., Cambridge, Mass., 1926-28, Fed. Telegraph Co., Palo Alto, Cal., also Newark, 1928-30; party chief Geophys. Service, Inc., Dallas, 1930-36, supr., 1936-41, v.p., 1941-50, pres., 1950-56, chmn. bd., 1956-59, hon. chmn., 1959—; founder dir. Tex. Instruments, Inc.; Hon. lectr. earth and planetary scis. MIT, 1973—; cons. prof. earth scis. Stanford U. Trustee Scripps Clinic and Research Found., Woods Hole Oceanographic Inst., S.W. Med. Found.; trustee So. Meth. U. Found. for Sci. and Engring., pres., 1964-66; trustee, past pres. St. Mark's Sch. Tex.; trustee Tex. Christian U.; trustee, mem. exec. com. Austin Coll.; membership com., life mem. corp., mem. vis. com. dept. physics, vis. com. earth and planetary scis. Mass. Inst. Tech.; mem. com. earth scis. Stanford; chmn. Excellence in Edn. Found. Recipient Santa Rita award U. Tex. System; with Ida Green Linz award City of Dallas, 1974; with Ida Green Internat. Ednl. and Research Tribute Nat. Acad. Scis., 1978; with Ida Green Pub. Welfare medal Nat. Acad. Scis., 1979; award for excellence in humanities North Dallas C. of C., 1978; citation So. Meth. U. Inst. for Study Earth and Man, 1979. Fellow Am. Acad. Arts and Scis.; mem. MIT Alumni Assn. (pres. 1968-69), Soc. Exploration Geophysicists (past pres., hon. life mem., Kaufman medal 1966, Maurice Ewing medal 1978), Am. Assn. Petroleum Geologists (Human Needs medal 1974), European Assn. Exploration Geophysicists, Mexican Assn. Petroleum Geologists, Tex. Assn. Grad. Edn. and Research (hon. chmn.), Dallas Geol. Soc. (hon. life), Dallas Geophys. Soc. (hon. life), IEEE (hon.), AIA (hon.), Explorers Club. Clubs: Dallas Country, Dallas Petroleum. Home and Office: 3525 Turtle Creek Blvd. Dallas TX 75219

GREEN, CHARLES WALTER, newspaper editor; b. Longmont, Colo., Jan. 11, 1947; s. Walter C. and Esther M. (Hansen) G. B.A., U. Colo., 1969. Reporter Denver Post, Inc., 1968-72, city editor, 1972-74, exec. city editor, 1974-80, asst. mng. editor, 1980-83, editorial page editor, 1983—; instr. U. Colo., 1977-79. Named Colo. Journalist of Yr. Sigma Delta Chi, 1978, Outstanding Alumnus U. Colo., 1982. Mem. Colo. Press Assn. (dir.), Am. Soc. Newspaper Editors, Nat. Conf. Editorial Writers, Denver Press Club (pres. 1978-79). Club: Oxford. Office: PO Box 1709 Denver CO 80201

GREEN, CLIFFORD SCOTT, judge; b. Phila., Apr. 2, 1923; s. Robert Lewis and Alice (Robinson) G.; m. Mabel Wood, June 20, 1959; children—Terri Alice, David Scott. B.S., Temple U., 1948, J.D., 1951. Bar: Pa. bar 1952. Practiced law, Phila., 1952-64; dep. atty. gen. State of Pa., 1954; judge County Ct., Phila., 1964-68, Ct. Common Pleas, 1968-71, U.S. Dist. Ct. for Eastern Dist. Pa., Phila., 1972—; lectr. in law Temple U. Bd. dirs. Children's Aid Soc. of Pa., Crime Prevention Assn. Phila.; mem. bd. mgrs. Children's Hosp., Phila. Served with USAAF, 1943-46. Recipient awards for community service Women's Christian Alliance, Health and Welfare Council, Opportunities Industrialization Center. Mem. Sigma Pi Phi. Presbyterian. Home: 2311 N 50th St Philadelphia PA 19131 Office: US Courthouse 6th Market Sts Philadelphia PA 19106

GREEN, DALE MONTE, judge; b. Outlook, Wash., Apr. 27, 1922; s. Carey W. and Minnie M. (Gunness) G.; m. Maxine Spencer, June 30, 1946; children—Judith Louise, Frederick William. B.A. in Econs. and Bus, U. Wash., 1948, B.S. in Law, 1949, J.D., 1950. Bar: Wash. bar 1950. Practiced in, Spokane, 1954; asst. U.S. dist. atty. Eastern Dist. Wash., 1954-56; trial atty. civil div. Dept. Justice, Washington, 1956-58; U.S. dist. atty. Eastern Dist. Wash., 1958-60; mem. firm Sherwood, Tugman & Green, Walla Walla, Wash., 1960-69; judge Wash. Ct. Appeals Div. III, Spokane, 1969—, chief judge, 1972-74, 78-80; Mem. Wash. Pattern Jury Instrn. Com., 1971—, State Adv. Bd. Jud. Edn., 1974-77, Wash. State Jud. Council, 1972-75. Editorial bd.: Wash. Law Rev, 1949-50. Served with AUS, 1943-46. Mem. Am., Fed., Wash. bar assns., Nat. Legal Aid and Defender Assn., Nat. Council on Crime and Delinquency, Am. Judicature Soc. Methodist. Clubs: Rotarian, Mason. Home: S 3914 Cook Spokane WA 99203 Office: Court of Appeals 500 N Cedar St Spokane WA 99201

GREEN, DALLAS *See* **GREEN, GEORGE DALLAS**

GREEN, DAN, publisher; b. Passaic, N.J., Sept. 28, 1935; s. Harold and Bessie (Roslow) G.; m. Jane Oliphant, Sept. 20, 1959; children—Matthew Kenan, Simon Pom. B.A., Syracuse (N.Y.) U., 1956. Publicity dir. Dover Press, 1957-58; sta. WNAC-TV, 1958-59, Bobbs-Merrill Co., 1959-62; with Simon & Schuster Inc., 1962—, asso. publisher, 1976-80, v.p., pub., 1980—; founder, pub. Kenan Press, 1979-80. Office: 1230 Ave Americas New York NY 10020

GREEN, DANIEL G., ophthalmology, electrical engineering and psychology educator, researcher; b. N.Y.C., Sept. 3, 1937; s. Gilbert and Lillian (Gannes) G.; m. Norma Alyne Anderson, Jan. 26, 1957; children: Peter, Rebecca. B.S.E.E., U. Ill., 1959; M.S., Northwestern U., 1961, Ph.D., 1964. Asst. prof. ophthalmology U. Mich, Ann Arbor, 1966-71; asst. prof. elec. engring. U. Mich., Ann Arbor, 1969-71, assoc. prof. psychology, 1971-76, assoc. prof. ophthalmology and elec. engring., 1971-76, prof. ophthalmology, elec. engring. and psychology, 1976—; vis. prof., scientist U. Calif.-San Francisco, 1980-81, Cambridge U., (Eng.), 1980-81; cons. neurobiology sect. NSF, 1968—; editorial cons. Sci. Jour. Optical Soc. Am., 1966—, Vision Research, 1966—. Magnavox scholar U. Ill., 1958-59; recipient Gold Scholarship Key, 1959; Cabell fellow Northwestern U., 1963-64. Fellow Optical Soc. Am. (past chmn. com. vision and phys., optics); mem. Assn. Research in Vision and Ophthalmology (past chmn. electrophysiology sect.), Optical Soc. Am., Soc. Neurosci., Am. Physiol. Soc., AAAS, AAUP, IEEE, Sigma Xi. Home: 516 Sunset Rd Ann Arbor MI 48103 Office: U Mich 3002 Neurosci Bldg 1103 E Huron St Ann Arbor MI 48109

GREEN, DAVID, insurance company executive; b. N.Y.C., Mar. 31, 1899; s. Joseph and Sarah (Rosenstein) G.; m. Jeannette Katchen, Mar. 25, 1926; children: Joan (Mrs. Michael Miron) (dec.), Alice (Mrs. Robert Fried). Naval Engr., Lehigh U., 1922; J.D., Rutgers U., 1926. Bar: N.J. bar 1926. Engr. Fed. Shipbldg. Co., 1923; practiced in, Newark, 1926-46; incorporator Motor Club of Am. Ins. Co., Newark, 1928, dir., 1928—, pres., 1954—; pres., dir. Motor Club Am. Trustee N.J. State Safety Council. Served with U.S. Army, 1918; from lt. to lt. comdr. USNR, 1942-45. Recipient Service award Def. Research Inst., 1968; Lehigh U. Alumni Assn. award, 1972; Man of Year award Ins. Brokers Assn. N.J., 1975. Mem. Fedn. Ins. Counsel (pres. 1964-65, chmn. bd. 1965-66, Man of Year award 1974), ABA (publs. vice chmn., asso. editor Forum 1966-67), N.J. Bar Assn., Essex County Bar Assn., Nat. Assn. Ind. Insurers (gov. 1953—, past chmn.), Nat. Conf. Lawyers (past chmn.), N.J. Joint Underwriting Assn. (dir.), N.J. Property Liability Ins. Guaranty Assn., N.J. Ins. Underwriting Assn. (past chmn. bd.), Pi Lambda Phi. Republican. Jewish. Clubs: Masons, Kiwanis (past pres.). Home: 320 S Harrison St Apt 4-H East Orange NJ 07018 Office: 484 Central Ave Newark NJ 07107

GREEN, DAVID EZRA, educator; b. N.Y.C., Aug. 5, 1910; s. Herman and Jennie (Marrow) G.; m. Doris Cribb, Apr. 15, 1935; children—Rowena (Mrs. Larry Matthews), Pamela (Mrs. Joseph Baldwin, Jr.). B.A., N.Y. U., 1930, M.A., 1932; Ph.D., Cambridge (Eng.) U., 1934. Beit Meml. Research fellow Cambridge, Eng., 1934-40; fellow Harvard, 1940-41; with enzyme lab. Coll. Phys. and Surg., Columbia, 1941-48; asso. prof. biochemistry Columbia, 1947; co-dir. Inst. Enzyme Research, U. Wis., 1948—, prof. enzyme chemistry, 1948—. Author: Mechanisms of Biological Oxidations, 1939, Molecular

Insights into the Living Process, 1967. Recipient Paul-Lewis Labs. award enzyme chemistry, 1946. Fellow Am. Acad. Arts and Scis.; fgn. fellow Royal Flemish Acad. Arts and Scis.; mem. Am. Soc. Biol. Chemists, Nat. Acad. Scis., Am. Chem. Soc., Harvey Soc., Biochem. Soc., Am. Soc. Cell Biology, Phi Beta Kappa, Sigma Xi. Home: 5339 Brody Dr Madison WI 53705

GREEN, DAVID HENRY, manufacturing company executive; b. Worcester, Mass., Feb. 8, 1921; s. Herbert H. and Florence (Knapp) G.; m. Betty Jeppson, June 23, 1951; children: Anne L., Susan E., David Henry, Charles J., Sarah C. B.A., Wesleyan U., Middletown, Conn., 1942; M.B.A., Harvard, 1943. Asst. treas. Valley Bank & Trust Co., Springfield, Mass., 1946-51; sr. v.p. Worcester County Nat. bank, 1952-65, New Eng. Mchts. Nat. Bank, Boston, 1965-73; chmn. L.G. Balfour Co., Attleboro, Mass., 1973—; dir. Mass. Higher Edn. Assistance Corp., L.G. Balfour Co. Trustee New Eng. Aquarium, Worcester Found. Exptl. Biology; hon. trustee Concord Acad.; bd. dirs. Bristol County Devel. Council, Attleboro Scholarship Found.; bd. assos. Wheaton Coll. Served as capt. AUS, 1943-46. Home: 675 Sudbury Rd Concord MA 01742 Office: 25 County St Attleboro MA 02703

GREEN, DAVID MARVIN, psychologist, educator; b. Jackson, Mich., June 7, 1932; s. George Elmer and Carrie Ruth (Crawford) G.; m. Clara Loftstrom, Jan. 2, 1953 (dec. July 1978); children: Allan, Phillip, Katherine, George; m. Marian Heinzmann, June 7, 1980. B.A., U. Chgo., 1952, U. Mich., 1954, M.A., 1955, Ph.D., 1958; NSF predoctoral fellow, M.I.T., 1956-57. Grad. research asso. Electronic Def. Group, U. Mich., 1954-56, 57-58; asst. prof. psychology M.I.T., 1958-63; cons. Bolt, Beranek & Newman, Inc., Cambridge, Mass., 1958—; asso. prof. psychology U. Pa., 1963-66, vice chmn. dept. psychology, 1964-66; prof. psychology U. Calif., San Diego, 1966-73; prof. psychophysics Harvard U., Cambridge, 1973—, chmn. dept. psychology and social relations, 1978-81; mem. exec. com. NRC Com. on Hearing, Bioacoustics and Biomechanics, 1968-71, chmn., 1970-71; mem. communicative scis. study sect. NIH, 1970-73; mem. sci. adv. group on noise Calif. Environ. Quality Study Council, 1970-72; chmn. CHABA Subcom. 9 Adoption of Composite Noise Scale, 1972—; mem. NRC Assembly of Behavioral and Social Scis., 1973—. Author: (with J.A. Swets) Signal Detection Theory and Psychophysics, 1966, Introduction to Hearing, 1976; Cons. editor: Psychol. Bull, 1965-68, Perception and Psychophysics, 1972—; mem. editorial bd.: Cognitive Psychology, 1970-73. Guggenheim fellow, 1973-74; overseas fellow St. Johns Coll., Cambridge, Eng., 1973-74. Fellow Am. Psychol. Assn., Acoustical Soc. Am. (Biennial award 1966, chmn. com. psychol. and physiol. acoustics 1970-73, exec. council 1972-75, pres. 1981-82), AAAS; mem. Soc. Exptl. Psychologists, Psychonomic Soc., Psychometric Soc., AAUP, Nat. Acad. Scis. Home: 9 Lakeview Terr Winchester MA 01890 Office: 33 Kirkland St Cambridge MA 02138

GREEN, DAVID O., educational administrator; b. Chgo., Feb. 14, 1923; s. David and Gertrude (Strauss) G.; m. Nova Muir, Sept. 12, 1948 (div. 1971); children: Katherine, Nova. B.S., DePaul, U., 1947; M.B.A., U. Chgo., 1948, Ph.D., 1956. C.P.A., Ill., 1951. Mem. faculty U. Chgo., 1949-81, prof. acctg., 1963-81, dir., 1974-78; v.p. adminstrn. Bernard Baruch Coll., City U. N.Y., 1979—; vis. prof. acctg. Fla. State U., 1963-64, 70, Middle East Tech U., 1967-68, U. Birmingham, 1968, London Grad. Sch. Bus. Studies, 1971-72, U. Canterbury, N.Z., 1973, Fla. Internat. U., 1977-78; fiscal and accounting cons. City of Chgo., 1957-63. Editor: Jour. Accounting Research, 1963-67; mem. editorial bd., 1968-82. Served with AUS, 1943-45. Home: 30 Waterside Plaza New York NY 10010 Office: 17 Lexington Ave New York NY 10010

GREEN, DONALD EARL, manufacturing company executive; b. Drumright, Okla., Oct. 16, 1934; m. Dorothy M. Reis, Sept., 1954 (div. 1975); children: Michele, Rebecca, Lawrence, Patrick, Kevin; m. Linda Lou Caton, Sept. 10, 1977. B.B.A., U. Tex.-Austin, 1958. Indsl. engr. Montgomery Wards, Ft. Worth, 1958-60; mfg. mgr. Texstar Plastics, Ft. Worth, 1960-63; master scheduler Bell Helicopter, Hurst, Tex., 1963-64; mfg. mgr. Frigiking, Dallas, 1964-67; exec. v.p. ARA Mfg., Grand Prairie, Tex., 1967. Republican. Episcopalian. Home: 705 Portofino Arlington TX 76012 Office: ARA Mfg Co 606 Fountain Pkwy Grand Prairie TX 75050

GREEN, EDITH, former congresswoman; b. Trent, S.D., Jan. 17, 1910; d. James Vaughn and Julia (Hunt) Starrett; children: James S., Richard A. Student, Willamette U., 1927-29; B.S., U. Oreg., 1939; postgrad., Stanford U., 1944; 33 hon. degrees including, Linfield Coll., Boston Coll., Reed Coll., Oberlin Coll., Georgetown U., Yale U., Williamette U., U. Portland, Tex. Christian U. Tchr. sch., Salem, Oreg., 1930-41; comml. radio work KALE, Portland, 1944-45, free lance, 1943-47; dir. pub. relations Oreg. Edn. Assn.; mem. of 84th-93d congresses from 3d Oreg. Dist., mem. appropriations com., edn. and labor com.; Congl. del. NATO Conf., London, 1959, WHO, 1973, World Population Conf., 1974; mem. U.S. Commn. UNESCO., Pres.' Commn. on Status of Women. Del. Democratic Nat. Conv., 1956, 60, 64, 68, 72, chmn. state delegation, 1960-68. Recipient Brotherhood award B'nai B'rith, 1956; Women of Year award Amvets, 1958; Community service award Nat. Assn. Colored Womens Clubs, 1962; Edn. Service award Am. Coll. Pub. Relations Assn., 1964; Top Hat award Bus. and Profl. Women's Clubs Am., 1965; President's award Nat. Rehab. Assn., 1967; Disting. Service award U. Oreg., 1967, Oreg. State U., 1972; AAUW Woman of Achievement award, 1974; 1st Citizen award Portland, 1978; others. Office: 8031 Sacajawea Way Wilsonville OR 97070

GREEN, EDWARD FAIRCHILD, lawyer; b. Cleve., Oct. 10, 1918; s. Otis and Harriet Louvan (Hoyle) G.; m. Martha Jane Smith, June 12, 1944. A.B., Swarthmore Coll., 1940; LL.B., Western Res. U., 1948. Bar: Ohio 1948. Claim examiner Conn. Gen. Life Ins. Co., 1940-41; practice law, Cleve., 1948-61; with White Motor Corp., Cleve. and Eastlake, Ohio and Farmington Hills, Mich., 1961—, asst. sec., 1966-75, asst. gen. counsel, 1970-75, v.p., gen. counsel, 1975—, also dir. subs. Served with USNR, 1942-44. Mem. Am., Ohio bar assns., Bar Assn. Greater Cleve., Am. Soc. Corp. Secs., Order of Coif. Republican. Baptist. Clubs: Eastern Cleve., Rotary. Home: 1134 S Belvoir Rd South Euclid OH 44121 Office: 837 E 79th St PO Box 5757 Cleveland OH 44101

GREEN, ERNEST, business executive; b. Columbus, Ga., Oct. 15, 1938; s. Albert and Susie (Marshall) G.; m. Wylene Jackson, June 14, 1956; children: Zachary, Derek, Ernest II. B.S., U. Louisville, 1962. Football player Cleve. Browns, 1962-68; pres. Ernie Green Inc.; dir. Church's Fried Chicken.; mem. East All Star Football Squad, 1966-67. Trustee Vocational Guidance and Rehab. Service, Cleve. Scholarship Program, Big Bros. Cleve.; vis. com. Sch. Dentistry, Case Western Res. U., also vis. com. phys. edn. and athletics; active Gov. Nelson Rockefeller's presdl. campaign. Named One of 10 Outstanding Young Men in Cleve. Cleve. Jr. C. of C., 1970. Home: 23450 Shaker Blvd Shaker Heights OH 44122 Office: 7016 Corporate Way Suite 208 Dayton OH 45459

GREEN, GARETH MONTRAVILLE, physician; b. Boston, Apr. 16, 1931; s. Robert Montraville and Dorothy Bradford (Summers) G.; m. Joan Allison Erskine, Sept. 5, 1953; children: Jennifer Joy, Geoffrey Ware, Alan Bradford. A.B. cum laude, Harvard, 1953, M.D., 1957. Intern U. Wash., Seattle, 1957-58, resident, 1958-60; research and tng. fellow Harvard, Channing and Thorndike Labs. Boston City Hosp., Med. Research Council U.K., 1960-64; instr. bacteriology and immunology, asso. medicine Harvard, 1964-68; asso. prof. Coll. Medicine, U. Vt., 1968-70, prof., 1970-76; practice medicine specializing in thoracic medicine, Burlington, 1968-76; asso. attending physician Med. Center Hosp. Vt., Burlington, 1970-72, attending physician, 1972-76; dir. Vt. Lung Center, 1974-76; prof., chmn. dept. environ. health scis. Johns Hopkins Sch. Hygiene and Pub. Health, 1976—; dir. respiratory medicine Johns Hopkins Sch. Medicine, 1983—; Mem. Nat. Adv. Health Service Council, 1970-74; mem. Nat. Heart, Lung and Blood Adv. Council, 1975-79, Nat. Environ. Health Sci. Adv. Council, 1981-84; chmn. EPA Health Effects Research Rev. Com., 1979-82; ad hoc cons. NIH, Nat. Acad. Scis. Adv. Panel Manned Space Flight, 1969-74; vice chmn. Md. Council Toxic Substances, 1978-82. Editor: Am. Rev. Respiratory Diseases, 1979-84. Trustee Vt. Lung Assn., 1969-76; bd. dirs. Am. Lung Assn., 1973-76; mem. research rev. com. Health Effects Inst., 1982—. NIH grantee. Mem. Am. Thoracic Soc. (J. Burns Amberson lectr. 1970, pres. 1974-75), Am. Soc. Clin. Investigation, Am. Fedn. Clin. Research, Infectious Diseases Soc. Am., Mass. Med. Soc., Boylston Med. Soc., Lodge of St. Andrew. Research concepts of lung defense mechanisms against environ. agts. Home: 2943 N Charles St Baltimore MD 21218 Office: 1102 Johns Hopkins Sch Hygiene and Pub Health 615 N Wolfe St Baltimore MD 21205 *Consider life as a long term investment; create and respond to opportunity; pursue quality and excellence in yourself and others.*

GREEN, GARY LEE, hockey coach; b. Tillsonburg, Ont., Can., Aug. 23, 1953; s. Harry James and Margaret G.; married; children: Jennifer Lee, Melissa Ann. B.A. in Psychology, U. Guelph, (Ont.), 1974. Coach Washington Capitals of Nat. Hockey League, Landover Md., 1979—. Named Coach of the Year, 1978-79. Office: Can Am PO Box 634 Guelph ON Canada*Because of my age, I cannot come to Washington to coach this team expecting the respect of my players; I'm going to have to earn it day by day.*

GREEN, GEORGE DALLAS (DALLAS GREEN), manager professional baseball team; b. Newport, Del., Aug. 4, 1934; s. George Dallas and Mayannah Sealy (Jones) G.; m. Sylvia Lowe Taylor, Jan. 31, 1958; children: Dana, John, Kim, Douglas. Student, U. Del., 1952-55, B.B.A., 1981. Asst. dir., then dir. minor leagues and scouting Phila. Phillies Profl. Baseball Team, 1969-79, mgr. parent team, 1979-82; exec. v.p., gen. mgr. Chgo. Cubs, 1982—. Trustee Del Found. Retarded Children. Office: Chgo Cubs Wrigley Field Chicago IL 60613 *

GREEN, GEORGE J., publishing company executive; b. N.Y.C., May 6, 1938; s. Monroe and Ruth (Gast) G. B.A., Yale U., 1960. Trainee advt. dept. Burlington Industries, N.Y.C., 1961-62; with The New Yorker Mag., 1962-84, N.Y.C. retail advt. salesman, 1962-64, Atlanta advt. sales in so. states, 1964-66, N.Y.C. advt. major accounts, 1966-67, asst. treas., 1967-71, circulation dir., v.p., dir., 1971-75, pres., 1975-84; exec. v.p., group publishing dir. Hearst mags., 1984—. Served with U.S. Army Res., 1960-65. Mem. Mag. Pubs. Assn. (chmn., dir.). Office: Hearst Mags 959 8th Ave New York NY 10019

GREEN, GERALD, author; b. Bklyn., 1922; (m); 3 children. Grad., Columbia, Columbia Sch. Journalism. Formerly with Internat. News Service; with NBC, intermittently 1950—. Producer: Today show with Dave Garroway; also: Chet Huntley Reporting; producer, writer various TV documentaries.; Author: Sword and the Sun, 1954, The Last Angry Man, 1957, The Lotus Eaters, 1959, The Heartless Light, 1961, The Portofino PTA, 1962, The Legion of Noble Christians, 1965, (with Lawrence Klingman) His Majesty O'Keefe, 1948, To Brooklyn With Love, 1968, The Artist of Terezin, 1968, Faking It, 1971, The Stones of Zion, 1971, Blockbuster, 1972, Tourist, 1973, My Son the Jock, 1975, An American Prophet, 1977, Girl, 1977, Holocaust (Emmy award for best screenplay, NCCJ Media award 1979), 1978 (Prix Internat. Dag Hammarskjold award 1979), The Healers, 1979, Cactus Pie, 1979, The Hostage Heart, 1976, The Chains, 1980, Murfy's Men, 1981. Mem. Writers Guild Am., Authors League, PEN Club, Phi Beta Kappa. Address: care Scott Meredith 845 3d Ave New York NY 10022

GREEN, GUY, film director; b. Somerset, Eng. Dir. photography: Great Expectations (Acad. award), Oliver Twist, Captain Horatio Hornblower, I Am a Camera; dir. films including: Sea of Sand, The Angry Silence, The Mark, Light in the Piazza; dir. filming including: Diamond Head; writer, dir.: films including A Patch of Blue, 1965; dir.: The Magus, 1967, A Walk in the Spring Rain, John Brown's Body, 1968-69, Luther, Once Is Not Enough, 1974, The Devil's Advocate, 1976, Luther for, Am. Film Theatre, 1972, The Outlander, 1978; several TV movies. Address: care Henry J Bamberger 2049 Century Park E Suite 1980 Los Angeles CA 90067

GREEN, HAROLD FRANCIS, oil company executive; b. Utica, N.Y., Jan. 4, 1916; s. Frank Percy and Mary (Coakley) G.; m. Corena Grace Crase, Dec. 16, 1950; children: Elizabeth (Mrs. D. Marr Duncan), James, Richard. B.A. maxima cum laude, U. Santa Clara, 1937, J.D. cum laude, 1940. Bar: Calif. bar 1941. Atty. Standard Oil Co., Calif., 1945-54; sr. v.p., dir. Res. Oil and Gas Co., Los Angeles, 1954-80; v.p., gen. counsel Hilliard Oil & Gas, Inc., Menlo Park, Calif., 1981-83, pres., chief exec. officer, New Orleans, 1983—. Served with USNR, 1941-45; PTO. Decorated Bronze Star. Mem. Calif. State Bar, Am. Bar Assn., Ind. Petroleum Assn. Am. (past dir.), Calif. Ind. Petroleum Assn. (dir.). Clubs: Univ. (Palo Alto); Los Altos Golf and Country. Home: 10410 Albertsworth Ln Los Altos Hills CA 94022 Office: 1440 Canal St New Orleans LA 70112

GREEN, HARRY, newspaper publisher; b. Phoenix, Jan. 14, 1906; s. Samuel Steele and Alice (Kay) G.; m. Mercedes Reussenzehn, Jan. 6, 1934; 1 dau., Floradel. A.B. in Econs, U. Redlands, 1922-26. Editor trade papers Western Canner and Packer and West Coast Builder, 1926-32; bus. mgr. Ventura County Star-Free Press, 1934-45; gen. bus. mgr. John P. Scripps (newspapers), 1945-73, v.p., dir., 1973—; pres. Watsonville Newspapers, Inc., Tulare Newspapers, Inc. Chmn. Draft Bd. SSS. 145., 1940-45. Mem. Audit Bur. Circulation (bd. dirs. 1965-73), Calif. Newspaper Pubs. Assn. (pres. 1963), Calif. Newspaperboy Found., Inc. (pres. 1949-50), Ventura C. of C. (pres. 1939). Club: Kiwanis (Ventura) (pres. 1939). Home: 9801 Sierra Vista Ave La Mesa CA 92041 Office: 306 Scripps Bldg 525 C St San Diego CA 92101

GREEN, HARRY EDWARD, lawyer; b. Coshocton, Ohio, Sept. 19, 1911; s. William and Jenny (Mobley) B.; m. Molly Morse Leachman, June 1, 1946; children: William Strother, Sara McLaurin, Nancy M. B.S. summa cum laude, Princeton, 1933; LL.B. cum laude, Harvard, 1936. Bar: Ohio bar 1936, N.Y. bar 1947, Ill. bar 1958. Asso. firm Squire, Sanders & Dempsey, Cleve., 1936-42, Armstrong & Keith, N.Y.C., 1946-47; gen. counsel, dir. W.I. Sugar Corp., 1947-52, v.p., sec., gen. counsel, dir., 1952-58; practiced in N.Y.C., 1946-58; dir., gen. counsel Melchior, Armstrong, Dessau Co., Ridgefield, N.J., 1948-59; gen. counsel Container Corp. Am., Chgo., 1958-59, v.p., gen. counsel, 1960-63, sr. v.p., 1963-76. Chmn. bd. dirs. Nat. Found., 1972—; bd. dirs., pres. Windham Children's Service, 1955-58. Served from 2d lt. to lt. col. USAAF, 1942-46; now col. Res. Decorated Legion of Merit. Mem. Am., Ill. bar assns., Bar Assn. City N.Y., Am. Arbitration Assn. (dir., chmn. Chgo. adv. council). Clubs: Mid-Day (Chgo.); Indian Hill (Winnetka, Ill.). Home: 181 Birch St Winnetka IL 60093 Office: 205 W Wacker Dr Suite 1100 Chicago IL 60606

GREEN, HILTON A., motion picture producer; b. Hollywood, Calif., Mar. 3, 1929; s. Alfred E. and Vivian (Reed) G.; m. Helen Harker, June 6, 1952; children: Wendolyn, Bradley, Pamela. B.S., U. So. Calif., 1952. Asst. dir. Revue Prdns., Hollywood, Calif., 1955-60; unit prodn. mgr. Universal City Studios, (Calif.), 1960-68, pridn. mgr., 1968-78; exec. prodn. mgr. Universal city Studios, (Calif.), 1978-82; producer Universal City Studios, (Calif.), 1982—. Producer: motion picture Psycho II, 1982, 16 Candles, 1983. Served with U.S. Army, 1952-54. Republican. Roman Catholic. Home: 3625 Locksley Dr Pasadena CA 91107 Office: Universal City Studios Universal City CA 91608

GREEN, HOWARD, cellular physiologist, educator, administrator; b. Toronto, Ont., Can., 1925. M.D., U. Toronto, 1947; M.S. in Physiology, Northwestern U., 1950. Research asst. dept. physiology Northwestern U., Evanston, Ill., 1948-50; research assoc., instr. biochemistry U. Chgo., 1951-53; instr. pharmacology NYU Sch. Medicine, 1954-55, asst. prof. chem. pathology, 1956-59, assoc. prof. pathology, 1959-65, prof., 1965-68, prof., chmn. cell biology dept., 1968-70; prof. cell biology MIT, Cambridge, 1970-80; Higgins prof. cellular physiology, chmn. dept. physiology and biophysics Harvard U. Med. Sch., Boston, 1980—; lectr. in field. Served to capt. M.C. USAR, 1955-56. Recipient Mr. And Mrs. J. N. Taub Internat. Meml. award, 1977, Selman A. Waksman award, 1978, Lewis S. Rosenstiel award, 1980, Lila Gruber Research award Am. Acad. Dermatology, 1980. Mem. Am. Acad. Arts and Scis., Nat. Acad. Scis. Home: 82 Williston Rd Brookline MA 02146 Office: Dept Physiology and Biophysics Harvard Med Sch 25 Shattuck St Boston MA 02115

GREEN, JACK PETER, med. scientist; b. N.Y.C., Oct. 4, 1925; s. Maurice and Tillie (Herman) G.; m. Arlyne Genevieve Frank, Oct. 25, 1958. B.S., Pa. State U., 1947, M.S., 1949; Ph.D., Yale, 1951, M.D., 1957; postgrad., Poly. Inst., Copenhagen, 1953-55, Inst. de Biologie Physico-Chimique, Paris, 1964-65. Vis. scientist Poly. Inst., Copenhagen, 1953-55, Inst. de Biologie Physico-Chimique, Paris, 1964-65; asst. prof. Yale, 1957-61, asso. prof., 1961-66, Cornell U. Med. Coll., 1966-68; prof., chmn. dept. pharmacology Mt. Sinai Sch. Medicine, 1968—; Mem. research grant rev. com. USPHS; mem. N.Y.C. Health Research Council, Dysautonomia Found., Irma T. Hirsch Trust. Contbr. articles profl. jours.; Mem. editorial bds. profl. jours. Recipient Claude Bernard Vis. Professorship U. Montreal, 1966. Mem. N.Y. Acad. Sci., Am. Chem. Soc., Am. Soc. Biol. Chemists, Soc. Drug Research, N.Y. Acad. Medicine, Harvey Soc., A.A.A.S., Am. Soc. Pharmacology and Exptl. Therapeutics, Internat. Soc. Quantum Biology, Am. Coll. Neuropsychopharmacology, Am. Soc. Neurochemistry, Soc. for Neurosci., Sigma Xi, Alpha Omega Alpha, Phi Lambda Upsilon, Gamma Sigma Delta. Home: 1212 Fifth Ave New York City NY 10029 Office: Mt Sinai Sch Medicine Dept Pharmacology Fifth Ave at 100th St New York City NY 10029

GREEN, JAMES COLLINS, state official; b. Halifax County, Va., Feb. 24, 1921; s. John Collins and Frances Sue (Oliver) G.; m. Alice McAulay Clark, 1943; children: Sarah Frances, Susan Clark, James Collins. Student, Washington and Lee U. Mem. Bladen County (N.C.) Bd. Edn., 1955-61; mem. N.C. Ho. of Reps., 1961-65, 69-73, speaker, 1975-76; mem. N.C. State Senate, 1967; lt. gov. N.C., 1977—; farmer, tobacco warehouse operator. Served with USMC, 1944-46. Presbyterian. Clubs: Masons (32 deg.), Shriners.). Office: Office of Lt Gov State Legis Office Bldg Raleigh NC 27611 *

GREEN, JAMES WESTON, educator, physiologist; b. Elkins, W.Va., May 16, 1913; s. James Weston and Adah (Harshbarger) G.; m. Erika Roth, July 8, 1961; children—James Philip, Stephen Henry. B.S., Davis-Elkins Coll., 1935; postgrad., U. Pa., 1940-41; Ph.D., Princeton, 1948. Faculty Rutgers U., New Brunswick, 1948—, prof. physiology, 1961—, chmn. dept. physiology and biochemistry, 1962-67, chmn. dept. physiology, 1967-73, dir. grad. physiology program, 1968-74, acting dean grad. sch., 1974-75, emeritus, 1980. Editor: New Developments in Tissue Culture, 1961. Bd. dirs. Wesley Found., Rutgers U. Served to capt. AUS, 1942-46. Ford Found. fellow, 1953-54. Mem. N.J. Acad. Sci. (exec. sec. 1980), Am. Physiol. Soc., Soc. Gen. Physiologists. Methodist (bd. stewards). Home: 409 Grant Ave Highland Park NJ 08904 Office: Rutgers U New Brunswick NJ 08903

GREEN, JAMES WILDER, association executive; b. Paris, Apr. 17, 1927; s. Thomas Samuel and Maud (Gutterson) G. (parents Am. citizens). Student, Yale U., 1945-47, Ill. Inst. Tech., 1947-48; B.Arch., Yale U., 1952. Lic. architect, N.Y. State. With Office of Paul Rudolph (Architect), Sarasota, Fla., 1952-53, Office of Philip Johnson (Architect), N.Y.C., 1953-54; asst. prof. Yale Sch. Architecture, 1956-57; asst. dir. dept. architecture and design Mus. Modern Art, N.Y.C., 1957-61, coordinator planning for bldg. program, 1961-63, coordinator program, 1963-67, dir. exhbn. program, 1967-69, 70-71, dep. to acting dir., 1969-70; dir. Am. Fedn. Arts, N.Y.C., 1971—; chmn. visual arts adv. com. Center for Inter-Am. Relations, 1972—. Bd. dirs. Sara Roby Found.; trustee MacDowell Colony. Served with Security Agy. AUS, 1954-56. Mem. Drawing Soc. (v.p. 1970—), Archtl. League N.Y. (mem. exec. com. 1973-80). Home: 20 E 74th St New York NY 10021 Office: 41 E 65th St New York NY 10021

GREEN, JAMES WYCHE, sociologist/anthropologist consultant; b. Alton, Va., Aug. 5, 1915; s. William Ivey and Mary (Crowder) G.; m. Pearl O'Neal Cornett, Mar. 2, 1940 (dec. 1982); 1 dau., Margaret Lydia.; m. Arlene Borkenhagen, Mar. 26, 1983. B.S. with honors, Va. Poly. Inst., 1938, M.S., 1939; postgrad., Duke U., 1947-48; Ph.D., U. N.C., 1953; student, Sch. Advanced Internat. Studies, Johns Hopkins U., 1959. Research fellow Va. Poly. Inst., 1938-39; research field supr. Va. Expt. Sta., 1939; asst. specialist program planning N.C. State Coll. Extension Service, 1939-42; v.p. Greever's, Inc., 1946; tchr. high sch., farm operator, 1946-47; asst. prof. rural sociology N.C. State Coll., 1949-54; from asso. chief to chief community devel. adv. to Govt. of Pakistan, Karachi, 1954-59; prof. rural sociology dept. Cornell U., Ithaca, N.Y., 1960; community devel. adviser to Govt. of So. Rhodesia, AID, 1960-64; chief community devel., local govt. adviser to Govt. of Peru, 1964-67; chief urban community devel. adviser to Govt. of Panama, 1967-69; prof., chmn. dept. sociology and anthropology U. N.C., Charlotte, 1969-70; chief methodology div. Bur. Tech. Assistance, AID, Washington, 1970-74; sociologist/anthropologist cons. AID, Washington, 1974-75, contractor, Yemen Arab Republic, 1975. Contbr. book chpts. and articles to profl. jours., also monographs. Served from 1st lt. to capt. AUS, 1942-46; lt. col. Res. ret., 1975. Decorated Croix de Guerre with silver star, France; Croix de Guerre with palm, Belgium; Bronze Star with cluster; named Outstanding Alumnus Hargrave Mil. Acad., 1979. Fellow Am. Anthrop. Assn., AAAS, Soc. Applied Anthropology; mem. Res. Officers Assn., Public Citizen, ACLU, Common Cause, Amnesty Internat., Alpha Kappa Delta, Omicron Delta Kappa, Alpha Zeta, Phi Kappa Phi. Conglist. Home and Office: 6430 Lily Dhu Ln Falls Church VA 22044 *I have found few joys in life which are as deep and lasting as "cracking a culture," i.e. understanding how it really works, and then using that understanding for its people's good as they see the good.*

GREEN, JASHA, sculptor, painter; b. East Boston, Mass., May 1, 1930; s. Benjamen and Mary (Malliaros) G.; m. Dian Mary Pitts, Jan.

15, 1962. Student, Boston Mus. Sch., 1947-50, Fernand Leger Sch., Paris, 1951-53. One-man shows, Everson Mus., Syracuse, N.Y., 1977, H.F. Johnson Mus.-Cornell U., Ithaca, N.Y., 1980, Chrysler Mus., Norfolk, Va., 1978, group shows, Grey Gallery-N.Y.U., 1979, Seitz Collection Princeton Mus., N.J., 1981, Israeli Mus., Jerusalem, 1980, Roanoke Coll. Mus., Va., 1982, represented in permanent collections, Guggenheim Mus., N.Y.C., represented in permanent colelctions, Phila. Mus. Art, represented in permanent collections, Bklyn. Mus. Home: 117 E 18th St New York NY 10003 *The summary of my life lies with my output as an artist.*

GREEN, JEROME FREDERIC, journalist; b. N.Y.C., Apr. 15, 1928; s. Frank Charles and Sylvia K. G.; m. Nancy Jane Hamilton, Dec. 18, 1961; 1 dau., Jennifer Elizabeth. A.B., Brown U., 1950; M.S., Boston U., 1952. Reporter, New York Jour.-Am., 1952, L.I. Star-Jour., 1956; writer, Mich. sports editor Ap, Detroit, 1956-63; sports writer Detroit News, 1963-73, sports columnist, 1973—; free lance mag. writer Sports Illustrated, Sporting News; commentator WOMC-FM, Detroit. Author: Year of the Tiger, 1969, The Detroit Lions-Great Teams, Great Years, 1972. Served to lt. (j.g.) USN, 1953-56. Recipient Mich. AP Sportswriting award, 1973, 79, UPI Mich. Sportswriting award, 1981, 82, 83, 84; named Mich. Sports Writer of Year, 1972, 79, 80, 81, 82; nominated for Pulitzer prize, 1982. Office: Detroit News 615 Lafayette Blvd Detroit MI 48231 *I write about games and people who play games for a daily newspaper. Nothing I write will change the world, make it better or worse. But it is a pleasant way to earn a living and I like to believe I bring some enjoyment to the people who read what I write.*

GREEN, JEROME GEORGE, ofcl. NIH; b. Bklyn., June 20, 1929; s. Samuel N. and Esther (Deiber) G.; m. Marie Charlotte Roder, Aug. 2, 1952; children—Karen Ann, Paul Jonathan. B.S. magna cum laude, Bklyn. Coll., 1950; M.D., Albany Med. Coll., 1954. Intern Albany (N.Y.) Hosp., 1954-55; mem. staff br. grants and tng. Nat. Heart Inst., NIH, Bethesda, Md., 1955-57, asso. dir. extramural research and tng., 1965-72; resident USPHS Hosp., San Francisco, 1957-59; spl. fellow in cardiopulmonary research Cardiovascular Research Inst., U. Calif., San Francisco, 1959-60; research div. Cleve. Clinic, 1960-65; dir. div. extramural affairs Nat. Heart, Lung and Blood Inst., NIH, Bethesda, 1972—. Fellow Am. Coll. Cardiology, Am. Heart Assn.; mem. Phi Beta Kappa, Alpha Omega Alpha. Home: 8304 Loring Dr Bethesda MD 20817 Office: Nat Heart Lung and Blood Inst Westwood Bldg NIH Bethesda MD 20205

GREEN, JEROME KEITH, manufacturing company executive; b. Highland, Ill., July 5, 1936; s. I. Frank and Florence Lydia (Kircher) G.; m. Kathy Jane Haefelin, June 26, 1965; children: Keith Edward, Julie Katherine. B.A. in Econs., Dartmouth Coll., 1958; M.B.A. in Bus. Acctg., Amos Tuck Sch. Bus. Adminstrn., 1959. C.P.A., Ill. Sr. accountant Price Waterhouse & Co., Chgo., 1960-64; With J.I. Case Co., Racine, Wis., 1964—, group v.p. internat., 1975-76, exec. v.p. internat., 1976-78, pres., chief operating officer, 1978-79, pres., chief exec. officer, 1979—; also dir.; dir. First Wis. Bank of Racine, Poclain, S.A. Served with Adj. Gen. Corps U.S. Army, 1959-60. Mem. Farm and Indsl. Equipment Inst. (dir.). Office: JI Case Co 700 State St Racine WI 53404

GREEN, JOE M., JR., lawyer; b. Houston, Apr. 10, 1912; s. Joseph Morris and Helen Mildred (Richardson) G.; m. Bennie Marie Pellerin, Feb. 22, 1975; children: Vicki, Bennie Pellerin. LL.B., South Tex. Coll. Law, Houston, 1938. Bar: Tex. 1938. Atty. Gulf Oil Corp., Houston, 1933-77, ret., 1977; individual practice law, Houston, 1977—; pres. Rockwell Fund, Inc.; v.p. Rockwell Lumber Co.; trustee, chmn. bd. trustees South Tex. Coll. Law. Served with Calvary U.S. Army, 1940-42; Served with M.P., U.S. Army, 1942-45. Methodist. Home: 4626 Bryn Mawr Ln Houston TX 77027 Office: 1921 Bank of the Southwest Bldg Houston TX 77002

GREEN, JOHN ALDEN, educator; b. Cardston, Alta., Can., Nov. 4, 1925; came to U.S., 1952, naturalized, 1961; s. John H.F. and Olivia (Thornhill) G.; m. Michele Therese Jugant, Aug. 27, 1954; children: John Scott, Jeffrey Paul (dec.), Evan Curtis, Alan Merrill, Kerry Anne, Cammie Suzanne, Nicole Renée, Brent Eric, Richard Derrin. B.A., Brigham Young U., 1954, M.A., 1955; Ph.D., U. Wash., 1960. Spl. instr. French, Boeing Aircraft Co., Renton, Wash., 1958-59; asst. prof. U. N.D., 1960-63; dir. Summer NDEA Inst., 1962; asso. prof., chmn. dept. U. Wichita, 1963-64; asso. prof. Brigham Young U., Provo, Utah, 1964-68, prof., 1968—, chmn. dept., 1969-71, dir. semester abroad program, 1979. Appeared in: The Miser, 1974, 76, 79, The Would-be Gentleman, 1977; Author: (play) That's the Spirit, 1969, French Reaction to Shakespeare, 1972, Albert Roustit, 1974, Liberty vs. Authority: The Gallant Assault in France, 1975, At the Top, 1977, Together, 1977, A Remarkable Discovery, 1977, Chroniques de Marcel Schwob, 1981; translator: L'Avare (Moliere), 1973, 76, 79; play Le Bourgeois Gentilhomme, 1974, 77, Prophecy in Music (Albert Roustit), 1975, Tartuffe, 1978, Knocking at Heaven's Door, 1982; dir. and actor film, 1982; Contbr. to: play Research on Language Teaching: An Annotated International Bibliography for 1945-61 (H.L. Nostrand), 1962; Knocking at Heaven's Door; contbr. articles and revs. to profl. jours. Served with RCAF, 1944-46. Home: 623 S 590 E Orem UT 84057 Office: 4015 JKBH Brigham Young U Provo UT 84602

GREEN, JOHN CAWLEY, lawyer; b. Washington, Mar. 2, 1910; s. Kirt and Linda (Cawley) G.; m. June Lazenby, Sept. 5, 1936. B.S., U.S. Naval Acad., 1934; J.D., Georgetown U., 1940. Bar: D.C. bar 1939. Examiner U.S. Patent Office, 1936-40; chief engr. Nat. Inventors Council (examining and analyzing civilian inventions directed to def. effort in cooperation with Armed Services), 1940-56, exec. dir., 1956-63; exec. sec. Publ. Bd., 1945-63; also in charge release of fed. research data; adviser Dept. State and ICA; dir. Office Tech. Services, U.S. Dept. Commerce, Washington, 1945-63; charge release fgn. sci. reports; dir. Research and Devel. div. Office Emergency Planning, 1963-66; dir. Office Analysis and Research, 1966-67; practice law, Washington, 1967—; pres. John C. Green Assos., 1968-77; cons. tech. adviser Internat. Conf. on Alien Patents, London, 1946. Recipient His Majesty's medal for services in cause of freedom, U.K., 1948; award for sci. efforts U.S. Sec. Army and Navy; exceptional service medal Sec. Commerce; medal Royal Swedish Acad. Engring. Scis., 1963. Fellow AAAS; mem. D.C., Fed. bar assns. Nat. Fedn. Sci. Abstracting and Indexing Services (pres. 1963-64). Clubs: Cosmos, Army Navy Country (Washington). Home: 464 Joyce Ln Arnold MD 21012 also 550 N St NW Washington DC 20024

GREEN, JOHN ORNE, lawyer, pharm. co. exec.; b. Erie, Pa., Jan. 1, 1922; s. John Orne and Harriot Cox (O'Brien) G.; m. Phyllis Booth, Jan. 13, 1945; children—John Orne 3d, Edward Townsend, George Thomas. Grad., Lawrenceville Sch., 1940; A.B., Yale, 1943; J.D., Harvard, 1948. Bar: N.Y. bar 1950, N.J. bar 1960, Conn. bar 1975. Asso. firm Mudge, Rose, Guthrie & Alexander, N.Y.C., 1948-51; gen. atty., asst. sec. Johnson & Johnson, New Brunswick, N.J., 1951-62; asst. sec., asst. gen. counsel Richardson-Merrell Inc., N.Y.C., 1962-65, sec., asst. gen. counsel, 1965-66, gen. counsel, 1966—, v.p., 1970—; Mem. Bd. Improvement Assessors, Princeton Twp., 1961-62; mem. Township Com., Princeton, 1963-65. Served to lt. USNR, 1943-46. Mem. Am., N.J., N.Y. State, Conn. bar assns., Assn. Bar City N.Y., Am. Soc. Corporate Secs., Pharm. Mfrs. Assn., Proprietary Assn., Westchester-Fairfield Corporate Counsel Assn., Food and Drug Law Inst. (dir.). Clubs: Yale (N.Y.C.); Capitol Hill (Washington); Redding (Conn.) Country, Mink Meadows Golf, Wilton Riding. Home: 45 Pin Oak Ln Wilton CT 06897 Office: Ten W Port Rd Wilton CT 06897

GREEN, JOHN ROOT, physics educator; b. Alameda, Calif., Sept. 19, 1920; s. John Doughty and Helen Mary (Root) G.; m. Anna Vallevik, Sept. 13, 1951; children: John Vallevik, Mary Alice, Jane Katherine. B.S. in Chemistry, U. Calif.-Berkeley, 1941, M.A., 1950, Ph.D. in Physics; Westinghouse, Whiting fellow, 1950. Research chemist Calif. Ink Co., Berkeley, 1941-42; teaching asst. U. Calif. at Berkeley, 1946-48; asst. prof. physics U. N.Mex. at Albuquerque, 1950-55, asso. prof., 1955-62, prof. physics, 1962-81, prof. emeritus, 1981—; mem. staff Los Alamos Sci. Lab., 1951; NSF sci. faculty fellow U. Oslo, Norway, 1957-58; Fulbright prof. physics U. Aleppo, Syria, 1966-67, U. Jordan, Amman, 1973-74. Mem. Albuquerque Legal Aid Soc., 1969—; arbitrator Albuquerque Mediation Ctr., 1983—; Mem. Sandoval County Democratic Grass Roots Com., 1963-69. Served with USAAF, 1942-46; capt. Res., 1946-52. Mem. AAUP, Am. Phys. Soc., Sigma Xi, Phi Beta Kappa, Pi Mu Epsilon. Research in cosmic radiation, dielectric properties and phase transformations in the organic solid state. Home: S S Box 712 Corrales NM 87048

GREEN, JOSEPH BARNET, neurologist; b. Phila., Aug. 2, 1928; s. Charles and Bella (Hurwitz) B.; (div.)children—Charna Alice Green Neal, Robert I. B.S., St. Joseph's Coll., Phila., 1950; M.D., Jefferson Med. Coll., Phila., 1954. Intern Wilkes-Barre (Pa.) Gen. Hosp., 1954-55; resident in neurology Georgetown U. Med. Center, 1955-58; asst. neurologist Pa. Hosp., Phila., 1960-64; asst. prof., then prof. neurology Ind. U. Med. Sch., 1964-72; prof. neurology and pediatrics, chmn. dept. neurology Med. Coll. Ga., Augusta, 1972-82; prof., chmn. dept. psychiatry and neurology Tulane U. Sch. Medicine, New Orleans, 1982—; cons. VA Med. Center, Augusta; chmn. profl. adv. bd. Epilepsy Assn.; mem. profl. adv. bd. Assn. Children with Learning Disabilities, Ga. chpt. Nat. Multiple Sclerosis Soc.; Fulbright lectr., Denmark, 1969; NIH project dir. Ga. Comprehensive Epilepsy Program, 1976. Author articles in field. Served with M.C. USNR, 1958-60. Fogarty Internat. Research fellow, Israel, 1981. Mem. AMA, Am. Acad. Neurology, Child Neurology Soc., Am. Neurol. Assn., Am. EEG Soc., Am. Epilepsy Soc. (sec. 1972), Assn. U. Profs. Neurology (v.p. 1981). Democrat. Jewish. Club: B'nai B'rith. Home: 4524 Bancroft Dr New Orleans LA 70122 Office: Dept Psychiatry and Neurology Tulane Med Center 1415 Tulane Ave New Orleans LA 70112

GREEN, JOSHUA, III, banker; b. Seattle, June 30, 1936; s. Joshua, Jr. and Elaine (Brygger) G.; m. Pamela K. Pemberton, Nov. 1, 1974; children: Joshua, Jennifer Elaine, Paige Courtney. B.A. in English, Harvard U., 1958. With Peoples Nat. Bank Wash., Seattle, 1960—, exec. v.p., 1972-75, pres., 1975—, chief exec. officer, 1977—, chmn. bd., 1979—, also dir.; v.p., dir. Joshua Green Corp. Vice pres., trustee Joshua Green Found.; trustee Seattle Found., Downtown Seattle Devel. Assn., U. Puget Sound, Tacoma. Mem. Seattle C. of C. (dir., v.p. 1980—). Clubs: Univ., Rainier, Seattle Tennis, Wash. Athletic (Seattle). Home: 1932 Blenheim Dr E Seattle WA 98112 Office: 1415 5th Ave Seattle WA 98171

GREEN, JOYCE HENS, federal judge; b. N.Y.C., Nov. 13, 1928; d. James S. and Hedy (Bucher) Hens; m. Samuel Green, Sept. 25, 1965 (dec. Oct. 23, 1983); children: Michael Timothy, June Heather, James Harry. B.A., U. Md., 1949; J.D., George Washington U., 1951. Bar: D.C. 1951, Va. 1956, U.S. Supreme Ct. 1956. Practice law, Washington, 1951-68, Arlington, Va., 1956-68; mem. firm Green & Green, 1966-68; judge Superior Ct., D.C., 1968-79, U.S. Dist. Ct. for D.C., 1979—. Trustee D.C. div. Am. Cancer Soc., 1963-76. Named Woman Lawyer of Yr., 1979. Fellow Am. Acad. Matrimonial Lawyers; mem. Am. Bar Assn., Va. Bar Assn., Bar Assn. D.C., D.C. Bar, D.C. Women's Bar Assn. (pres. 1960-62), Exec. Women in Govt. (chairperson 1977), Nat. Lawyers Club, Kappa Beta Pi, Phi Delta Phi (hon.). Office: US Dist Ct US Courthouse 3d and Constitution Ave NW Washington DC 20001

GREEN, JUNE LAZENBY, fed. judge; b. Arnold, Md., Jan. 23, 1914; d. Eugene H. and Jessie T. (Briggs) Lazenby; m. John Cawley Green, Sept. 5, 1936. J.D., Am. U., 1941. Bar: Md. bar 1943, D.C. bar 1945. Practiced in, Washington, 1947-68, Annapolis, Md., 1950-68; claims adjuster Lumbermans Mut. Casualty Co., Washington, 1942-43, claims atty., 1943-47; judge U.S. Dist. Ct. for D.C., 1968—; Bar examiner, Washington, 1963-68. Named Woman Lawyer of Year, 1965. Fellow Am. Acad. Matrimonial Lawyers; mem. Am. Bar Assn., Md. Bar Assn., Bar Assn. D.C. (dir. 1966-68), Women's Bar Assn. D.C. (pres. 1955-57), Kappa Beta Pi. Clubs: Nat. Lawyers, Zonta. Home: 464 Joyce Ln Arnold MD 21012 also 550 N St SW Washington DC 20024 Office: U S Courthouse Washington DC 20001

GREEN, KENSEY BASS, association executive, consultant, writer; b. Richmond, Va., June 8, 1938; d. Jesse Carroll and Kinsey (Bass) G. B.S., Mary Washington Coll., 1960; M.S., U. Md., 1965, Ph.D., 1969. Cert. asst. exec. Home econs. tchr. Prince William Pub. Schs., Nokesville, Va., 1960-64; prof., admisntr. U. Md. Colls. Edn. and Home Econs., 1964-75; exec. dir. Am. Home Econs. Assn., Washington, 1975—; v.p. and treas. G.L. Crandall Lapidary, Inc., Annapolis, Md., 1976—; bd. dirs. Future Homemakers Am., Reston, Va., 1975—; mem. Accrediting Council Journalism and Mass Communications, 1983—. Author: The World of Food - Tchrs. Guide, 1977; auhtor: the World of Food - Tchrs. Guide, rev., 1980; author: Relationships - Tchrs. Guide, 1979, Dicisions in Contemporary Living - Tchrs. Guide, 1976; monographs, 1979, 82. Dir. Ctr. for Handicapped, Silver Springs, Md., 1975-78; chmn. fin. com. Heritage Baptist Ch., Annapolis, 1980-83. Named Outstanding Alumnus Mary Washington Coll., 183. Mem. Am. Soc. Assn. Execs. (dir. 1976—, chmn. bd. 1982-83, Key 1982), Am. Home Econs. Assn., Md. Home Econs. Assn., World Future Soc. Democrat. Home: 5003 W Chalk Point Rd West River MD 20778 Office: American Home Econs Assn 2010 Massachusetts Ave NW Washington DC 20036

GREEN, LEON, JR., mechanical engineer; b. Austin, Tex., Aug. 13, 1922; s. Leon and Notra (Anderson) G.; m. Eleanor Broome Samuels, Apr. 14, 1951; children: John Anderson, Emily Broome, Charles Leon. B.S. in Physics, Calif. Inst. Tech., 1944, M.S. in Mech. Engring, 1947, Ph.D., 1950. With N.Am. Aviation, Inc., 1949-51, Aerojet-Gen. Corp., 1951-59, Aeronutronic div. Ford Motor Co., 1959-62; chief scientist Lockheed Propulsion Co., 1962-64; sci. dir. research and tech. div. Air Force Systems Command, Washington, 1964-67; dir. planning Washington area Lockheed Aircraft Corp., 1967-70; exec. sec. Def. Sci. Bd., Dept. Def., 1970-73; sr. staff engr. applied physics lab. Johns Hopkins U.; also cons. AEC, 1973-74; mem. tech. staff Mitre Corp., McLean, Va., 1974-77; cons. Gen. Atomic Co., 1977-80; pres. Energy Conversion Alternatives, Ltd., Washington, 1980—. Contbr. articles to profl. jours. Mem. ASME, Combustion Inst., AAAS, Sigma Xi. Club: Cosmos (Washington). Home and Office: 2101 Connecticut Ave NW Suite 67 Washington DC 20008

GREEN, LEWIS COX, lawyer; b. St. Louis, Oct. 14, 1924; s. John Raeburn and Elisabeth Haskell (Cox) G.; m. Louise Stewart Goold, Mar. 6, 1954; children—Lewis Cox, Mary Emily, Anne Raeburn, Kathleen Goold. A.B. cum laude, Harvard U., 1945, LL.B. magna cum laude, 1950. Bar: Mo. bar 1950. Law clk. Judge William E. Orr, U.S. Ct. of Appeals, 9th Circuit, 1950-51, Mr. Justice Stanley Reed, Supreme Ct. of U.S., 1951-52; atty. Office Gen. Counsel, NLRB, 1952-54; law clk. Chief Judge George H. Moore, U.S. Dist. Ct., Eastern Dist. Mo., 1955-56; partner firm Green, Hennings & Henry, St. Louis, 1954—; lectr. St. Louis U. Law Sch., 1954-55, Washington U. Law Sch., 1955-56; dir. Gen. Metal Products Co. Chmn. Air Conservation Commn. Mo., 1965-69; commr. Nat. Conf. Commrs. on Uniform State Laws, 1967—; del. Democratic Nat. Conv., 1976; mem. com. on human environ. Dem. Nat. Policy Com., 1970-72; mem. Mo. Dem. State Com., 1966-70; chmn. Mo. 2d Congl. Dist. Dem. Com., 1970-72; committeeman Bonhomme Twp., St. Louis County, Mo., 1958-74; pres. Coalition for Environ., St. Louis Region, 1972-74; bd. dirs. Conservation Fedn. Mo., 1970-74, Psychiat. Research Found., 1968-74, Mental Health Assn. St. Louis, 1960's, ACLU Eastern Mo. Served with AUS, 1943-46. Recipient Air Conservationist of Year award Conservation Fedn. Mo., 1970, Page One Civic award St. Louis Newspaper Guild, 1972, Environ. Quality award U.S. EPA, 1978. Mem. Am. Bar Assn., Mo. Bar Assn., Bar Assn. Met. St. Louis, Am. Law Inst., Am. Judicature Soc., World Peace Through Law Center. Club: Mo. Athletic. Home: 11 Litzsinger Ln Ladue MO 63124 Office: 314 N Broadway Room 1830 Saint Louis MO 63102

GREEN, M. EDWIN, architect; b. Kerhonkson, N.Y., July 1, 1896; s. Moses E. and Viola J. (Haskin) G.; m. Gladys W. Wilson, Sept. 1, 1922; children—Andrew Wilson, Moses Edwin, Elizabeth DeWitt. A.B., Carnegie Inst. Tech., 1920; grad. student, Fountainbleu Sch. Fine Arts, France, 1932. Asst. dir., bur. sch. bldgs. Dept. Pub. Instrn. Commonwealth of Pa., 1920-22; partner Lawrie & Green, Harrisburg, 1922—; Past pres. bd. of architectural registration Commonwealth Pa. Prin. archtl. works include Dauphin County Ct. House, Harrisburg, Hunt Meml. Library at Carnegie Inst. Tech, Commonwealth of Pa. William Penn Meml. Mus. and Archives Bldg; numerous hosps., schs., indsl. bldgs., hotel, coll. bldgs. Mem. bd. trustees Kiskiminetas Springs Boys Prep. Sch.; treas. Historical Found. Pa. Served as 1st lt. 94th Aero Squadron, 1st Pursuit Group. Decorated Croix de Guerre, France).; Recipient Alumni Merit award Carnegie Inst. Tech. Fellow A.I.A. (past pres. Central Pa. chpt.); mem. Pa. C. of C. (past dir.), Harrisburg C. of C., Pa. Soc. Architects (past pres.), Harrisburg Art Assn., Pa. Dept. Labor and Industry (mem. bldg. adv. bd.), Modular Bldg. Standards Assn., Order of Daedalians, Beta Theta Pi. Methodist (past pres. ch. bd. trustees). Clubs: Mason., Kiwanis, Torch, Country (Harrisburg); Wing. Address: RFD 1 Dauphin PA 17018

GREEN, MARGUERITE, educator; b. Chgo., Sept. 2, 1922; d. Edward A. and Mary (Prindeville) G. B.A., Barat Coll., 1943; M.A., Cath. U. Am., 1953, Ph.D., 1956; postgrad., U. Mich., U. London, Sophia U., Tokyo, Japan. Joined Religious of Sacred Heart, 1944; tchr. high sch. Acad. Sacred Heart, Chgo., 1946-49; prof. history and Am. studies Barat Coll., Lake Forest, Ill., 1949—, chmn. dept. history, 1958—. Author: The National Civic Federation and the American Labor Movement, 1900 to 1925, 1956. Nat. Endowment for Humanities scholar, 1975. Mem. Am. Hist. Assn., Am. Studies Assn., AAUP, Inst. of Women Today. Address: Barat Coll Lake Forest IL 60045

GREEN, MARK JOSEPH, lawyer, author; b. Bklyn., Mar. 15, 1945; s. Irving Arthur and Anna Constance (Suna) G.; m. Denisse Michele Frand, Aug. 13, 1977; 1 dau., Jenya Frand-Green. B.A. magna cum laude, Cornell U., 1967; J.D. cum laude, Harvard U., 1970. Bar: D.C. bar 1971. Dir. Corp. Accountability Research Group, Washington, 1970-75; campaign mgr. Ramsey Clark for Senate, 1976; dir. Public Citizen's Congress Watch, Washington, 1977-80. Author: (with others) The Closed Enterprise System, 1972, The Other Government: The Unseen Power of Washington LaWyers, 1975, (with Ralph Nader and Joel Seligman) Taming the Giant Corporation, 1972, Who Runs Congress?, 1972, 3d edit., 1979; editor: (with Bruce Wasserstein) With Justice For Some, 1971, The Monopoly Makers, 1973, (with Ralph Nader) Corporate Power in America, 1973, Verdicts on Lawyers, 1976. Bd. dirs. Citizen-Labor Energy Coalition, Fund for Class Action Costs; pres. The Democracy Project. Democrat. Jewish.

GREEN, MARSHALL, consultant, former ambassador; b. Holyoke, Mass., Jan. 27, 1916; s. Addison Loomis and Gertrude (Metcalf) G.; m. Lispenard Seabury Crocker, Feb. 14, 1942; children: Marshall Winthrop, Edward Crocker, Brampton Seabury. A.B., Yale U., 1939. Pvt. sec. to Am. ambassador to Japan, 1939-41; vice consul career, sec. Diplomatic Service, 1945; assigned, Wellington, N.Z., 1946-47; acting officer in charge Japanese affairs Dept. State, 1947-50; 1st sec. embassy, consul, Stockholm, 1950-55; assigned Nat. War Coll., 1955-56; regional planning adviser for Far East Dept. State, 1956-59, acting dep. asst. sec. of state, 1959-60; minister counselor Am. embassy, Korea, 1960-61; Am. consul gen., Hong Kong, personal rank of minister, 1961-63; dep. asst. sec. for Far Eastern affairs Dept. State, 1963-65; A.E. and P., Indonesia, 1965-69, to Australia and Nauru, 1973-75, asst. sec. state for East Asian-Pacific affairs, Washington, 1969-73, personal rank of career minister, 1966-79, cons., 1979—; dir. population crisis com., chmn. adv. com. Asia Soc., Washington.; Mem. U.S. team in Paris for Vietnam negotiations, 1969; chmn. task force on population Nat. Security Council, 1975—; chief U.S. del. to UN Population Commn., 1977, 79; bd. dirs. Nat. Com. U.S.-China Relations. Served to lt. USNR, 1942-45. Recipient Nat. Civil Service award, 1965, Disting. Service award, 1979. Mem. Japan-Am. Soc. Washington (pres.). Episcopalian. Clubs: Metropolitan, Chevy Chase (Washington); York Golf and Tennis (Maine). Home: 5063 Millwood Ln NW Washington DC 20016 Office: Dept State Washington DC 20520

GREEN, MEYER H., dentist, educator; b. Kolno, Poland, Mar. 22, 1917; came to U.S., 1928, naturalized, 1929; s. Louis A. and Bessie (Fellander) G.; m. Hilda Rosenberg, Sept. 30, 1944; children: Marc Stephen (dec.), Janice Beth. Student, Wayne U., 1935-40; D.D.S., U. Detroit, 1943. Diplomate: Am. Bd. Oral Medicine, Am. Bd. Clin. Hypnosis in Dentistry. Gen. practice dentistry, Detroit, 1946; sr. asso. attending med. staff teaching dental residents Sinai Hosp., Detroit, 1962—; lectr., writer in field. Bd. dirs. past v.p. Young Israel of Oak Woods, Mich. Served to capt. AUS, 1943-46. Recipient Achievement award Alpha Omega, 1980. Fellow Acad. Gen. Dentistry, Royal Soc. Health, Am. Acad. Oral Medicine (hon. and acad., nat. rec. sec., trustee 1958—, nat. pres. 1978—, gen. chmn. ann. meeting 1977, Cert. of Merit 1978); mem. Detroit Clinic Club, Mich. Soc. Oral Medicine (past pres. Mich. sect.), Mich. Soc. Psychosomatic Dentistry (past pres.), Am. Med. Writers Assn., Am. Soc. Preventive Dentistry, Acad. Gen. Dentistry, Internat. Acad. Orthodontics, Bunting Periodontal Study Club., Neurostimulation Study Group. Clubs: Century U., Detroit. Home: 2014 Waldon's Ct West Bloomfield MI 48033 Office: 14110 Gratiot Ave Detroit MI 48205 *While man's uniqueness is his ability to think and be rational, his true humanity does not come forth until he reaches out with his heart as well as his mind and thus forms a totally enduring and unbreakable bond between himself and the very purpose of Creation itself.*

GREEN, MORRIS, educator, physician; b. Indpls., May 27, 1922; s. Coleman and Rebecca (Oleinick) G.; m. Janice Barber Gorton, Mar. 11, 1955; children: David Schuster, Alan Coleman, Carolyn Ann, Susan Elaine, Marcia Ruth, Sylvia Rebecca. A.B., Ind. U., 1942, M.D., 1944. Intern Ind. U. Med. Center, 1945; resident pediatrics U. Ill. Research and Ednl. Hosps., 1947-49; instr. pediatrics U. Ill. Coll.

Medicine, 1949-52; asst. prof. Yale Sch. Medicine, 1952-57; faculty Ind. U. Sch. Medicine, Indpls., 1957—, prof. pediatrics, 1963—; chmn. dept. pediatrics, Perry W. Lesh prof. pediatrics, physician-in-chief James Whitcomb Riley Hosp. for Children, Indpls., 1967—. Author: Pediatric Diagnosis; 3d edit, 1980; co-editor: Ambulatory Pediatrics, 1968, 2d edit., 1977, 3d edit., 1983; editorial bd.: Social Work in Health Care; nat. adviser: Children Today. Served to capt. M.C. AUS, 1945-47. Recipient C. Anderson Aldrich award in child devel., 1982. Mem. Am. Pediatric Soc., Soc. Pediatric Research, Am. Fedn. Clin. Research, Am. Acad. Pediatrics, AMA, Am. Orthopsychiat. Assn., Inst. Medicine, Soc. Research Child Devel., Phi Beta Kappa, Sigma Xi, Alpha Omega Alpha. Home: 1840 Brewster Rd Indianapolis IN 46260

GREEN, NORMAN KENNETH, business executive, former naval officer; b. Columbus, Ind., July 1, 1924; s. Otto and Bernice Escalene (Snyder) G.; m. Mary Ann McCarthy, Mar. 12, 1949; children: David Bruce, Norman K., Penny Ann, Michael Anthony, Patricia Elizabeth. B.S., U.S. Naval Acad., 1947; M.S., Naval Postgrad. Sch., 1959. Joined U.S. Navy, 1943, advanced through grades to rear adm., 1974; comdg. officer USS St. Louis, 1970-72, comdg. officer USS Ticonderoga, 1972-73, capt. aviation assignment officer Bur. Naval Personnel, Washington, 1973-74, comdr. Sea Based ASW Wings Atlantic Fleet, 1974-77, comdr. Carrier Group 6 and Carrier Strike Force, Mayport, Fla., 1977-79, dep. dir. command and control Office Chief Naval Ops., Navy Dept., Washington, 1979-80, ret., 1980; sr. v.p. Charter Co., Jacksonville, Fla., 1980—. Mem. Com. of 100, Jacksonville, Fla., 1974-77; mem. exec. bd. United Way, 1974-77. Decorated Def. Superior Service medal, Legion of Merit.; recipient Brotherhood award NCCJ, 1979. Mem. Jackson C. of C. (bd. govs. 1974-77, 83—). Methodist. Clubs: Army-Navy, Ponte Vedra, Sawgrass, River. Home: 550 Granada Terr Ponte Vedra Beach FL 32082 Office: Charter Security Life Bldg One Charter Plaza Jacksonville FL 32202

GREEN, OLIVER FRANCIS, JR., lawyer; b. Cambridge, Mass., Aug. 17, 1924; s. Oliver Francis and Cleora M. (Perry) G.; m. Gloria J. Coscia, June 24, 1955; children—Elaine, Catherine, Matthew, Michael, Lisa. A.B., Harvard U., 1946; LL.B., U. Pa., 1951. Bar: Calif. bar 1953. Asso. firm Paul, Hastings, Janofsky & Walker, Los Angeles, 1952-60, partner, 1960-80, mng. partner, 1980—. Served with USN, 1943-46. Mem. State Bar Calif., Am. Bar Assn., Los Angeles County Bar Assn. Club: Jonathan. Office: 555 S Flower St 22d Floor Los Angeles CA 90071

GREEN, ORVILLE CRONKHITE, III, educator, physician; b. Oak Park, Ill., Jan. 14, 1926; s. Orville Cronkhite and Ellen (Carswell) G.; m. Nancy Gwendolyn Jones, May 15, 1954; children: Robert Vernon, Richard Cronkhite, James Carswell. B.A., Harvard, 1949; M.D., Northwestern U., 1954. Diplomate: Am. Bd. Pediatrics, Am. Bd. Pediatric Endocrinology. Intern Evanston (Ill.) Hosp., 1954-55; resident physician Children's Meml. Hosp., Chgo., 1955-57; clin. research fellow Johns Hopkins Hosp., 1957-60; asso. prof. pediatrics Ohio State U. Med. Sch., 1960-63, Northwestern U. Med. Sch., 1963-68, prof. pediatrics, 1968—; head div. endocrinology Children's Meml. Hosp., 1963—. Contbr. articles to med. jours. and books. Served with AUS, 1944-46. USPHS fellow, 1958-60; USPHS research support grantee, 1958—. Mem. Am. Pediatric Soc., Endocrine Soc., Lawson Wilkins Pediatric Endocrine Soc., Am. Diabetes Assn., Royal Soc. Medicine, Am. Soc. Human Genetics, Am. Acad. Pediatrics, Northwestern U. Med. Alumni Assn. (pres. 1969-71). Presbyn. Clubs: Harvard, University (Chgo.); Michigan Shores (Wilmette, Ill.). Office: 2300 Children's Plaza Chicago IL 60614

GREEN, PAUL EDGAR, marketing educator, author; b. Glenolden, Pa., Apr. 4, 1927. A.B., U. Pa., 1950, A.M., 1953, Ph.D., 1961. Statistician Sun Oil Co., Phila., 1950-53; comml. research analyst Lukens Steel Co., Coatesville, Pa., 1953-54, supr. opns. research group, sr. market analyst, 1955-58; instr. stats. Wharton Sch., U. Pa., Phila., 1954-55, guest lectr. mktg., 1961-62, assoc. prof. mktg., dep dir. Mgmt. Sci. Center, 1962-65, prof., 1965-71, S. S. Kresge prof., 1971—; market planning cons. E. I. duPont deNemours & Co., Wilmington, Del., 1958-62; guest lectr. stats. U. Del., 1959-60; lectr. numerous univs. and colls. Author: (with D.S. Tull) Research for Marketing Decisions, 1966, Research for Marketing Decisions, 4th edit., 1978, (with R.E. Frank) Quantitative Methods in Marketing Analysis, 1967, (with J.D. Carroll) Mathematical Tools for Applied Multivariate Analysis, 1976, Analyzing Multivariate Data, 1978, (with Martin Christopher) Brand Positioning, 1973; numerous book chpts., articles; mem. editorial bd. Mktg. Sci., 1965—; Jour. Mktg. Research, 1965—, Jour. Consumer Research, 1973—, Jour. Bus. Research, 1973—, Jour. Mktg., 1978—, Jour. Market Research Soc., 1981—. Recipient Alpha Kappa Psi award, 1963, 81, 1st prize Am. Psychol. Assn. (Div. 23) Research Design Competition, 1972, Paul D. Converse award Am. Mktg. Assn., 1978. Fellow Am. Statis. Assn., Am. Inst. for Decision Scis.; mem. Am. Mktg. Assn. (v.p. Mktg. Edn. div. 1967-68, mem. ednl. adv. com. on pharm. mktg. 1967-68, bd. dirs. Phila. chpt. 1976-78, Parlin award 1977), Inst. Mgmt. Scis., Psychometric Soc., Assn. Consumer Research, AAAS.

GREEN, PAUL ELIOT, JR., electrical engineer; b. Durham, N.C., Jan. 14, 1924; s. Paul Eliot and Elizabeth Atkinson (Lay) G.; m. Dorrit L. Gegan, Oct. 30, 1948; children: Dorrit Green Rodemeyer, Nancy E., Judy J., Paul M., Gordon M. A.B., U. N.C.-Chapel Hill, 1943; M.S., N.C. State U., 1948; Sc.D., MIT, 1953. Group leader MIT Lincoln Lab., Lexington, 1951-69; sr. mgr. IBM Research Div., Yorktown Heights, N.Y., 1969-80, mem. corp. tech. com., Armonk, N.Y., 1980—. Served to lt. comdr. USNR, 1943-60; ret. Named Disting. Engring. Alumnus N.C. State U., 1983. Fellow IEEE (Aerospace Pioneer award 1981); mem. Nat. Acad. Engring. Home: Roseholm Pl Mount Kisco NY 10549 Office: IBM Old Orchard Rd 3A-57 Armonk NY 10504

GREEN, PAULA, advertising agency executive; b. Hollywood, Calif., Sept. 18, 1927; d. Myron and Elizabeth (Grobstein) G.; m. John Glucksman, July 1, 1948; 1 son, Joel. B.A., U. Calif., 1943. Vice pres., creative mgmt. supr. Doyle, Dane, Bernbach, N.Y.C., 1956-69; pres., creative dir. Paula Green Inc. (Advt.), N.Y.C., 1969—. Creator, lyricist: N.Y. Times Home Delivery and Look for the Union Label for ILGWU (both included in Great Songs of Madison Ave. 1977); Contbr. feature articles to, Advt. Age. Chmn. nat. pub. info. com. Am. Cancer Soc., also bd. dirs., mem. exec. com., chmn. pub. info. com., bd. dirs., exec. com., N.Y.C. div.; mem. Gov. N.Y. Breast Cancer Adv. Com. Named Copywriter of Year Am. TV Festival, 1961; recipient Gold Key Copy Club N.Y.; Andy award, 1970, 76; Minerva award AWARE Internat., 1971; award Saturday Rev. mag., 1971; Big Apple award NYMRAD, 1976; Nat. Ann. Divisional award Am. Cancer Soc., 1978. Mem. Dirs. Guild Am., AFTRA. Office: Paula Green Inc Advt 134 W 26th St 5th Floor New York NY 10001 *I said it all in an advertising campaign I created for what was until then an unknown company in a not very highly regarded industry Avis Renta Car: "We try harder."*

GREEN, PETER LEROY, directory company executive; b. Prosser, Wash., Oct. 18, 1939; s. Walter Peter and Mildred (Brooks) G.; m. Judith Rae Hamilton, Aug. 3, 1963; 1 son, Christian. B.A. in Econs., Wash. State Coll., Ellensburg, 1963. Mgr. purchasing Boeing Corp., Renton, Wash., 1963-67; mgr. materials Gen. Telephone of Northwest, Everett, Wash., 1967-71, asst. sec., treas., 1971-76; sec., treas. Gen. Telephone of Mich., Muskegon, 1976-79; v.p. adminstrn., treas. GTE Directories Corp., Des Plaines, Ill., 1979—, also dir., Des Plaines. Mem. Nat. Cutting Horse Assn. (Ft. Worth), No. Ill. Cutting Horse Assn. (dir. 1982-83). Republican. Office: GTE Directories Corp 1865 Miner St Des Plaines IL 60016

GREEN, PETER MORRIS, classics educator, writer, translator; b. London, Dec. 22, 1924; U.S., 1971; s. Arthur and Olive Emily (Slaughter) G.; m. Lalage Isobel Pulveraft, July 28, 1951 (div.); children: Timothy Michael Bourke, Nicholas Paul, Sarah Francesca; m. Carin Margreta Christensen, July 18, 1975. B.A., Cambridge U., 1950, M.A., 1954, Ph.D., 1954. Dir. studies in classics Selwyn Coll., Cambridge, Eng., 1952-53; freelance writer, journalist, translator, London, 1954-63; lectr. Greek history and lit. Coll. Yr. in Athens, 1966-71; prof. classics U. Tex., Austin, 1971—, James R. Dougherty prof., 1982—; vis. prof. classics UCLA, 1976. Fiction critic: Daily Telegraph, London, 1954-63; sr. cons. editor: Hodder & Stoughton Ltd., London, 1959-63; cons.: (Odyssey project) Nat. Radio Theatre, Chgo., 1980-81; author: The Sword of Pleasure, 1975 (Heinemann award for Lit. 1957), The Shadow of the Parthenon, 1972, Alexander of Macedon 356-323 BC: A Historical Biography, 1974; translator, editor: Ovid: The Erotic Poems, 1982. Served to sgt. RAF, 1943-47. NEH fellow, 1983-84; Craven scholarship Cambridge U., 1950. Fellow Royal Soc. Lit. (council 1959-63); mem. Soc. for Promotion of Hellenic Studies (U.K.), Classical Assn. (U.K.), Am. Philol., Archaeol. Inst. Am. Mem. Liberal Party. Club: Savile (London). Home: 1505 Sunny Vale 219 Austin TX 78741 *Prime aims, then, now always; to have maximum possible time for writing, travel, sport, relationships; to avoid any job that threatens my solitude or independence; to shun mature opinions; to go on, forever if possible, finding every day exciting, new, a fresh challenge, mentally and physically; to love and be loved alsways to write all the books I have in me, and be healthy in mind and body until I die, preferably at well over the century, in Greeece.*

GREEN, PHILIP BEVINGTON, publishing company executive; b. Cambridge, Mass., Apr. 8, 1933; s. M. Thomas and Mary Margaret (Bevington) G.; m. Yolanda Verzulli, Mar. 14, 1960; children: Rebecca, Mark, Philip, Michael. Grad., Phillips Exeter Acad., 1951; B.A., Georgetown U., 1955; postgrad., Cath. U., 1955. Promotion dir. Jubilee mag., N.Y.C., 1959-62; circulation mgr. Reader's Digest, Pleasantville, N.Y., 1962-73; account supr. Wunderman Ricotta & Kline, N.Y.C., 1973-76; circulation dir. McCall's mag., N.Y.C., 1976-79; chmn., pub. Cath. Digest, St. Paul, N.Y.C., 1980—; dir. Am. Family Pubs., 1976-79, Select Mags., Inc., 1976-78. Served with AUS, 1956-58. Mem. Mag. Pubs. Assn., Cath. Press Assn., Direct Mail Mktg. Assn. Roman Catholic. Clubs: Scarsdale (N.Y.) Golf, St. Paul Athletic. 100 E Hartsdale Ave Apt 6ME Hartsdale NY 10530 Office: Catholic Digest St Paul's Sq Saint Paul MN 55164 also 815 2d Ave New York NY 10017 *Do the right things right.*

GREEN, RALPH J., JR., plant pathologist; b. Naylor, Mo., Aug. 17, 1923; s. Ralph J. and Beulah F. G.; m. Betty Jean Smith, Oct. 4, 1944; children—Robert Wayman, William Neill, Susan Elizabeth. B.S., Ind. State U., 1948; M.S., Purdue U., 1950, Ph.D., 1953. Instr. dept. botany U. Chgo., 1953-55; asst. prof. plant pathology Purdue U., 1955-58, asso. prof., 1958-66, prof., 1966—; cons. agr. Served with inf. U.S. Army, 1943-46. Decorated Bronze Star; recipient Silver Beaver award Boy Scouts Am., 1969. Fellow Ind. Acad. Sci., Am. Phytopath. Soc.; mem. Council Agrl. Sci. and Tech., Sigma Xi, Gamma Sigma Delta. Republican. Presbyterian. Club: Optimists. Research, numerous publs. in field. Home: 680 Vine St West Lafayette IN 47906 Office: Dept Botany and Plant Pathology Lilly Hall Purdue U Lafayette IN 47907

GREEN, RAYMOND S(ILVERNAIL), radio station executive; b. Torrington, Conn., Jan. 1, 1915; s. Percy Alexander and Amy (Silvernail) G.; m. Rose Basile, June 20, 1942; children: Carol Rae Green Hoffman, Raymond Ferguson. Student, Julius Hartt Sch. Music, 1934-37, Sarah Newton, 1925-33; voice with, Royal Dadmun, 1934-38, Giuseppe Boghetti, 1938-41, Alfredo Martino, 1942-50; coached with, Frederick Kitzsinger, 1946, Stuart Ross, 1947, Dr. Ernst Knoch, 1947-50; D.H.L., 1982; hon. degrees, 1984; hon. degrees, 1984. Producer, dir. musical programs NBC, N.Y.C., 1941-47, prodn. mgr., 1948; gen. mgr. Sta. WFLN, Phila., 1949-66, pres., 1966—, Franklin Broadcasting Co., 1966—; chmn. bd. Magnetik Prodns.; owner, operator conservation tree farm, Washington, Vt. Pres. Phila. Art Alliance, 1966-73, chmn. bd., 1973-77, hon. pres., 1977—; exec. v.p. Schuylkill Valley Nature Center, 1970—; bd. dirs. World Affairs Council Phila., 1974—; mem. adv. bd. Phila. Orch. Assn., LaSalle Coll., Cabrini Coll. Served as maj. USAAF, 1942-46. Recipient William Penn Human Rights award, 1982, George Washington Medal Freedoms Found. at Valley Forge. Fellow Royal Soc. Arts (London); mem. Broadcast Pioneers (pres. 1965-66, life dir.), Musical Fund Soc. Phila. (pres. 1983—), Am. Forestry Assn., Pa. Soc. Clubs: Peale, Franklin Inn, Philobiblon, Union League, Phila. Cricket (Phila.). Home: 308 Manor Rd Philadelphia PA 19128 Office: 8200 Ridge Ave Philadelphia PA 19128 *Success is the victory of principle over any compromise of quality.*

GREEN, REBECCA MCMULLAN, violinist; b. Mobile, Ala., Sept. 17, 1953; d. Melton Lee and Fannie Will (Clark) McMullan; m. Mitchell W. Green, Mar. 21, 1977. Mus.B., Memphis State U., 1975; postgrad., U. Cin. Coll. Conservatory Music, 1976-78. Adj. faculty U. Cin. Coll. Conservatory Music. Violinist, Mobile Symphony Orch., 1969-70; 1st violinist, Memphis Symphony Orch., 1971-75; asso. concertmaster, Cin. Symphony Orch., 1978—. Mem. Phi Kappa Phi, Phi Kappa Lambda. Home: 607 McAlpin St 15 Cincinnati OH 45220 Office: c/o Cin Symphony Orch 1243 Elm St Cincinnati OH 45210

GREEN, RICHARD ALAN, lawyer; b. Springfield, Mass., Apr. 25, 1926; s. Herman and Emma (Rudnick) G.; m. Lorna H. Paul, Sept. 6, 1957; children: Charles C., Thomas F. A.B. cum laude, Harvard U., 1947, LL.B., 1952. Bar: N.Y. 1954, D.C. 1975. Assoc. Steinberg & Patterson, N.Y.C., 1954-57; asst. U.S. atty. So. Dist. N.Y., 1957-59; 1st asst. counsel N.Y. State Commn. Investigation, 1960; individual practice law, N.Y.C., 1961-64; dir. ABA Project on Standards for Criminal Justice, 1964-73; dep. dir. Nat. Commn. on Reform of Fed. Criminal Laws, 1967-71; lectr. U. Va. Sch. Law, 1971; dep. dir. Fed. Jud. Center, Washington, 1971-74; partner Rowley and Green, Washington, 1974-80, Stohlman, Beuchert, Egan & Smith, 1981—. Served with USN, 1944-46. Mem. Am. Law Inst., ABA, D.C. Bar Assn., Assn. Bar City N.Y. Clubs: Harvard (N.Y.C.); Metropolitan (Washington). Home: 2725 N St NW Washington DC 20007

GREEN, RICHARD CALVIN, JR., utility company executive; b. Kansas City, Mo., May 6, 1954; s. Richard Calvin and Ann (Gableman) G.; m. Nancy Jean Risk, Aug. 6, 1977; 1 dau., Allison Thompt. B.S.B.A., So. Methodist U., 1976. With Mo. Pub. Service, 1976—, dist. mgr., Grandview, 1978-80, dir. fin., Kansas City, 1980-82, exec. v.p., 1982—; adv. dir. Green Securities, Kansas City, Mo., 1978—, Johnson County Broadcasters, Warrensburg, Mo., 1978—, Commerce Bank Kansas City, Mo., 1982—. Mem. Kansas City C. of C. (bd. dirs. 1983), Mo. C. of C. (bd. dirs. 1983), Assoc. Industries Mo. (bd. dirs. 1983). Republican. Mem. Christian Ch. (Disciples of Christ).

GREEN, RICHARD JAMES, securities company executive; b. Waterbury, Conn., Mar. 21, 1933; s. John Joseph and Anna Pearl (Vestro) G.; m. Syvia Irene Crawford, Oct. 9, 1953; children: Richard James, David Crawford, Mary Kathleen. B.S., U. Conn., 1959; postgrad., U. Wis. Banking Sch., 1966-69. C.P.A., Tex. Sr. acct. Payne Harrison and Co., C.P.A.s, Dallas, 1959-62; asst. controller Tex. Commerce Bank, Houston, 1962-65; sr. v.p., sec., treas. Federated Capital Corp., Houston, 1965-76; exec. v.p., sec., treas., dir. Hibbard, O'Connor & Weeks, Inc., Houston, 1976—; dir. Hibbard & O'Connor Govt. Securities, Inc., Hibbard & O'Connor Mcpl. Securities, Inc. Served with USAF, 1951-55. Mem. Bank Adminstrn. Inst. (chpt. pres. 1969-70), Am. Inst. C.P.A.s. Roman Catholic. Club: Jouston Met. Racquet. Home: 502 W Friar Tuck St Houston TX 77024 Office: Hibbard O'Connor & Weeks Inc 1300 Main St Houston TX 77002

GREEN, ROBERT EDWARD, JR., educator, physicist; b. Clifton Forge, Va., Jan. 17, 1932; s. Robert Edward and Hazle Hall (Smith) G.; m. Sydney Sue Truitt, Feb. 1, 1962; children: Kirsten Adair, Heather Scott. B.S., William and Mary Coll., 1953; Ph.D., Brown U., 1959; postgrad. (Fulbright grantee), Aachen (Germany) Technische Hochschule, 1959-60. Physicist underwater explosions research div. Norfolk (Va.) Naval Shipyard, 61959; asst. prof. mechanics Johns Hopkins, Balt., 1960-65, asso. prof., 1965-70, prof., 1970—, chmn. mechanics dept., 1970-72, chmn. mechanics and materials sci. dept., 1972-73, chmn. civil engring./materials sci. and engring. dept., 1979—; Ford Found. resident sr. engr. RCA, Lancaster, Pa., 1966-67; cons. U.S. Army Ballistic Research Labs., Aberdeen Proving Ground, Md., 1973-74; physicist Center for Materials Sci., U.S. Nat. Bur. Standards, Washington, 1974—. Author: Ultrasonic Investigation of Mechanical Properties (Treatise on Materials Science and Technology, Vol. 3), 1973; also articles. Mem. Am. Phys. Soc., Acoustical Soc. Am., Am. Inst. Mining, Metall. and Petroleum Engrs., Am. Soc. for Metals, Am. Soc. Nondestructive Testing, A.A.A.S., Sigma Xi, Tau Beta Pi, Alpha Sigma Mu, Sigma Nu. Methodist. Research in underwater shock waves, recovery, recrystallization, elasticity, plasticity, crystal growth and orientation, X-ray diffraction, electro-optical systems, linear and non-linear elastic wave propagation, light-sound interactions, high-power ultrasonics, ultrasonic attenuation, dislocation damping, fatigue, acoustic emission, non-destructive testing, polymers, biomaterials. Home: 936 Ellendale Dr Towson MD 21204 Office: Materials Sci and Engring Dept Johns Hopkins U Baltimore MD 21218

GREEN, ROBERT LAMAR, consulting agricultural engineer; b. Moultrie, Ga., Nov. 15, 1914; s. Louis Pinkney and Bessie (Tillman) G.; m. Frances Cowan, June 7, 1940; 1 son, Robert Lamar. B.S., U. Ga., 1934; M.S., Iowa State Coll., 1939; grad., Command and Gen. Staff Coll., 1944; Ph.D.; fellow Gen. Edn. Bd., Mich. State U., 1953. Registered profl. engr., Ga., Md. Terracing foreman Soil Erosion Service, Athens, Ga., 1934; camp engr. Civilian Conservation Corps., Bartow County, Ga., 1935; jr. agrl. engr. Soil Conservation Service, Lawrenceville and Americus, Ga., 1936-38, work unit conservationist, Lawrenceville, 1939-47; asst. prof. agrl. engring. La. State U., 1947-50, 53-54; agrl. engr. U.S. Spl. Tech. and Econ. Mission to Indonesia (ECA, MSA, TCA, FOA), Djakarta, 1951-53; supt., agrl. engr. S.E. Tidewater Expt. Sta., Dept. Agr., 1954-58; state drainage engr., Md., 1958-73; prof., head dept. agrl. engring. U. Md., 1958-73; coordinator Water Resources Research Center, 1965-79, prof. emeritus agrl. engring., 1979; acting dir. Md. Agrl. Expt. Sta., 1972-76; cons. agrl. engr., Central African Republic, 1979, Guyana, 1981. Contbr. articles to profl. and trade jours. Chmn. Spl. Gov.'s Com. to study shore erosion Md., 1960-66, Spl. Gov's Com. for Conservation and Devel. Natural Resources, 1960-66; mem. Md. Water Resources Commn., 1964—, chmn., 1975—; chmn. Md. Water Scis. Adv. Bd., 1968-73; bd. suprs. Dorchester County (Md.) Soil Conservation Dist., 1979. Served from 1st lt., cav. to maj., armor AUS, 1941-46; col. Res., ret. Md. Life fellow Am. Soc. Agrl. Engrs. (chmn. D.C.-Md. sect. 1961-62, rep. to NRC 1959-66, dir. 1969-71, rep. Agrl. Research Inst., Nat. Acad. Scis.-NRC 1974-76, del. Pan Am. Union Engrs., hon. v.p. 1972, rep. XII-XVI Congresses); mem. Sigma Xi, Tau Beta Pi, Phi Kappa Phi, Epsilon Sigma Phi. Episcopalian. Home and Office: Apt 3A 15310 Beaverbrook Ct Silver Spring MD 20906 also 312 Country Club Dr Rehoboth Beach DE 19971

GREEN, ROBERT THOMAS, lawyer; b. Shelby, Ohio; s. Thomas Jefferson and Blanche (Skiles) G.; m. Ruth Judd, June 22, 1935 (dec. 1958); childrenRobert Thomas, James J., Jeffrey S., Judith E.; m. Ann Kirkby, Feb. 14, 1964 (dec. 1975); m. Dorothy Walker, Sept. 23, 1976; childrenRobert Thomas, James J., Jeffrey S., Judith E. B.A., Amherst Coll., 1927; LL.B., Harvard, 1931. Bar: Ohio bar 1931. Practice in Shelby, 1936—; partner firm Long, Green & Long, 1936—; Chmn. bd. Autocall Co., Shelby, 1950-68; Mem. Ohio Bd. Bar Examiners, 1957-62, chmn., 1962-63; mem. Nat. Conf. Bar Examiners, 1962-66, chmn., 1965-66. Mem. Phi Beta Kappa. Home: 13 E Gaylord Ave Shelby OH 44875 Office: Insurance Bldg Shelby OH 44875

GREEN, RONALD WILLIAM, medical center administrator; b. East St. Louis, Ill., July 2, 1944; s. William Merritt and Jesse Blanche (Bowles) G.; m. Barbara Ruth Graebler, Dec. 21, 1970; children: William Jonathon, Jason Alexander. B.S., So. Ill. U., 1966; M.H.A., St. Louis U., 1971. Asst. adminstr. St. Louis U. Hosps., 1971-73, assoc. adminstr., 1973-77; adminstr. Tulane U. Hosp. and Clinic, New Orleans, 1977-82; v.p. Tulane Med. Ctr., 1982—; chmn. Met. Hosp. Council, New Orleans, 1982-83. Served with U.S. Army, 1966-68. Lutheran. Office: Tulane Med Ctr 1415 Tulane Ave New Orleans LA 70112

GREEN, S. WILLIAM (BILL GREEN), congressman; b. N.Y.C., Oct. 16, 1929; s. Louis A. and Evelyn (Schoenberg) G.; m. Patricia Freiberg, May 29, 1966; children: Catherine Ann, Louis Matthew. A.B. magna cum laude, Harvard U., 1950, J.D., 1953. Bar: D.C. bar 1953, N.Y. bar 1954. Law sec. Ct. Appeals for D.C., 1955-56; atty. firm Cleary, Gottlieb, Steen & Hamilton, N.Y.C., 1956-66, Paul, Weiss, Rifkind, Wharton & Garrison, 1966-68; counsel N.Y. Joint Legislative Com. on Housing and Urban Devel., 1961-64; mem. N.Y. State Assembly, 1965-68; regional adminstr. HUD, N.Y.C., 1970-77; chmn. Fed. Regional Council, 1971-77; mem. 95th-98th Congresses from N.Y. 18th Dist.; ex officio mem. Tri-State Regional Planning Commn., 1970-77; Del., N.Y. State Republican Conv., 1962, 66, del. Rep. Nat. Conv., 1980; mem. U.S. Holocaust Meml. Council; sec. Franklin D. Roosevelt Meml. Commn. Contbr. articles to legal jours. Bd. dirs. N.Y. Cancer Research Inst., Citizens Union Research Found.; bd. overseers Grad. Sch. Mgmt. and Urban Professions, New Sch. for Social Research, Albert Einstein Coll. Medicine; mem. adv. council N.Y. U. Grad. Sch. Public Affairs, Harvard U. Kennedy Sch. Govt.; founding trustee Jewish Assn. for Services to Aged; trustee Montefiore Hosp. and Med. Center. Served as 1st lt. U.S. Army, 1953-55. Mem. Am., N.Y. State bar assns., Assn. Bar City N.Y. (treas. 1966-68), N.Y. County Lawyers Assn., Harvard Law Sch. Assn. N.Y.C., Signet Soc., Phi Beta Kappa. Club: Harvard (N.Y.C.). Mem. Harvard Law Rev. Home: 755 Park Ave New York NY 10021 Office: 1110 Longworth House Office Bldg Washington DC 20515 also 110 E 45th St New York NY 10017

GREEN, STEVEN JAY, business executive; b. Phila., July 15, 1945; s. Carl and Sylvia G.; m. Dorothea Augusta, Mar. 19, 1967; children: Andrea Jacqueline, Kimberly Joy. B.B.A., U. Miami, 1967; postgrad., N.Y. Inst. Fin., 1967-68. Chmn. bd. Sterling Capital Investments, Inc., Miami, Fla., 1971—; chmn. bd., pres. Inprojet Corp., Miami, Fla., 1975-78; chmn. MultiNat. Trading Co., Miami, Fla., 1980—, KDT

Industries, Inc., Newton, Mass., 1980—; cons. Rapid Am. Co., N.Y.C., 1980—. Contbr.: articles to mags., including Fin. Exec., Am. Banker, Burroughs Clearing House. Mem. citizens bd. U. Miami, Fla., 1981—; asst. to mayor Dade County, Fla.; bd. dirs. Variety Children's Hosp.; apptd. Met. Dade County Zoning Appeals Bd., Fal. Mem. Young Pres. Orgn. Democrat. Jewish. Clubs: Standard, Grove Isle (Miami, Fla.). Office: KDT Industries Inc 150 California St Newton MA 02158

GREEN, THEODORE, III, engineering educator; b. Buffalo, Mar. 7, 1938; s. Theodore and Adelaide Roberta (Thompson) G.; m. Margaret Louise Harrison, Aug. 16, 1965; children: Theodore, Wendelin. A.B. in Physics, Amherst Coll., 1959; M.S. in Civil Engrng., Stanford U., 1965; Ph.D. in Engring. Mechanics, Stanford U. Assoc. prof. oceanography U.S. Naval Postgrad. Sch., Monterey, Calif., 1965-69; assoc. prof. civil engrng. and meteorology U. Wis., Madison, 1969-73, prof., 1974—. Contbr. articles to profl. jours. Grantee in field. Mem. ASCE, Am. Geophys. Union, Internat. Assn. Great Lakes Research, Wis. Acad. Sci. Arts and Letters, Sigma Xi. Episcopalian. Home: 3830 Council Crest Madison WI 53711 Office: Dept Civil and Environ Engrng U Wis Madison WI 53706

GREEN, THOMAS GEORGE, architect; b. Ackley, Iowa, July 12,1931; s. Thomas Chalmers and Marie Angeline (Dentel) G. B.A., U. Chgo., 1951, B.D., 1955; M.Arch., Yale U., 1959. Ordained to ministry United Ch. of Christ, 1955. With Architects Collaborative, 1959-65, assoc., 1964-65; ptnr. Benjamin Thompson & Assocs., architects, Cambridge, Mass., 1966-80; assoc. Wallace, Floyd, Assocs., Architects, Boston, 1981—; commd. minister United Ch. Bd. of Homeland Ministries, 1962-69, mem. archtl. adv. panel, 1979—; vis. critic Harvard Grad. Sch. Deisgn, 1981, Yale Sch. Architecture, 1983-84. Architect, Greylock Residential Houses, Williams coll., high sch., Bennington, Vt., Design Research Bldg., Harvard Sch. edn. Library, Cambridge, music bldg., Amherst Coll., Amherst Coll., Berkshire Community Coll., Pittsfield, Mass., Soldiers Field ParK Harvard U., Faneuil Hall Markets, Boston, Inter-Continental Hotels, Abu Dhabi, Al Ain, Cairo. Mem. Boston Zoning Commn. Eliel Saarinen Traveling fellow Yale U., 1959. Fellow AIA, Delta Upsilon. Democrat. Club: Yale (Boston).

GREEN, WARREN HAROLD, publisher; b. Auburn, Ill., July 25, 1915; s. John Anderson Logan and Clara Christina (Wortman) G.; m. Joyce Reinerd, Oct. 8, 1960. Student, Presbyn. Theol. Sem., 1933-34, Ill. Wesleyan U., 1934-36; M.B., Southwestern Conservatory, Dallas, 1938; M.M., St. Louis Conservatory, 1940, Ph.D., 1942; H.L.D. (hon.), Southeastern U., New Orleans, 1983, L.L.D., Institut de Droit Practique, Limoges, France, 1983. Prof. voice, composition, conducting and aural theory St. Louis Conservatory, 1938-44; program dir. U.S.O., Highland Park, Ill., Brownwood, Tex., Orange, Tex., Waukegan, Ill., 1944-46; community service specialist Rotary Internat., Chgo., 1946-47; editor in chief Charles C. Thomas, Pub., Springfield, Ill., 1947-66; pub., pres. Warren H. Green, Inc., St. Louis, 1966—, Warren H. Green Internat., Inc., 1970—; sec. John R. Davis Assos., Chgo., 1955—; exec. v.p. Visioneering Advt., St. Louis, 1966—; mng. dir. Pubs. Service Center, St. Louis, Chgo. and Longview, Tex., 1967—; Cons. U.S., European pubs., profl. socs.; lectr. med. publs. Civil War. Contbr. articles to profl. jours., books on Civil War history, writing, editing. Mem. Mayor's Com. on Water Safety, Met. St. Louis Art Mus., Mo. Bot. Gardens; exec. officer Affirmative Action, Inc., St. Louis. Recipient Presdl. citation for outstanding contbn. export expansion program U.S., 1973. Mem. Civil War Round Table (v.p. 1969—), Am. Acad. Criminology, Am. Acad. Polit. and Social Sci., Am. Assn. Med. Book Pubs., Am. Judicature Soc., Great Plains Hist. Soc., Co. Mil. Historians, Am. Soc. Personnel Adminstrs., University City C. of C. (pres. 1978—), Internat. Assn. Chiefs of Police. Clubs: Mo. Athletic, Elks, World Trade, Direct Mktg. (St. Louis); Clayton (Mo.). Home: 12120 Hibler Dr Creve Coeur MO 63141 Office: 8356 Olive Blvd Saint Louis MO 63132 *As God gives us the ability to seek the truth, know the truth, and be true to others as well as ourselves, and as God gives us the understanding to maintain a high sense of values in our work and in our relations with all fellowmen, it naturally follows that attitudes, endeavor, love of people and all other living things, cause one to like and be liked, which is the first step toward any worthwhile goal.*

GREEN, WAYNE SANGER, II, publisher; b. Littleton, N.H., Sept. 3, 1922; s. Wayne Sanger and Cleo (Willson) G.; m. Sherry Smythe; children—Tully, Sage. B.S., Rennselaer Poly. Inst., 1948. TV dir. sta. WXEL, Cleve., 1951-52; pres. Karlson Assos. (mfr. hi-fis), Bklyn., 1952-55; editor CQ mag., N.Y.C., 1955-60; editor, pub. 73 mag., Peterborough, N.H., 1960—; pub. BYTE mag. (computers), Peterborough, 1975-76; editor, pub. Kilobaud Microcomputing mag., Peterborough, 1976—; pub. Instant Software (microcomputer software), Peterborough, 1978—; editor, pub. Microcomputing Industry mag., Peterborough, 1979—, 80-Microcomputing mag., 1980—; rep. U.S. radio amateurs Internat. Telecommunications Union, Geneva, 1959; organizer amateur radio, Jordan, 1970. Author books on amateur radio, computers. Served with USNR, 1942-46. Mem. Peterborough C. of C. (pres. 1981), Mensa (a founder). Home: Peterborough NH 03458 Office: 73 Magazine Peterborough NH 03458

GREEN, WILLIAM JOSEPH, mayor of Philadelphia; b. Phila., June 24, 1938; s. William Joseph and Mary E. (Kelly) G.; m. Patricia Anne Kirk; children: William Joseph, Katherine Kirk, Anne Patricia, Maura Elizabeth. B.S., St. Joseph's Coll., 1960; J.D., Villanova Law Sch., 1974. Bar: Pa. 1977, D.C. 1978. Asso. mem. firm Wolf, Block, Schorr & Solis-Cohen, Phila., 1977-79; mem. 88th-94th congresses from 3d Dist. Pa.; mayor, City of Phila., 1980—. Democrat. Office: Office of Mayor City Hall Broad and Market Philadelphia PA 19107

GREEN, WILLIAM PORTER, lawyer; b. Jacksonville, Ill., Mar. 19, 1920; s. Hugh Parker and Clara Belle (Hopper) G.; m. Rose Marie Hall, Oct. 1, 1944; children: Hugh Michael, Robert Alan, Richard William. B.A., Ill. Coll., 1941; J.D., Northwestern U., 1947. Bar: Ill. 1947, Calif. 1948, Ct. Customs and Patent Appeals 1948, U.S. Patent and Trademark Office 1948, U.S. Ct. Appeals (fed. cir.) 1982, U.S. Ct. Appeals (5th and 9th cirs.), U.S. Supreme Ct. 1948, U.S. Dist. Ct. (cen. dist.) Calif. Practice patent, trademark and copyright law, Los Angeles, 1947—; mem. firm Wills, Green & Mueth, 1974—; del. Calif. State Bar Conv., 1982, 83. Bd. editors: Ill. Law Rev, 1946. Mem. Los Angeles World Affairs Council, 1975—. Served to lt. USNR, 1942-46. Mem. Am., Calif., Los Angeles County bar assns., Am. Patent Law Assn., Los Angeles Patent Law Assn. (past sec.-treas., bd. govs.), Lawyers Club Los Angeles (past treas., past sec., bd. govs., pres.-elect 1983–84), Am. Legion (past post comdr.), Phi Beta Kappa, Phi Delta Phi, Phi Alpha. Republican. Presbyn. (deacon 1961-63). Clubs: Big Ten of So. Calif., Northwestern U. Alumni of So. Calif., Phi Beta Kappa Alumni of So. Calif., Town Hall of Calif. Home: 3570 E Lombardy Rd Pasadena CA 91107 Office: 700 S Flower St Suite 1120 Los Angeles CA 90017

GREENAGEL, FRANK LOUIS, publisher; b. Fergus Falls, Minn., Oct. 7, 1939; s. Frank Henry and Vivian Louise (Larson) G.; m. Heather Arling, Aug. 23, 1963; children—Jill Heather, Frank Louis. B.A., U. Minn., 1961, M.A., 1963, Ph.D., 1965. Instr. communication U. Minn., 1961-64; asst. prof. U. Colo., Boulder, 1964-66; corp. mgr. employee communication Litton Industries, Beverly Hills, Calif., 1966-67, corp. mgr. orgn. research, staffing and devel., 1967-69, dir. indsl. relations, Hartford, Conn., 1969-70; gen. mgr. Litton Office Products Co. Ltd., Montreal, Que., Can., 1969-71; v.p. D. Van Nostrand div. Litton Industries, N.Y.C., 1971-75; mng. dir. VNU Am., Inc., N.Y.C., 1975—; pres. Arete Pub. Co., Princeton, N.J., 1977—. Committeeman, Tewksbury (N.J.) Twp., 1975-77, mayor, 1977. Address: Princeton Forrestal Center 101 College Rd E Princeton NJ 08540 *

GREENAGEL, JOHN PHILIP, public relations company executive; b. Fergus Falls, Minn., Jan. 24, 1941; s. Frank Henry and Vivian (Larson) G. B.A., U. Minn., 1962; postgrad., William Mitchell Coll. Law, St. Paul, 1962-64. Asst. dir. Bur. Mcpl. Research, St. Paul, 1962-64; pub. affairs dir. C. of C., St. Paul, 1964-66; asst. legis. mgr. U.S. C. of C., Washington, 1966-67; pub. affairs mgr. San Francisco C. of C., 1967-72; prin. John Greenagel PR, San Francisco, 1972—. Mgr. numerous polit. compaign, Calif., 1972—. Mem. Pub. Relations Soc. Am. (accredited, pres. San Francisco Bay chpt. 1978), Bay Area Pub. Affairs Council, Pub. Relations Round Table. Republican. Lutheran. Office: John Greenagel Pub Relations 1485 Bayshore Blvd San Francisco CA 94124

GREENAWALT, DAVID FRANKLIN, food processing and marketing company executive; b. Phila., July 6, 1933; s. Lloyd Nelson and Elizabeth Inez (Oberholtzer) G.; m. Doris Anne Coyle, May 5, 1956; children: Denise, David III. B.S. in Econs., Wharton Sch., U. Pa., 1955. Exec. v.p. Dairylea Coop., Pearl River, N.Y., 1973-77; v.p. prodn. and engrng. Wm. Underwood Co., Westwood, Mass., 1977-79; sr. v.p. Knudsen Corp., Los Angeles, 1979-81, exec. v.p., 1981-82, pres., chief operating officer, 1982—; dir. Mchts. and Mfg. Assn., Los Angeles, 1979—, Internat. Assn. Ice Cream Mfrs., Washington, 1973—, Knudsen Corp., Los Angeles, 1980—. Bd. dirs. Nat. Safety Council, Los Angeles, 1979—. Served to capt. USMC, 1956-59. Honored Dir.'s Table Beta Gamma Sigma, 1982. Republican. Roman Catholic. Clubs: California (los Angeles); Jonathan (Los Angeles). Lodge: KC. Home: 1346 Lida Ln Pasadena CA 91103 Office: Knudsen Corp 231 E 23d St Los Angeles CA 90051

GREENAWALT, H. SAMUEL, JR., banker; b. Grand Rapids, Mich., Nov. 9, 1928; s. H. Samuel and Bonnie Lockhard (Newcomb) G.; m. Diane L. Hubert, Nov. 2, 1980; children by previous marriage: Sheri, Tami, H. Samuel. B.S. in Econs, U. Pa., 1951; cert., Sch. Banking, U. Wis., 1960. With MacNaughton-Greenawalt Investment Bankers, 1954-56, U.S. Dept. Treasury, 1956-58; asst. v.p. Mich. Nat. Bank, Grand Rapids, 1958-61; exec. v.p. Mich. Nat. Bank of Detroit, 1961-80; chmn. of bd., chief exec. officer Mich. Nat. Bank-Mid Mich., Flint, 1980—; dir. DownRiver Internat., Flint Genesee Corp., Mich. Nat. Bank. Trustee U. Pa., 1975, 81—, Detroit Country Day Sch., 1972-80; mem. adv. bd. Hurley Hosp.; bd. dirs. DeWaters Trust, Flint Inst. Arts, Flint Goodwill Industries, Flint Area Econ. Council, Alliance of Greater Flint, Flint Downtown Devel., Flint Renaissance, Inc., Huron Valley Hosp.; chmn. bd. dirs. United Way Corp. Served with USMC, 1951-54. Decorated Purple Heart; recipient NCAA Silver Anniversary award U.S. Olympic Ski Found., 1976. Mem. Robert Morris Assoc., Flint C. of C. (bd. dirs.). Republican. Clubs: Detroit Athletic, Flint City, Univ., of Flint, Flint Golf, Wawrick Hills Country, Orchard Lake Country, Deepdale Golf, U. Pa. Alumni, Mich. Ski Assn. (pres.), Sigma Chi.). Office: PO Box 589 Bloomfield Hills MI 48013

GREENAWALT, KENNETH WILLIAM, lawyer; b. Town of Wall Street, Colo., Oct. 9, 1903; s. William Eckert and Cora May (Cornell) G.; m. Martha Frances Sloan, Sept. 3, 1929; children: William Sloan, Robert Kent, Ann Cornell Greenawalt Abernethy, Kim Chandler. LL.B., Cornell U., 1927. Bar: N.Y. 1929, U.S. Supreme Ct. 1933. Since practiced in N.Y.C.; asso. Sackett, Chapman, Brown & Cross, 1927-30, Davies, Auerbach & Cornell, 1930-44, mem., 1944-49,, Davies, Hardy Ives & Lawther (now Windels, Marx, Davies & Ives), 1949—; mem. faculty Practising Law Inst., 1981. Contbr. to legal publs.; guest participant radio, TV programs. Mem. Edgemont Sch. Dist. Bd. Edn., Scarsdale, N.Y., 1957-62, Met. Opera Guild; mem. bd. regents L.I. Coll. Hosp.; mem. Gen. Council Congregational Christian Chs., 1952-58. Recipient Woodford prize Cornell U., 1927, ABA Gavel award, 1962, George Washington Honor medal Freedoms Found., 1962. Fellow Am. Coll. Trial Lawyers, Soc. Values in Higher Edn. (dir.); mem. Acad. Polit. Sci., Am. Acad. Polit. and Social Sci., ABA (coms.), N.Y. Bar Assn. (coms.), Am. Judicature Soc., Bar Assn. City N.Y. (coms.), Cornell Law Assn., N.Y. State Vet. Med. Soc. (hon.), Vet. Med. Assn. N.Y.C. (hon.), Sigma Delta Chi, Phi Sigma Kappa, Phi Delta Phi, Sphinx Head (Cornell). Conglist. (trustee). Clubs: Cornell of N.Y. City and Westchester County, Westchester County Tennis (past pres.); Fox Meadow Tennis (Scarsdale); Harbor View (N.Y.C.). Home: 65 Highridge Rd Hartsdale NY 10530 Office: 51 W 51 St New York NY 10019

GREENAWALT, ROBERT KENT, lawyer; b. Bklyn., June 25, 1936; s. Kenneth William and Martha (Sloan) G.; m. Sanja Milic, July 14, 1968; children: Robert Milic, Alexander Kent Anton, Andrei Milenko Kenneth. A.B. with honors, Swarthmore Coll., 1958; Ph.B.; Keasbey fellow, Oxford (Eng.) U., 1960; LL.B.; Kent scholar, Columbia U., 1963. Bar: N.Y. bar 1963. Law clk. to Justice Harlan, U.S. Supreme Ct., 1963-64; spl. asst. AID, Washington, 1964-65; mem. faculty Columbia U. Law Sch., 1965—, prof. law, 1969—, Cardozo prof., 1979—; dep. solicitor gen. U.S., 1971-72; asso. dir. N.Y. Inst. Legal Edn., 1969; vis. prof. Stanford U. Law Sch., 1970, Northwestern U. Law Sch., 1983; atty. Lawyers Com. Civil Rights, 1965; mem. staff Task Force Law Enforcement N.Y.C., 1965; vis. fellow All Souls Coll. Oxford (Eng.) U., 1979. Co-author: The Sectarian College and The Public Purse, 1970; author: Legal Protections of Privacy, 1976, Discrimination and Reverse Discrimination, 1983; Editor-in-chief: Columbia U. Law Rev, 1962-63; Contbr. articles to legal jours. Recipient Ivy award Swarthmore Coll., 1958; fellow Am. Council Learned Soc., 1972-73, Clare Hall and Inst. Criminology, Cambridge (Eng.) U., 1972-73. Fellow Am. Acad. Arts and Sci.; mem. Am. Law Inst., Am. Soc. Polit. and Legal Philosophy. Home: 435 Riverside Dr New York City NY 10025 Office: Columbia Univ Law Sch 435 W 116th St New York City NY 10027

GREENAWAY, DONALD, hotel administration educator; b. Frankfort, Mich., Apr. 14, 1911; s. George Henry and Mary Elizabeth (Orr) G.; m. Louise Constance Wadsworth, June 27, 1936; 1 dau., Jeanne Elizabeth Greenaway Des Camp; m. Lorraine Katherine Muellenbach, July 6, 1958 (dec. Feb. 1983); 1 dau., Karen. B.A., Mich. State U., 1934; LL.D., Northwood Inst., 1970. Hotel adminstrn. and mgmt., 1934-41; food service exec. Trans World Airlines, 1946-47; prof. hotel adminstrn. Coll. Bus., Wash. State U., 1947-51; prof. adminstr.-dir. Sch. Hotel, Restaurant and Instl. Mgmt., Coll. Bus., Mich. State U., 1951-58; exec. v.p. Nat. Restaurant Assn., Chgo., 1958-70; asso. dean Sch. Hotel and Restaurant Mgmt., U. Houston, 1970-76; asst. to exec. v.p. Tex. Restaurant Assn., 1976—; Dir. Wilkensburg Hotel Co., Pa., Hotel Elkhart, Ind.; Mem. Gov.'s Com. for Devel. State Wash., 1950-51; pres., founder Nat. Council Hotel and Restaurant Edn., 1946; adviser to bd. dirs. Army and Air Force Exchange Service; adviser USPHS, USAF, World-Wide Food Service; mgmt. cons. Soc. Advancement Food Service Research; mem. 5th Internat. World Food Congress, U.S. Travel Service; also trade assn. adv. com. U.S. C. of C.; trade missions to Europe auspices Dept. Commerce.; Disting. vis. prof. Fla. Internat. U.; First Westin Hotels Disting. prof. Wash. State U. Author: Manual for Resort Operations, 1950, also monographs, papers, articles. Bd. dirs. Govs. Confs. Tourism Pacific N.W., 1947-49, Pacific N.W. Trade Assn., 1947-48. Served to capt. USAAF, 1942-46. Mem. AAUP, Am. Soc. Assn. Execs., Execs. Forum, Mich., Resort Assn., Mich. Pa. hotel assns., Am. Standards Assn. (com. standards for food service industry), Food Execs. Assn., Internat. Ho-Re-Ca, Confrerie de la Chaine des Rotisseurs, Theta Chi, Alpha Kappa Psi. Club: Rotarian. Home: 18526 83d Ave W Edmonds WA 98020 *In retrospect, historians will probably identify my generation as the "age of the executive." Men in my generation conceived, managed, and built worldwide enterprises which carried American technology throughout the globe. But it is also the age of instantaneous giants who do instantaneous disappearing acts. Who remembers yesterday's heroes in the business world? My generation will probably also be charged with ending rather than preserving the American dream. This is because we failed to preceve that personal business success was meaningless because we failed to contribute to America's overall intellectual and social growth.*

GREENAWAY, EMERSON, former librarian; b. Springfield, Mass., May 25, 1906; s. James and Sara Elizabeth (Lilley) G.; m. Helen Kidder, June 18, 1938; children: Ann (Mrs. Robert C. Pugh), Jane (Mrs. John G. Sampson). A.B. in L.S, U. N.C., 1935; B.S., U. Mass., 1927, L.H.D., 1952; Litt.D., Western Md. Coll., 1950, Drexel Inst. Tech., 1959, Wheaton Coll., 1973; LL.D., Temple U., 1958. Reference asst. City Library Assn., Springfield, Mass., 1928-30; supr. brs. and asst. librarian Pub. Library, Hartford, Conn., 1930-34, 36; spl. asst. Enoch Pratt Free Library, Balt., 1935, librarian, 1945-51, Pub. Library, Fitchburg, Mass., 1937-40, Free Pub. Library, Worcester, Mass., 1940-45; lectr. library adminstrn. Simmons Coll. Sch. Library Sci., Boston, 1942-45, Columbia U. Grad. Sch. Library Service, 1963-64, Drexel Inst. Library Sch., 1965, Library Sch., Kent State U., 1977; dir. Free Library of Phila., 1951-69; Dir. Forest Press, Inc.; Cons. in pub. libraries for UNESCO, 1947-49; Mem. Adult Ednl. Council, Mus. Council, Spl. Library Council, all Phila., Nat. Adv. Commn. Libraries, 1967; adv. com. U.S. Internat. Book and Library Programs; Pa. Adv. Council Library Devel., 1957-68; books across the sea com. English Speaking Union; chmn. Library vis. com. Wheaton Coll., Norton, Mass., 1967—. Trustee Schuylkill Valley Nature Center, hon. chmn., 1970—; trustee Harcum Jr. Coll., Union Library Catalog, Phila., 1952-69, Phila. Art Alliance, Tracy Meml. Library, New London, N.H., 1979—. Recipient 1954 Good Govt. award, 1955; Citation Phila. Jr. C. of C. and; U.S. C. of C.; Lippincott award ALA, 1955; Centennial citation, 1976; Disting. Achievement award Drexel Inst., 1965; Merit award Phila. Art Alliance, 1969; Disting. Alumni award U. N.C. Sch. Library Sci., 1981. Mem. ALA (council 1954—, exec. bd. 1954-60, pres. 1958-59), Mass. Library Assn. (life mem.), N.H. Library Trustees Assn. (dir. 1982—), Pa. Library Assn., Md. Library Assn. (life mem.), Assn. Friends N.H. Libraries (dir. 1982—), Am. Philos. Soc. (councilor, library com.), Internat. Fedn. Library Assns. Clubs: Franklin Inn, Philobiblon; Science and Arts (Germantown); Boy's (New London, N.H.); Balt. Bibliophiles, Appalachian Mountain. Home: N Pleasant St Rural Route 2 Box 1095 New London NH 03257

GREENBACKER, JOHN EVERETT, lawyer; b. Meriden, Conn., Oct. 4, 1917; s. Charles and Isabel Alice Francis G.; m. Carolyn Robertson Perrow, July 25, 1942; children—Susan Brown, John Everett, Florence Linn, Christopher F. Student, U. Conn., 1935-36; B.S., U.S. Naval Acad., 1940; J.D., Georgetown U., 1949, LL.M., 1969; M.A., George Washington U., 1964, U.S. Naval War Coll., 1964. Commd. ensign U.S. Navy, 1940, advanced through grades to capt., 1960; comdg. officer subchaser, 1942-43, comdg. officer destroyer escorts, 1943-46, comdg. officer destroyer, 1955-57, comdg. officer attack transport, 1962-63, comdr. destroyer div. 262, 1961-62, comdr. destroyer squadron 6, 1965-66, ret., 1969; sr. atty. legal dept. Balt. Gas & Electric Co., 1969-72, mem. finance dept., 1972-74, treas., 1974-76; practice law, Halifax, Va., 1976—; mem. firm J.E. Greenbacker & Son, 1978—. Home: Route 1 Box 614 Halifax VA 24558 Office: 15 S Main St Halifax VA 24558

GREENBAUM, JAMES RICHARD, liquor distributing company executive, real estate developer; b. Cleve., July 3, 1933; s. Harold and Miriam (Lion) G.; m. Peggy Strauss, Jan. 29, 1955; children: Robert Strauss, James R., Clifford Harold. B.A., Tulane U., 1955. Vice pres. Strauss Distbrs., Ark., 1961—; chmn. bd. TeleMktg. Communications of Las Vegas, Inc.; exec. v.p. Strauss Distbrs. of Monroe, 1957—, Gulf Inland Corp., Houston, 1959—; v.p. F. Strauss & Son, Inc., New Orleans, 1961—; dir. Bank of Palm Springs, S & D Realty, Little Rock. Regional chmn. Tulane Alumni Fund. Bd.; bd. govs., v.p. Desert Hosp. Found., Palm Springs; bd. dirs., pres. Jewish Welfare Fedn., Palm Springs. Served as lt. AUS, 1955-57. Mem. Zeta Beta Tau. Jewish (past pres., dir. temple). Clubs: Vail (Colo.) Racquet; Tamarisk, Racquet (Palm Springs, Calif.). Home: 432 W Hermosa Pl Palm Springs CA 92262

GREENBAUM, LOWELL MARVIN, pharmacologist, educator; b. Bklyn., June 13, 1928; s. Benjamin and Belle (Gordon) G.; m. Gloria Rubin, June 13, 1950; children: Matthew, Daniel, Jessica. B.S., CCNY, 1949; Ph.D., Tufts U., 1953. Am. Cancer Soc. fellow Yale U., 1954-56; instr. SUNY Downstate Med. Center, Bklyn., 1956-58, asst. prof. pharmacology, 1958-64; asst. prof. Columbia U. Coll. Physicians and Surgeons, 1964-66, asso. prof., 1966-70, prof., 1970-79, dir. med. scientist tng., 1972-79; prof., chmn. dept. pharmacology Med. Coll. Ga., 1979—, acting v.p. for research, acting dean Sch. Grad. Studies, 1984; vis. prof., NSF fellow Osaka (Japan) U., 1970-71; exchange scientist U.S.-Japan Coop. Cancer Program, 1977; pres. Internat. Kinin Congress, 1984. Contbr. numerous articles to profl. publs. Grantee NIH, 1965—, Health Research Council N.Y.C., 1965-70, Am. Cancer Soc., 1971-75. Mem. Am. Soc. Pharmacology and Exptl. Therapeutics (chmn. public affairs com. 1973-79), Assn. Med. Sch. Pharmacologists (pres. 1982—), Am. Soc. Biol. Chemistry, Am. Coll. Clin. Pharmacology, Am. Chem. Soc., Harvey Soc., AAAS, AAUP, Internat. Soc. Biochem. Pharmacology, Fedn. Am. Socs. Exptl. Biology (chmn. public affairs com. 1977-78), Southeastern Pharmacology Soc. (founder 1980). Research in polypeptides. Discovered leukokinins and T-kinin. Office: Dept Pharmacology Med Coll Ga Augusta GA 30912

GREENBAUM, STUART I., economist, educator; b. N.Y.C., Oct. 7, 1936; s. Sam and Bertha (Freimark) G.; m. Margaret E. Wache, July 29, 1964; children—Regina Gail, Nathan Carl. B.S., NYU, 1958; Ph.D., Johns Hopkins U., 1964. Instr. Johns Hopkins U., Balt., 1960-61, Loyola Coll., 1961-62; fin. economist Fed. Res. Bank of Kansas City, Mo., 1962-66; sr. economist Office of the Comptroller of the Currency, 1966-67; assoc. prof. econs. U. Ky., Lexington, 1968-74, prof., 1974-76, chmn. dept. econs., 1975-76; vis. prof. fin. Kellogg Grad. Sch. Mgmt., Northwestern U., Evanston, 1974-75, prof. fin., 1976—, Harold L. Stuart prof. banking and fin., 1978—; bd. dirs. Banking Research Ctr., 1976—; dir. First Fed. Savs. and Loan Assn. of Chgo., First Family Mortgage Corp. of Fla.; vis. prof. banking and fin. Leon Recanati Grad. Sch. of Bus. Adminstrn., Tel Aviv U., Israel, 1980-81; cons. to various fin. instns., public regulatory agys., and public acctg. firms, 1968—. Assoc. editor: So. Econ. Jour., 1977-79, Jour. of Finance, 1977-83, Jour. of Banking and Finance, 1980—, Jour. Fin. Research, 1981—, Nat. Banking Rev., 1966-67; Contbr. numerous articles on econs. and banking to profl. jours. Served with U.S. Army, 1958. Mem. Am. Econ. Assn., Am. Fin. Assn. Office: Banking Research Center Kellogg Grad Sch Mgmt Northwestern Univ Evanston IL 60201

GREENBERG, ALAN COURTNEY, stock broker; b. Wichita, Kans., Sept. 3, 1927; s. Theodore H. and Esther (Zeligson) G.; div., Aug. 1976; children: Lynne, Theodore. Student, U. Mo., 1949. With Bear, Stearns & Co., N.Y.C., 1949—, gen. ptnr., 1958—, also chief exec. officer. Recipient Lehman award Am. Jewish Com.; named Man of Yr. NCCJ; winner Nat. Bridge Championship, 1977. Mem. Am. Stock Exchange (gov.), Securities Industry Assn. (governing council), Soc. Am. Magicians. Jewish. Clubs: Harmonie; Bond (N.Y.C.); Sunningdale Country (Scarsdale, N.Y.). Office: Bear Stearns & Co 55 Water St New York NY 10041 *

GREENBERG, ALFRED HENRY, magazine editor; b. N.Y.C., Apr. 13, 1924; s. Edward and Sadie C. (Selwyn) G.; m. Adele Z. Rodbard, July 10, 1960; children—Danielle, Michele, Suzanne. A.B., Columbia, 1947; postgrad., U. Paris, 1947-49; M.S., Yeshiva U., 1958. Asst. mng. editor Cotton Trade Jour., Memphis, 1951-54; mng. editor Hosiery and Underwear Rev., 1954-55; sect. editor Women's Wear Daily, 1955-56; editor Chronicle of the UN, 1957-58, McCall Corp., 1958-64; exec. editor Skiing mag., N.Y.C., 1964-70, editor, 1971-74, editor-in-chief, 1974—. Co-author: Comeback, 1974; Translator: Sartre on Cuba, 1961; Contbr. articles to profl. jours. Served with AUS, 1942-45. Home: 71 Beach Ave Larchmont NY 10538 Office: 1 Park Ave New York City NY 10016

GREENBERG, ALLAN, cons.; b. N.Y.C., Dec. 8, 1917; s. Solomon and Rose (Honik) G.; m. Rosalie Katz, Nov. 7, 1943; children—Barbara L. Greenberg Gutman, Roy J. B.S., Coll. City N.Y., 1942; postgrad., U. Wis., 1944, New Sch. for Social Research, 1946-54. Actuary Psychol. Corp., N.Y.C., 1937-38; research analyst Serutan, Inc., Jersey City, 1939-41; research mgr./asst. dir. research Grey Advt., Inc., N.Y.C., 1948-55; sr. v.p., dir. research and planning Doyle Dane Bernbach, Inc., N.Y.C., 1955-74; research cons. to advt. agys. and mfrs., 1974—; faculty City U. N.Y. Grad. Sch.; former chmn. tech. research com. Advt. Research Found. Author: (with Mary Joan Glynn) A Study of Young People; booklet, 1966; Contbr. articles to profl. jours. Pres. mems. council Community Health Program Queens-Nassau. Served with AUS, 1942-45. Mem. Am. Assn. Pub. Opinion Research Am. Marketing Assn. (past dir. N.Y. chpt.), Travel Research Assn. (past dir.), Am. Psychol. Assn., Vol. Urban Cons. Group., B'nai Zion (past mem. nat. exec. bd.; past pres. L.I. region). Home and office: 7 Briarwood Dr Glen Cove NY 11542

GREENBERG, ARTHUR NORMAN, lawyer; b. Detroit, Oct. 4, 1927; s. Nathan and Eva (Magid) G.; m. Audrey Wittert, Aug. 15, 1955; children: Jonathan David, Daniel Lewis, Robert Joel. Student, Stanford, 1945; A.B. with honors, UCLA, 1949, LL.B., 1952. Bar: Calif. 1953. Partner law firm Greenberg, Glusker, Fields, Clamon & Machtinger, Los Angeles, 1959—. Contbr. articles to profl. jours. Bd. govs. Performing Arts Council, Music Center of Los Angeles County, 1980—; chmn. Los Angeles chpt. Am. Jewish Com., 1966-69, mem. nat. exec. bd., 1966—, chmn. nat. interreligious affairs com., 1969-73, nat. v.p., 1970-73, bd. govs., 1970-83, chmn. Western region, 1974-83, mem. dels. to, Israel and Europe, 1965, mem. dels. to, Mexico, 1967, mem. dels. to, S.Am., 1968, mem. dels. to, Israel and Rumania, 1976, mem. dels. to, Egypt and Israel, 1980; Bd. overseers Calif. Sch., Hebrew Union Coll.-Jewish Inst. Religion, 1969—; bd. dirs., mem. exec. com. Los Angeles Jewish Fedn., 1970-74, chmn. legal com., 1970—, mem. community relations com., 1961-73; chmn. Los Angeles attys. div. United Jewish Welfare Fund, 1969, 70; trustee Free Pub. Theatre Found., 1974—; mem. chancellors assos. U. Calif. at Los Angeles; trustee U.C.L.A. Found., 1979—. Served with AUS, 1945-47. Named Alumnus of Year Sch. Law, U.C.L.A., 1978. Mem. Los Angeles Bar Assn., Am. Bar Assn., State Bar Calif., Los Angeles County Mus. Art, Mus. Modern Art N.Y.C., Los Angeles County Bar Found. (dir. 1977-83), Order of Coif, Phi Beta Kappa, Pi Kappa Delta, Pi Sigma Alpha, Pi Gamma Mu. Jewish religion (pres. temple 1970-73). Club: Hillcrest Country (Los Angeles) (dir. 1976—). Office: 1900 Ave of the Stars 20th fl Los Angeles CA 90067

GREENBERG, BEN NORTON, surgeon; b. Omaha, May 30, 1903; s. Samuel and Rose (Coren) G. A.B., U. Nebr., 1925, B.Sc. in Medicine, 1926, M.D., 1928. Diplomate: Nat. Bd. Med. Examiners. Intern U. Nebr. Hosp., 1928-30; postgrad. Manhattan Eye and Ear Hosp., N.Y.C., 1930-32; resident Babies Hosp.-Columbia U. Med. Center, 1933; ship surgeon Am. Export and Grace Steamship Lines, 1934; practice medicine, specializing in eye, ear, nose and throat, York, Nebr., 1934—; staff York Gen. Hosp.; cons. in ophthalmology student health U. Nebr. Chmn. Coordinating Council for Pub. Higher Edn. in Nebr.; mem. nat. adv. council Center Disease Control, Atlanta.; Bd. dirs. Nebr. div. Am. Cancer Soc.; trustee Nebr. Med. Found.; regent U. Nebr., 1953—, pres. bd., 1957, 63, 68, v.p., 1967-70; mem. adv. council Nebr. Center for Regional Progress.; Alt. del. Nat. Republican Conv., 1972. Recipient Distinguished Service award Nat. Assn. Governing Bds. State Univs., 1962, Service to Mankind award Sertoma Internat., 1964, Builders award U. Nebr., 1973, Distinguished Service award U. Nebr. Alumni Assn., 1974. Fellow A.M.A.; mem. A.C.S., Nebr. Med. Assn. (councilor 1955-61), Nat. Assn. Governing Bds. State Univs. and Allied Insts. (pres. 1961-62, pres. found. 1961—), York County Med. Soc. (past pres.). Clubs: Mason, Rotarian (Cadwallader award 1969). Home: 1935 Lincoln Ave Apt B104 York NE 68467 Office: First Nat Bank Bldg York NE 68467

GREENBERG, BERNARD, entomologist, educator; b. N.Y.C., Apr. 24, 1922; s. Isidore and Rose (Gordon) G.; m. Barbara Muriel Dickler, Sept. 1, 1949; children: Gary, Linda, Deborah, Daniel. B.A., Bklyn. Coll., 1944; M.A., U. Kans., 1951, Ph.D., 1954. Asst. prof. biology U. Ill. Med. Center, Chgo., 1954-61, asso. prof., 1961-66, prof., 1966—; vis. sci. Istituto Superiore di Sanitá, Rome, 1960-61, Fulbright-Hays sr. research scholar, 1967-68; vis. sci. Instituto de Salubridad y Enfermedades Tropicales, Mexico City, 1962, 63; cons. in field. Author: Flies and Disease, vol. 1, 1971, vol. 2, 1973; contbr. articles to profl. jours. Served with USAF, 1944-46. NSF grantee, 1959-60, 79-81; NIH grantee, 1960-67; U.S. Army Med. Research and Devel. Command grantee, 1966-72; Electric Power Research Inst. grantee, 1976—; Office Naval Research grantee, 1977-78. Fellow AAAS; mem. Entomol. Soc. Am., AAAS, Scientists Inst. Pub. Info. Home: 1463 E 55th Pl Chicago IL 60637 Office: Dept Biol Scis U Ill Chgo Chicago IL 60680

GREENBERG, BERNARD GEORGE, educator; b. N.Y.C., Oct. 4, 1919; s. Samuel and Lillie (Kidansky) G.; m. Ruth Esther Marck, Apr. 7, 1946; children—Stanley Marc, Frances Kay, Raymond Seth. B.S., CCNY, 1939; Ph.D., N.C. State U., 1949. Chmn. dept. biostats. Sch. Pub. Health, U. N.C., 1949-72, dean, 1972-82, Kenan prof., 1969—; cons. WHO, NIH. Editor: (with A.E. Sarhan) Contributions to Order Statistics; contbr. articles profl. jours. Served to capt., inf. AUS, 1941-46; ETO. Recipient Bronfman prize Am. Pub. Health Assn., 1966; Watson S. Rankin award N.C. Public Health Assn., 1980; Oliver Max Gardner award U. N.C. Bd. Govs., 1981. Fellow Internat. Statis. Inst.; mem. Biometric Soc. (pres. 1971), Am. Statis. Assn., Am. Pub. Health Assn., Inst. Medicine of Nat. Acad. Scis. Jewish. Home: 425 Brookside Dr Chapel Hill NC 27514

GREENBERG, BRADLEY SANDER, educator; b. Toledo, Aug. 3, 1934; s. Abraham and Florence (Cohen) G.; m. Delight Thompson, June 7, 1959; children: Beth, Shawn, Debra. B.A. in Journalism; Univ. scholar, Bowling Green State U., 1956; M.S. in Journalism; Univ. fellow, U. Wis., 1957, Ph.D. in Mass Communications, 1961. Student asst. to pres. Bowling Green State U., 1955-56; project asst., dir. pub. info. Extension div. U. Wis., 1958-59; research asst. Mass Communications Research Center, 1959-60, postdoctoral fellow, 1960-61; lectr. Sch. Journalism, 1960-61; research asso. Inst. Communication Research, Stanford U., 1961-64; vis. asst. prof. dept. journalism U. Calif., Berkeley, 1962-63; asst. prof. Mich. State U., East Lansing, 1964-66, asso. prof., 1966-71, prof. dept. communication, 1971—, chmn. dept., 1977—, prof. telecommunication, 1975—; vis. prof. dept. social psychology London Sch. Econs. and Polit. Sci., 1971-72; vis. prof. dept. sociology Lund U., 1972; vis. prof. Annenberg Sch. Communications, U. So. Calif., 1979; sr. fellow East-West Center, Communication Inst., Honolulu, 1978-79, 81; cons. U.S. Army, Office Chief Info., 1962-72, Pres.'s Commn. on Causes and Prevention Violence, 1968-69, Surgeon Gen.'s Sci. Adv. Com. on TV and Social Behavior, 1970-72, BBC, 1971-72, Corp. Public Broadcasting, 1972-77, Inst. Medicine, Nat. Acad. Sci., 1979-80. Author: (with E.B. Parker) The Kennedy Assassination and the American Public: Social Communication in Crisis, 1965, (with Brenda Dervin) Use of the Mass Media by the Urban Poor, 1970, (with others) An Ascertainment Handbook for Public Broadcasting Facilities, 1975, Life on Television, 1980, Mexican Americans and the Mass Media, 1983; Mem. editorial bds.: Jour. Communication; contbr. chpts. to books, articles to profl. jours. Served to maj. U.S. Army Res., 1973. Recipient Chancellors award for disting. service in journalism U. Wis., 1978, Disting. Faculty award Mich. State U., 1979; named to Journalism Hall of Fame Bowling Green State U., 1980; research grantee NIH, NSF, Office Child Devel., Am. Assn. Advt. Agys., Nat. Assn. Broadcasters, states of Ill., Mich., Wis. Mem. Internat. Communications Assn., Assn. for Edn. in Journalism. Home: 2049 Ashland Ave Okemos MI 48864 Office: Dept Communication 473B Communication Arts and Scis Mich State U East Lansing MI 48824

GREENBERG, BYRON STANLEY, newspaper and business executive, consultant; b. Bklyn., June 17, 1919; s. Albert and Bertha (Getleson) G.; m. Helena Marks, Feb. 10, 1946; children: David, Eric, Randy. Student, Bklyn. Coll., 1936-41. Circulation mgr. N.Y. Post, 1956-62, circulation dir., 1962-63, bus. mgr., 1963-72, gen. mgr., 1973-79; sec. N.Y. Post Corp., 1966-75, treas., 1975-76, v.p., 1976—; v.p., dir. Leisure Systems, Inc., 1978-80; pres., chief exec. officer, dir. Games Mgmt. Services, Inc., 1979-80. Bd. dirs. 92d St YMHA, 1970-71, Friars Nat. Found., 1981-82. Served with AUS, 1942-45. Club: Friars. Home: 2560 S Grade Rd Alpine CA 92001 Office: 210 South St New York NY 10002

GREENBERG, CARL, journalist; b. Boston, Aug. 19, 1908; s. Harry and Fannie (Herman) G.; m. Gladys Bilansky, July 12, 1930; 1 son, Howard Allan. Student extension div., UCLA, 1927. Reporter Los Angeles Evening Express, 1926-28, City News Service of Los Angeles, 1928-33, Los Angeles Examiner, 1933-43, polit. editor, 1943-62; polit. writer Los Angeles Times, 1962-66, 68-73, polit. editor, 1966-68, mem. editorial bd., 1962-68. Disaster acting gov., Calif., 1959-67; past bd. dirs. 8-Ball Welfare Found. Served as coxswain USCGR, World War II. Recipient 1st prize for best news story So. Calif. Newspaper Writers, Los Angeles chpt. Theta Sigma Phi, 1944; Silver award Calif.-Nev. Asso. Press, 1957; co-recipient Pulitzer prize for gen. local reporting, 1966. Mem. Order of Hound's Tooth (charter), Coast Guard League, Eureka (Ill.) Community Assn. (hon. life), Soc. Profl. Journalists, Sigma Delta Chi, Kappa Tau Alpha., B'nai B'rith. Club: Greater Los Angeles Press (hon. life). Home: 6001 Canterbury Dr Culver City CA 90230 *In nearly a half-century of reporting, I, as others of my profession, have sought to preserve a free press against the assaults such as we now are witnessing.*

GREENBERG, CARL, lawyer; b. Newark, Oct. 13, 1934; s. Isadore and Mollie (Starr) G.; m. Barbara Fisher, June 9, 1959; children—Jill Robin, Wendy Beth, Deborah Amy. A.B., Rutgers U., 1956, J.D., 1959. Bar: N.J. bar 1960. Law sec. to judge N.J. Superior Ct., 1960-61; asso. firm Schreiber, Lancaster & Demos, Newark, 1961-64, partner, 1964-67; asso. firm Samuel A. Gennett, Newark, 1967-68; partner firm Porzio, Bromberg and Newman, Morristown, N.J., 1968—; lectr. trial practice and procedure N.J. Inst. Continuing Legal Edn., 1965—; adj. prof. Rutgers Law Sch., 1969—. Editor: Rutgers Law Rev, 1957-59. Served with U.S. Army, 1959. Fellow Am. Coll. Trial Lawyers, Am. Bar Found.; mem. Am. Arbitration Assn. (panel), Am., N.J., Essex County, Morris County bar assns., N.J. Trial Attys. Assn. Home: 5 Lenox Terr South Orange NJ 07079 Office: 163 Madison Ave Morristown NJ 07960

GREENBERG, DANIEL BEN, rental and leasing company executive; b. Mpls., May 14, 1941; s. Mayer and Ruth (Cooperman) G. A.B., Reed Coll., Portland, Oreg., 1962; J.D., U. Chgo., 1965. Bar: Calif. 1966. Staff atty. Calif. Dept. Water Resources, Sacramento, 1965-67; with Telecor Inc., Beverly Hills, Calif., 1967-80, sr. v.p., then sec., 1971-79, pres., chief exec. officer, 1979-80; also dir.; chmn. bd., chief exec. officer Electro Rent Corp., 1979—; dir. Nev. Savs. and Loan Assn. Trustee Center Law in Public Interest, 1973-78, Reed Coll., 1975—, Sierra Club Legal Def. Fund, 1978—; mem. contemporary arts council Los Angeles County Mus. Art, 1977-82; bd. dirs. CARE, Inc., 1981. Mem. Calif. Bar Assn., Los Angeles County Bar Assn., Am. Bus. Conf. (founding). Clubs: Calif. Yacht, Regency. Address: 3340 Ocean Park Blvd Suite 1000 Santa Monica CA 90405

GREENBERG, FRANK S., textile company executive; b. 1929;. Ph.B., U. Chgo., 1949. Asst. to pres. Charm Tred Mills, 1949, v.p., 1953, pres., 1953-59; v.p. Charm Tred Mills div. Burlington Industries, Inc., 1959-61, pres., 1961-62, pres. Monticello Carpet Mill div., 1962-70, group v.p., mem. mgmt. com. parent co. Monticello Carpet Mill div., Greensboro, N.C., 1970-72, exec. v.p. Monticello Carpet Mill div., 1972-78, pres. Monticello Carpet Mill div., 1978—. Served with AUS, 1951-53. Address: Burlington Industries Inc 3330 W Friendly Ave Greensboro NC 27410 *

GREENBERG, GEORGE, mill company executive; b. 1922; married. With Seaberg, Inc. (acquired by Guilford Mills Inc.), to 1967; v.p. mktg. Guilford Mills, Inc., Greensboro, N.C., 1967-70, exec. v.p., 1970-76, pres., chief operating officer, 1976—, also dir. Office: Guilford Mills Inc 4925 W Market St Box U-4 Greensboro NC 27402 *

GREENBERG, HOWARD, consultant; b. N.Y.C.; s. Jacob Mayer and Rose (Stein) G.; m. Rose Kaufman; 1 dau., Cynthia Irene. B.C.S. with highest honors, Benjamin Franklin U., 1937, M.C.S., 1938. Chief budget and finance Civilian Conservation Corps, Dept. Interior, 1935-41; financial and adminstrv. mgmt. OPA, 1942-46; owner retail food market, 1946; dep. dir. budget War Assets Adminstrn., 1946-48; pres. wholesale-retail liquor corp., 1949; with budget office HHFA, 1950; with Gen. Services Adminstrn., 1951-53, 54-62, 63-66, commnr. utilization and disposal service, 1963-66; dep. comptroller Small Bus. Adminstrn., 1953, dep. adminstr. for investment, 1966-67, dep. adminstr., 1967-69; dir. found. study, com. on small bus. U.S. Ho. of Reps., 1969-70, staff and exec. dir., 1970-74, cons., 1974-75, pvt. cons., 1976—; asso. dir. charge mgmt. Peace Corps, 1962-63; asst. prof. accounting Benjamin Franklin U., 1937-44; lectr. Civil Service Commn., insts., 1959-69; cons. chief staff U.S. Army, 1949. Recipient Outstanding Achievement award Fed. Govt. Accountants Assn., 1963; Meritorious Service award Gen. Services Adminstrn., 1961; Distinguished Service award, 1967; Adminstrs. Spl. Service award, 1968; both Small Bus. Adminstrn.; Outstanding and Meritorious Service award Com. on Small Bus., U.S. Ho. of Reps., 1974. Democrat. Jewish. Home: 15121 Glade Dr Silver Spring MD 20906 *Awareness of others' needs and ambitions—Striving to perform beyond my capabilities and not demeaning other persons' performances- Equal treatment of superiors, peers and subordinates—Diplomatically requiring professional and personal respect.*

GREENBERG, IRWIN MORTON, psychiatrist; b. Bklyn., Sept. 21, 1930; s. Max and Clara (Passweg) G. B.A. summa cum laude, N.Y. U., 1951, M.D., 1955; D.M.S.; USPHS fellow, SUNY, Downstate Med. Center, 1968. Intern L.I. Coll. Hosp., 1955-56; resident Bronx Municipal Hosp. Center-Albert Einstein Coll. Medicine, 1956-58, NIMH, 1959-60, clin. assoc., 1958-60; psychiatrist Hillside Hosp., Glen Oaks, N.Y., 1960-67; chief of service Bronx State Hosp., 1967-68, dep. dir., 1968-69; dir. Creedmoor State Hosp., Queens Village, N.Y., 1969-72; dir. psychiat. services Waterbury (Conn.) Hosp., 1972—; asst. clin. prof. psychiatry Albert Einstein Coll. Medicine, 1967-72; adj. prof. psychology York Coll., Queens, N.Y., 1970-72; assoc. clin. prof. psychiatry Yale U. Sch. Medicine, 1972—; fellow Pierson Coll., Yale, 1972-78; cons. staff Yale-New Haven Hosp., 1972—, West Haven VA Hosp., 1972, St. Mary's Hosp., 1975, St. Raphael's Hosp., 1976; Mem. com. Conn. Ambulatory Care Study, 1973; mem. Northwest Conn. Regional Mental Health Bd., 1975—, Central Naugatuck Valley Mental Health Council, 1975—, N.W. Conn. Region V Task Force, 1977; mem. regional program planning com. Conn. Dept. Mental Health, 1979; bd. dirs. N.W. Conn. Health Systems Agy., 1980—; mem. Conn. Gov.'s Spl. Task Force on Mental Health Policy, 1982. Dedication of Irwin M. Greenberg Adminstrn. Bldg. Creedmoor Psychiat. Center, Queens Village, N.Y., 1981. Fellow Am. Psychiat. Assn.; mem. AMA, AAAS, Am. Psychol. Assn., Conn. Hosp. Assn. (chmn. mental health com., council on mgmt. and planning 1981—). Address: Waterbury Hospital Robbins St Waterbury CT 06720

GREENBERG, JACK, lawyer; b. N.Y.C., Dec. 22, 1924; s. Max and Bertha (Rosenberg) G.; m. Sema Ann Tanzer, Feb. 19, 1950 (div. 1970); children: Josiah, David, Sarah, Ezra; m. Deborah M. Cole, 1970; children: Suzanne, William Cole. A.B., Columbia, 1945, LL.B., 1948; LL.D., Morgan State Coll., Central State Coll., 1965, Lincoln U., 1977. Bar: N.Y. 1949. Research asst. N.Y. State Law Revision Commn., 1949; asst. counsel NAACP Legal Def. and Ednl. Fund, 1949-61, dir.-counsel, 1961—; argued in sch. segregation, sit-in, employment discrimination, poverty, capital punishment, other cases before U.S. Supreme Ct.; adj. prof. Columbia Law Sch., 1970—; vis. lectr. Yale Law Sch., 1971; vis. prof. CCNY, 1977; lectr. Harvard Law Sch., 1983, Shikes fellow, 1981; cons. Center Applied Legal Studies, U. Witwatersrand, 1978. Author: (with H. Hill) Citizens Guide to Desegregation, 1955, Race Relations and American Law, 1959, Judicial Process and Social Change, 1976; contbg. author: Race, Sex and Religious Discrimination in International Law, 1981; Contbr. articles to legal jours. Bd. dirs. N.Y.C. Legal Aid Soc., Internat. League for Human Rights, Mexican Am. Legal Def. Fund, 1968-75, Asian Am. Legal Def. Fund, 1980—. Served to lt. (j.g.) USNR, 1943-46. Co-recipient Grenville Clark prize, 1978; Hon. fellow U. Pa. Law Sch., 1975. Fellow Am. Coll. Trial Lawyers; mem. ABA (commn. to study FTC, adv. com. to spl. com. on crime prevention, sect. on individual rights and responsibilities), N.Y. State Bar Assn. (exec. dir. spl. com. study state antitrust laws 1956), Am. Law Inst., Bar Assn. City N.Y. (Cardozo lectr. 1973), Adminstrv. Conf. U.S. Home: 1172 Park Ave New York NY 10128 Office: 99 Hudson St New York NY 10015

GREENBERG, JERROLD SELIG, health education educator; b. N.Y.C., Jan. 19, 1942; s. David and Bess G.; m. Karen Lider, Aug. 29, 1970; children: Todd, Keri. B.S., CCNY, 1964, M.S., 1965; Ed.D., Syracuse U., 1969. Tchr. N.Y.C. and Syracuse Pub. Sch. Dists., 1964-67; instr. Syracuse U., 1968-69; asst. prof. Boston U., 1969-71; prof. health edn. SUNY, Buffalo, 1971-79, U. Md., 1979—. Author: Student Centered Health Instruction: A Humanistic Approach, 1978, Health Through Discovery, 1980, 2d edit., 1983, Sex Education: Theory and Practice, 1981, Comprehensive Stress Management, 1983; assoc. editor: Jour. of Sch. Health, 1978-80; contbg. editor: Health Education, 1974-76; Contbr. articles to profl. jours. Served with U.S. Army, 1967. Western N.Y. chpt. Am. Heart Assn. grantee, 1977-78; Research Found. of SUNY grantee, 1979-80. Fellow Am. Sch. Health Assn., Soc. Sci. Study Sex; mem. Am. Public Health Assn., Assn. Advancement Health Edn. Jewish. Home: 9412 Reach Rd Potomac MD 20854 Office: U Md College Park MD 20742

GREENBERG, JOANNE, author; b. Bklyn., Sept. 24, 1932; d. Julius Lester and Rosalie (Bernstein) Goldenberg; m. Albert Greenberg, Sept. 4, 1955; children—David, Alan. B.A., Am. U., 1955. Tchr. exptl. class etymology Jefferson County (Colo.) Sch. System, 1963—. Author: The King's Persons, 1963 (Daroff Meml. award fiction 1963), I Never Promised You A Rose Garden, 1964 (Fromm-Reichmann award Am. Acad. Psychoanalysis 1967), The Monday Voices, 1965, Summering, 1966, In This Sign, 1970 (Kenner and Christopher awards 1971), Rites of Passage, 1972, Founder's Praise, 1976, High Crimes and Misdemeanors, 1979, Season of Delight, 1981 (Rocky Mountain Woman's Inst. award 1983), The Far Side of Victory, 1983. Address: 29221 Rainbow Hills Rd Golden CO 80401

GREENBERG, JOSEPH H., anthropology; b. Bklyn., May 28, 1915; s. Jacob and Florence (Pilzer) G.; m. Selma Berkowitz, Nov. 23, 1940. A.B., Columbia, 1936; Ph.D. in Anthropology, Northwestern U., 1940; D.Sci. (hon.), Northwestern U., 1982. Faculty U. Minn., 1946-48; asst. prof. Columbia, 1948-53, asso. prof., 1953-57, prof. anthropology, 1957-62; prof. Stanford, 1962—, Ray Lyman Wilbur prof. social scis. in anthropology, 1971; dir. Nat. Def. Edn. Act. African Lang. and Area Center, 1967—; Vis. prof. Summer Linguistic Inst., Mich. U., 1957, U. Minn., 1960; mem. panel anthropology and philosophy and history of sci. NSF, 1959-61; vis. prof. summer inst. U. Colo., 1961; dir. West African Langs. Survey, 1959—; Linguistic Soc. Am. prof. Summer Linguistic Inst., Oswego, N.Y., 1976. Author: Languages of Africa, 1963, Essays in Linguistics, 1957, Universals of Language, 1963, Influence of Islam on a Sudanese Religion, 1946, Anthropological Linguistics: An Introduction, 1968, Language, Culture and Communication: Essays by Joseph H. Greenberg, 1971, Language Typology, 1974, A New Invitation to Linguistics, 1977, Universals of Human Language, 4 vols, 1978; co-editor: Word, 1950-54. Served with Signal Intelligence Corp. AUS, 1940-45. Social Sci. Research Council fellow Northwestern U., 1940; Stanford fellow, 1958-59; Ford Found. grantee, 1952, 57-62; recipient Demobilization award Social Sci. Research Council, 1945-46; Guggenheim award, 1954-55; Haile Selassie award for African research, 1967; award in behavioral scis. N.Y. Acad. Scis., 1980. Mem. Am. Anthrop. Assn. (rep. to gov. bd. Internat. Inst. 1955—, 1st distinguished lectr. 1970), Linguistic Soc. Am. (exec. com. 1953-55, v.p. 1976, pres. 1977), West African Linguistics Soc. (chmn. 1965-66), African Studies Assn. (exec. com., also com. on langs. and linguistics 1959—, pres. 1964-65), Nat. Acad. Scis., Am. Acad. Arts and Scis., Am. Philos. Soc., Phi Beta Kappa. Home: 860 Mayfield Ave Stanford CA 94305

GREENBERG, JOSHUA F., lawyer, law educator; b. Bklyn., Feb. 27, 1933; s. Emil and Betty (Fierer) G.; m. Reva Frances Messeloff, June 28, 1959; children: Elizabeth, James, Anne. B.A., Columbia U., 1954, LL.B., 1956. Bar: N.Y. 1956. Assoc. firm Kaye, Scholer, Fierman,

Hays & Handler, N.Y.C., 1956-65, ptnr., 1966—; chmn. antitrust workshop Practising Law Inst., N.Y.C., 1969—; adj. prof. NYU Law Sch., N.Y.C., 1970—. Pres. Camp Ella Fohs, N.Y.C., 1965—. Mem. ABA (council antitrust law sect. 1981—), N.Y. State Bar Assn. (chmn. antitrust law sect. 1971). Jewish. Office: Kaye Scholer Fierman Hays & Handler 425 Park Ave New York NY 10022

GREENBERG, LEONARD ELI, recreational products company executive; b. New Haven, 1927. Grad., Trinity Coll., 1948. Chmn. Coleco Industries, Inc., Hartford, Conn. Office: Coleco Industries Inc 945 Asylum Ave Hartford CT 06105 *

GREENBERG, MARTIN GARY, broadcasting company executive; b. Bklyn., Apr. 6, 1941; s. Aaron W. and Beatrice (Hirschklau) G.; m. Elin Bank, Apr. 7, 1963; children: Corey Jon, Mark David, Jennifer Char. Student, Bklyn. Coll., 1958-62; B.A., N.Y. Inst. Tech., 1962. Promotion asst. Radio Sta. WMCA, N.Y.C., 1962-64; promotion dir. Radio Sta. WXYZ, Detroit, 1964, local salesman, 1965, nat. sales mgr., 1966-67, gen. sales mgr., 1971-73, Radio Sta. KXYZ, Houston, 1968-71; v.p., gen. mgr. Radio Sta. WLS, Chgo., 1973-79; pres. ABC FM Stas., N.Y.C., 1979-82; v.p., dir. Belo Broadcasting, Dallas, 1982—; dir. WLS, Inc.; bd. govs. ABC Contemporary Network. Bd. dirs. Nr. North Family Guidance Center, Chgo. Recipient Five to Watch award Detroit chpt. Am. Women in Radio and Television, 1966, First Place award Chgo. Women in Broadcasting, 1976; named Gen. Mgr. of Year Hall Radio Report, 1976. Pres. Greater Chgo. Radio Broadcasters Assn.; bd. dirs. Ill. Broadcasters Assn. Jewish. Club: Ill. Racquetball. Home: 3525 Hanover Dallas TX 75225 Office: 1330 Ave of Americas New York NY

GREENBERG, MAURICE RAYMOND, insurance company executive; b. N.Y.C., May 4, 1925; s. Jacob and Ada (Rheingold) G.; m. Corinne Phyllis Zuckerman, Nov. 12, 1950; children: Jeffrey W., Evan G., Lawrence S., Cathleen J. Pre-law cert., U. Miami, Fla., 1948; LL.B., N.Y. Law Sch., 1950, J.D. (hon.), 1972, New Eng. Sch. Law, 1970. Bar: N.Y. 1953. With Continental Casualty Co., 1952-60; v.p. C.V. Starr & Co., Inc., 1961-66, exec. v.p., 1966-68, pres., dir., 1968—, Am. Internat. Group, 1967—, also chief exec. officer; chmn., dir. Transatlantic Reins. Co., N.Am. Mgrs. Inc. Trustee N.Y. Hosp., N.Y.U. Served to capt. U.S. Army, World War II, Korea. Decorated Bronze Star. Mem. N.Y. Bar Assn., Fgn. Policy Assn., Council Fgn. Relations, Sigma Alpha Mu. Clubs: City Athletic, Sky, India House (N.Y.C.); Georgetown. Office: 70 Pine St New York NY 10270

GREENBERG, MAXWELL ELFRED, lawyer; b. Los Angeles, Mar. 11, 1922; s. Abe Lewis and Annette Friedman G.; m. Marcie Caplan, Mar. 27, 1945; children: Jan (Mrs. Meldon E. Levine), Richard E. A.B. cum laude, UCLA, 1941; LL.B. magna cum laude, Harvard U., 1949. Bar: Calif. 1950, Ill. 1959. Practiced law, Los Angeles, 1950—; research atty. Justice Roger Traynor, Calif. Supreme Ct., San Francisco, 1949-50; assoc. Pacht, Warne, Ross & Bernhard, Los Angeles, 1950-53; sr. mem. Greenberg, Bernhard, Weiss, Rosin & Fern, Inc., Los Angeles, 1954—; pres. Greater Ariz. Savs. & Loan Assn., Phoenix, 1961-66, chmn. bd., 1966-72, chmn. exec. com., 1972-73; adj. prof. law UCLA, 1972-74; dir. United Realty Investors, Inc. Author, editor, pub.: various legal outlines Calif. Bar Rev. Course, 1953-73. Nat. chmn. Anti-Defamation League, 1978-82; hon. chmn., 1983—; chmn. community relations com., v.p. Jewish Fedn.-Council Greater Los Angeles, 1975-77; chmn. bd. Rural Devel. Corp., 1969-70; v.p. Los Angeles Police Commn., 1980—. Served to 1st. lt. AUS, 1942-46. Mem. State Bar Calif., Ill., Am. bar assns., Phi Beta Kappa, Pi Gamma Mu, Pi Lambda Phi. Democrat. Home: 10701 Wilshire Blvd Los Angeles CA 90024 Office: Greenberg Bernhard Weiss Rosin & Fern Inc 1880 Century Park East Los Angeles CA 90067

GREENBERG, MELVIN NATHANIEL, lawyer; b. Newark, Oct. 22, 1928; s. Irving and Lena (Vinocur) G.; m. Elsa Stein, Jan. 20, 1957; children: Dianne, Carol Anne, Michael Ivan. B.A., N.Y. U., 1949, LL.M.; Kennison fellow, 1955; LL.B. with honors, U. Fla., 1952, J.D., 1967. Bar: Fla. 1952. Partner firm Morehead, Forrest, Gotthardt & Greenberg, Miami, Fla., 1955-60, Greenberg & Saks, Miami, 1960-67; partner, pres. firm Greenberg, Traurig, Askew, Hoffman, Lipoff, Rosen & Quentel, P.A., Miami, 1967; lectr. bus. law Fla. State U., 1953-54; bd. visitors; adj. prof. law U. Miami, 1966-75, N.Y. U., 1978—; adv. com. N.Y. U. Ann. Inst. Fed. Taxation, Nat. Citizens Adv. Com. for Support of Med. Edn., U. Miami Inst. Estate Planning; lectr. in field. Trustee U. Miami, chmn. vis. com. med. div.; bd. dirs. Nat. Children's Cardiac Hosp.; mem. Pres.'s Council U. Fla.; chmn. Citizens Advisory Bd., Miami.; trustee Jackson Meml. Hosp. Served to capt. USAF, 1952-54. Fellow Am. Coll. Tax Counsel; mem. Am., Dade County bar assns.; Mem. Fla. Bar, Greater Miami Tax Inst. Jewish. Clubs: Standard, Royal Palm Tennis, Westview Country., City. Home: 4770 Davis Rd Miami FL 33143 Office: 1401 Brickell Ave Miami FL 33131

GREENBERG, MICHAEL JOHN, zoologist, educator; b. N.Y.C., Sept. 28, 1931; s. Abraham S. and Lena (Kirsch) G.; m. Rima Robbins, June 10, 1954; children: Peter A., John K., Karl P. A.B., Cornell U., 1953; M.A., Fla. State U., 1955; Ph.D., Harvard U., 1958. Instr. zoology U. Ill., Urbana, 1958-60, asst. prof., 1960-64; asso. prof. biol. scis. Fla. State U., Tallahassee, 1965-73, prof., 1973-81, dir. marine lab., 1978-80; sci. dir. C.V. Whitney Lab. for Exptl. Marine Biology and Medicine, U. Fla., St. Augustine, 1980—; prof. pharmacology U. Fla. Coll. Medicine, 1981—; vis. prof. Hiroshima U. Med. Sch., 1978; vis. prof. zoology U. Hong Kong, 1981; instr. exptl. invertebrate zoology Marine Biol. Lab., Woods Hole, Mass., summers 1969-73, course dir., 1975-77; mem. adv. screening com. Internat. Exchange of Scholars, 1976-78; mem. regulatory biology panel NSF, 1983—. Editorial bd.: Jour. Exptl. Zoology, 1974-77, 83—, Comparative Gen. Pharmacology, 1970—, Physiol. Zoology, 1975—, The Physiology Tchr, 1977-78, Molecular and Cellular Neurobiology, 1979—, Marine Biology Letters, 1979—, Ency. of Sci. and Tech, 1979-81. Mem. Dangerous Drugs and Alcohol Abuse, 1970-72. Recipient grants Nat. Heart and Lung Inst., NIH, 1960—; NSF sr. postdoctoral fellow U. Melbourne, Australia, 1964-65, Misaki Marine Lab., Japan, 1965. Fellow AAAS (mem.-at-large sect. G com. 1979—); mem. Am. Soc. Zoologists (div. program officer 1969-70, div. chmn. 1976-77, co-chmn. joint task force with Am. Physiol. Soc. 1977-78), Am. Physiol. Soc., Am. Soc. Pharmacology and Exptl. Therapeutics, Soc. Gen. Physiologists, Marine Biol. Lab., Woods Hole, Soc. Exptl. Biology (U.K.), Tallahassee, Sopchoppy and Gulf Coast Marine Biol. Assn. (pres. 1967—), Sigma Delta Chi. Home: Rt 1 Box 112B Saint Augustine FL 32086

GREENBERG, MILTON, corporation executive; b. Carteret, N.J., Apr. 21, 1918; s. David and Eva (Salzer) G.; m. Maxine Carol Baer, June 30, 1948; children: Eve Diane, David Max, Alan Baer. Student, CCNY, 1934-40; B.A., NYU, 1943; M.P.A., Harvard U., 1954; Sc.D. (hon.), Canaan Coll., 1961, Merrimack Coll., North Andover, Mass., 1981. Research and devel. planner Air Force Cambridge Research Center, 1947-49, dep. dir. operations and planning, 1947-54, dir., 1954-58; pres. GCA Corp., 1958-80, pres., chmn., chief exec. officer, 1980—; First chmn. tech. mgmt. council Air Research and Devel. Command, 1957-58; U.S. del. to XIth Gen. Assembly, Internat. Union Geodesy & Geophysics, 1957; mem. Upper-Air Rocket & Satellite Research Panel; mem. central radio propagation lab. adv. panel of Nat. Acad. Scis., 1963-1968; dir., mem. exec. com. Mass. Tech. Park Corp., 1982—. Editor-in-chief: Planetary and Space Science, 1957-62; editorial adv. bd., 1962-75. Bd. dirs. Mass. High Tech. Council, 1978—, mem. exec. com., 1981—; Selectman Town of Andover, Mass., 1971-77; Trustee Canaan (N.H.) Coll., 1960-72, Merrimack Coll., 1983—. Served from cadet to maj. USAAF, 1943-47; geophysicist. Recipient Exceptional Civilian Service medal USAF, 1957. Asso. fellow AIAA; fellow AAAS; mem. Am. Geophys. Union, Am. Meteorol. Soc., Presidents Assn., Sigma Xi, Mu Chi Sigma, Beta Lambda Sigma. Home: 46 Sagamore Dr Andover MA 01810 Office: GCA Corp Burlington Rd Bedford MA 01730

GREENBERG, MILTON, political science educator; b. Bklyn., Feb. 20, 1927; s. Samuel and Fannie (Schnell) G.; m. Sonia B. Brown, June 20, 1948; children: Anne Greenberg Bookin, Nancy R. B.A., Bklyn. Coll., 1949; M.A., U. Wis., 1950, Ph.D. (univ. scholar), 1955. Instr. polit. sci. U. Tenn., Knoxville, 1952-55; asst. prof. Western Mich. U., Kalamazoo, 1955-59, asso. prof., 1959-64, prof., 1964, chmn. polit. sci. dept., 1965-69; dean Coll. Arts and Scis., Ill. State U., Normal, 1969-72; v.p. acad. affairs, dean faculties Roosevelt U., Chgo., 1972-80; provost, v.p. acad. affairs Am. U., Washington, 1980—; research asso. Cleve. Met. Services Commn., 1957; cons. Citizens for Mich. (constl. reform movement), 1960. Author: (with J.C. Plano) The American Political Dictionary, 1962, 6th edit., 1982, (with others) The Political Science Dictionary, 1973; contbr. to Colliers Yearbook, 1959—; contbr. articles to profl. jours. Mem. Mich. Gov.'s Commn. on Legis. Apportionment, 1962, Kalamazoo Community Relations Bd., 1964-65; mem. council Combined Health Appeal of Nat. Capital Area, 1982, v.p., 1983—. Social Sci. Research Council grantee, 1959, 61. Mem. Am. Polit. Sci. Assn., Midwest Polit. Sci. Assn. (exec. council 1972-75), Law and Soc. Assn., AAUP, Am. Assn. Higher Edn., N. Central Assn. Colls. and Schs. (commn. on instns. higher edn. 1975-80, exec. bd. 1979-80, cons.-evaluator 1975-80), Nat. Council Chief Acad. Officers, Am. Council on Edn. (exec. com. 1983—). Office: Am U Massachusetts and Nebraska Aves NW Washington DC 20016

GREENBERG, NAT, orchestra administrator; b. Warsaw, Poland, May 25, 1918; came to U.S., 1928, naturalized, 1943; s. Henry and Polly (Luj) G.; m. Anne Goodhart, July 19, 1941; 1 dau., Betty Jeanne. B.S., CCNY, 1941. Gen. mgr. Ft. Wayne (Ind.) Philharm., 1959-66, Rochester (N.Y.) Philharm., 1966-68; mgr. Columbus (Ohio) Symphony, 1968-76; mng. dir. San Antonio Symphony, 1976-82; mgr. Kansas City (Mo.) Symphony, 1982—; cons. Nat. Endowment for Arts, N.Y. State Arts Council, Ohio Arts Council. Bass player, Pitts., Buffalo, Kansas City, N.Y. symphonies, 1940-59. Bd. dirs. Am. Symphony Orch. League. Mem. Internat. Soc. Performing Arts Adminstrs., Assn. Coll., Univ. and Community Arts Adminstrs. Club: Rotary. Home: 801 E Armour Blvd Kansas City MO 64109 Office: 1029 Central St Kansas City MO 64105

GREENBERG, NATHAN, accountant; b. Worcester, Mass., May 17, 1919; s. Samuel and Ida (Katz) G.; m. Mimi Aaron, Mar. 12, 1950 (dec.); children: Henry Aaron, Ruthanne; m. Barbara Rudnick, Feb. 9, 1979. B.S. in Bus. Adminstrn, Boston U., 1942. C.P.A., Mass. With Internal Revenue Service, 1945-47; v.p. finance, dir. Gt. Am. Plactics Co., Worcester, Mass., 1948-68, Gt. Am. Chem. Corp., Fitchburg, Mass., 1968-80; chmn. Greenberg, Rosenblatt & Assos., P.C., C.P.A.s, Worcester, 1958—. Trustee Nathan and Barbara Greenberg Charitable Trust, Jewish Home for Aged, Jewish Community Center, Jewish Fedn. Served with AUS, 1942-45; ETO. Decorated Bronze Star. Fellow Am. Inst. C.P.A.'s, Mass. Soc. C.P.A.'s, Controllers Inst. Am.; mem. Mu Sigma. Club: Mt. Pleasant Country (Boylston, Mass.) (v.p. 1962—). Home: 85 Aylesbury Rd Worcester MA 01609 Office: 390 Main St Worcester MA 01608

GREENBERG, OSCAR WALLACE, educator, physicist; b. N.Y.C., Feb. 18, 1932; s. Joseph Jacob and Betty (Sklower) G.; m. Yael Shapiro, May 27, 1969; children—Joshua Daniel, Jeremy Hillel, Benjamin Gideon. B.S., Rutgers U., 1952; A.M., Princeton, 1954, Ph.D., 1957. Instr. Brandeis U., 1956-57; NSF postdoctoral fellow Mass. Inst. Tech., 1959-61; faculty U. Md., College Park, 1961—, prof. physics, 1967—; Mem. Inst. Advanced Study, fall 1964-65; vis. asso. prof. Rockefeller U., 1965-66; vis. prof. Tel-Aviv U., 1968-69, Johns Hopkins U., fall, 1977, NASA/Goddard Space Flight Center, spring 1978. Divisional asso. editor: Phys. Rev. Letters, 1976-78. Served to 1st lt. USAF, 1957-59. Recipient award in phys. scis. Washington Acad. Scis., 1971; Sloan research fellow, 1964-66; Guggenheim fellow, 1968-69. Fellow Am. Phys. Soc.; mem. Am. Math. Soc., Phi Beta Kappa. Home: 902 Kenbrook Dr Silver Spring MD 20902 Office: Dept Physics Astronomy Univ Md College Park MD 20742

GREENBERG, PAUL, newspaperman; b. Shreveport, La., Jan. 21, 1937; s. Ben and Sara (Ackerman) G.; m. Carolyn Levy, Dec. 6, 1964; children: Daniel, Ruth Elizabeth. B. Journalism, U. Mo., 1958, M.A. in History, 1959; student, Columbia Grad. Sch., 1960-62. Lectr. Am. history Hunter Coll., 1962; editorial page editor Pine Bluff (Ark.) Comml., 1962-66, 67—; syndicated columnist, 1970—; editorial writer Chgo. Daily News, 1966-67; adj. faculty in history U. Ark., Pine Bluff, 1978-82. Served to capt. U.S. Army, 1969. Recipient Grenville Clark award for best editorial, 1964, Pulitzer prize editorial writing, 1969, award Nat. Newspaper Assn., 1968, U. Mo. Sch. Journalism award, 1983. Republican. Jewish. Office: 300 Beech St Pine Bluff AR 71601

GREENBERG, PAUL WILLIAM, television journalist; b. N.Y.C., Apr. 6, 1933; s. Henry and Rose (Perlmutter) G.; m. Alice Pullman, Nov. 23, 1956; children: Judith, Seth. B.A., U. Mich., 1954; M.S. in Journalism, Columbia U., 1957. Writer, Sta. WIIC-TV, Pitts., 1957-61; reporter, writer, producer, ABC News, N.Y.C., 1961-64; writer, producer, CBS-NEWS, N.Y.C., 1964-72, 75-78; exec. producer, 1972-75; spl. events exec. producer, NBC News, N.Y.C., 1978-79; exec. producer: Nightly News, 1979—. Served with U.S. Army, 1954-56. Mem. Writers Guild Am., Dirs. Guild Am. Club: The Coffee House. Home: 165 West End Ave New York NY 10023 Office: NBC News 30 Rockefeller Plaza New York NY 10020

GREENBERG, ROBERT I., newspaper editor; b. N.Y.C., Aug. 26, 1930; s. Aaron and Ida (Miller) G.; m. Gail Ruth Fischer, Aug. 31, 1958; children: Laurence, Tedi. B.A. in Journalism, U. Okla., 1952; postgrad., Columbia U., 1952-53. Reporter, sports editor Lawton (Okla.) Constn.-Press, 1955-56, White Plains (N.Y.) Reporter-Dispatch, 1956-57; reporter Phila. Daily News, 1957; successively reporter, night, day, city and met. editor, asst. mng. editor features Phila. Inquirer, 1957—; cons. Acad. Natural Scis., 1967-68. Contbr. articles to mags. Served with AUS, 1953-55. Mem. Phia. Art Alliance, Pa. AP Mng. Editors Assn. (dir.), Assn. Am. Artists, Newspaper Features Council Am. (vice-chmn.), U. Okla. Assn., Sigma Delta Chi. Jewish. Home: 602 Stratford Dr Moorestown NJ 08057 Office: 400 N Broad St Philadelphia PA 19101

GREENBERG, SANFORD DAVID, corp. exec.; b. Buffalo, Dec. 13, 1940; s. Carl and Sarah (Fox) G.; m. Susan Beth Roseno, Aug. 12, 1962; children—Paul Eric, James Albert, Kathryn Lynne. A.B., Columbia, 1962, M.B.A., 1966; M.A., Ph.D.; Woodrow Wilson fellow Woodrow Wilson Dissertation fellow, Harvard, 1965; postgrad., Law Sch., 1965-66; Marshal scholar, Oxford (Eng.) U., 1964-65. Mng. partner Compressed Speech Co., 1961—; asst. prof. govt. Columbia, N.Y.C., 1965; research asso. Center for Internat. Affairs, Harvard, Cambridge, Mass., 1966; univ. research prof. U. Md., 1971-73; asst. to Pres.'s sci. adviser White House, Washington, 1966-67; dir. corp. devel. System Devel. Corp., Washington, 1967-68; chmn. bd., chief exec. officer EDP-Tech., Inc., Washington, 1968-71, Am. Metals and Alloys, 1970—, Realty Capital Inc., 1975—; dir., fin. adviser Tishman Realty & Constrn. Co., Inc., N.Y.C., 1973-78, Capital Centre, Washington, 1974—. Editor: (with T. Cronin) The Presidential Advisory System, 1969. Pres. Columbia Coll. Class of 1962.; Trustee Nat. Braille Press, Opera Soc., Washington; bd. dirs. Interdisciplinary Communications Inc. (Smithsonian Instn.), Nat. Com. on U.S.-China Relations, 1968—; chmn. bd. Communications Found.; bd. govs. Ben Gurion U. Negev. Named One of 10 Outstanding Young Men of Boston, One of 4 Outstanding Young Men of Mass., One of 10 Outstanding Young Men Am., 1966; White House fellow, 1966. Mem. Young Presidents Orgn. (Man of Year award 1974), Am. Polit. Sci. Assn., Council on Fgn. Relations, Japan Soc., Am. Hist. Assn., Oxford Union Soc., Phi Beta Kappa. Clubs: Federal City, Cosmos, Internat. (Washington); Harvard, Harmonie (N.Y.C.); Bay (Boston). Patentee device for compression and expansion of speech. Home: 700 New Hampshire Ave NW Washington DC 20037 Office: 600 New Hampshire Ave NW Washington DC 20037

GREENBERG, SIMON, rabbi, educator; b. Horoshen, Russia, Jan. 8, 1901; came to U.S., 1905, naturalized, 1924; s. Morris and Bessie (Chaidenko) G.; m. Betty Davis, Dec. 13, 1925; children: Moshe, Daniel Asher. Student, U. Minn., 1920-21; A.B., Coll. City N.Y., 1922; Rabbi, Jewish Theol. Sem., N.Y.C., 1925; Ph.D., Dropsie Coll., Phila., 1932; D.D., Jewish Theol. Sem. Am., 1950; postgrad., Hebrew U. in Jerusalem, Am. Sch. for Oriental Research, Jerusalem, 1924-25. Rabbi Har Zion Temple, Phila., 1925-46; lectr. Jewish edn. Jewish Theol. Sem., 1932-41, asso. prof. edn., 1941-48, provost, 1946, prof. edn. and homiletics, 1947—, acting pres., 1948-49, vice chancellor, v.p. faculties, 1951; dir. U. Judaism, Los Angeles, 1948-58, pres., 1958-66, chancellor, 1966-72; dir. Sem. Israel Project, 1973-82. Author: Living as a Jew Today, 1939, The Harishon Series, 1942, Ideas and Ideals in the Jewish Prayer Book, 1940, The First Year in the Hebrew School; A Teacher's Guide, 1945, The Conservative Movement in Judaism, 1954, Israel and Zionism, Conservative Approach, 1955, Foundations of a Faith, 1968, Words of Poetry, 1970, Ethics, Religion and Judaism; spl. supplement to Conservative Judaism, summer 1972, fall 1972; The Ethical in the Jewish and the American Heritage, 1977, A Jewish Philosophy and Pattern of Life, 1981, Year of the Bible: A Guide to Daily Bible Study for the Jewish Community, 1983. Bd. dirs. Phila. Psychiat. Hosp.; Pres. Rabbinical Assembly Am., 1937-39; past pres. Avukah-Intercoll. Zionist Orgn., Phila. br. United Synagogue, Phila. Bd. Jewish Ministers; mem. nat. exec. com. Zionist Orgn. Am., pres. Phila. br., 1941-44, chmn. nat. edn. com., 1943-45; exec. dir. United Synagogue Am., 1950-53; mem. exec. com. World Zionist Orgn., 1964-68; chmn. United Synagogue Commn. on Jewish Edn., 1962-67; mem. praesidium World Council on Jewish Edn., 1964-68; past mem. chaplains religious council U. Pa. Recipient Sam Rothberg award Hebrew U., 1977; Mordecai M. Kaplan medal U. of Judaism, 1977; Distinguished Service certificate Religious Edn. Assn. U.S. and Can.; Sem. medal, 1981; Solomon Schechter award United Synagogue, 1983. Fellow Conf. on Sci., Philosophy and Religion. Home: 420 Riverside Dr New York NY 10025 Office: 3080 Broadway New York NY 10027
I have admired many, envied no one.

GREENBERG, STEPHEN JAY, lawyer; b. Bayonne, N.J., Sept. 2, 1941; s. Louis and Jeanette Hilda (Steinberg) G.; m. Lillian D. Fekety, June 16, 1963; children—Joshua Bennett, Suzanne Lynne. B.A., Rutgers U., 1963; LL.B., U. Pa., 1966. Bar: N.Y. bar 1967, Pa. bar 1971. Asso. firm Strasser, Spiegelberg, Fried & Frank, N.Y.C., 1966, Schnader, Harrison, Segal & Lewis, Phila., 1971-72, partner, 1973—. Research editor: U. Pa. Law Rev, 1965-66. Served to capt. JAGC U.S. Army, 1967-71. Decorated Meritorious Service medal. Mem. Am. Bar Assn., Pa. Bar Assn., Phila. Bar Assn., Am. Law Inst., Order of Coif. Home: 725 S Highland Ave Merion PA 19066 Office: 1719 Packard Bldg Philadelphia PA 19102

GREENBERGER, ELLEN, social ecology educator; b. N.Y.C., Nov. 19, 1935; d. Edward Michael and Vera (Brisk) Silver; m. Michael Burton, Aug. 26, 1979; children by previous marriage—Kari Greenberger, David Greenberger. B.A., Vassar Coll., 1956; M.A., Harvard U., 1959, Ph.D., 1961. Instr. Wellesley (Mass.) Coll., 1961-63, asst. prof., 1963-67; sr. research scientist Johns Hopkins U., Balt., 1967-75; prof. social ecology U. Calif., Irvine, 1975—, dir. program in social ecology, 1975-80. Contbr. articles to profl. jours. USPHS fellow, 1956-59; Margaret Floy Washburn fellow, 1956-58; Ford Found. grantee, 1979-81; Spencer Found. grantee, 1979-81. Mem. Am. Psychol. Assn., Soc. Research in Child Devel., Am. Anthrop. Assn. Office: Program in Social Ecology Univ Calif Irvine CA 92717

GREENBERGER, ERNEST, lawyer; b. Sarospatak, Hungary, Mar. 16, 1923; came to U.S., 1939, naturalized, 1944; s. Solomon and Esther (Weinberger) G.; m. Stacia Pleva, May 17, 1956; children—James J., Daniel A. B.A., Roosevelt U., 1945. Bar: Ill. bar 1948. J.D., U. Chgo., 1947; assoc. firm Lawrence, Goldberg, Lawrence & Lewin, Chgo., 1947-55; ptnr. Antonow & Fink, Chgo., 1955-62; mem. firm Greenberger, Krauss & Jacobs, Chgo., 1962—; lectr. law U. Chgo. Downtown Center, 1960-61. Editor: U. Chgo. Law Rev, 1946-47. Bd. dirs. Am. Found. for Continuing Edn., 1953-65; bd. dirs. Jewish Community Centers Chgo., 1959-81, v.p., 1964-81; mem. Evanston Econ. Devel. Com., 1975-76. Mem. Am., Ill., Chgo. bar assns., Am. Arbitration Assn. (mem. nat. panel arbitrators 1962—), Order of Coif. Democrat. Jewish. Club: Standard (Chgo.). Home: 1314 Forest Ave Evanston IL 60201 Office: Suite 2700 180 N La Salle St Chicago IL 60601

GREENBERGER, HOWARD LEROY, lawyer, educator; b. Pitts., July 16, 1929; s. Abraham Harry and Alice (Levine) G.; m. Bette Jo Bergad, June 15, 1959. B.S. magna cum laude, U. Pitts., 1951; J.D. cum laude; Root-Tilden grantee, N.Y. U., 1954; diploma in law (Fulbright scholar), Oxford (Eng.) U., 1955. Bar: Pa. bar 1955, D.C. bar 1954, N.Y. bar 1969, U.S. Supreme Ct 1964. Law clk. U.S. Ct. Appeals 3d Circuit, 1958-60; asso. firm Kaufman & Kaufman, Pitts., 1960-61; asso. prof. law N.Y. U., 1961-65, prof., 1965—, asso. dean, 1968-72; dean and dir. Practising Law Inst, 1972-75; dir. Fgn. Law Insts., 1975—; cons. in field; v.p. Nat. Center Para-Legal Tng.; Pres. N.Y.C. chpt. Am. Jewish Com., 1977-79, nat. bd. govs., 1979—; pres. Early Am. Industries Assn., 1979—; vice chmn. N.Y. Conf. Soviet Jewry, 1977—. Author: (with G. Cole) The Meriden Experiment, (1973) Study of the Quality of Continuing Legal Education in the U.S, (1980); contbr. articles to legal publs.; chmn. editorial bd.: Jour. Legal Edn, 1974-77. Served to capt., JAGC U.S. Army, 1955-58. Recipient Sr. award U. Pitts., 1951; Sommer award N.Y. U., 1954; Alumni Meritorious Service award, 1977; Stanley Isaacs award Am. Jewish Com., 1979; Sesquicentennial award, 1982. Mem. Am. Law Inst., Am. Bar Assn., N.Y. State Bar Assn., Assn. Bar City N.Y., Assn. Am. Law Schs., Order of Coif, Phi Epsilon Pi. Democrat. Jewish. Clubs: N.Y. U. (pres. 1981—), Masons, Sojourners. Home: 4 Washington Sq Village Apt 16M New York NY 10012 Office: 343 Vand Hall 40 Washington Square S New York NY 10012

GREENBERGER, NORTON JERALD, physician; b. Cleve., Sept. 13, 1933; s. Sam and Lillian (Frank) G.; m. Joan Narcus, Aug. 10, 1964; children: Sharon, Rachel, Wendy. A.B., Yale U., 1955; M.D., Western Res. U., 1959. Diplomate: Am. Bd. Internal Medicine (sec.-treas. 1980-

82). Intern Univ. Hosps., Cleve., 1959-60, resident internal medicine, 1960-62; USPHS fellow in gastroenterology Harvard U., 1962-65, Mass. Gen. Hosp., Boston, 1962-65; with Ohio State U., Columbus, 1965-72, dir. div. gastroenterology, 1967-72, prof., 1971-72; prof., chmn. dept. medicine U. Kans., Kansas City, 1972—; mem. Nat. Bd. Med. Examiners, 1971-75; mem. gen. medicine study sect. A, NIH, 1973-76. Author: (with Daniel Winship) Gastrointestinal Disorders: A Pathophysiologic Approach, 1976, (with others) Drug Treatment of Gastrointestinal Disorders; editor: gastroent. sect. Yearbook of Medicine, 1969—; contbr. articles to med. jours. Recipient Outstanding Teaching award House Staff Dept. Medicine Ohio State U., 1970-71, Kans. U. Med. Sch. Class of 1978. Fellow A.C.P. (editorial com. gastroenterology sect. 1975-77); mem. Am. Fedn. Clin. Research (pres. Midwestern sect. 1973-74), Central Soc. Clin. Research (councilor 1975, pres. 1979-80), N.Y. Acad. Scis., AAAS, Midwestern Gut Club, Am. Gastroent. Assn. (pres.-elect 1983-84, pres. 1984), Am. Soc. Clin. Investigation, Am. Soc. Pharmacology and Exptl. Therapeutics, Assn. Am. Physicians, Assn. Profs. Medicine, Phi Beta Kappa, Sigma Xi, Alpha Omega Alpha. Home: 2611 W 70th Terr Mission Hills KS 66208 Office: 39th and Rainbow Sts Kansas City KS 66103

GREENBLATT, MILTON, psychiatrist; b. Boston, June 29, 1914; s. Julius and Sophia (Bolonsky) G.; m. Gertrude Anna Rogers, June 10, 1941; children: David John, Daniel Lawrence. A.B. summa cum laude, Tufts U., 1935, M.D. cum laude, 1939. Charleston research fellow, instr. physiology Tufts U. Sch. Medicine, 1939-40, prof. psychiatry, 1963-73, Alpha Omega Alpha lectr., Bergendahl Meml. lectr., 1963; intern gen. medicine Beth Israel Hosp., Boston, 1940-41; resident in psychiatry Mass. Mental Health Center, Boston, 1941-42; dir. Electroencephalography Lab., 1942-63, sr. physician, 1943-45, dir. labs., research, 1946-63, dir. clin. psychiatry, 1953-57, asst. supt., 1957-63; practice medicine specializing in psychiatry, Boston, 1941-73; supt. Boston State Hosp., 1963-67; assoc. clin. prof. psychiatry Harvard Med. Sch., 1958-63, lectr. psychiatry, 1963-73, lectr. dept. social relations, 1957-63; Eugene Barrera Meml. lectr. Albany Med. Sch., 1955; Israel Strauss Meml. lectr. Hillside Hosp., N.Y.C., 1962; lectr. div. psychiatry Sch. Medicine Boston U., 1963-73; prof. psychiatry, vice chmn. dept. psychiatry, dir. social and community psychiatry UCLA, 1973-79, asst. dean, 1977-79, prof., exec. vice chmn. dept. psychiatry and biobehavioral scis., dir. Neuropsychiatric Inst. Hosp. and Clinics, 1979—; dir. psychiatry Sepulveda VA Hosp., 1973-77; chief staff VA Med. Center Brentwood, 1977-79; commr. Mass. Dept. Mental Health, 1967-73; Bd. dirs. Am. Bd. Psychiatry and Neurology, v.p., 1975, pres., 1976. Author: (with others) From Custodial to Therapeutic Patient Care in Mental Hospitals, 1955; author, editor: Studies in Lobotomy, 1950, (with Harry C. Solomon) Frontal Lobes and Schizophrenia, 1953, (with others) the Patient and the Mental Hospital, 1957, (with Benjamin Simon) Rehabilitation of the Mentally Ill: Social and Economic Aspects, 1959, (with others) The Prevention of Hospitalization, 1963, Drug and Social Therapy in Chronic Schizophrenia, 1965; Editor: Mental Patients in Transition, 1961, College Students in a Mental Hospital, 1962, Halfway House: A Sociocultural and Clinical Study of Rutland Corner House: A Transitional Aftercare Residence for Female Psychiatric Patients, 1965, Threat of Impending Disaster, 1965, Poverty and Mental Health, 1967, Adolescents in a Mental Hospital, 1968, Dynamics of Institutional Change, 1971, Drugs in Combination with Other Therapies, 1975, Alcoholism Problems in Women and Children, 1976, Psychopolitics, 1978; assoc. editor: Am. Jour. Psychiatry, 1965-74; referee, 1974—; assoc. editor: Am. Jour. Social Psychiatry, 1981—; editorial bd.: Quar. Jour. Studies on Alcohol, 1958—, Psychiatric Opinion, 1962-80, Comprehensive Psychiatry, 1965—, New Eng. Jour. Medicine, 1967-70, Jour. Psychiat. Treatment and Evaluation, 1981—; editor in chief: Seminars in Psychiatry, 1968-74; series editor, 1974—; asso. editor: Social Psychiatry, 1972-79; assoc. editor: Psychiat. Annals, 1975—. Fellow Am. Psychiat. Assn. (life, Hofheimer prize 1951, v.p. 1972-73, past pres. No. New Eng. Dist. br., chmn. com. community aspects psychiatry, councilor 1966-69, chmn. commn. on drug safety 1966-68, chmn. council on internal orgn. 1973-76, chmn. ad hoc com. to consider component on long range planning 1979, Disting. Service award 1981, Disting. Psychiat. lectr. 1983), Boston Med. Library, Am. Coll. Psychiatrists; mem. Mass. Soc. Research Psychiatry (past pres.), Mass. Med. Soc. (past chmn. sect. psychiatry, neurology), Am. Coll. Neuropsychopharmacology (past pres.), Group for Advancement Psychiatry, Am. Psychopath. Assn. (past pres.), Am. Assn. for Social Psychiatry (pres. 1974-76), Am. Acad. Psychoanalysis (sci. asso.), Am. Acad. Clin. Psychiatrists, World Fedn. Mental Health, Am. Coll. Mental Health Adminstrn. Home: 3326 Longridge Terr Sherman Oaks CA 91423 Office: Neuropsychiatric Inst 760 Westwood Plaza Los Angeles CA 90024

GREENBLATT, RAY HARRIS, lawyer; b. Milw., June 29, 1931; s. Charles and Ethel (Harris) G.; m. Betty Goldsmith, July 11, 1955 (div. Mar. 1967); children: Walter, Robert, Edward; m. Helen Judith Pick, Mar. 29, 1969 (div. Dec. 1969). B.S. in Econs., U. Pa., 1953; J.D. magna cum laude, Harvard U., 1956. Bar: Ill. 1956. Assoc. Mayer, Brown & Platt, 1956-64, ptnr., 1965—; arbitrator Am. Arbitration Assn., 1970—; lectr. U. Wis. Sch. for Bankers, Madison, 1964, 73, Ill. Inst. Continuing Legal Edn., 1973. Contbr. articles to profl. jours. Pres. Winnetka Bd. Edn., Ill., 1974-75, mem., Ill., 1969-74. Mem. ABA, Chgo. Bar Assn., Chgo. Council Lawyers. Jewish. Clubs: Economic, Clif Dwellers, Union League (Chgo.); Lake Shore Country (Clencoe, Ill.). Home: 1003 Westmoor Rd Winnetka IL 60093 Office: Mayer Brown & Platt 231 S LaSalle St Chicago IL 60604

GREENBURG, DAN, author; b. Chgo., June 20, 1936; s. Samuel and Leah (Rozalsky) G.; m. Nora Ephron, Apr. 9, 1967 (div.); m. Suzanne O'Malley, July 20, 1980. B.F.A., U. Ill., 1958; M.A., UCLA, 1960. Copywriter Lansdale Co., Los Angeles, 1960-61, Carson Roberts Advt., 1961-62; mng. editor Eros mag., N.Y.C., 1962-63; copywriter Papert, Koenig, Lois (advt.), N.Y.C., 1963-65; free-lance writer, N.Y.C., 1965—. Author: How to Be a Jewish Mother, 1964, Kiss My Firm But Pliant Lips, 1965, How to Make Yourself Miserable, 1966, Chewsday: A Sex Novel, 1968, Jumbo the Boy and Arnold the Elephant, 1969, Philly, 1969, Porno-Graphics, 1969, Scoring: A Sexual Memoir, 1972, Something's There: My Adventures in the Occult, 1976, Love Kills, 1978, What Do Women Want?, 1982, (with Suzanne O'Malley) How to Avoid Love and Marriage, 1983; films I Could Never Have Sex with Any Man Who Has So Little Regard for My Husband, 1973, Private Lessons, 1981, (with Suzanne O'Malley) Private School, 1983; plays Arf, 1969; The Great Airplane Snatch, 1969, also articles.; Contbr. to: Broadway rev. Oh, Calcutta, 1969. Recipient Silver Key award Advt. Writers Assn., N.Y.C., 1964, Playboy Humor award, 1964, 72, 76. Mem. Dramatists Guild, Authors Guild Am., AFTRA, Screen Actors Guild, Writers Guild Am., Mystery Writers Am. Home: 323 E 50th St New York NY 10022

GREENE, A. CRAWFORD, JR., lawyer; b. San Francisco, Sept. 18, 1922; s. A. Crawford and Natalie (Coffin) G.; m. Daphne DuVal Dibble, June 23, 1951; children: A. Crawford III, Isabelle B., Catherine D., Daphne C. B.A., Yale U., 1943, LL.B., 1949. Bar: Calif. 1950. Assoc. firm McCutchen, Doyle, Brown & Enersen, San Francisco, 1949-59, partner, 1959—; dir. Redlake Corp., Nat. Med. Fellowships, Inc. Trustee Ross Sch. Dist., 1963-71, Nat. Health and Welfare Mut. Life Ins. Assn., 1968-80, 81—, Grace Cathedral, 1969-71, 74-75; trustee St. Luke's Hosp., 1970—, San Francisco Legal Aid Soc., 1964—; pres. San Francisco Legal Aid Soc., 1971-72; bd. dirs. William Babcock Meml. Endowment, 1964—, pres., 1974-76; bd. dirs. Hospice of Marin, 1979—. Served to 1st lt. U.S. Army, 1943-46. Mem. Am., Calif., San Francisco bar assns., Am. Law Inst. Republican. Episcopalian. Clubs: Pacific-Union (San Francisco); Lagunitas Country. Home: Willow Hill Ross CA 94957 Office: 3 Embarcadero Center San Francisco CA 94111

GREENE, A(LVIN) C(ARL), author; b. Abilene, Tex., Nov. 4, 1923; s. Alvin Carl and Marie (Cole) G.; m. Betty Dozier, May 1, 1950; children: Geoffrey, Mark, Eliot, Meredith Elizabeth. B.A., Abilene Christian U., 1948. Mem. staff Abilene Reporter-News, 1948-52; book editor, editorial columnist Dallas Times Herald, 1960-68, 1960-68, editor editorial page, 1963-65; staff U. Tex., Austin, 1968-69, 73; exec. editor Southwestern Hist. Quar., 1968-69; exec. producer Sta. KERA-TV, Dallas, 1970-71; editorial bd. KAAM, KAFM, 1979-81; radio commentator A.C. Greene's Historic Moments Sta. WFAA, 1982—; book reviewer MacNeil/Lehrer News Hour, 1983—. Author: A Personal Country, 1969, Living Texas, 1969, The Last Captive, 1972, Santa Claus Bank Robbery, 1972, Dallas: The Deciding Years, 1973, A Christmas Tree, 1973, Views in Texas, 1974, A Place Called Dallas, 1975, The Highland Park Woman, 1983, (with Roger Horchow) Elephants in Your Mailbox, 1980, One of 50 Best Books on Texas, 1982, Dallas USA, 1984. Served with USNR, 1943-46; PTO, CBI. Recipient award Nat. Conf. Christians and Jews, 1964; Dobie-Paisano fellow, 1968. Fellow Tex. Inst. Letters (pres. 1969-71, Mem., award 1964, 73), Tex. Electric Railroaders Assn. Presbyn. Home: 4359 Shirley Dr Dallas TX 75229

GREENE, ANTHONY STORM, constrn. equipment co. exec.; b. Aurora, Ill., Apr. 28, 1925; s. William B. and Jane (Smith) G.; m. Barbara Anderson, Aug. 31, 1946; children—Christopher Storm, Mary Kimberly. B.S., U. Calif. at Los Angeles, 1948. With Barber-Greene Co. (and subsidiaries), Aurora, 1948—; pres. B/G Can., Toronto, 1956-63, v.p. internat., Aurora, 1963-69, dir., 1966—, exec. v.p., 1969-71, pres., chief exec. officer, 1971—, chmn. bd., 1976—; dir. B/G Americas, B/G do Brazil, B/G Europa, Netherlands, B/G Eng., Growth Industry Shares, Inc., Chgo. Mem. Asso. Equipment Distbrs.; Industry Round Table, 1973, 74. Mem. exec. bd. Boy Scouts Am. Bd.; dirs. Internat. Road Fedn., 1976—. Served with USMCR, 1943-46. Mem. Constrn. Industry Mfrs. Assn., Conveyor Equipment Mfrs. Assn., Ill. C. of C., Aurora C. of C. (v.p. 1966-67). Home: 17 Buckingham Dr Prestbury Aurora IL 60504 Office: 400 N Highland Ave Aurora IL 60507

GREENE, BALCOMB, artist; b. Millville, N.Y., May 22, 1904; s. Bert Stillman and Florence (Stover) G.; m. Gertrude Glass, 1926 (dec. 1956); m. Terry Trimpen, 1961. A.B., Syracuse U., 1926; A.M., N.Y.U., 1940; postgrad., U. Vienna, 1926-28. Tchr. Dartmouth Coll., 1928-31; asso. prof. Carnegie Inst. Tech., Pitts., 1942-59. Exhibited in one man shows, Gallery, Paris, J.B. Neumann's New Art Circle, N.Y.C., 1947, Arts and Crafts Center, Pitts., 1953, Bertha Schaefer Gallery, annually 1950-61, Am. U., Washington, 1957, Brookhaven Nat. Lab., 1959, Centre Culture American, Am. embassy, Paris, 1960, A.C.A. Gallery, N.Y.C., 1980, exhbns. retrospective at, Whitney Mus. Am. Art, N.Y.C., 1961, Carnegie Inst. Tech., Munson-Williams-Proctor Inst., Utica, N.Y., Saidenberg Gallery, N.Y.C., 1962-68, Feingarten Galleries, Los Angeles, 1963, 64, Feingarten Galleries, Chgo., 1963, La Jolla (Calif.) Art Center, 1964, Tampa (Fla.) Art Inst., 1965, James David Gallery, Coral Gabels, Fla., 1965-66, Santa Barbara (Calif.) Mus. Art, 1966, Phoenix Art Mus., Berenson Gallery, Bay Harbor Islands, Fla., 1968, 70, Fairweather-Hardin Gallery, Chgo., 1969, Adele Bednary Galleries, Los Angeles, 1966-73, Forum Gallery, N.Y.C., 1970-73, Harmon Gallery, Naples, Fla., 1974, 75, A.C.A. Gallery, N.Y.C., 1977, Guild Hall, Easthampton, L.I., N.Y., 1978, Yares Gallery, Scottsdale, Ariz., 1979, others; represented in permanent collections, Mus. Modern Art, Whitney Mus. Am. Art, Solomon Guggenheim Mus., Met. Mus., all N.Y.C., Carnegie Inst., Pitts., Walker Art Center, Mpls., U. Nebr., Joselyn Mus., Omaha, Smithsonian Inst., Washington, U. Va., U. N.C., numerous others; also pvt. collections; represented by, ACA Gallery, N.Y.C., Harmon Gallery, Naples, Fla.; Editor: Art Front, 1935-36; Contbr. to profl. publs. works included in numerous art books. Recipient awards Art News Magazine. Mem. Am. Fedn. Arts, Am. Abstract Artists (chmn. 1936-67, 38-39, 40-41), Theta Beta Phi. Club: Cosmopolitan of Syracuse U. Subject of The Art of Balcomb Greene (Robert Beverly Hale), 1977. Home: Montauk Point Long Island NY 11954 also 2 Sutton Pl S New York NY 10022 Studio: 345 E 52d St New York NY 10022

GREENE, BERNARD HAROLD, lawyer; b. Bklyn., Sept. 21, 1925; s. Max and Clara (Pasweg) G.; m. Magda C. Schwartz, Sept. 19, 1948; children: Michael, Edith, Susan, Jonathan, David. B.B.A. magna cum laude, CCNY, 1948; LL.B. cum laude, Yale U., 1951. Bar: N.Y. 1952. Assoc. Paul, Weiss, Rifkind, Wharton & Garrison, N.Y.C., 1951-60; ptnr. paul, Weiss, Rifkind, Wharton & Garrison, 1960—; vis. lectr. Yale Law Sch., New Haven, 1972-78, 82-83; dir. First Sterling Corp., N.Y.C. Chmn. deferred giving and estate planning com. Community Service Soc., N.Y.C., 1975-82. 1st lt. U.S. Army, 1943-47. Mem. Assn. Bar City N.Y. (mem. surrogate's ct. com. 1958-61). Home: 153 Union St Montclair NJ 07042 Office: Paul Weiss Rifkins Wharton and Garrison 345 Park Ave New York NY 10154

GREENE, BETTE, novelist; b. Memphis, June 28, 1934; d. Arthur and Sadie (Steinberg) Evensky; m. Donald Sumner Greene, June 14, 1959; children: Carla, Jordan Joshua. Student, U. Ala., 1952, Memphis State U., 1953, Columbia U., 1955. Author: novels Summer of My German Soldier, 1973, Philip Hall Likes Me I Reckon Maybe, 1974, Morning Is A Long Time Coming, 1978, Get On Out Of Here, Philip Hall!, 1981, Them That Glitter and Them That Don't, 1983, I've Already Forgotten Your Name, Phillip Hall, 1984. Office: 338 Clinton Rd Brookline MA 02146 *As a writer, I always attempt to go beyond the "write about what you know" dictum. That's good as far as it goes, but it doesn't go far enough. Not nearly far enough. For I believe that the serious novelist must write about what makes her burst out into song... or into tears because that's where all the real writing resides. But to strike at it, the writer must have all the courage, all the conviction, and certainly all the passion of a Kamikazi pilot.*

GREENE, BRADFORD MARSON, landscape architect; b. Springfield, Mass., Jan. 24, 1920; s. Chester Marson and Louie Day (Mallette) G.; m. Mary Louise Cobb, Jan. 2, 1944; children—Christopher Marson, Elizabeth Bradford. B.S. magna cum laude, U. Mass., 1942. Jr. archtl. draftsman C.E. Port Engrs. Office, Boston Port of Embarkation, 1942-43; prin. planning draftsman Balt. Dept. Parks and Recreation, 1946-48; asst. landscape architect N.Y.C. Housing Authority, 1948-50; landscape architect Clarke & Rapuano, Inc., N.Y.C., 1950—, v.p. for landscape architecture, 1981—, also dir.; bd. dirs. S.I. Inst. Arts and Scis.; rec. sec. S.I. Citizens Planning Com. Treas., Fine Arts Fedn., 1972-80; landscape architecture mem. Art Commn. of City of N.Y., 1980-83. Important works include Travelers Ins. Co, Boston, Lehigh U. Master Plan and Sitework, Moravian Coll. Master Plan, Woods Hole Oceanographic Inst; site work for Ednl. Testing Center, Princeton, N.J.; comml. revitalization Port Richmond, S.I. Bd. dirs. S.I. Planning Found. Served with M.I. AUS, 1943-46. Decorated Army Commendation medal; recipient Community Service award Jr. C. of C., 1962. Fellow Am. Soc. Landscape Architects (exec. com., past pres. N.Y. chpt.); mem. N.Y. State Bd. for Landscape Architecture, Landscape Materials Info. Service (vice chmn.), Nat. Constrn. Industry Arbitration Com., Am. Vets. Com., Phi Kappa Phi. Democrat. Unitarian. Home: 62 Potter Ave Staten Island NY 10314 Office: Clarke and Rapuano Inc 215 Lexington Ave New York NY 10016

GREENE, CARLA, writer; b. Mpls., Dec. 18, 1916; d. William L. and Charlotte (Wunderman) G. Author: numerous children's books including How to Know Dinosaurs, 1966, Animal Doctors, 1967, Lighthouses, 1969, Los Camioneros, 1969, Before the Dinosaurs, 1970, How Man Began, 1972 (named Best Book of Year, Jr. Sci. Tchrs. Am. 1972), Cowboys, 1972, Our Living Earth, 1974, Man and Ancient Civilizations, 1977; contbr. adult articles and stories to mags. Mem. Authors League Am., Calif. Council on Children's Lit., Los Angeles County Mus., Los Angeles Music Center, PEN Internat., Reading Is Fundamental. Office: 8300 Sunset Blvd Los Angeles CA 90069

GREENE, CHARLES CASSIUS, advertising agency executive; b. Sullivan, Ill., June 6, 1897; s. Cassius Wilbur and Katherine (Mouser) B.; m. Ursula Lally. Ph.B., U. Chgo., 1919, J.D., 1921; postgrad., Sch. Commerce Northwestern U., 1932-33. Bar: Ill. Account exec. Albert Frank (advt.), Chgo., 1926-31; v.p. Carroll Dean Murphy (advt.), Chgo., 1931-36, Critchfield & Co. (advt.), 1936-40, Buchanan & Co. (advt.), 1940-44; v.p., resident mgr., dir. Doremus & Co. subs. BBDO Internat., Chgo., 1944-70, cons., 1970-77. Served as 2d lt., inf. U.S. Army, World War I. Mem. Pub. Relations Soc. Am. (past pres. Chgo., nat. v.p.), Phi Beta Kappa, Phi Kappa Psi, Phi Delta Phi. Republican. Clubs: Rotarian., Chgo. Athletic Assn., Chicago Press, Executives. Home: 1642 E 56th St Apt 1205 Chicago IL 60637 Office: 500 N Michigan Ave Suite 400 Chicago IL 60611

GREENE, DAVID GORHAM, physician; b. Buffalo, Feb. 5, 1915; s. Clayton W. and Emma (Walmsley) Otis) G.; m. Edith M. Albertson, Dec. 14, 1946; children: Amy A., Stephen G., Eleanor O., Constance C. A.B., Princeton U., 1936; M.D., Harvard U., 1940. Fellow Banting Inst., Toronto, Ont., Can., 1940-41, Columbia U. Coll. Phys. and Medicine, 1945-48; intern, then asst. resident in medicine Presbyn. Hosp., N.Y.C., 1941-46; mem. faculty SUNY Med. Sch., Buffalo, 1948—, prof. medicine, 1956—, asso. prof. physiology, 1970—; attending physician Buffalo Gen. Hosp.; hon. prof. medicine Autonomous U., Puebla, Mex., 1961; Litchfield lectr. Oxford (Eng.) U. Faculty Medicine, 1967; MacArthur lectr. U. Edinburgh (Scotland) Faculty Medicine, 1967; lectr. Keio U., Tokyo, 1978. Contbr. articles to med. jours., chpts. to books. Served as officer M.C. AUS, 1942-45. Mem. Am. Coll. Cardiology, Am. Coll. Chest Physicians, ACP, Am. Heart Assn., Am. Physiol. Soc., Am. Fedn. Clin Research, Assn. Univ. Cardiologists, N. Am. Soc. Cardiac Radiology, Soc. Cardiac Angiography (pres. 1983-84). Democrat. Home: 88 Ashland Ave Buffalo NY 14222 Office: 100 High St Buffalo NY 14203

GREENE, DAVID LEE, physical anthropologist, educator; b. Denver, Aug. 23, 1938; s. Ralph Francis and Dorothy Elizabeth (Allen) G.; m. Kathleen Ann Kerger, Sept. 4, 1962; 1 son, Andrew David. B.A., U. Colo., 1960, M.A., 1962, Ph.D. in Anthropology (NSF fellow). Asst. prof. anthropology and orthodontics SUNY, Buffalo, 1964-65; asst. prof., head dept. anthropology U. Wyo., 1965-67; asst. prof. U. Colo., Boulder, 1967-69, asso. prof., 1969-71, prof., 1971—, chmn. dept. anthropology, 1974-77, 81-83; dir. NSF Summer Inst. in Anthropology, 1970-71; outside grad. examiner U. Toronto, 1974, field research in Sudan, 1963-64, Micronesia, 1969. Author: Genetics, Dentition and Taxonomy, 1967, (with G.J. Armelagos) The Wadi Halfa Mesolithic Population, 1972; contbr. articles to profl. jours. NSF grantee, 1978-80. Fellow Am. Anthrop. Assn.; mem. Am. Assn. Phys. Anthropologists, AAAS, Sigma Xi. Democrat. Office: Dept Anthropology U Colo Boulder CO 80309

GREENE, DAVID MASON, English educator; b. Washington, Mar. 16, 1920; s. David Thomas and Eliza Beverly (Mason) G.; m. Helen Mildred Howard, June 10, 1944; 1 dau., Dana Mason. Student, Corcoran Art Sch., 1938; B.A., San Diego State Coll., 1951; M.A., U. Calif.-Berkeley, 1952, Ph.D., 1958. Lectr. English U. Calif.-Berkeley, 1955-57; instr. Pa. State U., 1957-58; asst. prof. Lehigh U., Bethlehem, Pa., 1958-64, assoc. prof., 1964-69; prof. Leghigh U., Bethlehem, Pa., 1969—; writer on music. Contbg. editor: Musical Heritage Soc.; author: Greene's Dictionary of Composers, 1984; numerous articles. Mem. Phi Beta Kappa, Omicron Delta Kappa, Phi Mu Alpha Sinfonia. Democrat. Home: Fire Ln Rte 3 Bethlehem PA 18015 Office: Dept English Lehigh Univ Bethlehem PA 18015

GREENE, DONALD JOHNSON, educator, author; b. Moose Jaw, Sask., Can., Nov. 21, 1916; s. Waldron Joseph and Katharine Annie (Beaton) G. B.A., U. Sask., 1941; M.A., U. London, 1948, D.Lit., 1973; Ph.D., Columbia U., 1954. Instr. English U. Sask., 1948-52; asst. prof. U. Calif., Riverside, 1954-57, Brandeis U., 1958-60; asso. prof. U. N.Mex., 1960-63; prof. U. Toronto, Ont., 1963-66; Vilas research prof. U. Wis., 1967-68; Leo S. Bing prof. English U. So. Calif., Los Angeles, 1968—. Author: The Politics of Samuel Johnson, 1960, The Age of Exuberance, 1970, (with James L. Clifford) Samuel Johnson: A Survey and Bibliography of Critical Studies, 1970; Editor: Samuel Johnson: A Collection of Critical Essays, 1965, Samuel Johnson, Political Writings, 1977. Served with Can. Army, 1941-45. Guggenheim fellow, 1957-58, 79-80; Can. Council sr. fellow, 1965-66. Fellow Royal Soc. Can.; mem. Am. Soc. for Eighteenth-Century Studies (sec. 1969-73, v.p. 1979), Internat. Soc. for Eighteenth-Century Studies (exec. com. 1967-73, v.p. 1975-79), MLA (editorial com. 1968-73, nominating com. 1972-73, chmn. English Group VIII 1964), Internat. Assn. U. Profs. English, Conf. on Brit. Studies (rec. sec. 1963-65). Clubs: Athenaeum (London); Johnson (Eng.) (hon. mem.). Office: Dept English U So Calif Los Angeles CA 90007

GREENE, EDWARD FORBES, chemistry educator; b. N.Y.C., Dec. 29, 1922; s. Roger Sherman and Kate (Brown) G.; m. Hildegarde Forbes, June 11, 1949; children: Susan Curtis, Judith Elizabeth, David Forbes, Roger Cobb. A.B., Harvard U., 1943, A.M., 1947, Ph.D., 1949. Jr. research chemist Shell Oil Co., Wood River, Ill., 1943-44; mem. staff Los Alamos Sci. Lab., 1949; research assoc. Brown U., Providence, 1949-51, instr., 1952-53, asst. prof. chemistry, 1953-57, assoc. prof., 1957-63, prof., 1963—; vis. prof. Tougaloo (Miss.) Coll., 1965; resident visitor Bell Labs., Murray Hill, N.J., 1976-77. Co-author: (with J.P. Toennies) Chemical Reactions in Shock Waves, 1964. Served with USN, 1944-46. NSF fellow, 1959-60, 66-67. Fellow Am. Phys. Soc.; mem. Am. Chem. Soc. Home: 10 Patterson St Providence RI 02906

GREENE, FRANCIS THORNTON, lawyer; b. N.Y.C., May 29, 1908; s. Frederick Stuart and Grace Emily (Clapp) G.; m. Byrd Harrison Tucker, Oct. 28, 1933; children: Frances Bland, Stuart Thornton. Student, St. Paul's Prep. Sch.; grad., Albany Acad., 1926; A.B., Va. Mil. Inst., 1930; LL.B., Harvard U., 1933. Bar: N.Y. 1934. Asso. Haight, Smith, Griffin & Deming, N.Y.C., 1933-34; staff gen. counsel's office SEC, Washington, 1934-37, asst. dir. trading and exchange div., 1937-41; partner firm Tucker, Mays, Cabell & Moore, Richmond, Va., 1946-49; spl. counsel Sec. Def., Washington, 1949-50; dep. gen. counsel Fed. Maritime Bd., 1950-52, gen. counsel, 1952; exec. v.p. Washington office Am. Mcht. Marine Inst., 1953-55, pres., 1955-56; mem. Surrey, Karasik & Greene, 1956-71; counsel Kirkpatrick,

Lockhart, Hill, Christopher & Phillips, 1972—. Contbr. numerous articles to profl. jours. Served as comdr. USNR, 1941-45. Mem. Am., Va., D.C., Fed. bar assns. Episcopalian. Clubs: Metropolitan (Washington); Whitehall, Harvard (N.Y.C.); Fauquier (Va.). Home: Hunting Ridge Warrenton VA 22186 Office: 1900 M St NW Washington DC 20036 also Cal Bldg Warrenton VA 22186

GREENE, FREDERICK DAVIS, II, educator; b. Glen Ridge, N.J., July 9, 1927; s. Phillips Foster and Ruth (Altman) G.; m. Theodora Elizabeth Whatmough, June 5, 1953; children—Alan, Carol, Elizabeth, Phillips. Grad., Phillips Andover Acad., 1944; B.A., Amherst Coll., 1949, D.Sc. (hon.), 1969; Ph.D., Harvard, 1952. Research asso. U. Calif., Los Angeles, 1952-53; instr. dept. chemistry Mass. Inst. Tech., Cambridge, 1953-55, asst. prof., 1955-58, asso. prof., 1958-62, prof., 1962—. Editor-in-chief: Jour. Organic Chemistry, 1962—; Contbr. articles sci. jours. Served with USNR, 1945-46. Alfred P. Sloan fellow, 1958-62; NSF Sr. Postdoctoral fellow, 1965-66. Mem. Am. Chem. Soc., Chem. Soc. (London), Am. Acad. Arts and Scis., Phi Beta Kappa. Home: Winchester MA 01890 Office: Dept Chemistry Mass Inst Tech Cambridge MA 02139

GREENE, GEORGE BENJAMIN, JR., air force officer; b. Laurens, S.C., Apr. 20, 1914; s. George Benjamin and Helen Louise (Crisp) G.; m. Jane Drake, Jan. 20, 1940; children—Susan, Charles Drake, Jacquelin. B.S., Clemson U., 1935; grad. flying tng., Kelly Field, Tex., 1938, Air War Coll., 1953. Commd. 2d lt. USAAF, 1935; advanced through grades to maj. gen. USAF, 1962; pilot and group engring. officer (8th Pursuit Group), Va. and N.Y., 1938-41, comdr., New Guinea, 1941-43, group exec. officer, 1942-43, group Comdg. officer, La., 1943, Fla., 1943, asst., 1943-44, Fla. and Va., 1944-46, Langley Field, Va., 1946-47, asst. chief staff, later chief staff, C.Z., 1947- 48, asst. dep. chief, then dep. chief staff operations, Hdgrs., Cairo, C.Z., 1948-50, chief combat operations, operations and tng., 1950-51, wing comdr., Del., 1951-52, Mich., 1953-56, dep. chief staff personnel, Ent AFB, Colo., 1956-59, chief staff, 1959-60, dep. comdr., Ramstein AFB, Germany, 1960-61, dep. chief staff operations, Wiesbaden, Germany, 1961-63, dir. mil. personnel, 1963-67, comdr., Tex., 1967—. Decorated D.S.C., Silver Star, Legion of Merit, D.S.M., Air medal, numerous area and service ribbons. Mem. Air Force Assn., Night Fighters Assn., Order Daedalians. Home: 8358 Windway Dr San Antonio TX 78239

GREENE, GRAHAM, author; b. Berkhamsted, Hertfordshire, Eng., Oct. 2, 1904; s. Charles Henry and Marion (Raymond) G.; m. Vivien Dayrell-Browning, 1927; 1 son, 1 dau. Ed., Berkhamsted Sch., Balliol Coll., Oxford, Eng.; Litt.D. (hon.), Cambridge (Eng.) U., 1962, Edinburgh (Scotland) U., 1967, D.Litt., Oxford U., 1979. Sub-editor London Times, 1926-30; lit. editor Spectator, 1940-41; with (Fgn. Office), 1941-44; dir. Eyre & Spottiswoode, Ltd., 1944-48, Bodley Head, London, 1958-68. Author: books Babbling April, 1925, The Man Within, 1929, The Name of Action, 1930, Rumour at Nightfall, 1932, Stamboul Train, 1932, It's a Battlefield, 1934, England Made Me, 1935, The Basement Room; short stories The Bear Fell Free, 1935; Journey Without Maps, 1936, A Gun for Sale, 1936, Brighton Rock, 1938, The Lawless Roads, 1939, The Confidential Agent, 1939, The Power and the Glory, 1940 (Hawthornden prize), British Dramatists, 1942, The Ministry of Fear, 1943; short stories Nineteen Stories, 1947; The Heart of the Matter, 1948, The Third Man, 1950, The Lost Childhood and Other Essays, 1951, The End of the Affair, 1951, Essais Catholiques, 1953; short stories Twenty-one Stories, 1954; Loser Takes All, 1955, The Quiet American, 1955, Our Man in Havana, 1958, A Burnt-Out Case, 1961, In Search of a Character, 1961, A Sense of Reality, 1963, The Comedians, 1966; film 1967 May We Borrow Your Husband? and Other Comedies of the Sexual Life; Collected Essays, 1969, Travels with My Aunt, 1969, A Sort of Life, 1971, The Pleasure Dome: The Collected Film Criticism 1935-40; short stories Collected Stories, 1972; The Honorary Consul, 1973, Lord Rochester's Monkey, 1974, An Impossible Woman, 1975, The Human Factor, 1978, Dr. Fischer of Geneva or The Bomb Party, 1980, Ways of Escape, 1980, Monsignor Quixote, 1982, J'Accuse, the Darker Side of Nice, 1982, Getting to Know the General, 1984; plays The Living Room, 1953, The Potting Shed, 1957, The Complaisant Lover, 1959, Carving a Statue, 1964, The Return of A.J. Raffles, 1975, For Whom the Bell Chimes and Yes and No, 1980; children's books The Little Train, 1947, The Little Fire Engine, 1950, The Little Horse Bus, 1952, The Little Steamroller, 1953 (Recipient Black Meml. prize 1949, Shakespeare prize, Hamburg 1968). Decorated Companion of Honour, Companion of Lit.; chevalier Legion of Honor; Grand Cross Order Vasco Nunez de Balboa (Panama); commandeurdes Arts et des Lettres (France); named hon. citizen Anacapri, 1978; hon. fellow Balliol Coll.; recipient Thomas More medal, 1973, John Dos Passos prize, 1980, medal City of Madrid, 1980, Jerusalem prize, 1981. Address: care Bodley Head 9 Bow St London WC2 England

GREENE, HAROLD H., judge. B.S., J.D., George Washington U. Judge U.S. Dist. Ct. for D.C., 1978—. Office: US Dist Ct 3d and Constitution Ave NW Washington DC 20001

GREENE, HENRY VINCENT, JR., manufacturing company executive; b. Weston, Mass., July 13, 1922; s. Henry V. and Josephina Virginia (Hayes) G.; m. May Hewitt, Feb. 3, 1945; children: Henry Vincent, Matthew William, Rita S. Student, Boston U., 1948-51; cert., Sloan Sch. Mgmt., MIT, 1966; M.B.A., Pace U., 1977. With Westinghouse Broadcasting Co., N.Y.C., 1946-66; with RKO Gen., N.Y.C., 1967—, sr. v.p., dir., 1978—; chmn., pres., dir. RKO Hotels; v.p., dir. RKO Pictures. Mem. Bd. Edn., Greenwich, Conn., 1977—; trustee YMCA, Leukemia Soc. Am. Served as naval aviator USN, 1941-45, 51-53; comdr. Res. ret. Republican. Roman Catholic. Clubs: Wings, Indian Harbor Yacht. Home: 40 Park Ave Greenwich CT 06830 Office: 1440 Broadway New York NY 10018 *Industrious, total application of your capability. Keep a sense of humor. Don't lose touch. Kipling was right in his poem "If".*

GREENE, HERBERT BRUCE, lawyer, merchant banker; b. N.Y.C., Apr. 13, 1934; s. Joseph Lester and Shirley (Kasen) G.; m. Judith Jean Metricks, Dec. 31, 1958; children: Pamela S., Scott L. A.B., Harvard U., 1955; J.D., Columbia U., 1958. Bar: N.Y. 1959, Conn. 1975. Asst. U.S. atty So. Dist. N.Y., Dept. Justice, N.Y.C., 1958-61; asso. firm Kaye, Scholer, Fierman, Hays & Handler, N.Y.C., 1961-66; asst. to gen. counsel CIT Fin. Corp., N.Y.C., 1966-67; group gen. counsel Xerox Corp., Rochester, N.Y., 1967-68, v.p. adminstrn., 1968-71; sr. v.p. Xerox Edn. Group, Stamford, Conn., 1971-75; v.p., gen. counsel, sec. Lone Star Industries, Inc., Greenwich, Conn., 1976-79, sr. v.p., asst. to chmn., 1979-82; ptnr. Earle and Greene & Co., Stamford, Conn., 1982—; dir. KCOR Corp. Mem. N.Y. State Bar Assn., ABA, Conn. Bar Assn., Bar Assn. City N.Y., Assn. Asst. U.S. Attys. for So. Dist. N.Y., Am. Mgmt. Assn., Phi Delta Phi. Republican. Home: 44 N Bulkley Ave Wesport CT 06880 Office: Three Landmark Sq Suite 400 Stamford CT 06901

GREENE, JACK PHILLIP, educator, historian; b. Lafayette, Ind., Aug. 12, 1931; s. Ralph Beamon and Nellie (Miller) G.; m. Sue Lucille Neuenswander, June 27, 1953; children: Jacqueline Megan, Granville. A.B., U. N.C., 1951; M.A., Ind. U., 1952, Litt.D. (hon.), 1977; postgrad., U. Nebr., 1952-53, 54-55, Bristol (Eng.) U., 1953-54; Ph.D., Duke, 1956. Instr. history Mich. State U., 1956-59; asst. prof. Western Res. U., 1959-62, asso. prof., 1962-65; vis. asso. prof., also vis. editor William and Mary Quar., Coll. William and Mary, 1961-62; vis. asso. prof. Johns Hopkins U., 1964-65; asso. prof. U. Mich., 1965-66; prof. history Johns Hopkins U., 1966-75, Andrew W. Mellon prof. humanities, 1975—, chmn. dept. history, 1970-72; Mem. Inst. Advanced Study, 1970-71; vis. prof. Columbia, 1973-74, 77; Harmsworth prof. Oxford (Eng.) U., 1975-76; Fulbright prof. Hebrew U., Jerusalem, 1979. Author: The Quest for Power: The Lower Houses of Assembly in the Southern Royal Colonies, 1689-1776, 1963, The Diary of Colonel Landon Carter of Sabine Hall, 1752-1778, 2 vols, 1965, Settlements to Society, 1584-1763, 1966, Colonies to Nation, 1763-1789, 1967, The Reappraisal of the American Revolution in Recent Historical Literature, 1967, The Ambiguity of the American Revolution, 1968, The Reinterpretation of the American Revolution, 1968, The American Colonies in the Eighteenth Century 1689-1763, 1969, Great Britain and The American Colonies 1606-1763, 1970, The Nature of Colony Constitutions, 1970; author: The First Continental Congress: A Documentary History, 1974, All Men are Created Equal, 1976; Joint editor: Preconditions of Revolution in Early Modern Europe, 1971, Neither Slave nor Free: The Freedmen of African Descent in the Slave Societies of the New World, 1972; joint editor: British Colonial America: Essays in the New History of the Early Modern Era, 1983. Served with AUS, 1957. Fulbright fellow, U.K., 1953-54; Lilly Found. fellow Clements Library, 1964; Guggenheim fellow, 1964-65; John Carter Brown Library fellow, 1969; fellow Woodrow Wilson Internat. Center for Scholars, 1974-75, Center for Advanced Study Behavioral Scis., 1979-80. Fellow Royal Hist. Soc.; mem. Am. Antiquarian Soc., Am. Hist. Assn., Orgn. Am. Historians, So. Hist. Soc., Phi Beta Kappa. Home: 1010 Bellemore Rd Baltimore MD 21210

GREENE, JAMES COFFIN, lawyer; b. San Francisco, Feb. 18, 1915; s. A. Crawford and Natalie (Coffin) G.; m. Elizabeth Rollins, June 20, 1940; children: Natalie Whittier Jennings, Carl Rollins (dec.), Sarah Elizabeth, James Coffin. B.A., Yale U., 1936, LL.B., 1939. Bar: Calif. 1940. Assoc. O'Melveny & Myers, Los Angeles, 1939-53, ptnr., 1953—; dir. Gt. Western Fin. Corp., Gt. Western Savs. and Loan Assn., Am. Mut. Fund, Inc. Pres. Honnold Library Soc., Claremont, Calif., Los Angeles Com. Fgn. Relations; trustee Claremont Univ. Center, Pacific Oaks, Pasadena, Calif., Thacher Sch., Ojai, Calif., U. Calif., Santa Barbara Found., Mus. Contemporary Art, Los Angeles. Mem. Am., Los Angeles County bar assns., State Bar Calif. Home: 1085 Glen Oaks Blvd Pasadena CA 91105 Office: 400 S Hope St Los Angeles CA 90071

GREENE, JEFFREY ALDEN, advertising agency executive; b. N.Y.C., June 6, 1925; s. Stanley R. and Constance (Murray) G.; m. Dorothy Anne Quimby, Feb. 3, 1951; children: Kim Elizabeth, John Scott, Hilary Virginia. B.A. magna cum laude, Colgate U., 1949. Account exec. Albert Frank-Guenther Law, Inc., N.Y.C., 1949-56; v.p., account exec. Kenyon & Eckhardt, Inc., N.Y.C., 1956-63; sr. v.p., mgmt. supr., mem. exec. com. William Esty Co. Inc., N.Y.C., 1963—. Served with USAAF, 1943-46. Mem. Phi Beta Kappa, Sigma Chi. Episcopalian (vestryman 1967-72). Clubs: Larchmont Shore (Larchmont); Winged Foot Golf (Mamaroneck, N.Y.). Home: 27 Willow Ave Larchmont NY 10538 Office: 100 E 42d St New York NY 10017

GREENE, JERRY GEORGE, physician; b. Regina, Sask., Can., May 13, 1937; came to U.S., 1962, naturalized, 1981; s. David Robert and Fae (Woodman) G.; m. Waltra Laguniak, Feb. 27, 1960; children: Deidre, Cheryl, Michael. M.D., U. Man., 1960. Diplomate: Am. Bd. Internal Medicine. Rotating intern St. Boniface Hosp., Winnipeg, Man., Can., 1960-61, jr. asst. resident medicine, 1961-62; teaching fellow U. Man., 1961-62; fellow in medicine Mayo Clinic, 1962-66, asst. in pulmonary diseases, 1966; chief pulmonary lab. St. Joseph's Hosp., St. Paul, 1966-69; asst. prof. medicine U. Minn., St. Paul, 1968-71, practice medicine specializing in internal medicine, 1966-68, Med. Assos. Saranac Lake, N.Y., 1972-78; asso. cardiac catheterization lab. St. Mary's Hosp., Mpls., 1967, dir. inhalation therapy program, 1967; chief pulmonary disease St. Paul Ramsey Hosp., 1968-71; med. dir. Will Rogers Hosp., Saranac Lake, N.Y., 1971-72, chief inhalation therapy, 1973, chief dept. medicine, 1977-78; chief pulmonary disease sect. VA Hosp., Fargo, N.D., 1978—; asst. prof. medicine in internal medicine U. Minn., 1968-71; prof. medicine U. N.D. Sch. Medicine; chief pulmonary service VA Hosp., Fargo, 1978—; cons. N.D. Lung Assn., PSRO, Blue Cross/Blue Shield N.D.; mem. adv. com. med. edn. NIH, 1980—, mem. pulmonary acad. award com. on pulmonary testing, 1979—. Contbr. articles to profl. jours. Bd. dirs. N.D. Lung Assn., 1979. Served with RCAF, 1960-62; to lt. col. M.C., USAF, Air N.G., 1982. Recipient Recognition award Mayo Clin. Fellow's Assn., 1966, Pulmonary Acad. award NIH, 1978. Fellow A.C.P., Am. Coll. Chest Physicians (com. on respirator pathophysiology); mem. Am. Soc. History Medicine, Am. Thoracic Soc., AMA, VA Pulmonary Physicians, N.D. Lung Assn., Mayo Clinic Alumni Assn. Office: 1919 Elm St Fargo ND 58102

GREENE, JOE (CHARLES EDWARD GREENE), former football player; b. Temple, Tex., Sept. 24, 1946. Student, N. Tex. State U. Defensive tackle Pitts. Steelers, 1969—; played in Pro Bowl, 1975, 76, 78, 82; color commentator CBS-NFL Today, 1983; private business, 1983. Named to Sporting News NFL Eastern Conf. All-Star Team, 1969; Sporting News AFC All-Star Team, 1970-74, 79. *

GREENE, JOHN CLIFFORD, dentist, university dean; b. Ashland, Ky., July 19, 1926; s. G. Norman and Ella R. G.; m. Gwen Rustin, Nov. 17, 1957; children: Alan, Lisa, Laura. A.A., Ashland Jr. Coll., 1947; student, Marshall Coll., 1948; D.M.D., U. Louisville, 1952, Sc.D. (hon.), 1980; M.P.H., U. Calif., Berkeley, 1961; Sc.D. (hon.), U. Ky., 1972, Boston U., 1975. Diplomate: Am. Bd. Dental Public Health (pres.). Intern USPHS Hosp., Chgo., 1952-53, staff, San Francisco, 1953-54; asst. regional dental cons. Region IX, San Francisco, 1954-56, asst. to chief dental officer, Washington, 1958-60; chief epidemiology program Dental Health Center, 1961-66; dep. dir. Div. Dental Health, 1966-70, acting dir., 1970, dir., 1970-73; acting dir. Bur. Health Resources Devel., 1973-74, dir., 1974-75; chief dental officer USPHS, 1974-81, dep. surgeon gen., 1978-81; with Epidemic Intelligence Service, Communicable Disease Center, Altanta and Kansas City, Mo., 1956-57; epidemiology and biometry br. Nat. Inst. Dental Research, NIH, Bethesda, Md., 1957-58; dean. Sch. Dentistry,U. Calif., San Francisco, 1981—; spl. cons. WHO, India, 1957; faculty Calif., U. Mich., U. Pa.; cons. Am. Dental Assn. Council, Nat. Health Professions Placement Network. Contbr. writings to profl. publs. Served with USN, 1945-46. Recipient citation Sch. Grad. Dentistry Boston U., 1971, U. of the Pacific, 1977, Meritorious and Disting. Service awards HEW, 1972, 75, Outstanding Alumnus award U. Louisville, 1980, award of merit FDI, 1978. Fellow Am. Coll. Dentists; mem. ADA, Calif. Dental Assn., San Francisco Dental Soc., Internat. Assn. Dental Research, Am. Assn. Public Health Dentists, Am. Acad. Periodontology, Am. Assn. Dental Schs. (v.p.), Inst. of Medicine of Nat. Acad. Sci., Federation Dentaire Internationale (chmn. commn. on public dental health, mem. WHO panel of experts on dental health), Omicron Kappa Upsilon, Delta Omega. Home: 103 Peacock Dr San Rafael CA 94901 Office: U Calif Sch Dentistry: San Francisco CA 94143

GREENE, JOHN THOMAS, JR., lawyer; b. Salt Lake City, Nov. 28, 1929; s. John Thomas and Mary Agnes (Hindley) G.; m. Kay Buchanan, Mar. 31, 1955; children: Thomas B., John B., Mary Kay. B.A., U. Utah, 1952, J.D., 1955. Bar: Utah 1955. Law clk. Supreme Ct. Utah, Salt Lake City, 1954-55; asst. U.S. atty. Dist. Utah, Salt Lake City, 1957-59; partner firm Marr, Wilkins & Cannon, Salt Lake City, 1959-69, Cannon, Greene & Nebeker, 1969-74, Greene, Callister & Nebeker, 1974—; spl. asst. atty. gen. State of Utah, 1965-69; spl. grand jury counsel Salt Lake County, 1970; pres. Utah Bar Found., 1971-74, trustee, 1971—. Author: sect. on mining rights American Law of Mining, 1965; editor: Utah Law Rev, 1954; contbr. articles to profl. jours. Pres. Community Services Council, Salt Lake City area, 1971-73; Republican chmn. Voting Dist. 47, Salt Lake County, 1969-73; chmn. Utah Bldg. Authority, 1980—. Mem. Utah State Bar (pres. 1970-71, chmn. judiciary com. 1971-76), Am. Bar Assn. (ho. of dels. 1975—, mem. spl. com. delivery legal service 1975-81, council gen. practice sect. 1974-82, chmn. spl. com. on environ. law 1971-75, mem. adv. com. Nat. Legal Service Corp. 1975-81), Am. Inn Ct. II (pres. 1983—), U. Utah Alumni Assn. (dir. 1968-69), Order of Coif, Phi Beta Kappa, Phi Kappa Phi. Mormon. Clubs: Ft. Douglas Country, Salt Lake Tennis. Home: 1923 Browning Ave Salt Lake City UT 84108 Office: 800 Kennecott Bldg Salt Lake City UT 84133

GREENE, JOSEPH ARTHUR, JR., univ. dean; b. Johnson City, Tenn., Oct. 19, 1920; s. Joseph Arthur and Cozie Josephine (Carpenter) G.; m. Sarah Virginia Jessee, Aug. 20, 1946; children—Kathryn Ann, Jacqueline Lee, Michael Joseph, Alan Vince. B.A., Berea (Ky.) Coll., 1941; M.A., U. Va., 1943, Ph.D., 1951. With traffic dept. Tenn. Eastman Corp., Kingsport, 1944-46; co-owner, prof. Cecil's Inst. Accountancy, Greenville, S.C., 1947; dean Sch. Bus. Adminstrn., U. So. Miss., Hattiesburg, 1949—. Served with AUS, 1943. Mem. Am., So. econ. assns., So. Bus. Adminstrn. Assn. (pres.), Hattiesburg C. of C. (dir.), Beta Gamma Sigma, Phi Kappa Phi, Delta Sigma Pi, Omicron Delta Kappa. Republican. Methodist. Club: Lion. Home: 401 S 32d Ave Hattiesburg MS 39401

GREENE, JOSEPH NATHANIEL, JR., foundation executive, former diplomat; b. N.Y.C., Apr. 9, 1920; s. Joseph N. and Nanine (Pond) G.; m. Edith Cowles, Mar. 21, 1942 (div. Aug 1960); children: Alice W., Nancy W., Edith E.; m. Christine O'Hara, Apr. 22, 1961; children—Joanna, John, stepdau. Susan O'Hara. Grad., Hotchkiss Sch., 1937; B.A., Yale U., 1941. Asst. instr. Phillips Acad., 1941; U.S. fgn. service officer, 1942-73, assigned to, Montreal, Ottawa, Rome, Trieste, desk officer for Italy, Dept. State, Washington, assigned to, Singapore, Bonn; dep. dir. exec. secretariat Dept. State, Washington, 1956; spl. asst. to Sec. State, 1957-59; assigned Imperial Def. Coll., London, 1960; counselor embassy, dep. chief mission, Lagos, Nigeria, 1961-63; minister-counselor, dep. chief mission Am. embassy, New Delhi, 1963-68; dep. adminstr. Bur. Security and Consular Affairs, 1968-69, dep. asst. sec. state internat. orgn. affairs, 1969-70; minister-counselor, dep. chief mission Am. embassy, London, 1970-71; diplomat-in-residence Brandeis U., Waltham, Mass., 1971-72; minister-counselor in charge U.S. interests, Cairo, 1972-73; pres. Seven Springs Center, Mt. Kisco, N.Y., 1973-82; mem. internat. adv. com. Am. Security Bank, 1978-82. Mem. Byram Com., Nature Conservancy, 1973-81. Served with USNR, 1944-46. Mem. Council Fgn. Relations. Clubs: Met. (Washington); Century, Yale (N.Y.C.). Home:: Joshuatown Rd Lyme CT 06371

GREENE, JULE BLOUNTE, lawyer; b. Dublin, Ga., Aug. 15, 1922; s. Jule B. and Bette (O'Neal) G.; m. George Williams, Aug. 22, 1952; children: James Herschel, Bradley O'Neal. A.B., Mercer U., 1949, LL.B., 1950. Bar: Ga. 1950, Supreme Ct. 1960. Atty. SEC, Atlanta, 1950-53, Washington, 1956-58, atty.-in-charge, Miami, Fla., 1958-69, regional adminstr., Atlanta, 1969-82; regional counsel Nat. Assn. Securities Dealers, Atlanta, 1982—; pvt. practice law, Macon and Waycross, Ga., 1953-56; Former mem. Atlanta Fed. Exec. Bd., Interagy. Bd. U.S. Civil Service Examiners; former v.p., dir. Peachtree Fed. Credit Union.; Former treas., dir. Mental Health Assn. Met. Atlanta. Served with A.C. AUS, 1942-46. Recipient award for exemplary achievement in pub. adminstrn. William A. Jump Meml. Found., 1958. Mem. Fed. Bar Assn. (pres. South Fla. chpt. 1961), Ga. Bar Assn., Kappa Alpha. Baptist. Club: Rotarian. Home: 9670 Roberts Dr NE Atlanta GA 30338 Office: #1100 250 Piedmont Ave Atlanta GA 30308

GREENE, KENNETH M., association executive; b. Cleve., Aug. 16, 1920; s. William E. and Rose (Fuerst) G.; m. Anne F. Ziemba, Sept. 5, 1949; children: Jocelyn Anne, Janet Elizabeth, Kenneth M. Jr. B.A., Brown U., 1942; M.A., Columbia U., 1947, Ph.D., 1964. Mem. faculty Simmons Coll., Boston, 1947-62, prof. English, 1962-70, dir. sch. edn., 1964-70; pres. Lasell Jr. Coll., Newton, Mass., 1970-75; exec. sec. United Chpts. Phi Beta Kappa, Washington, 1975—, Phi Beta Kappa Found., 1975—; dir. NDEA Inst. Advanced Study English, 1965-69. Mem. exec. com. Assn. Ind. Coll. and Univs. Mass., 1972-75; bd. mem. pub.-pvt. forum Commonwealth Mass. Bd. Edn., 1971-75; trustee Lasell Jr. Coll., 1970-76; mem. adv. council nursing program Newton-Wellesley Hosp., 1972-75, Mayor's Ednl. Adv. Com., Newton, 1974-75. Served to capt. AUS. Decorated Croix de Guerre with Bronze Star, Silver Star, Purple Heart; John Hay scholar Brown U., 1938-42; James Manning scholar, 1941; recipient Ratcliffe Hicks prize, 1940. Mem. Am. Soc. 18th Century Studies, AAUP, Am. Assn. Advancement Humanities, MLA. Home: 6206 Cheryl Dr Falls Church VA 22044 Office: United Chapters of Phi Beta Kappa 1811 Q St NW Washington DC 20009

GREENE, LAURENCE FRANCIS, educator; b. Chgo., Jan. 11, 1912; s. Morris and Rose (Fiedler) G.; m. Rosalyn R. Ravits, June 24, 1951; children: Edith, Richard, Nancy, James. B.S., U. Chgo., 1932; M.D., Harvard, 1936; Ph.D. in Urology, U. Minn., 1942. Diplomate: Am. Bd. Urology. Intern St. Luke's Hosp., Chgo., 1936-38; fellow Mayo Found., 1938-42; cons. urology Mayo Clinic, Rochester, Minn., 1942-78; mem. faculty Mayo Grad. Sch. Med., U. Minn., 1943-73, prof. urology, 1963-73, Mayo Med. Sch., 1973-74, Anson L. Clark prof. urology, 1974-78, prof. emeritus, 1978—; also mem. adv. bd. for continuing edn., 1973—; prof. clin. surgery/urology U. Calif. Sch. Medicine, San Diego; urologic cons. Univ. Hosp., VA Hosp.; vis. prof. U. Okla., 1968, U. S.C., 1976, U. So. Calif., 1979, Stanford U., 1980; mem. adv. bd. Am. Family Physician GP. Author: Transurethral Surgery, 1979; contbr. articles to profl. jours. Bd. dirs. Minn. Orch. Assn., 1966—; chmn. Rochester com., 1965-71; bd. dirs. Rochester Festival Music, 1965-66; pianist, mgr., Notochords Orch., Rochester, 1958—. Fellow A.M.A.; mem. Am. Urol. Assn., Am. Fertility Soc., Minn. Surg. Soc., Am. Soc. Nephrology, Soc., Univ. Urologists, Internat. Soc. Urologists, Univ. Urologic Forum, Sigma Xi; corr. mem. La Soc. Mexicana de Urologia, Soc. Medico-Quirurgica del Guayas. Home: 558 San Lucas Dr Solana Beach CA 92075 Office: 3350 LaJolla Village Dr San Diego CA 92161

GREENE, LEE SEIFERT, political scientist; b. Esbon, Kans., May 31, 1905; s. Eugene C. and Margaret E. (Cline) G.; m. Dorothy H. Kuersteiner, Dec. 24, 1932; children: Harriet Lee, Robert Everist. B.M., U. Kans., 1927, A.B., 1930; postgrad. (German-Am. exchange fellow), U. Leipzig, 1930-31; A.M., U. Wis., 1932, Ph.D., 1934, Brookings Instn., 1933-34, U. Mich., summer 1935. Social Sci. Research Council post-doctoral fellow, 1937-38; instr. music U. Kans., 1926-30; instr. U. Wis., 1934-36; research asso. and supr. pub. adminstrn. TVA, 1936-37, 1938-41; lectr. U. Tenn., Knoxville, 1937, asst. prof. polit. sci., 1938-39, asso. prof., 1939-45, prof., 1945—, Distinguished prof., 1965-75, prof. emeritus, 1975—, acting head dept.

polit. sci., 1942-46, head, 1946-71; dir. Bur. Pub. Adminstrn., 1945-71; exec. dir. Harris County (Houston) Home Rule Commn., 1956-57; exec. sec., Knoxville, Knox County Met. Charter Commn., 1957-59; cons. Knoxville Met. Planning Commn., 1960; vis. prof. U. Ala., summer 1948, U. Calif. at Los Angeles, summer 1949, Duke, summer 1950, Syracuse U., 1950-51, U. Ga., 1961, 65; Mem. civil service bd., Knoxville, 1941-47, chmn., 1945-47; Cons. TVA, 1941-42, So. Regional Edn. Bd., 1952-53, FOA, 1954; Chmn. research com. Constl. Conv., Tenn., 1953; cons. ICA, 1955, Memphis Charter Com., 1967, Shelby County Structure Com., 1969; Public panel mem. and labor arbitrator Nat. War Labor Bd., Nat. Wage Stblzn. Bd., U.S. Conciliation Service, Fed. Mediation and Conciliation Service; arbitrator TVA; mem. nat. panel arbitrators Am. Arbitration Assn. Author: (with V.H. Brown and Evan A. Iverson) Administration of Natural Resources in Tennessee, 1948, (with D.R. Grant) A Future for Nashville, 1952, Metropolitan Harris County, 1957, (with R.S. Avery) Government in Tennessee, 1962, 2d edit., 1966, (with D. Grubbs, V. Hobday) Government in Tennessee, 3d edit., 1975, (with George Parthemos) American Government: Policies and Functions, 1967, (with M.E. Jewell, D.R. Grant) The States and the Metropolis, (with Dye and Parthemos) American Government: Theory, Structure and Process, 1969, 2d edit., 1972, Governing the American Democracy, 1980, Lead Me On: Frank Goad Clement and Tennessee Politics, 1982, (with Montgomery and Folmsbee) History of U. of Tenn., 1984; editor: (with R. deV. Williamson) Five Years of British Labour, 1945-50, 1950, Resources and Policy, 1951, Jour. of Politics, 1953-57; assoc. editor (with R. deV. Williamson), 1949-52; spl. editor: Conservatism, Liberalism, and Natl. Issues (Annals Am. Acad.), 1962, City Bosses and Political Machines, 1964; Contbr. articles to profl. jours. Mem. Am. Polit. Sci. Assn., So. Polit. Sci. Assn. (pres. 1957-58), Nat. Mcpl. League, Am. Soc. Pub. Adminstrn., Nat. Inst. Pub. Affairs (trustee 1961-71), Phi Beta Kappa, Phi Kappa Phi, Pi Kappa Lambda, Beta Theta Pi, Phi Mu Alpha. Club: Masons. Home: 1410 Tugaloo Dr Knoxville TN 37919 Office: 106 Main Library U Tenn Knoxville TN 37916

GREENE, LORNE, actor; b. Ottawa, Ont., Can., Feb. 12, 1915; s. Daniel and Dora G.; m. Rita Hands, 1940 (div. 1960); children: Belinda and Charles (twins); m. Nancy Anne Deale, Dec. 1961; 1 child. Ed., Queen's U., Neighborhood Playhouse Sch. of Theatre, N.Y.C. Am. debut in: The Prescott Proposals, N.Y.C., 1953; starred in, Stratford (Ont.) Shakespeare Festival, 1955; Broadway appearances include Speaking of Murder, 1956, Edwin Booth, 1958; appeared with, New Play Soc., Earl Grey Players, Toronto, Ont.; founder, dir., actor, Jupiter Theater, Toronto; commentator documentary film: Churchill's Island; acted: in motion pictures including The Silver Chalice, 1954, Tight Spot, 1955, Autumn Leaves, 1956, Peyton Place, 1957, The Hard Man, 1957, Gift of Love, 1958, The Buccaneer, 1958, The Trap, 1959, Earthquake, 1974, Tidal Wave, 1975; regular on: TV series Bonanza, 1959-73, Griff, 1973-74, Lorne Greene's Last of the Wild, 1974-79, Battlestar Gallactica, 1978-79, Galactica, 1980, Code Red, 1981-82; TV movies include Man on the Outside, 1975, Nevada Smith, 1975; regular on: SST-Death Flight, 1977; played in: mini-series The Moneychangers, 1976, Roots, 1977, The Bastard, 1978; spls. Swing Out, Sweet Land, 1971, The Great American Music Celebration, 1976; animated feature Heidi's Song; appearances various other TV shows. Former chmn. Nat. Wildlife Found.; bd. dirs. Am. Horse Protection Assn.; chmn. Am. Freedom from Hunger Found.; spl. civilian adv. Office Tech. Assessment. Served with RCAF. Mem. Actors Equity Assn., Screen Actors Guild, AFTRA. Address: care Artists Group 10100 S Santa Monica Blvd Los Angeles CA 90067 *

GREENE, MARK RICHARD, marketing educator; b. Imbler, Oreg., Oct. 28, 1923; s. Homer Cooper and Adah (Hicks) G.; m. Fanney Runolfs, Dec. 31, 1946; children: Irving Edward, Robert, Erik. A.B., Stanford, 1947, M.B.A., 1949; Ph.D., Ohio State U., 1955. Asst. prof. bus. adminstrn. U. Oreg., 1949-51; lectr. Stanford, 1952; asst. Ohio State U., 1952-53; asst. prof. marketing Washington U., 1953-55; asso. prof. bus. adminstrn., Oreg., Eugene, 1955-58, asso. prof. ins., 1958-61, prof., head dept. marketing, ins. and transp., 1961-67; dir. Center For Internat. Bus. Studies, 1967-70, Acting dean, 1964-65; Distinguished prof. ins., Ga., Athens, 1970—; Inst. Basic Math. for Application to Bus. fellow Harvard, 1959-60; vis. prof. marketing Denver U., summer 1955; vis. prof. ins. U. Calif., Los Angeles, summer 1965; Exec. sec. Am. Assn. Collegiate Schs. Bus., 1953-55; bd. govs. Internat. Ins. Seminars, Inc. Author: Risk and Insurance, 1962, co-author 5th edit., 1981, The Role of Employee Benefit Structures in Manufacturing Industry, 1964, Risk Aversion, Insurance and the Future, 1971; Co-Author: Mathematical Methods and Models in Marketing, 1962, Insurance Insights, 1974, Risk Management: Text and Cases, 1978, 2d edit., 1983, Personal Financial Management, 1983; Contbr. articles to profl. jours. Served with USAAF, 1943-46. Mem. Acad. Internat. Bus., Am. Risk and Ins. Assn. (pres. 1968-69), Phi Theta Kappa, Beta Gamma Sigma, Gamma Iota Sigma, Alpha Kappa Psi. Conglist. Home: 335 St George Dr Athens GA 30606

GREENE, MICHAEL JOSEPH LENIHAN, foundation executive, retired army officer; b. West Point, N.Y., July 4, 1919; s. Douglass Taft and Eleanora (Lenihan) G.; m. Ruth Eileen Conner, Jan. 1, 1946; children: Mary, Rebecca Greene Fellows, Michael J.L., Katharine Greene Gray. Student, Drexel Inst. Tech., 1936-37; B.S., U.S. Mil. Acad., 1941; M.A., U. Va., 1951; grad., Army Command and Gen. Staff Coll., 1943, U.S. Naval War Coll., 1959, U.S. Naval War Coll., 1969. Commd. 2d lt. U.S. Army, 1941, advanced through grades to brig. gen., 1968; sec. Gen. Staff, U.S. 7th Army, Ger., 1956-58; asst. African affairs Office Asst. Sec. Def., 1959-63; exec. asst., sec. Joint Staff Mil. Assistance Command, Vietnam, 1963-65; comdr. 2d Brigade, 1st Armored Div., Ft. Hood, Tex., 1965-66; asst. to chmn. Joint Chiefs Staff, 1967-68; dep. comdt. Army War Coll., 1968-70; asst. comdr. 25th Div., Vietnam, 1970-71; comdg. gen. Army Hdqrs. Area Command for Saigon, 1971; ret., 1971, research analyst, McLean, Va., 1971-74, law firm adminstr., 1976-80, planning analyst, Washington, 1980; exec. dir. Army Distaff Found., Washington, 1981—. Decorated Silver Star, Legion of Merit with 2 oak leaf clusters, D.F.C., D.S.M., Bronze Star, Air medal with 17 oak leaf clusters, Army Commendation medal, Purple Heart. Mem. Assn. Grad. U.S. Mil. Acad., Alumni Assn. U. Va., Assn. U.S. Army. Home: 8501 Cyrus Pl Alexandria VA 22308

GREENE, NATHANAEL, historian, university official; b. Providence, Apr. 4, 1935; s. Nathanael Bowden and Doris Marcia (Wilde) G.; m. Anne B. Frank, Jan. 12, 1980; children: Jonathan N., Jeffrey P., ElizabethD., Matthew H. A.B., Brown U., 1957; Fulbright fellow, Fond. Nat. des Scis. Politiques, Paris, 1961-62; Ph.D., Harvard U., 1964. Mem. faculty Wesleyan U., Middletown, Conn., 1963—, prof. history, 1974—, v.p. acad. affairs, 1977—. Author: Crisis and Decline, 1968, Fascism: An Anthology, 1968, European Socialism Since World War I, 1971, From Versailles to Vichy, 1970. Fellow Am. Council Learned Socs., 1968-69; Guggenheim Found., 1971-72. Mem. Am. Hist. Assn., Soc. French Hist. Studies, Soc. Spanish and Portuguese Hist. Studies. Democrat. Episcopalian. Home: 574 Ballfall Rd Middletown CT 06457 Office: North Coll Wesleyan Univ Middletown CT 06457

GREENE, NICHOLAS MISPLEE, physician, educator; b. Milford, Conn., July 11, 1922; s. Joseph N. and Nanine W. (Pond) G.; m. Elizabeth R. Miller, May 21, 1946; children: Nicholas P., Cynthia R., Joseph Nathaniel II. B.S., Yale U., 1944, M.A., 1955; M.D., Columbia U., 1946. Diplomate: Am. Bd. Anesthesiology. Intern Presbyn. Hosp., N.Y.C., 1946-47; resident anesthesiology Mass. Gen. Hosp., Boston, 1949-51; vis. fellow U. Edinburgh (Scotland) and Royal Infirmary, 1951; asst. anesthetist Mass. Gen. Hosp.; also instr. anesthesia Harvard Med. Sch., 1951-53; asso. prof. anesthesiology, asst. prof. pharmacology U. Rochester Sch. Medicine; also dir. anesthesia Strong Meml. Hosp., 1953-55; prof. anesthesiology Yale Sch. Medicine, 1955—, chmn. dept. anesthesiology, 1955-73; chmn. dept. and dir. dept. anesthesiology Yale-New Haven Hosp., 1955-73. Author books and articles in field.; Editor: Anesthesiology, 1964-73; editor-in-chief, 1973-76, Anesthesia and Analgesia, 1977—. Served to lt. (j.g.), M.C. USNR, 1947-49. Mem. Assn. Univ. Anesthestists, Am. Soc. Anesthesiologists, Internat. Anesthesia Research Soc., N.E. Soc. Anesthesiologists, Am. Ornithologic Union, Nature Conservancy, Sigma Xi. Home: 1220 Ridge Rd Hamden CT 06517 Office: 333 Cedar St New Haven CT 06510

GREENE, PETER ALAN, advt. agy. exec.; b. N.Y.C., June 25, 1946; s. Richard Coleman and Marion Phyllis (Bader) G.; m. Rosemarie Christine Gambale, July 19, 1970. B.A. in English, Trinity Coll., Hartford, Conn., 1968; M.B.A. in Mktg, Columbia U., 1969. Asst. account exec. S.S.C.&B., Inc., N.Y.C., 1969-71; account exec. Ted Bates & Co., Inc., N.Y.C., 1971-72; account supr. Case & McGrath, Inc., N.Y.C., 1972-74; v.p., account supr. Benton & Bowles, Inc., N.Y.C., 1974-76, mgmt. supr., sr. v.p., 1979—; v.p. Benton & Bowles Ltd., Toronto, Ont., Can., 1976-79. Served with U.S. Army, 1969-70. Home: 30 Fifth Ave New York NY 10011 Office: 909 3d Ave New York NY 10022

GREENE, ROBERT ALLAN, univ. adminstr.; b. Boston, Nov. 6, 1931; s. Merrill Francis and Alice Josephine (Anderson) G.; m. Mary E. Mahoney, July 20, 1957; children—Robert, Merrill, Helen, Priscilla. B.A., Boston Coll., 1953, M.A., 1954; Ph.D., Harvard U., 1961. Lectr. dept. English Univ. Coll., U. Toronto, Ont., Can., 1958-61, asst. prof., 1962-65, asso. prof., 1966-69, prof., 1969-80, dean, 1972-77; Leverhulme vis. lectr. Durham (Eng.) U., 1962-63; vice-chancellor for acad. affairs, provost U. Mass., Boston, 1980—. Editor: (With H.R. MacCallum) Nathaniel Culverwell's Discourse of the Light of Nature, 1652, 1971. Home: 19 Centre St Apt 5 Cambridge MA 02139 Office: U Mass Harbor Campus Boston MA 02125

GREENE, ROBERT BERNARD, JR. (BOB GREENE), journalist, author; b. Columbus, Ohio, Mar. 10, 1947; s. Robert Bernard and Phyllis Ann (Harmon) G.; m. Susan Bonnet Koebel, Feb. 13, 1971; 1 dau., Amanda Sue. B.S., Northwestern U., 1969. Reporter Chgo. Sun-Times, 1969-71, columnist, 1971-78; syndicated columnist Field Newspaper Syndicate, Irvine, Calif., 1976-81, Tribune Co. Syndicate, N.Y.C., 1981—; contbg. corr. ABC News Nightline, 1981—; columist Chgo. Tribune, 1978—; lectr. fine arts U. Chgo. Contbg. editor: Esquire Mag., 1980—; books include We Didn't Have None of Them Fat Funky Angels on the Wall of Heartbreak Hotel and Other Reports from America, 1971; Running: A Nixon-McGovern Campaign Journal, 1973, Billion Dollar Baby, 1974, Johnny Deadline, Reporter: The Best of Bob Greene, 1976, (with Paul Galloway) Bagtime, 1977, American Beat, 1983. Recipient Nat. Headliner award for best newspaper column in U.S., 1977, Peter Lisagor award, 1981. Office: Chicago Tribune 435 N Michigan Ave Chicago IL 60611 *

GREENE, ROBERT WILLIAM, newspaper editor; b. Jamaica, N.Y., July 12, 1929; s. Francis McLaughlin and Mary Virginia (Clancy) G.; m. Kathleen A. Greene, Jan. 28, 1951; children: Robert William, Lea Marie. Student, Fordham U., 1947-50. Reporter Jersey Jour., 1949-50; sr. investigator N.Y.C. Anti-Crime Com., 1950-55; reporter Newsday, Garden City, N.Y., 1955, leader investigative team, 1967-73, sr. editor, from 1970, now asst. mng. editor; staff investigator U.S. Senate Select Com. on Unfair Practices in Labor/Mgmt. Field, 1957; lectr. in field. Author: Naked Came the Stranger, 1969, The Heroin Trail, 1973, The Sting Man, 1981. Chmn. publicity Smithtown Tercentenary, 1967; Founding mem. bd. dirs. Suffolk County Happy Landings Fund. Recipient George Polk award L.I. U.; Peter Zenger award U. Ariz.; James Wright Brown award; Gold Medal Pulitzer prize, 1970, 73; Mo. medal for disting. service to Am. journalism, 1979. Mem. Investigative Reporters and Editors Group (pres. 1976-77, chmn. exec. bd.). Republican. Roman Catholic. Club: L.I. Press (pres. 1976). Office: care Newsday Inc 235 Pinelawn Rd Melville NY 11747 *

GREENE, SHECKY, entertainer; b. Chgo., Apr. 8, 1926; s. Carl and Bessie (Harris) Greenfield; m. Nalani Kele, Dec. 6, 1972. Student public schs., Chgo. Entertainer in night clubs, 1947—, on TV, 1953—, also in movies, night club appearances at all major clubs throughout, U.S., 1947—, night club appearances, Las Vegas, 1953—; films include The Love Machine, 1970, Tony Rome, 1967; co-star: TV series Combat, 1956; host: Johnny Carson and Merv Griffin TV shows; co-host: numerous TV guest appearances on talk, variety and game shows Mike Douglas TV show; author all materials and songs for appearances. Recipient Las Vegas Best Lounge Entertainer award, 1972, 1st Jimmy Durante award as best comedian, Miami, Fla., 1975; named Comedy Performer of Yr. South Fla. Entertainment Writers Assn., 1978, Male Comedy Star of Yr. Las Vegas Acad. Variety and Cabaret Artists, 1977. Jewish. Club: Las Vegas Country. Office: care Regency Artists Ltd 920 Sunset Blvd Suite 823 Los Angeles CA 90012 *It took me many years to find out who I am—not in my occupation, but me personally. Though I was accepted by the public and my peers for many years, I never truly appreciated the gift with which I was blessed—to be able to get up on a stage and entertain people. Then I learned to respect and love myself and appreciate my blessings—and, in learning to do this, I also learned to love those who deserve to be loved, and to have the strength to walk away from those who do not enhance my life.*

GREENE, STEPHEN, painter; b. N.Y.C., Sept. 19, 1918; s. William and Augusta (Lasky) G.; m. Sigrid de Lima, 1953; 1 dau., Alison de Lima. Art student, Nat. Acad. Design, 1936-37, Art Student's League, 1937-38; B.F.A., U. Iowa, 1942, A.M., 1945. Instr. art Ind. U., 1945-46, Washington U., St. Louis, 1946-47, Parsons Sch. Design, N.Y.C., 1947-56, Pratt Inst., N.Y.U., Art Students League; artist in residence Princeton U., 1956-59; guest critic Columbia U., 1961-64, asst. prof., 1964-67; assoc. prof., then prof. Tyler Sch. Art, Temple Univ., 1968—. One man shows, Durlacher Bros., N.Y.C., 1947, 49, 52, Grace Borgenicht Gallery, 1955, 58, 59, Staempfli Gallery, 1961, 64, 66, 69, William Zierler Gallery, N.Y.C., 1971, 72, 73, 75, Marilyn Pearl Gallery, N.Y.C., 1977, 78, 79, 80, 82, Galeria Ponce, Mexico City, 1977, 79, 82, retrospectives, Dana and De Cordova Mus., 1953, Dana and De Cordova Mus., Princeton, 1956, The Corcoran Gallery of Am. Art, 1963, Akron Art Inst., 1978, Columbus Gallery Fine Arts, Ohio, N.C. Mus. Art, Raleigh, Currier Gallery Art, Manchester, N.H., exhbns., Whitney Mus., Art Inst. Chgo., Nat. Acad. Design, Milw. Art Inst., Va. Mus. Fine Arts, Met. Mus., Bklyn. Mus., Mus. Modern Art, Carnegie Internat., Musee d'Art Moderne of Paris, Found., Maeght, France, Am., São Paolo Biennial, (Brazil), 1961; Painters in, Europe, Prato, Italy, 1973; represented permanent collections, Wadsworth Athenaeum, Hartford, Conn., St. Louis City Art Mus., Pasadena (Calif.) Art Mus., Va. Mus. Fine Arts, Rockhill Nelson Gallery, Detroit Inst. Art, Whitney Mus., Met. Mus., Corcoran Gallery, Washington, San Francisco Art Mus., Art. Inst. Chgo., Fogg Art Inst., Addison Gallery, Mus. Modern Art, Tate Gallery, London, Guggenheim Mus., High Art Mus., Atlanta, Chase Manhattan Bank, Tenn. Fine Arts Center, Rose Art Mus. Brandeis U., others, also in pvt. collections. Recipient Recipient purchase prize Va. Mus. Fine Arts, 5th biennial contemporary Am. painting, 1946, 2d prize Kearney Meml., Milw. Art Inst., 1964, bd. dirs. award John Herron Art Mus., 1946, 1st prize ann. contemporary Am. painting Calif. Palace Legion of Honor, 1947, Prix de Rome, 1949, purchase prize Contemporary Am. Painting Exhibit, Isaac Delgado Mus., New Orleans, 1958, Corcoran Fourth prize, 1965, 2,500 award Nat. Inst. Arts and Letters, 1967, 5,000 grant Council of the Arts, 1967, Andrew Carnegie prize Nat. Acad. Design, 1971. Home: Box 408 A Storms Rd Valley Cottage NY 10989

GREENE, STEWART, advt. agy. exec.; b. N.Y.C., June 24, 1928; s. Harry and Yetta (Katz) Greenbaum; m. Iris Katz, Feb. 6, 1950; children—Lisa, Eric. B.S., N.Y. U., 1949; postgrad., Parsons Sch. Design. Co-founder Wells, Rich, Greene, Inc., N.Y.C., 1966. (Recipient Art Dirs. Gold medal Internat. Broadcasting Finest Comml. in World Award, Andy award for Alka-Seltzer stomach comml., Am. Film Festival's Best Campaign award for Alka-Seltzer, Art Dirs. Gold medal, Andy award for Benson & Hedges disadvantages comml., Am. Film Festival's Best Campaign award for Benson & Hedges.); Created: Braniff colored airplanes. Clubs: Corinthians (L.I.); Knickerbocker Yacht (Port Washington, L.I.); N.Y. Yacht. Home and Office: 1815 Heritage Way Manhasset NY 11030

GREENE, THEODORE PHINNEY, historian, educator; b. N.Y.C., May 20, 1921; children: 3. B.A., Amherst Coll., 1943; M.A., Columbia U., 1948. Lectr. Am history Columbia U., 1950-52; asst. prof. to assoc. prof. history Amherst Coll, Mass., 1952-57; prof. history Amherst Coll., Mass., 1973—, Winthrop H. Smith prof. history. Editor: American Imperialism in 1898, 1955, Wilson at Versailles and Roger Williams and the Massachusetts Magistrates, 1962, American Heroes: The Changing Models of Success in American Magazines, 1970. Mem. Am. Hist. Assn., Am. Studies Assn. Office: Dept History Amherst Coll Amherst MA 01002 *

GREENE, THOMAS MCLERNON, educator; b. Phila., May 17, 1926; s. George Durgin and Elizabeth (McLernon) G.; m. Liliane Massarano, May 20, 1950; children: Philip James, Christopher George, Francis Richard. B.A., Yale U., 1949, Ph.D., 1955; student, U. Paris, France, 1949-51. Mem. faculty Yale U., 1954—; prof. English and comparative lit. Yale, 1966—, chmn. directed studies program, 1965-68, chmn. dept. comparative lit., 1972-78; chmn. Renaissance Studies Program, 1980—, Frederick Clifford Ford prof. English and Comparative lit., 1978—. Author: The Descent From Heaven: A Study in Epic Continuity, 1963, Rabelais: A Study in Comic Courage, 1970, The Light in Troy: Imitation and Discovery in Renaissance Poetry, 1982; also articles.; Co-editor: The Disciplines of Criticism: Studies in Literary Theory, Interpretation and History, 1968. Served with AUS, 1945-47. Recipient Harbison prize for distinguished teaching, 1968, Harry Levin prize, 1982; grantee Am. Council Learned Socs., 1963-64; Guggenheim fellow, 1968-69; grantee NEH, 1978-79. Mem. MLA, Dante Soc. Am., Mediaeval Acad. Am., Renaissance Soc. Am. (v.p. 1981—), Am. Comparative Lit. Assn. (adv. bd. 1971-77, v.p. 1980—), Acad. for Lit. Studies, Spenser Soc. Home: 125 Livingston St New Haven CT 06511

GREENE, WARREN KEELER, mutual fund executive; b. Portland, Oreg., Feb. 3, 1936; s. Elbert Hinnish and Bernice (Hamilton) G.; m. Barbara Jean McReynolds, Feb. 7, 1959; 1 son, Warren Keeler. B.S. in Indsl. Engring., Oreg. State U., 1958; M.B.A., NYU, 1963. Investment analyst First Boston Corp., N.Y.C., 1959-62, instl. sales mgr., 1963-64; investment portfolio mgr. Am. Investors Corp., Greenwich, Conn., 1965-67, v.p., 1967-76, sr. v.p., 1976—, dir., Greeenwich, Conn.; v.p., dir. Am. Investors Fund, Inc., Greenwich; founder, p¢res., dir. Am. Investors Income Fund, Inc., Greenwich; founder, pres., dir. Am. Investors Money Fund, Inc., Greenwich; v.p., dir. Cascade Airways, Inc., Spokane, Wash. Mem. Republican Town Meeting, Greenwich, 1971-73. Served to lt. C.E. U.S. Army, 1959-67. Mem. No-Load Mut. Fund Assn. (pres. 1977-79, dir. 1969—), Investment Co. Inst., No-Load Mut. Fund Com. (chmn. 1979-81), Beta Theta Pi. Episcopalian. Clubs: NYU (N.Y.C.); Milbrook; Rotary (both Greenwich). Home: 249 Overlook Dr Greenwich CT 06830 Office: Am Investors Corp PO Box 2500 88 Field Point Rd Greenwich CT 06836

GREENFIELD, BRUCE HAROLD, lawyer, banker; b. Phila., Mar. 12, 1917; s. William I. and Bertha (Kauffman) G.; m. Adele Gersh, Sept. 18, 1955; children: Gregory Richard, Elizabeth Susan, Margaret Alison. B.A., Duke U., 1938; LL.B., Yale U., 1941. Bar: Pa. 1941. Atty. Office Tax Legis. Counsel, Treasury Dept., 1941-48; partner firm Folz, Bard, Kamsler, Goodis & Greenfield, Phila., 1949-53; v.p. Bankers Securities Corp., Phila., 1953-59, exec. v.p., 1959-70, pres., 1970-82; v.p., treas., dir. Sta. WSMB, Inc., New Orleans, 1957-82; pres., dir. Albert M. Greenfield & Co., Inc., unitl 1982; dir. City Stores Co., Continental Bancorp., Phila.; Lectr. N.Y. U., Tulane U., Am. U. tax insts. Contbg. author: Taxes mag. Treas., trustee Albert M. Greenfield Found.; bd. dirs., Phila., Am. Jewish Com., Assn. Jewish Children, Girl Scouts U.S.A. Served to maj. USAAF, 1942-46. Mem. Phila. Bar Assn., Tax Execs. Inst. (pres. Phila. 1964-65), Res. Officers Assn., Phi Beta Kappa. Democrat. Clubs: Yale (Phila. and N.Y.C.); Locust; Army and Navy (Washington). Home: 210 Barker Rd Wyncote PA 19095 Office: 1401 Walnut St Philadelphia PA 19102

GREENFIELD, ELOISE LITTLE, author; b. Parmele, N.C., May 17, 1929; d. Weston Wilbur Sr. and Lessie Blanche (Jones) Little; m. Robert Joseph Greenfield, Apr. 29, 1950; children: Steven Robert, Monica Joyce. Student, Miner Tchrs. Coll., Washington, 1946-49. With U.S. Patent Office, Washington, 1949-60, Washington Unemployment Compensation Bd., 1963-64, Washington Dept. Occupations and Professions, 1968; free-lance writer, 1958—; writer-in-residence D.C. Commn. Arts, 1973; mem. staff D.C. Black Writers Workshop, 1971-74. Author: juveniles Bubbles, 1972, Rosa Parks, 1973 (Carter G. Woodson award 1974), Sister, 1974, She Come Bringing Me That Little Baby Girl, 1974 (Irma Simonton Black Book award 1974), Paul Robeson, 1975 (Jane Addams Children's Book award 1976), Me and Neesie, 1975, First Pink Light, 1976, Mary McLeod Bethune, 1977, Good News, 1977, Africa Dream, 1977 (Coretta Scott King award 1978), Honey, I Love, 1978, Talk About a Family, 1978, (with Lessie Jones Little) I Can Do It By Myself, 1978, (with Lessie Jones Little and Pattie Ridley Jones) Childtimes: A Three Generation Memoir, 1979, Grandmama's Joy, 1980, Darlene, 1980, Daydreamers, 1981, Alesia, 1981; also short stories, articles. (Recipient citation Council Interracial Books for Children 1975); producer: children's rec. Honey, I Love 1982. Mem. Authors Guild. Office: care Honey Prodns Inc PO Box 29077 Washington DC 20017

GREENFIELD, GEORGE B., physician; b. N.Y.C., May 4, 1928; s. Jacob and Rose (Wolf) G.; m. Barbara Anne O'Driscoll, Mar. 3, 1956; children: Edward James, Sheelagh Anne. B.A., NYU, 1949; M.D., State U. Utrecht, Netherlands, 1956. Diplomate: Am. Bd. Radiology, Am. Bd. Nuclear Medicine. Intern Bridgeport (Conn.) Hosp., 1956-57; resident radiology Presbyn.-St. Lukes Hosp., Chgo., 1957-60; practice medicine, specializing in radiology, Chgo., 1960—; radiologist Cook County Hosp., 1961-66, asst. dir. diagnostic radiology, 1966-69; asso.

prof. radiology U. Ill., 1966-69; prof., chmn. dept. radiology Chgo. Med. Sch., 1969-74, Mt. Sinai Hosp. Med. Center, 1969—, pres. med. staff, 1983—; prof. diagnostic radiology Rush Med. Coll.; prof. radiology Cook County Grad. Sch. Medicine. Author: Radiology of Bone Diseases, 3d edit, 1980; sr. author: A Manual of Radiographic Positioning, 1973; contbr. articles to profl. jours. Served with U.S. Army, 1951. Fellow Am. Coll. Radiology; mem. AMA, Chgo. Med. Soc., Chgo. Roentgen Soc., Am. Roentgen Ray Soc., Radiol. Soc. N.Am., Inst. Medicine Chgo., Assn. Univ. Radiologists, AAAS, Internat. Skeletal Soc. Office: Mt Sinai Med Center 15th St and California Ave Chicago IL 60608

GREENFIELD, GORDON KRAUS, business executive; b. Phila., June 16, 1915; s. Albert Monroe and Edna Kraus (Paine) G.; m. Harriet F. Copelin, Feb. 6, 1945; children: Juliet Greenfield Six, Gordon Kraus, Faith Greenfield Lewis, Hope, James Donald. A.B., Princeton U., 1937. Pres., dir. City Splty. Stores, N.Y.C., 1953-60, Am. Corp., 1960-64, Franchard Corp., 1965-68; v.p., dir. Penson Freight Corp., 1968-69; pres. Q-Co Industries Inc., N.Y.C., 1968—. Chmn. bd., trustee Manhattan Sch. Music; bd. dirs. N.Y. chpt. Arthritis Found.; trustee Harlem Sch. Arts, NCCJ; trustee, pres. Albert M. Greenfield Found.; bd. dirs. Opera Orch. of N.Y., Young Concert Artists. Served to lt. USNR, 1940-45. Mem. Confrerie des Chevaliers du Tastevin, Met. Opera Club (v.p., dir.). Clubs: Univ. (N.Y.C.); Woodstock (Vt.) Country. Home: 179 E 70th St New York NY 10021 also Cobb Hill Rd Hartland VT 05048 Office: 33 W 60th St New York NY 10023

GREENFIELD, IRWIN GILBERT, college dean; b. Phila., Nov. 30, 1929; s. William and Sara (Baumbor) G.; m. Barbara Shapiro, June 16, 1951; children: Richard, Hermine, Steven. A.B. in Metallurgy, Temple U., Phila., 1951; M.S. in Metall. Engring, U. Pa., 1954, Ph.D., 1962. Registered profl. engr., Del. Metallurgist, Naval Air Exptl. Sta., Phila., 1951-53; sr. scientist Franklin Inst. Labs. Research and Devel., Phila., 1953-63; mem. faculty U. Del., Newark, 1963—, prof. metallurgy and mech./aerospace engring., 1968—, dean Coll. Engring., 1975—, interim dir. Materials Durability Ctr.; vis. lectr. univs. in Japan, 1965; vis. prof. Stanford U., 1969—, Oxford U., 1970—, Tech. U. Eindhoven, Netherlands, 1978; mem. uniform exams. com. Nat. Council Engring. Examiners, 1981—. Author papers in field., Research surfaces, electron microscopy, mech. properties, fatigue, diffused surface layers, erosion, wear, photovoltaic materials. Mem. U.S. Senator Roth's Energy Advisory Com., Del. Energy Resources Commn. conf.; keynote speaker. Chmn. exec. com. Del. Program Minority Engrs., 1974—. Grantee U. Del., 1963-64, NSF, 1964-69, 70-74, 78-81, Air Force Office Sci. Research, 1970-74, NASA, 1969-70; NSF travel grantee, 1965, 73. Mem. Am. Inst. Mining, Metall. and Petroleum Engrs., Electron Microscope Soc. Am., Am. Soc. Metals, Am. Soc. Engring. Edn., Soaring Assn. Am., Del. Assn. Profl. Engrs. (council), Sigma Xi. Home: 605 Country Club Rd Newark DE 19711 Office: Coll Engring Univ Del Newark DE 19711

GREENFIELD, JAMES LLOYD, newspaper exec.; b. Cleve., July 16, 1924; s. Emil and Belle (Speiser) G.; m. Margaret Ann Schwertley, July 16, 1954. B.A., Harvard, 1949. With Cleve. Press, 1939-41, Voice of Am., 1949-50; corr. for Time mag. in, Korea and Japan, 1951-55, bur. chief, New Delhi, India, 1956-57, dep. bur. chief, London, Eng., 1958-61; chief diplomatic corr. Time-Life, Washington, 1961-62; dep. asst. sec. state pub. affairs, 1962-64, asst. sec. state for pub. affairs, 1964-66; asst. v.p. internat. affairs Continental Airlines, Los Angeles, 1966-68; v.p. Westinghouse Broadcasting Co., N.Y.C., 1968-69; fgn. editor N.Y. Times, 1969-77, asst. mng. editor, 1977—. Clubs: Reform (London, Eng.); Century (N.Y.C.). Home: 850 Park Ave New York NY 10021 Office: New York Times New York NY 10036

GREENFIELD, JAMES ROBERT, lawyer; b. Phila., Mar. 31, 1926; s. Milton and Katherine E. (Rosenberg) G.; m. Phyllis Chaplowe, Aug. 17, 1947 (dec. May 1978); m. Joyce MacDonald Koehler, Mar. 22, 1980. B.S., Bates Coll., 1947; J.D., Yale U., 1950. Bar: Conn. 1950, U.S. Supreme Ct. 1959. Prin. firm Greenfield, Krick & Jacobs (P.C.), New Haven, 1958—; dir. So. New Eng. Telephone Co.; lectr. U. Conn. Law Sch., 1966-67, 71-72, 75-76. Mem. editorial bd.: Conn. Bar Jour, 1963-77. Pres. New Haven Symphony, 1976-78, Conn. Bar Found., 1976-77; bd. dirs. Nat. Jud. Coll., 1978—. Served with USNR, 1944-46. Fellow Am. Bar Found.; mem. ABA (state del. 1975-78, bd. govs. 1978-81, ho. of dels. 1972-83, spl. com. on governance 1983—), Conn. Bar Assn. (pres. 1973-74), New Haven County Bar Assn. (pres. 1969-70), Judicature Soc. (bd. dirs. 1983—), Yale Law Sch. Assn. (sec. 1977-80). Clubs: Graduate, Quinnipiack, New Haven Lawn. Home: 230 Blake Rd Hamden CT 06517 Office: 205 Church St New Haven CT 06510

GREENFIELD, JOHN CHARLES, bio-organic chemist; b. Dayton, Ohio, Ar. 10, 1945; s. Ivan Ralph and Mildred Louis (House) G. B.S. cum laude, Ohio U., 1967; Ph.D., U. Ill., 1974. High sch. sci. instr., Dayton, 1968-71; grad. research asst. U. Ill., 1971-74; postdoctroal reserch fellow Swiss Fed. Inst. Tech., Zurich, 1975-76; research chemist infectious diseases research Upjohn Co., Kalamazoo, 1976—. Am.-Swiss Found. for Sci. Exchange fellow, 1975; NSF-NATO postdoctoral fellow, 1975-76. Mem. Am. Chem. Soc., AAAS, Am. Soc. Microbiology, Sigma Xi. Home: 10618 Dandale St Kalamazoo MI 49002 Office: The Upjohn Co Infectious Diseases Research Kalamazoo NI 49001

GREENFIELD, JOSEPH CHOLMONDELEY, JR., physician, educator; b. Atlanta, July 20, 1931; s. Joseph Cholmondeley and Agnes (Game) G.; m. Mary Ruth Fordham, Aug. 13, 1955; children—Mary Agnes, Ruth Ann, Susan Lee. A.B. in History, Emory U., 1954, M.D., 1956. Intern, resident in medicine Duke Med. Center, Durham, N.C., 1956-59, asst. prof. medicine, 1962-65, asso. prof. medicine, 1965-70, prof. medicine, 1970—, James B. Duke disting. prof., 1981—; clin. asso. NIH, USPHS, 1959-62, mem. cardiovascular and pulmonary study sect., 1974-78, chmn. sect., 1975-78, cardiovascular rev. com., 1980-84, chmn. cardiovascular rev. com., 1983-84; mem. staff Duke Med. Center, 1962—, chief cardiovascular div., 1981—, chmn. dept. medicine, 1983—; mem. staff, chief cardiovascular div. VA, Durham, N.C., 1962—. Mem. editorial bd.: Circulation Research, Am. Jour. Physiology; contbr. numerous articles profl. jours. Fellow A.C.P., Am. Coll. Cardiology; mem. Am. Heart Assn. (fellow council clin. cardiology), Am., So. socs. clin. investigation, Am. Physiol. Soc., Assn., Physicians, Assn., U. Cardiologists, Phi Beta Kappa, Alpha Omega Alpha, Kappa Alpha. Methodist. Home: 1212 Virginia Ave Durham NC 27705 Office: Box 3246 Duke Medical Center Durham NC 27710

GREENFIELD, LAZAR JOHN, surgeon, educator; b. Houston, Dec. 14, 1934; s. Robert G. and Betty B. (Greenfield) Heath; m. Sharon Dee Bishkin, Aug. 29, 1956; children: John, Julie, Jeff. Student, Rice U., 1951-54; M.D., Baylor U., 1958. Diplomate: Am. Bd. Surgery (dir. 1976-82), Am. Bd. Thoracic Surgery, cert. gen. vascular surgery. Intern Johns Hopkins Hosp., Balt., 1958-59, resident, 1961-66; chief surgery VA Hosp., Oklahoma City, 1966-74; prof. dept. surgery U. Okla. Med. Center, 1971-74; Stuart McGuire prof., chmn. dept. surgery Med. Coll. Va., Richmond, 1974—; mem. surgery A study sect. NIH. Author: Surgery in the Aged, 1975; also chpts., articles, abstracts.; editor Complications in Surgery and Trauma, 1983. Served with USPHS, 1959-61. Thomas R. Franklin scholar, 1952; John and Mary Markle scholar in med. sci., 1968-73. Mem. Am. Surg. Assn., Am. Assn. Thoracic Surgery, Assn. Acad. Surgery, Soc. Univ. Surgeons, Phi Delta Epsilon. Home: Swift Creek Ln Box 422L Manakin-Sabot VA 23103 Office: Box 645 Med Coll Va Richmond VA 23298

GREENFIELD, MEG, journalist; b. Seattle, Dec. 27, 1930; d. Lewis James and Lorraine (Nathan) G. B.A. summa cum laude, Smith Coll., 1952; Fulbright scholar, Newnham Coll., Cambridge (Eng.) U., 1952-53; D.H.L., Smith Coll., 1978. With Reporter mag., 1957-68, Washington editor, 1965-68; editorial writer Washington Post, 1968-70, dep. editorial page editor, 1970-79, editorial page editor, 1979—; columnist Newsweek, 1974—. (Recipient Pulitzer prize for editorial writing 1978). Mem. Am. Soc. Newspaper Editors, Phi Beta Kappa. Club: Federal City (Washington). Home: 3318 R St NW Washington DC 20007 Office: 1150 15th St NW Washington DC 20005

GREENFIELD, NORMAN SAMUEL, psychologist, educator; b. N.Y.C., June 2, 1923; s. Max and Dorothy (Hertz) G.; m. Marjorie Hanson Klein, May 17, 1969; children—Ellen Beth, Jennifer Ann, Susan Emery. B.A., N.Y. U., 1948; M.A., U. Calif.-Berkeley, 1951, Ph.D., 1953. Fellow med. psychology Langley Porter Clinic, U. Calif. Med. Center, 1949-50; VA Mental Health Clinic trainee, San Francisco, 1950-53; instr. clin. psychology U. Oreg. Med. Sch., 1953-54; from asst. prof. to prof. psychiatry U. Wis. Med. Sch. at, Madison, 1954—; assoc. dir. Wis. Psychiat. Inst., U. Wis. Center for Health Scis., 1961-74. Co-editor: The New Hospital Psychiatry, Handbook of Psychophysiology. Served with USAAF, 1943-46. Mem. Am. Psychol. Assn., Soc. Psychophysiol. Research, Am. Psychosomatic Soc., AAUP. Office: Dept Psychiatry University Hosps Madison WI 53792

GREENFIELD, ROBERT KAUFFMAN, lawyer; b. Phila., Mar. 30, 1915; s. William I. and Bertha (Kauffman) G.; m. Louise Rose Stern, June 20, 1937; children: Linda (Mrs. Marvin C. Baldwin), Mary (Mrs. Larry W. Davenport), William Stern, James Robert. A.B., Swarthmore Coll., 1936; LL.B., Harvard, 1939. Bar: Pa. 1939. Practiced in, Phila., 1939—; with firm Goodis, Greenfield, Henry & Edelstein (and predecessors), 1939-77; of counsel firm Montgomery, McCracken, Walker & Rhoads, 1977—; chmn. bd. Phila. Co., 1983—; dir. Unicorp Am. Corp. Bd. dirs. Conv. and Tourist Bur., Phila., 1942-84; commr., v.p. Phila. Fellowship Commn., 1965-74; pres. Jewish Community Relations Council Phila., 1962-65, Moss Rehab. Hosp., 1969-74; chmn. bd. Moss Rehab. Hosp., 1974-77; finance chmn. Inst. Contemporary Art, 1974-83; exec. com. Council Performing Arts Phila., 1964-70; v.p. Nat. Community Relations Adv. Council, 1965-68; pres. Phila. chpt. Am. Jewish Com., 1966-68; bd. dirs. Pa. Coll. Podiatric Medicine, 1967—; 2d v.p. Marriage Council of Phila., 1980-83. Served with USNR, 1945. Mem. Am., Pa., Phila. bar assns., Phi Beta Kappa. Club: Racquet (Phila.). Home: 8221 Fairview Rd Elkins Park PA 19117 Office: 3 Parkway 20th Floor Philadelphia PA 19102

GREENFIELD, SANFORD RAYMOND, architect; b. N.Y.C., Feb. 3, 1926; s. Harry Leon and Dorothy (Shaefer) G.; m. Stella Berger, Oct. 12, 1952; children—Lise, Daniel, Stefanie. Student, Mich. State Coll. Liberal Arts, 1946-48; B.Arch., M.I.T., 1952, M.Arch., 1954; postgrad., New Sch. Social Research, N.Y.C., 1953, L'Inst. d'Urbanisme, Paris, 1954-55; Ed.M., Harvard U., 1975. Faculty Sch. Architecture and Planning, M.I.T., 1955-57; with Samuel Glaser, Boston, 1958-60; partner Carroll & Greenfield (architects), Boston, 1960-73; research mgr. AIA Research Corp., 1975-76; cons. Sanford R. Greenfield & Asso., Boston; chmn. dept. architecture Iowa State U., Ames, 1976-81; dean Sch. Architecture, N.J. Inst. Tech., 1981—; lectr. Inst. Urban Design, Krakow (Poland) Poly Technica, 1978; dir. edn. Boston Archtl. Center; cons. ednl. planning; lectr. Mass. Coll. Art. Editor: Architecture and the Computer, 1964, Forces Shaping the Role of The Architect, 1966, Systems, 1968; Contbr. articles to profl. jours.; Important works include Library St. John's Sem. Mem. 5-Presidents' Task Force on Edn., 1972-73; chmn. Nat. Adv. Council Continuing Edn., 1972-73. Served with USNR, 1944-46. Fulbright scholar, 1954-55; Nat. Endowment for Arts grantee, 1978. Fellow AIA; mem. Iowa Assn. Architects, Assn. Collegiate Schs. Architecture (v.p. 1972-73, pres. 1973-74, also dir.). Jewish. Club: Rotary.

GREENFIELD, SEYMOUR STEPHEN, mechanical engineer; b. Bklyn., July 9, 1922; s. Herman and Yetta (Silfen) G.; m. Eleanor Levy, Oct. 30, 1949; children—Meryl Joy, Bruce Howard. Student, N.Y. U., 1939-40; B.Mech. Engring., Poly. Inst. N.Y., 1944. Registered profl. engr., Calif., Conn., Mass., N.J., N.Y., La., Tex., Ohio. Engr. Percival R. Moses Assos., N.Y.C., 1946-47; sr. engr. and asso. Parsons, Brinckerhoff, Quade & Douglas, N.Y.C., 1947-64, partner, 1964—, chmn. bd., 1979—; Adviser Manhattan Coll., N.Y.C., 1974—; mem. devel. council Tex. A&M Sch. Architecture, 1981. Served to lt. USNR, 1944-46. Mem. Soc. Am. Mil. Engrs. (nat. pres. 1977, dir. 1975—, pres. N.Y.C. post 1974-75), Nat. Acad. Engring. Bldg. Research (mem. adv. bd. 1972—), N.Y. C. of C. and Industry (vice chmn. Transp. Council 1973—), N.Y. State Soc. Profl. Engrs., ASME, Am. Soc. Heating, Refrigerating and Air Conditioning Engrs., Moles (trustee). Home: 215 E 68th St Apt 18F New York NY 10021 Office: 1 Penn Plaza New York NY 10119

GREENFIELD, TAYLOR HATTON, former government official; b. Balt., Dec. 17, 1905; s. Amos Hatton and Lillian Estelle (Taylor) G.; m. Mildred Sophia Albert, Sept. 15, 1928; children: Lillian Greenfield Tilles, Millette Greenfield Barber. LL.B., U. Balt., 1940. Bar: Md. bar 1949. Exec. Glenn L. Martin Co., 1929-43, Gen. Motors, 1944-45; field dir. A.R.C., Germany, 1945-46; property and supply supr. War Assets Adminstrn., 1946-48; practice law, Balt., 1949-51; with Hayes Aircraft Co., Birmingham, Ala., 1951-55; adviser to Govt. Vietnam, 1955-62; mem. tech. adv. staff AID, Far East Bur., 1962-67; dir. Far East Logistics Office, 1965-67; chief logistics USOM, supply mgmt. officer, Bangkok, Thailand, 1969-72. Recipient Meritorious Honor award AID, 1966. Mem. Md. Bar, Hawaii Malocological Soc., Am. Forestry Assn., Nat. Audubon Soc., Nat. Wildlife Fedn., Internat. Transactional Analysis Assn. Club: Civitan. Home: 8623 Starcrest Dr San Antonio TX 78217 *I have long followed a rule to admit no answer to a problem more than tentative status inevitably subject to modification. Too often the truth of today proves to be the fallacy of tomorrow.*

GREENHILL, ROBERT FOSTER, investment banker; b. Mpls., June 20, 1936; s. J. Raymond and Mary (Foster) G.; m. Mary Gayle Gussett, Sept. 13, 1958; children: Sarah B., Robert Foster, Mary B. A.B., Yale U., 1958; M.B.A., Harvard U., 1962. Assoc. Morgan Stanley & Co., Inc., N.Y.C., 1962-70, mng. dir., 1970—. Trustee Whitney Mus. Am. Art, N.Y.C., NYU Med. Ctr. Served to lt. (j.g.) USNR, 1960-62. Mem. Council on Fgn. Relations. Clubs: Ausable (Keene Valley, N.Y.); Field (Greenwich); Links; Union (N.Y.C.). Home: 433 Riversville Rd Greenwich CT 06830 Office: Morgan Stanley and Co 1251 Ave of the Americas New York NY 10020

GREENHUT, MELVIN LEONARD, economist, educator; b. N.Y.C., Mar. 10, 1921; s. Ab and Lillian (Frudman) G.; m. Elmara Margaret Griffith, Mar. 24, 1944; children: Margaret Lee, Pamela Jo, John Griffith, Patricia Lynn. Ph.D., Washington U., 1951. Asst. prof. econs. Auburn (Ala.) U., 1948-52; asso. prof. econs. Miss. State U., 1952-53; prof. bus. and econs., chmn. social relations div. Rollins Coll., 1953-57; prof. econs. Fla. State U., 1957-59, 62-66; asso. dean Sch. Bus., U. Richmond, 1959-62; prof., head dept. econs. Tex. A. and M. U., College Station, 1966-69, distinguished prof. econs., 1969—; Vis. prof. Mich. State U., 1963, U. Cape Town, 1971, univs. Mannheim, Karlsruhe, Münster, 1972, 73, U. Pitts., 1976; cons. Rountree Assos., Richmond, Va., 1959, A.T. & T. (risk and uncertainty com.), 1961-62, Atlantic Research Corp., 1962; cons. to pres. Amerad Corp., 1962-64; cons. So. Conf. Council State Govts., 1964-66, Bur. Bus. Research, Memphis State U., 1965-66. Author: Plant Location in Theory and in Practice, 1956 (transl. into Japanese, 2 vols., 1973), (with Frank Jackson) Intermediate Income and Growth Theory, 1961, Full Employment, Inflation and Common Stocks, 1961, (with Marshall R. Colberg) Factors in the Location of Florida Industry, 1962, Microeconomics and the Space Economy, 1963, (with Tate Whitman) Essays on Southern Economic Development, 1964, A Theory of the Firm in Economic Space, 1970, (with H. Ohta) A Theory of Spatial Prices and Market Areas, 1975, (with Charles Stewart) Economics for the Voter, 1981, From Basic Economics to Supply Side Economics, 1983; Editor: So. Econ. Jour, 1966-68; cons. editor: Indsl. Devel, 1959-62; Contbr. articles to profl. jours. Mem. nat. econ. policy com. and econ. adv. council U.S. C. of C., 1960-63. Served to maj. AUS, World War II. Mem. Am. Econ. Assn., So. Econ. Assn. (past v.p.), Regional Sci. Assn. (councillor), Econometric Soc., Delta Chi, Omicron Delta Gamma. Lutheran (trustee). Home: 3107 Camelot Bryan TX 77801 Office: Dept Econs Tex A and M U College Station TX 77843

GREENKORN, ROBERT ALBERT, chemical engineering educator; b. Oshkosh, Wis., Oct. 12, 1928; s. Frederick John and Sophie (Phillips) G.; m. Rosemary Drexler, Aug. 16, 1952; children: David Michael, Eileen Anne, Susan Marie, Nancy Joanne. Student, Oshkosh State Coll., 1951-52; B.S., U. Wis., 1954, M.S., 1955, Ph.D., 1957. Postdoctoral fellow Norwegian Tech. Inst., 1957-58; research engr. Jersey Prodn. Research Co., Tulsa, 1958-63; lectr. U. Tulsa, 1958-63; asso. prof. theoretical and applied mechanics Marquette U., Milw., 1963-65; asso. prof. Sch. Chem. Engring., Purdue U., Lafayette, Ind., 1965-67; prof., head Sch. Chem. Engring., 1967-72, asst. dean engring., 1972-76; asso. dean engring., dir. Engring. Expt. Sta., 1976-80; v.p., asso. provost, v.p. for programs Purdue Research Found., 1980—. Author: (with D.P. Kessler) Transfer Operations, 1972, (with K.C. Chao) Thermodynamics of Fluids: An Introduction to Equilibrium Theory, 1975, (with D.P. Kessler) Modeling and Data Analysis for Engineers and Scientists, 1980, Flow Phenomena in Porous Media, 1983; Contbr. articles to profl. jours. Served with USN, 1946-51. Decorated D.F.C., Air medal with two oak leaf clusters. Fellow Am. Inst. Chem. Engrs.; Mem. Soc. Petroleum Engrs., Am. Inst. Mining, Am. Soc. Engring. Edn., Metall. and Petroleum Engrs., Am. Chem. Soc., Am. Geophys. Union, Sigma Xi, Phi Eta Sigma, Tau Beta Pi, Phi Gamma Delta. Roman Catholic. Patentee in field. Home: 151 Knox Dr West Lafayette IN 47906

GREENLAND, LEO, advt. exec.; b. N.Y.C., Mar. 4, 1920; s. Jack and Ida (Abrams) G.; m. Rita Levine, June 29, 1955; children—Seth, Andrew. Student, New Sch. for Social Research, 1945-47. Pres. Sherwood Prodns., 1949-52; exec. various advt. agys., 1952-59; pres. Smith/Greenland Co., Inc., N.Y.C., 1959—, chmn., chief exec. officer, 1974—; guest lectr. Fordham U. Sch. Communication Arts, 1967—. Nat. commr. Anti-Defamation League, chmn. radio-TV dept.; bd. dirs., sec. Friars Found. Served with AUS, 1943-46. Mem. Am. Advt. Agys. (bd. govs. N.Y.), Am. Mgmt. Assn. (lectr. 1969—), Am. Arbitration Assn., Nat. Businessmen's Council, Fgn. Policy Assn., Interracial Businessmen's Council, Eastern Frosted Foods Assn. (pres. 1965-67), Sales Execs. Club N.Y., Newcomen Soc. N.Am. Clubs: Harmonie, Sierra, Friars (N.Y.C.); Metropolis Country. Home: 20 Dolma Rd Scarsdale NY 10583 Office: 1414 Ave Americas New York NY 10019

GREENLEAF, JONATHAN WHITMAN, realty management executive; b. N.Y.C., July 28, 1939; s. Joseph Whitman and Fruma Sorrel (Winer) G.; m. Barbara Louise Kaye, July 29, 1965; children: Caroline, Catherine. B.A., Cornell U., 1961; M.B.A., U. Calif., Berkeley, 1964. Account exec. J. Walter Thompson Co., N.Y.C., 1963-69; partner Cadwell, Davis, Greenleaf, Inc., N.Y.C., 1969-70; v.p., dir. mktg. service Smith/Greenland, Inc., N.Y.C., 1970-71; exec. v.p. de Garmo, Inc., N.Y.C., 1971-79; sr. v.p. mktg. Merrill Lynch Realty Assocs., Stamford, Conn., from 1979, now pres. Calif. region, Los Angeles. Active Big Bros. N.Y., 1966-69; campaign mgr., mem. exec. com. North Castle Democratic Party, 1974; bd. dirs. Carver Center, White Plains, N.Y., 1968-69. Served with AUS, 1962. Club: Westchester Country. Home: 6742 Marina City Dr Marina Del Rey CA 90202 Office: 6033 W Century Blvd Los Angeles CA 90045

GREENLEE, HERBERT BRECKENRIDGE, physician, educator; b. Rockford, Ill., Sept. 6, 1927; s. Harvey James and Abbie (McCathran) G.; m. Shirley Claire Rurik, June 12, 1955; children: Herbert, William, Kenneth, Anne. A.B., Beloit Coll., 1951; M.D., U. Chgo., 1955. Diplomate: Am. Bd. Surgery. Intern U. Chgo. Clinics, 1956, resident in surgery, 1956-62; practice medicine specializing in surgery, Chgo., 1964-66; staff surgeon VA Hosp., Madison, Wis., 1966-67, asst. chief surg. service, Hines, Ill., 1967-72, chief surg. service, 1972—; asso. prof. surgery Stritch Sch. Medicine, Loyola U., Maywood, Ill., 1967-72, prof. surgery, 1972—. Author: Surgery of the Small and Large Intestine, 1973, Spanish edit, 1976; contbr. articles to sci. jours. Served with M.C. AUS, 1962-64. Recipient Raymond W. McNealy award Chgo. Surg. Soc., 1956. Fellow Am. Cancer Soc., A.C.S. (coordinator gen. surgery film sessions 1976—, chmn. motion picture com. 1978—, mem. program com. 1978—), Inst. Medicine Chgo.; mem. Am. Gastroenterology Assn., AMA, Soc. Surgery Alimentary Tract, Midwest Gut Club, Chgo. Soc. Gastroenterology (pres. 1973-74, counselor 1974-75), Am. Surg. Assn., Ill. Surg. Soc. (pres. 1975-76, trustee 1976—), Chgo. Surg. Soc. (sec. 1974-77, pres. 1980-81), Charles B. Puestow Surg. Soc., N.Y. Acad. Sci., Assn. VA Surgeons (pres. 1981-82), Assn. Acad. Surgery, Collegium Internat. Chirurgiae Digestivae, Western, Midwest, Central surg. assns., Internat. Soc. Surgery, Pancreas Club, Phi Beta Kappa, Sigma Xi, Alpha Omega Alpha. Home: 807 Keystone St River Forest IL 60305 Office: VA Hosp 112 Hines IL 60141

GREENLEE, HOWARD SCOTT, graphics executive; b. Chgo., Feb. 13, 1919; s. James T. and Edith (Scott) G.; m. Helen L. Schwarz, Oct. 4, 1941; children: Sarah, David Scott. A.B., U. Chgo., 1939, A.M., 1941, Ph.D., 1950; postgrad, Columbia, 1953-54. Tchr. pub. schs., Woodstock, Ill., 1941-42; asst. Salzburg Seminar in Am. Studies, 1948; vis. asst. history U. Chgo., 1950; asso. prof. history, asso. dean Simpson Coll., 1950-55; asso. dean, prof. history Southwestern U., 1955-56; dean coll., prof. history Park Coll., 1956-58; dean Coe Coll., 1958-65; prof. history Tuskegee Inst., Ala., 1965-68, acting dean, 1967-68; dean faculty Antioch Coll., Yellow Springs, Ohio, 1968-71; acad. dean, prof. history Windham Coll., Putney, Vt., 1971-73; with semi-subsistence Farming Community Graphics and Community Service, 1973—; organizer David Scott Press, 1978; Cons.-examiner (N. Central Assn. Colls. and Secondary Schs.). Mem. Planning Commn., Town of Royalton, Vt.; moderator Town of Royalton, 1980—; mem. long range planning com. Episcopal Diocese of Vt.; Bd. dirs. Hanover Coop. Soc. Served to lt. USNR, 1942-46. Faculty fellow Fund for Advancement Edn., 1953-54; travel grantee Carnegie Corp. Ednl. Adminstrn., 1960. Episcopalian. Address: Box 38 South Royalton VT 05068

GREENLEE, JOHN ALDEN, coll. pres.; b. Richland, Iowa, Sept. 7, 1911; s. John Amzi and Martha Denny (Logsdon) G.; m. Lillian Ruth Witte, Dec. 13, 1955. B.A., U. Iowa, 1930, M.A., 1931, Ph.D., 1934.

Prof., asst. to dean scis. Iowa State U., 1940-59; dir. engring. personnel and edn. Collins Radio Co., Cedar Rapids, Iowa, 1959-65; v.p. acad. affairs Calif. State U., Los Angeles, 1965-66, pres., 1966-79, pres. emeritus, 1980—; higher edn. cons., 1980—; Mem. Nat. Commn. on State Workmen's Compensation Laws, 1971-72. Served with USNR, World War II. Decorated Bronze Star. Mem. Phi Delta Kappa, Phi Kappa Phi, Alpha Kappa Psi, Beta Gamma Sigma. Home: 50 Oak Hill Ln South Pasadena CA 91030

GREENLICK, MERWYN RONALD, health services researcher; b. Detroit, Mar. 12, 1935; s. Emanuel and Fay (Ettinger) G.; m. Harriet Cohen, Aug. 19, 1956; children—Phyllis, Michael, Vicki. B.S., Wayne State U., 1957; M.S., U. Mich., 1961, Ph.D., 1967. Pharmacist, Detroit, 1957-60; spl. instr., instr. pharmacy adminstrn. Coll. Pharmacy Wayne State U., 1958-62; dir. of research Kaiser-Permanente Med. Care Program, Oreg. region, Portland, 1964—; v.p. (research) Kaiser Found. Hosps., 1981—; adj. prof. sociology Portland State U., 1965—; asso. clin. prof. preventive medicine and pub. health U. Oreg. Med. Sch., 1971—; mem. study com. on health delivery systems Gov.'s Comprehensive Health Planning Council; cons. Gov.'s Health Manpower Council. Bd. dirs. Washington County Community Action Orgn., 1966-70; pres. Jewish Edn. Assn., Portland, 1976-78; bd. dirs. Jewish Fedn., Portland, 1975-79. USPHS trainee, 1962-63, 63-64. Fellow Am. Pub. Health Assn. (governing council); mem. AAAS, Am. Sociol. Assn., Am. Statis. Assn., Group Health Assn. Am., Nat. Acad. Scis., Inst. Medicine. Jewish. Home: 712 NW Spring Portland OR 97229 Office: 4610 SE Belmont Portland OR 97215

GREENLY, B. COLIN, artist; b. London, Jan. 21, 1928; U.S., 1939, naturalized, 1948; s. Arthur John and Caroline Matilda (Fantini) G.; m. Laurie Ann Zadek, May 8, 1976; 1 dau., Katharine Lydia Caro. A.B., Harvard U., 1948; postgrad., Columbia U. Sch. Painting and Sculpture, 1951-53, Am. U. Grad. Sch. Fine Arts, 1956. Dir. art Madeira Sch., Greenway, Va., 1955-68; Dana prof. fine arts Colgate U., 1972-73; vis. artist numerous colls., univs. One-man shows, Corcoran Gallery Art, Washington, 1968, Royal Marks Gallery, N.Y.C., 1968, 70, Everson Mus., Syracuse, N.Y., 1971, Andrew Dickson White Mus., Cornell U., 1972, Picker Gallery, Colgate U., 1973, Finch Coll. Mus., N.Y.C., 1974, group shows include, Mus. Modern Art, N.Y.C., 1953, 73, De Cordova Mus., Lincoln, Mass., 1965, Des Moines Art Center, 1967, Nat. Collection Fine Arts, Washington, 1968, Krannert Art Mus., Champaign, Ill., 1969, 74, Emmerich Gallery Downtown, N.Y.C., 1972, John Weber Gallery, N.Y.C., 1975, Whitney Mus. Am. Art, N.Y.C., 1978, N.Y. State Mus., Albany, 1981; represented in permanent collections, Albright Knox Art Gallery, Buffalo, Corcoran Gallery Art, Des Moines Art Center, Everson Mus., High Mus. Art, Atlanta, Mus. Modern Art, N.Y.C., Phila. Mus. Art, Nat. Gallery Art, Washington, Nat. Collection Fine Arts, Washington, Herbert F. Johnson Mus., Ithaca, N.Y.; restoration and contemporary adaptation of: Hulse Barn, Campbell Hall. Nat. Endowment Arts grantee, 1967; Com. for Visual Arts grantee, 1974; Creative Artists Public Service program fellow N.Y.C., 1972, 78. Patentee in field of playground, shelter, sculpture. Address: RD 1 Box 545 Campbell Hall NY 10916 *Developing one's abilities may require a measure of commitment and excellence, but committing excellence to indiscriminate ends is artless. The synthesis of life and art is art.*

GREENMAN, MARTIN ALLEN, educator; b. Chgo., Apr. 12, 1917; s. Charles Edward and Matilda (Blue) G.; m. Mary Clare Gregory, Mar. 19, 1943 (dec. Nov. 1963); children—Margaret (Mrs. John A. Barmack), Charles, John, Martin, Matthew, Mark (dec.); m. Justine Litchfield, Oct. 20, 1964. B.A., U. Chgo., 1942, Ph.D., 1950; postgrad., Harvard, 1945-47. Ordained to ministry Unitarian Ch., 1957; teaching fellow in English Harvard, 1946-47; instr. philosophy Syracuse (N.Y.) U., 1948-50, U. Rochester (N.Y.), 1950-51, asst. prof., 1951-57; asso. minister 1st Unitarian Ch., St. Louis, 1957-59; minister Old Ship Ch., Hingham, Mass., 1959-64; asso. prof. philosophy, Morehead, Ky.; State U., 1964-65, prof., 1965-68; prof. philosophy Youngstown (Ohio) State U., 1968—, chmn. dept., 1968-78. Contbr. articles to profl. jours. Served to 1st lt. AUS, 1941-43; Served to 1st lt. USAAF, 1943-45. Mem. Nat. Humanities Faculty, Am. Philos. Assn., AAUP. Home: 327 Redondo Rd Youngstown OH 44504

GREENOUGH, WILLIAM CROAN, economist, pension executive; b. Indpls., July 27, 1914; s. Walter Sidney and Katharine (Croan) G.; m. Doris Decker, Jan. 4, 1941; children: David William, Walter Croan, Martha Alice. A.B., Ind. U., 1935, LL.D., 1966; M.A., Harvard U., 1938, Ph.D., 1949. Asst. to dean, instr. Ind. U. Sch. Bus., 1937-38, asst. to pres., 1938-41, Tchrs. Ins. and Annuity Assn. Am., 1941-43, 46-48, v.p., 1948-55, exec. v.p., 1955-57, pres., 1957-67, chmn., chief exec. officer, 1963-79, trustee, 1955—; chmn., chief exec. officer, trustee Coll. Retirement Equities Fund, 1952-79, chmn. fin. com., 1979-81; ret., 1981; pub. dir. N.Y. Stock Exchange, 1972-81; trustee Dry Dock Savs. Bank, 1961-83; dir. Turner Constrn. Co.; mem. adv. bd. Atlantic Richfield Retirement Plans. Author: College Retirement and Insurance Plans, 1948, A New Approach to Retirement Income, 1951, (with F. P. King) Retirement and Insurance Plans in American Colleges, 1959, Benefit Plans in American Colleges, 1969, Pension Plans and Public Policy, 1976; Editor: Pension Planning in the U.S, 1952; also numerous articles in field. Mem. Pres.'s Commn. Pension Policy, Washington, 1979-81; mem. various commns. Am. Council Edn., Assn. Am. Colls., U.S. Office Edn., 1958-70; mem. council Rockefeller U., 1973—; Trustee Com. for Econ. Devel., Russell Sage Found., 1967-77, Devereux Found., Ind. U. Found., The Aspen Inst., Carnegie Inst., Washington., Radcliffe Coll., Acad. for Ednl. Devel. Served from ensign to lt. USNR, 1943-45. Recipient Disting. Alumni Service award Ind. U., 1960, Elizur Wright award for variable annuity, 1961; Decorated Bronze Star medal. Mem. Life Office Mgmt. Assn., Regional Plan Assn. N.Y.C. (dir. 1967-76), Am. Pension Conf., Am. Econs. Assn., Am. Finance Assn., AAUP, Am. Risk and Ins. Assn., Council on Fgn. Relations, Phi Beta Kappa. Clubs: Harvard, Century Assn. (N.Y.C.). Home: 870 UN Plaza New York NY Office: 730 3d Ave New York NY 10017

GREENOUGH, WILLIAM TALLANT, psychobiologist; b. Seattle, Oct. 11, 1944; s. Harrison and Maryon C. (Whitten) G.; 1 dau., Jennifer Anne. B.A., U. Oreg., 1964; M.A., UCLA, 1966, Ph.D., 1969. Instr. U. Ill., Urbana-Champaign, 1968-69, asst. prof., 1969-73, assoc. prof., 1973-77, prof., 1977—, prof. psychology and anatomical scis., 1978—; vis. prof. psychobiology U. Calif., Irvine, 1972; vis. prof. psychology U. Wash., 1975-76. Cattell Found. fellow, 1975-76; USPHS and NSF grantee, 1969—. Mem. AAAS, Soc. Neurosci., Soc. Devel. Neurosci., Soc. Devel. Psychobiology, James G. Blaine Soc., Sigma Xi. Home: 2303 Southmoor Dr Champaign IL 61820 Office: Dept Psychology U Ill 603 E Daniel St Champaign IL 61820

GREENSPAN, ALAN, economist; b. N.Y.C., Mar. 6, 1926; s. Herman Herbert and Rose (Goldsmith) G. B.S. summa cum laude, NYU, 1948, M.A., 1950; Ph.D., N.Y. U., 1977. Pres., chief exec. officer Townsend-Greenspan and Co., Inc., N.Y.C., 1954-74, 77—; cons. Council Econ. Advisers, 1970-74, chmn., 1974-77; cons. Congressional Budget Office, 1977—; mem. Pres.'s Econ. Policy Adv. Bd., 1981—; chmn. Nat. Commn. on Social Security Reform, 1981-83; mem. Task Force on Econ. Growth, 1969, Pres.'s Fgn. Intelligence Adv. Bd., 1982—; co-founder Greenspan O'Neil, Inc., N.Y.C., 1984—; Commn. on an All-Vol. Armed Force, 1969-70; Commn. on Fin. Structure and Regulation, 1970-71; cons. U.S. Treasury, 1971-74, Fed. Res. Bd., 1971-74; mem. econ. adv. bd. Sec. of Commerce, 1971-72; mem. central market system com. SEC, 1972; mem. GNP rev. com. Office Mgmt. and Budget; sr. adviser panel on econ. acitivity Brookings Instn., 1970-74, 77—; mem. bd. economists Time mag., 1971-74, 77—; dir. Gen. Foods Corp., J.P. Morgan & Co., Morgan Guaranty Trust Co., Mobil Corp., Alcoa, Automatic Data Processing, Inc.; adj. prof. Grad. Sch. Bus. Adminstrn., N.Y. U., 1977—. Mem. Nixon for Pres. Com., 1968-69, dir. domestic policy research; personal rep. of Pres.-elect to Bur. Budget for transition period, chmn. task force on fgn. trade policy.; Bd. overseers Hoover Instn. on War, Revolution and Peace, 1973-74, 77—. Recipient John P. Madden medal, 1975; joint recipient Pub. Service Achievement award, 1976, William Butler Meml. award, 1977. Fellow Nat. Assn. Bus. Economists (past pres.); mem. Council Fgn. Relations, Conf. Bus. Economists. Clubs: Economic of N.Y.; Hillcrest Country (Los Angeles); Harmonie, Metropolitan (Washington); Century Country, Recess, University. Office: One New York Plaza New York NY 10004

GREENSPAN, DONALD, mathematician, educator; b. N.Y.C., Jan. 24, 1928; s. Louis and Jessie (Scholnick) G.; m. Ruth Lucas, July 3, 1957; children: James, Marc, Rona; m. Bonita Bowman, Jan. 23, 1979. B.S., NYU, 1948; M.S., U. Wis., 1949; Ph.D., U. Md., 1956. Instr. U. Md., 1948-56; research engr. Hughes Aircraft Co., 1956-57; asst. prof. Purdue U., 1957-61, asso. prof., 1961-62; permanent mem. U. Wis. Math. Research Center, Madison, 1962-68; prof. computer scis., cons. to U. Wis. Computing Center, 1965-78; prof. math. U. Tex., 1978—; lectr. Am. Math. Assn., 1963-64, U. Mich. Summer Conf., 1964; referee NRC, NSF. Author: Theory and Solution of Ordinary Differential Equations, 1960, Introduction to Partial Differential Equations, 1961, Introductory Numerical Analysis of Elliptic Boundary Value Problems, 1965, Introduction to Calculus, 1968, Lectures on the Numerical Solutions of Linear, Singular, and Nonlinear Differential Equations, 1968, Introduction to Numerical Analysis and Application, 1970, Discrete Models, 1973, Discrete Numerical Methods in Physics and Engineering, 1974, Arithmetic Applied Mathematics, 1980, Computer-Oriented Mathematical Physics, 1981; editor: Numerical Solutions of Nonlinear Differential Equations, 1966; contbr. articles to profl. jours. Served with USAF, 1953. Mem. Am. Math. Soc., Am. Phys. Soc., Assn. Computing Machinery, ACLU, NAACP, Ams. for Democratic Action. Office: Math Dept U Texas Arlington TX 76019

GREENSPAN, FRANCIS S., physician; b. Perth Amboy, N.J., Mar. 16, 1920; s. Philip and Francis (Goldensohn) G.; m. Bonnie Jean Fisher, Oct. 25, 1945; children—Richard L., Robert H., Susan L. B.A., Cornell U., 1940, M.D., 1943. Diplomate: Am. Bd. Internal Medicine. Mem. endocrinology staff U. Calif., Berkeley; chief endocrinology Stanford (Calif.) Hosp., 1949-59; chief thryoid clinic U. Calif. Med. Center, San Francisco, 1959—; practice medicine specializing in endocrinology, San Francisco; now clin. prof. medicine and radiology U. Calif. Med. Center; chief staff U. Calif. Hosps. and Clinics, San Francisco, 1976-78. Editor: Textbook of Endocrinology; contbr. articles to med. jours. Served with USNR, 1944-45. Mem. San Francisco Med. Soc., Calif. Med. Assn., AMA, Endocrine Soc., Am. Thyroid Assn., Western Soc. Clin. Research, Western Assn. Physicians, Calif. Acad. Medicine. Office: U Calif Medical Center San Francisco CA 94143

GREENSPAN, HARVEY PHILIP, applied mathematician, educator; b. N.Y.C., Feb. 22, 1933; s. Louis and Jessie (Scholnick) G.; m. Mirian Gordon, Sept. 6, 1953; children—Elizabeth, Judith. B.S., Coll. City N.Y., 1953; M.S., Harvard, 1954, Ph.D., 1956. Asst. prof. applied math. Harvard, 1957-60; faculty Mass. Inst. Tech., Cambridge, 1960—, prof. applied math., 1964—. Author: Theory of Rotating Fluids, 1968, Calculus: An Introduction to Applied Mathematics, 1973; Editor: Studies in Applied Mathematics, 1969. Home: 15 Chatham Circle Brookline MA 02146 Office: Mass Inst Tech Cambridge MA 02139

GREENSPUN, HERMAN MILTON, newspaper publisher; b. Bklyn., Aug. 27, 1909; s. Samuel J. and Anna (Fleischman) G.; m. Barbara Joan Ritchie, May 21, 1944; children: Susan Gail, Brian Lee, Jane Toni, Daniel Alan. Student, St. John's Coll., 1930-32; LL.B., St. John's Sch. Law, 1934; L.H.D. (hon.), U. Nev., Las Vegas, 1977. Bar: N.Y. bar 1936. Practice law, N.Y.C., 1936-46; pub. mag. Las Vegas Life, 1946-47; owner, pub. Las Vegas Sun, North Las Vegas Sun, 1950—; owner Colorado Springs Sun, 1970-75; editorial writer, columnist Las Vegas Sun, 1950—; pres. Las Vegas Sun, Inc., 1950—, KLAS-TV, Las Vegas TV, Inc., 1954-68; owner, pres. CATV-Las Vegas; former owner Sun Outdoor Advt. Co. Author: autobiography Where I Stand. Bd. dirs. Sun Youth Found. Served from pvt. to maj. AUS, 1941-46; ETO. Decorated Croix de Guerre with silver star; Conspicuous Service cross State N.Y.; recipient Outstanding Journalist award Jewish War Vets, 1957. Mem. Am. Newspaper Pubs. Assn., Am. Soc. Newspaper Editors, Fed. Bar Assn., Nev. Press Assn. (pres. 1957), Internat. Platform Assn., Calif. Newspaper Pubs. Assn., Am. Legion, VFW, DAV. Clubs: Nat. Press, Overseas Press, Variety, Friars; Las Vegas Country (dir.). Office: Las Vegas Sun 121 S Highland St Las Vegas NV 89106

GREENSTADT, MELVIN, investor, retired educator; b. N.Y.C., Jan. 18, 1918; s. Sol Max and Sadie (Rosenberg) G.; m. Helen Levy, June 22, 1941; children—Laurie (Mrs. Mason C. Brown), Kenneth, Judy. B.S., Coll. City N.Y., 1938; A.B., U. So. Calif., 1948, A.M., 1949; Ph.D., 1956. Chemist Littauer Pneumonia Research Fund, N.Y. U. Coll. Medicine, N.Y.C., 1938-40, War Dept., Radford, Va., 1941-42; tchr. chemistry and math. Fairfax High Sch., Los Angeles, 1950-66, 69-80; now real estate and fin. co. investor; assoc. prof. chemistry Calif. State Coll.-Long Beach, 1966-69; cons. sci. and math. edn. Co-author: CHEM Study Text, 1960, SMSG Math. Text, 1963. Served to lt. comdr. USNR, 1942-46. Recipient award Com. for Advanced Sci. Tng., 1962; Western Regional award in high sch. chemistry teaching Am. Chem. Soc., 1972; James Bryant Conant award high sch. chemistry teaching, 1973; award for chemistry teaching So. Calif. sect., 1974, 77, 78, 79; High Sch. Chemistry Tchr. Regional award Mfg. Chemists Assn., 1978; other awards including Los Angeles County Bd. Suprs., 1978. Home and Office: 6531 W 5th St Los Angeles CA 90048

GREENSTEIN, FRED IRWIN, political science educator; b. N.Y.C., Sept. 1, 1930; s. Arthur Aaron and Rose (Goldstein) G.; m. Barbara Elferink, July 14, 1957; children: Michael, Amy, Jessica. B.A., Antioch Coll., 1953; M.A., Yale U., 1956, Ph.D., 1960. Instr. Yale U., New Haven, 1959-62, vis. prof., 1965-68; mem. faculty Wesleyan U., Middletown, Conn., 1963-73, prof. polit. sci., 1966-73; Henry Luce prof. politics, law and society Princeton U., 1973-81, prof. politics, 1973—; vis. prof. U. Essex, Eng., 1968-69. Author: The American Party System and the American People, 1970, Children and Politics, 2d edit., 1969, Personality and Politics, 2d edit., 1975; co-author: (with R.E. Lane and J.D. Barber) Introduction to Political Analysis, 2 edit., 1965, (with M. Lerner) A Source Book for the Study of Personality and Politics, 1971, (with N.W. Polsby) The Handbook of Political Science, 8 vols., (with R. Wolfinger and M. Shapiro) Dynamics and American Politics, 1976, (with L. Berman and A. Felzenberg) The Evolution of the Modern Presidency: A Bibliographical Review, 1977; author: The Hidden-Hand Presidency: Eisenhower as Leader, 1982, The Reagan Presidency: An Early Appraisal, 1983. Served with AUS, 1953-55. Fellow Ctr. Advanced Study Behavioral Scis., 1964-65; NSF sr. postdoctoral fellow, 1968-69. Fellow Am. Acad. Arts And Scis.; mem. Am. Polit. Sci. Assn. (editorial bd. 1968-72, sec. 1976-77). Homme: 340 Jefferson Rd Princeton N.J. 08540 Office: Dept Politics Princeton Univ Princeton NJ 08940

GREENSTEIN, JESSE LEONARD, astronomer, emeritus educator; b. N.Y.C., Oct. 15, 1909; s. Maurice and Leah (Feingold) G.; m. Naomi Kitay, Jan. 7, 1934; children: George Samuel, Peter Daniel. A.B., Harvard U., 1929, A.M., 1930, Ph.D., 1937. Engaged in real estate and investments, 1930-34, Nat. Research fellow, 1937-39; assoc. prof. Yerkes Obs., U. Chgo., 1939-48; research assoc. McDonald Obs., U. Tex., 1939-48; mil. research under OSRD (optical design), Yerkes Obs.), 1942-45; prof. Calif. Inst. Tech., 1948-70, Lee A. DuBridge prof. astrophysics, 1971-81, prof. emeritus, 1981—; also staff mem. Hale Obs., 1949—, Palomar Obs., 1979—, exec. officer for astronomy, 1949-72; chmn. of faculty of inst., 1965-67; mem. obs. com. Hale Observatories; mem. staff Owens Valley Radio Obs.; cons., also com. mem. NASA and NSF on astronomy and radio astronomy; chmn. astronomy survey Nat. Acad. Scis., 1969-72; spl. cons. NASA, 1978—; vis. prof. Princeton, 1955, Inst. for Advanced Studies, 1964, 68-69, U. Hawaii, 1979, Niels Bohr Inst., 1979, NORDITA, Copenhagen, 1972, U. Del., 1981; lectr. in field; cons. Sci. Adv. Bd. USAF; dir. Itek Corp., Hycon Corp.; Chmn. bd. dirs. Associated Univs. Research in Astronomy, 1974-77; bd. overseers Harvard, 1965-71; bd. dirs. Pacific Asia Mus. Author sects. of treatises, 380 tech. papers.; Editor: Stellar Atmospheres, 1960; Contbr. sci. articles; author govt. reports. Named Calif. Scientist of Yr., 1964; recipient Apollo award, Disting. Public Service medal NASA, 1974. Mem. Royal Astron. Soc. (asso., gold medal 1975), Astron. Soc. Pacific (Bruce medalist 1971), Am. Astron. Soc. (councillor 1947-50, v.p. 1955-57, Russell lectr. 1970), Internat. Astron. Union (pres. commn. on spectroscopy 1952-58, chmn. U.S. del. 1969-72, Rennie Taylor award 1982), Nat. Acad. Scis. (councillor, sect. chmn. com. on sci. and pub. policy), Am. Philos. Soc., Am. Acad. Arts and Scis., Phi Beta Kappa. Club: Athenaeum (Pasadena) (bd. govs.). Home: 2057 San Pasqual St Pasadena CA 91107 *A long and happy life, in which scientific discovery was like breath. With age one faces the question—was it worth doing? Were the uncomfortable thousand nights at the large telescopes drudgery or drama? Was the blood in the committee-room necessary? Yes, Yes, Yes*

GREENSTEIN, JULIUS SIDNEY, college president, biologist; b. Boston, July 13, 1927; s. Samuel and Helen (Shriber) G.; m. Joette Mason, Aug. 23, 1954; children: Gail Susan, Jodi Beth, Jay Mason, Blake Jeffrey, Joette Elise. B.A., Clark U., 1948; M.S., U. Ill., 1951, Ph.D., 1955; postdoctoral study, Harvard U. Med. Sch., 1966. Mem. faculty U. Mass., Amherst, 1954-59; faculty Duquesne U., Pitts., 1959-70, chmn. dept. biol. scis., 1961-70, prof., 1964-70; prof., chmn. dept. biology State U. N.Y., Fredonia, 1970-74, acting dean arts and scis., 1973-74; dean math. and natural scis. Shippensburg (Pa.)U., 1974-80; also dir. Center for Sci. and the Citizen; pres. Central Ohio Tech. Coll., 1980—; dean, dir. Ohio State U., Newark, 1980—; vis. lectr. Am. Inst. Biol. Scis., 1966—. Author: Contemporary Readings in Biology, 1971, Readings in Living Systems, 1972; Spl. editor: Internat. Jour. Fertility, 1958-71; publs. profl. jours. Mem. Carnegie Civic Symphony Orch.; Mem. sci. adv. bd. Human Life Found.; trustee Licking Meml. Hosp., Licking County Symphony Orch.; mem. campaign cabinet United Way Licking County. Served in armored div. AUS, World War II. Recipient Wisdom award honor, 197O. Mem. Am. Assn. Acad. Deans, Am. Assn. Univ. Adminstrs., Am. Assn. Anatomists, Am. Inst. Biol. Scis., Internat. Fertility Assn., AAAS, Am. Soc. Zoologists, Am. Fertility Soc., Soc. Study Fertility (Eng.), Council Biol. Editors, Pa. Acad. Sci. (editorial bd. 1963—), N.Y. State Acad. Sci., Soc. Study Reprodn., AAUP (pres. Duquesne chpt.), Soc. Developmental Biology, Newark C. of C., Sigma Xi, Phi Sigma. Club: Rotary. Contbr. to understanding of causes and prevention of reproductive failure in mammals by studying early developmental stages of embryo, nature of male and female reproductive organs and endocrine glands; developed new techniques for staining specimens and smears; first to demonstrate that estradiol injections cause corpus luteum regression, hence early termination of pregnancy; investigated relationship of specific diseases to normal reproductive performance. Home: 1284 Howell Dr Newark OH 43055 *I have faith in the ability of men to reason together, if the truth is shared among them.*

GREENSTEIN, RUTH LOUISE, lawyer; b. N.Y.C., Mar. 28, 1946; d. Milton and Beatrice (Zutty) G.; m. David Seidman, May 19, 1972. B.A., Harvard U., 1966; M.A., Yale U., 1968; J.D., George Washington U., 1980. Bar: D.C. 1980. Fgn. service info. officer USIA, Washington and Tehran, Iran, 1968-70; adminstrv. asst. Export-Import Bank U.S., Washington, 1971-72; asst. dean Woodrow Wilson Sch. Pub. and Internat. Affairs, Princeton U., 1972-75; budget examiner U.S. Office Mgmt. and Budget, Washington, 1975-79; budget coordinator U.S. Internat. Devel. Coop. Agy., 1979-81; dep. gen. counsel NSF, 1981—. Mem. ABA, D.C. Bar Assn. Home: 2737 Devonshire Pl NW Apt 511 Washington DC 20008 Office: NSF 1800 G St NW Washington DC 20550

GREENWALD, CAROL SCHIRO, political consultant; b. Phila., Mar. 2, 1939; d. Sidney L. and Adele R. (Rosenheim) Schiro; children: David Bruce, William Michael. B.A. cum laude, Smith Coll., 1961; M.A., Hunter Coll., 1965; Ph.D. in Polit. Sci., CUNY, 1972. Instr. polit. sci. Queen's Coll., CUNY, 1970-73; asst. prof. Richmond Coll., CUNY, 1973-76, Bklyn. Coll., CUNY, 1976-77; research assoc. Bunting Inst., Radcliffe Coll., 1977-79; project dir. Jobs in the 1980s Pub. Agenda Found., N.Y.C., 1979-81; asst. dir. Evaluation N.Y.C. Adminstrv. Decentralization, 1971-73. Author: Group Power: Lobbying and Public Policy, 1977; contbr. articles on polit. sci. to profl. jours. Lilly Found. fellow. Mem. Northeastern Polit. Sci. Assn. (pres. 1981-82), Common Cause (chmn. N.Y. 1981-83, nat. dir. 1978-84), LWV (dir. N.Y. State 1967-69). Home: 688 Forest Ave Larchmont NY 10538

GREENWALD, CAROLINE MEYER, artist; b. Madison, Wis., Jan. 30, 1936; d. Frank Gustave and Linda Doris (Logemann) Meyer; children: Elaine Kathryn, Geraldine Lynn. B.S., U. Wis., 1957, M.A. in Arts, 1975, M.F.A., 1977; student, U. Notre Dame Art Workshop, 1976. Vis. artist Carleton Coll., 1982; lectr. univs. and seminars. Exhibitor one-woman shows, U. Wis.-Madison, 1975, 77, Source Gallery, San Francisco, 1977, Cin. Acad. Art, Galeria Kin, Mexico City, 1979, Loyola U.-Chgo., Getler-Pall Gallery, N.Y.C., 1980, 82, Evanston (Ill.) Art Ctr, 1980, Fendrick Gallery, Washington, 1981, Carleton Coll., Northfield, Minn., 1982, American Ctr., Tokyo, 1983, group shows, Nat. Collection Fine Arts, Washington, 1977, Pratt Graphics Ctr., N.Y.C., 1978, Detroit Inst. Arts, 1979, Visual Arts Ctr., Beer-Sheva, Israel, Seibu Mus Art, Toyko, Alice Simsar Gallery, Ann Arbor, Mich., Rockland Ctr. for Arts, West Nyack, N.Y., 1980, New Eng. Found. Arts touring exhbn., 1980-81, Printmaking Council N.J. touring exhbn., 1981, Centre International de la Tapisserie Ancienne et Modern Lausanne (Switzerland), Mus. Applied Arts, Belgrade, Yugoslavia, New American Paperworks internat. travelling exhbn., 1982-84, Am. Craft Mus., N.Y.C., 1982, Arts Council Gt. Britain touring exhbn., Australian Nat. Gallery, Canberra, Fine Arts Mus. L.I., Hempstead, 1982-83, Eve Mannes Gallery, Atlanta, 1983, Gallery Beni, Kyoto, Japan; represented in permanent collections, Art Inst. Chgo., Australian Nat. Gallery, Conn. Wesleyan U., Elvehjem Mus. Art, U. Wis.-Madison, Indpls. Mus. Art, Jessie Besser Mus., Alpena, Mich., Madison Art Ctr., Mpls. Inst. Arts, Mus. Modern Arts, N.Y.C.,

Phila. Mus. Art, EPA, San Francisco. Grantee Nat. Endowment Arts, 1983. Address: 3400 Cross St Madison WI 53711

GREENWALD, GERALD, automotive company executive; b. St. Louis, Sept. 11, 1935; s. Frank and Bertha G.; m. Glenda Lee Gerstein, June 29, 1958; children: Scott, Stacey, Bradley, Joshua. B.A. Cumlaude (Univ. scholar), Princeton U., 1957; M.A., Wayne State U., 1962. With Ford Motor Co., 1957-79; pres. Ford Venezuela, dir. non-automotive ops., Europe; vice chmn. Chrysler Corp., Highland Park, Mich., 1979—. Chmn. Meadowbrook Festival; bd. dirs. Detroit United Fund. Served with USAF, 1957-60. Mem. Young Presidents Orgn., Econ. Club Detroit. Clubs: Princeton, Detroit Athletic.

GREENWALD, GILBERT SAUL, physiologist; b. N.Y.C., June 24, 1927; s. Morris M. and Celia G.; m. Pola Gorsky, Sept. 9, 1950; children—Susan Greenwald Waxman, Elizabeth Greenwald Jordan, Douglas. A.B. with honors, U. Calif., Berkeley, 1949, Ph.D. in Zoology, 1954. Instr., then asst. prof. anatomy U. Wash. Med. Sch., Seattle, 1956-61; mem. faculty U. Kans. Med. Center, Kansas City, 1961—, disting. prof. physiology, chmn. dept., 1977; prof. Ob-Gyn, 1964—, prof. anatomy, 1965-77, research prof. in human reprodn., 1961-77; mem. reproductive biology study sect. NIH, 1966-70, mem. population research adv. com., 1967-71. Editor: Biology of Reprodn, 1974-77. Served with USNR, 1944-45. Mem. Soc. Study Reprodn. (pres. 1971), Endocrine Soc., Brit. Soc. Study Fertility, AAAS, Am. Physiol. Soc., Soc. Exptl. Biology and Medicine, Am. Assn. Anatomists, Sigma Xi. Office: Univ Kans Med Center 39th and Rainbow Blvd Kansas City KS 66103

GREENWALD, GUY PRESTON, JR., lawyer; b. Falls City, Nebr., Jan. 16, 1914; s. Guy Preston and Blanche (Maddox) G. A.B., Stanford U., 1935, LL.B., 1938. Bar: Calif. 1938. Pvt. practice law, Los Angeles, 1938—; partner Greenwald, Hoffman, Meyer & Guy, Los Angeles, 1958—; Lectr. continuing edn. series State Bar Calif., 1956; local counsel Celotex Corp.; counsel, dir. Los Angeles By-Products Co., Los Angeles Steel Casting Co., Shredded Steel Co. Bd. dirs. Child Guidance Clinic, Parsons Otis Art Inst. Assos. Fellow Am. Coll. Probate Counsel; mem. Am., Los Angeles bar assns., Am. Judicature Soc., State Bar Calif., Phi Beta Kappa, Delta Theta Phi. Clubs: University, Jonathan, Stanford (Los Angeles) (dir., treas. 1956). Home: 432 S Curson Ave 5H Los Angeles CA 90036 Office: 3345 Wilshire Blvd Suite 1106 Los Angeles CA 90010

GREENWALD, JAMES L., broadcasting and communications executive; b. N.Y.C., Apr. 2, 1927; s. Lester David and Ruth Amelia (Leberman) G.; m. Patricia Braunstein, Dec. 18, 1960; 1 son, Thomas. B.A., Columbia U., 1949; D.Comml. Sci., St. John's U., 1980. With Katz Agy., N.Y.C., 1956—, mem. radio sales staff, 1956-63, asst. sales mgr. radio, also dir., 1963-70; pres. Katz Radio, 1970-74; exec. v.p. Katz Communications, Inc., 1974-75, pres., chmn. bd., 1975—. Served with U.S. Army, 1945, 52-53. Mem. Internat. Radio and TV Soc. (bd. govs.), Broadcast Pioneers. Clubs: City Athletic; Old Oaks Country (Purchase, N.Y.). Office: 1 Dag Hammarskjold Plaza New York NY 10017

GREENWALD, JOSEPH ADOLPH, mfg. co. exec., former ambassador; b. Chgo., Sept. 18, 1918; s. Jacob and Lena (Corman) G.; m. Mary Virginia Doyle, Dec. 12, 1942; children—John, Bruce, Jane. Student, U. Pa., 1936-38; B.A. in Econs, U. Chgo., 1941; LL.B., Georgetown U., 1951. Bar: D.C. bar 1951. Internat. economist Dept. State, 1947, U.S. resident rep. internat. economist orgns., Geneva, Switzerland, 1952-55; chief comml. policy br. Office Internat. Trade, Dept. State, 1955-58; 1st sec., asst. comml. attache Am. embassy, London, Eng., 1958-63; dir. Office of Internat. Trade, Dept. State, 1963-65, dep. asst. sec. state for internat. trade policy, 1965-69; ambassador to OECD, Paris, 1969-72, European Communities, Brussels, 1972-76; asst. sec. state for econ. and bus. affairs, 1976; v.p. internat. planning The Bendix Corp., Southfield, Mich., 1976-79; pres. Bendix Japan, Ltd., Tokyo, 1979—; Chmn. U.S. del. UN Conf. on Trade and Devel., 1968. Mem. D.C. Bar, Phi Beta Kappa. Home: Town House Akasaka 5-25 Akasaka 8-Chome Minato-ku Tokyo 107 Japan Office: Time and Life Bldg 3-6 Ohtemachi 2-Chome Chiyoda-ku Tokyo 100 Japan

GREENWALD, MARTIN, publishing company executive; b. Bronx, N.Y., Apr. 25, 1942; s. David and Jean (Kaufman) G.; m. Beth Susan Greenwald, Feb. 7, 1965; children: Karen Sue, Craig Mitchell. A.B., Lafayette Coll., 1963; M.B.A., Columbia U., 1965. Mgr. acquisition planning, fin. analyst Macmillan Inc., N.Y.C., 1965-69, bus. mgr., trade div., 1970-72; new bus. devel. analyst Holt div. CBS, N.Y.C., 1969-70; v.p., gen. mgr. Hagstrom Co. Inc., N.Y.C., 1972-76; pres. Paddington Press, N.Y.C., 1976-80; dir.mktg. Facts On File, Inc., 1980-82, v.p. mktg., 1982—. Mem. Nassau County (N.Y.) Republican Com., 1973-80; v.p. Green Acres Library Bd., Hempstead, N.Y., 1976—, Green Acres Civic Assn., 1976—. Mem. Assn. Am. Pubs. Jewish. Home: 80 Riverdale Rd Valley Stream NY 11581 Office: 460 Park Ave S New York NY 10016

GREENWALD, ROBERT, public relations executive; b. N.Y.C., Jan. 14, 1927; s. Louis and Rebecca (Shapiro) G.; m. Genevieve Kushnir, Apr. 15, 1957 (div. 1960); m. Dorothy Pearl Brand, Apr. 19, 1963; children: Liza, Mark. B.A., NYU, 1949, postgrad., 1951-54; postgrad, Columbia U., 1950, New Sch., 1950-51. Account exec. Ruder, Finn & Rotman Inc., N.Y.C., 1954—, sr. assoc., 1955-56, v.p., 1957-65; sr. v.p. Ruder, Finn & Rotman, Inc., N.Y.C., 1965-79; exec. v.p. Ruder, Finn & Rotman Inc., N.Y.C., 1980-83, sr. counsel, 1982—. Author: (with Dorothy Brand) Learning To Live with The Love of Your Life, 1979. Chmn. pub. relations com. UNICEF, N.Y.C., 1976-82, dir., N.Y.C., 1976-82; bd. dirs. Jewish Family Services, N.Y.C., 1972-75. Served with U.S. Army, 1945-46; ETO. Recipient Silver Anvil award Pub. Relations Soc. Am., 1955, 73, 81, Paul B. Zucker award Ruder & Finn Inc., 1976, 82. Democrat. Jewish. Home: 1 Erwin Park Montclair NJ 07042 Office: Ruder Finn & Rotman Inc. 110 E 59th St New York NY 10012

GREENWALL, FRANK KOEHLER, mfg. exec.; b. N.Y.C., May 6, 1896; s. Henry and Hattie (Koehler) G.; m. Anna Alexander, Jan. 4, 1921; children—Susan (dec.), Nancy (Mrs. C. Richard MacGrath) (dec.). Student pub. schs., N.Y.C. With Nat. Starch & Chem. Corp. (and predecessor firms), 1920—, beginning as salesman, successively treas., v.p. sales, 1920-38, pres., dir., 1938-58, chmn. bd., chief exec. officer, 1958-64, chmn. bd., 1964-69, chmn. exec. com., 1969—, chmn. fin. com., 1978—. Hon. trustee Corn Refiners Assn., Inc.; trustee Susan Greenwall Found., Keep Am. Beautiful, Monmouth Med. Center. Served USNRF, World War I. Mem. Adhesive Mfrs. Assn. Clubs: Pinnacle, Marco Polo, Madison Sq. Garden, Turf and Field, Sky 7. (N.Y.C.). Home: 2 E 61st St New York NY 10021 also Tip Top Farm Holmdel NJ Office: 245 Park Ave New York NY 10017

GREENWALT, CLIFFORD LLOYD, utility executive; b. Solano, N. Mex., Jan. 12, 1933; s. Lloyd E. and Floral (Slover) G.; m. Shirley A. Ferrguson, June 7, 1958; children: David F., Karla Anne. Diploma, Draughton's Bus. Coll., 1951; B.A. in Civil Engring., U. Mo., 1960; M.B.A., U. Ill., 1977. Registered profl. engr., Mo., Ill. Engr. No. Ill. Gas Co., Bellwood, 1960-63; engring. supr. Central Ill. Pub. Service Co., Marion and West Frankfort, 1963-71, mgr. gas dept., Springfield, 1971-76, mgr. info. systems, 1976-78, v.p. corp. services, 1978-80, sr. v.p. ops., 1980—; dir. Electric Energy, Inc., Joppa, Ill. Bd. dirs. Lincolnwood Goodwill, Springfield, 1978—. Served with USAF, 1952-56. Lodge: Rotary. Office: 607 E Adams St Springfield IL 62701

GREENWALT, HARLAN EDWARD, electric co. exec.; b. Canfield, Ohio, Sept. 8, 1905; s. Orville and Clara (Lawrence) G.; m. Lola B., May, 1928, children—Lucille Greenwalt Parsons, Linda Greenwalt Lungstrom. Student, Ohio Bus. Inst., 1921-28. Factory mgr. Standard Transformer Co., Warren, Ohio, 1925-46; prodn. mgr. Kuhlman Corp., Troy, Mich., 1946-49, v.p., dir., 1949-55; exec. v.p., gen. mgr., dir., 1955-65, named pres., 1965, chief exec. officer, 1968-77, chmn. bd., 1977—. Clubs: Oakland Hills Country, Elks, Masons. Home: 1073 Stratford Ln Bloomfield Hills MI 48013 Office: 2565 E Maple Rd Troy MI 48084

GREENWALT, LYNN ADAMS, conservationist; b. Reno, Mar. 15, 1931; s. Ernest Jagger and Lyndel (Adams) G.; m. Judith Ann Cunningham, Nov. 18, 1955; children: Mark L., Grant L. B.S., U. Okla., 1953; M.S., U. Ariz., 1955. With Fish and Wildlife Service, Dept. Interior, 1957-81; refuge mgr. Salt Plains Nat. Wildlife Refuge, Okla., 1957, Bosque del Apache Nat. Wildlife Refuge, N.Mex., 1958, Fish Springs Nat. Wildlife Refuge, Utah, 1959-62, asst. regional supr. wildlife refuges, Albuquerque, 1962-68, asso. regional supr., Mpls., 1968-71, regional supr. law enforcement, Portland, Oreg., 1971-72, chief div. wildlife refuges, Washington, 1971-73; dir. U.S. Fish and Wildlife Service (formerly Bur. Sport Fisheries and Wildlife), 1973-81; cons., 1981—, regional exec. Nat. Wildlife Fedn.; guest lectr. Nat. Park Service, Albright Tng. Acad., Grand Canyon Nat. Park, Ariz., 1965-67. Served with U.S. Army, 1955-57. Mem. Wildlife Soc. (v.p. Minn. chpt. 1971), Am. Fisheries Soc. Home: 16412 Keats Terr Rockville MD 20855

GREENWALT, TIBOR JACK, physician; b. Budapest, Hungary, Jan. 23, 1914; came to U.S., 1920, naturalized, 1943; s. Bela and Irene (Foldes) G.; m. Shirley Johnson, Aug. 6, 1960 (dec. Sept. 1970); 1 son, Peter H.; m. Pia Glas, Feb. 27, 1971. B.A. summa cum laude, NYU, 1937, M.D., 1937. Diplomate: Am. Bd. Internal Medicine. Intern pathology and bacteriology Mt. Sinai Hosp., N.Y.C., 1937-38; rotating intern Kings County Hosp., Bklyn., 1938-40; resident medicine Montefiore Hosp., N.Y.C., 1940-41; research asso. New Eng. Med. Center, Boston, 1941-42; med. dir. Milw. Blood Center, 1947-66; faculty medicine Marquette U. Sch. Medicine, 1948-66, prof. medicine, 1963-66; cons. hematology VA Hosp., Wood, Wis., 1946-66, Milw. County Gen. Hosp., 1948-66; cons. Clin. Center, NIH, 1967-78, Bethesda Naval Med. Center, 1975-79; dir. blood program ARC, 1967-78, sr. sci. adviser blood programs, 1978-79; clin. prof. medicine George Washington U. Sch. Medicine, 1967-79; prof. medicine U. Cin. Med. Center, 1979—; dir. Paul I. Hoxworth Blood Center, 1979—; chmn. com. blood and transfusion problems Nat. Acad. Scis.-NRC, 1963-66; mem. hematology study sect. NIH, 1960-63, chmn., 1970-72; mem. research com. Am. Blood Commn., 1976-78; vis. prof., speaker throughout, U.S., 1960—; mem. Med. Research Service Merit Rev. Bd. for Hematology, VA, 1981—; mem. blood diseases and resources adv. com. Nat. Heart, Lung and Blood Inst., 1983—. Author: (with others) Hemolytic Syndromes, 1942, (with Shirley Greenwalt) Coagulation and Transfusion in Clinical Medicine, 1965; editor: (with Graham A. Jamieson) The Red Cell Membrane, 1969, Formation and Destruction of Blood Cells, 1970, Glycoproteins of Plasma and Membranes, 1971, The Human Red Cell in Vitro, 1974, Transmissible Disease and Blood Transfusion, 1974, Trace Proteins of Plasma, 1976, The Granulocyte, 1977, Blood Substitutes and Plasma Expanders, 1978, The Blood Platelet in Transfusion Therapy, 1978; editor, contbr.: Immunogenetics, 1967; editor-in-chief: Transfusion, 1960-66, assoc. editor, 1966—; editorial bd.: Gen. Principles of Blood Transfusions, 1962—, Vox Sanguinis, 1956-76, Haematologia, 1968—, Blood, 1979—; contbr. articles to profl. lit. Served to maj. M.C., AUS, 1942-46. Recipient Gold medal Caduceus Soc., NYU, 1933; Jr. Achievement award for outstanding contbn. sci., 1958; 1st Charles R. Drew award, Washington; Disting. Citizen's award Allied Vets. Council, 1963; award pioneer blood group research Center for Immunity, SUNY, Buffalo, 1976. Fellow N.Y. Acad. Scis., AAAS; mem. AMA, Am. Assn. Blood Banks (v.p. 1959-60, med. dir. central file rare donors 1960-66, John Elliot award 1966), Internat. Soc. Hematology, ACP, Internat. Soc. Blood Transfusion (pres. 1966-72, historian 1975—), Am. Soc. Clin. Pathologists, Central Soc. Clin. Research, Am. Soc. Hematology (treas. 1963-67), Am. Assn. Immunologists, Soc. Exptl. Biology and Medicine, Am. Soc. Human Genetics, Sigma Xi, Alpha Omega Alpha. Club: Cosmos. Home: 328 Compton Hills Dr Cincinnati OH 45215 Office: Hoxworth Blood Center 3231 Burnet Ave Cincinnati OH 45267

GREENWAY, HUGH DAVIDS SCOTT, journalist; b. Boston, May 8, 1935; s. James Cowen and Helen Livingston (Scott) G.; m. Joy Beverly Brooks, June 11, 1960; children—Julia Livingston, Alice Lauder, Sarah Davids. B.A., Yale U., 1958; postgrad., Oxford U., Eng., 1960-62. Corr. Time mag., London, 1962-63, Washington, 1963-64, Boston, 1964-66, Saigon, 1967-68, Bangkok, 1968-70, UN, N.Y.C., 1970-72; corr. Washington Post, Hong Kong, 1973-76, Jerusalem, 1976-78; asst. mng. editor for nat. and fgn. news Boston Globe, 1978—. Served with USNR, 1958-60. Nieman fellow Harvard U., 1971-72. Home: 634 Charles River St Needham MA 02192 Office: 135 Morrissey Blvd Boston MA 02107

GREENWAY, JOHN SELMES, hotel exec.; b. Santa Barbara, Calif., Oct. 11, 1924; s. John Campbell and Isabella Dinsmore (Selmes) G. B.A., Yale, 1949; LL.B., U. Ariz., 1954. Owner Ariz. Inn, Tucson, 1958—.

GREENWOOD, ALLAN NUNNS, electrical engineering educator; b. Leeds, Eng.; s. William Nunns and Ethel May (Burrell) G.; m. Grace Ruth Neville, July 24, 1944; children: Janet Penelope, Stephen Richard, Hilary Jane. B.A., Cambridge U., 1943, M.A., 1948; Ph.D., Leeds U., 1952. Devel. engr. Imperial Chem. Industries, Stourport, Eng., 1946-48; lectr. U. Leeds, 1948-54; vis. prof. U. Toronto, Ont., Can., 1954-55; cons. engr. sr. cons. engr. Gen. Electric Co., Phila., 1955-72; Philip Sporn prof., dir. Center Electric Power Engring., Rensselaer Poly. Inst., Troy, N.Y., 1972—; cons., industry, govt. Author: Electrical Transients in Power Systems, 1971, (with Lafferty et al) Vacuum Arcs, 1980, (with Tanaka) Advanced Power Cable Technology, Vols. I and II, 1983; contbr. articles to profl. jours. Served to lt. Royal Navy, 1943-46. Fellow IEEE; mem. Conf. Internat. des Grands Reseaux Electriques, Sigma Xi, Eta Kappa Nu. Unitarian. Patentee in power-switching technology. Office: Rensselaer Poly Inst Troy NY 12181

GREENWOOD, ALLEN HAROLD CLAUDE, aerospace executive; b. London, June 4, 1917; s. Thomas Claude G. (Hilda Letitia) and Knight (Greenwood). Student, Cheltenham Coll., 1930-35, Coll. Aero. Engring., London, 1936-39. Chartered engr. Exptl. flight test observer Vickers-Armstrongs Ltd., Wybridge, Surrey, U.K., 1940-42, 1946, service mgr., 1949, dir., 1960—; dep. mng. dir. Brit. Aricraft Corp., Webridge, 1969-72; dep. chmn. Brit. Aircraft Corp., 1972-75, chmn., 1975-77; dep. chmn. Brit. Aerospace, Weyridge, 1977-83; chmn., dir. Brit. Aerospace Inc.(U.S.A.), 1960-83; dir. Brit. Aerospace Australia Ltd., Sydney. Served to lt. comdr. Royal Navy, 1942-52. Decorated comdr. Order Brit. Empire, 1974. Fellow Royal Ero. Soc., Can. Aeros. and Astronautics (assoc.), AIA. Clubs: White's; Royal Automobile (London); Royal Lymington (Hampshire) Yacht. Address: 2 Rookcliff Park Ln Milford-on-Sea UK Lymington, Hampshire

GREENWOOD, DONALD THEODORE, educator; b. Clarkdale, Ariz., Dec. 8, 1923; s. Arthur Irving and Elizabeth Alma (Swanson) G.; m. Esther Marie Harju, Mar. 17, 1951; children: Anne Elizabeth, Brian William. B.S. in Mech. Engring, Calif. Inst. Tech., 1944; M.S. in Physics, 1948; Ph.D. in Elec. Engring, 1951. Engr. Engring. Research Assocs., St. Paul., 1946-47; teaching fellow Calif. Inst. Tech., Pasadena, 1948-51; head analog computation Lockheed Aircraft Corp., Burbank, Cal., 1951-56; lectr. U. So. Calif., 1954-56; mem. faculty U. Mich., Ann Arbor, 1956—, prof. aerospace engring., 1963—; vis. prof. U. Calif. at San Diego, 1969-70. Contbr.: Computer Handbook, 1962, Principles of Dynamics, 1965, Classical Dynamics, 1977. Served with USNR, 1943-46. Mem. AAAS, Am. Inst. Aero. and Astronautics, ASME, Sigma Xi, Tau Beta Pi. Presbyterian. Home: 1630 Hanover Rd Ann Arbor MI 48103

GREENWOOD, EL CAROL VOIGHTMAN, lawyer; b. Seward, Nebr., Oct. 2, 1920; s. James Charles and Ella Roline (Voightman) G.; m. Ernestine Hopson, Nov. 19, 1945 (div.); 1 son, Richard H.; m. Betty Schlesinger, June 12, 1983. A.B., Hastings Coll., 1941; J.D., U. Mich., 1949. Bar: Tex. 1950. Assoc. Fulbright & Jaworski, Houston, 1949-63, ptnr., 1963—. Served to lt. (s.g.) USNR, 1942-46. Mem. Maritime Law Assn. U.S. (exec. com. 1970-73), Internat. Bar Assn., ABA, Houston Bar Assn., State Bar Tex. Republican. Methodist. Clubs: Champions Golf, Plaza (Houston). Home: 6223 Rolling Water Dr Houston TX 77069 Office: Fulbright & Jaworski Bank of the SW Bldg Houston TX 77002

GREENWOOD, HAROLD WRIGHT, JR., savings and loan association executive; m. Carol Moses; 4 children. Ed., U. Minn., Acad. Accountancy, Mpls.; postgrad., LaSalle Correspondence Law Sch., 1955. Operating mgr. Midwest Fed. Savs. and Loan Assn. of Mpls., 1955-59, v.p., gen. mgr., 1959-65, chmn., pres., 1965—; chmn. bd. subs. Green Tree Acceptance, Inc., 1975—; owner Bank of Mpls. and Trust Co., Regal Savs. and Loan Assn., Balt., 1980—; dir. Security Savs. and Loan Assn., Milw.; apptd. Task Force on Housing, 1980; dir. Fed. Home Loan Bank Bd., Des Moines; apptd. Nat. Commn. on Neighborhoods; advisor Joint Com. of U.S. Congress, 1972-75. Recipient Am. award Am. Acad. Achievement, 1970. Mem. UN Assn. Mpls. (pres.), Savs. and Loan Council of Mpls. and St. Paul (pres.), Minn. Savs. and Loan League (pres.), U.S. Savs. and Loan League (chmn. legis. steering com. 1965-68), Nat. Savs. and Loan League (pres. 1979). Lodge: Kiwanis. Traveled to 37 countries representing White House and AID on internat. housing and fin. Home: 4869 E Lake Harriet Pkwy Minneapolis MN 55409 Office: Midwest Federal Savings and Loan Association of Mpls 801 Nicollet Mall Minneapolis MN 55402

GREENWOOD, HUGH JOHN, geologist, educator; b. Vancouver, C., Can., Mar. 17, 1931; s. John Marshall and Joan (Sampson) G.; m. Mary Sylvia Ledingham, Oct. 5, 1955; children—Bruce, Kelly, Lynn. B.A.Sc., U. B.C., 1954, M.A.Sc., 1956; Ph.D., Princeton U., 1960. Registered profl. engr., B.C. Geologist Ventures, Ltd., Noranda, Que., 1956-57; phys. chemist Carnegie Inst., Washington Geophys. Lab., 1960-63; asso. prof. geology Princeton U., 1963-67; prof. geology U. B.C., Vancouver, 1967—, head dept. geol. scis., 1977—. Contbr. articles to profl. jours. Recipient Steacie prize NRC, 1970; Siscoe fellow, 1959-60; Jacobus fellow, 1958-59; both Princeton U.; NSF grantee, 1963-67; NRC (Can.) grantee, 1967-81. Fellow Royal Soc. Can., Geol. Soc. Am., Geol. Assn. Can.; mem. Mineral. Soc. Am., Mineral. Assn. Can., Am. Geophys. Union, Geochem. Soc. (pres.). Office: U BC Faculty Sci Dept Geol Scis Vancouver BC V6T 1W5 Canada

GREENWOOD, JAMES RAYMOND, aircraft company executive; b. Washington, June 2, 1920; s. Ernest and Laura (Mandeville) G.; m. Stella Dixon (div.); 1 dau., Karen Greenwood Kraus; m. 2d Virginia eloise Hoyt, Oct. 27, 1946 (div.); children: Roxanne Greenwood Cable, Jeanne Greenwood Plant; m. 3d Helen Maxine Condon, Sept. 11, 1970. Student, La. State Normal Coll., 1943-44, U. Ga., 1943-44. Mgr, pub. relations Am. Airmotive, Miami, Fla., 1950-51; coordinator tng. Hawthorne Sch. Aeros, Moultrie, Ga., 1951-55; mgr. press relations Beech Aircraft Corp., Wichita, Kans., 1955-64; dir. pub. relations Gates Learjet Corp., Wichita, 1964-70, sr. v.p., Tucson, 1973—; dir. pub. affairs Fed. Aviation Adminstrn., Washington, 1970-73; adv. bd. U. Tex. Aviation Library, Dallas, 1974—, 99's Resource Ctr., Oklahoma City, 1982—, Pima Air Mus. Found., Tucson, 1981—; industry adv. council U. Ariz. Coll. Engring., 1982—; industry adv. com. Enbry-Riddle Aero. U., Prescott, Ariz., 1982—; industry adv. bd. Wichita State U., 1983—; aviation adv. com. Kans. Dept. Transp., Topeka, 1982—; mem. Nat. Def. Exec. Res., U.S. Dept. Transp., 1982—; trustee Aviation-Space Writers Found., 1977—. Author: Parachuting for Sport, 1962 (Fairchild award 1963), Parachute, 1964, Stunt Flying in the Movies, 1982 (AWA award 1983). Bd. dirs. Met. Tucson Conv.-Visitors Bur., Tucson, 1982—. Served with USN, 1941-46. Recipient Paul Tissandier diploma Fedn. Aeronautique Internationale, Belgium, 1982, George Washington Honor medal Freedoms Found., 1957. Mem. Nat. Press Club, Aviation-Space Writers Assn. (dir. 1975-79, N. Lever award 1980, B. Case award 1977, Pub. Relations trophy 1963), Wings Club, Tucson C. of C. (mil. affaris com. 1982—). Republican. Episcopalian. Clubs: Aero of Washington, Nat. Aviation, OX5 Aviation Pioneers, Quiet Birdmen. Home: 415 El Valle Green Valley AZ 85614 Office: Gates Learjet Corp PO Box 1186 Tucson AZ 85734

GREENWOOD, JAMES, JR., physician; b. Seguin, Tex., July 19, 1907; s. James and Ella L. (Harris) G.; m. Mary Pedan Cox, June 22, 1935; children—James, Alexander William, Mary Grace, Marvin Harris, Nancy Lee Greenwood Riddle, Andrew Pedan. A.B., Rice Inst., 1927; M.D., U. Tex., 1931. Diplomate: Am. Bd. Neurol. Surgery. Postgrad. work Phila. Gen. Hosp., 1931-35; pvt. practice neurosurgery, Houston, 1935—; clin. prof. neurosurgery Baylor U. Coll. Medicine, 1943—, acting chmn. div. neurosurgery, 1943-55, chmn., 1956-57; chief div. neurosurgery Meth. Hosp., 1936-81, sr. cons., 1981—; chmn. Jefferson Davis Hosp., 1940-46, St. Joseph's Infirmary, 1940-49; pres. staff Meth. Hosp., 1957-59; Prof. Hugo Krayenbuhl lectr., Zurich, 1973; cons. neurosurgery VA Hosp., M.D. Anderson Hosp. Cancer Research. Contbr. articles neurosurg. publs.; Amateur radio (W5PB) operator since, 1920. Recipient Ashbel Smith Distinguished Alumnus award U. Tex. Med. Br., Galveston, 1975, Distinguished R Man award Rice U., 1975. Fellow A.C.S.; mem. Harvey Cushing Soc., S.W. Surg. Congress, Am. Acad. Neurol. Surgery, Tex. Surg. Soc. (past pres.), So. Neurosurg. Soc. (past. pres.), Tex. Neurosurg. Soc. (Neurosurgeon of Yr. 1980), Tex. Neuropsychiat. Soc. (past pres.), Soc. Brit. Neurol. Surgeons (hon.), Alpha Omega Alpha, Phi Rho Sigma. Democrat. Episcopalian. Home: 1839 Kirby Dr Houston TX 77019 Office: 6560 Fannin Suite 830 Houston TX 77030 *A person cannot be happy without hard work and service to others. Everyone should do some work without pay. To raise children you need only to spend some time with them, and never let them forget that you love them.*

GREENWOOD, LAWRENCE GEORGE, banker; b. Briercrest, Sask., Can., June 16, 1921; s. Goerge Tuckfield and Mildred Jane (Clifford) G.; m. Margaret Purser, June 28, 1947. Grad., Regina Central Collegiate, 1938. With Cn. Bank Commerce, Regina, Sask.,

1938—, merged to form Can. Imperial Bank Commerce, 1961, pres., Toronto, 1968-71; vice chmn. Toronto, Montreal, 1971-76; chmn., prs., dir. Kinross Mortgate Co., 1977; pres., dir. Edifice Dorchester-Commerce Inc., 1978; exec. v.p. Can. Imperial Bank Commerce, Toronto, 1978; chmn. bd. Mortgage Corp.; dir. Imperial Life Assurance Co. Can.; mem. Can. adv. bd Liberty Mut. Ins. Co., Bd. Trade Met. Toronto. Dir., mem. Can. council Internat. C. of C.; mem. Nat. Trust for Scotland; trustee Queen's U. Hosp. for Sick Children; bd. dirs. Multiple Sclerosis Soc. Can. Served with RCAF, 1941-45. Mem. Am. Mgmt. Assn., Can. Netherlands Council, Unionville Home Soc. Clubs: York, Toronto; Empire of Can. (Toronto); Canadian. Home: 330 Spanina Rd Apt 2004 Toronto On Canada M5R 2V9 Office: CIBC Mortgage Corp Commerce Ct W Suite 2500 PO Box 115 Toronto On Canada M5L 1E5

GREENWOOD, PAT MINTER, insurance company executive; b. Sulphur Springs, Tex., Oct. 4, 1906; s. Elmore Patrick and Edna (Minter) G.; m. Isabelle Denker Norquist, Mar. 9, 1968; children: Betty Reese, Jimmy M., Kay Brown, William Sexton, Mary Ann. Student, U. of South, Sewanee, Tenn., 1924-25. With Gt. So. Life Ins. Co., Houston, 1925-76, exec. v.p., 1946-53, pres., 1953-67, chmn. bd., 1967—, also dir.; chmn. bd., dir., chmn. exec. com. Gt. So. Corp., 1977—; dir. First City Nat. Bank, Houston, Columbian Universal Life Ins. Co., State Savs. & Loan Assn., Salt Lake City. Mem. Delta Tau Delta. Clubs: Salesmanship (Dallas) (past pres.); River Oaks Country (Houston) (past v.p., dir.). Home: 3 Briarwood Ct Houston TX 77019 Office: 4151 Southwest Freeway Suite 480 Houston TX 77027

GREENWOOD, WILLIAM WARREN, broadcasting correspondent; b. Richmond, Va., Mar. 28, 1942; s. William Rogers and Gloria Vivian (Brown) Warren; m. Marsha Ann Sheppard, Dec. 21, 1968; 1 dau., Kelly. Student, Fla. State U., 1960-63; B.A., Am. U., 1970. Announcer Sta. WZRO, Jacksonville Beach, Fla., 1956-60; newscaster Sta. WMBR, Jacksonville, Fla., 1960-64, Sta. WPDQ, Jacksonville, 1964-66, Sta. WWDC, Washington, 1966-67; dir. pub. affairs Nat. Edni. Radio, Washington, 1967-68; news corr. U.P.I., Washington, 1968-70; corr. MBS, Washington, 1970-74, v.p. news, 1974-76; news corr. Sta. WCBS-TV, N.Y.C., 1976-79; White House corr. ABC News, Washington, 1979—80, Senate corr., 1980—; guest lectr. N.Y. U., 1975, 76; chmn. Congl. Radio-TV Galleries, Washington, 1975; lectr. Am. U., 1967; v.p. Nat. Press Bldg. Corp., 1974. Recipient award of merit ARC, 1960, 61, Jaycees, 1964, 65, Sch. Bell award Fla. Edn. Assn., 1965, AP award, 1965, Distinguished Service award Am. U., 1968; Media Merit award Am. Trial Lawyers Assn., 1977; Emmy award, 1978; Emmy nomination, 1979; N.Y.C. Firefighters award, 1979; Am. Bankers Assn. award, 1981. Mem. Radio and Television Corrs. Assn. (pres. 1975), Radio-Television News Dirs. Assn. (v.p. Washington chpt. 1976), White House Corrs. Assn., Fla. State U. Alumni Assn. (v.p. Washington chpt. 1974-75), State of Fla. Soc. Episcopalian. Clubs: Nat. Press (v.p. 1974, award 1974), Washington Press, Federal City (Washington); Ponte Vedra (Fla.). Home: 1605 44th St NW Washington DC 20007 Office: ABC 1717 DeSales St Washington DC 20036

GREER, CARL CRAWFORD, petroleum co. exec.; b. Pitts., June 12, 1940; s. Joseph Moss and Gene (Crawford) G.; m. Jerrine Ehlers, June 16, 1962; children—Caryn, Michael, Janet. B.S., Lehigh U., 1962; Ph.D., Columbia U., 1966. Asso. in bus. Columbia U., 1964-66, asst. prof. banking and finance, 1966-67; retail mktg. mgr. Martin Oil Service Inc., Alsip, Ill., 1967-68, exec. v.p., 1968, pres., dir., 1968-76, chmn. bd., pres., 1976—; dir. Pullman Bank & Trust Co., Heritage Bancorp. Inc., MSV Co., VSM Co., Colo. Energy Corp. Mem. Beta Theta Pi, Tau Beta Pi, Beta Gamma Sigma, Omicron Delta Kappa. Presbyterian.

GREER, DAVID S., physician, educator, univ. dean; b. Bklyn., Oct. 12, 1925; s. Jacob and Mary (Zaslawsky) G.; m. Marion Clarich, June 25, 1950; children—Jeffrey, Linda. B.S., U. Notre Dame, 1948; M.D., U. Chgo., 1953; M.A. (hon.), Brown U., 1975, L.H.D., Southeastern Mass. U., 1981. Diplomate: Am. Bd. Internal Medicine. Intern Yale-New Haven Med. Center, 1953-54; resident in medicine U. Chgo. Clinics, 1954-57; instr. endocrinology and medicine U. Chgo., 1957; practice medicine specializing in internal medicine, Fall River, Mass., 1957-74; chief staff dept. medicine Fall River Gen. Hosp., 1959-62; med. dir. Earle E. Hussey Hosp., Fall River, 1962-75; chief staff dept. medicine Truesdale Clinic and Truesdale Hosp., Fall River, 1971-74, pres. med. staff, 1968-70; sr. clin. instr. medicine Tufts U. Coll. Medicine, 1969-71, asst. clin. prof., 1971-78; clin. asso. prof. community health Brown U., 1973-75, dir. family practice residency program, 1975-78, prof. community health, 1975—, asso. dean medicine, 1974-81, dean medicine, 1981—, chmn. sect. community health, 1978-81; mem. Gov.'s Task Force on Quality of Care, Medicaid Program, Commonwealth of Mass., 1969-70; del. White House Conf. Aging, 1971, 81; Pres. Ind. Living Authority, State of R.I., 1975—; mem. exec. com. Cancer Control Bd. R.I., 1975-80; mem. R.I. Gov.'s Task Force for Inst. of Mental Health, 1976—; bd. dirs. Health Planning Council, Inc., Providence, 1976—; chmn. com. on aging Jewish Fedn. R.I., 1978-80; chmn. Gov.'s Commn. on Provision of Comprehensive Mental Health Services in R.I., 1980-81; trustee Southeastern Mass. U., 1970-81, chmn., 1973-74, Providence Mayor's Sr. Citizens Task Force, 1975; bd. dirs. Assn. Home Health Agys. R.I., 1975—; mem. Internat. Physicians for Prevention of Nuclear War, Inc., 1980—. Contbr. articles to profl. jours. Recipient Outstanding service award Mass. Easter Seal Soc., 1970; Outstanding Citizens award Jewish War Vets. Aux., 1973; Disting. Service award U. Chgo. Med. Alumni Assn.; Cutting Found. medal Andover Newton Theol. Sem., 1976. Fellow A.C.P.; mem. Inst. Medicine, Gerontol. Soc., Am. Congress Rehab. Medicine, Internat. Soc. Rehab. Medicine, R.I. Med. Soc. Jewish. Office: Brown U Box G Providence RI 02912

GREER, GERMAINE, author; b. nr. Melbourne, Australia, Jan. 29, 1939; d. Eric Reginald and Margaret May Mary (Lafrank) G. B.A. with honors in English and French Lit, U. Melbourne, 1959, M.A., U. Sydney, Australia, 1961; Ph.D. (Commonwealth scholar), Newnham Coll. of Cambridge U., Eng., 1964. Lectr. English U. Warwick, Eng., 1967-72; instr. poetry, dir. Center for Study of Women's Lit., U. Tulsa, 1979—. Author: The Female Eunuch, 1970, The Obstacle Race, 1979, others.

GREER, HOWARD EARL, former naval officer; b. Tyler, Tex., May 1, 1921; s. Earl Abner and Ollie (Lightfoot) G.; m. Suzanne Johnson, May 1, 1965; children—Margaret, Darby, David, Briand, Holly, Howard. Student, Tyler Jr. Coll., 1939-40; B.S., U.S. Naval Acad., 1943; M.B.A., George Washington U., 1965. Commd. ensign U.S. Navy, 1943, advanced through grades to vice adm., 1975; comdr. (Aircraft Carrier Hancock), 1967-69, Vietnam, (4 tours), Norfolk, Va., 1975-78; dir. CEDAM Internat.; with Convair Gen. Dynamics. Decorated D.S.M. (2), Legion of Merit (4), Knights of Malta Order St. John of Jerusalem. Mem. Assn. Naval Aviation (trustee), Assn. Early Pioneer Naval Aviators (pres.) (Golden Eagles), Tailhook Assn., Naval Res. Assn. Republican. Methodist. Clubs: Army-Navy (Washington); Lomas Santa Fe Country (San Diego). Home: 5481 Soledad Rd La Jolla CA 92037 Office: Gen Dynamics Convair San Diego CA 92138

GREER, MELVIN, medical educator; b. N.Y.C., Oct. 14, 1929; s. Aaron and Ceil (Cohen) Jefkel; m. Arline Ebert, Dec. 16, 1951; children: Jonathan, Richard, Alison, David. B.A. magna cum laude, N.Y. U., 1950, M.D., 1954. Intern, resident Bellevue Hosp., N.Y.C., 1954-56; fellow N.Y. Neurol. Inst., Columbia, 1958-61; prof., chmn. dept. neurology U. Fla. Coll. Medicine, Gainesville, 1963—; Cons. NIH, 1971—, Fla. Div. Corrections, 1971—; lectr., cons. Navy Dept.; Chmn. med. adv. com. Community Clinic, Gainesville, 1971-73. Author: Mass Spectrometry of Biologically Important Aromatic Acids, 1969, Differential Diagnosis of Neurological Diseases, 1977; also articles.; Editorial bd.: Neurology, Geriatics, 1968—. Served to lt. comdr. USNR, 1956-58. Recipient Medallion award Columbia, 1968, Hippocratic award U. Fla., 1970, Outstanding Clin. Tchr. award, 1975, 79; NIH grantee, 1962-71. Fellow Am. Acad. Neurology (councillor, sec.-treas. 1977—, pres. elect 1983—), Am. Acad. Pediatrics; mem. Am. Neurol. Assn. (councillor), Soc. Pediatric Research, Am. Pediatric Soc., Phi Beta Kappa, Alpha Omega Alpha. Home: 2058 NW 14th Ave Gainesville FL 32601

GREER, MONTE ARNOLD, physician, educator; b. Portland, Oreg., Oct. 26, 1922; s. William Wallace and Rose (Rasmussen) G.; m. Margaret Johnson, Dec. 31, 1943; children: Susan Elizabeth, Richard Arnold. Student, Oreg. State U., 1940-43; A.B., Stanford U., 1944, M.D., 1947. Intern San Francisco Gen. Hosp., 1946-47; research fellow endocrinology New Eng. Med. Center, Boston, 1947-49; resident internal medicine Mass. Meml. Hosp., Boston, 1949-50; research assoc. in endocrinology New Eng. Med. Center Hosp., 1950-51; sr. investigator, sr. asst. surgeon USPHS, Nat. Cancer Inst., NIH, Bethesda, Md., 1951-55; chief radioisotope unit VA Hosp., Long Beach, Calif.; clin. asst. prof. U. Calif. at Los Angeles, 1955-56; faculty, head div. endocrinology U. Oreg. Med. Sch., Portland, 1956-80, prof. medicine, 1962—; head div. endocrinology, metabolism and clin. nutrition Oreg. Health Scis. U., 1981—. Author: (with H. Studer) the Regulation of Thyroid Function in Iodine Deficiency, 1968, (with P. Langer) Antithyroid Drugs and Naturally Occurring Goitrogens, 1977; Editor: (with D.H. Solomon) The Thyroid, 1974; Mem. editorial bd.: Endocrinology, 1960-72, (with D.H. Solomon) Neuroendocrinology, 1965-76; Contbr. articles to profl. jours. Recipient Ciba (Oppenheimer) award Endocrine Soc., 1958, Research Career award NIH, 1962-81. Mem. Am. Fedn. for Clin. Research (chmn. Western sect. 1958-59), Western Soc. for Clin. Research (v.p. 1963-64, pres. 1967-68), Endocrine Soc. (mem. council 1966-68, v.p. 1976-77), Am. Thyroid Assn. (past v.p., dir. 1974-77, pres. 1980), Am. Soc. Clin. Investigation, Soc. Exptl. Biology and Medicine, Western Assn. Physicians (sec.-treas. 1974-77), Assn. Am. Physicians, Internat. Brain Research Orgn., Internat. Soc. Neuroendocrinology, AAAS, Sigma Chi. Home: 2706 Glen Eagles Rd Lake Oswego OR 97034 Office: Oreg Health Scis U Portland OR 97201

GREER, THOMAS HOAG, educator, historian; b. Bklyn., Apr. 18, 1914; s. Thomas H. and Lillian E. (Marmion) G.; m. Margarette M. Cheney, Dec. 17, 1939; children—Thomas M., Margarette E. A.B., U. Calif. at Berkeley, 1935, M.A., 1936, Ph.D., 1938. Instr. San Diego State Coll., 1938-42; chief hist. studies Air Hist. Office, USAAF, 1946-47; faculty Mich. State U., East Lansing, 1947—, prof. humanities, 1956—, chmn. dept., 1963-68. Author: American Social Reform Movements, 1949, USAAF in World War II, vol. VI, 1955, Development of Air Doctrine in Army Air Arm, 1955, What Roosevelt Thought, 1958, Curriculum Building in General Education, 1960, Brief History of the Western World, 1982; Gen. editor: Classics of Western Thought, 4 vols, 1980. Served to capt. USAAF, 1943-46. Faculty fellow Am. Council Learned Socs., 1952; recipient Disting. Faculty award Mich. State U., 1960. Mem. Am. Hist. Assn., Orgn. Am. Historians, AAUP, Phi Beta Kappa, Pi Gamma Mu. Home: 427 Collingwood Dr East Lansing MI 48823

GREER, THOMAS VERNON, business consultant and educator; b. Burnet, Tex., Oct. 13, 1932; s. Vernon Otho and Mattye Ether (Cashen) G.; m. Joanne Marie Greer, Apr. 23, 1966; children: Marc Bernley, Carl Mathieu Cashen. B.A., U. Tex., 1953, Ph.D., 1964; M.B.A., Ohio State U., 1957. Acct., So. regional hdqrs. J.C. Penney Co., Dallas, 1957-59; planner N. Am. Rockwell, Downey, Calif., 1959-61; asst. prof. La. State U., Baton Rouge, 1964-66, asso. prof., 1967-69; Fulbright prof. Universidad de las Americas, Mexico City, 1966-67; asso. prof. U. Md., College Park, 1969-73, prof., chmn. dept. mktg., 1973—; vis. scholar UN, fall 1982; cons. govt. agys., pvt. corps. Author: Marketing in the Soviet Union, 1973, Cases in Marketing: Orientation, Analysis and Problems, 1975, 3d edit., 1983; contbr. articles to profl. jours. Served with U.S. Army, 1954-55. Ford Found. fellow, 1963-64; Frost Found. fellow, Soviet Union, summer 1965, Costa Rica, summer 1966, Panama, summer 1967, Spain, summer 1969. Mem. Am. Mktg. Assn., So. Mktg. Assn. (pres.), Acad. Internat. Bus., Assn. Consumer Research, Product Devel. Assn., Soc. for Internat. Devel. Home: 12420 Kuhl Rd Silver Spring MD 20902 Office: Coll Bus Univ Md College Park MD 20742

GREEVER, WILLIAM ST. CLAIR, educator, historian; b. Lexington, Va., July 22, 1916; s. Gustavus Garland and May St. Clair (Stocking) G.; m. Janet Elizabeth Groff, Aug. 24, 1951; 1 dau., Barbara Clair. B.A., Pomona Coll., 1938; M.A., Harvard U., 1940, Ph.D., 1949. Instr. bus. history Northwestern U., 1947-49; mem. faculty U. Idaho, 1949—, chmn. dept. history, 1956-82, prof. history, 1958-82, prof. emeritus, 1982—. Author: Arid Domain: The Santa Fe Railway and Its Western Land Grant, 1954 (prize Pacific history Pacific Coast br. Am. Hist. Assn. 1954), The Bonanza West: The Story of the Western Mining Rushes, 1963 (Spur award best nonfiction Western, Western Writers Am. 1963); bd. editors: Pacific Hist. Rev., 1956-58; Bd. editors: Idaho Yesterdays, 1976—; Contbr. articles to profl. jours. Served with AUS, 1942-46. Guggenheim fellow, 1958-59. Mem. Am. Hist. Assn. (council Pacific Coast br. 1957-59), Western Hist. Assn. (council 1980-83), Orgn. Am. Historians, AAUP (pres. local chpt. 1955-56), Phi Beta Kappa. Home: 315 S Hayes St Moscow ID 83843

GREFE, RICHARD, public broadcasting executive; b. Buffalo, May 21, 1945; s. Richard W. and Marjorie Louise (Sine) G.; m. Karen Lee Vogel, Oct. 8, 1978; 1 son, Justin Sine. A.B., Dartmouth Coll., 1967; M.B.A., Stanford U., 1973. Book designer Stinehour Press, Lunenburg, Vt., 1967; writer Time Mag., N.Y.C., 1972; pres. Richard Grefe Assocs., San Francisco and Washington, 1973—; dir. policy devel. and planning Corp. of Pub. Broadcasting, Washington, 1983—. Editor: A Dartmouth Literary Tradition, 1966. Trustee Fiberworks Sch. Textile Arts, Berkeley, Calif., 1974-76; bd. dirs. Chgo. Children's Mus., 1976; mem. Gov.'s Task Force on Design, Calif., 1977. Lt. USN, 1967-71. Mem. Am. Planning Assn., Am. Inst. Cert. Planners, Am. Assn. Museums. Club: Detroit Athletic. Home: 1313 Constitution Ave NE Washington DC 20002 Office: 1111 16th St NW Washington DC 20036

GREFE, ROLLAND EUGENE, lawyer; b. Ida County, Iowa, June 27, 1920; s. Alfred William and Zoma Corrine (Lasher) G.; m. Mary Arlene Cruikshank, June 12, 1943; 1 son, Roger Frederick. B.A., Morningside Coll., 1941; J.D., State U. Iowa, 1946. Bar: Iowa 1946. Assoc. Schaetzle, Williams & Stewart, Des Moines, 1946-48, Schaetzle, Swift, Austin & Stewart, 1948-52; ptnr. Schaetzle, Austin & Grefe (and related firms), Des Moines, 1952-60, Austin, Grefe & Sidney, 1960-71; sr. ptnr. Grefe & Sidney, Des Moines, 1971—; dir. Freeman Decorating Co., Des Moines, Register & Tribune Syndicate, Inc. Bd. dirs. Des Moines Area Community Coll., 1966-76, pres., 1967-76; bd. dirs. Iowa State Bar Found., 1979—. Served to lt. USNR, 1942-45. Fellow Am. Bar Found., Am. Coll. Probate Counsel; Mem. Polk County Bar Assn. (pres. 1971-72), Iowa State Bar Assn. (bd. govs. 1972-76, pres. 1978-79, Merit award 1982), ABA (ho. f dels. 1982—), Des Moines Estate Planning Council, Lincoln Inne. Republican. Presbyterian. Clubs: Sertoma, Des Moines, Wakonda (Des Moines). Home: 4116 Beaver Ave Des Moines IA 50310 Office: 1980 Financial Center Des Moines IA 50309

GREGATH, JAMES REED, oilwell drilling company executive; b. Kansas City, Mo., Mar. 24, 1925; s. Eric Albert and Pauline (Reed) G.; m. Christeen Greer, Dec. 11, 1954; children: Christian Ann, James Reed. B.S.M.E., U. Kans., Lawrence, 1946. Drilling engr. Gulf Oil Corp., Kuwait, 1948-53, Helmerich & Payne, Okla. and Tex., 1953-61; v.p., drilling engr. Anson Corp., U.S. and S.Am., 1961-67; pres. Calvert-Gregath Drilling, Oklahoma City, 1967-71; exec. v.p. Magness Petroleum Co., Oklahoma City, 1971-73; pres. Grace Drilling Co., Oklahoma City, 1973—; v.p. W.R. Grace & Co., N.Y.C., 1981—. Served to ensign USNR, 1943-47. Mem. Internat. Assn. Drilling Contractors (dir. Houston chpt. 1980—). Republican. Methodist. Home: 10905 Maple Grove Oklahoma City OK 73120 Office: Grace Drilling Co 205 NW 63d Suite 100 Oklahoma City OK 73116

GREGG, ALVIS FORREST, professional football coach; b. Birthright, Tex., Oct. 18, 1933. B.S. in Phys. Edn., So. Methodist U., 1959. Player Green Bay Packers, NFL, Wis., 1956, 58-70, Dallas Cowboys, NFL, 1971; asst. coach Green Bay Packers, 1969-70, San Diego Chargers, 1972-73; asst. coach, then head coach Cleve. Browns, 1974-77; head coach Toronto Argonauts, CFL, 1979, Cin. Bengals, NFL, 1980-83, Green Bay Packers, NFL, 1984—; played in NFL Pro Bowl, 1960-64, 66-68, NFL Championship Game, 1960-62, 65-67, Super Bowl, 1966-67, coach, 1981. Address: 200 Riverfront Stadium Cincinnati OH 45202 *

GREGG, ARTHUR JAMES, former army officer, business executive; b. Florence, S.C., May 11, 1928; s. Robert Lee and Ethel (Howard) G.; m. Charlene S. McDaniel, Sept. 2, 1950; children: Sandra R., Alicia G. B.S. summa cum laude, St. Benedict Coll., 1964; postgrad., Command and Gen. Staff Coll., 1964, Army War Coll., 1968. Commd. 2d lt. U.S. Army, 1950; advanced through grades to lt. gen.; asst. sec. gen. staff Hdqrs. U.S. Army Materiel Command, Washington, 1965-66; comdg. officer 96th Supply and Service Bn., Vietnam, 1966-67; staff officer Joint Petroleum Office, Hdqrs. U.S. European Command, 1968-69; comdg. officer Nahbollenbach Army Depot, 1970-71; Dept. of Army staff positions, 1971-73; comdr. Army and Air Force Exchange Service, Europe, 1973-75; dep. chief staff for logistics Hdqrs. U.S. Army, Europe, 1975-77; dir. logistics Orgn. Joint Chiefs of Staff, 1977-79; dep. chief staff logistics Dept. Army, 1979-81; ret., 1981; pres. UCI, Inc., Springfield, Va., 1981—. Decorated Def. Disting. Service medal, Army Disting. Service medal, Legion of Merit with 2 oak leaf clusters, Joint Service Commendation medal, Army Commendation medal with 2 oak leaf clusters. Office: UCI Inc Springfield VA 22150

GREGG, DAVIS WEINERT, educator; b. Austin, Tex., Mar. 12, 1918; s. Davis Alexander and Lorene (Murff) G.; m. Mildred Grace McDaniel, May 15, 1942; children: Mary Cynthia, Davis William. B.B.A., U. Tex., 1939; M.B.A., U. Pa., 1940, Ph.D., 1948. Underwriter Aetna Casualty & Surety Co., Hartford, Conn., 1940-41; asst. prof. naval sci. U. Minn., 1945-46; prof. ins. Ohio State U., 1948-49, Grad. Sch. Bus. Stanford, 1949; asst. dean The Am. Coll., Bryn Mawr, Pa., 1949-51, dean, 1952-53, trustee, 1951-74, life trustee, 1974—, pres., 1954-82, Disting. prof. econs., 1982—; dir. Dow Jones & Co., Inc., Richard D. Irwin Inc., Aspis Pronia, Athens, Greece.; Dir. 1st Internat. Ins. Conf., Internat. Ins. Seminars; past chmn. Commn. on Ins. Terminology; trustee Kynett Found.; chmn. governing com. McCahan Found., 1965—; bd. dirs. Bryn Mawr Hosp. Author: An Analysis of Group Life Insurance, 1950, Group Life Insurance, 1964, Insurance Courses Outside the United States, 1960; Editor: World Insurance Trends, 1960, Property and Liability Insurance Handbook, 1965. Mem. Am. Risk and Ins. Assn. (pres. 1961), Am. Soc. C.L.U.s, AAUP, Beta Gamma Sigma (Dir.'s Table). Presbyterian (ruling elder). Clubs: Merion Golf Club; Union League (Phila.). Home: 820 Castlefinn Ln Bryn Mawr PA 19010 Office: 270 Bryn Mawr Ave Bryn Mawr PA 19010 *The dark side of the human condition is always brightened by the light of learning. From our first to our last years, learning enriches our lives with freedom of mind and spirit.*

GREGG, DONALD CROWTHER, educator; b. Marlboro, N.H., June 25, 1913; s. Arthur E. and Ida May (Crowther) G.; m. Florence Bentley Green, May 29, 1943 (dec. 1973); children—Bentley Crowther, Fulton Mills; m. Elizabeth Moulton, Dec. 21, 1974. B.S., U. Vt., 1935; M.S., U. N.H., 1937; Ph.D., Columbia, 1941. Asst. chemistry U. N.H., 1935-37, Columbia, 1937-39; research chemist Wallace & Tiernan Products, Belleville, N.J., 1940-41; faculty Harvard, 1940; vis. lectr., summer 1946; instr., asst. prof. Amherst (Mass.) Coll., 1941-46; prof. U. Vt., 1952—, Pomeroy prof. chemistry, 1963-78; vis. prof. U. Fla., 1962-63; sci. faculty fellow NSF, 1962-63. Author: Principles of Chemistry, 3d edit, 1968, College Chemistry, 2d edit, 1965, Chemistry in the Laboratory, 1966. Trustee Fletcher Free Library, 1964—, Pine Ridge Sch., 1972—, St. Johnsbury Acad., Vt. Inst. Community Involvement. Fellow Am. Inst. Chemists, Vt. Acad. Arts and Scis. (trustee); mem. Am. Chem. Soc. (chmn. Western Vt. sect. 1953), AAUP (pres. Vt. chpt. 1953-55), New Eng. Assn. Chemistry Tchrs. (hon.), New Eng. Acad. Sci. (pres. 1965-66), Vt. Library Trustees Assn. (pres. 1968-69), Sigma Xi (pres. Vt. chpt. 1952-53), Alpha Chi Sigma, Phi Lambda Upsilon, Sigma Delta Psi, Sigma Alpha Epsilon. Clubs: Sagamore Beach Colony, Burlington Tennis (v.p.), Burlington Tennis (dir. 1959-62). Home: Box 217 Hyde Park VT 05655

GREGG, DUANE LAWRENCE, editor; b. Hiawatha, Kans., Dec. 23, 1926; s. Albert Best and Margaret Emily (Lawrence) G.; m. Corinne Elizabeth Holm, June 17, 1951; children—David Lawrence, Kent Steven. B.S. in Engring, Kans. State U., 1950. Tchr. Hamlin (Kans.) pub. schs., 1950-52, Manhattan (Kans.) pub. schs., 1952-63; with Meredith Corp., Des Moines, 1963—, adminstrv. editor mag. div., 1973-76, publishing group adminstrv. editor, 1976-80, publishing group editorial services dir., 1980—. Served with USN, 1944-46. Mem. Sigma Nu. Republican. Presbyterian. Home: 1501 41st Pl Des Moines IA 50311 Office: 1716 Locust St Des Moines IA 50336

GREGG, HUGH, cabinet manufacturing company executive, former gov. N.H.; b. Nashua, N.H., Nov. 22, 1917; s. Harry A. and Margaret R. (Richardson) G.; m. Catherine M. Warner, July 24, 1940; children: Cyrus Warner, Judd Alan. Grad., Phillips Exeter Acad., 1935; A.B., Yale U., 1939; LL.B., Harvard U., 1942; LL.D., U. N.H., 1953; M.A., Dartmouth Coll., 1953; D.C.L., New Eng. Coll., 1954. Bar: N.H. 1942, Mass 1948. Practice law, Nashua, 1942—; mem. Sullivan, Gregg & Horton; former pres., treas. Gregg & Son, Inc., Nashua, N.H.; gov. of N.H., 1953-55; chmn. bd. Indian Head Banks, Inc., Nashua; chmn. bd., treas. Gregg Cabinets Ltd., Chambly, Que.; dir. N.H. Indian Head Nat. Bank, Nashua; owner Greggs Greenhouse Restaurant, Sarasota, Fla.; clk., former co-pub. N.H. Profiles; former mem. advisory bd. Am. Mut. Liability Ins. Co.; v.p. Forum N.H.'s Future, 1977—; mgr. Resources of N.H., Nashua; sec. Graphic 100, Inc., Nashua. Mem. Nat. Exec. Res.; Past pres. Nashua Fresh Air Camp; alderman-at-large, Nashua, 1948-50, mayor, 1950; Bd. dirs. Crotched Mountain Found.; bd. dirs. New Eng. Council, 1952-55, pres., 1955-57; trustee Waumbek Village Properties, Jefferson, N.H., 1970—; pres. Channel 21 TV. Served as spl. agt. Army CIC, 1942-46, 50-52. Mem. Nat.

Kitchen Cabinet Assn. (past first v.p.), Canadian Kitchen Cabinet Assn. (dir.), VFW. Home: RFD 5 Gregg Rd Nashua NH 03062 Office: 14 Church St Nashua NH 03060

GREGG, JAMES CALVIN, lawyer; b. Ebensburg, Pa., Dec. 26, 1924; s. Oliver E. and Sophia G.; m. Dora Osterstock, June 9, 1951; children: Gregory Michael, Watson W. Student, Ind. State Tchrs. Coll., 1946-47; LL.B., George Washington U., 1950. Bar: D.C. 1950, Va. 1953. Partner firm Gregg & Tait, Washington, 1950-57, MacLeay, Lynch, Bernhard & Gregg, 1957—. Served with USAAF, 1943-46. Mem. Bar Assn. D.C., Va. State Bar, Va. Assn. Def. Attys., D.C. Def. Lawyers Assn., The Counselors, Defense Research Inst., Phi Delta Phi. Home: 3156 N 21st St Arlington VA 22201 Office: 1625 Eye St NW Washington DC 20006 also 1401 Wilson Blvd Arlington VA 22209

GREGG, MAURICE W., casual apparel chain stores executive; b. 1932; married. B.A., U. Mich., 1954; M.B.A., Wayne State U., 1957. Staff auditor Ernst & Ernst C.P.A.s, 1956-61; asst. to treas. Gilchrist Co., 1961-63; asst. controller Gimbel Bros.-Pitts., 1963-69; v.p. fin. Joseph Magnin Co., 1969-70; with Touche, Ross & Co. C.P.A.'s, 1970-72; v.p. fin. Gimbel Bros., 1972-78; exec. v.p. fin., treas., chief fin. officer The Gap Stores Inc., San Bruno, Calif., 1978—. Office: The Gap Stores Inc 900 Cherry Ave Box 60 San Bruno CA 94066 *

GREGG, RICHARD ALEXANDER, educator; b. Paris, France, Aug. 22, 1927; s. Alan and Eleanor (Barrows) G.; m. Francoise Bouriez, June 6, 1953; 1 son, Jonathan Alan. Grad., Deerfield (Mass.) Acad., 1945; A.B., Harvard, 1951, M.A., 1952; Ph.D., Columbia, 1962. Instr. Russian lang. Amherst (Mass.) Coll., 1957-58; instr. Russian lang. and lit. Brown U., 1959-60; from instr. to asso. prof. Russian lang. and lit. Columbia, 1960-69; prof. Russian, John Guy Vassar chmn. dept. Vassar Coll., 1970—. Author: F.I. Tiutchev: The Evolution of a Poet, 1965, (with others) Major Soviet Writers; Essays in Criticism, 1973, Alexander Pushkin: A Symposium on the 175th Anniversary of His Birth, 1976; also articles. Served with USAAF, 1946-47. Ford Found. fellow, 1955-56; U.S. Govt. fellow, Leningrad, 1958-59; Guggenheim fellow, 1965-66. Mem. Modern Lang. Assn., Am. Assn. Advancement Slavic Studies. Home: 64 Boardman Rd Poughkeepsie NY 12603

GREGG, RICHARD NELSON, museum dir.; b. Kalamazoo, Sept. 4, 1926; s. Sherman U. and Elizabeth (Dye) G.; m. Patricia Dunbar, June 17, 1952 (div. 1972); children—William S., Joel D. Student, Western Mich. U., 1945-47; B.F.A., Cranbrook Acad. Art, 1949, M.F.A., 1950. Instr. Cranbrook Sch. Boys, 1950-51; instr. Worcester (Mass.) Art Mus., 1951-54; dir. Kalamazoo Art Inst., 1954-56; curator Toledo Art Mus., 1956-59; head edn. Art Inst. Chgo., 1959-61; dir. Paine Art Center, Oshkosh, Wis., 1961-69, Joslyn Art Mus., Omaha, 1969-72, Allentown (Pa.) Art Mus., 1972—. Served with USAAF, 1945-46. Mem. Am. Assn. Museums, Assn. Art Mus. Dirs. Address: Allentown Art Museum Box 117 Allentown PA 18105

GREGG, WILLIAM PAUL, insurance company executive; b. Fresno, Calif., Jan. 25, 1925; s. Paul Shirley and Margaret Sloan (Gordon) G.; m. Jerry Lee Narmore, Feb. 22, 1952; children: Frederick Paul, Jeffrey L., Nancy L. B.A., Stanford U. With Farmers Ins. Group, Los Angeles, 1949-60; dist.sales mgr. Allstate Ins. Co., Northbrook, Ill., 1960-62, field sales mgr., 1962-63, regional sales mgr., 1963-66, asst. gen. sales mgr., 1966-67, regional sales mgr., 1967-69, zone sales mgr., 1969-71, regional assoc. v.p., 1971-72, asst. v.p. advt. and sales promotion, 1972-73, v.p. mktg. devel., 1973-74, v.p. mktg., dir., 1974-78, sr. v.p. claims dir., tech. coordinator, 1978-81; exec. v.p. Capital Holding Corp., Louisville, Ky., 1981-82; pres. Agy. Group Allstate Ins. Co., Northbrook, Ill., 1982—; dir. Peoples Life Ins. Co., Washington, Nat. Standard Life Ins. Co., Orlando, Fla., Home Security Life Ins. Co., Durham, N.C., Ga. Internat. Life Ins. Co., Atlanta, Capital Enterprise Ins. Group, Louisville; chmn. Commonwealth Life Ins. Co., Louisville, 1982—. Div. chmn. Met. United Way, Louisville, 1982. Served to lt. (j.g.) USN, 1942-46. Mem. Life Ins. Mktg. and Research Assn. (bd. dirs. 1977-81, chmn. 1979-80), Agy. Mgmt. Tng. Council (bd. dirs. 1981—), Soc. C.L.U.s. Clubs: Jefferson, Louisville Boat. Home: 610 McCready Ave Louisville Ky 40206 Office: Capital Holding Corp 680 4th Ave Louisville Ky 40202

GREGOR, ARTHUR, poet; b. Vienna, Austria, Nov. 18, 1923; came to U.S., 1939, naturalized, 1945; s. Benjamin and Regine (Reiss) Goldenberg. B.S. in Elec. Engring., Newark Coll. Engring., 1945. Engaged in engring., 1954, journalism, 1956-61; sr. editor Macmillan Co., 1962-70; vis. prof. Calif. State U., Hayward, 1972-73; prof., dir. creative writing program Hofstra U., 1973—. Author: Octavian Shooting Targets, 1954, Declensions of a Refrain, 1957, Basic Movements, 1966, Figure in the Door, 1968, A Bed by the Sea, 1970, The Selected Poems of Arthur Gregor, 1971, The Past Now, 1975, Embodiment and Other Poems, 1982, A Longing in the Land, Memoir of a Guest, 1983; also books for children.; contbr. maj. lit. revs. and mags. Recipient 1st Appearance prize Poetry mag., 1948. Mem. PEN. Home: 131 W 78th St New York NY 10024 *The struggle for poetic and spiritual sustenance is as urgent and as natural as that of a creature needing air. America is in the process of spiritual recognition. The struggle continues.*

GREGOR, HOWARD FRANK, educator, geographer; b. Two Rivers, Wis., Apr. 7, 1920; s. Stephen Phillip and Emily (Drissen) G.; m. Marjorie Evelyn Onley, Dec. 26, 1950; 1 dau., Marsha Evelyn. B.S., U. Wis., 1946, M.S., 1947; Ph.D., U. Calif. at Los Angeles, 1950. Instr. geography Ind. U., 1950-51; analyst CIA, Washington, 1951-53; vis. asst. prof. geography U. Oreg., 1953-54; asst. planner Los Angeles County Regional Planning Commn., 1954-55; asst. prof. geography San Jose (Calif.) State Coll., 1955-60, U. Calif. at Davis, 1960-64, asso. prof., 1964-69, prof., 1969—. Author: Environment and Economic Life, 1963, Geography of Agriculture: Themes in Research, 1970, An Agricultural Typology of California, 1974, Industrialization of U.S. Agriculture: An Interpretive Atlas, 1981; Contbr. articles to profl. jours. Served with USAAF, 1942-45. Decorated D.F.C., Air Medal with 1 silver and 3 bronze oak leaf clusters. Mem. Assn. Pacific Coast Geographers (pres. 1960), Assn. Am. Geographers (pres. Pacific coast div. 1960), Am. Geog. Soc., Sigma Xi, Pi Gamma Mu, Phi Delta Kappa. Home: 1309 Beech Ln Davis CA 95616

GREGOR, TIBOR PHILIP, association executive; b. Levoca, Czechoslovakia, Apr. 25, 1919; s. Philip and Emma (Aufricht) G.; m. Helen Frances Lorenz, Sept. 15, 1942; children: Jan Michael, Charlotte Anne. Student, U. London, 1938-41. Gen. sales mgr. Eastern Steel Products Ltd., Toronto, Ont., Can., 1952-57; pres., gen. mgr. Roneo Co. Ltd., Toronto, 1957-63, also Roneo, Inc., Phila.; pres. Municipal Sand & Gravel Co., Kingston, Ont., 1964-71; exec. dir. Can. Soft Drink Assn., Toronto, 1972—. Author: On the Employment of Mentally Handicapped, 1971. Pres. Met. Toronto Assn. Mentally Retarded, 1961-64, Can. Assn. Mentally Retarded, 1969-71; vice chmn. Toronto Centennial Com., 1964-67. Served with Czechoslovak Armoured Brigade Group, British Forces, 1940-45. Decorated Medal of Merit; Paul Harris fellow, 1980. Mem. Can. Assn. Mentally Retarded (life), Inst. Assn. Execs., Am. Soc. Assn. Execs., Health League Can. Mem. United Ch. Clubs: Royal Can. Mil. Inst., Rotary (past treas., dir.), Toronto Bd. Trade, Toronto Lawn Tennis (dir.), Masons.). Home: 218 Glen Rd Toronto ON M4W 2X3 Canada Office: 443 University Ave Toronto ON M5G 1T8 Canada

GREGORIAN, VARTAN, library adminstr.; b. Tabriz, Iran, Apr. 8, 1934; came to U.S., 1962; s. Samuel B. and Shushanik G. (Mirzaian) G.; m. Clare Russell, Mar. 25, 1960; children—Vahe, Raffi, Dareh. Grad., Coll. Armenien, 1955; B.A., Stanford U., 1958, Ph.D., 1964; M.A. (hon.), U. Pa., 1972. Instr., asst. prof., asso. prof. history San Francisco State Coll., 1962-68; asso. prof. history U. Calif. at Los Angeles, 1968; asso. prof., prof. history U. Tex. at Austin, 1968-72, dir. spl. programs, 1970-72; Tarzian prof. Armenian and Caucasian history U. Pa., Phila., 1972-80, dean, 1974-79, provost, 1978-80; pres. N.Y. Public Library, 1981—; mem. Nat. Humanities Faculty, 1970—. Author: The Emergence of Modern Afghanistan, 1880-1946, 1969; editorial bd.: Armenian Rev, 1973—; contbr. articles to profl. jours. Chmn. Univ. Profs. for Sissy Farenthold for Gov. Tex., 1972; bd. dirs. Council Internat. Visitors. Recipient award of distinction Phi Lambda Theta and Phi Delta Kappa, 1980; Silver Cultural medal Italian Ministry Fgn. Affairs, 1977; Gold medal of honor City and Province of Vienna (Austria), 1976; Am. Philos Soc. grantee, 1965, 66; Danforth E.H. Harbison Teaching award, 1969; Cactus Teaching award, 1971; Social Sci. Research Council fellow, 1960; Ford Found. Fgn. Area Tng. fellow, 1960-62; Am. Council Learned Socs.-Social Sci. Research Council fellow, 1965; John Simon Guggenheim fellow, 1971-72; Social Sci. Research Council fellow, 1971-72; Am. Council Edn. fellow, 1973. Mem. Am. Hist. Assn. (program chmn. 1972), Assn. Advancement Slavic Studies (program chmn. Western Slavic Conf. 1967), World Affairs Council Phila., Mid East Studies Assn., Phi Beta Kappa, Sierra Club. Office: NY Public Library 42d St and Fifth Ave New York NY 10018

GREGORY, ANNE ELIZABETH, editor; b. Leamington, Ont., Can., Nov. 2, 1936; d. Herbert Thorp and Helen Elizabeth (Ewald) G. (mother Am. citizen). B.A. in Psychology with honors, Hollins (Va.) Coll., 1958. With Merrill, Lynch, Pierce, Fenner & Smith, N.Y.C., 1958—; exec. editor Investor's Reader (bus. news mag.), 1972-74, publs. mgr. individual investment div., 1974—, asst. v.p., 1975-77, v.p., 1977—; pub. Merrill Lynch Market Letter, 1976, stockfinder, 1982. Mem. Fin. Women's Assn., Pi Epsilon Mu. Republican. Episcopalian. Club: Meadow (Southampton, N.Y.). Office: 1 Liberty Plaza 165 Broadway New York NY 10006

GREGORY, ARTHUR STANLEY, chemist; b. Benton County, Oreg., Oct. 22, 1914; s. Arthur Donald and Edith Florence (Self) G.; m. Rosemary Faire Larsen, June 16, 1939; children—Garth L., Sharon Lynette, Gwyneth Faire. B.S., Oreg. State U., 1936; Ph.D., Ohio State U., 1940. Research chemist E.I. duPont de Nemours & Co., Wilmington, Del., 1940-42; with Weyerhaeuser Co., Longview, Wash., 1946-60, dir. research, Tacoma, 1960-76, research mgmt. cons., 1976—; past mem. research adv. bds. Inst. Paper Chemistry, Wash. State U., Oreg. Forest Products Lab.; mem. adv. and cons. coms. NSF, Nat. C. of C., Canadian Pulp and Paper Inst. Contbr. chem. articles to tech. jours. Served to lt. col. AUS, 1942-45; ETO. Decorated Bronze Star medal. Mem. Forest Products Research Soc., TAPPI, Canadian Pulp and Paper Assn., Am. Chem. Soc., Am. Forestry Assn., Indsl. Research Inst., N.Y. Acad. Sci., Am. Mgmt. Assn. Clubs: Kiwanis (past pres. Longview), Elks.). Patentee in field. Home: 920 Fairview Dr S Tacoma WA 98465

GREGORY, BETTINA LOUISE, journalist; b. N.Y.C., June 4, 1946; d. George Alexander and V. Elizabeth Friedman; m. John P. Flannery, II, 1981. Student, Smith Coll., 1964-65; diploma in acting, Webber-Douglas Sch. Dramatic Art, London, 1968; B.A. in Psychology, Pierce Coll., Athens, Greece, 1972. Reporter Sta. WVBR-FM, Ithaca, N.Y., 1972-73, Sta. WCIC-TV, Ithaca, 1972; reporter, anchorwoman Sta. WGBB, Freeport, N.Y., 1973, Sta. WCBS, N.Y.; freelance reporter, writer AP, N.Y.C., 1973-74; freelance reporter N.Y. Times, 1973-74; with ABC News, 1974—, corr., Washington, 1977-79, White House corr., 1979—, sr. gen. assignment corr., 1980—. Recipient 1st Place award Nat. Feature News, Odyssey Inst., N.Y., 1978, Clarion award Women in Communications, Inc., 1979, hon. mention Nat. Commn. on Working Women, 1979; named one of top 10 investigative reporters TV Guide, 1983. Mem. Newswomen's Club N.Y. (recipient Front Page award 1976), Washington Press Club, Radio TV Corrs. Assn., White House Corrs. Assn. Office: 1717 De Sales St NW Washington DC 20036

GREGORY, BOBBY LEE, lab. adminstr.; b. Allen, Okla., Sept. 30, 1938; s. Jessie Lee and Sylvia Sylvoy (Caldwell) G.; m. Margaret E. Brown, July 15, 1961; children—Gwen, Ginger, Elizabeth. B.S., Carnegie Inst. Tech., Pitts., 1960, M.S., 1961, Ph.D., 1963. With Sandia Nat. Lab., Albuquerque, 1963—, dir. microelectronics, 1981—; vis. asst. prof. Carnegie Mellon U., 1969. Asso. editor: IEEE Jour. of Solid-State Circuits, Solid State Electronics, 1978-81; contbr. articles in field to profl. jours. Fellow IEEE. Republican. Home: 1614 Bayita Ln NW Albuquerque NM 87107 Office: Sandia National Laboratories Albuquerque NM 87185

GREGORY, CYNTHIA KATHLEEN, ballerina; b. Los Angeles, July 8, 1946; d. Konstantin and Marcelle (Tremblay) G.; m. Terrence S. Orr, May 14, 1966 (div.); m. John Hemminger, 1976. Grad. high sch. Ford Found. scholar San Francisco Ballet, 1961. Soloist, 1962-65; with, Am. Ballet Theatre, N.Y.C., 1965—; soloist, 1966; prin. dancer, 1967—; appeared on TV with, San Francisco Opera, 1963-64; in film Girl Most Likely, 1955; made TV appearance on: The Edge of Night, 1981. Recipient Silver Bowl Dance mag., 1975. Office: care Am Ballet Theatre 888 7th Ave New York NY 10019 *

GREGORY, DICK, comedian, civil rights activist; b. St. Louis, Oct. 12, 1932; m. Lillian Smith, 1959; children: Michele, Lynne, Paula, Pamela, Stephanie, Gregory, Christian, Ayanna, Miss, Yohance. Student, So. Ill. U., 1951-53, 55-56. Lectr. univs. throughout U.S. Entertainer, Esquire Club, Chgo.; opened night club, Apex, Robbins, Ill.; master ceremonies, Roberts Show Club, Chgo., 1959-60; night club appearances, Akron, Milw., Chgo., 1960, San Francisco, Hollywood, numerous other cities, 1961—, comedy act, Playboy Club, Chgo., 1961; TV guest appearances: others Jack Paar show; record albums Dick Gregory: The Light Side-Dark Side; others; Author: Nigger, 1964, What's Happening, 1965, The Shadow That Scares Me, Write Me In, No More Lies, 1971, Dick Gregory's Political Primer, 1971, Dick Gregory's Natural Diet for Folks Who Eat, Cookin' With Mother Nature, 1973, Dick Gregory's Bible Tales, with Commentary, 1974, Up From Nigger, 1976, (with Mark Lane) Code Name Zorro: The Murder of Martin Luther King, Jr, 1977. Peace and Freedom Party presdl. candidate, 1968. Served with AUS, 1953-55. Winner Mo. mile championship, 1951, 52; named Outstanding Athlete So. Ill. U., 1953; recipient Ebony-Topaz Heritage and Freedom award, 1978. Office: PO Box 3266 Tower Hill Farm Plymouth MA 02361

GREGORY, DONALD MUNSON, lawyer; b. San Francisco, Jan. 21, 1897; s. Warren and Sarah (Hardy) G.; m. Josephine Wallace, May 21, 1924; children—Joan (Mrs. Thomas C. Benet), Donald Munson. A.B., U. Calif. at Berkeley, 1920; LL.B., Harvard U., 1923. Bar: Calif. bar 1924. Since practiced in, San Francisco; mem. firm Chickering & Gregory, 1926—. Del. Commn. for Relief in Belgium, 1916-17. Served as 2d lt. F.A. U.S. Army, 1917-19; lt. col. Adj. Gen. Dept. AUS, 1942-45. Mem. Astron. Soc. Pacific, Am., San Francisco bar assns., State Bar of Calif., Am. Judicature Soc. Clubs: Pacific Union, Sierra, Commonwealth (San Francisco). Home: 940 Green St San Francisco CA 94133 Office: Three Embarcadero Center Suite 2300 San Francisco CA 94111

GREGORY, GEORGE TILLMAN, JR., justice S.C. Supreme Ct.; b. McConnellsville, S.C., Dec. 13, 1921; s. George T. and Inez Anderson G.; m. Willie Mae Elliott, Dec. 27, 1951; children—George Tillman III, William Elliott. A.B., U. S.C., 1943, LL.B., 1944. Bar: bar 1944. U.S. commr., 1945-46, city recorder, Chester, 1946-50; judge S.C. Circuit Ct., 6th Jud. Circuit, 1956-78; asso. justice S.C. Supreme Ct., 1975—. Mem. S.C. Ho. of Reps., 1951-52, 55-56; Trustee Furman U., 1968-72. Mem. Am. Bar Assn., Law Fedn. and Euphradian Library Soc. (pres.). Office: Supreme Ct SC 1231 Gervais St Columbia SC 29201 *

GREGORY, GUSTAV ROBINSON, educator, natural resource economist; b. Cass City, Mich., Sept. 1, 1915; s. William Alfred and Erna May (Roeser) G.; m. Edna Ann Hano, Mar. 26, 1943; children: Bonnie Ann, Robin Scott, Sharolyn Kay. B.S., Central Mich. U., 1938, LLD. (hon.), 1977; B.S. in Forestry, U. Mich., 1940; M.F., 1940; Ph.D., U. Calif. at Berkeley, 1953. Timber cruiser U.S. Forest Service, West Coast, 1940; jr. research forester Allegheny Forest Expt. Sta., Beltsville, Md., 1941-42; forest economist East Tex. br. So. Forest Expt. Sta., Nacogdoches, 1945-49; George Willis Pack asst. prof. resource econs. Sch. Natural Resources, U. Mich., Ann Arbor, 1952-55, asso. prof., 1955-60, prof., 1960—; chief analysis, survey sect., forestry div. FAO, Rome, 1960-61, forestry coordinator world indicative plan, 1966-67; cons. Dept. Treasury, 1962, UN spl. fund, Mexico, 1963, Mexican Govt., summer 1964, 65, 66, Harvard Center Internat. Affairs, Liberia, 1965, World Bank, Portugal, 1966, Ford Found., India, 1970, 71, 72, India and Nepal, 1975, 76, 77, Pakistan, 1977, India, Burma and Indonesia, 1978, World Bank, 1973, 74, Provincial Govt. of N.S., Can., 1973, 74, 75, Provincial Govt. of Que., 1975, G. Banzhaf & Co., 1979, 80; co-dir. Seminar Tropical Hardwood Marketing, West Berlin, 1961; sr. economist timber study Pub. Land Law Rev. Commn.; co-dir. UN-FAO Seminar Forestry and Econ. Devel., Rome, 1971, Bradford, Eng., 1972. Author: Forest Resource Economics, 1972; Contbr. articles to profl. jours. Served to lt. USNR, 1942-45. Fellow Soc. Am. Foresters (past chmn. div. econs.); mem. Am. Econ. Assn., Finnish Forestry Soc. (hon.), Nat. Acad. Forest Sci. Mex. (hon.), Phi Beta Kappa, Sigma Xi, Phi Kappa Phi, Phi Sigma, Xi Sigma Pi, Gamma Alpha. Home: 3530 Woodland Rd Ann Arbor MI 48104

GREGORY, HARDY, JR., justice Georgia Supreme Court; b. Vienna, Ga., Aug. 11, 1936; s. Hardy and Mary Wood (Gaither) G.; m. Carolyn Burton, June 14, 1959; children: Hardy III, Elizabeth Marywood. B.S., U.S. Naval Acad., 1959; LL.B., Mercer U., 1967. Bar: Ga. 1966. Atty. Adams & O'Neal, Macon, Ga., 1966-71, Davis & Gregory, Vienna, Ga., 1971-76; judge Superior Cts., Cordale Cir., Ga., 1976-81; justice Ga. Supreme Ct., Atlanta, 1981—. Chmn. Democratic Exec. Com. Dooly County, Ga., 1971-76; mem. Bd. Edn. Dooly County, 1972. Served to capt. USAF, 1959-64; served to capt. USN, 1955-59. Democrat. Methodist. Home: 6140 Rivershore Pkwy NW Atlanta GA 30328 Office: Supreme Ct Ga Judicial Bldg Atlanta GA 30334

GREGORY, HEROLD LA MAR, orchestra administrator; b. Farmington, Utah, Nov. 9, 1923; s. Elijah B. and Julia Ellen (Tree) G.; m. Mary Ethel Eccles, Aug. 15, 1951; children—Vicki McGregor, Walter E., Suellen. B.A., U. Utah, 1949. Exec. dir. Utah Symphony, Salt Lake City, 1957—; pres. East German mission Ch. of Jesus Christ of Latter-day Saints, Berlin, 1953-57, mission sec., 1949-51; asso. prof. arts adminstrn. U. Utah, 1976—. Served with AUS, 1943-45. Home: 3215 Skycrest Circle Salt Lake City UT 84108 Office: 123 W S Temple Salt Lake City UT 84101 *The guiding light in my life has been an abiding faith in the eternal destiny of man and a never ending quest to determine or identify my earthly mission and achieve it, thus reaching my full human potential.*

GREGORY, IAN WALTER, educator, psychiatrist; b. London, Eng., July 14, 1926; came to U.S., 1959, naturalized, 1964; s. Ernest Walter and Anna (Buckner) G.; m. Eleanor Jean Dingwall, June 10, 1950; children: Robert Dalziel, Mary Elizabeth, Heather Jean, Roderick Ian. B.A., U. Cambridge (Eng.), 1946, M.B., 1948, M.A., 1951, M.D., 1956; D. Psychiatry, U. Toronto (Can.), 1954; M.P.H., U. Mich., 1959. Instr. psychiatry U. Western Ont., 1955-58; Commonwealth Fund fellow U. Mich., 1958-59; asst. prof., then asso. prof. psychiatry U. Minn., 1959-65; prof. psychiatry, chmn. dept. Ohio State U., Coll. Medicine, 1965—; Cons. div. research grants NIH, 1963-65. Author: Psychiatry: Biological and Social, 1961, (with others Abnormal Psychology, 2d edit.) Psychiatry: Biological and Social, 1972, Fundamentals of Psychiatry, 2d edit, 1968, Psychiatry: Essentials of Clinical Practice, 1977, 2d edit., 1983; also articles. Gold medal in psychiatry U. Toronto, 1954. Fellow Am. Psychiat. Assn., Royal Coll. Physicians (Can.), Royal Coll. Psychiatrists; mem. Delta Omega, Phi Kappa Phi. Home: 2019 Upper Chelsea Rd Columbus OH 43221

GREGORY, JAMES, librarian; b. Hendersonville, N.C., Dec. 24, 1923; s. James Parker and Hattie (Cochran) G. A.B., Eastern Ky. State U., 1944; M.A., U. N.C., 1945; M.S. in L.S, Columbia, 1955. Head catalogue N.Y. Hist. Soc., 1956-64, librarian, 1965-80. Compiler: Narratives of the Revolution in New York, 1975; editor: Papers of Horatio Gates, 1979. Trustee Frank Gavin Found. Mem. N.Y. Tech. Services Libraries (pres. 1965-66), Am. Library Assn. (chmn. history sect. 1972-73), Bibliog. Soc. Am., N.Y. Geneol. and Biog. Soc. Episcopalian (trustee). Club: Grolier (N.Y.C.). Home: 224 Riverside Dr New York NY 10025

GREGORY, JAMES, actor; b. N.Y.C., Dec. 23, 1911; s. James Gillen and Axemia Theresa (Ekdahl) G.; m. Ann Catherine Miltner, May 25, 1944. Grad. high sch. Appeared with Summer Stock cos., Deer Lake Pa., 1936, 37, 39, Millbrook, N.Y., 1938, Braddock Heights, Md., 1940, Buck's County Playhouse, New Hope, Pa., 1941, Ivy Tower Playhouse, Spring Lake, N.J., 1951; appeared in: Broadway shows Key Largo, 1939, Journey to Jerusalem, 1940, Dream Girl, 1945, Dead Pigeon, 1954, In Time to Come, 1941, All My Sons, 1947, Death of a Salesman, 1948-49, Desperate Hours, 1956-57, Fragile Fox, 1955; motion pictures include The Young Strangers, 1955, Al Capone Story, 1955, Gun Glory, 1956, Nightfall, 1956, The Big Caper, 1956, A Distant Trumpet, 1961, Underwater Warrior, 1962, PT-109, 1965, Sons of Katie Elder, 1967, Manchurian Candidate, 1967, Captain Newman, M.D, 1967, Million Dollar Duck, 1968, Clam Bake, Secret War of Harry Frigg, Shoot Out, Strongest Man in the World, 1974, Main Event, 1979, Wait Til Your Mother Gets Home, 1982; also 5 Matt Helm pictures; appeared on: television shows Gunsmoke; as Inspector Luger in: Barney Miller, TV series. Served with USNR, USMCR, 1942-45; PTO. Mem. Soc. Preservation and Encouragement Barber Shop Quartet Singing Am. Club: Hollywood Hackers. Home: 23 Oakmont Dr Los Angeles CA 90049 Office: care Internat Creative Mgmt Inc 8899 Beverly Blvd Los Angeles CA 90048

GREGORY, JAMES MICHAEL, profl. hockey league exec.; b. Port Colborne, Ont., Can., Nov. 4, 1935; s. Henry Joseph and Catherine Cecilia (Gandour) G.; m. Rosalie Donna Bruno, May 1959; children—Andrea, David, Valerie, Maureen. Student, St. Michael's Coll., Toronto. Formerly trainer, coach, mgr. and coach various hockey teams; mgr.-coach Vancouver (B.C.) Canucks; gen. mgr. Toronto

Maple Leafs, 1969-79; dir. scouting NHL, Rexdale, Ont., 1979—; gen. mgr. 3 Can. Jr. championship teams. Recipient (with team) Meml. Cup, 1961, 64, 67. Address: NHL 1 Greensboro Dr Rexdale ON M9W 1C8 Canada

GREGORY, JAMES PETER, scientific instrumentation manufacturing executive; b. Hartford, Conn., May 27, 1934; m. Joan Senior, Sept. 9, 1957; children: Clayton S., Mark S., Karen L. A.B., Brown U., 1956; J.D., George Washington U., 1961. Bar: D.C. 1961, Conn. 1963. Chief law clk. U.S. Ct. Claims, 1961-62; atty. firm Cummings & Lockwood, Stamford, Conn., 1962-64, Pfizer, Inc., N.Y.C., 1964-66; v.p., sec., gen. counsel Perkin-Elmer Corp., Norwalk, Conn., 1966—. Trustee Danbury (Conn.) Hosp. Served with AUS, 1957-59. Mem. Conn. Bar Assn., D.C. Bar Assn. Home: 45 St Johns Rd Ridgefield CT 06877 Office: Perkin-Elmer Corp Main Ave Norwalk CT 06856

GREGORY, JOHN MASON MOODY, JR., tobacco co. exec.; b. Durham, N.C., Feb. 5, 1907; s. John Mason Moody and Mary (Barksdale) G.; m. Katherine Jamieson, Apr. 18, 1936; children—John Mason Moody III, Andrew Jamieson. A.B., Duke, 1929. With Am. Leaf Orgn. Imperial Tobacco Co. Gt. Britain and Ireland, Ltd. (and predecessor), 1929—, pres., 1963-72, Brit. Leaf Tobacco Co. Can., Ltd., 1964-72. Mem. Durham City Council, 1945-57; bd. dirs. N.C. Citizens Assn.; Trustee Atlantic Christian Coll., Greenfield Acad.; bd. dirs. Wilson Community Fund, Wilson Planning and Zoning Com. Served with USNR, World War II. Mem. Wilson C. of C. (v.p. 1971-72, pres. 1972, dir.), Alpha Tau Omega. Democrat. Episcopalian. Clubs: Dunes Golf and Beach (Myrtle Beach, S.C.); Commonwealth (Richmond, Va.); Wilson Country. Home: 400 Wilshire Circle Wilson NC 27893 Office: 1st Union Bank Bldg Wilson NC 27893

GREGORY, JOSEPH TRACY, educator, paleontologist; b. Eureka, Calif., July 28, 1914; s. Frank C. and Edith (Tracy) G.; m. Jane Everest, Feb. 21, 1949; children: Carl Douglas, Sarah Jane. A.B., U. Calif. at Berkeley, 1935, Ph.D., 1938; postgrad., Inst. Meteorology, U. Chgo., 1943-44. Lectr. zoology Columbia U., 1939; WPA paleontology lab. supr. Tex. Bur. Econ. Geology, 1939-41; instr. geology U. Mich., 1941-46; asst. prof., then asso. prof. geology Yale, 1946-60; curator vertebrate paleontology Peabody Mus., 1946-60; prof. paleontology, also curator lower vertebrates Mus. Paleontology, U. Calif. at Berkeley, 1960-79, prof. emeritus, 1979—, chmn. dept. paleontology, 1960-65, 71-75, dir. mus., 1971-75. Co-editor: Am. Jour. Sci, 1955-60; editor: Bibliography of Fossil Vertebrates, 1969—. Served with AUS, 1942-46. Fellow Geol. Soc. Am.; mem. Am. Soc. Mammalogists, Am. Soc. Zoologists, Soc. Study Evolution, Soc. Vertebrate Paleontology (sec.-treas. 1954-57, pres. 1958), Paleontol. Soc., Phi Beta Kappa, Sigma Xi. Office: Mus Paleontology U Calif Berkeley CA 94720

GREGORY, MEL HYATT, insurance company executive; b. Frankfort, Ky., Mar. 29, 1936; s. Mel Hyatt and Audrey (Fraley) G.; m. Joyce Klein, Sept. 9, 1955; children: Susan Gregory lawson, Scott, Beth. B.S., Stetson U., 1958. Mgr., agt. Equitable Life Ins. Co., Louisville, 1959-66, agy., mgr., Dayton, Ohio, 1966-70, Atlanta, 1970-73, v.p., Cin., 1974-77, sr. v.p., N.Y.C., 1978—. Bd. dirs. Clark Coll., Atlanta, 1982—, USO, Greater N.Y. Served to capt. U.S. Army, 1958-62. Mem. Gen. Agts. and Mgrs. (pres. 1966-74). Republican. Clubs: Cherokee Country (Atlanta); Canoe Brook Country (Summit, N.J.). Home: 139 Rotary Dr Summit NJ 07901 Office: Equitable Life Assurance Soc of US 1285 Avenue of the Americas New York NY 10019

GREGORY, MICHAEL STRIETMANN, educator; b. Oakland, Calif., Oct. 6, 1929; s. Walter and Alexine (Mitchell) G.; m. Ora Thorson, Feb. 2, 1952 (div.); children: Alexa, Tanya; m. Jan. Louise Rosenthal, June 27, 1962; 1 dau., Erika. A.B., U. Calif., Berkeley, 1952, Ph.D. in Cultural Anthropology, 1969. Instr. in English San Jose (Calif.) State U., 1956-57; mem. faculty dept. English San Francisco State U., 1959—, prof., 1971—, dir. NEXA sci.-humanities convergence program, 1975—; founding mem. Nat. Bd. Cons., Nat. Endowment Humanities, 1974—; cons. NSF. Author: Sociobiology and Human Nature, 1978, The Recombinant DNA Controversy: Public Policy at the Frontier of Knowledge, 1978; Contbr. articles on sci. and humanities, history of ideas. Served with USNR, 1951-53. NIMH grantee, Hong Kong, 1965-66; Calif. Council for Humanities in Public Policy grantee, 1977, 80, 82-83; Andrew W. Mellon Found. grantee, 1978-81. Fellow Am. Anthrop. Assn.; mem. Amnesty Internat., MLA, AAAS, Hastings Inst., Joseph Conrad Soc., AAUP. Home: 351 Melrose Ave Mill Valley CA 94941 Office: Sch Humanities San Francisco State U San Francisco CA 94132 *The most important insight into life has come, for me, from the great Polish-English novelist, Joseph Conrad. Conrad understood the role of illusion: that illusions can kill us or save us, and sometimes they do both. Illusions that aggrandize us, and lend justification for cruelty and heartlessness, almost certainly will one day destroy us. Other illusions make us not more powerful than we really are, but better: duty, steadfastness, pride of craft, truth, and above all, love. These illusions create light and sustain life, and as such they must be cherished, for without them the world would be dark — too dark altogether.*

GREGORY, MITCHELL V., steel company executive; b. N.Y.C., Dec. 3, 1935; s. Nicholas and Costandino (Pino) G.; m. Diane C. Brahms, June 7, 1964; children: Michele, William. B.A., Adelphi U., 1957. C.P.A., Pa. With Mathieson Aitken & Co. (C.P.A.s), until 1968; supr., sr. acct. Peat, Marwick, Mitchell, Phila., 1968-72; corp. controller Sharon Steel Co., Miami Beach, Fla., 1972-74, v.p., 1974—; (also affiliated companies: DWG Corp.),,,,; trustee Universal Housing and Devel. Co., 1976—. Elder Miami Shores Presbyn. Ch. Mem. Am. Inst. C.P.A.s, Pa. Inst. C.P.A.s.

GREGORY, NOBLE K., lawyer; b. Los Angeles, Apr. 19, 1918; s. James Noble and Hazel (Veach) G.; m. Sara Dunlap, Feb. 21, 1947; children: James, Carol. B.A., UCLA, 1939; J.D., U. Calif.-Berkeley, 1946. Bar: Calif. 1946. Law clk. presiding justice Calif. Supreme Ct., 1946-48; assoc. Pillsbury, Madison & Sutro, San Francisco, 1948-56, ptnr., 1956—; instr. San Francisco Law Sch., 1947; mem. Calif. Law Rev. Commn., 1970-75. Served to lt. USAAF, 1943-45. Deocrated D.F.C.; decorated Air medal with 3 clusters, Purple Heart. Mem. State Bar Calif. (chmn. com. on appellate cts. 1974-75), ABA, San Francisco Bar Assn. (chmn. adminstrn. of justice com. 1966), Am. Judicature Soc. Clubs: Commonwealth, San Francisco Comml. Home: 225 Maywood Dr San Francisco CA 94127 Office: 225 Bush St San Francisco CA 94104

GREGORY, NORMAN WAYNE, chemistry educator, researcher; b. Albany, Oreg., June 23, 1920; s. Arthur Donald and Edith Florence (Self) G.; m. Lillian Virginia Larsson, May 21, 1943; children: Norman Wayne Jr., Martha Jean, Brian Neil. Student, Lower Columbia Jr. Coll., 1936-38; B.S., U. Wash., Seattle, 1940, M.S., 1941; Ph.D., Ohio State U., 1943. Research chemist Radiation Lab., U. Calif., Berkeley, 1944-46; instr. U. Wash., Seattle, 1946-47, asst. prof., 1947-53, assoc. prof., 1953-57, prof. chemistry, 1957—, chmn. dept. chemistry, 1970-75. Author: Physical Chemistry, 1964; contbr. articles to profl. jours. Mem. Am. Chem. Soc. (chmn. Puget Sound sect. 1964), Am.Chem. Soc. (treas, 1962), Sigma Xi. Office: U Wash Chemistry Dept BG-10 Seattle WA

GREGORY, PAUL (JASON GREGORY LENHART), producer; b. Waukee, Iowa, Aug. 27, 1920; s. James Clifford and Esther May (Taylor) Lenhart; m. Janet Gaynor, 1965. Student, Drake U. Head concert div. Music Corp. Am., 1947-48; prof. drama dept. San Diego State U. Started Charles Laughton reading tours, 1948; Produced: Don Juan in Hell, 1951, John Brown's Body, 1952, The Caine Mutiny Court Martial, 1953, Elsa Lancaster's Pvt. Music Hall, 1953, That Fabulous Redhead, 1954, Three for Tonight, 1955; motion picture The Night of the Hunter, 1954, The Rivalry, 1957, The Naked and the Dead, 1958, The Marriage-Go-Round, 1958-60, The Pink Jungle, 1959, Captains and the Kings, 1961, Prescription Murder, 1962, Lord Pengo, 1963, Seven Ways of Love, 1963, Dame Judith Anderson as Hamlet, 1970, The Grapes of Wrath, 1978; producer: Ray Bradbury's Martian Chronicles, 1978-79; (co-recipient Emmy award for best TV adaptation of Caine Mutiny Court Martial 1955). Recipient N.Y. Critics award, 1952, Outer Circle Critics award, 1954; Alumni Distinguished Service award Drake U., 1959. Hon. mem. Theta Alpha Phi.

GREGORY, PAUL, insurance executive, negotiations consultant; b. N.Y.C., Feb. 25, 1935; s. Alexander and Fania (Fine) Chigrinsky; m. Phyllis Gregory, Aug. 30, 1979; children by pervious marriage: Andrea, Richard, Michele. B.A., CCNY, 1958; LL.D., Hebrew U., Jerusalem, 1972. Sr. v.p., dir. Alexander & Alexander Inc., N.Y.C., 1966-83; vice chmn. Frank B. Hall Re Inc., N.Y.C., 1983—; dir. Leasco Inc., Puritan Fashions Corp., Reliance Group Holdings, Reliance Ins. Co., United Pacific Ins. Co., United Pacific Life Ins. Co., Bank Leumi Trust Co. N.Y., Alexander & Alexander Internat. Inc. Composer: Misfortune of Being Clever (opera), 1966. Bd. dirs. Anti-Defamation League of B'nai B'rith, 1967. Served to maj. U.S. Army, 1957-59. Recipient various maj. sales awards. Office: 261 Madison Ave New York NY 10016

GREGORY, ROBERT EARLE, JR., apparel company executive, lawyer; b. Greenville, S.C., May 8, 1942; s. Robert E. and Ellen (Robinson) G.; m. Suzanne Hodges, June 20, 1965 (div. 1982); children: Scott, Kelly; m. 2d Karen Marie Howard, Apr. 24, 1982. B.A., Wofford Coll., 1964; J.D., U. S.C., 1968; Advanced mgmt. program, Harvard Grad. Bus. Sch., Cambridge, Mass., 1978-79. Bar: S.C. 1968, Fed. 1968, U.S. Supreme Ct. 1974. Legal asst. to chief justice S.C. Supreme Ct., Columbia, 1968-70; div. counsel Akzona, Inc., Asheville, N.C., 1970-72; gen. counsel Spartan Mills, Spartanburg, S.C., 1972-79, group v.p., gen. counsel, 1977-79; exec. v.p., pres. Lee Co. div. VF Corp., Wyomissing, Pa., 1980-83; pres., chief operating officer VF Corp., Wyomissing, Pa., 1983—, dir.; dir. United Mo. Bank Kansas City, N.A., Mo., 1982—. Alumni dir. Wofford Coll., Spartanburg, 1976-81, sec., Spartanburg, 1979-80, pres. elect, Spartanburg, 1981. Mem. S.C. Bar Assn. Episcopalian. Clubs: Harvard (N.Y.C.); Harvard Bus. Sch. (Phila.). Home: 320 Wyomissing Blvd Wyomissing PA 19610 Office: VF Corp 1047 N Park Rd Wyomissing PA 19610

GREGORY, ROBERT TODD, mathematics educator; b. Owensboro, Ky., Mar. 19, 1920; s. Richeson Todd and Jennie (Howard) G.; m. Margaret Kathryn Bentzinger, Dec. 29, 1944; children: Rosalie Jane, Carl Richeson. Student, Georgetown Coll., Ky., 1937-38; B.S., U.S. Naval Acad., 1942; M.S., Iowa State U., 1948; Ph.D., U. Ill., 1955. Instr. math. Fla. State U., 1949-50; research asst. U. Ill., 1950-55; asst. prof. math. U. Calif., Santa Barbara, 1955-59; asso. prof., prof. math. U. Tex., Austin, 1959-75, sr. research mathematician Computation Ctr., 1959-70, prof. math., 1963-75, prof. math. and computer sci., 1966-75, acting chmn. dept. computer sci., 1966-68, asso. dir. Ctr. for Numerical Analysis, 1970-75; prof., head dept. computer sci., prof. math. U. Tenn., Knoxville, 1975-80, prof. computer sci. and math., 1980—. Author: Numeral Systems, 1963, Error-Free Computation, 1980; co-author: A Collection of Matrices for Testing Computational Algorithms, 2d edit, 1978, A Survey of Numerical Mathematics, 2 vols, 1972, Methods and Applications of Error-free Computation, 1983; Contbr. articles to profl. jours. Served with USN, 1942-46. Mem. Am. Math. Soc., Math. Assn. Am., Soc. for Indsl. and Applied Math. (editorial bd. Jour. on Applied Math.), Assn. for Computing Machinery, Sigma Xi. Home: 3311 Mt Vernon Dr Knoxville TN 37920

GREGORY, ROSS, history educator; b. Washington, Ind., Feb. 11, 1933; s. Norrell and Bertha Beatrice (Jones) G.; m. Shirley Ann Heines, Dec. 15, 1961; children: Theresa M., Graham T., Darren M. A.B., Ind. U., 1959, M.A., 1961, Ph.D. (U. fellow), 1964. Asst. prof. history W.Va. Inst. Tech., Montgomery, 1963-66; asst. prof. history Western Mich. U., Kalamazoo, 1966-69, asso. prof., 1969-73, prof., 1973—. Author: Walter Hines Page: Ambassador to St. James's, 1970 (Frederick Jackson Turner award), The Origins of American Intervention in the First World War, 1971; contbg. author: To Do Good in the World: Woodrow Wilson and America's Mission in Makers of American Diplomacy, 1974, The Domino Theory in Ency. Am. Fgn. Policy, 1978; Contbr. articles to profl. jours. Served with AUS, 1954-56. Am. Philos. Soc. grantee, 1967; Western Mich. U. fellow, 1969, 83. Mem. Orgn. Am. Historians, Am. Hist. Assn. Home: 2812 Romence Rd Kalamazoo MI 49002

GREGORY, RUTH WILHELMENE, librarian; b. West Point, Nebr., Feb. 20, 1910; d. Edward George and Wilhelmene (Plieth) G. A.B., U. Nebr., 1933; M.L.S., U. Wis., 1938. Gen. library asst. Lincoln (Nebr.) City Library, 1934-36; librarian editorial dept. Rotarian mag., Chgo., 1937; acting librarian Stevens Point (Wis.) Pub. Library, 1938-39; asso. librarian Waukegan (Ill.) Pub. Library, 1939, head librarian, 1939-76, library cons., 1976—; exec. sec. div. pub. libraries ALA, 1946-48. Author: Anniversaries and Holidays, 3d edit., 1975, 4th edit., 1983; co-author: Public Libraries in Cooperative Systems, 1971; editor: Public Libraries, 1947-48. Sec. Waukegan City Planning Commn., 1950-57; sec. bd. dirs. Lake County Mus. of History. Mem. Round Table (v.p., editor 1948-49), ALA (council 1951-54, chmn. jury on citation of trustees 1952-53, pres. pub. libraries div. 1954-55, exec. bd. 1956-60), Ill. Library Assn. (pres. 1947-48, mem. planning bd. 1951-54), AAUW (pres. Waukegan br. 1949-51, Ednl. Found. Name award 1980), P.E.O., LWV, Kappa Delta. Clubs: Chgo. Library; Woman's (Waukegan); Altrusa. Home and Office: 2035 Walnut St Waukegan IL 60087

GREGORY, WILLIAM HAMILTON, mag. editor; b. Kansas City, Mo., Apr. 15, 1924; s. Wesley Hall and Margaret (Rempe) G.; m. Virginia Marie Gregg, Sept. 4, 1946; children—Robert, Peter, Susan, Nancy, Martha, Kathryn. B.S. in Journalism, Creighton U., Omaha, 1947. Reporter Clinton (Iowa) Herald, 1946-50; reporter, copy editor Kansas City (Mo.) Times, 1950-56; with Aviation Week and Space Tech., N.Y.C., 1956—, mng. editor, 1958-72, exec. editor, 1972-79, editor-in-chief, 1979—. Mem. Westport (Conn.) Planning and Zoning Commn., 1963-71; Westport rep. S.W. Regional Planning Agy., 1970. Served as aviator USNR, 1942-46. Recipient Robert S. Ball award Aviation and Space Writers Assn., 1975, Eugene Dubois award N.Y. Airline Public Relations Assn., 1978. Roman Catholic. Clubs: Nat. Press, Army and Navy, Cosmos (Washington). Home: 227 Falcon Ridge Rd Great Falls VA 22066 Office: 1777 N Kent St Suite 710 Arlington VA 22209

GREIDINGER, B. BERNARD, accountant, educator; b. N.Y.C., Mar. 30, 1906; s. Max and Fannie (Oster) G. B.B.A., CCNY, 1928; M.S., Columbia U., 1932, Ph.D., 1939. C.P.A., N.Y. Ptnr. Beame & Greidinger C.P.A., N.Y.C., 1929-42; sr. partner Greidinger and Co. (C.P.A.), 1946-71; partner Hertz, Herson & Co., N.Y.C., 1971—; prof. accounting grad. sch. bus., N.Y. U., 1948-74, prof. emeritus, 1974—; prof. accounting U. Calif. at Los Angeles, summer 1947; lectr. accounting Coll. City N.Y., 1930-39, Rutgers U., 1940-46; Disting. vis. prof. acctg. Rider Coll., Lawrenceville, N.J., 1980—; past dir., mem. exec. com. U.S. Hoffman Machinery Corp.; Rep. dir. gen. UNRRA at inception Internat. Refugee Orgn., 1946; financial adv., chief financial operations UNRRA, 1946-47; cons. budget adv. com. Army-Air Force Post Exchange Serv., 1948; cons. to chief ordnance Dept. of Army, N.Y. dist., 1952—, spl. cons. to comptroller N.Y., 1955; coordinator N.Y.U., U.S. Operation Mission (internat. cooperation adminstrn.), Israel, 1956. Author: Accounting Requirements of the Securities and Exchange Commission, 1941, Preparation and Certification of Financial Statements, 1950, (with others) Big Business Methods for Small Business, 1952, Filings with the Securities and Exchange Commission, 1966, Handbook for Auditors, 1971; Contbr. chpts. to books; articles to profl. jours. Business, 1952. Mem. Temp. Commn. City Finances, N.Y.C., 1965-66; mem. citizens' commn. on future of City U. N.Y., 1970—; chmn. transition com. Mayor of N.Y.C., 1974; mem. Mayor's Com. on Judiciary, 1974—, Mayor's Council Econ. and Bus. Advisers, 1974—, Commn. Cultural Affairs City of N.Y., 1976—, Indsl. and Comml. Incentive Bd. City of N.Y., 1977—. Served with finance dept. AUS, 1942-44; from maj. to lt. col. USAAF, 1944-46; col. USAFR. Mem. Am. Inst. C.P.A.'s, N.Y. State Soc. C.P.A.'s, Am. Accountants Assn., Nat. Assn. Accountants, Acad. Polit. Scis. Clubs: Mason., Columbia, New York University Faculty. Home: 2 Washington Sq Village New York NY 10012 Office: 2 Park Ave New York NY 10016

GREIG, THOMAS CURRIE, Canadian govt. ofcl.; b. Edinburgh, Scotland, Dec. 16, 1931; s. Thomas Currie and Elsie E. (Bell) G. M.A., U. Edinburgh, 1953. Chartered accountant. With Peat, Marwick, Mitchell & Co., Toronto, Can., 1956-62, acting mgr., 1961-62; with M. Loeb Ltd., Ottawa, 1962—, v.p., treas., 1965-67, sr. v.p., treas., 1967-71, exec. v.p. finance, 1971-72; asst. dep. minister finance Canadian Dept. Nat. Def., Ottawa, 1972-77; asst. dep. minister customs program Canadian Dept. Nat. Revenue, Ottawa, 1977—. Served to lt. Royal Navy, 1953-56. Club: Rideau (Ottawa). Home: 1943 Marquis Ave Ottawa ON K1J 8J1 Canada Office: Connaught Bldg MacKenzie Ave Ottawa ON K1A 0L5 Canada

GREIG, WALTER, college president; b. Austin, Tex., Nov. 16, 1906; s. Walter and Elizabeth (Kopperl) G.; m. Shirley Jean Coker, Dec. 7, 1946; children: Carol Ann, Walter Coker. Student, U. Tex., 1924-30; B.S., Cleary Coll., 1949, B.B.A., 1960, M.B.A., 1961, Sc.D., 1962; D.C.Sc., Drake Coll., 1964. Bar: Tex. bar 1931, Mich. bar 1946, U.S. Supreme Ct. bar 1942. Pvt. practice law, Austin, Tex., 1931-41, Detroit, 1946-47; exec. sec. Mich. Liquor Control Commn., 1947-49; asst. to pres. Cleary Coll., 1949, trustee, sec. bd., 1950-51, exec. v.p., 1951-70, pres., treas. bd. trustees, 1970-74, pres. emeritus, 1974—, sec. bd., 1974—. Mich. indsl. ambassador, 1962-64; mem. Ypsilanti Civil Service Commn., 1963-71; chmn. Ypsilanti Compensation Com., 1972-80; mem. City Police and Fire Pension Bd., 1973—; chmn. City Tax Bd. Rev., 1977-79; Bd. dirs. Ypsilanti Area Indsl. Devel. Corp., 1970-71, pres., 1973-74. Served to capt. AUS, 1941-46. Recipient proclamation as outstanding citizen Mayor Ypsilanti and Mich. Legislature, Legion of Honor Kiwanis Club; named Ky. Col.; recipient Gold honor award York Rite. Mem. Ypsilanti Bd. Commerce (v.p. 1956-57, dir. 1955-58), Washtenaw Ave. Bus. and Profl. Assn. (chmn. 1970-73), Mil. Order Fgn. Wars (Mich. comdr. 1958-59), Tex., Mich. bar assns., Tex. U. Ex-students Assn., Am. Legion (comdr. post 88). Presbyterian. Clubs: Masons (K.T., Shriner, 33 deg., Jester, Royal Order Scotland), Kiwanis, Washtenaw Country. Home: 1223 Washtenaw Ave Ypsilanti MI 48197 *I believe that we all came into this world with the talents given by God to use wisely for the benefit of all and we must leave this world more enriched for the next generation that follows us. Therefore we must in our lifetime do many things to improve our surroundings and the human race. This is the way to find joy and happiness in the time allotted us.*

GREIG, WILLIAM TABER, JR., publishing company executive; b. Mpls., Apr. 16, 1924; s. William Taber and Margaret Naomi (Buckbee) G.; m. Doris Jane Walters, June 23, 1951; children: Kathryn Ann Greig Rowland, William Taber, III, Gary Stanley, Doris Jane. B.Arch., U. Minn., 1945. Jr. exec. Bur. Engraving, Mpls., 1946-48; partner, mgr. Praise Book Publns., Mound, Minn., 1948-50; v.p., exec. v.p., gen. mgr. Gospel Light Publs., 1950-76, pres., owner, Ventura, Calif., 1976—; dir. Lighthouse Partners Bookstores, World Impact, Inc., Latin Am. Mission, Gospel Lit. Internat.; vice chmn. Samuel Zwemer Inst.; trustee John Perkins Found. Bd. dirs. Alcoholics Hope Found. Served to lt. (j.g.) USNR, 1943-46. Mem. Evang. Christian Pubs. Assn. (dir., pres. 1981-83). Republican. Presbyterian. Club: Verdugo. Home: 347 Lupine Way Ventura CA 93001 Office: 2300 Knoll Dr Ventura CA 93003

GREIN, RICHARD FRANK, bishop, educator; b. Bemidji, Minn., Nov. 29, 1932; s. Lester Edward and LaVina Minnie (Frost) G.; m. Joan Dunwoody Atkinson, Nov. 25, 1961; children: David, Margaret, Mary Leslie, Sara. B.A. in Geology, Carlton Coll., 1955; M. Div., Hashotah House Sem., Wis., 1959, S.T.M., 1970. Ordained priest Episcopal Ch., 1959; priest-in-charge Elk River mission field, Minn., 1959-64; rector St. Mathew's Ch., Mpls., 1964-69, St. David's Ch., Minnetonka, Minn., 1969-73; prof. pastoral theology Nashotah House House Theol. Sem., 1973-74;; rector St. Michael and All Angel Ch., Mission, Kans., after 1974; bishop The Episcopal Ch., Tepeka, kans. Co-author: Preparing Younger Children for First Communion, 1972. Priest assoc. Order Holy Cross; pres. Guardian Angels Found., Elk River, 1963-64. Mem. Council Assoc. Parishes. Office: Episcopal Ch Benthany Pl Topeka KS 66612

GREINER, EDWARD DAVID, industrial manufacturing company executive; b. Peoria, Ill., Mar. 11, 1920; s. Fritz O. and Ethel K. (Mohn) G.; m. Dorothy M. Janssen, July 31, 1943; children: David (dec.), Joel, Dan, Mark A., John R. Student, U. Ill., 1937-38; B.S., Bradley U., 1941. Acct. R.G. LeTourneau, Inc., Peoria, 1941-42, asst. treas., 1946-53; sec.-treas. LeTourneau-Westinghouse Co., Peoria, 1953-59; v.p. finance Westinghouse Air Brake Co., Pitts., 1959-63; v.p. Cherry-Burrell Corp., Chgo., 1963-64; asst. to pres. Masonite Corp., Chgo., 1965-70, v.p. adminstrn., 1970-77, exec. v.p., 1977-83, vice chmn., 1983—, also dir.; dir. Binks Mfg. Co., Franklin Park, Ill. Bd. dirs. Met. YMCA, Chgo. Served to lt. USNR, 1942-46. Home: 34 Princeton Rd Hinsdale IL 60521 Office: 29 N Wacker Dr Chicago IL 60606

GREINER, MORRIS ESTY, JR., TV executive; b. Mpls., Nov. 7, 1920; s. Morris Esty and Irene Marie (O'Connell) G.; m. Dorothy J. Carter, May 23, 1946; 1 son, Derek Carter. A.B., Duke, 1942. Promotion mgr. Sta. WHB, Kansas City, Mo., 1946-50; editor Swing mag., 1946-50; copy dir. Rogers & Smith (advt. agy.), Kansas City, Mo., 1950-51, radio and TV dir., 1951-53; mgr. Sta. WHB-TV, Kansas City, Mo., 1953-54, Sta. KMBC-TV, 1954-64, Sta. WMC-TV, Scripps-Howard Broadcasting Co., Memphis, 1964-66, v.p., 1966—, also dir.; gen. mgr. stas. WMC-TV, WMC, WMC-FM, Memphis, 1966—; dir. NBC TV Affiliates Bd. Dels., 1969-73; faculty Memphis State U., 1968-70. Pres. Red Balloon Players, 1969-70, bd. dirs., 1968-75; pres. Greater Memphis State, 1970-72, bd. dirs., 1966—; bd. dirs. Memphis

Speech and Hearing Center, 1968-80, pres., 1973-77; steering chmn. United Memphis, 1970-71; pres. United Way of Greater Memphis, 1976-77, chmn., 1977-78, life trustee, 1978—; mem. president's round table LeMoyne-Owen Coll.; selection chmn. Leadership Memphis, 1982; trustee Memphis State U. Found., Scripps-Howard Found., Memphis Acad. Arts; vice chmn. Memphis Acad. Arts, 1980—; bd. dirs. Mid-South Fair Assn., Jobs for High Sch. Grads., 1982—; mem. chancellor's round table U. Tenn. Center Health Scis., Pres.'s Club Christian Bros. Coll., Pres.'s Council Memphis State U.; adv. council Memphis Cotton Carnival Assn.; mem. exec. bd. Memphis NAACP. Served to lt. USNR, 1942-46. Named Boxer Breeder of Year, 1955; Regional Emmy winner Nat. Acad. TV Arts and Scis., 1971; Iris award Nat. Assn. TV Program Execs., 1980; Disting. Service award NAACP, 1981. Mem. Nat., Tenn. assns. broadcasters, Maximum Service Telecasters. Home: 18 Morningside Park Memphis TN 38104 Office: 1960 Union Ave Memphis TN 38104

GREISEN, KENNETH INGVARD, physicist; b. Perth Amboy, N.J., Jan. 24, 1918; s. Ingvard C. and Signa (Nielsen) G.; m. Elizabeth C. Chase, Apr. 12, 1941 (dec.); children: Eric Winslow, Kathryn Elise; m. Helen A. Leeds, Mar. 27, 1976. Student, Wagner Coll., 1934-35; B.S., Franklin and Marshall Coll., 1938; Ph.D., Cornell U., 1942. Instr. Cornell U., 1942-43, asst. prof., 1946-48, asso. prof., 1948-50, prof. physics, 1950—, chmn. dept. astronomy, 1976-79, univ. ombudsman, 1975-77, dean faculty, 1978-83; scientist Manhattan Project, Los Alamos, 1943-46. Fellow Am Phys. Soc.; mem. Am. Astron. Soc., Internat. Astron. Union, Nat. Acad. Sci., AAUP. Research cosmic rays. Home: 336 Forest Home Dr Ithaca NY 14850

GREITZER, HERMAN S., lawyer; b. N.Y.C., Nov. 30, 1919; s. William and Ida (Wolfe) G.; (div.)1 dau., Elizabeth. B.S.S., CCNY, 1941; LL.B. (Harlan Fiske Stone scholar Legis. Drafting Research Fund), Columbia U., 1949. Bar: D.C. 1950, N.Y. 1950, U.S. Supreme Ct. 1953. Pub. relations officer Supreme Comdr. Allied Powers, Tokyo, Japan, 1946; legis. atty. Commerce Dept., Washington, 1949-50; trial atty. Justice Dept., Washington, 1950-51, appellate atty., 1951-55; pvt. practice law, N.Y.C., 1955-64; atty. R.H. Macy & Co., Inc., N.Y.C., 1964-73; v.p., gen. counsel, sec., dir. Marcade Group Inc., Jersey City, 1973—. Served to capt. F.A. AUS, 1942-46. Mem. Am. Bar Assn. Home: 55 W 11th St New York NY 10011 Office: 21 Caven Point Ave Jersey City NJ 07305

GREMBAN, JOE LAWRENCE, utilities executive; b. Goodman, Wis., June 3, 1920; s. Joseph and Anna (Kryzyak) G.; m. V. June Smith, June 8, 1945; children: Ronald D., Keith D., Brian D. B.B.A., U. Wis., 1948; postgrad., U. Mich., 1973. Spl. accountant Central Ill. Electric & Gas Co., Rockford, Ill., 1948-62; asst. treas. Sierra Pacific Power Co., Reno, 1962-63, corp. sec., 1963-69, v.p., 1969-71, v.p., sec., treas., 1971-72, fin. v.p., treas., 1972-73, exec. v.p., 1973-75, pres., 1975-76, pres., chief exec. officer, 1976-80, chmn., pres., chief exec. officer, 1980—. Past pres. Nev. Area council Boy Scouts Am.; past dir. Nev. Taxpayers Assn., Reno Better Bus. Bur. Served with USAAF, 1942-45. Mem. Nat. Assn. Accountants (past pres.), Reno Execs. Club (past pres.), Edison Electric Inst., Pacific Coast Gas Assn. (past dir.), Pacific Coast Electric Assn. (dir.). Club: Rotarian. Home: 2865 Juliann Way Reno NV 89502 Office: Sierra Pacific Power Co 100 E Moana Ln Reno NV 89520 *

GREMILLION, CURTIS LIONEL, JR., psychologist; b. Slaughter, La., Feb. 26, 1924; s. Curtis Lionel and Beatrice (Watson) G.; m. Rosemary Duhon, Dec. 8, 1951; children: Suzanne Lynelle Gremillion Walden), Curtis Lionel III, Monique Angele. B.A. in Psychology and Music, U. Southwestern La., 1948; postgrad. in psychology, La. State U., 1948-49, 53. Profl. musician, 1940-43, 46-51; staff psychologist East La. State Hosp., Jackson, 1949-83, dir. psychology and social service depts., 1953- 57, asst. supt., 1957-62, adminstr., 1961, 62-64, acting supt., 1964-66, asso. adminstr., 1966-81, patient advocate, 1981-83; cons. psychology, 1983—; dir. regional council Alcoholism and Drug Abuse, 1972-76. Author: History of The East Louisiana State Hospital. Bd. dirs. La. State Credit Union, 1962-68; chmn. East Feliciana Parish United Givers Fund, 1960; regional chmn. Am. Heart Assn., 1968—, ARC, 1954-55, 62, Boy Scouts Am., 1964-69, Am. Cancer Soc., 1963-64; bd. dirs. So. Behavioral Research Found., 1970-76. Served with USNR, 1943-46. Recipient Outstanding Leadership and Service award La. Dept. Hosps., 1966. Mem. La. Psychol. Assn. (charter), So. Sociol. Assn., La. Music Therapy Assn. (dir. 1966—), Am. Legion, Internat. Platform Assn., Psi Chi, Sinfonia, Pi Gamma Mu, Kappa Delta Pi. Democrat. Baptist. Clubs: New Orleans Jazz, Lions. Address: PO Box 306 Slaughter LA 70777

GRENANDER, M.E., educator, critic; b. Rewey, Wis., Nov. 21, 1918; d. Carl John and Mary Matilda (Whitney) G.; m. James William Corbett, May 5, 1972. A.B., U. Chgo., 1940, A.M., 1941, Ph.D., 1948; D.H.L. (hon.), King Meml. Coll., Columbia, S.C., 1977. Mem. faculty dept. English, SUNY, Albany, 1948—, prof., 1961—, dir. Inst. Humanistic Studies, 1977-80; vis. prof. Am. lit. Facultes des lettres et des scis. humaines Lille and Toulouse, France, 1960-61; vis. prof. Chinese univs., summer 1979, lectr., France, Switzerland, USSR, Poland. Author: Ambrose Bierce, 1971, Helios: From Myth to Solar Energy, 1978, Apollo Agonistes: The Humanities in a Computerized World, 1979, Asclepius at Syracuse: Thomas Szasz, Libertarian Humanist, 1980; editorial bd.: Jour. Humanities and Tech., Lit. of Liberty; author: numerous articles. Served in USN, 1942-46. Mem. N.Y. State Am. Studies Assn. (pres. 1973-74), MLA, N.E. MLA, Law and Humanities Inst., Am. Studies Assn., Internat. Assn. Univ. Profs. of English, Humanities and Tech. Assn. (v.p. 1978-81), Internat. Assn. Philosophy and Lit., DAR, Phi Beta Kappa. Home: 269 Brookhaven Dr East Berne NY 12059 Office: Dept English SUNY Albany NY 12222

GRENDLER, PAUL FREDERICK, historian, educator; b. Armstrong, Iowa, May 24, 1936; s. August Paul and Josephine Lucy (Girres) G.; m. Marcella T. McCann, June 16, 1962; children: Peter, Jean. A.B., Oberlin Coll., 1959; M.A., U. Wis., 1961, Ph.D., 1964. Instr. history U. Pitts., 1963-64; lectr. history U. Toronto, Ont., Can., 1964-65, asst. prof., 1965-69, assoc. prof., 1969-73, prof. history, 1973—; postdoctoral fellow Inst. for Research in Humanities, U. Wis., 1967-68. Author: Critics of the Italian World 1530-1560, 1969, The Roman Inquisition and the Venetian Press 1540-1605, 1977, rev. Italian transl., 1983, Culture and Censorship in Late Renaissance Italy and France, 1981; editorial bd., exec. com.: Collected Works of Erasmus, 1976—; Contbr. articles to profl. jours. Fulbright fellow to Italy, 1962-63; Can. Council leave fellow, 1970-71; Am. Council Learned Socs. fellow, 1971-72; I Tatti fellow Harvard U. Center for Italian Renaissance Studies, Florence, Italy, 1970-72; sr. fellow Soc. for Humanities, Cornell U., 1973-74; Guggenheim Meml fellow, 1978-79; Social Scis. and Humanities Research Council Can. fellow, 1979-80; Woodrow Wilson Internat. Ctr. for Scholars fellow, 1982-83. Mem. Renaissance Soc. Am., Am. Hist. Assn., Am. Cath. Hist. Assn. (Marraro prize 1978), Soc. Italian Hist. Studies, Toronto Renaissance and Reformation Colloquium. Home: 115 Sheldrake Blvd Toronto ON Canada M4P 2B1 Office: Dept History U Toronto Toronto ON Canada M5S 1A1

GRENELL, JAMES HENRY, manufacturing company executive; b. Mpls., Feb. 19, 1924; s. Harrison Morton and Harriet Elizabeth (Kuch) G.; m. Naomi Betty Callerstrom, Sept. 15, 1945; children—Bonita (Mrs. Michael Wolfe), Suzanne Naomi, Andrea (Mrs. Edward Mendes). B.B.A., U. Minn., 1947; A.M.P., Sch. Bus. Harvard, 1974. With Honeywell Inc., Mpls., 1951—, accountant, 1951-56, div. controller, 1956-68, group controller, 1968-71, asst. corp. controller, 1971-74, v.p., controller, 1974-82, v.p., staff exec., 1982—; Instr. Mgmt. Inst. U. Wis.-Madison, 1960-69, Inst. Tech. U. Minn., Mpls., 1963-65; asso. dir. Mgmt. Center Coll. St. Thomas, 1959-69. Contbr. articles to profl. jours. Bd. dirs. Mpls. Soc. for Blind, 1963-71, pres., 1970-71; bd. dirs. U. Minn. Coll. Bus. Alumni Bd., 1975—. Served to 1st lt., 1943-46; ETO. Mem. Fin. Execs. Inst., Alpha Kappa Psi. Republican. Conglist. Clubs: Harvard of Minn., Edina (Minn.) Country. Home: 6200 Wyman Ave Edina MN 55436 Office: Honeywell Plaza Minneapolis MN 55408

GRENET, CLAUDE JULIEN, transport executive; b. Paris, Apr. 17, 1931; U.S., 1951, naturalized, 1957; s. Julien Claude and Suzanne (Guillemot) G.; m. Dorisanne Michael, Dec. 29, 1951; children: Daniel, Christianne, Michele, Philippe. B.S. in Bus. Adminstrn., U. Nebr., 1953. C.P.A., Nebr. Staff acct. Deloitte, Haskins & Sells (various locations), 1955-60, prin., nat. and internat. officer, 1961-75; Caribbean controller Bordens Co., San Juan, 1960-61; v.p. fin., treas. Refrigerated Transport Co., Inc., Atlanta, 1975—. Mem. Nat. Acctg. and Fin. Council (chmn. edn. com. So. region, pres.), Am. Inst. C.P.A.s. Home: 2247 Oxbow Circle Stone Mountain GA 30087 Office: 3901 Jonesboro Rd Forest Park GA 30050

GRENGA, HELEN EVA, educator; b. Newnan, Ga., Apr. 11, 1938; d. Angelo and Eva Jane (Kelley) G. A.B., Shorter Coll., 1960; Ph.D. in Chemistry, U. Va., 1967. Postdoctoral fellow Ga. Inst. Tech., Atlanta, 1967, asst. prof. chem. engring., 1968-72, asso. prof., 1972-77, prof., 1977—, asso. dean, 1978—. Contbr. articles to profl. jours. NSF grantee, 1969-70, 71-79; Office of Edn. grantee, 1978—. Mem. Am. Soc. Metals, AIME, Soc. Women Engrs. (council sect. reps. 1975-76, nat. chmn. career info. center and indsl. support 1976-77, exec. com. 1977-79, nat. student activities chmn. 1977-78, nat. sec. 1978-79, nat. 1st v.p. 1980-81, nat. pres. 1981-82), Am. Soc. Engring. Edn., Sigma Xi (pres. 1978-79), Alpha Delta Kappa. Baptist. Home: 6139 Hickory Dr Forest Park GA 30050 Office: Georgia Institute Tech 225 North Ave Atlanta GA 30332

GRENIER, (GEORGE) THOMAS, publisher; b. N.Y.C., July 1, 1938; s. Charles Edard and Helen Treasa (Stoken) G.; m. Vieva Fisher Cristy, May 15, 1965; children. Vieva, Jennifer, Emilie. B.A., Rutgers U., 1961. Media buyer Young & Rubicam, N.Y.C., 1961-63; sales rep. Time, Inc. Life, N.Y.C., 1963-69; account mgr. Downe Communications, N.Y.C., 1969-71; category mgr. Bus. Week, McGraw Hill, N.Y.C., 1971-78; pres. Harper Atlantic Sales, N.Y.C., 1978-81; publisher Conde Nast Pubs., Inc., N.Y.C., 1981—. Mem. Delta Phi (pres. 1960-61). Republican. Presbyterian. Clubs: Baltusrol (Springfeild, N.J.); N.Y. Athletic (N.Y.C.); Essex Hunt (Peapack, N.J.). Home: PO Box 567 Far Hills NJ 07931 Office: Conde Nast Publs 350 Madison Ave New York NY 10017

GRENQUIST, PETER CARL, publisher; b. East Orange, N.J., Feb. 15, 1931; s. Ernst Alexander and Carmela (Anastasia) G.; m. Barbara Ross Krone, Dec. 20, 1967; children: Carl Robert, Louisa Beatrice. B.A., Dartmouth Coll., 1953; M.A., Columbia U., 1957, Ph.D., 1963. Vice pres. Am. Assembly, Columbia U., 1957-62; dir. Spectrum Books, Prentice-Hall, Inc., 1962-70; v.p. coll. div. Prentice-Hall, Inc., 1970-72, corp. v.p., 1972—, pres. Trade Book div., 1972-80; chief exec. officer Arco Pub., Inc. (subs.), 1981—. Served to lt. (j.g.) USNR, 1953-56. Woodrow Wilson fellow, 1956-57. Mem. Phi Beta Kappa, Sigma Nu. Office: Prentice-Hall Inc Englewood Cliffs NJ 07632

GRENVIK, AKE NILS ADOLF, medical educator; b. Sunne, Sweden, July 10, 1929; came to U.S., 1968; s. Anders J. and Elsa M. (Jansson) G.; m. Inger Margareta Valley, May 31, 1952; children: Anders, Monica, Christer, Stefan. B. Medicine, Carolinska Inst., Stockholm, Sweden, 1951, M.D., 1956; Ph.D., U. Uppsala, Sweden, 1966. Diplomate: Am. Bd. Anesthesiology. Docent surgeon U. Uppsala, 1966-68; assoc. prof. anesthesiology U. Pitts. Sch. Medicine, 1970-74, prof., 1975—, prof. surgery, 1981—, dir. critical care medicine Univ.-Health Center, 1980—. Author: Effects fo Respiratory Treatment, 1966; editor: Brain Failure and Resuscitation, 1982, Medico-Legal Aspects of Critical Care Medicine, 1984; book series Clinics in Critical Care Medicine, 1981—. Served to capt. Swedish Air Force, 1960-70. Recipient Cert. of merit Am. Coll. Chest Physicians, 1971, Cert. Appreciation Ministry Pub. Health, Managua, Nicaragua, 1972. Fellow Am. Thoracic Soc., ACP, European Soc. Intensive Care Medicine; mem. Swedish Med. Assn., AMA, Soc. Critical Care Medicine (pres. U.S.A. 1977-78), World Fedn. Soc. of Intensive and Critical Medicine (mem. council, treas. 1981-85). Home: 2629 Thorntree Dr Pittsburgh PA 15241 Office: Presbyn-Univ Hosp 230 Lothrop St Pittsburgh PA 15213

GRESHAM, GLEN EDWARD, physician; b. Ft. Worth, Dec. 1, 1931; s. Perry Epler and Elsie Inez (Stanbrough) G.; m. Phyllis Elaine Kilmer, Nov. 9, 1957; children: Stephen Deane, David Epler, Elizabeth Anne Kilmer, Jennifer Gordon. B.A., Harvard Coll., 1953; M.D., Columbia U., 1958. Intern, Univ. Hosps., Cleve., 1958-59, resident internal medicine, 1959-60, 62-64; asst. prof. preventive medicine Ohio State U., Columbus, 1964-69; asst. prof. medicine Yale U., New Haven, 1969-70; asso. prof. rehab. medicine, medicine and community medicine Tufts U., Boston, 1970-78; prof., chmn. dept. rehab. medicine SUNY-Buffalo, 1978—. Served with USPHS, 1960-62. Nat. Found. fellow rehab., 1962-64; recipient Disting. Service award Mass. Council Orgns. Handicapped, 1972. Fellow ACP; mem. Am. Congress Rehab. Medicine, Am. Rheumatism Assn., Am. Fedn. Clin. Research, Am. Spinal Injury Assn. Congregationalist. Clubs: Harvard (Boston); Saturn (Buffalo). Researcher epidemiology chronic disease, functional assessment. Office: 462 Grider St Buffalo NY 14215

GRESHAM, NEWTON, lawyer; b. Jewett, Tex., July 21, 1905; s. Edward Alexander and Beulah Benton (Selman) G.; m. Mary Frances Stone, July 3, 1933; 1 dau., Susan Frances. A.B., Sam Houston State Tchrs. Coll., 1924; LL.B., U. Tex., 1930. Bar: Tex. 1930. Practiced in Houston; ptnr., counsel to firm Fulbright & Jaworski (and predecessor), 1937—. Mem. bd. regents State Tchrs. Colls. Tex., 1959-65, pres. bd., 1963-65; mem. coordinating bd. Tex. Coll. and Univ. System, 1965-83, vice chmn., 1965-80, chmn., 1983; trustee Killson Ednl. Found., Sam Houston Found. Fellow Am. Bar Found., Am. Coll. Trial Lawyers; mem. Internat. Assn. Ins. Counsel, Fedn. Ins. Counsel, State Bar Tex. (pres. 1956-57), Order of Coif, Phi Delta Phi, Alpha Chi, Alpha Tau Omega. Clubs: Coronado, River Oaks Country (Houston) (pres. 1950). Home: 1935 Olympia Dr Houston TX 77019 Office: 800 Bank of Southwest Bldg Houston TX 77002

GRESHAM, PERRY EPLER, university official, philosophy educator; b. Covina, Cal., Dec. 19, 1907; s. George Edward and Mary Elizabeth (Epler) G.; m. Elsie Stanbrough, Dec. 9, 1926 (dec. Mar. 1947); 1 son, Glen Edward; m. Alice Fickling Cowan, May 6, 1953; 1 dau., Nancy. A.B. summa cum laude, Tex. Christian U., 1931, B.D., 1933, LL.D., 1949; postgrad., U. Chgo., 1932-33, Columbia, 1931-41; Litt.D., Culver-Stockton Coll., 1954, Findlay Coll., U. Cin., 1966, W. Va. U., 1971; L.H.D., Chapman Coll., 1964, Concord Coll.; Ed.D., Transylvania, 1965, Rio Grande Coll.; LL.D., Alderson-Broaddus Coll.; Pd.D., Youngstown U., 1966; D.B.A., Lawrence Inst. Tech., 1973. Prof. philosophy Tex. Christian U., 1936-42; minster U. Christian Ch., Ft. Worth, 1933-42, Seattle, 1942-45, Central Woodward Christian Ch., Detroit, 1945-53; feature writer Detroit Free Press, 1950-52; pres. Bethany (W.Va.) Coll., 1953-72, chmn. bd., 1972-76, distinguished prof. philosophy, 1973—; former adj. prof. U. Wash.; former lectr. U. Mich.; Mem. study com. Commn. on Faith and Order, World Council Chs., 1948-60; pres. W.Va. Found. Colls., 1954-58; mem. clergy industry commn. N.A.M., 1957-65; commn. on liberal edn. Assn. Am. Colls., 1963—; chmn. North Central Assn. Colls. and Univs., 1964-66; pres. Internat. Conv. Christian Chs., 1960-61; dir. emeritus Chesapeake & Potomac Telephone Cos., Cooper Tire and Rubber Co., Findlay, Ohio.; Westbanco Corp., Wheeling Dollar Bank.; Bd. dirs. Found. for Econ. Edn., 1960—, pres., 1983—, chmn. bd., 1966-68; bd. dirs. Lawrence Inst. Tech., Detroit, John A. Hartford Found., N.Y.C. Author: Incipient Gnosticism in the New Testament, 1933, Disciplines of the High Calling, 1954, The Sage of Bethany, 1960, Answer to Conformity, 1961, Abiding Values, 1972, Campbell and the Colleges, 1973, With Wings As Eagles, 1980. Mem. Am. Philos. Soc. Internat. Robert Burns Soc., Internat. Platform Assn., Alpha Chi. Mason (Shriner). Clubs: University (N.Y.C.); Duquesne (Pitts.); Williams Country (Weirton); Rotary (Wheeling); Skytop (Pa.); Royal Scottish (Glasgow); Authors (London). Home: Highland Hearth Bethany WV 26032

GRESHAM, ROBERT COLEMAN, government official; b. Booneville, Miss., Nov. 12, 1917; s. J.F. and Pearl (Bellamy) G.; m. Katherine Wootten, Oct. 8, 1955; children: Robin (Mrs. Keith T. Groseclose), D. Jackson. A.A., Sunflower Coll., Miss., 1938; B.C.S., Southeastern U., Washington, 1942. Spl. agt., exec. FBI, 1938-53; asst. dir. research Council State Chambers Commerce, Washington, 1953-65; Republican staff dir. Ho. Appropriations Com., U.S. Congress, 1965-69; commr. ICC, Washington, 1969—; vice chmn. U.S. Ry. Assn., 1982—. Republican. Episcopalian. Home: PO Box 4524 Silver Spring MD 20904 Office: 12th and Constitution Ave NW Washington DC 20423

GRESOV, BORIS (VLADIMIR), economist; b. St. Petersburg, Russia, Aug 7, 1914; s. Paul Vladimir and Maria (de Suzor) G.; m. Letitia Coxen Graham, June 21, 1945; children: Winston Graham, Christopher Leo. B.A. with honors, Cambridge U., Eng., 1938, M.A., 1952. With Office Econ. Warfare (unit War Prodn. Bd.); prodn. mgr. Compania Nacional Minera de Taxco S.A., Mex., 1941-45; v.p. Industrias y Minas S.A., Mex., 1945-49; cons. economist Shields & Co., N.Y.C., 1949-52, G.H. Walker & Co., 1952-58; dir., mem. exec. com. Western Devel. Co. of Del., Santa Fe, 1954-61; mem., adv. bd. Axe Sci. & Electronics Corp., N.Y.C., 1957-61; cons. economist E.W. Axe & Co., N.Y.C., 1957-61; dir., chmn. bd./chief exec. officer Shattuck Denn Mining Corp., N.Y.C., 1958-60, dir., chmn. exec. com., 1961-66; founder, pres. Excelsior Fund, Inc., N.Y.C., 1963—; chmn. Standard Metals Corp., 1963—, pres., chief exec. officer, 1965—; dir. Flying Tiger Line, Inc., Burbank, Calif., 1957-65, Axe-Templeton Growth Fund of Can., Ltd., N.Y.C., 1958-61, Internat. Oil & Gas Corp., Denver, 1961-66, USLIFE Income fund, Inc., N.Y.C. Mem. Nat. Econ. N.Y., Nat. Economists Club (Washington), N.Y. Soc. Security Analysts, AIM (president's council), N.Y. Assn. Bus. Economists, Union Soc. (Cambridge), Conferie de la Chaine des Rotisseurs (chevalier). Roman Catholic. Clubs: Metropolitan, University, Met Opera (N.Y.C.); L.I. Country (Eastport, N.Y.); Westhampton Country (Westhampton Beach, L.I.); Surf (Quogue, L.I.); La Coquille (Palm Beach, Fla.). Home: 45 E 72d St New York NY 10021 Office: Olympic Tower 645 Fifth Ave New York NY 10022

GRESSAK, ANTHONY RAYMOND, JR., hotel executive; b. Honolulu, Jan. 22, 1947; s. Anthony Raymond and Anne Tavares (Ferreira) G.; m. Catherine Streb, Apr. 11, 1981; children: Danielle Kirsten, Anthony Raymond III. A.A., Utah State U., 1967; postgrad., U.S. Army Inf. Officers Candidate Sch., 1968. Restaurant mgr. Ala Moana Hotel, Honolulu, 1970-72; gen. mgr. Fred Harvey, Inc., Ontario, Calif., 1972-73; regional mgr. So. Calif., 1972-73, regional mgr. tollway ops., 1973; divisional mgr. Normandy Lanes, 1973; resident mgr. Royal Inns of Am., San Diego, 1974; food and beverage dir. Asso. Inns & Restaurant Co. of Am. (Aircoa), Big Sky, Mont., 1974-75; condomium mgr. Big Sky, 1975; asst. gen. mgr. Naples (Fla.) Bath and Tennis Club, 1975-76; food and beverage dir. Nat. Parks, Grand Canyon, Ariz., 1976-77; gen. mgr. Grand Canyon Nat. Park Lodges, 1977-79; divisional v.p. food services The Broadway, Carter Hawley Hale, Inc., Los Angeles, 1979-82; exec. v.p. Silco Corp., Los Angeles, 1982—; maitre de table Chaine des Rotisseurs-Napa Valley. Served with U.S. Army, 1967-70. Decorated Silver Star medal, Bronze Star medal, Purple Heart. Mem. Nat. Restaurant Assn., Les Amis d'Escoffier, Internat. Order DeMolay (life mem., chevalier), Smithsonian Assos., Humane Soc. U.S. Roman Catholic. Club: Industry Hills Country. Home: 17775 Nearbank Dr Rowland Heights CA 91748 Office: 2029 Century Park E Los Angeles CA 90067 *Common sense isn't so common. Self discipline and respect for yourself will achieve success. Strive for perfection and you will attain it. Never give up.*

GRESSENS, ROBERT J., electrical equipment company executive; married. B.S. in Physics, Harvard U.; B.S.E.E., Ill. Inst. Tech. With GTE Products Corp., 1951—; exec. asst. to v.p. mfg. GTE Automatic Electric, 1951-57, mgr. indsl. products, 1957-58; v.p. mfg. GTE Lenkurt, 1958-63, pres., 1963-66; exec. v.p. GTE Automatic Electric, 1966-67, pres., 1967-76, group pres. communications products, 1976-80, corp. v.p., 1980-81; pres., dir. GTE Internat. Inc., Stamford, Conn., 1981—. Office: GTE Internat Inc One Stamford Forum Stamford CT 06904 *

GRESSMAN, EUGENE, lawyer; b. Lansing, Mich., Apr. 18, 1917; s. William Albert and Bess Beulah (Nagle) G.; m. Nan Alice Kirby, Aug. 6, 1944; children: William, Margot and Nancy (twins), Eric. A.B., U. Mich., 1938, J.D. with distinction, 1940. Bar: Mich. 1940, U.S. Supreme Ct. 1945, D.C. 1948, Md. 1959. Atty. SEC, Washington, 1940-43; law clk. to Justice Frank Murphy, U.S. Supreme Ct., 1943-48; partner firm Van Arkel, Kaiser, Gressman, Rosenberg & Driesen, Washington, 1948-77, of counsel, 1977-81, Bredhoff & Kaiser, Washington, 1981—; spl. counsel U.S. Ho. of Reps., 1976—; William Rand Kenan, Jr. prof. law U. N.C., Chapel Hill, 1977—; Disting. vis. prof. Fordham U. Law Sch., 1982-83; vis. prof. law Ohio State U., 1967, Mich. Law Sch., 1969, George Washington U., 1971-77, Ind. U., 1976, Catholic U. Am., 1977; judge Appeal Tax Ct. Montgomery County, Md., 1959-62. Author: (with Robert L. Stern) Supreme Court Practice, 5th edit, 1978, (with Charles A. Wright and others) Federal Practice and Procedure, vol. 16, 1977; contbr. articles to legal jours. Mem. Am. Bar Assn., Fed. Bar Assn., Am. Law Inst., Am. Judicature Soc., D.C. Bar, Order of Coif, Order of Barristers, Phi Beta Kappa. Home: 325 Glendale Dr Chapel Hill NC 27514 Office: Sch Law U NC Chapel Hill NC 27514

GRETEMAN, FRANK HENRY, bishop; b. Willey, Iowa, Dec. 25, 1907; s. Bernard and Mary (Meissner) G. A.B., Loras Coll., 1929; S.T.L., N.Am. Coll., Rome, Italy, 1932; J.C.L., Cath. U., 1937. Asst. pastor St. Augustine Ch., Spokane, Wash., 1933-35; pastor Assumption Ch., Merrill, Iowa, 1937-41, St. Michael's Ch., Sioux City, Iowa, 1941-50, Holy Spirit Ch., Carroll, Iowa, 1950-65; aux. bishop, vicar gen. Sioux City Diocese, 1965-70, bishop, 1970—. Office: PO Box 1530 1821 Jackson St Sioux City IA 51102

GRETHER, DAVID MACLAY, economics educator; b. Phila., Oct. 21, 1938; s. Ewald T. and Carrie Virginia (Maclay) G.; m. Susan Edith Clayton, Mar. 24, 1961; children: Megan Elizabeth, John Clayton. B.S., U. Calif., Berkeley, 1960; Ph.D., Stanford U., 1969. Research staff economist Cowles Found., Yale U., 1966-70; lectr. econs. Yale U., 1966-68, asst. prof., 1968-70; assoc. prof. econs. Calif. Inst. Tech., Pasadena, 1970-75, prof. econs., 1975—, exec. officer for social scis., 1978-82, chmn. Dir. Humanities and Social Scis., 1982—. Author: (with M. Nerlove and J.L. Carvalho) Analysis of Economic Time Series: A Synthesis, 1979; contbr. articles to profl. jours. Mem. Econometric Soc., Am. Statis. Assn., Am. Econ. Assn. Home: 2116 N Craig Ave Altadena CA 91001 Office: Calif Inst Tech Pasadena CA 91125

GRETHER, HENRY MORONI, JR., univ. dean; b. Salt Lake City, Jan. 29, 1920; s. Henry Moroni and Grace (Howell) G.; m. Jane Child, June 16, 1944; children—Deborah, Henry Moroni III, Sharon Elise. B.A., U. Utah, 1943, J.D., 1947; LL.M., U. Minn., 1948. Bar: Nebr. bar 1949, U.S. Supreme Ct. bar 1949. Practiced in, Lincoln, 1949—; instr. law U. Nebr., 1948-51, asst. prof., 1951-54, asso. prof., 1954-57, prof., 1957—, dean, 1966—; asst. atty. gen., Nebr., 1950; spl. atty. Nebr. Rds. and Irrigation, 1954-57; spl. asst. atty. gen., Nebr., 1957-60; minority counsel U.S. Senate Judiciary Com., 1960. Author: Cases and Materials on Water Rights, 1949, Restatement of the Law of Security. Nebraska Annotation, 1950; Contbr. articles to profl. jours. Pres. Cornhusker Dairy Queen, Inc., 1970—; dir. Lincoln Agr. Credit Corp.; trust cons. Union Bank & Trust Co.; arbitrator Fed. Mediation and Conciliation Service; hearing officer FAA; mem. exec. bd. Nebr. State Bar Assn., 1976—; Mem. Lincoln City Zoning Commn., 1950-60; Trustee Rocky Mountain Mineral Law Found.; bd. dirs. Nebr. Continuing Legal Edn. Inc., 1974-77. Served with USAAF, 1943-46. Recipient Outstanding Mem. award Nebr. Bar Assn., 1968. Mem. Nat. Conf. Commrs. Uniform State Laws (Neb. commr.), Am. Law Inst., Am. Bar Assn., Am. Judicature Soc., Am. Arbitration Assn. (nat. labor panel), Am. Legion, Delta Phi, Phi Alpha Delta. Mem. Ch. of Jesus Christ of Latter-day Saints. Club: Elk. Home: 6721 Rexford Dr Lincoln NE 68506

GRETZKY, WAYNE, professional hockey player; b. Brantford, Ont., Can., Jan. 26, 1961; s. Walter and Phyllis G. Center Peterborough Petes, Jr. Ont. Hockey Assn., 1977-78, Sault Ste. Marie Greyhounds, 1977-78, Indpls. Racers, World Hockey Assn., 1978-79, Edmonton Oilers (Alta., Can.), NHL, 1979—. Player NHL All-Star Game, 1980-83; named Rookie of Yr. World Hockey Assn., 1979, Most Valuable Player NHL, 1980-83, Sportsman of Yr. Sports Illus., 1982; recipient Lady Byng Meml. Trophy NHL, 1980. Adress: care Edmonton Oilers Northlands Coliseum Edmonton AB Canada T5B 4M9 *

GREULICH, RICHARD CURTICE, anatomist, gerontologist; b. Denver, Mar. 22, 1928; s. William Walter and Mildred Almena (Libby) G.; m. Betty Brent Mitchell, Dec. 19, 1948 (div. 1955); children: Christopher, Robert; m. Leonora Faye Colleasure, Dec. 27, 1958; children: Jeffrey, Hilary. A.B., Stanford U., 1949; Ph.D. (AEC fellow), McGill U. (Can.), 1953. Instr. Sch. Medicine, UCLA, 1953-55, asst. prof. anatomy, 1955-61, asso. prof. anatomy, 1961-64, prof. anatomy, 1964-66, asso. prof. oral biology Sch. Dentistry, 1961-64, prof. oral biology, 1964-66; sci. dir. Nat. Inst. Dental Research, NIH, Bethesda, Md., 1966-74; acting dir. Nat. Inst. Aging, Bethesda, 1975-76; dir. Gerontology Research Center and sci. dir. Nat. Inst. Aging, Balt., 1976—; staff dir. U.S. Pres.'s Biomed. Research Panel, 1974-75; vis. investigator Karolinska Inst., Stockholm, 1955-57, U. London, 1962-63, McGill U., 1963; vis. prof. anatomy U. Va., 1966-73. Served with F.A., U.S. Army, 1946-48. Recipient award for basic research in oral sci. Internat. Assn. Dental Research, 1963, Superior Service award HEW, 1971; Bank of Am.-Giannini Found. fellow, 1955-57; USPHS spl. fellow, 1962-63. Mem. Am. Assn. Anatomists, Gerontol. Soc., Am. Inst. Biol. Scis., AAAS, Am. Soc. Cell Biology, Sigma Xi. Club: Cosmos (Washington). Research, publs. on growth, differentiation and aging at cellular and organismic level. Office: Gerontology Research Center Balt City Hosps Baltimore MD 21224

GREVELLE, JAMES VERNON, lawyer; b. Waco, Tex., Sept. 2, 1938; s. James and Jimmie Elna (Lee) G.; m. Garnett Dowell Brown, Sept. 15, 1971; children: Garnett Anne, Caroline Elizabeth. B.A., U. Tex., 1961, LL.B., 1963. Bar: Tex. bar 1963, Calif. bar 1968. Asso. firm Baker & Botts, Houston, 1963-67; corp. counsel Teledyne, Inc. (and others), Los Angeles area, 1967-72; partner firm Shank, Irwin, Conant, Williamson & Grevelle, Dallas, 1972-81; pres. James V. Grevelle, P.C., Dallas, 1981. Bd. dirs. Alliance Française, Dallas. Served with AUS, 1964; with Res., 1964-69. Mem. Am., Tex., Calif., Dallas bar assns., Am. Soc. Internat. Law, Dallas Internat. Law Assn., Phi Beta Kappa, Beta Theta Pi. Club: Lancer's (Dallas). Home: 5815 Joyce Way Dallas TX 75225 Office: 8300 Douglas Ave Suite 800 Dallas TX 75225

GREVILLE, THOMAS N(ALL) E(DEN), educator; b. N.Y.C., Dec. 27, 1910; s. Algernon Palgrave Eden and Hermione Rockwell (Nall) G.; m. Esther Christine Bagnall, Sept. 3, 1934 (div. 1950); children: Alice Eden, Edgar Murdock Eden; m. Florence Nusim, July 23, 1951. B.A., U. of South, 1930; M.A., U. Mich., 1932, Ph.D., 1933. Actuarial asst. Acacia Mut. Life Ins. Co., Washington, 1933-37; instr. U. Mich., 1937-40, vis. prof., 1962-63; actuarial mathematician U.S. Bur. Census, 1940-46, USPHS, 1946-52; statis. cons. U.S. Ops. Mission to Brazil, 1952-54; asst. chief actuary U.S. Social Security Adminstrn., 1954-57; chief mathematician U.S. Army Q.M.C., 1957-61; v.p. S.A. Miller Co., Washington, 1961-62; prof. Math. Research Center and Sch. Bus. U. Wis., Madison, 1963-81, prof. emeritus, 1981—; actuarial adviser Nat. Center for Health Statistics, 1973-76; pres. Psychical Research Found., Chapel Hill, N.C., 1980—; Fulbright lectr., Brazil, 1971. Author: United States Life Tables and Actuarial Tables 1939-41, 1946, (with A. Ben-Israel) Generalized Inverses: Theory and Applications, 1974; editor: Theory and Applications of Spline Functions, 1969. Fellow Soc. Actuaries, Am. Statis. Assn.; mem. Inter-Am. Statis. Inst., Parapsychol. Assn.

GREY, ALAN LEWIS, psychoanalyst; b. N.Y.C., May 20, 1919; s. Louis and Rose Edith (Saphir) G.; m. Hilda Aranow, Sept. 15, 1941 (div. June 1982); children: Constance, Daniel. B.S.S., CCNY, 1939; M.A., Columbia U., 1940; Ph.D., U. Chgo., 1949. Pvt. practice psychoanalysis, N.Y.C., 1962—; assoc. prof. Tchrs. Coll. Columbia U., 1951-62; prof. psychology Fordham U., Bronx, 1976—; mem. faculty White Inst., 1976—, Westchester Ctr., 1977—; Fulbright sr. lectr., India, 1970-71, 62-63; pre council on legis. N.Y. State Psychologists, 1956. Editor: Man, Woman and Marriage, 1970, Class and Personality in Society, 1969; cons. editor: Contemporary Psychoanalysis, Psychoanalytic Psychology; contbr. articles to profl. jours. Mem. N.Y. State Psychol. Assn. (sec. treas. 1953-54), Am. Psychol. Assn., Am. Acad. Psychoanalysis, William A. White Psychoanalytic Assn., Am. Group Therapy Assn., Sigma Xi. Home: 147 Mercer Ave Hartsdale NY 10530 Office: Fordham Univ Bronx NY 10468 *Considering the state of my world and my own bumpy past, it seems premature to produce guidelines. I am only age 65 and still trying to figure it all out.*

GREY, JAMES DAVID, clergyman; b. Princeton, Ky., Dec. 18, 1906; s. George Lindsay and Lucy Ann (Keeney) G.; m. Lillian Gaines Tooke, Sept. 16, 1927; children: Martha Ann, Mary Beth. A.B., Union U., Jackson, Tenn., 1929, D.D., 1938; Th.M., Southwestern Bapt. Theol. Sem., Ft. Worth, 1932; LL.D., La. Coll., Pineville, 1952; D.D., Baylor U., 1953. Ordained to ministry Bapt. Ch., 1925; pastor Tabernacle Ch., Ennis, Tex., 1931-34, First Ch., Denton, Tex., 1934-37, New Orleans, 1937-72, emeritus, 1972; minister radio program The Gospel Hour, New Orleans, 1941-72, Bapt. Hour, 1949, 52. Author: Epitaphs for Eager Preachers, 1972; also religious booklets and contbr. to Bapt. periodicals. Bd. dirs. Met. Area Com., New Orleans, 1966—; organizer, bd. dirs. La. Moral and Civic Found., 1943-56, pres., 1953-56; pres. bd. trustees La. Coll., 1960-61; bd. dirs. United Fund Greater New Orleans, Council for a Better La., Salvation Army, gulf states area, Info. Council of Americas; pres. New Orleans Fedn. Chs., 1957; dir. Met. New Orleans Crime Commn.; pres. La. Bapt. Conv., 1948-50, So. Bapt. Conv., 1951-53; mem. Bold Missions Task Force, 1976—; mem. exec. com. Bapt. World Alliance, 1950-70; pres. Met. Crime Commn., New Orleans, 1968-69; mem. La. Commn. on Law Enforcement and Adminstrn. Justice, 1968-70, New Orleans Council on Naval Affairs, State Bd. Corrections, 1971—; bd. dirs. Pratt-Stanton Manor, Inc., So. Bapt. Hosps., Affiliated Bapt. Hosps., So. Bapt. Hosp. Found., Health Care Cons. and Mgmt. Services; adv. bd. Big Bros., New Orleans. Named Ky. col., 1950; Recipient Times-Picayune Loving Cup, 1971; named One of 10 Outstanding Persons, New Orleans Inst. Human Understanding, 1976. Mem. Alpha Tau Omega. Club: Kiwanis (dir. 1946-47). Home: 4524 S Galvez St New Orleans LA 70125 *Men may misjudge your aim, think they have cause to blame; say you are wrong. Go on your quiet way; God is your judge-not they. Fear not, be strong*

GREY, JERRY, aerospace and energy system scientist, publisher; b. N.Y.C., Oct. 25, 1926; s. Abraham and Lillian (Danowitz) G.; m. Florence Maier, 1974; children by previous marriage—Leslie Ann, Jacquelyn Eve. B.S., Cornell U., 1947, M.S., 1949; Ph.D., Calif. Inst. Tech., 1952. Instr. thermodynamics Cornell U., 1947-49; engine devel. engr. Fairchild Co., 1949-50; hypersonic aerodynamicist Guggenheim Aerospace Lab., Pasadena, Calif., 1950-51; sr. engr. Marquardt Co., 1951-52; prof., dir. Nuclear Propulsion Research Lab., Princeton Sch. Engring. and Applied Sci., 1952-67; pres. Greyrad Corp., N.Y.C., 1959-71; adminstr. tech. activities and pub. policy AIAA, 1971-82; pub. Astronautics and Aeronautics, 1982—; pres. Calprobe Corp., 1972-82; chmn. solar adv. panel Office of Tech. Assessment, U.S. Congress, 1974-81; adj. prof. environ. sci. L.I. U., 1976-83; dir. Applied Solar Energy Corp. Editor: (with Vivian Grey) Space Flight Report to the Nation, 1962, The Race For Electric Power, 1972, The Facts of Flight, 1973, (with J.P. Layton) New Space Transportation Systems, 1973, (with Arthur Henderson) Exploration of the Solar System, 1974, Aircraft Fuel Conservation, 1974, (with H. Killian and G. Dugger) Solar Energy for Earth, 1975, Noise, Noise, Noise!, 1975, (with R. Downey and B. Davis) Space: A Resource for Earth, 1976, Space Manufacturing Facilities (Space Colonies), 1975, 77, 79, 81, (with R.L. Salkeld and D. Patterson) Space Transportation: 1980-2000, 1978, (with Martin Newman) Aerospace Technology Transfer to the Public Spector, 1978, Alternative Fuels for Transportation, 1979, Enterprise, 1979, (with Christine Krop) Aerospace Technology and Marine Transport, 1979, Aeronautics in China, 1981, (with Lawrence Hamden) Space Tracking and Data Systems, 1981, Internat. Aerospace Rev., 1982, (with Lawrence Levy) Global Implications of Space Activities, 1982; editor: Beachheads in Space, 1983. Bd. dirs. Scientists Inst. for Pub. Info., 1979—. Served with USNR, 1944-46. Fellow Explorers Club; mem. AIAA (past v.p.), Am. Astronautical Soc. (dir.), ASME, ASTM, Am. Rocket Soc. (past chpt. pres.), Am. Nuclear Soc., IEEE, Internat. Astron. Fedn. (v.p.), Am. Assn. Engring. Socs. (past chmn. coordinating com. on energy), Internat. Acad. Astronautics, Internat. Solar Energy Soc., N.Y. Acad. Sci., Sigma Xi, Tau Beta Pi, Phi Kappa Phi. Address: 1 Lincoln Plaza 250 New York NY 10023

GREY, JOEL, actor; b. Cleve., Apr. 11, 1932; s. Mickey and Grace Katz; m. Jo Wilder, June 29, 1958; children: Jennifer, Jimmy. Litt.D. (hon.), Cleve. State U., 1974. Began stage career in childhood, traveling with father as song and dance man; played, Chez Paris, Chgo., at age 18; N.Y. stage debut in: The Littlest Revue, 1956; appeared with nat. touring co. of: Stop the World; on Broadway in, 1963, Come Blow Your Horn, 1961, Half a Sixpence, 1965, George M, 1969, Harry, Noon and Night, 1965, Marco Polo Sings a Solo, 1977; appeared: on stage in The Grand Tour, 1979; role in: Broadway musical Cabaret, 1966-67, also motion picture, 1972; TV appearances on: Evening at Pops, 1979, others; TV spls. include George M, 1970, Twas the Night Before Christmas, 1974, Jubilee!, 1976, Night of 100 Stars, 1982, The Yeoman of the Guard, 1984; films include About Face, 1952, Calypso Heat Wave, 1957, Come September, 1961; TV appearances on: Man on a Swing, 1974, Buffalo Bill and the Indians, 1975, The Seven Percent Solution, 1976 (Recipient Tony award for performance in Cabaret 1967, Acad. award for best supporting actor in film 1972). Address: care ICM 40 W 57th St New York NY 10019 *

GREY, JOEL STANLEY, apparel company executive; b. Bklyn., Jan. 13, 1938; s. Louis and Florence G.; m. Rochelle Saporta, Oct. 21, 1961; children: Gary, Fredda. Student, Bklyn. Poly. Inst., Rensselaer Poly. Inst.; B.S., Hofstra U., 1961. Partner Parkway Electric Service, Merrick, N.Y.; engr. Dworman Assos. (builders), N.Y.C., Ruby Philite Co., Long Island City; exec. v.p., dir. Russ Togs, Inc., N.Y.C., 1972—. Served to capt. AUS, 1961-63. Office: 1411 Broadway New York NY 10018 *Surround yourself with bright, enthusiastic people who care. Give them credit where it's due and care for them enthusiastically as well. Enthusiasm makes the difference in all endeavors—personal and business*

GREY, JOHN R., oil company executive; b. 1922; married. B.S. in Chem. Engring, Stanford U., 1943. With Standard Oil Co. Am., from 1944, engr., El Segundo, Calif., 1944-57, mgr. Salt Lake Refining Co. subs., 1957-61, v.p. Salt Lake Pipe Line Co. subs., 1961-62, mgr. ops. Richmond refinery, 1962-65, chief engr. Standard Oil Co. Calif., San Francisco, 1965-66, v.p. mfg. Standard-Western Ops., Inc., 1966-69, corp. v.p. Standard Oil Co. Calif., San Francisco, 1969-74, pres., from 1974; dir. Standard Oil Co. Am., also others. Office: care Standard Oil Co Calif 225 Bush St San Francisco CA 94104 *

GREYSER, STEPHEN ABEL, business and marketing educator; b. Boston, Mar. 17, 1935; s. Morris and Gladys (Koven) G.; m. Linda L. Segel, June 30, 1968; 1 dau., Naomi. A.B., Harvard U., 1956, M.B.A. (Chirurg Advt. fellow), 1958, D.B.A., 1965. Radio-TV producer O'Leary Advt., Boston, 1952-58; research asst., research assoc. Harvard Bus. Sch., 1958-61, asst. prof., 1966-68, assoc. prof., 1968-72, prof. bus. adminstrn., 1972—; asst. editor, research dir. Harvard Bus. Rev., 1961-66, sec. editorial bd., 1966—; exec. dir. Mktg. Sci. Inst., Cambridge, Mass., 1972-80, trustee, 1972—; Disting. lectr. mktg. York U., Toronto, Ont., 1974, U. Western Ont., 1975, U. Houston, 1979; Kellwood lectr. Washington U., St. Louis, 1980; dir. Doyle Dane Bernbach Internat. Inc.; faculty prin. Mgmt. Analysis Center, Cambridge, 1968—; co-chmn. Penney Consumer Affairs Forum, 1975, 79; Bd. dirs. Advt. Research Found., 1977—; trustee Arts Adminstrn. Research Inst., 1966—; chmn. Internat. Research Seminar in Mktg., 1978; mem. acad. adv. bd. Am. Assn. Advt. Agys. Ednl. Found., 1978—, chmn., 1981—. Author: (with R.A. Bauer) Advertising in America: The Consumer View, 1968, (with E.C. Bursk) Advanced Cases in Marketing Management, 1968, (with T.C. Raymond and D. Schwalbe) Cases in Arts Administration, 1970, Cases in Advertising and Communications Management, 2d edit, 1981, (with E.C. Bursk) Cases in Marketing Management, 1975, (with J.G. Myers and W. Massy) Marketing Research and Knowledge Development—An Assessment for Marketing Management, 1980; author: (with R. Young) Managing Cooperative Advertising: A Strategic Approach, 1983; editor: Toward Scientific Marketing, 1964, Cultural Policy and Arts Administration, 1973, Understanding and Meeting Consumerism's Challenges, 1975, Advertising: Better Planning, Better Results, 1980; mem. editorial bd.: Jour. Mktg, 1969-74, 76—. Am. Assn. Advt. Agy. Ednl. Found. grantee, 1969-71. Mem. Am. Mktg. Assn. (nat. dir. 1967-69, pres. Boston chpt. 1964-65), Am. Acad. Advt. (regional dir. 1964-67, nat. pres. 1972-74, chmn. 1974-76), Assn. for Consumer Research (mem. adv. bd. 1974-81), Am. Assn. for Pub. Opinion Research., Market Research Council. Club: Harvard (Boston). Home: 46 Campbell Rd Wayland MA 01778 Office: Harvard Bus Sch Morgan 343 Soldiers Field Boston MA 02163

GREYTAK, THOMAS JOHN, physics educator; b. Annapolis, Md., Mar. 24, 1940; s. John Joseph and Cecilia Felicia (Schwartz) G.; m. Elizabeth Ann Bardeen, June 25, 1966; children: Andrew Bardeen, Matthew Bardeen. S.B., M.I.T., 1963, M.S., 1963, Ph.D., 1967. Instr. M.I.T., Cambridge, 1967, asst. prof. physics dept., 1967-70, assoc. prof., 1970-77, prof., 1977—; vis. scientist physics dept. U. Calif., San Diego, 1972-73. Alfred P. Sloan Research fellow., 1971-73. Fellow Am. Phys. Soc. Home: 29 Acacia Ave Chestnut Hill MA 02167 Office: Mass Inst Tech Room 13-2074 Cambridge MA 02139

GRIBBON, DANIEL MCNAMARA, lawyer; b. Youngstown, Ohio, Jan. 27, 1917; s. James Edward and Loretta (Hogan) G.; m. Jane Retzler, Sept. 13, 1941; children: Diana Jane Gribbon Motz, Deborah Ann Gribbon Alt. A.B., Western Res. U., 1938; J.D., Harvard U., 1941. Bar: D.C. 1946. Law clk. Judge Learned Hand, 1941-42; asso. firm Covington & Burling, Washington, 1946-50, partner, 1950—; dir. 1st Am. Bank N.A. Served with USN, 1942-46; to lt. comdr. Res. Fellow Am. Bar Found.; mem. Am. Coll. Trial Lawyers, D.C. Bar Assn. (chmn. bd. profl. responsibility 1976—). Roman Catholic. Clubs: Metropolitan, Chevy Chase, City Tavern; Harvard (N.Y.C.). Home: 4655 Hawthorne Ln Washington DC 20016 Office: 1201 Pennsylvania Ave NW Washington DC 20004

GRIBBS, ROMAN S., judge, former mayor of Detroit; b. Detroit, Dec. 29, 1925; s. Roman and Magdeline (Widziszewski) Grzyb; m. Katherine Stratis, June 12, 1954; children: Paula, Carla, Christopher, Rebecca, Elizabeth. B.S. magna cum laude, U. Detroit, 1952, LL.D., 1954. Bar: Mich. 1954. Tchr. law and acctg. U. Detroit, 1953-56; asst. pros. atty., Wayne County, Mich., 1956-64; pvt. practice law Shaheen, Gribbs & Shaheen, 1964-66; presiding referee Traffic Ct., 1966-68; sheriff, Wayne County, 1968-69, mayor of, Detroit, 1970-73; partner firm Fenton, Nederlander, Dodge, Barris & Gribbs, 1974; adj. prof. U. Mich., 1974; dir. Bank of Commonwealth, 1974—; judge Wayne County Circuit Ct., 1975-82, chief judge pro tem, 1980-82; judge Mich. Ct. Appeals, 1983—; Mem. Presdl. Commn. CD Adv. Commn., 1970-74. Trustee U. Detroit, 1974—. Served as sgt. AUS, World War II. Mem. Nat. League of Cities (pres. 1973), Mich. Judges Assn. (dir. 1978—), U.S. Conf. Mayors (trustee), Mich. Conf. Mayors (pres.), Delta Sigma Phi, Blue Key. Democrat. Roman Catholic.

GRICE, HARWOOD VINSON, banker; b. Dallas, Aug. 15, 1915; s. Harwood Newman and Ada May (Vinson) G.; m. Elsie Irene Grice, Mar. 12, 1976; children by previous marriage—Harwood Vinson, Edward Cowan. B.S. with honors, So. Meth. U., 1935. Asst. v.p. Republic Nat. Bank, Dallas, 1934-48; with United Calif. Bank, Los Angeles, 1948—, sr. v.p., 1959-63, exec. v.p., 1963-74, vice chmn., 1974-77. Served to lt. (s.g.) USNR, 1942-45. Mem. Robert Morris Assos., Mchts. and Mfrs. Assn. (dir.), Lambda Chi Alpha, Beta Gamma Sigma, Phi Eta Sigma, Alpha Theta Phi. Methodist. Clubs: Wilshire Country, Stock Exchange. Home: 5355 Alta Bahia Ct San Diego CA 92109

GRICH, ROBERT ANTHONY, baseball player; b. Muskegon, Mich., Jan. 15, 1949. Student, UCLA, Fresno State U. Infielder with Balt. Orioles, 1970-76, Calif. Angels, 1977—; mem. Am. League All-Star Team, 1972, 74, 76, 79, 80, 82. Named to Sporting News Am. League All-Star Team, 1976, 81. Office: Calif Angels 2000 State College Blvd Anaheim CA 92806 *

GRIDER, GEORGE WILLIAM, lawyer; b. Memphis, Oct. 1, 1912; s. John McGavock and Marguerite (Samuels) G.; m. Ann Elizabeth Curlin, June 18, 1936; children: George William, Gail Ann (Mrs. James Gurley), Sally Elizabeth (Mrs. Morton Weiss), Wilson Northcross. Student, Southwestern at Memphis, 1931-32; B.S., U.S. Naval Acad., 1936; LL.B., U. Va., 1950. Bar: Tenn. 1949, N.Y., U.S. Supreme Ct. Commd. ensign USN, 1936, advanced through grades to capt., 1947; ret., 1947, practice in, Memphis, 1950-64; v.p., sec., gen. counsel Carborundum Co., Niagara Falls, N.Y., 1967-75; pres. Niagara River White Waters Tours, 1972-75; partner firm Apperson, Crump, Duzane & Maxwell, Memphis, 1975—; Mem. 89th Congress from Tenn. Author: (with Lydel Sims) War Fish, 1958. Chmn. Travelers Aid Soc., Memphis, 1950-52; mem. pres.'s adv. bd. Southwestern at Memphis, 1955-64; mem. Memphis and Shelby County Planning Commn., 1958-60, Shelby County Quar. Ct., 1960-64; chmn. Memphis and Shelby County chpt. ARC, 1960-62; chmn. USO, Memphis, 1952-58, nat. bd. dirs., 1956-66; trustee Memphis Acad. Arts, 1975—, LeMoyne-Owen Coll., Memphis, 1975—; chmn. LeMoyne-Owen Coll., 1980-82; bd. visitors U.S. Naval Acad., 1967-82. Decorated Navy Cross, Silver Star medal, Bronze Star medal; recipient Citizen of Year award Memphis Newspaper Guild, 1962. Mem. Raven Soc., Phi Delta Phi, Omicron Delta Kappa. Democrat. Methodist. Clubs: Rotary, Engrs. (Memphis). Home: 235 Windover Grove Memphis TN 38111 Office: 100 N Main Bldg Suite 2610 Memphis TN 38103

GRIDER, JOSEPH KENNETH, theology educator, writer; b. Madison, Ill., Oct. 22, 1921; s. William Sanford and Elizabeth Mary (Krone) G.; m. Virginia Florence Ballard, July 4, 1942; children: Linda Lucille (dec.), Jennifer Elizabeth, Joseph Kenneth II, Carol Christine. Th.B., Olivet Nazarene Coll., Kankakee, Ill., 1944, A.B., 1945; M.D., Nazarene Theol. Sem., Kansas City, Mo., 1947; M.Div. summa cum laude, Drew U., Madison, N.J., 1948, M.A., 1950; Ph.D., Glasgow U., Scotland, 1952; student, Oxford U., Eng., 1964. Ordained to ministry Ch. of the Nazarene, 1944, pastor, Wilmington, Ill., 1944-45, Federated Ch., Kingston, Mo., 1945-47, Methodist Circuit, Colesville, N.J., 1948-50, Nazarene Mission, Glasgow, 1951-52; tutor in systematic theology, Bibl. lit. and Greek Hurlet Nazarene Coll., Glasgow, 1950-52; assoc. prof. theology Pasadena Coll., Calif., 1952-53, Nazarene Theol. Sem., Kansas City, 1953-64, prof., 1964—. Author: books Repentance Unto Life, 1964, Taller My Soul, 1965, Commentary on Ezekiel, 1966, Commentary on Zechariah, 1969, Commentary on Daniel and Ezekial, 1968; translator: New International Version of the Bible, 1978; assoc. editor: Beacon Dictionary of Theology, 1984; contrb. articles to encys., jours., chpts. in books. Named Alumnus of Yr. Olivet Nazarene Coll., 1966. Mem. Wesleyan Theol. Soc., Kansas City Soc. Theol. Studies. Democrat. Club: Kansas City Breakfast (sec.). Office: Nazarene Theol Seminary 1700 E Meyer St Kansas City MO 64131

GRIEBEL, PAUL GUNTHNER, tractor company executive; b. Goldlauther, Thuringen, Germany, Dec. 20, 1919; s. Arnold and Lydia (Stormer) G.; m. Elizabeth Weiss, Oct. 18, 1942; children: Paul,

Paulette, Melissa. B.S.M.E., Ill. Inst. Tech., 1942; Dr.Engr. hon., S.D. Sch. Mines and Tech., 1974. Trainee Caterpillar Tractor Co., Peoria, Ill., 1942, staff and supr. in tng. mfg. and planning supt. factory, 1959, asst. factory mgr., 1960, planning mgr., 1963, asst. dir. European mfg., 1965, facilities planning mgr., 1967, personnel devel. mgr., 1970, labor relations mgr., 1973, v.p. employee relations, 1980—. Mem. Conf. Bd. Adv. Council on Mgmt. and Personnel Research, N.Y.C., 1980—. Mem. Labor Policy Assn. (dir.), Machinery and Allied Products Inst. Club: Country of Peoria. Office: 100 NE Adams Peoria IL 61629

GRIEBEL, RICHARD H., corp. exec.; b. Liberty, N.Y., Apr. 4, 1924; s. Joseph F. and Libbie R. (Henry) G.; m. Elaine A. Gretzkowski, Jan. 26, 1946; children—R. Nelson, Douglas M., Barbara E. A.B., Dartmouth, 1946; postgrad., Columbia, 1946; Grad., Exec. Devel. Program, Ind. U., 1956. With RCA, 1946-53, ITT Farnsworth Electric Co., 1953-58, Raytheon Co., 1958-59; v.p. ITT, 1960-62, also pres.; group exec. Comml. Telecommunications group and pres., gen. mgr. Kellogg Switchboard & Supply Co.; pres., chmn. bd., dir. Fairbanks, Morse and Co., N.Y.C., 1963-67; v.p., dir. Fairbanks Whitney Corp., N.Y.C., 1963-64; v.p., group exec., dir. Colt Industries, Inc., 1964-67; chmn. bd. Canadian Locomotive Co., Ltd., Kingston, Ont., Can., 1963-67, Pratt & Whitney Machine Tool Co., Hartford, Conn., 1963-64, Colt Firearms Co., Hartford, 1963-64; pres., chief exec. officer, dir. P. Ballantine & Sons, 1967-69, Lehigh Valley Industries, Inc., 1969-72, chmn. bd., 1972-73; pres. Tassaway, 1973-77; mgr. 1st Found. Capital Corp., 1974-77, Allied Investment Co., 1977—; overseer Hanover Inn, Hanover, N.H., 1968-79; dir. Panelgraphic Corp., West Caldwell, N.J.; pvt. investment cons. Served to capt. USMCR, 1942-46, 51-52. Mem. Am. Inst. Indsl. Engrs., Am. Soc. Tool Mfg. Cos., Am. Soc. Naval Engrs., Assn. U.S. Army, Armed Forces Communications and Electronics Assn., Nat. Def. Transp. Assn. (dir.), Am. Ordnance Assn. Clubs: Rockaway River Country (Denville, N.J.) (pres. 1976-80); Union League (N.Y.C.)). Home: Claridge House II Apt 8HE Verona NJ 07044 Office: 122 E 42d St New York NY 10017

GRIEFEN, JOHN ADAMS, artist, educator; b. Worcester, Mass., Nov. 24, 1942; s. Robert John and Faith (Adams) G.; m. Paulette Joy Hunsicker, Sept. 27, 1970; 1 dau., Katherine Abigail Jacqueline. Student, Chgo. Art Inst., 1964-65, Bennington Coll., 1965-66; B.A., Williams Coll., 1966; postgrad., Hunter Coll., 1966-68. Instr. Bennington Coll., 1968-69, Great Neck Adult Edn., N.Y., 1971-76. One-man shows, Kornblee Gallery, 1969, 70, 73, one- man shows, Deitcher O'Reilly Gallery, N.Y.C., one-man shows, William Edward O'Reilly Inc., N.Y.C., Martha Jackson Gallery, N.Y.C., Frnak Watters Gallery, N.Y.C., 1979, Salander O'Reilly Galleries, N.Y.C., 1981, 82, 84, Harcus-Hrakow Gallery, Boston, Phyllis Kind Galley, Chgo., B.R. Kornblatt Gallery, Balt., Diane Brown Gallery, Washington, 1978, Sunne Savage Gallery, Boston, 1979, Frank Watters Gallery, Sydney, Australia, Williams Coll. Mus. Art, Williamstown, Mass., 1980, Martin Gerard Gallery, Edmonton, Alta., Can., 1981, Gallery Moos Ltd., Toronto and Calgary, exhibited group shows, Indpls. Mus. Art, Phoenix Mus., Sydney Mus., Whitney Mus. Purdue U., N.Y. Mus. Modern Art, exhibitied group shows, Santa Barbara Mus., exhibited group shows, Boston Mus. Fine Arts, represented in pub. collections, Larry Aldrich Mus. Contemporary art, represnented in pub. collections, Allen Art Mus., represented in pub. collections, Arthur A. Anderson Co., represented in pub collections, Bank of Ill., represented in pub. collections, Calary (Can.), represented in pub. collections, Boston Mus. Fine Arts, Bklyn. Mus., represented in pub. collections, Carnegie Inst. Mus. Art, represented in pub collections, Chase Manhattan Bank, represented in pub. collections, Continental Resources Inc., Hines Indsl., represented inpub. collections, Boston, represented in pub. collections, N.Y.C., Washington, Dallas, Hirshhorn Mus. and Sculpture Garden, Washington, Met. Mus. Art, Michner Collections-U. Tex., Musnson-William-Proctor Art Inst., Mus. Modern Art, Newark Mus. Fine Arts, Reader's Digest Assn. Inc., Rose Art Mus., Brandeis U., Rothmans Art Gallery, St. Lawrence U., Sydney Mus., Australia, Whitney Mus., Williams Coll. Art Mus., Worcester Mus. Art, Mass. Home: 57 Laight St New York NY 10013 Home: Box 109 RD 2 Greenwich NY 12834

GRIEM, MELVIN LUTHER, educator, physician; b. Milw., May 22, 1925; s. Milton E. and Breta (Luther) G.; m. Sylvia Marie Fudzinski, Aug. 25, 1951; children—Katherine Leslie, Robert Corbin, Melanie Elizabeth. B.S., U. Wis., 1948, M.S., 1950, M.D., 1953. Intern U. Kan. Med. Center, 1953-54; resident U. Chgo. Clinics, 1954-57; mem. faculty U. Chgo., 1957—; prof., dir. Chgo. Tumor Inst., 1967—; cons. Argonne (Ill.) Nat. Lab., 1967—; Mem. cancer research tng. com. Nat. Cancer Inst., 1969-72; chmn. radiation study sect. HEW, 1977-79; mem. med. adv. bd. Nuclear Regulatory Commn., 1980—. Editorial bd.: Jour. Radiation Research, 1971-73, Jour. Radiology, 1969—, Jour. Investigative Radiology, 1973—; Contbr. articles to profl. jours. Commr. Ogden Dunes (Ind.) Water Dept., 1960-68; Bd. dirs. Am. Cancer Soc. Ill., 1971—. Served with AUS, 1943-45. Am. Cancer Soc. advanced clin. fellow, 1957-60; recipient Career Research Devel. award Nat. Cancer Inst., 1963-67. Mem. Am. Soc. Therapeutic Radiologists (chmn. edn. com. 1968-70), Radiol. Soc. N.Am. (program com. 1969-73). Club: Quadrangle (Chgo.). Home: Box 453 Ogden Dunes IN 46368 Office: 950 E 59th St Chicago IL 60637

GRIER, HERBERT EARL, scientist, consultant; b. Chgo., July 3, 1911; s. Herbert Earl and Martha (Sleeter) G.; m. Dorothy Jean Whitcomb, Sept. 5, 1954; children: Herbert Earl III, Joan, David Louis. B.S., MIT, 1933, M.S., 1934; D.Sc. (hon.), U. Nev., 1967. Elec. engr. Mass. Inst. Tech., 1934-47; founder, sr. v.p., pres., dir. EG&G, Boston and Las Vegas, 1947-76; pres. CER Geonuclear Corp., Las Vegas, 1965-76, now dir.; dir. AVX Corp.; Pres. So. Nev. Indsl. Found., 1965-66; chmn. nat. adv. bd. Desert Research Inst. of U. Nev., 1965-76; chmn. aerospace safety adv. panel NASA, 1973-81, mem., 1981—, Nev. Bd. Registered Profl. Engrs. Vice pres., trustee Nev. So. U. Land Found., 1967-77. Recipient Certificate of Appreciation Sec. Army, 1954, NASA Pub. Service medal, 1981. Mem. MIT Alumni Assn. Research in ultra high-speed photography and devel. of stroboscopic and flash lighting techniques, atomic weapons. Office: 2223 Avenida de la Playa Suite 304 La Jolla CA 92037

GRIER, JOSEPH WILLIAMSON, JR., lawyer; b. Charlotte, N.C., Aug. 5, 1915; s. Joseph Williamson and Beulah Mae (Wallace) G.; m. Catherine Langdon Smart, Oct. 28, 1949; children—Joseph Williamson, III, Catherine Witherspoon, Susan Grier Phillips, Roy Smart, Bruce Taliaferro, Robin Wallace. A.B. in Econs, U. N.C., Chapel Hill, 1937; J.D., Harvard U., 1940. Bar: N.C. bar 1940, U.S. Supreme Ct. bar 1947. Law clk. 4th Circuit Ct. Appeals, 1941-42; practiced law, Charlotte, 1946—; sr. partner firm Grier, Parker, Poe, Thompson, Bernstein, Gage and Preston, 1946—; chmn. Charlotte Charter Revision Com.; vice chmn. Charlotte-Mecklenburg Consol. Commn. Mem. N.C. Bd. Higher Edn., 1964-65; chmn. bd. trustees Queens Coll., Charlotte, 1974—; chmn. permanent jud. commn. Presbyterian Ch., 1966-71; chmn. Charlotte Parks and Recreation Commn., 1959-63. Served with U.S. Army, 1942-45. Decorated Bronze Star; recipient Man of Yr. award Civitan Club of Charlotte, 1967. Mem. N.C. Bar Assn. (bod. govs., v.p.), ABA, Am. Judicature Soc., 26th Jud. Dist. Bar Assn. (pres.), Am. Legion (dept. comdr. N.C. 1948-49), Phi Delta Theta. Democrat. Clubs: Charlotte Country, Charlotte City. Home: 1869 Queens Rd W Charlotte NC 28207 Office: 1100 Cameron-Brown Bldg Charlotte NC 28204

GRIES, DAVID JOSEPH, computer science educator; b. Flushing, N.Y., Apr. 26, 1939; s. Konrad and Anne (Zeeb) G.; m. Elaine White, Nov. 26, 1961; children: Paul Christian, Susan Norene. B.S., Queens Coll., 1960; M.S., U. Ill., 1963; Dr. rer. nat., Munich Tech. U., W.Ger., 1966. Mathematician, programmer U.S. Naval Weapons Lab., Dahlgren, Va., 1960-62; tech. asst. Munich Tech. U., 1963-66; asst. prof. computer sci. Stanford U., Palo Alto, Calif., 1966-69; asst. prof. Cornell U., Ithaca, N.Y., 1969-73, assoc. prof., 1973-77, prof., 1977—, chmn. dept. computer sci., 1982—. Author: Compiler Construction for Digital Computers, 1971, (with Richard Conway) Introduction to Programming, 1973, The Science of Programming, 1981; editor: Programming Methodology, 1978; text and monograph series, 1975—; editorial bd.: Acta Informatica, 1972—, IFIP (Jour. Internat. Fedn. Info. Processing), 1976—. Guggenheim fellow, 1983-84. Mem. Asn. Computing Machinery (Best Paper in Systems and Programming award 1977). Home: 112 Glenside Rd Ithaca NY 14850 Office: Dept Computer Sci Cornell U Ithaca NY 14853

GRIES, GEORGE ALEXANDER, biology educator; b. Cambridge, Mass., May 2, 1917; s. John Mathew and Ethel (Goff) G.; m. Mary Lou Carpenter, May 26, 1939; children: James C., Judy L. A.B., Miami U., Oxford, Ohio; M.S., Kans. State U., 1940; Ph.D., U. Wis., 1942. Asst. plant pathologist Conn. Agr. Expt. Sta., 1942-45; asso. prof., then prof. plant physiology Purdue U., 1945-60; research demonstrator U. Wales, Swansea, 1957-58; prof. plant pathology, head dept. U. Ariz., 1960-66, prof. head biol. scis., 1966-68; dean arts and scis. Okla. State U., Stillwater, 1968-80, Service prof., 1981-82; Mem. Commn. Edn. in Agr. and Natural Resources, 1961-69, Commn. Undergrad. Edn. in Biol. Scis., 1969-71; cons. evaluator Commn. Instns. Higher Edn. North Central Assn. Colls. and Schs., 1968-83. Contbr. articles to profl. jours. Mem. commn. on arts and scis. Nat. Assn. State Univs. and Land-Grant Colls. Recipient Silver Beaver award Boy Scouts Am. Mem. Am. Phytopathol. Soc. (councillor-at-large 1966-68), Am. Inst. Biol. Sci. (governing bd. 1968-74, exec. com. 1973-78, chmn. edn. com. 1974-76, pres. 1977), Bot. Soc. Am., Nat. Assn. Coll. Tchrs. Agr., Phi Beta Kappa, Sigma Xi, Phi Kappa Phi, Phi Sigma. Presbyterian. Home: 501 Ocotillo Pl NBU 4603 Green Valley AZ 85614

GRIES, JOHN PAUL, geologist; b. Washington, June 7, 1911; s. John Matthew and Ethel Martha (Goff) G.; m. Virginia Overbeck, July 5, 1933; children—John Charles, Donald Alan. A.B., Miami U., Ohio, 1932; M.S., U. Chgo., 1933, Ph.D., 1935. Geologist Ill. Geol. Survey, 1935-36; from instr. to asst. prof. geology S.D. Sch. Mines and Tech., Rapid City, 1936-44; from asso. prof. to prof., 1946—, dir. grad. studies, 1951-66, dean grad. div., 1966-76; geologist Magnolia Petroleum Co., Midland, Tex., 1944-46; now geol. cons. in groundwater, engrng. geology non-metallics, mineral fuels. Participant Am. Geol. Inst., Internat. Field Inst., Paris Basin, summer 1965. Contbr. articles to profl. jours. Mem. Geol. Soc. Am., Am. Inst. Mining, Metall. and Petroleum Engrs., Am. Assn. Petroleum Geologists, Paleontol. Soc., Rapid City Astron. Soc. (treas.), Sigma Xi, Sigma Tau. Club: Rotary. Home: 238 St Charles St Rapid City SD 57701

GRIESA, THOMAS POOLE, U.S. district judge; b. Kansas City, Mo., Oct. 11, 1930; s. Charles Henry and Stella Lusk (Bedell) G.; m. Christine Pollard Meyer, Jan. 5, 1963. A.B. cum laude, Harvard U., 1952; LL.B., Stanford U., 1958. Bar: Wash. 1958, N.Y. 1960. Atty. Justice Dept., 1958-60; with firm Symmers, Fish & Warner, N.Y.C., 1960-61, Davis Polk & Wardwell, 1961-72, partner, 1970-72; judge U.S. Dist. Ct. So. Dist. N.Y., 1972—. Mem.: Stanford Law Rev., 1956-58. Bd. visitors Stanford Law Sch., 1982-84. Served to lt. (j.g.) USCGR, 1952-54. Mem. ABA, Bar Assn. City N.Y. Christian Scientist. Clubs: Union, Harvard (N.Y.C.). Office: US Ct House Foley Sq New York NY 10007

GRIESE, ROBERT ALLEN, football player; b. Evansville, Ind., Feb. 3, 1945. B.S., Purdue U., 1967. Quarterback with Miami Dolphins, 1967-81; mem. Am. Football League All-Star Team, 1967-68; played in Pro Bowl, 1970-71, 73-74, 77, 78. Author: (with Gale Sayers) Offensive Football, 1972. Named Sporting News AFC Player of Year, 1971, Sporting News AFC All-Star Team, 1970, 71, 73. Office: care Miami Dolphins 330 Biscayne Blvd Bldg Miami FL 33132 *

GRIESEMER, ALLAN DAVID, museum executive; b. Mayville, Wis., Aug. 13, 1935; s. Raymond John and Leone Emma (Fisher) G.; m. Nancy Jean Sterenberg, June 6, 1959; children: David, Paul, Steven. A.B., Augustana Coll., 1959; M.S., U. Wis., 1963; Ph.D., U. Nebr., 1970. Curator; coordinator ednl. services U. Nebr., Lincoln State Museum, 1965-77, assoc. prof., assoc. dir., 1977-79, acting dir., 1980-81, assoc. dir. and coordinator, 1981-82, interim dir., 1982—; mem. faculty dept. geology U. Nebr., Lincoln, 1968-80; lectr. in geology U. Nebr., Lincoln State Mus., 1968-80. Contbr. articles to sci. jours., mus. publs., 1965—. Recipient Hon. award Sigma Gamma Epsilon, 1958; grantee in field. Mem. Paleontol. Soc., Nebr. Mus. Conf. (pres. 1976-79), Nebr. Geol. Soc., Nebr. Acad. Scis., Mountain Plains Conf., Mountain Plains Mus. Assn. (pres. 1979), Am. Assn. Museums (v.p. 1983). Lutheran. Home: 2112 Harrison Ave Lincoln NE 68502 Office: U Nebr State Museum 14th and U Sts Lincoln NE 68588

GRIEVE, PIERSON MACDONALD, specialty chemicals company executive; b. Flint, Mich., Dec. 5, 1927; s. P.M. and Margaret (Leamy) G.; m. Florence R. Brogan, July 29, 1950; children: Margaret, Scott, Bruce. B.S. in Bus. Adminstrn., Northwestern U., 1950; postgrad., U. Minn., 1955-56. With Caterpillar Tractor Co., Peoria, Ill., 1950-52; staff engr. A.T. Kearney & Co. (mgmt. consultants), Chgo., 1952-55; pres. Rap-in-Wax, Mpls., 1955-62; exec. AP Parts Corp., 1962-67; pres., chief exec. officer Questor Corp. (formerly Dunhill Internat. Inc.), Toledo, 1967-81; cons, entrepreneur in venture capital, 1981-82; chmn. bd., chief exec. officer Econ. Lab., St. Paul, 1983—. Adv. council J.L. Kellogg Grad. Sch. Mgmt., Northwestern U.; bd. overseers Sch. Mgmt., U. Minn.; bd. dirs. Guthrie Theatre, St. Paul Chamber Orch. Served with USNR, 1945-46. Mem. Chevaliers du Tastevin; Mem. Beta Gamma Sigma (bd. dirs.). Episcopalian. Clubs: St. Paul Athletic; Minnesota, Pool and Yacht (St. Paul); Economic (N.Y.C.). Office: ECONOMICS LABORATORY INC OSBORN BLDG Saint Paul MN 55102

GRIEVES, ROBERT BELANGER, engineering educator; b. Evanston, Ill., Oct. 15, 1935; s. Roy and Marie (Belanger) G.; m. Sandra Lee Artman, Dec. 10, 1966; children: Christopher Robert, Jaime Robert. B.A. in Russian, Northwestern U., 1956, M.S. in Chem. Engrng, 1959, Ph.D., 1961. Asst. prof. civil engrng. Northwestern U., Evanston, 1961-63; from asst. prof. to asso. prof. civil and environmental engrng. Ill. Inst. Tech., Chgo., 1963-67; prof., chmn. chem. engrng. dept. U. Ky., Lexington, 1967-79, dir. Ky. Water Resources Research Inst., 1973-82, assoc. dean adminstrn., grad. programs and research coll. Engrng., 1976-82; dean Coll. Engrng., prof. civil engrng. U. Tex.-El Paso, 1982—; cons. to industry in air and water pollution control. Author articles on phys.-chem. separations, indsl. waste treatment. Mem. Am. Inst. Chem. Engrs., Water Pollution Control Fedn., Phi Beta Kappa, Sigma Xi, Tau Beta Pi. Home: 705 Cresta Mira Dr El Paso TX 79912

GRIFFEN, CLYDE CHESTERMAN, historian; b. Sioux City, Iowa, July 29, 1929; s. Clyde Rumbaugh and Rosanna Susan (Chesterman) G.; m. Sarah Goldsborough Donoho, Feb. 14, 1959; children: John Winslow, Sarah Bolling, Robert Henry. B.A., State U. Iowa, 1952; M.A., Columbia U., 1953, Ph.D., 1960. Lectr. Columbia U., N.Y.C., 1954-57; instr. history Vassar Coll, Poughkeepsie, N.Y., 1957-61, asst. prof., 1961-67, asso. prof., 1967-75, Lucy Maynard Salmon prof. Am. history, 1975—, chmn. dept. history, 1982—, dir. Am. culture program, 1977-79. Author: (with Sally Griffen) Natives and Newcomers: The Ordering of Opportunity in Mid-Nineteenth-Century Poughkeepsie, 1978. NSF grantee, 1973-74; Nat. Humanities Inst. fellow, 1976-77. Mem. Am. Hist. Assn., Orgn. Am. Historians, Social Sci. History Assn. (editorial bd. 1976—). Home: 9 MacCracken Ln Poughkeepsie NY 12601 Office: Dept History Vassar Coll Poughkeepsie NY 12601

GRIFFEN, WILLIAM BEDFORD, anthropologist; b. Los Angeles, Jan. 30, 1928; s. Bedford Baxter and Glayds Dudley (MacClatchie) G.; m. Joyce Olive Jones, Aug. 28, 1964; 1 dau. by previous marriage, Cynthia Ann. B.A., Whittier Coll., 1951; M.A., Mexico City Coll., 1955; Ph.D. (U.S. Steel Found. fellow), U. Ariz., 1965. Export clk. Gen. Paint Corp., San Francisco, 1952; asst. mgr. Pintura Gen., Panama City, Panama, 1953; historian St. Augustine (Fla.) Hist. Soc., 1957-59; asst. dir. Sch. Inter-Am. Studies, U. Fla., 1959-60; asst. prof. anthropology No. Ariz. U., 1964-66, asso. prof., 1966-68, 71-76, prof., 1976—, chmn. dept. anthropology, 1965-68, 71—; asso. prof. St. Louis U., 1968-71; cons. Ariz. Commn. Indian Affairs, 1966-68. Author: Culture Change and Shifting Populations in Central Northern Mexico, 1969, Indian Assimilation in the Franciscan Area of Nueva Vizcaya, 1979. NSF grantee, jr. investigator, 1962-64; Nat. Endowment for Humanities grantee, jr. scholar, 1968-69. Fellow Am. Anthrop. Assn.; mem. Soc. Humanistic Anthropology, No. Ariz. Soc. Sci. and Art, Southwestern Anthropol. Assn., Am. Soc. Ethnohistory, Union Concerned Scientists, Danforth Assos., Phi Kappa Phi (corr. sec. chpt. 1977-79), Sigma Delta Pi. Home: Route 4 Box 902 Flagstaff AZ 86001 Office: No Ariz U Dept Anthropology Box 15200 Flagstaff AZ 86011

GRIFFENHAGEN, GEORGE BERNARD, trade association executive; b. Portland, Oreg., June 9, 1924; s. Richard Bernard and Clara (Schoenian) G.; m. Joan Helen Houston, June 21, 1946; children: Gary Bernard, Gordon Wesley, Barbara Clare. B.S. in Pharmacy, U. So. Calif., 1949, M.S., 1950; student, Fresno State Coll., 1946, U. London, 1948. Dir. research Nion Corp., Hollywood, Calif., 1950-52; curator div. med. scis. Smithsonian Instn., 1952-59; sec. sect. history of pharmacy Am. Pharm. Assn., Washington, 1952-59, pres. Washington chpt., 1958-59, asso. exec. dir., 1959—, editor Jour., 1969-76; sec.-gen. 4th Pan Am. Congress Pharmacy and Biochemistry, Washington, 1957; sec. organizing com. 31st Internat. Congress Pharm. Scis., Washington, 1971; sec.-gen. Internat. Congress History of Pharmacy, Washington, 1983; v.p. Pan Am. Pharm. and Biochem. Fedn., 1963-82; U.S. del. Internat. Pharm. Fedn. Gen. Assemblies, London, 1955, Brussels, 1958, Copenhagen, 1960, Vienna, 1962, Amsterdam, 1964, Hamburg, 1968, Geneva, 1970, Lisbon, 1972, Rome, 1974, Warsaw, 1976, Cannes, 1978, FIP Council, Bucharest, 1969, Dublin, 1975; congress coordinator, The Hague, 1977; U.S. del. Pan Am. Congress Pharmacy and Biochemistry Congresses, Mexico City, 1963, Buenos Aires, 1966, Caracas, 1969, Panama, 1972, Internat. Congress History of Pharmacy, Budapest, Hungary, 1981, Fedn. Asian Pharm. Assns. Congress, Seoul, Korea, 1982; mem. Nat. Action Com. on Drug Edn., Office of Edn., 1970-71, Va. Gov.'s Council on Narcotic and Drug Abuse Control, 1970-72. Editor: Scalpel and Tongs, 1972-73; Contbr. articles to profl. jours. Mem. Fairfax County (Va.) Republican Com., 1962-80; adminstrv. asst. to chmn. Va. State Rep. Com., 1969-71; life mem. Rep. Nat. Com., 1979—; Founding pres. Nat. Coordinating Council on Drug Edn., 1968-69, trustee, 1969-72. Served with C.E. AUS, World War II; ETO. Recipient Pfizer Merit award U.S. CD Council, 1964, U. So. Calif. Alumnus award, 1969. Mem. Am. Inst. History of Pharmacy (pres. 1960-61, mem. council, Edward Kremers award 1969), Friends of Hist. Pharmacy (pres. 1957-58), Pharm. Wholesalers Assn. (Distinguished Service award 1971), Am. Topical Assn. (1st v.p. 1972-75, pres. 1976-79, pres. med. subjects unit 1969-72, Distinguished Topical Philatelist award 1970, Myrtle Watt Med. Philately Topicalist award 1980), Am. Philatelic Congress (Jere Hess Barr award 1969), Am. Philatelic Soc. (sec.-treas. Writers Unit 1982—, U.S. commr. to Internat. Exhbn. Thematic Philately, Basel, Switzerland 1983), Am. Revenue Assn. (named to Sterling Meml. Roll of Disting. Fiscalists 1979), Philatelic Lit. Assn., Academie Internationale d'Histoire de la Pharmacie (treas. 1971-81), Pharm. Soc. Gt. Britain (hon.), Sigma Xi, Rho Chi, Phi Kappa Psi. Home: 2501 Drexel St Vienna VA 22180 Office: 2215 Constitution Ave NW Washington DC 20037

GRIFFETH, PAUL LYMAN, counseling and personnel educator; b. Sturgis, Mich., Aug. 3, 1919; s. Shirley C. and Edna M. (Kaechele) G.; m. Phyllis Mae Dean, Jan. 17, 1942; children: Gary Dean, Lindsey Jo. B.A., Mich. State U., 1941; M.A., U. Iowa, 1955; Ph.D., 1958. Officer Walstrom-Griffeth Co., Harbor Springs, Mich., 1946-52; asst. dean men U. Iowa, 1953-56, dean men, 1956-58; dean students Western Mich. U., Kalamazoo, 1958-66, v.p. student services, 1966-70, prof. counseling and personnel, 1970—, chmn. dept. counseling and personnel, 1980—. Dir. First Fed. Savs. & Loan Assn. Kalamazoo.; Past pres. Constance Brown Speech and Hearing Center. Served with USNR, 1941-46. Mem. Am. Coll. Personnel Assn., Mich. Coll. Personnnel Assn. (past pres.), Council Mich. Guidance and Personnel Assns. (past pres.), Am. Personnel and Guidance Assn., Sigma Nu, Omicron Delta Kappa, Phi Delta Kappa. Presbyterian (elder). Club: Kiwanis. Home: 22569 Sunset Dr Kalamazoo MI 49009

GRIFFIES, HIRAM FARRELL, service industry executive; b. Flint, Mich., Oct. 28, 1932; s. Hiram Franklin and Mary Ruth (McClanahan) G.; m. Barbara Lucille Edwards, Aug. 22, 1959; children: Todd Edward, Trayce Drake. B.A., Gen. Motors Inst., 1955; M.B.A., U. Detroit, 1958. Mfg. rep. Gen. Motors Corp., Atlanta, Detroit and St. Louis, 1955-62; personnel rep. Lockheed-Ga., Marietta, Ga., 1962-64; head indsl. services br. Ga. Inst. Tech., 1964-66; sr. cons. Fry Cons., Atlanta, 1966-68; pres. Munford, Inc., Atlanta, 1968-77; group v.p. Nat. Service Industries, Inc., Atlanta, 1977—. Served with USNR, 1950-56. Republican. Methodist. Clubs: Cherokee Town and Country, Kiwanis. Home: 6134 Riverside Dr NW Atlanta GA 30328 Office: 1180 Peachtree St NE Atlanta GA 30309

GRIFFIN, BOB FRANKLIN, lawyer, state legislator; b. Braymer, Mo., Aug. 15, 1935; s. Benjamin Franklin and Mildred Elizabeth (Cowan) G.; m. Linda Charlotte Kemper, Aug. 18, 1957; children: Julie Lynn, Jeffrey Scott. B.S. in Bus. Adminstrn., U. Mo., 1957, J.D., 1959. Atty. dept. judge adv. gen. U.S. Air Force, Iceland, 1959-62; sole practice Griffin Law Firm, Cameron, Mo., 1963-82; prosecuting atty. Clinton County, Plattsburg, Mo., 1963-70; mem. Mo. Ho. of Reps., 1977—; mem. firm Linde Thomson Fairchild Langworthy Kohn & Van Dyke, P.C., Kansas City, Mo., 1983—; speaker pro tem Mo. Ho. of Reps., Jefferson City, Mo., 1977-80, speaker, 1981—. Mem. exec. com. Nat. Conf. State Legislators, 1981—; mem. Dem. Legis. Leaders Caucus, 1981—, Dem. Nat. Com. Served to capt. USAF, 1959-62. Decorated Air Force Commendation medal, 1960. Mem. Mo. Bar Assn., Clinton County Bar Assn. Methodist. Office: Griffin Law Office 223 E Third St Cameron MO 64429

GRIFFIN, CAMPBELL ARTHUR, JR., lawyer; b. Joplin, Mo., July 17, 1929; s. Campbell Arthur and Clara M. (Smith) G.; m. Margaret Ann Adams, Oct. 19, 1958; children: Campbell A., Larara Ann. B.A.,

U. Mo., 1951, M.A. in Acctg., 1952; J.D., U. Tex., 1957. Bar: Tex. 1957. Assoc. firm Vinson & Elkins, Houston, 1957-68, ptnr., 1968—. Mem. ofcl. bd. Bethany Christian Ch., Houston, 1962-65, 66-69, chmn. bd. elders, Houston, 1968. Mem. ABA, Tex. Bar Assn., Houston Bar Assn., State Bar Tex. (chmn. sect. corp. banking and bus. law 1974-75). Office: Vinson & Elkins First City Tower Houston TX 77002

GRIFFIN, CARLETON HADLOCK, accountant; b. Richmond Heights, Mo., Oct. 30, 1928; s. Merle Leroy and Bernice Hilder Edwards (Nelson) G.; m. Mary Lou Goodrich, Dec. 26, 1953; children: Julia, Anne. B.B.A., U. Mich., 1950, J.D., 1953, M.B.A., 1953. Mem. audit and tax staff Touche Ross & Co., Detroit, 1955-59, adminstrv. partner, Denver, 1959-71, nat. tax dir., N.Y.C., 1971-72, nat. dir. ops. and adminstrn., 1972-74, chmn. bd., 1974-82, sr. ptnr., 1982—, regional ptnr., 1983—. Contbr. articles to profl. jours. Sr. warden St. Paul's Episcopal Ch., Darien, Conn., 1979-81. Served with Fin. Corps AUS, 1953-55. Mem. Am. Inst. C.P.A.s, Colo. Soc. C.P.A.s (pres. 1970-71), N.Y. Soc. C.P.A.s. Republican. Club: University (N.Y.C.). Home: 77 Middlebrook Farm Rd Wilton CT 06897 Office: 1633 Broadway New York NY 10019

GRIFFIN, CLAIBOURNE EUGENE, chemistry educator, university dean; b. Rocky Mount, N.C., Oct. 15, 1929; s. Claibourne Eugene and Virginia (Perry) G.; m. Dorthella L. McArthur, June 14, 1972. Student, Phillips Andover Acad., 1946-47; B.A., Princeton, 1951; M.S., U. Va., 1953, Ph.D., 1955. USPHS fellow Cambridge U., 1955-57; instr. U. Pitts., 1957-58, asst. prof., 1958-62, asso. prof., 1962-66, prof. dept. chemistry, 1966-69; adj. sr. fellow Mellon Inst., 1966-69; prof., chmn. dept. chemistry U. Toledo, 1969-74; dean grad. studies and research, prof. chemistry U. Akron, 1974-77, dean arts and scis., prof. chemistry, 1977—; adj. prof. chemistry Bowling Green State U., 1973-74; cons. Stauffer Chem. Co., 1962-82. Contbr. articles to profl. jours. Mem. Sigma Xi, Phi Lambda Upsilon. Home: 1100 Merriman Rd Akron OH 44303

GRIFFIN, DEWITT JAMES, architect; b. Los Angeles, Aug. 26, 1914; s. DeWitt Clinton and Ada Gay (Miller) G.; m. Jeanmarie Donald, Aug. 19, 1940; children: Barbara Jean Griffin Holst, John Donald, Cornelia Caulfield Claudius, James DeWitt. Student, UCLA, 1936-38; B.A., U. Calif., 1942. Designer Kaiser Engrs., Richmond, Calif., 1941; architect CF Braun & Co., Alhambra, Calif., 1946-48; pvt. practice architecture, Pasadena, Calif., 1948-50; prin. Goudie & Griffin Architects, San Jose, Calif., 1949-64, Griffin & Murray, 1964-66, DeWitt J. Griffin & Assocs., 1966-69; pres. Griffin/Joyce Assocs., Architects, 1969-80; chmn. Griffin Balzhiser Affiliates (Architects), 1974-80; founder, pres. Griffin Cos., 1980—; founder, dir. San Jose Savs. and Loan Assn., 1965-75, Capitol Services Co., 1964-77, Esandel Corp., 1965-77. Publisher: Sea Power mag, 1975-77; Archtl. works include U.S. Post Office, San Jose, 1966, VA Hosp, Portland, 1976, Bn. Barracks Complex, Ft. Ord, Calif., 1978. Dir. San Jose Symphony Assn., 1973—, exec. v.p., 1977-79, pres., 1979-81; bd. dirs. Coast Guard Acad. Found., 1974—; founder, bd. dirs. U.S. Navy Meml. Found., 1978-80, trustee, 1980—; trustee Montalvo Ctr. for Arts, 1982—. Served to comdr. USNR, 1942-46, 50-57. Recipient Navy Meritorious Pub. Service award, 1971, Disting. Service award Navy League of U.S., 1973; Coast Guard Meritorious Pub. Service award, 1975; Navy Distinguished Pub. Service award, 1977; Coast Guard Distinguished Pub. Service award, 1977. Fellow Soc. Am. Mil. Engrs.; emeritus mem. AIA; mem. U.S. Naval Inst., Navy League U.S. (pres. Santa Clara Valley council 1963-66, Calif. state pres. 1966-69, nat. dir. 1967—, exec. com. 1968—, pres. 12th region 1969-71, nat. v.p. 1973-75, nat. pres. 1975-77, chmn. 1977-79), Phi Gamma Delta. Republican. Congregationalist. Clubs: St. Francis Yacht, Commonwealth of San Francisco. Home and Office: 17653 Tourney Rd Los Gatos CA 95030

GRIFFIN, DONALD R(EDFIELD), zoology educator; b. Southampton, N.Y., Aug. 3, 1915; s. Henry Farr and Mary Whitney (Redfield) G.; m. Ruth M. Castle, Sept. 6, 1941 (div. Aug. 1965); children: Nancy Griffin Jackson, Janet Griffin Abbott, Margaret, John H.; m. Jocelyn Crane, Dec. 16, 1965. B.S., Harvard U., 1938, M.A., 1940, Ph.D., 1942. Jr. fellow Harvard U., Cambridge, Mass., 1940-41, 46, research assoc., 1942-45, prof., 1953-65; asst. prof. Cornell U., Ithaca, N.Y., 1946-47, assoc. prof., 1947-52, prof., 1952-53, Rockefeller U., N.Y.C., 1965—, trustee, 1973-76; pres. Harry Frank Guggenheim Found., 1979-84. Author: Listening in the Dark, 1958 (Nat. Acad. Scis. Elliot medal 1961), Echoes of Bats and Men, 1959, Animal Structure and Function, 1962, Bird Migration, 1964 (Phi Beta Kappa prize 1966), The Question of Animal Awareness, 1976. Mem. Am. Ornithologists Union, Am. Soc. Zoologists, Am. Physiol. Soc., Ecol. Soc. Am., Am. Acad. Arts and Scis., Nat. Acad. Scis., Am. Philos. Soc., Am. Soc. Naturalists, Phi Beta Kappa, Sigma Xi. Office: Rockefeller U 1230 York Ave New York NY 10021

GRIFFIN, F. O'NEIL, banker; b. Osceola, Ark., Sept. 10, 1926; s. Samuel Y. and Lydia I. (Ingram) G.; m. Elaine Bode, Jan. 2, 1974; children: S. Clifton, Richard D. B.S., Ark. State U., Jonesboro, 1948; postgrad. in acctg., U. Tex., Austin, 1949-50. C.P.A., Tex. With Arthur Andersen & Co. (C.P.A.s), Houston, Dallas and Denver, 1950-57; v.p., treas., dir. Western Nuclear, Inc., Rawlins, Wyo., 1957-59; v.p. fin. Colo. Oil & Gas Corp., Denver, 1959-61; pres. Uptime Corp., Golden, Colo., 1961-66; sr. asso. corp. fin., then gen. partner Eastman Dillon, Union Securities & Co., 1966-79; pres., chief exec. officer TeleCom Corp., 1969-71; exec. v.p., vice chmn. First City Bancorp. Tex., Inc., Houston, 1971-75; chmn. bd., chief exec. officer Mountain Banks, Ltd., Denver, 1975—; dir. Conquest Exploration Co. Trustee Meml. Hosp. System, Houston, 1973-75, Mt. Airy Hosp., Denver, 1976-78. Served with USNR, 1943-46. Mem. Tex. Bd. Public Acctg. Republican. Baptist. Clubs: River Oaks Country, Ramada (Houston); Riverhill (Kerrville, Tex.); Garden of Gods, Cheyenne Mountain Country (Colorado Springs, Colo.); Cherry Hills Country, Denver Country (Denver). Home: 206 Spring Mill Dr Kerrville TX 78028 Office: 522 Fairway Dr Kerrville TX 78028

GRIFFIN, GERALD DUANE, aeronautical engineer; b. Athens, Tex., Dec. 25, 1934; s. Herschel Hayden and Helen Elizabeth (Boswell) G.; m. Sandra Jo Huber, Apr. 19, 1958; children: Kirk Laurence, Gwendolyn Diane. B.S. in Aero. Engring, Tex. A. and M. U., 1956. With Douglas Aircraft Co., Long Beach, Calif., 1956, Lockheed Missiles and Space Co., Sunnyvale, Calif., 1960-62, Gen. Dynamics Co., Ft. Worth, 1962-64; with NASA, 1964-81, 82—; dir. NASA Johnson Space Center, Houston, 1982—; v.p. systems engring. and mgmt. Scott Sci. and Tech., Inc., Lancaster, Calif., 1981-82. Served as navigator USAF, 1956-60. Recipient Exceptional Service medal, Outstanding Leadership medal NASA; Presdl. rank Meritorious Sr. Exec.; Presdl. Medal of Freedom group award; named Old Master Purdue U. Asso. fellow AIAA; mem. Tau Beta Pi. Office: Office of Dir Johnson Space Ctr Houston TX 77058

GRIFFIN, GILROYE ALFRED, JR., pharmaceutical company executive; b. Columbia, S.C., Aug. 22, 1938; s. Gilroye Alfred and Rachel Precious (Carr) G.; m. D. Lynne White, Dec. 10, 1983; 1 son, Gilroye Alfred. A.B., Dartmouth Coll., 1959; J.D., Columbia U., 1962. Bar: N.Y. 1966. Legal counsel N.Am. div. Mobil Oil Corp., N.Y.C., 1964-68; mgr. labor relations and urban affairs Bristol-Myers Co., 1968-70; v.p. corp. adminstrn., asso. gen. counsel Kenyon & Eckhardt, Inc., 1970-74; also dir.; v.p. mgmt. planning CBS, Inc., N.Y.C., 1974-79; v.p. employee relations Bristol-Myers Co., N.Y.C., 1979—; mem. N.Y. State Fin. Control Bd., 1979-81; dir. Freedom Nat. Bank, 1973-77, Unity Broadcasting, Inc. Mem. White House Operation Awareness Task Force, 1972; Bd. dirs. Inter-racial Council on Bus. Opportunity; trustee Benedict Coll.; chmn. adv. bd. Nat. Urban Black Exec. Exchange Program, Studio Mus. of Harlem, 1974-77; v.p., bd. dirs. Coll. Placement Services, Inc. Served to 1st lt. U.S. Army, 1962-64. Mem. Am. Soc. for Personnel Adminstrn. (dir. 1969-72), Am., N.Y. State bar assns., Internat. Radio and Television Soc. (dir. 1971-74), Council Concerned Black Execs. (dir. 1970-74), Am. Mgmt. Assn. Clubs: One Hundred Black Men., Board Room. Office: 345 Park Ave 43d Floor New York NY 10022

GRIFFIN, HENRY LUDWIG, press photographer; b. Balt., May 19, 1916; s. Harry and Teresa (Grill) G.; m. Barbara Hupp, July 14, 1937 (dec. 1976); children—Ronald Edward, Carole Roberta; m. E. Josephine Steiniger, 1978. Student high sch., Balt. With AP, 1932-78, news photographer, 1934-78; war corr., 1942-45; chmn. Senate Press Photographers Gallery, 1956-62, chmn. legislative com., 1962—. Recipient of citation War Dept., commendation Navy Dept. Mem. White House News Photographers Assn. (life). Club: Moose. Home: 3214 Gumwood Dr University Hills MD 20783

GRIFFIN, HERSCHEL EMMETT, educator, ednl. adminstr.; b. Valley City, N.D., July 28, 1918; s. Herschel Raymond and Olive Buckley (Whalian) G.; m. Frances Helen Nye, June 6, 1943; children—Bruce Nye, Karen Lynn. A.A., Chaffey Jr. Coll., Ontario, Calif., 1937; B.A., Stanford, 1939; M.D., U. Calif., San Francisco, 1943. Diplomate: Am. Bd. Preventive Medicine (sec., treas. 1978-79). Intern in surgery U. Calif. Hosp., 1944; resident surgery San Francisco Hosp., 1945; practice medicine, Upland, Calif., 1947-50; became 1st lt., M.C. U.S. Army, 1943, advanced through grades to col., 1962; regtl. surgeon, div. preventive medicine officer Calif., comdg. officer med. bn., Japan, div. surgeon Korea, 1950-52, comdg. officer, Sasebo, Japan, 1952-53; fellow in epidemiology Walter Reed Army Research and Grad. Sch., 1954-55; chief communicable disease br. Office Surgeon Gen., Dept. Army, 1955-58; theater epidemiologist U.S. Army, Europe, dep. for profl. services, Germany, 1959-62; asst. for profl. services Office Dep. Asst. Sec. Def., 1963-65; exec. officer Office Surgeon Gen., Dept. Army, 1965-66, chief preventive medicine div., 1966-69; ret., 1969; prof. epidemiology, dean Grad. Sch. Pub. Health, U. Pitts., 1969-80; asso. dir., prof. epidemiology Grad. Sch. Public Health, San Diego State U., 1980—; U.S. Army rep. Gorgas Meml. Inst., 1966-69, Leonard Wood Meml., 1966-69; cons. Walter Reed Army Inst. Research, 1972—, WHO, 1972-77, chmn. expert com. on recommended requirements for schs. pub. health, 1972—; del. Pa. Health Conf. Com., U. Health Center of Pitts., 1970-73, Pa. Health Council, 1972-74; sci. adviser U.S. EPA, 1973—; pres. Pa. Health Council, 1973-74; cons. Uniformed Services U. of Health Scis., 1975—; chmn. Pa. Health Conf. Com., 1973-74; chmn. com. on med. and biol. effects of environ. pollutants NRC/Nat. Acad. Scis., 1972-76; chmn. infectious disease adv. com. Nat. Inst. Allergy and Infectious Diseases, NIH, 1974-76; mem. Gov.'s Task Force on Health Edn. in Pa., 1974-76; mem. adv. com. Gov.'s Energy Council, 1974-79; bd. dirs. Pa. Health Research Inst., 1973-75; mem. Armed Forces Epidemiological Bd., 1973—, pres., 1977-79, chmn. ad hoc study team on procurement standards, 1974-75; chmn. com. to study health effects of air pollution Allegheny County Bd. Health/Allegheny County Health Dept., 1974-76. Contbr. articles to profl. jours. Decorated Legion of Merit, Bronze Star medal, Army Commendation medal. Fellow A.C.P., Am. Coll. Preventive Medicine, Am. Pub. Health Assn.; mem. AMA (mem. Ho. Dels.), Assn. Schs. of Pub. Health (pres. 1971-73, exec. com. 1973-75), Soc. Med. Cons. to Armed Forces (chmn. preventive medicine com. 1970-73, pres. 1975-76). Home: 11274 Pabellon Ct San Diego CA 92124 Office: Grad Sch Pub Health San Diego State U San Diego CA 92182

GRIFFIN, JAMES ANTHONY, bishop; b. Fairview Park, Ohio, June 13, 1934; s. Thomas Antohny and Margaret Mary (Hanousek) G. B.A., Borromeo Coll., 1956; J.C.L. magna cum laude, Pontifical Lateran U., Rome, 1963; J.D. summa cum laude, Cleve. State U., 1972. Ordained priest Roman Catholic Ch., 1960, bishop, 1979; asso. pastor St. Jerome Ch., Cleve., 1960-61; sec.-notary Cleve. Diocesan Tribunal, 1963-65; asst. chancellor Diocese of Cleve., 1965-68, vice chancellor, 1968-73, chancellor, 1973-78, vicar gen., 1978-79; pastor St. William Ch., Euclid, Ohio, 1978-79; aux. bishop Diocese of Cleve., vicar of western region, Lorain, Ohio, 1979-83; bishop of Columbus Diocese of Columbus (Ohio), 1983—; mem. clergy relations bd. Diocese of Cleve., 1972-75, mem. clergy retirement bd., 1973-78, mem. clergy personnel bd., 1979—. Author: (with A.J. Quinn) Thoughts for Our Times, 1969, Thoughts for Sowing, 1970, (with others) Ashes from the Cathedral, 1974, Sackcloth and Ashes, 1976. Bd. dirs. Holy Family Cancer Home, 1973-78; trustee St. Mary Sem., 1976-78; bd. dirs., mem. pension com. Cath. Cemeteries Assn., 1978-83; bd. dirs. Meals on Wheels, Euclid, 1978-79. Mem. Am. Canon Law Soc., Am. Bar Assn., Ohio Bar Assn., Euclid Ministerial Assn. (pres. 1978-79). Office: 198 E Broad St Columbus OH 43215

GRIFFIN, JAMES BENNETT, anthropologist, educator; b. Atchison, Kan., Jan. 12, 1905; s. Charles Bennett and Maude (Bostwick) G.; m. Ruby Fletcher, Feb. 14, 1936; children—John Bennett, David Moss, James Chapman. Ph.B., U. Chgo., 1927, A.M., 1930; Ph.D. (fellow in aboriginal N.Am. ceramics 1933-36), U. Mich., 1936; D.Sc., Ind. U., 1971. Research asso. Mus. Anthropology, U. Mich., Ann Arbor, 1936-41, asst. curator archaeology, 1937-42, asso. curator, 1942-45, curator, 1945-75, curator emeritus, 1976—, dir. Mus. Anthropology, 1946-75, sr. research scientist, 1976—, lectr. econ. and polit. geography, war tng. program, 1943-44; asso. prof. anthropology, 1945-49, prof., 1949-76, Russel lectr., 1972, prof. emeritus, 1976—, chmn. dept., 1972-75; Chmn. anthropology sect. Mich. Acad. Sci., Arts and Letters, 1936-37, 43-44; field research in, Ill., 1928, 29, 48, in, Pa., 1930, in, Ind., 1933, in, Miss. and, Ark., 1940, 41, in, Mexico, 1946, in, Mich., 1948, Ill. and Mo., 1950; mem. faculty field sch. univs. Calif., Mich., Tex. in 26th Summer Sch. of Nat. U., Mexico City, 1946. Author: Archaeological Survey in the Lower Mississippi Alluvial Valley, 1940-47, Vol. 25 (with others), 1950; Author, editor: Archeology of Eastern United States, 1952; Contbr. articles to profl. jours. Mem. Permanent Council of Internat. Union of Prehistoric and Protohistoric Scis., 1948-76, mem. exec. com., 1962-76; pres. com. on anthropology Pan-Am. Inst. Geography and History, 1954-59; pres. Conf. on Mich. Archeology, 1966-76. Recipient Viking Fund medal and award in archeology, 1957, Distinguished Service award U. Mich., 1976. Fellow AAAS (sect. H., 1945, past sect. com. and v.p.), Am. Anthrop. Assn. (pres. Central States br. 1948-49), Soc. for Am. Archaeology (asst. editor 1936-46, asso. editor 1946-50, 1st v.p. 1945-46, exec. com. 1945-46, 195O-53, pres. 1951-52, Fryxell award 1980), Nat. Acad. Sci., Am. Quaternary Assn. (sec. 1970-72), Sociedad Mexicana de Antropologia, Assos. Field Archeology (exec. com. 1972-77), Soc. Profl. Archeologists, Soc. Archeol. Scis. (exec. bd. 1978), Southeastern Archaeol. Conf. (pres. 1980-81), Sigma Xi, Phi Sigma. Office: University Museums Bldg Ann Arbor MI 48109

GRIFFIN, JAMES DONALD, mayor Buffalo; b. Buffalo, June 29, 1929; s. Thomas J. and Helen M. (O'Brien) G.; m. Margaret Ellen McMahon., May 4, 1968; children—Maureen, Megan, Thomas. Grad., Erie County Tech. Inst., 1958. With feed mills and grain elevators, Buffalo; now engr. Buffalo Creek R.R.; mem. Ellicott Dist. Council, 1961-65, N.Y. State Senate, 1967-77; mayor City of Buffalo, 1977—. Served to lt. U.S. Army, 1951-53; Korea. Mem. Buffalo C. of C. Democrat. Roman Catholic. Club: K.C. Office: 65 Niagara Sq Buffalo NY 14202 *

GRIFFIN, JAMES EDWARD, educator; b. Columbus, Ohio, Dec. 17, 1922; s. Don Wallace and Belle (Eason) G.; m. Frances Lenora Roberts, Sept. 22, 1948; children—Karl Edward, Bruce William, Karen Lorraine. B.A., Western Md. Coll., 1944; certificate phys. therapy, Duke U., 1946, M.A., 1948; Ph.D., U. Pa., 1959. Staff phys. therapist Duke Med. Center, 1946-48; sr. phys. therapist Hosp. Chronic Illness, Rocky Hill, Conn., 1948-53; mem. faculty U. Pa., 1953-70, prof. phys. therapy, 1969-70; prof. phys. therapy, chmn. dept. SUNY, Buffalo, 1970-74; chmn. Northeastern region Council Phys. Therapy Sch. Dirs., 1971—; dir. program in phys. therapy, prof. physiology and health sci. Ball State U., Muncie, Ind., 1980—. Fellow Internat. Soc. Med. Hydrology and Climatology; mem. Am. Phys. Therapy Assn. (chmn. sect. research 1968-70), Phila. Physiol. Soc., Am. Congress Rehab. Medicine, N.Y. Acad. Scis., Assn. Schs. Health Related Professions (chmn. com. equivalency 1969-71). Home: Rural Route 12 Box 302 Muncie IN 47302 Office: Ball State U Muncie IN 46306

GRIFFIN, JAMES EDWIN, utilities executive; b. Langhorne, Pa., Dec. 11, 1927; s. James Edwin and Freda Martha; children: James, Bruce, Roger. B.S., Pa. State U., 1952, M.S., 1954. Research analyst Commonwealth Pa., 1953-55; econ. analyst Pa. R.R., 1955-59; area devel. dir. Central Vt. Public Service Co., Rutland, 1958-65, v.p., 1965-71, exec. v.p., 1971, pres., dir., 1972—; chmn. bd., chief exec. officer, dir. Vt. Electric Power Co., Inc. and; pres., chief exec. officer, dir. Conn. Valley Electric Co., 1972—; dir., exec. v.p. Vt. Yankee Nuclear Power, 1973, pres., 1974; dir. Vt. Nat. Bank, Yankee Atomic Electric Co., Maine Yankee Atomic Power Co., Conn. Yankee Atomic Power Co. Chmn., Rutland County chpt. ARC; bd. dirs. Vt. Heart Assn.; trustee Green Mountain Coll., Rutland Devel. Corp., New Industries, Inc.; bd. dirs. Eastern States Exposition; trustee Green Mountain council Boy Scouts Am. Mem. NAM (com. natural resources mgmt. and conservation), Electric Council New Eng. (dir.), Edison Electric Inst., Alpha Sigma Phi. Republican. Episcopalian. Home: 81 Lincoln Ave Rutland VT 05701 Office: 77 Grove St Rutland VT 05701

GRIFFIN, JERALD LEE, chem. mfg. co. exec.; b. Detroit, Feb. 21, 1926; s. J. A. and Beulah (Childers) G.; m. Valetta May Batchelor, Dec. 25, 1944; children—Steve, Kathleen (Mrs. Gary Allen Fenwick), Christine (Mrs. Gary Egleson), Janet (Mrs. Craig Potts). Student, Central Mich. U., 1943, Lawrence Coll., 1944; B.B.A., U. Mich., 1952, M.B.A., 1952; P.M.D., Harvard, 1964. Ind. contractor Mich. Bell Telephone Co., 1950-52; asst. credit mgr., div. controller, internat. controller, treas., v.p., auditor Dow Corning Corp., Midland, Mich., 1952—; dir. Chem. Bank & Trust Co., Midland Bahamas Co., Ltd. Chmn. Sen. Griffin Finance Com. Republican Party, 1966. Served to lt. USNR, 1943-49. Mem. Midland C. of C., Alpha Kappa Psi. Home: 1421 Airfield Ln Midland MI 48640 Office: Dow Corning Center Midland MI 48640

GRIFFIN, JOHN ARNOLD, III, jazz musician, tenor saxophonist; b. Chgo., Apr. 24, 1928. Jazz musician with, Lionel Hampton, Joe Morris, Art Blakey, Thelonious Monk; co-leader with, Lockjaw Davis jazz group, 1960's; joined, Kenney Clarke-Francy Boland Big Band, toured extensively, Europe; feature, Montreux Jazz Festival, 1975; albums include NYC Underground. Office: care Ms Management 130 E 31st St New York NY 10016 *

GRIFFIN, JOHN DOUGLAS, association executive; b. Hamilton, Ont., Can., June 3, 1906; s. Herbert Spohn and Edith Moore (Robinson) G.; m. Erica Maude Withrow, Sept. 22, 1934; children: Charles Peter Morecroft, John David Anthony.; m. Barbara Mary Solan, Mar. 16, 1982. Student, Hamilton Collegiate Inst.; B.A., U. Toronto, 1929, M.D., 1932, M.A., 1933, postgrad. psychology, 1932-33; postgrad., Hosp. for Sick Children in Toronto, 1933; Rockefeller fellow postgrad. psychiatry, 1934-36. Staff Nat. Com. Mental Hygiene (now Canadian Mental Health Assn.), 1936-39, med. dir., 1939-41, gen. dir., 1953-72; asst. psychiatrist Clinic Psychol. Medicine, Hosp. Sick Children, 1937-41; cons. personnel devel. Moore Corp., Inc., 1945-51; cons. mental health program Canadian Broadcasting Corp., 1945-56; spl. lectr. Sch. Social Work, U. Toronto, 1946-56; mem. psychiat. panel Def. Research Bd., 1949-57; mem. Canadian adv. com. mental health to Fed. Govt., 1950-70; mem. Inter-Am. Council Psychiat., 1967-69, Ont. Mental Health Found., 1976-82. Author: (with W. Line and S.R. Laycock) Mental Hygiene-A Manual for Teachers, 1938, (with Tyhurst, Chalke, et al.) More for the Mind, 1963, (with B. Swadron, Chalke, et al.) The Law and Mental Disorder, 1968; popular, sci. articles. Served to col. M.C. Canadian Army, 1941-45. Recipient Bowis award Am. Coll. Psychiatry, 1974. Fellow Am. Psychiat. Assn. (council, life mem.), Canadian Psychiat. Assn. (pres. 1967-68, life mem.), Ont. Psychiat. Assn. (life mem.), Royal Coll. Physicians and Surgeons; hon. fellow Toronto Acad. Medicine; mem. Can. Med. Assn., Ont. Med. Assn.; hon. mem. Canadian Coll. Family Practice. Clubs: Faculty (U. Toronto), National Yacht. Home: 18 Bracondale Hill Rd Toronto ON M6G 3P4 Canada

GRIFFIN, JOHN TOOLE, broadcasting company executive; b. McAlester, Okla., May 3, 1923; s. John T. and Ada (Toole) G.; m. Martha L. Watson, Apr. 25, 1959; children: John W., David F. B.S. in Bus, Okla. U., 1947. Chmn. bd. Griffin Grocery Co., Muskogee, Okla., 1943—, Griffin TV, Inc. (and predecessors), Muskogee, 1943—; dir. Citizens Nat. Bank, Muskogee, Okla. Gas & Electric Co. Pres. Five Civilized Tribes Mus., Muskogee; pres., bd. dirs. Okla. Heritage Assn.; trustee Oklahoma City U., 1981—; bd. dirs. Okla. Med. Research Found. Served with AUS, 1943-45. Mem. Phi Gamma Delta, Beta Gamma Sigma, Phi Eta Sigma. Methodist. Home: 600 Robb St Muskogee OK 74401 Office: 111 S Cherokee St Muskogee OK 74401

GRIFFIN, LELAND MILBURN, speech educator; b. Kansas City, Kans., Apr. 9, 1920; s. Herbert Lester and Cliffe (Connell) G.; m. Dorothy M. Schlotzhauer, July 4, 1943; children: Dorothy Lee, Charles James Grant, Andrew Dion Crispin. A.B., U. Mo., 1941, M.A., 1942; Ph.D., Cornell U., 1950. Asst. prof. speech Washington U., St. Louis, 1950-54; asso. prof., chmn. dept. speech Boston U., 1954-56; asso. prof. speech Northwestern U., Evanston, Ill., 1956-64, prof. speech, 1964—, Van Zelst research prof. in communication, 1982-83; prof. speech Garrett Theol. Sem., 1958-68. Asso. editor: Quar. Jour. Speech, 1954-59, 69-71, Central States Speech Jour, 1950-52, 64-66, Bicentennial Monograph Series, 1972-78; Contbr. articles to profl. jours. Bd. dirs. Rhetoric Soc. Am., 1972-74. Served to lt (j.g.) USNR, 1943-46. Recipient Citation of Merit award U. Mo., 1971. Mem. Am., Central States speech assns., AAUP, Rhetoric Soc. Am., Internat. Soc. History Rhetoric, Phi Kappa Phi. Republican. Episcopalian. Home: 1940 Orrington Ave Evanston IL 60201

GRIFFIN, MARTIN IGNATIUS JOSEPH, JR., historian, univ. dean; b. Phila., Nov. 13, 1933; s. Martin Ignatius Joseph and Constance Mary (Magee) G. A.B. (Benjamin Franklin scholar 1951-55), U. Pa., 1955; M.A. (Woodrow Wilson fellow), Yale U., 1956; Ph.D. (Jr. Sterling fellow), Yale U., 1963; postgrad. (Fulbright fellow), U. London, 1958-59. Instr. history Yale U., New Haven, Conn., 1960-63, asst. prof., 1963-68, Morse fellow, 1965-66, dir. undergrad. studies history, 1966-72, lectr. history, 1968—, resident fellow Saybrook Coll.,

1960—, acting dean, 1966-67, dean, 1968-71, asst. dean Yale Coll., asso. dean undergrad. affairs, 1971-73, asso. dean Yale Coll., 1973—, dean undergrad. studies, 1976—. Mem. Am. Hist. Assn., Conf. Brit. Studies, Phi Beta Kappa (sec. Yale chpt. 1970—). Clubs: Yale (N.Y.C.); Elizabethan. Home: 979 Saybrook Coll Yale U New Haven CT 06520 Office: Deans Office Yale College 1604A Yale Station New Haven CT 06520

GRIFFIN, MARVIN ANTHONY, naval engineering company, executive; b. Butler Springs, Ala., Mar. 28, 1923; s. Randolph Simpson and Linnie (Barrett) G.; m. Jane Pearle A. L'Herisson, Sept. 4, 1949; children: Margaret Lynn, John Marvin, Barbara Lee, Elizabeth Ann. B.S., Auburn U., 1949; M.S. Engring, U. Ala., 1952; D.Eng., Johns Hopkins, 1960. Registered profl. engr., Ala. Chief ops. analysis Anniston Ordnance Depot, Ala., 1949-51; sr. mfg. engr. Western Electric Co., Winston-Salem, N.C., 1952-55; chief engring. Cumberland Mfg. Co., Chattanooga, 1955-57; instr. Johns Hopkins, 1957-60; chief indsl. engr. Matson Navigation Co., San Francisco, 1960-61, v.p. corporate devel., 1977-78, group v.p., 1978—; prof. indsl. engring. U. Ala., 1961-76, chmn. dept., 1965-71, chmn. dept. computer sci. and operation research, 1971-76, dir. computer sci., 1969-76; mem. maritime transp. research bd., maritime info. com. Nat. Acad. Sci., 1976—; mgmt. cons. to industry, govt.; labor arbitrator Fed. Mediation and Conciliation Service, Am. Arbitration Assn. Contbr. articles to profl. jours. Served to comdr. USNR, 1943-47; PTO. Sr. postdoctoral fellow Johns Hopkins U., 1969. Mem. Operations Research Soc. Am., Am. Inst. Indsl. Engrs. (dir. 1954-55, chpt. pres. 1959-60), Am. Soc. Engring. Edn., Inst. Mgmt. Sci., Assn. Computing Machinery. Home: 93 Claymont Circle Tuscaloosa AL 35404 Office: PO Box 6316 University AL 35486

GRIFFIN, MARY, English educator; b. Chgo., Dec. 25, 1916; d. Michael Anthony and Margaret (O'Connor) G. B. Music Edn, Mundelein Coll., Chgo., 1939, A.B., 1947; A.M., Catholic U. Am., 1950; Ph.D. (scholarship 1958-59, fellowship 1961), Fordham U., 1961. Mem. Congregation of Sisters of Charity, 1939-75; instr. piano and English Clarke Coll., Dubuque, Iowa, 1944-53; asst. prof. English Mundelein Coll., 1953-60, acad. dean, 1960- 67; research fellow English Yale, 1968-69; prof. English Alcorn A. and M. Coll., Lorman, Miss., 1969-73, Mundelein Coll., Chgo., 1970—, dir. Grad. Program in Liberal Studies, 1983—; Mem. upperclass awards com. Ill. Scholarship Commn., 1963-65; mem. Deans' Workshop, Harvard, 1964; mem. planning com. Johnston Coll., U. Redlands (Calif.), 1968-69. Author: The Courage to Choose, 1975; Editor: (Charles Burney) The Trial of Midas II, 1961. Summer scholar U. London (Eng.), 1961; Nat. Endowment for the Humanities grantee Alcorn U., 1973. Mem. AAUW, Modern Lang. Assn., Am. Conf. Acad. Deans (exec. com. 1964-68), Assn. Higher Edn. (exec. com. 1966- 68), Am. Council on Edn. (com. on acad. affairs 1965-68), Kappa Gamma Pi. Address: Mundelein Coll 6363 Sheridan Rd Chicago IL 60660

GRIFFIN, MELVIN WILLIAM, distilling company executive; b. Winnipeg, Man., Can., Mar. 16, 1923; s. Aylmer and Elma G.; m. Kathleen Ann Devine, Oct. 27, 1947; children: Lorna Griffin Smith, Patrick, Richard, Bruce, David. B.Sc., U. Man.; P.Eng., Queen's U., Kingston, Ont., Can. With Def. Industries Ltd., 1944-45; with Distillers Corp. Ltd., 1945-75, served in, Jamaica, B.W.I., until 1963, v.p., dir., 1967-70, exec. v.p., chief operating officer, 1970-75; pres. House of Seagram Ltd. (name later changed to Joseph E. Seagram & Sons, Ltd.), Montreal, Que., Can., 1975-78; exec. v.p. mfg. Seagram Co. Ltd., 1978—; dir. Seagram Co. Ltd., Joseph E. Seagram & Sons, Ltd., Rowett, Legge & Co., Ltd., Montreal Baseball Club Ltd., Glenlivet Distillers Ltd., Donwood Inst. Mem. Internat. C. of C. (Can. council), Montreal Bd. Trade, Province Que. C. of C., La Chambre de Commerce du District de Montreal, Queen's U. Alumni, Winnipeg C. of C., Montreal Amateur Athletic Assn. Roman Catholic. Club: Beaconsfield Golf. Office: Seagram Co Ltd 1430 Peel St Montreal PQ Canada H3A 1S9

GRIFFIN, MERV EDWARD, entertainer, TV producer; b. San Mateo, Calif., July 6, 1925; s. Mervyn Edward and Rita (Robinson) G.; m. Julann Elizabeth Wright, May 18, 1958 (div. June 1976); 1 son, Anthony Patrick. Student, San Mateo Coll., 1942-44; L.H.D., Emerson Coll., 1981. Owner MGP (Merv Griffin Prodns.), TAV, Hollywood, Calif.; owner 3 radio stas., 1965—; v.p., dir. spl. promotions Camelot Inc. subs. Am. Leisure Corp., 1981—; also dir.; owner Teleview Racing Patrol Inc., Miami, Fla. Performer, Merv Griffin Show radio sta. KFRC, San Francisco, 1945-48; vocalist, Freddy Martin's Orch., 1948-52; contract player, star: So This is Love, Warner Bros., 1953-55; TV master ceremonies, 1958—, Merv Griffin Show, NBC-TV, 1962-63, Westinghouse Broadcasting Co., 1965-69, CBS-TV, 1969-72, Metro Media Prodns.. syndicated TV, 1972—; currently producing: Dance Fever and Wheel of Fortune. Trustee Dr. Armand Hammer United World Coll. of Am. S.W. Club: Bohemian (San Francisco). Address: 1541 N Vine St Hollywood CA 90028

GRIFFIN, MICHAEL DANIEL, investment couselor; b. New Haven, May 26, 1939; s. Michael F. G. and Mae S. (Griffin); m. Allice N. Griffin, June 15, 1963; children: Michael S., Peter G., Geoffrey S. B.A., Yale U., 1960; M.B.A., Columbia U., 1962. Chartered fin. analyst. Research analyst Scudder Stevens & Clark, N.Y.C., 1963-70, v.p. fin. and adminstrn., 1969—. Bd. govs. Lawrence Hosp., Bronxville, N.Y., 1979—, treas., Bronxville, N.Y., 1982—; pres., dir. Bronxville Community Fire Dept., 1975-79; mem. Bd. Zoning Appeals, Bronxvill, 1980—. Mem. Investment Counsel Assn. Am. (bd. govs.). Office: Scudder Stevens & Clark 345 Park Ave New York NY 10154

GRIFFIN, NORRIS SAMUEL, fin. exec.; b. Winston Salem, N.C., Sept. 2, 1931; s. Jesse L. and Ola (Styers) G.; m. Jeanette Priddy, Mar. 6, 1954; children—Neil Styers, David Louis. B.B.A., Wake Forest U., 1958. Pres. Southeastern Fin. Co., Charlotte, N.C., 1971-73; pres., chief exec. officer Bank Va. BVA Credit Corp., Richmond, 1974-80; chmn. bd., pres. Canadian Fin. Co., Montreal, Va., 1974-80; exec. v.p., dir. Bank Va. Co., Richmond, 1975-80; exec. v.p. Associated Comml. Corp., Charlotte, 1980—. Served with USAF, 1950-53. Mem. Nat. Comml. Fin. Conf. (chmn. bd., dir., past pres.). Republican. Lutheran. Clubs: Union League (N.Y.C.); Myers Park Country, Charlotte City (Charlotte). Office: 400 S Tryon St Charlotte NC 28285

GRIFFIN, OSCAR O'NEAL, JR., oil company executive; b. Daisetta, Tex., Apr. 28, 1933; s. Oscar O'Neal and Myrtle Ellen (Edgar) G.; m. Patricia Lamb, July 28, 1955; children: Gwendolyn Ann, Amanda Karen, Gregory O'Neal, Marguerite Ellen. B. Journalism, U. Tex., 1958. Editor Canyon (Tex.) News, 1959-60, Pecos (Tex.) Ind., 1960-62; reporter Houston Chronicle, 1962-66, White House corr., 1966-69; asst. dir. pub. affairs U.S. Dept. Transp., Washington, 1969-74; pres. Griffin Well Service, Inc., El Campo, Tex., 1974—, Cross Roads Drilling Services, Inc., 1980—; chmn. Cross Roads Oil Field Supply, Inc., 1980—; dir. United Gen. Ins. Co. Served with AUS, 1953-55. Recipient award for investigative reporting Southwest Journalism Forum, 1963; Pulitzer prize for local reporting not under pressure of edit. time, 1963. Mem. Sigma Delta Chi. (Distinguished Service in Journalism award Ft. Worth chpt. 1962, Courage in Journalism award Des Moines chpt. 1963, award for gen. reporting nat. orgn. 1963), Assn. Well Servicing Contractors (dir.), El Campo Museum Soc. (trustee), El Campo C. of C. (pres.). Clubs: National Press, Houston Press. Home: PO Box 1301 El Campo TX 77437 Office: 2004 N Wharton St El Campo TX 77437

GRIFFIN, ROBERT P., lawyer, former U.S. senator; b. Detroit, Nov. 6, 1923; s. J.A. and Beulah M. G.; m. Marjorie J. Anderson, 1947; children—Paul Robert, Richard Allen, James Anderson, Martha Jill. A.B., B.S., Central Mich. U., 1947, LL.D., 1963; J.D., U. Mich., 1950, LL.D., 1973; LL.D., Eastern Mich. U., 1969, Albion Coll., 1970, Western Mich. U., 1971, Grand Valley State Coll., 1971, Detroit Coll. Bus., 1972, Detroit Coll. Law, 1973; L.H.D., Hillsdale (Mich.) Coll., 1970; J.C.D., Rollins Coll., 1970; Ed.D., No. Mich. U., 1970; D. Pub. Service, Detroit Inst. Tech., 1971. Bar: Mich. Practiced in, Traverse City, 1950-56, mem. 85th-89th congresses from 9th Dist. Mich.; U.S. senator from Mich., 1966-79; vis. fellow Am. Enterprise Inst. Public Policy Research, 1979—; counsel firm Miller, Canfield, Paddock & Stone, Traverse City, 1979—; dir. Pacesetter Bank and Trust. Chmn. bd. trustees Gerald R. Ford Found.; mem. World bd. govs. USO. Served with inf. AUS, World War II; ETO. Named 1 of 10 Outstanding Young Men of Nation U.S. Jaycees, 1959. Mem. Am., Mich., D.C. bar assns., Am. Legion. Republican. Club: Kiwanian. Office: Miller Canfield Paddock & Stone 13999 W Bay Shore Dr Traverse City MI 49684

GRIFFIN, ROBERT THOMAS, automotive company executive; b. Somerville, Mass., July 3, 1917; s. Michael and Cecilia (Rourke) G.; m. Mary Ellen Mulcahy, Sept. 10, 1960; children: Mary Catherine, Christiane Marie, Justine Dufresne, Joseph Michael. B.S., Boston Coll., 1939; M.A. in Pub. Adminstrn, Boston U., 1954; postgrad., Harvard U. Grad. Sch. Pub. Adminstrn., 1954-55. Regional mgr. War Assets Adminstrn., 1946-49; with GSA, Washington, 1950-56, 58-80, spl. asst. to adminstr., 1961-62, asst. adminstr., 1962-70, asst. commr. property mgmt., 1970-73; spl. asst. to adminstr. for coordination John F. Kennedy Library, 1973-77, acting adminstr., 1977—; dep. adminstr. GSA, 1977-78; sr. advisor Pres.'s Spl. Trade Rep., White House, 1977-78; sr. advisor to Personal Rep. of Pres. to Middle East Negotiations, White House, 1978-80; staff exec. to pres. Chrysler Corp., 1980—; dir. Van Pool Services, Inc.; mem. Pres.'s Inflation Task Force, 1978-79; conferee White House Conf. Natural Beauty, 1964, Pres.'s Fed. Agy. Task Force on Cost Reduction, 1965; adminstrv. cons. Govt. of Iran, 1956-58; mem. Pres.'s Com. Minority Enterprise. Bd. dirs. Hamlet Citizens Assn., Chevy Chase, Md., 1981—. Served with USCGR, 1943-46. Mem. Am. Soc. Pub. Adminstrn., DAV. Clubs: Washington Athletic, Columbia Country. Office: 1100 Connecticut Ave NW Washington DC 20036

GRIFFIN, TOM, editor; b. Charlotte, N.C., June 26, 1926; s. Richard C. Mathis (stepfather) and Ruby Mathis; m. Dorothy Virginia Hewitt, Oct. 22, 1949; children—Steven Thomas, Diane Patricia. B.S.B.A. in Journalism, U. Tenn., 1951. Night mgr. United Press (now U.P.I.), Ala., 1951-54; mng. editor Cotton Trade Jour., 1954-59; asst. advt. mgr. E. L. Bruce Co. (flooring and floor care products co.), 1959-62; copy desk Memphis Comml. Appeal, 1962; exec. editor Ross Publs., 1963-64; advt. mgr. John Blue Co. (mfr. agrl. equipment), 1965-67; asso. editor Delta Farm Press, 1968-69; freelance writer, photographer, 1970-72; editorial dir. Cotton Farming, Rice Farming and Custom Applicator mags. Little Publs., Memphis, 1973—. Served with USNR, 1944-46. Mem. Am. Agrl. Editors Assn., Am. Theosophical Soc. Republican. Methodist. Home: 6086 Fox Ridge Dr Memphis TN 38115 Office: 6263 Poplar Ave Memphis TN 38119

GRIFFIN, VILLARD STUART, JR., geology educator; b. Birmingham, Ala., May 19, 1937; s. Villard Stuart and Myra (Justice) G.; m. Raija Tuulikki Nikander, June 12, 1966; children: Victoria Sirkka, Elizabeth Roosa-Maria, Anna Kristina, Ester Kaarina. B.A., U. Va., 1959, M.S., 1961; Ph.D., Mich. State U., 1965. Grad. asst. U. Va., Charlottesville, 1960-61, Mich. State U., East Lansing, 1961-63; geologist Little Bob Mining Co., Marietta, Ga., summer 1960; geologic aide Roland F. Beers, Inc., Alexandria, Va., summer 1960, Va. Div. Mineral Resources, Charlottesville, summers, 1961, 62, 64; mem. faculty Clemson U. (S.C.), 1964—, prof. geology, 1975—; vis. research investigator Geol. Survey Finland, Helsinki, 1975; project geologist S.C. Geol. Survey, Columbia, 1965—; cons. Bechtel Corp., 1966, John Wiley & Sons., 1971, C. D'Appolonia Engrs., Inc., 1973, S.C. Electric and Gas Co., 1973-76, Chevron Corp., 1976; cons. dept. energy E.I. duPont de Nemours Co., 1978; cons. Fulton Nat. Bank, 1980, Ga. Geol. Survey, 1980; lectr. Geologisk-Mineralogisk Mus. and Inst., Oslo, Norway, 1975, Mineral. Soc. Stockholm, 1975, Geologiska-Mineralogika Inst. Uppsala, Sweden, 1975, Turku U. Geol. and Mineral. Inst., 1975, others; assoc. investigator U.S. Office Water Resources Research, 1965-66. Cons. editor: Rocks and Minerals, 1976-79; mem. editorial bd.: Geolgic Notes, 1976-80; contbr. articles to profl. jours. Recipient W.A. Tarr award Sigma Gamma Epsilon, 1960, J.K. Roberts Geology dept. award U. Va., 1961; Mich. State U. scholar, 1961-63; Phillip Francis du Pont fellow, 1960-61; NSF grantee, 1968, 70, 72. Fellow Geol. Soc. Am.; mem. AAAS, Nat. Geog. Soc., Am. Inst. Profl. Geologists (sect. v.p. 1981), Geol. Soc. Finland, Carolina Geol. Soc. (v.p. 1968), Ga. Geol. Soc., Sigma Xi (grantee 1963). Home: PO Box 1204 Clemson SC 29631

GRIFFIN, W(ILLIAM) L(ESTER) HADLEY, shoe company executive; b. Edwardsville, Ill., May 17, 1918; s. Ralph D. and Julia (Hadley) G.; m. Phoebe M. Perry, Apr. 1, 1942; children: Dustin H. II, Lockwood Perry, Peter Burley. A.B., Williams Coll., 1940; LL.B., Washington U., 1947. Bar: Mo. 1947. Counsel Wohl Shoe Co., St. Louis, 1947-51, asst. sec. treas., 1950-51; sec. Brown Shoe Co. (name changed to Brown Group, Inc. 1972), St. Louis, 1954-64, v.p., 1964-66, exec. v.p., 1966-68, pres., 1968-72, chief exec. officer, 1969-72, 79-82, chmn. bd., 1972—, pres., 1972-79, chmn. exec. com., 1971—, also dir.; chmn. bd. Fed. Res. Bank St. Louis; dir. Gen. Am. Life Ins. Co., Owens-Corning Fiberglas Corp., TransWorld Corp., TWA Inc., Ralston Purina Co. Chmn. bd. trustees Washington U.; chmn. nat. bd. Smithsonian Assocs.; trustee Williams Coll., 1975-80; chmn. bd. trustees St. Louis Symphony Soc. Assn.; pres. United Fund Greater St. Louis, 1973, campaign chmn., 1972; mem. emeritus, former pres. St. Louis Civic Progress. Served from ensign to lt. USNR, 1941-45; as lt. comdr., 1951-52; Korea. Mem. Am. Footwear Industries Assn. (past chmn.). Republican. Office: 8400 Maryland Ave Saint Louis MO 63105

GRIFFIN, WILLIAM MARVIN, insurance company executive; b. Hartford, Conn., June 20, 1926; s. Samuel M. and Florence E. (Smith) G. A.A., U. Hartford, 1949; B.S., U. Pa., 1952. Sec. investments Conn. Gen. Life Ins. Co., Hartford, 1952-64; sr. v.p. Hartford Fire Ins. Co., 1964-73, exec. v.p., 1973—, chmn. fin. com., 1977—, also dir., dir. subsidiaries; dir. Eaton & Howard, Vance Sanders Mut. Funds; pres. Hartford Securities Co., Inc., Hartford Real Estate Co.; dir. Tex. Utilities Co. Served with AUS, 1945-46. Clubs: Hartford Golf., University. Office: Hartford Plaza Hartford CT 06115

GRIFFIN, WILLIAM THOMAS, lawyer; b. N.Y.C., Sept. 27, 1905; s. John and Alice (Doonan) G.; m. Joan Mannix, Jan. 10, 1934; children: Christine, William, Gabrielle, Peter. A.B. summa cum laude, Holy Cross Coll., 1927; LL.B. cum laude, Fordham U., 1930. Bar: N.Y. 1931. Practiced in N.Y.C.; former v.p. law N.Y., New Haven and Hartford Ry. Co. Corp.; dir. New Eng. Transp. Co., Am. Trust Co.; dir., v.p., gen. counsel Roper Realization Co., Inc., John L. Roper Lumber Co., Norfolk So. Land Co.; dir., v.p., atty. Providence Produce Warehouse Co. Member Am., Fed., Richmond County bar assns., Am. Judicature Soc., Nat. Lawyers Club, N.Y. Law Inst., N.Y. County Lawyers Assn., Assn. ICC Practitioners, Internat. Assn. Barristers. Clubs: New York Athletic (N.Y.C.); Quinipiack (New Haven); Richmond County Country (S.I., N.Y.); Princess Anne Country (Virginia Beach, Va.). Home and Office: 37 Howard Ave Grymes Hill NY 10301

GRIFFING, CLAYTON ALLEN, building materials company executive; b. Pine Bluff, Ark., Oct. 20, 1940; s. Hugh Milton and Vernon Frances (Cates) G.; m. Jean Ann Lack, Nov. 21, 1962; children: C. Lance, Kimberly. B. in Ceramic Engring, Ga. Inst. Tech., 1963; M.B.A., Emory U., 1965. With Atlantic Steel Co., Atlanta, 1965-80, asst. treas. finance, 1969-71, treas., 1971-78, v.p. fin., 1978-80; sr. v.p. Lowe's Cos. Inc., North Wilkesboro, N.C., 1980—. Trustee Fernbank, Inc., 1975-80; Mem. Leadership Atlanta, 1972-73. Mem. Fin. Execs. Inst., Exchange Club (dir. 1971-72, pres. 1975-76), Emory Bus. Sch. Alumni Assn. (pres. 1975-76), Leadership Ga., Beta Gamma Sigma. Home: Route 4 Box 64D Wilkesboro NC 28697 Office: Box 1111 North Wilkesboro NC 28656

GRIFFING, JOSEPH BRUCE, educator; b. Tempe, Ariz., Feb. 24, 1919; s. John B. and Anna M. (Kelly) G.; m. Penelope M. Scott, Sept. 1, 1950; children—Cynthia, Steven, Joan, Deborah. B.S., Ia. State U., 1941, M.S., 1947, Ph.D., 1948; Roosevelt fellow, U. San Marcos, Lima, Peru, 1941-42; NRC fellow, U. Cambridge, Eng., 1953-55. Instr. genetics Iowa State U., 1947-48, asst. prof., 1948-53; prin. research officer plant industry Commonwealth Sci. and Indsl. Research Orgn., Australia, 1955-57, sr. research fellow, 1957-59, sr. prin. research scientist, 1959-65, chmn. genetic sect., 1960-62; Mershon prof. genetics Ohio State U., 1965—, chmn. dept., 1967—. Bd. dirs. Ohio State U. Research Found. Served with AUS, 1943-46. Chilean-Pan.-Am. fellow, 1942. Mem. Genetics Soc. Am., Am. Soc. Naturalist, AAAS, Ohio Acad. Sci., Sigma Xi, Gamma Sigma Delta. Home: 4235 Clairmont Rd Columbus OH 43220

GRIFFITH, ANDY, actor; b. Mt. Airy, N.C., June 1, 1926; m. Barbara Edwards; children—Andy Sam, Dixie Nan. Grad., U. N.C. at Chapel Hill. Performed for civic clubs, night clubs; TV debut as monologuist: Ed Sullivan show, 1954; Broadway debut as illiterate hillbilly draftee in: No Time for Sergeants, 1955; also in motion picture, 1958; motion pictures include Onionhead, 1958, Second Time Around, Savages, 1974, Winter Kill, 1974, Adams of Eagle Lake, 1975, The Treasure Chest Murder, 1975, Hearts of the West, 1975, Six Characters in Search of an Author, Hollywood TV Theatre, 1976, The Girl in the Empty Grave, 1977; role: Broadway musical comedy Destry, 1959; recording What It Was Was Football; TV star: Andy Griffith Show, 1960-69; series Headmaster, 1970-71, The New Andy Griffith Show, 1970, Washington behind Closed Doors, 1977; TV movie From Here to Eternity; TV movie series Centennial; also numerous TV appearances. Home: Studio City CA 91604 *

GRIFFITH, B(EZALEEL) HEROLD, physician, educator; b. N.Y.C., Aug. 24, 1925; s. Bezaleel Davies and Henrietta (Herold) G.; m. Jeanne B. Lethbridge, 1948; children: Susan, Nancy. Student, Johns Hopkins U., 1943-44; M.D., Yale U., 1948. Diplomate: Am. Bd. Plastic Surgery (dir. 1976—, chmn. 1981-82). Intern Grace New Haven Community Hosp.-Yale U., 1948-49; resident in surgery VA Hosp., Newington, Conn., 1949-50; asst. resident in surgery 2d (Cornell) Surg. Div., Bellevue Hosp., N.Y.C., 1952-53; resident in plastic surgery VA Hosp., Bronx, 1953-55, U. Glasgow, Scotland, 1955, N.Y. Hosp. Cornell Med. Center, N.Y.C., 1956; research fellow in plastic surgery Cornell U. Med. Coll., 1956-57; practice medicine specializing in plastic surgery, Chgo., 1957—; attending plastic surgeon Northwestern Meml., Children's Meml., VA Lakeside hosps., Rehab. Inst. Chgo.; instr. surgery Northwestern U., 1957-59, asso. in surgery, 1959-62, asst. prof. surgery, 1962-67, asso. prof., 1967-71, prof., 1971—, chief div. plastic surgery, 1970—; cons. plastic surgeon Nantucket (Mass.) Cottage Hosp. Assoc. editor: Plastic and Reconstructive Surgery; Contbr. articles to profl. jours. Trustee Roycemore Sch., Evanston, 1966-79. Served to lt., M.C. USNR, 1950-52. Fellow A.C.S., Am. Assn. Plastic Surgeons, Chgo. Surg. Soc., Royal Soc. Medicine; mem. Am. Soc. Plastic and Reconstructive Surgeons (sec. 1972-74), Brit. Assn. Plastic Surgeons, Plastic Surgery Research Council (chmn. 1969), Am. Cleft Palate Assn., N.Y. Acad. Scis., AAAS, AMA, Ill., Chgo. med. socs., Assn. Am. Med. Colls., Midwestern Assn. Plastic Surgeons, Soc. Head and Neck Surgeons, Ill., Chgo. hist. socs., Civil War Round Table, Evanston Hist. Soc. (trustee 1974-78), Sigma Xi. Club: Yale (Chgo.). Lodge: Masons. Research in transplantation, skin tumors, cleft palate, paraplegia. Office: 251 E Chicago Ave Chicago IL 60611

GRIFFITH, CALVIN ROBERTSON, baseball executive; b. Montreal, Que., Can., Dec. 1, 1911; came to U.S., 1921; adopted by Clark C. Griffith, 1923; m. Natalie N. Niven, Feb. 1, 1940; children: Clark C., N. Corinne, Clare. Ed., Staunton Mil. Acad., 1928-32, George Washington U., 1932-35. Sec. Chattanooga Baseball Club, 1935-37, pres., 1937, mgr., 1937; pres., mgr., treas. Charlotte Club, 1938-41; v.p. Washington Am. League Baseball Club, 1943-55, pres., 1955-61, Minn. Twins, Am. League, 1961—; v.p. Am. League Profl. Baseball, 1973—; Mem. planning com. Profl. Baseball, also rules com. Named Baseball exec. of Year, 1965. Presbyterian. Address: care Minn Twins Metropolitan Stadium 8001 Cedar Ave Bloomington MN 55420 *

GRIFFITH, CLARK CALVIN, II, baseball club executive; b. Charlotte, N.C., Oct. 17, 1941; s. Calvin Robertson and Natalie Norris (Niven) G.; m. Karen Holmquist, Nov. 20, 1968; 1 son, Clark Calvin III. A.B., Dartmouth Coll., 1966. With Minn. Twins Baseball Club, Mpls., 1966—, exec. v.p.; treas., 1978—; chmn. bd. Major League Baseball Promotion Corp. Served with USN, 1961-63. Club: Minneapolis. Office: 501 Chicago Ave Minneapolis MN 55415

GRIFFITH, DONALD RAYMOND, physician; b. Kalamazoo, July 10, 1926; s. Lester James and Agnes Louise (DeYoung) G.; m. Constance Lee Newcomer, June 11, 1949; children: Pamela Jean, Curtis Alan (dec.). Student, Notre Dame U., 1944-45; A.B., Kalamazoo Coll., 1947; M.D., U. Mich., 1951. Diplomate: Am. Bd. Internal Medicine. Intern Univ. Hosp., Ann Arbor, 1951-52, resident internal medicine, 1954-57; physician Midelfort Clinic, Eau Claire, Wis., 1957—, bd. dirs., 1963—, pres. bd. dirs., 1970-77, med. dir., 1981—; preceptor U. Wis. Med. Sch., 1967—. Served with USNR, 1952-54. Mem. Am. Group Practice Assn. (trustee 1972-75, v.p. 1975-76, pres. 1977-78), A.C.P., Am. Soc. Internal Medicine, Wis. State Med. Soc., AMA. Republican. Congregationalist. Home: 1356 Priory Rd Eau Claire WI 54701 Office: 733 W Clairemont Eau Claire WI 54701

GRIFFITH, EDWIN CLAYBROOK, educator; b. Hague, Va., May 24, 1915; s. Richard Lee and Sarah Lee (Brown) G.; m. Mary Owen Hill, Dec. 28, 1940; children—Martha Anne, Richard Lee III. A.B., Hampden-Sydney Coll., 1936; M.A., U. Va., 1939, Ph.D., 1940. Instr. govt. Marshall (Va.) High Sch., 1936-37; instr. econs. Berea Coll., summer 1940; prof. econs. U. Ga., 1940-46; faculty Washington and Lee U., Lexington, Va., 1946-80, prof., 1950-80, prof. econs. emeritus, 1980—, head dept., 1959-80. Labor arbitrator Fed. Mediation and Conciliation Service, 1950—; pres. Community Chest, Lexington, 1956-57; mem. planning commn. Lexington, 1957-62, chmn., 1957-60;

mem. Lexington Sch. Bd., 1960-71, chmn., 1968-71; hon. chmn. Lexington United Fund, 1968; pres. Stonewall Jackson Hosp., Lexington, 1964-68. Mem. So. Econs. Assn., Va. Social Sci. Assn., Am. Arbitration Assn., Phi Beta Kappa, Omicron Delta Kappa, Beta Gamma Sigma. Episcopalian (vestryman). Club: Lion (past pres. Lexington). Home: 29 Sellers Ave Lexington VA 24450 *Our lives must be consistent with our responsibilities to God, to whom we are accountable, and to other people, to whom we are indebted for most of our opportunities.*

GRIFFITH, ELWIN JABEZ, lawyer, univ. adminstr.; b.; b. Barbados, W.I., Mar. 2, 1938; came to U.S., 1956, naturalized, 1963; s. Vincent and Ermie G.; m. Norma Joyce Rollins, June 9, 1962; 1 dau., Traci. B.A., L.I. U., 1960; J.D., Bklyn. Law Sch., 1963; LL.M., N.Y. U., 1964. Bar: N.Y. bar 1963. Asst. counsel Chase Manhattan Bank, N.Y.C., 1964-68, 68-71; asst. prof. law Cleveland Marshall Law Sch., 1968; asst. counsel Tchrs. Ins. and Annuity Assn., N.Y.C., 1971-72; asst. dean Drake U. Law Sch., 1972-73; asso. prof. U. Cin., 1973-76, prof., 197-61976-78, asso. dean, 1974-78; prof., dean DePaul U. Law Sch., 1978—; legal counsel Bedford-Stuyvesant Jaycees, 1968-71; vis. prof. colls.; vis. prof. Black exchange program Nat. Urban League, 1970-75. Contbr. articles to law revs. Bd. dirs. Leadership Council for Met. Open Communities, Chgo. Mem. N.Y. State Bar Assn., Am. Bar Assn. Office: 25 E Jackson St Chicago IL 60604

GRIFFITH, ERNEST RALPH, physician, educator; b. Bklyn., Aug. 20, 1928; s. Wesley and Dollie (Rutter) G.; m. Anna Santell, Aug. 22, 1981; children—Ann Griffith, Price, Jean Ellen. B.S., Dickinson Coll., 1952; M.D., Jefferson Med. Coll., 1956; M.S., U. Wash., 1970. Practice medicine specializing in family medicine, Colo., 1958-67; asst. dir., asst. then asso. prof. dept. phys. medicine and rehab. U. Cin., 1969-75; prof., chmn. dept. rehab. medicine Med. Coll. Va., Va. Commonwealth U.; now med. dir. Inst. Rehab. Medicine Good Samaritan Hosp., Phoenix.; Chmn. ad hoc com. Am. Congress Rehab. Medicine, 1980—. Contbr. articles to profl. jours. Served with AUS, 1946-48. Prin. investigator HEW grant; co-investigator Nat. Cancer Inst. grant, others. Mem. Am. Acad. Phys. Medicine and Rehab., Am. Congress Rehab. Medicine, Am. Acad. Electrodiagnosis and Electromyography. Address: Inst Rehab Medicine Good Samaritan Hosp 1111 E McDowell Rd PO Box 2989 Phoenix AZ 85062

GRIFFITH, FRANK WELLS, utility executive; b. Ft. Dodge, Iowa, July 1, 1921; s. Frank Whitcombe and Gladys (Wells) G.; m. Betty Marie Harrelson, Sept. 12, 1945; children: Clark Wells, Steven Harrelson, Jon Lance. B.S. in Gen. Engring, Iowa State U., 1947; student in utility mgmt., U. Mich., 1960. Gen. engr. U.S. Gypsum Co., Sweetwater, Tex., 1947-48; with Iowa Pub. Service Co., Sioux City, 1948—, asst. to pres., 1961-63, v.p. operations, 1963-65, exec. v.p., 1965-66; pres., chmn. bd., also dir.; pres., chmn. bd., dir. Midwest Energy Co.; dir. Security Nat. Corp.; Bd. dirs. Edison Electric Inst., 1970-84, vice chmn., 1980-81, chmn., 1981-82; bd. dirs. Electric Power Research Inst., 1981-84, Electric Info. Council, 1983-84. Trustee Iowa Natural Heritage Found.; gen. chmn. United Fund, 1968; commr. Iowa Devel. Commn., 1970-76; Bd. dirs. Sioux City Symphony Assn., Sioux City Art Center, Siouxland Blood Bank; chmn. bd. trustees Westmar Coll., 1967-74. Served to maj. USAAF, 1941-45; CBI. Mem. ASME, Am. Gas Assn., Midwest Gas Assn. (chmn. 1971-72), Nat. Assn. Electric Cos. (dir. 1974-77), N. Central Electric Assn. (pres. 1969), Sioux City C. of C. Episcopalian (vestryman). Clubs: Sioux City Engrs., Sioux Racquet (Sioux City); Masons, Shriners, Rotary. Home: 4019 Hiawatha St W Sioux City IA 51104 Office: PO Box 778 Sioux City IA 51102

GRIFFITH, GARTH ELLIS, lawyer, holding company executive; b. Cleve., July 1, 1928; s. Arthur Elza and Marguerite Mary (Ellis) G.; m. Julia Ellen Wilson, Oct. 29, 1971. A.B., Ohio Wesleyan U., 1950; J.D., U. Mich., 1953; LL.M., Case Western Res. U., 1964. Bar: Ohio 1953, Va. bar 1981. Atty. Chesapeake & Ohio Ry. Co., Cleve., 1957-64, gen. atty., 1964-75, sec., gen. solicitor, 1975-77, Chessie System, Inc., 1975-77, gen. solicitor, 1977-80; gen. counsel CSX Corp., 1980—. Served in U.S. Army, 1953-57. Mem. ABA, Greater Cleve. Bar Assn., Va. Bar Assn., Va. State Bar Assn., Richmond Bar Assn., ICC Practitioners Assn. Democrat. Methodist. Clubs: Cleve. Athletic.; Commonwealth (Richmond,). Home: 1517 Harborough Rd Richmond VA 23233 Office: 1500 Federal Reserve Bldg PO Box C-32222 Richmond VA 23261

GRIFFITH, HAROLD MELVIN, steel co. exec.; b. Clinton, Ill., July 4, 1904; s. Melvin M. and Anna (McGaw) G.; m. Fredrica Schneider, Sept. 14, 1927; children—Gretchen (Mrs. Harold R. Skeels), Shirley (Mrs. George Russell). B.S. in Elec.Engring, Chgo. Tech. Coll., 1926; student, Advanced Mgmt. Program, Harvard, 1949. Steel works metallurgist Bethlehem Steel Co., 1926-30, Jones and Laughlin Steel Co., 1930-36; with The Steel Co. of Can., Ltd., Hamilton, 1936—, beginning as metallurgist, successively asst. open hearth supt., open hearth supt., asst. works mgr., works mgr., asst. to the pres., 1936-53, v.p., 1953-64, exec. v.p., 1964-66, pres., 1966-71, chief exec. officer, 1968-73, chmn. bd., 1971-76, chmn. exec. com. of bd., 1976-79, dir., 1960-79; dir. Toronto, Hamilton & Buffalo Ry. Co. Mem. Am. Iron and Steel Inst., Internat. Iron and Steel Inst., Am. Inst. Mining, Metall. and Petroleum Engrs. (past chmn. open hearth steel com.). Office: Stelco Inc PO Box 205 Toronto-Dominion Centre Toronto ON M5K 1J4 Canada

GRIFFITH, JAMES WILLIAM, consulting engineer; b. Waco, Tex., Apr. 11, 1922; s. Paul Isaac and Willie Elizabeth (Rawlin) G.; m. Dorothy Louise Cannon., Oct. 17, 1949; children: Pamela D. (Mrs. John Fletcher Freeman), James William. B.S., So. Meth. U., 1949, M.S., 1956; student, Tex. Tech. U., 1940-41, U. Utah, 1943-44. Dir. engring. grad. div. So. Meth. U., 1960-67, chmn. dept. indsl. engring., 1965-67, prof., chmn. dept. systems engring., 1967-69; mgmt. cons. James W. Griffith Inc., Dallas, 1970—; U.S. expert in daylighting Commn. Internationale de l'Eclairage, 1957—; cons. to govt. agys. including HUD, HEW, Nat. Acad. Scis. Contbr. articles to profl. jours. Served with USAAF, 1942-46. Named to Engrs. of Distinction Engrs. Joint Council, 1970. Fellow Illuminating Engring. Soc. (nat. pres.), AAAS; mem. Bldg. Research Inst. (dir. 1965-67, 73-75), Nat., Tex. socs. profl. engrs., Sigma Tau, Eta Kappa Nu. Home: 3921 Caruth Blvd Dallas TX 75225 Office: PO Box 7596 Dallas TX 75209

GRIFFITH, JOHN FRANCIS, pediatrics educator; b. Humboldt, Sask., Can., Feb. 14, 1934; came to U.S., 1963; s. J. Stuart and Grayce M. (Reid) G.; m. Shirley Shaw, Sept 2, 1961; children: Kathleen Ann, Karen Elizabeth, Kristine M., James Stuart. B.A., U. Sask., 1956, M.D., 1958. Diplomate: Am. Bd. Pediatrics. Intern Montreal Gen. Hosp., Oue., Can., 1958-59, resident, 1959-60, gen. practice medicine, Westhill, Ont., Can., 1960-61; pediatric resident Montreal Children's Hosp., 1961-63, Case Western Res.U., Cleve., 1963-64, Mass. Gen. Hosp., Boston, 1964-67; research fellow neurology Harvard U. Med. Sch., Boston, 1964-66, research fellow neurophysiology, 1966-67, teaching fellow neurology, 1967-69; research infectious diseases Children's Hosp. Med. Ctr., Boston, 1967-69; asst. prof. pediatrics Duke U. Med. Ctr., Durham, N.C., 1969-71, assoc. prof., 1971-76, assoc. prof. medicine, 1975-76; prof. and chmn. pediatrics U. Tenn., Memphis, 1976—; med. dir. Le Bonheur Hosp., Memphis, 1976—, exec. com. med. staff, 1976—, exec. com. long range planning, 1981—; mem. staff City of Memphis Hosp., 1976—, exec. com. med. staff; cons. St. Jude Hosp., Memphis, 1976—; examiner Am. Bd. Pediatrics, Chapel Hill, N.C., 1979—, mem. task force on recert., mem. written exam. com., co-chmn. com., Chapel Hill, 1982—; mem. residency rev. com. Accreditation Council, Chgo., 1982—. Contbr. articles to profl. jours. Howard Hughes Found., 1971-74; Multiple Sclerosis grantee, 1969-71; Benjamen Miler Meml. grantee, 1971-74; FDA grantee, 1978-80. Mem. Memphis Epilepsy Found., Memphis and Mid-South Pediatric Soc., Memphis Acad. Neurology, Irish-Am. Pediatrics Soc., So. Soc. Pediatric Research, Mid-South Med. Ctr. Council, Soc. Pediatrics Research, Am. Pediatric Soc., Memphis-Shelby County Med. Soc., ABA, Am. Acad. Pediatrics, Assn. Med. Sch. Pediatrics Dept. Chairmen, Royal Coll. Physicians and Surgeons, Sigma Xi. Office: Le Bonheur Children's Med Center 848 Adams Memphis TN 38103

GRIFFITH, ORAN HEATON, ret. editor; b. Gary, Tex., Nov. 24, 1914; s. Wyatt Greer and Frances Ethel (Heaton) G.; m. Alice Marie Bradbury, July 13, 1935; 1 son, Charles Leo. B.S., Stephen F. Austin State U., Nacogdoches, Tex., 1949; Th.D., Tex. Bapt. Inst. and Sem., Henderson, 1960. Tchr., prin., supt. Tex. pub. schs., 1937-48; ordained to ministry Baptist Ch., 1938; pastor rural chs., 1938-48, White Oak (Tex.) Bapt. Ch., 1948-55, Lowell St. Bapt. Ch., Texarkana, Tex., 1955—; editor-in-chief Am. Bapt. Assn. Publs., 1955-80; chaplain Texarkana Fire Dept., 1961-62. Author: Successful Sunday School Administration, 1957, Child Evangelism, 1961, Here's How to Have a Better Sunday School, 1963, The Unity of the Trinity, 1976; Editor, pub.: The Soul Winner, 1952-55; writer quar.: Young People's Sunday Sch, 1955-57. Fund raiser Bogg Springs Bapt. Youth Encampment, Wickes, Ark., 1960; pres. trustees, 1960-67. Club: Lion (dir. White Oak club 1953-55). Home: 3012 Post St Texarkana TX 75501

GRIFFITH, RICHARD THOMAS, banker; b. Kansas City, Mo., Jan. 20, 1943; s. Harry Richard and Marie C. (Doyle) G.; m. Edna Elizabeth Miller, July 9, 1966; children: Cynthia Marie, Jennifer Denise. Student, Pepperdine U., 1960-61; cert., Grad. Sch. Banking, Stanford U. With First State Bank of Lynwood, Calif., 1961-64; asst. v.p., asst. mgr. corr. banking Crocker Citizens Nat. Bank, Los Angeles, 1964-66, v.p. data processing, 1966-70, v.p. mgr. data processing and systems adminstrn., San Francisco, 1971-73, v.p., asst. to pres., 1973, v.p., dep. adminstr. systemwide ops., 1974-75; exec. v.p. banking div. Teknekron, Bereley, Calif., 1975; sr. v.p. data processing Fed. Res. Bank of San Francisco, 1975-76, sr. v.p. bank ops., 1976-78, exec. v.p. dist. ops., 1981-83, 1st v.p., chief operating officer, 1983—. Served with USMC, 1962. Mem. Town Hall of Los Angeles. Clubs: Tiburon (Calif.) Peninsula, Commonwealth of Calif. Office: Fed Res Bank of San Francisco 101 Market St San Francisco CA 94105

GRIFFITH, ROBERT FREDERICK, former state justice; b. Claremont, N.H., June 12, 1911; s. Murrie Daniel and Grace Lavinia (Bickford) G.; m. Mabel Gertrude Brown, June 18, 1938; children: John Perry, Nancy Griffith Bjorkgren. B.A., U. N.H., 1933; J.D., Boston U., 1936. Bar: N.H. 1936. Since practiced in Nashua; asso. Hamblett & Hamblett, 1938-47; partner Hamblett, Griffith, Moran & Hamblett, 1947-52; asso. justice N.H. Superior Ct., 1952-67, N.H. Supreme Ct., 1967-77; dir. 2d Nat. Bank, Nashua, 1956-60. Chmn. Nashua chpt. ARC, 1954-56; pres. bd. dirs. YMCA, 1948-52; bd. dirs. Meml. Hosp., 1968-70. Served to 1st lt. inf. AUS, 1944-46. Recipient Centennial award Boston U., 1972; Silver Shingle, 1972; decorated Commendation medal. Mem. ABA, N.H. Bar Assn., Nashua Bar Assn. (past pres.). Republican. Unitarian. Clubs: Nashua Country, 20 Associates; Jacaranda West Country (Venice, Fla.). Home: 12 Berkeley St Nashua NH 03060 also 329 Coral St Venice FL 33595

GRIFFITH, ROBERT KENASTON, fabricated metal products company executive; b. Canton, Ohio, Mar. 5, 1917; s. Louis Eugene and Mary Wygant (Kenaston) G.; m. Edna Adele Roth, Nov. 1, 1942; children: Robert Kenaston, Adele Harley, Louis Eugene II, Mary Anne, Martha Wygant. B.S., Lafayette Coll., 1940; night student, Wharton Sch., U. Pa., 1953-55. With Riley Stoker Corp., Worcester, Mass., 1940-41, 46—, v.p., treas., 1956-60, pres., treas., 1960-69, chief exec. officer, 1966-69; v.p., treas., dir. Badenhausen Co., Cornwells Heights, Pa., 1956—; asst. sec., dir. A.W. Cash Co., Decatur, Ill., 1956—; pres., treas. Robert K. Griffith & Assos., Inc., Putnam, Conn., 1971—, Griffith Distbn. Co. Inc., Putnam; dir. Mechanics Bank, Worcester. Incorporator Hahnemann Hosp., Worcester; chmn. bd. fin. Town of Woodstock, Conn. Served to lt. col. USNR, 1941-46. Mem. ASME, Am. Soc. Ins. Mgmt., Zeta Psi. Republican. Home: 1300 Wahoo Ct Naples FL 33962

GRIFFITH, SAMUEL BLAIR, II, author, lectr., cons.; b. Lewistown, Pa., May 31, 1906; s. Henry Foster and Marguerite (Fitzgerald) G.; m. Belle Gordon Nelson, Dec. 21, 1929; children—Belle Gordon (Mrs. Harry Bailey Heneberger), Jane Serrill. B.S., U.S. Naval Acad., 1929; D.Phil., Oxford U., Eng., 1961; L.H.D., U. Maine, 1977. Commd. 2d lt. USMC, 1929, advanced through grades to brig. gen., 1956; staff, corps comdr., Tientsin, China, staff (7th Fleet), 1945-46, comdg. officer, Tsingtao, China, 1946-47, staff, Newport, R.I., 1947-50, chief of staff, 1951-52, mem. staff, Europe, 1953-56, ret., 1956; research fellow Council on Fgn. Relations, N.Y., 1964-67; research asso. Hoover Instn., Stanford, 1967-68; cons. aerospace systems div. Bendix Corp., Ann Arbor, Mich., 1965-67, Stanford Research Inst., Menlo Park, Cal. and; Washington, 1968-70, Hoover Instn., Stanford, 1967-68, Inst. for Def. Analysis, Washington, 1968-69; lectr. Nat. War Coll., Washington, 1966-68, Air War Coll., Maxwell AFB, Ala., 1967-70, Naval War Coll., Newport, R.I., 1975, 68, Army War Coll., Carlisle, Pa., 1970; U.S. Mil. Acad., 1966, 77, U.S. Naval Acad., 1968, U. Calif. at Berkeley, 1969, Stanford, 1968, Commonwealth Club, San Francisco, 1967, League Women Voters, Washington, 1968, Washington and Lee U., 1969, U. Va., 1969; Mem. Nat. Com. on U.S.-China Relations, N.Y.C., 1966-71; mem. vis. com. East Asian Studies, Harvard, 1967-70. Author: Mao Tse-tung: On Guerrilla War, 1962, Sun Tzu: The Art of War, 1963, The Battle for Guadalcanal, 1963, Peking and People's Wars, 1966, The Chinese People's Liberation Army, 1968, In Defense of the Public Liberty; Britain, America and the Struggle for Independence, from 1760 to the Surrender of Yorktown in 1781, 1976, also articles. Decorated D.S.C., Navy Cross, Purple Heart. Mem. Inst. for Strategic Studies, London, Eng., New Coll. Soc., 1st Marine Div. Assn., 1st Marine Raider Assn., U.S. Naval Acad. Alumni Assn., Marine Corps Assn. Address: 4 Elm St Newport RI 02840

GRIFFITH, STEVE CAMPBELL, JR., lawyer; b. Newberry, N.C., June 14, 1933; s. Steve Campbell and Bertie (Hambright) G.; m. Mary Stanley Salley, Dec. 22, 1962 (div. 1975); children: Mary Salley, Elizabeth Jane; m. Elizabeth Earhardt, May 22, 1976. B.S., Clemson U., 1954; LL.B., U. S.C., 1959. Ptnr. Blease & Griffith Attys., Newberry, 1959-64; asst. gen. counsel Duke Power Co., Charlotte, N.C., 1964-71, sec., assoc. gen. counsel, 1971-74, gen. counsel, 1975-77, v.p., gen. counsel, 1977-82, sr. v.p., gen. counsel, 1982—, dir., mem. exec. com., 1982—. Mem. S.C. Gen. Assembly, 1961-62. Served to 1st lt. U.S. Army, 1955-57. Mem. ABA, N.C. Bar Assn., S.C. Bar Assn., Mecklenberg Bar Assn. Democrat. Episcopalian. Club: Charlotte City. Lodge: Masons. Office: Duke Power Co 422 S Church St Charlotte NC 28242

GRIFFITH, THOMAS, editor; b. Tacoma, Dec. 30, 1915; s. Thomas and Anne (O'Reilly) G.; m. Caroline Coffman, Sept. 26, 1937. A.B., U. Wash., 1936; postgrad. (Nieman fellow), Harvard, 1942-43. Reporter, asst. city editor Seattle Times, 1936-42; contbg. editor Time Mag., 1943-49, nat. affairs editor, 1949-51, fgn. news editor, 1951-60, asst. mng. editor, 1960-63; sr. staff editor Time, Inc. (publs.), 1964-67; editor Life mag., 1968-72; essayist, newswatch columnist Time mag., 1973—; columnist, contbg. editor Atlantic mag., 1974-81; spl. writer Fortune mag., 1973—. Author: The Waist High Culture, 1959, How True, A Skeptic's Guide to Believing the News, 1974. Mem. Council Fgn. Relations, Hammer and Coffin, Fir Tree, Sigma Delta Chi. Clubs: University, Century Assn., Coffee House (N.Y.C.). Home: 25 East End Ave New York NY 10028

GRIFFITH, WAYLAND COLEMAN, mechanical engineer, educator; b. Champaign, Ill., June 26, 1925; s. Coleman Roberts and Mary Louise (Coleman) G.; m. Sylvia Brigitte Kuhn, May 27, 1961; children: Susan Jane, Rachel Diane. A.B., Harvard U., 1945, M.M.E., 1946, Ph.D., 1949. Registered profl. engr., N.C. Engr. Pratt & Whitney Aircraft Corp., summers 1945, 48; instr., then asst. prof. Princeton U., 1950-57; successively asst. dir., dir., v.p. research Lockheed Missiles & Space Co., 1957-71; asst. dir. new bus., 1971-73; R.J. Reynolds prof. mech. engring., dir. Engring. Design Center, N.C. State U., Raleigh, 1973—; vis. lectr. Stanford U., 1957-73; mem. various fed. and state sci. adv. panels, 1964—, Mem. citizens adv. com. transp., Raleigh, 1976-80. Author articles shockwaves, research adminstrn., energy systems, dust explosions.; Asso. editor: Jour. Fluid Mechanics, 1956—; co-editor: Recent Developments in Shock Tube Research, 1973. Recipient Gov.'s award N.C., 1978; AEC postdoctoral fellow, 1949; NSF postdoctoral fellow, 1955. Mem. Am. Phys. Soc., Am. Inst. Aeros. and Astronautics (chmn. Carolina sect. 1983-85), Royal Aero. Soc., AAAS (mem.-at-large sect. M 1981-84), Phi Beta Kappa, Sigma Xi, Pi Tau Sigma. Democrat. Methodist. Club: Cosmos (Washington). Home: 809 Rosemont Ave Raleigh NC 27607 Office: 2405 Broughton NC State U Raleigh NC 27650

GRIFFITH, WILLIAM ALEXANDER, mining co. exec.; b. Sioux Falls, S.D., Mar. 28, 1922; s. James William and Adeline Mae (Reid) G.; m. Gratia Frances Hannan, Jan. 27, 1949; children—Georgeanne Reid, James William, Wade Andrew. B.S. in Metall. Engring, S.D. Sch. Mines and Tech., 1947; M.S. in Metallurgy, M.I.T., 1950; Mineral Dressing Engr. (hon.), Mont. Coll. Mineral Sci. and Tech., 1971. With N.J. Zinc Co., 1949-57, chief milling and maintenance, 1956-57; metallurgist Rare Metals Corp. Am., Tuba City, Ariz., 1957-58; dir. research and devel. Phelps Dodge Corp., Morrenci, Ariz., 1958-68; with Hecla Mining Co., Wallace, Idaho, 1968—, exec. v.p., 1978, pres., 1979—; pres., dir. Chester Mining Co.; dir. Granduc Mines Ltd., Consol. Silver Corp. Served with USNR, 1943-46. Mem. AIME (Gaudin award 1977, Richards award 1981), Am. Mining Congress (dir.), Idaho Mining Assn. (pres.), Sigma Tau, Theta Tau. Republican. Clubs: Elks, Gyro. Home: PO Box 654 Osburn ID 83849 Office: PO Box 320 Wallace ID 83873

GRIFFITH, WILLIAM EDGAR, educator; b. Remsen, N.Y., Feb. 19, 1920; s. William G. and Sarah G. (Mitchell) G.; m. Ingeborg Maria Ehrhardt, 1948; children—Evelyn Elizabeth, Dorothy Isabelle, Oliver William. A.B., Hamilton Coll., Clinton, N.Y., 1940; M.A., Harvard U., 1941, Ph.D., 1950. Teaching fellow Harvard U., 1948-50; asst. to pres. Free Europe Com., 1950-51; polit. adviser Radio Free Europe, Munich, Germany, 1951-58; research asso. Center Internat. Studies, Mass. Inst. Tech., 1958-65, prof. polit. sci., 1965-72, Ford prof. polit. sci., 1972—; adj. prof. diplomatic history Fletcher Sch. Law and Diplomacy, 1962—; roving editor The Reader's Digest, 1973—. Author: Albania and the Sino-Soviet Rift, 1963, The Sino-Soviet Rift, 1964, Sino-Soviet Relations, 1964-1965, 1967, The Ostpolitik of The Federal Republic of Germany, 1978, The Superpowers and Regional Tensions, 1981; Editor: Communism in Europe, 2 vols, 1964, 66, The World and The Great Power Triangles, 1975, The Soviet Empire: Expansion and Detente, 1976, The European Left, 1979. Served to 1st lt. AUS, 1942-46. Mem. Council Fgn. Relations. Home: 19 Peacock Farm Rd Lexington MA 02173 Office: 30 Wadsworth St Cambridge MA 02139

GRIFFITHS, DANIEL EDWARD, university dean; b. Bridgeport, Conn., May 8, 1917; s. Frederick George and Helen (Quist) G.; m. Priscilla Tomlinson, June 22, 1946; children: Priscilla Ann Griffiths Russel, Michael Edward. B.Ed., Central Conn. State Coll., 1940; M.Ed., U. N.H., 1949; Ph.D., Yale, 1952. Asst. prof. edn. Colgate U., 1949-52; prof. edn. State Coll. Tchrs., Albany, N.Y., 1952-55; dir. coop. devel. pub. sch. adminstrn., asso. coordinator ednl. research N.Y. State Dept. Edn., 1955-56; asso. prof., then prof. edn. Columbia Tchrs. Coll., 1956-61; assoc. dean Sch. Edn. NYU, N.Y.C., 1961-65, dean Sch. Edn., Health, Nursing and Arts Professions, 1965—, spl. asst. to provost, 1983—; Dir. devel. criteria of success in sch. adminstrn. project, coop. research br. U.S. Office Edn., 1957-61, dir. devel. taxonomies of orgnl. behavior in edn. project, 1964; dir. N.Y.C. Study Tchr. Mobility, 1963; pres. N.Y. State Tchr. Edn. Conf. Bd., 1973-83. Author: Human Relations in School Administration, 1956, Administrative Theory, 1959, Organizing Schools for Effective Education, 1962, Administrative Performance and Personality, 1962, The School Superintendent, 1967; editor: Behavioral Science and Educational Administration, 1964, Developing Taxonomies of Organizational Behavior in Education, 1969, The Dilemma of the Deanship, 1980; chmn. editorial bd.: N.Y. U. Edn. Quar., 1968-83; editor: Ednl. Adminstrn. Quar, 1975-79; Editorial bd.: Library of Edn, 1961-67; chmn. Library of Edn, 1964-67. Pres. Sch. Bd. Greenburgh, N.Y., 1961-64. Served with USAAF, 1943-46. Mem. Am. Ednl. Research Assn., Nat. Conf. Profs. Ednl. Adminstrn., Am. Assn. Colls. Tchr. Edn. (dir. 1975-78), Assn. of Colls. and Schs. of Edn. in State Univs. and Land Grant Colls. and Affiliated Pvt. Univs. (exec. bd. 1972-83), Assn. Deans of Edn. in Pvt. Univs. (chmn. 1972-83), Univ. Council of Ednl. Adminstrn., NEA, Kappa Delta Pi, Phi Delta Kappa. Clubs: Scarsdale Golf (pres. 1980), Westchester Srs. Golf Assn. (pres. 1978-80). Home: 54 Clarendon Rd Scarsdale NY 10583 Office: NYU New York NY 10003

GRIFFITHS, FRANK A., professional sports team executive. Chmn. bd. Vancouver Canucks, Nat. Hockey League, B.C., Can. Office: Care Vancouver Canucks 100 N Renfrew St Vancouver BC Canada V5K 3N7§

GRIFFITHS, IORWERTH DAVIS ACE, educator; b. Raised, Idaho; s. Iorwerth Vivian and Katherine (Lewis) G.; m. Dorothea Ohs. B.S., U. Idaho; M.S., U. Ariz.; Ed.D., No. Colo. U.; postgrad., Wash. State U., U. Minn. With Sears Roebuck & Co., Dick Graves, Inc., Nev. and Idaho; tchr. public schs., Potlatch, Idaho, counselor public sch., Port Townsend, Wash.; dean of students Eastern Ariz. Coll., Thatcher, Reedley (Calif.) Coll.; prof. edn. Calif. State U., Fresno, 1959—; dir. U.S. Govt. Counselor Tng. Workshops, 1962, 64. Contbr. articles to profl. jours.; co-author: Principles of Retailing, 1956. Mem. Am. Personnel and Guidance Assn. (membership chmn. 1961-63), Am. Psychol. Assn., NEA, Calif. Personnel and Guidance Assn. (McDaniel award), Nat. Vocat. Guidance Assn., Assn. Counselor Edn. and Supervision, Calif. State Employees Assn., Kings-Tulare Guidance Assn., San Joaquin Valley Guidance Assn., Fresno Counselors Assn., Kappa Delta Pi, Delta Psi Omega, Phi Delta Kappa. Republican. Unitarian. Home: 6462 N Remington St Fresno CA 93704 Office: Calif State U N Maple Ave Fresno CA 93740

GRIFFITHS, PHILLIP A., mathematics educator, university provost. B.S., Wake Forest U., 1959; Ph.D., Princeton U., 1963. Miller fellow U. Calif.-Berkeley, 1963-64, asst. prof., 1964-66, assoc. prof., 1966-68; prof. math. Princeton U., N.J., 1968-72, Harvard U., 1972-83; Dwight Parker Robinson prof. math. Princeton U.; provost, James B. Duke prof. math. Duke U., Durham, N.C., 1984—. Recipient LeRoy P. Steel prize Am. Math. Soc., 1971. Office: Office of Provost Duke U Durham NC 27706 *

GRIFFITHS, RICHARD REESE, oil service corporation executive; b. Youngstown, Ohio, July 6, 1931; s. Frank Reese and Louis Mary (Hoffman) G.; m. Alma M. Mackin, June 22, 1957; children: Richard Reese, Gregory, Douglas. B.S., Youngstown U., 1957; M.B.A., Kent State U., 1960. Mgr. personnel Babcock & Wilcox, Barberton, Ohio, 1959-69; indsl. relations mgr. Dresser Industries, Chgo., 1969-77; v.p. human resources Trane Co., La Crosse, Wis., 1977-79; sr. v.p. human resources Geosources Inc., Houston, 1979—. Served with USMC, 1952-54. Mem. Am. Soc. Personnel Adminstrn., Machinery and Allied Products Inst. (vice-chmn. 1983-84). Republican. Roman Catholic. Clubs: Kingwood Country(Tex.); University (Houston). Office: Geosource Inc Suite 2000 2700 Post Oak Blvd Houston TX 77056

GRIFFITHS, ROBERT BUDINGTON, physics educator; b. Etah, India, Feb. 25, 1937; s. Walter Denison and Margaret (Hamilton) H. A.B., Princeton, 1957; M.S., Stanford, 1958, Ph.D., 1962. Postdoctoral fellow U. Calif. at San Diego, 1962-64; asst. prof. Carnegie-Mellon U., Pitts., 1964-67, asso. prof., 1967-69, prof. physics, 1969—, Otto Stern prof., 1979—. NSF postdoctoral fellow, 1962-64; Alfred P. Sloan research fellow, 1966-68; J.S. Guggenheim fellow, 1973; recipient Sr. Scientist award Humboldt Found., 1973, A. Cressy Morrison award Acad. Scis., N.Y., 1981. Mem. Am. Phys. Soc., Am. Sci. Affiliation, Phi Beta Kappa, Sigma Xi. Presbyn. Research in thermodynamics and statis. mechanics. Office: Physics Dept Carnegie Mellon Univ Pittsburgh PA 15213

GRIFFITHS, SYLVIA PRESTON, physician; b. London, Dec. 25, 1924; d. Wheeler Bate and Dorothy (Hartley) Preston; m. Raymond B. Griffiths; 1 dau., Wendy Elizabeth. B.A., Hunter Coll., 1944; M.D., Yale U., 1948. Intern Grace-New Haven Community Hosp., 1948-49, resident, 1949-52; fellow in pediatric cardiology Yale U., 1952-54; asst. to prof. clin. pediatrics Columbia U., N.Y.C., 1955, prof. clin. pediatrics, 1977—. Recipient career scientist award Health Research Council, City of N.Y., 1963-69. Mem. N.Y. Heart Assn. (dir. 1977—), Am. Acad. Pediatrics, Am. Pediatric Soc., Am. Heart Assn., Am. Coll. Cardiology. Office: Columbia-Presbyterian Med Center 622 W 168th St New York NY 10032

GRIFFO, JAMES VINCENT, JR., biology educator, educational administrator; b. Bklyn., Sept. 17, 1928; s. James Vincent and Delsie (Ceruti) G.; m. Sally Jean Stieren, Nov. 20, 1954; children: James Vicent III, Lauren Carol, Kenneth Charles. B.S., U. Ky., 1952, M.S., 1953; Ph.D., U. Fla., 1960. Teaching and research asst. U. Fla., 1956-60; instr. biology Fairleigh Dickinson U., Madison, N.J., 1960-61, asst. prof., Madison, 1962-63, chmn. dept. biology, Madison, N.J., 1963-66, acting campus dean, 1966, assoc. prof., Madison, 1967-69, campus dean, Madison, N.J., 1967—, prof., 1969—, campus provost, 1971—; project leader Wildlife Diseases U.S. Dept. Interior Fish and Wildlife Service, Laurel, Md., 1961-62. Served with AUS, 1953-55. Mem. Am. Soc. Mammalogists, Wildlife Fedn. Republican. Roman Catholic. Home: 33 Sherbrooke Dr Florham Park NJ 07932 Office: Office of Provost Fairleigh Dickinson U 285 Madison Ave Madison NJ 07940

GRIGG, JOSEPH WILLIAMS, newspaper correspondent; b. Bangor, Maine, Aug. 23, 1910; s. Joseph Williams and Anna Prentiss (Stearns) G.; m. Jerry Abbott, Apr. 4, 1944 (dec. 1959); children: Margaret, Richard Abbott; m. Margaret Meikle, November 19, 1960. Grad., Westminster Sch., London, England, 1929; student of, Trinity Coll., Cambridge, England, 1929-32; B.A., Cambridge U., 1932, M.A., 1966. Corr. London office N.Y. Sun, 1932-34; corr. United Press, London, 1934-39, 1957, Berlin, 1939-42, Washington, 1942-43, war corr., 1943-45, chief corr. and mgr. for France, Paris, 1945-51, chief corr. and mgr. for Germany, Frankfurt and Bonn, 1951-57; chief European corr. United Press Internat., 1957-60, news mgr. Western Continental Europe and North Africa, 1960-66, chief European corr., 1966-83; now freelance corr. newspapers including Atlana Jour.-Constn., St. Petersburg Times. Co-author: This is the Enemy, 1942. Mem. Anglo-Am. Press Assn. Paris (pres. 1965), Fgn. Press Assn. (Germany), Assn. Am. Corres. (pres. 1978) (London), Fgn. Press Assn. (London). Clubs: Wig and Pen (London); Overseas Press of Am. Home: 80A Oakwood Ct London W 14 England Office: United Press Internat 8 Bouverie St London EC 4 England

GRIGG, MILTON LATOUR, architect; b. Alexandria, Va., Apr. 18, 1905; s. James Fossett and Mary Emily (Glasgow) G.; m. Grace Vestal Thomas, Sept. 1, 1930; m. Ella Albian Repass, May 18, 1940. Student, U. Va., 1924-29. Cons. Nat. Council Chs.; commn. architecture Luth. Ch. Am., U.S. Park Service; mem. citizens adv. panel GSA.; Mem. Planning Commn. Charlottesville; chmn. Bldg. Code Rev. Bd. Draftsman, designer, Perry, Shaw & Hepburn, Boston, architects for restoration, Colonial Williamsburg, Va., 1929-33; pvt. practice architecture, Alexandria and Charlottesville, Va., 1933—; specializing: estates, chs., restoration, including Edgemont; other historic sites; sr. partner, Grigg, Wood, Browne, Eichman & Dalgliesh, to 1980; archtl. cons., 1980—; architect Am. embassy, Canberra, Australia.; Contbr. numerous papers to tech. lit. Pres. Interfaith Research Center, N.Y.; comptroller Internat. Congress on Religious Architecture.; Bd. dirs. Va. Archtl. Found. Civilian service with C.E., 1942-45; chief design hosps., mil. structures. Fellow AIA (religious bldg. com., regional dir. Middle Atlantic region); mem. Ch. Archtl. Guild Am. (pres.), Guild for Religious Architecture (pres.), Delta Sigma Phi, Theta Tau, Omicron Delta Kappa (hon. mem.), Scarab. Episcopalian. Clubs: Cosmos (Washington); Farmington, Colonade (Charlottesville). Home: 2033 Hessian Rd Meadowbrook Hills Charlottesville VA 22903 Office: 206 5th St NE Charlottesville VA 22901 *

GRIGG, WILLIAM HUMPHREY, utility executive; b. Shelby, N.C., Nov. 5, 1932; s. Claud and Margy (Humphrey) G.; m. Margaret Anne Ford, Aug. 11, 1956; children: Anne Ford, John Humphrey, Mary Lynne. A.B., Duke U., 1954, LL.B., 1958. Bar: N.C. 1958. Gen. practice, Charlotte, 1958-63; with Duke Power Co., 1963—, v.p. finance, 1970-71, v.p., gen. counsel, 1971-75, sr. v.p. legal and finance, Charlotte, 1975-82, exec. v.p. fin. and adminstrn., 1982—, also dir. Editor-in-chief: Duke Law Jour, 1957-58; Contbr. articles to profl. jours. Dir. Hatteras Income Fund, Inc.; Trustee Charlotte Latin Sch., Methodist Home Aged, Eugene M. Cole Found.; bd. dirs. Charlotte-Mecklenburg YMCA. Served to capt. USMCR, 1954-56. Mem. Am., N.C. bar assns. Methodist. Club: Charlotte Country. Home: 2301 Hopedale Ave Charlotte NC 28207 Office: 422 S Church St Charlotte NC 28202

GRIGGS, DOUGLAS MERIWETHER, JR., physiologist, medical educator; b. Portland, Maine, Aug. 14, 1928; s. Douglas Meriwether and Mackye (Reed) G.; m. Anne Lee Hager, May 26, 1956; children: Douglas, Stephen. B.A., Harvard U., 1949; M.D., U. Va., 1953. Intern, St. Lukes Hosp., N.Y.C., 1953-54, resident, 1954-58; asst. prof. internal medicine Hahnemann Med. Coll., Phila., 1962-66, asso. prof., 1966-67; asso. prof. physiology U. Mo. Med. Sch., Columbia, 1967-70, prof., 1970—; mem. research com. Mo. Heart Assn., 1972; study sect. cardiovascular and pulmonary NIH. Contbr. articles on cardiovascular research to profl. jours.; editorial bd.: Circulation Research, Am. Jour. Physiology: Heart and Circulation Physiology. USPHS Research Career Devel. awardee, 1963-72. Mem. Am. Physiol. Soc. Address: 1016 Yale St Columbia MO 65201

GRIGGS, HAROLD WARNER, banker; b. Duluth, Minn., July 23, 1918; s. Richard L. and Neva (Warner) G.; m. Barbara Ware, Mar. 31, 1943; children—Harold Warner, Richard W., Betsy H. Student, Dartmouth, 1938, 39; B.A., U. Minn., 1942. Asst. v.p. Duluth Nat. Bank, 1946-48; v.p. No. City Nat. Bank, Duluth, 1948-61, Union Bank, Los Angeles, 1961-63, regional v.p., Pasadena (Calif.) office, 1963-70, sr. v.p. pub. affairs, Los Angeles, 1970—; dir. First Nat. Bank, Hibbing, Minn., Virginia, Minn., Gilbert, Minn. Mem. Pasadena Tournament Roses, 1963—; Bd. dirs., pres. Caltech. Assos., 1973-75; bd. dirs., chmn. Los Angeles chpt. ARC, 1972—. Served to lt. USNR, 1942-45; PTO. Mem. Pasadena C. of C. (pres., dir. 1967-70), Psi Upsilon. Club: Altadena (Calif.) Town and Country. Home: 2085 Fox Ridge Dr Pasadena CA 91107 Office: Union Bank 445 S Figueroa St Los Angeles CA 90071

GRIGGS, JAMES HENRY, educator; b. New Monmouth, N.J., Oct. 21, 1912; s. James Edward and Deborah Ann (Roberts) G.; m. Anne Elizabeth Cameron, Sept. 1, 1936; children—Carol Ann, Nancy Jane. A.B., Harvard, 1932; M.A., Columbia Tchrs. Coll., 1933, Ed.D., 1940. High sch. tchr. Middletown (N.J.) Township High Sch., 1933-34; elementary sch. tchr., Des Moines, 1934-36; successively demonstration sch. tchr., asst. dir. demonstration sch., dean instrs. Nat. Coll. Edn., Evanston, Ill., 1936-48; dir. tchr. edn. Western Mich. U., Kalamazoo, 1948-56, dean, 1956-70, prof. edn., 1970-79, prof. emeritus, 1979—. Contbg. author: Curriculum Readers, 1937-38. Served to 2d lt. AUS, 1944-46. Mem. Phi Delta Kappa, Kappa Delta Pi. Baptist. Club: Rotarian. Home: 2609 Bruce Dr Kalamazoo MI 49008

GRIGGS, LEONARD LEROY, JR., airport administrator; b. Norfolk, Va., Oct. 13, 1931; s. Leonard LeRoy and Mary (Blair) G.; m. Denise Ziegler, Mar. 18, 1977; children: Margaret Rosalyn, Virginia Lorraine, Julia Blair, Deborah Branham. B.S., U.S. Mil. Acad., 1954; M.S. in Aero. Engring., Air Force Inst. Tech., 1960, George Washington U., 1967; disting. grad., Naval War Coll., 1967, Army War Coll., 1971. Registered profl. engr., Ohio. Commd. 2d lt. U.S. Army, 1954; advanced through grades to col. USAF, 1970; served in Vietnam, ret., 1977; dir. Lambert St. Louis Internat. Airport, 1977—. Decorated Silver Star, D.F.C. with 4 oak leaf clusters, Bronze Star, Meritorious Service medal, Air medal with 22 oak leaf clusters, Purple Heart, Air Force Commendation medal with 2 oak leaf clusters, Army Commendation medal; Medal of Honor; Medal of Gallantry (Vietnam); recipient Aviation Engring. Safety award FAA, 1979. Mem. Airport Operators Council Internat., Am. Assn. Airport Execs., Profl. Engring. Soc. St. Louis, Order of Dadelians. Clubs: Mo. Athletic (St. Louis); Order DeMolay. Home: 1609 Tradd Ct St Louis MO 63017 Office: PO Box 10212 Lambert Station St Louis MO 63145

GRIGGS, ROBERT CHARLES, physician; b. Wilmington, Del., Jan. 8, 1939; s. Albert Bertin and Virginia (Robertson) G.; m. Rosalyne Hoggard, June 16, 1964; children—Jennifer, Heather. A.B., U. Del., 1960; M.D., U. Pa., 1964. Intern Case Western Reserve U., Cleve., 1964-65, resident, 1965-66, Nat. Inst. Neurol. Disease and Blindness, Bethesda, Md., 1966-68; resident in medicine, neurology U. Rochester, N.Y., 1968-71, prof. neurology, medicine, pathology, pediatrics, dir. neuromuscular disease clinic, 1972—; practice medicine specializing in neurology, Rochester, 1971—. Author: Treatment of Neuromuscular Diseases, 1977. Served to lt. comdr. USPHS, 1966-68. A.C.P. Research and Teaching grantee, 1971-74. Office: PO Box 673 Dept of Neurology Strong Meml Hosp Rochester NY 14642

GRIGGY, KENNETH JOSEPH, food company executive; b. Suffield, Ohio, Mar. 7, 1934; s. Edward F. and Margaret M. (Rothermel) G.; m. Janice Marie Doetzel, July 30, 1960; children: Jill, Matthew, Mark, Jennifer. B.A., Athenaeum of Ohio, 1956; M.Ed., Xavier U., 1961. With Am. Heart Assn., Cin., 1960-61, Mead Johnson & Co., Evansville, Ind., 1962-64; v.p., dir. consumer product group Ralston Purina Co., St. Louis, 1964-73; pres., dir. domestic ops. Riviana Foods, Inc., Houston, 1973-75; chmn. bd., pres., chief exec. officer Wilson Foods Corp., Oklahoma City, 1975—. Bd. dirs. State Fair Okla. Served with U.S. Army, 1959-60. Mem. Am. Meat Inst. (dir.), Okla. C. of C. (dir.), Young Pres.'s Orgn. Clubs: Oklahoma City Golf and Country, Oak Tree Golf, Whitehall. Office: 4545 Lincoln Blvd Oklahoma City OK 73105

GRIGSBY, HENRY JEFFERSON, JR., editor; b. Denver, Dec. 29, 1930; s. Henry Jefferson and Thelma Pearl (Nispel) G.; m. Joan Shirley Rinker, Sept. 6, 1953; children: Kevin, Lisa, Lincoln. B.A., U. Colo., 1954. Reporter Sterling (Colo.) Jour.-Advocate, 1954-55; reporter, Sunday editor Lewiston (Idaho) Morning Tribune, 1955-58; reporter Denver bur. UPI, 1958-59, bur. mgr., Cheyenne, Wyo., 1959-61, mgr. Denver bur., 1961-66, S.W. div. news editor Dallas bur., 1966-69, mgr. San Francisco bur., 1969-72, night mng. editor, N.Y.C., 1972-74, mng. editor for news, 1974-75; asso. editor Forbes mag., N.Y.C., 1976-77, sr. editor, 1977-81, exec. editor, 1981—. Pres. Dallas chpt. Nat. Soc. Autistic Children, 1967-69. Served with USAF, 1950-52. Mem. N.Y. Fin. Writers Assn., Sigma Delta Chi, Phi Delta Theta. Home: 160 W 16th St Apt 1E New York NY 10011 Office: 60 Fifth Ave New York NY 10011

GRIGSBY, JEFFERSON EUGENE, JR., artist, educator; b. Greensboro, N.C., Oct. 17, 1918; s. Jefferson Eugene and Purry (Dixon) G.; m. Rosalyn Thomasena Marshall, June 12, 1943; children: Jefferson Eugene, Marshall Cephas. B.A., Morehouse Coll., 1938; student, J.C. Smith U., 1934-35, Am. Artists Sch., 1938-39; M.A., Ohio State U., 1940; Ph.D., NYU, 1963; D.F.A. (hon.), Phila. Coll. Art, 1965; postgrad., Ariz. State U., 1947, 49, Columbia U., 1950, 51. Artist in residence Johnson C. Smith U., Charlotte, N.C., 1940-41; art instr. Bethune-Cookman Coll., Daytona Beach, Fla., 1941-42; head art dept. Carver High Sch., Phoenix, 1946-54; tchr. Phoenix Union High, 1954-58, head art dept., 1958-66; prof. Ariz. State U., Tempe, 1966—; tchr. Children's Creative Ctr., Brussels World's Fair, 1958; co-dir. S.W. region 2d World Fest of Black and African Arts and Culture, Lagos, Nigeria, 1977; chmn. Four Corners Art Edn. Conv., Scottsdale, Ariz., 1982. One-man shows, Wirshemm Gallery, Luxembourg City, 1944, Morehouse Coll., Atlanta, 1967, J.C. Smith U., 1967, Central State Coll., Wilberforce, Ohio, 1967, Winston-Salem State U., 1971, No. Colo. U., Tex. So. U., 1966, Atlanta Pub. Schs., 1983, group shows, Balt. Mus., 1940, Atlanta U., 1938, Ariz. State Fair, 1952; group shows, Am. Negro Expn., Chgo., 1940; group shows, Black Artists-South Huntsville Mus., 1979, Artists of the Black Community, Ariz., 1981, Nat. Cof. Artists, represented in permanent collections, Richmond Pub. Schs., Va., Malcolm X Coll., Chgo., Nat U.-Ghana, Cape Castle, Tex., So. U.; auhtor: Art & Ethnics, 1970; cons. editor: African Arts Mag.; contbg. editor: School Arts Mag. Bd. dirs. Phoenix Art Mus., Opportunities Industrialization Ctr., Booker T. Washington Child Devel. Ctr., Phoenix Arts Coming Together. Served with AUS, 1942-45. Recipient 75th Anniversary medallion U. Ariz., 1960, 25th Anniversary medallion Nat. Gallery Art, 1966, E.C. Morra award of excellence Nat. Conf. Artists, 1977, Merit award Phoenix, Urban League, 1974, Disting. Research Scholar award Ariz. State U., 1982-83; elected Danforth Assn., 1974. Fellow African Studies Assn.; mem. Nat. Art Edn. Assn. (v.p. Pacific region 1972-74, co-chmn. minority concerns com. 1978, mem. Grigsby award com. 1980, award for contbn. to art edn. 1980), Ariz. Art Edn. Assn., Ariz. Artists Guild, Am. Assn. Aesthetics, Internat. Soc. Edn. through Art, Nat. Conf. Artists, NEA, Coll. Art Assn., African Heritage Assn., Alpha Phi Alpha, Nat. Found. Advancement of Art (mem. visual arts selection com.). Home: 1117 N 9th St Phoenix AZ 85006 Office: Art Deptz Ariz State U Temple AZ 85281 *It has been my great fortune to have had support and encouragement from my relatives, my wife and children. My parents instilled a sense of integrity, a love of learning, and confidence in myself. My wife and sons have creatively reinforced these attributes. My first art teacher gave me insights into teaching that cannot be found in texts. My students have been among my greatest teachers.*

GRIGSBY, JOHN LYNN, electronics company executive; b. Tulsa, Apr. 28, 1924; s. James Arnette and Lynette (Kimmons) G.; m. Virginia Ruth Eck, July 15, 1950; children—David A., Sharon L., Susan E., Gloria J. B.S. in Elec. Engring, U. Colo., 1949; M.S., Stanford, 1956, Ph.D., 1959. Radio operator FCC, Tex., Neb., 1942, 43; engr. Gen. Electric Co., Pittsfield, Mass., Syracuse, N.Y., 1949-52; research asso. Stanford, 1953-59; chief engr., v.p. applied tech. div. Itek Corp., Palo Alto, Cal., 1960-70, exec. v.p., 1970-75, pres., 1975-80, corp. v.p. for def. electronics ops., 1980—. Served with USAAF, 1943-46. Mem. IEEE (sr.), Sigma Xi, Tau Beta Pi, Eta Kappa Nu, Sigma Tau. Research and devel. in active and passive electronic countermeasures systems. Home: 729 Viola Pl Los Altos CA 94022 Office: 645 Almanor Ave Sunnyvale CA 94086

GRIGSBY, MARGARET ELIZABETH, physician; b. Prairie View, Tex., Jan. 16, 1923; d. John Richard and Lee (Hankins) G. B.S., Prairie View State Coll., 1943; M.D., U. Mich., 1948. Diplomate: Nat. Bd. Med. Examiners, Am. Bd. Internal Medicine. Intern Homer G. Phillips Hosp., St. Louis, 1948-49, asst. resident medicine, 1949-50; asst. resident Freedmen's Hosp., Washington, 1950-51, asst. physician, 1952-56, attending physician, 1956; practice medicine specializing in internal medicine, Washington, 1953-54; instr. medicine Howard U., Washington, 1952-57, asst. prof., 1957-60, asso. prof., 1960-66, prof., 1966—, chief of infectious diseases, 1952-71, lectr., 1955-59, adminstrv. asst. dept. medicine, 1961-63; epidemiologist USPHS, Ibadan, Nigeria, 1966-68; hon. vis. prof. preventive and social medicine U. Ibadan, 1967-68; cons. AID, Dept. State, 1970-71; mem. adv. com. anti-infective agents FDA, 1970-72. Contbr. articles to med. jours. Rockefeller Found. fellow Harvard U., 1951-52; research fellow Thorndike Meml. Lab., Boston City Hosp., 1951-52; China Med. Bd. fellow tropical medicine U. P.R., 1956; Commonwealth Fund Fellow U. London, 1962-63. Fellow A.C.P.; mem. AMA, Nat. Med. Assn., Med. Soc. D.C., AAUP, Royal, Am. socs. tropical medicine and hygiene, Am. Pub. Health Assn., Medico-Chirug. Soc. D.C., Assn. Former Interns and Residents Freedman's Hosp., Bus. and Profl. Women's Club, Pasteur Med. Reading Club, Prairie View, U. Mich. alumni assns., Sigma Xi, Alpha Epsilon Iota, Alpha Kappa Alpha. Home: 3265 Chestnut St NW Washington DC 20015 Office: Howard U Washington DC 20059

GRIKA, LARRY ARNOLD, musician; b. Chgo., Oct. 14, 1932; s. Samuel and Celia (Goldberg) G.; m. Pearl Millman, Aug. 8, 1966; children: Marc U., Lauren J., Deborah J. Mus.B., Chgo. Mus. Coll., 1954; Mus.M., Roosevelt U., 1955; postgrad., Cath. U., DePaul U. Instr. music history and violin Antioch (Ohio) Coll., 1959-62; mem. Phila. Orch. Com., 1967-68, 68-69, chmn. mems.' com., 1978-79; mem. faculty Temple U., Phila., 1982—; del. Internat. Conf. Symphony and Opera Orchs., 1979; faculty Glassboro (N.J.) State Coll., 1975-77. With, Lyric Opera, Chgo., 1954, 55; 1st violinist, Cin. Symphony Orch., 1962-64, Phila. Orch., 1964—; mem., Amerita String Ensemble, 1966—; participant, Casals Festival, P.R., 1982. Served with AUS, 1956-59. Recipient Oliver Ditson award, 1953-54, 54-55. Home: 215 Philellena Rd Cherry Hill NJ 08034 Office: 1420 Locust St Philadelphia PA 19102

GRILICHES, ZVI, educator, economist; b. Kaunas, Lithuania, Sept. 12, 1930; came to U.S., 1951, naturalized, 1960; m. Diane Asseo, Apr. 26, 1953; children—Eve, Marc. Student, Hebrew U., Jerusalem, 1950-51; B.S., U. Calif. at Berkeley, 1953, M.S., 1954; M.A., U. Chgo., 1955, Ph.D., 1957. Asst. prof. econs. U. Chgo., 1956-59, asso. prof., 1960-64, prof., 1964-69, Harvard U., 1969-78, Nathaniel Ropes prof. polit. economy, 1979—, chmn. dept. econs., 1980—; research asso. Nat. Bur. Econ. Research, 1959-60, 78—; vis. prof. Econometric Inst., Netherlands Sch. Econs., Rotterdam, 1963-64, Hebrew U., 1964, 72, 77; cons. Rand Corp., Brookings Instn.; Bd. govs. Fed. Res. System, Ford Found., NSF; mem. Pres. Sci. Adv. Council Panel on Youth, 1970-73. Author: Price Indexes and Quality Change, 1971, Economies of Scale and the Form of the Production Function, 1971; Contbr. articles to profl. jours. Served with Israeli Army, 1948-49. Fellow Am. Acad. Arts and Scis., Econometric Soc. (pres. 1975), Am. Statis. Assn., AAAS.; mem. Nat. Acad. Scis. (com. on ability testing 1979-81, com. on nat. stats. 1980-82), Am. Econ. Assn. (mem. exec. com. 1979—, J.B. Clark medal 1965), Am. Farm Econ. Assn. (award of merit 1958, 59, 60, 65), Royal Econ. Soc. Home: 89 Dorset Waban MA 02168

GRILL, LAWRENCE J., lawyer, business company executive; b. Chgo., Nov. 5, 1936; s. Samuel S. and Evelyn (Wollack) G.; m. Joan V. Krimston, Dec. 16, 1961; children: Steven Eric, Elizabeth Anne. B.S. with honors, U. Ill., 1958; postgrad., U. Chgo., 1959-60; LL.B., Northwestern U., 1963. Bar: Ill. bar 1963, Cal. bar 1965; C.P.A., Ill. Audit and tax mgr. Arthur Anderson & Co., Chgo., 1959-60; with firm Aaron, Aaron, Schimberg & Hess, Chgo., 1963-64, Gendel, Raskoff, Shapiro & Quittner, Los Angeles, 1964-66; sec., gen. counsel Traid Corp., Los Angeles, 1966-69; v.p., sec., gen. counsel Kaufman & Broad, Inc., Los Angeles, 1969-78; pres. Kaufman & Broad Asset Mgmt., dir. subs.; v.p., sec., gen. counsel AM Internat., Inc., Century City, 1978-82, dir. subs.; sr. v.p., group ops. officer Wickes Cos., Inc., Santa Monica, 1982—. Served with AUS, 1958-59. Home: 4622 Via Apuesta Tarzana CA 91356 Office: 3340 Ocean Park Blvd Santa Monica CA 90405

GRILLO, HERMES CONRAD, surgeon; b. Boston, Oct. 2, 1923; s. Giacomo and Rose G.; m. Dorothy Whittier, July 5, 1958; children—Andrea York, Hermes Conrad, Paula, Amy Whittier. A.B., Brown U., 1943; M.D., Harvard U., 1947. Diplomate: Am. Bd. Surgery, Am. Bd. Thoracic Surgery (dir. 1979—). Intern Mass. Gen. Hosp., Boston, 1947-48, resident, 1948-51, 53-55, mem. surg. staff, 1955—, chief gen. thoracic surgery, 1969—; practice medicine, specializing in thoracic surgery, Boston, 1955—; prof. surgery Harvard U. Med. Sch., 1973—. Mem. editorial bd. Jour.: Thoracic and Cardiovascular Surgery, 1975-82; contbr. sci. articles to profl. jours. Served with USMC, 1951-52; Served with USN, 1952-53. Decorated Commendation medal with Combat V, cavaliere Dell'Ordine al Merito della Repubblica Italiana, Order Civil Merit (Korea). Mem. Am. Assn. Thoracic Surgery, Soc. Thoracic Surgeons, Am. Surg. Assn., A.C.S., Am. Coll. Chest Physicians, Am. Thoracic Soc., N.E. Surg. Soc., Belgian Surg. Soc. (hon.), Italian Thoracic Surg. Soc. (hon.), Assn. Thoracic Surgeons (hon.), Phi Beta Kappa, Sigma Xi, Alpha Omega Alpha. Office: Mass Gen Hosp Boston MA 02114

GRILLO, JOANN, mezzo soprano; b. Bklyn., May 14, 1939; d. John D. and Lucile (DePierre) G.; m. Richard Kness, 1967; 1 son, John Richard. Grad., Hunter Coll., 1976; student, N.Y. Coll. Music, Am. Acad. Dramatic Arts; studied voice with, Marinka Gurewich, Kathryn Long, Daniel Ferro, Lorenzo Anselmi, Joan Dornemann; also courses, Met. Opera. Appeared in: Aida, Madame Butterfly, N.Y. City Opera, 1962; European debut in: Werther at, Gran Teatro Liceo, Barcelona, 1963, 78; appeared with, Paris Opera, Teatro San Carlo, Naples, Zurich Stadttheatre, Bellas Artes of Mexico City, 1963, 78, Israel Nat. Opera, Opera of Marseille, 1964, Frankfort Opera-Carmen, Amneris, Jocasta, 1967-68; debut with, Met. Opera, N.Y.C., 1963; resident artist, 1963—; debut with Vienna Staatsoper as Carmen, 1978; performed Carmen with, Paris Opera, 1981; appearances, Opera Nice, Washington Opera Soc., Amsterdam Opera, Phila. Opera, Cin. Opera, 1978; toured U.S. for, Civic Concert Orgn., 1959, 1961; presented concerts in, Europe, Latin Am., Far East. Roman Catholic. Office: care Eric Semon Assocs Inc 111 W 57th St New York NY 10019 *I pray that God is with me in all that I do; that He gives me the courage to face life with a total honesty; that He provides me with renewed enthusiasm every time that I fall.* *

GRIM, JERRY, union ofcl.; b. Athens County, Ohio, Dec. 27, 1922; s. Jerry and Ethel (Handley) G.; m. Marjorie Dudley, Aug. 26, 1944; 6 children. Student, Ohio U., 1938-41. With Western Union Telegraph Co., 1943—; regional pres. (Lake region United Telegraph Workers), 1972-73, nat. sec.-treas., 1974-75, internat. sec.-treas., Rockville, Md., 1975—. Served with AUS, 1944-46. Democrat. Office: 701 Gude Dr Rockville MD 20850

GRIM, SAMUEL ORAM, chemistry educator; b. Landisburg, Pa., Mar. 11, 1935; s. Oram Michael and Esther Blanche (Gable) G.; m. Faith H. Rojahn, June 8, 1957 (div. 1982); children: Stephen W., Amy R., Lucy G.; m. Caren L. Klarman, Mar. 11, 1983. B.S., Franklin and Marshall Coll., 1956; Ph.D., Mass. Inst. Tech., 1960. Faculty U. Md., College Park, 1960—, prof. chemistry, 1968—, chmn. inorganic chemistry div., 1970-77, 80—. Contbr. articles to profl. jours. Union Carbide Co. scholar, 1954-56; NSF fellow, 1958-60; summer teaching fellow, 1960; research fellow Imperial Coll., London, 1961-62; Sir John Cass's Found. sr. research fellow City of London Poly., 1979-80. Fellow Am. Inst. Chemists, Royal Soc. Chemistry (London); mem. Am. Chem. Soc., AAAS, N.Y. Acad. Scis., Chem. Soc. Washington, Phi Beta Kappa, Sigma Xi (Sci. Achievement award 1983), Phi Lambda Upsilon, Alpha Chi Sigma. Republican. Clubs: Mason., Terrapin (College Park). Home: 4205 Sheridan St University Park MD 20782 Office: Dept Chemistry U Md College Park MD 20742

GRIMBALL, WILLIAM HEYWARD, lawyer; b. Charleston, S.C., Feb. 6, 1917; s. William Heyward and Panchita (Heyward) G.; m. Frances Lucas Ellerbe, Aug. 9, 1944; children—William Heyward, Henry E., Arthur, Francis E. A.B., Coll. of Charleston, 1938; LL.B., U. Va., 1941. Bar: S.C. bar 1941. Since practiced in, Charleston; asso. firm Mitchell & Horlbeck, 1941-50; individual practice law, 1950-59, 63-64; mem. firm Figg, Gibbs & Grimball, 1959-63; partner firm Grimball, Cabaniss, Vaughan & Guerard, 1964-80, Grimball, Cabaniss, Vaughan & Robinson, 1981—. Pres. Preservation Soc., Charleston, 1974-75; mem. S.C. Legislature, 1952-58; chmn. Charleston County del., 1955-58; alderman City of Charleston, 1960-72, mayor pro tem, 1969; mem. Charleston County Election Commn., 1978-81. Served with USNR, 1942-46; to lt. comdr., 1962. Fellow Am. Coll. Trial Lawyers, Am. Bar Found.; mem. Am. Law Inst., Am. Bar Assn., S.C. Bar Assn., Charleston County Bar Assn. (past pres.), Maritime Law Assn., Alumni Assn. Coll. of Charleston (pres. 1953), Soc. of Cin., S.C. Soc., St. Andrews Soc., St. Cecilia Soc. Republican. Episcopalian. Clubs: Masons (past grand master S.C., 33 deg.), Shriners, Carolina Yacht. Home: 107 Chadwick Dr Charleston SC 29407 Office: 39 Broad St Charleston SC 29402

GRIMES, DALE MILLS, electrical engineering educator; b. Marshall County, Iowa, Sept. 7, 1926; s. LeRoy and Helen (Mills) G.; m. Janet LaVonne Moore, Mar. 22, 1947; children: Prudence Rae, Craig Alan. B.S. in Physics, Math. and Chemistry, Iowa State U., 1950, M.S. in Physics and Math, 1951; Ph.D. in Elec. Engring, U. Mich., Ann Arbor, 1956. From research asso. to prof. elec. engring. U. Mich., 1951-76; chief scientist Conductron Corp., Ann Arbor, 1960-63; prof. elec. engring., chmn. dept. U. Tex., El Paso, 1976-79; prof. elec. engring., head dept. Pa. State U., 1979—; cons. to govt. and industry. Author: Electromagnetism and Quantum Theory, 1969, Automotive Electronics, 1974; also articles on radar, biconical antennas, electromagnetic radiation. Served with USNR, 1943-46. Mem. IEEE, Am. Phys. Soc., AAAS, Am. Soc. Engring. Edn. Patentee ferrite radar absorbing material, magnetic absorbers. Home: 2548 Sleepy Hollow Dr State College PA 16801 Office: Elec Engring Dept Pa State Univ University Park PA 16802

GRIMES, HOWARD RAY, management consultant; b. Manilla, Iowa, July 24, 1918; s. Ray Herb and Sarah Alice (Saunders) G.; m. Dorothy Mae Bergren, Apr. 12, 1941; children: Patricia, Susan, Nancy, Sarah, Laura. Student, U. Wis., 1939; B.A., Grinnell Coll., 1940. With Aetna Life & Casualty Co., 1940—, field supr., regional mgr., Boston, 1950-74, regional dir., v.p. field, 1974-82; mgmt. cons., 1983—; v.p. Aetna Casualty Am.; dir. Treasure Masters Corp., Derry, N.H., Waterville Co., Inc. Bd. mem., sr. deacon Wellesley Hills Congregational Ch., 1975—; mem. Wellesley Town Meeting, 1973—; asst. treas., bd. dirs. Silver Anniversary All-Am. Found., 1964—; bd. dirs., former pres. Human Relations Service of Wellesley, 1960-70. Served with USAAF, 1942-45. Named Sports-Illustrated Silver Anniversary All-Am., 1964. Clubs: Down Town (bd. govs., v.p. Boston), Weston (Mass.) Golf; Bald Peak Colony (N.H.); Wellesley (pres., dir.). Home: 81 Arnold Rd Wellesley Hills MA 02181 West Branch Rd Waterville Valley NH 03223

GRIMES, IRVIN LORENZO, publisher; b. Chgo., Apr. 4, 1918; s. Irvin L. and Agnes E. (Shellhammer) G.; m. Nancy O. Ellis, Jan. 6, 1946; children: Sharon, Cynthia, Richard. B.S., Ind. U., 1942. With Richard D. Irwing Inc., Homewood, Ill., 1946—, pres., 1963-75, vice chmn. bd., 1975-77, chmn. bd., chief exec. officer, 1977—, dir.; pres. subs. Dorsey Press, 1959-64, dir., 1959—; v.p. subs. Dow Jones Irwin Inc., 1965-75, dir., 1965—. Bd. dirs. Ingall Meml. Hosp., Western Golf Assn., Calumet council Boy Scouts Am. Mem. Am. Acctg. Assn., Am. Mgmt. Assn., Am. Mktg. Assn., Am. Econ. Assn., Homewood C. of C. (dir.). Episcopalian. Club: Olympia Fields Country (dir.). Home: 20348 Ithaca Rd Olympia Fields IL 60461 Office: Richard D Irwin Inc 1818 Ridge Rd Homewood IL 60430

GRIMES, J. WILLIAM, cable television executive; b. Wheeling, W.Va., Mar. 7, 1941; s. John Bauer and Elizabeth (Hartshorn) G.; m. Barbara Leathers, Dec. 19, 1964; children: Spencer, Leland, Colby. B.English, W. Va. Wesleyan U., 1963; postgrad., St. John's U. With CBS, Inc., 1968, dir. sales WCAU, Phila., 1971-72, v.p., gen. mgr. CBS Radio Spot Sales, 1972-73, v.p., gen. mgr. WEEI Radio, Boston, 1973-74, v.p. AM stas., 1974-77, v.p. personnel, 1977-79, sr. v.p. AM and FM Stas., 1979-81, v.p. Broadcast Group; exec. v.p., chief operating officer ESPN, Inc., Bristol, Conn., 1981, pres., chief exec. officer, 1982—; dir. Cable Television Advt. Bur., N.Y.C., 1982—; mem. Nat. Acad. TV Arts and Scis., 1983—; com. mem. New Sch. for Social Research, 1983—. Bd. dirs. YMCA, Darien, Conn., 1981-82, Darien Jr. Football League, 1976-80. Mem. Nat. Assn. Broadcasters (dir. 1979-81). Clubs: Wee Burn Country, Tokeneke Tennis (Darien). Home: 20 Maywood Rd Darien CT 06820 Office: ESPN Inc ESPN Plaza Bristol CT 06010

GRIMES, STEPHEN HENRY, judge; b. Peoria, Ill., Nov. 17, 1927; s. Henry Holbrook and June (Kellar) G.; m. Mary Fay Fulghum, Dec. 29, 1951; children: Gay Diane, Mary June, Sue Anne, Sheri Lynn. Student, Fla. So. Coll., 1946-47; B.S. in Bus. Adminstrn, U. Fla., 1951, LL.B., 1954; LL.D., Stetson U., 1980. Bar: Fla. 1954. Since practiced in, Bartow; partner firm Holland and Knight, 1956-73; judge Ct. Appeal 2d Dist. Fla., 1973—, chief judge, 1978—; chmn. Conf. Fla. Dist. Cts. Appeal, 1978-80; mem. Fla. Council on Criminal Justice., 1979-82, Fla. Jud. Qualifications Commn., 1982—. Bd. dirs. Bartow Meml. Hosp., 1958-61, Bartow Library, 1968-78; trustee Polk Jr. Coll., Winter Haven, Fla., 1967-70, chmn., 1969-70; bd. govs. Polk Pub. Mus., 1976—. Served with USNR, 1951-53. Fellow Am. Coll. Trial Lawyers; mem. ABA, 10th Circuit Bar Assn. (pres. 1965), Fla. Bar, Bartow C. of C. (pres. 1964). Episcopalian (sr. warden 1964-65, 77). Clubs: Rotarian (Bartow) (pres. Bartow 1957-58, dist. gov. 1960-61); Peace River Country (Bartow) (pres. 1966-67). Home: 1950 El Paso St E Bartow FL 33830 Office: PO Box 327 Lakeland FL 33802

GRIMES, TAMMY, actress, singer, comedienne; b. Lynn, Mass., Jan. 30, 1936; d. Luther Nichols and Eola Willard (Niles) G.; m. Christopher Plummer, Aug. 16, 1956 (div. 1960); 1 dau., Amanda Michael. Grad., Beaver Country Day Sch., 1951, Stephens Jr. Coll., 1953. Mem. staff Westport Playhouse, Conn., 1954. N.Y. debut in, Neighborhood Playhouse, 1955; appeared in: Look After Lulu, 1959 (Theatre World award); singer, actress: Littlest Review, Off Broadway Phoenix Theatre, 1956; appeared, Stratford (Ont.) Shakespeare Festival, 1958; performed, Cambridge (Mass.) Drama Festival; in: Shakespeare's Twelfth Night, summer 1959; role of Moll in: Marc Blitzstein's opera The Cradle Will Rock, N.Y.C. Center, 1960; role in: on Broadway Unsinkable Molly Brown, 1961-62; later on tour; TV performer, NBC-TV on, Omnibus, 1959, Hollywood Sings, 1960; series Hour of Great Mysteries, 1960; in: Four Poster, CBS-TV, 1962, Horror at 35,000 Feet (Movie of the Week), CBS-TV, 1973, The Borrowers, Hallmark Hall of Fame, 1974; appeared in: Broadway prodn. Rattle of A Simple Man, 1964, High Spirits, 1965-66, Jubilee, 1973; starred in: Mollie, 1978, Tartuffe, 1977, California Suite, 1976-77; appeared in: films Three Bites of the Apple, 1966, Play It As It Lays, 1972, Somebody Killed Her Husband, 1977, The Runner Stumbles, 1979, Can't Stop the Music, 1980; musical 42d Street, 1980; theatrical appearances in Father's Day, 1979, A Month in the Country, 1979-80; mem., Potter's Field Theatre Co. (Recipient Comoedia Matinee Club award 1961), Potter's Field Theatre Co. (Antoinette Perry award 1960), Potter's Field Theatre Co. (Variety Drama Critics award 1961), Potter's Field Theatre Co. (Tony award for Private Lives 1970). Republican. Office: care Rifkin-David Agy 9301 Wilshire Blvd Suite 306 Beverly Hills CA 90210 *

GRIMES, WILLIAM ALVAN, retired chief justice N.H. Supreme Court; b. Dover, N.H., July 4, 1911; s. Frank J. and Annie (Ash) G.; m. Barbara Terry Parsons, June 22, 1940; children: Gail Terry, Gordon Francis. B.S., U. N.H., 1934, LL.D., 1969; LL.B., Boston U., 1937; LL.D., William Mitchell Coll. Law, 1979, Calif. Western Sch. Law, 1981. Bar: N.H. 1937. Assoc. firm Cooper & Hall, Rochester, N.H., 1937-41; partner firm Cooper, Hall & Grimes, Rochester, 1941-47; solicitor, City of Dover, 1946-47; justice N.H. Superior Ct., Concord, 1947-66, Supreme Ct. of N.H., 1966-79, chief justice, 1979-81; mem. faculty Nat. Coll. State Judiciary; disting. vis. prof. Calif. Western Sch. Law; mem. exec. com., past chmn. Appellate Judges Conf.; chmn. N.H. Vocat. Rehab. Planning Commn., N.H. Gov.'s Commn. on Crime and Delinquency; mem. council judges Nat. Council Crime and Delinquency; chmn. edn. com. Appellate Judges Conf.; mem. adv. council Nat. Center for State Cts. Mem. N.H. Ho. of Reps., 1933-35, 37-39. Served to lt. USNR, World War II. Mem. Am. Bar Assn. (past chmn. div. jud. adminstrn., chmn. drug abuse com. criminal law sect.), Stafford County Bar Assn., Bar Assn. State N.H. Democrat.

GRIMLEY, LIAM KELLY, educator; b. Dublin, Ireland, Apr. 4, 1936; came to U.S., 1970; s. William and Eileen (Kelly) G.; m. Marie Sadon, Aug. 26, 1973; children: Kevin, Conor. B.A., Nat. U. Ireland, 1960; L.Ph., Faculte Libre, Paris, 1963; H.D.Ed., Clongowes Wood Coll., Ireland, 1964; Th.B., Inst. Philosophy and Theology, Dublin, 1968, S.T.L., 1970; M.Ed., Kent State U., 1971, Ph.D., 1973. Tchr. English Lycee Moderne, LePuy, France, 1961-62; asst. dir. Summer Sch. English, Observatorio del Ebro, Tortosa, Spain, 1961-62; tchr. math and modern langs. Clongowes Wood High Sch., Ireland, 1963-64; tchr. math, classical langs. St. Ignatius Elementary and Secondary Sch., Galway, Ireland, 1964-66; instr. statistics and probability theory Univ. Coll., Galway, 1965-66; prof. theology Conf. Major Religious Superiors, Dublin, 1969-70; counselor Newman Center, Syracuse U., 1970; tchr. social studies Walsh Jesuit High Sch., Cuyahoga Falls, Ohio, 1971; asst. dir. Ohio Soc. Crippled Children and Adults, Tiffin, summer 1971; intern sch. psychologist Kent State U., 1972-73, research and devel. dir. lab. schs., 1972-73; prof. spl. edn. Ind. State U., Terre Haute, 1973—, chmn. dept., 1975-81, dir. Inst. Continuing Edn. in Psychology,, 1976-78; cons. Joseph P. Kennedy Found., 1973—; mem. State Adv. Com., Div. Pupil Personnel, 1975-78; Mem. Ind. State Manpower Steering Com., 1977-80; chmn. State Adv. Bd. on Pupil Personnel Services, 1980—; mem. State Council on Edn. of Handicapped, 1979—. Editor: The Sch. Psychology Digest, 1976-79; contbr. articles to profl. jours. Mem. Am. Psychol. Assn., Ind. Psychol. Assn. (pres. div. sch. psychology 1980-81), Nat. Assn. Sch. Psychologists. Roman Catholic. Home: 43 Allendale Terre Haute IN 47802 Office: Dept Spl Edn Sch Psychology and Communication Disorders Ind State U Terre Haute IN 47809

GRIMLEY, SLATER SAMUEL, Canadian govt. ofcl.; b. Derby, Eng., Aug. 10, 1921; s. Thomas Burton and Gertrude Ethel G.; m. Anne Margaret Daunt Golden, Oct. 16, 1948; children—Eileen, Myra. B.Sc. in Chem. Engring, Imperial Coll. Sci. and Tech., London, 1943, Ph.D., 1945. Research chem. engr. Brit. Atomic Energy Project, Can./U.K., 1945-1954; tech. mgr. plastics div. Can. Industries Ltd., Montreal, 1958-60, v.p. corp. planning and research, 1969-72; gen. mgr. research and devel. dept. Imperial Chem. Industries Ltd., London, 1965-67; gen. mgr. devel. and evaluation Nat. Research Council Can., 1972—. Author. Fellow Chem. Inst. Can.; mem. Can. Soc. Chem. Engring. (chmn. 1962), Instn. Chem. Engrs. (Hinchley medal), N.Am. Soc. Corp. Planning. Patentee in field. Home: 26 Rothwell Dr Ottawa ON K1J 7G4 Canada Office: Nat Research Council Can Montreal Rd Ottawa ON K1A 0R6 Canada

GRIMM, BEN EMMET, librarian; b. Jersey City, Sept. 27, 1924; s. Benjamin Harrison and Eunice Blanche (Whitenack) G.; m. Jean Kay Bohrer, Aug. 19, 1950 (div. 1982); children: Jeffrey, Kevin, Mark, Wendy. B.A., Washington and Lee U., 1949; M.S., Columbia U., 1950. Librarian youth services Detroit Public Library, 1950-52; sr. librarian Fair Lawn (N.J.) Public Library, 1952-54; reference and reading librarian Montclair (N.J.) Public Library, 1955-56, asst. dir., 1956-61; dir. Belleville (N.J.) Public Library, 1961-72, Jersey City Public Library, 1973—; mng. editor Library Trustee Newsletter, 1978-80; chmn. Hudson County Audio-Visual Aids Commn., 1975—; cons. library bldgs. services and adminstrn., 1966—. Chmn. Hudson County Am. Revolution Bicentennial Celebration Com., 1973-74. Served with USAAF, 1942-45. Decorated D.F.C., Air medal with oak leaf clusters; recipient Better Belleville award, 1968. Mem. ALA, N.J. Library Assn. (pres. 1968-69). Club: Rotary. Home: 14 Forest St Montclair NJ 07042 Office: 472 Jersey Ave Jersey City NJ 07302

GRIMM, DONALD E., oil company executive; b. Charleston, W.Va., Feb. 23, 1930. With W. R. Grace & Co., Dallas, 1961—, sr. v.p., dir., 1983—. Address: 3400 Interfirst Two Dallas TX 75270

GRIMM, EDITH RAMBAR, merchandising/marketing consultant; b. Seneca Falls, N.Y., Jan. 17, 1908; d. Mitchel J. and Florence (Kutner) Rambar; m. Emery G. Grimm, Aug. 31, 1929 (dec. Mar. 19, 1959). Ph.B., U. Chgo., 1927; postgrad., U. Mich., 1927-28. Tchr. math. Detroit pub. schs., 1927-29; supr. personal shopping service Marshall Field and Co., Chgo., 1935; with Carson Pirie Scott and Co., Chgo., 1935—, asso. gen. mdsg. mgr., 1958-63, v.p. gen. merchandising, 1963-73; chmn. retail adv. bd. Bride's mag., 1946-48; Regional dir. Chgo. Fashion Group, 1949-50; mem. adv. council Tobé-Coburn Sch., 1965—; dir. seminars on retailing Am. Mgmt. Assn. Chmn. gen. mdse. div. Chgo. Heart Fund, 1964; Mem. U. Ill. Citizens Com., 1972—, Nat. Home Fashions League Fund. Com., 1969—. Recipient Victory award and citation for war bond sales, 1945; YWCA award for outstanding Chgo. woman in bus. and industry, 1972; named one of ten outstanding women bus. and community leaders in, Chgo., 1959. Mem. Home Fashions League, Am. Inst. Decorators (nat. jury mem. for design competition 1953, design awards jury 1964), U. Chgo. Alumni Assn. (exec. bd. and senate 1952-53, chmn. improved activities com. 1954), Fashion Group. Clubs: Arts, Economic (Chgo.). Home: 3170 Sheridan Rd Apt 521 Chicago IL 60657 *I believe that courage, hard work, knowledge and decency in working with all levels of people in the business world are necessary for one to be truly successful. I tried to give full measure of these qualities to achieve my goals and with a little bit of luck succeeded most of the time.*

GRIMM, EDWARD ELIAS, retired naval officer, retired banker; b. York, Pa., Dec. 1, 1910; s. Walter Elwood and Mary (Craumer) G.; m. Ernestine Bernardin, June 1, 1936; children: Edward Anthony, Diana Michelle (Mrs. Robert Dean Brotherton). B.S., U.S. Naval Acad., 1933; M.B.A., George Washington U., 1952. Commd. ensign U.S. Navy, 1934; advanced through grades to rear adm., 1964, comdg. officer U.S.S. Rupertus, 1949-51, assigned Office Chief Naval Ops., 1952-55, 60-63, comdg. officer U.S.S. Sierra, 1955-56, asst. dir. budget and reports Office Navy Comptroller, 1956-59, comdr. Destroyer Squadron 30, 1959-60, comdr. Destroyer Squadron 6, 1960, comdg. officer U.S.S. Des Moines, 1960, comdr. Cruiser Destroyer Flotilla 6, 1963-64, dep. dir. ops. Nat. Mil. Command Center, Joint Chiefs of Staff, 1964-65, dir. budget and reports Dept. Navy, 1965-68, comdr. Tng. Command, Pacific Fleet, San Diego, 1968-69, ret., 1969; asst. v.p. Wells Fargo Bank, San Diego, 1969-71, v.p., 1971-75, ret., 1975; sales rep. Dura-Bernardin, Inc., Bedford Park, Ill., 1976-82, ret., 1982. Decorated Legion of Merit (2), Purple Heart; Korean Presdl. citation; Order Prince Henry the Navigator, Portugal). Mem. U.S. Naval Acad. Alumni Assn., World Affairs Council San Diego. Clubs: Army-Navy Country (Arlington, Va.); Rest and Aspiration. Home: 3440 Bangor Pl San Diego CA 92106

GRIMM, GOETZ, automobile company executive; b. Gotha, Ger., May 16, 1928; s. Otto R. and Elfriede (Schmidt) G.; m. Ursula A. M. Schneider, Sept. 25, 1959; children: Andrea, Kathrin. Grad., Gymnasium Ernestinum, Gotha, 1948. Apprentice, Voigtlaender and Sohn, Braunschweig, Germany, 1948-50; exec. position in fin. field Volkswagenwerk AG, Wolfsburg, Germany, 1950-59; sec. Volkswagen Am., Inc., Englewood Cliffs, N.J., 1959-70, v.p. fin. and adminstrn., sec.-treas., 1978—, v.p. fin. services, Warren, Mich., 1978—. Home: 5336 Forest Way Bloomfield Hills MI 48013 Office: 888 W Big Beaver Rd PO Box 3951 Troy MI 48007

GRIMM, JAMES (RONALD GRIMM), transportation executive; b. Monroe, Mich., Nov. 5, 1935; s. Carl S. and Annie B. (Platt) G.; m. Carol Ann Forman, Aug. 24, 1957; children: James R., Phillip H. B.S. in Bus. Adminstrn, Ariz. State U., 1958. Dir. internal audit Motorola Inc., Phoenix, 1961-68; bus. and fin. mgr. Europe Motorola Semicondr. Co., Geneva, 1968-70; dir. internat. fin. Fairchild Camera & Instrument Co., Mountain View, Calif., 1970-71; v.p. internat. fin. Computer Scis. Corp., Los Angeles, 1971-74; sr. v.p., chief fin. exec. Pertec Computer Corp., Los Angeles, 1974-80; exec. v.p. fin. and adminstrn. MAPCO, Inc., Tulsa, 1980-84; v.p., chief fin. officer Greyhound Corp., Phoenix, 1984—. Contbr. articles to Inst. Internal Auditors publs., 1964-68. Inducted into Ariz. State U. Hall of Fame, 1982. Mem. Inst. Internal Auditors (founder and 1st pres. Phoenix chpt. 1963), Fin. Exec. Inst. Clubs: Southern Hills, Tulsa. Home: 4167 S Wheeling St Tulsa OK 74105 Office: 111 W Clarendon St Phoenix AZ 85077

GRIMM, REINHOLD, humanities educator; b. Nuremberg, Germany, May 21, 1931; s. Eugen and Anna (Käser) G.; m. Anneliese Schmidt, Sept. 25, 1954; 1 dau., Ruth Sabine. Student, U. Erlangen, Germany, 1951-56, Ph.D., 1956, U. Colo., 1952-53. Faculty German lit. U. Erlangen, 1957-61, U. Frankfurt, Germany, 1961-67; vis. prof. Columbia, also N.Y. U., spring 1967, U. Va., fall 1978; Alexander Hohlfeld prof. German and comparative lit. U. Wis., 1967-80, Vilas prof. comparative lit. and German, 1980—; mem. Inst. for Research in Humanities, U. Wis., spring 1981. Author: numerous books including Nach dem Naturalismus: Essays zur modernen Dramatik, 1978, Brecht und Nietzsche oder Geständnisse eines Dichters, 1979, Von der Armut und vom Regen: Rilkes Autwort auf die soziale Frage, 1981; editor: Monatshefte, 1979—, Deutsche Romantheorien, 2d edit, 1974, Deutsche Dramentheorien, 1971, 3d edit., 1980; co-editor: Basis, 1970-80, German Studies, 1968—, Brecht Yearbook, 1971-81; contbr. articles to profl. jours. Recipient Förderungspreis der Stadt Nürnberg, 1964; Guggenheim fellow, 1969-70. Mem. MLA, Am. Assn. Tchrs. German (pres. 1974-75). Home: 3983 Plymouth Circle Madison WI 53705

GRIMM, ROLAND DUBOIS, investment company executive; b. Kingston, N.Y., Jan. 7, 1926; s. Howard Hasbrouck and Lydia Ruth (Hardenbergh) G. B.A., Yale U., 1950; M.A., Columbia U., 1951. Asst. treas. Mass. Hosp. Life Ins. Co., Boston, 1954-56; industry specialist Mass. Investors Trust, Boston, 1956-61; v.p. Fidelity Fund, Inc., Fidelity Mgmt. and Research Co., Boston, also FMR Investment Service, Inc., Dow Theory Fund, Inc., Magellan Fund, Inc., 2d Congress St. Fund, Inc., Contrafund, Inc., Equity Fund, Inc., 1961-67; chmn. bd., dir. Endowment Mgmt. and Research Corp., Boston, 1967-79, Omega Fund, Inc., 1968-79; pres., dir. Faneuil Mgmt. Corp., 1979—, Faneuil Fund, Inc., 1979—; trustee NE Med. Center Hosp.; corporator New Eng. Deaconess Hosp., all Boston; dir. Affiliated Publs., Inc., Boston Globe, McCaw Communications Cos. Inc., Northland Investment Corp. Bd. dirs. Lend-A-Hand Soc., 1956—; trustee U. Notre Dame. Served with AUS, 1944-46. Mem. Boston Security Analysts Soc. Clubs: Somerset (Boston); Duxbury (Mass.) Yacht. Office: PO Box 5000 Duxbury MA 02331

GRIMSLEY, JAMES ALEXANDER, JR., univ. adminstr., ret. army officer; b. Florence, S.C., Nov. 14, 1921; s. James Alexander and Anne (Darby) G.; m. Jessie Lawson, Dec. 8, 1945; children—James Alexander III, Anne, William. B.S., The Citadel, 1942; M.A., George Washington U., 1964. Mgr. Peoples Gas Co., Florence, 1946-48;

commd. 2d lt. U.S. Army, 1942, advanced through grades to maj. gen., 1974; ret., 1975; v.p. adminstrn. and finance The Citadel, Charleston, S.C., 1975-80, pres., 1980—. Decorated Silver Star medal, D.S.M., Legion of Merit, Bronze Star medal, Purple Heart, Combat Inf. badge. Mem. Assn. U.S. Army. Episcopalian. Address: The Citadel Charleston SC 29409

GRIMSLEY, WILL HENRY, author; b. Monterey, Tenn., Jan. 27, 1914; s. Alvis Chilton and Bertie Eliza (Elrod) G.; m. Nellie Blanchard Harris, Feb. 12, 1937; children: Aleena Gayle, William Kelly, Nellie Blanchard. Student pub. schs., Nashville. Sports writer, then sports editor Eve. Tennessean, Nashville, 1933-39; sports writer Nashville Tennessean, 1940-42; corr. AP, Memphis, 1943-47, sports writer, N.Y.C., 1947—, spl. corr., 1969, nat. sports columnist, 1977—. (Recipient Bronze Hugo award for documentary Olympics, The Eternal Torch, Chgo. Internat. Film Festival 1974); Author: Golf-Its History, People and Events, 1966, Tennis-Its History, People and Events, 1971, Football-Greatest Moments of the Southwest Conference, 1968; supervising editor: A Century of Sports, 1971, Sports Immortals, 1971. Named Nat. Sportswriter of Yr., Nat. Sportscasters and Sportswriters Assn. Am., 1978, 80, 81, 83. Mem. Golf Writers Assn. Am. (pres. 1977-78), Baseball Writers Assn. Am. Democrat. Baptist. Clubs: Casino (Garden City); Winged Foot (Mamaroneck, N.Y.); Westchester Country (Rye, N.Y.). Home: 2 Prescott St Garden City NY 11530 Office: 50 Rockefeller Plaza New York NY 10020

GRIMSON, KEITH SANFORD, ret. physician, educator; b. Munich, N.D., Apr. 21, 1910; s. Judge Gudmundur and Ina (Sanford) G.; m. Ardyce Mozelle Johnson, Oct. 16, 1934; children—Roger Connell, Baird Sanford, Keith Sanford. B.A., U. N.D., 1930, B.S., 1931; M.D., U. Chgo., 1934. Intern Presbyn. Hosp., Chgo., 1934; fellow, resident surgery U. Chgo., 1935-39, instr. dept. surgery, 1940- 42; Belgian Am. Ednl. Found. Research fellow with Prof. C. Heymans, Ghent, Belgium, 1939-40; asst. prof. surgery Duke U. Sch. Medicine, Durham, N.C., 1943-48, prof., 1948—; prof. surgery Duke Hosp.; cons. AMA, HEW, Am. Heart Assn., surg. and med. socs. Asso. editor: Ann. Revs. of Internal Medicine, 1952-, The Am. Surg. Jour, 1953-, Modern Medicine, 1955—; Contbr. profl. jours. Fellow A.C.S.; mem. Am., So. surg. assns., Am. Physiol. Soc., Am., So. socs. clin. research, Am. Heart Assn., Am. Soc. Pharmacology and Exptl. Therapeutics, Soc. U. Surgeons, Sigma Xi, Phi Delta Theta, Alpha Kappa Kappa. Presbyn. Home: 3313 Devon Rd Hope Valley Durham NC 27707

GRIN, S. SPENCER, publisher, lawyer, educator; b. N.Y.C., Jan. 14, 1928; s. Bernard Boris and Clara (Kane) G.; m. Anne Zabol, Oct. 16, 1955; children: Caron, Milton, Robert, Jennifer. B.A., N.Y. U., 1948; J.D., Bklyn. Law Sch., 1952; Ph.D., Union Grad. Sch., Antioch (Ohio) U., 1971. Bar: N.Y. 1952. Partner firm Gorode, Grin & Samuels, N.Y.C., 1953-70; dir. internat. studies Acad. for Ednl. Devel., N.Y.C., 1971-72, cons., 1972—; exec. v.p., pub. Saturday Rev., 1972—; vice chmn., dir. Saturday Review Inc., N.Y.C., 1972-77; counsel Delson & Gordon, N.Y.C. and Washington, 1977-82, Hartke and Hartke, 1982—; chmn. bd. dirs. Hartke and Hartke Cons., Falls Church, Va., 1983—; cons. Inst. on Man and Sci., Borlan Industries, R.S.V.P. Cinema, Atlanta/Sosnoff Capital; adj. prof. internat. relations and communications Friends World Coll., Westbury, N.Y., 1967-71; adj. prof. communications Adelphi U., 1980, Don Bolles vis. lectr., 1981; adj. prof. Grad. Sch. Bus. Hofstra U., 1982; del. UNESCO Internat. Ednl. Yr. Author: World Education, 1971; co-author: World Education, Emerging Concepts, 1978; editor: (with Richard L. Tobin) The Golden Age Essays, 1974, Jour. World Edn, 1967-70. Trustee Pan Am. Devel. Found., Washington, Am. Mus. Immigration, Liberty Island, N.Y., NCCJ; asso. bd. S. Nassau Communities Hosp.; bd. dirs. Am. Field Service, N.Y.C., NCCJ, N.Y.C. Served with USCGR, 1951-52. Mem. Am. Bar Assn., Am. Arbitration Assn., Soc. Internat. Law, World Peace Through Law Center, Mag. Pubs. Assn. (chmn. com. on responsibilities and freedom of press 1972), UN Assn., Overseas Press Club. Office: 2 Pennsylvania Plaza New York NY 10001

GRINDLAY, JONATHAN ELLIS, astrophysics educator; b. Richmond, Va., Nov. 9, 1944; s. John Happer and Elizabeth (Ellis) G.; m. Sandra Kay Smyrski, Oct. 10, 1970; children: Graham Charles, Kathryn Jane. A.B., Dartmouth Coll., 1966; M.A., Harvard U., 1969, Ph.D., 1971. Jr. fellow Harvard U., Cambridge, Mass., 1971-74, asst. prof., 1976-81, prof. astrophysics, 1981—; astrophysicist Smithsonian Obs., Cambridge, Mass., 1974-76; cons. MIT Lincoln Lab., Bedford, Mass., 1982—; mem. vis. com. astronomy U. Chgo., 1983—; mem. users com. Cerro Tololo Interam. Obs., La Serena, Chile, 1981—; mem. astrophysics program com. Aspen Ctr. for Physics, Colo., 1983—. Contbr. articles to profl. jours.; patentee (identification new technique for imaging hard x-rays with minimal distortion), 1976. Recipient Bart J. Bok prize dept. astronomy, Harvard U., 1976; NSF, NASA research grantee, 1978—. Mem. Am. Astron. Soc. (nat. sec.-treas. high energy astrophysics div. 1982—), Am. Phys. Soc., Internat. Astron. Union. Unitarian-Universalist. Home: 9 Grantwood Rd Arlington MA 02174 Office: Harvard Obs 60 Garden St Cambridge MA 02138

GRINELL, SHEILA, science exhibition developer; b. N.Y.C., July 15, 1945; d. Richard N. and Martha (Mimiless) G.; m. Thomas E. Johnson, July 15, 1980; 1 son, Michael; stepchildren: Kathleen, Thomas. B.A., Radcliffe Coll., 1966; M.A., U. Calif.-Berkeley, 1968. Co-dir. exhibits and programs The Exploratorium, San Francisco, 1969-74; promotion dir. Kodansha Internat., Tokyo, 1974-77; traveling exhbn. coordinator Assn. Sci. Tech. Ctrs., Washington, 1978-80, exec. dir., 1980-82, project dir., Oakland, N.J., 1982—; cons. The Computer Mus., Boston, 1983—, Nat. Zool. Park, Washington, 1981, Sesame Pl., Langhorne, Pa., 1980, U.S. Geol. Survey, 1979; project dir. traveling exhibition Chips and Changes, 1984. Editor: A Stage for Science, 1979. Fulbright teaching asst. AAAS, 1966; hon. Woodrow Wilson fellow, 1967. Mem. AAAS, Am. Assn. Museums-Internat. Council Museums, Phi Beta Kappa. Office: 16th St NW Washington DC 20036

GRINER, PAUL FRANCIS, physician; b. Phila., Jan. 1, 1933; s. John Archibald and Josepha (Snyder) G.; m. Miriam Millard, Aug. 25, 1956; children—Laura, Paul Francis. B.A., Harvard U., 1954; M.D. (Doran Stevens Alumni prize 1959, Life Ins. Found. award 1959), U. Rochester, N.Y., 1959. Mem. faculty U. Rochester Sch. Medicine and Dentistry, 1967—, prof. medicine, 1973—, now Samuel E. Durand prof., acting chmn. dept. medicine, 1977-79, head gen. medicine unit, 1976—, asso. chmn. clin. services dept. medicine; cons. in field. Author articles in field, chpts. in books. Served as officer M.C. USAF, 1961-63. Decorated Commendation medal; grantee HEW, others. Fellow A.C.P. (gov.); mem. Assn. Am. Med. Colls., Am. Soc. Hematology, Am. Fedn. Clin. Research, Clin. Chemistry Data Communications Group, Soc. Research and Edn. in Primary Care Internal Medicine (pres. 1981—), Am. Clin. and Climatol. Assn., Interurban Club, Sigma Xi, Alpha Omega Alpha. Episcopalian. Club: Harvard of Rochester (dir. 1973—). Home: 220 Kilbourn Rd Rochester NY 14618 Office: 601 Elmwood Ave Rochester NY 14642

GRINGS, WILLIAM (WASHBURN GRINGS), educator; b. Superior, Wis., Mar. 19, 1918; s. William Welker and Jessie (Washburn) G.; m. Hilda Balster, Aug. 27, 1942; children—Carol Ann, Janet Marie, Steven Frederick (dec.), Elaine Ethel. A.B., U. Dubuque, 1940; M.A., U. Iowa, 1941, Ph.D., 1946. Asst. prof. psychology U. Denver, 1946-47; faculty U. So. Calif., Los Angeles, 1947—, prof. psychology, 1960—, chmn. dept., 1960-68; Cons. govt. mil. depts., also mem. assns. Author: Laboratory Instrumentation in Psychology, 1954, Emotions and Bodily Responses, 1978; Contbr. research papers to profl. lit. Served to 1st lt. USAAF, 1942-45. Fellow Am. Psychol. Assn., A.A.A.S.; mem. Psychometric Soc., Calif. Psychol. Assn., Los Angeles County Psychol. Assn. (pres. 1960-61), Soc. Psychophysiol. Research (pres. 1967-68), Sigma Xi. Home: 7806 Cowan Ave Los Angeles CA 90045

GRINKER, ROY RICHARD, SR., psychiatrist, psychoanalyst; b. Chgo., Aug. 2, 1900; s. Julius and Minnie (Friend) G.; m. Mildred Barman, July 24, 1924; children: Roy Richard, Joan Richman. S.B., U. Chgo., 1919; M.D., Rush Med. Coll., 1921. Instr. neurology Northwestern U., 1925; instr. neurology U. Chgo., 1927-29, asst. prof., 1929-31, asso. prof., 1931-35, asso. prof. psychiatry, 1935-36, also chief psychiat. div., 1935-36; chmn. dept. neuropsychiatry, also dir. Inst. for Psychosomatic and Psychiat. Research and Tng., Michael Reese Hosp., Chgo., 1946—; clin. prof. psychiatry U. Ill., 1951-66; prof. psychiatry Pritzker Med. Sch., U. Chgo., 1969—; sr. ednl. prof. Northwestern U. Med. Sch., 1980—. Author: also numerous other sci. publs. 50 Years in Psychiatry; co-author: The Borderline Patient; Editor: Mid-Century Psychiatry, Toward a Unified Theory of Human Behavior. Served as student Army Tng. Corps, 1917; col. M.C., 1942-45. Decorated Legion of Merit.; Recipient Maj. Raymonds Longacre award for sci. contbn. to aviation medicine, 1955; Profl. Achievement award U. Chgo. Alumni Assn., 1969; Gold Medal award Soc. Biol. Psychiatry, 1970; Salmon medal N.Y. Acad. Medicine, 1970. Fellow AAAS, N.Y. Acad. Scis., Am. Coll. Neuropharmacology; mem. Am. Psychopathology Assn., Acad. Psychoanalysis (pres. 1961), Am. Assn. Research in Nervous and Mental Diseases, Am. Assn. Neuropathologists, Am. Neurol. Assn., Am. Psychiat. Assn., Am. Psychoanalytic Soc., AMA (editor-in-chief archives neurology, psychiatry 1956-59, archives of gen. psychiatry 1959- 69), Sigma Xi. Club: Standard. Home: 910 N Lake Shore Dr Chicago IL 60611 Office: Michael Reese Hosp 29th and Ellis Ave Chicago IL 60616

GRINKER, ROY RICHARD, JR., psychiatrist; b. Chgo., Apr. 25, 1927; s. Roy Richard and Mildred (Barman) G.; m. Florence Schwartz, Oct. 19, 1958; children—Jennifer, Roy Richard III. Ph.B., U. Chgo., 1947; M.D., Harvard, 1952; postgrad., Chgo. Inst. Psychoanalysis, 1956-62. Intern Mary Hitchcock Meml. Hosp., Hanover, N.H., 1952-53; resident Michael Reese Hosp. and Med. Center, Chgo., 1953-54, 55-56; now attending physician; resident U. Ill. Hosp., 1954-55; instr. neurology and psychiatry Northwestern U. Med. Sch., 1962-63; mem. faculty Chgo. Inst. Psychoanalysis, 1966—, tng. and supervising analyst, 1974—. Contbr. articles to profl. jours. Served with USNR, 1945-46. Fellow Am. Psychiat. Assn.; mem. Am. Psychoanalytic Assn., AMA, Nu Sigma Nu. Home: 237 E Delaware Pl Chicago IL 60611 Office: 676 St Clair St Chicago IL 60611

GRINSTEAD, EUGENE ANDREWS, naval officer; b. Durham, N.C., Sept. 12, 1923; s. Eugene A. and Ann B. (Childress) G.; m. Gayle Marie Kane, Sept. 22, 1944; children: Eugene Andrews, Mary K., Kurt M., Mark, Karen A., Matthew, Robert, Michele, John. Student, U. N.C., 1941-44; grad., Advanced Mgmt. Program, Harvard U., 1967. Commd. ensign U.S. Navy, 1944, advanced through grades to vice adm., 1981; service in, Italy, Panama; asst. chief staff supply comdr. Naval Air Force, Atlantic Fleet, 1970-72; dir. material div. Office Chief Naval Ops., Washington, 1972-75; vice comdr. Naval Supply Systems Command, Washington, 1975-77, comdr., 1977-81; chief Naval Supply Corps., 1977-81; dir. Def. Logistics Agy., Alexandria, Va., 1981—. Decorated D.S.M., Legion of Merit (2), Meritorious Service medal, Navy Commendation medal. Mem. Am. Soc. Naval Engrs., Nat. Def. Transp. Assn., Naval Hist. Assn. Office: Def Logistics Agy Cameron Sta Alexandria VA 22314

GRINSTEAD, WILLIAM CARTER, JR., coal company executive; b. Houston, Aug. 8, 1930; s. William Carter and Lee Tevis (Poyner) G.; m. Linda Ruth Rowe, Oct. 24, 1953; children—Cynthia Gaye, William Carter. Student, Rice U., 1948-50; B.S. in Petroleum Engring, U. Tex., 1953. Instr. U.S. Naval Acad., 1955-57; with Exxon USA, 1957—, prodn. ops. mgr., Los Angeles, 1971-72, New Orleans, 1972-73, govt. relations mgr., Houston, 1973-76, mgr. East Tex. prodn. div., 1976-78; sr. v.p. Exxon Coal USA, Inc., Houston, 1978-80, pres., 1980—; mem. adv. com. on coal and lignite Tex. Energy and Natural Resources Adv. Council; mem. petroleum engring. vis. com. Coll. Engring., U. Tex. Bd. dir. Soc. for the Performing Arts, Houston. Served with USN, 1953-57. Mem. AIME, Am. Petroleum Inst., Tex. Soc. Profl. Engrs., Nat. Coal Assn. (dir.), Delta Kappa Epsilon. Republican. Episcopalian. Clubs: Houston Country, Allegro, Petroleum. Office: PO Box 2180 Houston TX 77001

GRINSTEIN, GERALD, airline executive; b. 1932. Grad., Yale U., 1954; LL.B., Harvard U., 1957. Bar: D.C. Counsel to merchant marine and transp. subcoms., chief counsel U.S. Senate Commerce Com., Washington, 1958-67; adminstrv. asst. U.S. Senator Warren G. Magnuson, Washington, 1967-69; ptnr. Preston Thorgrimson Ellis & Holman, 1969; with Western Air Lines Inc., Los Angeles, 1969—, chmn. bd., 1983—, dir.; dir. Econ. Devel. Council Puget Sound, Gen. Telephone Co. of Northwest. Club: Washington Jockey (bd. dirs.). Office: Western Air Lines Inc 6060 Avion Dr Los Angeles CA 90009 *

GRIP, CARL MANFRED, JR., institute official; b. Rockford, Ill., May 21, 1921; s. Carl Manfred and Nora Elizabeth (Bostrum) G.; m. Janet Wolter, Feb. 1973; children by previous marriage: Jeffrey Carl, Jeremy Alan, Timothy Harris. A.B., Beloit Coll., 1946; Ph.D., U. Chgo., 1956. Research asst. U. Chgo., 1946, dir. univ. house system, 1950-54, asso. dir. community orgn. research project, 1953-54, lectr., 1954-56; asst. dean men U. Ill., 1947-50; dean men; asso. dept. psychiatry Temple U., 1956-66, clin. asst. prof. dept. psychiatry, 1966-68; dean (Coll. Liberal Arts); chmn. Met. Studies Center, Ill. Inst. Tech., Chgo., 1968-75, asst. v.p. planning, 1975-78; pres. South Side Planning Bd., Chgo., 1976—; faculty Phila. Psychoanalytic Inst., 1956-66. Weekly TV program The Adolescent, 1957-58. Bd. dirs. Fellowship House, 1958-68, Neighborhood Redevel. Assistance Corp.; commr. Phila. Fellowship Commn., 1963-68; vestryman St. James Cathedral, 1975—. Mem. Am. Psychol. Assn., AAAS, Am. Assn. for Higher Edn., Sigma Xi, Beta Theta Pi. Club: University (Chgo.). Home: 900 Lake Shore Dr Chicago IL 60611 Office: Southside Planning Bd Glessner House 1800 S Prarie Ave Chicago IL 60616

GRIPPE, PETER, sculptor, printmaker, painter; b. Buffalo, Aug. 8, 1912; s. Leonardo and Josephine (Orlando) G.; m. Florence Berg, Apr. 21, 1940; 1 stepson, Ronald Roseman. Student, Albright Art Sch., Buffalo, 1923-25, Art Inst. Buffalo, 1929-35, Atelier 17, N.Y.C., 1944-47. Student tchr. sculpture Art Inst. Buffalo, 1934-35; instr. sculpture, drawing Fed. Arts Project, N.Y.C., 1939-42; instr. sculpture Black Mountain Coll., 1948; instr. drawing design Pratt Inst., 1949-50; instr. sculpture Smith Coll., 1951- 52; dir., instr. etching and engravings Atelier 17, 1951-53; now prof. fine arts Brandeis U. Author: 21 Etchings and Poems; contbr.: Palette to Palate, 1978; One-man show, Orrefors Gallery, N.Y.C., 1942, Willard Gallery, N.Y.C., 1944, 45, 46, 48, Brandeis U., 1957, Paridot Gallery, 1957, 59, Nordness Gallery, N.Y.C., 1960, 63, group exhibitions, Whitney Mus. Am. Art, Wildenstein Gallery, Library of Congress, Art Inst. Chgo., Bklyn. Mus., Worcester Art Mus., U. Chgo., Met. Mus. Art, Mus. Modern Art, Carnegie Inst. Borgenicht Gallery, Pa. Acad. Fine Art, Stable Gallery, Addison Gallery Am. Art, outdoor sculpture Guild Hall, Easthampton, N.Y., Whitney Mus. Am. Art, 1980, Boston Athenaeum Gallery, 1981; group exhibitions, Zabriskie Gallery, 1983; group exhibitions, numerous others, prints exhibited, Achenbach Found. of Graphic Arts, San Francisco, Nat. Gallery Art, Washington, Boston Mus. Fine Arts, Balt. Mus. Art, Met. Mus. Art, Mus. Modern Art, others; rep. permanent collections, Albright Art Gallery, Addison Gallery Am. Art, Library of Congress, N.Y. Pub. Library Print Collection, Tel Aviv Mus., Met. Mus. Art, Whitney Mus. Art, Mus. Modern Art, N.Y.C., Nat. Gallery, Washington, others. (Recipient purchase prize Bklyn. Mus. 1947), others. (prize for print Met. Mus. Art), others. (Charles M. Lea award Print Club. Phila. 1953), others. (1st prize for sculpture Boston Arts Festival 1955), others. (sculpture award Nat. Council U.S. art 1955), others. (R.I. Arts Festival 1961); Two sculpture murals, Puerto Rican Info. Center, N.Y.C., 1959; participant, Days Lumberyard Studios, Provincetown Art Assn. and Mus., 1978. Guggenheim fellow for sculpture, 1964-65. Club: Artists (N.Y.C.). Commn. to design medallion for ann. creative arts award Brandeis U., 1957, 7 1/2 ft. bronze figure for Theodore Shapio Forum, 1963, 7 ft. laminated wood sculpture "Figure in Movement" for Sci. Bldg. Simmons Coll., Boston, 1972. Address: 1190 Boyslton St Newton MA 02164 also Main Rd Orient LI NY 11957 *Over the past forty years my principle ideas and goal has centered on two concepts of "space" and "movement" hoping to enlarge the scope of sculpture and forge a new path for American art.*

GRIPPI, SALVATORE WILLIAM, painter; b. Buffalo, Sept. 30, 1921; s. Leonardo and Josephine (Orlando) G.; m. Rosalind Ratzenberg, Apr. 14, 1945. Student, Mus. Modern Art, N.Y.C., 1944-45, Art Students' League, N.Y.C., 1945-48, Atelier 17, N.Y.C., 1951-53, Istituto Statale d'Arte, Florence, Italy, 1953-55. Instr. Atelier 17, summer 1953, Cooper Union Art Sch., 1956-59, Sch. Visual Arts, N.Y.C., 1961-62; asso. prof. art Claremont Grad. Sch., 1962-68, Pomona Coll., 1962-68; prof., founder art dept. Ithaca Coll., 1968—; invited participant Ford Found. Conf. Visual Artists, 1961. One-man shows include, N.Y. U., N.Y.C., 1958, Zabriskie Gallery, N.Y.C., 1956, 59, Krasner Gallery, N.Y.C., 1962, 64, 79, 81, Feingarten Galleries, 1967, 70, Everson, Mus., Syracuse, N.Y., 1978, Handwerker Gallery, Ithaca Coll., group shows include, Met. Mus. Art, N.Y.C., 1952, Schneider Gallery, Rome, 1954, Galleria La Fontanella, Rome, 1955, Whitney Mus. and Smithsonian Inst. Traveling show, 1958-59, Corcoran Gallery Art, Washington, 1959, 63, Whitney Mus., N.Y.C., 1960, Mus. Modern Art, N.Y.C., 1962; represented in permanent collections, Whitney Mus., Met. Mus. Art, N.Y. Pub. Library, N.Y.C., Joseph Hirshorn Collection, Washington, Milw.-Downer Coll., Ithaca Coll., St. Lawrence U., Everson Mus. Served with USNR, 1942-45. Mem. Art Students' League (life, treas. 1961-62, bd. control 1961-64), Coll. Art Assn. Office: Art Dept Ithaca Coll Ithaca NY 14850

GRISANTI, EUGENE PHILIP, flavors and fragrances company executive; b. Buffalo, Oct. 24, 1929; s. Nicholas D. and Victoria (Pantera) G.; m. Anne Couming, June 29, 1953; children: Marylee, Christopher, Eugene Paul. A.B. magna cum laude, Holy Cross Coll., 1951; LL.B., Boston U., 1953; LL.M., Harvard U., 1954. Bar: Mass. 1953, N.Y. 1954. Mem. firm Fulton, Walter & Halley, N.Y.C., 1954-60; gen. atty. Internat. Flavors & Fragrances Inc., N.Y.C., 1960-64, sec., gen. atty., 1964-70, v.p., sec., gen. atty., 1970-74; pres. Internat. Flavors & Fragrances, U.S., 1974-79; sr. v.p., dir. Internat. Flavors & Fragrances Inc., 1979—. Mem. Fragrance Found. (dir.), Fragrance Materials Assn. (pres., dir.), Flavor and Extract Mfrs. Assn. (dir.), N.Y.C. Bar, Research Inst. for Fragrance Materials (dir.). Clubs: Larchmont Yacht, Winged Foot Golf; University (N.Y.C.). Office: Internat Flavor & Fragrances Inc 521 W 57th St New York NY 10019 *

GRISANTI, FRANK ANTHONY, management consultant; b. Buffalo, Oct. 21, 1920; s. Salvatore and Marian (Palermo) G.; m. Dorothy Louise Stolzenberg, July 14, 1951; children: Melanie Louise, Mari-Jo. B.S., Okla. A & M Coll., 1943. Vice-pres. Segal Lock and Hardware Co., N.Y.C., 1949-52; asso. Robert Heller and Assos., Cleve., 1952-58; v.p. Young Spring and Wire Corp., Detroit, 1958-61, Mordy & Co. (Mgmt. Cons.), 1961-67; pres. Grisanti and Galef, Inc., Los Angeles, 1967—; chmn., chief exec. officer Mid-Atlantic Coca-Cola Bottling Co. Inc.; chmn. Spectrum Group Inc. Served with USNR, 1945-46. Mem. World Affairs Council., Town Hall of Calif. (life). Republican. Episcopalian. Clubs: Jonathan, Regency, Los Angeles Country. Home: 12845 Hanover St Los Angeles CA 90049 Office: 16000 Ventura Blvd Encino CA 91436

GRISHAM, FRANK PHILLIPS, educator, librarian; b. Birmingham, Ala., Aug. 28, 1928; s. James Ernest and Evie Elizabeth (Phillips) G.; m. Louise Fly, Sept. 23, 1950; children: Elizabeth, Phillip, David, Brian. A.B., Birmingham So. Coll., 1949; M.Div., Vanderbilt U., 1952; M.L.S., George Peabody Coll., 1958. Dir. religious life Birmingham So. Coll., 1954-56; div. librarian, asso. prof. Vanderbilt U., Nashville, 1956-64, asst. dir. Joint Univ. Libraries, asso. prof., 1965-67, asso. dir., asso. prof., 1967-68, dir. Joint Univ. Libraries, asso. prof., 1968-79, asso. prof., dir. univ. library, 1979-82; exec. dir. SOLINET, Atlanta, 1982—; ordained minister N. Ala. Conf. Meth. Ch., 1949; Bd. dirs. Southeastern Library Network, 1975—, chmn., 1978-79; mem. Tenn. Adv. Council Libraries, 1974-82. Vice chmn. Met. Nashville Davidson County Bd. Edn., 1964-75. Mem. ALA, Tenn. Library Assn. (pres. 1975-76), Southeastern Library Assn., Assn. Research Libraries (dir. 1977-80). Home: 408 Lakes Dr Atlanta GA 30339

GRISHAM, JACK EDWIN, lawyer; b. Jerico Springs, Mo., Sept. 20, 1921; s. Opal Francis and Merle Maude (Yeates) G.; m. Patricia Davis; children: Julie A., Jonathan E. B.A., UCLA, 1943; J.D., U. So. Calif., 1948. Bar: Calif. 1949. Mem. Grisham & Cannon, Long Beach, Calif., 1953—, sr. partner, 1968—. Served with USN, 1943-45; PTO. Mem. Long Beach Bar Assn. (pres. 1972), Am., Los Angeles County bar assns., Am., Calif., Los Angeles trial lawyers assns., Am. Bd. Trial Advocates. Democrat. Lutheran. Office: 13872 Harbor Blvd Suite 1D Garden Grove CA

GRISHAM, JOE WHEELER, pathologist, educator; b. Smith County, Tenn., Dec. 5, 1931; s. William Wince and Grace (Allen) G.; m. Jean Evelyn Malone, July 2, 1955. B.A., Vanderbilt U., 1953, M.D., 1957. Intern Washington U.-Barnes Hosp., St. Louis, 1957-58, resident in pathology, 1958-60; mem. faculty Washington U., Med. Sch., 1960-73, prof. pathology and anatomy, 1969-73; asso. pathologist Barnes Hosp., 1969-73; vis. instr. Makerere Med. Coll., Kampala, Uganda, 1961; prof. pathology, chmn. dept. U. N.C. Med. Sch., Chapel Hill; also pathologist-in-chief N.C. Meml. Hosp., 1973—; mem. pathology study sect. NIH, 1969-73, chmn., 1970-73, 79-83; bd. sci. counsellors Nat. Inst. Environ. Health Scis., 1974-78; mem. sci. advisory panel Chem. Industry Inst. Toxicology, 1977—, chmn., 1980—; adv. bd. Given Inst. Pathobiology, 1983—. Contbr. articles to med. jours. Served to lt. comdr. USNR, 1961-63. John and Mary R. Markle scholar acad. medicine, 1964-69; fellow Life Ins. Med. Research Fund, 1959-61, Nat. Cancer Inst., 1958-59. Mem. Am. Assn. Pathologists, Am. Assn. Cancer Research, Am. Assn. Study Liver Diseases, Am. Soc. Cell Biology, Tissue Culture Assn., Internat. Acad. Pathology, AMA, AAAS. Home: 1703 Curtis Rd Chapel Hill NC 27514 Office: Dept Pathology Univ NC Med Sch Chapel Hill NC 27514

GRISHAM, WAYNE R., congressman; b. Lamar, Colo., Jan. 10, 1923; m. Mildred Grace Watt, 1944; children—Cathy, Randall, Kellie. A.A., Long Beach City Coll., 1947; B.A., Whittier Coll., 1949; postgrad., U. So. Calif., 1950-51. Pres. Wayne Grisham Realty; chmn. First Mut. Mortgage Co.; mayor, City of La Mirada, Calif., 1973-74, 77-78; mem. La Mirada City Council, 1970-78, 96th and 97th Congresses from 33d Dist., Calif. Served with AC U.S. Army, 1942-46. Decorated Air medal, Purple Heart. Mem. Calif. Jaycees, C. of C., YMCA, Whittier Coll. Alumni Assn., City of Hope, VFW. Republican. Methodist. Club: Kiwanis.

GRISKEY, RICHARD GEORGE, educator; b. Pitts., Jan. 9, 1931; s. George and Emma (Maskell) G.; m. Pauline Anne Becker, June 11, 1955; children: Paula Louise, David Richard. B.Ch.E., Carnegie-Mellon U., 1951, M.Ch.E., 1955, Ph.D., 1958. Registered profl. engr., Wis. Sr. engr. E. I. duPont Co., Seaford, Del., 1958-60; asst. prof. U. Cin., 1960-62; assoc. prof. Va. Poly. Inst., 1962-64, prof., 1964-66; prof., head chem. engring. dept. U. Denver, 1966-68; dir. research and found. research prof. Newark Coll. Engring., 1968-71; prof. chem. engring., dean U. Wis.-Milw., 1971-82; prof. chem. engring., dean engring. U. Ala.-Huntsville, 1982—; vis. scientist Polish Acad. Sci.-U.S. Nat. Acad. Sci., 1971; OAS vis. prof. Multi Nat. Food Project, Brazil, 1973; vis. prof. Monash U., Australia, 1974, Algerian Inst. Petroleum, 1975, 76; chem. engring. cons. Editor, Marcel Dekker Inc., 1974—; referee, reviewer: Canadian Jour. Chem. Engring, Am. Inst. Chem. Engrs. Jour., Jour. Polymer Sci., Jour. Fluid Mechanics, Jour. Heat Transfer; Author: Chemical Engineering for Chemists; Contbr. numerous articles to sci. jours. Served with AUS, 1951-53. Fellow Am. Inst. Chemists; mem. Am. Inst. Chem. Engrs., Soc. Rheology, Am. Soc. Engring. Edn., Am. Assn. Higher Edn., Soc. Plastics Engrs., Am. Chem Soc. (Congressional counselor), ASME, Tau Beta Pi, Sigma Xi, Triangle, Scabbard and Blade. Roman Catholic. Home: 4633 N Cramer St Milwaukee WI 53211

GRISSINGER, JAMES ADAMS, speech and drama educator; b. Bklyn., Oct. 5; s. James Leroy and Ethel (Adams) G.; m. Jo Ann Smith, July 8, 1950; children: Lynnan, Beth. B.S., Ohio State U., 1946, M.A., 1947, Ph.D., 1957. Grad. asst. Ohio State U., 1946-47; instr. Coll. Wooster, Ohio, 1949-50; asst. prof. Otterbein Coll., 1950-55, assoc. prof., 1955-58, prof., 1958—, chmn. dept. speech and theatre, 1951—; cons. bus. and profl. speech. Contbr. articles to profl. jours. Mem. Westerville (Ohio) City Council, 1958-70, chmn., 1968-70; presiding judge Westerville Election Precinct, 1960—. Served to 2d lt. USAF, 1943-46; ret. lt. col., 1969. Recipient Outstanding Tchr. award Ohio Speech Communication Assn., 1977. Mem. Ohio Speech Assn. (pres. 1966), Nat. Carousel Assn., Pi Kappa Delta (recipient province distinguished service award 1968, nat. v.p. 1969-73), Sigma Alpha Epsilon. Presbyn. (elder). Clubs: Antique Auto Am. (state pres. 1979-80), Craft Antique Boat). Home: 111 Central Ave Westerville OH 43081

GRISSOM, DONALD BAUER, life insurance company executive; b. Judsonia, Ark., Mar. 12, 1919; s. Walter J. and Mayme (Bauer) G.; m. Medora E. Beal, Dec. 27, 1945; children—Jane Elizabeth, Robin Bauer. Student, U. Ark., 1946-47. Cashier So. Nat. Ins. Co., Little Rock, 1936-46, dir., v.p., 1946-48; asst. to pres. Midwestern United Life Ins. Co., Fort Wayne, Ind., 1949-50, sec., 1950-72, dir., 1952—, v.p., 1955-64, 1st v.p., 1964-70, exec. v.p., 1970-72, pres., 1972-78, vice chmn. bd., 1978—; also dir.; v.p. Am. Travelers Life Ins. Co., Indpls., 1960-61; dir., pres. Ill. Mid-Continent Life Ins. Co., Chgo., 1964-65; dir., v.p., treas. Transcontinental Motor Inns, Inc., 1959-72, pres., 1972; dir., sec., treas. Varied Industry Plan, 1960-73; dir., pres. Exec. Mgmt. Corp., 1960-73; dir. Ft. Wayne Nat. Bank.; First v.p. Assn. Ind. Legal Res. Life Ins. Cos., 1975-76, pres., 1977—. Mem. world services com. YMCA, 1962-70; Bd. dirs. Am. Cancer Soc., 1970-72, Ft. Wayne Fine Arts Found., 1975-78. Served with AUS, 1942-45. Decorated Bronze Star. Mem. Ft. Wayne-Allen County Hist. Soc. (dir. 1977). Conglist. (moderator, deacon, trustee). Clubs: Columbia (Indpls.); Fort Wayne Country, Summit. Home: 1407 Three Rivers N Fort Wayne IN 46802 Office: 1812 Fort Wayne Nat Bank Fort Wayne IN 46802

GRISSOM, J. DAVID, banker; b. Portsmouth, Ohio; 3 children. B.A., Centre Coll.; LL.B., U. Louisville. Partner firm Greenebaum, Grissom, Doll, Matthews & Boone, Louisville, to 1969; exec. v.p., sec. Humana, Inc., until 1969; now dir.; now chmn., chief exec. officer, dir. Citizens Fidelity Corp. and Citizens Fidelity Bank & Trust Co.; dir. Louisville br. Fed. Res. Bank, Capital Holding Co., Porter Paint Co., Churchill Downs, Systems Assocs., Inc. Trustee Ky. Ind. Coll. Found.; mem. exec. com. Ky. Econ. Devel. Com., Epilepsy Assn. Ky.; nat. corp. com. United Negro Coll. Found.; mem. Ky. Council Economic Edn. Mem. Ky. Bankers Assn. (dir.), Assn. Res. City Bankers, Council Higher Edn., Louisville Area C. of C. (dir.), Ky. C. of C. (dir.). Address: Citizens Fidelity Corp Citizens Plaza Louisville KY 40202

GRISSOM, JOSEPH CAROL, former merchandising co. exec.; b. Lufkin, Tex., Apr. 29, 1931; s. B. R. and Carolyn (Riley) G.; m. Audrey Pedarre, Dec. 23, 1952; children—Joseph Carol, David Scott. B.S., La. State U., 1952. Asst. store mgr. Western Auto Supply Co., Kansas City, Mo., 1954-55, territorial sales mgr., store mgr., 1955-59, wholesale sales mgr., 1959-60, retail sales mgr., 1960-64, regional promotions mgr., 1964-65, div. mgr., 1965-67, regional v.p., 1967-73, corp. v.p. ops., 1973-76, exec. v.p., 1976, pres., 1976—, chief exec. officer, 1977—, chmn. bd., 1978-80, also dir.; dir. 1st Nat. Bank Kansas City. Exec. dir. Heart of Am. council Boy Scouts Am.; bd. govs. Am. Royal; bd. dirs. Starlight Theatre, United Fund. Served with USAF, 1952-54. Republican. Methodist. Clubs: Indian Hills Country, Brookridge Country, Ponte Vedra. Home: 10516 England Dr Overland Park KS 66212 Office: 8500 College Blvd Suite 135 Overland Park KS 66210

GRISSOM, LEE ALAN, association executive; b. Pensacola, Fla., Sept. 7, 1942; s. Levi Aaron and Virginia Sue (Olinger) G.; m. Sharon Kay Hasty, May 14, 1966; children: David, Jonathon, Matthew. B.A., San Diego State U., 1965, M.City Planning, 1971. Sr. research assoc. Western Behavioral Scis. Inst., La Jolla, Calif., 1965-73; mgr. planning div., then gen. mgr. San Diego C. of C., 1973-75, exec. v.p., gen. mgr., 1975-81, pres., 1981—; instr. urban planning U. Calif.-San Diego, 1973; host TV program The City Game, 1972-75. Contbr. articles to profl. jours. Chmn. Boy Scouts Am. Fair, San Diego, 1977-78, San Diego Boy Scouts Am. Council; trustee, v.p., mem. exec. com. Western Behavioral Scis. Inst.; mem. Gov. Calif.'s Planning and Adv. Assistance Council, 1977-79; mem. integration com. San Diego City Schs.; bd. dirs. Econ. Devel. Corp.; chmn. San Diego Housing Commn., 1983—, Pres.'s Adv. Bd., San Diego State U., 1983—; mem. Calif. Econ. Devel. Task Force, 1983—. Named Outstanding Young Citizen San Diego Jaycees, 1976, Calif. Jaycees, 1977, U.S. Jaycess, 1978. Mem. Am. Soc. Planning Ofcls., San Diego County Cultural Heritage Commn., Am. Inst. Planners (award recognition Calif. chpt. 1973), Calif. Assn. C. of C. Execs. Club: Rotary. Office: San Diego C of C 110 W C St San Diego CA 92101

GRISWOLD, CHARLES LANIER, foundation executive; b. Erie, Pa., July 16, 1920; s. Roger Wolcott and Mary Lanier (Turnure) G.; m. Nancy Rogers Leslie, July 12, 1947; children: Leslie Griswold Carrington, Charles Lanier, Elizabeth Rogers, Stephen Spence. Student, Yale U., 1940-42; B.A., Wesleyan U., Conn., 1947. Salesman Alcoa, Cleve. and N.Y.C., 1948-52; sales mgr. Alcomex, S.A., Mexico City, 1953-57, gen. mgr., 1957-60; dir. mktg. Alcoa Internat., Lausanne, Switzerland, 1960-65; comml. dir. Alcoa Gt. Britain, London, 1966-68, exec. dir., 1968-71; area mgr. Alcoa, San Francisco, 1971-76; sr. v.p. Alcoa Found., Pitts., 1976-77, pres., 1978—. Vice pres. bus. Com. for Arts, N.Y.C., 1968—; bd. dirs. Pitts. Symphony Orch., Pub. Broadcasting System Sta. WQED, Pitts.; mem. corp. adv. com. NAACP. Served to lt. USNR, 1943-46. Mem. Conf. Bd. N.Y. (contbns. council). Episcopalian. Clubs: Duquesne, Pitts. Golf, Fox Chapel Country (Pitts.); Yale (N.Y.C.); Bohemian (San Francisco); Burlingame Country (Hillsborough, Calif.); Mill Reef (Antigua). Office: 1501 Alcoa Bldg Pittsburgh PA 15219 *

GRISWOLD, DONALD JOHN, cutting chain manufacturing executive, lawyer; b. Lebanon, Ohio, June 28, 1919; s. Ray Clarence and Bertha Ellen (Garrison) G.; m. Betsy Alana Siegle, Dec. 7, 1945; children: G. Scott, Bruce Curtis, Ann Elizabeth. B.S., U. Oreg., 1949, LL.B., 1951. Bar: Oreg. 1951. With M.H. Keelar (public acctg.), Lebanon, 1946-47; atty. gen. State of Oreg., 1952-58; partner firm Pattullo, Gleason, Griswold & Hinson, Portland, Oreg., 1959-67; with Omark Industries, Inc., Portland, 1967—, v.p., sec., gen. counsel, 1973—. Served with USMCR, 1941-45. Mem. Oreg. Bar Assn. Republican. Baptist. Clubs: Lake Oswego Country, Masons. Office: 5550 SW Meadow Ave Portland OR 97201

GRISWOLD, ERWIN NATHANIEL, lawyer; b. East Cleveland, Ohio, July 14, 1904; s. James Harlen and Hope (Erwin) G.; m. Harriet Allena Ford, Dec. 30, 1931; children: Hope Eleanor Griswold Murrow, William Erwin. A.B., A.M., Oberlin Coll., 1925; LL.B., Harvard U., 1928, S.J.D., 1929; L.H.D., Tufts Coll., 1949, Case Inst. Tech., 1950; LL.D., U. B.C., 1949, Brown U., 1950, U. Sidney, U. Melbourne, 1951, Dalhousie U., 1952, Harvard, Amherst Coll., 1953, Columbia U., U. Richmond, 1954, Brandeis U., 1956, U. Mich., 1959, Northwestern U., 1960, Notre Dame U., Allegheny Coll., 1961, U. Toronto, 1962, Williams Coll., 1966, Tulane U., Boston Coll., Princeton U., 1968, Ripon Coll., 1972, Suffolk U., 1973, N.Y. Law Sch., 1978, U. Bridgeport, 1982, Oberlin Coll., 1982; D.C.L., U. Western Ont., 1961, U. Toronto, 1962, U. Edinburgh, Georgetown U., 1963, Oxford U., 1964; D.Litt., Western Res. U., 1967. Bar: Ohio 1929, Mass. 1935, D.C. 1973. With Griswold, Green, Palmer & Hadden, Cleve., 1929; atty. office solicitor gen., spl. asst. to atty. gen., Washington, 1929-34; asst. prof. law Harvard U., 1934-35, prof., 1935-46, dean, Charles Stebbins Fairchild prof. law, 1946-50, dean, Langdell prof. law, 1950-67; solicitor gen. U.S., 1967-73; partner Jones Day Reavis & Pogue, Washington, 1973—; mem. Alien Enemy Hearing Bd. for Mass., 1941-45; cons. expert U.S. Treasury Dept., 1942; mem. U.S. Civil Rights Commn., 1961-67; trustee Oberlin Coll., Bradford Jr. Coll., 1942-49, Tchrs. Ins. and Annuity Assn., 1942-46, Harvard Law Rev. Assn., 1938-67; bd. dirs. Am. Bar Found., pres., 1971-74, Assn. Am. Law Schs., 1957-58. Author: Spendthrift Trusts, 1936, 2d edit., 1947, Cases on Federal Taxation, 1940, 6th edit., 1966, (with others) Cases on Conflict of Laws, 1941, rev. edit., 1964, The Fifth Amendment Today, Law and Lawyers in the United States. Fellow Am. Acad. Arts and Sci. (v.p. 1946-48), Brit. Acad. (corr.); hon. bencher Inner Temple; mem. ABA (ho. of dels. 1957—), Mass. Bar Assn., Am. Law Inst., Am. Coll. Trial Lawyers, Am. Philos. Soc., Phi Beta Kappa. Clubs: Harvard (N.Y.C.); Burning Tree, Cosmos, Metropolitan (Washington); Century Assn. (N.Y.); Charles River Country. Home: 36 Kenmore Rd Belmont MA 02178 Office: 655 15th St NW Washington DC 20005-5701

GRISWOLD, JOHN CARROLL, business executive; b. Decatur, Ill., Oct. 3, 1901; s. Harry Ross and Edna Cantrell (Graves) G.; m. Marguerite Bessire, July 22, 1922 (dec. 1971); children: Jacqueline Louise Griswold Moore, David Ross; m. Anita Lihme de Lobokowicz, 1972 (dec. 1976). Student, Millikin U., 1919-21, LL.D., 1964; D.H.L., N.Y. Inst. Tech.; spl. courses, Chgo.-Kent Coll. Law, 1921-23. Clk., Continental Casualty Co., Chgo., 1922-25, resident v.p. in charge, Chgo. office, 1931-36; with Rollins Burdick Hunter Co., 1925-31; dir., v.p. Fred. S. James & Co., Chgo., 1936, mgr., 1939-45; founder, pres., dir. Griswold & Co., Inc., N.Y.C., 1945-62; exec. com., dir. Marsh & McLennan, Inc., 1962-69; v.p. W.R. Grace & Co., 1949-55, dir., 1950, exec. v.p., 1955-64; gen. partner Eastman Dillon, Union Securities & Co., 1964-72, sr. v.p., dir., 1971-72; dir., chmn. exec. com. Metromedia, Inc.; dir. Chemed, Inc., Safety First Shoes, Inc. Trustee Athens (Greece) Coll., Millikin U., Postgrad. Inst. Osteo. Medicine and Surgery; Trustee emeritus Brick Presbyn. Ch., N.Y.C.; co-chmn. bd. govs. N.Y. Coll. Osteo. Medicine. Mem. Griswold Family Assn. Am., U.S. Srs. Golf Assn., The Pilgrims, Sigma Alpha Epsilon, Phi Delta Phi. Presbyterian. Clubs: Links, Wall Street, River (N.Y.C.); Chicago; Bohemian, Pacific-Union (San Francisco). Home: 435 E 52d St New York NY 10022 Office: 211 E 51st St Suite 5D New York NY 10022

GRISWOLD, LYMAN DWIGHT, lawyer; b. Hanford, Calif., Sept. 14, 1914; s. Alpheus E. and Henrietta V. (Center) G.; m. Olga Telonicher, Aug. 30, 1942; children—Charlotte, Craig George, Margot. B.S. in Econs, U. Calif., 1937, LL.B., J.D., 1940. Bar: Calif. bar. Asst. dist. atty., Kings County, Hanford, 1942-46, individual practice, Hanford, 1946—; sec., gen. counsel Ranchers Cotton Oil Co., Fresno, Calif., 1955—; gen. counsel Calcott, Ltd., Bakersfield, Calif., 1950—; dir. Imperial Corp. Am., San Diego, 1979—. Mem. Am. Bar Assn., Am. Coll. Trial Lawyers, Kings County Bar Assn., Chancellors Club, Deans Club, Navy League U.S., Kings County Sheriff's Posse, Internat. Food and Wine Soc. Democrat. Methodist. Clubs: The Family, Elks. Office: 311 N Douty St Hanford CA 93232

GRITTON, EUGENE CHARLES, nuclear engineer; b. Santa Monica, Calif., Jan. 13, 1941; s. Everett Mason and Matilda (Benne) G.; m. Sandra Jennie Kelley (div.); children: Dennis Mason, Kathleen Wanda; m. Betty Jane Verdick (div.); m. Gwendolyn Owen, Jan. 1, 1980. B.S., UCLA, 1963, M.S., 1965, Ph.D., 1966. Research engr. environ. simulation modelling and poser systems engring. Rand Corp., Santa Monica, Calif., 1966-73, project leader advanced undersea tech. program, 1973-76, program dir. marine tech., 1974-76, head phys. scis. dept., 1975-77, head engring. and applied scis. dept., 1977—; kvis. lectr. dept. mech. engring. U. So. Calif., Los Angeles, 1967-72; vis. lectr. dept. energy and kinetics UCLA, 1971, 73. AEC fellow, 1963; NSF Coop. Grad. fellow, 1964-66. Mem. Am. Nuclear Soc. (mem. exec. com. aerospace and hydrospace div. 1974-75), AIAA. Home: 8221 Delgany Ave Playa del Rey CA 90291 Office: The Rand Corp 1700 Main St Santa Monica CA 90406

GRIVAS, THEODORE, historian; b. Cambridge, Mass., July 11, 1922; s. John T. and Angelina (Jahalidis) G.; m. Jacqueline Smith, June 17, 1955 (div. 1983); children: Deborah L., Melanie C., T. Gregory. A.B. magna cum laude, U. So. Calif., 1952, A.M., 1953, Ph.D., 1958. Instr. history U. So. Calif., 1956-57; asst. prof. History Calif. State U., Fresno, 1957-62; prof., 1962-72, chmn. dept. history and div. social scis., 1962-72; prof. history Calif. State U., Sonoma, 1972—; cons. in field. Author: History of the Los Angeles YMCA, 1957, History of Western Civilization Handbook, 1958, California's Military Government, 1846-50, 1963; Contbr. articles to profl. jours. Served with USNR, 1942-45; PTO. John Randolph Haynes fellow, 1957; Am. Philos. Soc. fellow, 1963. Mem. Am. Hist. Assn., Western History Assn., Phi Beta Kappa, Phi Alpha Theta, Phi Kappa Phi, Pi Gamma Mu, Phi Delta Kappa. Home: 3854 Montecito Ave Santa Rosa CA 95404 Office: Dept History Calif State U 1801 E Coati Ave Rohnert Park CA 94928

GRIZZLE, JAMES ENNIS, educator; b. Coeburn, Va., Apr. 20, 1930; s. Joseph Jackson and Jeanette Ellen (Bise) G.; m. Barbara Ann Huntsman, Aug. 18, 1951; children—William Joseph, Linda Jean, Thomas Bruce. B.S., Berea Coll., 1951; M.S., Va. Poly. Inst., 1954; Ph.D., N.C. State U., 1960. Asst. prof. U. N.C., Chapel Hill, 1960-64, asso. prof., 1964-69, prof., chmn. dept. biostatistics, 1969—; cons. NIH and pharm. firms, 1970—. Contbr. articles to sci. jours. Served with U.S. Army, 1956-57. Recipient various grants. Fellow Am. Statis. Assn., AAAS, Am. Heart Assn.; mem. Internat. Statis. Inst., Am. Public Health Assn., Biometric Soc., Soc. Clin. Trials. Home: Route 2 Box 310 Graham NC 27253 Office: Biostatistics Sch of Pub Health U North Carolina Chapel Hill NC 27514

GROB, GERALD N., historian, educator; b. N.Y.C., Apr. 25, 1931; s. Sidney and Sylvia G.; m. Lila Kronick, Dec. 25, 1954; children: Bradford S., Evan D., Seth A. B.S., CCNY, 1951; M.A., Columbia U., 1952; Ph.D., Northwestern U., 1958. Instr. history Clark U., Worcester, Mass., 1957-59, asst. prof., 1959-61, assoc. prof., 1961-66, prof., 1966-69, chmn. dept. history, 1967-69; prof. history Rutgers U., New Brunswick, N.J., 1969—, chmn. dept., 1969-71, 72-73, 81—; vis. prof. history Princeton U., spring 1979; mem. fellowship adv. com. NEN, 1975-76; chmn. study sect. history of medicine NIH, 1975-77. Author: books including Ed Jarvis and The Medical World of 19th Century America, 1978, Workers and Utopia, 1961, The State and The Mentally Ill, 1966 (ann. prize Am. Assn. for State and Local History 1965), Mental Institutions in America, 1973, Mental Illness and American Society, 1875-1940, 1983; contbr. articles to profl. jours. Served with C.E. U.S. Army, 1955-57. NIH grantee, 1960-65, 67-81; NEH fellow, 1972-73; Am. Council Learned Socs. fellow, 1976-77; Guggenheim fellow, 1980-81. Mem. Am. Assn. for History of Medicine (council 1978-81), Am. Antiquarian Soc., Am. Hist. Assn., Orgn. Am. Historians. Jewish. Home: 821 Starview Way Bridgewater NJ 08807 Office: Dept History Rutgers U New Brunswick NJ 08903 *My philosophy of history is essentially a tragic one; a study of the past, if undertaken in as honest and objective a manner as is humanly possible, should render us less certain about our omniscience and ability to control the future.*

GROB, HOWARD SHEA, biologist, univ. dean; b. Oakland, Calif., June 18, 1932; s. Jacob Nathan and Rose Leah (Berger) G.; m. Helen B. Mandel, Aug. 12, 1960; children—Matthew Adam, Douglas Benson. B.S., CCNY, 1957; M.S., N.Y. U., 1958, Ph.D., 1962. Instr. biology Hunter Coll., City U. N.Y., 1962-64; asst. prof. physiology N.Y. U. Coll. Dentistry, 1964-69, asso. prof., 1969-71; asso. prof. biology Adelphi U., Garden City, N.Y., 1971-75, prof. biology, 1975—, chmn. dept. biology, 1975-80, dean, 1980—, 1981—; cons. Roche Clin. Labs and Endocrine Research Labs.; mem. Scientists Com. for Public Info., 1969-72. Contbr. articles to sci. jours. Chmn. com. Manhattan council Boy Scouts Am., 1966-71. Served with AUS, 1951-55. USPHS grantee, 1965-73. Mem. Am. Physiol. Soc., Soc. Study Reprodn., Internat. Soc. Psychoneuroendocrinology, Tissue Culture Assn., Harvey Soc., Am. Soc. Zoologists, N.Y. Acad. Scis., AAAS. Jewish. Home: 675 West End Ave New York NY 10025 Office: Grad Sch Arts and Scis Adelphi U Garden City NY 11530 *Subject your own ideas and beliefs to the most penetrating analyses.*

GROBE, CHARLES STEPHEN, lawyer, accountant; b. Columbus, Ohio, May 5, 1935; s. Harry A. and Bertha S. (Swartz) G.; m. Ila Silverman, Aug. 30, 1964; children—Eileen, Kenneth. B.S., U. Calif. at Los Angeles, 1957; J.D., Stanford, 1961. Bar: Calif. bar 1962; C.P.A., Calif.; certified specialist taxation law, Calif. Tax accountant, Beverly Hills, Calif., 1961-63, tax atty., Los Angeles, 1963—; Lectr. Sch. of Public Health, UCLA, 1972, Loma Linda (Calif.) U. Sch. of Medicine, 1971-76, Calif. C.P.A. Found., 1974. Author: Guide to Investing Pension and Profit-Sharing Trust Funds, 1973, Guardianship, Conservatorship and Trusts on Behalf of Persons Who Are Mentally Retarded—An Assessment of Current Applicable Laws in the State of California, 1974, Using an Individual Retirement Savings Plan and the Related Rollover Provisions of the Pension Reform Act of 1974, 1975, Guide to Setting Up a Group Term Life Insurance Program Under IRC Section 79, 1976, also articles. Served to 2d. lt. AUS, 1957-58. Mem. State Bar Calif., Am., Los Angeles, Beverly Hills bar assns., Calif. Soc. of C.P.A.'s, Nat. Health Lawyers Assn., Soc. Hosp. Attys. of Am. Hosp. Assn. Home: 501 N Cliffwood Ave Los Angeles CA 90049 Office: 2029 Century Park East Suite 1260 Los Angeles CA 90067

GROBE, JAMES LESTER, physician; b. Huntington, W.Va., Apr. 16, 1921; s. James Waitman and Emma Jane (Kearns) G.; m. Rosalind June Evans, Dec. 9, 1943; children: James Lester, Jeffrey, Lori, Lisa. B.S., W.Va. U., 1950; M.D., Med. Coll. Va., Richmond, 1952. Diplomate: Am. Bd. Family Practice (pres. 1977-78). Intern Good Samaritan Hosp., Phoenix, 1952-53; practice family medicine, Phoenix, 1953—; assoc. prof. U. Ariz. Coll. Medicine, 1972—; pres. Ariz. Blue Shield Corp., 1966-70; mem. Council Med. Splty. Socs., 1971-77; dir. family practice residency program Phoenix Bapt. Hosp., 1978-82; mem. Liaison Com. Continuing Med. Edn., 1975-78, Am. Bd. Med. Spltys., 1976-78; cons. surgeon gen. U.S. Army, 1974—; pres. Ariz. Mental Health Assn., 1964-66; chmn. Gov. Ariz. Com. Mental Health, 1964-66; bd. dirs. Nat. Assn. Mental Health, 1965-67, Pres.'s Commn. Mental Health Children, 1965-68; exec. com. Pres.'s Commn. on Stroke, 1969-70. Served with USAAF, 1943-46. Recipient Pinel award Ariz. Psychiat. Assn., 1966; Alumni award U. Ariz., 1977. Fellow Royal Australian Acad. Gen. Practitioners; charter fellow Am. Acad. Family Physicians (pres. 1972-73); mem. AMA, Ariz. Med. Assn. (pres. 1971), Maricopa County Med. Assn. (Joseph Banks Gold medal 1965), Ariz. Acad. Family Physicians (pres. 1963), Soc. Tchrs. Family Medicine, Inst. Medicine. Office: 5422 W Thunderbird Rd Glendale AZ 85306

GROBMAN, ARNOLD BRAMS, educator, museum curator; b. Newark, Apr. 28, 1918; s. Samuel H. and Sophia (Brams) G.; m. Hulda Gross, Feb. 20, 1944; children: Marc Ross, Beth Allison. B.S., U. Mich., 1939; M.S., U. Rochester, 1941, Ph.D., 1943. Instr. zoology U. Rochester, 1943-44; research asso. Manhattan project, 1944-46; from asst. prof. to asso. prof. biology U. Fla., 1946-59, research specialist, med. center study, 1951-52; dir. Fla. State Mus., 1952-59; dir. biol. scis. curriculum study U. Colo., 1959-65; dean (Coll. Arts and Scis.); prof. zoology Rutgers U., New Brunswick, N.J., 1965-67, dean Rutgers Coll., prof. zoology Rutgers Coll., 1967-72; vice chancellor for acad. affairs, prof. biol. scis. U. Ill., Chgo., 1973-74, spl. asst. to pres., 1974-75; chancellor U. Mo.-St. Louis, 1975—, prof. biology, 1975—; adj. curator Fla. State Mus., 1982—; vis. lectr. Utah State U., Nat. Taiwan Normal U., U. Campinas, Brazil, U. New Delhi, India, U. Sind, Pakistan, Chulalongkorn U., Bangkok, Thailand, U. Singapore, Sophia U., Japan, Chiang Mia U., Thailand; cons. to govt., industry, founds. and ednl. instns., 1954—; Mem. div. biology and agr. NRC-Nat. Acad. Scis., 1954-58, com. adult edn., 1956-58; sec. U.S. nat. com. Internat. Union Biol. Scis., 1966-69; Chmn. Ednl. Opportunity Center of Met. St. Louis, 1976-78; mem. advisory team sci. soc., Thailand, 1971; fgn. observer Treaty Plebiscite, Gov. Panama, 1977-78; mem. Commn. on Adult Learner. Author: (with others) Island Life: A Study of the Land Vertebrates of Eastern Lake Michigan, 1948, Our Atomic Heritage, 1951, Genetics Effects of Chronic X-irratiation Exposure in

Mice, 1960, BSCS Biology Implementation in the Schools, 1964, The Changing Classroom, 1969; Editor: Social Implications of Biological Education, 1970; contbr. articles to profl. jours. and encys. Bd. dirs. in St. Louis United Way Laumeier Sculpture Park, Narcotics Service Council, Regional Commerce and Growth Assn., Conf. on Edn.; v.p. Conf. on Edn., 1980—; Bd. dirs. in St. Louis Higher Edn. Center. Recipient Fred H. Stoye prize Am. Soc. Ichthyologists and Herpetologists, 1941; A Cressy Morrison prize N.Y. Acad. Scis., 1943; Macalaster award Nat. Assn. Biology Tchrs., 1966; award of merit Urban League, 1984. Mem. Acad. Zoology in India (exec. com. 1967-69), Am. Assn. Higher Edn., AAAS (council 1961-65), Am. Assn. Museums (mus. tng. com. 1960-63), Am. Assn. State Colls. and Univs. (urban affairs com. 1977—), Am. Ednl. Research Assn., Am. Inst. Biol. Scis. (exec. com. 1958-61, Disting. Service award 1984), Am. Soc. Ichthyologists and Herpetologists (bd. govs. 1952—, pres. 1964), Am. Soc. Naturalists, Am. Soc. Zoologists, Assn. Am. Med. Colls., Assn. Southeastern Biologists, Assn. Supervision and Curriculum Devel., Asian Assn. Biol. Edn., Biol. Scis. Curriculum Study (chmn. steering com. 1965-69), Biol. Soc. China, Biol. Soc. Washington, Council on Fgn. Relations, NEA, Edn. Programs Improvement Corp. (trustee 1970-74), Colo.-Wyo. Acad. Sci., AAUP, Explorers Club, Fla. Acad. Sci., Fla. Found. Future Scientists (chmn. 1957-59), Mo. Council Pub. Higher Edn. (exec. com. 1977-82, v.p. 1978, pres. 1979), Mo. Bot. Garden, Nat. Council Accreditation Tchr. Edn. (chmn. 1970-71), Genetics Soc. Am., Herpetologists League, Philippine Assn. Sci. Tchrs., Nat. Assn. Biology Tchrs. (pres. 1966, editorial bd. 1974-77, dir. 1978-80), Nat. Assn. Research Sci. Teaching, Nat. Assn. State Univs. and Land Grant Colls. (exec. com. 1979-80, council on acad. affairs 1974-76, chmn. div. urban affairs 1978-79), Nat. Sci. Tchrs. Assn., Nature Conservancy, Newcomen Soc., N.J. Acad. Scis., Sci. Soc. Thailand, Soc. Study Amphibians and Reptiles, Soc. Study Evolution, Soc. Systematic Zoology, Soc. Vertebrate Paleontology, Southeastern Museums Conf. (pres. 1955-57), Assn. Tropical Biology, Phi Beta Kappa, Sigma Xi, Phi Kappa Phi, Phi Sigma, Alpha Epsilon Delta. Office: Office of the Chancellor University of Mo-St Louis MO 8001 Natural Bridge Rd Saint Louis MO 63121

GROBMAN, HULDA GROSS (MRS. ARNOLD B. GROBMAN), educator; b. Phila., Aug. 2, 1920; d. Joseph and Dora (Abrahams) Gross; m. Arnold B. Grobman, Feb. 20, 1944; children—Marc Ross, Beth Alison. A.B., U. Pa., 1940; M.Pub. Adminstrn., U. Mich., 1941; Ed.D., U. Fla., 1958. Research asso. Western Interstate Commn. on Higher Edn., Boulder, Colo., 1959-60; staff cons. Biol. Scis. Curriculum Study, Boulder, 1960-65; also editor newsletter, Biology: Implementation in the Schools; dir. evaluation Joint Council on Econ. Edn., N.Y., 1965-66; prof. edn. N.Y. U., 1966-72, Bklyn. Coll., City U. N.Y., 1972-73; sr. research asso. Am. Dental Assn., Chgo., 1973-74; dir. edn./career mobility, area health edn. system, prof. med. edn. U. Ill. Med. Center, 1973-75; prof. health edn. St. Louis U. Med. Center, 1975—, also cons. ednl. policies; cons. Sci. Edn. Center, U. Sao Paulo, Brazil; vis. prof. Asian Assn. Biol. Edn., Hebrew U. Jerusalem Inst. on Test Writing, 1972; cons. Fundacao Carlos Chagos, Sao Paulo, Brazil. Author: Developmental Curriculum Projects, 1970, Evaluation Activities of Curriculum Projects, 1968; cons. editor: Jour. Ednl. Research, Am. Ednl. Research Jour, 1975-80, also articles. Mem. bd. League Women Voters Fla., 1950-55; candidate for City Commn., Gainesville, Fla., 1955. Recipient A Individual Achievement award 3d Army Res. Command, 1965. Fellow AAAS (council 1967-73); mem. Asian Assn. Biology Edn. (charter hon. mem.), Am. Ednl. Research Assn. (sec. div. I 1979—), John Dewey Soc. (dir. 1978-81), Nat. Council Measurement in Edn., Am. Assn. Med. Colls. (rep. group on med. edn.). Home: 9 Bellerive Acres Saint Louis MO 63121 Office: St Louis Med Center Saint Louis MO 63104

GROBSTEIN, CLIFFORD, biological scientist, author, educator; b. N.Y.C., July 20, 1916; s. Aaron Joshua and Birdie (Yurdin) G.; m. Rose Gruver, Aug. 6, 1938; children: Paul, Joan; m. Ruth Hirsch Beloff, June 12, 1966. B.S., CCNY, 1936; M.A., UCLA, 1938, Ph.D., 1940. Instr. zoology Oreg. State Coll., 1940-43; sr. research fellow USPHS, 1946-47; biologist Nat. Cancer Inst., 1947-57; prof. biology Stanford, 1957-65; exec. head dept. biol. scis. Stanford U., 1963-65; chmn. dept. biology U. Calif. at San Diego, 1965—, dean Sch. Medicine, vice chancellor health scis., 1966-73, vice chancellor univ. relations, 1973-77, prof. biol. sci. and pub. policy, 1977—, also mem. coordinating council on med. edn.; cons. NSF; Cons. NIH, Am. Cancer Soc., Guggenheim Found., Macy Found. Served to capt. USAAF, 1943-46. Recipient Brachet award Royal Acad. Scis. Belgium, 1959. Fellow Am. Acad. Arts and Scis.; mem. Am. Soc. Zoologists (past pres.), Am. Soc. Cell Biologists, Internat. Inst. Embryology, Soc. Study Devel. and Growth (past pres.), Nat. Acad. Scis. Inst. Medicine. Home: La Valle Plateada Rancho Santa Fe CA 92067

GRODEN, JOHN FRANCIS, lawyer; b. Watertown, Mass., Mar. 16, 1908; s. Michael F. and Flavia D. (Grady) G.; m. Helen Mead Wires, Aug. 12, 1940; children: Sarah, Helen, Frances, Edith, John Frances. A.B., Boston Coll., 1930; LL.B., Harvard U., 1933. Bar: Mass. 1933. Since practiced in, Boston; ptnr. firm Withington, Cross, Park & Groden, 1947—; Sec.-treas. U.S. Figure Skating Assn., 1961-67. Served to comdr. USNR, World War II. Decorated Sec. Navy Spl. Commendation. Fellow Am. Coll. Trial Lawyers; mem. Am., Boston, Cambridge bar assns., Boston Coll. Alumni Assn. (treas. 1958- 59), Mass. Arms Collectors, Company Mil. Collectors. Club: Varsity, Skating, Harvard (Boston). Office: 73 Tremont St Boston MA 02108

GRODIN, CHARLES, actor, writer, dir.; b. Pitts., Apr. 21, 1935; s. Ted and Lana (Grodin); (div.)1 dau., Marion. Student, U. Miami; grad., Pitts. Playhouse Sch.; pupil acting, Lee Strasberg, Uta Hagen. Made: N.Y. stage debut in Tchin-Tchin, 1962; films include Catch 22, Rosemary's Baby, The Heartbreak Kid, Heaven Can Wait, Real Life, Sunburn, Seems Like Old Times, King Kong, It's My Turn, The Great Muppet Caper, 1981, The Incredible Shrinking Woman, 1981; appeared in: numerous plays including Steambath, Absence of a Cello, Same Time Next Year; co-author, dir.: It's a Glorious Day. . ..and All That, Off Broadway, 1966; author, lyricist, dir.: Hooray! It's a Glorious Day. . .And All That; dir.: Lovers and Other Strangers; producer, dir.: Thieves, Unexpected Guests; author: One of the All Time Greats; dir.: Marlo Thomas TV spl. Acts of Love and Other Comedies; writer, dir.: Simon and Garfunkel Spl; dir., producer: Paradise (Recipient Outer Critics Circle award 1975, Actors' Fund award of merit 1975). Address: care Ufland Agy 190 N Canon Dr Beverly Hills CA 90210 *

GRODINS, FRED SHERMAN, educator, physiologist, biomedical engineer; b. Chgo., Nov. 18, 1915; s. Abe E. and Minnie (Levine) G.; m. Sylvia Johnson, Mar. 28, 1942. B.S., Northwestern U., 1937, M.S., 1940, M.D., 1942, Ph.D., 1944. Instr. Northwestern U., 1942-44, assoc. prof., 1947-50, prof. physiology, 1950-67; asst. prof. U. Ill., 1946, assoc. prof., 1947; prof. elec. engring. and physiology U. So. Calif., 1967-76, prof., chmn. dept. biomed. engring., 1976—, Z.A. Kaprielian prof., 1982—; Mem. physiology tng. com. NIH, 1964-68, biomed. engring. tng. com., 1968-72, mem. pulmonary diseases adv. com., 1973-77, mem. cardiovascular and pulmonary study sect., 1979-80; cons. Rand Corp., 1964—. Author: Control Theory and Biological Systems, 1963, Respiratory Function of the Lung and Its Control, 1978. Served to capt. USAAF, 1944-46. Mem. Am. Physiol. Soc., Biomed. Engring. Soc., Soc. Exptl. Biology and Medicine, AAAS, Sigma Xi, Phi Beta Kappa, Alpha Omega Alpha, Phi Lambda Upsilon. Research in physiology, biomed. engring. Home: 26 Chuckwagon Rd Rolling Hills CA 90274 Office: Univ So California Los Angeles CA 90089

GRODSKY, GEROLD MORTON, biochemistry educator; b. St. Louis, Jan. 18, 1927; s. Louis and Goldie (Feldacker) B.; m. Kayla Deane Wolfe, Dec. 6, 1952; children: Andrea, Jamie. B.S., U. Ill., 1946, M.S., 1947; Ph.D., U. Calif.-Berkeley, 1954; postgrad., Cambridge U., Eng., 1954-55. Research biochemist U. Calif. Med. Sch., San Francisco, 1955-61, prof. biochemistry, 1961—; vis. prof. U. Geneva, 1968-69; cons. U.S. Naval Hosp., Oak Knoll, Calif., 1959—, VA Hosp., Martinez, Calif., 1964-68, USPHS Hosp., San Francisco, 1964-66; cons. various pharm. houses; Somogyi Meml. lectr., 1972, Helen Martin lectr., 1976. Editorial bd.: Diabetes, 1965-73, Am. Jour. Physiology, 1977—; contbr. chpts. to books; contbr. 150 articles on diabetes and storage, secretion of insulin to profl. jours. Mem. med. adv. bd. Juvenile Diabetes Found., 1974-77, 80—; chmn. Am. Diabetes Nat. Research Com., 1977; program dir. NIH Diabetic Animal Program, 1978—; chmn. research adv. bd. to Sec. Health, 1982—. Served to lt. (s.g.) USNR, 1944-54. NIH Pub. Health grantee, 1955—. Mem. Am. Soc. Biol. Chemists, Soc. Exptl. Biology, Am. Fedn. Clin. Research, European Diabetes Assn., Am. Diabetes Assn. (research bd. 1974—), San Francisco Sponsors (pres. 1966), Sigma Xi. Club: San Francisco Yacht. Home: 3969 Washington St San Francisco CA 94118 Office: Dept Biochemistry and Biophysics Sch Medicine U Calif San Francisco CA 94143

GRODY, DONALD, lawyer; b. N.Y.C., Dec. 18, 1927; s. Charles E. and Jeannette (Kessler) G.; m. Svetlana McLee, Dec. 12, 1958; children: Dion, Gordon, James, Jeremy. Student, Royal Acad. Dramatic Art, 1949-50; B.A. cum laude, Hunter Coll., 1951; LL.B., N.Y. Law Sch., 1959. Bar: N.Y. State bar 1959. Profl. actor, singer, 1950-58; atty. U.S. Dept. Labor, Washington, 1959-60; labor union atty., N.Y.C., 1960-65; atty.-advisor Nat. Labor Relations Bd., Washington, 1965-67; asst. gen. counsel Retail Clerks Internat. Assn., Washington, 1967-69; gen. counsel Distributive Workers Am., N.Y.C., 1970-73; exec. sec. Actors Equity Assn., N.Y.C., 1973-80; asst. exec. dir. NFL Players Assn., Washington, 1980-81; sole practice law, N.Y.C., 1981—; Mem. theatre adv. panel Nat. Endowment for the Arts; mem. exec. bd., dept. profl. employees AFL-CIO.; Chmn. Equity-League Pension and Welfare Trust Funds, 1975—. Served with AUS, 1945-47. Mem. Am. Bar Assn., Assn. Bar City N.Y., Internat. Fedn. Actors. Democrat. Office: 113 University Pl New York City NY 10003

GROEBLI, WERNER FRITZ (MR. FRICK), profl. ice skater; b. Basel, Switzerland, Apr. 21, 1915; s. Fritz and Gertrud (Landerer) G.; m. Yvonne Baumgartner, Dec. 30, 1954. Student architecture, Swiss Fed. Inst. Tech., 1934-35. Chmn. pub. relations com. Profl. Skaters Guild Am., 1972—. Performed in ice shows, Patria, Brighton, Eng., 1937; command performance in, Marina, London, 1937, Symphony on Ice, Royal Opera House, 1937; mem., Ice Follies, 1939—; partner (with Hans Mauch); in comedy team Frick & Frack, 1939-53; solo act as Mr. Frick, 1953—; numerous TV appearances including Snoopy on Ice, 1973, Snoopy's Musical on Ice, 1978, Sportsworld, NBC-TV, 1978, Donnie and Marie Osmond Show, 1978, Mike Douglas Show, 1978, Dinah Shore Show, 1978; films include Silver Skates, 1942, Lady Let's Dance, 1943, Jinxed, 1981; (Named Swiss Jr. skating champion 1934). Served with Swiss Army, 1934-37. Named to Madison Sq. Garden Hall of Fame for 10,000 performances in Ice Follies, 1967; recipient Hall of Fame Ann. award Ice Skating Inst. Am. Mem. Swiss Friends of U.S., Am. Swiss Hist. Soc. Clubs: American (Zurich); Swiss (San Francisco) (hon.). Has now passed 15,000 performances in Ice Follies; originator cantilever spread-eagle skating movement. Office: care US Figure Skating Assn 20 1st St Colorado Springs CO 80906

GROEGER, JOSEPH HERMAN, metal company executive; b. Bethlehem, Pa., Nov. 5, 1925; s. Joseph A. and Mary (Gitschier) G.; m. Dorothy Rumble, Dec. 20, 1947; children: Joseph Herman, David J. B.S., Lehigh U., 1950. Trainee, tube mill foreman Revere Copper & Brass, Inc., N.Y.C., 1950-54, metall. mgr. West Coast div., 1954-62, gen. process mgr., 1965-67, gen. project mgr., 1967-69, asst. gen. mfg. mgr., 1969-72, v.p., gen. mfg. and engring. mgr., 1972-76, v.p. copper and brass ops., 1976—, dir., 1977—; pres. Revere Copper Products, 1980—; chmn. bd. Revere Research Inc.; works mgr. Laminaçã Nacional de Metais, Brazil, 1962-65; dir. Multimetals Ltd., Kota, India. Served with USMCR, 1943-46. Mem. Copper Club, Lambda Chi Alpha. Home: 800 N George St Rome NY 13440 Office: PO Box 300 Rome NY 13440

GROENING, WILLIAM ANDREW, JR., lawyer, former chemical company executive; b. Saginaw, Mich., Nov. 20, 1912; s. William Andrew and Rose (Egloff) G.; m. Virginia Jane Gann, July 27, 1940; children: Mary R. Groening Flores), William Andrew III, Janet R. Groening Marsh, Phyllis L. Groening Beehr), Theodore J. B.A., U. Mich., 1934, J.D., 1936; LL.D., Saginaw Valley Coll., 1974. Bar: Mich. 1936. With legal dept. Dow Chem. Co., Midland, Mich., 1937-51, asst. gen. counsel, 1951-67, gen. counsel, 1968-77, asst. sec., 1955-71, v.p., 1971-77, mem. finance com., 1972-77; sec., dir. Dow Corning Corp., 1961-77, KartridgPak Co., 1966-77. Author: The Modern Corporate Manger: Responsibility and Regulation, 1981. Mem. Regina High Sch. Bd., 1963-67; bd. arbitrators Roman Catholic Province of Mich., 1970-71; chmn. pension com. Mich. Cath. Conf.; chmn. bd. Saginaw Valley Coll., 1963-73; charter commr. City of Midland, 1944, city councilman, 1946-50; trustee Willard and Martha Dow Meml. Ednl. Fund, 1949-75, pres., 1951-75; nat. chmn. U. Mich. Law Sch. Fund, 1979-80. Mem. State Bar Mich. (chmn. anti-trust law sect. 1967-68), Mich. Conf. Bar Pres. (chmn. 1952-53), ABA, Midland County Bar Assn. (past pres.), Am. Judicature Soc. (past dir., v.p., exec. com.). Republican. Roman Catholic. Clubs: KC, Midland Country, Saginaw Valley Torch, Rotary. Home: 4204 Arbor Dr Midland MI 48640

GROENNERT, CHARLES WILLIS, electric company executive; b. Nashville, Ill., Aug. 30, 1937; s. Melvin William and Helen Louise (Gaebe) G.; m. Margy Lu Duensing, June 21, 1958; children: Todd C., Gaye L., Brett D. B.S., So. Ill. U., 1958. C.P.A., Mo.; C.P.A., Ill. C.P.A. Peat, Marwick, Mitchell & Co., St. Louis, 1958-65; auditor, treas., v.p. Emerson Electric Co., St. Louis, 1965—. Served with AUS, 1958-59. Mem. Am. Inst. C.P.A.s, Fin. Execs. Inst. Club: Glen Echo Country. Home: 3812 Baville Ct Florissant MO 63034 Office: 8000 W Florissant Ave Saint Louis MO 63136

GROESCHEL, AUGUST HERMAN, hosp. adminstr., physician; b. Jersey City, May 31, 1908; s. August Herman and Margaret (Murphy) G.; m. Mary T. Molloy, Feb. 21, 1933 (dec. 1945); children—Peter, Moya, Noel; m. Eileen D. Bosquett, Jan. 3, 1946; children—Margaret, Catherine. A.B., Holy Cross Coll., 1927; M.D., Columbia, 1931, M.S., 1947. Intern French Hosp., N.Y.C., 1931-33, N.Y. Nursery and Child's Hosp., 1933-34; pvt. practice, Sussex, N.J., 1934-40; asst. med. dir. Health Ins. Plan Greater N.Y., 1947-48; asst. dir. N.Y. Hosp., 1948-52, asso. dir., 1954-66, adminstr., 1967-69; exec. dir. Phila. Gen. Hosp., 1952-54; v.p. N.Y. Hosp.-Cornell Med. Center, 1970-73; dir. N.J. Blood Services, 1973-75; asst. prof. pub. health and preventive medicine Cornell U. Med. Coll., 1954-73; spl. cons. surgeon gen. USPHS, 1959—; surgeon gen. U.S. Army, 1954—; Pres. Community Blood Council Greater N.Y., 1959-73, pres. emeritus, 1973—, exec. asso., 1975-79; bd. dirs. Group Health Ins., Inc., N.Y., 1961-80; med. control bd. Health Ins. Plan Greater N.Y., Inc., 1957-75, bd. dirs., 1963-75; treas. Career Center Social Services, 1966-70; mem. nat. health resources adv. com. Office Emergency Planning, Exec. Offices President, 1963-68, also chmn. com. blood, health adviser to dir., 1969-79, chmn. nat. health resources adv. com., 1969-79; chmn. nat. adv. com. on selection physicians, dentists and allied specialists SSS, 1969-73, chmn. adv. com. on selection of drs., dentists and allied specialists, 1973-76; bd. dirs. Am. Bur. Med. Aid to China, 1968-80, 1st v.p., 1969, pres., 1970, hon. pres., 1971; mem. Nat. Bd. Med. Examiners, 1970-74. Author: (with Emanuel Hayt and Lillian R. Hayt) Law of Hospital, Physician and Patient, 2d edit, 1972, (with Emanuel Hayt and Dorothy McMullan) Law of Hospital and Nurse, 1958. Trustee La Guardia Hosp., N.Y.C. Served to lt. col. AUS, 1941-45; brig. gen. Res., ret., 1967. Decorated Legion of Merit. Fellow AMA, N.Y. Acad. Medicine, Am. Pub. Health Assn., Am. Coll. Hosp. Adminstrs.; mem. Am. Hosp. Assn. Home: 715 Boston Blvd Sea Girt NJ 08750

GROGAN, HUGH, business consultant; b. Kansas City, Mo., Nov. 2, 1923; s. Hugh and Gladys Carroll (Cox) G. Student, Loyola U., Los Angeles, U. So. Calif. Pres. Piedmont Life Ins. Co., Atlanta, 1967-72; chmn. bd. Pacific Fidelity Life Ins. Co., Los Angeles, 1970-71, pres., treas., 1971-74; prin. Grogan & Assos., Los Angeles, 1974-75; pres., chief exec. officer USLIFE Life Ins. Co., Pasadena, 1975-77, All Am. Life Ins. Co., Chgo., 1977-81; v.p. USLIFE Equity Sales, 1975-81. Served with U.S. Army, 1943-45. Home: 11750 Sunset Blvd Apt 501 Los Angeles CA 90049

GROGAN, KENNETH AUGUSTINE, pub. co. exec.; b. N.Y.C., May 20, 1924; s. Kenneth Augustine and Mildred Beatrice (Kean) G.; m. Gertrude Catherine Healy, Dec. 28, 1946; children—Kimberly Ann, Kenneth Augustine, Lawrence Edward, Thomas John. Student, Fordham U., 1941-42; B.S., N.Y. U., 1948. With Modern Salon mag. Vance Pub. Corp., 1946—, Eastern sales mgr., N.Y.C., 1953-62, gen. mgr., Chgo., 1962-64, pub., 1964—, corp. v.p., 1965—. Mem. Wheeling Twp. (Ill.) Republican Club, 1962-78, Elk Grove Village (Ill.) Rep. Club, 1978—. Served with USAF, 1942-45; ETO. Recipient several industry awards. Mem. Nat. Beauty and Barber Mfrs. Assn. (mktg. com. 1978-80). Roman Catholic. Clubs: Union League of Chgo., Elks. Home: 531 Easy St Des Plaines IL 60016 Office: Modern Salon mag Vance Pub Corp 300 W Adams St Chicago IL 60606

GROGAN, STEVEN JAMES, professional football player; b. San Antonio, July 24, 1953; s. James White and Doris Joan (Anderson) G.; m. Roberta Dale Hewson, Apr. 2, 1977. B.S. in Phys. Edn, Kans. State U., 1975. Quarterback New Eng. Patriots of NFL, Foxboro, Mass., 1975—. Sports ambassador Kans. Easter Seal Soc., 1976, chmn., 1978. Recipient Inspiration and Leadership award New Eng. Patriots, 1975, 76; named most valuable offensive player, 1976, 77. Mem. Nat. Football League Players Assn. Baptist. Office: New Eng Patriots Schaffer Stadium Route 1 Foxboro MA 02035 *

GROGAN, WILLIAM ROBERT, university dean; b. Pittsfield, Mass., Aug. 2, 1924; s. William Patrick and Irene A. (Finch) G.; m. Mae Jean Kafer, Jan. 26, 1966. B.S., Worcester Poly. Inst., 1945, M.S., 1949. Instr. elec. engring. Worcester Poly. Inst., Mass., 1946-49, asst. prof., 1949-56, assoc. prof., 1956-62; prof. WorcesterPoly. Inst., 1962—; dean undergrad. studies Worcester Poly. Inst., 1970—; engring. cons. Gen. Electric Co., Pittsfield, Mass., 1953-61; cons. U.S. Navy, Washington, 1963-66, Bell Telephone Labs., Holmdeli, N.J., 1964-65; trustee Bay State Savs. Bank, Worcester, 1973—. Patentee in field. Chmn. Diocese of Worcester bd. edn., 1974-76. Lt. USN, 1942-46, 51-52. Recipient Outstanding Teaching award Worcester Poly. Inst. Trustees, 1969, Sci. Achievement award Worcester Engring. Soc., 1979, Chester F. Carlson award Am. Soc. Engring. Edn., 1979, William Wickenden award, 1980. Fellow IEEE; mem. Worcester Econ. Club, Sigma Xi, Tau Beta Pi, Eta Kappa Nu; Phi Kappa Theta nat. pres. (1960-64). Roman Catholic. Home: 10 Laconia Rd Worcester MA 01609 Office: Worcester Poly Int Dept Undergrad Studies Worcester MA 01604

GROH, CLIFFORD JOHN, lawyer; b. Ramapo, N.Y., Apr. 1, 1926; s. Marcel and Helen (Jaworski) G.; m. Lucy Bright Woodruff, Aug. 22, 1949; children: Clifford John II, Paul Woodruff, Lucy Elizabeth. B.S., St. Lawrence U., 1948; J.D., U. N.Mex., 1951. Bar: N.Mex. 1952, Alaska 1953. Ptnr. firm Groh, Eggers & Price, 1955—; mem. Alaska Senate, 1970-74. First pres. Operation Statehood, 1953; chmn. Alaska Constl. Research Com., 1955; mem., pres. Anchorage Ind. Sch. Bd., 1955-59, 62-63; assemblyman Greater Anchorage Area Borough, 1964-66; mem. Anchorage City Council, 1963-67, acting mayor, 1966-67; chmn. Greater Anchorage Charter Com., 1968-69; mem. Republican Nat. Com., 1976-78. Served to lt. USNR, 1943-46, 50-52. Named Outstanding Legislator, 1972. Fellow Am. Bar Found.; Mem. ABA, Alaska Bar Assn. (bd. govs. 1958-61, pres. 1960-61), Anchorage Bar Assns., Am. Judicature Soc. Episcopalian. Home: 1576 Coffey Ln Anchorage AK 99501 Office: 550 W 7th Ave Suite 1250 Anchorage AK 99501

GROH, DAVID LAWRENCE, actor; b. N.Y.C., May 21, 1941; s. Benjamin and Mildred G. B.A., Brown U., 1961; postgrad. (Fulbright scholar), London Acad. Music and Dramatic Art, 1962-63. Appeared: on Broadway Chapter Two, 1978, Antony and Cleopatra, Elizabeth the Queen; Off-Broadway Hot L Baltimore, 1973; TV series Rhoda, 1974-77, Another Day, 1978; TV movies Smash-Up on Interstate 5, 1976, Victory at Entebbe, 1977, Murder at the Mardi Gras, 1978, Child Stealer, 1979, Power, 1979; feature films Change in the Wind, 1972, Two Minute Warning, 1976, A Hero Aint Nothin' But A Sandwich, 1977. Served with U.S. Army, 1963-64. Mem. Phi Beta Kappa. Office: care Phil Gersh Agy 222 N Canon Dr Beverly Hills CA 90210 *

GROHMAN, ROBERT T., clothing company executive; b. 1924; (married). Student, S.D. State Coll., U. Nebr., U. Calif., Davis. Gen. mgr. weaving ops. Duplex, 1946-57; gen. mgr. ops. Internat. Playtex Corp., 1957-69; pres. BVD Co., 1969-74; v.p. parent co., pres. internat group Levi Strauss & Co., 1974—, exec. v.p., chief operation officer, 1976-81, pres., chief exec. officer, 1981—, dir. Address: 1155 Battery St San Francisco CA 94106

GROJEAN, THOMAS FRANCIS, business executive; b. Chgo., July 25, 1938; s. Francis Thomas and Veronica Mary (Brown) G.; m. Therese Mary Frystak, May 6, 1961; children: Thomas F., William M., Janet L., Elizabeth A. B.B.A. cum laude, U. Notre Dame, 1960. C.P.A., Ill. Sr. accountant Price, Waterhouse & Co., Chgo., 1960-64; treas. So. Airways, Inc., Atlanta, 1964-67; v.p. finance Tiger Internat. (formerly Flying Tiger Corp.) and Flying Tiger Line, Los Angeles, 1967-71; also dir.; pres., chief exec. officer, dir. N.Am. Car Corp., Chgo., 1971-78; exec. v.p., dir. Tiger Internat., 1975-78, pres., dir., 1978-83; dir. Stepan Chem.; Founding chmn. adv. council Coll. Bus., Loyola-Marymount U.; chmn. adv. council Coll. Bus., U. Notre Dame. Mem. Am. Inst. C.P.A.'s, Nat. Freight Transp. Assn., Young Pres.'s Orgn. Clubs: Notre Dame, Los Angeles Country (Los Angeles); Mid-America (Chgo.).

GROLNICK, HERBERT NORMAN, insurance company executive; b. Bklyn., Oct. 11, 1932; s. Abraham and Hilda (Karp) G.; m. Barbara Drebotick, Nov. 10, 1969; children: Ronald, George. B.B.A., CUNY, 1954. Personnel asst. Phelps Dodge Refining Corp., N.Y.C., 1956-59; asst. personnel mgr. Resistoflex Corp., Roseland, N.J., 1959-61, planning analyst, 1961-74, adminstrv. asst., 1974-76, asst. sec., 1976-

78; corp. sec. The Guardian Life Ins. Co., N.Y.C., 1978—. Served with U.S. Army, 1954-56. Address: 201 Park Ave S New York NY 10003

GROMAN, NEAL BENJAMIN, microbiology educator; b. Chisholm, Minn., May 21, 1921; s. Raphael Simon and Jenny Rebecca (Levine) G.; m. Elaine Ruth Spigle, Nov. 19, 1943; children: Jo Ann Tamarin, Nancy (Mrs. Meir Sheffer), Richard, Ellen. B.S., U. Chgo., 1947, Ph.D., 1950. Instr. U. Wash., Seattle, 1950-53, asst. prof., 1953-58, assoc. prof., 1958-63, prof. microbiology, 1963—, dir. office biology edn., 1971-75, acting chmn. dept. microbiology, 1981-82. Contbr. articles to profl. pubs. Served with AUS, 1942-46. John and Mary Markle Found. scholar, 1955-60; John Simon Guggenheim fellow, 1958-59; USPHS fellow, 1966-67. Fellow Am. Acad. Microbiology; mem. Am. Soc. Microbiology (chmn. virology sect. 1963-64), N.Y. Acad. Scis., Sigma Xi. Home: 4805 NE 40th Seattle WA 98105 Office: Dept Microbiology Univ Wash Seattle WA 98195

GROMEN, RICHARD JOHN, educator, university dean; b. Cleve., Dec. 3, 1930; s. John Rudolph and Rena Marie (Calcagni) G.; m. Joyce Margaret Pawlak, Jan. 27, 1951; children: Margot Lynn, Doreen Rae, Richard John. B.A., Adelbert Coll., 1953; M.A., Western Res. U., 1961; Ph.D., 1969. Salesman Beck Shoe Store, Parma, Ohio, 1946-48; cowboy Minor Cattle Ranch, Hyannis, Nebr., 1949; with classified advt. dept. Cleve. News, 1949-50; office mgr. Parma Cut Stone, 1950-60; part-time bookkeeper, Cleve., 1960-64; acct., bookkeeper Broadview Savs. and Loan, Cleve., 1960-64; tchr., summer sch. dir. Brunswick (Ohio) High Sch., 1960-64; mem. faculty Edinboro U. of Pa., 1964—, prof., dean faculty arts and scis. Author: British Historians and Their View of the British Policy of Appeasement, 1931-39, 1969; contbr. to: Hist. Abstracts, 1972-78. Treas. Edinboro Found.; bd. dirs. Edinboro State Coll. United Cerebral Palsy Joint Council; v.p. Ams. for Competitive Enterprise System; pres. Tri-Boro Little League, 1979—. Tuition scholar, 1949-55. Mem. NEA (life), Am. Hist. Assn., Orgn. Am. Historians, Conf. Brit. Studies, AAUP, Phi Alpha Theta. Lutheran. *The standards one sets should be for oneself and not for others. Nor should one express a view on a controversial issue until one can understand why someone as sincere and honest as oneself can hold the opposite view.*

GROMER, FRANK JOSEPH, JR., advertising executive; b. N.Y.C., June 1, 1925; s. Frank Joseph and Mary (Derrick) G.; m. Carol Marie Maloney, June 1, 1947; children: Ellen Gromer Schiavone, Mark, Paul, Jean. Student, Lafayette Coll., 1943-44, NYU, 1948-49. With Foote, Cone & Belding Advt. Inc., N.Y.C., 1947—, chmn. strategy bd., 1970, sr. v.p., also dir., 1970—; dir., chmn. bd. Advt. Research Found., N.Y.C., Advt. Info. Services, Luxo Lamp Corp., Port Chester, N.Y. Served with USAAF, 1943-47; PTO. Recipient Bronze plaque Media/Scope mag., 1964. Mem. Media Dirs. Council (pres. 1963—), Radio and TV Research Council, Am. Assn. Advt. Agys. (media policy com.). Office: 101 Park Ave New York NY 10178

GROMMESH, DONALD JOSEPH, aerospace engr.; b. Fargo, N.D., Aug. 13, 1931; s. Ralph H. and Eva N. (Rademacher) G.; m. Joanne Margaret Herman, Nov. 26, 1952; children—Michael, Mark, Melinda, Belinda, Joseph, Kristine. B.S., N.D. State U., 1953. Aerodynamics engr. Cessna Aircraft Co., Wichita, Kans., 1953-55, structures engr., structures engring. group leader, 1957-62; chief structures engring., chief engr., v.p. research and engring. Gates Learjet Corp., Wichita, 1962—. Served with USAF, 1955-57. Mem. Soc. Automotive Engrs., Am. Inst. Aeronautics Astronautics, Aerospace Industries Assn. Am., Gen. Aviation Mfrs. Assn. Roman Catholic. Home: 3101 Wilma St Wichita KS 67218 Office: 8220 W Harry St Wichita KS 67277

GRONER, PAT NEFF, hospital administrator; b. Dallas, Dec. 21, 1920; s. Frank Shelby and Laura (Wyatt) G.; m. Louise Mary Rugg, May 5, 1944; children: Josephine Louise, Frank Shelby III. Student, East Tex. Bapt. Coll.; also LL.D.; A.B., Baylor U., 1941. Pilot Colonial Airlines (now Eastern Airlines), 1946-47; asst. adminstr. Mary Fletcher Hosp., Burlington, Vt., 1947-48; adminstr. Barre (Vt.) City Hosp., 1948-50; chief exec. officer Baptist Hosp., Pensacola, Fla., 1950-80; pres. Bapt. Regional Health Services, 1980-83; pres. emeritus Bapt. Care Inc., 1984—; pres. Hosp. Research and Devel. Inst., 1964—; v.p., treas. Multihosp. Mut. Ins. Ltd., 1975-84; cons. holding co., 1984—; mem. exec. com. Vol. Hosps. of Am., 1977-84, sr. cons., 1984—; Dir. First Mut. Savs. of Fla.; mem. fed. hosp. council HEW, 1972-76. Exec. com. Blue Cross-Blue Shield Fla., 1952-81; chmn. Greater Pensacola United Fund, 1966; pres. Greater Pensacola United Way, 1977-79. Served with USMC, 1941-45. Recipient Good Govt. award Pensacola Jaycees, 1960, George Washington medal Freedom Found., 1961, Liberty Bell award Soc. Bar 1st Jud. Circuit Fla., 1970, award of merit Fla. Hosp. Assn., 1971, Disting. Service award Southeastern Hosp. Conf., 1972; named Civitan of Year, 1971-72, Disting. Alumnus award East Tex. Bapt. Coll., 1974, award for disting. community service United Way, 1980, Kiwanis Man of Year, 1980. Fellow Am. Coll. Hosp. Adminstrs. (bd. regents 1966-70); mem. Am. Hosp. Assn. (trustee 1967-70, 82—), Fla. Hosp. Assn. (pres. 1954-55), Southeastern Hosp. Conf. (pres. 1958-59). Club: Rotary (pres. 1966-67). Home: 2200 Banquo's Trail Pensacola FL 32503 Office: 1717 N E St Pensacola FL 32501 *"Faith is a higher faculty than reason," ... Will Durant.*

GRONER, STANLEY, sporting goods company executive. Exec. v.p. AMF, Inc., White Plains, N.Y. Office: AMF Inc 777 Westchester Ave White Plains NY 10604§

GRONERT, BERNARD GEORGE, editor; b. Prairie du Chien, Wis., June 22, 1920; s. George M. and Irene J. (Kimball) G.; m. Laura Cahalan, Dec. 2, 1942; children: Paula Gronert Hayes, John, Monica. A.B., Wabash (Ind.) Coll., 1942; M.A., U. Wis., 1948. Reporter Dayton Herald, 1946-47; Field editor Ronald Press, N.Y.C., 1950-61; history editor Macmillan Co., 1961-63; exec. editor Columbia U. Press, N.Y.C., 1964—. Served with USAF, 1942-46. Home: 394 Branch Ave Little Silver NJ 07739 Office: 562 W 113th St New York NY 10025

GRONINGER, DONALD LYNN, rubber company executive; b. Middleton, Ohio, Dec. 4, 1941; s. Jacob Kelly and Nancy Lee (Berry) G.; m. Carol Ann Purdy, Sept. 20, 1969; children—Jennifer, Adam, Greg. B.A., U. Cin., 1963, J.D., 1966. Bar: Ohio. Assoc. firm Baker, Hostetler & Patterson, Cleve., 1973-75; asst. counsel Firestone Tire & Rubber Co., Akron, Ohio, 1975-80, asst. sec., 1980, sec., 1980-82, v.p., 1982, v.p. human resources, 1982—. Served with U.S. Army, 1966-68. Decorated Bronze Star. Mem. Am. Soc. Corp. Secs., Cleve. Bar Assn., Order of Coif. Methodist. Office: 1200 Firestone Pkwy Akron OH 44317

GRONOWICZ, ANTONI, author; b. Rudnia, Poland, July 31, 1913; came to U.S., 1938, naturalized, 1962; s. Antoni and Paulina (Dorocinska) G.; m. Sophia Shymanska, June 8, 1940; children: Anthony Boleslaw, Gloria Andrea. Ph.D., U. Lwow, Poland, 1937. Author: poetry Prosto w Oczy, 1936; Bunt Walki, 1937, Melodia Switow, 1939, The Quiet Vengeance of Words, 1968, Polish Poems, 1972; essays Byki Czystej Poezji, 1936; Pattern For Peace, 1951; novels I Chlopi Ida od Wschodu, 1937; Bolek, 1942, Hitler's Woman, 1942, Four From The Old Town, 1944, The Piasts, 1945, Gallant General, 1946, Virtue in Four Positions, 1965, An Orange Full of Dreams, 1972, The Hookmen, 1973, American Sextet, 1974; art theory Harmonizm, 1938; plays Niedroga Recepta, 1938; A Comedy of Angels, 1957, Chiseler's Paradise, 1958, Modjeska, 1962; biog. novels Paderewski, 1942; Chopin, 1943, Tchaikovsky, 1944, Rachmaninoff, 1946, Modjeska-Her Life and Loves, 1956; biography Béla Schick and the World of Children, 1954; play Greta, 1967, The United Animals, 1967 (1st prize Internat. Competition, Geneva 1970); The Great Society, 1968, Forward Together, 1969; essays Polish Profiles, 1976; Rocos, 1977, Shores of Pleasure, Shores of Pain, 1978 (1st prize Provincetown Acad. Arts Competition 1979); play Colors of Conscience, 1979; biography God's Broker (John Paul II), 1984. Decorated Polonia Restituta Order, Poland; recipient Polish Nat. Lit. prize, 1938; Ford Found. grantee, 1959. Mem. Authors League Am., P.E.N., Dramatists Guild, Cath. Poetry Soc. Am., Cath. Press Assn. Address: 132 E 82d St New York NY 10028 *Hard work is the essence of my life. Through work I find the reason for existence and even some enjoyment in daily life.*

GROOM, DALE, educator, physician; b. Tulsa, Nov. 6, 1912; s. Fernando Hooker and Mary (Dale) G.; m. Marjorie Ruth Tweed, Jan. 26, 1944; children: Shelley Ann, Lincoln Dale, Randall Tweed. A.B., Hiram Coll., 1936; M.D., Med. Coll. Va., 1943; M.S. in Medicine, U. Minn., 1948. Diplomate: Am. Bd. Internal Medicine (subsplty. cardiovascular disease). Intern Northwestern U. Passavant Hosp., Chgo., 1943; fellow in medicine Mayo Clinic, 1945-49; pvt. practice internal medicine, Miami, Fla., 1949-53; asso. prof. medicine, asst. dean Med. Coll. S.C., 1953-68; prof. medicine, asso. dean continuing edn. U. Okla. Med. Center, Oklahoma City, 1968-78, prof. emeritus, 1978—; mem. staff Univ. Hosp.; cons. Oklahoma City VA, Presbyn., Mercy hosps.; nat. cons. cardiology USAF, 1965—, FAA, 1970-74. Author: Clinics in Electrocardiography, 1961; editorial bd.: Am. Heart Jour, 1977—; contbr. articles on coronary heart disease, EKG and cardiovascular sounds to profl. jours. Trustee Ednl. Resources Found. Served to lt. M.C., USNR, 1944-45. Fellow ACP (regent 1969-75, chmn. bd. govs. 1968, 69), Am. Coll. Cardiology; mem. Am. Heart Assn. (fellow council clin. cardiology), AMA (council on sci. assembly 1965-74), Mayo Cardiovascular Soc. (pres. 1971-73), Mayo Alumni Assn. (pres. 1969-71), The Doctors Mayo Soc., Sigma Xi, Alpha Omega Alpha. Home: 8330 E Cholla Rd Scottsdale AZ 85260

GROOM, JOHN MILLER, food company executive; b. Washington, Dec. 12, 1936; s. Charles Francis and Marjorie (Miller) G.; m. Carolyn Anderson, Sept. 22, 1962; children: John Michael, David Allen. Student, U. of South, 1954-55; B.S., Miami U., Oxford, Ohio, 1958. C.P.A., Ill. With John Morrell & Co. (meat packers), Chgo., 1960-70; v.p., controller Hygrade Food Products Corp., Detroit, 1970-81, Wilson Foods Corp., Oklahoma City, 1981—. Mem. Am. Inst. C.P.A.s, Am. Inst. Corporate Controllers. Home: 2513 Stamford Ct Edmond OK 73034 Office: PO Box 26724 Oklahoma City OK 73126

GROOM, JONATHAN DANIEL, manufacturing company executive; b. N.Y.C., Jan. 29, 1928; s. Daniel Michael and Olga (Kroner) G.; m. Jean Hackley, Sept. 2, 1961; children: Kathy, Samuel. B.S., Northwestern U., 1951; M.B.A., Columbia U., 1958. With IBM Corp., White Plains, N.Y., 1953-75, mgr. basic systems mktg., v.p., 1965-73, exec. v.p., White Plains, 1973-75; with Philip Morris, N.Y.C., 1975—, exec. v.p., 1980—; dir. Philip Morris Indsl., Inc. Bd. dirs. N.Y. Found. Ind. Colls., United Performing Arts Fund, United Way, Salvation Army; vice chmn. N.Y. region NCCJ, 1978-80. Served to capt. U.S. Army, 1951-53. Mem. Am. Paper Inst., Am. Mgmt. Assn., Conf. Bd. Club: University. Home: Werik Complex 266 Pearl St Hartford CT 06103

GROOME, REGINALD K., hotel executive; b. Montreal, Que., Can., Dec. 18, 1927; s. Cyril T. and Muriel H. (Forbes-Toby) G.; m. Christina M. Walker, June 20, 1953; children: Reginald A., Roderick, Richard. Ed., McGill U., Cornell U. With Montreal Pub. Co., 1945-53; broadcaster CBC Internat. Service; also overseas corr. Can. daily newspapers, 1951; dir. advt. and public relations, then personnel mgr. hotel chain, Montreal, 1953-57; with Hilton Can., from 1957, v.p., then exec. v.p., 1965-72, pres., from 1972, chmn. bd. dirs., from 1978; pres., dir., also gen. mgr. Queen Elizabeth Hotel, Montreal, until 1983; v.p. Hilton Internat., N.Y.C., 1982—; past pres. Montreal Bd. Trade; Can. dir. Crum & Forster Can. Ltd., Herald Ins. Co., U.S. Fire Ins. Co., North River Ins. Co., Alliance Compagnie Mutuelle d'Assurance Vie, Dustbane Enterprises Ltd., L.W. Biegler Can. Ltd. Past pres., internat. commr. Nat. council Boy Scouts Can.; life gov. Montreal Gen. Hosp.; gov. Concordia U. Decorated officer Order of Can.; recipient Silver Wolf award Boy Scouts Can.; Outstanding Citizenship award Montreal Citizenship Council, 1976. Mem. Advt. and Sales Execs. Club Montreal, Tourist Industry Assn. Can. (bd. dirs., past chmn.), Que. C. of C. (dir.). Address: Bonaventure Hilton 1 Place Bonaventure Montreal PQ Canada H5A 1E4

GROOMS, HARLAN HOBART, judge; b. Jeffersonville, Ky., Nov. 7, 1900; m. Angeline M. Grooms; children: Harlan Hobart, Ellen Elizabeth, John Franklin, Angeline. J.D., U. Ky.; LL.D. (hon.), Samford U. Bar: Ky. bar and Ala. bar. Practiced in, Birmingham, Ala., 1926-53; former mem. Spain, Gillon, Grooms & Young; U.S. dist. judge No. Dist. of Ala., 1953—. Trustee Samford U. Mem. Am., Ala. bar assns., Phi Alpha Delta, Omicron Delta Kappa, Pi Kappa Alpha. Baptist. Club: Civitan. Office: 332 Federal Courthouse Birmingham AL 35203 *

GROOMS, RED, artist; b. Nashville, June 2, 1937. Student, Peabody Coll., Chgo. Art Inst., New Sch. Social Research, Hans Hofmann Sch., Provincetown, Mass. One-man exhbns. include, Sun Gallery, Provincetown, 1958, Reuben Gallery, N.Y.C., 1960, Tibor de Nagy Gallery, 1963, 65-67, 69-70, Artists Guild, Nashville, 1962, Allan Frumkin Gallery, Chgo., 1967, John Bernard Myers Gallery Discount Store, 1971, Happenings: A Play Called Fire, Sun Gallery, 1958, Burning Bldgs, N.Y.C., 1958, Rutgers Gallery Art, New Brunswick, N.J., 1973, N.Y. Cultural Center, Mus. de Arte Contemporaneo, Caracas, Venezuela, Brooke Alexander Gallery, N.Y.C., 1975, Ft. Worth Art Mus., 1976, Whitney Mus. Am. Art, 1973, Stanford Mus., 1976, SUNY-Purchase, 1978, Hudson River Mus., Yonkers, N.Y., 1979, Lowe Art Mus., U. Miami, 1980, Aspen Ctr. Visual Arts, 1981, Seibu Mus., Tokyo, 1982, Marlborough Gallery N.Y.C., 1984, group exhbns. include, Chgo. Art Inst., 1964, Delancey St. Mus., N.Y.C., 1959, 60, also, Provincetown/Chrysler Mus., Tibor de Nagy Gallery, N.Y.C., 1969, Walker Art Center, Mpls., 1970, Guggenheim Mus., N.Y.C., 1972, Ruckus Manhattan, N.Y.C., 1975-76, 81, SUNY, Purchase, 1978, Lowe Art Mus. U., Miami (Fla.), 1980, The New Gallery, Cleve., 1982, ICA, Phila., others; (with Rudy Burckhardt) movie Shoot the Moon, 1962, Big Sneeze, 1965, Before "n' After, 1966, Washington's Wig Whammed!, 1966, Fat Feet, 1966, (with Rudi Burckhardt) Meow, Meow!, 1967; commd.: (with Mimi Gross) Meow, Meow!, for mural, Centre Modern Culture, Florence, Italy; represented in: permanent collections Meow, Meow!, Mint Mus. Art, Charlotte, N.C., Chgo. Art Inst., Mus. Modern Art, N.Y.C., Chrysler Mus. Art, Provincetown, Mass., Cheekwood Fine Arts Mus., Nashville, Raleigh (N.C.) Mus. Art. Address: care Marlborough Gallery Inc 40 W 57th St New York NY 10019 *

GROOMS, THOMAS ALBIN, biological chemist; b. Dayton, Ohio, Apr. 6, 1943; s. Byron Edwin and Thelma Florence (Albin) G.; m. Geraldine Francis Madill, Nov. 1, 1969; children: Aaron, Evan, Ian, Sarah. B.S., Baldwin-Wallace Coll., 1965; Ph.D., U. Cin., 1973. Postdoctoral fellow Northwestern U., 1972-73; sr. investigator Wilson Labs., Inolex Corp., Park Forest South, Ill., 1973-75; scientist Leeds and Northrup Co., North Wales, Pa., 1975-76; dir. chemistry research and devel. Yellow Springs Instrument Co., (Ohio), 1976—; instr. Am. Sch. Corr., 1973, Wittenberg U., 1978, Antioch Coll., 1982. Contbr. articles to profl. jours. Mem. Am. Assn. for Clin. Chemistry, Internat. Soc. Artificial Organs, Sigma Xi. Mem. Christian Ch. Office: Yellow Springs Instrument Co Inc Box 279 Yellow Springs OH 45387

GROOS, ARTHUR BERNHARD, JR., German literature educator, academic administrator; b. Fullerton, Calif., Feb. 5, 1943; s. Arthur Bernhard and Nancy Elizabeth (Stowe) G.; m. Bonnie Cleo Buettner, Apr. 16, 1979; children: Peter, Jan. A.B. magna cum laude, Princeton U., 1964; M.A., Cornell U., Ithaca, N.Y., 1966, Ph.D., 1970; postgrad., Freie Universitat Berlin, 1966-67. Asst. prof. UCLA, 1969-73; asst. prof. German lit. Cornell U., 1973-76, assoc. prof., 1976-82, prof., 1982—, dir. medieval studies, 1974—; chmn. German dept. adv. council Princeton U., N.J., 1981—; vis. prof. Universitat Paderborn, W.Ger., 1982. Editor: Dichtkinst und Lebenskunst, 1981. Fulbright fellow Berlin, 1966; Fulbright sr. fellow Munich, 1979; Guggenheim fellow Munich, 1979. Mem. MLA, Internat. Arthurian Soc., Medieval Acad. Am., Wolfram v. Esenchbach Gesellschaft, Internat. Courtly Lit. Soc., Phi Beta Kappa. Home: 492 Valley Rd Brooktondale NY 14817 Office: Dept German Lit 185 Goldwin Smith Hall Cornell U Ithaca NY 14853

GROPP, LOUIS OLIVER, editor; b. LaPorte, Ind., June 6, 1935; s. Hosea Howard and Carol Gladys (Pagel) G.; m. Jane Margaret Goodwin, Aug. 15, 1965; children—Amy Alison, Lauren Elizabeth. B.A. in Communication Arts, Mich. State U., 1957. Design editor Home Furnishings Daily, Chgo. and N.Y.C., 1960-67; v.p. Milo Baughman Design, Wellesley, Mass., 1967; exec. editor House and Garden Guides (Conde Nast Co.), N.Y.C., 1968-72, editor-in-chief, 1973-80, House and Garden, 1981—. Author: Solar Houses, 1978. Chmn. bd. deacons Riverside Ch., N.Y.C., 1973-75. Home: 488 2d St Brooklyn NY 11215 also Old Depot Rd Quoque NY 11959 Office: 350 Madison Ave New York NY 10017

GROPPER, MITCHELL HAROLD, lawyer; b. Saskatoon, Sask., Can., Oct. 2, 1942; s. Nathan Frank and Zora Elka (Rose) Grooper; m. Arlene Lana Ruth Gladstone, Aug. 26, 1964 (div. 1979); children: Daniel Benjamin, Naomi Laura. B.A. in Econs. magna cum laude, U. Sask., 1964, LL.B. magna cum laude, 1964; LL.M. (hon.), London Sch. Econs. and Polit. Sci., 1967. Called to bar B.C., Ont. Hon. lectr. U. B.C., Vancouver, Can.; asst. prof. faculty of law U. Western Ont., London; sr. v.p. Daon Devel. Corp., Vancouver; now ptnr. firm Shrum, Liddle & Hebenton, Vancouver; counsellor Counselling Service, London, Ont., 1968-70; mem. Com. on Personel Property Security Legis. Law Reform Commn., Vancouver. Chmn. Heritage Adv. Com. City of Vancouver, 1975-77. Mem. Can. Bar Assn., Can. Tax Found., Law Soc. B.C., Law Soc. Upper Can. (Ont.). Home: 2469 Point Grey Rd Vancouver BC Canada V6K 1A1

GROSE, ROBERT FREEMAN, psychology educator; b. Norwood, Mass., July 12, 1924; s. Arthur Dester and Alice Buck (Littlefield) G.; m. Ann Bawden Huntington, Aug. 9, 1947; children: Peter Huntington, Catherine Littlefield, Margaret Susan, Amy Tarrant. B.A., Yale U., 1944, M.S., 1947, Ph.D., 1953; M.A. hon., Amherst Coll., Mass., 1970. From instr. to prof. psychology Amherst Coll., 1950—, registrar, 1956-78, dir. instl. research, 1974—, affirmative action officer, 1980-83; adj. prof. Grad. sch. Edn. U. Mass., Amherst, 1975—; cons. Silliman U., Dumaguet City, Philippines, 1963-64. Co-author: Data Book 1, 1978, Data Book 11, 1983; co-editor: Transfer of Learning, 1936. Vice chmn. Town Amherst Zoning Bd., 1975-82; mem. town meeting Town of Amherst, 1964—. Served to lt. (j.g.) USNR, 1944-46. Mem. Am. Assn. Coll. Registrars, New Eng. Assn. Coll. Registrars (pres. 1972), Assn. Instl. Research, N.E. Assn. Instl. Research (pres. 1979-80), Am. Psychol. Assn., Am. Ednl. Research Assn., Sigma Xi. Democrat. Mem. Ch. of Christ. Club: Rotary Internat. (chmn. internat. found. 1978-81). Home: 132 Farmington Rd Amherst MA 01002 Office: Amherst Coll Amherst MA 01002

GROSE, ROBERT WARFIELD, printing and publishing company executive; b. Balt., June 20, 1941; s. William Edwin and Sara Ruth (Cox) G.; m. Patricia Macmanus, June 18, 1964; children: Peter Kingman, David Spencer, Kathryn Hollister. B.E., Yale U., 1963; M.B.A., U. Chgo., 1965; M.Sc. in Econs. (U. Chgo. Internat. fellow), London Sch. Econs., U. London, 1966. Fin. analyst Exxon Corp., N.Y.C., 1966-68; mgmt. cons. Case and Co., N.Y.C., 1968-71; asst. to pres. Cooper Labs., Bedford Hills, N.Y., 1971-74; mgmt. cons. Ernst and Ernst, Balt., 1974-75; pres. Williams & Wilkins Co. (med. book pub. div.), Balt., 1975-81; pres. printing and pub. services div. Waverly Press, 1981—, chief operating officer, 1983—. Trustee Gilman Sch., Balt., 1976—, Assn. Ind. Md. Schs., 1980—; chmn. devel. council Johns Hopkins U. Children's Center, 1978—. Mem. Am. Mgmt. Assn. Club: Maryland. Home: 207 Woodlawn Rd Baltimore MD 21210 Office: 428 E Preston St Baltimore MD 21202

GROSE, WILLIAM RUSH, publishing executive; b. Charleston, W.Va., Jan. 29, 1939; s. William Ellis and Mary W. (Morrison) G. Grad., Haverford Coll., 1961. With Prentice-Hall, Inc., Englewood Cliffs, N.J., 1962-70, Warner Communications, Inc., N.Y.C., 1970-72; editor-in-chief Dell Pub. Co., Inc., N.Y.C., 1972-79; v.p., pub. Jove Publs., Inc., N.Y.C., 1979-81; v.p., editorial dir. Berkeley/Jove Pub. Group, 1981-82; v.p., editor-in-chief New Am. Library Inc., 1982-83; v.p., editorial dir. Pocket Books, 1983—. Democrat. Episcopalian. Club: Knickerbocker. Home: 929 Park Ave New York NY 10028 Office: 1230 Ave of the Americas New York NY 10020

GROSECLOSE, ELGIN, economist, author; b. Waukomis, Okla., Nov. 25, 1899; s. M. Clarence and Della (Wishard) G.; m. Louise Elizabeth Williams, June 25, 1927; children: Sarah Jane (Mrs. Peter Theodoropoulos), Nancy Margaret (Mrs. Herold Witherspoon), Hildegarde Elsa (Mrs. Earl Bender), Suzy French (Mrs. Paul San Soucie). A.B., U. Okla., 1920; M.A., Am. U., 1924, Ph.D., 1928. Tchr. Presbyn. Mission Sch., Tabriz, Persia (now Iran); spl. agt. U.S. Dept. Commerce, 1923-26; with Guaranty Trust Co., N.Y.C., 1927-30; assoc. editor Fortune; also lectr. City Coll. N.Y., 1930-32; asst. prof. bus. adminstrn. U. Okla., 1932-35; economist telephone investigation FCC, 1935-38; economist U.S. Treasury Dept., 1938-43; treas.-gen., Iran, 1943; head firm Elgin Groseclose, Econ. Counsel, 1944-59, Groseclose, Williams and Broderick (fin. analysts and cons.), 1959—; founder, exec. dir. Inst. for Monetary Research, 1961—. Author: Money: The Human Conflict, 1934, rev. edit. pub. as Money and Man, 1961, 67, 76, The Persian Journey of the Rev. Ashley Wishard and His Servant Fathi, 1937, Ararat, 1939, 74, 77, The Firedrake, 1942, Introduction to Iran, 1947, The Carmelite, 1955, The Scimitar of Saladin, 1956, Fifty Years of Managed Money, The Story of the Federal Reserve, 1966, The Kiowa, 1978, America's Money Machine, The Story of the Federal Reserve, 1980, Olympia, 1980, Comanche Country, 1982, also monographs. Founder Welfare of Blind, Inc., 1956, pres., 1956-66, 78—. Recipient Nat. Book award, 1939; Found. for Lit. award, 1940; gold medallion Christian Book Publishers, 1978. Mem. Okla. Soc. Washington (pres. 1945-46), Washington City Bible Soc. (pres. 1966-72, dir. 1950—), Phi Beta Kappa, Phi Delta Phi, Alpha Kappa Psi, Delta Sigma Rho, Delta Tau Delta. Episcopalian. Clubs: Nat. Economists, Cosmos (Washington); Kenwood Country. Home: 4813

Woodway Ln NW Washington DC 20016 Office: 1200 15th St NW Washington DC 20005

GROSECLOSE, EVERETT HARRISON, editor; b. Childress, Tex., June 25, 1938; s. Everett Jackson and Eula Margaret (Snider) G.; m. Edna Kathryn Hunter, Dec. 24, 1962; children—Kirsten Lee, Megan Margaret. B.A. in Journalism, Tex. Tech. U., Lubbock, 1961. Reporter Wall St. Jour., Dallas and N.Y.C., 1965-70, asst. mng. editor, Cleve., 1970-76; dir. public affairs Dow Jones & Co., N.Y.C., 1976-80; mng. editor Dow Jones News Services, N.Y.C., 1980—. Served with AUS, 1961-64. Decorated Army Commendation medal. Unitarian. Home: 218 Richards Rd Ridgewood NJ 07450 Office: 22 Cortlandt St New York NY 10007

GROSENBAUGH, DOWNEY A., lawyer; b. Fort Dodge, Iowa, Apr. 4, 1915; s. Frederick A. and Julia (Downey) G.; m. Lois Margaret Wilkins, Apr. 24, 1942; children—Charles, Diana. J.D., U. Iowa, 1939. Bar: Calif. bar 1940, U.S. Supreme Ct. bar 1961. With Douglas Aircraft Co., 1940-45; individual practice law, Hollywood, Calif., 1947-60; partner firm Meserve, Mumper & Hughes, Los Angeles, 1960—; dir. Forest Lawn Co. Served with AUS, 1945-46. Mem. Los Angeles County Bar Assn., Hollywood Bar Assn. (pres. 1956), Calif. Bar Assn., Am. Bar Assn., Los Angeles Trial Lawyers Assn. (pres. 1959), Am. Coll. Trial Lawyers, Better Bus. Bur. Los Angeles-Orange Counties (dir.). Republican. Roman Catholic. Clubs: Big Canyon Golf (Newport Beach, Calif.); Jonathan, Kiwanis, Lakeside Golf (Los Angeles). Home: 885-37 S Orange Grove Pasadena CA 91105 Office: 333 S Hope St 35th Fl Los Angeles CA 90071

GROSFELD, JAY LAZAR, pediatric surgeon, educator; b. N.Y.C., May 30, 1935; m. Margie Faulkner; children: Lisa, Denise, Janice, Jeffrey, Mark. A.B. cum laude, NYU, 1957, M.D., 1961. Diplomate: Am. Bd. Surgery. Intern in gen. surgery dept. surgery Bellevue and Univ Hosps. NYU, N.Y.C., 1961-62; resident in gen. surgery Bellevue and Univ. Hosps. NYU, N.Y.C., 1962-66; resident in pediatric surgery Ohio State U. Coll. Medicine, Children's Hosp., 1968-70; clin. instr. surgery NYU Sch. Medicine, N.Y.C., 1965-66, asst. prof. surgery and pediatrics, 1970-72; instr. surgery Ohio State U. Coll. Medicine, 1968-70; prof., dir. pediatric surgery Ind. U. Sch. Medicine, Indpls., 1972—, Lafayette F. Page prof., 1981—; surgeon-in-chief James Whitcomb Riley Hosp. Children. Author numerous papers, reports, book chpts., articles for med. jours. Served to capt. M.C. U.S. Army, 1966-68. Decorated Commendation medal; recipient numerous fellowships, grants, teaching awards. Fellow Am. Acad. Pediatrics, ACS; mem. AMA, Assn. Acad. Surgery, N.Y. Cancer Soc., Am. Pediatric Surg. Assn., Soc. Univ. Surgeons, Marion County Med. Soc., Ind. State Med. Assn., Pediatric Surgery Biology Club, Am. Trauma Soc., Soc. Surgery Alimentary Tract, Central Surg. Assn., Brit. Assn. Pediatric Surgeons, Western Surg. Assn., Internat. Soc. Surgery, Am. Surg. Assn., Phi Beta Kappa, Sigma Xi, Alpha Omega Alpha. Office: J W Riley Children's Hosp 702 Barnhill Dr Indianapolis IN 46223

GROSH, RICHARD JOSEPH, manufacturing company executive; b. Ft. Wayne, Ind., Oct. 29, 1927; s. Joseph A. and Vera (Vogeding) G.; m. Susan Marie Ankenbruck, June 24, 1950; children: Katherine (Mrs. Craig Johnson), Anton, Richard, John, Jane, Suzanne. B.S., Purdue U., 1950, M.S., 1952, Ph.D., 1953. Registered profl. engr., N.Y., Ind. Research, devel. Capehart Farnsworth Corp., Ft. Wayne, 1950-51; asst. prof. mech. engring. Purdue U., Lafayette, Ind., 1953-56, asso. prof., 1956-58, prof., 1958-71, head, 1961-65, asso. dean engring., 1965-67, dean, 1967-71; pres. Rensselaer Poly. Inst., Troy, N.Y., 1971-76; chmn. bd., chief exec. officer Ranco, Inc., Dublin, Ohio, 1976—, also dir., Dublin; dir. Sterling Drug Inc., Transway Internat. Cons. editor, Charles E. Merrill Book Co.; Contbr. articles to profl. jours. Served with CIC USAAF, 1946-47. Fellow ASME; mem. Nat. Acad. Engring., AIAA, Pi Tau Sigma, Sigma Pi Sigma, Tau Beta Pi. Home: 818 Bluffview Dr Worthington OH 43085 Office: Ranco Inc 555 Metro Pl N Suite 550 Dublin OH 43017

GROSHANS, RUSSELL GLEN, utility company executive; b. Minot, N.D., Feb. 14, 1929; s. Louis Christian and Elizabeth Claire (Bosse) G.; m. Barbara Joan Mottley, June 27, 1953; children: Maris, Barbara, Russell Glen. B.S., U.S. Mil. Acad., 1953; M.S., Georgetown U., 1964, Ph.D., 1967. Program physicist Office Aerospace Research, Washington, 1963-67; systems engr. RCA Corp., Hightstown, N.J., 1967-68, tech. adviser corp. research and engring. staff, Princeton, N.J., 1969-77; dir. market planning COMSAT Gen. Corp., Washington, 1978-79, div. dir. bus. devel., 1979-80; tech. planning and devel. Central Telephone & Utilities, Chgo., 1980—; grad. physics lectr. RCA Corp., 1968-69. Mem. Monmouth County Environ. Council, 1972-78. Served with USAF, 1953-67. Mem. IEEE, Am. Geophys. Union. Republican. Roman Catholic. Clubs: Golf (Spring Lake, N.J.); West Point Soc., Georgetown Club (N.Y.C.). Home: 1 Old Coach Rd Barrington IL 60010 Office: Central Telephone & Utilities 5725 E River Rd Chicago IL 60631

GROSHANS, WERNER, artist; b. Eutingen, Germany, July 6, 1913; came to U.S., 1927; s. Emil and Anna (Jung) G.; m. Yetta Abramowitz, June 3, 1944. Grad., Newark Sch. Fine and Indsl. Arts, 1932. Chmn. fine arts dept. Jersey City Mus., 1966-69. Exhibited group shows, Whitney Mus., 1948-50, 52-53, Carnegie Inst., 1953, Met. Mus., 1950, 52, Butler Inst., NAD, Montclair Mus. Art, Parrish Art Mus., Newark Mus., Audubon Artists, Silvermine Guild, AFA Traveling Exhbn., Hirschl-Adler Gallery, Springfield (Mass.) Mus. Fine Arts, Kennedy Gallery, Wadsworth Atheneum, U. Md., 1966-67, Quinata Gallery, Nantucket, Mass., 1969, Centenary Coll., 2-man exhbn., Hackettstown, N.J., 1969, Okla. Mus. Art, New Britain Mus. Am. Art, retrospective, 1973, Babcock Galleries, one-man show, N.Y.C., 1973, Canton (Ohio) Art Inst., 4-man show, 1971, Nat. Inst. Arts and Letters Exhbn., 1975, 80, Montclair (N.J.) Art Mus., retrospective, 1976, Mus. Art, Industry and Sci., Bridgeport, Conn., Rutgers U., Newark, 1980, Mus. Fine Art, Roslyn, N.Y., U. Del., others; represented permanent collections, Davenport (Iowa) Municipal Art Gallery, Ct. Gen. Sessions, Washington, Newark Mus., Newark Pub. Library, NAD Collection, Ency. Brit. collection, New Britain (Conn.) Mus. Am. Art, William Benton Mus., U. Conn., Storrs, Canton Art Inst., Dresden (E. Ger.) Mus. State Collection, Montclair Art Mus., also pvt. collections. Recipient Thomas B. Clarke award NAD, 1960, Henry Ward Ranger Fund purchase prize, 1961-74, 1st prize Montclair Art Mus., 1961, Pauline Wick award, 1961, Painters and Sculptors award, 1964, Silver medallion N.J. Tercentenary Exhbn., 1964, Famous Artists Sch. award, 1965, Margaret C. Cooper award, 1966, Gold medal., Ligonier, Pa., 1966, N.J. Artist of Year award, 1966, Edward C. Roberts Meml. award New Britain Mus. Am. Art, 1969, N.J. State Council on Arts fellow, 1980-81. Nat. academician N.A.D. (council 1970-73); Mem. Audubon Artists, Conn. Acad. Fine Arts, Allied Artists, Asso. Artists N.J., Painters and Sculptors Soc. N.J. (v.p. 1967-71), Pastel Soc. Am. Home: R D #1 Box 57 Catskill NY 12414 Office: Babcock Galleries 20 E 67th St New York City NY *Often the search for one's identity leads to the frantic striving, at all costs, for originality and newness; the desire to be contemporary, avant garde. This searching usually produces its opposite, a counterfeit originality, sterile conformity, and imitation. I would like to look back upon my life's work and be able to say I have not succumbed to the negative pressures artists face in our dollar-oriented society. If it will be said of my paintings, that they reflect a love of nature and the humanist tradition in art, my life will have served some purpose.*

GROS LOUIS, KENNETH RICHARD RUSSELL, university official; b. Nashua, N.H., Dec. 18, 1936; s. Albert W. and Jeannette Evelyn (Richards) Gros L.; m. Dolores K. Winandy, Aug. 28, 1965; children: Amy Katherine, Julie Jeannette. B.A., Columbia U., 1959, M.A., 1960; Ph.D. (Knapp fellow), U. Wis., 1964. Asst. prof. Ind. U., Bloomington, 1964-67, assoc. prof. English and comparative lit., 1967-73, prof., 1973—, assoc. chmn. comparative lit. dept., 1967-69, assoc. dean arts and scis., 1970-73, chmn. dept. English, 1973-78, dean arts and scis., 1978-80, v.p., 1980—. Editor: Yearbook of Comparative and Gen. Literature, 1968—; Editor Vol. I: Literary Interpretations of Biblical Narratives, 1974; editor Vol. II, 1982; Contbr. articles to profl. jours. Mem. Ind. Com. Humanities, chmn., 1980-81; bd. dirs. Blue Cross. Recipient Disting. Teaching award Ind. U., 1970. Mem. MLA, Nat. Council Tchrs. Eng., Phi Beta Kappa. Home: 1119 E 1st St Bloomington IN 47401

GROSS, ABRAHAM, rabbi, educator; b. Bklyn., June 29, 1928; s. Joseph and Tillie (Lauer) G.; m. Hannah Leah Stern, Dec. 18, 1952; children—Israel Meyer, Elijah Moses, Vitel, Adel Binah, Hilda Mindy, Solomon Abel. Rabbi, Ch'san Sofer Rabbinical Sem., 1952; B.B.A., Coll. City N.Y., 1951; M.S. Edn, Yeshiva U., 1959; 6th yr. profl. certificate, Hunter Coll., 1968. Rabbi Young Israel of Coll. Av., Bronx, N.Y., 1953-63, Congregation Adath Jeshurum, Bronx, 1963-68, Young Israel of Vanderveer Park, Bklyn., 1968-72, Congregation Shaare Hatikvah, N.Y.C., 1972—; asst. prin. pub. schs., N.Y.C., 1966-73, prin., 1973—. Mem. Community Planning Bd. 4, Bronx, 1966-69; active Bonds for Israel, Yeshiva, Beth Jacob movements.; Treas. Charles and Ana Elenberg Found. Mem. Rabbinical Alliance Am. (pres. 1969-71), Met. Bd. Orthodox Rabbis (treas. 1965-69). Home: 2720 Ave J Brooklyn NY 11210 Office: 711 W 179th St New York City NY 10033

GROSS, AL, electronics, electrical engineer; b. Toronto, Ont., Can., Feb. 22, 1918; came to y, 1919; s. Nathan and Bertha (Rappaport) G.; m. Helen Mary Makse, Dec. 15, 1979 (dec. 1980); m. Ethel Marie Stanka, May 9, 1982. B.S. in Elec. Engring., Case Sch. Applied Sci., 1939. Chief engr. Gilmore Industries, Cleve., 1974-76; staff engr. Hickok Elec. Instrument Co., Cleve., 1976; nat. sales mgr., engr. Fiberglass Div. True Temper Corp., Cleve., 1976-78; sr. engr. controls Parson-Peebles Electric Products, Cleve., 1979-82; specialist product design ITT Cannon Electric, Phoenix, 1983—. Contbr. (articles to profl. jours.); patentee (antenna, high frequency transmitter and receiver, radio tuning apparatus, radio frequency oscillator, others). Recipient Presdl. commendation for affirmative contbns. in telecommunications field. Fellow IEEE, Radio Club Am.; mem. World Citizens Band Union (hon.), European Citizens Band Fedn., Fedn. Citizens Band Italiano, Nat. Citizens Band Council of Ireland, U. U.K. Citizens Band Fedn. (hon.), Fraternal Order Police. Roman Catholic. Office: ITT Cannon Electric 2801 Air Ln Phoenix AZ 85034

GROSS, CHARLES GORDON, psychologist; b. N.Y.C., Feb. 29, 1936; s. Frank and Sara (Gordon) G.; m. Gaby Ellen Peierls, Sept. 23, 1961; children—Melanie, Monica, Derek, Rowena. B.A., Harvard U., 1957; Ph.D., Cambridge (Eng.) U., 1961. From postdoctoral fellow to asst. prof. psychology M.I.T., 1961-65; vis. lectr., asst. prof., then lectr. Harvard U., 1963-70; prof. psychology Princeton U., 1970—. Author papers on brain and visual function. Grantee NIH, NSF, Spencer Found. Home: 45 Woodside Ln Princeton NJ 08540 Office: Green Hall Princeton Univ Princeton NJ 08540

GROSS, CHARLES WAYNE, physician, educator; b. Covington, Va., Nov. 9, 1930; s. Charles Calvin and Frances Hattie (Field) G.; m. Catherine McCombs; children: Charles Edward, William Elsworth, Alice Carey, Nicholas Fleming, Catherine Elizabeth. B.S., U. Ky., 1953; M.D., U. Va., 1961. Diplomate: Am. Bd. Otolaryngology. Instr. Midway (Ky.) Jr. Coll., 1956-57; intern U. Va. Hosp., Charlottesville, 1961-62; resident Buckley (W.Va.) Meml. Hosp., 1962-63, Mass. Eye and Ear Infirmary, Boston, 1963-66; teaching fellow, then asst. otolaryngology Harvard Med. Sch., 1966-67; asst. prof. U. Cin. Med. Sch., 1967-68; prof., chmn. dept. otolaryngology and maxillofacial surgery U. Tenn. Med. Sch., 1970-77; Past chmn. advisory bd., now v.p. Better Hearing Inst.; past pres. bd. regents Hearing Instruments Inst. Contbr. articles to profl. jours. Served to lt. USNR, 1953-56. Mem. AMA (pres. 1984), Am. Acad. Otolaryngology, Am. Acad. Facial Plastic and Reconstructive Surgeons (dir., chmn. edn. com. 1975-82), ACS (otolaryngology program rep. trauma com. 1977-83), So., Mid South, Tenn. med. assns., Memphis and Shelby County Med. Soc. (del. to AMA Ho. of Reps. 1979-83), Memphis Soc. Otolaryngology (pres. 1979-81), Am. Cancer Soc., Am. Council Otolaryngology (past nat. membership chmn.), Triological Soc., Tenn. Acad. Otolaryngology, Am. Soc. Head and Neck Surgery. Home: 1508 Goodbar St Memphis TN 38104

GROSS, DAVID JONATHAN, physicist; b. Washington, Feb. 19, 1941; s. Bertram M. and Nora (Faine) G.; m. Shulamith Toaff, Mar. 30, 1962; children—Ariela, Elisheva. B.Sc., Hebrew U., Jerusalem, 1962; Ph.D., U. Calif., Berkeley, 1966. Harvard Soc. of Fellows jr. fellow Harvard U., 1966-69; asst. prof. physics Princeton U., 1969-71, asso. prof., 1971-73, prof., 1973—. Alfred P. Sloan fellow, 1970-74. Fellow Am. Phys. Soc.; mem. AAAS. Research, numerous publs. in field; discovered asymptotic freedom, 1973; proposal of non-Abelian gauge theories of the strong interactions, 1973. Home: 264 Hartley Ave Princeton NJ 08540 Office: Jadwin Hall Princeton U Princeton NJ 08544

GROSS, DEAN COCHRAN, librarian; b. Waterville, Ohio, Feb. 21, 1922; s. William Martin and Opal Florence (Cochran) G.; m. Gertrude Sharpe, Apr. 23, 1967; children: David Paul, Terrie Louise. A.B., Miami U., 1947; M.S., Drexel U., 1952. Dir. Harrisburg (Pa.) Pub. Library, 1966-71; state librarian State of Kans., Topeka, 1971-73; dir. Citizens Library, Washington, Pa., 1973-76, Norfolk (Va.) Pub. Library, 1977-83; condr. weekly radio program of reading from great books. Book reviewer for newspapers. Bd. dirs. Order of Cape Henry, 1607, Urban League, Salvation Army, Washington, Pa.; chmn. Greater Harrisburg Area Arts Council (Pa.); chmn. Catawba dist. Boy Scouts Am.; ruling elder Ch. of Covenant Presbyn. Ch., Washington, Pa. Served with U.S. Army, 1943-45. Decorated Bronze Star; Cross of War Merit, Italy). Mem. ALA, Va. Library Assn., English Speaking Union. Clubs: Rotary, Torch. Office: 301 E City Hall Ave Norfolk VA 23510 *I have devoted my life to education as a librarian, to religion as a church worker, and to music as a singer in church. I believe the preservation of the world and the realization of the destiny of mankind of fellowship with God, as St. Paul wrote, require the continuous inspiring of hearts and the informing of minds. We need to merge now religion, science, and humanism.*

GROSS, ERIC TARAS BENJAMIN, elec. engr.; b. Vienna, Austria, May 24, 1901; came to U.S., 1939, naturalized, 1943; s. Berthold and Sophie (Gerstman) G.; m. Catharine B. Rohrer, Aug. 14, 1942; children—Patrick Walter, Elizabeth Sophia, Margaret Joan. E.E., Tech. U., Vienna, 1923, D.Sc., 1932. Registered profl. engr., Ill., N.Y., Vt.; Chartered engr., U.K. Elec. engr. in industry with emphasis on heavy electric power engring., 1923-42; asst. prof. elec. engring. Cornell U., 1942-45; prof. elec. engring. Ill. Inst. Tech., 1945-62; chmn. electric power engring., 1962-73; Philip Sporn prof. engring. Rensselaer Poly. Inst., Troy, N.Y., 1962—; cons. War Dept., 1942-45; Vis. scholar Va. Polytech. Inst. and State U., 1972. Contbr. numerous articles to profl. jours. Recipient citation Am. Power Conf., 1972; Distinguished Faculty award Rensselaer Poly. Inst., 1972; Western Electric Fund award Am. Soc. for Engring. Edn., 1972; spl. citation Edison Electric Inst., 1976; Austrian Cross of Honor in Sci. and Arts 1st class, 1980. Fellow N.Y. Acad. Scis., IEEE (citation and silver plaque Brazil Council 1974, Northeastern Region award 1976, Power Generation Com. award 1977, Edn. Com. award 1978), AAAS, Inst. Elec. Engrs. (London); mem. Nat. Acad. Engring., Am. Arbitration Assn. (mem. nat. panel), Am. Soc. Engring. Edn., Panamerican Congress on Engring. (v.p. for U.S. 1970-78), Sigma Xi, Tau Beta Pi, Eta Kappa Nu (nat. pres. 1953-54, eminent mem. award 1975). Home: 2525 McGovern Dr Schenectady NY 12309 Office: Rensselaer Poly Inst Troy NY 12181

GROSS, EUGENE P., physics educator. Edward and Gertrude Swartz prof. theoretical physics Brandeis U., Waltham, Mass. Office: Brandeis U Dept Physics Waltham MA 02154§

GROSS, FRANZ BRUNO, educator; b. Vienna, Austria, July 29, 1919; came to U.S., 1940, naturalized, 1944; s. Max and Alice (Koref) G.; m. Margaret M. Chappell, Dec. 5, 1952; 1 son, Christopher John. Diploma, U. Rome, Italy, 1938; M.A., Harvard, 1943, Ph.D., 1952; postgrad., Grad. Inst. Internat. Relations, Geneva, Switzerland, 1947-50, Acad. Internat. Law, The Hague, Netherlands, 1958. Lectr. Grinnell (Ia.) Coll., 1943-44; with UN Secretariat, 1950-51; vis. prof. Babson Coll., Mass., 1951-52, Coll. City N.Y., 1953-54; acting chmn. Bradford Coll., 1954-59; mem. faculty, head polit. sci. dept. Widener Coll., Chester, Pa., 1959-71, chmn. liberal arts div., 1962-67, also chmn. polit. sci. dept., Distinguished prof., coordinator internat. affairs program, 1967-71; prof. internat. affairs and African studies, dean Grad. Sch. Duquesne U., Pitts., 1971-76; prof. polit. sci. U. New Haven, 1978—, dean arts and scis., 1978-80; vis. prof. U. Pa. Grad. Sch., 1961-63, U. Dakar, Senegal, W. Africa, 1966-67, Free U. Berlin, Spring 1977; guest lectr. univs. in, Western and Eastern Europe, North and West Africa, Madagascar, India, Mexico; mem. acad. deans com. Pitts. Council Higher Edn., 1971-76; cons. on UN U. Pa. Fgn. Policy Inst., 1962-67. Editor, contbg. author: The United States and the United Nations, 1964; editor, writer: Des Moines Register and Tribune, 1944, UN Bulletin, 1950-51, N.Y. Sunday Times, 1960; editorial bd.: Polity, 1976-79. Served with M.I. AUS, 1944-46; press officer U.S. Mil. Govt., 1946-47, Germany. Recipient Outstanding Teaching award Widener Coll., 1965; Fulbright fellow Summer Inst. Indian Civilization, India, 1965; Fulbright Ednl. expert, Germany, 1975. Fellow African Studies Assn.; mem. Internat. Studies Assn. (exec. com. Middle Atlantic region 1968-70, 74-78, pres. Phila. area 1971-72), Pa. Polit. Sci. Assn. (exec. com. 1972-74, v.p. 1974-75, pres. 1975-77), North Eastern Polit. Sci. Assn. (exec. com. 1970-72, exec. com. 74-76, v.p. 1976-78, pres. 1978-79), Am. Polit. Sci. Assn., Am. Assn. U. Adminstrs., AAUP, Pa. Assn. Grad. Schs. (pres. 1975-76), Am. Soc. Internat. Law, Profs. for Peace in Middle East (exec. com. 1970-73, v.p. 1973—), Internat. Soc. for Ednl., Cultural and Sci. Interchanges (exec. sec. 1974-77), Nat. Com. on Fgn. Policy, World Federalists (mem. bd. Pitts. area council). Club: Harvard-Yale-Princeton (Pitts.). Home: 31 Edgehill Rd New Haven CT 06511 *In the present world, peace is the most important concern. With permanent change, caused mainly by nationalism, ordinary people all over the world are dislocated and deprived of their homes and their countries. A peaceful world might stabilize our economy and give hope and guarantee economic development.*

GROSS, FRITZ A., electronics co. exec.; b. Germany, Oct. 8, 1910; came to U.S., 1912, naturalized, 1920; s. Fritz and Anna (Hörmann) G.; m. Olive Nelson, Aug. 14, 1937; children-Jane, Martha, Susan. Grad., Lowell (Mass.) Inst. Tech., 1930, 1931; D.Eng. (hon.), Northeastern U., 1975. Registered profl. engr., Mass. Design engr. S.H. Couch Co., Quincy, Mass., 1932-34; with Raytheon Co., Lexington, Mass., 1934—, mgr. heavy electronic equipment operations, 1958-60, vice pres., gen. mgr. equipment div., 1960-68, v.p. engring., 1968—, tech. cons., 1975; tech. adviser radio aids to navigation USN, 1946. Recipient Certificate of Merit commendation USN, 1946. Fellow IEEE; mem. Am. Soc. Naval Engrs., Armed Forces Communications and Electronics Assn. Home: 71 Westland Rd Weston MA 02193 Office: Raytheon Co Lexington MA 02173

GROSS, HAL RAYMOND, bishop; b. Walla Walla, Wash., Jan. 15, 1914; s. John J. and Millie (Hale) G.; m. Evelyn Blythe Kerr, July 22, 1933; 1 dau., Patricia Ann Gross Ernst. Student, Oreg. State U., 1931-36; J.D., Willamette U., 1939, Ch. Div. Sch. of Pacific, 1946, D.D., 1965. Bar: Oreg. bar 1939. Pvt. practice in, Corvallis, 1939-42; atty. Oreg. Unemployment Compensation Commn., 1942-44; ordained to ministry Episcopal Ch., 1946; pastor U. Oreg., 1946-47; rector St. Paul's Ch., Oregon City, 1947-61; archdeacon Episcopal Diocese Oreg., 1961-65; suffragan bishop, Oreg., 1965-79, ret., 1979; mem. exec. council Episcopal Ch., 1975-79; vice chmn. Ho. of Bishops, 1976-79. Trustee Ch. Div. Sch. of Pacific, 1950-55, 72-73. Mem. Oreg. Bar Assn., Phi Delta Theta. Democrat. Club: Rotarian (hon.). Home: 8255 Fairway Dr Wilsonville OR 97070

GROSS, JOHN BIRNEY, minister; b. Barbourville, Ky., Aug. 24, 1924; s. John Owen and Harriet (Bletzer) G.; m. Lois Feldkircher, July 8, 1948; children: John Birney II, Steven Louis. A.B., DePauw U., 1948; B.D., S.T.M., Drew U., 1953; Ph.D. (Kellog fellow 1956-58), George Peabody Coll., 1958. Ordained to ministry Methodist Ch., 1950; minister, Mendham, N.J., 1950-53; dean chapel Centenary Coll. Women, Hackettstown, N.J., 1953-56; asst. to pres. Fla. So. Coll., Lakeland, 1958-59, dean acad. affairs, 1959-65; dean coll. Mt. Union Coll., Alliance, Ohio, 1965-67, v.p., 1967-68; dean coll. Tex. Wesleyan Coll., Ft. Worth, 1968-79, prof. religion, 1979-82; assoc. minister First United Meth. Ch., Clearwater, Fla., 1982—. Co-chmn. membership drive Community Concerts, Alliance, 1968; mem. Crandel alumni scholarship com. DePauw U., 1967; Bd. dirs. Lakeland chpt. ARC, 1963-65, Community Concerts, Lakeland, 1963-65, Casa Manana Playhouse, Ft. Worth, 1968—. Served with AUS, 1943-46. Mem. Am. Assn. Acad. Deans, Assn. Acad. Deans, So. Assn. Schs. and Colls., Phi Delta Kappa, Kappa Delta Pi, Phi Mu Alpha. Democrat. Club: Kiwanian. Home: 1876 Albright Dr Clearwater FL 33575

GROSS, JOHN HAMMES, metallurgical engineer; b. Hummelstown, Pa., Jan. 27, 1923; s. Charles Franklin and Anna Elda (Hammes) G.; m. Phyllis Jean McKelvie, Sept. 12, 1942; 1 son, Jeffrey John. B.S., Lehigh U., 1944, M.S., 1948, Ph.D., 1955. With Bethlehem Steel Corp., Pa., 1940-44; mem. faculty Lehigh U., Bethlehem, 1946-59; with U.S. Steel Corp., Monroeville, Pa., 1959-83, asst. dir., 1967-68, mgr. steel products devel., 1968-72, dir. research, 1972-81, dir. tech. implementation, 1981-83; exec. dir. Am. Welding Tech. Application Ctr., 1983—; pres. John H. Gross Assocs., 1983—. Contbr. articles to various publs. Served with USNR, 1944-46. Am. Soc. for Metals fellow, 1972. Home and Office: 1766 Mountainview Dr Monroeville PA 15146

GROSS, JONATHAN LIGHT, computer scientist educator; b. Phila., June 11, 1941; s. Nathan K. and Henrietta E. (Light) G.; m. Susan Fay Kodner, Aug. 29, 1976; children: Aaron, Jessica, Joshua, Rena Lea. B.S., M.I.T., 1964; M.A., Dartmouth Coll., 1966, Ph.D., 1968. Instr. math. Princeton (N.J.) U., 1968-69; asst. prof. math. stats. Columbia U., N.Y.C., 1969-72, asso. prof., 1973-78, prof., 1978-79; prof. computer sci., math., 1979—, vice chmn. computer sci., 1982—; cons.

Russell Sage Found., Inst. Def. Analyses., Bell Labs., Alfred P. Sloan Found. Co-author: Fundamental Programming Concepts, 1972, FORTRAN 77 Programming, 1978, Introduction to Computer Programming, 1979, Pascal Programming, 1982, Measuring Culture, 1984, PASCAL, 1984; adv. editor: Columbia U. Press, Jour. Graph Theory, Computers and Electronics; Contbr.: Jour. Graph Theory; articles to profl. jours. IBM postdoctoral fellow, 1972-73; Sloan fellow in math., 1973-75. Mem. Am. Math. Soc., Assn. Computing Machinery, Soc. Indsl. and Applied Math. Jewish. Home: 150 Hightstown Rd Princeton Junction NJ 08550 Office: 450 Computer Sci Bldg Columbia U New York NY 10027

GROSS, LEROY, sugar company executive; b. N.Y.C., Aug. 11, 1926; s. Morris and Sarah (Leichter) G.; m. Betty Koch, Aug. 28, 1949; children: Michael Stephen, Kenneth Richard, Emily Jayne. B.S. in Accounting, N.Y. U., 1948; postgrad., Fordham U. Sch. Law, 1951-53; M.B.A. in Accounting, N.Y. U., 1955. With SuCrest Corp., N.Y.C., 1948-77, internal audit mgr., 1962-65, corp. accounting mgr., 1965-69, controller, 1969-75, asst. sec., 1971-77; v.p., 1975-77; v.p., controller Revere Sugar Corp., 1977—; lectr. N.Y. U., 1968-71. Served with USAAF, 1946-47. Mem. Inst. Internal Auditors, Nat. Assn. Accountants, Fin. Execs. Inst. Home: 121 McKeel Ave Tarrytown NY 10591 Office: 210 Clay Ave Lyndhurst NJ 07071

GROSS, LUDWIK, physician; b. Cracow, Poland, Sept. 11, 1904; came to U.S., 1940, naturalized, 1943; s. Adolf and Augusta (Alexander) G.; m. Dorothy L. Nelson, Oct. 7, 1943; 1 dau., Augusta H. M.D., Iagellon U., Cracow, 1929; Prix Chevillon, Acad. Medicine, Paris, 1937; Dr.Sci. honoris causa, Mt. Sinai Sch. Medicine, CUNY, 1983. Diplomate: Am. Bd. Internal Medicine. Intern and resident St. Lazar Gen. Hosp., Cracow, 1929-32; part time research exptl. cancer Pasteur Inst., Paris; postgrad. clin. tng. Salpetriere, U. Paris, 1932- 39; cancer research Christ Hosp., Cin., 1941-43; chief cancer research VA Med Center, Bronx, 1946—, Distinguished physician, 1977; research prof. dept. medicine Mt. Sinai Sch. Medicine, N.Y.C., 1971-73, emeritus prof., 1973—; cons. Sloan Kettering Inst., Meml. Center, N.Y.C., 1955-57, assoc. scientist, 1957-60; Distinguished Leukemia lectr. U. So. Ala., 1976; 17th G.H.A. Clowes Meml. lectr., 1977. Author: Oncogenic Viruses, 1961, 3d edit., 1983; author numerous papers on cancer and leukemia in profl. jours. Served from capt. to maj. M.C. AUS, 1943-46. Decorated chevalier Legion of Honor, France; recipient Robert R. De Villiers award for research on leukemia Leukemia Soc. N.Y., 1953, Walker prize Royal Coll. Surgeons Eng., 1962, Pasteur Silver medal Pasteur Inst., 1962, Lucy Wortham James award James Ewing Soc., 1962, WHO UN prize, 1962, The Bertner Found. award, 1963, Albert Einstein Centennial medal, 1965, Albion O. Bernstein award Med. Soc. N.Y. State, 1971, Spl. Virus Cancer Program award Nat. Cancer Inst., 1972, William S. Middleton award VA, 1973, Albert Lasker Basic Med. Research award, 1974, Founders award Cancer Research Inst., 1975; prin. Paul Ehrlich-Ludwig Darmstaedter prize, 1978; Prix Griffuel, Paris, 1978; Exceptional Service award VA, 1979; VA Disting. physician, 1977-81. Fellow A.C.P., AAAS, Internat. Soc. of Hematology, N.Y. Acad. Scis.; mem. Am. Soc. Hematology, AMA, Nat. Acad. Scis., Am. Assn. Cancer Research (dir. 1973-76), Assn. Mil. Surgeons U.S., Soc. of Exptl. Biology and Medicine, Bronx County, N.Y. State med. socs. Home: 29 Ramona Ct New Rochelle NY 10804

GROSS, MARTIN LOUIS, editor, author; b. N.Y.C., Aug. 15, 1925; s. Samuel and Anna (Bachrach) G.; m. Anita Garil, Nov. 24, 1946 (dec.); children: Amy, Ellen; m. Anita Klang Rush, Sept. 1, 1974; stepchildren: Louis Rush, Jane Rush, William Rush. B.S., CCNY, 1947; postgrad., Columbia U., 1950-52. Author, syndicated columnist, mag. writer, 1953—; editor, pub. Intellectual Digest, N.Y.C., 1970-72; editor-in-chief Book Digest mag., N.Y.C., 1974-81; pres., editor-in-chief Empire books, N.Y.C., 1981—; mem. faculty New sch. Social Research, 1963—; adj. asst. prof. social history NYU, 1974—. Author: The Brain Watchers, 1963, The Doctors, 1966, The Psychological Society, 1979; contbr. numerous articles to nat. mags. Served as flight officer USAAF, 1943-46. Recipient Sch. Bell award NEA, award Am. Heritage Found. Mem. PEN, Internat. Authors Guild. Office: Emprie Books 527 Madison Ave New York NY 10022

GROSS, MAX S., investment brokerage company executive; b. Trenton, N.J., Apr. 13, 1928; s. I. Irving and Hildred (Ehrlich) G.; m. Josephine Marie Briggs, Dec. 30, 1979; children: Caren, James, Gary, Steven; stepchildren: Jan, Susan David. Diploma, N.Y. Inst. Fin., 1956. Dist. mgr. Reeds Stores Corp., 1946-56; registered rep. Engerleider & Co., N.Y.C., 1956-58; with Bache Halsey Stuart Shields Inc., 1959—, exec. v.p. br. system, 1974-76, dir., 1974-77, pres., 1975-78; sr. v.p., regional mgr. parent co., N.Y.C., 1976-83, v.p. Princeton office (N.J.), 1983—; v.p., dir. Md. Diamond and Jewelry Exchange; mem. Mid-West Stock Exchange., 1975-78. Bd. dirs., treas. Jewish Community Center, Washington, 1964-69. Mem. Wall St. Mgrs. Assn., Washington Soc. Investment Analysts, Security Traders Assn. Washington (past officer), Bond Club Washington (past officer). Club: World Trade Center (N.Y.C.). Home: 13 Garrison Pl Newtown PA 18940 Office: 104 Carnegie Ctr Princeton NJ 08540

GROSS, PATRICK WALTER, business executive, management consultant; b. Ithaca, N.Y., May 15, 1944; s. Eric T. B. and Catharine B. (Rohrer) G.; m. Sheila Eve Proby, Apr. 12, 1969; children: Geoffrey Philipp, Stephanie Lovell. Student, Cornell U., 1962-63; B.Engring. Sci., Rensselaer Poly. Inst., 1965; M.S.E. in Applied Math., U. Mich., 1966; M.B.A., Stanford U., 1968. Cons. info. mgmt. operation Gen. Electric Co., Schnectady, 1965-67; sr. staff mem. Office Sec. Def., Washington, 1968-69, spl. asst., 1969-70; founder, chmn. exec. com., prin. exec. officer Am. Mgmt. Systems, Inc., Arlington, Va., 1970—, also dir.; dir. Washington Healthcare Corp., Capital Health Resources, Inc. Trustee Washington Hosp. Center, 1977—, Sidwell Friends Sch., 1980—; mem. Econ. Policy Council UNA-USA. Mem. Fgn. Policy Assn. (bd. govs., dir., mem. exec. com. 1977—), World Affairs Council Washington (dir., founding vice chmn. 1980—), Council Fgn. Relations, Washington Inst. Fgn. Affairs, Internat. Inst. Strategic Studies (London), Nat. Economists Club, Am. Econ. Assn., Pres. Assn., Sigma Xi, Tau Beta Pi. Clubs: Metropolitan (Washington); Chevy Chase; University (N.Y.C.). Home: 7401 Glenbrook Rd Bethesda MD 20814 Office: 1777 N Kent St Arlington VA 22209

GROSS, PAUL, physician, educator; b. Berlin, June 8, 1902; s. Martin and Julia (Baumgarten) G.; m. Dorothy J. Mulac, Aug. 4, 1930; children: Julianne Gross Sauvageot, Paul James, Peter Martin, John Edwin. A.B., Western Res. U., 1924, M.D., 1927, M.A. (Crile research fellow pathology 1928-29), 1929. Intern St. Vincent's Charity Hosp., Cleve., 1927-28; resident pathology Cleve. City Hosp., 1929-31; pathologist St. Vincent's Charity Hosp., 1931-35; vol. asst. to Prof. Erdheim, Vienna, Austria, 1931-32; pathologist West Pa. Hosp., Pitts., 1935-44, St. Joseph's Hosp., 1944-54; dir. research lab. Indsl. Health Found., Mellon Inst., also sr. fellow Inst., 1948-68, adv. fellow, 1968—; adj. prof. pathology indsl. diseases Grad. Sch. Pub. Health. U. Pitts., 1960-68; research prof. Grad. Sch. Pub. Health, U. Pitts., 1968-71, adj. prof., 1971-76; disting. research prof. pathology Med. U. S.C., 1971-76, adj. prof., 1976—. Author: (with T.F. Hatch) Pulmonary Deposition and Retention of Inhaled Aerosols, 1964, (with D.C. Braun) Toxic and Biomedical Effects of Fibers with Special Reference to Asbestos, Man-Made Vitreous Fibers and Organic Fibers, 1983; also numerous articles. Recipient Adolph G. Kammer merit in authorship award Indsl. Med. Assn., 1967. Fellow ACP; mem. Am. Coll. Chest Physicians, Indsl. Med. Assn., Coll. Am. Pathologists, Am. Thoracic Soc., Am. Indsl. Hygiene Assn. (hon.), Am. Assn. Pathologists and Bacteriologists, Internat. Acad. Pathology, Am. Soc. Clin. Pathologists, AMA, Am. Soc. Exptl. Pathology. Spl. research chronic pulmonary diseases. Home: 28 Maui Circle Naples FL 33942

GROSS, PAUL ALLEN, corporate executive; b. Richmond, VA, Oct. 1, 1937; s. Albert and Cynthia (Saxe) G.; m. Gail Byrd, Nov. 19, 1966; children: Lorri, Garry, Randy. Student, U. Richmond, 1956-59; B.A., U. Ga., 1961; M.H.A., Va. Commonwealth U., 1964; cert. in hosp. adminstrn., U. Miami. Cert. hosp. adminstrn., Fla. Resident Tampa Gen. Hosp., Fla., 1964; adminstrv. asst. Dallas County Hosp. Dist., 1964-66, asst. adminstr., 1966-69, sr. asst. adminstr., 1969-70, assoc. adminstr., 1971-72; clin. assoc. prof. hosp. med. care U. Tex. Southwestern Med. Sch., 1964-72, Sch. Allied Health Scis., Dallas, 1964-72; exec. dir. Humana Inc. Suburban Hosp., Louisville, 1972-76; v.p. Fla. region Humana Inc., Miami, 1976-81; sr. v.p. Pacific region Humana Inc., Newport Beach, Calif., 1981—, trustee acute care gen hosps., 1983—. Contbr. articles to profl. jours. Mem. health adv. com. Senator Paul Carpenter, Cypress, Calif., 1983; mem., asst. chmn. U.S. Selective Service System Local Bd. 154, 1983. Served with USNR, 1955-63. Recipient Humana Club award Suburban Hosp. Central Region, Louisville, 1975, 76; named Outstanding Adminstr. of Yr., 1974. Fellow Am. Coll. Hosp. Adminstrs.; mem. Am. Hosp. Assn., Tex. Hosp. Assn., Hosp. Council So. Calif. (chmn. multi-instl. corp. liason com. 1983—), United Hosp. Assn. Calif., Fedn. Am. Hosps. (trustee 1980-81). Office: Humana Inc 450 Newport Ctr Dr Suite 550 Newport Beach CA 92660

GROSS, PAUL RANDOLPH, biologist, laboratory administrator; b. Phila., Nov. 27, 1928; s. Nathan and Kate (Segal) G.; m. Mona Lee Feld, Mar. 27, 1949; 1 dau., Wendy Loren. B.A., U. Pa., 1950, Ph.D. (Harrison and NSF fellow), 1954; M.A., Brown U., 1963; D.Sc., Med. Coll. Ohio, 1979. Asst. prof. biology N.Y. U., 1954-58, asso. prof., 1958-61; asso. prof. biology Brown U., 1962-65; prof. biology M.I.T., 1965-71; prof., chmn. dept. biology U. Rochester, 1972-78, dean grad. studies, 1975-78, chmn. sci. adv. com., 1974-78; pres., dir. Marine Biol. Lab., Woods Hole, Mass., 1978—; prin. investigator research and tng. grants from NSF and NIH, 1955—; mem., advisor to doctoral council N.Y. State Edn. Dept.; mem. adv. com. cell and developmental biology Am. Cancer Soc.; mem. oversight com. Assn. Am. Colls.; mem. nat. adv. council Nat. Inst. Child Health and Human Devel.; mem. sci. adv. com. Tufts U. Sch. Vet. Medicine; mem. council U. Va. Ctr. for Advanced Studies. Contbr. sci. articles to profl. jours. Mem. Indsl. Devel. Corp., Town of Falmouth (Mass.); trustee U. Rochester. Lalor fellow, 1954-55; NSF fellow U. Edinburgh, 1961-62. Fellow Am. Acad. Arts and Scis.; mem. Internat. Soc. for Developmental Biology, Am. Physiol. Soc., Am. Soc. Zoologists (chmn. sect. on developmental biology), AAAS, Am. Soc. Cell Biology. Clubs: Woods Hole Yacht, Cosmos. Office: Marine Biological Laboratory Woods Hole MA 02543

GROSS, RICHARD EDMUND, teacher educator; b. Chgo., May 25, 1920; s. Edmund Nicholas and Florence (Gallistel) G.; m. Jane Clare Hartl, May 25, 1943; children: Kathryn Ann, Elaine Clare, Edmund Ralph, John Richard. B.S., U. Wis., 1942, M.S., 1946; Ed.D., Stanford, 1951. Jr. personnel officer FSA, Milw., 1942-43; tchr. Central High Sch., Madison, Wis., 1943-48; instr. Menlo Sch. and Coll., Menlo Park, Calif., 1948-51; asso. prof. Fla. State U., 1951-55; mem. faculty Sch. Edn., Stanford U., 1955—, prof., 1965—, chmn. curriculum and tchr. edn., 1977—; chief cons. central com. social studies Calif. Dept. Edn., 1958-60; Fulbright lectr. tchr. edn. U. Wales, Swansea, 1961-62; guest prof. Am. Inst., U. Frankfurt, Germany, 1968-69; ednl. adviser World Bank Pilot Center project U. Santiago, Spain, 1973; vis. prof. Monash U., Melbourne, Australia, 1976; curriculum cons. to schs., 1952—; adv. bd. Edn. Policy Com., 1958-68; chmn. nat. advisory bd. E.R.I.C. Social Sci. Center, U. Colo., 1969-71; dir. social studies, adviser Addison-Wesley Publs.; Bd. dirs. Calif. Inst. Internat. Studies, Inst. Devel. Human Resources. Author: How to Handle Controversial Issues, 1952, The Problems Approach and the Social Studies, 1955, The Sociology of the School, 1957, The United States Congress, 1957, Educating Citizens for Democracy, 1958, The Heritage of American Education, 1962, British Secondary Education, 1965, Civics in Action, 1966, Man's World: A Physical Geography, 1966, The History of Education: A Timeline, 1967, Teaching the Social Studies, 1969, Profile of America, 1971, Quest for Liberty, 1971, Teaching Social Studies Skills, 1973, The Human Experience, 1974, What Should We Be Teaching in the Social Studies, 1983; editor: Phi Delta Kappa Bi-centennial Fast-Backs, 1976, Social Studies for Our Times, 1978, American Citizenship: How We Govern, 1979, Learning to Live in Society, 1980; Editor: Calif. Social Sci. Rev, 1962-68; Contbr. articles to encys., profl. jours.; Creator: Scholastic World-Affairs Multitext Publs, 1963; K. and E. overhead viewer transparencies for U.S. History, 1964. Mem. Nat. Council Social Studies (pres. 1967), Nat. Soc. Study Edn., AAUP, Am. Acad. Polit. and Social Sci., History of Edn. Soc., Assn. Supervision and Curriculum Devel., NEA, World Assn. Civic Edn. (exec. com.), Phi Alpha Theta, Kappa Delta Tau, Phi Delta Kappa. Home: 26304 Esperanza Dr Los Altos Hills CA 94022 Office: Cubberley Hall Stanford Univ Stanford CA 94305

GROSS, ROBERT ALAN, history educator; b. New Haven, Feb. 17, 1945; s. Samuel and Roslyn (Chadys) G.; m. Ann Leslie Goldman, May 22, 1966; children: Matthew Benjamin, Stephen Alexander, Eleanor Elizabeth. B.A., U. Pa., 1966; M.A. (Woodrow Wilson nat. fellow), Columbia U., 1968, Ph.D., 1976. Gen. sec. U.S. Student Press Assn., Washington, 1966-67; asst. editor Newsweek, N.Y.C., 1968-70; NIMH trainee in social history Columbia U., 1970-72; adj. asst. prof. Worcester Poly. Inst., 1973-76; asst. prof. history and Am. studies Amherst Coll., 1976-78, asso. prof., 1980—; prof. Am. studies U. Sussex, Brighton, England, 1982-83. Author: The Minutemen and Their World, 1977 (Nat. Hist. Soc. Book award); (Bancroft prize). Columbia U. Pres.'s fellow, 1969-70; Nat. Endowment for Humanities fellow, 1978; Guggenheim fellow, 1979-80; Charles Warren fellow Harvard U., 1979-80; Amherst Coll. Trustees faculty fellow, 1979-80. Mem. Am. Hist. Assn., Orgn. Am. Historians, Am. Studies Assn., MLA, Am. Antiquarian Soc., Phi Beta Kappa. Democrat. Jewish. Research in 19th century U.S. social and cultural history. Home: 14 Nutting Ave Amherst MA 01002 Office: Dept Am Studies Amherst Coll Amherst MA 01002

GROSS, ROBERT ALFRED, physics educator; b. Phila., Oct. 31, 1927; s. John and Esther (Schwartz) G.; m. Elee B. Kauffmann, Nov. 21, 1952; children: David Andrew, John Henry. B.S., U. Pa., 1949; M.S., Harvard U., 1950, Ph.D., 1952. Chief research engr. Fairchild Engine & Airplane Co., 1954-59; mem. faculty Columbia U., N.Y.C., 1960—, prof. engring. sci., 1960-78, prof. applied physics, 1978—, Vera and Percy Hudson prof., 1980—, dean Sch. Engring. and Applied Sci., 1982—; founder Plasma Physics Lab., 1961, chmn. plasma physics program, 1960-70, chmn. mech. engring. dept., 1970-76, chmn. dept. applied physics and nuclear engring., 1978—; prof. Internat. Sch. Physics, Enrico-Fermi-Varenna, Italy, 1969; Dir. Fairfield Tech., 1962-66, Samson Fund, 1963-70, Fundamatic Investors, Inc., 1970-71; sr. vis. fellow Australian Acad. Scis., U.S.-USSR exchange scientist, 1967; vis. prof. Sydney (Australia) U., 1974, 79; cons. indsl., govt. agencies, 1950—; mem. nat. com. fluid mechanics films NSF, 1964-70; mem. rev. com., mechanics div. Nat. Bur. Standards, 1971-76; mem. fusion power coordinating com. U.S. Dept. Energy, 1980-82, mem. magnetic fusion adv. com., 1982—; mem. Fulbright-Hayes adv. screening com. Council Internat. Exchange Scholars, 1976-78; mem. vis. com. Brookhaven Nat. Lab., 1979—, Lehigh U., 1982—. Asso. editor: Physics of Fluids Jour, 1970-73; corr. editor: Jour. Comments on Plasma Physics and Controlled Fusion, 1978—; Contbr. articles to tech. lit. Served with AUS, 1945-46. Recipient Waverly Gold medal Combustion Inst., London, Eng., 1959; Great Tchr. award Columbia U., 1975; NSF sr. post-doctoral fellow U. Calif. at Berkeley, 1959-60; Guggenheim Found. fellow, Fulbright-Hays fellow, 1966-67; Fulbright-Hayes sr. fellow, 1974. Fellow AIAA (v.p. 1965-66), Am. Inst. Aeros. and Astronautics (editor-in-chief selected reprint series 1968-77, Pendray award 1967), Am. Phys. Soc. (chmn. exec. com. fluid dynamics div. 1970-71, exec. com. plasma physics div. 1974-75); mem. AAAS, Univ. Fusion Assn. (exec. com. 1980-82), Sigma Xi, Tau Beta Pi. Home: 14 Sunnyside Way New Rochelle NY 10804

GROSS, RONALD MARTIN, forest products company executive; b. 1933. B.A., Ohio State U., 1955, postgrad., 1955-58; M.B.A., Harvard U., 1960. Info. specialist Battelle Meml. Inst., Columbus, Ohio, 1957-58; with U.S. Plywood-Champion Papers, Inc., Hamilton, Ohio, 1960-63, Chgo., 1963-66, N.Y.C., 1966-68; v.p. planning and adminstrn., sec. Columbia Cellulose Co. Ltd., Vancouver, B.C., Can., 1968-69, sr. v.p., sec., 1969-70, exec. v.p., 1970-73; pres., chief exec. officer, dir. Canadian Cellulose Co., Ltd., 1973-78; pres., chief operating officer, dir. ITT Rayonier, Inc., Stamford, Conn., 1978-81, pres., chief exec. officer, dir., 1981—, chmn., 1984—. Office: ITT Rayonier Inc 1177 Summer St Stamford CT 06904

GROSS, RUTH TAUBENHAUS, physician, educator; b. Bryan, Tex., June 24, 1920; d. Jacob and Esther (Hirshenson) Taubenhaus; m. Reuben H. Gross, Jr., Aug. 22, 1942 (div. June 1952); 1 son, Gary E. B.A., Barnard Coll., 1941; M.D., Columbia U., 1944. Intern Charity Hosp., New Orleans, 1944; resident in pediatrics Tulane U., New Orleans, 1945, Columbia U., N.Y.C., 1946, 47; instr. Radcliffe Infirmary, Oxford, Eng., 1949-50; instr. pediatrics Stanford (Calif.) U., 1950-53, asst. prof., 1953-56, assoc. prof., 1956-60, prof., 1973—, Katharine Dexter and Stanley McCormick prof. pediatrics, 1976—, acting exec. pediatrics, 1957-59, asso. dean student affairs, 1973-75, dir. div. gen. and ambulatory pediatrics, 1975—, dir. Stanford-Children's Ambulatory Care Center, 1980—; assoc. prof. pediatrics, co-dir. div. human genetics Albert Einstein Coll. Medicine, Yeshiva U., N.Y.C., 1960-64, prof. pediatrics, 1964-66; clin. prof. pediatrics U. Calif. Med. Center, San Francisco, 1966-73; dir. dept. pediatrics Mt. Zion Hosp. and Med. Center, San Francisco, 1966-73; prin. investigator for gen. pediatrics Acad. Devel. Program, Robert Wood Johnson Found., 1983—, nat. program dir. Infant Health and Devel. Program, 1983—. Contbr. articles to profl. jours. Commonwealth fellow human genetics Instituto de Genetica, Pavia, Italy, 1959-60. Mem. Nat. Acad. Scis. (Inst. Medicine), Am. Fedn. Clin. Research, Am. Pediatric Soc., Soc. Pediatric Research, Am. Acad. Pediatrics, Ambulatory Pediatric Assn., Soc. Adolescent Medicine, Internat. Soc. Study Behavioral Devel., Phi Beta Kappa, Alpha Omega Alpha, Sigma Xi. Office: Dept Pediatrics Stanford U Med Sch Stanford CA 94305

GROSS, SAMSON RICHARD, geneticist, biochemist, educator; b. N.Y.C., July 27, 1926; s. Isidor and Ethel (Mermelestein) G.; m. Helen Hudi Steinmetz, Sept. 16, 1952; children—Deborah Ann, Michael Robert, Eva Elizabeth. B.A., N.Y.U., 1949; A.M., Columbia, 1951, Ph.D. (USPHS fellow), 1953. Asst. prof. genetics Stanford, 1956-57, Rockefeller U., N.Y.C., 1957-60; asso. prof. dept. microbiology and immunology Duke, Durham, N.C., 1960-65, prof. genetics and biochemistry, 1965—, dir. div. genetics dept. biochemistry, 1965-77, dir. univ. program in genetics, 1967-77; Bd. dirs. Cold Spring Harbor (N.Y.) Lab. Quantitative Biology, 1967-72. USPHS Spl. fellow Weizmann Inst., 1969-70; Josiah Macy Found. fellow Hebrew U., 1977-78. Mem. Genetic Soc. Am., AAAS, Am. Soc. Microbiology, Am. Soc. Biol. Chemists, Phi Beta Kappa. Home: 2411 Prince St Durham NC 27707

GROSS, SEYMOUR LEE, educator; b. N.Y.C., Jan. 28, 1926; s. Joseph Lee and Henrietta Lee (Weinreb) G.; m. Elaine Linford, Dec. 25, 1951; children—Thelma Lee, Thomas Linford, James Linford. B.A., U. Denver, 1949, M.A., 1950; Ph.D., U. Ill., 1954. Instr. Ind. U., South Bend, 1955-57; asst. prof. U. Notre Dame, 1957-60, asso. prof., 1960-66, prof., 1966-69; Burke O'Neill prof. Am. lit. U. Detroit, 1969—; prof. extraordinary U. Skopje, Yugoslavia, 1962-63. Author: American Literature Survey, 3d edit, 1975, Images of the Negro in American Literature, 1966; also handbooks. Served with AUS, 1944-46. Mem. Modern Lang. Assn., Am. Studies Assn., Internat. Assn. U. Profs. English, Soc. Study So. Lit., Phi Beta Kappa. Home: 19519 Shrewsbury Rd Detroit MI 48221

GROSS, SHELLY, theatrical producer, author; b. Phila., May 20, 1921; s. Samuel W. and Anna (Rosenblum) G.; m. Joan Seidel, May 1, 1946; children: Byron, Frederick, Daniel. A.B., U. Pa., 1942; M.S. in Journalism, Northwestern U., 1947. Local news dir. and commentator WFPG, Atlantic City, 1948-49; spl. events dir. and announcer WFIL-AM and TV, Phila., 1949-58; chief exec. officer Music Fair Group Inc., Devon, Pa., 1955—, N.Y.C., 1955—. Author: The Crusher, 1970, Havana X, 1978. Served to lt. USN, 1942-46; PTO. Named Outstanding Comml. Announcer TV Guide, 1954; recipient Super Achiever award Juvenile Diabetes Found., 1976. Mem. League of N.Y. Theatres and Producers, Phi Beta Kappa, Phi Gamma Mu, Sigma Delta Chi. Office: Music Fair Group Inc 176 Swedeford Rd Devon PA 19333

GROSS, SIDNEY, editor; b. Dusseldorf, Germany, Jan. 17, 1920; came to U.S., 1938, naturalized, 1944; s. David and Helen (Klausner) G.; m. Lillian Nee Zlotnick, Mar. 21, 1948; children—Jane Alice, Nancy Ellen. B.S., Princeton, 1942; M.A., Columbia, 1950. Mng. editor Boland & Boyce Pubs., Montclair, N.J., 1950-52, Breskin Pubs., Inc., N.Y.C., 1952-63; with McGraw Hill, Inc., N.Y.C., 1963—, editor in chief, 1968—, chmn. editorial bd., 1970—; editor Modern Plastics; editorial dir. Modern Plastics Ency., 1975—, Modern Plastics Internat., Lausanne; chmn. bd. trustees Plastic Inst. Am., 1979—; dir. Plastics Hall Fame, 1975—. Served with communications system USAAF, 1942-47. Recipient Jesse Neal award, 1978. Mem. Soc. Plastics Engrs. (dir. 1972—), Soc. Plastics Industry, Plastics Pioneers, Soc. Bus. Paper Editors, Am. Chem. Soc., Phi Beta Kappa. Home: 65-43 181th St Flushing NY 11365 Office: 1221 Ave of Americas New York NY 10020

GROSS, SIDNEY, public relations executive, journalism educator; b. Cleve., Sept. 7, 1923; s. Ernest and Katherine (Ney) G.; m. Zenith Henkin, Dec. 9, 1946; children: Kenneth, Lawrence, Kathy. B.A., Ohio State U., 1949, LL.B., 1950. Reporter Elyria (Ohio) Chronicle Telegram, 1938-41; reporter-deskman Press, Cleve., 1941-44; with AP, Columbus, Ohio, 1945-48; publicist, Ted Bates, N.Y.C., 1951-54; public relations exec. Vernon Pope Co., N.Y.C., 1955-70; founder Gross & Assos., N.Y.C., 1971—; prof. journalism and mass communications NYU, N.Y.C., 1983—. Mem. Sch. Bd., Dumont and Tenafly, N.J., 1957-59; candidate for mayor, Tenafly, 1968. Mem. Public Relations Soc. Am., Overseas Press Club, Nat. Investor Relations Soc. Home: 400 E 56th St New York NY 10022 Office: 592 Fifth Ave New York NY 10036

GROSS, SIDNEY W., neurosurgeon, educator; b. Cleve., Aug. 28, 1904; s. Joseph and Frieda (Weiss) G.; m. Bobbie Bruce, 1983; 1 son by previous marriage, Samuel. A.B., Western Res. U., (now Case Western Res. U.), 1925, M.D., 1928. Diplomate: Am. Bd. Neurol. Surgery. Intern Michael Reese Hosp., Chgo., 1928-29; resident Neurol. Inst., N.Y.C., 1929-31; asst. neurosurgery Washington U., St. Louis, 1931-33; vol. Neuropath. Lab. U. Chgo., 1933; neurosurgeon Mt. Sinai Hosp., Cleve., 1933-34; now emeritus prof. neurosurgery Mt. Sinai Sch. Medicine, N.Y.C.; emeritus dir. dept. neurosurgery City Hosp., Elmhurst, N.Y.; dir. emeritus dept. neurosurgery Mt. Sinai Med. Center, N.Y.C.; prof. neurology U. So. Fla. Coll. Medicine, 1978-79; sr. neurosurg. cons. Tampa (Fla.) VA Hosp., 1978-79; cons. Wadsworth VA Hosp., Los Angeles, 1980—; neurosurgeon Serra Meml. Health Ctr., Sun Valley, Calif.; clin. prof. neurology UCLA Sch. Medicine, 1981—. Author: Diagnosis and Treatment of Head Injuries, 1940; Contbr. numerous articles to profl. jours. Served with AUS, World War II; chief neurosurg. sect. Halloran Gen. Hosp.; maj. M.C. U.S. Army, 85th Evacuation Hosp., 180th and 116th gen. hosps.; ETO. Fellow A.C.S., N.Y. Acad. Medicine; mem. Am. Neurol. Assn., Harvey Cushing Soc., N.Y. Soc. Neurosurgery (sec.), Phi Beta Kappa, Alpha Omega Alpha. Address: 330 Alta Ave Santa Monica CA 90402

GROSS, STANLEY CHARLES, auditors association executive; b. Louisville, Feb. 21, 1922; s. Herbert Allen and Loretta M. (Koch) G.; m. Mary Louise Metcalfe, Apr. 10, 1948; children: Elaine M., Deborah A., Barry R. B.S., Cleve. State U., 1969. Cert. internal auditor. Dir. internal auditing Sherwin-Williams Co., Cleve., 1947-79; pres. Inst. Internal Auditors, Altamonte Springs, Fla., 1980—. Served to capt. USAF, 1942-46; China, Burma, India. Mem. Inst. Internal Auditors (chmn. 1976-77, Disting. Service award 1981). Republican. Roman Catholic. Clubs: Sweetwater County (Longwood, Fla.); Citrus (Orlando, Fla.). Home: 143 Wild Oak Circle Longwood FL 32779 Office: Inst Internal Auditors Inc 249 Maitland Ave Altamonte Springs FL 32701

GROSS, STEPHEN MARK, pharmacist, university dean; b. Bklyn., July 31, 1938; s. Arthur S. and Hazel F. (Marks) G.; m. Susan S. Farber, Nov. 5, 1961; children: Julie S. (1 dau.). B.S., Columbia U., 1960, M.A., 1969, Ed.D., 1975. Pharmacist/mgr. C.O. Bigelow Chemists Inc., N.Y.C., 1960-65, Bigelow-Americana Chemists Inc., 1963-65; asst. to dean Coll. Pharm. Scis., Columbia U., 1965-68, asst. dean, 1968-71, asso. dean, 1971-72, acting dean, 1972-74, dean, 1974-76; dean grad. studies Arnold & Marie Schwartz Coll. Pharmacy and Health Scis. L.I. U., 1976-79; acting dean Sch. Bus. and Pub. Adminstrn., Bklyn. Ctr. L.I.U., 1983—; dean grad. studies and research Conolly Coll., 1979—; Mem. adv. council Project Respect for Drugs, 1966-70; dir. Arden House Confs. on Indsl. Pharmacy, 1966-79; v.p. Pond Assn., 1972, pres., 1976-78. Editorial bd.: New Environment in Pharmacy program, 1974-77, U.S. Pharmacist, 1978-80; Contbr. articles to profl. publs. Recipient numerous grants instnl. improvement. Mem. Am. Pharm. Assn., Acad. Pharm. Scis., Am. Assn. Colls. Pharmacy (chmn. sect. continuing edn. 1979-80), Pharm. Advt. Council, Pharm. Soc. State N.Y., Soc. Am. Magicians (v.p. N.Y. Assembly 1981-83, pres. 1983—). Home: 43 Knott Dr Glen Cove NY 11542 Office: 1 University Plaza Brooklyn NY 11201

GROSS, THEODORE LAWRENCE, university dean, author; b. Bklyn., Dec. 4, 1930; s. David and Anna (Weisbrod) G.; m. Selma Bell, Aug. 27, 1955; children: Donna, Jonathan. B.A., U. Maine, 1952; M.A., Columbia U., 1957, Ph.D., 1960. Mem. faculty Coll. City N.Y., 1958-78, prof. English, 1971-78, chmn. dept., 1970-72, assoc. dean and dean humanities, 1972-78; provost Capitol Campus, Pa. State U., Middletown, 1979-83; dean Sch. Letters and Sci. SUNY Coll., Purchase, 1983—; vis. prof., Fulbright scholar, Nancy, France, 1964-65, 68-69, Dept. State lectr., Nigeria, Israel, Japan, Austria. Author: Albion W. Tourgée, 1964, Thomas Nelson Page, 1967, Hawthorne, Melville, Crane: A Critical Bibliography, 1971, The Heroic Ideal in American Literature, 1971, Academic Turmoil: The Reality and Promise of Open Education, 1980; also essays, revs.; editor: Fiction, 1967, Dark Symphony: Negro Literature in America, 1968, Representative Men, 1969, A Nation of Nations, 1971, The Literature of American Jews, 1973; gen. editor: Studies in Language and Literature, 1974, America in Literature, 1978. Served with AUS, 1952-54. Grantee Rockefeller Found., 1976-77, Am. Council Learned Socs. Mem. Nat. Council Tchrs. English (chmn. lit. com.), MLA, P.E.N. Club: Century Assn. Home: 113 Old Mill Rd Great Neck NY 11023 Office: SUNY Coll at Purchase Purchase NY 10577

GROSS, WILLIAM ANTHONY, consumer finance company executive; b. Orange, N.J., Apr. 12, 1928; s. Anthony Bernard and Henrietta Marie (Gatfield) G.; m. Dolores Mary Rebar, July 21, 1951; children: William Anthony, Patricia Ellen, John Francis, Karen Ann. B.S. in Bus. Adminstrn, Seton Hall, 1950; postgrad., U. Tex., 1951-53, Rutgers U., 1953, Sloan Sch. Mgmt., 1979. Sr. auditor Haskins & Sells, Newark, 1953-63; with Beneficial Corp., Wilmington, Del., 1963—, sr. v.p. financing, accounting, 1974-82, sr. v.p. taxes and acctg. policies, 1982—; dir. Western Auto Supply Co., Midland Internat. Corp. Served from pvt. to 1st. lt. USAF, 1951-53. Mem. N.J. Soc. C.P.A.'s, Am. Inst. C.P.A.'s, Financial Execs. Inst., Nat. Assn. Accountants. Home: 9 Burlington Rd Livingston NJ 07039 Office: 300 Beneficial Ctr Peapack NJ 07977

GROSS, WILLIAM JOSEPH, ret. city mgr.; b. Toledo, Apr. 27, 1926; s. Clarence W. and Olive (Smith) G.; m. Donna J. Munson, June 28, 1947; children—Marcia, Jeffery, James, Jacqueline. B.S. in Civil Engring, U. Toledo, 1950. Registered surveyor, Ohio.; Registered land surveyor, Mich.; Registered profl. engr., Ohio, Mich. Asst. to city mgr., City of Toledo, 1954-56, dir. pub. service, 1956-59; dep. dir. Ohio Hwy. Dept., Columbus, 1959-63; adminstr., Lucas County, Toledo, 1963-66, cons. civil engr., Toledo, 1966-68, city mgr., 1968-71, safety-service dir., City of Oregon, Ohio, 1971-81. Contbr. articles to tech. jours. Served with USNR, 1944-46. Recipient merit award Toledo Area San. Dist., 1959. Fellow Am. Soc. C.E. (past pres. Toledo); mem. Nat. League Cities (del.), Profl. Ofcls. N.W. Ohio (past chmn.), Municipal Finance Officers Assn., Nat. Assn. County Adminstrs., Am. Assn. State Hwy. Officers, Internat. City Mgmt. Assn., Am. Right-of-Way Assn. (past regional dir.), Am. Pub. Works Assn., Nat. Soc. Profl. Engrs., Am. Water Works Assn., Water Pollution Control Fedn. Address: 3243 Shakespeare Lane Toledo OH 43615

GROSSBERG, SIDNEY EDWARD, educator; b. Miami, Fla., Nov. 13, 1929; s. Lazar and Anita (Mandell) G.; m. Josette Micheline Brugerolle, May 20, 1959; children: Daniel Eliot, Leslie David. B.S., Emory U., 1951, M.D., 1954. Resident Duke U. Hosp., Durham, N.C., 1954-55, 57-58; fellow in medicine Johns Hopkins U., Balt., 1958-59; asst. prof. U. Minn. Med. Sch., Mpls., 1959-62, Cornell U., N.Y.C., 1962-66; vis. investigator Pasteur Inst., Paris, 1964-65, 74-75; prof. microbiology Marquette U. and Med. Coll. Wis., Milw., chmn. dept., 1966—, Walter Schroeder prof. microbiology, 1983—; cons. WHO, Geneva, 1982—, NIH, 1973—, U. Tex. Grad. Sch., 1977, others. Patentee in field. Bd. dirs. Friends of Music, U. Wis., Milw., 1980—. Capt. U.S. Army, 1955-57. Recipient Research Career Devel. award NIH, 1961-66; John and Mary Markle scholar, 1965-70; European Molecular Biol. Orgn. sr. fellow, 1974-75. Fellow Infectious Diseases Soc. Am.; mem. Am. Soc. Virology, Central Soc. Clin. Research, Am. Assn. Immunologists, Soc. Microbiology Gt. Britain, Phi Beta Kappa. Office: Dept Microbiology Med Coll Wis 8701 Watertown Plank Rd Milwaukee WI 53226

GROSSCHMID-ZSOGOD, GEZA BENJAMIN, educator; b. Budapest, Hungary, Oct. 29, 1918; came to U.S., 1947, naturalized, 1950; s. Lajos de Grosschmid and Jolan de Szitanyi; m. Leonora Martha Nissler, Nov. 8, 1946; 1 dau., Pamela Ann. J.U.D., Royal Hungarian Pazmany Peter U., Budapest, 1943. Adminstrv. asst. German mission UNRRA, 1946-47; mem. faculty Duquesne U., 1948—, prof. econs., 1955—, dir., 1959-70, 1960-74, acting acad. v.p., 1970-71, acad. v.p., 1971-75, chmn. div. economic scis., 1978—; cons., field reader U.S. Office Edn., 1965—. Author: (with others) Principles of Economics, 1959; also numerous monographs, translations, articles, book revs. Bd. dirs. Afuture Fund; bd. visitors Coll. Arts and Scis. of U. Pitts.; bd. dirs. Battle of Britain Found. Served with Royal Hungarian Army, 1944-45. Decorated knight of obedience Sovereign Mil. Order Malta, 1974; knight justice Constantine Order St. George, Naples, 1959; Nat. Order Valor, Fed. Rep. of Cameroon; knight comdr. with star Order St. Gregory Great Holy See; officer Order of Equatorial Star, Gabon; knight Nat. Order Zaire; officer Order of Lion, Senegal). Republican. Roman Catholic. Clubs: Duquesne (Pitts.); Middlesex County Cricket, Squash Racquets Assn., Athenaeum (London); Royal Forth Yacht (Edinburgh, Scotland); Metropolitan, Army and Navy (Washington). Home: 3115 Ashlyn St Pittsburgh PA 15204

GROSSE, EDUARD, advertising executive, publisher; b. Berlin, July 1, 1928; U.S., 1950; s. Eduard Georg and Hildegard (Drude) G.; m. Angelika Bestehorn, Apr. 10, 1966; children: Patricia, Barbara, Eduard Douglas, Vanessa. Student, U. Frankfurt, Ger., 1948-50; M.A., U. Minn., 1951; Ph.D., U. Berlin, 1956. Sr. econ. analyst Dept. State, 1953-56; sr. project dir. BBDO (advt.), Mpls., 1956-58; research group head Ogilvy, Benson & Mather, N.Y.C., 1958-59; mgmt. supr., dir. J. Walter Thompson, Frankfurt, 1959-65; mng. dir., head European ops., chmn. bd. Foote, Cone & Belding Internat., Chgo., 1965—; pres. Grosse & Crain Verlag, Pub. Co., Berlin and Frankfurt, 1983—; dir. Foote, Cone & Belding Communications Inc., Chgo.; pub. Grosse Pub. Co., Berlin. Author: Universalistic and Regional Economic Integration, 1956, 100 Years of European Advertising, 1980. Chmn. bd. dirs. Internat. Visitors Ctr. of Chgo., 1982—. Mem. Internat. Advt. Assn., Assn. European Advt. Agys., German Am. C. of C. (dir. 1974—), Am. C. of C. in Ger. (dir. 1971—), Steuben-Schurz Soc. (dir. 1971—). Evang. Lutheran. Clubs: Tavern, Racquet (Chgo.); Union Internat. (Frankfurt). Office: 401 N Michigan Ave Chicago IL 60601

GROSSE, EDWARD MILTON, mag. exec.; b. Los Angeles, Mar. 31, 1925; s. Peter and Gisela G.; m. Dorothy Jane Blackburn, Sept. 18, 1948; children—Robert, Stephen, Frederick. D.D.S., U. Pa., 1948. Practice dentistry, Norwood, Pa., 1947-79; exec. dir. nat. hdqrs. Psi Omega, Prospect Park, Pa., 1960—; v.p. ops. Indsl. mag., 1979—. Mem. William Penn Sch. Bd., 1967-73, pres., 1971-73; pres. Lansdowne Bd. Health, 1958-73, Allied Youth Council. Served with USN, 1943-46, 48-50, 52-54. Fellow Interat. Coll. Dentists, Am. Coll. Dentists; mem. Am. Dental Interfraternity Council (exec. sec. 1969—), ADA. Republican. Presbyterian. Clubs: Kiwanis (past pres.), Springhaven.). Office: 1030 Lincoln Ave Prospect Park PA 19074

GROSSI, OLINDO, educator, architect; b. N.Y.C., July 17, 1909; s. Alexander and Ferdinanda (Bartalini) G.; m. Martha Seymour, Sept. 26, 1940; childrenSusan, John, Thomas. A.B., Columbia U., 1930, B.Arch., 1932, M.S. in Architecture, 1933; student, Am. Acad. Rome, 1933-36. Assoc. architecture and fine arts Bard Coll., 1938-42, Columbia, 1944-45; dean sch. architecture Pratt Inst., 1946, dir. internat. programs, 1969; dean architecture and arts N.Y. Inst. Tech., 1971-83, dir., 1979; pvt. practice architecture, N.Y.C., 1945—; cons. N.Y.C. Planning Commn., Office of Information, U.S. Govt., L.I.U., N.Y.U.; adviser on tropical architecture and archtl. edn. in S.E. Asia for Asia Found. Author: Downtown Brooklyn Civic Center, 1963; Contbr. articles and designs in miscellaneous publs. Chmn. Goals for Nassau Com.; Mem. Mayor's Panel of Architects, N.Y.C. Recipient Brunner scholarship, 1949, Rome prize in Architecture, 1933; Carnegie scholarship to Paris, 193O; first prize Residential Design at Conv. N.Y. Assos. Architects, 1950; first prize beach house design Archtl. League; Strauss Meml. award for contbn. to profession, 1954. Fellow A.I.A., Beaux Arts Inst. Design (trustee), Am. Acad. Rome Alumni (pres.), Assn. N.Y. State Architects (dir.), Archtl. Historians, N.Y. Soc. Architects, Assn. Collegiate Schs. Architecture (pres.), Archtl. League N.Y. (pres.), Municipal Art Soc., Fine Arts Fedn. Club: Architect League. Home: 234 Manhasset Ave Manhasset NY 11030 Office: NY Inst Tech Old Westbury NY 11568

GROSSINGER, PAUL, hotel executive; b. N.Y.C., Sept. 17, 1915; s. Harry and Jennie (Grossinger) G.; m. Ricelle Persky, June 17, 1947; children: Richard, Michael, James. B.S. in Hotel Adminstrn, Cornell U., 1936. Gen. mgr. Grossinger Hotel and Country Club, N.Y., 1954-55, exec. v.p., 1958-63, pres., 1964—; mgr. Grossinger Beach Hotel, Miami Beach, Fla., 1941-42; gen. mgr. Grossinger Pancoast Hotel, Miami Beach, 1947-53; v.p., dir. Monticello Raceway, N.Y., 1958—; dir. Sullivan County Nat. Bank, Liberty, Neighborhood Realty; chmn. adv. com. Hotel Sch., Sullivan County Community Coll.; pres. Internat. Hospitality Advisors, 1979-81. Pres. Community Gen. Hosp., 1967; mem. alumni adv. com. Cornell U. Council, 1967—; active Boy Scouts Am.; area chmn. United Jewish Appeal, 1958-59, hon. chmn. Catskill region, 1966; N.E. regional chmn., v.p. Anti-defamation League.; patron Class of 1982 Shannon Coll. Hotel Mgmt., Ireland. Served with AUS, 1944-46. Mem. Hospitality Mag.-Hotelmen's Hall of Fame. Mem. N.Y. State Hotel and Motel Assn. (pres. 1960-62), Am. Hotel and Motel Assn. (dir. 1964-65), Sullivan County Hotel Assn. (pres. 1955-57), Alpha Epsilon Pi.; mem. B'nai B'rith. Club: Friars (N.Y.C.). Lodges: Masons; Elks; Rotary (hon.). Address: Grossinger Hotel Grossinger NY 12734

GROSSINGER, RICHARD SELIG, publisher, writer, editor; b. N.Y.C., Nov. 3, 1944; s. Paul Leonard and Martha Washington (Rothkrug) G.; m. Lindy Downer Hough, June 21, 1966; children: Robin, Miranda. B.A., Amherst Coll., 1966; M.A., U. Mich., 1968, Ph.D. in Anthropology, 1975. Lectr. in anthropology-geography U. Maine, Portland, 1970-72; mem. faculty dept. cultural history Goddard Coll., Plainfield, Vt., 1972-77; founder, editor, pub. Io mag., 1965—, North Atlantic Books, Richmond, Calif. Author: books Solar Journal: Oecological Sections, 1970, Spaces Wild and Tame, 1971, Book of the Earth and Sky, 1971, Mars: A Science Fiction Vision, 1971, The Continents, 1973, Early Field Notes From the All-American Revival Church, 1973, The Windy Passage from Nostalgia, 1974, The Book of Being Born Again into the World, 1974, Martian Homecoming at the All-American Revival Church, 1974, The Long Body of the Dream, 1974, Book of the Cranberry Islands, 1974, The Provinces, 1975, The Unfinished Business of Doctor Hermes, 1976, Planet Medicine from Stone Age Shamanism to Post-Industrial Healing, 1980, The Night Sky, 1981, Embryogenesis, 1984; editor: (with Kevin Kerrane) Baseball I Gave You All The Best Years of My Life, 1977, Ecology and Consciousness, 1978, Alchemy: pre-Egyptian Legacy, Millennial Promise, 1979. NIH fieldwork fellow, 1969; Nat. Endowment for Arts writer's fellow, 1976. Mem. Soc. for Study Native Arts and Scis. (dir. 1980—).

GROSSMAN, BURTON JAY, physician, educator; b. Chgo., Nov. 27, 1924; s. Paul and Neva (Sonnenschein) G. B.S., U. Chgo., 1945, M.D., 1949. Diplomate: Am. Bd. Pediatrics. Intern Billings Meml. Hosp., U. Chgo. (Clinics), 1949-50; resident Bobs Roberts Meml. Hosp., 1950-51, 53-54, attending physician, 1955—; med. dir. La Rabida Children's Hosp. and Research Center, Chgo., 1961—, attending physician, 1957—; instr. pediatrics U. Chgo. Med. Sch., 1954-57; asst. prof., 1957-61, asso. prof., 1961-66, prof. pediatrics, 1966—; Co-chmn. rheumatic fever prevention com. Chgo. Heart Assn., 1962-72. Served to capt. M.C. USAF, 1951-53. Recipient Joseph P. Brenneman award Chgo. Pediatric Soc., 1981. Fellow Am. Acad. Pediatrics; mem. Am. Pediatric Soc., Soc. for Pediatric Research, Midwest Soc. Pediatric Research, Chgo. Rheumatism Soc. (pres. 1969-71), Arthritis Found. (med. sci. com. 1968-77, vice chmn. 1972-75). Home: 5300 South Shore Dr Chicago IL 60615 Office: La Rabida Children's Hosp and Research Center 65th at Lake Michigan Chicago IL 60649

GROSSMAN, EVERETT PHILIP, retail exec.; b. Boston, June 10, 1924; s. Joseph B. and Esther L. G.; m. Cynthia E. Rich, Mar. 31, 1979; children—Linsey Grossman Selvitella, Heidi Grossman Soderstrom. A.B., Harvard U., 1946. Exec. v.p. Grossman's, Braintree, Mass., 1970; exec. v.p. retail group Evans Products Co., Braintree, 1970; dir. Quincy Coop. Bank, Mass. Trustee Temple Emanuel, Newton. Served with AUS, 1943-46. Mem. Am. Assn. Mil. Engrs., Northeastern Lumbermen's Assn., Mass. Retail Lumber Dealers Assn. (past pres.), S. Shore C. of C., Boston C. of C. Clubs: Harvard (Boston); Masons, B'nai B'rith. Office: 200 Union St Braintree MA 02184

GROSSMAN, FRANK NEWTON, transportation holdoing company executive; b. Galveston, Tex., Oct. 29, 1927; s. Frank A. and Frances (Newton) G.; m. Jacqueline Ann Mosher, June 12, 1954; children: Mark M., F. Reid, Neil N. B.S. in Journalism, U. Tex., 1950. Asst. to pres. Sante Fe Ry., Chgo., 1972-75; asst. v.p. Santa Fe Ry., Washington, 1975-77; v.p. SFI & Santa Fe Ry., Chgo., 1977-83; sr. v.p. corp. communications Santa Fe Industries, Chgo., 1983—; pres. Santa Fe Industries Found., Chgo., 1983; v.p. corp. communications Santa Fe So. Pacific Corp., 1984. Served with USNR, 1944-46. Mem. Soc. Profl. journalists. Republican. Methodist. Home: 1206 Indian Tr Hinsdale IL 60521 Office: Santa Fe Industries Inc 224 S Michigan Ave Chicago IL 60604

GROSSMAN, GORDON WILLIAM, direct marketing cons.; b. Cleve., Sept. 26, 1932; s. Clarence George and Helen Catherine (Swartzel) G.; m. Mary Ann Creel, June 19, 1954; children—Linda Jeanne, Earl Martin. B.A. (NROTC regular scholar), Princeton, 1954; Fulbright scholar, Exeter U., Eng., 1954-55. Sr. v.p., mktg. dir. Readers Digest Assn., Inc., Pleasantville, N.Y., 1958-74, dir., 1967-74; pres. Gordon W. Grossman, Inc., Chappaqua, N.Y., 1974—; dir. Select Mags., 1966-73. Bd. dirs. Westchester Childrens Assn., 1960-68, Am. Cancer Soc., Better Bus. Bur. Westchester. Served with USN, 1955-56. Mem. Direct Mail Mktg. Assn. Club: Princeton (N.Y.C.). Address: 606 Douglas Rd Chappaqua NY 10514

GROSSMAN, HERBERT LELAND, trade association executive; b. Alliance, Ohio, Sept. 4, 1930; s. Homer Sherman and Lula Kathryn (Zartman) G.; m. Donna Jean Haas, Jan. 18, 1953; children: Robert Owen, Catherine Ann, William Howard. B.S. in Journalism, Northwestern U., 1952. Asst. exec. dir. Stark County Lung Assn., Canton, Ohio, 1955-59; asst. exec. dir. D.C. Lung Assn., Washington, 1959-65; asst. gen. mgr. Nat. Assn. Bedding Mfrs., Washington, 1965-69, exec. v.p., 1970—. Pres. East Falls Church Civic Assn., Arlington, Va., 1963; pres. Birches Homeowners Assn., Arlington, 1977. Served with USN, 1952-55; Korea. Mem. NAM (mem. exec. com. trade assns. dept. 1979-81), Am. Soc. Assn. Execs., Washington Soc. Assn. Execs., U.S. C. of C. Presbyterian. Home: 4716 N 24th St Arlington VA 22207 Office: 1235 Jefferson Davis Hwy Suite 601 Arlington VA 22202

GROSSMAN, IRVING, architect; b. Toronto, Ont., Can., July 12, 1926; s. Benjamin and Jenny (Appel) G.; m. Helena Derwinger, Feb. 28, 1971; children: Adam, Jonas. B.Arch. with honors, U. Toronto, 1950. Pvt. practice architecture, Toronto, 1954—; mem. faculty U. Toronto Sch. Architecture, 1954-62; chmn. Stratford Seminar Civic Design, 1966. Prin. works include Flemingdon Park; residential community, Toronto, 1959-65, The Highlands, Ottawa, Ont., 1971, Crombie Apts, Toronto, 1980, Expo '67 Adminstrn. Bldg; various synagogues, libraries; pvt. residences. Recipient Hobbs Glass prize U. Toronto, 1948; Toronto Brick prize, 1949; Archtl. Gold medal, 1950; Regional Design award Canadian Housing Design Council, 1957, 1957; Nat. Design award, 1962, 71; Research award Canadian Council, 1959; Massey medal, 1967; Canadian Centennial medal, 1967; Ont. Masons Relations award, 1970, 73; Design award Scarborough Planning Bd., 1972; award of excellence Canadian Architects Yearbook, 1970, 72, 78; Pilkington Glass fellow, 1950; academician Royal Canadian Acad. Arts. Fellow Royal Archtl. Inst. Can.; mem. Ont. Assn. Architects (scholarship 1947, Design award 1967). Home: 21 Chestnut Park Rd Toronto ON M4W 1W4 Canada Office: 7 Sultan St Toronto ON M5S 1L6 Canada

GROSSMAN, JACK, advt. agy. exec.; b. N.Y.C., Mar. 22, 1925; s. Benjamin Robert and Sarah Dora (Bender) G.; m. Esther Arline Goldman, Nov. 23, 1949; children—Barbara Ruth, Neil David. B.Sc., N.Y. U., 1950, postgrad., 1952. With Biow Co., Inc., N.Y.C., 1951-56, mgr. sales research, 1954-56; with William Esty Co., In., N.Y.C., 1956—, mgr. research dept., then v.p. research, 1964-73, sr. v.p., dir. research, 1973—; adj. asso. prof. mktg. Pace U., 1962-74. Bd. dirs. L.I. Cons. Center, 1979—. Served with AUS, 1943-47. Decorated Bronze Star with oak leaf cluster, Purple Heart. Mem. Am. Mktg. Assn., World Futurist Soc., Advt. Agy. Research Dirs. Council. Jewish. Home: 1025 Fifth Ave New York NY 10028 Office: 100 E 42d St New York NY 10017

GROSSMAN, JACOB, physician, educator; b. N.Y.C., Aug. 6, 1916; s. Isaac and Anna (Toner) G.; m. Frances Gaezer, July 9, 1948; children—Arthur B., Victor G., Daniel K., Walter D. B.S., Coll. City N.Y., 1935; M.A., Columbia, 1936; M.D., U. Louisville, 1940. Intern Morrisania City Hosp., N.Y.C., 1940-42; resident neurology, medicine Montefiore Hosp., 1946-48, research asso., attending physician medicine, 1948-65; dir. medicine Hosp. for Joint Diseases and Med. Center, N.Y.C., 1966-80; prof. clin. medicine Mt. Sinai Sch. Medicine, N.Y.C., also City U. N.Y., 1968—; vis. prof. medicine Albert Einstein Coll. Medicine, N.Y.C. Contbg. editor: Fed. Am. Soc. Exptl. Biology. Served to maj., M.C. AUS, 1942-45. Fellow A.C.P.; mem. Am. Physiol. Soc., Soc. for Exptl. Biology and Medicine, Am. Soc. Nephrology, Alpha Omega Alpha. Research cardio-vascular, renal, metabolism. Home: 64 Fayette Rd Scarsdale NY 10583

GROSSMAN, JEROME BARNETT, income tax preparation co. exec.; b. Kansas City, Kans., Sept. 9, 1919; s. Harry and Dora (Cohen) G.; m. Marian R. Navran, Sept. 19, 1945; children—Jean, Janet. B.A., U. Mich., 1941. Registered prin. Nat. Assn. Security Dealers, 1969-72. Exec. v.p., gen. mgr. Helzberg's Diamond Shops, Kansas City, Mo., 1941-66; dir. mktg. H & R Block, Inc., Kansas City, Mo., 1966-69, asst. to pres., 1969-71, exec. v.p., chief operating officer, 1971—, dir., 1973—. Trustee Menorah Med. Center, Kansas City, 1975—, Temple B'nai Jehudah, 1953-56. Served with USAAF, 1942-45. Mem. NCCJ,

Internat. Franchise Assn. (dir. 1974—), Sales and Mktg. Execs., Nat. Assn. Realtors, Kansas City Real Estate Bd. Jewish. Clubs: Oakwood Country (v.p. 1969-71), B'nai B'rith.). Home: 1251 W 63rd Terr Kansas City MO 64113 Office: 4410 Main St Kansas City MO 64111

GROSSMAN, JOEL BARRY, political science educator; b. N.Y.C., June 19, 1936; s. Joseph and Selma G.; m. Mary Hengstenberg, Aug. 23, 1964; children: Alison, Joanna, Daniel. B.A., Queens Coll., 1957; M.A., U. Iowa, 1960, Ph.D., 1963. Faculty dept. polit. sci. U. Wis., Madison, 1963—, prof., 1971—, chmn. dept., 1975-78; fellow in law and polit. sci. Harvard Law Sch., Cambridge, Mass., 1965-66; Fulbright lectr. U. Strathclyde, Glasgow, 1968-69; vis. prof. law U. Stockholm, 1973. Editor: Law and Soc. Review, 1978-82; author: Lawyers and Judges, 1965, Frontiers of Judicial Research, 1969, Law and Change in Modern America, 1971, Constitutional Law and Judicial Policy Making, 1972, 80; contbr. articles in field to profl. jours. Bd. trustees Center for Pub. Representation, Madison, 1977—. Served with USAR, 1960-66. Mem. Wis. Civil Liberties Union (vice chmn. 1970-72), Am. Polit. Sci. Assn., Midwest Polit. Sci. Assn., So. Polit. Sci. Assn., Law and Soc. Assn. Democrat. Home: 5318 Russett Rd Madison WI 53711 Office: Dept Polit Sci U Wis Madison WI 53706

GROSSMAN, KARL H., journalist; b. Bklyn., Feb. 1, 1942; s. Herbert and Ruth (Hyman) G.; m. Janet Kopp, May 25, 1961; children: Kurt, Adam. Student, Antioch Coll., 1959-61, Adelphi Suffolk Coll., 1961-64; B.S. in Social Sci., Empire State Coll., SUNY, 1976; M.A. in Media Studies, New Sch. Social Research, 1981. Copyboy Cleve. Press and News, 1960; reporter Babylon (N.Y.) Town Leader, 1962-64; reporter, columnist L.I. Press, Jamaica, N.Y., 1964-77; founder, editor Island Closeup News Service, Sag Harbor, N.Y., 1977—; freelance writer, 1970—; faculty SUNY Coll. Old Westbury, 1978—; adj. assoc. prof. Southampton Coll., 1979—; contbg. editor The Sun, Chapel Hill, N.C., 1976-78; program host Long Island World, Sta. WLIW-TV (pub. service TV channel), 1972-73; appearances on news and documentary programs Long Island World WLIW-TV L.I. (pub. service TV channel), 1973-79; program host, reporter Suffolk Cablevision, 1977-78; reporter, commentator WRCN radio, 1979—; news anchor, program host WSNL-TV, 1979—; creator, commentator ten-part environ. TV series Can Suffolk Be Saved, 1974-75. Author: Cover Up: What you are not supposed to know about Nuclear Power, 1980, The Poison Conspiracy, 1983; contbr. articles to mags., lit. and profl. jours., short stories to mags. Nat. dir. League Against Obnoxious TV Commls., 1961-63; council mem.-at-large Suffolk County council Boy Scouts Am., 1972-77; bd. dirs. Transitional Services N.Y., 1978-79; mem. Eagle Scout Assn. Suffolk County; Mem. Order of Arrow. Recipient George Polk Meml. award, 1970; annual award finalist Sigma Delta Chi, 1971; citation EPA, 1978; cert. of merit N.Y. State Senate, 1979; environ. citation Concerned Citizens of Montauk, 1979; named Conservation Communicator of Yr., Suffolk County Fish and Game Assn., 1971; recipient Environ. Writing award Suffolk Am. Legion, 1971, Photography award N.Y. Press Assn., 1963, Journalism award Suffolk Parks Assn., 1974; Journalism award Friends of the Earth, 1979; award for best news story N.Y. Press Assn., 1979; award for best continuing feature column Press Club L.I., 1981. Jewish. Club: Press of L.I. (founder, pres. 1974-75). Home: 347A Noyac Rd Sag Harbor NY 11963 Address: Box 1680 Sag Harbor NY 11963 *Through my career as a journalist I have tried to adhere to the philosophy of the first newspaper at which I was employed, a Scripps-Howard paper which lived by the chain's motto: "Give light and the people will find their own way." In a world where now many aim to twist and suppress the press, cover up the truth; because of the army of PR people and other assorted media-manipulators out there, and the awesome and sweeping power of media in society today, it is of crucial import. Our survival and that of democracy depends on it.*

GROSSMAN, LAWRENCE, biochemist, educator; b. Bklyn., Jan. 23, 1924; s. Isidor Harry and Anna (Lipkin) G.; m. Barbara Meta Mishen, June 24, 1949; children—Jon David, Carl Henry, Ilene Rebecca. Student, Coll. City N.Y., 1946-47; B.A., Hofstra U., 1949; Ph.D., U. So. Cal., 1954. Scientist NIH, Bethesda, Md., 1956-57; asst. prof. biochemistry Brandeis U., Waltham, Mass., 1957-62, asso. prof., 1962-67, prof., 1967-75; E.V. McCollum prof., chmn. dept. biochemistry Johns Hopkins Sch. Hygiene and Pub. Health, Balt., 1975—; Mem. sci. adv. com. Am. Cancer Soc.; adviser in biochemistry NIH. Author: Method in Nucleic Acids, 2 vols, 1968, 2 vols., 1971, 2 vols., 1974, 3 vols., 1979, 2 vols., 1980; asso. editor: Cancer Research; contbr. articles to profl. jours. Trustee Brandeis U. Served to lt. USNR, 1942-45. Decorated D.F.C., Air medal.; Research grantee NSF, NIH, Am. Cancer Soc., Dept. Energy; Commonwealth fellow, 1963; Guggenheim fellow, 1973; USPHS Career Devel. awardee, 1964-74. Mem. Am. Soc. Biol. Chemists, Am. Biophys. Soc., Am. Soc. Photobiology. Home: 5723 Uffington Rd Mount Washington Baltimore MD 21209 Office: 615 N Wolfe St Baltimore MD 21218

GROSSMAN, LAWRENCE KUGELMASS, communications executive; b. N.Y.C., June 21, 1931; s. Nathan F. and Rose (Goldstein) G.; m. Alberta S. Nevler, Mar. 1, 1954; children: Susan Lee, Jennifer Nancy, Caroline Ann. B.A., Columbia, 1952; student, Harvard Law Sch., 1953. Editor, promotion exec. Look mag., 1953-56; advt. exec. CBS-TV, 1956-62; v.p. advt. NBC, 1962-66; pres. Lawrence K. Grossman, Inc., N.Y.C., 1966-76, Forum Communications, Inc., 1969-76, Pub. Broadcasting Service, Washington, 1976-84, NBC News, N.Y.C., 1984—. Assos. Editor: A Candid Portrait of the 1964 Presidential Election, 1965. Mem. Phi Beta Kappa. Office: NBC News 30 Rockefeller Plaza New York NY 10020

GROSSMAN, LAWRENCE MORTON, nuclear engineering educator; b. N.Y.C., Aug. 2, 1922; (married); 1 child. B.Chem. Engring., City Coll. N.Y., 1942, M.Sc. (Standard Oil Co. Calif. fellow), 1944; Ph.D. in Engring. Sci., U. Calif. at Berkeley, 1948. Chem. engr. E.I. du Pont de Nemours & Co., Niagara Falls, N.Y., 1942-43; instr. mech. engring. U. Calif. at Berkeley, 1944-46, lectr., 1946-48, asst. prof., 1948-54, asso. prof. nuclear engring., 1954-60, prof., chmn. dept. nuclear engring., 1960—; Fulbright lectr. U. Delft, 1952-53; NSF Sr. research fellow Saclay Nuclear Research Center, France, 1961-62; NATO sr. fellow, 1974. Mem. A.A.A.S., Am. Nuclear Soc. Office: Etcheverry Hall U Calif Berkeley CA 94720

GROSSMAN, MARSHALL BRUCE, lawyer; b. Omaha, Mar. 24, 1939; s. Lee and Elsie (Stalmaster) G.; m. Marlene Belle Delson, Aug. 19, 1962; children: Rodger Seth, Leslie Erin. Student, U. Calif. at Los Angeles, 1957-59; B.S.L., U. So. Calif., 1964, LL.B., 1964. Bar: Calif. 1965. Mem. firm Alschuler, Grossman & Pines, Los Angeles, 1965-67, partner, 1967—; Lectr. law U. So. Calif., Los Angeles, 1966-69; lectr., author on comml. litigation, 1968—. Mem. Calif. Coastal Commn., 1981—. Mem. ABA, Los Angeles Bar Assn., Beverly Hills Bar Assn. (bd. govs. 1971-76), Barristers Bar Assn. (pres. 1972-73), Assn. Bus. Trial Attys. (bd. govs. 1974-75), Los Angeles Jewish Fedn. (chmn. commn. on law and legislation 1973-74, chmn. commn. on Soviet Jewry 1981), Order of Coif, Tau Delta Phi, Phi Alpha Delta. Club: Mason. Office: 1880 Century Park E 12th Floor Los Angeles CA 90067

GROSSMAN, MICHAEL, economist; b. Bklyn., July 12, 1942; s. Mortimer and Doris (Orent) G.; m. Ilene Joy Gordon, Sept. 11, 1966; children: Sandra Diane, Barri Lynn. B.A., Trinity Coll., Hartford, Conn., 1964; Ph.D, Columbia U., 1970. Asst. prof. Ctr. Health Adminstrn. Studies, Grad. Sch. Bus., U. Chgo.,, 1969-71; research assoc., co-program dir. health econs. research Nat. Bur. Econ. Research, N.Y.C., 1972—; prof. econs. CUNY Grad. Sch., 1974; cons. in field. Author: The Demand for Health: A Theoretical and Empirical Investigation, 1972; contbr. articles to profl. jours. Ford Found. fellow, Columbia U. Mem. Am. Econ. Assn., Population Assn. Am., Am. Pub. Health Assn., Health Econs. Research Assn., Phi Beta Kappa, Pi Gamma Mu. Research on teenage smoking and alchol use, U.S. neonatal mortality, health and pollution. Home: 200 Linwood Ave Fort Lee NJ 07024 Office: Nat Bur Econ Research 269 Mercer St New York NY 10003

GROSSMAN, MOSES, physician, educator; b. Kiev, Russia, Oct. 14, 1921; came to U.S., 1941, naturalized, 1944; s. Gregory and Klara (Kaufman) G.; m. Verle Anne Campbell, July 14, 1951; children—Deborah, Pamela, David, Daniel. A.B., U. Calif. at Berkeley, 1943; M.D., U. Calif. at San Francisco, 1946. Faculty U. Calif. at San Francisco, 1951—, prof. pediatrics, 1964—; chief pediatrics San Francisco Gen. Hosp., 1959—; asso. dean U. Calif. Sch. Medicine, 1964-73. Contbr. articles to profl. jours. Mem. Am. Acad. Pediatrics, Am. Pediatric Soc., Soc. for Pediatric Research, Infectious Disease Soc. Am. Home: 1001 Ulloa St San Francisco CA 94127

GROSSMAN, NANCY, artist; b. N.Y.C.; s. Murray and Josephine G. B.F.A., Pratt Inst., 1962. Mem. jury sculpture N.Y. State Council on Arts, 1973, Prix de Rome fellowships Am. Acad. in Rome, 1974. Exhibited in one-woman shows, Krasner Gallery, N.Y.C., 1964, 65, 65, 67, Cordier & Ekstrom, N.Y.C., 1968, 69, 71, 73, 75, 76, Church Fine Arts Gallery, U. Nev., Reno, 1978, Barbara Gladstone Gallery, N.Y.C., 1980, 82, Heath Gallery, Atlanta, 1981; exhibited in numerous group shows, including, Whitney Mus. Am. Art, N.Y.C., 1968, 69, 69, 73, 80, 81, Fogg Art Mus., Cambridge, Mass., 1972, Am. Acad. Arts and Letters/Nat. Inst. Arts and Letters invitational, N.Y.C., 1974, New American Painting exhbn., Hungary, Czechoslovakia, Poland, 1978, Bettė Stoler, 1983; represented in permanent collections, Whitney Mus. Am. Art, Hirshhorn Mus., Washington, Smithsonian Inst., Dallas Mus. Fine Arts, Balt. Mus., Larry Aldrich Mus., Ridgefield, Conn., Mus. Boymans Van Benningen, Rotterdam, Netherlands, U. Calif., Berkeley, Princeton U. Art Mus., N.J. Recipient Inaugural Contemporary Achievement award Pratt Inst., 1966, Am. Acad. Arts and Letters/Nat. Inst. Arts and Letters award, 1974; Ida C. Haskell scholar, 1962; John Simon Guggenheim Meml. Found. fellow, 1965. Mem. Sculptors Guild. Address: 105 Eldridge St New York NY 10002

GROSSMAN, ROBERT GEORGE, physician, educator; b. N.Y.C., Jan. 24, 1933; s. Ferenc and Vivian (Isenberg) G.; m. Ellin Friedman, June 26, 1955; children—Amy, Kate, Ruth. B.A., Swarthmore Coll., 1953; M.D., Columbia U., 1957. Diplomate: Am. Bd. Neurosurgery. Intern Strong Meml. Hosp., Rochester, N.Y., 1957-58; resident Presbyn. Hosp., Columbia U., N.Y.C., 1960-63; practice medicine, specializing in neurol. surgery, Houston, 1973—; instr., assoc. prof. neurol. surgery U. Tex. S.W. Med. Sch., 1963-68; assoc. prof., prof. neurol. surgery Albert Einstein Coll. Medicine, 1969-73; prof., chmn. div. neurol. surgery U. Tex. Med. Br., Galveston, 1973-80; prof., chmn. dept. neurol. surgery Baylor Coll. Medicine, 1980—; chief neurosurg. service Meth. Hosp., Houston, 1980—; chmn. neurology B study sect. USPHS, NIH, 1972-74. Author: (with W. D. Willis) Medical Neurobiology, 3d edit, 1981; editorial bd.: Jour. Neurosurgery, 1981—, Neurol. Research, 1979—. Served with AUS, 1958-60. Mem. Am. Assn. Neurol. Surgeons, A.C.S., Soc. Univ. Surgeons. Home: 1821 South Blvd Houston TX 77098 Office: Baylor Coll Medicine 1200 Moursund Houston TX 77030

GROSSMAN, SANFORD, lawyer; b. N.Y.C., July 4, 1929; s. Philip and Irene (Hare) G.; m. Barbara Rothman, May 23, 1951; children: Daniel J., Donna A. Student, NYU, 1947-49; LL.B., Bklyn. Law Sch., 1952. Bar: N.Y. 1953, U.S. Supreme Ct. 1964. Pvt. practice law, N.Y.C., 1954-79; ptnr. Simpson Thacher & Bartlett, N.Y.C., 1979—; dir. Bellemead Devel. Corp., Lyndhurst, N.J. Served with U.S. Army, 1952-54. Mem. N.Y. County Lawyers Assn., Westchester Bar Assn. Clubs: India House, Princeton (N.Y.C.). Home: James Rd Chappaqua NY 10549 Office: 1 Battery Park Plaza New York NY 10004

GROSSMAN, SEBASTIAN PETER, psychologist, educator; b. Coburg, Bavaria, Jan. 21, 1934; came to U.S., 1954, naturalized, 1955; s. Otto and Arnet (Peipers) G.; m. Lore Bensel, June 30, 1955. B.A., U. Md., 1958; M.S., Yale, 1959, Ph.D., 1961. Asst. prof. psychology U. Iowa, 1961-64; asso. prof. psychology U. Chgo., 1964-67, prof., 1967—, chmn. dept. biopsychology, 1968-72, 76—. Author: A Textbook of Physiological Psychology, 1967, Essentials of Physiological Psychology, 1973; Regional editor: Jour. Physiology and Behavior, 1965—, Pharmacology, Biochemistry and Behavior, 1973—, Neurosci. and Biobehavioral Revs; cons. editor: Psychopharmacologia, 1968-78, Psychobiology, 1969—; editorial bd.: Biochem. Psychology, 1970—, Jour. Life Sci, 1970—; Contbr. articles profl. jours. Fellow AAAS, Am. Psychol. Assn.; mem. Am. Physiol. Soc., Royal Soc. Medicine, Phi Kappa Phi. Home: 1159 E 56th St Chicago IL 60637

GROSSMANN, MARIA, librarian; b. Vienna, Austria, June 12, 1919; came to U.S., 1940; d. Fritz and Adele (Geiringer) Schweinburg; m. Walter Grossmann, Oct. 5, 1945; children—John, Carol, Barbara. B.A., Smith Coll., 1942; M.A., Radcliffe Coll., 1943; M.L.A., Simmons Coll., 1956; Ph.D., Harvard U., 1959. Order librarian, head tech. services, asst. librarian, librarian Andover-Harvard Theol. Library, Harvard Divinity Sch., Cambridge, Mass., 1956-73, 79—; faculty Harvard Divinity Sch., 1956-73, 79—; librarian for collection devel. Harvard U. Library, Faculty Arts and Scis., 1974-79; cons. various theol. schs; mem. library com. Boston Theol. Inst.; Fellow Am. Council Learned Socs., 1964-65, Am. Philos. Soc., 1964-65, Deutsche Forschungsgemeinschaft, 1964. Bibliographer: for English lang. publs. ann. Luther Bibliography, Luther Jahrbuch; contbr. writings to European, U.S. publs. Fellow Am. Theol. Library Assn. (pres. 1968-69, bd. of microtext 1972—); mem. Am. Assn. Theol. Schs. (accrediting com., commn. on accrediting), Am. Soc. Ch. History, Renaissance Soc. Am., Verein fuer Reformationsgeschichte, Luther Gesellschaft, ALA. Quaker. Home: 97 Waverly St Belmont MA 02178 Office: 45 Francis Ave Cambridge MA 02138

GROSSMANN, WALTER, librarian; b. Vienna, June 5, 1918; U.S., 1939, naturalized, 1941; s. Otto and Valerie G.; m. Maria Schweinburg, Oct. 6, 1945; children—John, Carol, Barbara. B.A., Yankton (S.D.) Coll., 1941; M.A., Harvard, 1943, Ph.D., 1951; M.S., Simmons Coll., Boston, 1962. Asso. prof. history Simmons Coll., 1947-52; asst. librarian book selection Harvard, 1952-64, lectr. history and lit., 1961-64, Archibald C. Coolidge bibliographer, 1964-66; prof. history U. Mass., Boston, 1966—, dir. libraries, 1969—; vis. lectr. McGill U. Sch. Library Sci., 1966-78. Author: Johann Christian Edelmann: From Orthodoxy to Enlightenment, 1976; Editor: Edelmann Sämtliche Schriften, 12 vols, 1969—. Guggenheim fellow, 1964-65; Humboldt Gesellschaft fellow, 1970. Mem. Am. Hist. Assn., MLA, ALA, Soc. 18th Century Studies, Société Européenne— de Culture. Home: 97 Waverley St Belmont MA 02178 Office: Univ Mass Harbor Campus Boston MA 02125

GROSSVOGEL, DAVID I., comparative literature educator; b. San Francisco, June 19, 1925; s. Israel and Ada (Bloom) Gur; m. Jill Elyse, June 22, 1974; children: Steven Michael, Deborah Amanda. B.A., U. Calif., Berkeley, 1946-49; postgrad. (Fulbright fellow), U. Grenoble, France, 1950; M.A., Columbia U., 1951; Ph.D. (Univ. fellow), Columbia U., 1954. Instr. Columbia U., 1954-56; mng. editor Romanic Rev., 1954-56; asst. prof. Harvard U., 1956-61; assoc. prof. Cornell U., Ithaca, N.Y., 1961-64, dir. grad. studies Romance lit., 1961-65, prof., 1964—, Goldwin Smith prof. comparative lit. and Romance studies, 1970—, chmn. dept. Romance studies, 1970-73; founder, editor Diacritics, 1971-76. Author: The Selfconscious Stage, 1958, reprinted as Twentieth-Century French Drama, 1961, Jean Anouilh's Antigone, 1959, Four Playwrights and a Postscript, 1962, reprinted as The Blasphemers, 1964, Sagan's Bonjour Tristesse, 1965, Limits of the Novel, 1968, Divided We Stand, 1970, Mystery and Its Fictions, 1979. Served with USAAF, 1943-45. Recipient Clark research award Harvard U., 1959; CRB fellow, Brussels, 1952-53; Fulbright fellow, Paris, 1959-60; Guggenheim fellow, Paris, 1964-65. Mem. MLA, Phi Beta Kappa. Office: 282 Goldwin Smith Cornell U Ithaca NY 14853 *There is a difference between individuality and demonstrative non-conformity: if the non-conformist is looking for ways to be different, he will be a victim of his misguided efforts and as much beholden as the compliant. The poet, explorer, seer can be only himself. He may live in worlds that are underpopulated, but they are worlds encountered at dawn. His friends may be few, but they are disinterested. He experiences the freedom that others talk about.*

GROSSWEINER, LEONARD IRWIN, physicist, educator; b. Atlantic City, Aug. 16, 1924; s. Jules H. and Rae (Goldberger) G.; m. Bess Tornheim, Sept. 9, 1951; children-Karen Ann, Jane (dec.), James Benjamin, Eric William. B.S., Coll. City N.Y., 1947; M.S., Ill. Inst. Tech., 1950, Ph.D., 1955. Asst. chemist Argonne (Ill.) Nat. Lab., 1947-50, asso. physicist, 1950-57; asso. prof. physics Ill. Inst. Tech., Chgo., 1957-62, prof. physics, 1962—, chmn. dept. physics, 1970-81, Sang Exchange lectr., 1972-73; vis. prof. radiology Stanford U. Sch. Medicine, 1979; cons. Donner Lab. U. Calif., Berkeley, Chgo. Med. Sch.; North Chicago, Ill., Hines (Ill.) VA Hosp., Michael Reese Med. Center, Chgo.; Mem. U.S. Nat. Com. Photobiology, 1977-81, chmn., 1980-81. Author: Organic Photoconductors in Electrophotography, 1970; Contbr. articles to profl. jours. Served with AUS, 1944-46. Fellow Am. Phys. Soc. (sec.-treas. div. biol. physics 1973-76, chmn. 1977-78), N.Y. Acad. Scis.; mem. Am. Chem. Soc., AAAS, Radiation Research Soc., Am. Soc. Photobiology (council 1977-80, sec.-treas. 1981—), Biophys. Soc., Inter-Am. Photochem. Soc. (exec. com. 1976-78), Sigma Xi (distinguished faculty lectr. 1970). Home: 231 Wentworth Ave Glencoe IL 60022 Office: Ill Inst Tech IIT Center Chicago IL 60616

GROSVENOR, EDWIN STUART, magazine editor and publisher; b. Washington, Sept. 17, 1951; s. Melville Bell and Anne Elizabeth (Revis) G. B.A., Yale Coll., 1974; M.S. in Journalism, Columbia U., 1975, M.B.A., 1976. Freelance photographer Nat. Geog. Soc., Washington, 1967-76; staff photographer Miami News, Fla., 1975; pres. Grosvenor Publs., Inc., N.Y.C., 1977—; editor and pub. Portfolio Mag., N.Y.C., 1979—. Assoc. felllow Saybrook Coll. (Yale Coll.), 1979—; dir. Earth Soc. Found., N.Y.C., 1979—; mem. adv. com. Nat. Mus. Women's Art, Washington, 1982—; mem. corp. Curry Coll., Milton, Mass., 1983—. Recipient 1st place Graphic Arts Award Competition for 2 issues of Portfolio Mag. Printing Industries Am., 1980, 81; finalist gen. excellence category Printing Industries Am., 1983; recipient Nat. Mag. awards, 1983. Fellow Am. Geog. Soc.; mem. Am. Soc. Mag. Editors, Art Deco Soc., Internat. Ctr. of Photography, Nat. Press Photographers Assn., Nat. Trust for Hist. Preservation. Clubs: Metropolitan, Nat. Press (Washington); Yale (N.Y.C.); Wolf's Head (New Haven). Home: 211 W 56th St Apt 31D New York NY 10019 Office: Grosvenor Publs Inc 156 Fifth Ave New York NY 10010

GROSVENOR, GILBERT MELVILLE, editor, business executive; b. Washington, May 5, 1931; s. Melville Bell and Helen (Rowland) G.; m. Donna C. Kerkam, June 16, 1961; children: Gilbert Hovey, Alexandra Rowland; m. Wiley Jarman, June 1, 1979; 1 son, Graham Dabney. B.A., Yale U., 1954; D.Pub. Service (hon.), George Washington U., 1983; L.H.D. (hon.), U. Colo., 1983, Curry Coll., 1984; LL.D. (hon.), Coll. Wooster (Ohio), 1983. With Nat. Geog. Soc., 1954—, trustee, 1966—, v.p., 1966-80, asso. editor, 1967-70, editor, 1970-80, pres., 1980—; dir. Am. Security and Trust Co., Peoples Life Ins. Co., Chesapeake & Potomac Telephone Co.; mem. com. on oceans and internat. environ. and sci. affairs Dept. State; fellow Yale Corp. Trustee B.F. Saul Real Estate Trust, N.Y. Zool. Soc., Internat. Oceanographic Found., William H. Donner Found., Inc.; bd. dirs. World Wildlife Fund-U.S.; governing bd. Potomac Sch.; ann. corp. mem. Children's Hosp.; mem. Washington Cathedral Bldg. Com. Served with AUS, 1954-56. Recipient Editor of Year award Nat. Press Photographers Assn., 1975; Disting. Achievement award U. So. Calif. Sch. Journalism and Alumni Assn., 1977. Mem. Assn. Am. Geographers, Explorers Club, Newcomen Soc. Clubs: Alfalfa, Overseas Writers (Washington); Chevy Chase (Md.). Home: 8456 Holly Leaf Drive McLean VA 22102 Office: Nat Geographic Soc 17th and M Sts NW Washington DC 20036

GROSVENOR, ROBERT STRAWBRIDGE, sculptor; b. N.Y.C., Mar. 31, 1937; s. Ted Phinney and Anita (Strawbridge) G.; m. Jacqueline Gardner, Jan. 18, 1966; children: Kali, Marina, Jeremy. Grad. high sch.; student, Ecole des Beaux Arts, France, 1956, Ecole Superièure des Arts Decoratifs, Paris, 1957-59, Università di Perugia, Italy, 1958. One man exhbns. include, Park Pl. Gallery, N.Y.C., 1965, 67, Dwan Gallery, Los Angeles, 1966, Ricke Gallery, Cologne, Germany, 1969, Fischbach Gallery, N.Y.C., 1970, Paula Cooper Gallery, N.Y.C., 1970-75, 78-81, La Jolla Mus. Contemporary Art, Calif., 1971, Galerie Stampa, Basel, Switzerland, 1975, Galerie Eric Fabre, Paris, 1975, 77, Inst. Art and Urban Resources, N.Y.C., 1976, 84, group exhbns. include, Mus. Modern Art, N.Y.C., Whitney Mus., Walker Art Center, R.I. Sch. Design, Albright-Knox Gallery, Mus. Contemporary Art, Houston, Los Angeles Mus., Aldrich Mus. Contemporary Art, Ridgefield, Conn., MIT, Cambridge, Mass., numerous others; rep. permanent collections, Mus. Modern Art, Whitney Mus., Larry Aldrich Mus., Walker Art Center, Lannon Found., Storm King Art Center, M. Nornick Collection. Nat. Endowment grantee, 1969; Guggenheim fellow, 1970; recipient award Am. Acad. Arts and Letters, 1973. Address: care Paula Cooper Gallery 115 Wooster St New York NY 10012

GROTE, EDWIN O., financial company executive; b. Evansville, Ind., Mar. 16, 1924. Student, Evansville Coll. Past exec. v.p., ops. Chrysler Fin. Corp., Troy, Mich., pres., chief operating officer, 1980—; v.p. Chrysler Corp., Highland Park, 1981—. Office: Chrysler Fin Corp 900 Tower Dr Troy MI 48098

GROTEN, BARNET, research co. exec.; b. Bklyn., Oct. 25, 1933; s. Irving and Pearl G.; m. Iris Diane Brand, Aug. 1955; children—Eric Allen, Kurt David, Jessica Amy. B.S., Bklyn. Coll., 1954; Ph.D., Purdue U., 1961. With Exxon Co., various locations, 1961—; dir. research and bus. devel. Tex. Eastern Corp., Houston, 1977—; exec. v.p. Tex. Eastern Dėvel., Inc., 1980—; sec. Gulf Univs. Research Consortium, 1980-81. Contbr. articles to profl. jours. Mem. AAAS, Am. Chem. Soc., Am. Inst. Chem. Engrs., Am. Mgmt. Assn., Indsl.

Research Inst., Soc. Petroleum Engrs. Office: PO Box 2521 Houston TX 77001

GROTH, JOHN, artist, journalist; b. Chgo., Feb. 26, 1908; s. John and Ethel (Bragg) G. Student, Art Inst. Chgo., 1926-27, Art Student's League N.Y., 1937-38; D.Arts (hon.), Eastern Mich. U., 1976. Art dir. Esquire, 1933-36, Broun's Nutmeg, 1939; European war corr. Chgo. Sun, 1944, Am. Legion, 1945; lectr., 1945-46; art instr. Art Student's League N.Y., 1946—; artist-war corr. Met. Group Syndicate Korea, French Indo-China, 1951; USAF corr., Congo-Central Africa, 1960, artist, war. corr., Dominican Republic, 1965, Vietnam, 1967; art instr. Pratt Inst., 1952—, Parsons Sch. Design, 1954-55, N.A.D., 1962—; corr. Sports Illustrated, Asia, 1954; artist in residence U. Tex., 1970. Illustrator: (by Kurt Sprague) The Promise Kept, 1975; Works represented, Mus. Modern Art, Library of Congress, Met. Mus. Art, Chgo. Art Inst., Bklyn. Mus., Butler Art Inst., Youngstown, Ohio, U. Tex. collection, U. Ga. collections, U.S. Army, Navy, Marines, Air Force; others, Surgeon Gen.'s Office; series of drawings of Jack Ruby trial, acquired Dallas Pub. Library, 1977; Illustrator: Grapes of Wrath (Steinbeck), 1947, Men Without Women (Hemingway), 1946, World of Wood, Field & Stream (Randolph), 1956, The Well Tempered Angler (Gingrich), 1959, War and Peace (Tolstoy), 1961, Exodus (Uris), 1962, Black Beauty, 1962, A Christmas Carol, 1963, The Stories of O'Henry (Ltd. Edits. Club), 1965, Gone With the Wind (Mitchell), 1967, War Prayer (Mark Twain), 1968, All Quiet on the Western Front (Erich Maria Remarque), 1969, John Groth's World of Sport, 1970, Life and Death of a Brave Bull, 1972, The Brave Men, 1972, Puddin' Head Wilson (Mark Twain), 1974, The Last Running (John Graves), 1974, The Fishing in Print (Arnold Gingrich), 1974, Biography of an American Reindeer (Alice Hopf), 1976, Journey to Pleasant Hill (Elijah Petty), 1982; illustrator-author: Studio: Europe, 1945, Studio: Asia, 1952. Recipient Allied Artist award, 1961. Fellow Explorers Club; mem. Audubon Artists. (dir.); Mem. Soc. Illustrators, Am. Water Color Soc., N.A.D. (asso.). Clubs: Overseas Press, Illustrators, Lotos, Salmagundi (N.Y.C.). Address: 61 E 57th St New York NY 10022 *When a boy, I wanted to be a soldier, an athlete, a traveler, and to be present at the great events of my time. Through art I've been able to be all of them and was enabled to sketch and paint most of the great events of the past forty years.*

GROTTEROD, KNUT, paper company executive; b. Sarpsborg, Norway, Feb. 12, 1922; emigrated to Can., 1945, naturalized, 1954; s. Klaus and Maria Magdelena (Thoresen) G.; m. Isabel Edwina MacMaster, Feb. 25, 1950; children: Ingrid, Christopher, Karen. Grad., Tech. Coll., Horten, Norway, 1945; B.M.E., McGill U., Can., 1949, postgrad, 1951. With Consol. Bathurst Ltd., Que., 1951-70; v.p. prodn., gen. mgr. N.S. Forest Industries, Port Hawkesbury, 1970-73; v.p. mfg. Fraser Cos. Ltd., Edmundston, N.B., Can., 1973-75, sr. v.p. ops., 1975-76; exec. v.p. Fraser Inc., Edmundston, 1980-82, pres., chief operating officer, 1982—; dir. Island Paper Mills, New Westminster, B.C., 1983—; chmn. bd. J.P. Levesque & Sons Inc., Ashland, Maine, 1982—; mem. local adv. bd. Central Trust Co., Edmundston, N.B., 1979—; dir. Pulp and Paper Research Inst. Can., Montreal, 1983—. Bd. dirs. Canadian-Scandinavian Found., Montreal, 1974-75, v.p., Montreal, 1975-77, pres., Montreal, 1978. Served with Norwegian Underground Army, 1941-45. Mem. N.B. Forest Products Assn. (dir. 1983—), Canadian Pulp and Paper Assn., Corp. of Profl. Engrs. of Province of Que., Tech. Assn. Pulp and Paper Industry, Paper Industry Mgmt. Assn., Am. Mgmt. Assn. Lodge: Rotary. Home: 28 Lawson St Edmundston NB Canada E3V 1Z4 Office: Fraser Inc 27 Rice St Edmundston NB Canada E3V 1S9

GROTZ, WILLIAM ARTHUR, r.r. cons.; b. N.Y.C., July 1, 1904; s. William and Edythe Eleanor (Love) G.; m. Helen Van Dusen, July 4, 1934; children—Patricia Ann (Mrs. Daniel Baker), W. Arthur. B.C.S. summa cum laude, N.Y. U., 1929. In selling and statis. work, 1921-30; investment analyst, later in charge railroad reorgn. and bus. relations with railroads Chase Nat. Bank, 1930-45, v.p., 1945-52; pres., dir., mem. exec. com. Western Md. Ry. Co., Balt., 1952-69; spl. adviser to trustees Boston & Me. Corp., 1970; profl. r.r. cons.; v.p. Pa. Co., 1974-80; Chmn. Met. Transit Authority Md., 1961-69. Former Mem. exec. com. Greater Balt. Com.; trustee Goucher Coll.; former dir. Balt. Symphony, Balt. Opera. Mem. Nat. Def. Transp. Assn. (life), Balt. Assn. Commerce. Presbyn. Clubs: Elkridge, Baltimore Country. Home: 3900 N Charles St Baltimore MD 21218 Office: 101 E Redwood St Baltimore MD 21202

GROTZINGER, LAUREL ANN, university dean; b. Truman, Minn., Apr. 15, 1935; d. Edward F. and Marian Gertrude (Greeley) G. B.A., Carleton Coll., 1957; M.S., U. Ill., 1958, Ph.D., 1964. Instr., asst. librarian Ill. State U., 1958-62; asst. prof. Western Mich. U., Kalamazoo, 1964-66, assoc. prof., 1966-68, prof., 1968—, asst. dir. Sch. Librarianship, 1965-72, dean/chief research officer Grad. Coll., 1979—, interim dir. Sch. Library and Info. Sci., 1982—. Author: The Power and the Dignity, Scarecrow, 1966; editorial bd.: Jour. Edn. for Librarianship, 1973-77, Dictionary Am. Library Biography, 1975-77; contbr. articles to profl. jours. Mem. AAUW, ALA (sec. treas. Library History Roundtable 1973-74, vice chmn., chmn.-elect 1983-84), Acad. Mgmt., Assn. Library Info. Sci. Edn., Am. Assn. Higher Edn., Council Grad. Schs., Mich. Council Grad. Deans (chmn. 1983—), Nat. Council Research Adminstrs., Soc. Research Adminstrs., Mich. Acad. Sci., Arts and Letters (mem.-at-large, exec. com. 1980—, pres.-elect 1981—), Phi Beta Kappa (pres. SW Mich. chpt. 1977-78), Beta Phi Mu, Pi Delta Epsilon, Alpha Beta Alpha, Delta Kappa Gamma. Home: 2729 Mockingbird Dr Kalamazoo MI 49008

GROUSSMAN, RAYMOND G., diversified utility and energy company executive; b. Price, Utah, Dec. 15, 1935; s. Raymond K. and Gene E. (Goetzman) G.; m. Marilyn Kaye Jensen, Mar. 16, 1964; children: Katherine Anne, Laura Kaye, Daniel Ray, Adam J. B.S., U. Utah, 1961, J.D., 1966. Bar: Utah 1965, U.S. Supreme Ct. 1978. Police officer Salt Lake City Police Dept., 1962-66; mem. firm Amoss & Groussman, Salt Lake City, 1966-69; staff atty. Utah Legal Services, 1969-70; chief dep. Salt Lake County atty., 1970-71; assoc. Pugsley, Hayes, Watkiss, Campbell & Cowley, Salt Lake City, 1971-74; gen. counsel Mountain Fuel Supply Co., Salt Lake City, 1974—, v.p., 1977—; dir. Wexpro Co. Bd. dirs. Children's Service Soc. Utah, 1976-77; trustee Ft. Douglas Mil. Mus., 1976—; bd. advisers Energy Law Center, U. Utah Coll. Law, 1978—; mem. criminal law revision com. Utah Legis. Council; bd. dirs. Utah Legal Services, 1970-78, United Way of Salt Lake City, 1982—. Served with U.S. Army, 1957-60; lt. comdr. USCGR, 1967—. Mem. Am. Bar Assn., Fed. Energy Bar Assn., Am. Gas Assn., Pacific Coast Gas Assn. (chmn. legal adv. council 1979-80), Salt Lake County Bar Assn., Salt Lake Legal Defenders Assn. (dir. 1978—), Salt Lake City C. of C., Sigma Alpha Epsilon, Delta Theta Phi. Office: Mountain Fuel Supply Co 180 E 100 S St Salt Lake City UT 84139

GROUT, GORDON S., banker; b. 1937. B.A., Westminister Coll., 1959. With Wells Fargo Bank N.A., 1963—, asst. v.p., 1970-73, v.p., 1973-77, mgr., 1977-79, mgr. consumer credit div., then v.p. credit mgmt., 1979-80, mgr. credit tng. dept., 1980-81, with credit policy group, then dep. group head, 1981, sr. v.p., 1981-83, exec. v.p., 1983—. Served to capt. U.S. Army, 1959-63. Office: Wells Fargo Bank NA 464 California St San Francisco CA 94163 *

GROUT, VERNON M., manufacturing company executive; b. 1918; married. A.B., Clark U., 1928; M.B.A., Harvard U., 1941. C.P.A., N.Y. Mem. staff Lybrand, Ross Bros. & Montgomery, 1946-55; with Diamond Internat. Corp., N.Y.C., 1955—, asst. treas., 1962-65, comptroller, 1965-68, treas., 1968-70, v.p., treas., 1970-77, v.p., fin., from 1977, now exec. v.p., chief fin. officer, also dir. Served with USNR, World War II. Office: Diamond Internat Corp 733 3d Ave New York NY 10017 *

GROVE, ANDREW S., electronics company executive; b. 1936; m. With Fairchild Camera and Instrument Co., 1963-67; pres., chief operating officer Intel Corp., Santa Clara, Calif., 1968—, dir. Office: Intel Corp 3065 Bowers Ave Santa Clara CA 95051 *

GROVE, BRANDON HAMBRIGHT, JR., diplomat; b. Chgo., Apr. 8, 1929; s. Brandon Hambright and Helen Julia (Gasparska) G.; m. Marie Cheremeteff, 1959 (div. 1983); children: John C., Catherine C., Paul C., Mark C. A.B., Bard Coll., 1950; M.P.A., Princeton U., 1952. Joined U.S. Fgn. Service, 1959; vice consul, Abidjan, Ivory Coast, also Upper Volta, Niger, and Dahomey, 1959-61, staff asst. to undersec. state, 1961-62, spl. asst. to dep. undersec. state for adminstrn., 1962-63, spl. asst. to Am. ambassador, New Delhi, India, 1963-65, U.S. liaison officer to city govt., Berlin, Germany, 1965-69; dir. Office Panamanian Affairs, State Dept., 1969-71; mem. Sr. Seminar in Fgn. Policy, 1971-72; dep. dir. State Dept. policy planning staff, Washington; also staff dir. Under Secretaries Com. of Nat. Security Council, 1972-74; chargé d' affaires, then dep. chief of mission Am. Embassy to German Dem. Republic, 1974-76; fgn. service sr. insp. Dept. State, 1976-78, acting insp. gen., 1978; dep. asst. sec. state for Inter-Am. affairs, 1978-80, consul gen., Jerusalem, 1980-83; asst. instr. Princeton U., 1953. Served to lt. USNR, 1954-57. Recipient Meritorious Honor award State Dept., 1970. Mem. Am. Fgn. Service Assn. Club: Princeton of N.Y.C. Office: Dept of State Washington DC 20520

GROVE, DAVID LAWRENCE, economist; b. Boston, Apr. 25, 1918; s. Lawrence Roger and Emily (Becker) G.; m. Lois Pawlowski, May 13, 1942; 1 dau., Carolyn Anne. Grad., Boston Latin Sch., 1935; A.B. magna cum laude, Harvard, 1940, M.A., 1942, M.P.A., 1942, Ph.D., 1952. Economist Fed. Res. Bd., 1944-52; adviser monetary and banking problems, Paraguay, 1944, 51, Ecuador, 1947, 57, 58, Guatemala, 1945, 46, 56, 62, 65, Philippines, 1948, 49, Colombia, Chile, 1950, Israel, 1964; chief economist Bank Am., San Francisco, 1952-58, v.p., head internat. relations, 1961-62, v.p., head bond investment dept., 1962-63, v.p., 1959-63; v.p., econ. advisor Fed. Res. Bank San Francisco, 1963-64; v.p., economist Blyth & Co., N.Y., 1965-66; chief economist IBM, 1966-69, v.p., chief economist, 1969-78; pres. David L. Grove Ltd., 1978—; sr. economic advisor Marine Midland Bank, 1978-83; lectr. Am. U., 1952, Center of Latin Am. Monetary Studies, Mexico, 1954-56, 58, 64, 66; dir. Internorth Co., Gen. Pub. Utilities Corp., Aetna Variable Fund, Inc., Aetna Encore Fund, Inc., Aetna Income Shares, Inc.; Mem. Time Mag. Bd. of Economists, 1969-80, N.Y. State Council Econ. Advisers, 1973-74, several U.S. Govt. adv. coms.; bd. dirs. Nat. Bur. Econ. Research; trustee Com. Econ. Devel., N.Y. Med. Coll., 1972-75. Author articles in field.; Mem. editorial bd.: Fin. Analysts Jour. Served with OSS, 1942-44. Decorated officer Order of Merit, Ecuador). Mem. Am. Econ. Assn., Internat. C. of C. of U.S. (dir. 1967-78), U.S. Council Internat. Bus. (pres. 1978—), Phi Beta Kappa. Episcopalian. Home: 5 The Knoll Armonk NY 10504 Office: 1212 Ave of Americas 21st Floor New York NY 10036

GROVE, EDWARD RYNEAL, artist, sculptor; b. Martinsburg, W.Va., Aug. 14, 1912; s. Harry Muth and Bertha Mae (Sigler) G.; m. Jean Virginia Donner, June 24, 1936; children: David Donner, Eric Donner. Art studies, Nat. Sch. Art, Washington, 1933-34, Corcoran Sch. Art, Washington, 1934-37, 40-45, Robert Brackman, 1946. Die sinker, 1936-40; vignette and portrait engraver Bur. Engraving and Printing, Washington, 1940-47, Security-Columbian Banknote Co., Phila., 1947-62; sculptor-engraver U.S. Mint, Phila., 1962-65. Free lance artist, West Palm Beach, Fla., 1965—, one-man shows, Nat. Philatelic Mus., Phila., 1954, Phila. Art Alliance, 1960, Norton Gallery Art, West Palm Beach, 1971, works exhibited, Cayuga Mus. History and Art, Auburn, N.Y., 1964, Episcopal Acad. Gallery, Phila., 1966, nat. and regional ann. exhibits; represented in permanent collections, Met. Mus. Art, Carnegie Inst., Corcoran Art Gallery, Miami Heart Inst., Mus. Medallic Art, Cracow, Poland, U. Pa. Div. Grad. Medicine, Pangborn Corp., Hagerstown, Md., Pa. Hist. Soc., Phila., Am. Bag & Paper Corp., Phila., U.S. Dept. Navy, Smithsonian Instn., Rehab. Inst. Chgo., The Citadel, Charleston, S.C., Washington Cathedral, Ch. of Bethesda-by-the-Sea, Palm Beach, Fla., Coventry (Eng.) Cathedral, Imperial Palace, Tokyo, Dr. Armand Hammer, Los Angeles, Portsmouth Royal Naval Mus., (Eng.); instr. drawing and portraiture, Flagler Art Center, West Palm Beach, 1972-73; works include Congressional gold medal for Bob Hope, 1963, World War II medal series, 1966-70; works include (with Jean Donner Grove) mural Ch. of Holy Comforter, Drexel Hill, Pa.; works include four coin set for Knights of Malta, 1965; instr.: alphabet medal Soc. Medalists, 1973, Imperial Japanese visit medal, 1975, Soyuz-Apollo medal, 1975, Am. Legion armed forces bicentennial medal series, 1975, bronze Bicentennial monument; E. Sterling Nichol meml. plaque, Miami Heart Inst. Benefactor award, 1978, John Paul Jones nat. medal, U.S. Capital Hist. Soc. medal, 1979, Natural World medal Soc. Medalists, 1980, Norton Gallery medal of Honor, 1981; works include (with J.F. Clapp, Jr.) 91st anniversary medal Am. Numis. Assn., 1982; works include (with Jean Donner Grove) Am. Express goldpiece, 1983; works include others; Contbr. articles to profl. jours. and books. Pres. Palm Beach Animal Rescue League, 1979-80. Recipient bronze medals Washington Landscape Club, 1945, 53, Grumbacher watercolor award Cumberland Valley Art Exhibit, Hagerstown, 1965, Lindsey Morris meml. prize Nat. Sculpture Soc., 1967, Bennett meml. prize, 1971; gold medal Am. Numis. Assn., 1969; Heath Lit. cert. of merit, 1979. Fellow Nat. Sculpture Soc.; mem. NAD (assoc.), Artists Equity Assn. (nat. v.p. 1965-67), Engravers Guild, Steel and Copper Plate Engravers League Phila. (pres. 1957-59), Phila. Sketch Club, Am. Numis. Assn., Token and Medal Soc., Am. Medallic Sculpture Assn., Art Mus. Palm Beaches, Soc. Four Arts, English-Speaking Union, Mensa, Knights Malta (Chevalier, congress del. Florence, Italy 1983). Episcopalian. Home and Studio: Sea Lake Studio 3215 S Flagler Dr West Palm Beach FL 33405

GROVE, ERNEST L., JR., utility executive; b. Martinsburg, W.Va., 1924; (married). B.A., Denison U., Granville, Ohio, 1947; M.B.A., U. Pa., 1949; J.D., U. Conn., 1959. Vice pres., chief fin. and acctg. officer Conn. Light & Power Co., 1965-66, All N.E. Utilities Systems Co., 1966-72; exec. v.p. N.E. Utilities Service Co., 1972-75; sr. exec. v.p. fin. Detroit Edison Co., 1975-80, vice chmn. bd., chief fin. officer, 1980—, also dir.; v.p., dir. Midwest Energy Resources Co., St. Clair Energy Corp., Edison Illuminating Co., Detroit, Peninsula Electric Light Co., Washtenaw Energy Corp.; dir. Asso. Electric and Gas Services Ltd. Office: Detroit Edison Co 2000 2d Ave Detroit MI 48226 *

GROVE, JEAN DONNER (MRS. EDWARD R. GROVE), sculptor; b. Washington, May 15, 1912; d. Frederick Gregory and Georgia V. (Gartrell) Donner; m. Edward R. Grove, June 24, 1936; children: David Donner, Eric Donner. Student, Cornell U., 1932, Hill Sch. of Sculpture, 1934-35, Corcoran Sch. of Art, 1935-37, 42-44, Cath. U. Am., 1936-37, Phila. Mus. Art Sch., 1967; B.S., Wilson Tchrs. Coll., 1939. Exhibited one-man shows, Wilson Tchrs. Coll., Washington, 1939, Grove Family Exhbns., Cayuga Mus. History and Art, Auburn, N.Y., 1964, Episcopal Acad. Gallery, Phila., 1966, group shows, Pa. Acad. Fine Arts, Phila., 1947, 48, 51, 53, N.A.D., N.Y.C., 1949, 78, 81, 83, Nat. Sculpture Soc. at Archtl. League, N.Y.C., Topeka, 1957, Lever House, N.Y.C., 1974, 75, Equitable Gallery, N.Y.C., 1976, 78, 83, Art U.S.A., Madison Sq. Garden, N.Y.C., 1958, Corcoran Gallery Art, Washington, 1943-47, Internat. Gallery, Washington, 1946, Phila. Mus. Art, 1955, 59, 62, Phila. Art Alliance, 1957, 60, 66, Phila. Civic Ctr., 1968, Flagler Art Ctr., West Palm Beach, Fla., 1972, Norton Gallery Art, West Palm Beach, 1974, 81; represented in permanent collections, Rosenwald Collection, Phila., Ch. of Holy Comforter, Drexel Hill, Pa., Fine Arts Commn., City Hall, Phila.; sculptor numerous portrait commns., garden figures and fountains, 1940—; (with E.R. Grove) Am. Express Goldpiece, 1982. Recipient 1st prize sculpture Nat. Mus. Washington, 1946, 1st Prize Sculpture Arts Club, 1946, Portrait Prize, 1947, Morris Goodman award John Herron Art Mus., Indpls., 1957, Competition prize for design and sculpture Artists Equity Phila. award, 1960, Human award Animal Rescue League of Palm Beach, 1974, 80, Tallix Foundry award NSS Bicentennial Exhbn. Equitable Gallery, N.Y.C., 1976, Acad. of Italy with gold medal, 1979, Golden Centaur award, 1982. Mem. Nat. Sculpture Soc., Artists Equity Assn. (dir. Phila. chpt. 1964-66), Phila. Art Alliance, Soc. of Four Arts, Norton Gallery Art, Soc. Washington Artists, English Speaking Union, Animal Rescue League of Palm Beach (com. chmn. 1972—, dir. 1975—), St. Mary's Guild of Episcopal Ch. Women (v.p. 1974-76), Nat. Acad. Design (assoc.), Kappa Delta Pi. Club: Poinciana (Palm Beach). Home and Studio: Sea-Lake Studio 3215 S Flagler Dr West Palm Beach FL 33405

GROVE, WILLIAM JOHNSON, physician, medical educator; b. Ottawa, Ill., Mar. 23, 1920; s. Joseph Roy and Florence (Johnson) G.; m. Betty Pedigo, Mar. 23, 1944; children: William Johnson, Pamela J. Holly Lynn. B.S., U. Ill., 1941, M.D., 1943, M.S. in Surgery, 1949. Intern U. Ill. Research and Ednl. Hosps., 1944, asst. resident surgery, 1949-50, chief resident surgery, 1951-52; asst. resident surgery Hines VA Hosp., 1950-51; mem. faculty U. Ill. Coll. Medicine, 1951—, prof. surgery, 1964-81, prof. emeritus, 1981—, dean, 1968-70, exec. dean, 1970-76, vice chancellor for acad. affairs, 1976-80, vice chancellor emeritus, 1981—, acting dir., 1980-81; attending surgeon U. Ill. Hosp.; cons. W.K. Kellogg Found., 1981—. Author numerous articles in field. Served to capt. AUS, 1944-46. Fellow A.C.S.; mem. AMA, Assn. Am. Med. Colls., Central, Chgo. surg. socs., Soc. Univ. Surgeons, Am. Heart Assn., Warren H. Cole Soc., Soc. Clin. Surgery, Am. Surg. Assn., Inst. Medicine Chgo., Sigma Xi, Alpha Omega Alpha, Phi Delta Epsilon. Home: 1152 Lakeside Dr Battle Creek MI 49015 Office: 400 North Ave Battle Creek MI 49016

GROVENSTEIN, ERLING, JR., educator, chemist; b. Miami, Fla., Nov. 12, 1924; s. Erling and Lois (Nesbitt) G.; m. Catherine Gangwer, Sept. 4, 1954 (dec. 1961); children: John Nesbitt, Alfred Enloe; m. Lillian Anne Enloe, June 23, 1962. B.S. in Chemistry, Ga. Sch. Tech., 1944; Ph.D. in Organic Chemistry, M.I.T., 1948. Research assoc. M.I.T., Cambridge, summer 1948; mem. faculty Ga. Inst. Tech., 1948—, Julius Brown prof. chemistry, 1965—; research participant Oak Ridge Nat. Lab., summers 1949, 54. Mem. Am. Chem. Soc. (vis. asso. com. profl. tng.), Chem. Soc. (London), Ga. Acad. Sci., AAUP, Sigma Xi (Monie Ferst research award Ga. Inst. Tech. chpt. 1956), Phi Kappa Phi, Alpha Chi Sigma. Presbyterian (elder). Home: 2424 Briarmoor Rd NE Atlanta GA 30345

GROVER, CHARLES WYMAN, diplomat; b. Waltham, Mass., July 24, 1928; s. Eugene Sears and Louise (Wyman) G.; m. Janet Hilma Halsten, Aug. 25, 1957; children: Marisa, Charles, Michael, Ellen. B.A., Antioch Coll., 1951; M.A., U. Oreg., 1953; postgrad. in Latin Am. studies, Tulane U., 1965-66, Stanford U., 1970-71. Joined fgn. service Dept. State, 1956; consul, Medellin, Columbia, 1971-73; dep. exec. dir. Bur. Latin Am. Affairs, Dept. State, Washington, 1973-75, personnel officer, 1975-78; dep. chief of mission, Santiago, Chile, 1978-82, consul gen., Guavaquil, Ecuador, 1982—. Served as cpl. U.S. Army, 1953-55. Mem. Am. Fgn. Service Assn., New Eng. Historic Geneal. Soc. Home: Mills Shore Rd Hampstead NH 03841 Office: Am Consulate Gen 9 de Octubre y Garcia Moreno Guayaquil Ecuador Office: Am Consulate Gen APO Miami FL 34039

GROVER, EDWARD D., actor; b. Huntington Park, Calif., Oct. 23, 1932; s. A.D. and Edna Florence (Rhoads) G.; m. Brita G. Brown, June 7, 1965; children—Tony, Heidi. B.S., U. Toledo, 1957; postgrad. in drama, U. Tex., 1957-58. Appeared with, Antioch Shakespeare Festival, 1957, Hedgerow Theatre, Moylan, Pa., Oreg. Shakespeare Festival, 1958-59, various Broadway and off-Broadway appearances; appeared on: TV, including series Baretta; also films, including Serpico. Served with U.S. Army, 1954-56. Office: care Beakel & Jennings Agy Artists' Mgrs 427 N Canon Dr Suite 205 Beverly Hills CA 90210

GROVER, EVE RUTH, banker; b. Germany, Mar. 9, 1929; came to U.S., 1946, naturalized, 1951; d. George and Gisa (Deutsch) Bergmann;, Sept. 19, 1948; children—Ronald George, Jeffrey Louis. Grad. degree in bank mgmt, U. Va., 1974; grad., Am. Inst. Banking, 1973. With 1st Nat. City Bank, N.Y.C., 1946-51, Citizens Bank of Takoma Park, Md., 1956-60, Am. Security & Trust Co., Washington, 1960-64; asst. br. mgr. Public Nat. Bank, Washington, 1964-69; asst. treas., br. mgr. Union Trust Co. of Md., Balt., 1969-71; v.p. State Nat. Bank, Bethesda, Md., 1971-78, dir. women's hdqrs., 1975-78; pres., chief exec. officer 1st Women's Bank Md., Rockville, 1978—; mem. Md. Small Bus. Devel. Financing Authority. Mem. Women's Commn., Montgomery County, Md.; bd. dirs. Montgomery County Community Child Care Council, 1976-77, Girls Clubs of Greater Washington, 1976-77; mem. adv. bd. Mt. Vernon Coll.; mem. Rockville Econs. and Amenity Adv. Com.; vice chmn. Md. Small Bus. Devel. Financing Authority. Recipient award for contbns. during Fed. Women's Week Naval Sea Systems Command, 1976, award of appreciation for participation in Internat. Women's Year program Md.-Nat. Capital Park and Planning Commn. Mem. Am. Inst. Banking (dir., award for service as trustee 1975-76), Nat. Council Career Women (dir. 1976-77), Nat. Assn. Bank Women, Assn. Women Bus. Owners, Federally Employed Women (hon.), Rockville C. of C. (dir. 1979-81), Bus. and Profl. Women. Democrat. Coordinator, speaker at seminars related to women and fin. Office: 1800 Rockville Pike PO Box 2022 Rockville MD 20852

GROVER, NORMAN LAMOTTE, theologian, philosopher; b. Topeka, Feb. 9, 1928; s. LaMotte and Virginia Grace (Alspach) G.; m. Anne Stottler, June 24, 1950; children: Jennifer Jean, Peter Neal, Rebecca Louise, Sandra Christine. B. Mech. Engring., Rensselaer Poly. Inst., 1948; B.D., Yale, 1951, S.T.M., 1952, Ph.D., 1957. Mem. faculty, chaplain Hollins (Va.) Coll., 1954-57, asst. prof. religion, 1956-57; ordained to ministry Presbyn. Ch., 1952; head dept. philosophy and religion Va. Poly. Inst. and State U., 1957-75, prof. philosophy and religion, 1961—; Mem. supervising com. So. leadership tng. project Fund for Republic, 1955-56; asso. Danforth Found., 1958—, sr. asso., 1962—, chmn. Va., N.C. and S.C. conf., 1962—; psychotherapeutic counsellor Blacksburg Community Counselling Center, 1962-65. Mem. AAUP (pres. Va. Poly. Inst. and State U. chpt. 1961-62, 81-82, sec.-treas. chpt. 1959-60, 77-80, v.p. chpt. 1960-61, 80-81), NAACP, Am. Philos. Assn., Va. Philos. Assn. (pres. 1969), So. Soc. Philosophy and Psychology, Am. Acad. Religion, Va., Montgomery County councils human relations, ACLU, Am. Acad. Arts and Scis. Club: Yale (Va.). Home: 705 Burruss Dr NW Blacksburg VA 24060 Office: Dept Religion 310 Patton Hall Va Poly Inst and State U Blacksburg VA 24061

GROVER, ROBERT JOHN, university official; b. LaPorte, Ind., Oct. 27, 1942; s. John Thomas and Gladys Marie (Hartnett) G.; m. Susan Katherine Shaw, Nov. 11, 1966 (div. July 1973); 1 son, Robert Shawn; m. Connie Lou Peeples, June 7, 1975. B.A. in Edn., Ball State U., 1965; M.L.S., Ind. U., 1970, Ph.D., 1976. Media coordiantor Westville Pub. Schs. (Ind.), 1968-70; librarian Oak Park River Forest High Sch., Oak Park, Ill., 1970-74; asst. prof. Sch. Library Sci. U. So. Calif., Los Angeles, 1976-79, asst. dean Sch. Library and Info. Mgmt., 1979-81; dean Sch. Library and Info. Mgmt. Emporia State U. (Kans.), 1981—. Editor: periodical Children's Film Internat., 1977, 79, 80, Great Plains Libraries, 1982. Exec. bd. Am. Ctr. Films for Children, Los Angeles, 1979—; dep. dir. 8th Los Angeles Internat. Children's Film Festival, 1979; co-chmn. Internat. Children's Film Festival, Emporia, 1983; mem. C. of C.-Emporia State Univ. High Tech. Task Force, 1983. Mem. ALA, Assn. for Library Service to Children (chmn. film evaluation com. 1981-83), Calif. Media and Library Educators Assn. (hon. pres. So. sect. 1980-81), Beta Phi Mu (exec. bd. internat. 1983—), Pi Lambda Theta. Lodge: Lions (Emporia exec. council 1982—). Office: Sch Library and Info Mgmt Emporia State U Emporia KS 66801

GROVER, ROBERT LAWRENCE, tool co. exec.; b. Chgo., Sept. 28, 1910; s. Donald and Martha (Bates) G.; m. Ruth W. Dean, May 12, 1934; children—Kathleen C., Patricia R., Barbara E., Robert Lawrence, Donald D., Margaret E. B.S., Northwestern U., 1931, J.D., 1934; LL.D., Carthage Coll., 1973; D.B.A., Piedmont Coll., 1978. Bar: Ill. bar 1934, Wis. bar 1943. Practice in, Chgo., 1934-42; with Snap-on Tools Corp., Kenosha, Wis., 1942—, exec. v.p., 1964-66, pres., 1966-74, chmn. bd., 1974-77, also dir.; dir. Twin Disc, Inc. Pres. Kenosha County council Boy Scouts Am., 1960-65. Recipient Silver Beaver award Boy Scouts Am. Mem. SAR, Order of Coif, Phi Beta Kappa. Congregationalist. Home: 4 Belleview Blvd Belleair FL 33516 Office: 8028 28th Ave Kenosha WI 53140

GROVES, FRANKLIN NELSON, business executive; b. Mpls., Dec. 28, 1930; s. Frank Malvon and Hazel Olive (Nelson) G.; m. Carolyn Mary Thomas, July 31, 1954; children: Catherine Mary Groves Gangelhoff, Franklin Nelson, Elizabeth Ann. B.A., U. Minn., 1954. With S.J. Groves & Sons Co., Mpls., 1954—, v.p., treas., 1964-69, pres., 1969—, chmn. bd., 1971—, also dir., pres. subs. corps., 1964—. Pres. trustees Groves Found.; bd. dirs. Groves Learning Center. Served to 1st lt. USAF, 1954-56. Mem. Am. Saddle Horse Breeders Assn. (dir.), Moles, Beavers. Mem. Community Ch. Clubs: Mpls. Athletic, Thoroughbred of Am. Home: 1482 Hunter Dr Wayzata MN 55391 Office: PO Box 1267 10000 Highway 55 W Minneapolis MN 55440

GROVES, GEORGE L., JR., air freight service co. exec.; b. Springfield, Mass., Sept. 22, 1928; s. George L. and Elida Octavia (Thulin) G.; m. June E. Kohler, Aug. 26, 1950; children—Craig George, Thomas Edward, Nancy Lynn. B.S. in Bus. Adminstrn, Am. Internat. Coll., 1949. Vice pres. sales Asso. Transport, Inc., N.Y.C., 1949-67; exec. v.p., chief exec. officer Adley Express, Inc., New Haven, 1967-70; exec. v.p. Acme Fast Freight, Inc., N.Y.C., 1970-73; pres. Air Cargo, Inc., Annapolis, Md., 1973—. Office: Air Cargo Inc 1819 Bay Ridge Ave Annapolis MD 21403

GROVES, HARRY EDWARD, lawyer, educator; b. Manitou Springs, Colo., Sept. 4, 1921; s. Harry A. and Dorothy A. (Cave) G.; m. Dolores Ruth Hale (div. 1947); 1 son, Sheridon Hale; m. Evelyn Frances Apperson, Dec. 23, 1949. B.A., U. Colo., 1943; J.D., U. Chgo., 1949; LL.M., Harvard, 1959. Bar: N.C., Tex. and Ohio, also U.S. Supreme Ct. Staff asst. Am. Council Race Relations, Chgo., 1949; asst. prof. law N.C. Coll. Law, 1949-51; pvt. practice law, Fayetteville, N.C., 1952-56; prof., dean Sch. Law, Tex. So. U., 1956-61; head dept. law U. Singapore, 1962-64, dean, 1963-64; dir. minority groups project Assn. Am. Law Schs., 1964-67; vis. prof. constl. law U. Malaya, Singapore, 1960-62; vis. prof. law U. Wash., 1965-66; pres. Central State U., Wilberforce, Ohio, 1965-68; pvt. practice law, Dayton, Ohio, 1970-74; prof. law U. Cin., 1968-70, U. Dayton, 1974-76; dean N.C. Central U. Law Sch., 1976-81; Henry P. Brandis prof. law U. N.C. Sch. Law, 1981—; vis. prof. U. Utah, 1968, U.N.C., 1970; referee Montgomery County Domestic Relations Ct., 1972-74. Author: The Constitution of Malaysia; Contbr. articles to profl. jours. City councilman, Fayetteville, 1955-56; Chmn. bd. dirs. Dayton-Miami Valley Consortium, 1968; pres. bd. dirs. Legal Services of N.C., 1982—. Served with AUS, 1943-46, 50-51. Home: Route 3 Box 274-A Durham NC 27713 Office: Sch Law U NC Chapel Hill NC 27514 *I have tried to deal lovingly with my family, thoughtfully with my friends, honestly with my clients and associates.*

GROVES, JOHN TAYLOR, III, chemist, educator; b. New Rochelle, N.Y., Mar. 27, 1943; s. John Taylor and Frances (Gaylor) G.; m. Karen Joan Morrison, Apr. 15, 1967; children—Jay, Kevin. B.S., M.I.T., 1965; Ph.D., Columbia U., 1969. Asst. prof. U. Mich., Ann Arbor, 1969-76, asso. prof., 1976-79, prof. organic chemistry, 1979—; cons. in field; dir. Mich. Center for Catalytic and Surface Scis., Ann Arbor, 1981—. Contbr. articles to profl. jours. Recipient Phi Lambda Upsilon award for outstanding teaching and leadership, 1978. Mem. Am. Chem. Soc., N.Y. Acad. Sci., Sigma Xi. Office: Univ of Mich Dept Chemistry Ann Arbor MI 48109

GROVES, MICHAEL, banker; b. London, Jan. 2, 1936; U.S., 1969; s. Percy Reginald and Lily Sarah (Bentley) G.; m. Monica Rosario, June 8, 1963; children: Christopher, Carolyn, Jonathan. Grad., Inst. Chartered Accts., London, 1958; licentiate and teaching cert., Royal Acad. Music, 1959, Sch. Bank Adminstrn., U. Madison, Wis., 1976. Chief acct. Malaysian Estate Agys. Group Ltd., Kuala Lumpur, Malaysia, 1959-61; chief acct. Flour Mills Nigeria, Ltd., Lagos, 1961-62; asst. fin. mgr. Fábrica de Tejidos La Union Ltda, Lima, Peru, 1963-69; asst. to comptroller internat. First Wis. Corp., Milw., 1969-70, asst. auditor, 1970-72, loan rev. officer, 1972-79; sr. v.p. Am. South Bancorp., Birmingham, 1979-82; v.p., mgr. credit review Mercantile Trust Co., St. Louis, 1982—; mem. faculty Sch. Bank Adminstrn., U. Madison, 1979—. Author: Loan Review: A Guide, 1978, mus. compositions, arrangements. Mus. dir., com. mem. Selangor Philharm. Soc., Kuala Lumpur, 1959-61, Brit. Council Activities, Lima, 1963-69. Fellow Inst. Chartered Accts. Eng. and Wales; mem. Robert Morris Assos. (mem. faculty loan rev. seminars 1977-80, chmn. 1978-79), Bank Adminstrn. Inst. (faculty, audit course 1970-74). Office: PO Box 524 St Louis MO 63166

GROVES, RAY JOHN, accountant; b. Cleve., Sept. 7, 1935; m. Anne Keating, Aug. 18, 1962; children: David, Philip, Matthew. B.S., Ohio State U., 1957. C.P.A., Ohio. With Ernst & Whinney, Cleve., 1957—, ptnr., 1966-71, nat. ptnr., 1971-77, chmn., chief exec. officer, 1977—; mem. adv. com. corp. disclosure SEC, 1976-78; mem. adv. council Coll. Adminstrv. Sci., Ohio State U., U. Chgo. Grad. Sch. Bus. Councilman, City of Lyndhurst (Ohio), 1969-72; chmn. bd. trustees Leadership Cleve., 1977-79; trustee Hawken Sch.; vice chmn. bd. trustees Ursuline Coll. Mem. Am. Inst. C.P.A.s (dir., SEC com.), Nat. Assn. Securities Dealers (bd. govs.); mem. Nat. Assn. Accts. Republican. Clubs: Union, Cleve. Athletic, Pepper Pike Country, Mayfield Country (Cleve.); Board Room, Links (N.Y.C.); Metropolitan, Internat., Capitol Hill (Washington); Laurel Valley Country. Home: 50 Windrush Dr Moreland Hills OH 44022 680 Madison Ave New York NY Office: 2000 National City Center Cleveland OH 44114 also 153 E 53 St New York NY 10022

GROVES, WALLACE, financier; b. Norfolk, Va., Mar. 20, 1901; s. James S. and Lillie (Edwards) G.; m. Georgette Cusson; children: Gordon, Gene, Graham, Gary, Gayle. M.A., B.Sc., J.D., LL.M., Georgetown U., Washington, 1924, D.Hum. (hon.), 1981, LL.D., Ursinus Coll., Collegeville, Pa. Bar: Admitted Md. bar 1925. Practiced law, until 1931; then went to N.Y. to engage in reorganization and mgmt. industrial and financial concerns; formerly pres. and chmn. bd. Phoenix Securities Corp.; ret. chmn. bd. Grand Bahama Port Authority Ltd.; Founder Wallace Groves Aquaculture Found. Address: PO Box 5 Freeport Grand Bahama Island Bahamas

GROWE, JOAN ANDERSON, state ofcl.; b. Mpls., Sept. 28, 1935; d. Arthur F. and Lucille M. (Brown) Anderson; children: Michael, Colleen, David, Patrick. B.S., St. Cloud State U., 1956; cert. in spl. edn, U. Minn., 1964; exec. mgmt. program State and local govt., Harvard U., 1979. Tchr. elem. pub. schs., Bloomington, Minn., 1956-58, tchr. for exceptional children elementary pub. schs., St. Paul, 1964-65; spl. edn. tchr. St. Anthony (Minn.) Pub. Schs., 1965-66; mem. Minn. Ho. of Reps., 1973-75; sec. of state Minn., St. Paul, 1975—; mem. adv. com. Fed. Election Commn.; mem. Judicial Planning Com.; exec. council Minn. State Bd. Investment. Active Minn. Nuclear Freeze Campaign. Recipient Minn. Sch. Bell award, 1977, YMCA Outstanding Achievement award, 1978. Mem. Nat. Assn. Secs. of State (pres. 1978-79), Bus. and Profl. Women, Women's Polit. Caucus, League Women Voters, Common Cause, Women Against Mil. Madness, Democratic Statewide Elected Ofcls., Citizen's League, Minn. Shares for Hunger, Minn. Assn. Retarded Citizens, AAUW, Zonta. Mem. Democratic Farm Labor Party. Roman Catholic. Office: 180 State Office Bldg Saint Paul MN 55155

GRUB, PHILLIP DONALD, business educator; b. Medical Lake, Wash., Aug. 8, 1936; s. Carl Dryer and Barbara Rosalie (Johnson) G. B.A. in Econs. and Bus. Edn. with highest honors, Eastern Wash. State Coll., 1953; M.B.A. (Scottish Rite Found. fellow), George Washington U., 1960; D.B.A. (Am. Security and Trust scholar), George Washington U., 1964. Pres. Phillip D. Grub, Inc., Spokane, Wash., 1953-54; cons. to small businesses, Spokane, 1956-62; co-owner, co-mgr. 7G Ranch, Medical Lake, 1962-70; asso. prof., dir. programs in internat. bus. George Washington U., Washington, 1964-70, chmn. dept. bus. adminstrn., 1968-70, prof. bus. adminstrn., 1971-73, Aryamehr prof. multinat. mgmt., 1974—, spl. asst. to pres., 1974-80; mgmt. cons. to industry and govts.; vis. prof. internat. bus. adminstrn., acting dir. Ohio World Trade Edn. Center, Cleve. State U., 1972-73; dir., chmn. exec. com. Diplomat Nat. Bank, 1978-80; mem. bd. advisors Donaldson, Luftkin & Jenrette, 1980-83. Author: A Guide to Personnel Development, 1966, (with others) A Handbook for Term Papers, Theses and Dissertations, 1974, American-East European Trade: Controversy, Progress, Prospects, 1968, (with Norma M. Loeser) Executive Leadership: The Art of Successfully Managing Resources, 1969, (with Mika S. Kaskimies) International Marketing in Perspective, 1971, (with Ashok Kapoor) The Multinational Enterprise in Transition, 1972, 2d edit., 1983; (with Ghadar and Khambata) Asia Dimensions of International Business, 1982; contbr. articles to profl. jours. Served with U.S. Army, 1954-56. Mem. Acad. Internat. Bus. (pres. 1975-77), Acad. of Mgmt., Orgn. for African Econ. Devel. (co-chmn. bd. govs.), U.S. Japan Soc. (dir., exec. sec.), Fellows Acad. Internat. Business, Alpha Kappa Psi. Lodges: Kiwanis (internat. relations chmn.); Masons; Scottish Rite. Home: 2342 S Rolfe St Arlington VA 22202 Office: George Washington U Washington DC 20052

GRUBB, DONALD HARTMAN, paper industry supplies company executive; b. West Chester, Pa., Oct. 22, 1924; s. Donald C. and Bessie (Hanthorne) G.; m. Jean Louise Flounders, Sept. 7, 1946; children: Donna Jean (Mrs. John H. Miller), Deborah Anne (Mrs. James R. Jackson), Donald Philip. B.A., U. Pa., 1949; M.A., Am. U., 1954; postgrad., N.Y. U., 1963-64. With U.S. Treasury Dept., Washington, 1949-57, recruitment officer, 1951-53, dir. personnel, 1953-57; mgr. personnel Westvaco Corp., N.Y.C., 1957-59, regional adminstrv. mgr., Hoboken, N.J., 1959-61, mgr. sales, 1961-64; asst. to v.p. Huyck Corp., Stamford, Conn., 1964, v.p. adminstrn. and mktg., 1969-70, exec. v.p., 1970-73, pres., dir., chief exec. officer, 1973-81; chmn. BTR Paper Group, 1981-82; pres. Gedon Enterprises, 1982—; v.p., gen. mgr. Formex Co. of Can., Kentville, N.S., 1965-67; also dir.; v.p., gen. mgr. Huyck Formex Co. of U.S., Greeneville, Tenn., 1967-69; dir. Overton Corp., Bluebird Champions, Inc., Morganite, Inc., Wake County Hosp. System; mem. adv. bd. Peden Steel. Bd. dirs. Blanchard-Fraser Meml. Hosp., Kentville, N.S., Can., 1966-67, N.C. State U. Pulp and Paper Found. Served with AUS, 1943-46. Mem. Raleigh C. of C. (dir. 1976-78), Phi Beta Kappa. Presbyterian. Office: Huyck Corp Wake Forest NC 27587

GRUBB, WILLIAM FRANCIS X., consumer software executive, marketing executive; b. N.Y.C., Aug. 11, 1944; s. William Martin and Eileen F. (Donnelly) G.; m. Eileen B. O'Leary, Apr. 4, 1964; children: Catherine E., William M., Kerri A., Christopher. B.A., Fordham U., 1966; M.B.A., Seton Hall U., 1972. Mktg. and sales exec. Black & Decker, Towson, Md., 1968-79; v.p. mktg. Atari, Sunnyvale, Calif., 1979-81; chmn., pres. New West Mktg., Mountain View, Calif., 1981; pres., chief exec. officer, chmn. Imagic, Los Gatos, Calif., 1981—. Home: 12421 Fredericksburg Dr Saratoga CA 95070 Office: Imagic 981 University Ave Los Gatos CA 95030

GRUBB, WILSON LYON, physician, educator; b. Balt., Nov. 26, 1910; s. Harry and Eleanor (Chaney) G.; m. Margot J. Carter, 1967; 1 son, James Carter. Grad., St. Albans Sch., Washington, 1929; A.B., Johns Hopkins, 1932, M.D., 1937. Diplomate: Am. Bd. Pediatrics. Intern bacteriology and pathology Boston Children's Hosp. Med. Center, 1937-38, intern pediatrics, 1938-40; asst. resident pediatrics Johns Hopkins Hosp., 1940-41; practice medicine specializing in pediatrics, Balt., 1941—; pediatrician-in-chief Union Meml. Hosp., Balt., 1961-81; attending pediatrician Greater Balt. Med. Center, 1943—, U. Md. Hosp., 1970—, Ch. Home and Hosp., Balt., 1942—, chief pediatrics, 1956-61; pediatric cons. Childrens Hosp.; asst. prof. pediatrics Johns Hopkins Med. Sch., 1957—; asso. prof. pediatrics Sch. Medicine, U. Md. Fellow Am. Acad. Pediatrics (chmn. for Md. 1966-70, alternate dist. chmn. 1970-75), A.M.A., Md. Diabetes Assn. (pres. 1966-75), Med. and Chirurgical Faculty Edn., Nat. Kidney Found., Md. Hist. Soc., Phi Beta Kappa, Phi Kappa Psi. Episcopalian. Clubs: Pithotomy (Johns Hopkins Med. Sch.); Johns Hopkins, Churchmens, Tudor and Stuart, Baltimore Country (Balt.); St. Petersburg (Fla.) Yacht. Spl. research juvenile diabetes, adoptions, infant feeding. Home: 3607 Greenway St Baltimore MD 21218 Office: 5820 York Rd Baltimore MD 21212

GRUBBE, KENNETH S., grain company executive; b. Boone, Iowa, Aug. 21, 1935; s. Roy M. and Verna L. (Johnson) G.; m. Ruth E. Grempel, Oct. 14, 1961; children: Jeffrey, Jill. A.A., Webster City Jr. Coll., 1955; B.A., Buena Vista Coll., 1959. With Farmland Industries Inc., Kansas City, Mo., 1962-79; fin. v.p., treas. Far Mar Co. Inc., Kansas City, 1980—; sec.-treas., dir. Farmers Commodities Co., Des Moines, 1981—; dir. Ill. Coop. Futures Co., Chgo., Kansas City Terminal Co., Mo.; sec.-treas., dir. Farmland Securities Co., Kansas City, 1976, Far Mar Co. Export Elevator Inc., 1981—, Far Mar Co. Internat. Ltd., 1982—. Served with USN, 1956-57. Home: Rural Route 22 Kansas City MO 64152 Office: Far Mar Co Inc One Ward Pkwy Box 619 Kansas City MO 64141

GRUBBS, ELVEN JUDSON, publisher; b. Taylor County, Fla., Dec. 26, 1930; s. Judson Omer and Nancy Lourainie (Lundy) G.; m. Loretta Caruthers, June 4, 1950; 1 son, Russell Elven. Student public schs., Ocala, Fla. With Ocala Star-Banner, 1947-77, advt. dir., 1964-77, gen. mgr., 1968-77; v.p., publisher The Ledger, Lakeland, Fla., 1977-82; pub. Sarasota (Fla.) Herald-Tribune, 1982—. Mem. Am. Newspaper Publs. Assn., Fla. Press Assn. Democrat. Baptist. Lodges: Elks; Lions (pres. 1973-74). Home: 5104 Flicker Field Circle Sarasota FL 33581 Office: 801 S Tamiami Trail Sarasota FL 33577

GRUBBS, JAMES LEE, chem. co. exec.; b. Little Rock, May 4, 1944. B.S. in Aerospace Engring, U. Tex., 1966; M.B.A. in Fin, U. Pa., 1971. Vice pres. Citibank (N.A.), N.Y.C., 1971-79; v.p. fin. Pantasote Inc, Greenwich, Conn., 1979—. Mem. Fin. Execs. Inst., Beta Gamma Sigma. Office: PO Box 1800 Greenwich CT 06830

GRUBE, GERALD GEORGE, retail executive; b. Sheboygan, Wis., Aug. 10, 1919; s. Harry A. and Louise (Tegaauntvert) G.; m. Selma Ibe, July 5, 1941; children: Judith Ann Grube Gardner, Kathleen Jean Grube Warren. Student pub. schs., Sheboygan. With Schultz Sav-O Stores, Inc. (and predecessors), Sheboygan, 1939—, sec.-treas., then v.p., treas., 1959-73, sr. v.p. fin., treas., 1973—; also mem. exec. com., dir.; dir. Piggly Wiggly Racine, Inc., 1951-59, sec., 1953-59; treas. Piggly Wiggly Gt. Lakes, Inc., 1955-59; sec., dir. Piggly Wiggly Kenosha, Inc., 1957-59; sec.-treas., dir. Sav-O Corp., 1961—; vice chmn. bd. Wis. Mchts. Fedn., 1970—; pres. Wis. Food and Tobacco Inst., 1963-64. Chmn. bd. Sheboygan Meml. Hosp., 1977-83, bd. assocs., 1983—, v.p. found., 1982—; vice chmn. budget com. Sheboygan United Fund, 1960-63; pres. Sheboygan Emergency Services, Inc., 1983—. Served with AUS, World War II. Mem. Nat. Assn. Food Chains, Food Mktg. Inst. Lutheran. Club: Sheboygan Country. Home: 4145 S 16th St Sheboygan WI 53081 Office: 2215 Union Ave Sheboygan WI 53081

GRUBE, LEWIS BLAINE, coal company financial executive; b. Punxsutawney, Pa., Feb. 6, 1917; s. George Peter and Lorena (Korb) G.; m. Bernice Bonner, July 5, 1941; children: Judith Elaine, Jean Ann, Jacquelyn Lee, James Bonner. B.A., Pa. State U., 1938. With Rochester & Pittsburgh Coal Co., Indiana, Pa., 1938—, treas., 1966—, controller, 1969-75, v.p., 1975—. Treas. Indiana Sch. Bd., 1955-73, Indiana Sch. Authority, 1974—; pres. Indiana Hosp. Authority, 1975—. Served to 1st lt. Q.M.C. U.S. Army, 1942-46, 50-51. Mem. Financial Execs. Inst. Republican. Presbyterian. Lodges: Kiwanis; Masons; Elks. Home: 1511 Woodland Rd Indiana PA 15701 Office: 655 Church St Indiana PA 15701

GRUBER, ALAN RICHARD, insurance company executive; b. N.Y.C., Nov. 2, 1927; s. Abraham and Esther Lucille (Hiller) G.; m. Harriet C. Mandel, Nov. 7, 1948; children: James Mark, Marian Amy Gruber Montgomery, Steven Bennett. S.B., M.I.T., 1945, S.M., 1946; M.A., Harvard U., 1948. Treas., mgr. engring. Nuclear Devel. Corp. Am., White Plains, N.Y., 1948-57; div. mgr. Marquardt Corp., Van Nuys, Calif., 1958-61; exec. v.p. Capital for Tech. Industries, Inc., Santa Monica, Calif., 1961-64; dir. corp. planning Xerox Corp., Stamford, Conn., 1965-70; v.p. corp. devel. Heublein Inc., Farmington, Conn., 1970-72; pres. Triumph Am. Inc., N.Y.C., 1972-75; v.p. Internat. Basic Economy Corp., N.Y.C., 1975-76; chmn., pres. Orion Capital Corp., N.Y.C., 1976-82, chmn., chief exec. officer, 1982—; dir. Guardian Mut. Fund, Inc., N.Y.C., Math. Applications Group, Inc., Elmsford, N.Y., Mountain Med. Equipment, Inc., Littleton, Colo.; mem. SEC Adv. Com. on Tender Offers, 1983—. Mem. Am. Econs. Assn., N.Y. Soc. Security Analysts, Assn. Corp. Growth. Clubs: Harmonie, Econ. (N.Y.C.); Metropolis Country (White Plains). Home: 876 Park Ave New York NY 10021 Office: 30 Rockefeller Plaza New York NY 10112

GRUBER, FREDRIC FRANCIS, business executive; b. Pekin, Ill., July 16, 1931; s. Louis Simon and Lillian Frances (Klein) G.; m. Dolores Rae Hanson, Aug. 15, 1960; children: Darrell Grant, Eric Tyson. B.S. in Acctg., Bradley U., 1956; postgrad., Northwestern U. C.P.A. Audit mgr. Arthur Young & Co., Chgo., 1956-63; controller Associated Coca-Cola Bottling Co., Inc., Daytona Beach, Fla., 1963-66, asst. treas., 1964-66, treas., 1966—, v.p., 1976-83; exec. v.p. United Home Services Fla., Inc., 1983—. Active Daytona Beach Comm. of 100. Served with USCG, 1950-53. Mem. Fin. Execs. Inst., Am., Fla. insts. C.P.A.s, Daytona Beach C. of C. Lutheran. Clubs: Rotary, Halifax. Office: PO Drawer G Sanford FL 32772

GRUBER, JOHN BALSBAUGH, physics educator, university official; b. Hershey, Pa., Feb. 10, 1935; s. Irvin John and Erla R. (Balsbaugh) G.; m. Judith Anne Higer, June 20, 1961; children: David Powell, Kean Leigh, Mark Balsbaugh. B.S., Haverford (Pa.) Coll., 1957; Ph.D., U. Calif. at Berkeley, 1961. NATO postdoctoral fellow Inst. Tech. Physics, Tech. U. Darmstadt, Germany, 1961-62, gastdozent, 1961-62; asst. prof. physics U. Calif. at Los Angeles, 1962-66; asso. prof. physics Wash. State U., Pullman, 1966-71, prof. chem. physics, 1971-75, asst. dean, 1968-70, asso. dean, 1970-71; prof. physics, dean Coll. Sci. and Math., N.D. State U., Fargo, 1975-80; prof. physics and chemistry, v.p. for acad. affairs Portland (Oreg.) State U., 1980—; vis. prof. Joint Center Grad. Study, Richland, Wash., 1964, 65, 66, Ames Lab., Dept. of Energy, Iowa State U., 1976, 77, 78, 79, 80, invited lectr., U.S., Can., Europe, 1966—; cons. in solid state physics and spectroscopy Aerospace Corp., El Segundo, Calif., 1962-65, Douglas Aircraft and McDonnell Douglas Astronautics Co., Santa Monica, Calif., 1963-69, N.Am. Aviation, Space and Info. Systems, Downey, Calif., 1964-66, Battelle-Northwest, Richland, Wash., 1964-69, Los Alamos (N.Mex.) Sci. Lab., 1969-71, 73-74; Mem. task force lunar exploration sci. Apollo, NASA, 1964-69, 71-73; mem. Rare Earth Research Conf. Com., 1976—, exec. com., 1977—, sec. bd. dirs., 1979—; gen. conf. chmn. XIV Internat. Rare Earth Research Conf., 1979; exec. sec. Internat. Frank H. Spedding Award, 1979, 83. Contbr. articles to profl. jours., chpts. to books. Trustee Symphony Bd. Fargo-Moorhead Symphony Orch., 1978-80; Pres. Franklin Elementary Sch. PTA, Pullman, 1973-74; pres. elect PTA coordinating council, City of Pullman, 1974-75; v.p. Horace Mann Elementary Sch. PTA, Fargo, 1975-76, pres., 1976-77; mem. PTA coordinating council, City of Fargo, 1976-77, N.D. State Bd. PTA; chmn. Univ., Coll. and Pub. Sch. Relations Bd., 1979-80; active Boy Scouts Am.; trustee Pullman Pub. Library, 1973-75, N.D. Symphony Orchestras Assn., 1978-80; bd. dirs. Westminster Found., 1982—. Grantee AEC-ERDA, 1963-75, NSF, 1966-72, 76-78, 79—, NASA, 1966-72, 76-78, U.S. Army Research Office, Durham, 1979-80, Am. Chem. Soc. Petroleum Research Funds, 1979-80, also Dept. Energy, 1979—. Fellow Am. Phys. Soc. (chmn. nat. meeting sessions); mem. N.Y. Acad. Scis., AAAS, N.D. Acad. Sci., Oreg. Acad. Sci., Council Colls. Arts and Scis., Phi Beta Kappa, Phi Kappa Phi, Sigma Xi, Sigma Pi Sigma. Presbyterian (ruling elder). Clubs: Mason (Shriner), Kiwanian.). Home: 12 DaVinci Lake Oswego OR 97034 Office: Vice Pres for Acad Affairs Office 308 Neuberger Hall Portland State U PO Box 751 Portland OR 97201

GRUBER, WILLIAM PAUL, journalist; b. Chgo., May 2, 1932; s. Frank and Gisella (Rudelitch) G. B.S. in Journalism, U. Ill., 1954. Asst. editor Community News, Woodstock, Ill., 1954-55; reporter, markets editor U.P.I., 1958-63; mem. staff Chicago's Am., 1963—; financial editor Chgo. Today, 1968-74; financial writer Chgo. Tribune, 1974—. Served with AUS, 1955-57. Mem. Am. Soc. Bus. Writers, Sigma Delta Chi. Club: Chgo. Press. Home: 6030 N Sheridan Rd Chicago IL 60660 Office: 435 N Michigan Ave Chicago IL 60611

GRUBERG, CY, educational administrator; b. Kingston, N.Y., Aug. 23, 1928; s. Joseph and Sara J. (Jacobson) G. B.S., Rider Coll.; M.A., Syracuse U., 1949; postgrad. guidance and counseling, Columbia U., NYU, Hofstra U., Harvard U., Adelphi U., U. Maine, U. Vt.; Ph.D., Columbia Pacific U., 1980. Guidance counselor, dean and dir. guidance Lynbrook (L.I.) High Sch., 1960-66; asst. prof. State U. N.Y. at New Paltz, 1966-67; dir. pupil personnel services Hastings-on-Hudson (N.Y.) Pub. Schs., 1967—; group leader summer resident camps, 1950—; mem. faculty Inst. Beau Soliel, Villars, Switzerland, 1955; tour dir. summer tours, U.S., Europe, Russia, Israel, Mexico, Can., 1961—; instr. adult edn. Mepham High Sch., 1950-55; mem. faculty Roosevelt Sch., summers 1949-50. Cons. N.C.C.J.; Active local drives Nat. Cerebral Palsy Assn., Am. Cancer Soc., Muscular Dystrophy Found., Cystic Fibrosis Found., Leukemia Soc. Am., also, Community Scholarship drives; exec. bd. Nassau County Boys and Girls Week Com.; adv. com. Hastings Youth Employment Service; adv. council Graham Home; chmn. Hastings Student Project Com.; Mem. Hastings Safety Commn.; Bd. dirs. Echo Hills Mental Hill Clinic, Dobbs Ferry, N.Y. Served to 1st lt. AUS, World War II. Recipient Nat. citation Parents' mag., 1960-65; scholar workshop human relations U. Maine, 1958; recipient William O. Hamilton award Key club N.Y. State, 1964, 72. Mem. N.Y. State Tchrs. Assn., N.Y. State Personnel and Guidance Assn., Am. Guidance and Personnel Assn., Westchester-Putnam-Rockland Personnel and Guidance Assn., NEA, Assn. Coll. Admissions Counselors, Am. Ednl. Research Assn., Am. Legion, VFW, Phi Delta Kappa, Zeta Beta Tau. Clubs: B'nai B'rith, Kiwanis. Home: 445 Broadway Hastings-on-Hudson NY 10706 Office: Hastings High Sch Hastings-on-Hudson NY 10706 *Counseling is not advice-giving pep talks or lectures—this may be the most important thing we can say about it. Counseling is an art that takes much training, understanding, and practice. Counseling is an interaction between two people to produce change. In schools it is a process of relationship and interaction between an adult and an adolescent through which the youngster may achieve goals personal to himself. The concern is always a personal one and frequently private to the pupil concerned. Progress comes through the thinking that the individual-with-the-problem does for himself rather than through solutions suggested by the counselor. The counselor's function is to make this kind of thinking possible rather than to do it himself.*

GRUBERG, MARTIN, political science educator; b. N.Y.C., Jan. 28, 1935; s. Benjamin and Mollie (Stolnitz) G.; m. Rosaline Kurfirst, Mar. 25, 1967 (dec. 1980); m. Humaira Sayeed, Aug. 15, 1983. B.A., CCNY, 1955; Ph.D., Columbia U., 1963. Agt.-adjudicator Passport Agy., Dept. State, N.Y.C, 1960-61; tchr. social studies Pelham (N.Y.) High Sch., 1961-62; instr. polit. sci. Hunter Coll., 1961-62; tchr. social studies James Monroe and Seward Park High Schs., N.Y.C., 1962-63; asst. prof. polit. sci. U. Wis. at Oshkosh, 1963-66, assoc. prof., 1966-69, prof., chmn. dept., 1969-72, dir. pre-law program, 1966-69, coordinator criminal justice program, 1983—. Author: Women in American Politics, 1968; newspaper column: Women: Our Largest Minority, The Paper for Central Wisconsin, 1970-71, Spotlight on Women for Oshkosh Northwestern, 1971-73; Broadcast 16 weeks Civil Rights Revolution, Wis. State FM Network, 1969, The American Presidency, State FM Network, 1974; Contbr. articles to encys., profl. jours. Pres. Oshkosh Human Rights Council, 1966-68; v.p. Winnebago chpt. NOW, 1970-71; sec. Oshkosh chpt., 1980-81, pres., 1981—; pres. Women's Caucus of Midwest Polit. Scientists, 1980-81. Recipient Am. Legion Aux. Americanism award, 1949, N.Y. State Scholarship, 1952, Buckvar award, 1955, Steigman award, 1955, Columbia grantee, 1961, 62, Wis. Regents' Research grantee, 1964-70, 73-75. Mem. Am. Polit. Sci. Assn., Midwest Polit. Sci. Assn., Wis. Polit. Sci. Assn. (pres. 1974-75), Law and Soc. Assn., AAUP (state sec. 1975—, pres.-elect 1981-82, pres. 1982-83), Aurelian Soc. Optimist. Home: 1660 Westhaven Dr Oshkosh WI 54901 Office: Clow Hall U Wis Oshkosh WI 54901

GRUBMAN, WALLACE KARL, chemical company executive; b. N.Y.C., Sept. 12, 1928; s. Samuel and Mildred G.; m. Ruth R. Winer, July 29, 1950; children: Steven L., Eric P. B.S. in Chem. Engring, Columbia U., 1950; M.S., N.Y. U., 1954. With Nat. Starch and Chem. Corp., 1950—, corp. v.p., gen. mgr. adhesive div., Bridgewater, N.J., 1972-77, group v.p., 1977-78, pres., chief operating officer, dir., 1978-83, pres., chief exec. officer, 1983—; dir. United Nat. Bank, Plainfield, N.J., Unilever U.S. Inc., N.Y.C. Mem. Chem. Mfrs. Assn., Soc. Chem. Industry, Am. Inst. Chem. Engrs. Clubs: Princeton (N.Y.C.); Roxiticus Golf (Mendham, N.J.); Mid-Ocean (Bermuda). Office: 10 Finderne Ave Bridgewater NJ 08807

GRUCHACZ, ROBERT S., food co. exec.; b. Bloomfield, N.J., May 15, 1929; s. Stanley A. and Mae (Zalenski) G.; m. LaVerne T. Stein, Mar. 2, 1957; children—Robert S., Thomas A., Christopher J. B.S., Seton Hall U., 1950; M.B.A., N.Y. U., 1971; student, Advanced Mgmt. Program, Harvard, 1973. C.P.A., N.J. With Arthur Young & Co., C.P.A.'s, 1955-58, Sterling Drug Inc., N.Y.C., 1958-65; controller Nabisco Inc., 1965-72, asst. to pres., 1973-74, 76—, v.p., 1979—; exec. v.p. Aurora Products, 1974-76. Served as 1st lt. USAF, 1952-54. Mem. Am. Inst. C.P.A.'s, Fin. Execs. Inst. Home: 61 Rockledge Dr Livingston NJ 07039 Office: East Hanover NJ 07936

GRUEN, DAVID HENRY, banker; b. Buffalo, Aug. 12, 1929; s. Edward Charles and Florence (Knoche) G.; m. Joan Willard, Jan. 3, 1976; children by previous marriage: David E., Stephen P., Cathryn E., Edward Charles II, William A. B.A., Cornell U., 1951, M.B.A., 1954. C.P.A., N.Y. Sr. accountant Arthur Andersen & Co., N.Y.C., 1954-59; asst. treas. Marine Midland Banks, Inc., 1959-60, asst. v.p., 1960-63, v.p., treas., 1963-69; sr. v.p. Marine Midland Bank-Western, 1969-74; sr. v.p., treas. Marine Midland Banks, Inc., Buffalo, 1974-80; sr. v.p., gen. auditor, 1980—. Served from 2d lt. to 1st lt. USAF, 1951-53. Mem. Am. Inst. C.P.A.s, Tax Execs. Inst., N.Y. Soc. C.P.A.s, Am. Accounting Assn., Financial Execs. Inst. Home: 34 Middlesex Rd Buffalo NY 14216 Office: 1 Marine Midland Center Buffalo NY 14240

GRUEN, GERALD ELMER, psychologist; b. Granite City, Ill., July 19, 1937; s. Elmer George and Velma Pearl G.; m. Karol Jane Selvidge, Mar. 20, 1960; children—Tami Jane, Christy Lynn. B.A., So. Ill. U., 1959; M.A., U. Ill., 1963, Ph.D., 1964. Postdoctoral fellow Heinz Werner Inst. of Developmental Psychology, Clark U. and Worcester (Mass.) State Hosp., 1964-66; asst. prof. dept. psychol. scis. Purdue U., West Lafayette, Ind., 1966-69, asso. prof., 1969-74, prof., 1974—. Author: (with T. Wachs) Early Experience and Human Development; contbr.: chpt. to The Structuring of Experience, 1977; articles to profl. jours. Deacon Calvary Baptist Ch., West Lafayette. Recipient USPHS research awards, 1968-71, Nat. Research Service award NIMH, 1976-80, Research award Nat. Insts. Child Health and Human Devel., 1981-83. Fellow Am. Psychol. Assn.; mem. Midwestern Psychol. Assn., Soc. for Research in Child Devel., Sigma Xi. Home: 1001 Eton St West Lafayette IN 47906 Office: Purdue U West Lafayette IN 47907

GRUENBERG, ROBERT, newspaperman; b. Chgo., Sept. 13, 1922; s. Samuel and Fannie (Cohen) G.; m. Ruth Jonathan, Sept. 18, 1943; children: Mark Jonathan, Jeremy Ethan. B.Ph., Northwestern U., 1953. Reporter, Chgo. Daily News, 1941-61; Reporter Evening Star, Washington, 1961-62; Washington corr. Chicago's Am., 1962-66; reporter Chgo. Daily News, 1966-78, Washington corr., 1968-78; mem. press staff NEA, 1978—; chmn. Chgo. Daily News unit of the Chgo. Newspaper Guild, AFL-CIO, 1956, mem. exec. bd. guild, 1957. Editor: NEA report Tragedy in Puerto Rico; contbr.: articles to Progressive mag., Nation. Served with inf. AUS, 1943-46. Recipient Page One award Chgo. Newspaper Guild, 1955, 6O, 69, 70; 1st Ann. James P. McGuire Meml. award Ill. div. ACLU, 1968; Marshall Field award, 1969; Ill. A.P. Spot News award, 1972. Home: 4018 Ingersol Dr Silver Spring MD 20902

GRUENBERG, ROBERT PERSHING, exposition building manager; b. Bklyn., July 29, 1918; s. James and Mary (Debrowsky) G.; m. Imogene Chandler, June 10, 1941; children: James Chandler, Imogene Mary, Peter Colby. B.S., U. Ill., 1940, M.S. in Commerce, 1941. With Nat. Home Furnishings Assn., Chgo., 1941-72, v.p. charge service, 1960-65, exec. v.p., sec., 1965-72; v.p., treas., gen. mgr. So. Furniture Expn. Bldg., High Point, N.C., 1972—. Bd. dirs. United Community Service, 1974-75; chmn. Downtown Devel. Com., 1976-77; mem. exec. com., chmn. phys. improvements com. Econ. Devel. Bd., 1977-78, bd. dirs., 1977—; bd. visitors High Point Coll., 1977-79, trustee, 1980—; mem. Home Econs. Found., U. N.C., 1977-79, v.p., 1978-79. Served to lt. USNR, World War II; PTO. Mem. Home Furnishings Council (dir. 1966-72), High Point C. of C. (bd. dirs. 1975-78), CEO Roundtable (vice chmn. 1981—), So. Furniture Club (sec.-treas. 1972-82). Clubs: High Point Execs. (bd. dirs. 1976-78), High Point Rotary.). Home: 304 Edgedale Dr High Point NC 27262 Office: Southern Furniture Exposition Bldg PO Box 828 High Point NC 27261

GRUENISEN, ALLAN GEORGE, insurance executive; b. Oshkosh, Wis., Dec. 19, 1919; s. George Wesley and Jeanett (Noe) G.; m. Shirley Ruth Flath, Nov. 22, 1947; children: Gary, Gayle. Ph.B., U. Wis., 1944, J.D., 1946. With Am. Family Ins. Group, Madison, Wis., 1946—; exec. v.p. Am. Standard Ins. Co. of Wis., Madison, 1960-66, v.p. legal, 1967—, sec., 1965—, dir., 1968—; sec., v.p. legal, dir. Am. Family Mutual Ins. Co., Madison, Wis., 1968—, Am. Family Life Ins. Co., Madison, 1968—, Am. Family Fin. Services, Inc., 1969—; dir. Wis. Healthcare Liability Plan, Wis. Ins. Plan, Wis. Security Fund., Southwestern Ins. Info. Service. Active Boy Scouts Am., Madison, 1968-71; vice chmn. Dane County (Wis.) Cancer Dr., 1975; bd. dirs. YMCA, Madison, 1965-70. Mem. ABA, State Bar of Wis., Internat. Assn. Ins. Counsel, Wis. Ins. Alliance (chmn. 1968, 69, 74), Minn. Ins. Guaranty Assn. (dir.), State Hist. Soc. Wis. Clubs: Mendota Yacht, Madison, Civil War Round Table. Home: 6437 Antietam Ln Madison WI 53705 Office: 3099 E Washington Ave PO Box 7430 Madison WI 53783

GRUENTZIG, ANDREAS ROLAND, cardiologist, educator; b. Dresden, Germany, June 25, 1939; s. Wilmar and Charlotte G.; m. Margaret Anne Thornton, May 28, 1983; 1 dau., Sonja. M.D., U. Heidelberg, Germany, 1964. Privat dozent U. Zurich, 1977-80; prof. medicine and radiology, dir. interventional cardiovascular medicine Emory U., Atlanta, 1980—. Contbr. articles to med. jours. Recipient Goetz prize U. Zurich. Mem. Am. Heart Assn., Deutsche Gesellschaft fuer Herz und Kreislaufforschung, Schweizerische, Angiologische Gesellschaft. Office: 1364 Clifton Rd NE Atlanta GA 30322

GRUENWALD, GEORGE HENRY, new products management consultant; b. Chgo., Apr. 23, 1922; s. Arthur Frank and Helen (Duke) G.; m. Corrine Rae Linn, Aug. 16, 1947; children: Helen Marie Gruenwald Orlando, Paul Arthur. B.S., Northwestern U., 1947; student, Evanston Acad. Fine Arts, 1937-38, Chgo. Acad. Fine Arts, 1938-39, Grinnell Coll., 1940-41. Asst. to pres. Uarco, Inc., Chgo., 1947-49; creative dir., mgr. mdse. Willy-Overland Motors Inc., Toledo, 1949-51; brand and advt. mgr. Toni Co., Chgo., 1951-53; v.p., creative dir., account supr. E.H. Weiss Agy., Chgo., 1953-55; exec. v.p., supr. mgmt. North Advt., Chgo., 1955-71; pres., treas., dir. Pilot Products, Chgo., 1964-71; pres., dir. Advance Brands, Inc., Chgo., 1963-71; exec. v.p., dir. Campbell Mithun Inc., Mpls. and Chgo., 1971-72, pres., dir., 1972-79, chmn., dir., 1980-81, chief exec. officer, dir., 1981-83, chief creative officer, 1983-84; mgmt. cons. new products. Editor-in-chief: Oldsmobile Rocket Circle mag, 1955-65, Hudson Family mag, 1953-55; author: New Products, 1984, New Products, What Really Works, 1984. Trustee Chgo. Pub. TV Assn., 1971-78, Mpls. Soc. Fine Arts, 1975-83; trustee Twin Cities Pub. TV Corp., 1971—, pres., 1975-76, chmn., 1977-79, chmn. exec. com., 1980—; trustee Minn. Pub. Radio Inc., 1973-77, vice chmn., 1974-75; bd. dirs., exec. com. Public Broadcasting Service, Washington, 1978—; bd. dirs. St. Paul Chamber Orch., 1982—; bd. advisors Linus Pauling Inst. Sci. and Medicine, Palo Alto, 1983—. Served with USAAF, 1943-45. Recipient Hermes award Chgo. Federated Advt. Clubs, 1963; Ednl. TV awards, 1969, 71. Mem. Am. Assn. Advt. Agencies (mgmt. com. 1976—). Clubs: Wayzata, Minneapolis; Tavern (Chgo.); Metropolitan, Canadian (N.Y.C.). Home: 1725 Hunter Dr Wayzata MN 55391 also Rancho Santa Fe CA Office: PO Box 1696 Rancho Santa Fe CA 92067 111 E Wacker Dr Chicago IL 60601 *To learn. To teach. To make a difference.*

GRUETZMACHER, ALFRED HENRY, commodity broker; b. Chgo., Apr. 14, 1919; s. Alfred H. and Eleanor H. (Meyer) G.; m. Marcella Stoegbauer, July 5, 1940; children: Gail Gruetzmacher Stuedemann, Alfred H., III. Student, Ripon (Wis.) Coll., to 1942. Ind. commodity broker Chgo. Bd. Trade, 1953-61; partner Geldermann & Co., Chgo., 1961-69, v.p., 1969—; chmn. Chgo. Bd. Trade, 1980—. Author papers in field. Mem. adv. council sch. bus. U. Ill.-Chgo., No. Ill. U. Served to 2d lt. U.S. Army, 1942-45. Decorated Bronze Star, Purple Heart. Mem. Nat. Grain Dealers Assn., Am. Legion. Club: Union League (Chgo.). Address: Geldermann & Co 141 W Jackson Blvd Chicago IL 60604

GRULEE, CLIFFORD GROSSELLE, JR., physician, educator; b. Chgo., June 9, 1912; s. Clifford Grosselle and Margaret (Freer) G.; m. Mary Evelyn Lewis, Feb. 14, 1943; 1 son, Clifford Grosselle III. B.A., Williams Coll., 1933; M.D., Northwestern U., 1937. Diplomate: Am. Bd. Pediatrics. Rotating intern St. Luke's Hosp., Chgo., 1937-38; house officer bacteriology, pathology and clin. pediatrics Boston Childrens Hosp., 1938-42, chief resident pediatrics, 1942; Rockefeller fellow pediatrics U. Minn., 1946-47; asst., then assoc. prof. pediatrics U. Tex. Med. Sch., 1947-49; mem. faculty Tulane U. Sch. Medicine, 1949-63, prof. pediatrics, 1956-63, dir. grad. medicine, 1956-63, assoc. dean, 1958-63, acting dean, 1960, mng. editor bull. med. faculty, 1952-63; prof. pediatrics, dean Coll. Medicine, U. Cin., 1963-73; dean La. State U. Sch. Medicine at Shreveport, 1973-75; vice-chancellor Med. Center Shreveport, 1975-76; dean Rockford Sch. Medicine, U. Ill. Coll. Medicine, Rockford, 1976-82; assoc. dean Coll. Medicine, U. Cin., 1982—; cons. to surgeon gen. Brooke Gen. Hosp., San Antonio, 1948-49; cons. pediatrics Keesler Field, Miss., 1952-59; chmn., directing med. staff Cin. Gen. Hosp., Christian R. Holmes Hosp.; chmn. deans com. Cin. VA Hosp.; physician cons. VA, 1970-71. Served to capt., M.C. AUS, 1942-45. Mem. Am. Acad. Pediatrics (chmn. com. juvenile delinquency 1962-65), Soc. Pediatric Research, Am. Pediatric Soc., Assn. Am. Med. Colls. (chmn. Midwest-Great Plains region 1969-70, exec. com. 1970—), A.M.A., Alpha Omega Alpha (chpt. councillor), Phi Delta Theta, Phi Rho Sigma. Office: Assoc Dean U Cin Coll Medicine 231 Bethesda Ave. Cincinnati OH 45267

GRUM, CLIFFORD J., publishing executive; b. Davenport, Iowa, Dec. 12, 1934; s. Allen F. and Nathalie (Cate) G.; m. Janelle Lewis, May 1, 1965; 1 son, Christopher J. B.A., Austin Coll., 1956; M.B.A., Wharton Sch., U. Pa., 1958. Formerly with Republic Nat. Bank, Dallas; former v.p. finance Temple Industries, Diboll, Tex.; with Time, Inc., N.Y.C., treas., 1973-75, v.p., 1975-80, exec. v.p., 1980—; pub. Fortune, 1975-79; dir. Cooper Industries, Inc. Trustee Austin Coll. Office: Time Inc Time and Life Bldg Rockefeller Center New York NY 10020

GRUMAN, ROBERT CLAYTON, prosthetist; b. Mpls., Mar. 1, 1922; s. Adelbert Paul and Charlotte (Blanchard) G.; m. Beverly Jane Taylor, Dec. 21, 1947; children: Gregory, William, Nancy. Student, Carleton Coll., 1940-43, U. Mich., 1943; B.B.A., U. Minn., 1947. With Winkley Artificial Limb Co., Mpls., 1947—, pres., 1957—, Protheses Orthipedique, Inc., Quebec, Can., 1957-64, Marks Artificial Limb Co., N.Y.C., 1957-72; sec.-treas. Am. Prosthetics, Inc., Des Moines, Davenport, Iowa, Iowa City, Ft. Lauderdale, Fla., and Buffalo, 1963-72, v.p., 1972-80, sec., 1974-80; partner Bevard Co., 1963—. Area vice chmn. Mpls. United Fund, 1962. Served with USAAF, 1943-46. Mem. Am. Orthotics and Prosthetics Assn. (regional dir. 1960-61, pres. 1964), Am. Acad. Orthotists and Prosthetists, Minn. Rehab. Assn. (pres. 1960), Am. Legion, Am. Bd. Certification Orthotists and Prosthetists. Clubs: Kiwanis (pres. 1975-76, lt. gov. div. 5 Minn.-Dakota Dist. Home: 19140 Ramsey Rd Deephaven MN 55391 Office: 740 Douglas Dr Golden Valley MN 55422

GRUMBACH, DORIS, novelist, editor, critic, educator; b. N.Y.C., July 12, 1918; d. Leonard and Helen Isaac; (div.)children: Barbara (Mrs. Samuel Wheeler), Jane (Mrs. Robert Emerson), Elizabeth (Cale), Kathryn. B.A., N.Y. U., 1939; M.A., Cornell U., 1940; D.H.L., Russell Sage Coll., 1980. Title writer MGM, N.Y.C., 1940-41; asso. editor Archtl. Forum, Time, Inc., 1941-43; prof. English Coll. St. Rose, Albany, N.Y., 1952-72; vis. prof. Empire State Coll., State U. N.Y., Saratoga Springs, 1972-73; contbg. and lit. editor The New Republic, Washington, 1971-73, lit. editor, 1973-75; prof. Am. lit. Am. U., Washington, 1975—; adj. prof. English U. Md., 1974-75; vis. prof. Iowa Writers' Workshop, 1980, 83, Johns Hopkins U. (writing seminars), 1983. Freelance critic: Washington Star, Washington Post, Los Angeles Times, Chgo. Tribune; non-fiction columnist: N.Y. Times Book Review, 1976-81; fiction columnist: Chronicle Higher Edn, 1979-81; columnist: Fine Print, Sat. Rev, 1977-78; Author: The Spoil of the Flowers, 1962, The Short Throat, The Tender Mouth, 1964, The Company She Kept, 1967; contbr. author: Book Reviewing, 1978, Chamber Music, 1979, The Missing Person, 1981; book critic: Morning Edition, Nat. Pub. Radio, Writer's Choice, MacNeil-Lehrer News Hour. Served with USNR, 1943-44. Mem. PEN, Phi Beta Kappa. Home: 909 North Carolina Ave SE Washington DC 20003

GRUMBACH, MELVIN MALCOLM, physician, educator; b. N.Y.C., Dec. 21, 1925; s. Emanuel and Adele (Weil) G.; m. Madeleine F. Butt, Dec. 1, 1951; children: Ethan Malcolm, Kevin Lawrence, Anthony Havemeyer. Student, Columbia Coll.; M.D., Columbia U., 1948. Diplomate: Am. Bd. Pediatrics (mem. com. on subsplty. pediatric endocrinology 1975—), Nat. Bd. Med. Examiners. Resident in pediatrics Babies Hosp., Presbyn. Hosp., N.Y.C., 1949-51; vis. fellow Oak Ridge Inst. Nuclear Studies, 1952; postdoctoral fellow, asst. pediatrics Johns Hopkins Sch. Medicine, 1953-55; mem. faculty Columbia Coll. Physicians and Surgeons, N.Y.C., 1955-66, assoc. prof. pediatrics, 1961-66; from asst. attending pediatrician to asso. attending pediatrician, head pediatric endocrine div. and postdoctoral tng. program pediatric endocrinology Babies Hosp. and Vanderbilt Clin., Columbia-Presbyn. Med. Center, 1955-66; prof. pediatrics, chmn. dept. U. Calif. Sch. Medicine, San Francisco, 1966—; dir. pediatric service U. Calif. Hosps., 1966—; vis. prof. Vanderbilt U., 1961, Emory U., 1962, U. Western Ont., 1962, U. N.C., 1963; Alpha Omega Alpha lectr. State U. N.Y. Downstate Med. Center, 1961, U. Calif. at San Francisco, 1966; univ. lectr. U. Zurich, 1971; Clausen vis. prof. U. Rochester, 1972; Richard E. Weitzman vis. prof. UCLA, 1981; Culpeper vis. prof. U. N.C., 1982; Moll lectr. U. Wash., 1979; vis. prof. U. Tex.-Dallas, 1983; univ. lectr. Assembly of Profs., College de France, Paris, 1979; Eley lectr. Harvard U. Med. Sch., Children's Med. Center, Boston, 1979; domestic lectr. Jour. Pediatrics Edn. Found., 1962, 79; Mali Dittman lectr. U. Chgo., 1980; Frederick M. Kenny lectr. Children's Hosp. Pitts., 1981; Winthrop award lectr. Am. Fertility Soc., 1981; Grover Powers lectr. Yale U., 1981; univ. lectr. Assembly of Profs., College de France, Paris, 1979; Meredith Campbell lectr. Am. Urol. Soc., 1982; Prader lectr. Tel Aviv U. Med. Sch., 1982; Hopkins-Maryland lectr., 1983; cons. Letterman Gen. Hosp., Children's Hosp., San Francisco, U.S. Naval Hosp., Oakland, Calif., HEW, Welfare, NIH, Nat. Bd. Med. Examiners, 1964-68; mem. human embryology and devel. study sect. NIH, 1962-66, endocrinology study sect., 1967-71; bd. sci. counselors Nat. Inst. Child Health and Human Devel., 1971-75; mem. gen. clin. research centers com., div. research resources NIH, 1976-80; mem. sci. adv. com., clin. research adv. com. Nat. Found.-March of Dimes, 1969—, chmn. clin. research adv. com., 1974—; mem. awards com. Lita Annenberg Hazen Awards for Excellence in Clin. Research, 1981—; San Francisco chpt. trustee; mem. sci. adv. bd. Scripps Clinic and Research Found., 1977-78; mem. sci. adv. bd. Princesse Marie Christine Found., Brussels, 1981—, U. Mich. Ctr. for Human Growth and Devel., 1982—; mem. adv. bd. Nat. Pituitary Agy., 1965-69, NIH Evaluation of Endocrinology and Metabolic Diseases, 1977-79; mem. sci. council Aid Pour la Recherche Medicole a l'enfance, Paris, 1981—. Asso. editor, mem. editorial bd.: Jour. Clin. Endocrinology, 1957-70; adv. editor: Jour. Pediatrics, 1966-73; editorial bd., 1973-79; asso. editor: Pediatric Research, 1970—; assoc. editor: Barnett Pediatrics, 14th-17th edits.,, Rudolph Pediatrics, 16th-17th edits., Current Topics in Experimental Endocrinology 1968—; internat. editorial bd. pediatrics and pediatric surgery: Excerpta Medica, 1974—; editorial bd.: Biology of Reproduction, 1968-70, Monographs on Endocrinology, Springer-Verlag, 1975—; Contbr. articles to med. and sci. books and jours. Served to capt. M.C. USAF, 1951-53. Postdoctoral fellow Nat. Found. Infantile Paralysis, 1953-55; recipient Joseph M. Smith prize Columbia U., 1962; Career Scientist award Health Research Council City N.Y., 1961-66; Silver medal Bicentennial Columbia Coll. Physicians and Surgeons, 1967; Borden award Am. Acad. Pediatrics, 1971; Robert H. Williams Disting. Leadership award, 1980. Fellow Am. Acad. Pediatrics, N.Y. Acad. Sci.; mem. AAAS, Am. Pediatrics Soc., Assn. Med. Sch. Pediatric Dept. Chairmen (exec. council 1967-72, pres. 1973-75), Am. Soc. Clin. Investigation, Assn. Am. Physicians, Am. Soc. Human Genetics, Harvey Soc., Lawson Wilkins Pediatric Endocrine Soc. (pres. 1975-76), Western Soc. Pediatric Research (pres. 1978-79), Soc. Pediatric Research, Teratology Soc., Endocrine Soc. (council 1968-71, 80-83, pres. elect 1980-81, pres. 1981-82), Internat. Endocrine Soc. (del. to central com. 1976—), Soc. Study Reprodn., European Soc. Pediatric Endocrinology (corr.), Société Française de Pediatrie (corr.), Internat. Neuroendocrinology Soc., Argentine Soc. Endocrinology and Metabolism (hon.), Western Assn. Physicians, Calif. Acad. Medicine, Western Soc. Clin. Research, Pacific Coast Fertility Soc. (hon.), Sigma Xi, Alpha Omega Alpha. Club: Univ. (N.Y.C.). Office: Dept Pediatrics U Calif Sch Medicine San Francisco San Francisco CA 94143

GRUNAU, PAUL EDWARD, engineering company executive; b. Milw., Aug. 31, 1911; s. Paul John and Alma Charlotte G.; m. Lenore Anderson, June 3, 1935; children: Gary, Susan, Gretchen. Student, U. Wis., 1936-37. With Grunau Co., Inc., Milw., 1930—, pres., 1948-74, chmn. bd., chief exec. officer, 1974—; dir. Oil Gear Co., Bay View State Bank. Chmn. Airport Improvement Council County of Milw. Named Constrn. Man of Yr. Allied Constrn. Employers Assn., 1975. Mem. Assoc. Mech. Contractors Assn., Profl. Engrs. Soc., Nat. Constructors Assn. Clubs: Wis., Milw. Athletic, Western Racquet, Pinetree Golf, Bluemound Golf. Lodges: Masons; Shriners. Home: 1505 Sunset Dr Elm Grove WI 53122 Office: Grunau Co Inc 307 W Layton St Milwaukee WI 53207

GRUNBAUM, ADOLF, philosophy educator, author; b. Cologne, Germany, May 15, 1923; came to U.S., 1938, naturalized, 1944; s. Benjamin and Hannah (Freiwillig) G.; m. Thelma Braverman, June 26, 1949; 1 dau., Barbara Susan. B.A., Wesleyan U., Middletown, Conn., 1943; M.S. in Physics, Yale, 1948; Ph.D in Philosophy, Yale, 1951. Mem. faculty Lehigh U., 1950-60, prof. philosophy, 1955-56, Selfridge prof. philosophy, 1956-60; vis. research prof. Minn. Center Philosophy of Sci., 1956, 59; Andrew Mellon prof. philosophy U. Pitts., 1960—, research prof. psychiatry, 1979—, dir. Center Philosophy of Sci., 1960-78, now chmn.; Chmn. sect. philosophy of phys. scis. Internat. Congress for Logic and Philosophy of Sci., Jerusalem, Israel, 1964, Bucharest, Rumania, 1971, Salzburg, Austria, 1983; Physicist div. war research Columbia, World War II. Author: Philosophical Problems of Space and Time, 1963, 2d edit., 1973, Modern Science and Zeno's Paradoxes, 2d edit, 1968, Geometry and Chronometry in Philosophical Perspective, 1968, The Foundations of Psychoanalysis: A Philosophical Critique, 1984; also over 100 articles.; Editorial bd.: Ency. Philosophy, 1961—; bd. editors: Philosophy Sci, 1959—, Am. Philos. Quar, Erkenntnis, Psychoanalysis and Contemporary Thought, Studies in History and Philosophy of Science, The Philosopher's Index; co-editor: Pitts. Series in Philosophy and History of Sci. Served with M.I.S. U.S. Army, 1944-46. Recipient J. Walker Tomb prize Princeton, 1958; honor citation Wesleyan U., 1959. Fellow AAAS (v.p. sect. L 1963), Philosophy Sci. Assn. (rep. to Internat. Union for History and Philosophy of Sci.), Am. Philos. Assn. (pres. Eastern div. 1982-83), Philosophy of Sci. Assn. (pres. 1965-70), Am. Acad. Arts and Scis., Phi Beta Kappa, Sigma Xi. Home: 2270 McCrea Rd Pittsburgh PA 15235 Office: 2510 Cathedral of Learning U Pitts Pittsburgh PA 15260

GRUNDMAN, IRVING, professional hockey club executive; b. Montreal, Que., Can., July 23, 1928; s. Morris and Bessie (Epstein) G.; m. Gail Schreiber, Mar. 19, 1950; children: Howard Steven, Gary Neil, Pamela Ann. Student public and high schs., Montreal. With M. Grundman & Sons Ltd., Montreal, 1945-59; later v.p.; pres. Laurentian, Pare, Blvd. & Iberville Lanes, Montreal, McArthur Lanes, Ottawa, Ont., Can. and; Cloverleaf Lanes, Kingston, Ont., 1959—, Montreal Forum, 1971—; exec. v.p., mng. dir. Club de Hockey Canadien, Montreal, 1979—. Mem. Saint-Laurent (Que.) City Council, 1968—. Clubs: Gatineau Rod and Gun, Masons, B'nai B'rith (pres. St.-Laurent lodge 1961-62). Office: 2313 Saint Catherine St W Montreal PQ H3H 1N2 Canada *

GRUNDMANN, CHRISTOPH JOHANN, educator; b. Berlin, Germany, Dec. 29, 1908; s. Bruno Johann and Mathilde (Bolomey) G.; m. Lieselotte M. Mieth, Mar. 1, 1963; 1 son by previous marriage, Henning J. Dipl. Chem., U. Berlin, Germany, 1931, Ph.D., 1933; Dr.Phil. Habil, U. Heidelberg, Germany, 1937. Chem. researcher acad. instns. and pvt. cos., Germany, 1933-51; staff Research Found., Ohio State U., 1952-58; dir. research and devel. Gen. Cigar Co., Lancaster, Pa., 1958-60; sr. fellow Mellon Inst., Pitts., 1961—; prof. chemistry Carnegie-Mellon U., Pitts., 1967-76; patent cons., 1961—; research cons. Olin Mathieson Chem. Corp., 1952-58; Mem. patent adv. com. Dept. Interior, 1960-62. Mem. N.Y. Acad. Scis., Am. Chem. Soc., Gesellschaft Deutscher Chemiker, Sigma Xi. Club: R.K. Duncan (Pitts.). Research and numerous publs. and patents in organic, medicinal, polymer chemistry. Home: 1518 Williamsburg Pl Pittsburgh PA 15235 Address: Mellon Institute Carnegie-Mellon University Pittsburgh PA 15213

GRUNDSTEIN, NATHAN DAVID, management science educator; b. Ashland, Ohio, Sept. 19, 1913; s. Samuel Lewis and Rose J. (Kolinsky) G.; m. Dorothy Deborah Davis, Nov. 12, 1938; children: Miriam R. (Mrs. Bruce R. Levin), Margaret J. (Mrs. Stewart Helvey), Leon D., Robert H. B.A., Ohio State U., 1935, M.Sc., 1936; Ph.D., Syracuse U., 1943; LL.B., George Washington U., 1951. Bar: Mich. bar 1954, Ohio bar 1981. Legal research asst. Office Head Atty., Dept. Agr., 1939-40; adminstrv. asst. to asst. commr. FDA, 1940-41; adminstrv. officer, exec. asst. to vice chmn. for labor prodn. WPB, 1941-47; prof. pub. law and adminstrn. Wayne State U., 1947-58; prof. adminstrn. Grad. Sch. Pub. and Internat. Affairs, U. Pitts., 1958-64; prof. mgmt. policy, dir. grad. program pub. mgmt. sci. Case Western Res. U., 1964—; sr. vis. scholar Canberra Coll. Advanced Edn., Canberra, Australia, 1979; cons. to govt. and industry; lectr. in field. Author: Adminstrative Practice and procedure Under the Federal Plant Quarantine Act, 1940, Administrative Practice and Procedure Under the Federal Food, Drug and Cosmetic Act, 1941, Industrial Mobilization for War, Vol. I, Part III, 1947, Cases and Readings on Administrative Law, (with J.F. Davison), 1952, Administrative Law and the Regulatory System, 1966, Presidential Delegation of Authority in Wartime, 1961, Ethical Concerns and the City Managers Code of Ethics, 1967, Administrative Law and the Regulatory System, rev. edit, 1968, The Managerial Kant, 1982, New Work: A Theory of Pure Strategy, 1984; Donor book collection to, Memphis State U. Chmn. Citizens Com. for Cleveland Heights Progress, 1979-81, 83-84. Mem. Inst. Mgmt. Sci. (exec. com. Coll. Philosophy 1980—), Soc. Gen. Systems Research, Am. Soc. Legal Philosophy, Mich. Bar Assn., Ohio Bar Assn., Order of Coif, Phi Beta Kappa. Jewish. Home: 2872 Washington Blvd Cleveland Heights OH 44118 Office: Sears Bldg Sch Mgmt Case Western Res Univ Cleveland OH 44106

GRUNDY, KENNETH WILLIAM, political science educator; b. Phila., Aug. 6, 1936; s. William and Alma (Hahn) G.; m. Martha Jonet Paxson, June 25, 1960; children: William MacIntyre, Thomas Paxson, Anne Edmunds. B.A. with honors, Ursinus Coll., 1958; M.A., Pa. State U., 1961, Ph.D., 1963. Asst. prof. polit. sci. San Fernando Valley State Coll., Northridge, Calif., 1963-66; assoc. prof. Case Western Res. U., Cleve., 1966-74, prof., 1974—, chmn. dept. polit. sci., 1974-76; vis. sr. lectr. Makerere U. Coll., Kampala, Uganda, 1967-68; vis. scholar Inst. Social Studies, The Hague, Netherlands, 1972-73; vis. Fulbright prof. U. Zambia, Lusaka, 1977, Nat. U. Ireland, Galway, 1979-80; mem. editorial adv. bd. Center Internat. Race Relations, 1968—. Author: Conflicting Images of the Military in Africa, 1968, Guerrilla Struggle in Africa, 1971, Confrontation and Accommodation in Southern Africa, 1973, (with Michael Weinstein) The Ideologies of Violence, 1974, We're Against Apartheid, But, 1974, Defense Legislation and Communal Politics, 1978, (with V. McHale and B. Hughes) Evaluating Transnational Programs in Government and Business, 1980, Soldiers Without Politics, 1983; contbr. articles to profl. jours.; book rev. editor: Internat. Jour. Comparative Sociology, 1973-83; contbg. editor: Current History, 1982—; editorial adv. bd.: African Affairs, 1983—. NDEA fellow, 1959-62; Rockefeller Found. grantee, 1967-68; Center Internat. Race Relations fellow, 1969-70; Social Sci. Research Council grantee, 1972, 79-80; Earhart Found. grantee, 1979; 1st Bradlow fellow S. African Inst. Internat. Relations, 1982. Mem. African Studies Assn. (exec. council), Inter-Univ. Seminar on Armed Forces and Soc., Internat. Studies Assn. Home: 2602 Exeter Rd Cleveland Heights OH 44118 Office: Dept Polit Sci Case Western Res U Cleveland OH 44106

GRUNER, GEORGE FRANK, editor; b. Alameda, Calif., Feb. 13, 1925; s. George F. and Alberta (Potter) G.; m. Irene Obermiller, May 8, 1949; 1 son, Richard. Reporter Oakland (Calif.) Tribune, 1942, 45-52; desk man Stars and Stripes (U.S. Army daily newspaper), Darmstadt, Germany, 1952-55; with Fresno (Calif.) Bee, 1955—, asst. mng. editor, 1970, mng. editor, 1971-81, exec. editor, 1981—. Served with AUS, 1943-45. Mem. Am. Soc. Newspaper Editors. Office: 1626 E St Fresno CA 93786

GRUNEWALD, DONALD, college president; b. N.Y.C., Feb. 9, 1934; s. Harry A. and Tina (Gegner) G.; m. Barbara Susan Frees, Feb. 7, 1981; children: 1 son, Donald Frees. A.B., Union Coll., 1954; M.A., Harvard U., 1955, M.B.A., 1959, D.B.A., 1962; LL.D., Emerson Coll., 1973; Litt.D., Suffolk U., 1974; D.Sc., Far East U., 1979, Medaille Coll., 1983; Ph.D. honoris causa, U. Mindanao, 1981. Instr. U. Kans. Sch. Bus., 1959-60; lectr. Boston U. Coll. Bus. Adminstrn., 1961-62; research agt. Harvard U. Grad. Sch. Bus., 1962; asst. prof. Rutgers U. Grad. Sch. Bus., 1962-65, asso. prof., 1965-67; dean, prof. Suffolk U. (Coll. Bus. Adminstrn., Grad. Sch. Adminstrn.), 1967-69, v.p., dean, 1969-72; pres. Mercy Coll., Dobbs Ferry, N.Y., 1972—; ednl. cons., propr. Boston Athenaeum.; Life gov. Manchester Coll., Oxford, Eng.; trustee Trinity Coll., Washington. Author: Cases in Business Policy, 1962, (with Moranian and Reidenbach) Business Policy and Its Environment, 1964, (with H. Bass) Public Policy and the Modern Corporation, 1966, Small Business Management, 1966, (with Fenn, Katz) Business Decision Making and Government Policy, 1966, (with Flink) Managerial Finance, 1969. Trustee Dobbs Ferry Hosp., Lab. Inst. Merchandising, Westchester Conservatory of Music. Served as lt. USAF, 1955-57. Decorated Knight Sovereign Order St. John of Jerusalem. Fellow Royal Soc. Arts, Inst. Commerce; mem. Am. Econ. Assn., Acad. Mgmt., Internat. Assn. Univ. Pres.'s (exec. com.). Clubs: Rotarian (N.Y.C. and Boston) (bd. dirs. Boston 1971-72, pres. Hastings club 1975-76); Harvard (N.Y.C. and Boston); Cosmos (Washington); Ardsley Country. Home: 2 Hudson Rd E Ardsley-on-Hudson NY 10503 Office: Mercy Coll 555 Broadway Dobbs Ferry NY 10522 *I have always relied on the old motto: "Never rest until you have made the good better and the better best."*

GRUNWALD, HENRY ANATOLE, editor, writer; b. Vienna, Austria, Dec. 3, 1922; came to U.S., 1940, naturalized, 1948; s. Alfred and Mila (Loewenstein) G.; m. Beverly Suser, Jan. 7, 1953 (dec. 1981); children: Peter, Madeleine, Lisa. A.B., N.Y.U., 1944, L.H.D., 1975; LL.D., Iona Coll., 1981; L.H.D., Bennett Coll., 1983. Editorial staff Time mag., 1945—, sr. editor, 1951—, fgn. editor, 1961—, asst. mng. editor, 1966-68, mng. editor, 1968-77, corp. editor, 1977-79, editor in chief, 1979—. Author: Salinger, a Critical and Personal Portrait, 1962, Churchill, The Life Triumphant, 1965, The Age of Elegance, 1966; Contbr. to: Life and Horizon mags. Trustee Am. Austrian Found., Scientists' Inst. Pub. Info. Mem. Council on Fgn. Relations, Am. Council on Germany, World Press Freedom Com. (dir.), Met. Opera Guild (dir.), Met. Opera Assn., ASCAP, Phi Beta Kappa. Club: Century Assn. (N.Y.). Home: 50 E 72d St New York NY 10021 Office: Time and Life Bldg Rockefeller Center New York NY 10020

GRUPPE, KARL HEINRICK, sculptor; b. Rochester, N.Y., Mar. 18, 1893; s. Charles Paul and Helen Elizabeth (Mitchell) G.; m. Betty A. Clarke, Oct. 9, 1948; 1 dau., Elizabeth Mitchell. Student art, Royal Acad., Antwerp, Belgium,, Art Student League, N.Y.C.; pupil of, Karl Bitter, N.Y.C., 1912-15. Chief sculptor monument restoration project, Dept. Parks, N.Y.C., 1934-37. Served with USMC, 1918-19. Recipient St. Gaudens prize Art Students League, 1912, Avery prize Archtl. League, 1920, Helen Foster Barnett prize, 1926; Saltus gold medal NAD, 1952; Dessie Greer prize 131st Ann. Exhbn. NAD, 1956; Lindsey Morris Meml. prize Nat. Sculpture Soc., 1968; Gold medal, 1975; Elizabeth Watrous Gold medal for sculpture NAD, 1969, 76; Daniel Chester French award, 1974; medal of honor Nat. Arts Club, 1970, Nat. Sculpture Soc., 1980. Mem. N.A.D. (1st v.p. 1956-59), Art Commn. Assos. (dir.), Nat. Sculpture Soc. (pres. 1950, Therese and Edwin H. Richard Meml. prize 1977). Clubs: Century Assn., Nat. Arts (N.Y.C.). Home: Box 926 Southold NY 11971

GRUSKIN, ALAN BURTON, physician, educator; b. Springfield, Mass., June 30, 1937; s. Irving and Ida G.; m. Alberta Mandell, June 28, 1959; children: Karen, Glenn. B.S., U. Mass., Amherst, 1959; M.D. cum laude, U. Vt., Burlington, 1963. Diplomate: Am. Bd. Pediatrics (pediatric nephrology; chmn. subspecialty bd. 1980). Intern, then resident in pediatrics Bronx (N.Y.) Mcpl. Hosp. Center, 1963-65; postdoctoral fellow Albert Einstein Coll. Medicine, 1965-68; mem. faculty Temple U. Med. Sch., Phila., 1968—, prof. pediatrics, 1979—; dir. renal div. St. Christopher's Hosp. Children, 1973—, exec. dir. end stage renal disease program, 1977, chmn. edn. com., 1974-77, pres. med. staff, 1981-83, bd. mgrs., 1981-84; cons. Cherry Hill (N.J.) Hosp., 1972—, Cooper Hosp., Camden, N.J.; mem. Internat. Study Kidney Disease in Children, 1971—; exec. com. Chronic Renal Disease Network 24, 1976-81; bd. dirs. Phila. Renal Youth Rehab. Program, 1976, United Hosps., Inc., Phila., 1981-84, Greater Del. Valley Kidney Found., 1971, treas., 1973-76; pres. 1980 Internat. Pediatric Nephrology Symposium, 1977; chmn. bd. dirs. Kidney Found. Southeastern Pa., 1979. Editor Internat. Jour. Pediatric Nephrology; editorial bd. Perspectives in Peritoneal Dialysis; Contbr. numerous articles to med. jours. Mem. Internat. Soc. Pediatric Nephrology, Internat. Soc. Nephrology, Soc. Pediatric Research (chmn. nephrology session 1980), Am. Soc. Nephrology, Am. Acad. Pediatrics, Am. Fedn. Clin. Research, Am. Soc. Pediatric Nephrology, Phila. Pediatric Soc., Am. Heart Assn., Soc. Pediatric Research, Heart Assn. Southeastern Pa., Heart Assn. Pa. Home: 1922 Huntington Dr Cherry Hill NJ 08003 Office: St Christopher's Hosp for Children 5th and Lehigh Aves Philadelphia PA 19133

GRUSKIN, MARY J. (MRS. ALAN D. GRUSKIN), art dealer; b. Italy; d. Mauro Bovio and Tina Simone; m. Alan D. Gruskin, July 16, 1940; children—Richard B., Robert A. Student, Cooper Union, Traphagen Sch. Design, Grand Central Art Sch., N.Y. Sch. Design, Art Students League. Designer for china; dress buyer Martin's, Bklyn., 1937-40; partner Midtown Galleries, 1944—, dir., 1970—. Assembled paintings for Art-in-Industry collections; assisted arrangement contemporary Am. artists group for design of print fabrics; illustrated: book jacket and story for book House That Runs Itself. Mem. Trenton, Friends of N.J. State Mus., Trenton. Mem. Art Dealers Assn., Nat. Council Women U.S. Home: 200 E 57th St New York NY 10022 Office: 11 E 57th St New York NY 10022

GRUSKOFF, MICHAEL SAUL, film producer; b. N.Y.C., Aug. 27, 1935; s. Max G. and Lillian (Brodsky) Wortman; m. Aloma Ichinose, Dec. 7, 1963 (div. 1972); children: Shawn, Peter, Jennifer. Agt. William Morris Agy., N.Y.C., 1958-60, Creative Mgmt. Assocs., Los Angeles, 1964-70; ind. film producer, Los Angeles, 1971—. Served with Presdl. Honor Guard, 1955-57. Recipient comedy award Acad. Humor, 1976, Caesar award Acad. Arts and Techniques of Cinema (France), 1982, Outstanding Achievement award Acad. Sci. Ficiton, 1982, Golden Globe nomination Hollywood Fgn. Press, 1982. Mem. Acad. Motion Picture Arts and Scis. Democrat. Jewish. Office: Gruskoff Film Orgn 10202 W Washington Blvd Culver City CA 90230

GRUSON, SYDNEY, newspaper executive; b. Dublin, Ireland, Dec. 16, 1916; came to U.S., naturalized, 1962; s. Harry and Edith (Black) G.; m. Marit Bergson Gentele, Aug. 25, 1975; 1 dau., Kerry; children by previous marriage: Sheila Clare, Lindsey David. Privately educated. Rewrite man, reporter, fgn. corr. Can. Press, Toronto, 1932-44; mem. staff N.Y. Times, 1944-67, 69—; editor, chief exec. officer Paris edit., 1966-67, v.p., then sr. v.p., 1970-79, vice chmn., 1979—; asso. pub. Newsday, 1968-69; dir. N.Y. Times Co. Jewish. Club: Sands Point Golf. Office: NY Times 229 W 43d St New York NY 10036 *

GRUTKA, ANDREW GREGORY, bishop; b. Joliet, Ill., Nov. 17, 1908. Student, St. Procopius Coll. and Sem., Lisle, Ill., Urban U. and Gregorian U., Rome. Ordained priest Roman Catholic Ch., 1933; moderator of lay activities Diocese of Gary, Ind., 1955; first bishop of, Gary, 1957; mem. Pontifical Marian Acad., 1970; pres. Cath. Communications Found., 1971-76, chmn. bd., 1976—. Office: PO Box 80428 San Diego CA 92138 *

GRUVER, BERNARD FRANCIS, animated film designer, educator; b. Long Beach, Calif., June 25, 1923; s. Joseph and Ethel (Warshafsky) G.; m. Adah Coropoff, Aug. 18, 1946 (div. Aug. 1978); children: Nancy, Allison,; m. Jan Green, Sept., 1978. Student, Long Beach City Coll., 1941-42; grad., Art. Ctr. Sch., 1950. Mem. tech. staff Graphic Films co., Los Angeles, 1950-56; designer TV commls. Kling Studios, Los Angeles, 1954; designer Acad. Pictures, N.Y.C., 1954; film dir. story and design John Sutherland Prodns., Los Angeles, 1955-56; adj. prof. animation design U. So. Calif., Los Angeles, 1963, 65, 68, 69-76. Film designer: The Spray's The Thing, 1955, The Golden River, 1956; designer, dir. TV comls., Bill Melendez Prodns., Los Angeles, 1965—, Bill Melendez Prodns., Los Angeles; films A Charlie Brown Christmas, 1965 (George Foster Peabody award), It's The Great Pumpkin, Charlie Brown, 1966. Recipient numerous award, Internat. Broadcasting award, 1963, Golden Eagle award, 1964, Venice Film Festival award, 1954. Mem. Acad. Motion Picture Arts and Scis., Internat. Animation Soc. (dir. 1963-76), Screen Cartoonist Guild (pres. 1955-57), TV Acad., U. So. Calif. Alumni Assn., Art Center Alumni Assn. Home: 5010 Sunnyslope Ave Sherman Oaks CA 91423 Office: 439 N Larchmont Blvd Los Angeles CA 90004

GRUZLESKI, JOHN EDWARD, mining and metallurgical engineering educator, scientist; b. Sudbury, Ont., Can., Dec. 10, 1941; s. Alexander Leo and Beatrice Elizabeth (Zettel) G.; m. Olga Korec, Aug. 30, 1969. B.Sc., Queen's U., Kingston, Ont., 1964, M.Sc., 1965; Ph.D., U. Toronto (Ont.), 1967. Asst. prof. mining and metall. engring. McGill U., Montreal, Que., 1969-72, assoc. prof., 1972-82, prof., 1982—, chmn. dept. mining and metall. engring., 1980—. Contbr. articles to profl. jours.; co-inventor non destructiv foundry control device. Mem. Am. Soc. Metals (pres. Montreal chpt. 1977-78), Metall. Soc. (treas. Montreal chpt. 1978-81), Ordre des Ingenieurs du Quebec, Can. Inst. Mining and Metallurgy, Am. Founderymen's Soc. Roman Catholic. Office: Dept Mining and Metall Engring McGill U 3450 University St Montreal PQ Canada H3A 2A7

GRYDER, JOHN WILLIAM, chemistry educator; b. Los Angeles, Nov. 6, 1926; s. William Thomas and Myrtle (Bogart) G.; m. Rosa Meyersburg, Sept. 1, 1949; children: David Jonas, Katherine Ann, Thomas William. B.S., Calif. Inst. Tech., 1946; Ph.D., Columbia, 1950. Jr. scientist Brookhaven Nat. Lab., 1948-49; mem. faculty Johns Hopkins, 1949-, prof. chemistry, 1966—, exec. officer dept., 1966-70, assoc. dean Sch. Arts and Scis., 1982—; Mem. steering com. Baltimore County-City Sci. Seminars, 1958-73. Contbr. articles to profl. jours. Bd. govs. Center Research Instrn. and Curricuium in Sci. and Math., 1965-68; chmn. bd. mgrs. Levering Hall YMCA, 1966-72; trustee People's Community Health Center, 1981-82. Mem. Am. Chem. Soc., AAUP, Am. Phys. Soc., Sigma Xi, Tau Beta Pi. Democrat. Home: 2006 W Rogers Ave Baltimore MA 21209

GRYDER, ROSA MEYERSBURG, toxicologist; b. Bklyn., Aug. 23, 1926; d. Reuben and Dorothy Meyersburg; m. John William Gryder, Sept. 1, 1949; children: David, Katherine, Thomas. B.S. in Biology, Bucknell U., 1947; M.S. in Microbiology, Yale U., 1949; Ph.D. in Biochemistry, Johns Hopkins U., 1955. Fellow in ophthalmology Wilmer Inst., Johns Hopkins U. Sch. Medicine, 1954-55, NIH postdoctoral fellow, 1956-59, research asso. dept. physiol. chemistry, 1961-64; asst. prof. biochemistry U. Md. Sch. Medicine, 1966-74; sci. adv. Office Health Affairs FDA, Rockville, Md., 1974-79; assoc. dir. research ops. and planning Nat. Center Toxicological Research, 1979-82; toxicologist FDA, Washington, 1982—. Mem. N.Y. Acad. Scis., Am. Soc. Microbiology, Am. Coll. Toxicology, Soc. Risk Assessment, Soc. Study Social Biology. Office: 200 C St SW Washington DC 20204

GRYSON, JOSEPH ANTHONY, orthodontist; b. Rahway, N.J., Feb. 11, 1932; s. Elmer Joseph Anthony and Joyce Asher (Toms) G.; m. Patricia Ann Huddleston, Nov. 22, 1961; children—Karen Ann, David Joseph. B.Chem. Engring., Cornell U., 1954; D.D.S., U. Calif., San Francisco, 1964. Diplomate: Am. Bd. Orthodontics. Engr. div. refinery tech. service Standard Oil of Calif., Richmond, 1954, 58-60; individual practice dentistry specializing in orthodontics, San Rafael, Calif., 1964—; clin. prof. orthodontics U. Calif., San Francisco, 1965—. Contbr. articles to profl. jours. Treas., pres., dir. Homeowners Assn., San Rafael, 1970—. Served as pilot USN, 1954-58. Mem. Pacific Coast Soc. Orthodontists (com. chmn. 1976-78, treas. 1970-76, program chmn. 1978-79, dir. 1980—), Am. Assn. Orthodontists, ADA, Calif. Dental Assn., E.H. Angle Soc. Home: 1060 Lea Dr San Rafael CA 94903 Office: 750 Las Gallinas Ave San Rafael CA 94903

GRZYBOWSKI, KAZIMIERZ, legal educator; b. Czortków, Poland, June 19, 1911; came to U.S., 1950; s. Ludwik and Maria (Wieckowska) G.; m. Zofia Szczerbowska, Aug. 5, 1936. LL.M., U. Lwow, Poland, 1933, Dr.Jur., 1935; S.J.D., Harvard U., 1934. Bar: Poland 1936. Asst. prof. law Lvov (Poland) U., 1936-39; judge dist. ct., Lvov, 1936-39; dir. Polish Info. Service, Middle East, Jerusalem, 1942-45; exec. officer Govt. Com. Polish Affairs, 1945-48; free-lance journalist, London, 1948-50; editor law library Library of Congress, Washington, 1950-60; vis. prof. law U. Mich., Ann Arbor, 1960-61, Yale Law Sch., New Haven, 1961-62, Leiden (Holland) U., 1963-64; sr. research asso. Duke U., Durham, N.C., 1964—, prof. law and polit. sci., 1970—; Cons. Rand Corp., Washington, 1961-63, State Dept., 1961, ACDA, Washington, 1964. Author in Polish) Article 18 of the Covenant of the League of Nations, 1934; (in Polish) Article 18 of the Covenant of the League of Nations International Tribunals and Municipal Law, 1937, General Principles of Private International Law Conflicts, 1939; (with V. Gsovski) (in English) Government Law and Courts in the Soviet Union and Eastern Europe, 2 vols, 1959, The Draft of the Civil Code in Poland, 1962; Economic Treaties and Agreements of the Soviet Bloc, 1952, Soviet Legal Institutions, Their Doctrines and Social Functions, 1962, Soviet Private International Law, 1965, The Socialist Commonwealth of Nations: Organization and Institutions, 1964, Soviet Public International Law: Doctrines and Diplomatic Practice, 1970, East West Trade, 1974, Trade with China, 1975. Served with Polish Army, 1939-42. Decorated Mil. Cross.; grantee Gregory and Kosciuszko Found., 1933-34; Recipient grants Fulbright Found., Leiden, 1963-64, Fulbright Found., Strasbourg, France, 1967-68,

Carnegie Endowment, 1964-67. Mem. Am. Soc. Study Comparative Law (bd. govs. 1970—). Home: 2605 University Dr Durham NC 27707

GSCHNEIDNER, KARL ALBERT, JR., metallurgist, educator, editor, consultant; b. Detroit, Nov. 16, 1930; s. Karl and Eugenie (Zehetmair) Gschneiner; m. Melba. E. Pickenpaugh, Nov. 4, 1957; children: Thomas, David, Edward, Kathryn. B.S., U. Detroit, 1952; Ph.D., Iowa State U., 1957. Mem. staff Los Alamos Sci. Lab., 1952-62, sec. chief, 1961-62; vis. asst. prof. U. Ill., Urbana, 1962-63; assoc. prof. materials sci. and engring. Iowa State U., Ames, 1963-67, prof., 1967-69, Disting. prof., 1979—, metallurgist, 1963-67, sr. metallurgist, 1967—, dir. Rare-Eath Infto. Ctr., 1966—; vis. prof. U. Calif.-San Diego, La Jolla, 1979-80; cons. Los Alamos Nat. Lab., 1981—. Author: Rare Earth Alloys, 1961, Scandium, 1975; other books, numerous articles to profl. publs., numerous chpts. to profl. publs.; editor: (5 vol.) book Handbook on the Physics and Chemistry of Rare Earths, 1979-82, Industrial Applications of Rare Earth Elements, 1981; other books. Recipient William Hume-Rothery award AIME, Warrendale, Pa., 1978, Outstanding Sci. Accomplishment in Metallurgy and Ceramics award Dept. Energy, Washington, 1982. Mem. Am. Chem. Soc., Am. Soc. Metals, Am. Crystallographic Assn., Metall. Soc. (former chmn. coms., awards 1979—), AAAS. Roman Catholic. Office: Iowa State U Ames Lab Ames IA 50011

GSCHWIND, DONALD, automotive corporation executive; b. Youngstown, Ohio, July 3, 1933; s. Mark Leon and Esther Lillian (Wauschek) G.; s. Eleanor Ann Tyken, May 27, 1961; children: Sandra J., Kurt L. B.S. in Mech. Engring., Case Westen Res. U., 1955; M.S. in Auto Engring., Chrysler Inst. Engring., 1957; M.B.A., Mich. State U., 1975. With Chrysler Corp., Detroit, 1968—, mgr. steering and suspense engring., 1968-72, mgr. product engring., 1972-74, mgr. quality control, 1974-76, dir. chassis engring., 1976-80, v.p. product planning, 1980—. Served to 1st lt. USAF, 1957-59. Mem. Soc. Auto Engring., Tau Beta Pi. Office: Chrysler Corp PO Box 857 Detroit MI 48288

GSCHWIND, JOHN KARL, industrial products company executive; b. Reedsburg, Wis., Feb. 9, 1934; s. Alfred Edward and Mary Elizabeth (Donahoe) G.; m. Regina Crane, June 22, 1957; children: John C., Paul C., Maria, Julie R., Clare T. B.S. in Chem. Engring. cum laude, U. Notre Dame, 1956. Process engr. Kimberly Clark, 1960-62, prodn. supt., 1963-65; prodn. mgr. John Strange Paper Co., 1965-67, gen. mgr., 1967-70, v.p. adminstrn., 1970-72; gen. mgr., asst. to pres. Menasha Corp., 1972-74, corp. v.p., 1974-78; pres. plastics div. Albany Internat. (N.Y.), 1978-79, group v.p. indsl. products, 1980—. Served with USN, 1956-60. Mem. Am. Mgmt. Assn., Albany C. of C., NAM, Notre Dame Alumni Northeastern N.Y. Office: Albany Internat One Sage Rd Albany NY 12204

GSTALDER, HERBERT WILLIAM, pub.; b. New Rochelle, N.Y., Dec. 27, 1942; s. HerbertHerbert Charles and Mary Jane (McDonald) G.; m. Barbara Elizabeth Kraus, Sept. 11, 1965; children—Karen Elizabeth, Steven Herbert, Ellen Catherine. B.A., Georgetown U., 1965; M.B.A., N.Y. U., 1968. With Kraus Periodicals, Millwood, N.Y., 1965—; mgr. Kraus Reprint Co., Millwood, 1970—; v.p. Kraus-Thomson Orgn., Millwood, 1974, pres., 1976—, also dir. Mem. ALA. Roman Catholic. Home: 15 Cross Ridge Rd Chappaqua NY 10514 Office: Route 100 Millwood NY 10546

GUADIERI, MILLICENT HALL, association executive; b. East Liverpool, Ohio, Jan. 26, 1941; d. John Thompson and Sara (Pollock) Hall; m. Alexander V.J. Guadiere, June 10, 1967; 1 son, Alexandre Barclay Everson. A.A., Centenary Coll., Hackettstown, N.J., 1961; postgrad., U. Pitts., 1962. Polit. researcher U.S. embassy, Paris, 1964-65; asst. to pres. RTV Internat., Inc., N.Y.C., 1966-71; adminstr. Assn. Art Mus. Dirs., Savannah, Ga., 1973—. Bd. dirs. Ga. Pub. Radio, Savannah, 1978-79. Mem. N.Y. Jr. League (dir. 1973-75, Vol. of Yr. award 1978), Am. Assn. Mus. Republican. Presbyterian. Home: 311 W York St Savannah GA 31401 Office: Assn Art Mus Dirs PO Box 10082 Savannah GA 31401

GUALTIERI, JOSEPH PETER, museum dir.; b. Royalton, Ill., Dec. 25, 1916; s. Simone and Teresa (Toracca) G.; m. Marie E. MacDonald, Nov. 21, 1939; children—Ricardo Simone, Renee Marie. Diploma, Art Inst. Chgo., 1939; postgrad. study in, Italy, 1969-70. Tchr. art Hull House, Chgo., 1942, Lyman Allyn Mus., New London, Conn., 1945-46, Willimantic State Coll., Willimantic, Conn., summers 1950-52, Hillyer Coll., Hartford, Conn., eves. 1957-58, Norwich (Conn.) Art Sch., also Norwich Free Acad., 1943-79; dir. Slater Meml. Mus., Norwich, 1962—. One-man exhbns. include, Chgo. Art Inst., 1941, Contemporary Art Gallery, N.Y.C., 1951, Nexus Gallery, Boston, 1965, Parnassus Gallery, Chgo., 1941-42, Cummings Art Center, New London, Conn., 1979. Bd. dirs. Otis Library, Norwich, 1975—; mem. Norwich Charter Revision Com. Recipient 1st prize Chgo. Art Inst., 1941, Logan medal, 1941; purchase prize Pa. Acad. Fine Arts, 1948, 51; prize Eastern States Exposition Conn. Artists, 1951. Mem. Conn. Acad. Fine Arts. Home: 60 Warren St Norwich CT 06360 Office: 108 Crescent St Norwich CT 06360

GUANDOLO, JOHN, lawyer; b. Beaver County, Pa., Sept. 11, 1919; s. Vincent and Tommasina (Meta) G.; m. Elizabeth Wade, Feb. 13, 1942; 1 son, Joseph Wade. A.B. in Econs, U. Ill., 1940; J.D., U. Md., 1943; transp. courses, Northwestern U., 1962. Bar: D.C. bar 1944, Md. bar 1952, Ill. bar 1956, Mo. bar 1962, U.S. Supreme Ct. bar 1949. Trial atty. Dept. Justice, 1948-56; gen. atty. Rock Island R.R., 1956-57; practice law specializing in transp. and antitrust law, Washington, 1957-62, 63—; commerce atty. M.P. R.R., 1962-63; gen. ptnr. Macdonald, McInerny, Guandolo, Jordan & Crampton, Washington, 1963—; lectr. Am. U., 1967-73. Co-author: Federal Procedure Forms, Vol. 1, 1949, author 3 vols., 1961, also supplements; co-author: Regulation of Transportation, 1964, Transportation Regulation, 1972, 79, 83; author: Transportation Law, 1965, 73, 79, 83, (with others) Coordinated Transportation: Problems and Requirements, 1969; also articles; editor-in-chief: ICC Practitioners Jour, 1959-75. Mem. Am., Fed., D.C. bar assns., Assn. ICC Practitioners (pres. 1976-77), Am. Soc. Traffic and Transp. Club: University (Washington). Home: 10905 Rosemont Dr Rockville MD 20852 Office: 1090 Vermont Ave NW Washington DC 20005

GUARD, DAVE, musician; b. Honolulu, Oct. 19, 1934; s. Carl Jackson and Marjorie Elizabeth (Kent) G.; m. Gretchen Ballard, Nov. 4, 1957 (div. Nov. 1979); children: Catherine Kent, Thomas Jonathan, Sarah. B.A. in Econs., Stanford U., 1956; student, Swami Muktananda, 1976—. Lived in, Australia, 1962-68; pres. Britannia Enterprises, Ltd., 1960—; dir. Granada Music BMI, 1961-66; final judge Am. Song Festival, 1978—; Univ. lectr. Deirdre, 1978—. Leader, Kingston Trio, 1957-61, Whiskeyhill Singers, 1962; folk music adviser: TV series for Jazz Meets Folk, Australian Broadcasting Commn., 1964; host: TV music series Dave's Place, 1965-66; leader, The Expanding Band, 1978—; mem. singing group, Hassilev, Settle & Guard, 1974; songwriter, arranger, tchr.; recording artist for, Capitol Records; also albums recorded in Australia as accompanist; Whiskeyhill Singers recorded: sound track for film How The West Was Won, 1962 (Acad. award); Kalimba soloist, 1967; featured performer: ABC-TV Spl. Great Folk Revival, 1974; accompanist: Manhattan Transfer Singing Group, 1977; vocalist: John Stewart album Bombs Away Dream Babies, 1979; corr.: Peninsula mag, 1977; producer: Hawaiian album Pure Gabby, 1979 (Recipient 7 Gold Record awards, 2 Grammy awards.); Author: Colour Guitar, 1967, Colour Guitar Primer, 1971, Colour Guitar Reader, 1972, (with Gretchen Guard) Deirdre: A Celtic Legend, 1977, (with Caridad Sumile) Hale-Mano: A Legend of Hawaii, 1981; Editor: Baba Company Mag, 1981, Siddha Path mag., 1983; Reviewer: Hawaiian album Whole Earth Catalog, 1968-69. Recipient 7 Gold Record awards, 2 Grammy awards, Hoku-Hano-Hano award. Inventor musicolor system. Address: 1023 Mercedes Ave Los Altos CA 94022

GUARD, RAY WESLEY, educator, metallurgist; b. Lafayette, Ind., Nov. 28, 1927; s. Arthur Thomas and Cleo (Gross) G.; m. Edwina Louise Nichols, Oct. 16, 1948; children—Daniel Thomas, Neil Russell, Randall Brian, Alan Edward, Celia Louise; m. Sue Ann Russell, Aug. 10, 1979; children—William Anton Russell, Michael Aaron Russell, Nicole Alexis Russell. B.S. in Metall. Engring, Purdue U., 1947, Ph.D., 1952; M.S., Carnegie Inst. Tech., 1948. Instr. Purdue U., 1948-50; research asso. Gen. Electric Co., 1952-60, mgr. diamond process devel., 1960-62; mgr. metallurgy br. Gen. Precision Ind., 1962-63; group leader metall. service N.Am. Aviation Sci. Center, 1963-66; prof. metall. engring., head dept. Mich. Tech. U., 1966-70; dean Coll. Engring., U. Tex. at El Paso, 1970-76, prof. metall. engring., 1976—; adj. asso. prof. metall. engring. Rensselaer Poly. Inst., 1956-60; Dir. Copper Industries Devel. Corp., 1967-70. Bd. dirs. Portage Lake United Fund, 1968-70. Federated Metals Co. scholar, 1947; recipient Best Paper award Am. Inst. Chem. Engring., 1960. Mem. Am. Inst. Mining, Metall. and Petroleum Engrs. (chmn. high temperature materials com. 1959-60), Am. Soc. Metals (chmn. trans. com. 1959-60), Acta Metallurgica (dir. 1972-75), Tau Beta Pi, Phi Kappa Phi. Patentee in field. Home: 1018 Blanchard St El Paso TX 79902

GUARDINO, HARRY, actor; b. Bklyn., Dec. 23, 1925. Ed., Haaren High Sch. Movie debut, 1951; films include Pork Chop Hill, 1959, Hell is for Heroes, 1962, Madigan, 1968, Lovers and Other Strangers, 1969, Red Sky at Morning, 1971, Dirty Harry, 1971, Capone, 1975, St. Ives, 1976, The Enforcer, 1976, Roller Coaster, 1977, Any Which Way You Can, 1980; TV movies include Indict and Convict, 1974, Street Killing, 1976, Contract on Cherry St, 1977, Evening in Byzantium, The Sophisticated Gents, 1981; TV appearances include Police Story; appeared on: Broadway in Woman of the Year, 1980-81; also others. Mem. Acad. Motion Picture Arts and Scis. Office: care Internat Creative Mgmt 40 W 57th St New York NY 10019 *

GUARDO, CAROL J., university administrator; b. Hartford, Conn., Apr. 12, 1939; d. C. Fred and Marion (Biase) G. B.A., St. Joseph Coll., 1961; M.A., U. Detroit, 1963; Ph.D., U. Denver, 1966. Asst. prof. psychology Eastern Mich. U., Ypsilanti, 1966-68; asso. prof., staff psychologist U. Denver, 1968-73; asso. prof., dean coll. Utica Coll. of Syracuse U., Utica, N.Y., 1973-76; prof., dean Coll. Liberal Arts, Drake U., Des Moines, 1976-80; provost, prof. U. Hartford, 1980—; Mem. Iowa Humanities Bd., 1976-80, pres., 1978-80; bd. dirs. Assn. Am. Colls. Author: The Adolescent As Individual: Issues and Insights, 1975; contbr. articles to profl. jours. Trustee St. Joseph Coll. NSF fellow, 1964; NIMH fellow, 1964-66. Mem. Am. Assn. Higher Edn., Am. Psychol. Assn., Assn. Gen. and Liberal Studies (pres. 1979-81), Soc. Research in Child Devel., Phi Beta Kappa. Office: U Hartford West Hartford CT 06117

GUARE, JOHN, playwright; b. N.Y.C., Feb. 5, 1938; s. John and Helen Clare (Grady) G.; m. Adele Chatfield-Taylor. Grad., Georgetown U.; M.A., Yale U. Lectr. NYU; seminar in writing fellow Saybrook Coll., Yale U., 1977-78. Author: (plays) Muzeeka, 1968; plays Cop-out, 1969, House of Blue Leaves, 1970, Rich and Famous, 1977, Bosoms and Neglect, 1979, Lydie Breeze, 1982, Gardenia, 1982; co-adapter, lyricist: Two Gentlemen of Verona, 1971; Marco Polo Sings a Solo, 1973, Landscape of the Body, 1977; co-author: (screenplay) Taking Off, 1970; author: Atlantic City, 1981; playwright-in-residence, N.Y. Shakespeare Festival, 1976-77. Bd. dirs. N.Y. Mcpl. Arts Soc. Recipient Obie award for Muzeeka, 1968, Variety Poll award N.Y. Drama Critics Most Promising Playwright, 1968-69, N.Y. Drama Critics award for Best Am. Play, 1971, Obie award for Best Play, 1971, Outer Critics Circle prize for Playwriting, 1971, N.Y. Drama Critics award for Best Musical, 1972, Tony awards for Best Musical and Best Libretto, 1972, Jefferson award, 1971, Best Screenplay award N.Y. Film Critics, Los Angeles Film Critics, Nat. Film Critics, 1981. Mem. Dramatist Guild Council, Authors League; fellow N.Y. Inst. Humanities. Address: care R. Andrew Boose 1 Dag Hammarskjold Plaza New York NY 10017 *

GUARINI, FRANK J., congressman; b. Jersey City, Aug. 20, 1924; s. Frank J. and Caroline (Critelli) G. Student, Columbia U.; B.A., Dartmouth Coll., 1947; LL.B., N.Y.U., 1950, LL.M., 1955; postgrad., The Hague Acad. Internat. Law, Netherlands. Bar: N.J. 1951, U.S. Supreme Ct. 1951, Ct. Internat. Trade 1979. Partner firm Guarini & Guarini, Jersey City, 1951—; mem. 96th-98th Congresses from 14th N.J. Dist.; mem. ways and means com., subcom. on trade, subcom. on select revenue measures, oversight subcom., select com. on narcotics abuse; mem. N.J. Senate, 1966-72, chmn. air and water pollution and pub. health com., appropriations com., 1967-68. Co-author: New Jersey Rules of Evidence. Mem. council on govt. Fairleigh Dickinson U.; mem. exec. com. Christ Hosp., Jersey City; fund chmn. Urban League Hudson County.; Bd. dirs. Hudson County Mental Health Assn., Hudson County Health and Tb League; mem. nat. bd. govs. ARC, also pres. Jersey City chpt.; chmn. bd. regents St. Peter's Coll., Jersey City; trustee Hudson County Bar Found. Served to lt. USNR, 1942-46; PTO. Mem. ABA, Fed. Bar Assn., Inter-Am. Bar Assn., Hudson County Bar Assn. (trustee), N.J. State Bar Assn. (gen. council), Hudson County C. of C., Hague Acad. Internat. Law (trustee), Assn. Am. Trial Lawyers (nat. bd. govs.), N.J. Assn. Trial Lawyers (chmn. exec. com.), Dante Alighieri Soc., UNICO, Phi Delta Phi (pres.), Alpha Delta Phi. Clubs: Rotary (dir.), Columbus Citizens, Bergen Carteret; University, Hudson County (Jersey City) (bd. govs.). Office: 610 Newark Ave Jersey City NJ 07306 also Longworth House Office Bldg Washington DC 20515

GUARINO, JOHN RALPH, physician, scientist; b. N.Y.C., Aug. 17, 1915; s. Joseph J. and Marie (Ferrara) G.; m. Kathleen Paff, Aug. 2, 1947; children: Christopher John, Joseph Charles, Edward James. B.S., L.I. U., 1937; M.D., Coll. Physicians and Surgeons, Boston, 1943. Diplomate: Am. Bd. Internal Medicine. Intern Wyckoff Hosp., Bklyn., 1943-44; resident in internal medicine VA Hosp., Buffalo, N.Y., 1955-57; practice medicine, Westford, Mass., 1947-52, research on simplified artificial kidney, 1947-52; inaugurated artificial kidney service Harlem Hosp., N.Y.C., 1952-53, chief artificial kidney service, 1952-53, L.I. Coll. Medicine Hosp., 1952-53; asst. chief medicine VA Hosp., Livermore, Calif., 1959-69, chief medicine, Poplar Bluff, Mo., 1969-72, Topeka, Kans., 1972-74, internist, Boise, Idaho, 1974—; clin. asst. prof. medicine U. Wash., 1977-79, clin. asso. prof., 1979-83, clin. prof., 1983—; cons. dialysis and treatment uremia, 1952—, guest lectr. nephrology, 1952—. Contbr. articles on internal medicine to profl. jours. Served to capt., M.C. USAF, 1953-55. Fellow A.C.P.; mem. Am. Soc. Artificial Internal Organs (charter), Mass. Med. Soc., AMA. Roman Catholic. Pioneer in development of artificial kidney, lung and heart; developed auscultatory percussion method of chest examination, auscultatory percussion exam. of head to detect intracranial masses, auscultatory percussion exam. of urinary bladder to detect urinary retention. Address: 2404 Ormond St Boise ID 83705

Creative research cannot be programmed, directed, or hired. A fat budget often perpetuates sterile output. It is no substitute for a hungry mind.

GUARINO, ROGER CHARLES, brokerage company executive; b. N.Y.C., July 2, 1929; s. Nicholas Joseph and Gloria (Briatico) G.; m. Gloria O'Toole, June 2, 1956; children—Roger Charles, Jr., Barbara, Stephen (dec.). B.S., Columbia U., 1951; M.B.A., Hofstra U., 1960. Systems engr. Am. Machine & Foundry Co., Greenwich, Conn., 1951-53, 55-56; sr. project engr. Am. Bosch Arma Corp., Garden City, N.Y., 1956-60; mgr. mgmt. systems dept. AVCO Missile Systems, Wilmington, Mass., 1960-66; dir. corp. systems and data processing Kelsey Hayes Co., Romulus, Mich., 1966-71; v.p. data processing and communications Am. Express Co., N.Y.C., 1971-75; exec. v.p. Fed. Home Loan Bank N.Y., N.Y.C., 1975-81; v.p. Bear, Stearn's & Co., N.Y.C., 1981—. Mem. Am. Inst. Indsl. Engrs., Assn. Systems Mgmt. Home: 1010 Bloomfield St Hoboken NJ 07030 Office: 55 Water St New York NY 10041

GUARRERA, FRANK, concert baritone; b. Phila., Dec. 3, 1924; s. Anthony and Rosaria (Cavallaro) G.; m. Adelina Di Cintio, Oct. 14, 1944. Grad., Curtis Inst. Music, 1948. Now prof. voice and opera U. Wash., Seattle. Made debut in U.S. at, Phila. Pop Concert, 1946; sang with, Norfolk (Va.) Symphony, 1947; operatic debut as Silvio in: Il Pagliacci, N.Y.C. Center, 1947 (recipient award Met. Opera Auditions of the Air), N.Y.C. Center (sponsored by Farnsworth Radio and Television Corp.), N.Y.C. Center (also contract with Met. Opera for 1948-49). Served with USNR, 1943-46. Invited by Arturo Toscanini to La Scala, Italy, for anniversary program dedicated to Boito, and there made debut in role of Fanuel in Nerone, also sang leading role in The Pearl Fishers and role in The Love of Three Kings, 1948; has sung over 35 leading roles at Met. Opera House and in every Opera Co. in U.S. Address: 4514 Latona Ave NE Seattle WA 98105

GUASTAFERRO, ANGELO, federal agency administrator; b. Hoboken, N.J., June 4, 1932; s. Carlo and Rafaela Nancy (Gioffi) G.; m. Eleanor Lago, Sept. 12, 1954; children: Carl, Mark, John Brian. B.S. in Mech. Engring, N.J. Inst. Tech., 1954; M.B.A., Fla. State U., 1963. With NASA, 1963—, dep. project mgr., 1974-76, dir. planetary programs, Washington, 1979-81; dep. dir. Ames Research Center, Moffett Field, Calif., 1981—; v.p., bd. dirs. Langley Fed. Credit Union, 1977-79; cons. in field. Served with USAF, 1955-58. Recipient Langley Spl. Achievement award NASA, 1974, 77, 78, Outstanding Leadership medal, 1977, Superior Performance award, 1980, Exceptional Service medal, 1981, Presdl. Meritorious rank, 1982. Fellow AAAS; Mem. AIAA (Space Systems medal 1982), Planetary Soc., Mars First Landing Soc. (pres. 1978-79). Roman Catholic. Clubs: Toastmasters (Eglin AFB, Fla.) (past pres.); K.C. (grand knight). Office: Ames Research Center Code 200-2 Moffett Field CA 94035

GUAY, EDWARD, financial economist, investment advisor; b. Pitts., Mar. 31, 1943; s. John William and Minnie Catherine (Rohn) G.; m. Joye Nakamura, Dec. 7, 1968; childrenD: Robert Edward, Keiko Ann, David Yukio. B.S. in Fgn. Service, Georgetown U., 1965; M.B.A., U. Pitts., 1968. Fin. analyst Conn. Gen. Corp., Hartford, 1968-71, sr. econ. analyst, 1971-73, economist, 1973-77, chief economist, 1977-82, CIGNA Corp., 1982—; econ. cons. Congl. Adv. Panel, Washington, 1982-83. Justice of peace Bloomfied, Conn., 1981—; mem. Bloomfield Republican Town Com., 1975-83. Served to 1st lt. U.S. Army; 1965-67. Mem. Am. Fin. Assn., Nat. Assn. Bus. Economists, Hartford Soc. Fin. Analysts. Roman Catholic. Office: Econs Dept CIGNA Corp Hartford CT 06152

GUBA, EGON GOTTHOLD, educator; b. Chgo., Mar. 1, 1924; s. Oswald and Rosina (Schell) G.; m. Elaine Vivian Thompson, June 21, 1947 (div.); children—Christianne Joan, Susan Carol, Philip Paul; m. Yvonna Sessions Lincoln, Aug. 7, 1980. A.B., Valparaiso U., 1947; M.A., U. Kans., 1950; Ph.D., U. Chgo., 1952. Instr. math. physics Valparaiso U., 1947-48; research asso. U. Chgo., 1951-53, instr., 1952-56, asst. prof. edn., 1956-57; asso. prof. edn. U. Kansas City, 1957-58; research asso. Community Studies, Inc., Kansas City, Mo., 1957-58; successively research asso., asso. prof., prof. bur. ednl. research and service Ohio State U., 1958-66, dir. bur. ednl. research and service, 1961-65, asst. dir. Sch. Edn., 1965-66; prof. edn. Ind. U., 1966—, asso. dean acad. affairs, 1968-74; Dir. Nat. Inst. for Study Ednl. Change, 1966-68. Editor: Theory into Practice, until 1966. Served with C.E. AUS, 1943-46. Mem. Am. Psychol. Assn., Am. Ednl. Research Assn., Phi Delta Kappa. Home: 942 Waterloo St Bloomington IN 47401

GUBELMANN, WALTER STANLEY, corporate executive; b. N.Y., June 16, 1908; s. William S. and Juliette E. (Metz) G.; m. Barton Green, Nov. 1, 1941; children: William Samuel II, James Barton. Student, Philips Andover Acad.; A.B., Yale U., 1931; postgrad. bus. adminstrn, Columbia U., 1931-33. Pres. Realty & Indsl. Corp., 1935—,. Trustee, pres. Soc. Four Arts, Palm Beach, Fla.; mem. Trust Fund Bd. Library of Congress, Washington, 1973—. Served as capt. AUS, World War II. Mem. Palm Beach Civic Assn. (dir.). Clubs: Racquet and Tennis, N.Y. Yacht (organizer and mgr. Constellation syndicate, winner Am.'s cup 1964), Cruising of Am., Leash (N.Y.C.); Seawanhaka Yacht (Oyster Bay, N.Y.); Pilgrims (N.Y.); L.I. Wyandach Country (Eastport); Corinthian Yacht (Phila.); Royal Swedish Yacht Club (Stockholm, Sweden); Clambake, Bailey's Beach, Newport Country, Reading Room (Newport, R.I.); Bar Harbor (Maine) Yacht; Everglades (gov., v.p.), Seminole, Bath and Tennis (Palm Beach, Fla.). Home: 160 Via del Lago Palm Beach FL 33480 summers Starboard House Narragansett Ave Newport RI 02840 Office: 235 S County Rd Palm Beach FL 33480

GUBSER, CHARLES S., government official, former congressman; b. Gilroy, Calif., Feb. 1916; s. Charles Henry and Ella Oma (Matlack) G.; m. Jean Ella Gordon, Dec. 9, 1972. Student, San Jose (Calif.) State Jr. Coll., 1932-34; A.B., U. Calif., 1937, postgrad., 1937-39. Tchr. secondary sch. Gilroy Union High Sch., 1939-43; operator truck farm, Calif., 1940-50; assemblyman from 29th Dist., Calif. Legislature, 1950-52; mem. 83d-93d congresses from 10th Calif. Dist.; chmn. U.S. sect. Can.-U.S. Permanent Joint Bd. on Def., 1975-77, 82—. Mem. Kappa Alpha. Clubs: Masons, Sertoma. Office: 395 Tam O'Shanter Way Monument CO 80132

GUCCI, ALDO, retail stores executive; b. Florence, Italy, May 26, 1909; s. Guccio G. Now owner Gucci Shops Inc., N.Y.C., Chgo., Beverly Hills, Palm Beach; chmn. bd. Guccio Gucci Soc. r.l, Florence, Rome, Milan, Montecatini, Italy; dir. Gucci Ltd., London, Gucci Soc. Resp. Ltd., Paris. Office: 8 Via Condotti 00187 Rome Italy also care Hamra Assocs 2 E 54th St New York NY 10022 *

GUCCIONE, ROBERT CHARLES JOSEPH EDWARD SABATINI, publisher; b. Bklyn., Dec. 17, 1930; m. Muriel Hudson, 1954; 5 children. Mng. editor London American; founder, pub. Penthouse Mag., N.Y.C., 1965—; also pub. Forum, Viva, PhotoWorld, Omni. Artist, 1948-55; formerly cartoonist and greeting card designer; producer, dir.: film Caligula, 1979. Office: care Penthouse Internat Ltd 909 3d Ave New York NY 10022 *

GUCKIEN, JOHN V., food company executive; b. 1925; married. B.A., St. Joseph's Coll., 1952. With Dean Foods Co., Inc., Franklin Park, Ill., 1952—, exec. v.p. mktg., 1967—, dir. Office: Dean Foods Co Inc 3600 River Rd Franklin Park IL 60131 *

GUDEFIN, MICHEL J., aluminum company executive; b. St. Cloud, France, 1923. B.S.M.E., Columbia U., 1943. With Lazard Freres, 1946-55, Pimax Inc., 1955-59; chmn. Instel Corp., 1959-75; chmn. bd. Howmet Aluminum Corp., Greenwich, Conn.; pres. Pechiney Ugine Kuhlmann Corp.; chmn., chief exec. officer Inisel Corp. Served with U.S. Army, 1944-46. Address: Howmet Aluminum Corp 475 Steamboat Rd Greenwich CT 06830 *

GUDENBERG, HARRY RICHARD, bus. exec.; b. Frankfurt, Germany, May 20, 1933; s. Albert and Erna (Bacharach) G.; m. Sharon Rickey, Nov. 23, 1978; children—Lori, Bruce. B.S., N.Y. U., 1960, M.B.A., 1964; J.D., Seton Hall U., 1970. Bar: N.J. bar 1970, U.S. Supreme Ct 1973. With ITT, N.Y.C., 1970—, dir. indsl. relations, 1977-78, v.p., dir. indsl. relations, 1978-79, v.p., dir. indsl. and employee relations, 1979—. Served with U.S. Army, 1953-55. Mem. Am. Bar Assn., N.J. Bar Assn., Bergen County Bar Assn., Labor Policy Assn., Bar Assn. City N.Y., Machinery and Allied Products Inst., N.Y. Indsl. Relations Assn., Indsl. Relations Research Assn. Office: 320 Park Ave New York NY 10022

GUDGER, LAMAR, lawyer, former congressman; b. Asheville, N.C., Apr. 30, 1919; s. Vonno Lamar and Mary Elizabeth (Wilson) G.; m. Eugenia Reid, Oct. 25, 1947; children—Carol Eugenia, Martha Elizabeth, Lamar, Eugene Reid. A.B., U. N.C., 1940, LL.B., 1942. Bar: N.C. bar 1942. Practiced in Asheville, 1942-77, 81—; mem. N.C. Ho. of Reps., 1951-52, N.C. Senate, 1971-77; solicitor 19th Dist. N.C., 1952-54; mem. 95th-96th Congresses from 11th Dist. N.C.; mem. N.C. Bar Prison Study Com., 1970-74, N.C. Ports Authority, 1967-68, N.C. Legis. Research Commn., 1971-72. Bd. dirs. Buncombe County Mental Health Assn., 1972, Children's Home Soc. N.C., 1972-74; sec. Buncombe County Democratic Party, 1961-62. Served with USAAF, 1942-45. Methodist. *

GUDINAS, DONALD JEROME, retired army officer, banker; b. Sheboygan, Wis., Apr. 15, 1933; s. Frank E. and Margaret A. G.; m. Patricia Roesner, Nov. 22, 1952; children—Allen, Jean, Karen. B.S., Benedictine Coll., 1970; M.B.A., St. Mary's U., 1972; postgrad. exec. mgmt. program, Pa. State U., 1978, Army War Coll., 1978. Cert. comptroller, securities broker/dealer. Entered U.S. Army as capt., 1960, advanced through grades to brig. gen., 1980; comptroller, Ft. Carson, Colo., 1972-76, Ft. Hood, Tex., 1976-78; program, budget officer U.S. Army Forces Command, Ft. McPherson, Ga., 1978-79, dep. comptroller, 1979-80, comptroller, 1980-83; pres. Eisenhower Nat. Bank, San Antonio, 1983—; prof. pub. adminstrn. U. Colo., 1973-77. Author: Automation of Medium Size Commercial Banks, 1972; contbr. articles to profl. jours. Chmn. div. United Way, Atlanta, 1980-82. Decorated DSM, Legion Merit, Bronze Star, others. Mem. Am. Soc. Mil. Comptrollers (pres. chpt.), Assn. U.S. Army., Am. Bankers Assn. Roman Catholic. Club: Ft. Sam Houston Officers. Home: 1207 High Rock Circle San Antonio TX 78282 Office: Eisenhower Nat Bank Fort Sam Houston TX 78234

GUDORF, KENNETH FRANCIS, energy company executive; b. Minster, Ohio, Mar. 3, 1939; s. Norbert Herman and Freda Elizabeth (Moorman) G.; m. Evelyn Margaret Sommer, Aug. 31, 1962; children: Eric, Craig, Caroline. A.B., U. Dayton, 1961; M.B.A., U. Mich., 1967. Dep. treas. Gulf Oil Corp., London, 1970-74; fin. rep. Gulf Corp., Washington, 1974-76; v.p. planning Gulf Oil Corp., Reston, Va., 1976-78, sr. dir. mergers, acquisitions and divestments, Pitts., 1978-81; sr. v.p. fin., chief fin. officer Diversified Energies Inc., Mpls., 1981—; mem. council Minn. State Bd. Investments Adv. Council, St. Paul, 1983—; bd. dirs. Minn. Council Econ. Edn., Mpls., 1982—. Served to capt. U.S. Army, 1962-65. Mem. Fin. Execs. Inst. Clubs: Minneapolis, Mpls. Athletic; Interlachen Country (Mpls.). Home: 5210 Green Farms Rd Edina MN 55436 Office: Diversified Energies Inc 201 S. 7th St Minneapolis MN 55402

GUE, LESLIE ROBB, educator; b. Medicine Hat, Alta., Can., Aug. 5, 1918; s. Dell Irvin and Annie Matilda (Robb) G.; m. Lillian Maud Dutton, Sept. 15, 1943 (div.); children: David, Linda, Alison. B.Ed., U. Alta., 1947, postgrad., 1948-49, Ph.D. (Univ. fellow), 1967; B.S.W., U. B.C., Can., 1960. Clk. Imperial Bank Can., Sangudo, Alta., 1936-40; tchr. Lethbridge (Alta) Sch. Div., 1947-48, Edmonton (Alta.) Public Sch. Bd., 1949-51; editor dept. edn. Govt. of Alta., Edmonton, 1951-52, supr. sch. broadcasts, 1952-54, supt. schs., 1961-64; coordinator rehab. services Alta. Dept. Welfare, Edmonton, 1954-61; prof. dept. ednl. adminstrn. U. Alta., Edmonton, 1966—; cons. on native edn. Can. Edn. Assn., Council of Ministers of Edn. Can.; dir. Thailand-Can. Comprehensive Sch. Projects, 1966-82. Author: An Introduction to Educational Administration in Canada, 1977. Bd. dirs. Goodwill Rehab. Services of Alta., 1963-79, pres., 1967-69; mem. leadership com. Internat. Intervisitation Program, 1978-Canada, 1974-78. Served with RCAF, 1940-45. Can. Council travel grantee, 1974. Mem. Amnesty Internat. (nat. exec. com. 1974-77), Can. Soc. Study of Edn., Can. Assn. Study of Ednl. Adminstrn., Can. Assn. Social Workers, Commonwealth Council for Edn. Adminstrn., Phi Delta Kappa. Unitarian Universalist. Home: PO Box 4453 Edmonton AB Canada T6E 4T5 Office: Dept Ednl Adminstrn U Alta Edmonton AB Canada T6G 2G5 *Life has been good to me, but not easy. I have a deeply rewarding calling—the professorship. I have three fine children, stable and productive people. My goals in life have been to maintain a connectedness with the Central Power and with my fellow human beings, and to be productive and happy in private and public life.*

GUEDEL, JOHN, radio and TV writer, producer; b. Portland, Ind., Oct. 9, 1913; s. Walter Morris and Hazel McKee (Bimel) G.; m. Beth Pingree, Aug. 15, 1936; children—John Kenneth, Heidi Beth; m. Helen Parrish, Aug. 3, 1956; m. Valerie McDonald, June 27, 1968. Student, U. Calif. at Los Angeles, 1931-32. V.p. in charge radio Dan B. Miner Advt. Co., Los Angeles, 1937-41; Russel M. Seeds Advt. Co., Chgo., 1942-44; pres. John Guedel Radio Prodns., Hollywood, 1942—; Partner Peterson-Guedel Family Center, 1959-72; chief exec. officer Tanner Electronics Systems Tech., Inc., 1973—. Motion picture writer: Bohemian Girl (Laurel and Hardy), Hal Roach Studio, Culver City, Calif., 1933-37; writer, producer: People Are Funny, 1938-60, House Party, 1945-70 (Emmy award 1954), Tommy Dorsey show, 1943-44, Charlotte Greenwood show, 1944, Life With Linkletter TV show, 1950-52, 70, Earn Your Vacation show, 1949-50; producer Groucho Marx radio and TV shows, 1947-61 (Emmy and Peabody awards 1952), Red Skelton show, 1943-46; former producer: TV show For Better or Worse; Author: Tornado, 1942; Originator singing comml. radio spots, 1938. Cons. U.S. Dept. State, 1952. Mem. Radio Writers Guild, Radio and TV Dirs. Guild (pres. 1949-50), Nat. Acad. TV Arts and Scis. (pres. Hollywood chpt.), Pacific Pioneer Broadcasters (pres. 1973-74). Home: 8455 Fountain Ave Los Angeles CA 90069 *Don't put seat covers on your life.*

GUEDRY, JAMES WALTER, paper corporation executive, lawyer; b. Morgan City, La., Jan. 7, 1941; s. J. Walter and P. Marie (McNulty) G. A.B. magna cum laude, Georgetown U., 1962; postgrad., U. Brussels, 1962-63; LL.B., U. Va., 1966. Bar: N.Y. 1967. Assoc. Lord, Day & Lord, N.Y.C., 1966-76; counsel Internat. Paper Co., N.Y.C., 1976—. Mem. Assn. Bar City N.Y. Home: 79 Charles St New York NY 10014 Office: Internat Paper Co 77 W 45th St New York NY 10036

GUEDRY, LEO J., agricultural economics educator; b. Baton Rouge, Nov. 2, 1940; s. Leo J. and Beulah LaCour (Monger) G.; m. Nealea Ann Vosbury, Jan. 25, 1964; children: Leigh Ann, Grechen. B.S., La. State U., 1962; M.S., U. Ill.-Urbana, 1965; Ph.D., Oreg. State U.-Corvallis, 1970. Asst. prof. agrl. econs. La. State U., 1969-74, assoc. prof., 1974-81, prof. agrl. econs., Baton Rouge, 1981—, head dept. agrl. econs., 1981—; trustee Gulf South Research Inst., Baton Rouge, 1982—. Mem. editorial council: So. Jour. Agrl. Econs., 1977-79; editor, 1981. Mem. Am. Agrl. Econs. Assn., Am. Econs. Assn., So. Agrl. Econs. Assn., Western Agrl. Econs. Assn. Office: Dept Agrl Econs and Agribus La State U 101 Agrl Adminstrn Bldg Baton Rouge LA 70803

GUELICH, ROBERT VERNON, management consultant; b. Dayton, Ohio, Oct. 30, 1917; s. Lewis M. and Pearl B. (Brown) G.; m. Jane E. Schory, Dec. 6, 1941; children: Susan Jeanne Guelich Mackenzie, Robert Vernon, Helen Jane. B.A., Ohio Wesleyan U., 1938; M.B.A., Harvard U., 1940. Reporter Dayton Jour., 1935-37; writer-editor Air Force mag., 1942-46; asst. dir. public relations Firestone Tire & Rubber Co., Akron, Ohio, 1946-57; v.p. public relations Montgomery Ward & Co., Chgo., 1957-81; sr. mgmt. cons. Hill & Knowlton, Chgo., 1981-83; asst. to chmn. Nat. Fitness Found. and Acad., 1981—; trustee Found. Public Relations Research and Edn., 1978-80; chmn. Nat. Public Relations Seminar, 1981; mem. Exec. Service Corps, 1983—. Bd. dirs. Nat. 4-H Service Com. Council, 1972-81; bd. dirs. Freedoms Found. at Valley Forge, 1978-80; pres. bd. edn. New Trier Twp. High Sch., 1966-70. Served to maj. USAAF, 1941-46. Recipient George Washington Honor medal Freedoms Found., 1977. Mem. Public Relations Soc. Am. (dir. 1976-79, 3 Silver Anvil awards, 4 Presdl. citations, 1976, Outstanding Film award), Phi Beta Kappa, Omicron Delta Kappa, Sigma Delta Chi., Phi Gamma Delta. Republican. Presbyterian. Clubs: Nat. Press (Washington); Chgo. Yacht, Mid-Am. (Chgo.). Home: 380 Sterling Rd Kenilworth IL 60043 Office: Executive Service Corps 25 E Washington Chicago IL 60602

GUEMPEL, GROVER A., finance corporation executive; b. Teaneck, N.J., Sept. 5, 1930; s. Walter Allen and Etta Mae (Whitney) G.; married; children: Walter, Cheryl Ann, Glenn, Kelly. With various fin. cos., to 1964, Fin. Am. Corp., Allentown, Pa., 1964—, now sr. v.p. northeast region. Served with USN, 1948-52. Republican. Home: 1610 N 26th St Allentown PA 18104 Office: Fin Am Corp 1621 Cedar Crest Suite 109 Allentown PA 18104

GUENDEL, THOMAS JOSEPH, machinery manufacturing company executive; b. N.Y.C., July 1, 1927; s. Cornelius Herman and Helen Rose (Sommer) G.; m. Ann Marino, May 26, 1951; children: Douglas, Richard, Stephen. B.S. in Mech. Engring, Pratt Inst., 1950; M.B.A., NYU, 1960. Sales engr. sales, mgmt. cons. service Gen. Electric Co., N.Y.C., 1950-62; mgr. distbn. Westinghouse Air Brake Co., Peoria, Ill., 1962-65, v.p. internat. div., 1965-69; v.p. constrn. equipment div. J.I. Case Co., Racine, Wis., 1969-72, pres., 1972-79, chmn. bd., 1979—, chief exec. officer, dir., 1972—; chmn. bd., chief exec. officer Portec, Inc., 1980—, also dir.; dir. Modine Mfg. Co., Ceco Corp. Mem. adv. council U. Ill., 1981—; Bd. dirs. Nat. Chamber Found.; vice chmn. Spl. Com. for U.S. Exports. Served with USNR, 1945-46. Mem. NAM (dir., exec. com.), Chgo. Council Fgn. Relations, Traffic Club Detroit. Roman Catholic. Clubs: Chgo. Golf, Mid-Am.; Somerset (Racine). Home: 156 Briarwood N Oak Brook IL 60521 Office: Portec Inc 300 Windsor Dr Oak Brook IL 60521

GUENTHER, ARTHUR HENRY, physicist; b. Hoboken, N.J., Apr. 20, 1931; s. George G. and Florence B. (Roberts) G.; m. Joan Eileen Roth, Nov. 21, 1954; children: Tracie Katherine, Wendy Katherine. B.S., Rutgers U., 1953; Ph.D., Pa. State U., 1957; D.Sc., U. Albuquerque, 1973. Supervisory physicist Air Force Weapons Lab., Kirtland AFB, N.Mex., 1959-62, supervisory research physicist, 1962-65, sci. advisor, chief simulation group, 1965-66, chief scientist support group, 1966-69, chief tech. div., 1969-70, sci. dir., tech. div., 1970-74, chief scientist, 1974—; cons. Ctr. Occupational Research and Devel., 1970—; bd. dirs. Tech. Edn. Research Center S.W., 1976—; mem. N.Mex. Sci. and Tech. Com.; adj. prof. physics Air Force Inst. Tech., Wright-Patterson AFB, Ohio, 1967—; adj. prof. elec. engring. Tex. Tech. U., 1971; adj. prof. chemistry U. N.Mex., 1978—. Contbr. articles to profl. jours. Served with USAF, 1957-59. Recipient Disting. Scientist of Yr. award N.Mex. Acad. Sci., 1977; Harry Diamond award IEEE, 1971; Disting. Pub. Service award State of N.Mex., 1981; Arthur L. Schawlow medal, 1983. Fellow Optical Soc. Am., IEEE; mem. Am. Inst. Physics, Am. Chem. Soc., N.Mex. Acad. Scis., ASTM (vice chmn. com. on lasers), Sigma Xi, Phi Lambda Upsilon. Patentee in field. Home: 6304 Rogers Ave NE Albuquerque NM 87110 Office: Air Force Weapons Lab Kirtland AFB NM 87117

GUENTHER, CHARLES JOHN, librarian, author; b. St. Louis, Apr. 29, 1920; s. Charles Richard and Hulda Clara (Schuessler) G.; m. Esther G. Klund, Apr. 11, 1942; children—Charles John, Cecile Anne, Christine Marie. A.A., Harris Tchrs. Coll., 1940; student, St. Louis U., 1952-54; B.A., Webster Coll., 1973, M.A., 1974; L.H.D. (hon.), So. Ill. U., Edwardsville, 1979. Editorial asst. St. Louis Star-Times, 1938; various positions Social Security Commn. Mo., Dept. Labor, U.S. Employment Service, War Dept., C.E., St. Louis, 1941-43; head archives unit USAAF Aero Chart Service, St. Louis, 1943-45, head research unit, 1945-47; asst. chief, chief of library, translator, historian, geographer, supervisory cartographer, librarian USAF Aero Chart and Info. Center (name changed to DMA Aerospace Center), St. Louis, 1947-57, chief tech. library, 1957-75; Civilian library specialist Project Crossroads, USAF, 1946; instr. creative writing Peoples Art Center, St. Louis, 1953-56; lectr., poetry workshop leader McKendree Writers Confs., McKendree Coll., 1955—, dir., 1970-73. Author: Modern Italian Poets, 1961, Paul Valery in English, 1970; poems Phrase/Paraphrase, 1970, Voices in the Dark, 1974; Translator: with others Selected Poems of Alain Bosquet, 1963; Contbr. to: Anthology of Spanish Poetry, 1961, Modern European Poetry, 1966, New Directions, 1968-80, Roots and Wings, 1976; Contbr. articles to profl. jours.; Book reviewer: St. Louis Post-Dispatch, 1953—, Globe-Democrat, 1972—. Decorated commendatore Ordine al Merito della Repubblica Italiana; recipient Shell Co. Found. grant for book Phrase/Paraphrase, 1970; Lit. award Mo. Library Assn., 1974. Mem. Poetry Soc. Am. (Midwest regional v.p., James Joyce award 1974), St. Louis Writers Guild (v.p. 1958, pres. 1959, 76-77), St. Louis Poetry Center (chmn. bd. chancellors 1965-72, pres. 1974-76), Mo. Writers Guild (v.p. 1971-73, pres. 1973-74), Spl. Libraries Assn. (pres. Greater St. Louis chpt. 1969-70), Rose Soc. Greater St. Louis; corr. mem. Academie d'Alsace (diplome d'honneur 1957); hon. mem. Les Violetti Picards et Normands, Paris, Academia de Ciencias Humanisticas y Relaciones, Mexico, Academie Chablaisienne, Thonon-les-Bains, France, Biblioteca Partenopea, Naples; asso. mem. Internat. Am. Inst. Home: 2935 Russell Blvd Saint Louis MO 63104 *A poet's relation to his time is complex and mutable. A poet's temperament, attitudes, and sense of the function of poetry are all changeable and conflict with each other throughout his life. In a world which tends to be imitative, regimented, and standardized, each poet is his own definition of poet, his own conscience, his own value.*

GUENTHER, GEORGE CARPENTER, travel co. exec.; b. Reading, Pa., Aug. 27, 1931; s. John H. and Eleanor (Carpenter) G.; m. Kathleen Lance Coyle, Oct. 20, 1962; children—George Carpenter, Todd C., John E., Gregory C. A.B. in Psychology, Amherst Coll., 1952. Pres. John H. Guenther Hosiery Co., Reading, 1955-67; dep. sec. Pa. Dept. Labor and Industry, 1967-69; dir. Bur. Labor Standards, Dept. Labor, 1969-71, asst. sec. labor for occupational safety and health, 1971-73; sr. v.p. Ins. Co. N. Am., Phila., 1973-75; v.p. Talmage Tours, Inc., Phila., 1975-77; pres. 1977. Served with USNR, 1952-55. Home: 470 Bair Rd Berwyn PA 19312 Office: 1223 Walnut St Philadelphia PA 19107

GUENTHER, JACK EGON, lawyer; b. San Antonio, Dec. 14, 1934; s. Egon E. and Camilla (Mallepell) G.; m. Valerie Urschel, Feb. 1, 1964; children: Charles Urschel, Abigail Camilla, Jack Egon. B.B.A., U. Tex. at Austin, 1956; LL.B. magna cum laude, St. Mary's U., 1959; LL.M. in Taxation, N.Y. U., 1960. Bar: Tex. 1959; C.P.A., Tex. Practice pub. accounting, San Antonio, 1957-59, practiced in, 1960—; asso. firm Cox & Smith (and predecessor firm), 1961-65, partner, 1965—; chmn. bd. North Loop Volkswagen, Inc., 1965—, Subaru South, Inc., 1976—, Universal Datsun, Inc., 1976—; dir. San Antonio Spurs Basketball Team; adj. prof. law St. Mary's U.; lectr. various tax insts. Bd. dirs. San Antonio Economic Devel. Found. Served to capt., JAG Corps AUS, 1957. Mem. Am., Tex. bar assns., Tex. Soc. C.P.A.'s, Sigma Chi, Phi Delta Phi. Episcopalian. Office: 600 Nat Bank of Commerce Bldg San Antonio TX 78205

GUENTHER, KENNETH ALLEN, trade association executive, economist; b. Rochester, N.Y.; s. Walter K. and Erna (Ahrenz) G.; m. Lilly Hoesli, Jan. 11, 1964; 1 dau., Christine R. B.A. cum laude, U. Rochester, 1957; postgrad., Johns Hopkins U. Sch. Advanced Internat. Studies, 1957-58, Rangoon Hopkins Ctr., Burma, 1958-59, Yale U., 1959-60. Internat. economist Dept. Commerce, Washington, 1960-65; fgn. service officer Dept. State, Washington, 1965-69, Santiago, Chile, 1965-69; spl. asst. to Senator Jacob Javits U.S. Senate, Washington, 1969-73; exec. dir. Inter-Am. Devel. Bank, Washington, 1973-74; asst. spl. trade rep. White House, Washington, 1974-75; assoc. dir. Ind. Bankers Assn. of Am., Washington, 1980-82, exec. dir., 1982—; mem. exec. com. Small Bus. Legis. Council, Washington, 1982—; mem. adv. com. Consumers for World Trade, Washington, 1982—. Contbr. articles on econs. to profl. jours. Served with U.S. Army, 1961-66. Recipient spl. achievement award FRS, 1977. Clubs: Bretton Woods (Potomac, Md.); Exchequer. Office: Ind Bankers Assn Am 1625 Massachusetts Ave NW Washington DC 20036

GUENZEL, PAUL WALTER, corporate executive; b. Chgo., Jan. 8, 1910; s. Louis and Alice (Paepcke) G.; m. Elizabeth Skinner, Sept. 10, 1938; children: Elizabeth Alice Carlin, William Skinner. A.B., Williams Coll., 1931. With Container Corp. Am., Chgo., 1931-73, asst. sec., 1947-48, asst. sec. and asst. treas., 1948-49, then v.p., treas., dir., 1949-73; ret., 1973; asst. treas. 1630 Sheridan Corp. Bd. dirs. Lawson YMCA, Albany Park Community Center, Donors Forum Chgo., Sr. Citizens Agy. of No. Door County, Wis.; trustee North Shore Country Day Sch. Found., Taxpayers Fedn. Ill. Mem. Phi Delta Theta. Clubs: University, Mid Day, Commercial, Chgo. Commonwealth (Chgo.); Indian Hill (Winnetka, Ill.). Home: 1630 Sheridan Rd Wilmette IL 60091 Office: 77 W Washington St Room 1604 Chicago IL 60602

GUENZEL, RUDOLF PAUL, banker; b. N.J., Apr. 4, 1940; s. Rudolf Edwin and Charlotte (Klein) G.; m. Marquerite Baker, Aug. 15, 1964; children: Douglas E., Kristen M. B.S. in Econs., Fairleigh Dickinson U., 1963, M.B.A. in Acctg. and Taxation, 1968. Asst. mgr. Chem. Bank, N.Y.C., 1967-68, asst. sec., 1968-69, asst. controller, 1969-71, asst. v.p., 1971; v.p. European Am. Bank, N.Y.C., 1971-75, sr. v.p., 1975-80, exec. v.p., 19806. Mem. Fin. Exec. Inst., Robert Morris Assocs. Office: European American Bancorp 10 Hanover Sq New York NY 10015

GUERARD, ALBERT JOSEPH, writer, educator; b. Houston, Nov. 2, 1914; s. Albert Leon and Wilhelmina (Macartney) G.; m. Mary Maclin Bocock, July 11, 1941; children—Catherine Collot, Mary Maclin, Lucy Lundie. A.B., Stanford U., 1934, Ph.D., 1938; A.M., Harvard U., 1936. Faculty instr. Amherst (Mass.) Coll., 1935-36; faculty Harvard U., 1938-61, beginning as instr. English, successively faculty instr., asst. prof., asso. prof., 1948-54, prof. English, 1954-61, Stanford U., 1961-65, Albert L. Guerard prof. lit., 1965—. Author: The Past Must Alter, 1937, Robert Bridges, 1942, The Hunted, 1944, Maquisard, 1945, Joseph Conrad, 1947, Thomas Hardy, 1949, Night Journey, 1950, Andre Gide, 1951, Conrad the Novelist, 1958, The Bystander, 1958, The Exiles, 1963, The Triumph of the Novel: Dickens, Dostoevsky, Faulkner, 1976, The Touch of Time: Myth, Memory and the Self, 1980; Co-editor: The Personal Voice, 1964. Served as tech. sgt. psychol. warfare br. AUS, World War II. Rockefeller fellow, 1946-47; Fulbright fellow, 1950-51; Guggenheim fellow, 1956-57; Ford fellow, 1959-60; Nat. Found. Arts fellow, 1967-68; Nat. Found. Humanities fellow, 1974-75; Recipient Paris Review Fiction prize, 1963. Mem. Am. Acad. Arts and Scis., Phi Beta Kappa. Home: 635 Gerona Rd Stanford CA 94305

GUERIN, DEAN PATRICK, investment banker; b. St. Paul, Feb. 21, 1922; s. Joseph H. and Della (Booth) G.; m. Jo Alice Maryman, Sept. 3, 1959; children: Dean William, Susan Jane, Stephen Patrick, Mark Joseph. B.S. in Bus. Adminstrn, Boston U., 1949. With Sperry Gyroscope Co., N.Y.C., 1940-42; registered rep. Chas. A. Day & Son, Boston, 1946-49, Dallas Rupe & Son, 1949-51; chmn. Eppler, Guerin & Turner, Inc., Dallas, 1951—; dir. Circle K Corp., Redman Industries, Inc., Seagull Pipeline Corp., Trinity Industries, Howard B. Wolf, Inc., Zale Corp., Components Corp. Am. Asso. Mem. Municipal Adv. Council Tex., 1955—. Served with USMCR, 1942-46; PTO. Mem. Am., Midwest, N.Y. stock exchanges.; Mem. Investment Bankers Am. Home: 9400 Rockbrook Dr Dallas TX 75220 Office: 2001 Bryan Tower 23d Floor Dallas TX 75201

GUERIN, GILLES G., college adminstrator; b. Epernay, Marne, France, May 23, 1943; emigrated to Can., 1964; s. Gaston and Therese (Coillard) G.; m. Rose A. Rouquette, Aug. 18, 1966; children: Laetitia, Ivan. Engr., Inst. Nat. Scis. Appliques, M.Sc., M.A.; Ph.D., U. Montreal. Mem. Ecole de Relations Industrielles, U. Montreal, dir. sci., 1983—. Author: Le Systems de Planification des Resources Hamaines, 1978, Des Series Chronologiques au Systems Statisque Canadien, 1983. Grantee Boursier France Can., 1964-66, Boursier France Que., 1966-68, Conseil des Arts du Can., 1970-72. Mem. Can. Assn. Indsl. Relations, Human Resource Planning Soc. Office: Ecole de Relations Industrielles U Montreal 3150 Jean Brillant St Montreal PA Canada H3C 3J7

GUERIN, JOHN WILLIAM, artist; b. Houghton, Mich., Aug. 29, 1920; s. Omer Francis and Mildred Montague (Miller) G.; m. Anne Walden Dewey, Dec. 28, 1948 (dec. 1979); m. Martha Macashan, Apr. 10, 1982. Student, Am. Acad. Art, Chgo., Art Students League, N.Y.C., Escuela de Bellas Artes, San Miguel, Mexico. Prof. art U. Tex., 1953-80, prof. emeritus, 1980—. Artist in residence, Skowhegan (Maine) Sch. Painting and Sculpture, 1960; one-man shows, Kraushaar Galleries, N.Y.C., 1960, 63, 68, Ft. Worth Art Center, 1956, 64, 65, Marion Kooglar McNay Art Inst., San Antonio, 1961, 65, Centennial Mus., Corpus Christi, Tex., 1963, Carlin Galleries, Ft. Worth, 1962, 64, 67, 70, 77, 81, one-man retrospective show, Nave Mus., Victoria, Tex., 1982, group exhbns. include, Met. Mus. Art, Whitney Mus. Art, Art Inst. Chgo., Corcoran Mus. Art, Carnegie Inst.; represented in permanent collections, Chrysler Mus., Provincetown, Mass., Joslyn Mus., Omaha, New Britain (Conn.) Mus., Houston Mus., Dallas Mus., U. Notre Dame Art Gallery, Colorado Springs (Colo.) Fine Art Center., Archives Am. Art, Smithsonian Instn., Washington. Served with USAAF, 1942-45. Grantee Am. Acad Arts, 1959, Am. Acad Arts, U. Tex., 1960, Ford Found., 1978; recipient Henry Ward Ranger Fund Purchase prize NAD, 1958; Research Inst. grant U. Tex., 1960, 66. Mem. Art Students League, N.Y.C. (life). Episcopalian. Home: 3400 Stoneridge Rd Austin TX 78746

GUERINDON, PIERRE CLAUDE, heavy construction equipment company executive; b. Paris, Apr, 24, 1927; U.S., 1980; s. Georges Jean and Marie Antoinette Claudia (Pilon) G.; m. Arlette Jeanne Lagacherie, Aug. 11, 1949; 1 son, Philippe. M.E.,C.E., Ecole National Superieur Arts et Metiers aix France, 1949. Mgr. mfg. Caterpillar France S.A., Grenoble, France, 1961-68, asst. plant mgr., 1969, pres., 1968-76; mng. dir. Caterpillar Belgium S.A., Gosselies, 1976-80; v.p. Caterpillar Tractor Co., Peoria, Ill., 1980—; dir. Ateliers de Constructions Electriques de Charleroi, Brussels. Bd. dirs. Bus. Sch. Inst. Adminstrn. Enterprise, Grenbole, France, 1968-76; v.p. Amis de L' Universite, Grenble, 1970-76; bd. dirs. Greater Peoria YMCA, 1982. Served with French Army, 1949-50. Mem. French Civil Engrs., Nat. Engr. Arts et Metiers, Fabrimetal Nat. Metallurgh Profl. Assn. (bd. dirs.), Am. C. of C. (pres. S.E. Region France 1970-76). Roman Catholic. Clubs: Ivy (Peoria); Royal Ocean Racing (London); Am. Radio Relay (Newington Conn.). Lodge: Rotary. Home: 242 Detweiller Dr Peoria IL 61615

GUERNSEY, LOUIS HAROLD, oral and maxillofacial surgeon, educator; b. Port Chester, N.Y., Sept. 22, 1923; s. Harold Allen and Odette Marcelle (Caillat) G.; m. Isabelle Margaret Napoli, Mar. 15, 1946; children: John Allen, Nancy Jean, Paula, Louis Harold. B.S., N.Y. U., 1959; D.D.S., U. Pa., 1947, M.Sc. in Dentistry, 1956. Diplomate: Am. Bd. Oral and Maxillofacial Surgery. Gen. practice dentistry, Gooding, Idaho, 1947-52; commd. 1st lt. Dental Corps U.S. Army, 1953, advanced through grades to col., 1967; service in, W. Ger., ret., 1974; prof. oral surgery, chmn. dept. oral and maxillofacial surgery U. Pa. Sch. Dental Medicine, 1974-80, prof. oral/maxillofacial surgery, 1980—, dir. postgrad. oral surgery programs, 1974-80; dir. oral surgery U. Pa. Hosp., 1974—; con. VA, Children's, Pa. hosps.; mem. staff Presbyn. Hosp., U. Pa. Med. Center. Contbr. articles profl. jours. Decorated Legion of Merit; recipient Harold Krogh Oral Cancer award Washington chpt. Am. Cancer Soc., 1974. Fellow Internat. Coll. Dentists, Am. Coll. Dentists, Am. Dental Soc. Anesthesiology; mem. ADA, Am. Soc. Oral and Maxillofacial Surgeons, Brit. Assn. Oral Surgeons, Internat. Assn. Oral Surgeons, Am. Assn. Hosp. Dentists, Pa. Soc. Oral and Maxillofacial Surgeons. Republican. Roman Catholic. Home: 6408 City Ave Philadelphia PA 19151 Office: Oral-Maxillofacial Surg Assos Hosp of Univ Pa 3400 Spruce St Philadelphia PA 19104

GUERNSEY, OTIS LOVE, JR., critic, editor; b. N.Y.C., Aug. 9, 1918; s. Otis L. and Margaret (Henderson) G.; m. Dorianne Downe, Dec. 11, 1943. Student, Taft Sch., Watertown, Conn.; B.A., Yale, 1940. With N.Y. Herald Tribune, 1941-60, successively copy boy, reporter, asso. film and drama critic, film critic and drama critic, arts editor, 1955-60; story cons. CBS, 1957-59; free lance writer, 1960—; editorial cons. New Eng. Guide, 1960-80; drama critic and sr. editor Show mag., 1963-64; arts editor Diplomat mag., 1965-67; lectr. on modern theater. Author original film stories, also articles on stage and screen.; Editor: The Dramatists Guild Quar, 1964—, Dramatists Guild Newsletter, 1978—, Best Plays; series of theater yearbooks, 1965—, Directory of the American Theater, 1971; anthology Playwrights/Lyricists/Composers on Theater, 1974. Mem. N.Y. Newspaper Guild, N.Y. Film Critics (past chmn.), Am. Theater Critics Assn. (charter mem.), Dramatists Guild, Phi Beta Kappa. Club: Century Assn. (N.Y.C.). Address: North Pomfret VT 05053

GUERRANT, DAVID EDWARD, food company executive; b. Elizaville, Ky., Sept. 27, 1919; s. William Upton and Claire (Jordan) G.; m. Charlotte L. Lander, Feb. 6, 1942; children: Stephen, Jeffrey. B.S., Kans. State U., 1941. With Potts-Turnbull Agy., Kansas City, Mo., 1941-48; creative dir. Campbell-Ewald Co., Chgo., 1948-51; with John W. Shaw Advt., Inc., Chgo., 1951-61, pres., 1959-61, MacFarland, Aveyard & Co., Chgo., 1961-64; v.p. marketing Libby, McNeill & Libby, Chgo., 1964-68, pres., chief exec. officer, 1968-73, chmn. bd., 1971-77; also dir.; pres., chief exec. officer Nestlé Co., Inc., White Plains, N.Y., 1973—; chmn. Nestlé Enterprises Inc. (holding co. for Nestlé Co. Inc., Libby, McNeill & Libby and Stouffers Inc.), 1977—. Presbyn. Clubs: Chicago; Westmoreland Country (Wilmette, Ill.); Woodway Country (Darien, Conn.). Home: 102 Ludlowe Rd New Canaan CT 06840 Office: 100 Bloomingdale Rd White Plains NY 10605

GUERRANT, EDWARD OWINGS, emeritus educator; b. Danville, Va., Feb. 2, 1911; s. Peter Dutois and Grace (Owings) G.; m. Helen Louise Daggett, Feb. 14, 1936 (dec.); 1 dau., Helen Louise (Mrs. Stewart A. Toy); m. Charlotte Edwina Tompkins, Aug. 12, 1944; children—Lucy Allison, Edward Owings. A.B., Davidson Coll., 1933; M.A., U. So. Calif., 1939, Ph.D., 1942. Instr. history Calif. Inst. Tech., 1942-44; polit. analyst Office Coordinator Inter-Am. Affairs, 1944-45, State Dept., 1945-46; asso. prof., then prof history Davidson Coll., 1946-54; mem. faculty Calif. State U. at Los Angeles, 1954—, head dept., 1957-64, prof. history, 1960-79, prof. emeritus, 1979—, chmn. dept. history, 1966-69; vis. summer prof. U. So. Calif., 1947-54; vis. prof. history U. Hawaii, 1963. Author: Roosevelt's Good Neighbor Policy, 1950, Modern American Diplomacy, 1954, Herbert Hoover and Franklin D. Roosevelt: Comparisons and Contrasts, 1960, (with K.A. Martyn) Toward A More Perfect Union, 1967. Ford fellow, 1952-53. Mem. Phi Beta Kappa, Phi Delta Theta. Presbyn. (ruling elder). Home: 2266 Midwick Dr Altadena CA 91001

GUERRI, WILLIAM G., lawyer; b. Higbee, Mo., Mar. 30, 1921; S. Grant and Pearl (Zambelli) G.; m. Millicent K. Branding; children—Paula Ann (Mrs. Baker), Glenda Kay, William Grant. A.B., Central Meth. Coll., 1943; LL.B., Columbia, 1946. Bar: N.Y. bar 1946, Mo. bar 1947. Mem. firm Thompson & Mitchell, St. Louis. Mem. bd. editors: Columbia Law Rev, 1945-46. Bd. dirs. St. Louis Heart Assn., chmn., 1972—; bd. dirs. United Way Greater St. Louis, curator, Central Meth. Coll. Mem. Am. Bar Assn., Am. Law Inst., Am. Judicature Soc., Mo. Bar, Bar Assn. Met. St. Louis, Assn. Bar City N.Y., Phi Delta Phi. Clubs: Noonday, Round Table. Home: 1993 Windmoor Pl Saint Louis MO 63131 Office: One Mercantile Center Saint Louis MO 63101

GUESS, WALLACE LOUIS, university dean; b. Durham, N.C., July 18, 1924; s. Vernon Ernest and Sara Elizabeth (Glenn) G.; m. Betty Jo Leifeste, June 21, 1947 (dec. 1979); children: Ginnylu, Gerrysu.; m. Betty Banks, May 30, 1981. B.S. in Pharmacy, U. Tex., 1949, M.S., 1951; Ph.D., U. Wash., 1959. Instr. pharmacy U. Tex., 1949-51, asst. prof., 1953-61, asso. prof., 1961-68, prof., 1968-71; dean, prof. pharmaceutics U. Miss., University, 1971—; cons. Baxter Labs, Morton Grove, Ill.; Chmn. FDA Antimicrobiol Panel II. Contbr. articles to profl. jours. Served with AUS, 1943-45. NIH grantee. Fellow AAAS; mem. Am. Assn. Colls. Pharm., Soc. Toxicology, Mexican Pharm. Assn. (hon.), Sigma Xi, Rho Chi. Office: Sch Pharmacy U Miss University MS 38677

GUEST, JAMES ALFRED, association executive; b. Montclair, N.J., Dec. 25, 1940; s. J. Alfred and Elizabeth Laney (Montignani) G.; m. Priscilla Frances Beach, Mar. 1, 1974; children: Benjamin, Betsey. B.A., Amherst Coll., 1962; postgrad., MIT, 1963-64; LL.B., Harvard U., 1967. Bar: Mass. 1967. Legis. asst. to Sen. Edward Kennedy of Mass., 1968-71; commr. banking and ins., State of Vt., 1973-76; sec. State of Vt., 1977-81; pres. Consumers Union, Inc., 1980—. Woodrow Wilson fellow, 1963-64. Democrat. Home: 20 Woodcrest Ln Burlington VT 05401

GUEST, JUDITH ANN, author; b. Detroit, Mar. 29, 1936; d. Harry Reginald and Marion Aline (Nesbit) G.;, Aug. 22, 1958; children: Larry, John, Richard. B.A. in Edn., U. Mich., 1958. Elem. sch. tchr. Birmingham (Mich.) Pub. Schs., 1959-60, Royal Oak (Mich.) Pub. Schs., 1969-70; continuing edn. tchr. Troy (Mich.) Pub. Schs., 1974-75. Author: Ordinary People, 1976 (Janet Heidinger Kafka prize), Second Heaven, 1982. Mem. Detroit Women Writers, Authors Guild, PEN Am. Center. Office: care Viking Press 40 W 23d St New York NY 10010

GUEST, MAURICE MASON, scientist, educator; b. Fredonia, N.Y., July 30, 1906; s. Maurice S. and Daisy (Mason) G.; m. Alice Rhoda Avery, Aug. 16, 1936; children—Avery Mason, John Andrew. A.B., U. Mich., 1930; Ph.D., Columbia, 1941. Field asst. U.S. Dept. Agr. Bur. of Entomology, 1930-31; sci. tchr. Sherman (N.Y.) High Sch., 1931-36; instr. physiology Columbia, 1936-40, research asso., 1940-42; asso. prof. physiology Wayne U. Coll. Medicine, 1946-51; prof., chmn. dept. physiology U. Tex. Med. Br., Galveston, 1951-73, Ashbel Smith prof. physiology, 1973—; Mem. Med. Adv. Bd. Film Prodn. Contbr. articles to profl. jours. Served to maj. USAAF, 1942-46. Mem. Am. Physiol. Soc., AAAS, AAUP, Soc. for Exptl. Biology and Medicine, Internat. Hematol. Soc. Home: 1409 Harbor View Dr Galveston TX 77550

GUEST, ROBERT HENRY, management educator; b. East Orange, N.J., May 3, 1916; s. James Henry and Charlotte (Newbould) G.; m. Kate Hay, Dec. 18, 1942; children: David Hartley, Gregory Alan, John Hay, Peter Staples. A.B. cum laude, Amherst Coll., 1939, L.H.D., 1974; M.A., Columbia U., 1941, Ph.D., 1960; M.A. (hon.), Dartmouth Coll., 1963. Dir. indsl. relations Limerick Yarn Mills, Me., 1941-42; sr. field examiner NLRB, 1946-47; mem. field research staff Labor and Mgmt. Center Yale, 1948-52; assoc. dir. research tech. project, 1952-60; ptnr. Charles R. Walker Assocs. (mgmt. cons.), New Haven, 1952-61; prof. organizational behavior Amos Tuck Sch. Dartmouth, 1960—; mng. dir. Health Mgmt. Assos. (mgmt. cons.), 1975—; asso. Stanley Peterfreund Assos. (mgmt. cons.), 1979—; Mediator Conn. Labor-Mgmt. Com. Econ. Devel., 1960; mem. N.H. Gov's. Mental Health Com., 1964, N.H. Aeros. Commn., 1968; mem. mgmt. adv. panel NASA, 1969. Author: (with C. R. Walker) The Man on the Assembly Line, 1952, (with C. R. Walker and A. N. Turner) The Foreman on the Assembly Line, 1957, Organizational Change: The Effect of Successful Leadership, 1962, (with others) Hospital Policy: Process and Action, Robotics: The Human Dimension, 1984; Contbg. editor: Changing Forces In American Society, 1964, Organizational Research in Health Institutions, 1973, IL Mutamento Della Organizzazione Aziendale, 1976, (with Paul Hersey and Kenneth H. Blanchard) Organizational Change Through Effective Leadership, 1977, Innovations in the Workplace, 1981. Mem. exec. com. N.H. Democratic Party. Served with USNR, 1942-45. Recipient Book of Year award Nat. Orgn. Devel. Council, 1963, Article of Year awards Can. Assn. Mgmt., 1967, Am. Coll. Hosp. Adminstrs., 1974. Mem. Alpha Delta Phi. Club: Royal and Ancient Golf (St Andrews, Scotland). Home: 8 Barrett Rd Hanover NH 03755 *A fundamental assumption, convincingly proven through a lifetime of research in America and 16 industrial nations, is that the capacity for creativity among ordinary men and women in modern industrial enterprise is far greater than what managers are willing to admit to. The task of the future is to discover why our complex technological bureaucracies stifle initiative and to act on it.*

GUETTEL, HENRY ARTHUR, arts executive; b. Kansas City, Mo., Jan. 8, 1928; s. Arthur Abraham and Sylva (Hershfield) G.; 1 dau. by previous marriage, Laurie C.; m. Mary Rodgers, Oct. 14, 1961; children: Matthew Rodgers (dec.), Adam Arthur, Alexander Burton. Student, Wharton Sch. of U. Pa., 1944-47, U. Kansas City, 1947-48. Stage mgr. on Broadway and TV, also stock cos., 1949-60; gen. mgr. Royal Ballet, Canada, 1953-54; producer nat. touring cos. The Best Man, Sound of Music, Camelot, Oliver; then also gen. mgr. Music Theatre of Lincoln Center; touring cos. The Merry Widow, Kismet, Carousel, Annie Get Your Gun, Show Boat, 1964-67; mng. dir., then v.p. Am. Nat. Opera Co., 1967-68; prodn. supr. exploratory music theatre prodns., forum Vivian Beaumont Theater and theatre concerts Music Theatre, Lincoln Center, 1966-69; Assoc. Kaplan Veidt, Ltd., 1970-72; v.p., prodn. asso. Cinema 5, Ltd., 1972-78; v.p. creative affairs Columbia Pictures, 1978-80; sr. v.p. East Coast Prodn. Twentieth Century-Fox, 1980-82; exec. dir. Theatre Devel. Fund, 1982—; Mem. theatrical advisory panel N.Y. State Council of Arts, 1965-70; cons. theatre to State U. N.Y., 1969-70; bd. dirs. Chelsea Theatre Center, N.Y.C., 1966-72, Performing Arts Repertory Theatre, 1971-82, Theatre Devel. Fund, 1980—. Served with AUS, 1954-56. Mem. League N.Y. Theatres, Internat. Assn. Concert Mgrs. Club: Century. Address: 115 Central Park W New York NY 10023

GUFFEY, JAMES ROGER, banker; b. Kingston, Mo., Sept. 11, 1929; s. John William and Elsie M. (Palmer) G.; m. Sara C. Carmack, Feb. 7, 1959; children—James Michael, Sara Elizabeth. B.S. in Bus. Adminstrn, U. Mo. at Columbia, 1952, LL.B., J.D., 1958; grad. advanced mgmt. program, Harvard Bus. Sch., 1974. Bar: Mo. bar 1958. Practice in, Kansas City, 1958-68; partner firm Fallon, Guffey & Jenkins, 1965-68; sr. v.p., gen. counsel, sec. Fed. Res. Bank, Kansas City, 1968-76, pres., 1976—; instr. bus. law U. Mo. at Columbia, 1956-57; instr. uniform comml. code Am. Inst. Banking, 1968-69; instr. Colo. Sch. Banking, 1976-77. Served with U.S. Army, 1952-54. Mem. Am., Mo., Kansas City bar assns., Kansas City Lawyers Assn., Am. Judicature Soc., Phi Gamma Delta, Phi Delta Phi. Home: 5207 Sunset Dr Kansas City MO 64112 Office: 925 Grand Ave Kansas City MO 64198

GUFFIN, GILBERT L., clergyman, educator; b. nr. Marietta, Ga., Aug. 5, 1906; s. William Thomas and Nora (Eubanks) G.; m. Lorene Parrish, Aug. 23, 1930; children: Gilbert Truett, Orville Thomas. A.B., Mercer U., 1930, D.D., 1955; B.D., Eastern Bapt. Theol. Sem., 1935; Th.M., 1938; Th.D., 1941; LL.D., Atlanta Law Sch., 1951; L.H.D., Eastern Coll., 1972. Ordained to ministry Bapt. Ch., 1927; prin. Jr. High Sch., Mabelton, Ga., 1927-28, Elizabeth Jr. High Sch., Marietta, 1930-33; pastor various chs. in, Ga., 1927-33, First Ch., Merchantville, N.J., 1935-42, Jasper, Ala., 1942-47; dean Bapt. Seminar, Walker Coll., 1942-47; dir. extension div. Christian tng. Howard Coll. (now Samford U.), Birmingham, 1947-49, dean of religion, chmn. extension div., 1961-71, dean emeritus, 1971—; pres. Eastern Bapt. Theol. Sem., Phila., 1950-61, trustee, 1941-44, 1961-77, bd. dir. emeritus, 1977—; pres. Eastern Coll., 1952-61, trustee, 1961-72, bd. dirs. emeritus, 1972—; Layne lectr. New Orleans Bapt. Theol. Sem., 1958; former mem. bd. lectrs. Freedom's Found.; Bd. dirs. Ala. Bapt. Conv., 1942-47, mem. exec. com., 1945-47, chmn. Christian life and public affairs commn., 1974-82; exec. bd. N.J. Bapt. Conv., 1938-42; bd. dirs. Birmingham Council of Christian Edn., 1970-73, 75, now life mem.; bd. dirs. Ala. Baptist Ministers Benefit Soc., 1974—, The Lord's Day Alliance U.S., 1976—; bd. advisers Bible Land Tours Assn., 1956-57; bd. dirs. Pa. Theol. Sem. Found., Inc., 1955-61; bd. dirs. trustee Watchman-Examiner Found., N.Y., 1960-71; trustee Ala. Temperance League (now Ala. Christian Action Program), 1943-49, 61—; bd. mgrs. Council Missionary Coop., Am. Bapt. Conv., 1953-61, pres. sem. presidents and deans, 1958-59; mem. Guatemala-Ala. Partners of Alliance, 1969-72; messenger Bapt. World Alliance, Atlanta, 1939, Copenhagen, 1947, Cleve., 1950, London, 1955, Rio de Jenario, 1960, Miami, 1965, Tokyo, 1970; tours in 45 countries; condr. European tours, 1947, Holy Land tour, 1955, 63, Around-the-World tour, 1970. Author: How To Run A Church, 1948, Called of God, 1951, Pastor and Church, 1955, El Pastor La Iglesia, 1955, The Gospel in Isaiah, 1968, El Evangelio En Isaias, 1968, The Bible: God's Missionary Message to Man, vol. I, 1973, vol. II, 1974; Editor: Walker Bapt. Herald, 1944-47, What God Hath Wrought, 1960; Writer: Monthly Bible Studies for, Royal Service, 1964-68; co-author: The Pentateuch: Joshua to Malichi; Contbr. to: religious publs. Life and Work Ann, 1966-67, 67-68, for Bapt. Sun. Sch. bd. So. Bapt. Conv. Recipient Freedoms Found. awards, 1960, 61. Mem. Greater Birmingham Pastors' Assn. (exec. com. 1962-63, 67-72, 82-83), Birmingham Bapt. Assn. (exec. bd.), Birmingham Bpt. Assn. (chmn. com. on Christian life and pub. affairs 1981—), Ala. Writer's Conclave, Omicron Delta Kappa. Clubs: Mason, Rotarian (past pres.). Originator Howard Plan extensive edn. Home: Kirkwood by the River 3605 Ratliff Rd Box 70 Birmingham AL 35210 *Life is a trust given to each of us, a trust to be administered with accountability to the Giver. To use it only for self is to waste it. To invest it for the good of humanity - by relieving suffering, by promoting virtue, by strengthening the home, itself the keystone of society and of civilization, and by encouraging reverence toward God - is both to preserve it and to transform it into eternal riches.*

GUGELOT, PIET CORNELIS, physics educator; b. Bussum, The Netherlands, Feb. 24, 1918; came to U.S., 1947, naturalized, 1954; s. Pieter Cornelis and Anna (Arnold) G.; m. Ursula Federspiel, June 27, 1944; 1 son, Oliver C. Physics degree, Fed. Sch. Tech., Zurich, Switzerland, 1940, Ph.D., 1945. Research asso. Phys. Inst., Fed. Sch. Tech., Zurich, 1940-47; research asso. Princeton, 1947-49, asst. prof., 1949-56; dir. Inst. for Nuclear Research, Amsterdam, The Netherlands; prof. nuclear physics U. Amsterdam, 1956-66; prof. physics U. Va., Charlottesville, 1966—; vis. prof. U. Wash., 1954; vis. scientist Oak Ridge Nat. Lab., 1959, U. Calif., Livermore, 1960; vis. prof. Stanford, 1963-64, Fermi Inst., U. Chgo., 1970; dir. NASA Space-Radiation Lab., 1966; cons. NASA Langley Research Center, Los Alamos Sci. Lab.; vis. scientist dept. nuclear physics Saclay CERN, 1975-76; vis. prof. U. Lyon, France, 1977. Contbr. articles to profl. jours. Recipient Alexander von Humboldt award. Fellow Am. Phys. Soc.; mem. Swiss, European phys. socs., Gesellschaft Ehemaliger Polytechn., Sigma Xi, Sigma Pi Sigma (hon.). Office: Dept Physics U Va Charlottesville VA 22901

GUGGENHEIM, MALVINA HALBERSTAM, lawyer, educator; b. Poland, May 2, 1937; came to U.S., 1947, naturalized, 1952; d. Marcus and Pearl (Halberstam) Halberstam; m. Wolf Z. Guggenheim, Aug. 13, 1963; children—Arye, Achiezer. B.A. cum laude, Bklyn. Coll., 1957; J.D. (Kent scholar, Stone scholar), Columbia U., 1961, M.I.A., 1964. Bar: N.Y. 1962, Calif. 1968, U.S. Supreme Ct. 1966. Law clk. to fed. dist. judge So. Dist. Ct., N.Y.C., 1961-62; research asso. Columbia U. Project on Internat. Procedure, 1962-63; asst. dist. atty., N.Y. County, 1963-67; mem. firm Rifkind & Sterling, Los Angeles, 1968-69; sr. atty. Nat. Legal Program on Health Problems of Poor, UCLA., 1969-70; asso. prof. law Loyola U., Los Angeles, 1970-71, prof., 1971-76; prof. law Benjamin N. Cardozo Sch. Law, Yeshiva U., N.Y.C., 1976—; vis. prof. law U. So. Calif., Los Angeles, 1972-73, U. Tex., summer 1974, U. Va., 1975-76; reporter Am. Law Inst. Model Penal Code, 1977-79; univ. seminar asso. Columbia U. Seminar in Human Rights, 1978—. Articles and rev. editor: Columbia Law Rev, 1960-61; Contbr. articles to profl. jours. Mem. Am. Bar Assn. (criminal justice, internat. law, individual rights and responsibilities sects.), Internat. Law Assn. (exec. com., human rights com.), Am. Soc. Internat. Law, Columbia Law Sch. Alumni Assn., Phi Beta Kappa. Office: 55 Fifth Ave New York NY 10003

GUGGENHEIM, RICHARD E., lawyer, shoe co. exec.; b. Cin., Ján. 5, 1913; s. Eli F. and Eva (Stransky) G.; m. Carol J. Rice, Sept. 21, 1942 (dec. 1958); children—Jane, Polly, Richard R.; m. Alice W. Joseph, Feb. 27, 1967. A.B., U. Mich., 1934; LL.B., Harvard, 1937. Bar: Ohio bar 1937, Supreme Court of U.S 1942. With Dept. Justice, 1940-42, 46-50, atty. civil and anti trust div., 1946-50; dep. gen. counsel ESA, 1950-51; with U.S. Shoe Corp., 1951-71, v.p., 1960-71, sec., 1964-71; dir. FHLB, Cin., 1965-70, Dept. Liquor Control, State of Ohio, 1971-75; cons., service coordinator U.S. Shoe Corp., 1976-79; mem. Cin. CSC, 1976—; Mem. Mayor Cin. Friendly Relations Com., 1958-59; chmn. Ohio Civil Rights Commn., 1959-62; mem. Ohio Constl. Rev. Commn., 1970-79. Served to maj. AUS, 1942-46. Mem. Am., Ohio, Cin. bar assns., Miami Soc., Pub. Health Fedn., Ohio Folk Art Assn. (pres. 1980—). Jewish. Home: 2470 Grandin Rd Cincinnati OH 45208 Office: 1658 Herald Ave Cincinnati OH 45212

GUGGENHEIMER, HEINRICH WALTER, mathematician, educator; b. Nurnberg, Germany, July 21, 1924; came to U.S., 1959; s. Siegfried and Marguerite Erna (Bloch) G.; m. Eva Auguste Horovicz, June 6, 1947; children: S. Michael, Esther H., Tobias I.S., Hanna Y. Diploma math, Swiss Fed. Inst. Tech., Zurich, 1947, Dr.Sc. Math., 1950. Lectr. Hebrew U., Jerusalem, 1954-56; prof. Bar Ilan (Israel) U., 1956-59; asso. prof. Wash. State U., Pullman, 1959-60, U. Minn., Mpls., 1960-62, prof., 1962-67, Poly. Inst. N.Y. (formerly Poly. Inst. Bklyn.), 1967—. Author: (2d edit.) Differential Geometry, 1977, Plane Geometry and Its Groups, 1967, Mathematics for Engineering and Science, 1976, Applicable Geometry, 1977; Mem. cons. bd.: Dialectica, internat. jour, 1955—; Contbr. articles to profl. jours. Served with Swiss Army, 1944-54. Mem. Am. Math. Socs., Swiss Math. Soc. (life), Math. Assn. Am., Soc. Indsl. and Applied Math., Institut de la Methode. Home: 426 Wilson St West Hempstead NY 11552 Office: Route 110 Farmingdale NY 11735

GUGGENHIME, RICHARD ELIAS, lawyer; b. San Francisco, Sept. 19, 1908; s. David J. and Elsa (Triest) G.; m. Charlotte M. Johnson, Mar. 2, 1939; children: Richard J., David J. A.B., Stanford U., 1929; LL.B., Harvard U., 1932. Bar: Calif. 1932. Assoc. Heller, Ehrman, White & McAuliffe, San Francisco, 1932-33, 34-39, partner, 1939-41, 46-79, of counsel, 1980—; mng. ptnr. Fresno-Kern Assocs.; emeritus dir. Wells Fargo Bank, N.A.; SMV Minerals, Inc. Pres. San Francisco Community Chest, 1952; pres. Rosenberg Found., 1954-57; Trustee Stanford U., 1958-78, pres. bd., 1964-67. Served from lt. (j.g.) to comdr. USNR, 1941-45. Decorated Bronze Star medal with gold star. Mem. Am., San Francisco bar assns., Phi Beta Kappa. Home: 65 Raycliff Terr San Francisco CA 94115 Office: 44 Montgomery St San Francisco CA 94104

GUICE, JOHN THOMPSON, retired air force officer; b. Kosciusko, Miss., Nov. 5, 1923; s. Gustave Nathaniel and Anne Maei (McCool) G.; m. Charlotte Webb, Mar. 8, 1949; children—John Thompson, James G., Steven L., Thomas A., Joseph D. B.S. in Engring, U.S. Mil. Acad., 1947; M.S. in Internat. Relations, George Washington U., 1966; disting. grad., Air Command and Staff Coll., 1962, Air War Coll., 1966. Commd. 2d lt. U.S. Army, 1947; advanced through grades to maj. gen. USAF, 1974; tactical and interceptor pilot, 1947-55; officer Air N.G. and N.G., 1956—; dep. dir. Air N.G., 1974-77, dir., 1977-81, ret., 1981. Decorated Legion of Merit, Air Force D.S.M. Mem. Air Force Assn., N.G. Assn., Sigma Chi. Home: 4901 N Calle Luisa Tucson AZ 25718

GUIDOTTI, GUIDO, educator, biochemist; b. Florence, Italy, Nov. 3, 1933; came to U.S., 1951, naturalized, 1959; s. Mario and Jiun (Casano) G.; 1 son, Guido. M.D., Washington U., St. Louis, 1957; Ph.D., Rockefeller U., 1963; M.S. (hon.), Harvard, 1968. Intern, then asst. resident Barnes Hosp., St. Louis, 1957-59; mem. faculty Harvard, 1963—, prof. biochemistry, 1969—. Mem. Am. Soc. Biol. Chemists, AAAS, Am. Acad. Arts and Scis., Harvey Soc., Sigma Xi. Home: 50 Bennington St Newton MA 02158

GUIDRY, FREDERICK HOLLIES, journalist, editor; b. New Orleans, July 25, 1924; s. Louis Charles and Winifred (Hollies) G.; m. Nannette Harriet Fontaine, Dec. 18, 1965. B.A., Tulane U., 1947, LL.B., 1949. Bar: La. bar 1949. Asso. firm Dart, Guidry & Price, New Orleans, 1950; journalist Christian Sci. Monitor, Boston, 1951—, asst. editor, 1966-67, asst. bus. and fin. editor, 1968-74, book editor, 1975-78, arts and entertainment editor, 1978-79, wire editor, 1979, computer supr., 1979—. Served with U.S. Army, 1944-45, 50-51. Decorated Bronze Star medal. Home: 355 Chestnut St Ashland MA 01721 Office: 1 Norway St Boston MA 02115

GUIDRY, MARION ANTOINE, educator; b. Lafayette, La., Oct. 1, 1925; s. Bertin and Elizabeth (Theriot) G.; m. Mary Margaret Boudreaux, Aug. 17, 1946; children—Joy Marie, Janet Raye, John Bertin. B.S. in Chemistry, Tulane U., 1947, M.S. in Biochemistry, 1949, Ph.D., 1952. Asst. prof. chemistry U. Southwestern La., Lafayette, 1951-53; research asso. ophthalmology Tulane U. Sch. Medicine, New Orleans, 1953, asst. prof. ophthalmology, 1954-56; research asso. pathology La. State U. Sch. Medicine, New Orleans, 1956-58, asst. prof. pathology, 1958-65; prof. chemistry, biology W. Tex. State U., Canyon, 1965—; Cons. biochemistry clin. chemistry hosps. in, Lafayette, New Orleans, Amarillo, Tex., 1951—. Contbr. articles to profl. jours. Served with USNR, 1943-45. Mem. Am. Chem. Soc., Soc. Exptl. Biology and Medicine, Am. Assn. Pathologists, Am. Heart Assn. (council arteriosclerosis 1964—), Tex. Acad. Sci., Am. Oil Chemists Soc., Sigma Xi. Roman Catholic. Home: 3300 Conner Dr Canyon TX 79015

GUIDRY, RONALD AMES, profl. baseball player; b. Lafayette, La., Aug. 28, 1950; s. Roland Ames and Mary Grace G.; m. Bonnie Lynn Rutledge, Sept. 23, 1972; children—Jamie Racheal, Brandon. Student in archtl. drafting, U. Southwestern La., 1968-71. Minor league player N.Y. Yankees, Johnson City, Tenn., Ft. Lauderdale, Fla., West Haven, Conn. and Syracuse, N.Y., 1971-75, major league pitcher, 1975—; pres. Ron Guidry Enterprises, Inc. Served with U.S. N.G., 1971-77. Mem. Major League Baseball Players Assn. Democrat. Roman Catholic. Office: care John Schneider Enterprises Inc 515 S College Rd Suite 200 Lafayette LA 70503

GUIHER, JAMES MORFORD, JR., publisher; b. Clarksburg, W.Va., Feb. 21, 1927; s. James Morford and Ruth Holt (Souders) G.; m. Elizabeth Ewing Hart, Aug. 20, 1954; children: Catharine Brownfield, Deborah Hart. B.A., Princeton U., 1951; postgrad., Harvard U., 1951-52, Boston Mus. Sch. Fine Arts, 1953-54. Editor coll. textbooks Prentice-Hall, Inc., Englewood Cliffs, N.J., 1954-66, exec. editor Ednl. Book div., 1966-68, editor-in-chief, 1968-74, v.p., gen. mgr., 1974-76; publishing cons., 1976—. Served with AUS, 1945-47. Mem. Assn. Am. Pubs. Home: 4 E 88th St New York City NY 10028 Office: Prentice-Hall Inc Englewood Cliffs NJ 07632

GUILD, ALDEN, life insurance company executive; b. Boston, July 3, 1929; s. Howard Redwood and Frances Allen (Warren) G.; m. Ruth Ineta Creighton, Sept. 14, 1957; 1 dau., Heather Louise. B.A., Dartmouth Coll., 1952; J.D., U. Chgo., 1957; LL.D. (hon.), Norwich/Vt. Coll., 1977. Bar: Vt. 1958. With law dept. Nat. Life Ins. Co., Montpelier, Vt., 1957—, asst. v.p., counsel, corp. sec., 1974-83, v.p., gen. counsel, 1983—. Contbr. legal jours. Trustee Norwich U., 1972—, Vt. Coll., 1967—, Kimball U. Acad., 1972-74, Wood Art Gallery, 1961-72; mem. Dartmouth Coll. Alumni Council, 1975-78. Served with USAF, 1950-53; Korea. Recipient Distinguished Service award Montpelier Jr. C. of C., 1962. Mem. Am., Vt. bar assns., Assn. Life Ins. Counsel, Am. Soc. Corp. Secs., Phi Beta Kappa, Order of Coif, Theta Chi. Republican. Clubs: Lake Mansfield Trout, Masons, Elks. Home: Murray Rd Montpelier VT 05602 Office: Nat Life Ins Co Nat Life Dr Montpelier VT 05602

GUILD, NELSON PRESCOTT, coll. pres.; b. Keene, N.H., Nov. 20, 1928; s. Louis F. and Hope (Mason) G.; m. Margaret Adele Graf, June 24, 1950; children—Douglas, Matthew. B.A., U. N.H., 1953; M.A., Pa. State U., 1955, Ph.D., 1958. Asst. prof. govt. Hamilton Coll., Clinton, N.Y., 1958-64, asso. prof., 1964-66; dean Frostburg (Md.) State Coll., 1966-69, pres., 1969—. Author: (with Kenneth T. Palmer) Essays and Readings, 1968. Served with USAF, 1946-49.

GUILDEN, IRA, corporate executive; b. N.Y.C. Dir., chmn. bd. dirs. Baldwin Securities Corp., John B. Stetson Co., Devel. Corp. for Israel; pres., treas. North Ocanic Securities Co., Inc. Office: 19 W 44th St New York NY

GUILDS, JOHN CALDWELL, JR., university dean; b. Columbia, S.C., Feb. 27, 1924; s. John Caldwell and Lucille (Folk) G.; m. Carolee Green Heriot, July 3, 1947; children: Carolee Heriot, Reba Lucille, John Caldwell III. A.B., Wofford Coll., 1947; A.M., Duke U., 1949, Ph.D., 1954. Instr. Duke U., 1949-52; asst. prof Clemson U., 1952-54; asso. prof. E. Central State Coll., 1954-56; mem. faculty Tex. Tech. U., Lubbock, 1956-64, prof. English, chmn. dept., 1962-64; prof. English, head dept. U. S.C., Columbia, 1964-70, vice provost, 1970-75; dean Coll. Humanities and Fine Arts, U. Houston, 1975-79; dean J. William Fulbright Coll. Arts and Scis. U. Ark., 1979—; Smith-Mundt prof. Am. lit. U. Damascus, 1959-60; vis. William Gilmore Simms research prof. U. S.C., 1979; Pres. S. Atlantic Assn. Depts. English, 1971. Gen. editor: The Centennial Edition of the Writings of William Gilmore Simms; Contbr. to profl. jours. Served with AUS, 1943-46; ETO. Decorated Purple Heart, Bronze Star. Mem. Modern Lang. Assn. Am., Internat. Assn. U. Profs. English, Phi Beta Kappa. Address: 37 Garvin Ave Fayetteville AR 72701

GUILFOYLE, GEORGE H., bishop; b. N.Y.C., Nov. 13, 1913; s. James J. and Johanna (McGrath) G. A.B., Georgetown U., 1935; student, St. Joseph's Sem., 1939-44; J.D., Fordham U., 1939, NYU School Banking, 1945; LL.M., Columbia U., 1946; LL.D., St. Francis College, 1958, Manhattan Coll., 1962, Iona Coll., 1966; Lit.D., St. Joseph's Coll., Phila., 1968. Bar: N.Y. 1940. Ordained priest Roman Cath. Ch., 1944, named papal chamberlain, 1955, domestic prelate, 1958; asst. St. Patrick's Cathedral, 1944-45, St. Andrew's Ch., 1944-46; asst. chancellor, also asst. St. Elizabeth's Ch., N.Y.C., 1946-47; with Catholic Charities, N.Y.C., 1947-66, exec. dir., 1956-66; episcopal vicar Richmond County (S.I.), also; pastor St. Peter's Ch., 1966-68; bishop of Camden, N.J., 1968—; Asso. moderator coordinating com. Cath. Lay Orgns. Archdiocese N.Y., 1954-57; archdiocesan consultor, 1960-68; nat. spiritual dir. Soc. St. Vincent de Paul, 1966—; Pres. Nat. Conf. Cath. Charities, 1959-61, bd. dirs., 1959-67; mem. N.Y.C. Adv. Bd. Pub. Welfare, 1960-66, Archdiocesan Commn. for Community Planning, 1964- 68. Bd. dirs. Nat. Shrine Immaculate Conception; trustee Seton Hall U. Recipient John Carroll award Georgetown U., 1963; Knight grand cross Equestrian Order Holy Sepulchre Jerusalem. Office: 1845 Haddon Ave Camden NJ 08101 *

GUILFOYLE, JOHN W., communications co. exec.; b. Burbank, Calif. Ed., Wilson Jr. Coll., Northwestern U. With ITT, 1951—; v.p., indsl. relations dir., then v.p. ops. Fed. Electric Corp., 1956-59, pres., 1959-64, Am. Cable and Radio Corp., 1964; group exec. U.S. Def./Space Group, 1964-66, v.p., 1966-79, group exec., 1966-68, 1968-78, 1978-79; pres. ITT Europe, 1979-83, Pres and CEO, ITT Telecommunications Corp. 1983— sr. v.p. parent co., 1979-80, exec. v.p., 1980—. Served with U.S. Army, World War II. Mem. NAM (past vice chmn. nat. def. com.), Council of Americas (dir., exec. com.), Navy League, Air Force Assn., Nat. Aviation Club. ITT Corp. 320 Park Ave. New York, NY 10022 *

GUILFOYLE, RICHARD JOSEPH, insurance company executive; b. St. John's, Nfld., Can., July 5, 1935; came to U.S., 1939; s. Thomas Joseph and Anastisa (Woodford) G.; m. Helen E. Walsh, July 1, 1961; children: Jane, Tom. B.A., St. Francis Coll., 1961; advanced mgmt. program, Harvard U., 1982. Regional controller Allstate Ins. Co., 1961-71; budget dir. Allstate Enterprises, Northfield, Ill., 1971; v.p. fin. planning Prudential Property & Casualty Co., Holmdel, N.J., 1971-78; v.p., dir. planning Reliance Ins. Co., Phila., 1978-82, sr. v.p., dir. planning and human resources, 1982—; dir. Cananwill Consumer Discount Co., Phila., Pilot Ins. Co., Reliance Corp. Services Inc., Reliance Reins. Mgmt. Inc., Reliance Underwriting Mgmt. Inc. Served to sgt. USAF, 1953-57. Mem. Planning Exec. Inst., Assn. Internat. Mgmt. Cons. (midwest regional dir. 1981—). Roman Catholic. Club: Harvard Bus. Sch. (Phila.). Home: 1220 Foxglove Ln East Goshen PA 19380 Office: Reliance Ins Cos 4 Penn Ctr Philadelphia PA 19103

GUILLEMIN, ROGER, physiologist; b. Dijon, France, Jan. 11, 1924; came to U.S., 1953, naturalized, 1963; s. Raymond and Blanche (Rigollot) G.; m. Lucienne Jeanne Billard, Mar. 22, 1951; children—Chantal, Francois, Claire, Helene, Elizabeth, Cecile. B.A., U. Dijon, 1941, B.Sc., 1942; M.D., Faculty of Medicine, Lyons, France, 1949; Ph.D., U. Montreal, 1953; Ph.D. (hon.), U. Rochester, 1976, U. Chgo., 1977, Baylor Coll. Medicine, 1978, U. Ulm, Germany, 1978, U. Dijon, France, 1978, Free U. Brussels, 1979, U. Montreal, 1979. Intern, resident univs. hosps., Dijon, 1949-51; asso. dir., asst. prof. Inst. Exptl. Medicine and Surgery, U. Montreal, 1951-53; asso. dir. dept. exptl. endocrinology Coll. de France, Paris, 1960-63; prof. physiology Baylor Coll. Medicine, 1953—; adj. prof. medicine U. Calif. at San Diego, 1970—; resident fellow Salk Inst., 1970—. Decorated Legion of Honor, France, 1974; recipient Gairdner Internat. award, 1974; U.S. Nat. Medal of Sci., 1977; co-recipient Nobel prize for medicine, 1977; recipient Lasker Found. award, 1975; Dickson prize in medicine, 1976; Passano award med. sci., 1976; Schmitt medal neurosci., 1977; Barren gold medal, 1979; Dale medal Soc. for Endocrinology, U.K., 1980. Fellow AAAS; Mem. Am. Physiol. Soc., Endocrine Soc. (council), Soc. Exptl. Biology and Medicine, A.A.A.S., Internat. Brain Research Orgn., Internat. Soc. Research Biology Reprodn., Soc. Neuro-scis., Nat. Acad. Scis., Am. Acad. Arts and Scis., Club of Rome. Office: Salk Inst Box 85800 San Diego CA 92138

GUILLEN, CLAUDIO, comparative literature educator; b. Paris, Sept. 25, 1924; s. Jorge and Germaine (Cahen) G.; m. Elfie Karzke, Dec. 12, 1958. B.A., Williams Coll., 1943; M.A., Harvard U., 1947, Ph.D. in Comparative Lit., 1953. Teaching fellow Harvard U., Cambridge, Mass., 1948-50, 1952-53, instr. summr sch., 1967, prof. comparative lit. and Romance Langs., 1978—, chmn. dept. comparative lit., 1979—, chmn. lit. maj., 1981—; instr. spanish Cologne, 1950-52; asst. prof. Spanish Princeton U., 1953-60, assoc. prof.Spanish, 1960-65, dir. program in comparative lit., 1963-65; prof. comparative lit. U. Calif.-San Diego, 1965-76, dir. Center for Iberian and Latin Am. Studies, 1975-76; vis. prof. Bryn Mawr, 1956-57, Johns Hopkins U., 1964-65, Ecole Normale d'Auteuil, 1954, Malaga, 1977-78; instr. summer schs. Middlebury, 1953, 1955, 1957, Malaga, 1975, 1980, Salamanca, 1976, Santander, 1978, 1979, dir. Calif. Edn. Abroad Program, Madrid, 1972-74; mem. Com. on Comparative History of Lit. in European Langs., 1980—; dir. Clasicos Alfaguara, Madrid, 1974—; editorial council mem. PMLA, Princeton Series in European and Comparative Lit. Author: Lazarillo de Tormes and El Abencerraje, 1966, Literature as System: Essays Toward the Theory of Literary History, 1974, (essays, reprinted anthologies), Germany, Spain, Italy; contbr. (articles to pubs. in field). Served with Free Franch Forces, Worl War II. Mem. MLA (exec. council 1970-74), Internat. Comparative Lit. Assn. (exec. com. 1973-79), Am. Comparative Lit. Assn. (exec. com. 1966-72), Spanish Soc. Comparative Lit. (pres. 1983), Am. Acad. Arts and Scis. Office: Harvard U 402 Boylston Cambridge MA 02138

GUILLERMIN, JOHN, film director; b. London, Nov. 11, 1925. Student, Cambridge U. Dir.: films The Waltz of the Toreadors, 1962, Guns at Batasi, 1964, Rapture, 1965, The Blue Max, 1966, House of Cards, 1969, The Bridge at Remagen, 1969, El Condor, 1970, Skyjacked, 1972, Shaft in Africa, 1973, The Towering Inferno, 1974, King Kong, 1976, Death on the Nile, 1978, Mr. Patman, 1978. Address: Internat Creative Mgmt 8899 Beverly Blvd Los Angeles CA 90048 *

GUILLERY, RAINER WALTER, anatomy educator; b. Greifswald, Germany, Aug. 28, 1929; came to U.S., 1964; s. Hermann and Eva (Hackel) G.; m. Margot Cunningham Pepper, Dec. 21, 1954; children: Peter, Edward, Philip, Jane. B.Sc. in Anatomy, U. Coll., London, Eng., 1951; Ph.D., 1954. Asst. lectr. Univ. Coll., London, Eng., 1953-57, lectr., 1957-63, reader, 1963-64; asso. prof. U. Wis. at Madison, 1964-68, prof. anatomy, 1968-77; prof. dept. pharm. and physiol. Scis. U. Chgo., 1977-84; Dr. Lee's prof. anatomy Oxford U., Eng., 1984—. Mem. editorial bd.: Jour. Comparative Neurology, 1971—, Jour. Neurocytology, 1972-76, Jour. Neurophysiology, 1975-81, Neurosci, 1979—, Jour. Neurosci, 1980—. Fellow Royal Soc.; Mem. Am. Assn. Anatomists, Soc. for Neurosci., Am. Soc. Cell Biology, Anatom. Soc. Gt. Britain. Research on central nervous system, synapses, degeneration, devel. visual pathways. Home: 5805 S Blackstone Ave Chicago IL 60637

GUILLET, JAMES EDWIN, chemistry educator, research scientist; b. Toronto, Ont., Can., Jan 14, 1927; s. Edwin Clarence and Mary Elizabeth (Scott) G.; m. Helen Ann Bircher, July 4, 1953; children: Edwin, Barbara, Patricia, Carolyn. B.A., U. Toronto, 1948; Ph.D. in Phys. Chemistry, Cambridge U., 1955; Sc.D., Cambridge U., 1974. Research chemist Eastman Kodak Co., Rochester, N.Y., 1948-50; sr. research chemist Tenn. Eastman Co., Kingsport, 1950-52, research assoc., 1963; assoc. prof. chemistry U. Toronto, 1963-69, prof., 1969—, assoc. dean. for research and planning Scarborough campus, 1983—; pres. Ecoplastics Ltd., Toronto, 1975—; vis. prof. CNRS, Strasbourg, France, 1970-71, Kyoto (Japan) U., 1974, U. Calif.-San Diego, 1978-79, U. Mainz (W.Germany), 1981; cons. Glidden Co. Ltd., 1964—, Imperial Oil Enterprises Ltd., 1965, Royal Packaging, Holland, 1972-79. Author Plastics and Ecological Problems, 1973; Photophysics and Photochemistry, 1984; contbr. articles to sci. publs.; inventor 55 products including photodegradable plastics. Recipient Dunlop award in polymer chemistry, 1978; Guggenheim fellow, 1981-82. Fellow Chem. Inst. Can., Royal Soc. Can.; mem. Am. Chem. Soc., Chem. Soc. (London). Mem. United Ch. Can. Home: 31 Sagebrush Ln Don Mills ON Canada M3A 1X4 Office: Dept Chemistry U Toronto Toronto ON Canada M5S 1A1

GUILLOT, ROBERT MILLER, univ. pres.; b. Headland, Ala., Jan. 2, 1922; s. Clarence Miller and Ruth (Lindsay) G.; m. Patty Shirley, Sept. 1, 1947; children—Patricia Ann, Shirley Lynne, Robert Miller. B.S., Auburn (Ala.) U., 1943; J.D., U. Ala., 1948. Bar: Ala. bar 1948. Practice in, Dothan, 1948-51; sr. v.p., sec. Vulcan Life & Accident Ins. Co., Birmingham, 1952-66; chmn. bd. Am. Educators Life Ins. Co., Birmingham, 1966-72; pres. U. North Ala., 1972—; Pres. Ala. League Municipalities, 1971-72, Assn. Ala. Life Ins. Cos., 1970-71. Mayor Vestavia Hills, Ala., 1960-72; Trustee Troy (Ala.) State U., 1964-72. Served with USAF, 1951-52; C.L.U. Baptist. Clubs: Mason (Shriner), Rotarian.).

GUIMOND, JOHN PATRICK, financial consultant; b. Green Bay, Wis., June 5, 1927; s. Herbert A. and Elizabeth M. G.; m. Avyce L. Veek, Aug. 20, 1949; children: John Patrick, James T., Cheryl L., Lisa M., Leanne M. B.B.A., U. Wis., Madison, 1951. Controller Rayovac div. ESB Inc., Madison, Wis., v.p. adminstrn., 1974-77; treas. ESB Inc., Phila., 1977-79; sr. v.p. Rayovac Corp., Madison, Wis., 1979-83; fin. cons., Madison, 1983—; dir. Sub-Zero Freezer, Inc.; lectr. U. Wis. Grad. Sch. Bus. Served with USAF, 1945-47. Mem. Fin. Execs. Inst. Clubs: Madison, Nakoma Golf. Office: 3100 Lake Mendota Dr Suite 805 Madison WI 53705 *

GUIN, JUNIUS FOY, JR., judge; b. Russellville, Ala., Feb. 2, 1924; s. Junius Foy and Ruby (Pace) G.; m. Dorace Jean Caldwell, July 18, 1945; children—Janet Elizabeth Smith, Judith Ann Mullican, Junius Foy III, David Jonathan. Student, Ga. Inst. Tech., 1940-41; A.B. magna cum laude; J.D., U. Ala., 1947; LL.D., Magic Valley Christian Coll., 1963. Bar: Ala. bar 1948. Practiced in, Russellville; sr. partner firm Guin, Guin, Bouldin & Porch, 1948-73; fed. dist. judge, Birmingham, Ala., 1973—; commr. Ala. Bar, 1965-73, 2d v.p., 1969-70; Pres. Abstract Trust Co., Inc., 1958-73; sec. Iuka TV Cable Co., Inc., Haleyville TV Cable Co., Inc., 1963-73; former dir., gen. counsel First Nat. Bank of Russellville, Franklin Fed. Savs. & Loan Assn. of Russellville.; Lectr. Cumberland-Samford Sch. Law, 1974—, U. Ala. Sch. Law, 1977—. Chmn. Russellville City Planning Com., 1954-57; 1st chmn. Jud. Commn. Ala., 1972-73; mem. Ala. Supreme Ct. Adv. Com. (rules civil procedure), 1971-73; mem. adv. com. on standards of conduct U.S. Jud. Conf., 1980—; Republican county chmn., 1954-58, 71-72, Rep. state fin. chmn., 1972-73; candidate for U.S. Senator from, Ala., 1954; Ala. Lawyers' Finance chmn. Com. to Re-elect Pres., 1972; trustee Ala. Christian Coll. Served to 1st lt., inf. AUS, 1943-46. Named Russellville Citizen of Year, 1973; recipient Dean's award U. Ala. Law Sch., 1977. Mem. Am. Radio Relay League, ABA (mem. spl. com. on residential real estate transactions 1972-73), Ala. Bar Assn. (com. chmn. 1965-73, award of Merit 1973), Jefferson County Bar Assn., Fed. Bar Assn., Am. Law Inst., Ala. Law Inst. (dir. 1969-73, 76—), Am. Judicature Soc., World Peace Through Law Center, Farrah Law Soc., Farrah Order Jurisprudence, Quarter Century Wireless Assn., Phi Beta Kappa, Delta Chi. Mem. Ch. of Christ (elder). Club: Rotarian. Home: 3400 Stoneridge Dr Birmingham AL 35243 Office: 106 Federal Courthouse Birmingham AL 35203

GUIN, RUSSELL LOWELL, pub. co. exec.; b. Mt. Cory, Ohio, Feb. 18, 1897; s. Albert and Elizabeth (McKinley) G.; m. Elizabeth Hudson, Aug. 14, 1920; children—Jane Ann, Gretchen; m. Alice Lee Morrison, Aug. 24, 1976. B.A., Ohio Wesleyan U., 1917; M.A., U. Ill., 1928. Athletic coach schs., Iowa and Ohio, 1917-20, prin. high sch., supt. schs., Ill., 1920-31; chmn. bd. Interstate Printers and Pubs., Inc., Danville, Ill., 1931—; dir. 1st Nat. Bank; pres. bd. 1st Savs. & Loan. Trustee Danville Jr. Coll.; mem. Ill. State Vocat. Adv. Council; nat. pres. Am. Bus. Clubs. Served with USN, 1918-19. Named Danville Citizen Number One, 1977. Mem. Chi Phi. Republican. Methodist. Clubs: Elks, Masons. Home: 212 Denvale Dr Danville IL 61832 Office: 19 N Jackson St Danville IL 61832 *I have conducted business for 50 years on the basis of "if it isn't good for both of us, it isn't good for either one".*

GUINDON, RICHARD GORDON, cartoonist; b. St. Paul, Dec. 2, 1935; s. John Edgar and Dorothy Lillian (Powell) G.; married; 1 son, Grey Burrell. Student public schs., St. Paul. Cartoonist The Realist Mag., N.Y.C., 1962-67; syndicated cartoonist Guindon, 1977—, Mpls. Tribune, 1968-81, Los Angeles Times, 1977—, Detroit Free Press, 1981—. Author: Guindon, 1976, Cartoons by Guindon, 1979, The World According to Carp, 1983; also datebooks, calendars, T-shirts, other items. Served with U.S. Army, 1953-56. Mem. Newspaper Guild. Office: 321 W Lafayette Blvd Detroit MI 48231

GUINDON, ROGER, university administrator; b. Ville-Marie, Que., Can., Sept. 26, 1920; s. Alderic and Germaine (Morisset) G. B.A., U. Ottawa, Can., 1942, L.Ph., 1943, B.Th., 1945, L.Th., 1947; D.Th., U. Fribourg, Switzerland, 1954; LL.D., Trent U., 1968, Laurentian U., 1969, U. Western Ont., 1975, Royal Mil. Coll., Kingston, 1981, York U., 1983; D.U., U. Montreal, 1982. Ordained priest Roman Catholic Ch., 1946; prof. theology U. Ottawa, Ont., 1947-51, 54-64, dean faculty of theology, 1961-64, rector, from 1964, now vice chancellor.; Mem. Ont. Council Health, 1967—, exec. mem., 1971—; mem. Tribunal on Bilingual Higher Edn. in N.S., 1969-70; chmn. Ottawa Health Sci. Complex Co-ordinating Com., 1973—; mem. Ont. Task Force on Health Planning, 1973, Assn. Commonwealth Univs., 1964—, exec. mem., 1966-68; mem. Assn. Univs. and Colls. of Can., 1964—, chmn., 1966-68; mem. Council of Ont. Univs., 1966—, vice chmn., 1973—; bd. govs. Labour Coll. Author: Beatitude et Theologie morale chez saint Thomas d'Aquin, 1956. Trustee Ont. Cancer Treatment and Research Found., 1964—, Ottawa Civic Hosp., 1965-69, Forum for Young Canadians, 1975—; hon. chmn. United Way Campaign, 1981-83; mem. Comml. and Indsl. Devel. Corp., 1980—. Decorated companion Order of Can. Office: 550 Cumberland St Ottawa ON K1N 6N5 Canada

GUINDON, WILLIAM G., theological association executive. Chmn. dept. physics Boston Coll., 1953-64; v.p., dean Holy Cross Coll., 1966-68; Regional provincial superior S.J. New Eng., 1968-74; sabbatical Collegio Internazionale del Gesu, Rome, 1974-75; del. 32d gen. congregation S.J., Rome, 1974-75; dean Jesuit Sch. Theology, Chgo., 1975-79, pres., 1977-81; spl. asst. to provincial superior S.J. New Eng., 1982—. Address: Provincial Offices 761 Harrison Ave Boston MA 02118 *I have enjoyed immensely the variety of substantial responsibilities entrusted to me by and for the Society of Jesus (the "Jesuits"), mostly in the New England region. Certainly a large part of this enjoyment has come from the students and others I have been privileged to serve, but the splendid education I received both by the Society of Jesus and M.I.T. has laid the groundwork.*

GUINN, DONALD EUGENE, telephone company executive; b. Wellington, Kans., Oct. 26, 1932; s. Cecil William and Avis Velma (Scoles) G.; m. Marlene Darhl, Mar. 21, 1953; children: Debra Michele, Damon Jeffrey, David Leslie. B.S. in Civil Engring, Oreg. State U., 1954. Various mgmt. positions Pacific Tel. & Tel., Portland, Oreg., 1954-75; v.p. engring. and network sers. Pacific N.W. Bell, 1976; asst. v.p. engring., asst. v.p. customer sers. AT&T, N.Y.C., N.J., 1976-78, v.p. customer services, v.p. network services, 1978-80; chmn., chief exec. officer Pacific Tel & Tel, San Francisco. Bd. dirs. Pacific Sci. Center, Seattle, 1975-76. Mem. Profl. Engrs. Oreg., IEEE (communications policy bd.). Republican. Lutheran. Office: Pacific Tel and Tel 140 New Montgomery St San Francisco CA 94105 *

GUINN, GEORGE EARL, clergyman, educator; b. Mossville, Miss., Aug. 21, 1912; s. David Howard and Martha Irene (Easterling) G.; m. Gail Holmes, July 13, 1937 (dec. 1969); 1 dau., Peggy Elaine (Mrs.

Herschel Wood Crump); m. Neva Norsworthy DeMoss, June 12, 1970. A.B., La. Coll., 1937; student, Southwestern Bapt. Theol. Sem., 1938-39; Th.M., New Orleans Bapt. Theol. Sem., 1942, Th.D., 1944; D.D., Mercer U., Ga., 1961; LL.D., William Jewell Coll., 1970. Ordained to ministry Bapt. Church, 1933; pastor First Ch., Sterlington, La., 1937-41, Jennings, La., 1941-45, Bossier City, La., 1945-48; head dept. homiletics Southwestern Bapt. Theol. Sem., Fort Worth, 1948-51; pres. La. Coll., Pineville, 1951-74; prof. Christian preaching So. Bapt. Theol. Sem., Louisville, 1974—; Mem. La. Bd. Instns. (chmn. 1956-58), La. Found. Pvt. Colls., (pres. 1954-55, 60-61, 64-65, 67-68), So. Baptist Conv. edn. commn., 1952-58, 68—, Assn. of So. Baptist Colls. and Schs., 1961-67, 68—, pres., 1970-71. Co-author: So. Bapt. Preaching, 1959. Mem. Pi Kappa Delta. Clubs: Mason, Rotarian. Address: 3108 Claiborne Circle Monroe LA 71201

GUINN, LESLIE WAYNE, singer; b. Conroe, Tex., Apr. 29, 1935; s. Leslie and Sybil Vernon (Henry) G.; m. Mary Ellen Jackson, Dec. 2, 1961; children: Robin, Jonathan, Rachel. B.Mus., Northwestern U. Currently prof. voice U. Mich., Ann Arbor. Debut with Leopold Stokowski in: Carmina Burana, N.Y.C., 1966; European debut in: Wozzeck, Stuttgart Opera, 1983; performances include solo recitals; Debut with Leopold Stokowski in chamber music concerts; appearances with, U.S. symphony orchs.; rec. artist, Nonesuch Records; (Winner Am. Opera Auditions). Served with U.S. Army, 1959-62. Martha Baird Rockefeller grantee. Mem. Nat. Assn. Tchrs. Singing. Office: Sch Music U Mich Ann Arbor MI 48109

GUINNESS, ALEC, actor; b. London, Apr. 2, 1914; m. Merula Salaman; 1 son, Matthew. Student, Pembroke Lodge, Southbourne, Roborough Sch., Eastbourne, Fay Compton Studio Dramatic Art; D.F.A. (hon.), Boston Coll., 1962, D.Litt., Oxford U., 1978. Copywriter, Arks Publicity, 1933. Debut with walk-on role in Libel!, 1934; Shakespearean debut in Hamlet, 1934; appeared with Old Vic Co., 1936-37; toured Europe and Egypt, 1938-39; with John Gielgud's Co., 1937-38; appeared in Romeo and Juliet, Perth, Scotland, 1939; Great Expectations (also adapted), 1939, Cousin Muriel, The Tempest, Thunder Rock, all 1940, Flare Path, N.Y.C., 1942; appeared in own adaptation of: The Brothers Karamazov, 1946; in; Vicious Circle, 1946; with, Old Vic Co., 1946-48; dir.: Twelfth Night, 1948; appeared in: The Human Touch, 1949, The Cocktail Party, N.Y.C. and Edinburgh, Scotland, 1949-50, Under the Sycamore Tree, 1952; Richard III and All's Well That Ends Well, Stratford Shakespeare Festival, Ont., Can., 1953, The Prisoner, 1954, Hotel Paradiso, 1956, Ross, 1960 (London Evening Standard award), Exit the King, 1963, Dylan, N.Y.C., 1964, Incident at Vichy and Macbeth, 1966, Wise Child, 1967, Time Out of Mind, 1970, A Voyage Round My Father, 1971, Habeas Corpus, 1973, A Family and a Fortune, 1975, Yahoo, 1976, The Old Country, 1977-78; actor, dir.: The Cocktail Party, 1968; film appearances Great Expectations, 1945; Oliver Twist, 1948, Mudlark, 1950, Kind Hearts and Coronets, 1951, The Lavender Hill Mob, 1951 (Acad. award nomination), The Man in the White Suit, 1951, Captain's Paradise, 1953, The Prisoner, 1956, The Bridge on the River Kwai (Acad. award, Golden Globe award, Brit. Film Acad. award 1957), The Horse's Mouth, 1958 (Venice Film Festival award), Our Man in Havana, 1960, Tunes of Glory, 1960, Lawrence of Arabia, 1962, Dr. Zhivago, 1965, The Comedians, 1967, Cromwell, 1970, Scrooge, 1970, Hitler: The Last Ten Days, 1973, Brother Sun, Sister Moon, 1973, Murder by Death, 1976, Star Wars, 1977 (Acad. award nomination), Lovesick, 1982, Passage to India, 1984; Am. TV debut in The Wicked Scheme of Jebal Deeks, 1959; Brit. TV appearances include The Actor, 1968; Twelfth Night, 1969, The Gift of Friendship, 1974, Caesar and Cleopatra, 1975, Tinker Tailor Soldier Spy, 1979 (Brit. Film Acad. TV award), Little Lord Fauntleroy, 1980, Smiley's People, 1981, Edwin, 1983. Served in Vol. Res., Royal Navy, 1941-45; commd. lt., 1942. Created comdr. Order Brit. Empire, 1955; knight bachelor, 1959; recipient Acad. award for services to cinema, 1980.

GUINTHER, HARRY PHILIP, retail clothing company executive; b. Toledo, Mar. 7, 1923; s. Harold and Dorothy (MacLane) G.; m. Virginia Ann Kujawa, Jan. 19, 1946; children: David Harry, John Philip. Student, Toledo U., 1946-48, Northwestern U., 1952-56, Baldwin Wallace Coll., 1956-62. With Richman Bros. Co., Cleve., 1945-76, gen. mgr., exec. v.p., 1976; pres. Hart, Schaffner & Marx Retail Stores, Chgo., 1976-78; pres., chief exec. officer Richman Bros. Co., Cleve., 1978—; dir. Kinney Shoe Corp., Richman Bros. Co., Precision Pattern Corp. Served with USAF, 1942-45. Decorated D.F.C. with Oak leaf cluster, Air medal with eight oak leaf clusters, Purple Heart with Oak Leaf cluster. Mem. Nat. Assn. Mens Sprotswear Buyers, Menswear Retailers Am. Republican. Lutheran. Clubs: N.Y. Athletic, Cleve. Yachting, Chagrin Valley Country, Rotary. Office: Richam Bros Co 1600 E 55th St Cleveland OH *

GUION, ROBERT MORGAN, psychologist, educator; b. Indpls., Sept. 14, 1924; s. Leroy Herbert and Carolyn (Morgan) G.; m. Mary Emily Firestone, June 8, 1947; children: David Michael, Diana Lynn, Keith Douglas, Pamela Sue, Judith Elaine. B.A., State U. Iowa, 1948; M.S., Purdue U., 1950, Ph.D., 1952. Vocat. counselor Purdue U., 1948-51, research fellow, 1951-52; mem. faculty Bowling Green (Ohio) State U., 1952—, prof. psychology, 1964—, chmn. dept., 1966-71; vis. prof. U. Calif. at Berkeley, 1963-64, U. N.Mex., summer 1965; tech. adviser Dept. Personnel Services, State Hawaii, summer 1970; vis. research psychologist Ednl. Testing Service, 1971-72; cons. in field, 1954—. Author: Personnel Testing, 1965. Served with AUS, 1943-46. Recipient James McKeen Cattell award Am. Psychol. Assn., 1965, 81. Mem. Am. Psychol. Assn. (pres. div. 14 1972-73, pres. div. 5 1982-83), Midwestern Psychol. Assn., Internat. Assn. Applied Psychology, Am. Edn. Research Assn., Nat. Council on Measurement in Edn., Sigma Xi, Psi Chi. Methodist. Home: 632 Haskins Rd Bowling Green OH 43402

GUIORA, ALEXANDER ZEEV, psychologist; b. Nyiregyhaza, Hungary, June 13, 1925; came to U.S., 1963, naturalized, 1968; s. Solomon and Theresa (Gottlieb) G.; m. Susie N. Neuser, Jan. 20, 1955. Docteur d'Universite, Sorbonne U., Paris, 1951. Prof. psychiatry, psychology and linguistics U. Mich., Ann Arbor, 1964—; vis. prof. U. Negev, Israel, 1971; vis. prof., chmn. dept. med. psychology Technion Israel Inst. Tech., 1976-77; vis. prof. Hebrew U., Jerusalem, 1983—. Editor: (with Marrvin Brandwin) Perspectives in Clinical Psychology, 1968, Epistemology for the Language Sciences, 1983; contbr. articles to profl. jours. Mem. Am. Psychol. Assn. Jewish. Club: Azazels. Home: 2115 Londonderry Rd Ann Arbor MI 48104 Office: U Mich Ann Arbor MI 48109

GUISE, DAVID EARL, architect, educator; b. N.Y.C., Dec. 29, 1931; s. Jack I. and Frances (Haberman) G.; m. Gretchen Grurnfelder, Nov. 21, 1962; children: Gabrielle Ann, John George, Jacqueline Alexis, Ursula Claire. B. Arch. with honors, U. Pa., 1957. Job capt. Kahn & Jacobs, Architects, N.Y.C., 1957-60; designer draftsman E.J. Robin, Architect, N.Y.C., 1961; architect David Guise, Architect, N.Y.C., 1962—; asst. prof. Sch. Architecture, CCNY, 1966-70, assoc. prof., 1970-76, prof., 1976—; adj. prof. Columbia U., 1983—. Contbr. articles to profl. jours.; architect numerous comml. and residential bldgs. Mem. nat. panel Am. Arbitration Assn., 1967—; sec. Irvington Planning Bd., N.Y. Mem. AIA, Constrn. Specifications Inst., Bldg. Research Inst., Assn. Collegiate Schs. Architecture. Home: Fargo Ln Irvington NY 10533 Office: 250 W 57th New York NY 10019

GUITE, HAROLD FREDERICK, classics educator; b. Clayworth, Notts., Eng., Mar. 12, 1920; s. Frederick William and Amy Eliza (White) G.; m. Janetta Inglis Keith Murray, Mar. 26, 1951; children: Candace Jane Elizabeth, Ayodeji Malcolm. Exhibitioner, St. Catharine's Coll., Cambridge, 1939-40; B.A. Gen., U. London, 1944, 1946, Arthur Platt student, 1946-47, M.A., 1952. Coll. supr. St. Catharine's Coll., Cambridge, 1946-47; asst. lectr. classics, lectr. in Latin U. Manchester, 1947-56; lectr., sr. lectr. classics U. Ibadan, Nigeria, 1956-63; prof., head of classics, dean arts, mem. council exec. U. Rhodesia, 1963-67; prof. classics McMaster U., Hamilton, Ont., Can., 1967—, bd. govs., Hamilton, Ont., Can., 1983-85; assoc. mem. Darwin Coll., Cambridge (Eng.) U., 1980-81; gov. Hartley Victoria Coll., Manchester, 1950-56; hon. inspector edn. Western Region, Nigeria, 1958-63; gov. Waddilove Tng. Inst., Rhodesia, 1964-67; Methodist rep. Joint Com. Chs. on Tchr. Tng., Rhodesia, 1964-67; Chmn. com. on tng. of lay preachers Manchester and Salford Meth. Mission, 1952-56; treas. Manchester br. China Christian Univs. Assn., 1951-56; sr. friend Student Christian Movement, 1947—. Author: What Kind of Classics?, 1965; Editor: Proceedings of the African Classical Assns, 1963-67; Mem. editorial bd.: Phoenix, 1970-74; Dir.: Plautus's Mostellaria in Latin, 1958; Played Charlie in: Muriel Spark's Doctors of Philosophy, 1969. Bd. govs. McMaster U., 1983—. Mem. Fellowship of Reconciliation (mem. internat. council, chmn. youth com. 1951-56), McMaster U. Faculty Assn. (pres. 1977-79), Cambridge Union Soc., Youth Hostel Assn. Office: Classics Dept McMaster University Hamilton ON Canada

GUITTAR, LEE JOHN, newspaper executive; b. St. Louis, May 4, 1931; s. LeRoy and Edna Mae (Johnston) G.; m. Elizabeth Madden Shedrick, Aug. 23, 1980; children—David Lee, Stephen Joseph, Mitchell John, Jeanne Marie, Richard Laughran; step-children: Elisabeth F. Shedrick, Kathryn S. Shedrick, Daniel C. Shedrick. A.B. program, Columbia U., 1953; M.B.A. program, U. Mass., 1962. With Gen. Electric Co., 1955-65, mgr. community and govt. relations programs, N.Y.C., 1963-65; mgr. employee and pub. relations Tidewater Oil Co., N.Y.C., 1965-66; personnel dir., then circulation dir. Miami (Fla.) Herald, 1967-72; v.p., bus. mgr. Detroit Free Press, 1972-74, v.p., gen. mgr., 1974-75, pres., dir., 1975-77; pub. Dallas Times Herald, 1977-81; Publisher The Denver Post, 1981-83; chmn. Denver Post, 1983—; chmn., chief exec. officer Dallas Times Herald, 1983; Group v.p. newspaper Times Mirror Co., 1981—. Bd. dirs. Dallas Citizens Council, Goals for Dallas, ARC, United Way, Central Bus. Dist. Assn. Served to lt. (j.g.) USNR, 1953-55; Korea. Mem. Am. Newspaper Pubs. Assn., Am. Mgmt. Assn., Am. Press Inst., Dallas C. of C. (dir.), Phi Beta Kappa. Republican. Roman Catholic. Clubs: City, Plaza of the Ams. Athletic (Dallas); Tower, Bent Tree Country., Las Colinas Country; Cherry Hills Country (Denver); Castle Pines Country (Colo.). Home:: 3620 Colgate Ave Dallas TX 75225 Office: 1101 Pacific Dallas TX 75202 *

GULBRANDSON, L.C., justice Montana Supreme Court; b. Vida, Mont., Oct. 28, 1922; s. E.O. and May (Farnham) G.; m. Wilma Loomans, Apr. 20, 1976; 1 son by previous marriage, Stephen. B.S.L., U. Minn., 1950, LL.B., 1952. Bar: Mont. 1953. Judge U.S. Dist. Ct. 7th Dist. Mont., 1959-83; justice Mont. Supreme Ct., Helena, 1983—. Served to capt. USAAF, 1942-48; PTO. Home: 2034 Gold Rush Ave Helena MT 59601 Office: Montana Supreme Court Sanders St Helena MT 59601

GULCHER, ROBERT HARRY, aircraft company executive; b. Columbus, Ohio, Aug. 26, 1925; s. Alban H. and Beatreice (Plohr) G.; m. Anne Cummings, Dec. 14, 1950 (dec.); children: Jeffrey, Donald; m. Suzanne K. Kane, Apr. 12,1969; children: Andrew, Kristin. B.S., U.S. Marine Acad., 1945; B.E.E., Ohio State U., 1950. Third asst. engr. Am. Petroleum Transp. Co., N.Y.C., 1945-46; engr. Capital Elevator & Mfg. Co., Columbus, Ohio, 1949-51, Columbus div. N. Am. Aviation, 1951-53, various mgmt. engring. positions, 1953-66; chief engr. Columbus div. Rockwell Internat., 1966-79; v.p. research and engring. N. Am. Aircraft ops., El Segundo, Calif., 1979—. Fellow AIAA (assoc.); mem. IEEE (sr.). Republican. Lutheran. Office: Rockwell Internat 201 N Douglas St El Segundo CA 92045

GULDEN, SIMON, lawyer, foods company executive; b. Montreal, Que., Can., Jan. 7, 1938; s. David and Zelda (Long) G.; m. Ellen Lee Barbour, June 12, 1977. B.A., McGill U., Montreal, 1959; LL.L., U. Montreal, 1962. Bar: Que. Ptnr. Genser, Philips, Friedman & Gulden, Montreal, 1963-68; sec., legal counsel Pl. Bonaventure, Inc., 1969-72; legal counsel real estate Steinberg Inc., Montreal, 1972-74; solicitor, prime atty. Bell Can., Montreal, 1975-76; v.p., gen. counsel, sec. Nabisco Brands Ltd., Toronto, 1976—. Mem. Internat. Assn. Lawyers and Jurists, Internat. Fiscal Assn., Can. Bar Assn., Internat. Bar Assn., Lord Reading Law Soc. Que., Montreal Bd. Trade, Toronto Bd. Trade, Assn. Conseils Francization Que., Advt. and Sales Execs. Club, Am. Mgmt. Assn. Clubs: Island Yacht, Cambridge (Toronto); Canadian. Home: 15 Morning Gloryway Willowdale ON M2H 3M1 Canada Office: 1 Dundas St W Suite 2900 Toronto ON M5G 2A9 Canada

GULICK, JACK A., insurance company executive; b. Wilkes-Barre, Pa., June 21, 1929; s. Andrew and Marcella G.; m. Jeanne Marie Durkin, June 19, 1954; children: John, Ann, James, Margaret. A.B. in Journalism, U. Ga., 1950. Claims adjuster Nationwide Ins. Cos., Harrisburg, Pa., 1955-57, group sales, Columbus, Ohio, 1957-64, Buffalo and Atlanta, 1957-64, assn. group sales mgr., Columbus, 1964-68, dir. group sales, 1968-70, v.p. bus. accounts, 1970-81, v.p. sales and fin. services, 1981—; dir. Pub. Employee Benefit Services Corp., Oklahoma City. Served to 1st lt. U.S. Army, 1950-52. Mem. Columbus Health Underwriters Assn. Democrat. Roman Catholic. Club: St. Anthony's Men's (Columbus, Ohio). Home: 5414 Rockwood Rd Columbus OH 43229 Office: Nationwide Ins Cos Nationwide Plaza Columbus OH 43216

GULICK, JOHN, anthropology educator; b. Newton, Mass., Apr. 18, 1924; s. Millard Burr and Alida (Carey) G.; m. Margaret G. Eaton, Apr. 10, 1946 (dec. Sept. 1979); children: Stephen M., James C., Anne S.; m. Betty E. Cogswell, June 23, 1982. A.B. magna cum laude, Harvard U., 1949, A.M., 1951, Ph.D., 1953. Teaching fellow Harvard U., 1951, 53; lectr. Am. U. Beirut, 1952, vis. prof. anthropology, 1961-62; instr. Adelphi Coll., 1953-55; asst. prof., asso. prof., prof. anthropology U. N.C.-Chapel Hill, 1955—, chmn. dept. anthropology, 1965-70; dir. Cross-Cultural Lab., Inst. Research Social Sci., U. N.C., 1955-59; bd. dirs. Human Relations Area Files, 1959-66; vis. prof. anthropology U. Isfahan, Iran, 1970-71, Shiraz U., 1978. Author: Social Structure and Culture Change in a Lebanese Village, 1955, Cherokees at the Crossroads, 1960, rev. edit., 1973, (with Charles E. Bowerman) Adaptation of Newcomers in the Piedmont Industrial Crescent, 1961, Tripoli: A Modern Arab City, 1967, The Middle East: an Anthropological Perspective, 1976, repub., 1983; editor: Dimensions of Cultural Change in the Middle East, 1965; co-editor: Symposium on Cherokee and Iroquois Culture, 1961. Served with Am. Field Service, 1943-44; with AUS, 1944-46. Fellow Am. Anthrop. Assn., Middle East Studies Assn.; mem. So. Anthrop. Soc. (pres. 1968-69), Phi Beta Kappa. Home: 1029 Highland Woods Chapel Hill NC 27514

GULICK, SIDNEY LEWIS, univ. ofcl.; b. Kobe, Japan, Aug. 17, 1902; s. Sidney L. and Cara May (Fisher) G.; m. Evelyn Mary Bade, July 31, 1931; children—Marian G. Wilson, Sidney Lewis III. A.B., Oberlin Coll., 1923, M.A., 1925; Ph.D., Yale U., 1931. Tchr. English, piano Doshisha U., Kyoto, Japan, 1923-24; asso. pub. speaking U. Calif. at Berkeley, 1927-30; instr. English U. Rochester, 1931-35; asst., then asso. prof. English, Mills Coll., 1935-45; asso. prof. English Calif. State U. at San Diego, 1945-49, prof. English, 1949-69, prof. emeritus, 1969—, dean arts and scis., 1959-69, emeritus, 1969—, adminstrv. adviser, 1969—. Author: A Chesterfield Bibliography to 1800, 1935, rev. edit., 1979, Some Unpublished Letters of Lord Chesterfield, 1937, Gulick Vocabulary Survey, 1957, 61; Contbr. essays, articles to learned publs. Served as chief procurement and placement dist. postal censor San Francisco Office of Censorship, 1942-45. Mem. Modern Lang. Assn., AAUP, Philol. Assn. Pacific Coast, Phi Kappa Phi. Conglist. Club: Calif. Writers. Home: 10301 Sierra Vista La Mesa CA 92041 Office: San Diego State U San Diego CA 92182

GULICK, WALTER LAWRENCE, psychologist, coll. pres.; b. Summit, N.J., July 4, 1927; s. Walter Lawrence and Carol (Dewey) G.; m. Winifred Bourn Frazee, Oct. 18, 1952; children—Hans, Tod, Kristina. A.B., Hamilton Coll., Clinton, N.Y., 1952; M.A. (Theta Delta Chi fellow), U. Del., 1955, Dartmouth, 1968; Ph.D. (psychology scholar 1955-57), Princeton, 1957. Mem. faculty U. Del., 1957-65, prof. psychology, 1963-65, chmn. dept., 1964-65; prof. psychology Dartmouth, Hanover, N.H., 1965-74, chmn. dept., 1970-73, 74-75, Distinguished Class of 1925 prof., 1973-75; dean of coll. Hamilton Coll., 1975-79, prof. psychology, 1975—, William R. Kenan prof., 1979-81; pres. St. Lawrence U., 1981—; vis. prof. U. Vt., summer 1966; cons. Presbyn. Hosp., Phila., 1961-63; editorial cons. Oxford U. Press, 1963—, McGraw-Hill Pub. Co., 1966-67, Harper & Row, 1971-73, Cambridge U. Press, 1979—. Author: Hearing: Physiology and Psychophysics, 1971, Human Stereopsis: Psychophysical Analysis, 1976; Contbr. articles to profl. jours. Mem. Hanover Sch. Bd., 1972-75, Dresden Bd. Sch. Dirs., 1972-75; Mem. grad. council Princeton U., 1972-75; mem. adv. council Nat. Inst. for Humanities, 1975—; mem. teaching evaluation project HEW. Served with AUS, 1946-48. Recipient Nat. Service award, 1955, 81; Dale prize music Hamilton Coll., 1952. Mem. N.Y. Acad. Scis., Eastern Psychol. Assn., Psychonomic Soc., Phi Beta Kappa, Sigma Xi (pres. Dartmouth chpt. 1967-68), Psi Chi (pres. U. Del. chpt. 1954-55). Research vision and hearing. Home: 54 E Main St Canton NY 13617

GULINO, ATEO LOUIS, specialty chemical company executive; b. Cin., Feb. 12, 1917; s. Emil G. and Celeste (Pagnatti) G.; m. Virginia P. Plogsted, Apr. 17, 1941; children: Denis G., Talia C. B.A., U. Cin., 1950. With DuBois Chems., Cin., 1940-70, exec. v.p., 1969-70; sr. v.p. Chemed Corp., Cin., 1970, exec. v.p., 1970—; pres. Total Group, Cin., 1982—. Pres. Cin. Speech and Hearing Ctr., 1970-74; trustee Cin. Symphony Orch., Good Samaritan Hosp., Cin. Mem. Soap and Detergent Assn. (trustee). Clubs: Hyde Park Golf and Country (trustee), Queen City (trustee 1970—), Banker's (trustee 1975—). Office: Chemed Corp 511 Walnut St Cincinnati OH 45202

GULKIN, HARRY, film producer; b. Montreal, 2Que., Can., Nov. 14, 1927; s. Peter Oliver and Raya (Shinderman) G. Portrait photographer, 1942-44, mcht. seaman, trade union organizer, 1944-49, labour journalist, critic, trade union organizer, 1950-56, market researcher, cons., 1956-71, ind. film producer, 1971—; challenger Nat. Film Bd., Can., 1979. Dir., Can. Film Inst.; producer: Penny and Ann (2d prize Film Festival Internat. Congress Rehab. Centres 1976, award Amtec Media Festival 1977), 1974 (Red Ribbon Am. Film Festival 1977), Lies My Father Told Me (Hollywood Fgn. Critics award as best fgn. film 1975, Canadian Film award 1976, Grand prize Virgin Islands Internat. Festival 1975, Christopher awards for writing, direction, prodn. 1975, Actra award for best original screenplay 1976, Canadian Motion Picture Distbrs. Assn. award 1976), 1975 (others), Jacob Two Meets The Hooded Fang, 1976 (Gold medallion spl. jury award Miami Internat. Film Festival 1978, Spl. Jury award 8th Internat. Children's Film Festival, Los Angeles 1979), Two Solitudes, 1977; Editor: The Marketer Jour, 1966. Bd. dirs. Saidye Bronfman Centre. Mem. Motion Picture Inst. Can. (pres. 1977), Can. Film Inst. (pres.), Assn. Que. Film Producers, Cinematheque Québecoise, Am. Mktg. Assn. (past chtp. pres.). Home: 111 Saint Joseph Blvd W Montreal PQ Canada H2T 2P2

GULLANDER, WERNER PAUL, consultant, ret. corp. exec.; b. Big Rapids, Mich., July 19, 1908; s. Paul and Elvira Esther (Werner) G.; m. Dorothy Mae Becker, July 12, 1930 (div. 1971); children: Barbara Louise Gullander Weinberger, Judith Maria; m. Elizabeth B. Famme, Sept. 16, 1971. B.S., U. Minn., 1930; LL.D. (hon.), U. Puget Sound, 1966. Acctg. trainee Gen. Electric Co., 1930-33, traveling auditor, 1933-38, supervising auditor, 1938-44; sec., treas. Gen. Electric Supply Corp., 1945-48, dist. mgr., 1948-51; fin. v.p. Weyerhauser Co., Tacoma, 1952-60; exec. v.p., dir. Gen. Dynamics Corp., 1960-62; pres. NAM, N.Y.C., 1962-72, now bd. dirs.; cons.; dir. Zurn Industries, Inc.; mem. Conf. Bd., Bus. and Industry Advisory Com. OECD. Mem. Financial Execs. Inst., Tau Kappa Epsilon. Clubs: Washington Athletic, 101 (Seattle); Port Ludlow Yacht. Home: 221 N Bay Ln Apt 5 Port Ludlow WA 98365

GULLEDGE, CHARLES GLENN, diversified technical services company executive; b. Marion, Ill., Oct. 4, 1919; s. Basyle Glenn and Ethel Minnie (Binkley) G.; m. Patricia M. Moore, Jan. 19, 1944; children: Ann Dee, Patrick Forrest, Christopher Moore; m. Elizabeth Ann Wright, Dec. 29, 1960; stepchildren: Allen Wright Price, Suz-Ann Price Stephenson. B.S. in Mech. Engring, Washington U., St. Louis, 1941, postgrad., 1949; postgrad., Harvard U.-M.I.T., 1944. With Emerson Electric Mfg. Co., St. Louis, 1946-60, v.p., gen. mgr. electronics and avionics div., 1956-60; pres., vice chmn., chief exec. officer, dir. Dynalectron Corp. (and predecessor), McLean, Va., 1960—; chmn., dir. Dynalectric Co., Dynalectric Supply Co., Dynalectric Co. Nev., State Electric Co. Ltd., Fuller-Austin Insulation Co.; chmn., pres. Fleetwood Contractors, Inc.; dir. (numerous other affiliated cos.). Chmn., commr. Fairfax County, Va., County Econ. Devel. Authority, 1980—; vice chmn. Nat. Council Synthetic Fuels Prodn., 1980—; bd. dirs. Fairfax Symphony Orch., 1983—. Served to capt. USMCR, 1943-46. Mem. Am. Mgmt. Assn. (Pres.'s Assn.), Internat. Mgmt. and Devel. Inst. (corp. strategic planning council), Nat. Aviation Club (gov.), Nat. Aero. Assn., Air Force Assn., Army Aviation Assn. Am., Assn. Naval Aviation, Am. Petroleum Inst., Fairfax County C. of C. (dir. 1981—). Home: 1701 N Kent St Arlington VA 22209 Office: 1313 Dolley Madison Blvd McLean VA 22101

GULLEY, WARREN L.(BILL), business executive; b. Wetaug, Ill., Nov. 16, 1922; s. J. Walter and Doss M. (Goodman) G.; m. Nancy J. Redmond, May 7, 1947; children: Joseph Michael, William Patrick, John Walter, Timothy James. Student pub. schs., Ill. Adminstrv. asst., then dep. asst. to mil. asst. President U.S., 1966-75; dir. White House Mil. Office, 1976-77; pres. Internat. Six Inc., Washington, RPA Group Internat., Inc. Author: Breaking Cover. Served to sgt. maj. USMC, 1939-68. Decorated Legion of Merit, Purple Heart. Address: 7831 Welch Ct Alexandria VA 22310

GULLEY, WILBUR PAUL, JR., savings and loan executive; b. Little Rock, Aug. 8, 1923; s. Wilbur Paul and JaJa Douglas (Ashburn) G.; m. Mary Elizabeth Bragg Hunt, Mar. 13, 1971; children by previous marriage: Wilbur Paul III and William H. (twins), James Ransom, Michael. A.B. in Bus. Adminstrn., Duke U., 1947. With Gulley Ins. Agy., Little Rock, 1947, partner, mng. officer, 1947-58; with Savers

Fed. Savs. & Loan Assn., Little Rock, 1947—, sec., 1948-52, v.p., 1952-58, pres., 1959-83, chmn. bd., 1983—, also dir.; Pres. Better Bus. Bur. Ark., 1962; gen. chmn. United Fund campaign, Pulaski County, Ark., 1963-64; v.p. Little Rock Boys Club, 1970-71, pres., 1971-72. Trustee, pres. George W. Donaghey Found., 1969-72; commr. Metrocentre Improvement Dist., 1977-81, chmn., 1981; trustee Ark. State U., 1968-73, sec.-treas., 1971-72, chmn., 1972-73; trustee Savs. and Loan Found., 1977-81; Trustee Hendrix Coll., Conway, Ark., 1980—. Served with USNR, 1943-46. Mem. Southwestern Savs. and Loan Conf. (pres. 1960-61), Savs. Assn. Retirement Fund (trustee 1960-65), U.S. Savs. and Loan League (mem. exec. com. 1963-66), Pulaski County Savs. and Loan League, pres. 1964), Ark. Savs. and Loan League (pres. 1965-66), League Savs. Instns. (exec. com. 1963-66), Little Rock C. of C. (pres. 1968), Phi Beta Kappa, Sigma Alpha Epsilon, Beta Omega Sigma. Methodist (bd. stewards). Clubs: Little Rock Country, Little Rock, Capital (Little Rock). Home: 2 Sunset Dr Little Rock AR 72207 Office: Capitol Ave at Spring St Little Rock AR 72203

GULLI, FRANCO, violinist; b. Trieste, Italy, Sept. 1, 1926; m. Enrica Cavallo. Tchr. Accademia Chigiana, Siena, Italy, Conservatory of Music, Lucerne, Switzerland; prof. music Ind. U., Bloomington, 1972—; mem. juries internat. violin competitions. Am. debut with, Dallas Symphony, 1968, numerous appearances with leading orchs. in U.S. and Can., including, Chgo., Cleve., Cin., Dallas, Detroit, Pitts., Milw., Washington and, Ottawa; appears with leading orchs. and at all prin. festivals in Europe, (with wife, pianist) joint recitals, Enrica Cavallo, at Met. Mus. Art, also world tours; rec. artist, Musical Heritage, RCA, Decca, Angelicum and, Audio Fidelity records. Recipient critics prize for rec. Mendelssohn Double Concerto and F Major Concerto. Address: care Columbia Artists Mgmt 165 W 57 St New York NY 10019

GULLICKSON, GLENN, JR., physician, educator; b. Mpls., July 9, 1919; s. Glenn and Grace (Stellwagen) G.; m. Glenna A. Swore, May 18, 1957; children: Mary, Glenn III. B.A., U. Minn., 1942, M.D., 1945, Ph.D., 1961. Diplomate: Am. Bd. Phys. Medicine and Rehab. Intern Gallinger Municipal Hosp., Washington, 1944-45; faculty U. Minn. Med. Sch., Mpls., 1946—, assoc. prof. phys. medicine and rehab., 1961-66, prof. phys. medicine and rehab., 1966—, acting head dept., 1974-75, interim head, 1982—, asst. dir. Rehab. Center, 1954-61, dir., 1961—; Exec. dir. Am. Congress Phys. Medicine and Rehab., 1960-66; Mem. exam. com. phys. therapists Minn. Bd. Med. Examiners, 1961-71, pres., 1968-71; mem. med. adv. com. Minn. Soc. for Crippled Children and Adults, 1967-72; fellow stroke council Am. Heart Assn., mem. exec. com., 1971-74; mem. neurol. scis. research tng. com. Nat. Inst. Neurol. Diseases and Blindness, 1965-69; exec. com. Joint Com. Stroke Facilities, 1969-78. Served to lt. (s.g.), M.C. USNR, 1945-46, 53-54. Mem. A.M.A. (prin. rep. intersplty. com. 1968-72, mem. residency review com. phys. medicine, rehab. 1971-79), Minn., Hennepin County med. socs., AAAS, AAUP, Nat., Minn. rehab. assns., Minn. Med. Found., Am. Acad. Phys. Medicine and Rehab. (gov., v.p. 1968-69, pres. 1970-71), Am. Bd. Phys. Medicine and Rehab. (chmn. 1976-81), Am. Congress Rehab. Medicine (v.p. 1978—), Assn. Acad. Physiatrists, N.Y. Acad. Scis., Sigma Xi. Home: 217 Holly Rd Hopkins MN 55343 Office: Health Sciences Center Univ Minn Minneapolis MN 55455

GULLICKSON, STUART GLASS, law educator, university dean; b. St. Paul, July 19, 1924; s. Oscar Samuel and Zillah (Glass) G.; m. Janet Margaret Maxwell, May 30, 1947; children: Lynn, Ann, Beth. B.A., U. Wis., 1950. Bar: Wis. 1950, U.S. Dist. Ct.(we. dist.) Wis. 1950. Assoc. Schmitt and Gullickson, Merrill, Wis., 1950-56; ptnr. Hoffman, Tembath and Gullickson, Wausau, Wis., 1957-67; lectr., vis. prof. law U. Wis. Law Sch., Madison, 1967-70, prof., 1971—, assoc. dean, 1980—, legal counsel, 1976-78; cons. Coll. Law, Sydney, Australia, 1980; dir. Gen. Practice Course, Madison, 1967-75; chancellor Wis. Conf. United Methodist Ch., 1972-76. Author: Structuring a General Practice Course, 1976, General Practice, 3 vols., 1974-83; co-editor: Workbook for Wisconsin Estate Planners, 1965-69. Served to 1st lt. U.S. Army, 1943-46. Fellow Am. Bar Found.; mem. State Bar Wis. (gov. 1952-53, 74-76), Dane County Bar Assn. (pres. 1983-84), Order of Coif. Club: Torske Klubben (Madison). Home: 206 Blue Ridge Pkwy Madison WI 53705 Office: U Wis Law Sch Madison WI 53706

GULLIVER, ADELAIDE CROMWELL, sociology educator; b. Washington, Nov. 27, 1919; d. John Wesley, Jr. and Yetta Elizabeth (Mavritte) Cromwell; m. Philip H. Gulliver, May 12, 1973; 1 son by previous marriage, Anthony C. Hill. A.B., Smith Coll., 1940; M.A., U. Pa., 1941; certificate social work, Bryn Mawr Coll., 1943; Ph.D., Radcliffe Coll., 1952; L.H.D., U. Southwestern Mass., 1972. Mem. faculty Hunter Coll., 1942-44, Smith Coll., 1945-46; mem. faculty Boston U., 1951—, now prof. sociology.; Mem. adv. com. vol. fgn. aid AID, 1964-80; mem. Nat. Council Humanities, 1968-70; adv. com. corrections Commonwealth Mass., 1955-68, mem. commn. instns. higher edn., 1973-74; adv. com. to dir. IRS, 1970-71, to dir. census, 1972-75. Mem. bd. Wheelock Coll., 1971-72, Nat. Center Afro-Am. Artists, 1971-80, African Am. Scholars Council, 1971—, Nat. Fellowship Fund, 1974-75. Mem. African Studies Assn. (dir. 1966-68), Am. Acad. Arts and Scis., Am. Sociol. Assn., Council on Fgn. Affairs (bd. fgn. scholarships 1980—), Phi Beta Kappa. Home: 51 Addington Rd Brookline MA 02146 Office: 138 Mountfort St Brookline MA 02146

GULMI, JAMES SINGLETON, apparel and clothing mfg. co. exec.; b. Schenectady, Mar. 16, 1946; s. Henry Charles and June (Singleton) G.; m. Susan Janet Cole, Aug. 24, 1968; children—Bradford Charles, Leah Cole. B.A., Baldwin Wallace Coll., 1968; M.B.A., Emory U., 1971. With Genesco, Inc., 1971—, asst. treas., Nashville, 1974-79, dir. fin. ops., 1978-79, treas., 1979—; mem. young exec. council Nashville City Bank. Mem. Fin. Execs. Inst. (chpt. dir. 1979-80). Episcopalian. Office: Genesco Inc Genesco Park Room 450 Nashville TN 37202

GUMBEL, BRYANT CHARLES, broadcaster; b. New Orleans, Sept. 29, 1948; s. Richard Dunbar and Rhea Alice (LeCesne) G.; m. June Carlyn Baranco, Dec. 1, 1973; 1 son, Bradley Christopher. B.A., Bates Coll., 1970. Writer Black Sports mag, N.Y.C., 1971, editor, 1972; sportscaster KNBC-TV, Burbank, Calif., 1972-76, sports dir., 1976-81; sports host NBC Sports, N.Y.C., 1975-82; co-host Today Show NBC, N.Y.C., 1982—. Recipient Emmy award, 1976, 77; Golden Mike award, Los Angeles Press Club, 1978, 79. Mem. AFTEA. Office: 30 Rockefeller Plaza Suite 1508 New York NY 10020 *

GUMBLETON, THOMAS J., bishop; b. Detroit, Jan. 26, 1930. Student, St. John Provincial Sem., Mich., Pontifical Lateran U., Rome. Ordained priest Roman Catholic Ch. 1956. Ordained titular bishop Ululi and aux. bishop, Detroit, 1968—. Office: 1234 Washington Blvd Detroit OI 48226 *

GUMMERE, JOHN, insurance company executive; b. Mt. Holly, N.J., Feb. 12, 1928; s. John Westcott and Ruth (Clark) G.; m. Eleanor Frances Greene, Oct. 9, 1954; children: Cynthia Clark, John Greene. B.A., Yale U., 1948. With Phoenix Mut. Life Ins. Co., Hartford, Conn., 1949—, sec. charge underwriting dept., 1961-64, 2d v.p., 1964-65, v.p., 1965-72, sr. v.p., 1972-78, exec. v.p., 1978-81, pres., chief exec. officer, 1981—, also dir.; dir. Phoenix Equity Planning Corp., N.Y. Casualty Ins. Co., Phoenix Life Ins. Co., Conn. Nat. Bank, Phoenix Gen. Ins. Co., Phoenix Investment Counsel Boston. Mem. exec. com. Med. Info., 1972-77, chmn., 1977; bd. dirs. Hartford Grad. Ctr., Inst. of Living, Old State House, Jr. Achievement. Fellow Soc. Actuaries; mem. Greater Hartford C. of C. (dir.), Sigma Xi. Office: 1 American Row Hartford CT 06115

GUMMERE, WALTER COOPER, manufacturing company executive; b. Columbus, Ohio, Apr. 24, 1917; s. Walter Cooper and Glenn (Becker) G.; m. Virginia Lee Jeffries, Jan. 10, 1942; children: Virginia Glenn Stewart, Deborah (Mrs. Charles W. Lilgendahl) (dec.), Rebecca Jane (Mrs. Richard S. Carey). A.B., Brown U., 1940; M.B.A., U. Louisville, 1953. Chief indsl. engr. Colgate Palmolive Co., 1947-53; gen. supt., dir. Rich's Inc., Atlanta, 1953-57; personnel adminstr. Montgomery Ward & Co., Chgo., 1957-60; v.p., gen. mgr. Plasti-Line Inc., Knoxville, Tenn., 1960- 62; mgmt. cons., 1962-63; with Tappan Co., 1963-73, exec. v.p., 1966-72, pres., chief exec. officer, 1972-73; also dir.; chmn., chief exec. officer The Vendo Co., 1974-78; pres. Square Pegs Assos., Inc., 1978—. Served to capt. AUS, 1942-46. Mem. Newcomen Soc., Acad. Mgmt., Delta Upsilon, Phi Beta Kappa. Presbyn. Home and Office: Rebel Run Farm 14 Grassy Lake Rd Archer FL 32618

GUMP, FRANK ERNST, surgeon; b. St. Louis, Feb. 16, 1928; s. William Simon and Ilse (Ernst) G.; m. Elizabeth Cannon, July 18, 1959; children: John, William, Sarah. B.A., Harvard U., 1951; M.D., NYU, 1955. Diplomate: Am. Bd. Surgery. Intern, resident surgery Presbyn. Hosp., N.Y.C., 1955-63; practice medicine, specializing in surgery, N.Y.C., 1963—; instr. Columbia div. Bellevue Hosp., 1963-66; asst. prof. surgery Columbia U., 1966-69, prof., 1976—. Contbr. articles to med. jours. Served with USN, 1946-48. Fellow ACS; mem. AMA, Soc. Univ. Surgeons, Am. Surg. Assn., Am. Assn. Surgery of Trauma. Home: 33 Prospect Hill Ave Summit NJ 07901 Office: 161 Fort Washington Ave New York NY 10032

GUMP, RICHARD ANTHONY, lawyer; b. Tulsa, Nov. 22, 1917; s. HArry Allen and Mary (Hanrahan) G.; m. Billie Louise Nail, Feb. 18, 1941; children: Marilyn Virginia Gump Stewart, Richard Anthony. B.B.A., U. Tex., 1939, LL.B., 1940. Bar: Tex. bar 1940, D.C. bar 1971. Spl. agt. FBI, 1940-45; partner firm Akin, Gump, Strauss, Hauer and Feld, Dallas, 1945—. Mem. Dallas Bar Assn., D.C. Bar Assn., State Bar Tex., ABA, Tex. Bar Found., Salesmanship Club Dallas. Roman Catholic. Clubs: Dallas, Chaparral, Northwood; Headliners (Austin, Tex.); Serra. Office: 2800 Republic Bank Bldg Dallas TX 75201

GUMPERT, GUNTHER, painter; b. Krefeld, Ger., Apr. 17, 1919; came to U.S., 1967, naturalized, 1971; s. Karl and Erna (Cordes) G.; m. Anita Von Kahler, Nov. 28, 1967. Grad., Human. Gymnasium, Krefeld, 1937, Sch. Fine Arts, Krefeld, 1938, Sch. Fine Arts, Wuppertal, 1939. Numerous one-man shows in, Europe and U.S. including: Zurich, 1955, Winterthur, 1959, Paris, 1960, Vienna, 1961, Rome, 1962, N.Y.C., 1963, Chgo., 1963, 64, London, 1963, Pforzheim, 1964, Seattle, 1965, 68, 70, 73, 76, Denver, 1972, Washington, 1966, 68, 69, 72, 75, 79, Cleve., 1971, Santo Domingo, 1978, group shows include, Suermondt Mus., Aachen, Ger., 1948, Kaiser-Wilhelm Mus., Krefeld, 1949, 50, 51, Internat. Exhibit Abstract Art, Pistoia, Italy, 1961, Salon Realites Nouvelles, Paris, 1959, 60, 61, Salon De Mai, Paris, 1962, Gruppe Z, Wuppertal, 1960, Internat. Exhbn. Contemporary Art, London, 1964; represented in permanent collections, Met. Mus. Art, N.Y.C., Victoria and Albert Mus., London, Albertina, Vienna, Kaiser-Wilhelm Mus., Krefeld, Museo Nacional de Bellas Artes, Santiago, Chile, Sch. Design, Providence, R.I., Princeton U. Art Mus., Mus. Fine Arts, Dallas, Denver Art Mus., Finch Coll. Mus., N.Y.C., Wesleyan U., Middletown Conn., Roosevelt House, New Delhi, India, Museo de Arte Moderno, Santo Domingo, Phillips Collection, Washington, and others; FIlm for TV Gumpert At Work, 1963. Address: 3752 McKinley St NW Washington DC 20015

GUMUCIO, FERNANDO RAUL, foods and beverage company executive; b. Bolivia, Sept. 9, 1934; s. Julio F. G.; children: Linda, Julie, Cynthia, Beverly. B.S., U. San Francisco, 1957; M.B.A., St. Mary's Coll., 1977. Dir. mktg. Latin Am. Del Monte, Mexico, 1963-68, group product dir., San Francisco, 1971-73, dir. sales and product mgmt., 1973-74, v.p. mktg., 1973-80, pres. dry grocery and beverage products group, 1980—; dir. Basic Am. Foods, San Francisco; mem., exec. bd. Nat. Food Producers Assn., Washington. Active Boy Scouts Am.; bd. regents St. Mary's Coll. Republican. Roman Catholic. Clubs: St. Francis Yacht; World Trade (San Francisco). Office: Del Monte Corp 1 Market Plaza San Francisco CA 94119

GUNAJI, NARENDRA NAGESH, civil engineer, educator; b. Belgaum, India, Jan. 9, 1931; came to U.S., 1954, naturalized, 1962; s. Nagesh V. and Saraswati N. (Manage) G.; m. Georgianna P. Boyle, May 28, 1958; children: Rajini, Monica, Greg, Kim, Shannon. B.C.E., U. Poona, India, 1953; M.S., U. Wis., 1955, Ph.D., 1958. Registered profl. engr., Ohio, N.Mex. Research asst. U. Wis., Madison, 1954-55, Wis. Alumni Research Found. fellow, 1955-58, corr. study instr., 1955-58; asst. prof. civil engring. Ohio No. U., Ada, 1958-60; asst. prof. N.Mex. State U., Las Cruces, 1960-61, asso. prof., 1961-64, prof., 1964—, dir. Engring. Expt. Sta., 1966-82, dir. Bldg. Materials Reserch and Testing Inst., 1976-82. Mem. Nat. Soc. Profl. Engrs., Internat. Assn. Hydraulic Research, Am. Geophys. Union, ASCE, Water Pollution Control Fedn., Am. Soc. Engring. Edn., AAAS, Am. Meteorol. Soc., Nat. Water Well Assn., Am. Water Works Assn., Sigma Xi, Tau Beta Pi, Chi Epsilon. Club: Rotary. Office: New Mexico State U Las Cruces NM 88003

GUND, GEORGE, III, financier; b. Cleve., May 7, 1937; s. George and Jessica (Roesler) G.; m. Mary Theo Feld, Aug. 13, 1966; children—George, Gregory. Student, Western Res. U., Menlo (Calif.) Sch. Bus. Engaged in personal investments, San Francisco, 1967—, cattle ranching, Lee, Nev., 1967—; partner Calif. Seals, San Francisco, 1976-77; pres. Ohio Barons, Inc., Richfield, 1977-78; chmn. bd. Northstar Fin. Corp., Bloomington, Minn., 1978—, Minn. North Stars, Bloomington; dir. Ameritrust Cleve.; vice-chmn. Gund Investment Corp., Princeton, N.J.; chmn. North Stars Met Center Mgmt. Corp., Bloomington; v.p. hockey Sun Valley Ice Skating, Inc., Idaho. Chmn. San Francisco Internat. Film Festival, 1973—; mem. sponsors council Project for Population Action; adv. council Sierra Club Found.; mem. internat. council Mus. Modern Art, N.Y.C.; collectors com. Nat. Gallery Art; bd. dirs. Calif. Theatre Found., Bay Area Ednl. TV Assn., San Francisco Mus. Art, Cleve. Health Museum, George Gund Found., Cleve. Internat. Film Festival, Sun Valley Center Arts and Humanities, U. Nev. Reno Found. Served with USMCR, 1955-58. Clubs: Calif. Tennis, University, Olympic (San Francisco); Union, Cleve. Athletic, Rowfant (Cleve.); Ranier (Seattle). Office: 1821 Union St San Francisco CA 94123

GUNDERSHEIMER, HERMAN SAMUEL, art historian; b. Wurzburg, Germany, Apr. 25, 1903; came to U.S., 1940, naturalized, 1945; s. Samuel and Sofie (Salzer) G.; m. Frieda Siegel, May 21, 1935; children: Werner L., Ann E. Student, U. Munich, Germany, 1921-22, U. Wurzburg, 1922-23, U. Berlin, 1923-24; Dr. phil., U. Leipzig, Ger., 1925. Museum asst., Ulm, Germany, 1926-28, asst. curator mus., Frankfurt on the Main, Germany, 1929-32; dir. Rothchild Mus., Frankfurt on the Main, 1933-39; lectr. in art history Am. U., 1940; asst. prof. art history Temple U., 1941-43, asso. prof., 1943-47, prof., 1948-70, chmn. dept. art history, 1943-70, dir. art history study tours, through Europe, 1951-67; dir. Temple U. Abroad, Rome, 1970-73; guest prof. U. Tel Aviv, 1973-74, LaSalle Coll., 1974-82. Author: books, including Fresco Painting in 18th Century Churches of Southern Germany; contbr. articles on art history, especially of 18th century, to profl. jours. Recipient Lindback award Temple U., 1964. Mem. Coll. Art Assn., Renaissance Soc., AAUP, Pa. Acad. Art, Phila. Mus. Art, Rosenbach Mus., Franklin Inn. Jewish. Club: Peale. Home: 2 Franklin Town Blvd Apt 2403 Philadelphia PA 19103 *Two experiences have most deeply affected my adult life: the "expulsion" from Germany in 1939 after the years of struggling to stay physically and mentally alive amidst the horror of Nazi destruction, and the reconstruction of my and my family's lives with the understanding help of colleagues and students in the United States. I have seen the abyss and the heights man can reach, and have not lost faith in his basic goodness. My cherished field of studies and my teaching have strengthed my hopeful outlook.*

GUNDERSHEIMER, WERNER LEONARD, historian; b. Frankfurt/am/Main, Germany, Apr. 7, 1937; came to U.S., 1940, naturalized, 1945; s. Herman Samuel and Frieda (Siegel) G.; m. Karen Rosenwald, June 23, 1963; children—Joshua, Benjamin. Jr. B.A. magna cum laude, Amherst Coll., 1959; M.A., Harvard U., 1960, Ph.D., 1963; M.A. (hon.), U. Pa., 1971. Fellow Soc. Fellows Harvard U., 1963-66; asst. prof. history U. Pa., Phila., 1966-68, asso. prof., 1968-71, prof., 1971—, chmn. dept. history, 1977-79, dir. Center for Italian Studies, 1980-83; vis. prof. U. Wis., 1963-64, Johns Hopkins U., 1967-68; vis. scholar Swarthmore Coll., 1970-72, Harvard U., 1983-84; dir. New Concepts Fund. Author: The Italian Renaissance, 1965, The Life and Works of Louis Le Roy, 1966, French Humanism, 1970, Art and Life at the Court of Ercole I d'Este, 1972, Ferrara: The Style of a Renaissance Despotism, 1973; contbr. articles to scholarly jours. Mem. Carter-Mondale Task Force on Arts and Humanities, 1976; trustee Rosenbach Mus. and Library, 1967-70, chmn. bd., 1970-80; mem. adv. com. Otto von Kienbusch Collection, Phila. Mus. Art. Decorated cavaliere Stella della Solidarietà Italiana Fgn. Ministry of Republic of Italy; Guggenheim fellow, 1974-75; I Tatti fellow, 1975; Am. Philos. Soc. grantee, 1967; grantee Inst. for Advanced Study, Princeton, N.J., 1970-71. Mem. Am. Hist. Assn., Renaissance Soc. Am., Medieval Acad. Am., Royal Hist. Soc. (Gt. Britain), Soc. Italian Hist. Studies, Am. Jewish Hist. Soc. (exec. council, acad. council). Democrat. Home: 220 St Mark's Sq Philadelphia PA 19104 Office: Dept History U Pa Philadelphia PA 19104

GUNDERSON, ELMER MILLARD, state justice; b. Mpls., Aug. 9, 1929; s. Elmer Peter and Carmaleta (Oliver) G.; m. Lupe Gomez, Dec. 29, 1967; 1 son, John Randolph. Student, U. Minn., U. Omaha, 1948-53; LL.B., Creighton U., 1956; LL.M., U. Va., 1982; LL.D., Calif. Western Sch. Law; student appellate judges seminar, N.Y. U., 1971; LL.D., U. Pacific. Bar: Nebr. bar 1956, Nev. bar 1958. Atty.-adviser FTC, 1956-57; pvt. practice, Las Vegas, 1958-71; justice Nev. Supreme Ct., 1971—, chief justice, 1975-76, 81-82; instr. bus. law So. regional div. U. Nev.; lectr., author bulls. felony crimes for Clark County Sheriff's Dept.; counsel Sheriff's Protective Assn.; mem. legal staff Clark Council Civil Def. Agy.; legal counsel Nev. Jaycees. Compiler, annotator: Omaha Home Rule Charter; project coordinator: Jud. Orientation Manual, 1974. Chmn. Clark County Child Welfare Bd., Nev. central chpt. Nat. Multiple Sclerosis Soc.; hon. dir. Spring Mountain Youth Camp. Served with U.S. Army. Recipient A.J.S. Herbert Harley award. Mem. Am., Nebr., Nev. bar assns.; Mem. Inst. Jud. Adminstrn., Am. Law Inst., Am. Trial Lawyers Assn., Am. Judicature Soc., Phi Alpha Delta, Alpha Sigma Nu. Home: 1240 Custer Circle Carson City NV 89701 Office: Supreme Ct Bldg Carson City NV 89701

GUNDERSON, GERALD AXEL, economics educator, administrator; b. Seattle, May 24, 1940; s. Marian A. and Ethel Ann (Hamon) G.; m. Margaret Jean Overway, Sept. 10, 1965; children: David Eric, Laura Lynn. B.A. in Econs., U. Wash., 1962, M.A., 1966, Ph.D., 1967. Asst. prof. econs. U. Mass., Amherst, 1967-74; vis. assoc. prof. econs. Mt. Holyoke Coll., South Hadley, Mass., 1974-75; spl. lectr. econs. N.C. State U., Raleigh, 1975-78; prof. econs. Trinity Coll., Hartford, Conn., 1978-82, Shelby Cullom Davis prof. Am. bus. and econ. enterprise, Hartford, 1982—, dir. Davis Endowment, 1982—. Author: A New Economic History of America, 1976; contbg. author: Explorations in Econs. History, 1973—, Jour. Econ. History, 1974, Social Sci. History, 1977. Grantee Freedom Found. at Valley Forge, 1981. Mem. Assn. Pvt. Enterprise Edn., Econ. History Assn., Am. Econ. Assn. Home: 6 Andrew Dr Weatogue CT 06089 Office: Trinity Coll 300 Summit St Hartford CT 06106

GUNDERSON, HERBERT EDMOND, speech pathologist; b. San Francisco, Aug. 7, 1923; s. Herbert Wilhelm and Violet Olga (McNevin) G.; m. Amelia Carol Risdon, Aug. 5, 1943; 1 dau., Mary Ellen Gunderson Traylor. Student, Drury Coll., 1953; B.A., Central Bible Coll., 1954; postgrad., Pasadena Coll., Berkeley Baptist Div. Sch., 1954-55; M.S. with honors, U. Oreg., 1964, Ph.D., 1971. Lic. spl. edn. tchr., Oreg. Instr. speech and homiletics Eugene (Oreg.) Bible Coll., 1955-61; asst. prof. speech Eastern Wash. U., Cheney, 1965-69, asso. prof. speech, chmn. dept., 1973-75, prof. speech, 1976-82, prof. emeritus speech pathology and audiology, 1982—, chmn. dept., 1976-78, 81-82; founder, dir. Ann. Insts. in Laryngectomee Rehab., 1968—; cons. speech pathology. Bd. dirs. Spokane County Cancer Assn.; 1st v.p., bd. dirs. Spokane Vis. Nurse Assn. Served with U.S. Army, 1942-46, 47-50. Mem. Am. Speech and Hearing Assn., Wash. Speech and Hearing Assn., Surg. and Prosthetic Speech Rehab. Group. Republican. Home: PO Box 71 Valley WA 99181

GUNDERSON, LEE E., banker; b. Sioux Falls, S.D., Apr. 11, 1930; s. Lee E. and Grace (Cougshall) G.;, Nov. 30, 1953; children: Jay, Karl. Student, U. S.D., 1948-51, Grad. Sch. Banking, U. Wis., 1962-65. Cashier Chancellor State Bank, S.D., 1952-60; cashier, dir. Farmers and Mchts. Bank, Greenwood, Wis., 1960-64; pres., dir. Bank of Osceola (Wis.), 1964—, also chief exec. officer.; pres., dir. Grad. Sch. Banking, U. Wis.-Madison, 1981—. Chmn. Housing Authority of Osceola, 1970—; treas. Osceola Indsl. Devel., Inc., 1968—. Mem. Am. Bankers Assn. (chmn. communications council 1975-77, pres. 1980-81), Wis. Bankers Assn. (pres. 1974-75). Republican. Methodist. Clubs: St. Paul Athletic, Masons. Office: PO Box 188 Osceola WI 54020

GUNDERSON, NORMAN GUSTAV, educator; b. Schenectady, May 29, 1917; s. Ole Andrew and Martha Marie (Christiansen) G.; m. Shirley Elizabeth Mosher, Oct. 6, 1945; children—Sharon E., Wendy C., Karen M. Student, N.Y. State Coll. for Tchrs., Albany, 1933-37; A.M., Cornell U., Ithaca, N.Y., 1941, Ph.D., 1948. Tchr. high sch., Walden, N.Y., 1937-40; instr. math. Cornell U., part time 1942-45, 45-46; sr. research asso. Allegany Ballistics Lab., Cumberland, Md., 1945; successively instr., asst. prof., asso. prof. math. U. Rochester, 1946-66, prof. math. and edn., 1966-80, prof. emeritus, 1980—; lectr. math. Nazareth Coll., 1980—; cons. various sch. systems on math. edn. Mem. Assn. Math. Tchrs. N.Y. State (pres. 1968-69), Math. Assn. Am. (sec. Upper N.Y. State sect. 1950-67), Am. Math. Soc., Nat. Council Tchrs. Math. Home: 2085 W Henrietta Rd Rochester NY 14623

GUNDERSON, STEVE C., congressman; b. Eau Claire, Wis.; May 10, 1951; s. Arthur E. and Adeline C. G. B.A., U. Wis., 1973. Mem. Wis. Assembly, 1974-79; legis. dir. Rep. Toby Roth, 1979; mem. 97th-98th Congresses from Wis. 3d dist.; Dir. spl. projects Wis.'s Gov.

Dreyfus campaign, 1978. Republican. Lutheran. Club: Pleasantville Lions. Office: 416 Cannon House Office Bldg Washington DC 20515

GUNDLACH, HEINZ LUDWIG, investment banker; b. Dusseldorf, Germany, July 6, 1937; came to U.S., 1969, naturalized, 1980; s. Heinrich Otto and Ilse (Schuster) G.; children: Andrew, Annabelle. M.Law, U. Heidelberg, 1962, D.Law, 1962. Vice pres. Thyssen A.G. Dusseldorf, 1964-68; v.p., partner Loeb, Rhoades & Co., N.Y.C., 1969-75; vice chmn., chief exec. officer Fed-Mart Corp., San Diego, 1975-81; vice chmn. successor cos. Sunbelt Properties, Inc., 1981—, Trucolor Foto Inc., 1981—. Served with W. Ger. Army, 1958-59. Republican. Clubs: Annabelle's, St. James's (London); Recess (N.Y.C.). Office: 375 Park Ave New York NY 10152

GUNDRUM, JAMES RICHARD, clergyman; b. Muscatine, Iowa, Nov. 30, 1929; s. Otto and Margaret Isabel (Black) G.; m. Frances Ellen Lathrop, June 14, 1954; children—Cameron Michael, David William, Carolyn Anne. B.A., Iowa Wesleyan U., 1951; M.Div., Seabury Western Theol. Sem., Evanston, Ill., 1954, D.D., 1976. Ordained priest Episcopal Ch., 1954; vicar chs. in, Western Iowa, 1954-58; rector St. Michael's Ch., Cedar Rapids, Iowa, 1958-69; mission cons. Episcopal Diocese Iowa, 1969-75, canon, 1976—; sec.-treas. Episcopal Gen. Conv., 1975-77, exec. officer, 1977—, sec. exec. council, 1977—; sec. Domestic and Fgn. Missionary Soc., 1977—; trustee Seabury Western Theol. Sem., 1975; chaplain Cedar Rapids Police Dept., 1961-69. Editor jour., canons gen. conv. Bd. dirs. chmn. personnel com. Cedar Rapids chpt. A.R.C., 1960-64; bd. dirs. Cedar Rapids Mental Health Assn., 1961-65; Mem. Iowa N.G., 1946-48. Recipient Disting. Service Cross St. Michael's Ch., 1968; named Hon. Cedar Rapidian, 1969. Mem. Soc. Advancement Mgmt. Democrat. Club: Rotary (past v.p., dir. Cedar Rapids). Home: 1301 The Colony Hartsdale NY 10530 Office: 815 2d Ave New York NY 10017

GUNDY, HOWARD B., state education official, consultant; b. Syracuse, N.Y., Sept. 2, 1915; s. Ernest G. and Mae S. (Sidley) G.; m. Janet Prime, Oct. 13, 1941; children: Charles, Susan, Barbara. A.B., Syracuse U., 1939; Ph.D. in Public Adminstrn, Maxwell Sch. Citizenship and Public Affairs, 1961; M.S.S.W., U. Buffalo, 1948; LL.D. (hon.), U. Ala., 1981. Dir. Sch. Social Work, Syracuse (N.Y.) U., 1948-57, dean, 1962-64, prof., 1948-64; dean., prof. Sch. Social Work, Sacramento State U., 1964-66; dean, prof. Sch. Social Work, U. Ala., University, 1966-71, acad. v.p., 1971-78, dir. Washington office, 1978-80, v.p. research and service, 1978-80, acting pres., chief exec. officer, 1980-81, spl. cons. devel. office, 1981—; Chancellor Dept. Postsecondary Edn. State of Ala., 1982—; spl. cons. on post-secondary edn. to gov. Ala., 1981; chmn. So. Regional Edn. Bd., Commn. on Human Services. Pres. Ala. State Conf. Social Work; chmn. gov.'s com. on children and youth, N.Y. chmn. gov.'s com. on children and youth, Calif. chmn. gov.'s com. on children and youth, Ala.; mem. West Ala. Health Planning Council. Served with USAAF, 1941-45. Named Man of Year Tuscaloosa C. of C., 1981, Educator of Year Phi Delta Theta, 1981; recipient Algernon Sidney Sullivan award Omicron Delta Kappa, 1981. Mem. Acad. Cert. Social Workers, Ala. Conf. Social Work, Am. Public Welfare Assn., Nat. Assn. State Univs. and Land Grant Colls., Am. Assn. Higher Edn., Am. Soc. Public Adminstrn., Jasons, Omicron Delta Kappa. Clubs: University, Indian Hills Country. Home: 17 High Forest Tuscaloosa AL 35406 Office: 305 S Lawrence St Montgomery AL 36104

GUNKLER, CARL ANDREW, JR., banker; b. Ft. Wayne, Ind., Jan. 23, 1920; s. Carl A. and Bertha C. (Niebergall) G.; m. June B. Denton, May 23, 1946; 1 son, Andrew C. Student, Grad. Sch. Banking, Rutgers U., 1951. With Lincoln Nat. Bank & Trust Co., Ft. Wayne, 1939-81, pres., dir., 1977-81, chief exec. officer, 1979-81; banking cons., 1981—; asso. dir. Shipshewana State Bank, Ind. Pres. Ft. Wayne Conv. Bur., 1963-64; pres. Jr. Achievement, Ft. Wayne, 1971-73; chmn. Ind. Council for Econ. Edn., 1971-73; pres. bd. dirs. Ft. Wayne Urban League. Served with USAAF, 1942-46. Recipient Bronze Leadership award. Mem. Fin. Execs. Inst. (past pres. Ft. Wayne chpt.), Ind. Bankers Assn., Ft. Wayne C. of C. Episcopalian. Clubs: Orchard Ridge Country (pres. Ft. Wayne 1966-67), Ft. Wayne Country, Rotary. Home and office: 5615 Indiana Ave Fort Wayne IN 46807

GUNN, GEORGE F., JR., state supreme court associate justice; b. Ft. Smith, Ark., Oct. 29, 1927. A.B., Westminster Coll., 1950; J.D., Washington U., St. Louis, 1955. Assoc. firm Gleick & Strauss, St. Louis, 1955-56; atty. Wabash R.R. Co., St. Louis, 1956-58; ptnr. firm Rebman La Tourette & Gunn, St. Louis, 1958-68; city atty. City of Brentwood (Mo.), 1963-71; counsel Terminal R.R. Assn., St. Louis, 1968-71; county counselor St. Louis County (Mo.), 1971-73; judge Rock Hill (Mo.) Mcpl. Ct., 1971, Eastern Dist. Mo. Ct. Appeals, Clayton, 1973-82; assoc. justice Mo. Supreme Ct., Jefferson City, 1982—. Chmn. South County region ARC, St. Louis, 1971-74; bd. mgrs. Mid County YMCA, St. Louis, 1961—; bd. dirs. World Congress Equality and Freedom, 1975. Mem. ABA, Mo. Bar Assn., Met. St. Louis Bar Assn., Washington U. Law Alumni (pres. 1974), Phi Delta Phi. Office: Mo Supreme Ct PO Box 150 Jefferson City MO 65102

GUNN, JAMES EDWARD, astrophysicist; b. Livingstone, Tex., Oct. 21, 1938; s. James Edward and Rhea (Mason) G. B.S., Rice U., Houston, 1961; Ph.D., Calif. Inst. Tech., 1966. Sr. space scientist Jet Propulsion Lab., 1966-69; asst. prof. Princeton (N.J.) U., 1969-70, Eugene Higgins prof. astrophysics, 1980—; asst. prof., then prof. astrophysics Calif. Inst. Tech., 1970-80; dep. prin. investigator space telescope wide field camera NASA, 1977—. Served with C.E. USAR, 1967. Sloan Found. fellow, 1972-76. Mem. Am. Astron. Soc., Astron. Survey Com., Nat. Acad. Scis. Democrat. Office: Peyton Hall Princeton U Princeton NJ 08544

GUNN, MOSES, actor, theatrical director; b. St. Louis, Oct. 2, 1929; s. George and Mary (Briggs) G. (foster mother, Jewel C. Richie); m. Gwen Landes, July 25, 1966; 1 dau., Kirsten Sarah. A.B., Tenn. State U., 1959. Former tchr. speech and drama Grambling Coll. Theatrical appearances include The Blacks, 1962-63, In White America, 1963-64, Day of Absence, 1965, Measure for Measure, 1965, A Hand is on The Gate, 1966, Aaavron in Titus Andronicus, 1957, Negro Ensemble Co, 1967-68, Twelfth Night, Othello, Sky of the Blind Pig, 1971, The Poison Tree, 1973, 76, The First Breeze of Summer, 1975; TV appearances include Kung Fu; movie Haunts of the Very Rich, 1972; dramatic spl. The First Breeze of Summer, 1976; films include Nothing But a Man, 1962, WUSA, 1970, The Great White Hope, 1970, Shaft, 1971, Shaft's Big Score, 1972, Eagle in a Cage, 1972, Hot Rock, 1972, Amazing Grace, 1974, The Iceman Cometh, 1973, Rollerball, 1975, Aaron Loves Angela, Remember My Name, Wild Rovers, 1971, The Ninth Configuration, 1980. Served with AUS, 1954-57. Recipient Obie award, 1967-68; Jersey Jour. award for best actor, 1967-68. Mem. Theta Alpha Phi. Address: care Blalee Agy Ltd 409 N Camden Rd Suite 202 Beverly Hills CA 90210

GUNN, THOM(SON WILLIAM), poet; b. Gravesend, Eng., Aug. 29, 1929; came to U.S., 1954; s. Herbert Smith and Ann Charlotte (Thomson) G. B.A., Trinity Coll., Cambridge (Eng.) U., 1953. Tchr. English, U. Calif.-Berkeley, 1958-66. Author: Fighting Terms, 1954, The Sense of Movement, 1957, My Sad Captains, 1961, Touch, 1967, Moly, 1971, Jack Straw's Castle and Other Poems, 1976, Selected Poems, 1979, The Passages of Joy, 1982, The Occasions of Poetry, 1982. Address: 1216 Cole St San Francisco CA 94117

GUNN, WENDELL W., presidential assistant; 3 children. A.B., Florence State U., 1965; M.B.A., U. Chgo., 1971. Asst. prof. fin. Tex. So. U.; v.p. Chase Manhattan Bank, 1974-79; asst. treas., dir. investor relations Pepsi Co., Inc., 1979-82; spl. asst. to pres., asst. dir. for commerce and trade Office Policy Devel., Washington; exec. sec. Cabinet Council on Commerce and Trade, Exec. Office of Pres., Washington. Mem. adv. council on econ. affairs and subcom. on tax policy and monetary affairs Republican Nat. Com.; bd. dirs. New Coalition for Econ. and Social Change; mem. adv. bd. Lincoln Inst. for Research and Edn. Office: Office of Policy Devel 1600 Pennsylvania Ave NW Washington DC 20500 *

GUNNELLS, JAMES CAULIE, JR., physician; b. Greenwood, S.C., Feb. 4, 1931; s. James Caulie and Mary Frances (Rearden) G.; m. Virginia McGowan Burns, June 16, 1956; children—Virginia Burns, Mary Madge, Michael Francis. B.S., Furman U., 1952; M.D., Med. U. S.C., 1956. Bar: Diplomate Am. Bd. Internal Medicine (nephrology). Intern and jr. resident First Med. (Columbia) Div., Bellevue Hosp., N.Y.C., 1956-58; fellow and sr. resident in medicine Duke U. Med. Center, Durham, N.C., 1958-60, mem. faculty, 1962—, prof. medicine, nephrology div., 1972—; cons. VA Hosp., Fayatteville, N.C., Durham County Hosp.; cons. biomed. div. New Eng. Nuclear Corp., 1967-71. Author articles in field, chpts. in books; editorial bd.: Kidney Internat, 1971-73. Served to lt. comdr. M.C. USNR, 1960-62. Fellow A.C.P.; mem. AMA, Am. Heart Assn., Am. Fedn. Clin. Research, Am. Soc. Nephrology, Internat. Soc. Nephrology, So. Soc. Clin. Investigation, Am. Soc. Artificial Internal Organs, Am. Heart Assn. (med. adv. bd. council high blood pressure research), Am. Clin. and Climatological Assn., Transplanatation Soc., Alpha Omega Alpha, Sigma Alpha Epsilon. Episcopalian. Home: 3317 Devon Rd Durham NC 27707 Office: Box 2991 Duke Univ Med Center Durham NC 27710

GUNNERSON, ROBERT MARK, lawyer, manufacturing company executive; b. Washington Island, Wis., Apr. 6, 1949; s. Roger William and Ester Victoria (Rosengren) G.; m. Mary Beth Fischer, Oct. 28, 1978. B.B.A., U. Wis. at Milw., 1971; J.D., Marquette U., 1974. Bar: Wis. 1974. Staff atty. Modine Mfg. Co., Racine, Wis., 1974-77, asst. sec., 1977, sec., 1977-79, sec., asst. treas., 1979-80, treas., 1980—; ad hoc. instr. U. Wis., Parkside, 1976-78. Treas. Racine Environ. Com., 1980-81, pres., 1982-84. Mem. Wis. Bar Assn., Wis. Inst. C.P.A.s (asso.). Home: 9101 W Grange Ave Hales Corners WI 53130 Office: 1500 Dekoven Ave Racine WI 53401

GUNNERUD, PER-BJORN, chemical company executive; b. Oslo, June 29, 1932; U.S., 1965; s. Per-Bjorn and Borghild Helene (Hansen) G.; m. Caron Catherine Cashman, June 29, 1968; children: Kirsten H., Per-Bjorn, Christian Jon. Student, U. Oslo; B.A., Oslo Hardelsgymnasium. Div. mgr. Lehmkuhl A-S, Oslo, 1954-59; mng. dir. Soilax A-S, Oslo, 1960-64; v.p. mktg. El Internat., N.Y.C., 1965-68; pres. ELMCO, SICA, ECLAB, P.R., 1968-70, Magnus Maritec Inc., St. Paul, 1971-80; sr. v.p. internat. Econs. Lab., Inc., St. Paul, 1981—. Office: Econs Lab Inc 370 Wabas Ave Osborn Bldg Saint Paul MN 55102

GUNNESS, ROBERT CHARLES, chemical engineer; b. Fargo, N.D., July 28, 1911; s. Christian I. and Elizabeth (Rice) G.; m. Beverly Osterberger, June 18, 1936; children: Robert Charles, Donald Austin, Beverly Anne. B.S., U. Mass., Amherst, 1932; M.S., MIT, 1934, D.Sc., 1936. Asst. prof. chem. engring. MIT, 1936-38; research dept. Standard Oil Co. Ind., 1938-47, mgr. research, 1947-51, asst. gen. mgr. mfg., gen. mgr. supply and transp., 1952-56, exec. v.p., 1956-65, pres., 1965-74, vice chmn., 1974-75, dir., 1953-75; dir. Oakbrook Consol., Inc.; Vice chmn. research and devel. bd. Dept. Def., 1951. Trustee U. Chgo., Rush-Presbyn.-St. Lukes Hosp.; life mem. Mass. Inst. Tech. Corp.; past chmn. Nat. Merit Scholarship Corp.; past pres., trustee John Crerar Library. Fellow Am. Inst. Chem. Engrs. (council 1951); mem. Nat. Acad. Engring., Am. Chem. Soc., Am. Acad. Arts and Scis., Sigma Xi, Phi Kappa Phi, Kappa Sigma. Clubs: Commercial, Chicago, Mid-Am. (Chgo.); Chemists (N.Y.C.); Pauma Valley Country, Old Elm, Augusta Nat. Home: PO Box 538 Rancho Santa Fe CA 92067

GUNNING, FRANCIS PATRICK, lawyer, ins. assn. exec.; b. Scranton, Pa., Dec. 10, 1923; s. Frank Peter and Mary Loretta (Kelley) G.; m. Nancy C. Hill, Aug. 10, 1951; 1 son, Brian F. Student, City Coll. N.Y., 1941-43; LL.B., St. John's U., 1950. Bar: N.Y. bar 1950. Legal editor Prentice Hall Pub. Co., N.Y.C., 1950-51; legal specialist Tchrs. Ins. & Annuity Assn. Am., Coll. Retirement Equities Fund, N.Y.C., 1951-53, asst. counsel, 1953-57, asso. counsel, 1957-60, counsel, 1960-65, asst. gen. counsel, 1965-67, asso. gen. counsel, 1967, v.p., asso. gen. counsel, 1967-73, sr. v.p., gen. counsel, 1973-74, exec. v.p., gen. counsel, 1974—; mem. N.Y. adv. bd. Chgo. Title Ins. Co.; trustee, mem. exec. and audit coms. Mortgage Growth Investors. Contbr. articles on mortgage financing to profl. jours. Served with USAAF, 1943-46. Mem. Am., N.Y. bar assns., Am. Land Title Assn., Am. Law Inst., Assn. Bar City of N.Y., Assn. Life Ins. Counsel, Nat. Assn. Coll. Univ. Attys. Republican. Roman Catholic. Home: 32 Kewanee Rd New Rochelle NY 10804 Office: 730 3d Ave New York NY 10017

GUNNING, HARRY EMMET, chemistry educator; b. Toronto, Ont., Can., Dec. 16, 1916; s. Lorenzo Edward and Ledo Beryl (Shangrew) G.; m. Donna Marie Beahan, Jan. 30, 1943; 1 dau., Judith Gunning Dumont. B.A. with first class honors in Chemistry, U. Toronto, 1939, M.A. in Phys. Chemistry, 1940, Ph.D., 1942; D.Sc. (hon.), U. Guelph, 1969, Queen's U., 1974; LL.D., U. Victoria, 1978. NRC postdoctoral fellow Harvard U., 1942-43; asst. research chemist div. pure chemistry Nat. research Council Can., 1943-44; assoc. research chemist Nat. Research Council Can., 1944-46; asst. prof. chemistry U. Rochester, 1946-48; assoc. prof. chemistry Ill. Inst. Tech., 1948-51, Ill. Inst. Tech, 1951-54; prof., chemistry Ill. Inst. Tech., 1954-57; prof., chmn. dept. chemistry U. Alta., Edmonton, Can., 1957-74, Killam Meml. prof. chemistry, 1968—, pres. univ., 1974-79; cons. Dept. Econ. Devel., Alta., 1979—; chmn. adc. com. on water Alta. Dept. Transp., Alta., 1979—; chief exec. officer CHEMBIOMED Ltd.; mem. bd. Alta. Oil Sands Tech. and Research Authority; chmn. Winspear Found.; mem. MERBANCO Corp.; chmn. Edmonton Research and Devel. Park; chmn. nat. advisors com. New Can. Ency.; chmn. adv. bd. sci. and tech. CBC. Contbr. numerous articles to profl. jours,. Decorated officer Order of Can., 1979; recipient medal Brit. Assn. for Advancement Sci., 1939, achievement award Province of Alta., 1971, 79; Ruben Wells Leonard fellow, 1939; Reuben Wells Leonard scholar, 1936. Mem. Chem. Inst. Can. (pres. 1973-74, medal 1967). Home: 14815 64th Ave Edmonton AB Canada T6H 4Y1 Office: Suite E3-44 Chemistry Center Univ Alta Edmonton AB Canada T6G 2E1

GUNNING, JOHN THADDEUS, supt. schs.; b. Pontiac, Ill., May 9, 1917; s. Thaddeus John and Wanda Louise (Riess) G.; m. Jean Gara Gregory, Dec. 30, 1941; children—John G., Gara Jean. Ed.B., Ill. State U., 1938; M.S., U. Ill., 1942; Ed.D., Ind. U., 1964; postgrad., Western Ill. State U., 1939, U. Akron, 1941, U. Ill., 1946, 48, 51, 53, U. Minn., 1949, Columbia Tchrs. Coll., 1963. Tchr. pub. schs., Jacksonville, Ill., 1938-41, Old Trail Sch., Akron, Ohio, 1941-42; prin. Lab. Sch., State Coll., St. Cloud, Minn., 1946-50; successively asst. prin., prin., asst. supt. Gary (Ind.) pub. schs., 1950-61; supt. Calumet Twp. schs., Gary, 1961-63, Sch. Dist. 189, East St. Louis, Ill., 1964-67, Unified Sch. Dist., Racine, Wis., 1967-70, City Sch. Dist., Syracuse, N.Y., 1970-73, Duval County Schs., Jacksonville, Fla., 1973-76; lectr. edn. Ind. U., 1952-58, So. Ill. U., 1966, U. Wis.-Milw., 1968, State U. N.Y. at Oswego, 1973, U. North Fla., 1974, 75, Stetson U., 1979—. Mem. Gov.'s Area Council, State Div. for Youth, Syracuse, 1970-73, City-County Drug Abuse Commn., 1971-73, Mayor's Commn. on Problems of Aging, 1971-73; chmn. United Way campaign Syracuse pub. schs., 1972; pres. Sch. Facilities Council for Architecture, Edn. and Industry, 1971-75; Bd. dirs. Syracuse Pub. Library, UN Assn. Central N.Y., YMCA, Jr. Achievement Jacksonville, 1973-76, Jacksonville Council Citizen Involvement, 1974-76, Jacksonville Bicentennial Commn., 1974-76. Served with USAAF, 1943-45. Mem. Am. Assn. Sch. Bus. Ofcls., Am. Assn. Sch. Adminstrs., Century Club, Ednl. League Ill., Phi Delta Kappa. Clubs: San Jose Country, Torch. Home: 2817 Village Grove Dr N Jacksonville FL 32217

GUNNING, ROBERT CLIFFORD, mathematician, educator; b. Longmont, Colo., Nov. 27, 1931; s. Clifford Henry and Inez (Wilhelm) G.; m. Wanda S. Holtzinger, July 9, 1966. A.B., U. Colo., 1952; M.A., Princeton, 1953, Ph.D., 1955. NSF fellow U. Chgo., 1955-56; mem. faculty Princeton, 1956—, prof. math., 1966—, chmn. dept., 1976-79; vis. prof. U. Saõ, Paulo, Brazil, 1957; Sloan fellow, 1958-61; asst. dir. studies, math. St. Catharines Coll., Cambridge U., 1959-60; vis. prof. U. Munich, 1967; mem. editorial bd. Princeton U. Press, 1969-73. Author: Lectures on Modular Forms, 1962, (with H. Rossi) Analytic Functions of Several Complex Variables, 1965, Lectures on Riemann Surfaces, Vol. I, 1966, Vol. II, 1967, Vol. III, 1972, Complex Analytic Varieties, Vol. I, 1970, Vol. II, 1974, Generalized Theta Functions, 1976, Uniformization of Complex Manifolds, 1978, also articles. Fellow AAAS; mem. Am. Math. Soc., Phi Beta Kappa, Sigma Xi. Episcopalian. Clubs: Princeton (N.Y.C.); Nassau (Princeton). Office: Fine Hall Washington Rd Princeton NJ 08544

GUNNISON, GALE W., reinsurance executive; b. Moline, Ill., Oct. 20, 1924; s. August Victor and Jennie (Landstrom) G.; m. Catherine E. Lackland, Apr. 16, 1949; children: Robert, Scott, Mark. B.A., Knox Coll., 1949. Casualty and bond analyst Hartford A&I, Chgo., 1948-53; v.p. Leslie N. Cook, Inc., Chgo., 1953-66; sr. v.p. Employers Reinsurance Corp., Overland Park, Kans., 1966—, dir. Office: Employers Reinsurance Corp 5200 Metcalf Overland Park KS 66201

GUNSBERG, SHELDON, entertainment industry executive; b. Jersey City, Aug. 10, 1920. Student, St. Peters Coll., N.J. State Normal, N.Y. U. With Night of Stars, Madison Sq. Garden, N.Y.C., 1942; fgn. publicity 20th Century-Fox, 1942, United Artists, 1945-47; with Universal roadshows; asst. advt. and publicity dir. Rank Prodns., 1947-54; v.p. Walter Reade Theatres; exec. v.p., dir. Walter Reade Orgn., 1962-71, chief operating officer, 1971-73, pres., chief exec. officer, 1973—, also; chmn. exec. com. Bd. dirs. Will Rodgers Meml. Hosp. Office: Walter Reade Orgn 241 E 34th St New York NY 10016 *

GUNSON, LEO JOSEPH, ret. business exec.; b. Phila., July 5, 1896; s. John D. and Mary F. (Cahill) G.; m. Florence G. Cullen, June 29, 1922; children—Mary Elizabeth, Leo Joseph, Jr. Student, Notre Dame Acad., Phila., 1902-08, St. Joseph's Coll., 1908- 12, U. Pa., 1914-17. With Publicker Industries, Inc., 1924-76, treas., until 1976; pres., dir. Continental Distilling Corp., until 1976; ret., 1976. Served to 1st lt. 312th Machine Gun Bn., World War I. Decorated knight grand cross Order Holy Sepulchre. Mem. Am. Legion. Club: Phila. Country. Home: 1801 JF Kennedy Blvd Philadelphia PA 19103

GUNSUL, BROOKS R.W., architect; b. Seattle, Aug. 7, 1928; s. Frank Justus and Phyllis (Webster) G.; m. Marilyn Thompson, Aug. 26, 1950; children: Robin, Karen, David, Jana. B.S. in Archtl. Engring., Wash. State U., 1952. Registered architect, Oreg., Wash., Ill., N.Y. Architect Stewart & Richardson architect, Portland, 1952-57, Scott & Payne, 1957-59, Wolff & Zimmer, 1959-65; ptnr. Wolff, Zimmer Gunsul. Frasca, Portland, 1966-77, Zimmer Gunsul Frasca, 1977—; mem. adv. com. Washington State U. Dept. Architecture, Pullman, 1983—; dir., founder Architecture Found., Portland, 1980—. Contbr. articles to profl. jours. Served with U.S. Army, 1946-47. Fellow AIA. Clubs: Portland Yacht, Multnomah. Office: Zimmer Gunsul Frasca Partnership 320 SW Oak St Suite 500 Portland OR 97204

GUNTER, ANNIE LAURIE, treas. of Ala.; b. N.C., June 23, 1919; d. Samuel Franklin and Daisy (Callahan) Cain; m. William A. Gunter, Oct. 14, 1946; 1 son, William A., IV. Student public schs., Lake Wales, Fla. Sec. Lake Wales Public Sch. System, then exec. sec. citrus and real estate devel. co., until 1946; coordinator Ala. Office Hwy. and Traffic Safety, Montgomery, 1971-72; dir. Ala. Office Consumer Protection, 1972-78; treas. State of Ala., Montgomery, 1978—; Mem. platform com. Nat. Democratic Conv., 1972, 76; mem. Ala. Dem. Exec. Com., 1974—, Montgomery County Dem. Exec. Com. Mem. Women in Communications, Nat. Assn. Consumer Affairs Adminstrs., DAR, Daus. Am. Colonists, Eagle Forum. Presbyterian. Club: Soroptomists. Office: State Capitol Montgomery AL 36130

GUNTER, FRANK ELLIOTT, artist; b. Jasper, Ala., May 8, 1934; S. Frank Marion and Lucy Ellen (Butler) G.; m. Dora Carolyn Carlton, Aug. 9, 1958; 1 dau., Lisa Cameron. B.F.A., U. Ala., 1956; M.A., Fla. State U., 1960. Tchr. art Birmingham (Ala.) Public Schs., 1956-58; asst. prof. art Murray State U., 1960-62; prof. U. Ill., 1962—; chmn. painting programs; asso. U. Ill. Center Advanced Study, 1974-75. One-man shows, 1957—, including, Cultural Center for Am. Embassy, Paris, 1971, Am. Library, Brussels, 1972, Maison Descarte, Amsterdam, 1973, Ill. Arts Council, Chgo., 1970, Joy Horwich Gallery, Chgo., 1978, 80, group shows include, No. Ariz. U. Art Gallery, Flagstaff, 1975, Madison (Wis.) Art Center, 1977; represented in permanent collections, Birmingham Mus. Art, Evansville (Ind.) Mus., Swope Gallery, Terre Haute, Ind., Ill. State Mus., Springfield, Bank of Ind., Merrillville, Union League Club, Chgo., H.F. Corp., Chgo., Purdue U., St. Paul Art Center, U. N.D. U. Ill. travel fellow, 1964, 66, 68, 74, 77. Episcopalian. Home: 806 S Elm Blvd Champaign IL 61820 Office: Sch Art and Design Univ Ill Champaign-Urbana IL 61820

GUNTER, FRANKLIN DELANO, retail executive; b. McLeansboro, Ill., July 25, 1933; s. Ernest George and Velma (Veach) G.; m. Dolores Ann Schmulbach, Mar. 19, 1955; children: Tracy, Kreg. B.S., So. Ill. U., 1963. Tax acct. Phillips Petroleum Co., St. Louis, 1954-60, Peabody Coal Co., 1960-66; v.p. taxes Continental Telephone Co., St. Louis, 1966-73, The May Dept. Stores Co., 1973—. Served with USN, 1951-54. Mem. Am. Retail Fedn, Mo. Retail Assn., Ill. Retailers Assn., Tax Execs. Inst., Tax Found. Inc., Tax Council, Fin Execs. Inst. Christian Ch. Lodge: Masons. Home: 36 Clover Dr Belleville IL 62221 Office: May Dept Stores Co 6th and Olive Sts Saint Louis MO 63101

GUNTER, JOHN BROWN, JR., real estate executive; b. Johnstown, Pa., May 22, 1919; s. John Brown and Mary (Barr) G.; m. Dorothy Mulhollen, July 5, 1942; 1 dau., Jerrol Louise. Student, Valley Forge Mil. Acad. Jr. Coll., 1937-39; B.S., U. Md., 1941. Exec. dir. Johnstown Community Chest, 1946-48; trainee, mgr. Sears, Roebuck & Co., 1948-52; adminstrv. asst. Penn Traffic Co., Johnstown, 1952-58, controller, 1958-62, asst. treas., 1962-65, sec., 1965—, corp. v.p., 1976—; pres. Dept. Store div., 1976-78; pres., dir. Winston Corp., real estate devel., Johnstown, 1978—; v.p., dir. Johnstown Tribune Pub. Co.; dir.

Internat. Refractories Inc., Johnstown Savs. Bank; instr. mgmt. U. Pitts., Johnstown. Served to lt. col. AUS, 1941-46; ETO. Decorated Order Brit. Empire, Bronze Arrowhead. Mem. Nat. Retail Mchts. Assn. (past dir.), Pa. Retailers Assn. (past dir.), Mensa, Phi Delta Theta. Republican. Presbyterian. Lodge: Masons. Home: 2215 Crabtree Ln Johnstown PA 15905 Office: WJAC Bldg Johnstown PA 15905

GUNTER, WILLIAM DAWSON, JR., state official; b. Jacksonville, Fla., July 16, 1934; s. William Dawson and Tillie G.; m. Teresa Arbaugh, June 26, 1971; children—Bart, Joel, Rachel, Rebecca. B.S.A., U. Fla., 1956. Tchr. public schs., Live Oak, Fla., 1956; ins. agt. Central Fla.; mem. Fla. State Senate, 1966-72, 92d Congress from Fla. 5th Dist.; treas. and ins. commr. State of Fla., 1976—; sr. v.p. Southland Equity Corp., Orlando, Fla.; pres. Southland Capital Investors, Inc., Orlando. Deacon Baptist Ch.; bd. dirs. Central Fla. Fair Assn. Served with U.S. Army. Recipient good govt. award Fla. State Jaycees, 1972. Mem. Nat. Assn. State Treasurers (pres.), Nat. Assn. Ins. Commrs. (v.p.), Nat. Assn. State Auditors, Comptrollers and Treasurers (intergovtl. relations com.), Orlando C. of C. (past dir.). Democrat. Clubs: Jaycees, Kiwanis, Masons. Office: The Capitol Plaza Level Tallahassee FL 32301

GUNTHER, GERALD, lawyer, educator; b. Usingen, Germany, May 26, 1927; came to U.S., 1938, naturalized, 1944; s. Otto and Minna (Floersheim) Gutenstein; m. Barbara Kelsky, June 22, 1949; children: Daniel Jay, Andrew James. B.A., Bklyn. Coll., 1949; M.A., Columbia, 1950; LL.B., Harvard, 1953. Bar: N.Y. bar 1955. Law clk. Judge Learned Hand, 1953-54; Chief Justice Earl Warren, 1954-55; asso. firm Cleary, Gottlieb, Friendly & Hamilton., N.Y.C., 1955-56; asso. prof. law Columbia, 1956-59, prof., 1959-62; prof. law Stanford, 1962-72, Wm. Nelson Cromwell prof., 1972—; Lectr. polit. sci. Bklyn. Coll., 1949-50; vis. prof. Harvard Law Sch., 1972-73; mem. faculty Salzburg Seminar in Am. Studies, 1976; W.W. Crosskey Meml. lectr. U. Chgo., 1976; John A. Sibley Meml. lectr. U. Ga., 1979; research dir. com. constl. simplification N.Y. Inter-law Sch., 1957-58; cons. Ford Found., 1974—; dir. Columbia Fed. Cts. History Project, 1957-59; mem. bd. overseers com. to visit Harvard Law Sch., 1974-80; bd. overseers Harvard Law Rev., 1967-72; mem. steering com. Citizens for Constn., 1979-81; adv. com. on experimentation in law Fed. Jud. Center, 1978-81. Author: John Marshall's Defense of McCulloch versus Maryland, 1969, Cases and Materials on Constitutional Law, 10th edit, 1980, Cases and Materials on Individual Rights in Constitutional Law, 1970, 3d edit., 1981; Mem. editorial bd., Found. Press, 1972—; Contbr. articles to profl. jours. Served with USNR, 1945-46. Recipient distinguished alumnus award Bklyn. Coll., 1961; Guggenheim fellow, 1962-63; Center Advanced Study in Behavioral Scis., fellow, 1969-70; Fulbright-Hays lectr., Ghana, 1970; Nat. Endowment Humanities Fellow, 1980-81. Fellow Am. Acad. Arts and Scis.; mem. Am. Philos. Soc., Am. Law Inst., Am. Hist. Assn. (mem. com. Littleton-Griswold Fund 1968-73), Orgn. Am. Historians. Office: Stanford Law Sch Stanford CA 94305

GUNTHER, JANE PERRY (MRS. JOHN GUNTHER), editor, writer; b. N.Y.C., Aug. 17, 1916; d. Reginald and Hilda (Hedley) Perry; m. John W. Vandercook, June 20, 1938 (div. Sept. 1947); m. John Gunther, Mar. 3, 1948 (dec. May 1970); 1 son, Nicholas. B.A., Vassar Coll., 1938. With Am. Film Center, N.Y.C., 1941-42, Duell, Sloan & Pearce publishers, 1945-48; mem. editorial staff Reader's Digest, N.Y.C., 1973-77. Trustee The Asia Soc., N.Y.C., 1966-79, Huxley Inst., N.Y.C., 1972-82, Mannes Coll. Music, 1979—. Club: Cosmopolitan (N.Y.C.). Home: 1 East End Ave New York NY 10021

GUNTHER, JOHN JOSEPH, association executive; b. Leavenworth, Kans., Dec. 18, 1925; s. John Joseph G. and Margaret (Houllahan) Bartlett; m. Rita Xavier, Oct. 19, 1963; 1 dau., Rita St. John. B.A., U. Notre Dame, 1947; M.P.A., U. Kans., 1947; J.D., George Washington U., 1954. Bar: D.C. 1954, U.S. Supreme Ct. 1956. Instr. U. Kans., 1946; intern Nat. Inst. Pub. Affairs, 1947-48; asst. to U.S. Sec. of Labor, 1947, U.S. Senator, 1947-48; sole practice law, Washington, 1949-58, lobbyist, 1949-58; exec. dir. U.S. conf. of Mayors., Washington, 1958—; founder Nat. Urban Coalition; chmn. several bds. state and local govt. ofcls.; lectr. London U., Am. U. Contbr. articles in field. Adv. bd. John F. Kennedy Sch. Govt.; chmn. D.C. Redevel. Land Agy., 1963-76. Served with AC U.S. Army, 1943-44. Mem. ABA, D.C. Bar Assn., Am. Pub. Health Assn., Am. Soc. Pub. Adminstrn., Internat. Union Local Authorities. Democrat. Roman Catholic. Clubs: Sun Valley Ctr; Internat. (Washington).

GUNTHEROTH, WARREN GADEN, physician; b. Hominy, Okla., July 27, 1927; s. Harry William and Callie (Cornett) G.; m. Ethel Haglund, July 3, 1954; children: Kurt, Karl. Sten. M.D., Harvard U., 1952. Diplomate: Am. Bd. Pediatrics, Am. Bd. Pediatric Cardiology, Nat. Bd. Med. Examiners. Intern Peter Bent Brigham Hosp., Boston, 1952-53; fellow in cardiology Children's Hosp., Boston, 1953-55, resident in pediatrics, 1955-56; research fellow physiology and biophysics U. Wash. Med. Sch., Seattle, 1957-58, mem. faculty, 1958—, prof. pediatrics, 1969—, head div. pediatric cardiology, 1964—. Author: Pediatric Electrocardiography, 1965, How to Read Pediatrics ECGs, 1981, Crib Death (Sudden Infant Death Syndrome), 1982; also numerous articles; editorial bd.: Am. Heart Jour, 1977-80, Circulation, 1980-83; sect. editor: Practice of Pediatrics, 1979—. Served with USPHS, 1950-51. Spl. research fellow NIH, 1967; research grantee, 1958—. Mem. Am. Physiol. Soc., Soc. Pediatric Research, Biomed. Engring. Soc. (charter), Soc. Exptl. Biology and Medicine, Am. Heart Assn. (chmn. N.W. regional med. research adv. com. 1978-80), Cardiovascular System Dynamics Soc. (charter), Am. Coll. Cardiology. Democrat. Home: 13201 42d Ave NE Seattle WA 98125 Office: Dept Pediatrics RD-20 Univ Wash Med Sch Seattle WA 98195 *My career includes medical practice, teaching and research; my hobby is mountain climbing. Both work and hobby benefit from courage. Encouraging students to ask difficult—and even embarrassing—questions, reaching a timely diagnosis, starting treatment in a dangerously ill patient, and raising challenging questions in research that may provoke anger or scorn; all require courage. Silent convictions are not enough.*

GUNZBERG, ARTHUR S(AMUEL), men's clothing company executive; b. Buffalo, Dec. 24, 1911; s. Ben and Jeannette (Wile) G.; m. Aline Du Bin, June 3, 1936; children: Guy, Lynn. B.S.E., Wharton Sch., U. Pa., 1934. With M. Wile & Co. Inc., Buffalo, 1934—, pres., 1960-71, chmn. bd., 1971—; dir. Hartmarx Corp. (name formerly Hart Schaffner & Marx). Mem. Clothing Mfrs. Assn. U.S.A. (dir.). Office: 2020 Elmwood Ave Buffalo NY 14207

GUNZENHAUSER, GERARD RALPH, JR., tobacco company executive; b. Mt. Vernon, N.Y., Sept. 26, 1936; s. Gerard Ralph and Helen Elizabeth (Carey) G.; m. Alfa Marjorie Vendetti, Sept. 17, 1960; children: Cathy Susan, Michael Gerard, Christopher John, Eric David. B.B.A., Iona Coll., 1965; postgrad., NYU Sch. Bus. Adminstrn., 1967-68. Asst. mgr. fin. analysis Gen. Foods Corp., White Plains, N.Y., 1962-68; dir. fin. planning and analysis RJR Foods, Inc., Winston-Salem, N.C., 1968-76; area fin. dir. R.J. Reynolds Tobacco Internat., Winston-Salem, 1976-79; comptroller R.J. Reynolds Tobacco. Co., Winston-Salem, 1979-81; v.p., comptroller R.J. Reynolds Tobacco Co., Winston-Salem, 1981-83, v.p. fin., chief fin. officer, 1983—; bd. dirs. Reynolds Carolina Credit Union, Winston-Salem, 1973-83, Consumer Credit Counseling Service, 1983—. Chmn. St. Leo's Parish Council, Winston-Salem, 1974-77; exec. v.p. Winston-Salem Nat. Little League, 1981—; mem. Bishop McGuinness Meml. High Sch. Bd. Edn., Winston-Salem, 1983—. Named to Hon. Order Ky. Cols., 1983. Mem. C. of C. of Winston-Salem (chmn. sch. budget task force 1976). Roman Catholic. Office: R J Reynolds Tobacco Co 401 N Main St Winston-Salem NC 27102

GUNZENHAUSER, KEITH, insurance company executive; b. Humeston, Iowa, Oct. 19, 1933; s. Carl John and Ella (Fight) G.; m. Kathleen Joyce, Apr. 19, 1964; children: Bruce, Bonnie. B.A., Simpson Coll., 1956. With Central Life Ins. Co., Des Moines, 1956—, v.p. securities, 1972-76, sr. v.p., 1976—; dir. Frontense Capital Corp., Chgo., Iowa Bus. Devel. Credit Corp., Des Moines; bd. dirs. Iowa Pub. Employees Retirement System, Des Moines, 1971-83. Bd. dir. YMCA; bd. dirs. Van Meter Bd. Edn., 1978—. Served with U.S. Army, 1953-55. Mem. Des Moines Soc. Fin. Analysts (pres. 1971-72), Chartered Fin. Analyst, Fin. Exec. Inst. Methodist. Club: Des Moines. Home: Route 1 PO Box 250 Van Meter IA 50261 Office: Central Life Assurance Co 611 5th Box 1555 Des Moines IA 50261

GUNZENHAUSER, STEPHEN CHARLES, conductor; b. N.Y.C., Apr. 8, 1942; s. M(ax) Kurt and Ruth (Sorsky) G.; m. Rochelle E. Davis, June 14, 1970; children—Marisa, Amy. B.Mus., Oberlin Coll., 1963; diploma, Salzburg (Austria) Mozarteum, 1962; M.Mus., New Eng. Conservatory Music, 1965; artist diploma, Hochschule, Cologne, W. Ger., 1968. Guest condr., Rhenish Chamber Orch., Cologne, 1967-69, City of Gelsenkirchen Orch., 1972, Nat. Orch. Costa Rica, 1975, Del. Pro Musica, 1974-75, Lancaster (Pa.) Symphony, 1979, Radio Orch. Ireland, Dublin, 1979, 82; condr., Hessian State Broadcasting Network Orch., 1969, RIAS Orch. of Berlin, Knoxville (Tenn.) Symphony, 1982, Duluth-Superior (Wis.) Symphony, Ala. Symphony, 1983, Spokane Symphony, Laredo Symphony (Tex.); asst. condr., Monte Carlo Nat. Orch., 1968-69, Am. Symphony Orch., N.Y.C., 1969-70; music dir., Bklyn. Center Chamber Orch., 1970-72, Kennett (Pa.) Symphony Orch., 1974-78, Wilmington (Del.) Chamber Orch., 1976—, Del. Symphony, 1978—; prin. condr., Lancaster Symphony; music dir., Lancaster Symphony, 1981; exec. dir., Wilmington Music Sch., 1974—; artistic dir., Wilmington Music Sch., 1983; clarinettist; rec. artist. Trustee Nat. Guild Community Schs. Arts, 1977—. Fulbright grantee, 1965-68; recipient 1st prize Santiago (Spain) Competition, 1967. Mem. Musicians Union, Condrs. Guild, Am. Symphony Orch. League, Music Tchrs. Nat. Assn. Home: 901 Shallcross Ave Wilmington DE 19806 Office: PO Box 1870 Wilmington DE 19899 *As musician, I can neither build nor repair the tangible aspects of life. My hope is to minister successfully to the spirit.*

GUPTA, SHANTI SWARUP, statistician; b. Saunasi, India, Jan. 25, 1925; s. Sitaram and Ramphali G.; m. Marianne Heinicke, Feb. 20, 1974; 1 dau., Maya Erika. B.A. with honors, St. Stephen's Coll., Delhi, 1946; M.A. in Math, Delhi U., 1949; Ph.D. in Statistics, U. N.C., 1956. Lectr. Delhi Coll., 1949-53; research statistician Bell Telephone Labs., 1956-57, 58-61; asso. prof. math. U. Alta., 1957-58; vis. asso. prof. Stanford U., 1961-62; prof. statistics and math. Purdue U., West Lafayette, Ind., 1962—, head dept., 1968—. Co-author 2 books in field; editor 2 books; contbr. articles to profl. jours. Fulbright fellow, 1953-54. Fellow Am. Statis. Assn., Inst. Math. Statistics, Royal Statis. Soc., Internat. Statis. Inst., AAAS; mem. Bernoulli Soc. for Probability and Statistics, Math. Assn. Am., Sigma Xi. Home: 104 Tecumseh Park Ct West Lafayette IN 47906 Office: Dept Statistics Purdue Univ West Lafayette IN 47907

GUPTA, SURAJ NARAYAN, physicist, educator; b. Haryana, India, Dec. 1, 1924; came to U.S., 1953, naturalized, 1963; s. Lakshmi N. and Devi (Goyal) G.; m. Letty Gupta, July 14, 1948; children—Paul, Ranee. M.S., St. Stephen's Coll., India, 1946; Ph.D., U. Cambridge, Eng., 1951. Imperial Chem. Industries fellow U. Manchester, Eng., 1951-53; vis. prof. physics Purdue U., 1953-56; prof. physics Wayne State U., 1956-61, Distinguished prof. physics, 1961—; vis. physicist Argonne Nat. Lab., Brookhaven Nat. Lab., NRC Can. Author: Quantum Electrodynamics, 1977. Fellow Am. Phys. Soc., Nat. Acad. Scis. India. Research on relativity, gravitation, quantum electrodynamics, nuclear physics, high-energy physics. Home: 1300 E Lafayette Blvd Detroit MI 48207 Office: Dept Physics Wayne State U Detroit MI 48202

GUPTILL, LEIGHTON, real estate exec.; b. Bklyn., May 27, 1920; s. Arthur Leighton and Ethel M. (Weir) G.; m. Louise Post Hubert, July 14, 1945; children—Ann Louise, William Leighton. B.A., Colgate U., 1942. Publisher Am. Artist mag., 1956-63; pres. Watson-Guptill Publs., Inc. (pubs. art and music books), N.Y.C., 1956-62, v.p., 1963-78, dir. publs. music book div., 1963-78; exec. v.p. Relotech, Inc., Westport, Conn., 1978—. Mem. Vets. Hosp. Radio and TV Guild, Am. Legion, Am. Theatre Organ Enthusiasts, Am. Fedn. Musicians, Phi Gamma Delta. Clubs: Mason (32 deg., Shriner), University, Darien, Conn. Home: 86 Hills Point Rd Westport CT 06880

GURAK, STANLEY, foundry company executive; b. Scranton, Pa., Apr. 3, 1923; s. Thomas and Catherine Gurak D.; m. Evelyn Jane, Mar. 18, 1952; children: Stanley T., Stacie Jo, Christy Lynn. B.S.M.E., Pa. State U., 1949. With U.S. Pipe & Foundry Co., Birmingham, Ala., v.p. mfg., 1974-76, div. pres., 1976-79, corp. pres., 1979—; group v.p. Jim Walter Corp., Tampa, Fla. Served to sgt. U.S. Army, 1943-45; ETO. Office: US Pipe & Foundry Co 3300 First Ave N Birmingham AL 35202

GURALNICK, SIDNEY AARON, univ. provost; b. Phila., Apr. 25, 1929; s. Philip and Kenia (Dudnik) G.; m. Eleanor Alban, Mar. 10, 1951; children—Sara Dian, Jeremy. B.Sc., Drexel Inst. Tech., Phila., 1952; M.S., Cornell U., 1955, Ph.D., 1958. Instr., then asst. prof. Cornell U., 1952-58, mgr. structural research lab., 1956-58; mem. faculty Ill. Inst. Tech., Chgo., 1958—, prof. civil engring., 1967—, dir. structural engring. labs., 1968-71, dean, 1971-75, exec. v.p., provost, 1975—, trustee, 1976—; devel. engr. Portland Cement Assn., Skokie, Ill., 1959-61; participant internat. confs.; cons. to govt. and industry. Author numerous papers in field. Trustee Inst. Gas Techs., 1976—. Served with AUS, 1950-51. McGraw fellow, 1952-53; Faculty Research fellow Ill. Inst. Tech., 1960; European travel grantee, 1961. Fellow Am. Concrete Inst.; mem. ASCE (Collingwood prize 1961), Internat. Assn. Bridge and Structural Engring., Soc. Exptl. Stress Analysis, Sigma Xi. Office: 3300 S Federal St Chicago IL 60616

GURALNIK, DAVID B(ERNARD), lexicographer, publishing executive; b. Cleve., June 17, 1920; s. Julian and Rose (Chanes) G.; m. Shirley Nashkin, June 14, 1942; 1 dau., Eve Rachel Guralnik Harrington. B.A., Western Res. U., 1941, M.A., 1946; postgrad., Oreg. State U., 1943-44. From asst. editor to dictionary editor-in-chief and v.p. World Pub. Co., Cleve. and N.Y.C., 1941-74; dictionary editor-in-chief, v.p. William Collins & Sons, Cleve. and Glasgow, Scotland, 1974-80, Simon & Schuster, Inc., Cleve. and N.Y.C., 1980—. Author: Making of a New Dictionary, 1952; editor-in-chief: Webster's New World Dictionaries including College Edit., 1953, 2d College Edit., 1970, Student Edit., 1976, Young Readers Edits., 1961, 79; adv. bd.: The Gamut, 1983—, Cuyahoga Rev., 1982—, Jewish Lang. Rev., Haifa, Israel, 1983—. Pres. Jewish Community Ctr., Cleve., 1976-79; v.p. Cleve. Jewish News, 1974-83, Cleve. Chamber Music Soc., 1977—; bd. overseers Case Western Res. U., 1982—; trustee ACLU, Cleve., 1981—. Served with U.S. Army, 1943-45; ETO. Decorated Bronze Star; recipient Ohioana citation Ohioana Library Assn., Columbus, Ohio, 1953. Mem. PEN, Am. Name Soc., Nat. Council Tchrs. of English, Am. Dialect Soc., Dictionary Soc. N.Am. (exec. com.). Club: Rowfant (Cleve.). Home: 14014 Shaker Blvd Shaker Heights OH 44120 Office: New World Dictionary Div Simon & Schuster Inc 850 Euclid Ave Cleveland OH 44114

GURD, FRANK ROSS NEWMAN, biochemist, educator; b. Montreal, Que., Can., Jan. 20, 1924; came to U.S., 1946, naturalized, 1954; s. Fraser Baillie and Jessie (Newman) G.; m. Ruth Sights, June 12, 1956; children: Fraser, Kathleen, Martha, Charles. Grad. cum laude, Phillips Exeter Acad., 1941; B.S., McGill U., 1945, M.S., 1946; Ph.D., Harvard, 1949. Asst. dir. Bur. Med. Research, Equitable Life Assurance Soc., N.Y.C., 1955-59; asst. prof. clin. biochemistry Med. Coll. Cornell U., 1955-60; prof. biochemistry Sch. Medicine, Ind. U., 1960-66, prof. chemistry, 1965-79, disting. prof. biochemistry and chemistry, 1979—; Chmn. biophysics and biophys. chemistry B study sect. NIH, 1968-70. Author: Chemical Specificity in Biological Interactions, 1954, (with D.J. Hanahan) Chemistry of the Lipides, 1960; Editorial bd.: Jour. Biol. Chemistry, 1966-72, 76-81. John Simon Guggenheim and Helen Hay Whitney fellow dept. biochemistry Sch. Medicine, Washington U., 1954-55. Mem. Am. Soc. Biol. Chemists, Am. Chem. Soc., Biophys. Soc., N.Y. Acad. Scis., A.A.A.S., Sigma Xi. Research, publs. on lipoprotein isolated from blood; combination of proteins with certain metal salts; identification of sites of binding and effects on conformation; modes of combination of metal ions with peptides; chem. modification of proteins to correlate structure in solution with that in crystalline state, Sequence determinations on myoglobins of different Species; Specific enrichment proteins with carbon-13 for nuclear magnetic resonance studies, semisynthesis of proteins; interactions of carbon dioxide with peptides and proteins; analysis of electrostatic effects and internal motions in proteins. Home: 2600 Fairoaks Ln Bloomington IN 47401

GURDIN, MICHAEL MEYER, plastic surgeon; b. Pine Bluff, Ark., Sept. 15, 1910; s. Nathan and Millie (Nichols) G.; m. Marlene Seghetti, Oct. 2, 1963; children—Julie (Mrs. Robert Findley), Jonathan M. Student, U. Ark., 1927-29; M.D., Tulane U., 1933. Diplomate: Am. Bd. Plastic Surgery. Intern Cedars of Lebanon Hosp., Los Angeles, 1933-34, resident in surgery, 1935-36; practice medicine specializing in plastic and reconstructive surgery, Beverly Hills, Calif.; cons. plastic surgery VA Hosp., Sawtelle, Calif.; asso. clin. prof. plastic surgery U. Calif. at Los Angeles Med. Center, 1946—. Served to comdr. M.C. USNR, 1940-46. Fellow A.C.S., Internat. Coll. Surgeons; mem. Am. Soc. Aesthetic Plastic Surgery (pres. 1975-76), Am. Soc. Plastic and Reconstructive Surgeons (pres. 1972-73), Calif. Soc. Plastic Surgeons (pres. 1957-58). Office: 436 N Roxbury Dr Beverly Hills CA 90210

GURECK, WILLIAM ALEXANDER, naval officer; b. Mineola, N.Y., July 2, 1929; s. William Richard and Elisabeth Anna (Girnt) G.; m. Phyllis C. Rein, Feb. 11, 1957; children: William Scott, Kristin Elisabeth. Student, Columbia U., 1946-48, Naval War Coll., 1961-62; B.S., Naval Postgrad. Sch., Monterey, Calif., 1964. Commd. ensign U.S. Navy, 1950, advanced through grades to rear adm., 1975; ops. officer (Fighter Squadron 51), 1960-61, 1964-65, exec. officer, then comdg. officer, 1965-67, head aviation jr. officer assignment sect., 1967-68, comdr., 1968-69, ops. officer, 1969-71, exec. asst. to dir., 1971-72, comdg. officer U.S.S. Shreveport, 1972-73, asst. chief of staff for readiness with comdr., 1973-74, comdg. officer U.S.S. John F. Kennedy, 1974-75, dep. chief of staff, readiness and resources on staff comdr. in chief, 1976-77, comdr., 1978-80, dep. dir., 1980—. Decorated Legion of Merit with 4 gold stars, D.F.C., Bronze Star, Air medal with 24 gold stars, Meritorious Service medal, Joint Service Commendation medal, Navy Commendation medal with 4 gold stars. Mem. U.S. Naval Inst., Assn. Naval Aviation. Club: Commonwealth. Home: 6003 Roxbury Ave Springfield VA 22152 Office: OP-094B Navy Dept Washington DC 20350

GUREN, SHELDON BRUCE, lawyer, business executive; b. Cleve., Oct. 25, 1924; s. Nathan M. and Rose Lois (Gottfried) G.; m. Cynthia M. Wedding, Mar. 8, 1970; children: Jon D., Pamela E., Beth A., Laura L. B.B.A., Western Res. U., 1944; LL.B., Harvard U., 1948. Bar: Ohio 1948, Fla. 1979. Of counsel Burke, Haber, Berick (and predecessors), Cleve., 1984—; of counsel Smith and Mandler, Miami, Fla., 1984—; chmn. bd., treas., dir. Trans Investment Co.; pres., dir. Trans Comml. Industries, Inc.; pres. Mortgage Advisory Service Co., 1969-71, treas., 1971—; sec., pres., dir. Gt. Lakes Towing Co.; trustee, sec. U.S. Realty Investments, 1961-70, trustee, pres., chief exec. officer, 1970-77, chmn. bd., chief exec. officer, 1977-83. Served with U.S. Army, 1945-46. Mem. Ohio, Fla., Cleve. bar assns. Home: 190 Casuarina Coral Gables FL 33143 Office: 300 National City Bank Bldg Cleveland OH 44114 800 Brickell Ave Miami FL 33131

GURGIN, VONNIE ANN, social scientist; b. Toledo, Nov. 20, 1940; d. John and Pauline (Stoicer) G. B.A., Ohio State U., 1962; M.A., U. Calif., Berkeley, 1966; D.Criminology, 1969. Research asst. Calif. Dept. Mental Hygiene, San Francisco, 1962-64; research sociologist U. Calif., Berkeley, 1964-66; dir. cons. services Survey Research Center, 1967-68, asst. prof. criminology, 1968-71; research sociologist Social Sci. Research and Devel. Corp., Berkeley, 1966-67; sr. research criminologist Stanford Research Inst. (now SRI Internat.), Menlo Park, Calif., 1971-72; pres., research dir. Inst. Study Social Concerns, Berkeley, 1972—; asst. chief resource for cancer epidemiology sect. Calif. Tumor Registry, Calif. Dept. Health Services, Emeryville, 1981—; dir. survey research No. Calif. Cancer Program, Palo Alto, 1982—; cons. in field. Author reports, monographs, articles. Bd. dirs. Research Guild, Sacramento, 1983—. Mem. Am. Sociol. Assn., Pacific Sociol. Assn., AAUP, Am. Soc. Criminology, Nat. Council Crime and Delinquency, AAAS, Am. Acad. Polit. and Social Scientists, Soc. Epidermiol. Research, Nat. Soc. Lit. and Arts. Address: 1099 Sterling Ave Berkeley CA 94708

GURIAN, NAOMI, lawyer, labor union executive; b. N.Y.C., Mar. 1, 1933; d. Elias Jerome and Ethel (Lipman) G.; m. Burt Goldreich, Oct. 18, 1976; children by previous marriage: Mitchell, Vicki, Daniel. A.A., UCLA, 1952, B.A., 1955; J.D., San Fernando Valley Coll. Law, 1976. Bar: Calif. 1976. Assoc. councel Writers Guild Am., Los Angeles, 1976-78, asst. exec. dir., 1978-82, exec. dir., 1982—. Office: Writers Guild Am 8955 Beverly Blvd Los Angeles CA 90048

GURIN, ARNOLD, social work educator; b. N.Y.C., Dec. 5, 1917; s. Morris and Sarah (Nimetz) G.; m. Helen Bass, Dec. 27, 1942; children: Nathaniel, Naomi. B.S., CCNY, 1937; M.S., Columbia U., 1943; Ph.D., U. Mich., 1965. Dir. budget research Council Jewish Fedns. and Welfare Funds, N.Y.C., 1945-53, dir. field service, 1953-58; lectr. social work Mich. State U., 1958-62; prof. social adminstrn. Brandeis U., 1962-71, 76—; dean Florence Heller Grad. Sch., 1971-76; dir. community orgn. curriculum project Council Social Work Edn., 1965-68. Author: (with Robert Perlman) Community Organization and Social Planning, 1972, Community Organization Curriculum in Graduate Social Work Education: Report and Recommendations, 1970; Contbr. articles to profl. jours. Mem. tng. grants rev. panel Office Juvenile Delinquency, HEW, 1963-68; mem. task force on social services 1968; vis. prof. Hebrew U. Sch. Social Work, Jerusalem, 1980; chmn. Internat. Com. on Evaluation of Project Renewal in Israel,

1981. Mem. Nat. Conf. Social Welfare (nat. bd. 1972-75), Nat. Assn. Social Workers, Am. Sociol. Soc. Home: 63 Kingswood Rd Auburndale MA 02166 Office: 415 South St Waltham MA 02254

GURIN, SAMUEL, biochemist, educator; b. N.Y.C., July 1, 1905; s. Morris and Rose (Zwinig) G.; m. Celia Zall, June 14, 1930; children—Robert N., Richard S. B.A., Columbia, 1926, M.S., 1930, Ph.D., 1934; NRC fellow, U. Ill., 1935-37; D.Sc., LaSalle Coll., 1965, Phila. Coll. Pharmacy, 1961, U. Fla., 1979. Prof. biochemistry U. Pa., 1951-68, chmn. dept., 1954-62, dean, 1962-68; prof. biochemistry Med. Sch. and dept. biol. scis. U. Fla., Gainesville, 1970—; dir. Cornelius Vanderbilt Whitney-U. Fla. Marine Biol. Labs., 1972; mem. metabolism panel NRC. Editorial bd.: Jour. Biol. Chemistry. Mem. Am. Soc. Biol. Chemists, Am. Chem. Soc. Home: Route 1 Box 126B St Augustine FL 32084

GURLAND, ROBERT H., philosophy educator, consultant; b. N.Y.C., Oct. 14, 1933; s. Samuel Joseph and Bessie (Nozick) G.; m. Helen Bassett, Feb. 20, 1960; children: Sarah Elizabeth, Keith Porter. B.A., CCNY, 1955; M.A., Adelphi U., 1960; Ph.D., NYU, 1971. Tchr. math. Eastwoods Sch., Oyster Bay, N.Y., 1956-58, Roslyn pub. schs., N.Y., 1958-62; mem. faculty San Jose State Coll., Calif., 1962-64; prof. math. C.W. Post Coll., Brookville, N.Y., 1964-70; prof. philosophy NYU, N.Y.C., 1970—; vis. prof. U.S. Mil. Acad., West Point, N.Y., 1976-78, Hofstra U., Adelphia U.; cons., lectr. Gen. Electric Corp., Croton-on-Hudson, N.Y., Indsl. Coll. Armed Forces, Washington. Recipient Outstanding Civilian Service medal Dept. Army, West Point, 1978, Gt. Tchr. award Alumni Fedn. NYU, 1973; named Man of Yr. C.W. Post Coll. L.I.U., 1967; NSF grantee. Mem. Am. Philos. Assn., Assn. Symbolic Logic, Beta Lambda Sigma, Omega Epsilon. Home: 45 Brookfield Rd Northport NY 11768 Office: Dept Philosophy NYU 19 University Pl Room 305 New York NY 10003

GURLEY, FRANKLIN LOUIS, food company executive, lawyer; b. Syracuse, N.Y., Nov. 26, 1925; s. George Bernard and Catherine Veronica (Moran) G.; m. Elizabeth Anne Ryan, June 17, 1950. A.B., Harvard U., 1949, J.D., 1952. Bar: Mass. 1952, N.Y. 1956, Ill. 1956, Mich. 1956, D.C. 1956. Fgn. service staff officer Dept. State, Washington and Germany, 1953-55; atty. N.Y. Central R.R. Co., 1955-56; asst. dist. atty. New York County, 1956-57; atty. firm Dewey, Ballantine, Bushby, Palmer & Wood, N.Y.C., 1957-63; gen. counsel, sec. IBM Europe Corp., Paris; also mng. atty. IBM Corp., Armonk, N.Y., 1963-68; sr. v.p., gen. counsel Nestle S.A., Vevey, Switzerland, 1968-83, spl. legal adv., 1984—; Pres. Tappan Landing Assn., Tarrytown, N.Y., 1958-60. Author: 399th in Action, 1946, King Philip's War; play, 1952; Adv. bd.: Swiss Antitrust Rev, 1977—; Contbr. articles to profl. jours. Served with inf. AUS, 1944-46; ETO. Decorated Bronze Star, Combat Inf. Badge. Mem. Am., Ill., Internat. bar assns., Assn. Bar City N.Y., N.Y. County Lawyers Assn., Internat. Law Assn., Am. Soc. Internat. Law, S.A.R. (sec., bd. mgrs. N.Y. chpt. 1957-63), Harvard Law Sch. Assn., Harvard Law Sch. Assn. Europe. Clubs: Harvard (N.Y.C., France, Switzerland); Lausanne Golf, Montreux Golf; Am. Internat. (Geneva). SEt West Point and Heptagonal 1000-yard records in track, 1948. Home: 1681 Romanens Fribourg Switzerland Office: Nestle SA 1800 Vevey Switzerland

GURNETT, DONALD ALFRED, physics educator; b. Cedar Rapids, Iowa, Apr. 11, 1940; s. Alfred Foley and Velma (Trachta) G.; m. Marie Barbara Schmitz, Oct. 10, 1964; children: Suzanne, Christina. B.S. in Elec. Engring., U. Iowa, 1962, M.S. in Physics, 1963, Ph.D., 1965. Prof. physics U. Iowa, Iowa City, 1965-75, 76-79, 80—; research scientist Max-Planck Inst., Garching, W. Ger., 1975-76; vis. prof. UCLA, 1979-80; mem. space physics com. Nat. Acad. Sci., Washington, 1975-78, mem. com. on solar terrrestrial research, 1976-79, mem. com. on planetary and lunar exploration, 1982—. Recipient Alexander von Humboldt Found. award, 1975, Disting. Sci. Achievement award NASA, 1980. Fellow Am. Geophys. Union (assoc. editor Jour. Geophys. Research 1974-77); mem. Internat. Union Radio Sci. (Dellinger gold medal 1978), Am. Phys. Soc., Soaring Soc. Am. (Iowa State gov. 1983—). Home: 6 Durham Ct Iowa City IA 52240 Office: Dept Physics and Astronomy U Iowa Iowa City IA 52242

GURNEY, ALBERT RAMSDELL, JR., playwright, novelist, educator; b. Buffalo, Nov. 1, 1930; s. Albert Ramsdell and Marion (Spaulding) G.; m. Mary Forman Goodyear, June 8, 1957; children—George, Amy, Evelyn, Benjamin. B.A., Williams Coll., 1952; M.F.A., Yale, 1958. Mem. faculty Mass. Inst. Tech., 1960—, prof. lit., 1970—. Author: Best Short Plays, 1955-56, 57-58, 69, 70, Scenes From American Life, 1971, The Golden Fleece, 1969, Children, 1974, The Gospel According to Joe, 1974, Who Killed Richard Cory, 1976, The Middle Ages, 1977, Entertaining Strangers, 1977, The Wayside Motor Inn, 1977, O Youth and Beauty, TV adaptation of story by John Cheever, The Golden Age, 1980, The Dining Room, 1981, What I Did Last Summer, 1982—. Served with USNR, 1952-55. Recipient N.Y. Drama Desk award, 1971; Rockefeller Playwrights award, 1977, Playwriting award Nat. Endowment Arts, 1981-82. Mem. Dramatists Guild, Authors League Am., Writers Guild. Home: 120 W 70th St Apt 3C New York NY 10023 Office: Dept Humanities Mass Inst Tech Cambridge MA 02139

GURNEY, CHARLES EDWIN, III, naval officer; b. Chester, Pa., May 30, 1930; s. Marshall Barton and Mary Graham (Smith) G.; m. Ann Lowrey Malstrom, June 10, 1952; children—Laurie, Karen, Craig, Thomas. B.S., U.S. Naval Acad., 1952; M.A. in Polit. Sci, Stanford U., k1964. Commd. ensign U.S. Navy, 1952, advanced through grades to rear adm., 1978; comdg. officer (U.S.S. Hooper (FF 1026), 1965-66, 1969-71, 1972-73, duty in, 1975-78, comdg. officer, 1973-75, mem. staff Comdr. in Chief, 1971-72, dep. comdr., Ft. Sheridan, Ill., 1978-79, comdr., Gt. Lakes, Ill., 1979-81, comdr. Middle East Force, U.S. Navy rep., Persian Gulf, 1981—. Decorated Def. Superior Service medal, Bronze Star, Meritorious Service medal. Episcopalian. Office: Comdr Middle East Force FPO New York NY 09501

GURNEY, DANIEL SEXTON, race car manufacturing company executive, racing team executive; b. L.I., Apr. 13, 1931; s. John R. and Roma (Sexton) G.; m. Evi B., July 7, 1970; children: Justin B., Alexander R.; children by previous marriage: John, Lyndee, Danny, Jimmy. Grad., Menlo Jr. Coll., 1951. Profl. race car driver, 1955-70; pres., owner All Am. Racers, Inc. (doing bus. as); Dan Gurney Eagle Racing Cars, U.S.A., Santa Ana, Calif., 1964—; mgr. Eagle Racing Team (Indpls. 500 winners 1968, 75, U.S. Auto Club Nat. Championship winners 1968, 74), Formula A Championship winners 1968, 69); sports commentator CBS Sports; mem. Automobile Competition Com. for U.S.A. Served with U.S. Army, 1952-54; Korea. Recipient numerous racing awards. Mem. Screen Actors Guild, AFTRA, U.S. Auto Club, Sports Car Club Am., U.S. C. of C., Championship Auto Racing Teams, Inc., Soc. Automotive Engrs., Fedn. Internationale de L'Automobile, Internat. Motor Sports Assn. Clubs: Balboa Bay, Eagle. Office: All-Am Racers Inc 2334 S Broadway Santa Ana CA 92707

GURNEY, EDWARD JOHN, lawyer, former U.S. senator; b. Portland, Maine, Jan. 12, 1914; s. Edward J. and Nellie (Kennedy) G.; m. Leeds Dye, May 1979; children—Jill, Sarah. B.S., Colby Coll., 1935; LL.B., Harvard, 1938; LL.M., Duke, 1948. Bar: N.Y. bar 1939, Fla. bar 1949. Practiced law in, N.Y.C., 1938-41, Winter Park, Fla., 1948—; mem. 88th-90th congresses from 11th Dist. Fla., U.S. Senate from Fla., 1969-75; City commr., Winter Park, 1952-58, mayor, 1961-62. Served to lt. col. AUS, 1941-46; ETO. Decorated Silver Star medal, Purple Heart. Mem. Am., Fla., N.Y. bar assns. Home: 617 N Interlachen Ave Winter Park FL 32789

GURNEY, JAMES THOMAS, lawyer; b. Ripley, Miss., Jan. 24, 1901; s. James Andrew and Mary Jane (Shepherd) G.; m. Blanche Johnson, Mar. 5, 1925; 1 son, J. Thomas. A.B., Miss. Coll., 1919, LL.D., 1972; student, U. Chgo., 1919-20, Columbia U., 1919; LL.B., Cumberland U., Lebanon, Tenn., 1922, J.D., 1968; LL.D., Stetson U., 1970; D.H.L., U. Fla., 1978. Bar: Fla. 1922. Mem. faculty Miss. Woman's Coll., Hattiesburg, 1919-21; and since practiced in, Orlando; counsel Minute Maid Co. (div. Coca- Cola Co.); gen. counsel Orlando Utilities Commn., 1925—; dir. emeritus Beneficial Corp.; mem. Fla. Supreme Court com. for redrafting common law rules of procedure, 1945; mem. examining bd. Fla. Parole Commn., 1945; chmn. bd. control Fla. Insts. of Higher Learning, 1945-49, now bd. regents. Author: Life Insurance Law of Florida, 1934, Disability Claims Resort to Equity, 1940, World War II Construction of War clauses, 1946; Contbr. articles to Fla. Bar Jour. Trustee New Orleans Bapt. Theol. Sem., 1960-67; former bd. dirs. Children's Home Soc. of Fla.; mem. Fla. Council of 100. Recipient Cert. of Merit U. Fla., 1953; Distinguished Service award Stetson U., 1958; Distinguished Service citation New Orleans Bapt. Theol. Sem. and So. Bapt. Found., 1967; award Pres. Ind. Colls. Fla., 1970; Cert. of Appreciation Miss. Coll., 1984. Fellow Am. Bar Found., Am. Coll. Trial Lawyers; mem. ABA (com. on life ins. law, vice chmn. 1944-47, admissions 1944-48, ssn. and adv. spl. com. on pub. relations 1944-46, adminstrv. law 1945, chmn. Fla. membership com. on ins. sect. 1946-48), Fla. State Bar Assn. (pres. 1942-43), Orange County Bar Assn., Internat. Bar Assn., Am. Life Conv. (legal sect.), Assn. of Life Ins. Counsel (exec. com. 1946-48), Orange County Budget Commn. (chmn. 1935-42), Orlando Community Chest (gen. chmn.), C. of C. (pres. 1930, nat. council 1940-41, J. Thomas Gurney, Sr. ann. leadership award 1984), Internat. Platform Assn., Fla. Blue Key (hon.), Newcomen Soc., Alumni Assn. U. Fla. (hon.). Democrat. Baptist. Clubs: Lions (dist. gov. 35th dist. 1928), University, Orlando Country, Rotary (Orlando). Home: 1701 N Spring Lake Dr Orlando FL 32804 Office: 203 N Magnolia Ave The Gurney Bldg Orlando FL 32801

GURR, TED ROBERT, political science educator; b. Spokane, Wash., Feb. 21, 1936; s. Robert Lucas and Anne (Cook) G.; m. Erika Brigitte Klie, Feb. 20, 1960 (dec. May 1980); children: Lisa Anne, Andrea Mariel; m. Barbara Harff, Jan. 14, 1981. B.A. (Wilson Nat. fellow 1957), Reed Coll., 1957; postgrad., Woodrow Wilson Sch. Pub. and Internat. Affairs, Princeton, 1957-58; Ph.D., N.Y. U., 1965. Asst. editor, then asso. editor Am. Behavioral Scientist, 1961-64; asst. to dir. N.Y.U. office research services, N.Y.C., 1962-64; mem. faculty Princeton U., 1965-69, research asso., 1965-67, asst. prof. politics, 1967-69, asso. dir. workshop in comparative politics, 1966-69; asso. prof. polit. sci. Northwestern U., 1969-72, prof. polit. sci., 1972-74, Payson S. Wild prof. polit. sci., 1974—; chmn. dept., 1977-80; co-dir. hist. and comparative task force Nat. Commn. on Causes and Prevention of Violence, 1968-69; vis. fellow Inst. Criminology, Cambridge U., 1976. Author: (with A. de Grazia) American Welfare, 1961, Why Men Rebel, 1970, Politimetrics, 1972, (with C. Ruttenberg) Cross National Studies of Civil Violence, 1969, (with H.D. Graham) Violence in America: Historical and Comparative Perspectives, 1969, rev. edit., 1979, (with H. Eckstein) Patterns of Authority, 1975, Rogues, Rebels and Reformers, 1976, (with P. Grabosky and R.C. Hula) The Politics of Urban Crime and Conflict, 1977, Handbook of Political Conflict: Theory and Research, 1980; Editorial bd.: World Politics, 1970-73, Comparative Political Studies, 1968—; co-editor: Sage Professional Papers in Comparative Politics, 1969-73; editor: Comparative Political Studies, 1979-80. Recipient Woodrow Wilson Found. award for best book in polit. sci. Why Men Rebel, 1970; Ford Found. faculty fellow, 1970; Guggenheim fellow, 1972-73; German Marshall Fund sr. fellow, 1976; Fulbright sr. fellow, Australia, 1981. Fellow Internat. Soc. for Study Aggression.; mem. Am. Polit. Sci. Assn., Peace Sci. Soc., Internat. Studies Assn., Social Sci. History Assn., Phi Beta Kappa. Office: Scott Hall Northwestern U Evanston IL 60201

GURSEY, FEZA, physicist; b. Istanbul, Turkey, Apr. 7, 1921; s. Ahmet Reshid and Remziye (Hisar) G.; m. Suha Pamir, Oct. 9, 1952; 1 son, Yusuf S. B.S., Istanbul U., 1944; Ph.D., London U., 1950; Docent's Habilitation, Istanbul U., 1953, Ph.D. (hon.), 1981. Postdoctoral research fellow Cambridge (Eng.) U., 1950-51; docent in physics U. Istanbul, 1953-57; research asst. Brookhaven Nat. Lab., Upton, N.Y., 1957-58; mem. Inst. for Advanced Study, Princeton, N.J., 1958-60, 1963-64; prof. physics Middle East Tech. U., Ankara, Turkey, 1961-68, Yale U., New Haven, 1968-77, J.W. Gibbs prof. physics, 1977—; vis. prof. Columbia U., N.Y.C., 1960-61, Coll. de France, Paris, 1981. Contbr. articles to profl. jours. Served with Turkish Army, 1952-54. Recipient J.R. Oppenheimer prize U. Miami, 1977; A Cressy Morrison award in natural sci. N.Y. Acad. Sci., 1981. Mem. Am. Phys. Soc., Turkish Phys. Soc., Turkish Nat. Orgn. for Sci. and Tech. Research (mem. council 1964-68, Sci. prize 1969), Conn. Acad. Arts and Sci. Office: 217 Prospect St New Haven CT 06511

GURSKY, HERBERT, research exec., astrophysicist; b. Bronx, N.Y., May 27, 1930; s. Joseph Mayer and Sonia Pauline (Balen) G.; m. Flora Pauline Aronson, Sept. 13, 1958; children—David Meyer, Robert Aaron. B.S., U. Fla., 1951; M.S., Vanderbilt U., 1953; Ph.D., Princeton U., 1957. Staff scientist Am. Sci. and Engring. Inc., Cambridge, Mass., 1961-68; v.p., 1968-73; supr. astrophysics Smithsonian Astrophys. Obs., Cambridge, Mass., 1973-81; prof. astronomy Harvard U., Cambridge, 1974-81; asso. dir. Harvard/Smithsonian Center for Astrophysics, Cambridge, 1976-81; supt. space sci. div., chief sci. E.O. Hulburt Center for Space Research, Naval Research Lab., 1981—. Author: (with R. Ruffini) Neutron Stars, Black Holes and Super Nova, 1976, (with R. Giacoconi) X-Ray Astronomy, 1974; Contbr. numerous articles to profl. jours. Fellow Am. Phys. Soc., AAAS, Am. Astron. Soc. Home: 8340 Greensboro Dr Apt 812 McLean VA 22102 Office: Naval Research Lab Code 4100 Washington DC 20375

GURTIN, MORTON EDWARD, educator; b. Jersey City, Mar. 7, 1934; s. Saul Gurtin and Irene (Hoffman) Burns; children—Amy Lynn, William Robert. B.M.E., Rensselaer Poly. Inst., 1955; Ph.D., Brown U., 1961. Structures engr. Douglas Aircraft Co., 1955-56, Gen. Electric Co., 1956-59; research asso. Brown U., 1961-62, asst. prof., 1962-64, assoc. prof., 1964-66; prof. math. Carnegie Mellon U., 1966—; Sr. Fulbright-Hays fellow, Guggenheim fellow U. Pisa, Italy, 1974; lectr., Europe, South Am., Can., cons. to industry. Author: (with B.D. Coleman, I Herrera, and C. Truesdell) Wave Propagation in Dissipative Media, 1965, An Introduction to Continuum Mechanics, 1981; Assoc. editor: Archive for Rational Mechanics and Analysis, Jour. Elasticity; Contbr. articles to profl. jours., (with B.D. Coleman, I Herrera, and C. Truesdell) including Handbuch der Physik. Mem. Soc. Natural Philosophy, Am. Math. Soc., Sigma Xi. Office: Dept Math Carnegie-Mellon U Pittsburgh PA 15213

GURVITZ, MILTON SOLOMON, psychologist; b. Buffalo, Nov. 27, 1919; s. Isidor and Rebecca (Huravitz) G.; m. Sylvia Klein, June 20, 1948; children: Lynda Irene, Robert. B.S., SUNY, Buffalo, 1941; M.A., N.Y. U., 1948, Ph.D., 1950. Diplomate: Am. Bd. Profl. Psychology. Psychologist USPHS Hosp., Lewisburg, Pa., 1942-46, Center for Psychol. Services, N.Y.C., 1947-48; chief psychologist Hillside Hosp.-L.I. Jewish Med. Center, Glen Oaks, N.Y., 1949-55; clin. asso. prof. Adelphi U., Garden City, N.Y., 1950-55; cons. psychologist Jewish Community Services L.I., 1955-61; pvt. practice psychology, Great Neck, N.Y., 1950—; dir. Great Neck Consultation Center, 1960—; clin. prof. postdoctoral program in psychoanalysis Adelphi U., 1968—, chmn. child and adolescent faculty; cons. Conn. Commn. on Alcoholism, 1947-53. Author: Dynamics of Psychological Testing, 1950. Fellow Am. Psychol. Assn., Soc. Projective Techniques, mem., Nat. Psychol. Assn. for Psychoanalysis (sr.). Democrat. Jewish. Home and Office: 10 Vista Dr Great Neck Estates NY 11021

GURWITCH, ARNOLD ANDREW, assn. exec., lawyer; b. Hamburg, Germany, Jan. 29, 1925; came to U.S., 1946, naturalized, 1952; s. Max and Bertha I. (Schereschevsky) G.; m. Barbara A. Guthrie, July 21, 1961; children—Laurence Andrew, Sara Anne. Student in law, U. Basle, Switzerland, 1943-46; LL.B., Bklyn. Law Sch., 1955. Bar: N.Y. State bar 1955. Resident atty. Leeds Music Corp., N.Y.C., 1956-60; partner firm Rosen, Seton & Sarbin, N.Y.C., 1960-64; internat. rep. A.S.C.A.P., N.Y.C., 1964-74, head fgn. dept., 1974-78, fgn. mgr., 1978—. Editor: Guide to Jazz, 1956. Mem. Fed., N.Y. State bar assns., Copyright Soc. U.S.A., Am. Arbitration Assn. (nat. panel arbitrators). Home: 101 Hickory Grove Dr W Larchmont NY 10538 Office: 1 Lincoln Plaza New York City NY 10023

GURY, JEREMY, writer, advertising executive; b. N.Y.C., Mar. 2, 1913; s. Abraham and Rebecca (Silverman) G.; m. Louise Hutchison, Feb. 24, 1950; children: Michael Collister, Melissa Jeremie. M.A. with 1st honors, Columbia U., 1935. Contbg. editor The Spur, N.Y.C.; mng. editor Stage Mag., N.Y.C., 1936; sr. script writer We the People, 1937; copy chief Ferry Hanley Advt. Agy., N.Y.C., 1938-41; copy dir. Donahue & Coe, N.Y.C., 1941-47; sr. writer Ted Bates & Co., N.Y.C., 1948-53, creative supr., v.p., 1956-59, v.p., 1959—, creative dir., 1959-68, chmn. planning bd., 1965-67, dep. chmn. bd. dirs., creative services, 1968-71, creative cons., 1972—; creative dir. Benton & Bowles, N.Y.C., 1953-56; exec. dir. Quadrant Communications, Inc., 1973-75; creative cons. Mktg. Corp. Am., 1978-79; adv. bd. Software Technology Group, Inc. Author: (with Aldous Huxley) They Still Draw Pictures, (with Reginald Marsh) The Round and Round Horse, 1943; play The Hither and Thither of Danny Dither, 1956, (with Hilary Knight) The Wonderful World of Aunt Tuddy, 1958; Author, librettist: (with William Schuman) The Mighty Casey, 1953, 2d edit., 1983. Hon. trustee Inst. Internat. Edn.; creative dir. N.Y. Statue of Liberty Centennial Commn., 1983. Aide to surgeon gen. U.S. Army, 1941-44. Home: Orchard Hill Rd Katonah NY 10536

GUSBERG, SAUL BERNARD, physician, educator; b. Newark, Aug. 3, 1913; m. Dorothy Cushner, June 17, 1938; 1 son, Richard. Student, U. Mich., 1934; M.D., Harvard U., 1937; Sc.D, Columbia U., 1948. Research fellow Collis P. Huntington Hosp., Harvard; resident obstetrics, gynecology Sloane Hosp. for Women, Columbia-Presbyn. Med. Center, 1946; asst. attending obstetrician and gynecologist Sloane Hosp. for Women, Francis Delafield Hosp., Vanderbilt Clinic, 1946-53, asso. attending, 1954-62; asst. prof. clin. obstetrics and gynecology Coll. Phys. and Surg., Columbia, 1953, asso. prof., 1953-62, clin. prof., 1962-66; obstetrician and gynecologist-in-chief Mt. Sinai Hosp., N.Y.C.; prof., chmn. obstetrics and gynecology Mt. Sinai Sch. Medicine, City U. N.Y., 1965-80, disting. service prof., dir. emeritus, 1980—; mem. adv. com. div. cancer control Nat. Cancer Inst., 1976-79; Bd. dirs. N.Y. div. Am. Cancer Soc., chmn. adv. com. on research and therapy, 1962, pres.-elect N.Y. div., 1966, pres., 1967-70, nat. pres., 1979-80; now mem. nat. exec. com. Benjamin Franklin fellow Royal Soc. Arts. Editor-in-chief: Gynecologic Oncology; author, editor: Gynecologic Cancer, 5th edit; asso. editor: Obstetrics and Gynecology, 1963-67; editorial bd.: Obstetrics and Gynecological Survey, Cancer; now asso. editor.; Contbr. articles on pelvic surgery and cancer to profl. jours. Fellow Royal Belgian Soc. Obstetrics and Gynecology (hon.), N.Y. Acad. Sci., N.Y. Acad. Medicine (pres. 1975-76), A.C.S. (gov. 1975-80), Am. Gynecol. Soc., Am. Radium Soc. (v.p. 1968), Am. Coll. Obstetricians and Gynecologists (chmn. com. on malignant disease 1965-70), Am. Assn. Obstetricians and Gynecologists (council 1971-74, pres. 1978-79), Soc. Gynecologic Oncologists (pres. 1974), Royal Coll. Obstetricians and Gynecologists (London) (hon.), Venezuelan Gynecol. Soc. (hon.), Venezuelan Cancer Soc. (hon.), Ecuadorian Cancer Soc. (hon.); mem. Am. Profs. Obstetrics and Gynecology, Soc. Gynecol. Investigation, N.Y. Obstet. Soc. (pres. 1962-63), Am. Soc. Cytology (v.p. 1962), Soc. Pelvic Surgeons (pres. 1976), Fedn. Oncologic Socs. (pres. 1976), Central (hon.), S.W. (hon.), Am. Gynecology Club, N.W. Assn. Obstetricians and Gynecologists (hon. mem.), South Atlantic Assn. Obstetricians and Gynecologists (hon. mem.), Phi Beta Kappa, Sigma Xi. Clubs: Harvard (N.Y.C.); Ardsley Country. Research on gynec. cancer. Home: 257 Palisade Ave Dobbs Ferry NY 10522 Office: 1176 Fifth Ave New York City NY 10029

GUSEWELLE, CHARLES WESLEY, journalist; b. Kansas City, Kans., July 22, 1933; s. Hugh L. and Dorothy (Middleton) G.; m. Katie Jane Ingels, Apr. 17, 1966; children—Anne Elizabeth, Jennifer Sue. B.A. in English, Westminster Coll., 1955. Reporter Kansas City (Mo.) Star, 1955-66, editorial writer of fgn. affairs, 1966-76, fgn. editor, 1976-79, asso. editor, columnist, 1979—. Contbr. short stories to Brit., Am. lit. quars. Served to lt. AUS, 1956-58. Recipient Aga Khan prize for fiction, 1977. Home: 1245 Stratford Rd Kansas City MO 64113 Office: 1729 Grand Ave Kansas City MO 64108

GUSFIELD, JOSEPH ROBERT, sociologist, educator; b. Chgo., Sept. 6, 1923; s. Isidor Henry and Emma (Dauber) G.; m. Irma Geller, Sept. 14, 1946; children: Julia, Daniel, Ilene. B.Ph., U. Chgo., 1946, M.A., 1949, Ph.D. in Sociology, 1954. Instr. social sci. U. Chgo. Coll., 1949-51; asst. prof. sociology Hobart and William Smith Colls., 1951-55, U. Ill., Urbana, 1955-60, assoc. prof., 1960-64, prof., 1964-69, U. Calif., San Diego, 1969—; Fulbright lectr., India, 1962-63, 66, 81; cons. Nat. Inst. on Alcohol Abuse and Alcoholism, 1975—. Author: Symbolic Crusade, 1963, Protest, Reform and Revolt, 1970, Academic Values and Mass Education, 1970, Community, 1976, The Culture of Public Problems, 1981. Served with U.S. Army, 1943-46. Guggenheim fellow, 1973-74. Mem. Am. Sociol. Assn., Pacific Sociol. Assn. (pres. 1977-78), Asian Studies Assn. Office: Dept Sociology U Calif San Diego La Jolla CA 92037 *

GUSHMAN, JOHN LOUIS, corporation executive; b. Lima, Ohio, May 29 1912; s. Louis Alexis and Belle (Whitney) G.; m. Helen Louise Little, Sept. 11, 1937; children: Sally Gillespie, Susan Fetters, John Louis. B.A., Ohio State U., 1934, J.D., 1936; certificate of completion, Inst. Mgmt., Northwestern U., 1953. Bar: Ohio 1936. Practiced law with Williams, Eversman & Morgan, Toledo, 1936-47; with legal dept. and successively v.p., gen. mgr. internat. div. Owens-Ill., Inc., 1947-61; pres., chief operating officer, dir. Anchor Hocking Corp., 1961-67, pres., dir., chief exec. officer, 1967-71, chmn. bd., chief exec. officer, 1971-77, chmn. exec. com. of bd. dirs., 1977—; dir. Richman Bros. Co., Dana Corp., F.W. Woolworth Co. Former chmn. bd. trustees Ohio State U. Served as maj. USAAF, World War II. Mem. Order of Coif, Phi Beta Kappa, Phi Delta Theta. Presbyterian. Home: 925 Spyglass Ln Naples FL 33940 Office: Anchor Hocking Corp Lancaster OH 43130

GUSKIN, ALAN EDWARD, university chancellor; b. Bklyn., Mar. 22, 1937; s. David N. and Frances (Midler) G.; m. Judith Toby Greenstein, June 10, 1959; children: Sharon, Andrea. B.A. with honors, Bklyn. Coll., 1958; Ph.D., U. Mich., 1968. Peace Corps volunteer and instr. Chulalongkorn U., Thailand, 1961-64; dir. selection VISTA, 1964-65; dir. Fla. Migrant Farm Worker Program, 1965-66; asst. project dir. Inst. Social Research, U. Mich., 1966-68; asst. dir. Center Research on Utilization Sci. Knowledge, Inst. Social Research, 1968-69; lectr. dept. psychology and residental coll. U. Mich., 1968-71; dir. ednl. change team Sch. Edn., 1969-71; provost Clark U., Worcester, Mass., 1971-73, acting pres., 1973-74, prof. sociology and edn., 1973-75; prof. edn., chancellor U. Wis.-Parkside, Kenosha, 1975—; Bd. dirs. Am. Assn. State Colls. and Univs. Author: (with Samuel Guskin) A Social Psychology of Education, 1970; also numerous monographs, articles, reports; editor: New Directions in Teaching and Learning, The Administrator's Role in Effective Teaching, 1981. Mem. Soc. Psychol. Study Social Issues. Home: 4116 12th St Kenosha WI 53142 Office: U Wis-Parkside Kenosha WI 53141

GUSNARD, RAYMOND THOMAS, savings and loan executive; b. St. Louis, Nov. 19, 1926; s. Harry Raymond and Julia Elizabeth G.; m. Marilyn Rose Edison, May 22, 1977; children—Debra Ann, Gary Allyn. B.S., St. Louis U., 1949, M.B.A., 1952. C.P.A., Mo. Mgr., acct. Arthur Andersen & Co., St. Louis, 1954-60; v.p. fin. Gardner Advt. Co., St. Louis, N.Y.C., Brussels, Belgium, 1960-68, Edison Bros. Stores, Inc., St. Louis, 1968-75; exec. v.p. Roosevelt Fed. Savs. & Loan Assn., St. Louis, 1975-79, pres., 1979—, chief operating officer, 1975-82, chmn. bd., chief exec. officer, 1982—, vice chmn., dir., 1964—. Mem. fin. com. Greater St. Louis council Girl Scouts U.S.A.; trustee, mem. fin. com. Mo. Baptist Hosp. Served with USAF, 1952-54. Mem. Am. Inst. C.P.A.'s, Fin. Execs. Inst., Fin. Analysts Soc. Roman Catholic. Office: 900 Roosevelt Pkwy Chesterfield MO 63017

GUSSIN, ROBERT ZALMON, pharm. co. exec.; b. Pitts., Jan. 5, 1938; s. Carl and Yetta G. B.S. in Pharmacy, Duquesne U., 1959, M.S. in Pharmacology, 1961, Ph.D., U. Mich., 1965. Research fellow dept. pharmacology SUNY, 1965-67; research pharmacologist Lederle Labs., N.Y.C., 1967-69, group leader dept. cardiovascular renal pharmacology, 1969-73, dir. cardiovascular renal disease therapy sect., 1973-74; exec. dir. research McNeil Labs., Ft. Washington, Pa., 1974-78, v.p. research div., 1978, v.p. research and devel., 1978-79; v.p. sci. affairs Spring House, Pa., 1979—. Author: Introduction to Cardiovascular Pharmacology, 1976; mem. editorial bd.: New Drug Evaluations, Drug Devel; contbr.in field. Mem. Am. Soc. Pharmacology and Exptl. Therapeutics, Am. Soc. Nephrology, Am. Fedn. Clin. Research, AAAS, N.Y. Acad. Scis., Am. Heart Assn. Research, Pharmaco Therapy. Office: McNeil Pharmaceutical Spring House PA 19477

GUSSMAN, HERBERT, oil co. exec.; b. N.Y.C., Aug. 25, 1911; s. Samuel and Lottie (Simon) G.; m. Roseline Nadel, Apr. 14, 1935; children—Ellen J. Gussman Adelson, Barbara Gussman Heyman. A.B., Cornell U., 1933. With Res. Drilling Co., Tulsa, 1940—, chmn. bd., 1950—; chmn. exec. com. M.P.R.R. Co.; dir. exec. com. T.&P. Ry.; dir. 1st Nat. Bank and Trust Co., Tulsa; Miss. River Transmission Co., Mid-Am. Savs. & Loan Assn., Mo. Pacific Corp. Pres. Tulsa Philharmonic Soc.; trustee Philbrook Art Mus. Mem. Tulsa C. of C. (dir.), Phi Mu Alpha. Home: 4644 S Zunis Ave Tulsa OK 74105 Office: 1st Nat Bank Bldg Tulsa OK 74103

GUSSMAN, LAWRENCE, international business consultant; b. Irvington, N.J., Dec. 23, 1915; s. Samuel and Lottie (Simon) G; m. Catharine Raymond Moore, Dec. 31, 1939; children: William Raymond, Margaret Elaine, John Albert. B.A., Columbia, 1937, B.S., 1938, Chem. Engr., 1939. Chem. engr. Research Found., 1939-40; with Stein, Hall & Co., Inc. (and subsidiaries), N.Y.C., 1940-72, pres., dir., 1953-73, Eastern Maine Starch Co., Inc., 1955-73, Stein-Davies Co., 1952-73; chmn. bd. Stein, Hall So., Inc., 1958-73; dir. Partners Fund, Guardian Mut. Fund, Hindustan Gum & Chem. Co., India, Pakistan Gum & Chem. Co., Karachi. Mem. Columbia Engring. Sch. Council; also mem. adv. council Columbia Faculty of Engring. and Applied Sci.; bd. dirs., pres. Albert Schweitzer Fellowship; mem. Chief Execs. Forum. Decorated Knight of Malta; recipient Egleston medal Columbia Engring. Sch. Alumni Assn., 1970. Mem. Internat. Assn. for Work of Dr. Albert Schweitzer of Lambarene (pres.). Club: Quaker Ridge (Scarsdale, N.Y.). Home: 14 Cooper Rd Scarsdale NY 10583 Office: 1211 Ave of the Americas New York NY 10036

GUSSOW, ALAN, painter, sculptor; b. Bronx, N.Y., May 8, 1931; S. Don and Betty (Gussow) G.; m. Joan Dye, Oct. 21, 1956; children: Adam Stefan, Seth James. A.B., Middlebury Coll., 1952; postgrad., Cooper Union, 1953. Instr. in painting and drawing Parsons Sch. Design, N.Y.C., 1956-68; vis. artist and sr. lectr. U. Calif., Santa Cruz, 1975; adj. asso. prof. Pace U., Pleasantville, N.Y., 1977—; project dir. Artists-in-residence in Palisades Interstate Park, 1975-78. Contbr. articles on landscape beauty and preservation to various publs.; One-man shows include, Peridot Gallery, N.Y.C., 1962-72, Portland Mus. Art, Maine, 1971, Washburn Gallery, N.Y.C., 1973-80, group shows include, Joslyn Art Mus., Omaha, 1973, Sheldon Meml. Art Gallery, Lincoln, Nebr., Am. Acad. and Nat. Inst. Arts and Letters, N.Y.C., 1977; represented in permanent collections, Va. Mus., Richmond, Corcoran Gallery of Art, Washington, Sheldon Meml. Art Gallery, Lincoln. Del. to Democratic Nat. Conv., 1972; founding trustee Edward Hopper Landmark Preservation Found., Nyack, N.Y., 1971—, Artists for Environment Found., 1971; chmn. bd. Artists for Environment Found., 1971-74; trustee America the Beautiful Fund, 1970—, pres., 1979; trustee Friends of the Earth, v.p., 1976, pres. found., 1980—. Recipient Prix de Rome, 1953-55; Edward John Noble Found. grantee, 1974. Address: 121 New York Ave Congers NY 10920 *I believe we preach what we practice and not vice versa. My art is not a product but rather a by-product of my whole life—the things I do as well as the things I think.*

GUSSOW, DON, publisher, author; b. Pumpyan, Lithuania, Dec. 7, 1907; came to U.S., 1920, naturalized, 1923; s. Samuel (Simcke) and Anna (Chaia) Sonia (Luria) G.; m. Betty Gussow, Oct. 19, 1930; children: Alan, Mel, Paul. Student, CCNY, 1926-27, Maxwell Tng. Sch. Tchrs., Bklyn., 1927-28; tchr. tng. diploma, U. Vt., 1928-29; student, N.Y. U., 1929-31, B.A., 1977. Editor Butcher's Adv., N.Y.C., 1929-30, Confectionery-Ice Cream World, 1930-34, 39-44, Internat. Confectioner, 1935-39; founder, 1944; since chmn., editor-in-chief, chief exec. officer Magazines for Industry, Inc., N.Y.C.; v.p., editor Harcourt Brace Jovanovich, Inc., N.Y.C., 1982—; dir. Cowles Communications, Inc., 1966-70, Am. Bus. Press, 1968-71, 76—; pres. bus. and profl. mags. div. Cowles Communications, Inc., 1966-70. Author: Divorce Corporate Style, 1972, The New Merger Game, 1978, Chaia Sonia, A Family's Odyssey Russian Style, 1980, The New Business Journalism, 1983; also articles Chaia Sonia, A Family's Odyssey Russian Style; contbg. editor: Ency. Brit, 1939-63. Founder Am. Assn. Candy Technologists, 1948; created Kettle award of candy industry, 1946. Recipient Pub. Service award Nat. Confectioners Assn., 1971; Pres.'s award Am. Coll. Legal Medicine, 1974; Honor scroll Am. Bus. Press, 1979; Gallatin fellow N.Y. U., 1980; Disting. Pub. Service award Anti-Defamation League, 1983; Cert. of Distinction NYU, 1983. Clubs: N.Y. U., Overseas Press. Marco Polo (N.Y.C.). Home: 50 Sutton Pl S New York NY 10022 Office: 747 3d Ave New York NY 10017 *I don't believe in luck, but opportunity is something else. The key to success is to be aware of exceptional opportunities as they present themselves and act promptly and constructively.*

GUSSOW, MEL, drama critic, author; b. N.Y.C., Dec. 19, 1933; s. Don and Betty G.; m. Ann Meredith Beebe, Aug. 12, 1963; 1 son, Ethan. B.A., Middlebury (Vt.) Coll., 1955; M.S., Columbia U., 1956. Asso. editor Newsweek mag., N.Y.C., 1959-69; drama critic N.Y. Times, 1969—, also; Sta. WQXR (radio sta. of N.Y. Times); adj. asst. prof. cinema studies N.Y. U. Author: Don't Say Yes Until I Finish Talking: a Biography of Darryl F. Zanuck, 2d edit, 1980; Contbr. articles to nat. mags. Served with U.S. Army, 1956-58. Recipient George Jean Nathan award for dramatic criticism, 1977-78; Guggenheim fellow, 1979. Mem. N.Y. Drama Critics Circle, Am. Theater Critics Assn., Players Club. Office: care New York Times 229 W 43d St New York NY 10036

GUSSOW, ROY, sculptor, educator; b. Bklyn., Nov. 12, 1918; s. Abraham and Mildred (Jaffe) G.; m. Mary Maynard, Oct. 10, 1946; children: Olga, Mimi, Jill. Diploma ornamental horticulture, N.Y. State U., Farmingdale, 1938; B.A. in Product Design, Inst. Design, Chgo., 1948. Tchr. sculpture, design Bradley U., Peoria, Ill., 1948, Colorado Springs Fine Arts Center, 1949-51; asst. prof. to prof. Sch. Design, N.C. State Coll., 1951-62; adj. prof. sculpture Sch. Architecture, Pratt Inst., 1962-68, Sch. Art, Columbia U., N.Y.C., 1981—. Exhbns. include, Art Inst. Chgo., 1947-49, Joslyn Mus., Omaha, 1949-50, Pa. Acad., 1951-59, Detroit Inst. Art, 1959, Met. Mus., 1951, Whitney Mus., 1956, 62, 64, 66, 68, Kansas City Art Mus., 1950, Arts Club, Chgo., 1966, Colorado Springs Art Center, 1951, Grace Borgenicht Gallery, N.Y.C., 1964, 71, 73, 77, 80; represented in permanent collections, High Mus., Atlanta, N.C. State Art Mus., Ackland Mus., Chapel Hill, N.C., Bklyn. Mus., Whitney Mus., Mus. Modern Art, N.Y.C., Guggenheim Mus., N.Y.C., also pvt. collections, commns. include, Dept. Commerce, 1956, Lenoir Rhyne Coll., 1957, Coop. Savs. & Loan Assn., Wilmington, N.C., 1959, N.C. State Coll., 1961, Cal. Mus. Sci. and Industry, 1962, Phoenix Mut. Life Ins. Co., Hartford, Conn., 1963, Tulsa Civic Center, 1968, Xerox Corp., 1969, Creedmore State Hosp., Queens, N.Y., N.Y.C. Family Ct. Bldg., Manhattan, 1972, Heublein Corp., Farmington, Conn., 1975, Combustion Engring. Inc., Stamford, Conn., 1976, City of Reading, (Pa.), 1979; City of Harrisburg, (Pa.), 1983. Served with AUS, 1942-45; ETO. Recipient hon. mention Pa. Acad., 1958, N.C. Mus. Art, 1957, 61; purchase award N.C. Mus. Art, 1952, 61, Ford Found., 1960, 62. Mem. Sculptors Guild (pres. 1976-80, dir. 1967—), Artists Equity Assn. N.Y. (dir. 1977—, v.p. 1980—). Address: 4040 24th St Long Island City NY 11101 also care Grace Borgenicht Gallery 724 Fifth Ave New York NY 10019 *Equilibrium of tensions makes harmony... The forces creating this balance which is harmony are rhythmical. This is the essence of nature, of life. These are the elements with which I work. With the subject removed, the fundamentals are more clearly, more deeply viewed. The composition of such elements becomes a challenge to thinking and feeling. They provoke search, desire and hope—this is the creation of a civilization, and the measure of contentment comes from the degree to which these are experienced.*

GUSTAFSON, DALE RUDOLPH, life insurance company executive; b. Omaha, Mar. 25, 1924; s. Rudolph T. and Elizabeth S. G.; m. Jean Betty Shapland, May 31, 1946; children: James R., Kay V., John B. B.A., State U. Iowa, 1948, M.S., 1949. Actuarial trainee Ohio Nat. Life Ins. Co., Cin., 1949-51; with United Benefit Life Ins. Co., Omaha, 1951-65, v.p., chief actuary, 1962-65; actuary, v.p. adminstrn. Am. Council Life Ins., Chgo., 1965-73; v.p., actuary Northwestern Mut. Life Ins. Co., Milw., 1973-83, sr. v.p., 1983—. Author papers in field. Served with USAAF, 1942-45. Decorated Air medal. Fellow Soc. Actuaries (past v.p., dir.); mem. Am. Acad. Actuaries (dir., past pres.), Am. Risk and Ins. Assn. (past dir.). Republican. Presbyterian. Club: Racine (Wis.) Yacht. Home: 4907 W Parkview Dr Mequon WI 53092 Office: 720 E Wisconsin Ave Milwaukee WI 53202

GUSTAFSON, DWIGHT LEONARD, educator, university dean; b. Seattle, Apr. 20, 1930; s. Carl Leonard and Rachel Doris (Johnson) G.; m. Gwendolyn Anne Adams, May 28, 1952; children: Dianne, David, Donna, Gale. B.A., Bob Jones U., 1952, M.A., 1954; LL.D., Tenn. Temple Schs., 1960; D.Mus., Fla. State U., 1967. Grad. asst., depts. theory and voice, div. music Bob Jones U., 1952-54, acting dean sch. fine arts, 1954-56, dean, 1956—; condr. univ. orch. and univ. chorale U. Opera Assn. Composer: one-act opera The Hunted; also choral and instrumental works. Mem. Southeastern Composers League, Am. Choral Dirs. Assn. (state pres.), Mus. Edn. Nat. Conf., Pi Kappa Lambda. Address: Bob Jones U Greenville SC 29614

GUSTAFSON, JAMES ERIC, insurance corporation executive; b. Joliet, Ill., Oct. 21, 1946; s. G.R. and C.G. (Gnadinger) G.; m. Jeanne Duffy, Sept. 2, 1967. B.A., U. S.D., 1967. With Gen. Reinsurance Corp., Greenwich, Conn., 1969—, sr. v.p., 1982—. Office: Gen Reinsurance Corp 600 Steamboat Rd Greenwich CT 06830

GUSTAFSON, JAMES M., theology educator; b. Norway, Mich., Dec. 2, 1925; s. John O. and Edith (Moody) G.; m. Louise Roos, Sept. 3, 1947; children: Karl, Greta, John, Birgitta. B.S., Northwestern U., 1948; B.D., Chgo. Theol. Sem. and U. Chgo., 1951, D.D., 1980; Ph.D., Yale, 1955; D.H.L., Bloomfield Coll., 1972; D.L., Concordia Coll., 1983. Ordained to ministry United Ch. of Christ, 1951; pastor, Northford, Conn., 1951-54; asst. dir. Study Theol. Edn. in Am., 1954-55; mem. faculty Yale, 1955-72; Univ. prof. theol. ethics U. Chgo., 1972—. Author: (with H.R. Niebuhr and D.D. Williams) The Advancement of Theological Education, 1957, Treasure in Earthen Vessels: The Church as a Human Community, 1961, Christ and the Moral Life, 1968, The Church as Moral Decision Maker, 1970, Christian Ethics and the Community, 1971, Theology and Christian Ethics, 1974, Can Ethics Be Christian?, 1975, Protestant and Roman Catholic Ethics, 1978, Ethics from a Theocentric Perspective, Vol. 1, 1981. Served with AUS, 1944-46. Guggenheim fellow, 1959-60, 67-68. Mem. Am. Soc. Christian Ethics (pres. 1969), Am. Acad. Arts and Scis. Home: 5450 S Ridgewood Ct Chicago IL 60615

GUSTAFSON, JOHN ALFRED, biology educator; b. Boston, Mar. 31, 1925; s. Walter Alfred and Lilly Christine (Anderson) G.; m. Nancy Gay Johnson, June 30, 1951; children: Walter A., Laura E., Daniel D., Martha E., J. Olaf. A.B., Dartmouth, 1948; Ph.D., Cornell U., 1954. Asst. prof. biology State U. N.Y. Coll., Brockport, 1954-55, asst. prof. biology, Cortland, 1955-57, asso. prof. biology, 1957-63, prof. biology, 1963-81, chmn. dept. biol. scis., 1965-77; project dir. NSF Grant for Outdoor Sci. Edn., 1980-82; Participant NSF Inst., 1962; pres. Alliance for Environ. Edn., 1974; mem. Temporary State Commn. on Youth Edn. in Conservation, N.Y., 1969-73; owner, pub. Slingerland-Comstock Co., 1976—. Author: (with B.A. Hall) Laboratory Studies in Botany, 1960; Editor: Nature Study, Jour. Environ. Edn. and Interpretation, 1965-79, (with B.A. Hall) Alliance Exchange, 1975-76. Vice chmn. Planned Parenthood Cortland County, 1970; chmn. Town of Homer (N.Y.) Zoning Bd., 1959-69, Town of Homer Planning Bd., 1969-75; vice chmn. Eastern Susquehanna Water Resources Bd., 1969-76; pres. Highvista Nature Center, Inc., 1973—; chmn. Cortland County Environ. Mgmt. Council, 1980-82, Cortland County Anderson-Lucey campaign, 1980; Bd. dirs. N.Y. State Bapt. Found. for Campus Ministry. Served with USMCR, 1943-46, 51-53. Fellow AAAS (council 1968-73); mem. Am. Nature Study Soc. (pres. 1962-63, treas. 1964-75, 79—, Distinguished Service award 1969), Nature Conservancy (dir. and treas. central N.Y. chpt., chmn. N.Y. State bd. dirs. 1983—), Phi Delta Kappa. Republican. Baptist. Home: 5881 Cold Brook Rd Homer NY 13077 *As I think back over my life, I am impressed by the evidence that God, through my commitment to him, has given guidance and direction at those times when crucial decisions were made. So often what seemed at the time to be a relatively insignificant decision turned out to have been a key turning point. It is God's Spirit within me, and his love and concern, that gives meaning to what I do.*

GUSTAFSON, PHILIP FELIX, scientific laboratory executive; b. Ann Arbor, Mich., Apr. 2, 1924; s. Felix Gustav and Beulah Emily (Lewis) G.; m. Delores May Humecke, June 26, 1949; children: Bruce David, Cindy Dee. B.S., U. Mich., 1949; M.S., Ill. Inst. Tech., 1954, Ph.D., 1958. Research technician Argonne (Ill.) Nat. Lab., 1949-52, asst. physicist, 1952-59, asso. physicist, 1959-66; fallout specialist div. biology and medicine AEC, Washington, 1966-68; asso. dir. div. radiol. physics, 1968-71; sr. biophysicist Argonne Nat. Lab., 1970, mgr. environ. impact statement project, 1971-75, dir. environ. impact studies div., 1975-81, dir. environ. research div., 1983—; dir. Ill. Dept. Nuclear Safety, Springfield, 1981-83; mem. Ill. Com. Atomic Energy, 1971-76, vice chmn., 1976-81. Contbr. numerous articles on environ. radiation, fallout radioactivity, radio ecology, atmos. transport, environ. impact, and radioactive waste mgmt. to tech. jours. Served with U.S. Maritime Service, 1944-46. Recipient Glover award Dickinson Coll., Pa., 1971; recipient Cert. of Achievement U. Ghent, Belgium, 1979. Mem. AAAS, Am. Nuclear Soc. Republican. Presbyterian. Home: 413 Addison Rd Riverside IL 60546 Office: Argonne Nat Lab Argonne IL

GUSTAFSON, RALPH BARKER, poet, educator; b. Lime Ridge, Que., Can., Aug. 16, 1909; s. Carl Otto and Gertrude Ella (Barker) G.; m. Elisabeth Renninger, Oct. 4, 1958. B.A., M.A., Bishops U., 1930, D.C.L. (hon.), 1977; B.A., M.A., Oxford U., Eng., 1933; D.Litt. (hon.), Mt. Allison U., 1973. Music master Bishops Coll. Sch., 1930; master St. Alban's Boys Sch., Ont., 1934; with Brit. Info. Services, 1942-46; prof., univ. poet Bishop's U., Lennoxville, Que., 1963-79; music critic Canadian Broadcasting Corp., 1960—; Mem. various award juries Can. Council; rep. Can. poet to U.K., 1972, Can. poet to USSR, 1976, Can. poet to Washington, 1977, Can. poet to Italy, 1981, 82. Author: poetry The Golden Chalice, 1935, Alfred the Great, 1937, Epithalamium in Time of War, 1941, Lyrics Unromantic, 1942, Flight into Darkness, 1944, Rivers among Rocks, 1960, Rocky Mountain Poems, 1960, Sift in an Hourglass, 1966, Ixion's Wheel, 1969, Theme and Variations for Sounding Brass, 1972, Selected Poems, 1972, Fire on Stone, 1974, Corners in the Glass, 1977, Soviet Poems, 1978, Sequences, 1979, Gradations of Grandeur, 1982, Landscape with Rain, 1980, Manipulations on Greek Themes, 1983, Conflicts of Spring, 1981, The Moment is All: Selected Poems, 1944-83; short stories The Brazen Tower, 1975, The Vivid Air, 1980; Editor: Anthology of Canadian Poetry, 1942, A Little Anthology of Canadian Poetry, 1943, Canadian Accent, 1944, The Penguin Book of Canadian Verse, 1958, rev. edit., 1967, 75, 84. Recipient Arts award Can. Council, 1959, 71-72; Gov. Gen.'s award for poetry, 1974; A.J.M. Smith award Mich. State U., 1974; Queen's Silver Jubilee medal, 1978; Sr. fellow Can. Council, 1959-60. Mem. Keble Assn. Oxford (life), League Canadian Poets, Assn. Canadian U. Tchrs. English. Home: PO Box 172 North Hatley PQ J0B 2C0 Canada

GUSTAFSON, RICHARD CHARLES, rental and leasing co. exec.; b. Duluth, Minn., Nov. 23, 1942; s. Ernest Raymond and Ethel Florence G.; m. Judith Ann Voss, Aug. 20, 1966; children—David, Ann. B.S. in Acctg, U. Minn., 1964. C.P.A., Minn.; cert. internal auditor. Tax accountant Control Data Corp., Mpls., 1968-72; with Nat. Car Rental System, Inc., Mpls., 1972—, internal audit mgr., 1976-79, corp. v.p., treas., 1979—. Cubmaster local Cub Scouts, 1978-81; mem. council Community of Cross Lutheran Ch., 1979-81. Served as officer USNR, 1964-68. Mem. Inst. Mgmt. Accountants, Minn. Soc. C.P.A.'s. Home: 10009 Oxborough Rd Bloomington MN 55437 Office: 7700 France Ave S Minneapolis MN 55435

GUSTAFSON, WINTHROP ADOLPH, aeronautical and astronautical engineering educator; b. Moline, Ill., Oct. 14, 1928; s. Gustav A. and Katherine (Wenger) G.; m. Sarah Elizabeth Garner, Aug. 3, 1957; children: Charles Lee, Stanley Scott, John Winthrop, Richard Neil. B.S., U. Ill., 1950, M.S., 1954, Ph.D., 1956. Research scientist Lockheed Missiles & Space Co., Palo Alto, Calif., 1956-60; asso. prof. Sch. Aeros. and Astronautics, Purdue U., Lafayette, Ind., 1960-66, prof., 1966—, assoc. head sch., 1980—; vis. prof. U. Calif. at San Diego, 1968; research engr. Allison div. Gen. Motors Co., Indpls., summer 1962; mem. tech. staff Bell Telephone Labs., Whippany, N.J., summer 1966, NASA-Dryden Flight Research Center, summer 1976; cons. Goodyear Aerospace Corp., Akron, Ohio, 1964, Los Alamos Sci. Lab., 1977. Contbr. articles to profl. jours. Served to 1st lt. USAF, 1951-53. Mem. AIAA, Am. Soc. Engring. Edn., Sigma Xi. Home: 209 Lindberg Ave West Lafayette IN 47906 Office: Purdue U Lafayette IN 47907

GUSTAFSSON, BORJE KARL, veterinarian, educator; b. Varnamo, Sweden, Feb. 26, 1930; s. Albin Karl and Svea Gertrud (Andersson) G.; m. Gunilla A. Granzelius, July 11, 1958; children: Katarina, Charlotte, Lars. B.Vet. Sci., Royal Vet. Coll., Stockholm, 1953, D.V.M., 1960, Ph.D., 1966. Research assoc., instr., asst. prof. Royal Vet. Coll. Stockholm, 1960-67, tchr., researcher animal reproduction, head clinics dept. Ob-Gyn, 1967-75, acting prof., chmn. dept. Ob-Gyn, 1970-73; vis. prof. U. Minn. Coll. Agr., St. Paul, 1974; prof. theriogenology Coll. Vet. Medicine, 1976-78; dir. grad. edn. in theriogenology U. Minn., 1976-78; prof., head dept. vet. clin. medicine Coll. Vet. Medicine, U. Ill., Urbana-Champaign, 1978—. Contbr. numerous articles in field of animal reproduction to profl. jours. Served with Swedish Vet Corps, 1952-54. Lagerlof's fellow, 1974. Mem. Swedish Vet. Med. Assn., AVMA, Assn. Am. Vet. Med. Colls., Am. Assn. Vet. Clinicians, Soc. Study Reproduction, World Assn. Vet. Physiologists, Pharmacologists and Biochemists. Home: 2102 S Race St Urbana IL 61801 Office: 1008 W Hazelwood St Urbana IL 61801

GUSTAVE, HENRI *See* **FRANCO, JOHAN**

GUSTAVSON, CARL GUSTAV, educator; b. Vinton, Iowa, Aug. 3, 1915; s. Carl Linus and Edla (Gustafson) G.; m. Caryl Jennings, June 30, 1943; children: Carl, Eric, Martha. A.B., Augustana Coll., 1937; M.A., U. Ill., 1938; Ph.D. (Pres. White fellow 1938-40), Cornell U., 1942. Instr. Lake Forest Coll., 1942-43; asst. prof. Miami U., Oxford, Ohio, 1943-45; asst. to asso. prof. Ohio U., Athens, 1945-56, acting chmn. dept., 1955-56, prof. history, 1956-71, distinguished prof. history, 1971—, chmn. dept., 1961-65; vis. prof. summer Emory U., 1949, Cornell U., 1950, Wayne State U., 1955, U. Ill., 1961, U. Cin., 1964, Western Res. U., 1965, U. Ga., 1968, U. Pacific, 1969; Fulbright fellow U. Uppsala, Sweden, 1970. Author: A Preface to History, 1955, The Institutional Drive, 1966, Europe in the World Community Since 1939, 1970, The Mansion of History, 1976. Del. XI Internat. Congress Hist. Socs., Stockholm, 1960. Ford Found. Fellow, 1953-54; grantee Am. Philos. Soc., 1956, 64; recipient Baker Research award, 1965, Alumni outstanding achievement award Augustana Coll., 1972. Mem. Am. History Assn., Ohio Acad. History (pres. 1964-65, ann. award 1956, Disting. Service award 1978), French Hist.-Soc., Am.-

Scandinavian Found., Societe d'Histoire Moderne (Paris), Phi Beta Kappa, Phi Alpha Theta, Pi Gamma Mu, Lambda Chi Alpha. Episcopalian. Club: Swedish (Chgo.). Home: 14 Utah Pl Athens OH 45701 summer General Delivery Kenora ON Canada

GUSTAVSON, DEAN LEONARD, architect; b. Salt Lake City, June 27, 1924; s. Ernest L. and Leona (Hansen) G.; m. Barbara Knight, Apr. 28, 1944; children—Mark Steven, Lisa Ann, Clint Knight. Student, U. Utah, 1946-47; B.Arch., U. Calif-Berkeley, 1951. Individual practice architecture, Salt Lake City, 1953—; pres. Dean L. Gustavson Assos. (architects and planners), Salt Lake City, 1957—, Gustavson, Nelson and Panushka, Inc. (architects), 1976-82, Gustavson Group Inc. (design and constrn. mgrs.), 1978—; mng. architect U. Utah Med. Center Additions Project, 1975-82; pres. Nat. Council Archtl. Registration Bds., 1969-70; project mgr. U. Calif.-Berkeley Bioscis. Additions Complex, 1982—; co-chmn. Internat. Com. Archtl. Registration, 1970—; chmn. World Conf. on Edn. and Reciprocity of Architects, Amsterdam, Holland, 1971; Chmn. planning Salt Lake City's Second Century Plan, 1960-62. Served with USAAF, 1942-46. Fellow A.I.A. (pres. Utah chpt. 1959-60, chmn. chpt. task force on objectives and means 1974); mem. Salt Lake C. of C. (chmn. econ. devel. steering com.), U.S. C. of C., Am. Mgmt. Assn. Clubs: Ft. Douglas (Salt Lake City); Bloomington (Utah) Country. Dean L. Gustavson award established in his honor NCARB, 1974. Home: 5775 Highland Dr Salt Lake City UT 84121 Office: 630 E South Temple Salt Lake City UT 84102

GUSTE, WILLIAM JOSEPH, JR., lawyer, state ofcl.; b. New Orleans, May 26, 1922; s. William Joseph and Marie Louise (Alciatore) G.; m. Dorothy Schutten, Apr. 17, 1947; children: William Joseph III, Bernard Randolph, Marie Louise, Melanie Ann, Valerie Eve, Althea Marie, Elizabeth Therese, James Patrick, Anne Duchesne, John Jude (dec.). A.B., Loyola, New Orleans, 1942, LL.B., 1943, LL.D., 1974. Bar: La. bar 1943. Asso. firm Guste, Barnett & Redmann, 1943, 46-56, Guste, Barnett & Little, 1956-70, Guste, Barnett & Colomb, 1970-72; mem. La. Senate, 1968-72; atty. gen. State La., New Orleans, 1972—; Co-owner Antoine's Restaurant, New Orleans; chief counsel Housing Authority, New Orleans, 1957-71. Pres. New Orleans Cancer Assn., 1960-62; nat. pres. United Cancer Council, 1965-67; pres. Met. Crime Commn., 1956-57; Asso. Cath. Charities, 1960-62; chmn. Juvenile Ct. adv. com. Orleans Parish, 1961-63; Mem. City New Orleans Street Paving Study Com., 1965-66; Trustee Xavier U., 1967—, also chmn. bd. lay regents. Served with AUS, 1942-46; ETO. Named Outstanding Young Man City New Orleans, Nat. Jr. C. of C., 1951, comdr. Mil. and Hospitaller Order St. Lazarus of Jerusalem, 1978; recipient John F. Kennedy Leadership award Young Dems. La. State U., 1973; No. La. Polit. Action League award, 1975; Gautrelet award Springhill Coll., 1976; Housing Man of Yr. award Nat. Housing Conf., 1976; Nat. Penology award Am. Prison Ministry, 1979; Pelican award Ecology Center, 1980; Silver Torch award Anti-Defamation League; B'nai B'rith, 1980. Mem. Am. Assn. Small Bus. (dir.), Nat. Assn. Housing and Redevel. Ofcls. (dir.), Am. Judicature Soc., Legal Aid Bur., Am., La., New Orleans bar assns., St. Thomas More Cath. Lawyers Assn., Young Men's Bus. Club of Greater New Orleans (hon. life), Internat. House, Blue Key, Sigma Alpha Kappa, Phi Alpha Delta (hon.). Democrat. Roman Catholic. Clubs: Pickwick, Bienville. *

GUSTLIN, PHILIP RAYMOND, lawyer; b. Santa Ana, Calif., Sept. 25, 1934; s. Paul Raymond and Evelyn (Jumper) G.; m. Hansel C. Huss, 1958 (div.); children: Holly, Gretchen P., Caroline; m. Susan I. Sterne; children: Michelle, Stacey. B.S., U. Calif. at Los Angeles, 1957; J.D., U. So. Calif., 1963. Bar: Calif. bar 1964; C.P.A., Calif. Jr. auditor, sr. auditor Peat, Marwick, Mitchell & Co. (C.P.A.'s), 1957-59; with Electronic Specialty Co., 1959-68, asst. controller, controller, gen. counsel, gen. mgr., 1963-64, gen. mgr., 1964-66, asst. to pres., 1966-67; gen. mgr. Los Angeles Electronics, 1967-69; exec. v.p. Tasker Industries, 1969-71; with firm Gustlin, Gail & McCabe, Los Angeles, 1971-83, Gustlin, Golob and Bragin, 1983—; dir. Internat. Controls Corp. Served with AUS, 1957. Mem. Calif. Soc. C.P.A.s, Los Angeles, Beverly Hills bar assns., State Bar Calif., Am. Inst. C.P.A.s, Nat. Assn. Atty.-C.P.A.s, Sigma Nu. Clubs: Jonathan, Multnomah Athletic. Home: 13266 Ponderosa Dr Los Angeles CA 90049 Office: 11726 San Vicente Blvd #450 Los Angeles CA 90049

GUTCHÉ, GENE, composer; b. Berlin, Germany, July 3, 1907; came to U.S., 1925; s. Maxmillian and Flora (von Zerbst) G.; m. Marion Frances Buchan, Dec. 1, 1935. M.A., U. Minn., 1950, Ph.D., State U. Iowa, 1953. Guggenheim fellow, 1963-65. Contbr. articles to profl. jours.; World premieres include Piano Concerto Opus 24, Mpls. Summer Session, 1956, Third String Quartet Opus 12 No. 3, Arts Quartet, 1958, Holofernes Overture Opus 27 No. 1, Mpls. Symphony, 1959, Rondo Capriccioso Opus 21, N.Y. Chamber Orch., 1960, Concertino for Orch. Opus 28, Mpls. Summer Session, 1961, Fourth String Quartet Opus 29 No. 1, Fine Arts Quartet, 1962, Symphony IV Opus 30, Albuquerque Symphony, 1962, Timpani Concertante Opus 31, Oakland Symphony, 1962, Symphony V for Strings Opus 34, Chautauqua Festival, 1962, Bongo Divertimento Opus 35, St. Paul Chamber Orch., 1962, Raquel Opus 38, Tulsa Philharmonic, 1963, Genghis Khan Opus 37, Mpls. Symphony, 1963, Rites in Tenochtitlan Opus 39, St. Paul Chamber Orch., 1965, Gemini Opus 41, Mpls. Summer Session, 1966, Hsiang Fei Opus 40, Cin. Symphony, 1966, Rites in Tenochtitlan Opus 39 No. 1, New Orleans Symphony, 1967, Classic Concerto for Chamber Orch. Opus 44, St. Paul Chamber Orch., 1967, Aesop Fabler Suite Opus 43, Fargo-Moorhead Symphony, 1968, Epimetheus USA Opus 46, Detroit Symphony, 1969, Symphony VI, Opus 45, Detroit Symphony, 1971, Icarus, Opus 48, Nat. Symphony, 1976, Bi-Centurion, Opus 49, Rochester Philharmonic, 1976, Perseus & Andromeda XX, Opus 50, Cin. Symphony, 1977, Helios Kinetic, Opus 52, Fla. Philharmonic, 1978, Akhenaten, Opus 51, Milw. Symphony, 1980, Opus 51, No 2, St. Louis Symphony, 1983; works performed, U.S., Europe, also recs. (Recipient Minn. State Centennial prize 1958, Luria award 1959, prize Albuquerque Nat. Composition 1962, prize Oscar Espla Internat. Composition 1962, XVI Premio Citta di Trieste 1969, Louis Moreau Gottschalk Gold medal 1970, XIX Premio Citta di Trieste 1972), commns. include, St. Paul Philharmonic, 1962, St. Paul Arts and Scis., 1965, regents U. Minn., 1966, Fargo-Moorhead Symphony, 1967, St. Paul Chamber, Detroit Symphony, 1969, Nat. Symphony Orch., 1975, Rochester Philharmonic, 1976, Cin. Symphony Orch., 1977, Fla. Philharmonic, 1978, Fla. Philharmonic, Milw. Symphony, 1980 (nationwide broadcast of Akhenaten, Opus 51 by NPR/N/C radio 1980). NEA Bicentennial grantee, 1976, 77, 78; Ford Found. rec. grantee, 1976. Mem. Am. Fedn. Musicians, Am. Composers Alliance, Am. Music Center. Address: Regus Pub 10 Birchwood Ln White Bear Lake MN 55110 *I have always bent every effort to meet the public on common ground because music must involve a People. By that means only can it reflect what we are, what we do, and what culture, here in AMERICA, contributes to the World.*

GUTEK, GERALD LEE, educator; b. July 10, 1935; s. Albert Thomas and Irene Mildred (Novotney) G.; m. Patricia Ann Egan, June 12, 1965; children: Jennifer Ann, Laura Lee. B.A., U. Ill., 1957, M.A., 1959, Ph.D., 1964. Teaching asst. dept. history U. Ill., Urbana, 1959, div. gen. studies, 1961-62; instr., asst. prof., assoc. prof., prof., dean Sch. Edn.-Loyola U., Chgo., 1963—. Author: Education and Schooling: An Introduction, 1983, Basic Education: An Historical Perspective, 1981, Joseph Neef: The Americanization of Pestalozzianism, 1978. Bd. trustees Erikson Inst., Chgo., 1979—; mem. Bd. Edn. Cook County Sch. Dist. 102, 1978-81. Named Educator of Yr. Phi Delta Kappa, 1977, Grotelueschen Lectr. of Yr. Concordia Tchrs. Coll., 1979, Powell Meml. Lectr. U. Ill.-Chgo., 1982. Mem. Am. Ednl. Studies Assn. (bd. dirs. 1979-83), History of Edn. Soc., Midwest History of Edn. Soc. Roman Catholic. Office: Loyola U Chgo 820 N Michigan Ave Chicago IL 60611

GUTEKUNST, RICHARD RALPH, microbiology educator; b. Allentown, Pa., Jan. 20, 1926; s. George D. and Jennie L. (Alsop) G.; m. Anna Frances Fetterman, Dec. 27, 1946; children: Mary Jane Ellickson, Richard M., Jo Anne Loughery. B.S., Phila. Coll. Pharmacy and Sci., 1951; M.S., Cornell U., 1957, Ph.D., 1958. Commd. ensign U.S. Navy, advanced through grades to comdr., 1968; mem. faculty Hahnemann Med. Coll. and Hosp., Phila., 1968-80, prof. microbiology and immunology, 1974-80; dir. Clin. Micro Lab., 1968-75; dean Coll. Allied Health Professions, 1975-80, Coll. Health Related Professions; prof. dept. med. tech. and microbiology U. Fla., Gainesville, 1980—. Vice-pres. Lower Gwynedd (Pa.) Twp. Council, 1972-80; mem. council St. Peter's Luth. Ch., North Wales, Pa., 1972-77, pres., 1974-77. Recipient Lindback award, 1975; Faculty Achievement award Coll. Allied Health Professions, Hahnemann Med. Coll. and Hosp., Phila., 1980. Fellow Am. Acad. Microbiology; mem. Am. Soc. Allied Health Professions (pres.-elect 1981-82, pres. 1982-83), Assn. Practitioners Infection Control, Am. Soc. Microbiology, AAAS, Am. Public Health Assn., N.Y. Acad. Sci. Republican. Lutheran. Club: Masons. Home: 3705 NW 25th Ave Gainesville FL 32605 Office: Box J-185 JHMHC Gainesville FL 32610

GUTELIUS, JOHN ROBERT, surgeon, educator; b. Montreal, Que., Can., Jan. 18, 1929; s. Nelson Edward and Gertrude Regina (May) G.; m. Elizabeth Ann Timmins, July 23, 1955; children: Charles, Julie, Ann, John, Joan, Peter, Matthew, Kathryn. B.A., Loyola Coll., U. Montreal, 1950; M.D., McGill U., 1955, Dip. Surgery, 1961. Intern Royal Victoria Hosp., Montreal, 1955-56; resident McGill U. Teaching Hosp., Montreal, 1956-61; practice medicine, specializing in surgery, Kingston, Ont., 1973—; assoc. prof. surgery McGill U., 1965-69, assoc. dean, 1968-69; prof., head surgery dept. U. Sask., 1969-73, dean, 1970-73; head surgery dept. Queens U., Kingston, 1973-83; prof. Queen's U., Kingston, 1973—, co-chmn. div. vascular surgery, 1978—; hon. cons. Royal Victoria Hosp., Montreal.; Bd. dirs. U. Hosp., Saskatoon, South Sask. Hosp. Center, 1970-73. Markle Found. scholar, 1963-68; James IV Assn. traveller, 1973. Fellow Royal Coll. Physicians and Surgeons, A.C.S., Am. Coll. Chest Physicians, Royal Soc. Arts; mem. Assn. Canadian Med. Colls. (pres. 1973-74), Am. Surg. Assn., Can. Assn. Clin. Surgeons, Can. Soc. for Vascular Surgery, numerous others. Home: Rural Route 1 Kingston ON Canada K7L 4V1 Office: Kingston Gen Hosp Kingston ON Canada K7L 2V7

GUTERBOCK, HANS GUSTAV, educator; b. Berlin, Germany, May 27, 1908; U.S., 1949, naturalized, 1955; s. Bruno Gustav and Margarethe (Auer) G.; m. Frances Hellmann, Sept. 2, 1940; children—Walter Michael, Thomas Martin. Student, U. Berlin, 1926-27, U. Marburg, 1928-29; Ph.D., U. Leipzig, 1934, U. Uppsala, 1977. Asst. Berlin (Germany) Museum, 1933-35; prof. Hittitology U. Ankara, Turkey, 1936-48; guest lectr. U. Uppsala, Sweden, 1948-49; with Oriental Inst., U. Chgo., 1949—, prof. Hittitology, 1956—, Tiffany and Margaret Blake Distinguished Service prof., 1969-76, emeritus, 1976—. Author: Hittite text Kumarbi, 1946; Hittite seals Siegel aus Bogazkoy, 2 vols, 1942; also articles. Mem. German expdn., Boghazkoy, Turkey, 1933-35, U. Chgo. expdn., 1958, 59, 61, 64, 66, 68; pres. Am. Research Inst. in Turkey, 1968-77. Mem. Am. Oriental Soc., Am. Schs. Oriental Research, German Archaeol. Inst., Am. Acad. Arts and Scis., Am. Philos. Soc. Home: 5834 S Stony Island Ave Chicago IL 60637

GUTERMUTH, CLINTON RAYMOND, conservationist, naturalist; b. Fort Wayne, Ind., Aug. 16, 1900; s. Henry Christian and Alice Virtue (Zion) G.; m. Ila Bessie Horm, Mar. 4, 1922 (dec. Dec. 3, 1975); m. Marian Schutt Happer, Mar. 21, 1977. Student, U. Notre Dame, 1918-19; grad., Am. Inst. Banking, 1927, postgrad., 1927-28; D.Sc. (hon.), U. Idaho, 1972. Asst. cashier St. Joseph Valley Bank, Elkhart, Ind., 1922-34; dir. div. edn. Ind. Dept. Conservation, Indpls., 1934-40, dir. div. fish and game, 1940-42; Ind. rent dir. OPA, Indpls., 1942-45; exec. sec. Am. Wildlife Inst., Washington, 1945-46; v.p. Wildlife Mgmt. Inst., 1946-71; Chmn. Natural Resources Council Am., 1959-61, hon. mem., 1971; pres., dir. Wildfowl Found. Inc., 1956—; nat. adv. council Pub. Land Law Rev. Commn., 1964-70; Trustee, sec. N.Am. Wildlife Found., Inc., 1945-74; trustee, pres. Stronghold (Sugarloaf Mountain) Inc., 1947—; bd. dirs., pres. World Wildlife Fund, U.S., 1961-73, hon. pres., 1973—; internat. trustee, exec. com. World Wildlife Fund (Internat.), 1971-75; bd. dirs., pres. Nat. Inst. for Urban Wildlife, 1976—. Author: Official Lake Guide, 1938, Quips and Queries; page on natural history Outdoor Indiana, 1934-42; W.M.I. bi-weekly Outdoor New Bulletin, 1947-50; Co-author: The Fisherman's Encyclopedia, 1950, The Standard Book of Fishing, 1950; Numerous articles and, lectures on various phases of natural resource conservation. Program chmn. ann. N.Am. Wildlife and Natural Resources Conf., 1946-71. Recipient Leopold medal Wildlife Soc., 1957; Fishing Hall of Fame Sportsman's Club Am., 1958; Distinguished Service award Nat. Assn. Soil Conservation Dists., 1958; Meritorious service award Nat. Watershed Congress, 1963; Nat. Service award Keep Am. Beautiful, 1965; Nat. Conservation award Mich. United Conservation Clubs, 1967; Distinguished Service award Nat. Wildlife Fedn., 1969; Horace M. Albright medal Am. Scenic and Historic Preservation Soc., 1970; Order of Golden Ark Prince Netherlands, 1972; elected Hunting Hall of Fame, 1975; recipient Gold medal Camp Fire Club Am., 1977. Fellow AAAS; hon. mem. Am. Com. for Internat. Wildlife Protection; mem. Nat. Rifle Assn. (life mem.; dir. 1963—, pres. 1973-75, life mem. exec. council 1975—), African Safari (Conservation award 1977), Izaak Walton League Am. (life), Outdoor Writers Assn. Am., The Wildlife Soc. (hon. mem., trustee 1951—), Nat. Audubon Soc. (Audubon medal 1982), Wilderness Soc. (life), Am. Fisheries Soc., Internat. Assn. Game Fish and Conservation Commrs. (hon.), Am. Forestry Assn. (hon.), Am. Soc. Range Mgmt., Am. Inst. Biol. Scis., Conservation Edn. Assn., Nat. Parks Assn., Nature Conservancy, The 1001-Nature Trust, World Wildlife Fund, Polar Inst. N.Am., Soil Conservation Soc. Am. (hon.), Arctic Inst. N.Am., Safari Club Internat., Zool. Soc. (N.Y.). Clubs: Mason (32, K.T.), Cosmos, Nat. Press, University (Washington); Explorers, Boone and Crockett (hon. life); Camp Fire (N.Y.C.); Booneville (Ind.) Press (hon.); Elkhart (Ind.) Conservation (hon.); Miami (Fla.) Sailfish); Tanana Valley (Alaska) Sportsmen's (hon.); Outdoor Boating Am. (hon.). Home: 2111 Jefferson Davis Hwy Apt 605 S Arlington VA 22202 *A lifetime of long hours of hard work combined with a conscientious dedication to my natural resource goals for public betterment have overcome my many personal shortcomings.*

GUTFELD, NORMAN E., lawyer; b. Pitts., Dec. 8, 1911; s. Adolph and Fannie (Haupt) G.; m. Evelyn Kirtz, Aug. 9, 1938; children: Nancy Gutfeld Brown, Howard, Charles, Joan Gutfeld Miller, Rose, Steven. B.A., Case-Western Res. U., 1933, LL.B., 1935. Bar: Ohio 1935. Individual practice law, Cleve., 1935-43; atty. U.S. Regional War Labor Bd., Cleve., 1944; assoc. firm Benesch, Friedlander & Morris, Cleve., 1944-53; treas. Builders Structural Steel Corp., Cleve., 1953-59; partner Garber, Gutfeld & Jaffe, Cleve., 1959-73, Simon, Haiman, Gutfeld, Friedman and Jacobs, 1973-80; of counsel Hertz Kates Friedman & Kammer, Cleve., 1981—. Mem. Cleveland Heights-University Heights Bd. Edn., 1956-63, pres., 1958-59; treas. Bur. Jewish Edn. Cleve., 1974-79; trustee Cleve. Jewish Community Fedn., 1976-77. Mem. Bar Assn. Greater Cleve., Ohio State Bar Assn., Citizen's League Cleve. Club: Cleve. City. Home: 3189 Monmouth Rd Cleveland Heights OH 44118 Office: 1020 Leader Bldg Cleveland OH 44114

GUTFREUND, JOHN H., investment banker; b. N.Y.C., Sept. 14, 1929. B.A., Oberlin Coll., 1951. With Salomon Brothers, N.Y.C., 1953—, partner, 1963, exec. com., 1966, mng. partner, 1978—, chmn. bd., chief exec. officer, 1981—; co-chmn. Philbro-Salomon Inc., N.Y.C., 1981—, co-chief exec. officer, 1983—; dir. N.Y. Stock Exchange, 1981—. Trustee, exec. vice chmn. Montefiore Hosp. and Med. Center; treas., trustee Jewish Communal Fund; trustee Oberlin Coll., N.Y. Pub. Library.; chmn. Downtown-Lower Manhattan Assn., Inc. Served with U.S. Army, 1951-53. Mem. Securities Industry Assn. (dir.). Office: Salomon Brothers One New York Plaza New York NY 10004

GUTH, ALAN HARVEY, physicist; b. New Brunswick, N.J., Feb. 27, 1947; s. Hyman and Elaine (Cheiten) G.; m. Susan Tisch, Mar. 28, 1971; 1 son, Lawrence David. S.B. and S.M., MIT, 1969, Ph.D. in Physics, 1972. Instr. Princeton (N.J.) U., 1971-74; research assoc. Columbia U., N.Y.C., 1974-77, Cornell U., Ithaca, N.Y., 1977-79, Stanford Linear Accelerator Ctr., Calif., 1979-80; assoc. prof. Physics MIT, Cambridge, 1980—. Alfred P. Sloan fellow, 1981. Mem. Am. Phys. Soc. Office: Center Theoretical Physics MIT Cambridge MA 02139

GUTH, DONALD JOHN, retired corporation executive; b. Manning, Iowa, Mar. 24, 1916; s. T. R. and Laura (Guth) McCann; m. Josephine C. Lindsey, Mar. 16, 1934; 1 son, Donald D. Student, Capital City Comml. Coll., 1934, Am. Inst. Bus., 1935, Harvard, 1952. Clk. Mut. Benefit Life Ins. Co., Des Moines, 1934-35; accountant Ford Motor Co., Des Moines, 1935-42; comptroller, treas., chief financial officer Solar Aircraft Co., Des Moines, N.Y.C., San Diego, 1942-61; controller, chief accounting officer Collins Radio Co., Dallas, 1961-68; v.p. GF Industries, Inc., Dallas, 1969-71; v.p., dir. Gen. Earth Minerals Corp., Dallas, 1969-71; v.p., dir., sec., treas. Varo, Inc., Garland, Tex., 1971-80, vice chmn., dir., 1980-81; dir. Swift Ohio Corp., Kenton, 1970-71, Constrn. Products Corp., Miami, Fla., 1971-72, Varo-Semiconductor, Inc., Garland, 1971-81, Diagnostic Info., Inc., Sunnyvale, Calif., 1981-83. Pres. Taxpayers Assn., Des Moines and San Diego; mem. exec. com. bus. advisory com. U. Tex., Arlington. Served with Iowa State Guard, 1942-45. Recipient Remington Rand trophy as pres. Nat. Assn. Accountants, 1948. Mem. Fin. Execs. Inst. (nat. dir., past pres. Dallas and Ia. chpts., past nat. v.p.), Nat Assn. Accountants (past nat. v.p., mem. nat. exec. com., past pres. Des Moines chpt., council continuing ednl. policies 1965-68). Home: 117 Raleigh House Port Charlotte FL 33952 also 5301 Mathews Rd Middletown WI 53562

GUTH, JOHN ELIAS, JR., computer company executive, publisher; b. St. Louis, Jan. 16, 1929; s. John Elias and Helen Agnes (Yonkus) G.; m. Mary Jane Wolf, Sept. 15, 1951; children: James E., Patricia Ann. B.S. in Bus. Adminstrn, Washington U., St. Louis, 1950. With IBM Corp., Chgo., 1954—; now pres. Sci. Research Assos., subs. IBM; also dir.; dir. subs., also Nat. Blvd. Bank, Chgo., Nat. Standard Co., Niles, Mich.; Alderman, 2d Ward, City of Lake Forest, Ill., 1974-78. Mem. Mayor's Council on Econ. Devel., Chgo., 1974—; bd. dirs., v.p. devel. Open Land Project, Chgo., 1976-80. Mem. Chgo. Assn. Commerce and Industry. Presbyn. Club: Onwentsia. Home: 541 Douglas St Lake Forest IL 60045 Office: 155 N Wacker Dr Chicago IL 60611

GUTH, SHERMAN LEON, experimental psychologist, educator; b. N.Y.C., Dec. 9, 1932; s. Arthur and Caroline (Laub) G.; m. Diane Harper, Mar. 10, 1969; children (by previous marriage): Melissa, Victoria. B.S., Purdue U., 1959; M.A., U. Ill., 1961, Ph.D., 1963. Lectr. dept. psychology Ind. U., Bloomington, 1962-63, instr., 1963-64, asst. prof., 1964-67, asso. prof., 1967-70, prof., 1970—; dir. research and grad. devel. Sch. Optometry, 1980—, chmn. dept. visual scis., 1982—; vis. asso. prof. psychology Mich. State U., 1968-69; NIH spl. research fellow in psychology U. Calif., Berkeley, 1971-72; NSF program dir. for sensory physiology and perception, 1977-78. Served with U.S. Army, 1953-55. NIH research grantee, 1964-70, NSF research grantee, 1963—. Fellow Optical Soc. Am.; mem. Assn. for Research in Vision and Ophthalmology, Psychonomic Soc. Home: 3634 Longview St Bloomington IN 47401 Office: Dept Psychology or Sch Optometry Ind U Bloomington IN 47405

GUTHEIM, FREDERICK, writer, consultant; b. Cambridge, Mass., Mar. 3, 1908; s. August G. and Augusta (Meiser) G.; m. Mary Purdon, June 8, 1935; 1 son, Nicholas. A.B., U. Wis., 1931; postgrad., U. Chgo., 1933-35; D.Pub. Service, George Washington U., 1979. Mem. staff Brookings Instn., 1931-33; with fed. housing and planning agys., 1935-47; staff writer N.Y. Herald-Tribune, 1947-50; asst. exec. dir., A.I.A, 1950-53, pvt. practice as planning and hist. preservation cons., 1953—; chmn. internat. cons. Gutheim/Seelig/Erickson, 1971-81; staff dir. Joint Com. on Washington Met. Problems U.S. Congress, 1958-60; pres. Washington Center for Met. Studies, 1960-65, Sr. fellow, 1965-80; producer-dir. exhbns. Mus. Modern Art, 1939—, Nat. Gallery Art, 1956; vis. prof Williams Coll., 1969; disting. vis. prof. environ., studies Central Wash. U.,, 1970; adj. prof. Am. history and civilization, urban and regional planning George Washington U., 1971—, also research cons., dir. grad. program in historic preservation. Author: Houses for Family Living, 1948, (with Coleman Woodbury) Rethinking Urban Redevelopment, 1949, The Potomac, 1949, Housing as Environment, 1953, 100 Years of Architecture in America, 1957, Alvar Aalto, 1960, The Federal City, Plans and Realities, 1976, Worthy of the Nation, 1977; Editor: Frank Lloyd Wright On Architecture, 1941, In The Cause of Architecture, 1975; adv. editor for architecture and planning: Mag. of Art, 1935-40; asst. architecture editor: Federal Guide Series, 1936-37; corr. editor: Urbanistica, 1950-58, Progressive Architecture, 1954-59; Archtl. critic, Washington Post, 1960-62; contbg. editor, Chesapeake Country Life mag., 1983-84, Chesapeake Horizons, 1983, Potomac Reflections, 1984; Producer film: A Fatal Beauty, 1980. Commr. Upper Montgomery County (Md.) Planning Com., 1950-57; mem. Nat. Capital Regional Planning Council, 1952-57, Pres.'s Council on Pa. Ave, 1962-64, Pres.'s Task Force on Natural Beauty, 1964, U.S. Capitol Master Plan Group, 1976-82; chmn. Nat. Capital Transp. Agy. Bd., 1961-65; mem. Potomac Planning Task Force, Dept. Interior, 1965-67; chmn. Frederick Law Olmsted Sesquicentennial, 1972, Sugarloaf Regional Trails, Md., 1974—; cons. on environ., habitat confs. UN, 1965-78; mem. Montgomery County Historic Preservation Commn., 1979-81; adviser Nat. Assn. Olmsted Parks, 1980—. Served with AUS, 1943-45. Decorated Order of Lion, Finland; recipient Finlandia Found. award, 1964, Tapiola Medallion, 1974; Calvert prize Md. Hist. Trust, 1976; Guggenheim Found. fellow, 1965-66. Mem. Italian Town Planning Inst. (hon.), AIA (hon., Medallist 1978), Am. Inst. Cert. Planners, Internat. Fedn. for Housing and Planning (mem. council 1977—). Club: Cosmos (Washington). Home: 23720 Mt Ephraim Rd Dickerson MD 20842 Office: Am Studies Program George Washington U 2108 G St Washington DC 20052

GUTHEIM, ROBERT JULIUS, government official;; b. Washington, Dec. 30, 1911; s. August G. and Augusta (Meiser) G.; m. Bernice A.

Howard, June 19, 1937; children: George C., August W. B.S. in C.E, Harvard, 1933, M.B.A., 1935. Registered mech. and electrical engr. Travel in Europe, studying elec. cable mfg., 1935; mem. staff Gen. Cable Corp., 1935-39; asst. engr. system planning bur. Potomac Electric Power Co., Washington, 1939-43; civilian asst. to head guided missile and electronics program Bur. Ordnance, Dept. of Navy, 1946-55; mem. staff asst. sec. navy for material, 1956, staff spl. asst. to sec. def. for guided missiles, 1956- 57; staff dir. plans and coordination Office Dir. Guided Missiles, Office Sec. Def., 1957-59; chmn. spl. com. adequacy of range facilities Dept. Def., 1957-59; staff missiles Office Dir. Def. Research and Engring., 1959-60; mgmt. officer space scis. NASA, 1961-63, program planning officer space scis. and applications, 1963-73; lectr. on mgmt. problems, 1957—. Contbr. to: Ency. Brit. Served from lt. (j.g.) to lt. comdr. USNR, 1943-46; capt. USNR, 1962—; comdg. officer Naval Reserve Weapons Unit 664, 1963-64. D.C. Lutheran. Clubs: Kenwood Country (Bethesda, Md.); Harvard (Washington and N.Y.C.). Home: 5210 Goddard Rd Bethesda MD 20014

GUTHKE, KARL SIEGFRIED, foreign language educator; b. Lingen, Germany, Feb. 17, 1933; came to U.S., 1956, naturalized, 1973; s. Karl Hermann and Helene (Beekman) G.; m. Dagmar von Nostitz, Apr. 24, 1965; 1 son, Carl Ricklef. M.A., U. Tex., 1953; Dr.phil., U. Göttingen, Germany, 1956; M.A. (hon.), Harvard U., 1968. Mem. faculty U. Calif., Berkeley, 1956-65; prof. German lit. U. Calif. at Berkeley, 1962-65, U. Toronto, Ont., Can., 1965-68, Harvard U., 1968-78, Kuno Francke prof. German art and culture, 1978—; vis. prof. U. Colo., 1963, U. Mass., 1967. Author: Englische Vorromantik und deutscher Sturm und Drang, 1958, (with Hans M. Wolff) Das Leid im Werke Gerhart Hauptmanns, 1958, Geschichte und Poetik der deutschen Tragikomödie, 1961, Gerhart Hauptmann: Weltbild im Werk, 1961, rev. edit., 1980, Haller und die Literatur, 1962, Der Stand der Lessing-Forschung: Ein Bericht über die Literatur, 1932-1962, 1965, Modern Tragicomedy: An Investigation into the Nature of the Genre, 1966, Wege zur Literatur: Studien zur deutschen Dichtungs-und Geistesgeschichte, 1967, Hallers Literaturkritik, 1970, Die Mythologie der entgötterten Welt: Ein literarisches Thema von der Aufklärung bis zur Gegenwart, 1971, Das deutsche bürgerliche Trauerspiel, 1972,23d rev. edit., 1979, G.E. Lessing, 3d edit., 1979, Literarisches Leben im 18. Jahrhundert in Deutschland u. in der Schweiz, 1975, Das Abenteuer der Literatur, 1981, Haller im Halblicht, 1981, Der Mythes der Neuzeit, 1983, Erkundungen, 1983; transl.: Die moderne Tragikomödie: Theorie und Gestalt, 1968; Co-editor: (Hanser) Gotthold Ephraim Lessing, Werke, 1970-72, Joh. H. Füssli, Sämtliche Gedichte, 1973, Lessing Yearbook, Colloquia Germanica, Twentieth Century Literature. Guggenheim fellow, 1965; fellow Am. Council Learned Socs., 1972-73; Recipient Walter Channing Cabot prize, 1977; Nat. Endowment for Humanities fellow, 1979-80. Mem. Modern Lang. Assn., Lessing Soc. (past pres.), Lessing Akademie (senator), Acad. Lit. Studies. Home: Hillside Rd Lincoln MA 01773 Office: Boylston Hall Harvard Univ Cambridge MA 02138

GUTHMAN, EDWIN O., editor; b. Seattle, Aug. 11, 1919; s. Otto and Hilda (Leiser) G.; m. Jo Ann Cheim, July 6, 1947; children—Lester, Edwin, Gary, Diane. A.B., U. Wash., 1941. Reporter Seattle Star, 1946-47, Seattle Times, 1947-61; dir. pub. information Dept. Justice, 1961-64; press asst. Senator Robert Kennedy, 1965; nat. news editor Los Angeles Times, 1965-77; editor Phila. Inquirer, 1977—. Author: We Band of Brothers, 1971. Entered U.S. Army, 1941; commd. 2d lt., 1942; advanced to capt., 1945; served as reconnaissance officer, 339th inf. Regt., 85th Div.; ETO; disch., 1946. Recipient Purple Heart, Silver Star medal., Pulitzer prize for nat. reporting, 1949; Nieman fellow Harvard, 1950-51; Alumnus Summa Laude dignatus U. Wash., 1975. Office: Phila Inquirer Philadelphia PA 19101

GUTHMAN, JACK, lawyer; b. Cologne, Ger., Apr. 19, 1938; came to U.S., 1939, naturalized, 1945; s. Albert and Selma (Cahn) G.; m. Sandra Polk, Nov. 26, 1967. B.A., Northwestern U., 1960; LL.B., Yale U., 1963. Bar: Ill. bar 1963. Law clk. to dist. judge U.S. Dist. Ct. No. Ill., 1963-65; since practiced in, Chgo.; partner firm Sidley & Austin, 1970—. Chmn. City Chgo. Zoning Bd. Appeals, 1975—. Democrat. Jewish. Club: Standard (Chgo.). Home: 230 E Delaware Pl Chicago IL 60611 Office: 1 First Nat Plaza Chicago IL 60603

GUTHRIE, ALFRED BERTRAM, JR., author; b. Bedford, Ind., Jan. 13, 1901; s. Alfred Bertram and June (Thomas) G.; m. Harriet Larson, June 25, 1931 (dec.); children: Alfred Bertram III, Helen Larson; m. Carol B. Luthin, Apr. 3, 1969. Student, U. Wash., 1919-20; A.B., U. Mont., 1923, Litt.D., 1949; L.H.D., Ind. State U., 1975; Litt.D., Mont. State U., 1977. Reporter Lexington (Ky.) Leader, 1926-29, city editor, editorial writer, 1929-45, exec. editor, 1945-47; tchr. creative writing U. Ky., 1947-52. Author: The Big Sky, 1947, The Way West, 1949, These Thousand Hills, 1956, The Big It, 1960, The Blue Hen's Chick, 1965, Arfive, 1971; named to (Ky. Journalism Hall of Fame); Author: Wild Pitch, 1973; juvenile Once Upon a Pond, 1973; The Last Valley, 1975, The Genuine Article, 1977, No Second Wind, 1980, Fair Land, Fair Land, 1982; contbr. stories, articles to mags.; also author of screen plays. Recipient Pulitzer prize for distinguished fiction, 1950; Wrangler award Nat. Cowboy Hall of Fame, 1970; Distinguished Achievement award Western Lit. Assn., 1972; Golden Saddleman award Western Writers Am., 1978; Distinguished Contbn. award State of Ind., 1979; commemorative award Commonwealth of Ky., 1979; Mont. Gov.'s award for disting. achievement in arts, 1982; Nieman fellow Harvard, 1944-45. Home: The Barn Star Route Box 30 Choteau MT 59422

GUTHRIE, EUGENE HARDING, physician; b. Washington, Apr. 9, 1924; s. Marshall Crapon and Harriet Ellen (Harding) G.; m. Elizabeth Schultz, June 5, 1948; children—Stephen Harding, Linda Elizabeth, Michael Dustin, Matthew Chapin and Leslie Ann (twins), Melissa Ellen. Student, Haverford Coll., 1942, Duke, 1943, U. N.C., 1945-47; M.D., George Washington U., 1951; M.P.H., U. Mich., 1955. Intern USPHS Hosp., Balt., 1951-52, house officer, 1952-53; commd. USPHS, 1951, med. dir., 1959, chief sch. health and rural health activities, then chief program officer Bur. State Services, 1959-62, chief neurol. and sensory disease service br., div. chronic diseases, 1962, chief div., 1962-66, asst. surgeon gen. for operations, 1966, asso. surgeon gen., 1967-68; exec. dir. Md. Comprehensive Health Planning Agy., 1968-74; cons. in health systems planning and devel., 1974-77; asso. exec. dir. Am. Health Planning Assn., 1977-78; dep. state health officer, health officer Dorchester and Talbot Counties, Md., 1978—; clin. asso. prof. community medicine and internat. health Georgetown U. Sch. Medicine, 1968-71; asso. in pub. health adminstrn. Johns Hopkins U. Sch. Hygiene, 1969—; mem. Md. Planning and Adv. Council Developmental Disabilities Services and Facilities Constrn. Act, 1971-74; mem. regional adv. group metro. Washington Regional Med. program, 1973-76; regional adv. group Regional Med. Program Md., 1970-74; STaff dir. surgeon gen's adv. com. smoking and health, 1963-64. Asso. editor: Jour. Sch. Health, 1960-63. Mem. interdepartmental com. health sch. aged child HEW, 1957-59, com. agrl. migrants, 1957-59; alternate mem. interagy. adv. group Pres.' Council Youth Fitness, 1957-59; mem. working group Pres.' Com. Migratory Labor, 1957-59; cons. health and fitness Boy Scouts Am., 1958-59; mem. commd. officers awards bd. USPHS, 1963-64; mem. med. com. Pres.' Commn. Employment Handicapped, 1963-68; dir. Nat. Interagy. Council on Smoking and Health, 1964-68; mem. Adv. Council Emergency Med. Services Md. Dept. Health and Mental Hygiene, 1973-74; Mem. med. adv. com. ARC blood program, 1967-68; Bd. dirs. Hosp. Edn. and Research Found., 1970-72. Served with M.C. USCGR, 1942-45. Recipient Meritorious Service medal USPHS, 1964; named Asso. Press Man of Year in Science, 1964. Mem. Am. Acad. Comprehensive Health planning (chmn. bd. dirs. 1969-71), A.M.A., Am. Soc. Planning Officials, Am. Pub. Health Assn. (mem. program devel. bd. 1970-73), USPHS Commd. Officers Assn. (exec. com.), U.S.-Mexico Border Pub. Health Assn., Am. Sch. Health Assn., Smith-Reed-Russel Med. Soc., Armed Forces Relief and Benefit Assn. (dir. 1966-68), Am. Assn. for Comprehensive Health Planning (treas. 1971-72, dir. 1971-74), Assn. Mil. Surgeons, Am. Hosp. Assn. (mem. council on planning 1971-73), Chevy Chase Recreation Assn. (dir. 1964-69), Delta Omega, Phi Delta Theta, Nu Sigma Nu. Home: Route 1 Box 113 Teal Pt Rd Easton MD 21601

GUTHRIE, FRANK ALBERT, science educator; b. Madison, Ind., Feb. 16, 1927; s. Ned and Gladys (Glick) G.; m. Marcella Glee Farrar, June 12, 1955; children: Mark Alan, Bruce Bradford, Kent Andrew, Lee Farrar. A.B., Hanover Coll., 1950; M.S., Purdue U., 1952; Ph.D., Ind. U., 1962. Mem. faculty Rose-Hulman Inst. Tech., Terre-Haute, Ind., 1952—, asso. prof., 1962-67, prof. chemistry, 1967—, chmn. dept., 1969-72, chief health professions adviser, 1975—; Kettering vis. lectr. U. Ill., Urbana, 1961-62. Mem. exec. bd. Wabash Valley council Boy Scouts Am., 1971—, v.p. for scouting, 1976; selection chmn. Leadership Terre Haute, 1978-80. Served with AUS, 1945-46. Recipient Silver Beaver award Boy Scouts Am., 1980. Fellow Ind. Acad. Sci. (pres. 1970); mem. Am. Chem. Soc. (sec. 1973-77, editor directory 1965-77, chmn. div. analytical chemistry 1979-80, counselor Wabash Valley sect. 1980—), Coblentz Soc., Midwest Univs. Analytical Chemistry Conf., Nat. Assn. Advs. Health Professions, Hanover Coll. Alumni Assn. (pres. 1974, Alumni Achievement award 1977), Sigma Xi, Phi Lambda Upsilon, Phi Gamma Delta. Presbyterian. Club: Masons (32 deg.). Home: 19 S 21st St Terre Haute IN 47803

GUTHRIE, FRANK EDWIN, entomologist, educator; b. Louisville, Jan. 14, 1923; s. Blaine and Lera May (Waller) G.; m. Bernice Button, Dec. 26, 1947; children—Janet, Caroline. B.S., U. Ky., 1947; M.S., U. Ill., 1949, Ph.D., 1952. Asst. prof. entomology U. Fla., Quincy, 1952-54; asst. prof. entomology N.C. State U., Raleigh, 1954-59; asso. prof., 1959-62, prof., 1962—; asst. dean Grad. Sch., 1962-64, dir. research and tng. programs in pesticide toxicology, 1964—. Co-author: Concepts of Pest Management, 1970, Biochemical Toxicology, 1980, Environmental Toxicology, 1980; contbr. articles to profl. jours. Served with USMCR, 1943-46, 51-52. Mem. Entomol. Soc. Am., Am. Chem. Soc., Soc. Toxicology. Home: 823 Beaver Dam Rd Raleigh NC 27607 Office: Dept Entomology NC State U Raleigh NC 27695

GUTHRIE, FRANKLIN KIRNEY, wood products executive; b. Longview, Wash., Sept. 11, 1935; s. Leroy Roland and Eva Grace (Bowman) G.; m. Margery Ann Stockman, Sept. 8, 1956; children: Gary Franklin, Thomas Lowell, Gwendolyn Kristine. B.S. in Chem. Engring., Oreg. State U., 1958; M.S., Inst. Paper Chemistry, 1960, Ph.D., 1962. With Weyerhaeuser Co., 1962—, beginning as project engr., successively shift foreman, asst. supt., prodn. mgr., paperboard mill mgr., Springfield, Oreg., dir. fiber products research and devel., Tacoma, 1971-74, dir. wood products research and devel., 1974-82, dir. info. systems, 1982—; Bd. dirs. Jr. Achievement of Eugene-Springfield, Inc., 1967-71, pres., 1970-71; bd. dirs. McKenzie-Willamette Hosp., 1969-70. Mem. Indsl. Research Inst., TAPPI, Forest Products Research Soc., Springfield C. of C. (dir. 1971). Office: Weyerhaeuser Co Tacoma WA 98477

GUTHRIE, GEORGE RALPH, real estate development corporation executive; b. Phila., Mar. 12, 1928; s. George Ralph and Myrtle (Robertson) G.; m. Shirley B. Remmey; children: Mary Elizabeth, Brenda Ann. B.S. in Econs, U. Pa., 1948. With I-T-E Imperial Corp., Phila., 1948-70, controller, financial planner, 1960-68, treas., 1968-69, v.p. finance, 1969-70; pres. N. K. Winston Corp., N.Y.C., 1970-76; exec. v.p. Urban Investment and Devel. Co., Chgo., 1976-78, pres., 1978—, chmn., 1982—. Mem. Pres.'s Council Nat. Coll. Edn., Lutheran Social Services of Ill. Mem. Financial Execs. Inst., Am. Mgmt. Assn. (mem. finance planning council 1970-75), Urban Land Inst., Chgo. Assn. Commerce and Industry (bd. dirs.); mem. Soc. Indsl. Realtors, Nat. Assn. Indsl. and Office Parks, Nat. Realty Com. (bd. dirs.). Republican. Clubs: Glen View, Jupiter Hills, Carlton, Execs., Economics, Chicago. Home: 35 Linden Ave Wilmette IL 60091 Office: 845 N Michigan Ave Chicago IL 60611

GUTHRIE, HARVEY HENRY, JR., clergyman, seminary dean; b. Santa Paula, Calif., Oct. 31, 1924; s. Harvey Henry and Emma (Aubrey) G.; m. Doris Mignonette Peyton, Dec. 29, 1945; children: Lawrence Harvey, Lynn Frances, Stephen Temple, Andrew Simpson. B.A., Mo. Valley Coll., 1944; student, Union Theol. Sem., N.Y.C., 1944-45; S.T.B., Gen. Theol. Sem., N.Y.C., 1948, S.T.M., 1953, Th.D., 1958. Ordained to ministry Episcopal Ch., 1947; vicar St. Martha's Ch., White Plains, N.Y., 1947-50; fellow, instr. Gen. Theol. Sem., N.Y.C., 1950-58; mem. faculty Episcopal Div. Sch., Cambridge, Mass., 1958—, prof. O.T., 1964—, asso. dean, 1967-69, dean, 1969—; vis. lectr. Columbia U., 1955-56; vis. prof. Andover Newton Theol. Sch., 1966-67. Author: God and History in the Old Testament, 1960, Israel's Sacred Songs, 1966, Theology as Thanksgiving, 1981. Democrat. Home: 4 Berkeley St Cambridge MA 02138

GUTHRIE, HENRY BLANDY, lawyer; b. N.Y.C., June 6, 1902; s. HEnry Blandy and Ada (McMahan) G.; m. Elizabeth A. Guthrie, June 22, 1932. Grad., Hill Sch., 1920; A.B., Princeton U., 1924; J.D., Harvard U., 1927. Bar: N.Y. 1928. Asso. Shearman & Sterling, N.Y.C., 1927-41, mem. firm, 1941—; v.p., dir. Goelet Estate Co., 1950—, R.I. Corp., 1950—; dir. Doubleday & Co., 1963—. Chmn. bd. trustees Big Bros., 1948-55, sponsor, 1955—; v.p. Big Bros. Am., 1951-55; trustee St. Luke's Hosp. Center, 1952—, v.p., 1959-63, chmn. exec. com., 1963-66, pres., 1966-70, chmn., 1970-79; trustee Mt. Desert Island Hosp., 1962-71, Green-Wood Cemetery, 1962—; v.p. Green-Wood Cemetery, 1963-65, pres., 1965-75; bd. dirs. United Hosp. Fund N.Y. Decorated comdr. Order St. John. Mem. Am., N.Y. bar assns., Assn. Bar City N.Y., Phi Beta Kappa. Clubs: Racquet and Tennis, Downtown Association (N.Y.C.); Cap and Gown (Princeton, N.J.). Home: Rural Route 2 Box 173 Bedford NY 10506 Office: 53 Wall St New York NY 10005

GUTHRIE, JAMES WILLIAMS, educator; b. Chgo., Aug. 28, 1936; s. James Williams and Florence (Harvey) G.; m. Paula Humphreys Skene, Feb. 26, 1976; 1 son, James Kyle; children by previous marriage: Sarah Virginia, James Williams, Shanon Louise. B.A., Stanford U., 1958; M.A., 1960; Ph.D., 1968. High sch. tchr., Arcata, Calif., 1960-61, Palo Alto, Calif., 1961-64; asst. to dean Sch. Edn. Stanford U., 1965-66; spl. asst. to sec. Dept. HEW, Washington, 1966-67; prof. U. Calif., Berkeley, 1967-70; Alfred North Whitehead postdoctoral fellow Harvard U., 1970; dep. dir. N.Y. State Edn. Commn., 1971-72; edn. specialist U.S. Senate, Washington, 1972-73; prof. edn. U. Calif., Berkeley, 1973-80, chmn. dept. edn., 1981-83; cons. HEW, also N.Y., Fla., Calif., Alaska, Oreg., and Wash. state legislatures. Author: Schools and Inequality, 1970, New Models for American Education, 1971, State School Finance Alternatives, 1975, School Finance: Economics and Politics of Public Education, 1978, School Finance Policies and Practices, 1980. Mem. City of Berkeley Bd. Edn., 1975-82, pres., 1976-77; mem. Calif. Commn. on Tchr. Credentialing, 1982—; bd. dirs. Berkeley-Albany YMCA, 1977—, Alta Bates Hosp., 1981—. Recipient cert. of Merit Am. Public Adminstrn. Assn., 1976; U.S. Office of Edn. grantee, 1968-69; Ford Found. grantee, 1970-73; Hewlett Found. grantee, 1982—. Mem. Am. Ednl. Research Assn., Am. Assn. Sch. Adminstrs., Nat. Sch. Bd. Assn., Calif. Sch. Bd. Assn., Calif. Tchrs. Assn., Phi Delta Kappa. Episcopalian. Club: Rotary. Home: 52 Oakvale St Berkeley CA 94705 Office: Room 1501 Tolman Hall U Calif Berkeley CA 94720

GUTHRIE, JANET, racing driver; b. Iowa City, Iowa, Mar. 7, 1938; d. William Lain and Jean Ruth (Midkiff) G. B.S. in Physics, U. Mich., 1960. Comml. pilot and flight instr., 1958-61; research and devel. engr. Republic Aviation Corp., Farmingdale, N.Y., 1960-67; publs. engr. Sperry Systems, Sperry Corp., Great Neck, N.Y., 1968-73; racing driver Sports Car Club Am. and Internat. Motor Sports Assn., 1963—; profl. racing driver U.S. Auto Club and Nat. Assn. for Stock Car Racing, 1975—. Recipient Curtis Turner award Nat. Assn. for Stock Car Racing-Charlotte World 600, 1976; First in Class, Sebring 12-hour, 1970; North Atlantic Road Reacing champion, 1973; named to Women's Sports Hall of Fame, 1980. Mem. Madison Ave. Sports Car Driving and Chowder Soc. First woman to qualify for and race in Indpls. 500, 1977, finished 9th, 1978.

GUTHRIE, JOHN REILEY, retired army officer; b. Phillipsburg, N.J., Dec. 20, 1921; s. John Milton, Jr. and Claire (Reiley) G.; m. Rebecca Jane Jeffers, June 18, 1947; children: Rebecca Claire, Michael Reiley, John Jeffers, Peter Blair, Margaret, Kevin McCammon. Grad., Blair Acad., 1938; A.B. with honors, Princeton, 1942; grad., Command and Gen. Staff Coll., 1944, Nat. War Coll., 1961. Commd. 2d lt. U.S. Army, 1942, advanced through grades to gen., 1977; served in, Hawaii and, Japan, World War II, asst. to mil. attache, London, Eng., 1946-49, with, U.S., Japan and Korea, 1949-51, comdr., 1952-53, mem. staff and faculty, 1953-56, staff officer, 1956-58, mil. asst., asst. exec. officer to sec. of army, 1958-60, staff, 1961-64, comdr., chief of staff, asst. div. comdr., 1964-65; mem. Orgn. Joint Chiefs of Staff, 1965-66; dir. developments Dept. of Army, 1966-67; asst. div. comdr. (2d Inf. Div.), 1967-68, dir. research, devel. and engring., Washington, 1969-71, dep. comdr. for materiel acquisition, 1971-73, dep. chief staff, 1973-75; comdr. U.S. Army Japan and IX Corps, 1975-77, U.S. Army Materiel Devel. and Readiness Command, 1977-81. Decorated D.S.M. with 1 oak leaf cluster; Legion of Merit with 2 oak leaf clusters; Bronze Star medal with 2 oak leaf clusters; Joint Service Commendation medal; Army Commendation medal; recipient Disting. Service award Federally Employed Women, 1980; Eagle award Nat. Guard Bur., 1981. Mem. Assn. U.S. Army, Am. Def. Preparedness Assn., Soc. Logistics Engrs., Soc. Mil. Engrs., Res. Officers Assn. (Minuteman Hall of Fame award 1981). Presbyterian. Clubs: Princeton (Washington and N.Y.C.); Nassau (Princeton). Army staff action officer for devel. and launching of 1st U.S. artificial earth satellite, Explorer I (Jupiter C29), 1958. Home: 7420 Walton Ln Annandale VA 22003 office: association of us army 2425 wilson blvd arlington va 22211

GUTHRIE, MEARL RAYMOND, JR., educator; b. Eldorado, Kans., Oct. 4, 1922; s. Mearl Raymond and Pauline Marie (Benz) G.; m. Lolita Ann Thayer, July 21, 1946; children—Scott Raymond, Carla Ann. Student, U. Tulsa, 1941-43; B.S., Ball State U., 1948, M.A., 1949; Ph.D., U. Minn., 1953. Property accountant for constrn. firm, customer service rep. Pub. Service Co. of, Okla., 1940-43; grad. asst. Ball State U., 1948-49; teaching asst. U. Minn., 1949-50; mem. faculty U. Cin., 1950-54, Bowling Green (Ohio) State U., 1954—, chmn. dept. bus. edn., 1957—; chmn. div. bus. adminstrn. Coll. of V.I., 1965-66; producer film strips on gen. and bus. math. Ednl. Devel. Labs., 1961. Author: Workbook for Briefhand, 1958, Alphabetic Indexing, 4th edit, 1981; Co-author: Today's Business Mathematics, 1967, Business Mathematics for the Consumer, 1975, 3d edit., 1983; Contbr. articles to ednl. periodicals. Chmn. fund dr. Boy Scouts, Bowling Green. Served with AUS, 1943-46. Named Outstanding Bus. Educator in Ohio, 1973. Mem. Ohio Archaeol. Soc., Black Swamp Archaeol. Assn. (pres.), Nat. Assn. Bus. Tchr. Edn. (pres. 1975-77, mem. exec. bd.), Nat. Bus. Edn. Assn. (treas., nat. council, state membership chmn., dir. nat. student membership), Ohio Bus. Tchrs. Assn. (pres.), Am. Mgmt. Soc. (chpt. pres. 1975-76, Diamond Merit award 1979), Asso. Orgns. for Tchr. Edn. (chmn. 1978), Am. Assn. Colls. for Tchr. Edn. (dir. 1977-79), Consumer Econ. Assn. Ohio (governing bd. 1980—), Delta Pi Epsilon (chpt. pres.), Pi Omega Pi, nat. organizer, nat. v.p., nat. pres., Beta Gamma Sigma, Sigma Zeta, Kappa Delta Pi, Phi Kappa Phi, Sigma Phi Epsilon. Presbyterian (elder; chmn. Christian edn. com.; trustee). Home: 123 N Grove St Bowling Green OH 43402 *If you do anything, you will be criticized; if you do not do anything, you will be criticized; so you might as well do something.*

GUTHRIE, RANDOLPH HOBSON, lawyer; b. Richmond, Va., Nov. 5, 1905; s. Joseph Hobson and Thomasia Harris (Parkinson) G.; m. Mabel Edith Welton, Mar. 24, 1934; children: Randolph Hobson, Jo Carol, George Gordon. B.S., The Citadel, 1925, LL.D., 1976; LL.B. magna cum laude, Harvard U., 1931. Bar: N.Y. 1932. Since practiced in, N.Y.C.; sr. partner Mudge, Rose, Guthrie, Alexander and Ferdon; chmn. bd. Studebaker Corp., Studebaker-Worthington, Inc., 1963-71, chmn. exec. com., 1971-81; chmn. bd. UMC Industries, Inc., 1969-76, chmn. exec. com., 1976-81. Mem. ABA, N.Y. Bar Assn., Assn. Bar City N.Y. Episcopalian. Clubs: Knickerbocker, Harvard (N.Y.C.). Home: 43 S Beach Lagoon Road Sea Pines Plantation Hilton Head SC 29928 Office: 20 Broad St New York NY 10005

GUTHRIE, RICHARD ALAN, physician; b. Nov. 13, 1935; s. Merle Pruitt and Cleona Marie (Weaver) G.; m. Diana Fern Worthington, Aug. 18, 1957; children—Laura, Joyce, Tamara. A.A., Graceland Coll., 1955; M.D., U. Mo., 1960. Diplomate Am. Bd. Pediatrics. Intern U.S. Naval Hosp., Camp Pendleton, Calif., 1960-61, dir. dependent services, Sangley Point, Philippines, 1961-63; asst. instr., resident in pediatrics U. Mo., 1963-65, NIH fellow in endocrinology and metabolism, 1965-68, asst. prof., dir. newborn services, 1968-71, assoc. prof. pediatrics, 1971-73; prof., chmn. dept. pediatrics U. Kans. Med. Sch., Wichita, 1973-82; exec. dir. Kans. Regional Diabetes Center. Co-author: Nursing Management in Diabetes Mellitus; The Child with Diabetes; contbr. articles to profl. jours. Mem. health ministries bd. Reorganized Ch. Jesus Christ Latter-day Saints. Served with USN, 1960-63. Recipient grants NIH, 1968—; Outstanding Faculty award U. Kans., Wichita, 1976. Fellow Am. Acad. Pediatrics; mem. Am. Diabetes Assn. (dir. 1972-77), Kans. Diabetes Assn. (pres. 1974, chmn. bd. 1974-77), Sedgewick County med. socs., Soc. Med. Sch. Pediatric Dept. Chairmen, Soc. Pediatric Research, Lawson Wilkins Pediatric Endocrinology Soc., Midwest Soc. Pediatric Research, Alpha Omega Alpa, Lambda Delta Sigma, Sigma Xi. Home: 4967 Hillcrest St N Wichita KS 67220 Office: Kans Regional Diabetes Center 1122 N Topeka Wichita KS 67214

GUTHRIE, ROBERT VAL, psychologist; b. Chgo., Feb. 14, 1930; s. Paul Lawrence and Lerlene Yvette (Cartwright) G.; m. Elodia S. Guthrie, Sept. 15, 1952; children: Robert S., Paul L., Michael V., Ricardo A., Sheila E., Mario A. B.S., Fla. A&M U., 1955; M.A., U. Ky., 1960; Ph.D., U.S. Internat. U., 1970. Tchr. San Diego City Schs., 1960-63; instr. psychology San Diego Mesa Coll., 1963-68, chmn. dept., 1968-70; asso. prof. U. Pitts., 1971-73; sr. research psychologist Nat. Inst. Edn., Washington, 1973-74; asso. dir. organizational effectiveness and psychol. scis. Office of Naval Research, Arlington, Va., 1975; supervising research psychologist Naval Personnel, Research and Devel. Center, San Diego, 1975-82; pvt. practice psychology National City, Calif., 1982—; Adj. asso. prof. George Washington U., Washington, 1975; lectr. Georgetown U., 1975; adj. asso. prof. U. Pitts., San Diego State U., 1977. Author: Psychology in the World Today, 1968, 2d edit., 1971, Encounter, 1970, Black Perspectives, 1970, Man and Society, 1972, Psychology and Psychologists, 1975, Even the Rat Was White, 1976. Served with USAF, 1950-59; Korea. Mem. AAAS, Am., Western, Calif. psychol. assns., Fedn. Am. Scientists, Am. Acad. Polit. and Social Scis., Kappa Alpha Psi. Research on social psychol., organizational and personnel psychol. variables in small groups. Home: 4636 Baxter Ct San Diego CA 92117 Office: 502 S Euclid Ave National City CA 92050

GUTIERREZ, HORACIO TOMAS, concert pianist; b. Havana, Cuba, Aug. 28, 1948; came to U.S., 1961; s. Tomas A. and Josephine (Fernandez) G.; m. Patricia A. Asher, July 1, 1972. Diploma, Juilliard Sch. Music, 1970; student, Sergei Tarnowsky, Los Angeles. Debut (at age 11), Havana Symphony Orch., 1959; performed maj. recital halls with maj. symphony orchs. throughout world; appeared: Music Nights BBC-TV, London; PBS, U.S.; tours, U.S., Can., Europe, S. Am., Israel, USSR, recs., EMI; Angel, Liszt, Tschaikowsky, Schumann, Grieg. Recipient 2d prize Tschaikowsky Competition, 1970, Avery Fisher award for outstanding achievement in music, 1982. Office: care Columbus Artists Mgmt Inc 165 W 57th St New York NY 10019

GUTIERREZ, MAX, JR., lawyer; b. San Salvador, May 26, 1930; U.S., 1930, naturalized, 1959; s. Max J. and Elva (Sol) G.; m. Mary Juanita O'Hearn, Jan. 26, 1957; children—Michele M., Michael E., Paul F., William F., Laurelle M., Maxmillian J. A.B., U. Calif., Berkeley, 1953; J.D. cum laude, U. San Francisco, 1959; LL.M., Georgetown U., 1960. Bar: Calif. bar 1960. Asso. firm Brobeck, Phleger & Harrison, San Francisco, 1960-67, mem. firm, 1967—; lectr. U. San Francisco Sch. Law, 1963-72. Bd. dirs. Florence Crittenton Services. Served with AUS, 1953-55. Mem. Am. Bar Assn., San Francisco Bar Assn. (judiciary com. 1970—, chmn. 1972), State Bar Calif. (family law com. 1967-69, chmn. 1969, chmn. probate and trust law com. 1973), Am. Judicature Soc., Am. Bar Found., Am. Coll. Probate Counsel, Internat. Acad. Estate and Trust Law (pres. 1978-80), St. Thomas More Soc., Phi Delta Phi, Sigma Chi. Republican. Office: Spear St Tower One Market Plaza San Francisco CA 94105

GUTIERREZ, RAUL, advertising agency executive; b. Mexico City, Mex., Feb. 18, 1913; s. Raul Gutierrez Velasco and Ana (Escalante) de Gutierrez; m. Sylvia Wanless, June 12, 1958; children: Fabian, Juanmarco, Silvia. Student, Instituto Politecnico Nacional, Mex. Film producer Clasa Films Mundiales, Mexico City, 1945-50; mgr. ARS-UNA Publicistas, Mexico City, 1945-50; gen. mgr. Publicidad Interamericana, Mexico City, 1951-57; founder, owner Panamericana de Publicidad, Mexico City, from 1956; merged Ogilvy and Mather Internat., 1969; pres., chmn. bd. Panamericana Ogilvy & Mather, S.A., Mexico City, 1969—; founder Lineas Unidas del Norte; v.p. Instituto de Investigaciones Publicitarias, 1975, Consejo Nacional de la Publicidad, 1969-72; organizer, lectr. profl. seminars, confs. in field. Author writings in field. Negotiator Mexican Senate. Served to lt. Mexican Army, 1942-45. Named Unique Advertiser Life Mag., 1958; interviewed Life Mag., 1958. Mem. Asociacion Nacional de la Publicidad (pres. 1954-56, 1st award 1957, 2d award 1981), Asociacion Mexicana de Agencias de Publicidad (founder 1950, v.p., pres. 1969-72), Colegio de Publicistas (founder). Club: Club de Golf Chapu Hepec (pres.). Home: Palermo 20 Lomas Hipodromo Naucalpan de Juarez MexicoMexico 53900 Office: Panamericana Ogilvy and Mather SA Bohia de Santa Barbara 43 Col Veronica Anzures Mexico D V Mexico 11300

GUTKIND, PETER CLAUS WOLFGANG, educator; b. Berlin, Germany, Sept. 16, 1925; emigrated to U.S., 1947; s. Erwin A. and Margarete (Jaffe) G.; m. Alice E. Kellogg, Sept. 4, 1951; children: Katherine A., Laetitia S., Gabriele B., Christopher John. B.A. with honors in Anthropology, Earlham Coll., 1950; M.A., U. Chgo., 1952; Ph.D., U. Amsterdam, 1963. Research fellow East African Inst. Social Research, Makerere U. Coll., Kampala, Uganda, 1953-59; sr. staff tutor Univ. Coll., West Indies, Jamaica, 1959-60; research asso. Florence Heller Sch., Brandeis U., 1960-61; reader in sociology Inst. Social Studies, The Hague, 1961-63; prof. anthropology McGill U., 1963—. Author: (with A.W. Southall) Townsmen in the Making-Kampala and Its Suburbs, 1957, The Royal Capital of Buganda, 1963, (with D.G. Jongmans) Anthropologists in the Field, 1967, Urban Anthropology: Perspectives on Third World Urbanization and Urbanism, 1974; editor: (with I. Wallerstein) The Political Economy of Contemporary Africa, 1976, (with P. Waterman) African Social Studies, 1977, (with R. Cohen and J. Copans) African Labor History, 1978, (with R. Cohen and P. Brazier) The Struggle of Third World Workers, 1979; sr. series editor Sage Publs. Series on African Modernization and Devel., 1975—. Can. Council grantee, 1966-67; Social Sci. Research Council grantee, 1966-67; Wenner-Gren Found. Anthrop. Research grantee, 1966-67; UN fellow, 1955-56. Fellow Royal Anthrop. Inst., Royal Africa Soc., African Studies Assn. U.S.A.; mem. African Studies Assn. U.K., Assn. Social Anthropologists of Commonwealth, Am. Anthrop. Assn. Home: 23 Winchester Ave Westmount PQ Canada Office: Dept Anthropology McGill U 855 Sherbrooke St W Montreal PQ H3A 2T7 Canada

GUTKNECHT, PAUL HERBERT, petroleum company executive; b. St. Louis, June 6, 1932; s. Clarence D. and Ella J. (Feddersen) G.; m. Mary Ellen Finegan, July 27, 1956; children—Beth E., Mark D., Barry F., Steven P. B.S. in Bus. Adminstrn, U. Denver, 1954, M.B.A., 1959. C.P.A., Colo. Various positions Colo. Oil & Gas Corp., Denver, 1956-65; controller Derby Refining Co., Wichita, Kans., 1965-70; v.p., treas. Total Petroleum, Alma, Mich., 1970-78, exec. v.p. fin., 1978—. Served with U.S. Army, 1954-56. Mem. Am. Inst. C.P.A.'s, Am. Petroleum Inst. Republican. Lutheran. Home: 11374 Quivas Way Westminster CO 80234 Office: Total Petroleum NAm Ltd One Denver Pl Denver CO 80202

GUTMAN, DAVID, chemistry educator, researcher; b. Valetta, Malta, Nov. 2, 1934; came to U.S., 1938; s. Herbert and Gertraud (Goldstein) G.; m. Robert A. Procker, May 15, 1965; children: Hiedi, Lorraine, Sarah. B.S., U. Calif.-Berkeley, 1960; Ph.D., U. Ill., 1965. Asst. prof. chemistry Ill. Inst. tech., Chgo., 1964-70, assoc. prof., 1970-75, prof., 1975—; program dir. NSF, Washington, 1976-77. Mem. Am. Chem. Soc., Am. Phys. Soc., Combustion Inst. Office: Ill Inst Tech 3300 S Federal St Chicago IL 60616

GUTMAN, EDWARD STUART, stockbroker; b. Bklyn., Feb. 9, 1943; s. Herman E. and Sylvia (Schiller) G.; m. Patricia Joyce Grossman, Dec. 4, 1966; children: Heidi Leigh, Robert Barry. Student, CCNY. Trader First Prudential Co., N.Y.C., 1966-69, Axelrod & Co., 1969-71, E.A. Viner & Co., 1971, Merkin & Co., 1971-73; gen. ptnr. Bear Stearns & Co., N.Y.C., 1973—; mem. Am. Stock Exchange, 1975—, mem. exchange specialist steering com., 1979—. Trustee Birch Nathen Sch., 1982—. Served with U.S. Army, 1960-61. Office: 55 Water St New York NY 10041

GUTMAN, HERBERT GEORGE, historian; b. N.Y.C., Mar. 18, 1928; s. Joseph and Anna G.; m. Judith Mara Gutman, June 20, 1950; children: Marta Ruth, Nell Lisa. B.A., Queens Coll., N.Y.C., 1949; M.A. in History, Columbia U., 1950, Ph.D., U. Wis., 1959. Instr. Fairleigh Dickinson U., 1956-59, asst. prof. history, 1959-63; asso. prof. history SUNY, Buffalo, 1963-65, prof., 1965-66; prof. history U. Rochester, 1966-72, CCNY, 1972-77, Grad. Sch. and Univ. Center, CUNY, N.Y.C., 1977-81, Disting. prof. history, 1981—, dir. Am. Working Class History Project, 1981—; mem. MacArthur Found. United Negro Coll. Fund Disting. Scholars Program, 1983—; Disting. prof. Ctr. N.Am. Studies, Ecole des Hautes Etudes en Sciences Sociales, Paris, 1982-83. Author: The Black Family in Slavery and Freedom, 1976, Slavery and the Numbers Game, 1975, Work, Culture, and Society in Industrializing America, 1976; mem. editorial bd.: Labor History, 1960—, Social History, 1975—. Mem. Nat. Hist. Publs. and Records Commn., 1974-78; bd. dirs. N.Y. Council for Humanities, 1976-80. Ford Found. fellow, 1978-79; Rockefeller Found. fellow, 1977-79; NEH fellow, 1975-76; Social Sci. Research Council fellow, 1970-71; Center Advanced Study in Behavioral Scis. fellow, 1966-67; Davis Center Hist. Studies fellow, 1975-76. Mem. Orgn. Am. Historians (exec. bd. 1975-78), N.Y. State Labor Historians Assn. (pres. 1976-77), Am. Acad. Arts and Scis. Jewish. Home: 97 6th Ave Nyack NY 10960 Office: Grad Sch and Univ Center City U NY 33 W 42d St New York NY 10036

GUTMAN, ROBERT WILLIAM, eductional administrator, educator; b. N.Y.C., Sept. 11, 1925; s. Theodore and Elsie G. B.A., N.Y. U., 1945, M.A., 1948. Instr. New Sch. for Social Research, 1955-57; founder, lectr. Bayreuth Festival Master Classes, 1959-61; lectr. design history art and design div. Fashion Inst. Tech., SUNY, N.Y.C., 1957-66, asst. prof., 1966-71, asso. prof., 1971-76, prof., 1971—, dean div. art and design, 1974-79, dean grad. studies, 1979—; lectr. PBS Telecast of Bayreuth Festival, 1983. Author: Richard Wagner, The Man, His Mind, and His Music, 1968, German transl., 1970; editor: Volsunga Saga (transl. by William Morris), 1961. Biography juror Nat. Book Awards, 1973; Guggenheim fellow, 1979. Mem. Victorian Soc. Clubs: Nat. Arts, Princeton, Andiron, Lotos (N.Y.C.). Home: 37 W 12th St New York NY 10011 Office: Fashion Inst Tech 127 W 27th St New York NY 10011

GUTMANN, DAVID LEO, psychology educator; b. N.Y.C., Sept. 17, 1925; s. Isaac and Masha (Agronsky) G.; m. Jeanna Redfield, Aug. 18, 1951; children: Stephanie, Ethan. M.A., U. Chgo., 1956, Ph.D., 1958. Lectr. psychology Harvard U., 1960-62; prof. U. Mich., 1962-76, Northwestern U., 1976—, chief of psychology, 1976-81, dir. older adult program, 1978—; cons. Ill. State Psychiat. Inst., Chgo., 1979—, VA Lakeside Hosp., 1978—. Co-author: (with Bardwick, Douvan and Horner) Feminine Personality & Conflict, 1979. Mem. Am. Profs. for Peace in the Middle East, N.Y.C., 1968—, Com. for the Free World, N.Y.C., 1980-83. Served with U.S. Merchant Marine, 1943-46. Recipient Career Devel. award NIMH, 1964-74. Fellow Gerontol. Soc. Am., Sigma Xi. Democrat. Jewish. Office: Northwestern U. Med School 303 E Chicago Ave Chicago IL 60611

GUTMANN, JOHN, artist, photographer, educator; b. Breslau, Germany, May 28, 1905; s. Julius and Ida (Fleischhauer) G. B.A., State Acad. Arts and Crafts, Breslau, 1927; M.A., State Inst. Higher Edn., Berlin, 1928. Asst. prof. art San Francisco State Coll., 1938-49, asso. prof., 1949-55, prof., 1955-73, prof. emeritus, 1973—. One-man shows, Gurlitt Gallery, Berlin, 1932, Paul Elder Gallery, San Francisco, 1935, San Francisco Mus. Art, 1937, Delphic Studios, N.Y.C., Wayne State U., Detroit, 1938, one-man shows of photographs, M.H. deYoung Meml. Mus., San Francisco, 1938, 41, 47, Light Gallery, N.Y.C., 1974, San Francisco Mus. Art, 1976, Castelli Gallery, N.Y.C., 1979, 81, Fraenkel Gallery, San Francisco, 1980, photographs appearing in nat. and internat. mags.; represented in permanent collections, Mus. Modern Art, N.Y.C., San Francisco Mus. Modern Art, New Orleans Mus. Art, Boston Mus. Fine Arts, Calif. Palace of Legion of Honor, Crocker Art Gallery, Sacramento, Mills Coll., Amon Carter Mus., Ft. Worth, Houston Mus. Fine Arts, Oakland (Calif.) Mus. Art, Oakland (Calif.), Nat. Gallery, Canberra, Australia, others. Served with U.S. Army, 1942-45. Guggenheim fellow in photography, 1977. Mem. Coll. Art Assn. Am. Home: 1543 Cole San Francisco CA 94117 Office: SFSU 1600 Holloway San Francisco CA 94132

GUTMANN, LUDWIG, neurologist, educator; b. Frankfurt, Germany, U.S., 1938; s. Solomon and Rosa (Kahn) G.; m. Sandra Siegel, 1954; children: Joan, Laurie, Richard. A.B., Princeton U., 1955; M.D., Columbia U., 1959. Am. Bd. Psychiatry and Neurology. Med. intern U. Wis. Med. Center, Madison, 1959-60, resident in neurology, 1960-63; chief neurology services USAF Hosp., Scott AFB, Ill., 1963-65; neurol. cons. Alton (Ill.) State Hosp., 1963-65; neurophysiology fellow Mayo Clinic, Rochester, Minn., 1965-66; ast. prof. dept. neurology W. Va. U. Med. Ctr., Morgantown, 1966-69, assoc. prof. and acting chmn., 1969-70; prof., chmn. W. Va. U. Med., 1970—; asst. prof. dept. physiology and biophysics W. Va. U. Med. Ctr., 1968-69; asoc. W/Va. U. Med. Ctr., 1970-73; prof. W. Va. U. Med. Ctr., 1973—, dir. Electromyograph Lab., 1966—; cons. VA Hosp., Clarksburg, W. Va., 1967-75; mem. adv. bd. Myasthenia Gravis Found., 1968—; mem. med. test com. Nat. Bd. Med. Examiners, 1983—. Contbr. (articles to profl. publs.), (abstracts to profl. publs.). Mem. Am. Acad. Neurology, Am. Neurol. Assn., Am. Assn. Electromyography and Electrodiagnosis (bd. dirs. 1974-76), Assn. for Research in Nervous and Mental Diseases, Assn. Univ. Profs. of Neurology (sec.-treas 1980-83, pres. elect 1983), W. Va. State Med. Assn., Monongalia County Med. Soc., Sigma Xi. Home: Woodland Rd Morgantown WV 26505 Office: Dept Neurology WV Sch Medicine Morgantown WV 26506

GUTMANN, MAX, department store executive; b. Germany, 1922. Chmn. bd. Elder-Beerman Stores Corp., dept. store chain; co-founder subs. Bee-Gee Shoe Corp., 1953, now chmn. bd.; chmn. bd. subs. Spare Change, Margo's LaMode, women's splty. chain, El-Bee Chargit Corp., El-Bee Office Outfitters; dir. Bank One of Dayton, Dayco Corp., Frederick Atkins, Inc. Bd. dirs. Good Samaritan Hosp., Urban League, Jewish Fedn. of Greater Dayton; mem. area progress council Downtown Devel. Council; mem. bus. adv. council U. Dayton. Club: One Hundred. Home: 9556 Bridlewood Trail Spring Valley OH 45370 Office: 3155 El-Bee Rd Dayton OH 45439

GUTMANN, REINHART BRUNO, clergyman, social worker; b. Munich, Bavaria, Germany, May 1, 1916; came to U.S., 1942, naturalized, 1946; s. Franz and Berta G.; m. Vivian Carol Brunke, Oct. 7, 1944; children: Robin Peter Edward, Martin Francis. Student, History Honours Sch., Manchester U., Eng., 1936-38; M.A. in Social Scis, St. Andrews U., Scotland, 1939, Coll. of Resurrection, Eng., 1939-41; postgrad., Coll. Preachers, Washington, 1948, 52, U. Wis., summer, 1951, St. Augustine's Coll., Eng., 1964. Ordained deacon Ch. of Eng., 1941, ordained priest, 1942; curate St. Michael's Parish, Golders Green, London, 1941-42; rector St. Mark's Parish, Green Island, N.Y., 1944-45, St. Andrew's Parish, Milw., 1952-54; chaplain and mem. faculty Hoosac (N.Y.) Sch., 1943-45; founder, exec. dir. Neighborhood House and Episcopal City Mission, Milw., 1945-60; priest-in-charge St. Peter's Mission, North Lake, Wis., 1958-60; exec. dir. Friendship House, Washington, 1960-62; cons. Indian social welfare Exec. Council of Episcopal Ch., N.Y.C., 1962-64, exec. sec. div. community services, 1964-68, exec. for social welfare and field services, 1968-71; part-time priest-in-charge St. Thomas of Alexandria, Pittstown, N.J., 1968-75; hon. asst. priest St. Martin's Ch., Pawtucket, R.I., 1980; mgr. spl. projects Human Resources Adminstrn., N.Y.C., 1971-72, spl. asst. to asst. adminstr., 1972-73, dir. mgmt. office community services, 1973, spl. asst. to dep. adminstr. social services, 1973-75; nat. exec. dir. Foster Parents Plan, Inc., Warwick, R.I., 1975-82. Chmn. dept. Christian social relations Province of Midwest, Episcopal Ch., 1954-60; chmn. social edn. and action Nat. Fedn. Settlements, 1960-62; hon. canon All Saints Cathedral, Milw., 1971. Mem. Acad. Cert. Social Workers, Nat. Assn. Social Workers, Am. Public Welfare Assn. Democrat. *Personal success is not measured by wealth or public recognition. It is the knowledge that one has done everything possible to help people achieve dignity, security, and fulfillment; and in so doing has transmitted a sense of personal caring for the needs of others.*

GUTOWSKY, HERBERT SANDER, chemistry educator; b. Bridgman, Mich., Nov. 8, 1919; s. Otto and Hattie (Meyers) G.; m. Barbara Stuart, June 22, 1949 (div. Sept. 1981); children: Daniel Kurt (dec.), Robb Edward, Christopher Carl.; m. Virginia Warner, Aug. 1982. A.B., Ind. U., 1940, D.Sc. (hon.), 1983; M.S., U. Calif.-Berkeley, 1946; Ph.D., Harvard U., 1949. Mem. faculty U. Ill. at Urbana, 1948—, prof. chemistry, 1956—, head div. phys. chemistry, 1956-63, head dept. chemistry and chem. engring., 1967-70; dir. Sch. Chem. Scis., head dept. chemistry, 1970—; mem. chemistry panel NSF, 1963-66, chmn. panel, 1965-66, mem. adv. com. on planning, 1971-74; mem. Ill. Bd. Natural Resources and Conservation, 1973—; G.N. Lewis Meml. lectr., 1976, G.B. Kistiakowsky lectr., 1980. Mem. adv. bd. Petroleum Research Fund, 1959-61; mem. selection and scheduling com. Gordon Research Conf., 1959-64, 68-72, trustee, 1969-72, chmn. bd. trustees, 1971-72. Served to capt., chem. warfare service AUS, 1941-45. Recipient 1966 $5000 Irving Langmuir award Am. Chem. Soc.; Midwest award St. Louis sect., 1973; 1974 $1000 prize Internat. Soc. Magnetic Research; Peter Debye award in phys. chemistry Am. Chem. Soc., 1975; Nat. medal of Sci., 1977; Guggenheim fellow, 1954-55. Fellow Am. Phys. Soc. (chmn. div. chem. physics 1973-74), AAAS, Am. Acad. Arts and Scis., mem., Nat. Acad. Scis. (mem. com. sci. and pub. policy 1972-75, chmn. panel on atmospheric chemistry 1975-77, mem. com. impacts of stratospheric change 1975-77), Am. Chem. Soc. (chmn. div. phys. chemistry 1966-67, com. on profl. tng. 1969-77, chmn. 1974-77), AAUP, Phi Beta Kappa, Sigma Xi. Home: 202 W Delaware Ave Urbana IL 61801 Office: Noyes Lab 505 S Mathews St Urbana IL 61801

GUTSCH, WILLIAM ANTHONY, astronomer; b. Newark, Jan. 14, 1946; s. William Anthony and Mary (Ellenback) G.; m. Mary F. Gutsch, Aug. 16, 1969. B.S., St. Peter's Coll., 1967; M.S., U. Va., 1973, Ph.D., 1978. Staff astronomer Rochester Museum and Sci. Ctr., N.Y., 1973-82; chmn. Am. Mus.-Hayden Planetarium, N.Y.C., 1982—; cons. in field, lectr. in field; news columnist Rochester Times-Union, 1980—; sci. reporter Sta.-WOKR-TV, Rochester, N.Y., 1976-82; sci. corr. Sta.-WABC-TV, N.Y.C., 1982—; cons. U. Santiago, Chile, 1982. Author newspaper articles, TV news and plantarium scripts. Recipient award of service U. Santiago, 1982, City of Buenos Aires, 1983. Mem. Am. Astron. Soc., Am. Meterol. Soc., Am. Assn. Physics Tchrs., Internat. Planetarium Soc. Office: 81st St and Central Park W New York NY 10024

GUTSCHE, CARL DAVID, chemistry educator; b. LaGrange, Ill., Mar. 21, 1921; s. Frank Carl and Vera (Mutchler) G.; m. Alice Eugenia Carr, June 4, 1944; children: Clara Jean, Betha Lynn, Christopher Glenn. B.A., Oberlin Coll., 1943; Ph.D., U. Wis., 1947. With U.S. Dept. Agr. Office Sci. Devel., 1943-44; instr. chemistry Washington U., St. Louis, 1947-48, asst. prof., 1948-51, asso. prof., 1951-59, prof., 1959—, chmn. dept., 1970-76; cons. to industry; chmn. medicinal chemistry study sect. NIH, 1978-81; Bd. dirs. St. Louis Conservatory and Schs. for Arts, 1978-82. Author: The Chemistry of Carbonyl Compounds, 1967, Carbocyclic Ring Expansion Reactions, 1968, Fundamentals of Organic Chemistry, 1975; mem. adv. bd.: Jour. Organic Chemistry, 1979—; mem. editorial bd.: Organic Preparations and Procedures Internat., 1968—; contbr. articles profl. jours. Guggenheim fellow, 1981. Mem. Am. Chem. Soc. (chmn. St. Louis sect. 1959, dir), Chem. Soc. (London), AAUP, Phi Beta Kappa, Sigma Xi. Home: 6933 Kingsbury Blvd University City MO 63130 Office: Washington Univ Saint Louis MO 63130

GUTTAY, ANDREW JOHN ROBERT, agronomy educator, researcher; b. Los Angeles, May 12, 1924; s. Andrew and Helmi M. (Nurmi) G.; m. Maisie S. Kahkonen, Sept. 10, 1948; children: Nancy G., Dorothy E., Kathy L., David A. B.S., Mich. State U., 1948, Ph.D., 1959; M.S., Iowa State U., 1950. Cert. profl. agronomist; cert. profl. soil scientist. Land use specialist Mich. Dept. Conservation, 1950-51; instr. Mich. State U., 1951-58; dist. agronomist Nat. Plant Food Inst., Chgo., 1958-61; prof. agronomy U. Conn., Storrs, 1961—, head dept. plant sci., 1961-74; Chmn. Conn. Adv. Com. Standards for Agrl. Chems., 1962—; Conn. Commn. Pesticides, 1963, Natural Area Preserves Adv. Com., 1969-71. Contbr. articles to profl. lit. Served with AUS, 1943-46; ETO. Decorated Combat Infantryman's Badge, Bronze Star. Fellow AAAS; mem. Am. Soc. Agronomy, Am. Soc. Hort. Sci., Soil Sci. Soc. Am., Council Agrl. Sci. and Tech., Mycol. Soc. Am., Conn. Forest and Park Assn., AAUP (sec.-treas. U. Conn. chpt. 1979-81), Sigma Xi, Alpha Zeta, Gamma Sigma Delta, Phi Kappa Phi (pres. chpt. 1980-81). Congregationalist (chmn. council 1966-67, deacon 1967). Clubs: Lion (pres. 1971-72), Willimantic Country, Storrs Rod and Gun (sec.-treas. 1964-65), Storrs Rod and Gun (pres. 1970-71), U. Conn. Faculty-Alumni Center (pres. 1974-75). Home: 15 Russett Ln Storrs CT 06268

GUTTENBERG, ALBERT ZISKIND, planning educator; b. Chelsea, Mass., Nov. 6, 1921; s. Harry and Edith (Bernstein) G.; m. Mariella Mascardi, June 29, 1964. A.B. in Social Relations, Harvard U., 1948; postgrad. in sociology, U. Chgo., 1949-51, U. Pa., 1958-59. Planner Planning Bd., City of Portland, Maine, 1954-56; planning analyst Planning Commn., City of Phila., 1956-60; chief gen. plans and programming sect. Comprehensive Planning div., 1960-61; sr. planner Nat. Capital Downtown Com., Washington, 1962-63; asso. prof. urban planning U. Ill., 1964-69, prof. urban and regional planning, 1969—; cons. in field. Author: (with others) Explorations Into Urban Structure, 1964, New Directions in Land Use Classification, 1965, Human Ecology, 1975; contbr. articles on land use planning to profl. publs. Served with U.S. Army, 1942-46. Guggenheim fellow, 1970-71; Brookings Inst. guest scholar, 1970-71; Gelderman Fund grantee Delft U. Tech., 1977. Mem. Am. Planning Assn., Am. Inst. Cert. Planners, Regional Sci. Assn., Nat. Com. Digital Geog. Data Standards (corr.). Home: 711 Hamilton Dr Champaign IL 61820 Office: 909 W Nevada St Urbana IL 61801

GUTTENPLAN, HAROLD ESAU, food co. exec.; b. Flushing, N.Y., Oct. 12, 1924; s. Adolph and Mollie (Penner) G.; m. Jeanette Harris, Apr. 17, 1948; children—Bruce David, Mark Stuart. B.A., Queens Coll., 1948; M.B.A., N.Y. U., 1951. Statistician printing ink div. Sun Chem. Corp., 1948-49; cost accountant, chief accountant, asst. treas. DCA Food Industries, Inc., N.Y.C., 1949-66, treas., 1966—, asst. sec., 1972-73, sec., dir., 1973—; dir. Nisshin-DCA. Cub Scout leader Nassau County Thunderbird council Boy Scouts Am., 1955-63. Served with USAAF, 1943-45; PTO. Recipient Anti-Defamation League citation award, 1968. Mem. Daus. of Jacob Relatives Assn. (pres. 1976-77), Alpha Phi Omega (pres. 1947-48), B'nai B'rith (pres.

Sagamore lodge 1963-64). Home: 26 Roberta Ln Syosset NY 11791 Office: 919 3d Ave New York NY 10022

GUTTENTAG, JACK MARK, economist, educator; b. Bklyn., Dec. 9, 1923; s. Sidney W. and Fannie (Coon) G.; m. Doris Wallach, June 5, 1955; children: William, Adam. B.S., Purdue U., 1948; Ph.D., Columbia, 1958. Market analyst FHA, 1952- 54; economist Fed. Res. Bank N.Y., 1954-62; prof. finance Wharton Sch., U. Pa., 1962—, holder chair in banking, 1969—; mem. sr. research staff Nat. Bur. Econ. Research, 1965-71; dir. Fed. Home Loan Bank Pitts.; cons. in field, 1962—. Mng. editor: Jour. Finance, 1974-76; Author: Lender of Last Resort in an International Context; also monographs, articles. Redlining and Public Policy. Served with inf. AUS, 1943-46; ETO. Mem. Am. Econ. Assn., Am. Finance Assn. (bd. dirs. 1968-70, 78-80). Home: Box 574 Valley Forge PA 19481

GUTTER, ROBERT HAROLD, orchestra conductor; b. N.Y.C., June 16, 1938; s. Jerome Sidney and Matilda (Bressler) G.; children: Deborah Carole, and Sheryl Lynn. B.Music, Yale U., 1959, M.Music, 1960. Asst. prof. U. Wis. at Madison, 1964-67; asso. prof. Drake U.; also lectr. Wittenberg U., 1969-70. Condr., Des Moines Symphony, 1967-69, SPringfield (Ohio) Symphony, 1969-71, Springfield (Mass.) Symphony, 1970—; guest condr., Albuquerque Symphony, 1970, Albuquerque Symphony, Colorado Springs, Colo., New Orleans Opera, 1969, New Orleans Opera, Siena, Italy, 1970, Palazzo Pitti, Austrian Tonkünstler Orch., 1978, Leonard Bernstein Festival of Am. Music, Vienna Volksopera Orch., 1981, Sarajevo (Yugoslavia) Philharm., Orguesta Sinfonica de Xalapa, Mex., 1979, 81, Seville Philharm., 1983, Bucharest Philharm., Ploesti Symphony, Irish Nat. Radio Orch.; recs. for Opus One; (U.S. State Dept. grantee, 1962, as condr. for Nat. Orch. of Uruguay.). Mem. Am. Fedn. Musicians, Am. Symphony Orch. League, AAUP. Home: 67 Maple St Springfield MA 01105 Office: Springfield Symphony Orch 284 State St Springfield MA 01105

GUTTERMAN, GERALD S., diversified manufacturing company executive; b. Wilkes-Barre, Pa., Jan. 29, 1929; s. Israel and Freda G.; m. Janet Jenkin, Aug. 26, 1954; children: Andrew, Lawrence, David. B.S., U. Scranton, 1950; M.B.A., N.Y. U., 1951. Sr. fin. analyst Allied Chem. Corp., N.Y.C., 1955-58; dir. divs. Am. Mgmt. Assn., N.Y.C., 1958-65; exec. v.p. fin. and adminstrn. Sun Chem. Corp., N.Y.C., 1965—; dir. Ault and Wiborg Group, Ltd., London. Served with USN, 1952-55. Mem. Fin. Execs. Inst. Club: Rolls Royce Owners. Home: 27 Pondfield Pkwy Mount Vernon NY 10552 Office: Sun Chem Corp 200 Park Ave New York NY 10017

GUTTMAN, HELENE NATHAN, science administrator; b. N.Y.C., July 21, 1930; d. Arthur and Mollie (Bergovoy) Nathan. B.A., Bklyn. Coll., 1951; A.M. (Andelot fellow), Harvard U., 1956; M.A., Columbia U., 1958; Ph.D. (Rutgers scholar), Rutgers U., 1960. Chartered chemist Royal Soc. Chemistry. Research technician Pub. Health Research Inst., N.Y.C., 1951-52; control bacteriologist Burroughs-Wellcome, Inc., Tuckahoe, N.Y., 1952-53; vol. researcher Haskins Labs., N.Y.C., 1952-53, research asst., 1953-56, research asso., 1956-60, staff microbiologist, 1960-64; lectr. dept. biology Queens Coll., N.Y.C., 1956-57; research collaborator Brookhaven Nat. Labs., Upton, L.I., N.Y., 1958; guest investigator Botanisches Institut der Technisches Hochschule, Darmstadt, Germany, 1960; research asso. dept. biol. scis. Goucher Coll., Towson, Md., 1960-62; vis. asst. research prof. dept. medicine Med. Coll. Va., Richmond, 1960-62; asst. prof., then asso. prof. dept. biology NYU, 1962-67; asso. prof. dept. biol. scis. U. Ill.-Chgo., 1967-69, prof., 1969-75; prof. dept. microbiology Med. Sch., 1969-75; asso. dir. for research Urban Systems Lab., 1975; expert Office of Dir., Nat. Heart, Lung and Blood Inst., NIH, Bethesda, Md., 1975-77; coordinator research resources Office Program Planning and Evaluation, Nat. Heart Lung and Blood Inst., 1977-79; dep. dir. Sci. Adv. Bd., Office of Adminstr., EPA, 1979-80; program coordinator, post-harvest tech., food safety and human nutrition, sci. and edn. adminstrn. Dept. Agr., 1980—. Sr. author: Experiments in Cellular Biodynamics, 1972; editorial bd.: Jour. Protozoology, 1972-75, Jour. Am. Med. Women's Assn, 1978-81; contbr. articles to profl. jours. and books. Mem. edn. com. Ill. Commn. on Status Women, 1974-75; cons. EPA, mem. sci. adv. bd., 1974-79; Bd. dirs. Du Page County Comprehensive Health Care Agy., 1974-75. Recipient Thomas Jefferson Murray prize Theobald Smith Soc., 1959; spl. award for work in Germany Deutscher Forschungs Gemeinschaft, 1960; Fellow Dazian Found., 1956; research grantee. Fellow AAAS, Am. Inst. Chemists (com. chmn.), Am. Acad. Microbiology, N.Y. Acad. Scis.; mem. Soc. Am. Bacteriologists (pres.'s fellow 1957), Tissue Culture Soc., Am. Soc. Neurochemistry, Am. Soc. Biol. Chemistry, Neuroscis. Soc., Am. Soc. Microbiologists, Am. Soc. Cell Biology (past com. chmn.), Am. Soc. Clin. Nutrition, Am. Soc. Plant Physiology, Am. Soc. Tropical Medicine and Hygiene, Soc. Indsl. Microbiologists, Soc. Gen. Microbiologists (Eng.), Soc. Protozoology (past mem. exec. com.), Soc. Exptl. Biology and Medicine, Biophysics Soc., Reticuloendothelial Soc., Assn. Women in Sci. (past mem. exec. bd., past com. chmn.), Fed. Orgn. Profl. Women (past task force chmn.), Univ. and Coll. Women Ill. (past v.p.), Sigma Xi, Sigma Delta Epsilon (past coordinator regional centers). Home: 5306 Bradley Blvd Bethesda MD 20814 Office: Science and Edn Coordination Office Sci and Edn Adminstrn US Dept Agr BARC W Beltsville MD 20705 *If it's worth having, it's worth fighting for.*

GUTTMAN, IRVING ALLEN, opera stage director; b. Chatham, Ont., Can., Oct. 27, 1928; s. Shea and Bernetta (Schaffer) G. Opera student, Royal Conservatory Music, Toronto, Ont., 1947-48. Asst. to Herman Geiger Torel of Can. Opera Co., Toronto, 1948-52; dir., under Pauline Donalda Montreal (Que., Can.) Opera Guild, 1959-68. Founding artistic dir., Vancouver (B.C., Can.) Opera Assn., 1960-74; artistic dir., Edmonton (Alta., Can.) Opera Assn., from 1966, Man. (Can.) Opera Assn., Winnipeg, from 1972; dir. numerous TV productions of opera, including first full-length TV opera for, CBC French Network, 1953, operatic productions for numerous U.S. opera cos., also Can. and European cos.; founding artistic dir., Opera Group, Courtenay Youth Music Camp. Decorated Centennial medal, Queen Elizabeth Jubilee medal. Mem. Canadian Equity, Am. Guild Musical Artists. Office: Edmonton Opera Assn 8540 69th Ave Edmonton AB Canada T6E 0R6 *

GUTWILLIG, ROBERT ALAN, publishing company executive; b. N.Y.C., Oct. 29, 1931; s. Bernard Henry and Marian (Born) G.; m. Rosemary Wallace, Sept. 22, 1956; m. Rosilyn Heller, Sept. 1, 1975; children: Katherine, Stephen, Anne. B.A. cum laude in English, Cornell U., 1953; postgrad., Stanford U., 1955-56. Exec. editor McGraw-Hill Book Co., N.Y.C., 1958-67; editorial v.p. New Am. Library, N.Y.C., 1967-69, World Pub. Co., 1969-70; sr. v.p. Playboy Enterprises, Inc., Chgo., 1970-75; pres., editor Look Mag., Inc., N.Y.C., 1978—; dir. Hollingsworth Group; partner Evans-Novak Polit. Report Co., Washington, New Mags. Verlagsgesellschaft M.b.H., Munich, W. Ger., Dresden Dr. Prodns., Inc., Dresden Dr. Pub., Inc.; dir. Hachette, Inc., Hachette Japan, Regents, Pub. Co, Inc., K.K. Regents Japan, Arista Corp. Writer; producer; Author: After Long Silence, 1956, The Fugitives, 1957; Contbr. to various publs. Served with USNR, 1953-54. Home: 2237 Nichols Canyon Rd Los Angeles CA 90046

GUTWIRTH, MARCEL MARC, French literature educator; b. Antwerp, Belgium, Apr. 11, 1923; s. Jacob Nahum and Frieda (Willner) G.; m. Madelyn Katz, June 20, 1948; children: Eve, Sarah, Nathanael. Student, N.Y.U., 1941-42; A.B., Columbia, 1947, M.A., 1948, Ph.D., 1950. Mem. faculty Haverford (Pa.) Coll., 1948—, William R. Kenan, Jr. prof. French lit., 1977-82, Jaan and John Whitehead prof., 1983—; vis. prof. Johns Hopkins, 1967, Queens Coll., 1968, Bryn Mawr Coll., 1969, 76; Andrew Mellon vis. prof. humanities Tulane U., 1980. Author: Molière ou l'invention comique, 1966, Jean Racine: un itinéraire poétique, 1970, Stendhal, 1971, Michel de Montaigne ou le pari d'exemplarité, 1977. Bd. dirs. Childbirth Edn. Assn. Greater Phila., 1961-64. Served with AUS, 1943-46; ETO. Fulbright postdoctoral fellow, Paris, France, 1953-54; Am. Council Learned Socs. fellow, 1964-65; Guggenheim fellow, 1971-72. Mem. ACLU, Modern Lang. Assn. (editorial bd. publs. 1973-76), Am. Assn. Tchrs. French, AAUP. Jewish. Home: 753 College Ave Haverford PA 19041

GUTWIRTH, SAMUEL WILLIAM, author; b. Austria, Mar. 10, 1903; U.S., 1910, naturalized, 1920; s. Henry and Regina (Wachsberger) G.; m. Sarah Fonstein, Dec. 24, 1943. D.D.S., Loyola U., Chgo., 1925. Practice dentistry, Chgo., 1925-44, author, educator, 1944—. Author: How to Free Yourself From Nervous Tension, 1955, You Can Stop Worrying, 1957, How to Sleep Well, 1959, You Can Learn to Relax, 1961; Contbr. articles to sci. jours. Mem. Am. Assn. for Advancement of Tension Control (chmn. div. dentistry), Royal Soc. Health (London, Eng.), Am. Dental Assn., Ill., Chgo. dental socs. Home: 6730 South Shore Dr Chicago IL 60649

GUY, DANIEL SOWERS, coll. dean, lawyer; b. Columbus, Ohio, July 12, 1928; s. Ralph Julian and Mary Elizabeth (Broyles) G.; m. Eleanor Bryenton, Dec. 22, 1962; children—Stanley, Sharon. B.A., Ohio Wesleyan U., 1949; J.D., Ohio No. U., 1952; LL.M., U. Mich., 1956, S.J.D. (Cook fellow), 1970. Bar: Ohio bar 1952. Gen. practice law, Canton, Ohio, 1956; asst. atty. gen. State of Ohio, 1957-58; asst. prof. law Ohio No. U. Coll. Law, 1959-62, asso. prof., 1962-65, prof., 1965-73, 77—, dean, 1978—; prof. Law Sch., U. N.D., 1973-77; Congl. fellow, Washington, 1961-62; fellow Inst. in Social Sci. Methods in Legal Edn., Denver, 1967; staff dir. Crime Prevention Task Force, N.D., Criminal Justice Com., 1974-75. Author: State Highway Condemnation Procedures, 1970; contbr. articles to profl. jours. Served with U.S. Army, 1952-54. Mem. Ohio State Bar Assn., Am. Bar Assn., Am. Judicature Soc., League Ohio Law Sch. (pres. 1968-69), Order of Coif, Phi Beta Kappa. Methodist. Clubs: Kiwanis, Masons. Home: 220 Grandview Ada OH 45810 Office: Coll Law Ohio No U Ada OH 45810

GUY, RALPH B., JR., judge; b. Detroit, Aug. 30, 1929; s. Ralph B. and Shirley (Skladd) G. A.B., U. Mich., 1950, J.D., 1953. Bar: Mich. bar 1953. Individual practice law, Dearborn, Mich., 1954-55; asst. corp. counsel City of Dearborn, 1955-58, corp. counsel, 1958-69; chief asst. U.S. atty., Eastern Dist., Mich., Detroit, 1969-70, U.S. Atty., 1970-76; judge U.S. Dist. Ct., Eastern Dist. Mich., 1976—; Treas. Detroit-Wayne County Bldg. Authority, 1966-73; chmn. sch. study com. Dearborn Bd. Edn., 1973; mem. Fed. Exec. Bd., 1970—, dir., 1971-73. Recipient Civic Achievement award Dearborn Rotary, 1971; Distinguished Alumni award U. Mich., 1972. Mem. ABA (state chmn. sect. local govt. 1965-70), Fed. Bar Assn. (pres. 1974-75), Detroit Bar Assn., Dearborn Bar Assn. (pres. 1959-60), State Bar Mich. (commr. 1975—), Am. Judicature Soc., Nat. Inst. Municipal Law Officers (chmn. Mich. chpt. 1964-69), Mich. Assn. Municipal Attys. (pres. 1962-64), Mich. Municipal League, Out-County Suprs. Assn. (pres. 1965), Phi Alpha Delta, Lambda Chi Alpha. Clubs: Rotary (local pres. 1973-74), U. Mich. Alumni (local pres. Dearborn 1961-62). Office: 252 Fed Bldg Detroit MI 48226

GUY, ROBERT DEAN, lawyer, soft drink company executive; b. Muncie, Ind., Jan. 22, 1934; s. Fred F. and Mary (Wiltrout) G.; m. Carol V. Fry, Apr. 5, 1955; children: Dani Sue, Robin, Kristin, James Stacy. A.B. in Exons. with distinction and honors, U. Mich., 1955, J.D. with distinction, 1957. Bar: Mich. 1958, N.C. 1961. Assoc. firm Kennedy, Covinton, Lobdell & Hickman, Charlotte, N.C., 1960-64; tax atty. Am. Oil Co., Chgo., 1964-66; tax mgr. Amoco Chem. Corp., Chgo., 1966-72; v.p. taxes Quaker Oats Co., Chkgo., 1972-78; v.p., gen. tax counsel Coca-Cola Co., Atlanta, 1978—; mem. adv. bd. Tax Mgmt. Inc. Served to capt. USAF, 1957-60. Mem. ABA, Tax Execs. Inst., Nat. Fgn. Trade Council, Internat. Fiscal Assn., Arnold Air Soc., Order of Coif., Phi Beta Kappa, Phi Kappa Phi. Office: The Coca Cola Co 310 North Ave NW Atlanta GA 30313

GUYKER, WILLIAM CHARLES, JR., electrical engineer, researcher; b. Donora, Pa., Aug. 21, 1933; s. William Charles G. and Mary Kurylak (Guyker); m. Alice Jane Burns, June 26, 1971; 1 dau., Patricia Lynn. B.S. in E.E., MIT, 1959. Registered profl. engr., Pa. Controls-communications engr. West Pa. Power Co., Greensburg, 1959-62, tech. coordinator, 1962-66; liaison engr. nuclear Gulf Gen. Atomic & Gen. Electric, La Jolla and Sunnyvale, Calif., 1966-68; sr. staff engr. power supply Allegheny Power Service Corp., Greensburg, 1968-70, sr. engr. planning, 1970-73, sr. engr. research and devel., 1973—; adj. prof. W.Va. U., Morgantown, 1970—; lectr. U. Pitts., 1970—; accreditor Accreditation Bd. for Engring. and Tech., N.Y.C., 1977—. Contbr. in field. Fin. chmn. Christ Episcopal Ch., Greensburg, 1973-76; pres., dir W.Pa. Power Affiliated Fed. Credit Union, Greensburg, 1974-83. Served with U.S. Army, 1952-55. Fellow IEEE (chmn. Pitts. asct. 1973-74, Power Group award 1970, Centennial award medal 1984); mem. Electric Power Research Inst., Am. Mgmt. Assn., AAAS. Republican. Episcopalian. Lodge: Elks. Office: Allegheny Power Service Corp 800 Cabin Hill Dr Greensburg PA 15601 *The quiet professionalism that rules my behavior was hard sought. It was earned by rigorous training and forthright responsibility, as a response to my perception of injustice and intolerance in the many locales of my career, steel mill, coal mine, power plant, and my self-supported education in Chicago and Boston. People's attitudes, on the street and in board rooms, taught me how to do things and to take statisfaction from performance. Rewards come, but aren't expected. A leadership role is not a reward but a dutiful responsibility to serve.*

GUYNN, GEORGE CARROLL, banker; b. Waynesboro, Va., Dec. 10, 1942; s. Norman Carroll and Grace (Beane) G.; m. Becky H. Harris, June 12, 1964; children: Robyn, Michael Shawn. B.S. in Indsl. Engring., Va. Poly. Inst., 1964; M.S. in Indsl. Mgmt., Ga. Inst. Tech., 1969; P.M.D., Harvard U. Bus. Sch., 1972. With Fed. Res. Bank, 1964—, asst. v.p., Atlanta, Miami, New Orleans, 1969-72; v.p. Fec. Res. Bank, New Orleans, 1972-79; sr. v.p., mem. mgmt. com. Fed. Res. Bank, Atlanta, 1980—. Bd.dirs. N.W. Ga. council Girl Scouts U.S.A., 1980—; bd. dirs. S.W. La. council Girl Scouts U.S.A., 1975-78, S.W. La. council Boy Scouts Am., 1978-80. Named Young Man of Year Jaycees, New Orleans, 1979. Presbyterian. Club: Kiwanis (Coral Gables, Fla.). Home: 5034 Shadow Glen Ct Dunwoody GA 30338 Office: Fed Res Bank of Atlanta 109 Marietta St Atlanta GA 30303

GUYON, JOHN CARL, univ. adminstr.; b. Washington, Pa., Oct. 16, 1931; s. Carl Alexander and Sara Myrle (Bumgarner) G.; m. Elizabeth Joyce Smith, Nov. 12, 1955; children—Cynthia Joan, John Carl, II. B.A., Washington and Jefferson Coll., 1953; M.S., Toledo U., 1958; Ph.D., Purdue U., 1961. Mem. faculty U. Mo., 1961-71, prof. chemistry, chmn. dept., 1970-71, Memphis State U., 1971-74; dean Coll. Sci., So. Ill. U., Carbondale, 1974-75,, asso. v.p. research, 1976-80, v.p. acad. affairs and research, 1980—. Author: Aanlytical Chemistry, 1965, Qualitative Analysis, 1966, Solution Equilbria, 1969; also articles, abstracts.; Gen. editor: Instrumental Methods of Analysis. Served with AUS; 41954-56. Eli Lilly Co. fellow, 1959-61; Owens Ill. Co. fellow, 1958; Jesse W. Lazear scholar, 1953. Mem. Am. Chem. Soc., AAAS, Phi Beta Kappa, Sigma Xi, Phi, Lambda Upsilon. Home: Route 4 Carbondale IL 62901 Office: Anthony Hall So Ill Univ Carbondale IL 62901

GUYTON, ARTHUR CLIFTON, physician, educator; b. Oxford, Miss., Sept. 8, 1919; s. Billy Sylvester and Mary Katherine (Smallwood) G.; m. Ruth Alice Weigle, June 12, 1943; children—David Lee, Robert Allan, John Richard, Steven William, Catherine A., Jean M., Douglas, James, Thomas, Gregory Paul. A.B., U. Miss., 1939; M.D., Harvard, 1943. Intern Mass. Gen. Hosp., 1943, asst. resident, 1946; acting asso. prof. physiology U. Tenn. Med. Sch., 1947, asso. prof. pharmacology, 1947-48; prof. and chmn. dept. physiology and biophysics U. Miss., Jackson, 1948—; Mem. cardiovascular research study sect. NIH, 1954-58, mem. physiology tng. com., 1958-64, chmn., 1961-64; mem. adv. council Nat. Heart and Lung Inst., 1971-75; mem. physiology com. Nat. Bd. Med. Examiners, 1960-64, chmn., 1962-64. Author: Function of the Human Body, 5th rev. edit, 1979, Textbook of Medical Physiology, 6th rev. edit, 1981, Circulatory Physiology: Cardiac Output and Its Regulation, rev. ed, 1973, Circulatory Physiology II: Dynamics of the Body Fluids; Basic Human Physiology, 1972, 2d rev. edit., 1977, Circulatory Physiology III: Arterial Pressure and Hypertension; also textbooks.; Contbr. articles to profl. jours.; Cons. editor Jour.: Am. Jour. Physiology; editor: Internat. Rev. Physiology. Served in med. research USN, 1944-46. Recipient Commendation citation by Army for wartime research, One of Ten Outstanding Young Men of Am. award U.S. Jr. C. of C., 1951, Ida Gould award AAAS, 1959, Wiggers award Am. Physiol. Soc., 1972, ALZA award Biomedical Engring. Soc., 1972, Ross McIntyre award, 1972; Distinguished Research award Am. Heart Assn., 1976; Einthoven award, Leiden, Holland, 1979; CIBA award for hypertension research Am. Heart Assn., 1980. Fellow Am. Coll. Cardiology (v.p. 1965-66), AAAS; mem. Am. Heart Assn., Fedn. Am. Socs. Exptl. Biology (pres. 1975-76), Am. Physiol. Soc. (pres. 1974-75), Miss. Acad. Sci. (pres. 1963-64), So. Soc. for Clin. Research (pres. 1956-57), Circulation Soc. (chmn. 1970), Miss. Heart Assn. (pres. 1955-56), Alpha Omega Alpha, Pi Kappa Pi, Sigma Alpha Epsilon, Tau Kappa Alpha, Alpha Kappa Kappa, Phi Eta Sigma, Alpha Epsilon Delta, Omicron Delta Kappa. Home: 234 Meadow Rd Jackson MS 39206 Office: Miss Medical Center Jackson MS 39216

GUYTON, ROBERT POOL, banker; b. Blue Mountain, Miss., Mar. 31, 1937; s. Albert J. and Birma Elizabeth (Pool) G.; m. Katherine Cole Taylor, June 19, 1960; children: Robert Pool, Randall Taylor. B.B.A., U. Miss., 1958; M.B.A., Harvard U., 1966. With Deposit Guaranty Nat. Bank, Jackson, Miss., 1960-71; pres., dir. Nat. Bank of Ga., Atlanta, 1971-74, 77-79, First Miss. Nat. Bank, Jackson, 1974-77; pres., chief exec. officer, dir. Bank South, 1980; dir. First Miss. Corp. Jackson.; bd. dirs. Central Atlanta Progress, Inc., Met. YMCA, High Mus. Art. Mem. bd. visitors Emory U.; trustee The Westminster Schs. Served to 1st lt. AUS, 1958-60. Named Outstanding Young Man of Year Miss. Jr. C. of C., 1968. Mem. Young Pres. Orgn., Ga. Bus. and Industry Assn. (dir.), Atlanta C. of C. (dir., past pres.), Ga. C. of C. (dir.), Omicron Delta Kappa, Sigma Chi. Episcopalian. Clubs: Peachtree Golf, Piedmont Driving, Commerce. Home: 801 W Conway Dr NW Atlanta GA 30327 Office: Bank South Corp PO Box 5092 Atlanta GA 30302

GUYTON, WILLIAM JAMES, mgmt. cons.; b. Eau Claire, Wis., Nov. 22, 1922; s. Ernest Arnold and Goldie Marie G.; m. Marion Danielson, Oct. 21, 1950; children—Joanna, Carolyn, Pamela. B.S. in Elec. Engring, U. Pa., 1943; M.B.A., Harvard U., 1948. With A.T. Kearney, Inc., Chgo., 1952—, v.p., dir., 1952—; dir. Benefit Trust Life Ins. Co., Berghoff Restaurant Co., both Chgo., Wenger Corp., Owatonna, Minn. Author: Marketing-Production Teamwork, 1970. Served to lt. USNR, World War II. Mem. Inst. Mgmt. Cons. Republican. Lutheran. Clubs: Met., Mich. Shores. Home: 2512 Iroquois Rd Wilmette IL 60091 Office: 222 S Riverside Plaza Chicago IL 60606

GUZE, SAMUEL BARRY, psychiatrist, educator, univ. ofcl.; b. N.Y.C., Oct. 18, 1923; s. Jacob and Jenny (Berry) G.; m. Joy Lawrence Campbell, June 7, 1946; children—Jonathan, Ann. Student, Coll. City N.Y., 1939-41; M.D., Washington U., 1945. Diplomate: Am. Bd. Internal Medicine, Am. Bd. Psychiatry and Neurology. Faculty Washington U. Sch. Medicine, St. Louis, 1951—, prof. psychiatry, asso. prof. medicine, 1964—, asst. to dean, 1965-71, vice chancellor for med. affairs, 1971—, co-head dept. psychiatry, 1974-75, head dept., 1975—, Spencer T. Olin prof., 1974—; pres. Washington U. Med. Center, 1971—; staff Barnes Hosp., St. Louis, 1951—, psychiatrist-in-chief, 1975—; staff Renard Hosp., 1953—, psychiatrist-in-chief, 1975—; asst. dir. Psychiatry Clinic, Washington U. Sch. Medicine, 1951-55, dir., 1955-75. Contbr. articles to profl. jours. Fellow A.C.P., Am. Psychiat. Assn., Royal Coll. Psychiatry, Am. Coll. Psychiatry; mem. Am. Fedn. for Clin. Research, Psychiat. Research Soc., AMA, Am. Psychosomatic Soc., Assn. for Research in Nervous and Mental Diseases, Am. Psychopathol. Soc., Soc. Biol. Psychiatry, Soc. Neurosci., Inst. of Medicine of Nat. Acad. Scis., Sigma Xi, Alpha Omega Alpha. Home: 17 Ridgemoor Dr St Louis MO 63105 Office: 4940 Audubon Ave St Louis MO 63110

GUZMÁN, ROGELIO I., cons., retired banker; b. San Juan, P.R., Nov. 24, 1920; s. Nicolás and Belén (Belaval) G.; m. Elba Lloveras, Feb. 8, 1947; children: Gladys Socorro, Rogelio Ismael, Luz Belén, Carlos Manuel. Grad., Stonier Grad. Sch. Banking, 1957. Accountant Royal Bank of Can., 1940-53; successively v.p., gen. mgr., exec. v.p., exec. v.p. Banco de San Juan, Santurce, from 1953; dir. Banco de Caguas. Mem. Philatelic Soc. P.R. (pres. 1958-60), P.R. Bankers Assn. (treas. 1951, hon. v.p. 1982). Home: D-12 Cambridge Santa Ana Rio Piedras PR 00927 Office: 32 Acosta St Caguas PR 00626

GWALTNEY, CORBIN, editor, publishing executive; b. Balt., Apr. 16, 1922; s. Howell Corbin and Margaret (Bell) G.; m. Doris Jean Kell, July 13, 1946; children—Margaret Kell, Jean Corbin, Thomas Stewart; m. Jean Caryl Wyckoff, June 20, 1973. B.A., Johns Hopkins U., 1943; hon. L.H.D., L.I. U., 1970. Instr., English Johns Hopkins U., 1946; with indsl. relations dept. Western Electric Co. and Locke div. Gen. Electric Co., 1946-49; editor Johns Hopkins Mag., 1949-59; editor, exec. dir., pres. Editorial Projects for Edn., Inc., Balt. and Washington, 1959-78; editor, pres. Chronicle Higher Edn., Washington, 1966—. Served with AUS, 1943-45. Recipient Robert Sibley award Am. Alumni Council, 1951, 56, 59, Disting. Service to Higher Edn. awards Columbia U. Alumni Fedn., 1964, Am. Coll. Public Relations Assn., 1971; George Polk award for edn. reporting, 1979. Home: 5104 Brookview Dr Bethesda MD 20816 Office: Chronicle Higher Edn 1333 New Hampshire Ave NW Washington DC 20036

GWALTNEY, JACK MERRIT, JR., physician, educator; b. Norfolk, Va., Dec. 24, 1930; s. Jack Merrit and Mary Gordon (Weck) G.; m. Sarah Bullock Parrott, June 26, 1954; children: Elizabeth Cromwall, Jack Merrit. B.A., U. Va., 1952, M.D., 1956. Diplomate: Am. Bd. Internal Medicine. Rotating intern Univ. Hosps., Cleve., 1956-57, resident internal medicine, 1957-59; chief resident internal medicine U. Va. Hosp., Charlottesville, 1959-60; prof. asst. respiratory virus research U. Va. Sch. Medicine, 1962-63, research fellow preventive medicine and medicine, 1963-64, instr. preventive medicine and medicine, 1964-66, asst. prof., 1966-70, asso. prof. internal medicine, 1970-75, Wade Hampton Frost prof., 1975—, head sect. epidemiology and virology, 1970—; asso. mem. Commn. Acute Respiratory Diseases, Armed Forces Epidemiol. Bd., 1968-73; mem. adv. panel infectious disease therapy U.S. Pharmacopeia, 1970—; cons. NSF, 1976-79; chmn. bd. trustees Am. Type Culture Collection, 1976-78. Editorial bd.: Antimicrobial Agents and Chemotherapy; contbr. numerous articles to profl. jours. Served to capt. U.S. Army, 1960-62. Postdoctoral fellow Nat. Inst. Allergy and Infectious Diseases, NIH, 1963-64; Edward Livingston Trudeau fellow Am. Thoracic Soc., 1964-67; recipient Research Career Devel. award NIH, 1969-73. Fellow A.C.P.; mem. Am. Type Culture Collection (trustee 1972-77), Am. Epidemiol. Soc., Albemarle County Med. Soc., Am. Fedn. Clin. Research, Am. Soc. Microbiology, Am. Thoratic Soc., Va. Thoratic Soc. (sec. treas., governing council 1973-75, v.p. 1975-76, pres. 1977—), AAUP, AAAS, Infectious Diseases Soc. Am., Med. Soc. Va., So. Soc. Clin. Investigations, Am. Clin. and Climatol. Assn., Soc. Epidemiologic Research, Sigma Xi, Alpha Omega Alpha. Home: 1454 Rugby Rd Charlottesville VA 22903 Office: U Va Sch Medicine Box 473 Charlottesville VA 22908

GWALTNEY, JOHN LANGSTON, anthropologist; b. Orange, N.J., Sept. 25, 1928; s. John Stanley and Mabel (Harper) G. B.A., Upsala Coll., 1952; M.A., New Sch. Social Research, 1957; Ph.D., Columbia U., 1967; D.Sc. (hon.), Bucknell U., 1979, D.Litt., Upsala Coll., 1980. Prof. anthropology SUNY, Cortland, 1967-71; prof. anthropology Syracuse (N.Y.) U., 1971—. Author: The Thrice Shy: Cultural Accomodation to Blindness and other Disasters in a Mexican Community, 1970, Drylongso: A Self-Portrait of Black America, 1980. Recipient Ansley Dissertation award Columbia U., 1967; Nat. Endowment Humanities fellow, 1973-74, Black Anthropologists Publ. award, 1980, Unity award in Media, 1983, Syracuse U. Chancelor's Citation, 1983; Am. Council Learned Socs. fellow, 1975-76. Mem. Am. Anthrop. Assn., Soc. Applied Anthropology, Am. Ethnological Assn., Assn. Black Anthropologists, Am. Folklore Soc., Latin Am. Area Group, Com. on Opportunity in Sci., AAAS. Office: Dept Anthropology 500 University Pl Syracuse Univ Syracuse NY 13210 *Life has taught me with the rod of reason that self-betrayal is the vilest treason from which most consequent deception flows.*

GWATHMEY, CHARLES, architect; b. Charlotte, N.C., June 19, 1938; s. Robert and Rosalie Dean (Hook) G.; m. Bette-Ann Damson, Dec. 15, 1974. Student, U. Pa., 1956-59; M.Arch., Yale U., 1962. Partner firm Gwathmey and Henderson, N.Y.C., 1968-70, Gwathmey, Henderson & Siegel, 1970-71, Gwathmey-Siegel Architects, 1971—; vis. profl. archtl. design Pratt Inst., Yale U., Princeton U., Harvard U., Columbia U., Cooper Union, U. Calif., Los Angeles.; Eliot Noyes prof. architecture Harvard U., 1984. Pres. bd. trustees Inst. Architecture and Urban Studies, N.Y.C., 1978. Recipient Arnold Brunner prize Am. Nat. Inst. Arts and Letters, 1970; William Wirt Winchester travelling fellow, 1962-63; Fulbright grantee, France, 1962-63, AIA Nat. Honor awards for Straus residence, Purchase, N.Y., 1969, Whig Hall, Princeton U., 1976, dormitory, dining and student union State U. N.Y., Purchase, 1976, Progressive Architecture design awards. Fellow AIA (firm award 1982, Medal of honor 1983); mem. Am. Nat. Inst. Arts and Letters. Address: 1115 Fifth Ave New York NY 10028

GWATHMEY, ROBERT, artist; b. Richmond, Va., Jan. 24, 1903; s. Robert and Eva Mortimer (Harrison) G.; m. Rosalie Dean Hook, Nov. 2, 1935; 1 son, Charles. Student, N.C. State Coll., 1924-25, Md. Inst., 1925-26, Pa. Acad. Fine Arts, 1926-30. Represented permanent collections, Carnegie Mus., Pitts., Telfair Mus., Savannah, Ga., Boston Mus., Va. Mus., Richmond, Pa. Acad., Phila., San Diego Mus., Los Angeles Mus., Springfield Mus., Mass., IBM Corp., U. Tex., U. Okla., Ala. Poly. Inst., Butler Art Inst., Youngstown, Ohio, Rochester Meml. Gallery, N.Y., U. Ga., U. Ill., Whitney Mus., Mus. Modern Art, Sao Paulo, Brazil. Recipient First prize Contemporary Water Color Ann., San Diego Mus., 1941, Second prize Carnegie Inst. ann., 1943, Pepsi-Cola Ann., 1946, Birmingham Mus., 1956, Fourth prize Corcoran Gallery, 1957; Nat. Acad. Arts and Letters grantee, 1946; Pa. Acad. Fine Arts fellow, 1958. Mem. Nat. Inst. Arts and Letters, NAD. Home and Office: PO Box 108 Amagansett NY 10023

GWIAZDA, STANLEY JOHN, university dean; b. Phila., Feb. 14, 1922; s. Nicholas and Pauline (Stanczak) G.; m. Regina R. Grzeskowiak, Nov. 26, 1944; 1 dau., Marianne C. B.S. in Mech. Engring., Drexel Inst. Tech., 1944, M.S., 1952. Mem. faculty Drexel U., 1946—, asso. prof. mech. engring., 1952—, dean, 1963—; Bd. dirs. Phila. Govt. Tng. Inst., 1963—. Author: (with J. H. Billings) Advanced Machine Design, 1958. Mem. adv. bd. Holy Family Coll., Phila., 1982—. Served to lt. (j.g.) USNR, 1944-46; PTO; lt. comdr. Res. Mem. Assn. Univ. Evening Colls. (chmn. com. on faculty devel. 1971-72), Am. Soc. Engring. Edn., Assn. Continuing Higher Edn. (dir. 1976-79, chmn. ethics com. 1979-83), Engrs. Club Phila., Res. Officers Assn. (pres. N.J. dept. 1973-74), Ret. Officers Assn., Cross Keys, Pi Tau Sigma, Alpha Sigma Lambda. Roman Catholic. Home: 2001 Wayne Ave Haddon Heights NJ 08035 Office: Drexel Univ Evening Coll Philadelphia PA 19104

GWILLIAM, GILBERT FRANKLIN, college administrator; b. Park City, Utah, Aug. 28, 1925; s. Gilbert Franklin and Marion (Dunbar) G.; m. Marjorie Gardner, Apr. 25, 1950; children: Gilbert Franklin, III, Tassie Katherine. A.B., U. Calif., Berkeley, 1950, Ph.D., 1956. Mem. faculty Reed Coll., Portland, Oreg., 1957—, prof. biology, 1968—, v.p., provost, 1979-82; mem. corp. Marine Biol. Lab., Woods Hole, Mass. Author papers in field. Served with USNR, 1943-46, 50-51. Recipient Nat. Research Service award Nat. Inst. Neurol. and Communicative Disorders and Stroke, 1978, spl. postdoctoral fellow, 1970; fellow Rockefeller Found., 1956, NSF, 1964. Mem. AAAS, Soc. Neurosci., Soc. Gen. Physiologists, Am. Soc. Zoologists, Western Soc. Naturalists, Phi Beta Kappa. Democrat. Office: 3203 SE Woodstock Blvd Portland OR 97202

GWINN, JOHN L., pediatric radiologist; b. Gallipolis, Ohio, Oct. 15, 1922; s. Harry and Edna (Birtcher) G.; m. Patricia Ruth Emerson, June 21, 1945; children: Sharon E., Barbara S., J. Steven, Jeffrey M. A.B., Denison U., 1944; M.D., U. Louisville, 1946; M.S., U. Minn., 1954. Intern Indpls. Gen. Hosp., 1947; resident Mayo Clinic, Rochester, Minn., 1950-54; gen. practice medicine, Corydon, Ind., 1947-48, practice medicine specializing in pediatrics, Long Beach, Calif., 1955; resident Ind. U. Med. Center, 1956-58; pediatric radiologist Children's Hosp., Los Angeles, 1959—, radiologist-in-chief, 1961—, dir., 1974-75; prof. radiology and pediatrics U. So. Calif., 1969—. Contbr. articles to profl. jours.; editorial bd.: Radiology. Served to capt., M.C. USNR, 1943-45, 50-52. Fellow Am. Coll. Radiology (bd. chancellors 1981—), Am. Acad. Pediatrics; mem. AMA, Assn. Am. Physicians, Calif., Los Angeles County med. assns., Calif. Radiol. Soc. (sec. 1970—, pres.-elect 1975, pres. 1976), Los Angeles Radiol. Soc. (pres. 1971-72), Soc. Pediatric Radiology (sec. 1961—, pres. 1975), Western Soc. Pediatric Research, Radiol. Soc. N. Am. (2d v.p. 1974), Am. Roentgen Ray Soc. (1st v.p. 1979), Radiol. Soc. So. Calif. (pres. 1968). Clubs: Masons, Elks. Home: 1524 Hillcrest St Glendale CA 91202 Office: 4650 Sunset Blvd Los Angeles CA 90027

GWINN, ROBERT P., electrical appliance manufacturing executive; b. Anderson, Ind., June 30, 1907; s. Marshall and Margaret (Cather) G.; m. Nancy Flanders, Jan. 20, 1942; 1 son, Richard Herbert. Ph.B., U. Chgo., 1929. With Sunbeam Corp., 1936—, gen. sales mgr. elec. appliance div., 1951-52, v.p., dir., 1952, pres., 1955-71, chmn. bd., chief exec. officer, 1971-82; pres. Sunbeam Appliance Service Co., 1952-82; chmn. bd. Ency. Brit., Titan Oil Co., Exploration, Inc.; dir. Continental Casualty Co., Continental Assurance Co., CNA Financial Corp. Trustee Hanover Coll., U. Chgo., U. Chgo. Cancer Research Found. Mem. Elec. Assn. Chgo. (dir.), Ill. C. of C. (dir., v.p.), Brit.-Am. C. of C. in Midwest (dir.), Alpha Sigma Phi. Clubs: Chicago, University (Chgo.); Riverside (Ill.) Country, Commercial, Economic. Office: 310 S Michigan Ave Chicago IL 60506

GWINN, WILLIAM DULANEY, phys. chemist, educator; b. Bloomington, Ill., Sept. 28, 1916; s. Walter E. and Allyne (Dulaney) G.; m. Margaret Boothby, July 11, 1953; children—Robert B., Ellen, Kathleen. A.B., U. Mo., 1937, M.A., 1939; Ph.D., U. Calif. at Berkeley, 1942. Teaching asst. U. Calif. at Berkeley, 1939-42, mem. faculty, 1942—, prof. phys. chemistry, 1955-79, prof. emeritus, 1979—; research prof. Miller Research Inst., 1961-62; Vis. prof. chemistry U. Minn., Mpls., 1969-70. Asso. editor: Jour. Chem. Physics, 1962-64. Guggenheim fellow, 1954; Sloan fellow, 1955-59; recipient citation merit U. Mo., 1964. Fellow Am. Phys. Soc.; mem. Am. Chem. Soc., Phi Beta Kappa, Sigma Xi, Pi Mu Epsilon. Spl. research molecular structure, microwave spectroscopy, quantum mechanics, direct digital control. Home: 8506 Terrace Dr El Cerrito CA 94530 Office: Dept Chemistry Univ California Berkeley CA 94720

GWINNER, ROBERT FRED, JR., educator; b. Canton, Miss., Oct. 19, 1935; s. Robert Fred and Muriel Elizabeth (Murphy) G.; m. Mary Christine Martin, Nov. 17, 1952; children—Kevin Patrick, Karen Pamela. B.S., U. So. Miss., 1958; M.B.A., U. Ark., 1960, Ph.D., 1963. Instr. U. Ark., Fayetteville, part time, 1959-61; asst. prof. U. Wyo., Laramie, 1961-64; asso. prof. U. Ala., Tuscaloosa, 1964-70; prof. mktg. Ariz. State U., Tempe, 1970—; mktg. mgmt. cons. Union Carbide, Knoxville, Tenn., 1964-65, Sperry Rand, Phoenix, 1970-71, Talos Systems, 1971-72, Motorola, 1972-75. Author: Sales Strategy: Cases and Readings, 1969, Marketing: An Environmental Perspective, 1977. Served with AUS, 1954-56. Mem. So. Mktg. Assn., Southwestern Social Sci. Assn., Alpha Tau Omega, Alpha Kappa Psi, Beta Gamma Sigma, Pi Sigma Epsilon, Phi Kappa Phi. Home: 3000 Fairway Dr Tempe AZ 85282

GWYNN, JOHN BRIND, business information services company executive; b. Cheam, Surrey, Eng., Jan. 7, 1937; s. John William and Christina A. (Yeaxlee) G.; m. Ann-Marie Gibbs, Oct. 14, 1972; 1 dau.: Olivia I. B.A., Cambridge U., 1960, M.A., 1963. Account exec. Mather & Cowther, U.K., 1960-63; sr. economist Confedn. of Brit. Industry, U.K., 1965-66; project dir. Economist Intelligence Unit, 1966-67, mng. dir., 1967-71, Commodities Research Unit, 1971-73; gen.mgr., mng. dir., v.p. exec. v.p. and pres for Europe Dun & Bradstreet Ltd., Dunn & Bradstreet Internat., London, 1974—, dir., 1975-81, Donnelley Mktg. Services Ltd., London, 1978—, D & H Group Ltd., N.Y.C., 1976—, Dun & Bradstreet Stubbs Ltd., Dublin, Ireland, 1975—. Served Royal Army Service Corps, 1955-57. Ch. of Eng. Club: Royal Automobile (London).

GWYNNE, FRED, actor; b. N.Y.C., July 10, 1926; m. Jean Reynard; 4 children. Attended, Phoenix Sch. Design, N.Y.; B.A., Harvard U., 1951. Broadway debut in Mrs. McThing, 1952, Love's Labour's Lost, 1953, The Frogs of Spring, 1953, Irma la Douce, 1953, Here's Love, 1963, The Lincoln Mask, 1972; with, Am. Shakespeare Festival in, Cat on a Hot Tin Roof and, Twelfth Night, 1974, Our Town, 1975, The Winter's Tale, 1975, A Texas Trilogy, 1976, Angel, 1978, Grand Magic, 1979 (Obie award); appeared in: films On the Waterfront, 1954, Munster Go Home, 1966, Luna, 1979, Simon, 1980; TV series Car 54, Where Are You?, 1961-63, The Munsters, 1964-66; other TV appearances include Harvey, 1958, The Hasty Heart, 1958, The Old Foolishness, 1961, The Lesson, 1966, Infancy, 1967, Arsenic and Old Lace, 1969, The Littlest Angel, 1969, Paradise Lost, 1971, The Police, 1971, Dames at Sea, 1971, Bound for Freedom, 1976; copywriter, J. Walter Thompson, 1955-60; Author: What's a Nude?; author: children's books God's First World, Best in Show, Battle of the Frogs and Mice, The King Who Rained *

GYFTOPOULOS, ELIAS PANAYIOTIS, engineering educator, consultant; b. Athens, Greece, July 4, 1927; came to U.S., 1953, naturalized, 1963; s. Panayiotis Elias and Despina (Louvaris) G.; m. Artemis S. Scalleri, Sept. 3, 1962; children: Vasso, Maro, Rena. Diploma in Mech. and Elec. Engring., Tech. U. Athens, 1953; Sc.D. in Elec. Engring., M.I.T., 1958. Registered profl. engr., Mass. Instr. M.I.T., Cambridge, Mass., 1955-58, asst. prof., Cambridge, 1958-61, assoc. prof., 1961-64, prof., 1964-69, Ford prof. engring., 1969—; chmn. Nat. Energy Council Greece, 1975-78; dir. Thermo Electron Corp., Waltham, Mass., 1976—; cons. to various U.S. corps. Author: (vol. 1) Thermionic Energy Conversion, 1973, (vol. 2) Thermionic Energy Conversion, 1979, Fuel Effectiveness in Industry, 1974; editor: Energy Conversation Manuals, 1982. Served with Greek Navy, 1948-51. Fellow Am. Nuclear Soc. (bd. dirs. 1966-69), Am. Acad. Arts and Scis., Acad. Athens, Nat. Acad. Engring. Greek Orthodox. Office: MIT Dept Nuclear Engring Massachusetts Ave Cambridge MA 02139

GYSBERS, NORMAN CHARLES, educator; b. Waupun, Wis., Sept. 29, 1932; s. George S. and Mabel (Landaal) G.; m. Mary Lou Ziegler, June 23, 1954; children—David, Debra, Daniel. A.B., Hope Coll., 1954; M.A., U. Mich., 1959, Ph.D., 1963. Tchr. Elem. and Jr. High Sch., Muskegon Heights, Mich., 1954-56; lectr. edn. and psychology U. Mich., 1962-63; prof. edn. U. Mo., Columbia, 1963—; cons. U.S. Office Edn.; mem. nat. adv. coms. ERIC Clearinghouses in Career Edn. and Counseling and Personnel Services; research and devel. com. for CEEB, Am. Insts. for Research Project on Career Decision Making, Comprehensive Career Edn. Model, TV Career Awareness Project KCET-TV, Los Angeles; dir. 10 nat. research projects and 11 state projects in career devel.-guidance. Editor: (with L. Sunny Hansen) Vocat. Guidance Quar; spl. issue Personnel and Guidance Jour, May 1975; Jour. Career Edn, 1979—, (with E. Moore and W. Miller) Developing Careers in the Elementary School, 1973, (with E. Moore and H. Drier) Career Guidance: Practices and Perspectives, 1973, (with E. Moore) Improving Guidance Programs, 1981; contbr. articles to profl. jours. and chpts. to textbooks. Elder Presbyn. Ch. Served with arty. U.S. Army, 1956-58. Mem. Am. Personnel and Guidance Assn. (pres. 1977-78, disting. profl. service award 1983), Nat. Vocat. Guidance Assn. (pres. 1972-73, nat. merit award 1981), Assn. for Counselor Edn. and Supervision, Am. Sch. Counselor Assn., Am. Vocat. Assn. (v.p. 1979-82, merit award guidance div. 1978), Mo. Guidance Assn. (outstanding service award 1978), Internat. Assn. Ednl. and Vocat. Guidance. Home: 1701 Kathy Dr Columbia MO 65201 Office: Room 111 Edn Bldg Coll Edn U Mo Columbia MO 65211

GYURKO, MICHAEL G., banker; b. Mar. 23, 1947; s. E.P. and Olga G.; m. Christine Siwa, June 30, 1968; children: Kristin, Angela. B.S., Ohio State U., 1970; M.B.A., U. Toledo, 1972. Div. controller Owens-Corning Fiberglas, 1968-73; treas. Goslin-Envirotech, 1973-74; comptroller First Nat. Bank of Birmingham, 1974-77, sr. v.p., from 1977, now exec. v.p. ops. and adminstrn. div.; dir. Harris Transfer and Warehouse, Engel Mortgage Co. Treas. Hoover Homeowners Assn., 1979-80, pres., 1980-81; asst. treas. Ala. Symphony; bd. dirs. ARC. Mem. Fin. Execs. Inst. (chpt. pres. 1983-84), Nat. Assn. Accountants, Am. Bankers Assn., Ala. Bankers Assn. (ops. com.). Roman Catholic. Clubs: Green Valley Country, Downtown, Riverchase. Home: 2659 Apollo Circle Birmingham AL 35216 Office: 1900 5th Ave N Birmingham AL 35203

HAAB, LARRY DAVID, utility company executive; b. Fairbury, Ill., Sept. 28, 1937; s. Samuel Frances and Sarah Louise (Steidinger) H.; m. Ann Geddes, Aug. 2, 1958; children: Sheryl, David, Julie. B.S., Millikin U., 1959. C.P.A., Ill. Sr. acct. Price Waterhouse, St. Louis, 1959-65; with Ill. Power Co., Decatur, 1965—; now sr. v.p. Pres. Milliken U. Alumni Bd., 1981, Macon County Mental Health Bd., Decatur, 1983—. Mem. Edison Electric Inst. (fin. com.), Am. Inst. C.P.A.s. Club: Country of Decatur. Office: 500 S 27th St Decatur IL 62525

HAACKE, HANS CHRISTOPH, artist, educator; b. Cologne, Germany, Aug. 12, 1936; came to U.S., 1961; m. Linda Snyder, Oct. 5, 1965; children: Carl, Paul. M.F.A., State Art Acad., Kassel, Germany, 1960; student (DAAD scholar), Atelier 17, Paris, 1960, Tyler Sch. Art, Phila., 1961. Adj. instr. art Cooper Union, N.Y.C., 1967-71, asst. prof., 1971-75, asso. prof., 1975-79, prof., 1979—. Author: Werkmonographie, 1972, Framing and Being Framed, 1975; One-man shows, including, Paul Maenz Gallery, Cologne, W. Ger., 1971, 74, 81, Mus. Haus Lange, Krefeld, W. Ger., 1972, Françoise Lambert Gallery, Milan, 1972, 76, John Weber Gallery, N.Y.C., 1973, 75, 77, 79, 81, 83, Lisson Gallery, London, 1976, Max Protetch Gallery, Washington, Kunstverein Frankfurt, W. Ger., Galerie Durand-Dessert, Paris, 1977, 78, Badischer Kunstverein, Karlsruhe, W. Ger., 1977, Wadsworth Atheneum, Hartford, Conn., Museum Modern Art, Oxford, Eng., 1978, Stedelijk van Abbemuseum, Eindhoven, Netherlands, 1979, Mus. Contemporary Art, Zagreb, Yugoslavia, 1980, Galerie France Morin, Montreal, 1983, exhibited in group shows, including, Tokyo Biennal, 1970, Documenta, Kassel, 1972, 82, Venice (Italy) Biennial, 1976, 78, Stedelijk Mus. Amsterdam, 1962, 65, 82. Guggenheim fellow, 1973; NEA grantee, 1978. Office: care John Weber Gallery 420 W Broadway New York NY 10012

HAAD, REUBEN PIERCE, JR., utility company executive; b. Barnesville, Ga., May 14, 1927; s. Reuben Pierce and Mary Julia (Chandler) H.; m. Jeanne Carolyn Stokes; children: Steven Lloyd, David Mitchell, Mary Margaret. B.B.A., Ga. State U., 1952; J.D., Emory U., 1961. Bar: Ga. 1961. Ins. mgr. Ga. Power Co., 1961-66, mgr. tng. and devel., Atlanta, 1969-70, asst. to exec. v.p., 1972-74, asst. v.p., 1974-75, v.p., 1975-79, sr. v.p., 1979—; mgr. fueld supply So. Co. Services, Inc., Birmingham, Ala., 1970-72; dir. Blue Cross-Blue Shield, Atlanta. Bd. dirs. Greater Atlanta Coalition, 1983, Pvt. Industry Council, Atlanta, Atlanta Lung Assn.; pres. Ga. Lung Assn., Atlanta, 1983. Served with USN, 1945-46. Mem. Edison Electric Inst., Ga. Bar Assn. Methodist. Club: Mason. Home: 1166 Lullwater Rd NE Atlanta GA 30307 Office: Georgia Power Company 333 Piedmont Ave Atlanta GA 30308

HAAG, EVERETT KEITH, architect; b. Cuyahoga Falls, Ohio, Jan. 27, 1928; s. Arnold and Lois (Martz) H.; m. Eleanor Jean Baker, Nov. 1, 1961; children—Kurt, Paula, Pamela. B.S. in Architecture, Kent State U., 1951; B.Arch., Western Res. U., 1953. Founder, prin. firm Keith Haag & Assos. (architects), Cuyahoga Falls, 1955-72; founder, pres. Keith Haag Assos. Inc. (architecture-engring.-planning), Cuyahoga Falls, 1972-81; archtl. and planning cons., Cuyahoga Falls, 1981—; instr. Kent State U., 1952-54. Pres. Tri-County Planning Commn., 1960-61; chmn. Urban Renewal Review Commn., Cuyahoga Falls, 1971—, Regional Planning Group, Northampton Twp., 1970—; mem. Akron Regional Devel. Bd.; Bd. dirs. Goodwill Industries, Akron, Stan Hylvett Hall Found., Inc.; mem. alumni bd. Kent State U., 1970-72. Recipient 31 archtl. design awards. Fellow AIA (past pres. Akron chpt., nat. com. on office practice); mem. Architects Soc. Ohio (exec. com., sec. 1975-76, v.p. 1977-78, pres. 1979), Northampton C. of C. (pres. 1972), Summit County Hist. Soc. (dir. 1974—). Clubs: President's (Kent State U.), Hilltoppers (Akron U.). Home: 1007 Steel Corners Rd Cuyahoga Falls OH 44223 Office: PO Box 1147 Cuyahoga Falls OH 44223

HAAG, WALTER M(ONROE), JR., research institute executive, industrial engineer; b. Williamsport, Pa., Apr. 25, 1940; s. Walter Monroe and Julia Maria (Halabura) H.; m. Joanne Marie Spudis, May 2, 1971. B.I.E., Pa. State U., 1962, M.S. in Indsl. Engring., 1968; M.P.H., U. Mich., 1971. Indsl. engr. Sylvania, Montoursville, Pa., 1962-64, supr. quality control, 1965-66; commd. lt. (j.g.) U.S. Pub. Health Services, 1966; advanced through grades to capt., 1977; mgmt. analyst NIH, Bethesda, Md., 1966-69; global community health career fellow USPHS, Washington, 1969-71; tech. officer WHO, Geneva, 1972-73; br. chief resource mgmt. Nat. Inst. Occupational Safety and Health, Rockville, Md., 1973-74, dep. dir. planning, 1974-76, dir. phys. scis. and engring., Cin., 1976—; cons. Assn. Media-Based Continuing Edn. for Engrs., Atlanta, 1979; adminstr. research for instruments, fibrous aerosol monitor Indsl. Research 100 award, 1972. Speaker Am. Lung Assn., Las Vegas, Nev., 1979, Air Pollution Control League, Cin., 1982. Recipient Commendation medal USPHS, Rockville, 1976; named Supr. of Yr. Federally Employed Women, Cin., 1980. Mem. Inst. Indsl. Engrs. (sr. treas. chpt. 1964-65, v.p. chpt. 1966), Am. Mgmt. Assn., Soc. Research Adminstrs., Am. Conf. Govtl. Indsl. Hygienists. Republican. Roman Catholic. Office: Nat Inst Occupational Safety and Health 4676 Columbia Pkwy Cincinnati OH 45226

HAAG, WILLIAM GEORGE, anthropologist, educator; b. Henderson, Ky., Aug. 15, 1910; s. William George and Lillian (Kreipke) H.; m. Hope Sullivan, Dec. 25, 1937 (dec. 1974); children: William George 3d, John Martin (dec.), Forrest Kreipke, Alaric Sullivan.; m. Olinde V. Smith, May 22, 1983. B.S., U. Ky., 1932, M.S., 1933; Ph.D., U. Mich., 1948. Field archeologist TVA, 1934, 36-37; curator Mus. Anthropology, U. Ky., 1937-49, asst. prof. anthropology, 1938; asso. prof. U. Miss., 1949-52; mem. faculty La. State U., Baton Rouge, 1952—, prof., 1955-66; curator Museum Anthropology, Alumni prof. anthropology, 1966-78, Alumni prof. emeritus, 1978—, chmn. dept. geography and anthropology, 1961-63, acting dir., 1975-76; state archaeologist La., 1972-77, cons. archaeologist, 1978—; field expdns. in, Tenn., 1934, Ala., 1936-37, Ky., 1937-41, Miss., 1950-51, Cape Hatteras, 1954-55, Carolina coast, 1956-57, Mexico, 1959, St. Lucia and Martinique, 1960-61, Nicaragua, 1970, Costa Rica, 1977. Author: Aboriginal Dogs, 1948, Archeology of Coastal North Carolina, 1958; Editor: Southeastern Archaeol. Conf, 1939-59; asst. editor: Am. Antiquity, 1947-50. Served to 1st lt. USAAF and; Served to 1st lt. AUS, 1942-45. Named Ky. col., 1978; Southeastern Archaeol. Conf. award, 1977, 78; James A. Ford award for outstanding contbn. to La. Archaeology, 1979. Fellow A.A.A.S.; mem. Soc. Am. Archaeology, La., Ark., Tenn. archeol. socs., Sigma Xi, Gamma Alpha, Beta Beta Beta, Phi Sigma, Sigma Gamma Epsilon, Delta Tau Delta, Omicron Delta Kappa, Phi Kappa Phi. Club: Explorers. Home: 330 Magnolia Wood Ave Baton Rouge LA 70808

HAAK, HAROLD HOWARD, university president; b. Madison, Wis., June 1, 1935; s. Harold J. and Laura (Kittleson) H.; m. Betty L. Steiner, June 25, 1955; children—Alison Marie, Janet Christine. B.A., U. Wis., 1957, M.A., 1958; Ph.D., Princeton U., 1963. Asst. prof., assoc. prof. polit. sci., pub. adminstrn. and urban studies San Diego State Coll., 1962-69, dean, 1969-71; acad. v.p. Calif. State U., Fresno, 1971-73, pres., 1980—; v.p. U. Colo., Denver, 1973, chancellor, 1974-80. Mem. County of San Diego Employee Relations Panel, 1969-71; chmn. Denver Met. Study Panel, 1976-77; bd. dirs. Fresno Econ. Devel. Corp., 1981—, Fresno Philharm., 1981—. Recipient U. Colo. medal, 1980. Mem. Phi Beta Kappa, Phi Kappa Phi. Home: 4411 N Van Ness Blvd Fresno CA 93704

HAAKENSTAD, OTTO, life ins. co. exec., lawyer; b. Havnik, Norway, Dec. 7, 1901; came to U.S., 1907, naturalized, 1934; s. Ole and Marie (Olson) H.; m. Lillian Peterson, June 30, 1925; children—Dale L., Ardith L. (Mrs. Harlan Holly), Alan Otto. Student, N.D. Agrl. Coll. Bar: N.D. bar 1926, also Fed. Ct. bars 1926, U.S. Supreme Ct. bar 1926. Mem. firm Burnett, Bergesen & Haakenstad, Fargo, 1926-1953; spl. atty. U.S. Dept. Justice, Fargo, 1935-44; co-founder Western States Life Ins. Co., Fargo, 1930, sec., 1930-44, pres., 1944-68, chmn., 1968-81, chmn. emeritus, 1981—; dir. Fargo Nat. Bank, N.D., 1953-75. Vice pres. Am. Life Conv., 1948-57, mem. exec. com., 1957-60, pres., 1960-61; Past mem. bd. admissions and budget, past chmn. Fargo United Fund. Mem. Fargo C. of C. (past dir.), N.D. C. of C. (dir. 1965-69), Inst. Life Ins. (dir. 1965-69), Am. N.D. bar assns. Lutheran (trustee). Clubs: Mason (grand master N.D. 1969-70), Lion (past dep. dist. gov.), mem. Red Cross of Constantine., Fargo Country. Office: Western States Life Bldg 700 S 7th St Fargo ND 58108

HAALAND, GORDON ARTHUR, psychologist, university administrator; b. Bklyn., Apr. 19, 1940; s. Ole E. and Ellen R. (Hansen) H.; m. Carol E. Anderson, Jan. 19, 1963; children: Lynn, Paul. A.B., Wheaton (Ill.) Coll., 1962; Ph.D., SUNY, Buffalo, 1966. Asst. prof. to prof. U. N.H., Durham, 1965-74, chmn. dept. psychology, 1970-74, dean Coll. Arts and Scis., 1974-79, v.p. for acad. affairs, 1979—, interim pres., 1983—; vis. prof. U. Bergen, Norway, 1972-73. Contbr. papers to profl. publs. and confs. Mem. Council of Colls. of Arts and Scis., Nat. Assn. State Univs. and Land-Grant Colls. (commn. on arts and scis., exec. com. council on acad. affairs), Am. Psychol. Assn. (div. 8 and 26), Eastern Psychol. Assn., AAAS, AAUP, Sigma Xi, Phi Kappa Phi. Office: Thompson Hall Academic Affairs Univ New Hampshire Durham NH 03824

HAAN, CHARLES THOMAS, agricultural engineering educator; b. Randolph County, Ind., July 10, 1941; s. Charles Leo and Dorothy Mae (Smith) H.; m. Janice Kay Johnson, June 3, 1967; children: Patricia Kay, Christopher Thomas, Pamela Lynn. B.S. in Agrl. Engring, Purdue U., 1963, M.S., 1965; Ph.D. in Agrl. Engring, Iowa State U., 1967. Grad. asst. Purdue U., W. Lafayette, Ind., 1963-64; research asso. Iowa State U., Ames, 1964-67; asst. prof., asso. prof., prof. U. Ky., Lexington, 1967-78; prof., head agrl. engring. dept. Okla. State U., Stillwater, 1978—; cons. in area of hydrology various firms and govtl. orgns. Author: Statistical Methods in Hydrology, 1977, Hydrology and Sedimentology of Surface Mined Lands, 1978; editor: Hydrologic Modeling of Small Watersheds, 1981; contbr. tech. papers and reports to publs. and confs. Recipient and or adminstr. various research grants. Mem. Am. Soc. Agrl. Engrs. (Young Researcher of 1975, research paper award 1969), Am. Geophys. Union, Nat. Soc. Profl. Engrs., Okla. Soc. Profl. Engrs., Am. Soc. for Engring. Edn., Am. Inst. Hydrologists, Sigma Xi, Tau Beta Pi, Alpha Epsilon, Gamma Sigma Delta, Phi Kappa Phi. Roman Catholic. Home: 720 Lakeshore Dr Stillwater OK 74075 Office: Oklahoma State Univ Stillwater OK 74078

HAAS, ANDREW THOMAS, labor union official; b. Phila., Mar. 22, 1924; m. Alice, 1947; 7 children. Student, Iowa State Tchrs. Coll., 1943-45, St. Joseph's Coll. Indsl. Relations, 1952-55. Mem. Internat. Assn. Heat and Frost Insulators and Asbestos Workers, Washington, 1942—; fin. sec. local 14, Internat. Assn. Heat and Frost Insulators and Asbestos Workers, Phila., 1953-54; corr. sec., bus. agt. local 14, Internat. Assn. Heat and Frost Insulators an Asbestos Workers, Phila., 1955-64; internat. v.p. Internat. Assn. Heat and Frost Insulators and Asbestos Workers, Washington, 1957-67, gen. sec.-treas., 1967-72, gen. pres., 1972—. Served with U.S. Army, 1943-45. Office: Internat Assn Heat and Frost Insulators and Asbestos Workers 1300 Connecticut Ave NW Washington DC 20036 *

HAAS, EDWARD LEE, accounting firm executive; b. Camden, N.J., Nov. 9, 1935; s. Edward David and Mildred (Wynne) H.; m. Mary Ann Lind, Dec. 27, 1958; children: John Eric, Gretchen Lind. B.A., LaSalle Coll., 1958; postgrad., Temple U., 1960-62. Mgr. systems devel. RCA Corp., Cherry Hill, N.J., 1966-71; mgr. computer tech. services Gen. Tire & Rubber Co., Akron, Ohio, 1971-74; mgr. computer applications research and devel. Ernst & Whinney, Cleve., 1974-75, dir. nat. systems group, 1976-77, nat. dir. data processing and software products, 1977, nat. ptnr., 1978—, cons. ptnr., 1984—. Served to 1st lt., arty. U.S. Army, 1958-59. Mem. Soc. Cert. Data Processors, Data Processing Mgmt. Assn., Assn. Systems Mgmt., Assn. Computing Machinery. Republican. Roman Catholic. Clubs: Cleve. Athletic, Hudson Country, Hudson Tennis, Mid-Day, Greater Cleve. Growth, Cotillion Soc. Cleve., Western Res. Racquet.

HAAS, FELIX, univ. ofcl.; b. Vienna, Austria, Apr. 20, 1921; came to U.S., 1939, naturalized, 1943; s. Adolf and Marianne (Schick) H.; m. Violet Bushwick, Apr. 17, 1948; children—Richard Allen, Elizabeth Ann, David Robert. B.S., Mass. Inst. Tech., 1948, M.S., 1949, Ph.D., 1952. Instr. Lehigh U., 1952-53; Fine research lectr. Princeton, 1953-55; asst. prof. U. Conn., 1955-56; mem. faculty Wayne State U., 1956-61, asso. prof. math., 1957-60, chmn. dept., 1960-61; head div. math. sci. Purdue U., 1961-62, dean, 1962-74, provost univ., 1974—, exec. v.p., provost, 1975—, prof. math., 1961—; math. cons. to industry, 1952—; dir. Barber-Greene and Co. Contbr. articles to profl. jours. Served with AUS, 1943-46. Mem. Am. Math. Soc., Am. Math. Assn., Am. Soc. Engring. Edn., AAUP, AAAS. Office: Purdue Univ West Lafayette IN 47907

HAAS, FREDERICK CARL, paper and chemical company executive; b. Buffalo, Feb. 16, 1936; s. Karl A. and Marie S. (Shilling) H.; m. Dorothy A. Wittlief, Aug. 31, 1957; children—Kenneth Karl, Lawrence Frederick, Sandra Dorothy. B.S. in Chem. Engring, Purdue U., 1957; M.S. in Nuclear Engring, Rensselaer Poly. Inst., Troy, N.Y., 1959; Ph.D. in Chem. Engring, Rensselaer Poly. Inst., Troy, N.Y., 1960; grad., Advanced Mgmt. Program, Harvard U., 1978. Registered profl. engr., N.Y. Research engr. Cornell Aero. Lab., 1960-63; with Westvaco Corp., 1963—, corp. research dir., then v.p., 1978-81, sr. v.p., N.Y.C., 1982—; asst. prof. Potomac State Coll., 1966; mem. curriculum com., research com. U. Maine; research adv. com. Inst. Paper Chemistry. Author papers in field. AEC fellow, 1957. Mem. Am. Mgmt. Assn. (research and devel. council), Am. Inst. Chem. Engrs., Am. Chem. Soc., TAPPI, Nat. Soc. Profl. Engrs., Indsl. Research Inst., Dirs. Indsl. Research, Can. Pulp and Paper Assn., Bearded Collie Club Eng., Bearded Collie Club Am., Sigma Xi. Methodist. Office: Westvaco Corp 299 Park Ave New York NY 10017

HAAS, FREDERICK PETER, ret. corp. exec.; b. Yonkers, N.Y., Oct. 16, 1911; s. John George and Margaret Mary (McDevitt) H.; m. Mary Helen Parke, Feb. 8, 1941; children—Susanne Phyfe (Mrs. Bruce W. Harned), Margaret McDevitt (Mrs. Edward J. Vayda), Harriet Parke (Mrs. Ralph Levesque). Grad., Phillips Acad., Andover, Mass., 1931; B.A., Yale, 1935, LL.B., 1938. Bar: N.Y. bar 1939. Asso. firm Webster & Garside, N.Y.C., 1938-46; partner firm Webster & Sheffied (and predecessors), N.Y.C., 1946-65; counsel, dir. Liggett Group, Inc. (and predecessors), N.Y.C., 1965-76, v.p., 1967-76; ret., 1976; pres. Tobacco History Corp., Durham, N.C., 1976—; past dir. Paddington Corp., N.Y.C., Austin-Nichols, Nat. Oats Co., Inc., Brite Industries, Inc., Earl Grissmer Co., Inc. Served to lt. USNR, 1943-46. Fellow Am. Coll. Trial Lawyers; mem. Am., N.Y. State bar assns., Assn. Bar City N.Y. (sec. 1949-51). Clubs: Yale (N.Y.C.); Croasdaile Country (Durham). Home: 1917 Front St Durham NC 27705

HAAS, GEORGE AARON, lawyer; b. N.Y.C., July 6, 1919; s. Herman Joseph and Violet (Cowen) H.; m. Miriam Durkin, Aug. 1942; children—Thomas Leonard, Karen Ann (Mrs. Michael Davenport), James G.D. A.B., Princeton, 1940; LL.B., Yale, 1947. Bar: Ga. bar 1947. Since practiced in, Atlanta; partner Dunaway, Haas & Broome (and predecessor firms), 1947—; Sec., dir. Lucerne Corp., East Freeway Corp., Crescent View Corp., Mountain View Corp., Lake Placid Corp. Mem. hosp. and health div. Atlanta Community Council, 1962-68; mem. tech. assistance com., del. White House Conf. on Children and Youth, 1970; state trustee from Ga. Nat. Easter Seal Soc. for Crippled Children and Adults, 1959-65, mem. exec. com., 1961-65, v.p., 1963-65, 1st v.p., 1965-66, mem. ho. of dels., 1965-73; bd. dirs. 1965-73, chmn. formula rev. bd., mem. relations and standards rev. com., 1967-69, pres., 1969-71; trustee Ga. Easter Seal Soc. for Crippled Children and Adults, 1955-65, 78—, sec., 1957-58, pres., 1959-61, chmn. ho. of dels., 1967-69; Bd. dirs. Fulton-DeKalb chpt. Nat. Found.; mem. med. adv. bd. Ga. chpt. Am. Phys. Therapy Assn. Served to capt. F.A. AUS, World War II. Mem. Am., Ga., Atlanta bar assns., Lawyers Club Atlanta, Atlanta C. of C. (past chmn. health com.). Clubs: Kiwanian., Standard (Atlanta) (past sec., dir.). Home: 2860 Ridgewood Circle NW Atlanta GA 30327 Office: 2964 Peachtree Rd NW Atlanta GA 30305

HAAS, HAROLD, ch. ofcl.; b. Union City, N.J., Nov. 9, 1917; s. Joseph August and Magdalena (Bonin) H.; m. Evelyn Johnsen, May 23, 1942; children—Marilyn Susan, Carolyn Sandra (Mrs. Paul E. Henry, Jr.). Student, U. Jena, Germany, 1938, U. Oslo, Norway, 1947; A.B., Wagner Coll., Staten Island, N.Y., 1939, D.D., 1958; M.A., U. Pa., 1942; Ph.D., Drew U., 1952. Ordained to ministry Lutheran Ch., 1942; pastor in, Rochester, N.Y., Linden, N.J. and, Jersey City, 1942-57; exec. sec. bd. social missions United Luth. Ch. Am., 1957-62, bd. social ministry, 1963-66; dean of coll. Wagner Coll., 1966-70; exec. dir. div. of mission and ministry Luth. Council in U.S.A., 1971-77; pres. Tressler Luth. Service Assn., Camp Hill, Pa., 1977—; Mem. gen. bd. Nat. Council Chs., 1956-65; rep. to Luth. Council U.S.A., 1967—; mem. bd. world missions Luth. Ch. Am., 1968-70; del. and visitor Luth. World Fedn. assemblies, Sweden, 1947, Germany, 1952, U.S., 1957, Finland, 1963; del. numerous confs. Nat. Council Chs.; Mem. nat. bd. Nat. Conf. Social Welfare, 1963-66; mem. bd. Nat. Assembly Nat. Vol. Health and Social Welfare Agys., 1973—. Author: Marriage, 1960, also articles, chpts. in books. Home: 402 Lamp Post Ln Camp Hill PA 17011

HAAS, HAROLD MURRAY, motion picture exec.; b. Jamaica, N.Y., Apr. 20, 1925; s. Ludwig and Sadie (Borish) H.; m. Henny Notowitz, Dec. 25, 1949 (div. Mar. 1980); children—Gilda Susan, Linda Deborah; m. Beverly Rabinowitz Weingard, Apr. 20, 1980. B.S., Columbia, 1948, M.S., 1951. C.P.A., N.Y., Calif. Jr. acct. Arthur Young & Co. (C.P.A.'s), N.Y.C., 1948-49; audit mgr. Harry Berman & Co. (C.P.A.'s), N.Y.C., 1949-55; asst. controller MCA Inc., N.Y.C., 1955-60, controller agy. div., Chgo., 1960-62, chief acct., Universal City, Calif., 1962-65, controller, 1965-75, treas., 1975—, v.p., treas., 1979—; dir. Yosemite Park & Curry Co., 1974—. Bd. dirs. Ebony Showcase Theatrical Workshop, 1971-72, adv. bd., 1972; mem. entertainment industry bd. United Jewish Welfare Fund, 1970-71. Served with AUS, 1943-45. Decorated Combat Inf. Badge. Mem. Columbia U. Grad. Sch. Bus. Alumni Assn. (asso.). Home: 1945 N Normandie Ave Los Angeles CA 90027 Office: 100 Universal City Plaza Universal City CA 91608

HAAS, HOWARD GREEN, bedding manufacturer; b. Chgo., Apr. 14, 1924; s. Adolph and Marie (Green) H.; m. Carolyn Werbner, June 4, 1949; children: Jody, Jonathan. Student, U. Chgo., 1942; B.B.A., U. Mich., 1948. Promotion dir. Esquire, Inc., Chgo., 1949-50; advt. mgr. Mitchell Mfg. Co., Chgo., 1950-52, v.p. advt., 1952-56, v.p. sales, 1956-58; sales mgr. Sealy, Inc., Chgo., 1959-60, v.p. marketing, 1960-65, exec. v.p., 1965-67, pres., treas., 1967—, also dir. Mem. nominating com. Glencoe Sch. Bd.; mem. print and drawing com. Art Inst. Chgo.; chmn. parent's com. Washington U., St. Louis; bd. dirs. Jewish Children's Bur.; pres. Orch. of Ill. Assn.; mem. vis. com. Sch. Social Service Administrn. U. Chgo. Served to 1st lt. USAAF, 1943-45; ETO. Decorated Air medal with 3 oak leaf clusters; recipient Brotherhood award NCCJ, 1970, Human Relations award Am. Jewish Com., 1977. Mem. Nat. Assn. Bedding Mfrs. (past vice chmn., trustee), Soc. Contemporary Art. Democrat. Jewish religion. Clubs: Mason., Birchwood Tennis (Highland Park, Ill.). Office: 525 West Monoroe Street Chicago IL 60606

HAAS, JOSEPH F., lawyer; b. Atlanta, 1911; m. Betty L. Geismer; children: Jeffrey, Susan Haas Reinach. A.B., U. Mich.; J.D., Harvard U. Bar: Ga. Practiced in, Atlanta; now sr. partner Arnall Golden & Gregory. Author: Liability of Social Agencies, 1952. Mem. exec. com., legal counsel Voter Edn. Project, 1967-73; mem. Ga. Council for the Arts, 1973-78, White House Conf. on Children and Youth, 1960; chmn. Ga. Com. for Children and Youth, 1963-64; mem. Atlanta Mayor's Commn. on Crime and Delinquency, 1966-67, Community Relations Commn., 1967-68, Central Atlanta Progress; mem. budget com. Bur. Cultural and Internat. Affairs of City of Atlanta; pres. Hebrew Benevolent Congregation, 1960-62, Community Council of Atlanta Area, 1962-64, Atlanta Legal Aid Soc., 1961, Jewish Childrens Service, 1959-62, Child Service and Family Counseling Center, 1970-71, Theatre Atlanta, Inc., 1965-68; bd. dirs. Child Welfare League Am., 1952-58, gen. counsel, 1953—; bd. dirs. Community Chest, 1968-70, Ga. Conservancy; pres. bd. sponsors Atlanta Symphony Orch., 1973-74; trustee Atlanta Arts Alliance. Mem. ABA; Mem. Ga., Atlanta bar assns., Am. Judicature Soc., Nat. Com. for an Effective Congress, World Assn. Lawyers, World Peace Through Law (charter mem.), Phi Beta Kappa, Phi Kappa Phi. Office: 1000 Fulton Fed Bldg Atlanta GA 30335 *To paraphrase Eleanor Roosevelt's biographer's statement about her: "It is better to light a candle than to curse the darkness."*

HAAS, JOSEPH MARSHALL, petroleum consultant; b. Alexandria, La., June 21, 1927; s. Samuel and Lulu Susan (Haupt) H.; m. Mary Louise Nance, June 4, 1949 (dec. Jan. 1950); 1 son, Samuel Douglas; m. Marion Barker, Apr. 9, 1954; children—Joseph Marshall, Suzanne M., Thomas B., Katherine L. B.Mech. Engring., Ga. Inst. Tech., 1949. With Gen. Am. Oil Co., Dallas, 1949-78, asst. v.p. prodn. and engring., 1957-60, v.p. engring., 1960-78; petroleum cons. Haas Engring., 1978—; v.p., dir. Haas Investment Co., La. Central Land and Improvement Co.; pres., dir. Avoyelles Wholesale Grocery Co., Ltd. Served with USNR, 1945-46. Mem. Am. Petroleum Inst., Am. Inst. Mining and Metall. Engrs., Ind. Petroleum Assn. Am., Tau Beta Pi, Sigma Chi, Pi Tau Sigma. Methodist. Clubs: Mason (32 deg., Shriner), Northwood, Engineers, North Tex. Georgia Tech. Home: 6830 Orchid Ln Dallas TX 75230 Office: Meadows Bldg Dallas TX 75206

HAAS, KENNETH GREGG, orchestra manager; b. Washington, July 8, 1943; s. Philip and Eunice (Dillon) H.; m. Barbara Dooneief, Feb. 14, 1964; children: Elizabeth, Amanda. A.B., Columbia U., 1964. Asst. to mng. dir. N.Y. Philharm., 1966-70; asst. gen. mgr. Cleve. Orch., 1970-75, gen. mgr., 1976—, Cin. Symphony Orch., 1975-76; mem. music panel Ohio Arts Council, 1975-79; co-chmn. orch. panel Nat. Endowment Arts, 1982—; trustee Cleve. Ballet, 1974-77. Mem. Am. Symphony Orch. League (dir. 1980-82, exec. com. 1981—), Mgrs. Maj. Orchs. U.S. and Can. (chmn. 1980-82). Office: Severance Hall Cleveland OH 44106

HAAS, LEONARD CLARENCE, university chancellor emeritus; b. Eau Claire, Wis., Feb. 17, 1915; s. Lee Leon and Laura (Brown) H.; m. Dorellen Marie Lambert, May 31, 1941; children: Karen Marie, Kristine Kay. B.E., Wis. State Coll., Eau Claire, 1935; M.A. in History, U. Wis., 1938; student, Columbia, 1939, U. So. Calif., 1940; Ph.D., U. Minn., 1954; LL.D., St. Olaf Coll., Northfield, Minn., 1968. Tchr. elementary sch., Watertown, S.D., 1935-37; grad. asst. history U. Wis., 1937-38; dir. guidance, faculty Wausau (Wis.) Sr. High Sch., 1938-41; faculty Inst. Hist. and Polit. Sci., Wis. State U., Eau Claire, 1941-44, 46-48, dir. tchr. tng. and placement, 1944-46, prof. history, dean of instrn., registrar, 1948-59, pres., 1959-71; exec. v.p. U. Wis. System, 1971-73; chancellor U. Wis. at Eau Claire, 1973—. Vice pres. Eau Claire City Council, 1949-55, pres., 1955-57; mem. Eau Claire Downtown Devel. Com., 1978; bd. dirs. Eau Claire United Way, United Cerebral Palsy, Grace Luth. Found., 1979—; v.p. Grace Luth. Found., 1980—, pres., 1982-83; trustee Eau Claire Public Library; adv. council Luther Hosp.; mem. Com. Protection Human Subjects; bd. dirs. Bd. of Coll. Edn. of Am. Luth. Ch.; com. div. coll. and univ. work Nat. Luth. Council; chmn. Council Chancellors U. Wis. System, 1974-75, West Central Wis. Consortium of Univs., 1977-78; mem. Service Acad. Selection Commn. Recipient Luth. layman's award, 1957; Kiwanis Achievement award for civic service, 1957; Distinguished Alumnus award U. Wis. at Eau Claire, 1966. Mem. Wis. League Municipalities (dist. v.p. 1954), N.E.A., Wis. Com. Gen. Edn. (chmn. 1956), Wis. Assn. Higher Edn. (pres. 1968), Am. Assn. Coll. Registrars, Hesperia Lit. Soc., Mortar Bd., Omicron Delta Kappa, Phi Kappa Phi, Phi Delta Kappa, Kappa Delta Pi, Pi Kappa Delta, Phi Alpha Theta. Lutheran (bd. edn.). Clubs: Kiwanian (pres. Eau Claire 1952, lt. gov. 1952. Home: 1819 Drummond St Eau Claire WI 54701

HAAS, LESTER CARL, architect; b. Shreveport, La., Apr. 9, 1913; s. Jacob and Hanna (Kahn) H.; m. Niki Kal, Nov. 1, 1942; children: Dale Frances, Catherine Kal (Mrs. Fred Donald Youngswick). B.A., Johns Hopkins, 1933; B.Arch., U. Pa., 1936; postgrad., Ecole Des Beaux-Arts, N.Y.C., 1936-37, diplome, 1939; student, Am. Acad., Rome, Italy, 1940. Archtl. apprentice W. Pope Barney, Phila., 1936-39; architect Robert & Co., 1940-41; practice architecture in, Shreveport, 1946-65; ptnr. Haas & Massey & Assos. (architects), Shreveport, 1966—; mng. partner TAG-The Archtl. Group, 1978—. Co-author: weekly column Ark-La-Tecture, 1967-71; Principal works include, Pioneer Bank and Trust Co., Shreveport main office and 9 br. banks, 1948-78, KTBS offices, radio and TV studios, Shreveport, 1948-76, Caddo Sch. Exceptional Children, Shreveport, 1956, also addition, 1977, La Sands Western Hills Motel, Bossier City, La., 1957, St. Pius X Sch., convent and sanctuary alterations, N. Shreveport, 1962, Barksdale Officer Club, Barksdale AFB, La., 1965, Northwestern State U. at Shreveport, 1966, Restoration and Renovation of the Strand Theatre, Shreveport, 1978-81, C-Barc Adult Workshop, Shreveport, 1970, additions, 1979, Adminstrv. Center, Caddo Parish Sch. Bd., Shreveport, 1971, Master Plan and Adminstrn. Bldg., Delgado Coll., New Orleans, 1979-81. Chmn. rev. com. N.W. La. Areawide Health Planning Council, 1973-75, pres., 1975-76; pres. Travelers Aid, 1951, Children's Service Bur., 1952, Courtyard Players Civic Theatre, 1954, ARC, 1963-65, NCCJ, 1965-69; nat. bd., 1970-73, St. Vincent Acad. Parents Club, 1966-67, Lyric Ball, 1967, Caddo Found. for Exceptional Children, 1972-74; v.p. Caddo-Bossier Assn. Retarded Children, 1957, United Fund, 1963-67, Caddo Found. Exceptional Children, 1967—; adv. bd. Congregation Daughters of Cross, 1965-69; community adv. com. Jr. League, 1973-76 community adv. com. Jr. League, all Shreveport; mem. Shreveport Bldg. Bd., 1979-83; pres. Mental Health Assn. Caddo-Bossier, 1981-82. Served from ensign to lt. USNR, 1942-45. Decorated Navy Commendation medal; recipient Merit award 2d Internat. Lighting Exposition, 1947; Ann. Brotherhood citation Shreveport chpt. NCCJ, 1974; John Stewardson Travelling scholar architecture, 1939. Fellow AIA (pres. N.La. chpt. 1955, exec. com. Gulf States regional council 1956); mem. Constrn. Specifications Inst. (cert. constrn. specifier 1979, pres. Shreveport chpt. 1970-71, Nat. Jury Fellows 1974-76), La. Architects Assn. (rep. to Gov.'s Com. to Rewrite Fire Marshal's Act 1973), Shreveport Jr. C. of C. (past v.p.), Shreveport C. of C. (past officer), Am. Legion, D.A.V., Tau Sigma Delta. Jewish (pres. congregation 1967, 68). Club: Greater Shreveport Racquet. Home: 1031 Dudley Dr Shreveport LA 71104 Office: Haas & Massey 504 Texas St Shreveport LA 71101

HAAS, MARC, industrial executive; b. Cin., Mar. 16, 1908; s. Marc and Alice (White) H.; m. Helen Hotze, Feb. 3, 1951. Grad., Horace Mann Sch., 1925, Princeton U., 1929. Ptnr. Emanuel & Co., mems. N.Y. Stock Exchange, 1933-42; dept. dir. Office Def. Transp., Washington, 1942-45; asso. Allen & Co., N.Y.C., 1945-55; pres. Am. Transp. Enterprises, Inc. and subs., N.Y.C., 1955—, Am. Diversified Enterprises, Inc. and subs.; dir. Golden Cycle Corp., Cave Laurent Perrier. Named Knight Order of St. John. Episcopalian (warden). Club: Princeton (N.Y.C.). Home: 14 E 75th St New York NY 10021 Office: 711 Fifth Ave New York NY 10022

HAAS, PAUL RAYMOND, petroleum company executive;; b. Kingston, N.Y., Mar. 10, 1915; s. Frederick J. and Amanda (Lange) H.; m. Mary F. Diedrick, Aug. 30, 1936; children: Rheta Marie, Raymond Paul, Rene Marie. A.B., Rider Coll., 1934, LL.D., 1976. C.P.A., Tex. Acct. Arthur Andersen & Co. (C.P.A.s), N.Y.C. and Houston, 1934-41; with La Gloria Oil & Gas Co., Corpus Christi, Tex., 1941-59, v.p., treas., dir., 1947-59; adminstrv. v.p. Tex. Eastern Transmission Corp., Houston, 1958-59; pres., chmn. bd. Prado Oil & Gas Co., 1959-66, Wiltex Corp., 1950-65, Garland Co., 1956-65, Citronelle Oil & Gas Co., 1967-69, Corpus Christi Oil and Gas Co., 1968—; ltd. partner Salomon Bros., 1973—; dir. Corpus Christi Nat. Bank, Kaneb Services, Inc., Tex. Commerce Bancshares, Houston Natural Gas Corp.; ind. oil and gas operator, 1959—. Trustee Corpus Christi Ind. Sch. Dist., 1951-58, pres., 1956-58; mem. Tex. Bd. Edn., 1962-72, vice chmn., 1970-72; mem. Gov.'s Com. Edn., 1966-69; Trustee Paul and Mary Haas Found., 1954—, Robert T. Wilson Found., 1954-72, Rider Coll., 1959-67, Moody Found., 1966-73, Found. Center, 1970-75, Council on Founds., 1970-76, Commn. on Philanthropy and Pub. Needs, 1973-75, Univ. Cancer Found. M.D. Anderson Hosp. and Tumor Inst., 1975—. Presbyn. (elder). Home: 4500 Ocean Dr Apt 9A Corpus Christi TX 78412 Office: PO Box 779 Corpus Christi TX 78403

HAAS, PETER E., manufacturing company executive; b. San Francisco, Dec. 20, 1918; s. Walter A. and Elise (Stern) H.; m. Mimi Lurie, Aug. 31, 1981; children: Peter E., Michael Stern, Margaret Elizabeth. Student, Deerfield Acad., 1935-36; A.B., U. Calif., 1940;

postgrad., Harvard, 1943. Asst. prodn. mgr. Levi Strauss & Co., San Francisco, 1946-51, v.p., dir., 1951-58, exec. v.p., 1958-71, pres., 1971-81, chief exec. officer, 1978-81, chmn. bd., 1981—; dir. Crocker Nat. Corp., Crocker Nat. Bank, AT&T, Levi Strauss Internat. Mem. Golden Gate Nat. Recreation Area Adv. Com.; Former bd. dirs. Jewish Welfare Fedn.; former trustee Stanford U.; trustee San Francisco Bay Area Council. Republican. Jewish. Office: Levi Strauss & Co Levi's Plaza 1155 Battery St San Francisco CA 94106

HAAS, ROBERT GREEN, advertising agency executive; b. Chgo., Sept. 14, 1921; s. Adolph R. and Marie (Green) H.; m. Carolyn Buhai, June 29, 1947; children: Andrew Robert, Mari Beth, Betsy Ann, Thomas Michael, Karen Sue. Student, U. Ill., 1940-41, Western Mich. U., 1944-45. Pres. Robert Haas Advt., 1960-63, Bronner & Haas Advt., 1963-67; exec. v.p. Grey-North Advt. Agy., Chgo., 1967-80; pres. CEE & H Co., Inc., 1981-82, Haas & Assocs., Inc., 1983—, Maxwell's & Maxwell's Too Restaurants, Denver, The Vail Cookie Co.; mng. ptnr. JEB Leasing Co., 1980—. Served with USNR, 1942-46. Home: 280 Sylvan Rd Glencoe IL 60022 Office: 666 Dundee Rd Suite 604 Northbrook IL 60062

HAAS, VINTON BENJAMIN, JR., educator; b. Terre Haute, Ind., Aug. 30, 1923; s. Vinton Benjamin and Mayme Catherine (Hartzler) H.; m. Jeanne Reak, Mar. 25, 1944; children—Catherine Elizabeth (Mrs. David Francis Bean), Vinton Benjamin III, Douglas Francis, Marjorie Ellen (Mrs. John E. Kalliongis). B.S., Rose Poly. Inst., 1943; M.S., Mass. Inst. Tech., 1949, Sc.D., 1956. Test engr. Gen. Electric Co., 1946-47; instr. Mass. Inst. Tech., 1947-49, 53-56; asst. prof. N.D. State Coll., 1949-50, U. Conn., 1950-53, asso. prof., 1956, prof., 1957-79, prof. emeritus, sr. lectr., 1979—; head elec. engring. dept., 1968-74; vis. prof. Imperial Coll., U. London, 1963, 78, M.I.T., 1970; dir. research project IBM Corp., 1961-63. Served with C.E. AUS, 1943-46. Mem. I.E.E.E., Am. Soc. Engring. Edn., Sigma Xi, Tau Beta Pi, Eta Kappa Nu. Home: 180 Puddin Ln Willimantic CT 06226

HAAS, WALTER ABRAHAM, JR., retired apparel company executive, professional baseball executive; b. San Francisco, Jan. 24, 1916; s. Walter Abraham and Elise (Stern) H.; m. Evelyn Danzig, 1940; children: Robert D., Elizabeth Haas Eisenhardt, Walter J. B.A., U. Calif., 1937; M.B.A., Harvard U., 1939; hon. degree, Wheaton Coll., 1983. Chmn. exec. com. bd. dirs. Levi Strauss & Co., San Francisco; owner Oakland Athletics Baseball Co., Calif.; dir. Bank of Am., Bank Am. Corp., UAL, Inc., United Airlines. Mem. Trilateral Commn. Served in mil., World War II. Named a Leader of Tomorrow Time mag., 1953, Chief Exec. Officer of Yr. Fin. World mag., 1976; recipient Jefferson award Am. Inst. Pub. Service, 1977, Alumni Achievement award Harvard Grad. Sch. Bus., 1979. Office: Levi Strauss & Co 1155 Battery St San Francisco CA 94111

HAAS, WALTER J., JR., professional sports team executive. Exec. v.p. Oakland A's Am. League, Calif. Office: Care Oakland A's Oakland-Alameda County Coliseum Oakland CA 94621§

HAAS, WARD JOHN, business executive; b. N.Y.C., Aug. 26, 1921; s. M.A. and Pauline (Ward) H.; m. Jane Corya, Dec. 25, 1943; children: Margaret C., Jeffrey W., Elizabeth C. B.S., M.I.T., 1943, Ph.D., 1949. Biochemist E.I. duPont de Nemours & Co., 1949-51; fgn. service attache Am. Embassy, London, 1951-54; asst. to dir. Agrl. Research and Devel. Center, Charles Pizer & Co., Inc., Terre Haute, Ind., 1954-56, asst. to pres., N.Y.C., 1957-60; dir. ops. Pfizer Labs. div., N.Y.C., 1959-64; asso. prof. mgmt., dir. Space Scis. Research Center, U. Mo., 1964-68; dir., pres. Warner-Lambert Research Inst., Morris Plains, N.J., 1968-69; v.p. research and devel. Warner-Lambert Co., 1969-72; corp. v.p. research and devel. S.C. Johnson & Son, Inc., Racine, Wis., 1972-75; v.p. research and devel. Chesebrough-Pond's, Inc., Greenwich, Conn., 1975—. Served with U.S. Army, 1943-46. Fellow AAAS; Mem. Am. Inst. Chemists, Am. Chem. Soc., AIAA, Indsl. Research Inst. (dir. 1979-82), Assn. Dirs. Indsl. Research, Am. Mgmt. Assn. (research and devel. council 1976-82), Sigma Xi. Home: 768 Sasco Hill Rd Fairfield CT 06430 Office: 40 Merritt Blvd Trumbull Indsl Park Trumbull CT 06611

HAAS, WARREN JAMES, librarian, association executive; b. Racine, Wis., Mar. 22, 1924; s. Samson Henry and Laura (Jacobson) H.; m. Peggy Anne Tinker, June 14, 1947; children: Anne Bruington, Warren James, William Henry. A.B., Wabash (Ind.) Coll., 1948, D.Litt. hon., 1983; B.L.S., U. Wis., 1950. Asst. librarian Racine Pub. Library, 1950-52, Johns Hopkins, 1952-59; cons. Council Higher Ednl. Instns. in, N.Y.C., 1959-60; asso. librarian Columbia, 1961-66, dir. libraries, 1970-72, v.p. for information services and univ. librarian, 1972-77; v.p. Council on Library Resources, 1976-78, pres., 1978—; dir. libraries U. Pa., 1966-69; Cons. on library bldgs.; pres. Assn. Research Libraries, 1970. Served with USAAF, 1943-46. Recipient Henry Elias Howland meml. prize Yale U., 1980. Assn. Research Libraries (dir. 1967-71, pres. 1970); Mem. ALA. Clubs: Cosmos (Washington); Century, Grolier (N.Y.C.). Address: 105 7th St SE Washington DC 20003

HAAS, WILLIAM PAUL, coll. pres.; b. Newark, May 31, 1927; s. Joseph J. and Elizabeth (Ryan) H. A.B., Providence Coll., 1948; S.T.L., Pontifical Inst., Washington, 1954; Ph.D., U. Fribourg, Switzerland, 1962; D.B.A. (hon.), Bryant Coll., Providence, 1966; LL.D., U. R.I., 1967, Brown U., 1969; D.D., Conn. Wesleyan U., 1969; D.H.L., R.I. Coll., 1970, Salve Regina Coll., 1971. Ordained priest Roman Cath. Ch., 1953, laicized, 1973; prof. theology and philosophy Emmanuel Coll., Boston, 1954-60; prof. philosophy Providence Coll., 1962-63, 71-72, pres., 1965-71; asso. prof. U. Notre Dame, 1963-65; on leave as post-doctoral research asso. Boston U., 1972-73; vice chancellor for acad. affairs Mass. State Coll. System, 1973-79; pres. North Adams (Mass.) State Coll., 1979—; inaugurated spl. program religious studies Purdue U., 1963-65; vis. prof. contemporary theology Wabash Coll., Crawfordsville, Ind., 1964-65; vis. distinguished prof. U. R.I., 1971-72; Mem. R.I. Council Arts, 1967-70, R.I. Adv. Council State Tech. Services Act, 1965, 1967-71; mem. commn. learning Assn. Am. Colls., 1966-69; adv. council extension and continuing edn. Dept. Health, Edn. and Welfare, 1966-70; mem. commn. humanities in schs. Nat. Found. on Arts and the Humanities, 1967-71; chmn. R.I. Higher Edn. Council, 1969-71. Author: The Conception of Law and the Unity of Peirce's Philosophy, 1964, The Contemporary Arts, 1965; Contbr. articles to profl. jours. Bd. dirs. R.I. Philharmonic Orch., 1965-68, R.I. Found. Repertory Theatre, 1966-71, R.I. Urban Coalition, 1969-71, Packard Manse (center ecumenical studies), Boston, 1965-67; trustee John F. Kennedy Meml. Fund R.I., 1966-71, New Eng. Colls. Fund, 1970-71, Rocky Hill Sch., 1971-73, Bryant Coll., 1971-79; bd. dirs. United Fund R.I., 1967-71, Howard Found., Brown U., 1969-73; chmn. R.I. com. Rhodes Scholarship Trust, 1969, mem., 1970. Mem. Am. Soc. Aesthetics, Nat. Cath. Edn. Assn. (exec. com. coll. and univ. dept. 1970-73). Home: 375 Church St North Adams MA 01247 Office: Office of Pres North Adams State Coll Church St North Adams MA 01247

HAASE, GUNTER ROLAND, physician, educator; b. Chemnitz, Germany, Sept. 30, 1924; s. Max Hermann and Eugenie (Hantke) H.; m. Virginia Potter, July 15, 1949; children—Christopher, Stephanie, Leslie, Peter. Student, U. Berlin, 1943-45; M.D., Ludwig-Maximilians U., lMunich, Germany, 1949. Intern St. Luke's Hosp., Denver, 1950-51; resident psychiatry U. Colo., 1951-54; clin. asso. NIH, USPHS, 1954-56; fellow clin. neurology and neuropathology Queen Sq. Hosp., London, Eng., 1957; asso. neurologist NIH, 1958-59; asso. prof. neurology U. Okla. Sch. Medicine, 1960-64; prof. neurology Temple U. Sch. Medicine, Phila., 1964-73, chmn. dept., 1966-73; prof. neurology U. Pa., Phila., 1974—; dir. dept. neurology Pa. Hosp., Phila., 1974—. Served with German Air Force, 1942-45; Served with USPHS, 1954-59. Mem. Am. Acad. Neurology, Assn. Research and Nervous and Mental Diseases, AMA, Am. Neurol. Assn. Home: 799 Robin Hood Rd Rosemont PA 19010 Office: Pennsylvania Hospital 8th and Spruce Sts Philadelphia PA 19107

HAASE, RICHARD HENRY, educator; b. Cleve., Feb. 27, 1924; s. Harold M. and Fern (Dyer) H.; m. Kathleen I. Deane, June 9, 1951; children-Deane D., David R., Diane M. B.S. in Aero. Engring, Purdue U., 1945; M.B.A., Tulane U., 1949; Ph.D., U. Calif. at Los Angeles. With CONVAIR Corp., 1946-47, Gen. Electric Co., 1947-51, 65-67; lectr. engring., asst. head engring. extension U. Calif. at Los Angeles, 1951-61; mem. tech. staff RAND Corp., 1961-65; prof. statistics, head finance and statistics dept. Drexel U., 1967—; cons. in field. Served with USNR, 1943-46. Faculty fellow NSF, 1959-60. Mem. Sigma Xi, Pi Tau Sigma, Tau Beta Pi, Alpha Kappa Psi, Beta Gamma Sigma. Home: 138 Woodgate Ln Paoli PA 19301 Office: Drexel Univ Philadelphia PA 19104

HAASE, WALTER, association exec.; b. Appleton, Wis., Jan. 27, 1920; s. Walter Godfrey and Elisabeth (Sauer) H.; m. Evelyn Hope Stoll, Aug. 31, 1946; children: Gretchen Elizabeth, David, Amy. Student, Northwestern Coll., Watertown, Wis., 1937-38; B.B.A., U. Minn., 1941. Auditor Touche, Niven & Co., Mpls., 1941-42; financial analyst Equity Corp. (and affiliates), N.Y.C., 1946-49; with Am. Assn. Advt. Agencies, Inc., N.Y.C., 1949—, exec. sec.-treas., 1955-74, v.p., 1974-83, sr. v.p., 1983—. Served with Ordnance Corps AUS, 1942-46. Mem. Beta Gamma Sigma. Lutheran. Home: 64 Tunstall Rd Scarsdale NY 10583 Office: 666 Third Ave New York NY 10017

HAASE, WILLIAM EDWARD, professional baseball executive; b. Highland Park, Mich., Dec. 26, 1943; s. Byron C. and Vera Ethel (Techow) H.; m. Sandra Lee Berg, Aug. 24, 1974; 1 son, John William. B.B.A., Western Mich. U. Sr. acct. Copper & Brass Sales, Inc., Detroit, 1971-75; auditor Detroit Baseball Club, 1975-76, bus. mgr., 1976-78, v.p. ops., 1978-83, exec. v.p., chief operating officer, 1983—. Served with USMC, 1963-66. Mem. Western Mich. U. Vets. Assn. (pres. 1970-71), VFW, Western Mich. U. Alumni Assn. Lodges: Masons; Shriners. Office: Detroit Baseball Club 2121 Trumbull St Detroit MI 48216

HAASS, ERWIN HERMAN, lawyer; b. Detroit, Feb. 18, 1904; s. Otto C. and Minnie (Peters) H.; m. Virginia Allmand, Oct. 5, 1937; children: Frederick, Robert, Stephen, Susan, Sandra. A.B., U. Mich., 1925, J.D., 1927. Bar: Mich. bar 1927. Asso. Race, Haass & Allen, Detroit, 1927-30; partner Hitt, Brewer & Haass, Detroit, 1930-41, Haass, Lungershausen, Frohlich & Lawrence (and predecessor firms), 1941-77; of counsel Dickinson, Wright, Moon, VanDusen and Freeman, Detroit, 1977—; dir. Ross Roy, Inc., Detroit, The First Bankers N.A., Pompano Beach, Fla., Pettibone Corp., Chgo. Served to lt. col. AUS, 1942-46. Clubs: Country, Detroit, Boat, Detroit Athletic, Grosse Pointe (Detroit); Royal Palm Yacht and Country (Boca Raton, Fla.). Home: 991 Hillsboro Beach Pompano Beach FL 33062 Office: PO Box 2795 Pompano Beach FL 33072

HAAYEN, RICHARD JAN, ins. co. exec.; b. Bklyn., June 30, 1924; s. Cornelius Marius and Cornelia Florence (Muskus) H.; m. Marilyn Jean Messner, Aug. 30, 1946; children—Richard Jan, Peter Wyckoff, James Carell. B.Sc., Ohio State U., 1948. With Allstate Ins. Co., 1950—, v.p. underwriting, 1969-75, exec. v.p., Northbrook, Ill., 1975-80, pres., 1980—, also dir.; dir. Ins. Info. Inst., N.Y.C., Tech-Cor, Wheeling, Ill., Ins. Inst. Am., Malvern, Pa. Bd. sponsors Evang. Hosp. Assn. Mem. Nat. Assn. Ind. Insurers, Property Casualty Ins. Council, Phi Delta Theta. Republican. Club: Chgo. Union League. Home: 1410 Lake Shore Dr S Barrington IL 60010 Office: Allstate Ins Co Allstate Plaza Northbrook IL 60062

HABBE, DONALD EDWIN, univ. exec.; b. Milw., Jan. 20, 1931; s. John Edwin and Anna May (Lewis) H.; m. Lois Ann Preucil, Dec. 27, 1953; children—Donald, Peter, Susan, Thomas. B.A., Denison U., 1952; M.S., U. Wis., 1954, Ph.D., 1957. Fgn. service officer Dept. State, Washington, and, Mexico, 1956-59; from asst. prof. to prof. polit. sci. U. S.D., Vermillion, 1959-67; asso. dean Coll. Arts and Scis., 1967-69, dean, 1970-77; acad. v.p. U. Mont., 1977—; Rockefeller fellow Fgn. Policy Assn. UN, 1961-62; vis. prof. Grad. Sch. Internat. Studies, U. Denver, 1964-65. Mem. Nat. Assn. State Univs. and Land Grant Colls. (mem. commn. on arts and scis.), Am. Polit. Sci. Assn., Internat. Studies Assn. Home: 10405 Grant Creek Rd Missoula MT 59801

HABECKER, EUGENE BRUBAKER, college administrator; b. Hershey, Pa., June 17, 1946; s. Walter Eugene and Frances (Miller) H.; m. Marylou Napolitano, July 27, 1968; children: David, Matthew, Marybeth. A.B., Taylor U., 1968; M.A., Ball State U., 1969; J.D., Temple U., 1974; Ph.D., U. Mich., 1981. Bar: Pa. 1974. Asst. dean Eastern Coll., St. Davids, Pa., 1970-74; dean students, asst. prof. polit. sci. George Fox Coll., Newberg, Oreg., 1974-78; exec. v.p. Huntington Coll., (Ind.), 1979-81, pres., 1981—; evaluation cons. North Central Assn., Chgo., 1982—; dir. Christian Coll. Coalition, Washington, 1982—, ICUI Inc., Indpls., 1983—; sec., mem. bd. Assoc. Colls. Ind., Indpls., 1982—. Author: Affirmative Action in Independent College, 1977; contbr. articles to profl. jours. Mem. steering com. Christians for Polit. Alternatives, Fort Wayne, Ind., 1979—. Mem. ABA, Christian Legal Soc., Assn. for Advancement of Higher Edn., Huntington C. of C. (mem. exec. devel. com. 1982—), Phi Delta Kappa. Republican. Mem. United Brethren Ch. Lodge: Rotary. Office: Huntington Coll 2303 Coll Ave Huntington IN 46750

HABEEB, VIRGINIA THABET, editor; b. Charleston, W.Va.; d. Mitchell Joseph and Rose M. (Couri) Thabet; m. Mitchell H. Habeeb. B.A. in Home Econs., Marshall U., 1946. Home service adviser Appalachian Electric Power Co., Abingdon, Va., 1946-49; with Crosley div. Avco Mfg. Corp., Cin., 1949-54; staff mem. field home econs. program, regional home economist, dir. nat. home econs. tng. program; women's editor daily show WCHS-TV, Charleston, 1954-55; asso. home equipment editor Am. Home mag., N.Y.C., 1955-58, home equipment editor, 1958-62, food and equipment editor, 1962-69, mng. editor, 1969-70; dir. Editorial Services, N.Y.C., 1970—; contbg. editor Ladies Home Jour., 1972—, Modern Bride mag., 1972—, Girl Talk mag., 1972—, Family Health Mag., 1975—. Author: The Little Chef's Book, 1953; editor: Handbook of Household Equipment Terminology, 1956-60; Editor: American Home All-Purpose Cook Book, 1966; author: Ladies Home Journal Art of Homemaking, 1973, Macap's Handbook for the Informed Consumer, 1973, Thousands of Creative Kitchen Ideas, 1976, The Complete Blender Cookbook, 1978, Remodeling Your Kitchen, 1980. Former mem. home com. Greater N.Y. Safety Council; mem. home conf. com. Nat. Safety Council; bd. dirs. Talbot-Perkins Children's Services, 1976—. Recipient Disting. Alumna award Dept. Home Econs., Marshall U., 1981, Marshall U. Alumni Assn., 1982. Mem. Am. Home Econs. Assn., Elec. Women's Round Table (chmn. N.Y. chpt. 1962-63), nat. dir. elec. women, nat. v.p. (1964-66), Advt. Women N.Y. (dir. 1971-72), Home Economists in Bus. (nat. chmn. housing and household equipment com. 1959-60), Maj. Appliance Consumer Action Panel (chmn. 1975-79), Home Appliance Mfrs. Assn. (hon. life). Office: 200 E 62d St New York NY 10021 also 1121 Crandon Blvd Suite D-608 Key Biscayne FL 33149

HABEL, ROBERT EARL, veterinary educator; b. Toledo, Aug. 8, 1918; s. Earl Urs and Grace (Vaughan) H.; m. Wilma Jane Fulks, June 6, 1942; children: Stephanie (Mrs. Montgomery T. Shaw), Gareth Robert. D.V.M., Ohio State U., 1941, M.Sc., 1947; M.V.D., State U. Utrecht, The Netherlands, 1956. Mem. faculty Cornell U., 1947—, asso. prof., 1950-60, prof. vet. anatomy, 1960-78, prof. emeritus, 1978, head dept., 1960-76; vice chmn. Internat. Com. Vet. Anatomical Nomenclature, 1963-80, mem. editorial com., 1967—; chmn. Internat. Com. Vet. Gross Anat. Nomenclature, 1980—. Author: (with J.R. Rooney and W.O. Sack) Guide to the Dissection of the Horse, 1977, Guide to the Dissection of Domestic Ruminants, 1977, Applied Veterinary Anatomy, 1981; Translator: (with E. Biberstein) Histology of Domestic Animals, 1952. Served to capt. AUS, 1942-46. NIH research fellow State U. Utrecht, 1953-54; Nat. Library Medicine research fellow Vienna (Austria) Vet. Coll., 1967-68, 75-76. Mem. Am. Assn. Anatomists, Am. Assn. Vet. Anatomists, World Assn. Vet. Anatomists (pres. 1971-75), Am., N.Y. State vet. med assns. Clubs: Adirondack Mountain (Glens Falls, N.Y.); Cayuga Trails (Ithaca). Home: 1529 Ellis Hollow Rd Ithaca NY 14850

HABER, EDGAR, physician, educator; b. Berlin, Germany, Feb. 1, 1932; came to U.S., 1939, naturalized, 1944; s. Fred Siegfried and Dorothy Judith (Bernstein) H.; m. Carol Avery, Nov. 16, 1958; children: Justin, Graham, Eben. A.B., Columbia U., 1952, M.D., 1956; M.A. (hon.), Harvard U., 1968. Diplomate: Am. Bd. Internal Medicine. Intern in medicine Mass. Gen. Hosp., Boston, 1956-57, asst. resident in medicine, 1957-58, resident in medicine, 1961-62, asst. in medicine, 1963-64, asst. physician, 1965-68, physician, 1969—, chief cardiac unit, 1964—; assoc. Lab. Cellular Physiology, Nat. Heart Inst., Bethesda, Md., 1958-61; hon. clin. asst. cardiac dept. St. George's Hosp., London, Eng., 1962-63; instr. medicine Harvard Med. Sch., Boston, 1963-64, asso. in medicine, 1964-65, asst. prof., 1965-68, assoc. prof., 1968-71, prof., 1972—; Mem. study sect. allergy and immunology NIH, 1965-68, vice chmn. panel on heart and blood vessel diseases, 1972-73, mem. arteriosclerosis task force, 1978; mem. task force on immunology and disease Nat. Inst. Allergy and Infectious Disease, 1972-73; mem. tissue and organ biology interdisciplinary cluster President's Biomed. Research Panel, 1975—; mem. U.S. del. to U.S.-USSR Health Exchange, 1975; vis. prof. Stanford U., 1967, 78, Emory U., 1971, U. Ala., 1971, 76, Mayo Clinic, 1972, U. Calif., San Francisco, 1972, Am. U., Beirut, Lebanon, 1972, Duke U., 1976, U. Mass., 1978; guest lectr. Biol. Soc. and Cardiol. Soc., Copenhagen, Denmark, 1971; WHO lectr., Santiago, Chile, 1973; Jennifer Jones Simon lectr. in med. scis. Calif. Inst. Tech., 1974; Alpha Omega Alpha lectr. La. State U., 1975; George C. Griffith sci. lectr., 1975; Centennial lectr. Meharry Med. Sch., 1976; John Kent Meml. lectr. Stanford U., 1978; Ives lectr. Soc. of Fellows, Scripps clinic and Research Found., 1979; Bunn Meml. lectr. Youngstown Hosp. Assn., N.E. Ohio Univs., 1979; John J. Sampson lectr. Mt. Zion Hosp. and Med. Center, San Francisco, 1979; 1st internat. lectr. Internat. Soc. and Fedn. of Cardiology. Co-author: Digitalis, 1974, The Future of Antibodies in Human Diagnosis and Therapy, 1976, The Practice of Cardiology, 1980; Editor: Hypertension, 1984-89; mem. editorial bd.: Jour. Clin. Investigation, 1969-70, Immunochemistry, 1970-74, Jour. Immunology, 1971-73, Clin. Immunology and Immunopathology, 1971—, New Eng. Jour. Medicine, 1978-81, Herz, 1979—, Circulation, 1978-81, Circulation Research, 1981; contbr. numerous articles to sci. jours., also chpts. to books. Trustee Boston Biomed. Research Inst., Inc. Served with USPHS, 1958-62. Named One of 10 Outstanding Young Men Boston Jr. C. of C., 1966; recipient medal of excellence Columbia U., 1976. Fellow Am. Coll. Cardiology, Am. Acad. Arts and Scis.; mem. Royal Soc. Medicine (London), Am. Soc. Biol. Chemists (membership com. 1971-73), Mass. Med. Soc., AAAS, Am. Assn. Immunologists, Am. Soc. Clin. Investigation (nominating com. 1972, councillor 1975), Am. Fedn. Clin. Research, Brit. Soc. Immunology, Assn. Am. Physicians, Internat. Soc. Hypertension (Volhard Prize 1980), Am. Heart Assn. (fellow council on clin. cardiology, research com. 1970—, v.p. for research 1973-74, pub. policy and govt. relations working group 1973—, George E. Brown meml. lectr. 1973), Internat. Union Immunological Socs. (chmn. edn. com. 1971-73), New Eng. Cardiovascular Soc. (pres. 1978-79), Assn. Univ. Cardiologists (pres. 1979-80), Phi Beta Kappa, Alpha Omega Alpha. Club: Harvard (Boston). Home: 83 Ridgeway Rd Weston MA 02193 Office: Cardiac Unit Mass Gen Hospital Boston MA 02114

HABER, FRANCIS COLIN, educator; b. Flint, Mich., Apr. 21, 1920; s. Arthur and Amelia (Glenfield) H.; m. Ruth E. Owens, 1943 (div.); 1 son, Robert O. Student U. Iowa, 1940-41; B.A., U. Conn., 1948; M.A., Johns Hopkins, 1951, Ph.D., 1957. Asso. editor Md. Hist. Mag., 1952-53; reference librarian Peabody Inst. Library, 1953-55; editor Md. Hist. Mag.; librarian Md. Hist. Soc., Balt., 1955-58; asst. prof. U. Fla., 1958-63, asso. prof., 1963-66; prof. U. Md., College Park, 1966—, chmn. dept. history, 1968-71. Author: Age of the World: Moses to Darwin, 1959, (with others) Forerunners of Darwin, 1959; Contbr. articles profl. jours. Served with U.S. Mcht. Marine, 1941-45. Am. Philos. Soc. grantee, 1958-64; Folger fellow, 1962. Fellow Royal Hist. Soc. (London); mem. History of Sci. Soc., Soc. History Tech., Internat. Soc. for Study of Time. Club: Cosmos (Washington). Home: 3026 R St NW Washington DC 20007 Office: Dept History U Md College Park MD 20742

HABER, IRA JOEL, artist, art educator; b. N.Y.C., Feb. 24, 1947; s. Oscar and Rosalind (Tilzer) H. Student public schs. Instr. art SUNY, Stony Brook, 1981—, U. Calif. (San Diego), 1982, Ohio State U. (Columbus), 1984. Exhibited one-man shows, Fischbach Gallery, N.Y.C., 1971, 72, 74, Kent (Ohio) State U., 1977, Pam Adler Gallery, N.Y.C., 1978, 80, 82, Rutgers U., 1980, SUNY, Stony Brook, 1981, one man shows, Ohio State U., 1984, group shows include, Mus. Modern Art, N.Y.C., 1970, Whitney Mus., N.Y.C., 1971, 73, Public Sch. One, L.I., N.Y., 1976, Albright-Knox Gallery, Buffalo, 1979; represented in permanent collections, N.Y. U., Guggenheim Mus., N.Y.C., Hirshhorn Mus., Washington, Allen Meml. Art Mus., Oberlin (Ohio) Coll., Albright-Knox Gallery, Buffalo. Nat. Endowment for Arts fellow, 1974, 77; Creative Artists Public Service grantee, 1974, 77; Ariana Found. grantee, 1982. Address: 105 W 27th St New York NY 10001

HABER, JACK N., editor; b. Bklyn., Feb. 26, 1939; s. Michael H. and Ada (Weiss) H. Attended, Bklyn. Coll., 1956-58. Asso. editor Men's Wear mag., 1962-65; editor Scene mag., Esquire publ., 1965-68; sr. editor Clothes mag., 1968-69; editor Gentlemen's Quar. (acquired by Condé Nast Publs. 1979), N.Y.C., 1969-77, editor-in-chief, 1977—; instr. exec. seminars in men's wear store mgmt. N.Y. U. Inst. Retail Mgmt., 1970-74; lectr. Field Studies Center N.Y., 1980—, Wharton Exec. Lifestyles lecture series Wharton Sch., 1980-81. Served with AUS, 1958-60. Recipient Lulu award for excellence in reporting men's fashion news Men's Fashion Assn.-Menswear Retailers Am., 1971, 72. Mem. Am. Soc. Mag. Editors. Home: 25 Fifth Ave New York NY 10003 Office: 350 Madison Ave New York NY 10017

HABER, JOYCE, writer, columnist; b. N.Y.C., Dec. 28, 1932; d. John Sanford and Lucille (Buckmaster) H.; m. Douglas S. Cramer, Jr., 1966 (div. 1974); children: Douglas S. III, Courtney Sanford. Student, Bryn Mawr Coll., 1949-50; A.B., Barnard Coll., 1953. Researcher, Time Mag., 1953-63, Los Angeles corr., 1963-66; columnist Los Angeles

Times and Los Angeles Times Syndicate, 1966-75; contbg. editor Los Angeles mag., 1977-79; freelance writer. Author: Caroline's Doll Book, 1962, The Users, 1976; contbr.: articles to numerous popular mags. including New West Mag. *God's gift to art and life is truth: the Devil's curse is hypocrisy. Let the truth be told. Let Shakespeare and Shaw and Dickens and Hemingway and O'Hara be read. But let us also read Russell Baker and Theodore White and Art Buchwald. And never forget the wit of Dorothy Parker, or the sainted prose (if not the ideology) of Simone de Beauvoir. Let us not be depressed by their genius, but take compensation in what is often facetiously called the great American Puritan ethic—work. Believe that if you work longer and harder than they, you will succeed, and satisfy, and entertain. Entertainment—through honesty—and love—is all.*

HABER, MERYL HAROLD, physician, educator, author; b. Cleve., Dec. 28, 1934; s. Harry J. and Sadie (P.) H.; m. Virginia J. Jackson, Oct. 1, 1959; children: Michael, Jeffrey, Deborah. B.S., Northwestern U., 1956, M.S., 1958, M.D., 1959. Diplomate: Am. Bd. Pathology. Intern Los Angeles County Gen. Hosp., 1959-60; resident Chgo. Wesley Meml. Hosp., 1960-61; fellow in pathology Univ. Coll. Med. Sch., London, 1961-62; resident Passavant Meml. Hosp., Chgo., 1962-64, head anatomic pathology, 1964-66; instr. pathology Northwestern U. Med. Sch., 1963-66, prof. clin. pathology, 1981—; dir. labs. St. Francis Hosp., Honolulu, 1966-73; asso. prof. pathology U. Hawaii, 1966-71, prof., 1971-73, U. Nev., 1973-80, chmn. dept. pathology and lab. medicine, 1973-80; program dir. Sch. Med. Tech., 1973-80; prof. Rush Med. Coll., Chgo., 1980—, assoc. chmn. dept. pathology, 1980—; exec. v.p. Am. Soc. Clin. Pathologists, Chgo., 1980-82. Author: Urine Casts: Their Microscopy & Clinical Significance, 1976, The Urinary Sediment, A Textbook Atlas, 1981; mem. editorial bd.: Am. Jour. Clin. Pathology, 1976-82, The Pathologist, 1984—; cover editor: Lab Medicine, 1978-82. Bd. dirs. Makana Found., Hawaii, 1970-73; bd. dirs. Nev. div. Am. Cancer Soc., 1976-80. USPHS fellow, 1958-64. Fellow Am. Soc. Clin. Pathologists, Coll. Am. Pathologists. Office: 1753 W Congress Pkwy Chicago IL 60612

HABER, RALPH NORMAN, educator; b. Lansing, Mich., May 15, 1932; s. William and Fannie (Gallas) H.; m. Ruth Lea Boss, 1961 (div. 1974); children—Sabrina Beth, Rebecca Ann; m. Lyn R. Roland, 1974. B.A., U. Mich., 1953; M.A., Wesleyan U., Middletown, Conn., 1954; Ph.D., Stanford, 1957; Postdoctoral fellow, Med. Research Council, Applied Psychology Unit, Cambridge, Eng., 1970-71. Research asso. Inst. for Communication Research, Stanford, 1957-58; instr. psychology San Francisco State Coll., 1957-58; asst. prof. psychology Yale, 1958-64; asso. prof. psychology U. Rochester, N.Y., 1964-67, prof. psychology, 1967-70, prof. psychology and visual sci., 1970-79, chmn. dept. psychology, 1967-70, mem. faculty senate, 1968-70, sec., mem. steering com., 1969-70; prof. psychology U. Ill., Chgo., 1979—; vis. prof. Air Force Human Resources Lab., Williams AFB, Ariz., 1981—; vis. scientist Med. Research Council Applied Psychology Unit, Cambridge, Eng., 1970-71; chmn., divisional maj. III Yale, 1959-64; vis. asst. prof. New Sch. for Social Research, 1963; research cons. VA, 1967-71; adv. editor for exptl. psychology Holt, Rinehart & Winston Book Pubs., 1969-77. Author: (with Hershenson) The Psychology of Visual Perception, 1973, 2d edit., 1980, (with Fried) An Introduction to Psychology, 1975, (with others) Discovering Psychology, 1977; Editor: Current Research on Motivation, 1966, Contemporary Theory and Research on Visual Perception, 1968, Information Processing Approaches to Visual Perception, 1969; Contbr. articles to profl. jours. Mem. Nat. Acad. Sci.-NRC Com. on Vision, 1970—; Committeeman 18th Ward, Brighton (N.Y.) Democratic Com., 1967-70; Founding mem., trustee Coll. Admission Prep. Program, Rochester, 1968-70. Recipient Outstanding Achievement award U. Mich., 1977; Behavioral Sci. fellow Ford Found., 1953-54; Fellow NSF; fellow NIMH, Nat. Inst. Edn., Air Force Office Sci. Research. Fellow Am. Psychol. Assn., A.A.A.S.; mem. Eastern Psychol. Assn., Psychonomics Soc., Optical Soc. Am., Sigma Xi, Pi Lambda Phi. Home: 3268 Summit Ave Highland Park IL 60035 Office: Dept Psychology U Ill at Chgo Circle Chicago IL 60680

HABER, WARREN H., business executive; b. Mar. 9, 1941; m.; 2 children. B.A. in Adminstrn., CUNY, 1962. Chmn. bd. Kenai Corp., N.Y.C., 1973—; chmn bd. Ocilla Industries, Inc., N.Y.C., 1981—; ptnr. Founders Equity, Inc., N.Y.C., 1969—, Founders Property Mgmt. Co., Inc., 1980—; a founder New Am., Inc. (now Campanelli Industries, Inc.), Braintree, Mass., 1970, dir. Bd. dirs., treas. 1070 Park Ave. Corp., N.Y.C.; bd. dirs., trustee Allen-Stevenson Sch., N.Y.C.; bd. dirs. Internat. Ctr. for Disabled, N.Y.C. Served with M.C. USAR, 1962. Club: Athletic. Home: 1070 Park Ave New York NY 10028

HABER, WILLIAM, educator, economist; b. Rumania, Mar. 6, 1899; U.S., 1909; s. Leon and Anna (Stern) B.; m. Fannie Gallas, Aug. 31, 1924; children—Ralph, Alan. B.A., U. Wis., 1923, M.A., 1926, Ph.D., 1927; postgrad., U. Wis. and Harvard, 1924-25; L.H.D. honoris causa, Hebrew Union Coll., 1961, Mich. State U., 1970; Ph.D. (hon.), Hebrew U., Jerusalem, 1971; LL.D., Brandeis U., 1974. Labor mgr. Hart, Schaffner & Marx, 1923; instr. econs. U. Wis., 1926-27; asso. prof. econs. Mich. State Coll., 1927-36; prof. econs. U. Mich., 1936—, chmn. dept., 1962-63; dean Coll. Lit., Sci. and Arts, 1963-68, spl. adviser to exec. officers, 1968—; dir. Oakland Housing, Inc., 1935—, chmn., 1970—; dir. Huron Valley Nat. Bank; impartial chmn. Kaiser UAW Retirement Fund, 1951—; state emergency welfare relief adminstr., 1933-36; state dir. Nat. Youth Adminstrn. for Mich., 1935-36; dep. dir. WPA, 1934-36; chmn. Unemployment Ins. Study Commn., 1936; mem. Mich. Unemployment Compensation Commn., 1936-37; cons. Social Security Bd., 1939-45, Nat. Resources Planning Bd., 1940-44, chmn. com. long-range work and relief policy, 1941-44; spl. asst. to dir. Bur. Budget, 1942, mem. conf. post war relief readjustment of civilian and mil. personnel, 1943, chief planning div., 1942; dir. Bur. Program Requirement, War Manpower Commn., 1943, asst. exec. dir., 1944; adviser on manpower to dir. Office War Moblzn. and Reconversion, 1945, cons., 1945- 46; mem. Am. Assn. Social Security (com. post-def. planning), 1941, U.S. Employment Service (tech. bd. on occupational research program), 1940; chmn. Fed. Adv. Council on Employment Security, 1948—; mem. Manpower Cons. Com., Nat. Resources Security Bd., Nat. Def. Agy., 1947- 48; mem. pub. adv. com. Area Redevel. Adminstrn., Dept. Commerce, 1962, mem. regional export expansion council, 1962; panel Am. Arbitration Assn.; mem. Nat. Acad. Arbitrators, Social Science Research Council (com. on econ. security), 1941—; mem. indsl. com. (for paper products, rubber and textiles) Wage and Hour Adminstrn., 1941; mem. Adv. Council on Social Security, 1938-39; cons. on manpower to sec. of labor, and Def. Manpower Adminstrn.; Adviser on Jewish affairs to comdr.-in-chief U.S. Forces in Germany and Austria., 1948-49; mem. Pres.'s Task Force on Depressed Areas, 1961; Exec. com. Am.-Jewish Com., 1945—; chmn. nat. Hillel commn. B'nai B'rith, 1949-64, hon. chmn., 1964—; pres. Am. ORT Fedn. (rehab. through training), 1951; pres. central bd. World ORT Union, 1955—. Author: Industrial Relations in the Building Industry, 1930, Unemployment Relief and Economic Security, 1936, The Cost of Financing Unemployment Insurance in Michigan, 1952, Labor Relations and Productivity in the Building Trades, (with H.L. Levinson), 1955; co-author: Post War Economic Reconstruction, 1945, The Michigan Economy: Its Potentials and Its Problems, 1960, (with Wilbur J. Cohen) Social Security Program Problems and Policies, 1961, (with others) Michigan in the 1970s, 1965, (with Merrill G. Murray) Unemployment Insurance in the American Economy, 1966; Editor: Readings in Social Security, 1948, Labor in a Changing America, 1966; co-editor: Manpower in the United States, 1954; Contbr. to: others. Bd. dirs. United Service for New Americans, 1947—; bd. govs. Hebrew U., Jerusalem, 1968—; trustee Brandeis U., 1969—. Recipient John Dewey award League Indsl. Democracy, 1960, John Lendrum Mitchell award indsl. relations U. Wis., 1924; Wertheim fellow for research indsl. relations Harvard, 1925. Mem. Am. Econ. Assn., Am. Pub. Welfare Assn., Soc. Pub. Adminstrn., Indsl. Relations Research Assn. (pres. 1960). Home: 530 Hillspur Rd Barton Hills Ann Arbor MI 48105

HABERECHT, ROLF REINHOLD, electronics company executive; b. Germany, June 4, 1929; s. Max F. and Olga H.; m. Ute Haberecht, Aug. 21, 1961; children: Michael, Caroline. M.S., Tech. U., Berlin, 1954, Ph.D., 1956; M.B.A., So. Meth. U., 1967. Research scientist P.R. Mallory & Co., Inc., Indpls., 1956-61; with Tex. Instruments, Inc., Dallas, 1962-83, v.p., 1975-83; chmn. bd. Semicon Advanced Tech., Inc., Richardson, Tex., 1983—. Trustee St. Mark's Sch. of Tex., Dallas, 1978—, Episcopal Sch. of Dallas, 1979—, Lamplighter Sch. Patentee in field. Office: 1850 N Greenville Ave Suite 140-R Richardson TX 75081

HABERKERN, ROY CONRAD, JR., lawyer; b. Winston-Salem, N.C., Nov. 14, 1915; s. Roy Conrad and Esther (Hampton) H.; m. Maria Carlota Isabel Garfias, Sept. 27, 1941; children: Roy Conrad, Richard G., Charles M., John H. B.S. summa cum laude, Haverford Coll., 1937; LL.B. cum laude, Yale U., 1940. Bar: N.Y. 1941, D.C. 1960. Assoc. Milbank, Tweed, Hadley & McCloy, N.Y.C., 1940-42, 46-48, ptnr., 1948—; dir. various affiliates Chase Manhattan Bank, N.Am. Pres. Garden City Sch. Bd., N.Y., 1955-69; 1st v.p. bd. dirs. Nassau Hosp., Mineola, N.Y.; mem. Cathedral chpt. Cathedral of the Incarnation, Garden City. Served with USAAF, 1942-46. Decorated Legion of Merit. Mem. ABA, N.Y. State Bar Assn., N.Y.C. Bar Assn., Nassau County (N.Y.) Bar Assn., Am. Law Inst. Episcopalian. Clubs: Downtown Assn., Cherry Valley, Yale of N.Y., Wall St. Lodge: Masons. Home: 80 Brook St Garden City NY 11530 Office: Milbank Tweed Hadley & McCloy 1 Chase Manhattan Plaza New York NY 10005

HABERLER, GOTTFRIED, economist; b. Purkersdorf, Austria, July 20, 1900; came to U.S., 1936. D. in Law and Econs., U. Vienna, Austria, 1925. Lectr, later prof. econs. and stats., Vienna U., Austria, 1928-36; vis. lectr. Harvard U., 1931-32; attached to fin. sect. League of Nations, Geneva, 1934-36; prof. internat. trade Harvard U., 1936-71, prof. emeritus, 1971—; resident scholar Am. Enerprise Inst., Washington, 1971—; bd. govs. FRS, Washington, 1943. Mem. Internat. Econ. Assn. (pres. 1950-51), Nat. Bur. Econ. Research (pres. 1955), Am. Econs. Assn. (v.p. 1948), Royal Econ. Soc., Econometric Soc. Home: 4108 48th St NW Washington DC 20016 Office: Am Enterprise Inst 1150 17th St NW Washington DC 20036

HABERMAN, FREDERICK WILLIAM, educator; b. Duquesne, Pa., May 11, 1908; s. Louis Henry and Maude (McLaughlin) H.; m. Helen Louise Power, June 16, 1934; children—Frederick William IV, Ann Marwood (Mrs. Gene L. Armstrong). A.B., Allegheny Coll., 1930; A.M., U. Wis., 1936; Ph.D., Cornell U., 1947. Tchr. Harborcreek (Pa.) High Sch., 1930-32; instr. Allegheny Coll., 1932-36, asst. prof., 1942-43; instr. Princeton, 1938-42; faculty U. Wis., Madison, 1947—, successively asst. prof., asso. prof., 1949-52, prof., 1952-79, Andrew T. Weaver prof. communication arts, 1973-79, Andrew T. Weaver prof. emeritus, 1979—; chmn. dept. speech, 1954-70. Author: (with James W. Cleary) A Bibliography, 1947-61, 1964, Nobel Lectures—Peace, 3 vols, 1972; Editor: (with others) An Historical Anthology of Select British Speeches, 1967; Contbr. essays to profl. jours. and books. Mem. bd. edn. Joint dist. 1, towns of, Middleton and Madison, Wis., 1951-54. Served to lt. USNR, 1943-46. Mem. AAUP, Speech Communication Assn., Central States, Wis. speech communication assns., Phi Kappa Phi, Delta Sigma Rho, Phi Delta Theta. Home: 5760 Bittersweet Pl Madison WI 53705

HABGOOD, ANTHONY JOHN, management consultant; b. Woodbastwick, Eng., Nov. 8, 1946; s. John Michael and Diana Margaret (Dalby) H.; m. Nancy Ray Atkinson, June 29, 1974; children: Elizabeth Ann, John Alan, George Michael. B.A. in Econs., Gonville and Caius Coll., Cambridge U., 1968; M.A., Cambridge U., 1971; M.S. in Indsl. Adminstrn., Carnegie-Mellon U., Pitts., 1970. With Boston Cons. Group Inc., 1970—, v.p., dir., 1977—, mem. mgmt. com., 1980-82, mem. exec. com., 1983—. W.L. Mellon fellow, 1968-70. Mem. Ch. of Eng. Club: Royal Norfolk and Suffolk Yacht. Office: 68 Knightsbridge London SW1 England

HABIB, PHILIP CHARLES, former foreign service officer; b. Bklyn., Feb. 25, 1920; s. Alex and Mary (Spiridon) H.; m. Marjorie W. Slightam, Aug. 27, 1942; children: Phyllis A., Susan W. B.S., U. Idaho, 1942, LL.D., 1974; Ph.D., U. Calif. at Berkeley, 1952. Fgn. service officer, 1949-78, 3d sec. Am. embassy, Ottawa, Can., 1949-51, 2d sec. Am. embassy, Wellington, N.Z., 1952-54; research specialist Dept of State, Washington, 1955-57; Am. consulate gen., Port of Spain, Trinidad, 1958-60, fgn. affairs officer Dept. State, 1960-61, counselor for polit. affairs Am. embassy, Seoul, Korea, 1962-65, Saigon, Vietnam, 1965-67, personal rank of minister, 1966-67; dep. asst. sec. State for East Asian and Pacific affairs, 1967-69; mem. U.S. delegation to meetings on, Vietnam, Paris, 1968-71, personal rank of ambassador, 1969-71; ambassador to Republic of Korea, Seoul, 1971-74; asst. sec. state for East Asian and Pacific affairs, 1974-76, undersec. of state for polit. affairs, 1976-78; diplomat-in-residence Stanford U., 1978-79; sr. advisor to Sec. of State, 1979-80; personal rep. of Pres. to Middle East, 1981—; sr. research fellow Hoover Instn., 1980—. Served from pvt. to capt. AUS, 1942-46. Recipient Rockefeller Pub. Service award, 1969; Nat. Civil Service League award, 1970; Dept. State Disting. Honor award, 1977; Pres.'s award for disting. fed. service, 1979; Presdl. Medal of Freedom, 1982; Lebanon's Order of Cedars, 1982. Roman Catholic. Address: 1606 Courtland Rd Belmont CA 94002

HABICHT, CHRISTIAN HERBERT, history educator; b. Dortmund, Ger., Feb. 23, 1926; came to U.S., 1972; s. Hermann Christian and Emile Julie (Diefenbach) H.; m. Freia Renate Wilkowski, Aug. 15, 1952; children: Susanne, Christoph, Nikolaus. Dr.Phil., U. Hamburg, 1952, Habil, 1957. Asst. to assoc. prof. U. Hamburg, 1952-61; prof. ancient history U. Marburg/Lahn, 1961-65; prof. U. Heidelberg, 1965-73, dean, 1966-67; prof. Inst. Advanced Study, Princeton, N.J., 1973—; vis. prof. Princeton U., 1973—. Author books; contbr. articles to profl. jours. Mem. Am. Philos. Soc., Acad. Heidelberg, German Archeol. Inst., Austrian Archeol. Inst., Am. Inst. Archeology, Assn. Ancient Historians. Office: Sch Hist Studies Inst Advanced Study Princeton NJ *

HABICHT, FRANK HENRY, II, lawyer; b. Oak Park, Ill., Apr. 10, 1953; s. Frank Henry and Jeanne Ellen (Patrick) H.; m. Wendy Louise Wilson, June 14, 1980; 1 dau., Jennifer Alane. A.B., Princeton U., 1975; J.D., U. Va., 1978. Bar: D.C. 1978, U.S. Supreme Ct. 1983. Assoc. Kirkland & Ellis, Washington, 1978-81; spl. asst. to atty. gen. U.S., Dept. Justice, Washington, 1981-83; dep. asst. atty. gen. for natural resources Dept. Justice, Washington, 1982-83, asst. atty. gen. for land and natural resources, 1983—; mem. faculty Am. Law Inst.-ABA Continuing Edn., 1983. Editor: Va. Jour. Internat. Law, 1977-78. Mem. transition team Dept. Justice, 1980. Dillard Legal Writing fellow, 1977-78; Nat. Merit scholar, 1971. Mem. ABA, U. Va. Alumni Assn. Republican. Presbyterian. Club: Princeton Rugby (pres. 1974-75). Office: Dept Justice 10th and Constitution Ave NW Washington DC 20530

HABICHT, JEAN-PIERRE, public health researcher, educator, consultant; b. Geneva, Dec. 15, 1934; U.S., 1974; s. Max H. and Elizabeth (Peterson) Herzog; m. Pat Hinxman, Jan. 3, 1959; children: Heidi, Christopher, Oliver. M.D., U. Zurich, 1962, Dr. Medicine, 1964; M.P.H., Harvard U., 1968; Ph.D., MIT, 1969. Cert. in clin nutrition Am. Bd. Nutrition. Biochem. research asst. Merck, Sharpe & Dohme, Rahway, N.J., 1958-59; pediatric intern Children's Hosp. Med. Ctr., Boston, 1965-66; med. officer WHO, Guatemala, 1969-74; prof. maternal and child health U. San Carlos, Guatemala, 1972-74; spl. asst. Nat. Ctr. for Health Stats., Washington, 1974-77; James Jamison prof. nutritional epidemiology Cornell U., Ithaca, N.Y., 1977—; cons. on pub. health issues to internat. agys., nat. govts., 1975—; mem. expert com. on nutrition WHO, Geneva, 1975—; mem. Task Force WHO Reproductive Unit, Geneva, 1978-80; mem. epidemiology and disease control study sect. NIH, Washington, 1980-83; mem. food and nutritional bd. Nat. Acad. Scis., Washington, 1981—; mem. UN Coordinating Subcom. Nutrition, 1983—. Contbr. articles to profl. jours., chpts. in books. Fellow Am. Coll. Epidemiology; mem. AAAS, Am. Inst. Nutrition, Am. Pub. Health Assn., Soc. for Epidemiologic Research, Internat. Epidemiol. Assn., Sigma Xi, Delta Omega. Democrat. Quaker. Office: Div Nutritional Sci Savage Hall Cornell U Ithaca NY 14853

HABIF, DAVID V., surgeon, educator; b. Cin. M.D., Columbia, 1939. Diplomate: Am. Bd. Surgery (mem. bd. 1966-72, vice chmn. 1971-72). Successively intern, asst. resident surgery, resident surgery, attending surgery Presbyn. Hosp., N.Y.C., 1939-47; Morris and Rose Milstein prof. surgery Columbia Coll. Phys. and Surg., 1972—. Served with AUS, 1942-45. Decorated Bronze Star, Presdl. Citation with 2 oak leaf clusters. Fellow A.C.S.; mem. A.M.A., Soc. Exptl. Biology and Medicine, Am. Surg. Assn., Soc. Univ. Surgeons, Halsted Soc., Soc. Surgery Alimentary Tract, Allen O. Whipple Surg. Soc. (pres. 1968-70), N.Y. Surg. Soc. (pres. 1974-75). Address: 161 Fort Washington Ave New York City NY 10032

HABIG, ARNOLD FRANK, piano, organ, furniture mfg. exec.; b. Jasper, Ind., May 2, 1907; s. Frank A. and Sarah (Rottet) H.; m. Barbara T. Cukierski.; children—Thomas, John, Douglas, Nancy, Margaret Ann, Barbara, Marilyn. Grad., Spencerian Bus. Coll., 1926; LL.B., U. Evansville, 1978. With Jasper Wood Products Co., 1928-50; co-founder, pres. Jasper Corp., 1950-63, chmn., 1963-74, Kimball Internat., Inc., 1974-82, asst. to chief exec. officer, 1982—; with Spring Valley Bank and Trust Co., 1958—, now chmn. bd. Office: Jack Schneider Kimball Internat Inc 1549 Royal St Jasper IN 57546

HABIG, DOUGLAS ARNOLD, manufacturing company executive; b. Louisville, 1946; s. Arnold F. and Mary Ann (Jahn) H. B.S., St. Louis U., 1968; M.B.A., Ind. U., 1972. Comml. loan officer Ind. Nat. Bank, Indpls., 1972-75; exec. v.p., treas., chief fin. officer Kimball Internat. Inc., Jasper, Ind., 1975-81, pres., dir., 1981—. Office: Kimball Internat Inc 1600 Royal St Jasper IN 47546

HABIG, THOMAS LOUIS, piano, organ, furniture manufacturing executive; b. Jasper, Ind., June 18, 1928; s. Arnold Frank and Mary Ann (Jahn) H.; m. C. Roberta Snyder, Jan. 31, 1953; children: Randall, Julia, Brian, Sandra, Paul. B.B.A., Tulane U., 1950. With Kimball Internat., Inc. (predecessor firm), Jasper, and, 1952; (predecessor firm), 1952—, exec. v.p., 1960-63, pres., 1963—, chmn., chief exec. officer, 1981—, also dir.; dir. Springs Valley Nat. Bank. Served with AUS, 1950-52. Mem. Am. Legion, Sigma Chi. Roman Catholic. Club: K.C. Office: 1600 Royal St PO Box 460 Jasper IN 47546 *I learned from experience and have continued the philosophy of hiring or promoting exceptionally qualified people into key executive positions and delegating to them virtually complete responsibility for profit performance in line with an agreed to "game plan" of operation.*

HACAULT, ANTOINE JOSEPH LEON, bishop; b. Bruxelles, Man., Can., Jan. 17, 1926; s. Francois and Irma (Mangin) H. B.A., U. Man., 1947; theol. student, St. Boniface Maj. Sem., 1947-51; S.T.D., Angelicum U., Rome, 1954; D.C.L. honoris causa, St. John's Coll., Winnipeg, Man., 1977. Ordained priest Roman Cath. Ch., 1951; chaplain St. Boniface Sanatorium, 1954; prof. theology St Boniface Maj. Sem., 1954-64; dir. diocesan rev. Les Cloches de Saint Boniface, 1961; personal theologian to archbishop of St. Boniface; also council expert 2d Vatican Ecumenical Council, 1962-64; bishop titular of, Media, aux. bishop of, St. Boniface, 1964-72, coadjutor bishop, 1972-74, archbishop of, St. Boniface, 1974—; rector Coll. St. Boniface, 1967-69. Address: 151 Ave de la Cathedrale Saint Boniface MB Canada R2H 0H6 *

HACHEY, THOMAS EUGENE, British and Irish history educator, consultant; b. Lewiston, Maine, June 8, 1938; s. Leo Joseph and Margaret Mary (Johnson) H.; m. Jane Beverly Whitman, June 9, 1962. B.A., St. Francis Coll., 1960; M.A., Niagara U., 1961; Ph.D., St. John's U., 1965. Asst. prof. history Marquette U., Milw., 1964-69, assoc. prof., 1969-77, prof., 1977—, chmn. dept. history, 1979—; vis. prof. history Sch. Irish Studies, Dublin, 1977-78, U. Vt., Burlington, 1978; cons. investments in Ireland Frost & Sullivan, N.Y.C., 1978—; pres. Am. Conf. Irish Studies, 1983—. Author: Problem of Partition: Peril to World Peace, 1972, Britain and Irish Separatism, 1977; editor: Voices of Revolution, 1972, Confidential Despatches, 1974. Fellow Anglo-Am. Assocs. Roman Catholic. Home: 663 N 75th St Wauwatosa WI 53213 Office: Dept History Marquette U Milwaukee WI 53213

HACHTEN, WILLIAM ANDREWS, journalism educator, author; b. Wichita, Kans., Nov. 30, 1924; s. George Charles and Emma Elizabeth (Andrews) H.; m. Harva Kaaren Sprager, Apr. 5, 1952; children: Elizabeth, Marianne. B.A., Stanford, 1947; M.S., UCLA, 1952; Ph.D., U. Minn., 1961. Profl. football player N.Y. Giants, 1947; reporter Santa Paula (Calif.) Chronicle, 1948-49, Long Beach (Calif.) Press-Telegram, 1952-54, Santa Monica (Calif.) Outlook, 1954; copy editor Los Angeles Examiner, 1955-56; prof. Sch. Journalism and Mass Communication, U. Wis.-Madison, 1959—, asst. dir., 1973-75, dir., 1975-80. Author: The Supreme Court on Freedom of the Press, 1968, Muffled Drums: The News Media in Africa, 1971, Mass Communication in Africa: An Annotated Bibliography, 1971, World News Prism, 1981; assoc. editor: Journalism Quar, 1972-75. Served with USMCR, 1943-46. Recipient Sigma Delta Chi award for research in journalism, 1968, Fulbright-Hays Research award for Africa, 1968; Fulbright lectr. U. Ghana, 1972-73. Mem. Assn. Edn. Journalism, Internat. Press Inst., Internat. Assn. Mass Communication Research. Unitarian. Home: 2130 Chamberlain Ave Madison WI 53705

HACK, JOHN TILTON, geologist; b. Chgo., Dec. 3, 1913; m. Clare Ferriter, 1942; children: Katherine Ferriter Hack Parker, John Tilton. A.B., Harvard, 1935, M.A., 1938, Ph.D. in Geomorphology, 1940. Geologist Awatovi Expdn., Peabody Mus. Harvard, 1937-39; instr. geology Hofstra Coll., 1940-42; geologist U.S. Geol. Survey, Interior Dept., Washington, 1942—, asst. chief geologist for environ. geology, 1966-71, research geologist, 1971-84; professorial lectr. George Washington U., Washington, 1980-83. Contbr. articles to profl. jours. Recipient Kirk Bryan award Geol. Soc. Am., 1961; Disting. Service award Dept. Interior, 1972; G.K. Warren prize Nat. Acad. Sci., 1982. Fellow Geol. Soc. Am.; mem. AAAS. Club: Cosmos (Washington). Office: 4722 Rodman St NW Washington DC 20016 *Throughout my professional career I have been fortunate in having superiors and close colleagues who were in sympathy with my scientific goals. On my part I was willing to take on some of the less rewarding tasks that have to be done in a large organization. Whatever the reason, my professional life has been very rewarding to me.*

HACK, MARVIN H., educator; b. Rochester, Feb. 25, 1917; s. James W. and Dorothy (Bennett) H. B.S., Roosevelt Coll., 1949; Ph.D., U. Chgo., 1951. Mem. faculty Tulane U., New Orleans, 1952—, prof. histochemistry, 1964—; prof., chmn. dept. biochemistry King Faisal U., Dammam, Saudi Arabia, 1977-78; biochemist NIH, 1955. Editorial bd.: Cellular and Molecular Biology, 1977—. Mem. Am. Assn. Anatomists, Soc. Exptl. Biology and Medicine, Am. Soc. Biochemists, Sigma Xi. Research and publs. on biochemistry, histochemistry, methodology and physiology of lipids using comparative techniques. Home: 1430 Tulane Ave New Orleans LA 70112

HACKBERT, DONALD MICHAEL, printing company executive; b. Chgo., Mar. 14, 1933; s. Louis James and Ruth Miriam (Zoleski) H.; m. Sherele A. Glenn, Jan. 28, 1956; children: Michael, Virginia, Judy. Student, Western Ill. U., 1950-51; M.B.A., U. Chgo., 1974-75. With R.R. Donnelley & Sons Co., 1955—, dir. mfg. div., Lancaster, Pa., 1965-68, v.p. mfg., Warsaw, Ind., 1968-72, sales v.p., Chicago, 1972-80, group v.p., 1980—. Republican. Presbyterian. Club: Union League (Chgo.). Home: 606 Lakeview Terr Glen Ellyn IL 60137 Office: RR Donnelley & Sons Co 2223 King Dr Chicago IL 60616

HACKBIRTH, DAVID WILLIAM, aluminum company executive; b. Butler, Ind., Jan. 25, 1935; s. Ernest William and Bessie Mae (Snyder) H.; m. Anna Katherine Shaffer, July 19, 1959; children: Cynthia Kay, David William. Student, Defiance Coll., 1953; B.S., Ind. U., 1959; J.D., Wayne State U., 1963, postgrad., 1965; M.B.A., U. Detroit, 1965. Bar: Mich. bar 1963. Auditor Ernst & Ernst, Indpls., 1958-59; fin. and budget analyst Ford Motor Co., Dearborn, Mich., 1959-62; legal adminstr. Chrysler Corp., Detroit, 1962-63, tax atty., 1963-66, Glidden Co., Cleve., 1966-67; asst. to treas. Alcan Aluminum Corp., Cleve., 1967-70, asst. to group v.p. ops., 1970-73; pres., dir. Aluminio de Colombia S.A., 1973-75; v.p. Alcan Bldg. Products div. Alcan Aluminum Corp., Warren, Ohio, 1975-78, pres., 1978-83, Alcan Sheet and Plate div., 1983—; dir. Alcan Aluminum Corp., Cleve. Served with U.S. Army, 1954-56. Mem. Aluminum Assn. (vice chmn. sheet and plate div.), Mich. Bar Assn., ABA, Cleve. Growth Assn., Can Mfrs. Inst. (dir.), Beta Alpha Psi, Delta Theta Phi. Clubs: Country of Hudson, Walden Golf and Tennis, Western Res. Racquet, Cotillion Soc. Cleve., Clevelander, Scottish Rite. Home: 290 Bicknell Dr Hudson OH 44236 Office: Alcan Sheet and Plate 100 Erieview Plaza Cleveland OH 44114

HACKEL, EMANUEL, science educator; b. Bklyn., June 17, 1925; s. Henry N. and Esther (Herbstman) H.; m. Elisabeth Mackie, June 24, 1950 (dec. Apr. 1978); children: Lisa M., Meredith Anne, Janet M.; m. Rachel A. Fisher, Oct. 18, 1981; stepchildren: Daniel E., Tabitha A., and Jessica K. Harrison. Student, N.Y. U., 1941-42; B.S., U. Mich., 1948, M.S., 1949; Ph.D., Mich. State U., 1953. Fisheries biologist Mich. Dept. Conservation, 1949; mem. faculty Mich. State U., East Lansing, 1949—, prof. natural sci., 1962-74, chmn. dept. natural sci., 1963-74, prof. medicine, 1974—, prof. zoology, 1974—; asst. dean coll., 1958-63; research fellow Galton Lab., Univ. Coll., London, Eng., 1970-71, 77-78; vis. investigator blood group research unit Lister Inst., London, Eng., 1956-57; cons. Mpls. War Meml. Blood Bank, 1983—. Author: Guide to Laboratory Studies in Biological Science, 1951, Studies in Natural Science, 1953, Natural Science, 1955, Vols. 1, 2, 3, 1952-63; Editor, 1963, The Search for Explanation-Studies in Natural Science, Vols. 1, 2, 3, 1967-68, Laboratory Manual for Natural Science, Vol. 1, 2, 3, 1967-68, Human Genetics, 1974, Theoretical Aspects of HLA, 1982, Bone Marrow Transplantation, 1983; Contbr. articles on genetics, human blood group immunology and chem. nature of blood group antigens, human biochem. genetics, tissue typing, human histocompatability antigens to sci. jours. Served to lt. (j.g.) USNR, 1943-47. Recipient Cooley Meml. award Am. Assn. Blood Banks, 1969. Mem. Assn. Gen. and Liberal Studies (sec.-treas. 1962-65), AAUP, AAAS, Genetics Soc. Am., Am. Soc. Human Genetics, Am. Assn. Blood Banks (dir. 1983—, chmn. sci. sect. 1983—), Mich. Assn. Blood Banks (v.p. 1970, pres. 1975-77), Am. Inst. Biol. Sci., Biometric Soc., Transplantation Soc. Mich. (dir. 1975—), Am. Assn. for Clin. Histocompatability Testing, N.Y. Acad. Scis., Sigma Xi, Phi Kappa Phi. Home: 244 Oakland Dr East Lansing MI 48823 Office: Dept Medicine Mich State U East Lansing MI 48824

HACKEL-SIMS, STELLA BLOOMBERG, lawyer, former government official; b. Burlington, Vt., Dec. 27, 1926; d. Hyman and Esther (Pocher) Bloomberg; m. Donald Herman Hackel, Aug. 14, 1949; children: Susan Jane, Cynthia Anne; m. Arthur Sims, Aug. 28, 1980. Student, U. Vt., 1943-45; J.D. cum laude, Boston U., 1948. Bar: Vt. 1948, Mass. 1948, D.C. 1979, Va. 1982. Individual practice law, Burlington, 1948-49, Rutland, Vt., 1949-59, 73—; city prosecutor City of Rutland, 1957-63; commr. Vt. Dept. Employment Security, 1963-73; treas. State of Vt., 1975-77; dir. U.S. Mint, Dept. Treasury, Washington, 1977-81; chmn. Vt. Municipal Bond Bank, 1975-77. Mem. Vt. Adv. Com. on Mental Retardation, Interdept. Council on Aging, Commn. on Status Women, Human Resource Inter-Agency Com., Emergency Resource Priorities Bd., Info. Planning Council, Legis. Council Equal Opportunity Com., Vt. Indsl. Devel. Authority, Vt. Housing Fin. Agy., Vt. Claims Commn., Vt. Tchrs. Retirement Fund. Bd., Vt. Home Mortgage Guaranty Bd.; chmn. Vt. State Employees Retirement Fund; ex-officio mem. Nat. Manpower Adv. Com., 1971-72, Fed. Adv. Council on Unemployment Ins., 1971-72; Pres. Rutland Girl Scouts Leaders Assn., 1949-50, Rutland League Women Voters, 1951-52, Rutland Council Jewish Women, 1955-56; chmn. womens div. Rutland Community Chest Dr., 1952, Rutland County-Vt. Assn. for Blind, 1953-56; pres. Rutland County Democratic Women's Assn., 1956-63; treas. Rutland City Dem. Com., 1957-63; former rep. office women's activities Dem. Nat. Com., Regional Council I., Women's CD Councils; mem. Vt. bd. Girl Scouts U.S.A. Mem. Vt. Bar Assn., Rutland County Bar Assn. (pres. 1973), Bus. and Profl. Women's Club, AAUW (pres. Rutland county br. 1961-62), Vt. Council Social Agys., League Women Voters, Am. Soc. Pub. Adminstrn., Interstate Conf. Employment Security Agencies (v.p. region I 1966-68, legis. com. 1969, sr. v.p. 1970-71, pres. 1971-72), Delta Phi Epsilon. Clubs: Emblem (dir. 1960-63), Woodmont Country; Internat. (Washington). Office: 2701 N Pershing Dr Arlington VA 22201

HACKENBROCK, CHARLES R., cell biologist, educator; b. Bklyn., Dec. 23, 1929; s. Arthur and Stella H.; m. children—Laura, Sheila, Sandra. B.S., Wagner Coll., 1961; Ph.D. (univ. acad. scholar, 1961, NIH fellow, 1962-66), Columbia U., 1966. Asst. prof. anatomy Sch. Medicine, Johns Hopkins U., 1965-68, asso. prof. anatomy, 1968-71; prof. cell biology U. Tex. Health Sci. Center, Dallas, 1971-77; prof., chmn. anatomy Sch. Medicine, U. N.C., Chapel Hill, 1977—; dir. Labs. for Cell Biology, Electron Microscope Labs. Editor: Jour. of Cell Biology, 1981—; adv. editor: Electron Microscopy in Biology, 1980—; contbr.: research articles to Cell Biology and Bioenergetics, 1965—. Served with U.S. Army, 1951-53. Mem. Am. Soc. Biol. Chemists, Am. Soc. Cell Biology, Biophys. Soc., Electron Microscopy Soc., Am., N.Y. Acad. Scis., Am. Assn. Anatomists, Assn. Anatomy Chairmen, Council Nat. Soc. for Med. Research. Office: School Medicine U NC Chapel Hill NC 27514

HACKER, ANDREW, political science educator; b. N.Y.C., Aug. 30, 1929; s. Louis Morton and Lilian (Lewis) H.; m. Lois Sheffield Wetherell, June 17, 1955; 1 dau., Ann. A.B., Amherst Coll., 1951; M.A., Oxford (Eng.) U., 1953; Ph.D., Princeton U., 1955. Instr. govt. Cornell U., Ithaca, N.Y., 1955-56, asst. prof., 1956-60, asso. prof., 1960-66, prof., 1966-71; prof. polit. sci. Queens Coll., CUNY, 1971—; cons. Conf. Bd., Brookings Instn., Rockefeller Bros. Fund, Nat. Council Chs., Am. Jewish Com., NBC, Ency. Brit. Author: Ideology, Science, 1960, Congressional Districting, 1963, The Study of Politics, 1973, The Corporation Take-Over, 1964, The End of the American Era, 1970, The New Yorkers, 1975, Free Enterprise in America, 1977, U.S.: A Statistical Portrait of the American People. Mem. Am. Polit. Sci. Assn., AAUP, Phi Beta Kappa. Home: 20 W 64th St New York NY 10023 Office: Dept Polit Sci Queens Coll City U NY Flushing NY 11367

HACKER, BENJAMIN THURMAN, naval officer; b. Washington, Sept. 19, 1935; s. Coleman Leroy and Alzeda (Crockett) H.; m. Jeanne Marie House, May 7, 1958; children: Benjamin Thurman, Bruce, Anne. B.A., Wittenberg U., 1957; grad. in engring. sci., U.S. Naval Postgrad. Sch., 1963; M.S.A., George Washington U., 1978. Commd. ensign U.S. Navy, 1958, advanced through grades to rear adm., 1980; comdg. officer Naval Facility, Barbados, W. I., 1967-69; comdg. officer, prof. naval sci. Fla. A&M, Tallahassee, 1972-73; comdg. officer Patrol Squadron 24, Jacksonville, Fla., 1974-75, U.S. Naval Air Sta., Brunswick, Maine, 1978-80; comdr. U.S. Mil. Enlistment Processing Command, Ft. Sheridan, Ill., 1980-82, Fleet Air, Mediterranean, Naples, Italy, 1982—. Decorated Legion of Merit. Mem. U.S. Naval Inst., Nat. Naval Officers Assn., Alpha Phi Alpha. Office: COMFAIRMED FPO New York NY 09521

HACKER, HILARY BAUMANN, bishop; b. New Ulm, Minn., Jan. 10, 1913; s. Emil and Sophia (Baumann) H. Student, Nazareth Hall, St. Paul, Minn., 1928-32, St. Paul Sem., 1932-38; J.C.B., Gregorian U., Rome, Italy, 1939. Ordained priest Roman Cath. Ch., 1938; asst. pastor Ch. of Nativity, St. Paul, June-Oct. 1938; asst. pastor Ch. of Most Holy Trinity, Winsted, Minn., 1939-41; vice chancellor Archdiocese of St. Paul, June-Sept. 1941, chancellor, 1941-45, vicar gen., 1945-56; bishop, Bismarck, N.D., 1956-82. Home: 505 10th Ave NW Mandan ND 58554

HACKERMAN, NORMAN, university president, chemist; b. Balt., Mar. 2, 1912; s. Jacob and Anna (Raffel) H.; m. Gene Allison Coulbourn, Aug. 25, 1940; children: Patricia, Stephen, Sally, Katherine. A.B., Johns Hopkins U., 1932, Ph.D., 1935; LL.D. (hon.), Abilene Christian U., 1978, St. Edward's U., 1972; D.Sc. (hon.), Tex. Christian U., 1978, Austin Coll., 1975. Asst. prof. Loyola Coll., Balt., 1935-39; research chemist Colloid Corp., 1936-40; asst. chemist USCG, 1939-41; asst. prof. chemistry Va. Poly. Inst., Blacksburg, 1941-43; research chemist Kellex Corp., 1944-45; asst. prof. chemistry U. Tex., Austin, 1945-46, asso. prof., 1946-50, prof. chemistry, 1950-70, chmn. dept., 1952-61, dir. corrosion research lab., 1948-61, dean research and sponsored programs, 1960-61, v.p., provost, 1961-63, vice chancellor acad. affairs, 1963-67, pres., 1967-70; prof. chemistry Rice U., Houston, 1970—, pres., 1970—; trustee Mitre Corp., 1980—; cons. in corrosion, 1946—, in surface chemistry, 1948—; Chmn. Gordon Research Conf. on Corrosion, 1950; on Chemistry at Interfaces, 1959, mem. bd. trustees, 1970-73; chmn. Inter Soc. Corrosion Com., 1956-58; mem. bd. on energy studies Nat. Acad. Scis./NRC, chmn., 1974-77; mem. Nat. Bd. on Grad. Edn., 1971-76, Nat. Sci. Bd., 1968-80, chmn., 1974-80; mem. Def. Sci. Bd., 1978—, Energy Research Adv. Bd., 1980—; mem. environ. pollution panel Pres.'s Sci. Adv. Com., 1965-66; cons. Assn. Univs. for Research in Astronomy, 1964-70; mem. sci. and ednl. adv. com. Lawrence Berkeley Lab., 1974-81; chmn. bd. trustees Argonne Univs. Assn., 1969-73. Contbr. numerous articles to sci. jours.; Tech. editor: Jour. Electrochem. Soc, 1950-68; editor, 1969—; interim editor: Electrochem. Tech, 1965-68; adv. editorial bd.: Corrosion Sci, 1965—; editorial bd.: Catalysis Reviews, 1968-73. Bd. dirs. Oak Ridge Asso. Univs., 1978—; chmn. sci. adv. bd. Robert A. Welch Found., 1982—; mem. Tex. Gov.'s Task Force on Higher Edn., 1981—. Recipient Whitney award Nat. Assn. Corrosion Engrs., 1956; Joseph J. Mattiello Meml. lectr. Fedn. Socs. Paint Tech., 1964; Southwest Regional award Am. Chem. Soc., 1965; Palladium medalist Electrochem. Soc., 1965; Am. Inst. Chemists gold medal, 1978; Mirabeau B. Lamar award Assn. Tex. Colls. and Univs., 1981; Disting. Alumnus award Johns Hopkins U., 1982. Fellow N.Y. Acad. Scis., AAAS, Am. Acad. Arts and Scis.; mem. Nat. Acad. Scis., Am. Chem. Soc. (bd. editors monograph series 1956-62, exec. com. colloid div. 1955-58), Electrochem. Soc. (hon. mem.; pres. 1957-58), Faraday Soc., Am. Philos. Soc., Nat. Assn. Corrosion Engrs. (dir. 1952-55, chmn. A.B. Campbell Young Authors Award com. 1960—), Internat. Soc. Electrochemistry, Sigma Xi, Phi Lambda Upsilon, Alpha Chi Sigma, Phi Kappa Phi.

HACKES, PETER SIDNEY, radio-TV news corr.; b. N.Y.C., June 2, 1924; s. John R. and Ruth (Misch) H.; children—Pamela T. Hackes Thurston, Carole Austin, Peter Quinn. B.A., Grinnell (Iowa) Coll., 1948, L.H.D. (hon.), 1967; M.A., U. Iowa, 1949; Litt.D. (hon.), Newberry (S.C.) Coll., 1967. With radio stas. in, N.Y., Iowa and Ky., 1947-52; Washington corr. CBS, 1952-55, NBC, 1955—, Dept. Def. corr., 1956-67; anchorman NBC World News Roundup, 1957-61. Bd. govs. Nat. USO; bd. dirs. Cheshire Found., Wolf Trap Farm Park, Performing Arts, 1975-78; mem. trustees council Met. Washington YMCA; commr. Nat. Commn. Fire Prevention and Control, 1971-73. Served with USNR, 1943-46; capt. Res. Recipient Emmy award for Apollo space flight coverage, 1969-70, Peabody award for Second Sunday Series, 1972. Mem. AFTRA, Acad. Ind. Scholars, Naval Res. Assn., S.P.E.B.S.Q.S.A. Address: 4001 Nebraska Ave NW Washington DC 20016

HACKETT, BUDDY, actor; b. Bklyn., Aug. 31, 1924; s. Philip and Anna (Geller) Hacker; m. Sherry Cohen, June 12, 1955; children—Sandy Zade, Ivy Julie, Lisa Jean. Ed. pub. schs., Bklyn. Theatrical appearances include: Call Me Mister, 1946, Lunatics and Lover, 1954, I Had A Ball, 1964; motion picture appearances include: Walking My Baby Back Home, 1953, Gods Little Acre, 1958, Music Man, 1962, The Wonderful World of The Brothers Grimm, 1961, All Hands on Deck, 1961, Everything's Ducky, 1961, It's a Mad, Mad, Mad, Mad World, 1962, Golden Head, 1963, Muscle Beach Party, 1964, The Love Bug, 1969; star TV series Stanley, 1956-57; TV, cafe and nightclub appearances throughout, U.S.; Recipient (Donaldson award 1955, Venice Film Festival award 1961) *

HACKETT, EARL RANDOLPH, neurologist; b. Moulmein, Burma, Feb. 16, 1932; s. Paul Richmond and Martha Jane (Lewis) H.; m. Shirley Jane Kanehl, May 25, 1953; children—Nancy, Raymond, Susan, Lynn, Laurie, Richard, Alicia. B.S., Drury Coll., Springfield, Mo., 1953; M.D., Western Res. U., 1957. Diplomate: Am. Bd. Psychiatry and Neurology. Intern, then resident in neurology Charity Hosp., New Orleans, 1957-62; resident in internal medicine VA Hosp., New Orleans, 1958-59; mem. faculty La. State U. Med. Sch., New Orleans, 1962—, prof. neurology, 1973—, head dept., 1977—; mem. med. adv. bd. Myasthenia Gravis Found. Mem. AMA, Am. Acad. Neurology, Am. Assn. EMG and Electrodiagnosis, Soc. Clin. Neurologists, La. Med. Soc., Orleans Parish Med. Soc. Methodist. Home: 10125 Suzanne Dr River Ridge LA 70123 Office: 1542 Tulane St New Orleans LA 70112

HACKETT, JOHN BYRON, advertising agency executive; b. N.Y.C., Dec. 28, 1933; s. John Joseph and Cecelia Elizabeth (Meehan) H.; m. Patricia P. Briordy, May 23, 1964 (div. 1980); children: Kimberly, John. B.B.A., Iona Coll., 1956; LL.B., St. Johns U., 1960. Bar: N.Y. 1961. Sales adminstr. NBC, N.Y.C., 1962-65; with J. Walter Thompson Co., N.Y.C., 1965—, v.p. legal dept., 1971-76, sr. v.p. adminstrn., 1976-80, sr. v.p., gen. mgr. entertainment div., 1980-83, sr. v.p., dir. spot broadcasting U.S.A., 1983—; faculty mem. Practising Law Inst. Mem. U.S. Trademark Assn. (dir.), Am. Bar Assn., Assn. Bar City N.Y. Home: 1 Toms Point Ln Port Washington NY 11050 Office: 466 Lexington Ave New York NY 10017

HACKETT, JOHN FRANCIS, bishop; b. New Haven, Dec. 7, 1911; s. Thomas J. and Anna (Whalen) H. Student, St. Thomas Sem., Bloomfield, Conn., 1929-31, Seminaire St. Sulpice, Issy and Paris, France, 1931-36; LL.D., Fairfield University, 1953, Providence College, 1960. Ordained priest Roman Cath. Ch., 1936; asst. pastor St. Aloysius Ch., New Canaan, Conn., 1936-45; sec. Bishop of Hartford, 1945-52; asst. chancellor Diocese of Hartford, 1945-51, vice chancellor, 1951-52, chancellor, 1953-59, vicar-gen., 1954—; consecrated titular bishop of Helenopolis in Palaestina; aux. bishop of, Hartford, 1952. Home: 872 Farmington Ave West Hartford CT 06119 Office: 134 Farmington Ave Hartford CT 06105

HACKETT, JOHN THOMAS, economist; b. Fort Wayne, Ind., Oct. 10, 1932; s. Harry H. and Ruth (Greer) H.; m. Ann E. Thompson, July 24, 1954; children: Jane, David, Sarah, Peter. B.S., Ind. U., 1954, M.B.A., 1958; Ph.D., Ohio State U., 1961. Instr. Ohio State U., 1958-61; asst. v.p., economist Fed. Res. Bank, Cleve., 1961-64; dir. planning Cummins Engine Co., Columbus, Ind., 1964-66, v.p. finance, 1966-71, exec. v.p., 1971—, also dir.; dir. Ransburg Corp., Heritage Venture Corp., Irwin Union Corp., Corp. for Innovation Devel.; Mem. finance council Nat. Indsl. Conf. Bd.; pres. Ind. Secondary Market for Edn. Loans.; Bd. dirs. Cummins Engine Found.; mem. Ohio State U. Alumni Adv. Council. Served to 1st lt. AUS, 1954-56. Mem. Am. Econ. Assn., Financial Execs. Inst., Am. Finance Assn., Financial Mgmt. Assn., Bus. Economists Assn., Beta Gamma Sigma. Home: 1005 Hawthorne Dr Columbus IN 47201 Office: 1000 5th St: Columbus IN 47201

HACKETT, LEEDS, banker; b. Easton, Pa., Aug. 16, 1940; s. Bruce and Ann (Gerhardt) Beisel; m. Veronica Walker, Apr. 9, 1976; 1 dau., Elizabeth. B.S., Babson Coll., 1965; postgrad., N.Y. U., 1966-68. With Marine Midland Bank N.A., 1965—; now exec. v.p. OIC Internat. Banking div. Served with U.S. Army, 1959-62. Mem. Robert Morris Assn. Republican. Episcopalian. Office: 140 Broadway New York NY 10015 *

HACKETT, RANDALL WINSLOW, advertising executive; b. N.Y.C., June 6, 1935; s. Montague H. and Flavia (Riggio) H.; m. Lela Lee Ottley, June 22, 1957 (div. 1975); children: Randall, Holly, Welles; m. Eleanor Gay Cumings, Oct. 9, 1976; stepchildren: Samantha McLean, Stuart McLean. A.B., Harvard U., 1957; M.B.A., Columbia U., 1959. Sr. product mgr. Colgate Palmolive, N.Y.C., 1964-68; sr. v.p. Grey Advt., N.Y.C., 1964-68; v.p. mktg. ITT Continental Baking, Rye, N.Y., 1968-78; sr. v.p. Norton Simon Inc., N.Y.C., 1978-80; exec. v.p. Ted Bates Advt., N.Y.C., 1980—. Republican. Episcopalian. Clubs: Racquet and Tennis, River (N.Y.C.); Porcellian (Cambridge, Mass.). Home: 150 E 73d St New York NY 10021 Office: 1515 Broadway New York NY 10036

HACKETT, ROGER FLEMING, history educator; b. Kobe, Japan, Oct. 23, 1922; s. Harold Wallace and Anna Luena (Powell) H.; m. Caroline Betty Gray, Aug. 24, 1946; children: Anne Marilyn, David Gray, Brian Vance. B.A., Carleton Coll., 1947; M.A., Harvard U., 1949, Ph.D., 1955. Prof. history Northwestern U., Evanston, Ill., 1953-61; prof. history U. Mich., Ann Arbor, 1961—, chmn. dept., 1975-77; dir. Center for Japanese Studies, 1968-71, 78, 79; cons. Office of Edn., HEW; mem. sub-com., joint com. Social Sci. Research Council. Author: Yamagata Aritomo in the Rise of Modern Japan 1838-1922, 1971; Editor: Jour. Asian Studies, 1959-62; contbr. articles and chpts to profl. jours. and books. Served with USMC, 1942-46. Social Sci. Research Council fellow; Japan Found. fellow; Fulbright-Hays fellow; fellow St. Antony's Coll. Oxford U. Mem. Am. Hist. Assn., Japan Soc., Assn. for Asian Studies (exec. com., bd. dirs. 1966-69), Internat. House of Japan, Phi Beta Kappa. Club: Racquet (Ann Arbor). Home: 2122 Dorset Rd Ann Arbor MI 48104 Office: Dept History U Mich Ann Arbor MI 48109

HACKETT, THOMAS PAUL, psychiatrist; b. Cin., July 6, 1928; m. Mary Ann Kamuf, 1951 (div. 1960); 1 dau., Melissa; m. Eleanor Mayher, 1961; children: Laura, Shelagh, Thomas. B.S., U. Cin., 1948, M.D., 1952. Diplomate: Am. Bd. Psychiatry and Neurology. Intern USPHS Hosp., San Francisco, 1952-53; clin. and research fellow in psychiatry Mass. Gen. Hosp., Boston, 1955-58; resident in psychiatry Boston Psychopathic Hosp., 1957-58; asst. in psychiatry Mass. Gen. Hosp., 1958-59, asst. psychiatrist, 1959-64, asso. psychiatrist, 1964-72, chief psychiat. consultation service, 1968-76, psychiatrist, 1972—, acting chief psychiatry, 1974-76, chief psychiatry, 1976—; clin. and research fellow Harvard Med. Sch., Boston, 1955-58, asst. in psychiatry, 1958-59, instr. psychiatry, 1959-67, clin. asso. in psychiatry, 1967-69, asst. prof. psychiatry, 1969-72, asso. prof., 1972-76, prof., 1976—, Eben S. Draper prof. psychiatry, 1977—; cons. in psychiatry Div. of Legal Medicine, Commonwealth of Mass., 1955-74; spl. fellow in legal psychiatry Law-Medicine Inst., Boston U. Med. Sch., 1964-65, vis. prof., 1977—; cons. Indsl. Accidents Bd., Commonwealth of Mass., 1970—, VA Hosp., Bedford, Mass., 1974—; cons. internat. rehab. research program Social and Rehab. Service, HEW, 1974—; cons. NIMH, NIH, 1975—; cons. Nat. Heart, Lung & Blood Inst., 1977—. Editor: (with N.H. Cassem) Massachusetts General Hospital Handbook of General Hospital Psychiatry, 1978; Contbr. chpts. to books, articles to profl. jours.; Asso. editor: Psychosomatics, 1979—; cons. editor: Psychiat. Medicine Update, 1978—; mem. editorial bd.: Annals of Internal Medicine, 1977—, Jour. of Affective Disorders, 1978—; contbg. editor: Med. Econs, 1967—; mem. rev. bd.: Jour. Cardiac Rehab, 1979—. Fellow ACP, Am. Coll. Psychiatry, Am. Psychiat. Assn.; mem. Mitchell Pediatrics Soc., Mass. Med. Soc., Am. Psychosomatic Soc., Assn. Psychiat. Treatment Offenders, No. New Eng. Psychiat. Soc., AAAS, Am. Psychopath. Assn., Internat. Soc. and Fedn. Cardiology (mem. council on cardiac rehab.), Phi Eta Sigma. Office: Dept Psychiatry Mass Gen Hosp Fruit St Boston MA 02114

HACKFORD, TAYLOR, film director, producer; b. Santa Barbara, Calif., Dec. 31, 1944; s. Joseph and Mary (Taylor) H.; m. Georgie Lowres; 1 child, Rio; m. Lynne Littman (div. 1972); 1 son, Alexander. B.A. in Internat. Relations, U. So. Calif. Vol. Peace Corps, Bolivia, 1968-69; dir., producer, reporter, writerr Sta.-KCET, Community TV of So. Calif., Los Angeles, 1970-77; dir., producer, writer Hackford Littman Films, Los Angeles, 1977-79; dir. United Artists Films, Los Angeles, 1979-80, Paramount Pictures, 1981-82; producer, dir. Columbia Pictures, Los Angeles, 1983—. Producer, dir., writer: short dramatic film Teenage Father, 1978 (Oscar 1979); dir.: feature film The Idolmaker, 1980, An Officer and A Gentleman, 1982, Agains All Odds, 1984. Recipient Silver Reel award San Francisco Film Festival, 1972, Emmy award Acad. TV Arts and Scis., 1974, 1977, Acad. award Acad. Motion Picture Arts and Scis., 1979. Mem. Dir.'s Guild Am., Writers Guild Am.

HACKING, IAN MACDOUGALL, philosophy educator; b. Vancouver, B.C., Can., Feb. 18, 1936; s. Harold Eldridge and Margaret Elinore (MacDougall) H.; m. Laura Anne Leach, Jan. 4, 1962 (div. 1969); children: Jane Frances, Daniel Rachel; m. Judith Polsky, Aug. 14, 1983. B.A., U.B.C., 1956, Cambridge U., 1958, M.A., 1962; Ph.D., Cambridge FU., 1962. Research fellow Peterhouse Coll., Cambridge U., Eng., 1962-64; assoc. prof. U. B.C., Vancouver, 1964-69; univ. lectr. Cambridge U., 1969-75; Henry W. Stuart prof. Stanford U., Calif., 1975-82; prof. U. Toronto, Ont., Can., 1982—. Author: Logic of Statistical Inference, 1965, Why Does Language Matter to Philosophy, 1975, The Emergence of Probability, 1975, Representing and Intervening, 1983. Fellow Ctr. Advanced Study in Behavioral Scis. Stanford U., 1974. Office: Inst History and Philosophy of Sci U Toronto Toronto ON Canada M5S 1K7

HACKL, ALPHONS J., publisher; b. Warman, Can., Mar. 31, 1917; s. John J. and Anna (Moser) H.; m. Muriel J. Forster, Feb. 2, 1946; 1 son, John Raymond. Grad., Handelsschule, Salzburg, Austria, 1934; student, Nat. U., 1937-38, Corcoran Sch. Art, 1938-40, U. Chgo., 1941; B.A., Sussex Coll. Tech., 1945; postgrad., Internat. Summer Sch., St. Peter Coll., Oxford U., 1976. Apprentice Funder & Mueller, printers, Salzburg, 1934-36; advt. copywriter, art dir., account exec. advt. agy. and dept. store, Washington, 1936-40; founder, owner Colortone Press, Washington, 1946—; founder, pres., pub. Acropolis Books, Ltd., Washington, 1965—; Lectr., instr. George Washington U., 1974-78; Past mem. adv. council SBA; mem. adv. bd. specialist program George Washington U.; adv. bd. Washington Tech. Inst. Contbr. articles to profl. publs. Bd. dirs. Met. Sch. Printing; adv. bd. Montgomery Coll.; bd. dirs. Friends Nat. Zoo. Served to capt. AUS, 1940-45. Decorated Bronze Star.; Recipient George Washington Honor medal Freedoms Found. Fellow Corcoran Art Gallery; mem. Pub. Relations Soc. Am., Printing Industry Am., Nat. Assn. Photo-Lithographers, U.S. C. of C., Ednl. Press Assn., Assn. Am. Publishers, Printing Industry Washington, AAAS, Washington Writers Group. Mem. Soc. of Friends. Clubs: Capitol Hill, Nat. Press, Washington Art Dirs. (dir. Washington). Patentee programmed instrn. device. Home: 3077 Cleveland Ave NW Washington DC 20008 Office: 2400 17th St Washington DC 20009 *Always do more than is expected of you, and keep your promises.*

HACKL, DONALD JOHN, architect; b. Chgo., May 11, 1934; s. John Frank and Frieda Marie (Weichmann) H.; m. Bernardine Marie Becker, Sept. 29, 1962; children: Jeffrey, Scott, Craig Michael, Cristina Lynn. B.Arch., U. Ill., 1957, M.S. in Architecture, 1958. Project architect Loebl Schlossman & Bennett (architects-engrs.), Chgo., 1962-64; asso. Loebl, Schlossman Bennett & Dart, Chgo., 1967—, partner, 1970—, exec. v.p., dir., 1974—; pres., dir. Loebl Schlossman & Hackl, 1975—, Dart-Hackl Internat. Ltd., 1975—; mem. Nat. Council Archtl. Registration Bds.; chmn. Midwest Architecture Design Conf., 1983; guest design critic dept. architecture U. Ill., 1975, 76, 81; guest lectr. U. Notre Dame, 1977, 78, 80, 82; cons. Public Service Adminstrn., Washington, 1974-76; v.p. Chgo. Bldg. Congress, 1983, 84. Prin. works include Samsonite Corp. Hdqrs., Denver, 1968, Water Tower Place, Chgo., 1974, HFC World Hdqrs., Northbrook, Ill., 1978, Square D Internat. Hdqrs., Palatine, Ill., 1978, Cancer Research Inst., King Faisal Specialist Hosp. and Research Center, Riyadh, Saudi Arabia, 1978, Allstate Ins. Co., Barrington, Ill., 1981, Shriners Hosp. Crippled Children, Chgo., 1979, West Suburban Hosp., Oak Park, Ill., 1981; Contbr. articles to profl. jours. and trade publs. Mem. Chgo. Met. Cancer Crusade, 1973; trustee AIA Found., 1981—, pres. Chgo. chpt., 1983; bd. dirs., mem. exec. com. AIA Service Corp., 1981—; bd. dirs. Chgo. Archtl. Assistance Ctr., 1982; trustee West Suburban Hosp., Oak Park, Ill., 1983; mem. adv. bd. Constrn. Law Inst., Kent Coll. Law, 1982, 83. Fellow AIA (dir. 1982-84, v.p., exec. com. 1985, treas., dir., v.p., pres. Chgo. chpt. 1976-82, dir. Ill. council 1979-81); mem. Chgo. Bldg. Congress (dir. 1978-79), Nat. Trust Hist. Preservation, Chgo. Assn. Commerce and Industry, Greater North Michigan Ave. Assn., Art Inst. Chgo., Field Mus. Natural History. Roman Catholic. Clubs: Tavern, Carlton, Economic, Lake Zurich. Office: 845 N Michigan Ave Chicago IL 60611

HACKLER, JOHN BYRON, III, architect; b. Pekin, Ill., Mar. 31, 1925; s. John Byron and Josephine (Walters) H.; m. Patricia Ann Baum, June 29, 1948 (div.); children: Catherine Frances, John Byron, Ann Frost. B.Arch., Carnegie-Mellon U., 1949. Pvt. practice architecture, 1950-53; with Foley, Hackler, Thompson, Lee, 1953-65; pres. John Hackler & Co., Peoria, Ill., 1965—; vis. prof. Grad. Sch. Architecture, U. Ill.; Bd. dirs. Upgrade, Inc., pres., 1973-77; nat. adv. bd. Am. Hearing Research Found. Served with USAAF, 1943-45. Fellow AIA. Home: 2431 W Madera Ct Peoria IL 61614 Office: 504 Fayette St Peoria IL 61603

HACKLEY, FLOYD VINCENT, university chancellor, retired air force officer; b. Roanoke, Va., June 14, 1940; s. David Walton and Ernestine H. H.; m. Brenda Stewart, June 12, 1960; children: Dianna M., Michael R. Student, Northwestern Mich. Coll., 1962-63; B.A. magna cum laude, Mich. State U., 1965; postgrad., U. Colo., 1966-67; Ph.D. with honors, U. N.C., 1975. Served as enlisted man U.S. Air Force, 1958-78, commd. 2d lt., 1965, advanced through grades to maj., 1976, comdr. Officer Tng. Sch. 3436 Student Squad, 1966-67, exec. officer 20th Spl. Squad, Vietnam, 1967-68; analyst for Middle East, North Africa, NATO South Flank, Hdqrs. USAF, Europe, 1968-71; assoc. prof. internat. relations USAF Acad., 1974-78, ret., 1978; assoc. v.p. U. N.C., Chapel Hill, 1978-81; chancellor U. Ark.-Pine Bluff, 1981—. Counselor, treas. Denver Area council Boy Scouts am., 1966-67; instr. AAU, 1976-78; mem. Pres.'s Council on Phys. Fitness, 1975-81; coach USAF Acad. men's and women's cross-country and track, 1975-78; bd. dirs. United Fund, Chapel Hill, 1979-81; mem. adv. com. U. Ark. Grad. Inst. Tech., 1983—; mem. adv. bd. Nat. Ctr. for Toxicol. Research, 1983; mem. Ark. Edn. Standards Com. for Elem. and Secondary Schs., 1983—; mem. exec. com. Triangle World Affairs Ctr., Chapel Hill, 1978-81. Decorated Bronze Star, Meritorious Service medal, U.S., Cross of Gallantry, Vietnam. Mem. Polit. Sci. Assn. N.C., Phi Beta Kappa, Phi Kappa Phi, Pi Sigma Alpha. Office: Office of Chancellor U Ark Pine Bluff AR 71601

HACKMAN, GENE, actor; b. San Bernardino, Calif., Jan. 30, 1930; s. Eugene Ezra H.; m. Faye Maltese, 1956; children: Christopher, Elizabeth, Leslie. Appeared in stage prodn.: The Natural Look, others; film roles include Lilith, 1964; Bonnie and Clyde, 1967, First to Fight, 1967, Hawaii, 1966, Riot, 1969, The Split, 1968, The Gypsy Moths, 1969, Downhill Racer, 1969, Marooned, 1970, I Never Sang for My Father, 1969, Doctor's Wives, 1971, The French Connection (N.Y. Film Critics award), 1971 (Acad. award best actor, Golden Globe award, Brit. Acad. award, N.Y. Film Critics award), Cisco Pike, 1971, Scarecrow, 1973 (Cannes Film Festival award), The Poseidon Adventure, 1972 (Brit. Acad. award), The Conversation, 1974, Zandy's Bride, 1974, The French Connection II, 1975, Bite the Bullet, 1975, Night Moves, 1975, Lucky Lady, 1975, A Bridge Too Far, 1977, The Domino Principle, 1977, March or Die, 1977, Superman, 1978, All Night Long, 1980. Named Star of Year, Nat. Assn. Theatre Owners, 1974. Address: care Stein & Stein Suite 707 9200 Sunset Blvd Los Angeles CA 90069

HACKMYER, ARNOLD A(BNER), lawyer; b. N.Y.C., July 15, 1925; s. Morris and Tillie (Gilbert) H.; m. Selma Kleinfeld, Mar. 17, 1949; children: Ilene, Carol, Gary, Lester. B.A., CCNY, 1946; J.D., Harvard U., 1949. Bar: N.Y. 1949. Assoc. firm Glen N. W. McNaughton, N.Y.C., 1949-50; partner firm Perl, Hackmyer & Tishelman, N.Y.C., 1950-54; assoc. firm Hirson & Bertini, N.Y.C., 1954-59; v.p., sec., gen. counsel Mastan Co. Inc., N.Y.C, 1960-68; partner firm Bresler & Hackmyer (and predecessors), N.Y.C., 1969—; Spl. asst. atty. gen., asst. counsel N.Y. Crime Commn., N.Y.C., 1951-53; asst. counsel N.Y. Moreland Commn. on Harness Racing, N.Y.C., 1953-54. Mem. joint bd. edn. Valhalla (N.Y.) Sch. Dist., 1957-58; Chmn. Greenburgh (N.Y.) Democratic Com., 1959-60; Trustee Thornton Donovan Sch., New Rochelle, N.Y., 1975-78. Served with inf. AUS, 1943-45. Decorated Purple Heart. Mem. ABA, N.Y. County (N.Y.) Lawyers' Assn., Assn. Comml. Finance Attys., Jewish Community Center of White Plains (N.Y.), Odd Fellows. Home: 8 Antony Rd White Plains NY 10605 Office: 747 3d Ave New York NY 10017

HACKNEY, JAMES ACRA, III, engineer, manufacturing company executive; b. Washington, N.C., Sept. 27, 1939; s. James Acra and Margaret Dunston (Hodges) H.; m. Constance Garrenton, June 5, 1961; children: Kenneth Ross, Jane Mather. B.S. in Mech. Engring, N.C. State U., 1961, 1962. Registered profl. engr., N.C., Kans. With Hackney Industries, Inc., Washington, N.C., 1961—; chief engr. Hackney & Sons, Inc., 1961-63, asst. gen. mgr., 1963-65, exec. v.p., gen. mgr., 1965-70, pres., chief exec. officer, 1970—; also pres. subs. Hackney & Sons Inc., Washington, Hackney & Sons (Midwest), Inc., Independence, Kans.; chmn. bd. Consol. Switchgear & Elec. Systems, Inc., Harvey, La.; dir. N.C. Nat. Bank, Washington. Chmn., Blackbeard dist., pres. East Carolina council Boy Scouts Am., 1976-77, chmn. Boy Scout program com. Southeast region, 1979-83; chmn. bus. curriculum adv. com. Beaufort County Tech. Inst., 1969-72; mem. engring. adv. council N.C. State U., 1973-76, chmn., 1975-76; pres. Coastal Plain Devel. Assn., 1969; vice chmn. Zoning and Planning Commn., Washington, 1966-73; v.p., bd. dirs. N.C. Engring. Found., 1977-82; mem. adminstrv. bd. local Meth. Ch., 1976—; chmn. bd. trustees Beaufort County Hosp., 1975-77; trustee N.C. State U., Raleigh, 1979—. Served to 1st lt. Ordnance Corps AUS, 1963-65. Recipient Disting. Service award (young man of year) Washington (N.C.) Jaycees, 1970; named N.C. Small Businessman of year SBA, 1971; Outstanding Young Engr. N.C. Profl. Engrs. N.C., 1970-71; Young Engr. of Yr. Nat. Soc. Profl. Engrs., 1971; Outstanding Young Alumnus N.C. State U., 1975. Mem. Truck Body and Equipment Assn. (dir.), Beverage Body Mfrs. Assn. (pres. 1969-70), Washington C. of C. (pres. 1972-74), Inst. Indsl. Engrs. (chpt. pres. 1967-68), Profl. Engrs. N.C. (pres. Eastern Carolina chpt. 1971-72), N.C. Citizens for Bus. and Industry (dir. 1979—), N.C. State U. Alumni Assn. (dir. 1976—). Club: Rotarian (pres. 1978-79). Home: 220 Alderson Rd Washington NC 27889 Office: 400 Hackney Ave PO Box 880 Washington NC 27889

HACKNEY, WILLIAM PENDLETON, lawyer; b. Uniontown, Pa., June 5, 1924; s. Henry Eastman and Elisabeth Moore (Pendleton) H.; m. Doris M. Fast, June 28, 1947; children: W. Penn, Peter E., Jeanne S. A.B., Princeton U., 1946; LL.B., Harvard U., 1951. Bar: Pa. 1951. Asso. firm Reed Smith Shaw & McClay, Pitts., 1951-64, partner, 1964—; adv. Gov.'s Banking Law Commn., Pa., 1964-65; mem. Gov.'s Commn. on Constl. Revision, 1964; com. counsel Pa. Constl. Conv., 1967-68. Author: Pennsylvania Corporations Law Practice, 1966; contbr. articles to profl. jours. Bd. pensions United Presbyn. Ch. U.S.A., Phila.; bd. dirs. YMCA Pitts.; pres. Arts and Crafts Center, 1972-73; dir. Chamber Music Soc. Served with USAAF, 1943-46. Mem. ABA (chmn. acctg. standards, mem. com. on law and acctg.), Pa. Bar Assn. (past chmn. sect. on corp., banking and bus. law, past chmn. corp. law com.), Allegheny Bar Assn. (past chmn. corp. law sect.). Republican. Clubs: Duquesne, Fox Chapel Golf, Harvard-Yale-Princeton (Pitts.). Home: 5024 Castleman St Pittsburgh PA 15232 Office: 747 Union Trust Bldg Pittsburgh PA 15219

HACKWORTH, DONALD E., automotive manufacturing company executive; b. 1937. B.S. in Bus. Adminstrn., Ohio State U., 1963; grad. exec. program, Stanford U. With Gen. Motors Corp., Detroit, 1963—, various supervisory position, later mgr. Delco Moraine div., Dayton, 1973-78, dir. mfg. facility planning worldwide product planning, Detroit, 1978-79, gen. mgr. mfg. Oldsmobile div., 1979-81, corp. v.p., pres., gen. mgr. mfg. Oldsmobile div., 1981, corp. v.p., 1981—; pres., gen. mgr. Gen. Motors of Canada Ltd. Office: Gen Motors Corp 3444 W Grand Blvd Gen Motors Bldg Detroit MI 48202 *

HADAS, PAMELA WHITE, author; b. Holland, Mich., Oct. 31, 1946; d. James Floyd and Phyllis Elizabeth (Pelgrim) White; m. David Elkus Hadas, Dec. 31, 1970. Student, Interlochen Acad. Arts, 1962-64; B.A., Washington U., St. Louis, 1968, M.A., 1970, Ph.D., 1973. Lectr. Washington U., St. Louis, part time 1976-79, vis. prof., 1983; Lectr. Webster Coll., part time, 1978; asst. prof. Middlebury Coll., 1982; faculty Bread Loaf Sch. English, 1982-83; staff assoc. Bread Loaf Writers' Conf., 1980-83. Poetry editor: Webster Rev, 1978-83; Author: works include Marianne Moore: Poet of Affection, 1977; poetry Designing Women, 1979, In Light of Genesis, 1980, Beside Herself: Pocahontas to Patty Hearst, 1983. Recipient Witter Bynner award Am. Acad. and Inst. Arts and Letters, 1980, Oscar Blumenthal award Poetry; Robert Frost fellow Bread Loaf Writers Conf., 1979. Mem. Poetry Soc. Am., PEN, Poets and Writers. Home: 6628 Pershing Ave St Louis MO 63130

HADDAD, ABRAHAM HERZL, electrical engineering educator, researcher; b. Baghdad, Iraq, Jan. 16, 1938; came to U.S., 1963; s. Moshe M. and Masuda (Cohen) H.; m. Carolyn Ann Kushner, Sept. 9, 1966; children: Benjamin, Judith, Jonathan. B.S. in Elec. Engring., Technion-Israel Inst. Tech., Haifa, 1960, M.S., 1963, M.A., Princeton U., 1964, Ph.D., 1966. Asst. prof. elec. engring. U. Ill., Urbana, 1966-70, assoc prof., 1970-75, prof., 1975-81; sr. staff cons. Dynamics Research Corp., Wilmington, Mass., 1979; program dir. NSF, Washington, 1979-83; prof. Ga. Inst. Tech., Atlanta, 1983—; advisor U.S. Army Missile Command, Huntsville, Ala., 1969-79; vis. assoc. prof. Tel Aviv U., 1972-73. Editor: Non-linear Systems, 1975. Fellow IEEE (editor Trans. on Automatic Control 1983—); mem. AAAS, Ops. Research Soc. Am. Jewish. Office: Sch Elec Engring Ga Inst Tech. Atlanta GA 30332

HADDAD, EUGENE, tech. co. exec.; b. Tampa, Fla., Aug. 10, 1925; s. Simon Farrage and Mary (Lutz) H.; m. Barbara Eloise Brown, June 23, 1951; children—Mary Elizabeth, Thomas Eugene, Geoffrey Allen, Susan Eloise, Barbara Jane. A.A., U. Fla., Gainesville, 1947; B.S. in Engring. Physics, Ala. Poly. Inst. Tech., Auburn, 1948; M.S. in Physics, UCLA, 1951; Ph.D., U. Utah, 1959. Teaching asst. U. So. Calif., Los Angeles, 1949, UCLA, 1950-51; teaching fellow, research fellow U. Utah, 1953-55; mem. staff Los Alamos Sci. Lab., 1951-60; asst. group leader Gen. Dynamics Co., San Diego, 1960-66; instr. physics UCLA extension, San Diego, 1963-66; mem. staff AEC research div., 1966-68; vis. prof. physics Catholic U. Am., Washington, 1966-67; asst. to dep. dir. sci. and tech. U.S. Def. Atomic Support Agy., Washington, 1968-69; lectr. U. Tex. at Austin, 1969-71; exec. v.p. Columbia Sci. Research Inst., Austin, Tex., 1969-71; exec. v.p., dir. Columbia Sci. Industries Co., Austin, 1969-76, pres., chief exec. officer, dir., 1976—. Contbr. articles to profl. publs. Fellow Am. Phys. Soc.; mem. Am. Nuclear Soc., Sigma Xi, Sigma Pi Sigma, Phi Kappa Phi. Clubs: Cosmos (Washington); Balcones Country (Austin). Home: 3606 Highland View Dr Austin TX 78731 Office: PO Box 9908 Austin TX 78766

HADDAD, GEORGE ILYAS, research scientist, educator; b. Aindara, Lebanon, Apr. 7, 1935; came to U.S., 1952, naturalized, 1961; s. Elias Ferris and Fahima (Haddad) H.; m. Mary Louella Nixon, June 28, 1958; children—Theodore N., Susan Anne. B.S. in Elec. Engring, U. Mich., 1956, M.S., 1958, Ph.D., 1963. Mem. faculty U. Mich., Ann Arbor, 1963—, asso. prof., 1965-69, prof. elec. engring., 1968—, dir. electron physics lab., 1968-75, chmn. dept. elec. and computer engring., 1975—; cons. to industry. Contbr. articles to profl. jours. Recipient Curtis W. McGraw research award Am. Soc. Engring. Edn., 1970. Fellow IEEE (editor proc. and trans.); mem. Am. Soc. Engring. Edn., Am. Phys. Soc., Sigma Xi, Phi Kappa Phi, Eta Kappa Nu, Tau Beta Pi. Office: Dept Elec and Computer Engring Univ Mich Ann Arbor MI 48109

HADDAD, GEORGE RICHARD, musician, educator; b. East End, Sask., Can., May 11, 1918; s. Richard and Labeeby (Salloum) H.; m. Lilyan Aboud, May 20, 1949; children: Constance Haddad Frecker, Diane, Carolyn. Asso., Toronto Conservatory Music, 1931, 1941; Mus.B., U. Toronto, 1940; M.A., Ohio State U., 1954; student, Royal Conservatory Music Toronto, 1936-40, Julliard Grad. Sch., N.Y.C., 1940-43, Paris Conservatoire, 1950-52. Tchr. piano Bay View Summer Coll. Music, summers 1948-51; prof. Sch. Music Ohio State U., Columbus, 1952—. Appeared in various recitals; guest appearances throughout, U.S., Can., Europe, 1944—; guest artist, Detroit Symphony, Toronto Symphony, Luxembourg Symphony, and, others. Mem. Music Tchrs. Nat. Assn., Nat. Music Guild Piano Tchrs., Ohio Music Tchrs. Assn., Musicians Union, Pi Kappa Lambda. Clubs: Faculty, Kinsmen of Can., Torch. Home: 2689 River Park Dr Columbus OH 43220 *I have found from experience that the chief ingredients which contribute towards a successful career are (1)To be highly motivated (2)To have a disciplined life (3)To persevere and persist throughout all obstacles, and (4)To have an ambition that is under control but yet does not lose sight of the goal.*

HADDAD, HESKEL MARSHALL, physician; b. Baghdad, Iraq, Sept. 26, 1928; came to U.S., 1953, naturalized, 1962; s. Moshe M. and Masuda (Cohen) H.; m. Doris I. Fatzer, July 4, 1963; children: Ava Masuda, Andreas Moshe, Albert Michael. Student, Royal Baghdad Coll. Medicine, 1945-50; M.D., Hebrew U., Jerusalem, 1953. Diplomate: Am. Bd. Pediatrics, Am. Bd. Ophthalmology. Intern Donolo Hosp., Jaffo-Tel Aviv, Israel, 1950-51; rotating intern Hadassah U. Hosp., Jerusalem, 1951-53; pediatric resident Children's Med. Center, Boston, 1953-56; fellow in pediatric endocrinology Johns Hopkins Hosp., Balt., 1956-58; fellow in clin. endocrine br. Nat. Inst. Arthritis and Metabolic Diseases, NIH, Bethesda, Md., 1958-59, pediatrician sect. clin. endocrinology, 1959-60; asst. prof. pediatrics sch. medicine Howard U., Washington, 1959-60; resident, asst. dept. ophthalmology sch. medicine Washington U., St. Louis, 1960-64; leave of absence, 1962-63; fellow pediatric ophthalmology Inst. Visual Sci., San Francisco, 1962; research fellow Hôpital des Quinze-Vingts, Laboratoire de Physiologie de Vision, Ecole des Hautes Etudes, Paris, 1962-63; ophthalmologist Hôpital Beni Messous, Algiers, Algeria, 1964; asst. attending ophthalmic surgeon, also asst. prof. ophthalmology Mt. Sinai Hosp. and Sch. Medicine, N.Y.C., 1964-67; dir. dept. ophthalmology Beth Israel Med. Center, N.Y.C.; also asso. prof. ophthalmology Mt. Sinai Sch. Medicine, 1967-71; clin. prof. ophthalmology N.Y. Med. Coll., 1971—. Author: Endocrine Exophthalmos, 1973, Metabolic Eye Diseases, 1974, Metabolic-Pediatric Eye Diseases, 1979; Editor-in-chief: Metabolic Ophthalmology, 1976-79, Metabolic and Pediatric Ophthalmology, 1979-82, Metabolic, Pediatric and Systemic Ophthalmology, 1982—; Contbr. numerous articles and revs. to profl. jours. Pres. Am. Com. for Rescue and Resettlement of Iraqui Jews, World Orgn. Jews from Arab Countries, Parents' Assn. of Sch. of Performing Arts, 1980-83. Fellow A.C.S., Am. Inst. Chemists; mem. Am. Endocrine Soc., Am. Fedn. Clin. Research, Assn. Research Ophthalmology and Vision, AMA, New York County Med. Soc., AAAS, Am. Acad. Ophthalmology, N.Y. Acad. Medicine, N.Y. Acad. Scis., N.Y. Soc. Clin. Ophthalmology, Soc. Eye Surgeons, Société Française d' Ophthalmologie, German Ophthal. Soc., Internat. Soc. Metabolic Eye Disease (founder, sec.-treas. 1973—), World Soc. on Systemic Ophthalmology (founder, sec.-treas. 1982). Office: 9 E 96th St New York NY 10028 *The Commandment of "loving ones' neighbor" should read "Thou shalt love for thy neighbor as for thy self." Whereas we cannot always control the emotion of love, we are consciously able to stop doing unto others what we do not like for ourselves*

HADDAD, JAMIL RAOUF, physician; b. Mosul, Iraq, Aug. 18, 1923; U.S., 1952, naturalized, 1965; s. Raouf Sulaiman and Fadhila (Shaya) H.; m. Mary Lou Scorsone, Aug. 1, 1959; children—Ralph J., John L., James M. M.B., Ch.B., Iraqi Royal Coll. Medicine, Baghdad, Iraq, 1946. Med. officer Khanaqin (Iraq) Hosp., 1946-52; asst. resident pathology Crawford W. Long Meml. Hosp., Atlanta, 1953-54; resident Bellevue Hosp., N.Y.C., 1954-56; practice medicine specializing in pathology, N.Y.C., 1963—; chmn. dept. anatomic and clin. pathology St. Clare's Hosp. and Health Center, N.Y.C., 1971-81; dir. pathology and clin. lab. Passaic (N.J.) Gen. Hosp., 1981—; asso. Sloan-Kettering Inst. for Cancer Research, N.Y.C., 1960-66; asst. prof. pathology N.Y. U. Coll. Medicine, 1959-65, asst. clin. prof. pathology, 1965-67, asso. clin. prof. pathology, 1967-70, clin. prof. pathology, 1970—; asst. prof. exptl. cell biology Mt. Sinai Grad Sch. Biol. Scis., N.Y.C., 1966-70, lectr., 1971—. Mem. Coll. Am. Pathologists, Am. Soc. Clin. Pathologists, AMA, N.Y. Pathol. Soc., N.Y. State, New York County med. socs. Home: 420 E 23d St New York NY 10010 Office: 350 Boulevard Passaic NJ 07055

HADDAD, JERRIER ABDO, engineering management consultant; b. N.Y.C., July 17, 1922; s. Abdulmassih Abdo and Rashida Helen (Shaker) H.; m. Carol Jane McCowen, Sept. 7, 1974; children: Mary Degarmo, Helen Abushaheen, Suzanne Baktash, Albert John, Alexander Lansdowne. B.E.E., Cornell U., 1945; S.C.D. (hon.), Union Coll., 1971, Clarkson Coll., 1978. Various engring. positions IBM, 1945-67, v.p., Armonk, N.Y., 1967-74, v.p. engring. programming and tech., 1974-77, v.p. tech. personnel devel., 1977-81; cons. NRC, Washington, 1981—; dir. Am. Dist. Telegraph Co. Fellow IEEE; mem. AAAS, Nat. Acad. Engring., Sigma Xi., Tau Beta Pi, Eta Kappa Nu. Patentee in field. Home: 162 Macy Rd Briarcliff Manor NY 10510

HADDAD, ZACK HAROUN, pediatrician; b. Cairo, Egypt, Jan. 27, 1938; came to U.S., 1961, naturalized, 1967; s. Haroun and Lella (Wahba) H.; m. Eveline Sylvia Lifton, Mar. 21, 1964; children: Ari, Lara. B.Sc., U. Cairo, 1956; M.D., U. Paris, 1961. Diplomate: Am. Bd. Pediatrics, Am. Bd. Allergy and Immunology. Intern Meml. Hosp., Niagara Falls, N.Y., 1961-62; resident Cook County Hosp., Chgo., 1962-63, Children's Hosp., Los Angeles, 1963-64, N.Y.C.-Bellevue Hosp., 1964-65, Children's Hosp., Pitts., 1965-66, U. Calif. Med. Center, San Francisco, 1966-67; asst. prof. pediatrics U. So. Calif. Sch. Medicine, Los Angeles, 1967-70, asso. prof., 1970-79, prof., 1979—; dir. pediatric allergy and immunology div. Los Angeles County-U. So.

Calif. Med. Sch., 1967—; mem. staff Los Angeles County Hosp., chief pediatric allergy and immunology clinics, 1967—; cons. Nat. Asthma Center, 1974—; bd. dirs. Am. Assn. Convalescent Hosps. for Asthmatic Children, 1971—. Author numerous research articles, also chpts. in books.; Editorial bd.: Western Jour. Medicine; bd. editors: Annals of Allergy. Fellow Am. Acad. Pediatrics, European Soc. Allergy and Clin. Immunology, Internat. Assn. Allergy, Am. Coll. Allergists (regent, Bela Schick lectureship award 1981), Am. Acad. Allergy; mem. Soc. Pediatric Research, Western Soc. Pediatric Research, Mex. Soc. Allergy and Immunology, Calif. Med. Assn. (adv. panel on allergy), AMA.

HADDEN, ALEXANDER HAWTHORNE, sports agency executive, lawyer; b. Cleve., Dec. 23, 1924; s. John Alexander and Marianne (Millikin) H.; m. Susan Margaret Heiser, June 21, 1966; children: Jane Hawthorne, David Alexander, Elisabeth Severance (dec. 1976), John Alexander II, Katherine Spring. B.A., Yale U., 1948; J.D., Western Res. U., 1951. Bar: U.S. Supreme Ct. bar, Ohio bar. Asso. to partner firm Baker, Hostetler & Patterson, Cleve., 1951-70; sec.-treas., gen. counsel Office Baseball Commr., N.Y.C., 1970—; Bd. dirs. Hadden Found. Served to 1st lt., inf. AUS, 1942-46; ETO. Home: Route 3 Box 303 Grafton VT 05146 Office: 75 Rockefeller Plaza New York NY 10019

HADDOCK, AUBURA GLEN, educator; b. Jasper, Ark., May 29, 1935; s. Walter Lee and Zada (Owens) H.; m. Bobbie Sue Fugett, Oct. 1, 1954; children—Debbie Sue, Glen David, Vicky Denise, Dee Ann. B.S. in Math, State Coll. Ark., 1954, M.S., Okla. State U., 1958, Ph.D., 1961. Tchr. Carlisle (Ark.) High Sch., 1955-57; asso. prof. Ark. Coll., 1961-64, prof., dean, 1964-66; asso. prof. math. U. Mo., Rolla, 1966-68, prof., 1968—, chmn. math. dept., 1968-81; Dir. Batesville Devel. Corp., 1964-65. Contbr. articles to profl. jours. Recipient Outstanding Service award Ark. Coll., 1966. Mem. Am. Math. Soc., Math. Assn. Am. (gov. 1970-73), Am. Soc. Engring. Edn., Sigma Xi. Baptist. Club: Rotarian. Home: Route 4 Box 159 Rolla MO 65401

HADDON, HAROLD ALAN, lawyer; b. Flint, Mich., Dec. 2, 1940; s. Russell Daniel and Virginia Sibyl (Johnston) H.; m. Beverly Jean Reading, July 2, 1966. A.B., Albion Coll., 1962; A.M., U. Mich., 1963; J.D., Duke U., 1966. Bar: Colo. bar 1966; Cert. trial counsel U.S. Cts. Martial. Asso. firm Davis, Graham & Stubbs, Denver, 1966-70; chief trial dep. Colo. Pub. Defender, 1970-73; partner firm Haddon, Morgan & Foreman, Denver, 1974—; adj. prof. law in criminal trial advocacy U. Denver Sch. Law, 1972-73; spl. prosecutor Colo. State Grand Jury, 1976-78. Editor-in-chief Duke Law Jour., 1965-66. Sec. Nat. Multiple Sclerosis Soc., 1970-76; mem. Colo. U.S. Jud. Selection Com., 1977; campaign mgr. U.S. Sen. Gary W. Hart, 1974-80; fin. chmn. Colo. Gov. Richard D. Lamm, 1978. Mem. Am., Colo., Denver bar assns., Nat. Assn. Criminal Def. Lawyers, Order of Coif, Phi Beta Kappa. Democrat. Episcopalian. Home: 409 21st St Denver CO 80205 Office: 1034 Logan St Denver CO 80203

HADDON, SAM ELLIS, lawyer; b. West Monroe, La., June 19, 1937; s. James Charlie and Letha (Daughtry) H.; m. Betty G. Loyd, Dec. 22, 1958; children—Elizabeth Anne Haddon Alexander, Steven Craig, Allison Lee. B.S., Rice U., 1959; student, Border Patrol Acad., El Paso, 1959-60, Treasury Law Enforcement Sch., Washington, 1961; J.D. with honors (Univ. scholar), U. Mont., 1965. Bar: Mont. 1965, U.S. Supreme Ct. 1975. Immigration patrol insp. U.S. Border Patrol, 1959-61; agt. Fed. Bur. Narcotics, 1961-62; research asst. in law U. Mont., 1964-65; law clk. to judge U.S. Dist. Ct., 1965-66; assoc. firm Anderson, Symmes, Forbes, Peete and Brown, Billings, Mont., 1966-69; ptnr. firm Boone, Karlberg and Haddon, Missoula, Mont., 1969—; instr. U. Mont. Sch. Law, 1971, 72-73, 74—; chmn. Mont. Supreme Ct. Commn. on Rules of Evidence, 1975—; judge pro tem Mont. Dist. Ct. for 4th Jud. Dist., 1975; spl. master Mont. Supreme Ct., 1978; del. Jud. Conf. 9th Circuit, 1975, rep., 1977-80; mem. com. on rules U.S. Dist. Ct. for Dist. Mont. Mem. staff: Mont. Law Rev, 1963-64; editor-in-chief, 1964-65. Recipient Allen Smith award U. Mont. Law Sch.; Justin Miller award; Outstanding Student award Phi Delta Phi. Mem. ABA, Am. Judicature Soc. (dir. 1976-79), Am. Bd. Trial Advocates (advocate), Am. Law Inst., Mont. Bar Assn. (chmn. sect. young lawyers 1967-68, exec. com. 1968-69), State Bar Mont. (trustee 1976-78), Western Mont. Bar Assn. Office: 301 Central Sq 201 W Main St Missoula MT 59802

HADDON, WILLIAM, JR., profl. inst. exec., physician; b. Orange, N.J., May 24, 1926; s. William and Anna (Herrstrom) H.; m. Gene Billo, June 16, 1956; children—Jonathan, Charles, Robert. S.B., Mass. Inst. Tech., 1949; M.D., Harvard, 1953, M.P.H. magna cum laude, 1957. Research fellow microbiology, postdoctoral fellow Nat. Found. Infantile Paralysis, Harvard Sch. Pub. Health, 1954-55, research asso., 1955-56; dir. driver research center N.Y. Dept. Health, 1957-61, dir. epidemiology residency program, 1961-65, acting asst. commr. pub. health research, devel. and evaluation, 1963-64, asso. dir. div. chronic disease services, 1964-66; asst. prof., then asso. prof. epidemiology Albany (N.Y.) Med. Coll., Union U., 1960-66; spl. asst. for traffic safety planning to undersec. transp. Dept. Commerce, 1966; adminstr. Nat. Hwy. Safety Agy., also; Nat. Traffic Safety Agy., Dept. Commerce, 1966-67; dir. Nat. Hwy. Safety Bur., Dept. Transp., 1967-69; pres. Ins. Inst. Hwy. Safety, Washington, 1969—, Highway Loss Data Inst., 1972—; Mem. com. mil. accidents Armed Forces Epidemiological Bd., 1965-69; mem. U.S. delegation com. on challenges of modern society North Atlantic council NATO, 1969; mem. com. emergency med. services Nat. Acad. Sci./NRC, 1970-73. Author: (with E. A. Suchman and D. Klein) Accident Research, Methods and Approaches, 1964; also articles. Served with USAAF, 1944-45. Recipient Modern Medicine award for distinguished achievement, 1969; Bronfman prize Am. Pub. Health Assn., 1969; Stone award Am. Trauma Soc., 1977. Mem. Am. Pub. Health Assn. (council on environment 1970-72, chmn. reference com. on resolutions on environment 1972), Sigma Xi, Delta Omega. Home: 7506 Hamilton Spring Rd Bethesda MD 20817 Office: Ins Inst Hwy Safety Watergate 600 Washington DC 20037

HADDOX, BENJAMIN EDWARD, educator, sociologist; b. Orlando, Fla., Dec. 11, 1923; s. James Henry and Lily (Caldwell) H.; m. Geraldine Hayes, Sept. 14, 1942; children: Benjamin Edward, Cheryl Ann, John Stephen. A.B., Stetson U., 1945; B.D., So. Bapt. Theol. Sem., 1950; M.A., U. Fla., 1960, Ph.D., 1962. Ordained to ministry Baptist Ch., 1945; minister in Fla., 1950-62; asst. prof. sociology Miss. State U., 1962-64; asst. prof., acting chmn. dept. sociology Stetson U., 1964-66; prof., head dept. sociology Butler U., Indpls., 1966—; research in Bogota, Colombia, 1961. Author: Sociedad y Religión en Colombia, 1965, Joint Decision Making Patterns and Related Factors Among Low Income Families, 1965; also articles. Miss. rep. regional research project low income families, 1962-64. U.S. Steel Found. fellow, 1960-62. Mem. A.A.U.P. (pres. Butler U. chpt. 1968-69), A.A.A.S., Am. Sociol. Assn., North Central Midwest, So. sociol. socs., Latin Am. Studies Assn., Nat. Council on Family Relations, Council on Religion in Internat. Affairs, Soc. Sci. Study of Religion, Ind. Council on World Affairs, Phi Beta Kappa, Phi Kappa Phi. (pres. Butler chpt. 1971-72). Democrat. Mem. Christian Ch. Home: 327 Buckingham Dr Indianapolis IN 46208

HADDY, FRANCIS JOHN, physician, educator; b. Walters, Minn., Sept. 6, 1922; s. Thomas J. and Frances (Shaheen) H.; m. Theresa Eileen Brey, Sept. 21, 1946; children: Richard, Carol, Alice. Student, Luther Coll., Decorah, Iowa, 1940-42; B.S., U. Minn., 1943, B.M., 1946, M.D., 1947, M.S. in Physiology, 1949, Ph.D. in Physiology (Am. Heart Assn. fellow), 1953. Diplomate: Am. Bd. Internal Medicine. Intern Mpls. Gen. Hosp., 1946-47; fellow internal medicine Mayo Found., 1949-51; asst. prof. physiology and medicine Northwestern U. Med. Sch., 1953-61; clin. investigator VA Research Hosp., Chgo., 1957-59; prof. physiology, chmn. dept., asso. prof. medicine U. Okla. Med. Center, 1961-66; prof. physiology, chmn. dept. Mich. State U., East Lansing, 1966-76; prof. physiology and medicine Uniformed Services U., Bethesda, Md., 1976—, chmn. dept. physiology, 1976—; mem. cardiovascular study sect. NIH, 1963-69; tng. com. Nat. Heart and Lung Inst., NIH, 1970-73; mem. atherosclerosis and hypertension adv. com. Nat. Heart, Lung and Blood Inst., NIH, 1983—; research com. Am. Heart Assn., 1974-80. Mem. editorial bd.: Am. Jour. Physiology, 1963-69, 80—, Jour. Applied Physiology, 1963-69, Procs. Soc. Exptl. Biology and Medicine, 1969-72, Circulation Research, 1975-81, Microvascular Research, 1978-81, Hypertension, 1978-81. Mem. Am. Physiol. Soc. (steering com. circulation group 1972-75, chmn. com. on coms. 1974-77, mem. council 1976-79, pres. 1981, fin. com. 1983—, Carl J. Wiggers award 1966), Am. Soc. Clin. Investigation.; mem. Fedn. Am. Socs. Exptl. Biology (bd. dirs. 1980-83), Internat. Union Physiol. Scis. (U.S. nat. com. 1976-79, 81—), Nat. Acad. Scis. (basic biomed. scis. panel, com. on nat. needs for biomed. and behavioral research personnel, inst. medicine 1983—). Home: 4701 Willard Ave Apt 1005 Chevy Chase MD 20815

HADEN, CHARLES, jazz bassist, composer; b. Shenandoah, Iowa, Aug. 6, 1937. Formed group with Ornette Coleman, Biley Higgins and Don Cherry; performing debut, N.Y.C., 1959. Performed throughout, U.S., Europe; played with, Archie Shepp, Keith Jarrett, Alice Coltrane, Pee Wee Russell, Liberation Music Orch., others; recs. include Escalator Over the Hill, (with Carla Bley) Relativity Suite, (with Don Cherry) Expectations, (with Keith Jarrett) Tribute, Ballad of the Fallen; appeared at, Newport Jazz Festival, 1966-67, 70-72, Monterey Jazz Festival, 1966-67. Recipient Downbeat Critic's New Star award, 1961; Guggenheim Found. grantee, 1970; Nat. Endowment Arts grantee, 1973. *

HADEN, CHARLES H., II, judge; b. Morgantown, W.Va., Apr. 16, 1937; s. Charles H. and Beatrice L. (Costolo) H.; m. Priscilla Ann Miller, June 2, 1956; children: Charles H., Timothy M., Amy Sue. B.S., W.Va. U., 1958, J.D., 1961. Partner Haden & Haden, Morgantown, W.Va., 1961-69; state tax commr. W.Va., 1969-72; justice Supreme Ct. Appeals W.Va., 1972-75, chief justice, 1975; judge U.S. Dist. Ct. No. and So. Dists. W.Va., Parkersburg, 1975-82; chief judge U.S. Dist. Ct. So. Dist. W.Va., 1982—; mem. W.Va. Ho. of Dels., 1963-64; asst. prof. Coll. Law, W.Va. U., 1967-68; mem. com. adminstrn. probation system Jud. Conf., 1979—. Mem. Bd. Edn., Monongalia County, W.Va., 1967-68. Mem. W.Va. Bar Assn., Monongalia-Kanawha Counties Bar Assn., W.Va. Jud. Assn. Office: PO Box 1139 Parkersburg WV 26101 *

HADEN, CLOVIS ROLAND, engineer, university dean; b. Houston, Apr. 10, 1940; s. Clovis Newton and Mary Aline (Baker) H.; m. Joyce Elaine Haden, Aug. 8, 1956; children: Cathy, Kimberly, Clay. Student, Navarro Jr. Coll., 1958-59; B.S.E.E., Arlington State Coll., 1961; M.S.E.E., Calif. Inst. Tech., 1962; Ph.D., U. Tex., 1965. Asst. prof. U. Okla., 1965-68; dir. Sch. Elec. Engring. and Computing Scis., 1972-78; asso. prof. Tex. A&M U., College Station, 1968-71, prof., 1971-72; dir. Inst. Solid State Electronics, 1969-72; dean Coll. Engring. and Applied Scis., Ariz. State U., Tempe, 1978—; bd. dirs. Ariz. Transp. Research Center, 1980—; mem. Gov.'s Commn. on Sci. and Tech., 1980—, chmn. transp. subcom., 1981—, mem. adv. council for engring., 1979—; bd. dirs. Harrington Arthritis Research Ctr. Exec. editor: Electric Power Systems Research jour, 1978—. Bd. mgrs. Tempe YMCA. Bur. Engring. research fellow, 1964. Mem. IEEE (Oklahoma City Engr. of Yr. award 1977), Ariz. Soc. Profl. Engrs. (Engr. of Yr. award 1983), Am. Soc. Engring. Edn., Nat. Soc. Profl. Engrs., Ariz. Assn. Indsl. Devel., Soc. Mfg. Engrs., Sigma Xi, Phi Kappa Phi, Eta Kappa Nu, Tau Beta Pi. Republican. Mem. Ch. of Christ. Office: Coll Engring and Applied Scis Ariz State Univ Tempe AZ 85281

HADEN, PATRICK CAPPER (PAT HADEN), former professional football player, sports commentator; b. Westbury, N.Y., Jan. 23, 1953. B.A. in English, U. So. Calif. Quarterback Los Angeles Rams, NFL, 1976-81; player Pro Bowl, Nat. Football League All-Star Game, 1977; color commentator CBS-TV, 1982—. Office: CBS Sports 51 W 52nd St New York NY 10019 *

HADIDIAN, DIKRAN YENOVK, librarian, clergyman; b. Aintab, Turkey, June 9, 1920; came to U.S., 1946, naturalized, 1956; s. Yenovk Haroutune and Helen (Koundakjian) H.; m. Jean Root Wackerbarth, June 9, 1948; children: Eric Dikran, Andrew Dikran. B.A., Am. U. Beirut, 1944; B.D., Hartford Theol. Sem., 1948; M.A., Hartford Sch. Religious Edn., 1949; S.T.M., Hartford Sem. Found., 1950; M.S. in L.S, Columbia U., 1960. Instr. Oak Grove Sch., Vassalboro, Me., 1950-52, Sweet Briar Coll., 1952-55; librarian Hartford Sem. Found., 1957-66, Pitts. Theol. Sem., 1966—; vis. lectr. U. Pitts., 1969—; Mem. corp. bd. United Ch. World Ministries, 1971-77; Bd. dirs. Pitts. Chamber Music Soc. Chmn. editorial bd.: Perspective, 1967-72; editor series: Bibliographia Tripotamopolitana, 1969—; gen. editor: Pitts. Theol. Monograph Series, 1974—; dir., gen. editor: Pickwick Publs.; Contbr. articles to profl. jours. Mem. Studiorum Novi Testamenti, Soc. Bibl. Lit., Am. Theol. Library Assn. Home: 4137 Timberlane Dr Allison Park PA 15101 Office: 616 N Highland Ave Pittsburgh PA 15206

HADLEY, ELMER BURTON, botanist, educator; b. Iola, Kans., Oct. 24, 1936; s. Elmo A. and Bertha E. (Mock) H. B.S., U. Calif., Santa Barbara, 1958; M.S., U. Ill., 1960, Ph.D., 1963. Asst. prof. U. N.D., 1964-65; asst. prof. U. Ill., Chgo., 1965-67, asso. prof., 1967-70, prof., 1970—, head dept. biol. scis., 1969-74; dean Coll. Liberal Arts and Scis., 1974-79; fellow Brookhaven Nat. Lab., 1963-64. Contbr. articles to profl. jours. Mem. Ecol. Soc. Am., Phi Beta Kappa, Phi Kappa Phi. Office: Dept Biol Scis U Ill at Chicago Circle Chicago IL 60680

HADLEY, MARLIN LEROY, direct sales financial consultant; b. Mankato, Kans., Jan. 5, 1931; s. Charles LeRoy and Lillian Fern (Dunn) H.; m. Clarissa Jane Payne, Sept. 17, 1949; children: Michael LeRoy, Steven Lee. B.S., U. Denver, 1953; postgrad., Harvard U., 1966. Pres. Jewel Home Shopping Service div. Jewel Cos., Inc., Barrington, Ill., 1953-72; pres., chief exec. officer, dir. Beeline Fashions, Inc., Bensenville, Ill., 1972-82; chmn. bd. HAS Originals, Blairstown, NJ, 1984—; fin., bus. cons.; pres., dir. Beeline Real Estate Corp., Act II Jewelry, Inc., Home Galleries, Inc.; dir. Goulder Co., Inc., Climax Spltys., Inc. Club: Economics (Chgo.). Home: 4298 West Lake Circle Littleton CO 80123 Office: PO Box 179 Blairstown NJ 07825

HADLEY, PAUL ERVIN, educator; b. South Ovid, Mich., July 17, 1914; s. Ervin C. and Viola M. (Barnes) H.; m. Virginia Faye Last, May 15, 1945; 1 dau., Deborah Faye. A.B., Occidental Coll., Los Angeles, 1934; A.M., U. So. Calif., 1946, Ph.D. in Comparative Lit, 1955; L.H.D., Nat. U., 1980. Tchr. El Monte (Calif.) Union High Sch., 1935-42; exec. sec. Centro Cultural Paraguayo Americano, Asunción, Paraguay, 1943-44; head Cultural Insts. unit U.S. Dept. State, Washington, 1945; instr. internat. relations U. So. Calif., Los Angeles, 1945-47, asst. prof., 1947-55, asso. prof., 1955-64, prof., 1964-81, emeritus prof., 1981—; dean summer session, 1960-73; dean U. Coll. and summer session, 1966-73, asso. v.p. acad. adminstrn., 1973-77, interim acad. v.p., 1975-77, acad. v.p., 1977-81; exec. sec. Inst. World Affairs, 1948—; chmn. Pacific Coast Council Latin Am. Studies, 1956-57; mem. Woodrow Wilson Fellowship selection com. Region XV, 1960-67; fgn. leader and specialist program Am. Council on Edn., 1960-62; mem. State Com. on Continuing Edn., 1966-76; mem. adv. com. Servicemembers Opportunity Colls., 1978-81; Chmn. edn. sect. Town Hall of Calif., 1965-68, chmn. internat. relations sect., 1969-71; Trustee Latin Am. Scholarship Program Am. Univs., 1972-74. Mem. Assn. U. Summer Sessions (pres. 1970-71), Inst. Internat. Edn. (adv. bd. West Coast region), Nat. U. Extension Assn. (chmn. region VI 1970-71, pres. 1976-77), Adult Educators Greater Los Angeles (chmn. 1970-71), Phi Beta Kappa, Pi Sigma Alpha, Sigma Alpha Epsilon, Phi Kappa Phi. Presbyn. (elder, stated clk. Presbytery). Home: 3098 Menlo Dr Glendale CA 91208

HADLEY, ROLLIN VAN NOSTRAND, museum executive; b. Westboro, Mass., Dec. 13, 1927; s. Rollin Van Nostrand and Arabelle (McKinstry) H.; m. Shelagh Grace Pratt, Sept. 23, 1961; children: Susan Olmstead Hadley Garruthers, Jane Houghton Hadley Preziose, Hope McKinstry, Peter Van Nostrand, James Broughton, Sarah Hamilton. Grad., St. Mark's Sch., 1945; A.B., Harvard U., 1950, M.A., 1981. Reporter Harrisburg newspapers, (Pa.), 1950-52; with Corning Glass Works, 1952-60, mgr. budgets, 1957-59, dir., 1957-60; treas., dir. Corning Glass Internat., 1959-60; faculty U. Bocconi, Milan, Italy, 1960-62; adminstr. Isabella Stewart Gardner Mus., Boston, 1963-70, dir., 1970—. Author: Drawings: Isabella Stewart Gardner Museum, 1968, Sculpture in the Gardner Museum (Renaissance Section), 1977, Museums Discovered: Isabella Stewart Gardner Museum, 1981. Trustee emeritus Corning Mus. Glass; pres. Save Venice, Inc., 1974—; bd. dirs. Boston Fulbright Com., Inc.; mem. vis. com. dept. fine arts Boston U., 1977—. Served with AUS, 1946-47. Decorated comdr. Order of Merit, (Italy). Mem. Assn. Art Mus. Dirs. Episcopalian. Clubs: Tavern, Club of Odd Volumes (Boston); Grolier (N.Y.C.). Home: 2 Palace Rd Boston MA 02115 Office: Isabella Stewart Gardner Museum 2 Palace Rd Boston MA 02115

HADLEY, STANTON THOMAS, building materials company executive, lawyer; b. Beloite, Kans., July 3, 1936; s. Robert Campbell and Helen (Schroeder) H.; m. Charlotte June Holmes, June 9, 1962; children: Gayle Elizabeth, Robert Edward, Stanton Thomas, Steven Holmes. B.S. in Metall. Engring., Colo. Sch. Mines, 1958; LL.B., U. Colo., 1962. Bar: Colo. 1962, U.S. Dist. Ct. 1962, U.S. Patent Office 1963. Metallurgist ASARCO, Leadville, Colo., 1957; tng. engr. Allis-Chalmers Co., West Allis, Wis., 1958-61; adminstrv. engr. Ball Corp., Boulder, Colo., 1961-62, atty., 1962-65; patent counsel Scott Paper Co., Phila., 1965-71, U.S. Gypsum Co., Chgo., 1971-76; gen. mgr. metals div., 1976-79, group v.p. indsl. group, 1979-84, sr. v.p. adminstrn., sec., 1984—; patent counsel Nat. Mfrs. Assn.; dir. Durabond Products Co.; bd. dirs. WJE Assocs., Inc., U.S. Gypsum Found.; mem. founders' council Field Mus.; mem. Chgo. United, Chgo. Assn. Commerce and Industry. Bd. dirs. Greater Chgo. Safety Council, North Suburban YMCA, Northbrook Symphony Orch. Served with U.S. Army, 1959. Mem. Am. Soc. Metals, Licensing Execs. Soc., Assn. Corp. Patent Counsel. Republican. Clubs: Union League, Sunset Ridge Country, Executives. Home: 2416 Colony Ct Northbrook IL 60062 Office: 101 S Wacker Dr Chicago IL 60606

HADLEY, SUSAN JANE, physician; b. Madison, Wis., Sept. 30, 1919; d. Frederick Brown and Jenny Elizabeth (Potts) H.; m. David S. Biberman, May 23, 1951; children—David Hadley, Elizabeth Anne. B.A., U. Wis., 1941; M.D., Cornell U., 1944. Intern Bellevue Hosp., 1944-45, resident in pulmonary disease, 1945-46; resident in medicine N.Y. Hosp., 1946-48, asst. dir. central labs., 1951-64, dir. lab. microbiology, 1964-70, chief pulmonary clinic, 1964—; fellow, instr. N.Y. U., 1948-51; asst. prof. medicine Cornell U., 1952-68, asso. prof., 1968-72, prof., 1972—, asst. to chmn. dept. medicine, 1965—; mem. clin. labs. adv. com. N.Y.C. Dept. Health, 1968-73. Mem. Harvey Soc., Am. Thoracic Soc., N.Y. Acad. Medicine, N.Y. Trudeau Soc., Phi Beta Kappa, Alpha Omega Alpha. Club: Cosmopolitan (N.Y.C.). Home: 1035 5th Ave New York NY 10028 Office: 1300 York Ave New York NY 10021

HADSEL, FRED LATIMER, found. exec., former ambassador; b. Oxford, Ohio, Mar. 11, 1916; s. Fred Latimer and Mary (Perine) H.; m. Winifred Nelson, Oct. 21, 1942; children—Mary C., Winifred R., Jane L. A.B., Miami U., Oxford, 1937, LL.D. (hon.), 1977; M.A., Clark U., 1938; Ph.D., U. Chgo., 1942; grad. student, U. Grenoble, France, 1933, Freiburg U., Germany, 1938. Instr. Rutgers U., 1946; with Dept. of State, 1946—; assigned hist. research German Affairs Office; exec. secretariat Bur. Near Eastern, South Asian and African Affairs, 1946-56; dir. Office So. Africa Affairs, 1956-57; 1st sec. Am. embassy, London, Eng., 1957-61, dep. chief mission Am. embassy, Addis Ababa, Ethiopia, 1961-62; adviser Bur. African Affairs, Dept. State, 1963-64; dir. Office Inter-African Affairs, 1964; U.S. ambassador to Somalia, 1969-71, to Ghana, 1971-74; dir. George C. Marshall Found., Lexington, Va., 1974—; Professorial lectr. polit. sci. George Washington U., 1947-57, 1974—; mem. Grad. Council, 1947-57; lectr. African affairs Columbia, summer 1962, Johns Hopkins, 1968-69, Howard U., 1968-69; George C. Marshall distinguished prof. internat. studies Va. Mil. Inst., 1976—. Contbr. articles to profl. jours. Served from pvt. to maj. AUS, 1942-46. Mem. Phi Beta Kappa, Beta Theta Pi, Omicron Delta Kappa, Phi Eta Sigma. Address: Marshall Found Drawer 1600 Lexington VA 24450

HADZI, DIMITRI, sculptor, educator; b. N.Y.C., Mar. 21, 1921; s. Theodore and Christina H.; married; children: Christina, Stephen. Student, Bklyn. Poly. Inst., 1940-43, Cooper Union, 1946-50; M.A. (hon.), Harvard U., 1977. Studio prof. visual and environ. studies Harvard U., Cambridge, Mass., 1977—. One-man shows, Galleria Schneider, Rome, 1958, 60, Galerie Van de Loo, Munich, W. Ger., 1961, Radich Gallery, N.Y.C., 1961-62, MIT, 1963, Richard Gray Gallery, Chgo., 1972, Mekler Gallery, Los Angeles, 1978, Gruenebaum Gallery, N.Y.C., group shows include, Venice Biennale, 1956, 58, 62, Guggenheim Mus., N.Y.C., 1979, represented in permanent collections, Mus. Modern Art, N.Y.C., Guggenheim Mus., Whitney Mus., N.Y.C., Hirshhorn Mus., Washington, Yale U. Gallery, Fogg Art Mus., Cleve. Mus., Phila. Mus. Art, Dallas Mus. Art, UCLA, Albright-Knox Art Gallery, Buffalo; archtl. Commns. include Bronze doors, St. Paul's Ch., Rome, 1962-76, Fed. Res. Bank, Mpls., 1971-73; archtl. Commn. include Johnson Wax, Racine, Wis., 1978-79; archtl. commns. include fountain, Toledo and Boston, 1982-83. Served with USAAF, 1943-46. Fulbright fellow, 1950; Louis Comfort Tiffany award, 1954; Guggenheim Found. fellow, 1957. Fellow Am. Acad. Arts and Scis.; mem. Nat. Inst. Arts and Letters. Home: 7 Ellery Sq Cambridge MA 02138 Office: Carpenter Center Harvard Univ 19 Prescott St Cambridge MA 02138

HAEBEL, ROBERT EDWARD, marine corps officer; b. Marcus Hook, Pa., July 18, 1927; s. William John and Blanche Harriet H.; m. Barbara Louise Shellenberger, Sept. 1, 1951; children: Deborah L., Lisa L., Jeffrey C. B.A. in Edn, West Chester (Pa.) State Tchrs. Coll., 1951, M.A., U. N.Mex., 1967, George Washington U., 1971. Enlisted in USMC, 1945, commd. 2d lt., 1951, advanced through grades to maj.

gen., 1979; service in, Korea, Okinawa, Taiwan and Vietnam; comdg. gen. Force Troops, 1976-78; dir. personnel mgmt. Div. Hdqrs. USMC, 1978-80, asst. dep. chief staff manpower, 1979-80; comdg. gen. Marine Corps Recruit Depot, Parris Island, S.C., 1980-82, 3d Marine Amphibious Force, 1982—. Decorated Legion of Merit with Combat V, Bronze Star with combat V, Purple Heart with gold star. Roman Catholic. Home: Quarters TA-1 Camp Courtney FPO San Francisco CA 96606 Office: Comdg Gen 3d Marine Amphibious Force FPO San Francisco CA 96606

HAEBERLIN, JOHN BENJAMIN, JR., physician, educator; b. Chgo., Sept. 25, 1909; s. John Benjamin and Carolyn (Parrott) H.; m. Clare Rogerson, Mar. 21, 1936; children—Susan, John. B.Sc., U. Chgo., 1930; M.D., C.M., McGill U., 1935. Diplomate: Am. Bd. Dermatology and Syphilology. Intern Ill. Research and Edn. Hosp., Chgo., 1936-37; practice of medicine, 1937—, specializing in dermatology, 1943—; fellow dermatology U. Ill., 1946-49, clin. asst. prof. dermatology, 1948—; chmn. dept. dermatology Presbyn. Hosp., 1953-59, Presbyn.-St. Lukes Hosp., Chgo., 1959-68; adj. prof. dermatology U. N.Mex., Albuquerque, 1972—; hon. staff Bernalillo County Med. Center, 1973—. Served from lt. to maj. AUS, 1942-46. Mem. A.M.A., Albuquerque, Bernalillo County med. assns., Chgo. Dermatol. Soc. (pres. 1967), N.Mex. Dermatol. Soc., Am. Acad. Dermatology, N.Mex. Med. Soc., Am. Dermatol. Assn., Psi Upsilon. Home: 6508 Katson Ave NE Albuquerque NM 87109

HAECKEL, GERALD BURSETH, financial consultant; b. Lewistown, Mont., Oct. 20, 1929; s. Christopher A. and Anne (Burseth) H.; m. Joanne L. Dings, Mar. 17, 1956; children: John, Peter, Stephen. Student, Mont. State Coll., 1947-48; B.S., U. Pa., 1952. With N.Y. Life Ins. Co., N.Y.C., 1952-66, v.p., 1965-66; v.p. finance Fla. Gas Co., Winter Park, 1966-68; v.p., dir. Hamilton Bros. Oil Co., Denver, 1968-74; pres., dir. Hamilton Bros. Exploration Co., 1972-74; sr. v.p. finance Transco Cos., Inc., Houston, 1974-77, exec. v.p., 1977-81, dir., 1975-81; v.p. fin. Ensource Inc., Houston, 1981-82; fin. cons., Scottsville, Va., 1983—; dir. Quanex Corp. Served with USNR, 1948-49. Home: Rt 1 Box 273 Scottsville VA 24590

HAEFELE, EDWIN THEODORE, political scientist; b. Burnt Prairie, Ill., Oct. 5, 1925; s. Monroe Edwin and Lola Amanda (Coles) H.; m. Ruth Anne Woods, Dec. 23, 1948; children: Ann Katherine, Douglas Monroe, John Joseph. Student, Mich. State U., 1943, Ill. Wesleyan U., 1946-48, U. Chgo., 1948-50. Staff asst. Pub. Adminstrn. Clearing House, Chgo., 1951-54; asst. dir. Transp. Center, Northwestern U., 1954-62; mem. sr. staff Brookings Instn., Washington, 1962-67; mem. sr. research staff Resources for Future, Inc., Washington, 1967-73; prof. polit. sci. and pub. policy U. Pa., Phila., 1973-82, prof. emeritus, 1982—; v.p. Consortium Govtl. Counselors, Inc., 1983—. Author: Government Controls on Transport, 1965, Representative Government and Environmental Management, 1973; Editor: Transport and National Goals, 1967, The Governance of Common Property Resources, 1974. Served with AUS, 1943-46. Decorated Purple Heart, Presdl. Unit citation. Mem. AAAS. Republican. Congregationalist. Home: 2 Red Cross Ave Newport RI 02840

HAEGELE, JOHN ERNEST, leasing company executive; b. Phila., July 11, 1941; s. Ernest F. and Cecilia (Wheeler) H.; m. Victoria J. Brasten, July 31, 1965; children: John, Scott, Lisa. B.S. in Acctg. and Fin., 1964. C.P.A., N.Y. Acct. Arthur Young & Co., N.Y.C., 1964-68, mgr., 1968-71; asst. controller Indian Head Inc., N.Y.C., 1971-76, v.p., controller, 1976-82; exec. v.p. dir. Interpool, Ltd., N.Y.C., 1982—. Served with U.S. Army; 1964-69. Mem. Am. Inst. C.P.A.s, N.Y. Soc. C.P.A.s, Fin. Execs. Inst. Republican. Roman Catholic.

HAEGER, PHYLLIS MARIANNA, association management company executive; b. Chgo., May 20, 1928; d. Milton O. and Ethel M. B.A., Lawrence U., 1950; M.A., Northwestern U., 1952. Midwest editor TIDE mag., 1952-55; exec. v.p. Smith, Bucklin & Assos., Inc., Chgo., 1955-78; pres. P.M. Haeger & Assos., Inc., Chgo., 1978—. Mem. Am. Soc. Assn. Execs., Chgo. Soc. Assn. Execs., Inst. Assn. Mgmt. Cos., Nat. Assn. Women Bus. Owners, Chgo. Execs. Club, Chgo. Fin. Exchange, Chgo. Network, Nat. Assn. Bank Women (exec. v.p.).

HAEHL, HARRY LEWIS, lawyer; b. Palo Alto, Calif., July 6, 1912; s. Harry Lewis and May Ada (Burrel) H.; m. Helen Dungan, Apr. 18, 1936; children: John Hilton, Susan Jane Haehl Rapp, Elizabeth Anne Haehl Bushnell. A.B., Stanford U., 1933, J.D., 1936. Bar: Calif. 1936. Asso. firm Lillick, Geary, Olson & Charles, San Francisco, 1936-41; U.S. sp. prize commr. Pacific Ocean Area, 1945-46; partner firm Lillick, McHose & Charles, San Francisco, 1946-80, sr. partner, 1974-80, mng. partner, 1978-80, of counsel, 1980—; lectr. Admiralty Inst., Tulane U. Law Sch., 1966; Chmn. bd. dirs. Childrens Hosp. at Stanford, 1970-73; sec.-treas. San Francisco Consular Corps, 1980—; trustee Peninsula Endowment, San Francisco Bar Assn. Found., World Affairs Council No. Calif., pres., 1963-64. Contbr. chpts. to: Ocean Transportation, 1954. Served to comdr. USNR, 1941-46. Decorated Johan Mangku Negara (Malaysia); Hon. consul gen. for Malaysia in Calif., 1967—. Mem. Am., Calif., San Francisco bar assns., Am. Soc. Internat. Law, Fgn. Policy Assn., Maritime Law Assn. of U.S. Clubs: Bohemian, Pacific Union, Menlo Country, Lahaina Yacht. Home: 2373 Sharon Oaks Dr Menlo Park CA 94025 Office: Two Embarcadero Center 2600 San Francisco CA 94111

HAEHL, JOHN GEORGE, JR., utility executive; b. Bklyn., Aug. 16, 1922; s. John George and Madeline (Hamilton) H.; m. Alice Norton; children: Constance, Victoria. B.S. cum laude, U. So. Calif., 1949. C.P.A., N.Y. Mgr. Price Waterhouse & Co. (C.P.A.'s), N.Y.C., Rochester and Syracuse, N.Y., 1949-61; with Niagara Mohawk Power Corp., Syracuse, 1961—, controller, 1965-68, v.p., 1968-73, exec. v.p., 1973, pres., chief exec. officer, 1973, chmn. bd., chief exec. officer, 1980—, also dir.; mng. dir. Niagara Mohawk Fin. Co. N.Y.; dir. Key Bank Central N.Y., Can. Niagara Power Co. Ltd., Utilities Mut. Ins. Co., Hydro-Co. Enterprises, Inc., Empire State Power Resources, Inc. Bd. dirs. N.Y. State Coll. Forestry Found., Inc.; trustee Canal Mus., Syracuse U. Served with USNR, 1942-46. Mem. Am. Inst. C.P.A.s, N.Y. State Soc. C.P.A.s, Edison Electric Inst., Assn. Edison Illuminating Cos., Energy Ass. N.Y. State, N.Y. Power Pool, Gyro Internat. Episcopalian. Club: Onondaga Golf and Country (Fayetteville, N.Y.). Office: Niagara Mohawk Power Corp 300 Erie Blvd W Syracuse NY 13202 *

HAEHNEL, WILLIAM OTTO, JR., telephone co. exec., orgn. exec.; b. San Antonio, July 30, 1924; s. William Otto and Marie Helena (Fricke) H.; m. Mildred E. Engelken, June 25, 1947; children—William Haehnel III, Nancimarie. Student, Tulane U., 1944-47; B.S. in Bus. Adminstrn., Bus. in Bus. Mgmt, U. Tex., 1949. With Southwestern Bell Telephone Co., 1949—, pub. information mgr., Austin, Tex., 1969—; lectr. bus. to colls. and univs. Mem. Civitan, 1958—; dir. Austin club, 1960, pres., 1964-65; life mem., 1969—, lt. gov. Tex. dist., 1965-66, gov., 1966-67, internat. chmn. 50th anniversary year extension com., 1968-69, chmn. internat. contest and awards com., 1969-70, v.p., 1970-72, sr. v.p. internat. exec. bd., 1971-72, internat. pres., 1972-73. Active Boy Scouts Am., Boys Club of Austin and Travis County, Austin State Sch. Council, Travis State Sch. Vol. Council, Austin Council Retarded Children, United Fund., Tex. Youth Conf., P.T.A., Austin Aqua Festival, Austin Civic Club Council, YMCA, Travis County Jr. Coll. Bd., Travis County Grand Jury Assn. Served with AUS, 1943-45. Named Civitan of Year, 1962; recipient Club Honor Key, 1964; Recipient numerous awards; George Washington Honor medal Freedoms Found. at Valley Forge, 1973, 74; named Austin Citizen of Yr., 1973. Mem. U. Tex. Ex-Students Assn., Austin C. of C., San Antonio C. of C. (red carpet com.). Republican. Lutheran (chmn. finance com., mem. ch. council, membership and long range planning coms., pres. ch.). Home: 2607 Greenlawn Pkwy Austin TX 78757 Office: 1600 Guadalupe St Austin TX 78701

HAELTERMAN, EDWARD OMER, vet. microbiologist, educator; b. Norway, Mich., Oct. 14, 1918; s. Omer and Hortanse Agnes (Smith) H.; m. Violet Marie Raiche, Aug. 10, 1946. D.V.M., Mich. State U., 1952; M.S., Purdue U., 1955; Ph.D., 1959; Ph.D. Doctor Honoris Causa, State U. Ghent, Belgium, 1974. Instr. Purdue U., West Lafayette, Ind., 1952-59, asso. prof., 1959-64, prof. microbiology, 1964—; asst. dean Sch. Vet. Medicine, 1958-61; Vis. investigator Rockefeller U., 1958; research officer East African Vet. Research Orgn., 1967-68. Contbr. articles to profl. jours. Served with USNR, 1942-45. Mem. Am. Soc. Microbiology, AVMA, AAAS, AAUP, U.S. Animal Health Assn., Sigma Xi, Phi Kappa Phi, Phi Zeta, Gamma Sigma Delta. Democrat. Club: Torch. Home: 3006 Soldiers Home Rd West Lafayette IN 47906

HAENICKE, DIETHER HANS, university administrator, educator; b. Hagen, Germany, May 19, 1935; came to U.S., 1963, naturalized, 1972; s. Erwin Otto and Helen (Wildfang) H.; m. Carol Ann Colditz, Sept. 29, 1962; children: Jennifer Ruth, Kurt Robert. Student, U. Gottingen, 1955-56, U. Marburg, 1957-59; Ph.D. magna cum laude in German Lit. and Philology, U. Munich, 1962. Asst. prof. Wayne State U., Detroit, 1963-68, assoc. prof., 1968-72, prof. German, 1972-78, resident dir. Jr. Year in Freiburg (Ger.), 1965-66, 69-70, dir. Jr. Year Abroad programs, 1970-75, chmn. dept. Romance and Germanic langs. and lits., 1971-72, assoc. dean Coll. Liberal Arts, 1972-75, provost, 1975-77, v.p., provost, 1977-78; dean Coll. Humanities Ohio State U., 1978-82, v.p. acad. affairs, provost, 1982—; asst. prof. Colby Coll. Summer Sch. of Langs., 1964-65; lectr. Internationale Ferienkurse, U. Freiburg, summers 1961, 66, 67. Author: (with Horst S. Daemmrich) The Challenge of German Literature, 1971, Untersuchungen zum Versepos des 20. Jahrhunderts, 1962; editor: Liebesgeschichte der schonen Magelone, 1969, Der blonde Eckbert and andere Novellen, 1969, Franz Sternbalds Wanderungen, 1970; contbr. articles to acad. and lit. jours. Fulbright scholar, 1963-65. Mem. Modern Lang. Assn. Am., AAUP, Am. Assn. Tchrs. of German, Am. Council Teaching of Fgn. Langs., Mich. Acad. Arts and Scis., Internationale Vereinigung fur Germanische Sprach-und Literaturwissenschaft, Hoelderlin Gesellschaft. Home: 2827 Pickwick Dr Columbus OH 43221 Office: Office of Provost Ohio State U Columbus OH 43210

HAENLEIN, GEORGE FRIEDRICH WILHELM, dairy scientist, educator; b. Mannheim, Germany, Oct. 27, 1927; came to U.S., 1953, naturalized, 1957; s. Albrecht P. and Elizabeth (von Kameke) H.; m. Elizabeth R. Zeitler, Feb. 20, 1954; children: Theodore, Elizabeth, Alice, Walter, Carl. Dipl. Eng. Agr. U. Hohenheim, 1950, Dr. Sci. Agr., 1953; M.S., U. Del., 1960; Ph.D., U. Wis., 1972. Tchr., research asst. animal nutrition U. Hohenheim, 1948-53; asst. mgr., herdsman Zeitler Dairy Farms, Inc., Newark, Del., 1953-57; research asso. U. Del., Newark, 1957-64, supr. dairy herds, 1957—, asst. prof. animal sci. and agrl. biochemistry, 1964-69, asso. prof., 1969-74, prof., 1974—, acting chmn. animal sci. and agrl. biochemistry, 1977, state dairy extension specialist, 1978—; residence dir. U. Del. Study Abroad, Vienna, Austria, 1977; abstractor fgn. jours. Biol. Abstracts, Phila., 1958—; dairy judge Md. Fair Bd., 1958—; chmn. com. on nutrition goats NRC, 1975—; N.E. regional steering com. on dairy research U.S. Dept. Agr., 1976—; AID rep., Panama, 1978; lectr. on dairy cows and goats various internat. symposia. Assoc. editor: Internat. Goat and Sheep Research Jour., 1981; chmn. and editor: USDA Extension Dairy Goat Handbook, 1979; Contbr. articles to profl. jours. Bd. dirs. New Castle County Civic League, 1973; chmn. citizen participation adv. council Del. Hwy. Dept., 1974. U.S. State Dept. exchange scholar, 1951; NSF fellow, 1965. Fellow AAAS; Mem. N.Y. Acad. Sci., Internat. Goat Assn., Am. Soc. Animal Sci., Am. Dairy Sci. Assn., German Soc. Animal Breeding, Holstein-Friesian Assn. Am., N.Y. Mus. Natural History, Nat. Mastitis Council, Nat. Geog. Soc., Am. Grasslands Council, Eastern Guernsey Breeders Assn. (dir. 1964—), Del. Guernsey Breeders Assn. (sec. 1954-57), N.Y. Zool. Soc., Council Agrl. Sci. and Tech. (task force 1982), Dairy Council (dir. 1978—), Am. Guernsey Cattle Club (life), Am. Dairy Goat Assn. (chmn. internat. symposia 1977, 79), Internat. Oceanographic Found., Smithsonian Instn. Assos. (charter), Internat. Platform Assn., Suburban Newark Civic League (sec. 1972), Sigma Xi, Phi Kappa Phi, Delta Phi Alpha. Lutheran (mem. ch. council 1974, v.p.). Home: 2071 S College Ave Newark DE 19702 *A broad foundation in the basic sciences and classic humanities together with practical experiences and a slow start may be more productive in the long run than early specialization and a fast rise to recognition.*

HAENSZEL, WILLIAM MANNING, epidemiologist, educator; b. Rochester, N.Y., June 19, 1910; s. William Edward and Myrtle (Manning) H.; m. Helen Margery Clark, July 26, 1946; children: Charles Edward, Priscilla Clark, James Irving. B.A., U. Buffalo, 1931, M.A., 1932. Statistician N.Y. State Dept. Health, 1934-47; dir. bur. vital statistics Conn. Dept. Health, Health, 1947-52; head biometrics sect. Nat. Cancer Inst., 1952-57, asst. chief biometry br., 1957-62, chief, 1962-76; sr. epidemiologist Ill. Cancer Council, 1976—; lectr. pub. health Yale Sch. Medicine, 1949-52; adj. prof. biostatistics U. Pitts. Grad. Sch. Pub. Health, 1966-82; prof. epidemiology U. Ill. Sch. Pub. Health, 1976—; mem. U.S. Nat. Com. Vital and Health Statistics, 1964-68; mem. com. human adaptability Nat. Acad. Sci., 1965—; mem. Commn. Epidemiology and Cancer Prevention, Internat. Union Against Cancer, 1966-70; mem. working party methodology of cancer epidemiology WHO, 1965—; chmn. com. studies migrant populations Internat. Union Against Cancer, 1966-70; cons. U.S. Joint Com. Cancer Staging and End-Results, 1961—, WHO, 1961—, Colombia Nat. Com. Against Cancer, 1963—; chmn. orgn. com. Internat. Assn. Cancer Registries, 1967; mem. com. epidemiology and statistics Am. Cancer Soc., 1960-70. Editor: Epidemiological Study of Cancer and Other Chronic Diseases, 1966; Contbr. articles to profl. jours. Recipient Superior Service award HEW, 1967. Fellow AAAS, Am. Statis. Assn. (chmn. biometrics sect. 1965-66); mem. Am. Pub. Health Assn. (chmn. statis. sect. 1955-56), Am. Epidemiological Soc., Biometrics Soc. (regional adv. bd. 1955-57). Home: 341 E Hawthorne Blvd Wheaton IL 60187 Office: Ill Cancer Council 36 S Wabash Ave Chicago IL 60603

HAERER, CAROL, artist; b. Salina, Kans., Jan. 23, 1933; d. Alfred Vesper and Helen Margaret (Bozarth) H.; m. Philip W. Wofford, Nov. 1962; 1 dau., Sara Gwyn Haerer-Wofford. Student, Doane Coll., 1950-51; B.F.A. cum laude, U. Nebr., 1954, Chgo. Art Inst., Summers 1952, 53; M.A., U. Calif., Berkeley, 1958. Dir., instr. Summer Painting Workshop, Bennington Coll., 1976-80; resident Yaddo, 1982. One-person shows include, Galerie Prismes, Paris, 1956, Berkeley Gallery, 1958, Albright Coll., Reading, Pa., 1964, Max Hutchinson Gallery, N.Y.C., 1971, 73, Bennington (Vt.) Coll., 1978, Landmark Gallery, N.Y.C., 1979, Oscarsson-Hood Gallery, N.Y.C., 1981, 83, group shows include, Whitney Mus., N.Y.C., 1970-72, Syracuse (N.Y.) U. Mus., Bklyn. Mus., 1980-81; represented in numerous permanent pvt., mus. collections including, Guggenheim Mus., N.Y.C., Whitney Mus., N.Y.C., Bklyn. Mus., Oakland Art Mus. (Calif.), Sheldon Art Galleries, U. Nebr., Lincoln. MacDowell Colony fellow, 1969, 79; Woolley fellow, Paris, 1955; Fulbright scholar, Paris, 1954. Home: 90 Bedford St New York NY 10014 Office: RD 2 Box 63 B Hoosick Falls NY 12090

HAERING, RUDOLPH ROLAND, physics educator, researcher; b. Basle, Switzlerland, Feb. 27, 1934; emigrated to Can., 1947; s. Rudolph and Selma (Tschudin) H.; m. Mary P. Peatfield, Aug. 6, 1954; Susan J., Linda J. B.A., U. B.C., 1954, M.A., 1955; Ph.D., McGill U., 1957. Head dept. physics Simon Fraser U., Burnaby, B.C., 1964-68, v.p. acad., 1968-69, prof. physics, 1964-72; head dept. physics U. B.C., 1973-77, prof. physics, 1973—; pres. CTF systems, Post Coquitlam, B.C., 1970-73; chmn. bd. CTF Systems, Port Coquitlam, B.C., 1973-77; dir. Moli Energy Ltd., Burnaby, 1977—, cons., 1977—. Editor: Can. Jour. Physics, 1968-72. Decorated Order of Can. Fellow Royal Soc. Can.; mem. Can. Assn. Physicists (pres. 1978-79, Herzberg medal 1970, pres. 1978-79, CAP medal 1982), Am. Phys. Soc. Office: Dept Physics U British Columbia Vancouver BC Canada V6T 1W5

HAESKE, HORST, physicist; b. Breslau, Germany, May 27, 1925; m. Gisela Werner; 2 children. Diploma in physics, Goettingen U., 1952, Ph.D., 1955. Mem. staff Battelle Inst., Frankfort/Main, 1956—, assoc. dir., then exec. assoc. dir., 1972-74, mng. dir., 1974—; v.p. Battelle Meml. Inst., Columbus, Ohio, 1976—. Author papers in field. Mem. German Phys. Soc. Address: 35 Am Römerhof D-6000 Frankfort/Main 90 Federal Republic of Germany

HAESSLE, JEAN-MARIE GEORGES, painter; b. Buhl/Haut/Rhin, France, Sept. 12, 1939; came to U.S., 1967; s. Georges and Marguerite H. Student, Ecole Nationale des Beaux Arts, Paris, France, 1965-67, Ecole de la Grande Chaumiere, Paris, 1966-67. Painter, Paris, France, 1965-67, N.Y.C., 1967—, one man shows include, Panoras Gallery, N.Y.C., 1968, West Broadway Gallery, N.Y.C., 1973, Atlantic Gallery, Washington, 1979, Nat. Acad. Sci., Washington, RR Gallery, N.Y.C., 1980, Gabrielle Bryers Gallery, N.Y.C., 1981; exhibited groups shows, U.S. and abroad including, Salon de la Jeune Peinture, Musee d'Art Moderne, Paris, France, 1968, Palace of Fine Arts, Mexico City, Mex., 1972, Aldrich Mus. Contemporary Art, Ridgefield, Conn., 1978; represented in permanent collections, U.S. and abroad including, So. Ill. U., Edwardsville, Bank of N.Y., N.Y.C., Atlantic-Richfield, Los Angeles, Am. Express, Fla., IBM, Los Angeles, Exxon, Fla., Chase Manhattan Bank, Los Angeles, Citibank, Los Angeles, Oven Corning Fiberglass, Toledo., Works reviewed in profl. and popular publs. Roman Catholic. Home: 106-112 Spring St New York NY 10012

HAFER, FREDERICK DOUGLASS, utility executive; b. West Reading, Pa., Mar. 12, 1941; s. Charles Frederick and Irene Naugle (Renninger) H.; m. Martha Louise Gartner, Apr. 6, 1963; children: Frederick, Craig, Keith. Student, Drexel Inst. Tech., 1959-62. With Met. Edison Co., Reading, Pa., 1962-68; with Gen. Pub. Utilities Corp., N.Y.C., 1968—, asst. treas., 1970, treas., 1970-78; v.p. rates GPU Service Corp., 1977—; v.p., dir. Met. Edison Co., Pa. Electric Co., 1982—; dir. Jersey Central Power & Light Co. Office: 100 Interpace Pkwy Parsippany NJ 07054

HAFERBECKER, GORDON MILTON, former educator, labor arbitrator; b. Antigo, Wis., July 19, 1912; s. August A. and Elizabeth (Becker) H.; m. Erma R. Groth, May 29, 1937 (dec. Mar. 1982); children: Judith (Mrs. John A. Miller), John. B.E., U. Wis., Stevens Point, 1939; M.A., Northwestern U., 1942; Ph.D., U. Wis., 1952. Rural tchr. nr., Antigo, 1931-37, high sch. tchr., 1939-42, Beloit, Wis., 1942-45; instr. U. Wis., La Crosse, 1945-46, prof. econs., Milw., 1946-56; dean, instr. U. Wis. at Stevens Point, 1956-62, v.p. acad. affairs, 1962-71, asst. chancellor for acad. affairs, 1971-73, vice chancellor acad. affairs, 1973-74, acting pres., 1967, prof., 1974-80; fact-finder, labor arbitrator, 1964—; dir. First Financial Savs. & Loan Assn., Stevens Point; mem. Gov.'s Tax Adv. Com., Wis., 1959-60; sec. North Central Wis. Labor-Mgmt. Council, 1977—. Author: Wisconsin Labor Laws, 1958. Chmn. Portage County chpt. A.R.C., 1963-64. Mem. Indsl. Relations Research Assn. Club: Rotarian (pres. Stevens Point 1962-63). Home: 1600 Brawley St Stevens Point WI 54481

HAFFNER, ALDEN NORMAN, university official; b. Bklyn., Oct. 3, 1928; s. Irving and Irene (Gutfleisch) H. A.B., Bklyn. Coll., 1948; O.D., Pa. Coll. Optometry, 1952; M.P.A., NYU, 1960, Ph.D., 1964; D.O.S. (hon.), Mass. Coll. Optometry, 1960, Sc.D., Pa. Coll. Optometry, 1973. Exec. dir. Optometric Center of N.Y., N.Y.C., 1957—; acting chief adminstrv. officer State Coll. Optometry, SUNY, N.Y.C., 1970-71, dean, 1971-76, pres., 1976-78; assoc. chancellor for health scis. SUNY, Albany, 1978-82, vice chancellor for research, grad. studies and profl. programs, 1982—; cons. in field. Contbr. articles in field to profl. jours. Mem. adv. com. Commn. for Blind and Visually Handicapped, State Dept. Social Services, 1966-70; mem. bd. nat. study commn. on optometry Nat. Commn. on Accrediting, 1968-70; mem. health manpower planning com. Comprehensive Health Planning Agy., N.Y.C., 1969-73; project dir. Fed. Program of Identification, Counseling, Guidance and Recruitment of Minority Students in Profession of Optometry, 1968-74; mem. Mayor's Com. for Study of Aging, N.Y.C., 1958; chmn. bd. trustees Manhattan Health Plan, Inc., 1976—. Served to 1st lt. M.C. U.S. Army, 1953-55. Recipient Albert Fitch Meml. award, 1962; Prof. Frederick A. Woll Meml. award, 1961; Distinguished Achievement award Alumni Assn., N.Y. U. Grad. Sch. Pub. Health Adminstrn., 1974. Fellow Am. Pub. Health Assn., AAAS, Am. Sch. Health Assn., Am., N.Y. acads. optometry; mem. N.Y. Acad. Sci., Group Health Assn. Am., Am. Pub. Welfare Assn., Am. Soc. Pub. Adminstrn., Nat. Rehab. Assn., Illuminating Engring. Soc., Am. Optometric Assn., N.Y. State Optometric Assn., Gerontol. Soc., Am. Assn. Univ. Adminstrs., Pub. Health Assn. City of N.Y. (dir. 1967—), Nat. Assn. Land Grant Colls. and State Univs. (com. health affairs 1981). Home: 201 E 36th St New York NY 10016 Office: State U NY Albany NY 12246

HAFFNER, ALFRED LOVELAND, JR., lawyer; b. Bklyn., Sept. 11, 1925; s. Alfred Loveland and Mary Ellen (Myers) H.; m. Mary Dolores Hyland, July 10, 1965; children: Mary Elizabeth, Anne Dolores, Jeanne Marie, Catherine Dianne. B.S. in Engring, U. Mich., 1950, J.D., 1956. Bar: N.Y. 1958. Draftsman-engr., indsl. engr., asst. plant engr. Owens-Ill. Glass Co., Bridgeton, N.J., 1950-53, Streator, Ill., 1953-54; since practiced, N.Y.C.; asso. firm Kenyon & Kenyon, N.Y.C., 1957-60, Ward, McElhannon, Brooks & Fitzpatrick, 1960-61, partner, 1961-71, Brooks Haidt Haffner & Delahunty, N.Y.C., 1971—; Chmn. Nat. Council Patent Law Assns., 1973-74; bd. dirs. Nat. Inventors Hall of Fame Found., 1972—, pres., 1973-74, sec., 1980—. Served with USNR, 1943-46. Mem. ABA, N.Y. State Bar Assn., Am. Patent Law Assn., N.Y. Patent Law Assn. (sec. 1964-68, dir. 1968-70, 71-72, pres. 1970-71), Strathmore Assn. Westchester (treas. 1976-79, v.p. 1980-82, pres. 1982-83, exec. com. 1983—), Phi Gamma Delta, Phi Alpha Delta. Club: Westchester Country. Home: 1 Gainsborough Rd Scarsdale NY 10583 Office: 99 Park Ave New York NY 10016

HAFFNER, CHARLES CHRISTIAN, III, printing company executive; b. Chgo., May 27, 1928; s. Charles Christian and Clarissa (Donnelley) H.; m. Anne P. Clark, June 19, 1970. B.A., Yale U., 1950.

With R.R. Donnelley & Sons Co., Chgo., 1951—, treas., 1962-68, v.p. and treas., 1968-83, vice-chmn. and treas., 1983-84, vice-chmn., 1984—, also dir.; chmn. bd. dirs. Lakeside Bank, 1970; dir. DuKane Corp., Protection Mut. Ins. Co. Chmn. Morton Arboretum; trustee Sprague Found., Art Inst. of Chgo., Newberry Library, Latin Sch., Chgo., 1978-84, Ill. Cancer Council, 1984—; bd. govs. Nature Conservancy., 1973-84, chmn. Ill. chpt., 1984—. Served to 1st lt. USAF, 1952-54. Clubs: Chicago, Comml., Commonwealth, Racquet, Caxton (Chgo.); Saddle and Cycle. Home: 1524 N Astor St Chicago IL 60610 Office: 2223 S Martin Luther King Jr Dr Chicago IL 60616

HAFNER, ARTHUR WAYNE, librarian; b. Ft. Wayne, Ind., June 1, 1943; s. Elmer and Dora Henrietta (Alfeld) H.; m. Ruth Theresa Austin, June 18, 1967; children: Tamar Gisela, Zachary Paul, Ethan Daniel, Jeremy Micah. B.S. in Math., Purdue U., 1965, M.S., U. Minn.-Mpls., 1967, M.A. in Library Sci., 1970; Ph.D., U. Min.-Mpls., 1974. Cert. med. librarianship. Bus. researcher Goodyear Tire & Rubber Co., Akron, Ohio, 1967-68; instr. math. Northland Coll., Ashland, Wis., 1968-69; chief med. Librarian Mt. Siani Hosp., Mpls., 1970-71; dir. health sci. library and clin. assoc. prof. U. Minn., Duluth, 1971-80; dir. library services, assoc. prof. library sci. Chgo. Coll. Osteo. Medicine, 1980-82; dir. div library and archival services AMA, Chgo., 1982—; cons. in field, lectr. in field. Author: Descriptive Statistics for Librarians, 1982; contbr. articles to profl. jours. Faculty trainer Minn. chpt. Am. Heart Assn., Mpls., 1974-80; instr., tchr. Northland chpt. ARC, 1973-80; patrolman St. Louis County Sheriff's Vol. Rescue Squad, Duluth, 1972-80. USPHS fellow, 1969-70. Mem. Am. Assn. Med. Soc. Execs., ALA, Med. Library Assn., Minn. Council Health Sci. Libraries (chmn. 1979-80), Health Sci. Librarians of Ill., Ill. Library Assn., Beta Phi Mu. Republican. Jewish. Club: Downtown Ct. Lodge: Masons (32 degree). Home: 3523 Maple Leaf Dr Glenview IL 60025 Office: AMA 535 N Dearborn St Chicago IL 60610-4377

HAGAN, CLIFFORD OLDHAM, athletic director; b. Owensboro, Ky., Dec. 9, 1931; m. Martha Milton; children—Lisa Hagan Thaxton, Laurie Hagan Hill, Amy Hagan Burdette, Clifford Oldham. B.S., U. Ky., 1954; M.S. in Edn, Washington U., St. Louis, 1958. Mem. St. Louis Hawks Profl. Basketball Team, 1956-66; player-coach Dallas Chapparals Profl. Basketball Team, 1967-70; asst. dir. athletics dir. U. Ky., 1972-75, dir. athletics, 1975—. Served as officer USAF, 1954-56. Recipient numerous sports awards, also service awards; named to Basketball Hall of Fame, 1977. Address: Athletic Dept Univ Ky Memorial Coliseum Lexington KY 40506

HAGAN, JOHN AUBREY, financial exec.; b. Pulaski, Tenn., Sept. 30, 1936; s. Edwin Jackson and Rebecca Maria (Smith) H.; m. Nicole Emilie Thiltges, Sept. 7, 1958; children—Mark, Alex, Micheline. A.B., Harvard, 1958, M.B.A., 1963. With R. J. Reynolds Tobacco Co. (name later changed to R. J. Reynolds Industries), Winston-Salem, N.C., 1963—, asst. controller, 1970-75, controller, chief accounting officer internal auditing and fin. info. system, 1975-79, v.p., controller, 1979—. Bd. dirs. United Way of Forsyth County, 1976—, pres., 1979. Served with USN, 1958-61. Mem. Fin. Execs. Inst. (com. on corp. reporting 1979—, pres. N.C. chpt. 1981-82), Nat. Assn. Accts., Common Cause Greater Winston-Salem C. of C. (speakers bur. 1977—), Am. Mgmt. Assn. (fin. council 1981—). Home: 2565 Woodberry Dr Winston-Salem NC 27106 Office: PO Box 2959 Winston-Salem NC 27102

HAGAN, JOSEPH HENRY, college president; b. Providence, Mar. 2, 1935; s. Joseph Henry and Claire Veronica (Gorman) H.; m. Patrice O'Malley, June 21, 1975; 1 son, Kevin O'Malley. A.B., Providence Coll., 1956; Ed.M., Boston U., 1960; LL.D., Salve Regina Coll., 1968; D.P.A., Mount St. Joseph Coll., 1976. Tchr. Providence Public Schs., 1958-61; legis. asst. to Congressman F.J. St Germain, 1961-64; staff asst. Pres.'s Com. on Juvenile Delinquency, 1964-65; spl. asst. OEO, 1965-68; dir. planning, devel. and fed. relations Bryant Coll., Smithfield, R.I., 1968-70, v.p. for public affairs, 1970-73, lectr. public adminstrn., adj. prof. social scis., 1971-73; spl. asst. Nat. Endowment for Humanities, Washington, 1973-78; pres. Assumption Coll., Worcester, Mass., 1978—, lectr. politics, 1981—. Trustee St. Vincent Hosp. Mem. Assn. Cath. Colls. and Univs. (dir.), Am. Polit. Sci. Assn., Am. Soc. for Public Adminstrn., Worcester Com. on Fgn. Relations, AAUP, Knights of Malta. Roman Catholic. Clubs: University (Washington, Providence); Worcester. Office: Office of Pres Assumption Coll Worcester MA 01609

HAGAN, PAUL WANDEL, priest, organist, educator, composer; b. Spencer County, Ind., Nov. 18, 1930; s. George Wandel and Cassie Alice (Byrne) H. B. Music Edn. magna cum laude, U. Evansville, 1954; M.S., Ind. State U., 1955; Th.M. cum laude, Sacred Heart Sem. Tchr., Ft. Wayne (Ind.) Community Schs., 1963-76; organist St. Joseph Ch., 1968-76; prof. St. Francis Coll., Ind. U. Extension, Ft. Wayne. Composer: Psalm Chorale Preludes, 1970, Swedish Suite, 1975, Scottish Suite, 1975, Trois Petite Elegies, 1973, Sketches of Paris Churches, 1974, Apostolic Suite, 1976. Recipient govt. grants to study music with M. Dupre, J. Langlais, A. Marchal, R. Falcinelli, F. Peeters, A. Heiller, M.C. Alain. Club: Masons. Home: St Paul's Ch 1031 Kem Rd Marion IN 46952

HAGAN, ROBERT LESLIE, consulting company executive; b. Kansas City, Kans., Sept. 15, 1923; s. Daniel Leslie and Mary Kathryn (Schneiders) H.; m. Betty Jean Downey, Oct. 7, 1950; children—Daniel, Debora, David, John. B.S. in Econs, Rockhurst Coll., Kansas City, Mo., 1947. Dist. mgr. Bur. Census, Commerce Dept., Kansas City, Kans., 1948-52, regional asst., Kansas City, Mo., 1952-55, regional dir., St. Louis, 1956-58, asst. chief geography div., Washington, 1958-69, project mgr., 1970; census, Jeffersonville, Ind., 1969-72; dep. dir. Bur. Census, Washington, 1972-76, Suitland, Md., 1977-79, acting dir., Washington, 1976-77; pres. Robert L. Hagan & Assos. (data and mktg. cons.), 1979—, CENEX, Inc. (statis. and info. cons.), 1981—. Served with USAAF, 1942-45. Home and office: 3703 Riverwood Ct Alexandria VA 22309

HAGAN, WALLACE WOODROW, geologist; b. Griggsville, Ill., Feb. 3, 1913; s. Warren L. and Mabel Rea (Bruner) H.; m. Mary Elizabeth Levan, Nov. 30, 1940; children—Elizabeth Annette, Karen Rea (Mrs. James A. Wade). B.S., U. Ill., 1935, M.S. (grad. scholar), 1936, Ph.D. (grad. fellow), 40-41), 1942; postgrad., U. Mo., summer 1937. Cert. profl. geologist. Park geologist Mesa Verde Nat. Park, summer 1935; field asst. Geol. Soc. Am. studies, summers 1935, 36; asst. petroleum geologist J.V. Wicklund Devel. Co., Detroit, 1937-39; cons. geologist, Greenville, Ky., Urbana, Ill., 1939-40; geologist charge ground water sect., div. geology Ind. Dept. Conservation, 1942-44; geologist Sohio Petroleum Co., 1945-48, Felmont Oil Corp., 1948-52; cons. geologist, Owensboro, Ky., 1952-58; dir., state geologist Ky. Geol. Survey U. Ky., 1958-78, state geologist emeritus Ky. Geol. Survey, 1978—; cons. geologist, 1978—; Mem. topographic mapping com. Ky. C. of C., 1947-51; mem. adv. bd. Ky. Geol. Survey, 1952-58, ex officio mem., 1958-78, mem., 1978—; Am. Assn. State Geologists rep. to Dept. Interior Geol. Survey div. com. water data for pub. use, Washington, 1968-78; rep. gov. of Ky. research com. Interstate Oil Compact Commn., 1958—, chmn. research com., 1965-66; bd. dirs. Ky. Conservation Congress, also mem. natural resources devel. com. and mineral resources subcom., 1961-64; chmn. quality water com. Ky. Water Resources Study Commn., 1959; rep. gov. Ky. Nat. Water Research Symposium, 1961; mem. research and policy adv. com. Ky. Water Resources Research Inst., 1964-78, mem. fed.-state adv. council, 1973-78; mem. adv. council Inst. for Mining and Mineral Research, U. Ky., 1972-78; mem. Ky. Water Resources Council; mem. subcom. on Maxie Flats radioactive waste disposal site Ky. Sci. and Tech. Commn., 1971-75; mem. adv. com. on underground injection wastewaters Ohio River Valley Water Sanitation Commn., 1970-78; mem. mineral resources subcom. Lower Mississippi Region Comprehensive Study, 1970-76; ex-officio mem. Ky. Devel. Cabinet, 1973-78. Contbr. articles to profl. jours. Recipient John Wesley Powell award U.S. Geol. Survey, Dept. Interior, 1972. Fellow Geol. Soc. Am. (vice chmn. S.E. sect. 1957); mem. Am. Assn. Petroleum Geologists (dist. rep. Great Lakes 1954, mineral econs. symposium com. 1969-72, pub. service award 1982), Ind.-Ky. Geol. Soc. (hon.; exec. officer 1955-56), Lexington Geol. Soc., Assn. Am. State Geologists (statistician 1963-66, v.p. 1966-67, pres. 1968-69, chmn. liaison com. 1966-68), Am. Inst. Profl. Geologists (mem. adv. bd. 1983-84, pres. Ky. sect. 1982-83), Geol. Soc. Ky. (hon. life mem., pres. 1966-67), Ky. Acad. Sci. (Disting. Scientist award 1977), Ky. Oil and Gas Assn. (State regulatory com. 1982-84, Disting. Service award 1978), Ky. Mining Inst., Ill. Mining Inst., Phi Beta Kappa, Sigma Xi, Phi Kappa Phi, Sigma Gamma Epsilon. Methodist (ofcl. bd., vice chmn. 1974, chmn. edn. commn. 1979-81). Club: Rotarian. Home and Office: 317 Jesselin Dr Lexington KY 40503

HAGAN, WILLIAM THOMAS, history educator; b. Huntington, W.Va., Dec. 19, 1918; s. William Fleming and Verna (Grass) H.; m. Charlotte Evangeline Nix, Jan. 31, 1943; children: Thomas M., Martha D., Daniel B., Sarah E. B.A., Marshall U., 1941; Ph.D., U. Wis., 1950. From assoc. prof. to prof. North Tex. State U., 1950-65; from prof. to disting. prof. State Univ. Coll., Fredonia, N.Y., 1965—, chmn. dept. history, 1965—; acting acad. v.p. North Tex. State U., Fredonia, N.Y., 1970-71; vis. disting. prof. U. Houston, 1977. Author: The Sac and Fox Indians, 1958; auhtor: American Indians, 1961, Indian Police and Judges, 1966, United States-Comanche Relations, 1976; bd. editors: Western Hist. Quar., 1973-78; editorial cons.: Arizona and the West, 1978—. Mem. adv. bd. Newberry Library's Ctr. Indian History, Chgo., 1972—. Served to 1st lt. AUS, 1942-45; PTO. Mem. Am. Hist. Assn., Orgn. Am. Historians, Western History Assn. (pres. 1979-80, council 1980-82), Am. Soc. Ethnohistory (pres. 1963). Democrat. Home: 8 Bryant Pl Fredonia NY 14063 Office: State University Coll Fredonia NY 14063

HAGEDORN, DOROTHY LOUISE, librarian; b. McKeesport, Pa., Sept. 4, 1929; d. Emil and Catherine (Middlemiss) H. B.A., Seton Hill Coll., 1950; M.S., Fordham U., 1952, Columbia U., 1957. Tech. info specialist Lawrence Rdiation Lab., Berkeley, Calif., 1961-63; head adult services New Orleans Pub. Library, 1964-71; sci., engring. librarian Tulane U., New Orleans, 1971-81, acting univ. librarian, 1981-82, assoc. univ. librarian, 1983—. Mem. ALA, La. Library Assn. Address: Howard-Tilton Meml Library Tulane Univ New Orleans LA 70118

HAGEGARD, HAKAN, baritone; b. Karlstad, Sweden, Nov. 25, 1945; 2 children. Student, Music Acad., Stockholm; pupil, of Tito Gobi, Gerald Moore, Erik Werba. Debut as Papageno in: The Magic Flute, Royal Opera Sweden, 1968; Met. Opera debut, 1978; appearances with major opera cos. throughout world; appearance in: film The Magic Flute, 1975; recitalist throughout world. Address: care Thea Dispeker Artists Mgmt 59 E 54th St New York NY 10022

HAGEL, RAYMOND CHARLES, business executive, educator; b. Jersey City, Sept. 5, 1916; s. Morris and Theresa (Feigenbaum) H.; m. Ruth Block, May 30, 1941; children: Keith W., Wendy A. B.S. cum laude, NYU, 1937. Promotion mgr. McGraw-Hill Pub. Co., 1937-38, 41-42, 45-46; with bus. dept. N.Y. World-Telegram, 1939-40; with Asso. Mag. Contbrs., Inc., 1947-48; pres. Smith, Hagel & Knudsen, Inc., N.Y.C., 1948-59, P.F. Collier & Son Corp., 1959-60, chmn. bd., 1961-65; exec. v.p. Crowell-Collier Pub. Co. (name changed to Crowell Collier and Macmillan, Inc. 1965, Macmillan Inc.; 1973), 1959-60, pres., 1960-76, chief exec. officer, 1963-80, chmn. bd., 1964-80, also dir.; pres., chief exec. officer Raymond C. Hagel, Inc., Westport, Conn., 1980—; David L. Tandy exec.-in-resident, vis. prof. M.J. Neeley Sch. Bus., Tex. Christian U., 1980—, mem. adv. bd. dept. journalism, 1981—; prof. mgmt. Barney Sch. Bus. and Public Adminstrn., U. Hartford, 1981—, chmn. dept. mgmt., 1983—; mem. Rockefeller Center adv. bd. Chem. Bank, N.Y.C.; mem. council Internat. Exec. Service Corps.; disting. adj. prof. Coll. Bus. and Pub. Adminstrn., NYU, 1972—, mem. dean's adv. council, 1973. Trustee, Coll. of New Rochelle, 1970-76, 77-80. Served with USNR, 1942-45. Recipient John T. Madden Meml. medal NYU, 1972; Disting. Service award in investment edn. Investment Edn. Inst. of Nat. Assn. Investment Clubs, 1973; Madden asso., Gallatin asso. NYU. Mem. Fgn. Policy Assn., Am. Assn. Higher Edn., Dirs. Table, Assn. Am. Pubs., Alpha Delta Sigma, Beta Gamma Sigma, Beta Alpha Psi. Clubs: Economic, Metropolitan, Publisher's Lunch (N.Y.C.). Office: 4 Whitney St Extension Westport CT 06880

HAGEL, ROGER S., retail stores company executive. Owner, mgr. supermarket, 1944-59; regional v.p. Arden-Mayfair, Inc., 1959-67; dir. store ops. A.J. Bayless Markets Inc., Phoenix, 1967-68, sr. v.p., dir. retail ops., 1968-69, pres., chief exec. officer, dir., 1969—. Office: A J Bayless Markets Inc 111 E Buckeye Rd Phoenix AZ 85036 *

HAGELMAN, CHARLES WILLIAM, JR., educator; b. Houston, Nov. 9, 1920; s. Charles William and Anna Marie (Griffin) H.; m. Elizabeth Drisler Sloan, Sept. 7, 1946; children: Lucy Ann, Charles William III, John Francis. B.A., U. Tex., 1942, Ph.D. (fellow 1952-53), 1956; M.A., Columbia U., 1947; postgrad., Washington U., St. Louis, 1942, Va. Mil. Inst., 1943-44. Part-time instr. English Columbia, 1946-47; instr. Muhlenberg Coll., 1947-51, U. Tex., 1953-55; instr., then asst. prof. to assoc. prof. U. Houston, 1955-59; prof. English, head dept. Lamar State Coll., Beaumont, Tex., 1959-66; prof. English, assoc. dean humanities Coll. Arts and Scis. U. Toledo, 1966-68; prof. English No. Ill. U., Dekalb, 1968—, chmn. dept., 1968-74; tech. writing cons., 1956-66; editorial cons. Survival Planning Project Houston-Harris County Area, 1956-57, Business Rev. mag., 1957-59; cons. North Central Assn. Colls. and Secondary Schs., 1970-80; Rep. Lamar State Coll. to So. Humanities Conf., 1961-66. Editor, author: introduction A Vindication of the Rights of Woman, 1966, (with Robert J. Barnes) A Concordance to Byron's Don Juan, 1967; Contbr. articles to profl. jours. Served with AUS, 1942-46. Recipient U.S. Steel Co. award for outstanding achievement teaching U. Houston, 1958. Mem. MLA, Midwest Lang. Assn. (exec. com. 1972-74, v.p. 1977-78, pres. 1978-79), South Central Lang. Assn., Keats-Shelley Assn., Byron Soc., Conf. Coll. Tchrs. English (past pres.), Phi Kappa Phi, Sigma Tau Delta. Episcopalian. Office: Dept English No Ill U Dekalb IL 60115

HAGELSTEIN, ROBERT PHILIP, publisher; b. N.Y.C., Dec. 15, 1942; s. H. Robert and E. Ann (Buhrow) H.; m. Ann G. Linguvic, Apr. 26, 1970; children: Christopher R., Jonathan W. B.A. in English Lit., L.I. U., 1964. Prodn. mgr. Johnson Reprint Corp., N.Y.C., 1965-68, editor-in-chief, 1968-70; v.p. Greenwood Press, Inc., Westport, Conn., 1970-73, pres., 1973—; dir. Aldwych Press, London; v.p. Congressional Info. Service; pub. cons. Contbr. articles to scholarly and profl. jours.; author Converticalc computer software program. Mem. Info. Industry Assn., Am. Soc. Info. Sci., Nat. Microfilm Assn., Spl. Libraries Assn. (George Polk Awards com.). Office: 88 Post Rd W Westport CT 06881

HAGEMAN, HOWARD GARBERICH, clergyman, sem. pres.; b. Lynn, Mass., Apr. 19, 1921; s. Howard G. and Cora E. (Derfler) H.; m. Carol Christine Wenneis, Sept. 15, 1945. Grad., Albany Acad., 1938; A.B., Harvard, 1942; B.D., New Brunswick Sem., 1945; D.D. (hon.), Central Coll., 1957, Knox Coll., Toronto, 1977, Litt.D., Hope Coll., 1975; L.H.D., Ursinus Coll., 1975. Ordained to ministry Reformed Ch., 1945; minister North Reformed Dutch Ch., Newark, 1945-73; pres. New Brunswick (N.J.) Sem., 1973—; exchange lectr., South Africa, 1956; lectr. Princeton Sem. Author: Lily Among the Thorns, 1952, We Call This Friday Good, 1961, Pulpit and Table, 1962, The Book that Reads You, 1962, Predestination, 1963, That the World May Know, 1965, Advice to Mature Christians, 1965, Easter Proclamation, 1974, Celebrating the Word, 1977; Editor: de Halve Maen. Pres. gen. synod Reformed Ch. Am., 1959-60. Mem. Societas Liturgica (internat. treas. 1967-73), N. Am. Acad. Liturgy, Holland Soc. N.Y. (domine), St. Nicholas Soc. (chaplain), Colonial Order of Acorn, Phi Beta Kappa. Club: Harvard (N.Y.C.). Address: 17 Seminary Pl New Brunswick NJ 08901

HAGEMEYER, RICHARD HERMAN, coll. pres.; b. Toledo, Dec. 15, 1917; m. Janet Stump, Aug. 10, 1940; children—Richard Herman, Carol Jean. B.S., Bowling Green State U., 1939; M.A., U. Mich., 1951; Ed.D., Wayne State U., 1961. Tchr. Waterville (Ohio) High Sch., 1939-41, Fordson High Sch., Dearborn, Mich., 1946-52, Wayne State U., Detroit, 1958-60; coordinator related instrn. div. Henry Ford Community Coll., Dearborn, Mich., 1952-62; asst. supt. Charlotte (N.C.) Mecklenburg Schs., 1962-63; pres. Central Piedmont Community Coll., Charlotte, 1963—; dir. So. Nat. Bank N.C., Charlotte.; Mem. adv. council N.C. Bd. Edn., 1967—, N.C. Joint Com. Dental Edn., 1969-72; cons. Nat. Apprenticeship Adv. Council, 1951-52. Bd. dirs. Nat. Lab. Higher Edn., Charlotte Symphony; bd. advisers Johnson C. Smith U. Served with USAAF, 1941-46. Recipient Meritorious Service award U.S. Dept. Labor, 1962, Alumni Community award Bowling Green State U., 1975; Danforth Fund grantee, 1972. Mem. Am. Council on Edn. (dir. 1979—), Am. Assn. Community and Jr. Colls. (commn. curriculum 1968-71, commn. adminstrn. 1970-72, bd. dirs. 1974—, chmn. bd. 1976-77), N.C. Assn. Jr. Colls. (pres. 1966-68), So. Assn. Jr. Colls. (exec. com. 1971-73, pres. 1972-73), League for Innovation in Community Coll. (bd. dirs. 1969—, pres. 1976-77), Charlotte C. of C. (bd. dirs. 1968-71, 74—), Sigma Alpha Epsilon, Phi Delta Kappa. Club: Rotarian (bd. dirs. Charlotte 1970—). Home: 3201 Landerwood Dr Charlotte NC 28210

HAGEN, CHARLES WILLIAM, JR., botany educator; b. Spartanburg, S.C., Mar. 21, 1918; s. Charles William and Florence Marie (Follmar) H.; m. Mary M. Swan, Dec. 20, 1942; children: Charles William III, David Carl, Ronald Eric. A.B., Cornell U., 1939; Ph.D., Ind. U., 1944. Asst. in botany Ind. U., Bloomington, 1939-43, instr., 1946-47, asst. prof., 1947-51, asso. prof., 1951-59, prof., 1959-83, prof. emeritus, 1983—, acting chmn. dept. botany, summer 1950, 65-66, acting chmn. div. biol. scis., 1964-65, asso. dean, 1965-66, 1966-69, asso. dean acad. affairs and facilities planning, 1969-72, dean for resource devel., 1972-75, dir. long-range planning, 1975-81; Mem. war research staff OSRD, Columbia and Ft. Benning, Ga., 1943; asst., asso., staff biologist Metall. Labs., Manhattan Dist., Chgo., 1943-46. Contbr. articles to profl. jours. Mem. Environmental Quality and Conservation Commn., Bloomington, 1971-72, land use com., 1971-74; Bd. dirs. Ednl. Projects, Inc., 1965-76, Ind. U. Retirement Community, Inc., 1977—. Guggenheim fellow, 1957-58; Fulbright research scholar, 1957-58. Fellow Ind. Acad. Scis.; mem. AAAS, Am. Inst. Biol. Scis., AAUP, Phi Beta Kappa, Sigma Xi, Theta Xi. Home: Route 1 Box 175 Nashville IN 47448 Office: Morrison Hall 110 Ind U Bloomington IN 47405 *I have attempted to perform effectively in every responsibility assigned to me and have declined opportunities for which I questioned my competence. In a favorable environment, this approach to life has led to varied and satisfying professional experiences. At this point, I do not plan to change my style appreciably.*

HAGEN, GEORGE LEON, business consultant; b. Bancroft, Idaho, Sept. 8, 1924; s. George William and Mabel (Waddell) H.; m. Anita Louise Rowe, Aug. 31, 1946; children—Richard Lee, Judy Ann, Paul Evan, Phillip Bradley. Student, Mont. Sch. Mines; B.Sc. in Chem. Engring, U. Wash., 1948, U. Wash., 1951. Registered profl. engr., Wash., B.C. Indsl. engr. methods Boeing Airplane Co., 1948-51; with Reichhold Chems. Inc., Seattle, 1951-61, plant engr., sales rep., 1956-61; with Reichhold Ltd., Vancouver, B.C., Can., 1961—, v.p., 1963—, exec. v.p., 1964-66; pres. Reichhold Ltd. Toronto, 1966-81, chief exec. officer, 1971-81, also dir.; pres. G.L. Hagen Assocs., Inc., bus. and computer cons., 1981—. Mem. Toronto Bd. Trade. Served with USNR, 1943-45. Mem. Am. Inst. Chem. Engrs., Forest Products Research Soc., Soc. Plastic Engrs., TAPPI, Can. Chem. Producers Assn., Advanced Mgmt. Research, Am. Mgmt. Assn. (pres.'s assn.), Phi Kappa Psi. Club: Markland Wood Golf and Country. Patentee formaldehyde mfg. Home: 296 Mill Rd E-8 Etobicoke ON M9C 4X8 Canada also 3226 Palm Aire Dr Sarasota FL 33580

HAGEN, JAMES ALFRED, marketing executive; b. Forest City, Iowa, Mar. 27, 1932; s. Archie M. and Catherine E. (McGuire) H.; m. Mary King, Aug. 16, 1958; children: Jospeh Patrick, Margaret Mary. B.A., St. Ambrose Coll., 1956; M.A., Iowa State U., 1958. Asst. gen. freight agt. Mo. Pacific R.R., St. Louis, 1958-62; dir. mktg. research, v.p. corp. devel. So. Rwy., Washington, 1963-71, 76-77; assoc. adminstr. econs. Fed. R.R. Adminstrn., Washington, 1971-74; pres. U.S. Rwy. Assn., Washington, 1974-76; sr. v.p. mktg. and sales Consol. Rail Corp., Phila., 1977—. Mem. Nat. Freight Transp. Assn. Roman Catholic. Home: 224 French Rd Newton Square PA 19073 Office: Consolidated Rail Corp 1808 Six Penn Center Philadelphia PA 19103

HAGEN, JOHN WILLIAM, psychology educator; b. Mpls., May 11, 1940; s. Wayne Sigvart and Elfie Marie (Erickson) H.; adopted children—Darus Gene, Lonny John. B.A., U. Minn., 1962; Ph.D., Stanford U., 1965. Asst. prof. psychology U. Mich., Ann Arbor, 1965-69, assoc. prof., 1969-73, prof., 1973—, chmn. developmental program, 1971-83, dir. Ctr. Human Growth and Devel., 1982—; Mem. Mich. Gov.'s Spl. Commn. on Age of Majority, 1970-71; mem. adv. council Mich. Dept. Edn., 1972-74; chmn. Univ. Com. on Internat. Year of Child, 1979-80; mem. research rev. com. Nat. Inst. Child Health and Human Devel., 1980—. Co-author: Perspectives on the Development of Memory and Cognition, 1977; Cons. editor: Merrill Palmer Quar, 1968-80, Child Devel, 1972—; contbr. articles to profl. jours. Bd. dirs. Guild House Campus Ministry, Ann Arbor, 1972—. Recipient Standard Oil Found. award, 1967; USPHS trainee, 1963-65; Woodrow Wilson fellow, 1962-63. Fellow Am. Psychol. Assn.; mem. Midwestern Psychol. Assn., Soc. Research in Child Devel. (chmn. program com. 1981-83), Internat. Soc. Study of Behavioral Devel., Phi Beta Kappa. Unitarian Universalist. Clubs: Univ., Alumni (Ann Arbor). Home: 3421 Burbank Dr Ann Arbor MI 48105

HAGEN, PAUL BEO, physician; b. Sydney, Australia, Feb. 15, 1920; emigrated to Can., 1959, naturalized, 1965; s. Conrad and Mary (McFadzean) von H.; m. Jean Himms, Sept. 29, 1956; children—Anna, Nina. M.B., B.S., U. Sydney, 1945. Intern, resident New South Wales Dept. Health, Sydney, 1945-48; lectr. physiology U. Sydney, 1948-50; sr. lectr. physiology U. Queensland, 1950-52; research fellow

Oxford U., 1952-54; asst. prof. pharmacology Yale U., 1954-56, Harvard U., 1956-59; head biochemistry dept. U. Man., 1959-64, Queens U., 1964-67; dir. NRC, Ottawa, Ont., 1967-68; prof. pharmacology, dean grad. studies U. Ottawa, 1968-83; mem. med. bd. Muscular Dystrophy Assn. Can., 1961—, chmn., 1976—, nat. pres., 1980-83; vice chmn. Med. Research Council, 1967; trustee Can. Inst. Particle Physics, 1971-79. Editorial bd.: Biochem. Pharmacology, 1961-66, Jour. Pharmacology and Exptl. Therapeutics, 1960-64, Can. Jour. Biochemistry, 1963-67; Contbr. to books and periodicals on physiol., biochem. and pharm. subjects. Chmn. Ont. Bd. Library Coordination, 1971-73. Recipient Lederle Faculty award Yale U., 1956, Centennial medal Govt. of Can., 1967; C.J. Martin fellow Oxford U., 1952; J.H. Brown fellow Yale U., 1954; Fulbright fellow, 1954. Fellow Chem. Inst. Can. (v.p., pres. biochem. div. 1962-64); mem. Physiol. Soc., Brit. Pharm. Soc., Am. Soc. Pharmacologists, Can. Assn. Grad. Schs. (pres. 1973). Home: 233 Tudor Pl Ottawa ON K1L 7Y1 Canada Office: Dept Pharmacology U Ottawa Health Scis Center 451 Smyth Rd Ottawa ON K1H 8M5 Canada

HAGEN, RONALD HENRY, publisher; b. Gettysburg, S.D., Aug. 11, 1941; s. Henry William and Otilla Marie (Trefz) H.; children: Ronda Anne, Racquel Kristie. B.S., Drake U., 1963; M.A., U. San Francisco, 1965. Nat. sales mgr. Berkley Pub. Co., 1963-64; sales mgr. Sunset mag., San Francisco, 1964-68; v.p., gen. mgr. KoraCorp Industries, San Francisco, 1968-70; pres. The Hagen Group, San Francisco, 1970—, also chmn. Hagen Mktg. and Communications div.; pub. Arts and Leisure Publs., San Francisco, 1974—, U.S. Football League mag. Kickoff, 1983—; pres., editor The Exec. mag., 1983—; editor-in-chief San Francisco Mag., 1983—; dir. Performing Arts Services. Bd. dirs. Performing Arts Services., Los Angeles Theater Alliance; nat. bd. dirs. Aid to Adoption Spl. Kids. Served with USAF, 1964-65. Mem. Western Pubs. Assn., San Francisco C. of C. Republican. Home: 1843 Pine St San Francisco CA 94115 Office: 950 Battery San Francisco CA 94111 *To have contributed to the improvement of any area I have an involvement in is the prime goal.*

HAGEN, UTA, actress; b. Gottingen, Germany, June 12, 1919; d. Oskar F. L. and Thyra A. (Leisner) H.; m. Herbert Berghof, Jan. 24, 1951; 1 dau., Leticia. D.F.A. (hon.), Smith Coll., 1978, L.H.D., De Paul U., 1981, Wooster Coll., 1982. Tchr. acting Herbert Berghof Studio, N.Y.C., 1947—. Played: Ophelia, Dennis, Mass., 1937, Nina in Sea Gull, N.Y.C., 1938, Key Largo, 1939, Vicki, 1942, Othello, 1943-45; appeared in: plays Masterbuilder, 1947, Angel Street, 1948, Street Car Named Desire, 1948, 50, Country Girl, 1950, G.B. Shaw's Saint Joan, 1951-52, Tovarich, City Center, 1952, In Any Language, 1952, The Deep Blue Sea, 1953, The Magic and the Loss, 1954, The Island of Goats, 1955, A Month in the Country, 1956, Good Woman of Setzuan, 1957, Who's Afraid of Virginia Wolff, 1962-64, The Cherry Orchard, 1968, Charlotte, 1980; also univ. tour 1981-82; appeared in: films The Other, 1972, The Boys from Brazil, 1978; TV appearances include: A Month in the Country, 1956, Out of Dust, 1959; appeared in numerous TV spls.; numerous guest star appearances including: Lou Grant, 1982, A Doctor's Story, 1984; Author: Respect for Acting, 1973, Love for Cooking, 1976, Sources, a Memoire, 1983. Recipient Antoinette Perry award, 1951, 63; N.Y. Drama Critics award, 1951, 63; Donaldson award best actress, 1951; London Critics award for best actress, 1963-64 season; Outer Circle award; named to Theatre Hall of Fame, 1981. Address: Herbert Berghof Studio 120 Bank St New York NY 10014

HAGENAH, WILLIAM JOHN, JR., chewing gum manufacturing company executive; b. Chgo., Aug. 3, 1920; s. William John and Florence (Doyon) H.; m. Marjorie Clark; children: William, Philip, Blanny, John. A.B., Princeton, 1942. With Wm. Wrigley Jr. Co., Chgo., 1945—, asst. to treas., 1953-59, v.p., asst. treas., 1959-71, v.p., treas., 1971-79, sr. v.p., 1979—, also dir.; pres., treas., dir. Chgo. Nat. League Ball Club, Inc., 1978-81; dir. Wrigley Import Co., Four-Ten Corp., Wallace Computer Services. Served to lt. USNR, 1942-45. Home: 92 Woodley Rd Winnetka IL 60093 Office: 410 N Michigan Ave Chicago IL 60611

HAGENDORN, WILLIAM, lawyer; b. Bklyn., Sept. 1, 1925; s. William V. and Florence (Hull) H.; m. Patricia Yarvote, Apr. 6, 1974; children: Katherine Florence, Patricia Ann. A.B., Princeton U., 1944; J.D., Harvard U., 1949; LL.M., NYU, 1952. Bar: N.Y. 1949. Practiced in N.Y.C., 1949—; assoc. firm Debevoise, Plimpton & McLean, N.Y.C., 1953-61, Carter, Ledyard & Milburn, 1961-65; gen. counsel Am. Express Co., 1965-72, Wells Fargo & Co., 1965-68, Equitable Securities, Morton & Co., N.Y.C., 1966-72; asso. firm Shearman & Sterling, N.Y.C., 1973—; Adviser to com. uniform consumer credit code Nat. Conf. Uniform State Laws, 1966-68. Served with inf. AUS, 1944-46. Mem. Assn. Bar City N.Y. Club: University (N.Y.C.). Home: 5 Sherman Ave Bronxville NY 10708 Office: Citicorp Center 153 E 53d St New York NY 10022

HAGENSTEIN, WILLIAM DAVID, consulting forester; b. Seattle, Mar. 8, 1915; s. Charles William and Janet (Finigan) H.; m. Ruth Helen Johnson, Sept. 2, 1940 (dec. 1979); m. Jean Kraemer Edson, June 16, 1980. B.S. in Forestry, U. Wash., 1938; M. Forestry, Duke, 1941. Registered profl. engr., Wash., Oreg.; registered forester, Calif. Field aid in entomology U.S. Dept. Agr., Hat Creek, Calif., 1938; logging supt. and engr. Eagle Logging Co., Sedro-Woolley, Wash., 1939; tech. foreman U.S. Forest Service, North Bend, Wash., 1940; forester West Coast Lumbermen's Assn., Seattle and Portland, Oreg., 1941-43, 45-49; sr. forester FEA, South and Central Pacific Theaters of war and Costa Rica, 1943-45; mgr. Indsl. Forestry Assn., Portland, 1949-80, exec. v.p., 1956-80, hon. dir., 1980—; pres. W. D. Hagenstein & Assos., Inc., Portland, 1980—; H.R. MacMillan lectr. forestry U. B.C., 1952, 77; Benson Meml. lectr. U. Mo., 1966; S.J. Hall lectr. indsl. forestry U. Calif. at Berkeley, 1973; cons. forest engr. USN, Philippines, 1952; mem. U.S. Forest Products Trade Mission, Japan, 1968; del. VII World Forestry Congress, Argentina, 1972, VIII Congress, Indonesia, 1978; mem. U.S. Forestry Study Team, West Germany, 1974; mem. sec. Interior's Oreg.-and Calif. Multiple Use Adv. Bd., 1975-76; Trustee Wash. State Forestry Conf., 1948—; trustee Keep Oreg. Green Assn., 1957—, v.p., 1970-71, pres., 1972-73; adv. trustee Keep Wash. Green Assn., 1957—; dir. Western Forestry Center, 1965—, v.p., 1965-79. Author: (with Wackerman and Michell) Harvesting Timber Crops, 1966; Assoc. editor: Jour. Forestry, 1946-53; Contbr. numerous articles to profl. jours. Trustee Oreg. Mus. Sci. and Industry, 1968-73. Recipient Forest Mgmt. award Nat. Forest Products Assn., 1968; Western Forestry award Western Forestry and Conservation Assn., 1972, 79. Fellow Soc. Am. Foresters (mem. council 1958-63, pres. 1966-69); mem. Am. Forestry Assn. (life, hon. v.p. 1966-69, 74—), Commonwealth Forestry Assn. (life), Internat. Soc. Tropical Foresters, Portland C. of C. (mem. forestry com. 1949-79, chmn. 1960-62), Nat. Forest Products Assn. (mem. forestry adv. com. 1949-80, chmn. 1972-74, 78-80), West Coast Lumbermen's Assn. (v.p. 1969-79), Hoo Hoo Club, Xi Sigma Pi (named outstanding alumnus Alpha chpt. 1973). Republican. Home: 3062 SW Fairmount Blvd Portland OR 97201 Office: 225 SW Broadway Room 412 Portland OR 97205

HAGER, GEORGE PHILIP, educator; b. Balt., Mar. 16, 1916; s. George Philip and Marie Theresa (Zilch) H.; m. Margaret Kathryn League, Dec. 24, 1938; children—Philip (dec.), Priscilla, Deborah, Andrew. B.S. in Pharmacy, U. Md., 1938, M.S., 1940, Ph.D., 1942; postgrad., U. Colo., 1938-39. Postdoctorate fellow Northwestern U., 1941-42; research organic chemist Lilly Research Labs., 1942-45; asst. prof. chemistry U. Md., 1945-48, prof. pharm. chemistry, head dept., 1948-55; sr. sci. Smith Kline & French Labs., 1955-57; dean U. Minn Coll. Pharmacy, 1957-66, Sch. Pharmacy, U. N.C., Chapel Hill, 1966-74, dean emeritus, 1974—, prof., 1974-81, prof. emeritus, 1981—; mem. Nat. Health Resources Adv. Com., 1968-79; mem. com. on chem. information Nat. Acad. Scis.-NRC, 1961-68, chmn., 1961-66; adv. com. research in biol. and phys. scis. FDA, 1966-69; cons. chem. information program Office Sci. Information Service NSF, 1965-72; pharmacist dir. USPHS, 1967; nat. civilian cons.-pharmacy surg. gen. USAF, 1967-76. Bd. regents Augsburg Coll., Mpls., 1964-66; mem. bd. devel. Lenoir-Rhyne Coll., Hickory, N.C., 1973-77, chmn., 1976-77, trustee, 1977-80. Mem. Am. Pharm. Assn. (chmn. sci. sect. 1956-57, trustee 1968-71), N.C. Pharm. Assn., Am. Chem. Soc., Md. Biol. Soc. (pres. 1952), Pharm. Mfrs. Assn. (mem. com. on sales tng. programs 1976-78), Am. Assn. Colls. Pharmacy (pres. 1965-66), Sci. Research Soc. Am., Acad. Pharm. Scis. (pres. 1968-69), Sigma Xi (pres. U. N.C. chpt. 1976-77), Rho Chi. Home: Rt 1 Box 221-D Pittsboro NC 27312

HAGER, JOSEPH ARTHUR, retired chemical coatings manufacturing executive; b. Chgo., Jan. 4, 1900; s. Adam and Wanda (Erdmann) H.; m. Margaret Mabel Walbaum, Jan. 5. 1929. Student, Northwestern U., 1919; LL.B., Kent Coll. Law, 1920; D.B.A. (hon.), Detroit Coll. Bus., 1976. Tchr. pub. sch. system, Chgo., 1920; purchasing agt. Great Atlantic & Pacific Tea Co., 1920-21; mfrs. rep., 1921-22; spl. agt. Bradley & Vrooman Co., Chgo., 1922-24; with Grand Rapids Varnish Corp. (now Guardsman Chems. Inc.), Mich., 1924-78, ret., 1978; v.p., dir. sales (now Guardsman Chems. Inc.), 1944-61, pres., chief exec. officer, 1961-66, chmn. bd. and chief exec. officer, dir., 1966-70; v.p. Grand Rapids Varnish Corp., N.C., 1952-61, pres., chief exec. officer, 1961-70; chmn. bd., chief exec. officer Lambert Corp., Houston, 1962-70, pres., 1965-70; chmn. bd. Lambert Corp. Fla., 1962-70, Schaefer Varnish Co., 1964-70, pres., chief exec. officer, 1965-70; pres. Alma-Guard Ltd., 1963-69; Cons. paint, varnish and lacquer, sect. chems. bur. WPB, 1942-43, Smaller War Plants, 1943-44. Emeritus chmn. bd. trustees Davenport Coll. Bus., Grand Rapids. Served with U.S. Army, 1917-19. Recipient George Baugh Heckel award of Paint Industry, 1954; named Ky. col., 1961; recipient Top Mgmt. award Sales and Marketing Execs., Grand Rapids, 1964. Mem. Nat. Paint, Varnish and Lacquer Assn. (past dir., pres., chmn. bd., chmn. exec. com. 1964-66), Grand Rapids Assn. Furniture Designers, Sales and Marketing Exec. Club Internat., Grand Rapids Sales and Marketing Execs. Club (founder), Internat. Platform Assn. Clubs: Elk., Blythefield Country (bd. dirs. 1955-58), Peninsular (bd. dirs. 1933-48), Peninsular (Grand Rapids) (pres. 1937-41). Home and Office: 2002 Robinson Rd SE Grand Rapids MI 49506 *God's greatest gift is the opportunity to serve one's fellowman.*

HAGER, LARRY STANLEY, book editor, publishing executive; b. Elmira, N.Y., May 23, 1942; s. Howard Mark and Merle E. (Woodard) H.; m. Anita K. Liedtke; children: Larry Mark, Lori Ann. B.A., Mansfield U. Editor Internat. Textbook Co., Scranton, Pa., 1969-72; sr. editor Intext Inc., N.Y.C., 1972-74, Thomas Y. Cromwell, 1974-77, Van Nostrand Reinhold, 1977-82, editor-in-chief, 1982-83, editorial dir. profl. reference div., 1983—. Exec. bd., dist. chmn. Thomas A. Edison council Boy Scout Am., 1982-83. Served with U.S. Army, 1964-66; Vietnam. Recipient as pub. Best Tech. Book award Am. Assn. Pubs., 1980, Best Engring. Book Am. Assn. Pubs., 1981, Best Phys. Sci. Book, 1982. Mem. ASME, Am. Inst. Indsl. Engrs. Methodist. Home: 403 Prospect Ave Avenel NJ 07001 Office: Van Nostrand Reinhold 135 W 54th St New York NY 10020

HAGER, LOWELL PAUL, educator, biochemist; b. Girard, Kans., Aug. 30, 1926; s. Paul William and Christine (Selle) H.; m. Frances Erea, Jan. 22, 1949; children—Paul, Steven, JoAnn. A.B., Valparaiso U., 1947; M.A., U. Kans., 1950; Ph.D., U. Ill., 1953. Postdoctoral fellow Mass. Gen. Hosp., 1953-55; asst. prof. biochemistry Harvard, 1955-60; Guggenheim fellow Oxford (Eng.) U., also Max Planck Inst. Zellchemie, 1959-60; mem. faculty U. Ill. at Urbana, 1960—, prof. biochemistry, 1965—, head biochem. div., 1967—; Chmn. physiol. chemistry study sect. NIH, 1965—; vis. scientist Imperial Cancer Research Fund, 1974; cons. NSF, 1976. Editor: life scis. Archives Biochemistry and Biophysics, 1966—; asso. editor: Biochemistry, 1973—; mem. editorial bd.: Jour. Biol. Chemistry, 1974—. Served with USAAF, 1945. Mem. Am. Chem. Soc., Am. Soc. Biol. Chemists, Am. Soc. Microbiology (chmn. physiology div. 1967). Research enzyme mechanisms, intermediary metabolism, tumor virus. Home: 801 W Delaware St Urbana IL 61801

HAGER, ROBERT, journalist; b. N.Y.C. Ed., Dartmouth Coll., 1960. Broadcaster minor league baseball Sta.-WBUY, Lexington, N.C., 1960-61; reporter on state govt. Sta.-WPTF, Raleigh, N.C., 1961-63; polit. reporter Sta.-WBTV, Charlotte, N.C., 1963-65; Corr. and local news anchorman for Sta.-WRC-TV, NBC News, Washington, 1965-69; corr. NBC Network News, Saigon, Vietnam, 1969-70, Berlin, 1970-73, N.Y.C., 1973-79, 1979—. Office: care NBC News 4001 Nebraska Ave NW Washington DC 20016 *

HAGER, ROBERT WORTH, aerospace company executive; b. Longview, Wash., June 20, 1928; s. Josiah Denver and Merle (Worth) H.; m. Margaret Goodnough, Aug. 25, 1950; children: Stephen M., Sandra L. Hager Dahl, Shane D. B.S. in Civil Engring, U. Wash., 1949, M.S., 1950. Research fellow U. Wash., 1949-50; research engr. U.S. Navy Civil Engring. Lab., Port Hueneme, Calif., 1950-53; mem. staff Sandia Corp., Albuquerque, 1953-55; with Boeing Aerospace Co., Seattle, 1955—, Minuteman program mgr., 1973-78, v.p., gen. mgr. ballistic missile and space div., 1978-80, v.p. engring., 1980—. Mem. AIAA, Air Force Assn. Methodist. Club: Sahalee Golf and Country. Office: PO Box 3999 Seattle WA 98129

HAGERTY, WILLIAM WALSH, university president; b. Holyoke, Minn., June 10, 1916; s. William Walsh and Alice Amanda (Lindberg) H.; m. Mary Elizabeth McKay, Sept. 30, 1939; children: William Walsh III, Catherine Mary (Mrs. Richard Garnett, III), Michael McKay. B.Sc. in Mech. Engring, U. Minn., 1939; M.S., U. Mich., 1943, Ph.D., 1947; D.Sc., Pa. Coll. Optometry, 1965; LL.D., Phila. Coll. Textiles and Sci., 1968, Temple U., 1968. Registered profl. engr., Tex. With pumping sta. operation Gt. Lakes Pipe Line Co., St. Paul, 1935-39; jr. engr. U.S. Gypsum Co., St. Paul, 1939-40, Wright Field, Dayton, Ohio, 1940; instr. mech. engring. Villanova Coll., 1940-41, U. Cin., 1941-42; instr. engring. and mechanics U. Mich., 1942-47, asst. prof., 1947-49, assoc. prof., 1949-51, prof., 1951-55; dean U. Del. Sch. Engring., 1955-58; prof., dean Coll. Engring., U. Tex., 1958-63; pres. Drexel U., Phila., 1963—; Dir. Communications Satellite Corp., Central-Penn. Nat. Bank, Drexel Bond Debenture Trading Fund, Phila. Electric Co., Selas Corp., Martin-Marietta Corp., Mut. Benefit Life Ins. Co., AAA; vice chmn. West Phila. Corp.; bd. mgrs. Germantown Savs. Bank, 1971-81; cons. to adminstr. NASA, 1964-70; mem. Nat. Sci. Bd., 1964-70; now mem. Phila. Commn. Higher Edn. Author: (with H.J. Plass, Jr.) Engineering Mechanics, 1967; also articles. Mem. Commn. Presdl. Scholars, 1964-69; chmn. Southeastern Pa. Devel. Fund, 1964-69; mem. Phila. council exec. bd., nat. council Boy Scouts Am.; Trustee Jefferson Med. Coll., 1965-69; bd. visitors Air U., USAF, 1964-67; mem. adv. com. USCG Acad., 1964-74, chmn., 1968-74; mem. exec. com. Univ. City Sci. Center. Named Delaware Valley Engr. of Year, 1970; recipient Sesquicentennial award U. Mich., 1967; Outstanding Achievement award U. Minn. Alumni Assn., 1969. Mem. ASME, Am. Soc. Engring. Edn., Nat. Soc. Profl. Engrs., Tex. Soc. Profl. Engrs., Sigma Xi, Pi Tau Sigma, Phi Kappa Phi, Tau Beta Pi, Sigma Gamma Tau. Methodist. Clubs: Aronimink Golf; Mid-Ocean (Bermuda). Address: Drexel Univ 32d and Chestnut Sts Philadelphia PA 19104

HAGFORS, TOR, astronomy center administrator, electrical engineering and astronomy educator; b. Oslo, Dec. 18, 1930; U.S., 1963; s. Vidar Johan and Hanna Viktoria (Edmundson) H.; m. Gillian Patricia Hart, Jan. 3, 1953; children: John, Toril, Martin, Vivien. M.Engring., U. Trondheim, Norway, 1955; Ph.D., U. Oslo, 1959. Scientist Norwegian Def. Research Labs., Kjeller, 1955-59, 61-63; research asst. Stanford U., Calif., 1961-63; staff mem. Lincoln Labs. MIT, Lexington, Mass., 1963-69, 71-73; dir. Jicamarca Obs., Lima, Peru, 1969-71; prof. elec. engring. and astronomy U. Trondheim, 1973-82; dir. Nat. Astronomy and Ionosphere Ctr. Cornell U., Ithaca, N.Y., 1982—; mem. Fachbeirat Max-Planck Inst. fuer Astronomie, Lindau-Hanz, Ger., 1977-82, Swedish Space Research Bd., Stockholm, 1978-82. Author, editor: Radar Astronomy, 1967, High Latitude Space Plasma Physics, 1983. Mem. IEEE, Am. Astron. Soc., Am. Geophys. Union, Internat. Union Radio Sci. Office: Astronomy and Ionosphere Ctr Space Scis Bldg Cornell Univ Ithaca NY 14853

HAGGARD, FORREST DELOSS, minister; b. Trumbull, Nebr., Apr. 21, 1925; s. Arthur McClellan and Grace (Hadley) H.; m. Eleanor V. Evans, June 13, 1946; children—Warren A., William D., James A., Katherine A. A.B., Phillips U., 1948; M.Div., 1953; D.D. (hon.), 1967; M.A., U. Mo., 1960. Ordained to ministry Christian Ch., 1948; minister Overland Park (Kans.) Christian Ch., 1953—; pres. Kansas City Area Ministers Assn., 1959, Kans. Christian Ministers Assn., 1960; mem. adminstrn. com., gen. bd. Christian Ch., 1968-72; pres. World Conv. Chs. of Christ (Christian/Disciples of Christ), 1975—; chmn. Grad. Sem. Council, Enid, Okla., 1970; pres. Nat. Evangelistic Assn., 1972. Author: The Clergy and the Craft, 1970, also articles. Pres. Johnson County (Kans.) Mental Health Assn., 1962-63; mem. council Boy Scouts Am., 1964-69; bd. dirs. Kans. Home for Aged, 1960-65, Kans. Children's Service League, 1964-69; pres. bd. dirs. Kans. Masonic Home, 1974-75; mem. bd. dirs. Kans. Masonic Found, 1970—. Club: Masons (grand master Kans. Chaplain Genl. Grand Chpt. Royal Arch Internat. 1975—). Home: 6816 W 78th Terr Overland Park KS 66204 Office: 7600 W 75th St Overland Park KS 66204 *Early confronted with a basic decision to serve myself only or others also, I determined to use time and energy as felt led by God to do. Success has had the component of personal well being and freedom as well as the feeling of being useful.*

HAGGARD, MERLE RONALD, songwriter, recording artist; b. Bakersfield, Calif., Apr. 6, 1937; s. James Frances and Flossie Mae (Harp) H.; m. Leona Williams, Oct. 7, 1978 (div.); children: Dana, Marty, Kellie, Noel. Grad. high sch. Rec. artist Tally Records, 1977—, MCA Records, 1977-78, Capitol Records, 1963-76; pres. Shade Tree Music Pub. Co., 1970—, Hag Prodns. Inc., 1973—. Appeared in: TV spls. The Waltons; writer, composer: TV mus. scores including Movin' On (Recipient 12 awards Acad. Country and Western Music, 26 Achievement awards Broadcast Music Inc., 7 awards Shade Tree Music Pub., 5 gold album awards, 1 platinum album award, 2 awards Music City News, named Songwriter of Yr., Nashville Songwriters Assn. 1970, also 5 outstanding writer achievement awards.); Author: Sing Me Back Home, 1981. Mem. Country Music Assn. (5 awards), Am. Fedn. TV and Rec. Artists, Screen Actors Guild, Am. Fedn. Musicians. Address: care Tex Whitson Shade Tree Music Inc 901 Lake Blvd Redding CA 96003

HAGGERTY, DAN, actor; b. Hollywood, Calif., Nov. 19, 1941; s. Don H.; m. Diane Rooker; children—Tracey, Tammy. Grad. high sch. Animal trainer for: films Lt. Robin Crusoe, USN, 1966, Monkeys, Go Home!, 1967, The Christmas Tree, 1969, for; TV series Tarzan, 1966-68, Daktari, 1966-69; actor: films including Easy rider, 1969, Wild Country, 1971, Tender Warrior, 1971, Grasslands, Snow Tigers, Where the North Wind Blows, The Life and Times of Grizzly Adams, 1976, The Adventures of Frontier Fremont, 1977, King of the Mountain, 1981; regular TV series The Life and Times of Grizzly Adams, 1977-78; TV appearance in Terror Out of the Sky *

HAGGERTY, JOHN EDWARD, former army officer, research center administrator; b. Reading, Mass., Sept. 9, 1918; s. Timothy Steven and Kathryn Margaret (Kyle) H.; m. Elizabeth Penn hammond, Sept. 29, 1945; children: John Edward, William S., Thomas M., David B., Richard K. LL.B. cum laude, Suffolk U., 1941; postgrad., N.C. State U., 1972; grad., Command and Gen. Staff Coll., Ft. Leavenworth, Kans., 1954, Army War Coll., Carlisle Barracks, Pa., 1961; postgrad. in advanced mgmt., Harvard U., 1964; B.S., U. Md., 1971. Enlisted U.S. Army, 1941-42, commd. 2d lt., 1942, advanced through grades to brig. gen., 1973, troop comdr., ETO, 1942-45; instr. health care Baylor U., Ft. Sam Houston, Tex., 1945-50; congl. liason officer Dept. Army gen. Staff, Washington, 1950-54; dir. med. personnel Dept. Army Gen. Staff (European Command), 1954-57, dir. spl. projects and med. legis., Washington, 1957-60; exec. officer, chief adminstr. Med. Research and Devel. Command, Washington, 1961-63; exec. officer, chief adminstrv. services U.S. Army Hosp., Ft. knox, Ky., 1963-66; exec. asst., dir. med. plans and ops. Pacific Command, Hawaii, 1966-69; U.S. med. rep. SEATO, Bangkok, 1966-69; exec. officer, chief adminstrv. services U.S. Army Hosp., Airborne Ctr., Ft. Bragg, N.C., 1969-72; dir. civilian health and med. program of uniformed services Office Sec. Def., Washington, 1972-73; dir. resource mgmt. Army Med. Dept., Washington, 1973-77; chief Med. Service Corps, Washington, 1973-77; ret. U.S. Army, 1977; assoc. dir. New Eng. Regional Primate Research Ctr., Harvard U. Med. Sch., Southborough, Mass., 1978—. Decorated Disting. Service medal, Legion of Merit medal, Meritorious Service medal, Joint Commendation medal, Army Commendation medal; decorated Army Med. Dept. medallion; recipient Presdl. citation Baylor U., 1977, Ray Brown award Assn. Mil Surgeons U.S., 1978; named hon. alumni Harvard U. Med. Sch., 1981. Mem. U.S. Army War Coll. Alumni Assn., Fed. Health Care Exec. Inst., Baylor U. Alumni Assn., Harvard Bus. Sch. Alumni Assn., Am. Coll. Hosp. Adminstrs. Home: 9 North St Grafton MA 01519 Office: New Eng Regional Primate research Ctr One Pine Hill Dr Southborough MA 01772

HAGGERTY, JOHN RICHARD, banker; b. Elizabeth, N.J., Sept. 15, 1935; s. John R. and Mary Alice (Keogh) H.; m. Marilyn McGurgan, May 25, 1957; children: Kathleen, Teresa, Eileen, John. B.S., St. Peter's Coll., 1957. C.P.A., N.J. Audit supr. Peat, Marwick, Mitchell & Co., Newark, 1960-67; fin. v.p. Unimusic Inc., Linden, N.J., 1967-72; auditor United Jersey Banks, Princeton, N.J., 1972-76, comptroller, 1976-78, sr. v.p., chief fin. officer, 1978-82, exec. v.p., 1982—; dir. United Jersey Bank-Central, Elizabeth, N.J. Trustee Youth and Family Counselling Service, Westfield, N.J., 1970-73. Served to capt. USMC, 1957-60; PTO. Mem. Fin. Execs. Inst., Am. Inst. C.P.A.'s, N.J. Soc. C.P.A.'s. Office: United Jersey Banks PO Box 2066 Princeton NJ 08540

HAGGERTY, LAWRENCE GEORGE, business executive; b. Harvey, N.D., Aug. 10, 1916; s. Michael Eugene and Lillian Marie (Evenson) H.; m. Mary Ellen Sweeney, Oct. 17, 1942; children: Michael Eugene, Catherine Ann (Mrs. James Lenahan), Eileen Mary (Mrs. John

Mundy), Patrick Bernard, Margaret Ellen, Sheila Bridget (Mrs. Timothy Mahoney), Maureen Elizabeth, Timothy James, Monica Louise. B.M.E., Marquette U., 1940. Successively student engr., mgmt. trainee to mgr. mfg. RCA Victor, Indpls., 1940-48; gen. mgr. appliance and parts mfg. divs. F.L. Jacobs Co., Indpls., Traverse City, Mich., 1948-50; with Internat. Tel. & Tel., 1950-58; successively dir. mfg., v.p. mfg., v.p. and gen. mgr. tech. products div., pres., dir. Capehart-Farnsworth Co., 1950-56; pres. Farnsworth Electronics Co., 1956-58; also dir.; pres., dir., chief exec. officer Warwick Electronics Inc. (formerly Warwick Mfg. Corp.), 1958-66; pres., dir. Lawrence G. Haggerty & Assos., Inc., Chgo., 1967—; chmn. dir. Haggerty Enterprises; chmn. bd., pres., dir. Lava-Simplex Internationale; dir. Wilton Corp. Trustee Marquette U. Decorated knight of Holy Sepulchre. Mem. Tau Beta Pi, Alpha Sigma Nu, Pi Tau Sigma. Roman Catholic. Clubs: Lyford Cay (New Providence, Bahamas); North Shore Country (Glenview, Ill.); Bob O'Link Golf (Highland Park, (Ill.). Home: 1420 Sheridan Rd Apt 9-C Wilmette IL 60091 Office: 1650 W Irving Park Rd Chicago IL 60613

HAGGERTY, ROBERT JOHNS, physician, educator; b. Saranac Lake, N.Y., Oct. 20, 1925; s. Gordon Abbott and Nina (Johns) H.; m. Muriel Ethel Protzmann, Oct. 29, 1949; children: Robert, Janet, Richard, John. A.B., Cornell U., 1946, M.D., 1949; A.M. (hon.), Harvard U., 1975. Intern Strong Meml. Hosp., Rochester, N.Y., 1949-51; from resident to chief resident pediatrics Children's Hosp. Med. Center, Boston, 1953-55; med. dir. family health care program Harvard Med. Sch., also asst. prof. pediatrics, 1953-64; prof. pediatrics, chmn. dept. U. Rochester Sch. Medicine, 1964-75; Roger I. Lee prof. health services, chmn. dept. health services Harvard Sch. Pub. Health, 1975-78; prof. pediatrics Harvard Med. Sch., Boston, 1975-78, clin. prof., 1978-80; pres. Wm. T. Grant Fedn., N.Y.C., 1980—; clin. prof. pediatrics Cornell U. Med. Sch., N.Y.C., 1980—; dir. gen. pediatrics acad. devel. program Robert Wood Johnson Found., 1978—; mem. health services research sect. USPHS, 1964-70, 82—, chmn., 1968-70, 82—; mem. N.Y. State Health Planning Adv. Council, Carnegie Council on Children, 1972-77; chmn. panel health scis. research, com. on nat. needs for biomed. and behavioral research personnel NRC, 1975-78; Mem. bd. U.S. Com. on UNICEF, 1981—. Editor: (with M. Green) Ambulatory Pediatrics, 1968, 2d edit., 1977, 3d edit., 1983; Co-editor: (with J. Lucey) Pediatrics, 1973-80; editor-in-chief: Pediatrics in Rev, 1978—; contbr. articles to med. jours. Mem. U.S. com. UNICEF. Served to capt. USAF, 1951-53. Recipient Martha M. Eliot award Am. Public Health Assn., 1976; Markle scholar acad. medicine, 1962-67; fellow Center for Advanced Study Behavioral Scis., Stanford, Calif., 1974-75. Mem. Assn. Med. Sch. Pediatric Dept. Chairmen (pres. 1969-70), Am. Assn. Poison Control Centers (pres. 1962-64), Am. Acad. Pediatrics (Grulee award 1981, v.p., pres.-elect 1983-85), Am. Pediatric Soc., Ambulatory Pediatric Assn. (chmn. 1963-64, George Armstrong award 1969), Assn. Am. Med. Colls., Internat. Epidemiological Assn., Soc. Pediatric Research (v.p. 1970-71), Inst. Medicine (council 1974-77, chmn. steering com. nat. study quality assurance programs 1975-76), Phi Beta Kappa, Alpha Omega Alpha.

HAGGETT, WILLIAM E., shipbuilding company executive. Pres., chief exec. officer Bath Iron Works Corp., Maine. Office: Bath Iron Works Corp 700 Washington St Bath ME 04530§

HAGGSTROM, OLLE EDWARD, industrial design executive; b. Burea, Norland, Sweden, May 14, 1925; came to U.S., 1929; s. Edward and Ruth Volberg (Lindh) H.; m. Elaine Susan Porter, Sept. 16, 1950; children: Susan lynn, Carl Eric. B.S. in Indsl. Design, U. Bridgeport, 1974; cert. in indsl. design, Pratt Inst., 1950. Indsl. designer Gen. Electric Co., Bridgeport, Conn., beginning 1946, Louisville, until 1952, account mgr. dishwasher indsl. design, 1952-53, account mgr. range devel. indsl. design, 1953-54, account mgr. home laundry indsl. design, 1954-60, mgr. housewares idsl. design, Bridgeport, Conn., 1960—. Patentee in field. Served with U.S. Army, 1943-46. Fellow Indsl. Designers Soc. Am. (treas. 1963-69). Republican. Methodist. Lodges: Masons; Shriners. Office: Gen Electric Co 1285 Boston Ave Bridgeport CT 06602

HAGIN, ROSA A., psychologist, educator; b. Elizabeth, N.J., June 14, 1921; d. William N. and Jennie B. (Smith) H. B.S., Trenton State Coll., 1941; M.A., N.Y. U., 1944, Ph.D., 1955. Diplomate: Am. Bd. Profl. Psychology. Dir. spl. services Roselle (N.J.) Bd. Edn., 1951-58, Irvington (N.J.) Bd. Edn., 1958-61; fellow clin. psychology N.Y. U. Med. Center, 1949-51, instr., 1961-64, asst. prof., 1964-69, research asso. prof. psychology, 1969-76, research prof., 1976—, co-dir. learning disorders unit, 1964-83; prof. div. psychol. and ednl. services Fordham U. at Lincoln Center, N.Y.C., 1979—; pvt. practice psychology, N.Y.C., 1955—. Contbr. articles to profl. jours. Fellow Am. Psychol. Assn., Am. Orthopsychiat. Assn.; mem. Am. Assn. Mental Deficiency, Orton Soc., NEA (life), N.J. Psychol. Assn., N.Y. Psychol. Assn. Home: 15 Canterbury Pl Cranford NJ 07016 Office: 200 E 33d St New York NY 10016

HAGIS, PETER, JR., educator; b. Phila., Jan. 16, 1926; s. Peter and Irene (Supper) H.; m. Jeanie Clelland MacGregor, Mar. 28, 1953; children—Joann, Peter Scott. B.S. in Edn, Temple U., 1950, M.A. in Math, 1952; Ph.D., U. Pa., 1959. Mem. faculty Temple U., 1952—, asso. prof. math., 1963-68, prof., 1968—; cons. Remington Rand Univac, Blue Bell, Pa., 1957-62. Contbr. articles to profl. jours. Served with USMCR, 1944-46. Mem. Am. Math. Soc., Math. Assn. Am. Methodist. Home: 880 Edison Ave Philadelphia PA 19116

HAGLE, GEORGE HERBERT, JR., oil company executive, lawyer; b. Ponca City, Okla., Mar. 27, 1936; s. G. Herbert and Earline (Proctor) H.; m. Antonia S. Day, Aug. 29, 1959 (div. Sept. 1981); children: Mary Scott, George H.; m. Catherine A. Manganiello, Dec. 31, 1981. B.E., Yale U., 1958; LL.B., U. Tex., 1962. Bar: Tex. 1962, Calif. 1977. V.p., gen. counsel BP Pipelines Inc., San Francisco, 1977-80, BP N.America Inc., N.Y.C., 1980—. Bd. dirs. Rice Design Alliance, 1973-74; pres. Citizens Environ. Coalition, 1972-74. Home: 45 W 60th St New York NY 10023 Office: BP North America Inc 620 Fifth Ave New York NY 10020

HAGLER, ERWIN HARRISON (SKEETER), photojournalist; b. Ft. Worth, Aug. 7, 1947; s. Erwin Harrison and Alice V. (Hornbeck) H.; m. Becky Ann Weatherly, Sept. 24, 1977; children—Casey, Cody. B.Arch., U. Tex., Austin, 1971. Staff photographer Waco (Tex.) News Tribune, 1971-72, Ft. Worth Star-Telegram, 1972-74, Dallas Times Herald, 1974—. Recipient Pulitzer prize feature photography, 1980; named Regional Photographer of Year Nat. Press Photographers Assn. Inc., 1972, 74. Home: PO Box 628 Red Oak TX 75154 Office: 1101 Pacific St Dallas TX 75202

HAGLER, JON LEWIS, investment executive; b. Harlingen, Tex., May 28, 1936; s. John Arthur and Helen (Starkey) H.; m. Jo Ann Winchester, Dec. 21, 1958; children: Elizabeth Ayn, Karin Jill. B.S., Tex. A&M, 1958; M.B.A., Harvard U., 1963. Investment analyst, portfolio mgr. Waddell & Reed, Inc., Kansas City, Mo., 1963-69; pres., chmn. Jennison Mgmt. Corp., N.Y.C., 1969-77; v.p., treas. Ford Found., N.Y.C., 1977-81; chmn. Hagler, Mastrovita & Hewitt, Inc., Boston, 1982—. Trustee Bennington Coll., 1976-80. Served with U.S. Army, 1958-61. Mem. N.Y. Soc. Security Analysts, Investment Tech. Assn. Methodist. Club: Harvard of N.Y. Home: 2 Pleasant St Dover MA 02030 Office: One Post Office Sq Boston MA 02109

HAGLER, MARVELOUS MARVIN, professional boxer; b. Newark, May 23, 1954; s. Robert James H. and Ida Mae (Lang) Sims; m. Bertha Joann Dixon, June 21, 1980; children: Gentry, James, Celeste, Marvin Jr., Charelle. Profl. middleweight boxer World Boxing Assn. World Boxing World Champion, 1980—; profl. record 57 wins, 2 losses, 2 draws. Named Outstanding Boxer of Yr. Nat. Amateur Boxing Assn., 1973; winner Championship Belts World Boxing Assn., Panama, 1980, World Boxing Council, Mex., 1980, Ring mag. N.Y.C., 1981, U.S. Boxing Assn. Internat., 1983. Mem. World Boxing Assn., U.S. Boxing Assn., World Boxing Council. Am. Baptist. Lodge: Kiwanis (Brockton, Mass.). Office: Marvelous Enterprises Inc PO Box 336 Brockton MA 02403

HAGLUND, GERHARD OSCAR, machinery manufacturing company executive; b. St. Paul, Jan. 17, 1916; s. Oscar and Ingeborg (Olson) H.; m. Mary Elizabeth Vellenga, Nov. 12, 1944; children: Mary Lynn, Gerhard Oscar. B.S. in Mech. Engring, U. Minn., 1937, M.S., 1939. Registered profl. engr., Minn. Engrs. asst. Allis Chalmers Mfg. Co., Milw., 1937-38, asst. engr., 1939-41; engring. instr. U. Minn., 1938-39; head mech. design sect. Naval Ordance Lab., Washington, 1941-45; mgr. instrument sect. Cornell Aero. Lab., Buffalo, 1945-46; chief engr. aero. research lab. Gen. Mills, Mpls., 1946-47, dir. bus. research, dir. sales, dir. research, 1951-56, dir. planning, 1956-57, dir. nuclear equipment, 1957-61; mgr. engring., physics div. Fredrick Flader, Inc., Buffalo, 1947-51; v.p. Vitro Corp. Am., 1961-63; sr. v.p., dir. Allis Chalmers Mfg. Co., Milw., 1963-72; v.p., mem. exec. com. Crompton & Knoules Corp., N.Y.C.; pres. Textile Machinery Group, Charlotte, N.C., 1972-74, George J. Meyer Co. div. ATO, Inc., Cudahy, Wis., 1974—; group exec., v.p. Figgie Internat., Inc., Richmond, Va.; dir. Meyer Dumore, Ltd., London, Eng., Meyer do Brazil, Sao Paulo, Meyer de Mexico, Guadalajara, TK Internat., Tulsa, SDS Systems Corp., Nuclear Equipment, Ltd., London, Eng. Contbr. to tech. papers airborne and indsl. instrumentation. Active in Jr. Achievement; bd. dirs. United Community Service Greater Milw.; pres. Geo. J. Meyer Found.; chmn. adv. com. mech. engring. dept. U. Minn.; mem. pres.'s exec. senate Marquette U. Recipient two citations Dept. Navy; nat. award ASME, 1937. Fellow Am. Inst. Mgmt.; mem. Inst. Aero. Scis., Instrument Soc. Am. (chmn. control elements div., dir.), Am. Nuclear Soc., ASME, Am. Assn. Cost Engrs., Am. Ordnance Assn., Air Force Assn., U.S. Figure Skating Assn. (governing council), Newcomen Soc. N.Am., Sigma XI. Episcopalian (vestryman). Clubs: Advertising, Executive, Figure Skating (Mpls.) (pres.); Univ. (Milw.); Chenequa Country. Patentee instrumentation and controls. Home: 35245 W Fairview Rd Oconomowoc WI 53066 Office: Figgie Internat Inc 200 Executive Dr Suite 142 Brookfield WI 53005 *Unshakeable belief in divine guidance and prayer; Dedication of life to Christ and needs of others; Hard work and motivation of associates to achievement; In-depth business planning; Absolute need for free enterprise system.*

HAGMAN, HARLAN LAWRENCE, teacher educator; b. DeKalb, Ill., Sept. 8, 1911; s. Gus Carl and Emily Sophia (Peterson) H.; m. Mary Anna Cassels, May 23, 1943; children—William Gordon, Richard Harlan, Jean Cassels, Thomas Lawrence; foster children—James Evanson, Donald Jones. Ed.B., No. Ill. U., 1936; M.A., Northwestern U., 1939, Ph.D., 1947. Formerly tchr. pub. schs., prin. and supt.; instr. Northwestern U., 1940-41; asso. prof. Drake U., Des Moines, 1947-49, prof. edn., 1949-50, dean coll. edn., 1950-57; prof. edn. Wayne State U., 1957-60, dean adminstrn., 1960-72; prof. higher edn., 1972—; Moderator fgn. policy radio broadcasts, nat. network. Author: A Handbook for the Schoolboard Member, 1941, The Administration of American Public Schools, 1951, (with Alfred Schwartz) Administration in Profile for School Executives, Administration of Elementary Schools, 1956, (with Alfred Schwartz), 1955, September Campus, 1977, Bright Michigan Morning: The Years of Governor Tom Mason, 1981, The Academic Life, 1983; Editorial cons., McGraw-Hill Book Co., Internat. City Mgrs. Assn.; Contbr. to: Am. Peoples Ency; also contbr. to ednl. jours. Bd. dirs. Youth for Understanding. Served as lt. comdr. USNR, World War II. Mem. AAUP. Club: Players. Home: 1017 Kensington Rd Grosse Point Park MI 48230 Office: Wayne State U Detroit MI 48202

HAGMAN, LARRY, actor; b. Weatherford, Tex., Sept. 21, 1931; s. Benjamin and Mary (Martin) H.; m. Maj Axelsson, 1954; children: Heidi, Preston. Student, Bard. Coll. Began career in off-Broadway shows; appeared in: Broadway shows God and Kate Murphy, 1959, The Nervous Set, 1959, The Warm Peninsula, 1959-60, The Beauty Part, 1962-63; numerous TV appearances from late 1950's to mid 1960's, including The Edge of Night; starred in: TV series I Dream of Jeannie, 1965-70, The Good Life, 1971-72, Here We Go Again, 1973, Dallas, 1978—; motion picture debut in Ensign Pulver, 1964; other films include Fall Safe, 1964; other films The Group, 1966; other films include In Harm's Way, 1965; also dir.: Beware! the Blob, 1972; Harry and Tonto, 1974, Mother, Jugs and Speed, 1976, The Eagle Has Landed, 1977, S.O.B., 1981; has appeared in TV films; dir. of USO shows for U.S. Air Force in Europe. Office: care Lorimar Prodns 10202 W Washington Blvd Culver City CA 90230 *

HAGMANN, JOHN SHUGART, architect; b. Bronxville, N.Y., Apr. 11, 1938; s. Raymond Louis and Adele Bernice (Schneider) H.; m. Lee Yee Hsu, Sept. 20, 1970; 1 dau., Katherine Hsu. B.A., Amherst Coll., 1959; M.Arch., Yale U. Sch. Architecture, 1966. Archtl. designer Greater London Council, 1966, I.M. Pei and Partners, N.Y.C., 1967-68, Edward L. Barnes (Architect), 1968-69; prin. Stern and Hagmann (Architects), N.Y.C., 1969-76, John S. Hagmann (Architect), 1976-77; assoc. Abramovitz-Harris-Kingsland, Architects, N.Y.C., 1977-83; prin. Hagmann/Mitchell, Architects, N.Y.C., 1983—. Vestryman Christ and St. Stephens Ch., N.Y.C. Recipient award of honor N.Y. Soc. Architects, 1974, certificate of merit N.Y. State Assn. Architects, 1975, 76, Nat. Housing Design Competition 1st pl. award N.Y. State Urban Devel. Corp., 1975, citation Progressive Architecture Design Awards Program, 1976, award Internat. Competition for Victoria Peak, 1983. Mem. AIA (N.Y. chpt. citation 1972, 74, chpt. residential design award 1977, nat. honor award 1980), Archtl. League of N.Y. Episcopalian. Home: 336 Central Park W New York NY 10025 Office: 853 Broadway New York NY 10003

HAGNER, ARTHUR FEODOR, geologist, educator; b. Union City, N.J., May 26, 1911; s. Feodor H.S. and Ernestine (Geggis) H.; m. Dorothy Damon, Aug. 11, 1967; children by previous marriage: Dorothy K. (Mrs. Craig Baker), Thomas P. A.B., NYU, 1934; Ph.D. (Univ. Fellow, NRC fellow), Columbia U., 1939. Instr. Columbia U. Ext., 1935-37; Instr. to asso. prof. U. Wyo., 1939-47; asst. state geologist, Wyo., 1941-48; research asso. U. Chgo., 1947-48; asso. prof. U. Ill., Urbana, 1948-53, prof. geology, 1953—; geologist U.S. Geol. Survey.; Co-dir. NSF Summer Inst. in Geology for Coll. Tchrs., 1957, 58. Contbr. articles to profl. jours. Trustee Nat. Hemophilia Found., 1950-67. Fellow Geol. Soc. Am., Mineral. Soc. Am., Geol. Soc. London; mem. Nat. Assn. Geology Tchrs. (pres. central sect. 1961-62), Ill. Earth Sci. Assn. (pres. 1973-74), Geol. Soc. Stockholm, Geol. Soc. Norway, Geol. Soc. Finland, Soc. Econ. Geologists. Home: 70 Strawberry Hill Ave 2-A Fairfield Bldg Stamford CT 06902

HAGOOD, ANNABEL DUNHAM, speech communication educator; b. Hattiesburg, Miss., Feb. 7, 1924; d. John H. and Isabella (Smith) Dunham; m. William Knox Hagood, June 6, 1950 (div. Sept. 1969). A.B., Southwestern La. Inst., 1944; M.A., U. Wis., 1946; postgrad., 1947-49. Asst. dir. debate and drama Southwestern La. Inst., 1944-45; asst. counselor U. Wis., 1945-46; instr. U. Ala., Tuscaloosa, 1946-49, asst. prof. speech, 1949-57, assoc. prof., 1957-63, prof., 1963—, dir. forensics, 1946-77, chmn. area rhetoric and speech communication, 1973-76, chmn. dept. speech communication and theatre, 1976-79, chmn. dept. speech communication, 1979, chmn. student acad. affairs Coll. Arts and Scis., 1969-71; chmn. arts and scis. faculty senate (U. Ala.), 1972-73; pres. Coll. Arts and Scis. U. Ala., 1975-77; Mem. adv. com. contests and awards Alexander Hamilton Bicentennial Commn., 1956-57; trustee Nat. Debate Tournament Com., 1967-77, chmn., 1968-69, 74-76, treas., 1972-73. Editor: The Register, 1956, 57; Contbr. chpts. to books, articles to profl. jours. Mem. Am. Forensic Assn. (past nat. pres.), Speech Communication Assn. (chmn. com. in internat. discussion and debate 1953-55), So., Ala. speech assns., Phi Kappa Phi, Pi Kappa Delta, Tau Kappa Alpha (past nat. pres.). Home: 35 Academy Dr Tuscaloosa AL 35406 Office: Dept Speech Communication Box 1965 University of Alabama Tuscaloosa AL 35401

HAGOORT, THOMAS HENRY, lawyer; b. Paterson, N.J., May 30, 1932; s. Nicholas Hugh and Rae (Sytsma) H.; m. Lois Ann Bennett, Sept. 6, 1954; children: Nancy Lynn, Susan Audrey. A.B. cum laude, Harvard U., 1954, LL.B. magna cum laude, 1957. Assoc. firm Cleary, Gottlieb, Steen & Hamilton, N.Y.C., 1957-67, ptnr., 1968—; dir. Rhone-Poulenc, Inc., Monmouth Junction, N.J., 1979—. Note editor, Harvard Law Rev., 1956-57. Pres. Mountainside Hosp., Montclair, N.J., 1983—, Internat. Bacalaureat of N. Am., N.Y.C., 1980—, Montclair Bd. Edn., 1966-70; mem. exec. com., council of found. Internat. Baccalaureate Orgn., Geneva, 1982—. Mem. ABA, N.Y. State Bar Assn., N.Y. County Bar Assn. Democrat. Clubs: Harvard of N.J. (pres. 1977-78), Montclair Golf, Shelter Island Yacht, Broad St. Home: 77 S Mountain Ave Montclair NJ 07042 Office: 1 State Street Plaza New York NY 10004

HAGOPIAN, LOUIS THOMAS, advertising executive; b. Pontiac, Mich., June 1, 1925; s. Thomas and Sarah (Uligian) H.; m. Joanne Kelly, Dec. 31, 1955; children: Susan, Thomas, Matthew. Student, Northwestern U., 1944; B.A. in Bus. Adminstrn, Mich. State U., 1947. With Pontiac Motor Car Co., 1948-53; successively service rep., dist. sales mgr.; with Chrysler Corp., 1953-60, sales promotion exec. Dodge div., 1953-56, dir. advt. and sales promotion Plymouth div., 1956-60; account supr. NW Ayer Inc., 1960-62, v.p., 1962-66, Detroit mgr., 1963-66, exec. v.p., gen. mgr. N.Y. region, 1967-73, vice chmn., 1973-76, chmn., chief exec. officer, 1976—, also dir. Mem. exec. com., bd. dirs. Hwy. Users Fedn. for Safety and Mobility; mem. sports com. USIA; N.Y. State chmn. Nat. Com. for Employer Support of Guard and Res., 1982-84; chmn. Automotive Safety Found., 1978-80. Served to lt. (j.g.) USNR, World War II. Recipient Disting. Alumnus award Mich. State U., 1978. Mem. Am. Assn. Advt. Agys. (nat. vice chmn. 1984), Am. Council on Arts (dir. 1982-84), Assn. Nat. Advertisers, Adcraft Club Detroit, Kappa Sigma. Clubs: Wee Burn Country, Pine Valley Golf, Jupiter Hills, University. Office: 1345 Ave of Americas New York NY 10105

HAGSTROM, WARREN OLAF, educator; b. Mpls., May 27, 1930; s. Andrew and Borghild Ingebjorg (Aune) H.; m. Lois Eleanor Mendum, July 30, 1956; children—Eric, Susan. B.A., U. Minn., 1952, M.A., 1954; Ph.D., U. Calif. at Berkeley, 1963. Instr., research asso. U. Calif. at Berkeley, 1961-62; asst. prof. sociology U. Wis. at Madison, 1962-65, asso. prof., 1965-68, prof., 1968—, chmn. dept. sociology, 1973-76; Mem. NSF adv. panel on sociology and social psychology, 1969-71, NRC adv. coms., 1969-73; cons.-evaluator North Central Assn. Colls. and Secondary Schs., 1973—. Author: The Scientific Community, 1965. Served with AUS, 1954-56. Mem. Am. Sociol. Assn., A.A.A.S., Soc. for Study Social Problems, Soc. for Social Studies Sci. (pres. 1976-78). Home: 916 Shorewood Blvd Madison WI 53705

HAGSTRUM, HOMER DUPRE, physicist; b. St. Paul, Mar. 11, 1915; s. Andrew and Sadie Gertrude (Fryckberg) H.; m. Bonnie Doone Cairns, Aug. 29, 1948; children—Melissa Billings, Jonathan Tryon. B.E.E., U. Minn., 1935, B.S., 1936, M.S., 1939, Ph.D., 1940. Teaching and research asst. U. Minn., 1935-40; research physicist Bell Telephone Labs., Inc., Murray Hill, N.J., 1940—, head surface physics research dept., 1954-78; gen. chmn. Phys. Electronics Conf. Com., 1976-80. Fellow Am. Phys. Soc. (chmn. div. electron and atomic physics 1957, Davisson-Germer prize 1975); mem. Am. Vacuum Soc. (dir. 1976-78, Welch award 1974), Nat. Acad. Scis., Sigma Xi, Tau Beta Pi, Eta Kappa Nu. Author research articles, rev. chpts. mass spectrometry, microwave magnetrons, surface physics, electron spectroscopy, interaction of ions and metastable atoms with surfaces. Home: 30 Sweetbriar Rd Summit NJ 07901 Office: 600 Mountain Ave Murray Hill NJ 07974

HAGSTRUM, JEAN HOWARD, educator; b. St. Paul, Mar. 26, 1913; s. Andrew and Sadie Gertrude (Fryckberg) H.; m. Ruth Pritchett, June 29, 1941; children: Katherine Jeanne, Phyllis Ann. A.B. summa cum laude, U. Minn., 1933; M.A., Northwestern U., 1938; Ph.D., Yale U., 1941. Instr. English and speech North Park Coll., Chgo., 1934-38; chief allocation sect. U.S. Office Censorship, 1942-44; mem. faculty Northwestern U., Evanston, Ill., 1940-42, 46—, prof. English, 1957—, chmn. dept., 1958-64, 73-74, John C. Shaffer prof., 1970—; vis. lectr. at univs., Copenhagen, Lund, Stockholm, Uppsala, Gothenburg, Aix-en-Provence, Delhi, Bombay, Srinagar; mem. presdl. adv. com. Yale Center for Brit. Art and Brit. Studies, 1972—; Phi Beta Kappa vis. scholar, 1983-84. Author: Samuel Johnson's Literary Criticism, rev. edit, 1967, The Sister Arts, 1958, William Blake: Poet and Painter, 1964, (with others) A Community of Scholars, 1968, (with James Gray) Sermons of Samuel Johnson, 1979, Sex and Sensibility: Ideal and Erotic Love from Milton to Mozart, 1980. Trustee Newberry Library, 1964—. Served with AUS, 1944-46. Recipient Disting. Service award Phi Beta Kappa Assn., Chgo.; Fulbright research fellow, Italy, 1953-54, India, 1972, 82; grantee Am. Philos. Soc., 1952, 59, 76; fellow Newberry Library, Chgo., 1953, 57; sr. fellow Clark Library, UCLA, 1970; fellow Huntington Library, 1974, 83, Guggenheim Found., 1974-75, NEH, 1976-77. Mem. MLA (exec. council 1968-72), Swedish Hist. Soc. Spl. research 18th century lit., romantic lit., lit and psychology, relations of the arts. Home: 819 Michigan Ave Evanston IL 60202

HAGUE, DONALD VICTOR, museum dir.; b. Salt Lake City, Dec. 28, 1926; s. Roger Frank and Fawn (Robison) H.; m. Lorna Dangerfield, Aug. 27, 1947; children—Alan, Kevin, Steven, Bryan, Karen. B.S. in Zoology, U. Utah, 1951, M.A. in Art History (Nat. Endowment Arts fellow 1973), 1975; grad., Mus. Mgmt. Inst., U. Calif., Berkeley, 1979. Archtl. draftsman Scott & Beecher, Salt Lake City, 1948-50; artist, designer Mus. Anthropology, U. Utah, 1950-51; designer Salt Lake Cabinet & Fixture Co., 1952-54; chief artist Ft. Worth Mus. Sci. and Industry, 1954-58; graphic arts supr. Sperry Rand Corp., Salt Lake City, 1958-65; curator exhibits Utah Mus. Natural History, U. Utah, 1965-73, dir. mus., 1973—, univ. instr. zoology, 1966—; guest lectr. mus. studies, sci. illustrators, cons. in field, 1954—; chmn. task force public edn. Utah Antiquities Com., 1976; mem. adv. bd. Hansen Planetarium, 1970-73. Author articles in field. Mem. Salt Lake Sister Cities Com., 1975-78; chmn. community council South High Sch., 1975-79. Served with USNR, 1945-46. Mem. Am. Assn. Museums, Internat. Council Museums, Assn. Sci. Mus.

Dirs., Western Museums Assn. (v.p., 1972-74), Utah Museums Assn. (pres. 1972-74, award excellence 1976), Nat. Wildlife Fedn. Club: U.Utah Faculty. Office: U Utah Salt Lake City UT 84112

HAGUE, RAOUL, sculptor; b. Constantinople, 1905; U.S., 1921, naturalized, 1930; s. Nazar and Satenig Heukelekian. Student, Robert Coll. Prep. Sch., Constantinople, Iowa State Coll., 1921, Beaux-Arts Inst. of Design, N.Y.C., 1926-27, Art Students League, N.Y.C., 1927-28, Courtauld Inst., London, 1950-51. One-man shows, Egan Gallery, N.Y.C., 1962, 65, Washington Gallery Modern Art, 1964, Xavier Fourcade Gallery, N.Y.C., 1979; exhibited in group shows including, Mus. Modern Art, 1933, Curt Valentin Gallery, 1945, Whitney Mus. Am. Art, 1945-48, 52, 57, 58, Mus. Modern Art, 1956, London County Council Anglo-Am. Sculpture Show, London, 1963, 35, Americans, Paris, 1965, Xavier Fourcade Gallery, 1981, Grey Art Gallery and Study Ctr., NYU; represented in permanent collection, Albright Art Gallery, Mus. Modern Art, Whitney Mus. Am. Art, Met. Mus. Art, Art Inst. Chgo., Miller Co. Served as pvt. AUS, 1941-43. Recipient Audubon prize, 1945; Kleinert award, 1956; Woodstock Found. grantee, 1949; Ford Found. grantee, 1959; Am. Acad. Arts and Letters grantee, 1971; Rothko Found. grantee, 1972. Office: Xavier Fourcade Gallery 36 E 75th St New York NY 10021 *

HAGUE, WILLIAM EDWARD, JR., editor, author; b. Duquesne, Pa., Feb. 2, 1919; s. William Edward and Edith (Osburn) H.; m. Margaret Cleland Anderson, July 22, 1950 (div.). A.B., Princeton U., 1940; postgrad., U. Pitts. Sch. Law, 1940-41. Asso. editor Tide mag., 1947-49; promotion dir. Living for Young Homemakers mag., 1949-50, copy editor, 1951-54, mng. editor, 1954-61; editor Living's Guide to Home Planning mag., 1958-61; with Conde Nast Publs., N.Y.C.; sr. editor House & Garden, 1961; editor-in-chief House & Garden Guides, 1962-72; asst. account exec. Fitzgerald Advt. Agy., New Orleans, 1950-51. Author: How to Decorate With Color, 1964, What You Should Know About Furniture, 1965, Planning Your Vacation Home, 1968, Plan Your Baths for Beauty and Efficiency, 1969, Plan The Kitchen That Suits You, 1969, Making The Most of The One-Room Apartment, 1969, Your Vacation House, How To Plan It, 1972, Doubleday's Complete Basic Book of Home Decorating, 1976, Know Your America, California, 1978, Remodel, Don't Move, 1981, The New Complete Basic Book of Home Decorating, 1983. Recipient Dorothy Dawe award for disting. journalistic coverage in home furnishings field, 1969. Home: 1640 20th St San Francisco CA 94107

HAHN, BETTY, artist, photographer; b. Chgo., Oct. 11, 1940; d. Eugene Joseph and Esther Josephine (Krueger) H.; m. Daniel Andrews, Mar. 26, 1970. A.B., Ind. U., 1963, M.F.A., 1966. Asst. prof. photography Rochester (N.Y.) Inst. Tech., 1969-75; asso. prof. art U. N.Mex., Albuquerque, 1976—. One-woman shows, Smithsonian Instn., Washington, 1969, Sandstone Gallery, Rochester, N.Y., 1978, Blue Sky Gallery, Portland, Oreg., Susan Spiritus Gallery, Newport Beach, Calif., 1977, 82, Witkin Gallery, N.Y.C., 1973, 79, Ctr. Creative Photography, Tucson, 1981, Columbia Coll. Gallery, Chgo., 1982. Nat. Endowment Arts grantee, 1977-78, 82-83; N.Y. State Council Arts grantee, 1976. Mem. Soc. Photog. Edn., Coll. Art Assn., Evidence Photographers Internat. Council. Office: Art Dept Univ of New Mexico Albuquerque NM 87131

HAHN, EMILY, author; b. St. Louis, Mo., Jan. 14, 1905; d. Isaac Newton and Hannah (Schoen) H.; m. Charles R. Boxer, Nov. 28, 1945; children: Carola, Amanda. B.S., U. Wis., 1926; postgrad., Columbia U., 1928-29, Oxford U., 1934-35. Mining engr. Deko Oil Co., St. Louis, 1926; courier, Santa Fe, 1927-28; instr. geology Hunter Coll., N.Y.C., 1929-30; with Red Cross in, Belgian Congo, 1930-31; instr. English, writing Customs Coll., Shanghai, China, 1935-38, Chungking, China, 1940; instr. Customs U., Hong Kong, 1941. Writer of stories and scenarios, N.Y.C. and Hollywood, also travels and newspaper work in, Eng., Continent and North Africa, 1931-32; Author: books including Hongkong Holiday, 1946, China A to Z, 1946, Picture Story of China, 1946, Raffles of Singapore, 1946, Miss Jill, 1947, England to Me, 1949, Purple Passage, 1950, Love Conquers Nothing, 1952, Chiang Kai-Shek, 1955, Diamond, 1956, The Tiger House Party, 1959, China Only Yesterday, 1963, China to Me, 1963, Indo, 1964, Africa to Me, 1964, Animal Gardens, 1967, Times and Places, 1970, On the Side of the Apes, 1971, Once Upon a Pedestal, 1974, Mabel, 1977, Look Who's Talking, 1978, Love of Gold, 1981. Interned by Japanese govt. Dec. 1941; returned to U.S. on Gripsholm Dec. 1943. Address: 16 W 16th St Apt 12 N South New York NY 10011

HAHN, ERWIN LOUIS, physicist, educator; b. Sharon, Pa., June 9, 1921; s. Israel and Mary (Weiss) H.; m. Marian Ethel Failing, Apr. 8, 1944 (dec. Sept. 1978); children: David L., Deborah A., Katherine L.; m. Natalie Woodford Hodgson, Apr. 12, 1980. B.S., Juniata Coll., 1943, D.Sc., 1966; M.S., U. Ill., 1947, Ph.D., 1949; D.Sc., Purdue U., 1975. Asst. Purdue U., 1943-44; research asso. U. Ill., 1950; NRC fellow Stanford, 1950-51, instr., 1951-52; research physicist Watson IBM Lab., N.Y.C., 1952-55; asso. Columbia, 1952-55; faculty U. Calif. at Berkeley, 1955—, prof. physics, 1961—; asso. prof. Miller Inst. for Basic Research, Berkeley, 1958-59, prof., 1966-67; vis. fellow Brasenose Coll., Oxford (Eng.) U., 1981-82; cons. Office Naval Research, Stanford, 1950-52, AEC, 1955—; spl. cons. USN, 1959; adv. panel mem. Nat. Bur. Standards, Radio Standards div., 1961-64; mem. Nat. Acad. Sci./NRC com. on basic research; adv. to U.S. Army Research Office, 1967-69. Author: (with T.P. Das) Nuclear Quadrupole Resonance Spectroscopy, 1958. Served with USNR, 1944-46. Recipient Oliver E. Buckley prize Am. Phys. Soc., 1971; prize Internat. Soc. Magnetic Resonance, 1971; award Humboldt Found., Germany, 1976-77; co-winner Wolf Found. prize in physics, 1983-84; named to Calif. Inventor Hall of Fame, 1984; Guggenheim fellow, 1961-62, 69-70; NSF fellow, 1961-62; vis. fellow Brasenose Coll., Oxford, 1969-70; lifetime hon. fellow Brasenose Coll., Oxford, 1984. Fellow Am. Phys. Soc. (past mem. exec. com. div. solid state physics); mem. Am. Acad. Arts and Scis., Nat. Acad. Scis., Slovenian Acad. Scis. and Arts (fgn.). Home: 69 Stevenson Ave Berkeley CA 94708 Office: Dept Physics U Calif Berkeley CA 94720

HAHN, GEORGE LEROY, agrl. engr., biometeorologist; b. Muncie, Kans., Nov. 12, 1934; s. Vernon Leslie and Marguerite Alberta (Breeden) H.; m. Clovice Elaine Christensen, Dec. 3, 1955; children—Valerie, Cecile, Steven, Melanie. B.S., U. Mo., Columbia, 1957, Ph.D., 1971; M.S., U. Calif., Davis, 1961. Agrl. engr., project leader and tech. advisor Agrl. Research Service, U.S. Dept. Agr., Columbia, Mo., 1957, Davis, Calif., 1958-61, Columbia, 1961-78, Clay Center, Nebr., 1978—. Contbr. articles to tech. jours. and books on impact of climatic and other environ. factors on livestock prodn. and evaluation of methods of reducing impact. Recipient award Am. Soc. Agrl. Engrs.-Metal Bldgs. Mfrs. Assn., 1976. Mem. Am. Meteorol. Soc. (award for outstanding achievement in bioclimatology 1976), Am. Soc. Agrl. Engrs., Internat. Soc. Biometeorology, AAAS. Office: US Meat Animal Research Center PO Box 166 Clay Center NE 68933

HAHN, GILBERT, JR., lawyer; b. Washington, Sept. 12, 1921; s. Gilbert and Hortense (King) H.; m. Margot Hess, June 29, 1950; children: Gilbert III, Amanda B., Polly K. Grad., Phillips Exeter Acad., 1939; A.B. with high honors, Princeton U., 1943; LL.B., Yale U., 1948. Bar: D.C. 1948. Partner firm Amram & Hahn, Washington, 1954—; dir. U.S. Shoe Corp., Security Nat. Bank. Alt. del. Republican Nat. Conv., 1952; pres. Washington Young Rep. Club, 1949; mem. Rep. nat. finance com., 1964-68; chmn. D.C. Rep. Com., 1968-69, D.C. City Council, 1969-72; Pres. bd. dirs. Washington Hosp. Center, 1966-69, Washington Hosp. Center Research Found., 1964-66; chmn. D.C. Gen. Hosp. Commn., 1977-83. Served to 1st lt. AUS, 1942-46; ETO. Decorated Purple Heart. Mem. D.C., Md., U.S. Supreme Ct. bar assns. Clubs: Cannon, Corby Court, Federal City, University. Address: 3022 University Terr NW Washington DC 20016

HAHN, JACK ALBERT LOUIS, hospital and health care consultant; b. Evansville, Ind., Apr. 24, 1922; s. Albert George and Grace (Osborn) H.; m. Lois A. Walther, June 13, 1946 (dec. 1979); children: Susan Louise, Louis Albert, Joan Katheryn.; m. Barbara Lea Webb, Nov. 7, 1981. B.A., U. Evansville, 1943, LL.D., 1958; M.H.A., Northwestern U., 1948; LL.D., De Pauw U., 1970. Adminstrv. asst. Chgo. Wesley Meml. Hosp., 1946-47; adminstr. Meml. Hosp., Fremont, Ohio, 1948-52; asst. supt. Meth. Hosp. of Ind., Inc., Indpls., 1952-53, exec. dir., 1954-69, pres., 1969-81; hosp./health care cons., 1981—; vis. lectr., residency preceptor George Washington U., 1949, Washington U., 1956, Trinity U., 1971, Ind. U., 1975—; cons. AID, 1962, 68; mem. Surgeon Gen.'s Com. Emergency Planning, 1963-70, Certification Council, 1964—, chmn., 1968-70. Contbr. articles to hosp. and nursing jours. Mem. Bd. Health and Welfare Ministries, Methodist Ch., 1964-72, treas., 1968-72; v.p. Assn. Health and Welfare United Meth. Ch., 1973, pres.-elect, 1974-75, pres., 1975—, recipient adminstrs. award, 1970; Commr. Joint Commn. Accreditation Hosps., 1973-78, chmn., 1976; mem. Ind. State Health Coordinating Council, 1977—, pres., 1984—; trustee Tri-State Hosp. Assembly, 1973-80, treas., 1975-77, pres., 1979-80. Served to lt. (j.g.) USNR, 1943-46. Recipient Jackson award Northwestern U., 1966, Alumni Merit award, 1974. Fellow Am. Coll. Hosp. Adminstrs. (regent 1964-66); mem. Am. Hosp. Assn. (dir. 1977—, sec. 1980—, Ind. del. 1955-60, chmn. council asso. services 1962-65, vice chmn. council adminstrv. practice 1959-62, gen. council 1962-65, 70-72, chmn. 1970, trustee 1965-68, 70-72, pres. 1971, distinguished service award 1973, chmn. com. commrs. 1975), Ind. Hosp. Assn. (pres. 1962-63), Nat. Assn. Practical Nurse Edn. and Service (dir. 1956-62, chmn. hosp. adv. council 1955-60), Am. Protestant Hosp. Assn. (v.p. 1959, dir., pres. 1965-66, award of merit 1977), Nat. Health Council (dir. 1967-70). Methodist. Club: Rotary. Home: 4000 N Meridian St 2E Indianapolis IN 46208 Methodist Hosp Ind 1604 N Capitol Ave Indianapolis IN 46202

HAHN, JAMES MAGLORIE, librarian; b. Grey Eagle, Minn., June 2, 1936; s. Frank John and Mabel Leone H.; m. Ellen MacMonagle, Sept. 7, 1976; children by previous marriage: Michele Diane, Nichola Darcy, Jennifer Deirdre, Gillian Dana, Kristan Desiree. B.A., U. Minn., 1960, M.A., 1962, M.L.S., 1962. Dir. Libraries and Information Center, Minn. Dept. Corrections, 1961-63; chief librarian Royal Air Force, Lakenheath, Eng., 1963-68; asst. command librarian Hdqrs. U.S. Air Force Europe and Near East, Wiesbaden, Ger., 1968-69; staff librarian Hdqrs. 1st Air Force, Newburgh, N.Y., 1969; asst. chief for network devel. Library of Congress, Washington, 1970-75; chief library div. VA, Washington, 1975-79, dir. learning resources service, 1979-81, dir. continuing edn. resources services, 1981—; treas. SABIL Inc., 1983—; asso. prof. library sci. Cath. U. Am., Washington, 1977—; adviser on libraries and patient edn. Am. Hosp. Assn., 1977—; bd. regents Nat. Library Medicine, 1980—. Mem. ALA, Va., Med. library assns., Health Scis. Communication Assn. Home: 11663 Newbridge Ct Reston VA 22091 Office: Continuing Education Resources Service VACO 142 810 Vermont Ave NW Washington DC 20420

HAHN, K. ROBERT, aircraft manufacturing company executive; b. Clear Lake, S.D., Feb. 7, 1921; s. Clement Freeman and Mildred S. (Hannested) H.; m. Mary L. Crawford, Sept. 25, 1943; children: Marsha C., Nancy G., Susan K. A.B., Oberlin Coll.; J.D., Cornell U. Bar: D.C. Atty. firm Elmore, Moss & Moore, Washington, 1948-49; gen. counsel Lake Central Airlines, Indpls., 1949-51; contracts mgr. Lear Inc., Grand Rapids., Mich., 1951-54, v.p. mktg., 1954-59, exec. v.p., Santa Monica, Calif., 1959-62; pres. power equipment div. Lear Siegler Inc., Cleve., 1962-65, corp. v.p., Santa Monica, 1962-71, exec. v.p., dir., 1971—; dir. Rohr Inc., San Diego. Mem. Def. Policy Adv. Com. on Trade, Washington, 1981—. Served to 1st lt. USAF, 1943-45. Mem. Am. Def. Preparedness Assn. (pres. Los Angeles chpt. 1983—). Home: 55 Misty Acres Rolling Hills Estates CA 90274 Office: Lear Siegler Inc 2850 Ocean Park Blvd Santa Monica CA 90405

HAHN, LEWIS EDWIN, retired philosophy educator; b. Swenson, Tex., Sept. 26, 1908; s. Edwin D. and Ione (Brewster) H.; m. Elizabeth Herring, June 30, 1932; children: Helen Elizabeth, Mary, Sharon. B.A., U. Tex., 1929, M.A., 1929; Ph.D., U. Calif., 1939. Teaching fellow U. Calif., 1931-34; instr. philosophy U. Mo., 1936-39, asst. prof., 1939-46, assoc. prof., 1946-49; vis. lectr. Princeton, 1947; prof. philosophy Washington U., 1949-63, chmn. dept., 1949-63, assoc. dean Grad. Sch. Arts and Scis., 1953-54, dean Grad. Sch. Arts and Scis., 1954-63; research prof. philosophy So. Ill. U., Carbondale, 1963-77, prof. emeritus, 1977—, vis. prof., editor, 1981—; disting. vis. prof. Baylor U., 1977, 79, 80; Mem. U.S. Nat. Commn. UNESCO, 1965-67. Author: A Contextualistic Theory of Perception, 1942, (with others) Value: A Cooperative Inquiry, 1949; co-author: Guide to the Works of John Dewey, 1970; editor: Library of Living Philosophers, 1981—; Contbr. articles to profl. jours. Fellow AAAS; mem. Am. Philos. Assn. (exec. bd. 1950-54, 70-73, chmn. com. placement, available personnel 1951-54, sec.-treas. West div. 1949-51, sec.-treas. 1960-66, com. on internat. coop. 1967-80), AAUP, Am. Soc. Aesthetics, S.W. Philos. Soc. (pres. 1955), Mo. Philos. Assn. (pres. 1949-50), So. Soc. for Philosophy and Psychology (pres. 1958-59), Ill. Philosophy Conf. (pres. 1969-71), Phi Beta Kappa. Home: Reed Station Rd Route 2 Carbondale IL 62901

HAHN, RICHARD FERDINAND, lawyer; b. Chgo., May 20, 1909; s. Ernest Theodore and Emily (Sattler) H.; m. Grace Elizabeth Jepsen, Sept. 1, 1935; children—Nancy (Mrs. Noel G. Fischer), Lawrence. B.S., U. Ill., 1930, J.D., 1933. Bar: Ill. bar 1933. Since practiced in, Chgo.; mem. firm Halfpenny, Hahn & Roche, Chgo. and Washington. Mem. Woodstock (Ill.) City Council, 1965-67, 73-79; mem., sec. Woodstock Police Commn., 1968-71; mem. Woodstock Indsl. Devel. Commn., 1967-69, Woodstock City Planning Commn., 1957-62, 79—, Woodstock Community High Sch. Bd., 1952-55, 56-62; pres. Woodstock Community High Sch. Bd., 1958-62; Bd. dirs. Woodstock Fine Arts Assn., 1963-67. Mem. Am., Ill., Chgo. bar assns., Am. Judicature Soc., Phi Alpha Delta. Republican. Club: Mason. Home: 415 Laurel Ave Woodstock IL 60098 Office: 20 N Wacker Dr Chicago IL 60606

HAHN, RICHARD R., mfg. co. exec.; b. Rapid City, S.D., July 12, 1930; m. Joan Fager, May 24, 1953; children—David H., Carol L., Donald R., Kathleen J. B.S., Bethany Coll., 1952; M.S., Kans. State U., 1954, Ph.D., 1957. With Harvest Queen Mills, 1956-67; with A.E. Staley Mfg. Co., Decatur, Ill., 1967—, now v.p. research and devel. Mem. Am. Chem. Soc. Office: AE Staley Mfg Co Corporate R & D Center 2200 E Eldorado St Decatur IL 62525 *

HAHN, ROGER, historian, educator; b. Paris, Jan. 5, 1932; U.S., 1941, naturalized, 1953; s. John P. and Thérèse E.L. (Lévy) H.; m. Ellen Isabel Leibovici, Sept. 11, 1955; children: Elisabeth L., Sophie A. B.A. magna cum laude, Harvard U., 1953, M.A. in Teaching, 1954; certificate, Ecole Pratique des Hautes Etudes, Paris, 1955; Ph.D., Cornell U., 1962. Instr. history U. Del., 1960-61; mem. history faculty U. Calif. at Berkeley, 1961—, prof., 1974—; spl. asst. to dir. sci. affairs Bancroft Library, Berkeley, 1972—; chief U.S. del. XVth Congress History of Sci., Edinburgh, 1977; Bd. dirs. Centre de Synthèse, Paris, 1976—. Author: L'Hydrodynamique au XVIIIè Siècle, 1965, Laplace as a Newtonian Scientist, 1967, The Anatomy of a Scientific Institution: The Paris Academy of Sciences 1666-1803, 1971, A Bibliography of Quantitative Studies on Science and Its History, 1980, Calendar of the Correspondence of Laplace, 1982; adv. editor: Isis, 1971-75, 18th-Century Studies, 1976-80; cons. editor: History of Sci, 1972—; editorial advisor: Social Studies of Science, 1974—. Served with AUS, 1955-57. Fulbright scholar, 1954-55, 83-84; NSF fellow, 1959-60, 64-65; Am. Council Learned Socs. fellow, 1973-74; decorated chevalier Ordre des Palmes Académiques, 1977; recipient book prize Pacific Coast br. Am. Hist. Assn., 1972. Fellow AAAS (council 1967-73); mem. History Sci. Soc. (council 1967-70, 77-80), Am. Soc. 18th Century Studies (pres. 1982-83), Western Soc. 18th Century Studies (pres. 1977-78), West Coast History of Sci. Soc. (pres. 1982-84), Acad. Internat. d'histoire des Scis.

HAHN, SAMUEL WILFRED, educator; b. Columbia, S.C., Mar. 21, 1921; s. Samuel W. and Doris (Becker) H.; m. Martha Ann Strowd, June 24, 1947; children—Stephen S., Dale B., Carol C. A.B., Lenoir Rhyne Coll., Hickory, N.C., 1941; M.A., Duke, 1942, Ph.D., 1948. Vis. instr. math. Duke, 1946-47; instr. U. Mich., 1947-49; asst. prof. math. Wittenberg U., Springfield, Ohio, 1949-51; prof. math., 1960—, chmn. dept., 1961-67, asso. dean, 1963-65; prof. math., head dept. Winthrop Coll., Rock Hill, S.C., 1951-59; vis. prof. Fla. State U., summer 1960; prof. Hampden-Sydney Coll., 1959-60. Served to lt. USNR, 1942-46. Fellow Ohio Acad. Sci. (v.p. 1967-68); mem. Am. Math. Soc., Math. Assn. Am. (chmn. Ohio sect. 1972-73, bd. govs. 1979—), AAUP, Phi Beta Kappa., Sigma Xi. Lutheran. Home: 1019 Redbud Ln Springfield OH 45504

HAHN, THOMAS MARSHALL, JR., forest products corporation executive; b. Lexington, Ky., Dec. 2, 1926; s. Thomas Marshall and Mary Elizabeth (Boston) H.; m. Margaret Louise Lee, Dec. 27, 1948; children: Elizabeth Hahn McKelvy, Anne Hahn Clarke. B.S. in Physics, U. Ky., 1945; Ph.D., MIT, 1949; LL.D., Seton Hall U., 1976. Teaching asst. U. Ky., Lexington, 1944-45, assoc. prof., 1950-52; prof., dir. grad. studies physics, also dir. Nuclear Accelerator Labs., 1952-54; physicist U.S. Naval Ordnance Lab., 1946-47; research asst. MIT, 1947-50; prof. physics, head dept. Va. Poly. Inst. and State U., Blacksburg, 1954-59; dean arts and scis. Kans. State U., 1959-62; pres. Va. Poly. Inst. and State U., 1962-75; exec. v.p. Ga.-Pacific Corp., 1975-76, pres., 1976-82, pres., chief operating officer, 1982-83, pres., chief exec. officer, 1983-84, chmn. bd., pres., chief exec. officer, 1984—, also dir.; physicist N.Am. Phillips Co., summer 1945; staff mem. div. indsl. coop. MIT, summer 1950; research participant Oak Ridge Nat. Lab., summer 1951; cons. Reynolds Metals Co., 1958-59, Leeds and Northrup Co., 1958, AEC, 1959; mem. Nat. Sci. Bd., 1972-78. Chmn. Va. Met. Area Study Commn., 1966-68; bd. visitors Air U., 1966-69; chmn. Va. Cancer Crusade, 1972; dir. adv. bd. Salvation Army, 1972-74; Bd. dirs. Keep Am. Beautiful; chmn. Atlanta Area Services for Blind; mem. exec. bd. Peach Bowl; adv. bd. Atlanta Area Council Boy Scouts Am.; hon. chmn. March of Dimes/Walk Internat., 1984; trustee Emory U. Served with USNR, 1945-46. Named Va.'s Outstanding Citizen Toastmasters Internat., 1966; recipient MIT Corporate leadership award, 1976. Fellow Am. Phys. Soc.; mem. AAAS, Am. Assn. Physics Tchrs., So. Regional Edn. Bd. (dir. 1973-74), So. Assn. Land-Grant Colls. and State Univs. (pres. 1965-66), Am. Paper Inst. (chmn. 1982-83); Mem. Atlanta C. of C., Atlanta Arts Alliance, Central Atlanta Progress; mem. Phi Beta Kappa, Sigma Xi, Omicron Delta Kappa, Sigma Pi Sigma, Pi Mu Epsilon. Republican. Methodist. Clubs: Piedmont Driving, Links, Shenandoah, Capital City. Office: 133 Peachtree St Atlanta GA 30303

HAHNE, HENRY VICTOR, cons. engring. co. exec.; b. Riga, Latvia, Jan. 16, 1924; s. Harold Adolf and Lydia Maria (Aleksejev) H.; m. Iris Helen Suppik, Dec. 31, 1962; 1 dau., Victoria Ann. Dipl., Ingenieur, Technische Hochschule Graz, Austria, 1949; Ph.D., Stanford, 1954. Registered profl. engr., Calif. Engr. Ed. Ast & Co., Graz, 1949-51; engr. Pacific Car & Foundry Co., Seattle, 1951-52; asso. prof. dept. applied mechanics Washington U., St. Louis, 1954-56; research engr. Lockheed Missile & Space Div., Palo Alto, Calif., 1956-59; prof., head dept. civil engring. and applied mechanics U. Santa Clara, Calif., 1959-73; pres. Henry V. Hahne, Inc. (cons. engrs.), Los Altos, Calif., 1973—. Contbg. author: Handbook of Engineering Mechanics, 1961. Mem. Soc. Automotive Engrs., ASTM, ASCE. Home: 422 Cherry Ave Los Altos CA 94022 Office: 160 Main St Los Altos CA 94022

HAIDT, HAROLD, lawyer; b. Bklyn., Dec. 6, 1926; s. Samuel and Rebecca (Davidson) H.; m. Elaine Meredith Kaplan, July 4, 1954; children: Rebecca, Jonathan, Samantha. B.S. in Chem. Engring, Purdue U., 1947; J.D., George Washington U., 1950. Bar: D.C. 1951, N.Y. State 1965. Examiner U.S. Patent Office, Washington, 1947-51; practiced in, N.Y.C., 1964—; trial atty. antitrust div. U.S. Dept. Justice, 1951-53; corp. patent counsel Airco, Murray Hill, N.J., 1953-56; patent counsel Johnson & Johnson, New Brunswick, N.J., 1956-64, dir., 1961-64; partner firm Brooks Haidt Haffner & Delahunty, N.Y.C., 1971—; cons., lectr. in field. Mem. U.S. del. U.S.-USSR Exchange in Patents and Licensing, 1972-73; cons. working group on intellectual property Joint U.S.-USSR Commn. on Sci. and Tech. Cooperation, 1975-77; chmn. U.S. del. to Poland and E.Ger. on patents and licensing, 1975. Author: U.S. Government Policies Relating to Technology, 1975; contbr. articles to profl. jours. Bd. govs. Old Scarsdale (N.Y.) Assn., 1969—. Mem. Licensing Execs. Soc. (trustee 1971-74, v.p. 1973-74), Am., N.Y. patent law assns., Phi Lambda Upsilon. Home: 35 Church Ln Scarsdale NY 10583 Office: 99 Park Ave New York NY 10016

HAIG, ALEXANDER MEIGS, JR., former secretary state, former army officer, business executive; b. Phila., Dec. 2, 1924; s. Alexander Meigs and Regina Anne (Murphy) H.; m. Patricia Antoinette Fox, May 24, 1950; children: Alexander P., Brian F., Barbara E. Student, U. Notre Dame, 1943; B.S., U.S. Mil. Acad., 1947; M.A., Georgetown U., 1961; grad., Naval War Coll., 1960, Army War Coll., 1966, Niagara U.; LL.D. (hon.), U. Utah. Commd. 2d lt. U.S. Army, 1947, advanced through grades to gen., 1973; staff officer Office Dept. Chief of Staff for Ops. Dept. of Army, 1962-64; mil. asst. to sec. of army, 1964, dep. spl. asst. to sec. and dep. sec. of def., 1964-65; bn. and brigade comdr. 1st Inf. Div., Vietnam, 1966-67; regtl. comdr., dep. comdt. U.S. Mil. Acad., 1967-69; mil. asst. to asst. to the Pres. for Nat. Security Affairs, 1969-70; dep. asst. to the Pres. for Nat. Security Affairs, Washington, 1970-73; vice chief of staff U.S. Army, Washington, 1973; asst. to Pres., chief White House staff, 1973-74; comdr.-in-chief U.S. European Command, 1974-79; supreme allied comdr. Europe SHAPE, 1974-79; ret., 1979; pres., chief operating officer, dir. United Technologies Corp., Hartford, Conn., 1979-81; sec. state, Washington, 1981-82; dir. MGM/UA Entertainment Group, Leisure and Tech. Inc., Allegheny Internat. Inc., Commodore Internat. Trustee Loyola Coll., Balt. Decorated D.S.C., Silver Star with oak leaf cluster, Legion of Merit with 2 oak leaf clusters, D.F.C. with 2 oak leaf clusters, Bronze Star with oak leaf cluster, Air medal with 23 oak leaf clusters, Army Commendation medal, Purple Heart, U.S.; Nat. Order 5th Class; Gallantry Cross with palm; Civil Actions Honor medal 1st Class;

grand officer Nat. Order of Vietnam, Republic of Vietnam; medal of King Abdel-Aziz, Saudi Arabia; grand cross Order of Merit, W. Ger.; recipient Disting. Service medal Dept. of Def., U.S. Army; Man of Yr. award Air Force Assn.; James Forrestal Meml. award. Mem. Soc. of 1st Div. (v.p.). Office: Suite 800 1155 15th St NW Washington DC 20005

HAIGH, GEORGE WHYLDEN, banker; b. Toledo, Aug. 4, 1931; s. Frederick Dwight and Annette (Lipe) H.; m. Joan DuBois, Oct. 15, 1954; children—Constance, Stephen. B.A., Dartmouth Coll., 1953; postgrad., Fgn. Service Sch., Georgetown U., 1953-54. With DeVilbiss Co., Toledo, 1956-76, pres., 1972—, Toledo Trust Co., 1976—, Toledo Trustcorp., Inc., 1976—; dir. Champion Spark Plug Co., LST Corp., Inc.; bd. dirs. Internat. Fin. Conf. Pres. Family Services Greater Toledo, 1971-73; chmn. Toledo Economic Planning Council; dirs. A.R.C., Toledo, Toledo Mus. Art; trustee Toledo Hosp. Served with Signal Corps U.S. Army, 1954-56. Mem. Toledo C. of C. (pres. 1977-78). Republican. Episcopalian. Clubs: Toledo Country, Toledo; Belmont Country, Carranor Hunt and Polo (Perrysburg, Ohio); Rockwell Springs Trout (Sandusky, Ohio); Georgetown (Washington). Home: 4206 Bonnie Brae Circle Toledo OH 43606 Office: Three Seagate Toledo OH 43603

HAIGH, ROBERT WILLIAM, business executive, educator; b. Phila., Aug. 22, 1926; s. Harry E. and Mildred (Elliott) H.; m. Jane Stanton Sheble, June 19, 1948; children: Cynthia Jane, Anne Sheble, Robert William, Barbara Lynne. Student, Muhlenberg Coll., 1944-45; A.B. cum laude, Bucknell U., 1948; M.B.A. with high distinction, Harvard U., 1950, D.C.S., 1953. Research and teaching faculty Harvard U. Grad Sch. Bus. Adminstrn., 1950-56, asst. prof., 1953-56; asst. to pres. Helmerich & Payne, Inc., Tulsa, 1956, controller and asst. to pres., 1956-57, fin. v.p., dir., 1957-61, White Eagle Internat. Oil Co., 1957-60; dir. planning Standard Oil Co. (Ohio), Cleve., 1961, v.p. planning, 1961-63, v.p. corp. planning and devel., 1963-64, v.p. chems. and plastics bus., 1964-66, Vistron Corp. subs., 1966-67; group v.p., pres. edn. group, dir. Xerox Corp., Stamford, Conn., 1967-72; exec. v.p. Swedlow Corp., 1973-74, pres., chief exec. officer, dir., 1974; pres. Hillsboro Assocs., 1974-75; sr. v.p. Freeport Minerals Co., 1975-76; chmn. bd., chief exec. officer Photo Quest, Inc., Cognitrex, Inc., Seidel-Farris-Clark, Inc., 1977-78; dir. Wharton Applied Research Ctr., lectr. U. Pa., Phila., 1978-79; now Disting. prof. bus. adminstrn. Colgate Darden Grad. Sch. Bus. Adminstrn., U. Va.; dir. Landmark Communications, Inc.; adv. bd. Atlantic Venture Ptnrs. Author: (with John G. McLean) The Growth of Integrated Oil Companies, 1954. Served with USNR, 1944-45. Mem. Am. Petroleum Inst., Cleve. C. of C., Cleve. Council World Affairs, Phi Beta Kappa, Phi Lambda Theta. Home: 404 Ednam Dr Charlottesville VA 22901 Office: Colgate Darden Grad Sch Bus Adminstrn Box 6550 Charlottesville VA 22906

HAIGHT, CHARLES SHERMAN, JR., federal judge; b. N.Y.C., Sept. 23, 1930; s. Charles Sherman and Margaret (Edwards) H.; m. Mary Jane Peightal, June 30, 1953; children: Nina E., Susan P. B.A., Yale U., 1952, LL.B., 1955. Bar: N.Y. State 1955. Trial atty., admiralty and shipping dept. Dept. Justice, Washington, 1955-57; assoc. firm Haight, Gardner, Poor & Havens, N.Y.C., 1957-68, partner, 1968-76; judge U.S. Dist. Ct. for So. Dist. N.Y., 1976—. Bd. dirs. Kennedy Child Study Center; adv. trustee Am.-Scandinavian Found., chmn., 1970-76; bd. mgrs. Havens Fund. Mem. Maritime Law Assn., U.S., N.Y. State Bar Assn., Bar Assn. City N.Y., Fed. Bar Council. Episcopalian. Office: US Courthouse Foley Sq New York NY 10007

HAIGHT, EDWARD ALLEN, lawyer; b. Rockford, Ill., July 2, 1910; s. John T. and Augusta (Granger) H.; m. Valerie E. Haight, Jan. 1, 1935; children—Edward Allen, George Ives II, Edith Diane, Stephen Holmes. B.A., U. Wis., 1931; LL.B., Harvard U., 1934. Bar: Ill. bar 1934. Since practiced in, Chgo.; mem. firm Haight, Hofeldt Davis & Jambor and (predecessor firms), Chgo., 1956—. Served as lt. USNR, 1943-46. Mem. Am., Ill., Chgo., 7th Circuit bar assns., Am., Chgo. patent law assns., Am. Coll. Trial Lawyers. Clubs: Union League (Chgo.); Skokie Country. Home: 159 Abingdon Ave Kenilworth IL 60043 Office: 55 E Monroe St Chicago IL 60603

HAIGHT, FULTON WILBUR, lawyer; b. Los Angeles, July 9, 1923; s. Raymond Leroy and Heloise Marie (Davis) H.; m. Dorothy Cornelia Fitger, Oct. 4, 1952; children—Fulton Wilbur, Maureen Elizabeth, Hilary Josephine, Talis Susanne. LL.B., U. So. Calif., 1948. Bar: Calif. bar 1949. Practiced in, Los Angeles, 1949-50; sr. dep. city atty. City of Los Angeles, 1950-52; asso. mem. law firm Moss, Lyon & Dunn (name changed to Haight, Lyon & Smith 1967, now Haight, Dickson, Brown & Bonesteel, 1976), Los Angeles, 1952-59, partner, 1959-67, sr. partner, 1967—; lectr. Mem. Calif. Jud. Council Arbitration Adv. Com., 1972; organizer, def. chmn. Los Angeles Attys. Spl. Arbitration Plan, 1972; mem. bench and bar com. Los Angeles Superior Ct., 1970-72; mem. adminstrv. com. Arbitration Com., 1976—. Author: (with Cotchett) California Courtroom Evidence, 1972. Served to 1st lt. USAF, 1943-45. Decorated Air medal with 3 oak leaf clusters. Fellow Am. Coll. Trial Lawyers; mem. Assn. So. Calif. Def. Counsels (pres. 1970-71), State Bar Assn. Calif. (bd. govs. 1977-81, chmn. com. on arbitration 1974-77, v.p., bd. govs. 1977-78, 81—), Los Angeles Bar Assn. (chmn. co. for rev. jury procedure 1976—). Home: 1725 San Vicente Blvd Santa Monica CA 90402 Office: 201 Santa Monica Blvd Santa Monica CA 90406

HAIGHT, GILBERT PIERCE, JR., chemistry educator; b. Seattle, June 8, 1922; s. Gilbert Pierce and Ruth (Gazzam) H.; m. Shirley Myers Grapek, June 30, 1946; children: Jennifer Lea, Loisanne Fox, Charlene Ellen, Charles Pierce, Stephanie Louise, Christopher Warren. A.B., Stanford U., 1943; Ph.D., Princeton U., 1946; research fellow, Ohio State U., 1946-47; Rhodes scholar, Oxford (Eng.) U., 1947-48. Asst. prof. U. Hawaii, 1948-49, George Washington U., 1949-52, U. Kans., 1952-54; asso. prof. Swarthmore Coll., 1954-65; prof. chemistry Tex. A. and M. U., 1965-66, U. Ill. at Urbana, 1966—; vis. scientist Tech. U. Denmark, 1960-61; vis. fellow Australian Nat. U., 1981-82; cons. in field, 1951—; lectr. UNESCO Conf. Lab. Instrn., Perth, Australia, 1978, Chemistry Found. lectures, S. Africa, 1978; Dodge lectr. Franklin Inst., 1956; others.; Mem. Rhodes scholar selection com. for Kans., 1965-71, 73-79, 83, Rhodes scholar selection com. for Ill. (Ill.), 1972, 82. Author: Introduction to Physical Science, 1964, (with H.B. Gray) Basic Principles of Chemistry, 1967, (with R.E. Dickerson and H.B. Gray) Chemical Principles, 1970, 3d edit., 1979; also articles and lab. manuals; editorial bd.: Jour. Coll. Sci. Teaching, Coordination Chemistry Revs., Inorganic Chemistry. Recipient vis. scientist award in chem. edn. Western Conn. sect. Am. Chem. Soc., 1974; nat. award in chem. edn. Mfg. Chemists Assn., 1976; Chem. Edn. award Am. Chem. Soc., 1979. Mem. Am. Chem. Soc. (vis. scientist, chmn. div. chem. edn. 1976, mem. edn. and sci. commns.), Danish Chem. Soc., AAAS, Ill. Assn. Chemistry Tchrs. (pres. 1980), Am. Inst. Chemists, N.Y. Acad. Scis., Phi Beta Kappa, Sigma Xi, Phi Lambda Upsilon.

HAIGHT, JAMES THERON, corporation executive, lawyer; b. Racine, Wis., Dec. 10, 1924; s. Walter Lyman and Geraldine (Foley) H.; m. Patricia Aloe, Apr. 26, 1952; children: Alberta, Barbara, Catherine, Dorothy, Elaine. Student, U. Nebr., 1943-44, U. Bordeaux, France, 1947; diplome d'Etudes, U. Paris, 1948; B.A., U. Wis., 1950, LL.B., 1951. Bar: D.C. 1952, U.S. Supreme Ct 1952. Atty. Covington & Burling, Washington, 1951-56, Goodyear Tire & Rubber Co., Goodyear Internat. Corp., Akron, Ohio, 1956-61; gen. counsel, sec. George J. Meyer Mfg. Co., Milw., 1961-66; v.p., sec., chief corp. counsel Thrifty Corp., Los Angeles, 1966—; Mem. adv. bd. Internat. and Comparative Law Center, Southwestern Legal Found. Author: A Community Mental Health Services Act for Ohio, 1961, United States Regulation of East-West Trade, 1964; also articles.; Editor: Current Legal Aspects of Doing Business with Sino-Soviet Nations, 1973; mem. bd. editors: Internat. Lawyer, 1967-76. Served with C.E. AUS, 1943-46. Fellow Am. Bar Found.; mem. ABA (vice chmn. 1965-67, chmn. 1974-75, internat. law sect., chmn. nat. inst. on legal aspects of doing business in Europe 1971), Inter-Am. Bar Assn., Calif. Bar Assn., Los Angeles Bar Assn., Pasadena Bar Assn., Los Angeles Town Hall, Los Angeles World Affairs Council, Internat. Law Assn., Am. Fgn. Law Assn., Am. Corp. Counsel Assn., Am. Soc. Corp. Secs., Order of Coif. Home: 1390 Ridge Way Pasadena CA 91106 Office: 5051 Rodeo Rd Los Angeles CA 90016

HAIGHT, WARREN GAZZAM, land devel./mgmt. co. exec.; b. Seattle, Sept. 7, 1929; s. Gilbert Pierce and Ruth (Gazzam) H.; m. Suzanne H., Sept. 1, 1951; children—Paula Lea, Ian Pierce. A.B. in Econs, Stanford U., 1951; grad. various seminars, Am. Mgmt. Assn. Asst. Treas. Hawaiian Pineapple Co., Honolulu, 1955-64; v.p., treas. Oceanic Properties, Inc., Honolulu, 1964-67, pres., 1967—; dir. Oceanic Calif., Mililani Town, Inc.; trustee TransAm. Realty. Bd. dirs. Downtown Improvement Assn., Oahu Devel. Conf.; mem. Transit Coalition, Honolulu; active Jr. Achievement, Aloha United Way, C. of C. Hawaii. Served to lt. USNR, 1951-55. Mem. Land Use Research Found., Housing Coalition, Calif. Coastal Council. Clubs: Outrigger Canoe, Round Hill Country. Home: PO Box 2780 Honolulu HI 96803 Office: 130 Merchant St Honolulu HI 96813

HAIGNEY, JOHN EUSTACE, lawyer, corp. exec.; b. N.Y.C., Feb. 15, 1912; s. John J. and Susan (Lawlor) H.; m. Dorothy Anne Monahan, Aug. 18, 1943; children—Anne, John Eustace, Kathlyn, Mark, Paul, Jennifer and Courtney (twins). B.S., N.Y. U., 1933; LL.B., St. John's U., 1936. Bar: N.Y. bar 1936. Since practiced in, N.Y.C.; asso. firm Scandrett, Tuttle & Chalaire, N.Y.C., 1936-42, partner, 1946-49; partner firm Ide & Haigney, 1949—; legal counsel Rheingold Corp., N.Y.C., 1957-67, pres., dir., 1967-71, chmn., 1971—, dir.; dir. W.R. Grace & Co. Inc., Clevepak Corp., Glyco Chems., Inc., Chas. L. Huisking & Co., Richard Klinger, Inc. Bd. dirs. Leonard Tingle Found.; pres., dir. Huisking Found., N.Y.C; trustee Fordham U., 1971-76; mem. lay council St. John's U.; bd. govs. New Rochelle Hosp. Med. Center, 1979—. Served to maj. AUS, 1942-46. Mem. Assn. Bar City N.Y. (mem. com. on profl. responsibility 1973-76), N.Y. State, N.Y. County bar assns., Nat. Inst. Social Scis. Roman Catholic. Clubs: N.Y. Yacht, Union League (N.Y.C.); Larchmont Yacht. Home: 37 Larchmont Ave Larchmont NY 10538 Office: 41 E 42 St New York NY 10017

HAIGWOOD, PAUL BENTLEY, manufacturing company executive, former marine corps officer; b. N. Wilkesboro, N.C., Dec. 25, 1922; s. Thomas Jefferson and Octavia (Bentley) H.; m. Nancy Dobbins, Apr. 21, 1945; 1 dau., Nancy Logan Haigwood. B.S. in Commerce, U. N.C., 1947; M.A. in Personnel Mgmt., George Washington U., 1963; M.S. in Internat. Affairs, George Washington U., 1969. Bus. mgmt. trainee Gen. Electric Co., Schenectady, 1947-51; commd. 1st lt. U.S. Marine Corps, 1951, advanced through grades to col., 1968; sr. marine advisor Thai Marine Corps., 1960-63; comdr. bn. 6th Marines, 1963-65, regimental comdr., 1969-70; plans officer, Vietnam, 1965-66, chief staff 2d marine div., 1970-71; chief staff III Marine Amphibious Forces, Vietnam, 1972-73; ret., 1973; asst. sec. AMF Inc., White Plains, N.Y., 1973-76, v.p., sec., 1976—; also dir. numerous subs. Decorated Legion of Merit. Mem. Am. Soc. Corporate Secs., Ret. Officers Assn. Republican. Presbyterian. Home: 115 Hemlock Hill Rd New Canaan CT 06840 Office: 77 Westchester Ave White Plains NY 10604

HAILE, H. G., German language and literature educator; b. Brownwood, Tex., July 31, 1931; s. Frank and Nell (Goodson) H.; m. Mary Elizabeth Huff, Sept. 1, 1952; children: Jonathan, Christian, Constance. B.A., U. Ark., 1952, M.A., 1954; student, U. Cologne, Germany, 1955-56; Ph.D., U. Ill., 1957. Instr. U. Pa., 1956-57; asst. prof., then asso. prof. U. Houston, 1957-63; mem. faculty U. Ill., Urbana, 1963—, prof. German, 1965—, head dept., 1964-73, asso. mem., 1969—; vis. prof. U. Mich., U. Ga. Author: Das Faustbuch nach der Wolfenbuttler Handschrift, 1963, The History of Doctor Johann Faustus, 1965, Artist in Chrysalis: A Biographical Study of Goethe in Italy, 1973, Invitation to Goethe's Faust, 1978, Luther: An Experiment in Biography, 1980, 1983, From Humanism to Humanity: A History of Germany in the Early Modern, 1983; contbr. numerous articles on German lit. and higher edn. in Am. to profl. and popular jours. Fulbright fellow, 1955; Fellow Am. Council Learned Socs., 1961-62. Office: 437 Library Univ Ill Urbana IL 61801 *A child of the Dust Bowl who became a foreign language teacher, I was naturally critical of my native heritage. But in the eyes of European friends I stood for America, and I had to stand up for the gentler, nobler people we shall become. This gave me a vision to follow, and to serve.*

HAILE, JAMES FRANCIS, hospital administrator; b. Shamokin, Pa., Jan. 8, 1920; s. Philip J. and Mary (Brennan) H.; m. Betty Jane Kinnaw, May 19, 1943; children: Patricia, Peter, Peggy, Pamela, Karen. Student, U. Tenn., 1950-51. Finance officer VA hosps. at, Thomasville, Ga., Montgomery, Ala., Memphis, 1945-50; hosp. adminstrn. field rep. VA Hosp., Atlanta, 1950-53, adminstr., Montgomery, 1953-55, Minot, N.D., 1955-58, Hampton, Va., 1958-62, Wadsworth, Kans., 1962-69, dir., Indpls., 1969-72, VA Med. Center, Bay Pines, Fla., 1972-79, Seminole, Fla., 1979—. Bd. dirs. Leavenworth (Kans.) United Fund, 1962-65. Served to capt. USAAF, 1942-45; ETO. Mem. Am. Acad. Med. Adminstrs. (charter), Am. Legion, Fed. Hosp. Adminstrs. Inst. Alumni Assn. Lodges: Elks; Rotary (dir. Leavenworth Kans. chpt. 1965-68). Address: 13941 88th Ave N Seminole FL 33542 *"It is nice to be important, but more important to be nice."*

HAILE, LAWRENCE BARCLAY, lawyer; b. Atlanta, Feb. 19, 1938; m. Ann Springer McCauley, March 28, 1984; children: Gretchen Vanderhoof, Eric McKenzie, Scott McAllister; m. Sondra Lee Dangott, July 4, 1967. B.A. in Econs, U. Tex., 1958, LL.B., 1961. Bar: Calif. 1962. Law clk. to U.S. Judge Joseph M. Ingraham, Houston, 1961-62; pvt. practice law, San Francisco, 1962-67, Los Angeles, 1967—; mem. firm Hartman, Haile & Hughes, 1977—; instr. U. Calif. at Los Angeles Civil Trial Clinics, 1974, 76; lectr. law Calif. Continuing Edn. of Bar, 1973-74, 80-83; mem. nat. panel arbitrators Am. Arbitration Assn., 1965—. Asso. editor: Tex. Law Rev, 1960-61; Contbr. articles profl. publs. Mem. adv. bd. Inglewood Gen. Hosp. Mem. State Bar Calif., Tex., U.S. Supreme Ct. bar assns., Internat. Assn. Property Ins. Counsel (founding mem., pres. 1980), ASTM, London World Trade Centre Assn., Phi Delta Phi, Delta Sigma Rho. Club: Marine (London). Home: 9925 Lancer Ct Beverly Hills CA 90210 Office: 1910 Huntington Dr South Pasadena CA 91030 *Gold is like brass/Except less crass.*

HAILE, RAYMOND ALDERSON, JR., lawyer; b. Los Angeles, Jan. 10, 1930; s. Raymond Alderson and Alda Ruth (Turner) H.; m. Jeanne Hall Woods, June 23, 1956; children—Natalie Jeanne Haile, Jefferey Alderson. A.B., Stanford, 1952; J.D., Harvard, 1957. Bar: Calif. bar 1958, also U.S. Supreme Ct 1958. Counsel Kaiser Industries Corp., Oakland, Calif., 1960-69; asst. chief counsel Kaiser Industries Corp. and Kaiser Cement & Gypsum Corp., 1970-71; v.p., sec., gen. counsel Kaiser Steel Corp., Oakland, 1972-80; partner firm Reilly Jackson & Haile, San Francisco, 1980—. Bd. dirs. Oakland Mus. Served with AUS, 1954-55. Mem. Am., Calif. bar assns., Sigma Chi. Episcopalian. Home: 43 Farragut Ave Piedmont CA 94610 Office: 120 Montgomery St San Francisco CA 94104

HAILEY, ARTHUR, author; b. Luton, Eng., Apr. 5, 1920; emigrated to Can., naturalized, 1947 (also Brit. citizen); s. George and Elsie (Wright) H.; m. Sheila Dunlop, July 28, 1951; children: Roger, John, Mark (by previous marriage), Jane, Steven, Diane. Student pub. schs., Eng. Author novels: (with John Castle) Runway Zero-Eight, 1958, The Final Diagnosis, 1959, In High Places, 1962, Hotel, 1965, Airport, 1968, Wheels, 1971, The Moneychangers, 1975, Overload, 1979, Strong Medicine, 1984; Author novels pub. in 30 langs.; collected plays Close-up on Writing for Television, 1960; motion pictures include Zero Hour, 1956, Time Lock, 1957, The Young Doctors, 1961, Hotel, 1966, Airport, 1970, The Moneychangers, 1976, Wheels, 1978. Served as pilot/flight lt. RAF, 1939-47. Mem. Writers Guild Am., Authors League Am., Assn. Canadian Television and Radio Artists (hon. life). Home: Lyford Cay PO Box N-7776 Nassau Bahamas Office: Seaway Authors Ltd First Canadian Pl Suite 6000 Toronto ON Canada M5X 1A4

HAIMAN, FRANKLYN SAUL, author, communications educator; b. Cleve., June 23, 1921; s. Alfred Wilfred and Stella (Weiss) H.; m. Louise Goble, June 11, 1955; children—Mark David, Eric Saul. B.A., Case Western Res. U., 1942; M.A., Northwestern U., 1945, Ph.D., 1948. Mem. faculty Northwestern U., Evanston, Ill., 1948—, chmn. dept. communication studies, 1964-75, prof. communication studies and urban affairs, 1970—. Author: Group Leadership and Democratic Action, 1951, Freedom of Speech: Issues and Cases, 1965, Freedom of Speech, 1976, Speech and Law in a Free Society, 1981; co-author: The Dynamics of Discussion, 1960, 2d edit., 1980; editor: book series to Protect These Rights, 1976-77; contbr. articles to profl. jours. Pres. Ill. div. ACLU, 1964-75, nat. bd. dirs., 1965—, nat. corp. sec., 1976-82. Served with USAAF, 1942-45. Mem. Speech Communication Assn., Am. Psychol. Assn., AAUP, Phi Beta Kappa. Home: 824 Ingleside Pl Evanston IL 60201 Office: 1815 Chicago Ave Evanston IL 60201

HAIMAN, IRWIN SANFORD, lawyer; b. Cleve., Mar. 19, 1916; s. Alfred W. and Stella H. (Weiss) H.; m. Jeanne D. Jaffee, Mar. 8, 1942; children: Karen H. Schenkel, Susan L. B.A., Western Res. U., 1937; LL.B., Cleve. Marshall Law Sch., 1941; J.D., Cleve. State U., 1969. Bar: Ohio 1941. Asst. to pres. Tremco Mfg. Co., Cleve., 1936-42; house counsel William Edwards Co., Cleve., 1947-48; pvt. practice, Cleve., 1948-68; ptnr. firm Garber, Simon, Haiman, Gutfeld, Friedman & Jacobs, 1968-80; ptnr. McCarthy, Lebit, Kleinman, Crystal & Haiman, 1981—; lectr. in speech Western Res. U., 1948-70; dir. Washington Fed. Savs. and Loan Assn.; asst. law dir., prosecutor City of Lyndhurst, Ohio, 1965-79, law dir., 1979—. Trustee Montefiore Home, Cleve., 1974—, East End Neighborhood House, Cleve., 1962-68; councilman City of South Euclid, 1948-54, pres., 1952-54; pres. Young People's Congregation, Fairmount Temple, 1951-52; sec., trustee Surburban Temple, 1962-65; chmn. speakers div., bd. dirs. Cleve. chpt. ARC, 1959-62; chmn. speaker and film div. Cleve. United Appeal, 1961-62; chmn. speakers div. Jewish Welfare Fund Cleve., 1973-79. Served as 1st lt. AUS, 1943-47. Mem. Ohio, Cleve. bar assns., Am. Assn. Trial Lawyers, Zeta Beta Tau. Clubs: Oakwood Country, Lake Forest Country (pres. 1971-72, 75-79). Home: 20201 North Park Blvd Shaker Heights OH 44118 Office: 900 Illuminating Bldg Cleveland OH 44113

HAIMAN, ROBERT JAMES, newspaper editor, journalism educator; b. Norwich, Conn., May 6, 1936; s. Albert and Letta (Cone) H.; m. Elizabeth Royce Greenlaw, Sept. 26, 1964; 1 son, Robert Greenlaw. Student, U. Conn., 1953-55; B.S., U. Fla., 1957; postgrad., Am. Press Inst., Columbia U., 1963. Reporter St. Petersburg (Fla.) Times, 1958-60, copy editor, 1962-63, nat. editor, 1964-66, mng. editor, 1966-76, exec. editor, 1976-83; pres., mng. dir. Poynter Inst. Media Studies, 1983—; dir. Times Pub. Co., St. Petersburg, Semit Corp., St. Petersburg, Fla., Trend May. Inc., Times Holding Co., Congressional Quar., Inc., Washington.; Mem. pres. round table Eckerd Coll.; trustee Poynter Inst. Media Studies, St. Petersburg. Mem. pres.'s council U. Fla., U. South Fla. Served with USMC, 1961. Mem. A.P. Mng. Editors (pres. 1982), Am., Fla. socs. newspaper editors, Internat. Press Inst. Zurich, Sigma Delta Chi. Democrat. Presbyterian (elder). Clubs: Racquet, St. Petersburg Yacht, University (St. Petersburg); Bath (Redington Beach, Fla.). Home: 961 31st Terr NE Saint Petersburg FL 33734 Office: 556 Central Ave Saint Petersburg FL 33701

HAIMANN, THEO, author, management science educator; b. Koblenz, Germany, Nov. 17, 1911; came to U.S., 1936, naturalized, 1943; s. Hermann and Auguste (Oppenheimer) H.; m. Ruth G. Treiman, Dec. 31, 1941; children: Carolyn A., Mark H. Ph.D., U. Bonn, Germany, 1934; M.B.A., Washington U., St. Louis, 1956. Pres. Lennox Mfg. Co., 1936-57; mem. faculty U. Ariz., 1957-58, St. Louis U., 1958—, Mary Louise Murray prof. mgmt. sci., 1969—. Author: Professional Management, 1962, Supervisory Management for Hospitals, 1965, Management in the Modern Organization, 1970, 2d edit., 1974, Supervision: Concepts and Practices of Management, 1972, 3d edit., 1982, Supervisory Management For Health Care Institutions, 1973, Managing the Modern Organization, 1978, Management, 1982, Supervisory Management for Health Care Organizations, 3d edit., 1983. Bd. dirs. St. Mary's Hosp., St. Louis. Mem. Acad. Mgmt., Am. Econ. Assn., Beta Gamma Sigma, Alpha Kappa Psi. Home: 4 Robin Hill Saint Louis MO 63124

HAIMES, YACOV YOSSEPH, systems and civil engineering educator, consultant; b. Baghdad, Iraq, June 18, 1936; came to U.S., 1965, naturalized, 1972; s. Yosseph and Rose (Elani) H.; m. Sonia E. Jamison, June 16, 1968; children: Yosef, Michelle. B.S., Hebrew U., Jerusalem, 1964; M.S., U. Calif., 1967, Ph.D. with distinction, 1970. Jr. petroleum engr. Ministry of Devel., Jerusalem, 1962-65; asst. prof. engring. Case-Western Reserve U., Cleve., 1970-71, asso. prof. systems engring., 1971-76, dir. grad. program water resources and systems engring., 1972—, prof. systems engring. and civil engring., 1976—, dir. Center for Large Scale Systems and Policy Analysis, 1980—, chmn. systems engring. dept., 1983—; pres. Environ. Systems Mgmt. Inc., Ohio, 1974—; mem. staff Office of Sci. and Tech. Policy, Exec. Office of President, 1977, Com. on Sci. and Tech., Ho. of Reps., 1978; cons. in field.; chmn. UNESCO Working Group on Water Resources Planning, 1980—; mem. bd. on water sci. and tech. NRC, 1982-84. Author: (with W.A. Hall and H.T. Freedman) Multiobjective Optimization in Water Resources Systems, 1975, Hierarchical Analyses of Water Resources Systems, 1977, (with V. Chanbong) Multiobjective Decision Making: Theory and Methodology, 1983, (with P. Laconte) Water Resources and Land Use Planning, 1982; editor: Energy Auditing and Conservation, 1980, Risk/Benefit Analysis in Water Resources Planning and Management, 1981, Large Scale Systems, 1982; assoc. editor: IEEE Trans. on Systems, Man and Cybernetics, 1979—, Automatica, 1981—, Large Scale Systems: Theory and Applications, 1981—. Fellow IEEE, AAAS, ASCE; mem. Am. Water Resources Assn. (pres. Ohio sect. 1974-75), Univs. Council on Water Resources (chmn. com. on environ. quality 1977-79, dir. 1979—), ASCE (mem. com. on water resources systems 1975-80),

Internat. Fedn. Automatic Control (chmn. working group on water resources 1973—), Am. Automatic Control Council (vice chmn. systems engring. com. 1976-79), Am. Geophys. Union (mem. com. on water resources systems 1970-74, chmn. water resource environ. mgmt. com. 1980-82), Ops. Research Soc. Israel, Ops. Research Soc. Am., Internat. Water Resources Assn., Sigma Xi (past pres. local chpt.), Tau Beta Pi. Home: 14361 Washington Blvd University Heights OH 44118 Office: Dept Systems Engring Case Western Reserve U Cleveland OH 44106

HAIMO, DEBORAH TEPPER, mathematics educator; b. Odessa, Ukraine, July 1, 1921; d. Joseph Meir and Esther (Vodovoz) Tepper; m. Franklin Haimo, Feb. 27, 1944; children: Zara Tepper, Ethan Tepper, Leah Tepper, Nina Tepper, Varda Tepper. A.B. magna cum laude, Radcliffe Coll., 1943, A.M., 1943; Ph.D., Harvard, 1964. Acting head math. dept. Lake Erie Coll., 1943-44; instr. Northeastern U., 1944-45; lectr. Washington U., St. Louis, 1948-61; lectr., asst. prof., asso. prof. So. Ill. U., Edwardsville, 1961-68; prof. math. U. Mo., St. Louis, 1968—, chmn. dept. math., 1969-76; mem. Inst. Advanced Study, 1972-73; mem. coll. level exam. program Ednl. Testing Service, 1976—; Mem. team for feasibility study grad. programs Seoul Nat. U., Korea, 1974. Editor: Orthogonal Expansions and their Continous Analogues, 1968; Editorial bd.: Am. Math. Monthly, 1978—, Soc. Indsl. and Applied Math. Jour. on Math. Analysis, 1971—; Contbr. articles to profl. jours. Trustee Radcliffe Coll., 1975—. NASA research grantee, 1966-69; NSF grantee, 1969-71; NSF sci. faculty fellow, 1964-65; USAF Sci. Research grantee, 1971-74. Mem. Am. Math. Soc., Math. Assn. Am. (gov. at large 1974-77), Soc. Indsl. and Applied Math., AAUP, Assn. for Women in Math., Assn. Mems. Inst. Advanced Study (trustee), Phi Beta Kappa., Sigma Xi, Phi Kappa Phi. Home: 7201 Cornell Ave Saint Louis MO 63130

HAINES, COLIN ARTHUR, manufacturing company executive; b. Rugby, Eng., Nov. 17, 1922; s. Arthur and Winifred (Cobleigh) H.; m. Wanda Valerie Ferrier, Nov. 6, 1944; 1 dau., Gretchen.; m. Lorna Jean Cave, Sept. 26, 1981. B.A., Balliol Coll., Oxford U., 1942, M.A., 1950. Cert. gen. accountant, Ont. With Hawker Siddeley Can. Inc., Toronto, 1950—, corp. sec., 1976—, also dir. Served as pilot RAF, 1942-50. Fellow Inst. Chartered Secs. and Adminstrs. Anglican. Office: 7 King St E Toronto ON M5C 1A3 Canada

HAINES, LEWIS FRANCIS, emeritus humanities educator; b. Endicott, N.Y., Oct 28, 1907; s. William Joseph and Teresa Irene (Lewis) H.; m. Helen Mary Steere, Sept 1, 1930; 1 son, James Lewis. A.B., U. Mich., 1930, A.M., 1932, Ph.D., 1941. Instr. English Boys' Tech. High Sch., Milw., 1930-34; teaching fellow English U. Mich., 1935-41, instr. English, summer 1941; acting instr. English U. Fla., 1941-42, asst. prof., 1942-46, prof. humanities, 1946-67, prof. humanities and comprehensive logic, 1967-73, prof. humanities and behavioral studies, 1973-77, prof. emeritus, 1977—; editor U. Fla. Press, 1945-67, dir., 1949-67; cons. specialist New Century Cyclopedia of Names. Contbr. to: New Century Handbook of English Literature, World Book Ency., Collier's Ency.; Contbr. also to scholastic and lit. jours. Mem. Gov's Hwy. Safety Conf. Recipient Rockefeller research grant, summer 1962. Mem. MLA, South Atlantic MLA, AAUP, Nat. Council Tchrs. English, Fla. Hist. Soc., Newcomen Soc. N.A., Assn. Am. U. Presses, Am. Book Pubs. Council, Acad. Polit. Sci., Assn. for Latin Am. Studies, Phi Kappa Phi, Kappa Phi Sigma. Home: 23 SW 26th St Gainesville FL 32607 Office: Little Hall U Fla Gainesville FL 32611

HAINES, PERRY VANSANT, cattle company executive; b. Middletown, Ohio, Mar. 14, 1944; s. John Percy and Pendery (Spear) H.; m. Sidonie M. Sexton, 1982. A.B., Princeton U., 1967; M.B.A., Harvard U., 1970. Research asst. Harvard U., 1970-71; cons. Boston Cons. Group, 1971-74; exec. v.p. IBP, Inc. (formerly Iowa Beef Processors), Dakota City, Nebr., 1974—; v.p. Occidental Petroleum, Los Angeles, 1981—. Served with USMCR, 1967-68. Office: PO Box 515 Dakota City NE 68731

HAINES, RICHARD FOSTER, psychologist; b. Seattle, May 19, 1937; s. Donald Hutchinson and Claudia May (Bennett) H.; m. Carol Taylor, June 17, 1961; children: Cynthia Lynn, Laura Anne. Student, U. Wash., 1955-57; B.A., Pacific Luth. Coll., Tacoma, 1960; M.A., Mich. State U., 1962, Ph.D., 1964. Predoctoral research fellow NIH, 1964; Nat. Acad. Sci. postdoctoral resident research assoc. Ames Research Ctr. NASA, Moffett Field, Calif., 1964-67, research scientist, 1967—; cons. Stanford U. Sch. Medicine, 1966-67, TRW-Systems Group, 1969-70; mem. adv. com. on vision NRC; founding mem. advanced tech. applications com. Calif. Council AIA, 1975-80, NASA, 1975-80; mem. adv. bd. Space Scis. Ctr.-Foothill Coll., 1976-78; bd. advisors Fund for UFO Research, Washington. Author: UFO Phenomena and the Behavioral Scientist, 1979, Observing UFOs, 1980; contbr. articles to profl. jours.; patentee device for advanced detection of glaucoma, optical projector of vision performance data for design engrs. Mem. Palo Alto (Calif.) Mayor's Com. on Youth Activities, 1967; chmn. adv. council Christian Community Progress Corp., Menlo Park (Calif.); v.p., dir. Ctr. Counseling for Drug Abuse, Menlo Park; bd. dirs., chmn. sci. adv. team Threshold Found. Named Alumnus of Yr. Pacific Luth. U., 1972. Fellow Aerospace Med. Assn. (assoc.); mem. Optical Soc. Am., Midwestern Psychol. Assn., Assn. Aviation Psychologists, Internat. Soc. Air Safety Investigators, Soc. for Sci. Exploration, Sigma Xi. Home: 825 Langton Ave Los Altos CA 94022 Office: Ames Research Ctr NASA Moffett Field CA 94035

HAINES, ROBERT EARL, industrial construction executive; b. Kingston, N.Y., Mar. 27, 1929; s. Willis Holcomb and Helen (Earl) H.; m. Roxanne Weber, Oct. 29, 1976; children—Rebecca, Peter, Sarah, Martha. B.S. in C.E, Duke U., 1949. Lic. profl. engr., N.Y., Pa., Ohio, Ind., Ill., Tenn. With J. M. Foster, Inc., Gary, Ind., 1957—, v.p. engring., 1963-70, pres., 1970—. Mem. Ind. Gov.'s Water Resources Commn. Served with C.E. AUS, 1951-53. Mem. Nat. Soc. Profl. Engrs., Assn. Iron and Steel Engrs. Clubs: Gary Country (Merrillville, Ind.); Hunkee Hollow Athletic (Hobart, Ind.); Gary (Ind.) Country; Duquesne, Oakmont Country (Pitts.). Home: 4866 W 84th Terr Crown Point IN 46307 Office: J M Foster Inc PO Box M 750 Gary IN 46401

HAINES, WALTER WELLS, educator; b. Stamford, Conn., Dec. 1, 1918; s. Thomas Kelly Peterson and Carrie Hooker (Williams) H.; m. Hazel Ellen Maxwell, Jan. 1, 1945; children: Jennifer Jean, Deborah Lee, Pamela Ann, Christopher Alan, Liseli Ellen, Timothy Maxwell. B.A., U. Pa., 1940, M.A., 1941; M.A., Harvard, 1942, Ph.D. (Lehman nat. fellow 1941-43), 1943. Instr. econs. Kenyon Coll., 1946-47; mem. faculty N.Y. U., 1947—, prof. econs., 1960—, chmn. dept., 1956-68, dir. undergrad. studies, 1983—; adminstr. Friends Hosp., Tiriki, Kenya, 1969-70; Fulbright prof. econs. U. Peshawar, Pakistan, 1962-63; Fulbright prof. environ. conservation Middle East Tech. U., Ankara, Turkey, 1973-74. Author: Money, Prices and Policy, 1961, also articles. Fellow Internat. Inst. for Social Econs.; mem. AAAS, Am. Econ. Assn., Atlantic Econ. Assn., Eastern Econ. Assn., Fellowship of Reconciliation, Soc. Internat. Devel., Fedn. Am. Scientists, Scientists Inst. Pub. Info., Assn. for Social Econs., Phi Beta Kappa. Mem. Religious Soc. of Friends. Home: 30 Dogwood Ln Pomona NY 10970 Office: New York U New York NY 10003 *The wellspring of my life is a belief that there is something of God in every person. From this universality of the divine spark emerge many principles of faith; the brotherhood of man, the importance of the golden rule, the primacy of love. These in turn call for social action to promote civil rights, nondiscrimination, peace, cooperation, democracy, world equality, the preservation of a quality environment, and conservation of resources for future generations. I have no illusion that this belief has brought me "success," but it has contributed much to the richness of life.*

HAINES, WILLIAM WISTER, author; b. Des Moines, Sept., 1908; s. Diedrich Jansen and Ella Eustis (Wister) H.; m. Frances Tuckerman, Sept., 1934; children William Wister, Laura Tuckerman (Mrs. Murray Belman). B.S., U. Pa., 1931. Author: Slim, 1934, High Tension, 1938, Command Decision, 1947, The Honorable Rocky Slade, 1957, The Winter War, 1961, Target, 1964, The Image, 1968; also mag. stories, motion picture scripts, play Command Decision. Commd. 1st lt. AC AUS, 1942; relieved of active duty as lt. col., 1945. Address: 33751 Brigantine Dr Laguna Niguel CA 92677

HAINEY, RICHARD WILLIS, educator, former newspaper editor; b. McCook, Nebr., June 1, 1922; s. Conrad Patrick and Esther (Skoog) H.; m. Helene Starkey, June 16, 1945; 1 son, Mark F. B.S. in Journalism, Northwestern U., 1945, M.S., 1945. Mem. staff Chgo. Tribune, 1947-61; exec. editor Chgo. Today, 1961-74; lectr. Medill Sch. Journalism Northwestern U., 1947-74, prof., 1974—. Mem. City News Bur., Chgo. (pres.), Mid-Am. Press Inst. (pres.), Sigma Delta Chi. Home: 6768 Dowagiac Ave Chicago IL 60646 Office: Fisk Hall Northwestern U Evanston IL 60201

HAINFELD, FREDERICK, JR., banker; b. Oyster Bay, N.Y., June 10, 1909; s. Frederick and Margaret (Taylor) H.; m. Aletheia Garrison, May 3, 1942; children: Linda Carol, James Frederick. Student, Am. Inst. Banking, also Bankers Inst. Advanced Mgmt., 1952; LL.D., Adelphi U., 1975. With Corn Exchange Bank & Trust Co., N.Y.C., 1925- 27, State Bank of Sea Cliff, N.Y., 1927-29; with L.I. Trust Co. (formerly Garden City Bank & Trust Co.), 1929-43, 45—, pres., 1954-68, chief exec. officer, dir., chmn. bd., 1968-74, dir., 1975-81, dir. emeritus, 1981—; with Southside Bank of Bay Shore, L.I., N.Y., 1944-45; trustee Roosevelt Savs. Bank, 1970—; chmn. bd. Litco Corp., Garden City, N.Y., 1972-74, dir., 1975—, Vicon Industries Inc., Plainview, N.Y.; mem. adv. council L.I. Better Bus. Bur., 1960—. Mem. com. on pub. library service N.Y. State commr. edn., 1956-57; treas. ann. appeal Salvation Army, Garden City, 1954-59; pres. Tax and Estate Planning Council L.I., 1949; mem., chmn. fin. com. Nassau County council Boy Scouts Am., 1957-64, v.p., 1962, exec. bd., 1957—, chmn. trust fund, com., 1968-77; treas. Health and Welfare Council Nassau County, 1957-58, now mem.; pres., dir. L.I. Fund Industry, Labor and Commerce for Hosps., Health and Welfare, 1959-65, chmn. bd., 1963-65; Trustee Garden City Library, 1956-59; trustee Adelphi U., 1961—, treas., 1962-65, mem. exec. com., 1962—, finance com., 1964—, vice chmn. bd. trustees, 1965; trustee United Way L.I., 1965—; mem. governing bd. Human Resources Center, 1971—. Recipient awards Garden City Jr. C. of C., Silver Beaver award Boy Scouts Am. Mem. L.I. Pub. Relations Assn., Garden City C. of C. (pres., dir. 1957-58, award 1970), L.I. Bankers Assn. (chmn., dir. 1959-61). Clubs: Mason, Rotary; Garden City Golf, Cherry Valley (Garden City); Ponte Vedra (Fla.). Home: 20 Cedar Pl Garden City NY 11530 Office: 1401 Franklin Ave: Garden City NY 11530

HAIPLIK, THEODOR WILLIAM, paperboard packaging executive; b. Hamilton, Ont., Can., Apr. 10, 1934; s. Theodor Isidor and Mary (Braun) H.; children: Brenda Mary, Susan Kirsten. B.Sc., U. Toronto, 1956; M.B.A., McMaster U., 1966; postgrad., Harvard Bus. Sch., 1977. Registered profl. engr., Ont. Various positions in line and staff mfg. TRW (Can.), St. Catharines, Ont., 1957-66; dir. mfg. Container div. Bathurst Paper Ltd., Montreal, 1966-67; dir. mktg. services Consol. Bathurst Packaging Ltd., Montreal, 1967-69, area mgr. Container div., 1973-74, v.p. Container div., 1977-83, sr. v.p., gen. mgr. Container div., Mississauga, Ont., 1974-83; pres., chief exec. officer MacMillan Bathurst Inc., Mississauga, Ont., 1983—; mem. mgmt. com. Europa Carton AG, Hamburg, W. Ger., 1969-73. Mem. Assn. Prof. Engrs. Ont., Tech. Assn. Pulp & Paper Industries, Packaging Assn. Can. (dir.), Can. Corrugated Case Assn. (dir.), Internat. Corrugated Case Assn. Home: 577 Cochise Crescent Mississauga Ont. Canada L5H 1Y4 Office: MacMillan Bathurst Inc 2070 Hadwen Rd Mississauga Ont Canada L5K 2C9

HAIR, JAY DEE, association executive; b. Miami, Fla., Nov. 30, 1945; s. Wilbur R. and Ruth A. Johnson; m. Rebecca McDaniel, May 17, 1970; children: Whitney, Lindsay. B.S., Clemson U., 1967, M.S., 1969; Ph.D., U. Alta., 1975; postgrad., Govt. Execs. Inst., Sch. Bus. Adminstrn., U. N.C., 1980. Grad. teaching asst. entomology/zoology Clemson (S.C.) U., 1968-69, asst. prof. wildlife biology, 1977-81; grad. research fellow zoology U. Alta., Can., 1969-70; assoc. prof. zoology/forestry, adminstr. fisheries and wildlife scis. N.C. State U., Raleigh, 1977-81, adj. prof. zoology and forestry, 1982—; exec. v.p. Nat. Wildlife Fedn., Washington, 1981—; research and mgmt. cons. S.C. Wildlife/Marine Resources Dept., 1976-77; spl. asst. to asst. sec. for fish, wildlife and parks Dept. Interior, 1978-80; mem. Nat. Petroleum Council, Dept. Energy, 1981. Editor: Ecological Perspectives of Wildlife Management, 1977; contbr. articles to profl. jours. Bd. govs. Nat. Shooting Sports Found., 1981—; mem. conservation com. Boy Scouts Am., 1981; pres. N.C. Cued Speech Assn., 1978-81; chmn. bd. dirs. Cued Speech Ctr., Inc., 1979-81; bd. dirs. Parents and Profls. for Handicapped Children, N.C., 1979-81; mem. Wake County Hearing-Impaired Assn., (N.C.), 1978—; pres. Alexander Graham Bell Nat. Assn. Deaf, 1979. Served to 1st lt. U.S. Army, 1970-71. Named S.C. Wildlife Conservationist of Yr. Gov.'s Annual Conservation Awards Program, 1977; N.C. Conservationist of Yr., 1980; N.C. Gov.'s award for pub. service. Mem. Wildlife Soc. (Disting. Service award Southeastern sect. 1980), Soc. Am. Foresters, AAAS, Internat. Assn. Fish and Wildlife Agys., Ducks Unltd., Am. Wildlife Assn. for Resource Edn., N.C. Acad. Scis., N.C. Wildlife Fedn., S.C. Wildlife Assn. for Resource Edn., N.C. Acad. Scis., N.C. Wildlife Fedn., S.C. Wildlife Fedn. (F. Bartow Culp disting. service to conservation award 1978, Disting. Service award Southeast sect. 1980, Nat. Wildlife Fedn. Outstanding Affiliate award 1978), Am. Fisheries Soc., Am. Forestry Assn., Assn. Univ. Fisheries and Wildlife Program Adminstrs., Scabbard and Blade, Tiger Brotherhood, Blue Key, Phi Kappa Delta. Methodist. Office: 1412 16th St NW Washington DC 20036

HAIRE, BILL MARTIN, fashion designer; b. N.Y.C., Sept. 30, 1936; s. William Francis and Margaret Ann (Beatty) H.; m. Hazel Jean Keleher, Feb. 26, 1956. Asso. Applied Sci., Fashion Inst. Tech., 1955. Asst. designer Sam Friedlander, Inc., N.Y.C., 1956-58; designer Victoria Royal, Ltd., N.Y.C., 1960-74; v.p., designer Friedricks Sport, N.Y.C., 1974—; founder Bill Haire Ltd., 1981—. Designer costumes for, John Butler/Giancarlo Menotti Ballet, Sebastian, 1978; lic. collection for Matsuzakaya, Tokyo Style Co. Ltd., 1980; designer uniforms for, Eastern Airlines, 1980—. Recipient Mortimer C. Ritter award, 1976; Flying Colors award Braniff Airlines, 1977; Gold Coast award, 1979; Image of yr. award for Eastern Airline uniforms Nat. Assn. Uniform Mfrs. and Distbrs., 1982, 83. Mem. Fashion Designers of Am. (council). Clubs: Atrium, Galleria (N.Y.C.). Office: 205 W 39th St New York NY 10018

HAIRE, JAMES, stage mgr.; b. Phoenix, Oct. 21, 1940; s. James Clifford and Dorothy (Crum) H. B.F.A., U. Ariz., 1960; M.A., Northwestern U., 1962. Cons. in field. Producer: Little Eyolf, Actors Playhouse, 1964, Arms and the Man, E. End Theater, N.Y.C., 1964; stage mgr., Nat. Repertory Theater, 1965-67, Ford's Theater, Washington, 1968-69, Woody Allen's Don't Drink the Water, nat. tour, 1969, 70; new musical Georgy, Wintergarden, N.Y.C., 1969, Slow Dance on the Killing Ground, 1970, And Miss Reardon Drinks a Little, 1971; prodn. stage mgr., tour coordinator, Am. Conservatory Theater, San Francisco, 1971—. Overall winner Chgo. Mackinac race, 1981. Address: 450 Geary St San Francisco CA 94102

HAIRE, JOHN RUSSELL, organization executive, lawyer; b. Newport, R.I., Feb. 11, 1925; s. J. Russell and Pauline (Houghton) H.; m. Doris J. Buttry, Aug. 26, 1945; children: Elizabeth, Paul, Lynn. Student, Brown U., 1942-43; LL.B. cum laude, Harvard U., 1950. Bar: Mass. 1950. Assoc. Nutter, McClennen & Fish, Boston, 1950-51; legal, exec. asst. to Hon. William H. Vanderbilt, 1951-53; spl. asst. to pres. N.Y. Stock Exchange, 1953-54, sec., 1955-56, v.p. charge relations govtl. agencies and nat. orgns., 1956-59; v.p., sec. Hugh W. Long & Co., Inc., Fundamental Investors, other investment cos., 1959-62; exec. v.p., sec. Anchor Corp., Fundamental Investors, other investment cos., 1962-64; chmn. Anchor Corp., 1964-78; pres. Council Fin. Aid to Edn., 1978—; bd. mem. Ind. Coll. Funds Am., United Student Aid Funds, Joint Council on Econ. Edn., Investment Co. Inst.; dir. Washington Nat. Corp., Washington Nat. Life Ins. Co. N.Y., Anchor Nat. Life Ins. Co., Bowne & Co., Dean Witter/Sears Mutual Funds; past chmn. Investment Co. Inst. Past pres. Family and Children's Soc., Vail-Deane Sch., Elizabeth, N.J.; past trustee N.J. Symphony, Pingry Sch.; past chmn. Elizabeth Gen. Hosp.; past pres. Internat. Childbirth Edn. Assn., Inc. Served with AUS, 1943-47; ETO; sgt. maj. 18th Mechanized Cav. Squadron, 1945-47. Clubs: Univ.; Econ. (N.Y.C.). Home: 439 E 51 St New York NY 10022 Office: 680 Fifth Ave New York NY 10019

HAIRSTON, NELSON GEORGE, animal ecologist; b. Davie County, N.C., Oct. 16, 1917; s. Peter Wilson and Margaret Elmer (George) H.; m. Martha Turner Patton, Aug. 19, 1942; children: Martha Patton, Nelson George, Margaret Elmer. A.B., U. N.C., 1937, M.A., 1939; Ph.D., Northwestern U., 1948. Instr. U. Mich., 1948-52, asst. prof., 1952-57, asso. prof., 1957-61, prof., 1961-75; dir. Mus. Zoology, 1967-75; William R. Kenan, Jr. prof. zoology and ecology U. N.C., Chapel Hill, 1975—; adviser, cons.; mem. expert adv. com. on parasitic diseases WHO, Philippines, Iraq, Switzerland, Egypt, Sudan, Kenya, Tanzania, Rhodesia, South Africa, Ghana, Western Samoa, 1964-81; mem. tropical medicine and parasitology study sect. NIH, Bethesda, Md., 1965-70; chmn. adv. com. on biol. and med. scis. NSF, Washington, 1972. Contbr. articles on ecology to profl. jours. Served with AUS, 1941-46. NSF research grantee, 1960-68. Mem. Am. Soc. Naturalists, Ecol. Soc. Am., Soc. for Study Evolution, Brit. Ecol. Soc., Am. Soc. Ichthyologists and Herpetologists, AAAS, Am. Inst. Biol. Scis., Sigma Xi. Home: 1008 Highland Woods Chapel Hill NC 27514 Office: Dept Biology Wilson Hall 046A U NC Chapel Hill NC 27514

HAIRSTON, WILLIAM RUSSELL, JR., public administrator; b. Goldsboro, N.C., Apr. 1, 1928; s. William Russell and Malissa (Carter) H.; m. Enid Carey, June 2, 1957; 1 dau., Ann Marie. B.A., U. No. Colo. Editor D.C. Pipeline, 1973-78; pub. adminstr. city govt., Washington, 1978—. Author, producer: plays Walk in Darkness; author: Swan Song of the 11th Dawn; author, producer, dir.: Curtain Call Mr. Aldridge, Sir; dir.: Jerico-Jim Crow; writer films and TV shows for, USIA, Social Security Adminstrn.; theatre mgr., adminstr., N.Y. Shakespeare Festival, 1963-66, Greenwich Mews Theatre, 1963, Arena Stage, Washington, 1965-66; actor: film Take the High Ground, 1953; also appeared TV shows, off-Broadway, tour and summer stock appearances. Chmn. D.C. Police and Firefighters Retirement and Relief Bd.; Active Nat. Capital Area council Boy Scouts Am. Ford Found. grantee, 1965; Nat. Endowment for the Arts grantee, 1967. Mem. Am. Soc. Pub. Adminstrn., Am. Soc. Tng. and Devel., Authors League, Dramatists Guild. Address: 9909 Conestoga Way Potomac MD 20854 *Determine your ambition, set your goal, then be prepared to accept change and embrace opportunity in order to achieve success.*

HAISE, FRED WALLACE, JR., aerospace company executive, former astronaut; b. Biloxi, Miss., Nov. 14, 1933; s. Fred Wallace and Lucille (Blacksher) H.; m. Mary Griffin Grant, June 4, 1954; children: Mary Margaret, Frederick Thomas, Stephen William, Thomas Jesse. A.A., Perkinston Jr. Coll., 1952; B.S. in Aero Engring, U. Okla., 1959; D.Sc. (hon.), Western Mich. U. Naval aviation cadet USN, 1952-54; fighter pilot USMC, 1954-56, Air N.G., Okla., Ohio, 1957-63; capt. USAF, 1961-62; research pilot NASA Lewis Research Center, Cleve., 1959-63, NASA Flight Research Center, Edwards AFB, Calif., 1963-66; astronaut NASA Manned Spacecraft Center, Houston, 1966-77; comdr. Space Shuttle Orbiter Crew, 1977-79; v.p. for space programs Grumman Aerospace Corp., Bethpage, N.Y., 1979—; mem. crew Apollo 13, 1970; backup comdr. Apollo 16, 1972. Active Indian Guides YMCA, Lancaster, Calif. Recipient AB Honts trophy USAF Aerospace Research Pilot Sch., Edwards AFB, 1964; Presdl. Medal Freedom; Miss. Distinguished Civilian Service Medal; Jeff Davis award; Pine Burr award; City Houston Medal Valour. Mem. Soc. Exptl. Test Pilots, Phi Theta Kappa, Tau Beta Pi, Sigma Gamma Tau. Address: Grumman Aerospace Corp 1111 Stewart Ave Bethpage NY 11714 *

HAIT, GERSHON, pediatric cardiologist; b. May 10, 1927; U.S., 1952, naturalized, 1965; s. Nahum and Leah H.; m. Doris J. Coburn, Mar. 20, 1957; children: Jonathan, Yael. M.D., U. Lausanne, Switzerland, 1952. Intern Michael Reese Hosp., Chgo., 1952-53; resident Cook County Hosp., Chgo., 1961-62, fellow in pediatric cardiology, 1954-56, 59-60; instr. pediatrics, NIH fellow in pediatric cardiology Albert Einstein Coll. Medicine, Bronx, N.Y., 1962-64, dir. pediatric cardiology, 1966—, prof. pediatrics, 1979—, also mem. med. staff; mem. staff Bronx Mcpl. Hosp. Center, Montefiore, Booth Meml., New Rochelle, Flushing, and Arden Hill hosps., cardiac cons. to depts. of health of, Bronx, S.I., and; Rockland counties. Contbr. articles to profl. jours. Served to lt. M.C. Israeli Army, 1956-59. Grantee NIH, Am. Heart Assn., others. Mem. Am. Physiology Soc., Soc. for Pediatric Research, Am. Acad. Pediatrics, Am. Fedn. Clin. Research, Am. Heart Assn., Am. Coll. Cardiology, N.Y. Heart Assn. Jewish. Home: 14 Withington Rd Scarsdale NY 10583 Office: 1300 Morris Park Ave Bronx NY 10461

HAIT, RICHARD SCOTT, packaged goods manufacturing executive; b. Detroit, Dec. 17, 1926; s. France Scott and Helen (Brown) H.; m. Jean Kathleen Leonard, Aug. 19,1949; children: Stephen, Judith, Andrew, Winston. B.B.A., U. Mich., Ann Arbor, 1949. Mgr. advt. food div. Procter & Gamble Co., Cin., 1962-69, v.p. Can., Toronto, 1969-71, dir. pub. and community relations, Cin., 1971-81, exec. dir. Cin. Resource Devel. Com., 1981—. Editor: Eyes on Tomorrow, 1981. Vice chmn. Southwest Ohio Transit Authority, Cin., 1973-77; chmn. Sta. WCET-TV Pub. Broadcasting, Cin., 1979-82, Pub. Affairs Council Conf. Bd., N.Y.C., 1979-80; chmn. exec. com. Jobs for Cin. Grads., Inc., 1982—. Served with U.S. Navy, 1945-46; Korea. Republican. Episcopalian. Clubs: Cin. Country, Univ. (Cin.). Home: 3434 Principio St Cincinnati OH 45226

HAIZLIP, HENRY HARDIN, JR., former banker, real estate consultant; b. Pine Bluff, Ark., Dec. 18, 1913; s. Henry Hardin and Rebecca (Porter) H.; m. Emily Williamson, Feb. 15, 1947; children: Henry Hardin III, Wilson, Jean Hunter, Selden. Student, Tulane U., 1932-33. With W.N. Ballou Cotton Co., Memphis, 1933-36; with First

Nat. Bank Memphis, 1936-73, exec. v.p., 1968-70, chmn. exec. com., 1970-73; pres. First Memphis Realty Trust, 1970-73, chmn., 1973—; pres. First Tenn. Corp., 1973—; real estate cons. Haizlip/Lovitt, Memphis, 1979—; dir. Valmac Industries, Inc., Union Service Industries Inc.; vice chmn. First Tenn. Nat. Corp., until 1979; ret.; instr. in mortgage financing La. State U., Ohio State U. Pres. Memphis Cotton Carnival Assn., 1966, bd. dirs., 1967—; vice chmn. Shelby United Good Neighbors, 1967-68; mem. Chickasaw council Boy Scouts Am.; pres. Future Memphis, Inc., 1974—; Bd. dirs. Memphis and Shelby County unit Am. Cancer Soc., 1967-68; trustee Memphis Plough Community Found.; mem. pres.'s council Tulane U., New Orleans. Served to capt. AUS, 1941-46. Mem. Am. Bankers Assn., Downtown Assn. Memphis (chmn. bd.), Kappa Alpha. Episcopalian. Clubs: Memphis Country; Menasha Hunting and Fishing (Turrell, Ark.); Memphis Hunt and Polo. Home: 965 Audubon Dr Memphis TN 38117 Office: 6070 Quince Rd Memphis TN 38119

HAJEK, OTOMAR, mathematics educator; b. Beograd, Serbia, Jugoslavia, Dex. 22, 1930; came to U.S., 1966, naturalized, 1974; s. Frantisek Josef and Ruzena (Houdekova) H.; m. Olga Barbara Memcova, Jan. 23, 1928; 1 son, Michael F.A. Diploma math., Caroline U., Prague, Czechoslovakia, 1953, Candidate sci., 1953, R.N.Dr., 1965. Asst. prof. Czechoslovak Inst. Tech., Prague, 1953-56; sci. officer Research Inst. Computing Machinery, Prague, 1960-65; sr. sci. officer Caroline U., Prague, 1965-66; assoc. prof. Case Western Res. U., Cleve., 1966-69, prof. math., 1969—. Author: (with N.P. Bhatia) Dynamical Systems in the Plane, 1968, Local Semi-Dynamical Systems, 1969, Pursuit Games, 1975; co-editor: Global Differentiable Dynamics, 1970. Recipient Von Humboldt award, 1975; Deutsche Forschungsgemeinschaft fellow, Bonn., 1979. Mem. Am. Math. Soc., Union Czechoslovakian Mathematicians and Physicists (math. com. 1965-66), Gesellschaft Ang Math und Mechanik. Lutheran. Office: Math Dept Case Western Res U University Circle Cleveland OH 44106

HAJIM, EDMUND A., investment company executive; b. Los Angeles, July 26, 1936; s. Jack and Sally H.; m. Barbara E. Melnick, Aug. 8, 1965; children: Geoffrey Blair, Jon Bradley, Corey Brooke. B.S., U. Rochester, 1958; M.B.A., Harvard U., 1964. Research analyst Capital Research Co. subs. Capital Group, Inc., N.Y.C., 1964-66, office mgr., 1966-67; v.p., dir. Capital Mgmt. Service, 1967-69; pres. Greenwich Mgmt. Co., Conn., 1969; pres., dir. Growth Fund Am., 1969-70, Income Fund Am., 1970; sr. v.p. E.F. Hutton, Nat. Instl. Equity, N.Y.C., 1974-77; partner, mng. dir. Lehman Bros., N.Y.C., 1977, pres. securities div., 1977-79; partner, mng. dir., dir. Lehman Bros. Kuhn Loeb & Kuhn Loeb Lehman Bros. Internat., N.Y.C.; chmn. Lehman Mgmt. Co., Inc., N.Y.C.; chmn., dir. Lehman Corp., One William St. Fund, Lehman Cash Mgmt. Fund; chmn. Lehman Capital Fund, Furman Selz Mager Dietz & Birney, Furman Selz Asset Mgmt.; dir. Clabir Corp., Greenwich, Conn. Past chmn. bd. trustees Brunswick Sch., Greenwich; mem. pres. council U. Rochester, 1975—. Served with USN, 1958-61. Mem. Inst. Chartered Fin. Analysts, Fin. Analysts Fedn., N.Y. Soc. Security Analysts (past dir.). Clubs: Bond, Harvard, Wall Street (N.Y.C.); Greenwich Skating, Burning Tree Country (Greenwich). Office: Furman Selz Mager Dietz & Birney Inc 110 Wall St New York NY 10005

HAKALA, THOMAS RICHARD, urological surgeon; b. Sault Ste. Marie, Mich., June 15, 1936. B.A. in Biology, Stanford U., 1958; M.D., Harvard U., 1961. Diplomate: Am. Bd. Urology. Intern, then resident in gen. surgery Mass. Gen. Hosp., Boston, 1961-63, resident in urology, 1965-68; vis. investigator div. immunology, surgery br. Nat. Cancer Inst., 1969-71; asso. chief urology sect. Mpls. VA Hosp., 1971-75, chief, 1975; asst. chief urology sect. Oakland VA Hosp., Pitts., 1975—; instr. surgery U. Calif. Med. Sch., Davis, 1958-69, asst. prof., 1969; dir. dept. urology Sacramento Med. Center, 1968-69; asso. rpof. U. Minn. Med. Sch., 1975; mem. faculty U. Pitts., 1975—, prof. urol. surgery, 1975—, chief div., 1975—. Contbr. numerous articles to med. jours. Served with USPHS, 1963-65. Mem. A.C.S., Am. Soc. Transplant Surgeons, Am. Urol. Assn., Assn. Acad. Surgery, Pa. Med. Soc., Soc. Internat. D'urologie, Soc., Surg. Oncology, Soc. U. Urologists, Urology Investigators Forum. Office: 230 Lothrop St Suite 4414 Pittsburgh PA 15213

HAKEEM, MICHAEL, sociologist, educator; b. Fall River, Mass., Sept. 5, 1916; s. Joseph and Sophia (Daghir) H.; m. Helen Louise Cook, June 8, 1949. B.S., Ohio State U., 1942, M.A., 1945, Ph.D., 1950. Sociologist Ill. Div. Criminology, 1943-46; instr. State U. Iowa, 1946-47; instr., then asst. prof. Ohio State U., 1948-52; mem. faculty U. Wis., Madison, 1952—, prof. sociology, 1962—. Contbr. articles to profl. jours. Fellow Am. Sociol. Assn.; mem. Soc. Study Social Problems (exec. com. 1961-64), Nat. Conf. Delinquency and Crime. Home: 517 Caldy Pl Madison WI 53711

HAKEMIAN, JOHN PRESTON, financial services company executive; b. Chgo., May 7, 1939; s. George M. and Lillie Mae (Holcomb) H.; m. Janice Margaret Welch, Aug. 17, 1973; children: Thomas, Jennifer, James, Elizabeth; 1 step-dau., Sandra Terry. B.S., Ariz. State U., 1961; M.B.A., U. Mich., 1972. With Ill. Bell., Chgo., 1961-67, Chrysler Corp., Highland Park, Mich., 1968-72; v.p. Chrysler Fin. Corp., Troy, Mich., 1973-77; treas. Pullman Inc. (Trailmobile), Chgo., 1977-79; pres. Trailmobile Fin. Co. Corp., 1977-80, Harvest Fin. Services, Inc., Barrington, Ill., 1980-81, Interet Corp., Phila., 1981—; sr. v.p. fin. Geothermal Resources Internat., 1983—. Home: One Hunt Club Ln Malvern PA 19355 Office: 1700 Three Penn Center Philadelphia PA 19102

HAKIMI, S. LOUIS, electrical engineering educator; b. Meshed, Iran, Dec. 16, 1932; came to U.S., 1952, naturalized, 1967; s. A. Moshe and Miriam (Nabavian) H.; m. Mary Yomtob, Aug. 22, 1965; children: Alan, Carol, Diane. B.S. in Elec. Engring., U. Ill., Urbana, 1955, M.S., 1957, Ph.D., 1959. Asst. prof. elec. engring. U. Ill., 1959-61; asso. prof. Northwestern U., Evanston, Ill., 1961-66, prof., 1966—, chmn. dept. elec. engring., 1972-77. Asso. editor: Networks, 1975—; Assoc. editor: IEEE Transactions on Circuits and Systems, 1975-77. Fellow IEEE; mem. Soc. Indsl. and Applied Math., Sigma Xi, Tau Beta Pi, Phi Kappa Phi. Home: 2651 Oak Ave Northbrook IL 60062 Office: Dept Elec Engring and Computer Sci Northwestern U Evanston IL 60201

HAKIMOGLU, AYHAN, electronics company executive; b. Erbaa, Turkey, Aug. 19, 1927; came to U.S., 1955; s. Mekki and Mediha H.; m. Geraldine An Crilley, Nov. 19, 1982; children by previous marriage: Zeynep B., Incigul R., Deborah A., Leyla P. B.S.E.E., Robert Coll., Istanbul, 1949; M.S.E.E., U. Cin., 1950. Founder, pres., chmn. bd. Dynaplex Corp., Princeton, N.J., 1962-67; gen. mgr. Teledyne Telemetry Co., Los Angeles, 1966-67; founder, chmn. bd., pres. Aydin Corp., Ft. Washington, Pa., 1967—; dir. Fischer & Porter Co. Served to lt. Turkish Army, 1951-52. Moslem. Office: Aydin Corp 700 Dresher Rd PO Box 349 Horsham PA 19044

HALABY, NAJEEB E., lawyer, financier; b. Dallas, Nov. 19, 1915; s. Najeeb Elias and Laura (Wilkins) H.; m. Doris Carlquist, Feb. 9, 1946 (div. 1977); children: Lisa (Queen Noor of Jordan), Christian, Alexa; m. Jane Allison Coates Frick, Oct. 1, 1980. A.B., Stanford U., 1937; student, U. Mich. Law Sch., 1937-38; LL.B., Yale, 1940; LL.D., Allegheny Coll., 1967, Loyola U., Los Angeles, 1968. Bar: Calif. 1940, D.C. 1948, N.Y. 1973. Practiced in, Los Angeles; with O'Melveny & Myers, 1940-42; test pilot Lockheed Aircraft Corp., Burbank, Calif., 1942-43; fgn. affairs adviser to sec. def., 1948-53, dep. asst. sec. def., 1952-54; with L. S. Rockefeller and Bros., 1953-56; exec. v.p. Servomechanisms, Inc., 1956-58; pres. Am. Tech. Corp.; sec.-treas., counsel Aerospace Corp.; faculty lectr. UCLA, dir. def. studies program; chmn.; individual practice law, Calif., 1959-61; adminstr. FAA, 1961-65; sr. v.p., dir. Pan Am World Airways, N.Y.C., 1965-68, pres., 1968-72, chmn., chief exec. officer, 1969-72; pres. Halaby Internat. Corp., 1973—; dir. Bank America Corp., Menlo Fin. Corp., Chrysler Corp., Interasia Mgmt. Co. Ltd., Hong Kong. Mem. Adv. Council U.S.-Japan Econ. Relations; bd. dirs. Eisenhower Exchange Fellowships, Internat. Exec. Service Corps; vice chmn. Bus. Council Internat. Understanding; trustee Aspen Inst.; chmn. bd. trustees Am. U. Beirut. Served as naval aviator USN, World War II; asst. chief fighter sect. Naval Air Test Center; Patuxent River, Md. Decorated Legion of Honor, France; Order of Cedars, Lebanon; medal of Independence, Jordan; recipient Arthur Fleming award; Godfrey L. Cabot award; Monsanto Air Safety award. Fellow Am. Inst. Aeros. and Astronautics; mem. Am. Arbitration Assn., Soc. Exptl. Test Pilots, Corbey Ct., Council Fgn. Relations, Beta Theta Pi, Phi Delta Phi. Clubs: Met., Chevy Chase (Washington); Bohemian (Los Angeles); River, Explorers (N.Y.C.). Office: 239 Glenville Rd Greenwich CT 06830

HALABY, SAMIA ASAAD, painter, educator; b. Jerusalem, Dec. 12, 1936; d. Asaad Saba and Foutounie Assad (Atallah) H. B.S. in Design, U. Cin., 1959; M.A. in Painting, Mich. State U., 1960, M.F.A., Ind. U., 1963. Teaching asst. Ind. U., Bloomington, 1962-63, assoc. prof., 1969-72; instr. U. Hawaii, Honolulu, 1963-64, vis. lectr., summer 1966; asst. prof. Kansas City (Mo.) Art Inst., 1964-66, U. Mich., 1967-69; vis. lectr. art Yale U., 1972-73, assoc. prof., 1973-76, adj. assoc. prof., 1976-82; lectr. in field; artist-in-residence Tamarind Lithography Workshop, 1972; dir. (with 5 other artists) 22 Wooster Gallery, N.Y.C. One-man shows, Gima Gallery, Honolulu, 1964, The Gallery, Bloomington, 1970, Phyllis Kind Gallery, Chgo., 1971, Yale Sch. Art Gallery, 1972, Spectrum Gallery, N.Y.C., 1973, Marilyn Pearl Gallery, N.Y.C., 1978, Wooster Gallery, 1982, 83, Tossan-Tossan Gallery, N.Y.C., 1983, Housatonic Mus., Bridgeport, exhibited in group shows, including, Solomon R. Guggenheim Mus., N.Y.C., 1975, Susan Caldwell Gallery, N.Y.C., 1977, Iraqi Cultural Center, London, 1979, Kunsternes Hus, Oslo, Norway, 1981; represented in permanent collections, Solomon R. Guggenheim Mus., Indpls. Mus. Art, Art Inst. Chog., Nelson Rockhill Gallery Art, Kansas City, Ind. U. Mus., Mich. State U. Mus., Ft. Wayne (Ind.) Mus. Art, Detroit Inst. Art, Cleve. Mus. Art, Cin. Art Mus., Yale U. Gallery, Tamarind Inst. Collection, Albuquerque, Cooper-Hewitt Mus., N.Y.C., corp. collections, U.S. Steel, ATT Longlines, First Nat. Chgo, Kemper Ins. Chgo., S.E. Banking Corp. Fla., Wilko Chem. Corp. Kansas City Council for Faculty Devel. traveling fellow, 1965; Creative Artists Public Service Program grantee, 1978-79. Subject of profl. publs.

HALASI-KUN, GEORGE JOSEPH, hydrologist, educator; b. Zagreb, Austria-Hungary, July 28, 1916; came to U.S., 1958, naturalized, 1963; s. Tibor and Priscilla (Tholt) Halasi-K.; m. Elisabeth Christina Szorad., Mar. 10, 1945; children: Beatrice, Georgie. B.A. summa cum laude, Coll. of Budapest, 1934; M.S. in Civil Engring. summa cum laude, Mil. Inst. Tech., Ludovika, Budapest, 1938; C.E., Slovak Tech. U., Bratislava, Czechoslovakia, 1949; D.Engring. Sci. cum laude, Tech. U., Braunschweig, Germany, 1968. Registered profl. engr., Conn., N.J.; registered profl. hydrologist. Dir. water engring., asso. prof. Tech. U.; also prof. Coll. Water Engring., Kosice, Czechoslovakia, 1948-53; mgr.-chief engr. Pozemne Stavby Constrn. Co., Kosice, 1954-57; project mgr., assoc. Columbia, N.Y.C., 1958—, chmn. seminar water resources, 1967—; research assoc. Tech. U., Braunschweig, 1969-71; adj. prof. N.Y. Inst. Tech., 1971-76; vis. prof. Rutgers U., 1976—; adj. prof. Fairleigh Dickinson U., 1979—; state topographic engr. N.J. Environ. Protection Dept., 1971—. Author: Hydrology, 1949, Water Economy, 1952, Water in Agricultural Engineering, 1954, Analysis of Maximum Flood in Smaller Watershed Area-Computations, 1968, Hydrogeological Aspects of Pollution and Water Resources in Urbanized and Industrialized Areas, 1971, Ground Water Computations in New Jersey, 1974, Land Oriented Water Resources Data System in New Jersey, 1978; editor: publs. Columbia Seminar on Pollution and Water Resources. Fellow ASCE, Geol. Soc. Am.; mem. Internat., Am. water resources assns., Am. Congress Surveying and Mapping, Am. Inst. Hydrology, Société des Ingénieurs et Scientifiques de France, AAAS, AAUP. Home: 31 Knowles Ave Pennington NJ 08534 *Without high ideals, honesty, hard work, luck, and circumspectance in one's acting, even the smartest man will seldom succeed. In choosing ambitious goals and high standards one should be intransigent; but immediate adjustment of plans to changing situations is essential to any success. Solidarity and care about co-workers is a further step in maintaining of ideals and is part of any effective work.*

HALASZ, LASZLO, musical director, conductor; b. Debrecen, Hungary, June 6, 1909; came to U.S., 1926, naturalized, 1943; s. Ferdinand and Regine (Eichhorn) H.; m. Suzette F. Forgues; children: Georges, Suzanne. Student and grad. piano and conducting, Royal Hungarian Conservatory of Music, Budapest, 1929. Founder, artistic and music dir. N.Y.C. Opera, 1943-52; also Chgo. Opera Co., 1949-52; founder Peabody Art Theatre Balt.; also head conducting dept. Eastman Sch. Music, U. Rochester, 1965-67; dir. music, prof. N.Y. State U. Coll. at Old Westbury, 1968-71; program dir. teacher preparation in music SUNY, Stonybrook, 1971—. Piano soloist, Royal Hungarian Philharmonic Soc., 1928, gave piano concerts and conducted orchs. in, Europe, 1928-36; musical and artistic dir., St. Louis Grand Opera Assn., 1937-42; guest condr., Les Concerts Symphoniques, Montreal, Can., Aug. 1940, N.B.C. Symphony, Aug. 1941; musical and artistic dir., Havana Operatic Festivals, Sept. 1940, 41; debut as condr., Chgo. Opera in Falstaff (Eng. version), Nov. 1941; reengaged for, 1942 season; musical dir. and condr., Am. Symphony Orch.; performing under sponsorship of U.S.O., exclusively for the armed forces at camps, forts and bases, Dec. 1942-July 1943; guest condr., N.Y. Philharmonic Orch., Lewisohn Stadium, 1946, Montreal Festivals, N.B.C. Symphony and Les Concerts Symphoniques, Montreal, June 1952; recordings for, MGM and Remington records; music dir., Remington Records, Inc., 1953-55; music dir. German wing, Gran Teatro del Liceo, Barcelona, 1955-59; condr., Empire State Festivals, Summer 1957; artistic and music dir., Empire State Music Festival Inc., Music Festival of L.I., Inc., 1957-65; guest condr., Boston Opera, Royal Philharmonic Orch., London, 1962-63; condr., Eastman Philharmonic Orch. of Rochester; guest condr., Budapest State Opera, 1964-66, Teatro Liceo, Barcelona, 1967, 68, 70-72, Villa Lobos Meml. Concert, Rio de Janiero, Brazil Nat. Symphony of Caracas, Venezuela and Lima, Peru, 1969-70, Villa-Lobos Festival, Rio de Janeiro, 1972, 75; debut with, Orch. Sinfonica Nacional, Mexico City, 1976, Orch. Sinfonica Sodre, Montevideo, Uruguay, 1976, 78, 79, Sociedad de Conciertos de Buenos Aires, Argentina, 1976; condr., Kodaly Meml. Concerts, Hungary, 1971; music dir., Concert Orch. of Choir of L.I., Inc., 1971—, Nat. Grand Opera, Inc., 1983, 84; debut with, Frankfurt (Germany) Opera conducting, Strauss' Frau Ohne Schatten, 1974, 75; debut, Santiago Symphony Orch., 1979; condr. with, Am. Opera Center, Juilliard at Lincoln Center, 1980, 81. Recipient Page One award Newspaper Guild N.Y., 1968, Merit award Nat. Assn. Am. Composers and Condrs., Arturo Toscanini award JFK Library for Minorities, 1972; named Condr. of Year Nat. Orch. Montevideo (Uruguay), 1976, 78, 79. Mem. Central Opera Service. Home: 3 Leeds Dr Port Washington NY 11050 *Looking back on my life spanning seven decades I came to the conclusion, that if given the chance to start living again, I would not change an iota of the principles I lived by. Neither would I seek a different profession, career or way of life. As a conductor and university professor I had much contact with today's youth. I wish to advise them to set their life goals early; to follow the path to success in as straight a line as possible. Happiness and satisfaction in life do not come easily; but it is easier to absorb the ups and downs if one does not deviate from the principles of not compromising with honesty.*

HALASZ, NICHOLAS ALEXIS, surgeon; b. Budapest, Hungary, Mar. 13, 1931; came to U.S., 1948, naturalized, 1954; s. Elek and Lilly (Boehm) H.; m. Margaret Diane Hinshaw, Dec. 5, 1964; children—Katherine Ann, Peter Nicholas. B.S., Trinity Coll., 1950; M.D., Yale U., 1954. Diplomate: Am. Bd. Surgery, Am. Bd. Thoracic Surgery. Intern Yale-New Haven Med. Center, 1954-55, resident, 1956-62; asst. prof. UCLA, 1962-65, asso. prof., 1965-67; prof. surgery U. Calif., San Diego, 1967—, head div. anatomy, 1968—; dir. transplantation service Univ. Hosp., San Diego; cons. U.S. Naval Hosps., San Diego and Camp Pendleton, Calif. Contbr. articles to profl. jours. Served as capt., M.C. U.S. Army, 1956-58. NIH grantee, 1962—; NSF grantee, 1963-66; Am. Heart Assn. grantee, 1966-68; Markle Found. scholar in acad. medicine, 1966-71. Mem. AMA, Calif. Med. Assn., Am. Surg. Assn., Soc. Univ. Surgeons, Transplantation Soc., A.C.S., San Diego County Med. Soc., Phi Beta Kappa, Alpha Omega Alpha. Office: 225 Dickinson St San Diego CA 92103

HALBACH, EDWARD CHRISTIAN, JR., legal educator; b. Clinton, Iowa, Nov. 8, 1931; s. Edward Christian and Lewella (Sullivan) H.; m. Janet Elizabeth Bridges, July 25, 1953; children: Kristin Lynn, Edward Christian III, Kathleen Ann, Thomas Elliot, Elaine Diane. B.A., U. Iowa, 1953, J.D., 1958; LL.M., Harvard U., 1959; LL.D., U. Redlands, 1973. Assoc. prof. Sch. Law, U. Calif. at Berkeley, 1959-62, prof., 1963—, dean, 1966-75. Co-author: Materials on Decedents' Estates and Trusts, 1965, 73, 81, California Will Drafting, 1965; Reporter: Uniform Probate Code, 1969, Materials on Future Interests, 1977, Death, Taxes and Family Property, 1977; author: Use of Trusts in Estate Planning, 1975, Income Taxation of Estates and Trusts, 1978, 81, Fundamentals of Estate Planning, 1983; also articles in legal publs. Income Taxation of Estates and Trusts. Served from 2d to 1st lt. USAF, 1954-56. Mem. ABA (chmn., vice chmn. various coms. sect. individual rights and responsibilities and sect. real property probate and trust law, dir. probate and trust div., sect. chmn.), Iowa Bar Assn., Am. Law Inst. (advisor restatement 2d property), Am. Acad. Polit. and Social Scis., Am. Bar Found., Am. Coll. Probate Counsel, Internat. Acad. Estate and Trust Law (v.p., exec. com., pres.-elect), Beta Theta Pi. Democrat. Roman Catholic. Home: 679 San Luis Rd Berkeley CA 94707

HALBACH, JOSEPH JAMES, consumer products corp. exec.; b. Clinton, Iowa, Sept. 14, 1930; s. Edward Christian and Lewella Mary (Sullivan) H.; children—Joseph James, Daniel, Robert, John, Stephen. B.A., U. Iowa, 1953, J.D., 1956. Bar: Iowa bar 1956, Tex. bar 1966, Fed. bar 1961. Corp. counsel, dir. indsl. relations Tex. Instruments Inc., Dallas, 1961-68, Kaiser Aluminum and Chem. Corp., Balt. and Ravenswood, W.Va., 1956-60; v.p. indsl. and pub. relations Harnischfeger Corp., Milw., 1968-69; v.p. employee relations Questor Corp., Toledo, 1969-70; dir. econ. devel. OEO, Exec. Office of Pres., Washington, 1970-72; v.p., gen. counsel Riviana Foods Inc., Houston, 1972—. Served with AUS, 1953-55. Mem. Tex., Iowa, Fed., Am. bar assns. Home: 1201 Bering Dr 74 Houston TX 77057 Office: 2777 Allen Pkwy Houston TX 77019

HALBERG, CHARLES JOHN AUGUST, JR., educator; b. Pasadena, Calif., Sept. 24, 1921; s. Charles John August and Anne Louise (Hansen) H.; m. Ariel Arfon Oliver, Nov. 1, 1941 (div. July 1969); children—Ariel (Mrs. William Walters), Charles Thomas, Niels Frederick; m. Barbro Linnea Samuelsson, Aug. 18, 1970 (dec. Jan. 1978). B.A. summa cum laude, Pomona Coll., 1949; M.A. (William Lincoln Honnold fellow), UCLA, 1953, Ph.D., 1955. Instr. math. Pomona Coll., Claremont, Calif., 1949-50; assoc. math. UCLA, 1954-55; instr. Math. U. Calif.-Riverside, 1955-56, asst. prof. Math., 1956-61, assoc. prof. Math., 1961-68, prof. math., 1968—, vice chancellor student affairs, 1964-65; dir. Scandinavian Study Center at Lund (Sweden) U., 1976-78; docent U. Goteborg, Sweden, 1969-70; bd. dirs. Fulbright Commn. for Ednl. Exchange between U.S. and Sweden, 1976-79. Author: (with John F. Devlin) Elementary Functions, 1967, (with Angus E. Taylor) Calculus with Analytic Geometry, 1969. Served with USAAF, 1945-46. NSF fellow U. Copenhagen, 1961-62. Mem. Math. Assn. Am. (chmn. So. Calif. sect. 1964-65, gov. 1968), Am. Math. Soc., Sigma Xi, Phi Beta Kappa. Home: 267 Juniper Ave Carlsbad CA 92008

HALBERSTADT, ERNST, artist; b. Germany, Aug. 26, 1910; s. Albert and Johanna (Sichel) H.; m. Luba Hershman (dec.); children: Jerome, Jon, Steven, David; m. Catherine Cameron Capp. Asst. to Ezra Winter, 1932, to Diego Rivera, 1933; head dept. murals Sch. Mus. Fine Arts, Boston, 1947-51; instr. photography, Penland, N.C., 1973; instr. painting Mass. Maritime Acad., 1974. Illustrator: Shore Road to Ogonquit, 1969; one-man shows, Fed. Art Gallery, Boston, 1934-37, Cape Cod Art Assn., 1937, Kraushaar Gallery, N.Y.C., 1946, Inst. Contemporary Art, Boston, 1951, Marion (Mass.) Art Center, 1970, Onset Bay Art Assn., 1972, N.H. Coll., Manchester, 1977, exhibited in over 50 mus. group shows; represented in permanent collections, Addison Gallery Am. Art, Andover, Mass., Brockton (Mass.) Art Mus., Cleve. Mus. Art, DeCordova Mus., Lincoln, Mass., Fogg Mus. Art, Cambridge, Mass., Met. Mus. Art, Mus. Modern Art, New Britain (Conn.) Mus., U. Ga. Mus., Rose Art Mus., Brandeis U., Library of Congress, Boston Mus. Fine Arts; commd. works include: sculpture and murals, Irving Trust Co., N.Y.C., Hong Kong and London, murals, Met. Life Ins. Co., Warwick, R.I., 1977. Pepsi Cola Corp. fellow, 1946; recipient medal Art Dirs. Club Boston, 1956, 57. Mem. New Eng. Artists Equity Assn. (dir. 1949-52). *In my work I have tried to produce things that exist in their own right and have a life of their own.*

HALBERSTAM, DAVID, journalist, author; b. N.Y.C., Apr. 10, 1934; s. Charles A. and Blanche (Levy) H.; m. Elzbieta Tchizevska, June 13, 1965 (div. 1977); m. Jean Sandness Butler, June 29, 1979; 1 dau., Julia Sandness. A.B., Harvard U., 1955; various hon. degrees. Reporter West Point (Miss.) Daily Times Leader, 1955-56, Nashville Tennessean, 1956-60; mem. staff N.Y. Times, 1960-67, corr., Congo, 1961-62, Vietnam, 1962-63, N.Y.C., 1964-65, Warsaw, Poland, 1965-66, expelled, 1966, assigned, N.Y.C., 1966-67; contbg. editor Harper's mag., 1967-71. Author: The Noblest Roman, 1961, The Making of a Quagmire, 1965, One Very Hot Day, 1968, The Unfinished Odyssey of Robert Kennedy, 1969, Ho (Ho Chi Minh), 1971, The Best and the Brightest, 1972, The Powers That Be, 1979, The Breaks of the Game, 1981. Recipient Pulitzer prize for internat. reporting, 1964, George Polk Meml. award, 1964; Louis Lyons award, 1964; Page One award for Congo reporting, 1962; Overseas Press Club award, 1973. Address: care Alfred Knopf 201 E 50th St New York NY 10022

HALBERSTAM, HEINI, mathematician; b. Most, Czechoslovakia, Sept. 11, 1926; came to Eng., 1939, naturalized, 1947; s. Michael and Judith (Honig) H.; m. Heather M. Peacock, Mar. 11, 1950 (dec. 1971); children: Naomi Deborah, Judith Marion, Lucy Rebecca, Michael

Welsford; m. Doreen Bramley, Sept. 28, 1972. B.S. with honours, Univ. Coll., London U., 1946, M.S., 1948, Ph.D., 1952. Lectr. math. U. Exeter, 1949-57; reader Royal Holloway Coll., London U., 1957-62; Erasmus Smith prof. Trinity Coll., Dublin, Ireland, 1962-64; prof. Nottingham U., England, 1964-80; prof. math., head dept. U. Ill., Urbana-Champaign, 1980—; vis. lectr. Brown U., 1955-56; vis. prof. U. Mich., 1966, U. Tel Aviv, 1973, U. Paris-South, 1972. Co-author: Sequences, 1966, 2d edit., 1983, Sieve Methods, 1975; co-editor math. papers of, W.R. Hamilton, H. Davenport; contbr. articles to profl. jours. Mem. London Math. Soc. (v.p. 1962-63, 74-77), Math. Assn. Am., Edinburgh Math. Soc., Am. Math Soc. *

HALBERT, SHERRILL, fed. judge; b. Terra Bella, Calif., Oct. 17, 1901; s. Edward Duffield and Ellen (Rhodes) H.; m. Verna Irene Dyer, June 7, 1927; children—Shirley Ellen (Mrs. Stanley J. Eager), Douglas James. A.B., U. Calif. at Berkeley, 1924, J.D., 1927; LL.D., McGeorge Coll. Law, 1962. Bar: Calif. bar 1927. Practiced in, Porterville, 1927-41, San Francisco, 1942-44, Modesto, 1944-49, dist. atty., Stanislaus County, 1949; judge Superior Ct. of Calif., 1949-54; U.S. dist. judge Eastern Dist. Calif., 1954—; Chmn. bd. advisers McGeorge Sch. Law, Sacramento. Contbg. author: Lincoln for the Ages, 1960, Lincoln: A Contemporary Portrait, 1962. Mem. Am. Camellia Soc. (pres. emeritus), Native Sons of Golden West, Nat. Pony Express Centennial Assn. (pres.), Selden Soc., Calif. Hist. Soc., Alpha Chi Rho, Phi Delta Phi. Clubs: Lion (hon.), Ambassador's (Sacramento); Book of Calif., Commonwealth (San Francisco). Home: 4120 Los Coches Way Sacramento CA 95825 Office: US Courthouse 650 Capital Mall Sacramento CA 95814

HALBOUTY, MICHEL THOMAS, geologist, petroleum engineer, petroleum operator; b. Beaumont, Tex., June 21, 1909; s. Tom Christian and Sodia (Manolley) H.; 1 dau., Linda Fay. B.S., Tex. A. and M. U., 1930, M.S., 1931, Profl. Degree in Geol. Engring, 1956; D.Eng. (hon.), Mont. Coll. Mineral Sci. and Tech., 1966. Geologist, petroleum engr. Yount-Lee Oil Co., Beaumont, 1931-33, chief geologist, petroleum engr., 1933-35; v.p., gen. mgr., chief geologist and petroleum engr. Glenn H. McCarthy, Inc., Houston, 1935-37; owner firm cons. geologists and petroleum engrs., Houston, 1937—, discoverer numerous oil and gas fields, La. and Tex.; adj. prof. Tex. Tech U.; vis. prof. Tex. A. and M. U. Author several books.; Contbr. numerous papers on geology and petroleum engring. to profl. jours. Served as lt. col. AUS, 1942-45. Recipient Tex. Mid-Continent Oil and Gas Assn. distinguished service award for an ind., 1965; named engr. of year Tex. Soc. Profl. Engrs. and Engrs. Council, 1968; Distinguished Alumni award Tex. A. and M. U., 1968; Michel T. Halbouty Geoscis. Bldg. named for him, 1977; DeGolyer Distinguished Service medal Soc. Petroleum Engrs. of Am. Inst. Mining, Metall. and Petroleum Engrs., 1971; hon. mem. Spindletop sect., 1972; hon. mem. inst., 1973; Anthony F. Lucas Gold medal, 1975; Pecora award NASA, 1977; Horatio Alger award Am. Schs. and Colls. Assn., 1978. Mem. Am. Assn. Petroleum Geologists (hon., pres. 1966-67, Human Needs award 1975, Sidney Powers Meml. medal 1977), Am. Soc. Oceanography, Internat. Assn. Sedimentology, Inst. Petroleum, London, Am. Petroleum Inst., Am. Inst. Mining and Metall. Engrs., Soc. Paleontologists and Mineralogists, Soc. Econ. Geologists, Mineral. Soc. Am., Geol. Soc. Am., Soc. Exploration Geophysicists, Nat. Acad. Engring., Houston Geol. Soc. (hon.), N.Y., Tex. acads. scis., A.A.A.S., Am. Inst. Profl. Geologists, Am. Geol. Inst., Tex., Nat. socs. profl. engrs. Episcopalian. Clubs: Ramada, Houston, Petroleum, River Oaks Country (Houston); Dallas Petroleum; Eldorado Country, Vintage (Palm Desert, Calif.); New Orleans Petroleum; Cosmos (Washington); Broadmoor, Kissing Camels (Colorado Springs, Colo.). Home: 49 Briar Hollow Houston TX 77027 Office: Halbouty Center 5100 Westheimer Rd Houston TX 77056

HALCROW, HAROLD GRAHAM, agricultural economics educator; b. Bowesmont, N.D., Oct. 11, 1911; s. John and Winifred (McIntosh) H.; m. Eleanor Virginia Fearn, June 14, 1941; children: Meribel, Stephen, Beth, Ronald, Gayle. B.S.A., N.D. State U., 1937; M.S. in Agrl. Econs, Mont. State Coll., 1938; Ph.D. in Econs. (Farm Found. fellow 1941-42), U. Chgo., 1948. Instr., then asst. prof. Mont. State Coll., 1938-41, asst. prof., then prof., 1946-49; prof. agrl. econs. U. Conn., 1949-57; profl. agrl. econs. U. Ill., Champaign, 1957—, head dept., 1957-70; vis. prof. agrl. econs. Stanford, 1971, U. Calif. at Berkeley, 1971; cons. U.S. Bur. Census, 1953-56; Dir. Nat. Bur. Econ. Research, 1956-76. Author: Agricultural Policy of the United States, 1953, Readings in Agricultural Economics, 1955, (with R. J. Saulnier, Neil H. Jacoby) Federal Programs of Lending and Loan Insurance, 1957, Food Policy for America, 1977, Economics of Agriculture, 1980, Agricultural Policy Analysis, 1984; also articles.; Editor: Jour. Farm Economics, 1955-57. Served to lt. USNR, 1943-46. Mem. Phi Kappa Phi, Alpha Zeta, Alpha Phi Sigma, Alpha Gamma Rho. Home: 1011 Mayfair Rd Champaign IL 61820

HALDEMAN, HARRY R. (BOB HALDEMAN), business executive, former government official; b. Los Angeles, Oct. 27, 1926; s. Harry F. and Katherine (Robbins) H.; m. Jo Horton, Feb. 19, 1949; children: Susan Ward, Harry Horton, Peter Robbins, Ann Kurtz. Student, U. Redlands, 1944-45, U. So. Calif., 1945-46; B.S. in Bus. Adminstrn., UCLA, 1948. Account exec. J. Walter Thompson Co., Los Angeles and N.Y.C., 1949-59, v.p., mgr. Los Angeles office, 1960-68; asst. to Pres. U.S., chief White House staff, 1969-73; sr. v.p. Murdock Devel. Co., Los Angeles, 1979—; pres. Murdock Hotels Corp., 1984—; dir. Haldeman, Inc., Los Angeles, Family Steak Houses of Miami, Inc.; Chief staff Nixon presdl. campaign, 1968. Author: The Ends of Power, 1978. Bd. regents U. Calif., 1965-67, 68-69; trustee Calif. Inst. Arts, 1966-68, chmn. bd., 1968; former chmn. bd. trustees Nixon Found.; mem. Commn. White House Fellows, 1969-73; former mem. exec. com., trustee Kennedy Center for Performing Arts. Served with USNR, 1944-46. Mem. Beta Theta Pi, Pi Delta Epsilon.

HALDEMAN, JOE WILLIAM, novelist; b. Oklahoma City, June 9, 1943; s. Jack Carroll and Lorena (Spivey) H.; m. Mary Gay Potter, Aug. 21, 1965. B.S. in Physics and Astronomy, U. Md., 1967; M.F.A. in English, U. Iowa, 1975. Assoc. prof. writing program MIT, 1983-84. Author: War Year, 1972, Cosmic Laughter, 1974, The Forever War, 1975, Mindbridge, 1976, Planet of Judgment, 1977, All My Sins Remembered, 1977, Study War No More, 1977, Infinite Dreams, 1978, World Without End, 1979, Worlds, 1981, (with Jack C. Haldeman, II) There is No Darkness, 1983, Worlds Apart, 1983; editor: Nebula Awards 17, 1983. Served with U.S. Army, 1967-69. Decorated Purple Heart; Recipient Hugo award, 1976, 77, Nebula award, 1975. Mem. Sci. Fiction Writers Am. (treas. 1970-73, chmn. grievance com. 1977-79), Authors Guild, AAAS, L-5 Soc., Poets and Writers, Inc., Nat. Space Inst. Home: 345 Grove St Ormond Beach FL 32074

HALDEMAN, LLOYD HERBERT, communications company executive; b. Columbia, Pa., July 28, 1933; s. Lloyd H. and Anna Hilda (Frank) H.; m. Jeanene Millard, July 12, 1958; 1 dau., Janet. B.S., Westchester (Pa.) State Coll., 1955. Gen. mgr. Cin. Symphony Orch., 1963-71; pres. Arts and Edn. Mgmt. Corp., N.Y.C., 1971-74, Dallas Symphony Orch. Assn., 1974-79, Inovision, Dallas, 1979-80, HVC Corp. (home terminal networks), 1980—. Named Entrepreneur of Yr. Cox Sch. Bus., So. Meth. U., 1977; Disting. Civil Service award North Dallas C. of C., 1979. Republican. Methodist. Home: 4 Royal Terrace Ct Dallas TX 75225 Office: 4825 LBJ Freeway Dallas TX 75234

HALE, CHARLES FRANKLIN, finanical services company executive; b. Betsy Layne, Ky., Jan. 4, 1931; s. Charles E. and Bessie Lee (Vest) H.; m. Joy Lorraine Turner, Aug. 7, 1954; children: Holly Lee, Suzanne. B.S., La Salle U., 1954; J.D., Temple U., 1976. C.P.A., Pa. Mgr. internal audit Ins. Co. N.Am., Phila., 1963-67, asst. controller, 1967-72, controller, 1972-74, v.p., controller, 1974-76; v.p., gen. auditor INA Corp., Phila., 1977-82, CIGNA, 1982—; dir. various INA Corp. cos. Pres. bd. commrs. Lower Gwynedd Twp., Pa., 1969-83. 1st lt. Fin. Corps. U.S. Army, 1956-58. Recipient Outstanding Achievement award La Salle Acctg. Assn., Phila., 1978; named Citizen of Week Ambler Gazette, Involved Neighbor INA Corp. Mem. Am. Inst. C.P.A.s, Pa. Inst. C.P.A.s, ABA, Pa. Bar Assn. Republican. Presbyterian. Home: 912 Forest Dr GwyneddValley PA 19437 Office: CIGNA 1600 Arch St Philadelphia PA 19101

HALE, CHARLES RUSSELL, lawyer; b. Talpa, Tex., Oct. 17, 1916; s. Charles L. and Exa (Evans) H.; m. Clementine L. Moore, Jan. 5, 1946; children: Robert R., Norman B. A.B., Stanford U., 1939; J.D., Fordham U., 1950. Bar: N.Y. 1950, Calif. 1953. Supr., United Geophys. Co., Pasadena, Calif., 1940-46; mem. patent staff Bell Telephone Labs., N.Y.C., 1947-48, Sperry Gyroscope Co., Great Neck, N.Y., 1948-51; practiced in Pasadena, 1951-54; mem. firm Christie, Parker & Hale, Pasadena, 1954—. Mem. ABA, Los Angeles Bar Assn., Pasadena Bar Assn. (v.p. 1960-61), Am. Patent Law Assn., AAAS, Am. Soc. Internat. Law, IEEE. Clubs: University, Annandale Golf (Pasadena); Rancho Santa Fe (Calif.) Golf. Home: 60 N Golden West Ave PO Box 1546 Arcadia CA 91006 PO Box 616 Rancho Santa Fe CA 92067 Office: 201 S Lake Ave Pasadena CA 91101

HALE, ELMER, JR., wholesale and retail grocery company executive; b. 1919. With Hale-Halsell Co., Inc., Tulsa, 1940—, now chmn. bd., dir. Address: Hale-Halsell Co Inc Box 1026 McAlester OK 74501 *

HALE, EZRA ANDREWS, retired business executive, former publisher; b. Rochester, N.Y., Apr. 6, 1895; s. William Barton and Clara Louise (Andrews) H.; m. Josephine Booth, Oct. 6, 1919; children: William Barton II, Anne Booth (Mrs. Arthur W. Johnson), Andrews Brooks. A.B., U. Rochester, 1916. With Lawyers Coop. Pub. Co., Rochester, 1916-60, exec. v.p., 1946-48, pres., treas., 1948-60; dir., treas. Baker-Voorhees Co., Inc., Mt. Kisco, N.Y., 1940-60; dir. Central Trust Co., Rochester, 1930-70, chmn. bd., 1959-66, chmn. exec. com., 1966-70, hon. chmn. bd., 1970—; dir. Bancroft Whitney Co., San Francisco, 1942-52. Author: (with H.D. Shedd, George Chapman) Co-ops and You, 1945. Bd. dirs. Rochester Gen. Hosp., 1934-65, hon. dir., 1965—, pres. bd., 1944—; trustee Rochester Inst. Tech., 1935-65, 1st vice chmn., 1961-65, hon. trustee, 1965—, hon. vice chmn. bd. trustees, 1967-76, hon. chmn., 1976—; trustee U. Rochester, 1954-65, hon. trustee, 1965—; trustee Rochester Friendly Home, Bergen Swamp Preservation Soc., 1955-66. Served with U.S. Army, 1917-19; 1st lt. 307th F.A. AEF, 1918. Recipient Distinguished Eagle Badge award Otetiana council Boy Scouts Am., 1973; Nathaniel Rochester Soc. award, 1976; elected to Naismith Basketball Hall of Fame, 1979. Mem. Rochester C. of C. (dir. 1950-62), U. Rochester Alumni Assn. (past pres.), Am. Legion, V.F.W., Newcomen Soc. N. Am., Delta Kappa Epsilon. Republican. Presbyn. Clubs: University, Rochester Country. Home: 61 Douglas Rd Rochester NY 14610

HALE, GERALD ALBERT, natural resources and industrial products company executive; b. Kalamazoo, May 9, 1927; s. Edwin M. and Helen M. (Hinrichs) H.; m. Emma Jean Hamilton, Aug. 22, 1953; children—Jeffrey, Kathleen, John. B.S., Western Mich. U., 1952. Salesman Edgar Bros. Co., Metuchen, N.J., 1952-56; with Minerals & Chems. Philipp Corp. (and predecessors), 1956-67, v.p. sales minerals and chems. div., 1964-66, corp. v.p., 1965-69; (co. merged with Engelhard Industries to form Engelhard Minerals & Chems., 1967), exec. v.p. minerals and chems. div., asst. sec., 1967-69, pres. minerals and chems. div., 1969-78, sr. v.p. corp., 1969-70, exec. v.p. corp., dir., mem. exec. com., 1971-78; pres. gen. industry group, exec. v.p., corp. dir. Allegheny Ludlum Industries, Inc., Pitts., 1978-80; pres. Hale Resources, Summit, N.J., 1980—; dir. Summit & Elizabeth Trust Co., Sci. Mgmt. Corp., N.J. Mfrs. Ins. Co., Lenox, Inc., Oakite Products, Inc., Elizabeth Trust Co., Atlantic City Electric Co. Served with USAAF, 1945-47. Mem. Delta Upsilon. Clubs: Union League, Economic (N.Y.C.); Baltusrol Golf (Springfield, N.J.); Ocean Reef (Key Largo, Fla.); Duquesne (Pitts.). Home: 11 Glendale Rd Summit NJ 07901 Office: Hale Resources PO Box 6 Summit NJ 07901

HALE, HAMILTON ORIN, lawyer; b. Crystal Lake, Ill., Sept. 15, 1906; s. Alva Harry and May Gale (Hamilton) H.; m. J. Elizabeth Hale, June 29, 1946; children: Jean, Hamilton, Jamie. B.S., U. Ill., 1931; J.D., Northwestern U., 1931. Bar: Ill. bar 1931, N.Y. bar 1940, D.C. bar 1965. Practiced in, McHenry County, Ill., 1931; assoc. firm Pruitt & Grealis, Chgo., 1932-40; ptnr. firm Pruitt, Hale & MacIntyre, N.Y.C., 1940-48; founder Hale & Stimson (now Hale, Russell & Gray), N.Y.C. and Washington, 1948, ret., 1971; mem. firm Joslyn & Green, Woodstock, Ill., 1970-77, Wardell & Johnson, 1977-84; Dir. emeritus USAir, Inc.; faculty lectr. on air law Northwestern U. Law Sch., 1934-35. Mayor Village of Roslyn Estates, 1963-67; trustee Village of Bull Valley; vice pres. bd. trustees Buckley Country Day Sch., N.Y. Decorated knight of Order of St. Olav, Norway). Mem. Am., Ill. bar assns., Order of Coif, Theta Chi, Phi Alpha Delta. Republican. Methodist. Club: Woodstock (Ill.) Country. Home: 317 S Valley Hill Rd Woodstock IL 60098 Office: 451 Coventry Green Crystal Lake IL 60014

HALE, JAMES RUSSELL, clergyman, religious educator; b. Phila., Dec. 14, 1918; s. Robert Gifford and Dorothy Emma (Graham) H.; m. Marjorie Elinor Hoerman, June 10, 1944; children: Douglas Graham, Dean Edward. A.B., Muhlenberg Coll., 1940; B.D., Luth. Theol. Sem., Gettysburg, Pa., 1944, S.T.M., 1950; Ed.D., Union Theol. Sem. and Columbia U., N.Y.C., 1970. Ordained to ministry Lutheran Ch. Am., 1944. Parish pastor Gethsemane and Reformation Luth. chs., Keyport and Long Branch, N.J., 1944-46, Our Savior Luth. Ch., Balt., 1946-50, Redeemer Luth. Ch., Ramsey, N.J., 1950-59, St. Paul's Luth. Ch., Collingswood, N.J., 1959-62; instr. ch. and community Luth. Theol. Sem., Gettysburg, 1962-63, asst. prof., 1963-69, assoc. prof., 1969-70, prof., 1970—, editor Sem. Bull., 1965-69, dir. advanced studies program, 1975-80, dir. Town and Country Ch. Inst., 1980—; theologian-in-residence Horthorpe Hall, Leicestershire, Eng., 1980-81; chmn. acad. com. ch. and soc. Washington Theol. Consortium, 1971-74; bd. dirs. Council on Luth. Theol. Edn. in N.E., 1975-80; mem. urban policy panel Ctr. for Theology and Pub. Policy, Washington, 1983—. Author: To Have and to Hold, 1972, Who Are the Unchurched? An Exploratory Study, 1977, Lutherans and Social Action, 1979, The Unchurched: Who They Are and Why They Stay Away, 1980; contbr. articles to profl. jours. Sec., bd. dirs. Tressler Luth. Social Services, Camp Hill, Pa., 1973-77, 80—; chmn. bd. dirs. Tressler Luth. Home for Children; bd. dirs. Adams York Mental Health Clinic, Hanover, Pa., 1975-77; chmn. Adams County Com. for Family Food, Gettsburg, Pa., 1971-72; del. White House Conf. on Aging, 1981. Served with Civilian Public Service, 1943-44. Case Study Inst. fellow, Cambridge, 1973-75; Gerontolgy in Sem. Tng. Program fellow Nat. Interfaith Coalition on Aging, 1979; Danforth Found. assoc., 1963-65; recipient Luth. Brotherhood Faculty Research, 1963-64, 80, award Luth. Ch. Am., 1968-70, 80-81, grants. Mem. Am. Acad. Religion, AAUP, Am. Sociol. Assn., Religious Research Assn., Soc. Sci. Study Religion, Soc. Sociology of Religion, Rural Sociol. Soc. Democrat. Home: 153 S Hay St Gettysburg PA 17325 Office: Luth Theol Sem 61 W Confederate Ave Gettysburg PA 17325 *My life, career, and relationships seek to contribute to the humanization of persons and institutions in the American society. My passionate concern and consuming hope is that the common life of humankind be marked by the mutual acceptance by all people of others in the bonds of peace and justice. The highest fulfillment in life is not the enhancement of self but of the other.*

HALE, JAMES THOMAS, retail company executive; b. Mpls., May 14, 1940; s. Thomas Taylor and Alice Louise (Mc Connon) H.; m. Sharon Sue Johnson, Aug. 27, 1960; children: David Scott, Eric James, Kristin Lynn. B.A., Dartmouth Coll., 1962; LL.B., U. Minn., 1965. Bar: Minn. Law clk. Chief Justice Earl Warren, U.S. Supreme Ct., 1965-66; asso. firm Faegre & Benson, Mpls., 1966-73, partner, 1973-79; v.p., dir. corp. growth Gen. Mills, Inc., 1979-80, v.p. fin. and control consumer non-foods, 1981; sr. v.p., gen. counsel, corp. sec. Dayton-Hudson Corp., 1981—; adj. prof. U. Minn., 1967-73. Bd. dirs. Met. Econ. Devel. Assn.; co-chmn. Atty. Gen. Warren Spannaus Election Com., 1970-80; chmn. bd. Fund Legal Aid Soc., others. Mem. Hennepin County Bar Assn., Order of Coif, Phi Beta Kappa. Mem. Democratic-Farm-Labor party. Lutheran. Office: 777 Nicollet Mall Minneapolis MN 55402 *

HALE, JOHN DEWEY, chemist; b. Salt Lake City, Mar. 26, 1937; s. C. Dewey and Arta P. (Mathews) H.; m. Norma D. Perkins, Nov. 17, 1963; children: Eric, Anthony, Celia. Student, U. Utah, 1954-56; B.S., Brigham Young U., 1957, Ph.D., 1963; postgrad., Oxford U., 1963-65. Research group leader Kerr-McGee Corp., Oklahoma City, 1967-69, mgr. bus. analysis, 1969-72, sr. planning analyst, 1972-75, mgr. tech. devel., 1975-77, mgr. research and devel., 1977-79, mgr. tech. center, 1979-83, pres. tech. ops., 1983—. Contbr. articles to profl. jours. NIH fellow, 1963-65. Mem. Am. Chem. Soc., Am. Inst. Chem. Engrs. Office: PO Drawer 25861 Oklahoma City OK 73125

HALE, JOSEPH RICE, church organization executive; b. Texarkana, Tex., Mar. 25, 1935; s. Alfred Clay and Bess (Akin) H.; m. Mary Richey, June 2, 1964; 1 son, Jeffrey Glen. B.A., Asbury Coll., Wilmore, Ky., 1957; B.D., So. Methodist U., 1960; D.D., Asbury Theol. Sem., 1978. Ordained to ministry Meth. Ch., 1958, pastor, Sunset, Tex., 1958-60; evangelist, 1960-66; asso. dir. dept. evangelism Bd. Evangelism, Meth. Ch., 1966-68, dir. ecumenical evangelism, 1968-74; dir. evangelization devel. Bd. Discipleship, United Meth. Ch., 1975-76; gen. sec. World Meth. Council, 1976—; mem. exec. com. Key 73, 1970-73; sec. working group evangelism Nat. Council Chs., 1972; pres. Communications Found., Inc., 1974-75; world ambassador Internat. Prayer Fellowship, 1974; exec. com. Evangelization Forum, 1973-75; registrar World Meth. Evangelism Convocation, Jerusalem, 1974; mem. Conf. Secs. Christian World Communions, 1976—, chmn. Author: Design for Evangelism, 1970, Christ Matters!, 1971, God's Moment, 1972, also articles, chpts. books, encys.; producer: film The Spirit is Moving, 1980; video prodn To Live to God, 1984. Recipient Key to City of Daytona Beach, Fla., 1963, 64; named Ky. col., 1977. Home: 301 Forest Park Dr Waynesville NC 28786 Office: World Methodist Council PO Box 518 Lake Junaluska NC 28745

HALE, JUDSON DRAKE, editor; b. Boston, Mar. 16, 1933; s. Roger Drake and Marian (Sagendorph) H.; m. Sara Huberlie, Sept. 6, 1958; children: Judson Drake, Daniel, Christopher. B.A., Dartmouth Coll., 1958; D.Jour. (hon.), New England Coll., 1984. Asst. editor Yankee, Inc., Dublin, N.H., 1958-61, assoc. editor, 1961-63, mng. editor, 1963-69, editor, v.p., 1969—, also dir.; editor, v.p. Old Farmers Almanac; dir. Solar Environ. Scis., Inc. Editor: That New England, 1968. Author Inside New England, 1982; Trustee MacDowell Colony; chmn. Task Force for Hist. Preservation in N.H.; pres. bd. trustees Monadnock Community Hosp. Served with AUS, 1955-57. Mem. Cheshire County Dartmouth Alumni Club, Phi Kappa Psi. Republican. Episcopalian (moderator ch.). Club: Dublin Lake. Home: Valley Rd Dublin NH 03444 Office: Main St Dublin NH 03444

HALE, LAURENCE SWART, press association executive; b. Jamestown, N.Y., May 25, 1925; s. Earle Spring and Mildred (Swart) H.; m. Angeline Calanni, Sept. 4, 1950; children—Laurie Ann (dec.), Lisa Ann, Melissa Ann. B.J., U. Mo., 1950. Reporter Jamestown (N.Y.) Post-Jour., 1950-53; with Binghamton (N.Y.) Press, 1953-76, reporter, 1953-61, asst. city editor, 1961-65, city editor, 1965-67, asst. mng. editor, 1967-70, mng. editor, 1970, editor, 1971-76; asso. dir. Am. Press Inst., Reston, Va., 1977—. Served with USNR, 1943-45. Mem. N.Y. A.P. Assn. (pres. 1973), N.Y. State Soc. Newspaper Editors (pres. 1976), A.P. Mng. Editors Assn., Am. Soc. Newspaper Editors, Kappa Tau Alpha. Home: 2366 Tumbletree Way Reston VA 22091 Office: 11690 Sunrise Valley Dr Reston VA 22091

HALE, NANCY, author; b. Boston, May 6, 1908; d. Philip L. and Lilian (Westcott) H.; m. Fredson Bowers, Mar. 16, 1942; children (by former marriages)—Mark Hardin, William Wertenbaker. Grad., Winsor Sch., Boston, 1926; student, Sch. of Boston Mus. Fine Arts, 1927-28; studied in father's studio several years. Asst. editor Vogue, 1928-32, Vanity Fair, 1933-34; news reporter N.Y. Times, 1935; adv. capacity to advt. agy., 1930-35; lectr. short story Bread Loaf Writers Conf., 1957-65. (Recipient O. Henry prize for short-short story 1933, Benjamin Franklin spl. citation for short story 1958, Henry H. Bellaman award for lit. 1969); Author: The Young Die Good, 1932, Never Any More, 1934, The Earliest Dreams, 1936, The Prodigal Women, 1942, Between the Dark and the Daylight, 1943, The Sign of Jonah, 1950, The Empress's Ring, 1955, Heaven and Hardpan Farm, 1957, A New England Girlhood, 1958, Dear Beast, 1959; short stories The Pattern of Perfection, 1960; essays The Realities of Fiction, 1962, Black Summer, 1963, New England Discovery; anthology, 1963, The Life In The Studio, 1969, Secrets, 1971; biography Mary Cassatt, 1975, The Night of the Hurricane; juvenile, 1978; author: short stories which have appeared in over 40 anthologies, including the Foley and O. Henry collections, Va. Quar. Sarah Josepha Hale award, 1974; Phi Beta Kappa vis. scholar, 1971-72. Club: Cosmopolitan (N.Y.C.). Home: Route 11 Charlottesville VA 22901 *After a long and reflective life, my impression is that the life itself is seeking a goal & whether in art or in reality, the sign of creation having been present, as has been said, is a sensation of pure joy.*

HALE, NEWTON JOHNSTON, merchant; b. San Francisco, Jan. 10, 1902; s. Reuben Brooks and May (Johnston) H.; m. Betty Caughey, July 29, 1922; children: Betty May (Mrs. Edward H. McLaughlin, Jr.), Janet (Mrs. C. E. Havard). Student, Hitchcock Mil. Acad., 1920, Stanford U., 1920-22, N.Y. U. Sch. Retailing, 1925-26. With Hale Bros., Inc., 1922, R. H. Macy Co., Franklin Simon, 1925-26; with Hale Bros., 1926, dir., 1931, treas., 1934-43, Chmn. bd., dir., 1943-48; v.p., dir. Hale Bros. Assocs., Inc. (name now Hale Tech. Corp.); sec., dir. O. C. Field Gasoline Corp., 1922-44; dir. Broadway-Hale Stores, Inc., 1948-72; hon. dir. Carter Hawley Hale Stores Inc. Mem. Retail Mchts. Assn. (former pres., dir.), Retail Dry Goods Assn. (former pres., dir.), Retail Credit Assn. San Francisco (former pres., dir.), Sigma Alpha Epsilon. Republican. Clubs: Pacific-Union, Bohemian, Burlingame Country, Electric. Home: 45 Downey Way Hillsborough CA 94010 Office: 150 Stockton St San Francisco CA 94108

HALE, ORON JAMES, historian, educator; b. Goldendale, Wash., July 29, 1902; s. William Robert and Frances Isabella (Putnam) H.; m.

Annette Van Winkle, Aug. 7, 1929 (dec. 1968); m. Virginia S. Zehmer, July 9, 1970. A.B., U. Wash., 1926; A.M., U. Pa., 1928, Ph.D. (George Leib Harrison fellow history 1928-29), 1930; studied in, France and Germany, summers 1927, 28; Social Sci. Research Council fellowship in, London and Berlin, 1932-33; Litt. D., Hampden-Sydney Coll., 1958. Instr. history U. Pa., 1926-28; asst. prof. European history U. Va., 1929-38, asso. prof., 1938-46, prof., 1946-65, Corcoran prof. history, 1965—, chmn. dept., 1955-62, emeritus prof., 1972—; dir. Inst. Pub. Affairs, 1942, 53; acting chmn. Woodrow Wilson Sch. Fgn. Affairs, 1947-48; vis. prof. Duke, summers, 1934, 38, 39, U. Mo., 1937, U. N.C., 1946, Harvard, 1955; prof. Inst. Advanced Study, Princeton, 1963-64. Author: Germany and the Diplomatic Revolution, 1904-1906, 1931, Publicity and Diplomacy, 1890-1914, 1940, The Captive Press in the Third Reich, 1964 (spl. Polk award 1965), The Great Illusion, 1900-1914, 1971; Contbr. to hist., lit. and mil. periodicals. Served to col. AUS, 1942-46; served intelligence div. War Dept. Gen. Staff, 1942-45; mem. War Dept. Gen. Staff Hist. Mission in, 1945; Germany; hist. div. War Dept. spl. staff, 1945-46; col., M.I. Res., 1946-62; mem. Sec. Army's Adv. Com. on Mil. History, 1958-62; with U.S. High Commn. for Germany as dep. state commr. for Bavaria, 1950-51; commr., 1951-52. Recipient George Louis Beer prize diplomatic history Am. Hist. Assn., 1931; comdr.'s cross Order of Merit; Fed. Republic Germany, 1969; Thomas Jefferson award U. Va., 1969. Mem. Am., So. hist. assns., Soc. Am. Historians, Va. Soc. Sci. Assn., Phi Beta Kappa. Democrat. Presbyn. Club: Colonnade. Home: 1600 Westbrook Ave Apt 342 Richmond VA 23227

HALE, RALPH WEBSTER, obstetrician, gynecologist; b. Princeton, W.Va., Nov. 30, 1935; s. Ralph and Mabel (Burton) H.; m. Jane Esther Towner, Sept. 2, 1956; 3 children. B.S., U. Ill., 1957, M.D., 1960. Diplomate: Am. Bd. Obstetrics and Gynecology (examiner). Intern Akron (Ohio) Gen. Hosp., 1960-61; resident Kapiolani Hosp., Honolulu, 1965-68; student researcher dept. biochemistry U. Ill., 1956-60; clin. instr. dept. ob-gyn U. Hawaii (John A. Burns Sch. Medicine), Honolulu, 1968-70, instr., 1970-71, asst. prof., 1971-72, asso. prof., 1973-76, asso. dean student affairs, 1972-73, asso. dean clin. affairs, 1973-77, prof., chmn. dept. ob-gyn, 1976—, dir. continuing med. edn., 1979—; chief ob-gyn service (Kapiolani-Children's Med. Center), 1974—, program dir., 1976—, acting dir. perinatal services, 1979—, cons. gynecologist dept. pediatrics, 1979—. Mem. editorial bd.: Western Jour. Medicine, 1975; contbr. articles in field to profl. jours. Mem. Am. Coll. Obstetricians and Gynecologists (chmn. course coordinating com. 1980, ex-officio mem. com. on sci. program 1980-81), Am. Assn. Gynecol. Laparoscopists (mem. adv. bd.), Am. Fertility Soc., AMA, Assn. Profs. Gynecology and Obstetrics (v.p. 1978-79), Am. Coll. Sports Medicine, Pacific Coast Ob-Gyn Soc., Pacific Coast Fertility Soc. (pres. 1980), Hawaii Med. Assn., Honolulu Ob-Gyn Soc. (chmn. 1976-79). Office: U Hawaii John A Burns Sch Medicine Dept Obstetrics and Gynecology 1960 East West Rd Honolulu HI 96822

HALE, ROBERT BEVERLY, art educator, retired curator; b. Boston, Jan. 29, 1901; s. Herbert Dudley and Margaret Curzon (Marqu) H.; m. Barbara Barnes, Nov. 11, 1941 (div.); m. Niké Mylonas, Dec. 8, 1962; children—Alexander Curzon, Evelyn Everett. A.B., Columbia U., 1923; postgrad., Columbia Sch. Architecture, Fontainebleau, Art Students League. Asso. editor Art News, 1941-49; organizer dept. Am. art Met. Mus., N.Y.C., 1948, asso. curator, head dept., 1949-57, curator Am. painting and sculpture, 1958-66, curator emeritus, 1968—, mem. vis. com., 1973—; lectr. artistic anatomy Pa. Acad. Fine Arts, 1968—; instr. drawing, lectr. anatomy Art Students League, 1943—; adj. prof. drawing Columbia U., 1945-67; lectr. artistic anatomy Cooper Union, 1973—, prof. art, 1976—; Pres. Louis Comfort Tiffany Found., 1959-66, trustee, 1966—; v.p. N.Y.C. Art Festival, 1961—; mem. art com. Chase Manhattan Bank, 1960—. Author: 100 American Painters of the 20th Century, 1950, Drawing Lessons from the Great Masters, 1964, Snowland, 1971, (with Terry Coyle) Anatomy Lessons from the Great Masters, 1977, Albinus on Anatomy, 1979; editor, translator: Anatomie Artistique (Dr. Paul Richer), 1971, Rhys Caparn, 1972, (with Niké Hale) Balcomb Greene, 1977; Contbr. to: mags. of art, article Ency. Brit, 1956; one-man shows, Stamford (Conn.) Mus., 1959, Staempfli Gallery, N.Y.C., 1960; represented in permanent collections, Whitney Mus., Met. Mus., U. Ariz., others, many pvt. collections; exhbn. Tribute to a Curator: Robert Beverly Hale, Met. Mus., 1979. Recipient N.Y.C. Mayor's award honor for arts, 1977; Benjamin Franklin fellow Royal Soc. Arts, 1969. Mem. Art Students League (v.p. 1941-43, hon. life mem.), Am. Fine Arts Soc. (trustee), Am. Fedn. Arts (internat. com.), Am. Water Color Soc. (hon. mem., Dolphin gold medal 1981). Clubs: Columbia University Faculty, Century (N.Y.C.). Home: Curzon Mill Rd Newburyport MA 01950 summer Hydra Greece Office: Art Students League 215 W 57th St New York NY 10019

HALE, ROGER LOUCKS, manufacturing company executive; b. Plainfield, N.J., Dec. 13, 1934; s. Lloyd and Elizabeth (Adams) H.; m. Sandra Johnston, June 10, 1961; children: Jocelyn, Leslie, Nina. B.A., Brown U., 1956; M.B.A., Harvard U., 1961. With Tennant Co., Mpls., 1961—, pres., 1975—, chief exec. officer, 1976—, also dir.; dir. 1st Nat. Bank of Mpls., Donaldson Co., St. Paul Cos., Dayton Hudson Corp.; vice chmn. Minn. Bus. Partnership. Party sec. Democratic Farm Labor Party, 1968-70; bd. dirs. Citizens League, 1966-68, 81, research study chmn., 1970, 72; bd. dirs. Walker Art Center, 1970—; mem. Met. Planning Commn. Mpls., 1965-67. Served with USN, 1956-59. Office: Tennant Co 701 N Lilac Dr Minneapolis MN 55440

HALES, DAVID FOSTER, natural resources educator; b. Fort Worth, Tex., Nov. 14, 1944; s. Hubert William and Callie Bell H.; m. Claudia Beth Kamas; children: Lisa, Nathaniel, Joshua. B.S., Hardin-Simmons U., 1966; M.A. in Polit. Sci, U. Okla., 1970. Instr. polit. sci. U. Okla.; asst. prof. polit. sci. Stephen F. Austin State U., 1970-71; exec. asst. Okla. State Park System, 1971-75; Midwest regional coordinator Carter-Mondale Presdl. campaign, 1975-76; dep. asst. sec. Fish and Wildlife and Parks, Dept. Interior, Washington, 1977-81; Dana prof. natural resources, dir. Wildlife Mgmt. Ctr. U. Mich., Ann Arbor, 1981—; chmn. U.S.-USSR Bilateral Agreement on Protection of Nature; mem. Pres.'s Adv. Council on Hist. Preservation; mem. exec. bd. U.S. Com. of Internat. Council Monuments and Sites. Mem. Pinelands (N.J.) Planning Commn. Office: U Mich Sch Natural Resources Ann Arbor MI 48109

HALEVY, SIMON, physician, educator; b. Bucharest, Romania, June 5, 1929; came to U.S., 1963, naturalized, 1970; s. Meyer Abraham H. and Rebecca (Landau) H.; m. Hilda M. Valdes, 1968; 1 son, Daniel Abraham. M.D., U. Bucharest, 1953. Diplomate: Am. Bd. Anesthesiology. Intern Univ. Hosp., Coltzea, Romania, 1952-53, resident, 1953-54; practice medicine specializing in anesthesiology, 1955—; instr. anesthesia Postgrad. Inst. Medicine, Bucharest, 1955-57, chief lab. in anesthesia, 1957-60; preparator, instr. anatomy U. Bucharest Med. Sch., 1950; attending anesthesiologist Univ. Hosp., Fundeni, Bucharest, 1960-63; intern Community Hosp., Glen Cove, N.Y., 1964-65; resident Mt. Sinai Hosp., N.Y.C., 1965-67; asst. prof. anesthesiology Mt. Sinai Sch. Medicine, 1967-68; asst. prof. Albert Einstein Coll. Medicine, 1969-74; assoc. prof. Coll. Physicians and Surgeons, Columbia U., 1974-75; prof. SUNY, 1976—; asst. attending anesthesiologist Mt. Sinai Hosp. Services and Bronx Mcpl. Hosp. Center, 1967-71, attending anesthesiologist, 1973-74; attending anesthesiologist, assoc.-anesthesiologist-in-chief, dir. obstet. anesthesiology Nassau County Med. Center, 1976—; Chmn. com. on sci. exhibits Postgrad. Assembly in Anesthesiology, N.Y.C., 1971-80. Mem. editorial bd.: Microcirculation, Convergences Médicales; Contbr. articles to sci. jours. Fellow Am. Coll. Anesthesiologists; mem. AMA, Am. Soc. Anesthesiologists, Assn. des Anesthesiologistes Français, Deutche Gesellschaft für Anaesthesiologie und Intensivmedizin; Fellow Société Française d'Anesthesie et de Reanimation; mem. Association Internationale des Anesthesiologistes d'Expression (v.p., mem. adminstrv. council), N.Y. Acad. Scis., AAAS, Am. Soc. Pharmacology and Exptl. Therapeutics, N.Y. Acad. Scis. Office: Nassau County Med Center 2201 Hempstead Turnpike East Meadow NY 11554

HALEY, ALEX PALMER, author, foundation executive; b. Ithaca, N.Y., Aug. 11, 1921; s. Simon Alexander and Bertha George (Palmer) H.; m. Nannie Branch, 1941 (div. 1964); children: Lydia Ann, William Alexander; m. Juliette Collins, 1964 (div. 1972); 1 dau., Cynthia Gertrude. Student, Elizabeth City (N.C.) Tchrs. Coll., 1937-39; Litt.D., Simpson Coll., Indianola, Iowa, 1970. Author: The Autobiography of Malcolm X, 1965, Roots, 1976, Roots: The Saga of an American Family, 1979; Contbr. articles to periodicals. Founder, pres. Kinte Found., Washington, 1972—. Enlisted USCG, 1939; advanced to chief journalist, 1949; ret., 1959. Recipient Spl. Pulitzer prize, 1977. Mem. Authors Guild, Soc. Mag. Writers. Kinte Corp PO Box 3338 Beverly Hills CA 90212 *

HALEY, GEORGE, educator; b. Lorain, Ohio, Oct. 19, 1927; s. George and Mary (Haley). A.B., Oberlin Coll., 1948; M.A., Brown U., 1951, Ph.D. (Pres.'s fellow), 1956. Prof. U. Chgo., 1968—, chmn. dept. Romance langs., 1970-74. Author: Vicente Espinel and Marcos de Obregón, 1959, The Narrator in Don Quixote, 1965, Diario de un Estudiante de Salamanca, 1977; editorial bd.: Modern Philology, 1967—, Boletin Menéndez Pelayo. Guggenheim fellow, 1962-63. Mem. Modern Lang. Assn. Am., Hispanic Soc. Am., Phi Beta Kappa. Home: 901 S Plymouth Ct Chicago IL 60605 Office: 1050 E 59th St Chicago IL 60637

HALEY, JACK (JOHN J.), JR., director, producer, writer, exec.; b. Los Angeles, Oct. 25, 1933; s. Jack and Florence (McFadden) H.; m. Liza Minnelli, Sept. 15, 1974. B.S. in English, Loyola U., Los Angeles, 1956; postgrad., UCLA, U. So. Calif., also work in cinema arts. TV actor, 1955-56; joined David L. Wolper to form Wolper Prodns. Inc., 1959; pres. television Twentieth Century-Fox, 1975—; Co-founder The Thalians, 1955, bd. dirs., 1955-65; pres. Jack Haley Found., 1962—. Co-producer: TV show The Race for Space, 1959; producer-dir.: TV spl. Project: Man in Space, 1959, Hollywood: The Golden Years, 1960-61, Hollywood: The Great Stars, 1962, Hollywood: The Fabulous Era, 1962; producer, dir.: And Away We Go, 1963-64, The Incredible World of James Bond, 1965; writer, producer, dir., exec. charge prodn.: TV series Hollywood and the Stars (segment won Silver Lion award Venice Film Festival 1963-64); series Biography, 1962 (George Foster Peabody Broadcasting award); exec. producer, dir.: TV spl. The General, 1965; prodn. supr.: The Legend of Marilyn Monroe, 1966; supervising producer, Wolper Prodns. Inc. on all, Nat. Geog. Spls, 1966; producer, cowriter: A Funny Thing Happened on the Way to the White House, 1966; sr. v.p. charge all live entertainment, Wolper Prodns., Inc., 1967; writer, producer, dir.: TV spl. The Hidden World (grand Prix Monte Carlo Internat. TV Festival, Silver Lion award Venice Film Festival), 1967 (George Foster Peabody Broadcasting award); exec. producer: The Highlights of the Ice Capades, 1967, With Love, Sophia, 1967; producer, co-writer: A Funny Thing Happened on the Way to Hollywood, 1967; producer, dir.: Movin' With Nancy, 1967 (Emmy award); exec. producer: Monte Carlo, C'est La Rose, 1968, The Highlights of the Ice Capades, 1968; producer, dir.: The Beat of Brass, 1968; exec. producer: The Highlights of the Ice Capades, 1969, Life Goes to the Movies, 1976 (Emmy nomination); series That's Hollywood, 1977, 78, 79; producer, dir., co-writer: Bob Hope's World of Comedy, 1976, Heroes of Rock 'N' Roll, 1979; producer, co-writer, co-dir.: Frank Sinatra, Jr. . .With Family and Friends, 1969; dir.: film Norwood, 1969; writer-producer, dir.: documentary That's Entertainment, 1973, Life Goes to War: Hollywood and the Homefront, 1977; dir.: 1969 Acad. Awards Presentation; producer: 1979 Acad. Awards; dir.: The Love Machine, 1970; creative affairs, MGM, 1972-75; writer, exec. producer: 50 Years of MGM, 1975 (Emmy nomination); exec. in charge prodn.: Sherlock Holmes in N.Y; co-exec. producer: America Salutes Richard Rodgers, 1976 (Emmy nomination); producer: TV spls. Acad. Awards Show, 1974, The Mac Davis Christmas Special, 1975, The Mac Davis Special, 1975; American Movie Awards, 1981, 82; producer, dir., writer: Hollywood: The Gift of Laughter, 1982; producer series: Ripley's Believe It or Not!. Four of his documentaries presented by invitation at Moscow Film Festival. Address: 8489 W 3d St Los Angeles CA 90048

HALEY, JOHN CHARLES, banker; b. Akron, Ohio, July 24, 1929; s. Arthur and Katherine (Moore) H.; m. Rheba Hopkins, June 11, 1951; children: Alyson, Susan, John, Thomas. A.B., Miami U., Oxford, Ohio, 1950; M.S., Columbia Grad. Sch. Bus., 1951. With Chase Manhattan Bank, N.Y.C., 1953—, asst. treas., 1959-62, asst. v.p., 1962-64, v.p., 1964-70; exec. v.p. Chase Manhattan Corp, 1975—; group pres. Orion Banking Group, London, 1970-73; dir. Armco Corp., Netherlandse Credietbank. Trustee Pace U., Siemens Found.; chmn. bd. Nat. Corp. Fund for Dance, Inc. Served with AUS, 1951-53. Mem. Am. Bankers Assn. (chmn. internat. div.), Res. City Bankers Assn., German-Am. C. of C. (vice chmn.), Council Fgn. Relations, Beta Theta Pi. Clubs: Union, New Canaan Country. Home: 146 Lambert Rd New Canaan CT 06840 Office: 1 Chase Manhattan Plaza New York NY 10081

HALEY, PRISCILLA JANE, artist, printmaker; b. Boston, June 22, 1926; d. Arthur Benjamin and Jessamy (Fountain) H.; m. Thadeusz Bilous, May 21, 1961. B.A., Oberlin Coll., Ohio, 1948; grad., Brklyn. Mus. Sch., 1955. Resident artist Yaddo Found., Saratoga Springs, N.Y., 1957. Artist (one-man show), Village Art Ctr., N.Y.C., 1960, (represented in permanent collection), N.Y. Pub. Library, Nat. Acad. Galleries, Brklyn. Mus., Library of Congress, Bowdoin Coll. Art Mus., Oberlin Coll., Addison Gallery Art, Wesleyan U. Library, others, portfolio of prints and poems by Maine poets, The Island, 1961. Recipient Medal of Honor Audubon Artists, 1957; Louis Confort Tiffany Found. grantee, 1959. Mem. Soc. Am. Graphic Artists. Home: 133 Livingston Ave Babylon NY 11702

HALEY, ROGER KENDALL, librarian; b. Boston, Oct. 29, 1938; s. John F. and Rose (Walker) H.; 1 son, Michael J. A.B., Georgetown U., 1960; M.L.S., U. Md., 1976. Reference asst. U.S. Senate Library, Washington, 1964-71, asst. librarian, 1971-73, librarian, 1973—. Mem. Spl. Libraries Assn. Office: US Senate Library Room S-332 The Capitol Washington DC 20510

HALF, ROBERT, personnel agency executive, franchisor, author; b. N.Y.C., Nov. 11, 1918; s. Sidney and Pauline (Kahn) H.; m. Maxine Levison, June 17, 1945; children: Nancy Half Asch, Peggy Half Silbert. HB.S., N.Y. U., 1940. C.P.A., N.Y. Staff acct. S.D. Leidesdorf & Co. (now Ernst & Whinney), 1940-43; office and personnel mgr. Kayser-Roth Corp., 1943-48; chmn. bd. Robert Half of N.Y., Inc., N.Y.C., 1948—; pres. Robert Half Internat., Inc., 1964—, Accountemps Inc., U.S., Can., Eng., 1964—; guest speaker Am. Mgmt. Assn., Nat. Assn. Accts.; guest on TV and radio shows in, U.S. and Can.; mem. panel of experts Boardroom Reports. Author: The Robert Half Way To Get Hired in Today's Job Market, Robert Half on Hiring, Robert Half's Success Guide for Accountants, How to Hire Smart, How to Keep Your Best People; editorial adv.: Jour. Accountancy; editorial bd.: CPA Personnel Report; pub.: Prevailing Starting Salaries for Financial and Data Processing Positions, annually 1950—, Tax Rate Card, annually 1967—; contbr. numerous articles to mags. and newspapers. Expert witness subcoms. U.S. Senate.; Mem. Bd. Appeals Village of Saddle Rock, Great Neck, N.Y., 1956-62. Mem. Am. Acctg. Assn., Assn. Personnel Consultants N.Y. (pres. 1963-64, dir. 1960-65), Nat. Assn. Personnel Consultants, N.Y. State Soc. C.P.A.s, Am. Inst. C.P.A.s, Nat. Assn. Accts., Am. Mgmt. Assn., Assn. Human Resources Cons., Accts. Club Am., U.S. C. of C. Pioneer in specialized personnel recruiting. Office: 522 Fifth Ave New York NY 10036 *Life is unending: only individuals die. But their contributions, for good or bad, live on, and segments of these contributions are passed on from generation to generation.*

HALFEN, DAVID, publishing executive; b. Newark, July 23, 1924; s. Abraham and Rachael (Sudit) H.; m. Genevieve Alberte Martin, Jan. 15, 1948; children: Daniel William, Alexandre Anthony. B.S. with high honors, U. Wis., 1948; Diploma in French Civilization with high honors, U. Paris, 1949; Ph.D. with highest honors, U. Paris, 1954. From asst. editor to editor-in-chief Hart Pub. Co., N.Y.C., 1954-56, 58-62; fgn. affairs editor Scholastic mag., N.Y.C., 1956-58; from field editor to v.p., gen. mgr. Coll. div. Scott, Foresman and Co., Glenview, Ill., 1962-78, v.p., gen. mgr. Lifelong Learning div., 1978—; cons. Coalition for Literacy, 1982-83; participant Am. Productivity Ctr. Conf. for White House Conf. on Productivity, 1983; cons. U.S. Dept. Edn. Round Table on Adult Illiteracy, 1983. Author: La Plume: Revue Symbolists 1889-1899, 1954. Served with AUS, 1943-46; PTO. Mem. Am. Assn. Ret. Persons (cons.), Coalition Adult Edn. Orgns. (cons., dir.), Am. Assn. Adult and Continuing Edn. (cons., panelist).

HALFORD, ROBERT LAVELLE, architect; b. El Dorado, Ark., May 13, 1930; s. Robert Bradley and Algie Lee (Shedd) H.; m. Jean Elizabeth Hayes, Feb. 25, 1956; 1 dau., Lauren Elizabeth; m. Helen Blackmon, Dec. 14, 1974. Student, U. Miss., 1947-49, Fla. State U., 1951-52; B.Arch., U. Tex., 1955-59. Project architect Grayson Gill, 1961-65; partner Enslie O. Oblesby (Architects), 1968; mng. dir., pres. The Oglesby Group, Inc., Dallas, 1970-76; pres. Halford, Summers, Surles & Johnson (now HSJ Architects), 1976—, Halford A/E Systems Corp.; Mem. Nat. Council Archtl. Registration Bds. Served with USNR, 1947-49; Served with USAF, 1951-53. Mem. AIA (commr. Dallas chpt. 1971, 78, treas. 1975, nat. task force and com. 1974, 75, 76). Episcopalian. Home: 8827 Lanarkshire Dallas TX 75238 Office: 5207 McKinney Ave Dallas TX 75205

HALIO, JAY LEON, educator; b. N.Y.C., July 24, 1928; s. Samuel and Anna (Cohen) H.; m. June Doris Cohen, June 4, 1957; children: Brian, Amy. B.A., Syracuse U., 1950; M.A., Yale, 1951, Ph.D., 1956. Instr. English U. Calif. at Davis, 1955-57, asst. prof., 1957-63, asso. prof., 1963-68, prof., 1968, U. Del., 1968—, asso. provost for instrn., 1975-81; mem. central exec. com. Folger Inst. Renaissance Studies, 1975—; Fulbright-Hays sr. lectr. U. Malaya, 1966-67, Buenos Aires, Argentina, fall 1974. Author: Angus Wilson, 1964; Editor: Approaches to Macbeth, 1966, Twentieth Century Interpretations of As You Like It, 1968, Volpone (Jonson), 1968, Macbeth (Shakespeare), 1972, King Lear (Shakespeare), 1973, Shakespeare: Pattern of Excelling Nature, 1978, 1978, British Novelists Since 1960: Dictionary of Literary Biography, Vol. 14, 1983, (with Kenneth Muir, D.J. Palmer) Shakespeare, Man of the Theater, 1983; contbr. essays and revs. to lit. jours. Mem. MLA, English Speaking Union (chpt. dir.), Shakespeare Assn. Am., Renaissance Soc. Am., Phi Beta Kappa. Club: Blue and Gold. Home: 9 Radcliffe Dr Newark DE 19711 Office: Dept English U Del Newark DE 19711

HALKIN, HUBERT, mathematics educator, research mathematican; b. Liege, Belgium, June 5, 1936; came to U.S., 1960; s. Leon E. and Denise (Daude) H.; m. Carolyn Mulliken, June 22, 1964; children: Christopher, Sherrill-Anne. Ingenieur, Universite de Liege, 1960; Ph.D., Stanford U., 1963. Mem. tech. staff Bell Telephone Labs., Whippany, N.J., 1963-65; assoc. prof. math. dept. U. Calif., San Diego, 1965-69, prof., 1969—, dept. chmn., San Diego, 1981—. Editor: Jour. Optimization Theory and Applications, 1968—, Revue Francaise d'Automatique de Recherche Operationnelle, 1973—. Guggenheim fellow, 1971-72. Club: Sierra. Office: Dept Math Univ Calif San Diego La Jolla CA 92093

HALKYARD, EDWIN MILTON, diversified industrial company executive; b. N.Y.C., July 20, 1934; s. Edwin Milton and Edna Alice (Franklin) H.; m. Joan Sherwin, Sept. 15, 1956; children: Edwin, Martin, Christopher, Jonathan. A.B. in Econs., Princeton U., 1956. In various employee relations positions PPG Industries, Pitts., 1956-67; mgr. indsl. relations Allied Corp., Morristown, N.J., 1967-68, dir. indsl. relations, labor relations and employee relations, 1968-78, v.p., corp. relations, 1978-79, sr. v.p. human resources, 1979—; mem. employee relations com. Bus Roundtable, Washington, 1973—. Trustee St. Clare's Hosp., Denville, N.J., 1972—; pres. Arts Council Morris Area, Madison, N.J.; bd. overseers Found. at N.J. Inst. Tech., 1980—; trustee N.J. Symphony Orch. Served to capt. U.S. Army, 1957. Republican. Episcopalian. Club: Princeton (N.Y.C.). Office: Allied Corp PO Box 3000R Morristown NJ 07960

HALL, ADRIENNE ANN, advertising executive; b. Los Angeles; d. Arthur E. and Adelina P. Kosches; m. Maurice Hall; children: Adam, Todd, Stefanie, Victoria. B.A., UCLA. Founding ptnr. HaLL & Levine Advt., Los Angeles, 1960-80; vice-chmn. bd. Eisaman, Johns & Laws Advt. Inc., Los Angeles, 1980—; founding mem. Advt. Industry Emergency Fund, Los Angeles. Trustee UCLA; bd. regents Loyola-Marymount U., Los Angeles; mem. Blue Ribbon of the Music Center, Los Angeles, Pres. Circle, Los Angeles County Mus. Art. Recipient Nat. Headliner award Women in Communications, 1982, Profl. Achievement award UCLA Alumni, 1979; named Woman of Yr. Am Advt. Fedn., 1973, Ad Person of the West award Mktg. and Media Decisions, 1982. Mem. Nat. Women's Forum, Western States Advt. Agys. Assn. (pres.), Los Angeles Advt. Club (pres.), Hollywood Radio and TV Soc. (dir.), Overseas Edn. Fund, Com. 200 (western chmn.). Clubs: Calif. Yacht; Stock Exchange (Los Angeles). Office: Eisaman Johns & Laws Advt 6255 Sunset Blvd Los Angeles CA 90028

HALL, ALBERT CARRUTHERS, cons.; b. Port Arthur, Tex., June 27, 1914; s. Albert Bright and Eva (Carruthers) H.; m. Barbara Johnson, July 6, 1941. B.S., Tex. A. and M. Coll., 1936; Sc.D., Mass. Inst. Tech., 1943. Asst. elec. engring. Mass. Inst. Tech., 1937-39, instr., 1939-43, asst. prof., 1943-46, asso. prof., dir. dynamic analysis and control lab., 1946-50; asso. dir research labs. Bendix Aviation Corp., 1950-52, tech. dir., 1953-54, gen. mgr., 1954-57; dir. engring. (Denver div.); also dir. research Martin Co., 1958-60, v.p. engring., 1960-61, v.p., gen. mgr. space systems div., Balt., 1962-63; dep. for space tech. Office of Dir. Def. Research and Engring., Washington, 1963-65; v.p. advanced tech. Martin Marietta Corp., 1965-67, v.p. engring., 1967-71; asst. sec. def. (intelligence) Office Sec. Def., Washington, 1971-76; asst. to sec. Air Force for strategic and command and control systems, 1976-77, cons., 1977—; mem. torpedo study panel com. undersea warfare Nat. Acad. Sci.-NRC, 1963; chmn. sci. adv. com. Def. Intelligence Agy., 1970-71; mem. arms control bd. Def. Sci. Bd., 1968-

69. Trustee Severn Sch., Severna Park, Md., 1966-75, chmn. bd., 1966-71; trustee Western Md. Coll., Westminster, 1975—. Recipient certificate of merit Naval Ordnance Dept., 1964; Meritorious Civilian Service award Dept. Def., 1965; Exceptional Civilian Service award Def. Intelligency Agy.; Disting. Public Service medal Dept. Def., 1973, 75; Exceptional Service award U.S. Air Force, 1977. Fellow IEEE, Am. Inst. Aeros. and Astronautics; mem. Nat. Acad. Engring., Internat. Acad. Astronautics, Sigma Xi, Eta Kappa Nu (Outstanding Young Elec. Engr. award 1947), Tau Beta Pi. Clubs: Cosmos, Annapolis Yacht. Office: Box 315 C Queenstown MD 21658

HALL, ALBERT LEANDER, JR., lawyer; b. Chgo., June 17, 1926; s. Albert L. and Orpah (Starratt) H.; m. Catherine Ann Comstock, Sept. 27, 1947; children: Terry Lee, David M., Margaret Ruth, Diane Marie. Grad., Lake Forest Acad., 1944; B.S., U. Ill., 1949, M.S., 1950; J.D., Northwestern U., 1955. Bar: Ill. 1955. Tchr. Washington Park High Sch., Racine, Wis., 1950-52; partner firm Hall, Holmberg, Sloan, Roach, Johnston & Fisher (and predecessors), Waukegan, Ill., 1958—; arbitrator Am. Arbitration Assn., 1975—. Trustee Lake County Crippled Children, Inc., pres., 1979-81. Served with USNR, 1944-46. Mem. Lake County, Ill., Am. bar assns., Am. Judicature Soc., Waukegan-North Chicago C. of C. (pres. 1968-69), Delta Tau Delta, Phi Alpha Delta. Club: City of Waukegan (pres. 1970). Home: 2048 Hickory St Waukegan IL 60085 Office: 25 N County St Waukegan IL 60085

HALL, ANDREW DOUGLASS, financial cons.; b. Flushing, N.Y., June 17, 1910; s. Emlen Trenchard and Louisa Frances (Field) H.; m. LeMoyne Noyes, July 31, 1938; children—Andrew D., Emlen F., Anne D., Linda L., Benjamin T. A.B., Princeton U., 1932. With Bonbright & Co., 1932-36, Morgan Stanley & Co., 1936-45; with Diamond Match Co., N.Y.C., 1946-59, asst. to pres., 1946-48, v.p., asst. treas., 1949-50, financial v.p., 1950-59, dir., 1952-59; partner Morgan Stanley & Co., 1959-62; v.p., dir. Stauffer Chem. Co., 1962-68; pres., dir. Internat. Knitlock Corp., N.Y.C., 1969-70; chmn. Waran Assos., Inc., 1970—. Home and office: David's Hill Rd Bedford Hills NY 10507

HALL, ARNOLD ALEXANDER, mechanical and electrical manufacturing executive; b. Liverpool, Eng., Apr. 23, 1915; married; 3 daus. Grad. with honors, Clare Coll., Cambridge. Mem. staff Royal Aircraft Establishment, 1938-45; dir. Farnborough, 1951-55; Zaharoff prof. aviation U. London, head dept. aero., 1946-51; tech. dir. Hawker Siddeley Group, 1955-58, dir., 1958-63, vice chmn., mng. dir., 1963-67, chmn., mng. dir., 1967-81, chmn., 1981—; mng. dir. Bristol Siddeley Engines, Ltd. (merger Bristol Aero-Engines and Armstrong Siddeley Motors 1959), 1958-63, vice chmn., 1963-66; dir. Lloyds Bank Ltd., 1966—, Imperial Chem. Industries Ltd., 1970—, Phoenix Assurance Co. Ltd., 1969—, Onan Corp., U.S.A., 1976-80, Lloyd Bank U.K. Mgmt. Ltd., 1979—, Fasco Industries, Inc., 1980-81. Created knight, 1954; recipient Dutch A.G. von Baumhauer medal for contbn. to understanding problems of fatigue in aircraft structures, 1959; Gold medal Royal Aero. Soc., 1962. Fellow Royal Soc. (v.p., council 1978-79), Royal Aero. Soc. (hon., pres. 1958-59, council 1947-66), Soc. Brit. Aero-Space Cos. (council 1963-77), Soc. Aero-Space Cos. U.K. (pres. 1972-73), Am. Inst. Aeros. and Astronautics (hon.), Instn. Mech. Engrs. (hon.), Instn. Elec. Engrs. (hon.), Clare Coll.; mem. Nat. Acad. Engring. (fgn. affiliate), ASME (hon.), Locomotive and Allied Mfrs. Assn. (pres. 1968-69). Address: Hawker Siddeley Group PLC 18 St James Sq London SW1 England

HALL, ARTHUR RAYMOND, JR., clergyman; b. Danville, Ill., Apr. 16, 1922; s. Arthur Raymond and Hetta Ada (Wheeler) H.; m. Lou Ann Benson, Mar. 16, 1946; children: Janet Marie Hall Graff, Laura Ann Hall Scott, Nancy Marion. A.B., U. Ill., 1946, M.A., 1948; M.Div. cum laude, Union Theol. Sem., N.Y.C., 1951; D.D., Hanover Coll., 1961. Staff asst. McKinley Meml. Ch. and Found., Champaign, Ill., 1946-48; student asst. First Presbyn Ch., N.Y.C., 1948-50; ordained to ministry Presbyn. Ch., 1951; pastor First Presbyn. Ch., Monmouth, Ill., 1951-58, Central Presbyn. Ch., Louisville, 1958-67, Bradley Hills Presbyn. Ch., Bethesda, Md., 1967—; pres. bd. Christian edn. United Presbyn. Ch., 1968-73; sec., bd. dirs. Louisville Presbyn. Sem., 1962-70; chmn. renewal and extension of ministry (United Presbyn. Gen. Assembly), 1965-68, mem. joint com. on Presbyn. Reunion, 1969-83; moderator Synod of Piedmont, 1974-75; trustee U.P. Ch., 1974-83; bd. dirs. U.P. Found., 1974-83; del. Uniting Assembly of World Alliance of Ref. Chs., Nairobi, Kenya, 1970. Contbr. articles to periodicals. Pres. Citizens Met. Planning Council, Louisville, 1962; chmn. Mayor's Adv. Com. for Community Devel., Louisville, 1963-67; v.p. Louisville YMCA Downtown bd., 1963; bd. dirs. Louisville Health and Welfare Council, 1963-67, Greater Washington Council Chs., Johnson C. Smith Theol. Sem., Interdenominational Theol. Center, Atlanta, 1973; trustee Centre Coll. Ky., 1959-73, Union Theol. Sem., N.Y.C., 1975—, Travelers Aid Soc., Louisville, 1959-67; v.p. Travelers Aid Soc., 1961-67. Served to lt. (j.g.) USNR, 1943-46. Mem. Am. Guild Organists, Beta Theta Pi, Phi Delta Phi. Democrat. Clubs: Rotary, Interchurch (Washington). Home: 8400 Whitman Dr Bethesda MD 20817 Office: 6601 Bradley Blvd Bethesda MD 20817

HALL, ASAPH HALE, bus. exec.; b. Elmira, N.Y., Nov. 22, 1933; s. Asaph Bloomfield and Sarah Elizabeth (Lowman) H.; m. Dorothy Ann Mayes, Aug. 26, 1961; children—Jonathan Hale, Elizabeth Anne, Christopher Mayes, Jennifer Lynne. A.B., Dartmouth, 1955, M.S., 1956. With Westinghouse Electric Corp., 1956-69, mktg. mgr., 1964-69; spl. asst. to under sec. Dept. Transp., Washington, 1969-70, spl. asst. to dep. under sec., 1970-73, spl. asst. to sec. transp., 1973-74; dep. adminstr. Fed. R.R. Adminstrn., 1974-75, adminstr., 1975-77; staff v.p. corp. planning Gen. Dynamics Corp., St. Louis, 1977—; pres. Fore River R.R., 1977—. Mem. Dartmouth Coll. Alumni Council, 1976-79. Served with AUS, 1956-58. Pub. Affairs fellow Brookings Instn., 1966. Mem. IEEE, Phi Beta Kappa. Republican. Presbyn. Clubs: Dartmouth of Md. (pres. 1968-70), Dartmouth (St. Louis); Town and Country Racquet. Home: 3003 Westham Dr Saint Louis MO 63131 Office: Gen Dynamics Corp Pierre Laclede Center Saint Louis MO 63105

HALL, BERNARD, univ. ofcl.; b. N.Y.C., May 7, 1925; m. Evelyn Pimentel, Feb. 11, 1954. B.A., Bklyn. Coll., 1948; Ph.D., U. Calif. at Berkeley, 1955. Teaching asst., then research asst. U. Calif. at Berkeley, 1948-53, vis. grad. research economist, summer 1955; asst. prof. econs. Humboldt State Coll., 1953-57; asst. prof. bus. adminstrn. Fresno State Coll., 1958-60, vis. asso. prof., summer 1963; mem. faculty Kent (Ohio) State U., 1957-58, 60—, prof. econs., 1966—, asso. provost, 1969-70, exec. v.p., provost, 1970-74. Served with AUS, 1943-46. Address: Kent State U Kent OH 44240

HALL, BRIAN KEITH, educator; b. Port Kembla, N.S.W., Australia, Oct. 28, 1941; s. Harry J. and Doris (Gerrado) H.; m. June Denise Priestley, May 21, 1966; children: Derek Andrew, Imogene Elizabeth. B.Sc., U. New Eng., Australia, 1963, 1965, Ph.D., 1968, D.Sc., 1978. Teaching fellow U. New Eng., Armidale, 1965-68; asst. prof. biology Dalhousie U., Halifax, N.S., Can., 1968-72, assoc. prof., 1972-75, prof., 1975—, chmn. dept. biology, 1975—; vis. prof. U. Guelph, 1975, U. Queensland, Australia, 1981, Southampton U., Eng., 1982. Author: Development and Celluar Skeletal Biology, 1979; editor: Cartilage, 3 vols., 1983. Recipient Young Scientist of Yr. award Atlantic Provinces Interuniv. com. in Scis., 1974; fellow Nuffield Found., 1982. Mem. Council Biology of Can. (council 1979-81), AAAS. Club: Dalhousie Faculty. Home: 2384 Armcrescent E Halifax NS Canada B3L 3C7 Office: Dalhousie U Coburg Rd Halifax NS Canada B3H 4J1

HALL, BRINLEY MORGAN, investment co. exec.; b. Boston, Jan. 4, 1912; s. John Loomer and Dorothy Brinley (Morgan) H.; m. Elizabeth Jaques, June 10, 1939; children—Brinley Morgan, Dorothy B., Denison M., Robert T. Grad., St. Mark's Sch., 1930; B.A., Yale, 1934; student, Corpus Christi Coll., Cambridge (Eng.), U., 1934-35, Harvard Law Sch., 1935-37; LL.B., Northeastern U., 1947. Bar: Mass. bar 1947. Investment banker Whiting Weeks & Stubbs, Inc. (now Moseley Hallgarten, Estabrook & Weedon), Boston, 1937-42; since practiced in, Boston; with Choate, Hall & Stewart, 1947-62, partner, 1951-62; asst. atty. gen. Commonwealth of Mass., 1948-49; exec. dir Com. Central Bus. Dist., 1962-70; v.p., treas., sec. Hubbard Real Estate Investments, 1970—; also trustee; dir. Amstar Corp., N.Y.; trustee Provident Instn. for Savs., Boston. Served as maj. USAAF, 1942-46. Mem. Mass., Boston bar assns. Home: 218 Hart St Beverly Farms MA 01915 Office: 125 High St Boston MA 02110

HALL, CARL WILLIAM, mechanical and agricultural engineer, scientific research foundation executive; b. Tiffin, Ohio, Nov. 16, 1924; s. Lester and Irene (Routzahn) H.; m. Mildred Evelyn Wagner, Sept. 5, 1949; 1 dau., Claudia Elizabeth. B.S., B. in Agrl. Engring. summa cum laude, Ohio State U., 1948; M.M.E., U. Del., 1950; Ph.D., Mich. State U., 1952. Registered profl. engr., Mich., Ohio, Wash. Instr. U. Del., 1948-50, asst. prof., 1950-51, Mich. State U., 1951-53, asso. prof., 1953-55, prof., 1955-70, research adviser, 1957-64, chmn. dept. agrl. engring., 1964-70; dean, dir. research (Coll. Engring.); prof. mech. engring. Wash. State U., Pullman, 1970—, pres. Research Found., 1973—; asst. dir. Directorate for Engring. NSF; with ESCOE, Inc., Washington, 1979; research cons. U. P.R., 1957, 63; cons. U. Nacional de Colombia, 1960; cons. dairy engring., India, 1961, cons. food engring., China, 1961, Mission to Ecuador, 1966; U. Nigeria, 1967; cons. UNDP/SF Project 80 (higher edn. Latin Am.), 1964-70, Council Grad. Schs., Washington, 1970, Brazil project world food and nutrition study Nat. Acad. Sci., 1976-77, mem. engring. edn. del. to, People's Republic of China, 1978; co-chmn. Nat. Acad. Sci.-India Nat. Sci. Acad. Workshop, New Delhi, 1979; with ACA, Inc. (cons. engring.), 1956-70, pres., 1962-70; chmn. Nat. Dairy Engring. Conf., 1953-66; mem. U.S. sci. exchange del. to USSR, 1958; mem. postgrad. edn. select com. U.S. Navy, Monterey, Calif., 1975. Author: Drying Farm Crops, 1957, Agricultural Engineering Index 1907-1960, 1961-70, 71-80, (with others) Drying of Milk and Milk Products, 1966, 71, Agricultural Mechanization for Developing Countries, 1973; co-editor: Agricultural Engineers Handbook, 1960, Processing Equipment for Agricultural Products, 1963, 2d edit., 1979, Spanish edit., 1968, Milk Pasteurization, 1968, Ency. of Food Engineering, 1971, 84, Drying Cereal Grains, 1974, Dairy Technology and Engineering, 1976, Errors in Experimentation, 1977, Dictionary of Drying, 1979, Drying and Storage of Agricultural Products, 1980, Biomass as an Alternative Fuel, 1981, Dictionary of Energy, 1983; editor: Drying Technology:Marcel Dekker, Inc; Contbr. yearbooks, encys., handbooks. Sec. Tefft Found. for Bible Study, 1960-70. Served with AUS, 1943-46; ETO. Decorated Bronze Star; recipient outstanding tchr. award Alpha Zeta, 1957, 58; Distinguished Faculty award Mich. State U., 1963; Centennial Achievement award Ohio State U., 1970; Massey-Ferguson Edn. medal, 1976; Max Eyth medal, Germany, 1979; medal du Merite, France, 1979; La Medaille d'Argent, Paris, 1980. Fellow AAAS; Mem. ASME (chmn. central Mich. 1959-60), Am. Soc. Agrl. Engrs. (chmn. electric power and processing div. 1960, div. dir. 1962-64, 67-69, pres. 1974-75, Engr. of Year award Mich. chpt. 1964, Pacific Northeast region 1973), Am. Soc. Engring. Edn., Am. Inst. Biol. Scis., Nat. Soc. Profl. Engrs., Wash. Soc. Profl. Engrs. (nat. dir. 1975-79), Internat. Commn. Agrl. Engrs. (v.p. 1965-74), Engrs. Council for Profl. Devel. (exec. com., dir., sec. 1973-74, chmn. engring. accreditation comm. 1979-80), 99th Inf. Div. Assn., Inst. Food Tech., Sigma Xi, Alpha Zeta, Tau Beta Pi, Phi Kappa Phi, Gamma Sigma Delta, Phi Lambda Tau. Home: 3017 N Nottingham St Arlington VA 22207 Office: NSF Washington DC 20225

HALL, CARLYLE WASHINGTON, JR., lawyer; b. N.Y.C., Feb. 6, 1943; s. Carlyle Washington and Anzonette Marguerite (Asmussen) H.; Aug. 28, 1964 (div.); 1 son, Carlyle Washington III; m. Joanne Jackson, Jan. 1, 1977; children: Christopher Jackson, Andrew Jackson. B.A., Yale U., 1963; J.D. magna cum laude, Harvard U., 1966. Bar: Cal. bar. Tchr. law, adminstr. Internat. Legal Center, Sudan, Uganda, 1966-69; asso. firm O'Melveny and Myers, Los Angeles, 1969-71; co-founder, staff atty. Center for Law in Pub. Interest, Los Angeles, 1971—; Commr. Tahoe Regional Planning Agy., 1981-83. Mem. citizens adv. com. Los Angeles Central Bus. Dist. Plan, 1976; mem. land use task force Planning and Conservation League, 1975; bd. dirs. Pub. Counsel, Inc., 1977-79, Calif. Common Cause, 1980—. Recipient Environ. Activist of Year award Ventura County Environ. Coalition, 1975; Clean Air award Calif. Lung Assn., 1978; Durfee award for Contbn. to Advancement of Human Dignity, Durfee Found., 1982. Litigated pub. interest cases in Calif. Home: 2711 Anchor Ave Los Angeles CA 90064 Office: 10951 W Pico Blvd Los Angeles CA 90064

HALL, CHARLES DENIS, telecommunications equipment executive; b. Lennoxville, Que., Can., July 1, 1938; s. Charles Wayne and Grace Elizabeth H.; m. Florence May Falkingham, Nov. 23, 1963; 1 son, Jeffrey. B.Engring., McGill U., Montreal, 1960; M.Sc., U. Sask., 1961, Ph.D., 1964. Registered profl. engr., Ont. With No. Electric Co. Ltd., Montreal, 1964-71, exec. v.p. devel., 1974-76; v.p. switching devel. Bell-No. Research Ltd., Ottawa, 1972-74, exec. v.p. devel., 1974-76, pres., 1976-81; exec. v.p. mktg. and tech. No. Telecom Can. Ltd., Islington, Ont., 1981-82, sr. v.p. tech., Mississauga, Ont., 1982—. Author articles in field. Mem. Engring. Inst. Can., IEEE, Assn. Profl. Engrs. Ont. Christian Scientist. Address: 33 City Centre Dr Mississauga ON L5B 2N5 Canada

HALL, CHARLES FREDERICK, space scientist, govt. adminstr.; b. San Francisco, Apr. 7, 1920; s. Charles Rogers and Edna Mary (Gibson) H.; m. Constance Vivienne Andrews, Sept. 18, 1942; children—Steven R., Charles Frederick, Frank A. B.S., U. Calif., Berkeley, 1942. Aero. research scientist NACA (later NASA), Moffett Field, Calif., 1942-60, mem. staff space projects, 1960-63, mgr., 1963-80. Recipient Disting. Service medal NASA, 1974, Achievement award Am. Astronautical Soc., 1974, Spl. Achievement award Nat. Civil Service League, 1976, Astronautics Engr. award Nat. Space Club, 1979. Research, reports on performance of wings and inlets at transonic and supersonic speeds, on conical-cambered wings at transonic and supersonic speeds, 1942-60; Pioneer Project launched 4 solar orbiting, 2 Jupiter and 2 Venus spacecraft. Home: 817 Berry St Los Altos CA 94022

HALL, CHARLES WASHINGTON, lawyer; b. Dallas, June 30, 1930; s. Albert Brown and Eleanor Pauline (Hopkins) H.; m. Mary Louise Watkins, Aug. 3, 1957; children—Kathryn Louise, Allison Ash, Charles Washington III. B.A., U. of South, 1951; J.D., So. Methodist U., 1954, LL.M. in Taxation, 1959. Bar: Tex. 1954. Asso. firm Story, Armstrong & Steger, Dallas, 1954-56, partner, 1957; asso. firm Fulbright & Jaworski, Houston, 1957-66, partner, 1967—; dir. Friedman Industries, Inc. Pres., trustee Sarah Campbell Blaffer Found., Houston; bd. dirs. Goodwill Industries, Houston; trustee Southwestern Legal Found., Dallas, S.W. Research Inst., San Antonio, Tex. Fellow Am. Bar Found.; mem. Houston Bar Assn., Dallas Bar Assn., State Bar Tex., Am. Bar Assn., Internat. Bar Assn., Am. Coll. Tax Counsel, Am. Law Inst. Episcopalian. Clubs: River Oaks Country, Coronado, Houston City (Houston); Met. (Washington). Home: 3417 Ella Lee Ln Houston TX 77027 Office: 8th Floor Bank of SW Bldg Houston TX 77002

HALL, CHARLES WILLIAM, medical educator; b. Gage, Okla., Feb. 8, 1922; s. Cecil A. and Helen (Greene) H.; m. Sheila Ann Fowler, Dec. 3, 1979; children by previous marriage—Daniel C., Kendall W., Gregory A., Patrick C., Conan L. A.B., Kans. U., 1950, M.A. in Comparative Anatomy, 1952, M.D., 1956. Diplomate: Am. Bd. Surgery. Rotating intern Kans. U. Med. Center, 1956-57, resident surgery, 1957-62; fellow cardiovascular surgery Baylor U. Coll. Medicine, 1962-64; project dir. artificial heart program Nat. Heart Inst., 1964; project dir., artificial heart program Baylor U. Coll. Medicine, 1964-68, asst. prof. surgery, also asst. prof. physiology, 1964-68; cons. S.W. Research Inst., San Antonio, 1966-68, mgr. artificial organs research dept. bioengring., 1968-70, dir. dept. bioengring., 1970-75, inst. med. scientist, 1975—; clin. asst. prof. surgery U. Tex. Med. Sch. at San Antonio, 1969—. Editorial bd.: Jour. Biomed. Materials Research, Artificial Organs; Contbr. articles to profl. jours. Served with USAAF, 1942-46. Recipient 1st place prize essay contest Houston Surg. Soc., 1963, 64, S.W. Surg. Soc., 1964; Medalla de Oro Minister Bienestar Sociale, Argentina, 1975; Outstanding Contbn. Biomaterials award Clemson U., 1977; prof. honoris causa Cath. U. Cordoba, Argentina, 1965. Fellow Am. Coll. Cardiology, Am. Coll. Chest Physicians; mem. Am. Soc. Artificial Organs, Am. Burn Assn., Am. Heart Assn., N.Y. Acad. Sci., Assn. Advancement Med. Instrumentation, Instrument Soc. Am., AAAS, AMA, Biomed. Engring. Soc., Soc. Plastics Engrs., Tex. Heart Assn., Soc. for Biomaterials (founding pres.), Internat. Cardiovascular Soc., Soc. Surg. Rosario (Argentine), Sigma Xi (pres. Alamo chpt. 1981), Phi Beta Pi, Phi Sigma. Club: Mason. Co-inventor artificial heart; developer artificial skin used as bioadherent dressing for 3d deg. burns; developer permanently attached artificial limb; introduced velour fabrics into fields of biomaterials and surgery. Home: 8733 Cross Mountain Trail San Antonio TX 78255 Office: PO Drawer 28510 San Antonio TX 78284

HALL, CLAUDE HAMPTON, historian, educator; b. Proffit, Va., Sept. 29, 1922; s. Robert Montgomery and Josephine (Rodes) H.; m. Mary Inez Wingfield, Aug. 19, 1951; children—Claude Hampton, David Bruce. B.A., U. Va., 1947, M.A., 1949, Ph.D., 1954. Asst. reference librarian U. Va., 1947-51; instr. history Tex. A&M U., College Station, 1951-55, asst. prof., 1955-59, asso. prof., 1959-64, prof., 1964—; vis. asso. prof. U. Va., 1960-61, U. Mo., 1964. Author: Abel Parker Upshur: Conservative Virginian, 1790-1844, 1964; contbr. articles to profl. jours. Served with U.S. Army, 1942-45. Mem. AAUP, ACLU, Am. Hist. Assn., So. Hist. Assn., Va. Hist. Soc., Orgn. Am. Historians, Tex. State Hist. Assn. (H. Bailey Carroll award 1968), East Tex. Hist. Assn. (pres. 1977), Soc. Historians Am. Fgn. Relations, Soc. Historians Early Am. Rep., Phi Kappa Phi (past chpt. pres.). Republican. Baptist. Office: Dept History Tex A&M U College Station TX 77843

HALL, CONRAD, cinematographer; b. Tahiti, 1926; s. James Norman H. Student, U. So. Calif. Early career in indsl. and TV films, commls.; films include The Wild Seed, 1965, Morituri, 1965, Harper, 1966, The Professionals, 1966, Cool Hand Luke, 1967, In Cold Blood, 1967, Hell in the Pacific, 1968, Butch-Cassidy and the Sundance Kid, 1969, Tell Them Willie Boy is Here, 1969, The Happy Ending, 1969, Fat City, 1972, Electra Glide in Blue, 1973, Smile, 1975, The Day of the Locust, 1975, Marathon Man, 1976. Recipient Oscar award for Butch Cassidy and the Sundance Kid, 1969. Office: care Am Soc Cinematographers 1782 N Orange Dr Hollywood CA 90028 *

HALL, CYNTHIA HOLCOMB, judge; b. Los Angeles, Feb. 19, 1929; d. Harold Romeyn and Mildred Gould (Kuck) Holcomb; m. John Harris Hall, June 6, 1970 (dec. Oct. 1980); 1 son, Harris Holcomb; 1 dau. by previous marriage, Desma Letitia. A.B., Stanford U., 1951, J.D., 1954; LL.M., N.Y. U., 1960. Bar: Ariz. bar 1954, Calif. bar 1956. Law clk. to judge U.S. Ct. Appeals 9th Circuit, 1954-55; trial atty. tax div. Dept. Justice, 1960-64; atty.-adviser Office Tax Legis. Counsel, Treasury Dept., 1964-66; mem. firm Brawerman & Holcomb, Beverly Hills, Calif., 1966-72; judge U.S. Tax Ct., Washington, 1972-81, U.S. Dist. Ct. for central dist. Calif., 1981—. Served to lt. (j.g.) USNR, 1951-53. Office: US Courthouse 312 N Spring St Los Angeles CA 90012

HALL, DANIEL RAY ACOMB, educator, college dean; b. Dansville, N.Y., June 17, 1927; s. Daniel Ray Acomb and Louise (Schudoma) H.; m. Pauline Ruth Steinkamp, June 3, 1950; 1 dau., Ruth Alice. B.A., Wesleyan U., 1948; M.A., Columbia, 1949, Ed.D., 1958; postgrad., U. S.C., 1969, U. N.C., 1969. Asst. to dean adminstrn. Newark Coll. Engring., then asst. to pres., 1952-59; dir. admissions N.Y. State U. Coll. at Geneseo, 1959, prof. econs., 1959-67, then dir. summer session, dir. extension div., dean grad. studies, to 1967; prof. econs. Madison Coll., Harrisonburg, Va., 1967-76, dean coll., provost, dir. Center for Econ. Edn.; prof. econs. Trenton (N.J.) State Coll., 1976—, dean grad. study, 1976-83, dir. Ctr. Econ. Edn., 1983—; cons. Am. Assn. Colls. Tchr. Edn. Trustee N.J. Council on Econ. Edn.; mem. div. profl. ministry and continuing edn. com. N.J. Synod Luth. Ch. Am., until 1981; v.p. Tri State Commn. on Edn., 1979—. Named outstanding Educator Am., 1971. Mem. Phi Delta Kappa, Kappa Delta Pi (nat. commn. on plans for future), Delta Sigma Rho, Alpha Phi Omega, Delta Sigma Pi, Phi Nu Theta, Phi Chi Theta, Pi Gamma Mu, Omicron Delta Epsilon. Home: 14 Metekunk Dr Trenton NJ 08638

HALL, DARYL, musician; b. Pottstown, Pa., Oct. 11, 1949; s. Walter F. and Betty W. (Wanner) H. Ed., Temple U. Mem.: Hall and Oates Duo, 1972—; albums include: Sacred Songs, War Babies, Hall and Oates, No Goodbyes, Live Time, Rock and Soul, Whole Oates, Back Street; songs include: Sara Smile. Recipient Am. Music award for favorite pop group, 1984. Address: care Am Talent Internat 888 7th Ave New York NY 10106

HALL, DAVID, sound archivist, writer; b. New Rochelle, N.Y., Dec. 16, 1916; s. Fairfax and Eleanor Rayburn (Remy) H.; m., Sept. 8, 1940; children: Marion Hall Hunt, Jonathan, Peter, Susannah. B.S., Yale U., 1939; postgrad., Columbia U., 1940-41. Advt. copy writer Columbia Records, Bridgeport, Conn., 1940-42; music program annotator NBC, N.Y.C., 1942-48; classics music dir. Mercury Record Corp., N.Y.C., 1948-56; music editor Stereo Rev., N.Y.C., 1957-62, contbg. editor, 1962—; pres. Composers Rec., Inc., N.Y.C., 1963-67; curator Rodgers and Hammerstein Archives of Recorded Sound., N.Y. Pub. Library, N.Y.C., 1967-83; cons. Rodgers and Hammerstein Archives of Recorded Sound., N.Y. Pub. Libarry, N.Y.C., 1983—; dir. Music Center Am.-Scandinavian Found., N.Y.C., 1950-57; Fulbright vis. scholar Copenhagen U., 1956-57; free-lance writer, lectr., cons. in field. Author: The Record Book, 1940-48. Trustee Wilton Library Assn., Conn., 1975-79. Decorated knight Order of Lion, Finland. Mem. Nat. Acad. Red. Arts and Scis. (trustee 1965-67), Nat. Music Council (dir. 1968-80), Assn. for Recorded Sound Collections (pres. 1980-82). Democrat. Club: Yale (N.Y.C.). Home: 155 Catalpa Rd Wilton CT 06897 Home: Castine ME 04421 Office: NY Public Library Performing Arts Research Ctr 111 Amsterdam Ave New York NY 10018

HALL, DEREK HARRY, drug company sales executive; b. Darfield, Eng., May 31, 1945; came to U.S., 1960; s. vincent H. and Dathleen (Hinchliffe) Hamblin; m. Shelby Thompson, May 5, 1967; children: Bradley D., Trevor T., Allison S., Amanda S. Student, pub. schs., Ogden, Utah. Sales rep. McKesson Drug Co., Salt Lake City, 1968-74, dist. sales mgr., 1974-79, regional sales mgr., Walnut Creek, Calif., 1979-80, zone gen. mgr., Salt Lake City, 1980-83, sr. v.p. sales, San Francisco, 1983—. Author: Retail Account Manager Handbook, 1979. Missionary Mormon ch., Toronto, Ont., Can., 1964-67; troop chmn. Boy Scouts Am., Salt Lake City, 1980-82, scoutmaster, Danville, Calif., 1982-83. Recipient Sales Mgmt. award of excellence Glenbrook Labs., 1975, 76, award for Service of Pharmacy Marion Labs, 1983; named to Hall of Fame McKesson Drug co., 1976. Mem. Utah Pharm. Assn., Idaho Pharm Assn., Nat. Wholesale Druggist Assn. (chmn. mktg. com. 1980-81). Republican. Home: 661 Derbyshire Pl Danville CA 94526 Office: McKesson Corp 1 Post St San Francisco CA 94104

HALL, DON ALAN, newspaper editor; b. Indpls., Aug. 7, 1938; s. Oscar B. and Ruth Ann (Leak) H.; m. Roberta Louise Bash, Apr. 30, 1960; children: Alice Leigh, Nancy Elizabeth. B.A., Ind. U., 1960, M.A., 1968. News editor Rock Springs (Wyo.) Daily Rocket-Miner, 1960-63; mag. editor, picture editor Waukegan (Ill.) News-Sun, 1964-66; reporter, copy editor Salem (Oreg.) Capital Jour., 1966-70; free lance journalist, Victoria, B.C., Can., 1970-74; copy editor, sci. writer, music reviewer Corvallis (Oreg.) Gazette-Times, 1974-78, copy desk chief, 1978-82, news editor, 1983—; author weekly nature column for Oreg. newspapers, 1976—. Author: On Top Of Oregon, 1975. Recipient Westinghouse-AAAS Sci. Writing award, 1977. Office: Corvallis Gazette Times PO Box 368 Corvallis OR 97339

HALL, DONALD, writer; b. New Haven, Sept. 20, 1928; s. Donald Andrew and Lucy (Wells) H.; m. Kirby Thompson, Sept. 13, 1952 (div. Feb. 1969); children: Andrew, Philippa; m. Jane Kenyon, Apr. 17, 1972. B.A., Harvard U., 1951; B. Litt. (Henry fellow), Oxford U., 1953; postgrad., Stanford U., 1953-54; L.H.D. (hon.), Plymouth State Coll, D. Litt., Presbyn. Coll. Creative writing fellow Stanford U., 1953; jr. fellow Soc. Fellows, Harvard U., 1954-57; asst. prof. U. Mich., Ann Arbor, 1957-61, asso. prof., 1961-66, prof., 1966-77; poetry editor Paris Review, 1953-61; mem. poetry bd. Wesleyan U. Press, 1958-64; cons. Harper & Row, 1964-81; judge Bollingen Prize for Poetry, 1958, 59, Lamont Poetry Competition, 1967-69, Nat. Book Awards, 1968, Edgar Allen Poe and Copernicus awards Acad. Am. Poets, 1975, Nat. Poetry Series, 1979. Author: poems Exiles and Marriages, 1955, The Dark Houses, 1958, A Roof of Tiger Lilies, 1963, The Alligator Bride, 1969, The Yellow Room, 1971, The Town of Hill, 1975, A Blue Wing Tilts at the Edge of the Sea, 1975, Kicking the Leaves, 1978, The Toy Bone, 1979; criticism Marianne Moore: The Cage and the Animal, 1970, Goatfoot, Milktongue, Twinbird, 1978, To Keep Moving, 1980, The Weather for Poetry, 1982; juvenile Andrew the Lion Farmer, 1959, Riddle Rat, 1977; Oxcart Man, 1979; memoir String Too Short to be Saved, 1961, 79, Remembering Poets, 1978; biography Henry Moore, 1966, Dock Ellis in the Country of Baseball, 1976, (with David Finn) As the Eye Moves, 1970; limericks The Gentleman's Alphabet Book, 1972; prose Writing Well, 1973, 3d edit., 1979, 4th edit., 1982, Playing Around, 1974; editor: Harvard Adv. Anthology, 1950, (with L. Simpson and R. Pack) The New Poets of England and America, 1957, (with R. Pack) New Poets of England and America, Second Selection, 1962, A Poetry Sampler, 1962, Contemporary American Poetry, 1962, 2d edit., 1971, (with W. Taylor) Poetry in English, 1963, 2d edit., 1970, (with S. Spender) A Concise Ency. of English and American Poets and Poetry, 1963, 2d edit., 1970, Faber Book of Modern Verse, 1966, The Modern Stylists, 1968, A Choice of Whitman's Verse, 1968, Man and Boy, 1968; Anthology American Poetry, 1969, Pleasures of Poetry, 1971, (with D. Emblen) A Writer's Reader, 1976, 2d edit., 1979, 3d edit., 1982, To Read Literature, 1981, rev., 1983, To Read Poetry, 1982, Oxford Book American Literary Anecdotes, 1981, Claims for Poetry, 1982. Deacon South Danbury Ch. Recipient Lloyd McKim Garrison prize for poetry Harvard, 1951; John Osborne Sergeant prize for Latin translation Harvard, 1951; Newdigate prize for poetry Oxford U., 1952; Lamont Poetry Selection Acad. Am. Poets, 1955; Edna St. Vincent Millay Meml. award Poetry Soc. Am., 1955; Longview Found. award, 1960; Sarah Joseph Hale award, 1983; Guggenheim fellow, 1963, 72. Mem. MLA, AAUP, Authors Guild. Home: Eagle Pond Farm Danbury NH 03230

HALL, DONALD H., geophysicist; b. Maple Creek, Sask., Can., Nov. 23, 1925; s. John R.H. and Gertrude (Reid) H.; m. Esther B. Crabbe, June 2, 1955; children: Bernard J., Norman G., Judith D. B.Sc. with honors, U. Alta., 1948; M.A., U. Toronto, 1950; Ph.D., U. B.C., 1959. Lectr. geophysics U. B.C., 1957-59; asst. prof. U. Sask., 1959-62; research officer (Sask. Research Council), 1959-62; asso. prof. geophysics U. Man., Winnipeg, 1962-69, prof., 1979—, head dept. earth scis., 1978—. Author: History of the Earth Sciences in the Scientific and Industrial Revolutions, 1976; contbr. articles to profl. jours.; regional editor: Geoexploration, 1965—; editor: Can. Geophys. Bull., 1980—. Served with Can. Armed Forces, 1944-45. Mem. Am. Geophys. Union, Canadian Geophys. Union, Canadian Soc. Exploration Geophysicists, Geol. Assn. Can. Jewish. Home: 841 Borebank St Winnipeg MB R3N 1G5 Canada Office: Dept Eart Scis U Man Winnipeg R3T 2N2 Canada

HALL, DONALD JOYCE, greeting card company executive; b. Kansas City, Mo., July 9, 1928; s. Joyce Clyde and Elizabeth Ann (Dilday) H.; m. Adele Coryell, Nov. 28, 1953; children: Donald Joyce, Margaret Elizabeth, David Earl. A.B., Dartmouth, 1950; LL.D., William Jewell Coll., Denver U., 1977. With Hallmark Cards, Inc., Kansas City, Mo., 1953—, adminstrv. v.p., 1958-66, pres., chief exec. officer, 1966-83, chmn. bd., chief exec. officer, 1983—, also dir.; dir. Dayton-Hudson Corp., Mut. Benefit Life Ins. Co., William E. Coutts Co., Ltd.; past dir. Fed. Res. Bank Kansas City, Business Men's Assurance Co., Commerce Bank Kansas City, 1st Nat. Bank Lawrence. Pres. Civic Council Greater Kansas City; past chmn. bd. Kansas City Assn. Trusts and Founds.; Bd. dirs. Am. Royal Assn., Friends of Art, Eisenhower Found.; bd. dirs. Harry S. Truman Library Inst., Kansas City Symphony; past pres. Pembroke Country Day Sch., Civic Council of Greater Kansas City; trustee, past chmn. exec. com. Midwest Research Inst.; trustee Nelson-Atkins Museum of Art. Served to 1st lt. AUS, 1950-53. Recipient Eisenhower Medallion award, 1973; Parsons Sch. Design award, 1977; 3d Ann. Civic Service award Hebrew Acad. Kansas City, 1976; Chancellor's medal U. Mo., Kansas City, 1977; Disting. Service citation U. Kans., 1980. Mem. Kansas City C. of C. (named Mr. Kansas City 1972, dir.), AIA (hon.). Home: 6320 Aberdeen Rd Shawnee Mission KS 66208 Office: Hallmark Cards Inc 25th and McGee Sts Kansas City MO 64141

HALL, DONALD KEITH, lawyer; b. Ely, Nev., Aug. 24, 1918; s. Edward Clyde and Mabel Louise H.; m. Alla T. Puchalsky, Apr. 27, 1947; children—Melanie, Matthew, Natalie, Kristina, Theodore. B.S., U. Calif. at Los Angeles, 1940; J.D., U. So. Calif., 1949. Bar: Calif. bar 1949. Since practiced in, Los Angeles; law clk. U.S. Ct. Appeals 9th Circuit, Los Angeles, 1949-50; staff atty. Western Air Lines Inc., Los Angeles, 1950-52; mem. firm Darling, Hall, Rae & Gute, Los Angeles, 1953-79; sr. v.p., gen. counsel, sec. Western Air Lines, Inc., Los Angeles, 1979-81; mem. firm. Darling, Hall & Rae, Los Angeles, 1982—. Pres. South Pasadena Unified Sch. Dist., 1964. Served to capt. AUS, 1942-47. Mem. Los Angeles County Bar Assn. (pres. 1972-73), ABA, State Bar Calif., Order of Coif, Phi Kappa Phi. Home: 1315 Chelten Way South Pasadena CA 91030 Office: 523 W South St Los Angeles CA 90014

HALL, DONALD S., planetarium administrator; b. Columbus, Ohio, June 3, 1940; s. William Kenneth and Irene Myra (Beltzhoover) H.; m. Judith Elaine Isaacs, Sept. 4, 1965; 1 dau., Elizabeth Elaine. A.B., Stetson U., 1962; M.Ed., U. N.C., 1965. Adminstrv. asst. Morehead Planetarium, Chapel Hill, N.C., 1962-64, asst. dir., 1965-67; edn. dir. Strasenbrugh Planetarium, Rochester, N.Y., 1968-69, dir., 1970—; astronomy instr. U. N.C., 1966-67; U.S. astronaut instr. Morehead Planetarium, 1962-67; cons. planetariums, St. Louis, Tucson, 1971-73, Nat. Air and Space Mus.,, 1971-76, Smithsonian Instn., 1978; program cons. Ontario Place, Toronto, 1973; astronomy cons. Sci. Kit, Buffalo, 1969—; cons., San Francisco, 1982, Newport News, Va., 1983; program producer Hartford (Conn.) Children's Mus. and Perception Lab., Fairport, N.Y., 1969-70, 1969-70. Creator: Star Dome, 1969. Bd. dirs. Am. Theatre Organ Soc.; bd. dirs., program chmn. Rochester Theatre Organ Soc.; bd. dirs. Girl Scouts Genessee Valley; mem. adv. bd. dirs. Earth-Space-Sci. Edn. Center. Mem. Internat. Planetarium Soc. (pres. 1977-78), Middle Atlantic, Great Lakes planetarium socs. Home: 6987 Palmyra Rd Fairport NY 14450 Office: 663 East Ave Box 1480 Rochester NY 14603

HALL, E. EUGENE, educator; b. Mansfield, La., June 19, 1932; s. Alvin and Rose Marie (White) H.; m. Reba Hobby, Dec. 27, 1955; children—David, Laurie Ann, Steven. B.A., La. Coll., 1953; B.D., So. Bapt. Theol. Sem., 1956; M.A., La. State U., 1959, Ph.D., 1963. Asst. prof. speech Georgetown (Ky.) Coll., 1962-65, asso. prof., chmn. dept. speech, 1968-71; staff asst. to dean Coll. Arts and Humanities Western Ky. U., Bowling Green, also assoc. prof. speech, 1971-73; assoc. prof., chmn. dept. speech La. Coll., Pineville, 1965-68, dean coll., 1963-76, interim adminstr., 1974-75, v.p. acad. affairs, 1976-77; pres. Okla. Bapt. U., Shawnee, 1977-82; prof. New Orleans Bapt. Theol. Sem., 1982—. Author: Remember to Live, 1980; contbg. editor: La. Bapt. Message, 1974-75; contbr. articles to profl. jours. Served with USN, 1956-58. Recipient Disting. Alumni award La. Coll., 1978. Mem. Am. Assn. Univ. Adminstrs., Assn. So. Bapt. Coll. and Univ. Presidents, Am. Assn. Higher Edn., Nat. Collegiate Honors Council, Assn. Gen. and Liberal Studies, AAUP, Phi Mu Alpha Sinfonia., Phi Kappa Phi, Kappa Alpha. Home: 6841 Dorchester St New Orleans LA 70126

HALL, EDWARD BYRON, librarian; b. Mt. Sterling, Ky., Nov. 10, 1928; s. Byron Augustus and Mary Catherine (McGuigan) H.; m. Elizabeth Caroline Kinard, Feb. 4, 1956; children: Charles Byron, Edward Benjamin. B.A., U. Ky., 1951, M.S. in L.S, 1954. Br. librarian Free Library, Phila., 1956-59; dir. So. Md. Regional Library Assn., La Plata, 1959-62, Washington County Free Library, Hagerstown, Md., 1962-71; adminstr. Pub. Library Annapolis and Anne Arundel County, Md., 1971—; Cons. Law Library, Hagerstown, Mercersburg Acad. Library, 1965. Served to 1st lt. USAF, 1951-53; Europe. Mem. ALA, Md. Library Assn. (co-chmn. legis. and planning com., Md. Library award), Beta Phi Mu. Home: 300 F Hilltop Ln Annapolis MD 21403 Office: Library Headquarters 5 Harry S Truman Pkwy Annapolis MD 21401 *People and personal relationships most important in administration; always believe in being considerate of people's problems. Believe it is important to do best job possible rather than be concerned with getting to know important people.*

HALL, EDWARD TWITCHELL, anthropologist, educator, author; b. Webster Groves, Mo., May 16, 1914; s. Edward Twichell and Jessie Gilroy (Warneke) H.; m. Mildred Ellis Reed, Dec. 16, 1946; children: Ellen McCoy, Eric Reed. Student, Pomona Coll., 1929-30; A.B., U. Denver, 1936; M.A., U. Ariz., 1938; Ph.D., Columbia U., 1942. Asst. staff archeologist Lab. Anthropology, Santa Fe, 1937; staff dendroconologist Peabody Mus. Awatovi expdn., 1937-39; dir. Columbia Governador expdn., 1941; field work in, Micronesia, 1946, Southwestern U.S., 1933-43, Europe, 1952—, econ. and cultural survey, Micronesia, 1946; asso. prof. anthropology, chmn. dept. U. Denver, 1946-48; faculty Bennington (Vt.) Coll., 1948-51; dir. Point IV tng. program Fgn. Service Inst., State Dept., 1950-55; dir. research and dep. dir. (Washington office, Human Relations Area Files), 1955-57; pres. Overseas Tng. and Research, Inc., 1955-60; dir. communications research project Washington Sch. Psychiatry, 1959-63; mem. exec. com., council fellows; prof. anthropology Ill. Inst. Tech., 1963-67; prof. anthropology Northwestern Univ., 1967-77; partner Edward T. Hall Assos., 1960—; cons. intercultural relations internat. bus. and govt., 1955—; Leatherbee lectr. Harvard Bus. Sch., 1962; dir. Ansul Corp., Marinette, 1968-79; mem. small grants com. NIMH, 1962-65; mem. bldg. research adv. bd. NRC, 1964-68. Author: Earl Stockaded Settlements in Governador, N.M, 1942, The Silent Language, 1959, The Hidden Dimension, 1966, Handbook for Proxemic Research, 1975, The Fourth Dimension in Architecture, 1975, Beyond Culture, 1976, The Dance of Life, 1983, Hidden Differences: How to Communicate with the Germans. Bd. dirs. Mus. Bldg. Arts, 1978—; founding dir. Nat. Bldg. Mus., 1978—. Served to capt., C.E. AUS, 1942-46; ETO; PTO. Fellow Am. Anthrop. Assn.; mem. Soc. Applied Anthropology, Am. Ethnol. Assn., Explorers Club. Club: Century Assn. Office: 642 Camino Lejo Santa Fe NM 87501 *The most difficult task in the world is to know one's self. But knowing others can aid in the performance of that task.*

HALL, EMMETT MATTHEW, univ. chancellor; b. St. Columban, Que., Can., Nov. 29, 1898; s. James and Alice (Shea) H.; m. Isabel Mary Parker, June 26, 1922; children—Marian Hall Wedge, John E. Grad., U. Sask., 1919; D.C.L. (hon.), 1964, M.D., U. Ottawa, 1966, LL.D., U. Windsor, 1968, U. Man., 1968, Queen's U., 1974, Law Soc. Upper Can., 1975, Dalhousie U., 1977, York U., 1977, U. Regina, 1979; D.S. in Jurisprudence (hon.), Francis Xavier U., Antigonish, N.S., 1974. Bar: Called to Sask. bar 1922, king's counsel 1935. Pvt. practice law, Saskatoon, 1922-57; chief justice Queen's Bench Ct. for Sask., 1957-61; chief justice of, Sask., 1961-62; justice Supreme Ct. Can., 1962-73; chmn. Royal Commn. Health Services, 1961-64, Com. on Aims and Objectives for Edn. in Ont., 1961—; chancellor U. Guelph, 1971-77; lectr. law U. Sask. Coll. Law, 1948-58, mem. univ. senate, 1942-54, univ. chancellor, 1980—; Goodman lectr. U. Toronto Law Sch., 1975; chief commr. Grain Handling and Transp. Commn., 1975-77; labor arbitrator and concillator, 1973—. Trustee St. Paul's Separate Sch. Dist., Saskatoon, 1937-57, chmn., 1949-59; resident Catholic Sch. Trustees Sask., 1945-52; exec. com. Sask. Sch. Trustees Assn., 1952-57; chmn. bd. St. Paul's Hosp., Saskatoon, 1947-63. Decorated companion Order Can., 1974, knight of malta, 1958, knight Order St. Gregory, 1968, knight Holy Sepulchre, 1969; recipient Bronfman award Am. Public Health Assn., 1966. Hon. mem. U. Sask. Faculty Club; hon. nat. pres. Can. Civil Liberties Assn.; Mem. Can. Bar Assn. (v.p. for Sask. 1943-45), Law Soc. Sask. (pres. 1952), Can. Inst. Adminstrn. Justice (dir.), Internat., Commn. Jurists (past pres. Can. sect.). Clubs: Rideau (Ottawa); Saskatoon. Address: Apt 1205 620 Spadina Crescent E Saskatoon SK S7K 3T5 Canada

HALL, ERNEST E., retired government agency administration; b. Dayton, Nov. 17, 1901; s. Ozni and Julia (Schlotterbeck) H.; m. Florence M. Byrnes, Oct. 29, 1948; children: Kendra Elizabeth, Kevin Ernest. With Ozni Hall and Co., 1917-22; jr. acct. George P. Jackson and Co., 1922-25; asst. sec., treas. Hyde Motor Sales Co., 1925-29; asst. to sec. U.S. Dept. Agr., Washington, 1929-33; asst. chief div. control U.S. Bur. Pub. Rds., 1933-42; exec. officer Fed. Works Agy., 1942-47; v.p. C.F. Lytle Co. (heavy constrn.), Sioux City, Iowa, 1947-52; asst. adminstr. for ops. control services FCDA, Battle Creek, Mich., 1952-55; chief industry asst. br. Office Indsl. Devel. AEC, 1956-59; chief reports and statistics br. Div. Reactor Devel., 1959-64; chief reports staff Office Asst. Gen. Mgr. Reactors, Germantown, Md., 1965-70; ret. Chmn. Washington Grove Planning Commn., 1957-60, town treas., 1961-72. Mem. Am. Cheviot Sheep Soc. (dir. emeritus), Eastern Seaboard Sheep Council (pres. 1978-80), Natural Colored Wool Growers Assn. (pres. 1979-83). Home: 13140 Hiney Rd Red Rock Farm Frederick County Keymar MD 21757 *1) The Golden Rule. (2) Teddy Roosevelt: "Do the best you can, with what you have, wherever you are." (3) The Apostle Paul: "My grace is sufficient unto you." (4) From Lost Horizon: "Moderation in all things—even in virtue." (5) William H. Danforth's book: I DARE YOU. (6) From the BOOK OF JAMES: "Whoever, then, knows what is right to do and does not do it, that is a sin for him."*

HALL, ESTHER JANE WOOD, pharmacy educator; b. Gadsden, Ala., Sept. 18, 1911; d. Henry William and Emma Virginia (Crowe) Wood; m. Julian Kennis Hall, Jan. 13, 1949 (dec. 1974); 1 dau., Virginia Ann. B.S., Samford U., Birmingham, Ala., 1939; M.S., U. Tex., 1953, Ph.D., 1957; postdoctoral studies in jurisprudence, U. Tenn., 1969, 71. Pharmacist Fairview Pharmacy, Birmingham, 1929-39; prodn. control mgr., statistician Warren-Teed Products Co., Columbus, Ohio, 1939-44; label cons., dir., asst. prodn. control mgr. S.E. Massengill Co., Bristol, Tenn., 1944-46; asst. prof. Howard Coll., Birmingham, 1946-47; asst. prof. pharmacy U. Tex., Austin, 1947-61, asso. prof., 1961-75, prof., 1975—, dir. area pharmacy and health care adminstrn., cons. extension div., 1981—; cons. Am. Public Health Assn., Washington, 1961; spl. researcher Walgreen Co., Chgo., 1960; dir. Tex. Prescription Survey, Gosselin, Dedham, Mass., Hall & Assos., Profl. Research Cons.; chmn. manpower com. The Pharm. Found., U. Tex. Coll. Pharmacy, 1956—; friends hist. pharmacy Med. Coll. Va., 1965-70; mem. com. Pharmacy Edn. State Tex. Coordinating Bd. Schs.; faculty fellow Am. Found. Pharm. Edn., 1953-57. Author: (with A.H. Chute) The Pharmacist in Retail Distribution, 1953, 55, 60, 63, Teachers Guide, 1960, Study Guide for Pharmaceutical Jurisprudence, 1951, 56, 67, (with Henry M. Burlage) Pharmaceutical Abstracts, 1963-69, (with C.A. Walker) Manuals for Pharmacy Adminstration, 1969; various other manuals; contbr.: Southwestern Hist. Quar., 1959—. Recipient Lederle Lab. faculty award, 1965, 67, spl. commendation Am. Inst. History of Pharmacy, U. Wis.; participant Pharmacy Industry Forum, Princeton, 1959, Pharmacy Adminstrv. Seminar, Walgreen Co., Chgo., 1953, 60, 67, Dept. Justice Bur. Narcotics and Dangerous Drugs Nat. Tng. Inst., 1972, U. Okla. Health Care Adminstrn. Tng. Inst., 1972; visitation program Pharm. Mfrs. Assn., Stuart Labs., Wilmington, Del., 1976; others. Fellow AAAS; faculty fellow Am. Coll. Apothecaries; mem. Am. Assn. Colls. of Pharmacy, Am. Pharm. Assn., Capital Area Pharm. Assn., Am. Inst. History of Pharmacy (council), W. Tex. Hist. Soc., Am. Inst. Indsl. Engrs., Am. Soc. Hosp. Pharmacists, Am. Assn. Indsl. Engrs. (asso.), Royal Soc. Health Eng., Tex. Pharm. Assn. (historian 1979-80), Rho Chi, Kappa Epsilon, Sigma Iota Epsilon, Phi Mu. Episcopalian. Club: Faculty Center (Austin). Home: 3404 Exposition Blvd Colorado Foothills Austin TX 78703

HALL, E(UGENE) RAYMOND, zoologist, educator; b. Imes, Kans., May 11, 1902; s. Wilber Downs and Susan Effie (Donovan) H.; m. Mary Frances Harkey, Aug. 9, 1924; children—William Joel, Hubert Handel, Benjamin Downs. A.B., U. Kans., 1924; M.A., U. Calif. at Berkeley, 1925, Ph.D., 1928. Field biologist U.S. Bur. Biol. Survey, 1924-25; acting in charge Bur. Research, Calif. Dept. Fish and Game, 1926; curator of mammals U. Calif. Mus. of Vertebrate Zoology, 1927-1944; asst. prof. vertebrate zoology U. Calif., 1930-37, asso. prof., 1937-44; prof. zoology U. Kans., 1944-72, chmn. dept. zoology, 1944-61; dir. Mus. Natural History, 1944-67, editor mus. publs., 1946-67, research asso., 1967—, Summerfield Distinguished prof. zoology, 1958-72; dir. Kans. Biol. Survey, 1946-67, sr. biologist, 1967-73; state zoologist, 1959-67; prin. investigator office Naval Research, also NSF, 1950—; Mem. Nat. Parks Adv. Bd., 1954-60, council, 1961—; Maytag Disting. prof. zoology Ariz. State U., 1972; Mem. bd. councillors, bd. dirs. Save the Tallgrass Prairie, Inc., 1972—. Author: The Mammals of North America, 1959, 2d edit., 1981, others; contbr. articles to sci. jours. Recipient certificate of merit Nash Conservation Award, 1956; Proud Kansan award Outdoor Writers Kans., 1974; named Conservationist of Year Kans. Wildlife Fedn., 1972; Guggenheim fellow, 1942-43; Fulbright research prof., Turkey, 1968. Fellow AAAS (v.p. and chmn. sect. zool. scis. 1957), Calif., Wash. acads. sci.; mem. Am. Soc. Mammalogy (hon. mem.; pres. 1944-45), Am. Wildlife Soc., Am. Com. for Internat. Wildlife Protection (exec. com. 1946-70), Prairie Nat. Park Natural History Assn. (pres. 1968—), Am. Soc. Systematic Zoologists, Defenders of Wildlife (v.p. 1967-71), Soc. for Study Evolution, Cooper Ornith. Club, Am. Ornithol. Union, Kans. Acad. Sci. (council 1969-72), Am. Assn. Museums, Biol. Soc. Washington, Sigma Xi. (pres. Kans. chpt. 1959-61). Home: 1637 W 9th St Lawrence KS 66044 Office: Mus Natural History University Kans Lawrence KS 66045 *Those who love our world urge restraint in managing nature because lack of restraint shortens the existence of the animal component, including Homo sapiens. Current political systems focus too much on Homo alone, annually decreasing our planet's chances of return to health. Blessings on those to whom nature is their goddess and to her welfare bind their services.*

HALL, FREDERICK KEITH, chemist; b. Leeds, Eng., Jan. 3, 1930; naturalized, 1976; s. Frederick Stanley and Mary Elizabeth (Stocks) H.; m. Patricia Ellison, Aug. 25, 1956; children: Simon Keith, Stephanie Jane, Andrew Nicholas. B.S. with 1st class honors, U. Manchester, 1951; Ph.D., U. Leeds, 1954; grad., Advanced Mgmt. Program, Harvard U., 1979. Research chemist Courtaulds (Can.) Ltd., 1956-58, asst. tech. mgr., 1958-60, tech. mgr., 1960-63, plant mgr., 1963-66; dir. tech. service Internat. Paper Co., 1966-70, asst. dir. research center, 1970-72, dir. primary process, 1972-75, corp. dir. research, 1975-77; dir. S & T labs., 1977-79, chief scientist, 1979—. Served with Brit. Army, 1953-55. Fellow Royal Inst. Chemists, Textile Inst., Am. Inst. Chemistry; mem. Chem. Inst. Can., TAPPI, Can. Pulp and Paper Assn. Club: Tuxedo. Office: PO Box 797 Tuxedo Park NY 10987 *

HALL, FREDERICK LEONARD, writer, lecturer, conservationist; b. Seneca, Mo., Oct. 30, 1899; s. Frederick Bagby and Corinne (Steele) H.; m. Frances Mabley, Apr. 1923 (dec. 1937); m. Virginia Watson, May 28, 1941; 1 son, Frederick Leonard. Student, Washington U., St. Louis, 1920, LL.D., 1970, U. Wis., 1921-22; LL.D., Westminster Coll., Fulton, Mo., 1950. With R.R. Donnelley & Sons Co., 1930-45; columnist St. Louis Post Dispatch, 1943-59, St. Louis Globe Democrat, 1959-80; conservation lectr. Nat. Audubon Soc., others, 1944—. Author: Possum Trot Farm, 1948, Country Year, 1958, Stars Upstream, 1962, 63, 67, 87, Ozark Wildflowers, 1969, Journal of the Seasons, 1980, Earth's Song, 1981, also numerous articles in nat. mags.; Wildlife films An Ozark Anthology, 1960, Audubon's Wilderness, 1962, Forever Yours, 1966, Birds Over Florida, 1967, Country Year, 1971. Chmn. adv. commn. Ozark Nat. Scenic Riverways, 1965-69. Served with USNR, 1917-19. Named Master Conservationist in Mo., 1948; recipient Thomas Stokes award Nieman Fellows of Harvard, 1959, award for Outstanding Environ. Leadership Mo. Bot. Garden, 1982; named State Conservationist by Gov. Mo., 1966; appointed to Govs. Acad. Mo. Squires, 1967. Mem. Wilderness Soc., Nat. Audubon Soc., Nat. Parks Assn. (trustee), Am. Forestry

Assn., Defenders of Wildlife (past dir.), Humane Soc. U.S. (past dir.), Mo. Nature Conservancy (past dir.), Mo. Conservation Fedn. (dir.), Mo. Parks Assn. (dir.), Sierra Club, Sigma Delta Chi. Address: Possum Trot Farm Caledonia MO 63631 *Our objective has been to prove that man can live at peace with nature through cooperation rather than exploitation—a necessary prelude to living at peace with his fellowmen. We have proved neither except in our small corner of the Universe. Yet the years have been rich in values that make life worthwhile. Years like the recurring swing of the seasons and an ever-growing circle of good friends. Thus, today we can hope to have made some small contribution to a world that needs help if it is to survive.*

HALL, GAINES BRUCE, architect; b. Dothan, Ala., Apr. 25, 1938; s. Horatio Bruce and Blanch Auline (Foster) H.; 1 son, Gaines Bruce; m. 2d Sharon Ann Donaldson, Mar. 24, 1983; children: Shari, Trey. B.Arch., Auburn U., 1961. Registered architech, Ala., Ga., Fla. Architect intern Biggers & Neal, Dothan, Ala., 1963-65, Waid & Holmes, Dothan, 1965-67; jr. ptnr. Biggers & Neal, Dothan, 1967-68; v.p. Spann, Hall, Ritchie, Dothan, 1968-83, Peckham Guyton Albers and Viets, St. Louis, 1983—. Pres. Dothan Camp, Gideons Internat., 1969. Mem. AIA (Ala. council pres. 1976, regional dir. 1979-81, nat. pres. 1983-84), Jr. C. of C., C. of C. Soc., Am. Mil. Engrs. Baptist. Club: Bi-Racial Study Group (Dothan). Home: 7550 York Dr Clayton MO 63105 Office: Peckham Guyton Albers and Viets 200 N Broadway St. Louis MO 63102

HALL, GARY CURTIS, experimental test pilot, aerospace engineer and executive; b. Miami, Fla., Dec. 31, 1932; s. Clarence R. and Mary Lou (Schofill) H.; m. Carole Creech, July 12, 1970; children: Carol Jo, Johnna Rae, Mary Christine. B.S., U.S. Mil. Acad., 1956; M.S. in Aerospace Engring, U. Tex., Austin, 1961. Enlisted in U.S. Army, 1951; commd. 2d lt. inf., 1956, advanced through grades to lt. col.; airplane and helicopter pilot, 1958; grad. USN Test Pilot Sch., 1965; two tours of duty in, Vietnam; dep. comdr. U.S. Army Engring. Flight Test Activity, 1972-74, ret., 1975; dir. Mojave Flight Test Facility, Flight Systems, Inc., 1975-76; flight test project engr. A-10 fighter Fairchild Republic Co., Edwards AFB, Calif., 1977-79; supr. test team sect. Kentron Internat., Edwards AFB, 1979-82; mgr. aircraft flight test dept. Computer Scis. Corp., 1983—. Mayor, Rosamond, Calif., 1975. Decorated D.F.C., Legion of Merit, Bronze Star (2), others; named SE Kern County Citizen of Yr., 1980-81. Fellow Soc. Exptl. Test Pilots (1st army aviator asso. fellow); mem. Soc. Flight Test Engrs., Am. Helicopter Soc., U.S. Army Aviation Assn., Rosamond C. of C. (pres. 1974, 76, 77, 79-82). Pioneer devel. armed fighter helicopter. Home: PO Box 715 Rosamond CA 93560 *An early decision of what I wanted to do with my life and monumental dedication and perseverance enabled me to be successful. I have always been honest and straight-forward in everything I do.*

HALL, GEORGE ATWATER, book publisher; b. Boston, Nov. 12, 1925; s. Francis C. and Priscilla (Perry) H.; m. Alice Newberry, July 23, 1949; children: Marion, George Atwater, Susannah, William. B.A., Harvard U., 1948. Clk. New Eng. Trust Co., Boston, 1948-51; asst. treas. Little, Brown & Co., Boston, 1952-61, tres., 1961-66, v.p., 1966-79, sr. v.p., 1979-82, exec. v.p., 1982—. Trustee Wheelock Coll., Boston, 1959—, treas., Boston, 1959—; dir. Harvard U. Press, Cambridge, Mass., 1944-45. Club: Union (Boston). Home: 201 Willow Rd Nahant MA 01908 Office: Little Brown and Co 34 Beacon St Boston MA 02106

HALL, GEORGE HENRY GALE, insurance company executive; b. San Antonio, Sept. 27, 1945; s. Francis Garrison and Gale (Robinson) H.; m. JoNell Mays, Nov. 22, 1980; children: Leo, John. A.B., Ind. U., 1966; M.B.A., Harvard U., 1972. C.P.A., N.Y. Various positions USLife Corp., N.Y.C., 1973-79; v.p. corp. systems Protective Life Ins. Co., Birmingham, Ala., 1979-81; sr. v.p. and chief fin. officer Nat. Benefit Life Co., N.Y.C., 1981-83, Transamerica Life Cos., Los Angeles, 1983—. Served to capt. U.S. Army, 1966-69; Korea. Home: 13761 Stampede Circle Irvine CA 92714 Office: Transamerica Life Cos 1150 S Olive St Los Angeles CA 90015

HALL, GORDON R., state supreme court chief justice; b. Vernal, Utah, Dec. 14, 1926; s. Roscoe Jefferson and Clara Maud (Freestone) H.; m. Doris Gillespie, Sept. 6, 1947; children: Rick Jefferson, Craig Edwin. B.S., U. Utah, 1949, LL.B., 1951. Bar: Utah 1952. Sole practice, Tooele, Utah, 1952-69, city atty., City of Grantsville, Utah, 1954-69, town atty., Town of Wendover, Utah, 1955-69, Town of Stockton, Utah, 1955-69; legal adviser Tooele Army Depot, 1953-58; county atty. Tooele County, 1958-69; judge 3d Jud. Dist. Utah, 1969-77; assoc. justice Supreme Ct. Utah, 1977-81, chief justice, 1981—; pres. Utah Assn. Counties, 1965; mem. Pres's. Adv. Com. OEO, 1965-66. Served with U.S. Maritime Service, 1944-46. Mem. ABA, Utah Bar Assn. Office: Supreme Ct Utah 332 State Capitol Salt Lake City UT 84114

HALL, GUS (ARVO KUSTA HALBERG), political party official; b. Iron, Minn., Oct. 8, 1910; s. Matt and Susanna Halberg; m. Elizabeth Turner, Sept. 13, 1934; children: Barbara, Arvo. Student, Lenin Inst., Moscow, 1931-33. Mem. nat. com. Young Communist League, 1926-33; mem. Communist Party of U.S.A., 1934—, nat. sec., 1950-59, gen. sec., 1959—; gen. sec. Communist Party of Ohio, 1947-52; Communist Party candidate for Pres., 1972, 76. Author: pamphlets including For a Radical Change: The Communist View, 1966, On Course: The Revolutionary Process, 1969, Ecology: Can We Survive Capitalism?, 1972, Imperialism Today, 1972, The Energy Rip-Off: Cause and Cure, 1974, The Crisis of U.S. Capitalism and the Fight Back, 1975; Basics for Peace, Democracy and Social Progress, 1980. Served in USN, 1942-46. Office: Communist Party USA 235 W 23d St 7th Floor New York NY 10011 *

HALL, HAL OGDEN, cons., ret. govt. ofcl.; b. Springfield, Ill., Nov. 20, 1907; s. Harry Ogden and Pearl Emma (Porter) H.; m. Hazel Ann Bonhard, May 28, 1933; children—Hal Stephen, John Michael. B.E., So. Ill. U., 1930; M.B.A., Northwestern U., 1934; Ed.D., N.Y. U., 1943. Supt. schs., Greenview, Ill., 1930-36; asst. prof., then asso. prof. So. Ill. U., 1936-45; supt. schs., Belleville, Ill., also pres. jr. coll., 1945-57, supt. schs., Villa Park, Ill., 1957-61; civil def. adviser Ill. Dept. Edn., 1961; ednl. adminstrn. adviser AID, State Dept., Indonesia, 1962-65, South Vietnam, 1965-71, Washington, 1971-72, 1973-74, 1975-76; cons. internat. edn., 1977—; prof. grad. courses in sch. adminstrn. Washington and Ill. univs., 1954-55; lectr. Far East Tech. Center, 1967; legis. liaison officer Alexandria (Va.) Condominium Assn., 1978—; chmn. energy com. AKW Condominium Assn., 1979-81. Contbr. articles to profl. jours. Lobbyist Ill. Gen. Assembly) for fin. assistance for jr. colls., 1948-57. Recipient letters of commendation AID, 1967; Culture and Edn. medal 1st class Ministry Edn., 1969. Mem. NEA, Am. Assn. Sch. Adminstrs., Ill. Edn. Assn., Fgn. Service Assn., Alumni Assn. U. Ill. Home: 6101 Edsall Rd Alexandria VA 22304

HALL, HAROLD EMILE, lectr., cons., educator, ret. fgn. service officer; b. Logan, Utah, July 1, 1916; s. Emil Pearson and Violet (Peterson) H.; m. Rosa Hankey, Aug. 26, 1944; children—Barbara N., Stephen B. B.A., Utah State U., 1938; M.A., Stanford, 1943; postgrad., Oxford (Eng.) U., 1949. Instr. Stanford, 1943; internat. trade economist Dept. Commerce, 1944-48; consul, Sydney, Australia, 1949-53; internat. economist Dept. State, 1954; 1st sec., New Delhi, India, 1955-58; fgn. aid coordinator Dept. State, 1959-61, chief, 1963; counselor, London, Eng., 1964-68, spl. asst. to ambassador, 1969; diplomat-in-residence U. S.D., 1970; faculty Fed. Exec. Inst., Charlottesville, Va., 1971; prof. govt. U. Calgary, Alta., Can., 1972—; consul gen., Calgary, 1972-76. Served to lt. (j.g.) U.S. Mcht. Marines, 1945. Home: 311 S Samuel St Charles Town WV 25414

HALL, HAROLD HERSHEY, Office equipment company executive; b. Kinsman, Ohio, July 18, 1924; s. Emory and Ethel Gertrude (Hershey) H.; m. La Von Cameron Doner, June 8, 1949; children: Kathryn, Bruce, Harold, Jonathan, David. B.S. in Physics, S.D. State U., 1948, M.S., U. Oreg., 1949; Ph.D., U. Wis.-Madison, 1952. Sr. scientist Lawrence Livermore Lab., Calif., 1952-54, Lockheed Corp., Van Nuys, Calif., 1954-56; dir. research and devel. Aeronutronic Div., Philco-Ford, Newport Beach, Calif., 1956-68; pres. HRB-Singer Corp., State College, Pa., 1968-70; v.p. Aerospace Group, Singer Corp., N.Y.C., 1970-72; v.p. corp. research staff Xerox Corp., Palo Alto, Calif., 1972—; chief scientist ARPA AGILE Dept. Def., Washington, 1954-66; research and devel. panel Commn. on Govt. Procurement, Washington, 1970; trustee Univs. Research Assocs. Fermilab, Batavia, Ill., 1979—. Co-chmn. 1983 symposium com. Physicians for Social Responsibilty, 1983. Named Disting. Alumnus S.D. State U., 1979. Home: 580 Arastradero #506 Palo Alto CA 94306 Office: Xerox Palo Alto Research 3333 Coyote Hill Rd Palto Alto CA 94304

HALL, HENRY KINGSTON, JR., educator; b. N.Y.C., Dec. 7, 1924; s. Henry Kingston and Agnes (Furrer) H.; m. Alene Winifred Brown, Mar. 3, 1951; children—Joan, Douglas, Lillian. B.S., Poly. Inst. Bklyn., 1944; M.S., Pa. State U., 1946; Ph.D., U. Ill., 1949. Sr. research chemist textile fibers dept. E.I. DuPont de Nemours & Co., Inc., Wilmington, Del., 1952-65, group leader central research dept., 1965-69; prof. chemistry U. Ariz., Tucson, 1969—, chmn. dept., 1970-73; cons. Eastman Kodak Co., Rochester, Chevron Research Co., Richmond, Calif., Celanese Research Co., Summit, N.J., Amoco Chems. Co., Naperville, Ill., Ethicon Co., Somerville, N.J., Exxon Co., Linden, N.J.; vis. prof. Imperial Coll., London, 1976; sr. vis. fellow Japan Soc. for Promotion Sci., summer 1981. Contbr. articles profl. jours. Mem. Am. Chem. Soc. Research in mechanisms of organic reactions and synthesis of new high polymers. Home: 1230 E Seneca St Tucson AZ 85719

HALL, HOMER JAMES, chemist, information research consultant; b. Uniontown, Pa., Dec. 12, 1911; s. Homer) Maxwell and Susan (Newman) H.; m. Juliet McCarrell Leiper, June 7, 1941; children: David A., Stephen C., Eleanor L., Deborah M., B. Welling. A.B. magna cum laude, Marietta Coll., 1931; M.Sc., Ohio State U., 1932, Ph.D., 1935. Teaching asst. chemistry Ohio State U., 1931-35; research chemist Standard Oil Devel. Co., 1935, head patent search, 1937-41, head lab. group in hydrocarbon separations, 1943-48; chmn. open house Esso Research and Engring. Co., Linden, N.J., 1948, tech. adviser patent div., 1948-59, gen. sec. patent com., 1953, registered patent agt., 1954, tech. info. div., 1959-67, spl. editor, research assoc., 1964; sr. info. analyst, project mgr., asst. govt. contracts environ. research Govt. Research Lab., 1967-76; NSF project dir. Rutgers U. Sch. Library and Info. Studies, 1977-83, vis. research prof., 1982—; Acting sec. adv. com. Am. Petroleum Inst., 1944-46. Author: also numerous pamphlets, govt. reports. Evaluation and Analysis of Technical Information; Contbr. articles to profl. jours. Chmn. Cranford (N.J.) Tercentenary, 1961-64; mem. Centennial Steering Com., 1968-71; fund chmn. Cranford United Way, 1966; pres. Cranford chpt. Am. Field Service, 1968-70, host family, 1967; charter mem. Union County (N.J.) Cultural and Heritage Commn., 1970—; Bd. dirs. Wainwright Center for Devel. Human Resources, Rye, N.Y., 1971—, trustee, 1979—. Fellow Am. Inst. Chemists (chpt. pres. 1968-70, nat. dir. 1970-80, sec. bd. dirs. 1972-74, chmn. 1974-76, nat. sec. 1976-80, v.p. 1983—); mem. Am. Chem. Soc., AAAS (nat. council 1971-78), Am. Soc. Info. Sci. (group chmn. 1981—), Research Soc. Am., Cranford Hist. Soc. (trustee 1951—, pres. 1962-64, chmn. 1964-81), Phi Beta Kappa, Sigma Xi, Beta Beta Beta. Methodist (sec., chmn. bldg. com. 1951-62; trustee, chmn. adminstrv. bd. 1963-75). Club: Deer Lake. Patentee in petroleum field. Home: 310 Prospect Ave Cranford NJ 07016 Office: Rutgers Univ Sch Communication and Info Studies New Brunswick NJ 08903

HALL, HOWARD TRACY, chemist; b. Ogden, Utah, Oct. 20, 1919; s. Howard and Florence (Tracy) H.; m. Ida Rose Langford, Sept. 24, 1941; children—Sherlene, Howard Tracy, David Richard, Elizabeth, Virginia, Charlotte, Nancy. A.S., Weber Coll., 1939; B.S., U. Utah, 1942, M.S., 1943, Ph.D., 1948; D.Sc. (hon.), Brigham Young U., 1971. Registered patent agt. Chemist U.S. Bur. Mines, Salt Lake City, 1942-44, 46; research asso. Gen. Electric Research Lab., Schenectady, 1948-55; dir. research, prof. chemistry Brigham Young U., 1955-67, disting. prof. chemistry, 1967-80, disting. prof. emeritus, 1980—. Contbr. articles to profl. jours. Served as ensign USNR, 1944-46. Co-recipient Research medal Am. Soc. Tool Mfg. Engrs., 1962; Modern Pioneers Creative Industry award NAM, 1965; Engring. Materials Achievement award Am. Soc. Metals, 1973; Man of Yr. award Abrasive Engring. Soc., 1980; Alfred P. Sloan Found. research fellow, 1959-63. Fellow Am. Inst. Chemists (Chem. Pioneer award 1970), AAAS; mem. Am. Chem. Soc. (Creative Invention award 1972), Am. Phys. Soc. (co-winner Internat. Prize for New Materials 1977), Sigma Xi, Phi Kappa Phi. Republican. Mormon. Club: Timpanogos. Patentee in field. Pioneer in synthesizing of diamond. Home: 1711 N Lambert Ln Provo UT 84601 Office: Dept Chemistry Brigham Young Univ Provo UT 84602

HALL, HUGH DAVID, dentist, physician, educator; b. Henryetta, Okla., May 15, 1931; s. Hugh Colford and Mary Isabelle (Sadler) H.; m. Katherine Ayers Suydam, Feb. 20, 1960; children—Steven David, Andrew Durland, Brian Sadler. B.S., U. Okla., 1953; postgrad., U. Kansas City Sch. Dentistry, 1952-53; D.M.D., Harvard, 1957; M.D., U. Ala., 1977. Diplomate: Am. Bd. Oral and Maxillofacial Surgery. Practice dentistry, Birmingham, Ala., 1961-68, Nashville, 1968—; instr. oral surgery U. Ala. Sch. Dentistry, Birmingham, 1961-62; asst. prof. oral surgery, 1962-64, asso. prof. oral surgery, 1964, chmn. dept. oral surgery, 1965-68; prof., chmn. dept. oral surgery Vanderbilt U., Nashville, 1968—; vis. asso. prof. physiology and biophysics U. Ala. Med. Center, Birmingham, 1970—; mem. adv. com. Am. Bd. Oral Surgery, 1969-70, 81—. Mem. editorial bd.: Jour. Oral Surgery, 1974-82; contbr. articles on salivary gland physiology and oral surgery to tech. jours. Recipient Research Career Devel. award Nat. Inst. Dental Research, 1962-64; USPHS Research grantee, 1960-68. Fellow Internat. Assn. Oral Surgeons, AAUP; mem. Am. Dental Assn., Am. Assn. Oral and Maxillofacial Surgeons, Southeastern Soc. Oral and Maxillofacial Surgeons, Am. Physiol. Soc., AAAS, Internat. Assn. for Dental Research, Sigma Xi, Omicron Kappa Upsilon. Home: 3609 Knollwood Nashville TN 37215

HALL, J. PARKER, III, investment counselor; b. N.Y.C., June 13, 1933; s. J. Parker and Frances (Ferris) H.; m. Julia Alice Lange, June 23, 1956; children: Martha S., J. Parker IV, Alison G. Student, U. Chgo., 1950-52; B.A. in Econs, Swarthmore Coll., 1955; M.B.A. in Fin, Harvard U., 1957. Chartered fin. analyst. Fin. analyst Harris Trust & Savs. Bank, Chgo., 1957-61; fin. analyst Security Suprs., Chgo., 1961-63; investment mgr. Montgomery Ward & Co., Chgo., 1963-66; v.p. Harris Trust & Savs. Bank, Chgo., 1966-71; pres. Lincoln Capital Mgmt. Co., Chgo., 1971—; dir. LaSalle St. Fund. Contbr. articles to profl. jours. Former trustee, vice chmn., mem. exec. com. Ravinia Festival; former mem. bd. mgrs., mem. exec. com. YMCA Met. Chgo.; bd. mgrs. Swarthmore Coll. Mem. Fin. Analysts Fedn., Investment Analysts Soc. Chgo. (past pres.). Republican. Clubs: Economic, Executive, Chgo. Commonwealth, Mid-Day. Office: 200 S Wacker Dr Chicago IL 60606

HALL, JACK GILBERT, lawyer, business exec.; b. Joplin, Mo., Dec. 21, 1927; s. Oliver Perry and Emma Bertha H.; m. Barbara Jean Smith, Nov. 20, 1951; children: Stephen, Linda, Kathleen, Nancy, Julie. B.S. in Indsl. Relations, U. So. Calif., 1953; LL.B., LaSalle U., 1964. Bar: Calif. Gen. personnel dir. Carnation Co., 1953-60; labor relations mgr. Am. Potash & Chem. Co., Los Angeles, 1961-62, corp. dir. indsl. relations, 1967-68; labor relations specialist Aerojet Gen. Co., Azusa, Calif., 1963; asst. dir. labor relations Rexall Drug & Chem. Co., Los Angeles, 1964-66; labor counsel Dart Industries Inc., Los Angeles, 1969-79, corp. group v.p. labor relations, 1979—; staff v.p. labor relations Dart & Kraft Inc., 1981—; of counsel Jackson, Lewis, Schnitzler & Krupman, 1983—; vis. lectr. Calif. Inst. Tech., Pasadena, 1968-79; Mem. Equal Employment Adv. Council. Served with USNR, 1945-48. Mem. Am. Bar Assn., NAM, Labor Policy Assn., U.S. C. of C., Calif. Bar Assn., Los Angeles County Bar Assn. Republican. Mormon. Office: PO Box 3157 Los Angeles CA 90051 *

HALL, JAMES ALEXANDER, elec. engr.; b. Providence, Apr. 25, 1920; s. James Alexander and Leila (Tucker) H.; m. Marie Pauline Wassel, Sept. 22, 1945; children—James A., John Joseph, Jerome Michael. B.S. in Elec. Engring, Brown U., 1942; postgrad., Johns Hopkins U., 1946-50; Ph.D. in Elec. Engring, U. R.I., 1971. Engr. A.B. DuMont Labs., Passaic, N.J., 1942-46; jr. instr. physics, research asso. Johns Hopkins U., 1946-50; engr. sect. engring. mgr., adv. engr. Westinghouse Co., Bloomfield, N.J., Elmira, N.Y. and Balt., 1950-71; sr. adv. engr. (Advanced Tech. div.), 1972—; asso. prof. U. R.I., 1971-72, adj. prof., 1972; lectr. The Technion, 1971, Louvain la Neuve, 1975, Am. U., 1976. Contbr. articles to profl. jours., chpts. to books. Fellow IEEE; mem. Optical Soc. Am., Am. Vacumn Soc. Republican. Roman Catholic. Patentee in field. Home: 468 Lymington Rd Severna Park MD 21146 Office: PO Box 1521 MS 3525 Baltimore MD 21203

HALL, JAMES BYRON, univ. provost, author; b. Midland, Ohio, July 21, 1918; s. Harry and Florence (Moon) H.; m. Elizabeth Cushman, Feb. 14, 1946; children—Elinor, Prudence, Kathryn, Millicent, James M.M. Student, Miami U., Oxford, Ohio, 1938-39, U. Hawaii, 1938-40; B.A., State U. Iowa, 1947, M.A., 1948, Ph.D., 1953; postgrad., Kenyon Coll., 1949. Writer-in-residence Miami U., 1948-49, U. N.C., Greensville, 1954, U. B.C., 1955, U. Colo., 1963; instr. Cornell U., 1952-53; asst. prof. English U. Oreg., 1954-57, asso. prof., 1958-60, prof., 1960-65; prof. English, dir. The Writing Center, U. Calif. at Irvine, 1965-68; provost U. Calif. at Santa Cruz, 1968-75; Cons. editor Doubleday & Co., 1960-65. Author: Not by the Door, 1954, The Short Story, 1955, 15X3, 1957, Racers to the Sun, 1960, Us He Devours, 1964, Realm of Fiction, 1965-77, Modern Culture and Arts, 1967-75, Mayo Sergeant, 1967, The Hunt Within, 1973; stories The Short Hall, 1981; contbr. stories, poetry to anthologies. Founder Summer Acad. Contemporary Arts, 1959; cultural specialist U.S. Dept. State, 1964. Served with AUS, 1941-46. Recipient Octave Thanet prize, 1950, Oreg. Poetry prize, 1958, Emily Clark Balch Fiction prize, 1967, Chapelbrook award, 1967, Inst. Creative Arts award.; Rockefeller grantee, 1955. Mem. AAUP. Democrat. Methodist. Home: 31 Hollins Dr Santa Cruz CA 95060

HALL, JAMES CURTIS, univ. dean; b. Galax, Va., Feb. 12, 1926; s. Alonzo A. and Clara (Crissman) H.; m. Mary Anne Jones, Mar. 13, 1954; children—Michael Crissman, Suzanne King. Student, U. N.C., 1943-44; A.B., Duke, 1947; M.S., Va. Poly. Inst. and State U., 1952; Ed.D., Columbia, 1956. Tchr. Galax High Sch., 1947-50; instr. Va. Poly. Inst. and State U., 1951-54, Montclair State Coll., 1955; research asst. Columbia, 1955-56; asst. prof. Va. Poly. Inst. and State U., 1956-57; prof. Auburn U., 1957-62; dean Sch. of Bus., Va. Commonwealth U., 1962—; cons. to So. sch. systems; nat. lectr. econ. edn.; pres. Investment Enterprises, Inc.; dir. Richmond Investment Properties. Author: (with E.M. Robinson) College Business Organization and Management, 1964, (with others) General Business for Everyday Living, 3d edit, 1966, 4th edit., 1972, Business and You, 5th edit, 1979. Trustee Joint Council on Econ. Edn. Served with USNR, 1943-46. Mem. Va. Council Econ. Edn. (pres.), Nat. Bus. Edn. Assn. (pres. 1970-71), So. Bus. Edn. Assn. (pres. 1967), Adminstrv. Mgmt. Soc. (pres. Richmond chpt. 1969-70), Phi Beta Kappa, Phi Kappa Phi, Beta Gamma Sigma, Beta Alpha Psi. Home: 10408 Saxony Rd Richmond VA 23235 *Since I can remember, my desire has been to learn something new or to have some new experience every day that I live. I have tried always to treat every other person just as I would want to be treated under the same circumstance. I ask nothing of any person except that he tell the truth and that he treat every other human being with respect.*

HALL, JAMES FAY, JR., lawyer; b. Greenwood, Miss., Aug. 30, 1916; s. James Fay and Lois (Wilson) H.; m. Catherine Keller, May 17, 1941; children—Marianne Lois, Geraldine Catherine. A.B., U. Miss., 1936; LL.B., Georgetown U., 1945. Bar: D.C. bar 1945, Pa. bar 1958. Atty. legal staff Tax Ct. U.S., 1945-48; pvt. practice, Washington, 1948-57; with Rohm and Haas Co., Phila., 1957-76, gen. counsel, 1962-76, v.p., 1972-76, dir., 1963-76; pvt. practice, Wynnewood, Pa., 1976—. Mem. Am., D.C., Phila. bar assns. Home and office: 926 Remington Rd Wynnewood PA 19096

HALL, JAMES FREDERICK, coll. pres.; b. Detroit, Dec. 30, 1921; s. Cortez Rogers and Bertha Wilhelmina H.; m. Betty Louise Stark, Sept. 17, 1949; children—Kristine Martha, Jay Charles. Student, U. Mich., 1939-41; B.A., Wayne State U., 1942, M.A., 1948; Ed.D., Tchrs. Coll., Columbia U., 1953. Instr. Highland Park Jr. Coll., 1948-49; adminstrv. asst., instr. N.Y.C. Community Coll., 1950-51; dir. student personnel services, dept. head Orange County Community Coll., Middletown, N.Y., 1952-55; dean collegiate tech. div., exec. asst. to pres. Ferris State Coll., 1955-57; pres. Dutchess Community Coll., 1957-72, Cape Cod Community Coll., 1972—; Trustee, Mass. rep., Gov.'s appointment New Eng. Bd. Higher Edn., 1975—; chmn. Pres.'s Council of Regional Community Colls. in Mass., 1976-78; mem. Mass. Postsecondary Edn. Commn., 1978—; trustee Middle States Assn. Schs. and Colls., 1966-72; mem. mgmt. team Labor Negotiations for Regional Bd. Community Colls., 1978; bd. incorporators Bass River Savs. Bank, 1979—. Bd. dirs. Cape Cod Conservatory, West Barnstable, Mass., 1973—; trustee Cape Cod Hosp., Hyannis, Mass., 1978—. Served to lt., j.g. USNR, 1943-46. Mem. New Eng. Assn. Schs. and Colls. (accreditation teams 1975-77), Southeastern Assn. Cooperation in Higher Edn. in Mass. (dir. 1972-79, pres. 1976, treas. 1978), Mass. Adminstrs. in Community Colls. (pres. 1974-75), Associated Colls. of Mid-Hudson Area (chmn. bd. trustees 1963-64, 72 trustee 1963-72). Home: 29 Liverpool Dr Yarmouth MA 02675 Office: Cape Cod Community Coll West Barnstable MA 02668

HALL, JAMES LEO, JR., lawyer; b. St. Paul, Mar. 29, 1936; s. James L. and Mary Z. (Hitch) H.; m. Carol Rae Marshall, May 16, 1959; two children. B.A. with distinction, U. Okla., 1958; J.D., Harvard U., 1963. Bar: Okla. 1963. Mem. Crowe & Dunlevy, Oklahoma City, 1963—, pres., 1981-83; lectr. numerous symposia, convs. and instns., 1964—; instr. Okla. Bar Rev., Inc., 1972—; dir. Allied Nursing Care, Community Nat. Bank Okarche, Inc., MetroBank, N.A.; mem. Okla.

Health Care Corp. Contbr. articles tp legal jours. Vice chmn. bd. global ministries Okla. conf. United Methodist Ch., 1978—, chancellor, 1981—; trustee Crown Heights United Meth. Ch., 1978—, lay leader, 1978-80, chmn. adminstrv. bd., 1976-77; trustee Oklahoma City U. Served to lt. comdr. USN, 1958-60. Fellow Am. Bar Found.; mem. ABA, Fed. Bar Assn., Oklahoma County Bar Found. (pres. 1979-82), Oklahoma County Bar Assn. (treas. 1974-77), Okla. Bar Assn. (chmn. labor law sect. 1972), Am. Soc. Hosp. Attys., Phi Beta Kappa (pres. Oklahoma City alumni 1979). Republican. Clubs: Men's Dinner, Economic of Okla., Oklahoma City Golf and Country, Petroleum. Lodge: Kiwanis. Home: 1713 Elmhurst Ave Oklahoma City OK 73120 Office: Crowe & Dunlevy 1800 Mid Am Tower Oklahoma City OK 73102

HALL, JAMES STANLEY, jazz guitarist, composer; b. Buffalo, Dec. 4, 1930; s. Harold S. and Louella (Cowles) H.; m. Jane Susan Yuckman, Sept. 9, 1965; 1 dau., Debra Jean. Mus.B., Cleve. Inst. Music, 1955. Joined, Chico Hamilton, 1955; mem., Jimmy Giuffre Trio, 1957, tour, U.S. and Europe with, Jazz at Philharmonic, 1958, 59, Europe and S.A. with, Ella Fitzerald, 1959, 60; featured by, Sonny Rollins, 1961-62; formed quartet with, Art Farmer, 1962-64; leader own trio, 1962—; performed at, White House, 1969; motion picture appearance in Jazz on a Summer's Day, 1958; on: Ralph Gleason's TV Show, 1962-63, BBC, 1964, tour, Europe, 1967, 69, 79, 80, 81, 82, Japan, 1970, 76, 79; recording artist for, Pacific Jazz, United Artists, Atlantic, Verve, RCA, SABA, Milestone, CTI, Horizon, Concord., Concord., Concord., Concord. Recipient award Downbeat Critics Poll, 1963-65, 74, 76, 77, 78, 79, 80, 82, 83, Downbeat Readers' Poll, 1965-66, Playboy Mag. All-Star Poll for Guitar, 1968-71; named Best Performer Jazz Mag., 1965-66. Mem. Broadcast Music, Inc., Nat. Assn. Recording Arts and Scis. Subject of profile in New Yorker, Mar. 1975, cover story in Guitar Player Mag., May 1983.

HALL, JAMES WILLIAM, college president; b. Chester, Pa., Oct. 14, 1937; s. James William and Margaret (Crothers) H.; m. Wilma Bauer, May 20, 1961; children—Laura, Janet, Carol. B. Mus., Bucknell U., 1959; M.S., Union Theol. Sem., 1961; M.A., U. Pa., 1964, Ph.D., 1967. Instr. Cedar Crest Coll., Allentown, Pa., 1961-66; vis. asst. prof. SUNY, Albany, 1966-71, asst. acad. personnel, central adminstrn., 1966-68; asso. univ. dean univ.-wide activities, 1968-70, asst. vice chancellor policy and planning, 1970-71; pres. Empire State Coll., SUNY, Saratoga Springs, 1971—; acting pres. SUNY Coll., Old Westbury, N.Y., 1981-82. Editor: Am. Problem series Forging the American Character, 1971; (with B. Keules) Alternative Models for Undergraduate Education, 1982. Danforth fellow, 1959-67. Mem. Am. Hist. Assn., Am. Studies Assn., Soc. Values in Higher Edn., Am. Assn. Higher Edn. Methodist.

HALL, JEROME, lawyer, educator, author; b. Chgo., Feb. 4, 1901; s. Herbert and Sarah (Rush) H.; m. Marianne Cowan, July 2, 1941; 1 dau., Heather Adele. Ph.B., U. Chgo., 1922, J.D., 1923; Jur.Sc.D., Columbia, 1935; S.J.D., Harvard U., 1935; LL.D., U. N.D., 1958, U. Tübingen (W.Ger.), 1978. Bar: Ill. 1923. With firm Kixmiller & Baar, 1923-26; pvt. practice, 1926-29; lectr. Ind. U. Extension, Gary, 1924-29; prof. law U. N.D., 1929-32; asst. state's atty. Cook County, Ill., summer 1931; Spl. fellow Columbia Law Sch., 1932-34; Benjamin research fellow Harvard Law Sch., 1934-35; prof. criminal law and criminology La. State U., 1935-39; prof. law Ind. U., 1939-57, distinguished service prof. law, 1957-70; prof. law U. Calif. Hastings Coll. Law, San Francisco, 1970—; Hillman lectr. Coll. Pacific, 1947; Mitchell lectr. U. Buffalo, 1958; Fulbright lectr., U.K., 1954-55, U. Freiburg, Germany, 1961; Ford Found. lectr., Mex. and S. Am., 1960; Edward Douglass White lectr. La. State U., 1962; Murray lectr. U. Iowa, 1963; U.S. specialist State Dept. program, Far East and India, summers 1954, 68. Author: Readings in Jurisprudence, 1938, General Principles of Criminal Law, 2d edit., 1960, Cases and Readings on Criminal Law and Procedure, 4th edit., 1983, Living Law of Democratic Society, 1949, Theft, Law and Society, 2d edit., 1952, Studies in Jurisprudence and Criminal Theory, 1958, Comparative Law and Social Theory, 1963, Foundations of Jurisprudence, 1973, Law, Social Science and Criminal Theory, 1982; Editor: 20th Century Legal Philsophy Series, 8 vols; Contbr. articles to profl. jours. Recipient Lieber award for distinguished teaching, 1956. Mem. China Acad., Am. Bar Assn., Am. Fgn. Law Assn., Internat. Acad. Comparative Law, Societé Européenne de Culture, Soc. Pub. Tchrs. Law, Am. Soc. Polit. and Legal Philosophy (pres. 1967-69), Internat. Assn. Legal and Social Philosophy (pres. Am. sect. 1966-68), Latin-Am. Assn. Sociology (hon. pres. 1960), Council on Religion and Law (dir. 1977—). Home: 1390 Market St San Francisco CA 94102 Office: 198 McAllister St San Francisco CA 94102

HALL, JOE BEASMAN, coach, educator; b. Cynthiana, Ky., Nov. 30, 1928; s. Charles Curtis and Ruth (Marshall) H.; m. Katharine Roberta Dennis, Oct. 27, 1951; children—Judith Morton, Katharine Jo, Stephen Dennis. B.S., U. Ky., 1955; postgrad., Sewanee U., 1949-50; M.A., Colo. State Coll., 1963. Sales rep. H.J. Heinz Co., 1951-53; prodn. planner Kawneer, 1955-56; coach football, basketball, baseball Shepherdsville (Ky.) High Sch., 1956-58; athletic dir., basketball, baseball coach, dir. phys. edn. Regis Coll., Denver, 1958-64; asso. prof. phys. edn., basketball coach Central Mo. State U., 1964-65; asst. basketball coach U. Ky., Lexington, 1965-72, head basketball coach, 1972—; dir. Nat. Bank, Cynthiana. Recipient Coach of Year award Southeastern Basketball Conf., 1973, 75, 78; Peachbasket award, 1978. Mem. Nat. Assn. Basketball Coaches. Democrat. Office: Memorial Coliseum Lexington KY 40506 *

HALL, JOE E., trucking company executive; b. 1938; married. Student, Memphis State U. Dist. mgr. Roadway Express Inc., 1968-73; regional mgr. Spector Freight System Inc., 1973, PIE, 1973-76; terminal mgr. Mason Dixon Lines, 1976-77; with Transcon Lines, 1977—, mgr. Western div., 1978-79, sr. v.p. ops., 1979-82, pres., chief operating officer, 1982-83, pres., chief exec. officer, 1983—, Transcon Inc., 1983—. Office: Transcom Lines 101 Continental Blvd El Segundo CA 90245

HALL, JOHN ALLEN, international nuclear consultant; b. Benton Harbor, Mich., Sept. 22, 1914; s. Maurice John and Dora (Ferry) H.; m. Alice Greenidge, June 24, 1939; children: John Allen, Sheila Greenidge Hall Swift. B.S., Northwestern U., 1936; A.M., Harvard U., 1940, Ph.D., 1941. Instr. govt. U. Rochester, 1941-43; adviser U.S. del. UN, Washington, 1946, N.Y.C., 1947; chief Office Spl. Projects, AEC, Washington, 1948-52; dir. Office Internat. Affairs, 1952-55, dir. div. internat. affairs, 1955-58, asst. gen. mgr. internat. activities, 1958-61; dep. dir. gen. IAEA, 1961-64; asst. gen. mgr. U.S. AEC, Washington, 1964-67; dep. dir. gen. IAEA, Vienna, Austria, 1967-80; cons. Resources for the Future, Washington; joint sec. Combined Devel. Agy., Washington, 1949-55, U.S. mem., 1955; adviser to U.S. rep. UN Tech. Adv. Com., 1955, 58, 59, 60; chief liaison and protocal First Internat. Conf. on Peaceful Uses Atomic Energy, Geneva, Switzerland, 1955; sr. adviser U.S. rep. Conf. on Statute, IAEA, 1956; alt. U.S. rep. Inter-Am. Nuclear Energy Commn., 1959, 60; sr. adviser to chmn. U.S. del. First Gen. Conf., IAEA, Vienna, 1957, First Gen. Conf., Internat. Atomic Energy Agy. (2d Conf.), 1958, 1960, 1965, 1966; alt. U.S. rep. Inter-Am. Nuclear Commn., 1966; U.S. rep. Inter-Am. Sci. Symposium, Brazilia, Brazil, 1960. Served to lt. comdr. USNR, 1943-46. Decorated comdr. Papal Order of St. Sylvester. Clubs: Congl. Country, Harvard (Washington); Confrerie des Chevaliers du Tastevin (comdr.). Home: 8713 Cranbrook Ct Bethesda MD 20817

HALL, JOHN EMMETT, orthopedic surgeon, educator; b. Wadena, Sask., Can., Apr. 23, 1925; came to U.S., 1971; s. Emmett Matthew and Isobel Mary (Parker) H.; m. Frances Norma Walsh, May 31, 1952; children—Maureen, Susan, Bruce, Peter, Martha, Thomas, David. B.A., U. Sask., 1948; M.D., C.M., McGill U., Montreal, 1952. Diplomate: Am. Bd. Orthopedic Surgery. Orthopedic surgeon Hosp. Sick Children, Toronto, 1958-71, chief orthopedic surgeon, 1966-71; asst. prof. U. Toronto Faculty Medicine, 1966-71; prof. orthopedic surgery Harvard U. Med. Sch., 1971—; clin. chief orthopedics Children's Hosp. Med. Center, Boston, 1971-81, sr. assoc. in orthopedic surgery, 1981—. Contbr. articles med. jours. Served with RCAF, 1942-46. Fellow A.C.S., Royal Coll. Surgeons Can.; mem. AMA, Can. Med. Assn., Am. Orthopedic Assn., Can. Orthopedic Assn., Acad. Orthopedic Surgeons, Scoliosis Research Soc. (pres. 1968-70), Pediatric Orthopedic Assn. (pres. 1978-80), Royal Can. Mil. Inst. Roman Catholic. Club: Harvard. Home: 36 Codman Rd Brookline MA 02146 Office: 300 Longwood Ave Boston MA 02115

HALL, JOHN FRY, educator; b. Phila., Apr. 24, 1919; s. Harry R. and Alta (Herner) H.; m. Jean Midlam, May 14, 1943; 1 son, John. B.S., Ohio U., 1946; M.A., Ohio State U., 1947, Ph.D., 1949. Mem. faculty Pa. State U., University Park, 1949—, prof. psychology, 1958—; Program dir. psychobiology NSF, Washington, 1966-67; vis. prof. U. Va., 1952, U. Wis., 1954, U. Calif. at Berkeley, 1962, U. Hawaii, 1968, Fla. State U., 1975-76. Author: Psychology of Motivation, 1961, Psychology of Learning, 1966, Readings in the Psychology of Learning, 1967, Verbal Learning and Retention, 1971, Classical Conditioning and Instrumental Learning, 1976, An Invitation to Learning and Memory, 1982; contbr. articles to profl. jours. Mem. Am. Psychol. Assn., Psychonomics Soc., A.A.A.S., Sigma Xi. Home: 1288 Penfield Rd State College PA 16801 Office: Pa State U University Park PA 16802

HALL, JOHN HOPKINS, lawyer; b. Dallas, May 10, 1925; s. Albert Brown and Eleanor Pauline (Hopkins) H.; m. Marion Martin, Nov. 23, 1957; children—Ellen Martin, John Hopkins. Student, U. Tex., 1942, U. of South, Sewanee, Tenn., 1942-43; LL.B., So. Meth. U., 1949. Bar: Tex. bar 1949. Partner firm. Strasburger & Price, Dallas, 1957—. Served with U.S. Army, 1943-45. Fellow Tex. Bar Found., Am. Bar Found., Am. Coll. Trial Lawyers; mem. Am. Bar Assn., Tex. Bar Assn., Dallas Bar Assn., Tex. Assn. Def. Counsel, Def. Research Inst. Episcopalian. Clubs: City of Dallas, Royal Oaks Country, Fin and Feather. Office: 1200 One Main Pl Dallas TX 75250

HALL, JOHN LEWIS, lawyer; b. Woodville, Fla., July 26, 1904; s. Thomas Milton and Ola (Page) H.; m. Martha Buford, Aug. 24, 1927; children—John Lewis, Thomas Munroe. A.B. in Edn, U. Fla., 1927. Bar: Fla. bar 1936. Tchr. pub. schs., Fla., 1927-35, since practiced in, Tallahassee; mem. Fla. Capitol Center Planning Commn., Tallahassee, 1972-77; county atty. Leon County, 1939-66; atty. Fla. Assn. County Commrs., 1941-64; Mem. Fabisinski Com. of Fla., 1956-57; Adv. Commn. Revision Fla. Constn., 1957-59, Fla. Gov.'s Adv. Com. Race Relations, 1957-58. Bd. dirs. Tallahassee Symphony Assn. Mem. ABA, Tallahassee Bar Assn. (pres. 1946), Fla. Bar (gov. 1954-60, pres. 1959-60), Fla. County Attys. Assn. (pres. 1942), Blue Key, Beta Theta Pi, Sigma Delta Chi. Methodist (pres. legal adv. council Fla. conf. United Meth. Ch. 1973). Clubs: Mason (grand master Fla. 1958), Lions (pres. 1945). Home: 1204 Firethorn Ln Tallahassee FL 32303

HALL, JOHN RICHARD, oil company executive; b. Dallas, Nov. 30, 1932; s. John W. and Agnes (Sanders) H.; m. Donna S. Stauffer, May 10, 1980. B.Chem. Engring., Vanderbilt U., 1955. Chem. engr. Esso Standard Oil Co., Balt., 1956-58, Ashland Oil Co., Ky., 1959-63, coordinator carbon black div., Houston, 1963-65, exec. asst. v.p., 1965-66, v.p., 1966-68, sr. v.p., 1970-71; also dir.; pres. Ashland Chem. Co., 1971-74; exec. v.p. Ashland Oil, Inc., 1974—, group operating officer, 1976—, chief exec. officer petroleum and chems., 1978—, vice chmn., chief operating officer, 1979-81, chmn., chief exec. officer, 1981—. Trustee Franklin U., Columbus, Ohio; mem. com. visitors Vanderbilt U. Engring. Sch., Nashville.; bd. curators Transylvania U., Lexington, Ky. Served as 2d lt., Chem. Corps AUS, 1955-56. Mem. Mfg. Chemists Assn., Nat. Petroleum Refiners Assn., Am. Petroleum Inst., Ky. Soc. Profl. Engrs., Tau Delta Pi, Sigma Chi, Delta Kappa. Republican. Home: 99 Stoneybrook Dr Ashland KY 41101 Office: PO Box 391 Ashland KY 41114

HALL, JOSEPH EDGAR, scientific consultant; b. Bluefield, W.Va., Nov. 24, 1934; s. George Clarence and Beulah Mae (Gullion) H.; m. Donna Sue Scyphers, Dec. 31, 1954; children—Carter, Joseph, David, Martha, Jonathan, Michel, Laura. B.S., Concord Coll., 1957. C.P.A. W.Va., D.C. Jr. acct. John Heins & Co., Bluefield, 1957-59; audit mgr. Arthur Young & Co., Washington, 1959-66; treas., then v.p., now pres. Flow Labs., Rockville, Md., from 1966; pres. Flow Gen. Inc. (and subs.), McLean, Va., 1976—; dir. Flow Gen. Inc. and subs., 1976-83; cons. Flow. Gen. Inc. and subs., 1983—. Pres., founder Vienna Youth Inc. Mem. Am. Inst. C.P.A.s. Republican. Home: 10021 Lochness Ct Vienna VA 22180 Office: 7655 Old Springhouse Rd McLean VA 22101 *My basic tenet has been: "When in doubt, tell the truth." Everthing else seems to follow.*

HALL, KATIE BEATRICE GREENE, congresswoman; b. Miss., Apr. 3, 1938; d. Jeff Louis and Bessie Mae (Hooper) Greene; m. John H. Hall, Aug. 12, 1957; children: Jacqueline, Junifer. B.S., Miss. Valley State U., 1960; M.S., Ind. U., 1968, postgrad., 1972. Mem. Ind. Ho. of Reps. from 5th Dist., 1974-76, Ind. Senate, 1976-82, chmn. edn. com.; mem. 98th Congress from 1st Ind. Dist. Recipient numerous civic awards. Mem. AAUW, Nat. Council Negro Women, Nat. Council Social Studies, Nat. Council Black Legislators, Phi Delta Kappa. Democrat. Office: US Ho of Reps Washington DC 20515

HALL, KENNETH KELLER, judge; b. Greenview, W.Va., Feb. 24, 1918; s. Jack and Ruby (Greene) H.; m. Gerry Tabor, Apr. 6, 1940; 1 son, Kenneth Keller. J.D., W.Va. U., 1948. Bar: W.Va. 1948. Practiced law, Madison, W.Va., 1948-52; mem. firm Garnett & Hall, 1948-50; judge 25th Jud. Circuit Ct. W.Va., Madison, 1953-69, U.S. Dist. Ct. for So. Dist. W.Va., Charleston, 1971-76, U.S. Ct. Appeals (4th Circuit), 1976—. Served with USNR, 1942-45. Recipient Silver Beaver award Boy Scouts Am., 1962. Democrat. Baptist. Club: Rotary Internat. (past dist. gov.). Home: Charleston WV Office: PO Box 2549 Charleston WV 25329

HALL, LARKIN NEEL, implement manufacturing executive; b. El Paso, Tex., Mar. 31, 1933; s. Arthur and Helen Adams (Neel) H.; m. Eleanor Louise Dougall, June 30, 1956; children: Mark, Kathryn, Michael, Davidson, John. B.A., Stanford U., 1957, M.B.A., 1959. Various positions Deere & Co., 1956—; assigned to JD Intercontinental Ltd., also, Mex., 1956-66; sales mgr. JD Argentina, 1966-67; gen. mgr. Intercontinental, Moline, Ill., 1967-70, dir. sales brs., Germany, 1970, dir. mktg., Europe, Africa, Middle East, 1970-72, mng. dir., 1972-75, mng. dir. overseas ops., 1975, v.p. overseas ops., 1975-77, sr. v.p. overseas ops., 1977-83, sr. v.p. farm equipment and consumer products div., U.S. and Can., 1983—, dir., 1978—. Served with U.S. Army. Mem. Phi Delta Gamma. Address: Deere & Co John Deere Rd Moline IL 61265

HALL, LAURANCE DAVID, chemist, educator; b. London, Mar. 18, 1938; emigrated to Can., 1962; m. Winifred Margaret Golding, Aug. 1, 1962; children: Gwendolen, Juliet, Dominic Courtney, Brecken G. D'Arcy. B.Sc., U. Bristol, Eng., 1959, Ph.D., 1962. Postdoctoral fellow Ottawa (Ont., Can.) U., 1962-63; mem. faculty U. B.C., Vancouver, Can., 1963—, prof. chemistry, 1974—; Van Cleave lectr. U. Regina, 1983. Contbr. to profl. publs. Royal Soc. and Nuffield Found. scholar, 1967; Alfred P. Sloan Found. research fellow, 1971-73; recipient Jacob Biely Faculty research prize U. B.C., 1974; Cecil Green scholar U. Tex., Galveston, 1983; U. B.C. Killam Found. sr. fellow, 1979-80; Can. Council Killam research fellow, 1982-83, 83-84. Fellow Chem. Inst. Can. (Merck, Sharp and Dohme lectr. 1975); mem. Chem. Soc. London (Carbohydrate Chemistry award 1974, Corday-Morgan medal and prize 1976), Am. Chem. Soc., Spectroscopy Soc. Can. (Barringer award 1981). Home: 3959 W 36th Ave Vancouver BC V6N 2S7 Canada Office: Dept Chemistry Univ BC Vancouver BC V6T 1W5 Canada

HALL, LAWRENCE WILBUR, JR., tobacco company executive; b. Fairmont, W.Va., June 1, 1940; s. Lawrence Wilbur and Helen Louise (Hartley) H.; m. Diana Evelyn Shaw, Apr. 3, 1960; childern: Deborah Lynn, Wendy Leigh. B.S. in Bus. Adminstrn., W.Va. U., 1963. Dir. mktg. research R.J. Reynolds Tobacco Internat., Winston-Salem, N.C., 1977-78, dir. mktg., 1978-80; dir. mktg. research R.J. Reynolds Tobacco Co., 1980-81, v.p. brand mktg., 1981-82, v.p. mktg. devel., 1982—; bd. advisors mktg. research program U. Ga., Athens, 1980-81. Served to capt. USAF, 1963-68. Decorated Air Force Commendation medal. Mem. Am. Mktg. Assn. Republican.

HALL, LEE, educator, artist, design school president; b. Lexington, N.C., Dec. 15, 1934; d. Robert Lee and Florence (Fitzgerald) H. B.F.A., U. N.C., 1955; M.A., N.Y. U., 1959, Ph.D., 1965; postgrad., Warburg Inst. U. London, 1965; D.F.A. (hon.), U. N.C.-Greenville, 1976. Asst. prof. N.Y. State U. Coll., Potsdam, 1958-60; asso. prof., chmn. art dept. Keuka Coll., 1960-62; asso. prof. art Winthrop Coll., 1962-65; asst. prof., chmn. art dept. Drew U., Madison, N.J., 1965-67, asso. prof., chmn. art dept., 1967-70, prof., chmn. art dept., 1970-74; dean visual arts State U. N.Y. Coll. at Purchase, 1974-75; pres. R.I. Sch. Design, Providence, 1975-83. Exhibited in group shows in, London, N.Y.C., Winston-Salem, Eugene, Oreg., also others; represented by, Betty Parsons Gallery, N.Y.C., Armstrong Gallery, N.Y.C.; Dir. research on Pres. Kennedy's image in recent art, John F. Kennedy Meml. Library; panelist, Nat. Endowment for Humanities, 1972—; Contbr. articles to profl. jours. Recipient research grant Am. Philos. Soc., 1965, 68; Childe Hassam Purchase award Am. Acad. Arts and Letters, 1977; RISD Athena medal, 1983. Mem. AAUP, AAUW, Am. Soc. Aesthetics, Coll. Art Assn., Pi Lambda Theta. Home: Baker Ln RFD 2 Box 406 Old Lyme CT 06371

HALL, LEE BOAZ, publishing company executive, author; b. Little Rock, Oct. 8, 1928; s. Graham Roots and Louise (Boaz) H.; m. Mary Louise Reed, Nov. 29, 1951 (div.); children: Gwendolyn, Ann Valerie, Graham; m. Sarah Moore, Dec. 15, 1978. B.A., UCLA; M.A., U. N.Mex.; B.A., Yale U., 1950. Reporter Ark. Gazette, Little Rock, 1950-51, Dept. Def., Washington, 1951-52, W.Ger., 1952-53, Washington Post, 1953-55; with Life mag., 1955-70, bur. chief, Paris, 1963-66; editor Life en Espanol, 1966-69; editor internat. edits. Life, N.Y.C., 1970; pres. Tomorrow Pub. Co., N.Y.C., 1970-72; sr. v.p. internat. pub. Playboy Enterprises, Inc., Chgo., 1972—; dir. Boyle Realty Co., Little Rock, Hall Ledbetter Co. Author: International Magazine and Book Licensing, 1983. Served with U.S. Army, 1950-51. Mem. Federation Internationale de la Presse Periodique (liasion). Methodist. Clubs: Racquet (Chgo.); Yale (N.Y.C.). Home: 229 E Lake Shore Dr Chicago IL 60611 Office: Playboy Enterprises Inc 919 N Michigan Ave Chicago IL 60611 *Two words "fair play" define the principles and standards of conduct I try to adhere to in my life. Professionally, negotiating as I do with people of many cultures, fairness is of the essence. Too many Americans, isolated by oceans, guided by strict interpretation of the Puritan ethic and misled by the trappings of their power, lord their tastes, their customs and their wealth over those they percieve as less fortunate.*

HALL, MARION TRUFANT, botany educator, arboretum director; b. Gorman, Tex., Sept. 6, 1920; s. Frank Marion and Nora Gertrude (Wharton) H.; m. Virginia Riddle, Nov. 9, 1944; children: Susan, Alan Lee, John Lane. B.S., U. Okla., 1943, M.S., 1947; Ph.D. (Henrietta Heerman scholar 1951), Washington U., St. Louis, 1951; D.Sc. (hon.), North Central Coll., Ill., 1977. Ranger Nat. Park Service, Dept. Interior, 1942; instr. botany U. Okla., 1946-47; curator Bebb Herbarium, 1949; field botanist, instr. Tex. Nature Camp, Nat. Audubon Soc., Kerrville, Tex., 1948; grad. asst. zoology, teaching fellow Washington U., 1948-50; spl. lectr. genetics and evolution Henry Shaw Sch. Botany, 1952; botanist Cranbrook Inst. Sci., Bloomfield Hills, Mich., 1950-56, acting dir., 1955-56; prof., head dept. botany Butler U., 1956-62; vis. prof. botany U. Okla., 1962; dir. Stovall Mus. Sci. and History, 1962-66, Morton Arboretum, Lisle, Ill., 1966—; prof. botany, acting dir. U. Mich. Bot. Gardens, 1963-64; prof. horticulture U. Ill., Urbana; adj. prof. biology No. Ill. U.; Cons. Mich. Dept. Conservation, Handbook Biol. Materials for Museums. Contbr. numerous research articles to profl. jours. Bd. dirs. Joyce Found., Chgo.; governing mem. Forest Found. DuPage County; mem. environ. concerns com. DuPage County Regional Planning Commn. Served to lt. (j.g.) USNR, 1943-45. NSF grantee; recipient Alumni award for achievement U. Okla., 1953. Fellow Ind. Acad. Sci., Cranbrook Inst. Sci.; mem. Am. Soc. Plant Taxonomists, Internat. Assn. Plant Taxonomists, Ecol. Soc. Am., Asa Gray Meml. Assn., Soc. Study Evolution, Mich. Natural Areas Council, Okla. Acad. Sci., Bot. Soc. Am., Mich. Bot. Club (past pres. Detroit), Phi Beta Kappa, Sigma Xi, Phi Sigma. Home: Morton Arboretum Lisle IL 60532 Office: Morton Arboretum Lisle IL 60532

HALL, MARSHALL, JR., mathematics educator; b. St. Louis, Sept. 17, 1910; s. Marshall and Inez (Bethune) H. B.A., Yale U., 1932, Ph.D., 1936; postgrad., Cambridge (Eng.) U., 1932-33. Mem. Inst. Advanced Study, Princeton, 1936-37; instr., then asst. prof. Yale, 1937-46; asso. prof., then prof. Ohio State U., 1946-59; prof. math. Calif. Inst. Tech., Pasadena, 1959—, exec. officer for math., 1966-69, IBM prof. math., 1973—; vis. research fellow Merton Coll., Oxford, Eng., 1977; Lady Davis vis. prof. Technion-Israel Inst. Tech., Haifa, 1980; dir. Summer Inst. Finite Groups, Pasadena, 1960. Author: Theory of Groups, 1959, Combinatorial Theory, 1967. Served with USNR, 1943-46, 50-52. Recipient Wilbur Cross medal Yale, 1973; Henry fellow, 1932-33; Guggenheim fellow, 1955-56, 70-71. Fellow AAAS; mem. Am. Acad. Arts and Scis., Phi Beta Kappa, Sigma Xi. Clubs: Valley Hunt (Pasadena); Athenaeum (London). Home: 439 S Catalina 202 Pasadena CA 91106

HALL, MILES LEWIS, JR., lawyer; b. Ft. Lauderdale, Fla., Aug. 14, 1924; s. Miles Lewis and Mary Frances (Dawson) H.; m. Muriel M. Fisher, Nov. 4, 1950; children: Miles Lewis III, Don Thomas. A.B., Princeton U., 1947; J.D., Harvard U., 1950. Bar: Fla. 1951. Since practiced in, Miami; partner Hall & Hedrick, 1953—; dir. Gen. Portland, Inc., 1974-81. Author: Fla. Law and Practice, 1958. Chmn. 3d Appellate Dist. Ct. Nominating Commn., State Fla., 1972-75; Pres. Orange Bowl Com., 1964-65, dir., 1950—; vice-chmn., dir. Dade County (Fla.) A.R.C., 1961-62, chmn., 1963-64, dir., 1967-73; nat. fund cons. A.R.C., 1963, 66-68; bd. pres. Ransom Sch. Parents Assn., 1966;

chmn. South Fla. Gov.'s Scholarship Ball, 1966; mem. exec. bd. South Fla. council Boy Scouts Am., 1966-67; citizens bd. U. Miami, 1961-66; mem. Fla. Council of 100, vice chmn., 1961-62; mem. Coral Gables (Fla.) Biltmore Devel. Com., 1972-73; mem. bd. visitors Coll. Law, Fla. State U., 1974—; bd. dirs. Coral Gables War Meml. Youth Center, 1967—, pres., 1969-72; bd. dirs. Salvation Army, Miami, 1968-83. Served to 2d lt. USAAF, 1943-45. Mem. Am. Bar Assn. (Fla. co-chmn. membership com. sect. corp., banking and bus. law 1968-72), Dade County Bar Assn. (dir. 1964-65, pres. 1967), Fla. Bar, Am. Judicature Soc., Miami-Dade County C. of C. (v.p. 1962-64, dir. 1966-68), Harvard Law Sch. Assn. Fla. (dir. 1964-66), Alpha Tau Omega. Methodist (bd. stewards). Clubs: Kiwanis, Cottage, Harvard, The Miami, City of Miami (Miami); Princeton of So. Fla. (past pres., dir.). Home: 2907 Alhambra Circle Coral Gables FL 33134 Office: Suite 1104 Peninsula Fed Bldg 200 SE 1st St Miami FL 33131

HALL, MILTON REESE, energy company executive; b. Vicksburg, Miss., July 5, 1932; s. Alvin and Adelle (McKay) H.; m. Margaret Louise Bailey, Feb. 17, 1957; children: Mark Russell, Stacy Elaine. B.S. in Acctg., Miss. So. U., 1953, M.B.A., U. Miss., 1956; postgrad., La. State U., 1959-62. C.P.A., Miss. Trainee, div. controller Kaiser Aluminum, various locations, 1957-66; fin. analyst Tex. Instruments, Dallas, 1966-67; v.p. Koch Industries Inc., Wichita, Kans., 1967—. Served to cpl. U.S. Army, 1953-55. Recipient Silver medal Am. Inst. C.P.A.s, 1956. Mem. Nat. Assn. Accts. Republican. Baptist. Home: 8929 Crestwood Wichita KS 67206 Office: Koch Industries Inc 4111 E 37th St Wichita KS 67201

HALL, MONTY, television producer, actor; b. Winnipeg, Man., Can., 1925; s. Maurice Harvey and Rose (Rusen) Halparin; m. Marilyn Plottel, Sept. 28, 1947; children: Joanna, Richard David, Sharon Fay. B.S., U. Man., 1945. Lectr. broadcasting and fund raising various charities. Actor, U. Man., Canadian Army shows, NBC-Radio, NBC-TV, CBS-TV, ABC-TV; host: Let's Make a Deal, 1963—; Author: Emcee: Monty Hall, 1974. Bd. dirs. numerous charitable orgns.; bd. govs. NCCJ; hon. mayor, Hollywood, 1973—. Named Can. Univs. Grad. of Year, 1977. Mem. AFTRA, Screen Actors Guild, Variety Clubs (internat. pres. 1975-77, Internat. Humanitarian award 1983). Club: Hillcrest Country. Office: 7833 Sunset Blvd Los Angeles CA 90046 *The longer I live, the more I am obsessed with man's inhumanity directed against his fellow man. Is there a basic flaw in man's makeup which prevents the good from overtaking and defeating the evil? I have spent my adult life dedicated to helping children around the world, the diseased, handicapped and underprivileged. The rewards tangible and intangible have shaped my life, have given me an inner peace with myself, and yet a frustration at what could be — and is not. The same holds for nation against nation. What could be — and is not. Is this the order of things past and things to come? I pray with all my heart that the teachings of peace shall prevail.*

HALL, NANCY CHRISTENSEN, publishing company executive, author, editor; b. N.Y.C., Nov. 14, 1946; d. Henry Norman and Elvira (Dugan) Christensen; m. John R. Hall Jr., June 12, 1958; children: Jonathan Scott, Kirsten Marie. B.A., Manhattanville Coll., 1968; postgrad., Old Dominion U., 1970-71. Sr. assoc. editor Cahners Pub. Co., N.Y.C., 1972-74; freelance editor, N.Y.C., 1974-78; sr. editor Grosset and Dunlap, N.Y.C., 1978-81; exec. editor, asst. v.p. Macmillan Pub. Co., N.Y.C., 1981—. Author: Monsters: Creatures of Mystery, 1980, Macmillan Fairy Tale Alphabet Book, 1983; editor: Platt & Munk Treasury of Stories for Children, 1981. Mem. soc. Children's Book Writers. Home: 435 E 14th St New York NY 10009 Office: Macmillan Publishing Co 866 3d Ave New York NY 10009

HALL, NATHAN ALBERT, emeritus educator; b. Bozeman, Mont., July 3, 1918; s. Amos Cross and Myrtle (Lauffer) H.; m. Florence L. Turnbull, Dec. 14, 1960; children—Dennis Albert, Pamella Kathryn. B.Sc., U. Wash., 1939, Ph.D., 1948. Mgr. Pick & Pan Pharmacy, Sheridan, Mont., 1939-41; asst. prof. Phila. Coll. Pharmacy and Sci., 1949-50; pharm. chemist Eli Lilly & Co., Indpls., 1950-51; mem. faculty U. Wash., Seattle, 1951—, prof., 1962-81, prof. emeritus, 1981—, chmn. dept. pharmacy and pharmacy adminstrn., 1970-72; vis. prof. U. Malaya, Singapore, 1959-60, U. Sidney, Australia, 1968; sec.-treas. dist. 7 Am. Assn. Colls. Pharmacy-Nat. Assn. Bds. Pharmacy, 1969-76. Contbr. articles to profl. jours. Served to capt., inf. AUS, 1941-46; PTO. Decorated Combat Infantrymen Badge.; Fulbright lectr., 1959-60. Fellow AAAS. Home: 10553 41st Pl NE Seattle WA 98125

HALL, NEWELL J., chain drug store company executive; b. Clinton, Ind., 1932; married. Pharmacist Hook Drugs, Inc., Indpls., 1961-66, prescription drug buyer, 1966-69, asst. v.p., dir. profl. services, 1969-79, v.p., dir. profl. services, 1972-80, exec. v.p., 1980—, also dir. Office: Hook Drugs Inc 2800 Enterprise St PO Box 26285 Indianapolis IN 46226 *

HALL, NEWMAN A., mechanical engineer; b. Uniontown, Pa., June 14, 1913; s. Homer) Maxwell and Susan (Newman) H.; m. Eileen Creevey, Aug. 14, 1938; children: James Creevey, Elizabeth Arnold. A.B., Marietta (Ohio) Coll., 1934, D.Sc. (hon.), 1959; Ph.D., Calif. Inst. Tech., 1938; M.A., Yale, 1956. Registered profl. engr., Conn. Instr. in math. Queens Coll., Flushing, N.Y., 1938-41; engr. Chance Vought div. United Aircraft Corp., Stratford, Conn., 1941-42, supr. engrng. personnel, 1942-43; research engr. United Aircraft Corp., Hartford, 1944-47, head analysis sect., research div., 1946-47; prof. mech. engrng. and head heat power div., mech. engrng. dept. U. Minn., 1947-55; prof. mech. engrng., asst. dean charge Grad. Div. Coll. Engrng., N.Y. U., 1955-56; prof., chmn. dept. mech. engrng. Yale, 1956-64; cons. on ednl. facilities and adminstrn.; cons. engr. in thermodynamics, fluid dynamics, combustion; author, lectr. genealogy and local history. Exec. dir. Commn. Engrng. Edn., 1962-71; sci. adviser AID, Korea, 1972-73, Korea Ministry Sci. and Tech., 1974-76; ednl. cons., 1976—; dir. div. engrng. scis. Office of Ordnance Research, U.S. Army, 1952-53. Author: (with W.E. Ibele) Engineering Thermodynamics, 1960. Fellow ASME (chmn. bd. edn. 1959-61); mem. Soc. Automotive Engrs., Am. Soc. Engrng. Edn. (v.p. 1960-62), Combustion Inst. (dir.), Order of Founders and Patriots Am. (registrar gen.), Soc. Mayflower Desc., Nat. Geneal. Soc., Arnold Family Assn. South (pres. 1977-81), Phi Beta Kappa, Sigma Xi, Tau Beta Pi. Condr. engrng. research in thermodynamics, fluid mechanics, aerodynamics, heat transfer. Address: Esperanza Town Hill Rd Box 69 New Hartford CT 06057

HALL, O. GLEN, univ. dean; b. nr. Irvine, Ky., June 16, 1929; s. Dellie R. and Mattie (Colwell) H.; m. Doris Swingle, Dec. 31, 1948; children—Deborah Carol, Martha Lynne, Joel Glenn. B.S., Berea Coll., 1951; M.S., U. Ky., 1952; Ph.D., Iowa State U., 1955. Asst. prof. U. Ky., Lexington, 1952; asso. prof. U. Tenn., Knoxville, 1955-65, prof., head dept. agr., Martin, 1965-67, dean, Knoxville, 1967—; So. rep. Resident Instrn. Com. on Orgn. Policy in Agr. Contbr. articles to profl. jours. Mem. Am. Soc. Animal Sci., So. Agrl. Scientists Assn., Assn. State U. and Land Grant Colls., Assn. So. Deans and Dirs. Instrn. in Agr. (past chmn.), Tenn. Farm Bur., Sigma Xi, Omicron Delta Kappa, Phi Kappa Phi, Gamma Sigma Delta, Alpha Zeta. Methodist (adminstrv. bd. 1957—). Home: 9321 Briarwood Blvd Knoxville TN 37919 Office: PO Box 1071 Coll Agr Knoxville TN 37901

HALL, OGDEN HENDERSON, educator; b. Clayton, La., Nov. 8, 1922; s. William A. and Gladys (Denham) H.; m. Barbara Beale, Jan. 9, 1948; children—Michelle, Todd, Jennifer. B.S., La. State U., 1948, M.B.A., 1961, Ph.D., 1963. Office mgr. William Wolf Bakery, Baton Rouge, 1947-50; owner-mgr. Hall-Denham Hardware, Denham Springs, La., 1948-62; asso. prof. bus. Va. Poly. Inst., 1963-68; prof. dept. mgmt. and marketing U. New Orleans, 1968—; cons. in field. Pres. Denham Springs C. of C., 1958; bd. dirs. Credit Bur. Baton Rouge, 1959. Served with AUS, 1943-44; Served with USAAF, 1944-46. Mem. Acad. Mgmt., Eastern Acad. Mgmt. (pres. 1968), So. Mgmt. Assn. (pres. 1978), Am. Inst. Decision Scis., Inst. Gen. Semantics. Home: 1712 Killdeer St New Orleans LA 70122

HALL, PERRY EDWARDS, II, investment banker; b. S. Orange, N.J., Jan. 23, 1938; s. Herbert S. and Mary C. H.; m. Virginia Morgan, Oct. 9, 1965; children—Perry Edwards, III, Brooks C., Benjamin M. B.A., Princeton U., 1960. With Morgan Guaranty Trust Co. N.Y., 1963-81, sr. v.p., 1979-81; v.p., prin. Morgan Stanley & Co. Inc., San Francisco, 1981—. Served as officer USAR, 1961-63. Mem. Bond Club N.Y. Episcopalian. Address: 101 California St San Francisco CA 94111

HALL, PETER FRANCIS, physiologist; b. Sydney, Australia, Dec. 12, 1924; s. William and Ruby Alice (Price) H.; m. Helen Ruth Godfrey, Nov. 10, 1968; children: Philip Charles, Warwick David. M.B.B.S., U. Sydney, 1947, M.D., 1956; Ph.D., U. Utah, 1962. Sr. med. officer Royal Prince Alfred Hosp., Sydney, 1947-50; registrar Guys Hosp., 1954-59; hon. med. officer Sydney Hosp., 1954-59; NIH fellow U. Utah, 1959-62; asst. prof. dept. physiology U. Pitts., 1962-64; prof. biochemistry Melbourne U., 1964-71; prof., chmn. dept. physiology U. Calif., Irvine, 1971-78; prin. scientist Worcester Found. Exptl. Biology, Shrewsbury, Mass., 1978—. Author: Gynaecomastia, 1959, Function of the Endocrine Glands, 1959; Contbr. articles to med. jours. Recipient Merck prize for chemistry, 1959. Fellow Royal Australian Coll. Physicians, Royal Coll. Physicians (London); mem. Am. Physiol. Soc., Am. Soc. Cell Biology, Am. Soc. Biol. Chemistry, Endocrine Soc. Mem. Ch. of Eng. Home: 661 Main St Shrewsbury MA 01545 Office: Worcester Found for Exptl Biology 222 Maple Ave Shrewsbury MA 01545

HALL, RALPH MOODY, congressman; b. Tex., May 3, 1923; s. Hugh O. H.; m. Mary Ellen Murphy, Nov. 14, 1944; children: Hampton, Brett, Blakeley. Student, U. Tex., Tex. Christian U., So. Meth. U., LL.D. Bar: Tex. County judge, Rockwall County, Tex.; mem. Tex. Senate, 1962-72; past pres., chief exec. officer Tex. Aluminum Corp.; past gen. counsel Tex. Extrusion Co., Inc.; past organizer, chmn. bd. dirs., now dir. Lakeside Nat. Bank of Rockwall (now Lakeside Bancshares, Inc.); past vice-chmn. bd. dirs. Bank of Crowley; past chmn. bd. dirs. Lakeside News, Inc.; pres. North and East Trading Co.; chmn. bd. Linrock Inc.; v.p. Crowley Holding Co.; mem. U.S. Ho. Reps. from Tex., 1980—. Served with USNR, 1942-45. Mem. Am. Legion, VFW. Methodist. Lodge: Rotary (past pres.). Office: 1224 Longworth House Office Bldg Washington DC 20515

HALL, RICHARD NEAL, banker; b. Lockport, Ill., June 26, 1938; s. George F. and Mary C. (Fracaro) H.; m. Betty K. Gordon, Jan. 7, 1956; children: Rick, Michelle. B.A., Valparaiso U., 1960; M.A., U. Colo., 1962; postgrad., Stonier Grad. Sch. Banking, Rutgers U., 1976. Asst. v.p. United Calif. Bank, Los Angeles, 1962-69; v.p. Ariz. Bank, Phoenix, 1969-73, mgr. loan dept., 1973-75, mgr. corp. and internat. banking, 1975-78, exec. v.p., mgr. loan div., 1978-80; pres., chief exec. officer Westam. Bank, San Rafael, Calif., 1980—; dir. Newbery Energy Corp., Tempe, Ariz.; Treas. Robert Morris Assos., 1979. Pres. Trusteeship for St. Luke's Hosp., 1978; treas., bd. dirs. Goodwill Industries, 1979-80; bd. dirs. Luth. Hosps. and Homes Soc. Am., Fargo, N.D., 1981—; trustee Dominican Coll., San Rafael, 1981—. Mem. Phoenix C. of C. Clubs: Rotary (San Rafael); Meadow (Fairfax, Calif.). Home: 140 Main Dr San Rafael CA 94901 Office: 1108 5th Ave San Rafael CA 94901 *The qualities of perseverance and faith are most highly correlated with success especially when combined with common sense.*

HALL, ROBERT ANDERSON, JR., Italian language and literature educator; b. Raleigh, N.C., Apr. 4, 1911; s. Robert Anderson and Lolabel (House) H.; m. Frances L. Adkins, Aug. 31, 1936 (dec. Sept. 1975); children: Philip Adkins, Diana Katherine (Mrs. William C. Goodall), Caroline Amanda (Mrs. C.M. Erickson); m. Alice Mary Colby, May 8, 1976. A.B., Princeton, 1931; A.M., U. Chgo., 1935; Litt.D., U. Rome, 1934. Asst. prof. fgn. langs. U. P.R., 1937-39; instr. modern lang. Princeton, 1939-40; instr. Italian Brown U., Providence, 1940-42, asst. prof., 1942-46; lectr. internat. adminstrn. Columbia, 1943-44; vis. asst. prof. internat. adminstrn. Yale, 1943-44; asso. prof. linguistics Cornell U., Ithaca, N.Y., 1946-50, prof., 1950-76, prof. emeritus, 1976—, dir., Rome, 1966-67. Author: Bibliography of Italian Linguistics, 1941, The Italian Questione della Lingua, 1942, Melanesian Pidgin English, 1943, Hungarian Grammar, 1944, Descriptive Italian Grammar, 1948, Leave Your Language Alone, 1950, Short History of Italian Literature, 1951, Haitian Creole, 1953, Hands Off Pidgin English, 1955, Italian for Modern Living, 1958, Bibliografia della Linguistica Italiana, 1958, Italian Stories, 1961, Basic Conversational Italian, 1963, Cultural Symbolism in Literature, 1963, Introductory Linguistics, 1964, New Ways to Learn a Foreign Language, 1965, Pidgin and Creole Languages, 1966, Antonio Fogazzaro e la Crisi dell 'Italia Moderna, 1967, An Essay on Language, 1968, English Phrase and Clause Structure, 1969, La Struttura dell' Italiano, 1971, External History of the Romance Languages, 1974, The Comic Style of P.G. Wodehouse, 1974, Stormy Petrel in Linguistics, 1975, Proto-Romance Phonology, 1976, Antonio Fogazzaro, 1978, Language, Literature, and Life, 1979, Stormy Petrel Flies Again, 1980, The Kensington Rune-Stone is Genuine, 1982, Proto. Romance Morphology, 1983; contbr. numerous articles and book revs. to learned jours.; Composer: Missa Lanquan li jorn, 1972, Kyrie Praeparatio, 1981. Fulbright lectr. linguistics, Rome, 1950-51, 57-58; Guggenheim fellow, 1954, 70; recipient Profl. Achievement award U. Chgo., 1978. Mem. Linguistic Soc. Am. (v.p. 1961), Linguistic Assn. Can. and U.S. (pres. 1984-85), Am. Assn. Tchrs. Italian (v.p. 1945), Modern Lang. Assn. Am., Wodehouse Soc. (pres. 1983-85). Congregationalist. Home: 308 Cayuga Heights Rd Ithaca NY 14850

HALL, ROBERT BRUCE, bishop; b. Wheeling, W.Va., Jan. 27, 1921; s. Kent Bruce and Mary Ellen (Hazlett) H.; m. Dorothy Varner Glass, Jan. 26, 1949; children: Ellen Lynn, Kent Bruce II, Elizabeth Hazlett, Anne Louise, Susan Glass. B.A., Trinity Coll., Hartford, Conn., 1943, D.D., 1967; S.T.B., Episcopal Theol. Sem., Cambridge, Mass., 1949; D.D., Seabury Western Theol. Sem., 1966, Va. Theol. Sem., 1967, Kenyon Coll., 1969. Ordained to ministry Episcopal Ch., 1949; asso. minister, Huntington, W.Va., 1949-53, rector, Huntington, 1953-58, St. Chrysostom's Ch., Chgo., 1958-66; bishop coadjutor Episcopal Diocese Va., 1966-74, bishop of Va., 1974—; Trustee Va. Theol. Sem., 1967—, Blue Ridge Sch., Dyke, Va., 1968—. Served with AUS, 1943-46. Fellow Coll. of Preachers; mem. Delta Phi, Pi Gamma Mu. Home: 11 River Rd Richmond VA 23226 Office: 9006 Mooreland Ct Richmond VA 23229

HALL, ROBERT BURNETT, JR., geography educator; b. Ann Arbor, Mich., Dec. 4, 1923; s. Robert Burnett and Pauline Augusta (Fead) H.; m. Patricia M. Siller, Oct. 19, 1973; children by previous marriage: Robert III, Steven, Charles. A.B., U. Mich., 1947; M.A., 1948; Ph.D., 1952. Instr. Yale U., 1951-52; asst. prof. geography U. Rochester, N.Y., 1952-58, assoc. prof., 1958-65, prof. history and geography, 1965—, dir., 1967—, 1970—. Author: Japan: Industrial Power of Asia, 1963, rev. edit., 1976; also chpt. in book Ency. Brit. Trustee Am. Inst. Indian Studies, 1971-73. Served with AUS, 1942-45; ETO. Fulbright Research scholar Kobe U., Japan, 1954-55. Mem. Assn. Am. Geographers, Assn. Japanese Geographers, Assn. for Asian Studies (chmn. nat. membership com. 1964-66). Home: 167 Greystone Ln Rochester NY 14618 Office: U Rochester Rochester NY 14627

HALL, ROBERT C., grain products manufacuting company executive; b. Boston, 1915; married. B.A., Harvard U., 1936; postgrad. in econs., Oxford U., 1937. With Guaranty Trust Co., N.Y.C., 1937-41; vice chmn., chief fin. officer Bache & Co., 1945-73; chmn. Orion Pacific Ltd., Hong Kong, 1973-79; with Early & Daniel Indusrtires, Inc., 1974—; pres. Early & Daniel Industries, Inc., 1979—, treas., 1980—, dir.; vice chmn., dir. Fiduchiari & Gen. Corp.; v.p., dir. Hume Enterprises, Orion Multinat. Services Inc.; dir., treas. Gen. Grain Inc.; dir. Fla. Gen. Life Ins. Co., Tidewater Grain Corp., Japan Fund Inc., Puritan Fashions Inc., Logistics Control Group Internat. Ltd., Georgetown Life Ins. Co. Served to lt comdr. USN, 1941-45. Office: Early & Daniel Industries Inc 902 W Washington Ave Indianapolis IN 46204

HALL, ROBERT CARLTON, international grain merchant; b. Boston, Mar. 3, 1915; s. Francis T. and Lucy (Waterhouse) H.; m. Emma Gene Tucker, Nov. 23, 1946. B.A., Harvard, 1936; Dip. in Econs., Oxford (Eng.) U., 1937. Dist. rep. Guaranty Trust Co. N.Y., 1937-41; partner Bache & Co., 1945-64, treas., 1963—, dir., v.p., mem. exec. com., 1965—, vice chmn. bd., chief financial officer, 1968-73; chmn. Orion Pacific Ltd., 1973-79; exec. dir. Orion Bank Ltd., 1973-79; pres., dir. OMS Inc.; treas., dir. Gen. Grain Co., Early & Daniels, Tidewater Grain Co., Robemco Inc.; dir. Hume Enterprises, Early & Daniels Industries, Puritan Fashions Inc., Logistics Control Group, 130 E. 67th St. Corp. Bd. dirs. Japan Fund; adv. bd. Pace Coll. Served to lt. comdr. USNR, 1941-45. Mem. Japan Soc., Asian Soc. Clubs: River, Broad St. (N.Y.C.); Am., Jockey (Hong Kong); Portland, Achilles (London); Harvard Varsity (Cambridge, Mass.). Home: White Chimneys West Meeting House Rd New Milford CT 06776 also 130 E 67th St New York NY 10021 Office: 70 Pine St New York NY 10005

HALL, ROBERT CHAMBERS, satellite communications company executive; b. Ames, Iowa, May 20, 1931; s. Harry and Martha Marion (Smalley) H.; m. Joan Louis Summers, July 9, 1955; children: Ellen Hall McEllin, Kathryn, Elizabeth, Timothy, Laura, Margaret, Edward, Jean. B.S.M.E., Iowa State U., Ames, 1955. Vice-pres., group gen. mgr. computer systems, devel. and mfg. Control Data Corp., St. Paul, 1961-72; pres., chmn., chief exec. officer Securities Industry Automation Corp., N.Y.C., 1972-77; exec. v.p. N.Y. Stock Exchange, Inc., N.Y.C., 1977-79; pres., chief exec. officer Satellite Bus. Systems, McLean, Va., 1979—. Bd. dirs. United Fund Mpls., 1971-72. Served with USAF, 1951-52. Mem. Am. Mgmt. Assn. Clubs: Apawamis; Marursing Island (Rye, N.Y.). Office: 8283 Greensboro Dr McLean VA 22102 *

HALL, ROBERT ERNEST, educator; b. Palo Alto, CA, Aug. 13, 1943; s. Victor Ernest and Frances Marie (Gould) H.; m. Donna Pinsker, June 18, 1983; children by previous marriage: Christopher, Anne. B.A., U. Calif.-Berkeley, 1964; Ph.D., MIT, 1967. Asst. prof., acting assoc. prof. U. Calif., Berkeley, 1967-70; from asst. prof. to prof. MIT, Cambridge, 1970-78; prof., sr. fellow Stanford U. (Calif.), 1978—; dir. econ. fluctuation program Nat. Bur. Econ. Research, Cambridge, 1978—; adv. com. Exec. Office of Pres., Washington, 1981-82. Author: Low Tax, Simple Tax, Flat Tax, 1983; editor: Inflation, 1983. Woodrow Wilson fellow, 1964; Ford Found. faculty research fellow, 1969. Fellow Econometric Soc.; mem. Am. Econs. Assn., Am. Statis Assn. Democrat. Home: 726 Torreya Ct Palo Alto CA 94303 Office: Dept Econs Stanford Univ Stanford CA 94305

HALL, ROBERT HOWELL, U.S. district judge; b. Soperton, Ga., Nov. 28, 1921; s. Instant Howell, Jr. and Blanche (Mishoe) H.; m. Janice Kay Wren, July 15, 1982; children: Carolyn C., Patricia A., Howell A. B.S. in Commerce, U. Ga., 1941; LL.B., U. Va., 1948; LL.D. (hon.), Emory U., 1973. Bar: Ga. bar 1948, also U.S. Supreme Ct 1948. Prof. law Emory U., 1948-61; asst. atty. gen., Ga., 1953-61; head criminal div. Ga. Law Dept., 1959-61; judge Ga. Ct. Appeals, Atlanta, 1961-74; justice Ga. Supreme Ct., Atlanta, 1974-79; judge U.S. Dist. Ct. (No. Dist. Ga.), 1979—; Chmn. Jud. Council Ga., 1973-74, Gov.'s Commn. on Jud. Processes, 1971-73. Author 3 legal texts, also articles. Served with AUS, 1942-46; lt. col. Res.; ret. Recipient Leadership award Harvard Law Sch. Assn. Ga., 1971; Golden Citizenship award Fulton Grand Jurors Assn., 1975. Fellow Am. Bar Found.; mem. Am. Bar Assn. (ho. dels. 1971-73, chmn. com. Nat. Inst. Justice 1976-80), Am. Judicature Soc. (dir. 1964—, pres. 1971-73, Harley award 1974), Nat. Center State Cts. (adv. council 1971—, dir. 1977-79), Inst. Ct. Mgmt. (trustee 1976—), Am. Acad. Jud. Edn. (gov. 1964-71), Atlanta Lawyers Club, Delta Tau Delta, Delta Sigma Phi, Phi Delta Phi. Office: 2188 Russell Bldg 75 Spring SW Atlanta GA 30303

HALL, ROBERT JOSEPH, physician, medical educator; b. Buffalo, June 4, 1926; s. Joseph M. and Florence C. (Kirst) H.; m. Dorothy Nowak, Aug. 28, 1948; children: Thomas R., Kathleen A., Mary J. Hall Stuart, Michael F., Steven E. Student, Canisius Coll., Buffalo, 1943-45; M.D., U. Buffalo, 1948. Diplomate: Am. Bd. Internal Medicine, Sub Bd. Cardiovascular Disease (mem. cardiovascular disease sect. 1969-75). Intern Mercy Hosp., Buffalo, 1948-49; commd. 1st lt. M.C. U.S. Army, 1948, advanced through grades to col., 1966; resident in internal medicine Walter Reed Gen. Hosp., Washington, 1949-52, resident in cardiovascular diseases, 1956-57; asst. cardiovascular research Walter Reed Army Inst. Research, 1957-58; service in, Korea and Japan, 1952-55; chief cardiology service Brooke Gen. Hosp., Ft. Sam Houston, Tex., 1961-66, Walter Reed Gen. Hosp., 1966-69; ret., 1969; clin. assoc. prof. medicine Georgetown U. Med. Sch., 1967-69; clin. prof. medicine Baylor U. Coll. Medicine, Houston, 1969—, U. Tex. Med. Sch., 1977—; med. dir. Tex. Heart Inst., Houston, 1969—, chmn. exec. com. profl. staff, 1969—; dir. div. cardiology St. Luke's Episcopal Hosp., Houston, 1969—, chmn. cardiopulmonary resuscitation com., 1972—, assoc. chief med. service, 1970—; cons. Tex. Children's, VA, Brooke Gen. hosps., M.D. Anderson Hosp. and Tumor Inst.; mem. cardiovascular study sect. NIH, 1958-61; mem. phys. evaluation team Gemini project NASA, 1958-61; mem. nat. adv. heart counseil Dept. Def., 1966-69; adv. council Mended Hearts, 1970-78. Contbr. numerous articles med. jours. Mem. President's Adv. Panel Heart Disease. Decorated Legion of Merit. Fellow A.C.P., Am. Coll. Cardiology (gov. 1968-71-74, chmn. bd. govs. and trustee 1973-74); mem. Am. Heart Assn. (fellow council clin. cardiology; pres. Houston chpt. 1974-75, advisor corp. cabinet 1980—), Assn. Mil. Surgeons U.S., Assn. Advancement Med. Instrumentation, Pan Am. Med. Assn. (chmn. sect. cardiovascular diseases 1978—), Assn. Univ. Cardiologists, Tex. Med. Assn., Tex. Cardiology Club, Harris County Med. Soc., Houston Cardiology Soc. (chmn. 1976-77), Houston Soc. Internal Medicine. Home: 5504 Sturbridge St Houston TX 77056 Office: 1 Bates St Houston TX 77030

HALL, ROBERT LATANÉ, sociologist, educator; b. Atlanta, Feb. 25, 1924; s. James Augustus and Rachel (Rudd) H.; m. Joyce Engelking Goodwin, July 2, 1957; children—Annalisa, Karen Linda, Jeffrey Beck. B.A., Yale U., 1947; postgrad., U. Stockholm, 1947-48, U. So. Calif., 1950; M.A., U. Minn., 1950, Ph.D., 1953. Research asst. U. Minn., 1949-52, asst. prof., 1957-60, asso. prof. sociology, 1960-62; social psychologist Air Force Personnel and Tng. Research Center, San Antonio, 1952-54, 56-57, Tampa, Fla., 1954-56; program dir. sociology and social psychology NSF, 1962-65, mem. adv. panel on social sci. traineeships, 1966; assoc. prof. sociology and psychology, asst. to dean faculties U. Ill. at Chgo., 1965-66, prof. sociology, 1966—, head dept., 1966-71, 75-76, dir., 1974—; mem. (Com. on Sociol. Tng.), 1965-75; vis. scholar Center for Interdisciplinary Study Sci. and Tech., Northwestern U., 1971-72; mem. sci. adv. bd. (Center for UFO Studies), 1974—. Editorial cons.: Sociometry, 1966-70; assoc. editor, 1970-71; Contbr. articles to profl. jours. Pres. Hardy Home and Sch. Assn., Washington, 1964-65. Served with USAAF, 1943-45. Decorated D.F.C., Air medal with two oak leaf clusters. Fellow Am. Sociol. Assn.; mem. Am. Psychol. Assn., Common Cause, ACLU, U.S. Power Squadrons. Home: 435 Pine Manor Dr Wilmette IL 60091 Office: Dept Sociology U Ill at Chgo Box 4348 Chicago IL 60680

HALL, ROBERT THALLON, organization executive; b. N.Y.C., Sept. 22, 1933; s. Robert Scott and Barbara Thallon (Brown) H.; m. Kathleen Mary Egan, Aug. 30, 1958; children: Barbara Mary, Gregory John. B.A. in Econs, U. Tex., 1958; M.A. in Labor Econs, U. Ill., 1960. Economist Dept. Labor, 1960-63; budget examiner (Bur. Budget), 1965-68; manpower ofcl. Dept. Labor, 1968-73; adviser to (Australian minister labor), 1973-74, dir., Washington, 1974-77; asst. sec. econ. devel. Dept. Commerce, 1977-81; regional v.p. for western states Nat. Alliance Bus., San Francisco, 1981-83, sr. v.p. administration, Washington, 1983—. Served with AUS, 1952-54; Korea. Human Resources Devel. fellow OECD, 1963-64; recipient Sec. Labor Career Service award, 1973. Democrat. Office: Nat Alliance for Bus 1015 15th St NW Washington DC 20005

HALL, ROBERT WILLIAM, educator; b. Arlington, Mass., Apr. 6, 1928; s. Samuel Harry and Agness (Babikian) H.; m. Mary Alice Starritt, Oct. 25, 1958; children—Christopher Allen, Jonathan Brooks, Pamela Leigh, Timothy Randall, Jennifer Lane, Nicholas Ramsey. A.B., Harvard, 1949, M.A., 1951, Ph.D., 1953. Vis. asst. prof. philosophy Vanderbilt U., 1955-57; asst. prof. philosophy and religion U. Vt., Burlington, 1957-63, asso. prof., 1963-67, prof., 1967—, chmn. dept., 1963-72. Author: Plato and the Individual, 1963, Studies in Religious Philosophy, 1969, Plato, 1981; Editor: APEIRON, 1966—. Served with CIC AUS, 1953-55. Shedd fellow in religion in higher edn., 1968-69. Mem. Am. Philos. Assn., Soc. Ancient Greek Philosophy (sec.-treas. 1963-72), Am. Soc. Aesthetics, Phi Beta Kappa. Home: 165 N Prospect St Burlington VT 05401 Office: 70 S Williams St Burlington VT 05401

HALL, ROSS HUME, biochemist, educator; b. Winnipeg, Man., Can., Nov. 22. 1926; emigrated to U.S., 1954, naturalized, 1960; s. Reginald M. and Elizabeth (Hume) H.; m. Rachel May, Sept. 8, 1950 (div. 1979); children—Stewart, Donald, Mary Elizabeth; m. Anne Jones Haas, Sept. 1, 1979. B.A., U. B.C., 1948; Ph.D., U. Toronto, 1950, U. Cambridge, 1953. Research chemist Lederle Labs. div. Am. Cyanamid Co., 1954-58; prin. cancer research scientist Roswell Park Meml. Inst., Buffalo, 1958-67; asso. research prof. biochemistry State U. N.Y. at Buffalo, 1964-67; prof. dept. biochemistry McMaster U., Hamilton, Ont., 1967—, chmn. dept., 1967-73; co-founder, dir. En-Trophy Inst. Advanced Study; pub. Rev. Author: The Modified Nucleosides in Nucleic Acids, 1971, Food for Nought: the Decline in Nutrition, 1974; asso. editor: Jour. Holistic Medicine; contbr. articles to profl. jours. Mem. Am. Chem. Soc., Am. Soc. Biol. Chemists, Am. Assn. Cancer Research, A.A.A.S., Can. Biochem. Soc., Am. Soc. Plant Physiologists, Nat. Acad. Scis. (food safety com.). Office: Dept Biochemistry McMaster U Hamilton ON Canada

HALL, ROY CHARLES, lawyer; b. Seattle, Jan. 28, 1908; s. LeRoy Charles and Stella (Young) H.; children: Elizabeth (Mrs. S. Black), Robert Kilian. A.B., State Coll. Wash., 1929; M.B.A., U. Wash., 1931; postgrad., U. So. Calif., 1942; J.D., U. San Francisco, 1950. Bar: Calif., U.S. Supreme Ct. Tchr., athletic coach Centralia, Wash., 1929-35; tchr., athletic coach, Seattle, 1935-37; with SouthWestern Pub. Co., 1937-42, 1946-47; 1st dean coll. bus. adminstrn. U. San Francisco, 1947-54; sr. partner Hall & Assos.; prin. Federated Industries Trade Anslalt, Basel, Switzerland. Writer of miscellaneous articles bus. law. Mem. Mayor's Com. on Mental Health; bd. visitors Lincoln U. Law Sch., San Francisco. Served with U.S. Army, 1942-46; lt. col. Res.; ret. Mem. Am. Bar Assn., Calif. Bar, San Francisco Bar Assn. (mem. coms. on taxation, continued edn. bar), Am. Assn. Collegiate Schs. Bus. Adminstrn., Calif. Trial Lawyers Assn., Phi Delta Kappa. Republican. Clubs: Marines Meml. Assn. (San Francisco); Presidio Officers. Pvt. pilot. Home: 396 Marietta Dr San Francisco CA 94127 Office: 690 Market St San Francisco CA 94104

HALL, ROY DOUGLAS, III, real estate executive; b. Glen Ridge, N.J., Mar. 29, 1941; s. Roy Douglas, Jr. and Dorothy Howe (Wheildon) H.; m. Susan Elizabeth Dodge, Feb. 2, 1968; children: Lisa Susan, Sarah Elizabeth. B.A. in Econs, Yale U., 1963. With John Hancock Mut. Life Ins. Co., 1965-70; mgr. real estate fin. Ford Motor Credit Co., 1970-74; sr. v.p. Bay Colony Property Co., Boston, 1975-79, pres., dir., 1979—, Bay Fin. Corp., Boston, 1979—. Chmn. Manchester (Mass.) Fin. Com., 1980—. Home: 5 Running Ridge Rd Manchester MA 01944 Office: 2 Faneuil Hall Boston MA 02109

HALL, RUFUS GEORGE, educator; b. Sherman, Tex., Dec. 12, 1910; s. Rufus George and Mabel (Skiles) H.; m. Nancy Joline Furnace, Sept. 20, 1944; children—Nancy Jeanne, Robin James Rufus. B.A., U. Tex., 1933, M.A., 1935; Ph.D., Harvard, 1948. Mgr. Rufus G. Hall & Son Ins. Agy., Sherman, Tex., 1940-42; instr. polit. sci. U. Okla., Norman, 1946-48, asst. prof., 1948-52, asso. prof., 1952-59, prof., 1959-81, prof. emeritus, 1981—, chmn. dept. govt., 1951-60, asst. dean, 1968-79, chmn. univ. senate, 1971-72, asso. dean, 1979-81; cons. faculty asso.-in-residence Fgn. Service Inst., Washington, 1967. Author: Everthing One Needs to Know About American National Government, 1971, American National Government, 1974, rev. edit., 1979. Bd. dirs., chmn. Wesley Found., Norman. Served with USAAF, 1942-45. Mem. AAUP, Southwestern Social Sci. Assn., Internat. Studies Assn., Phi Beta Kappa, Pi Sigma Alpha. Democrat. Methodist. Home: 1031 Grover Ln Norman OK 73069

HALL, SUSAN, author, film producer; b. N.Y.C., Mar. 4, 1940; d. Isaac Davis and Marion; d. Isaac Davis and Dalton H.; 1 son, David. Grad., Milton (Mass.) Acad., 1957. Film writer, producer, Harvest Films, 1963-65, ABC, 1966-67; ind. producer, N.Y.C., 1967—; films include Summer's Children, 1963, The Smartest Kid in Town, 1963, Helping Hands, 1964, Cosmopolis, 1965, Children's Games, 1968; books include Encounter series, 1970, On and Off the Streets, 1970, Down Home, 1972, Street Smart, 1972, Gentleman of Leisure, 1973, Ladies of the Night, 1974, Out of Left Field, 1976 (Recipient awards Vancouver (B.C.) Film Festival 1964, Am. Film Festival 1964, San Francisco Film Festival 1965, Am. Inst. Graphic Arts 1973, Gold medal Venice Film Festival 1969). Mem. Authors Guild. Address: 200 W 58th St New York City NY 10019

HALL, THOMAS WILLIAM, religion educator; b. Portis, Kans., Sept. 20, 1921; s. Charles E. and Myrtle (DeWitt) H.; m. Ruth Helen Fisher, July 11, 1944; children: Carolyn Jane, Kristin Elaine, Douglas William. A.B., Kans. Wesleyan U., 1943; Th.M., Iliff Sch. Theology, Denver, 1946; Ph.D., Boston U., 1956. Asst. prof. Kans. Wesleyan U., 1946-48, Pittsburg (Kans.) State Coll., 1950-55; assoc. prof., chmn. dept. religion U. Denver, 1956-59; dean religion Stephens Coll., Columbia, Mo., 1959-66; chmn. dept. religion Syracuse U., 1966-74, prof., 1974—; Danforth tchr., 1955-56. Author: Introduction to Study of Religion, 1978. Grantee Syracuse travel and research, summer 1968. Mem. Am. Acad. Religion., Soc. for Values in Higher Edn, Soc. for Sociology of Religion. Research religious thought Europe and Asia. Home: 139 Lewis Ave Syracuse NY 13224

HALL, THOR, religion educator; b. Larvik, Norway, Mar. 15, 1927; came to U.S., 1957, naturalized, 1973; s. Jens Martin and Margit Elvira (Petersen) H.; m. Gerd Hellstrom, July 15, 1950; 1 son, Jan Tore. Diploma theology, Scandinavian Methodist Sem., 1950; postgrad., Selly Oak Colls., Birmingham, Eng., 1950-51; M.R.E., Duke U., 1959, Ph.D., 1962. Ordained to ministry Meth. Ch., 1952; minister Kongsvinger-Odal Meth. Ch., Norway, 1951-53; exec. sec. youth dept. Meth. Ch., Norway, 1953-57; minister Ansonville (N.C.) Meth. Ch., 1958-59; asst. minister 1st Presbyn. Ch., Durham, N.C., 1960-62; asst. prof. preaching and theology Duke U., 1962-68, assoc. prof., 1968-72; disting. prof. religious studies U. Tenn., Chattanooga, 1972—; vis. prof. Oslo U., 1977, Liberia, 1980, U. Copenhagen, 1984; mem. Gen. Bd. Evangelism, Meth. Ch., 1968-72, Oxford Inst. Meth. Theol. Studies, 1982—; cons. Ecumenical Prayer Seminars, 1967—, Army, Navy, Air Force Chaplains Corps, 1967, 68, 71, 72; James Sprunt lectr. Union Theol. Sem., Richmond, Va., 1970; Voigt lectr. So. Ill. Conf., United Meth. Ch., 1979; Goodson lectr. Va. Conf., United Meth. Ch., 1983; mem. Tenn. Com. for Humanities, 1978-82, chmn. subcom. on devel., mem. exec. com., 1979-82. Author: A Theology of Christian Devotion, 1969, A Framework for Faith, 1970, The Future Shape of Preaching, 1971, Whatever Happened to the Gospel, 1973, (with others) Proclamation: Aids for Interpreting the Lessons of the Church Year, 1975, Anders Nygren, 1978, Systematic Theology Today, Part I, 1978, The Evolution of Christology, 1981; editor: Var Ungdom, 1953-57, The Unfinished Pyramid (Charles P. Bowles), 1967, A Directory of Systematic Theologians in North America, 1977; contbr. articles to profl. jours. World Council Chs. scholar, 1950-51; Crusade scholar, 1957-59; Gurney Harris Kearns fellow, 1959-60; Angier Duke Meml. fellow, 1960-61; James B. Duke fellow, 1961-62; Am. Assn. Theol. Schs. faculty fellow, 1968-69; Fulbright-Hays travel grantee, 1984. Mem. Soc. Sci. Study Religion, Am. Acad. Religion (v.p. Southeastern region 1984-85), Soc. Philosophy of Religion, AAUP. Home: 1102 Montvale Circle Signal Mountain TN 37377 Office: Dept Philosophy and Religion U Tenn Chattanooga TN 37401 *The greatest factor contributing to personal growth and professional development is the full utilization of opportunities available at the present and the fulfillment of one's responsibilities, whatever they are.*

HALL, TOM T., songwriter, performer; b. Olive Hill, Ky., May 25, 1936; s. Virgil H.; m. Dixie Dean. Student, Roanoke Coll. Founder pub. co. Hallnote Music. With group, Tom Hall and the Kentucky Travelers; disc jockey, Sta. WMOR, Morehead, Ky.; songwriter with, Newkeys Music, Inc.; rec. artist with, Mercury Records, until 1977; with, RCA, 1977—; performed with band, The Storytellers, Carnegie Hall, N.Y.C., 1973; performed at, Smithsonian Instn., 1979, White House, 1980; albums include Magnificent Music Machine; many others. Served in U.S. Army, 1957-61. Office: Top Billing Internat 1003 18th Ave S Box 121089 Nashville TN 37212 *

HALL, TONY P., congressman; m. Janet Dick, 1973; children—Jyl, Matthew. A.B., Denison U., 1964. Realtor; mem. Ohio Ho. of Reps., 1969-72, Ohio Senate, 1973-78, 96th-98th Congresses from 3d Ohio Dist. Democrat. Clubs: Agonis, Trail's End. Office: 1728 Longworth House Office Bldg Washington DC 20515

HALL, WARREN ESTERLY, JR., lawyer; b. Atlanta, Ga., Dec. 2, 1910; s. Warren Esterly and Martha (Haygood) H.; m. Pauline Lewis, Feb. 3, 1934; children—Martha Anne (Mrs. John B. Byrne), Warren Esterly III (dec.). Student, Ga. Sch. Tech., 1929-30, 31-32; LL.B., Atlanta Law Sch., 1938. Bar: Ga. bar 1937, Fla. bar 1954. Engr. B.M. Hall & Sons, Atlanta, 1926-32; various positions including sales, office management and govt., 1932-37; labor relations adviser to OPA adminstr., Washington, also atty. and asst. adminstr., Atlanta, 1942-45; partner Prestwood & Hall, Atlanta, 1937-42, Poole, Pearce & Hall, 1946-61, Hall Sweeny, & Godbee, Deland, 1955-60, Adams, Hall, Sweeny & Godbee, Fort Lauderdale, 1958-60, Holland, Bevis, Smith, Kibler & Hall (and predecessors), Bartow and Lakeland, Fla., 1961-68, Holland & Knight, Bartow, Lakeland, Tallahassee and Tampa, Fla., 1968—; Gen. solicitor Econ. Stablzn. Agy., Washington, 1950-51; legal advisor to under sec. Navy, Washington, 1951; instr., lectr. labor law various law schs. Bd. editors: Fla. Law and Practice; Contbr. articles to legal publs. Mem. Fed., Am., Ga., Atlanta, 10th Jud. Circuit bar assns., Am. Judicature Soc., Ga. State Bar, Fla. Bar (del. jud. conf. of 5th circuit 1964-71, chmn. appellate ct. rules subcom. 1964-67, vice-chmn. Fla. ct. rules com. 1966-67), Am. Arbitration Assn. (nat. panel arbitration), Scribes, Phi Delta Theta. Episcopalian. Clubs: Lawyers (Atlanta); Peace River Country. Home: 1610 S Hibiscus Dr Bartow FL 33830 Office: 245 S Central Ave Bartow FL 33830

HALL, WILFRED MCGREGOR, engineering company executive;; b. Denver, June 12, 1894; s. Frederick Folsom and Annie L. (Thompson) H.; m. Anne Gertrude Jones, Apr. 4, 1921 (dec. Dec. 1976); children: Fredrick Folsom, Anne (dec.); m. Louise Hull Claire, June 23, 1978. B.S., U. Colo., 1916; D.Eng., Tufts U., 1955. Engr. hydroelectric constrn. Chas. T. Main Co., 1916-17, engr. hydroelectric investigation and design, 1920-22; with Chas. T. Main, Inc., 1941—, dir., 1943—, v.p., 1953-57, pres., chief exec. officer, 1957-72, chmn. bd., chief exec. officer, 1972—; Chmn. bd., chief exec. officer C.T. Main Corp.; chmn. bd., chief exec. officer Chas. T. Main Internat. Inc., Chas. T. Main N.Y. Inc.; chmn. bd., chief exec. bd. H.P.N. Cons. Inc.; chmn. bd., chief exec. officer Chas. T. Main Mich. Inc., Chas. T. Main Va. Inc., W.M. Hall & Assocs., Inc., Main Constructors Inc., Main Constrn. Mgmt. Inc.; engr. Chrisfield Contracting Co., 1919; supt. constrn., engr. U.G.I. Contracting Co., 1922-28; supt. constrn. Electric Bond & Share Co., 1929-31; cons. engr., 1932-33; engr. charge constrn. TVA, 1933-37; mgr. engring. and constrn., P.R., 1937-41; partner Uhl, Hall & Rich, 1953-62, mng. partner, 1962-80; chmn. bd. Main Erbauer Inc., C.T. Main Constrn Inc., Rite Equipment Co., Inc.; past dir. Arkwright-Boston Mfrs. Mut. Ins. Co.; Past dir. U.S. Com. Large Dams. Bd. dirs. Mass. Soc. Prevention of Blindness. Fellow Am. Soc. C.E.; mem. A.I.M. (fellow pres.'s council 1966), Am. Inst. Cons. Engrs. (past pres. New Eng. sect.), Cons. Engrs. Council New Eng. (past dir.), Soc. Mil. Engrs., Newcomen Soc. (trustee, chmn. Mass. com.), Royal Soc. Encouragement of Arts, Manufacture and Commerce, Engrs. Club (bd. govs.), Mass. Soc. Profl Engrs., Alpha Sigma Phi, Sigma Tau, Tau Beta Pi. Clubs: Metropolitan (N.Y.C.); Country (Brookline, Mass.); Algonquin, Rotary (past dir.), Hamilton Trust (Boston) (past pres.). Home: Penthouse D The Fairfield Prudential Center Boston MA 02199 Office: Prudential Tower Prudential Center Boston MA 02199 *Integrity, reasonable goals, careful selection of associates, and excellent health.*

HALL, WILLIAM DARLINGTON, lawyer; b. Elkins, W.Va., Jan. 12, 1914; s. Nathan I. and Grace (Darlington) H.; m. Louise Brown, Aug. 3, 1949; children—Carolyn L., Dorothy K., Beverly G. B.E.E., W.Va. U., 1934, M.E.E., 1935, E.E., 1940; J.D., George Washington U., 1946. Bar: D.C. 1945. Engr. Gen. Electric Co., Lynn, Mass., 1936-39; radio engr., patent adviser Signal Corps U.S. Army, Washington, 1939-47; chief patent sect., 1946-47, practiced in, Washington, 1945—; partner firm Hall, Myers and Rose, 1974—; arbitrator Am. Arbitration Assn., 1970—; mem. Army-Navy Parent Adv. Bd., 1946-47. Home: 10850 Stanmore Dr Potomac MD 20854 Office: Suite 200 Semmes Office Bldg 10220 River Rd Potomac MD 20854

HALL, WILLIAM DELANEY, acct.; b. Kansas City, Mo., June 16, 1922; s. Thomas N. and Ethel (Delaney) H.; m. Barbara Doane; children—Laurie E. Hall Hoover, Thomas D., J. Alexander, Andrew D. B.S., U. Ill., 1947, M.S., 1948. C.P.A., Ill., 6 other states. With Arthur Andersen & Co. (C.P.A.'s), 1948—, partner, 1958—, chmn. com. profl. standards. Bd. dirs. Chgo. Child Care Soc. Served to 1st lt. USAAF, World War II. Mem. Am. Inst. C.P.A.'s, Ill. Soc. C.P.A.'s, Mich. Assn. C.P.A.'s, Am. Acctg. Assn., Alpha Sigma Phi, Beta Alpha Psi, Beta Gamma Sigma. Presbyterian. Clubs: Mid-Day, Univ. (Chgo.). Home: 345 N Batavia Ave Batavia IL 60510 Office: 69 W Washington St Chicago IL 60602

HALL, WILLIAM EDWARD, JR., educator, journalist; b. Weston, W. Va., Mar. 21, 1923; s. William Edward and Olive Marion (McGee) H.; m. Lou Ann Jones, Nov. 27, 1946 (div.); children: Sharon Lou, Roberta Ann, William Philip; m. Carol Ann Cusick, Sept. 1, 1966; children: Kevin Dennis, Kimberlee Marian. B.A., U. N.Mex., 1944; M.S., Columbia, 1950; Ph.D., State U. Iowa, 1954. Reporter Albuquerque (N.Mex.) Tribune, 1939-46, sports editor, 1943, 46; dir. alumni relations U. N.Mex., 1947-52, instr. journalism part-time, 1950-51, asst. to pres., 1953; head dept. journalism, dir. pub. relations Tex. Tech. Coll., 1954-56; prof., dir. Sch. Journalism, U. Nebr., 1956-66; prof. Ohio State U., 1966—, dir. Sch. Journalism, 1966-78; Gannett vis. prof. journalism program U. Hawaii, winter 1978, 79, vis. prof., 1980-82; co-ordinator Iowa flow news study Internat. Press Inst., 1953. Editor: Journalism Abstracts, 1972-76. Nebr. cons. pub. relations, pub. info. ARC. Served with AUS, World War II; ETO. Winner Printer's Ink Silver Medal award with Am. Fedn. Advt., 1964. Mem. Am. Assn. Schs. and Depts. Journalism (pres. 1968-69), Assn. Edn. Journalism, Kappa Tau Alpha, Sigma Delta Chi, Pi Sgma Alpha, Pi Kappa Alpha. Club: Lincoln Advertising (chmn. bd. 1964-65). Home: 2494 Billiton Ct Columbus OH 43220 Office: Journalism Bldg 242 W 18th Ave Columbus OH 43210

HALL, WILLIAM JACKSON, statistician, educator; b. Beltsville, Md., Nov. 13, 1929; s. Reginald Foster and Lily (Hambleton) H.; m. Helen Bloxom Cox, Mar. 27, 1954 (div. 1981); children: Jacqueline Arden, Rebecca Clayton, Bryan Hambleton, Kay Randall.; m. Nancy T. Hufsmith, Jun. 1, 1982. A.B., Johns Hopkins U., 1950; M.A., U. Mich., 1951; Ph.D., U. N.C., 1955; postgrad., Manchester (Eng.) U., 1953, Cambridge (Eng.) U., 1954. Statistician Bell Telephone Labs., N.Y.C., 1954-55; asst. chief Polio Surveillance Unit, Communicable Disease Center, USPHS, Atlanta, 1955-57; lectr. U. Calif. at Berkeley, 1957, vis. prof., 1969; asst. prof. U. N.C., 1957-61, assoc. prof., 1961-66, prof. statistics, 1966-69; vis. prof. Stanford, 1967-69; prof. dept. stats. and div. biostats. U. Rochester, N.Y., 1969—, chmn. dept. stats., 1969-81; vis. prof. stats. and biostats. U. Washington, 1982. Asso. editor: Annals of Mathematical Statistics, 1968-73, Jour. Am. Statis. Assn, 1976-78. Fellow AAAS, Am. Statis. Assn., Inst. Math. Stats. (council 1973-76); mem. Royal Statis. Soc. Home: 75 Chelmsford Rd Rochester NY 14618

HALL, WILLIAM JOEL, educator, consulting civil engineer; b. Berkeley, Calif., Apr. 13, 1926; s. Eugene Raymond and Mary (Harkey) H.; m. Elaine Frances Thalman, Dec. 18, 1948; children—Martha Jane, James Frederick, Carolyn Marie. Student, U. Calif. at Berkeley, 1943-44, U.S. Mcht. Marine Acad., 1944-45; B.S. in Civil Engring, U. Kans., 1948; M.S., U. Ill., Urbana, 1951, Ph.D., 1954. Teaching asst. U. Kans., 1947-48; engr. Sohio Pipe Line Co., 1948-49; mem. faculty U. Ill., Urbana, 1949—, prof. civil engring., 1959—; cons. structural dynamics seismic, materials to govt. orgns. and industry. Author books, articles, chpts. in books, revs. Recipient A. Epstein Meml. award U. Ill., 1958; Halliburton Engring. Edn. Leadership award, 1980. Fellow ASCE (pres. Central Ill. sect. 1967-68, chmn. structural div. exec. com. 1973—, chmn. tech. council on lifeline earthquake engring. exec. com. 1982—, Kan. sect. award 1948, Walter L. Huber award 1963), AAAS; mem. Nat. Acad. Engring., Am. Concrete Inst., ASME, Am. Welding Soc. (Adams Meml. membership award 1967), Internat. Assn. Bridge and Structural Engrs., Earthquake Engring. Research Inst., Seismol. Soc. Am., ASTM, Soc. Exptl. Stress Analysis, Am. Soc. Engring Edn., Ill., Nat. socs. profl. engrs., Sigma Xi, Tau Beta Pi, Sigma Tau, Chi Epsilon, Phi Kappa Phi. Home: 3105 Valley Brook Dr Champaign IL 61821 Office: 1245 Newmark Civil Engring Lab 208 N Romine St Urbana IL 61801

HALL, WILLIAM STONE, mental health official; b. Wagener, S.C., May 1, 1915; s. Henry F. and Mary (Gantt) H.; m. Oxena Elizabeth Gunter, June 29, 1940; children: William Stone, Carol Lynn, Richard F. M.D., Med. U. S.C., 1937; student, Sch. Mil. Neuropsychiatry, 1944, Columbia U., 1947, U. Chgo., 1959. Diplomate: Am. Bd. Neurology and Psychiatry. Intern Columbia (S.C.) Hosp., 1937-38; mem. staff S.C. State Hosp., Columbia, 1938-52, supt., 1952-69, Pineland State Tng. Sch. and Hosp., 1953-66, Palmetto State Hosp. (name now Crafts-Farrow State Hosp.), 1952-66; commr. mental health S.C. Dept. Mental Health, 1963—; clin. prof. psychiatry Med. U. S.C., 1957—, U. S.C., 1976—; Mem. Presdl. Task Force on Mentally Handicapped, 1970; chmn. planning com. Surg. Gen.'s Conf. State and Ter. Mental Health Authorities, 1971, 72; liaison mem. Nat. Adv. Mental Health Council, Nat. Inst. Mental Health, 1972-73; mem. Gov.'s State Health Planning Council, 1973-74, Gov.'s Social Devel. Policy Council, 1973-74; mem. coordinating council S.C. Commn. on Aging, 1974—; mem. Adv. Council for Comprehensive Health Planning, 1967-75, 1st vice chmn., 1972, 73; councillor, accreditation council for psychiat. facilities Joint Commn. on Accreditation Hosps., 1973-79; mem. Gov.'s Com. on State Employees and their Employment, 1973—, S.C. Statewide Health Coordinating Council, 1976—, S.C. Gov.'s Interagy. Coordinating council on Early Childhood Devel. and Edn., 1980—, S.C. Pre-trial Intervention Adv. Com., 1980—. Trustee United Community Fund, 1968-71; bd. dirs. United Way of Midlands, 1976-80; adv. bd. Remotivation Technique Orgn., 1972-75. Served as maj. M.C. AUS, 1942-46. Recipient distinguished service plaque S.C. Mental Health Assn., 1960; recipient Orgnl. award S.C. Vocational Rehab. Assn., 1969; Ann. Distinguished Service award S.C. dept. Am. Legion, 1970; Distinguished Service award S.C. Hosp. Assn., 1972; Distinguished Alumnus award Med. U. S.C., 1974; named to S.C. Hall of Fame, 1975; named in his honor William S. Hall Diagnostic Ctr., Charleston, 1984. Fellow Am. Psychiat. Assn. (life, nominating com. 1968, chmn. program com. 12th Mental Hosp. Inst. 1960, com. certification in adminstrv. psychiatry 1972-80, pres. S.C. dist. br. 1957), Am. Coll. Psychiatrists (charter), Am. Coll. Mental Health Adminstrn.; mem. Am. Hosp. Assn. (chmn. governing council psychiat. hosp. sect. 1971), AMA (com. on nursing 1966-73), S.C. Mental Health Assn., Columbia Med. Soc. (pres. 1958), Assn. Med. Supts. Mental Hosps. (pres. 1964, 65, meritorious service award 1971), Nat. Assn. State Mental Health Program Dirs. (v.p. 1968,

69, pres. 1970, 71), S.C. State Employees Assn. (bd. dirs. 1968-76, v.p. 1971-73, pres. 1973-75, Outstanding State Employee 1967), Am. Assn. Psychiat. Adminstrs. (assoc. editor Jour. 1983—). Baptist (deacon). Club: Rotarian. Center for intensive treatment, research edn., Columbia, named William S. Hall Psychiat. Inst., 1964. Home: 1427 Summerville Ave Columbia SC 29201 Office: 2414 Bull St Columbia SC 29202

HALLADAY, LAURIE ANN, public relations executive; b. Monroe, Mich., Aug. 18, 1945; d. Alvin John and Florence (Lowrey) Kohler; m. Edward L. Howell, Aug. 27, 1966; m. 2d Fredric R. Halladay. B.J., U. Mo., 1967. Reporter, staff writer Copley Newspapers, Los Angeles, 1967-69; account exec. Furman Assocs., Los Angeles, 1969-71, v.p., 1971-74; account supr. Bob Thomas & Assocs., Los Angeles, 1974-76, v.p., 1976-78; v.p., sr. ptnr. Fleishman-Hillard, Inc., St. Louis, 1980—. Bd. dirs. Waterman Place Assn., St. Louis, 1983. Recipient Merit award Calif. Press Women, 1969, Lulu award Los Angeles Women's Ad Club, 1976. Mem. Pub. Relations Soc. Am. (Prism award 1977), Soc. Am. Travel Writers (assoc.), Women in Communications (dir. St. Louis 1980-82). Club: St. Louis Press. Home: 50 Waterman Pl Saint Louis MO 63112 Office: Fleishman-Hillard Inc 1 Memorial Dr Saint Louis MO 63102

HALLAM, BEVERLY LINNEY, artist; b. Lynn, Mass., Nov. 22, 1923; d. Edwin Francis and Alice (Linney) Hallam M. B.S. in Edn, Mass. Coll. Art, 1945; postgrad., Cranbrook Acad. Art, Mich., 1948; M.F.A., Syracuse U., 1953. Chmn. dept. art Lasell Jr. Coll., Auburndale, Mass., 1945-49; asso. prof. Mass. Coll. Art, 1949-62, lectr., 1962—; bd. dirs. Barn Gallery Assocs., Inc., Ogunquit, Maine, 1970—. One-woman shows, Joe and Emily Lowe Art Center, Syracuse U., 1953, DeCordova Mus., Lincoln. Mass., 1954, Shore Galleries, Boston, 1959, 62, 68, 73, 74, Witte Meml. Mus., San Antonio, 1968, U. Maine, 1969, Lamont Gallery, Exeter, N.H., Addison Gallery, Andover, Mass., 1971, Fitchburg Art Mus., 1972, Fairweather Hardin Gallery, Chgo., Hobe Sound (Fla.) Galleries, 1973, Inst. Contemporary Art, Boston, 1977, PS Galleries, Maine, 1981, Payson-Weisberg Gallery, N.Y.C., 1984, Farnsworth Mus., Rockland, Maine, others, two-person show, Inst. Contemporary Art, Boston, 1956, numerous group shows including, Barn Gallery, 1954—, Busch-Reisinger Mus., Harvard U., 1956, 59, 60, Portland (Maine) Mus., 1959, 84, Mus. Fine Arts, Boston, 1960, Inst. Contemporary Art, Boston, 1960, 63, 68, 77, Pace Gallery, Boston, 1962, DeCordova Mus., 1963, 64, 68, 69, 70, 71, 75, Fitchburg (Mass.) Art Mus., 1963, Ward-Nasse Gallery, N.Y.C., 1971-72, Ogunquit (Maine) Mus. Art, 1964, 70, 71, 78, 80, 84, R.I. Arts Festival, 1966, Smithsonian Instn., Washington, Farnsworth Mus., Rockland, Maine, 1967, Am. Water Color Soc. Traveling Exhibition, City Hall, Boston, 1970, Watercolor U.S.A., Springfield, Mo., 1968, Maine State Mus., 1976, Joan Whitney Payson Gallery of Art, Maine, 1980, PS Galleries, Tex., 1981-84, Bowdoin Coll. Mus. Art, 1984; represented in permanent collections, Rose Art Mus. Brandeis U., Worcester (Mass.) Art Mus., U. Mass., Corcoran Gallery Am. Art, Washington, Witte Meml. Mus., San Antonio, Kresge Art Gallery, Lansing, Mich., DeCordova Mus., Lincoln, Addison Gallery, Andover, Lamont Gallery, Exeter, Bowdoin Coll. Mus. Art, Fitchburg Art Mus., Mus. Art Ongunquit, Portland Mus., Colby Coll., U. Maine, Currier Gallery Art, Manchester N.H., Farnsworth Library and Art Mus., Rockland, Maine, U. N.H. Art Galleries, Durham, Everson Mus., Syracuse, First Nat. Bank, Boston, Ernst and Ernst, Chgo., Isham, Lincoln & Beale, Chgo., Carnegie Corp., N.Y., others, also, pvt. collections, U.S. Can., Paris, Switzerland; Publication Beverly Hallam, Paintings, Drawings and Monotypes, 1956-71, 1971. Recipient Pearl Safir award Silvermine Guild Artists, New Canaan, Conn., 1955; Painting Prize Boston Arts festival, 1957; Blanche E. Colman Found. award, 1960; Hatfield awards Boston Soc. Watercolor Painters, 1960, 64; 1st prize; Edwin Webster award, 1962; A.H. Benoit award Barn Gallery, Ogunquit, 1967. Mem. Ogunquit Art Assn. (past pres.). Pioneer use of polyvinyl acetate as painting medium. Address: RFD 2 Box 381 York ME 03909

HALLBERG, GARTH RAGNAR, advertising agency executive; b. Albany, N.Y., Jan. 31, 1944; s. Karl I. and Olga (Fagan) H.; m. Mary Adams Sampsell, May 25, 1968; 1 dau., Alexis. A.B., Columbia U., 1964, M.S. in Journalism, 1969, M.B.A., 1970. Account mgr. J. Walter Thompson, U.S.A. Inc., N.Y.C., 1970-79, v.p., 1974-79, sr. v.p., 1979-83. Served to lt. (j.g.) USNR, 1965-68. Clubs: Yale (N.Y.C.); Waccabuc Country (N.Y.). Home: East Ridge Rd Waccabuc NY 10597

HALLBERG, OWEN KENNETH, ednl. assn. exec.; b. Graceville, Minn., Apr. 26, 1923; s. Nels Gordon and Lillian Harmena (Johnson) H.; m. Geraldine Helen Rylander, Dec. 27, 1947; children—Stephen, Janicy (dec.), Judith (dec.), John. B.S. in Agr, U. Minn., 1946, M.S. in Agrl. Econs, 1947. Salesman Coop. Grange League Fedn., Ithaca, N.Y., 1947-51, Seldon-Watts Seed Co., St. Paul, 1951-53; asst. v.p. St. Paul Bank Coops., 1953-59; gen. mgr. Dairy Maid Products Coop., Eau Claire, Wis., 1959-65; mem., dir., mem. staff pub. relations Land O'Lakes, Inc., Mpls., 1965-73; pres. Am. Inst. Cooperation, Washington, 1973—. Recipient Dean Freeman award U. Minn., 1946, Alumni Service award U. Minn., 1955, Klinefelter award Coop. Editorial Assn., 1974; named hon. Minn. state farmer and hon. Am. farmer Future Farmers Am. Mem. Agrl. Coop. Devel. Internat., Grad. Inst. Coop. Leadership, Washington Soc. Assn. Execs., Pub. Relations Soc. Am., Farmhouse, Alpha Zeta. Home: 2110 S Rosewood Ln St Paul MN 55113 Office: 1800 Massachusetts Ave NW Washington DC 20036

HALLE, CLAUS M., beverage company executive; b. 1927; married. With Lemgol Lippe, W.Ger., 1946; with Coca-Cola Export Corp. subs., Atlanta, 1950—, Coca-cola GmbH, Essen, Germany, 1950-56, sales mgr., Germany, 1956-62, mgr., 1962-65, v.p. exprot, area mgr. Central Europe, 1965-70; corp. sr. v.p., pres., chief exec. officer Coca Cola Europe, 1970-73; pres., dir. Coca-Cola Export Corp., 1973; v.p. Coca-Cola Co., 1973-74, sr. v.p., 1974-76, exec. v.p., 1976-79; vice chmn. bd. Coca-Cola co., 1979-80; exec. v.p. Coca-Cola Co., 1980-81, sr. exec. v.p., 1981—. Office: Coca Cola Co 310 North Ave NW PO Drawer 1734 Atlanta GA 30301

HALLE, LOUIS JOSEPH, author, educator; b. N.Y.C., Nov. 17, 1910; s. Louis Joseph and Rita (Sulzbacher) H.; m. Barbara Mark, Mar. 16, 1946; children: John, Julia, Mark, Robin, Anne. B.S., Harvard, 1932, student Grad. Sch., 1937-38. With Internat. Rys. of C.Am. in, Guatemala and El Salvador, 1934; with Longmans, Green & Co. (pubs.), N.Y.C., 1935-36, Dept. State, 1941-54, staff inter-Am. affairs, 1941-51; assigned (Nat. War Coll.), 1951-52; mem. policy planning staff Dept. of State, 1952-54; research prof. Woodrow Wilson dept. fgn. affairs U. Va., 1954-56; prof. Grad. Inst. Internat. Studies, Geneva, 1956-77, prof. emeritus, 1977—; vis. prof. Bologna Center, Johns Hopkins U. Sch. Advanced Internat. Studies, 1977-80; Mem. Council Internat. Inst. Strategic Studies, 1964-75; Acad. adv. bd. NATO Defense Coll., 1973-76. (Recipient medal John Burroughs Assn. 1941, for book, Birds against Men, Paul Bartsch award for disting. contbns. to natural history 1979); Author: Transcaribbean, 1936, Birds against Men, 1938, River of Ruins, 1941, Spring in Washington, 1947, On Facing the World, 1950, Civilization and Foreign Policy, 1955, Choice for Survival, 1958, Dream and Reality, 1959, Men and Nations, 1962, Sedge, 1963, The Society of Man, 1965, The Cold War as History, 1967, The Storm Petrel and the Owl of Athena, 1970, The Ideological Imagination, 1971, The Sea and The Ice: A Naturalist in Antarctica, 1973, Out of Chaos, 1977, The Search for an Eternal Norm: as Represented by Three Classics, 1981, The Elements of International Strategy: A Primer for the Nuclear Age, 1984. Served as pvt. AUS, 1941; commd. lt. (j.g.) USCGR, 1943; asst. diplomatic adviser UNRRA, 1944. Home: Place de la Taconnerie 1 CH 1204 Geneva Switzerland

HALLE, MORRIS, linguist, educator; b. Liepaja, Latvia, July 23, 1923; s. Irving and Lisa (Kahan) H.; m. Rosamond Thaxter Strong, July 2, 1955; children—David S., John G., M. Timothy. Student, City Coll. N.Y., 1941-43; M.A., U. Chgo., 1948; postgrad., Columbia, 1948-49; Ph.D., Harvard, 1955. Mem. faculty Mass. Inst. Tech., Cambridge, 1951—, prof. modern langs. and linguistics, 1961-76, Ferrari P. Ward prof. modern langs. and linguistics, 1976-81, Inst. Prof., 1981—; James R. Killian, Jr. Faculty Achievement Award lectr., 1978-79. Author: (with R. Jakobson and C.G.M. Fant) Preliminaries to Speech Analysis, 1952, The Sound Pattern of Russian, 1959, (with N. Chomsky) The Sound Pattern of English, 1968, (with S.J. Keyser) English Stress: Its Form, Its Growth, and Its Use in Verse, 1971, (with G.N. Clements) Problem Book in Phonology, 1983. Served with AUS, 1943-46. Guggenheim fellow, 1960-61; Am. Acad. Arts and Scis. fellow, 1963—. Mem. Linguistic Soc. Am. (v.p. 1973, pres. 1974). Home: 206 Waverley Ave Newton MA 02158 Office: Mass Inst Tech Cambridge MA 02139

HALLECK, CHARLES A., lawyer; b. De Motte, Ind., Aug. 22, 1900; s. Abraham and Lura I. (Luce) H.; m. Blanche A. White, June 15, 1927; children—Charles White, Patricia. A.B. cum laude, Ind. U., 1922, LL.B., 1924. Bar: Ind. bar 1924. Practice in, Rensselaer; pros. atty. 30th Jud. Circuit, 1924-34; mem. 74th-90th congresses from 2d Ind. Dist.; majority leader U.S. Ho. of Reps. 80th and 83d Congresses; minority leader 86th to 88th Congresses.; Permanent chmn. Republican nat. conv., 1960. Served with inf. U.S. Army, World War I. Mem. Am. Legion, Order of the Coif, Phi Beta Kappa, Beta Theta Pi, Phi Delta Phi. Methodist. Club: Columbia (Indpls.). Home: Rensselaer IN 47978 Office: Courthouse Sq Rensselaer IN 47978

HALLECK, CHARLES WHITE, lawyer, former judge; b. Rensselaer, Ind., July 6, 1929; s. Charles Abraham and Blanche (White) H.; m. Carolyn L. Wood, Dec. 23, 1950 (div. Oct. 1969); children: Holly Louise, Charles White, Todd Alexander, Heather Leigh, Heidi Lynne, William Hemsley, Hope Leslie; m. Jeanne Wahl, May 16, 1970. A.B., Williams Coll., 1951; J.D., George Washington U., 1957; LL.D. (hon.), St. Joseph's Coll., 1971. Asst. U.S. atty. for D.C., 1957-59; asso. firm Hogan and Hartson, Washington, 1959-65; judge Superior Ct. D.C., 1965-77; mem. firm Lamb, Halleck & Keats, Washington, 1977-80; of counsel firm Kaswell, Perazich & Watson, Washington, 1980—. Served with USNR, 1951-55; Served to lt. USNR, ret.; lt. Res. Mem. Beta Theta Pi, Phi Delta Phi. Office: 1825 K St NW Washington DC 20006

HALLEN, PHILIP BURGH, foundation administrator; b. Buffalo, Oct. 11, 1930; s. Knute Philip and Ebba (Burgh) H.; m. Katharine Donna Eager, Jan. 21, 1955; children—Katrin Julia, Elissa, Diana, Margaret. B.A., Syracuse U., 1952, M.A., 1954; M.S., Yale, 1958. Adminstrv. resident Mass. Dept. Mental Health, Boston, 1957-58; asst. adminstr. Boston Dispensary Tufts-New Eng. Med. Center, 1959-61; clin. instr. pub. health Tufts U. Sch. Medicine, 1959-61; research assoc. Hosp. Planning Assn. Allegheny County, Pitts., 1961-63; pres. Maurice Falk Med. Fund, Pitts., 1963—; sr. assoc. Center Effective Philanthropy, Cambridge, Mass; Mem. Allegheny County Mental Health and Mental Retardation Bd., 1967—; cons. Staunton Farm Found. Trustee Am. Found. Mental Hygiene, Episcopal Div. Sch., Cambridge, Mass., 1978—; bd. dirs. Council on Founds., N.Y.C., 1974-79; vice chmn. Pa. Humanities Council; trustee Pub. Com. Mental Health, Washington.; chmn. Local Initiatives Service Corp., Pitts.; Bd. dirs. Pitts. Filmakers. Fellow Am. Pub. Health Assn., Am. Psychiat. Assn. (hon.); mem. Pa. Pub. Health Assn., Pitts. Oratorio Soc. (pres. 1966—). Democrat. Clubs: Harvard-Yale-Princeton, Junta (Pitts.); Yale (N.Y.C.). Home: 5633 Bartlett St Pittsburgh PA 15217 Office: 3317 Grant Bldg Pittsburgh PA 15219

HALLENBECK, GEORGE AARON, surgeon, educator; b. Rochester, Minn., June 29, 1915; s. Dorr Foster and Bessie (Graham) H.; m. Marian Mansfield, Dec. 16, 1938 (div. 1979); children: John M., George A., Christopher G. (dec.), Linda; m. Nancy Peek Chamberlin, 1979. B.S., Northwestern U., 1936, M.D., 1940; Ph.D. in Physiology, Mayo Found., U. Minn., 1943. Diplomate: Am. Bd. Surgery. Intern Virginia Mason Hosp., Seattle, 1939-40; cons. surgeon Mayo Clinic, Rochester, Minn., 1949-60, sect. surg. research, 1961-66, chmn. gen. surgery sects., 1966-68; prof. surgery and physiology Mayo Found., U. Minn., 1960-68; prof. surgery U. Ala., Birmingham, 1968-75; chmn. dept. surgery Scripps Clinic, La Jolla, Calif., 1976-80, sr. cons. surgery, 1980—. Author numerous sci. publs. Served to maj., M.C. AUS, 1943-46. Fellow A.C.S.; mem. Am., Central, Western, So. surg. assns., Am. Gastroenterol. Assn., Soc. Clin Surgeons, Am. Physiol. Soc., Soc. Exptl. Biology and Medicine, So. Surgeons Club, Phi Beta Kappa, Alpha Omega Alpha, Phi Delta Theta, Phi Rho Sigma. Home: Box 1108 Rancho Santa Fe CA 92067 Office: Dept Surgery 10666 N Torrey Pines Rd San Diego CA 92037

HALLENE, ALAN MONTGOMERY, elevator and escalator company executive; b. Moline, Ill., Mar. 12, 1929; s. Maurice Mitchell and Ruth (Montgomery) H.; m. Phyllis Dorene Welsh, June 16, 1951; children: Alan, Carol Louise, Janet Lee, James Norman. B.S., U. Ill., 1951; postgrad., Oak Ridge Sch. Reactor Tech., 1951-52. Reactor engr. U.S. AEC, Oak Ridge and Chgo., 1951-53; sales engr. Montgomery Elevator Co., Moline, Ill., 1953-54, mgr. accessories div., 1954-57, br. mgr., 1957-58, chief engr., Moline, 1958-60, v.p., dir., 1960-64, exec. v.p., dir., 1964-68, pres., dir., 1968—; dir. Moline Nat. Bank, Butler Mfg. Co., Ill. Bell Telephone., Rolscreen Co., First Midwest Bancorp., Inc. Mem. Moline Dist. 40 Bd. Edn., 1966-70; mem. Ill. Gov.'s Adv. Council; mem. adv. com. Tchr. Corps, HEW, 1970-73; mem. Ill. Commn. on Atomic Energy, 1968-73; Bd. dirs. Moline Luth. Hosp., 1967-80, Western Golf Assn., 1972-77, Am. Coll. Testing Program, 1975-81, U. Ill. Found., Quad-City Devel. Group, Augustana Coll., 1977-81; trustee Butterworth Meml. Trust.; mem. bus. adv. council U. Ill. Mem. U. Ill. Alumni Assn. (pres. 1973-75). Club: Rotary (pres. Moline 1961). Home: 1885 24th Ave A Moline IL 61265 Office: 30 20th St Moline IL 61265

HALLER, ARCHIBALD ORBEN, sociologist, educator; b. San Diego, Jan. 15, 1926; s. Archie O. and Eleanor (Brizzee) H.; m. Hazel Laura Zimmermann, Feb. 15, 1947; children—Elizabeth Ann, Stephanie Lynn, William John. B.A., Hamline U., 1950; M.A., U. Minn., 1951; Ph.D. (Univ. fellow), U. Wis., 1954. Project asso. U. Wis., Madison, 1954-56, prof. rural sociology, also sociology, 1965—, chmn. dept. rural sociology, 1970-72, chmn., 1976—; from asso. prof. to prof. sociology Mich. State U., East Lansing, 1956-65; Fulbright prof. Rural U. Brazil, 1962; Fulbright travel grantee univs. São Paulo, Brasília, Pernambuco, Ceará, 1974, Univs. São Paulo, Pernambuco, Paraiba and Ceará, Brazil, 1979; cons. in field Inter-Am. Inst. Agrl. Sci., 1959, OAS, 1963; Brazilian govt., 1965, AID, 1972, U. Sao Paulo, 1974-75, 76-77, Justice Dept., 1976-77, U. Ill., 1977. Author research monographs and tech. articles.; Contbr. articles to profl. jours. Mem. Mich. Com. Mental Health Policies, 1961-62; mem. Panel on Disasters and Devel., NRC, 1977—; sociology fellowship panel Council on Internat. Exchange Scholars, 1977—. Served with USNR, 1943-46. Fellow AAAS; mem. Rural Sociol. Assn. (pres. 1969-70, rep. to AAAS 1973—), Am. Sociol. Assn., Internat. Sociol. Assn., Internat. Rural Sociol. Assn., Latin Am. Rural Sociol. Assn., Midwest Sociol. Assn., Sociol. Research Assn., Latin Am. Studies Assn., Soc. Internat. Devel. Home: 529 Edward St Madison WI 53711

HALLER, CALVIN JOHN, banker; b. Buffalo, July 9, 1925; s. John Martin and and Emelia (George) H.; m. Yvette Ann Hogrewe, June 12, 1948; children: Cary John, Darlene Ann Haller Kalfahs. B.S. in Bus. Adminstrn. with distinction, U. Buffalo, 1949. With Buffalo Savs. Bank, 1949—, now pres. Western N.Y. dir.; dir. Blue Shield Western N.Y.; Mem. faculty ednl. programs Nat. Assn. Mut. Savs. Banking, 1966—. Bd. dirs. Niagara Lutheran Home, Cerebral Palsy Assn., Buffalo, Children's Found., Erie County, Neighborhood House; trustee past pres. Met. YMCA Buffalo and Erie County; trustee, chmn. bd. Keuka Coll. Served to lt. (j.g.) USNR, 1943-46. Mem. N.Y. Soc. Security Analysts, Am. Inst. Banking, Savs. Banks Assn. N.Y. State, Nat. Assn. Mut. Savs. Banks, U. Buffalo Alumni Assn., Buffalo Area C. of C., Newcomen Soc. N.Am., Nat. Assn. Bus. Economists, Beta Gamma Sigma. Lutheran. Clubs: Mason. Clubs, Country, Bond, Buffalo, Equality (Buffalo). Home: 235 Westfall Dr Tonawanda NY 14150 Office: 545 Main St Buffalo NY 14203

HALLER, GARY LEE, chemical engineering educator; b. Loup City, Nebr., July 10, 1941; s. Leo Edward and Carrie Dorothy (Obermiller) H.; m. Sondra Sue Krueger, Dec. 23, 1962; children: Jared Paul, Sarah Lynn, Joshua Nathaniel. B.S., Kearney State Coll., 1962; Ph.D., Northwestern U., 1966. Mem. faculty Yale U., New Haven, 1967—, asst. prof. engring. and applied sci., 1967-72, assoc. prof., 1972-80, prof., 1980-81, prof. chem. engring., 1981—. Bd. editors: Am. Scientist, New Haven, 1982—; author: (with Langford and Kellerman) Spectroscopy in Heterogeneous Catalysis, 1979; contbr. articles to profl. jours. Mem. AAAS, Am. Chem. Soc. (div. chmn. 1982), Am. Inst. Chem. Engrs., Catalysis Soc. (fgn. sec. 1984—), Royal Soc. Chemistry(London), Sigma Xi. Home: 841 Whitney Ave Hamden CT 06511 Office: Yale U 9 Hillhouse Ave New Haven CT 06520

HALLER, HENRY EDWIN, JR., manufacturing company executive; b. Pitts., Sept. 17, 1913; s. Henry Edwin and Emma (Burns) H.; m. Grace M. Horton, Aug. 15, 1942; children: Henry Edwin III, Marjorie Burns. B.S., U. Pitts., 1936. With Nat. Valve & Mfg. Co., Pitts., 1936—, former pres., now vice chmn., dir., 1956—. Past bd. dirs. Pa. AAA Fedn., Am. Automobile Assn.; Bd. dirs. Animal Rescue League, Boys Club Pitts.; Trustee Thiel Coll. Served with USNR, 1943-46. Clubs: Pitts. Athletic Assn. (past pres., dir.), West Penn Motor (assoc. dir., past pres.), Duquesne.). Lodge: Masons. Office: 701 Alpha Dr Pittsburgh PA 15238 also PO Box 100 Pittsburgh PA 15230

HALLER, JACOB ALEXANDER, JR., surgeon, educator; b. Pulaski, Va., May 20, 1927; s. Jacob Alexander and Julia (Allison) H.; m. Emily Merle Simms, June 16, 1951; children: Julia, Clare, Jacob Alexander. B.A., Vanderbilt U., 1947; M.D., Johns Hopkins U., 1951. Diplomate: Am. Bd. Surgery. Intern in surgery Johns Hopkins Hosp., 1951-52; Rotary Found. fellow in pathology U. Zurich, Switzerland, 1952-53; sr. asst. surgeon USPHS, 1953-55; asst. resident surgeon Johns Hopkins Hosp., 1955-58, resident surgeon, 1958-59; instr., then asst. prof. surgery U. Louisville, 1959-63; vis. asst. prof. surgery U. Pa., 1962-63; surg. fellow organ transplantation and tissue immunity Wistar Inst., Phila., 1962-63; assoc. prof. surgery Johns Hopkins U. and Hosp., 1963-67, prof. surgery, also Robert Garret prof. pediatric surgery, 1967—; children's surgeon-in-charge Johns Hopkins Hosp., 1965—; mem. active staff Balt. City Hosp., Loch Haven VA Hosp.; sr. asst. surgeon, surg. unit USCGR, 1953-54; sr. asst. surgeon, then clin. assoc. NIH, 1954-55. Author: Deep Thrombophlebitis: Pathophysiology and Treatment, 1967, The Hospitalized Child and His Family, 1967. Markle scholar acad. medicine, 1961-66; named Outstanding Clin. prof. U. Louisville Sch. Medicine, 1961; recipient Eagle Scout Boy Scouts am., 1945. Fellow ACS; mem. Am. Fedn. Clin. Research, Soc. Univ. Surgeons, So. Soc. Pediatric Research, Southeastern Surg. Congress, So. Surg. Assn., Am. Assn. Thoracic Surgery, Am. Acad. Pediatrics, Internat. Cardiovascular Soc., Soc. Vascular Surgery, Am. Assn. Surgery Trauma, Halsted Soc., So. Thoracic Surg. Assn., Kansas City Surg. Soc. (Mo.), Md. Heart Assn., Phi Beta Kappa, Sigma Xi. Office: Dept Pediatric Surgery Johns Hopkins U 600 N Wolfe St Baltimore MD 21205

HALLER, JOHN, geology educator; b. Basel, Switzerland, Mar. 6, 1927; s. Hans and Frieda (Meyer) H.; m. Susanna Margaretha Weisskopf, June 4, 1952; children: Daniel Urs, Patrick Renato. Ph.D., U. Basel, 1952, venia docendi, 1957. Geologist Lauge Koch's East Greenland Expdns., Greenland Dept., Copenhagen, Denmark, 1949-62; lectr. U. Basel, 1958-64; vis. lectr. Harvard U., Cambridge, Mass., 1964-65, assoc. prof., 1965-69, prof. geology, 1969-84. Author: Geology of the East Greenland Caledonides, 1971. Recipient Steno medal Geol. Soc. Denmark, 1974. Fellow Geol. Soc. Am., Arctic Inst. N.Am.; mem. Swiss Mineral. Soc. Home: 15 Homer Rd Belmont MA 02178 Office: 24 Oxford St Cambridge MA 02138

HALLETT, ARCHIBALD CAMERON HOLLIS, physics educator; b. Bermuda, Feb. 5, 1927; s. Rupert Carlyle Hollis and Jessie (Cameron) H.; m. Clara Frances Edith Gilbert, Sept. 5, 1950; children: William Langton Hollis, Mary Francis Hollis, James Archibald Hollis. Student, St. Andrew's Coll., Aurora, Ont., Can., 1943-44; B.A., Trinity Coll., U. Toronto (Ont., Can.), 1948; Ph.D., Kings Coll., Cambridge (Eng.) U., 1951. Mem. faculty dept. physics U. Toronto, 1951-77, prof., 1963—, asso. dean faculty, 1966-70; prin. University Coll., U. Toronto, 1970-77; pres. Bermuda Coll. Mem. bd. editors: Jour. Low Temperature Physics, 1969-79. Mem. Am. Phys. Soc. Home: Juniperhill Pembroke Bermuda

HALLETT, FRED NORTON, company executive; b. Mason City, Wash., Nov. 3, 1938; s. John L. and Alicemarie (Page) H.; m. Alice Harrington, Jan. 15, 1962; 2 children. B.S., Gonzage U., 1962; M.B.A., U.Calif.-Berkeley, 1967. Ops. mgr. Boise Cascade, 1968-72; program mgr. Sea Research Corp., 1972-73; asst. group controller Rohr Industries, Chula Vista, Calif., 1973-77; sr. v.p. Ribi Industries, Santa Ana, Calif., 1977-80; v.p. fin., treas. Nat. Steel and Shipbldg. Co., San Diego, 1980—; dir. Engine Tech. Corp., San Diego, 1981—. Bd. dirs. Salvation Army, 1983, San Diego Taxpayers Assn., 1983. Served to lt. USN, 1962-66. Mem. Calif. Mfg. Assn. (dir. 1982), San Diego C. of C. Office: Nat Steel and Shipbldg Co 28th and Harbor Dr San Diego CA 92138

HALLEY, JAMES HARVEY, natural resource executive; b. Phila., Apr. 2, 1926; s. Lawrence Ray and Elizabeth (Unruh) H.; m. Doris Ada Baust, Apr. 30, 1946; children: Janice E., Judith E., James H., Lawrence E. B.S. in Metall. Engring, N.Mex. Inst. Mining and Tech., 1954. Metallurgist Kennecott Copper Corp., Hurley, N.Mex., 1954-58, ops. gen. foreman, Hayden, Ariz., 1958-61; plant supt. Braden Copper Co., Caletones, Chile, 1961-67; asst. div. mgr. Western Knapp Engring. (div. Arthur G. McKee & Co.), San Francisco, 1967-71; exec. v.p. Bunker Hill Co., Kellogg, Idaho, 1971-73, pres., 1973-77; v.p. Gulf Resources & Chem. Corp., Houston, 1978-79; pres. BS&B Engring. Co. (Inc. subs.), 1979-81; sr. v.p. Davy-McKee Corp., San Ramon, Calif., 1981—. Served with USNR, 1944-46. Mem. Am. Inst. Mining, Metall. and Petroleum Engrs., Idaho Mining Assn. (pres. 1974-75), N.W. Mining Assn., Am. Mgmt. Assn. Home: 1208 Levin Ave

Mountain View CA 94040 Office: 2303 Camino Ramon Ramon CA 94583

HALLEY, JAMES WOODS, JR., physicist; b. Chgo., Nov. 16, 1938; s. James Woods and Faith (Fitzgerald) H.; m. Merile Antoinette Hobbs, June 6, 1970. Student, Principia Coll., 1956-58; B.S., M.I.T., 1961; Ph.D. (NSF fellow), U. Calif., Berkeley, 1965. Research asso. U. Calif., Berkeley, 1965, asst. prof., 1966-68; asso. prof. U. Minn., 1968-77, prof. physics, 1977—; vis. scientist U. Santiago, 1970, Oxford U., 1973, Atomic Energy Research Establishment, Harwell, 1973, U. Oreg., 1975, Brookhaven Nat. Lab., 1976, 79, Harvard U., 1979, Argonne Nat. Lab., 1981-83, Inst. Theoretical Physics, Santa Barbara, 1983; lectr. Yale U., 1976; chmn. Nat. Acad. Scis. Panel on NSF Fellowships, 1977-78; dir. NATO Summer Sch., 1977; referee NSF Phys. Rev., 1968—. Author: Physics of Human Motion, 1981; editor and contbr.: Correlation Functions and Quasiparticle Interactions, 1978; Contbr. articles on physics to profl. jours. Mem. Mpls. Adv. Coms. on Parks and Bicycle Paths, 1974-75; candidate Library Bd., Mpls., 1979; del. Democratic Nat. Conv., 1980; bd. dirs. Univ. Dist. Improvement Assn., 1974-75; mem. exec. council U. Minn. Edn. Assn., 1976—; chmn. bd. S.E. Food Corp., 1980-81; polit. action coordinator Farmer Labor Assn., 1980, state sec., 1982-83; mem. steering com. Minn. Interchange, 1980, 83, pres., 1981-82. Recipient George Taylor Teaching award U. Minn., 1979.; NSF postdoctoral fellow, Orsay, France, 1965-66; Research Corp. grantee, 1968; NSF grantee, 1972-79; Dept. Energy grantee, 1980—; Bush sabbatical fellow, 1983-84. Mem. Am. Phys. Soc., AAAS. Office: Sch Physics and Astronomy Minneapolis MN 55455

HALLGREN, RICHARD EDWIN, meteorologist; b. Kersey, Pa., Mar. 15, 1932; s. Edwin Leonard and Edith Marie H.; m. Maxine Hope Anderson, Apr. 17, 1954; children—Scott, Douglas, Lynette. B.S., Pa. State U., 1953, Ph.D., 1960. Systems engr. IBM Corp., 1960-64; sci. adv. to asst. sec. of commerce, 1964-66; dir. world weather systems ESSA, Rockville, Md., 1966-69, asst. adminstrn., 1969-70; asst. adminstr. NOAA, Rockville, 1970-71, asso. adminstr. environ. monitoring and prediction, 1971-73, asst. adminstr. for ocean and atmospheric scis., 1977-79; dep. dir. Nat. Weather Service, Silver Spring, Md., 1973-77, dir., 1979—; permanent U.S. rep. World Meteorol. Orgn. Contbr. articles to sci. jours. Served with USAF, 1954-56. Recipient Arthur S. Flemming award U.S. C. of C., 1968; Gold medal Dept. Commerce, 1969; named Meritorious Sr. Exec., 1980. Fellow Am. Meteorol. Soc. (pres.); mem. Am. Oceanic Orgn., Sigma Xi. Lutheran. Home: 6121 Wayside Dr Rockville MD 20852 Office: Nat Weather Service 8060 13th St Silver Spring MD 20910

HALLIDAY, IAN, astronomer; b. Lloydminster, Sask., Can., Nov. 10, 1928; s. Clarence Peter and Edith Victoria (Phillips) H.; m. Norma Lillian Mobley, July 7, 1951; children—John Douglas, Janet Elizabeth. B.A., U. Toronto, 1949, M.A., 1950, Ph.D., 1954. Sr. sci. officer Dominion Obs., Dept. Energy, Mines and Resources, Ottawa, 1952-70; sr. research officer Herzberg Inst. Astrophysics, Nat. Research Council Can., Ottawa, 1970—. Author research papers in field; editor: Jour. Royal Astron. Soc. Can, 1970-75; co-editor: Solid Particles in the Solar System, 1980. Recipient Queen's Silver Jubilee medal, 1977, Polish Medal of Merit, 1976. Fellow Royal Soc. Can.; mem. Internat. Astron. Union (pres. commn. 22 1976-79), Royal Astron. Soc. Can. (pres. 1980-82), Can. Astron. Soc., Am. Astron. Soc., Meteoritical Soc. Home: 825 Killeen Ave Ottawa ON K2A 2X8 Canada Office: Herzberg Inst Astrophysics Ottawa ON K1A 0R6 Canada

HALLIDAY, WALTER JOHN, lawyer; b. Bklyn., Feb. 7, 1907; s. Walter and Charlotte Estelle (Kelly) H.; m. Nancy Jane Fowler, Oct. 27, 1927. A.B., Harvard, 1928, LL.B., 1931; J.S.D., N.Y.U., 1950. Bar: N.Y. 1933. Practice in, N.Y.C., 1933—; partner firm Nims, Halliday, Whitman et al. (and predecessors), 1945-73, Halliday & Whitman, 1973—; counsel firm Bucknam & Archer, 1973-76. Author articles in field.; Editor: Trademark Reporter, 1947-52; chmn. editorial bd., 1952-53. Mem. planning bd. Rockville Centre, N.Y., 1937-43, trustee of village, 1941-43, mayor, 1943-45; mem. adminstrv. bd. St. Mark's Meth. Ch., 1964—, trustee, 1975—, v.p. bd. trustees, 1980-81. Served with AUS, 1943-44. Mem. Internat. Bar Assn., ABA (chmn. trademark div. 1957-58), N.Y. State Bar Assn., Assn. Bar City N.Y., Internat. Patent and Trademark Assn., U.S. Trademark Assn. (dir.; past chmn. lawyers adv. com.), Am. Mgmt. Assn. (lectr. 1968-69), N.Y. Patent Law Assn. (gov. 1957-60), Am. Legion. Republican. Clubs: Masons; Harvard (N.Y.C.); Chancery (Cambridge, Mass.); Wig and Pen (London); Rockville Links. Home: 245 Windsor Ave Rockville Centre NY 11570 Office: 49 Front St Rockville Centre NY 11570

HALLIDAY, WILLIAM ROSS, physician, author, speleologist; b. Emory U., Ga., May 9, 1926; s. William Ross and Jane (Wakefield) H.; m. Eleanore Hartvedt, July 2, 1951; children: Marcia Lynn, Patricia Anne, William Ross III. B.A., Swarthmore Coll., 1946; M.D., George Washington U., 1948. Intern Huntington Meml. Hosp., Pasadena, 1948-49; resident King County Hosp., Seattle, Denver Childrens Hosp., L.D.S. Hosp., Salt Lake City, 1950-57; practice medicine, Seattle, 1957-65, 83—; with Wash. Dept. Labor and Industries, 1965-76; med. dir. Wash. Div. Vocat. Rehab., 1976-82; dep. coroner, King County, Wash., 1964-66. Author: Adventure Is Underground, 1959, Depths of The Earth, 1966, 76, American Caves and Caving, 1974, 82; Editor: Jour. Spelean History, 1968-73; contbr. articles to profl. jours. Mem. Gov.'s North Cascades Study Com., 1967-76; mem. North Cascades Conservation Council, v.p., 1962-63; Dir. Western Speleological Survey, Seattle, 1955-81; pres., 1981—; Western Speleological Found. asst. dir. Internat. Glaciospeleological Survey, 1972—. Served to lt. comdr. USNR, 1949-50, 55-57. Fellow Am. Coll. Chest Physicians, Am. Acad. Compensation Medicine, Nat. Speleological Soc., Explorers Club; mem. Soc. Thoracic Surgeons, AMA, Am. Congress Rehab. Medicine, Am. Coll. Legal Medicine, Wash. State Med. Assn., King County Med. Soc., Am. Fedn. Clin. Research, Am. Spelean History Assn. (pres. 1968), Brit. Cave Research Assn., Nat. Trust (Scotland). Clubs: Mountaineers (past trustee), Seattle Tennis.). Home: 1117 36th Ave E Seattle WA 98112 Office: 1500 1st Ave S Seattle WA 98134

HALLIE, PHILIP PAUL, philosopher; b. Chgo., May 4, 1922; s. William I. and Nettie (Leibowitz) H.; m. Doris Ann Gabriele, Sept. 19, 1954; children—Michelena Louise, Louis Gabriele. B.A., Grinnell Coll., 1946, D.Litt. (hon.), 1968; M.A., Harvard U., 1948, Ph.D. (Fulbright scholar), 1951; B.Litt. (Harvard Traveling fellow), Oxford (Eng.) U., 1950. Tutor Trinity Coll. Oxford U., 1950-51; instr. Wesleyan U., Middletown, Conn., 1952-53, Griffin prof. philosophy, 1965—, chmn. philosophy dept., 1965-67, fellow, 1963-64, acting dir. Center, 1967—, dir., 1970—; prof. philosophy Vanderbilt U., Nashville, 1953-64; Am. rep. Internat. Philosophy Congress, Mysore, India, 1959. Author: Maine de Biran-Reformer of Empiricism, 1959, Scepticism, Man and God, 1963, The Scar of Montaigne, 1966, The Paradox of Cruelty, 1969, Lest Innocent Blood Be Shed, 1979, also articles, chpts. in books; editorial bd.: Am Scholar, 1965-69. Pres. Middletown PTA, 1964-65. Served with arty. AUS, 1941-44. Recipient Whitcomb Poetry prize, 1944; Guggenheim fellow, 1959-60; Am. Council Learned Socs. fellow, 1966-67; Nat. Endowment for Humanities ind. research fellow, 1981-82. Home: 137 Highland Ave Middletown CT 06457 Office: Wesleyan U Middletown CT 06457 *At least some of us in the Humanities should witness to a concern for those human beings amongst us who are fighting indignities with dignity.*

HALLIER, GERARD EDOUARD, hotel chain executive; b. Casablanca, Morroco, July 19, 1941; came to U.S., 1972; s. Marcel Edouard and Yvette Suzanne (Rousseau) H.; m. Michele Smadja, Sept. 30, 1964; children: Laurent, Brigitte, Isabelle. Grad., Coll. Montcel, Paris, 1958, Hotel Sch., Nice, France, 1964. Various exec. positions with Hotel Corp. Am., also Meurice Group Hotels, 1968-70; dir. devel. Esso Motor Hotels, 1970-72; with Ramada Inns Inc. (and affiliates), 1972—, pres. hospitality group, 1978-79, exec. v.p. parent co., 1979, chief operating officer, dir., Phoenix, 1979-82; pres., chief exec. officer MAG Internat., Phoenix, 1982—; dir. Promhote, France, 1968-72. Named Personity of Yr. Hotel Bus. sect. by French press, 1980. Office: 3838 E Van Buren St Phoenix AZ 85008

HALLIGAN, JAMES EDMUND, university administrator, chemical engineer; b. Moorland, Iowa, June 23, 1936; s. Raymond Anthony and Margaret Ann (Crawford) H.; m. Ann Elizabeth Sorenson, June 29, 1957; children: Michael, Patrick, Christopher. M.S. in Chem. Engring, Iowa State U., 1962, 1965, Ph.D., 1968. Process engr. Humble Oil Co., 1962-64; mem. faculty Tex. Tech U., 1968-77; dean engring. U. Mo., Rolla, 1977-79, U. Ark., Fayetteville, 1979-82, vice chancellor for acad. affairs, 1982-83, interim chancellor, 1983—; v.p. engring. Kandahar Cons. Ltd.; mem. Gov. Tex. Energy Adv. Council, 1972-74. Served with USAF, 1954-58. Recipient Disting. Teaching award Tex. Tech U., 1972, Disting. Research award, 1975, 76; Disting. Teaching award U. Mo., Rolla, 1978. Mem. Am. Inst. Chem. Engrs., Am. Soc. Engring. Edn., Tau Beta Pi, Phi Kappa Phi, Pi Mu Epsilon. Roman Catholic. Club: Rotary. Office: Adminstrn Bldg 422 U Ark Fayetteville AR 72701

HALLIGAN, JOSEPH WILLIAM, photographic inndustry executive; b. Boston, Sept. 10, 1944; s. Henry William and Marion (Neaves) H.; m. Nancy Jordan, June 28, 1969; 1 dau., Deborah. B.S. in Mgmt. and Bus. Adminstrn., Columbia Pacific U., San Rafael, Calif., 1983. Mgr. prodn. line maintenance Union Carbide, San Diego, Calif., 1969; maintenance control Fotomat Corp., La Jolla, Calif., 1970-74, nat. constrn. dir., 1974-76, v.p., Wilton, Conn., 1976-80, sr. v.p., 1980—; pres., dir. Fotomat Video Enterprises, Video Services of Am. Author: Maintenance and Construction Manuel, 1972. Served with USAF, 1965-69. Mem. Nat. Acad. Code Adminstrn., Internat. Conf. Bldg. Ofcls., Bldg. Ofcls. Code Adminstrs., So. Bldg. Code Congress Internat. Home: 29 Cob Dr Westport CT 06880 Office: Fotomat Corporation 64 Danbury Rd Wilton CT 06897

HALLIGAN, THOMAS WALSH, construction company executive; b. Davenport, Iowa, Oct. 20, 1922; s. Eugene Joseph and Gertrude (Walsh) H.; m. Mary E. McClelland, Apr. 17, 1947; children: Carol, Mary Beth, Susan, Nancy, Timothy, Kathleen. A.B., Georgetown U., 1943. With Walsh Constrn. Co., 1946-75, pres., 1975-80, now called Guy F. Atkinson Co. (subsidiary of Walsh Constrn. Co.), 1967, pres., chief operating officer, South San Francisco, 1982—. Recipient U. Minn. Sch. Pub. Health award, 1983. Office: Guy F Atkinson Co 10 W Orange Ave South San Francisco CA 94080

HALLIWELL, RICHARD EDWARD WINTER, veterinary medicine educator, researcher; b. Jersey, U.K., June 16, 1937; came to U.S., 1973; s. Authur Clare and Winifred Dorothea (Goode) H.; m. Jennifer Helen Roper, Sept. 7, 1963; children: Nicola Tracy, Jemma Victoria. B.A., U. Cambridge, Eng., 1958, M.A., 1958, Vet. M.B., 1961, Ph.D., 1973. Diplomate: Am. Coll. Vet. Dermatology (sec. 1982-84). Jr. fellow in vet. surgery U. Bristol, Eng., 1961-63; Wellcome fellow in immunology U. Cambridge, 1970-73; asst. prof. U. Pa., Phila., 1973-77; assoc. prof. dermatology Coll. Vet. Medicine, U. Fla., Gainesville, 1977-82, prof., 1982—, chmn. dept. med. scis., 1977—; cons. in field. Contbr. articles to profl. jours., 1962—; joint editor-in-chief vet. immunology and immunopathology, Elsevier Sci. Pub. Co., Amsterdam, Netherlands, 1979—; editorial bd.: Compendium of Continuing Education for the Practicing Veterinarian, 1979—. Recipient Small Animal Research award Ralston Purina Co., 1980; Morris Animal Found. fellow, 1980; NIH grantee, 1976, 82. Mem. Am. Assn. Vet. Immunologists (pres. 1983—), Internat. Union Immunologic Socs., Am. Acad. Vet. Allergy (pres. 1975-77), AVMA, Am. Animal Hosp. Assn., Brit. Small Animal Vet. Assn., Fla. Vet. Med. Assn., Pa. Vet. Med. Assn. Episcopalian. Home: 4232 NW 38th St Gainesville FL 32601 Office: U Fla Coll Vet Medicine Box J-126 JHMHC Gainesville FL 32610

HALLMAN, EUGENE SANBORN, educator, former Canadian government official.; b. Ettrick, Ont., Can., May 15, 1919; s. Ira Graybeil and Ruby Eliza (Sanborn) H.; m. Margaret McDonald Torrance, Sept. 25, 1943; children—Nancy, Margot, Mark. B.A. with honors in English, U. Toronto, 1942, also LL.B., student Faculty Law, 1974—. With Canadian Broadcasting Corp., Toronto, Ont., 1950—, prodn. planning, program dir. radio and TV, 1950-59, v.p. programming, 1960-68, v.p., gen. mgr., 1968-74, cons. broadcast communications, 1974—; with prosecutions sect. Dept. Justice, Can., 1979-82; lectr. in communication York U., Can., 1983-84. Mem. Internat. Broadcasting Inst. Home: 39 Old Mill Rd Toronto ON M8X 1G6 Canada

HALLMAN, GARY L., photographer, educator; b. St. Paul, Aug. 7, 1940; s. Jack J. and Helen A. H.; 1 son, Peter J. B.A., U. Minn., 1966, M.F.A., 1971. Mem. faculty dept. studio arts U. Minn., Mpls., 1970—, assoc. prof. photography, 1976—; vis. adj. prof. R.I. Sch. Design, 1977-78; Mem. visual arts adv. bd. Minn. State Arts Council, 1973-76. Exhbns. include, Internat. Mus. Photography, George Eastman House, 1974, Light Gallery, N.Y.C., 1975, Balt. Mus., Mus. Modern Art, N.Y.C., 1978; represented in permanent collections, Mus. Modern Art, N.Y.C., Internat. Mus. Photography, Rochester, N.Y., Nat. Gallery Can., Fogg Art Mus., Harvard U., Princeton U. Art Mus., Nat. Mus. Am. Art, Smithsonian Instn., Washington. Served with USN, 1958-61. Nat. Endowment Arts fellow, 1975-76; Bush Found. fellow, 1976-77; McKnight Found. fellow, 1982. Mem. Soc. Photog. Edn., Coll. Art Assn. Am. Office: Dept Studio Arts U Minn Minneapolis MN 55455

HALLMAN, GRADY LAMAR, JR., physician; b. Tyler, Tex., Oct. 25, 1930; s. Grady Lamar and Mildred (Kennedy) H.; m. Martha Suit, June 7, 1953; children—Daniel S., David L., Charles H. B.A., U. Tex., 1950; M.D., Baylor U., 1954. Diplomate: Am. Bd. Surgery, Am. Bd. Thoracic and Cardiovascular Surgery. Intern Chgo. Wesley Meml. Hosp., 1954-55; resident Baylor U. Coll. Medicine Hosps., 1955-56, 58-62; practice medicine specializing in cardiovascular surgery, Houston, 1962—; mem. staff St. Luke's Tex. Children's, Meth. hosps.; instr. dept. surgery Baylor U. Coll. Medicine, 1962-63, asst. prof., 1963-67, asso. prof., 1967-69, clin. asso. prof., 1969-71; sr. cons. cardiovascular surgery Tex. Heart Inst., 1971—; clin. prof. surgery U. Tex. Med. Sch. at Houston, 1977—; cons. cardiovascular surgery Brooke Army Hosp., also; Lackland Air Force Hosp. Author: Surgical Treatment of Congenital Heart Disease, 1966, 2d edit., 1976. Served with M.C. AUS, 1956-58. Mem. Am. Coll. Chest Physicians, Soc. U. Surgeons, A.C.S., Am. Coll. Cardiology, Am. Assn. for Thoracic Surgery, Soc. Thoracic Surgeons, Internat. Cardiovascular Soc., Soc. Vascular Surgery, Southwestern Surg. Congress, Tex., Houston surg. soc., Royal Soc. Health, So. Surg. Assn., Am. Surg. Assn., So. Thoracic Surg. Assn., Internat. Soc. Surgery, Phi Beta Kappa, Alpha Omega Alpha. Home: 3443 Inwood St Houston TX 77019 Office: 6621 Fannin PO Box 20345 Houston TX 77030

HALLMAN, H(ENRY) THEODORE, JR., textile designer; b. Bucks County, Pa., Dec. 23, 1933; s. H. Theodore and Mildred Eleanor (Brumbaugh) H. Certificate, Fountainebleau (France) Sch. Fine Arts, 1955; B.F.A., B.S. in Edn, Temple U., 1956; M.F.A. in Painting, Cranbrook Acad. Art, 1957, Cranbrook Acad. Art, 1958; Ph.D. in Edn, U. Calif., Berkeley, 1974. Workshop tchr. in design, textiles, handweaving, color, U.S., Eng., Can.; lectr. in design, textile structures; mem. faculty Ont. Coll. Art, Toronto, 1976—, Haystack Sch., Deer Island, Maine, 1958-60, Penland (N.C.) Sch., summers 1963-70, U. Calif., Berkeley, 1973-74, Calif. State U., San Francisco, 1970, Bklyn. Mus. Sch., 1973; chmn. dept. textile design Moore Coll. Art, 1963-69; summer prof. Florence Program (Italy) Ont. Coll. Art; bd. dirs. S.W. Craft Center, San Antonio, 1975—. One-man shows, Phila. Art Alliance, 1960, Loch Haven Art Center, Orlando, Fla., 1970, Woodmere Art Gallery, Phila., 1971, Royal Ont. Mus., Toronto, 1978, Renwick of Smithsonian, 1980; One-man shows, Centre des Arts Visuels, Mendel Art Gallery, Moore Coll. Art, McMillan Meml. Gallery, S.W. Craft Center, Fashion Inst. Tech., N.Y.C., 1983, Bklyn. Mus. Art, 1984; two-man show, Chgo. Art Inst., 1969, group shows include, Internationales Kunsthandwerk, Stuttgart, Germany; Group shows include, The Art Fabric: Mainstream; Miniature Weavings, London, Am. Fedn. Arts travelling exhbn., 1981-82, also numerous U.S. Govt. Agy. travelling shows; represented in permanent collections, Met. Mus. Art, N.Y.C., Victoria and Albert Mus., London, Bklyn., Mus. Art, Cooper Hewitt Mus., N.Y.C., Smithsonian Inst., Washington, Phila. Mus. Art, Oakland (Calif.) Mus. Art, Cin. Art Mus., Utah Mus. Fine Arts, Mus. Contemporary Crafts, N.Y.C., Addison Gallery Am. Art, Andover, Mass.; work represented in numerous art, design and craft jours. and books. Adv. bd. Pacific Basin Sch., Berkeley, Calif. L.C. Tiffany grantee, 1962. Mem. Internat. Soc. Arts and Letters (hon. life), World Craft Council (invited lectr. conf., Mexico 1976), Ont. Craft Council (dir.). 60 Ruddington Dr Apt 1604 Willowdale ON Canada M2K 2J9

HALLO, WILLIAM WOLFGANG, educator; b. Kassel, Germany, Mar. 9, 1928; came to U.S., 1940, naturalized, 1946; s. Rudolf and Gertrude (Rubensohn) H.; m. Edith Sylvia Pinto, June 22, 1952; children: Ralph Ethan, Jacqueline Louise. B.A. magna cum laude, Harvard U., 1950; M.A., U. Chgo., 1953, Ph.D., 1955; candidatus Litterarum Semiticarum, U. Leiden, Netherlands, 1951; M.A. (hon.), Yale U., 1965. Research asst. Oriental Inst., U. Chgo., 1954-56; from instr. to asst. prof. Bible and Semitic langs. Hebrew Union Coll.-Jewish Inst. Religion, Cin., 1956-62; mem. faculty Yale U., 1962—, prof. Assyriology, 1965-75, William M. Laffan prof. Assyriology and Babylonian lit., 1976—; curator Babylonian collection, 1963—; master Morse Coll., 1982—; chmn. dept. Near Eastern langs. and lits., 1975-82; vis. prof. Middle Eastern civilization Columbia U., 1970-71, 80; vis. prof. Jewish Theol. Sem., 1981-83. Author: (with J.J.A. van Dijk) The Exaltation of Inanna, 1968, Early Mesopotamian Royal Titles, 1957, (with W.K. Simpson) The Ancient Near East: A History, 1971, Sumerian Archival Texts, 1973, (with Briggs Buchanan) Early Near Eastern Seals in the Yale Babylonian Collection, 1981; co-author: The Torah: A Modern Commentary, 1981, (with James C. Moyer and Leo G. Perdue.) Scripture in Context II: More Essays on the Comparative Method, 1983; editor: Essays in Memory of E.A. Speiser, 1968, (with Carl D. Evans and John B. White) Scripture in Context: Essays on the Comparative Method, 1980; translator: The Star of Redemption, 1971; Contbr. numerous articles, revs. on Assyriology and Bibl. archeology.; Assoc. editor: Am. Oriental Soc, 1965-71; editorial com.: Yale Near Eastern Researches, 1967—; editor, 1970—. Mem. commn. Jewish edn. Union Am. Hebrew Congregations, 1967-71; co-founder, dir., mem. exec. com. Assn. Jewish Studies, 1970-71, v.p., 1972-74. Guggenheim fellow, 1965-66; Fulbright scholar, 1950-51; fellow Inst. Advanced Studies, Hebrew U., Jerusalem, 1978-79. Mem. Am. Oriental Soc. (chmn. Ancient Near East sect. 1971-78), Soc. Bibl. Lit., World Union Jewish Studies, Conf. Jewish Philosophy, Phi Beta Kappa. Club: Harvard (So. Conn.). Home: 99 Tower Pkwy New Haven CT 06511 Office: Babylonian Collection Yale Univ New Haven CT 06520

HALLOCK, C. WILES, JR., athletic official; b. Denver, Feb. 17, 1918; s. Claude Wiles and Mary (Bassler) H.; m. Marjorie Louise Eldred, Mar. 23, 1944; children: Lucinda Eldred Hallock Rinne, Michael Eldred. A.B., U. Denver, 1939. Sports info. dir. U. Wyo., 1949-60, track coach, 1952-56; sports info. dir. U. Calif.-Berkeley, 1960-63; dir. pub. relations Nat. Collegiate Athletic Assn., 1963-68; dir. Nat. Collegiate Sports Services, 1967-68; commr. Western Athletic Conf., 1968-71; exec. dir. Pacific-8 Conf., San Francisco, 1971-83; historian Pacific 10 Conf., 1983. Mem. Laramie (Wyo.) City Council, 1958-60. Served to lt. comdr. USNR, World War II. Decorated Air medal; mem. Nat. Football Found. and Hall of Fame Honors Ct. Mem. Nat. Collegiate Athletic Assn., Nat. Assn. Collegiate Dirs. Athletics (Corbett award 1983), Collegiate Commrs. Assn., Coll. Sports Info. Dirs. Am. (Arch Ward award 1963), Football Writers Assn. Am. (past dir.), U.S. Basketball Writers Assn., Lambda Chi Alpha. Presbyn. Home: 1333 Corte Madera Walnut Creek CA 94598 Office: 800 S Broadway Walnut Creek CA 94596

HALLORAN, BERNARD THORPE, lawyer; b. N.Y.C., May 27, 1931; s. James Francis and Frances Anne (Connor) H.; m. Ann R. Owings, May 15, 1965; children: Bernard Thorpe, James R., Susan C., Donna R., Elizabeth H. B.A. in Econs, U. So. Calif., 1953; LL.B., Columbia U., 1959; LL.M., Georgetown U., 1963. Bar: N.Y. 1960, D.C. 1964, Pa. 1967, Tex. 1971. Atty., adviser in office of legal adviser Dept. State, Washington, 1960-65; gen. counsel Hamilton Watch Co., Lancaster, Pa., 1965-69; v.p., gen. counsel subs. Univ. Computing Co., Dallas, 1969-70, asst. gen. counsel parent co., 1971-72; sec., gen. counsel Reed Tool Co., Houston, 1973-77; gen. counsel Baker Oil Tools group Baker Internat. Corp., 1976-77; sec., gen. counsel Creole Prodn. Services, Inc., Houston, 1977-79, BWT Corp., 1979-82; Sole practice, Houston, 1982—; dir. Gulf Coast Feeds, Inc. Served with AUS, 1953-55. Mem. Am., Tex. bar assns., Internat. Law Soc., Am. Arbitration Assn. (panel of arbitrators 1973—). Club: N.Y. Athletic. Home: 13318 Alchester Dr Houston TX 77079 Office: 10255 Richmond Fourth Floor West Houston TX 77042

HALLORAN, RICHARD COLBY, newspaper correspondent; b. Washington, Mar. 2, 1930; s. Paul James and Catherine (Lenihan) H.; m. Carol Prins, June 21, 1958; children: Christopher Paul, Laura Colby, Catherine Anne; m. Fumiko Mori, Nov. 11, 1978. A.B. with distinction, Dartmouth Coll., 1951; M.A., U. Mich., 1957. Staff writer, then asst. fgn. editor Business Week mag., 1957-61; Tokyo bur. chief McGraw-Hill World News, 1962-64; Asia specialist Washington Post, 1965-66, bur. chief, Tokyo, 1966-68, Washington corr., 1968-69, N.Y. Times, 1969-72, Tokyo bur. chief, 1972-76, Washington corr., 1976—. Author: Japan: Images and Realities, 1969, Conflict and Compromise: The Dynamics of American Foreign Policy, 1973. Served to 1st lt. AUS, 1952-55. Ford Found. fellow Columbia, 1964-65; recipient citation for interpretation fgn. affairs Overseas Press Club, 1969, George Polk award, 1982. Club: Foreign Corrs. (Tokyo). Home: 902 Van Ness East 2939 Van Ness St NW Washington DC 20008 Office: NY Times Washington Bur 1000 Connecticut Ave NW Washington DC 20036

HALLORAN, WILLIAM FRANK, univ. dean; b. Spearfish, S.D., Sept. 12, 1934; s. William Patrick and Frances Marie (Perrin) H.; m. Mary Helen Griffin, July 29, 1961; children—Julia Frances, William

David. B.A. magna cum laude, Princeton, 1956; M.A., Duke, 1959, Ph.D., 1965. Instr. English U. N.C., 1963-64; instr. English N.Y. U., 1964-66; asst. prof. English U. Wis.-Milw., 1966-68, asso. prof., 1968-72, prof., 1972—; asso. dean Coll. Letters and Sci., 1969-72, dean, 1972—; cons. North Central Assn., 1973—, Am. Inst. for Fgn. Study, 1980—. Served with U.S. Army, 1957. Recipient Uhrig Teaching award U. Wis.-Milw., 1968. Mem. Modern Lang. Assn., Midwest Modern Lang. Assn. (exec. com. 1971-74), AAUP, Council of Colls. of Arts and Sci., Phi Kappa Phi. Episcopalian. Club: University (Milw.). Home: 2611 E Beverly Rd Milwaukee WI 53211

HALLOWELL, BURTON CROSBY, business executive, educator; b. Orleans, Mass., May 2, 1915; s. William George and Sarah Frances (Crosby) H.; m. Pauline Russell, June 7, 1941; 1 son, Robert Crosby. B.A., Wesleyan U., Middletown, Conn., 1936, M.A., 1938, L.H.D., 1969; Ph.D., Princeton, 1949; L.H.D., Boston U., 1969, Tufts U., 1976; LL.D., Northeastern U., 1973, Am. Internat. Coll., 1975. Teller Windham County Nat. Bank, Danielson, Conn., 1936-37; Social Sci. Research Council pre-doctoral field fellow, 1940-41; instr. econs. Wesleyan U., 1941-42, asst. prof., 1946-50, asso. prof., 1950-56, Andrews prof. econs., 1956-67, v.p. for planning and devel., 1962-65, exec. v.p., 1965-67; on leave for research on fed. debt mgmt. Merrill Found. for Advancement Fin. Knowledge, 1956-57; on leave, 1956-57; on leave as staff mem. N.Y.C. Commn. for Money and Credit, 1960-61; pres. Tufts U., Medford, Mass., 1967-76; vice chmn. Keystone Custodian Funds, Inc., 1976, chmn. bd., 1977-79, chief exec. officer, 1978-79, also dir., 1971-79; dir. Loctite Corp., Home Fed. Savs. Bank, Worcester, Mass., Shaw Supermarkets Inc., East Bridgewater, Mass.; Oppenheimer & Co. Inc., N.Y.C., Thackeray Corp., N.Y.C., Miami, Fla.; Econ. cons. Conn. Gen. Life Ins. Co., 1949-62, Com. Econ. Devel., N.Y.C., Washington, 1953-54; Chmn. Mass. Housing Finance Agy., 1968-71; Mem. exec. com. New Eng. Colls. Fund, 1968-71; mem. exec. com. Assn. Ind. Colls and Univs. in Mass., 1968-73, pres., 1972-73. Contbr. articles to profl. jours. Trustee Cape Cod Mus., Brewster, Mass., 1982—; Trustee Medicenter Five, Inc., Harwich, Mass., 1983—; corporator New Eng. Med. Center, Boston, 1976—, Cape Cod Hosp., Hyannis, Mass., 1976—. With OPA and Civilian Supply, 1941; With OSS, 1942; Served to capt. AUS, 1942-46. Mem. Am. Econ. Assn., Am. Finance Assn., Phi Beta Kappa, Sigma Chi. Clubs: Commercial, Algonquin (Boston); Princeton (N.Y.C.). Home: PO Box 515 East Orleans MA 02643

HALLOWELL, HENRY RICHARDSON, investment banker; b. Phila., Aug. 12, 1898; s. J. Wallace and Bertinia (Essen) H.; m. Dorothy Saylor, June 25, 1919; children: Henry R., Dorothy (Mrs. Peter M. Fetterolf), Bertinia (Mrs. Omar Bailey), J. Wallace III. B.A., Yale, 1919. Agt. George H. McFadden & Bro., 1919-25; propr. Henry R. Hallowell & Son, 1925-31; registered rep. Lee Higginson & Co., 1931-32, Bryan, Penington & Colket, Phila., 1933-36; mgr. investment dept. Eastman Dillon & Co., 1937-45; partner Hallowell, Sulzberger & Co., Phila., 1945-57; sr. partner Hallowell, Sulzberger, Jenks & Co., 1958-73; v.p. Hoppin Watson, Inc., 1973-77; asso. Hopper Soliday & Co., 1977—; past pres., dir. Exchange Cold Storage Co.; dir. emeritus U.S. Air.; Former mem. N.Y. Stock Exchange, Am. Stock Exchange; asso. mem., gov. emeritus Phila. Stock Exchange. Bd. dirs. Merion Civic Assn., pres., 1945-47; dir. Bot. Soc. of Lower Merion, pres., 1971-72. Presbyn. Clubs: Union League, Rittenhouse, Penn (pres. 1964-69), Penn (dir.), Philadelphia Country.). Home: 600 E Cathedral Rd Philadelphia PA 19128 Office: 1401 Walnut St 12th Floor Philadelphia PA 19102

HALLOWELL, JOHN HAMILTON, political science educator; b. Spokane, Aug. 19, 1913; s. Harold Atlee and Anna Blanche (Williams) H.; m. Sarah Rebecca Rubin, Jan. 31, 1941; children: Carol Anne (Mrs. Thomas D. Hill), John Hamilton, Katherine Rebecca (Mrs. Irving Noyes). A.B. cum laude, Harvard U., 1935; M.A., Duke U., 1937; Ph.D., Princeton U., 1939; Litt.D., Coll. Holy Cross, 1963. Part-time instr. politics Princeton U., 1937-38; instr. polit. sci. UCLA, 1939-42; asso. communications analyst OWI, 1942; mem. faculty Duke U., 1942—, prof. polit. sci., 1950—, chmn. dept., 1964-71, James B. Duke prof., 1975-81, James B. Duke prof. emeritus, 1981—; vis. prof. Stanford U., 1950, U. Ill., 1964, U. Munich, Germany, 1955-56; Charles R. Walgreen Found. lectr. U. Chgo., 1952; del. Am. Council Learned Socs., 1964-70; dir. Nat. Endowment Humanities Summer Seminar for Coll. Faculty, 1975, 76; Dir. Lilly Endowment Research Program Christianity and Politics, 1957-68. Author: Decline of Liberalism as an Ideology, 1943, Main Currents in Modern Political Thought, 1950, The Moral Foundation of Democracy, 1953; also articles.; Editor: Prospects for Constitutional Democracy, 1976, From Enlightenment to Revolution, 1975; mem. editorial bd.: Jour. Ch. and State. Guggenheim fellow, 1955-56. Mem. Am. Polit. Sci. Assn. (council 1961-64, exec. com. 1963-64), So. Polit. Sci. Assn. (pres. 1964-65), Am. Soc. Polit. and Legal Philosophy, Phi Beta Kappa, Omicron Delta Kappa. Episcopalian. Club: Cosmos (Washington). Mailing Address: 3606 Darwin Rd Durham NC 27707

HALLOWELL, ROBERT EDWARD, French language educator; b. Charleston, Ill., Aug. 30, 1918; s. Edward Everett and Elizabeth (Stockover) H.; m. Mirzl Mueller, Aug. 11, 1949; 1 son, Eric Edward. B.S., Eastern Ill. U., 1939, Ped.D. (hon.), 1965; M.A., U. Ill., 1940, Ph.D., 1942; postgrad., U. Geneva, 1946-47. Spl. investigator War Dept., Ger., 1945-46; instr., then asst. prof. French U. Ill., 1948-60; asso. prof. French and Italian U. Wis., Milw., 1961-63, prof., 1963-68, chmn. dept., 1964-68; prof. French U. Ill., Chgo. Circle, 1968—, acting head dept, 1970; lectr. Centre d'Etudes Superieures de la Renaissance, Tours, France, summer 1964. Author: Ronsard and the Conventional Roman Elegy, 1954, French editor Modern Lang. Jour, 1960-64; contbr. articles to internat. profl. jours. Fulbright sr. research fellow, France, 1966-67. Mem. MLA (del. Assembly 1974-76), Am. Assn. Tchrs. French, Renaissance Soc., Am. Assn. Internat. des Etudes Francaises, Société Francaise des Seiziémistes, Phi Kappa Phi, Kappa Delta Pi, Pi Delta Phi. Club: Cliff Dwellers (Chgo.). Home: 1564 Bowling Green Dr Lake Forest IL 60045 Office: Univ Hall U Ill Chicago IL 60680

HALLOWELL, ROGER HAYDOCK, mfg. co. exec; b. Milton, Mass., Dec. 7, 1910; s. John White and Marian Hathaway (Ladd) H.; m. Frances Lee Weeks, Feb. 12, 1938; children—Roger Haydock, Beatrice W., Christian; m. Barbara Warner Noble. Student, Milton (Mass.) Acad., 1920-28; A.B., Harvard, 1933. Instr., coach Brooks Sch., N. Andover, Mass., 1933-36; with Incorporated Investors, Boston, 1936-38, Reed & Barton Corp., Taunton, 1938—, personnel dir., 1940-42, v.p., 1947-49, exec. v.p., 1951-53, dir., 1951—, pres., 1953-71, chmn. bd., 1971—; dir. First Bristol County Nat. Bank, Arkwright-Boston Ins. Co., Ludlow Corp. Pres. Boston council Boy Scouts Am., 1941, v.p., 1946-66; now dir. Annawon council.; Trustee Milton Acad. Served with USNR, 1942-46. Decorated Silver Star (2). Mem. N.A.M. (dir. 1957-64, regional v.p. 1961). Clubs: Porcellian, Cruising of America, Ski Hochgebirge (Boston); Essex Country, Manchester Yacht. Home: 10 Bridge St Manchester MA 01944 Office: Reed & Barton Corp Taunton MA 02780

HALLUM, JULES VERNE, microbiologist; b. Mpls., Mar. 18, 1925; s. Vernon Gerhard and Hulda Lorena (Gunderson) H.; m. Phyllis Hanson, June 22, 1945; children—Marcus V., Jessica B., Elizabeth C. A.B., U. Minn., 1948; Ph.D., U. Iowa, 1952. Fellow, chemistry dept. U. Minn., 1952-53; instr. chemistry dept. Ind. U., 1953-54; sr. fellow Mellon Inst., 1954-59, Columbian Carbon Corp., 1959-62; asst. prof. microbiology U. Pitts., 1962-70; asso. prof. microbiology Tulane U. Sch. Medicine, New Orleans, 1970-73; prof., chmn. dept. microbiology and immunology U. Oreg. Health Scis. Center, Portland, 1973—. Served with USMCR, 1942-45. Mem. Am. Soc. for Microbiology, Soc. Exptl. Biology and Medicine, Am. Acad. Microbiology, Sigma Xi. Democrat. Congregationalist. Home: 4231 SW 54th Pl Portland OR 97221 Office: U Oreg Health Scis Center 3181 SW Sam Jackson Park Rd Portland OR 97201

HALLY, JOHN RICHARD, lawyer; b. Cambridge, Mass., Feb. 26, 1923; s. Albert John and Isabel (Whitaker) H.; m. Barbara Livingston, July 1, 1950; 1 dau., Martha W. A.B. summa cum laude, Tufts U., 1947; LL.B. cum laude, Harvard U., 1949. Bar: Mass. bar 1949, U.S. Supreme Ct. bar 1959, 1st Fed. Ct. Appeal bar 1958, 2d Fed. Ct. Appeal bar 1971. Asso. firm Nutter, McClennen & Fish, Boston, 1949-60, partner, 1961—. Served with USNR, 1944-46. Fellow Am. Coll. Trial Lawyers, Mass. Bar Found., Am. Bar Found.; mem. Boston Bar Assn., Mass. Bar Assn., Am. Bar Assn. Office: 600 Atlantic Ave Boston MA 02210

HALMI, ROBERT, film producer; b. Budapest, Hungary, Jan. 22, 1924; s. Bela and Sarah (Deri) H.; m. Esther Szirmay, Sept. 9, 1980; children—Kevin Gorman, Kim Gorman, Robert, Bill. Grad., U. Budapest, 1946. Mag. photographer 1946-52; photographer Life mag., 1952-62; documentary producer, 1962-75. Producer movies for TV and theatres, 1975— (Recipient Spl. Jury award Houston Film Festival, Christopher award Internat. Film and TV.); Author: Zoos of the World. Clubs: Explorers, Adventurers.

HALPER, THOMAS, political science educator; b. Bklyn., Dec. 1, 1942; s. Albert and Pauline (Friedman) H.; m. Marilyn S. Snyder, Jan. 14, 1979; 1 dau., Pauline. A.B., St. Lawrence U., 1963; M.A., Vanderbilt U., 1967, Ph.D., 1970. Instr. Tulane U., 1967-68; asst. prof. polit. sci. Coe Coll., 1968-74, Baruch Coll., 1974-76, prof., chmn. dept., 1976—. Author: Foreign Policy Crises, 1971, Power, Politics and American Democracy, 1981; contbr. articles to profl. jours. Mem. Am. Polit. Sci. Assn. Home: 75 Livingston St Brooklyn NY 11201 Office: Dept Polit Sci Baruch Coll 17 Lexington Ave New York NY 10010

HALPERIN, BERTRAND ISRAEL, physics educator; b. Bklyn., Dec. 6, 1941; s. Morris and Eva (Teplitsky) H.; m. Helena Stacy French, Sept. 23, 1962; children: Jeffery Arnold, Julia Stacy. A.B., Harvard U., 1961; A.M., U. Calif., 1963, Ph.D., 1965; vis. grad. student, Princeton U., 1964-65. NSF postdoctoral fellow U. Paris, 1965-66; mem. tech. staff Bell Labs., Murray Hill, N.J., 1966-76; lectr. Harvard U., 1969-70, prof. physics, 1976—; cons. Bell Labs. Assoc. editor: Revs. Modern Physics, 1973-80. Fellow Am. Phys. Soc. (Oliver Buckley prize 1982), Am. Acad. Arts and Scis.; mem. Nat. Acad. Scis. Research in solid state theory, statis. physics. Office: Dept Physics Harvard U Cambridge MA 02138

HALPERIN, JOHN WILLIAM, educator; b. Chgo., Sept. 15, 1941; s. S. William and Elaine P. Halperin. A.B., Bowdoin Coll., 1963; M.A., U. N.H., 1966, Johns Hopkins U., 1968, Ph.D., 1969. Asst. prof. English, SUNY, Stony Brook, 1969-72, dir. summer session, 1969-72, asst. to acad. v.p., 1971-72; asso. prof. English, U. So. Calif., 1972-77, prof., 1977-83, dir. grad. studies in English, 1973-75; Centennial prof. English, Vanderbilt U., Nashville, 1983—; fellow Wolfson Coll., Oxford U., 1976; vis. prof. U. Sheffield (Eng.), 1979-80. Author: The Language of Meditation, 1973, Egoism and Self-Discovery in the Victorian Novel, 1974, (with Janet Kunert) Plots and Characters in the Fiction of Jane Austen, The Brontes and George Eliot, 1976, Trollope and Politics, 1977, Gissing: A Life in Books, 1982, C.P. Snow: An Oral Biography, 1983, The Life of Jane Austen, 1984; editor: Henry James, The Golden Bowl, 1972; Editor: The Theory of the Novel, 1974, Jane Austen: Bicentenary Essays, 1975, George Gissing, Denzil Quarrier, 1979, Anthony Trollope, Lord Palmerston, 1981, Anthony Trollope, Sir Henry Hotspur of Humblethwaite, 1981, Anthony Trollope, Dr. Wortle's School, 1984, George Meredith, The Ordeal of Richard Feverel, 1984; contbr. articles and essays to profl. jours. Served with U.S. Army, 1963-69. NDEA fellow, 1966-69; Rockefeller Found. fellow, 1976; Am. Philos. Soc. fellow, 1978; Guggenheim fellow, 1978-79; Am. Council Learned Socs. fellow, 1981. Mem. Am. Philos. Soc., MLA. Office: Dept English Vanderbilt U Nashville TN 37235

HALPERIN, MORTON H., political scientist, public interest group administrator; b. Bklyn., June 13, 1938; s. Harry and Lillian (Neubert) H.; m. Ina Elaine Weinstein, June 19, 1960 (div. Dec. 1979); children: David, Mark, Gary. A.B., Columbia U., 1958; M.A., Yale U., 1959, Ph.D., 1961. Research assoc. Harvard U., 1960-66, asst. prof., 1963-66; dep. asst. sec. U.S. Dept. Def., Washington, 1966-69; sr. staff mem. Nat. Security Council, Washington, 1969; sr. fellow Brookings Instn., Washington, 1969-73; research project dir. Twentieth Century Fund, Washington, 1974-75; dir. Ctr. Nat. Security Studies, Washington, 1975—; adj. prof. Columbia U., 1979—. Author: Limited War in the Nuclear, 1963, Contemporary Military Strategy, 1967, Bureaucratic Politics and Foreign Policy, 1976, Top Secret, 1977; editorial bd.: Fgn. Policy Mag., 1971—. Recipient Meritorious Civilian Service award U.S. Dept. Def., 1969, Hugh M. Hefner 1st Amendment Playboy Found., 1981, W. Lucius Cross medal Yale Grad. Sch. Alumni Assn., 1983. Mem. Council Fgn. Relations, Internat. Inst. Strategis Studies. Democrat. Jewish. Home: 1756 Swann St NW Washington DC 20009 Office: Ctr Nat Security Studies 122 Maryland Ave NE Washington DC 20002

HALPERIN, ROBERT MILTON, electrical machinery company executive; b. Chgo., June 1, 1928; s. Herman and Edna Pearl (Rosenberg) H.; m. Ruth Levison, June 19, 1955; children: Mark, Margaret, Philip. Ph.B., U. Chgo., 1949; B.Mech. Engring., Cornell U., 1949; M.B.A., Harvard U., 1952. Engr. Electro-Motive div. Gen. Motors Corp., La Grange, Ill., 1949-50; trust rep. Bank of Am., San Francisco, 1954-56; adminstr. Dumont Corp., San Rafael, Calif., 1956-57; pres. Raychem Corp., Menlo Park, Calif., 1957—, dir., 1961—. Served to lt. USAF, 1952-53. Club: Harvard of New York City. Home: 80 Reservoir Rd Atherton CA 94025 Office: 300 Constitution Dr Menlo Park CA 94025

HALPERIN, SAMUEL, educational institute administrator; b. Chgo., May 10, 1930; (married); 2 children. Student (scholar), Ill. Inst. Tech., 1948-49; A.B., A.M. (scholar 1950-52), Washington U., St. Louis, 1952; Ph.D. in Polit. Sci. (fellow 1954-56), Washington U., St. Louis, 1956; postgrad. (fellow), Columbia U., 1953-54. Asst. prof. polit. sci. Wayne State U., 1956-60; Am. Polit. Sci. Assn. congl. fellow Com. on Edn. and Labor, U.S. Ho. of Reps., 1960-61; legis. asst. to Hon. Cleveland M. Bailey and Adam C. Powell, 1960-61; cons. to subcom. on edn. and Senator Wayne Morse, Com. on Labor and Public Welfare, U.S. Senate, 1961, subcom. on reorgn., research and internat. orgns., 1970-73; specialist legis. services br. U.S. Office Edn., Washington, 1961-64, dir., 1963-64; asst. U.S. commr. edn. for legis., dir. office legis. and congl. relations, 1964-66; dep. asst. sec. for legis. HEW, Washington, 1966-69; dir. Ednl. Staff Seminar, Washington, 1969-74, Inst. for Ednl. Leadership, George Washington U., 1974-81, sr. fellow, 1981—, pres., 1981; fellow Jerusalem Ctr. Pub. Affairs, 1981-84; coordinator Relief Activities in South Lebanon, Am. Jewish Joint Distbn. Com., 1982; professorial lectr. Am. U., 1962-63; adj. prof. Tchrs. Coll. Columbia U., 1966-68; lectr. in edn. policy Duke U. Inst. Policy Scis. and Public Affairs, 1974-75; Alfred N. Whitehead fellow for advanced study in edn. Harvard U., 1969; mem. vis. com. Harvard Grad. Sch. Edn., 1973-79; mem. Urban Edn. Task Force, Nat. Urban Coalition; mem. profl. rev. panels; cons. speaker, guest lectr. in field; mem. nat. adv. bd. U.S. Peace Corps, Exec. High Sch. Internships Am., Nat. Sch. Vol. Program, HEW Steering Com. on Life-Long Learning, Nat. Student Ednl. Fund, Am. Council Edn.'s Nat. Identification Program for Advancement Women in Higher Edn. Adminstrn., United Student Aid Funds; mem. Sec. of Navy's Adv. Bd. on Edn. and Tng.; mem. adv. panel on human resources research Rand Corp. Author: The Political World of American Zionism, 1961, A University in the Web of Politics, 1960, Essays on Federal Education Policy, 1975; co-editor, contbg. author: Perspectives on Federal Educational Policy, 1976, Federalism at the Crossroads, Improving Educational Policymaking, 1976, A Guide for the Powerless, 1981; contbr. numerous articles, revs. to profl. publs.; cons.: Change mag; mem. nat. adv. bd.: Crossreference, Jour. Multi-Cultural Edn. Mem. nat. adv. bd. Am. Jewish Com. Served to maj. ROTC, 1948-52. Recipient Superior Service award HEW, 1964, 67, Disting. Service award, 1968; award of merit Nat. Assn. Public Sch. Adult Edn.; Disting. Service award Nat. Assn. State Bds. Edn., 1977; AFL-CIO grantee, 1959-60; Wayne State U. faculty research grantee, 1958-59. Mem. Phi Beta Kappa, Pi Sigma Alpha (pres.). Home: 3041 Normanstone Terr NW Washington DC 20008 Office: Inst Ednl Leadership 1001 Connecticut Ave NW Washington DC 20036

HALPERN, ABRAHAM LEON, psychiatrist; b. Warsaw, Poland, Feb. 2, 1925; U.S., 1957, naturalized, 1962; s. Rubin M. and Helen (Perelman) H.; m. Marilyn Lois Benjamin; children: Howard, Lon, Marnen, Heather Halpern Schneid, Mark, Emily, John. M.D., U. Toronto, Ont., Can., 1952. Diplomate: Am. Bd. Psychiatry and Neurology, Am. Bd. Forensic Psychiatry (dir. 1979—, v.p. 1983—). Intern Toronto Western Hosp., 1952-53; resident Warren (Pa.) State Hosp., 1957-60, Eastern Pa. Psychiat. Inst., Phila., 1959; asso. research scientist Mental Health Research Unit, Syracuse, N.Y., 1961-62; commr. mental health Onondaga County, 1962-67; practice medicine specializing in psychiatry, Port Chester, N.Y., 1967—; dir. psychiatry United Hosp., Port Chester, 1967—; attending psychiatrist Beth Israel Hosp., N.Y.C., 1968-73, Westchester County Med. Center, 1971—; cons. forensic psychiatry High Point Hosp., Port Chester, 1969—; cons. St. Vincent's Hosp., Harrison, N.Y., 1973—; clin. asst. prof. SUNY, Syracuse, 1964-67; asst. clin. prof. Mt. Sinai Sch. Medicine, 1970-74; clin. asso. prof. N.Y. Med. Coll., 1973-80, clin. prof. psychiatry, 1980—; clin. prof. forensic psychiatry, N.Y. Sch. Psychiatry, 1979—; mem. med. adv. com. Vis. Nurse Assn., Syracuse, 1962-67; mem. N.Y. State Mental Hygiene Med. Rev. Bd., 1982—. Assoc. editor: Bull. Am. Acad. Psychiatry and the Law, 1982—; mem. editorial bd.: Psychiat. Jour. of U. Ottawa, 1979—; mem. exec. editorial com.: Psychiat. Quar., 1982—. Chmn. Syracuse chpt. Com. to Abolish Capital Punishment, 1962-65; mem. profl. adv. com. N.Y. State Assn. for Mental Health, 1964-67; mem. N.Y. State Law Revision Adv. Com. on the Insanity Def., 1979-80, Westchester County Community Mental Health Bd., 1976-78; chmn. Westchester County Community Mental Health Bd., 1977-78; bd. visitors Harlem Valley Psychiat. Center, 1978-82; mem. N.Y. State Corrections Med. Rev. Bd., 1980—; bd. dirs. Westchester Council on Alcoholism, 1980—. Served to surgeon lt. comdr. Royal Can. Navy, 1942-45, 53-57. Recipient Citizenship award N.Y. State Bar Assn., 1966; Liberty Bell award Onondaga County Bar Assn., 1966. Fellow Am. Acad. Forensic Scis., A.C.P., Am. Coll. Psychiatrists, Am. Psychiat. Assn. (com. psychiatry and law 1973-75), Am. Assn. Psychoanalytic Physicians (dir. 1978—), Am. Public Health Assn.; mem. AMA, N.Y. State Med. Soc. (com. on mental health), Pan Am. Med. Assn. (mem. council sect. on psychiatry 1983—), Westchester County Med. Soc., Westchester Psychiat. Soc. (pres. 1973-74), Soc. Med. Jurisprudence (trustee 1980—), Internat. Soc. Law and Psychiatry (pres. 1983—), Am. Acad. Psychiatry and Law (councilor 1978-81, pres. 1982-83). Home: 720 The Parkway Mamaroneck NY 10543 Office: 406 Boston Post Rd Port Chester NY 10573

HALPERN, BENJAMIN, educator; b. Boston, Apr. 10, 1912; s. Solomon Leib and Fannie (Epstein) H.; m. Gertrude Elizabeth Gumner, Nov. 26, 1936; children: Elkan Frank, Joseph David. A.B., Harvard, 1932, Ph.D., 1936; B.J. Ed., Hebrew Tchrs. Coll., 1932. Mng. editor (Jewish Frontier), N.Y.C., 1943-49, mem. editorial bd., 1943-72; asso. dir. edn. and culture Jewish Agy., N.Y.C., 1949-56; research asso. Harvard Center for Middle East Studies, Cambridge, Mass., 1956-72; asso. prof. Near Eastern studies Brandeis U., Waltham, Mass., 1961-66, prof., 1966-80, prof. emeritus, 1980—. Author: The American Jew, A Zionist Analysis, 1956, 83, The Idea of the Jewish State, 1961, 69, Jews and Blacks, the Classic American Minorities, 1971. Exec. Jewish Agy., 1968-72; Trustee Hebrew Tchrs. Coll.; bd. govs. Tel Aviv U. Sr. fellow Nat. Endowment for Humanities, 1970; Guggenheim fellow, 1961-62. Home: 187 Mason Terr Brookline MA 02146

HALPERN, BRUCE PETER, educator; b. Newark, Aug. 18, 1933; s. Leo and Thelma (Rubin) H.; m. Pauline Touber Anklowitz, June 9, 1956; children—Michael Touber, Stacey Rachael. A.B., Rutgers U., 1955; M.Sc., Brown U., 1957, Ph.D., 1959. Asst. prof. physiology Upstate Med. Center, Syracuse, N.Y., 1961-66; asso. prof. psychology, neurobiology and behavior Cornell U., Ithaca, N.Y., 1966-73, prof., 1973—, chmn. dept. psychology, 1974-80; mem. Advisory Panel Sensory Physiology and Perception NSF. Editorial bd.: Chem. Senses; Contbr. articles to profl. jours. NIMH grantee, 1958-62; NIH grantee, 1963-72; NSF grantee, 1972—. Mem. Am. Physiol. Soc., AAAS, Assn. Chemoreception Scis. Home: 113 Winston Dr Ithaca NY 14850 *For those with power: As one's ability to influence or control the actions of others increases, one must become increasingly unwilling to use that ability. For scholars: Any generally accepted scientific idea is an ideal area for creative research, since the idea is almost surely wrong.*

HALPERN, DANIEL, poet, editor, educator; b. Syracuse, N.Y., Sept. 11, 1945; s. Irving and Rosemary (Glueck) H. B.A., Calif. State U., Northridge, 1969; M.F.A., Columbia U., 1972. Prof. New Sch. for Social Research, N.Y.C., 1971-76, Princeton U., 1975-76; prof. Columbia U., N.Y.C., 1976—, chmn. grad. writing div., 1981—; Bd. dirs., Assoc. Writing Programs, P.E.N., Columbia Translation Ctr., Art Without Walls. Author: Traveling On Credit, 1972; editor-in-chief: Antaeus, The Ecco Press, 1970—; editor: Borges on Writing, 1973, The Keeper of Height, 1973, Treble Poets, 1974, Songs of Mririda, 1975, Antaeus, The American Poetry Anthology, 1975, Street Fire, 1975, Life Among Others, 1978, Seasonal Rights, 1982. Nat. Endowment for Arts fellow, 1973-74; CAPS fellow, 1977-78; Robert Frost fellow at Breadloaf, 1974; others; recipient Gt. Lake Colls. Nat. Book award, 1973; Borestone Poetry award; others. Mem. Author's Guild, Poetry Soc. Am. Office: Writing Div Sch Arts 404 Dodge Hall Columbia U New York NY 10027

HALPERN, JACK, chemistry educator; b. Poland, Jan. 19, 1925; came to U.S., 1962; s. Philip and Anna (Sass) H.; m. Helen Peritz, June 30, 1949; children: Janice Deborah, Nina Phyllis. B.Sc., McGill U., 1946, Ph.D., 1949. Postdoctorate overseas fellow NRC, U. Manchester (Eng.), 1949-50; instr. chemistry U. B.C., 1950, prof., 1961-62; Nuffield Found. traveling fellow Cambridge (Eng.) U., 1959-60; prof. chemistry U. Chgo., 1962-71, Louis Block prof. chemistry, 1971—; vis. prof. U. Minn., 1962, Harvard, 1966-67, Calif. Inst. Tech., 1968-69, Princeton U., 1970-71, Max. Planck Institut, Mulheim, W.

Ger; external sci. mem. Max Planck Inst., Mulheim, W. Ger., 1983—; vis. prof. U. Copenhagen, 1978; Sherman Fairchild Disting. scholar Calif. Inst. Tech., 1979; guest scholar Kyoto U., 1981; Firth vis. prof. U. Sheffield, 1982; numerous guest lectureships; cons. editor Macmillan Co., 1963-65, Oxford U. Press; cons. Am. Oil Co., Monsanto Co., Argonne Nat. Lab., IBM, Air Products Co.; mem. adv. panel on chemistry NSF, 1967-70; mem. adv. bd. Am. Chem. Soc. Petroleum Research Fund, 1972-74; mem. medicinal chemistry sect. NIH, 1975-78, chmn., 1976-78; mem. chemistry adv. council Princeton U., 1982—; Mem. Art Inst. Chgo., 1964—. Asso. editor: Inorganica Chimica Acta, Jour. Am. Chem. Soc; co-editor: Collected Accounts of Transition Metal Chemistry, vol. 1, 1973, vol. 2, 1977; editorial bd.: Jour. Organometallic Chemistry; Contbr. articles to research jours.; Ency. Britannica, Accounts of Chem. Research; Catalysis Revs.; Jour. of Catalysis, Jour. Molecular Catalysis; contbr.: Jour. Coordination Chemistry; Contbr.: Gazzetta Chimica Italiana. Trustee Gordon Research Confs., 1968-70. Recipient Young Author's prize Electrochem. Soc., 1953; award in inorganic chemistry Am. Chem. Soc., 1968; award in catalysis Noble Metals Chem. Soc., London, 1976; Humboldt award, 1977; Richard Kokes award Johns Hopkins U., 1978; Alfred P. Sloan research fellow, 1959-63. Fellow Royal Soc. (London), AAAS, Am. Acad. Arts and Scis., Chem. Inst. Can., Royal Soc. Chemistry (London), N.Y. Acad. Scis.; mem. Am. Chem. Soc. (editorial bd. Advances in Chemistry series 1963-65, 78-81, chmn. inorganic chemistry div. 1971), Nat. Acad. Scis. (fgn. assoc.), Max Planck Soc., Sigma Xi. Home: 5630 Dorchester Ave Chicago IL 60637 Office: U Chgo Dept Chemistry Chicago IL 60637

HALPERN, JAMES BLADEN, lawyer; b. Buffalo, Apr. 20, 1936; s. Philip and Goldene P. (Friedman) H.; m. Jessie Malkoff, July 6, 1958 (div.); 1 dau., Jennifer; m. Niesa N. Brateman, Aug. 26, 1979. B.A., Harvard U., 1958, J.D., 1961. Bar: N.Y. 1961, D.C. 1970. Atty. corp. fin. div. SEC, Washington, 1961-64; chief counsel-instns., instl. investor study, 1969-70; asso. firm Proskauer Rose Goetz & Mendelsohn, N.Y.C., 1964-69, Arent, Fox, Kintner, Plotkin & Kahn, Washington, 1971-73, partner, 1974—; practice corp. and securities law, 1971—. Mem. ABA, Fed. Bar Assn., N.Y. State Bar Assn., D.C. Bar Assn., Assn. Bar City N.Y., Am. Law Inst. Democrat. Jewish. Club: Harvard N.Y.C. Home: 1350 19th Rd S Arlington VA 22202 Office: 1050 Connecticut Ave Washington DC 20036

HALPERN, MARTIN, author, educator; b. N.Y.C., Oct. 3, 1929; s. Louis and Edith (Eisinger) H.; m. Nancy M. Homer, July 5, 1959; children—Andrew Homer, Jessica M. B.A., U. Rochester, 1950, M.A., 1953; Ph.D., Harvard, 1959. Teaching fellow Harvard, 1954-56, 57-59; faculty U. Calif. at Berkeley, 1959-64, U. Mass., 1964-65, Brandeis U., 1965—, asso. prof. theatre arts, 1966-76, prof., 1976—, chmn. dept. theater arts, 1972-76, 82—; playwright-in-residence Circle Repertory Co., N.Y.C., 1978—. Author: Two Sides of an Island and Other Poems, 1963, William Vaughn Moody, 1964; play Tameem, 1973; Selected Poems, 1976; plays Total Recall in Best Short Plays, 1978, What The Babe Said, 1980; articles, plays and poems in jours.; plays produced, widely off Broadway in N.Y.C. and in regional and univ. theaters. Served with AUS, 1951-53. Fulbright scholar, 1956-57; Howard Found. fellow in writing, 1962-63. Mem. Phi Beta Kappa. Home: 14 Waban St Natick MA 01760 Office: Theatre Arts Dept Brandeis Univ Waltham MA 02154

HALPERN, NATHAN LOREN, industrialist; b. Sioux City, Iowa, Oct. 22, 1914; s. Aaron and Lena (Robin) H.; m. Edith Kessel, Oct. 7, 1938; 1 son, Michael. B.A., U. So. Calif., 1936; LL.B. cum laude, Harvard, 1939. Bar: Calif., D.C. 1939. Asst. to chmn. SEC, Washington, 1939-41; exec. asst. to dir. WPB, Washington, 1941-42, USIS, France, 1945; asst. to pres. CBS, N.Y.C., 1945-49; pres. TNT Communications, Inc., N.Y.C., 1949—; Former pres. Internat. Center Photography; pres. East Hampton Beach Preservation Soc.; trustee N.Y. Central Park Conservancy. Benefactor, mem. corp. Met. Mus. of Art. Served with USNR, 1942-44. Mem. Soc. Motion Picture and TV Engrs., Phi Beta Kappa. Clubs: Harvard, Players. Home: 993 Fifth Ave New York NY 10028 Office: 575 Madison Ave New York NY 10022

HALPERN, NORMAN GERALD, railroad executive; b. Bayonne, N.J., July 4, 1927; s. Joseph and Rose (Berman) H.; m. Diane Reiter, Sept. 12, 1953; children: Jeffrey A., Michael R., Peter M. B.S., Pa. State U., 1948; M.A., Case Western Res. U., 1954, postgrad. in indsl. psychology. Mgmt. cons. Psychol. Research Services, Cleve., 1952-56; with Chesapeake & Ohio Ry. Co.; v.p. labor relations, personnel and orgn. planning, sr. exec. v.p. adminstrn. Chessie System Railroads; dir. Chesapeake & Ohio Ry., B&O Ry., Western Md Co. and subs. Trustee Cleve. Ballet., Cleve. Opera, Cleve. Playhouse, Bellefaire, Leadership Cleve. Served to 1st lt. Armed Forces, 1949-52; Korea. Decorated Bronze Star, Commendation medal. Mem. Am. Mgmt. Assn., R.R. Personnel Assn., Ry. Systems Mgmt. Assn., Greater Cleve. Growth Assn., Ohio C. of C. Republican. Jewish. Clubs: Oakwood, Center (Balt.); Mid-Day. Home: 2726 Belvoir Blvd Shaker Heights OH 44122 Office: PO Box 6419 Cleveland OH 44101

HALPERN, RALPH LAWRENCE, lawyer; b. Buffalo, May 12, 1929; s. Julius and Mary C. (Kaminker) H.; m. Harriet Chasin, June 29, 1958; children: Eric B., Steven R., Julie B. LL.B. cum laude, U. Buffalo, 1953. Bar: N.Y. 1953. Teaching assoc. Northwestern U. Law Sch., 1953-54; assoc. firm Jaeckle, Fleischmann, Kelly, Swart & Augspurger, Buffalo, 1957-58; asso. firm Raichle, Banning, Weiss & Halpern (and predecessors), 1958-59, partner, 1959—. Pres. Buffalo Council World Affairs, 1972-74, Temple Beth Zion, Buffalo, 1981-83; chmn. Buffalo chpt. Am. Jewish Com., 1975-77; bd. govs. United Jewish Fedn., Buffalo, 1972-78. Served to capt. JAGC U.S. Army, 1954-57. Mem. ABA, N.Y. State Bar Assn. (chmn. com. profl. ethics 1971-76, chmn. com. jud. election monitoring 1983—), Erie County (N.Y.) Bar Assn., Am. Judicature Soc., Am. Law Inst. Home: 84 New Amsterdam Ave Buffalo NY 14216 Office: 1400 Main Place Tower Buffalo NY 14202

HALPERN, SHELDON WILLIAM, lawyer, consultant; b. N.Y.C., Dec. 16, 1935; s. Joseph and Bertha (Zins) H.; children: Joel Michael, Paul Benjamin. B.A., Cornell U., 1957, LL.B., 1959. Bar: N.Y. 1959, Minn. 1973. Mem. law firms, N.Y.C., 1959-73; v.p., gen. counsel, sec. Fingerhut Corp., Minnetonka, Minn., 1973-79; partner firm Robins, Davis and Lyons, Mpls., 1979-80; v.p., gen. counsel, sec. Viacom Internat., N.Y.C., 1980-82; tchr. U. Minn. Sch. Social Work, 1976. Editor: Cornell Law Rev. Bd. dirs. Jewish Community Relations Counsel, Anti-Defamation League Minn. and the Dakotas, Cricket Theatre. Mem. Assn. Bar City N.Y., Minn., N.Y. State bar assns., Corporate Counsel Assn. Minn., Phi Beta Kappa, Phi Kappa Phi, Order of Coif. *When someone asks, "what do you do?", we tend to answer by saying, "I am a . . .". That is, we respond to the objective "do" with the highly subjective "am". I have tried to live a life that is not defined solely by what I do. In the process, I hope to find more of who I am and to be less ready to judge others by what they do.*

HALPIN, ANNA MARIE, architect; b. Murphysboro, Ill., July 24, 1923; d. John William and Anna Christina (Weilmuenster) H. B.S. in Architecture, U. Ill., 1948. Mgr. editorial Sweet's div. McGraw-Hill Info. Systems Co., N.Y.C., 1967—; rep. to Constrn. Industries Coordination Com., Am. Nat. Metric Council, 1974-80. Designer, project architect various firms, San Francisco, Rome, N.Y.C., 1948-67. Mem. AIA (treas., dir. N.Y. chpt. 1974-78, coll. fellows 1976, nat. dir. 1977-79, nat. v.p. 1980, dir. Found. 1980), Women's Equity Action League (pres. N.Y. state orgn. 1976-77), Constrn. Specifications Inst., Alliance Women in Architecture. Home: 519 E 86th St New York NY 10028 Office: 1221 Ave of the Americas New York NY 10020

HALPIN, CHARLES AIME, archbishop; b. St. Eustache, Man., Can., Aug. 30, 1930; s. John S. and Marie Anne (Gervais) H. B.A., U. Man., 1950; B.Th., U. Montreal, 1956; Licentiate Canon Law, Gregorian U., Rome, 1960. Ordained priest Roman Catholic Ch., 1956; named monsignor Roman Cath. Ch., 1969, consecrated bishop, 1973; asst. St. Mary's Cathedral, Winnipeg, Man., 1956-58; vice chancellor, sec. to archbishop Archdiocese Winnipeg, 1960; officialis Archdiocesean Matrimonial Tribunal, 1962; vice-officialis Regional Matrimonial Tribunal, Regina, Sask.; chaplain to Pope, 1969-73; archbishop of Regina, 1973—. Mem. Western Cath. Conf. Bishops (pres.), Can. Conf. Cath. Bishops (dir.). Home: 2522 Retallack St Regina SK Canada Office: 3225 13th Ave Regina SK S4T 1P5 Canada

HALPIN, DANIEL WILLIAM, civil engineering educator, consultant; b. Covington, Ky., Sept. 29, 1938; s. Jordan W. and Gladys E. (Moore) H.; m. Maria Kirchner, Feb. 8, 1963; 1 son, Rainer. B.S., U.S. Mil. Acad., 1961; M.S.C.E., U. Ill., 1969, Ph.D., 1973. Research analyst Constrn. Engring. Research Lab., Champaign, Ill., 1970-72; faculty U. Ill.-Urbana, 1972-73; mem. faculty Ga. Inst. Tech., Atlanta, 1973—, prof., 1981—; cons. constrn. mgmt.; vis. assoc. prof. U. Sydney, Australia, 1981. Author: Design of Construction and Process Operations, 1976, Construction Management, 1980, Planung und Kontrolle von Bauproduktionsprozessen, 1979, Constructo - A Heuristic Game for Construction Management, 1973. Served with C.E. U.S. Army, 1961-67. Decorated Bronze Star; recipient Walter L.Huber prize ASCE, 1979; grantee NSF, Dept. Energy. Mem. ASCE (past sect. pres. 1981-82), Am. Soc. Engring. Edn., Sigma Xi. Methodist.

HALPORN, JAMES WERNER, classics educator; b. N.Y.C., Jan. 14, 1929; s. Robert and Louisa (Goldberg) H.; m. Roberta Krugman, June 1951 (div. 1958); 1 dau., Constance Hilary; m. Barbara Crawford, May 28, 1960; 1 son, Michael Friedrich. A.B., Columbia U., 1949, M.A., 1950; Ph.D., Cornell U., 1953. Instr. Greek and Latin Columbia U., 1954-58; vis. lectr. Carleton U., Ottawa, Can., 1958-59; vis. asst. prof. U. Mo.-Columbia, 1959-60; mem. faculty Ind. U., Bloomington, 1960—, prof. classical studies and comparative lit., 1968—, assoc. chmn. classical studies, 1976-78; vis. prof. classics and comparative lit. U. Calif., Berkeley, 1971-72; vis. scholar Harvard U., 1981-82; regional chmn. dist. IX Woodrow Wilson Nat. Fellowship Found., 1969—; rep. to adv. council Am. Acad. in Rome, 1965—. Author: Magni Aurelii Cassiodori De anima, 1973; co-author: The Meters of Greek and Latin Poetry, 1963, rev. edit., 1979, Lateinische Metrick, 3d edit., 1983; Contbr. articles to profl. jours. Fulbright scholar, Vienna, 1953-54; Am. Council Learned Socs./IBM Corp. fellow, 1965-66. Mem. Am. Philol. Assn. (chmn. com. on placement 1980-82), N.Am. Patristics Soc., Classical Assn. Gt. Britain, Soc. Promotion Hellenic Studies, Soc. Promotion Roman Studies, MLA. Club: Columbia Varsity C. Home: 702 Ballantine Rd Bloomington IN 47401

HALPRIN, ANNA SCHUMAN (MRS. LAWRENCE HALPRIN), dancer; b. Wilmette, Ill., July 13, 1920; d. Isadore and Ida (Schiff) Schuman; m. Lawrence Halprin, Sept. 19, 1940; children: Daria, Rana. Student, Bennington Summer Sch. Dance, 1938-39; B.S. in Dance, U. Wis., 1943. Founder, choreographer, dir., performer, Dancers' Workshop of San Francisco, N.Y.C., 1973; appeared in: films The Bed; master tchr., Esalen Inst., U. Calif. at Berkeley, U. Calif. at Los Angeles, U. Ill., Reed Coll., Harvard Sch. Design, Environmental Sch. Design, U. Calif., San Francisco State Coll., U. Mich.; coordinator, dir. Profl. Tng. Program, 1978—; choreographed: Jerusalem, 1973; films Golden Positions; others.; mem., Regional Bay Area Arts Council, San Francisco Arts Resource Devel. Com., Gestalt Inst., San Francisco; founder, dir., Marin Dance Coop.; dir., Tampala Inst.; workshop performances A Workshop for the People of San Francisco, 1975-76, Dances with the People of San Francisco, 1976-77, Am. Dance Festival, 1976, Search for Living Myths and Rituals through Dance and the Environment, 1982; Return to the Mountain, 2 day performance, 1983; Founder: Impulse mag; Author: Exit to Enter, 1973, Collected Writings, 1973, A School Comes Home, 1973, Collected Writings II, Movement Ritual I. Bd. dirs. East West Wholistic Healing Inst.; mem. Gov.'s Council on Phys. Fitness and Wellness. Recipient Guggenheim award, 1970-71; Nat. Endowment Arts Choreographers grantee, 1976; NEA choreography grantee, 1977; San Francisco Found. grantee, 1981. Mem. Assn. Am. Dance, Conscientious Artists Am. Home: 15 Ravine Way Kentfield CA 94904 Office: Fort Mason Laguna and Marina San Francisco CA 94114 *Coming to realize that truth, beauty and reality are what I am open and capable of experiencing. Furthermore, that whatever I truly experience is perfect—the perfection reflecting nature's manner of operation. I'm concerned with the evolution of the person in the artist, as well as the artist in the person, so that personal and artistic growth emerge as a whole.*

HALPRIN, LAWRENCE, landscape architect-planner; b. N.Y.C., July 1, 1916; s. Samuel W. and Rose (Luria) H.; m. Ann Schuman, Sept. 19, 1940; children: Daria, Rana. B.S. in Plant Scis, Cornell U., 1939, M.S., U. Wis., 1941; B. Landscape Architecture, Harvard U., 1942. Sr. asso. Thomas D. Church & Assos., San Francisco, 1946-49; prin. Lawrence Halprin & Assos., San Francisco, 1949-76; founder Lawrence Halprin Studios, 1976—; lectr. U. Calif.-Berkeley, 1960-65, Regents prof., 1982-83. Dir., Halprin Summer Workshop, 1966, 1968; prin. works include Ghirardelli Sq, San Francisco, Sea Ranch, Calif., Nicolett Mall, Mpls., Old Orchard Shopping Center, Skokie, Ill., Lovejoy Fountain, Pettigrove Park, Forecourt Fountain, Portland, Oreg., Market St. reconstrn, San Francisco, Seattle Freeway Park, Rochester Manhattan Park, Franklin Delano Roosevelt Meml, Washington, Levi Park and Plaza, San Francisco; Panelist, White House Conf. Natural Beauty, 1965; mem. bd. urban cons., Bur. Pub. Roads, 1966-67; design cons., Calif. Div. Hwys., 1963-65; landscape architect, urban cons., San Francisco Bay Area Rapid Transit Dist., 1963-66; mem., Gov. Calif.'s Conf. Calif. Beauty, 1966, Nat. Council Arts, 1966—; Adv. Council, Historic Preservation, 1967—; Bd. dirs., San Francisco Dancers Workshop Co., 1950—; (Named One of Leaders of Tomorrow, Time mag. 1953, recipient awards including Allied Professions Gold medal AIA 1964, Thomas Jefferson award in architecture 1979); Author: Cities, 1963; rev. edit., 1972, Freeways, 1966, New York, New York, 1968, The RSVP Cycles, 1970, Lawrence Halprin Notebooks, 1959-71, 1972; co-author: The Freeway in the City, 1968, Taking Part: A Workshop Approach to Collective Creativity, 1974, The Sketch Book of Lawrence Halprin, 1981. Served to lt. (j.g.) USNR, 1943-46. Fellow Am. Soc. Landscape Architects; mem. Am. Acad. Arts and Scis., Sierra Club. Democrat. Jewish. Address: 1620 Montgomery St San Francisco CA 94111

HALSEY, BRENTON SHAW, paper company executive; b. Newport News, Va., 1927. B.S. in Chem. Engring., U. Va.; postgard., Inst. of Paper Chemistry. Vice pres. planning Albemarle Paper Co., 1955-66; pres., gen. mgr. Interstate Bag. Co., 1966-68; co-founder James River Corp. of Va., Richmond, 1969, now chmn., chief exec. officer, dir.; dir. Dominion Bankshares, Dominion Nat. Bank, Westmoreland Coal Co. Office: James River Corp Va Tredegar St Box 2218 Richmond VA 23217

HALSEY, JAMES A., international entertainment impressario, theatrical producer, talent manager; b. Independence, Kans., Oct. 7, 1930; s. Harry Edward and Carrie Lee (Messick) H.; m. Minisa Crumbo; children: Sherman Brooks, Gina. Student, Independence Community Coll., 1948-50, U. Kans. Pres. Thunderbird Artists, Inc., producer shows for auditoriums, fairs, rodeos, TV, internat. music fests, also others in U.S. and internationally,, Independence, 1950—, Jim Halsey Co., Inc., Tulsa, 1952—, Jim Halsey Agy., James Halsey Property Mgmt. Co., Tulsa, Proud Country Entertainment, Stas. KTOW and KGOW, Silverline-Goldline Pub., J.H. Radio Mgmt., Cyclone Records, Tulsa Records, J.H. Lighting and Sound Co., Singin' T Prodns., NERECO Prodns., Norwood Advt. Agy.; bd. dirs. Roy Clark Celebrity Golf Classic; dir. Merc. Bank and Trust, Tulsa, Citizens Nat. Bank, Independence, Kans., Farmers & Mchts. Bank, Mound City, Kans.; gen. partner Parker Ranch, Tulsa; v.p. Gen. Artists Corp., Beverly Hills, Calif., 1956—; chmn. Churchill Recs. & Video Ltd., 1981—, Halsey Internat. Co., 1982—; personal mgr. various entertainment personalities; internat. jurist, Golden Orpheus Festival, Bulgaria, 1981-82. Producer shows for auditoriums, fairs, rodeos, celebrations in various cities throughout world; producer, Tulsa Internat. Music Festival, 1977-80, Neewollah Internat. Music Festival, 1981-83. Trustee Philbrook Art Center, Tulsa; bd. dirs. Thomas Gilcrease Museum Assn., Tulsa, Tulsa Philharm. Assn. Served with U.S. Army, 1954-56. Recipient Disting. Service award U.S. Jr. C. of, 1959, Jim Reeves Meml. award Acad. Country Music, 1977; Recipient Ambassador of Country Music award SESAC Corp., 1978, citation Cashbox Mag., 1980, Golden Orpheus Festival, 1982, Hubert Long award Mervyn Conn, Eng, 1982, FIDOF Oscar Midem 82, Cannes, France, 1982; Named Disting. Kansan Topeka Capital Jour. Mem. Country Music Assn. (dir. 1963-64, 70-71, v.p. 1979-80), Acad. Country Music (dir. 1969-70, 73-74, v.p. 1975-76, 78-79, 79-80, Jim Reeves Meml. award 1977). Home: 515 N 2d St Independence KS 67301 Office: 3225 S Norwood Tulsa OK 74135 Office: 9000 Sunset Blvd Los Angeles CA 90069 Office: 2 Music Circle S Nashville TN 37203 Office: 445 Park Ave New York NY 10022

HALSEY, RICHARD SWEENEY, university dean; b. Los Angeles, Apr. 8, 1929; s. John Calvin and Grace Thorne (Crossman) Sweeney; m. Patricia Siver, July 15, 1961; children: Rachel, Gabriela. B.Mus., New Eng. Conservatory, 1952, M.Mus., 1954; M.L.S., Simmons Coll., Boston, 1962; Ph.D. (U.S. Office Edn. fellow 1969-72), Case Western Res. U., 1972. Chief audio-visual dept. Olin Library, Washington U., St. Louis, 1962-65; dir. learning resources University City (Mo.) Sch. Dist., 1965-68; info. scientist Central Midwestern Regional Ednl. Lab., St. Ann, Mo., 1968-69; asst. prof. Sch. Library Sci., U. Toronto (Ont., Can.), 1972-73; asso. prof. library sci. Sch. Library and Info. Sci., SUNY, Albany, 1973—, dean, 1980—; cons. in field. Author: Classical Music Recordings for Home and Library, 1976; editor: CLiC Quar., 1982—; Author also articles. Coordinator steering com. for 28th Congressional Dist., Common Cause, 1979-80; sec. N.Y. State Common Cause, 1980-81; exec. dir. Citizens' Library Council N.Y. State, 1981—; mem. capital dist. adv. bd. Fund for Modern Cts., 1981—; mem. steering com. N.Y. State Parents as Reading Ptnrs., 1979—. Served with AUS, 1955-56. Mem. Soc. Am. Archivists, Assn. Info. and Image Mgmt., ALA (chmn. reference and subscription books rev. com. 1975-79, editorial adv. bd. booklist 1972-79), Am. Acad. Polit. and Social Sci., Am. Soc. Info. Sci., N.Y. State Library Assn. (pres. library edn. sect. 1979-80, sec. legis. com. 1980-81, outstanding service to libraries award 1983), Assn. Library and Info. Sci. Edn. (coordinator Legis. Alert Network 1983—, chmn. govtl. relations com. 1984—), Assn. Ednl. Communications and Tech., Pi Kappa Lambda. Democrat. Home: 239 Juniper Dr Schenectady NY 12306 Office: Sch Library and Info Sci SUNY Albany NY 12222 *The landscape of my mind was early lit by the printed word, and the book, for me, is a private place where unconventional ideas, insights, and passions may be met without fear of consequence. Like love and music-making, reading and learning are good even when they're bad because of their revivifying powers. And like the pursuit of happiness, the right to read must be defended to the death so that the fight against ignorance, inequity, unfeeling, and the fading of the light can continue.*

HALSEY, WILLIAM DARRACH, editor; b. Washington, Sept. 17, 1918; s. William D. and Mary Flagg (Price) H.; m. Frances Murlin, June 27, 1942; m. Elizabeth Darby, Apr. 11, 1966. Grad., Loomis Sch., 1936; B.S., Haverford Coll., 1940. Mng. editor Thorndike-Barnhart Comprehensive Desk Dictionary, 1951—, Thorndike-Barnhart Beginning Dictionary, 1952—, Thorndike-Barnhart Jr. Dictionary, 1952—, High Sch. Dictionary, 1952—, Thorndike-Barnhart Advanced Jr. Dictionary, 1957—; editorial dir. Collier's Ency., 1960, Merit Students Ency., 1965, Macmillan Dictionary, 1973, Macmillan Sch. Dictionary, 1974, Macmillan Dictionary for Children, 1975; v.p. Crowell-Collier Pub. Co., N.Y.C., 1962-65, Crowell Collier and Macmillan, Inc., 1965—; pres. Crowell-Collier Ednl. Corp., from 1964; sr. v.p. Macmillan, Inc., 1968—. Co-author: New Century Cyclopedia of Names, 1954, New Century Handbook of English Literature, 1956. Home: 40 E 9th St New York City NY 10028 Office: 866 3d Ave New York City NY 10003

HALSTEAD, BRUCE WALTER, biotoxicologist; b. San Francisco, Mar. 28, 1920; s. Walter and Ethel Muriel (Shanks) H.; m. Joy Arloa Mallory, Aug. 3, 1941; children: Linda, Sandra, David, Larry, Claudia, Shari. A.A., San Francisco City Coll., 1941; B.A., U. Calif.-Berkeley, 1943; M.D., Loma Linda U., 1948. Research asst. in ichthyology Calif. Acad. Scis., 1935-43; instr. Pacific Union Coll., 1943-44; mem. faculty Loma Linda U., 1948- 58; research asso. Lab. Neurol. Research, Sch. Medicine, 1964—; dir. World Life Research Inst., Colton, Calif., 1959—, Internat. Biotoxicol. Center; research asso. in ichthyology Los Angeles County Mus., 1964—; instr. Walla Walla Coll., summers 1964—; Cons. to govt. agys., pvt. corps; mem. editorial staff Exerpta Medica, 1959—, Toxicon, 1962—; mem. joint group experts on sci. aspects marine pollution UN; Dir. Nat. Assn. Underwater Instrs., Internat. Underwater Enterprises, Internat. Bots., Inc. Author: Poisonous and Venomous Marine Animals of the World, 4 vols., 1966; others.; contbr. numerous articles to profl. jours. Fellow AAAS, Internat. Soc. Toxicology (a founder), N.Y. Acad. Scis., Royal Soc. Tropical Medicine and Hygiene; mem. Am. Inst. Biol. Scis., Am. Micros. Soc., Am. Soc. Ichthyologists and Herpetologists, Am. Soc. Limnology and Oceanography, numerous others. Address: 23000 Grand Terrace Rd Colton CA 92324

HALSTEAD, DIRCK S., photographer, journalist; b. Huntington, N.Y., Dec. 24, 1936; s. William S. and Leslie (Munro) H. Ed., Haverford Coll., 1958. Staff photographer UPI, Dallas, 1958-60; spl. roving photographer Dept. of Army, Washington, 1960-61; photographer Black Star, Washington, 1961-62; picture bur. mgr. UPI, Phila., 1962-65, Saigon, Vietnam, 1965-66, roving spl. photographer, 1966-72; photographer Time mag., N.Y.C., 1972—, contract photographer, 1972-73, White House photographer, 1973-77, spl. color projects photographer, N.Y.C., 1977—. Pres. The Shooters, Inc., N.Y.C. Served with U.S. Army, 1960-61. Recipient 1st prize awards N.Y. Press Assn., 1973, 74, 75, 76, 77, Robert Capa award for exceptional photography from abroad requiring skill and courage, 1975, Front Page award Am. Newspaper Guild, 1975, 76, 1st prize color news, color features N.Y. Press Photographers, 1978, 1st pl. sports picture of year, 1982, others. Mem. White House News Photographers (1st prize news 1976, 1st prize for feature color 1977), N.Y., Nat. press photographers. Clubs: Nat. Press, Overseas Press.

Home: 322 W 57th St New York NY 10019 Office: Rm 2850 Time Life Bldg New York NY 10020

HALSTEAD, GEORGIA, educator; b. Lafayette, Ind., July 29, 1915; d. George E. and Alice (Switzer) H. B.S. in Home Econs, Purdue U., 1937; M.S. in Edn, Mich. State U., 1945; Ph.D., Pa. State U., 1954. Tchr. Brook (Ind.) High Sch., 1937-40, Washington Twp. Sch., Logansport, Ind., 1940-44; athletic dir. summer camps, Mich., 1943-44; tchr. Adrian (Mich.) High Sch., 1945-46; instr. Pa. State U., 1947-48; asst. prof. charge home econs. edn. Miami U., 1948-51; head home econs. edn. Winthrop Coll., 1953-58, chmn. home econs. dept., 1955-58, dir. tchr. edn., 1958-59; chmn. dept. home econs. Bowling Green State U., 1959—. Recipient distinguished alumni award Coll. Home Econs., Purdue U., 1972. Mem. Am. Assn. U. Women, Am. Assn. U. Profs., Am. Home Econs. Assn., Am. Hist. Assn., N.E.A., Am. Vocational Assn., D.A.R., Daus. Am. Colonists, Phi Lambda Theta, Omicron Nu, Kappa Delta Pi, Phi Kappa Phi, Phi Upsilon Omicron. Club: Purdue Sports Women. Home: 882 Scott Blvd Bowling Green OH 43402

HALSTEAD, HARRY MOORE, lawyer; b. Washington, Nov. 9, 1918; s. John Harry and Lucinda (Moore) H.; m. Carmella Ann LaRosa, Sept. 7, 1946; children—William, Lucinda, Christina, Concetta. A.B., Rutgers U., 1941; J.D., Yale U., 1948; LL.M., U. So. Calif., 1953. Bar: Calif. bar 1949. Pvt. practice, Los Angeles, 1949—; sr. ptnr. firm Halstead, Baker & Olson, 1959—; lectr. taxation, estate and trust law. Author several books; contbr. articles to profl. jours. Trustee Linfield Coll., McMinnville, Oreg., 1973-82, S. Pasadena United Methodist Ch. Served to maj. AUS, 1941-46. Mem. Am. Bar Assn. (vice chmn. com. tax and estate planning 1967-77, vice chmn. com. state death taxes 1977-80), State Bar Calif., U. So. Calif. Alumni Assn., Phi Gamma Delta. Clubs: Rutgers So. Calif. (past pres.), Yale of So. Calif. (past pres.), San Marino City, Arcadia Tennis. Home: 1400 Old Mill Rd San Marino CA 91108 Office: 615 S Flower St Los Angeles CA 90017

HALSTED, DONALD M., cement company executive; s. Donald M. and Barbara (Harris) H.; m. Helen Trent Harvey, June 14, 1950; children: Donald M., Amy M. A.B., Princeton U., 1950. With Atlantic Cement Co., Inc. subs. Newmont Mining Corp., Stamford, Conn., 1961-63, asst. v.p. mktg., 1961—, v.p., gen. sales mgr., 1963-65, v.p. mktg., 1966-67, pres., chief exec. officer, dir., 1967-79; press., chief operating officer Lone Star Industries Inc., Greenwich, Conn., 1979-83, vice chmn. spl. project, 1983—; dir. Bancroft Convertible Fund, N.Y.C., Trust Bd., Union Trust Co., Stamford Hydraulic Co., Bridgeport, Conn., subs. Bridgeport Hydraulic Co., 1975. Tower fellow, U. Bridgeport. Served with USAAF, 1945-46; to 2d lt. U.S. Army, 1949-58. Clubs: Landmark (Stamford); Mining (N.Y.C.); Nassau (Princeton, N.J.); Country of New Canaan (Conn.); Aspetuck Hunt and Fish (Easton, Conn.). Office: Lone Star Industries Inc 1 Greenwich Plaza Greenwich CT 06830

HALSTED, JOHN BURT, educator, historian; b. Antwerp, Belgium, Sept. 17, 1926; s. Henry Moore and Katharine (Holmes) H.; m. Betty Nilsen, May 14, 1949; children: Mark Nilsen, Brian Whittemore, Lorna Katharine. B.A., Wesleyan U., Middletown, Conn., 1948, M.A., 1949; Ph.D., Columbia U., 1954; M.A. (hon.), Amherst Coll., 1966. Instr. humanities Stevens Inst. Tech., 1950-52; mem. faculty Amherst Coll., 1952—, prof. history, 1966—. Editor: Romanticism: Problems in Definition, Explanation and Evaluation, 1965, Romanticism: A Collection of Documents, 1969, December 2, 1851, Contemporary Writings on The Coup d'Etat of Louis Napoleon, 1972. Served with USNR, 1944-46. Mem. Am. Hist. Assn., N.E. Victorian Studies Assn., AAUP (pres. Amherst 1967-69), Phi Beta Kappa, Psi Upsilon. Democrat. Episcopalian. Home: 254 Lincoln Ave Amherst MA 01002

HALSTED, JOHN G.H., educator, diplomat consultant; b. Vancouver, B.C., Can., Jan. 27, 1922; s. Frank Henry and Minnie Williams (Horler) Halstead; m. Jean McAllister Gemmill, June 20, 1953; children: Ian, Christopher. B.A., U. B.C., 1943; B.S., London Sch. Econs., 1950. Career dimplomat Dept. External Affairs, Can., 1946-82, asst. then dep. under sec. of state, 1971-75, ambassador to Bonn. W.Ger., 1975-80, ambassador to NATO, Brussels, 1980-82; vis. prof. Inst. for Study of Diplomacy, Georgetown U., Washington, 1983—; dir. DSMA Ltd., Toronto, Can.; mem. editorial bd. NATO's 16 Nations, Brussels, 1983. Served to lt. Royal Can. Navy, 1943-46; Europe. Mem. Atlantic Council Can. (dir.), Internat. Inst. Stretegic Studies, Can. Inst. Internat. Affairs, Can. Inst. Strategic Studies. Home: 187 Billings Ave Ottawa ON Canada K1H 5K8 Office: Inst for Study of Diplomac Georgetown U Washington DC 20057 *What is important is not what happens to a person in this life, but how he deals with it.*

HALSTED, JOHN MAC HARG, management consultant; b. Chgo., May 27, 1905; s. Joseph and Mary (Mac Harg) H.; m. Nancy Leahy, May 2, 1944; children: Joseph, Ellen, Henry, John Matthew; m. Dorothy Moore Benson, Dec. 8, 1962; stepchildren: Richard Benson, Virginia Benson, Lynda Benson, Diane Benson. B.A., U. Mich., 1927. With Colgate-Palmolive Co., 1927-69, dir. purchases, 1958-61, v.p. purchasing, 1961-69, cons., 1969; now mgmt. cons., N.Y.C. Pres. Alpine (N.J.) Bd. Edn., 1952, 53; mem. Alpine Town Council, commr. police, 1954-55. Mem. Oil Trades Assn. N.Y. (pres. 1970). Clubs: N.Y. Yacht, Riverside Yacht. Home: 2758 NE 30th Ave Lighthouse Point FL 33064 Office: Room 1001 310 Madison Ave New York NY 10017

HALSTON (ROY HALSTON FROWICK), fashion designer; b. Apr. 23, 1932. Student, Ind. U., Sch. Chgo. Art Inst. Designer custom millinery, 1958; fashion designer Bergdorf Goodman, N.Y.C., 1959-68; designer boutique Halston Ltd., 1968-76; designer, pres. dress mfg. firm Halston Originals, N.Y.C., 1972-75; pres. design firm Halston Enterprises, Inc., 1975—. Costume designer, Martha Graham ballets, Dance Theatre of Harlem, motion picture and theatre. Recipient Coty award (4), named to Coty Hall of Fame 1974, Martha Graham award (3). Address: 645 Fifth Ave New York NY 10022

HALTINER, GEORGE JOSEPH, educator; b. St. Paul, Nov. 26, 1918; s. Conrad and Elizabeth (Gardner) H.; m. Mary B. Wahl, June 21, 1947; children: Mary Louise, Jeffrey Peter, Kathleen Ann, Jean Marie, Michele Marie. B.S. summa cum laude, Coll. St. Thomas, St. Paul, 1940; Ph.M., U. Wis., 1942, Ph.D., 1948. Asst. prof. Naval Postgrad. Sch., Annapolis, Md., 1946; mem. faculty Navy Postgrad. Sch., Monterey, Calif., 1948—; prof., 1953—, distinguished prof., 1969—, chmn. dept. meteorology and oceanography, 1964-68, dept. meteorology, 1968-81; cons. in field, 1942—. Author: (with F.L. Martin) Dynamical and Physical Meteorology, 1957, Numerical Weather Prediction, 1971, (with R.T. Williams) Numerical Prediction and Dynamic Meteorology, 1980; also numerous articles. Served to lt. USNR, 1942-46; capt. Res. Fellow Am. Meteorol. Soc. (council); mem. Japanese, Royal meteorol. socs. Home: 1134 Alta Mesa Rd Monterey CA 93940

HALTIWANGER, ROBERT SIDNEY, JR., book publishing executive; b. Winston-Salem, N.C., Mar. 15, 1923; s. Robert Sidney and Janie Love (Couch) H. A.B., Harvard U., 1947. Coll. field rep. Prentice-Hall Inc., Atlanta, 1947-56, Southeast regional mgr., 1956-65, dir. Two Year div., Englewood Cliffs, N.J., 1965-71; v.p. sales Prentice-Hall Inc, Englewood Cliffs, N.J., 1971-80, exec. v.p. coll. div., 1980—. Served to 1st lt. USAF, 1943-46; PTO. Mem. Am. Assn. Pubs. (liason com. 1975-82). Democrat. Presbyterian. Home: 1 Horizon Rd Fort Lee NJ 07024 Office: Prentice-Hall Inc Englewood Cliffs NJ 07632

HALTOM, ELBERT BERTRAM, JR., U.S. dist. judge; b. Florence, Ala., Dec. 26, 1922; s. Elbert Bertram and Elva Mae (Simpson) H.; m. Constance Boyd Morris, Aug. 19, 1949; 1 dau., Emily Morris. Student, Florence State U., 1940-42; LL.B., U. Ala., 1948. Bar: Ala. bar 1948. Practiced in, Florence, 1948-80; mem. firm Bradshaw, Barnett & Haltom, 1948-58, Haltom & Patterson, 1959-80; U.S. dist. judge No. Dist. Ala., Birmingham, 1980—; bar commr. 11th Jud. Circuit Ala., 1976-80; Past chmn. Muscle Shoals Mental Health Center. Mem. Ala. Ho. of Reps., 1954-58; mem. Ala. Senate, 1958-62; candidate lt. gov. Ala., 1962; mem. Ala. Democratic Exec. Com., 1966-80. Served with USAAF, 1943-45. Decorated Air medal with four oak leaf clusters. Fellow Internat. Soc. Barristers, Am. Coll. Trial Lawyers; mem. Am., Ala. bar assns., Florence C. of C. (past pres.), Newcomen Soc. N.Am., Am. Legion, V.F.W., Phi Gamma Delta, Phi Delta Phi. Methodist. Office: Federal Courthouse Room 215 Huntsville AL 35801

HALVER, JOHN EMIL, nutritionist; b. Woodinville, Wash., Apr. 21, 1922; s. John Emil and Helen Henrietta (Hansen) H.; m. Jane Loren, July 21, 1944; children: John Emil, Nancy Lee Halver Hadley, Janet Halver Fix, Peter Loren, Deborah Kay. B.S., Wash. State U., 1944, M.S. in Organic Chemistry, 1948; Ph.D. in Med. Biochemistry, U. Wash., 1953. Plant chemist Asso. Frozen Foods, Kent, Wash., 1946-47; asst. chemist Purdue U., 1948-49; instr. U. Wash., Seattle, 1949-50, affiliate prof., 1960-75, prof. Coll. Fisheries, 1975—; dir. Western Fish Nutrition Lab., U.S. Fish and Wildlife Service, Dept. Interior, Cook, Wash., 1950-75, sr. scientist, nutrition, Seattle, 1975-78; cons. FAO, 1974—, S.E. Asia Fishery Devel. Center, Internat. Union Nutrition Scientists, Nat. Fish Research Inst., Hungary; affiliate prof. U. Oreg. Med. Sch., 1965-69; vis. prof. Marine Sci. Inst., U. Tex., Port Arkansas; pres. Fisheries Devel. Technology, Inc., 1980—. Served from pvt. to capt. U.S. Army, World War II; col. USAR. Decorated Purple Heart, Bronze Star; Croix d'Valeur, (France). Fellow Am. Inst. Fishery Research Biologists; mem. AAAS, Nat. Acad. Sci., Am. Sci. Affiliation, Am. Chem. Soc., Am. Fishery Soc., Am. Inst. Nutrition, Phi Lambda Upsilon, Pi Mu Epsilon, Alpha Chi Sigma. Methodist (lay leader). Club: Rotary. Determined vitamin and amino acid requirements for fish; identified aflatoxin B1 as specific carcinogen for rainbow trout hepatoma; identified vitamin C2 for fish. Home: Box 116 Underwood WA 98651 Office: U Wash Sch Fisheries Seattle WA 98195

HALVERSON, GEORGE CLARENCE, business administration educator; b. Greece, N.Y., Apr. 22, 1914; s. Nils and Bertha (Flodquist) H.; m. Thelma Lee Cunningham, Sept. 9, 1949; children: Kristine, John. A.B. in Govt. and Econs, Antioch Coll., Yellow Springs, Ohio, 1938; M.A. in Internat. Adminstrn, Columbia U., 1944; Ph.D. in Labor Econs, London Sch. Econs., 1952. Field examiner NLRB, 1938-41, 48-49; head bus. adminstrn. extension U. Calif., Berkeley, 1952-57, asst. dean, 1955-56; coordinator mgmt. devel. Ampex Corp., Redwood City, Calif., 1957-61; v.p. Hergenrather Assos., San Francisco, 1961-62; mem. faculty San Jose (Calif.) State U., 1962—, prof., 1965—, dean, 1974-81, chmn. manpower adminstrn. dept., 1963-68, asst. to pres., 1970-74. Co-author: Causes of Industrial Peace: Lockheed Aircraft Corp. and the Machinists, 1955; Contbr. articles to profl. jours. Hon. bd. dirs. Better Bus. Bur., San Jose, 1975—; bd. dirs. Industry Edn. Council Calif., 1977—, Center Creative Arts and Scis., 1978—, Applied Human Development, Inc., 1980—, Community Assn. for Retarded, 1982—. Served with USCGR, 1942-46. Fulbright fellow, 1949-51. Mem. Acad. Mgmt. Democrat. Unitarian. Home: 149 N Gordon Way Los Altos CA 94022 Office: San Jose State U San Jose CA 95192

HALVERSON, RICHARD CHRISTIAN, clergyman; b. Pingree, N.D., Feb. 4, 1916; s. Leroy Arthur and Edna Marie (Nielson) H.; m. Doris Seaton, Feb. 6, 1943; children: Richard C., Stephen S., Deborah. Student, Valley City (N.D.) State Tchrs. Coll., 1932-35; B.S., Wheaton Coll., 1939, LL.D. (hon.), 1958; Th.B., Princeton Theol. Sem., 1942; D.D. (hon.), Gordon Coll., 1981. Ordained to ministry United Presbyn. Ch. U.S.A., 1942; mng. dir. Forest Home Christian Conf. Grounds, 1942; asst. minister Linwood Presbyn. Ch., Kansas City, Mo., 1942-44; dir. Forest Home Christian Conf. Grounds, 1944; minister 1st Presbyn. Ch., Coalinga, Calif., 1944-47; minister leadership edn. 1st Presbyn. Ch. of Hollywood (Calif.), 1947-56; minister 4th Presbyn. Ch., Bethesda, Md., 1958-81; chaplain U.S. Senate, Washington, 1981—; asso. Internat. Prayer Breakfast Movement, Washington, 1956—; mem. adv. bd. African Enterprise, Campus Crusade for Christ, Community Bible Study, Inc., Inst. for Successful Ch. Leadership, Internat. Sch. Law, Kings Garden, Orient Crusades Mission, Radio of Free Asia, Today's Hope for Every Youth, Inc., United Presbyn. Center for Mission Studies; mem. nat. adv. bd. Christian Coll. Consortium; pres. Concern Ministries, Inc., Washington; chmn. U.S. bd. World Vision, Inc.; mem. bd. reference Bible Conf. Facilities, Inc., Chaplain of Waikiki Beach, Inc., Christian Coll. So. Africa, Christian Com. of Concern Bible Inst., Far East Broadcasting Co., Inc., Internat. Students, Inc., Latin Am. Mission, Westmont Coll., Yellows Boys Ranch. Author: Be Yourself. . . and God's, 1956, Perspective, 1957, Man to Man, 1961, The Quiet Man, 1963, God's Way out of Futility, 1964, Between Sundays, 1965, Relevance, 1968, A Living Fellowship - a Dynamic Witness, 1972, Manhood with Meaning, 1972, A Day at a time, 1974, Somehow Inside Eternity, 1980. Club: Kenwood Country (Bethesda, Md.). Office: SR-227C Russell Senate Office Bldg Washington DC 20510 *

HALVERSON, WENDELL QUELPRUD, assn. exec., clergyman, educator; b. Austin, Minn., July 11, 1916; s. Arthur Benjamin and Emma Josephine (Pederson) H.; m. Marian Lois Phypers, Aug. 3, 1940; children—Peder Quelprud, Ingrid Maud, Timothy Greenwood. B.A., State U. Iowa, 1940; M.Div., Union Theol. Sem., N.Y.C., 1943; student, Grad. Sch. Theology, Oberlin Coll., 1943-49, U. Oslo (Norway), 1949, U. Chgo., 1950; D.D. (hon.), Lake Forest U., 1956. Ordained to ministry Presbyn. Ch., 1943; pastor in, Clyde, Ohio, 1943-46, La Grange, Ill., 1949-58; asst. prof. philosophy religion Heidelberg Coll., Tiffin, Ohio, 1946-49; Chgo. corr. Christian Century, 1953; lectr. homiletics McCormick Theol. Sem., Chgo., 1957-58; gen. presbyter Presbytery N.Y., United Presbyn. Ch., 1958-61; pres. Buena Vista Coll., Storm Lake, Iowa, 1961-73, Iowa Assn. Ind. Colls. and Univs., Des Moines, 1973-80; exec. dir. Wis. Assn. Ind. Colls. and Univs., Madison, 1980—; mem. Wis. Gov.'s Adv. Council on Edn., 1980, Wis. Adv. Com. on Vocat. and Tech. Adult Edn.; dir. Iowa State Ednl. Radio and TV Broadcast, 1967-69; Sec. ch. extension bd. N.Y. Presbyn. Found., 1958-61; mem. bd. pensions Presbyn. Ch. U.S.A., 1956-58. Pres. Iowans for Better Justice, 1970-73; Chmn. bd. dirs. Iowa Coll. Found., 1972-73; pres. Des Moines chpt. Am.-Scandinavian Found., 1974-75. Clubs: Rotary, Madison, Ygdrasil Lit. (Madison). Home: 4767 Vosen Rd Middleton WI 53562 Office: 1002 Tenny Bldg 110 E Main St Madison WI 53703 *I have not always practiced it but it has been my experience that when I have walked the second mile, I have been fully blessed.*

HALVERSTADT, DONALD BRUCE, urologist, educator; b. Cleve., July 6, 1934; s. Lauren Oscar and Lillian Frances (Jones) H.; m. Margaret Ann Marcy, Aug. 4, 1956; children: Donna, Jeffrey, Amy. B.A. magna cum laude, Princeton U., 1956; M.D. cum laude, Harvard U., 1960. Diplomate: Am. Bd. Urology. Intern, then resident in surgery Mass. Gen. Hosp., Boston, 1960-62, resident in urology, 1964-67; practice medicine specializing in urology, Oklahoma City, 1967—; chief pediatric urology service Okla. Children's Meml. Hosp., Oklahoma City, 1967—, chief staff, 1974-79; clin. prof. urology and pediatrics U. Okla. Med. Sch., 1970—; interim provost U. Okla. for Health Scis., Oklahoma City, 1979-80; spl. asst. to pres. for hosp. affairs Oklahoma U., 1980—; exec. chief staff State of Okla. Teaching Hosps., 1980—, also bd. dirs. Contbr. articles to med. jours. Served with USPHS, 1962-64. Fellow A.C.S.; mem. AMA (Physicians Recognition award 1969, 72, 76, 79, 82), Am. Urol. Assn., Am. Acad. Pediatrics, Soc. Pediatric Urology, Am. Soc. Nephrology, Soc. Univ. Urologists, So. Med. Assn., Okla. Med. Assn., Okla. County Med. Soc. Presbyterian. Home: 2932 Lamp Post Ln Oklahoma City OK 73120 Office: 711 Stanton L Young Blvd Oklahoma City OK 73104

HALZEN, FRANCIS, physics educator; b. Tienen, Belgium, Mar. 23, 1944; came to U.S., 1971; s. Louis H. and Marthe Knap (Halzen); m. Nelly Debrier, Dec. 23, 1968; 1 son, David. Ph.D., U. Louvain, Belgium, 1969. Research fellow Cern U., Geneva, 1969-71; lector U. Louvain, 1971-83; prof. physics U. Wis.-Madison, 1972—. Author: textbook Quarks and Leptons, 1983. Home: 2320 Eton Ridge Madison WI 53705 Office: U Wis Dept Physics 1150 University Ave Madison WI 53706

HAM, JAMES MILTON, science educator; b. Coboconk, Ont., Can., Sept. 21, 1920; s. James Arthur and Harriet Boomer (Gandier) H.; m. Mary Caroline Augustine, June 4, 1955; chidren: Peter Stace, Mary Martha. B.A.Sc., U. Toronto, 1943; S.M., MIT, 1947, Sc.D., 1952; D.ès Sc.A., U. Montreal, 1973; D.Sc., Queen's U., 1974, U. N.B., 1979, McGill U., 1979, McMaster U., 1980; LL.D., U. Man., 1980, Hanyang U., Seoul, Korea, 1981, Concordia Coll., 1983; D.Eng., N.S. Tech. U., 1980, Meml. U., 1981; D.S.L., Wycliffe Coll., U. Toronto, 1983. Lectr., housemaster Ajax div. U. Toronto, 1945-46; research asso. Mass. Inst. Tech., 1949-51, asst. prof. elec. engring., 1951-52; mem. faculty U. Toronto, 1952—, head elec. engring., 1964-66, dean faculty applied sci. and engring., 1966-73, chmn. research bd., 1974-76, dean grad. studies, 1976-78, pres., 1978-83, prof. sci., tech. and pub. policy, 1983—; fellow New Coll., 1962; vis. scientist U. Cambridge (Eng.) and USSR, 1960-61; dir. Shell Can. Ltd.; fellow Brookings Instn., 1983-84. Author: (with G.R. Slemon) Scientific Basis of Electrical Engineering, 1961, Royal Commission on Health and Safety of Workers in Mines, 1976. Bd. govs. Ont. Res. Fedn. Served with Royal Canadian Navy, 1944-45. Decorated officer Order of Can.; recipient Sci. medal Brit. Assn. Advancement Sci., 1943; Centennial medal Can., 1967; Engring. Alumni medal, 1973; Engring. medal Assoc. Profl. Engrs. Ont., 1974; Queen's Jubilee medal, 1978; research fellow electronics MIT, 1950. Fellow Engring. Inst. Con. (Sir John Kennedy medal 1983), IEEE (McNaughton medal o61977); mem. Sigma Xi. Home: 135 Glencairn Ave Toronto ON M4R 1N1 Canada

HAM, JAMES RICHARD, clergyman; b. Chgo., July 11, 1921; s. James William and Loretta (Freely) H. B.Ed., Mundelein Maj. Sem., 1940-43; student, Maryknoll Sem. at N.Y., 1943-48, D.D. (hon.), 1968. Ordained priest Roman Cath. Ch., 1948; Maryknoll pub. relations work, Chgo., St. Louis, Phila. and Mpls., 1948-58, missionary, Guatemala and El Salvador region, 1958-68, ordained aux. Bishop of, 1968, vicar gen., 1968-80; rector Asumption Cathedral, 1967-70; pastor Our Lady of Guadalupe, Guatemala, 1970-80; aux. bishop of, St. Paul and Mpls., 1980—; dir. Prelature of Esquipulas, Nat. Lay Apostolate, Nat. Maj. Sem. Aux. chaplain mil. ordinariate, 1965-68; Guatemala. Club: K.C. Address: 226 Summit Ave Saint Paul MN 55102

HAM, JOE STROTHER, JR., educator; b. Okmulgee, Okla., Mar. 12, i928; s. Joe Strother and Eva Laura (Ludwick) H.; m. Florence Elaine Seeger, Feb. 23, 1952; children—Alice Rachel, Susan Elaine. Ph.B., U. Chgo., 1948, M.S., 1951, Ph.D., 1954. Research chemist E.I. DuPont de Nemours, Deepwater, N.J., 1953-56; mem. faculty. Tex. A. and M. U., College Station, 1956—, prof. physics, 1963—, prof. chemistry, 1967-78; cons. Shell Devel. Co., 1978-79; vis. fellow Mellon Inst., Pitts., 1959; research physicist Ford Motor Co., Dearborn, Mich., 1961-62; vis. scientist TNO Labs., Delft, The Netherlands, 1971, AFML, Wright-Patterson AFB, Ohio, 1980, 81. Contbr. profl. jours. Recipient Standard Oil Ind. Found. award for teaching, 1970-71. Mem. Am. Phys. Soc., Am. Assn. Physics Tchrs., Tex. Acad. Sci. (v.p. 1969-70), Soc. Plastics Engrs., Am. Chem. Soc., Sigma Xi, Sigma Pi Sigma, Phi Kappa Phi. Home: PO Box 3673 Bryan TX 77805 Office: Dept Physics Texas A and M U College Station TX 77841

HAM, LEE EDWARD, civil engr.; b. San Francisco, Dec. 19, 1919; s. Lloyd Burley and Helen Mary (Atkinson) H.; m. Elizabeth Jane Ridgway, Sept. 26, 1942; children—Elizabeth, Peter, Charles, Barbara. B.C.E., U. Calif., Berkeley, 1942. Civil engr. Wilsey & Broughton, S., San Francisco, 1946-52; v.p. Wilsey & Ham, Foster City, Calif., 1952-57, pres., 1957—. Author: The Corporate New Town, 1971. Vice pres. Western region Boy Scouts Am.; chmn. bd. Mills Meml. Hosp. Served with U.S. Army, 1941-46. Decorated Bronze Star. Fellow ASCE, Am. Cons. Engrs. Council; mem. Urban Land Inst., Lambda Alpha. Designer new town of Foster City, 1960. Home: 730 Chiltern Rd Hillsborough CA 94010 Office: 1035 E Hillsdale Blvd Foster City CA 94404

HAM, LESLIE GILMER, beverage company executive; b. Winnipeg, Man, Can., Mar. 3, 1930; s. Arthur Leslie and Frances Irene (Gilmer) H.; m. Anne Corris Dinsmore, June 12, 1954; children: Charles Keith, Susan Lesley, Cynthia Anne. B.A., McGill U., 1951, B.Commerce, 1953; M.B.A., U. Western Ont., 1956. Auditor Peat, Marwick, Mitchell, Montreal, Que., Can., 1953-55; brand mgr. Procter & Gamble Co., Can., Toronto, Ont., 1956-58; exec. v.p. Seven-Up Montreal Ltd., 1958-70; v.p. ops. Pepsi Cola Can. Ltd., Toronto, 1970-74; pres. Societe Internationale de Produits Alimentaires, Paris, 1974-75; exec. v.p. sales Pepsi-Cola Bottling Group, Purchase, N.Y., 1975-78; pres., chief exec. officer Pepsi-Cola Can. Ltd., Toronto, 1978-81; zone v.p. Far East-Can. Pepsico Internat., Toronto, 1981-82; v.p. Europe, Can. Pepsico Bottling Internat, Purchase, N.Y., 1982—. Mem. Inst. Chartered Accountants Que., Theta Delta Chi. Anglican. Clubs: Royal, Montreal Golf, Red Birds Ski (Montreal); Mississauga Golf, Granite (Toronto); St. Georges Golf; Country of Darien (Conn.). Office: Pepsico Bottling Internat Anderson Hill Rd Purchase NY

HAM, NORMAN DOUGLAS, educator, aero. engr.; b. Toronto, Ont., Can., Sept. 30, 1929; came to U.S., 1954, naturalized, 1963; s. Norman Herbert and Eileen Anna H.; m. Margaret Kathryn Appleby, May 23, 1953; children—Marilyn, Kathryn, Joslin. B.A.Sc., U. Toronto, 1951; S.M., M.I.T., 1952, Aero.E., 1957, Sc.D., 1968. Registered profl. engr., Mass. Engr. Avro Aircraft Co., Toronto, 1949-53; sr. engr. Fairey Aviation Co., London, 1953-54; project engr. Doman Helicopter Corp., Danbury, Conn., 1954-56; research engr., project leader M.I.T., Cambridge, 1956-60; project engr. Kaman Aircraft Corp., Bloomfield, Conn., 1960-61; prof. dept. aeros. M.I.T., Cambridge, 1961—; dir. Aerospace Systems Inc.; cons. Recipient Cierva Meml. prize Helicopter Assn. Gt. Britain, 1953; cert. AIAA, 1972; Army Research Office grantee, 1964-74; Naval Air Systems Command grantee, 1969-78; NASA grantee, 1968—. Mem. Assn. Profl. Engrs. Ont., Am. Helicopter Soc., U.S. Men's Curling Assn. Club: Canadian (Boston). Inventor helicopter individual-blade control system. Home: 128 Clinton Rd Brookline MA 02146 Office: Dept Aeronautics and Astronautics MIT Cambridge MA 02146

HAMADY, JACK AMEEN, retail food co. exec.; b. Baakline, Lebanon, May 10, 1909; came to U.S., 1920, naturalized, 1926; s. Albert A. and Yamna (Halabee) H.; m. Lily Richany, Feb. 24, 1935; children—Lloyd K., Grant F., Ronald N., Nawal (Mrs. Albert Alley). Student, Gen. Motors Inst., Internat. Corr. Schs., LaSalle Extension Bus. U. With Hamady Bros., Flint, Mich., 1920—, sr. v.p., sec., 1959-66, pres., chief exec. officer, 1966-69, chmn. bd. dirs., 1969—, chmn. bd. dirs. coordinating council, 1975. Pres. P.T.A. Council, 1949-50; mem. Flint Area Conf., Inc.; Bd. dirs. Jr. Achievement, Urban Coalition of Flint, Urban League of Flint, Mich. United Fund, Nat. Alliance of Businessmen; trustee Flint Inst. Music, Flint Community Players, United Fund Red Feather, Amalgamated Meat Cutters Employer and Employees Pension Fund, Retail Clks. Internat. Assn. Employer and Employees Health and Welfare Fund, Retail Clks. Internat. Assn. Employer and Employees Pension Trust Fund, Salvation Army; chmn. adv. bd. Salvation Army, 1973-75; mem. adv. bd. Coop. Extension Service, Genesee County, Mott Adult Edn.; mem. exec. council Boy Scouts Am. Recipient Americanization of Youth award, 1968, Distinguished Sales Achievement award, 1960, Sales Mgmt. Raymond Bill award, 1960, Hands of Mercy award Salvation Army, 1975; Citizen of Year Flint C. of C., 1979. Mem. Asso. Food Dealers Mich. (dir.), Sales and Mktg. Exec. Club Flint (past pres.), Super Market Inst., Mich. C. of C. (dir.), U.S. C. of C., Econ. Club Detroit. Clubs: Mason (Shriner), Elk, Rotarian (dist. gov. 1972-73), Birch Creek Hunt (Carran, Mich.); Flint City; Warwick Hills Golf and Country (Grand Blanc, Mich.). Home: 1009 Woodlawn Park Dr Flint MI 48503 Office: 3301 S Dort Hwy Flint MI 48501

HAMALAINEN, PEKKA KALEVI, historian, educator; b. Finland, Dec. 28, 1938; s. Olavi Simeon and Aili Aliisa (Laiho) H.; m. Patricia Beth Dunlap; 1965; children: Kim Ilkka, Leija-Lee Louise Aili, Timothy Pekka Olavi, Kai Kalevi Edward. A.B., Ind. U., 1961, Ph.D., 1966. Acting asst. prof. history U. Calif., Santa Barbara, 1965-66, asst. prof. history, 1966-70; assoc. prof. history U. Wis., Madison, 1970-76, prof., 1976—, chmn. Western European area studies program, 1977—; mem. nat. screening com. Scandinavian area Inst. Internat. Edn., Fulbright Hays Program. Author: Kielitaistelu Suomessa 1917-1939, 1968, Nationalitetskampen och sprakstriden i Finland 1917-1939, 1969, In Time of Storm: Revolution, Civil War and the Ethnolinguistic Issue in Finland, 1978, Luokka ja Kieli Vallankumouksen Suomessa, 1978; contbr. articles to profl. publs. and jours. Served to lt. Finnish Navy, 1957-58. Faculty research grantee U. Calif., 1966-69; faculty summer fellow, 1969; Ford Found. grantee, 1967; faculty research grantee U. Wis., Madison, 1970—; Am. Philos. Soc. research grantee, 1973; Am. Council Learned Socs. fellow, 1976; research grantee, 1978. Mem. Am. Hist. Assn., Soc. Advancement Scandinavian Study (adv. com. exec. council), AAUP, Fin. Hist. Assn. (corr. mem.), Ind. U. Alumni Assn. Office: Dept History U Wis Madison WI 53706

HAMALL, THOMAS KENNY, assn. exec.; b. Evanston, Ill., July 21, 1932; s. Thomas Eugene and Margaret Katherine (Kenny) H.; m. Barbara Ann O'Brien, Nov. 23, 1957; children—Mary, Eileen, Annette, Rosemary, Claire, Kenneth. Student, U. Miami, 1950-53, Columbia U., 1957-59. Edn. dir. Am. Cancer Soc., Miami, Fla., 1953-56, program coordinator med. affairs, N.Y.C., 1956-59, exec. dir., Omaha, 1959-61, Elizabeth, N.J., 1962-64; dir. pub. relations fund raising N.J. Assn. Mental Health, 1963-64; dir. devel. Preventive Medicine Inst. Strang Clinic, N.Y.C., 1964-67; dir. devel. and pub. affairs N.J. Coll. Medicine and Dentistry, Newark, 1967-70; corporate dir. civic affairs Borden, Inc., Columbus, Ohio, 1970-74; pres. Borden Found., 1970-74; fellow in met. governance and fin., dir. communications design center Acad. for Contemporary Problems, Columbus, 1974-75; exec. v.p. Atlanta C. of C., 1975—; pub. Atlanta mag., 1975-78; mem. adv. bd. Bus. Atlanta mag.; dir. Nat. Minority Supplier Devel. Council; lectr. in field. Mem. adv. bd. Corp. Policy Center, Grad. Sch. Bus., Emory U.; bd. dirs. Lenbrook Found.; mem. adv. bd. Internat. Bus. Inst., Grad. Sch. Bus., Atlanta U. Served with USNR, 1950-53. Fellow George Internat. Bus. Inst.; mem. Am. C. of C. Execs. (dir., past chmn. met. council), Nat. Assn. Fund Raisers, Ga. Indsl. Developers Assn. (pres., dir.), Ga. C. of C. Execs. (dir.), So. Assn. C. of C. Execs., Atlanta Regional Commn. Roman Catholic. Home: 2939 Ridge Valley Rd NW Atlanta GA 30327 Office: 1300 North-Omni Internat Atlanta GA 30303

HAMANN, DONALD ROBERT, physicist; b. Valley Stream, N.Y., May 16, 1939; s. Leonard Charles and Elsie Sophie (Hopfmuller) H.; m. Ruth Deborah Halpert, Feb. 27, 1966; 1 dau., Hillary Beth. B.S., M.I.T., 1961, Ph.D., 1965. Mem. tech. staff Bell Labs., Murray Hill, N.J., 1965-78, head dept. theoretical physics research, 1918-81, head dept. surface physics research, 1981—. Fellow Am. Phys. Soc. (Davisson-Germer prize 1979). Research, numerous publ. in theoretical solid-state physics. Home: 34 Valley View Ave Summit NJ 07901 Office: Bell Labs 600 Mountain Ave Murray Hill NJ 07974

HAMARNEH, SAMI KHALAF, historian of medicine and sci., author; b. Madaba, Jordan, Feb. 2, 1925; came to U.S., 1952, naturalized, 1957; s. Khalaf and and Nura A. (Zumut) H.; m. Nazha T. Ajaj, July 4, 1948; 1 son, Faris. B.Sc. in Pharmacy, Syrian U., Damascus, 1948; M.Sc. in Pharm. Chemistry, N.D. State U., Fargo, 1956; Ph.D. in History of Pharmacy and Medicine, U. Wis., 1959. Curator charge div. med. scis. Mus. History and Tech., U.S. Nat. Mus., Smithsonian Instn., Washington, 1959-72, historian dept. sci. and tech., 1972-77, curator emeritus, 1977—; med. historian King Fahd Med. Research Ctr., Jeddah, Saudi Arabia, 1982—; vis. asso. prof. George Washington U., 1963-64; vis. prof. history of sci. U. Pa., Phila., 1969; vis. prof. U. Aleppo, Syria, 1977-79; spl. research med. scis. and edn. in medieval Islam. Author: Bibliography of Medicine and Pharmacy in Medieval Islam, 1964, Index of Arabic Manuscripts on Medicine and Pharmacy at the National Library of Cairo, 1967, Index of Manuscripts on Medicine and Pharmacy in the Zahiriyah Library, 1969, Temples of the Muses and a History of Pharmacy Museums, 1972, Pharmacy Museums USA, 1972, Origins of Pharmacy and Therapy in the Near East, 1973, The Physician, Therapist and Surgeon Ibn al-Quff, 1974, Catalogue of Arabic Manuscripts on Medicine and Pharmacy at Brit. Library, 1975, Directory of Historians of Arabic-Islamic Science, 1980, also articles; editor: Jour. History Arabic Sci, 1976—. Recipient Star of Jordan medal, 1965; E. Kremers award for distinguished pharmaco-hist. writings, 1966. Mem. Inst. History Arabic Sci. (founding mem. 1976), Am. Inst. History Pharmacy, Arab Soc. for History Pharmacy (Cairo) (founding mem. 1976), Arab Acad. (corr. mem.), Islamic Civilization Inst. (corr. mem.). Home: 4631 Massachusetts Ave NW Washington DC 20016 Office: Smithsonian Instn NMAH Room 5119 Washington DC 20560

HAMBERG, DANIEL, economist, educator; b. Phila., Apr. 25, 1924; s. Isidor and Sophia (Kravitz) H.; m. Sylvia Gertrude Kaplan, July 1, 1949; 1 son, Kenneth. B.S. in Econs, U. Pa., 1945, M.A., 1947, Ph.D., 1952. Instr. econs. U. Del., 1946-47, 48-52, Princeton, 1947-48; from asst. prof. to prof. econs. U. Md., 1952-61; prof. econs. State U. N.Y. at Buffalo, 1961—, chmn. dept., 1966—; cons. sec. labor, 1962-64. Author: Business Cycles, 1951, Economic Growth and Instability, 1956, Principles of a Growing Economy, 1961, Essays in the Economics of Research and Development, 1966, Models of Economic Growth, 1971, The U.S. Monetary System, 1981. Ford faculty research fellow, 1962-63; Fulbright prof., 1956-57, 65-66. Fellow Royal Econ. Soc.; mem. Am. Econ. Assn., Pi Gamma Mu, Phi Kappa Phi. Home: 77 Wickham Dr Williamsville NY 14221 Office: John Lord O'Brien Hall State U of NY at Buffalo North Campus Buffalo NY 14260

HAMBIDGE, DOUGLAS WALTER, archbishop; b. London, Mar. 6, 1927; emigrated to Can., 1956; s. Douglas and Florence (Driscoll) H.; m. Denise Colvill Lown, June 9, 1956; children—Caryl Denise, Stephen Douglas, Graham Andrew. A.L.C.D., London U., 1953, B.D., 1958, D.D., 1969. Ordained deacon Church of England, 1953, priest, 1954, consecrated bishop, 1969; asst. curate St. Mark's Ch., Dalston, London, 1953-55, priest-in-charge, 1955-56; incumbent All Saints Ch., Cassiar, B.C., Can., 1956-58; rector St. James Parish, Smithers, B.C., 1958-64, North Peace Parish, Ft. St. John, B.C., 1964-69; canon St. Andrew's Cathedral, 1965; lord bishop of, Caledonia, 1969-80, New Westminster, B.C., 1980-81, lord archbishop of, New Westminster and metropolitan of B.C., 1981—. Office: 302-814 Richards St Vancouver BC Canada V6B 3AY

HAMBLEN, JAMES ERNEST, pharm. co. exec.; b. Big Stone Gap, Va., July 30, 1934; s. Ray Campbell and Elizabeth Crenshaw (Huff) H.; m. Judith Ann Edwards, May 25, 1968; 1 dau., Tara Elizabeth. B.A., Washington and Lee U., 1956; M.S., U. Tenn., 1960. Financial analyst Burlington Industries, Greensboro, N.C., 1956-57; treas. SmithKline Corp., Phila., 1960—. Served with AUS, 1957-59. Mem. Delta Upsilon. Republican. Presbyn. Home: 904 Longview Rd King of Prussia PA 19406 Office: 1500 Spring Garden St Philadelphia PA 19101

HAMBLEN, JOHN WESLEY, computer scientist; b. Story, Ind., Sept. 25, 1924; s. James William and Mary Etta (Morrison) H.; m. Brenda F. Harrod, Mar. 1, 1947 (div. 1979); 1 son, James. A.B., Ind. U., 1947; M.S., Purdue U., 1952; Ph.D., 1955. Tchr. math and sci. Kingsbury (Ind.) High Sch., 1946-48, Bluffton (Ind.) High Sch., 1948-51; asst. prof. math. Okla. State U., Stillwater, 1955-57; cons. in statis. methods for research staff Agrl. Expt. Sta., 1955-56, asso. prof. math., 1957-58; dir. Computing Center, 1957-58; asso. prof. stats., dir. Computing Center, U. Ky., Lexington, 1958-61; prof. math and technology Southern Ill. U., Carbondale, 1961-65; dir. Data Processing and Computing Center, 1961-65; project dir. computer scis. So. Regional Edn. Bd., Atlanta, 1965-72; prof. U. Mo., Rolla, 1972—, chmn. dept. computer sci., 1972-81; mem. tech. adv. com. Creative Application of Tech. to Edn., Tex. A. and M. U., 1966-68; mem. tech. adv. panel Western Interstate Commn. for Higher Edn., 1969-70; vis. scientist Ctr. for Applied Math. Nat. Bur. Standards, 1981-83; program chmn. World Conf. Computers in Edn., 1985; cons. FTC, 1978—, NSF, 1975-76. Editor: Ednl. Data Processing Newsletter, 1964-65; asso. editor: Jour. Ednl. Data Processing, 1965-67; editor: Jour. Assn. Ednl. Data Systems, 1967-68; asso. editor, 1968—; contbr. articles to profl. jours. Purdue Research Found. fellow, 1954-55; NSF grantee, 1966-81. Fellow AAAS; mem. Assn. Computing Machinery (sec. 1972-76, chmn. curriculum com. computer sci. 1976-80, gen. chmn. 1981 Computer Scis. Conf. 1979-81, chmn. Disting. Ser. Award com. 1980-81), IEEE Computer Soc., Inst. Math Stats., Data Processing Mgmt. Assn., Assn. Ednl. Data Systems (chmn. conv. adv. com. 1977-80, pres. 1968-69, sec. 1976-77, dir. 1965-70, 76-79), Am. Fedn. Info. Processing Socs. (dir. 1981—, chmn. edn. com. 1971-72, 79—), Soc. Indsl. and Applied Math, Am. Statis. Assn., Math. Assn. Am., Sigma Xi, Pi Mu Epsilon, Theta Chi, Upsilon Pi Epsilon, Alpha Chi Sigma. Club: Rotary. Home: Route 4 Box 436 Rolla MO 65401 Office: Dept Computer Science Univ Mo Rolla MO 65401 *It is difficult to improve upon the popular version of the "Golden Rule" for a succinct guide in life. A clear conscience and a good insurance program contribute greatly to a good night's sleep. With moderation in food and drink plus a good night's rest we should be able to handle most anything that comes our way.*

HAMBLET, NEWMAN, retail chain executive; b. Winchester, Mass., Aug. 20, 1914; s. Abel Martin and Marcia Leavit (Coburn) H.; m. Mae Catheryn Moynahan, Jan. 17, 1942; children: Barbara, Carolyn, Janice, Kenneth, Doreen, Shirley. B.A., Dartmouth Coll., 1935. With Macy's, N.Y.C., 1935-48, Bloomingdales, 1948-50; asst. gen. mgr. Lord & Taylor, N.Y.C., 1950-54; v.p. ops., then sr. v.p. ops. Thalhimer Bros., Inc., Richmond, Va., 1954-72, exec. v.p., 1972-82, also dir.; pres. NMH Assocs., Inc., 1982—; dir. Dominion Nat. Bank, both Richmond. Campaign chmn. Richmond United Way, 1962; bd. dirs. Met. Econ. Devel. Council, Richmond Eye Hosp., Central Richmond Assn., Downtown Devel. Commn.; past bd. dirs. Richmond chpt. ARC, Richmond Planning Commn.; mem. bd. visitors Mary Washington Coll., Fredericksburg, Va., vice rector. Served to lt. comdr. USNR, 1942-45. Recipient Good Govt. award Richmond First Club, 1979; named Outstanding Retailer of Year Richmond Retail Mchts. Assn., 1973. Mem. Nat., Richmond retail mchts. assns., Va. C. of C., Met. Richmond C. of C. (chmn. bd. 1976-77). Republican. Presbyn. Clubs: Hermitage Country, Kiwanis (past pres.), Commonwealth (Richmond); East Lake Woodlands Gulf and Racquet (Palm Harbor, Fla.); Bull and Bear (Richmond); Duck Woods Golf (Kitty Hawk, N.C.). Home: 11807 Sussex Sq Dr Richmond VA 23233 Office: 601 E Broad St Richmond VA 23219

HAMBLETON, BERT H., company executive; b. Cleve., Jan. 6, 1925; s. Bert H. and Beatrice (Richards) H.; m. Elizabeth Faught, June 11, 1946; children: Candace, Kenneth, Bert, James, Stephan. B.A., Ohio State U., 1949. Journalist Columbus Ohio Citizen, 1946-49; with Kroger Co., 1949-59, dir. merchandising, Shreveport, 1949-59; with Jewel Foods, Chgo., 1959-71, v.p. grocery ops., 1965-70; pres. Associated Grocers, Seattle, 1971—; dir. Union Bank, Tacoma, Mayne Nickless, Seattle. Bd. dirs. Corp. Council-Arts, Seattle, Seattle Symphony. Served with U.S. Army, 1943-46. Office: Associated Grocers Inc 3301 S Norfolk Seattle WA 98124

HAMBLETON, CHALKLEY JAY, retired banker; b. Chgo., June 22, 1912; s. Chalkley Jay and Elizabeth (McMurray) H.; m. Betty Moore Davis, Feb. 16, 1952; children—Chalkley Jay, Douglas McMurray. Student, Princeton, 1930-33; A.B., U. Chgo., 1934. With Harris Trust & Savs. Bank, Chgo., 1935-77, v.p., 1960-65, sr. v.p., 1965-71, sec., 1962-71, head trust dept., 1963-71, pres., 1971-76, vice chmn. bd., 1976-77, ret., 1977. Trustee Orchestral Assn. Chgo., 1963—, treas., 1967-72; trustee Berkshire Sch., Sheffield, Mass., 1968-72, Old Peoples Home, City of Chgo., 1955—; alternate mem. trustees com. Chgo. Community Trust, 1963-77; bd. dirs. Assn. House Chgo., 1936-66, pres., 1949; bd. dirs. Welfare Council Met. Chgo., 1954-66, treas., 1961-66; governing mem. Glenwood Sch. for Boys, 1966-77; trustee Latin Sch., Chgo., 1961-70, pres., 1967-70; bd. dirs. Mid-Am. chpt., A.R.C., 1972—; trustee Newberry Library, 1974—, chmn., 1979-82. Served to lt. comdr. USNR, 1942-46. Mem. Am. Bankers Assn. (exec. com. trust div. 1969-72, v.p., pres. trust div. 1973-74), Ill. Bankers Assn. (pres. trust div. 1968-69), Corp. Fiduciaries Assn. Ill. (pres. 1967-68, exec. com. 1963-72), Shedd Aquarium Soc. (treas. 1966-77). Clubs: Commercial, University, Casino, Commonwealth (treas., dir. 1971-77), Tavern (Chgo.)). Home: 70 E Cedar St Chicago IL 60611 Office: 115 S La Salle St Chicago IL 60603

HAMBLETON, THOMAS EDWARD, theatrical producer; b. Towson, Md., Feb. 12, 1911; s. Thomas Edward and Adelaide (McAlpin) H.; m. Caroline L. Hoysradt, 1936 (dec. 1947); children—Anne Crawford (dec.), Caroline Lucinda, Susan Sherwood; m. Merrell Hopkins, Feb. 1949; children—Thomas Edward, Mary, Mark. Student, St. Paul's Sch., Concord, N.H.; B.A., Yale, 1934. Producer: plays Once Upon A Mattress; mng. dir., Phoenix Theatre, N.Y.C., 1953—; where prodns. include Chemin de Fer; also numerous works by Shakespeare, Shaw, Gilbert and Sullivan, O'Neill, Chekov A Memory of Two Mondays, 1975-76, Ladyhouse Blues, Canadian Gothic/American Modern, Marco Polo, A Sorrow Beyond Dreams, G.R. Point, Scribes, 1976-77, Hot Grog, Uncommon Women and Others, Elusive Angel, One Crack Out, City Sugar, 1977-78, Getting Out, Later, Says I, Says He, Big and Little, Chinchilla, 1978-79, Winter Dancers, Shout Across the River, The Trouble With Europe, Save Grand Central, Second Ave. Rag, 1979-80, Bonjour La, Bonjour, Beyond Therapy, The Captivity of Pixie Shedman, Meetings, Isn't It Romantic, 1980-81; v.p., Theatre, Inc.; mng. dir., Phoenix, 1953-81; v.p., dir., Center Stage Balt. Pres. bd. dirs. Hampden-Booth Theatre Collection and Library; dir. Farrar, Straus & Giroux, Peale Mus., Balt. Served as lt. comdr. USNR, World War II. Mem. ASCAP (popular awards panel), League N.Y. Theatres (gov.), First Am. Congress of Theatre (pres.). Home: Timonium MD Office: 1540 Broadway New York NY 10036

HAMBRAEUS, BENGT, composer, educator; b. Stockholm, Sweden, Jan. 29, 1928; emigrated to Can., 1972; m. Enid Odenaes, Mar. 21, 1960; children: Michael, Elisabeth. M.A., Uppsala U., 1950, Ph.D., 1956. Librarian, amanuens Inst. of Musicology, Uppsala, 1948-56; program producer, head chamber music, head music prodn. Swedish Broadcasting Corp., Stockholm, 1957-72; prof. theory and composition McGill U., Montreal, Que., Can., 1972—, mem. senate, 1976-80; lectr. in field. Composer: Constellations I-V, 1958-83, Rota, 1962-63, Transfiguration, 1962-63, Rencontres, 1968-70; for organ and orch. Continuo, 1975; broadcast opera Sagan, 1979; Livre d'orgue, 1980-81; also numerous works for tape, choir, orch. and organ. Mem. Royal Swedish Music Acad., Swedish Composers Soc., Swedish Composers Performance Right Bur., Can. League Composers, Can. Coll. Organists. Office: Faculty of Music McGill University 555 Sherbrooke St W Montreal PQ H3A 1E3 Canada *Research and any creative work may need an ivory tower. But if there are no windows, or doors, or an emergency exit from such a tower, we may forget why we are here, as human beings, to share our achievements with other beings and help those who need help of any kind.*

HAMBRECHT, WILLIAM R., venture capitalist; b. 1935; married; 5 children. Student, Princton U. Broker Francis I. DuPont & Co., San Francisco; mng. ptnr. Hambrecht & Quist, San Francisco; dir. People Express, Inc. Office: Hambrecht & Quist 235 Montgomery St San Francisco CA 94104 *

HAMBRICK, GEORGE WALTER, JR., physician, educator; b. Charlottesville, Va., Dec. 4, 1922; s. George W. and Sallie Anna (McCallum) H. B.S., Concord Coll., 1944; M.D., U. Va., 1946. Intern State U. Iowa, 1946-47; asst. resident dermatology U. Va. Hosp., 1947-48; resident Columbia-Presbyn. Hosp., N.Y.C., 1950-51; fellow dermatology Duke Hosp., Durham, N.C., 1951-52, asso. dermatology, 1953; instr. Columbia, 1953-55, asso., 1955-57, asst. prof., 1957-62; asso. prof. U. Pa., 1962-66, Johns Hopkins Med. Sch., 1966-69, prof., 1969-76, dir. dermatology, 1967-76; prof. U. Cin., 1976-81, dir. dermatology, 1976-81; prof. Cornell U. Coll. Medicine, 1981—; chief dermatology N.Y. Hosp., 1981—. Served as capt., M.C. AUS, 1948-50. Fellow A.C.P.; mem. Soc. Investigative Dermatology (pres. 1971-72), Dermatology Found. (trustee, pres. 1974), Assn. Profs. of Dermatology, Am. Dermatol. Assn., AMA (del. 1981), Am. Acad. Dermatology (dir. 1978), Alpha Omega Alpha. Home: 1161 York Ave Apt 9-E New York NY 10021

HAMBRICK, JACKSON REID, lawyer, educator; b. Griffin, Ga., Nov. 14, 1917; s. Andrew Jackson and Susan Irene (Westmoreland) H.; m. Lucille Warden Rhudy, Sept. 6, 1941; children: Irene Frazier Olson, Kenton Warden. A.B., Wofford Coll., 1938; LL.B., Duke U., 1942. Bar: N.Y. 1943, D.C. 1958. Practiced law, N.Y.C., 1942-47; atty. Dept. Treasury, IRS, Washington, 1947-57; asso. prof. law George Washington U., Washington, 1957-61, prof., 1961-82; vis. prof. law Duke U., 1965; cons. on fed. taxation. Editor-in-chief: Duke U. Law Rev.; contbr. articles to law revs. Mem. ABA, D.C. Bar, Order of Coif. Democrat. Methodist. Home: 6022 Oakdale Rd McLean VA 22101

HAMBURG, BEATRIX ANN, medical educator and researcher; b. Jacksonville, Fla., Oct. 19, 1923; d. Francis Minor and Beatrix (Downs) McCleary; m., May 25, 1951; children: Eric N., Margaret A. A.B., Vassar Coll., 1944; M.D., Yale U., 1948. Diplomate: Nat. Bd. Med. Examiners. Intern Grace-New Haven Hosp., 1948-49; resident Yale Psychiat. Inst., New Haven, 1949-50; resident in pediatrics Children's Hosp., Cin., 1950-51; resident in psychiatry Inst. Juvenile Research, 1951-53; research assoc. Stanford U. Med. Sch. (Calif.), 1961-71, assoc. prof. psychiatry, 1976-80; assoc. prof. Harvard Med. Sch., Boston, 1980-83; exec. dir. Div. Health Policy Research, 1981-83; prof. psychiatry and pediatrics Mt. Sinai Hosp., N.Y.C., 1983—; assoc. dir. Lab. of Stress and Conflict, Stanford U. Med. Sch., 1974-76; sr. research psychiatrist NIMH, Bethesda, Md., 1978-80; dir. studies Pres.'s Commn. Mental Health, 1977-78; mem. vis. com. Sch. Pub. Health, Harvard U., 1977-80. Author: Behavioral and Psychosocial Issues in Diabetes, 1980; contbr. numerous sci. articles to profl. jours. Trustee W.T. Grant Found., 1978—; bd. dirs. New World Found., 1978-83; mem. Pub. Health Council State of N.Y., 1978-80. Vis. scholar Ctr. Advanced Study Behavioral Scis., 1967-68; recipient Outstanding Achievement award Alcohol, Drug Abuse and Mental Health Adminstrn., 1980. Fellow Am. Acad. Child Psychiatry; mem. Inst. Medicine of Nat. Acad. Scis., Soc. Profs. Child Psychiatry (program com. 1972-74), Am. Acad. Child Psychiatry (adolescent com. 1977-81), Soc. Adolesent Medicine, Am. Pub. Health Assn. (adolesent com. 1978-80), Soc. Study of Social Biology, Acad. Research in Behavioral Medicine (exec. council 1980), Phi Beta Kappa. Office: Mount Sinai Med Ctr One Gustave L Levy Pl New York NY 10029

HAMBURG, DAVID A., psychiatrist, foundation executive; b. Evansville, Ind., 1925. M.D., Ind. U., 1947, D.Sc. (hon.), 1976, Rush U., 1977. Diplomate: in Psychiatry, Am. Bd. Psychiatry and Neurology. Intern Michael Reese Hosp., Chgo., 1947-48, resident in psychiatry, 1949-50; asst. resident in psychiatry Yale U.-New Haven Hosp., 1948-49; practice medicine, specializing in psychiatry, 1950—; staff psychiatrist Brooke Army Hosp., 1950-52; research psychiatrist Army Med. Service Grad. Sch., 1952-53; asso. dir. Psychosomatic and Psychiat. Inst., Michael Reese Hosp., Chgo., 1953-56; fellow Center for Advanced Study in Behavioral Scis., Palo Alto, Calif., 1957-58, 67-68; chief Adult Psychiat. br. NIMH, Bethesda, Md., 1958-61; asst. in pathology Ind. U., 1946-47; asst. in psychiatry Yale U., 1948-49; prof., exec. head dept. psychiatry Stanford U. Med. Sch., 1961-72, Reed-Hodgson prof. human biology, 1972-76; Sherman Fairchild Distinguished scholar Calif. Inst. Tech., 1974-75; pres. Inst. Medicine Nat. Acad. Scis., Washington, 1975-80; dir. div. health policy research and edn. Harvard U., Cambridge, Mass., 1980-82, John D. Mac Arthur prof. health policy and mgnt. John F. Kennedy Sch. Govt., 1980-82; pres. Carnegie Corp., N.Y.C., 1983—; sr. adviser Center Social Policy Studies, Israel. Bd. dirs. Rockefeller U., Mt. Sinai Hosp., N.Y.C. Served as capt. M.C. AUS, 1950-53. Recipient numerous awards including; Pres.'s medal Michael Reese Med. Center, 1974; A.C.P. award, 1977; Mass. Inst. Tech. Bicentennial medal, 1977. Mem. Am. Psychiat. Assn. (Vestermark award 1977), Am. Psychosomatic Soc.,

Assn. Research Nervous and Mental Disease (pres. 1967-68), Internat. Soc. Research on Aggression (pres. 1976-78), Internat. Soc. Research in Psycho-neuroendocrinology, Psychiat. Research Soc. (chmn. 1965-66, 67-68), Am. Acad. Arts and Scis., AAAS (pres. elect), Phi Beta Kappa, Alpha Omega Alpha. Address: Carnegie Corp 437 Madison Ave New York NY 10002

HAMBURG, JOSEPH, physician, educator; b. Phila., Sept. 9, 1922; s. Thomas and Gertrude (Shulitzky) H.; m. Minerva Glickman, July 10, 1949; children: Jay, Marianne, Bonnie. Student, Temple U., 1938-42; M.D., Hahnemann Med. Coll., 1951, Sc.D., 1979. Diplomate: Am. Bd. Family Practice. Intern Stamford (Conn.) Hosp., 1951-52; pvt. practice medicine, Stamford, 1952-63; asst. prof. Coll. Medicine U. Ky., Lexington, 1963-66; dean Coll. Allied Health Professions, 1966—, prof. medicine, community medicine and allied health edn., 1971—; cons. in field. Pres. Ky. Peer Rev. Orgn., 1980. Gen. editor: Review of Allied Health Educations, Vols. 1-4, 1972-81. Served with U.S. Army, 1942-46. Mem. Am. Soc. Allied Health Professions (pres. 1972), AMA, Inst. Medicine, Ky. Med. Assn., Am. Acad. Family Practice, Ky. Acad. Family Practice. Home: 720 Kirkland Dr Lexington KY 40502 Office: U Ky Lexington KY 40506

HAMBURG, MARIAN VIRGINIA, educator; b. St. Louis, Oct. 20, 1918; s. Oliver John and Hazel (Klein) Miller; m. Morris Hamburg, Dec. 27, 1955; children: Jean, Jacalyn. Student, U. Wis., 1936-37; B.Sc., U. Mo., 1940; M.A., N.Y. U., 1945; Ed.D., Columbia U., 1955. Dir. health edn. YWCA, Chgo., 1946-48; health edn. coordinator Stephen F. Austin State U., Nacogdoches, Tex., 1948-49; sch. health cons. Nassau County Tb and Public Health Assn., Garden City, N.Y., 1949-51; asst. dir. pub. edn. Nat. Found., N.Y.C., 1951-54; sch. health cons. Am. Heart Assn., N.Y.C., 1954-64; mem. faculty N.Y. U., 1964—, asso. prof. edn., 1966-69, prof., 1969—, dir. health edn., 1967-73, chmn. dept. health edn., 1974—; dir. Alcohol Studies Project, 1975-79; dir. Nat. Inst. Sex Edn. in Elem. Sch., 1968-72; mem. White House Conf. Food, Nutrition, and Health, 1969; mem. com. sch. health and health careers Am. Heart Assn., 1964-66; mem. com. community programs Nat. Council YMCA, 1968; mem. task force sch. health edn. study Nat. Health Council, 1965-68; del. Nat. Interagency Council on Smoking and Health, 1967; dir. Sex. Info. and Edn. Council U.S. Author: (with Morris Hamburg) Health and Social Problems in Schools: Case Studies for School Personnel, 1968; mem. editorial bd.: Jour. Sch. Health, 1980—. Recipient award Mortar Bd., 1940, Women's Centennial Honor award U. Mo., 1968, Distinguished Service award N.Y. State Assn. Health, Phys. Edn., Recreation, 1970, U. Mo. Alumni award, 1978; Disting. Service award Assn. for Advancement Health Edn., 1981. Mem. Am. Sch. Health Assn. (Disting. Service award 1969), Am. Pub. Health Assn. (governing council 1979—), Soc. Pub. Health Edn., Am. Coll. Health Assn. (assoc. editor Jour. 1979—, v.p. 1983—), Internat. Union Health Edn. (pres. N.Am. region 1979—), Pi Lambda Theta (award 1940). Home: 933 Lincoln Ave Baldwin NY 11510 Office: New York U Sch Edn Health Nursing Arts Professions New York NY 10003

HAMBURGER, PHILIP (PAUL), writer; b. Wheeling, W. Va., July 2, 1914; s. Harry and Janet (Kraft) H.; m. Edith Iglauer, Dec. 24, 1942 (div. 1966); children: Jay Philip, Richard Shaw; m. Anna Walling Matson, Oct. 27, 1968. B.A., Johns Hopkins U., 1935; M.S., Grad. Sch. Journalism, Columbia, 1938. Mem. staff New Yorker mag., 1939—, writer Profiles, Talk of the Town, Reporter-at-Large articles, Notes for a Gazetteer, Letters from Fgn. Places, Casuals,, music critic, 1948-49, TV critic, 1949-55; on leave from New Yorker as writer, Office of Facts and Figures and O.W.I., 1941-43; Past mem. adv. bd. George Foster Peabody Radio and Television Awards; bd. dirs. Authors League Fund.; Condr. non-fiction workshop Ind. U. Writers' Conf., 1969, 75. Author (for govt.): Divide and Conquer; author: The Unconquered People, Tale of a City; Author: The Oblong Blur and Other Odysseys, 1949, J.P. Marquand, Esquire, 1952, Mayor Watching and Other Pleasures, 1958, Our Man Stanley, 1963, An American Notebook, 1965. Recipient 50th Anniversary Honors medal Grad. Sch. Journalism, Columbia, 1963. Mem. Authors League Am., Authors Guild (council), P.E.N. Clubs: Nat. Press (Washington); Century Assn., Coffee House (N.Y.C.). Home: 151 E 80th St New York NY 10021 also Wellfleet MA 02667 Office: care The New Yorker 25 W 43d St New York NY 10036

HAMBURGER, RICHARD JAMES, physician, educator; b. Phila., Feb. 2, 1937; s. W. Charles and Margaretha Gertrude (Schwab) H.; m. Mary Jane Murphy, Jan. 25, 1964; children: Ellen, Joan, Mary Lou, Richard, Maureen, James. B.S., Villanova U., 1958; M.D., Jefferson Med. Coll., 1962. Diplomate: Am. Bd. Internal Medicine. Intern Jefferson Med. Coll., Phila., 1962-63, resident in medicine, 1963-65, fellow in nephrology, 1965-66; practice medicine specializing in nephrology, Indpls., 1968—; mem. staff Ind. U. Hosp., Wishard Mem. Hosp., VA Hosp.; asst. prof. Ind. U. Med. Sch., 1968-72, asso. prof., 1972-77, prof., 1977—. Contbr. articles to profl. jours. Trustee Kidney Found. Ind., 1970-74, mem. med. adv. bd., 1969—. Served with AUS, 1966-68. Fellow A.C.P.; mem. Ind. Soc. Internal Medicine (trustee 1975-77), North Central Dialysis and Transplant Soc. (dir. 1972-75, 78-81), Am. Soc. Nephrology, Internat. Soc. Nephrology, Am. Soc. Artificial Internal Organs, Am. Fedn. Clin. Research, Nat. Kidney Found., Am. Soc. Internal Medicine, Renal Physicians Assn. (dir. 1977-84). Roman Catholic. Clubs: Indpls. Racquet, Meridian Hills Country. Home: 1215 Chessington Rd Indianapolis IN 46260 Office: 1120 South Dr FH108 Indianapolis IN 46223

HAMBURGER, STEPHEN CHARLES, medical educator; b. Atlantic City, Jan. 18, 1946; s. Jacob Robert and Freda (Lindenheim) H.; m. Linda Ireme Casper, June 9, 1968; children: Jfay Viktor, Melissa Sue. B.A., U. Conn., 1968; M.D., U. Conn.-Farmington, 1972. Diplomate: Am. Bd. Internal Medicine, sub-bd. endocrinology and metabolism. Intern Pa. Hosp., Phila., 1972-73; resident Med. Coll. Pa., 1973-77; asst. prof. medicine U. Mo. Sch. Medicine, Kansas City, 1977-80, assoc. prof., 1980-82, Edward Hasinger prof. medicine, 1983—, chmn. dept. medicine, 1982—; med. dir. Truman Med. Center, Kansas City, 1978-80; project dir. Western Mo. Area Health Edn. Center, U. Mo., Kansas City, 1980-82; acad. program dir. Consortium for Health Edn., 1982—. Author: Endocrine-Metabolic Emergencies, 1983; editor: Critical Care Quar., 1980, Topics in Internal Medicine, 1983. Bd. dirs. Mid Am. health Systems Agy., Kansas City, 1980-82. Fellow ACP; mem. Am. Soc. Internal Medicine (named young internist of yr. 1983, named young internist of yr. Mo. soc. 1982), Am. Endocrine Soc., Am. Diabetes Assn., Am. Assn. of Diabetes Edn. (bd. dirs. 1980-83, treas. 1982-83), Phi Beta Kappa, Phi Kappa Phi. Jewish. Home: 4409 W 93d St Prairie Village KS 66207 Office: U Mo-Kansas City Dept Medicine 2411 Holmes St Kansas City MO 64108

HAMBY, A. GARTH, beverage company executive; b. Oneota, Ala., 1938. B.A. in Journalism, U. Ala., 1959. Reporter Columbus Ledger News, 1959-61; various positions Ga. Power Co., 1961-67; staff rep. pub. reins. dept. Coca-Cola Co., Atlanta, 1967-70, mgr. editorial group pub. reins. dept., 1970-74, asst. to chmn. bd., 1974-78, v.p., sec., dir., corp. external affairs, 1978-79, sr. v.p., sec., dir. corp. external affairs, 1979-80, exec. v.p., sec., 1980-81, exec. v.p., Atlanta, 1981—. Office: Coca Cola Co 310 North Ave NW PO Drawer 1734 Atlanta GA 30301

HAMBY, ALONZO LEE, historian, educator; b. Humansville, Mo., Jan. 13, 1940; s. David Alonzo and Lila Lolita (Summers) H.; m. Joyce Ann Litton, June 6, 1967. Student, S.W. Mo. State Coll., 1956-57; B.A., S.E. Mo. State Coll., 1960; M.A., Columbia U., 1961; Ph.D. (Wilson fellow), U. Mo., 1965. Asst. prof. history Ohio U., Athens, 1965-69, asso. prof., 1969-75, prof., 1975—, chmn. dept. history, 1980-83; Orgn. Am. Historians rep. Joint Com. on Archives and Historians, 1975-78. Author: Beyond the New Deal: Harry S. Truman and American Liberalism (David D. Lloyd prize Truman Inst., Publ. award Ohio Acad. History, 1st book award Phi Alpha Theta 1973), The Imperial Years: The United States since 1939, 1976; editor: The New Deal: Analysis and Interpretation, 2d edit., 1980, Harry S. Truman and the Fair Deal, 1974, Access to the Papers of Recent Public Figures, 1977; contbr. articles and revs. to profl. jours. Woodrow Wilson fellow, 1960-61; NDEA fellow, 1962-64; John C. Baker fellow, 1969; NEH fellow, 1972-73; Evans Research fellow Harry S. Truman Inst., 1973-74; Harry S. Truman Inst. Research grantee, 1964, 66, 67, 69, 76; Ohio U. Research grantee, 1967, 76. Mem. Am. Hist. Assn. (nominating com. 1980-83), So. Hist. Assn. (membership com. 1982—), Orgn. Am. Historians, Soc. Historians of Am. Fgn. Relations, Ohio Acad. History (chmn. publ. award com. 1976-77). Home: 64 Eden Pl Athens OH 45701 Office: Dept History Ohio U Athens OH 45701

HAMEKA, HENDRIK FREDERIK, chemist, educator; b. Rotterdam, Holland, May 25, 1931; came to U.S., 1960, naturalized, 1963; s. Dirk C. and Johanna (Mannebeck) H.; m. Charlotte C. Procacci, Aug. 23, 1972. Drs., U. Leiden, Netherlands, 1953, D.Sc., 1956; M.A. (hon.), U. Pa., 1971. Research asso. U. Rome, Italy, 1956-57; fellow Carnegie Inst. Tech., 1957-58; research physicist N. V. Philips Lamps, Eindhoven, Netherlands, 1958-60; asst. prof. chemistry Johns Hopkins, 1960-62; asso. prof. chemistry U. Pa., 1962-67, prof. chemistry, 1967—. Mem. editorial bd.: Chem. Physics Letters; Author: Advanced Quantum Chemistry, 1965, Introductory Quantum Theory, 1967, Physical Chemistry, 1977; Contbr. numerous articles to sci. jours. Recipient Alexander von Humboldt prize, 1981; Alfred P. Sloan Research fellow, 1963—. Mem. Am. Phys. Soc. Research on theory of molecular structure and optical and magnetic properties of molecules; calculations of spin-orbit and spin-spin coupling; theory of resonance optical rotation, magneto-optical rotation and multiple-photon processes. Home: 1503 Argyle Rd Berwyn PA 19312 Office: Dept Chemistry U Pa Philadelphia PA 19104

HAMEL, DANA BERTRAND, educational administrator; b. Rumford, Maine, Aug. 9,1923; s. Donat H. and Louise (Kenison) H.; m. Shirley Elmeree Smith Knavel, Dec. 19, 1945; children—Dana Randolph, Michelle, April. A.B., Ashland (Ohio) Coll., 1951; M.A., Ohio State U., 1952; Ed.D., U Cin., 1962. Watchmaker Thomas J. Apryle & Sons, Johnstown, Pa., 1946; owner Hamels, Jewelers, Conemaugh, Pa., 1946-48; mem. mgmt. dept. Gen. Motors Inst., Flint, Mich., 1955-57; dean adminstrv. affairs Ohio Coll. Applied Sci. and Ohio Mechanics Inst., Cin., 1957-63, exec. v.p., dean of faculties, 1962-63; dir. Roanoke Tech. Inst., 1963-64, Va. Dept. Tech. Edn., Richmond, 1964-66; chancellor Va. Community Coll. System, Richmond, 1966—, cons., 1979-80; cons. to pres., dir. spl. acad. programs Va. State U., Petersburg, 1980—. Trustee, v.p. Southeastern Univs. Research Assn., Inc., 1981—; mem. Va. Adv. Council Vocat. Edn.; Bd. dirs. Richmond Eye Hosp., Center of Excellence, Inc., Richmond Community High Sch., 1981—. Served with USAAF, 1942-45. Mem. So. Assn. Schs. and Colls. (former pres.), Am. Assn. Jr. Colls. (commn. on legis.), Nat. Council State Dirs., Am. Soc. Engring. Edn., Am. Psychology and Guidance Assn., Nat. Assn. for Gifted Children, Am. Coll. Personnel Assn., Cin. Guidance and Personnel Assn., Phi Delta Kappa, Psi Chi, Iota Lambda Sigma. Clubs: Mason., Kiwanian. Home: 300 Coalport Rd Richmond VA 23229 Office: Va State U Box C Petersburg VA 23803

HAMEL, EDWARD EVERETT, transport co. exec.; b. St. Paul, Mar. 17, 1919; s. Edward Joseph and Pauline Marguerite (Lange) H.; m. Mary Jane Semotink, June 21, 1947; children—Edward, Mark, Nancy. Student, U. Minn., 1945-47. ICC practitioner lic., 1957. Traffic mgr. Dakota Transfer & Storage Co., Mpls., 1945-55; with Internat. Transport Inc., Rochester, Minn., 1955—, exec. v.p., 1972-76, pres., chief exec. officer, 1976—. Served with U.S. Army, 1941-45. Decorated Bronze Service Star, U.S.; Croix de Guerre with palm, France). Mem. Am. Trucking Assn., Nat. Assn. Specialized Carriers (past chmn. rate com.; pres.), Machinery Haulers Assn. (past chmn. rate com.). Office: 2450 Marion Rd SE Rochester MN 55901

HAMEL, JEAN-MARC, Canadian government official; b. Lotbinière, Que., Can., Feb. 19, 1925; s. Lorenzo and Hermine (Leclerc) H.; m. Jacqueline Lapointe, July 11, 1953; children—Pierre, Denis. B.Com., Laval U., 1948, M.Com., 1949; M.P.A., Syracuse (N.Y.) U., 1956. Asst. chief selection risks dept. Indsl. Life Ins. Co., 1949-50; with Canadian Civil Service Commn., 1950-64; dir. adminstrn. House of Commons, 1964-65, asst. to undersec. state, 1965-66, chief electoral officer Can., 1966—; sec. Can.-France Interparliamentary Assn., 1965-66; Mem. Collège d'Enseignement Général et Professionnel, Hull, Que., 1967-72, v.p., 1971; pres. Lyceé Claudel, 1972-77. Bd. govs. Hôpital Montfort, Ottawa, 1971—. Decorated chevalier Legion of Honor; recipient medal of merit French Nat. Assembly, 1965; Can. Centennial medal, 1967; Queen's Silver Jubilee medal, 1977. Mem. Assn. des Anciens de l'Université Laval (past pres. Ottawa chpt.), Inst. Pub. Adminstrn. Can., Canadian Polit. Sci. Assn., Pub. Personnel Assn. (past pres. Ottawa chpt.). Roman Catholic. Clubs: Le Cercle Universitaire (Ottawa) (pres. 1982-83); Richelieu (Hull) (pres. 1970). Home: 2376 Wyndale Crescent Ottawa ON K1H 7A6 Canada Office: 440 Coventry Rd Ottawa ON K1A 0M6 Canada

HAMEL, RODOLPHE, drug company executive; b. Lewiston, Maine, June 3, 1929; s. Rodolphe and Alvina Melanie (Bilodeau) H.; m. Marilyn Vivian Johnsen, June 10, 1957; children—Matthew Edward, Anne Melanie. B.A., Yale U., 1950; LL.B., Harvard U., 1953. Bar: Maine bar, D.C. bar 1953, N.Y. bar 1957. Assoc. firm Shearman & Sterling, N.Y.C., 1956-66; internat. counsel Bristol Myers Co., N.Y.C., 1966-72, 73, counsel internat. div., 1974-81, assoc. gen. counsel co., 1978—; v.p. Bristol-Myers Co., 1983—; v.p., sec., gen. counsel Macmillan Inc., N.Y.C., 1972-73. Served to 1st lt. AUS, 1953-56. Mem. Am., N.Y.C. bar assns. Clubs: Board Room, Yale (N.Y.C.). Home: 14 Coldstream Ln Upper Saddle River NJ 07458 Office: 345 Park Ave New York NY 10022

HAMELBERG, WILLIAM, physician, educator; b.; b. Chillicothe, Ohio, Dec. 13, 1925; s. William and Dora (Rosenberg) H.; m. Mary Louise Miller, Oct. 1, 1948; children—Lynne Louise, William Robert, Kim Scot, Mark Alan, Carol Leslie, Lisa Krista. Student, Ohio State U., 1943-44; B.S., Denison U., 1946; M.D., Ohio State U., 1948. Diplomate: Am. Bd. Anesthesiology. Intern U.S. Naval Hosp., Oakland, Calif., 1949-50; resident Ohio State U. Hosp., 1950-52; asst. instr. Ohio State U., 1950-51, instr., 1951-53; asst. prof., 1953-58; prof., chmn. dept. anesthesiology Med. Coll. S.C., 1958-59; prof., dir. div. anesthesia Ohio State U., 1959-68, prof., chmn. dept. anesthesiology, 1968-78, prof. emeritus, 1979—; dir. critical care St. Anthony's Hosp., Columbus, Ohio, 1978—. Served with USNR, 1943-45. Fellow Am. Coll. Anesthesiology; mem. A.M.A., Am. Soc. Anesthesiologists, Internat. Anesthesia Research Soc., Ohio Soc. Anesthesiologists, Columbus Acad. Medicine, Columbus Soc. Anesthesiologists, Am. Coll. Anesthesiologists, Ohio State Med. Assn., Assn. U. Anesthestists, Phi Chi. Home: 3077 Brandon Rd Columbus OH 43221

HAMELIN, LOUIS-EDMOND, educator; b. St. Didace, Que., Can., Mar. 21, 1923; s. Antonio and Maria (Desy) H.; m. Colette Lafay, Aug. 11, 1951; children: Philippe, Anne-Marie. B.A., U. Montreal, 1945; M.A. In Econs, U. Laval, 1948; Ph.D. in Geography, U. Grenoble (France), 1951; Doct. Lit., U. Paris, 1975; Sc.D. (hon.), McGill U., Montreal, 1976, U.D., Ottawa U., 1981. Prof., head dept. geography Laval U., 1955-62, prof., 1961—; dir. Centre d'Etudes Nordiques, 1962-72, dir. research, 1972; vis. prof. U. Montreal, 1961-64, U. Toulouse (France), 1968-69, U. Ottawa, 1970, U. Abidjan, 1975; prin. Université Trois-Rivières, 1978-83. Author: Glossary of Periglacial Phenomena, 1967, Canada (French), 1969, (English), 1973, Nordicity (French), 1975, (English, 1979). Mem. legis. assembly N.W. Territories, Yellowknife, 1971-75. Decorated Order Can., 1974; recipient Gov. Gen. Can. award, 1975, Molson prize, 1982. Fellow Royal Soc. Can.; mem. Que. Geog. Soc. (pres. 1952-54), Royal Canadian Geog. Soc., Hudson's Bay Record Soc., Assn. Canadian Geographers (pres. 1972). Home: 1244 Albert Lozeau Sillery PQ Canada G1T 1H4 Office: Univ Trois-Rivières Trois-Rivières PQ G9A 5H7 Canada

HAMELIN, MARCEL, educator; b. Saint-Narcisse, Que., Can., Sept. 18, 1937; m. Judy Purcell, Aug. 18, 1962; children—Danielle, Christine, Marc. Doctorat es Lettres, Universite Laval, Can. Faculty U. Ottawa, Ont., Can., prof. history, 1966—, chmn. dept. history, 1968-70, vice dean sch. grad. studies, 1972-74, dean faculty of arts, 1974—. Author: History of the Province of Quebec. Mem. Canadian Hist. Assn., Assn. Canadienne-francaise pour l'avancement des Scis. (pres. 1976-77), Royal Soc. Can. Home: 33 Woodlawn Ave Ottawa ON K1S 1S8 Canada Office: 165 Waller St Ottawa ON K1N 6N5 Canada

HAMERMESH, BERNARD, educator; b. Bklyn., Dec. 25, 1919; s. Isidore and Rose (Kornhauser) H.; m. Sylvia Molberger, Sept. 6, 1941; children—Judith Gay (Mrs. Arthur Springer), Richard George, Kenneth Scott. B.S., Coll. City N.Y., 1940; M.S., N.Y.U., 1942, Ph.D., 1944. Tutor physics Coll. City N.Y., 1940-41; grad. asst. N.Y.U., 1941-43, instr., 1943-46; sr. physicist Argonne (Ill.) Nat. Lab., 1948-59; sr. sci. adviser Phys. Research Center, TRW Systems, Redondo Beach, Calif., 1959-68; prof. physics, chmn. dept. Cleve. State U., 1968—; lectr. U. Ill. at Chgo., 1956-57, U. Calif. at Los Angeles, 1964. Mem. Sch. Bd. Sch. Dist. 163, Rich Twp.-Cook County, Ill., 1949-51; sch. trustee Rich Twp., 1951-57. NRC postdoctoral fellow Calif. Inst. Tech., 1946-48. Fellow Am. Phys. Soc.; mem. A.A.A.S., Fedn. Am. Scientists, Sigma Xi, Phi Beta Kappa. Research in cosmic ray neutrons, capture gamma rays, 7.7 meter bent crystal gamma ray spectrometer, micrometeoroid accelerator, high spin states from capture by nuclear isomers. Home: 18675 Parkland Dr Shaker Heights OH 44122

HAMERMESH, DANIEL SELIM, economist, educator; b. Cambridge, Mass., Oct. 20, 1943; s. Morton and Madeline (Goldberg) H.; m. Frances Witty, Dec. 18, 1966; children: David J., Matthew A. A.B., U. Chgo., 1965; Ph.D., Yale U., 1969. Asst. prof. econs. Princeton U., 1969-73; assoc. prof. econs. Mich. State U., East Lansing, 1973-76, prof., 1976—; dir. Office of Research, U.S. Dept. Labor, Washington, 1974-75; vis. prof. Harvard U., 1981; research assoc. Nat. Bur. Econ. Research, 1979—; mem. research adv. bd. Nat. Commn. on Unemployment Compensation, 1978-80. Author: Jobless Pay and The Economy, 1977; contbr. articles to profl. jours. Ford Found. dissertation fellow, 1967-68; NSF grantee, 1980-82; Dept. Labor grantee, 1971-74, 76-80. Mem. Am. Econ. Assn., Indsl. Relations Research Assn. Jewish. Office: Dept Econs Mich State U East Lansing MI 48824

HAMERMESH, MORTON, physicist, educator; b. N.Y.C., Dec. 27, 1915; s. Isador J. and Rose (Kornhauser) H.; m. Madeline Goldberg, 1941; children—Daniel S., Deborah R., Lawrence A. B.S., Coll. City N.Y., 1936; Ph.D., N.Y.U., 1940. Instr. physics Coll. City N.Y., 1941, Stanford, 1941-43; research asso. Radio Research Lab., Harvard, 1943-46; asst. prof. physics N.Y.U., 1946-47, asso. prof., 1947-48; sr. physicist Argonne Nat. Lab., 1948-50, asso. dir. physics div., 1950-59, dir. physics div., 1959-63, assoc. lab. dir. basic research, 1963-65; prof. U. Minn., Mpls., 1965-69, 70—; head Sch. Physics and Astronomy, 1965-69, 70-76; prof. physics, chmn. dept. physics State U. N.Y., Stony Brook, 1969-70. Translator: Classical Theory of Fields (by Landau and Lifshitz), 1951; Author: Group Theory, 1962; numerous papers in field. Fellow Am. Phys. Soc.; mem. Research Soc. Am. Office: Univ Minn Minneapolis MN 55455

HAMEROW, THEODORE STEPHEN, history educator; b. Warsaw, Poland, Aug. 24, 1920; came to U.S., 1930, naturalized, 1929; s. Haim Schneyer and Bella (Rubinlicht) H.; m. Margarete Lotter, Aug. 16, 1954; children—Judith Margarete, Helena Francisca. B.A., Coll. City N.Y., 1942; M.A., Columbia, 1947; Ph.D., Yale, 1951. Instr. Wellesley Coll., 1950-51, U. Md., 1951-52; instr., asst. prof., then asso. prof. U. Ill, 1952-58; mem. faculty U. Wis., 1958—, prof. history, 1961—, G. P. Gooch prof. history, 1978—, chmn. dept. history, 1973-76; cons. editor Dorsey Press, 1961-71. Author: Restoration, Revolution, Reaction, 1958, Otto von Bismarck: A Historical Assessment, 1962, The Social Foundations of German Unification 1858-1871, 2 vols, 1969-72, The Birth of a New Europe: State and Society in the Nineteenth Century, 1983; co-author: History of the World, 1960, A History of the Western World, 1969; Editor: Otto von Bismarck, Reflections and Reminiscences, 1968, The Age of Bismarck, 1973; editorial bd.: Jour. Modern History, 1967-70, Central European History, 1968-72, Revs. in European History, 1974-78. Served with inf. AUS, 1943-46. Mem. Am. Hist. Assn., Conf. Group Central European History (sec.-treas. 1960-62, chmn. 1976). Home: 466 S Segoe Rd Madison WI 53711

HAMES, CLIFFORD MOFFETT, banker; b. Atlanta, Jan. 17, 1926; s. William Cline and Gladys Falls (Moffett) H.; m. Ann Whitley, Dec. 7, 1946; children: Susan A. Hames Furner, Laurence C. B.A., Emory U., 1946; LL.B., Atlanta Law Sch., 1949; postgrad., Rutgers U. Grad. Sch. Banking, 1957. With mgmt. program Trust Co. of Ga., Atlanta, 1946-52; with Sun Bank N.A. of Orlando, (Fla.), 1952—; formerly trust officer, then sr. v.p. and trust officer, vice chmn. Sun First Nat. Bank of Orlando, 1975—; also dir.; sr. v.p. Sun Banks of Fla., Inc., 1979—; dir. Hubbard Constrn. Co., Hughes Supply, Inc.; Bd. suprs., treas. Reedy Creek Improvement Dist., 1975—. Bd. dirs., treas. Orlando Area C. of C., 1975-78; trustee, v.p. Winter Park Meml. Hosp. (Fla.), 1976—; trustee Winter Park Library, 1979—. Mem. Am. Bankers Assn., Fla. Bankers Assn. (past chmn. trust div.). Presbyterian. Clubs: Rotary, Univ., Country (Orlando); Citrus. Home: 780 Williams Dr Winter Park FL 32789 Office: 200 S Orange Ave Orlando FL 32801

HAMES, JERROLD FREDERICK, editor, journalist; b. Windsor, Ont., Can., Feb. 9, 1940; s. Frederick Thomas and Alfreda Mae (Cushman) H.; m. Vivian Patricia March, July 19, 1975. B.A., U. Windsor, 1964. Reporter Windsor Star, 1962-65, London (Ont.) Free Press, 1965-67; press and info. officer Anglican Ch. Can., Toronto, 1967-69; news editor ch. publn. Canadian Churchman, 1969-75, editor, 1975—. Mem. Religious Newswriters Assn. (asso.), Asso. Ch. Press.

Club: Toronto Press. Home: 17 Douville Ct Toronto ON M5A 4E7 Canada Office: 600 Jarvis St Toronto ON M4Y 2J6 Canada

HAMFF, LEONARD HARVEY, physician; b. West Blocton, Ala., Nov. 22, 1913; s. Christian F. and Meri (Harvey) H.; m. Elizabeth Anne Babington, Dec. 22, 1936; children—Mary Anne Mc Clemens, Catherine Willis. A.B., Emory U., 1932, M.D., 1938. Intern Univ. Hosp., Ann Arbor, Mich., 1938-39, asst. resident, 1939-40, resident in internal medicine, 1940-41, instr., 1941-42; practice medicine specializing in internal medicine, Atlanta, 1942—; dir. diabetic service Grady Meml. Hosp., 1945-68; clin. prof. medicine Emory U. Sch. Medicine, 1965. Fellow A.C.P., Am. Coll. Chest Physicians; mem. Ga. Diabetes Assn., Diabetes Assn. Atlanta, Am. Heart Assn., So. Med. Assn., Fulton County Med. Soc., Atlanta Clin. Soc. Methodist. Clubs: Capital City, Piedmount Driving. Office: 478 Peachtree St NE Atlanta GA 30308

HAMILL, DOROTHY STUART, profl. ice skater; b. Chgo.; d. Chalmers C. and Carolyn C. (Clough) H. Student, Colo. Acad., Greenwich High Sch. Profl. skater: Ice Capades, 1977—. Olympic Gold medalist, 1976; world figure skating champion, 1976. Address: care Ice Capades 6121 Santa Monica Blvd Hollywood CA 90038

HAMILL, JOHN P., bank executive; b. N.Y.C., 1940; married. A.B., Holy Cross Coll., 1961; Master's Degree in Taxation, NYU Sch. Law, 1964. Bar: N.Y., Ohio. Dep. gen. counsel legal dept. Chem. Bank N.Y.; pres., chief exec. officer Galbreath Mortgage Co.; pres., chief exec. officer trust affiliate, pres. mortgage banking affiliate Banc One Corp., Columbus, Ohio, prior to 1980; exec/ v.p., gen. counsel Shawmut Corp., Boston, 1980-81, pres., 1981—, Shawmut; dir. Shawmut Bank of Boston N.Am., 1981—. Office: Shawmut Corp 1 Federal St Boston MA 02211

HAMILL, MARK, actor; b. Oakland, Calif., Sept. 25, 1951; m. Marilou York, 1978; 1 son, Nathan Elias. Student, Los Angeles City Coll. Performed at, Renaissance Faire, Agoura, Calif., 3 seasons; appeared: TV series including Gen. Hosp., Tex. Wheelers, 1975, The F.B.I, Owen Marshall, Partridge Family; played: in TV movies Eric, 5, Sarah T. - Portrait of a Teen-Age Alcoholic, 1975, Delancey Street, 1975, The Crisis Within, 1975, Mallory: Circumstantial Evidence, 1976, The City, 1977; appeared: motion pictures Star Wars, 1977, Corvette Summer, 1978, The Big Red One, 1979, The Empire Strikes Back, 1980, Night the Lights Went Out in Georgia, 1981, Return of the Jedi, 1983; Broadway debut in: Elephant Man. Address: care Lucas Films Ltd PO Box 2009 San Rafael CA 94912 *

HAMILL, PETE (WILLIAM PETE HAMILL), journalist, author; b. Bklyn., June 24, 1935; s. William and Anne (Devlin) H.; m. Ramona Negron, Feb. 3, 1962 (div. 1970); children—Adriene, Deirdre. Student, Pratt Inst., 1952, Mexico City (Mexico) Coll., 1956-57. Comml. artist, 1957-60; reporter N.Y. Post, later columnist, 1960-74; columnist N.Y. Daily News, 1965-67, 69-79; contbg. editor Saturday Evening Post, 1963-64; contbr. Village Voice, N.Y.C., 1974—. Author: novels A Killing for Christ, 1968, The Gift, 1973, Flesh and Blood, 1977; non-fiction Irrational Ravings, 1972, The Invisible City: A New York Sketchbook, 1980; screenplays Doc, 1971, Badge 373, 1973; Contbr. articles to numerous mags. Served with USNR, 1952-54. Recipient Meyer Berger award Columbia Sch. Journalism, 1962, award Newspaper Reporters Assn., 1962. Mem. Writers Guild Am., Authors' Guild, Soc. Mag. Writers. Democrat. Office: care Random House Inc 201E 50th St New York NY 10022 *

HAMILTON, ALBERT CHARLES, educator; b. Winnipeg, Man., Can., July 20, 1921; s. George Ford and Mary (Briggs) H.; m. Mary E. McFarlane, July 2, 1950; children—Ian, Malcolm, Peter, Ross. B.A. with honors, U. Man., 1945; M.A., U. Toronto, 1948; Ph.D., U. Cambridge, Eng., 1953. Supr. English Cambridge (Eng.) U., 1950-52; prof. English U. Wash., 1952-68, Queen's U., Kingston, Ont., Can., 1968—; vis. fellow St. John's Coll., Cambridge, 1974-75; vis. prof. U. Toronto, 1961-62, Harvard U., 1969. Author: Structure of Allegory in Spenser's Faerie Queene, 1961, The Early Shakespeare, 1967, Sir Philip Sidney: a Study of his Life and Works, 1977; editor: Selected Poetry of Spenser, 1966, Spenser's Faerie Queene, 1977; sr. editor: The Spenser Ency. Huntington Library fellow, 1959-60. Fellow Royal Soc. Can.; mem. MLA, Renaissance Soc. Am., Assn. Can. U. Tchrs. of English, Spenser Soc. Am., Internat. Assn. U. Profs. Office: Dept English Queen's U Kingston ON K7L 3N6 Canada

HAMILTON, ALLAN CORNING, retired oil company executive; b. Chgo., June 9, 1921; s. Daniel Sprague and Mildred (Corning) H.; m. Edith Johnson, June 3, 1950; children: Kimball C., Scott W., Dean C., Gail W. B.S. in Econs., Harverford Coll., 1943. With Standar Oil Co., N.J., 1946-51, Esso Export Corp., 1951-56; treas. Internat. Petroleum co. Ltd., Coral Gables, Fla., 1956-61, Esso Internat. Inc., 1961-66; with Exxon Corp. (formerly Standard Oil Co., N.J.), N.Y.C., 1966-83; treas., prin. fin. officer Exxon Corp. (formerly Standard Oil co., N.J.), N.Y.C., 1970-85. Mem. vis. com. Grad. Sch. bus. U. Chgo.; mem. council Inst. Adminstrn. and Mgmt. Union Coll. Served to lt. USNR, 1943-46. Clubs: Woodway Country (Darien, Conn.); Explorers.

HAMILTON, ANTHONY R., electronics company executive; b. North Bergen, 1924. Mgr. purchasing dept. Lear Inc., 1947-56; mgr. Daystrom Pacific, 1956-57; salesman Hamilton Electronics Co., 1957-62; with Avnet Inc., N.Y.C., 1962—, sr. v.p., 1966-68, exec. v.p. electronic mktg. div., 1968-76, exec. v.p., vice chmn., dir., 1976-80, chmn. bd., chief exec. officer, dir., 1980—. Office: Avnet Inc 767 Fifth Ave New York NY 10153 *

HAMILTON, CALVIN SARGENT, city official; b. Lakeland, Fla., Dec. 12, 1924; s. Calvin Ralph and Francelia (Sargent) H.; m. Glenda Chapelle, Aug. 24, 1975; children: John, Hallam, Charles. B.A. in Landscape Architecture, U. Ill., 1949; M.City Planning, Harvard U., 1952; research fellow, U. Coll., U. London, 1953. Planning cons. Project East River, Dept. Def., Cambridge, Mass., 1952, Harland Bartholomew & Assos., St. Louis, 1953-55; exec. dir. Met. Planning Dept., Indpls., 1955-60, Pitts. Planning Dept., 1960-64; plan cons., Sao Paulo, Brazil, 1968; planning dir. Los Angeles City Planning Dept., 1964—; past mem. faculty Ind. U., U. Pitts., UCLA, U. So. Calif. Author papers, city plans. Founder Historic Landmarks Found., Indpls., 1959; co-founder Pitts. History and Landmarks Found., 1962; exec. com. Bldg. Research Adv. Bd., Nat. Acad. Scis., 1971-80; trustee Hubbard Trust, Boston, 1973—; bd. dirs. Los Angeles Conservancy, 1980, Ctr. for Mcpl. Planning, N.Y.C.; Vice pres., mem. gen. bd. Nat. Council Chs., 1963-70. Served with USAAF, 1942-46. Recipient Bronze tablet U. Ill., 1949, 1st Honor award for Los Angeles Planning Assn. Am. Planning Assn., 1983; Rotary Internat. Found. fellow, 1952; grantee W. German Govt., 1971. Fellow Am. Soc. Landscape Architects (Bradford Williams medal 1973), Am. Geog. Soc.; mem. Am. Inst. Cert. Planners, AIA (hon. asso. So. Calif. chpt.), Nat. Inst. Bldg. Scis. (exec. com. cons. council), Am. Shore and Beach Preservation Assn., Phi Kappa Phi, Chi Gamma Iota, Lambda Alpha, Chi Phi. Democrat. Presbyterian. Office: 200 N Spring St Los Angeles CA 90012 *I have always tried to reach for the highest professional goal even though it didn't seem possible at the time. I have often taken unpopular positions because I thought that they were right or at least in accordance with my own sense of justice or propriety.*

HAMILTON, CARL HULET, college administrator; b. Morris, Okla., Sept. 30, 1934; s. Alva Hulet and Olah Ethel (Pryor) H.; m. Gloria Joyce Gore, Sept. 3, 1954; children: Ray, Carla Jo, Deanna Jean. Th.B., Southwestern U., 1956; B.A., Oklahoma City U., 1957; M.A., U. Tulsa, 1962; Ph.D., U. Ark., 1968. Instr. English, Southwestern Coll., 1956-60; publs. mgr., editor Abundant Life Mag., Oral Roberts Evangelistic Assn., 1960-62; asst. prof. Oral Roberts U., Tulsa, 1966-77, asso. prof., 1977—, asst. dean acad. affairs, then acad. dean, until 1975, provost, v.p. acad. affairs, 1975—. Bd. dirs. Indian Nations Council Boy Scouts Am., Tulsa Met. YMCA. Mem. North Central Assn. Colls. and Schs., MLA, Am. Bar Assn., Am. Council Edn., Am. Assn. Presidents of Ind. Colls. and Univs., Phi Delta Kappa. Methodist. Clubs: So. Hills Country, Tulsa. Home: 2660 E 75th St Tulsa OK 74136 Office: 7777 S Lewis St Tulsa OK 74171

HAMILTON, CHARLES HENRY, newspaper consultant; b. Webster Springs, W.Va., Nov. 16, 1903; s. Alfred Patton and Cora Jane (Benedum) H.; m. Viola Belle Morrisette, Nov. 3, 1928 (dec. 1963); children: John Alfred, Barbara Morrisette (Mrs. Charles Fraley), Bette (Mrs. Lacey Jacobs, Jr.), Viola Lee; m. Muriel Marable Butler, 1964. Grad., Greenbrier Mil. Sch., 1923; A.B., Washington and Lee U., 1926. Reporter Clarksburg Exponent, 1925; sports writer Richmond News Leader, 1926-32, sports editor, 1932-36, city editor, 1936-51, mng. editor, 1951-69, asst. to pres., 1969-74; cons., 1974—; radio announcer, news commentator sta. WRVA, Richmond, 1927-34; pres. Dixie Profl. Football League, 1935-36; news commentator sta. WRNL, 1939-42; lectr. Am. Press Inst., Columbia, 1946-51; chmn. Va. Associated Press Newspapers, 1956-57; Dir. Fed. Home Loan Bank of Greensboro, 1963, chmn. bd., 1970. Author: Peter Francisco—Soldier Extraordinary; Contbr.: fiction, articles nat. mags., including Sat. Evening Post, Reader's Digest. Chmn. Va. adv. legislative com. unit to rewrite Va. hunting and fishing laws, 1962. Lt. col. AGC U.S. Army Res., 1949-54. Mem. Am. Soc. Newspaper Editors, Va. Press Assn. (pres. 1959, spl. plaque 1971, hon. life mem.), AP Mng. Editors Assn. (dir. 1955-58, bd. regents 1974—), Sigma Delta Chi, Lambda Chi Alpha, Delta Sigma Rho, Pi Delta Epsilon, Omicron Delta Kappa. Methodist. Club: Hermitage Country (pres. 1970-74). Home: 8207 Tyndale Rd Richmond VA 23227 Office: Richmond Newspapers Inc Richmond VA 23213

HAMILTON, CHARLES OWEN, physician; b. Delaware County, Ind., Aug. 27, 1922; s. Mark B. and Lucile E. (Lindsey) H.; m. Mary L. Fuller, June 29, 1941; June 29, 1941; childrenKaye, Charles Owen II, Philip F., Lucinda A., Mary Beth. B.S., Ind. U., 1943, M.D., 1945. Diplomate: Am. Bd. Anesthesiology. Intern Meml. Hosp., South Bend, Ind., 1945-46, resident, 1948-49, v.p. med. staff, 1976-78, pres. staff, 1978—, bd. dirs., 1976-78; practice medicine, specializing in anesthesiology, South Bend, 1949—. Del. Ind. Republican Conv., 1960; bd. dirs. South Bend Med. Found., Inc. Served to capt. AUS, 1943-48. Mem. Am. Soc. Anesthesiologists (sec. 1963-67), Ind. Med. Soc., St. Joseph County Med. Soc. (chmn. bd. trustees 1972-73), Ind. Med. Assn. (del.), Ind. Soc. Anesthesiology (pres. 1957-58, dir. 1968-73), No. Ind. Med. Found., AMA, Am. Coll. Anesthesiology, South Bend C. of C. Methodist (dir.). Home: 66288 Millet Rd Lakeville IN 46536 Office: 701 N St Joseph St Lower Level South Bend IN 46601

HAMILTON, CURTIS MANN, corporate executive; b. Buffalo, Feb. 21, 1924; s. George Robert and Esther (Mann) H.; m. Irene Bennett, July 9, 1948; children: Craig Adam, Jaye Foster, Charles Lee. B.S., Saint Meinrad Coll., 1952; grad., Advanced Mgmt. program, Harvard U., 1969. With Aluminum Co. Am., 1962-73, group v.p., 1973-75; exec. v.p. Trinity Industries Inc., Dallas, 1975—; dir. Hitchiner Mfg. Co.; bd. dirs., exec. com. Am. Paper Inst.; dir. Revere Copper & Brass Inc.; trustee Inst. Paper Chemistry. Served with U.S. Army, 1943-46. Mem. Am. Soc. Metals. Clubs: Economics, Sky (N.Y.C.); Rolling Meadows Country (Dallas). Address: Werik Bldg 5635 Yale Blvd 1st Fl Dallas TX 75206

HAMILTON, DANIEL STEPHEN, priest; b. Cedarhurst, N.Y., Jan. 7, 1932; s. Richard Samuel and Catherine Mary (Liston) H. B.A., Cathedral Coll., 1954; S.T.B., Cath. U. Am., 1958. Ordained priest Roman Catholic Ch., 1958; asst. pastor St. Anne's Ch., Garden City, N.Y., 1958-61; campus chaplain Adelphi U., Garden City, 1959-61; prof. St. Pius X Preparatory Sem., Uniondale, N.Y., 1961-68; campus chaplain Hofstra U., Hempstead, N.Y., 1961-66; columnist L.I. Catholic, Hempstead, 1962—, editor, 1975—; dir. Bur. Public Info., Diocese Rockville Centre, 1968—; chmn. Ecumenical Commn., 1968—; resident priest St. William the Abbot Parish, Seaford, N.Y., 1971—. Named hon. papal prelate, 1980. Mem. Cath. Theol. Soc. Am., Cath. Press Assn. U.S., Nat. Assn. Diocesan Ecumenical Officers. Home: 2000 Jackson Ave Seaford NY 11783 Office: 115 Greenwich St Hempstead NY 11551

HAMILTON, DAVID JOHN STUART, hotel executive; b. Eng., July 4, 1939; emigrated to Can., 1963; s. Eric Arthur and Ethel Ada (Dunthorne) H.; m. Beckett, Jan. 15, 1966; children: Eric, Britt. Student, Westminster Hotel Sch., 1956-58. Mgr. Holiday Inn, Calgary, Alta., 1968-72, St. Johns, Nfld., 1972-75, Holiday Inn-Downtown, Montreal, Que., 1975-80, Sheraton Centre of, Toronto, Ont., 1980—. Mem. Hotel Assn. Met. Toronto, Bd. of Trade. Clubs: Skal (Toronto); Variety (Ont.). Address: Sheraton Centre 123 Queen St W Toronto ON Canada

HAMILTON, DAVID PETER, writer; b. N.Y.C., Jan. 18, 1935; s. Frank and Elizabeth (Small) H. B.A., Princeton U., 1956, M.F.A., 1960; M.A., Harvard U., 1960. Music librarian Princeton U., 1960-65; asst. music editor W.W. Norton & Co. Inc., N.Y.C., 1965-66, music editor, 1967-74; music critic The Nation, 1968—; guest music critic New Yorker Mag., 1974; contbg. editor High Fidelity, 1970—; mem. faculty Aspen Music Sch., summer 1973, Juilliard Sch., 1980-81; mem. adv. council dept. music Princeton U., 1970-78; dir. Am. Music Center, 1970-78; bd. dirs., mem. editorial com. New World Records. Author: Listener's Guide to Great Instrumentalists, 1981. Recipient Deems Taylor award ASCAP, 1975; Woodrow Wilson Nat. fellow, 1956-57. Mem. Am. Musicol. Soc., Music Library Assn., Music Critics Assn., Phi Beta Kappa. Clubs: Princeton, Metropolitan Opera, Century (N.Y.C.). Home: 91 Central Park W New York NY 10023

HAMILTON, DAVID WHITMAN, anatomy educator; b. Anaconda, Mont., Nov. 29, 1935; s. David Whitman and Mary Ann (Syphers) H.; m. Donna Juhl Nelson, Dec. 20, 1959; children: David Whitman, Caitlin Linette. A.B., Harvard U., 1957; M.A., U. Kans., 1960; Ph.D., Cambridge (Eng.) U., 1963. Teaching fellow in anatomy Kans. U., 1957-59, instr. in anatomy, 1959-60; research fellow in anatomy Harvard U. Med. Sch., 1963-65, instr., 1965-67, asso. in anatomy, 1967-69, asst. prof. anatomy, 1969-71, asso. prof., 1971-77; mem. Lab. Human Reprodn. and Reproductive Biology, 1971-77; Rockefeller Found. spl. fellow in reproductive biology Cambridge U., 1970-71; Lawrence J. Henderson asso. prof. health scis. and tech. and asso. prof. joint program in health scis. and tech. Harvard U.-M.I.T., 1974-77; prof., head dept. anatomy U. Minn., 1977—; cons. in field. Contbr. articles to profl. publs.; asso. editor: Anat. Record, 1971-76, Internat. Jour. Andrology, 1983—; editorial bd.: Biology of Reprodn, 1975-77, Animal Reprodn. Sci, 1976-79, Jour. Andrology, 1980—; jour. reviewer. Mem. Wellesley (Mass.) Town Meeting, 1975-77; chmn. Wellesley Sch. Supt. Selection Com., 1976-77. Recipient Research Career Devel. award USPHS, 1970-75. Mem. Am. Assn. Anatomists, AAAS, Am. Soc. Cell Biologists, Endocrine Soc., Histochemistry Soc., Comitè Internat. d'Andrologie, Assn. Anatomy Chairmen (exec. council 1980—), Soc. Study Fertility (U.K.), Soc. Study Reprodn. Club: Harvard of Minn. Office: Dept Anatomy 4-135 Jackson Hall U Minn 321 Church St SE Minneapolis MN 55455

HAMILTON, DENNIS DIX, broadcasting executive; b. Detroit Lakes, Minn., July 24, 1951; s. Roger Gorden and Dorothy Ann (King) H. B.S. magma cum laude in Communications, Moorhead State U., 1973. Sales rep. Northrup King & Co.; with Melroe Mfg. Co.; producer, reporter Minn. Public Radio, 1973-77; gen. mgr. Sta. KCCM-FM, Moorhead, Minn. and Sta. KCRB-FM, Bemidji, Minn., 1977—; Bd. dirs. FM Area Modern Dance Co., 1977-78, That Dance Co., 1978, Community Arts, Inc., 1979—. Pres. Lake Agassiz Arts Council, 1983. Office: 920 S 8th St Moorhead MN 56560

HAMILTON, DONALD BENGTSSON, author; b. Uppsala, Sweden, Mar. 24, 1916; s. Bengt L.K. and Elise (Neovius) H.; m. Kathleen Stick, 1941; children: Hugo, Elise, Gordon, Victoria. B.S., U. Chgo., 1938. Writer and photographer, 1946—. Creator Matt Helm series; author: books, including Death of a Citizen, 1960, The Wrecking Crew, 1960, The Removers, 1961, The Silencers, 1962, Murderer's Row, 1962, The Ambushers, 1963, The Ravagers, 1963, The Shadowers, 1964, The Devastators, 1965, The Betrayers, 1966, The Menacers, 1968, The Interlopers, 1969, The Intriguers, 1972, The Intimidators, 1974, The Terminators, 1975, The Terrorizers, 1977, The Retaliators, 1976, The Poisoners, 1971, The Revengers, 1982, The Annihilators, 1983, The Infiltrators, 1984, Cruises with Kathleen, 1980, The Mona Intercept, 1980; contbr. articles on hunting, yachting and photography to mags. Mem. Mystery Writers Am., Western Writers Am. Office: 984 Acequia Madre PO Box 1045 Santa Fe NM 87501

HAMILTON, EARL JEFFERSON, economist, educator; b. Houlka, Miss., May 17, 1899; s. Joseph William and Frances Regina Anne (Williams) H.; m. Gladys Olive Dallas, June 2, 1923; 1 dau., Sita (Mrs. Joseph Halperin). B.S. with honors, Miss. State U., 1920; student, U. Tex., summers 1922, 23, M.A., 1924; A.M., Harvard, 1926, Ph.D., 1929; Dr. Honoris Causa, U. Paris, 1952, U. Madrid, 1967; LL.D., Duke, 1966. Athletic dir., football and track coach secondary schs., 1920-24; Thayer fellow econs. Harvard, 1925-26, Frederick Sheldon traveling fellow, 1926-27; asst. prof. econs. Duke, 1927-29, prof., 1929-44; dir. civilian staff Mil. Govt. Fiscal Sch., 1943-44; prof. econs. Northwestern U., 1944-47, U. Chgo., 1947-67, emeritus, 1968—; distinguished prof. econ. history State U. N.Y. at Binghamton, 1966-69, emeritus, 1970—; Prof. Universidad Internacional, Santander, Spain, summer 1933, Colegio de Mexico, summer 1943; mem. com. on research in econ. history Social Sci. Research Council, 1941-54, rapporteur, com. world regions of, Am. Council Learned Socs. and NRC, 1943; rapporteur 11th Congress Hist. Scis., Stockholm, Sweden, 1960. Author: American Treasure and the Price Revolution in Spain, 1501-1650, 1934, Money, Prices and Wages in Valencia, Aragon and Navarre, 1351-1500, 1936, War and Prices in Spain, 1651-1800, 1947, El Florecimiento del Capitalismo y Otros Ensayos, 1948; contbg. author: First Images of America: What the New World Gave the Economy of the Old, 1976; bd. editors: Jour. Modern History, 1941-43, Jour. Econ. History, 1941-52, Revista de Historia Económica, 1983—; editor: Jour. Polit. Economy, 1948-54; co-editor: Landmarks in Political Economy, 1962; Contbr. to Am., English, French jours. of econs. and history. Trustee Com. Research in Econ. History, Inc., 1956—. Recipient gold medal as world's greatest exhibitor N. Am. Gladiolus Council, 1978; Social Science Research fellow, 1929-30; Guggenheim Meml. fellow, 1937-38; faculty research fellow Ford Found., 1956-57. Fellow Royal Econ. Soc., AAAS, Am. Acad. Arts and Scis.; mem. Am. Econ. Assn. (v.p. 1955), Econ. Hist. Assn. (v.p. 1941-42, pres. 1951-52), Am. Hist. Assn., Hispanic Soc. Am. Home: 1438 Bunker Ave Flossmoor IL 60422 Office: 212 Kelly Hall U Chgo Chicago IL 60637

HAMILTON, EARLE GRADY, JR., architect; b. Greenville, Tex., Feb. 22, 1920; s. Earle Grady and Kate (Arnold) H.; m. EAnn Thut, Mar. 21, 1974; children: Kathryn Hamilton Harnden, Leigh Hamilton Miller, Sarah. B.Arch., Washington U., St. Louis, 1943, postgrad., 1946. Architect firms in, St. Louis and Dallas, 1946-54, pvt. practice, Dallas, 1954-56; ptnr. Harrell & Hamilton Architects, Dallas, 1956-70; pres., chmn. bd. Omniplan, Inc., Dallas, 1970—; mem. new exam. devel. com. Nat. Council Archtl. Registration Bds., 1969-72, treas., 1970-72, 1st v.p., 1971-73, pres., 1973-74; mem. Tex. Bd. Archtl. Examiners, 1965-71, chmn., 1969-70; Past mem. Dallas Planning Commn.; mem. planning group Dallas Arts Facilities Study, 1976. Designer: NorthPark Shopping Center and Expansion, Dallas, 1965, 75, Dallas, 1969, Mountain View Community Coll, Dallas, 1970, Tex. Tech Law Sch, Lubbock, 1970, Citizens Nat. Bank, Richardson, Tex., 1974, U.S. Mission, Geneva, 1978, Blue Cross-Blue Shield Hdqrs, Richardson, 1981, North Park IV, 1982. Bd. dirs. Dallas Mus. Fine Arts, 1966-73; bd. govs. Dallas Symphony Orch., 1978-81. Served with USNR, 1943-46. Recipient Arts and Sci. Alumni plaque Washington U., 1943, Alumni citation, 1969, citation Tex. Bd. Archtl. Examiners, 1972. Fellow AIA (medal 1943, pres. Dallas chpt. 1964), Alpha Rho Chi (medal 1943). Home: 4115 Hawthorne St Dallas TX 75219 Office: 1700 Republic Nat Bank Tower Dallas TX 75201

HAMILTON, FREDERIC CRAWFORD, oil company executive; b. Columbus, Ohio, Sept. 25, 1927; s. Ferris F. and Jean (Crawford) H.; m. Jane C. Murchison, Feb. 14, 1953; children: Christy, Frederic C., Crawford M., Thomas M. Grad., Lawrenceville Sch., 1945, Babson Coll., 1947. Pres. Hamilton Bros. Oil Co., Denver, 1957—, Hamilton Bros. Can. Gas Co., Ltd., Calgary, Alta., 1968—; chmn. bd. Hamilton Bros. Oil and Gas (Gt. Brit.), Ltd., London, Eng., 1964—, Hamilton Bros. Petroleum Corp., Denver; chmn., chief exec. officer, pres. Hamilton Oil Corp.; dir. Celanese Corp., Gates Learjet Corp., IntraWest Fin. Corp., U.S. Trust Co., Gulf Energy and; Devel. Co., Skandinaviska, Enskilda Banken Internat. Corp.; dir. First Matagorda Corp. Served with USAAF, 1944-46. Office: 1600 Broadway Denver CO 80202

HAMILTON, GEORGE E., JR., lawyer; b. Washington, Mar. 29, 1895; s. George E. and Louise (Merrick) H.; m. Marian Hamilton, Oct. 4, 1922. Student, Carlton Acad., 1909-13; A.B., Georgetown U., 1917, LL.B., 1920, Sc.D., 1971. Bar: D.C. bar 1920. Assoc. Hamilton & Hamilton, Washington, 1920-23, mem., 1923-46, sr. mem., 1946—; gen. counsel, dir. First Am. Bank N.A., Washington Terminal Co.; local counsel railroads; counsel Cath. Archdiocese of Washington. Trustee Corcoran Gallery Art. Served as sgt. U.S. Army, 1917-18. Decorated Knight of St. Gregory. Fellow Am. Bar Found.; mem. Am., D.C. bar assns., Soc. of Cincinnati. Clubs: Lawyers, Barristers, Chevy Chase (past pres.), Metropolitan (past pres.), Alfalfa (Washington) (past pres.); Rolling Rock, Alibi. Home: 2330 Wyoming Ave Washington DC 20008 Office: 734 15th St NW Washington DC 20005

HAMILTON, GEORGE HEARD, curator; b. Pitts., June 23, 1910; s. Frank Arthur and Georgia (Heard) H.; m. Polly Wiggin, Oct. 20, 1945; children: Richard, Jennet. B.A., Yale U., 1932, M.A., 1934, Ph.D., 1942; M.A., Cambridge U., 1971; Litt.D., Williams Coll., 1977. Research asso. Walters Art Gallery, Balt., 1934-36; instr. history art Yale U., 1936-43, asst. prof., 1943-47, asso. prof., 1947-56, prof., 1956-66; curator modern art Univ. Art Gallery, 1940-66; Robert Sterling Clark prof. art Williams Coll., Williamstown, Mass., 1963-64, prof. art,

1966-75, prof. emeritus, 1975—, vis. prof., 1976—; dir. Sterling and Francine Clark Art Inst., Williamstown, 1966-77, dir. emeritus, 1977—; Slade Prof. fine arts Cambridge U., 1971-72; Kress prof. in residence Nat. Gallery Art, Washington, 1978-79. Author: Manet and His Critics, 1954, Art and Architecture of Russia, 1954, European Painting and Sculpture 1880-1940, 1967, (with W.C. Agee) Raymond Duchamp-Villon, 1967, 19th and 20th Century Art: Painting, Sculpture, Architecture, 1970; editor: (catalogue) Collection Société Anonyme, Yale U. Art Gallery, 1950. Trustee Mus. Modern Art; v.p., trustee Hill-Stead Mus., Farmington, Conn., 1970-82; vice chmn., trustee Joseph H. Hirshhorn Mus. and Sculpture Garden, Washington, 1971-75. Fellow Am. Acad. Arts and Scis., Royal Soc. Arts (London); mem. Coll. Art Assn. Am. (pres. 1966-68), Internat. Assn. Art Critics (pres. Am. sect. 1967-69). Home: 121 Gale Rd Williamstown MA 01267

HAMILTON, GEORGE HENRY, JR., energy consultant; b. Gary, Ind., Apr. 7, 1939; s. George Henry and Tina Lauree (Magee) H. B.S. in Geology, George Washington U., 1968. Dir., Andean Found., Washington, 1970-72; mem. profl. staff Gen. Electric Co., Washington, 1972-73; pres. Solar Energy Co., Washington, 1973-77; prin. devel. mgr. Pullman Corp., Houston, 1977-78; now gen. mgr. no. hemisphere ops. Solar Energy Co., Barker, Tex.; cons. in energy policy devel. and advanced energy systems, 1978—. Contbr. articles to profl. jours. Served with U.S. Army, 1962-65. Mem. Am. Assn. Petroleum Geologists, Am. Geol. Soc., AAAS, Biometrics Soc. Club: Nat. Aviation (Washington). Patentee solar energy heating module, power generating array. Home: 5205 S Lake Rd Virginia Beach VA 23455

HAMILTON, GRACE TOWNS, state legislator; b. Atlanta, Feb. 10, 1907; d. George Alexander and Nellie (McNair) T.; m. Henry Cooke Hamilton, June 7, 1930; 1 dau., Eleanor Towns Payne. A.B., Atlanta U., 1927; M.A., Ohio State U., 1929; LL.D. (hon.), Emory U., 1984. Girls work sec. YWCA, Columbus, Ohio, 1927-28, mem. nat. program staff coll. responsible for interracial program devel. and univ. div., N.Y.C., 1936-43, cons. community relations for nat. bd., 1960-61; instr. Atlanta Sch. Social Work, 1928-29; instr. psychology Clark Coll., Atlanta, 1928-30, LeMoyne Coll., Memphis, 1930-34; dir. Survey White Collar and Skilled Negro Workers, Memphis, 1935-36; exec. dir. Atlanta Urban League, 1943-61; asso. dir. So. Regional Council, Atlanta, 1954-55; community relations cons. Hamilton Assos., Atlanta, 1961-67; dir. Atlanta Youth Council, 1966; mem. Ga. Ho. of Reps., 1965—, vice chmn. legis. and congl. reapportionment com., also mem. various others. Former mem. exec. com. Citizens Adv. Com. Urban Renewal, Atlanta; mem. bd. Gate City Day Nursery Assn.; former mem. Ga. Gov.'s Commn. on Status of Women, Gov.'s Spl. Council on Family Planning; mem. Nat. Citizens Adv. Commn. on Environ. Quality, 1966-71; vice chmn. Atlanta Charter Commn., 1972; former mem. nat. citizens adv. panel for community oriented met. govt. project Nat. Acad. Pub. Adminstrn.; mem. Fulton-DeKalb Hosp. Authority, 1971-75; former mem. exec. bd. Ga. div. NCCJ; Mem. Fulton County Democratic Exec. Com., 1970—; mem. Ga. exec. com. 5th Congl. Dist. Dem. Com., 1971—; former mem. Bd. dirs. Planned Parenthood Atlanta Area, Inc., Atlanta; trustee Meharry Med. Coll., Atlanta U.; former mem. Funds Appeal Rev. Bd., Atlanta; former vice chmn. Ptnrs. for Progress, Atlanta; former mem. bd. dirs. Atlanta Arts Festival, Multiple Sclerosis Soc., Atlanta; former mem. Nat. Dem. Com.'s Commn. on Presdl. Nomination and Party Structure (Winograd Commn.); mem. exec. bd. Atlanta Landmarks, Inc.; mem. Ga. Register Rev. Bd. (Nat. Historic Preservation), No. dist. Ga. Fed. Merits Rev. Council; at-large-mem. Commn. on Future of South (So. Growth Policies Bd.). Recipient Disting. Achievements award Atlanta U. Alumnae Assn., 1965, recognition of pub. service award Inquirers Club, Atlanta, 1966, Achievement award N.J. chpt. Links, Inc., 1966, Atlanta YWCA Gay Y's, 1967, Alumna of Yr. award Atlanta U., 1969, Achievement and Service award Atlanta Inquirer, 1969, cert. of appreciation Atlanta Urban League, 1970, appreciation for legis. support Ga. Vocat. Rehab. Assn., 1970, Nonpartisan Community Service award Fulton County Republican Women, 1971, Community Service award Iota Phi Lambda, 1972, citation for pub. service Sta. WSB-TV, 1972, Good Neighbor award NCCJ, 1973, Law Day-Liberty Bell award Atlanta Bar Assn., 1974; named President's award Assn. Pvt. Colls. and Univs. in Ga., 1980, legis. services award Ga. Mcpl. Assn., 1981, Towns-Hamilton award Atlanta U. Charter Day, 1981; recipient Disting. Community Service award Atlanta Urban League, 1983, Friend of Children award Council for Children Inc., 1984; named Atlanta Woman of Yr. in Professions, Ga. Speaker of Yr. Barkley Forum, Emory U., 1972, Legislator of Yr. Ga. Pub. Health Assn., 1984. Fellow So. Regional Council (life); mem. Nat. Order Women Legislators. Congregationalist. Home: 582 University Pl NW Atlanta GA 30314 Office: State Capitol Capitol Sq SW Atlanta GA 30334

HAMILTON, HAROLD PHILIP, foundation executive; b. High Point, N.C., Apr. 26, 1924; s. Alfred McKinley and Dora Elizabeth (Surratt) H.; m. Agnes Marie Kametz, Sept. 4, 1944; children: Dawn Elizabeth, Deborah Anne, Harold Philip, Elaine Denise. Student, Lehigh U., 1943-44; B.A. cum laude, High Point Coll., 1947, L.H.D., 1965; B.D. (Myers Park scholar), Duke, 1950, Ph.D., 1954. Asst. prof. philosophy and religion N.C. State Coll., 1953-55; dean of faculty, asso. prof. Christian thought Ky. Wesleyan Coll., 1955-58, dean of coll., prof., 1958-59, dean of coll., acting pres., 1959-60, pres., prof. Christian thought, 1960-70; pres. Central Meth. Coll., 1970-76; asst. state treas. Commonwealth of Ky., 1976-80; adminstr. Timken Mercy Med. Center, 1980-83; pres. Deaconess Hosp. Found., 1983—; Pres. Oxford Inst. Meth. Theol. Studies, 1958. Trustee Pop Warner Little Scholars. Served with AUS, World War II. Mem. Am. Renaissance Soc., Central States Faculty Conf. (exec. com.), Am. Soc. Ch. History, Inst. Higher Edn., Fayette C. of C., NEA, Nat. Assn. for Hosp. Devel., Newcomen Soc. N.Am., Phi Delta Theta, Phi Alpha Theta, Phi Beta Patron, Omicron Delta Kappa. Methodist (lay leader, ofcl. bd., tchr., elder). Clubs: Rotarian (v.p.), Round Table (Fayette)). Home: 7933 Marywood Dr Newburgh IN 47630 Office: Deaconess Hosp Found 611 Harriet St Evansville IN 47710

HAMILTON, H(ORACE) GEORGE, museum and planetarium administrator; b. Bordentown, N.J., May 15, 1925; s. Alexander and Gladys (Schwoebel) H.; m. Carleen Straus, Oct. 26, 1974; children by previous marriage: Roger John, Marianne Margaret, Alexander George; adopted children: Tia Moneé, Brock Jason, Brandon George, Faun Elyse. B.S., Trenton State Coll., 1948, M.A., 1960; grad. student, Temple U., 1963-65. Tchr. physics, math., chemistry William MacFarland High Sch., Bordentown, 1948-60; physics tchr. Cherry Hill (N.J.) High Sch., 1960-62; asst. prof. physics Trenton State Coll., 1962-68; asst. dir. edn. and operations Fels Planetarium of Franklin Inst., Phila., 1968-69, assoc. dir., 1969-71, dir., 1972—; assoc. dir. Franklin Inst. Sci. Mus., 1980-82, dep. dir., 1982—. Served with USMS, 1945-46. Recipient Shell Merit fellowship, 1962. Mem. Am. Astron. Soc., Astron. Soc. Pacific, Assn. Sci. and Tech. Ctrs., Internat. Soc. Planetarium Educators, Middle Atlantic Planetarium Soc., N.J. Astron. Soc., Sci. Research Soc. Am., AAAS, Am. Assn. Museums. Episcopalian. Club: Mason. Home: 1003 Kingston Dr Cherry Hill NJ 08034 Office: Franklin Inst Sci Museum and Planetarium 20th St and the Parkway Philadelphia PA 19103 *Never have I thought of my work as a teacher or director as a job. It is important to love what one is doing. The positions I have found myself in provide for a sharing with the world the Universe as I have come to know it. It is this sharing with my family, co-workers, and those I meet that makes my life really worth living. Success is a natural outcome of being happy with your daily activities.*

HAMILTON, HOWARD BRITTON, educator; b. Augusta, Kans., Oct. 28, 1923; s. Silas Howard and Ora (Barker) H.; m. Geraldine E. Karr, Jan. 27, 1943; children—Stephen P., Jana L., John V., Christopher H. B.S., U. Okla., 1949; M.S., U. Minn., 1955; Ph.D., Okla. State U., 1962; postgrad., U.S. Army Command and Gen. Staff Coll., 1969, Indsl. Coll. Armed Forces, 1971. Registered profl. engr., Pa., Ohio. Engr. Gen. Electric Co., Schenectady, 1949-53; prof., head elec. engring. dept. U. Wichita, 1955-64; unit chief mfg. research Boeing Co., Wichita, 1958-60; chief of party U. Pitts.-U.S. AID at U. Santa Maria, Valparaiso, Chile, 1964-66; prof., head elec. engring. dept. U. Pitts., 1966-73, prof. engring., 1973—; lectr. in power system interconnection, Bogota, Colombia, 1969; Ford Found. cons. U. Santa Maria, 1968; OAS lectr. computer analysis Santa Maria U., Chile, 1972. Author: Power Processing (Electric Machinery Analysis), 1970, Economic Control and Operation, Power Systems, 1971, Experiments and Principles of Systems Engineering, 1971. Served to capt. AUS, World War II; col. Res. ret. Decorated Air medal, Purple Heart. Fellow IEEE (student br. counselor, sec., treas., vice chmn., chmn. Wichita sect., dir., chmn. Pitts. sect. 1972-73, region II dir. 1977-78, mem. at large U.S. activity bd.); mem. Am. Soc. Engring. Edn., Phi Eta Sigma, Eta Kappa Nu, Sigma Tau, Tau Beta Pi. Home: 1422 Oak St Oakmont PA 15139 Office: 348 Benedum Hall U Pitts Pittsburgh PA 15261

HAMILTON, HOWARD LAVERNE, educator; b. Lone Tree, Iowa, July 20, 1916; s. Harry Stephen and Gertrude Ruth (Shibley) H.; m. Alison Phillips, Dec. 22, 1945 (dec. 1972); children: Christina Helen, Phillips Howard, Martha Jayne; m. Elizabeth Burnley Bentley, June 18, 1975; children: Elizabeth Marshall, Catherine Randolph. B.A. with highest distinction, State U. Iowa, 1937, M.S., 1938; postgrad., U. Rochester, 1938-40; Ph.D., Johns Hopkins U., 1941. Asst. prof. to prof. zoology Iowa State U., 1946-62, acting head, 1960-61, chmn. dept. zoology and entomology, 1961-62; prof. biology U. Va., 1962-82, prof. emeritus, 1982—. Author: Lillie's Development of the Chick, 1952; cons. editor, McGraw-Hill Ency. Sci. and Tech., 1962-78; mng. editor: The Am. Zoologist, 1965-70; Author: (with Viktor Hamburger) Citation Classic: A Series of Normal Stages in the Development of the Chick, 1951. Mem. Am. Soc. Zoologists, Am. Soc. Naturalists, Soc. Developmental Biology, Internat. Inst. Devel. Biology, Am. Inst. Biol. Sci., Nat. Soc. Ams. of Royal Descent (pres. gen. 1974-80, now hon. life pres. gen.), SAR (nat. exec. com., pres. Va. Soc. 1979-80, registrar gen. 1980—, pres. gen. 1982-83, recipient Minuteman award and Gold Good Citizenship medal), Order of Three Crusades 1096-1192 (historian gen. 1976—, 1st v.p. gen. 1983—), Assn. Preservation Va. Antiquities, Va. Hist. Soc., English Speaking Union, Order of Crown of Charlemagne in U.S.A. (pres. gen. 1982—), Order Ams. of Armorial Ancestry (councillor), Phi Beta Kappa, Sigma Xi, Phi Kappa Phi, Phi Sigma. Club: Farmington Country. Home: Jumping Branch Farm Route 5 Box 401 Charlottesville VA 22901 Office: Dept Biology Gilmer Hall U Va Charlottesville VA 22901 *Throughout my life I have always been ready to accept responsibilities when given and to do the best job that I could on any task assigned, never expecting or seeking prestige or aggrandizement. My research I followed through curiosity and interest. Teaching has been transferring excitement and enthusiasm for a subject, its reward being the satisfaction of preparing students for professional careers and helping them to become established. These guidelines have brought me happiness in my life and the rewards of gratitude, friendship, and respect.*

HAMILTON, HUGHBERT CLAYTON, psychologist, educator; b. Cedar Rapids, Iowa, Mar. 6, 1903; s. Leslie S. and H. Belle (Clayton) H.; m. Mildred Eckhardt, May 31, 1940. B.A., Cornell Coll., 1925; M.A., Columbia, 1926, Ph.D., 1929. Mem. faculty Temple U., 1928—, prof. psychology, 1946-70, chmn. dept., 1962-70, dir. psychology lab., 1930-70, editor univ. publs., 1945-69, prof. emeritus, 1970—. Contbr. articles to profl. jours. Fellow Am., Pa. psychol. assns., A.A.A.S.; mem. Eastern Psychol. Assn., Psychonomic Soc., AAUP, Midwestern Psychol. Assn., Sigma Xi. Home: 5720 Wissahickon Ave Philadelphia PA 19144

HAMILTON, IAIN ELLIS, composer; b. Glasgow, Scotland, June 6, 1922; emigrated to U.S., 1961; s. James and Catherine (Ellis) H. Mus.B., U. London (Eng.), 1950; Mus, D. (hon.), U. Glasgow, 1970. Engr., 1939-47; lectr. U. London, 1952-60, Morley Coll., London, 1951-60; Mary Duke Biddle prof. music Duke, 1961-78, chmn. dept., 1966-67; composer in residence, Tanglewood, Mass., 1962; Chmn. composers Guild Great Britain, 1958; chmn. sect. Inst. Contemporary Arts, London, 1958-60. Composer: operas Royal Hunt of the Sun, 1968, Agamemnon, 1961, 68, The Catiline Conspiracy, 1973, Tamburlaine, 1976, Anna Karenina, 1978; Raleigh's Dream, 1983; composer: Lancelot, 1983; Composer also symphonies, chamber works and vocal works. Recipient Koussevitsky Found. award, 1951; Royal Philharmonic prize, 1951; Arnold Bax gold medal, 1957; Vaughn Williams award, 1974. Fellow Royal Acad. Music; mem. Internat. Webern Soc. (founding mem.), Am. Soc. Univ. Composers (founding mem.). Home: 1 King St London WC2 England

HAMILTON, JAMES, lawyer, author; b. Chester, S.C., Dec. 4, 1938; s. Herman Prioleau and Edith Muriel (Gilchrist) H.; m. Siri Kristina Hagglund, July 14, 1979; 1 son, William James. A.B., Davidon Coll., 1960; LL.B., Yale U., 1963; LL.M., U. London, 1966. Bar: D.C. 1967, U.S. Ct. Appeals (9th cir.) 1977, U.S. Supreme Ct. 1978, U.S. Ct. Claims 1981, U.S. Ct. Appeals (4th cir.) 1983. Assoc. firm Covington & Burling, Washington, 1966-73; asst. chief counsel Senate Select Com. on Presdl. Campaign Activities (Watergate Commn.), U.S. Senate, Washington, 1973-74; ptnr. firm Ginsburg, Feldman & Bress, Washington, 1973—; chief counsel Spl. Joint Com. on Referendum Review, Congress of Micronesia, 1978; spl. counsel human resources subcom. for briefing book investigation Ho. of Rps., Washington, 1983-84; mem. D.C. jud. conf. U.S. Ct. Appeals D.C., 1978, 80. Author: The Power to Probe: A Study of Congressional Investigations, 1975; contbr. articles to profl. jours., articles to major newspapers. Issue coordinator, polit. organizer, advance man Presidential Campaign of Edmund S. Muskie, Washington, 1970-72. Served as 1st lt. U.S. Army, 1963-65. Decorated Army Commendation medal; Ford Found. travel and study grantee, 1974-75. Mem. ABA (individual rights subcom.), D.C. Bar (com. on legal ethics 1983—). Democrat. Presbyterian. Club: Mt. Vernon Tennis (Washington). Home: 3321 Rowland Pl NW Washington DC 20008 Office: Ginsburg Feldman & Bress Chartered 1700 Pennsylvania Ave NW Washington DC 20006

HAMILTON, JERALD, organist; b. Wichita, Kans., Mar. 19, 1927; d. Robert James and Lillie May (Rishel) H.; m. Phyllis Jean Searle, Sept. 3, 1954; children: Barbara Helen, Elizabeth Sarah, Catharine Sandra. B.Mus., U. Kans., Lawrence, 1948, M.Mus., 1950; postgrad., Royal Sch. Ch. Music, Croydon, Eng., summer 1955, Union Theol. Sem. Sch. Sacred Music, N.Y.C., summer 1960; pupil of, Laurel Everett Anderson, Andre Marchal, Catharine Crozier, Gustav Leonhardt. Instr., then asst. prof. organ and theory Washburn U., Topeka, 1949-59; dir. Washburn Singers and Choir, 1955-59; asst. prof. organ, dir. univ. singers and chorus Ohio U., Athens, 1959-60; asst. prof. organ and ch. music U. Tex., Austin, 1960-63; lectr. ch. music Episcopal Theol. Sem. S.W., Austin, 1961-63; mem. faculty U. Ill., Urbana-Champaign, 1963—, prof. music, 1967—; organist, choirmaster chs. in, Kans. and Tex., 1942-63; organist, choirmaster Episcopal Ch. St. John the Divine, Champaign, 1963—; mem., sometime chmn. commn. ch. music Epis. Diocese Kans., 1951-59; mem. bishop's commn. ch. music Epis. Diocese of Springfield, 1978-80, 82—; concert organist, 1955—. Fulbright scholar, 1954-55. Mem. Assn. Anglican Musicians, Am. Guild Organists, Omicron Delta Kappa, Pi Kappa Lambda, Phi Mu Alpha. Episcopalian. Home: Route 1 Box 137 Sidney IL 61877 Office: Sch Music Univ Ill Urbana IL 61801

HAMILTON, JOHN ROSS, financial consultant, educator; b. Winchendon, Mass., Oct. 3, 1924; s. Rollo Albert and May (Ross) H.; m. Roberta Frances Lowitz, Sept. 17, 1949; children—Heather Crawford, John Ross, Robert Anson, Hilary Beth. Student, Princeton U., 1944-45; B.S., Rensselaer Poly. Inst., 1947; M. B.A., Harvard U., 1949, postgrad. Cert. mgmt. accountant. Financial analyst Lever Bros. Co., 1952-54; controller Barnes Engring. Co., Stamford, Conn., 1954-57; asst. to treas. Colgate-Palmolive Internat., Inc., 1957-60; asst. treas. Lever Bros. Co., 1960-66; treas. Bulova Watch Co., N.Y.C., 1966-68; dir. fin. planning and analysis Crowell Collier & Macmillan, Inc., 1968-69, asst. controller, 1969-70; asst. treas. U.S. Industries, N.Y.C., 1970-73; prof. U. Hartford Sch. Bus. Adminstrn., 1975-81, Bentley Coll., Waltham, Mass., 1981—. Served as ensign USNR, 1945-46. Mem. Nat. Assn. Accts., Delta Tau Delta. Republican. Clubs: Princeton, Harvard Business School; Middlesex Swimming (Darien). Home: 41 Stanford Rd Wellesley Hills MA 02181 Office: Bentley Coll Forest and Beaver Sts Waltham MA 02154

HAMILTON, JOSEPH HANTS, JR., educator, physicist; b. Ferriday, La., Aug. 14, 1932; s. Joseph Hants and Letha (Gibson) H.; m. Jannelle Jauree Landrum, Aug. 5, 1960; children: Melissa Claire, Christopher Landrum. B.S., Miss. Coll., 1954, D.Sc. (hon.), 1982; M.S., Ind. U., 1956, Ph.D., 1958. Mem. faculty Vanderbilt U., 1958—, prof. physics, 1966—, Landon C. Garland prof. physics, 1981—, chmn. dept., 1979—; NSF postdoctoral fellow U. Uppsala, Sweden, 1958-59; research fellow Inst. Nuclear Studies, Amsterdam, 1962; vis. prof. U. Frankfort, 1979-80; mem. adv. panel Nat. Heavy Ion Labs., 1971-73; mem. nat. policy bd. Holifield Heavy Ion Facility, 1974—; organizer, chmn. exec. com., prin. investigator Univ. Isotope Separator, Oak Ridge, 1970—; cons. Oak Ridge Nat. Lab, 1972—; cons.; mem. council Oak Ridge Asso. Univs., 1974-80; organizer, dir. Joint Inst. for Heavy Ion Research, Oak Ridge, 1980—; chmn. Internat. Conf. Internal Conversion Processes, 1965, Internat. Conf. Radioactivity in Nuclear Spectroscopy, 1969; Internat. Conf. Future Directions in Studies Nuclei far from Stability, 1979. Co-author: Science: Faith and Learning, 1972, ORAU from the Beginning, 1980; co-author, editor: Internal Conversion Processes, 1966, Radioactivity in Nuclear Spectroscopy, 1972, Reactions Between Complex Nuclei, 1974, Future Directions in Studies of Nuclei Far from Stability, 1980; contbr. articles to profl. jours., chpts. to books. Mem. Mayor Nashville Citizens Adv. Com. Housing, 1970-74; bd. dirs. Vineyard Conf. Center, Louisville, 1972-77, Danforth asso., 1965—, So. Bapt. Conv. Hist. Commn., 1983—. Harvie Branscomb Disting. Prof. award Vanderbilt U., 1983-84; NSF grantee, 1959-76; ERDA-Dept. Energy grantee, 1975—; Humbolt prize W. Ger., 1979. Fellow Am. Phys. Soc. (vice chmn. Southeastern sect. 1972-73, chmn. Southeastern sect. 1973-74 1975, Jesse Beams gold medal for research 1975); mem. Sigma Xi (chpt. pres. 1970). Address: 305 Hildreth Ct Nashville TN 37215

HAMILTON, JOSEPH HEBERLING, textile co. exec.; b. Iowa City, Aug. 8, 1920; s. Clair E. and Prudence M. (Heberling) H.; m. Joan Van Gonsic, Oct. 8, 1952; children—Holly Heberling, Joseph Jeffrey. B.A., Harvard U., 1946, M.B.A., 1948. Asst. to chmn. bd. Burlington Industries, Greensboro, N.C., 1948-55; pres. Burlington Throwing Co., High Point, N.C., 1955-60; v.p. Madison Throwing Co., N.C., 1960-63; founder Textured Fibres, Inc. (name changed to Texfi Industries Inc. 1969), Greensboro, 1963, now chmn., chief exec. officer. Served to lt. USNR, 1942-45. Episcopalian. Home: 617 Blair St Greensboro NC 27408 Office: PO Box 20348 Greensboro NC 27420

HAMILTON, JOSEPH HENRY MICHAEL, JR., television producer; b. Los Angeles, Jan. 6, 1929; s. Joseph Henry Michael and Marie (Sullivan) H.; m. Carol Burnett, May 4, 1963 (div.); children: Kathleen, Dana, Joseph Henry Michael III, Jeffrey, Judith, John, Jennifer, Nancy, Carrie, Jody, Erin Kate. Grad., Los Angeles Conservatory Music and Arts, 1951. Musician and singer, 1948-51; engaged as a writer and asso. TV producer, 1951-57; TV producer, 1957—; prin. prodns. include: Carol Burnett & Co, Mama's Family. Recipient Emmy awards. Roman Catholic. Clubs: Bel Air Country; Westchester Country (Rye, N.Y.). Office: care NBC Press Dept 3000 W Alameda Burbank CA 91523 *

HAMILTON, LEE HERBERT, congressman; b. Daytona Beach, Fla., Apr. 20, 1931; m. Nancy Ann Nelson, Aug. 21, 1954; children: Tracy Lynn, Deborah Lee, Douglas Nelson. A.B., DePauw U., 1952; scholar, Goethe U., Frankfurt au Main, Germany, 1953; J.D., Ind. U., 1956. Mem. 89th-98th Congresses from 9th Dist. Ind.; vice chmn. congl. del. Interparliamentary Union, regional whip, mem. fgn. affairs com., chmn. subcom. on, Europe and Middle East, chmn. subcom. on econ. goals and intergovtl. policy, mem. permanent select com. on intelligence, mem. joint econ. com. Office: 2187 Rayburn House Office Bldg Washington DC 20515 *

HAMILTON, LINDA KAY, publishing company executive; b. Waukegan, Ill., May 13, 1945; d. Lloyd Henry and Vida May (Harms) Fruth; 1 dau., Arwen Elizabeth. B.A. cum laude, Mich. State U., 1966, M.B.A., 1972; A.M. in L.S., U. Mich., 1968. Sect. head Mich. State U. Libraries., 1969-73; head catalog dept. Wayne State U. Libraries, Detroit, 1973-75, network corrdinator, 1975-76; asst. dir. Mich. Library Consortium, 1976-77; mgr. bibliographic services Univ. Microfilms Internat., Ann Arbor, Mich., 1977-79; mgr. collections ops. Univ. Microfilms Internat., Ann Arbor, Mich., 1979-82; v.p. acad. micropublishing, dir. Research Publs. Inc., Woodbridge, Conn., 1982—. Editor: MLA Intellectual Freedom Newsletter, 1974-75, Cort Cat News, 1974-77; contbr. articles to profl. jours. Mem. ALA, Friends of Bethany Library Assn. (treas. 1983—), Advt. Club Greater New Haven (treas. 1983—). Office: Research Publs Inc 12 Lunar Dr Woodbridge CT 06525

HAMILTON, LYMAN CRITCHFIELD, JR., multi-industry executive; b. Los Angeles, Aug. 29, 1926; s. Lyman Critchfield and Lorraine (Gluck) H.; m. Mary Shepard, June 25, 1949; children: William, Richard, Douglas, David. B.A., Principia Coll., Elsah, Ill., 1947; student, U. Redlands, 1944-45; M.P.A., Harvard, 1949. With Bur. Budget, 1950-56, U.S. Civil Administrn. of, Ryukyu Islands, 1956-60, IBRD, also Internat. Finance Corp., 1960-62; with ITT, 1962—, treas., 1967-76, v.p., 1968-73, sr. v.p., 1973-74, exec. v.p., 1974-77, pres., 1977-79; chief operating officer, 1977, chief exec., 1978-79; formerly officer, dir. affiliated cos.; chmn., pres. Tamco Enterprises, Inc., N.Y.C., 1980—, also dir.; dir. Internat. Mobile Machines Corp., ETX Corp., Energy Assets Internat. Corp., Travelers Rest, Imperial Corp. Am. Mem. vis. com. J.F. Kennedy Sch. Govt., Harvard U. Served to ensign USNR, 1944-46. Office: Tamco Enterprises Inc 645 Fifth Ave New York NY 10022

HAMILTON, MARGARET LETITIA, publisher; b. Galt, Ont., Can., July 27; d. Norman and Venetia (Townley) H. Grad., Galt Collegiate Inst. and Vocat. Sch. Asso. Publisher, gen. mgr. Evening Reporter,

Galt, to 1954; exec. asst. to mng. dir. Thomson Newspapers Ltd., Toronto, Ont.; also Thompson Newspapers Inc., Des Plaines, Ill., 1955-69, v.p., asst. to mng. dir., 1969-75, sr. v.p., 1975-78, exec. v.p., 1979-80, pres., chief operating officer, 1981—. Mem. adv. bd. Sch. Bus. Adminstrn., U. Western Ont.; mem. governing council U. Toronto. Mem. Am. Newspaper Publishers Assn. (dir.), Canadian Press (v.p.), Advt. Bur. Canadian Daily Newspapers (dir.), Met. Bd. Trade (dir.), AP, Can. Press, Internat. Press Inst., Inter Am. Press Inst., Can. Daily Newspapers Assn., Ont. Provincial Dailies Assn., Commonwealth Press Union, Ont. Council U. Affairs. Mem. United Ch. Can. Clubs: Galt Country; Granite (Toronto). Home: 64 Blair Rd Galt ONT Canada N1S 2J1 Office: 65 Queen St W Toronto ON Canada M5H 2M8

HAMILTON, PAUL LARNELL, educator; b. Pueblo, Colo., Apr. 1, 1941; s. Arthur Reuben and Frances Susan (Price) H.; m. Emma Nell Lee, June 19, 1970 (div.); 1 son, John. B.A. in Sociology, U. Denver, 1964, M.A. in Secondary Edn, 1972; Ed.D. in Edn. and Black Studies, U. No. Colo., 1975. Tchr., curriculum cons. pub. schs., Denver, 1964—; dir. PUSH-EXCEL (on loan from Denver Public Schs.), 1979-81; asst. dir. Head Start Family Camp, 1967; assoc. dir. Denver Consortium on Teaching Minority History, 1969; lectr., research asst. U. Denver, 1971-72, adj. prof. history, 1982—; cons. Gen. Assistance Center, 1974—; sec., dir. Petro Energy Internat. Co., 1982—; Mem. adv. bd. Commn. Higher Edn., 1971-72; chmn. com. mil. acads. appts. Colo. 1st Congl. Dist., 1972-76. Mem. adv. bd. Colo. Common Cause, 1972-73; Mem. Colo. Ho. of Reps., 1969-73. Mem. Denver Fedn. Tchrs. (sec. 1966-68), Black Educators United (co-founder, pres. 1968), Kappa Delta Pi, Phi Kappa Delta. Democrat. Home: 2811 Vine St Denver CO 80205 Office: 451 Clermont St Denver CO 80220

HAMILTON, PETER BANNERMAN, lawyer; b. Phila., Oct. 22, 1946; s. William George and Elizabeth Jane (McCullough) H.; m. Elizabeth Anne Arthur Bannerman, May 8, 1982; 1 son, Peter. A.B., Princeton U., 1968; J.D., Yale U., 1971. Bar: D.C. 1972, Pa. 1972. Mem. staff Office Asst. Sec. Def. for Systems Analysis and Office Gen. Counsel, Dept. Def., Washington, 1971-74; mem. firm Williams & Connolly, Washington, 1974-77; gen. counsel Dept. Air Force, Washington, 1977-78; dep. gen. counsel HEW, Washington, 1979, exec. asst. to sec., 1979; spl. asst. to Sec. and Dep. Sec. Def., Washington, 1979-80; partner Califano, Ross & Heineman, Washington, 1980-82; v.p., gen. counsel, sec. Cummins Engine Co., Inc., 1983—. Articles editor: Yale Law Jour, 1970-71. Served to lt. USN, 1971-74. Recipient Exceptional Civilian Service decoration Dept. Air Force, 1978; Dept. Def. medal for Disting. Public Service, 1981. Democrat. Home: 2717 Riverside Dr Columbus IN 47201 Office: Cummins Engine Co Inc Columbus IN 47202

HAMILTON, RANDY HASKELL, university dean; b. N.Y.C., Dec. 27, 1921; s. Harry and Adelaide Beatrice (Haskell) H.; m. Louanne McKernan, Apr. 9, 1964; children: Leander Munhall, Sarah Beth, Jill Katherine, Jennifer Sabrina. A.B., U. N.C., 1943, M.A., 1947, M.C.R.P., 1949; Ph.D., Internat. U., Zurich, Switzerland, 1963. City mgr., Carolina Beach, N.C., 1949-52; Washington dir., asso. dir. Nat. League of Cities, Washington, 1952-56; v.p. McGregor & Werner Internat., Washington, 1956-58; city mgr., Bangkok, Thailand, 1958-64; dir. urban studies UN, N.Y.C., 1965-66; exec. dir. Inst. Local Self Govt., Berkeley, Calif., 1966-73; dean Grad. Sch. Pub. Adminstrn., Golden Gate U., San Francisco, 1973—; mem. regional rev. panel Harry S. Truman Scholarship Found., 1977-84. Author 2 books.; Contbr. articles to profl. jours. Served with USAAF, World War II. Decorated Comdr. Royal Order of Crown of Thailand, 1963; recipient Spl. Citation of Commendation U.S. CSC, 1975; named Man of Year N.C. Lions Clubs, 1949; recipient Achievement award Fed. Exec. Bd., San Francisco, 1952. Mem. Am. Soc. Pub. Adminstrn. (pres. 1975-76), Western Govtl. Research Assn. (pres. 1974-75), Calif. Assn. Pub. Adminstrn. Educators (pres. 1975-76), Internat. City Mgmt. Assn. (S.B. Sweeney award 1980), Nat. Acad. Pub. Adminstrn., Am. Consortium for Internat. Pub. Adminstrn. (v.p.), Nat. Mcpl. League (nat. council 1982-85), Internat. Assn. Schs. and Insts. of Adminstrn. (bd. govs. 1982-84). Clubs: Commonwealth, University (San Francisco). Home: 6101 Acacia Ave Oakland CA 94618 Office: 536 Mission St San Francisco CA 94105

HAMILTON, RICHARD DANIEL, neurosurgeon; b. Itasca, Tex., June 14, 1928; s. Richard McCrary and Maude Geneva (Fowler) H.; m. Edith Nelle Day, Dec. 31, 1948; children: Melanie Hamilton DeAngelis, Daniel, Melissa Hamilton Driscoll, David, John, Anna-Maria, Kristianna. M.D., Baylor U., 1950. Diplomate: Am. Bd. Neurol. Surgery. Intern Riverside Gen. Hosp., Arlington, Calif., 1950-51; resident in psychiatry and neurology Letterman Army Hosp., San Francisco, 1951-54; resident in gen. surgery Valley Forge Army Hosp., 1955-56; resident in neurosurgery Walter Reed Army Hosp., Washington, 1956-60, asst. chief neurosurgery, 1964-66; cons. neurosurgery U.S. Army, Korea, 1960-61, Europe, 1961-64; chief dept. neuroanatomy Walter Reed Army Inst. of Research, 1964-65; cons. neurosurgery U.S. Army, Vietnam, also comdg. officer, 1966-67; asst. chief neurosurgery Letterman Army Hosp., 1967-70, ret., 1970; private practice medicine specializing in neurosurgery, San Jose, Calif., 1970-80, Marysville, Calif., 1980—; mem. staff Santa Clara Valley Med. Center, San Jose, 1970—, chief div. neurosurgery, 1971-80, pres. staff, 1978-80; mem. staffs Rideout Hosp., Fremont Hosp.; prof. clin surgery Stanford Sch. Medicine, 1973-80; clin. asso. prof. San Jose State U., 1976-80. Bd. dirs. Calif. Regional Spinal Cord Injury Care System. Commd. 1st lt. M.C. U.S. Army, 1950; advanced through grades to col., 1967. Decorated Legion of Merit with oak leaf cluster. Fellow A.C.S.; mem. AMA, Calif. Med. Assn., Am. Assn. Neurol. Surgeons, Nat. Paraplegia Found., San Francisco Neurol. Soc., Am. Spinal Injury Assn. (dir.), Internat. Paraplegia Soc., Calif-Assn. Neurol. Surgeons (dir.), Yuba-Sutter-Colusa Med. Soc., Beta Beta Beta, Alpha Epsilon Delta. Republican. Presbyterian. Home: 519 Camino Cortez Yuba City CA 95991 Office: 414 G St Marysville CA 95901

HAMILTON, RICHARD FREDERICK, educator; b. Kenmore, N.Y., Jan. 18, 1930; s. Delmer Vernon and Ethelwyn Gertrude (Stevenson) H.; m. Irene Marie Elisabeth Wagner, Aug. 12, 1957; children: Carl Thomas, Tilman Michael. Student, U. Mich., 1947-48; B.A., U. Chgo., 1950; M.A., Columbia U., 1953, Ph.D., 1963. Instr. Skidmore Coll., Saratoga Springs, N.Y., 1957-59; instr. Harpur Coll., Binghamton, N.Y., 1959-64; asst. prof. Princeton U., 1964-66; assoc. prof., then prof. U. Wis., Madison, 1966-70; prof. McGill U., Montreal, Que., Can., 1970—. Author: Affluence and the French Worker in the Fourth Republic, 1967, Class and Politics in the United States, 1972, Restraining Myths, 1975, Who Voted for Hitler?, 1982. Mem. council Inter-univ. Consortium for Polit. and Social Research, 1975-79. Served with AUS, 1954-56. Mem. Council for European Studies (steering com. 1975-78). Home: 473 Argyle Ave Westmount PQ H3Y 3B3 Canada

HAMILTON, RICHARD PARKER, corporate executive; b. Worcester, Mass., Sept. 13, 1931; s. Ralph Ramsey and Doris Isabel (Waterhouse) H.; m. Nancy Marguerite Daniels, June 6, 1959; children: Jeffrey Richard, Jennifer Lynn, Kimberly Ann. B.B.A., U. Toledo, 1953; M.B.A., Ohio State U., 1954. Various positions Florsheim Shoe Co., Chgo., 1957-69, v.p., gen. mgr., 1969, pres., chief exec. officer, 1970-78; chmn., chief exec. officer retail stores div. Hart Schaffner & Marx, Chgo., 1978-80; pres., chief operating officer Hartmarx Corp., Chgo., 1981—. Served with U.S. Army, 1955-56. Congregationalist. Clubs: Chicago; Mid-Am. (Chgo.); Sunset Ridge Country (Northbrook, Ill.). Office: Hartmarx Corp 101 N Wacker Dr Chicago IL 60606

HAMILTON, ROBERT M., food company executive; b. Los Angeles, Mar. 29, 1926; s. Merle L. and Hazel D. (Fay) H.; m. Mildred M. Benedict, Apr. 5, 1947; children: John H., Robert, Susan R., Elizabeth A. B.S., U. Mass., 1952; M.S., Pa. State U., 1953. Div. mfg. plant mgr. H.P. Hood & Sons, Charlestown, Mass., 1959-62, mgr. new products mfg., 1962-64; dir. plants quality control Howard Johnson Co., Queens Village, N.Y., 1964-68, plant mgr., 1968-73, group v.p. mfg. plants, Braintree, Mass., 1973-81, sr. v.p. purchasing, mfg., dist. bn., 1981—. Served to cpl. USAF, 1944-47. Mem. Am. Mgmt. Assn. Republican. Club: Shriners. Office: Howard Johnson Co 220 Forbes Rd Braintree MA 02184

HAMILTON, ROBERT MORRISON, geophysicist; b. Houston, June 20, 1936; s. Robert Gilbert and Marieta Josephine (Heisser) H.; m. Mary Edith Hudson, Mar. 12, 1977; 1 dau. by previous marriage, Margaret Emily. Geophys. Engr., Colo. Sch. Mines, 1958; M.A., U. Calif., Berkeley, 1963, Ph.D., 1965. Research seismologist N.Z. Dept. Sci. and Indsl. Research, Wellington, 1965-68; geophysicist U.S. Geol. Survey, Menlo Park, Calif., 1968-72, dep. for earthquake geophysics then chief Office Earthquake Studies, Reston, Va., 1972-78, research geophysicist Office Earthquake Studies, 1978-82, chief geologist Office Earthquake Studies, 1982—, chmn. sci. adv. com., 1980-81. Served with AUS, 1959. Nat. scholar, 1954-58; Socony-Mobil Oil Co. scholar, 1958; Pan Am. Petroleum Found. scholar, 1963-64; recipient Cecil Green medal for outstanding geophysics grad., 1958, Dept. Interior Meritorious Service award, 1978. Fellow Geol. Soc. Am.; mem. Am. Geophys. Union, Seismological Soc. Am. (pres., bd. dirs.), Soc. Exploration Geophysics, Earthquake Engring. Research Inst., AAAS. Home: 2020 Mock Orange Ct Reston VA 22091 Office: US Geol Survey National Center Stop 911 Reston VA 22092

HAMILTON, ROBERT WILLIAM, business executive, lawyer; b. Los Angeles, Jan. 2, 1939; s. James Edwin and Margaret H.; m. Catherine Barre, Oct. 8, 1977. B.A., Stanford U., 1961; J.D., UCLA, 1964; M.C.L., U. Chgo., 1966; DES, U. Paris, 1969. Bar: Calif. 1964, N.Y. 1967. Asso. firm Cleary, Gotlieb, Steen & Hamilton, Paris and N.Y.C., 1967-71, Kaplan, Livingston, Goodwin, Berkowitz & Selvin, 1971-73; partner firm Samuel Pisar, Paris, 1973-77; v.p., gen. counsel Max Factor & Co., Los Angeles, 1977-80; asst. gen. counsel Norton Simon, Inc., 1980—. Mem. ABA, Los Angeles County Bar Assn. Home: 1060 Park Ave New York NY 10028 Office: 277 Park Ave New York NY 10017

HAMILTON, ROBERT WOODRUFF, business law educator; b. Syracuse, N.Y., Mar. 4, 1931; s. Walton Hale and Irene (Till) H.; m. Dagmar Strandberg, June 25, 1953; children: Eric Clark, Robert Andrew, Meredith Hope. B.A., Swarthmore Coll., 1952; J.D., U. Chgo., 1955. Bar: D.C. 1956. Law clk. Justice Clark, U.S. Supreme Ct., Washington, 1955-56; atty. firm Gardner, Morrison & Rogers, Washington, 1956-64; asso. prof. law U. Tex., Austin, 1964-67, prof., 1967—, Vinson and Elkins prof. law, 1972-81, James R. Dougherty prof., 1976-77, B.C. Schmidt prof. bus. law, 1981—; vis. prof. U. Minn., 1966, U. Ariz., 1971, U. Pa., 1978; John S. Lehmann disting. vis. prof. Washington U., St. Louis, 1982; research dir. Adminstrv. Conf. of the U.S., Washington, 1973-74, cons., 1970-78, Regulatory Council, 1979-80. Author: Texas Practice: Business Organizations, 2 vols, 1973, Cases and Materials on the Law of Corporations, 1976, 2d edit., 1981, The Law of Corporations in a Nutshell, 1980; Mng. editor: U. Chgo. Law Review, 1954; Contbr. articles to profl. jours. Mem. panel on new drug regulation HEW, 1975-77; Mem. equalization bd. Eanes Sch. Dist., Tex., 1975-77; mem. city council, West Lake Hills, Tex., 1967-70. Recipient Teaching Excellence awards U. Tex., 1970, 73. Mem. Am. Bar Assn. (chmn. rulemaking com. 1974-76), Order of Coif. Democrat. Home: 403 Allegro Austin TX 78746

HAMILTON, STUART, banker; b. Topeka, July 12, 1920; s. Clay and Ernestine (Klein) H.; m. Marian Patten, Nov. 7, 1941; children—Mark R., Scott A. B.S., Northwestern U., 1946; M.B.A., U. Chgo., 1950. With No. Trust Co., Chgo., 1946—, asst. auditor, 1957-60, auditor, 1960-63, v.p., auditor, 1963-65, v.p. operations, 1965-67, sr. v.p., 1967-75, exec. v.p., 1975—. Trustee Ill. Inst. Tech. Served to lt. comdr. USNR, 1941-46. Decorated Purple Heart, Silver Star. Mem. Phi Beta Kappa, Delta Upsilon. Clubs: Executive Program, Bankers, University, Exmoor Country (Chgo.). Home: 660 Bent Creek Ridge Deerfield IL 60015 Office: No Trust Co 50 S La Salle St Chicago IL 60675

HAMILTON, THOMAS EARLE, retired educator, honorary society executive; b. Savannah, Ga., June 10, 1905; s. Homer Francis and Catherine Clitheral (Langford) Hartwell; m. Juanita Vivian Adams, Aug. 2, 1933; children—Earle Hartwell, Charles Lee, Helen Catherine (Mrs. Paul A. Anthony). A.B., So. Methodist U., 1927, A.M., 1929; Ph.D. in Spanish and Classics (advanced fellow), U. Tex., 1940. Tchr. Garland (Tex.) High Sch., 1927-29, Highland Park High Sch., Dallas, 1929-37; instr. classical and Romance langs. Tex. Tech U., Lubbock, 1940-43, asst. prof., 1943-45, asso. prof., 1945-55, prof., 1955-71, prof. emeritus, 1971—; vis. prof. Spanish Tex. Woman's U., Saltillo, Mexico, 1945; vis. prof. Spanish and classics Austin Coll., 1962-63; cons. Houston Pub. Sch. System, 1953, Angelo State U., 1967-68; co-author grad. reading exams. in Spanish Ednl. Testing Service, Princeton, N.J., 1966-67. Editor: South Central Modern Lang. Assn. Bull, 1953-56; asso. editor, 1965-67; editor: El cardenal de Belen (Lope de Vega), 1948; Contbr. articles to profl. jours., various anthologies. Recipient award Sigma Delta Chi, 1965. Mem. MLA (life emeritus), South Central MLA (hon. life), Tex. Fgn. Lang. Assn. (hon. life, co-founder, pres. 1958, founder, editor Bull. 1953-57), Am. Assn. Tchrs. Spanish and Portuguese (emeritus, chmn. nominating com. 1956), Assn. Coll. Honor Socs. (chmn. com. on standards and definitions), Nat. Rifle Assn. (endowment), Eta Sigma Phi, Sigma Delta Pi (nat. v.p. 1950-59, nat. pres. 1959-68, 72-78, nat. hon. pres. 1979—), Sigma Delta Mu (founder, nat. pres. 1979—). Methodist. Home: 2303 N Celia Dr Cedar Park TX 78613 *If our life is to have meaning and we are to exert a healthful influence on others, then we must adopt as a guide a set of high principles rooted in the Christian faith.*

HAMILTON, THOMAS JAMES, college president; b. N.Y.C., July 31, 1932; s. Thomas J. and Margaret F. (Hildemann) H.; m. Lorraine Joseph, Aug. 1, 1961. B.A., St. John's U., 1954; M.A., Hunter Coll., 1960; Ph.D., U. Va., 1973. Asst. prof. humanities U. Va., Charlottesville, 1966-70; dir. devel. Longwood Coll., Farmville, Va., 1970-74; pres. Nazareth Coll., Kalamazoo, Mich., 1974-76; exec. v.p. Kendall Coll., Evanston, Ill., 1976-80; pres. Coll. of St. Teresa, Winona, Minn., 1980—. Bd. dirs. Group Homes of Winona, 1983—. Du Pont scholar U. Va., 1967. Mem. Winona C. of C. (dir. 1980—), Phi Beta Kappa, Phi Kappa Phi. Lodge: Kiwanis. Home: 870 Gilmore Ave Winona MN 55987 Office: Coll of St Teresa Winona MN 55987

HAMILTON, THOMAS STEWART, physician, hospital administrator; b. Detroit, June 19, 1911; s. J.T. Stewart and Lucy (Safford) H.; m. Amy Washburn, June 30, 1937; children: Ann Washburn Hamilton Cole, Barbara Hamilton Almy, Jeanne. Grad., Philips Exeter Acad., 1930; A.B., Williams Coll., 1934, D.Sc. (hon.), 1969; postgrad., Harvard, 1934-36; M.B., Wayne U., 1938, M.D., 1939; D.Sc. (hon.), Trinity Coll., 1962, U. Hartford, 1975. Intern, asst. resident Harper Hosp., Detroit, 1938-40; gen. practice medicine, Truro, Cape Cod, Mass., 1940-41; asst. dir. Mass. Gen. Hosp., Boston, 1941-42, 45-46; dir. Newton-Wellesley Hosp., Newton Lower Falls, Mass., 1946-54; exec. dir. Hartford (Conn.) Hosp., 1954-76, pres., 1969-76, pres. emeritus, 1976—; prof. U. Conn. Sch. Medicine, 1978—. Author articles in field. Trustee Soc. for Savs., 1961-70; Commr. Joint Commn. Accreditation Hosps., 1960-66; mem. cancer control com. USPHS, 1964-70; mem. liaison com. on med. edn., 1969-75; Regent U. Hartford, 1962-68; trustee McLean Fund, 1968—. Served from capt. to lt. col. M.C. AUS, 1942-45; adj., exec. officer 6th Gen. Hosp. Recipient Distinguished Service awards Am. Hosp. Assn., 1969, Conn. Hosp. Assn., 1970; Distinguished Alumnus award Wayne State U. Sch. Medicine, 1970; Gold Medal award Am. Coll. Hosp. Adminstrs., 1971, Pub. Service award Conn. Bar Assn., 1975; Gold Medal award New Eng. Hosp. Assembly, 1975. Fellow Am. Coll. Hosp. Adminstrs. (regent New Eng. 1953-57); mem. AMA (mem. internship rev. com. 1958-68), Mass., Conn., Hartford County med. assns., Assn. Am. Med. Colls. (sec.-treas. 1968-70), Council Teaching Hosps. (chmn. 1970), Am. Hosp. Assn. (pres., chmn. bd. trustees 1962-63), Conn. Hosp. Assn (pres. 1966), Mass. Hosp. Assn. (pres. 1951), Soc. Med. Adminstrs. (pres. 1968-70), Med. Adminstrs. Conf., Marine Hist. Soc. Clubs: Hartford, Farmington Country, Masons Island Yacht. Home: 50 Bayberry Hill Rd Avon CT 06001 Office: Hartford Hosp 80 Seymour St Hartford CT 06115

HAMILTON, VIRGINIA (MRS. ARNOLD ADOFF), author; b. Yellow Springs, Ohio, Mar. 12, 1936; d. Kenneth James and Etta Belle (Perry) H.; m. Arnold Adoff, Mar. 19, 1960; children: Leigh Hamilton, Jaime Levi. Student, Antioch Coll., 1952-55, Ohio State U., 1957-58, New Sch. for Social Research. Author: children's novels Zeely, 1967 (Nancy Block Meml. award Downtown Community Sch. Awards Com.), The House of Dies Drear, 1968 (Edgar Allan Poe award for best juvenile mystery 1969), The Time-Ago Tales of Jadhu, 1969, Planet of Junior Brown, 1971; W.E.B. Dubois: A Biography, 1972; children's novels Time-Ago Lost: More Tales of Jahdu, 1973, M.C. Higgins the Great (John Newbery medal 1974), 1974 (Nat. Book award 1975), Paul Robeson: The Life and Times of a Free Black Man, 1974, Arilla Sun Down, 1976; Illusion and Reality, 1976, The Justice Cycle: Justice and Her Brothers, 1978, Dustland, 1980, Gathering, 1980, Jahdu, 1980, Sweet Whispers, Brother Rush, 1982; Editor: Writings of W.E.B. Dubois, 1975. Recipient Ohioana Lit. award, 1969. Office: care Avon Books 1979 Broadway New York NY 10019 *

HAMILTON, WILLIAM, cartoonist, playwright, novelist; b. Palo Alto, Calif., June 2, 1939; s. Alexander and Ellen Truesdale (Ballentine) H.; m. Candida Darci Vargas, May 9, 1969; 1 dau., Alexandra Manuela Vargas. B.A., Yale U., 1962. Cartoonist: New Yorker mag, 1965—; syndicated cartoonist: Chronicle Features Syndicate; Author: Antisocial Register, 1974, Terribly Nice People, 1975, Husbands, Wives and Live Togethers, 1976, Introducing William Hamilton, 1977, Money Should Be Fun, 1979; (plays) Save Grand Central, 1976, Plymouth Rock, 1979, Happy Landings, 1981; (novels) The Love of Rich Women, 1981. Served with U.S. Army, 1963-65. Recipient Claude Moore Fuess medal, 1979. Mem. Dramatists Guild, Writers Guild Am., Am. Automobile Assn. Episcopalian. Home: 400 W 43d St New York NY 10036

HAMILTON, WILLIAM BERRY, JR., shipping company executive; b. Birmingham, Ala., Apr. 4, 1929; s. William Berry and Nettie (Whatley) H.; m. Jean Lucile Patteson, Feb. 1, 1951; children: Jean Lucile, Ann Elizabeth, William Berry III. B.A., Vanderbilt U., 1951. Accountant Hiwassee Constructors, Chattanooga, 1952; cert. pub. acct. O.E. Johnson & Assocs., Chattanooga, 1952-54; controller, gen. mgr. Spl. Products Co., Inc., Chattanooga, 1954-59; v.p., controller Ryder Truck Lines, Inc., Jacksonville, Fla., 1959-65; v.p. finance Chgo. Rawhide Mfg. Co., 1965-67; v.p., controller-treas. Sea-Land Service Inc., Elizabeth, N.J., 1967-69, exec. v.p. adminstrn., dir., 1969-75; v.p., treas., asst. sec. McLean Industries, Inc., Elizabeth, 1968-74; pres. Monterey Transp. Co., Inc. (subs. R.J. Reynolds Industries, Inc.), Winston-Salem, N.C., 1975-77; pres., dir. Security-First Corp., Jacksonville, Fla., 1977—; chmn. bd., pres. St. John's Marine Fin. Co. Inc., 1979—; chmn., chief exec. officer Port of Monmouth Devel. Corp.; dir., mem. exec. com. J.J. Henry Co., Inc., N.Y.C.; chmn. bd. Chemquip Distbrs., Inc.; dir. McCall Service Inc., Old Dominion Life Ins. Inc.; CEO, Inc.; instr. acctg. U. Chattanooga, 1953-54. Served with USAF, 1951-52. Recipient Guest Lectr. award U. Fla., 1965. Mem. Am. Bur. Shipping, Soc. Naval Architects and Marine Engrs., Am. Inst. C.P.A.s, Financial Execs. Inst., Am. Trucking Assn. (nat. bd. dirs., chmn. methods and procedures nat. accounting 1959—), Nat. Def. Transp. Assn., Nat. Assn. Accountants (named most valuable mem. Jacksonville 1959-60, chpt. v.p., bd. dirs. 1960-63), Tenn. Soc. C.P.A.s, Am. Accounting Assn., Nat. Officer Mgmt. Assn., Am. Mgmt. Assn., U.S. Power Squadron, USCG Aux., Propeller Club of U.S., Navy League, Phi Delta Theta, Pi Delta Epsilon. Episcopalian (vestryman). Clubs: Fla. Yacht, River (Jacksonville); Ponte Vedra, Sawgrass (Ponte Vedra Beach, Fla.); Sea Bright (N.J.) Beach; N.Y. Yacht, World Trade Center, Vanderbilt Alumni (N.Y.C.); Twin-City (Winston-Salem). Lodge: Kiwanis. Home: 417 Ponte Vedra Blvd Ponte Vedra Beach FL 32082 Office: 3308 Independent Sq Jacksonville FL 32202

HAMILTON, WILLIAM COWLES, foreign service officer; b. New Britain, Conn., July 23, 1922; s. Harold Ernest and Helen Mary (Cowles) H.; m. Jeanne Betty Lawton, June 22, 1946. B.A., Yale U., 1947, M.A., 1949, Ph.D., 1955. Instr. polit. sci. N.J. Coll. Women, New Brunswick, 1950-51; intelligence research specialist Dept. State, 1951-57; assigned U.S. Fgn. Service, embassy, Burma, 1957-59; dep. spl. asst. internat. affairs Supreme Allied Comdr. Europe, 1960-62; 1st sec., chief polit. sec. embassy, Laos, 1962-64; dep. dir. Far East region Internat. Security Affairs, Dept. Def., 1964-66; country dir. Laos, Dept. State, 1966-67; counselor of embassy for polit. affairs, Thailand, 1967-70; mem. Sr. Seminar in Fgn. Policy, 1970-71; minister Am. embassy, Philippines, 1971-73; dir. Office Research and Analysis for East Asia and Pacific, Dept. State, 1973-75; dir. internat. affairs Nat. War Coll., Ft. Leslie J. McNair, Washington, 1975-77; sr. insp. Office Insp. Gen., Dept. State, 1977-80; chargé d'affaires Am. Embassy, Stockholm, 1980-82; dir. systematic rev. classification/declassification ctr. Dept. State, Washington, 1983—. Mem. Am. Fgn. Service Assn., Internat. Studies Assn., Phi Beta Kappa. Office: care Fgn Service Mail Room Dept State Washington DC 20520

HAMILTON, WILLIAM FRANK, educator; b. Ridley Park, Pa., Apr. 28, 1939; s. William John and Anne Elizabeth (Pennypacker) H.; m. Marcia Krysa, June 20, 1964; children: William Michael, Robert Kyle. B.S., U. Pa., 1961, M.S., 1964, M.A., 1975; M.B.A., Wharton Sch., U. Pa., 1964; Ph.D., London Sch. Econs., 1967. Research engr. Sun Oil Co., Phila., 1961-67; asst. prof. Wharton Sch., U. Pa., Phila., 1967-73, assoc. prof., 1973-78, prof. mgmt. and tech., 1978—; assoc. dir. Davis Inst. Health Econs. U. Pa., 1975-78, dir. mgmt. and tech. program, 1978—; spl. asst. to sec. U.S. Dept. Transp., Washington, 1974-75; pvt. cons., Phila., 1967—; dir. Stevens. Conf. Trust, Phila., 1978—, Pierce Jr. Coll., 1978-83, Robinson-Halpern Co., Plymouth, Pa., 1977—. White House fellow, 1974-75; recipient Lindback award for Disting. Teaching U. Pa., 1972. Mem. AAAS, Ops. Research Soc. Am. (chpt. chmn. 1972), Inst. Mgmt. Scis.

HAMILTON, WILLIAM HOWARD, lab. exec.; b. Greenville, Pa., Apr. 2, 1918; s. Simeon Milo and Mary (Baer) H.; m. Ellinor Kistler, Feb. 9, 1944; children—William H., Nancy Hamilton Lopez. B.S. in Math. and Physics, Washington and Jefferson Coll., 1940, M.S., U. Pitts., 1948. With Westinghouse Electric Corp., 1945—; gen. mgr. Bettis Atomic Power Lab., West Mifflin, Pa., 1970-79; cons., 1979—. Pres. Edgewood Council, Pitts., 1971-77. Served to lt. comdr. U.S. Navy, 1942-45. Recipient Westinghouse Order of Merit, 1958. Fellow IEEE. Republican. Presbyterian. Clubs: University (Pitts.); Rolling Rock (Ligonier, Pa.). Patentee continous wave acoustic guidance system, 1965.

HAMILTON, WILLIAM MILTON, industrial company executive; b. Phila., Feb. 5, 1925; s. Louis Valentine and Elsie Marie (Walter) H.; m. Eidth Marie Busey, June 9, 1947; children: Barbara Marie, William Milton Jr., Patricia Ann. B.S. in Indsl. Mgmt., Ga. Inst. Tech., 1947. Asst. br. mgr. Swift & Co., Atlanta, 1947-48; treas. R.K. Price Co., Fayetteville, Ga., 1954-55; br. mgr. N.Y. Wire Cloth Co., Atlanta, 1955-56; from ops. mgr. to sr. v.p. Premier Indsl. Corp., Cleve., 1956—. Served to lt. USN, 1943-46, 48-54. Methodist. Club: Elyria Country (Ohio). Home: 1585 Greenleaf Circle Westlake OH 44145 Office: Premier Indsl Corp 4415 Euclid Ave Cleveland OH 44103

HAMILTON, WILLIAM T., petroleum company executive. Exec. v.p. exploration and prodn. Coral Petroleum, Inc. Office: Coral Petroleum Inc 980 Town and Country Rd Houston TX 77024§

HAMILTON, WILLIAM THORNE, aeronautical engineer; b. Marion Center, Pa., July 26, 1917; s. William Thorne and Jennie Irene (Mabon) H.; m. Ida Mae Dunn, Oct. 19, 1941; children: Richard James, Janet Gail, Nancy Jean. B.S. in Aero. Engring., U. Wash., 1941, M.S., 1947. Research scientist NASA Ames Aero. Lab., Moffett Field, Calif., 1941-45, 47-48; with Boeing Co., Seattle, 1948—; v.p. research and engring. div. Boeing Aerospace Co., 1974-77; v.p. research and devel. Boeing Comml. Airplane Co., 1978-80; v.p. engring. Boeing Mil. Airplane Co., Seattle, 1980-81, v.p., chief scientist, 1981-82; ret., 1982; mem. adv. com. NASA Research and Tech. Adv. Council, 1973-78; mem. Atlantic Group Aerospace Research and Devel., 1971-78. Author numerous publs. on aerodynamic stability and control. Served to ensign USN, 1945-46. Fellow AIAA; mem. Nat. Acad. Engring., Am. Def. Preparedness Assn. (corp.). Republican. Presbyterian. Office: PO Box 3707 M S 40-08 Seattle WA 98124

HAMISTER, DONALD BRUCE, electronics company executive; b. Cleve., Nov. 29, 1920; s. Victor Carl and Bess Irene (Sutherl) H.; m. Margaret Irene Singiser, Dec. 22, 1946; children: Don Bruce, Tracy. A.B. cum laude, Kenyon Coll., 1947; postgrad., Stanford U., 1948-49, U. Chgo., 1957. Application engr. S.E. Joslyn Co., Cin., 1947-48; regional sales mgr. Joslyn Mfg. and Supply Co., St. Louis, 1950-52, mktg. mgr., Chgo., 1953-55, asst. to pres., 1956-57, mgr. aircraft arrester dept., 1958-62, gen. mgr. electronic systems div., 1962-71, v.p., gen. mgr., dir., Goleta, Calif., 1973-78, group v.p. indsl. products, 1974-78, pres., chief exec. officer, 1978—, chmn., 1979—; pres. Joslyn Stainless; pres., dir. Joslyn Stamping Co.; pres., chmn., dir. Joslyn Def. Systems, Inc., 1981—; dir. Brewer Tichener Corp. Served to lt. USNR, 1942-46. Mem. IEEE, Airline Avionics Inst. (pres., chmn. 1972-74). Clubs: Univ. (Chgo.); Canadian (N.Y.C.). Home: 1141 Camino del Rio Santa Barbara CA 93110 Office: PO Box 817 Goleta CA 93017

HAMIT, HAROLD FRANCIS, physician; b. Stockton, Kans., Dec. 29, 1913; s. Claude Charles and Maude Leota (Laurie) H.; m. Ethel Cordelia Granger, Sept. 6, 1935; children—Francis Granger, Elaine Marie. A.B., N.Y. U., 1942, M.D., 1945; M.S., U. Colo., 1955. Diplomate: Am. Bd. Surgery, Am. Bd. Thoracic Surgery. Commd. 1st lt., M.C. U.S. Army, 1946, advanced through grades to col., 1963; regtl. surgeon (43d Inf.), Luzon, Philippines, 1946-47, post surgeon Tokyo Q.M. Depot, 1947-48; resident in surgery Oliver Gen. Hosp., Augusta, Ga., 1949-50, Brooke Gen. Hosp., San Antonio, 1950-51, Fitzsimons Gen. Hosp., Denver, 1953-55, Letterman Gen. Hosp., San Francisco, 1960-62; comdr. Army Hosp., Camp Leroy, Johnson, La., 1951-53, chief gen. surgery, Ft. Hood, Tex., 1955-57; postgrad. tng. Walter Reed Army Inst. Research, Washington, 1956-57; chief surg. br. (Army Research and Devel. Command), 1957-60; comdr. 121st Evacuation Hosp., Korea, 1962-63; chief gen. surgery (Brooke Gen. Hosp.), 1965-67; dir. div. surgery Walter Reed Army Inst. Research, 1967-68; ret., 1968; asso. dir. clin. research Travenol Labs., Morton Grove, Ill., 1968-70; asso. chmn. dept. gen. surgery Charlotte (N.C.) Meml. Hosp., 1970—; clin. prof. surgery U. N.C. Sch. Medicine, Chapel Hill, 1975—; research asso. prof. srugery Baylor U. Coll. Medicine, Houston, 1963-65; lectr. Northwestern Sch. Medicine, Chgo., 1968-70. Contbr. to profl. jours. Decorated Legion of Merit. Fellow Am. Assn. Surgery Trauma, A.C.S.; mem. AMA, Mil. Surgeons U.S., Am. Burn Assn., N.Y. Acad. Scis., AAAS, Corr. Soc. Surgeons, Internat. Platform Com., Mil. Order Carabao. Home: 1309 Providence Rd Charlotte NC 28207 Office: Charlotte Memorial Hosp Charlotte NC 28232 *When I think of all of the crossroads of opportunity of my life where decisions different from the ones I made would have resulted in a life and a career quite different from the one I have had, I am pleased with the paths I have chosen because they have led to a career of service to my country and to mankind. If I could live my life over I would hope to make essentially the same choices and hope for the same results.*

HAMLET, JAMES FRANK, former army officer, company director; b. Alliance, Ohio, Dec. 13, 1921; s. Frank James and Rhoda (Colbert) H.; m. Farice Mercedes Bray, July 8, 1951; 1 son, James Donald. Student, Tuskegee Inst., 1940-43; B.S., St. Benedict's Coll., Atchison, Kans., 1968; grad., Army War Coll., 1970. Commd. 2d lt. U.S. Army, 1944, advanced through grades to maj. gen.; comdr., Vietnam, 1966-67, 1970-71; asst. div. comdr. (101st Airborne Div.), Vietnam, 1971, comdg. gen., 1972, Ft. Carson, Colo., 1972-74; dep. insp. gen. U.S. Army, Washington, 1974-81; dir. United Services Automobile Assn., San Antonio, Wall St. Petroleum Corp., N.Y.C. Commr. Trenton City Mus., Mercer County Community Coll.; advisor Trenton YWCA. Decorated D.F.C., Distinguished Service Medal, Legion of Merit with 2 oak leaf clusters, Soldiers Medal, Bronze Star with 2 oak leaf clusters, Air medal with 49 oak leaf clusters. Episcopalian. Home: 20 Glenwood Ave Trenton NJ 08618

HAMLETT, SAMUEL BARKSDALE, educator; b. Farmville, Va., July 23, 1921; s. Samuel Hales and Nell (McCaughan) H.; m. Ethel Ruth Greer, Mar. 23, 1951; 1 son, Samuel Stephen. B.A., U. Tex. at Austin, 1947, M.A., 1949, Ph.D., 1966. Tchr. pub. schs., Alice, Tex., 1948-51, Austin, 1952-56; mem. faculty U. Tex. at Arlington, 1956—, prof. govt., 1969—, chmn. dept., 1966-77. Author: (with Luther Hagard, Jr. and August Spain) Legislative Redistricting in Texas, 1965. Chmn. bd. dirs. Wesley Found., U. Tex. at Arlington, 1968-70; chmn. bd. ch. and soc. Central Tex. conf. United Methodist Ch., 1973-75; mem. Arlington City Council, 1977-79; sec.-treas., bd. dirs. N.Tex. Higher Edn. Authority, 1979—, Higher Edn. Servicing Corp., Arlington, 1979—. Served with AUS, 1942-45. Decorated Air Medal, Purple Heart. Mem. Am. Polit. Sci. Assn., Southwestern Social Sci. Assn. Home: 1304 W Lavender Ln Arlington TX 76013

HAMLIN, ARTHUR TENNEY, librarian; b. Haverhill, Mass., Feb. 8, 1913; s. Christopher Robert and Edith (Redman) H.; m. Pauline L. Randolph, Sept. 16, 1939 (div. 1975); children: Peter R., Sally R. (Mrs. Richard Price), Rebecca R. (Mrs. Yutaka Sato); m. Jean Warren Boyer, 1976. A.B., Harvard U., 1934, postgrad., 1936-37; B.L.S. Columbia U., 1939. Asst. Harvard Coll. Library, 1934-36; curator Poetry Room, 1936-38, freshman proctor, adv., 1934-38; asst. gen. reference desk and econs. div. N.Y. Pub. Library, 1939-40; asst.-at-large U. of Pa. Library, 1940-42, chief service to readers and asst. librarian, 1945-49; research analyst Office Naval Intelligence, 1942-45; exec. sec. Assn. Coll. and Reference Libraries, 1949-56; univ. librarian U. Cin., 1956-68, prof. bibliography, 1962-68; dir. libraries, prof. Temple U., Phila., 1968-79, emeritus, 1979—; a founder, dir. Junto, Phila., 1941-42, 45-48; mem. Pa. Library Master Plan Com.; dir. Midwest Inter-Library Center, 1956-62; Fulbright lectr. U. Pavia, Italy, 1961-62; Fulbright research scholar U. Birmingham, Eng., 1966-67; mem. task force on a nat. periodicals system Nat. Commn. on Libraries and Info. Sci., 1975-77. Author: Harvard in Cincinnati, 1969, The University Library in the United States, 1981, St. Andrew's Church, Newcastle, Maine, a centennial history, 1983; Contbr. articles to profl. jours. Bd. dirs. City Charter Com., Cin., 1964-68. Mem. ALA (chmn. bldg. and equipment sect. 1957-58, chmn. adult services spl. projects com. 1959-60, mem. council 1958-62, 64-68, spl. rep. to flooded Italian libraries 1967, chmn. spl. com. to aid Italian libraries 1967-69, co-chmn. com. on flood damaged libraries 1972-73), Ohio Coll. Assn. (pres. libraries sect. 1960-61), Ohio Library Assn. (chmn. devel. com., mem. exec. bd.; v.p., pres. 1965), Pa. Library Assn. (chmn. conf. local arrangements com. 1969-70), Assn. Research Libraries (dir. 1973-74, chmn. task force on nat. periodicals resources plans 1973-75, chmn. com. on Negro acad. libraries 1971-75), Assn. Coll. and Reference Libraries (chmn. grants com. 1956-58, 64-66), Bibliog. Soc. Am., Union Library Catalog Pa. (treas. 1972-76), Alpha Beta Alpha. Episcopalian. Clubs: Franklin Inn, Harvard; Grolier (N.Y.C.). Home: RD 1 Box S-650 Wiscasset ME 04578 Office: Paley Library Temple U Philadelphia PA 19122 *As I look back on contacts with my fellow man the qualities of character that I place highest are integrity and a sense of stewardship. They are difficult qualities to hold fast, but they are essential to a truly useful, productive career.*

HAMLIN, HARRY ROBINSON, actor; b. Pasadena, Calif., Oct. 30, 1951; s. Chauncey Jerome and Bernice (Robinson) H.; 1 son, Dimitri Alexander. B.A., Yale U.; postgrad., Am. Conservatory Theatre, San Francisco. Appeared in: film Making Love, 1982, Clash of The Titans, 1981, Movie Movie, 1979, King of the Mountain, 1981; TV mini-series Studs Lonigan, Master of the Game, 1984. ITT Fulbright grantee, 1977.

HAMLIN, JAMES TURNER, III, physician, university dean; b. Danville, Va., Feb. 6, 1929; s. James T. and Nell (Davis) H.; m. Mary Caperton, June 9, 1955; children: Helen Austin, Mary Davis, James Turner. A.B., Va. Mil. Inst., 1951; M.D., U. Va., 1955. Intern Peter Bent Brigham Hosp., Boston, 1955; also resident; instr. medicine N.Y. Med. Coll., 1959-60; guest investigator Rockefeller Inst., N.Y.C., 1960-62; asst. prof. medicine Med. Coll. Ga., Augusta, 1962-64, asso. prof., 1964-66; asso. prof. medicine U. Va., Charlottesville, 1966-73, dir. clin. research center, 1966-71, asst. dean, 1970-71, acting dean sch. medicine, 1971-72, asso. dean, 1972-73; vice dean sch. medicine Tulane U., New Orleans, 1973-75, dean, 1975—, prof. medicine, 1973—. Contbr. articles to med. jours. Mem. Am. Fedn. for Clin. Research, So. Soc. for Clin. Investigation, AAAS, AMA, Med. Soc. Va., Albemarle County, La. State, Orleans Parish med. socs., Sigma Xi, Alpha Omega Alpha. Republican. Presbyterian. Home: 22 Park Island Dr New Orleans LA 70122 Office: 1430 Tulane Ave New Orleans LA 70112

HAMLIN, KENNETH ELDRED, JR., retired pharmaceutical company executive; b. Balt., Mar. 27, 1917; s. Kenneth Eldred and Julia (Gallup) H.; m. Janet Hoy, June 18, 1941; children: Kathleen Ann, Kenneth Thomas. B.S., U. Md., 1938, Ph.D., 1941. Research assoc. U. Ill., Urbana, 1941-42; instr. U. Md., 1942-43; research chemist, asst. head organic research, head organic research, asst. dir. chem. research Abbott Labs., North Chicago, Ill., 1943-61, dir. research, 1961-66; v.p. research and devel. Cutter Labs., Inc., Berkeley, Calif., 1966-73, v.p. research and quality assurance, 1973-74, sr. v.p. sci. ops., 1974-81, vice chmn. bd. dirs., 1980-81, dir., 1968-81; vol. tchr. gen. sci., computer sci. St. Patrick's Sch., Oakland, Calif., 1981—. Author: (with Jenkins, Hartung, Hamlin and Data) The Chemistry of Organic Medicinal Products, 1957. Mem. Am. Pharm. Assn., Am. Chem. Soc., AAAS, Sigma Xi, Rho Chi, Alpha Chi Sigma. Republican. Home: 41 Dos Posos Orinda CA 94563 Office: 4th and Parker Sts Berkeley CA 94710

HAMLIN, RICHARD EUGENE, former college president, banker; b. Royal, Iowa, June 2, 1925; s. Fred E. and Nancy Jane (Schuetz) H.; m. C. Joan Dahl, Aug. 14, 1949; children: Robert E., Elizabeth Ann. Student, Drury Coll., 1943; B.S., George Williams Coll., 1949; M.A., U. Omaha, 1952; Ph.D., U. Nebr., 1956. Exec. sec. South Omaha (Nebr.) YMCA, 1949-51, adult edn. dir., Omaha, 1951-53, asso. dir. research nat. bd., 1953-61; pres. George Williams Coll., 1961-83; chmn. bd. Bank of Yorktown, Lombard, Ill.; Tchr. summer conf. Am. Youth Found., summer sch. U. Omaha.; Chmn. bd. Asso. Colls. Ill., 1977-78; vice chmn. Fedn. Ind. Ill. Colls. and Univs., 1977-78, chmn., 1978-81. Author: Hi-Y Today, 1955, A New Look at YMCA Physical Education, 1957; Co-editor: YMCA Yearbook, 1958-61. Mem. Am., Ill. psychol. assns., Downers Grove (Ill.) C. of C. (past chmn. bd.). Conglist. Clubs: University, Economic (Chgo.). Address: One Yorktown Ctr Lombard IL 60148

HAMLIN, ROBERT HENRY, educator, management consultant; b. Cambridge, Mass., Apr. 2, 1923; s. Howard E. and Margaret E. (Henry) H.; m. Beate Kraschewski, Dec. 16, 1960; 1 son, Andrew Werner. A.B. summa cum laude, Ohio State U., 1944; B.S.M., Northwestern Med. Sch., 1945, B.M., 1946, M.D. with honors, 1947; M.P.H. magna cum laude, Harvard, 1952, LL.B., 1953. Diplomate: Am. Bd. Preventive Medicine. Intern Johns Hopkins Hosp., Balt., 1946-47; cons. Mass. commn. reporting, preparing and promulgating legislation on pub. and mental health and pub. welfare, 1950-53, 1st asst. to commnr. pub. health, Mass., 1952-53; asst. prof. legal medicine Harvard Law Sch., 1952-57; lectr. pub. health law and adminstrn. Harvard Sch. Pub. Health, 1952-57, asso. prof. pub. health adminstrn., 1959-62, Roger Irving Lee prof. pub. health, 1962-65, chmn. dept. pub. health practice, 1963-65; v.p. Booz, Allen and Hamilton (mgmt. cons.), 1965-67; ind. mgmt. cons., 1968; chmn. bd. MACRO Systems, Inc. (mgmt. cons.), Washington, 1969-80; clin. prof. comprehensive medicine Coll. Medicine, U. South Fla., 1980-83; acting dir., prof. pub. health program Coll. Pub. Health, U. South Fla., 1983—; pres. United Health Techs., Inc. (mgmt. cons.), 1981—; adj. prof. health adminstrn. Columbia U. Sch. Public Health and Adminstrv. Medicine, 1972-80; cons. Rockefeller Found., 1959-61; staff dir. spel. commn. Harvard health services, 1953-54; mem. U.S. Commn. for UNESCO; dir. pub. health, Brookline, Mass., 1953-57; cons. Hoover Commn. II, 1954-55; asst. to sec. health, edn. and welfare, 1957-59; vis. lectr. pub. health adminstrn. and law Harvard, 1957-59. Contbr. articles profl. publs. U.S. del. 10th session gen. conf. UNESCO, Paris, 1958; pub. health adminstrn. cons. to pvt. orgns., state and local govts. Served as apprentice seaman USN, 1943-46; lt. (j.g.) M.C. USNR, 1947-49. Fellow Am. Pub. Health Assn.; mem. Am. Pub. Welfare Assn., Am. Acad. Health Adminstrn. (dir. 1976-81), Mass. Med. Soc., Phi Beta Kappa, Phi Eta Sigma, Alpha Epsilon Delta, Alpha Omega Alpha, Delta Omega. Clubs: University, Fed. City (Washington). Home: 13300 Indian Rocks Rd Apt. 1904 Largo FL 33544 Office: Pub Health Program Coll Pub Health U South Fla MHC 6-238 13301 N 30th St Tampa FL 33612

HAMLISCH, MARVIN, composer; b. N.Y.C., June 2, 1944; s. Max and Lilly (Schachter) H. B.A., Queen's Coll., 1967; student, Juilliard Sch. Music, 1951-64. Accompanist and straight man on: tour with Groucho Marx, 1974-75; debut as pianist, Minn. Orch., 1975; composer: film scores for The Swimmer, 1968, Take the Money and Run, 1969, Bananas, 1971, Save The Tiger, 1973, Kotch, 1971, The Way We Were (Best Original Song and Best Original Dramatic Score, Am. Acad. Motion Picture Arts Scis. 1974), The Sting, (Best Scoring award Am. Acad. Motion Picture Arts Scis. 1974), Same Time Next Year, Ice Castles, 1979, Chapter Two, 1979, Starting Over, 1979, Ordinary People, 1980, Seems Like Old Times, 1980; popular songs Lollipops and Rainbows, 1960, Sunshine, Nobody Does It Better, 1977; Broadway musicals A Chorus Line, 1975 (Pulitzer and Tony awards), They're Playing Our Song, 1979; theme song for Good Morning, America, 1975. Address: care Rastar Films Inc Burbank CA 91505

HAMM, CHARLES JOHN, advertising company executive; b. Bklyn., May 11, 1937; s. Frank Coleman and Lisbeth (Higgins) H.; m. Irene Frail, Aug. 14, 1960; children: Charles William, Liza Higgins. B.A., Harvard U., 1959; M.B.A., N.Y. U., 1967. Vice pres., mgmt. supr. Wells Rich Greene Inc., N.Y.C., 1967-74; sr. v.p., mgmt. rep. Foote Cone & Belding Inc., N.Y.C., 1974-75; pres., chief operating officer F. William Free Inc., N.Y.C., 1975-77; exec. v.p. McCann-Erickson Worldwide, Inc., Atlanta, 1977-79, vice chmn. U.S.A., 1979-83, exec. v.p. internat., 1983—, also dir. Trustee Ind. Savs. Bank, N.Y.C., 1974—; Mem. alumni adv. council Phillips Exeter Acad., Exeter, N.H., 1980—. Served to 1st lt. C.E. U.S. Army, 1959-61. Clubs: Univ. (N.Y.C.); Bronxville (N.Y.); Field; Mashamack Fish and Game Soc. (Pine Plaines, N.Y.); Capital City (Atlanta). Office: 485 Lexington Ave New York NY 10017

HAMM, DONALD IVAN, educator; b. Wellington, Kans., Jan. 11, 1928; s. Cecil Randolph and Galys (Barker) H.; m. Jean Ann Ewing, Aug. 19, 1950; children: Jeffrey Lloyd, Cheryl Lynn, Dena Jo, David Ewing, James Ritchie. B.S., U. Okla., 1949, Ph.D., 1956; student, Southwestern U., 1945-46; M.S., Purdue U., 1951. Asst. prof. dept. chemistry Southwestern Okla. State U., Weatherford, 1951-53, assoc. prof., 1956-58, prof., 1958—, chmn. dept. chemistry, 1970-79, dean Sch. Arts and Scis., 1978—; vis. prof. chemistry Mich. State U., East Lansing, 1969-70; research assoc. Okla. Med. Research Found., Oklahoma City, 1953-55. Author: Chemistry: An Introduction to Matter and Energy, 1965, Fundamental Concepts of Chemistry, 1969. Mem. Am. Chem. Soc. (chmn. Okla. sect. 1972-73), Alpha Chi Sigma, Phi Lambda Upsilon, Sigma Pi Sigma. Democrat. Mem. Ch. of Christ. Club: Rotary (pres. 1960-61). Home: 1617 E Davis Rd Weatherford OK 73096 Office: 100 Campus Dr Weatherford OK 73096

HAMM, EDWARD FREDERICK, JR., bus. exec.; b. Chgo., Mar. 27, 1908; s. Edward Frederick and Sarah (Meek) H.; m. Joy Elizabeth Fairman, June 23, 1934; children—Julie Hamm Finley, Thornton Edward, Martha Joy Hamm Spencer. Student, Dartmouth Coll., 1930. Pres., treas. Traffic Service Corp., 1933—; pub. Traffic World, Traffic Bull., Daily Traffic World, 1944—; pres. Coll. Advanced Traffic, Inc., 1945—; cons. mag. sect. printing and pub. div. W.P.B., 1944-45; pres. Acad. Advanced Traffic; mem. distbn. council U.S. Dept. of Commerce; apptd. mng. dir. ICC, 1953. Mem. Chgo. Bus. Papers Assn. (pres. 1937), Asso. Bus. Papers (pres. 1948-49), Advt. Fedn. Am. (dir. 1948), Am. Soc. Traffic and Transp. (founder). Republican. Episcopalian. Clubs: Chicago (Chgo.); Metropolitan, Burning Tree, Nat. Press (Washington). Home: 2500 Virginia Ave NW Washington DC 20037 Office: 815 Washington Bldg Washington DC 20005

HAMM, WILLIAM GERALD, aerospace and electronics executive, engineer; b. Charlottesville, Va., May 27, 1931; s. Strother F. and Ruby (Barksdale) H.; m. Nancy B. Adkins, June 14, 1954 (div.); children: William G., Keith E., Alan R., David L.; m. Maria Laquer, Feb. 12, 1983. B.S. in Mech. Engring., U. Va., 1954. Engr. Douglas Aircraft Co., Santa Monica and Long Beach, Calif., 1954-61, Atlantic Research Corp., Alexandria, Va., 1961-71, v.p., 1971-80, exec. v.p., 1980—, dir. Mem. exec. bd., v.p. Boy Scouts Am. Nat. Capital Area, Washington, 1981—. Mem. AIAA, Am. Def. Preparedness Assn., Air Force Assn. (patron). Office: Atlantic Research Corp 5390 Cherokee Ave Alexandria VA 22314

HAMMAKER, PAUL M., business exec., educator, author; b. Dayton, Ohio, Jan. 25, 1903; s. Wilbur Emory and Willamine (Weihrauch) H.; m. Patricia Curry, Sept. 5, 1929 (dec. 1955); children—Robert, John, David; m. Adrienne V. S. Stokes, June 15, 1956 (dec. 1970). B.C.S., U. Ill., 1925; LL.D., MacMurray Coll., 1957. With Marshall Field & Co., 1943-57, divisional v.p., 1948; gen. mdse. mgr., sr. v.p., asst. gen. mgr. Chgo. and suburban stores, until 1957; exec. v.p., gen. mgr. Montgomery Ward, 1957-59, mem. bd. dir., 1958-61, pres., 1959-61; dir. The Fair Store, Montgomery Ward Real Estate Corp., Montgomery Ward Credit Corp., Standard T Chem. Co., Inc.; Prof. bus adminstrn. Grad. Sch. Bus. Adminstrn., U. Va., 1962-73; sr. fellow Center for Study Applied Ethics, 1973—; founder, partner Old Dominion Assos. (Mgmt. Cons.), 1964—. Author: (with Louis T. Rader) Plain Talk About Managing. Mem. Alpha Tau Omega, Beta Gamma Sigma. Presbyn. (elder). Clubs: Farmington Country, Boars Head Sports, Greencroft (Charlottesville, Va.); University, Chicago, Economic, Commercial, Mid-Am. (Chgo.); Westmoreland Country (Winnetka, Ill.). Home: 15 Farmington Dr Charlottesville VA 22901

HAMMAR, LESTER EVERETT, health care manufacturing company executive; b. Tillamook, Oreg., Dec. 15, 1927; s. Leo E. and Harriet L. (Parsons) H.; m. Margrit Steigl, May 9, 1964; children: Lawrence, Thomas, Stephanie. B.S., Oreg. State U., 1950; M.B.A., Washington U., 1964. With Montsanto Co., 1952-69; controller Monsanto-Europe, 1966-69; v.p., controller Smith Kline & French Labs., Phila., 1969-72, Abbott Labs., North Chgo., Ill., 1972—; dir. Hammar's Uniforms, Inc. Served to 1st lt., F.A. AUS, 1951-52. Mem. Fin. Execs. Inst. (com. mem.), Am. Mgmt. Assn. (finance council). Presbyn. Home: 809 Timber Ln Lake Forest IL 60045 Office: Abbott Labs North Chicago IL 60064

HAMMER, ARMAND, petroleum company executive, art patron; b. N.Y.C., May 21, 1898; s. Julius and Rose (Robinson) H.; m. Olga von Root, Mar. 14, 1927; m. Angela Zevely, Dec. 19, 1943; m. Frances Barrett, Jan. 26, 1956. B.S., Columbia U., 1919, M.D., 1921, LL.D., 1978; LL.D., Pepperdine U., 1978, Southeastern U., Washington, 1978, U. Aix-en-Provence, 1981; D.Public Service, Salem (W.Va.) Coll., 1979; H.H.D., U. Colo., Boulder, 1979. Pres. Allied Am. Corp., N.Y.C., 1923-25, A. Hammer Pencil Co., N.Y.C., London and Moscow, 1925-30, Hammer Galleries, Inc., 1930—, J. W. Dant Distilling Co., N.Y.C. and Dant, Ky., 1943-54; pres., chmn. bd. Mut. Broadcasting System, N.Y.C., 1957-58; chmn. bd., chief exec. officer Occidental Petroleum Corp., Los Angeles, 1957—; chmn. M. Knoedler & Co., Inc., N.Y.C., 1972—; dir. Nat. State Bank, Perth Amboy, N.J., 1949-56, City Nat. Bank, Beverly Hills, Calif., 1962-71, Can. Occidental Petroleum Ltd., Calgary, Alta., Raffinerie Belge de Petroles, Antwerp, Belgium, 1968-79, Cities Service Co., Tulsa; hon. dir. Fla. Nat. Bank of Jacksonville, 1966-72; mem. Nat. Petroleum Council, 1968—, Com. on Arctic Oil and Gas Resources, 1980—.

Author: The Quest of the Romanoff Treasure, 1936; subject of biography: The Remarkable Life of Dr. Armand Hammer (Robert Considine), 1975; Brit. edit. Larger than Life, 1976. Pres. N.J. Aberdeen Angus Assn., 1948-49; Bd. govs. Monmouth County Orgn. Social Service, Red Bank, N.J., 1949-61, Monmouth Meml. Hosp., Long Branch, N.J., 1946-58, Eleanor Roosevelt Cancer Found., N.Y.C., 1960—, Ford's Theatre Soc., 1970—, UN Assn. U.S.A., 1976—; trustee U. North Africa Assn., 1968-71, Los Angeles County Mus. Art, 1968—, UCLA Found., 1973-76, Nat. Symphony, 1977—, United for Calif., 1977—, Capitol Children's Mus., 1978—; chmn. wine and spirits div. Vis. Nurse Service Greater N.Y., 1946, Am. Aid to France, 1947; mem. Citizens Food Com., 1946-47, Cardinal Spellman's Com. of Laity for Catholic Charities, 1946-48, Public Adv. Com. on U.S. Trade Policy, 1968-69, Am. Com. for Nat. Archives, 1974-76, Los Angeles County-U. So. Calif. Cancer Assos., 1975—, George C. Marshall Assos., James Smithson Soc. of Smithsonian Nat. Assos., 1977—, U. Okla. Assos., 1981—, Bus. Adv. Commn. for 1984 Olympics, 1981—, Los Angeles Olympic Citizens Adv. Commn., 1981—; hon. trustee Denver Art Mus., 1980—; mem. adv. bd. Inst. of Peace, 1950-54, Los Angeles Beautiful, Inc., 1969-75, Com. for a Greater Calif., 1969—, Fogg Art Mus. and Fine Arts Library, Cambridge, Mass., 1977—, The Friendship Force, 1977—, Am. Longevity Assn., Inc., 1980—, Center Strategic and Internat. Studies, Georgetown U., 1981—; mem. fine arts com. U.S. Dept. State, 1981—; chmn. Pres.'s Cancer Panel, 1981—; mem. exec. com. Econ. Devel. Bd. City of Los Angeles, 1968-73; trustee, chmn. exec. com. Salk Inst. Biol. Studies, San Diego, 1969—; bd. dirs. Los Angeles World Affairs Council, 1969—, Planned Parenthood World Population/Los Angeles, 1970—, U.S.-USSR Trade and Econ. Council, 1973—, Assos. Harvard Bus. Sch., 1975—, Calif. Roundtable, 1976—, Century City Cultural Commn., 1977—, Corcoran Gallery Art, Washington, 1978—, Keep Am. Beautiful, Inc., 1979—, Bus. Com. for Arts, N.Y.C., 1980—; bd. visitors Grad. Sch. Mgmt., UCLA, 1957—, UCLA Sch. Medicine Center for Health Scis., 1980—; exec. mem. Energy Research and Edn. Found., 1978—; charter mem. Nat. Visiting Council of Health Scis. Faculties, Columbia U., 1978—; mem. univ. bd. Pepperdine U., 1979—; mem. fellows for life New Orleans Mus. Art, 1980—; mem. nat. support council U.S. Com. for UNICEF, 1980—; founder mem. Pepperdine Assos., 1976—; pres. Found. of Internat. Inst. Human Rights, Geneva, 1977—; mem. exec. bd. dirs. UN Assn. Los Angeles; mem. Bd. Mcpl. Arts Commrs. Los Angeles, 1969-73; mem. budget and fin. com. of bd. trustees Los Angeles County Mus. Art, 1972-74; sponsor Internat. Inst. Human Rights Peace Conf., Oslo, 1978, Campobello Peace Park sponsor Internat. Inst. Human Rights Peace Conf., Oslo, 1979 sponsor Internat. Inst. Human Rights Peace Conf., Warsaw, 1980 sponsor Internat. Inst. Human Rights Peace Conf., Aix-en-Provence, France, 1981. Served with M.C. U.S. Army, 1918-19. Endowed Armand Hammer Center for Cancer Biology, Salk Inst., 1969; Armand Hammer prof. bus. and public policy UCLA, 1968; Frances and Armand Hammer wing Los Angeles County Mus. Art, 1969; Armand Hammer Animal Facility Salk Inst., 1976; Calif. Inst. Cancer Research UCLA, 1976; Ann. Armand Hammer Cancer Conf. and Fund Salk Inst., 1976; Harvard/Columbia Russian Study Fund, 1977; Julius and Armand Hammer Health Scis. Center Columbia U., 1977; Five-Yr. Funding Program UN Assn., 1978, Corcoran Gallery Art, 1979, Jacquemart-André Mus., Paris, 1979; Ann. Armand Hammer Award Luncheon, Los Angeles, 1980; recipient Humanitarian award Eleanor Roosevelt Cancer Found., 1962; city commendation Mayor of Los Angeles, 1968; decorated comdr. Order of Crown, Belgium, 1962; comdr. Order of Andres Bellos, Venezuela, 1975; Order of Aztec Eagle, Mex., 1977; officer Legion of Honor, France, 1978; Order of Friendship Among Peoples, USSR, 1978; Disting. Honoree of Yr. Nat. Art Assn., 1978; Golden Plate award Am. Acad. Achievement, 1978; Aztec award Mexican-Am. Opportunity Fond., 1978; Appeal of Conscience award, N.Y.C., 1978; Spirit of Life award Oil Industry Council of City of Hope, 1979; Royal Order of Polar Star, Sweden, 1979; award Antique Monthly, 1980; Entrepreneur of Yr. award U. So. Calif., 1980; Maimonides award Los Angeles Jewish Community, 1980; Golden Achievement award Andrus Gerontology Center, U. So. Calif., 1981; Ambassador of Arts award State of Fla., 1981; officer Grand Order of Merit, Italy, 1981. Mem. Los Angeles Petroleum Club, Royal Acad. Arts (London), hon. corr., Am. Petroleum Inst. (dir. 1975—), Navy League U.S. (Los Angeles council 1980—), Fifty-Yr. Club Am. Medicine, Royal Scottish Acad. (hon.), AMA (life), N.Y. County Med. Assn., Internat. Inst. Human Rights, Alpha Omega Alpha, Mu Sigma, Phi Sigma Delta. Office: Occidental Petroleum Corp 10889 Wilshire Blvd Suite 1500 Los Angeles CA 90024

HAMMER, CARL, computer scientist, former computer co. exec.; b. Chgo., May 10, 1914; s. Karl Heinrich and Kaethe (Patzig) H.; m. T. Jeannette George, Sept. 23, 1944. Dipl. Math. Statistics, U. Munich, 1936, Ph.D. magna cum laude, 1938. Mathematician, statistician Tex. Co. Research Labs., Beacon, N.Y., 1938-43; statistician Pillsbury Mills Inc., N.Y.C., 1944-47; chmn. div. tech. edn. Walter Hervey Jr. Coll., 1947-51; sr. staff engr. Franklin Inst., Phila., 1951-55; dir. UNIVAC European Computing Center Sperry Rand Corp., Frankfurt/Main, Germany, 1955-57; staff cons., acting mgr. programming and analysis dept. Sylvania Electronic Products, Inc., Needham, Mass., 1957-59; sr. engrng. scientist surface communications div. RCA, N.Y.C., 1959-61, mgr. sci. computer applications, Washington, 1961-63; dir. computer sci. UNIVAC, Washington, 1963-81; instr. German for staff officers U.S. Mil. Acad., summer 1942; instr. math. Pratt Inst., 1945-46; instr. math. and statistics Sch. Gen. Studies, Hunter Coll., 1947-52; adj. prof. Am. U., 1962-80; vis. prof. Indsl. Coll. Armed Forces, Washington, 1967—. Author: Viscosity Index Tables, 1941, Rank Correlation of Cities, 1951, Univac Programming with Compilers, 1956, Computers and Simulation, Vol. IV, Number 4, 1961, High-Speed Digital Communication Networks, 1963, Statistical Validation of Mathematical Computer Routines, 1967, Signature Simulation and Certain Cryptographic Codes, 1971, Space Communications Procs., Panel Sci. and Tech, 1972, Computers in Research, Procs. Internat. Symposium, 1974; contbr. articles in field of computer tech. to profl. jours. Mem. Nat. Def. Exec. Res., 1970—. Recipient Computer Sci. Man of Year award Data Processing Mgmt. Assn., 1973. Fellow AAAS, N.Y. Acad. Scis., Assn. Computer Programmers and Analysts; mem. IEEE (sr.), AAUP, Am. Math. Soc., Am. Soc. for Cybernetics (sec. 1967, v.p. 1968, pres. 1969-72), Am. Statis. Assn., Assn. for Computing Machinery (chpt. chmn. Washington 1966-68, rep. Capital region 1968—, chmn. accreditation com. 1968-70, nat. lectr. 1969-70, chmn. nominating com. 1971-73, Disting. Service award 1979), N.Y. Acad. Scis., Assn. Systems Mgmt. (dir. Washington chpt. 1969-71), Inst. Math. Statistics, Math. Assn. Am., Soc. Indsl. and Applied Math. (treas. 1953-55), Research Soc. Am. Home: 3263 O St NW Washington DC 20007

HAMMER, CHARLES LAWRENCE, educator; b. Buffalo, N.Y., June 30, 1922; s. Charles L. and Maxine (Burdick) H.; m. Hazel Churchill Mills, Aug. 14, 1948; children—David, Alison, Carla, Bonnie. B.A., U. Mich., 1948, M.S., 1950, Ph.D., 1953. Instr. physics U. Mich., Ann Arbor, 1953-54; mem. faculty Iowa State U., Ames, 1954—, asso. prof., 1959-61, prof., 1961—; cons. Allis Chalmers Mfg. Co., Milw., 1956-68; mem. adv. council NSF, 1978—. Contbr. articles to profl. jours. Mem. Ames Goals and Priorities Com., 1974-76; mem. Community Theater, Ames, 1964—, Choral Soc., 1966-70; Chmn. Iowa Democratic Conf., 1970-72; mem. Iowa Dem. Central Com., 1974-80, Ames City Council, 1976—; bd. dirs. Midwestern U. Research Assn., Chgo. Served to 1st lt. USAAF, 1942-45; PTO. Decorated D.F.C. with oak leaf cluster, Air Medal with 3 oak leaf clusters. Fellow Am. Phys. Soc.; mem. Sigma Xi, Phi Beta Kappa, Phi Kappa Phi. Home: 1222 Scholl Rd Ames IA 50010

HAMMER, DONALD PRICE, librarian; b. Pottsville, Pa., Dec. 16, 1921; s. Edward Price and Gertrude May (Schaeffer) H.; m. Louise Eleanore Kohler, May 26, 1947; 1 son, Donald Edward. B.S., Kutztown (Pa.) State Coll., 1948; M.L.S., George Peabody Coll., 1955; postgrad., U. Pitts., Moody Bible Inst. Asst. librarian Gettysburg (Pa.) Coll. Library, 1948-50; gifts and exchange librarian, then law librarian Pa. State Library, Harrisburg, 1950-55; bookstack librarian U. Ill., Urbana, 1955-58; head serials unit, then head systems devel. Purdue U. Library, 1959-71; asso. dir. U. Mass. Library, 1972-73; exec. dir. Library and Info. Tech. Assn.-Library Adminstrn. and Mgmt. Assn., Chgo., 1973-79, Library and Info. Tech. Assn., 1979—; past mem. coms. Am. Nat. Standards Inst.; cons. in field. Author: The Information Age—Its Development, Its Impact, 1976; also articles, chpts. in books. Served with USAAF, 1942-44. Grantee Library Services and Constrn. Act, 1968-71. Mem. ALA (pres.-elect Info. Sci. and Automation Div. 1972-73), Am. Soc. Info. Sci. (chmn.-elect Ind. chpt. 1971-72), Beta Phi Mu. Baptist. Home: 203 Stafford Dr Wheeling IL 60090 Office: 50 E Huron St Chicago IL 60611

HAMMER, EMANUEL FREDERICK, clinical psychologist and psychoanalyst; b. N.Y.C., Aug. 15, 1926; s. Isadore and Rebecca (Lieberman) H.; m. Lila Maralyn King, June 4, 1950; children: Diane Robin, Cary Mark. Student, Bklyn. Coll., 1944-45, 46-47; B.A. magna cum laude, Syracuse U., 1948; Ph.D., N.Y. U., 1951. Diplomate: in clin. psychology Am. Bd. Profl. Psychology. Dir. intern tng. Lynchburg (Va.) State Colony, 1951-52; sr. research scientist N.Y. State Psychiat. Inst., 1952-55; dir. dept. psychology N.Y.C. Criminal Cts., 1955-72; chief psychologist Lincoln Inst. for Psychotherapy, N.Y.C., 1960-68; lectr. Bklyn. Coll., 1958-63, New Sch. for Social Research, 1972; adj. asso. prof. N.Y. U. Grad. Sch. Arts and Scis., 1966-76; clin. prof. Postdoctoral Inst. Advanced Psychol. Studies, Adelphi U., 1980—. Author: The Clinical Application of Projective Drawings, 1958, Creativity, 1961, Use of Interpretation in Treatment, 1968, Antiachievement: Perspectives on School Drop-Outs, 1970; others. Served with USAF, 1945-46; PTO. Fellow Am. Psychol. Assn.; liaison fellow Am. Anthrop. Assn.; mem. Nat. Psychol. Assn. for Psychoanalysis (dir.), N.Y. Soc. Clin. Psychology (pres. 1964-65). Home: 381 West End Ave New York NY 10024

HAMMER, FREDERICK S., banker; b. N.Y.C., June 17, 1936; s. Frederick P. and Rose H.; m. Ann Shaver, Nov. 7, 1958; children: Virginia, Kristin, Frederick P., Rebecca. A.B., Colgate U., 1958; M.S., Carnegie Mellon U., 1960, Ph.D., 1963. Vice-pres. Bankers Trust Co., N.Y.C., 1962-68; pres. Leasco Data Processing, Inc., Bethesda, Md., 1968-69, Integrated Systems Corp., N.Y.C., 1969-71; exec. v.p. fin. Assos. Corp. N.Am., South Bend, Ind., 1971-75; pres. MGT Ltd., Brussels, 1975-77; exec. v.p. consummer banking sect. Chase Manhattan Bank, N.Y.C., 1977—; dir. VISA U.S.A., Inc., VISA Internat. Author: Demand for Physical Capital, 1963, Analytical Methods in Banking, 1966; editor: Jour. Bank Research. Mem. Bd. Edn. Ridgewood, N.J.; trustee Colgate U., 1972-75, Wells Coll., 1969-75; vice chmn. United Way campaign, South Bend, 1974. Mem. Consumers Banking Assn., Assn. for a Better N.Y., Regional Plan Assn. Office: Chase Manhattan Bank One Chase Manhattan Plaza New York NY *

HAMMER, HAROLD HARLAN, oil company financial executive; b. Chgo., May 23, 1920; s. B. James and Frances (Halbren) H.; m. Hannah Richmond, Mar. 1, 1956; children: John, Elizabeth. B.S., Northwestern U., 1941; M.B.A., N.Y. U., 1950, J.D., 1955. Bar: N.Y. State 1955. Accountant U.S. Steel Corp., 1941-42; asst. sec.-treas. Duraloy Co., Scottdale, Pa., 1945-48; financial analyst, asst. controller Port of N.Y. Authority, 1948-50; investment counsel, N.Y.C., 1950—, since practiced in; v.p. finance, dir. Control Data Corp., Mpls., 1966-72; chmn. finance com., dir. Gen. Refractories Co., 1963-66; with Gulf Oil Corp., Pitts., 1972—, sr. v.p., 1972-73, exec. v.p., 1973-81, chief adminstrv. officer, 1981—; dir. La Salle Steel Corp., Lee Data Corp. Author: Financing the Port of New York Authority, 1957, also articles in field. Bd. govs. Midwest Stock Exchange.; Bd. dirs. W. Penn Hosp. Served as lt. USNR, World War II. Mem. Am., Fed., N.Y. bar assns., N.Y. Soc. Security Analysts, Financial Execs. Inst., V.F.W., Am. Legion, Phi Alpha Delta. Methodist. Clubs: Fox Meadow Tennis (gov. 1966); Duquesne, Fox Chapel Golf (Pitts.); Rolling Rock (Liqonier, Pa.). Home: 212 Schenley Rd Pittsburgh PA 15217 Office: Gulf Bldg Pittsburgh PA 15230

HAMMER, KENNETH FREDERICK, scale company executive; b. Seattle, Mar. 24, 1930; s. Karl E. and Marion A. (Flagler) H.; m. Gretchen H. Davis, July 12, 1958; children: Karin, Laurence, Karol, Peter, Richard. B.S. in Mech. Engring., U. Wash., 1952, M.S., Cornell U., 1954. Instr. Cornell U., Ithaca, N.Y., 1953-54; trainee Gen. Electric Co., Schenectady, 1954-55, mfg. mgr., Lynn, Mass., 1957-62; v.p. mfg. Computer Control div. Honeywell, Framingham, Mass., 1962-68; pres. Fairbanks Weighing div. Colt Industries, St. Johnsbury, Vt., 1968—; dir. Citizens Savs. Bank & Trust Co., St. Johnsbury. Trustee N.E. Vt. Regional Hosp., St. Johnsbury, 1982—, St. Johnsbury Acad., 1977—; chmn. bd. trustees Vt. Symphony Orch., Middlebury, 1970-72. Served with U.S. Army, 1955-57. Mem. Scale Mfg. Assn. (dir., pres. 1973-81), Vt. Indsl. Devel. Authority, Assn. Industry of Vt. (v.p. 1982—, dir. 1969-71, 72-75), Sigma Xi, Zeta Mu Tau, Tau Beta Pi, Phi Kappa Phi. Republican. Congregationalist. Office: Fairbanks Weighing Div Colt Industries Saint Johnsburg VT 05819

HAMMER, LAVERNE LOUIS, publisher, printer; b. Wellesley, Ont., Can., June 9, 1935; s. Adam Henry and Christina Margarette (Wagner) H.; m. Joyce Elizabeth Meyer, Oct. 6, 1956; children: Cheryl Joyce, Jeffrey Adam. B.A., Waterloo Lutheran U., 1966. From teller to asst. mgr. Canadian Imperial Bank Commerce (various locations), Ont., 1952-56; mgr. adminstrn. Dominion Electrohome Industries Ltd., Kitchener, Ont., 1956-64; dir., gen. mgr. Collier Macmillan Can., Ltd., Galt and Toronto, 1956-68; pres. Collier Macmillan Internat., N.Y.C., 1968-69; dep. mng. dir. Cassell & Collier Macmillan, Ltd., London, 1970-73; pres. Collier Macmillan Can., Ltd., Toronto, 1973-78, Brentano's Booksellers Ltd. Can., 1976-78; pres., owner Interprint Services (1978) Inc. Mem. Acad. Certified Adminstrv. Mgrs. (certified adminstrv. mgr.), Inst. Certified Adminstrv. Mgrs. Ont., Adminstrv. Mgmt. Soc. Lutheran. Club: Mayfair Racquet. Home: 28 Pepper Tree Dr West Hill ON Canada M1C 1Y7 Office: 187-17 Steelcase Rd W Markham ON Canada L3R 2R9

HAMMER, ROY ARMAND, lawyer; b. N.Y.C., Sept. 25, 1934; s. Joseph J. and Beatrice (Kopald) H.; m. Sylvia Goldberg, June 16, 1956; children: Julie, Beth. B.A., Yale U., 1956; M.A., Columbia U., 1957; LL.B., Harvard U., 1960. Bar: Mass. 1961. Since practiced in, Boston; partner firm Hemenway & Barnes, 1966—; spl. counsel City of Cambridge, Mass., 1966-68; Mem. Mass. Bar Overseers, 1974-78, vice chmn., 1977-78. Fellow Am. Bar Found. (chmn. Mass. 1982—); mem. Am. Bar Assn. (ho. dels. 1978—), Nat. Conf. Bar Presidents (exec. council 1980—), Mass. Bar Assn. (pres. 1978-79), Mass. Bar Found. (pres. 1981—), Boston Bar Assn. Democrat. Jewish. Clubs: Harvard, Yale (Boston). Office: 60 State St Boston MA 02109

HAMMER, SANFORD S., engineer, university administrator; b. Bklyn., Aug. 21, 1935; s. Murray and Gertrude H.; m. Marcia Rainer, June 22, 1958; children: Kenneth, Michele. B.S. in Physics, Poly. Inst. Bklyn., 1956, M.M.E., 1959, Ph.D. in Mech. Engring., 1966. Asst. prof. mech. engring. Poly. Inst. Bklyn., 1956-62, sr. research assoc., Farmingdale, N.Y., 1962-66; prof. engring. sci. Hofstra U., Hempstead, N.Y., 1966-75, exec. dean student services, 1975-82, provost, dean faculty, 1982—; engring. cons. various aerospace corps. and govt. agys., 1959-75. Office: Hofstra U Hempstead NY 11550

HAMMER, WADE BURKE, educator; b. Lakeland, Fla., Apr. 21, 1932; s. Orval Seown and Lilly Pearl (Wade) H.; m. Betty Dean Webb, June 22, 1956; children: Robert Burke, Joanna Wade. A.A., U. Fla., 1956; D.D.S., Emory U., 1960. Diplomate Am. Bd. Oral and Maxillofacial Surgery. Pvt. practice dentistry, Orange Park, Fla., 1960-61; resident in oral and maxillofacial surgery U. Pa., Phila., 1961-62, Grady Meml. Hosp., Atlanta and Emory U., 1962-65; pvt. practice oral surgery, Atlanta, 1965-68; mem. staff Talmadge Meml. Hosp., Augusta, Ga.; asst. prof. oral surgery Med. Coll. Ga., Augusta, 1968-71, assoc. prof., 1971-75, prof., 1975—; cons. Ft. Gordon Army Med. Center, Univ. Hosp., Augusta. Contbr. articles to profl. jours. Served with USN, 1950-54; served to col. USAR, 1976—. Fellow Am. Assn. Oral and Maxillofacial Surgeons, Am. Coll. Dentists, Am. Soc. Dental Anesthesiology; Mem. CADA; mem. Internat. Assn. Dental Research, Ga. Dental Assn., Eastern Dist. Dental Assn., Am. Assn. Dental Schs., Augusta Dental Soc., Ga. Soc. Oral and Maxillofacial Surgeons, Southeastern Soc. Oral and Maxillofacial Surgeons (pres. 1984-85), Res. Officers Assn., Assn. Mil. Surgeons, Exptl. Aircraft Assn., Omicron Kappa Upsilon. (pres. chpt. 1980-81). Methodist. Office: Medical Coll Ga Dept Oral and Maxillofacial Surgery Augusta GA 30912 *

HAMMERBECK, WANDA LEE, photographer; b. Lincoln, Nebr., Mar. 24, 1945; d. Thomas E. and Juanita (Arthur) Matthews. B.A. in Psychology, U. N.C., 1967, M.A., 1972; M.F.A. in Photography, San Francisco Art Inst., 1977. Gallery asst. Focus Gallery, San Francisco, 1974-75; darkroom asst. U. Calif. Extension, San Francisco, 1975; asst. Photog. Slide Library, San Francisco Art Inst., 1976, organizer slide and lecture tour photography, 1976, teaching asst. dept. photography, 1975-76; instr. photography Holy Names Coll., Oakland, Calif., 1976-81; dir. West Coast Visual Arts Archive, Camerawork Gallery, San Francisco, 1978-81; vis. lectr. various workshops and colls. in U.S., 1977-81; Bd. dirs. Camerawork Gallery, San Francisco, 1977—; Nat. Endowment for Arts grantee, 1979-80. One-woman shows of photography, San Francisco Mus. Modern Art, 1978, O.K. Harris, N.Y.C., 1979, Delahunty Gallery, Dallas, 1981; exhibited in group shows, 1975—, latest being, Santa Barbara (Calif.) Mus. Art, 1979, Calif. State U., Fullerton, Visual Studies Workshop, Rochester, N.Y., Mills Coll., Oakland, Calif., 1980, Jeffrey Fuller Fine Arts, Phila., 1980 81, U. Conn., Storrs, 1980, Tyler Sch. Art, Phila., DeCordova Mus., Lincoln, Mass.; represented in numerous public collections including, Fogg Mus., Harvard U., Cambridge, Mass., Mus. Modern Art, N.Y.C., Mpls. Inst. of Arts, Australian Nat. Gallery, UCLA, Center for Creative Photography, Tucson, Newport Harbor (Calif.) Art Mus., Atlantic Richfield Collection, San Francisco, R.I. Sch. Design, Providence, Santa Barbara Mus. Art, also, others. Mem. Soc. for Photog. Edn., Friends of Photography.

HAMMERLY, HARRY ALLAN, business executive; b. St. Paul, Feb. 23, 1934; s. Harry and Agnes (Iverson) H.; m. Lorraine M., May 18, 1957; children: Lynn, Matthew, Mary. B.B.A., U. Minn., 1955. C.P.A., Minn. With 3M, St. Paul, 1955-73; mng. dir. 3M Far East, Hong Kong, 1973-75; sr. mng. dir. Sumitomo 3M, Tokyo, 1975-79; v.p. Australia-Asia-Can. 3M, St. Paul, 1979-82, v.p. fin., 1982—. Served with U.S. Army, 1957-59. Mem. Fin. Execs. Inst., Nat. Assn. Accts. (chpt. v.p. 1972-83). Office: 3M 220 3M Center Saint Paul MN 55118

HAMMERSCHMIDT, JOHN PAUL, congressman, lumber company executive; b. Harrison, Ark., May 4, 1922; s. Arthur Paul and Junie (Taylor) H.; m. Virginia Sharp; 1 son, John Arthur. Student, The Citadel, 1938-39, U. Ark., 1940-41, Okla. State U., 1945-46. With Hammerschmidt Lumber Co., Harrison, 1946—; now chmn. bd.; dir. Harrison Fed. Savs. & Loan Assn.; Mem. Harrison City Council, 1948, 60, 62; mem. 90th-98th Congresses from 3d Ark. Dist. Chmn. Ark. Republican Com., 1964-66; mem. Rep. Nat. Finance Com., 1960-64; nat. Rep. committeeman from, Ark., 1976-80. Served as pilot USAAF, World War II; CBI. Decorated Air medal with 4 oak leaf clusters, D.F.C. with 3 oak leaf clusters. Mem. Ark. Lumber Dealers Assn. (past pres.), Southwestern Lumbermens Assn. (past pres.), Harrison C. of C. (named Man of Year 1965), Am. Legion. Presbyn. (ordained elder, deacon). Clubs: Mason (32 deg., Shriner), Elk, Rotarian (past pres. Harrison chpt.). Office: Rayburn House Office Bldg Washington DC 20515

HAMMES, GEORGE ALBERT, bishop; b. LaCrosse, Wis., Sept. 11, 1911; s. August Isidore and Caroline (Schumacher) H. Student, St. Lawrence Sem., Mt. Calvary, Wis., 1925-31, St. Louis Prep. Sem., 1931-33, Kenrick Sem., St. Louis, 1933-34, Sulpician Sem., Washington, 1934-37; M.A., Cath. U. Am., 1937; L.H.D. (hon.), Mt. Senario Coll., Ladysmith, Wis., 1969. Ordained priest Roman Cath. Ch., 1937; sec. to Bishop Alexander J. McGavick, LaCrosse, Wis., 1937-43; instr. Latin and religion Aquinas High Sch., LaCrosse, 1937-42; instr. ethics and religion St. Francis Sch. Nursing, LaCrosse, 1937-46; chancellor Diocese of LaCrosse, 1943-60; pastor Parish of St. Leo the Great, West Salem, Wis., 1957-60; bishop of, Superior, Wis., 1960—; Officialis Diocesan Matrimonial Tribunal, LaCrosse, 1943-60; diocesan dir. Cath. Lawyers' Guild, LaCrosse, 1956-60; pres. Tri-state Interfaith Devel. Enterprise, Superior, 1970-84. Adv. bd. Viterbo Coll., LaCrosse, 1954—, Cath. Social Service, La Crosse, 1954-60; trustee Mt. Senario Coll., Wis., 1969—; bd. dirs. Nat. Tech. Assistance Found., Mpls., 1971-84. Office: 1201 Hughitt Ave PO Box 969 Superior WI 54880

HAMMES, GORDON G., chemistry educator; b. Fond du Lac, Wis., Aug. 10, 1934; s. Jacob and Betty (Sadoff) H.; m. Judith Ellen Frank, June 14, 1959; children: Laura Anne, Stephen R., Sharon Lyn. A.B., Princeton, 1956; Ph.D., U. Wis., 1959. NSF postdoctoral fellow Max Planck Inst. fur physikalische Chemie, Göttingen, Germany, 1959-60; from instr. to asso. prof. Mass. Inst. Tech., Cambridge, 1960-65; prof. Cornell U., Ithaca, N.Y., 1965—, chmn. dept. chemistry, 1970-75, Horace White prof. chemistry and biochemistry, 1975—; Mem. physiol. chemistry study sect., tng. grant com. NIH; bd. counselors Nat. Cancer Inst., 1976-80; mem. adv. council chemistry dept. Princeton, 1970-75, Poly. Inst. N.Y., 1977-78, Boston U., 1977—. Author: Principles of Chemical Kinetics, (with I. Amdur) Enzyme Catalysis and Regulation, Chemical Kinetics: Principles and Selected Topics; (with I. Amdur) also articles. NSF sr. postdoctoral fellow, 1968-69; NIH Fogarty scholar, 1975-76. Mem. Am. Chem. Soc. (award biol. chemistry 1967, editorial bd. jours., exec. com. div. phys. chemistry 1976-79, exec. com. div. biol. chemistry 1977—), Am. Soc. Biol. Chemists (editorial bd. jour.), Nat. Acad. Scis., Am. Acad. Arts and Scis., Phi Beta Kappa, Sigma Xi, Phi Lambda Upsilon. Home: 107 Warwick Pl Ithaca NY 14850

HAMMING, RICHARD W., computer scientist; b. Chgo., Feb. 11, 1915; s. Richard J. and Mabel G. (Redfield) H.; m. Wanda Little, Sept. 5, 1942. B.S., U. Chgo., 1937; M.A., U. Nebr., 1939, Ph.D. in Math,

1942. With Manhattan Project, 1945-46; with Bell Telephone Labs., 1946-76; mem. faculty Naval Postgrad. Sch., Monterey, Calif., 1976—, adj. prof. computer sci., 1976—. Author books, papers in field. Fellow IEEE (Piore award 1979); mem. Assn. Computing Machinery (Turing prize 1968), Nat. Acad. Engring., Am. Math. Assn., AAAS. Office: Code 52 HG Naval Postgrad Sch Monterey CA 93940

HAMMITT, FREDERICK GNICHTEL, nuclear engineer; b. Trenton, N.J., Sept. 25, 1923; s. Andrew Baker and Julia (Stevenson Gnichtel) H.; m. Barbara Ann Hill, June 11, 1949; children: Frederick, Harry, Jane. B.S. in Mech. Engring., Princeton U., 1944; M.S., U. Pa., 1949, Stevens Inst., 1956; Ph.D. in Nuclear Engring, U. Mich., 1958. Registered profl. engr., N.J., Mich. Engr. John A. Roebling Sons Co., Trenton, 1946-48, Power Generators Ltd., 1948-50; project engr. Reaction Motors Inc., Rockaway, N.J., 1950-53, Worthington Corp., Harrison, N.J., 1953-55; research asso. U. Mich., Ann Arbor, 1955-57, asso. research engr., 1957-59, asso. prof., 1959-61, prof. nuclear engring., 1961—, mech. engring., 1965—, also prof. in charge Cavitation and Multiphase Flow Lab., 1967—; cons. govt. and industry; vis. scholar Electricité de France, Paris, 1967, Société Grenobloise Hydrauliques, Grenoble, France, 1971; Fulbright sr. lectr. French Nuclear Lab., Grenoble, 1974; Polish Acad. Sci. lectr. Inst. Fluid Mechanics, Gdansk, 1976. Author: (with R.T. Knapp, J.W. Daily) Cavitation, 1970, Cavitation and Multiphase Flow Phenomena, 1980; contbr. 400 articles to profl. jours., 5 chpts. to books. Served with USN, 1943-46. Fellow Inst. Mech. Engrs. (U.K.), ASME (past chmn. cavitation com. fluids div.), ASTM (past chmn. cavitation and liquid impingement); mem. Am. Nuclear Soc. (past chmn. S.E. Mich. sect.), Internat. Assn. Hydraulic Research (chmn. cavitation scale effects com.), Phi Beta Kappa, Sigma Xi, Tau Beta Pi. Republican. Presbyterian (elder). Patentee in field (5). Home: 1306 Olivia St Ann Arbor MI 48104

HAMMOCK, JOSEPH CULVER, educator, psychologist; b. Holly Pond, Ala., Sept. 20, 1926; s. Joseph Emmett and Katie Belle (Taylor) H.; m. Edna Hill Haynes, Sept. 10, 1947; children: Joseph Culver, Baxter Haynes, Margaret Anne. Student, Birmingham So. Coll., 1944; B.S., U. S.C., 1948, M.A., 1950; Ph.D., U. Tenn., 1953. Instr. U. S.C., 1949-50; psychometrician U. Tenn., 1951-52; research psychologist Human Resources Research Office, U.S. Army, 1952-55, dir. research, 1956-59; research psychologist Bell Telephone Labs., Inc., 1959-62; mem. faculty U. Ga., 1955—, prof. psychology, 1962—, head dept., 1962-69, dir. instructional research and devel., 1969-72; vice-chancellor for acad. devel. Univ. System Ga., 1974-76. Served with USNR, 1944-47. Mem. Am. Psychol. Assn. (rep. to council), Southeastern Psychol. Assn. (pres., exec. com.), Ga. Psychol. Assn. (pres., bd. dirs.), Soc. for Preservation and Encouragement Barbershop Quartet Singing in Am. (pres.), Sigma Xi, Psi Chi, Sigma Alpha Epsilon, Omicron Delta Kappa. United Methodist. Lodge: Kiwanis. Home: 367 Beechwood Dr Athens GA 30606

HAMMOND, BENJAMIN FRANKLIN, microbiologist, educator; b. Austin, Tex., Feb. 28, 1934; s. Virgil Thomas and Helen Marguerite (Smith) H. B.A., U. Kans., 1954; D.D.S., Meharry Med. Coll., 1958; Ph.D., U. Pa., 1962. Mem. faculty U. Pa. Sch. Dental Medicine, Phila., 1958—, prof. microbiology, 1970—, chmn. dept., 1972—; Pres.'s lectr. U. Pa., 1981, assoc. dean acad. affairs, 1984; Mem. oral medicine study sect. NIH, 1972-75; mem. Nat. Adv. Dental Research Council, 1975—; cons. in field. Recipient USPHS Research Career Devel. award, 1965, Lindback award U. Pa., 1969; Médaille d'Argent, City of Paris, 1978; NIH grantee, 1981—. Mem. Am. Soc. Microbiology, Internat. Assn. Dental Research (E.H. Hatton award 1959), Am. Assn. Dental Research (pres. 1978-79). Home: 560 N 23d St Philadelphia PA 19130

HAMMOND, CALEB DEAN, publisher, cartographer; b. Orange, N.J., June 24, 1915; s. Caleb Dean and Alice (Lindsley) H.; m. Patricia Treacy Ehrgott, July 20, 1940; children—Beth Lynn, Wendie Harrison, Caleb Dean 3d. B.S., Worcester Poly. Inst., 1937. Sales engr. Texas Co., N.Y.C., 1937-39; prodn. mgr. Hammond, Inc. (formerly C.S. Hammond & Co.), Maplewood, N.J., 1939-42, v.p. charge sales and mgmt., 1945-48, pres., 1948-67, chmn. bd., 1968-80, chmn. emeritus, 1981—; chmn. bd. Maplewood Bank & Trust Co. Trustee Orange Med. Center, Worcester Poly. Inst. Served from cadet to engring. lt. USCG, 1942-45. Mem. Assn. Am. Pubs., Am., Royal geog. socs., Phi Gamma Delta. Club: Baltusrol Golf (Springfield, N.J.). Home: 61 Woodland Rd Maplewood NJ 07040 Office: 515 Valley St Maplewood NJ 07040

HAMMOND, CHARLES AINLEY, clergyman; b. Asheville, N.C., Aug. 7, 1933; s. George Bradley and Eleanor Maria (Gantz) H.; m. Barbro Stigsdotter Laurell, July 16, 1960; children: Stig Bradley, Inga Allison. B.A., Occidental Coll., Los Angeles, 1955; B.D., Princeton Theol. Sem., 1958; D.D., Missouri Valley Coll., 1981, Wabash Coll., 1982. Ordained to ministry United Presbyn. Ch., 1958; pastor chs. in, Pa. and Calif., 1958-75; exec. presbyter Presbytery Wabash Valley, West Lafayette, Ind., 1975—; moderator 192d gen. assembly United Presbyn. Ch., 1980-81; founding dir. (United Presbyn. Center Mission Studies), 1973-74. Author: Newtonian Policy in an Age of Relativity, 1977, Seven Deadly Sins of Dissent, 1979. Sec. Hallam (Pa.) Borough Planning Commn., 1962-64, Westchester Community Plans, Los Angeles, 1966-68; chmn. zoning com. Pasadena (Calif.) Planning Commn., 1971-75, chmn. pvt. land use com., 1972-73, chmn. public land use com., 1973-74. Mem. Assn. Presbyn. Ch. Educators. Republican. Club: Lafayette Tennis. Office: 320 North St West Lafayette IN 47906

HAMMOND, CHARLES BESSELLIEU, obstetrician, gynecologist, educator; b. Ft. Leavenworth, Kans., July 24, 1936; s. Claude G. and Alice (Sims) H.; m. Peggy R. Hammond, June 21, 1958; children: Sharon L., Charles B. Student, The Citadel, 1957; B.S., M.D., Duke U., 1961. Intern Duke U., 1961-62, resident, 1962-63, 66-69, fellow in reproductive endocrinology, 1963-64, asst. prof. dept. ob-gyn, 1969-73, asso. prof., 1973-78, prof., 1978-81, E.C. Hamblen prof., 1981—, chmn., 1980—. Contbr. in field. Served with USPHS, 1964-66. Mem. Am. Bd. Ob-Gyn, Am. Fertility Soc. (dir. 1979—, pres. elect 1983), Am. Coll. Obstetricians and Gynecologists, Assn. Profs. Obstetrics and Gynecology, Am. Gynecologic Soc., Am. Assn. Obstetricians and Gynecologists, Soc. Gynecologic Investigation, N.C. Med. Soc., N.C. Soc. Obstetricians and Gynecologists. Presbyterian. Home: 2827 McDowell Rd Durham NC 27705 Office: PO Box 3143 Duke Med Center Durham NC 27710

HAMMOND, CHARLES TAYLOR, lawyer; b. Detroit, July 31, 1923; s. Maurice Eugene and Margaret Anne (Taylor) H.; m. Patricia Mary Baines, June 1, 1954; children—Susan, Charles, Sarah, Scott, Craig. A.B., Olivet Coll., 1947; LL.B., U. Mich., 1949. Bar: Mich. bar 1949. Since practiced in, Detroit; asso. firm Fitch, Hayes, Andes & Brown, 1949-52; partner firm Lewis & Watkins, 1954-64, Parsons, Tennent, Hammond, Hardig & Ziegelman, 1964-70, Donovan, Hammond, Ziegelman, Roach & Sotiroff (and predecessors), 1970—. Served with USNR, 1943-45, 52-54. Mem. State Bar Mich., Am. Bar Assn., Detroit Bar Assn. Home: 1465 Cedar Bend Bloomfield Hills MI 48013 Office: 400 Renaissance Center Suite 1100 Detroit MI 48243

HAMMOND, DAVID ALAN, stage director, educator; b. N.Y.C., June 3, 1948; s. Jack and Elizabeth Alida (Furno) H. B.A. magna cum laude, Harvard U., 1970; M.F.A., Carnegie-Mellon U., 1972. Mem. faculty Juilliard Theatre Center, N.Y.C., 1972-74; asst. conservatory dir. Am. Conservatory Theatre, San Francisco, 1974-81, asso. stage dir., 1974-78; dir. Summer Tng. Congress, 1976-80, resident stage dir., 1979-81; adj. asso. prof. acting and directing Yale Sch. Drama, New Haven, Conn., 1981—; guest artist Pacific Conservatory Performing Arts, 1976, U. Wash., 1977, SUNY, Purchase, 1979. Stage dir., Aspen Music Festival, Colo., 1974-75, San Francisco Opera, 1978, Carmel (Calif.) Bach Festival, 1979-80; artistic dir., Sherwood Shakespeare Festival, Oxnard, Calif., 1981. Recipient Drama-Logue critics award, Los Angeles, 1980, 81. Mem. Soc. Stage Dirs. and Choreographers, Actors' Equity, Am. Guild Mus. Artists, Am. Film Inst. Democrat. Jewish. Office: Yale Sch Drama PO Box 1903A Yale Sta New Haven CT 06520

HAMMOND, DEANNA LINDBERG, linguist; b. Calgary, Alta., Can., May 31, 1942; d. Albin William and Emma Lou (Thompson) Lindberg. B.A., Wash. State U., 1964; M.A., Ohio U., 1968; Ph.D., Georgetown U., 1977; student summer sch., U. Ariz., Guadalajara, Portland State U. With Peace Corps., Colombia, 1964-66; prof. English Universidad Industrial, Bucaramanga, Colombia, 1966-67; tchr. English, Spanish Pullman High Sch., Wash., 1969-74; lectr. Georgetown U., Washington, 1974-77, dir. summer sch. program, Quito, Ecuador, 1977; head lang. services Congl. Research, Library of Congress, Washington, 1977—; lectr. English as fgn. lang. No. Va. Community Coll., part-time, 1975—; mem. editorial bd. Modern Lang. Jour. Coordinator Washington Foster Parents Plan Vol. Support Group. Recipient Community Service award Sec. Califano, 1978. Mem. Am. Translators Assn. (Nat. sec. 1983—, editorial bd., rep. to joint nat. com. on langs., chmn. domestic liaison com., accreditation com.), Nat. Capital Area Translators Assn., Council Communication Socs. (pres. 1983-84, exec., govt. relations, publs. coms.), N.E. Conf. Teaching Fgn. Langs., Am. Assn. Tchrs. Spanish and Portuguese, Library of Congress Profl. Assn., Nat. Council Returned Peace Corps Vols., Phi Beta Kappa, Phi Kappa Phi. Democrat. Home: 3560 S George Mason Dr Alexandria VA 22302 Office: Congl Research Lang Services Library of Congress Washington DC 20540

HAMMOND, EDWIN HUGHES, educator; b. Ann Arbor, Mich., Jan. 8, 1919; s. Harry Emmons and Elizabeth Rose (Huddle) H.; m. Elizabeth Lapsley Mills, Dec. 28, 1940; children—Janet E. (Mrs. John Weigel), Richard Edwin, Lawrence Alan. A.B., U. Mo., 1939; M.A., U. Wis., 1940; Ph.D., U. Calif. at Berkeley, 1951; postgrad., Sch. Aerol. Engring., U.S. Naval Acad., 1943-44. Asst. geographer OSS, 1942; lectr. geography U. Calif. at Berkeley, 1946-47; instr. geography U. Nebr., 1948-49; instr. U. Wis., 1949-51, asst. prof., 1951-55, asso. prof., 1955-64; prof. geography Syracuse U., 1964-70, U. Tenn., 1970—, head dept., 1970-77; cons. (Ednl. Testing Service), 1965-69. Author: Procedures In The Descriptive Analysis Of Terrain, 1958, (with Trewartha and Robinson) Elements of Geography, 1957, 67, Fundamentals of Physical Geography, 1961, 68, (with Trewartha, Robinson, and Horn), 1977; Rev. editor: Annals Assn. Am. Geographers, 1969-71. Served from ensign to lt. USNR, 1942-46. Decorated Air medal; recipient award meritorious contbn. geography Assn. Am. Geographers, 1968. Mem. Assn. Am. Geographers (nat. council 1967-70, del. to NRC 1965-68), Am. Geog. Soc., AAAS, AAUP, Phi Beta Kappa, Sigma Xi. Democrat. Home: 7901 Corteland Dr Knoxville TN 37919

HAMMOND, FRANK JOSEPH, lawyer; b. Harvey, Ill., Dec. 9, 1919; s. William Ernest and Bessie (Seavey) H.; m. Frances Anderson, Feb. 13, 1945; children: Susan, Kent William. A.B., Carleton Coll., 1941; LL.B., Harvard U., 1948. Bar: Minn. 1948, U.S. Supreme Ct. 1970. Practice law, St. Paul, 1948—; mem. firms Briggs & Morgan, St. Paul, 1948—, pres., 1970-77; adj. prof. common law St. Paul Coll. Law, 1950-56; gen. counsel Bush Found., St. Paul, 1970—; dir. First Trust Co., St. Paul. Trustee Carleton Coll., Northfield, Minn., 1962—, United Theol. Sem., New Brighton, Minn., 1976-82, Alliss Ednl. Found., St. Paul, 1981—; bd. dirs. Minn. Orch. Assn., Mpls., 1979—, Minn. Found., St. Paul, 1975—; pres. Jr. C. of C., St. Paul, 1953-54; chmn. Operation 85, St. Paul, 1978-81; found. chmn. Minn. United Negro Coll. Fund, Mpls., 1979-80; mem. exec. com. Indianhead council/Boy Scouts Am., St. Paul, 1981—. Served to capt. USAF, 1941-45. Decorated D.F.C., Air medal with clusters, Purple Heart; recipient Christianson Meml. award St. Paul Jr. C. of C., 1980; named Boss of Yr. St. Paul Jr. C. of C., 1977, Citizen of Yr. UNICO, 1981, Disting. Eagle Boy Scouts Am., 1981. Mem. Minn. Bar Assn. (bd. govs. 1961-63, 68-70), Ramsey County Bar Assn. (pres. 1967), Phi Beta Kappa, Delta Sigma Rho. Clubs: Minnesota (St. Paul) (dir. 1960—); St. Paul Athletic (sec. 1949—); Informal (St. Paul)). Home: 1366 Fairmount Ave Saint Paul MN 55105 Office: Briggs and Morgan 2200 First National Bank Bldg Saint Paul MN 55101

HAMMOND, GEORGE DENMAN, physician, medical researcher, educator; b. Atlanta, Feb. 5, 1923; s. Percy W. and Elizabeth (Denman) H.; m. Florence Williams, Mar. 30, 1946; children: Lane Elizabeth Hammond Clark, Christopher Scott, Bruce Benedict, Kirk Denman. B.A., U. N.C.-Chapel Hill, 1944; M.D., U. Pa., 1948. Diplomate Am. Bd. Pediatrics. Intern Pa. Hosp., Phila., 1948-50; resident Children's Hosp., Phila., 1950, 52-53; research assoc. U. Calif. at San Francisco, 1954-55, instr. pediatrics, 1955-56, asst. prof., 1956-57; asst. prof. pediatrics U. So. Calif. Sch. Medicine, Los Angeles, 1957-60, assoc. prof., 1960-64, prof., 1964—, founding dir. Comprehensive Cancer Center, 1971—, founding dir. Kenneth Norris Cancer Research Hosp. and Inst., 1978—, assoc. dean planning, 1981—; assoc. hematologist Children's Hosp., Los Angeles, 1957-60, head div. hematology-oncology, 1960-71; chmn. children's cancer study group Nat. Cancer Inst., 1968—; mem. Cancer Research Center rev. com. Nat. Cancer Inst., 1972-74; mem. med. adv. bd. Cooleys Anemia Found., N.Y.C., 1967—; vis. investigator U. Turin, Italy, 1964-65; presdl. appointee Nat. Cancer Adv. Bd., 1974-80; gov.'s appointee Cancer Adv. Council, State of Calif. Editorial bd.: Am. Jour. Clin. Oncology, Internat. Jour. Oncology, Med. and Pediatric Oncology, Jour. Hematologic Oncology, Jour. Applied Physiology, Am. Jour. Physiology; Contbr. articles to profl. jours. Trustee Santa Barbara Med. Found.; memm. med. adv. bd. Nat. Leukemia Broadcast Council. Served to comdr. M.C. USNR, 1941-43, 50-52. Recipient Parver medal U. N.C., 1944, Patterson award U. N.C., 1944; Gianinni Found. fellow, 1954-56; Am. Cancer Soc. scholar, 1964-65; Disting. Alumnus award U. N.C., 1974; Navy League award for humanitarianism in medicine, 1979. Fellow Am. Acad. Pediatrics; mem. Leukemia Soc. Am. (med. bd. 1967-70), Am. Cancer Soc. (dir. Calif. div.), Am., Western socs. pediatric research, Am. Assn. Cancer Edn., Los Angeles Acad. Medicine, Internat. Union Against Cancer, Internat. Soc. Hematology, Am. Soc. Clin. Oncology, Am. Fedn. Clin. Research, Am. Soc. Hematology, Am. Assn. Cancer Research, Assn. Am. Cancer Insts., Soc. Surg. Oncology, Am. Pediatric Soc., Soc. Exptl. Biology and Medicine. Home: 851 S El Molino Pasadena CA 91106 Office: U So Calif Comprehensive Cancer Center 2025 Zonal Ave Los Angeles CA 90033 Children's Cancer Study Group 1721 Griffin Ave Los Angeles CA 90031 *Do what you can, where you are, with what you've got, and plan for success.*

HAMMOND, GEORGE SIMMS, chemist; b. Auburn, Maine, May 22, 1921; s. Oswald Kenric and Marjorie (Thomas) H.; m. Marian Reese, June 8, 1945 (div. 1977); children: Kenric, Janet, Steven, Barbara, Jeremy; m. Eva L. Menger, May 22, 1977; stepchildren—Kirsten Menger-Anderson, Lenore Menger-Anderson. B.S., Bates Coll., 1963; M.S., Ph.D., Harvard, 1947; D.Sc., Wittenberg U., 1972, Bates Coll., 1973; Dr. honoris causa, U. Ghent, 1973. Postdoctoral fellow U. Calif. at Los Angeles, 1947-48; mem. faculty Iowa State Coll., 1948-58, prof. chemistry, 1956-58; vis. asso. prof. U. Ill., summer 1953; prof. organic chemistry Calif. Inst. Tech., Pasadena, 1958-72, div. chemistry and chem. engring., 1968-72; Arthur Amos Noyes prof. chemistry; vice chancellor natural scis. U. Calif. at Santa Cruz, 1972-74, prof. chemistry, 1972-78; dir. Integrated Chem. Systems Lab. Allied Chem. Co., Morristown, N.J., 1978—; mem. chem. adv. panel NSF, 1962-65; fgn. sec. Nat. Acad. Scis., 1974-78. Author: (with J. S. Fritz) Quantitative Organic Analysis, 1956, (with D.J. Cram) Organic Chemistry, 1958, (with J. Osteryoung, T. Crawford and H. Gray) Models in Chemical Science, 1971; Editor: Advances in Photochemistry, 1961; Editorial bd.: Jour. Am. Chem. Soc, 1967—. Guggenheim fellow; NSF sr. fellow Oxford (Eng.) U. and U. Basel, Switzerland; Calif. Inst. Tech., 1956-57; Mem. Maine N.G., 1938-40; Recipient James Flack Norris award in phys. organic chemistry, 1968. Mem. Nat. Acad. Scis., Am. Chem. Soc. (award in petroleum chemistry 1960, Priestly medal 1976), Chemistry Soc. (London), Am. Acad. Arts and Scis., Phi Beta Kappa, Sigma Xi. Home: 43 Noe Ave Madison NJ 07940

HAMMOND, GUYTON BOWERS, educator; b. Birmingham, Ala., Nov. 7, 1930; s. Joseph Langhorne and Fanny (Bowers) H.; m. Alice Jean Love, June 27, 1959; children—Bruce Guyton, Mitchell Love. B.A., Washington and Lee U., 1951; postgrad., U. Utrecht, Netherlands, 1951-52, So. Baptist Theol. Sem., 1952-53; B.D., Yale, 1955; Ph.D., Vanderbilt U., 1962. Grad. teaching fellow Vanderbilt U., Nashville, 1955-57; instr. Va. Polytechnic Inst., Blacksburg, 1957-58, asst. prof., 1958-62, asso. prof., 1962-67, prof. philosophy and religion, 1967—, head dept., 1978—, pres. faculty senate, 1971-72, 75-76; Pres. Council on Human Relations, Montgomery County, Va., 1962-63. Author: Man in Estrangement, 1965, The Power of Self-Transcendence, 1966. Chmn. bd. advisers Va. Polytechnic Inst. chpt. YMCA, 1966-67. Mem. Am. Acad. Religion (nat. bd. dirs., pres. Southeastern region 1968-69), N.Am. Paul Tillich Soc. (pres. 1981-82), AAUP, Va. Philos. Assn., Lambda Chi Alpha. Presbyterian. Home: 508 Preston Ave Blacksburg VA 24060

HAMMOND, HARMONY LYNN, artist; b. Chgo., Feb. 8, 1944; d. William J. and Harmony R. H.; 1 dau., Tanya. Student, Milliken U., 1961-63; B.F.A., U. Minn., 1967, Alliance Francaise, Paris, summers 1967, 69. Tchr. U. Va., Charlottesville, 1980-81, U. N.C., Chapel Hill, 1981-82, U. N.Mex., Albuquerque, 1978-79, Tyler Sch. Fine Art, Phila., 1977-78, Hunter Coll., N.Y.C., 1982-83, Feminist Art Inst., 1982-83, Mason Gross Sch. Art, 1982-83; founding mem., feminist publ. on art and politics Heresies, 1976-80; founding mem. women's co-op. art gallery Artists in Residence, N.Y.C., 1972—. Exhibited one-woman shows, A.I.R. Gallery, N.Y.C., 1973, 82, LaMagna Gallery, N.Y.C., 1976, Real Artways, Hartford, 1982, Klein Gallery, Chgo., 1982, P.S.I., L.I., N.Y., 1979, Lerner-Heller Gallery, N.Y.C., 1979, 82, group shows include, N.Y. Cultural Center, 1973, Nancy Hoffman Gallery, N.Y.C., 1974, Vassar Coll., 1975, Douglas Coll., Rutgers, N.J., 1977, Sch. of Bklyn. Mus., 55 Mercer St. Gallery, Downtown Whitney Mus., 1978, 112 Green St. Gallery, N.Y.C., Renaissance Soc., Chgo., Haags Gementemuseum, Netherlands, 1980, Women's Bldg., Los Angeles, Sculpture Center, N.Y.C., 1981, Lerner-Heller Gallery, N.Y.C., N.Y. Coliseum, 1980, Bklyn. Mus., Phila. Mus. Contemporary Art; 10 yr. retrospective W.A.R.M and Glen Hanson Gallery, Mpls., 1980; resented in permanent collections, Walker Art Center, Mpls., Denver Art Mus., Indpls., Mus. Fine Art, Chgo., Mus. Contemporary Art, U. Mass., Amherst, U. Notre Dame, South Bend, Ind., Western Mich. U.; author: Wrappings: Essays on Feminism, Art and the Martial Arts; Contbr. articles to profl. jours. Nat. Endowment for Arts in Sculpture grantee, 1979-80; MacDowell Colony fellow, 1979, 81; Yaddo Colony fellow, 1979. Mem. U.S. Aikido Fedn.

HAMMOND, HAROLD EARL, educator, author, historian, gerontologist; b. Albany, N.Y., Nov. 28, 1922; s. Walter Earl and Mae V. (McKeever) H.; m. Helen Stegmann, Oct. 6, 1942; children: Susan Jane (Mrs. Christopher John Wray), Bruce Martin, April Thorne (Mrs. Charles Weed), Melody Joy (Mrs. David Bedell), Russell James. B.A., Wagner Coll., 1942; postgrad. in elec. engring., Newark Coll. Engring., 1943; M.A., Columbia U., 1945, Ph.D., 1951, St. Lawrence U., 1945-46, U. Conn., Boston U., U. N.H., 1978-79; Ed.D. candidate in gerontology, Boston U. History instr. Wagner Coll., Bergen Jr. Coll., 1946-48; asst. to pres. L.I. U.; asst. prof. history, dir. Eastern L.I. div. C.W. Post Coll., 1948-52; asst. prof. history, dir. pub. relations Union Coll., Schenectady, 1952-54; pres. Hammond, Beamish & Crannell, Inc., 1954-60; asst. dean Grad. Sch., Yeshiva U., 1958-60; prof. history Univ. Coll., N.Y. U., 1960-66, assoc. dean, 1960-66; dean Inter-Am. U. P.R., 1966; prof. history, chmn. dept. Franklin Pierce Coll., Rindge, N.H., 1967-70; prof. social and polit. sci. N.H. Coll., Manchester, 1970-74; pres. Hammond Promotions, Inc., 1974-80; adj. prof. gerontology Antioch/New Eng. Grad. Sch., 1979-80; dir. N.H. Gerontology Center, 1978-80; Bd. dirs. Monodnock Adult Edn. Center, Inc., Peterborough, N.H., 1974-77; Leverhulme fellow, prof. history St. David's Univ. Coll. U. Wales, Lampeter, Dyfed, 1972-73; justice of peace, 1973-80. Author: Pictorial Guidebook to Colleges and Universities in the Empire State, 1953, A Commoner's Judge, Life and Times of C. P. Daly, 1954, Diary of a Union Lady, 1962, We Hold These Truths, 1964, (with M.J. Belasko) A More Perfect Union, 1965, (with M.J. Belasko and E. Graff) The New Africa, 1966, (with E. Graff) Southeast Asia, 1967, (with M.J. Belasko) India-Pakistan, 1967, (with Rudolph Schwartz) China, Japan, and Korea, 1967, (with Thomas G. Kavunedus) The Middle East, 1968, (with M.J. Belasko) Soviet Russia, 1968; Contbr. articles to profl. jours. Recipient Great Scholars Am. award, 1971; mem. Exec. and Profl. Hall of Fame, 1970. Fellow Am. Geog. Soc.; mem. Am. Geriatrics Soc., Gerontol. Soc., Nat. Geriatrics Soc., Am. Hist. Assn., Polit. Sci. Acad., AAUP, New Eng. Assn., Soc. Aero. Flight Engrs., Am. Assn. Ret. Persons, Alpha Phi Omega, Phi Alpha Theta. Democrat. Lutheran (mem. laymen's movement stewardship). Lodges: Masons (32 deg.); Peterborough Lions. Home: 9 Vine St Peterborough NH 03458 also PO Box 1224 Lajas RR 287 La Parquera PR 00667 *My choice of a career was more than a quarter of a century in education, service in the communications field, and a new and second career in gerontology and it has been extremely rewarding. Ours has been a happy marriage, and we have launched five glorious children into adulthood. Our fires burn brightly and give warmth; we are prepared to meet the challenges of the future.*

HAMMOND, HAROLD FRANCIS, former association executive; b. Lynch, Nebr., June 1, 1908; s. Edward Francis and Lydia (Kallstrom) H.; m. Gertrude R. Rouse, Oct. 10, 1931; children:Harold Edward, Susan W. Student, Parsons Coll., Fairfield, Iowa, 1926-27; B.C.E., U. Mich., 1930; M.S., Harvard U., 1931. Registered profl. engr., N.J., D.C. Traffic engr. Gov. Mass. Com. St. and Hwy. Safety, 1931-34; traffic analyst Traffic Audit Bur., N.Y.C., 1934-35; dir. traffic and transp. div. Nat. Conservation Bur., 1935-44; mgr. Washington office Am. Transit Assn., 1944-47; asst. mgr. transp. and communication dept. U.S. C. of C., Washington, 1947-48; mgr. dept., 1948-55; exec. v.p., dir. Transp. Assn. Am., Washington, 1955-62, pres., dir., 1962-73, sr. adviser, 1973—; chmn. Nat. Cargo Security Council, 1971—; transp. cons. (Naval Operating Base), Norfolk, Va., also, 1940-44, former mem. adv. council fed. reports, mem. transp. adv. council, 1952. Author traffic and transp. manuals.; Co-editor: Traffic

Engineering Handbook. Mem. county council, Montgomery County, Md., 1949-53, pres., 1953-54. Mem. Nat. Inst. Traffic Engrs. (past pres., TAA-Seley awards 1972), Am. Soc. Traffic and Transp. (founder), Eno Found. Transp. (dir.). Republican. Presbyterian. Clubs: Univ., Congressional Country, Met. (Washington); Sea Pines (Hilton Head Island, S.C.); Harvard (N.Y.C.). Home: 12510 Pennyfield Lock Rd Potomac MD 20854

HAMMOND, J. EMMETT, financial executive; b. Norristown, Pa., June 30, 1938; s. John E. and Margaret (Dunbar) H.; m. Joan M. Coscia, Sept. 17, 1960; children: Michele, Kathleen, J. Emmett. B.S. in Econs., Villanova U., 1960. C.P.A., Ill. Staff mem. Arthur Andersen & Co., N.Y.C. and Phila., 1960-66, mgr. Hague office, 1966-69, ptnr., Phila., 1969-79; sr. v.p., chief fin. exec. Interstate United Corp., Chgo., 1979—; dir., treas. Thresholds, Chgo., 1980—. Mem. Union League of Phila., 1973—, Friends of Phila. Mus. Art, 1974-79. Mem. Am. Inst. C.P.A.s, Fin. Execs. Inst. Clubs: Tower, Economic (Chgo.); Union League (Phila.). Office: Interstate United Corp 120 S Riverside Plaza Chicago IL 60606

HAMMOND, JAMES WRIGHT, architect; b. Montclair, N.J., Apr. 12, 1918; s. Robert Stevens and Helen (Johnston) H.; m. Katrina Roy Boyden, Feb. 25, 1956 (div. June 1959); m. Helen Cheney Stuart Sloane, Nov. 27, 1976. B.S. in Architecture, Ill. Inst. Tech., 1942. Asso. Perkins, Wheeler & Will & Eliel Saarinen Asso. Architects, 1939-40; gen. partner Skidmore, Owings & Merrill, Chgo., 1946-61; partner Hammond and Roesch, Inc., Chgo., 1961-71, Hammond Beeby and Assocs., Inc., 1971-77, Hammond Beeby and Babka, Inc., 1977-82; now pvt. cons. Mem. facilities devel. com. Chgo. council Boy Scouts Am., 1958—; mem. Chgo. Crime Commn., 1955—; com. mem. Welfare Council Met. Chgo.; bd. dirs. Chgo. Planetarium Soc., Chgo. Commons Assos.; exec. bd. Auditorium Theatre Council Chgo.; trustee Thresholds, Chgo. Served with AUS, 1942-46. Fellow A.I.A. Bahai religion. Clubs: University, Casino, Chgo. Archtl. (pres.), Arts (Chgo.)). Home: 343 Green Bay Rd Glencoe IL 60022 Office: 1126 N State St Chicago IL 60610

HAMMOND, JANE LAURA, librarian, lawyer; b. nr. Nashua, Iowa; d. Frank D. and Pauline (Flint) H. B.A., U. Dubuque, 1950; M.S., Columbia U., 1952; J.D., Villanova U., 1965. Bar: Pa. 1965. Cataloguer Harvard Law Library, 1952-54; asst. librarian Sch. Law, Villanova (Pa.) U., 1954-62, librarian, 1962-76, prof. law, 1965-76; law librarian, prof. law Cornell U., Ithaca, N.Y., 1976—; Adj. prof. Drexel U., 1971-74; mem. depository library council to pub. printer U.S. Govt. Printing Office, 1975-78. Mem. Am. Assn. Law Libraries (sec. 1965-70, pres. 1975-76), Council Nat. Library Assns. (sec.-treas. 1971-72, chmn. 1979-80), Spl. Libraries Assn., ALA, ABA (com. on accreditation 1982—, chmn. com. on accreditation 1983-84), PEO. Episcopalian. Office: Cornell Law Library Myron Taylor Hall Ithaca NY 14853

HAMMOND, JAY STERNER, gov. of Alaska; b. Troy, N.Y., July 21, 1922; s. Morris Adelbert and Edna Brown (Sterner) H.; m. Bella W. Gardiner, Sept. 21, 1952; children—Heidi Lee, Dana E. B.S. in Biol. Scis, U. Alaska, 1948; LL.D., Alaska Methodist U., 1975. Govt. hunter, pilot U.S. Fish and Wildlife Service, Alaska, 1949-56; owner Lake Clark Lodge, Inc., 1956-74; gov., Alaska, 1974—; Mem. Alaska Ho. of Reps., 1960-66; mem. Alaska Senate, 1968-72, pres., 1970-72; mgr. Bristol Bay Borough, Alaska, 1965-67, mayor, 1972-74. Served to capt. USMCR, 1942-46. Office: Capitol Bldg Juneau AK 99811

HAMMOND, JOE PHIL, oil co. exec.; b. Hugo, Okla., May 18, 1922; s. Monroe Percy and Estelle Elizabeth (Afflerbach) H.; m. Margaret Elaine Huff, June 4, 1944; children—Joe Phil, Marilyn Lee. B.S., Okla. State U., 1943; LL.B., Columbia, 1948; grad., Advanced Mgmt. Program, Harvard, 1961. Bar: Okla. bar 1949, Ill. bar 1973. Practice in, Enid, Okla., 1949-50; atty. Stanolind Oil and Gas Co., 1952-61; gen. atty. Pan Am. Petroleum Corp., 1961-70; gen. counsel Amoco Prodn. Co., Tulsa, 1970-71, dir., 1970-73; asst. gen. counsel Standard Oil Co. (Ind.), Chgo., 1971-72, asso. gen. counsel, 1972-75, v.p., pub and govt. affairs, 1975—; dir. Wash. Nat. Corp. Served with AUS, 1943-46, 50-52. Mem. Sigma Mu. Methodist. Clubs: Westmoreland Country, Mid Am., International. Office: 200 E Randolph St Chicago IL 60601

HAMMOND, JOHN PAYNE, petroleum consultant; b. Okmulgee, Okla., Apr. 19, 1913; s. John Whitten and Grace (Payne) H.; m. Katharine Rees, 1937 (dec.); children—Grace (Mrs. Stanley Betzer, Jr.), Patricia (Mrs. Bryan Watt), Sara; m. Sarah M. Brietweiser, Oct. 25, 1975. B.S., U. Tulsa, 1936. With Amerada Petroleum Corp., 1941-69, asst. gen. prodn. supt., 1951-60, v.p., 1960-62, sr. v.p., 1962-67, exec. v.p., 1967-69; dir., mem. exec. com. of bd. dirs.; exec. v.p., dir. Amerada Hess Corp.; pres. Amerada div. Amerada Hess Corp., 1969-71; petroleum cons., Tulsa, 1971—; dir. First Nat. Bank Tulsa, Transok Pipe Line Co., Tulsa, Natomas Co., San Francisco. Bd. dirs. Goodwill Industries Tulsa. Mem. Am. Inst. Mining, Metall. and Petroleum Engrs. (past v.p., dir.), Soc. Petroleum Engrs. (past pres.), Am. Petroleum Inst., Mid-Continent Oil and Gas Assn., Tau Beta Pi, Phi Epsilon Tau. Presbyterian (trustee). Clubs: Southern Hills Country, Tulsa. Home: 3211 E 73d St Tulsa OK 74136 Office: PO Box 2902 Tulsa OK 74101

HAMMOND, PAUL YOUNG, political scientist, educator; b. Salt Lake City, Feb. 24, 1929; s. James Thaddeus and Hortense Clair (Young) H.; m. Merlyn Felt Simmons, Aug. 29, 1950; children: Paul Brett, Wendy Simmons, Robyn Simmons, Spencer Blair, Clifford Simmons. B.A., U. Utah, 1949; M.A., Harvard U., 1951, Ph.D., 1953; postgrad. Fulbright scholar, London Sch. Econs., 1952-53. Instr. govt. Harvard U., Cambridge, Mass., 1953-55; lectr. Columbia U., N.Y.C., 1956-57; asst. prof. polit. sci. Yale U., New Haven, 1957-62; research asso. Washington Center Fgn. Policy Research, Johns Hopkins U., 1962-64; mem. research staff Rand Corp., Santa Monica, Calif., 1964-76, head social sci. dept., 1973-76; vis. research polit. scientist U. Calif., Berkeley, 1971-72; Edward R. Weidlein prof. environ. and pub. policy studies U. Pitts., 1976-83, disting. service prof. pub. and internat. affairs, 1983—; dir. Energy and Environ. Center, 1979-81; lectr. U. Tex., U. So. Calif., U. Calif., Santa Barbara and Los Angeles; cons. in field. Author: Organizing for Defense: The Adminstration of the American Military Establishment, 1961, The Cold War Years: American Foreign Policy Since 1945, 1969, Cold War and Detente: The American Foreign Policy Process Since 1945, 1975; co-author: American Civil-Military Decisions, 1963, Information System Applications for a High Level Staff, 1972, Social Choice and Soviet Strategic Decision Making, 1977, Regional Energy Policy Alternatives, 1977, Administration of Security Assistance: Systems and Process, 1978, Individual Energy Conservation Behaviors, 1980, The Reluctant Supplier, 1983; co-editor: Political Dynamics in the Middle East, 1971. Trustee Inter-Univ. Case Program, Inc. Forrestal fellow in naval history, 1955; Stimson Fund fellow Yale U., 1959; Rockefeller fellow in internat. studies, 1963-64. Mem. AAAS, Am. Polit. Sci. Assn., Internat. Studies Assn. Mormon. Office: Grad Sch Pub and Internat Affairs Forbes Quad University of Pittsburgh Pittsburgh PA 15260

HAMMOND, R. PHILIP, chemical engineer; b. Creston, Iowa, May 28, 1916; s. Robert Hugh and Helen (Williams) H.; m. Amy L. Farmer, Feb. 28, 1941 (div. 1969); children: Allen L., David M., Jean Phyllis, Stanley W.; m. Vivienne Fox, 1972. B.S. in Chem. Engring., U. So. Calif., 1938; Ph.D. in Phys. and Inorganic Chemistry (Naval Research fellow), U. Chgo., 1947. Registered profl. engr., Ill., Calif. Chief chemist Lindsay Chem. Co., West Chicago, Ill., 1938-46; group leader Los Alamos Sci. Lab., 1947-62, asso. div. leader reactor devel. div., 1960-62; dir. nuclear desalination program Oak Ridge Nat. Lab., 1962-73; adj. prof. U. Calif. at Los Angeles, 1972; head energy group R & D Assos. Corp., Santa Monica, Calif., 1973—. Author articles on nuclear power reactors, nuclear wastes, reactor safety econs., energy centers, metallurgy of plutonium and refractory metals, rare earths, radiation chemistry, remote control engring.; contbr. to fusion energy concept using underground containment, to Ency. Brit. Mem. U.S. delegation Conf. on Peaceful Uses Atomic Energy, Geneva, Switzerland, 1955, 65, 71, IAEA Panel on Desalination, Vienna, Austria, 1964, 65, 66, 71; mem. U.S. team to USSR on desalination, 1964. Mem. Am. Nuclear Soc. (charter), Am. Chem. Soc., Am. Inst. Chem. Engrs., Sigma Xi, Phi Kappa Phi, Phi Lambda Upsilon. Patentee in field. Office: PO Box 1735 Santa Monica CA 90406 *With our achievements in desalination, efficient agriculture, and nuclear power, it is now clear that the food producing ability of the earth is not limited by technology. But our political and social institutions have not kept up. We are beset by poor leadership, indecision, tremendous waste and ignorance of the money value of time. Here is the challenge for youth.*

HAMMOND, ROBERT MORRIS, educator, author; b. N.Y.C., Dec. 29, 1920; s. John Farnsworth and Hazel Marguerite (Morris) H.; m. Marguerite Masius, June 12, 1943; children: Roberta Masius, Charles Edward. B.A., U. Rochester, 1942; M.A., Yale, 1947, Ph.D., 1952. Instr. French U. Ariz., Tucson, 1950-53, asst. prof., 1953-63, asso. prof., 1963-67; prof. French Harvard, summers 1965, 66; vis. prof. French lit. and cinema Wells Coll., Aurora, N.Y., 1967-68; prof. French lit. and cinema, also chmn. internat. communications and culture dept. State U. N.Y., Cortland, 1968—. Author: plays Solitaire, 1960, The Nursery, 1965, Beirut 75, 1976; Translator: plays by Pascal Vrebos Yalta 2000, 1976, Sade-Sack, 1980; Editor: Deux Films Francais, 1966, Creative French, 1969, Beauty and the Beast (Jean Cocteau), 1970; Contbr. articles on French cinema, teaching fgn. lang. by film to profl. jours. U.S. rep. Internat. Cine-Club Workshop, Marly-le-Roi, France, 1957, Congres Internat. des Arts et de la Litterature par le Cinema, 1971—; mem. jury Internat. Film Festival, Rheims, France, 1974 mem. jury Internat. Film Festival, Kranj, Yugoslavia, 1974 mem. jury Internat. Film Festival, Budapest, Hungary, 1975, Internat. Mil. Film Festival, Paris, 1981, Internat. Hist. Film Festival, Paris, 1983. Served with USAAF, 1942-46. Fulbright fellow; also French govt. fellow, 1950; U. Ariz. research grantee, 1966, 67; N.Y. State research grantee, 1971; Nat. Endowment for Humanities grantee for devel. interdisciplinary approach to study cinema, 1970-72. Mem. Modern Lang. Assn., N.E., Rocky Mountain modern lang. assns., Soc. Cinema Studies, Dramatists Guild. Club: Yale (N.Y.C.). Office: Internat Communications and Culture Dept State U NY Cortland NY 13045

HAMMOND, ROY JOSEPH, reins. co. exec.; b. St. Louis, Jan. 9, 1929; s. Edward Herman and Alvera Ann (Herzog) H.; m. Donna LaSalle Perkins, Apr. 12, 1951; children—Douglas Edward, Donald Erwin, Laura Ann Hammond Budniakiewicz. B.S., Northwestern U., 1954; J.D., DePaul U., Chgo., 1959. Bar: Ill. bar 1959. With Am. Mut. Reins. Co., Chgo., 1963—, v.p., then sr. v.p., gen. counsel and sec., 1967-76, pres., chief exec. officer, 1976—; also dir. Pres. Wheeling (Ill.) Mcpl. Park Dist., 1963-65. Served with AUS, 1946-48. Mem. Reins. Assn. Am. (dir. 1976—), Am. Bar Assn., Internat. Assn. Ins. Counsel, Fedn. Ins. Counsel, Ill. Bar Assn., Chgo. Casualty Adjusters Assn. (pres. 1972-73). Republican. Presbyterian. Club: Chgo. Yacht. Home: Whitehall Shores 207 Azalea Dr Camden NC 27921 Office: 1 E Wacker Dr Rm 3100 Chicago IL 60601

HAMMOND, STUART LINDSLEY, publishing executive; b. Orange, N.J., May 6, 1922; s. Caleb Dean and Alice (Lindsley) H.; m. Doris Virginia Fitchette, Apr. 6, 1946 (div. 1982); children: Gail Linda, Joan Ann, Dana Lindsley, Katherine Brooke. B.S., Lehigh U., 1946. Regional sales mgr. Hammond, Inc., Maplewood, N.J., 1946-49, mgr. sales/trade div., 1949-53, treas., 1953-57, v.p., treas., 1957-63, dir., 1954—, exec. v.p., 1964-67, pres., chief adminstrv. officer, 1968-75, pres., chief exec. officer, 1976-80, chmn. bd., 1980—; dir. Hammond Realty, Hammond Map Store, Hammond Almanac, Maplewood, N.J. Served to 1st lt. USAAF, 1942-45. Decorated Air medal. Mem. Alpha Tau Omega. Republican. Clubs: Baltusrol Golf, Short Hills, Skytop. Office: 515 Valley St Maplewood NJ 07040

HAMMOND, WILLIAM, dance company executive. Exec. dir. Alvin Ailey Am. Dance Theater, N.Y.C. Home: Alvin Ailey Am Dance Theater 1515 Broadway New York NY 10036§

HAMMOND, WILLIAM CHURCHILL, JR., former banker; b. Holyoke, Mass., July 4, 1903; s. William Churchill and Fanny (Reed) H.; m. Gertrude Green, June 24, 1935; children: Diana Churchill, Clarissa Reed, William Churchill. Grad., Groton Sch., 1921; Ph.B., Yale, 1925; M.B.A., Harvard, 1927. Statistician J & W Seligman, N.Y.C., 1927-29; research dept. Lehman Corp., 1929-36, Loomis Sayles & Co., Inc., Boston, 1936-42, asst. to pres., 1944-45; exec. asst. to Brig. Gen. Georges F. Doriot; chief research and devel. br. O.Q.M.G., Washington, 1942-43; mng. partner Boston office White, Weld & Co., N.Y.C., 1946-67, ret. ltd. partner, 1968-72; Selectman, Manchester, Mass., 1942; Trustee Mt. Holyoke Coll., 1951-61, Pine Manor Jr. Coll., 1962-74, New Eng. Aquarium. Mem. Mass. Audubon Soc. (dir. 1947-68), Elihu Club, Phi Beta Kappa, Delta Kappa Epsilon. Clubs: Bond (Boston); Myopia Hunt (Hamilton, Mass.); Anglers (N.Y.C.); Rod and Reel (Miami Beach, Fla.). Home: Hammondwood Hancock Point ME 04640

HAMMOND, WILLIAM ROGERS, educator; b. Atlanta, Oct. 19, 1920; s. Charles C. and Edna (Rogers) H.; m. Frances Estelle Turner, Mar. 22, 1947; children—Claren Charlotte, Alexandra Merlyn. B.S., Ga. State U., 1941; M.B.A., Harvard, 1943; D.B.A., Ind. U., 1954. Partner Brenner & Co. (C.P.A.'s), Atlanta, 1946-48; prof. bus. adminstrn., asso. dean Sch. Bus. Adminstrn., Ga. State U., Atlanta, 1948-75, dean grad. studies, 1958-73, Regent's prof., 1973—. Author accounting mgmt. and ins. books. Served to capt. AUS, 1943-46. Decorated Bronze Star medal. C.P.A., Ga. Mem. Am. Inst. C.P.A.'s, Acad. Mgmt., Am. Risk and Ins. Assn.

HAMMONDS, GEORGE HAMILTON, banker; b. Oklahoma City, Dec. 5, 1930; s. Homer Clare and Lucretia Eva (Decker) H.; m. Virginia Barnes, Sept. 7, 1957; children: Laura A., Tracy L., Nancy E. Student, Oklahoma City U., 1949; B.B.A., U. Okla., 1953. Auditor Okla. Tax Commn., 1953-54; sr. mgr. C.P.A. firm, Oklahoma City, 1956-67; controller Liberty Nat. Bank & Trust Co., Liberty Nat. Corp., Liberty Factors Inc., Liberty Real Estate Co., Liberty Property Mgmt. Co., Inc., Oklahoma City; sr. v.p. Liberty Nat. Bank & Trust Co., also Liberty Nat. Corp., 1980—. Trustee, Okla. Blood Inst.; bd. dirs. Liberty Nat. Found. Served as 1st lt. arty. U.S. Army, 1954-56. Mem. Oklahoma City C. of C., Fin. Execs. Inst. (pres., dir. chpt. 1983-84), Sigma Nu. Club: Quail Creek Golf and Country. Office: PO Box 25848 Oklahoma City OK 73125

HAMMONS, JAMES HUTCHINSON, chemistry educator, researcher; b. Chgo., Aug. 8, 1934; s. Harry Edgar and Rhoda Anita (Zimmermann) H.; m. Elisabeth Grant Netherwood, Aug. 18, 1956; children: Laura N., James B. B.A., Amherst Coll., 1956; M.A., Johns Hopkins U., 1958, Ph.D., 1962. Faculty Swarthmore Coll., Pa., 1964—, instr., 1964-66, asst. prof, 1966-70, assoc. prof., 1970-76, prof., 1976—, chmn. dept. chemistry, 1976-81. Contbr. chpts. to publs. in field. NSF sci. faculty fellow Yale U., 1981-82; research grantee Research Corp., Swarthmore, 1982, Petroleum Research Found., 1983—, Dreyfus Found., 1981-83. Mem. Am. Chem. Soc., Sigma Xi. Home: 17 Furness Ln Wallingford PA 19086 Office: Swarthmore College Swarthmore PA 19081

HAMMONS, RAY OTTO, research geneticist; b. Wesson, Miss., Oct. 2, 1919; s. William D. and Frances Lou (Douglas) H.; m. Ann R. Howell, Sept. 13, 1942; children: Mary Harmon, Lynda Eidson, Sue Hammons Bryner, Ray O. (dec.). A.A., Copiah Lincoln Jr. Coll., Wesson, Miss., 1941; B.S., Miss. State Coll.-State College, 1947, M.S., 1948; Ph.D., N.C. State U., Raleigh, 1953. Research instr. N.C. State U., 1949-53; asst. prof. Purdue U., 1953-55; geneticist Agr. Research Service U.S. Dept. Agr., Tifton, Ga., 1955-75, research leader crops Agr. Research Service, 1972—, supr. research geneticist Agr. Research Service, 1975—; cons. in field, speaker in field. Contbr. chpts. to books, numerous articles to profl. jours. Served to lt. USNR, 1941-45. Decorated D.F.C.; recipient Golden Peanut Research award Nat. Peanut Council, 1975, Disting. Sr. Faculty award Gamma Sigma Delta, 1980, Disting. Service award Ga. Peanut Commn., 1981. Fellow Am. Soc. Agronomy (vis. scientist 1981), Am. Peanut Research and Edn. Soc. Baptist. Home: 1203 Lake Dr Tifton GA 31794 Office: US Dept Agr Agr Research Service PO Box 748 Tifton GA 31793

HAMNER, EARL HENRY, JR., author, producer, TV and film writer; b. Schuyler, Va., July 10, 1923; s. Earl Henry and Doris Marion (Giannini) H.; m. Jane Martin, Oct. 16, 1954; children: Scott Martin, Caroline Spencer. Student, U. Richmond, 1940-43, Litt. D., 1974, Northwestern U., summer, 1946; B.F.A. in Radio Edn, Coll. Music of Cin., 1948; L.H.D., Berea Coll., 1975, Loyola U., 1975, De Paul U., 1976; D.F.A., Morris Harvey Coll., 1975. Radio writer sta. WLW, Cin., 1946-48; radio/TV writer NBC, N.Y.C., 1949-60; freelance TV and film writer, Hollywood, Calif., 1961—; pres. Amanda Prodns., Burbank, Calif., 19-—; Bd. assos. U. Richmond. Creator, co-exec. producer: The Waltons, CBS.; creator, exec. producer: Falcon Crest, CBS, Boone, NBC; Author: Fifty Roads to Town, 1953, Spencer's Mountain, 1961, You Can't Get There From Here, 1965, The Homecoming, 1970. Served with AUS, 1943-46. Recipient Annual award TV-Radio Writers, 1967, George Foster Peabody award, 1972, 5 Christopher awards, Virginian of Year Va. Press Assn., 1973, Emmy award, 1974, Virginian of Year Va. Assn. Broadcasters, 1975; named Man of Year Nat. Assn. TV Execs., 1974. Democrat. Episcopalian. Home: Studio City CA 91604 Office: Burbank Studios care Lorimar Prodns Inc 4000 Warner Blvd Burbank CA 91522

HAMNER, HOMER HOWELL, economist, educator; b. Lamont, Okla., Oct. 22, 1915; s. Homer Hill and Myrtle Susan (Edwards) H.; m. Winnie Elvyn Heafner, May 8, 1943 (dec. Aug. 23, 1946); 1 dau., Jean Lee (Mrs. Richard L. Nicholson); m. Marjorie Lucille Dittus, Nov. 24, 1947; 1 dau., Elaine. A.A., Glendale Coll., 1936; A.B., U. So. Calif., 1938; J.D., 1941; A.M., 1947; Ph.D., 1949. Fellow and teaching asst., dept. econs. U. So. Calif., 1945-49; prof. and chmn. dept. econs. Baylor U., 1949-55; editor research com. Baylor Business Studies, 1949-55, lectr. summer workshop, 1954; prof., chmn. dept. bus. adminstrn. and cons. U. Puget Sound, Tacoma, Wash., 1955-58, dir. sch. bus. adminstr. and econs., 1959-63, Edward L. Blaine chair econ. history, 1963—; also occasional lectr. Roman Forums, Ltd., Los Angeles, 1936-40; lectr. Am. Inst. Banking, 1949-50, Southwest Wholesale Credit Assn., 1949, James Connally AFB, 1950; cons. State of Wash. tax adv. council, 1957-58, State Wash. Expenditures Adv. Council, 1960. Author: Population Change in Metropolitan Waco, 1950; Reviewer, contbr.: to Jour. of Finance. Served with U.S. Army, 1941-44. Fellow Found. Econ. Edn., Chgo., 1953, Inst. on Freedom, Claremont Men's Coll., 1955; mem. AAUP, Am. Econ. Assn., Southwest Social Sci. Assn. (Tex. chmn. membership com.), Nat. Tax Assn., Am. Finance Assn., Am. Acad. Polit. and Soc. Sci., Order of Artus, Waco McLennan County Bar Assn. (hon.), Phi Beta Kappa, Phi Kappa Phi, Omicron Delta Gamma, Delta Theta Phi, Phi Rho Pi (degree highest achievement 1936). Methodist. Home: 4404 N 44th Tacoma WA 98407 *If physical resources grow scarce, it may become harder to live. If freedom wears too thin, it may become harder to survive.*

HAMOLSKY, MILTON WILLIAM, physician; b. Lynn, Mass., May 25, 1921; s. Israel and Sophie (Cremer) H.; m. Sandra Oelbaum, Feb. 18, 1979; children—Deborah Lynne, John Stephen, David James. A.B., Harvard U., 1943, M.D., 1946; Ad Eundum, Brown U., 1964. Diplomate: Am. Bd. Internal Medicine. Intern Beth Israel Hosp., Boston, 1946-47, resident, 1947-48, 50-51, asst. physician, dir. endocrine clinic, 1957-63; instr. Harvard U. Med. Sch., 1951-55, asst. prof. medicine, 1955-63; prof. med. sci. Brown U., 1963—; physician-in-chief R.I. Hosp., Providence, 1963—, W&I Hosp., 1981—; vis. asst. prof. biochemistry Brandeis U., 1958-59; vis. Commonwealth fellow College de France, 1960-61; cons. to hosps.; mem. exec. com. Diet Counselling Service Obstet. Health Care Com. Author: Thyroid Testing, 1968; contbr. numerous articles on endocrinology to profl. publs. Trustee Planned Parenthood, Providence, R.I. Child Guidance Clinic, Providence, Camp Jori, Providence. Served as capt. M.C. U.S. Army, 1948-50. Recipient Henry A. Christian award Harvard U. Med. Sch., 1946. Fellow A.C.P. (gov. R.I. chpt.); mem. AMA, Am. Thyroid Assn., Endocrine Soc., Am. Physiol. Soc., Soc. Clin. Investigation, Am. Fedn. Clin. Research, R.I. Diabetes Soc. (pres.), R.I. Heart Assn. (pres.). Home: 150 Arlington Ave Providence RI 02906 Office: RI Hosp Providence RI 02902

HAMOVITCH, WILLIAM, educator, univ. ofcl.; b. Montreal, Que., Can., Sept. 1, 1922; came to U.S., 1946, naturalized, 1953; s. Abraham and Tillie (Weisenfeld) H.; m. Mitzi Berger, May 30, 1946; children—Alan, Susan. B.Com., McGill U., 1943; M.P.A. (Adminstrn. fellow), Harvard, 1945, M.A., 1946, Ph.D., 1949. Lectr., asst. prof. U. Buffalo, 1946-53; asst. prof., asso. prof., prof. Queens Coll. City U. N.Y., Queens, 1953—, chmn. dept. econs., 1965—, provost, acad. v.p., 1976—; research scientist N.Y.C. Temp. Commn. on City Finances, 1965; Chmn. Commn. on Off-Track Betting in Nassau County, 1970. Author: Conflict and Stability in Labor Relations: A Case Study, 1952; Editor: The Federal Deficit: Fiscal Imprudence or Policy Weapon?, 1965, Monetary Policy: The Argument From Keynes' Treatise to Friedman, 1966, Employment and Occupation Projections for Nassau-Suffolk to 1985, 1968. Fellow Royal Econ. Soc.; mem. Am. Econ. Assn. Home: 77 Westminster Rd Great Neck NY 11020 Office: Queens Coll Flushing NY 11367

HAMP, ERIC PRATT, linguist; b. London, Nov. 16, 1920; U.S., 1925, naturalized, 1947; s. William Pratt and Edith (McConkey) H.; m. Margot Faust, Sept. 29, 1951; children: Julijana, Alexander. B.A., Amherst Coll., 1942, L.H.D., 1972; M.A., Harvard U., 1948, Ph. D. in Linguistics, 1954. Chief lend-lease govt. Union South Africa, 1942-46; mem. faculty U. Chgo., 1950—, prof. linguistics, 1962—, prof. behavioral scis., 1971—, prof. Slavic langs., 1980—, Robert Maynard Hutchins Disting. Service prof., 1973—, dir. Center Balkan and Slavic Studies, 1965—, chmn. dept. linguistics, 1966-69; vis. lectr. U. Mich., 1953; Vis. lectr. U. Wash., summer 1962; mem. staff Gaelic Dialect Survey, U. Edinburgh, Scotland, 1956, 57, 58; Collitz prof. U. Tex., summer 1960; vis. prof. linguistics U. Beograd, Yugoslavia, 1964, 67, Ind. U., summer 1964, U. Copenhagen, 1966, U. Bucharest, Romania,

1975, U. Salzburg, Austria, 1979, 82; U.S. cultural exchange lectr. Romania, summer 1966, USSR, spring 1975; asso. dir. Linguistic Inst. U. Ill., summer 1968; vis. scholar Inst. for Humanities, Pa. State U., 1969; Chmn. subcom. linguistics Com. Instnl. Coop., 1963-66; mem. com. automatic lang. processing Nat. Acad. Scis.-NRC, 1964—; mem. com. linguistic info. Center Applied Linguistics, 1964-68; chmn. com. lang. programs Am. Council Learned Socs., 1963-69; mem. linguistics com. Ind. U. Press, 1965-73; chmn. Com. for Ill. Place-Name Survey, 1966—; mem. area adv. com. for E. Europe, Council Internat. Exchange Scholars, 1966-78; mem. adv. subcom. for linguistics NSF, 1977-79; mem. Am. com. Assn. Internat. d'Etudes du Sud-Est Européen, 1968—, chmn., 1979—; mem. U.S. Nat. Commn. for UNESCO, 1972-77. Author: A Glossary of American Technical Linguistic Usage, 3d rev. edit., 1966, (with others) Language and Machines, 1966; editor: Readings in Linguistics II, 1966; Editor: Languages and Areas: Studies Presented to George V. Bobrinskoy, 1967, Themes in Linguistics: the 1970's, 1973; adv. editor: Foundations of Language, 1964-79; Adv. editor: Studies in Language, 1964-79, Gen. Linguistics, 1966—, Papers in Lang. and Lit., 1965—, Jour. Linguistics, 1971-81, Jour. Indo-European Studies, 1972—, Folia Linguistica Historica, 1978—, Ann. of Armenian Linguistics, 1978—, Anthrop. Linguistics, 1981—, Etudes celtiques, 1982—, Jour. Hist. Linguistics and Philology, 1982—, Glossologia (Athens), 1983—, Jewish Lang. Rev. (Haifa), 1983—; asso. editor: Internat. Jour. Am. Lingustics, 1967—, Native Am. Texts Series, 1974—; sect. head comparative and hist. linguistics: Celtic and Albanian sects. MLA Ann. Bibliography, 1969-82; adviser: Ency. Brit., 1969—, Braille Reading Program, Am. Printing House for the Blind, 1977—; contbr. to profl. jours. John Woodruff Simpson fellow from Amherst to U. Pa., 1946, to Johns Hopkins U., 1947; Sheldon Traveling fellow Harvard U., 1949-50; Fulbright sr. research scholar U. Athens, Greece, 1955-56; Social Scis. Research Council-Am. Council Learned Socs. grantee in Albanian dialectology, 1960-61; Fulbright-Hays fellow, 1966-67; Guggenheim fellow, 1973-74. Fellow Am. Acad. Arts and Scis. (membership com. 1982-84), AAAS, Am. Anthrop. Assn.; mem. Am. Philos. Soc., Linguistic Soc. Am. (exec. com. 1954-56, v.p. 1963, 70, pres. 1971, nominating com. 1960-62, 82—), MLA (sec. Celtic sect. 1954, 78, chmn. 1956, 79, chmn. gen. linguistics sect. 1970, lang. change 1976, nominating com. 1975, del. assembly 1976-77, PMLA adv. com. 1979-83), Philol. Soc. (London), Scottish Gaelic Texts Soc., Soc. de Linguistique de Paris, Soc. Linguistica Europaea, Soc. Italiana di Glottologia, Soc. Filologica Friulana, Acoustical Soc. Am., Am. Names Soc. (bd. mgrs. 1969-72), Internat. Phonetics Soc., Assn. Advancement of Baltic Studies, Am. Assn. Advancement of Slavic Studies, Am. Assn. Southeast European Studies, Bulgarian Studies Assn., Romanian Studies Assn. (dir. 1976-79), Soc. Slovene Studies (editorial com. 1979—), Soc. Albanian Studies (exec. com. 1978—), Soc. Armenian Studies, Phi Beta Kappa. Home: 5200 S Greenwood Ave Chicago IL 60615

HAMPE, KEITH ROBERT, process equipment company executive; b. Dryden, Ont., Can., Sept. 10, 1941; came to U.S., 1960; s. Leo and Zoelle M. (Merrill) H.; m. Suzanne Runden, Dec. 3, 1960; children: Robert, Margret. B.S. in Chemistry, Ariz. State U., 1963. Engr. Motorola Co., Phoenix, 1961-64; engring. supr. Fairchild Camera Co., Mt. View, Calif., 1965-67; with Nat. Semicondr. Co., 1968-79, group dir., Santa Clara, Calif., 1975-79; pres. Sertech Co., Salem, Mass., 1980, also; Airco Temescal div. Airco, Inc., Berkeley, Calif. Republican. Episcopalian. Office: 2850 7th St Berkeley CA 94710 *

HAMPSHIRE, SUSAN, actress; b. London, Eng., 1942; m. Pierre Granier-Deferre (div. dissolved 1974); 1 child.; m. Eddie Kulukundia, 1981. Actress: stage appearances in House Guest; rôles in: TV serials Dick Turpin, Barchester Chronicles; films include Bang (Winner Emmy award Best Actress in drama series 1970, 71, 73). Address: Midland Bank Ltd 92 Kensington High St London W1 England W8485H

HAMPSHIRE, WILLIAM R., metals company executive; b. Lancaster, Ohio, Mar. 23, 1928; s. Ernest A. and Georgia E. (Groff) H.; m. Jean C. Campbell, Aug. 22, 1951; children: Michael, Jennifer, Jonathan. B.S. in Chemistry, Miami U., Oxford, Ohio, 1950. With Howmet Aluminum Corp., Greenwich, Conn., group v.p., 1975-82, pres., chief exec. officer, 1982—, also dir.; dir. Intalco Aluminum Corp., Ferndale, Wash., 1975—, Eastalco Aluminum Corp., Frederick, Md., 1975—, Pechiney Uline Kuhlman, Greenwich, 1982—. Mem. Am. Mining Engrs. Republican. Episcopalian. Home: 165 Scarlet Oak Dr Wilton CT 06897 Office: Howmet Aluminum Corp 475 Steamboat Rd Greenwich CT 06830

HAMPSON, HAROLD ANTHONY, equity holding company executive; b. Montreal, Que., Can., Aug. 18, 1930; s. Harold Ralph and Geraldine Mary (Smith) H. B.A., McGill U., 1950; M.A. in Econs., Cambridge U., 1952. Mem. staff Royal Commn. of Can's Econ. Prospects, Ottawa, Ont., 1955-57; sec. Royal Commn. on Banking and Fin., Toronto, Ont., 1961-64; dir. research and underwriting Burns Bros & Denton, Toronto, 1957-61; v.p. Power Corp. Can. Ltd., Toronto, 1964-68; pres. Capital Mgmt. Ltd., Montreal, 1968-71; chmn. Can. Devel. Corp., Toronto, 1972-73, pres., chief exec. officer, 1973—; dir. Connaught Labs. Ltd., AES Data Ltd.; dir. Canterra Energy Ltd., Polysar Ltd., Kidd Creek Mines Ltd., Savin Corp., CDC Life Scis. Inc., CDC Data Systems. Bd. govs. York U.; chmn. exec. com., mem. policy analysis com. C.D. Howe Inst. Office: Suite 200-444 Yonge St Toronto ON M5B 2H4 Canada

HAMPTON, BENJAMIN BERTRAM, mfg. co. exec.; b. N.Y.C., Aug. 3, 1925; s. Max and Pauline (Weinberger) H.; m. Elizabeth Golub-Cohen, Oct. 16, 1975; 1 son by previous marriage, Roger Neil; stepchildren—Laurence, James, Lisa. B.Aero. Engring., N.Y.U., 1947; certificate mech. engring., Pa. State Coll., 1945; M.B.A., Harvard, 1949. Sales mgr. Carew Products, Inc., N.Y.C., 1949-51; project mgr. Emerson Radio & TV Corp., 1951-52; div. mgr. Paragon Oil Co., Mineola, L.I., 1952-55; mgmt. cons. E.N. Kagan & Co., N.Y.C., 1955-60; exec. asst. to pres. marketing Fed. Pacific Electric Co., Newark, 1960-62; asst. to pres. Seagrave Corp., N.Y.C., 1962-63; v.p. Swingline Inc., Long Island City, N.Y., 1963-68, exec. v.p., 1968-71, dir., 1970-71; exec. v.p., dir. Poloron Products Inc., New Rochelle, N.Y., 1971-73, pres., chief exec. officer, 1973-74; exec. v.p., dir. West Chem. Products, Inc., Long Island City, 1975—. Co-chmn. N.Y. State Finance Com. J.F. Kennedy presdl. campaign, 1960. Served with AUS, 1944-46. Mem. Am. Marketing Assn., Pi Lambda Phi. Club: Harvard (N.Y.C.). Home: 339 E Shore Rd Kings Point NY 11023 Office: 42-16 West St Long Island City NY 11101

HAMPTON, CLAUDE BLAINE, JR., food company executive; b. Newton, N.C., June 2, 1925; s. Claude Blaine; m. Edith Lingle, Nov. 1, 1947; children: Claude Blaine, III, Susan Gale. B.A., Catawba Coll., Salisbury, N.C., 1948; grad., Advanced Mgmt. Program, Harvard U., 1977. With Nabisco Brands, USA, 1949—, corp. sr. v.p., East Hanover, N.J., 1978—; dir. Chubb Life Ins. Co. Am. Served with USAAF, 1943-45. Decorated Air medal with 3 oak leaf clusters. Mem. Am. Logistics Assn., Sales Execs. Club. Home: 27 Douglas Dr Towaco NJ 07082 Office: NABISCO Inc DeForest Ave East Hanover NJ 07936

HAMPTON, COLIN CAMPBELL, insurance company executive; b. New Haven, Jan. 4, 1923; s. George W. and Jean (Stuart) H.; m. Marjorie A. Brown, June 16, 1951; children: Colin Campbell, Carolyn Fraser. B.S. in Bus. Adminstrn, Vanderbilt U., 1948; grad. student, N.Y.U.; M.B.A., U. Maine, 1972. With Mercantile Commerce Trust Co., St. Louis, 1948-49, McGraw-Hill Co., N.Y.C., 1949-50; bond trader Am. Security Corp., N.Y.C., 1951-52; securities analyst Bankers Trust Co., N.Y.C., 1952-55, Fiduciary Counsel, Inc., 1955-56; with Union Mut. Life Ins. Co., Portland, Maine, 1956—, pres., 1969—; corporator Portland Savs. Bank; dir. Central Maine Power Co. Trustee New Eng. Colls. Fund. Served to 1st lt. USAAF, 1943-45. Fellow Life Office Mgmt. Assn.; mem. Greater Portland C. of C. (dir.). Episcopalian. Clubs: Torch of Western Maine, Portland Country. Home: Ocean House Rd Cape Elizabeth ME 04107 Office: 2211 Congress St Portland ME 04102

HAMPTON, GORDON FRANCIS, lawyer; b. Fullerton, Calif., July 14, 1912; s. Lorenzo Arnie and Katharine (Twombly) H.; m. Virginia Rivers, Sept. 5, 1943 (dec. Jan. 1968); children: Roger Keith, Katharine Virginia (Mrs. Thomas M. Shenk), Wesley Gordon. A.B., Stanford U., 1935; LL.B., Harvard U., 1938. Bar: Calif. 1938. Since practiced in, Los Angeles; ptnr. firm Sheppard, Mullin, Richter & Hampton (and predecessors), 1945—; instr. Loyola U. Law Sch., Los Angeles, 1942-43; lectr. Calif. State Bar Continuing Edn. Program, 1950, 59; Vice chmn. Los Angeles County Republican Central Com., 1947-48; mem. Calif. Rep. Central Com., 1947-48. Editor: Los Angeles Bar Bull., 1950-51; contbr. articles to legal jours. Bd. dirs. Fellows Contemporary Art, 1975—, chmn., 1982-84; Chmn. Fellows Pasadena Art Mus., 1972-75; trustee Mus. Contemporary Art, Los Angeles, 1983—. Fellow Am. Bar Found.; mem. ABA (chmn. antitrust sect. com. supplementary antitrust sanctions 1964-67, lectr. Nat. Inst. Antitrust Law 1967, 69, 72, 78, chmn. nat. insts. antitrusts law subcom. 1967-71, mem. council antitrust law sect. 1971-75, budget officer antitrust law sect. 1975-77), D.C. Bar Assn., Calif. Bar Assn., Los Angeles Bar Assn. (trustee 1958-60), Am. Judicature Soc., Stanford U. Alumni Assn. (pres. 1961-62), Phi Beta Kappa. Presbyterian. Clubs: Valley Hunt (Pasadena); Chancery, California (Los Angeles). Home: 2665 Wallingford Rd San Marino CA 91108 Office: 333 S Hope St 48th Floor Los Angeles CA 90071

HAMPTON, GRACE RITA, union staff member, county commission administrator; b. Detroit, Oct. 2, 1925; d. Moses Sanford Ryan and Willie Mae (Hankerson) Price; children: Rita, Grace, Janeice, Hilliard, Sharain, Bryan. Clk. Detroit Ordinance U.S. Govt., 1944-48; clk.-typist UAW Local 142, Wayne, Mich., 1950-53, UAW Local 227, Detroit, 1955-57; sec., dir. Internat. UAW, Taylor, Mich., 1957-83, stenographer, Detroit, 1983—. Recording sec. Mich. Democratic Party, Lansing; bd. dirs. Wayne County Library Bd., Mich., 1962-80, Wayne County Rd. Commn., 1980—. Clubs: Inkster Democratic (Mich.); Nat. Orgn. Negro Women. Home: 27135 Yale Ave Inkster MI 48141 Office: Wayne County Road Commn 415 Clifford St Detroit MI 48141

HAMPTON, JOHN LEWIS, newspaper editor; b. Verda, Ky., Jan. 13, 1935; s. John Lewis and Ruby Lillian (Slagle) H.; children—Rachel McCauley, Jessica Morris, Jonathan Hugh. A.B. in Journalism (Outstanding Journalism Grad. award 1959), U. Ky., 1959; M.A. in Communications and Journalism (grad. fellow 1960), Stanford U., 1960. Staff writer AP, Lexington, Ky., 1960-61; bur. chief Louisville (Ky.) Courier-Jour., 1961-67; staff writer Nat. Observer, Washington, 1967-71, sr. editor, then asst. mng. editor, 1971-77; mem. editorial bd. Miami (Fla.) Herald, 1977, editor, 1978—. Mem. Commn. Ct. Costs and Delay, Fla. Bar, 1979-80. Served with AUS, 1953-56. Named to Hall Disting. Alumni U. Ky.; recipient Pulitzer prize in editorial writing, 1983. Mem. Am. Soc. Newspaper Editors, Inter Am. Press Assn., Fla. Soc. Newspapers Editors. Office: Miami Herald 1 Herald Plaza Miami FL 33101

HAMPTON, LEROY, chemical company executive; b. Ingalls, Ark., Apr. 20, 1927; s. Ed Levi and Kitty Annie (Larry) H.; m. Anne Neris Herndon, July 11, 1954; children: Mary Louise, Gloria, Stanley Lamar, Cedric Leroy, Candice La Neris. B.S., U. Colo., 1950; M.S., Denver U., 1960. Registered pharmacist, Colo., Mich. Registered pharmacist Rocky Mountain Drug Co., Denver, 1950-53; scientist-chemist Dow Chem. Co., Golden, Colo., 1953-58, profl. scientist-chemist in charge, 1958-61, devel. chemist, 1961-63, devel. leader, 1963-67, recruiting supr., Midland, Mich., 1967-68; recruiting mgr. N.E. Region, 1968-70, mgr. minority employee relations, 1970-75; pres. Dow Chem. Employees Credit Union, 1979; mgr. Issue Analysis, 1976-80, research asso., 1981—; owner, operator hardware store, Denver, 1965-67. Bd. dirs. Midland Kiwanis Club Found., 1973-74, Midland chpt. ARC, 1974-76, Dow Chem. Employees Credit Union, 1975—; mem. Midland Bd. Edn., 1978—, sec., 1979-80, v.p., 1981-82; bd. dirs. Midland Assn. Retarded Citizens, 1982—. Served with USNR, 1945-46. Mem. Am. Chem. Soc., Alpha Phi Alpha. Democrat. Presbyterian. Club: Kiwanian (pres. 1975-76). Home: 2206 Burlington Dr Midland MI 48640 Office: 2020 Dow Center Midland MI 48640

HAMPTON, LIONEL LEO, composer, condr., entertainer; b. Birmingham, Ala., Apr. 12, 1913; s. Charles and Gertrude (Whitfield) H.; m. Gladys Riddle, Nov. 11, 1936. Student, U. So. Calif., 1934; Mus.D. (hon.), Allen U., Columbia, S.C., Pepperdine Coll., 1975; Ph.D. in Music (hon.), Xavier U., 1975, Howard U., 1979. Mem., Benny Goodman Quartet, 1936-40; organized band, Lionel Hampton Orch., 1940. Recipient George Frederick Handel medallion. Mem. Alpha Phi Alpha. Clubs: Elk (grand band master), Mason (33 deg.), Friars, Grand Street Boys (N.Y.C.). Home: 1995 Broadway New York NY 10023 also 3808 W Adams Blvd Los Angeles CA 90018

HAMPTON, MARK GARRISON, architect; b. Tampa, Fla., July 17, 1923; s. Ham Stonewall and Laura (Bingenheimer) H. B.S., B.Arch., Ga. Inst. Tech., 1949. Owner Mark Hampton, Architect, Tampa, 1952-65, Miami, Fla., 1974—; partner Herbert H. Johnson Assos., Miami, 1966-73. Prin. works include Chemistry and Life Sci. bldgs, U. So. Fla., Tampa, 1961, First Fed. Office Bldg, Sarasota, 1973. Bd. dirs. Lannan Found., Palm Beach, Fla., 1972—; pres. Tampa Art Inst., 1958, 64; mem. Barrio Latino Commn., Tampa, 1960-67. Served with inf. AUS, 1943-46. Decorated Bronze Star, Purple Heart; recipient award Homes for Better Living competition, 1957, 62; Nat. Design award Horizon Home program, 1963. Fellow AIA (juror Nat. Honor awards 1963, 64, medal of honor for design Fla. Central chpt. 1974). Episcopalian. Clubs: University, Krewe of Gasparilla (Tampa). Address: 3900 Loquat Ave Coconut Grove FL 33133

HAMPTON, PHILLIP MICHAEL, consulting engineering company executive; b. Asheville, N.C., Sept. 5, 1932; s. Boyd Walker and Helen Reba (Smith) H.; m. Wilma Christine Gross, July 7, 1951; children: Philip Michael, Deborah Lynn, Gregg Ashley. A.B. in Geology, Berea Coll., 1954. Draftsman-designer Johnson & Anderson, Inc., Pontiac, Mich., 1955-57, designer, also project mgr., 1957-59, dir. bus. devel., 1962-76, v.p., 1966-74, exec. v.p., 1974-76; v.p. Spalding G. DeDecker & Assos., Inc., Madison Heights, Mich., 1976—; pres. HMA Consultants Inc., 1977—, Geo Internat., Inc., 1978—; v.p. JAVLEN Internat., 1971-73; co-founder, owner My World Shops and Hampton Galleries, Ltd., 1976—; co-owner Hampton-Tyedten Galleries Ltd., 1979—, mem. public adv. panel GSA, 1977—; chmn. task force of com. fed. procurement of architect/engr. services Am. Bar Assn., 1977—. Editor: Total Scope, 1963-71. Pres. Waterford Bd. Edn., 1969-71; mem. state resolution com. Democratic Conv., 1972; exec. com. Oakland County Dem. Com., 1973-74; precinct del., 1972-76; trustee Environ. Research Assos., sec.-treas., 1969-71, pres., 1971-73; chmn. Waterford Cable Communications Commn., 1981—. Fellow Am. Cons. Engrs. Council (internat. engring. com. 1971—, vice chmn. public relations com. 1970-72, chmn. publs. com. 1972-74, chmn. Am. Bar Assn. model procurement code com. 1977—); mem. Nat. Water Well Assn. (chmn. tech. div. 1969-71), ASCE, AAAS, Cons. Engrs. Council Mich. (awards com. 1970-74), Am. Arbitration Assn. (comml. panel 1977—). Presbyterian. Clubs: Pontiac Exchange, Pontiac-Detroit Lions Quarterback. Home and Office: 2440 Ostrum Pontiac MI 48055 Office: 655 W Thirteen Mile Rd Madison Heights MI 48071 *My first employment, at age 13, was as a janitor. The superintendent of facilities taught me to pay attention to detail. He advised, "clean under the stairwells and the entrance will take care of itself." I understood his meaning and adopted the philosophy as my own in many areas of my life and career.*

HAMPTON, REX HERBERT, realty company executive; b. Chgo., Aug. 3, 1918; s. John William and Alice Grace (Melling) H.; m. Ruth Lorraine Gibbons, Sept. 30, 1940; children: Hope, Rex Herbert, Robin Virgil, Maryalice. B.S. in Forest Mgmt, Utah State U., 1942; M.A. in Internat. Affairs, George Washington U., 1963; student, U.S. Air Force War Coll., 1963. Real estate broker, Colo. Commd. 2d lt. U.S. Army, 1942, advanced through grades to brig. gen., 1968; ret., 1972; mgr. Bennett Shellenberger Realty, Colorado Springs, Colo., 1975-80; pres., chief exec. officer Golden Cycle Gold Corp., Colorado Springs, 1980—. Decorated D.S.M., Legion of Merit with cluster, Bronze Star, others. Mem. Nat. Realtors Assn., Ret. Officers Assn. (pres. chpt.), VFW, DAV. Republican. Mormon. Clubs: Peterson Field Officers, Eisenhower Golf. Office: 228 N Cascade St Colorado Springs CO 80903

HAMPTON, ROBERT EDWARD, chem. co. exec.; b. Chattanooga, Sept. 21, 1922; s. Charles Alfred and Mary Lee (Plemons) H.; m. Geraldyne Ann Stivers, July 12, 1947; children—Adrienne Ann, Jeffrey Scott. Student, U. Tenn., 1946-48, B.A. in Bus. Adminstrn, 1949. Prin. Blackfox Sch., Cleveland, Tenn., 1949-50; vice consul, Munich, Germany, 1950-52; fgn. affairs officer exec. secretariat State Dept., 1952-53, staff asst. to sec. state, 1953-55; asst. dep. manpower, personnel and orgn. Dept. Air Force, 1955-57; spl. asst. to undersec. for adminstrn. State Dept., 1957-58; spl. asst. for personnel The White House, 1958-61; commr. CSC, 1961-69, chmn., 1969-77; dir. pub. affairs ICI Americas, Wilmington, Del., 1977-79, gen. mgr. public affairs, 1979—; mem. Bd. Fgn. Service, 1969; chmn. Fed. Labor Relations Council, 1970-77; mem. Pres.'s Commn. on White House Fellowships, 1969-77, Pres.'s Commn. Employment Handicapped, 1969-77, Pres.'s Econ. Adjustment Com., 1973-77, Internat. Civil Service Commn., 1970-77; mem. gen. adminstrn. bd. Dept. Agr. Grad. Sch., 1973-77. Served with USAAF, 1942-45; ETO. Named Young Republican of Year, 1960; recipient Silver Helmet award Amvets, 1970; Stockberger award Soc. for Personnel Adminstrn., 1971; Exec. Govt. award Opportunities Industrialization Centers, 1972; Merit award Fed. Adminstrv. Law Judges Conf., 1974. Mem. Nat. Acad. Pub. Adminstrn. Home: 635 Woodbine Rd Meadowcroft West Chester PA 19380 Office: ICI Americas Inc Wilmington DE 19897

HAMPTON, VERNE CHURCHILL, II, lawyer; b. Pontiac, Mich., Jan. 5, 1934; s. Verne Churchill and Mildred (Peck) H.; m. Stephanie Hall, Oct. 5, 1973; children: J. Howard, Timothy H., Julia C. B.A., Mich. State U., 1955; LL.B., U. Va., 1958. Bar: Mich. 1958. Since practiced in, Detroit; partner firm Dickinson, Wright, Moon, Van Dusen & Freeman, 1967—; sec. Douglas & Lomason Co.; dir. KPSI Radio Corp. Mem. Mich. Republican Fin. Com.; sec., dir. Detroit Bus./Edn. Alliance; corp. mem. Boy's Clubs Met. Detroit. Mem. State Bar Mich. (chmn. corp., fin. and bus. law sect. 1980—), Detroit Bar Assn., ABA, Sigma Alpha Epsilon, Phi Alpha Delta. Republican. Episcopalian. Clubs: Detroit, Country of Detroit. Home: 510 Oxford Rd Grosse Pointe MI 48236 Office: 800 First Nat Bldg Detroit MI 48226

HAMRICK, CLAUDE MEREDITH, transp. co. exec., lawyer; b. Rutherford County, N.C., July 27, 1926; s. Roland B. and Thelma H.; m. Lena Mae Lewis, July 6, 1957; children—Kent Lewis, Roland Mont. Student, Pfeiffer Jr. Coll., 1943-44; LL.B., Wake Forest U., 1950. Bar: N.C. bar 1950. Practiced law, Winston-Salem, N.C., 1953-59; partner firm Spry and Hamrick, Winston-Salem, 1959-69, Hamrick Doughton and Newton Winston-Salem, 1969-77; v.p., gen. counsel McLean Trucking Co., Winston-Salem, 1977—, also dir. Mem. N.C. Ho. of Reps., 1961-67. Served with JAGC U.S. Army, 1944-46, 50-52. Mem. N.C., 21st Jud. Dist. bar assns., Motor Carrier Lawyers Assn. Democrat. Baptist. Home: 360 Staffordshire Rd Winston-Salem NC 27104 Office: 1920 W 1st St Winston-Salem NC 27102

HAN, MOO-YOUNG, physicist; b. Seoul, Korea, Nov. 30, 1934; came to U.S., 1954; s. Sunghoon and Kiejer (Kim) H.; m. Changki Hong, Aug. 29, 1959; children: Grace, Chris, Tony. B.S., Carroll Coll., Waukesha, Wis., 1957; Ph.D., U. Rochester, 1964. Research assoc. Syracuse U., 1964-65; asst. prof. U. Pitts., 1965-67; asst. prof. physics Duke U., Durham, N.C., 1967-71, assoc. prof., 1971-77, prof., 1977—; vis. prof. Kyoto U., 1974. Recipient Outstanding Prof. award Duke U., 1971, Disting. Teaching award, 1972, Disting. Fgn. Scholar award Kyoto U., 1974. Mem. Am. Phys. Soc. Home: 615 Duluth St Durham NC 27705 Office: Dept Physics Duke U Durham NC 27706

HANAFEE, WILLIAM, radiologist; b. Louisville, Mar. 21, 1926; s. John F. and Mary (Crist) H.; m. Constance Gandolph, Nov. 25, 1948; children: William N., Linda, Patrick and Michael (twins). Student, Ind. Coll. Pharmacy, 1943-44; B.A., U. Rochester, 1946; M.D., U. Louisville, 1949. Faculty U. Calif., Los Angeles, 1953—; prof. radiology Sch. Medicine, 1966—, acting chmn. dept., 1966, chmn. dept., 1967-72; cons., Long Beach, VA, 1964—, Jules Stein Eye Inst., Los Angeles, 1966—; lectr. San Diego Naval Hosp., 1966. Fellow Am. Coll. Radiology; mem. AMA, Los Angeles Soc. Neurology and Psychiatry, Calif., Los Angeles County med. assns., N.Am., Pacific N.W., Calif., Los Angeles radiol. socs., Am. Soc. Head and Neck Radiology (sec.-treas.), Am. Roentgen Ray Soc., Pan Am. Med. Assn. Devel. computerized tomography and NMR scanning for cancer of larnyn, nasopharnyn and parotid gland and other areas of head and neck; noted for contrast studies of facial arteries, cavernous sinus and orbital veins; contbr. to investigation of trans-jugular cholangiography and controlled selective carotid angiography. Home: 547 Cashmere Terr Los Angeles CA 90049 Office: 405 Hilgard Ave Los Angeles CA 90024

HANAFUSA, HIDESABURO, virologist; b. Nishinomiya, Japan, Dec. 1, 1929; came to U.S., 1961; s. Kamehachi and Tomi H.; m. Teruko Inoue, May 11, 1958; 1 dau., Kei. B.S., Osaka (Japan) U., 1953, Ph.D., 1960. Research asso. Research Inst. for Microbial Diseases, Osaka U., 1958-61; postdoctoral fellow virus lab. U. Calif., Berkeley, 1961-64; vis. scientist College de France, Paris, 1964-66; asso. mem., chief dept. viral oncology Public Health Research Inst. of City N.Y. Inc., 1966-68, mem., 1968-73; prof. Rockefeller U., 1973—. Mem. editorial bd.: Internat. Jour. Cancer, 1974—, Jour. Virology, 1975—, BBA Rev. Cancer, 1973—, Intervirology, 1972—, Jour. Exptl. Medicine, 1976—, Cell, 1979—; contbr. articles to profl. jours. Recipient Howard Taylor Ricketts award, 1981, Albert Lasker Basic Med. Research award, 1982; Nat. Cancer Inst. grantee, 1966—; Am.

Cancer Soc. grantee, 1976—. Mem. Am. Soc. Microbiology, AAAS, N.Y. Acad. Sci. Research on RNA tumor viruses. Home: 500 E 63d St New York NY 10021 Office: Rockefeller U 1230 York Ave New York NY 10021

HANAHAN, DONALD JAMES, biochemist, educator; b. Springfield, Ill., May 13, 1919; s. James Francis and Clara (Schiller) H.; m. Lillian Marie Larsen, June 21, 1947; children—Douglas A., Laura J., Timothy J., Colleen J., Carolyn M. B.S., U. Ill., 1941, Ph.D., 1944. Research asso. Manhattan Project, 1944-45; postdoctoral fellow U. Calif., Berkeley, 1945-47; faculty U. Wash., Seattle, 1948-67, prof. biochemistry, 1958-67; prof., head dept. biochemistry U. Ariz., Tucson, 1967-76; prof. biochemistry U. Tex. Health Sci. Center, San Antonio, 1976—, chmn. dept., 1976—. Author: Lipid Chemistry, 1960; Contbr. articles to profl. jours. Guggenheim Found. fellow, 1955; NIH spl. fellow, 1965-66; Macy faculty scholar, 1974. Mem. Am. Chem. Soc., Am. Soc. Biol. Chemists. Home: 7904 Summit Circle Dr San Antonio TX 78255 Office: Dept Biochemistry U Tex Health Sci Center San Antonio TX 78242

HANAN, PATRICK DEWES, educator; b. New Zealand, Jan. 4, 1927; s. Frederick Arthur and Ida Helen (Dewes) H.; m. Anneliese Drube, July 1951; 1 son, Rupert Guy. B.A., Auckland U., 1948, M.A., 1949; B.A., U. London, 1953, Ph.D., 1960. Lectr. Sch. Oriental and African Studies, 1954-63; asso. prof., then prof. Stanford U., 1963-68; prof. Chinese lit. Harvard U., 1968—. Author: The Chinese Short Story, 1973, The Chinese Vernacular Story, 1981. Fellow Am. Council Learned Socs., Guggenheim Found.; Mem. Am. Acad. Arts and Scis. Office: 2 Divinity St Cambridge MA 02138

HANAU, RICHARD, emeritus physics educator; b. N.Y.C., Aug. 1, 1917; s. Leo and Stella (Bloch) H.; m. Laia Pearlmutter, Jan. 2, 1941; 1 dau, Loren Michael. S.B., Mass. Inst. Tech., 1939; M.S., U. Mich., 1940, Ph.D., 1947. Asst. Harvard Coll. Observatory, Cambridge, Mass., summers 1937-39; teaching fellow U. Mich., Ann Arbor, 1941-44, research assoc., 1944-46; assoc. prof. U. Ky., Lexington, 1947-60, prof. physics, 1960-83, prof. physics emeritus, 1983—; Vis. prof. U. P.R., Mayagüez, 1953-54; vis. assoc. prof. U. Conn., Storrs, summers 1954-55; prof. U. Indonesia, Bandung, 1956-58, acting head physics dept., 1957; research asst. U. Rochester, N.Y., 1958-59, summers, 1959-62; supr. Summer Sci. Inst. Coll. Physics, Delhi, India, summer 1966; cons. Am. Heritage Publ. Co., N.Y.C., 1964-67; vis. scholar Optical Scis. Center, U. Ariz., Tucson, 1973-74. Mem. Optical Soc. Am. (emeritus), Ky. Assn. Physics Tchrs. (pres. 1961-62), Sigma Xi, Sigma Pi Sigma.

HANBURY, GEORGE LAFAYETTE, II, city manager; b. Norfolk, Va., Sept. 20, 1943; s. Emmette Cecil and Adah Christine (Nelligar) H.; children: George Lafayette III, Melissa Lee. B.S. in Pub. Adminstrn, Va. Poly. Inst., 1965; M.P.A., Old Dominion U., 1977. Asst. to city mgr., Norfolk, 1967-70, asst. city mgr., Virginia Beach, Va., 1970-74, city mgr., 1974-82, Portsmouth, Va., 1982—. Mem. Internat. City Mgmt. Assn., Am. Soc. Pub. Adminstrs. Home: 4403 Point West Dr Portsmouth VA 23703 Office: Office of City Mgr City Hall Portsmouth VA 23703

HANBURY, UNA, sculptor; b. Eng., Oct. 8, 1909; d. Noel Hardwick and Violet Hilton (Cutbill) Rawnsley; m. Anthony H.R.C. Hanbury, Jan., 1926; children: Diana (Mrs. King), Jillian (Mrs. Richard A. Poole). Grad., Royal Acad.; studied sculpture Chelsea Poly., painting and drawing, La Grande Chaumiere L'Academie Julian, France. Exhibited, Royal Acad., London, Salon d'Automne, Paris, Nat. Sculpture Soc., Nat. Acad. Design, Nat. Arts Club, Mostra d'Arte Moderna, Camaiore, Italy, 1970, Corcoran Gallery of Art, Cowboy Hall of Fame; retrospective of portraits in bronze, Folger Shakespearean Library, 1971, St. John's Coll., Santa Fe, 1973; important works include: busts of Laura Gilpin (in Mus. Fine Arts, Santa Fe, Polingaysi (in Mus. No Ariz.); bust of Dato David Sung dedicated in, Kuala Lampur, 1971, Dr. Hans Bethe, Dr. Dr. Leonard Carmichael and Dr. Dillon Ripley, Smithsonian Instn., 1977, Julius Rudel in, J.F.K. Ctr., Faith and John Gau Meem, St. John's Coll., Santa Fe, N.Mex., Hugh Dryden in, Nat. Acad. Sci., Edwards AFB, Andres Segovia, Govt. of Spain; busts of Georgia O'Keefe, Rachel Carson, Buckminster Fuller, O. Robert Oppenheimer, Nat. Portrait Gallery; large sculptures appear on Wilson Blvd, Washington; St. Marks Lutheran Ch., Springfield, Va., also; Arandjelovac Sculpture Park, Yugoslavia, also, Le Bonheur Children's Med. Ctr., Memphis; important works include numerous pvt. gardens; Work included in: books Fifty Faces. Address: 1108 Calle Catalina St PO Box 2454 Santa Fe NM 87501 *For me a search for the eternal values and an endeavor to communicate to others what the artist may have been privileged to perceive is the role. To communicate the findings in a clear language is the struggle.*

HANCE, KENT R., congressman; b. Dimmitt, Tex., Nov. 14, 1942; m. Carol Hays, 1964; children—Ron, Susan. B.B.A., Tex. Tech. U., 1965; LL.B., U. Tex., 1968. Bar: Tex. 1968. Began practice law Lubbock; mem. faculty Tex. Tech U., 1968-73; mem. Tex. Senate, 1974-79, 96th-98th Congresses from 19th Tex. Dist. Bd. regents W. Tex. State U., 1972-74; an original incorporator Tex. Boys' Ranch, Lubbock. Mem. Tex. Bar Assn., Am. Bar Assn., C. of C., Water, Inc. Democrat. Baptist. Clubs: Lions (Lubbock); Rotary, Tex. Tech. Century. Office: 1214 Longworth House Office Bldg Washington DC 20515

HANCE, LACONLA HINSON, textile company executive; b. Lancaster, S.C., May 9, 1923; s. Hollis Louis and Ada Irene (Hinson) H.; m. Christine Royall Mobley, June 15, 1944; children: Rebecca Hance Price, Martha Hance Fields, John Patton. B.S., Clemson U., 1946; M.S., Inst. Textile Tech., Charlottesville, Va., 1949, Ph.D., 1951; grad. exec. program, U. N.C., 1966. Instr. Clemson U., 1946-47; chmn. acad. com. Inst. Textile Tech., 1951-53, exec. v.p., 1953, pres., 1953-64, trustee, chmn. adv. com., mem. exec. com., 1964—; div. v.p. Fieldcrest Mills Inc., Eden, N.C., 1964-69, corp. v.p., 1969-78, sr. v.p., 1979—; sec., v.p., pres. Nat. Council for Textile Edn., 1951-64; research collaborator So. Regional Research Labs., New Orleans, 1966—, N.C. State U., Raleigh, 1969—, EPA, Washington, 1971; chmn. research com. Am. Textile Mfrs. Inst., Washington, 1968-72, mem. environ. preservation com., 1972—. Author: American Cotton Handbook, 1966; mem. editorial staff: Man-Made Fiber Handbook, 1964; contbr. articles to profl. jours. Trustee Textile Research Inst., Princeton, N.J., 1982—, Meredith Coll., Raleigh, N.C., 1969—; mem. trustee orientiation com. N.C. Bapt. Assn., 1982-83; chmn. Eden Planning and Zoning Bd., 1967-72, Eden Recreation Com., 1972-76; bd. trustees, v.p., pres. Morehead Meml. Hosp., Eden, 1970-80; mem. Gov.'s Com. on Land Uses, 1968-72, Gov.'s Com. on Water Uses, 1980-81. Served to capt. inf. AUS, 1943-46; ETO. Mem. N.C. Textile Mfrs. Assn. (chmn. research com. 1968—), Am. Textile Managerial Engrs. Soc. (sec. 1979-80, v.p. 1980-81, pres. 1981-82). Democrat. Club: Meadow Greens Country (Eden). Lodge: Rotary. Home: 319 Pinewood Pl Eden NC 27288 Office: Fieldcrest Mills Inc 326 Stadium Dr Eden NC 27288

HANCE, MARGARET T., mayor; b. Spirit Lake, Iowa, July 2, 1923; (dec.)children: Richard, Glen. Student, U. Ariz., 1942-44; B.A., Scripps Coll., 1945. Producer pub. affairs documentaries for TV, 1967-69; writer, producer Holiday World Travel Show for radio, 1971-75; mem. Phoenix Parks and Recreation Bd., 1965-71, Phoenix City Council, 1971-75; mayor City of Phoenix, 1975—; dir. Valley Nat. Bank; confr. del. OCED, 1979. Mem. adv. commn. on intergovt. relations Presdl. Federalism Adv. Com; mem. Ariz. Justice Planning Supervisory Bd.; mem. community adv. bd. Salt-Gila Flood Control Study; bd. visitors St. Luke's Hosp.; advisor Women's Aux. Ariz. Kidney Found. Named Woman of Yr. Phoenix Advt. Club, 1978; recipient Don Bolles Meml. award Ariz. K.C., 1978, Centennial award Salvation Army, 1978, Alumni Achievement award U. Ariz., 1979. Mem. U.S. Conf. Mayors (trustee), Nat. League Cities (bd. dirs.), Nat. Conf. Republican Mayors and Elected Ofcls. (pres.), League Ariz. Cities and Towns (treas.). Office: Office of Mayor 251 W Washington St Phoenix AZ 95003 *

HANCE, WILLIAM ADAMS, geography educator; b. N.Y.C., Dec. 29, 1916; s. George Clifton and Grace (Adams) H.; m. Margaret Dorst, Mar. 23, 1940; children: Jean, Bronwen. A.B., Columbia, 1938, M.S., 1941, Ph.D., 1949. Mem. faculty Columbia, 1941—, asst. dean coll., 1942-43, 46-49, prof. econ. geography, 1959—, prof. emeritus, 1982—, chmn. grad. studies, 1961-64, chairman dept. geography, 1964-73; Field work in, Africa, 1951, 52, 56, 1962-63, 65, 69, 70, 74; chmn. joint com. African studies Am. Council Learned Societies-Social Sci.; Research Council, 1960-62. Author: African Economic Development, 1958, rev. edit., 1967, Location of Export Production in Tropical Africa (map), 1961, The Geography of Modern Africa, 1964, rev. edit., 1975, Population, Migration, and Urbanization in Africa, 1970, Black Africa Develops, 1977; also articles.; Editor, co-author: Southern Africa and the United States, 1968. Bd. mgrs. Uptown br. YMCA, 1949-61; v.p. Axe-Houghton Found., 1970-76, pres., 1976—; v.p. Nantucket Civic League, 1982—. Served to lt. (j.g.) USNR, 1944-46. Founding fellow African Studies Assn. (bd. dirs. 1958-61, exec. sec. 1959-60, vice president 1965-66, president 1966-67); honorary fellow American Geographic Society (pres. council 1972-73); member of the Royal African Soc., Assn. Am. Geographers, Royal Geog. Soc., Phi Beta Kappa. Episcopalian. Home: 15 Hinckley Ln Nantucket MA 02554

HANCHETT, WILLIAM, history educator; b. Evanston, Ill., May 25, 1922; s. William Francis and Alice (Trowbridge) H.; children: Thomas Forster, Emily Porter. Student, Black Mountain Coll., 1941-42, Roosevelt U., 1946-47; B.A., So. Methodist U., 1948; M.A., U. Calif. at Berkeley, 1949, Ph.D., 1952. Historian USAF, 1952-54; acting asst. prof. U. Colo., 1954-55; asst. prof. Colo. State U., 1955-56; mem. faculty San Diego State U., 1956—, prof. history, 1965—, chmn. dept., 1968-71. Author: Irish: Charles G. Halpine in Civil War America, 1970, The Lincoln Murder Conspiracies, 1983; also articles. Served with USAAF, 1942-45. Home: 3515 State St San Diego CA 92103

HANCHEY, RICHARD HOWARD, univ. dean; b. Dry Creek, La., Nov. 23, 1913; s. Sereno Lloyd and Pearl (Sigler) H.; m. Mary Marguerite Meadows, Dec. 24, 1939; 1 dau., Carrie Arthur (Mrs. Steve A. Alford III). B.S., Southwestern La. Inst., 1940; M.S., La. State U., 1942; Ph.D., Ohio State U., 1954. Asst. horticulturist U. Tenn., 1946-47; asst. prof., asst. horticulturist La. State U., Baton Rouge, 1947-51, asso. prof., asso. horticulturist, 1951-55, prof, 1955-60, dir. resident instrn., 1965, asso. dean, dir. resident instrn., 1972, dean, 1972—; Cons. Rosarian-Gulf Coast Dist., Am. Rose Soc.; hort. cons. flower show schs. com. Nat. Council State Garden Clubs, also; nat. hort. chmn. Contbr. articles to profl. jours. Served with AUS, 1942-45; ETO. Decorated Bronze Star medal; recipient citation for meritorious service La. Garden Club Fedn., 1964; Helena Chamberlain research fellow Ohio State U., 1951-52. Mem. Am. Soc. Hort. Sci., Am., La. (pres.) camellia socs., Am. Rose Soc., Nat. Hibiscus Soc., Sigma Xi, Phi Kappa Phi, Alpha Zeta, Phi Epsilon Phi, Pi Alpha Xi, Gamma Sigma Delta, Omicron Delta Kappa. Democrat. Methodist. Club: Mason (32 deg., Shriner). Home: 911 Magnolia Woods Baton Rouge LA 70808

HANCOCK, CHARLES CAVANAUGH, JR., scientific association administration; b. Riverside, Calif., Oct. 19, 1935; s. Charles Cavanaugh and Mary Elizabeth (Riordan) H.; m. Donna Ruth Dellwig, Apr. 12, 1958; children: Christopher Alan, Stephen Edward. B.S. in Chem. Engring, Stanford U., 1958; M.S. in Indsl. Engring, Tex. Tech U., 1967. Commd. 2d lt. U.S. Air Force, 1958, advanced through grades to lt. col., 1974; worldwide locations in research and devel. and logistics, to, 1979, ret., 1979; exec. officer Am. Soc. Biol. Chemists, Bethesda, Md., 1979—; also mgr. Jour. Biol. Chemistry. Decorated Meritorious Service medal with 3 oak leaf clusters. Mem. AAAS, Am. Inst. Indsl. Engrs. (sr.), Council Engring. and Sci. Soc. Execs., Sigma Xi, Alpha Pi Mu. Club: Country of Reston (Va.). Office: 9650 Rockville Pike Bethesda MD 20814

HANCOCK, ERNEST WILLIAM, physician, educator; b. Lincoln, Nebr., Apr. 6, 1927; s. Ernest Wilberforce and Eldrice Joy (Nelson) H.; m. Dagny Joan Egeberg, Mar. 16, 1963; children—William, Nelson, Adam. B.A., U. Nebr., 1948; M.D., Harvard U., 1952. Intern, then resident in medicine Harvard med. unit Boston City Hosp., 1952-57, chief resident in medicine, 1959-60; tng. in cardiology Guy's Hosp., London, 1957-59; mem. faculty Stanford U. Med. Sch., 1960—, prof. cardiology, 1972—. Office: Cardiology Div Stanford U Med Center Stanford CA 94304

HANCOCK, GEOFFREY WHITE, editor, writer, publisher; b. New Westminster, B.C., Can., Apr. 14, 1946; s. Jonas White and Margaret Eileen (Ramsbottom) H.; m. Theadora De Vos, June 30, 1972 (div. 1981); m. Gay Allison, Aug. 6, 1983. B.F.A., U. B.C., 1973, M.F.A., 1975. Editor-in chief Can. Fiction Mag., Toronto, Ont., Can., 1974—; lit cons. CBC Radio, Toronto, 1978—; dir. Nat. Mag. Awards, Toronto, 1979-82, UBC Alumni Chronicle, Vancouver, 1976-80. Editor: Magic Realism, 1980, Illusion One and Two, 1983, Metavision, 1983; author: Quebec Fiction Today, 1983. Recipient Fiona Mee award Quill & Quire, Toronto, 1979; Can. Council grantee, 1974—; Ont. Arts Council grantee, 1978—; UBC fellow, 1974-75. Mem. Periodical Writers of Can., Assn. Can. TV and Radio Actors. Anglican. Office: Canadian Fiction Mag PO Box 946 Station F Toronto ON Canada M4Y 2N9

HANCOCK, GERRE EDWARD, musician; b. Lubbock, Tex., Feb. 21, 1934; s. Edward Ervin and Flake (Steger) H.; m. Judith Duffield Eckerman, July 22, 1961; children: Deborah, Lisa. Mus.B., U. Tex., Austin, 1955; M.Sacred Music, Union Theol. Sem., N.Y.C., 1961. Asst. organist St. Bartholomew's Ch., N.Y.C., 1960-62; organist, choirmaster Christ Ch. Episcopal, Cin., 1962-71; mem. artist faculty Coll.-Conservatory Music, U. Cin., 1966-71; organist, master choristers St. Thomas Episcopal Ch., N.Y.C., 1971—; mem. faculty Juilliard Sch. Music, 1971—, Inst. Sacred Music, Yale U., 1973—; Am. rep. recitalist centenary celebrations Royal Coll. Organists, London, 1964; concert organist, U.S. and Europe. Composer: Book of Hymn Improvisations, 1975; also anthems, canatas, organ works. Served with AUS, 1956-58. Rotary Found. fellow, 1955. Fellow Royal Sch. Ch. Music; fellow Am. Guild Organists (past mem. council); mem. Assn. Anglican Musicians (past pres.), Phi Mu Alpha Sinfonia, Pi Kappa Lambda. Episcopalian. Club: St. Wilfred's (N.Y.C.). Home: 1170 Fifth Ave New York NY 10029 Office: 1 W 53d St New York NY 10019

HANCOCK, HERBERT JEFFREY, composer, pianist, publisher; b. Chgo., Apr. 12, 1940; s. Wayman Edward and Winnie (Griffin) H.; m. Gudrun Meixner, Aug. 31, 1968. Student, Grinnell (Iowa) Coll., 1956-60, Roosevelt U., Chgo., 1960, Manhattan Sch. Music, 1962, New Sch. Social Research, 1967. Owner-pub. Hancock Music Co.; pres. Harlem Jazz Music Center, Inc. Performed with, Chgo. Symphony Orch., 1952, Coleman Hawkins, Chgo., 1960, Donald Byrd, 1960- 63, Miles Davis Quintet, 1963-68; scored film Blow Up, 1966, Death Wish, 1974; has recorded with Chick Corea; Composer: Watermelon Man, 1962, Chameleon, 1973, Maiden Voyage, 1973; albums include Mwandishi, 1971, Sextant, 1972, Headhunters, 1973, Thrust, 1974, Feets Don't Fail Me Now, 1979, Monster, 1980, Lite Me Up, 1982, also others. Recipient citation of achievement Broadcast Music, Inc., 1963; Jay award Jazz mag., 1964; critics poll for talent deserving wider recognition Down Beat mag., 1967; 1st place piano category, 1968, 69, 70; composer award, 1971; All-Star Band New Artist award Record World, 1968; named top jazz artist Black Music mag., 1974. Mem. Nat. Acad. Rec. Arts and Scis., Jazz Musicians Assn., Nat. Acad. TV Arts and Scis., Broadcast Music. Club: Pioneer (Grinnel Coll.). Address: care William Morris Agy 151 El Camino Blvd Beverly Hills CA 90212 *

HANCOCK, IAN FRANCIS (O YANKO LE REDZOSKO), educator; b. London, Aug. 29, 1942; U.S., 1972; s. John Redzo and Kathleen Elsa (Hancock); m.; children: Julian Marko, Adrian Lee Imre, Meilinne Khim. Diploma in Oriental and African Studies, U. London, 1969, Ph.D., 1971. Reporter, photographer Daily Free Press, B.C., 1959-60; various positions, Europe, 1961-74; display advt. staff Sears Roebuck Co., B.C., 1964-65; compiler literary index Vancouver Pub. Library, 1971-72; prof. linguistics U. Tex., Austin, 1972—; mem. Adv. Council on Jewish Affairs, Haifa, 1983. Author: (with David De Camp) Pidgins and Greoles: Current Trends and Prospects, 1974, (with John Reinecke and others) Bibliography of Pidgin and Creole Languages, 1975, Problems in the Creation of Standard Dialect of Romanes, 1975; editor: Romani Sociolinguistics, 1979, Readings in Creole Studies, 1979; Editor: Jour. of Creole Studies, 1972; mem. editorial bd. Jour. of Gypsy Lore Soc., 1975, Roma, 1973, Jour. of Krio Literary Soc, 1970; Contbr.: articles to profl. jours. Jour. of Krio Literary Soc. Mem. Indian Inst. Romani Studies (bd. govs. 1971), Internat. Gypsy Com. (sec. gen. Am. div. 1970), Modern Lang. Assn., Gypsy Lore Soc., World Romani Union, Gypsy Soc. Chgo. (academic advisor), Am. Red Dress Gypsies Assn., Caribbean Linguistic Soc. Office: Dept English Parlin Hall University of Texas Austin TX 78712

HANCOCK, JOHN COULTER, electrical engineer, educator, university dean; b. Martinsville, Ind., Oct. 21, 1929; s. Floyd A. and Katherine (Coulter) H.; m. Betty Jane Holden, Feb. 6, 1949; children: Debbie, Dwight, Marilyn, Virginia. B.S. in Elec. Engring., Purdue U., 1951, M.S., 1955, Ph.D., 1957. Research engr. U.S. Naval Avionics Facility, Indpls., 1951-57; asst. prof. elec. engring. Purdue U., West Lafayette, Ind., 1957-60, asso. prof., 1960-63, prof., 1963—, head Sch. Elec. Engring., 1965-72, dean Schs. Engring., 1972—; dir. CTS Corp., Elkhart, Ind., Pub. Service Co. Ind., McClure Research Park, Lafayette, Ind., Schwab Safe Co., Lafayette, Ransburg Corp., Indpls., Hillenbrand Industries, Batesville, Ind. Author: An Introduction to the Principles of Communication Theory, 1961, Signal Detection Theory, 1966, An Introduction to Electrical Design, 1972. Bd. dirs. United Community Services, Lafayette, 1969-73; trustee Christian Theol. Sem., 1977—; chmn. commn. on new ch. devel. Christian Ch. Ind., 1975-78. Fellow IEEE (chmn. field awards com. 1979—); mem. Nat. Acad. Engring., Nat. Engring. Consortium (formerly Nat. Electronics Conf., dir. 1966-67, 74-77); fellow Am. Soc. Engring. Edn. (sec. elec. engring. div. 1969-70, vice chmn. 1971-72, chmn. 1972-73, exec. com. council profl. and tech. edn. 1973-74, dir. 1977-79, chmn. longrange planning com. 1977-79, pres.-elect 1982-83, pres. 1983-84); mem. Midwestern Program Minorities in Engring. (exec. com.), Eta Kappa Nu (nat. pres. 1969-70); Mem. Christain Ch. (elder, trustee 1974—). Home: 3829 Windward Pl West Lafayette IN 47906 Office: Engring Adminstrn Bldg Purdue U West Lafayette IN 47906

HANCOCK, JOHN D., film director; b. Kansas City, Mo., Feb. 12, 1939; s. Ralph David and Ella Mae (Rosenthal) H.; m. Dorothy Tristan, Dec. 29, 1975. B.A., Harvard. Dir.: play A Man's A Man, N.Y.C., 1962; artistic dir., San Francisco Actor's Workshop, 1965-66, Pitts. Playhouse, 1966-67; dir.: A Midsummer Night's Dream, N.Y.C., 1967; other plays off Broadway; various films, including Bang the Drum Slowly (Recipient Obie, Acad. award nomination, Brandeis citation). Home: 21531 Deerpath Ln Malibu CA 90265

HANCOCK, JOHN SHONK, lawyer, banker; b. Syracuse, N.Y., Sept. 28, 1914; s. Clarence E. and Emily (Shonk) H.; m. Frances Edwards, Sept. 21, 1946; children—Barbara, Charles, Elizabeth. B.A., Wesleyan U., Middletown, Conn., 1936; LL.B., Yale, 1939. Bar: N.Y. bar 1939, D.C. bar 1946. Asso. Hancock, Dorr, Ryan & Shove, Syracuse, 1939-40, Douglas, Proctor, MacIntyre & Gates, Washington, 1946-47; asst. in Office Sec. Air Force, Washington, 1948-55; trust officer, v.p. Key Bank of Central N.Y., Syracuse, 1955-81; ret. as sr. v.p.; dir. Can. Life Ins. Co. N.Y. Mem. Syracuse Airport Adv. Com.; Past pres. Onondaga County chpt. ARC; past pres. Central N.Y. Community Found.; bd. dirs., past chmn. Syracuse Boys Club; past trustee Wesleyan U. Served to maj. USAAF, 1941-46. Mem. N.Y. State Bankers Assn. (past chmn. trust div.). Republican. Episcopalian. Home: 221 Brattle Rd Syracuse NY 13203

HANCOCK, JOHN WALKER, III, banker; b. Long Beach, Calif., Mar. 8, 1937; s. John Walker and Bernice H.; m. Elizabeth Hoien, June 20, 1959; children: Suzanne, Donna, Randy, David. B.A. in Econs, Stanford U., 1958, M.B.A., 1960. With Security Pacific Nat. Bank, Los Angeles, 1960—, v.p., 1968-77, sr. v.p., 1977—. Bd. dirs. Long Beach (Calif.) Meml. Hosp., 1977—; pres., bd. dirs. Long Beach area council Boy Scouts Am., 1972-74. Mem. Am. Inst. Banking, Stanford U. Alumni Assn., Newcomen Soc. Republican. Clubs: California (Los Angeles); Virginia County. Home: 258 Roycroft Ave Long Beach CA 90803 Office: 333 S Hope St Los Angeles CA 90071

HANCOCK, M(ARION) DONALD, political scientist; b. McAllen, Tex., Aug. 20, 1939; s. Robert Nicklas and Florence Olive (Norquest) H.; m. Kay Abbie Lorans, May 29, 1965; children: Erik Lorans, Kendra Lee. B.A., U. Tex., 1961; postgrad., U. Bonn, Germany, 1959-60; M.A., Columbia U., 1962, Ph.D., 1966, U. Stockholm, 1963-64. Instr. Columbia U., spring 1965; asst. prof. polit. sci. U. Tex., Austin, 1965-69, assoc. prof., 1969-75, prof., 1975—, dir. Center for European Studies, 1970-79, assoc. dean, Coll. Social and Behavioral Scis., 1976-79; prof. Vanderbilt U., 1979—; dir. Center for European Studies, 1981—; co-chmn. Council for European Studies, 1981—; vis. prof. Columbia U., 1967, U. Bielefeld, 1973, U. Mannheim, 1977. Author: Sweden: The Politics of Postindustrial Change, 1972; editor: (with Gideon Sjoberg) Politics in the Post-Welfare State: Response to the New Individualism, 1972; co-editor: 10th ann. spl. issue Comparative Politics, 1978. Woodrow Wilson fellow, 1961-62; Dept. State Internat. Affairs fellow, summer 1962; Council Fgn. Relations internat. affairs fellow, 1972-73. Mem. Am. Polit. Sci. Assn., So. Polit. Sci. Assn., Council European Studies, Soc. Advancement Scandinavian Studies, Conf. Group on Nordic Soc. Democrat. Presbyterian. Office: Dept Polit Sci Vanderbilt U Nashville TN 37235

HANCOCK, RALPH LOWELL, author, specialist in Latin Am. affairs; b. Plainville, Ind., Nov. 23, 1903; s. John Hiram and Nancy (Cunningham) H.; m. Julia Ellen F. Ross, Dec. 25, 1924 (div.); 1 son,

David Lowell (dec.); m. Frances Fenster Iverson, 1948; children—Nancy Lowell, Bret Hiram. Ed., Springfield (Mo.) Bus. Coll.; student, Washington U., St. Louis, 1924-27. Resident news corr. covering, Latin America, 1936-40; organized publicity dept. Transportes Aereos Centro Americanos Airlines, 1940, dir., 1940-42; sr. economic analyst, specialist on Caribbean Area, Bd. Econ. Warfare, 1942-43; head of econ. mission to, Latin Am., 1942-43, Latin Am. adviser on editorial staffs of 3 publishing houses, 1943-49; Vice pres., dir. pub. relations in Latin Am. for Pan-Am. Found., Inc.; pres. Hemisphere Corp. Speaker 7th Ann. Conf. on Caribbean, U. of Fla., 1956. Author: Our Southern Neighbors, 1942, Mexico and Central Am, 1942, Latin America, 1943, Let's Look at Latin America, 1943, Opportunities in Latin America, 1946, Our Latin American Neighbors, 1946, The Rainbow Republics: Central America, 1947, The Magic Land: Mexico, 1948, Fabulous Boulevard, 1949, Caribbean Correspondent, 1951, Douglas Fairbanks: The Fourth Musketeer, 1953, Baja California, 1953, The Forest Lawn Story, 1955, Exploring American Neighbors, 1956, Laughter is a Wonderful Thing, 1956, Blondes, Brunettes and Bullets, 1957, Desert Living, 1958, Puerto Rico: A Success Story, 1960, The Lost Treasure of Cocos Island, 1960, Puerto Rico: A Travellers Guide, 1961, Mexico, 1964, The Compleat Swindler, 1968; authoritative articles on Book of Knowledge and Annual; Author and photographer of numerous ednl. films on Latin Am. and mag. and newspaper articles.; Latin Am. editor of: Invitation to Travel series; Editor-in-chief: Hemisphere Research. Lectr. Home: 11905 Handrich Dr San Diego CA 92131

HANCOCK, THOMAS, machinery manufacturing executive; b. Bloomington, Wis., Aug. 21, 1913; s. Herbert and Helen (Weeks) H.; m. Lena Vogel, Aug. 21, 1942; children: David G., Thomas C., Pamela E. Asst. to v.p. Trane Co., La Crosse, Wis., 1945-51, v.p. charge sales, 1951-55, exec. v.p., dir., 1955-63, pres., 1963—, chmn., chief exec. officer, 1968-78; dir. Employers Ins. of Wausau, Wis., Tenneco Inc., Houston, Northwest Bancorp., Mpls., No. Engraving Corp., Sparta, Wis., Norplex Corp., La Crosse. Chmn. La Crosse Redevel. Authority; bd. dirs. St. Francis Hosp., U. Wis.-La Crosse Found.; mem. council U. Chgo. Grad. Sch. Bus. Mem. Wis. Assn. Mfrs. and Commerce (dir.), N.A.M. (dir.). Home: 330 Indian Harbor Rd Vero Beach FL 32963 Office: Trane Co La Crosse WI 54601

HANCOCK, WALKER KIRTLAND, sculptor; b. St. Louis, June 28, 1901; s. Walter Scott and Anna (Spencer) H.; m. Saima Esther Natti, Dec. 4, 1943; 1 dau., Saima Deane (Mrs. Christopher French). Student Sch. Fine Arts, Washington U., 1918-20, U. Wis., 1920, Pa. Acad. Fine Arts, 1921-25, Am. Acad. in Rome, 1928; Dr. Fine Arts, Washington U., 1942. Trustee emeritus Am. Acad. in Rome, sculptor in residence, 1956-57, 62-63; sculptor in charge, Stone Mountain, Ga., 1964; head sculpture dept. Pa. Acad. Fine Arts, 1929-67. Sculptor: commissions include Maschmeyer Memorial Fountain, Forest Park, St. Louis, exterior reliefs, City Hall, Kansas City, Mo., Penn. War Memorial, 30th St. Station, Phila., Angel relief, Battle Monument Chapel, St. Avold, France, Bowker Memorial Fountain, All Saint's Ch., Worcester, Mass., bust Governor Percival P. Baxter, State House, Augusta, Maine, relief Andrew Mellon, Nat. Gallery of Art, Washington, James Madison, Library of Congress, Washington, John Paul Jones, Fairmount Park, Phila., wall fountain, Fed. Res. Bd. Bldg., Washington, General Douglas MacArthur, U.S. Mil. Acad., West Point, N.Y., Christ in Majesty, high altar, Nat. Cathedral, Washington, Chief Justice Earl Warren, U.S. Supreme Ct., Washington, Booth Tarkington, Nat. Portrait Gallery, Washington, Robert Frost, Nat. Portrait Gallery, Washington, Hubert Humphrey, U.S. Capitol, Washington, Chief Justice Warren E. Burger, Supreme Ct. Hist. Soc., Abraham Lincoln, Nat. Cathedral, Washington, Walter Annenberg, Eisenhower Med. Ctr., Rancho Mirage, Calif.; medals Dwight D. Eisenhower Inaugural medals, 1953, 57, The Air Medal, (Army and Navy), Frank P. Brown medal, Franklin Inst., numerous others. Mem. Mus. Am. Art Commn.; Trustee emeritus Saint-Gaudens Meml., Cornish, N.H.; hon. trustee Brookgreen Gardens. Served as capt. AUS, 1942-46; monuments, fine arts, archives officer, overseas, 2 years. Awarded Widener gold medal, Prix de Rome, 1925; fellowship prize Pa. Acad. Fine Arts, 1931; Helen Foster Burnett prize NAD, 1935; Anon. prize sculpture, 1949; Phila. Art Alliance medal of achievement, 1953; acad. medal of honor Pa. Acad. Fine Arts, 1953; Silver medal Archtl. League, 1955; J. Sanford Saltus medal, 1953; Herbert Adams Meml. award, 1954; Thomas R. Proctor prize NAD; Am. Acad. Achievement award, 1971; Academician NAD, Am. Acad. and Inst. of Arts and Letters; Benjamin Franklin fellow Royal Soc. Arts. Fellow Nat. Sculpture Soc. (Medal of Honor 1981, 75th Anniversary award for Outstanding Achievement); mem. Archtl. League N.Y., Alpha Tau Omega. Episcopalian. Clubs: Peale r21(Phila.); Century Assn. (N.Y.C.); St. Botolph (Boston). Home: Lanesville PO Box 133 Gloucester MA 01930

HANCOCK, WILLIAM HENRY, JR., motel co., exec.; b. Floyd County, Va., July 26, 1942; s. William Henry and Doris Tate (Hodges) H.; m. Ernestine Lee Poage; children—William Henry, Matthew Lee. B.S. in Acctg, Va. Poly. Inst. and State U., 1966. Branch asst. Creditway of Am., 1965-66; acct. Peat, Marwick, Mitchell & Co., 1966-70; sr. v.p. fin., dir. Am. Motor Inns, Inc., Roanoke, Va., 1970—; dir. First Va. Bank Roanoke-W., I.C. Ltd. Mem. Va. Soc. C.P.A.'s. Club: Masons. Home: 3410 Overhill Trail Roanoke VA 24018 Office: 1917 Franklin Rd Roanoke VA 24014

HANCOCKS, DAVID MORGAN, zoological gardens administrator; b. Kinver, Eng., May 5, 1941; came to U.S., 1975; s. Cecil and Eva Alice (Morgan) H. B.S. with honors, U. Bath, Eng., 1966, B.Arch., 1968. Registered architect, U.V. Asst. architect Zool. Soc. London, 1968-69; architect West of England Zool. Soc., Bristol, 1970-71; pvt. practice architecture, Seattle, 1972-74; dir. British Wildlife Park, Salisbury, Eng., 1974-75, Woodland Park Zool. Gardens, Seattle, 1976—; cons. in field. Author: Animals and Architecture, 1971, Master Builders of the Animal World, 1973; Contbr. articles in field to profl. jours. Recipient State of Wash. Gov.'s award for writing, 1975; Recipient chpt. award Am. Soc. Landscape Architects, 1977, Mcpl. League Seattle, 1983. Fellow (profl.) Am. Assn. Zool. Parks and Aquariums; mem. Royal Soc. Protection of Birds, Audubon Soc., Humane Soc. of U.S. Office: 5500 Phinney Ave N Seattle WA 98103

HANCOX, RALPH, publisher; b. Hampstead, Eng., Aug. 23, 1929; (married); 4 children. Student, Poly. Sch. Modern Langs., London, 1952-53, Harvard U., 1965-66, grad. program mgmt. devel., 1973. Can. corr. Observer Fgn. News Service, London, 1957-66; author radio and TV scripts, 1960-64; news editor Weekly Post Newspapers Ltd., Uxbridge, Middlesex, Eng., 1953-55; sr. reporter, daily columnist Kingston Whig-Standard Co. Ltd., Kingston, Ont., Can., 1955-57; asso. editor, then editor-in-chief Peterborough (Ont.) Examiner, 1957-67; editor Reader's Digest Assn. (Can.) Ltd., Montreal, 1967-73, v.p. adminstrn., then v.p. ops., 1973-78, pres., 1978—, Reader's Digest Mags. Ltd., 1978—, Pegatex Inc.; dir. Mags. Can.; judge editorial div. Nat. Newspaper Awards, 1972—. Trustee Peterborough Bd. Edn., 1962-66; gov. Conseil du Patronat du Que. Served with RAF, 1947-52. Recipient Nat. Newspaper award for editorial writing, 1966. Mem. Nat. Assn. Maj. Mail Users (pres.). Home: 631 Habitat 67 Cite du Havre Montreal PQ H3C 3R6 Canada Office: 215 Redfern Ave Montreal PQ H3Z 2V9 Canada

HAND, AVERY CHAPMAN, JR., banker; b. Mansfield, Ohio, Jan. 17, 1918; s. Avery Chapman and Reba Grace (Ackerman) H.; m. Mariann Stander, Feb. 23, 1946; children—Jo Lynn Wright, Jill Carla Hautzenroeder, Heidi Belinda, Holly Anne. Grad., Asheville (N.C.) Sch., 1937; student, Wharton Sch. of U. Pa., 1939; exchange student archeol. field work Irish Nat. Mus., Dublin, 1938. With Tracy & Avery Co., wholesale grocers, also Marchand Markets, supermarket chain, 1939-41; v.p. Mansfield Savs. Trust Nat. Bank, 1946-53; with First Buckeye Bank N.A., 1953—, pres., 1962—, chmn. bd., chief exec. officer, 1981—, also dir.; v.p., dir. Euclid Coffe Co., Cleve.; dir. Lynn Realty & Constrn. Co., Inc., Mansfield, United Telephone Co. Ohio, Indsl. & Tech. Sales & Service Co., Mansfield. Trustee Mansfield Gen. Hosp.; past pres. Soldiers and Sailors Mansfield Meml. Bldg., State Troopers Ohio; trustee Ashland Coll.; adv. bd. and found. Mansfield campus Ohio State U. Served to maj. AUS, 1941-46; ETO. Mem. Ohio C. of C. (chmn. bd. dirs.), Mansfield Area C. of C. (bd. dirs., past pres.), U.S. Power Squadron, 12th Army Group Assn., Richland County Hist. Soc. Conglist. Clubs: Westbrook Country (past pres.), University, Fifty-One, Our (past pres.), Bluecoats (Mansfield); Great Lakes Cruising (Chgo.); Huron (Ohio); Yacht; Plumbrook Country (Sandusky, Ohio); Rockwell Springs Trout (Castalia, Ohio). Home: 145 S Linden Rd Mansfield OH 44906 Office: 42-44 N Main St Mansfield OH 44901

HAND, CADET HAMMOND, JR., marine biologist, educator; b. Patchogue, N.Y., Apr. 23, 1920; s. Cadet Hammond and Myra (Wells) H.; m. Winifred Werdelin, June 6, 1942; children—Cadet Hammond III, Gary Alan. B.S., U. Conn., 1946; M.A., U. Calif. at Berkeley, 1948, Ph.D., 1951. Instr. Mills Coll., 1948-50, asst. prof., 1950-51; research biologist Scripps Inst. Oceanography, 1951-53; mem. faculty U. Calif. at Berkeley, 1953—, prof. zoology, 1963—; dir. Bodega Marine Lab., 1961—; Cons. NIH, 1964-66, NSF, 1964-69; mem. atomic safety and licensing bd. panel Nuclear Regulatory Commn., 1971—, adminstrv. judge atomic safety and licensing bd. panel, 1980—; NSF sr. postdoctoral fellow, 1959-60; Guggenheim fellow, 1967-68. Contbr. articles to profl. jours. Fellow Calif., Wash. acads. scis.; mem. No. Calif. Malacozool. Soc. (pres. 1963—), Soc. Systemic Zoology, Ecol. Soc. Am., Ray Soc. (Gt. Britain), Am. Soc. Zoologists (chmn. div. invertebrate zoology 1977-78), Soc. Limnology and Oceanography. Home: Star Route Bogeda Bay CA 94923 Office: Bodega Marine Lab Bodega Bay CA 94923

HAND, JOHN OLIVER, museum curator; b. N.Y.C., Aug. 17, 1941; s. John Osborn and LaBelle (Bridges) H.; m. Jane M. Gardner, June 22, 1968. B.A., Denison U., Granville, Ohio, 1963; M.A., U. Chgo., 1967; M.F.A. (Samuel Kress Found. fellow 1969-72), Princeton U., 1971; Ph.D. (Belgian Am. Found. fellow 1972-73), Princeton U., 1978. With edn. dept. Nat. Gallery Art, Washington, 1965-69, curator No. Renaissance painting, 1973—; preceptor Princeton U., 1971. Author papers in field. Office: Nat Gallery Art Washington DC 20565

HAND, ROGER, physician, educator; b. Bklyn., Sept. 25, 1938; s. Morton and Angela (Belevedere) H.; m. Abby Lippman, Dec. 24, 1961; children: Christopher, Jessica. B.S., NYU, 1959, M.D., 1962. Intern, then resident in internal medicine NYU Med. Center, 1962-68; postdoctoral fellow, asst. prof. Rockefeller U., N.Y.C., 1968-73; clin. asst. prof. medicine Cornell U. Med. Coll., N.Y.C., 1970-73; asst. prof., then assoc. prof. medicine McGill U., Montreal, Que., Can., 1973-80; prof. medicine, dir. McGill Cancer Center, 1980—; sr. physician Royal Victoria Hosp., Montreal, 1980—. Contbr. articles to profl. jours. Served with AUS, 1964-65. Decorated Air medal. Med. research grantee, fellow. Fellow ACP, Royal Coll. Physicians and Surgeons (Can.); mem. Am. Soc. Clin. Investigation, Am. Soc. Biol. Chemists, Am. Assn. Cancer Research, Am. Soc. Clin. Oncology, Infectious Disease Soc. Am., Can. Soc. Clin. Investigation, others. Office: McGill Cancer Center McGill U 3655 Drummond St Montreal PQ H3G 1Y6 Canada

HAND, WAYLAND DEBS, folklorist; b. Auckland, N.Z., Mar. 19, 1907; s. Hyrum and Margaret (Wride) H.; m. Viola White, June 8, 1932 (div. 1956); children: Jacqueline, Winifred Hand Marsh; m. Celeste Gilford, Dec. 19, 1957; 1 son, Sidney Gilford. A.B., U. Utah, 1933, M.A., 1934; Ph.D., U. Chgo., 1936. Instr. German, U. Minn., 1936-37; faculty UCLA, 1937-74, prof. German, folklore, 1952-74, prof. emeritus, 1974—; adv. editor Folklore Studies, U. Calif. Publs., 1952-72. Author: books, monographs including A Dictionary of Words and Idioms Associated with Judas Iscariot - A Compilation Based Mainly on the Germanic Languages, 1942 (Chgo. Folklore Soc. prize), (with Gustave O. Arlt) Humaniora - Essays in Literature, Folklore and Bibliography Honoring Archer Taylor on His Seventieth Birthday, 1960, Popular Beliefs and Superstitions from North Carolina, 2 vols, 1961-64 (4th Internat. Folklore prize 1965), American Folk Legend - A Symposium, 1971, American Folk Medicine - A Symposium, 1976, Magical Medicine, 1980; editor: (with Anna Casetta and Sondra B. Thiederman) Popular Beliefs and Superstitions: A Compendium of American Folklore from the Ohio Collection of Newbell Niles Puckett, 3 vols, 1981; contbr. numerous articles, revs. to profl. jours.; Editor: Dictionary of American Popular Beliefs and Superstitions, 1944—; asso. editor: Western Folklore, 1953-54, 54-66; adv. editor: Ethnomedizin, 1979. Trustee Am. Folklife Center, Library of Congress, 1976—, chmn. bd., 1976-77. Studies in History Am. Civilization stipend Library of Congress, 1946; grantee-in-aid Am. Council Learned Socs., 1945-46, 73, Am. Philos. Soc., 1951; John Simon Guggenheim Meml. Found. fellow, 1952-53, 60-61; research grantee NEH, 1968-75, 80-82; NIH; Nat. Library of Medicine, 1971-73; decorated knight 1st class Order of Lion of Finland.; Fife Honor lectr., 1981; Katharine M. Briggs Meml. lectr., 1982. Fellow Am. Folklore Soc. (pres. 1957-58, editor Jour., Memoirs 1947-51), So. Calif. Acad. Scis. (v.p. 1973-74), Folklore Soc. London (hon.); mem. MLA Am., Internat. Soc. for Folk-Narrative Research (v.p. 1964-74), Deutsche Gesellschaft fuer Volkskunde (hon.), Am. Dialect Soc., Am. Name Soc., Calif. Folklore Soc. (pres. 1969-70, rev. editor Quar. 1942-46, editor 1954-66), MLA So. Calif. (pres. 1955-56), Tex. Folklore Soc., N.Y. Folklore Soc. Home: 716 Courtland St Venice CA 90291 Office: Kinsey Hall 76 UCLA 405 Hilgard Ave Los Angeles CA 90024

HAND, WILLIAM BREVARD, federal judge; b. Mobile, Ala., Jan. 18, 1924; s. Charles C. and Irma W. H.; m. Allison Denby, June 17, 1948; children: Jane Connor Hand Dukes, Virginia Alan Hand Hollis, Allison Hand Peebles. B.S. in Commerce and Bus. Adminstrn, U. Ala., 1947, J.D., 1949. Bar: Ala. 1949. Mem. firm Hand, Arendall, Bedsole, Greaves & Johnston, Mobile, 1949-71; chief judge U.S. Dist. Ct. (so. dist.) Ala., 1971—. Chmn. Mobile County Republican Exec. Com., 1968-71. Served with U.S. Army, 1943-46. Decorated Bronze Star medal. Mem. Am., Ala., Mobile bar assns. Methodist. Office: PO Box 1964 Mobile AL 36633

HANDEL, MORTON EMANUEL, leisure products company executive; b. N.Y.C., Apr. 12, 1935; s. Benjamin and Mollie (Heller) H.; m. Irma Ruby, Aug. 5, 1956; children: Mark, Gary, Karen. B.A., U. Pa., 1956; postgrad., N.Y. U., 1957-59. Vice pres. Dale Plastic Playing Card Corp., N.Y.C., 1955-57; gen. mgr. Handel Nets & Fabrics Corp., N.Y.C., 1957-62; pres. A.M. Industries, Inc., Farmingdale, N.Y., 1962-68, Allan Marine, Inc., Deer Park, N.Y., 1969-71; chmn. bd. Marlow Yacht Corp., Deer Park, 1969-71; v.p. fin., sec.-treas. Aurora Products Corp. (subs. Nabisco Inc.), 1971-73, sr. v.p., chief fin. officer, 1973-74; v.p. Rowe Industries Inc., 1971-74; v.p., dir. Aurora Nederland N.V., 1971-74, Aurora Plastics Can. Ltd., 1971-74; v.p. fin., chief fin. officer Coleco Industries Inc., 1974-78, sr. v.p., chief fin. officer, 1978-82, exec. v.p. fin. and adminstrn., 1982-83, exec. v.p. corporate com., 1983—; Coleco Industries, Inc.; trustee Aurora Products Profit Sharing Trust, 1971-74, Coleco Industries Inc. Pension Fund, 1976—. Pres. Rochdale Vill. Civic Assn., 1964-65; bd. dirs. Jewish Children's Service Corp., 1976-78; corporator St. Francis Hosp., 1982—; bd. dirs. One Thousand Corp., 1983—. Mem. Am. Mgmt. Assn., Fin. Execs. Inst., Planning Execs. Inst., Alpha Epsilon Pi. Mailing address: 41 Ranger Ln West Hartford CT 06117 Office: 999 Quaker Ln S West Hartford CT 06110

HANDELMAN, BENJAMIN, newspaper company executive; b. 1924; married. B.B.A., CCNY, 1949. With N.Y. Times Co., 1942—, mgr. adminstrv. services circulation dept., 1965-68, bus. mgr. book and edn. div., 1968-69, asst. to exec. v.p., 1969-70, dir. subscription adminstrn., 1970-72, dir. subscription ops., 1972-73, v.p., 1973-75, sr. v.p., 1975—. Office: New York Times Co 229 W 43d St New York NY 10036 *

HANDELMAN, DAVID YALE, motion picture company executive; b. N.Y.C., July 2, 1938; s. Victor and Ruth (Goodman) H.; m. Janet K. Tarachow, June 11, 1961; children: Joanna Beth, Peter Henry. A.B., U. Pa., 1959; J.D., Harvard U., 1962. Bar: N.Y. 1963, Calif. 1977. With SEC, Washington, 1964-66; with firm Migdal, Low, Tenney & Glass, N.Y.C., 1966-68; with Laird Inc., investment bankers, N.Y.C., 1968-74; v.p., sec. Twentieth Century-Fox Film Corp., Beverly Hills, Calif., 1974—. Democrat. Home: 600 Bonhill Rd Los Angeles CA 90049 Office: Twentieth Century-Fox Flim Corp PO Box 900 Beverly Hills CA 90213

HANDELMAN, GEORGE HERMAN, mathematics educator; b. Pitts., Mar. 24, 1921; s. Morris and Sophia (Pincus) H.; m. Marcia Lee Mendelson, July 10, 1949; children: Nancy Miriam, Louise Sarah. A.B., Harvard U., 1941, A.M., 1942; Ph.D., Brown U., 1946. Asst. prof. engring. Brown U., 1947-48; asst. prof. math. Carnegie Inst. Tech., 1948-51, assoc. prof., 1951-55; prof. applied math. Rensselaer Poly. Inst., 1955—, chmn. dept. math., 1960-72, dean, 1972-78, Amos Eaton prof., 1978—; spl. research on elasticity, math. models in biology, wave motion, vibrations. Fellow ASME; mem. Am. Math. Soc., Soc. Indsl. and Applied Math., Math. Assn. Am., AAUP, Phi Beta Kappa, Sigma Xi. Home: 6 Clinton Pl Troy NY 12180

HANDELMAN, LAD, deep diving contractor, commercial fisherman; b. N.Y.C., Aug. 1, 1936; s. Louis and Barbara (Pirog) H.; m. Vesla Hovden, Oct. 7, 1975; children: Laurie, Roy, James, Anthea. Grad. advanced mgmt. program, Harvard U., 1972. Comml. abalone, albacore and lobster fisherman, Calif., 1953-63; partner Gen. Offshore Divers, Santa Barbara, Calif., 1963-65; chmn., chief exec. officer Calif. Divers, later Oceaneering Internat., Inc., Santa Barbara and Houston, 1965-79, Cal Dive Internat., 1979—. Chmn. Save Our Shellfish, Santa Barbara. Office: 219 E Stearns Wharf Santa Barbara CA 93101

HANDER, O. BENJAMIN, chemical company executive; b. Waco, Tex., Feb. 16, 1918; s. Edwin William and Katherine E. (Munz) H.; m. Clariece Sego, May 24, 1942; children: Howard Benjamin, Janet Clariece, Robert William. B.S. in Mech. Engring., Rice U., 1942. Chem. engr. Humble Oil Co., 1942-48; mgr. prodn. and control Office Synthetic Rubber, Washington, 1948-51; cons. Exec. Offices Pres. U.S., 1951-52; with Dewey & Almy Chem. Co., 1952-54, asst. to pres., 1953-54; co. merged with W.R. Grace & Co., N.Y.C., 1954, v.p. chem. group, 1962-65, v.p. gen. devel. group, 1965-71, corporate v.p., 1971-83, corporate sr. v.p., 1983—. Mem. ASME. Presbyn. Clubs: Baltusrol Golf (Springfield, N.J.); Princeton (N.Y.C.). Home: 30 Colt Rd Summit NJ 07901 Office: 1114 Ave of Americas New York NY 10036

HANDERSON, PAUL BARGAS, JR., bank operations consultant; b. McKees Rocks, Pa., Nov. 20, 1928; s. Paul Bargas and Viola Mae (Mullins) Henderson; m. Betty D. Langewisch, Aug. 25, 1951; children: Keith, Karen, Laura. B.S. in Mech. and Indsl. Engring., Washington U., St. Louis, 1948, 1948, M.S. in Bus. Adminstrn., 1950; Ph.D. in Indsl. Econs., MIT, 1960. Asst. for mgmt. U.S. Navy Bur. Ordnance, Washington, 1950-58; mgr. systems tech. Westinghouse Electric Corp., Pitts., 1960-67; program mgr. United Aircraft Corp., Hartford, Conn., 1967-68; dir. data services Allis-Chalmers Corp., Milw., 1968-74; v.p. Fed. Res. Bank N.Y., N.Y.C., 1974-77, sr. v.p., 1977-82, sr. adviser, 1982-84; bank ops. cons., N.Y.C., 1984—. Author: (with E.M. Heigler) Library Automation, 1970. Office: 110 Riverside Dr Suite 15B New York NY 10024 *There is a recurring necessity to induce change as the basis for comparative advantage; neglect makes it a matter of survival. There is also a constant and greater necessity to sustain existing operations; quality and efficiency depend on repetition. Anticipated change is thus compatible with stable management. Change for survival, and managers capable of inducing it, must be transitory for both are incompatible with sustained organizational success.*

HANDFORD, MORLEY G., oil company executive; b. Snowflake, Man., Can., Sept. 28, 1937; m. Carole Handford; children: Leslie, Heather, Leah, Bradley. B.Sc., U. Man., 1959, postgrad. in plant sci., 1960; M.B.A., U. Western Ont., 1965. Exec. v.p. Esso Chem. Can., Toronto, Ont., Can., 1974-76; v.p. Esso Chem. Europe, Brussels, 1976-79; asst. gen. mgr. mktg. dept. Imperial Oil Co., Toronto, 1979-80, v.p., gen. mgr. mktg. dept., 1980-81; exec. v.p. Esso Petroleum, Toronto, 1981—; dir. Montreal Pipe Line Ltd., Que., Portland Pipe Line Corp., Maine, Can. Standards Assocs., Toronto. Bd. dirs. Toronto Internat. Festival; mem. Wellesley Hosp. Advancement Fund, 1981. Mem. Bd. Trade Met. Toronto, Nat. Petoleum Refiners Assn. Club: Bayview Country (Thornhill, Ont.). Home: 251 Burbank Dr Willowdale ON Canada M2K 2S4 Office: 55 Saint Clair Ave W Toronto ON Canada M4V 2Y7

HANDIN, JOHN WALTER, geology and geophysics educator; b. Salt Lake City, Utah, June 27, 1919; s. Walter Hugo and Dolores (Peirce) H.; m. Frances Marie Robertson, Sept. 2, 1947; children: Diane, Katherine. A.B., UCLA, 1942; M.A., 1948; Ph.D., 1949. Research asso. Shell Devel. Co., Houston, 1950-66; prof. geology and geophysics Tex. A. and M. U., College Station, 1967—, assoc. dean Coll. Geoscis., 1973-82, dir. Center Tectonophysics, 1967-79, dir. Earth Resources Inst., 1979-81. Contbr. articles to profl. jours. Chmn. U.S. Nat. Com. Rock Mechanics, 1969-72; Cons. Terra Tek, 1970—, Los Alamos Sci. Lab., 1972-81, Sandia Labs., 1974-80, U.S. Geol. Survey, 1977-79, EPA, 1977-79, Lawrence Livermore Lab., 1976-81, Def. Nuclear Agy., 1976-77. Served with AUS, 1941-46. Recipient Distinguished Achievement award AIME, 1970. Fellow Am. Geophys. Union (Bucher medal 1983), Internat. Soc. Rock Mechanics (v.p. 1974-79). Home: 2614 Melba Circle Bryan TX 77802 Office: Center for Tectoro Physics Texas A and M U College Station TX 77843

HANDLAN, JOHN B., II, business executive; b. Wheeling, W.Va., Feb. 2, 1928; s. William C. and Sara (Jackson) H.; m. Elizabeth Corbin, Feb. 2, 1952; children: John B., Alfred C., Karen, Susan J., William C. A.B. in Liberal Arts, Washington and Lee U., 1952; postgrad., Goodyear Indsl. U., 1952-54. Regional sales mgr. Goodyear Tire & Rubber Co., Atlanta, 1952-60; sr. manpower coordinator Lockheed Aircraft Co., Marietta, Ga., 1960-66; sr. v.p. H.L. Yoh Co. subs. Day & Zimmermann, Inc., Phila., 1966-76, pres., 1976—; dir. Day & Zimmermann, Inc., 1977—. Mem. Phi Kappa Psi, Pi Alpha Nu. Clubs: Tavistock, Little Mill (Medford, N.J.). Home: 125 Wedgewood

Ln Haddonfield NJ 08033 Office: HL Yoh Co 1818 Market St Philadelphia PA 19103

HANDLEMAN, DAVID, audio products company executive; b. 1914; married. With Handleman Co., Inc., Clawson, Mich., 1937—, sec.-treas., 1946-66, chmn. dir., 1966—, also dir. Office: Handleman Co Inc 1055 W Maple Rd Clawson MI 48017 *

HANDLER, ALAN B., state justice; b. 1931. A.B., Princeton U.; LL.B., Harvard U. Bar: N.J. bar 1956. Asso. justice N.J. Supreme Ct. Office: NJ Supreme Ct Richard J Hughes Justice Complex CN 979 Trenton NJ 08625 *

HANDLER, EVELYN ERIKA, university president; b. Budapest, Hungary, May 5, 1933; d. Donald D. and Ilona Sass; m. Eugene S. Handler; children: Jeffrey, Bradley. B.A., Hunter Coll., 1954; M.Sc., N.Y. U., 1962, Ph.D., 1963; LL.D. (hon.), Rivier Coll., 1981. Research asst. Sloan Kettering Inst., N.Y.C., 1956-58; research asso. Merck Inst. Therapeutic Research, Rahway, N.J., 1958-60; mem. faculty, dept. biol. scis. Hunter Coll., N.Y.C., 1962-77, dean div. scis. and math, 1977-80; pres. U. N.H., Durham, 1980-83, Brandeis U., Waltham, Mass., 1983—; Mem. nat. adv. gen. med. sci. council NIH, 1981-84; mem. Am. Council Pharm. Edn., 1978-82; mem. exec. com. Nat. Assn. State Univs. and Land Grant Colls., 1981-83, mem. com. on policies and issues, 1981—. Contbr. articles and abstracts to profl. publs. Mem. New Eng. Bd. Higher Edn., 1980—, New Eng. Council Presidents, 1980-83, N.H. Coll. and Univ. Council, 1980-83, Post-Secondary Edn. Commn., 1980—; corp. mem. Woods Hole Oceanographic Instn., 1983-84.

HANDLER, HARRY, educational administrator. Suprt. Los Angeles Pub. Sch. System. Office: Office of Supt PO Box 3307 Terminal Annex Los Angeles CA 90051§

HANDLER, JEROME SIDNEY, anthropology educator; b. N.Y.C., Sept. 3, 1933; s. Sam and Sara (Wieder) H.; children—Joshua Martin, Lisa Frances. B.A., UCLA, 1956; M.A., 1959; Ph.D., Brandeis U., 1965. Asst. prof. anthropology So. Ill. U., Carbondale, 1964-68, assoc. prof., 1968-74, prof., 1974—; Olive B. O Connor vis. prof. Am. instns. Colgate U., Hamilton, N.Y., 1971-72; Hon. research asst. University Coll. London, 1966-67; staff archaeologist New World Archeol. Found., Chiapas, Mexico, 1957; cons. AID, fall 1964, Peace Corps, summer 1969; panelist Nat. Endowment for Humanities, 1977-79, 82. Author: A Guide to Source Materials for the Study of Barbados History, 1627-1834, 1971, The Unappropriated People: Freedmen in the Slave Society of Barbados, 1974; co-author: Plantation Slavery in Barbados: An Archaeological and Historical Investigation, 1978. Vis. research fellow U. W.I., Jamaica, 1969-70; research asso. Research Inst. for Study of Man, N.Y.C., summer 1978, 79; vis. scholar Center for Afro-Am. Studies, UCLA, summer, 1980; recipient research grants NSF, 1966-67, 71-73, Wenner-Gren Found. Anthrop. Research, 1971-72, Research Inst. Study Man, 1962, 70, NIH, 1965, Am. Philos. Soc., 1968; Nat. Endowment for Humanities fellow, 1969-70, 75-76, 79; Am. Council Learned Socs. travel grantee, 1977; grantee Social Sci. Research Council and Am. Council Learned Socs. Joint Com. on Latin Am. Studies, 1983. Fellow Am. Anthrop. Assn.; mem. Caribbean Studies Assn. (past mem. exec. council). Home: 201 S Maple St Carbondale IL 62901 Office: Dept Anthropology So Ill U Carbondale IL 62901

HANDLER, MARK S., business exec.; b. 1933; (married). Student, U. Ill.; B.S., Roosevelt U., 1957; M.S., N.Y. U., 1958. With R.H. Macy & Co. Inc., 1958—; mdse. adminstr. Bamberger's subs., 1962-65, v.p., mdse. adminstr., 1965-67, sr. v.p. merchandising, 1967-71, pres., 1979, chmn., chief exec. officer, 1979-80, pres. parent co., 1980—, also dir.; dir. Fidelity Union Bank. Served with U.S. Army, 1953-55. Address: 151 W 34th St New York NY 10001

HANDLER, MILTON, lawyer; b. N.Y.C., Oct. 8, 1903; s. George and Ray (Friedman) H.; m. Marion W. Kahn, Dec. 21, 1932 (dec.); 1 dau., Carole Enid; m. Miriam Adler, Feb. 3, 1955. A.B., Columbia U., 1924, LL.B. Ordronaux prize, 1926; LL.D., Hebrew U., 1965. Bar: N.Y. 1927. On staff Columbia U., 1927-72, now prof. law emeritus; engaged in pvt. practice law specializing in antitrust, trademark law; sr. partner firm Kaye, Scholer, Fierman, Hays & Handler; pres. N.Y. Majestic Corp., 1937-48; Gen. counsel Nat. Labor Bd., 1933-34; spl. asst. to gen. counsel Treasury Dept., 1938-40; asst. gen. counsel Lend Lease Adminstrn., 1942-43; spl. counsel Fgn. Econ. Adminstrn., 1943-44; asso. pub. mem. Nat. War Labor Bd., 1944; adviser Am. Law Inst. Restatement of Torts and Restatement of Torts second; arbitrator numerous important labor and comml. disputes; Mitchell lectr. Buffalo Law Sch., 1956-57; lectr. U. Leyden, The Netherlands, 1963; Mem. atty. gen.'s nat. com. to study antitrust laws, 1953-55. Author: books, articles including Antitrust in Perspective, 1957; Cases and Materials on Trade Regulation, 4th edit., 1967; Cases and Materials on Business Torts, 1972, Twenty-Five Years of Antitrust, 1973, (with others) Cases and Materials on Trade Regulation, 1975; Editor: Columbia Law Rev, 1924-26. Hon. chmn. bd. dirs. Am. Friends of Hebrew U., Jerusalem; dep. chmn., bd. govs. Hebrew U. Recipient bicentennial silver medallion Columbia, 1954; Scopus award Am. Friends of Hebrew U., 1963; medal of excellence Columbia Law Alumni, 1976; Outstanding Research in Law and Govt. award Fellows of Am. Bar Found., 1977; Human Relations award lawyers div. Anti-Defamation League Appeal, 1979; Milton Handler chair in trade regulation established at Columbia Law Sch., 1974; Joseph M. Proskauer award lawyers div. United Jewish Appeal, 1980; Handler Auditorium on Mt. Scopus Campus of Hebrew U., dedicated 1975. Fellow Am. Coll. Trial Lawyers, Am. Bar Found., Fed. Bar Council; mem. ABA (council antitrust sec. 1961-64), Fed. Bar Assn., N.Y. State Bar Assn. (chmn. spl. com. to study state antitrust laws 1956-66), Assn. Bar City N.Y., N.Y. County Lawyers Assn. (dir. 1953-56). Democrat. Jewish religion. Clubs: Men's Faculty (Columbia); Harmonie. Home: 625 Park Ave New York NY 10021 Office: 425 Park Ave New York NY 10022

HANDLERY, PAUL ROBERT, hotel executive; b. St. Helena, Calif., Apr. 8, 1920; s. Harry and Rose Helen (Braun) H.; m. Ardyce Arlene Lundquist, June 1, 1945; children: Barbara Kim (Mrs. David R. Metcalf), Michael Kent, Nancy Liane (Mrs. Jerry Newton), Jon Steven, Lane Ardyce. A.A., U. Calif. at Berkeley, 1940; B.S. with honors, Sch. Hotel Adminstrn., Cornell U., 1943. Cert. hotel adminstr. Vice pres. Handlery Hotels, Inc., San Francisco, 1946-63, pres., 1963—; Past pres., bd. dirs. San Francisco Conv. and Visitors Bur. Past chmn. adv. bd. San Francisco Salvation Army; past pres., trustee No. Calif. chpt. Leukemia Soc. Am.; hon. regent John F. Kennedy U., Martinez, Calif.; mem. adv. bd. Calif. Poly. U., Pomona, Golden Gate U., U. San Francisco; pres. Greater Union Square Assn., San Francisco, Am. Hotel Found.; v.p. Hotel and Restaurant Found.; chmn. adv. com. City Coll. San Francisco; past pres. East Bay Hotel Assn. Served to capt. AUS. Named to Men of Distinction Innkeeping mag., 1963, Hall of Fame Hospitality mag., 1966, Man of Year Pacific Hotel-Motel News, 1970, Nat. Jewish Hosp., Denver, 1973. Mem. Am. Hotel and Motel Assn. (pres. 1974, chmn. bd. 1975), Calif. Hotel and Motel Assn. (past pres., dir. emeritus), Hotel Employers Assn. San Francisco (pres.), Cornell Soc. Hotelmen. Clubs: Olympic, San Francisco Press, Commonwealth (San Francisco); Bermuda Dunes Country, Stardust Country, Diablo Country, Moraga Country. Home: 766 Augusta Dr Moraga CA 94556 Office: 351 Geary St San Francisco CA 94102

HANDLEY, G. KENNETH, holding company executive; b. 1906; married. B.A., Brigham Young U., 1928; M.B.A., NYU, 1931. V.p. Mfrs. Hanover Bank, 1930-57; ptnr. J.A. Hogle & Co., 1959-64; with Imperial Corp. Am., San Diego, 1961—, chmn. bd., chief exec. officer, 1979—, dir., Olson Farms Inc. Office: Imperial Corp Am 8787 Complex Dr San Diego CA 92123 *

HANDLIN, OSCAR, educator, historian; b. Bklyn., Sept. 29, 1915; s. Joseph and Ida (Yanowitz) H.; m. Mary Flug, Sept. 18, 1937; children: Joanna Flug, David Paltiel, Ruth Blume; m. Lilian Bombach, June 17, 1977. A.B., Bklyn. Coll., 1934; A.M., Harvard U., 1935, Ph.D., 1940; LL.D., Colby Coll., Waterville, Maine, 1962, U. Mass., Boston, 1982; L.H.D., Hebrew Union Coll., 1967, No. Mich. U., 1969; H.H.D., Oakland U., 1968; D.H.L., Seton Hall U., 1972; D.Letters, Bklyn. Coll., 1972; D.H.L., Boston Coll., 1975; L.H.D., Lowell U., 1980; Litt.D., U. Cin., 1981. Instr. history Bklyn. Coll., 1936-38; instr. history Harvard U., 1939-44, asst. prof., 1944-48, asso. prof., 1948-54, prof. history, 1954—, dir. Center for Study of Liberty in Am., 1958-66, Winthrop prof. history, 1962-65, Charles Warren prof. history, 1965-72, dir. Charles Warren Center for Studies in Am. History, 1965-72, Carl H. Pforzheimer Univ. prof., 1972—, dir. Univ. Library, 1979—. Author: Boston's Immigrants, 1941, Commonwealth, 1947, This Was America, 1949, The Uprooted, 2d edit., 1973, The American People in the Twentieth Century, 1954, Adventure in Freedom, 1954, Chance or Destiny, 1955, Race and Nationality in American Life, 1956, Readings in American History, rev. edit., 1970, Al Smith and His America, 1958, Immigration as a Factor in American History, 1959, The Newcomers-Negroes and Puerto Ricans in a Changing Metropolis, 1959, American Principles and Issues, 1961, The Dimensions of Liberty, 1961, The Americans, 1963, Fire-Bell in the Night, 1964, Children of the Uprooted, 1966, Popular Sources of Political Authority, 1967, History of the United States, 1967, America, A History, 1968, The American College and American Culture, 1970, Statue of Liberty, 1971, Facing Life-Youth and the Family in American History, 1971, A Pictorial History of Immigration, 1972, The Wealth of the American People, 1975, Truth in History, 1979, Abraham Lincoln and the Union, 1980, The Distortion of America, 1981; editor: Harvard Ethnic Ency.; contbr. hist. jours. Vice-chmn. U.S. Bd. Fgn. Scholarships, 1962-65, chmn., 1965-66; trustee N.Y. Pub. Library, 1973—. Recipient History prize Union League Club, 1934, J.H. Dumning prize Am. History Assn., 1941, award of honor Bklyn. Coll., 1945, Pulitzer prize for history, 1952, Christopher award, 1958, Bklyn. Coll. Alumni award, 1958; Robert H. Lord award, 1972; Guggenheim fellow, 1954; Brandeis U. fellow, 1965—; Harmsworth prof. U. Oxford, Eng., 1972-73. Fellow Am. Acad. Arts and Scis.; mem. Mass. Hist. Soc., Colonial Soc. Mass., Am. Jewish Hist. Soc. Jewish. Home: 18 Agassiz St Cambridge MA 02140 *My philosophy, such as it is, develops out of the study of the human past which persuades me that, despite the susceptibility to error and despite the frequent risks of failure, man has the capacity to make order and find purpose in the world in which he lives when he uses the power of his reason to do so.*

HANDS, WILLIAM ARTHUR, retired executive, educator; b. Bklyn., July 24, 1917; s. Arthur and Ottilie (Muller) H.; m. Grace Rita DeLapp, Aug. 21, 1943; children—James Albert, William Arthur, Bruce Cyril, Brian Thomas, Brent Edward, Carolyn Elizabeth. B.A., Bklyn. Coll., 1947; M.B.A., Harvard U., 1949. Asst. to controller Berger Bros. Co., New Haven, 1950-52; supr. cost accounting and inventory Ford div. Ford Motor Co., Detroit, 1952-57; controller MicroWave and Power Tube div. Raytheon Co., Boston, 1957-61; v.p., treas., dir. Nat. Casket Co., Inc., Boston, 1961-69; with Stanley Home Products, Inc., Westfield, Mass., 1969-82, fin. v.p., treas., dir., mem. exec. com., to 1982; prof. bus. adminstrn. Am. Internat. Coll., Springfield, Mass.; corporator Woronoco Savs. Bank, Westfield; mem. Westfield adv. bd. 3d Nat. Bank Hampden County. Served with USAAF, 1942-46. Mem. Nat. Assn. Accountants, Fin. Execs. Inst. Home: Meadowbrook Acres Granville MA 01034

HANDSAKER, MORRISON, economist, arbitrator, educator; b. Portland, Oreg., Nov. 20, 1907; s. John J. and Alice M. (Smith) H.; m. Marjorie Linfield, Aug. 25, 1934; 1 dau., Alice E. Handsaker Kidder. A.B., Reed Coll., 1929; Ph.D., U. Chgo., 1939. Code adviser NRA, 1934-36; instr. U. Wash., Seattle, 1937-38, Occidental Coll., Los Angeles, 1938-40, asst. prof., 1940-42, asso. prof., 1942-43; staff Nat. War Labor Bd., 1943-44; personnel rep. Lockheed Aircraft Corp., 1944-45; economist OPA, 1945-46; prof. econs. Lafayette Coll., 1946-76, chmn. dept. econs., 1946-70; arbitrator, 1941—; sr. Fulbright lectr. U. Sheffield, Eng., 1957-58, Waseda U., Tokyo, Yokohama (Japan) Nat. U., 1964-65. Author: The Chicago Cleaning and Dyeing Industry, 1939, Seasonal Farm Labor in Pennsylvania, 1953, (with Marjorie L. Handsaker) The Submission Agreement in Contract Arbitration, arbitration decisions pub. by reporting services; contbr. articles to profl. jours. Mem. emergency bds. under Ry. Labor Act, 1955, 57, 59, 61; mem. Bituminous Coal Operators Assn.-United Mine Workers Am. Dist. Panel Arbitration System, 1975-80; dist. arbitrator Consolidation Coal Co. and Dist. 31, United Mine Workers, 1982—; mediator, fact finder. Mem. Am. Econ. Assn., Internat. Indsl. Relations Assn., Indsl. Relations Research Assn., Am. Arbitration Assn. (mem. panel), Nat. Acad. Arbitrators (chmn. research and edn. com. 1959-60, mem. 1980-81, chmn. internat. corrs. com. 1973-75, research and edn. com. 1981), Soc. Profls. in Dispute Resolution. Presbyterian (elder). Home: 717 W Lafayette St Easton PA 18042 *In my thirty-six years as a professor of economics and labor-management relations, one of my main goals has been to give students an understanding of the economic system and its strengths and problems. I hope that in teaching concerning labor-management relations I have given my students an understanding of the collective bargaining process and some insights into the way the institutions of mediation and arbitration have helped bring more harmony between unions and management.*

HANDSCHUMACHER, ALBERT GUSTAVE, corporate executive; b. Phila., Oct. 20, 1918; s. Gustave H. and Emma (Streck) H.; m. Inger Stratton, Apr. 11, 1970; children by previous marriage: Albert, David W., Megan, Karin, Melissa. B.S., Drexel Inst. Tech., 1940; diploma, U. Pitts., 1941, Alexander Hamilton Inst., 1948. Prodn. mgr. Jr. Motors Corp., Phila., 1938-40; sales engr. Westinghouse Electric Co., Pitts., 1941; with Lear, Inc., Grand Rapids, Mich., 1945-57, beginning as sales mgr. central dist., successively asst. to pres., asst. gen. mgr., v.p. and gen. mgr., sr. v.p., dir. sales, pres., dir., 1959-62; v.p., gen. mgr. Rheem Mfg. Co., 1957-59; pres., dir. Lear Siegler, Inc., 1962-65; chmn. bd. Aeronca, Inc.; dir. First Exec. Corp., Lear Siegler, Inc., Golden West Financial Co., Actair Internat., Cramer Investment Co., World Savs. and Loan Assn., Exec. Life Ins. Co., Flight Dynamics Inc., Informatics Inc., Accounts Network Inc.; underwriting mem. Lloyd's of London. Trustee Drexel U.; vice chmn. bd. trustees City of Hope; nat. adv. chmn. Am. Heart Assn.; chmn. Los Angeles unit; mem. bus. adv. council UCLA Internat. Student Center; trustee Nat. Asthma Assn. Served to maj. USAAF, 1942-45. Recipient 60th Anniversary Alumni award for outstanding achievements and services field of indsl. mgmt. Drexel U., 1951, Outstanding Alumni award, 1971; Man of Year award City of Hope, 1970, Nat. Asthma Assn., 1978. Mem. Am. Mgmt. Assn., ASHRE. Clubs: Jonathan, Caiif. Yacht, Bel Air (Calif.) Country; Wings, Metropolitan (N.Y.C.); Confrerie de la Chaine des Rotisseurs, Beverly Hills; Le Mirador Country (Switzerland); Astro (Phila.). Home: 1100 Stone Canyon Rd Bel Air CA 90024 Office: 10100 Santa Monica Blvd Century City North Los Angeles CA 90067

HANDSCHUMACHER, ROBERT EDMUND, pharmacologist; b. Abington, Pa., Oct. 16, 1927; s. Gustav Heinrich and Emma (Streck) H.; children: Kurt Robert, Mark Davis. B.S., Drexel Inst., 1949; M.S., U. Wis., 1951, Ph.D., 1953. Asst. prof. Yale U., 1956-59, asso. prof., 1960-64, prof., 1964—, dir. div. biol. scis., 1969-72, chmn. dept. pharmacology, 1974-77; cons. Nat. Cancer Inst.; chmn. exptl. therapeutics study sect. NIH, 1979-83. Editorial bd., Cancer Research, 1962-68, 80—, Molecular Pharmacology, 1964-80, Pharm. Revs., 1978—. Sci. adviser Anna Fuller Fund; chmn. fellowship commn. Internat. Union Against Cancer, 1966-74; chmn. sci. rev. com. Brussels unit Ludwig Cancer Inst., 1980—. Served with USAAF, 1945-46. Am. Cancer Soc. scholar, 1957-62, Career research prof., 1964-74; Alexander Haddow research fellow, 1977-78. Mem. Am. Soc. Pharmacology and Exptl. Therapeutics, Am. Soc. Biol. Chemistry, Am. Assn. Cancer Research (dir. 1967-70, Sec.-treas. 1982—), Am. Chem. Soc., Sigma Xi, Tau Beta Pi; fellow AAAS. Home: 97 Great Harbor Guilford CT 06437 Office: 333 Cedar St New Haven CT 06510

HANDVILLE, ROBERT TOMPKINS, artist, illustrator; b. Paterson, N.J., Mar. 23, 1924; s. Robert Ray and Olive (Tompkins) H.; m. Marylee Pollock, Nov. 27, 1948; children: Robert C., David C. Cert., Pratt Inst., Bklyn., 1948; student, Bklyn. Mus. Art Sch., 1960-64. Asst. art dir. Ruthrauff & Ryan, N.Y.C., 1946-48; artist Kudner Advt. Agy., N.Y.C., 1948-50, Charles E. Cooper Studios, 1950-53; free lance artist, Pleasantville, N.Y., 1953—; mem. faculty Fashion Inst. Tech., N.Y.C., 1978—; mem. Joint Ethics Com., N.Y.C., 1983—; chmn. Artists in the Parks Program Nat. Park Service, Washinton, 1968-70. Designer: U.S. Commemmorative postal stamps: Yellowstone Nat. Park, 1972; Alfred Verille Air Mail, 1981. Chmn. Pleasantville Community Scholarship Fund, 1960-68; mem. United Fund Drive, Pleasantville, 1960-62. Served with USAF, 1942-46, 50-51. Recipient Ranger Fund Purchase prize Am. Watercolor Soc., 1960, Anonymous prize Audubon Artists, 1962, Am. Can. award 21st New Eng. Exhbn., 1976, Mario Cooper award Am. Watercolor Soc., 1983. Mem. Nat. Acad. Design (Sprayer prize 1982), Soc. Illustrators (treas. 1960-64, welfare chmn. 1972—), Am. Watercolor Soc. (dir. 1973-75, Pleissner award 1981), Pratt Inst. Alumni Soc. (dir. 1970-73). Presbyterian. Home: 99 Woodland Dr Pleasantville NY 10570

HANDY, CHARLES BROOKS, accountant, educator; b. Coffey, Mo., Apr. 26, 1924; s. Herbert Franklyn and Laura Ada Margaret (Mueller) H.; m. Donna Jean Peters, June 29, 1958; children: William Mark, Karen Lynne. B.A., Westminster Coll., Fulton, Mo., 1947; M.A., U. Iowa, 1956; Ph.D., Iowa State U., 1970. C.P.A., Iowa. Staff acct. McGladrey, Hansen, Dunn & Co. (name now McGladrey, Hendrickson & Pullen), Davenport, Iowa, 1955-58; instr. acctg. Iowa State U., Ames, 1958-60, asst. prof., 1960-70, asso. prof., 1970-75, prof., 1975—, chmn. supervisory com. indsl. adminstrv. scis., 1975-78, acctg. coordinator, 1977-78, chmn. dept. indsl. adminstrn., 1978-80, dir. Sch. Bus. Adminstrn., 1980-84, dean Coll. Bus. Adminstrn., 1984—. Served to lt. (j.g.) USNR, 1943-46. Mem. Am. Inst. C.P.A.s, Iowa Soc. C.P.A.s, Inst. Internal Auditors, Midwest Bus. Adminstrn. Assn., Beta Alpha Psi, Omicron Delta Epsilon. Republican. Presbyterian. Home: 1132 Johnson St Ames IA 50010 Office: 300 Carver Hall Iowa State U Ames IA 50011

HANDY, JOHN ABNER, JR., business executive; b. Mpls., Apr. 19, 1913; s. John Abner and Winnifred (Hammond) H.; m. Frances P. Slack, July 4, 1936; children: John Abner, Mary Eugenia. A.B., Hamilton Coll., 1935; M.B.A., Harvard U., 1937. Salesman Procter & Gamble Distbg. Co., 1937-40; dept. head, gen. office mgr., asst. controller Carborundum Co., Niagara Falls, N.Y., 1940-47; controller, later controller-asst. sec. Deering Milliken & Co., Inc.; sec. Pendleton Fabrics Corp.; controller numerous corps; sec. corp. Joseph E. Seagram & Sons, Inc., 1952-56, also; sec. subsidiary corps. Seagram Distillers Corp., Calvert Distilling Co., Carstairs Bros. Distilling Co., Inc., Frankfort Distilleries, Inc., Frankfort Distillers Corp., Gallagher & Burton, Inc., Hunter-Wilson Distilling Co., Inc., Julius Kessler Distilling Co., Inc., Lord Calvert Distilleries, Inc., Paul Jones & Co., Inc., Pharma-Craft Corp., Md. Distillery, Inc., Gen. Distillers Corp.; financial v.p., controller, dir. Chem. Constrn. Corp. (subsidiary Electric Bond & Share Co.), 1956-66; v.p., dir. Chem. Constrn. Internat. Del., Chem. Constrn. A.G. Zug, Switzerland; dir. Chem. Constrn. Ltd., Gt. Britain, Can., Linden Brunswick Corp., 1958-66; exec. v.p., dir. Fabergé, Inc., 1966-72; dir. planning Guideposts Assocs., Inc., 1977—. Contbr. articles to profl. publs. Mem. Fin. Execs. Inst., Am. Mgmt. Assn. (council), Nat. Office Mgmt. Assn. (past pres., dir. Buffalo chpt.), Am. Arbitration Assn. (panel), Tau Kappa Epsilon, Delta Sigma Rho. Clubs: Harvard (N.Y.C.); Gipsy Trail (Carmel, N.Y.). Home: Gipsy Trail Club Carmel NY 10512 Office: Guideposts Assocs Inc Carmel NY 10512

HANDY, LYMAN LEE, chemist, educator; b. Payette, Idaho, Aug. 4, 1919; s. Clarence Lee and Lillie (Hall) H.; m. Lenore E. Ross, Aug. 28, 1948; children—Mark Ross, Gail Eileen. Student, Western Wash. Coll., 1938-40; B.S., U. Wash., 1942, Ph.D., 1951. With Chevron Oil Field Research Co., 1951-66; mem. faculty U. So. Calif., 1966—, prof. chem. and petroleum engring., chmn. petroleum engring., 1966—, chmn. chem. engring., 1969-76, Omar B. Milligan prof. petroleum engring., 1976—; cons. in field. Mem. editorial bd., Trans. Am. Inst. Mining Engrs., 1960, 68, 69; Contbr. articles to profl. jours. Served to lt. USNR, 1942-46. Mem. Am. Chem. Soc. (chmn. Orange County sect. 1969), Soc. Petroleum Engrs. (dir. Los Angeles basin sect. 1971-75, chmn. 1974, nat. dir.-at-large 1978—), Am. Inst. Chem. Engrs., A.A.A.S., Phi Beta Kappa, Sigma Xi, Phi Lambda Upsilon, Tau Beta Pi. Home: 1401 Dana Pl Fullerton CA 92631 Office: University Park Los Angeles CA 90007

HANDY, RICHARD LINCOLN, civil engineer, educator; b. Chariton, Iowa, Feb. 12, 1929; s. Walter Newton and Florence Elizabeth (Shoemaker) H.; m. Charlsee Avonne Pitt, Apr. 18, 1964 (dec. 1980); 1 dau., Beth Susan.; m. Kathryn Etona Claussen, Feb. 13, 1983. B.S. in Geology, Iowa State U., 1951, M.S., 1953, Ph.D., 1956. Asst. prof. civil engring. Iowa State U., Ames, 1956-59, assoc. prof., 1959-63; prof., also dir. Geotech. Research Lab., 1963—; cons. in soil engring., soil and rock testing, landslide stabilization; v.p. research W.N. Handy Co., 1958—; pres. Handy Geotech. Instruments, Inc., 1980—. Author: (with M.G. Spangler) Soil Engineering, 3d edit, 1973, 4th edit., 82; contbr. articles to profl. jours. Recipient faculty citation Iowa State U., 1976. Fellow AAAS, Geol. Soc. Am., Iowa Acad. Sci.; mem. ASCE, ASTM, Soil Sci. Soc. Am., Internat. Soc. Soil Mech. and Found. Engrs. Patentee in soils field. Office: Geotech Research Lab Iowa State U Ames IA 50011

HANDY, ROBERT JOHN, insurance company executive; b. Long Prairie, Minn., Jan. 6, 1901; s. John Paul and Maude Louise (Baer) H.; m. Virginia Showalter, Jan. 14, 1927 (dec. Jan. 1949); children: J. Thomas, Susan (Mrs. Daniel Sass); m. Virginia Carver, Oct. 26, 1951 (dec. Apr. 1964); m. Marjory Sapp Swanson, June 14, 1969. B.A., U. Minn., 1923; postgrad., U. Wis., 1924; M.A., U. Wash., 1934. Dir. journalism Broadway High Sch., Seattle, 1924-26; editor Pacific Caterer; sec. Seattle Restaurant Assn., 1926-28; instr. math. and journalism Seattle Pub. Schs., 1928-45; treas., mgr. Wash. Tchrs. Credit Union, 1936—; pres., chmn. bd. Pub. Employees Mut. Ins. Co.,

1948—, Pub. Employees Mut. Casualty Co., 1949—; pres. Pemco Life Ins. Co., 1964—; dir. Tchrs. State Bank.; Mng. editor Ft. Monroe Coast Arty. Newspaper, 1922. Author: Money Management for Teachers, 1965—; also articles. Founder Tchrs. Found., 1966; bd. dirs. Wash. Ins. Council, 1968-69. Served to 2d lt. Coast Arty. Res., 1923-27. Recipient award of merit Wash. Credit Union League, 1972; Paul Harris fellow Rotary Internat., 1982. Club: Wash. Athletic. Home: 1620 34th Ct W Seattle WA 98199 Office: 325 Eastlake Ave E Seattle WA 98109

HANDY, ROBERT MAXWELL, patent lawyer; b. Buffalo, Apr. 1, 1931; s. John Abner and Yvonne Fernande (Blaise) H.; m. Berniece Emily Reist, July 2, 1955; children: Mary, Robert, David. B.S., Trinity Coll., 1953; M.S., Northwestern U., 1958, Ph.D., 1962; J.D., Ariz. State U., 1984. New product devel. research mgr. Westinghouse Electric Co., Pitts., 1961-69; product mgr. Semiconductor div. Motorola, Inc., Phoenix, 1969-72, corp. dir. research, 1972-75; exec. dir. Ariz. Solar Energy Research Commn., 1975-76; dir. bus. and tech. planning Integrated Circuits div. Motorola, Inc., Mesa, Ariz., 1976—, patent atty., Phoenix, 1980—; Instr. Carnegie Mellon U., 1967. Served to lt. (j.g.) USNR, 1954-57. Royall A. Cabell fellow, 1959-60. Mem. Am. Phys. Soc., IEEE, Phi Beta Kappa. Home: 4950 E Palomino St Phoenix AZ 85018 Office: Patent Law Dept Motorola Inc 4350 E Camelback Rd Phoenix AZ 85018

HANDY, ROBERT THEODORE, church historian, educator; b. Rockville, Conn., June 30, 1918; s. William Evans and Sarah (MacDonald) H.; m. Barbara Steere Mitchell, Dec. 29, 1941; children: Stephen William, Marilyn Barbara, David Robert. A.B., Brown U., 1940; M.Div., Colgate Rochester Div. Sch., 1943; Ph.D., U. Chgo., 1949; L.H.D. (hon.), Marietta Coll., 1977. Ordained to ministry Baptist Ch., 1943; pastor South Ch., Mt. Prospect, Ill., 1943-45; instr. Bapt. Missionary Tng. Sch., 1948-49, Shimer Coll., 1949-50; instr. ch. history Union Theol. Sem., N.Y.C., 1950-51, asst. prof., 1951-54, asso. prof., 1954-59, prof., 1959—, Henry Sloane Coffin prof. ch. history, 1981—, dir. studies, 1957-63, dean, 1970-71, dean grad. studies, 1974-76, acad. dean, 1976-78; adj. prof. dept. religion, Columbia U., 1973—. Author: We Witness Together, 1956, Members One of Another, 1959, (with others) American Christianity, 1960, 63, A Christian America: Protestant Hopes and Historical Realities, 1971, 2d edit., 1983, A History of the Churches in the United States and Canada, 1976; editor: The Social Gospel in America, 1966; Editor: Religion in the American Experience: The Pluralistic Style, 1972, The Holy Land in American Protestant Life, 1800-1948: A Documentary History, 1981; co-editor: Theology and Church in Times of Change, 1970. Mem. Faith and Order Commn., World Council Chs., 1954-75. Served from 1st lt. to capt. AUS, 1945-47; PTO. Mem. Am. Soc. Ch. History (past pres.), Am. Bapt. Hist. Soc. (pres. 1974-75), Am. Hist. Assn., Am. Acad. Religion, Assn. Theol. Schs. (task force on accreditation 1978-80). Home: 20 Holly Ln Cresskill NJ 07626 Office: 3041 Broadway New York NY 10027

HANDY, ROLLO LEROY, educator, research exec.; b. Kenyon, Minn., Feb. 20, 1927; s. John R. and Alice (Kispert) H.; m. Toni Scheiner, Sept. 17, 1950; children—Jonathan, Ellen, Benjamin. B.A., Carleton Coll., Northfield, Minn., 1950; M.A., Sarah Lawrence Coll., 1951; postgrad., U. Minn., 1951-52; Ph.D., U. Buffalo, 1954. Mem. faculty U. S.D., 1954-60, prof. philosophy, head dept., 1959-60; asso. prof. Union Coll., Schenectady, 1960-61; mem. faculty State U. N.Y. at Buffalo, 1961-76, prof. philosophy, 1964-76, chmn. dept., 1961-67, chmn. div. philosophy and social scis., 1965-67, provost faculty ednl. studies, 1967-76; pres. Behavioral Research Council, 1976—, Am. Inst. Econ. Research, 1977—. Author: Methodology of the Behavioral Sciences, 1964, Value Theory and the Behavioral Sciences, 1969, The Measurement of Values, 1970, (with Paul Kurtz) A Current Appraisal of the Behavioral Sciences, 1964; (with E.C. Harwood) rev. edit., 1973, Useful Procedures of Inquiry, 1973; Co-editor: Philosophical Perspectives on Punishment, 1968, The Behavioral Sciences, 1968, The Idea of God, 1968. Served with USNR, 1945-46. Mem. AAUP (chpt. pres. 1964-65), Am. Anthrop. Assn., Am. Philos. Assn., Mind Assn., Philosophy Sci. Assn. Home: Pine St Stockbridge MA 01262

HANDYSIDE, HOLSEY GATES, govt. ofcl.; b. Cleve., Aug. 23, 1927; s. Douglas P. and Edna (Gates) H. B.A., Amherst Coll., 1950; M. Pub. Affairs, Princeton U., 1953. Adminstrv. aide Dept. Interior, 1952; staff asst. to mil. advisor FOA (now AID), Washington, 1953-55; joined Fgn. Service, Dept. State, 1955; polit. officer, Cairo, 1955-57; detailed Arabic lang. and area tng. Fgn. Service Inst. Field Sch., Beirut, 1957-59; comml. attache, Baghdad, Iraq, 1960-62, staff asst. to asst. sec. state for internat. orgn. affairs, Washington, 1962-64, postmgmt. officer, 1964-65, chief polit. sect., Tripoli, Libya, 1965-70; dir. Office Atomic Energy and Aerospace, Bur. Politico-Mil. Affairs, State Dept., Washington, 1970-74; mem. 17th Sr. Seminar in Fgn. Policy, 1974-75; ambassador to Islamic Republic of Mauritania, 1975-77; dep. asst. sec. internat. nuclear and tech. programs Dept. Energy, Washington, 1978—. Served with USAAC, 1945-47. Fulbright fellow U. Grenoble Faculté de Droit, 1950-51. Mem. Am. Fgn. Service Assn., Middle East Inst., Phi Beta Kappa Assos.

HANEMAN, VINCENT SIERING, JR., consulting engineer, educator, university dean; b. Orange, N.J., Feb. 19, 1924; s. Vincent Siering and Helen (Harris) H.; m. Adelaide Russell, Oct. 3, 1961; children: Vincent Siering III, Charles Frederick, Rosalyn Tullos, Kaye Kavisic. S.B., MIT, 1947; M.S. in Aero. Engring, U. Mich., 1950, Ph.D., 1956. Registered profl. engr., Ohio, Okla., Tex., Ala., Alaska. Asst. head flight research Project Meteor, Mass. Inst. Tech., 1947-49; project head automatic wind tunnel data reduction U. Mich., 1949-51; project officer analogue computer research Wright Air Devel. Center, Ohio, 1951-52; asso. prof., asst. dept. head aero. engring. Air Force Inst. Tech., Wright Patterson AFB, Ohio, 1955-59; chief spl. projects div. guidance and control directorate Air Force Ballistic Missile Div., 1959-60; pres., sr. asso. Haneman Assos., Richardson, Tex., 1960-66, Stillwater, Okla., 1967-72, Auburn, Ala., 1972-73; chmn. bd. Haneman Assos., Inc., Richardson, Stillwater and Auburn, 1961-73, exec. v.p., Stillwater, 1966-67; prof. mech. engring., dir. engring. research, asso. dean Coll. Engring., Okla. State U., 1966-72; prof. aeros. engring., dean Sch. Engring., Auburn U., 1972-80; prof. mech. engring., dean Sch. Engring., U. Alaska, 1980—; cons. flight simulator project U. Mich., 1952-55, Gen. Electric Co., Gen. Dynamics, Space Tech. Labs., Chance Vought Corp., Ling Temco-Vought, Nat. Acad. Scis., Union Carbide, others. Contbr. articles on instrumentation, control and guidance, aircraft performance, engring. edn. to tech. jours. Mem. Army Sci. Adv. Panel, 1967-77; chmn. night low level com. Project Master, Point of Contact Airmobile. Served to 1st lt. USAAF, 1943-45; MTO; to maj. USAF, 1951-60; to maj. gen. Res., moblzn. asst. to dep. chief staff for research and devel. Decorated D.S.M., Legion of Merit with oak leaf cluster, D.F.C. with oak leaf cluster, Air medal with 7 oak leaf clusters, Air Force Commendation medal. Assoc. fellow Am. Inst. Aeros. and Astronautics; fellow Am. Soc. Engring. Edn. (past sec. mech. and aero. divs., past nat. chmn. aero. div., past mem. gen. council, past mem. exec. com., past chmn. engring. research council, past 1st v.p., chmn. dean's inst. 1978, mem., chmn. planning factors com. Engring. Coll. Council 1976-80, pres. 1980-81), Am. Astronautical Soc. (sr.), Am. Helicopter Soc., IEEE, Nat. Soc. Profl. Engrs. (ethics com. 1974-75, nat. chmn. Engring. Week 1977, 78, chmn. cost of engring. edn. com., nat. dir. 1979-80), Ala. Soc. Profl. Engrs. (state chmn. Engring. Week 1973-76), Alaska Soc. Profl. Engrs. (pres. Fairbanks chpt. 1982-83), Nat. Conf. Advancement Research (ad hoc mem. exec. com. 1977—), Sigma Xi, Tau Beta Pi, Sigma Tau, Phi Kappa Phi, Pi Epsilon Gamma, Sigma Nu. Home: SR Box 30320 F 5.5 Mile Farmers Loop Rd Fairbanks AK 99701 Office: Dean Engring U Alaska Fairbanks AK 99701

HANES, DAVID GORDON, lawyer; b. N.Y.C., July 7, 1941; s. John Wesley and Hope (Yandell) H.; m. Ann Derby Gulliver, Sept. 10, 1966; children: Allison, Jonathan. B.A. magna cum laude with exceptional distinction, Yale U., 1966; J.D. cum laude, Columbia U., 1969. Bar: N.Y. 1970, D.C. 1971, U.S. Supreme Ct. 1981. Law clk. to Mr. Justice Reed, U.S. Supreme Ct., 1969; sr. law clk. to Mr. Chief Justice Burger, U.S. Supreme Ct., 1970; asso. firm Wilmer, Cutler & Pickering, Washington, 1972-74; spl. asst. to John Doar, Counsel to House Judiciary Com. for Impeachment Inquiry, 1974; exec. asst. to adminstr. FEA, Washington, 1975-77; founding partner firm Colby, Miller & Hanes, Washington, 1977-79; partner firm Reid & Priest, N.Y.C. and Washington, 1979—; mem. Nat. Adv. Commn. on Criminal Justice Standards and Goals, Police Task Force, 1972-73. Author: The First British Workmen's Compensation Act, 1897, 1968; bd. editors: Columbia Law Rev, 1968-69. Bd. dirs. Family and Child Services, Washington, 1972-76, vice chmn., 1975-76; trustee Conn. Coll., 1973-83, chmn. audit and mgmt. com., 1978-83; trustee Sheridan Sch., 1983—. Served with USMC, 1961-64. Mem. Am. Bar Assn., Fed. Bar Assn., D.C. Bar Assn., Fed. Energy Bar Assn., Phi Beta Kappa. Republican. Roman Catholic. Clubs: Links, Knickerbocker (N.Y.C.); Capitol Hill (life), Metropolitan, Chevy Chase (Washington). Home: 5071 Sedgwick St NW Washington DC 20016 Office: 1111 19th St NW Washington DC 20036

HANES, FRANK BORDEN, shopping center executive, farmer, author; b. Winston-Salem, N.C., Jan. 21, 1920; s. Robert March and Mildred (Borden) H.; m. Barbara Mildred Lasater, Dec. 3, 1942; children: Frank Borden, Nancy Hanes White, Robin March Hanes Kent. B.A., U. N.C., 1942. Columnist, feature writer, reporter, copy editor Winston-Salem Jour. and Sentinel, 1946-49; vice chmn., dir. Mchts. Devel. Co.; shopping center Winston-Salem, 1964—; dir. Chatham Mfg. Co., Elkin, N.C., Hanes Dye & Finishing Co., Winston-Salem. Author: Abel Anders, 1951, The Bat Brothers, 1953, The Fleet Rabble, 1961, Journey's Journal, 1958, Jackknife John, 1964, The Seeds of Ares, 1977, The Garden of Nonentities, 1983. Chmn. com. for endowed professorships U. N.C., 1965-67; chmn. Friends of U. N.C. Library, 1966-68, Old Salem, Inc., 1968-70, Summit Sch., 1959-62; pres. Winston-Salem Operetta Assn., 1949-50, Winston-Salem Arts Council, 1955-56, N.C. Lit. and Hist. Assn., 1973-74; mem. bd. visitors U. N.C., 1980—; chmn. Arts and Sci. Found., 1976—; trustee John Motley Morehead Found.; chmn. John W. and Anna Hodgin Hanes Found.; bd. visitors U. N.C. Press, N.C. Soc.; bd. dirs. N.C. Children's Home Soc. Served with USNR, 1942-45. Recipient Roanoke Chowan award for poetry N.C. Lit. and Hist. Assn., 1953; award Winston-Salem Arts Council, 1957; Cum Laude Soc. award Woodberry Forest Sch., 1961; Sir Walter Raleigh award for fiction, 1961; Distinguished Alumnus award U. N.C., 1975; Distinguished Service medal U. N.C. Alumni Assn., 1978. Mem. P.E.N., N.C. Writers Conf. (chmn. 1951-52), N.C. Quarter Horse Assn. (pres. 1963-64), Order of Gimghoul (pres. 1940-41), Order of Minotaur (pres. 1941-42), Sigma Alpha Epsilon. Clubs: Rotarian., Old Town (Winston-Salem); Rancheros Visitadores (Santa Barbara, Calif.); Roaring Gap (N.C.) (pres. 1976-78); Cane River (Pensacola, N.C.); Rainbow Springs (Macon County, N.C.). Home: 1057 W Kent Rd Winston-Salem NC 27104

HANES, FRED WILLIAM, librarian; b. Vandalia, Ill., Aug. 21, 1920; s. Frederick Marion and Mildred (Yost) H.; m. Betty Louise Haines, June 14, 1947; children: Julia Rae, Daniel Bruce, Jennifer Gail. A.B., Earlham Coll., 1946; M.A., Ind. U., 1951. High Sch. tchr., Nevis, Minn., 1947-49; reference and circulation librarian Ind. U. Library, 1951-58; lectr. div. library sci., 1956; bibliographer Am. lit. group Modern Lang. Assn. in preparation publ., Am. Lit. Manuscripts, 1957-58; dir. libraries Ind. State U., Terre Haute, 1958-67, 68-71, dean library services, 1971-74; dir. libraries U. Tex. at El Paso, 1974—; librarian Humboldt State Coll., Arcata, Calif., 1967-68; library dir. Inst. Edn. and Research, U. Punjab, Lahore, West Pakistan, also; prof. library sci., auspices AID, 1961-63; exec. sec. S.W. Acad. Library Consortium, 1975-78. Trustee AMIGOS Bibliog. Council, 1977—. Served with USAAF, 1943-45. Decorated Belgium Fourragere. Mem. Am., Tex., Border-Regional, Southwestern library assns., Delta Sigma Phi. Home: 1012 Esplanada El Paso TX 79932 *In my own life I have seen that the greatest accomplishments have resulted from accepting tasks that seemed too big or too difficult. I think that the fear of failure expands the mind, sharpens the senses, increases creativity, hones the perceptions. Growth is never more rapid than when one seeks to fill a space that seems too large.*

HANES, GORDON, former hosiery manufacturing company executive; b. Winston-Salem, N.C., Mar. 3, 1916; s. James Gordon and Emmie (Drewry) H.; m. Helen Greever Copenhaver, Aug. 30, 1941; children: James Gordon III, Eldridge C., Margaret Drewry. B.A., Yale U., 1937; student, Pace Inst., 1937-39; H.H.D. (hon.), N.C. State U. Acct., Hanes Hosiery Mills Co., Winston-Salem, N.C., 1939-41, sec., 1947-48, v.p., 1948-53, exec. v.p., 1954-57, pres., 1958-65; pres., chief exec. officer Hanes Corp., 1967-74, chmn. bd., 1965-79, also dir., ret. 1979; dir. Hanes Dye & Finishing Co. State senator N.C., Forsyth County, 1963-65; chmn. bd. trustees N.C. Mus. Art; mem. assocs. exec. com. Smithsonian Instn.; trustee Folger Library; mem. nat. collectors' com. Whitney Mus. Art; mem. collectors' and adv. com. Nat. Gallery Art. Served as adminstrv. officer Ordnance USNR, 1941-45. Address: 480 Shepherd St Winston-Salem NC 27103

HANES, JAMES HENRY, chemical company executive; b. Houston, Dec. 23, 1922; s. Ralph Davis and Mable Mae (Anderson) H.; m. Doris Marilyn Hall, Sept. 1950; children: Douglas, Stephen, Barbara, Constance. B.S. with honors, Rose-Hulman Inst., 1944; J.D., U. Mich., 1951. Bar: Mich. 1951, Okla. 1955, Colo. 1974, U.S. Supreme Ct. 1976. With Dow Chem. Co., U.S.A., 1946-48, 51—, dir. indsl. relations, 1968-72, gen. mgr., Golden, Colo., 1972-74, gen. counsel, Midland, Mich., 1974—, v.p., 1976—, also mem. public issues com., retirement bd.; dir. Dorinco Reins. Co., First Nat. Bank, Boulder, Colo., 1973-74. Mem. gen. fund com. Saginaw Valley State Coll., 1976—; bd. dirs. Midland Hosp. Center, 1975—, chmn., 1977-79, chmn. fin. com., 1979-82, chmn. personnel com., 1982—; bd. dirs. Midland United Way, 1970-72; active local Boy Scouts Am. Served to lt. (j.g.) USNR, 1944-46. Recipient Individual Contbns. award Soc. Mfg. Engrs., 1974, Safety award Life is Fragile Club, 1974. Mem. NAM, Mich. Bar Assn., Colo. Bar Assn., Okla. Bar Assn., Midland County Bar Assn. (past pres.), Chem. Mfrs. Assn. (gen. counsel com.), Nat. Legal Center Public Interest (lawyers adv. com.). Presbyterian. Clubs: Rotary, Masons (32 deg.). Address: 2030 Dow Center Midland MI 46840

HANES, RALPH PHILIP, JR., textile company executive; b. Winston-Salem, N.C., Feb. 25, 1926; s. Ralph Philip and Dewitt (Chatham) H.; m. Joan Audrey Humpstone, Jan. 14, 1950 (dec. Jan. 1983). Grad., Woodberry Forest Sch., 1944; student, U. N.C., 1944-46; B.A., Yale U., 1949; L.H.D. (hon.), St. Andrews Coll., Laurinburg, N.C., 1981. With Hanes Co., Inc. (formerly Hanes Dye and Finishing Co.), Winston-Salem, N.C., 1950—; pres. Hanes Dye and Finishing Co., 1965-68, chmn. bd., 1968—, Ampersand, Inc., 1976—. Bd. dirs. Nat. Cultural Center for the Performing Arts, 1962-65; mem. Nat. Council Arts, 1965-70, mem. adv. music panel, 1970-72; bd. dirs. Am. Symphony Orch. League, 1958-61, Moravian Music Found., 1963-65; trustee Salem Coll., 1961-64; bd. dirs. Jargon Soc. Inc., 1968—, pres., 1968-75; chmn., founder N.C. State Arts Council, 1964-66; founder Am. Council Arts, bd. dirs., 1960-69, pres., 1964-66, vice chmn., 1967-69; bd. visitors Barter Theatre, State Theatre of Va., 1967-75; mem. nat. adv. com. Brevard Sch. Music, 1969-74; trustee, exec. com. N.C. Sch. Arts, 1966-78; mem. nat. adv. com. Am. Crafts Council, 1970-72, Appalachian Trail Conf., 1973-76; asso. fellow Jonathan Edward Coll., Yale U., 1971-74; chmn. Yale U. Council Com. on Music, 1970-73; bd. dirs. Nat. Audubon Soc., 1972-78, John W. and Anna H. Hanes Found., 1974—, S. Appalachian Highlands Conservancy, 1974-78, Old Salem, Inc., 1974-77, Izaak Walton League Am., 1974-78, Nature Conservancy, 1975-79, Kennedy Center for the Performing Arts, 1975-80; mem. internat. council Mus. Modern Art, 1978—; bd. dirs. Salzburg Seminar of Am. Studies, 1978—82, Spoleto Festival, 1979—; arts cons. govts. of, Austria, 1978 arts cons. govts. of, P.R., 1978; bd. dirs. Nat. Council Friends of Kennedy Center, 1975-80, Nat. Mus. Am. Art, Renwick Gallery, 1976—, Alliance for Arts Edn., 1976-79; mem. exec. com. Nat. Council for Arts and Edn., 1976-79; mem. adv. council on arts Fed. Res. Bank of Richmond (Va.), 1977-78; bd. dirs. Am. Land Trust, 1976—, Bus. Com. for Arts, 1980—; mem. Gov.'s Council Bus., Arts and Humanities, 1977—; mem. fine arts com. Fed. Res. Bank of Washington, 1979-81; mem. adv. bd. Pauline Koner Dance Consort, 1977-80; bd. dirs. Arts Internat., 1981—, Arts Resources Corp., 1981-83; adv. com. Am. Farmland Trust, 1983—. Named Young Man of Yr. Winston-Salem Jaycees, 1958, N.C. Jaycees, 1958; recipient Gov.'s award for preservation of natural areas, 1969, public service award State of N.C., 1976, Morrison award for the Arts, 1977, Swan award, 1979, N.C. Soc. of N.Y.C. award, 1979, Community Service award Winston-Salem Urban League, 1979, Conservation awardrd Gulf Oil Co., 1982, award for disting. service to arts Nat. Gov's Assn., 1982, N.C. Gov's award in fine arts, 1982, awards Winston-Salem chpt. NAACP, 1983. Mem. Am. League Anglers, Potomac Appalachian Mountain Club, S.E. Council on Founds., Trout Unlimited, World Bus. Council, Appalachian Consortium, East African Wildlife Soc., Izaak Walton League, Nat. Wildlife Fedn., N. Am. Mycological Assn., Pa. Acad. Fine Arts, Royal Soc. Arts, Wilderness Soc., Walpole Soc., Appalachian Trail Conf. Clubs: Century Assn., Yale (N.Y.C.); Met. (Washington); Peale for Visual Arts (Phila.); Cane River, Currituck, Roaring Gap, Old Town. Home: Box 749 Winston Salem NC 27102 Office: Ampersand Inc 820 Buxton St Winston Salem NC 27101

HANESIAN, DERAN, chemical engineering and chemistry educator, consultant; b. Niagara Falls, N.Y., Sept. 26, 1927; s. Vahan and Anna (Kabasakallian) H. B.Ch.E., Cornell U., 1952, Ph.D., 1961. Registered profl. engr., N.Y., N.J. Prodn. engr. E.I. duPont de Nemours, Niagara Falls, 1952-57, research engr., Deepwater, N.J., 1960-63; prof., chmn. dept. chem. engring. and chemistry N.J. Inst. Tech., 1963—; research engr. E.I. duPont, 1964-67, Exxon, Florham Park, N.J., 1967-70; tchr. Celanese, 1977, 80, Algerian Petroleum Inst., 1978; vis. prof. U. Edinburgh, 1981. Served with U.S. Army, 1946-46. Recipient Robert Van Houten award N.J. Inst. Tech., 1977; Fulbright grantee Erevan Poly. Inst., Armenia, USSR, 1981; Deutscher Akademischer Austauschdienst grantee; NSF grantee, 1967, 72. Fellow Am. Inst. Chem. Engring.; mem. Am. Chem. Soc., Am. Soc. Engring. Edn., Sigma Xi, Omega Chi Epsilon, Alpha Chi Sigma, Tau Beta Pi, Omicron Delta Kappa. Armenian Apostolic. Home: 230 Centre St Nutley NJ 17110 Office: New Jersey Institute of Technology 323 High St Newark NJ 07102

HANEY, PAUL DUNLAP, environ. engr.; b. Kansas City, Mo., Feb. 5, 1911; s. Wille Merrit and Mae (Dunlap) H.; m. Nell Cecilia Rezac, Feb. 2, 1935; 1 son, Paul Alan. B.S. in Chem. Engring, U. Kans., 1933; M.S. in San. Engring, Harvard U., 1937. Registered profl. engr., Kans., Mo., Ohio. With div. san. engring. Kans. State Dept. Health, Lawrence, 1934-47; asso. prof. san. engring. Sch. Public Health, U. N.C., Chapel Hill, 1947-48; commd. engr. officer USPHS, Cin., 1948-54; partner, engring. cons. Black & Veatch (Cons. Engrs.), Kansas City, Mo., 1954—; cons. in field. Contbr. articles to profl. jours. Mem. Nat. Acad. Engring., Am. Water Works Assn. (hon. mem., Diven medal 1971), Water Pollution Control Fedn. (hon. mem.; past pres., Bedell award 1970, Emerson award 1975, Orchard medal 1979), Am. Acad. Environ. Engrs. (Cleary award 1977), ASCE, Am. Inst. Chem. Engrs., Am. Chem. Soc., AAAS, Am. Public Health Assn., APWA, Nat. Soc. Profl. Engrs., Kans. Engring. Soc., Sigma Xi. Clubs: Carriage (Kansas City); Cosmos (Washington). Home: 18 LeMans Ct Prairie Village KS 66208 Office: 1500 Meadow Lake Pkwy Kansas City MO 64114

HANEY, RAYMOND LEE, gas and electric company executive; b. Piedmont, Kans., Dec. 9, 1939; s. Carl Wilburn and Imogene (Johnson) H.; m. Linda Jo Amis, Nov. 2, 1967; children: Laura Jo, Paul Lee, Kevin Seth, Kimberly Ann. B.S., Brigham Young U., 1970, M.B.A., 1972. Mgr. fin. services San Diego Gas and Electric Co., 1979-80, mgr. fin. services, asst. treas., 1980-81, treas., 1981-83, v.p. fin., treas., 1983—; dir. New Albion Resources, San Diego, Japatul Corp., Califia Co. Served with USN, 1957-60. Mem. Fin. Execs. Inst., Nat. Corp. of Corporate Treas. Republican. Mormon. Home: 10621 Queen Ave San Diego CA 92041 Office: San Diego Gas and Electric Co PO Box 1831 San Diego CA 92112 *I feel that devotion to and sucess in the home is much more important than any other award of honor.*

HANFLING, MARTIN A., business executive; b. Bklyn., July 26, 1934; s. Herman M. and Sadie (Smith) Henfling; m. Alisa Reich, Sept. 3, 1959; children: Dan, Jonathan. B.S., NYU, 1956, M.B.A. with distinction, 1963. Project mgr. Airco Inc. Comml. Research, N.Y.C., 1964, mgr. mktg. research welding products, 1965-67, asst. to chmn. bd., 1968-76, gen. mgr. ednl. services, Montvale, N.J., 1977-79, pres., 1979—. Served with U.S. Army, 1956-58. Mem. Am. Mktg. Assn., Nat. Assn. Trade and Tech. Schs., Assn. Ind. Schs. and Colls. Office: Airco Educational Services 85 Chestnut Ridge Rd Montvale NJ 07675

HANFLING, ROBERT IRWIN, energy/fin. cons., former govt. ofcl.; b. Bklyn., Apr. 12, 1938; s. Herman Milton and Sadie (Smith) H.; m. Phyllis Ann Schwartz, June 21, 1964; children—Joshua Lawrence, Diane Ruth, Benjamin George. B.Ch.E., Rensselaer Poly. Inst., 1959; M.S., W.Va. U., 1961; M.B.A., CCNY, 1966. With Union Nuclear Corp., 1961-71, dir. planning, until 1971; v.p., dir. Transfer Systems, Inc., 1971-72; investment mgr. Technol. Investment Mgmt. Corp., 1972-74, Fed. Energy Adminstrn., U.S. Dept. Energy, 1975-80; dep. under-sec. Dept. Energy, Washington, 1980—; pres. Robert I. Hanfling Assos. Ltd., cons. in energy and finance. Home: 5521 Chevy Chase Pkwy NW Washington DC 20015 Office: 1200 18th St NW Suite 610 Washington DC 20036

HANFMANN, GEORGE MAXIM ANOSSOV, archaeologist, curator, educator; b. Petersburg, Russia, Nov. 20, 1911; came to U.S., 1934, naturalized, 1940. Dr. Phil., U. Berlin, 1934; student, U. Jena, Munich U.; Ph.D., Johns Hopkins, 1935; M.A., Harvard, 1949. Successively jr. prize fellow, instr., asst. prof. Harvard, 1935-43, asst. prof., 1945-49, asso. prof. fine arts, 1949-56, prof., 1956—, John E. Hudson prof. archeology, 1971—; curator classical art Fogg Art Mus., 1946-74; dir. archeol. exploration, Sardis, 1958-78; mem. Inst. Advanced Study, Princeton, 1947-48, 71-72; visitor classical dept. Mus. Fine Arts, Boston; mem. mng. com. Am. Sch. Classical Studies in

Athens.; U.S. editor OWI, 1943-44; chief German sect. ABSIE, 1943-45. Author books, monographs; exhbn. catalogues, articles and revs. Fellow Am. Acad. Arts and Scis., Soc. Antiquaries London (Eng.), Brit. Acad. (corr.); mem. Instituto di Studi Etruschi Florence, German, Austrian archeol. insts., Archeol. Inst. Am. (gold medal for disting. archaeol. achievement 1979), Socs. Hellenic and Roman Studies, Am. Schs. Oriental Research, Am. Research Center Egypt, Acad. Mainz, Academie des Inscriptions et Belles Lettres France (corr.), Am. Philos. Soc., Brit. Inst. Persian Studies, Phi Beta Kappa. Address: Fogg Art Museum Cambridge MA 02138

HANFORD, GEORGE HYDE, educational administrator; b. Cambridge, Mass., July 29, 1920; s. Alfred Chester and Ruth Hyde H.; m. Elaine Halstead, Sept. 15, 1942; children: Anne Catherine Hanford Stossel, Mary Lee Hanford Brown. B.A., Harvard U., 1941, M.B.A., 1943. Asst. dean Harvard Grad. Sch. Bus. Adminstrn., 1946-48; treas., bus. mgr., tchr., coach N. Shore Country Day Sch., Winnetka, Ill., 1948-55; treas., then v.p., exec. v.p. Coll. Entrance Exam. Bd., N.Y.C., 1955-79, pres., 1979—. Former trustee Nat. Scholarship Service and Fund Negro Students, Dwight Sch., Ednl. Testing Service, United Bd. Coll. Devel.; Trustee Thomas A. Edison State Coll., Am. Council on Edn., Eastern Ednl. Consortium. Served with USNR, 1943-46. Episcopalian. Clubs: Harvard (N.Y.C.); Tenafly Tennis. Office: 888 Seventh Ave New York NY 10106

HANFT, RUTH S. SAMUELS (MRS. HERBERT HANFT), economist; b. N.Y.C., July 12, 1929; d. Max Joseph and Ethel (Schechter) Samuels; m. Herbert Hanft, June 17, 1951; children: Marjorie Jane, Jonathan Mark. B.S., Cornell U., 1949; M.A., Hunter Coll., 1963. Cons. Urban Med. Econs. Project, Hunter Coll., N.Y.C. and D.C. Dept. Health, 1962-63; health economist Office of Research and Stats., Social Security Adminstrn., Washington, 1964-66; chief grants mgmt., health div. Office Econ. Opportunity, Washington, 1966-68; sr. health analyst Office of Asst. Sec. Planning and Evaluation, HEW, Washington, 1968-71, spl. asst., asst. sec. health, 1971-72, dep. asst. sec. for health policy, research and stats., 1977-79, dep. asst. sec. for health reserach, stats. and tech., 1979-81; health care cons., 1982—; vis. prof. Dartmouth Med. Sch., 1976—; Sr. research asso. Inst. Medicine-Nat. Acad. Scis., Washington, 1972-76. Contbr. articles to profl. jours. Fellow Am. Public Health Assn., Royal Soc. Health, Hastings Inst. Bioethics; mem. Inst. Medicine of Nat. Acad. Sci. Jewish. Home: 3609 Cameron Mills Rd Alexandria VA 22305 Office: 2233 Wisconsin Ave NW Washington DC 20007

HANGA, FRED, JR., economist, educator; b. Cortland, N.Y., Sept. 4, 1931; s. Fred and Bertha (Rimkevicz) H.; m. Diane Moskowitz, Dec. 23, 1956; children—Lisan, Alex Evan. A.B., Syracuse U., 1957, Ph.D., 1963; M.A., New Sch. for Social Research, 1959. Fiscal economist U.S. Bur. Budget, Washington, 1962-63; asst. prof. econs. Lehigh U., 1963-64; prof. polit. economy, dir. polit. economy programs Grad. Sch. Pub. Affairs, State U. N.Y. at Albany, 1964-67; prof. econs. State U. N.Y. at Cortland, 1967—; fiscal adviser Harvard Adv. Group attached to Dept. Planning, Govt. of Liberia, 1969-70, UN Devel. Program, Govt. of Liberia, 1971, Harvard Inst. Internat. Devel. attached to Tehran Devel. Council Secretariat, Govt., Iran, 1977; cons. Joint Legislative Com. on Fiscal Analysis and Rev., N.Y. State Legislature, 1969. Served with inf. AUS, 1950-53; honor guard Tomb Unknown Soldier, 1953. Mem. Am. Econ. Assn. Home: 38 W Court St Cortland NY 13045

HANGEN, JOHN, JR., paper manufacturing company executive; b. Dayton, Ohio, Feb. 23, 1924; s. Cleo John and Glenna (Welsh) H.; m. Eleanor Mae Krauss, Mar. 2, 1946 (div. June 1976); children—Diane, Ronald; m. Beverly Arlene Hawn, May 7, 1977. Grad., Internat. Accountants Soc., 1950. With NCR Corp., Dayton, 1941-78, controller, 1961-64, v.p. finance, 1964-72, v.p. corp. affairs, 1972-75, sr. v.p. corp. affairs, 1975-77, sr. v.p. media products group, Appleton, Wis., 1977-78; also dir.; chmn. bd., chief exec. officer Appleton Papers Inc. subs. BAT Industries, 1978—; dir. Copeland Corp., Standard Oil Co. Ohio, 1st Nat. Bank, Appleton, Batus Corp. Home: 1511 Briarcliff Dr Appleton WI 54915 Office: Appleton Papers Inc Appleton WI 54911

HANGER, CHARLES ERNEST, lawyer; b. Oakland, Calif., Feb. 23, 1924; s. Samuel McLean and Mae Claudia (Stanifer) H.; m. Ann Folger, Sept. 4, 1948 (div.); children: Dean C., Susan S.; m. Faye Ellene Williams, Sept. 5, 1953; 1 dau., Julie; stepchildren: Gilbert Foerster, Deborah Clemmer. B.A., U. Calif.-Berkeley, 1948, LL.B., 1950. Bar: Calif. 1951, U.S. Supreme Ct. 1968. Assoc. Steinhart Office, San Francisco, 1951-59; assoc. Brobeck, Phleger & Harrison, San Francisco, 1959-61, ptnr., 1962—. Served to 1st lt. U.S. Army, 1943-45. Decorated Purple Heart. Fellow Am. Coll. trial Lawyers (state chmn. 1981-83), Am. Coll. Trial Lawyers (regent 1983—); mem. ABA, Calif. Bar Assn., San Francisco Bar Assn. Republican. Episcopalian. Clubs: St. Francis Yacht, Merchants Exchange (San Francisco). Home: 12 Woodside Way PO Box 1344 Ross CA 94957 Office: Brobeck Phleger & Harrison Spear St Tower San Francisco CA 94105

HANHAM, HAROLD JOHN, educator, dean; b. Auckland, New Zealand, June 16, 1928; came to U.S., 1968; s. John Newman and Ellie (Malone) H.; m. Ruth Soulé Arnon, Jan. 27, 1973. B.A., Auckland Univ. Coll., U. N.Z., 1948, M.A., 1950; Ph.D., Selwyn Coll., Cambridge (Eng.) U., 1954; A.M. (hon.), Harvard, 1968. Asst. to lectr. to sr. lectr. govt. U. Manchester, 1953-63; prof. politics, head dept. U. Edinburgh, Scotland, 1963-68; prof. history Harvard, 1968-73; prof. history and polit. sci., dean Sch. Humanities and Social Sci., Mass. Inst. Tech., Cambridge, 1973—; examiner African univs., 1964-69. Author: Elections and Party Management, 1959, The Nineteenth Century Constitution, 1969, Scottish Nationalism, 1969, Bibliography of British History, 1851-1914, 1976. Guggenheim fellow, 1972-73. Mem. Am. Acad. Arts and Scis., Royal Hist. Soc., Hist. Assn., Am. Hist. Assn., Econ. Hist. Soc., Polit. Studies Assn., Royal Commonwealth Soc. Clubs: St. Botolph (Boston); United Oxford and Cambridge Univ. (London); Harvard (N.Y.C.). Home: 4 Coolidge Hill Rd Cambridge MA 02138

HANIFAN, JAMES MARTIN MICHAEL, professional football coach; b. Compton, Calif., Sept. 21, 1933. B.A., U. Calif., 1955. Profl. football player CFL, Toronto, Ont., 1955; asst. coach Yuba Jr. Coll., 1959-61; head coach Charter Oak High Sch., Covina, Calif., 1962-63; asst. coach Glendale City Coll., 1964, 65, U. Utah, 1966-69, U. Calif., 1970-71, San Diego State U., 1972, St. Louis Cardinals, NFL, 1973-78, head coach, 1980—; asst. coach San Diego Chargers, 1979. Office: St Louis Cardinals 200 Stadium Plaza Saint Louis MO 63102 *

HANIFEN, RICHARD CHARLES, bishop; b. Denver, June 15, 1931; s. Edward Anselm and Dorothy Elizabeth (Ranous) H. B.S., Regis Coll., 1953; S.T.B., Cath. U., 1959, M.A., 1966; J.C.L., Pontifical Lateran U., Italy, 1968. Ordained priest Roman Catholic Ch., 1959; asst. pastor Cathedral Parish, Denver, 1959-66; sec. to archbishop Archdiocese Denver, 1968-69, chancellor, 1969-76; aux. bishop of, Denver, 1974—. Office: 29 W Kiowa St Colorado Springs CO 80903

HANIGAN, JOHN LEONARD, manufacturing executive; b. N.Y.C., Aug. 15, 1911; s. John P. and Winifred L. (Brennan) H.; (dec.)children: Joan C., John F. Student, Stevens Inst. Tech., 1930-33; grad. advanced mgmt. program, Harvard U., 1944. With R. H. Macy & Co., N.Y.C., 1933-35; with Corning Glass Works, N.Y., 1937-62, v.p., 1953-62; pres. Corning Glass Works Can., Ltd., 1957-62; exec. v.p. Dow Corning Corp., 1962-63; pres., dir., mem. exec. com. Brunswick Corp., 1963-76, chief exec. officer, 1966-76, chmn. exec. com., dir., 1976-83; chmn. bd. Genesco Inc., Nashville, 1977-84, also dir.; dir. Allis-Chalmers Corp., Nat. Can Corp. Office: Genesco Inc Genesco Park 230 Nashville TN 37202

HANIGAN, LAWRENCE, transit commn. exec.; b. Notre-Dame-de, Stanbridge, Can., Apr. 3, 1925; s. John Henry and Alice (Lareau) H.; m. Anita Martin, July 20, 1946; children—Carmen, Doris, Guy, Patricia, Michael. Sales mgr. Boisse Lumber Co., Montreal, 1950-52; regional mgr. Cooper-Widman Ltd., Montreal, 1952-70; mem. City of Montreal Exec. Com., 1970-78; chmn. Montreal Urban Community Exec. Com., 1972-78; chmn., gen. mgr. Montreal Urban Community Transit Commn., 1974—. Mem. Quebec Transport Adv. Council. Mem. Am. Pub. Transit Assn. Washington (v.p.), Transit Devel. Corp. Inc. Washington (dir.), Assn. des Commissaires du Transport urbain du Quebec (dir.), Internat. Union of Pub. Transport of Bruxelles (dir.), Can. Urban Transit Assn. (dir.). Roman Catholic. Club: Saint-Denis. Home: 2360 Charles-Gill St Montreal PQ H3M 1V7 Canada Office: 159 Saint Antoine St W Montreal PQ H2Z 1H3 Canada

HANIGAN, THOMAS EDWARD, JR., industrial executive; b. Schenectady, July 18, 1922; s. Thomas Edward and Jane M. (Fessette) H.; m. Olga Emervk, Oct. 19, 1946; children: Ian Thomas, Vitold Michel. B.A., Union Coll., Schenectady, 1946. With W.R. Grace & Co., N.Y.C., 1946—, beginning as trainee, successively mgr. ins. dept., asst. treas., asst. v.p., 1946-58, v.p., mem. appropriations com., 1958-69, exec. v.p., 1969—, cons., 1980—; dir. Sage Energy Co. Trustee, Trustee Union Coll. Served with AUS, 1943-46. Mem. Nat. Assn. Accountants, Psi Upsilon. Clubs: Lake George, Sky. Home: 41 Sunnybrook Rd Bronxville NY 10708 Office: 1114 Ave of Americas New York NY 10036

HANISH, GREGORY ALBERT, hotel and restaurant company executive; b. Hazelton, Pa., Feb. 7, 1943; s. Albert William and Elizabeth (Chervenak) H.; m. Helen Marie Nemchick, July 29, 1964; 1 dau., Elena. B.S., Pa. State U., 1964. Food and beverage mgr. Loew's Hotels, San Juan, 1964-67, ops. analyst, N.Y.C., 1967-68; owner, operator Guest House/Restaurant, San Juan, 1968-69; ops. mgr. Howard Johnson Co., Braintree, Mass., 1969-72, v.p. ops., 1972-80, group v.p., 1980—. Trustee Jordan Hosp., Plymouth, Mass., 1983. Mem. Am. Hotels and Motel Assn., Nat. Restaurant Assn. Lutheran. Club: Plymouth Country. Home: 5 Tinkertown Ln Duxbury MA 02332 Office: Howard Johnson Co 222 Forbes Rd Braintree MA 02184

HANKE, BYRON REIDT, land planning consultant; b. Mt. Pleasant, Pa., Oct. 28, 1911; s. Emil and Augusta T. (Graf) H.; m. Anne Damon Fisher, Oct. 12, 1938; children: Carol Elizabeth Hanke Teich, Emily Anne Hanke VanZee. B.A., Colgate U., 1933; M.Landscape Architecture, Harvard U., 1937, 1938; M.Urban Planning, 1940. Land planning cons. FHA, 1940-45, dir. land planning, 1945-72; dir. homes assn. study Urban Land Inst., Washington, 1962-64; pres. Byron R. Hanke Assocs., cons. residential land planning and community assns., Washington, 1972—; land planning cons. U.S. Govt. in Dominican Republic, 1967, Japan, 1970; cons. founding Community Assns. Inst., 1973-74. Author: The Homes Association Handbook, 1964, Urban Densities in the U.S. and Japan, 1971, Design Review . . . Architectural Control, 1978, Information System for Community Association Practitioners, 1983; co-author reports, handbooks. Recipient Merit award Nat. Assn. Home Builders, 1969. Fellow Am. Soc. Landscape Architects; mem. Am. Inst. Cert. Planners, Community Assns. Inst. (trustee, Disting. Service award 1978), Urban Land Inst. (exec. group), Phi Beta Kappa, Lambda Alpha (award innovations and publs. 1972). Address: 5320 39th St NW Washington DC 20015

HANKE, STEVEN HAROLD, economist; b. Macon, Ga., Dec. 29, 1942; s. Harold Elmer H. B.S., U. Colo., 1964, Ph.D., 1969. Asst. prof. Colo. Sch. Mines, Golden, 1966-69; mem. faculty Johns Hopkins U., Balt., 1969—, prof. applied econs., 1975—; assoc. prof. U. Calif., Berkeley, 1974-75; sr. economist Pres.'s Council Econ. Advisers, Washington, 1981-82; sr. fellow Heritage Found., Washington, 1983, Manhattan Inst., N.Y.C., 1984—; adj. scholar Cato Inst., Washington. Assoc. editor: Water Resources Bull; bd. advs.: Jour. Austrian Econs.; editorial bd.: The Cato Jour.; contbr. profl. publs. Grantee Urban Inst., EPA, HUD, Am. Water Works Assn. Research Found. Fellow Inst. for Humane Studies; Mem. Am. Econs. Assn., Am. Water Works Assn. Address: Dept Polit Economy Johns Hopkins Univ Baltimore MD 21218

HANKENSON, E. CRAIG, JR., performing arts company executive; b. Mankato, Minn., Apr. 12, 1935; s. Edward Craig and Ethel Irene (Favre) H.; m. Francis Joyce Hall, Mar. 23, 1957 (div. 1980); 1 dau., Meridith Joyce.; m. Catherine Ann Donaldson, 1981; 1 dau., Jennifer Leigh. Mus.B., Eastman Sch. Music, 1957, Mus.M., 1959. Head voice and opera dept. Auburn (Ala.) U., 1959-62; bus. mgr. Chautauqua (N.Y.) Opera Assn., 1958-61, stage mgr., 1957-59, stage dir., 1962; mgmt. intern San Francisco Opera Co., 1962-65; asso. dir. Brevard (N.C.) Mus. Center, 1965-68; gen. mgr. Saratoga (N.Y.) Performing Arts Center, 1968-75, dir., 1975-78; exec. dir. Wolf Trap Found. Performing Arts, Vienna, Va., 1978-81; dir., chmn. dept. arts mgmt. and events U. South Fla., Tampa, 1983—; pres. Producers, Inc. (PICASTAR), 1981—; dir. Rochester (N.Y.) Community Opera, 1957-59; mem. Title III adv. council N.Y. Dept. Edn., 1969-75, N.Y. Gov.'s Commn. on Arts in Edn., 1978; cons. N.Y. Council on Arts; council bd. Rensselaer Poly. Inst.; cons. theater constrn. and mgmt. Concord (Calif.) Pavillion, Robin Hood Dell, Phila. Producer or exec. producer: Great Jazz Pianists, PBS-TV, 1979-81; producer: Brigadoon, Majestic Theatre, N.Y.C., 1980-81; nat. tour of Show Boat, 1980, Kiss Me Kate and Taming of the Shrew, Washington Internat. Jazz Festival, 1980, nat. tour, Pete Fountain, Jerry Mulligan, Pete Fountain and Al Hirt, 1982, 83, Tom Paxton; Translator: Haydn's Lo Speziale, 1958, Smetana's Bartered Bride, 1964; Contbr. articles to profl. jours. Bd. dirs. Capitol Area Resident Opera Co., 1969-71; mem. alumni adv. bd. Eastman Sch. Music, 1974—; mem. com. performing arts Leukemia Soc. Am., Inc.; mem. spl. adv. com. on spl. projects and presenting orgns. Nat. Endowment for Arts, 1979-80. Recipient citation Central Theaters, Moscow, 1973. Mem. Internat. Assn. Concert and Festival Mgrs. (dir.), Performing Arts Assn. N.Y. (pres. 1972), Orgn. Summer Festival Mgrs. (moderator 1971—, dir), N.Y. Fedn. Music Clubs (dir.), Saratoga Springs C. of C. (dir. 1969-72, chmn. promotion com. 1970-72), Council of Pres.'s, Albany League Arts, Saratoga Springs PTA (pres. 1972-73), Phi Mu Alpha (life). Presbyterian (elder) 1969-75). Clubs: Nat. Press, Lions. Home: Tampa FL Office: Coll Fine Arts U South Fla Tampa FL 33620

HANKIN, BERNARD JACOB, lawyer; b. Ewen, Mich., Apr. 6, 1913; s. Harry and Mae (Chudacoff) H.; m. Beatrice Judith Berman, Mar. 17, 1946; children: Janet Ruth, James Alan. A.B., U. Wis., 1934, LL.B., 1937. Bar: Wis. bar 1937. Since practiced in, Milw.; partner firm Kluwin, Dunphy, and Hankin, 1958—. Served with inf. AUS, 1941-45; PTO. Decorated Bronze Star (2), Combat Inf. badge; recipient Vilas medal U. Wis., 1934. Mem. ABA, Milw. Bar Assn. (pres. 1965-66), State Bar Wis., Fedn. Ins. Counsel, Delta Sigma Rho., B'nai B'rith. Jewish religion. Home: 5814 N Kent Ave Milwaukee WI 53217 Office: 788 N Jefferson Milwaukee WI 53202

HANKIN, CHARLES DONALD, life insurance consultant; b. N.J., May 11, 1915. Grad. high sch. With Mut. Life Ins. Co. N.Y., 1933-46; with Occidental Life Ins. Co. Calif., 1946—, v.p., 1969-71, sr. v.p., 1971-80, cons., 1980—; Chmn. med. relations for So. Calif. Health Ins. Assn. Am., 1970-80, chmn. nat. dental relations, 1971-72, chmn. nat. council on consumer and profl. relations, 1974, mem. council on consumer and profl. relations, 1978-80, chmn. nat. health data policy and mgmt. com., 1979-80. Bd. dirs. Beverly Hosp., Montebello, Calif., 1977-80. Served with AUS, 1942-46. Mem. Internat. Claim Assn. (pres. 1970-71, sec. 1973-76, chmn. privacy com. 1977-80), Los Angeles Life and Accident Claim Assn. (pres. 1954). Office: Transam Occidental Life Ins Co 12th at Hill and Olive Sts Los Angeles CA 90015

HANKIN, JOSEPH NATHAN, coll. pres.; b. N.Y.C., Apr. 6, 1940; s. Harry and Beatrice H.; m. Carole G. Hankin, Aug. 20, 1960; children—Marc, Laura, Brian. B.A. in Social Scis, CCNY, 1961; M.A. in History, Columbia U., 1962; Ed.D. in Adminstrn. Higher Edn. (Kellogg fellow), Columbia U., 1967; postgrad. seminar, Harvard U. Grad. Sch. Bus., 1979; Litt.D., Mercy Coll., 1979. N.Y. State Regents coll. teaching fellow CCNY, 1961-63, fellow dept. history, 1962-63, lectr., 1963-65; lectr. history Bklyn. Coll., U. City N.Y., summer, 1963, Queens Coll., summer 1964; course asst. dept. higher and adult edn. Tchrs. Coll., Columbia U., spring 1965, occasional lectr., 1965—, adj. asso. prof. higher and adult edn., 1976—; dir. evening div. and summer session Harford Jr. Coll., 1965-66, dean continuing edn. and summer session, 1966-67, pres., 1967-71, Westchester Community Coll., 1971—; speaker, panelist and cons. in field. Contbr. articles and revs. to profl. publs. and newspapers. Mem. adv. com. Columbia U. Tchrs. Coll. Community Coll. Center, 1970—; bd. dirs., mem. exec. com. Westchester Community Coll. Found., 1971—; treas., 1975—; mem. Tri-State Coll. Consortium (now Eastern Ednl. Consortium), 1975—, pres., 1977—; mem. adv. com. SUNY Ednl. Opportunity Center, 1975—; mem. Council for Arts in Westchester, N.Y., 1971—, mem. coll. adv. com., 1971; mem. arts action plan for Westchester com., 1974-75; mem. Friends of Arts, 1976—; mem. religious sch. com. Congregation Emanu-El, Westchester, 1972-78, bd. dirs., 1975-81, v.p., 1977-79; mem. Westchester Rockland Newspapers Lend-A-Hand Adv. Bd., 1974—; trustee Westchester Econ. Understanding Found., 1979—. Recipient Disting. Service award Bel Air (Md.) Jaycees, 1968, Brotherhood award Westchester region NCCJ, 1975, Championship of Youth award Youth Services div. B'nai B'rith, 1978. Mem. Am. Assn. Jr. Colls. (v.p. 1971-74, pres.'s acad. 1976—), AAUP, Am. Assn. Higher Edn. (charter life), Assn. Pres.'s Public Community Colls., Faculty Student Assn. Westchester Community Coll. (dir. 1971-75), Lower Hudson Council Chief Sch. Adminstrs., N.Y. State Assn. Jr. Colls., Young Presidents Orgn., Phi Delta Kappa, Alpha Beta Gamma (hon.). Home: 4 Merion Dr Purchase NY 10577 Office: 75 Grasslands Rd Valhalla NY 10595 *In order to succeed, to do the best we can at whatever level on whatever path we choose, we do not need brilliance, nor money, nor luck, nor successful parents, nor benign climate, nor even perfect health. We do need belief and hope, imagination and inventiveness, foresight, preparation, and also motivation and perseverence, as well as hard work*

HANKIN, LEONARD J., merchant; b. Bklyn., Apr. 25, 1917; s. Harry and Jennie (Rubin) H.; m. Kathleen Keane, Mar. 14, 1953; children: Kim, Lyn. B.B.A., Coll. City N.Y., 1936; Am. Council Learned Socs. fellow, Cornell U., 1940. With Bergdorf & Goodman Co., N.Y.C., 1935-81, exec. v.p., to 1981; pres. Leonard Hankin Fur Assos., Inc.; dir. U.S. Fashion Exhibit, Moscow, 1959; sr. advisor Maximilian Fur Co. Bd. dirs. Adult Edn. Student League, N.Y.C., 1940; Vice pres. Ednl. Alliance, N.Y.C. Served with OSS, 1943-47. Mem. Beta Gamma Sigma. Home: 5297 Independence Ave Riverdale NY 10471 Office: 20 W 57th St 3d Floor New York NY 10001

HANKINS, JACK FRANKLIN, lawyer; b. Christiansburg, Va., Nov. 26, 1920; s. William Edward and Verna Lee (Griffith) H.; m. Mary Ann Brammer, Dec. 30, 1944; children: Jack Franklin, David G., Michael K., J. Stephen. B.S.B.A., Va. Poly. Inst., 1942; J.D., Washington and Lee U., 1950. Bar: Va. 1949. Staff accountant Leach, Calkins & Scott, 1945-47; instr. acctg. Washington and Lee U., 1947-50; chief accountant Ga.-Pacific Co., 1950-53; individual practice law, practice acctg., Martinsville, Va., 1953-55; sec.-treas. Am. Furniture Co., Martinsville, 1955-75; v.p. fin., treas., dir. Martin Processing, Inc., Martinsville, 1975-81; mem. Broaddus-Epperly-Broaddus, Martinsville, 1981—; dir. Am. Furniture Co., Inc., Va. Nat. Bank, Aldon Industries, Inc. Served to lt. USNR, 1942-45. Decorated D.F.C. with gold star, Air medal with 6 gold stars, Purple Heart. Mem. Fin. Exec. Inst., Martinsville-Henry County C. of C. (pres. 1975), Martinsville Jaycees (pres. 1955, Disting. Service award 1955). Republican. Presbyterian. Lodge: Kiwanis, Martinsville (pres. 1964). Home: 1219 Sam Lions Trail Martinsville VA 24112 Office: PO Box 4146 Martinsville VA 24115

HANKS, JOHN KENNEDY, music educator, singer; b. Purcell, Okla., Oct. 10, 1917; s. John Carl and Elizabeth (Kennedy) H.; m. Shirley Tillotson, 1946 (div. 1976); children: Nancy, Elizabeth, John; m. Joan Tetel, 1950. B.S., Juillard Sch. Music, 1948; M.A., Columbia U., 1950. Asst. prof. music Smith Coll., 1948-54; assoc. prof. Duke U., 1954-65, prof., 1965—; singer Am. art songs in concert worldwide. Author: (rec. anthology and book) The Art Song in America I, 1967, The Art Song in America II, 1975. Served in USAF, 1942-46; CBI; served to col. Res., 1946-75; ret. Recipient Eagle Scout award Boy Scouts Am., 1933; Juilliard fellow, 1941-48. Democrat. Episcopalian. Office: Duke U Dept Music Durham NC 27708

HANKS, ROBERT JACK, writer, consultant, former naval officer; b. Marysvale, Utah, June 28, 1923; s. Arthur Edward and Katherine Peggy (Winters) H.; m. Doris Louise, Nov. 27, 1946; children—Linda Lou, Karen Sue. B.S., U.S. Naval Acad., 1945. Commd. ensign U.S. Navy, 1945, advanced through grades to rear adm., 1972; service at sea, Pacific and Persian Gulf (Bahrain), also Indian Ocean area, comdr., 1972-75; dir. security assistance div. Navy Dept., 1975-76, dir. strategic plans and policy div., 1976-77; ret., 1977, free lance writer, cons., 1977—; sr. politico-mil. analyst Inst. Fgn. Policy Analysis. Author: The Unnoticed Challenge: Soviet Maritime Strategy and the Global Choke Points, 1980, The Cape Route: Imperiled Western Lifeline, 1981, The Pacific Far East: Endangered American Strategic Position, 1981, The U.S. Military Presence in the Middle East: Problems and Prospects, 1982; contbg. author: America Spreads Her Sails, 1972, Sea Power and Strategy in the Indian Ocean, 1981; also numerous articles, books on strategic and polit. affairs. Decorated Legion of Merit (2), Bronze Star; research fellow Center Internat. Affairs, Harvard U., 1970-71. Mem. U.S. Naval Inst. (life, Silver medal Essay contest 1968, 80, Bronze medal 1969, Gold medal 1970, 79), Middle East Inst., U.S. Strategic Inst., Internat. Inst. Strategic Studies. Republican.

HANLE, PAUL ARTHUR, museum administrator; b. Newark, Oct. 27, 1947; s. John Edward and Claire (Kane) H.; m. Joan duBois Burroughs, Oct. 1979. A.B. in Physics, Princeton U., 1969, M.S., Yale U., 1972, M.Phil., 1972, Ph.D. in History of Sci, 1975. Research fellow Smithsonian Instn., Washington, 1973-74, asso. curator, 1974-78, curator of sci. and tech., 1978-80, acting chmn. space sci. and exploration dept., 1980-81, chmn. dept., 1981—. Author: (with Paul Forman) Einstein. A Centenary Exhibition, 1979, Bringing Aerodynamics to America, 1980; Editor: High Technology on Earth, 1979, (with Van Del Chamberlain) Space Science Comes of Age, 1981. NSF intern, 1971; NSF traineeship, 1971-72; recipient Research award Smithsonian Instn., 1978; Robert H. Goddard Hist. Essay award, 1979. Mem. Am. Phys. Soc., History of Sci. Soc., Sigma Xi. Office: Dept Space Science and Exploration National Air and Space Museum Smithsonian Institution Washington DC 20560

HANLEN, JOHN GARRETT, artist; b. Winfield, Kans., Jan. 1, 1922; s. Homer Hartford and Etta Belle (Garrett) H. Student, Pa. Acad. Fine Arts, 1939-43, 46-50, Barnes Found., Merion, Pa., 1942, 43, 47. Gen. critic painting Pa. Acad. Fine Arts, 1953—; prof. drawing, painting Moore Coll. Art, Phila., 1954-83. Exhibited in group shows including, Pa. Acad. Fine Arts anns., 1948—, Detroit Art Inst., 1959, Moore Coll. Art, Phila., 1968, Penn Mus., Harrisburg, Pa., 1971, Rosenfeld Gallery, Phila., 1979, one-man shows include, Peale House, Phila., 1966; Woodmere Art Gallery, Chestnut Hill, Pa., 1973; represented in permanent collections, Library of Congress, Pa. Acad. Fine Arts, War Dept. of Combat Art. Served with Signal Corps, AUS, 1943-46. Decorated Chinese Bronze Star; Tiffany Found. fellow, 1950; Edwin Austin Abbey fellow, 1951; Moore Coll. Art grantee, 1980. Mem. Fellowship Pa. Acad. Fine Arts, Woodmere Art Gallery (fine arts com. 1975—). Home: Logan Sq East #2004 Philadelphia PA 19103

HANLEY, CHARLES, educator; b. Phoenix, May 2, 1920; s. Frank and Tillie (Besse) H.; m. Marilyn Lorrayne Lee, May 23, 1949; children—Lisa, Eve, Matthew, Lila, Charles. B.A., Ariz. State Coll., 1946; M.A., U. Calif. at Berkeley, 1950, Ph.D., 1954. Instr. psychology Mich. State U., East Lansing, 1954-55, asst. prof., 1956-58, asso. prof., 1959-63, prof., 1964—, asst. dean, 1969-76. Served with USNR, 1941-45. Mem. Am. Psychol. Assn., A.A.A.S., N.A.A.C.P., Sigma Xi. Home: 1203 W Grand River East Lansing MI 48823 Office: Dept Psychology Mich State U East Lansing MI 48824

HANLEY, FRANK XAVIER, labor union official; b. N.Y.C., July 5, 1930; s. Simon P. and Sally H.; m. Patricia Healy, 1959; 6 children. Student, U. Notre Dame, 1954-58, trade union program Harvard U., 1959. Mem. Internat. Union Operating Engrs., Washington, 1948—, asst. to gen. pres., 1959-74, v.p., 1974-79, sec.-treas., 1979—. Mem. VFW. Club: Notre Dame. Office: Internat Union Operating Engrs 1125 17th St NW Washington DC 20036 *

HANLEY, JAMES MICHAEL, congressman; b. Syracuse, N.Y., July 19, 1920; s. Michael Joseph and Alice (Gillick) H.; m. Rita Harrington, Aug. 12, 1950; children: Christine Mary, Peter James. LL.D. (hon.), LeMoyne Coll., Syracuse, 1967, Syracuse U., 1980. Funeral dir., Syracuse, 1939—; owner Callahan-Hanley-Mooney Funeral Home, Syracuse, 1953—; mem. 89th-92d congresses from 34d Dist. N.Y., 93d-98th Congresses from 32d Dist. N.Y., mem. banking, finance and urban affairs com., post office and civil service com. and small bus. com., ad hoc com. on Irish affairs. Hon. life comdr. Onondaga County Vets. Council.; Mem. Onondaga County Democratic Com., also campaign coordinator, 1963; trustee Maria Regina Coll., Syracuse, Coll. Environ. Sci. and Forestry, SUNY, Syracuse. Served with AUS, World War II. Named Humanitarian of Yr., Salvation Army, 1980; James M. Hanley Fed. Office Bldg. and Courthouse named in his honor, Syracuse, 1981. Mem. Am. Legion (past post comdr.), Holy Name Soc., Ancient Order Hibernians, Regular Vets. Assn. (past N.Y. comdr.), Nat., N.Y., Onondaga County funeral dirs. assns., Syracuse C. of C., Syracuse Police Benevolent Assn., Army and Navy Union, Order of Alhambra (past grand comdr. Navarre Caravan). Clubs: KC (Syracuse) (past grand knight Syracuse council, Man of Year 1960); Kiwanis, Elks, Antique Auto, All City Veterans (Syracuse). Home: 316 Coleridge Ave Syracuse NY 13204 Office: 1301 Pennsylvania Ave NW Suite 1150 Washington DC 20004

HANLEY, JOHN GERALD, clergyman; b. Read, Ont., Can., Feb. 21, 1907; s. Denis and Jessie (Bryson) H. B.A., U. Toronto, 1927; grad. theology, St. Augustine's Sem., Toronto, 1931; D.D. (hon.), Queen's U., 1973. Ordained priest Roman Cath. Ch., 1931; asst. in cathedral, Kingston, Ont., 1931-32, Trenton, Can., 1934-41; editor Canadian Register, 1941-70; prof. Jr. Sem., Vancouver, B.C., Can., 1932-34; chaplain Newman Club, Queen's U., Kingston, 1941-58; vicar-gen. Archdiocese Kingston, 1969—; nat. chaplain Canadian Newman Clubs, 1944-45, 52-55. Author: Across Canada with Newman, 1957. Chmn. Canadian Cath. Press Commn., 1958-67. Recipient Kingston award Queen's U. Alumni Assn., 1970; Queen Elizabeth II Silver Jubilee medal, 1977; Hon. Achievement award City of Kingston, 1982; hon. Canon St. George's Anglican Cathedral, 1983. Mem. Cath. Press Assn. U.S. and Can. (bd. dirs. 1961-64, sec. 1962-64, 65-68), Cath. Bibl. Assn. Am. (v.p. 1944-45). Address: 279 Johnson St Kingston ON K7L 1Y5 Canada

HANLEY, JOHN JOSEPH, publishing company executive; b. Holyoke, Mass., Oct. 2, 1939; s. John Joseph and Mary Ellen (Flynn) H.; m. Joyce Bernadette Juele, July 2, 1966; children: Kathryn, Mary, John, Anne, Jillean. B.S., U.S. Naval Acad., 1962. Med. editor W.B. Saunders Co., Phila., 1972-74, editor-in-chief, 1974-76, gen. mgr., 1976-80; pres. CBS Profl. Pub., 1980—; chmn., group exec. STM Internat. Pub. Assn. Mem. adv. bd. CARE/Medico. Served to lt. USN, 1959-67. Mem. Am. Med. Pubs. Assn. (pres. 1976-78). Roman Catholic. Clubs: Down Town (Phila.); N.Y. Athletic. Office: CBS Pub Co div W B Saunders Co W Washington Sq Philadelphia PA 19105

HANLEY, JOHN PATRICK, coll. pres.; b. N.Y.C., Feb. 15, 1933; s. John and Margaret H.; (married); children—Christopher, Ian. B.A., CCNY, 1955; M.A., Hunter Coll., 1961; M.B.A., N.Y. U., 1961, also postgrad. Mgmt. analyst Chem. Bank N.Y. Trust, N.Y.C., 1960-64; instr. English N.Y.C. Community Coll. and Sullivan County Community Coll., 1963-66; dean adminstrv. services Mercer County Community Coll., 1966-69, dean instructional research, 1969-70, asst. to pres., 1970-72, dean for planning and devel., 1972-76, pres., 1976—, also prof. bus. Served with U.S. Army, 1956. Office: Mercer County Community Coll Trenton NJ 08690

HANLEY, JOHN THOMAS, consulting engineer; b. Chgo., Mar. 26, 1923; s. William C. and Grace (Prindiville) H.; m. Mary Carolyn Duke, Oct. 22, 1945; children: Judith Ellen, Joan Marie, John Thomas, Barbara Brooks, Michael Davies. B.S., Dartmouth Coll., 1947, M.S., 1948; Ph.D., U. Ill., 1963. Served with C.E., USNR, 1948-58, advanced through grades to lt. comdr., 1956; asst. to chief blast br. (Armed Forces Spl. Weapons Project), Washington, 1949-52; resident officer in charge constrn. Skiffs Creek Annex, Yorktown, Va., 1952-53; pub. works officer, Lake Mead Base, Nev., 1954-56; staff civil engr. hdqrs. Allied Forces Mediterranean, Malta, 1956-58; instr. civil engring. U. Ill., Urbana, 1958-63; asso. head dept. civil engring. U. Minn., Mpls., 1963-71, dir. undergrad. studies Inst. Tech., 1968-71, prof., 1969-71; dir. planning, research and devel. Clark Engring. Co., 1971-73; chmn. bd. Environmental Services, Inc., 1971—; pres. Fowler Hanley, Inc., 1972-78, Hanley Assos., 1978—; cons. Office CD, Washington, 1961-63, Minn. Dept. CD, 1963—, Hart-Carter Co., Mpls., 1964-65, 3M Co., 1966—, Oak Ridge Nat. Lab., 1967-69. Vice pres. Minn. Profl. Engrs. Found., 1969-70, pres., 1970-71. Served to signalman 2d class USNR, 1942-45. Ford Found. fellow, 1960-61. Mem. Nat. Soc. Profl. Engrs. (nat. dir. 1972—), Minn. Soc. Profl. Engrs. (pres. 1971-72), ASCE, Quarter Racing Owners Am. (pres. 1980-81). Home: 5705 Lawndale Ln Plymouth MN 55446 Office: 1207 Harman Pl Minneapolis MN 55403

HANLEY, ROBERT FRANCIS, lawyer, educator; b. Spokane, Wash., June 26, 1924; s. Richard E. and Ada E. (St. Peter) H.; m. Margaret Lungren, June 12, 1947 (div.); children: Kathleen Hanley Creore, Marcia Hanley Hoover, Elizabeth; m. Joan McLaughlin, Mar. 26, 1982. B.S., Northwestern U., 1947, J.D., 1950. Bar: Ill. 1950, Colo. 1983. Asst. atty. gen. State Ill., Chgo., 1952-55; ptnr. Isham Lincoln & Beale, Chgo., 1959-68, Jenner & Block, 1968-82, Morrison & Foerster, Denver, 1982—; mem. faculty Northwestern U., Chgo., 1960-82. Contbr. articles to profl. jours. Served to lt. col. USMC, 1942-64. Fellow Am. Coll. Trial Lawyers, Internat. Soc. Barristers; mem. Nat. Inst. Trial Advocacy (chmn. bd. 1981—), ABA (chmn. sect. litigation 1975-76, ho. of dels. 1977—). Democrat. Clubs: University, Saddle and Cycle (Chgo.). Home: 2552 E Alameda 1 Denver CO 80209 Office: Morrison & Foerster 1670 Broadway Suite 3100 Denver CO 80202

HANLEY, ROBERT LEO, bank holding company executive; b. Milw., July 23, 1943; s. Leo Bernard and Sophia Joan (Wabiszewski) H.; m. Heidi Diane Keck, Aug. 12, 1967; children: Robert Neuman, Kathryn Courtenay. B.B.A. in Fin, U. Notre Dame, 1965; J.D., Marquette U., 1968; diploma, Stonier Grad. Sch. Banking, 1978. Bar: Wis. bar 1968. With Marine Nat. Exchange Bank of Milw., 1968—, asst. v.p., 1976-78, v.p., 1978-82, sec. bd. dirs., 1974-82; v.p., sec. Marine Corp., Milw., 1976-82, v.p., gen. counsel, 1982—; pres., dir. Red Bus Corp., Milw. Bd. dirs. United Performing Arts Fund, Milw., to 1980, Channel 10/36 Friends, Future Milw.; trustee Ripon Coll.; corp. mem. Curative Workshop of Milw. Cath. Home.; voting mem. Wis. Soc. to Prevent Blindness. Mem. State Bar Wis., Assn. Bank Holding Cos., Wis. Bankers Assn. Roman Catholic. Clubs: Univ. (Milw.); Blue Mound Golf and Country (Wauwatosa, Wis.). Home: 4515 N Frederick Ave Whitefish Bay WI 53211 Office: care Marine Corp 111 E Wisconsin Ave Milwaukee WI 53202

HANLIN, HUGH CAREY, life insurance company executive; b. Chattanooga, Mar. 16, 1925; s. Hugh Carey and Irene (Thompson) H.; m. Wilma Jean Deal, June 23, 1951; children: Timothy Carey, Chris Allan. Student, Emory U., 1942-44, 46-47; B.A., U. Mich., 1948. With Provident Life & Accident Ins. Co., 1948—, exec. v.p., 1973-77, pres., 1977—, chief exec. officer, 1979—, dir., 1973—; dir. Provident Gen. Ins. Co., Am. Nat. Bank & Trust Co., Chattanooga., Third Nat. Corp. Bd. dirs. Chattanooga Opera Assn., 1970-79, pres., 1973-74; past pres. Chattanooga-Hamilton County Speech and Hearing Center; bd. dirs. Allied Arts Fund of Chattanooga, pres., 1982-84; bd. dirs. Mocassin Bend council Girl Scouts U.S.A., 1971-75, Girls Club Chattanooga, 1976-77, United Fund Chattanooga, 1979—, Chattanooga YMCA, 1980—, Chattanooga Area Urban League, 1981-83; trustee U. Chattanooga Found., 1977—, Tenn. Ind. Colls. Fund, 1979-80, The Am. Coll., 1981; mem. Tenn. Council on Econ. Edn., 1978-80, Cherokee Area council Boy Scouts Am., 1980—; pres. Cherokee Area council Boy Scouts Am., 1981-82; bd. visitors Berry Coll., Rome, Ga. Served to lt. (j.g.) USNR, 1943-46. Fellow Soc. Actuaries; mem. Southeastern Actuaries Club (pres. 1956-57), Chattanooga C. of C. (downtown devel. com. 1980—), Phi Beta Kappa, Alpha Tau Omega. Presbyterian. Clubs: Mountain City (dir. 1977—), Chattanooga Golf and Country, Rotary. Home: 7472 Preston Circle Chattanooga TN 37421 Office: Provident Life and Accident Ins Co Chattanooga TN 37402

HANLON, C. ROLLINS, physician, educator; b. Balt., Feb. 8, 1915; s. Bernard and Harriet (Rollins) H.; m. Margaret M. Hammond, May 28, 1949; children: Philip, Paul, Richard, Christine, Thomas, Mary, Martha, Sarah. A.B., Loyola Coll., Balt., 1934; M.D., Johns Hopkins U., 1938; D.Sc. (hon.), Georgetown U., 1976. Diplomate Am. Bd. Surgery (chmn. 1966-67). Intern John Hopkins Hosp., 1939-40, W.S. Halsted fellow in surgery, 1939-40, instr. surgery, 1946-48, asst. prof., 1948-50; asst. resident, resident in surgery Cin. Gen. Hosp., 1940-41, 43-44; exchange fellow surgery U. Calif., 1941-42; prof. surgery, chmn. dept. St. Louis U., 1950-69; prof. surgery Northwestern U. Med. Sch., 1969—; Chmn. surgery study sect. NIH, 1965-66; pres. Council Med. Specialty Socs., 1974-75; chmn. Coordinating Council on Med. Edn., 1976-77. Contbr. articles to profl. jours. Served to lt. (j.g.) M.C. USNR, 1944-46; CBI. Recipient Fleur-de-lis award St. Louis U., 1968; Statesmen in Medicine award Airlie Found., 1974. Founder group Am. Bd. Thoracic Surgery (1949); Fellow A.C.S. (gov., regent 1967-69, dir. 1969—), Royal Australasian Coll. Surgeons (hon.), Royal Coll. Surgeons of Eng. (hon.), Royal Coll. Surgeons in Ireland (hon.), Am. Hosp. Assn. (hon.); mem. Am. Heart Assn. (surgery research study com. 1966-68), Internat. Cardiovascular Soc. (pres. N.Am. chpt. 1963-64), Soc. Vascular Surgery (pres. 1968), AMA, Am. Surg. Assn. (sec. 1968-69, pres. 1981-82), Western Surg. Assn., So. Surg. Assn., Soc. Thoracic Surgeons, Central Surg. Assn., Am. Assn. Thoracic Surgery (treas. 1962-68), Soc. U. Surgeons (pres. 1958), Soc. Clin. Surgery (pres. 1968-70), St. Louis Surg. Soc., Johns Hopkins Med. and Surg. Assn. (v.p. 1975-77), Johns Hopkins Soc. Scholars, Alpha Omega Alpha. Roman Catholic. Club: Serra (St. Louis) (1st v.p.). Address: 55 E Erie St Chicago IL 60611

HANLON, JAMES ALLISON, confectionery company executive; b. Oak Park, Ill., Nov. 27, 1937; s. James Graves and Frances (Allison) H.; m. June Weiland, May 30, 1959; children: Perian, Loretta, Jill, James. B.A., U. Notre Dame, 1959; postgrad., London Bus. Sch., 1979, Wharton Sch., 1980. Acct. exec. Needham Harper Steers Advt., Chgo., 1959-67; mktg. mgr. L.S. Heath & Sons, Inc., Robinson, Ill., 1967-70; v.p. mktg. Peter Paul Cadbury, Naugatuck, Conn., 1970-80, pres., 1983—; pres., dir. Cadbury Can., Rexdale, Ont., 1980-83; dir. Cadbury Schweppes & Powell, Rexdale. Served with USMCR, 1956-59. Named Mktg. Warrior of the Year AMR, Inc., N.Y.C., 1980. Clubs: New Haven Country, Farms Country (v.p., gov. 1975-80). Home: 36 Tall Pine Rd Milford CT 06460 Office: Peter Cadbury New Haven Rd Naugatuck CT 06770

HANLON, JOHN JOSEPH, public health administrator, educator; b. Boston, May 7, 1912; s. John Joseph and Florence (Livingston) H.; m. Frances E. Pizzo, June 24, 1939; children: Jon Jerrold, Donald Livingston. B.S., MIT, 1933, M.S., 1934; spl. student, Harvard Sch. Public Health, 1934; M.B., Wayne U., 1940, M.D., 1941; M.P.H., Johns Hopkins U., 1942. Diplomate Am. Bd. Preventive Medicine. Asst. san. engr., Eaton County, Mich., 1934; asst. epidemiologist, statistician Detroit Dept. Health, 1935-40; staff Harper Hosp., Detroit, 1940-41; health officer, Bradley County, Tenn., 1941; dir. nutrition Tenn. Public Health, 1942-43; assoc. prof. public health adminstrn. U. N.C., 1943-44; lectr. preventive medicine Duke U., 1943-44; assoc. prof. U. Mich., 1944-49, prof. public health, 1951-52; chief health Mission, Inst. Inter-Am. Affairs, Bolivia, 1949-51; med. dir. USPHS; chief public health div. U.S. Fgn. Aid Program, 1952-57; dir. public health services, City of Phila., 1957-64; prof., chmn. dept. preventive medicine and public health Temple U. Sch. Medicine, 1957-64; commr. pub. health, Detroit and Wayne County; adj. prof. public health adminstrn. U. Mich.; prof., chmn. dept. community medicine Wayne State U. Sch. Medicine, 1964-68; asst. surgeon gen. USPHS, Washington, 1968-76; prof. pub. health, health program coordinator San Diego State U., 1976—; mem. U.S. del. to World Health Assembly, 1953, 54, 56; chmn. Detroit-Wayne County Community Mental Health Bd., 1964-67. Author: (with Beeuwkes) Nutrition and Public Health, 1945, 47, Principles of Public Health Adminstration, 1950, 55, 60, 64, 69, 74, (with George E. Pickett) Public Health—Administration and Practice, 1979, 8th edit., 1984, Principios de Salud Pública, 1956, 63, Design for Health, 1963, 71, Guias Para La Salud de la Comunidad, 1967, (with others) A Strategy for a Livable Environment, 1967; also articles, bulls. Decorated Order of Condor, Bolivia, 1951; named hon. alumnus Coll. Human Services, San Diego State U., 1979; recipient Disting. Alumnus award Wayne State U., 1968. Fellow Am. Public Health Assn. (pres. 1967-68, presdl. citation 1977, 1st ann. award for excellence in health adminstrn. 1981); hon. fellow Royal Soc. Health, Coll. Medicine of Phila.; mem. Soc. Prospective Medicine (treas. 1976—), Alpha Omega Alpha, Sigma Xi, Delta Omega; hon. mem. Sociedad Boliviana de Salud Pública, Hellenic Public Health Soc. Home: 1553 Calle Candela La Jolla CA 92037

HANN, ROY WILLIAM, JR., civil engineer, educator; b. Oklahoma City, Mar. 21, 1934; s. Roy W. and Irene (Billups) H.; m. Ann Mullman, Dec. 27, 1960 (div. Apr. 1983); children: Kimberly Anne, Sharon Irene, Roy Lee, Karen Bea. B.S., U. Okla., 1956, M.C.E., 1957, Ph.D., 1963. Registered profl. engr., Okla., Tex.; lic. real estate broker, Tex.; lic. comml. pilot. Engr. C.H. Guernsey and Assos., Oklahoma City, 1959-60; asst. prof. civil engring U. S.C., Columbia, 1962-64; asst. prof. civil engring. dept. environ. engring. div. Tex. A&M U., College Station, 1965-67, asso. prof., 1967-71, prof., 1971—, head environ. engring. div., 1970-75, 81—, dir. sea grant program, 1976-77; pres. Civil Engring. Systems, Internat. Spill Tech. Corp., Hann Investments; owner, operator Spring Valley Ranches, cons. civil engring. to various indsl. and mfg. cos., and cons. engrs., 1960—, U.S. Army Corps Engrs., 1967-68, 75-76, Dept. of Justice, 1971-73, EPA, 1974-75, WHO, 1974-75, IMCO, 1978—. Author: Fundamental Aspects of Water Quality Management, 1972; Contbr. numerous articles on computer methods, oil pollution control and water supply, water pollution to profl. jours. Served with USPHS, 1957-59. Recipient Palladium medal Nat. Audubon Soc. and Am. Assn. Engring. Socs., 1983. Mem. ASCE (Paper award 1970, 71, 72), Am. Soc. Engring. Edn., Tex. Soc. Profl. Engrs. (Named Outstanding Young Engr. 1969), Am. Water Works Assn. (Outstanding Paper award 1969), Tex. Water Pollution Control Fedn., World Dredging Assn., Tex. Water Utilities Assn., Sigma Xi, Sigma Chi, Chi Epsilon, Bryan-College Station Apt. Assn. (pres. 1975-76, dir. 1977—), Omicron Delta Kappa, Tau Beta Pi. Home: 1300 Walton Dr College Station TX 77840 Office: Dept Civil Engring Texas A and M University College Station TX 77843

HANNA, ARCHIBALD, JR., librarian; b. Worcester, Mass., Sept. 24, 1916; s. Archibald and Rachel Sutherland (Knight) H.; m. Edith Sue Mensch, June 1, 1940; children—Stewart Billings, Jean, James Diener. A.B., Clark U., 1939; M.A., Yale, 1946, Ph.D., 1951; M.S., Columbia, 1949. Sr. cataloger Yale U. Library, 1949-52; William Robertson Coe curator Yale Collection Western Am., 1952-81; Fellow Ezra Stiles Coll.; Ordained deacon Protestant Episcopal Church, 1961. Served with USMCR, 1942-46; col. Res. ret. Mem. Am. Antiquarian Soc. Clubs: Odd Volumes, St. Botolph. Home: 6 Damascus Rd Branford CT 06405

HANNA, GEOFFREY CHALMERS, Can. govt. research adminstr.; b. Stretford, Lancashire, Eng., Oct. 5, 1920; s. Walter and Dorothy (Cross) H.; m. Barbara Helen Scott, Apr. 7, 1951; children—Christopher Scott, David Scott, Jeremy Scott. B.A., Trinity Coll., Cambridge (Eng.) U., 1941, M.A., 1943. Radar research U.K. Ministry of Supply, 1941-45; nuclear researcher U.K. Mission to Can., 1945-50; with NRC Can. and Atomic Energy Can. Ltd., 1950—; dir. physics div. Chalk River (Ont., Can.) Nuclear Labs., 1967-71, research dir., 1971—. Contbr. articles to profl. publs. Fellow Royal Soc. Can. Anglican. Home: 5 Tweedsmuir Pl Deep River ON K0J 1P0 Canada Office: Chalk River Nuclear Labs Chalk River ON K0J 1J0 Canada

HANNA, GORDON, newspaperman; b. Jack County, Tex., Feb. 22, 1920; s. John Grey and Ethyl (Wood) H.; m. Annie Lou Guidry, Apr. 22, 1941; children—Judith, Harriet. Student, Tex. Technol. Coll., 1936-39. Reporter Port Arthur (Tex.) News, 1939-42; reporter Houston Press, 1943-44, reporter, legislative corr., 1946-48, city editor, 1949-54; mng. editor Comml. Appeal, Memphis, 1954-59; editor Evansville (Ind.) Press, 1959-68, Comml. Appeal, Memphis, 1969-75; gen. editorial mgr. Scripps-Howard Newspapers, 1976—; v.p., dir. E.W. Scripps Co., 1976—. Served with USAAF, 1944-45. Mem. Am. Soc. Newspaper Editors. Office: 1100 Central Trust Tower Cincinnati OH 45202

HANNA, JACK BUSHNELL, zoo director; b. Knoxville, Tenn., Jan. 2, 1947; s. Edwin Ross and Caroline (Bushnell) H.; m. Suzanne Egli, Dec. 20, 1968; children: Kathleen, Suzanne, Julie. B.A., Muskingum Coll., New Concord, Ohio, 1969; postgrad., U. Tenn.; D.Sc. (hon.), Otterbein Coll., 1983. Head curator Knoxville Zool. Park, 1970-72; dir. Central Fla. Zool. Park, Sanford, Fla., 1973-75; v.p., asso. producer Stan Brock Wilderness Adventure Movie Co., 1975-78; exec. dir. Columbus (Ohio) Zool. Park, 1978—; speaker, cons. in field. Asso. producer: documentary The Forgotten Wilderness, 1975; co-host weekly: TV wildlife show Hanna's Ark, 1981. Trustee Muskingum Coll., 1981—, Ohio Leukemia Assn., 1980-81. Served with USAR, 1968-71. Recipient Disting. Alumni award Muskingum Coll., 1980, Citizen of Yr. award Columbus K.C., 1980; named Outstanding Citizen Columbus Jaycees, 1979, 80; recipient Disting. Service award, 1980. Fellow Internat. Wildlife Fedn.; mem. Am. Assn. Zool. Parks and Aquariums, Appalachian Zool. Soc. (dir.), Columbus Zool. Assn. (dir.). Presbyterian. Home: 8900 Turin Hill Ct Dublin OH 43017 Office: 9990 Riverside Dr Powell OH 43065

HANNA, JOHN PAUL, lawyer; b. N.Y.C., July 12, 1932; s. Paul Robert and Jean (Shuman) H.; m. Joyce Adams, June 18, 1955; children: Kristine, Katherine. Grad., Phillips Acad., Andover, Mass., 1950; B.A., Stanford U., 1954, J.D., 1959. Bar: Calif. 1959. Since practiced, Palo Alto; pres. John Paul Hanna (P.C.). Author: Teenagers and the Law, 1967, The Complete Layman's Guide to the Law, 1974, California Condominium Handbook, 1975; Editor, co-author: Youth and the Law, 1963. Mem. Santa Clara County Estate Planning Council, 1963-65; mem. Peninsula Estate Planning Council, 1962-65, chmn. com. new legislation, 1963-65; Vice pres. Univ. and Crescent Park Assn., 1967; sec. Palo Alto chpt. United Fund, 1966-68; founding mem. Palo Altans Town Hall, 1966; mem. Mayor's Com. Planning in the Foothills, 1964—; Mem. Calif. Republican Central Com., 1971—; Trustee Castilleja Sch. Served to 1st lt. AUS, 1954-56. Named Young Man of Year in Palo Alto, 1964; named one of Five Outstanding Young Men Calif., 1967. Mem. ABA, Palo Alto Bar Assn., State Bar Calif., Palo Alto C. of C. (v.p. 1967-68), Delta Tau Delta, Phi Delta Phi. Methodist. Clubs: Elk, Kiwanian (pres. Palo Alto 1968), Menlo Circus (Menlo Park, Calif.)). Home: 137 Atherton Ave Atherton CA 94025 Office: 525 University Ave Palo Alto CA 94301

HANNA, MELVIN WESLEY, educator; b. Glendale, Calif., Oct. 1, 1932; s. Melvin Edward and Juanita Christine (Stallings) H.; m. Sarah Louise Nordstrom, Aug. 31, 1956; children: Gregory James, Steven Russell, John Melvin. B.S., UCLA, 1954; Ph.D., U. Minn., 1959. NSF postdoctoral fellow Calif. Inst. Tech., 1959-60, Arthur A. Noyes teaching fellow, 1960-61; asst. prof. U. Colo. at Boulder, 1961-63, assoc. prof., 1963-66, prof. chemistry, 1966—. Author: Quantum Mechanics in Chemistry, 1969, rev. edit., 1980, Foundation Studies in

General Chemistry, 1976; Contbr. articles sci. jours. Alfred P. Sloan fellow, 1965-67. Mem. Am. Chem. Soc., Phi Beta Kappa. Home: 750 Lincoln Pl Boulder CO 80302

HANNA, MICHAEL GEORGE, JR., immunologist, institute administrator; b. Cleve., July 7, 1936; s. Michael George and Camilla Karem H.; m. Barbara Ann Pearson, Sept. 6, 1958; children: Michael George, Christina Louise, Suzanne Kathleen. B.S. in Biology, Baldwin-Wallace Coll., 1958, M.S., Notre Dame U., 1960; Ph.D., U. Tenn., 1964. Research biologist biology div. Oak Ridge Nat. Lab., 1964-68, dir. immunology of carcinogenesis group, 1968-75; dir. cancer biology, head host tumor interaction sect. cancer biology program Nat. Cancer Inst. Frederick (Md.) Cancer Research Facility, 1975-79; dir. Nat. Cancer Inst. Frederick (Md.) Cancer Research Facility, 1979-82; dir. Litton Inst. Applied Biotechnology, Kensington, Md., 1982—; mem. sci. com. Internat. Conf. on Lymphatic Tissue and Germinal Centers in Immune Response, 1971—. Gen. editor: Contemporary Topics in Immunobiology, 1971—; mem. editorial bd.: Immunopharmacology, 1978—. Mem. Soc. Exptl. Pathology, Am. Assn. Cancer Research, Am. Assn. Immunologists, AAAS, Reticuloendothelial Soc., Sigma Xi. Office: PO Box B Bldg 427 Frederick MD 21701

HANNA, NESSIM, educator, mktg. cons., educator; b. Assiut, Egypt, Apr. 30, 1938; came to U.S., 1961, naturalized, 1973; s. Yanni and Lulu (Shehata) H.; m. Gretchen Lelia Wright, Aug. 18, 1968. B.S. in Commerce, Cairo U., 1958; M.S. in Mktg., U. Ill., 1964, Ph.D. in Mktg, 1969. Asst. prof., chmn. dept. mktg. W.Va. Inst. Tech., Montgomery, 1968-69; asso. prof. bus. adminstrn. Middle Tenn. State U., Murfreesboro, 1969-70; prof. mktg. No. Ill. U., De Kalb, 1970—; mktg. cons. Arab Research and Admintrn. Center, 1975-77, Investments Cons. Internat., 1974-77. Author: Marketing Opportunities in Egypt: A Business Guide, 1977; contbr. articles to profl. jours. Named Outstanding Citizen Citizenship Council Met. Chgo., 1974. Mem. Southwestern Social Sci. Assn., Am. Mktg. Assn., Midwest Bus. Adminstrn. Assn., Assn. Egyptian Am. Scholars, Acad. Mktg. Sci., Am. Inst. Decision Scis., Phi Beta Lambda, Beta Gamma Sigma. Congregationalist. Home: 580 Normal Rd De Kalb IL 60115 Office: Dept Mktg No Ill U De Kalb IL 60115 *

HANNA, PAUL JOHNSTON, banker; b. Cannonsburg, Pa., Sept. 26, 1915; s. George J. and Ethel (Lyon) H.; m. Grace M. Gillen, June 22, 1946; children: Paul Johnston II, Lee E. B.S., U. Pitts., 1939; postgrad., Rutgers U., 1950, Dartmouth Grad. Sch. Credit and Financial Mgmt., 1955. With Citizen's Trust Co., Canonsburg, 1939-41; sr. v.p. nat. div. Mfrs. Hanover Trust Co., N.Y.C., 1946-72; exec. v.p. Mfrs. Hanover Corp., 1972-78, mem. adv. bd., 1978—; vice chmn. GEICO Corp., 1978-82, dir., vice chmn. inventory com., 1982—; dir. United Jersey Banks, a; Holding Co., Princeton, N.J., GEC, GEC of N.J., Govt. Employees Fin. Services Co. Md., GEICO Fin. Co. N.C., GEIBANK, Govt. Employees Fin. & Indsl. Loan Corp., Banner Life Ins. Co., Banner Life Ins. Co. N.Y., United Jersey Bank Hackensack, N.J.; chmn. Govt. Employees Fin. Corp.; vice chmn. Govt. Employees Ins. Co., 1978—; AVEMCO Corp., 1980, Resolute Reins. Co., 1981. Trustee, former chmn. bd. trustees Rider Coll. Served to lt. col. AUS, 1941-45. Decorated Bronze Star Belgian Croix de Guerre, Presdl. citation. Presbyn. (elder). Clubs: Baltusrol Golf (Springfield, N.J.) (gov., sec., pres.); Columbia Golf (Chevy Chase, Md.); Links (N.Y.C.); Burning Tree Golf (Va.); Ocean Reef (Key Largo, Fla.); Card Sound Golf, Harbor Course (Fla.). Home: 219 Oak Ridge Ave Summit NJ 07901 Office: GEICO Plaza Washington DC 20076

HANNA, PAUL ROBERT, educator; b. Sioux City, Iowa, June 21, 1902; s. George Archibald and Regula (Figi) H.; m. Jean Shuman, Aug. 20, 1926; children: Emily-Jean Hanna Johnson, John Paul, Robert Shuman. A.B., Hamline U., St. Paul, 1924, Ped.D., 1937; A.M., Columbia U., 1925, Ph.D., 1929. Asst. psychology Hamline U., 1923-24; supt. schs., West Winfield, N.Y., 1925-27; research asso. Lincoln Sch., Columbia, 1928-35; asst. prof. Columbia Tchrs. Coll., 1930-35; asso. prof. Stanford U., 1935-37, prof. edn., 1937-54, Lee L. Jacks prof. edn., 1954-67, emeritus, 1967—, dir., 1954-68, emeritus, 1968—, dir. Stanford Univ. Services, 1941-44, founding chmn. Assoc. Libraries, 1973-75; sr. research fellow Hoover Instn., 1975—; Cons. U.S. Office Edn., U.S. Mut. Security Agy., AID; staff, cons. Nat. Resources Planning Bd., 1939-42; cons. Army Specialized Training Div. of War, 1942-44, War Relocation Authority, 1942-45, Sec. of War on German reedn., 1947, U.S. Govt. for Panama Canal Zone, 1947; mem. UNESCO consultative ednl. mission to, Philippines, 1949; coordinator Philippine Dept. Edn.-Stanford U. contract financed by AID, 1953-60; cons. to coordinator Inter-Am. Affairs, assignments in, S.Am., 1940-41, C.Am., 1941-42; mem. staff ednl. policies commn. N.E.A., 1948; mem. internat. relations com. Am. Council on Edn., 1955-60; mem. com. on Atlantic studies Atlantic Council and Atlantic Inst., 1962-68; cons. Edn. and World Affairs, 1964-68; chmn. Yugoslavia team U.S. State Dept., 1966; Am. specialist assigned African nations on ednl. reform, 1967; dir. Stanford-Asia Found. seminar on higher edn. in nation bldg., Korea, 1968; chmn. Nat. Evaluation Com. Peace Corps/Univ. Relations, 1968-69; cons. coop. research br. U.S. Office Edn., 1963-69; mem. U.S. Nat. Commn. UNESCO, 1970-77; cons. numerous state and city bds. edn. Sr. author social sci. textbooks, Scott Foresman Co.; author numerous articles, profl. books, films for Ency. Britannica Films, World Book Ency. Bd. dirs. Internat. Bd. Atlantic Colls., 1966-69, Jessie V. and Clement W. Stone Found., 1969-72; trustee Castilleja Sch., 1957—, United World Colls., 1968-72; mem. W.K. Kellogg Found., 1944-58, Presdl. Task Force on Arts and Humanities, 1981-82. Fellow A.A.A.S.; mem. N.E.A. (life mem. several depts.), Nat. Soc. Study Edn., Soc. Internat. Devel., Asia Soc., Comparative Edn. Soc., Am. Acad. Polit. and Social Sci., Internat. House Japan, Nat. Planning Assn., Am. Forestry Assn., John Dewey Soc., Council Fgn. Relations, World Affairs Council, Sierra Club, Nat. Trust for Historic Preservation, Soc. Archtl. Historians, UN Assn. U.S., Redwood Region Conservation Council, Phi Beta Kappa, Theta Chi, Phi Gamma Mu, Phi Delta Kappa, Kappa Delta Pi. Republican. Clubs: Kiwanian., Cosmos (Washington); Bohemian (San Francisco). Home: 20 Mitchell Pl Stanford CA 94305

HANNA, ROBERT JOHN, automobile club executive; b. Hamilton, Ont., Can., June 5, 1928; s. Robert John and Mary Jane (McVeigh) H.; m. Carolyn Elizabeth King, Jan. 27, 1950; children: Martho Jo, Sarah Jane. Student, pub. schs. Tool and die maker Callander Mfg. /co., Guelph, Ont., 1946-50, A. C. Widkman Ltd., Etobicoke, Ont., 1950-53; ptnr. Autosport Equipment, Ltd., Cooksville, Ont., 1953-64; nat. service mgr. Can. Motor Industries, Toronto, Ont., 1964-68; exec. dir. Can. Automobile Sport Clubs, Toronto, 1968—; del. mem. com. Fedn. Internat. de l'Auto, Paris, 1968—; mem. exec. com. Fedn. Internat. Sport Auto, Paris, 1975—; mem. world council Fed. Internat. Sport Auto, Paris, 1983—; pres. FISA Safety Commn., Paris, 1977-78, World Cup Commn., 1982—; mem. organizing com. Can. Grand Prix, 1967—. Designer, builder, driver various sports racing cars, 1953-61. Clubs: British Empire Motor; Canadian Racing Drivers Assn. (Toronto) (pres. 1964-68). Home: 2585 Cliff Rd Mississauga ON Canada L5A 2P5 Office: Canadian Automobile Sport Clubs 5385 Yonge St Willowdale ON Canada M2N 5R7

HANNA, STANLEY SWEET, physicist, educator; b. Sagaing, Burma, May 17, 1920; s. Alexander Carson and Hazel (Ames) H.; m. Jane Reeves Martin, Dec. 27, 1942; children: David Stanley, Peter Alexander, Susan Lee. A.B., Denison U., 1941, D.Sc., 1970; Ph.D., Johns Hopkins U., 1947. Mem. faculty Johns Hopkins U., 1943-55, asst. prof. physics, 1948-55; asso. physicist Argonne Nat. Lab., 1955-60, sr. physicist, 1960-63, cons., 1963-68; prof. physics Stanford U., 1963—; cons. Los Alamos Sci. Lab., 1967-74. Chmn. nuclear physics panel, com. on physics Nat. Acad. Scis., 1964-65. Served with AUS, 1945-46. Guggenheim fellow, 1958-59; Humboldt awardee, 1977. Fellow Am. Phys. Soc. (organizing com. 1966-67, exec. com. 1967-68, 75—, vice chmn. 1975-76, chmn. 1976-77, councillor div. nuclear physics 1978-82, publ. com. 1980-83, chmn. com. 1981-83); mem. Phi Beta Kappa, Sigma Xi, Omicron Delta Kappa. Spl. research nuclear structure, giant resonances, polarizations of nuclear radiations, positron polarization, lifetimes of nuclear states, resonance absorption, analogue states, electron scattering, nuclear moments, hyperfine interactions, Mössbauer effect. Home: 784 Mayfield Ave Stanford CA 94305

HANNA, THOMAS LOUIS, philosopher, educator, author; b. Waco, Tex., Nov. 21; s. John Dwight and Winifred (Beaumier) H.; m. Susan Taff, May 12, 1950; children—Mary Alice, Michael John, Wendell France.; m. Eleanor Comp Criswell, June 25, 1974. B.A., Tex. Christian U., 1949; B.D., U. Chgo., 1954, Ph.D., 1958. Dir. Jean de Beauvais Club, U. Paris, France, 1951-52; chmn. dept. philos. and religious thought Hollins Coll.; also dir. Hollins Abroad, Paris, 1961-62; writer-in-residence Duke, 1964-65; prof., chmn. dept. philosophy U. Fla., 1965-73, prof., 1973—; dir., prof. Humanistic Psychology Inst., 1973-75; founder, dir. Novato Inst. for Somatic Research and Tng., 1975—. Author: The Thought and Art of Albert Camus, 1958, The Bergsonian Heritage, 1963, The Lyrical Existentialists, 1963, Bodies in Revolt: A Primer in Somatic Thinking, 1970, The End of Tyranny: An Essay on the Possibility of America, 1975, Explorers of Humankind, 1979, The Body of Life, 1980; Founder, editor: Somatics, 1976—. Fellow Am. Council Learned Socs., 1968-69. Mem. Somatics Soc. (founder, pres.). Office: 1516 Grant Ave Suite 220 Novato CA 94947

HANNA, V. LEONARD, legal administrator; b. Caldwell, Kans., Sept. 9, 1917; s. Leonard Barkley and Mary Frances (Key) H.; m. Edith Gertrude Bailey, Apr. 24, 1944; children—Joan Gertrude Hanna Hinchliffe, Janet Mary Hanna Evans, Constance Norma Hanna Smith, Beth Edith Hanna White, Mark Leonard. B.Ed., Western Ill. State Tchrs. Coll., 1939; M.B.A., U. Mich., 1961. C.P.A., Mich. With Carnegie Ill. Steel Corp., 1940-46, bur. chief procedures staff, 1945-46; instr. Duquesne U., Pitts., eves., 1945-47; systems specialist Price, Waterhouse & Co. (C.P.A.'s), Pitts., N.Y.C. and Detroit, 1947-50; controller Internat. Textbook Co., Scranton, Pa., 1950-53; treas., controller Allied Products Corp., Detroit, 1953-57; v.p. fin., treas., asst. sec. Fenestra Inc., Detroit, 1957-62; v.p. fin. and control Eve. News Assn., Detroit, 1962-82; adminstr. firm Butzel Long Gust Klein & Van Zile, Detroit, 1982—. Mem. Fin. Execs. Inst. (pres. Detroit chpt. 1963-64), Inst. Newspaper Controllers and Fin. Officers (dir. 1969-72, Walter F. Carley award 1975); mem. Assn. Legal Adminstrs.; Mem. Detroit C. of C. (president's club 1969-72), Am. Inst. C.P.A.'s, Mich. Assn. C.P.A.'s, Econ. Club Detroit, Beta Alpha Psi. Lutheran. Club: Elks. Home: 616 Suffield St Birmingham MI 48009 Office: 1881 First Nat Bldg. Detroit MI 48226 *I have enjoyed the luxury of integrity. That says it all.*

HANNA, WILLIAM BROOKS, book publisher; b. Montreal, Que., Can., Feb. 22, 1936; s. George Spencer and Phyllis Edith (Brooks) H.; m. Barbara Helen Jones, Dec. 19, 1960; children: Catherine Frances, Philip Spencer. Grad., Upper Can. Coll., 1954; B.A. in Modern History, U. Toronto, 1958. Successively coll. sales mgr., sch. sales mgr., editor-in-chief Collier-Macmillan-Can., Ltd., 19S8-65; pres. Pergamon of Can., Ltd., also dep. chmn. bd., Toronto, 1967-68; exec. v.p., dir. Pergamon Press, Inc., 1966-68; v.p., dir. Burns & MacEachern, Ltd., Toronto, 1968-70; pres., dir. GLC Pubs., Toronto, 1970-75; pres., chief exec. officer, dir. Holt Rinehart & Winston of Can., Ltd., Toronto, 1975-78; pub. joint UNICEF/Red Cross Com. for 1979 Internat. Yr. of Child, 1978—; v.p. Gen. Pub. Co. Ltd., Toronto, 1979—; dir. Beaufort Books Ltd., Toronto. Home: 51 Acacia Rd Toronto ON Canada M4S 2K6 Office: 30 Lesmill Rd Don Mills ON Canada M3B 2T6

HANNA, WILLIAM DENBY, animated cartoon producer; b. Melrose, N.M., July 14, 1910; s. William John and Avice Joyce (Denby) H.; m. Violet B. Wogatzke, Aug. 7, 1936; children—David William, Bonnie Janna (Mrs. Sidney Williams). Mem. story dept., also lyricist and composer, Harman-Ising Studios, 1930-37; with, Metro-Goldwyn-Meyer, (1937-57); created: (with Joseph Barbera) Tom and Jerry series; dir.-producer, sr. v.p., Hanna-Barbera Prodns., Inc., Hollywood, Calif., (1957); created series: TV Quick Draw McGraw, Ruff & Ready, Yogi Bear, Huckleberry Hound, The Flintstones, Top Cat, Jetsons, Johnny Quest; also producer for: theatrical release Loopy de Loop (Recipient 7 Acad. awards for Tom and Jerry series.). Office: 3400 W Cahuenga Blvd Hollywood CA 90068 *

HANNA, WILLIAM JOHNSON, electrical engineering educator; b. Longmont, Colo., Feb. 7, 1922; s. William Grant and Anna Christina (Johnson) H.; m. Katherine Fagan, Apr. 25, 1944; children: Daniel August, Paul William. B.S. in Elec. Engring, U. Colo., 1943, M.S., 1948, E.E., 1951. Registered profl. engr., Colo. Mem. faculty U. Colo., 1946—, prof. elec. engring., 1962—; cons. in field; mem. Colo. Bd. Engring. Examiners, 1973—. Author articles, reports. Served to 1st lt. AUS, 1943-46. Recipient Faculty Recognition award Students Assn. U. Colo., 1956, 61; named Colo. Engr. of Year Profl. Engrs. Colo., 1968; recipient Alfred J. Ryan award, 1978; Archimedes award Calif. Soc. Profl. Engrs., 1978; Outstanding Engring. Alumnus award U. Colo., 1983; Ky. col. Mem. IEEE, Am. Soc. Engring. Edn., Nat. Soc. Profl. Engrs. (pres. Colo. 1967-68), Nat. Council Engring. Examiners (pres. 1977-78), AIEE (chmn. Denver 1961-62). Republican. Presbyterian. Club: Masons. Home: Silver Spruce Nederland Star Route Boulder CO 80302 Office: Elec Engring Dept Box 425 Univ Colo Boulder CO 80309 *Honors and awards I have received are but a reflection of the character of my friends and assos. To them and my family go the accolades.*

HANNAFORD, MARK WARREN, business executive; b. Woodrow, Colo., Feb. 7, 1925; s. William Townsend and Ina (Owen) H.; m. Sara Jane Lemaster, Apr. 20, 1948; children: Mark William, Kim Karl, Robert Owen. B.A., Ball State U., 1950, M.A., 1955; postgrad. (John Hay fellow), Yale, 1961-62. Tchr. Lakewood (Calif.) High Sch., 1956-67; tchr. polit. sci. Long Beach (Calif.) City Coll., 1967-77; mem. 94th and 95th Congress from 34th Calif. Dist.; White House coordinator internat. trade policy U.S. Dept. Commerce, 1978; sr. assoc. Martin Haleey Co., Washington, 1980; pres. Bankcard Holders of Am., 1980, Window on Washington, Inc., 1983—. Mem. planning commn., Lakewood, 1960-61, councilman, Lakewood, 1966-68, mayor, 1968-70, 72, 74; mem. Los Angeles County Dem. Central Com., 1962-67, Calif. State Dem. Central Com. Served with USAAF, 1943-46. Address: 4944 N Stevely Ave Lakewood CA 90713

HANNAFORD, PETER DOR, public relations executive; b. Glendale, Calif., Sept. 21, 1932; s. Donald R. and Elinor (Nielsen) H.; m. Irene Dorothy Harville, Aug. 14, 1954; children: Richard Harville, Donald R. II. A.B., U. Calif., 1954. Account exec. Helen A. Kennedy Advt., 1956; v.p. Kennedy-Hannaford, Inc. (name changed to Kennedy, Hannaford & Dolman, Inc. 1965), San Francisco and Oakland, Calif., 1957-62, pres., 1962-67, Pettler & Hannaford, Inc., Oakland, 1967-69; v.p. Wilton, Coombs & Colnett, Inc., 1969-72; pres. Hannaford & Assos., Oakland, 1973—; asst. to Gov. of Calif.; dir. public affairs Govs.' Office, 1974; chmn. bd. Hannaford Co., Inc. (formerly Deaver & Hannaford, Inc.), 1975—; Nat. pres. Mut. Advt. Agy. Network, 1968-69; instr. advt. Merritt Coll., Oakland, 1964-67; vice chmn. Calif. Gov.'s Consumer Fraud Task Force, 1972-73. Pres. East Bay div. Republican Alliance, 1968-69; mem. Alameda County Rep. Central Com., Rep. State Central Com. Calif., 1968-74; Rep. nominee for U.S. Congress, 1972; mem. Piedmont Park Commn., 1964-68; Bd. dirs., mem. exec. com. Oakland Symphony Orch. Assn., 1963-69; bd. dirs. Children's Hosp. Med. Center No. Calif., 1967-70; mem. governing bd. Tahoe Regional Planning Agy., 1973-74; trustee White House Preservation Fund, 1981—; mem. pub. relations adv. com. USIA, 1981—. Served as 1st lt. Signal Corps AUS, 1954-56. Mem. Guardsmen San Francisco, Theta Xi. Presbyterian. Clubs: University (San Francisco); (Washington). Office: 444 S Flower St Los Angeles CA 90017

HANNAFORD, ROBERT VARLAN, educator; b. Anderson, Ind., Sept. 28, 1929; s. William T. and Ina (Owen) H.; m. Neola Cope, Aug. 26, 1951; children: Stephen Cope, Catherine Anne. A.B., Wabash Coll., 1950; Ph.D., Columbia U., 1955. Prof. philosophy Ripon Coll., Wis., 1956—. Editor: The Case for and Against Power for the Federal Government, 1978, Concept Formation and Explanation of Behavior, 1980. Bd. dirs. Ripon Coll. Philosophy Conf., 1970—. Served with U.S. Army, 1953-55. Recipient Palmer Chair for Leadership Values Ripon Coll., 1981; grantee NEH, ACLS, Wis. Humanities Com. Mem. Am. Philos. Assn. (grant), ACLU, Phi Beta Kappa. Democrat. Office: Ripon Coll Ripon WI 54971

HANNAH, JOHN ALFRED, educator, food and agr. cons.; b. Grand Rapids, Mich., Oct. 9, 1902; s. Wilfred Steele and Mary Ellen (Malone) H.; m. Sarah May Shaw, June 22, 1938; children—Mary Elizabeth, Robert W., Thomas A., David H. Student, Grand Rapids Jr. Coll., 1912-21, U. Mich., 1921-23; B.S., Mich. State U., 1923, D.Agr., 1941; LL.D., U. Mich., 1944, U. R.I., 1954, Central Mich. U., 1955, Albion Coll., 1957, U. Conn., 1960, Colo. State U., 1963, Alma Coll., 1964, U. Maine, 1965, Howard U., 1966, U. Md., 1966, Ariz. State U., 1966, Tuskegee Inst., 1967, Kalamazoo Coll., 1967, Western Mich. U., 1967, U. S.D., 1967, Ohio State U., 1968, U. Notre Dame, 1970, Akron U., 1970, Hope Coll., 1970, U. Am., 1970; H.H.D., U. Ryukyus, 1952, Mich. State U., 1979, Oakland U., 1969; L.H.D., U. Fla., 1953; D.Sc., Mich. Tech. U., 1953, U. Nigeria, 1961, Tri State Coll., 1967; D.Litt., No. Mich. U., 1957, Grand Valley State Coll., 1968. With Coop. Agrl. Extension Services, Mich. State U., 1923-35; sec. bd. trustees Mich. State U., 1935-41, pres., 1941-69, pres. emeritus, 1969—; asst. sec. Dept. Def., 1953-54; mng. agt. Fed. Hatchery Coordinating Com., 1933-35; Am. chmn. Permanent Joint Bd. for Def., Can. and U.S., 1954-64; chmn. U.S. Commn. on Civil Rights, 1957-69, Am. Council on Edn., 1967-68; adminstr. AID, 1969-73; dep. sec. gen. UN World Food Conf., Rome, Italy, 1974; exec. dir. UN World Food Council, Rome, 1975-78; chmn. Internat. Fertilizer Devel. Center, Muscle Shoals, Ala., 1974—; dir. Internat. Agrl. Devel. Services, 1974—. Del. Mich. Constl. Conv., 1961-62; chmn. adv. task force for State of Mich. Civil Service Reform, 1978-79. Mem. Nat. Assn. Land Grant Colls. and State Univs. (past pres., chmn. exec. com.), Phi Beta Kappa. Clubs: Cosmos (Washington); Detroit; Univ. (East Lansing, Mich.). Home: Box 215 Dansville MI 48819 Office: Mich State Univ 220 Nisbet Bldg East Lansing MI 48824

HANNAH, MARY-EMILY, university administrator, educator; b. Denver, Mar. 14, 1936; d. Stewart Whistler and Emily (Wight) H. A.B., Grinnell Coll., 1958; LL.D., Grineell Coll., 1982; M.A., U. Iowa, 1962; Ph.D., U Ill., 1967. Instr. Arvada High Sch., Denver, 1958-61; prof. speech St. Cloud (Minn.) State U., 1962-64, 67-78; asst. prof. speech Sacramento State U., 1966-67; acting. pres. Met. State U., St. Paul, 1977; vice chancellor acad. affairs Minn. State Univ. System, St. Paul, 1976-80; chancellor U. Wis.-Eau Claire, 1980-84; vice chancellor Pa State System of Higher Edn., Harrisburg, 1984—. Office: 301 Market St Harrisburg PA 17108

HANNAH, NORMAN BRITTON, former foreign service officer; b. Mattoon, Ill., Dec. 1, 1919; s. Harry Ingalls and Vivian (Britton) H.; m. Edna McCoy, Feb. 20, 1943 (dec.); children: Norman Britton, Harry Ingalls II; m. Elizabeth Anderson, Dec. 10, 1971; stepchildren: Harriet Anderson, Kathryn Elderkin, Wendy Fatoric. B.A. with honors, U. Ill., 1941; M.A., La. State U., 1942; postgrad., U. Minn., 1946-47. Instr. polit. sci. U. Minn., 1946-47; with Dept. of State, 1947—; beginning as vice consul Am. consulate gen., Shanghai, China; successively 2d sec., consul Am. embassy, Bangkok, Thailand; consul, prin. officer Am. consulate, Tabriz, Iran; 2d sec., consul Am. embassy, Tehran, Iran, 1947-55; officer charge Iranian affairs, Washington, 1955-57; spl. asst. to dep. under-sec. of state, 1957-58; assigned Nat. War Coll., 1958-59; dep. chief mission Am. embassy, Kabul, Afghanistan, 1959-62; dep. dir. S.E. Asian affairs, 1962-64; polit. adviser to comdr.-in-chief Pacific, Honolulu, 1964-66; U.S. minister Am. embassy, Bangkok, 1966-70; diplomat-in-residence, vis. prof. polit. sci. Haverford Coll., 1970-71; consul gen., Sydney, Australia, 1971-78. Contbg. editor: Nat. Review; contbr. to: Fgn. Service Jour., 1955-58. Served to lt. USNR, 1942-46; PTO. Mem. Delta Phi. Home: 5113 Scarsdale Rd Bethesda MD 20816

HANNAN, PHILIP MATTHEW, bishop; b. Washington, May 20, 1913; s. Patrick Francis and Lillian Louise (Keefe) H. Student, St. Charles Coll., 1931-33; A.B., Cath. U., 1935, M.A., 1936, J.C.D., 1949, N.Am. Coll., 1936-40; S.T.B., S.T.L., Gregorian U., Rome, 1940. Ordained priest Roman Catholic Ch., 1939; clerical appt. St. Thomas Aquinas Ch., Balt., 1940-42; vice chancellor Cath. Diocese Washington, 1948-51, chancellor, 1951-62, vicar gen., 1960-65; adminstr. St. Patrick's Ch., Washington, 1951-56, pastor, 1956-65; aux. bishop Archdiocese Washington; also editor-in-chief Catholic Standard of D.C., 1956-65; archbishop, New Orleans, 1965—; organizer housing program for elderly Christopher Homes, Inc.; Chmn. ad hoc com. Nat. Conf. Cath. Bishops Office Priestly Life and Ministry, 1971—; chmn. bd. trustees Cath. U. Am., Washington, 1973—; nat. chaplain Cath. Da's. Am., 1974-78; mem. communications com. U.S. Cath. Conf. Bishops, 1979—. Mem. goals com. Met. Area Com. New Orleans; mem. White House Conf. on Children and Youth, 1970—; mem. exec. bd. New Orleans council Boy Scouts Am., 1970—; mem. bd., past chmn. interfaith com. United Fund New Orleans, 1970—. Served as chaplain USAAF, 1942-46. Address: 7887 Walmsley Ave New Orleans LA 70125

HANNAWALT, WILLIS DALE, lawyer; b. Delaware, Ohio, Apr. 28, 1928; s. Othelloe Erwin and Dorothy (Sherbourne) H.; m. Vivian Nina Chaya, Sept. 8, 1950; children: Nina Jo, James Frederick, Rachel Beth. A.B., U. Chgo., 1950, J.D., 1954. Bar: Calif. 1955, U.S. Supreme Ct. 1970. Teaching fellow Stanford U., Palo ALto, Calif., 1954-55; assoc. Pillsbury, Madison & Sutro, San Francisco, 1955-65, ptnr., 1965—; mem. faculty Golden Gate Law Sch., San Francisco, 1958-68; cons. Hudson Inst., Tarrytown, N.Y., 1964. Chmn. State Bar Jour. Com., 1964. Served with USCG, 1946-47, 51-53. Fellow ABA; mem. Calif. Bar Assn., San Francisco Lawyer's Club. Democrat. Club: Olympic (San Francisco). Office: Pillsbury Madison & Sutro 225 Bush St San Francisco CA 94104

HANNAY, N(ORMAN) BRUCE, chemist, educator; b. Mt. Vernon, Wash., Feb. 9, 1921; s. Norman Bond and Winnie (Evans) H.; m. Joan Anderson, May 27, 1943; children: Robin, Brooke. B.A., Swarthmore Coll., 1942, D.Sc. (hon.), 1979; M.S., Princeton U., 1943, Ph.D., 1944; Ph.D. (hon.), Tel Aviv U., 1978, D.Sc., Poly. Inst. N.Y., 1981. With Bell Telephone Labs., Murray Hill, N.J., 1944-82, exec. dir. materials research div., 1967-73, v.p. research and patents, 1973-82, ret., 1982; dir. Plenum Pub. Co., Gen. Signal Corp., Flag Investors Fund, Rohm and Haas Co., Alex Brown Cash Res. Fund; Chmn. sci. adv. council Atlantic Richfield Corp., Gulf Applied Techs.; Regents' prof. UCLA, 1976, U. Calif., San Diego, 1979; cons. Alexander von Humboldt Found. Author: Solid State Chemistry, 1967, also articles.; Mem. numerous editorial bds.; editor: Semiconductors, 1959, Treatise on Solid State Chemistry, 1974. Recipient Acheson medal, 1976, Perkin medal, 1983. Fellow Am. Phys. Soc.; mem. Nat. Acad. Engring. (fgn. sec.), Nat. Acad. Scis., Am. Acad. Arts and Scis., Mexican Nat. Acad. Engring., Am. Chem. Soc., Electrochem. Soc. (past pres.), Indsl. Research Inst. (past pres., medal 1982), Dirs. of Indsl. Research (past chmn.). Research on dipole moments and molecular structure, thermionic emission, mass spectroscopy, analysis of solids, solid state chemistry, semiconductors, superconductors. Home: Mitchell Point Friday Harbor WA 98250 Office: Nat Acad Engring 2101 Constitution Ave Washington DC 20418

HANNEMAN, RODNEY ELTON, metallurgical engineer; b. Spokane, Wash., Mar. 14, 1936; s. Christie Luther and Viva Helen (Sugrue) H.; (married); children: David, Susan. B.S. in Phys. Metallurgy, Wash. State U., 1959; M.S. in Metallurgy, M.I.T., 1961, Ph.D., 1963. With Gen. Electric Co., Schenectady, 1963-81, mgr. materials characterization lab., 1977-80, mgr. materials programs, 1980-81; v.p. research, devel. and energy resources Reynolds Metals Co., Richmond, Va., 1981—; Mem. vis. com. dept. materials sci. and engring. M.I.T., 1975-80, mem. adv. bd. materials processing center, 1980—; mem. adv. bd. U. Va., 1982—; vice chmn. research bd. Gas Research Inst., 1983—; bd. dirs. Metals Properties Council, 1982—. Author. Recipient Alumni Achievement award Wash. State U., 1978. Mem. Am. Soc. Metals (Geisler award 1971, Engring. Materials Achievement award 1973), Am. Chem. Soc. (Chem. Innovator award 1970, Edison medallion 1979), AIME, AAAS, Sigma Xi. Patentee in field. Office: Reynolds Metals Co 6601 W Broad St Richmond VA 23261

HANNIGAN, JUDSON, paper manufacturing company executive; b. Boston, 1924; married. A.B., Dartmouth Coll., 1948. Pres. Internat. Paper Co., 1974-76; corp. v.p. The Continental Group, Inc., Stamford, Conn., 1976—, exec. v.p. Brown System ops. Continental Forest Industries div., 1976—; dir. Atlantic Ins. Group. Served to capt. USMC. Office: Continental Forest Industries 20 Harbor Plaza Stamford CT 06904 *

HANNON, BRUCE M., engineer, educator; b. Champaign, Ill., Aug. 14, 1934; s. Walter Leo and Kathleen Rose (Phalen) H.; m. Patricia Claire Coffey, Aug. 11, 1956; children—Christopher, Claire, Laura, Brian. B.S. in Civil Engring, U. Ill., 1956, M.S. in Engring. Mechanics, 1966, Ph.D., 1970. Engr. with chem. industry, 1957-66; instr. U. Ill., Urbana, 1966-71, assoc. prof. energy research, 1974-83, prof. regional sci., 1983—; cons. NSF, Nat. Acad. Sci., Nat. Acad. Engring., chem. industry, various fed. energy agencies.; mem. energy engring. bd. NRC. Contbr. articles to profl. jours. Served as 1st lt. C.E. AUS, 1956-57. Named Engring. Tchr. of the Yr. U. Ill., 1970; Man of the Yr. Sierra Club, 1971; recipient 10,000 1st prize Mitchell Award Club of Rome, 1975. Patentee in field. Home: 1208 W Union St Champaign IL 61820 Office: Geography Dept University of Illinois Urbana IL 61801

HANNUM, JOHN BERNE, U.S. judge; b. Chester, Pa., Mar. 19, 1915; s. John Berne and Helen (Weaver) H.; m. Nancy Penn Smith, Dec. 21, 1940; children: John Berne, Richard P.S., Carol A. (Mrs. Bruce O. Davidson). Grad., Lawrenceville Sch., 1934; student, Princeton U., 1934-37, Franklin and Marshall Coll., 1937-38; LL.B., Dickinson Sch. Law, 1941; LL.D. (hon.), Widener U., 1976, Lincoln U., 1978. Bar: Pa. 1942. Partner, trial lawyer firm Pepper, Hamilton & Scheetz, Phila., 1955-68; judge Superior Ct. Pa., 1968-69, U.S. Dist. Ct. Eastern Pa., 1969—; mem. com. on adminstrn. fed. magistrates system Jud. Conf. U.S., 1975—. Mem. commissary, past ch. advocate Episcopal Diocese Pa.; past mem. sch. bd., chmn. exec. com. Unionville-Chadds Ford Dist., Chester County, Pa., 1947-68; Mem. Electoral Coll., 1956; chmn. Chester County (Pa.) Republican Com., 1962-64; mem. Pa. Republican Exec. Com., 1962-64; del. Pa. Constl. Conv., 1967-68, Rep. Nat. Conv., 1960; Trustee Dickinson Sch. Law, Chester County Hosp., Widener U.; Mem. regional panel White House Fellows. Served to lt. USN, 1941-45. Mem. Am., Pa., county bar assns., Justinian Soc. (hon.), State Soc. Cincinnati Pa. (hon.). Episcopalian (vestry). Club: Mason. Home: Unionville PA 19375 Office: 12613 US Courthouse 6th and Market Sts Philadelphia PA 19106

HANOLD, TERRANCE, lawyer, food industry exec., capital mgmt. adviser; b. Mpls., June 22, 1912; s. Robert Arter and Dena (Tillotson) H.; m. Ruth Lorraine Evarts, June 17, 1939; children—Ruth Lorraine, John Terrence, Robert Evarts, Dena Gail, Thomas Tillotson, David Comstock, Lee Hinckley, Dennis Patrick. A.B., U. Minn., 1934, LL.B., 1936. Bar: Minn. bar 1936. Law sec. to chief justice Minn. Supreme Ct., 1936-38; pvt. practice law, Mpls., 1938-44; legal counsel Mpls. Star & Tribune Co., 1944-46; with Pillsbury Co., Mpls., 1946-75, atty., asst. sec., treas., asst. gen. counsel, 1946-56, treas., 1956-58, treas., controller, 1958-59, treas., prin. financial officer, 1959-60, v.p. finance, 1960-63, exec. v.p. internat. ops. and finance, 1963-67, pres., 1967-73, chmn. exec. com., 1973-75, dir., 1961-75; pres., dir. Arter Co., 1976—; dir. 1st Nat. Bank Mpls., 1969-76, Koppers Co. Inc., INA Investment Securities Co., ConAgra. Contbr. articles to profl. jours. Mem. food adv. com. Cost of Living Council, 1973-74; chmn. Food and Drug Law Inst., 1974-75, Council Better Bus. Burs., 1974-76; trustee Com. Econ. Devel., Minn. Symphony, Mpls. Inst. Arts, Inst. Ecumenical and Cultural Research, Council on Religion and Internat. Affairs. Clubs: Minakahda, Minneapolis. Home: 6566 France Ave S Minneapolis MN 55435 Office: 4900 IDS Tower Minneapolis MN 55402

HANRAHAN, EDWARD STEPHENSON, educator; b. Marietta, Ohio, Sept. 8, 1929; s. William Parnell and Veronica (Stephenson) H.; children—Veronica, Harriet Katherine, Elizabeth. Student, Marietta Coll., 1947-48; B.Sc., U. Miss., 1951; M.S., W.Va. U., 1956, Ph.D., 1959. Instr. W.Va. U., 1957-58; chemist E.I. duPont & Co., 1958-63; prof. chemistry Marshall U., Huntington, W.Va., 1963—, chmn. dept., 1967-77; dean Coll. of Sci., 1977—; cons. Polan Industries, Roberts Chem. Co., Pilgrim Glass Co., U.S. Naval Propellant Plant; vis. scientist Ohio Acad. Sci. Contbr. articles to sci. jours. Chmn. W.Va. Conf. on Higher Edn. and Chem. Industry, 1971-72. Served with USN, 1951-54. Danforth Asso. fellow. Mem. Am. Chem. Soc. (com. on chem. edn. 1971-78), Chem. Soc. (London), A.A.A.S., AAUP, Coblentz Soc., N.Y. Acad. Sci., W.Va. Acad. Sci. (pres. 1977-78), Sigma Xi, Phi Lambda Upsilon, Chi Beta Phi. Home: PO Box 2427 Huntington WV 25725

HANRAHAN, ROBERT JOSEPH, chemist, educator; b. Chgo., Jan. 7, 1932; s. James Richard and Lucille Florence (Granger) H.; m. Mary Ellen Hogan, Oct. 28, 1957; children: Ann Marie, Sheila Frances, Robert Joseph, Margaret Evyleen. B.S., Loyola U., Chgo., 1953; Ph.D., U. Wis., Madison, 1957. Research chemist Pure Oil Co., Crystal Lake, Ill., 1953; teaching asst., research asst. Monsanto research fellow U. Wis., Madison, 1953-57; NSF postdoctoral fellow Leeds (Eng.) U., 1957-58; asst. prof. phys. chemistry U. Fla., 1958-64, asso. prof., 1964-71, prof., 1971—, chmn. phys. chemistry div., 1977—; vis. sci. Hahn-Meitner Inst. Nuclear Research, Berlin, 1976; cons. in field. Contbr. articles to profl. jours. AEC research grantee, 1963-74; ERDA grantee, 1975-77; Dept. Energy grantee, 1977—; Dreyfus Found. grantee, 1983. Mem. Am. Chem. Soc., Am. Phys. Soc., Radiation Research Soc., AAAS, Am. Soc. Mass Spectrometry, Inter-Am. Photochem. Soc. Democrat. Roman Catholic. Research on chem. effects of nuclear radiation. Home: 3730 NW 16th Pl Gainesville FL 32605 Office: Dept Chemistry U Fla Gainesville FL 32611

HANRATTY, THOMAS JOSEPH, chemical engineer, educator; b. Phila., Nov. 9, 1926; s. John Joseph and Elizabeth Marie (O'Connor) H.; m. Joan L. Hertel, Aug. 25, 1956; children: John, Vincent, Maria, Michael, Peter. B.S. Chem. Engring., Villanova U., 1947, 1979; M.S., Ohio State U., 1950; Ph.D., Princeton U., 1953. Engr. Fischer & Porter, 1947-48; research engr. Battelle Meml. Inst., 1948-50; engr. Rohm & Haas, Phila., summer 1951; research engr. Shell Devel. Co., Emeryville, Calif., 1954; faculty U. Ill., Urbana, 1953—, asso. prof., 1958-63, prof. chem. engring., 1963—; cons. in field; vis. asso. prof. Brown U., 1962-63. Contbr. articles to profl. jours. Mem. U.S. Nat. Com. on Theoretical and Applied Mechanics. NSF sr. postdoctoral fellow, 1962; recipient Curtis W. McGraw award Am. Soc. Engring. Edn., 1963, Sr. Research award, 1979. Fellow Am. Phys. Soc., Am. Acad. Scis.; mem. Nat. Acad. Engrs., Am. Inst. Chem. Engrs. (Colburn award 1957, Walker award 1964, Profl. Progress award 1967), Am. Chem. Soc. Roman Catholic. Club: Serra Internat. Home: 1019 W Charles St Champaign IL 61820 Office: 205 Roger Adams Lab U Ill Urbana IL 61801

HANSARD, JAMES WILLIAM, librarian; b. Charleston, Ark., May 2, 1936; s. J.D. and Emma (Collier) H.; m. Ruth Avery Bishop, June 1, 1962; children: Will, Sharon, Rebecca. B.S. in Engring, U. Central Ark., 1958; M.S. in L.S, La. State U., 1966. Librarian, tchr. history, Corning, Ark., 1958-59; librarian, choral and band dir. Corning High Sch., 1959-60; dir. libraries Presbyn. Day Sch., Memphis, 1960-62, Memphis Univ. Sch., 1960-62, librarian, tchr. geography, 1962-64; acquisitions librarian Ark. State U., 1964-65, asst. librarian, then asso. librarian, 1965-78, library dir., 1978—, chmn. dept. library sci., 1965—. Mem. Council Library Edn. (past chmn.), ALA, N.E. Ark. Library Assn. (past. pres.), Ark. Library Assn. (past pres.). Baptist. Club: Exchange. Home: 209 Bush St Jonesboro AR 72401 Office: PO Box 2040 State University AR 72467

HANSBERGER, ROBERT VAIL, mfg. co. exec.; b. Worthington, Minn., June 1, 1920; s. Floyd L. and Edythe (Vail) H.; m. Klara K. Kille, Mar. 27, 1942; children: Roberta Ann, Carol Ann. A.A., Worthington Jr. Coll., 1940; B.M.E. with distinction, U. Minn., 1942; M.B.A. with high distinction, Harvard U., 1947; LL.D., Seattle U., 1963, U. Ida., Lewis and Clark Coll., Gonzaga U., U. Idaho. Asst. to exec. v.p. Container Corp. Am., 1947-50, div. chief engr., 1950-53, budget dir., 1953-54; exec. v.p., dir. Western Kraft Corp., Portland, Oreg., 1954-56; dir., mem. exec. com. Western Corrugated, Inc., 1955-56; pres., dir. Western Sales Co., 1956; dir. Boise Payette Lumber Co., Idaho, 1956-57; pres., dir., chmn. bd. Boise Cascade Corp., 1956-72; chmn., chief exec. officer, chmn. bd. Futura Corp., Boise, 1972—; chmn. bd. dirs., chief exec. officer, also dir. Futura Communications Corp.; dir. Albertson's Inc., First Charter Fin. Corp., Mackay Bar Corp., Heath Tecna Corp., VSI Corp., Idaho Power Co., Western Pacific R.R. Co., Western Pacific Industries, Trus Joist Corp., Fairchild Industries; Mem. Bus. Council; vis. prof. Boise State U. Mem. Bus. Com. for Arts, Arches of Sci. Award Selection Com.; adv. bd. Boise State U.; bd. dirs. Planned Parenthood Idaho; bd. dirs., vice chmn. bd. trustees St. Luke's Regional Med Center; trustee, mem. exec. com. Aspen Inst. Humanistic Studies; trustee Coll. of Idaho. Served to ensign USNR, 1945-46. Decorated asso. officer Grand Priory Hosp. St. John Jerusalem. Mem. Sun Valley Forum, Tau Beta Pi, Pi Tau Sigma, Alpha Kappa Psi. Home: 1305 Harrison Blvd Boise ID 83702 Office: Futura Corp Drawer F Suite 1010 One Capital Center Boise ID 83702

HANSCH, CORWIN HERMAN, educator; b. Kenmare, N.D., Oct. 6, 1918; s. Herman William and Rachel (Corwine) H.; m. Gloria J. Tomasulo, Jan. 8, 1944; children—Clifford, Carol. B.S., U. Ill., 1940; Ph.D., N.Y.U., 1944. Research chemist Manhattan project E.I. du Pont de Nemours & Co., Inc., 1944-45, research chemist, 1945-46; prof. chemistry Pomona Coll., 1946—; spl. research relationship chem. structure and drug action. Guggenheim fellow Fed. Inst. Tech., Zurich, Switzerland, 1952-53, Pomona Coll., 1966-67; Petroleum Research Fund fellow U. Munich, Germany, 1959-60; Recipient medal Italian Soc. Pharm. Sci., 1967; Coll. Chemistry Teaching award Mfg. Chemists Assn., 1969; Research Achievement award Am. Pharm. Assn., 1969; E.A. Smissman award Medicinal Chemistry Am. Chem. Soc., 1975; Tolman award Los Angeles sect., 1976. Home: 4070 Olive Knoll Pl Claremont CA 91711

HANSCH, THEODOR WOLFGANG, physicist, educator; b. Heidelberg, W.Germany, Oct. 30, 1941; came to U.S., 1970; s. Karl E. and Martha (Kiefer) H. Abitur, Helmholtz Gymansium, Heidelberg, 1961; M.S., U. Heidelberg, 1966, Ph.D., 1969. Asst. prof. physics U. Heidelberg, 1969-70; NATO fellow Stanford U., 1970-72, asso. prof. physics, 1972-75, prof., 1975—. Co-editor: Metrologia, 1975—; adv. editor: Optics Communications, 1975—; assoc. editor: Applied Physics B, 1983; contbr. articles to profl. jours. Named Calif. Scientist of Year, 1973; recipient Alexander von Humboldt Sr. U.S. Scientist award, 1978-79; Otto Klung award, 1980, Cyrus B. Comstock prize Nat. Acad. Scis., 1983; Alfred P. Sloan fellow, 1973-75. Fellow Am. Phys. Soc. (Herbert Broida prize 1983), Optical Soc. Am. (assoc. editor jour. 1982—); mem. Optical Soc. N. Calif. (dir. 1975—), Am. Acad. Arts and Scis., Deutsche Physikalische Gesellschaft, Sigma Xi. Roman Catholic. Researcher spectroscopy and quantum electronics, devel. powerful monochromatic pulsed dye lasers, high resolution nonlinear spectroscopy of atoms and molecules. Home: 1510 Oak Creek Dr Apt 405 Palo Alto CA 94304 Office: Dept Physics Stanford U Stanford CA 94305

HANSCOM, DANIEL HERBERT, lawyer, former government official; b. Chgo., Apr. 16, 1917; s. Louis Marion and Kathryn Cristina (Murphy) H.; m. Margaret Elizabeth Smith, Mar. 24, 1943; children: Barbara, Deborah, Michael, Constance, Stephanie. B.S. with honors, Northwestern U., 1939, J.D., 1942. Bar: Ill. bar 1942, Kans. bar 1949, U.S. Supreme Ct. bar 1967. Trial atty. FTC, Washington, 1956-68, asst. gen. counsel, 1969-72, adminstrv. law judge, 1972, chief adminstrv. law judge, 1973-80; pvt. practice, Washington, 1980—. Served to comdr. USN, 1942-47, 50-54. Mem. Am. Bar Assn., Conf. Adminstrv. Law Judges. Club: Nat. Lawyers. Home: 7701 Hackamore Dr Potomac MD 20854

HANSELMAN, RICHARD WILSON, shoe and apparel company executive; b. Cin., Oct. 8, 1927; s. Wendell Forest and Helen E. (Beiderwelle) H.; m. Beverly Baker White, Oct. 16, 1954; children: Charles Fielding, II, Jane White. B.A. in Econs, Dartmouth Coll., 1949. Vice pres. merchandising RCA Sales Corp., Indpls., 1964-66, v.p. product planning, 1966-69, v.p. product mgmt., 1969-70; pres. luggage div. Samsonite Corp., Denver, 1970-73, pres. luggage group, 1973-74, exec. v.p. ops., 1974-75, pres., 1975-77; sr. v.p. Beatrice Foods Co., Chgo., 1976-77, exec. v.p., 1977-80; pres., chief operating officer, dir. Genesco Inc., Nashville, 1980—, chief exec. officer, 1981—; dir. Becton Dickinson & Co., Arvin Industries, Third Nat. Corp. Served with U.S. Army, 1950-52. Mem. UN Assn. (econ. policy council), Phi Kappa Psi. Clubs: Denver Country., Belle Meade Country, Nashville City, Union League, Chicago, Shoal Creek. Office: Genesco Inc Genesco Park Nashville TN 37202

HANSEN, ANDREW MARIUS, library association executive; b. Storm Lake, Iowa, Mar. 25, 1929; s. Andrew Marius and Margaret Mary (Van Wagenen) H.; m. Rina M. Smith, Feb. 24, 1967; 1 son, Neil S. B.A., U. Omaha, 1951; postgrad., U. Md., 1955; M.A., U. Minn., 1962, U. Iowa, 1968-71. Librarian Bismarck (N.D.) Public Library, 1957-63, Sioux City (Iowa) Public Library, 1963-67; instr. Sch. of Library Sci., U. Iowa, Iowa City, 1967-71; exec. sec. ALA, Chgo., 1971-80, exec. dir. reference and adult services div., 1980—; vis. asst. prof. Ind. State U., Terre Haute, 1966. Served with USAF, 1951-55. Mem. N.D. Library Assn. (pres. 1958-59, sec., treas. 1962-63), Iowa Library Assn. (pres. 1967-68), Coalition Adult Edn. Orgns. (dir. 1972—), Chgo. Library Club (sec. 1983-84). Home: 314 Skokie Ct Wilmette IL 60091 Office: American Library Assn 50 E Huron St Chicago IL 60611

HANSEN, ARNE RAE, museum administrator; b. Fergus Falls, Minn., Mar. 4, 1940; s. Arnold Rudolph and Elma Mildred (Tolliver) H.; stepson L. R. Hinzmann; m. Diane Cecelia Bowman, Jan. 29, 1966; children: Kyla Kristine, Gueran Wray. A.A., Black Hawk Coll., 1968; B.F.A. (Kennedy scholar), U. Tex., 1970; M.F.A., U. Okla., 1972. Asst. to dir. museums Ill. State U., Normal, 1972-73, acting dir. mus's., 1973-74, dir. mus's., 1974-75, asst. prof. art, 1973-75; dir. Colorado Springs (Colo.) Fine Arts Center, 1975-79, Rocky Mountain Regional Art Conservation Center, U. Denver, 1979—. Artist, represented in permanent collections, Art Mus. of U. Okla., Ardmore (Okla.) Art Center. Bd. dirs. El Paso County (Colo.) Park and Recreation Dist., Broadmoor Ski Racing Acad.; pres. Colorado Springs Am. Athletic Union Swim Team. Served with USAF, 1958-65. Mem. Internat. Council Mus., Art Mus. Am (treas.), Colo.-Wyo. Assn. Mus., Assn. Art Mus. Dirs., Mountain Plains Mus. Assn. (v.p.), Am. Assn. Mus. (sr. examiner accreditation program), Western Assn. Art Museums (treas.), Colorado Springs C. of C., Phi Theta Kappa, Phi Kappa Phi. Home: Box 719 Avon CO 81620 Office: 2420 S University Blvd Denver CO 80208

HANSEN, ARTHUR GENE, university chancellor; b. Sturgeon Bay, Wis., Feb. 28, 1925; s. Henry A. and Ruth (Anderson) H. B.S. in Elec. Engring, Purdue U., 1946, M.S. in Math, 1948, D.Eng., 1970; Ph.D. in Math, Case Inst. Tech., 1958; D.Sc., Tri State Coll., 1972, Ind. U., 1982. Research scientist NASA, 1948-49, 50-58; tchr. U. Md., 1949-50; sect. head Cornell Aero. Lab., Buffalo, 1958-59; mem. faculty mech. engring. U. Mich., 1959-66; dean Ga. Inst. Tech., 1966-69, pres., 1969-71, Purdue U., 1971-82; chancellor Tex. A&M U. System, 1982—; prof. mech. engring. Tuskegee Inst., 1965; sr. research engr. Douglas Aircraft Co., 1964; cons. to industry, 1961-70; dir. Am. Electric Power Co., Inc., Internat. Harvester Co., Internat. Paper Co.; Chmn. Atlanta Civic Design Commn., 1967-69, Ga. Sci. and Tech. Commn., 1968-71, Ga. Ocean Sci. Center of Atlantic Commn., Atlanta, 1968-71; mem. adv. council Skidaway Oceanographic Inst. for Univ. System Ga., 1968-71; pres. Ind. Conf. Higher Edn., 1975; chmn. com. on minorities in engring. NRC, 1974-76; bd. dirs. Nat. Action Council for Minorities in Engring., Inc., 1980-81; mem. gen. adv. com. to ERDA, 1975-76; chmn. adv. council Electric Power Research Inst., 1973-79; mem. research adv. com. Dept. Energy, 1984. Author: Similarity Analyses of Boundary Value Problems in Engineering, 1964, Fluid Mechanics, 1967. Chmn. bd. visitors Air U., 1974-77; trustee Nat. Fund Minority Engring. Students, 1980-81; mem. acad. adv. bd. U.S. Naval Acad., 1975-79; chmn. Tex. Com. Employer Support of Guard and Res. Served with USMCR, 1943-46. Recipient Leather medal Sigma Delta Chi; named Ind. Engr. of Yr., 1979, Purdue Disting. Alumnus, 1979. Mem. AAAS, Gas Research Inst. (chmn. adv. council 1976-79), Nat. Acad. Engring. (council), Am. Soc. Engring. Edn., Sigma Xi, Eta Kappa Nu, Pi Tau Sigma, Tau Beta Pi, Phi Kappa Phi, Omicron Delta Kappa, Phi Eta Sigma, Kappa Kappa Psi. Home: 2405 Quail Hollow Bryan TX 77801 Office: Office of Chancellor Texas A&M Univ System College Station TX 77843

HANSEN, BARBARA CALEEN, university dean; b. Boston, Nov. 24, 1941; d. Reynold L. and Dorothy (Richardson) Caleen; m. Kenneth Dale Hansen, Oct. 8, 1976; 1 son, David Scott. B.S., UCLA, 1964, M.S., 1965; Ph.D., U. Wash., 1971. Asst. prof. then assoc. prof. U. Wash., Seattle, 1971-76; prof., assoc. grad. dean U. Mich., Ann Arbor, 1977-82; assoc. v.p. acad. affairs and research, dean grad. sch. So. Ill U., Carbondale, 1982—; mem. adv. com. to dir. NIH, Washington, 1979-83; mem. joint health policy com. Assn. Am. Univs., Nat. Assn. State Univs. and Land-Grant Colls., Am. Council on Edn., Washington, 1982—; mem. nutrition study sect. NIH, 1979—; mem. program com. Inst. Medicine-Nat. Acad. Scis., Washington, 1982—. Contbr. articles to profl. jours.; editor: Controversies in Obesity, 1983; chpts. on physiology. Mem. adv. com. Am. Bur. Med. Advancement China, N.Y.C., 1982—, Robert Wood Johnson Found., Princeton, N.J., 1982—. Fellow U. Pa. Inst. Neuroscis., 1966-68, Am. Acad. Nursing, 1977; Arthur Patch McKinley scholar Phi Beta Kappa, 1964. Mem. Am. Physiol. Soc., Inst. Medicine, Am. Inst. Nutrition, Am. Soc. for Clin. Nutrition, Phi Beta Kappa. Republican. Presbyterian. Home: 30 Meadowood Ln Carbondale IL 62901 Office: So Ill U Grad Sch Carbondale IL 62901

HANSEN, CHARLES, corporate executive; b. Jersey City, May 23, 1926; s. Charles Henry and Katherine (Bensch) H.; m. Carolyn P. Smith, Sept. 26, 1953; children: Mark, Melissa. B.S., U. Mich., 1946; J.D., Mich. Law Sch., 1950. Bar: N.Y. 1951, Wis. 1961, Mo. 1980. Engr. Westinghouse Electric Co., 1946; assoc. Mudge, Stern, Williams & Tucker, 1950-53; chief labor counsel, div. counsel Sylvania Electric Products, 1953-61; sec., gen. counsel Trane Co., La Crosse, Wis., 1961-69, exec. v.p., 1968-73; pres. Cutler-Hammer World Trade, Inc., 1973-77; v.p. Cutler-Hammer, Inc., 1973-77, exec. v.p., 1977-79; sr. v.p. law Emerson Electric Co., 1979-84, sr. v.p., sec., gen. counsel, 1984—. Served to lt. (j.g.) USNR, 1943-46. Mem. Am., Wis., Mo. bar assns., Order of Coif, Tau Beta Pi. Home: 8 Wydown Terr Clayton MO 63105 Office: 8000 W Florissant Saint Louis MO 63136

HANSEN, CLAIRE V., financial executive; b. Thornton, Iowa, June 3, 1925; s. Charles F. and Grace B. (Miller) H.; m. Renee C. Hansen, Aug. 17, 1946; children: Charles James, Christopher David, Peter Chrissis. B.Sc., U. Notre Dame, 1947; M.B.A., Harvard U., 1948. Chartered fin. analyst. With Salk, Ward & Salk, Inc.; v.p. Salk Inst. Agency, 1954-59; with Duff, Anderson & Clark, Chgo., 1959-67, v.p., dir., 1967-71; dir. Duff and Phelps, Inc., 1972—; exec. v.p., dir. Duff & Phelps, 1975, pres., dir., 1975—. Bd. dirs. Chgo. Lung Assn., 1962-80, pres., 1973-75; bd. dirs. Am. Lung Assn., 1971-83; trustee Glenwood Sch. Boys, 1974—; bd. dirs. Center Religion and Psychotherapy in Chgo., 1979—, Auditorium Theatre Council, Schwab Rehab. Hosp., 1978—; pres. Schwab Rehab. Hosp., 1980-82. Served with USMC, World War II. Mem. Investment Analysts Soc. Chgo., Fin. Analysts Fedn. Republican. Episcopalian. Clubs: Economic, Met., Mid-Am.,

Univ., Olympia Fields Country. Home: 73 Graymoor Ln Olympia Fields IL 60461 Office: 55 E Monroe St Chicago IL 60603

HANSEN, DONALD W., financial services executive; b. Chgo., June 9, 1924; s. Chris M. and Violet Louise (Anderson) H.; m. Nancy SanRoman, Dec. 21, 1944; children: Donald W. II, Scott D., Debra Anne. B.S. in Bus. and Econs, Ill. Inst. Tech., 1948; postgrad., U. Chgo. Grad. Sch. Bus., 1957. Fin. rep., mgr. bank relations Comml. Credit Co., Chgo., 1948-57; pres. Sears Roebuck Acceptance Co., Wilmington, Del., 1957-63; v.p. fin. services Allstate Ins. Co., 1963-75, v.p. money center and banking adminstrn., 1971-76; pres. Allstate Fin. Corp., 1964-74; chmn. bd. Allstate Savs. & Loan Assn., 1963-66; pres., chief exec. officer Allstate Enterprises Mortgage Corp., Anaheim, Calif., 1972-74; pres., chief exec. officer, dir. First Farwest Corp., Portland, Oreg., 1976-78, Midwestern United Life Ins. Co., Ft. Wayne, Ind., 1978—; pres., chief operating officer United Equitable Corp., Lincolnwood, Ill. Bd. dirs. Fine Arts Found. and Art Mus. of Ft. Wayne. Served with AUS, 1943-46. Mem. Newcomen Soc., U.S., Ind. chambers commerce, Ind. Soc. Chgo., Phi Kappa Sigma. Republican. Presbyterian. Clubs: Ft. Wayne Country, Summit (Ft. Wayne); Internat., Portland City. Home: 6 Court of Fox River Valley Lincolnshire IL 60015 Office: 733 N Cicero Ave Lincolnwood IL 60646

HANSEN, DONALD WALDEMAR, food products company executive; b. Washington, Oct. 16, 1927; s. Waldemar Conrad and Muriel (Bruggman) H.; m. Janet Eleanor Lines, Sept. 6, 1952; children: Kimberly, Philip, Jeffrey. B.S., Iowa State U., 1951, M.S., 1952; postgrad., NYU Sch. Bus., 1966. Vice pres. Stamats Pub. Co., Cedar Rapids, Iowa, 1953-62; gen. mgr. PDI Internat. (A.B.) Time Inc., London, 1962-67; v.p. Crosfield Electronics Inc., N.Y.C., 1967-68, dir.; with W.W. Grainger Inc., Chgo., 1970-81, v.p. mfg., 1973-76, v.p. ops., 1976-77, v.p. adminstrn. and planning, 1978-81, dir.; exec. v.p., dir. CFS Continental Inc., Chgo., 1981—; pres. Doerr Electric Corp., W. W. Grainger Inc. Served with USN, 1946-47. Mem. Internat. Foodservice Mfg. Assn. (bd. dirs. 1982—), Econ. Club Chgo., Sigma Alpha Epsilon, Sigma Delta Chi. Clubs: Lansdowne; Am. (London); Barrington Hills Country (Ill.). Office: CFS Continental Inc 100 S Wacker Dr Chicago IL 60606

HANSEN, FRANCIS EUGENE, clergyman; b. Underwood, Iowa, Oct. 30, 1925; s. John Alexander and Annie (Rasmussen) H.; m. Wanda Ann Hoss, Aug. 20, 1949; children: Blair, Cheryl. Student, Biarritz (France) Am. U., 1946; A.A., Graceland Coll., Lamoni, Iowa, 1948; B.S., U. Kans., 1950. Claim service rep. Mut. of Omaha, 1950-54; ordained to ministry Reorganized Ch. of Jesus Christ of Latter-day Saints, 1943, ordained bishop, 1956; asst. to Presiding Bishopric, World Hdqrs. Reorganized Ch. of Jesus Christ of Latter-day Saints, Independence, Mo., 1954-56, bishop, Los Angeles, 1956-66, counselor to presiding bishop, 1966-72, presiding bishop, 1972—; Vice pres., mem. bd. publs. Herald Pub. House.; dir. Charter Bank of Independence, Health Care Systems, Inc. Mem. Good Govt. League, 1969—; Mem. community adv. com. to Councilman John Cassidy, Los Angeles City Council, 1966—; v.p. Truman-Forest Pharmacy Bd.; pres. bd. suprs. Atherton Levy Dist.; mem. Jackson County Farm Bur. Treas.; trustee Independence Sanitarium and Hosp., 1966—; bd. dirs. Mound Grove Cemetery, Social Service Center, Central Devel. Assn., Central Profl. Bldg.; mem. corp. body H.S. Truman Neurol. Center, Casa Real Retirement Center; pres. bd. dirs. Elbert A. Smith Retirement Center. Served with AUS, 1944-46; ETO. Decorated Combat Inf. badge, Purple Heart. Hon. fellow Harry S. Truman Library Inst.; Mem. C. of C. (dir.), Jackson County Hist. Soc., Order of Bishops, Lambda Delta Sigma, Beta Gamma Sigma. Club: Rotarian (dir., com. chmn.). Home: 1308 N 6th St Blue Springs MO 64015 Office: The Auditorium PO Box 1059 River at Walnut Independence MO 64051

HANSEN, FRED GILLINGHAM, oil and gas company executive; b. Richland Center, Wis., June 15, 1935; s. Martin and Phyllis Ester (Gillingham) H.; m. Joyce Ann Walton, July 3, 1953; children: Shelley Hansen Tessen, Gregory Martin, Hans Eric. B.S.C.E., U. Wis., 1957; cert., Harvard U. Bus. Sch., 1967. Engr. officer Continental Pipeline Co., 1960-68; asst. div. mgr. Continental Oil Co., Denver, 1968-69; pres. Navajo Refining Co., Artesia, N.Mex., 1969-76, So. Union Refining Co., Hobbs, N.Mex., 1976-81, exec. v.p., chief operating officer, Dallas, 1981-82, pres., chief exec. officer, 1982—. Mem. N.Mex. Senate, 1975-76; chmn. United Fund, Artersia, 1974; pres. N.Mex. Taxpayers Assn., 1974. Served with U.S. Army, 1957-60. Mem. Nat. Peroleum Refiners Assn. (dir. 1970—), Ind. Refiners Assn. (dir. 1973-82), N.Mex. Assn. Commerce and Industry (dir. 1974-82), Am. Gas Assn. (dir. 1982—). Democrat. Methodist. Clubs: Petroleum, Elks. Lodge: Elks. Home: 3449 Courtyard Circle Dallas TX 75234 Office: So Union Co 1800 InterFirst Two Dallas TX 75270

HANSEN, GEORGE VERNON, congressman; b. Tetonia, Idaho, Sept. 14, 1930; s. Dean Erlease and Elmoyne Bendicta (Brewer) H.; m. Constance Sue Camp, Dec. 19, 1952; children—Steven, James, Patricia, William, Joanne. A.B. in History and Russian with honors, Ricks Coll., Rexburg, Idaho, 1956; grad., Grimms Bus. Coll., 1958; postgrad. edn., Idaho State U., 1962-63. Tchr. math. secondary pub. sch., 1956-58; guest lectr. ins. and estate planning colls. and high schs.; spl. agt. N.Y. Life Ins. Co., 1958—; mayor Alameda, Idaho, 1961-62, 1962, mem. city commn., 1962-65; mem. 89th-90th, 94th-96th Congresses, 2d Dist. Ida.; dep. under-sec. agr. for congl. relations and dep. adminstr. Agrl. Stblzn. and Conservation Service. (for state and county operations), 1969-71. Chmn. Bannock County Heart Assn., 1962-64. Served with USAF, 1951-54; Served with USNR, 1964-70. Recipient Distinguished Service award Pocatello Jaycees, 1961. Mem. Idaho Municipal League (bd. dirs. 1961-63), Pocatello C. of C., Am. Legion, Idaho Farm Bur., Life Ins. Underwriter Assn. Republican. Mem. ch. of Jesus Christ of Latter-Day Saints. Clubs: Kiwanian (bd. dirs.), Pocatello 20-30 (past pres.). Office: 1125 Longworth House Office Bldg Washington DC 20515

HANSEN, GRANT LEWIS, aerospace and info. systems executive; b. Bancroft, Idaho, Nov. 5, 1921; s. Paul Ezra and Leona Sarah (Lewis) H.; m. Iris Rose Heyden, Apr. 21, 1945; children: Alan Lee, Brian Craig, Carol Margaret, David James, Ellen Diane. B.S. in Elec. Engring., Ill. Inst. Tech., 1948; postgrad. engring. and mgmt., UCLA, Calif. Inst. Tech.; D.Sc., Nat. U., 1978. With Douglas Aircraft Co., 1948-60; v.p., program dir. for Centaur (Convair div.), 1960-65; v.p. launch vehicle programs Convair div. Gen. Dynamics Corp., 1965-69; asst. sec. air force for research and devel., 1969-73; v.p. Gen. Dynamics Corp., San Diego, 1974-78, v.p., gen. mgr., 1973-78; exec. v.p. System Devel. Corp., Santa Monica, Calif., 1978—; also pres. SDC Systems Group, 1978—; U.S. del. NATO (Adv. Group for Aerospace Research and Devel.), 1969-73; U.S. mem. sci. com. for nat. reps. SHAPE Tech. Center, The Hague, Netherlands, 1969-73; mem. research and tech. adv. council NASA, 1971-73; mem. sci. adv. bd. Dept. Air Force, 1976—. Served with USNR; World War II. Decorated Purple Heart; recipient Pub. Service award NASA, 1966, Disting. Pub. Service award, 1975; Alumni Recognition award Ill. Inst. Tech., 1967; USAF Exceptional Civilian Service medal, 1973, 83. Fellow AIAA (nat. pres. 1975), Am. Astronautical Soc., AAAS, Internat. Acad. Astronautics; mem. IEEE (sr.), German Soc. Air and Space Travel (corr.), Nat. Alliance Businessmen (nat. bd. dirs., dir. region IX), Nat. Acad. Engring. (aeros. and space engring. bd.), NRC, Eta Kappa Nu, Tau Beta Pi. Home: 10737 Fuerte Dr LaMesa CA 92041 Office: System Devel Corp 2500 Colorado Ave Santa Monica CA 90406 *I've given my whole self to each challenge I've accepted, believing that what's best for my future is an honest day's effort today. I have great faith in my God and my country.*

HANSEN, GROVER J., savings and loan association executive; b. Chgo., Sept. 29, 1923; s. Aage and Johanne (Rasmussen) H.; m. Geraldine Jones, Oct. 9, 1965; children: Michael E., Debra E., Denyse A., Robert H., Charles R. B.S. in Edn, No. Ill. U., DeKalb, 1949; M.B.A., U. Chgo., 1956; grad., Advanced Mgmt. Program, Harvard U., 1970. Exec. sec., edn1. dir. Am. Inst. Banking, 1951-61; asst. dir. banking edn. com. Am. Bankers Assn., 1961-62; gen. mgr. Produce Reporter Co., Wheaton, Ill., 1962-66; with First Fed. Savs. and Loan Assn., Chgo., 1966—, sr. v.p., 1967-71, pres., chief adminstrv. officer, dir., 1971—, pres., chief operating officer, 1976-83, pres., mng. officer, 1983—; dir. First Savs. Corp., Lawyers Title Ins. Corp., First Fed. Savs. of Chgo. Found., Life of Va., Investors Mortgage Ins. Co., Western Employers Ins., Ill. Power Co.; chmn. bd. Savs. Place, Inc., Appraisal Services, Inc., First Fed. Agy.; pres., dir. First Savs. Investment Corp.; chmn. bd., chmn. exec. com., dir. Chgo. Area Renewal Effort Service Corp., 1972-76. Bd. dirs. Mid-Am. chpt. ARC, 1973-83, chmn., 1979-81; trustee Met. Crusade Mercy, 1976-79, chief crusader bus. and profl. div., 1976-80; chief crusader United Way/ Crusade of Mercy, 1981-82; chmn. bd. Center Religion and Psychtherapy, Chgo., 1971-78; bd. dirs. Chgo. Theol. Sem., 1973-75, bd. assos., 1980—; chmn. devel. subcom. Cook County Econ. Devel. Adv. Com., 1977-79; bd. govs. Glenwood Sch. Boys, 1974—; bd. dirs. Ingalls Meml. Hosp., 1973-78; governing mem. Chgo. Symphony Orch., 1980—; mem. Cook County R.E. Tax Study Commn., 1977-79; vice chmn. spl. gifts campaign Chgo. YMCA, 1973-75; gen. fund dr. chmn. Chgo. Jr. Achievement, 1976. Served to lt. USAAF, 1942-45. Recipient Medal of Merit award from mayor of Chgo., 1976; Distinguished Service award Kiwanis Internat., 1977; Most Distinguished Alumni award No. Ill. U., 1977. Mem. Fed. Savs. and Loan Council Ill. (dir. 1977-79), Cook County Ins. Savs. Assns., Am. Inst. Banking (life), Am. Savs. and Loan Inst., Newcomen Soc. N.Am. Clubs: Union League (Chgo.) (dir. 1973-80, 1st v.p. 1977-78); Union League (pres. 1978-80), Econ., Harvard Bus. Sch. (Chgo.). Home: 1501 N State Pkwy Chicago IL 60610 Office: 1 S Dearborn St Chicago IL 60603 also First Federal of Chicago PO Box 4444 Chicago IL 60680

HANSEN, HERBERT EDWIN, retired oil company executive; b. Cleve., Oct. 29, 1920; s. Marius and Romaine (Christman) H.; m. Marietta Grider Hewitt, Jan. 5, 1946; children: Marian Romaine, Donna Hewitt, David Christman. B.A. summa cum laude, Oberlin Coll., 1942; M.B.A. with distinction, Harvard U., 1946, J.D., 1949. Bar: Mo. 1949. Asso. firm Dietrich, Tyler and Davis, Kansas City, Mo., 1949-52; zone landman Gulf Oil Corp., Tulsa and Wichita, Kans., 1952-56; adminstrv. asst. to gen. mng. dir. Iranian Oil Operating Co., Teheran, 1956-62; coordinator govt. agreements Eastern Hemisphere Gulf Oil Co., London, Eng., 1962-69; v.p. Gulf Oil Corp., Pitts., 1969-75; sr. v.p. Gulf Oil Exploration and Prodn. Co., Houston, 1975-83. Contbr. to: Jour. Energy and Devel. Served to lt. comdr. UNSR, 1943-46. Mem. Mo. Bar Assn., Houston Com. on Fgn. Relations, Harvard Law Sch. Assn., Phi Beta Kappa. Republican. Methodist. Club: Harvard (Houston). Home: 11839 Durrette St Houston TX 77024

HANSEN, HOBART GARFIELD, physician, hosp. supt.; b. Hancock, N.Y., Aug. 10, 1923; s. Hobart Garfield and Dorothy (Nielsen) H.; m. Archer Ellis, Sept. 3, 1949; children—Christian Stowe, Margaret Ellis. A.B., Columbia, 1945, M.A., 1946; M.D., U. Va., 1957. Intern research psychology N.Y. State Psychiat. Inst. and Hosp., 1945-46; intern clin. psychology N.Y. State Dept. Mental Hygiene, 1946-47; clin. psychologist Elmira (N.Y.) Reception Center and Elmira Reformatory, 1947-51; chief psychologist Western State Hosp., Staunton, Va., 1951-53; med. intern U. Va. Hosp., 1957-58; staff physician Western State Hosp., 1958-60; resident psychiatry St. Elizabeth's Hosp., Washington, 1960-63; clin. dir. Western State Hosp., 1963-65, asst, supt., 1965-67, supt., 1967-77; med. dir. Massanutten Mental Health Center, 1977—; psychiat. cons. Woodrow Wilson Rehab. Center, 1977-79; psychiatrist Rockbridge Mental Health Clinic, 1977-79; clin. asst. prof. psychiatry U. Va. Sch. Medicine, 1965—. Mem. Am. Psychiat. Assn., Neuropsy. Soc. Va. (pres. 1976-77). Home: 148 Fallon St Staunton VA 24401

HANSEN, HUGH JUSTIN, agricultural engineer; b. Thief River Falls, Minn., Mar. 30, 1923; s. Oscar Edward and Othelia C. (Olen) H.; m. JoAnne Skeim, Aug. 28, 1949; children: Susan Marie, Christopher Hugh, Mark Alexander. B.S. in Agrl. Engring, N.D. State U., 1951; M.S., Cornell U., 1952. Asst. prof. agrl. engring. Purdue U., 1952-55; with Reuben H. Donnelley Corp., N.Y.C., 1955-71, pub., 1962-71; with Dun-Donnelly Pub. Corp., N.Y.C., 1971-74; mgr. Western Regional Agrl. Engring. Service, Oreg. State U., Corvallis, 1974-78, extension energy engr., 1978—. Served with USMCR, 1942-46. Fellow Am. Soc. Agrl. Engrs. (bd. dirs. 1964-66, pres. 1971-72); Mem. Am. Soc. Engring. Edn., Am. Agrl. Editors Assn. Home: 3018 NW Lisa Pl Corvallis OR 97330 Office: Agrl Engring Dept Oreg State U Corvallis OR 97331 *Helping farmers do a good job of producing high quality food and fiber with a minimum of labor and a fair return on their investment with a reasonable profit has been and continues to be my lifetime professional objective.*

HANSEN, JAMES LEE, sculptor; b. Tacoma, June 13; s. Hildreth Justine and Mary Elizabeth H.; m. Annabelle Hair, Aug. 31, 1946; children—Valinda Jean, Yauna Marie. Grad., Portland Mus. Art Sch. Mem. faculty Oreg. State U., Corvallis, 1957-58, U. Calif., Berkeley, 1958, Portland State U., 1964—, U. Oreg., 1967. One-man shows include, Fountain Gallery, Portland, Oreg., 1966, 69, 77, U. Oreg. Art Mus., Eugene, 1970, Seligman (Seders Gallery), Seattle, Portland Art Mus., 1971, Cheney Cowles Meml. Mus., Spokane, Wash., 1972, Polly Freidlander Gallery, Seattle, 1973, 75, 76, group exhbns. include, N.W. Ann. Painters and Sculptors, Seattle, 1952-73, Oreg. Ann. Painters and Sculptors, Portland Art Mus., 1952-75, Whitney Mus. Am. Art, N.Y.C., 1953, Santa Barbara (Calif.) Mus. Art, 1959-60, Denver Art Mus., 1960, San Francisco Art Mus., Smithsonian Instn., Washington, 1974, Wash. State U., Pullman, 1975; represented in permanent collections, Graphic Arts Center, Portland, State Capitol, Olympia, Wash., U. Oreg., Eugene, Salem (Oreg.) Civic Center, Clark Coll., Vancouver, Wash., various banks and schs., numerous commns. Address: 6423 NE 284th St Battle Ground WA 98604 *

HANSEN, JAMES ROGER, musician; b. Joliet, Ill., Sept. 22, 1908; s. James and Minnie (Petersen) H.; m. Rita Ellen Williams, Aug. 30, 1947; children—Jane, Susan, Mary Joan. Mus.B., Cosmopolitan Sch. Music, Chgo., 1952; Mus.M., Chgo. Conservatory Music, 1955; student, Loyola U. at Chgo. Chmn. Chgo. Symphony Orch. mems'. com., 1970-71, 71-72; faculty Chgo. Conservatory Music. Violinist, Kansas City Philharmonic Orch., 1935-42, Pitts. Symphony Orch., 1945-46, Chgo. Symphony Orch., 1946—. Served with USAAF, 1942-45. Mem. Chgo. Fedn. Musicians (shopsteward 1970-71, 71-72). Club: Cliff Dwellers (Chicago). Home: 2332 Bryant Ave Evanston IL 60201 Office: 220 S Michigan Ave Chicago IL 60604

HANSEN, JOHN PAUL, engineering educator; b. Bain, Minn., Feb. 11, 1928; s. Charles George and Henrietta Eva (Taylor) H.; m. Doris Alma Dropps, Sept. 9, 1950; children: Steven Michael, Bradley Paul, Kurt Lewis. B.S., U. Minn., 1954, M.S., 1955, Ph.D., 1958. Registered profl. engr., Ala. Metall. engr. U.S. Bur. Mines, Mpls., 1958-63; prof. metall. engring. U. Ala., University, 1963-67, 73—, prof., head chem. and metall. engring. dept., 1970-73; chief metallurgy research lab. U.S. Bur. Mines, Tuscalossa, Ala., 1967-70; also lectr. U. Ala.; cons. Army Missile Command, Ala. Geol. Survey. Served with AUS, 1946-49, 50-52. Mem. AIME, Am. Inst. Chem. Engrs., Sigma Xi, Tau Beta Pi, Alpha Sigma Mu, Omega Chi Epsilon. Lutheran. Club: University Faculty (pres. 1973). Research reduction of iron ores and prereduced iron ore pellets. Home: 12 Twin Manor Northport AL 35476 Office: Dept Metallurgical Engring Univ Ala PO Box G University AL 35486

HANSEN, KENT FORREST, nuclear engineering educator; b. Chgo., Aug. 10, 1931; s. Kay Frost and Mary (Cummins) H.; m. Katherine Elizabeth Kavanagh, June 13, 1959 (dec. Dec. 1975); children—Thomas Kay, Katherine Mary; m. Deborah Lea Hill, June 26, 1977. S.B., Mass. Inst. Tech., 1953, Sc.D., 1959. Mem. faculty Mass. Inst. Tech., 1960—, prof. nuclear engring., 1969—, exec. officer nuclear engring. dept., 1972-76, acting head dept., 1975—, assoc. dean engring., 1979-81; dir. EG&G, Inc.; cons. to industry. Co-author: Numerical Methods of Reactor Analysis, 1964, Advances in Nuclear Science and Technology, Vol. 8, 1975. Ford postdoctoral fellow, 1960-61. Fellow Am. Nuclear Soc. (dir., Arthur Holly Compton award 1978); mem. Soc. Indsl. and Applied Math., Assn. Computing Machines, Am. Soc. Engring. Edn., Nat. Acad. Engring., Sigma Xi, Sigma Chi. Home: Baker Bridge Rd Lincoln MA 01773 Office: Mass Inst Tech Massachusetts Ave Cambridge MA 02139

HANSEN, KERMIT READ, former banker, financial company executive; b. Omaha, Feb. 26, 1917; s. Axel T. and Mary (Sarman) H.; m. Mary Rosborough, June 6, 1945; children: Kurt, Eric, Kristin, Lauren. A.B., U. Nebr., 1939; grad., Sch. Financial Pub. Relations, Chgo., 1962. Announcer radio sta. KOWH, Omaha, 1939-41; in advt. sales, editorial columnist Omaha World-Herald, 1946-50, asst. bus. mgr., 1951- 53; with Gardner Advt., Washington, 1950-51; partner Allen & Reynolds Advt., Omaha, 1953-59; with U.S. Nat. Bank Omaha, 1959-81, exec. v.p., 1967-73, pres., 1973-81, chmn., 1975-78; pres. Nebr. Electronic Transfer System, Inc., 1975-77, Fin. Perspectives Co., 1981—; instr., trustee Basic Sch. Banking, 1964-68; pres., instr. Intermediate Sch. Banking, 1968—, instr., 1976—. Pres. Omaha Symphony, 1956-62, United Community Services, 1969-71; pres. Omaha Safety Council, 1959-61, chmn., 1961-62; Bd. regents U. Nebr., 1971—, chmn., 1974. Served to col. AUS, World War II; brig. gen. Res.; ret. Decorated Silver Star, Legion of Merit, Bronze Star with 2 oak leaf clusters, Purple Heart, Combat Inf. Badge; recipient Silver Beaver award Boy Scouts Am., 1965; named Man of Year Omaha Jr. C. of C., 1948, Omaha Order Eagles, 1949; recipient Safety award Neb. B'nai B'rith, 1964. Mem. U.S. C. of C., Nebr. C. of C. (v.p., treas. 1963-65), Omaha C. of C., Bank Pub. Relations and Marketing Assn. (dir. 1964-67), Assn. Res. City Bankers, Ak-Sar-Ben (councilor 1968—), Beta Theta Pi. Clubs: Omaha, Omaha Country. Home: Quail Ridge 21935 Mayberry Circle Elkhorn NE 68022

HANSEN, LARRY LEE, electronics co. exec.; b. Ephraim, Utah, Aug. 19, 1928; s. Lester J. and Ethel Mary (Larson) H.; m. Barbara Louise Jones, Nov. 26, 1954; children—Jana Lee, Lizabeth Ann, Bradley L., Karen Lynne. B.S. in Elec. Engring, Utah State U., 1958. With Varian Assos., 1964—, plant mgr., Salt Lake City, 1964-70, corp. v.p., pres. indsl. equipment group, Palo Alto, Calif., 1975—; chmn. adv. com. semicondr. mfg. equipment Dept. Commerce, 1975. Served with USAF, 1950-54. Mem. Semicondr. Equipment and Material Inst. (dir. 1975—, pres., chmn. bd. 1980—). Mormon. Office: 611 Hansen Way Palo Alto CA 94033

HANSEN, LEROY JOHN, mag. editor; b. Eagle River, Wis., Mar. 10, 1922; s. Harry Forest and Angeline Barbara (Renk) H.; m. Michiko Iwata, June 15, 1954; children—Dane John, Mark Roy, Teresa Ann. Student, U. Wis., 1940-43; B.A. in Journalism, U. So.Calif., 1948. With Riverside (Calif.) Press-Enterprise, 1948; with UP and UPI, 1948-65, div. news editor in, Asia, 1958-62; with U.S. News & World Report, Washington, 1965—, fgn. editor, 1979—. Served with USMC, 1943-46. Office: 2400 N St NW Washington DC 20037

HANSEN, LOWELL C., II, state ofcl.; b. Oct. 11, 1939; (married); 5 children. B.S.B.A., U. Nebr. Mem. S.D. Ho. of Reps., 1972-78, speaker pro tem, 1974-76, speaker, 1976-78; lt. gov., State of S.D., Pierre, 1979—. Republican. Office: Office Lt Gov State Capitol Bldg Pierre SD 57501 *

HANSEN, MORRIS HOWARD, statistician, former govt. ofcl.; b. Thermopolis, Wyo., Dec. 15, 1910; s. Hans C. and Maud Ellen (Omstead) H.; m. Mildred R. Latham, Aug. 31, 1930; children—Evelyn Maxine, Morris Howard, James Hans, Kristine Ellen. B.S., U. Wyo., 1934; M.A., Am. U., 1940; LL.D., U. Wyo., 1959. Statistician Wyo. Relief Adminstrn., 1934; statistician U.S. Bur. of Census, Washington, 1935-43, statis. asst. dir., 1944-49, asst. dir. statis. standards, 1949-61; asso. dir. research and devel., 1961-68; sr. v.p. Westat, Inc., 1968—; instr. statistics grad. sch. Dept. Agr., 1945-50; formerly statis. cons. Nat. Analysts, Inc. Co-author: Sample Survey Methods and Theory, 2 vols, 1953; Contbr. articles to statis. jours. Recipient Rockefeller Pub. Service award, 1962. Fellow Am. Statis. Assn. (pres. 1960), Royal Statis. Soc. (hon.), A.A.A.S., Inst. Math. Statistics (pres. 1953); mem. Internat. Statis. Inst. (hon. mem.), Inter-Am. Statis. Inst., Population Assn. Am., Nat. Acad. Sci. (com. nat. statistics 1972-76), Internat. Assn. Survey Statisticians (pres. 1973-77), Sigma Xi, Alpha Tau Omega, Phi Kappa Phi. Home: 5212 Goddard Rd Bethesda MD 20014

HANSEN, NILES MAURICE, economics educator; b. Louisville, Jan. 2, 1937; s. Kristian and Alma (Jensen) H.; m. Josephine Drescher, Aug. 22, 1959; children: Karen, Eric, Laura. B.A., Centre Coll. Ky., 1958; M.A., Ind. U., 1959, Ph.D., 1963. Mem. research staff Center for Regional Econs., Ghent (Belgium) U., 1961-62; asst. prof. econs. U. Tex., Austin, 1963-65, prof., dir. Center for Econ. Devel., 1969—; prof. econs. U. Ky., Lexington, 1967-69; dir. research project Dept. Labor and Econ. Devel. Adminstrn., Dept. Commerce, 1967. Author: French Regional Planning, 1968, France in the Modern World, 1969, Rural Poverty and the Urban Crisis, 1970, Intermediate-Size Cities as Growth Centers, 1971, Growth Centers and Regional Devel, 1972, Location Preferences, Migration and Regional Growth, 1973, The Future of Nonmetropolitan America, 1973, Public Policy and Regional Development, 1974, The Challenge of Urban Growth, 1975, Improving Access to Economic Opportunity, 1976, The Border Economy, 1981; Editor: Human Settlement Systems: International Perspectives on Structure Change and Public Policy, 1977, The Border Economy: Regional Development in the Southwest, 1981; Contbr. articles to profl. jours. NSF fellow U. Paris, France, 1965-66. Mem. Am. Econ. Assn., So. Econ. Assn., Assn. Comparative Econs., Regional Sci. Assn., Assn. French Speaking Regional Economists. Home: 807 Rock Creek Dr Austin TX 78746 Office: Dept Econs U Tex Austin TX 78712

HANSEN, ORVAL, lawyer, former congressman; b. Firth, Idaho, Aug. 3, 1926; s. Farrel L. and Lily (Wahlquist) H.; m. June Duncan, Dec. 31, 1955; children: Margaret, Elizabeth, James, Katherine, John, Mary, Sarah. B.A., U. Idaho, 1950; J.D., George Washington U., 1954, LL.M., 1973, M.Phil., 1980. Bar: Idaho 1954. Practice law, Idaho Falls,

1956-68; staff asst. to Senator Henry Dworshak, 1950-54; mem. Idaho Ho. of Reps., 1956-62, 64-66, house majority leader, 1961-62; mem. Idaho Senate, 1966-68, chmn. manpower adv. com., 1963-68; mem. 91st-93d congresses from 2d Idaho Dist.; former mem. firm Cook, Purcell, Hansen & Henderson, Washington.; sole practice, Washington. Trustee John F. Kennedy Center for Performing Arts, Aerospace Edn. Found.; pres. Columbia Inst. for Polit. Research. Served with USNR, 1944-46. Rotary Found. fellow U. London (Eng.) Sch. Econs., 1954-55. Mem. Idaho, D.C. bar assns., Am. Legion, V.F.W., Phi Beta Kappa, Sigma Chi, Phi Alpha Delta, Sigma Delta Chi. Republican. Mormon. Home: 5555 Little Falls Rd Arlington VA 22207 Office: 8 E St Washington DC 20003

HANSEN, PETE, cartoonist; b. Denmark; s. Ernie and Kamma (Ruse) H.; m. June Alma Gurss; children: Steven, Brian, Matthew. Student, Newark Sch. Fine Art, 1934-37. Cartoonist, Walt Disney Studios, Burbank, Calif., 1938-40, M.G.M. Animation Studio, Hollywood, Calif., 1947-48; syndicated cartoon strip Lolly, Tribune Co. Syndicate, N.Y.C., 1955—. Mem. Cartoonists Soc. U.S. Office: Tribune Co Syndicate 220 E 42d St New York NY 10017

HANSEN, PETER SIJER, educator, harpsichordist; b. Hayward, Calif., Feb. 5, 1911; s. Peter and Anna (Christoffersen) H.; m. Doris L. Ballard, Dec. 30, 1942. A.B., U. Calif., 1931; M.Music, Eastman Sch. Music, 1934; Ph.D., U. N.C., 1939; exchange student, U. Munich, Germany, 1937-39. Head music dept. Stephens Coll., Columbia, Mo., 1946-53; prof., head music dept. Newcomb Coll.; also chmn dept. music Tulane U., 1953-75, emeritus, 1975—; prof. in charge Tulane-Newcomb Jr. Year Abroad, 1962-63. Pianist-accompanist, N.Y.C. and touring, 1945-46; Author: An Introduction to Twentieth Century Music, 1960, 4th rev. edit., 1977; weekly series lecture recitals on ednl. TV, WYES, New Orleans. Served to lt. (s.g.) USNR., 1942-45. Fulbright research fellow, Paris, 1951-52. Mem. Nat., La., New Orleans music tchrs. assns., Am. Musicol Soc., Coll. Music Soc. Home: 1331 Louisiana Ave New Orleans LA 70115

HANSEN, RICHARD ALAN, truck and trailer exec.; b. Berwyn, Ill., July 10, 1931; s. Melvin Alfred and Dorothy Lucille (Richey) H.; m. Joan Katharine Lacey, Sept. 10, 1955; children—Debra Ann, Richard Alan, David Andrew. B.A., DePauw U., 1953; M.B.A., Ind. U., 1956. With Ernst & Ernst (C.P.A.'s), Indpls., 1956-59; with Boozer Test Mgmt. Service, Indpls., 1959-62; sec., treas. Gen. Automotive Parts Corp., Dallas, 1962-80; v.p., sec. Tex. Kenworth Co., Dallas, 1980—. Served with AUS, 1953-55. Mem. Am. Inst. C.P.A.'s, Tex., Ind. socs. C.P.A.'s, Fin. Execs. Inst. Episcopalian. Club: Rotarian. Home: 4640 Allencrest Ln Dallas TX 75234 Office: 4040 Irving Blvd Dallas TX 75247

HANSEN, RICHARD FRED, architect; b. Mason City, Iowa, Apr. 20, 1932; s. R.P. and Florence Mary (Scherping) H.; m. Barbara Mound, July 20, 1957; children: Kristen, Steven, Mark. B.Arch., Iowa State U., 1955. Draftsman Waggoner & Waggoner, Architects, Mason City, Iowa, 1950-55, architect, 1957-62; prin. Hansen Lind Meyer, Iowa City, Iowa, 1962—; mem. prof. adv. bd. dept. architecture Iowa State U., 1970-75, 1979, mem. engring. adv. council, 1971-79; mem. Iowa Bd. Archtl. Examiners, 1978—, pres., 1980-81; chmn. Region IV Nat. Council Archtl. Registration Bds., 1980-81, mem. intern devel. program assessment com., 1980; pres. Bus. Devel., Inc., Iowa City, 1968-70; mem. Planning and Zoning Commn., Mason City, Iowa, 1959-62. Served to lt. (j.g.) USNR, 1955-57. Fellow AIA (co-chmn. edn. com. 1966, pres. Iowa chpt. 1971); mem. Am. Coll. Hosp. Adminstr. (affiliate), C. of C. Hosp. Adminstr. (chmn. 1971). Methodist. Home: 2026 Ridgeway Dr Iowa IA 52240 Office: Hansen Lind Meyer PC Plaza Centre One Iowa City IA 52244

HANSEN, RICHARD KING, lawyer; b. Modesto, Calif., May 28, 1938; s. Robert and Gretchen (King) H.; m. S. Loretta Young, Dec. 31, 1971; 1 dau., Kymberly Joy. B.S. in Bus. and Tech, Oreg. State U, 1961; J.D., U. So. Calif., 1969. Bar: Calif. bar 1971. With mktg./contracts Bendix Corp., North Hollywood, Calif., 1962-68; mgr. contracts Electonic Memories, Inc., Hawthorne, Calif., 1969; atty., contracts Pertec Computer Corp., Los Angeles, 1970-73, sec., gen. counsel, 1973-81, v.p., 1975-81; of counsel Riordan, Caps, Carbone & McKinzie, P.C., Los Angeles, 1981-82; sole practice, Torrance, Calif., 1982—. Mem. Am. Bar Assn., Calif. Bar Assn., Los Angeles County Bar Assn., Am. Soc. Corp. Secs., Phi Alpha Delta, Phi Kappa Tau. Republican. Congregationalist. Office: 19000 Hawthorne Blvd Torrance CA 90503

HANSEN, RICHARD W., foundation executive; b. Detroit, Oct. 4, 1919; s. Richard W. and Madeline Loba (Dickenson) H.; m. Jo Anne Huffman, Aug. 14, 1968. B.A., Wayne State U., Detroit, 1940. With Prentice-Hall Pub. Co., Engelwood Cliffs, N.J., 1946-64, asst. v.p., exec. editor, 1958-64; pres. Dickenson Pub. Co., Los Angeles, 1964-72, dir., 1965—; exec. dir. Ednl. Found. Am., Encino, Calif., 1972—. Pres. So. Calif. Assn. for Philanthropy. Served with AUS, 1941-46. Office: 16250 Ventura Blvd Encino CA 91436

HANSEN, ROBERT JOSEPH, civil engineer; b. Tacoma, May 27, 1918; s. Joseph and Olaug (Axness) H.; m. Eleanor Swaim Welch, Dec. 26, 1948; children: Eric Charles, Karen Welch. B.S., U. Wash., 1940; Sc.D., MIT, 1948. Research engr. NRC, 1940-43; Princeton, 1943-45, Arthur D. Little Co., Cambridge, Mass., 1945; NRC predoctoral fellow, 1946-47; research asso. MIT, 1947-48, mem. faculty, 1948—, prof. civil engring., 1957—, dep. dir. Project Transp., 1964-67; partner Hansen, Holley & Biggs, Inc. (cons. engrs.), Cambridge, 1955—, prin., 1975—; partner Newmark, Hansen & Assos., Cambridge and Urbana, Ill., 1958-68; cons. biomechanics Mass. Gen. Hosp., 1956-60; mem. security resources panel Exec. Office of Pres., 1957; mem. sr. adv. panel Air Force Ballistic Div., USAF, 1958-60; mem. exec. com. Adv. Com. CD, Nat. Acad. Scis., 1959—. Author: (with others) Structural Design for Dynamic Loads, 1959; also articles, chpts. in books.; editor: Seismic Design for Nuclear Power Plants, 1970. Recipient Army-Navy cert. of appreciation, 1948; Disting. Service citation Dept. Def., 1969. Fellow ASCE (Moisseiff award 1974, Raymond C. Reese research prize 1975); mem. Boston Soc. Civil Engrs., Sigma Xi, Tau Beta Pi. Home: 25 Cambridge St Winchester MA 01890 Office: MIT Cambridge MA 02139

HANSEN, ROBERT NOEL, savings and loan company executive; b. San Francisco, Dec. 27, 1943; s. Elwood Leslie and Thelma Marie (Cruz) H. (Switzer); m. Donna Darlene Albright, Aug. 7, 1971; children: Darin, Eric, Daryl, Hans, Clinton. B.S., Menlo Sch. Bus. Adminstrn., Palo Alto, Calif., 1966; cert., U. Wash. Sch. Exec. Devel., 1977. With Bay View Fed. Savs. & Loan Assn., San Mateo, Calif., 1972—, sr. v.p.-mgr. fin. div., 1978-79, sr. v.p., 1979-80; pres. Bay View Fed. Savs. & Loan, San Mateo, Calif., 1980—; dir. Bay View fed. Savs. & Loan Assn., San Mateo, Calif.; mem. banking adv. com. Coll. of San Mateo, 1981—. Mem. exec. bd. San Mateo County council Boy Scouts Am., Calif.; mem. San Mateo County Devel. Assn., 1980—; bd. govs. Mills Meml. Hosp. Found., San Mateo, 1979—; dep. sheriff Mounted Patrol, San Mateo County, 1980—. Recipient Key to City City of South San Francisco, 1983. Mem. Nat. Council Savs. Instns., U.S. League Savs. Assns., Calif. Savs. and Loan League, Bay Cities Savs. and Loan league (dir. 1982—). Clubs: Peninsula Golf and Country, The 100 (San Mateo). Office: Bay View Savs 2121 S El Camino Real San Mateo CA 94403

HANSEN, ROBERT SUTTLE, chemist, educator; b. Salt Lake City, June 17, 1918; s. Charles Andrew and Bessie (Suttle) H.; m. Gilda Cappannari, Apr. 8, 1939; 1 son, Edward Charles. B.S., U. Mich., 1940, M.S., 1941, Ph.D., 1948; D.Sc. (hon.), Lehigh U., 1978. Asst. prof. chemistry dept. Iowa State U., Ames, 1948-51, asso. prof., 1951-55, prof., 1955—, chmn., 1965-68, distinguished prof., 1967—; asso. chemist Ames Lab., Dept. Energy, 1948-55, sr. chemist, 1955—, chief chemistry div., 1965-68, dir., 1968—; cons. Union Carbide Corp., Procter & Gamble Co.; Mem. chemistry adv. panel NSF, 1971-75, materials research adv. com., 1976-80; mem. Gov.'s Sci. Adv. Council, 1977—, Iowa Energy Policy Council, 1978—. Fellow AAAS; mem. Am. Chem. Soc. (past sec.-treas., chmn. colloid div., Kendall Co. award colloid chemistry 1966, Midwest award 1980), Am. Phys. Soc., AAUP, Phi Beta Kappa, Sigma Xi, Phi Kappa Phi. Home: 2030 McCarthy Rd Ames IA 50010

HANSEN, ROBERT WILLIAM, painter, educator; b. Osceola, Nebr., Jan. 1, 1924; s. William Otto and Gladys Marie (Miller) H.; m. Margaret Helen Kuhlman, Mar. 21, 1948; children: Eric Pat, Fritz Gerald. A.B., U. Nebr., 1948, B.F.A., 1948; Maestro de Bellas Artes, Escuela U. de Bellas Artes, San Miguel de Allende, Mexico, 1949; postgrad., U. de Michoacan, Morelia, Mexico, 1952-53. Asst. prof. art Bradley U., 1949-55, U. Hawaii, 1955-56; asst. prof. Occidental Coll., 1955-60, asso. prof., 1960-67, prof., 1967—. One-man shows include, Comara Gallery, Los Angeles, 1964, 66, 68, 70, 72, 75, Castellane Gallery, N.Y.C., 1964, L.A. Munic. Gallery, 1973, Brand Gallery, 1976, Mich. State U. Gallery, 1980, Oranges/Sardines Gallery, Los Angeles, 1981, 82, group shows include, Mus. Modern Art, N.Y.C., 1961, Carnegie Internat., Pitts., 1961, 64, The New Vein Show, Europe and S. Am., 1969-71; represented in permanent collections, Mus. Modern Art, N.Y.C., Whitney Mus., N.Y.C., Fine Arts Gallery of San Diego. Served with U.S. Army, 1943-46. Guggenheim fellow, India, S.E. Asia, 1961-62; Fulbright sr. research grantee, India, 1961-62; Tamarind lithographic fellow, 1964-65. Mem. Coll. Art Assn., ACLU, Phi Beta Kappa. Home: 1974 Addison Way Los Angeles CA 90041 Office: Occidental Coll Art Dept Los Angeles CA 90041

HANSEN, ROGER GAURTH, university administrator, nutrition and food science educator; b. Smithfield, Utah, Aug. 18, 1920; s. Willard and Syble (Toolson) H.; m. Anna Lou Rees, Aug. 14, 1973; children: Roger, Ted, Lars. B.S., U. Wis., 1944, M.A., 1946, Ph.D., 1948. Grad research and teaching asst. biochemistry U. Wis., Madison, 1944-48; asst. prof. biochemistry U. Utah, Salt Lake City, 1948-50; assoc. prof., prof. biochemistry U. Ill-Urbana, 1950-57; prof., chmn. biochemistry Mich State U., East Lansing, 1957-68; provost, disting. prof. nutrition and food scis. and biochemistry Utah State U., Logan, 1968—; visitor Inst. Biochem. Genetics, U. Cologne, 1965; vis. prof. dept. biochemistry and biophysics U. Calif.-San Francisco, 1975; dir. nutrition and end. info. program U.S. Dept. Agr.-Sci. and Edn. Adminstr., 1980-82; chmn. task force to evaluate Senate Com. report on dietary goals for U.S. Council Agr. Sci. and Tech., 1977; biochem. cons. USPHS; mem. Nat. Nutrition Consortium, Inc., 1978—; mem. tech. adv. com. Thrasher Research Fund, 1978—; mem. sci. adv. com. Am. Inst. Banking, 1978—; bd. advisors Nutrition Research, Inc., 1978—; mem. nutrition research adv. com. Nat. Livestock and Meat Bd., 1978—. Author: (with B.W. Wyes and A. Sorenson) Nutritional Quality Index of Foods, 1979; contbr. articles to profl. jours. Recipient Sesquincentennial award U. Mich., 1967, Robinaward Utah State U., 1976. Mem. AAAS, Am. Chem. Soc., Am. Inst. Nutrition (Borden award 1968), Am. Soc. Biol. Chemists, Am. Soc. Exptl. Biology, Sigma Xi, Phi Kappa Phi, Phi Lambda Upsilon, Phi Sigma, Gamma Alpha. Lodge: Rotary. Home: 1676 E 1030 N Logan UT 84321 Office: Provost's Office UMC 14 Utah State U Logan UT 84322

HANSEN, RUSSELL A., retail company executive; b. 1926; married. Student, Augsburg Coll. With K Mart Corp., Troy, Mich., 1948—, asst. store mgr., 1949-55, store mgr., 1955-64, dist. mgr., 1964-69; sales promotion mgr. div. 1 Kresge Stores, 1969-70; sales dir. and mdse. mgr. Kresge and Jupiter Stores, 1970-72, v.p. and gen. mgr., 1972-73; corp. v.p., dir. sales promotion K Mart Corp., Troy, Mich., 1973-77, exec. v.p. merchandising, 1977-82, exec. v.p. subs., 1982—, dir., 1982—. Served with USAF, 1944-46. Office: K Mart Corp 3100 W Big Beaver Troy MI 48084 *

HANSEN, STEPHEN CHRISTIAN, banker; b. N.Y.C., July 3, 1940; s. Norbert C. and Harriet C. H.; m. Ethel Olmsted, June 12, 1971; 1 son, Lee Christian. A.B., Princeton U., 1962; LL.B., U. Va., 1966; postgrad., Brown U. Grad. Sch. Banking. Bar: N.Y. 1966. Assoc. Alexander & Green, N.Y.C., 1966-68; mem. N.Y. State Legislature, 1968-70; spl. asst. to undersec. HUD, Washington, 1970-73; sr. v.p. Dollar Bank, Pitts., 1976-78, pres., 1978—, chief exec. officer, 1982—. Mem. N.Y. State Bar Assn. Republican. Office: Dollar Bank 535 Smithfield St Pittsburgh PA 15222

HANSHAW, JAMES BARRY, pediatrician, educator; b. Scarsdale, N.Y., Dec. 23, 1928; s. George Lee and Kathryn Frances (Reilly) H.; m. Marian Christine Kernan, Aug. 14, 1954; children: Thomas, Lee, Elizabeth, John, Margaret. A.B., Syracuse U., 1950; M.D., SUNY, Syracuse, 1953. Intern Cin. Gen. Hosp., 1953-54; resident pediatrics U. Rochester Med. Center, 1956-58; Nat. Found. postdoctoral fellow virology Harvard U. Sch. Pub. Health, 1958-60; academic medicine, specializing in pediatrics, Rochester, N.Y., 1960-75, Worcester, Mass., 1975—; instr. to prof. pediatrics and microbiology U. Rochester Sch. Medicine, 1960-75; prof., chmn. dept. pediatrics U. Mass., 1975—; lectr. pediatrics Harvard U. Med. Sch.; vis. prof. Inst. Child Health, London U. and Hosp. for Sick Children, London, 1971-72; cons. USPHS, Am. Acad. Pediatrics, Mass. Dept. Pub. Health. Author: (with J.A. Dudgeon) Viral Infections Fetus and Newborn, 1978, 2d edit. (with Dudgeon and W.C. Marshall), 1984; editor: Am. Jour. Diseases of Children, 1972-82, New Eng. Pediatrician, 1981—. Served with USAF, 1953-56. Buswell fellow U. Rochester, 1960-62; NIH grantee, 1962-75. Mem. Am. Pediatric Soc., Soc. Pediatric Research, Am. Acad. Pediatrics, Infectious Diseases Soc. Am., New Eng. Pediatric Soc., Sigma Xi, Alpha Omega Alpha. Home: 18 Bay Path Dr Boylston MA 01505 Office: 55 Lake Ave N Worcester MA 01605

HANSLOWE, KURT LOEWUS, educator; b. Vienna, Austria, Oct. 15, 1926; came to U.S., 1940, naturalized, 1948; s. Ernst and Leopoldine (Olbrich) Loewus; m. Nannette Reese, Dec. 20, 1948; children—David, Nicholas, Theodora. B.A., Yale U., 1947; J.D., Harvard U., 1951. Bar: Mich. bar 1952. Asst. gen. counsel UAW, Detroit, 1951-58; prof. law, indsl. and labor relations Cornell U., Ithaca, N.Y., 1958—; labor arbitrator; cons., mediator N.Y. Public Employment Relations Bd., 1968—. Author: (with Oberer) Labor Law: Collective Bargaining in a Free Society, 1972; editor: Indsl. and Labor Relations Rev, 1962-65. Pres. Am. Unitarian Youth, 1948-49; mem. Unitarian-Universalist Council of Liberal Chs., Boston, 1954-56. Sr. Fulbright-Hays scholar, Vienna, 1977-78. Office: Cornell Law Sch Ithaca NY 14853 *

HANSMANN, RALPH EMIL, investment executive; b. Utica, N.Y., May 25, 1918; s. Emil C. and Friedericka (Fuchs) H.; m. Doris Macdonald, Oct. 16, 1943; children—Robert E., Jane C. A.B., Hamilton Coll., 1940; M.B.A., Harvard, 1942. Investment asso. Harold F. Linder, William T. Golden, N.Y.C., 1945-48, 53—; staff Gen. Am. Investors Co., Inc., 1949-52; dir. Standard Shares, Inc., Cheapside Dollar Fund Ltd., Verex Corp., Verde Exploration, Ltd. Trustee, treas. Inst. Advanced Study, Princeton, N.J.; trustee Hamilton Coll., Clinton, N.Y.; trustee, treas. N.Y. Pub. Library. Served as lt. USNR, 1942-45. Mem. Phi Beta Kappa. Clubs: Ridgewood (N.J.) Country; Wall Street (N.Y.C.). Home: 385 Manchester Rd Ridgewood NJ 07450 Office: 40 Wall St New York NY 10005

HANSON, ALLAN MORRIS, publishing co. exec.; b. Ladysmith, Wis., Aug. 4, 1934; s. Allen and Gladys Lenore (Morris) H.; m. Naomi Wolf, Aug. 10, 1959; children—Mark David, Hilary Ruth, Kimberly Ann. B.S. in Pharmacy, Oreg. State U., 1957. Mgr. various pharmacies, 1957-62; owner Webb & Rogers Drugs, San Rafael, Calif., 1963-68, H&R Pharmacies Inc., San Rafael, 1968-72; founder, 1973; pres. CM Publs.; pubs. Bicycling mag., San Rafael, 1973-78; pres. H & R Promotions, 1978—; v.p., dir. Software Module Mktg. Co., Sacramento, 1977—; sec., dir. R.C. Dick Geothermal Corp., 1976—; pub. cons., 1978—. Mem. Marin County Grand Jury, 1975-76. Served with AUS, 1958-59. Mem. Am., Calif. pharm. assns. Republican. Clubs: Marin Tennis, Terra Linda Rotary. Home: 51 Mt Muir Ct San Rafael CA 94903 Office: 22 Mitchell Blvd San Rafael CA 94903

HANSON, ANGUS ALEXANDER, geneticist; b. Chilliwack, C., Can., Jan. 1, 1922; s. Francis George and Orpha (McKenzie) H.; m. Helen Gertrude Crook, July 3, 1948; children—Bruce, Alexander, Brian Ernest, Margot Ruth. B.S.A., U. B.C., 1944; M.S., McGill U., 1946; postgrad., Va. Poly. Inst., summer 1947; Ph.D., Pa. State U., 1951. Grad. asst. agronomy dept. Macdonald Coll., Quebec, Can., 1944-46, lectr., 1946-48, asst. prof., 1948-49; agt. U.S. Regional Pasture Research Lab., University Park, Pa., 1949-52; research leader grass and turf investigation crops research div. Agrl. Research Service, U.S. Dept. Agr., 1953-65, chief forage and range br. crops research div., 1965-72, dir., Beltsville, Md., 1972-79; asso. dir. research Waterman-Loomis Co., Highland, Md., 1979-80; dir. research, v.p. W-L Research, Inc., 1980—. Trustee Hillandale Elem. Sch. Recipient Superior Service award Dept. Agr., 1961, Disting. Service award, 1979. Fellow AAAS, Am. Soc. Agronomy; mem. Am. Genetics Assn., Am. Soc. Agronomy, Crop Sci. Soc. Am. (pres.), Sigma Xi. Home: 10411 Sweetbriar Pkwy Silver Spring MD 20903 Office: 7625 Brown Bridge Rd Highland MD 20777

HANSON, ANNE COFFIN, art historian; b. Kinston, N.C., Dec. 12, 1921; d. Francis Joseph Howells and Annie Roulhac (Coffin) Coffin; m. Bernard Alan Hanson, June 27, 1961; children by previous marriage: James Warfield Garson, Robert Coffin Garson, Ann Blaine Garson. B.F.A., U. So. Calif., 1943; M.A. in Creative Arts, U. N.C., 1951; Ph.D., Bryn Mawr Coll., 1962. Instr. Albright Art Sch., U. Buffalo, 1955-58; vis. asso. prof. art Cornell U., 1963; asst. prof. Swarthmore Coll., 1963-64, Bryn Mawr Coll., 1964-68; dir. Internat. Study Center, Mus. Modern Art, N.Y.C., 1968-69; adj. asso. prof. NYU, 1969-70; prof. history art Yale U., New Haven, 1970—, chmn. dept., 1974-78; resident Am. Acad. Rome, spring, 1974. Author: Jacopo della Quercia's Fonte Gaia, 1965, Edouard Manet, 1966, Manet and the Modern Tradition, 1977; contbr. articles to profl. jours; editorial bd.: The Art Bull., 1971—; editor monograph series, Coll. Art Assn., 1968-70; governing bd., Yale U. Press, 1977—; editorial com.: Art Jour., 1979-83. NEH fellow, 1967-68; Am. Council Learned Socs. grantee, summer 1963, fellow, 1983-84; fellow Inst. Advanced Study, fall, 1983. Mem. Coll. Art Assn. Am. (pres. 1972-74), Comité Internationale de l'histoire de l'Art (nat. mem.). Home: 28 Lincoln St New Haven CT 06511 Office: Dept History Art 56 High St Yale U New Haven CT 06520

HANSON, ARTHUR WARREN, restaurant chain executive; b. Kittery, Maine, June 29, 1927; s. Howard Hartley and Bernice (Bonney) H.; m. Catherine Louise Brown, Mar. 6, 1954; children: Mark, Paul, Robin. Student, Emerson U., 1947-49. With Cleaves Food Service, Silver Spring, Md., 1949-59, v.p., to 1959; with Valle's Steak House Corp., Portland, Maine, 1959—, pres., chief exec. officer, owner, 1980—; dir. Prose, Inc.; pres. R & K Wholesalers. Mem. adv. trustee Humphrey Vocat. Sch., Boston. Served with USMC, 1945-49. Mem. Maine Restaurant Assn. (v.p., chmn. edn. com.), Mass. Restaurant Assn. Roman Catholic. Home: 33 Winding River Rd Needham MA 02192 Office: 40 Grove St Wellesley MA 02181

HANSON, BERTIL LENNART, polit. scientist; b. Chgo., Sept. 8, 1932; s. Birger Waldemar and Sofia Cecilia (Eriksson) H.; m. Adelia Nell Castor, Mar. 21, 1964; children—Jon Steffan, Peter. B.Sc., Northwestern U., 1953; A.M., U. Chgo., 1956, Ph.D., 1959. Mem. faculty Okla. State U., Stillwater, 1959—, prof. polit. sci., 1976—. Served with U.S. Army, 1953-55. Fulbright fellow, 1966-67, 73-74. Mem. Am. Polit. Sci. Assn., AAUP. Home: 2808 Sangre Rd Stillwater OK 74074 Office: Polit Sci Dept Okla State U Stillwater OK 74078

HANSON, CARL THOR, health agency executive, retired naval officer; b. Amarillo, Tex., May 7, 1928; s. Carl Joseph Emanuel and Lillian (Nelson) H.; m. Charlotte Ann Edens, Oct. 6, 1956; children: Inge Rew, Erica Karen, Ivor Carl, Lars Jon, Ursula Edens. B.S., U.S. Naval Acad., 1950; M.A., Oxford (Eng.) U., 1954. Commd. ensign U.S. Navy, 1950, advanced through grades to vice adm., 1979; service in, Korea and Vietnam, naval aide, exec. asst. to sec. Navy, 1970-72, comdg. officer Naval Sta., Pearl Harbor, 1973-74; chief U.S. Naval Mission to Brazil, 1974-76; comdr. Cruiser-Destroyer Group 8; also comdr. Attack Carrier Striking Group 2, U.S. 6th Fleet, 1976-77; mil. asst. to sec. def., 1977-79; dir. joint staff Office Joint Chiefs Staff, 1979-82, ret., 1982; mil. analyst (Cable News Network), 1982, pres., chief exec. officer, 1982—. Decorated Def. D.S.M. with oak leaf cluster, Legion of Merit, Bronze Star with combat V, Meritorious Service medal, Joint Service Commendation medal; Vietnam Navy Distinguished Service medal; Brazilian Naval Order of Merit; Rhodes scholar, 1951-54. Mem. Am. Assn. Rhodes Scholars, Council Fgn. Relations, U.S. Naval Inst., U.S. Naval Acad. Alumni Assn., Am. Fedn. Musicians (hon. life). Episcopalian. Clubs: N.Y. Yacht; Leander Rowing (Eng.); Gavea Golf and Country (Rio de Janeiro). Home: The Beresford 211 Central Park W Apt 5H New York NY 10024 Office: Nat Multiple Sclerosis Soc 205 E 42d St New York NY 10017

HANSON, DICK VINCENT, magazine editor; b. Bode, Iowa, Sept. 15, 1925; s. Lawrence Herman and Pearl (Watnem) H.; m. Marilyn Louise Taylor, Apr. 23, 1949; children—Dirk Taylor, Kimberly Ann, Richard Elliott. B.S., Iowa State U., 1948. Mem. editorial staff Successful Farming mag., Des Moines, 1949—, exec. editor, 1955-57, editor, 1957—, agrl. editorial dir., 1981—; mem. journalism curriculum com. U. Ill. at Urbana, 1969—. Mem. Gov. Iowa's Com. on Outdoor Recreation, 1965-67; adv. com. to council rural health A.M.A., 1963-65; chmn. Nat. Farm Inst., 1963. Mem. Am. Agrl. Editors Assn. (past pres.), Am. Assn. Agrl. Coll. Editors, Nat. Wildlife Fedn., Wilderness Soc., Outdoor Writers Assn. Am., Sigma Delta Chi, Gamma Sigma Delta, Alpha Zeta, Delta Upsilon. Home: Rural Route 1 Winterset IA 50273 Office: 1716 Locust St Des Moines IA 50313

HANSON, DONALD NORMAN, educator, chem. engr.; b. Minooka, Ill., Aug. 3, 1918; s. Charles M. and Nellie K. (Pope) H.; m. Sarah L. Hartman, Nov. 6, 1943; children—Charles Hartman, David Frederick, Kristin Ann. B.S., U. Ill., 1940; M.S., U. Wis., 1941, Ph.D., 1943. Mem. faculty U. Wis., 1943-44, Kans. State U., 1946; with Shell Devel. Co., 1944-46; mem. faculty U. Calif. at Berkeley, 1947—, prof. chem. engring., 1958—, chmn. dept., 1963-67; vis. prof. U. Philippines, 1956-

58. Author: (with others) Computation of Multistage Separation Processes, 1961. Mem. Am. Inst. Chem. Engrs., Am. Chem. Soc., Sigma Xi, Delta Sigma Phi, Alpha Chi Sigma, Tau Beta Pi. Home: 522 Moraga Way Orinda CA 94563 Office: Chem Engring Dept Univ California Berkeley CA 94720

HANSON, DONALD WAYNE, electronic engineer, consultant; b. Denver, Feb. 9, 1937; s. Melvin G. and Eleanor (Henning) H.; m. Patricia Lee Gregory, Mar. 16, 1963; children: Susan Ann, Pamela Cathleen. B.S. in Elec. Engring., U. Colo., 1959, M.S., Stanford U., 1961. Registered profl. engr. Colo. Scientist Lockheed Missile and Space Co., Sunnyvale, Calif., 1959-61; engr. Ford-Western Devel. Labs., Palo Alto, Calif., 1961-63; electronic engr. Nat. Bur. Standards, Boulder, 1963—; cons. BDM Corp., Albuquerque, 1983—. Contbr. articles to profl. jours.; patentee satellite controlled clock. Recipient IR-100 Indsl. Research Mag., 1977. Fellow IEEE (M. Barry Carlton 1975); mem. Eta Kappa Nu, Tau Beta Pi. Republican. Presbyterian. Home: 735 Jonquil Pl Boulder CO 80302 Office: Nat Bur Standards 325 Broadway St Boulder CO 80302

HANSON, DUANE ELWOOD, sculptor; b. Alexandria, Minn., Jan. 17, 1925; s. Dewey O. and Agnes N. (Nelson) H.; m. Janice Roche, Aug. 19, 1950; children—Craig Curtis, Paul Duane, Karen Liane; m. Wesla Host, June 15, 1968; children—Maja, Duane Elwood. Student, Luther Coll., 1943-44, U. Wash., 1944-45; B.A., Macalester Coll., 1946; M.F.A., Cranbrook Acad. Art, 1951; D.H.L., Nova U., 1979. Tchr. high schs., Idaho, 1946-47, Iowa, 1949-50, Conn., 1951-53, U.S. Army Dependent Schs., Germany, 1953-60, Atlanta, 1960-62; instr. art Oglethorpe U., 1962-65; asst. prof. Miami-Dade Jr. Coll., 1965-69; sculptor associated O.K. Harris Gallery, N.Y.C., 1969—. One man shows include, Würtembergischer Kunstverein, Stuttgart Germany, 1974, Neue Galerie, AAchen, Germany, Akademie der Künste, Berlin, 1975, Humleback, Denmark, Lousiana Mus., 1975, Edwin A. Ulrich Mus. Art, Wichita, Kans., 1976, U. Nebr. Art Galleries, Lincoln, Des Moines (Iowa) Art Center, Univ. Art Mus. U. Calif. at Berkeley, Portland (Oreg.) Art Mus., William Rockhill Nelson Gallery, Atkins Mus. of Fine Arts, both in Kansas City, Mo., Colo. Fine Arts Center, Colorado Springs, Colo., Va. Mus. Fine Arts, Richmond, Va., Corcoran Gallery of Art, Washington, all 1977, Whitney Mus. Am. Art, N.Y.C., 1978, Jacksonville (Fla.) Art Mus., 1980, Lowe Art Mus., Miami, Fla., 1981, Lock Haven Art Mus., Orlando, Fla., Norton Gallery, Palm Beach, Fla. Recipient Ella Lyman Trust grant, 1963; Blair award Art Inst. Chgo., 1974; D.A.A.D. grantee, Berlin, 1974. Home: 6109 SW 55th Ct Davie FL 33314 Office: OK Harris Gallery 383 W Broadway New York NY 10012

HANSON, DURWIN MELFORD, educator; b. Decorah, Iowa, Dec. 29, 1915; s. Melvin C. and Nickolena (Rasmusen) H.; m. Margorie Nell Kennard, May 15, 1937. B.S., Iowa State U., 1939, M.S., 1949, Ph.D., 1956. Tchr. pub. schs., Storm Lake, Iowa, 1939-41, Melvindale, Mich., 1941-42; tng. facilities officer VA, Des Moines, 1946-49; mem. faculty Iowa State U., Ames, 1949-60, asso. prof. vocational edn., 1949-55, prof., 1955-60; prof., head dept. N.C. State U., Raleigh, 1960—; bd. consultants Community Coll. of Air Force, 1973—. Chmn. United Fund, N.C. State U., 1968-69, chmn. adv. com., 1970—. Served with USNR, 1942-46. Named to Hall of Fame N.C. Bowling Assn.; recipient Outstanding Faculty award, 1971, Outstanding Extension Service award, 1978. Mem. Am. Vocat. Assn., Nat. Assn. Indsl. Tech. Tchr. Educators (pres. 1969-70, trustee 1976-78), So. Assn. Colls. and Schs. (research com., com. on occupational edn.), NEA, Assn. Supervision and Curriculum Devel., Southeastern Bowling Conf. (v.p.), Phi Kappa Phi, Psi Chi, Phi Delta Kappa. Home: 4513 Pamlico Dr Raleigh NC 27609 *Education is the future of the United States. Every effort must be made to provide all youth an opportunity to progress to their ultimate goal of worthy life membership.*

HANSON, EARL DORCHESTER, biology educator; b. Shahjahanpur, India, Feb. 15, 1927; s. Harry Albert and Jean (Dorchester) H.; m. Carlota Ferne Kinzie, June 10, 1948 (div. Aug. 1973); children: Mardi Jean, Stanley Royce, Kenric Mark; m. Evelyn Schenker, Jan. 4, 1975. A.B., Bowdoin Coll., 1949; Ph.D., Ind. U., 1954. Teaching fellow Ind. U., summer 1954; from instr. to asst. prof. Yale, 1954-60; asso. prof. Wesleyan U., Middletown, Conn., 1960-63, prof. biology, 1963-82, Fisk prof. natural sci., 1972—, prof. biology and sci. in soc., 1982—; Mem. Commn. Undergrad. Edn. in Biol. Scis., 1962-67, chmn., 1965-67; mem. regional bd. examiners Woodrow Wilson Fellowships, 1964-65; mem. discipline com. for biology Coll. Entrance Exam. Bd., 1974-76. Author: Animal Diversity, 3d edit, 1972; co-author: Biology: The Science of Life, 1979; Editor: (with others) The Lower Metazoa, 1963, The Origin and Early Evolution of Animals, 1977, Understanding Evolution, 1981. Served with USMCR, 1945-46. Recipient Harbison award for distinguished teaching, 1970; Fulbright fellow, 1960-61, 78-79; Guggenheim fellow, 1960-61. Mem. AAUP, AAAS, Am. Inst. Biol. Scis. (bd. govs. 1970-74), Soc. Protozoologists, Fedn. Am. Scientists, Nat. Assn. Sci. Tchrs. Home: 306 H Wheeler Hill Dr Durham CT 06422

HANSON, EUGENE NELSON, lawyer, educator; b. Iola, Wis., Sept. 27, 1917; s. Harris Gilbert and Delia (Nelson) H.; m. Katie Lou Craft, June 29, 1950; children: P. Louise (Mrs. Ronald F. Gossard), Jennifer Lou (Mrs. Kyle M. Wilhelm). B.A., Luther Coll., Decorah, Iowa, 1939; M.A., U. Wis., 1940, J.D., 1946; LL.M., U. Mich., 1948. Bar: Wis. 1946, Ohio 1954. Asst. prof. law Ohio No. U., Ada, 1947-51, asso. prof., 1951-54, prof., 1954-75, 76—, dean, 1958-73; Fulbright prof. U. Iceland, 1960; distinguished vis. prof. McGeorge Sch. Law, U. of Pacific, 1974-75, prof., 1975-76; judge Harding County Ct., 1983—. Pres. Village Council, 1960-61; Sec. Nat. Lutheran Campus Ministry, Luth. Ch. Am., 1964-67; mem. exec. bd. Ohio Synod, 1969-71. Recipient Distinguished Service award Luther Coll., 1966. Mem. Am., Ohio bar assns., Order of Coif. Democrat. Home: 604 Merrie Monte Ln Ada OH 45810

HANSON, GEORGE FULFORD, geologist; b. Schenectady, 1916; s. George F. and Barbara (Taylor) H.; m. Marguerite Gardner, Apr. 19, 1948; children: Hollis, Tracy, Lindley. Student, Oxford U., 1935; B.S., Union Coll., 1943; M.S., U. Wis., 1952. Asst. geologist Union Coll., 1940-43, instr., 1946-47; state geologist, Wis. and; dir. Wis. Geol. and Natural History Survey, U. Wis., 1953-72; prof. geology and geography U. Wis. Extension, 1972; Mem. U.S. Maritime Service, 1943-45. Fellow Royal Geog. Soc., Geol. Soc. Am.; mem. A.A.A.S., Assn. Am. State Geologists, Wis. Acad. Sci., Am. Inst. Profl. Geologists, Phi Beta Kappa, Sigma Xi. Home: Box 216 Route 1 Alstead NH 03602

HANSON, HAROLD PALMER, physicist, government official; b. Virginia, Minn., Dec. 27, 1921; s. Martin Bernhard and Elvida Elaine (Paulsen) H.; m. Mary Jean Stevenson, June 22, 1944; children: Steven Bernard, Barbara Jean. B.S., Superior (Wis.) State Coll., 1942; M.S., U. Wis., 1944, Ph.D., 1948. Mem. faculty U. Fla., 1948-54, dean grad. sch., 1969-71, v.p. acad. affairs, 1971-74, exec. v.p., 1974-78; mem. faculty U. Tex., Austin, 1954-69, prof. physics, 1961-69, chmn. dept., 1962-69; provost Boston U., 1978-79; exec. dir. Com. on Sci. and Tech., U.S. Ho. of Reps., Washington, 1979-82, 84—; provost Wayne State U., Detroit, 1982-84; summer research physicist Lincoln Labs., Mass. Inst. Tech., 1953, Gen. Atomic Co., San Diego, 1964; summer vis. lectr. U. Wis., 1957; Fulbright research scholar, Norway, 1961-62. Bd. dirs. N. Central Fla. Health Planning Council; mem. steering com. Fla. Ednl. Computer Network. Decorated St. Olav's medal, Norway, Order of North Star 1st class, Sweden; U. Fla. presdl. scholar, 1976. Fellow Am. Phys. Soc.; mem. Sigma Xi, Sigma Pi Sigma, Omicron Delta Kappa. Clubs: Town and Gown (Austin); Rotary. Office: 2321 Rayburn House Office Bldg Washington DC 20215

HANSON, JO, artist; b. Carbondale, Ill.; d. Thomas A. and Carrie M. H. M.A. in Art, San Francisco State U., U. Ill. Lectr. sculpture U. Calif., Berkeley, U. Calif. Extension Center, San Francisco, 1977; instr. sculpture Calif. Coll. Arts and Crafts, Oakland, 1978, 79; lectr. Otis Art Inst., Los Angeles, 1978, 79; guest lectr. art and photography various museums and univs., 1974—; grants evaluation cons. Calif. Arts Commn., 1975; participant art panel Internat. Women's Year Conf., Houston, 1977 and; ann. meetings Women's Caucus for Art and Coll. Art Assn., 1979, 81; guest curator U. Calif. Extension Center, San Francisco, 1977. Interview appearances on radio and TV programs, 1976—, one-woman shows of sculpture and multi-media installations include, Corcoran Gallery Art, Washington, 1974, Pa. Acad. Fine Arts, Phila., 1976, U. So. Ill., Carbondale, 1977, Utah Mus. Fine Arts, Salt Lake City, San Francisco Mus. Modern Art, 1976, 80; exhibited in numerous group shows, latest being, San Francisco Mus. Modern Art, 1978, Otis Art Inst., Craft Center, Worcester, Mass., 1979, De Anza Coll., Cupertino, Calif., 1980, Museau de Arte Contemporanea da U. de Sao Paulo, Brazil, Pratt Manhattan Center, N.Y.C., 1981. Chairperson Koshland Community Park Program and Design Com., 1975; commr. San Francisco Arts Commn., 1982—. Recipient commendation San Francisco Bd. Suprs., 1980; Nat. Endowment for Arts fellow, 1977. Mem. Artists Equity Assn. (chmn. com. on artist-mus. relationships 1975-76), Women's Caucus for Art, Coll. Art Assn. Subject of articles in numerous newspapers, mags. and books; subject 2 TV documentaries So. Ill. U., 1977.

HANSON, JOHN BERNARD, plant physiologist, educator; b. Denver, Mar. 24, 1918; s. Bernard and Emily (Vogt) H.; m. Rebecca Elizabeth Hanson, Jan. 30, 1943; children—Emily Frances, Elizabeth Louise, Lois Rebecca. B.A. in Botany magna cum laude, U. Colo., 1948, Ph.D., Wash. State U., 1952. NRC postdoctoral fellow Calif. Inst. Tech., 1952-53; mem. faculty U. Ill. at Urbana, 1953—, prof. botany, 1960—, head dept., 1967-77. Editorial bd.: Plant Physiology, 1964—, Crop Sci, 1963-66, Weed Sci, 1963-67, Ann. Rev. Plant Physiology, 1971-76. Served with AUS, 1940-45. Fulbright research scholar Waite Agrl. Research Inst., Australia, 1959-60; NATO sr. fellow, summer 1968, U. East Anglia, Norwich, Eng. Mem. Am. Soc. Plant Physiologists (pres. 1973-74, Barnes award 1980, trustee 1981—), Am. Soc. Agronomy (Crop Sci. award 1965), Sigma Xi. Conglist. Home: 610 Burkwood St Urbana IL 61801

HANSON, JOHN CONRAD, banker; b. N.Y.C., Feb. 4, 1921; s. John Conrad and Grace B. (Hucknall) H.; m. Gwenda Whomsley, Oct. 29, 1949; children:Lee, John. B.S. in Econs, U. Pa., 1946, M.B.A., 1947. With ins. brokerage firm, 1947-48; with Brown Bros. Harriman & Co., N.Y.C., 1948—, partner, 1971—; fin. adviser Comml. Union Assurance Cos., Boston. Served with USMCR, 1942-46. Mem. N.Y. Soc. Security Analysts, Sigma Nu, Beta Gamma Sigma. Republican. Conglist. Clubs: Broad Street (N.Y.C.); Canoe Brook Country (Summit, N.J.). Home: 19 Roland Dr Short Hills NJ 07078 Office: 59 Wall St New York NY 10005

HANSON, JOHN J., lawyer; b. Aurora, Nebr., Oct. 22, 1922; s. Peter E. and Hazel Marion (Lounsbury) H.; m. Elizabeth Anne Moss, July 1, 1973; children from their previous marriages—Mark, Eric, Gregory. A.B., U. Denver, 1948; LL.B. cum laude, Harvard U., 1951. Bar: N.Y. bar 1952, Calif. bar 1955. Asso. firm Dewey, Ballantine, Bushby, Palmer & Wood, N.Y.C., 1951-54; partner firm Gibson, Dunn & Crutcher, Los Angeles, 1954—, mem. exec. com., 1978—. Contbr. articles to profl. jours. Trustee Palos Verdes (Calif.) Sch. Dist., 1969-73. Served with U.S. Navy, 1942-45. Fellow Am. Coll. Trial Lawyers; mem. Am. Bar Assn., Los Angeles County Bar Assn. (chmn. antitrust sect. 1979-80). Clubs: Bel Air Country (Los Angeles); Mission Hills Country (Rancho Mirage, Calif.); Fox Acres Country (Red Feather Lakes, Colo.). Home: 953 Linda Flora Dr Los Angeles CA 90049 Office: 333 S Grand Ave Los Angeles CA 90017

HANSON, JOHN NILS, industrial high technology manufacturing company executive; b. Berwyn, Ill., Jan. 22, 1942; s. Robert and Stephanie Ann (Kazluskas) H.; m. Stephanie Morgan, June 5, 1965; children: Laurel, Mark Nils. B.S. in Chem. Engring., MIT, 1964, M.S. in Nuclear Engring., 1965; Ph.D. in Nuclear Sci. and Engring., Carnegie-Mellon U., 1969. Sr. scientist Westinghouse Electric Corp., Bettis Atomic Power Labs., West Mifflin, Pa., 1965-70, asst. to gen. mgr. advanced test core, 1971-73; fellow White House, Washington, 1970-71; asst. to pres. Gould Inc., Rolling Meadows, Ill., 1973-74, pres., gen. mgr. electric motor div., St. Louis, 1974-78, group v.p. elec. products, Rolling Meadows, 1978-80; v.p. Internat. Harvester, 1980-81; pres. Solar Turbines Internat., San Diego, 1980—; v.p. Caterpillar Tractor Co., Peoria, Ill., 1981—. Contbr. articles on indsl. tech. to profl. jours. Vice chmn. Friends of Scouting Fundraising-Boy Scouts Am., San Diego council, 1983—; mem. Judge Wallace Longrange planning com., 1983—, vice chmn. fin. adv. com., 1983—; mem. cabinet fund drive United Way, San Diego County Chpt., 1982—; mem. exec. fin. com. Pete Wilson for Senate campaign, San Diego, 1982; vice chmn. Children's Hosp. Research Ctr., San Diego, 1983—; mem. vis. com. sponsored research MIT, Cambridge, 1978—; mem. Pvt. Industry Council, 1983. Mem. White House Fellows Assn., Greater San Diego C. of C. (bd. dirs.). Office: Solar Turbines Inc PO Box 85376 San Diego CA 92138

HANSON, JOSEPH J., publishing executive; b. N.Y.C., Sept. 23, 1930; s. Isiah and Mary (Solodow) H.; m. Gloria Hanson; children: Melissa Ann, Leigh Caren, Meri Jenifer, Joshua Joseph. Student, Rochester Inst. Tech., 1950-52. Eastern sales mgr. Indsl. Pub. Corp., Cleve., 1954-58; v.p. Mgmt. Pub. Corp., Greenwich, Conn., 1958-65; pres. Market Publs., Inc., New Canaan, Conn., 1965-76; chmn. bd. Marketplace Publs., Inc., New Canaan, 1967-69, Internat. Advt., Inc., 1983—; pub., editor-in-chief Folio The Mag. for Mag. Mgmt., 1972—; chmn. Media Pub. Corp., 1978-80; dir. ann. Mag. Publishing Week, 1979-80; producer Face to Face (ann. pub. conf. and expn.); v.p., dir. Conf. Mgmt. Corp., 1976-80; U.S. del. Internat. Fedn. Periodical Press, 1982—; lectr. schs. journalism colls. and univs. Exec. dir. Assn. Supervisory Nurses, New Canaan, 1969-75; trustee Mead Sch., Greenwich, Conn., 1971-74. Recipient Jessie H. Neal award for disting. journalism, 1975; award for disting. journalism Fla. Mag. Assn., 1978; Lee C. Williams award for disting. contbns. to the periodical pub. field, 1979; Marie Archer award for mag. design, 1979. Mem. Am. Bus. Press (dir. 1974-77), Mag. Pubs. Assn. (edn. com.). Clubs: Metropolitan, Overseas Press, Nat. Press. Home: 76 Turtleback Ln W New Canaan CT 06840 Office: 125 Elm St PO Box 4006 New Canaan CT 06840

HANSON, KERMIT OSMOND, university dean emeritus, banking program executive; b. Troy Twp., Iowa, May 14, 1916; s. Gerhard Severin and Suniva Fosmark (Borge) H.; m. Jane Elizabeth Haugen, Aug. 17, 1940; children: James Stephen, Katherine Jane, Paul Richard, Daniel Gerhard. A.B. cum laude, Luther Coll., Decorah, Iowa, 1938; M.S., Iowa State U., 1940, Ph.D., 1950; D.Sc. (hon.), Luther Coll., 1981. Operations analyst Fed. Land Bank, Omaha, 1941-43; chief statis. service sect. (VA br. office), Seattle, 1946-47; mem. faculty Sch. Bus. Adminstrn., U. Wash., Seattle, 1948—, prof. accounting, finance and statistics, 1954—, chmn. dept. accounting, finance and statistics, 1955-60, asso. dean, 1959-64, dean, 1964-81, dean emeritus, 1981—; instr., ednl. dir. Pacific Coast Banking Sch., 1949-81, also mem. bd. dirs.; exec. dir. Pacific Rim Bankers Program, 1977—, also vice chmn. bd. dirs.; dir. Leckenby Co., Pacific Century Funds, Inc., Wash. Fed. Savs. & Loan Assn.; cons. GAO, 1970-78; chmn. Wash. Gov.'s Adv. Council on Productivity, 1974-75; bd. advisers Naval Postgrad. Sch., Monterey, Calif., 1976—. Author: Managerial Statistics, 1955, (with G. Brabb) Managerial Statistics, 2d edit, 1961; editor: (with T. Roehl) The United States and the Pacific Economy in the 1980's, 1980. Mem. adv. com. Chief Seattle council Boy Scouts Am., 1958—, pres., 1967-69, recipient Silver Beaver award, 1963; Bd. dirs. Journey for Perspective Found., 1964-76. Served to lt. USNR, 1943-46. Recipient Disting. Service award U. Wash., 1981. Mem. Am. Assn. Collegiate Schs. Bus. (pres. 1971-72), Am. Accounting Assn., Am. Finance Assn., Financial Execs. Inst., Beta Gamma Sigma, Beta Alpha Psi, Alpha Kappa Psi. Lutheran. Home: 17760 14th Ave NW Seattle WA 98177

HANSON, LYLE EUGENE, veterinarian, educator; b. Sarona, Wis., Oct. 2, 1920; s. Fred S. and Marion (Bergquist) H.; m. Ruth Allene Magruder, June 18, 1945; children—Bruce Lloyd, Karen Ruth, Craig Lyle, Jane Eileen. Ph.B., Northland Coll., Ashland, Wis., 1942; D.V.M., Mich. State Coll., 1950; M.S., U. Ill., 1953, Ph.D., 1957. Veterinarian Wis. Dept. Agr., 1950; mem. faculty U. Ill. at Urbana, 1950—, prof., 1961—, head dept. vet. pathology and hygiene, 1967-79, asso. dean, 1979—. Served with AUS, 1942-46. Mem. Am. Vet. Med. Assn., Ill. Vet. Med. Assn., Am. Assn. Avian Pathologists, Am. Soc. Microbiology, Am. Coll. Vet. Microbiology, U.S. Animal Health Assn., Sigma Xi, Phi Zeta, Gamma Sigma Delta. Home: 1908 Shelly Ct Box 287 Urbana IL 61801

HANSON, MARIE RUTH, publishing company executive, consultant; b. Lakewood, Ohio, Mar. 19, 1946; d. David T. and Edith Mervice (Craft) Hansen. B.S., Okla. State U., 1968; postgrad., Okla State U., 1970-71. Dir. jours. div. Johns Hopkins U. Press, Balt., 1972—. Mem. Balt. Pubs. Assn., Soc. Scholarly Pub., Women in Scholarly Pub., Assn. Am. Univ. Presses, Assn. Am. Pubs., Am. Council Learned Socs. Democrat. Presbyterian. Home: 3620 Rexmere Rd Baltimore MD 21218 Office: Johns Hopkins U Press Baltimore MD 21218

HANSON, MAURICE FRANCIS (MAURY HANSON), magazine editor, publisher; b. Phila., Oct. 14, 1907; s. Michael Francis and Sarah (O'Neill) H.; m. Margaret Ellen Hixon, Oct. 28, 1939; children: Robert Hixon, Michael Francis, Barbara Greenleaf (Mrs. Charles Eliot Pierce, Jr.). B.A., Yale, 1930. Fgn. corr., columnist Consol. Pubs. Newspapers, 1930-32; account exec., dept. head Benton & Bowles, Inc., 1932-38; with J. Walter Thompson Co., 1938-43, 46-60, v.p., 1947-60; cons. to Yale pres. A. Whitney Griswold, 1960-62; pub. relations cons. Gen. Motors Corp., 1963-67; founder, editor, pub. The Nutmegger mag. of Conn., Greenwich, 1967—; dep. dir. OWI, 1943-46. Author: Pierpont the Foxhound, 1939, College Reunion, 1955. Recipient Yale medal for outstanding service to univ., 1975. Republican. Roman Catholic. Clubs: Round Hill (Greenwich); Royal and Ancient Golf (St. Andrews, Scotland). Home: 21 Lauder Ln Greenwich CT 06830 Office: 6 W Putnam Ave Greenwich CT 06830

HANSON, PAUL DAVID, religion educator; b. Ashland, Wis., Nov. 17, 1939; s. Hans Victor and Lydia (Thompson) H.; m. Cynthia Jane Rosenberger, Aug. 20, 1966; children. Amy Elizabeth, Mark Christopher, Nathaniel Ross. B.A., Gustavus Adolphus Coll., 1961; B.S., Yale U., 1965; Ph.D., Harvard U., 1970. Asst. prof. O.T. Harvard Div. Sch., 1970-75, prof., 1975—, bussey prof. div., 1981—. Author: The Dawn of Apocalyptic, 1976, The Dawn of Apocalyptic, 2d edit., 1979, Dynamic Transcendence, 1978, The Diversity of Scripture, 1982, Visionaries and Their Apocalypses, 1983; mem. editorial bd.: Hermeneia Commentary Series, 1971—. Fulbright fellow, 1961-62; Woodrow Wilson fellow, 1965-66; Kent fellow, 1966-70; Am. Council Learned Socs. fellow, 1972-74; Alexander von Humboldt fellow, 1981-82. Mem. Am Schs. Oriental Research, Soc. Religion in Higher Edn., Soc. Bibl. Lit. Home: 27 Cushing Ave Belmont MA 02178 Office: Harvard U Divinity Sch Cambridge MA 02138

HANSON, PAULINE, poet; b. Mass. Resident sec. Yaddo, Saratoga Springs, N.Y., 1950-76. Author: The Forever Young and Other Poems, 1955, Across Countries of Anywhere, 1971; Contbr. poetry to mags., anthologies. Recipient Eunice Tietjens Meml. prize Poetry mag., 1965; Am. Acad. and Nat. Inst. Arts and Letters award for lit., 1972; Nat. Endowment for Arts grantee, 1972. Address: 219 Freeman St Brookline MA 02146

HANSON, RAYMOND LESTER, lawyer; b. San Francisco, Nov. 2, 1912; s. Raymond O. and Hilda (Beavis) H.; m. Eleanor E. Quandt, June 15, 1935; children—E. Lynne Dilling, Christine H. Cabot. A.B., Stanford U., 1933; J.D., U. Calif. Hastings Coll. Law, 1936; LL.D. (hon.), Whitworth Coll., 1977, L.H.D., Coll. of Idaho, 1980. Bar: Calif. bar 1936, U.S. Supreme Ct. bar 1956. Partner firm Hanson, Bridgett, Marcus, Vlahos & Stromberg, San Francisco, 1957—; mem. vol. adv. com. atty. gen. Calif., 1972—, asst. dist. atty., City and County of San Francisco, 1937-38, columnist, lectr. on trusts and estate planning. Elder, trustee Calvary Presbyn. Ch., San Francisco, 1939-41; ruling elder United Presbyn. Ch. in U.S.A., 1939—; pres. bd. of ch. extension Presbytery of San Francisco, 1946-49, moderator, 1953; justice Permanent Jud. Commn., Supreme Ct. of denomination, 1952-61; chmn. bd. San Francisco Theol. Sem., 1974—; chmn., mem. worship and music com. First Presbyn. Ch. of San Mateo, 1959-64; past pres., sec. Pacific Med. Center, Inc.; past pres. No. Calif. Presbyn. Homes, Inc.; past chmn. bd., dir. San Francisco Met. YMCA; pres., bd. dirs. Goodwill Industries San Francisco, 1972-73; bd. dirs. U. Calif. Hastings Coll. Law; mem. asso. bd. San Francisco council Boy Scouts Am.; mem. adv. bd. Golden Gate U. Center for Tax Studies; active U. Calif. Alumni Council, 1970-71. Served to lt. USNR, 1943-46. Recipient award of year for outstanding and distinguished service U. Calif. Hastings Coll. Law, 1975. Fellow Am. Coll. Probate Counsel (chmn. subcom. on adminstrn. estates, uniform probate code com. 1972); mem. Am. Judicature Soc., Nat. Assn. Coll. and Univ. Attys., Lawyers Club of San Francisco, San Francisco Estate Planning Council, ABA (state chmn. com. on charitable trusts 1972), Calif. Bar Assn. (chmn. com. on conf. resolution 1967-69), San Francisco Bar Assn. (past dir., past chmn. estate and trust law sect., chmn. publs. com. 1969-70), Am. Assn. Homes for Aging, Internat. Acad. Estate and Trust Law (academician). Clubs: Kiwanis Internat. (past chmn. boys and girls work com. Calif.-Nev.-Hawaii Dist., past pres. San Francisco), Commonwealth of San Francisco.). Home: care Sequoias 501 Portola Rd Box 8062 Portola Valley CA 94025 Office: 333 Market St San Francisco CA 94105

HANSON, RICHARD ARTHUR, investment firm executive; b. Mpls., Apr. 8, 1936; s. Rudolph Melvin and Opal Mae (Hills) H.; m. Carol May Jadick, June 28, 1958; children: Craig Arthur, Alexander Dean. A.B. in Econs, Cornell U., 1958; postgrad., Grad. Sch. Bus. Adminstrn. N.Y. U., 1960-62. With Chase Manhattan Bank (N.A.), N.Y.C., 1961-80, sr. v.p., group exec., 1971-77, dept. exec., 1977-80; pres., chief operating officer Thermasol Ltd., Leonia, N.J., 1980; pres. Merrill Lynch Indsl. Resources, N.Y.C., 1981—. Bd. dirs. Fifth Avenue Assn., N.Y.C., 1974-80; Chmn. Wyckoff (N.J.) Planning Bd.,

1970-71. Served to 1st lt. USMC, 1958-61. Clubs: Indian Trail (Franklin Lakes, N.J.); Arcola Country (Paramus, N.J.). Home: 417 Carriage Ln Wyckoff NJ 07481

HANSON, RICHARD STEPHEN, bacteriologist, educator; b. Platte, S.D., Nov. 14, 1935; s. James Walter and Mary Ann (Konechne) H.; m. Doreothe Ann Glynn, Dec. 27, 1956; children—Michael Orin, Stephen Francis, Thomas Edward. B.S., S.D. State Coll., 1959; Ph.D. (USPHS predoctoral fellow), U. Ill. at Urbana, 1962. Research scientist U.S. Dept. Agr., Peoria, Ill., 1962-63; USPHS postdoctoral fellow Laboitoire D'Enzymologie du CNRS, Gif-Sur-Yvette, France, 1963-64; asst. prof. biochemistry U. Ill. Med. Center, Chgo., 1965-67; asst. prof. dept. bacteriology U. Wis.-Madison, 1967-69, prof., 1972—, chmn. dept., 1973-77; prof. microbiology, dir. Gray Freshwater Biol. Inst., U. Minn., 1981—. Contbr. articles to profl. jours.; Mem.: Jour. Applied Microbiology. Served with AUS, 1954-56. USPHS sr. postdoctoral fellow, 1973. Mem. Am. Soc. Biol. Chemists, Am. Soc. Microbiology (pres. North Central br. 1975), Sigma Xi, Phi Kappa Phi. Research on bacterial sporogenesis, metabolic regulation, methane oxidation, microbial ecology. Home: 4162 Hillcrest Rd Wayzata MN 55391

HANSON, RICHARD WINFIELD, biochemist; b. Oxford, N.Y., Nov. 10, 1935; s. John Vincent and Agatha Helen H.; m. Gloria M. Lucchesi, June 10, 1961; children: Paul, Benjamin, Daria. B.S., Northeastern U., 1959; M.S., Brown U., 1961, Ph.D., 1963. Asst. prof., asso. prof., prof. Temple U. Sch. Medicine, Phila., 1965-78; prof., dir. dept. biochemistry Case Western Res. U. Sch. Medicine, Cleve., 1978—; cons. USPHS, FDA. Contbr. sci. articles to profl. jours. Served to capt., Med. Service Corps U.S. Army, 1963-65. Recipient Kaiser-Permanente award for excellence in teaching, 1982; USPHS fellow, 1965-66. Mem. Am. Soc. Biol. Chemists, AAAS, Biochemical Soc., Am. Inst. Nutrition (Mead-Johnson award 1971). Home: 2689 Berkshire Rd Cleveland Heights OH 44106 Office: Dept Biochemistry Case Western Res U Sch Medicine Cleveland OH 44106

HANSON, ROBERT ARTHUR, agricultural equipment executive; b. Moline, Ill., Dec. 13, 1924; s. Nels A. and Margaret I. (Chapman) H.; m. Patricia Ann Klinger, June 25, 1955. B.A., Augustana Coll., Rock Island, Ill., 1948. Various positions Deere & Co., Moline, 1950-62, gen. mgr., Mexico, 1962-64, Spain, 1964-66, dir. mktg. overseas, 1966-70, v.p. overseas ops., 1972, sr. v.p. overseas div., 1973, dir., 1974—, exec. v.p., 1975-78, pres., 1978—, chief operating officer, 1979-82, chmn. pres., chief exec. officer, 1982—; dir. Procter & Gamble Co., Internat. Council Morgan Guaranty Trust Co., N.Y.C., Dun & Bradstreet Corp., Agribus. Council; mem. Bus. Council; Adv. com. bus. programs Brookings Instn. Trustee Com. for Econ. Devel., Mayo Found.; bd. dirs. Farm and Indsl. Equipment Inst. Served with USMCR, 1943-46. Home: 2200 29th Avenue Ct Moline IL 61265 Office: John Deere Rd Moline IL 61265

HANSON, ROBERT CARL, sociologist, educator; b. Wichita, Kans., Nov. 5, 1926; s. Otto Albert and Alma Charlotta (Larson) H.; m. Margaret B. Bremner, Jan. 1, 1950; children—Steven, Holly, Juliana. Student, U. Wyo., 1944, Tex. A&M U., 1945; B.A., U. Calif., Berkeley, 1949, M.A., 1951, Ph.D., 1955; postgrad., Harvard U., 1951-52. Instr. Mich. State U., 1955-57, asst. prof., 1957-60, U. Colo., Boulder, 1960-62, asso. prof., 1962-65, dir. Bur. Sociol. Research, 1962-64, acting dir. Inst. Behavioral Sci., 1964-65, prof. sociology, 1965—, research program dir., 1965-75; cons. USPHS (Migrant Health Br.), 1963-65; mem. Com. on Acad. Disciplines for Study Commn. on Undergrad. Edn. U.S. Office Edn., 1972-75. Author: (with Richard Jessor, Theodore D. Graves and Shirley L. Jessor) Society, Personality and Deviant Behavior, 1968; Contbr. articles to profl. jours. Served with AUS, 1944-46. Russell Sage Found. residency grantee, 1960-62; USPHS research grantee, 1960-63; NIMH research grantee, 1960-63, 64-70; Council on Research and Creative Work fellow, 1964-65. Mem. AAAS (mem. com. on desert and arid zones research 1961-62), Peace Research Soc., AAUP, Am. Fedn. Tchrs., ACLU, Am. Sociol. Assn. (com. on social stats. 1964-66), Pacific Sociol. Assn. Address: Dept Sociology Univ Colo Boulder CO 80309

HANSON, ROBERT DUANE, civil engineering educator; b. Albert Lea., Minn., July 27, 1935; s. James Edwin and Gertie (Kvale) H.; m. Kaye Lynn Nielsen, June 7, 1959; children: Craig Robert, Eric Neil. Student, St. Olaf Coll., Northfield, Minn., 1953-54; B.S.E., U. Minn., 1957, M.S. in Civil Engring., 1958; Ph.D., Calif. Inst. Tech., Pasadena, 1965. Registered profl. engr., Mich., N.D. Design engr. Pitts.-Des Moines Stel, Des Moines, 1958-59; asst. prof. U. N.D., Grand Forks, 1959-61; research engr. Calif. Inst. Tech., 1965; asst. prof. U. Calif.-Davis, 1965-66; from asst. prof. to prof. civil engring. U. Mich., Ann Arbor, 1966—, chmn. dept. civil engring., 1976—; cons. Bechtel Corp., Ann Arbor, 1976—, Berg-Hanson-Wight, 1977—; cons., dir. CWA Walker, Inc., Kalamazoo, Mich., 1979—; cons. NSF, Washington, 1979—. Contbr. articles to profl. jours. Recipient Reese Research award ASCE, 1980, Disting. Service award U. Mich., 1969. Mem. ASCE (com. chmn. 1975—), Earthquake Engring. Research Inst. (v.p. 1977-79, dir. 1976-79), Am. Concrete Inst., Seismological Soc. Am. Lutheran. Lodge: Rotary (Ann Arbor). Home: 5564 Briar Glen Dr Saline MI 48176 Office: Dept Civil Engring Univ Mich Ann Arbor MI 48109

HANSON, ROBERT MILLER, association executive; b. St. Louis, Jan. 7, 1922; s. Perry McLean and Mabel (Miller) H.; m. Lynn M. McClurken, Sept. 17, 1955; 1 son, Craig McLean. Student, Washington U., St. Louis, 1940-41. Dir. tng. edn. and pub. affairs Exec. Office of Pres. U.S., Battle Creek, Mich., 1955-61; v.p. Blue Cross & Blue Shield Mich., Detroit, 1961-77; exec. dir. Motorists Info., Detroit, 1977-79, Am. Animal Hosp. Assn., Mishawaka, Ind., 1979—. Served to capt. USAAF, 1942-45. Mem. Pub. Relations Soc. Am. (chmn. health com. 1975), Am. Soc. Assn. Execs. Club: Knollwood (South Bend). Home: 16433 Foxcross Granger IN 46530 Office: Am Animal Hosp Assn 204 Lincolnway E Mishawaka IN 46544

HANSON, ROBERT WARREN, chemistry educator; b. Bemidji, Minn., Aug. 7, 1923; s. Thomas T. and Clara M. (Severson) H.; m. Margaret Fern Allen, Jan. 1, 1947; children: Terrill Allen, Rebecca Lee (Mrs. Carroll E. Miller), Mark Robert. B.A., Bemidji State Coll., 1948; M.S., U. Minn., 1949; Ph.D., U. Ia., 1961. Instr. chemistry Wis. State Coll., Platteville, 1949-51; research chemist 3M Co., St. Paul, 1951-52; instr. chemistry St. Cloud (Minn.) State Coll., 1952-59, asso. prof., 1961-63; instr. sci. U. Iowa, 1959-60, research asst., 1960-61; asso. prof. phys. sci. State Coll. Iowa, Cedar Falls, 1963-66; prof. chemistry and sci. edn. U. No. Iowa, Cedar Falls, 1966—; sec.-treas. Nat. Assn. Acads. Sci., 1976-79, pres., 1980; liaison officer Iowa Gov.'s Sci. Adv. Council, 1977-81. Editor: Iowa Acad. Sci. Bull, 1967—; mng. editor: Procs. Iowa Acad. Sci. and Iowa Soc. Tchrs. Jour, 1976—. Served with AUS, 1943-45. Fellow AAAS (Council 1982—), Iowa Acad. Sci. (exec. dir. 1967-83); mem. Nat. Sci. Tchrs. Assn., Assn. Edn. Tchrs. Sci., Phi Delta Kappa, Phi Lambda Upsilon. Designer transparency originals on chem. bonding and solutions and ionization, 1966. Home: 1400 W 18th St Cedar Falls IA 50613

HANSON, ROGER JAMES, physics educator; b. Hutchinson, Minn., Oct. 27, 1927; s. Arndt and Clara (Tange) H.; m. Marilyn Lois Juul, Aug. 13, 1950; children—Kathy, Bruce, Ralph, Mette. Student, Dana Coll., 1946-48; B.S., Gustavus Adolphus Coll., 1950; M.A., U. Nebr., 1953, Ph.D., 1956. Asst. prof. Grinnell Coll., 1956-60, asso. prof., 1960-63, prof., 1963-69; prof. physics U. No. Iowa, Cedar Falls, 1969—, head physics dept., 1969-80; research physicist U. Aarhus, Denmark, 1966-67, Ames Lab. of AEC, summers 1964, 65, 69. Contbr. articles to physics jours. NSF Sci. Faculty fellow Harvard, 1961-62. Mem. AAAS, Am. Phys. Soc., Am. Assn. Physics Tchrs., Acoustical Soc. Am., Catgut Acoustical Soc. Lutheran. Home: 2211 Greenwood Ave Cedar Falls IA 50613

HANSON, ROGER KVAMME, librarian; b. Aneta, N.D., Nov. 24, 1932; s. Torris R. and Thora (Kvamme) H.; m. Gretchen Leupp, July 9, 1960; children—Sharon, Carolyn, Ronald, Michael. B.S. in Edn, Mayville State Coll., 1961; M.L.S., U. Denver, 1966; M.P.A., Brigham Young U., 1978. Tchr./librarian Johnson County High Sch., Buffalo, Wyo., 1962, asst. librarian, 1963-66; dir. libraries U. N.D., Grand Forks, 1969-72; asst. to dir. libraries U. Minn., Mpls., 1967-69; asso. dir. libraries U. Utah, Salt Lake City, 1972-73, dir. libraries, 1973—. Served with USN, 1952-56. Recipient Outstanding Alumni award Mayville State Coll., 1974. Mem. Utah, Mountain Plains library assns., ALA. Lutheran. Club: Elks. Office: Marriott Library U Utah Salt Lake City UT 84112 *

HANSON, ROGER WAYNE, univ. dean; b. Frost, Minn., Sept. 3, 1922; s. Maynard P. and Hazel B. (Lund) H.; m. Bette Ruth Johnson, Dec. 27, 1948; children—Heidi, Eric. B.A., U. Iowa, 1946, M.A. in Protozoology, 1948; Ph.D. in Zoology and Physiology, U. Calif. at Los Angeles, 1952. Lectr. biology U. Calif. at Santa Barbara, 1952-53; NSF postdoctoral fellow U. Ala., 1953-54, pharmacology fellow, Birmingham, 1954-55, NIH fellow, 1955-57, instr., 1957-59, asst. prof., 1959-62, asso. prof., 1962-66, prof., 1966—, dean, 1973-81, dir. coordinated curricula for basic allied health sci., 1981—; prof. pharmacology U. Ala. Med. Center, 1967, prof. biology, chmn. div. natural scis. and math., 1966—; vis. asso. prof. U. Calif. Med. Coll., San Francisco; on contract to Indonesia-AID project, 1964-65. Editorial bd.: Jour. Coll. Sci. Teaching, 1972-74, 75-77; Contbr. articles to profl. jours. Mem. Ala. Council Human Relations, 1954-64; mem. Ala. bd. ACLU, 1968-72, Ala. adv. council U.S. Civil Rights Commn., 1968-69, Equal Employment Adv. Council for Transp. Dept. FAA, 1969-70. Served with AUS, 1943-46. Fellow A.A.A.S.; mem. Am. Physiol. Soc., Ala. Acad. Sci. (chmn. med. sect. 1960-61), A.A.U.P. (v.p. Ala. sect. 1963-64), Nat. Sci. Tchrs. Assn. (nat. bd. 1973-75, So. regional dir. 1973-75), Am. Inst. Biol. Scis., Sigma Xi. Home: 1734 Woodbine Dr Birmingham AL 35216

HANSON, VICTOR HENRY, II, newspaper publisher; b. Augusta, Ga., Aug. 17, 1930; s. Clarence Bloodworth, Jr. and Elizabeth (Fletcher) H.; m. Elizabeth Stallworth, Dec. 29, 1953; children: Clarence Bloodworth III, Victor Henry III, Elizabeth Mickel, Mary Fletcher, Robert Stallworth. Grad., Choate Sch., 1949; student, U. Va., 1949-51; B.A., U. Ala., 1954. With Birmingham (Ala.) News & Post Herald, 1946-54, 57—, gen. mgr., 1963—; with advt. and prodn. dept. WAPI-TV, Birmingham, 1954-55; v.p. Birmingham News Co., 1960-79, pres., pub., 1979—; pres. Mercury Express, Inc.; dir. AmSouth Bank, N.A., AmSouth Bancorp. Trustee Gordon Coll., Wenham, Mass., So. Research Inst., Birmingham. Served to capt. USAAF, 1955-57. Mem. Birmingham C. of C., Kappa Alpha. Presbyn. Clubs: Rotarian., Birmingham Country, Downtown, Mountain Brook, The Club (Birmingham). Home: 3404 Fieldstone Ln Birmingham AL 35243 Office: 2200 4th Ave N Birmingham AL 35203

HANSON, VIRGIL, pediatric rheumatologist, educator; b. Lima, Peru, June 30, 1920; m. Catherine Archer Low; children: Heather Hanson, Holly Hanson. B.A., UCLA, 1942; M.D., Johns Hopkins U., 1945. Intern Los Angeles County Gen. Hosp., 1945-46; resident in pediatrics Childrens Hosp. of Los Angeles, 1950-52; now head div. rheumatology and rehab. med. dir. Childrens Hosp. Rehab. Center, 1960—; asst. in pediatrics U. So. Calif. Sch. Medicine, Los Angeles, 1954-56, asst. prof. pediatrics, 1960-64, asso. prof., 1965-72, prof., 1972—; instr. pediatrics UCLA, 1956-58, asst. clin. prof., 1958-60; mem. subcom. on research Nat. Commn. on Arthritis, NIH, 1975-76; vice chmn. med. and sci. com. So. Calif. chpt. Arthritis Found. Mem. editorial bd.: Arthritis and Rheumatism, 1976-79; contbr. articles to profl. jours. Recipient Victor Stork award Childrens Hosp., Los Angeles, 1953, Disting. service award So. Calif. chpt. Arthritis Found., 1976. Mem. So. Calif. Rheumatism Soc. (pres. 1965-66), Am. Rheumatism Assn. (co-chmn. council on pediatric rheumatology 1975-77, mem.-at-large exec. com. 1976-79), Am. Acad. Pediatrics, Western Soc. Pediatric Research (mem. council 1979-82), Argentine Soc. Rheumatology (hon.), Los Angeles Pediatric Soc., N.Y. Acad. Scis., Council on Pediatric Rhematology (chmn.), Am. Pediatric Soc. Office: 4650 Sunset Blvd Los Angeles CA 90027 *

HANSON, WALTER EDMUND, consulting engineer; b. Lyndon, Kans., July 14, 1916; s. Andrew C. and Laura (Mickelson) H.; m. Sue Roling, Sept. 14, 1940; 1 dau., Karen Sue. B.S., Kans. State U., 1939; M.S., U. Ill., 1947. Draftsman computer Petty Geophys. Engring. Co., San Antonio, 1939-40; bridge detailer and designer Howard, Needles, Tammen & Bergendoff, Kansas City, Mo., 1940-42; instr. civil engring. U. Ill., 1942-43; asst., asso. prof. civil engring., 1946-51; engr. bridges Ill. Div. Hwys., 1951-54; cons. engr., Springfield, Ill., 1954—. Author: (with R.B. Peck and T.H. Thornburn) Foundation Engineering, 2d edit, 1974; Contbr. articles to profl. jours. Served to lt. (j.g.) USNR, 1943-46. Fellow Am. Cons. Engrs. Council; mem. ASCE, Ill. Engring. Council, Nat., Ill. socs. profl. engrs., Am. Concrete Inst., Am. Ry. Engrs. Assn., ASTM, Sigma Tau, Chi Epsilon. Republican. Presbyterian. Home: 81 Linden Ln Springfield IL Office: 1525 S 6th St Springfield IL 62703

HANSON, WALTER EDWARD, accountant; b. Adelphia, N.J., Oct. 17, 1925; s. Samuel and Ida (Clayton) H.; m. Frances Barber, Aug. 24, 1946 (div. July 1980); children: Katharine, Elizabeth, Barbara; m. Elizabeth Bowden, July 25, 1980. A.B., Lafayette Coll., 1949; postgrad., Lehigh U., summer 1949, U. Minn., 1951-52. C.P.A., N.Y., 15 other states. Sr. accountant Haskins & Sells, N.Y.C., 1949, Mpls., 1949-55; v.p., comptroller M. & St. L. R.R., 1955-57; partner Peat, Marwick, Mitchell & Co., N.Y.C., 1957-80, partner in charge N.Y.C. office, 1961-65, chmn. bd., chief exec. officer, 1965-80; dir. AM Internat., Chgo., Fidelity Group of Funds, Boston, CIGNA Corp., Phila., Northeast Energy Corp., Stamford, Conn. Mem. adv. council Stamford U. Grad. Sch. Bus.; Chmn. bd. trustees Lafayette Coll.; bd. overseers Harvard Bus. Sch.; bd. govs., exec. com. UN Assn. U.S. Served with USNR, 1943-45. Mem. Am. Inst. C.P.A.s (treas., dir.), N.Y. State Soc. C.P.A.s, Internat. C. of C. (trustee, exec. com. U.S. council), Beta Alpha Psi. Clubs: Downtown Assn., N.Y. Yacht, Board Room (N.Y.C.). Home: 126 Beachside Ave Westport CT 06880

HANSON, WILLIAM HERBERT, philosophy educator; b. Mpls., Sept. 23, 1936; s. William F. and Viola H. (Matthes) H.; m. JoAnn M. Lilja, June 15, 1957; children—Lynne M., Jillian K. B.A., Hamline U., 1958; M.A., Yale U., 1960, Ph.D., 1965. Research logician Univac div. Sperry Rand Corp., 1960-66; asst. prof. philosophy U. Minn., 1966-69, asso. prof., 1969-77, prof., 1977—, chmn., 1980—. Contbr. articles in field to profl. jours. Nat. Endowment for Humanities fellow, 1974-75. Mem. Am. Philos. Assn., Assn. for Symbolic Logic, AAUP. Office: 355 Ford Hall 224 Church St SE Minneapolis MN 55455

HANST, JOHN L., gas company executive; b. Olney, Ill., Jan. 11, 1940; s. Ferdnand H. and Georgia E. (Harden) H.; m. Clo Ann Hanst Ethridge, Dec. 23, 1961; children: Kristen L., Jon Mitchell. B.B.A. in Fin., Tex. Tech. U., 1963; postgrad., Columbia U., 1981. Sr. supply rep. Trunkline Gas Co., Houston, 1966-73, Natural Gas Pipe Line, 1973-76; mgr. gas supply Fla. Gas Transmission Co., Houston, 1976-78, v.p., 1978-81, exec. v.p., 1981-82, sr. v.p., 1982—. Served to 1st lt. U.S. Army, 1963-65. Mem. Natural Gas Men of Houston (pres. 1982). Republican. Presbyterian. Office: PO Box 27711 Houston TX 77227

HANTHO, CHARLES HAROLD, petrochemical executive; b. Lethbridge, Alta., Can., 1931. B.Sc. in Chem. Engring., U. Alta., Can., 1953; B.B.A., S.W. Tex. State U., 1958. Tech. asst. C-I-L Inc., Edmonton, Alta., 1953, with plastics sales dept., Toronto, 1954-61, Brampton, Ont., 1964-67, Montreal, Que., 1964-67, gen. mgr. plastics, Montreal, 1968-71, v.p., dir., 1973-81, pres., chief exec. officer, 1981—; dep. chmn. C-I-L Imperial Chem. Industries P.L.C., London, 1976-78. Office: C-I-L Inc 90 Sheppard Ave E North York ON Canada M2N 6H2

HANUSHEK, ERIC ALAN, economics educator; b. Lakewood, Ohio, May 22, 1943; s. Vernon F. and Ruth (Hostetler) H.; m. Nancy L. Keleher, June 11, 1965; children: Eric Alan, Megan E. B.S., U.S. Air Force Acad., 1965; Ph.D. in Econs., MIT, 1968. Sr. staff economist Council Econ. Advisers, Washington, 1971-72; assoc. prof. U.S. Air Force Acad., 1972-73; sr. economist Cost of Living Council, Washington, 1973-74; assoc. prof. econs. Yale U., 1975-78; dir. pub. policy analysis U. Rochester, 1978—, prof. econs., 1978—; cons. Mathematica Policy Research, Princeton, N.J., 1976—. Author: Education and Race, 1972, (with others) Statistical Methods for Social Scientists, 1977. Served to capt. USAF, 1965-74. Mem. Assn. Pub. Policy (analysis and mgmt. policy council), Am. Econ. Assn., Econometric Soc., Am. Statis Assn. Office: U of Rochester Dept Economics Rochester NY 14627

HANVEY, FORREST ROBERT, JR., communications co. exec.; b. San Diego, May 2, 1933; s. Forrest Robert and Clara Patricia (May) H.; m. Suzanne Monnett, June 9, 1957; children—Monnett, Jacqueline, Forrest, Dennis. Student, Calif. Inst. Tech., 1951-53; B.S. with honors, U.S. Naval Acad., 1957; M.S., M.I.T., 1959. Mgr. systems analysis Singer-Gen. Precision Aerospace, Wayne, N.J., 1962-66; with Western Union Telegraph Co., Upper Saddle River, N.J., 1966—, v.p. systems engring., 1980—. Mem. Bd. of Edn., Borough of Upper Saddle River, 1970-77, pres., 1973-77. Served to capt. USAF, 1957-62. Mem. IEEE, Assn. Computing Machinery. Home: 66 Timberlane Rd Upper Saddle River NJ 07458 Office: 1 Lake St Upper Saddle River NJ 07458

HANWAY, JOHN, II, multinational co. exec.; b. Mt. Vernon, N.Y., Oct. 23, 1924; s. John Howard and Marie Theresa (Fenlon) H.; m. Elena Gracia, May 8, 1950; children—John III, David Howard (dec.), Robert William, Linda, Thomas Edward. Grad., Hill Sch., 1942; B.A., Yale, 1948. With A.D. McKelvy Co., also Prince Matchabelli, Inc., 1948-53, Robert Heller & Assos., 1953-63; with Internat. Tel. & Tel. Corp., 1963—, v.p. adminstrn., 1964—, also sr. v.p., 1964—. Served to 1st lt., pilot USAAF, 1942-45; PTO. Office: ITT Corp 320 Park Ave New York NY 10022

HANZALEK, FREDERICK JOSEPH, mech. engr.; b. N.Y.C., Aug. 1, 1924; s. William Vincent and Julia Barbara (Seible) H.; m. Astrid Teicher, Nov. 11, 1955. B.S. in Mech. Engring, U. Louisville, 1945; M.S., Columbia U., 1947. Engr. Am. Sugar Refining Co., 1947-51; sect. mgr. Jefferson Chem. Co., N.Y.C., 1951-55; with Combustion Engring., Inc., Windsor, Conn., 1955—, dir. product design, 1968-74, dir. research, 1974-80, gen. mgr. controls div., 1980—; mem. exec. com. Metal Properties Council; bd. govs. Welding Research Council. Contbr. power plant tech. articles to profl. jours. Chmn. Bd. Finance, Town of Suffield, 1975—, chmn., 1978; chmn. Suffield Republican Town Com., 1968-72. Served with U.S. Navy, 1944-46. Mem. ASME (Prime Movers award 1966), Am. Nuclear Soc. Club: Suffield Country. Patentee power plant equipment. Home: 155 S Main St Suffield CT 06078 Office: 102 Addison Rd Windsor CT 06095

HANZLIK, RAYBURN DEMARA, lawyer, government official; b. Los Angeles, June 7, 1938; s. Rayburn Otto and Ethel Winifred (Membery) H.; m. Susan Evans, Sept. 28, 1963; children: Kristina, Rayburn, Alexander, Geoffrey. B.S., Principia Coll., 1960; M.A., Woodrow Wilson Sch. Fgn. Affairs, U. Va., 1968; J.D., U. Va., 1974. Bar: D.C., Va. Staff asst. to Pres. U.S., Washington, 1971-73; asso. dir. White House Domestic Council, 1975-77; of counsel firm Danzansky Dickey Tydings Quint & Gordon, Washington, 1977-78, Akin Gump Hauer & Feld, 1978-79; individual practice law, Los Angeles, 1979-81; adminstr. Econ. Regulatory Adminstrn., Dept. Energy, Washington, 1981—. Contbg. author: Global Politics and Nuclear Energy, 1971, Soviet Foreign Relations and World Communism, 1965. Alt. del. Republican Nat. Conv., 1980; dir. Calif. Rep. Victory Fund, 1980. Served to lt. USN, 1963-68; Vietnam. Mem. ABA, Va. Bar Assn., D.C. Bar Assn., U.S. Naval Inst. Republican. Christian Scientist. Club: Nat. Press. Office: Forrestal Bldg Room 5B-148 1000 Independence Ave Washington DC 20585 *

HAPALA, MILAN ERNEST, government educator; b. Hranice, Czechoslovakia, Sept. 19, 1919; came to U.S., 1938, naturalized, 1943; s. Vladimir and Marie (Mlcochova) H.; m. Adelaide E. Hamilton, Sept. 6, 1947; children: Milan Ernest, Mary Elizabeth. A.B., Beloit Coll., 1940; A.M., Nebr. U., 1941; Ph.D. in Polit. Sci, Duke, 1956. Mem. faculty Sweet Briar Coll., 1947—, asso. prof. govt., chmn. div. social studies, 1956-60, 70-73, prof. govt., 1960—, Carter Glass prof., 1962—, chmn. dept., 1952-63, 65-68, 72—, dir. Asian studies, 1980—; instr. Lynchburg (Va.) br. Am. Inst. Banking, 1955-59; vis. lectr. Lynchburg Coll., 1951; vis. prof. U. Va., 1967-68, Randolph-Macon Woman's Coll., 1972; dir. faculty seminar in India U.S. Office Edn., summer 1970; research assoc. Russian and East European Ctr., U. Ill., 1982-83. Author articles, book revs. Chmn. Amherst County Bicentennial Commn. Served with USAAF, 1942-45. Fgn. lang. (Hindi-Urdu) fellow Nat. Def. Fgn. Lang. U. Pa., 1964-65. Mem. Am. Polit. Sci. Assn., Assn. Asian Studies, Assn. Internat. Studies, Am. Assn. Advancement Slavic Studies, AAUP, Czechoslovakian Soc. Arts and Scis., Va. Soc. Sci. (mem. bd. 1966-69), Phi Beta Kappa. Club: Rotarian (pres. Amherst 1955). Home: Waugh's Ferry Rd Amherst VA 24521 Office: Box S Sweet Briar VA 24595

HAPGOOD, ROBERT, educator; b. Lompoc, Calif., Dec. 11, 1928; s. Arthur Richard and Elsie Rachel (Brown) H.; m. Marilyn Janelle Oliver, July 16, 1950; children—Miranda Kristin, Susanna Elizabeth. B.A. with highest honors, U. Calif., Berkeley, 1950, M.A., 1951, Ph.D., 1955. Instr. English Ind. U., 1955-57; vis. prof. Am. lit. and civilization Dijon (France) U., 1957-58; instr. U. Calif., Berkeley, 1958-59, asst. prof., Riverside, 1959-65; mem. faculty U. N.H., Durham, 1965—, prof. English, 1969—, chmn. dept., 1972-75; dir. U. N.H./Cambridge U. summer program, 1982—; exchange prof. Osaka (Japan) U., 1977-79; dir. Shakespeare Workshop, Bowdoin Coll., summers 1972-75; mem. editorial bd. Univ. Press New Eng., 1975-77. Contbr. to profl. jours. Served with AUS, 1953-55. Recipient essay prize English Inst., 1968; fellow Inst. Renaissance Studies, Ashland, Oreg., summer 1961; Mellon postdoctoral fellow, 1964-65; fellow Southeastern Inst. Medieval and Renaissance Studies, Chapel Hill, N.C., summer 1969; Am. Council Learned Socs. fellow, 1979-80. Mem. MLA, Shakespeare

Assn. Am., Internat. Shakespeare Assn. Home: Cove Road Cape Neddick ME 03902 Office: Dept English Univ New Hampshire Durham NH 03824

HAPP, HARVEY HEINZ, electrical engineer, educator; b. Berlin, June 27, 1928; U.S., 1947, naturalized, 1953; s. Harry and Hertha (Friedmann) H.; m. Ruth Hollander, Nov. 17, 1951; children: Deborah Ann, Sandra Eva. B.S. in Elec. Engring, Ill. Inst. Tech., 1953; M.E.E., Rensselaer Poly. Inst., Troy, N.Y., 1958; D.Sc., U. Belgrade, Yugoslavia, 1962. Registered profl. engr., N.Y. With Gen. Electric Co., 1954—, sr. application engr., Schenectady, 1968-72, mgr. analytical engring. services, 1972-77, mgr. advanced system tech., 1977-82, mgr. system analysis, 1982—, also mem. faculty power system engring. course; lectr. colls. Author: Diakoptics and Networks (translated into Russian and Romanian), 1971, Piecewise Methods and Applications to Power Systems, 1980; Editor: Gabriel Kron and Systems Theory, 1972; editorial bd.: Proc. IEEE; Contbr. numerous articles and book revs. to profl. jours., chpts. to tech. books. Fellow IEEE (Prize Paper award region 5 1962, power systems engring. com. 1977, region 1 award 1980); mem. Tensor Soc. Gt. Brit. (v.p. 1972—), Conf. International des Grands Reseaux Electrique a Haute Tension, Internat. Power Systems Computations Conf. (co-founder 1962), Gen. Electric Co. Engrs. and Scientists Assn. (chmn. policy com. 1968-70), Ill. Inst. Tech. Alumni Assn., Sigma Xi, Tau Beta Pi, Eta Kappa Nu. Home: 2211 Webster Dr Schenectady NY 12309 Office: Gen Electric Co Bldg 2-548 1 River Rd Schenectady NY 12345 *My driving force has been a strong desire to make a contribution, a sense of commitment, a disregard for the materialistic, and a recognition of a finite lifetime, but a work which transcends it.*

HAPPEL, JOHN, chemical engineer, educator; b. Bklyn., Apr. 1, 1908; s. John and Emilie (Weinkauf) H.; m. Dorothy Merriam, 1951; children: Jill, George, Ruth. B.S., MIT, 1929, M.S., 1930; D.Ch.E., Poly. Inst. Bklyn., 1948. Registered profl. engr., N.Y. With (Socony Vacuum Oil Co.), 1930-48; prof. chem. engring., chmn. dept. N.Y.U., 1949-73, prof. emeritus, 1973—; sr. research asso., Columbia, 1973—, adj. prof., 1976—; cons. to various cos. on petroleum chems.; pres. Catalysis Research Corp.; bd. mgrs. Mohonk Consultations, Inc.; Mem. petroleum industry war council, 1942-45, mem. tech. com. charge constrn. and operation world's largest butadiene plant for synthetic rubber, 1942-47; Mem. indsl. adv. bd. for chem. engring. U. Conn., Storrs, 1981—. Author: Chemical Process Economics, 1958, 2d edit. (with Donald Jordan), 1974, (with Howard Brenner) Low Reynolds Number Hydrodynamics, 1965, 2d edit., 1973, paperback edit., 1983; Translator: (with M.F. Delleo, Jr., G. Dembinski, A.H. Weiss) Catalysis by Non-Metals (from Russian by O.V. Krylov), 1970, (with Miguel Hnatow and Laimonis Bajars) Base Metal Oxide Catalysts, 1977; assoc. editor: Chem. Engring. Jour.; mem. editorial adv. bd.: Ency. Chem. Processing and Design; Contbr. articles to profl. jours., chpts. to tech. books. Recipient Certificate of Distinction Poly. Inst. Bklyn.; Tyler award N.Y. sect. Am. Inst. Chem. Engrs. Fellow N.Y. Acad. Scis. (v.p. 1977), Am. Inst. Chem. Engrs.; mem. Am. Chem. Soc. (honor scroll), Nat. Acad. Engring., Sigma Xi, Alpha Chi Sigma, Phi Lambda Upsilon, Tau Beta Pi. Episcopalian. Club: Chemists (N.Y.C.). Patentee in field. Home: 69 Tompkins Ave Hastings-on-Hudson NY 10706 Office: Columbia University New York NY 10027

HAPPER, WILLIAM, JR., physicist, educator; b. Vellore, India, July 27, 1939; came to U.S., 1941, naturalized, 1961; s. William and Gladys (Morgan) H.; m. Barbara Jean Baker, June 10, 1967; children—James William, Gladys Anne. B.S., U. N.C., 1960; Ph.D., Princeton U., 1964. Research asso. Radiation Lab., Columbia U., N.Y.C., 1964, asst. prof. physics, 1967-70, asso. prof., 1970-74, prof., 1974-80, dir., 1976-79; prof. Princeton (N.J.) U., 1980—; cons. in field. Alfred P. Sloan fellow, 1967; Recipient Alexander von Humboldt award Fed. Republic of Germany, 1976. Fellow Am. Phys. Soc. Democrat. Home: 559 Riverside Dr Princeton NJ 08540 Office: Dept Physics Princeton U Princeton NJ 08540

HARA, ARTHUR S(HIGERU), trading company executive; b. Vancouver, B.C., Can., Apr. 3, 1927; s. Takeo and Koki H.; m. Shizue Horii, Jan. 30, 1948; children: George T., Elaine J. B.Sc., Kobe U. (Japan), 1951; grad. advanced mgmt. program, Harvard U., 1980. Mgr. grains dept. Mitsubishi Can. Ltd., Vancouver, 1968-75, v.p., 1975-79; exec. v.p. Mitsubishi Can Ltd., Vancouver, 1979-83; chmn. bd. Mitsubishi Can. Ltd., Vancouver, 1983—; chmn. bd. United Oilseed Products Ltd., Lloydminster, Alta., Can., 1978—; dir. Lakeside Fram Industries, Brooks, Alta. Vice chmn. Vancouver Bd. Trade, 1983, Council for Can. Unity, Vancouver, 1983. Clubs: Vancouver, Vancouver Lawn Tennis and Badminton.

HARAGAN, DONALD ROBERT, educator; b. Houston, Apr. 15, 1936; s. Donald William and Mary (Thompson) H.; m. Willie Mae O'Berry, July 2, 1966; children—Shannon Lea, Shelley Jo. B.S., U. Tex., 1959, Ph.D., 1969; M.S., Tex. A & M U., 1960. Registered profl. engr., Tex. Research asst. Tex. A & M U., College Station, 1959-60; research scientist U. Tex., Austin, 1960-66, instr., 1966-69; asst. prof. Tex. Tech. U., Lubbock, 1969-72, asso. prof., 1972-78, prof. geosci., 1978—; dept. chmn., 1972-77, 80—. Contbr. articles in field to profl. jours. Mem. Nat. Soc. Profl. Engrs., AAAS, Am. Meteorol. Soc., Tex. Soc. Profl. Engrs., Tex. Acad. Sci. Home: 3204 53rd St Lubbock TX 79413 Office: Tex Tech U Dept Geosciences PO Box 4109 Lubbock TX 79409

HARARI, HANANIAH, artist; b. Rochester, N.Y., Aug. 29, 1912; s. Israel Ely and Sarah (Berger) H.; m. Freda Emanuel, May 10, 1936 (dec. 1977); 1 son, Michael John; m. Shirley Lewis, Sept. 1, 1979. Student, Coll. Fine Arts, Syracuse (N.Y.) U., 1930-32; in ateliers of, Fernand Leger, André Lhote, Marcel Gromaire, Paris, 1932-34; at, Fontainebleau Ecole de Fresque, Paris, 1933. Tchr. painting Am. Artists Sch., N.Y.C., 1938-40, New Sch. Social Research, 1974, Sch. Visual Arts, 1974-83; tchr. illustration Workshop Sch. Art, 1950-52. One-man shows, Mercury Gallery, 1939, Pinacotheca, 1941, 43, Laurel Gallery, 1948, 51, New Sch. Social Research, 1974, Nardin Galleries, 1979, Martin Diamond Fine Arts, Inc., 1981, exhbns. include, Mus. Modern Art, 1938, 42-43, Whitney Mus., 1942, 43, 44, 46, 47, 81, Met. Mus., 1943, Toledo Mus., 1947, San Francisco Palace Legion of Honor, Art Dirs. Ann., 1947-48, 1950, 52, Albright Art Gallery, Buffalo, Cleve. Mus. Art, Art Gallery of Toronto, Art. Mus. N.Mex., Albuquerque, 1977, Portsmouth Gallery (Va.), 1982, Lowe Art Mus., Miami, Fla., 1983, others; represented in permanent collections, Met. Mus., Phila. Mus. Art, Whitney, Mus., Albright Art Gallery, U. Ariz., Tucson; affiliated, Portraits, Inc., Nardin Galleries, Martin Diamond Fine Arts, Inc. Served with AUS, 1943-45. Recipient Hallgarten prize N.A.D., 1942, Emy Herzfeld award 4th Ann. Audubon Artists Exhbn., 1945. Home: 34 Prospect Pl Croton-on-Hudson NY 10520 *In appreciation of the gift of life, I aspire to leave some lively and harmonious tracks.*

HARARY, FRANK, mathematician, educator; b. N.Y.C., Mar. 11, 1921; s. Joseph and Mary (Laby) H.; children: Miriam, Natalie, Judith, Thomas, Joel, Chaya. B.A., Bklyn. Coll., 1941, M.A., 1945, D.A. (hon.), 1962; Ph.D., U. Calif., Berkeley, 1948; M.A. status, U. Oxford, Eng., 1973; D.Sc. (hon.), U. Aberdeen, Scotland, 1975; Fil.Dr. in Social Scis. (hon.), U. Lund, Sweden, 1978; M.A. status, U. Cambridge, Eng., 1981. Mem. faculty dept. math. U. Mich., Ann Arbor, 1948—, prof., 1964—; faculty asso. Research Center for Group Dynamics, Inst. Social Research, 1950-82; mem. Inst. Advanced Study, Princeton, N.J., 1957-59; vis. prof. Univ. Coll. London, 1962-63, London Sch. Econs., 1966-67, U. Melbourne, 1969, U. Waterloo, Ont., Can., 1970, U. Chile, Santiago, 1970, U. Copenhagen, 1970, Nanyang U., Singapore, 1972, Technion, Haifa, Israel, 1973, U. Niamey, Niger, 1975, U. Newcastle, Australia, 1976, Simon Bolivar U., Caracas, Venezuela, 1977; fellow Wolfson Coll., U. Oxford, 1973-74, Churchill Coll., Cambridge U., 1980-81; Colloquium lectr. Edinburgh Math. Soc., St. Andrews, 1972; inaugural lectr. S.E. Asian Math. Soc., Singapore, 1972, lectr., Penang, Malaysia, 1974, Inst. Mgmt. Scis., Phila., 1958, IRE, N.Y.C., 1958, AAAS, 1960, Linguistic Soc. Am., 1960, 1st Caribbean Combinatorial Conf., Kingston, Jamaica, 1970, 2d Caribbean Combinatorial Conf., Barbados, 1977, Soc. Indsl. and Applied Math., Santa Barbara, Calif., 1968, Math. Assn. Am., Bradenton, Fla., 1975, 5th Brit. Combinatorial Conf., Aberdeen, Scotland, 1975, 7th S.E., Conf. on Graph Theory and Computing, Baton Rouge, 1977, Ont. Math. Meetings, St. Catherine, 1977, Bremer Konferenz zur Chemie, Bremen, Germany, 1978, European Assn. for Theoretical Computer Sci., Udine, Italy, 1978, Math. Assn. Am., Valparaiso, Ind., 1980, Holland, Mich., 1980, Brookings, S.C., 1983, Serbian Chem. Soc., Kragujevac, Yugoslavia, 1980, Greek Math. Soc., Athens, 1983, Assn. for Math. Applied to Econ. and Social Scis., Catania, Sicily, 1983; disting. scientist in residence N.Y. Acad. Scis., 1977; Humboldt Found. fellow, Munich, Germany, summers 1978, 79. Editor, founder: Jour. Combinatorial Theory, 1966—; editor: Discrete Mathematics, 1970—, Jour. Math. Sociology, 1970-78, Bull. Calcutta Math. Soc, 1976—, Jour. Combinatorics, Info. and Systems Scis, 1976—; editor, founder: Jour. Graph Theory, 1977—, Social Networks, 1978-81, Networks, 1979—, Discrete Applied Mathematics, 1979—, Math. Modelling, 1980—, Math. Social Scis, 1980—; Author: (with R. Norman and D. Cartwright) Structural Models, 1965, Graph Theory, 1969, (with E. Palmer) Graphical Enumeration, 1973; (with Per Hage) Structural Models in Anthropology, 1983; Editor: (with E. Palmer) A Seminar on Graph Theory, 1967, Graph Theory and Theoretical Physics, 1967, Proof Techniques in Graph Theory, 1969, New Directions in the Theory of Graphs, 1973, (with R. Bari) Graphs and Combinatorics, 1974, Topics in Graph Theory, 1979, (with J. S. Maybee) Graphs and Applications, 1984. Mem. Am. Math. Soc., London Math Soc., Glasgow Math Soc., Edinburgh Math Soc., Can. Math Soc., S.E. Asian Math Soc., Malaysian Math Soc., Calcutta Math Soc. (v.p. 1978—), Math. Assn. Am., Soc. for Indsl. and Applied Math. Home: 1015 Olivia Ave Ann Arbor MI 48104 Office: Dept Math U Mich Ann Arbor MI 48109

HARBAUGH, GEORGE MILTON, hotel executive; b. Ashland, Ohio, May 29, 1930; s. Fred Ellston and Mary Mabel (Baldauf) H.; m. Mary Ferra, Jan. 20, 1962; children: Lynne, George Milton II. B.A. in Bus. Adminstrn, Pasadena Coll., 1954. Sales mgr. Edgewater Beach Hotel, Chgo., 1961-63; dir. sales Internat. Hotel, Los Angeles, 1963-69; v.p. sales Corrigan Hotels, Los Angeles, 1969-72; gen. mgr. Hyatt Regency Hotel, Los Angeles, 1972-83; founder Harbaugh Hotel Mgmt. Corp., Los Angeles, 1983—. Bd. dirs. Los Angeles Visitors and Conv. Bur., 1972-79. Served with USMCR, 1951-53. Mem. So. Calif. Businessmen's Assn. (treas. 1978-79). Roman Catholic. Office: Harbaugh Hotel Mgmt 9570 W Pico Blvd Los Angeles CA 90035

HARBAUGH, JANE WORTH, university administrator; b. Balt., Apr. 24, 1930; d. Vernon Leslie and Charlotte (Kirby) H. A.B., Tufts Coll., 1952; M.A., Fletcher Sch. Law and Diplomacy, 1953, Ph.D., 1957. Instr. history and polit. sci. U. Chattanooga, 1957-59, asst. prof., 1959-62, asso. prof., 1962-65, prof., chmn. dept. history, 1965-69; dean Coll. Arts and Scis., U. Tenn. at Chattanooga, 1969-75, vice chancellor for acad. affairs, 1975-81, assoc. provost, 1981—; chairperson Tenn. Rhodes Scholarship Com., 1977—. Mem. ad hoc com., adv. editorial bd. SUNY, 1965-66; v.p. Adult Edn. Council Chattanooga Area, 1962-64, dir., 1958-60; bd. dirs., exec. com. Allied Arts Council of Chattanooga, 1970-71, 73-79; bd. dirs. Appalachian Regional Arthritis Found., 1975-78, Chattanooga Nature Center, 1978-81; mem. nat. policy bd. CONDUIT, 1978—; mem. Tenn. planning com. Am. Council on Edn.; mem. adv. bd. PUSH-EXCEL, 1978, mem. exec. com., 1979—; chmn. Coca Cola Scholarship Com., 1982—. Rockefeller Found. research grantee, 1956; recipient Evans Found. award, 1963; fellow Center E. Asian Studies, Harvard U., 1960-61. Mem. Assn. Asian Studies (chmn. com. undergrad. edn. 1966-68), Greater Chattanooga C. of C. (dir. 1977—, 2d v.p. 1980, exec. com. 1980-81). Democrat. Club: Walden (bd. govs. 1981). Home: 720 Maryland Circle Chattanooga TN 37412

HARBAUGH, JOHN WARVELLE, applied earth sciences educator; b. Madison, Wis., Aug. 6, 1926; s. Marion Dwight and Marjorie (Warvelle) H.; m. Josephine Taylor, Nov. 24, 1951; children: Robert, Dwight, Richard. B.S., U. Kans.-Lawrence, 1948, M.S., 1950; Ph.D., U. Wis., 1955. Prodn. geologist Carter Oil Co., Tulsa, 1951-53; chmn. bd. Terrascis. Inc., San Francisco, 1979—; prof. applied earth sci. Stanford U., 1955—. Author: (with J.H. Doveton and J.C. Davis) Probability Methods in Oil Exploration, 1977, Computer Simulation in Geology, 1981. Recipient Haworth Disting. Alumni award U. Kans., 1968. Fellow Goel. Soc. Am.; mem. Am. Assn. Petroleum Geologists (Levorsen award 1970). Republican. Club: Cosmos (Washington). Home: 683 Salvatierra St Stanford CA 94305 Office: Stanford U Geology Bldg Stanford CA 94305

HARBAUGH, WILLIAM HENRY, historian, educator; b. Newark, Jan. 16, 1920; s. William K. and Emily (Wright) H.; m. Virginia Wayne Talbot, Aug. 15, 1953; children: Emelyn Hartridge, William Talbot, Henry Richmond. A.B., U. Ala., 1942; M.A., Columbia, 1947; Ph.D., Northwestern U., 1954. Instr. U. Conn., 1946-49, 53-56, asst. prof., 1956-61; instr. U. Md., 1952-53; sr. fellow Yale Law Sch., 1960-61; vis. asso. prof. Rutgers U., 1961-62; prof., chmn. dept. history Bucknell U., Lewisburg., Pa., 1962-66; prof. U. Va., 1966-77, Commonwealth prof., 1977-82, Langbourne M. Williams prof., 1982—. Author: Power and Responsibility: Life and Times of Theodore Roosevelt, 1961, The Life and Times of Theodore Roosevelt, 1963, Lawyer's Lawyer: The Life of John W. Davis, 1973; editorial adv. com.: The Papers of Woodrow Wilson, 1977. Served to capt. AUS, 1942-45; ETO. Decorated Croix de Guerre with gold star. Mem. Theodore Roosevelt Assn. (trustee 1976—), ACLU, Pa.-German Soc., Phi Beta Kappa, Chi Phi. Democrat. Unitarian. Home: 1930 Thomson Rd Charlottesville VA 22903 Chaplin CT 06235

HARBECK, WILLIAM JAMES, real estate executive, lawyer; b. Glenview, Ill., Dec. 16, 1921; s. Christian Frederick and Anna (Gaeth) H.; m. Jean Marie Allsopp, Jan. 20, 1945; children: John, Stephen, Timothy, Mark, Christopher. B.A., Wabash (Ind.) Coll., 1947; J.D., Northwestern U., 1950. Bar: Ill. 1950. Land acquisition atty. Chgo. Land Clearance Commn., 1950-51; with Montgomery Ward & Co., Chgo., 1951-81, asst. to pres., dir. corp. facilities, 1968-70, v.p., dir. facilities devel., 1970-81; v.p. Montgomery Ward Devel. Corp., 1972-81; pres., chief exec. officer Montgomery Ward Properties Corp., 1974-81; pres. William J. Harbeck Assocs., 1981—; dir. Randhurst Corp., 1972-81, exec. com., 1975-79, govt. affairs com., 1977—, urban com., 1980-83; bd. dirs. Internat. Council Shopping Centers, 1972-78, exec. com., 1975-78, lectr., 1969—. Author articles in field; mem. editorial bds. profl. jours. Bd. dirs. Chgo. Lawson YMCA, 1973—, chmn. devel. com., 1979—; bd. dirs. Greater North Michigan Ave. Assn., Chgo., 1979-81; chmn. constrn. com. Chgo. United, 1979-81; co-chmn. Chgo. Bus. Opportunities Fair, 1980-81; mem. real estate com. Chgo. Met. YMCA, 1982—; mem. pres.'s council Concordia Coll., River Forest, Ill., 1969—; youth Bible and Bethel instr. Redeemer Luth. Ch., Highland Park, Ill., 1965, congregation pres., 1968-70, chmn. ch. growth com., 1982—; trustee Lutheran Ch. Mo. Synod Found., 1975-76, 81—, mem. Synodical mission study commn., 1974-75, mem. research and planning com., 1981—, mem. task force on synodical constn. by-laws and structure, 1975-79; sponsor Luth. Chs. for Career Devel., 1979—; corp. chmn. U.S. Bond drive, Chgo., 1976; chief crusader Chgo. Crusade Mercy, 1976-78; div. chmn. Chgo. Cerebral Palsy campaign, 1977-78. Served to lt. (j.g.) USNR, 1942-46. Mem. Ill. Bar Assn., Luth. Layman's League, Alpha Sigma Kappa, Phi Alpha Delta, Pi Alpha Chi. Home and Office: 470 E Linden St Lake Forest IL 60045

HARBERGER, ARNOLD CARL, economist, educator; b. Newark, July 27, 1924; s. Ferdinand C. and Martha (Bucher) H.; m. Ana Beatriz Valjalo, Mar. 15, 1958; children: Paul Vincent, Carl David. Student, Johns Hopkins U., 1941-43; M.A., U. Chgo., 1947, Ph.D., 1950; Dr.h.c., U. Tucuman, 1979. Asst. prof. polit. economy Johns Hopkins U., 1949-53; asso. prof. econs. U. Chgo., 1953-59, prof., 1959—, chmn. dept., 1964-71, 75-80, Gustavus F. and Ann M. Swift disting. service prof., 1977—, dir. Center Latin Am. Econ. Studies, 1965—; vis. prof. MIT (Center Internat. Studies), New Delhi, 1961-62, Econ. Devel. Inst., IBRD, 1965, Harvard U., 1971-72, Princeton U., 1973-74, UCLA, 1983, 84; cons. IMF, 1950, 1951-52, U.S. Treasury Dept., 1961-75, Com. Econ. Devel., 1961-78, Planning Commn., India, 1961-62, 73, Pan Am. Union, 1962-76, Dept. State, 1962-76, Central Bank, Chile, 1965-70, Planning Dept., Panama, 1965-77, Colombia, 1969-71, Ford Found., 1967-77, Planning Commn., El Salvador, 1973-75, Budget and Planning Office, Uruguay, 1974-75, Can. Dept. Regional Econ. Expansion, 1975-77, Finance Ministry, Bolivia, 1976, Mex., 1976—, Can. Dept. Employment and Migration, 1980-82, Indonesian Ministry Fin., 1981-82, Can. Dept. Fin., 1982—, Chinese Ministry Fin., 1983. Author: Project Evaluation, 1972, Taxation and Welfare, 1974; Editor: Demand for Durable Goods, 1960, The Taxation of Income from Capital, 1968, Key Problems of Economic Policy In Latin America, 1970; Contbr. sci. papers to profl. jours. and govt. publs. Served with AUS, 1943-46. Guggenheim fellow; Fulbright scholar; faculty research fellow Social Sci. Research Council; Ford Found. faculty research fellow, 1968-69. Fellow Econometric Soc., Am. Acad. Arts and Scis.; mem. Am. Econ. Assn. (mem. exec. com. 1970-72), Royal Econ. Soc., Nat. Tax Assn., Phi Beta Kappa. Home: 4840 S Greenwood Ave Chicago IL 60615 Office: 1126 E 59th St Chicago IL 60637

HARBERT, GUY MORLEY, JR., obstetrician and gynecologist; b. Fredericksburg, Va., Dec. 19, 1929; s. Guy Morley and Hannah (Turman) H.; m. Peggy Ann Simpson, Sept. 8, 1951; children—Lucille Hannah, Guy Morley, III, Michael Simpson. B.A., U. Va., 1952, M.D., 1956. Diplomate: Am. Bd. Ob-Gyn (maternal-fetal medicine). Intern Barnes Hosp., St. Louis, 1956-57; resident in ob-gyn U. Va. Hosp., 1959-63; med. faculty U. Va. Med. Sch., 1963—, prof. ob-gyn, 1976—; mem. human embryology and devel. study sect. NIH, 1975-79. Author articles in profl. jours., chpts. in books. Served as officer M.C. USAF, 1957-59. Mem. Soc. Gynecol. Investigation (exec. council 1973-76), Perinatal Research Soc. (exec. council 1977-79), So. Perinatal Assn. (exec. council 1974-77), Am. Gynecol. Soc., Am. Assn. Obstetricians and Gynecologists, N.Y. Acad. Scis., Am. Coll. Obstetricians and Gynecologists, Assn. Profs. Ob-Gyn, S. Atlantic Assn. Obstetricians and Gynecologists, Sigma Xi. Presbyterian. Office: Box 387 Univ Hosp Charlottesville VA 22908

HARBIN, JOHN PICKENS, former service company executive; b. Waxahachie, Tex., July 17, 1917; s. E.P. and Mary Joy (Beale) H.; m. Dorothy Lee Middleton, Oct. 18, 1943; 1 dau., Linda Ann. B.B.A., U. Tex., 1939. Accounting tng. program Carter Oil Co. (Exxon Corp.), Tulsa, 1939-40; accountant Creole Petroleum Corp., Venezuela, 1940-42, 45-47; became controller, asst. sec. Halliburton Co., 1948, former chmn. bd., chief exec. officer, now dir.; dir. Citibank, Citicorp, N.Y.C., Burlington Industries, Greensboro, N.C., La. Land & Exploration Co., New Orleans, Petrolite Corp., St. Louis. Active Boy Scouts Am.; bd. dirs. Southwestern Med. Found.; trustee Southwestern Legal Found. Served as lt. USNR, 1943-45. Mem. Ind. Petroleum Assn. of Am., Am. Petroleum Inst. (dir.), Petroleum Equipment Suppliers Assn. (dir.), Conf. Bd. Bus. Roundtable, Tex. Research League (dir., past chmn.), Navy League U.S., Dallas C. of C., Nat. Petroleum Council, Dallas Council World Affairs, Dallas Citizens Council (dir.), Delta Tau Delta, Beta Alpha Psi. Clubs: Dallas Petroleum, Dallas Country; Tower (Dallas); Chaparral, Brook Hollow Golf; Brook (N.Y.C.). Home: 4816 Lakeside Dr Dallas TX 75205 Office: 2600 Southland Center Dallas TX 75201

HARBISON, JOHN HARRIS, composer, educator; b. Orange, N.J., Dec. 20, 1938; s. E. Harris and Janet R. (German) H.; m. Rose Mary Pedersen, Aug. 31, 1963. B.A. (Jr. fellow), Harvard U., 1960; M.F.A., Princeton U., 1963. Rockefeller composer in residence Reed Coll., 1968; asst. prof music M.I.T., Cambridge, Mass., 1969-72, assoc. prof., 1972-79, prof., 1979—; music dir. Cantata Singers and Ensemble, 1969-73; composer-in-residence Pitts. Symphony Orch., 1982-84, Tanglewood, 1984. Composer: opera Full Moon in March, Diotima; for large orch. Recipient award Am. Inst. Arts and Letters; Brandeis Creative Arts citation; Nat. Endowment for Arts award; Guggenheim fellow. Home: 563 Franklin St Cambridge MA 02139 Office: MIT 424 14th St N Cambridge MA 02139

HARBISON, WILLIAM JAMES, state judge; b. Columbia, Tenn., Sept. 11, 1923; s. William Joshua and Eunice Elizabeth (Kinzer) H.; m. Mary Elizabeth Coleman, June 14, 1952; children: William Leslie, Mary Alice. Student, The Citadel, 1943-44; B.A., Vanderbilt U., 1947, J.D., 1950. Bar: Tenn. 1950. Pvt. practice law, Nashville, 1950-74; spl. justice Tenn. Supreme Ct., Nashville, 1966-67, justice, 1974—, chief justice, 1980-82; adj. prof. law Vanderbilt Law Sch., Nashville, 1950—; chmn. civil rules com. Tenn. Supreme Ct., 1965-74. Editor-in-chief: Vanderbilt Law Review, 1949-50. Mem. Metro Nashville Bd. Edn., 1970-74. Served with AUS, 1943-46. Mem. ABA, Tenn. Bar Assn., Nashville Bar Assn. (pres. 1970-71), Order of Coif, Phi Beta Kappa. Democrat. Methodist. Clubs: Cedar Creek, Cumberland, Rotary. Home: 1031 Overton Lea Rd Nashville TN 37220 Office: 314 Supreme Ct Bldg Nashville TN 37219

HARBOURT, CYRUS OSCAR, electrical engineering educator; b. Baton Rouge, June 1, 1931; s. John Leslie and Marie (Berthelot) H.; m. Mary Josephine Heuvel, Dec. 27, 1952; children: Ellen Catherine, Joan Carol, Cyrus David, Anna Marie, Mary Alice. B.S. in Elec. Engring, La. State U., 1952; M.S., MIT, 1955; Ph.D., Syracuse U., 1961. Registered profl. engr., Mo. Instr. La. State U., 1954-55, Syracuse (N.Y.) U., 1957-61; asst. prof., then asso. prof. U. Tex. at Austin, 1961-67; prof. elec. engring. U. Mo.-Columbia, 1967—, chmn. dept. elec. engring., 1967-77, dir. continuing engring. edn., 1982—; elec. engr. Bonneville Power Adminstrn., Portland, Oreg., 1977-78; Asso. prin. engr. Radiation, Inc., Melbourne, Fla., summer 1965; cons. to industry. Co-author: Network Computer Analysis, 1969. Served with AUS, 1955-57. Recipient Engring. Teaching Excellence award Gen. Dynamics Co.-U. Tex., 1963. Mem. IEEE, Nat. Soc. Profl. Engrs., Mo. Soc. Profl. Engrs., Am. Soc. Engring. Edn., Sigma Xi, Tau

Beta Pi, Phi Kappa Phi, Omicron Delta Kappa. Roman Catholic. Home: 2306 Ridgefield Rd Columbia MO 65201

HARBRANT, ROBERT FRANCIS, labor union executive; b. Johnstown, Pa., Oct. 6, 1942; s. Berthol John and Helen Mary (Hankinson) H.; m. Anne Marie Pekala, Aug. 19, 1967; children: Christopher John, Mary Jeanne, Kathleen Marie, Julie Anne. Student, Cambria-Rowe Bus. Sch., 1960-61, George Meany Labor Studies Center, Am. U., 1967-70, LaSalle Extension U., 1973-74. With acctg. dept. AFL-CIO, 1962-67; public relations dir. Union Label and Service Trades Dept., 1967-72, asst. to sec.-treas., 1972-74, exec. asst., 1974-77; exec. dir. Food and Allied Service Trades Dept., Washington, 1977, sec.-treas., 1977-79, pres., 1979—; mem. com. on organizing, com. on community services AFL-CIO. Chmn. labor adv. com. Boy Scouts Am., mem. nat. exec. bd.; mem. exec. bd. Nat. Cath. Scouting Com. Mem. Consumer Fedn. Am. (dir.), Com. of Evolution of Work and Its Implications, United Food and Comml. Workers Internat. Union, Office and Profl. Employees Internat. Union, Hotel and Restaurant Employees Internat. Union. Club: K.C. Home: 19324 Madison House St Olney MD 20832 Office: Food and Allied Service Trades Dept 815 16th St NW Washington DC 20006

HARBUTT, CHARLES, photographer; b. Camden, N.J., July 29, 1935; s. Charles Henry and Catharine (McMahon) H.; m. Alberta Eleanor Steves, Aug. 8, 1958; children: Sarah, Charles, Damian; m. Joan Liftin, Dec. 22, 1978. B.S., Marquette U., 1956. Assoc. editor Jubilee Mag., N.Y.C., 1956-59; mem. Magnum Photos, N.Y.C. and Paris, 1963-81, Archive Pictures, 1981—; pres. Actuality Inc., N.Y.C., 1970—; cons. N.Y.C. Planning Commn., 1968-70. Author: Travelog, 1974 (Best Arles 1974); co-editor: Americans in Crisis, 1969; author: monograph I Grandi Photographi, 1983; curator: exhibit Am Pavilion, Salford, 1980. Office: Archive Pictures Inc 111 Wooster St New York NY 10012

HARCLEROAD, FRED FARLEY, educator; b. Cheyenne, Wyo., Nov. 22, 1918; s. Fred Farley and Ina Mary (Livermore) H.; m. Moyne Payne, Dec. 20, 1942; children: Patricia Irene, Fred Douglass. A.B., U. No. Colo., 1939, M.A., 1942; Ph.D., Stanford U., 1948. Tchr., coach Ault (Colo.) High School, 1939-42, prin., 1942-43; tchr., coach, counselor Menlo Sch. and Jr. Coll., 1943-46; asst., acting instr. Stanford, summers 1944, 45; staff San Diego State U., 1946-52, coordinator audio-visual service, 1947-50, co-ordinator secondary edn., 1949-51, chmn. div. edn., 1951-52; dean instrn. San Jose Jr. Coll., 1952-53, San Jose State U., 1952-57, dean of coll., 1957-59; pres. Calif. State U., Hayward, 1959-67; prof. higher edn. U. Iowa, Iowa City, 1968-74; pres. (Am. Coll. Testing Program), 1967-74; dir. Center for Study Higher Edn., U. Ariz., Tucson, 1974-80, prof. higher edn., 1974—; pres.-elect Am. Assn. State Colls. and Univs., 1967, bd. dirs., 1965-68, chmn. com. internat. edn., 1966-69, chmn. or mem. com. on purposes and policies, 1966-76; chmn. accreditation commn. Nat. Home Study Council, 1977—; mem. bd. Council on Postsecondary Accreditation, 1981—. Co-author: International Education in the Developing State Colleges and Universities, 1966, Audio-Visual Instruction: Media and Methods, 1959, rev. edits., 1964, 69, 73, 77, Educational Auditing and Voluntary Institutional Accreditation, 1975; sr. author: The Developing State Colleges and Universities: Historical Background, Current Status, and Future Plans, 1969, Continuing Studies Program in the Mass. State College System, 1972, Regional State Colleges and Universities Enter the 1970's, 1973; Editor: (with William Allen) Audio Visual Administration, 1951, The Education of the Audio Visual Communication Specialist, 1960, Learning Resources in Colleges and Universities, 1964, Issues of the Seventies: The Future of Higher Education, 1970, Higher Education: A Developing Field of Study, 1974, Educational Auditing and Accountability, 1976, (with others) The Regional State Colleges and Universities in the Middle Seventies, 1976, Financing Postsecondary Education in the 1980's, 1979, Voluntary Organizations in America and the Development of Educational Accreditation, 1980, Accreditation: History, Process, and Problems, 1980; author mag. articles edn., textbooks. Mem. Am. Council Edn. (mem. Pacific Coast com. 1955-58), Western Coll. Assn. (dir. 1963-67), Assn. Profs. Higher Edn. (chmn. 1973-75), N.E.A. (dept. audio visual instrn. com. on profl. edn. 1951-53, mem. adv. bd. ednl. policies commn. 1961-63, 65-68), Calif. Audio-Visual Edn. Assn. (pres. So. sect. 1950-51, sec. 1951-52), Calif. Council Tchr. Edn. (chmn. ednl. TV com.), Phi Delta Kappa, Phi Alpha Theta, Kappa Delta Pi, Phi Kappa Phi, Phi Mu Alpha, Sinfonia, Blue Key. Clubs: Rotarian., Commonwealth. Home: 840 E Via Linterna Tucson AZ 85718

HARCLERODE, JACK EDGAR, biologist; b. Everett, Pa., June 29, 1935; s. Thomas Carl and Alberta Suzanne (Schetrompf) H.; m. Joan Kathryn Yohn, July 3, 1960; children—Jolee, Jill, Jan. B.S., Shippensburg State Coll., 1957; M.S., Pa. State U., 1958, Ph.D., 1962. Asst. prof. zoology Ohio U., Athens, 1962-65; asst. prof. Bucknell U., Lewisburg, Pa., 1965-67, asso. prof., 1967-72, prof., 1972—, Herbert L. Spencer prof. biology, 1977—. Contbr. articles to profl. jours. NIH grantee, 1979-81; recipient Lindback award for disting. teaching, 1977. Mem. Am. Soc. Andrology, Endocrine Soc., AAAS, Am. Soc. Zoologists, Pa. Acad. Scis. Home: RD 1 Box 453 Lewisburg PA 17837 Office: 331 Taylor Hall Bucknell U Lewisburg PA 17837

HARCOURT, JOHN BERTRAM, educator; b. Providence, Oct. 20, 1922; s. Cyril Bennett and Mary Esther (Christian) H.; m. Mary Ellen Trueb, July 22, 1950; children: Kathryn Moseley, James Patton. A.B., Brown U., 1943, M.A., 1947, Ph.D., 1952. Instr. Brown U., 1946-51; instr. Cornell U., 1951-53; mem. faculty Ithaca (N.Y.) Coll., 1953—, prof., 1961—, Charles A. Dana prof. English, 1977—, trustee, 1974-77. Author: The Ithaca College Story, 1983; Contbr. articles to profl. jours. Bd. dirs. Tompkins County (N.Y.) chpt. ARC, 1963-68, chmn., 1967-68. Served with U.S. Army, 1943-46. Recipient Alumni Meritorious Service award Ithaca Coll., 1982; named Hon. Alumnus, 1983. Mem. AAUP, MLA, Shakespeare Assn. Am., Phi Beta Kappa, Phi Kappa Phi. Democrat. Episcopalian. Office: 329 Muller Faculty Center Ithaca Coll Ithaca NY 14850 *If I use my time and fill my space creatively, reasonably, lovingly, I have added something to the universe that otherwise would simply not be there. If I mess up, I've left a hole that will remain forever. To see time and space as eternally significant, as sacramental realities, is to live rather than merely exist.*

HARCOURT, MICHAEL FRANKLIN, lawyer, mayor of Vancouver; b. Edmonton, Alta., Can., Jan. 6, 1943; s. Frank Norman and Stella Louise (Good) H.; m. Mai-Gret Wibecke Salo, June 26, 1971; 1 son, Justen Michael. B.A., U. B.C., 1965, LL.B., 1968. Bar: B.C. 1969. Founder dir. Vancouver Community Legal Assistance Soc., 1969-71; partner firm Lew, Fraser & Harcourt, 1971-79; pres. Housing & Econ. Devel. Consulting Firm, Vancouver, 1977—; alderman, City of Vancouver, 1972-80, mayor, 1980—; Asst. dir. Justice Devel. Commn., Vancouver; dir. Housing Corp. of B.C. Mem. Law Soc. B.C. New Democrat. Mem. United Ch. Can. Office: 453 W 12th Ave Vancouver BC Canada V5Y 1V4

HARDAWAY, ROBERT MORRIS, III, physician, educator, ret. army officer; b. Camp John Hay, Philippines, Jan. 9, 1916; s. Robert Morris and Olive (Gray) H.; m. Lee H. Harkey, June 12, 1939; children—Robert Morris IV, Elizabeth J., Thomas G. II, Christopher. A.B., U. Denver, 1936; postgrad., U. Colo. Med. Sch., 1935-37; M.D., Washington U., St. Louis, 1939. Diplomate: Am. Bd. Surgery. Commd. 1st lt., M.C. U.S. Army, 1939, advanced through grades to brig. gen., 1970; ward officer, surg. service Fitzsimons Gen. Hosp., Denver, 1940-41, N. Sector Gen. Hosp., Hawaii, 1941-43; tchr. Med. Field Service Sch., Carlysle Barracks, Pa., 1943-45; surg. trainee Nichols Gen. Hosp., Louisville, 1945-46; resident surgery Madigan Gen. Hosp., Tacoma, 1946-47, Fitzsimons Gen. Hosp., 1949-50; chief surg. service 34th Gen. Hosp., Korea, 1947-49, Sta. Hosp., Ft. Belvoir, Va., 1950-54, 97th Gen. Hosp., Frankfurt, Germany, 1954-58, Martin Army Hosp., Ft. Benning, Ga., 1958-60; dir. div. surgery Walter Reed Army Inst. Research, Washington, 1960-67; comdg. officer 97th Gen. Hosp., Frankfurt, Germany, 1967-70; comdg. gen. William Beaumont Gen. Hosp., El Paso, 1970-75; prof. surgery Tex. Tech U. Sch. Medicine, El Paso, 1975—; staff R.E. Thomason Gen. Hosp., El Paso, 1975—. Author: Syndromes of Disseminated Intravascular Coagulation, 1966, Clinical Management of Shock, Surgical and Medical, 1968, Capillary Perfusion in Health and Disease, 1981; Contbr. articles on intravascular coagulation and hemorrhagic shock to jours. and books. Decorated Army Commendation medal with oak leaf cluster, Legion of Merit with oak leaf cluster, D.S.M.; recipient 2d prize for exhibit A.M.A., 1964; Silver award exhibit Am. Soc. Clin. Pathologists-Coll. Am. Pathologists, 1964; certificate of outstanding achievement U.S. Army Sci. Conf., 1964. Fellow A.C.S., Am. Coll. Angiology, Am. Assn. for Surgery Trauma, Microcirculation Assn.; mem. Assn. Mil. Surgeons U.S., A.M.A., Alpha Omega Alpha. Episcopalian. Office: 4815 Alameda Ave El Paso TX 79905 *Nothing we know, (or think we know) is the ultimate truth.*

HARDBECK, GEORGE WILLIAM, univ. dean; b. Edwardsville, Ill., Dec. 18, 1925; s. George Fred and Clara (Stahlhut) H.; m. Grete Olga Zipser, Apr. 17, 1947; 1 dau., Gail Leontine. B.S., U. Ill., 1954, M.S., 1956, Ph.D. in Labor Econs, 1958. Supr. Vienna Area Command Engr. Depot, U.S. War Dept., 1946-47; with Shell Oil Refinery, Wood River, Ill., 1947-49; teaching asst. U. Ill. at Urbana, 1955-58; asso. prof. econs. La. Poly. Inst., 1958-59; asst. prof. econs. St. Louis U., 1959-61; asso. prof. Kans. State U., Manhattan, 1961-64; resident dir. grad. program bus. U. Mo., 1964-66; prof. econs. Creighton U., 1966-71, asso. dean, 1966-68, dean, 1968-71; prof. econs. and indsl. relations, dean Coll. Bus. and Econs., U. Nev., Las Vegas, 1971—; cons. in field, also labor arbitrator, 1960—; Mem. arbitration roster Fed. Mediation and Conciliation Service. Author monographs and articles on labor and indsl. relations. Served with AUS, 1944-46; ETO. Decorated Purple Heart, Combat Inf. badge; H.B. Earhart fellow, 1957-58; fellow econs. U. Ill., summer 1956. Mem. Indsl. Relations Research Assn., Am. Arbitration Assn., Order Artus, Alpha Kappa Psi, Beta Gamma Sigma, Phi Kappa Phi. Home: 3659 Descanso St Las Vegas NV 89121

HARDBERGER, PHILLIP DUANE, lawyer, journalist; b. Morton, Tex., July 27, 1934; s. Homer Reeves and Bess (Scott) H.; m. Linda Morgan, May 1968; 1 dau., Amy. B.A., Baylor U., 1955; M.S., Columbia U., 1960; LL.B., Georgetown U., 1965. Reporter, Waco (Tex.) News Tribune, 1952-54; press rep. Tex. Baptist Conv., 1958-59; asso. editor Mil. Pub. Inst., N.Y.C., 1961; exec. sec. Peace Corps, 1962-66; spl. asst. to dir. Office Econ. Opportunity, 1967-68; trial lawyer, 1968—. Contbr. articles to profl. jours. Served to capt. USAF, 1955-58. Home: 470 Furr Dr San Antonio TX 78201 Office: 111 Soledad Suite 1490 San Antonio TX 78205

HARDCASTLE, KENNETH LLOYD, oil company executive; b. Gonzales, Tex., July 29, 1934; s. Lloyd Seth and Irene Helen H.; m. Sandra Delone Funk, Dec. 26, 1957; children: April Denise, Kendy Lin, Michael Lloyd. Jill Michelle. B.B.A., S.W. Tex. State U., 1958. Statis. cost acctg. supr. Cameron Iron Works., Inc., Houston, 1960-65, mgr. cost acctg. forged products, 1965-66, mgr. acctg., 1966-69, mgr. mfg. die forged products, 1969-73, ops. mgr. die forged products, 1973-79, v.p., 1979-81, sr. v.p. forged products div., 1981—. Mem. Forging Industry Assn. (dir. 1977-80). Office: Cameron Iron Works Inc PO Box 1212 13013 NW Freeway Houston TX 77251

HARDEE, WILLIAM COVINGTON, lawyer, banker; b. Florence, S.C., Mar. 2, 1919; s. Abram Lindsay and Cornelia (Covington) H.; m. Georgina Hazeltine, Sept. 5, 1942 (div. 1955); 1 dau., Pamela Graves Hardee Jackson; m. Joan Chappell Lamont, May 14, 1955 (dec. Aug. 1974); stepchildren: Thrae Harris, Robin Lamont, John E. Lamont; children: Felicity, Meredith, Nell, William.; m. Diana Faulkner Schereschewsky, June 12, 1976. A.B., Emory U., 1940; LL.B. magna cum laude, Harvard U., 1943. Bar: Mass. 1947, N.Y. 1955. Practiced law, Boston, 1947-54, N.Y.C., 1955—; assoc. firm Ropes & Gray, 1947-50; asst. prof. to prof. law Harvard U. Law Sch., 1950-55; assoc. firm Clark, Carr & Ellis, 1954-59, ptnr., 1957-69; gen. counsel U.P.R.R. Co., 1967-68; ptnr. firm Kelley, Drye, Warren, Clark, Carr & Ellis, N.Y.C., 1969-71; chmn., pres., chief exec. officer Lincoln Savs. Bank, N.Y.C., 1975—; mem. U.S.-U.S.S.R Trade Mission to Brazil for Dept. Commerce, 1967; trustee Savs. Banks Retirement System, 1978—. Editor: (with R. Amory Jr.) Materials on Accounting, 1953, (with Nell Dorr) Life Dance, 1976. Served to lt. comdr. USNR, 1942-46. Mem. N.Y.C. Bar Assn. (past com. chmn.), Am. Arbitration Assn., Order St. John, Nat. Assn. Mut. Savs. Banks (treas. 1982—), Phi Beta Kappa, Omicron Delta Kappa, Kappa Alpha. Espiscopalian. Clubs: Union League (N.Y.C.); Metropolitan (Washington); Rembrandt (Bklyn.). Home: Goose Hill Farm Mallory Brook Rd Washington CT 06793 Home: Las Columnas Mijas Malaga Spain Office: Lincoln Savings Bank 200 Park Ave New York NY 10166

HARDEEN, THEODORE, JR., lawyer; b. London, Eng., Dec. 20, 1905; s. Theodore and Elsie (Parsons) H.; m. Elizabeth Brett, Nov. 1, 1952; 1 son, Theodore Brett. LL.B., U. Va., 1930. Bar: Ill. bar 1930, Va. Bar 1964. Practiced in, Chgo., 1930-53; adminstr. Def. Air Transp., Dept. Commerce, Washington, 1953-64; gen. counsel Va. Trailways, 1964-67; v.p. Western Sales, Ltd., Geneva, 1967-70; counsel Export-Import Bank U.S., Washington, 1970—; Chmn., U.S. rep. NATO Civil Aviation delegation, 1958, 59, 60, 61, 62; Dir. Universal Motor Co., Universal Foundry Co., Lantana Aero Corp., Dr. Peter Fahrney & Sons Co., Palm Beach Aero Corp.; Bd. dirs., v.p. Chgo. Blackhawk Hockey Team. Served as maj. Air Transport Command USAAF, 1942-46. Decorated Air medal, Commendation medal. Mem. Chgo. Bar Assn., Phi Sigma Kappa. Clubs: Everglades (Palm Beach, Fla.); Tavern (Chgo.); Farmington Country, Farmington Hunt, Boar's Head (Charlottesville, Va.); University (Washington). Address: Bellair Charlottesville VA 22901

HARDEN, JOHN WILLIAM, publicist; b. Graham, N.C., Aug. 22, 1903; s. Peter Ray and Nettie Cayce (Abbott) H.; m. Josephine Holt, June 13, 1928 (dec. Dec. 1951); children: Glenn Abbott (Mrs. Fred Springer-Miller), John William; m. Sarah Plexico, Oct. 5, 1953; children: Holmes Plexico and Mark Michael (twins), Jonathan Holder. A.B., U. N.C., 1927. Circulation mgr., advt. mgr. Burlington (N.C.) Daily Times-News, 1922, also; editor (Graham news dept.); classified advt. mgr. Raleigh News and Observer, 1923; with U. N.C. News Bur., 1923-28; reporter, columnist Charlotte (N.C.) News, 1928-37; news editor Salisbury Evening Post., 1937-44, Greensboro Daily News, 1944; pvt. sec. Gov. R. Gregg Cherry, 1945-48; campaign mgr. for U.S. Senator William B. Umstead, 1948; dir. pub. relations Burlington Industries, 1948-58, asst. v.p., 1948, v.p., 1949-58; pub. relations counsellor and cons. John Harden Assocs., Greensboro, 1958—; asst. to pres. Cannon Mills Co., Kannapolis, N.C.; v.p., dir. Rowan Corp. Author: Alamance County: Economic and Social, 1928, The Devil's Tramping Ground and Other North Carolina Mystery Stories, 1949, Tar Heel Ghosts, 1954, North Carolina Roads and Their Builders, 1966, Cannon, 1977; Contbr. trade publs. Mem.-at-large Greensboro council Boy Scouts Am.; mem. vis. com. Guilford Coll.; bd. dirs., mem. exec. com. Penick Meml. Home; bd. dirs. N.C. Bus. Found., Carolina Regional Theatre; trustee Crossnore (N.C.) Sch. Mem. Greensboro C. of C. (dir., pres.), N.C. Historic Preservation Soc., N.C. Press Assn., Gen. Alumni Assn. U. N.C. (pres. 1955), Pub. Relations Soc. Am. Democrat. Episcopalian (chmn. 1958 every mem. canvass; vestryman, sr. warden). Clubs: Greensboro City, Rotary (dir., pres., dist. gov.), Greensboro Country, Carolina Motor (pres., dir., mem. exec. com.), Grandfather Golf and Country (dir.), Grandfather Mountain Lake (pres.), Linville Golf.). Home: 2700 Twin Lakes Dr Greensboro NC 27407 Office: 621 N Eugene St Greensboro NC 27401

HARDEN, MARVIN, artist, educator; b. Austin, Tex.; s. Theodore R. and Ethel (Sneed) H. B.A. in Fine Arts, UCLA, also M.A. in Creative Painting. Tchr. art Calif. State U., Northridge, 1968—, Santa Monica (Calif.) City Coll., 1968; mem. art faculty UCLA Extension, 1964-68. One-man shows include, Ceeje Galleries, Los Angeles, 1964, 66, 67, Occidental Coll., Los Angeles, 1969, Whitney Mus. Am. Art, N.Y.C., 1971, Eugenia Butler Gallery, Los Angeles, Irving Blum Gallery, Los Angeles, 1972, Los Angeles Harbor Coll., David Stuart Galleries, Los Angeles, 1975, Coll. Creative Studies, U. Calif., Santa Barbara, 1976, James Corcoran Gallery, Los Angeles, 1978, Newport Harbor Art Mus., 1979, Los Angeles Mcpl. Art Gallery, 1982, group shows include, U.S. State Dept. Touring Exhbn., USSR, 1966, Oakland (Calif.) Mus. Art, UCLA, Mpls. Inst. Art, 1968, San Francisco Mus. Art, 1969, Phila. Civic Center Mus., Mus. Art, R.I. Sch. Design, N.S. State Mus., Everson Mus. Art, Syracuse, La Jolla (Calif.) Mus., 1969, 70, High Mus. Art, Atlanta, 1969, Flint (Mich.) Inst. Arts, Ft. Worth Art Center Mus., Contemporary Arts Assn., Houston, 1970, U. N.Mex., 1974, U. So. Calif., 1975, Bklyn. Mus., 1976, Los Angeles County Mus. Art, 1977, Newport Harbor Art Mus., Frederick S. Wight Gallery, UCLA, 1978, Cirrus Editions, Ltd., Los Angeles, 1979, Franklin Furnace, N.Y.C., 1980, Art Ctr. Coll. Design, Los Angeles, 1981, Alternative Mus., N.Y.C., Laguna Beach Mus. (Calif.), 1982, Los Angeles Inst. Contemporary Art, Mus. Contemporary Art, Chgo., 1983, Mint Mus., Charlotte, N.C., DeCordova and Dana Mus. and Park, Lincoln, Mass.; represented in permanent collections, Whitney Mus. Am. Art, N.Y.C., Mus. Modern Art, N.Y.C., Metromedia, Inc., Los Angeles, San Diego Jewish Community Center, Berkeley (Calif.) U. Mus., Home Savs. & Loan Assn., Los Angeles, also pvt. collections. Bd. dirs. Images & Issues, 1980—; mem. artists adv. bd. Los Angeles Mcpl. Art Gallery Assn., 1983—. Recipient UCLA Art Council award, 1963; Nat. Endowment Arts fellow, 1972; awards in Visual Arts, 1983; Guggenheim fellow, 1983. Mem. Los Angeles Inst. Comtemporary Art (co-founder 1972). Home: PO Box 353 Chatsworth CA 91311 Office: Calif State U Northridge 18111 Nordhoff St Northridge CA 91330

HARDEN, NORMAN EUGENE, business services company executive; b. Fond du Lac, Wis., May 3, 1934; s. Russell J. and Norma M. (Mayer) H.; m. Sondra Willoughby, Dec. 23, 1976; children: Gary, Cheryl, Jeffrey. B.S. magna cum laude, Lawrence U., Appleton, Wis., 1958. With A.C. Nielsen Co., Northbrook, Ill., 1958—, exec. v.p., 1968-76, pres., 1976—, also dir. Trustee Lawrence U. Served with USAF. Mem. Am. Mktg. Assn. (presidents assn.), Econ. Club Chgo. Club: Biltmore Country. Office: AC Nielsen Co Nielsen Plaza Northbrook IL 60062 *

HARDEN, OLETA ELIZABETH, educator, univ. adminstr.; b. Jamestown, Ky., Nov. 22, 1935; d. Stanley Virgil and Myrtie Alice (Stearns) McWhorter; m. Dennis Clarence Harden, July 23, 1966. B.A., Western Ky. U., 1956; M.A. in English, U. Ark., 1958, Ph.D., 1965. Teaching asst. U. Ark., Fayetteville, 1956-57, 58-59, 61-63; instr. S.W. Mo. State Coll., Springfield, 1957-58, Murray (Ky.) U., 1959-61; asst. prof. English Northeastern State Coll., Tahlequah, Okla., 1963-65; asst. prof. Wichita (Kans.) State U., 1965-66; asst. prof. English Wright State U., Dayton, Ohio, 1966-68, asso. prof., 1968-72, prof., 1972—, asst. chmn. English dept., 1967-70, asst. dean, 1971-73, asso. dean, 1973-74; exec. dir. Gen. Univ. Services, 1974-76. Author: Maria Edgeworth's Art of Prose Fiction, 1971. Wright State U. research and devel. grantee, 1969, 78; Ford Found. grantee, 1971; Wright State sabbatical grantee Oxford (Eng.) U., 1978-79. Mem. Modern Lang. Assn., Coll. English Assn., AAUP, Women's Caucus for Modern Langs., Am. Com. Irish Studies. Home: 2618 Big Woods Trail Fairborn OH 45324 Office: Dept of English Wright State University 7751 Colonel Glenn Hwy Dayton OH 45431

HARDEN, PATRICK ALAN, journalist, news executive; b. Twickenham, Eng., Aug. 13, 1936; s. Ernest William and Annie Ceridwen (Jones) H.; m. Connie Marie Graham, Nov. 2, 1963; children: Marc Graham, Ceri Marie. Cert. in journalism, Ealing (Eng.) Tech. Coll., 1957. With UPI, 1960-78, regional exec., London, 1968-69, European picture mgr., London and Brussels, 1969-72, regional exec., Detroit, 1973-75; gen. mgr. UPI Can. Ltd., Montreal, 1976-78, UP Can., Toronto, 1979—, dir., sec., 1979-82; treas. UPI Can. Ltd.; gen. mgr. Edmonton (Alta.) Sun, 1982-84, pub., 1984—. Served with RAF, 1957-59. Office: 9405 50th St Edmonton AB T6P 2T4 Canada

HARDER, F. WILLIAM, investment banker; b. Delhi, N.Y., Aug. 16, 1904; s. William Henry and Alice L. (Every) H.; m. Myrtle P. Gerst, Feb. 28, 1925 (div.); children: Betty (Mrs. Donald M. McClellan), Phyllis Mae (Mrs. Richard Reininger), Alice Joanne (Mrs. Jay Woodward); m. Lois M. Chillingworth, May 16, 1952. Student, Del. Acad., 1921, Central City Bus. Sch., Syracuse, N.Y, 1922. Security trader E.G. Childs & Co., Inc., Syracuse, 1922-30, Eshelman-Harder Co., Inc., 1930-32, Harder-Mengarelli, Inc., 1932-36, Harder & Co., Inc., N.Y.C., 1936-38; with Allen & Co., Inc., 1938—, exec. asso., 1964-66, pres., dir., 1966-67, dir., chmn. exec. com., 1967-74, sr. cons., 1975—; dir. emeritus Airborne Freight Corp., Seattle; dir., chmn. exec. com. Arts-Way Mfg. Co., Armstrong, Iowa; dir. The Reading Co., Plymouth Meeting, Pa.; dir., chmn. exec. com. Weigh-Tronix Inc., Fairmont, Minn. Trustee Nat. Mus. Racing, Saratoga Springs, N.Y.; trustee emeritus Skidmore Coll., Saratoga Springs; trustee, mem. exec. com. Thoroughbred Owners and Breeders Assn., Jamaica, N.Y.; asso. mem. N.F.L. Alumni Assn., chmn. hon. mems., Ft. Lauderdale, Fla. Clubs: Carlton (Chgo.); Saratoga Golf and Polo (Saratoga Springs); Turf and Field, Cornell (N.Y.C.); Golf; Indian Creek Country (Indian Creek Village, Fla.); Surf (Surfside, Fla.); Seaview Country (Absecon, N.J.). Home: 10225 Collins Ave Bal Harbour FL 33154 also 50 Sutton Pl S New York NY 10022 Office: 711 Fifth Ave New York NY 10022

HARDER, HENRY UPHAM, insurance company executive; b. N.Y.C., Mar. 9, 1925; s. Lewis F. and Gertude B. (Harris) H.; m. Calista Lincoln, June 28, 1952; children: Frederic, Trudy, Christy, Holly, Henry. B.A., Yale U., 1948. With Chubb & Son, Inc., The Chubb Corp., and affiliates, N.Y.C., 1948—; exec. v.p. The Chubb Corp., N.Y.C., 1974-77, pres., 1977—, chief exec. officer, 1980—, chmn., 1981—; chmn., chief exec. officer, dir. Chubb & Son, Inc.; chmn., pres., chief exec. officer, dir. Fed. Ins. Co., Vigilant Ins. Co.; chmn., dir. Gt. No. Insurance Co., Pacific Indemnity Co.; dir. Piggly Wiggly So., Inc., East Point Reinsurance Co. of Hong Kong Ltd., Bellemead Devel. Corp., Am. Ins. Assn., The Cranston Print Works Co., Bellemead Devel. Corp. Trustee Presbyterian Hosp., N.Y.C., Coll. of Insurance, Geraldine R. Dodge Found., St. George's Sch. Served as lt. (j.g.), aviator USNR, 1943-45. Clubs: Econ. of N.Y., Down Town Assn. (N.Y.C.); Blind Brook (Purchase, N.Y.). N.Y.). Office: 15 Mountain View Rd Warren NJ 07061

HARDER, KELSIE BROWN, educator; b. Pope, Tenn., Aug. 23, 1922; s. Prince William and Belle (MaGee) H.; m. Louise Maron, Oct. 9, 1960; children: Kelsie Terry, Gerald William, Dennis Prince, Frank Maron, Thomas Brown, Ann Leslie, Marcia Louise. B.A. magna cum laude, Vanderbilt U., 1950, M.A., 1951; Ph.D., U. Fla., 1954. Asst. prof. English, Youngstown U., 1954-58, asso. prof., 1958-60, prof., 1960-64; Fulbright lectr., India, 1962-63; prof. English, SUNY, Potsdam, 1964—, chmn. English dept., 1964-78; Fulbright vis. prof. U. Lodz, Poland, 1971-72; cons. Office Edn., Washington, summers 1966, 67, Random House Dictionary of the English Lang.; mem. Com. on Place Name Survey of U.S., SUNY Awards Com., 1976-81. Guest appearances: Cable News Network, stas. WXYZ, WEWS.; Editor: Names, 1966-68, 81—, Illustrated Dictionary of Place Names: Canada and the United States, 1976; mem. adv. bd.: American Speech, 1960-61, 80-81; contbr. articles to profl. jours. Served with AUS, 1944-46. Mem. Am. Name Soc. (past exec. sec.-treas., v.p., pres.), MLA, Ohio Folklore Soc. (past pres.), Tenn. Folklore Soc., Miss. Folklore Soc., N.Y. Folklore Soc. (exec. com.), Nat. Council Tchrs. of English, Internat. Centre of Onomastics (Belgium), Am. Dialect Soc. (proverbs and usage com.), St. Lawrence County Hist. Assn. (past pres., trustee), Milton Soc. (life), Spenser Soc. (life), Phi Beta Kappa, Sigma Phi Epsilon (dist. gov. 1965-66), Eta Sigma Phi, Sigma Delta Pi, Phi Kappa Phi. Home: 5 Lawrence Ave Potsdam NY 13676

HARDER, LEWIS BRADLEY, business executive; b. N.Y.C., July 23, 1918; s. Lewis Francis and Gertrude Burbank (Harris) H.; m. Dorothy Dyer Butler, Sept. 7, 1941; children: Deirdre Butler, Diana. B.A., Harvard U., 1941. Analyst Morgan Stanley & Co., N.Y.C., 1941; customers man Harris Upham & Co., 1945-51, partner, 1951-54; pres. South Am. Gold & Platinum, 1954-63, dir., 1952-63; pres., dir. Colamer Co., Pacific Met Co., Colamerican Metals Corp.; chmn. bd., chief exec. officer Internat. Mining Corp.; dir. Panam. Capital Corp., Madison Fund, Canton Corp., Chgo., Pitts. and W.Va. Ry. Co., Brascan Ltd., Cerro-Marmon Corp., Bancroft Fund., Union Oil of Calif., Eberstadt Energy Resources Fund, Pacific Holding Corp., Flexi-Van Corp. Served to lt. USNR, 1942-45. Decorated D.F.C. Roman Catholic. Clubs: Brook (N.Y.C.); Bedford Golf and Tennis, Seminole. Home: 120 Mount Holly Rd Katonah NY 10536 Office: 101 Park Ave Room 4450 New York NY 10017

HARDER, ROBERT CLARENCE, state official; b. Horton, Kans., June 4, 1929; s. Clarence L. and Olympia E. (Kubik) H.; m. Dorothy Loy Welty, July 31, 1953; children: Anne, James David. A.B., Baker U., Baldwin, Kans., 1951; M.Th., So. Meth. U., 1954; Th.D. in Social Ethics, Boston U., 1958; L.H.D., Baker U., 1983. Ordained to ministry Meth. Ch., 1959; pastor East Topeka Meth. Ch., 1958-64; mem. Kans. Ho. of Reps., 1961-67; research asso. Memninger Found., Topeka, 1964-65; instr. Washburn U., Topeka, 1964, 68, 69; dir. Topeka Office of Econ. Opportunity, 1965-67; tech. asst. coordinator Office of Gov. of Kans., 1967-68; dir. community resources devel. League of Kans. Municipalities, 1968-69; dir. Kans. Dept. Social Welfare, Topeka, 1969-73, sec., 1973—; instr. Kans. U. Sch. Social Welfare, 1971—. Contbr. articles to profl. jours. Recipient Disting. Service award East Topeka Civic Assn., 1963; Romana Hood Award, 1965; others. Mem. Am. Soc. Public Adminstrs. (Public Adminstr. of Yr., Kans. chpt. 1980), Am. Public Welfare Assn., Kans. Council on Children and Youth, Kans. Conf. Social Welfare. Democrat. Office: Social and Rehab Services 6th Floor State Office Bldg Topeka KS 66612

HARDER, VIRGIL EUGENE, educator; b. Ness City, Kans., July 19, 1923; s. Walter J. and Fern B. (Pausch) H.; m. Dona Maurine Dobson, Feb. 4, 1951; children—Christine Elaine, Donald Walter. B.S., U. Iowa, 1950, M.A., 1950; Ph.D., U. Ill., 1958. Instr. bus. adminstrn. U. Ill., Urbana, 1950-55; instr. bus. adminstrn. U. Wash., Seattle, 1955—, asst. prof., 1955-59, asso. prof., 1959-67, prof., 1967—, asso. dean sch. bus. adminstrn., 1966-74; dir. Inst. Fin. Edn. Sch. for Exec. Devel., Seattle, 1974—; communications cons. bus. orgns. Author: (with Herta Murphy and Charles Peck) Building Favorable Impressions by Mail, 1961, Using PERT in Marketing Research, (with Frank Lindell) Marketing Management and Decision Sciences, 1971; Contbr. articles, monographs to profl. publs. Served with AUS, 1943-45. Fellow Am. Bus. Communications Assn. (pres. 1965). Club: Trail Blazers. Home: 6025 50th Ave NE Seattle WA 98115 Office: Sch Bus Adminstrn U Wash Seattle WA 98195

HARDESTY, BOYD ARCHER, biochemist; b. Cheney, Wash., May 15, 1932; s. Bonner K. and Mildred E. (Porter) H.; m. Willa Mae Boozer, June 10, 1952; children—Bruce, Brian, Diana. B.S., Wash. State U., 1953, M.S., 1956; Ph.D., Calif. Inst. Tech., 1961. NSF postdoctoral fellow Yale U. Med. Sch., New Haven, Conn., 1961-62, U. Ky. Med. Sch., Lexington, 1962-63, USPHS postdoctoral fellow, 1963-64; asst. prof. biochemistry U. Tex., Austin, 1964-68, asso. prof., 1968-73, prof., 1973—. Contbr. numerous articles in field to sci. jours.; editorial bd.: Archives Biochemistry Biophysics, 1972. Home: 1502 Harbor View Rd Austin TX 78746 Office: Clayton Found Biochem Inst Univ Texas Austin TX 78712

HARDESTY, CHRISTOPHER SCOTT, mining company executive; b. Bronxville, N.Y., Jan. 11, 1945; s. Egbert Railey and Martha Elizabeth (Josi) H. B.S., Bucknell U., 1967; M.B.A., U. Pa., 1972. With Exxon Corp., 1972-78; treas. Esso Caribbean, 1976-78; asst. treas. Newmont Mining Corp., N.Y.C., 1978-79, treas., 1979—. Served with USN, 1967-70. Club: Larchmont Yacht (N.Y.).

HARDESTY, EGBERT RAILEY, consulting engineer; b. Kansas City, Mo., July 25, 1915; s. Shortridge and Adelia V. (Ferrell) H.; m. Martha Elizabeth Josi, Oct. 11, 1940; children—Christopher, Pamela Hardesty Van Horn. B.C.E., Rensselaer Poly. Inst., 1940. Designer Waddell & Hardesty, N.Y.C., 1940-42; designer Hardesty & Hanover, N.Y.C., 1945-51, asso. engr., 1953-58, partner, 1958—. Mem. Town of Mamaroneck (N.Y.) Bd. Zoning, Appeals.; Vestryman St. John's Episcopal Ch., Larchmont, N.Y., 1972-75. Served to lt. Civil Engr. Corps USNR, 1942-45; to lt. comdr., 1951-53. Fellow ASCE (pres. met. sect. 1981-82, chmn. sects. 2d dist. councils 1983-84), Am. Cons. Engrs. Council; mem. Am. Rd. Transp. Builders Assn. (dir. 1976-80, pres. planning and design div. 1976-77), Am. Concrete Inst., N.Y. Soc. Profl. Engrs., Internat. Bridge Tunnel Turnpike Assn., Am. Ry. Engring. Assn., Sigma Xi, Tau Beta Pi. Republican. Club: Larchmont Yacht. Home: Chatsworth Gardens 4C Larchmont NY 10538 Office: 1501 Broadway New York NY 10036

HARDESTY, HIRAM HAINES, physician, educator; b. Paulding, Ohio, Jan. 16, 1914; s. Eugene and Ida (Underwood) H.: m. Mary Lee Bill, June 12, 1940; children—Susan Hardesty Corcoran, Thomas Haines, John Lee. A.B., Miami U., Oxford, Ohio, 1936; M.D., Western Res. U., 1940; postgrad., U. Pa., 1945-46. Diplomate: Am. Bd. Ophthalmology. Resident ophthalmology Univ. Hosps., Cleve., 1946-48, mem. teaching staff, 1948—, asso. clin. prof., 1960—. Contbr. articles to profl. jours. Active local United Appeal.; Bd. dirs. Cleve. Soc. for Blind, Allen Meml. Library. Served with USAAF, 1941-45. Fellow Am. Acad. Ophthalmology and Otolaryngology; mem. Cleve. Ophthalmology Club (past pres.), Ohio Soc. Prevention Blindness (bd. dirs.), Am. Orthoptic Council. Home: 3310 Warrensville Center Rd Shaker Heights OH 44122 Office: University Suburban Health Center 1611 S Green Rd Cleveland OH 44121

HARDESTY, ROBERT LOUIS, university president, government official; b. St. Louis, June 4, 1931; m. Mary Adelaide Roberts; 4 children. B.A., George Washington U., 1957. Assoc. (various newspapers and advt. agys.), 1957-64; spl. asst. to Postmaster Gen. John Gronouski, 1964-65, Pres. Lyndon B. Johnson, 1965-72; press. sec. to gov. Tex., 1973-76; vice chancellor U. Tex. System, Austin, 1976-81; pres. S.W. Tex. State U., San Marcos, 1981—; bd. govs. U.S. Postal Service, Washington, 1976—, vice chmn., 1979-81, chmn., 1981—; mem. Edn. Commn. of the States, 1983—. Mem. Democratic Nat. Platform Com., 1976. Clubs: Metropolitan; University (Washington); Headliners (Austin); Argyle (San Antonio). Office: SW Tex State U Office of Pres San Marcos TX 78666 *The best education and finest opportunity a person can have is being associated with great men and women at an early age; to learn from their confidence, to absorb their values, to profit from their mistakes and to draw wisdom from their sense of judgment.*

HARDGRAVE, ROBERT LEWIS, JR., government studies educator, writer; b. Greensburg, Pa., Feb. 6, 1939; s. Robert L. and Orlene (Pirtle) H. B.A., U. Tex.-Austin, 1960; M.A., U. Chgo., 1962, Ph.D., 1966. Asst. prof. government Oberlin Coll., Ohio, 1966-67; prof. U. Tex.-Austin, 1967—; cons. U.S. Dept. State, Washington, 1982-83. Author: The Dravidian Movement, 1965, The Nadars of Tamilnad, 1969, (with James A. Bill) Comparative Politics, 1971, Essays in the Political Sociology of South India, 1979, India: Government and Politics in a Developing Nation, 3d edit., 1980, India Under Pressure: Prospects for Political Stabilityf, 1984. Mem. Assn. Asian Studies, Am. Polit. Sci. Assn. Home: 1409 Flintridge Rd Austin TX 78746 Office: Dept Government U Tex Austin TX 78712

HARDIE, ROBERT HOWLE, astronomer; b. Lachine, Que., Can., Dec. 5, 1923; came to U.S., 1946, naturalized, 1960; s. Robert Howie and Catherine (Campbell) H.; m. Frances Harriet Isley, Aug. 23, 1950; children—James Alexander, Robert Stephen. B.Sc., McGill U., 1945, M.Sc., 1946; Ph.D., U. Chgo., 1950. Vis. asst. prof. Ohio State U., 1951-53; astronomer Lowell Obs., Flagstaff, Ariz., 1953-55; mem. faculty Vanderbilt U., 1955—, prof. astronomy, 1963—; dir. Dyer Obs., 1961-71. Mem. Royal Astron. Soc., Astron. Soc. Pacific, Soc. Mfg. Engrs. Spl. research stellar photometry, astron. instrumentation. Home: 5120 Wilmar Dr Nashville TN 37220 Office: Dyer Observatory Vanderbilt U Nashville TN 37235

HARDIMAN, JOSEPH RAYMOND, investment banker; b. Salisbury, Md., May 27, 1937; s. Leonard Roy and Virginia Mildred (Darden) H.; m. Katherine McCampbell, Mar. 23, 1963; children: Katherine Hughes, Elizabeth Gore. B.A., U. Md., 1959, LL.B., 1962. Bar: Md. 1962. Law clk. to Hon. Hall Hammond; chief judge Ct. of Appeals Md., 1962-63; asso. Miles & Stockbridge, Balt., 1963-68; exec. v.p., sec., dir. Robert Garrett & Sons, Inc., Balt., 1968-75; gen. partner Alex. Brown & Sons, 1975—; dir. Balt. Radio Show, Inc., Depository Trust Co., N.Y.C. Bd. dirs. Arthritis Found., Md., 1975—, pres., 1976-78; bd. dirs. Balt. Urban Coalition, 1975-78; vice chmn. Commn. on Govtl. Efficiency and Economy, 1975-76; mem. steering com. Baltimore County Charter Rev. Commn., 1977-78; mem. exec. and fin. adv. bd. U. Md. Hosp.; trustee St. Paul's Sch. for Girls. Mem. Securities Industry Assn. (chmn. firm and industry analysis com. 1981-82), Order of Coif, Phi Delta Theta, Omicron Delta Kappa. Clubs: Maryland, Merchants, Elkridge (Balt.). Home: 7814 Ellenham Ave Ruxton MD 21204 Office: 135 E Baltimore St Baltimore MD 21203

HARDIN, ADLAI STEVENSON, sculptor; b. Mpls., Sept. 23, 1901; s. Martin D. and Julia (Stevenson) H.; m. Carol Moore, Feb. 22, 1934; children: Carol J., Adlai Stevenson. A.B., Princeton U., 1923. With Quaker Oats Co., 1923-25, Z.L. Potter Co., 1925-33; v.p. Wm. Esty Co., 1933-60. Rep. permanent collections, Brookgreen Gardens, S.C., Pa. Acad. Fine Arts, New Britain (Conn.) Mus. Am. Art, IBM Collection of Sculpture of Western Hemisphere, McMaster Div. Coll., McMaster U., Interchurch Center, N.Y.C., Seamen's Bank for Savs., N.Y.C., Princeton, Aid Assn. for Lutherans, Appleton, Wis.; prin. works include: life-sized bronze figures of St. Peter and St. Paul, St. Patrick's Cathedral, N.Y.C., 1983. Winner Ecclesiastical Competition Nat. Sculpture Soc., 1950, Lindsey Morris Meml. prize, 1956; recipient Saltus medal N.A.D., 1945; Avery prize Archtl. League, 1940; Daniel Chester French medal NAD, 1968; gold medal for sculpture, 1976; medallion for Brookgreen Gardens S.C. N.A. Fellow Nat. Sculpture Soc. (pres. 1957-59, Mrs. Louis Bennett prize 1965). Club: Century Assn. (N.Y.C.). Address: Cove Rd Lyme CT 06371

HARDIN, CHARLES ROE, JR., lawyer; b. Newark, June 18, 1921; s. Charles Roe and Emma (Downer) H.; m. Jean Sherrill, May 19, 1951; 1 dau., Katharine. Grad., Phillips Exeter Acad., 1938; A.B., Princeton U., 1942; LL.B., Columbia U., 1948. Bar: N.J. bar 1949. Since practiced in Newark and Morristown; ptnr. firm Pitney, Hardin & Kipp, 1958—; law clk. N.J. Superior Ct., 1949-50. Candidate for N.J. Assembly, 1951; mem. Essex County (N.J.) Democratic Com., 1953-54, Chester Twp. Planning Bd., 1969-81; Trustee Babies Hosp., Newark, 1952-57, sec., 1957; trustee Florence Critenton League, Newark, 1952-57, 63-66. Served to lt. USNR, 1942-46. Mem. Am., N.J., Essex County, Morris County bar assns., Am. Geog. Soc. Episcopalian. Clubs: Princeton (N.Y.C.); Essex (Newark). Home: Old Gladstone Rd RFD 2 Box 1184 Chester NJ 07930 Office: 163 Madison Ave CN 1945 Morristown NJ 07960 33 Washington St Newark NJ 07102

HARDIN, CLIFFORD MORRIS, economist; b. Knightstown, Ind., Oct. 9, 1915; s. James Alvin and Mabel (Macy) H.; m. Martha Love Wood, June 28, 1939; children: Susan Carol (Mrs. L.W. Wood), Clifford Wood, Cynthia (Mrs. Robert Milligan), Nancy Ann (Mrs. Douglas L. Rogers), James. B.S., Purdue U., 1937, M.S., 1939, Ph.D., 1941, D.Sc. (hon.), 1952; Farm Found. scholar, U. Chgo., 1939-40; LL.D., Creighton U., 1956, Ill. State U., 1973; Dr. honoris causa, Nat. U. Colombia, 1968; D.Sc., Mich. State U., 1969, N.D. State U., 1969, U. Nebr., 1978, Okla. Christian Coll., 1979. Grad. asst. Purdue U., Lafayette, Ind., 1937-39, 40-41; instr. U. Wis., 1941-42, asst. prof. agrl. econs., 1942-44; asso. prof. agrl. econs. Mich. State Coll., 1944-46, prof., chmn. agrl. econs. dept., 1946-48, asst. dir. agrl. expt. sta., 1948, dir., 1949-53, dean agr., 1953-54; chancellor U. Nebr., 1954-69; sec. U.S. Dept. Agr., Washington, 1969-71; vice chmn. bd., dir. Ralston Purina Co., St. Louis, 1971-80; dir. Center for Study of Am. Bus., Washington U., St. Louis, 1981-83, scholar-in-residence, 1983—; chmn. instl. policy com. Stifel, Nicolaus & Co., St. Louis, 1980—; dir. Omaha br. Fed. Res. Bank of Kansas City, 1961-67, chmn., 1962-67. Editor: Overcoming World Hunger, 1969. Mem. ednl. adv. com. W.K. Kellogg Found, 1960; trustee Rockefeller Found., 1961-69, 72-81, Farm Found., 1973—, Freedoms Found. at Valley Forge, 1973—, Internat. Agr. Devel. Service, 1975—, Am. Assembly, 1975—, U. Nebr. Found., 1975—; U.S. del. Internat. Conf. Agrl. Economists, Eng., 1947; mem. Pres.'s Com. to Strengthen Security Free World, 1963; mem. exec. com. Council Higher Edn. in Am. Republics, 1963-69; mem. Nat. Sci. Bd., 1966-70; bd. dirs. F.C.A. of St. Paul, 1950-51. Mem. Assn. State Univs. and Land-Grant Colls. (pres. 1960, chmn. exec. com. 1961), Sigma Xi, Alpha Zeta, Alpha Gamma Rho. Home: 10 Roan Ln Saint Louis MO 63124 Office: 500 N Broadway Saint Louis MO 63102 Office: Washington U Campus Box 1208 Saint Louis MO 63130

HARDIN, DAVID KIMBALL, market research executive; b. Evanston, Ill., Apr. 26, 1927; s. Charles Marks and Louise Lytle (Kimball) H.; m. Diane Davies, Sept. 5, 1953 (dec. 1981); children: Nancy, Jan, Amy; m. Paula Cantwell, Aug. 1, 1982. B.S., MIT, 1949; M.B.A., U. Chgo., 1950; deacon, Seabury Western Theol. Sem., Northwestern U., Evanston, 1974. With Market Facts, Inc., Chgo., 1950—, v.p., then exec. v.p., 1957-64, pres., 1964-75, chmn. bd., 1974—; dir. Sterling Faucet Co.; lectr. DePaul U., Chgo., 1957-59, Northwestern U., 1958-60. Vice pres., bd. dirs. Chgo. Council Fgn. Relations, 1965-71; chmn. Multiple Sclerosis Soc., Chgo., 1976-78; v.p., trustee Chgo. Sunday Evening Club, 1972-80. Served with AUS, 1945-46. Mem. Am. Mktg. Assn. (pres. 1972-73). Episcopalian. Club: Westmoreland Country. Office: 100 S Wacker Dr Chicago IL 60606

HARDIN, EUGENE BROOKS, JR., banker; b. Wilmington, N.C., Oct. 18, 1930; s. Eugene Brooks and Roberta Gilmour (Sterling) H.; m. Olivia Lynch, Aug. 16, 1958; children—John Haywood II, Olivia Cary. B.S., U. N.C., 1952. With Wachovia Bank & Trust Co., 1956—, asst. v.p., 1957-60, v.p., 1962-68, sr. v.p., 1969-72; all Wilmington, N.C., sr. v.p., regional exec., Raleigh, 1972-79, regional v.p., 1979—, cashier, Burlington, N.C., 1961-62. Pres., bd. dirs. Babies Hosp., Wilmington, 1968-72; pres. United Fund, 1970; treas., trustee Episcopalian Diocese East Carolina, 1965—; chmn. Raleigh Civic Center Authority, 1978—; mem. Raleigh-Durham Airport Authority, 1981; chmn. bd. trustees St. Mary's Coll., 1979—; bd. dirs. Children's Home Soc. N.C. Served with USNR, 1948-49; to lst lt. USAF, 1952-56. Mem. Robert Morris Assos. Clubs: Civitan (pres. Wilmington 1971-72); Carolina Yacht (Wrightsville Beach); Carolina Country (Raleigh); Cape Fear Country (Wilmington). Home: 404 Drummond Dr Raleigh NC 27609 Office: Wachovia Bank & Trust Co PO Box 27886 Raleigh NC 27611

HARDIN, FRED A., labor union official; b. Greenville, S.C., Feb. 21, 1918; m. Eleanor Hardin; children: Frederick David, Carol R. Hardin Hayes, Jane Leslie. With So. Ry., Greenville, from 1940, local union officer, 1951-63, gen. chmn. on, from 1963; v.p. United Transp. Union, Lakewood, Ohio, 1968-79, pres., 1979—, also chief wage negotiator; chmn. health and welfare com. for cooperating ry. labor orgns. Bd. dirs. YMCA. Mem. Ry. Labor Execs. Assn. (chmn.). Democrat. Office: 14600 Detroit Ave Cleveland OH 44107

HARDIN, GEORGE CECIL, JR., petroleum consultant; b. Oakwood, Tex., Oct. 6, 1920; s. George Cecil and Pearl (Moore) H.; m. Virginia Howard, Nov. 21, 1942; children—George Howard, Susan. B.S. in Geology and Petroleum Engring, Tex. A. and M. U., 1941; Ph.D. in Geology (Van Hise fellow 1941), U. Wis., 1942. Registered engr., Tex., Okla. Mining engr. Victory Fluorspar Mine, Cave In Rock, Ill., 1942; geologist U.S. Geol. Survey, 1942-45, party chief, 1944-45; geologist Carter Gragg Oil Co., Palestine, Tex., 1945-46; geologist, petroleum engr. M.T. Halbouty Cons. Firm, Houston, 1946-51; exploration and prodn. mgr. M.T. Halbouty Oil and Gas Interests, Houston, 1951-59, gen. mgr., 1959-61; exec. v.p., dir. Halbouty Alaska Oil Co., 1957-61; partner Hardin and Hardin (cons. geologists), Houston, 1961-65; mgr. oil and gas expln. Kerr-McGee Oil Ind., Inc., 1964-65; v.p. N.Am. Oil & Gas Exploration, 1965-67, v.p. oil, gas and minerals exploration, 1967-68, group v.p. exploration, 1968; v.p. Kerr-McGee, Argentina, 1967-68, Kerr-McGee Can., Ltd., 1967-68, Kerr-McGee Australia, Ltd., 1967-68; pres. Royal Resources Corp., 1968-70, Ada Oil Exploration Corp., 1970-71, Ashland Exploration Co., 1971-80; sr. v.p. Ashland Oil Inc., 1971-80; dir. Ashland Oil Can Ltd., 1976-79, Allied Bank of Tex., Houston, 1956-78, mem. exec. com., 1956-62, chmn. auditing com., 1962-65; vice-chmn., dir. Integrated Energy, Inc., 1981-83; owner Quail Ridge Farm, Oklahoma City. Author articles in field. Fellow Geol. Soc. Am., A.A.A.S.; mem. Houston Geol. Soc. (pres. 1961-62), Soc. Econ. Paleontologists and Mineralogists, New Orleans, S. Tex. geol. socs., Gulf Coast Assn. Geol. Socs. (pres. 1959), Am. Assn. Petroleum Geologist (sec.-treas. 1964-66), Soc. Exploration Geophysicists Am. Inst. Profl. Geologists. Clubs: Petroleum (bd. dirs. 1956-58), River Oaks Country, Plaza, Grandfather Country, Brazos River Hunting and Fishing (W. Columbia, Tex.) (bd. dirs. 1961-64); Petroleum.). Home: 204 Arborway Houston TX 77057 Office: 115 Barkdull Houston TX 77006

HARDIN, HAL D., lawyer, former United States attorney; b. Davidson County, Tenn., June 29, 1941. B.S., Middle Tenn. State U., 1966; J.D., Vanderbilt U., 1968; attended, State Jud. Coll., Reno, 1976. Bar: Tenn. 1969, D.C. Fingerprint technician FBI, 1961; dir. St. Louis Job Corps Center, 1968; asst. dist. atty., Nashville, 1969-71; mem. firm Jack Norman & Assos., Nashville, 1970-75, Gracey and Maddin, 1975; presiding judge Nashville Trial Cts., 1976-77; U.S. atty. Middle Dist. Tenn., 1977-81; practice law, Nashville, 1981—; prof. govt. Aquinas Coll., 1975-76. Served in Peace Corps, 1963-65. Mem. Nashville Bar Assn. (dir.), Tenn. Bar Assn. (gen. counsel). Office: First American Center 14th Floor Nashville TN 37238

HARDIN, JAMES NEAL, educator; b. Nashville, Tenn., Feb. 17, 1939; s. James N. and Ina M. (Anderson) H.; m. Anne Farr. A.B., Washington and Lee U., 1960; postgrad., U. Berlin, 1960-61; Ph.D., U. N.C., 1967. Instr. U. N.C.-Chapel Hill, 1961-67; prof. German lit. U. S.C., Columbia, 1969—; co-dir. Camden House, Inc. Author: Die Heilige Johanna, 1975; editor: Der Verliebte Desterreicher, 1977; co-editor: Studies in German Lang., Lit. and Linguistics; contbr. articles to profl. jours. and mags. Recipient Alexander von Humbolt award, 1974-75; Fulbright scholar, 1960-61. Mem. MLA, Am. Assn. Tchrs. of German, South Atlantic MLA, Am. Soc. German Lit. 16th and 17th Centuries, Internat. Verein fuer Germanistik. Home: 132 Norse Way Columbia SC 29206 Office: Dept Foreign Langs U Sc Columbia SC 29208

HARDIN, JOHN ALEXANDER, broadcasting consultant; b. Montclair, N.J., Feb. 9, 1911; s. Joseph Lawson and Katharine (Womack) H.; m. Edith Kaletsch, June 26, 1937. Student, U. N.C., 1930-34, N.Y. U., 1936-37. Pub. accountant, 1934-41, financial cons., 1958—; former chmn. MBS; former pres., chmn. bd. Mut. Broadcasting Corp., N.Y.C.; now cons. Amway Communications, Inc.; officer, dir. Black Gold Corp., Narva Labs. Inc., Gilchemic Inc., deSeverskey Electronatom Corp. Mem. Montclair Police Res., 1941-42; active A.R.C., Community Chests.; Bd. dirs. Montclair Animal Welfare League, Community Hosp. at Montclair, Greenaway Found. Served with USNR, 1942-46. Mem. Sigma Chi. Clubs: Glen Ridge Country (past pres.); Essex County Country., Montclair Golf (N.J.); Sky (N.Y.C.). Home: 17 Wayside Pl Montclair NJ 07042 Office: 100 E 42d St New York NY 10017

HARDIN, LOWELL STEWART, economics educator; b. nr. Knightstown, Ind., Nov. 16, 1917; s. J. Fred and Mildred (Stewart) H.; m. Mary J. Cooley, Sept. 21, 1940; children: Thomas Stewart, Joyce Ann, Peter Lowell. B.S., Purdue U., 1939; Ph.D., Cornell U., 1943. Grad. asst., instr. Cornell U., 1939-43; instr., asst. and asso. prof., prof. Purdue U., 1943-65, adj. prof. agrl. econs., 1965-66, prof., 1981—, acting head dept. agrl. econs., 1954-57, head dept., 1957-65; also dir. Purdue Work Simplification Lab.; program adviser agr. Ford Found., 1965-66, program officer agr., 1966-81; trustee Internat. Food Policy Research Inst., Washington, Internat. Center for Agrl. Research in Dry Areas, Aleppo, Syria, Internat. Service for Notational Agrl. Research, The Hague, Netherlands, Agrl. Devel. Council, N.Y.C. Author: (with L.M. Vaughan) Farm Work Simplification, 1949. Mem.

Am. Agrl. Econ. Assn. (pres. 1963- 64), Internat. Assn. Agrl. Economists, Sigma Xi, Alpha Gamma Rho, Phi Kappa Phi, Alpha Zeta, Sigma Delta Chi. Presbyn. Home: Route 5 Box 540 Monticello IN 47960 Office: Dept Agrl Economics Purdue U West Lafayette IN 47907

HARDIN, PAUL, university president; b. Charlotte, N.C., June 11, 1931; s. Paul and Dorothy (Reel) H.; m. Barbara Russell, June 8, 1954; children: Paul Russell, Sandra Mikush, Dorothy Ruth. A.B., Duke U., 1952; J.D., 1954; L.H.D. (hon.), Clemson U., 1970, LL.D., Coker Coll., 1972, Litt.D., Nebr. Wesleyan U., 1978. Bar: Ala. 1954. Practiced in, Birmingham, 1954, 56-58; asst. prof. Duke Law Sch., 1958-61, assoc. prof., 1961-63, prof., 1963-68, univ. trustee, 1969-74; pres. Wofford Coll., Spartanburg, S.C., 1968-72, So. Methodist U., Dallas, 1972-74, Drew U., Madison, N.J., 1975—; vis. prof. U. Tex., summer 1960, U. Pa., 1962-63, U. Va., 1974; Dir. Summit Bancorp., Summit Trust Co., N.J. Bell Telephone Co., Shearson Daily Dividend, Inc. and related funds. Author: (with Sullivan, others) The Administration of Criminal Justice, 1966, (with Sullivan) Evidence, Cases and Materials, 1968; Contbr. articles to profl. jours. law revs. Chmn. Human Relations Com., Durham, N.C., 1961-62; mem. gen. conf. United Meth. Ch., 1968, 76, 80, 84; pres. Nat. Assn. Schs. and Colls. of United Meth. Ch., 1984; chmn. Nat. Commn. on United Meth. Higher Edn., 1975-77. Served with CIC AUS, 1954-56. Mem. Order of Coif, Phi Beta Kappa. Home: Campus Drew U Madison NJ 07940

HARDIN, WILLIAM DOWNER, lawyer; b. Newark, Sept. 27, 1926; s. Charles R. and Emma (Downer) H.; m. Rosemarie Koellhoffer, Jan. 19, 1952; children: William Downer, David Gerth, Peter Roe. A.B., Princeton, 1948; LL.B., Columbia, 1951. Bar: N.J. 1951. Law clk. N.J. Superior Ct., 1951-52; since practiced in, Newark and Morristown; mem. firm Pitney, Hardin, Kipp & Szuch, Newark and Morristown, 1957—; Mem. N.J. Bd. Bar Examiners, 1964-68, chmn., 1968; mem. local draft bd. SSS, 1953-74, chmn., 1970-74; Mem. Family Service Bur., Newark, 1953-75, pres., 1960-66; mem. Family Service Morris County, 1976—, pres., 1979-82; mem. membership com. Family Service Assn. Am., 1965-78, dir., 1971-79; mem. Nat. Budget and Consultation Com., 1966-71, Council on Accreditation Services for Families and Children. Trustee Newark Acad., 1952—. Served with USNR, 1944-46. Mem. Am., N.J., Essex, Morris County bar assns. Episcopalian (vestry). Clubs: Essex (Newark); Morristown (N.J.); Nassau (Princeton); Princeton (N.Y.). Home: 15 Gap View Rd Short Hills NJ 07078 Office: 163 Madison Ave Morristown NJ 07960

HARDING, BOYD WESLEY, medicine and biochemistry educator, researcher; b. Provo, June 4, 1926; s. Wesley Roe and Alice (Phillips) H.; m. Charlotte Virginia Knoepke, Dec. 27, 1955; children: Suzy, Frederick, Lotte, Lars. B.S. in Chemistry, Brigham Young U., 1950; M.D., U. Utah, 1954, Ph.D. in Biochemitry, 1961. Instr. medicine U. So. Calif., Los Angeles, 1960-62, asst. prof., 1962-66, assoc. prof., 1966-70, prof. medicine and biochemistry, 1970—. Served with USN, 1944-46. NIH grantee, 1965-69. Mem. Endocrine Soc., Am. Soc. Biol. Chemistry, AAAS, Am. Fedn. Clin. Research. Club: King Harbor Yacht (Redondo Beach, Calif.). Office: Univ So Calif 2505 Zonal Ave Los Angeles CA 90033

HARDING, CHARLES MALIM, industrialist; b. Toronto, Ont., Can., May 13, 1911; s. Charles Victor Malim and Minnie (Flavelle) H.; m. Constance Hope Magee, Sept. 10, 1947; children: Stephanie Constance Hope Brady, Charles Malim Victor, Debora Mary Malim. B.A., U. Toronto, 1931. Chmn. bd. Harding Carpets Ltd., Toronto, 1967; dir. Confederation of Life Ins. Co., 1964—. Chmn. U. Toronto Varsity Fund, past chmn. governing council; mem. U. Toronto Connaught Com. Served to col. Can. Army, 1939-45. Mem. Can. Carpet Inst. (past pres.), Can. Textiles Inst. (past chmn.), Kappa Alpha (past chmn.). Anglican. Clubs: Toronto, Toronto Golf, York, Queen's, Badminton & Racquet, Big Point. Home: 48 Rosedale Rd Toronto ON Canada M4W 2P6 Office: 11 Adelaide St W Suite 700 Toronto ON Canada M5H 1L9

HARDING, FANN, health science administrator; b. Henderson, Ky., Jan. 29, 1930; d. James Hilary and Lucy (Caldwell) H. Student, Western Coll., Oxford Ohio, 1947-48; A.B. in Biology, Coker Coll., Hartsville, S.C., 1951; M.S. in Anatomy, Med. U. S.C., Charleston, 1954, Ph.D., 1958. Research and teaching asst. dept. anatomy Med. U. S.C., 1951-53, teaching fellow, 1953-55, research fellow, 1955-58; analyst pub. health research program, research and tng. grants br. Nat. Heart Inst., Bethesda, Md., 1958-61, scientist adminstr. research and tng. grants br., 1961-64, chmn. nat. adv. heart council statements com., 1961-64, sr. health scientist adminstr. research grants br. (sect. chief), 1964-69, sr. health scientist adminstr. thrombosis and hemorrhagic diseases br. (acting chief), extramural program, also arteriosclerosis program arteriosclerosis diseases br., 1969-72, mem., 1966-68; sr. health scientist adminstr. thrombosis and hemorrhagic diseases program (acting chief), div. blood diseases and resources Nat. Heart and Lung Inst. (name changed to Nat. Heart, Lung and Blood Inst. 1976), Bethesda, 1972-74; asst. to dir. div. blood diseases and resources Nat. Heart, Lung and Blood Inst., 1974—, program dir. extramural research tng. and devel. program in blood diseases and transfusion medicine, exec. sec. blood diseases and resources adv. com.; asst. coordinator U.S.-USSR Health Exchange Program, 1974—; mem. Women's Action Program Adv. Com., HEW, 1971-72; cons. James H. Mitchell Found., Washington, 1962-67, Washington VA Hosp., 1968-70; environ. cons. Henderson (Ky.) Citizens Com., 1974-76. Organizer NIH Orgn. for Women, 1970; bd. dirs. Assn. Women in Sci. Edn. Found., 1973-77; bd. visitors Coker Coll., 1974-78; bd. dirs., treas. Nat. Children's Choir, Washington, 1981—. Recipient Ruth Patrick award, 1951; NIH award for sustained performance, 1973; Nat. award for contbns. to public policy Fedn. Orgns. for Profl. Women, 1977. Fellow Sigma Delta Epsilon; mem. Nat. Women's Polit. Caucus (charter), Assn. Women in Sci. (founding mem., exec. bd. 1973-75), Fedn. Orgn. Profl. Women (founding pres., exec. bd. 1972—), AAAS (panel on women in sci. 1973-77), Microcirculatory Soc. (charter), Reticuloendothelial Soc. (charter), Am. Assn. Blood Banks, Brit. Soc. Rheology, Am. Assn. Blood Banks, Internat. Soc. Thrombosis and Haemostasis. Home: 5306 Bradley Blvd Bethesda MD 20814 Office: National Heart Lung and Blood Institute NIH Bethesda MD 20205 *There are no rewards or punishments, only consequences.*

HARDING, HURSHEL RUDOLPH, lawyer; b. Texico, N.Mex., Oct. 22, 1929; s. Nathan Robert and Ethel (McQuatters) H.; m. Joyce Yvonne Hart, Nov. 10, 1954; children—Deborah Joyce, David Randolph. Student, Tex. Tech U., 1948-51; LL.B., J.D., Baylor U., 1954. Bar: Tex. bar 1954. County atty., Parmer County, Tex., 1957-75; partner firm Aldridge, Harding, Aycock & Atkinson, Farwell, Tex., 1961—. Contbr. articles to profl. jours. Served as 1st lt. USAF, 1954-56. Mem. Tex., 154th Jud. Dist. bar assns., Farwell C. of C. (pres. 1961-63, dir. 1963-66), Baylor Law Alumni Assn. (dir. 1974-76), Am. Rifle Assn., Phi Alpha Delta. Democrat. Mem. Christian Ch. Clubs: Mason, Lion (pres. 1959-60). Home: 901 9th St PO Box 606 Farwell TX 79326 Office: 402 3d St Farwell TX 79325

HARDING, JAMES GORDON, hosp. adminstr.; b. Warsaw, Ind., June 12, 1921; s. Claude A. and Mabel (James) H.; m. Phyllis Meyer, June 14, 1947; children—Susan M., James M., Phillip A., Thomas D. B.S., Wayne State U., 1949; M.Hosp. Adminstrn., Washington U., St. Louis, 1951. Adminstrv. resident Aultman Hosp., Canton, Ohio, 1950-51; asst. supt. St. Luke's Hosp., Cleve., 1951-52; adminstr. Cleve. Clinic Hosp., 1953-71; pres. Wilmington (Del.) Med. Center, 1971—; Chmn. Ohio Mgmt. Services Corp., 1968-70; Former mem. bd. Council and League for Nursing, Cleve.; former chmn. Community Regional Med. Program; former mem. bd. Blue Cross of N.E. Ohio Adv. Com.; Bd. dirs., sec., mem. exec. com. Hosp. Bur., Inc. Bd. dirs., past vice chmn. Del. div. Am. Cancer Soc.; bd. dirs. Greater Wilmington Devel. Council, Urban Coalition Met. Wilmington, Inc., Del. Inst. Med. Edn. and Research, Nat. Health Council, Inc.; mem. assembly council teaching hosps. of Am. Assn. Med. Colls.; bd. dirs., mem. exec. com. United Way of No. Del. Served with AUS, 1942-45. Fellow Am. Coll. Hosp. Adminstrs. (nominating com.); mem. Am. Hosp. Assn. (past del.), Ohio Hosp. Assn. (hon., pres. 1967-68), Greater Cleve. Hosp. Assn. (past dir.), Nat. League Nursing, Nat. Alliance Businessmen (adv. com.), Hosp. Adminstrs. Study Soc. Home: 400 Foulk Rd Wilmington DE 19803 Office: PO Box 1668 Wilmington DE 19899

HARDING, JAMES WARREN, finance co. exec.; b. Montoursville, Pa., Nov. 9, 1918; s. James John and Alda (Edkin) H.; m. Emily Sue Landes, Mar. 22, 1941; 1 dau., Connie Sue (Mrs. Richard E. Fisher). B.A., Lycoming Coll., 1937-38; M.A., U. Chgo., 1940. With Kemper Cos., Chgo., 1940—, accountant, 1940-50, comptroller, 1960-68, exec. v.p., 1969; chmn. bd. Bank of Chgo., from 1969; pres. Kemper Corp., Am. Underwriting Corp., Central Mortgage Co., Nat. Agts. Service Co., 1969—, also dir.; dir. Kemper Corp., Kemper Reins. Co. Contbr. articles to ins. and trade mags. Finance chmn. Crusade of Mercy, Chgo., 1964-65; trustee James S. Kemper Found., Mundelein Coll.; adv. bd. U. Chgo., Brigham Young U. Served with USNR, 1943-44. Recipient Hardy award Ins. Inst., 1946. Mem. Am. Mgmt. Assn., Econ Club, Financial Execs. Inst., Ins. Statis. Assn., Nat. Indsl. Conf. Bd., Ill. C. of C. (dir.), Phi Kappa Sigma. Republican. Methodist. Clubs: Chgo., University (Chgo.). Home: 1230 Thornbury Libertyville IL 60048

HARDING, ROBERT LEGRANDE, physician; b. Mannington, W.Va., Nov. 19, 1909; s. Lee Clevel and Margaret Ann (Cunningham) H.; m. Audrey Ariel Anderson, Nov. 16, 1940; 1 son, Robert L. Postgrad., Bucknell U., 1942-43; D.D.S., U. Mich., 1937, M.D., 1946. Intern Univ. Hosp., Ann Arbor, Mich., 1938-40, St. Joseph's Hosp., Ann Arbor, 1946-47; tng. surg. service George Washington U., 1953-54; practice medicine, specializing in plastic and reconstructive surgery, Harrisburg, Pa., 1954—; plastic surgeon Harrisburg Hosp., 1954—, Polyclinic Hosp., Harrisburg, 1954—; clin. prof. plastic surgery Pa. State U., 1969—; cons., lectr. in field. Author pubs. in field.; Former editor: Cleft Palate Jour. Served with M.C. U.S. Army, 1951-53. Nat. Inst. Dental Research grantee, 1967—. Fellow Am. Coll. Dentists, A.C.S.; mem. Am. Assn. Plastic Surgeons (pres. 1974-75), Am. Soc. Plastic and Reconstructive Surgeons, Am. Soc. Aesthetic Plastic Surgeons, Am. Cleft Palate Assn. (pres. 1953-54), Am. Soc. Maxillofacial Surgeons, AMA, Am. Dental Assn., Alpha Omega Alpha, Phi Kappa Phi, Omicron Delta Upsilon. Republican. Presbyn. Club: Rotarian. Research oral-facial communicative disorders. Home: 2815 Fairview Rd Camp Hill PA 17011 Office: Riverside Office Ctr Bldg 4 2101 N Front St Harrisburg PA 17110 *The best way to prepare for opportunities in any field of endeavor is to gain as much formal education and supervised training as possible. With this background, and together with a dedication to a high-principled doctrine and continuing self-education, a person is in the best position to accept opportunity and attain success in any field.*

HARDING, VICTOR MATHEWS, lawyer; b. Chgo., July 23, 1908; s. Victor Mathews and Mary M. (Boak) H.; m. Julia Burley, May 25, 1940; children: Julia Harding Weidman, Mary Elizabeth Harding Craft, Katherine DeBlois Harding Bohannon, Victor Clark, Nancy Jane Harding Winter, Burley. A.B. cum laude, Harvard U., 1931, LL.B., 1935; Harvard scholar, Emmanuel Coll., Cambridge U., 1931-32. Bar: Ill. 1935, Wis. 1944. Practiced in, Chgo., 1935-42, Milw., 1944—; with firm Bell, Boyd & Marshall, 1935-42; trial atty. for solicitor U.S. Dept. Labor, 1942-44; mem. firm Whyte, Hirschboeck, S.C., 1944—; Mem. bd. appeals and bd. health, Village of River Hills, 1948-65; mem. sch. bd. Nicolet High Sch., 1952-57, Mapledale Elem. Sch., 1950-56; mem. com. ct. reorgn. Milwaukee County Bd. Suprs., 1959-60, Joint Com. Bench and Bar to revise rules Circuit Ct. Milwaukee County, 1951-53; Trustee Milw. U. Sch., 1955-63. Mem. ABA, Fed., Wis., Milw. bar assns., Am. Judicature Soc., Legal Club Chgo. Clubs: Town, Wis., Harvard. Home: 7730 N River Rd Milwaukee WI 53217 Office: 2100 Marine Plaza Milwaukee WI 53202

HARDING, WALTER, retired American literature educator, writer; b. Bridgewater, Mass., Apr. 20, 1917; s. Roy Valentine and Mary Alice (MacDonald) H.; m. Marjorie Brook, June 7, 1947; children: David, Allen, Lawrence, Susan. B.S. in Edn., Bridgewater (Mass.) State Coll., 1939; M.A., U. N.C., 1947; Ph.D., Rutgers U., 1950. Instr. (Rutgers U.), 1947-51; asst. prof. U. Va., 1951-56; from assoc. prof. to disting prof. Am. lit. SUNY-Geneseo, 1956-82, disting. prof. emeritus, 1983—; dir. SUNY Research Found., 1970—; lectr. Dept. of State Am. Specialists Program, 1964, 67; dir. Nat. Endowment Humanties seminars, 1976, 77, 79, 83. Author: Days of Henry Thoreau, 1965, The Thoreau Handbook, 1959; editor: (with others) The Thoreau Correspondence, 1958, Variorum Walden, 1963; editor-in-chief: Writings of Thoreau, 1965-73. Fellow Am. Council Learned Socs., 1965. Mem. MLA, Thoreau Soc. (pres. 1963). Home: PO Box 115 Groveland NY 14462 Office: State University College Geneseo NY 14454

HARDINGE, HARLOWE, manufacturing company executive; b. Denver, Mar. 17, 1894; s. Hal Williams and Bertha (Wilson) H.; m. Florence Donnelly, Mar. 22, 1929 (dec. Dec. 1978); children: Byron Cantine, Harlowe De Forest; m. Madeline Baumbach, Sept. 19, 1980. Student, Collegiate Sch., N.Y.C., 1906-10, Tome Sch., Port Deposit, Md., 1910-12; M.E., Cornell U., 1916. Registered profl. engr., Pa. With Hardinge Conical Mill Co., N.Y.C., 1916-23; v.p., gen. mgr. Hardinge Co., Inc., York, Pa., 1923-39, pres., 1939-68, chmn., 1964—, also chief exec. officer; former dir. Nat. Central Bank Pa. Contbg. author: Zimmerman and Lavine Handbook of Engineering Costs. Trustee York Coll., Pa.; mem. council, former mem. adminstrv. bd. Cornell U. Served as capt., Signal Corps AUS, 1917-19. Mem. Am. Inst. Mining and Metall. Engrs. (Legion Honor, Richards award 1972, named disting. mem. class of 1975, Disting. Pennsylvanian 1981), York Mfrs. Assn. (past pres.), Pa. C. of C. (bd. dirs.), Mining and Metall. Soc. Am., York Art Assn. (life), Hist. Soc. York County, Laurel Fish and Game Assn., Sigma Xi, Phi Kappa Sigma. Republican. Clubs: Rotary (fellow), Lafayette, York Country; Monterey Peninsula Country (Pebble Beach, Cal.). Home: 556 Country Club Rd York PA 17403 150 Del Mesa Carmel Carmel CA 93921 Office: PO Box 867 York PA 17405

HARDINGS, JOHN HIBBARD, insurance company executive; b. Plainfield, N.J., Jan. 12, 1936; s. Ernest Reginald and Emily (Hibbard) Harding; m. Courtenay Main, July 11, 1959 (div. Nov. 1973); children: Robert, Brooke, Ashley; m. Joan Edith Drake, Nov. 29, 1973. B.A., Princeton U., 1958. Asst. actuary Nat. Life Ins. Co., Montpelier, Vt., 1965-67, assoc. actuary, Montpelier, 1967-69, actuary research and devel., 1969-72, v.p., actuary, 1972-80, sr. v.p., chief actuary, 1980-83, exec. v.p., 1983—; dir. Adminstrv. Services, Inc., Champlain Life Ins. Co., Equity Services, Inc., Nat. Life Investment Mgmt. Co., Nat. Pension Life Ins. Co., Sentinel Advisors, Inc., Vt. Life Ins. Co. Fellow Soc. Actuaries; mem. Am. Acad. Actuaries (dir. 1982—). Home: RD 2 PO Box 950 Plainfield VT 05667 Office: Nat Life Ins Co National Life Dr Montpelier VT 05604

HARDIS, STEPHEN ROGER, mfg. co. exec.; b. N.Y.C., July 13, 1935; s. Abraham I. and Ethel (Krinsky) H.; m. Sondra Joyce Rolbin, Sept. 15, 1957; children—Julia Faye, Andrew Martin, Joanne Halley. B.A. with distinction, Cornell U., 1956; M.P.A. in Econs, Woodrow Wilson Sch. of Pub. and Internat. Affairs, Princeton, 1960. Asst. to controller Gen. Dynamics, 1960-61; financial analyst Pfaudler Permutit Inc., 1961-64; staff asst. to controller, 1964; mgr. corp. long-range planning Ritter Pfaudler Corp., 1965-68, dir. corporate planning, 1968; treas. Sybron Corp., Rochester, N.Y., 1969—, v.p. fin., 1970-77, exec. v.p. fin. and planning, 1977-79; exec. v.p. fin. and adminstrn. Eaton Corp., Cleve., 1979—; dir. Centran Corp., Central Nat. Bank, Shlegal Corp.; mem. bd. econ. advisors Security N.Y. Corp., Univ. Circle Corp. Past mem. Gov.'s Spl. Task Force on High Tech. Industry; past bd. dirs. Rochester Area Hosp. Corp., Rochester Area Ednl. TV Sta., Genesee Hosp. Served with USNR, 1956-58. Mem. Fin. Execs. Inst., MAPI Fin. Council, Phi Beta Kappa. Home: 23276 Laureldale Rd Shaker Heights OH 44122 Office: 100 Erieview Plaza Cleveland OH 44114

HARDISON, OSBORNE BENNETT, JR., educator; b. San Diego, Oct. 22, 1928; s. Osborne Bennett and Ruth (Morgan) H.; m. Marifrances Fitzgibbon, Dec. 23, 1950; children: Charity Ruth, Sarah Frances, Laura Fitzgibbon, Agnes Margaret, Osborne Bennett, Mathew Fitzgibbon. B.A., U. N.C., 1949, M.A. in English Lit., 1950; Ph.D., U. Wis., 1956; Litt.D., Rollins Coll., 1970, Kalamazoo Coll., 1975, Georgetown U., 1977, Amherst Coll., 1979. Teaching asst. U. Wis., 1950-53; instr. English U. Tenn., 1954-56, Princeton U., 1956-57; mem. faculty U. N.C. at Chapel Hill, 1957-69, prof. English and comparative lit., 1967-69; dir. Folger Shakespeare Library, Washington, 1969-84; Univ. prof. English Georgetown U., 1985—; Chmn. Southeastern Inst. Medieval and Renaissance Studies, 1965, co-chmn., 1966. Author: Lyrics and Elegies, 1958, Modern Continental Literary Criticism, 1962, The Enduring Monument, 1962, English Literary Criticism: The Renaissance, 1964, Christain Rite and Christian Drama in the Middle Ages, 1965, Practical Rhetoric, 1966, (with Leon Golden) Aristotle's Poetics: A Translation and Commentary for Students of Literature, 1968, Toward Freedom and Dignity: The Humanities and the Idea of Humanity, 1973, Pro Musica Antiqua, 1977, Entering the Maze: Identity and Change in Modern Culture, 1981; Editor: (with others) The Encyclopedia of Poetry and Poetics, 1965, Medieval and Renaissance Studies, 1966, The Quest for Imagination, 1971, Film Scripts I-IV, 1971, (with Leon Golden) Classical and Medieval Criticism, 1974; adv. editor: Jour. Medieval and Renaissance Studies; also series editor for book pubs. Trustee U. Detroit, 1969-79. Decorated Cavaliere della Republic Italiana, Order Brit. Empire; Fulbright fellow, Rome, Italy, 1953-54; Folger Library fellow, summer, 1958; Guggenheim fellow, 1963-64; recipient Haskins medal Medieval Acad. Am., 1967. Mem. MLA (exec. council 1968-71), Renaissance Soc. Am., Am. Assn. Higher Edn. (dir. 1980—), Phi Beta Kappa. Office: Georgetown Univ Dept of English 37th and O St Washington DC 20052

HARDISON, RUTH INGE, sculptor; b. Portsmouth, Va.; d. William Lafayette and Evelyn Elizabeth (Jordan) H.; 1 dau., Yolande. Student, Tenn. State U., Vassar Coll. Artist's model, photographer, actress, tchr., counselor, poet, N.Y.C.; creator: series sculptured busts Ingenious Am.; sculptured portraits Negro Giants in History; outdoor mural New Generation, Intermediate Sch. 74, N.Y.C. Bd. Edn.; head Jackie Robinson, N.Y.C. Dept. Cultural Affairs; monument Frederick Douglass, Princeton U.; represented in permanent collections. Address: 444 Central Park W Apt 4B New York NY 10025 *My mother used to tell my brother and me: You must make the world a better place for having lived in it. I am still trying to do that by living as lovingly and creatively as I can. I enjoy my life and all its challenges. I hope my work contributes to the joy, encouragement and inspiration of all who view it.*

HARDISTY, HUNTINGTON, naval officer; b. Atlanta, Feb. 3, 1929; s. John Thomas and Mildred (Huntington) H.; m. Sally Ives, July 3, 1954; children: John Thomas, Robert Huntington. Student, U. N.C., 1947; B.S. in Engring., U.S. Naval Acad., 1952; M.A. in Internat. Relations, Harvard U., 1964. Commd. ensign U.S. Navy, 1952, advanced through grades to rear adm., 1978; comdg. officer VF-32, 1968-69, comdr. CAW-11, 1971-72, comdg. officer U.S.S. Savannah (AOR-4), 1973-74, comdg. officer U.S.S. Oriskany (CV-34), 1975-76; acting pres. Naval War Coll., Newport, R.I., 1977; comdr. U.S. Naval Forces, Philippines, 1978-79; comdr. Carrier Group Seven, 1980, comdr. Carrier Strike Force Seventh Fleet, 1981-82; chief ADCNO Plans/Policy/Ops, Navy Dept., Washington, 1983—. Decorated Silver Star, Legion of Merit with Combat V and 4 gold stars, D.F.C. with gold star, Air medal with 6 gold stars; recipient Disting. Service award Navy League, 1977. Mem. Sigma Chi. Episcopalian. Office: ADCNO Plans/Policy/Ops Navy Dept OP-06B Washiington DC 20350

HARDMAN, HAROLD FRANCIS, pharmacology educator; b. East Orange, N.J., Aug 2, 1927; s. Harold Maine and Agnes Lillian (McGovern) H.; m. Jean Ely Dettmer, June 27, 1950; children—David, Timothy, John, Susan. B.Sc. (Am. Found. Pharm. Edn. scholar), Rutgers U., 1949; M.Sc. (Am. Found. Pharm. Edn. fellow), U. Ill. at Chgo., 1951, Ph.D., U. Mich., 1954, M.D., 1958. Asst. prof. pharmacology U. Mich., 1958-60; asso. prof. pharmacology Marquette U., Milw., 1960-62; prof. pharmacology, chmn. dept. Med. Coll. of Wis. at Milw., 1962—, asso. dean basic scis., 1968-70; Bd. dirs. Med. Coll. Wis., 1980-82. Served to sgt. AUS, 1946-47. John and Mary Markle scholar academic medicine, 1958-63. Mem. Am. Soc. Pharmacology and Exptl. Therapeutics (chmn. program com. 1973-76, councillor 1976-79, pres.-elect 1981-82, pres. 1982-83), Fedn. Am. Socs. Exptl. Biology (pres. 1983-84), Assn. Med. Sch. Pharmacology Chairmen (sec. 1970-72, pres. 1978-80), Milw. Acad. Medicine (pres. 1974-75). Research in cardiovascular pharmacology, pharmacology of marijuana and derivatives. Home: 1120 Indianwood Dr Brookfield WI 53005

HARDMAN, JOEL GRIFFETH, pharmacologist; b. Colbert, Ga., Nov. 7, 1933; s. Joel Carlton and Ruby Lee (Griffeth) H.; m. Georgette Johnson, July 16, 1955; children: Pamela Hope, Frances Leigh, Mary George, Joel Carlton. B.S. in Pharmacy, U. Ga., 1954, M.S., 1959; Ph.D. in Pharmacology, Emory U., 1964. Instr. pharmacy U. Ga., Athens, 1957-60; predoctoral fellow dept. pharmacology Emory U., Atlanta, 1960-64; instr. physiology Vanderbilt U., Nashville, 1964-67, asst. prof., 1967-70, asso. prof., 1970-72, prof. physiology, 1972-75, prof., chmn. dept. pharmacology, 1975—; Francqui fgn. vis. prof. Free U. Brussels, 1974; mem. pharmacology study sect. NIH, 1975-79, chmn., 1977-79; mem. research com. Tenn. Heart Assn., 1976-79; mem. adv. Bd. Advances in Cyclic Nucleotide Research. Mem. editorial bd.: Jour. Biol. Chemistry, 1975-80, Jour. Cyclic Nucleotide Research, 1974—, Circulation Research, 1980—; contbr. sci. papers in field to profl. publs.; editor: Molecular Pharmacology, 1983—. Recipient H.B. Van Dyke award Columbia U., 1981. Mem. Am. Soc. Pharmacology and Exptl. Therapeutics, AAAS, Am. Heart Assn. (research com. 1979—), Am. Soc. Biol. Chemists.

Office: Dept Pharmacology Vanderbilt U Sch Medicine Nashville TN 37232

HARDMAN, JOHN MALEY, physician; b. Matheson, Colo., Jan. 15, 1933; s. John Maley and Agness Scott (Hill) H.; m. Margaret V. Nesom, Feb. 27, 1978; children by previous marriage—John S., Shari L. B.S., U. Colo., 1954, M.D., 1958; M.S., Baylor U., Waco, Tex., 1965. Commd. 1st lt. M.C. U.S. Army, 1958, advanced through grades to col., 1973; rotating intern (Walter Reed Army Med. Center), 1958-59, gen. pathology resident, 1959-63, neuro-pathology tng., 1965-69, service in, Korea, 1963-64, chief dept. pathology, Washington, 1975-77, ret., 1977; prof. pathology, chmn. dept. John A. Burns Sch. Medicine, U. Hawaii, Manoa, 1977—, dir. residency program univ. integrated pathology residency program, 1978—; dir. labs. Kapiolani-Children's Med. Center, Honolulu, 1978—; cons. neuropathology St. Francis Hosp., Straub Clinic and Hosp., Tripler Army Med. Center; dir.-at-large Hawaii div. Am. Cancer Soc., 1971-75; hosp. coordinator Tripler Army Med. Center, 1974; adv. com. Pacific S.W. Regional Med. Library Service, 1978—; chmn. Western Regional Assn. Pathology Chmn., 1979-80; chmn. med. adv. com. Hawaii chpt. Multiple Sclerosis Soc., 1979—. Editor: Compendium of Tests Available in HBS Clinical and Veterinary Laboratories, Vol. 5, 1976; contbr. articles med. to publs. Chmn. carnival com. Ft. Shafter Area Youth Activities Council, 1973; pres. Ft. Shafter-Tripler Dolphin Swim Club, 1972-73. Decorated Legion of Merit, Army Commendation medal, Army Meritorious Service medal; recipient Sir Henry Wellcome medal, 1968. Mem. Internat. Acad. Pathology, Coll. Am. Pathologists, Assn. Mil. Surgeons U.S., Am. Assn. Neuropathologists, Am. Assn. Pathologists and Bacteriologists, Assn. Pathology Chmn., Hawaii Soc. Pathologists, Sigma Xi, Alpha Omega Alpha, Alpha Epsilon Delta, Rho Chi, Nu Sigma Nu. Episcopalian. Club: Viking. Office: 1960 East-West Rd Honolulu HI 96822

HARDON, JOHN ANTHONY, clergyman, educator; b. Midland, Pa., June 18, 1914; s. John and Anna (Jevin) H. A.B., John Carroll U., 1936; M.A., Loyola U., Chgo., 1941; S.T.D., Gregorian U., Rome, 1951. Joined Soc. of Jesus, 1936; ordained priest Roman Cath. Ch., 1947; asso. prof. fundamental theology West Baden (Ind.) Coll., 1951-62; asso. prof. religion Western Mich. U., 1962-67; prof. fundamental theology Bellarmine Sch. Theology, North Aurora, Ill. and; Chgo., 1968-73; research prof. Jesuit Sch. Theology, Chgo., 1973—; prof. advanced studies in Cath. doctrine St. John's U., Jamaica, N.Y., 1974—; vis. prof. comparative religion St. Paul U., Ottawa, Can., 1968—; prof. Notre Dame Inst. (a Pontifical Catechetical Inst.), Va., 1981—; theol. dir. Mark Communications Corp., Toronto, 1973—; editorial dir. Cath. Home Study Inst.; v.p. Inst. on Religious Life; dir. retreats priests and religious; chmn. bd. Cath. Voice of Am., Inc.; cons. in field. Author: The Protestant Churches of America, 2d edit, 1968, rev. edit., 1981, Christianity in Conflict, 1959, All My Liberty, 1959, rev. edit., 1981, For Jesuits, 1963, Religions of the World, 2d edit, 1968, rev. edit., 1981, The Hungry Generation, 1967, The Spirit and Origins of American Protestantism, 1968, Religions of the Orient-A Christian View, 1970, American Judaism, 1971, Christianity in the Twentieth Century, 2d edit, 1972, rev. edit., 1978, The Catholic Catechism, 1975, Holiness in the Church, 1976, Religious Life Today, 1977, Modern Catholic Dictionary, 1980, Salvation and Sanctification, 1978, Theology of Prayer, 1979, The Question and Answer Catholic Catechism, 1981, Spiritual Life in the Modern World, 1982; Editor: Gospel Witness, 1971, Jour. Cath. Doctrine, 1977. Recipient Papal medal, 1951; award outstanding work in field history Cath. Press Assn., 1973; medal Slovak World Congress, 1978. Mem. AAUP, Am. Soc. Missiology, Instituto Slovaco, Internat. Assn. Mission Studies, Fellowship Cath. Scholars. Address: Loyola Residence 53 E 83d St New York NY 10028

HARDWAY, WENDELL GARY, coll. pres.; b. Bolair, W.Va., Mar. 5, 1927; s. Ressie Bruce and Elsie Clennen (Miller) H.; m. Hannah Lou Garrett, July 12, 1950. B.S., W.Va. U., 1949, M.S., 1953; Ph.D., Ohio State U., 1959. Tchr. Troy (W.Va.) High Sch., 1949-54; asst. prof. sci. Glenville (W.Va.) State Coll., 1954-57, asso. prof. edn., 1959-61, prof., chmn. div. edn., dir. student teaching, 1961-66; pres. Bluefield (W.Va.) State Coll., 1966-73, Fairmont (W.Va.) State Coll., 1973—; dir. City Nat. Bank, Fairmont. Pres. United Way, Fairmont, 1976; Mem. Glenville City Council, 1958-64; pres. W.Va. Intercollegiate Athletic Conf., 1977-78. Served with AUS, 1945-46. Named Man of Year Bluefield Jaycees, 1969. Mem. Fairmont C. of C. (1st v.p. 1976), Phi Delta Theta, Gamma Sigma Delta, Phi Delta Kappa, Kappa Delta Pi. Methodist. Home: Campus Dr Fairmont WV 26554 Office: Fairmont State Coll Fairmont WV 26554

HARDWICK, DAVID FRANCIS, pathologist; b. Vancouver, B.C., Can., Jan. 24, 1934; s. Walter H. W. and Iris L. (Hyndman) H.; m. Margaret M. Lang, Aug. 22, 1956; children: Margaret F., Heather I., David J. M.D., U. B.C., 1957. Intern Montreal (Que., Can.) Gen. Hosp., 1957-58; resident Vancouver Gen. Hosp., 1958-59, Children's Hosp., Los Angeles, 1959-62; research assoc. U. So. Calif., 1961-62; clin. instr. U. B.C., Vancouver, 1963-65, asst. prof. pathology, 1965-69, assoc. prof., 1969-74, prof., 1974—, head dept. pathology, 1976—; dir. labs. Children's Hosp., Vancouver, 1969—, Vancouver Gen. Hosp., 1976—; chief med. staff Children's Hosp., 1969—; mem. U. B.C. Senate, 1966-71. Author: Acid Base Balance and Blood Gas Studies, 1968, Intermediary Metabolism of Liver, 1971; contbr. numerous articles to profl. publs. Recipient Queen's Centennial medal Govt. Can., 1978. Fellow Royal Coll. Physicians (Can.), Coll. Am. Pathologists; mem. Can. Med. Assn., B.C. Assn. Lab. Medicine, B.C. Med. Assn., N.Y. Acad. Sci., Pediatric Pathology Club, Internat. Acad. Pathology, Alpha Omega Alpha. Home: 727 W 23d Ave Vancouver BC Canada V5Z 2A7 Office: Dept Pathology U BC 2211 Wesbrook Pl Vancouver BC Canada V6T 1W5

HARDWICK, ELIZABETH, author; b. Lexington, Ky., July 27, 1916; d. Eugene Allen and Mary (Ramsey) H.; m. Robert Lowell, July 28, 1949 (div. Oct. 1972); 1 dau., Harriet. A.B., U. Ky., 1938, M.A., 1939; postgrad., Columbia U., 1939-41. Adj. asso. prof. Barnard Coll. Author: novels The Ghostly Lover, 1945, The Simple Truth, 1955, Sleepless Nights, 1979; essays A View of My Own, 1962; Seduction and Betrayal, 1974; Editor: The Selected Letters of William James, 1960; adv. editor: N.Y. Rev. Books; Contbr.: to New Yorker. Guggenheim fellow, 1947; recipient George Jean Nathan award, dramatic criticism, 1966. Mem. Am. Acad. and Inst. Arts and Letters. Home: 15 W 67th St New York NY 10023

HARDY, ALAN M., diplomat; b. Orange, N.J., May 26, 1934; 6 children. B.A., U. Cin., 1959; M.A., UCLA, 1969; grad., Fgn. Service Inst., 1976. Intelligence research specialist Dept. State, 1956-57; consular officer, Toronto, 1959-61, adminstrv. officer, Tananarive, 1961-63, consular and econs. officer, Milan, 1963-65, econ. officer, Mogadishu, 1965-67, country officer for Nigeria, 1967-68, fgn. affairs polit. analyst, 1969-71, country officer for Kenya and Tanzania, 1971-73, polit. officer, Dakar, 1973-75, Budapest, Hungary, 1976-78, personnel officer, 1978-79, country officer for Mozambique and Namibia, 1979-81; U.S. Ambassador to Republic of Equatorial Guinea, Malabo, 1982—. Served with U.S. Army, 1957-59. Office: US Embassy Malabo Equatorial Guineau Dept State Washington DC 20520

HARDY, CHARLES LEACH, U.S. district judge; b. Los Angeles, Jan. 24, 1919; s. Charles Little and Dorothy (Leach) H.; m. Jean McRae, Jan. 26, 1947; children: Charles M., Caroline, Catherine, John L. Julianne, Eileen, Sterling A., Steven W., Janette. B.S., U. Ariz., 1947, LL.B., 1950. Bar: Ariz. 1949. Pvt. practice, Phoenix, 1949-66, dep. county atty., Maricopa County, Ariz., 1952-55, asst. atty. gen., State of Ariz., 1956-59; judge Ariz. Superior Ct., 1966-80; U.S. dist. judge Ariz. Dist., Phoenix, 1980—. Pres. Young Democratic Clubs Ariz., 1956-57, nat. committeeman, 1957-58; chmn. Maricopa County Dem. Central Com., 1958-59; mem. Ariz. Bd. Crippled Children's Services, 1965. Served with F.A. AUS, 1941-45. Decorated Bronze Star. Mem. ABA, Am. Judicature Soc., State Bar Ariz., Maricopa County Bar Assn. Mormon. Office: US Courthouse Bldg 230 N 1st Ave Room 6031 Phoenix AZ 85025 *

HARDY, DAVID, lawyer, corporate executive; b. Los Angeles, May 15, 1924; s. Rex Giffen and Dorothy Field (Simpson) H.; m. Constance Parrette (div. 1969); children—Francesca, David Kimberley, Robert Paul; m. Charlotte Broomberg (div. 1976); children—Varda, Crystine; m. Jane Myers, 1977; stepchildren—Bradley and Lauren Myers. Student, U. Calif. at Los Angeles, at Berkeley, 1947-50; B.A., LL.B. Bar: Calif. bar 1951. V.p. Kaiser Steel Corp., 1969-73, lawyer, exec. affiliated cos., Oakland, Calif., 1948-73; v.p. Kaiser Industries Corp., 1962-71; ptnr. Millikan, Montgomery, Olafson & Hardy, Pasadena, Calif., 1973-76; asso. gen. counsel Foremost-McKesson, Inc., 1976-79, dep. gen. counsel, 1979—. Served to lt. (j.g.) USNR, 1943-46. Mem ABA (chmn. com. corporate counsel sect. corporate banking and bus. 1983—); Mem. San Francisco Bar Assn., State Bar Calif., Order of Coif. Office: One Post St San Francisco CA 94104

HARDY, DAVID JERRY, lawyer; b. Crookston, Minn., Apr. 19, 1931; s. Jerry Melvinius and Camilla Helene (Lokensgard) H.; m. Elizabeth Ann Hills, Dec. 16, 1961; children: John, James, Susan. B.A., St. Olaf Coll., 1953; J.D., Harvard U., 1956. Instr. humanities MIT, Cambridge, 1953-56; assoc. firm Winston & Strawn, Chgo., 1956-62; ptnr. F.H. Prince & Co., Inc., Chgo., 1978—; dir. Winston & Strawn, Chgo., 1962—. Mem. Commn. for a New Luth. Ch., Mpls., 1982—; bd. regents St. Olaf Coll., Northfield, Minn., 1980—; mem. Com. on Luth. Unity, Mpls., 1981-82; bd. regents Augustana Coll., Sioux Falls, S.D., 1969-81; bd. govs. Luth. Inst. Human Ecology, Park Ridge, Ill., 1964-77; bd. dirs. Luth. Social Services of Ill., 1961-67. Recipient Dist. Alumnus award St. Olaf Coll., 1975. Mem. Phi Beta Kappa, Blue Key, Pi Gamma Mu, Pi Kappa Delta, Tau Kappa Alpha. Lutheran. Clubs: Mid-Day, Meadows. Home: 317 E Forest Ln Palatine IL 60067 Office: Winston & Strawn One First National Plaza Chicago IL 60603

HARDY, DEBORAH WELLES, history educator; b. Milw., Nov. 2, 1927; d. Frank M. Hursely and Doris (Berger) Hursley; (dec.)children: Scott, Jonathan, Bridget. B.A., Stanford U., 1949; M.A., U. Calif., 1950; Ph.D., U. Wash., 1968. TV writer, 1964-72; mem. faculty U. Wyo., Laramie, 1967—, prof. history, 1978—, head dept., 1980—; mem. Wyo. Council Humanities, 1972-76. Author: Petr. Tkachev: The Critic as Jacobin, 1977; also articles. Grantee Social Sci. Research Council, summer 1971, Am. Philos. Soc., 1976. Mem. Am. Hist. Assn., Am. Assn. Advancement of Slavic Studies, AAUP, NEA, Western Social Sci. Assn., Western Slavic Assn., Phi Beta Kappa. Home: 2450 Park Ave Laramie WY 82070 Office: History Dept U Wyo Laramie WY 82071

HARDY, DORCAS R., government official; b. Newark, N.J., July 18, 1946; d. Colburn and Ruth (Hart) H. B.A., Conn. Coll., 1964-68; M.B.A., Pepperdine U., 1976. Legis. research asst. U.S. Senator Clifford P. Case, Washington, 1970; spl. asst. White House Conf. Children and Youth, Washington, 1970-71; exec. dir. Health Services Industry Commn., Cost of Living Council, Washington, 1971-73; asst. sec. Calif. Dept. Health, Sacramento, 1973-74; assoc. dir. U. So. Calif. Ctr. Health Services Research, 1974-81; asst. sec. human devel. services HHS, Washington, 1981—. Bd. dirs. Vols. in Internat. Service and Awareness, Santa Barbara, Calif., Jr. League of Pasadena, All Saints Childrens Ctr., Girl Scouts U.S.A. Mem. Republican Women's Forum, Exec. Women in Govt. Office: US Dept Health and Human Services 200 Independence Ave SW Washington DC 20201

HARDY, GEORGE WILLIAM, airlines exec.; b. Groveland, Mass., May 7, 1922; s. Elvin N. and Marian E. H.; m. Vena Hamilton, Oct. 15, 1943; children—Anne E., Susan Hardy Cameron, Deborah J. Grad., Roosevelt Aviation Sch., 1941. With Eastern Air Lines, Inc., 1942—, v.p. line maintenance, Miami, Fla., 1980—. Served with U.S. Army, 1944-47. Republican. Office: International Airport Miami FL 33148

HARDY, GORDON ALFRED, educator; b. Hudson, Ind., Aug. 18, 1918; s. Carl Alfred and Gayle (Pike) H.; m. Lillian Studebaker, May 19, 1945; children—John Studebaker, Christopher Bartlett, Susan, Jeffrey Pike. B.A., B.Mus., U. Mich., 1941, M.Mus., 1946; B.S., Juilliard Sch. Music, 1952. Teaching fellow Juilliard Sch. Music, 1952-53, teaching asst., 1953-54, mem. faculty lit. and materials of music dept., 1954—, asso. dean, 1963-69, dean students, 1970-76; dean Aspen (Colo.) Music Sch., 1963-66, exec. v.p., 1966-75, pres., 1976—. Author: (with Arnold Fish) Music Literature-A Workbook for Analysis, vol. I, Homophony, 1963, vol. II, Polyphony, 1966. Bd. dirs. Juilliard Repertory Project, 1968, Juilliard Inst. Spl. Studies, 1969. Served to lt. USNR, 1942-45. Mem. Theta Chi. Home: 149 E 73 St New York City NY 10021

HARDY, HUGH GELSTON, architect; b. Spain, July 26, 1932; s. Gelston LaVenture and Barbara (Walton) Hardy LaV.; m. Tiziana Spadea, Jan. 29, 1966; children: Sebastian, Penelope. B.Arch., Princeton U., 1954, M.F.A. in Architecture, 1956. Archtl. asst. to Jo Mielziner, N.Y.C., 1958-62; founder Hugh Hardy & Assocs., N.Y.C., 1962-67; partner Hardy Holzman Pfeiffer Assocs., N.Y.C., 1967—; Davenport vis. prof. archtl. design Yale U., 1976; chmn. Design Arts Adv. Panel Nat. Endowment for the Arts; cons., lectr. in field. Co-designer: (with Holzman and Pfeiffer) Columbus (Ind.) Occupational Health Center, 1973, Orchestra Hall, Mpls., 1974, Cooper-Hewitt Mus., N.Y.C., 1976, St. Louis Art Mus, 1977, Best Products Corp. Hdqtrs., Richmond, Va., 1979, Madison Civic Center, Wis., 1980, The Joyce Theatre, N.Y.C., 1982, Hult Ctr. for the Performing Arts, Eugene, Ore., 1982; contbr. articles to profl. jours.; Author: (with Holzman and Pfeiffer) Reusing Railroad Stations, 1974. Bd. dirs. Municipal Art Soc. N.Y., N.Y.C., 1975-79; v.p. Municipal Art Soc., N.Y.C., 1975-83. Served with C.E. U.S. Army, 1956-58. Recipient D'Amata prize Princeton U., 1954; Brunner prize in architecture Nat. Inst. Arts and Letters, 1974. Fellow AIA (N.Y. chpt. medal of honor 1978, Archtl. Firm award 1981, several Honor awards); mem. Archtl. League N.Y. (v.p. for architecture 1977-81), N.A.D. (assoc.). Clubs: Century Assn., Players. Office: 257 Park Ave S New York NY 10010

HARDY, HUGH SPENCE, banker; b. Saskatoon, Sask., Can., Oct. 14, 1924; s. Edwin Thomas Spence and Emma (McMahon) H.; m. Betty J. Hillyard, Dec. 29, 1950; children: Richard, Bradford, Brenda, Scott. B.Comm., U. Sask., 1948. Mgmt., Hudson's Bay Co., Winnipeg, Man., Can., 1948-53; pres. Hugh S. Hardy & Assos., Vancouver, B.C., Can., 1954-57, Universal Mktg. Research Inc., N.Y.C., 1958-63; partner Touche Ross & Co., Montreal, Que., Can., 1964-65; v.p. mktg. Royal Bank of Can., Montreal, 1966-78, sr. v.p. public affairs, 1979—. Nat. dir. Boys and Girls Clubs of Can. Served to lt. Can. Army, 1943-45, 50-52. Mem. Can. Bankers Assn. (policy and planning com.), Bank Mktg. Assn. (speaker, panelist), Bank Mktg. Council (U.S.), Conf. Bd. in Can., Public Affairs Council. Mem. United Ch. of Can. Clubs: Mt. Stephen, Summerlea Golf and Country (dir.), Montreal Athletic Assn.). Office: Head Office Royal Bank of Canada Box 6001 Montreal PQ H3C 3A9 Canada

HARDY, JEROME SPILMAN, financial executive; b. Manhattan, Kans., Jan. 2, 1918; s. Cleo Clinton and Irene (Johnson) H.; m. Betty St. Clair, Dec. 13, 1946; children: Martha, James, Douglas, Gordon, Quentin. B.S., U. Md., 1939. Mem. hwy. edn. bd. Automotive Safety Found., 1939-43; partner Harris & Hardy (S.A., pub. relations firm), 1946; exec. Doubleday & Co., N.Y.C., 1947-59, v.p. for advt., 1956-59; dir. Time Life Books div. Time, Inc., N.Y.C., 1959-60; pub. Life Book div. Time, Inc. (Book div.), 1961-64; also v.p. corp.; pub. Life mag., 1964-70; exec. v.p. Dreyfus Corp., 1970, pres., 1970-80; dir. Doyle Dane Bernbach, Reeves Communications Corp., Ency. Brit., Futures Group, Nat. Demographics, Ltd., H.S. Stuttman, Energy Assets Internat. Corp.; chmn. Investment Co. Inst., 1976-78. Bd. dirs. Center for Public Resources; bd. dirs., 1st vice chmn. Salk Inst. Served from pvt. to 1st lt. USAAF, 1943-46. Clubs: University, Sky (N.Y.C.); Augusta Nat. Golf, Pine Valley Golf, Country of New Canaan. Home: 19 Fable Farm Rd New Canaan CT 06840 Office: 420 Lexington Ave Suite 2803 New York NY 10170 *Leave the people the hell alone, but pick up those who stumble.*

HARDY, JOHN CHRISTOPHER, physicist; b. Montreal, Que., Can., July 10, 1941; s. Noel Woodburn and Ethel May (Collins) H.; m. Lynn Helen Frederick, June 3, 1964; children: Ericka, Kirsten, Bruce, Alana. B.Sc., McGill U., Montreal, 1961, M.Sc., 1963, Ph.D. (D.W. Ambridge prize 1965), 1965. NRC Can. post-doctoral fellow Oxford (Eng.) Nuclear Physics Lab., 1965-67; Miller research fellow Lawrence Radiation Lab., Berkeley, Calif., 1967-70; asso. research officer Atomic Energy Can. Ltd., Chalk River, Ont., 1970-74, sr. research officer, 1975—, head nuclear physics br., 1983—; sci. asso. CERN, Geneva, 1976-77. Contbr. articles to profl. jours. Fellow Royal Soc. Can. (Rutherford medal in physics 1981); mem. Can. Assn. Physicists (Herzberg medal 1976), Am. Phys. Soc. Office: Chalk River Nuclear Labs Chalk River ON K0J 1J0 Canada

HARDY, JOHN EDWARD, educator, author; b. Baton Rouge, Apr. 3, 1922; s. Roger Barlow and Mary (McCoy) H.; m. Marie Elam, Dec. 30, 1942 (div.); children: Margot (Mrs. Timm Ferguson), Leonore (Mrs. David Dvorkin), Catherine (Mrs. Didier Pouligny), Laura, Anne (Mrs. George Biswell), Eve; m. Willene Schaefer, June 25, 1969. B.A., La. State U., 1944; M.A., State U. Iowa, 1946; Ph.D., Johns Hopkins U., 1956. Mem. English faculties U. Detroit, 1945-46, Yale U., 1946-48, U. Okla., 1948-52, Johns Hopkins U., 1952-54; mem. faculty U. Notre Dame, 1954-66, prof. English, 1964-66, mem. acad. council, 1963-66, grad. council, 1963-66; prof. English, chmn. dept. U. South Ala., 1966-69; prof. English U. Colo., Boulder, 1969-70; prof. English, chmn. dept. U. Mo., St. Louis, 1970-72; dir. grad. studies in English U. Ill.-Chgo. Circle, 1972-75, prof. English, 1972—, mem. grad. coll. exec. com., 1974-76, 81-82. Author: (with Cleanth Brooks) Poems of Mr. John Milton, 1951, The Curious Frame, 1962, Man in the Modern Novel, 1964, Katherine Anne Porter, 1973, Certain Poems, 1958; Editor: The Modern Talent, 1964, (with Seymour L. Gross) Images of the Negro in American Literature, 1966. Fulbright prof. Am. lit. U. Munich, Germany, 1959-61; Ford Faculty Study fellow, 1952-53; Rockefeller fellow poetry, 1954. Mem. MLA, Phi Beta Kappa. Home: 1115 N Ridgeland Oak Park IL 60302 Office: Dept of English U Ill-Chgo Circle Chicago IL 60680

HARDY, JOSEPH, actor; b. Arlington, Mass., Aug. 10, 1918; s. James Joseph and Nora (Curtin) H.; m. Lynne Emery, Aug. 17, 1966. Appeared on: Major Bowes Radio Amateur Hour, 1942, Arthur Godfrey Radio Talent Show, 1947, night club mimic act, 1945—; Broadway appearances include: Tempest, 1945, Detective Story, 1950, Small Hours, 1951, Male Animal, 1952, Mr. Roberts, 1956, Cut of the Axe, 1960, The Freaking Out of Stephanie Blake, 1967; motion picture appearances include: Middle of the Night, 1959, Tell Me in the Sunlight, 1963, Husbands, 1969, The Arrangement, 1969, Cops and Robbers, 1972, For Pete's Sake, 1973; The Magnificent 10, 1981; toured in: The Front Page, Fla.-Can. tour, 1970; appeared with wife in: Never Too Late, 1970, Masque of St. George and the Dragon, Actor's Studio, 1970; appeared in: Best of Families, PBS, 1977, Bob Fosse's All That Jazz, 1979. Mem. Screen Actors Guild, Actors Equity Assn., AFTRA. Democrat. Roman Catholic. Office: Box 238 Radio City Station New York NY 10101-0238 *People make a big deal about "Thank God It's Friday." Well, any day, life is a gift to treasure.*

HARDY, MARIE PAULA, educator; b. Kansas City, Feb. 24, 1926; d. Russell Charles and Agnes Esther (Cunningham) H. B.A., St. Mary Coll., 1962; M.A., U. Nebr., 1969; Ph.D., U. Ill., 1972. Joined Sisters of Charity of Leavenworth, Roman Catholic Ch., 1943; elem. tchr. parochial schs., Kans., Mo., Colo., Ill., Calif., Mont., 1945-57, secondary tchr. parochial schs., 1957-68; scholar-in-residence U. Newcastle Upon Tyne, Eng., 1970-71; mem. faculty St. Mary Coll., Leavenworth, Kans., 1971—; chmn. dept. edn., 1978—; mem. drama commn. York Internat. Conf., Eng., 1971; condr. workshop, seminars in field. Contbr. articles to profl. jours. Triple T fellow; NDEA grantee; grantee Kans. Regional Council Higher Edn., U.S. Dept. Edn. Mem. Nat. Council Tchrs. English, Am. Assn. Coll. Tchrs. of Edn., AAUW, NEA, Internat. Reading Assn., Kans. Assn. Higher Tchrs. English, Assn. Tchr. Educators, Kans. Internat. Reading Assn., Spl. Interst Group-A Network on Adolescent Lit., Nat. Assn. Elem. Sch. Prins., Nat. Assn. Secondary Sch. Prins., Kans. Reading Profls. Higher Edn., Kans. Assn. for Gifted, Talented, Creative, Assn. Ind. Liberal Arts Colls. for Tchr. Edn. Democrat. Roman Catholic. Home and Office: Saint Mary Coll Leavenworth KS 66048

HARDY, NORMAN E. PETER, food company executive; b. Toronto, Ont., Can., Jan. 4, 1917; s. George and Myrtle (Dunsmore) H.; m. Dorothy Walter, Apr. 6, 1939; children: Eleanor Gayle, Beverley Georgine. Student, Pickering Coll., Ont. With Hardy Cartage Co. Ltd., 1935, Brewers' Warehousing Co. Ltd., 1948-49; mgr. Toronto Brewery, John Labatt Ltd., 1949-56, gen. mgr., 1956-59, v.p. beverages div., 1959, chmn. bd., past., dir.; dir. Braxcan Ltd., Noma Ind. Ltd.; vice chmn., chief exec. officer Toronto Blue Jays Baseball Club; chmn. Ont. Racing Commn. Served to lt. RCNVR, World War II. Clubs: The London, Mississauga Gold and Country, London Hunt and Country, Granite, Primrose. Office: John Labatt Ltd 451 Ridout St N London ON Canada *

HARDY, RALPH W.F., biochemist; b. Lindsay, Ont., Can., July 27, 1934; s. Wilbur and Elsie H.; m. Jacqueline M. Thayer, Dec. 26, 1954; children: Steven, Chris, Barbara, Ralph, Jon. B.S.A., U. Toronto, 1956; M.S., U. Wis.-Madison, 1958, Ph.D., 1959. Asst. prof. U. Guelph, Ont., Can., 1960-63; research biochemist DuPont deNemours & Co., Wilmington, Del., 1963-67, research supr., 1967-74, assoc. dir., 1974-79, dir. life scis., 1979—; mem. exec. com. bd. agr. Nat. Acad. Sci.; editorial bd. sci. jours. Author: Nitrogen Fixation, 1975, A Treatise on Dinitrogen Fixation, 3 vols, 1977-79; contbr. over 100 articles to sci. jours. Recipient Gov. Gen.'s Silver medal, 1956; WARF fellow, 1956-58; DuPont fellow, 1958-59. Mem. Am. Chem. Soc. (exec.

com. biol. chemistry div., Del. award 1969), Am. Soc. Biol. Chemists, Am. Soc. Plant Physiology (exec. com.), Am. Soc. Agronomy, Am. Soc. Microbiology. Episcopalian. Patentee (2). Home: Box 364 Unionville PA 19375 Office: EI DuPont Co Wilmington DE 19898

HARDY, RICHARD EARL, rehabilitation counseling educator, psychologist; b. Victoria, Va., Oct. 11, 1938; s. Clifford E. and Mattie Louise (Hamilton) H.; 1 son, Jason Elliott. B.S., Va. Poly. Inst. and State U., 1960, M.S., 1962, Ed.D., 1966. Lic. psychologist Va., N.C., Ariz., Tex., diplomate: in counseling psychology. Rehab. counselor State of Va., Richmond, 1961-63; rehab. advisor HEW, Washington, 1964-66; chief psychologist S.C. Dept. Rehab., Columbia, 1966-68; prof. dept. rehab. counseling Va. Commonwealth U., Richmond, 1968—, chmn. dept., 1968—; internat. cons. to numerous countries including Turkey, Iraq, Peru, Uruguay, South Africa, Brazil, Thailand. Author: Vocational Rehabilitation: Profession and Process, 1972, International Rehabilitation: Approaches and Programs, 1981, Hemingway: A Psychological Portrait, 1983, numerous other books. Recipient Nat. award Nat. Rehab. Assn., 1976, Am. Assn. Workers for Blind, 1976. Mem. Am. Psychol. Assn.; fellow Am. Assn. Counseling and Devel., Am. Assn. Vol. Action Scholars. Office: Va Commonwealth U 921 Franklin St Richmond VA 23284

HARDY, ROBERT MACDONALD, civil engr.; b. Winnipeg, Man., Can., Sept. 25, 1906; s. Robert and Winnifred (Paterson) H.; m. France de Savoye, Aug. 24, 1939; children—Robert Henry, George Alexander, John Anthony. B.S.C.E., U. Man., Winnipeg, 1929, D.Sc. (hon.), 1957, Royal Mil. Coll. Can., 1972, LL.D., U. Alta., Edmonton, 1977. Instr. Faculty Engring., U. Alta., 1930-38, asst. prof. civil engring., 1938-42, asso. prof., 1942-46, prof., 1946-59, 63-71, dean, 1946-59, 63-71; cons., pres. R.M. Hardy & Assos. Ltd., Edmonton, Alta., Can., 1959-63; cons., chmn. bd. Hardy Assos. Ltd., Edmonton, 1978—; dir. Monenco Ltd., Montreal. Contbr. numerous articles on geotech. engring., Engring. Edn. and profl. engring. practice to profl. jours. Served with Can. Air Tng. Corps, 1943-46. Decorated officer Order Can.; recipient R.F. Leggett award Can. Geotech. Soc., 1971, Centennial award Can. Council Profl. Engrs., 1973, Achievement award Province Alta., 1974. Fellow Royal Soc. Can.; mem. Assn. Profl. Engrs., Geologists and Geophysicist Alta., Assn. Profl. Engrs. Man., ASCE. Unitarian. Clubs: Rotary, Masons. Home: 11615 Edinboro Rd Edmonton AB T6G 1Z7 Canada Office: PO Box 746 Edmonton AB T5J 2L4 Canada

HARDY, THOMAS AUSTIN, sculptor; b. Redmond, Oreg., Nov. 30, 1921; s. Orlando Buell and Marie Jane (Austin) H. B.S., U. Oreg., 1942, M.F.A., 1952. Lectr. U. Calif., Berkeley, 1956-58; assoc. prof. sculpture Tulane Univ., New Orleans, 1958-59; artist-in-residence Reed Coll., Portland, Oreg., 1959-61; prof. sculpture Univ. Wyo., Laramie, 1975-76. One man shows, De Young Mus., San Francisco, 1957, Oakland (Calif.) Art Mus., 1958, Pensacola (Fla.) Art Center, Columbia U., 1959, Seattle Art Mus., 1954, Stanford U. Gallery, 1955, group shows include, Met. Mus., N.Y.C., 1952, Am. Mus. Natural History, 1958, Pa. Acad., Phila., Mus. Modern Art, N.Y.C., 1959; represented in permanent collections, Whitney Mus. Am. Art, N.Y.C., Seattle Art Mus., Portland (Oreg.) Art Mus., Lloyd Art Center, Portland, Hilton Hotel, Portland, Chandler Meml. Pavilion, Los Angeles, Fed. Bldg., Juneau, Alaska, Western Forestry Center, Portland, One Civic Center, Salem, U. Calif., Berkeley, Clackamas Town Center, Portland, Seattle Center, High Desert Mus., Bend, Oreg. Bd. dirs. Art Advocates, 1975—, Friends of Timberline Lodge, 1976—, Portland Center for Visual Arts, 1977-81. Mem. Portland Art Assn., Audubon Soc., Am. Mus. Natural History, Kappa Sigma. Democrat. Home: 1422 SW Harrison St Portland OR 97201 Studio: 1023 N Killingsworth Portland OR 97217 Office: Kraushaar Galleries 724 Fifth New York NY 10019

HARDY, THOMAS CRESSON, insurance company executive; b. Hoisington, Kans., Jan. 17, 1942; s. C.C. and Delia H.; m. m. Jan C. Walters, June 15, 1963; children—Jay C., Glenn W. B.A., U. Kans., 1963; M.B.A., Wharton Sch., U. Pa., 1965. C.L.U., F.L.M.I. Sr. analyst treas. dept. Exxon Corp., N.Y.C., 1965-69; treas. Keene Corp., N.Y.C., 1969-73; exec. v.p. fin. Fidelity Union Life Ins. Co., Dallas, 1973-79; (co. acquired by Allianz of Am. 1979); v.p. Allianz of Am.; pres. Allianz Investment Corp., Dallas, 1979-82; exec. v.p. Lumberman's Investment Corp., 1982—; Dir. Gt. Am. Res. Ins. Co., Sunbelt Ins. Co., Oil Field Services Group. Mem. bus.-fin. adv. bd. N. Tex. State U. Sch. Fellow Life Mgmt. Inst. (chpt. pres.), Fin. Execs. Inst. (pres. chpt., nat. dir.). Republican. Methodist. Office: 1201 Elm St Dallas TX 75270

HARDY, WALTER LINCOLN, chem. co. exec.; b. Chgo., Feb. 28, 1916; s. Thomas Jefferson and Nellie J. (Collins) H.; m. Ruth Elizabeth Heinig, Nov. 10, 1944; children—Meridith Lynn, Thomas George, Elizabeth Ellen. B. Chemistry, Cornell U., 1937, M. Chem. Engring., 1938; M.B.A., U. Chgo., 1969. Registered profl. engr., N.Y. Devel. engr. and tech. asst. to research dir. Tide Water Oil Co., Bayonne, N.J., 1938-41; gen. mgr. Protective Coatings Corp., Nutley, N.J., 1945-48; v.p., gen. mgr. Leed Pak, Inc., N.Y.C., 1948-52; dir. engring. client relations Foster D. Snell Inc., N.Y.C., 1952-59; mgr. chem. research Internat. Minerals & Chem. Corp., Skokie, Ill., 1959-62; v.p. research and devel. Simoniz Co., Chgo., 1962-65; dir. research and devel. Richardson Co., Des Plaines, Ill., 1965-80; dir. indsl. relations dept. chemistry U. Calif., San Diego, 1981—; mem. Army-Navy Patent Adv. Bd., 1942-46, Nat. Prodn. Authority, 1950-52. Mem. Sch. Bd. Dist. 110, Deerfield, Ill., 1961-67, v.p., 1965-66, pres., 1967; mem. council Cornell U., Ithaca, N.Y., 1965-77; mem. Com. of Deerfield, 1960—, pres., 1972-74; trustee Village of Riverwoods, Ill., 1973-77; ordained permanent deacon Roman Catholic Ch., 1979. Served to lt. col. USAAF, 1941-46. Fellow Am. Inst. Chemists; mem. Indsl. Research Inst., TAPPI, Am. Assn. Cost Engrs. (charter), Am. Mgmt. Assn., Cornell Soc. Engrs. (pres. 1957-59, dir. 1959—), Alpha Chi Sigma. Clubs: Cornell of Chgo. (pres. 1966-68), Anchor and Saber of N.Y.C. (pres. 1957-58); Tennaqua (Deerfield)). Home: 17479 Fairlie Rd San Diego CA 92128 Office: Rm 2112 Urcy Hall Univ Calif-San Diego LaJolla CA 92093

HARDY, WALTER NEWBOLD, physics educator, researcher; b. Vancouver, B.C., Mar. 25, 1940; s. Walter Thomas and Julia Marquerite (Mulroy) H.; m. Shelia Lorraine Hughes, July 10, 1959; children: Kevin James, Steven Wayne. B. SC. in Math and Physics with honors, U. B.C., 1961, Ph.D. in Physics, 1965. Postdoctral fellow Centre d'Etudes Nucleaire de Saclay, France, 1964-66; mem. tech. staff N.Am. Rockwell, Thousand Oaks, Calif., 1966-71; assoc. prof. physics U. B.C., 1971-76, prof., 1976—; vic. scientists Ecole Normale Superieure, Paris, 1980-81. Contbr. articles to sci. jours.; patentee precision microwave instrumentation. Rutherford Meml. scholar, 1964; Alfred P. Sloan fellow, 1972-74; recipient Stacie prize NRC of Can., 1978. Mem. Can. Assn. Physicists (Herzberg medal 1978), Am. Phys. Soc. Office: U British Columbia Vancouver BC Canada V6T 1W5

HARE, DAVID, playwright; b. St. Leonards, Sussex, Eng., June 5, 1947; s. Clifford Theodore and Agnes (Gilmour) H.; m. Margaret Matheson, Aug. 1970 (div. 1980); children: Joe, Lewis, Darcy. M.A., Cambridge U., 1968. Author: (plays) Slag, 1970; plays The Great Exhibition, 1971, Knuckle, 1974, Fanshen, 1975, Teeth "n' Smiles, 1975, Plenty, 1978 (N.Y. Critics Circle award for Broadway prodn. 1983), A Map of the World, 1982; TV films include Licking Hitler (Best Play of Year award Brit. Acad. Film and TV Arts 1978), Dreams of Leaving, 1980, Saigon, 1983; plays performed in, U.S. at Public Theatre, N.Y.C., Goodman Theatre, Chgo., Arena Theatre, Washington,; writer, dir.: film Wetherby, 1984; writer: screenplay Plenty, 1984; assoc. dir., Nat. Theatre, 1984; stage dir., Royal Court Theatre. Recipient Drama award Evening Standard, 1979, John Llewellyn Rhys award, 1974. Club: Dramatists. Home: 33 Ladbroke Rd London W 11 England

HARE, DAVID, artist; b. N.Y.C., 1917. Doctorate, Md. Inst. Art. Artist-in-residence Delgado Mus., New Orleans, 1964; vis. instr. sculpture Phila. Coll. Art, 1964-65; vis. artist U. Oreg., Eugene, 1966; with Tamarind Inst., U. N.Mex., Albuquerque, from 1972—. One-man shows of sculpture, 1941—, latest being, Alessandra Gallery, N.Y.C., 1976, Guggenheim Mus., N.Y.C., 1977, Hamilton Gallery, N.Y.C., 1978, Zolla Lieberman Gallery, Chgo., Hamilton Gallery, 1979, 80, numerous group shows, 1946—, latest being, Whitney Mus. Am. Art, N.Y.C., 1976, Mus. Contemporary Crafts, N.Y.C., 1977, Renwick Gallery, Washington, Rutgers U., New Brunswick, N.J., 1977, Hayward Gallery, London, Albright Knox Art Gallery, Buffalo, N.Y., 1978, Max Davidson Gallery, N.Y.C., 1980, Hamilton Gallery, N.Y.C., Contemporary Arts Mus., Houston, 1981; represented in permanent collections, Mus. Modern Art, N.Y.C., Met. Mus., N.Y.C., Whitney Mus. Am. Art, N.Y.C., Bklyn. Mus., Albright-Knox Art Gallery, Buffalo, Guggenheim Mus., N.Y.C., Akron (Ohio) Art Inst., San Francisco Mus. Art, Yale U. Art Gallery, New Haven, Washington U. Gallery of Art, St. Louis, Wadsworth Atheneum, Hartford, Conn., Brandeis U., Mass., Delgado Mus. Art, also pvt. collections; sculpture includes The Cronus Series. Lanscapes; Contbg. editor: VVV mag, 1942-44 *

HARE, FREDERICK KENNETH, geography and physics educator, university official; b. Wylye, Eng., Feb. 5, 1919; s. Frederick Eli and Irene (Smith) H.; m. Suzanne Alice Bates, Aug. 23, 1941 (div. 1952); 1 son, Christopher John; m. Helen Nielson Morrill, Dec. 26, 1953; children: Elissa Beatrice, Robin Gilbert. B.S. 1st class honors, U. London, 1939; Ph.D., U. Montreal, 1950; LL.D., Queens U., 1964, U. Western Ont., 1968, Trent U., 1979; D.Sc., McGill U., 1969, Adelaide U., 1974, York U., 1978. Asst. prof. geography McGill U., 1945-49, prof., chmn. dept. geography, 1950-62, prof. geography and meteorology, dean faculty arts and scis., 1962-64; dir. Arctic Meteorology Research Group, McGill Sub-Arctic Research Lab., 1954-62; prof. geography King's Coll., U. London, 1964-66; master of Birkbeck Coll., U. London, 1966-68; pres. U. B.C., Vancouver, Can., 1968-69; prof. geography and physics U. Toronto, Ont., Can., 1969—, Univ. prof., 1976—, dir. Inst. Environ. Studies, 1974-79; provost Trinity Coll., 1979—; gov. Trinity Coll. Sch., 1979—; dir.-gen. research coordination Can. Dept. of Environment, 1972-73, sci. adviser, 1972-74; Mem. NRC, Can., 1962-64; mem. Natural Environment Research Council, U.K., 1965-68; Bd. dirs. Resources for the Future, 1968-80; chmn. spl. programme panel on ecoscis. NATO, 1972-75; mem. Can. Environ. Adv. Council, 1973-78; Mem. corp. Woods Hole Oceanographic Inst., 1976-79; Chmn. Canadian Climate Planning Bd., 1979—. Author: The Restless Atmosphere, 1953, On University Freedom, 1967, (with M.K. Thomas) Climate Canada, 1974, 2d edit., 1979; author, editor: (with R.A. Bryson) Climates of North America; Contbr. articles to sci. publs. Served as meteorologist Brit. Air Ministry, 1941-45; flight lt., meteorol. br. R.A.F.V.R., 1943-45; Gt. Britain. Fellow King's Coll., 1967; Recipient Patterson medal, 1973, Massey medal, 1974; Patron's medal Royal Geog. Soc., 1977; decorated officer Order Can., 1978; recipient U. Toronto Alumni Faculty award, 1982. Fellow Royal Soc. Can. (Centenary medal 1982), Royal Meteorol. Soc. (past pres.), Royal Geog. Soc., Am. Geog. Soc. (hon. mem.), Arctic Inst. N.Am. (past chmn.), Canadian, Am. meteorol. socs., AAAS; mem. Geologists Assn., Inst. Brit. Geographers, Can. Assn. Geographers (past pres.), Am. Geophys. Union, Am. Quatranary Assn. Office: Trinity College Toronto ON M5S 1H8 Canada

HARE, NATHAN, editor, publisher; b. Slick, Okla., Apr. 9, 1934; s. Seddie and Tishia (Davis) H.; m. Julia Reed, Dec. 27, 1956. A.B., Langston U., 1954; M.A., U. Chgo., 1957, Ph.D., 1962; Ph.D., Calif. Sch. Profl. Psychology, San Francisco, 1975. Instr. Va. State Coll., Petersburg, 1957-58; asst. prof. sociology Howard U., Washington, 1961-67; chmn. dept. Black studies San Francisco State Coll., 1968-69, dir., 1968; founding pub. Black Scholar.; founder, pres. Black World Found.; bd. dirs. N.Am. Zonal Com. on Second World Black and African Festival Arts and Culture, Lagos, Nigeria, 1974, San Francisco Local Devel. Corp. Author: The Black Anglo Saxons, 1965; editor: Black Male/Female Relationships, 1979—; Contbr. articles to profl. jours. Recipient Disting. Alumni award Langston U., 1975, Presdl. citation Nat. Assn. Equal Opportunity in Higher Edn., 1982; Community-Clin. Psychology award So. Regional Edn. Bd., Atlanta, 1978; Nat. award Nat. Council Black Studies, 1983; Profl. Person of Yr., San Francisco chpt. Nat. Assn. Negro Bus. and Profl. Women's Clubs, 1980. Office: 1801 Bush St San Francisco CA 94109 *My main aspiration in life has been to help make the world a better place, and I have found that, in trying to make the world a better place, it has been necessary, over and over again, to try to make myself a better person. But I keep on trying.*

HARE, ROBERT LEWIS, physician; b. Rockaway, Oreg., Sept. 28, 1923; s. Clarence Lewis and Ola May (Corcoran) H.; m. Helen Josephine Archbold, July 15, 1945; children: Patricia Lynn, Kathryn Ann, Steven Archbold, Cynthia Lee, Robert Craig. B.S., U. Ill., 1947, M.D., 1949; M.S., U. Minn., 1955. Diplomate: Am. Bd. Internal Medicine. Intern U. Chgo. Hosps., 1949-50; resident Mayo Clinic, 1951-52; practice medicine, specializing in internal medicine, Portland, Oreg., 1955—; mem. attending staff Good Samaritan Hosp., Physicians and Surgeons Hosp.; clin. prof. medicine U. Oreg. Med. Sch., 1975—; v.p. Portland Metro Health Plan, 1975—; pres. Multnomah Found. for Med. Care, 1983—; active Nat. Profl. Standards Rev. Council, 1976-79. Editorial bd.: Western Jour. Medicine, 1977—; contbr. articles to med. jours. Served with AUS, 1943-45; M.C., U.S. Army, 1952-53. Fellow ACP; mem. AMA, Oreg. Med. Assn. (past pres.), Am. Soc. Internal Medicine (Spl. Recognition award 1977, chmn. com. on assessment of performance, trustee 1979—), Oreg. Soc. Internal Medicine (past pres.), Diabetes Assn. Oreg. (past pres.), Alpha Omega Alpha, Phi Kappa Epsilon. Methodist. Club: Multnomah Athletic. Home: 1665 SW Highland Pkwy Portland OR 97221 Office: 2232 NW Pettygrove St Portland OR 97210

HARE, ROBERT YATES, music history educator; b. McGrann, Pa., June 14, 1921; s. Robert Deemar and Beulah (Yates) H.; m. Constance King Rutherford, Mar. 31, 1948; children: Stephen, Beverly, Madeleine. Mus.B., U. Detroit, 1948; M.A., Wayne State U., 1950; Ph.D., U. Iowa, 1959. Instr. Marietta (Ohio) Coll., 1949-51, Del Mar Coll., Corpus Christi, Tex., 1951-55; prof., chmn. grad. studies San Jose (Calif.) State U., 1956-65; prof., dean Eastern Ill. U. Music, 1965-74; prof. music history and lit. Ohio State U., Columbus, 1974—, dir. Sch. Music, 1974-78, dir. audio-rec. engring., 1979-82, arts adminstr. research and faculty devel., 1982—; cons. in field; Mem. council music edn. in higher edn. Ill. Music Educators Assn., 1969—. Condr. coll. symphony band, 1956-63; condr., San Jose Youth Symphony, 1957-59; condr. univ. symphony, 1968-74; Contbr. articles to profl. jours.; French horn recitals, Carnegie Music Hall, Pitts., 1940, 42; French hornist, Pitts. Symphony Orch., 1941-43, 44-45, Buffalo Philharmonic, 1943-44, Cin. Summer Opera Co., 1945, Indpls. Symphony Orch., 1945-46, San Antonio Symphony Orch., 1947-49; orchestrator, San Antonio Symphony Orch. Mem. com. grad. and profl. edn. in arts and humanities Ill. Bd. Higher Edn., 1969-70; mem. performing arts commn. Ill. Sesquicentennial, 1967; mem. exec. bd. Greater Columbus Arts Council, 1974-76, Ohio Alliance for Arts in Edn., 1974-76; trustee Columbus Symphony Orch., 1975-79. Recipient Profl. Promise scholarship Carnegie Inst. Tech., 1939. Mem. Music Educators Nat. Conf. (publs. planning com. 1970-76), Mus. Tchrs. Nat. Assn., Am. Musicol. Soc., Coll. Music Soc., Internat. Musicol. Soc., Phi Mu Alpha, Sinfonia (hon.), Pi Kappa Lambda. Lodges: Masons; Shriners. Home: 2494 Farleigh Rd Columbus OH 43221 Office: Coll of Arts 305 Mershon Auditorium Columbus OH 43210

HARE, WOODROW WILSON, plant pathologist, educator emeritus; b. nr. Scooba, Miss., Aug. 10, 1915; s. William Henry and Madie (Daws) H.; m. Mary Louise Eckles, June 23, 1940; children—Marjorie Jane (Mrs. William Lester Self Andrews), Julia Katherine (Mrs. Alney Austin Baham). A.A., E. Miss. Jr. Coll., 1934; B.S., Miss. State U., 1937, M.S., 1940; Ph.D., U. Wis., 1943. Instr. plant pathology and agronomy U. Wis., 1943-45, asst. prof., 1945-48; asso. prof. plant pathology Miss. State U., Mississippi State, 1948-57, prof. plant pathology, 1957-64, head plant pathology and weed sci., 1964-80, emeritus head and prof., 1981—; Vice pres., dir. Harson Growers, Inc., Wiggins, Miss. Contbr. articles to profl. jours. Trustee East Miss. Jr. Coll., 1977. Served from ensign to lt. (j.g.) USNR, 1944-46. Recipient award in plant pathology CIBA-Geigy Co., 1976; named Alumnus of Yr. East Miss. Jr. Coll., 1976. Mem. Bot. Soc. Am., AAAS, Am. Phytopathol. Soc. (pres. So. div. 1957, nat. council 1958-59, editorial bd. Phytopathology 1969-73), Sigma Xi, Beta Beta Beta, Kappa Mu Epsilon, Gamma Sigma Delta, Phi Kappa Phi. Developed and released disease-resistant varieties of vegetable crops. Home: 215 Bridle Path Starkville MS 39759 Office: Drawer PG Mississippi State MS 39762 *Remember that this is a brief trip and we are promised no tomorrows; enjoy a little, make a little progress, and do a little good for somebody every day.*

HARFORD, JAMES JOSEPH, association executive; b. Jersey City, Aug. 19, 1924; s. Thomas William and Jane Hume (Henderson) H.; m. Mildred Rita Waters, Apr. 19, 1952; children: Susan Gately, James Joseph, Peter Benedict (dec.), Jennifer, Christopher. B.S. in Mech. Engring, Yale, 1945. Sales engr. Worthington Corp., 1946-49; asso. editor Modern Industry, 1950-52; free-lance writer, Europe, 1952-53; exec. sec. Am. Rocket Soc., 1953-63; exec. dir. Am. Inst. Aeros. and Astronautics, 1963—; mem. U.S. del. Internat. Astronautical Congresses, 1959—. Served as ensign USNR, 1945-46. Fellow AIAA, AAAS, Brit. Interplanetary Soc., Royal Aero. Soc. (asso.); mem. Council Engring. and Sci. Soc. Execs. (v.p. 1978). Home: 601 Lake Dr Princeton NJ 08540 Office: 1633 Broadway New York NY 10019

HARGADON, BERNARD JOSEPH, JR., consumer goods company executive; b. Ardmore, Pa., Dec. 27, 1927; s. Bernard Joseph and Anna Mendenhall (Lancaster) H.; m. Mary Lee Jones, June 13, 1953; children: Geoffrey, Robert, Louise, Lawrence, David. B.S., Drexel U., 1952, M.B.A., 1959. Auditor Gen. Motors Corp., 1955-57; prof. acctg. Drexel U., 1957-59; with AID, Colombia, 1960-63, Foremost-McKesson, San Francisco, 1964—; pres. Foremost-McKesson Internat., 1980—; adj. prof. internat. bus. Golden Gate U. Author: in Spanish Principles of Accounting, 1964, Principles of Cost Accounting, 1971. Bd. govs. San Francisco Symphony.; trustee Golden Gate U. Served with USN, 1945-48. Roman Catholic. Clubs: San Francisco Tennis, Boundary Oaks Tennis (Walnut Creek, Calif.); World Trade. Office: 1 Post St San Francisco CA 94104

HARGER, ARTHUR JAMES, author, corp. exec., designer; b. Lansing, Mich., Dec. 9, 1941; s. Chester Arthur and Lucille (Wilkie) H. B.S., U. Oreg., 1963; M.S., UCLA, 1964; M.Arch., Interlochen Inst. Art. Co-founder, officer ELI Inc., Wilmington, 1963—, pres., 1970-71, chmn. bd., 1971—; dir., pres. Agritame, Inc., Wilmington, pres., 1972—; dir., pres. New Equity Generators Inc., Wilmington, 1977—; dir. Amiable Androids Inc., Satel-Strike Systems Inc., Weave-A-Loom Inc., Cheeselovers World, Inc., All Prins. Inc., Discotext, Inc., Elgin Marble Exchange, Inc., Frigid Midgets Inc., Gallimaufry Galleria Inc, Hydropon-Gro Inc., Insurage Inc., Lettuce Rutabaga U Inc., Librarie Hachure Ltd., numerous others. Author: Negative Heights; contbr. articles to mags. Sec. U. Oreg. chpt. Sierra Club, 1962; co-founder nat. chpt. Youth for Kennedy, 1960, Peace and Freedom Party, 1968, Civil Libertarian Party; trustee, sec. Harger Timber Trust; trustee Agricorps Found., Green Power Found. Machris fellow, 1963; Ford Found. fellow, 1964. Mem. Izaak Walton League (sec. 1966-67), Soc. Progressive Ams. Celestial Exploration, Dem. Activists Internat Sci., Aircraft Owners and Pilots Assn., Nat. Bus. Aircraft Assn. Clubs: Sun Valley (Ketchum, Idaho); South Coast Sailing (Newport Beach, Calif.); Sun Jupiter Island (Fla.) Sailing, Michilimackinac Sail Ski & Tee. Office: 130 Shepard St Lansing MI 48912

HARGER, ROBERT OWENS, elec. engr.; b. Flint, Mich., Sept. 15, 1932; s. Ervin Robinson and Vera May (Fisher) H.; children—Eric, Peter, Karl, Laura. B.S.E. in Math, U. Mich., 1955, M.S.E. in Elec. Engring, 1959, Ph.D., 1961. Research engr. Inst. Sci. and Tech., U. Mich., Ann Arbor, 1960-68, asst. prof. elec. engring., 1962-65; asso. prof. elec. engring. U. Md., College Park, 1968-75, prof., 1975—, chmn. elec. engring. dept., 1975-80; cons. in field. Author: Synthetic Aperture Radar Systems, 1970; editor: Optical Communication Theory, 1977. Served with USN, 1955-58. Fellow IEEE (Carlton award 1977); mem. AAAS. Office: Elec Engring Dept U Md College Park MD 20742

HARGETT, BILLY HOWELL, banker; b. Harris County, Ga., Nov. 7, 1928; s. Edwin Starr and Myrtice Mildred (Howell) H.; m. Eleanor Rosa Mehaffey, July 12, 1953; children: Linda C., Hargett DaSilva, Susan E. Hargett McElhannon, Betty H., Cynthia S. Student, North Ga. Coll., Dahlonega, 1945-47; B.B.A., U. Ga., 1949; cert. Stonier Grad. Sch. Banking, Rutgers U., 1958, Harvard U. Program Mgmt. Devel., 1961. With Fed. Res. Bank, Atlanta, 1949-66, Jacksonville, Fla., 1949-66, asst. v.p., Atlanta, 1966-68, v.p., 1968-74, sr. v.p., 1974—. Mem. Willing Hands, Jacksonville, 1961; Atlanta C. of C., 1968-70; mem.adminstrv. bd., fin. com. Briarcliff United Methodist Ch. Served to 1st lt. U.S. Army, 1951-53; Korea. Mem. U. Ga. Alumni Assn. (bd. mgrs. 1972-78), Am. Inst. Banking, Bank Adminstrn. Inst. Clubs: Harvard, Leslie Beach (Atlanta). Home: 2574 Sugarplum Ct Atlanta GA 30345 Office: Federal Reserve Bank of Atlanta 104 Marietta St NW Atlanta GA 30303

HARGIS, BILLY JAMES, clergyman; b. Texarkana, Tex., Aug. 3, 1925; s. Jimmie Earsel and Laura Lucille (Fowler) H.; m. Betty Jane Secrest, Dec. 21, 1951; children—Bonnie Jane, Billy James II, Becky Jean, Brenda Jo. Student, Ozark Bible Coll., 1943-45; B.A., Pikes Peak Bible Sem., 1957; Th.B., Burton Coll., 1958; LL.D., Bob Jones U., 1961. Ordained to ministry Christian Ch., 1943; pastor Christian chs., Sallisaw, Okla., 1944-46, Granby, Mo., 1946-47, Sapulpa, Okla., 1947-50, Ch. of Christian Crusade, Tulsa, 1966—; founder, pres. Christian Echoes Nat. Ministry, Inc., Tulsa, 1948—, Am. Christian Coll., 1970-74; Pub. Christian Crusade Newspaper, 1948—; speaker Christian Crusade network radio broadcasts, 1949—, syndicated TV series Pray for America, 1979-82; founder, chmn. bd. David Livingston Missionary Found., 1970-80, Soc., 1974-80; founder, pres. Billy James Hargis Evang. Assn., 1975—, Ch. of Christian Crusade, 1966—, Ams. Against Abortion, 1971—, Good Samaritan Children's Found., Inc., 1975—. Author: Communist America - Must It Be, 1960, Communism The Total Lie, 1961, Facts About Communism and Churches, 1962, The Real Extremists - The Far Left, 1964, Distortion By Design, 1965, Why I Fight For A Christian America, 1974, Thou Shalt Not Kill—My Babies, 1977, The Depth Principle, 1977, The Disaster File, 1978, Riches and Prosperity Through Christ, 1978, The National News Media, 1980, The Cross and the Sickle-Super Church, 1982, Abortion on Trial, 1982. Home: Rose of Sharon Farm Neosho MO 64850 Office: Suite 175 5800 E Skelly Dr Tulsa OK 74135 *If I have achieved any success in this life, it is because I take God at His Word and act upon it, and I love the free enterprise, democratic concept of the United States with all my heart and am willing to be branded an extremist in my defense of these ideals. It is because of my love of New Testament Christianity and the United States that I have tried to add my voice for God and Country.*

HARGRAVE, ALEXANDER DAVIDSON, banker; b. Canadaigua, N.Y., Mar. 17, 1920; s. Thomas J. and Catherine (Davidson) H.; m. Marcia; children: Susan Hargrave Hopeman, Alexander MacKenzie, Charles Crouch, Margaret. A.B., Princeton U., 1941; LL.B. cum laude, Harvard U., 1948. Bar: N.Y. 1948. With firm Nixon, Hargrave, Devans & Doyle, Rochester, N.Y., 1948-63, partner, 1953-63; exec. v.p. Lincoln First Bank Rochester, 1963-68, pres., 1968-74, chief exec. officer, 1970-74, also dir.; v.p., sec., treas. Lincoln 1st Banks Inc., 1967-74, pres., 1974-78, chief exec. officer, 1976-84, chmn., 1976—, also dir.; chief exec. officer Lincoln First Bank NA, 1979-84, chmn., 1979—; chmn. Visa U.S.A. Inc., 1975-84, Visa Internat., 1977-84; dir. Sybron Corp., Gleason Works, Rochester Telephone Corp., Bausch & Lomb Inc. Past pres., past bd. dirs. United Way of Greater Rochester; trustee Internat. Mus. Photography at George Eastman House; past pres. Highland Hosp., Rochester; trustee Rochester Inst. Tech.; bd. dirs. Rochester/Monroe County Conv. and Publicity Bur., Inc., Automobile Club Rochester. Served to lt. comdr. USNR, 1941-45; PTO. Mem. ABA, N.Y. State Bar Assn. Clubs: Country of Rochester, Genesee Valley (Rochester). Office: 1 Lincoln First Sq Rochester NY 14643

HARGRAVE, CAROLYN H., college administrator. Provost, vice chancellor for acad. affairs La. State U., Baton Rouge. Office: La State U Office of Provost Baton Rouge LA 70803§

HARGRAVE, ROBERT WEBB, banker; b. Evansville, Ind., May 8, 1920; s. William Jasper and Erma Christina (Fabian) H.; m. Florence Molyneaux, Nov. 11, 1944; children—Robert Webb, Christine (Mrs. Stuart Wolff), Thomas, Susan, John, Michael, Jane Ann. B.S., U. Notre Dame, 1942. With Haskins & Sells (C.P.A.'s), Chgo., 1945-47; accountant Bell & Gossett, Morton Grove, Ill., 1947-48; pres., dir. Citizens Nat. Bank, Evansville, 1948—; dir. Ryan Contracting Co. Mem. Sheriff's Merit Bd.; Bd. dirs. St. Marys Hosp. Found., Evansville Scholastic Soc. Served with USNR, 1942-45. Mem. Evansville C. of C., Evansville Estate Planning Council. Roman Catholic. Clubs: K.C., Evansville Country, Petroleum. Home: 2401 E Chandler St Evansville IN 47714 Office: 19 NW 4th St Evansville IN 47708

HARGRAVE, RUDOLPH, judge Oklahoma Supreme Court; b. Shawnee, Okla., Feb. 15, 1925; s. John Hubert and Daisy (Holmes) H.; m. Madeline Hargrave, May 29, 1949; children: Cindy Lu, John Robert, Jana Sue. LL.B., U. Okla., 1949. Began legal practice at, Wewoka, 1949; asst. county atty., Seminole County, 1951-55; judge Seminole County Ct., 1964-67, Seminole County Superior Ct., 1967-69; dist. judge Okla. Dist. Ct., Dist. 22, 1969-79; assoc. justice Okla. Supreme Ct., 1979—; news dir. Sta.-KWSH. Mem. adv. com. Boy Scouts Am. Mem. Seminole County Bar Assn., Okla. Bar Assn., ABA. Democrat. Methodist. Lodges: Lions; Masons. Office: Supreme Ct Okla State Capitol Lincoln Blvd Oklahoma City OK 73105 *

HARGRAVE, SARAH QUESENBERRY, corporate foundation executive; b. Mt. Airy, N.C., Dec. 11, 1944; d. Teddie W. and Lois Knight (Slusher) Quesenberry. Student, Radford Coll., 1963-64, Va. Poly. Inst. and State U., 1964-67. Mgmt. trainee Thalhimer Bros. Dept. Store, Richmond, Va., 1967-68; Central Va. fashion and publicity dir. Sears Roebuck & Co., Richmond, 1968-73, nat. decorating sch. coordinator, Chgo., 1973-74, nat. dir. bus. and profl. women's programs, 1974-76; v.p., treas., program dir. Sears-Roebuck Found., Chgo., 1976—, program mgr. corp. contbns. and memberships, 1981—. Bd. dirs. Am. Assembly Collegiate Schs. Bus., 1979-82, mem. vis. com., 1979-82, mem. fin. and audit com., 1980-82, mem. task force on doctoral supply and demand, 1980-82; mem. Com. for Equal Opportunity for Women, 1976; chmn., 1978-79, 80-81; mem. bus. adv. council Walter E. Heller Coll. Bus. Adminstrn., Roosevelt U., 1979—; co-dir. Ill. Internat. Women's Yr. Ctr., 1975. Named Outstanding Young Women of Yr., Ill., 1976, Women of Achievement State Street Bus. and Profl. Woman's Club, 1978. Mem. Assn. Humanistic Psychology, Am. Home Econs. Assn., Nat. Fedn. Bus. and Profl. Women's Clubs, Women and Founds.-Corp. Philanthropy, Eddystone Condominium Assn. (v.p. 1978—). Home: 421 W Melrose St Chicago IL 60657 Office: Sears-Roebuck Found Sears Tower Chicago IL 60684

HARGRAVE, VICTORIA ELIZABETH, librarian; b. Ripon, Wis., Aug. 22, 1913; d. Alexander Walter and Estelle Winifred (Swanson) H. A.B., Ripon Coll., 1934; library diploma, U. Wis., 1938; M.A., U. Chgo., 1947; postgrad., U. Cal. at Los Angeles, 1970. Tchr. Brandon (Wis.) High Sch., 1934-37; extension librarian Ia. State Coll. Library, 1938-44; librarian Ripon Coll., 1944-46, MacMurray Coll., 1947-78; Mem. adv. council librarians U. Ill. Grad. Sch. Library Sci., 1962-64. Mem. A.L.A., AAUW. Home: 141 Caldwell St Jacksonville IL 62650

HARGREAVES, ROBERT, educator, orchestra conductor; b. Baxenden, Lancashire, Eng., Aug. 20, 1914; came to U.S., 1923, naturalized, 1938; s. William and Mary Elizabeth (Hankinson); m. Katherine Elizabeth Benedict, Apr. 11, 1938; children: Hall Robert, Daniel Dewhurst, Mary LeValley. A.B. summa cum laude, Albion Coll., 1936, Mus. D. honoris causa, 1969; M.Mus., Eastman Sch. Music, U. Rochester, 1939, Ph.D., 1941; Mus.D. (hon.), Chgo. Coll. Conservatory Music, 1977; student, Ecole Monteux, summers 1951-52. Supr. music pub. schs., Chelsea, Mich., 1936-38; teaching fellow Eastman Sch. Music, 1938-41; dir. grad. studies Ill. Wesleyan U., 1941-45; guest lectr. Drake U. Coll. Fine Arts, 1942; founder Bloomington-Normal Symphony Orch., 1944, Nat. Orch. Arrangers' Festival, 1944; dir. sch. music Ball State U., 1945-81, dir. emeritus sch. music, 1981—; founder Muncie Symphony Orch., 1949; guest prof. U. Tex. Coll. Fine Arts, 1953; Examiner for Nat. Commn. Accreditation; Tchr. Edn. North Central Assn. Nat. Assn. Schs. of Music. Guest condr., String Symphony, Am. Symphony Orch. League, 1954; premiere season, French Lick Music Festival, 1957, Indpls. Philharmonic Orch., 1963, Nashville Symphony and Chamber Orch., 1967, Prague Symphony, 1972, Orquesta Sinfónico Provinciale de Santa Fe, Argentina, 1980, 81, Orquesta Sinfónico Provinciale de Santa Fe, also Chaco and Corrientes, Argentina, 1980, Orquesta Sinfónico Provinciale de Santa Fe, Rosario, 1981; condr. tours, Am. Allegro Ballet Co., 1958-66, premiere performances, Indpls. Civic Ballet, 1959, N.E. Regional Festival Ballet Gala (7 cos.), 1967, Chgo. Chamber Players, 1978—; columnist: The Indiana Musicator; Author: The Teaching of Brass Instruments in School Music Supervisors Training Courses, 1952, Survey of Available Data on the Violin Vibrato, 1939; Editorial asso.: Jour. of Research in Music Edn; Editorial com.: Music for Everybody; Contbr. articles music, edn. publs. Recipient awards Rockefeller Found., Kulas Found., A.S.C.A.P., Am. Symphony Orch. League for study of conducting with Eugene Ormandy, Alfred Wallenstein, and George Szell; Outstanding Young Man award Muncie Jaycees; Outstanding Faculty Service award Ball State U., 1978; Outstanding Faculty Creative Endeavor award, 1981. Mem. Nat. Assn. Schs. Music (regional v.p. 1956-57, chmn. com. research 1959-63, chmn. grad. commn. 1965, pres. 1966-70, hon. mem. 1980), Internat. Platform Assn., Ind. Music Educators Assn. (bd. dirs.), Am. String Tchrs. Assn. (pres. Ind. div. 1948-53), NEA, Symphony Orch. League, Nat. Sch. Orch. Assn., Music Tchrs. Nat. Assn., Nat. Music Council (bd. dirs. 1969—), Tau Kappa Epsilon, Phi Mu Alpha Sinfonia (province gov. 1949-51, nat. hon. mem., Orpheus award 1981), Pi Kappa Lambda, Phi Beta (nat. hon. patron 1962), Sigma Alpha Iota. Home: 2610 Bay Dr Bradenton FL 33507

HARGREAVES, WILLIAM JAMES, chemical company executive; b. Bay City, Mich., Apr. 1, 1921; s. Christopher and Grace H.; m. Julia L. Nikolai, May 29, 1947; children: Michael, Deborah. Student, Bay City Jr. Coll.; B.S. in Chem. Engring., Mich. State U., 1946; postgrad., Case Western Res. U., 1959; grad. Advanced Mgmt. Program, Harvard U., 1966. With Dow Corning Corp., Midland, Mich., 1946—, exec. v.p., 1977—, also dir. Trustee Delta Coll. Served with USN, 1943-46. Mem. Am. Inst. Chem. Engrs. Presbyterian. Lodge: Rotary. Home: 411 Arbor Dr Midland MI 48640 Office: Dow Corning Corp PO Box 1767 Midland MI 48640

HARGROVE, JAMES WARD, financial consultant; b. Shreveport, La., Oct. 31, 1922; s. Reginald H. and Hallie (Ward) H.; m. Marion Elizabeth Smith, Aug. 25, 1942; children: James W., Florence, Thomas M., William H. Grad., Sewanee Mil. Acad., 1939; B.A., Rice Inst., 1943. Sec., treas. Caddo Abstract Co., 1946-47; with Tex. Eastern Transmission Corp., 1947-69, successively office mgr., asst. sec., asst. treas., sec., treas., 1947-54, v.p., sec., 1954-58, v.p. finance, 1958-67, sec., 1958-63, sr. v.p., 1967-69; asst. postmaster gen. finance and adminstrn. U.S. Postal Service, Washington, 1969-71, sr. asst. postmaster gen. support, 1971-72; fin. cons., Houston, 1972-76, U.S. ambassador, Australia, 1976-77; chmn. Vaughan, Nelson & Hargrove, Inc. (investment counselors), 1977—83; fin. cons., 1983—; Gov.-adviser Rice U. Mem. Phi Beta Kappa. Home: 60 Tiel Way Houston TX Office: 6300 Tex Commerce Tower Houston TX 77002

HARGROVES, VERNON CARNEY, clergyman; b. Nansemond County, Va., Sept. 4, 1900; s. Robert Tatem and Emily Martha (Carney) H.; m. Narcissa Bruce Daniel, Dec. 1, 1928; children—Narcissa Daniel, Emily Carney, Jeannette Snead. A.B., Princeton, 1922, M.A., 1927; Th.G., So. Baptist Theol. Sem., 1925; D.D., U. Richmond, 1941; LL.D., Temple U., 1955. Instr. Am. Sch., Kuling, China, 1922-23; pastor Princeton (N.J.) Bapt. Ch., 1925-27, Weatherford Meml. Ch., Richmond, Va., 1928-32, 2d Bapt. Ch. of Germantown, Phila., 1932-71; preaching mission to, Russia, 1955, 58, Czechoslovakia and Hungary, 1964, fellowship mission to, Romania and Yugoslavia, 1966, to, Russia, 1971; Trustee, past moderator Phila. Bapt. Assn.; dir., past pres. Phila. Council Chs.; pres. Am. Bapt. Conv., 1954-55; v.p. Bapt. World Alliance, 1960-65, pres., 1970-75; chmn. N. Am. Bapt. Fellowship, 1966-68. Contbr. to various publs., nat. and denominational.; Chmn. editorial com.: The Secret Place, 1950-54. Chmn. Phila. Medal Honor Award Com., 1954-55, 66—; Past bd. dirs. Community Chest of Phila.; v.p. 1922 Found., Princeton U. Mem. Pa. Bible Soc. (pres. 1977—), Phi Kappa Sigma, Phi Alpha, Phi Beta Kappa (alumnus mem.). Clubs: Rotarian., Morgan Edwards (Phila.). Home: 7806 Linden Rd Philadelphia PA 19118 *I am an idealist and, I believe, a realist. It is possible that the only true realist is an idealist.*

HARI, KENNETH STEPHEN, painter; b. Perth Amboy, N.J., Mar. 31, 1947; s. Stephen John and Jeannette Anna (Matuszewski) H. Diploma, Newark Sch. Fine and Indsl. Arts, 1966; B.F.A., Md. Inst. Art, 1968. Cons. various cos. Exhibited in group shows at, Md. State Mus., 1967, Union Coll., Schenectady, 1969, Monmouth (N.J.) Coll., 1970, Newark Mus., 1971, Trenton State Coll., 1972, one-man exhbns. include, C.C. Price Gallery, N.Y.C., H.S. Graphics, Ltd., Keasbey, N.J.; represented in permanent collections, Vatican, Lincoln Center Gallery for Performing Arts, N.Y.C., Va. Poly. Inst., Blacksburg, N.J. State Mus., Trenton, Grand Ole Opry House, Nashville, other pub. and pvt. collections; Important works include portraits of, W.H. Auden, N.Y.C., 1969, M. Moore, N.Y.C., Pablo Casals, Marlboro, Vt., 1970, Andres Segovia, N.Y.C., 1972, James Michener, Pipersville, Pa., 1973, Marcel Marceau, N.Y.C., Donald Delue, N.Y.C., Dr. Allan Callow, Boston, Kurt Vonnegut, Jr., Buckminster Fuller, Lord Hailsham, London, 1978, Dr. Linus Pauling for Pauling Inst., Menlo Park, Calif., 1979, Paul Robeson for Paul Robeson Center, Rutgers U., Newark (Hay award recipients.); Original lithographs pub. Prophet, 1971, Lovers of Our Time, 1971, Vermont, 1972, Folk Singer, Marcel Marceau, 1973, Abraham, 1973, Ernest Hemingway, 1978, Homage to Virginia, 1980, Tropical Ladies, 1981. Bd. dirs. N.J. Art Festival, 1973—. Address: 228 Sherman St Perth Amboy NJ 08861 also Dr John Eastman care HSG Ltd Box 243 Keasbey NJ 08832 *Art is the soul of man, and without it he is lost.*

HARIG, ROBERT G., manufacturing corporation executive; b. Chgo., Sept. 1, 1921; s. Michael and Rose (Ruchs) H.; m. Joyce, May 25, 1974 (div.); children: James, Linda, Lois, Michael, Steven, Thomas. Pres. Darling Store Fixtures, Inc., Paragould, Ark. Home: PO Box 837 Paragould AR 82450 Office: Darling Store Fixtures PO Box 970 Paragould AR 92450

HARING, ELLEN STONE (MRS. E.S. HARING), educator; b. Los Angeles, Dec. 1921; d. Earl E. and Eleanor (Pritchard) Stone; m. Philip S. Haring, Dec. 1942 (div. June 1951). B.A., Bryn Mawr Coll., 1942; M.A., Radcliffe Coll., 1943, Ph.D. (AAUW fellow), 1959. Adminstrv. worker A.R.C., Boston, 1943; mem. faculty Wheaton Coll., Norton, Mass., 1944-45, Wellesley Coll., 1945-72, asso. prof., 1958-64, prof. philosophy, 1964-72, U. Fla., Gainesville, 1972—, chmn. dept., 1972-80. Mem. Am. Philos. Assn., Metaphys. Soc. Am. Office: ASB 240 U Fla Gainesville FL 32611

HARING, EUGENE MILLER, lawyer; b. Washington, May 16, 1927; s. Horace E. and Edith (Miller) H.; m. Janet K. Marshall, Apr. 10, 1971. A.B. summa cum laude, Princeton U., 1949, A.M. (Woodrow Wilson fellow), 1951; LL.B., Harvard U., 1955. Bar: N.J. 1955, N.Y., U.S. Dist Ct. N.J., U.S. Ct. Appeals (3d cir.), U.S. Supreme Ct. Asst. in instrn. Princeton U., 1950-52; assoc. firm McCarter & English, Newark, 1955-61, ptnr., 1961—; dir., mem. exec. com. Columbian Mut. Life Ins. Co., Binghamton, N.Y., 1962-80; mem. ct. computerization com. Supreme Ct. N.J., 1981-83. Contbr. articles to profl. jours. Chmn. United Campaign, Summit, N.J., 1966-67, trustee, 1967-69; trustee Princeton Prospect Found., 1965-69; chmn. Princeton Twp. Zoning Bd. Adjustment, 1979-80; vestryman Trinity Episcopal Ch., Princeton, 1975-79, warden, 1980—; mem. com. on constn. and canons Episc. Diocese of N.J., 1980—, chancellor, 1983—. Served with USNR, 1945-46. Mem. Fed. Bar Assn. (com. trial advocacy specialization 1978—), ABA, N.J. Bar Assn. (ins. com. 1972—, chmn. 1981—), Essex County Bar Assn., Mercer County Bar Assn., Am. Law Inst., Am. Judicature Soc., Internat. Assn. Ins. Counsel, Harvard Law Sch. Assn. N.J. (pres. 1971-72, nat. v.p. 1972-73), Phi Beta Kappa. Clubs: Princeton (N.Y.C.); Essex (Newark); Nassau (Princeton, N.J.). Home: 75 Rosedale Ln Princeton NJ 08540 also Office: 550 Broad St Newark NJ 07102

HARING, HOWARD JACK, magazine editor; b. Boyertown, Pa., Aug. 7, 1924; s. Howard and Beulah (Rose) H.; m. Rosalind Kenyon Hoyle, Dec. 10, 1949; children: Christopher, Jeffrey, Douglas, Andrea, Eric. A.B., Muhlenberg Coll., 1948; M.J., Columbia U., 1949. Reporter, Providence Jour.-Bull., 1949; editor Boyertown (Pa.) Times, 1950; reporter Allentown (Pa.) Morning Call, 1951-53; sports columnist, TV mag. editor Washington Star, 1954-58; asso. editor Saturday Evening Post, Phila., 1958-62; copy chief Ladies Home Jour., N.Y.C., 1963-69; exec. editor Boys' Life mag., North Brunswick, N.J., 1970-71; editor Exploring mag., 1972-74; sr. editor Guideposts mag., N.Y.C., 1975-81, mng. editor, 1982—; instr. editing newspapers and periodicals Am. U., Washington, 1955-58. Editor numerous books for, Curtis Pub. Co., Scribner's and Reader's Digest Books; revised, edited: Pete Martin's Jerry Giesler, 1957. Vice-chmn. Indsl. Commn. West Windsor Twp., N.J., 1970-72, chmn., 1973-74. Served with AUS, 1942-46. Decorated Purple Heart. Mem. Am. Soc. Mag. Editors. Home: 6 Piedmont Dr Cranbury NJ 08512 Office: Guideposts 747 3d Ave New York NY 10017

HARING, OLGA MUNK, medical educator, physician; b. Oradea, Bihor, Romania, Aug. 25, 1917; came to U.S., 1949; d. Moris and Ilona (Lindenbaum) Munk; m. Tibor J. Haring, Feb. 20, 1938 (div. Jan. 1961); 1 dau., Claire. B.A., Jewish Girls Gymnasium, Budapest, Hungary, 1932; M.D., U. Vienna, 1938, Leon U., Nicaragua, 1939; postgrad., Sorbonne U., Paris, 1947-49. Diplomate: Am. Bd. Internal Medicine. Med. dir. pub. health dept. Health Ctr. 1, Managua, Nicaragua, 1940-46; chief of service cardiology ward, fgn. asst. medicine and cardiology Gen. Hosp., Managua, 1946-47; trustee in medicine and cardiology Laribosiere Hosp., Paris, 1947-49; intern St. Francis Sanitorium for Cardiac Children, Roslyn, N.Y., 1950; research assoc. div. cardiology Chg. Med. Sch., 1950-57; clin. assoc. in medicine Chgo. Med. Sch., 1953-57; assoc. of chief of service Univ.-La Rabida Sanitarium, 1952-57; Hektoen Inst. fellow in pediatric cardiology Cook County Children's Hosp., 1951; rotating intern Mt. Sinai Hosp., Chgo., 1952, chief cardiac pediatric clinic, 1952-57; resident in medicine Chgo. Wesley Meml. Hosp., 1960-61, Cook County Hosp., Chgo., 1961-62; research assoc. in teratology Congenital Heart Disease Research and Tng. Ctr.-Hektoen Inst. Med. Research, Chgo., 1962-66; assoc. attending physician div. medicine Cook County Hosp.-Northwestern U. Med. Sch., Chgo., 1964—, mem. univ. faculty dept. medicine, 1965—, prof., 1974—, prof. dept. community health and preventive medicine, 1974—, dir. med. sch. cardio-pulmonary-renal clinics, 1965-75, dir. cardiac clinics, 1975—, prof. Grad. Sch., 1972—; attending staff physician Northwestern Meml. Hosp., Chgo., 1966—; attending physician VA Lakeside Hosp., Chgo., 1975—. Contbr. numerous articles, abstracts to profl. jours. Fellow in social pediatrics UN Children's Emergency Fund-U., Paris, 1948; grantee NIH, 1956-61, 67-73, Chgo. Heart Assn., 1962-66, Health Resources Adminstrn., 1972-76, Nat. Heart and Lung Inst., 1974-79, 77-82. Fellow ACP, Am. Coll. Cardiology, Am. Heart Assn. (council on circulation), Inst. Medicine in Chgo., Sigma Xi; mem. Am. Fedn. Clin. Research, AAAS, Assn. Computing Machinery, Assn. Health Records, AAUP, Am. Med. Women's Assn., Am. Geriatrics Assn., Am. Gerontology Soc. Democrat. Jewish. Home: 1201 Judson St Evanston IL 60202 Office: Dept Medicine Northwestern U Med Sch 303 E Chicago Chicago IL 60611

HARKARVY, BENJAMIN, ballet master, choreographer; b. N.Y.C. Student, New Sch., Sch. Am. Ballet; also ballet schs. of, Mme. Anderson-Ivantzova, Edward Caton, George Chaffee. Dir. Benjamin Harkarvy Ballet Sch. and Co., N.Y.C., 1951-57; Mem. com. awarding choreographic commns. Ministry Arts and Scis., Holland, 1967—. Artistic dir., Royal Winnipeg (Can.) Ballet, 1957-58; ballet master, Netherlands Ballet, 1958-59; founder, artistic dir., ballet master, Netherlands Dance Theatre, 1959-69; artistic dir., Harkness Ballet, 1969-70, Netherlands Nat. Ballet, 1970-71, Pa. Ballet, 1972—; choreographer, Canadian Broadcasting Co.-TV, 1957-58; Created: ballets Poems of Love and the Seasons, Recital for Cello and Eight Dancers, Madrigalesco, Grand Pas Espagnol, Visage, Time Passed Summer, Continuum, From Gentle Circles.

HARKE, DOUGLAS JAMES, physicist, educator, university dean; b. Edmonton, Alta., Can., Apr. 18, 1942; naturalized, 1976; s. Alvin Herbert and Donna (Henkelman) H.; m. Diana Archer, Aug. 21, 1964; children: Douglas, Russell, Andrew. B.S., U. Alta., 1963; M.A. in Edn, Washington U., St. Louis, 1964; M.S., Ph.D., Purdue U., 1969. High sch. physics tchr., Leduc, Can., 1964-65, South Bend, Ind., 1965-67; asst. prof. physics SUNY, Geneseo, 1969-74, dean grad. studies and research, 1974—. Author: Tests in Physics, 1972. NSF fellow, 1963-64; David Ross Found. fellow, 1969. Mem. Am. Assn. Physics Teachers, Nat. Council Univ. Research Adminstrs., Nat. Assn. for Research in Sci. Teaching. Office: Erwin 202 SUNY Geneseo NY 14454

HARKER, ROBERT IAN, geologist, educator; b. Glasgow, Scotland, Aug. 2, 1926; came to U.S., 1953, naturalized, 1961; s. George Percival and Hilda (McAldowie) H.; m. Marina Adele Pundt, June 5, 1955; children: Elizabeth, Jennifer, Christina. B.A., Cambridge (Eng.) U., 1949, M.A., 1953, Ph.D., 1954; M.A. (hon.), U. Pa., 1973. Asst. prof. geology Pa. State U., State College, 1953-56; sr. scientist Johns-Manville Corp., Manville, N.J., 1956-62; pres. Tem-Pres Research Inc. (materials research and devel.), State College, 1962-70; prof. geology U. Pa., Phila., 1970—, chmn. dept. geology, 1974-79; cons. in field. Contbr. articles to profl. jours. Served to sub-lt. Royal Navy, World War II. Fellow Geol. Soc. London, Am. Mineral. Soc.; mem. Phila. Mineral. Soc., Mineral. Soc. London. Patentee in field. Home: 37 Penarth Rd Bala-Cynwyd PA 19004 Office: Dept Geology D4 U Pa Philadelphia PA 19104 *Beware of vanity - it is the father of pomposity, and pomposity begets nincompoops.*

HARKEY, IRA BROWN, JR., journalist, educator, author; b. New Orleans, Jan 15, 1918; s. Ira Brown and Flora Broad (Lewis) H.; m. Marie Ella Gore, 1939 (; (separated 1959); children—Ira Brown III, Marie Ella (Mrs. Loran E. Bosarge), Erik G., Lewis, Amelie (Mrs. Rex Foster), William Millsaps; m. Marion Marks Drake, Dec. 10, 1963 (div. 1976); 1 dau., Katherine B.; m. Virgia Quin Mioton, Feb. 24, 1977. B.A., Tulane U., 1941; M.A., Ph.D. in Polit. Sci, Ohio State U. Reporter, feature writer Times-Picayune, New Orleans, 1939-42, 46-49; editor, pub., pres. The Chronicle, Pascagoula, Miss., 1949-63; pres. Gulf Coast Times, Ocean Springs, Miss., Advertiser Printing Inc., Pascagoula, 1949-63; mem. faculty Ohio State U., 1965-66; Carnegie vis. prof. U. Alaska, 1968-69; profl. lectr. journalism U. Mont., 1970; Allen lectr. U. Oreg., 1972; sec., v.p., dir. Okla. Coca-Cola Bottling Co., Inc., Oklahoma City, 1965-80, Gt. Plains Industries, 1979-80; pres. Indian Creek Co., Inc., 1981—. Author: The Smell of Burning Crosses, 1967, The Story of Noel Wein, 1974; Contbr. articles to mags. Served to lt. USNR, 1942-46. Recipient Pulitzer prize for distinguished editorial writing, 1963; Sidney Hillman Found. award, 1963; Sigma Delta Chi nat. award for distinguished pub. service in newspaper journalism, 1963; Media award Nat. Conf. Christians and Jews, 1963. Mem. A.A.U.P., Assn. Edn. Journalism, Am. Polit. Sci. Assn., Am. Acad. Polit. Sci., Authors Guild, Phi Beta Kappa, Delta Kappa Epsilon, Kappa Tau Alpha., Pi Sigma Alpha. Clubs: La., Boston (New

Orleans); Petroleum (Oklahoma City). Address: Star Route Box 574-540 Kerrville TX 78028

HARKEY, JOHN NORMAN, lawyer; b. Russellville, Ark., Feb. 25, 1933; s. Olga John and Margaret (Fleming) H.; m. Willa Moreau Charlton, May 24, 1959; children—John Adam, Sarah Leigh. A.S., Marion (Ala.) Inst., 1952; LL.B., U. Ark., 1959, B.S., 1959, J.D., 1969. Bar: Ark. bar 1959. Since practiced in, Batesville; pros. atty. 3d Jud. Dist. Ark., 1961-65; Ins. commr., Ark., 1967-68; chmn. Ark. Commerce Commn., 1968-69. Served to 1st lt. USMCR; Korea. Mem. Am., Ark. bar assns., Am. Assn. Trial Lawyers, Am. Judicature Soc., ACLU, Ark. Council Human Relations, U.S. Marine Corps League, Delta Theta Phi. Home: Route 4 Batesville AR 72501 Office: PO Box 2535 Batesville AR 72501

HARKIN, THOMAS R., congressman; b. Cumming, Iowa, Nov. 19, 1939; s. Patrick and Frances H.; m. Ruth Raduenz, 1968; children: Amy, Jenny. B.S., Iowa State U., 1958; J.D., Cath. U. Am., 1972. Mem. staff Ho. of Reps. Select Com. U.S. Involvement in S.E. Asia, 1970; mem. 94th-98th Congresses from 5th Iowa Dist., (Sci. and Tech. Com.). Served with USN, 1962-67. Named Outstanding Young Alumnus Iowa State U. Alumni Assn., 1974. Democrat. Office: 2411 Rayburn House Office Bldg Washington DC 20515

HARKINS, GEORGE FREDERICK, clergyman; b. Phila., Feb. 28, 1913; s. John and Jennie (Waters) H.; m. Janet I. Earhart, June 18, 1940; children—John Edgar, Paul Frederick. A.B., Gettysburg Coll., 1937, L.H.D., 1969; B.D., Gettysburg Sem., 1940; D.D., Muhlenberg Coll., 1954; Th.D., Midland Lutheran Coll., 1967; S.T.D., Thiel Coll., 1970; LL.D., Susquehanna U., 1971. Ordained to ministry Luth. Ch., 1941; pastor in, Penbrook-Harrisburg, Pa., 1941-49; asst. to pres. United Luth. Ch., 1949-60, sec., 1960-62; asst. to pres. Luth. Ch. in Am., 1962-68, sec., 1968-74; gen. sec. Luth. Council in U.S.A., 1974-79; v.p. Nat. Luth. Council, 1962-65, pres., 1965-66; Mem. Luth. Resettlement Com., 1951-54, chmn., 1953-54; mem. Joint Commn. on Luth. Unity; pres. U.S.A. nat. com. Luth. World Fedn., 1966-70; mem. commn. on world service, 1970-77; mem. gov. bd., exec. com. Nat. Council Chs. Christ U.S.A., 1961-75; v.p. Luth. Council in U.S.A., 1970-74; pres. Religion in Am. Life, 1973-78, sec., 1971-73. Author: The Church and Her Work, 1960, Handbook for Committees, 1966, Handbook on the Ordained Ministry, 1971; Contbr. to: religious periodicals. Luth. Ency. Trustee Wagner Coll., S.I., N.Y., 1972-76; v.p. Am. Immigration and Citizenship Assn., 1974—. Named Young Man of Year, Harrisburg, Pa., 1948. Mem. Alpha Kappa Alpha, Kappa Phi Kappa, Kappa Delta Rho. Home: 437 Meer Ave Wyckoff NJ 07481

HARKINS, JOHN GRAHAM, JR., lawyer; b. Phila., May 9, 1931; s. John Graham and Elizabeth Taylor (Bowers) H.; m. Beatrice Gibson McIlvain, June 30, 1955; children: John Graham III, Alida McIlvain. B.A. with honors, U. Pa., 1953, LL.B. summa cum laude, 1958. Bar: Pa. 1959, U.S. Supreme Ct. 1971. Asso. firm Pepper, Hamilton & Scheetz, Phila., 1958-63, partner, 1963—; instr. U. Pa., 1956-58, lectr. Law Sch., assoc. trustee-law; chmn. adv. com. Inst. Law and Econs., 1981—; dir. Globe Ticket Co. Supr., Easttown Twp., Pa., 1972-77. Editor-in-chief: U. Pa. Law Rev, 1957-58. Bd. dirs. Chester County Hosp.; trustee Curtis Inst. Music. Served with U.S. Army, 1953-55. Fellow Salzburg Seminar in Am. Studies, 1961. Mem. Am. Coll. Trial Lawyers, Am. Law Inst., Am. Bar Assn., Pa. Bar Assn., Phila. Bar Assn., Jud. Conf. U.S. Ct. of Appeals for 3d Circuit, Order of Coif, Phi Beta Kappa. Clubs: Merion Cricket, Radnor Hunt. Home: Lowbrook Devon PA 19333 Office: 2001 Fidelity Bldg Philadelphia PA 19109

HARKINS, JOSEPH FRANCIS, state official; b. Nowata, Okla., Dec. 5, 1938; s. Arthur Thomas and Patricia (Krampf) H.; m. Judy Cary, Aug. 17, 1961; children: Ross, Jeffrey, Ellen. B.A., U. Kans., 1960, M.P.A., 1962; postgrad., U. Mo., 1965-66, U. Minn., 1976. Administrv. asst. to state health officer Kans. Dept. Health, Topeka, 1962-63; research asso. Inst. Community Studies, Kansas City, Mo., 1963-64; asst. dir. for adminstrn. Cancer Research Center, Columbia, Mo., 1964-68; adminstr. Wayne Miner Neighborhood Health Center, Kansas City, 1968-69; asst. dir. Model Cities Agy., Kansas City, Mo., 1969-70; sr. urban specialist Inst. for Community Studies, Kansas City, Mo., 1970-73; asst. prof. U. Kans. Sch. Medicine, Kansas City, 1973-76; dir. div. planning and public edn. Kans. Dept. Health and Environment, Topeka, 1976-79, sec., 1979-83; dir. Kans. Water Office, Topeka, 1983—. Served with USAR, 1956-59; Served with USMCR, 1959-60. Democrat. Home: 1122 Avalon Rd Lawrence KS 66044 Office: 109 E 9th St Topeka KS 66620

HARKINS, WILLIAM DANIEL, hospital administrator; b. Hartford, Conn., June 1, 1943; s. Joseph Thomas and Margaret Mary (Ford) H.; m. Mary Ellen Conroy, Aug. 26, 1968; children: Eileen, Brian, Billy. B.A. in Polit. Sci., Providence Coll., 1965; M.P.H., Yale U., 1968. Planning assoc. in adminstrn. Yale U., New Haven, 1970-72; asst. adminstr. St. Mary's Hosp., Westbury, Conn., 1972-74; adminstr. Health Care, Inc., Bridgeport, Conn., 1974-75; assoc. adminstr. St. Mary's Hosp., Waterbury, 1975-79, St. Mary's Med. Ctr., Evansville, Ind., 1979-81, adminstr., 1981—; adminstrv. cons. Palm Grove Manor, Naples, Fla., 1977-79, Devereaux Group, Ltd., New Haven, 1972-75. Mem. Met. Evansville Progress Com., 1981—; bd. dirs. S.W. Ind. Pub. Broadcasting, Inc., 1980—. Capt. U.S. Army, 1968-70. Mem. Am. Coll. Hosp. Adminstrs., Met. Evansville C. of C. (dir. 1980-83). Clubs: Evansville Country, Petroleum. Office: St Marys Med Ctr of Evansville 3700 Washington Ave Evansville IN 47750

HARKINS, WILLIAM EDWARD, educator; b. State College, Pa., Nov. 10, 1921; s. John F. and Mary K. (Wagner) H. B.A., Pa. State U., 1942; M.A., Columbia, 1946, Ph.D., 1950; Litt.D., Susquehanna U., 1975. Instr. Slavic langs. U. Pa., 1948-49; mem. faculty Columbia, 1949—, prof. Slavic langs., 1964—, chmn. dept., 1964-71, 82—, asso. dir. Russian Inst., 1973-74, 76-77, dir., 1974-76, 80-81; Pres. Masaryk Inst., 1970-73. Author: Dictionary of Russian Literature, 1956, Karel Capek, 1962. Served as officer USNR., 1942-45. Guggenheim fellow, 1958-59. Mem. Am. Assn. Tchrs. Slavic and East European Langs. (pres. 1974-76). Home: 10 Monroe Pl Brooklyn NY 11201

HARKNA, ERIC, advertising executive; b. Tallinn, Estonia, June 24, 1940; came to U.S., 1947; s. Erich K. Harkna, Adelaide and Mender H.; m. Susan K. Holt, Aug. 30, 1972; children: Britt, Kristiana. B.A., Colgate U., 1962; M.B.A., Columbia U., 1964. Account exec. Benton & Bowles, N.Y.C., 1965-68; v.p., account supr. Kenyon & Eckhart, N.Y.C., 1969-71, BBDO, Inc., 1973-74, v.p., mgmt. supr., 1974-76, sr. v.p., dir., 1977-82; exec. v.p., dir., 1979-82; pres., dir. BBDO, Inc., Chgo., 1982—. Mem. corp. com. Juvenile Diabetes Found., Chgo., 1982. Colgate U. Norwegian Study grantee, 1961; recipient Internat. Bus. award Columbia U., 1964. Mem. Chgo. Advt. Club, Am. Mktg. Assn., Internat. Assn. Students in Econ. and Comml. Scis. (pres. 1962-64). Clubs: N.Y. Athletic (N.Y.C.); N.Y.A.C. Yacht (Pelham, N.Y.); Chgo. Yacht, East Bank (Chgo.). Office: 410 N Michigan Ave Chicago IL 60611

HARKNESS, BRUCE, educator; b. Beaver Dam, Wis., Apr. 16, 1923; s. Reuben Elmore Ernest and Ruth (Thomas) H.; m. Barbara McNutt White, Oct. 29, 1967; 1 son, Mark Andrew Joseph; children by previous marriage—Stephen W., Marguerite, Laura C., Jonathan C., Michael B. Student, Kalamazoo Coll., 1941-42, Swarthmore Coll., 1942-43; M.A. in English, U. Chgo., 1948, Ph.D., 1950. From instr. English to prof. U. Ill., 1950-63, 64-66, asso. dean liberal arts and scis., 1964-66; prof. English, chmn. dept. So. Ill. U., 1963-64; dean arts and scis. Kent (Ohio) State U., 1966-74, prof. English, 1974—; mem. (Center for Scholarly Edits.), 1976-80. Author: Bibliography and Novelistic Fallacy, 1959, Secret of the Secret Sharer Bared, 1965; Editor: (Conrad) Heart of Darkness, 1960, (Conrad) Secret Sharer, 1962; adv. editor: College English, 1964-70; gen. editor: Cambridge edit. Works of Joseph Conrad, 1977—. Served with USAAF, 1943-45. Carnegie fellow, 1949-50; Guggenheim fellow, 1957-58. Mem. Modern Lang. Assn. (exec. bd. Midwest sect. 1961-64), Nat. Council Tchrs. English (dir. at large 1964-68), Bibliog. Soc. Va. Home: 1295 Lake Martin Dr Kent OH 44240

HARKNESS, DONALD RICHARD, hematologist, educator; b. Mitchell, S.D., Aug. 23, 1932; s. Kenneth McKenzie and Marguerite (Sherwood) H.; m. Mary Hideko Nishi, Aug. 22, 1954; children: Laurel Jean, Kenneth Bruce, Susan Marie, Jane Elizabeth. B.A. with highest honors in Zoology, U. Calif.-Berkeley, 1954; M.D. magna cum laude, Washington U., St. Louis, 1958. Med. intern Barnes Hosp.-Washington U., 1958-59, med. resident, 1959-60; asst. prof. med. faculty U. Miami, Fla., 1964-68, assoc. prof., 1968-73, prof., 1973-80; Love prof. medicine U. Wis., Madison, 1980—, chmn. dept., 1980—; mem. adv. com. on sickle cell disease NIH, Bethesda, Md., 1974-75; dir. Miami Comprehensive Sickle Cell Ctr., 1973-78; program specialist in hematology VA Central Office, Washington, 1974-77. Researcher in hematology; contbr. writing to profl. publs. John and Mary Markle Found. scholar in acad. medicine, 1966-71. Fellow ACP; mem. Am. Soc. Hematology (councillor 1978-81), Am. Soc. Clin. Investigation, Assn. Am. Physicians, Central Soc. for Clin. Research, Midwest Blood Club (councillor 1982—), Nat. Blood Club (sec.-treas. 1976-77), So. Blood Club (pres. 1979-80), Alpha Omega Alpha. Republican. Presbyterian. Home: 110 Standish St Madison WI 53705 Office: Dept Medicine Univ Wis 600 Highland Ave Madison WI 53792

HARKNESS, JOHN CHEESMAN, architect; b. N.Y.C., Nov. 30, 1916; s. Albert and Sara (Cheesman) H.; m. Sarah Pillsbury, June 14, 1941; children: Sara (Mrs. Super), Joan (Mrs. Edwin Hantz), Nell, Timothy, Alice, Frederick, John P. A.B. cum laude, Harvard, 1938, B.Arch., 1941, M.Arch., 1941. Founding partner firm The Architects Collaborative, Cambridge, Mass., 1946—, pres., 1966-67, 77—; mem. archtl. faculty Grad. Sch. Design, Harvard, 1946-50; vis. lectr. Mass. Inst. Tech., 1950, also; Tulane U., Va. Poly. Inst., U. Pa. (others); archtl. advisor Minn. State Capitol Planning, City of Boston. Projects include Children's Hosp. Med. Center Boston (Nat. award AIA, Parker medal); various bldgs., Harvard, U. Tunis, Tunisia, Nat. Shawmut Bank, major office bldg. for, Conn. Gen. Life Ins. Co., Bloomfield, Charlestown Savs. Bank, Boston, pub. schs. Active Boston Arts Festival; mem. vis. com. R.I. Sch. Design., Harvard Grad. Sch. Design. Served with Am. Field Service, 1943-44; Served with AUS, 1944-45. Recipient 7 design awards Am. Assn. Sch. Adminstrs. Fellow AIA; mem. Boston Soc. Architects (bd. dirs., pres. 1973), Mass. Assn. Architects (pres. 1975), NAD, Archtl. League N.Y., Harvard Alumni Assn. (bd. dirs. 1965). Home: 34 Moon Hill Rd Lexington MA 02173 Office: 46 Brattle St Cambridge MA 02138

HARKNESS, MARY LOU, librarian; b. Denby, S.D., Aug. 19, 1925; d. Raleigh Everette and Mary Jane (Boyd) Barker; m. Donald R. Harkness, Sept. 2, 1967. B.A., Nebr. Wesleyan U., 1947; A.B. in L.S, U. Mich., 1948; M.S., Columbia U., 1958. Jr. cataloger U. Mich. Law Library, 1948-50; asst. cataloger Calif. Poly. Coll., 1950-52; asst. cataloger, then head cataloger Ga. Inst. Tech., 1952-57; head cataloger U. S.Fla., Tampa, 1958-67, dir. libraries, 1967—; sec.-treas., dir. Am. Studies Press, Inc.; cons. Nat. Library Nigeria, 1962-63. Bd. dirs. Southeastern Library Network, 1977-80. Recipient Alumni Achievement award Nebr. Wesleyan U., 1972. Mem. Am., S.E., Fla. library assns., Fla. Women's Network, Athena Soc. Democrat. Mem. United Ch. Christ. Home: 13511 Palmwood Ln Tampa FL 33624 Office: Univ South Fla Library Fowler Ave Tampa FL 33620

HARKNESS, SARAH PILLSBURY, architect; b. Swampscott, Mass., July 8, 1914; d. Samuel Hale and Helen (Watters) Pillsbury; m. John C. Harkness, June 14, 1940; children: Sara, Joan, Nell, Timothy, Alice, Frederick, John P. M.Arch., Smith Coll., 1940; M.F.A. (hon.), Bates Coll., 1974. Registered architect, Mass. Prin. The Architects Collaborative, Cambridge, Mass., 1945—. Author: (with James N. Groom, Jr.) Building Without Barriers, 1976. Recipient honor award for Bates Coll. Library AIA-ALA, 1976, honor award for Chase Learning Ctr., Eaglebrook Sch. AIA, 1967. Fellow AIA (dir. 1972-75, v.p. 1978); mem. Boston Soc. Architects (dir. 1979-80, v.p., pres.-elect. 1984). Address: 34 Moon Hill Rd Lexington MA 02173

HARKRADER, CARLETON ALLEN, lawyer; b. Bristol, Va., Dec. 17, 1917; s. Charles Johnston and Elva Louise (Moorman) H.; m. Julia Visetti, Jan. 1946 (div. 1949); 1 son, Richard; m. Doris Newman, Feb. 3, 1951; children—Carol, Elva, Deborah. A.B., Va. Mil. Inst., 1940; LL.B., Yale, 1953. Mailer, reporter, editorial writer Bristol Herald Courier, 1934-41; corr. Newsweek mag., Rome; (with Newbold Noyes Jr. interviewed Pope Pius XII on Vatican reaction to atomic bomb), 1945-46, also corr. in, Middle East and France, 1945; exec. editor and pub. Bristol Herald Courier and News Bull., 1946-51; appellate atty., legal adviser FTC, 1957-61; partner firm Wald, Harkrader & Ross (and predecessor firm), Washington, 1961—. Served from 2d lt. to maj. AUS, 1941-42; with II Corps on North African landing; served in Allied Force Hdqrs. in; North Africa and Italy. Decorated Bronze Star medal.; Recipient Lee Editorial award Va. Press Assn. and Lee Sch. of Journalism, Washington and Lee U. for distinguished editorial writing, 1941. Mem. Am., Fed., Va., D.C. bar assns., Sigma Delta Chi, Phi Delta Phi. Democrat. Club: Met. (Washington). Home: 10211 Forest Lake Dr Great Falls VA 22066 Office: 1300 19th St NW Washington DC 20036

HARKRADER, CHARLES JOHNSTON, JR., surgeon; b. Bristol, Tenn., Mar. 2, 1913; s. Charles Johnston and Elva Louise (Moorman) H.; m. Lucille Ferrell Teass, Feb. 5, 1940; children—Charles Johnston III, Nancy (Mrs. William Dorner Hargrave), Peg (Mrs. Michael Tinkler Stone). A.B., Va. Mil. Inst., 1933; M.D., U. Va., 1938. Diplomate: Am. Bd. Surgery. Intern U. Va. Hosp., 1938-39, resident, 1939-40, Charleston (W.Va.) Gen. Hosp., 1941-42, 46-48; vis. surgeon Bristol (Tenn.) Meml. Hosp., 1948—; Dir. Bank of Va. Southwest. Chmn. Charter Commn., Bristol, 1970-73; mem. City Council, Bristol, 1973-75, Bd. Edn., Bristol, 1957-60; Trustee Va. Intermont Coll., 1964—. Served to maj. AUS, 1942-45. Decorated Bronze Star medal. Fellow A.C.S.; mem. Am., Tenn. State med. assns., Med. Soc. Va., Southeastern Surg. Congress, Va. Surg. Soc., Phi Delta Theta, Nu Sigma Nu. Methodist. Club: Country Bristol. Home: 21 Compton Rd Bristol TN 37620

HARKRADER, MILTON KEENE, JR., advertising executive; b. Cranford, N.J., Apr. 8, 1937; s. Milton Keene and Elizabeth Dyer (Evans) H.; m. Nina B. Salo, June 25, 1960; children: Nina Elizabeth, Milton Keene III, Eric Scott. A.B., Hamilton Coll., 1958; M.B.A., Wharton Sch., U. Pa., 1960. Account exec. Dancer Fitzgerald Sample, Inc., N.Y.C., 1960-63; product mgr. Colgate Palmolive Co., N.Y.C., 1963-65; account exec. Foote Cone & Belding, Inc., N.Y.C., 1965-66; v.p., account supr. Young & Rubicam, Inc., N.Y.C., 1966-73; exec. v.p. Isidore Lefkowitz Elgort, Inc., N.Y.C., 1973-79; sr. v.p., mgmt. supr. Doyle Dane Bernbach, Inc., N.Y.C., 1979—. Chmn. bd. trustees Ch. of All Nations, N.Y.C., 1974-77; mem. parents' adv. council Kenyon Coll. Mem. Hamilton Coll. Alumni Assn. (bd. govs.). Clubs: Wharton, DKE (N.Y.C.); Weston Field (Weston, Conn.). Home: 83 Cavalry Rd Weston CT 06883 Office: 437 Madison Ave New York NY 10022

HARKRIDER, DAVID GARRISON, geology educator; b. Houston, Sept. 25, 1931; s. William Max and Wille Mae (Garrison) H.; m. Janna Lee Frazier, July 1, 1974; children by previous marriage: Claire Eleanor, John David. B.A. in Physics, Rice U., 1953, M.A. in Geology, 1957; Ph.D. in Geophysics, Calif. Inst. Tech., 1963. Asst. prof. Brown U., Providence, 1965-67, assoc. prof., 1967-70; assoc. prof. geology and planetary sci. Calif. Inst. Tech., Pasadena, 1970-79, prof., 1979—, assoc. dir. Seismol. Lab., 1977-80; cons. Geotech Teledyne, 1965-71, Sierra Geophysics, 1979-80, Woodward Clyde Cons., 1980—, S-Cubed, 1971-80. Contbr. articles to profl. jours. Lt. (j.g.) USNR, 1953-55. Fellow Am. Geophys. Union; mem. Seismol. Soc. Am. (dir. 1982—). Home: 611 Fillmore St Pasadena CA 91106 Office: Geol and Planetary Scis Calif Inst Tech 1201 E California Blvd Pasadena CA 91125

HARL, NEIL EUGENE, economist, lawyer, educator; b. Appanoose County, Iowa, Oct. 9, 1933; s. Herbert Peter and Bertha Catherine (Bonner) H.; m. Darlene Ramona Harris, Sept. 7, 1952; children: James Brent, Rodney Scott. B.S., Iowa State U., 1955, Ph.D., 1965; J.D., U. Iowa, 1961. Bar: Iowa 1961. Field editor Wallace's Farmer, 1957-58; research assoc. U.S. Dept. Agr., Iowa City and Ames, Iowa, 1958-64; assoc. prof. econs. Iowa State U., Ames, 1964-67, prof., 1967—, Charles F. Curtiss Disting. prof., 1976—; frequent lectr. in field. Author: Farm Estate and Bus. Planning, 1973, 9th edit., 1984, Agricultural Law, 15 vols., 1980-81; contbr. articles to profl. jours.; author/actor films and videotape programs. Trustee Iowa State U. Agrl. Found., 1969—. Served to 1st lt. AUS, 1955-57; capt. USAR. Recipient Outstanding Tchr. award Iowa State U., 1973; Outstanding Extension Program award Am. Agrl. Econ. Assn., 1970; award excellence in communicating research results, 1975; disting. undergrad. tchr. award, 1976; Disting. Service to Agr. award Am. Soc. Farm Mgrs. and Rural Appraisers, 1977; Faculty Service award Nat. Univ. Extension Assn., 1980. Mem. Iowa, Am. bar assns., Am. Agrl. Econs. Assn. (exec. bd. 1979-82, pres. 1983-84), Am. Agrl. Law Assn. (1980-81). Home: 2821 Duff Ave Ames IA 50010 Office: Dept Econs Iowa State U Ames IA 50011

HARLAN, JACK RODNEY, geneticist, educator; b. Washington, June 7, 1917; s. Harry Vaughn and Augusta (Griffing) H.; m. Jean Yocum, Aug. 4, 1939; children: Sue (Mrs. Robert Hughes), Harry, Sherry (Mrs. Mark Wilson), Richard Edwin. B.S. in Botany with distinction, George Washington U., 1938; Ph.D. in Genetics, U. Calif. at Berkeley, 1942. Research asst. Tela R.R. Co., Honduras, 1942; geneticist Dept. Agr., Woodward, Okla., 1942-51, Stillwater, Okla., 1951-61; prof. agronomy Okla. State U., 1951-66; prof. gentics U. Ill. at Urbana, 1966—; botanist Dept. of Agr. (plant exploration and introduction), Turkey, Syria and Iraq, 1948, Iran, Afghanistan, Pakistan, India and Ethiopia, 1960; sr. staff mem. Iranian prehistoric project Oriental Inst. U. Chgo., 1960, sr. staff mem. Turkish prehistoric project, 1964; mem. Dead Sea Archaeol. Project, 1977, 79, 83; plant exploration, Africa, Asia, Latin Am.; Cons. FAO, 1970-71. Mem. internat. bd.: Plant Genetic Resources, 1974-79; contbr. profl. jours. Fellow AAAS, Am. Soc. Agronomy, Am. Acad. Arts and Sci.; mem. Nat. Acad. Scis., Crop Sci. Soc. Am. (pres. 1966), Am. Inst. Biol. Scientists, Bot. Soc. Am., Am. Soc. Agronomy, Soc. for Econ. Botany, Phi Beta Kappa, Sigma Xi, Phi Kappa Phi. Presbyn. (elder). Home: 1822 Crescent Dr Champaign IL 61820 Office: care Dept Agronomy U Ill S-516 Turner Hall Urbana IL 61801

HARLAN, JAMES CLARKE, banker; b. Charlottesville, Va., May 1, 1928; s. John Frederick and Myrtle Mildred (Clarke) H.; m. Betty Ann Blakey, Apr. 16, 1955; children—James Clarke, Sally Blakey. B.A., U. Va., 1950, M.A. in Polit. Sci., 1952; certificate, Stonier Grad. Sch. Banking, Rutgers U., 1964. With United Va. Bank, Richmond, 1954—, sr. v.p. charge loan adminstrn. div., 1971—; instr. banking schs. U. Va. Served to 1st lt. AUS, 1952-54; Korea. Mem. Richmond Assn. Credit Mgmt. (past pres.), Robert Morris Assos. (past pres. Carolina-Va. chpt.), Smithsonian Assos., Va. Mus., Nat. Trust Hist. Preservation, Assn. Preservation of Va. Antiquities, Delta Upsilon. Presbyn. (elder). Clubs: Lion (past pres. Richmond Host club), Willow Oaks Country; Farmington Country (Charlottesville). Home: 8705 Shadow Ln Richmond VA 23229 Office: United Virginia Bank 9th and Main Sts Richmond VA 23219

HARLAN, JOHN FREDERICK, JR., hosp. adminstr.; b. Charlottesville, Va., Dec. 18, 1925; s. John Frederick and Myrtle (Clarke) H.; m. Doris Davis Driscoll, Nov. 22, 1974; children—Patricia Ann, John Frederick III, Dorothy Karol and Barbara Ellen (twins), Douglas Allen. B.A., U. Va., 1950; grad., Med. Coll. Va. Sch. Hosp. Adminstrn., 1952. Adminstrv. asst. U. Va. Hosp., Charlottesville, 1952-54; asst. dir., 1954-58, asso. dir., 1958-65, dir., 1965-81; asst. v.p. U. Va. Sch. Medicine, 1981—; dir. Va. Nat. Bank. Chmn. community drive Nat. Found. Infantile Paralysis, 1958; Mem. Charlottesville Sch. Bd., 1963-66; mem. Albemarle Dem. Com., 1956-60; Past pres. U. Va. Hosp. Employees Credit Union; bd. dirs. United Givers Fund, U. Va. Student Aid Found., Blue Cross/Blue Shield of Va., 1968-72. Served with AUS, 1944-46. Decorated Bronze Star medal.; Recipient Key Man award Jaycees, 1959. Mem. Med. Coll. Va. Sch. Hosp. Adminstrn. Alumni Assn. (past pres.), U. Va. Alumni Assn., Albemarle County Med. Soc., Charlottesville-Albemarle Jr. C. of C. (past pres.), Am. Hosp. Assn. (Va. del. 1972—), Va. Hosp. Assn. (past pres.). Methodist (bd. dirs.). Club: Lion (past pres.). Home: 26 Monterey Dr Charlottesville VA 22901 Office: U Va Hosp Box 192 Charlottesville VA 22908

HARLAN, NEIL EUGENE, business executive; b. Cherry Valley, Ark., June 2, 1921; s. William and Mary Nina (Ellis) H.; m. Martha Almlov, Sept. 27, 1952; children: Lindsey Beth, Neil Eugene, Sarah Ellis. Ed., U. Edinburgh, Scotland, 1946; B.S., U. Ark., 1947, LL.D., 1969; M.B.A., Harvard, 1950, D.B.A., 1956. Mem. faculty Grad. Sch. Bus. Adminstrn. Harvard, 1951-62, asst. prof., 1954-58, asso. prof., 1958-61, prof., 1962; asst. sec. air force, Washington, 1962-64; v.p., chief financial officer, dir. Anderson, Clayton & Co., 1964-66, exec. v.p., 1966-67; dir. McKinsey & Co., Inc., 1967-74; chmn. bd. Foremost-McKesson, Inc., San Francisco, 1974-79, chmn., 1979—, also dir.; dir. U.S. Leasing Internat., Inc. Author: Management Control in Air Frame Subcontracting, 1956, (with R.H. Hassler) Cases in Controllership, 1958, (with R.F. Vancil) Cases in Accounting Policy, 1961, (with Christenson and Vancil) Managerial Economics, 1962. Chmn. bd. trustees San Francisco Ballet; trustee Mills Coll.; Trustee World Affairs Council; chmn. Pvt. Industry Council of San Francisco; mem. bus. adv. com. San Francisco Edn. Fund; mem. vis. com. Harvard Bus. Sch. Served with AUS, 1943-46. Mem. Am. Inst. C.P.A.s, Conf. Bd. Clubs: Congressional Country (Bethesda, Md.); Webhannet Golf, Edgecomb Tennis (Kennebunk Beach, Maine); Bankers, Pacific Union (San Francisco); Menlo Country (Woodside, Calif.); Links (N.Y.C.). Home: 394 Golden Hills Dr Portola Valley CA 94025 Office: Crocker Plaza One Post St San Francisco CA 94104

HARLAN, ROBERT WARREN, charitable association executive; b. London Mills, Ill., Jan. 30, 1921; s. Custer and Louella (McElra) H.;

m. Effie Louella Henley, Aug. 26, 1945; children: Nancy Jane (Mrs. John Franklin Billings, Jr.), Linda Louella (Mrs. Phillip Ucciferri), Kathryn Louise (Mrs. Steven Hoxmeier), Betsy Ann (Mrs. Walter Haines). B.A., Whittier Coll., 1947; M.A., U. So. Calif., 1955; Ph.D., Ohio State U., 1970. Dir. YMCA's in So. Calif., 1943-61; asso. exec. Ohio-W.Va. area council YMCA's, Columbus, Ohio, 1961-67; exec. dir. Central Atlantic Area council YMCA's, Princeton, N.J., 1967-69, Pacific Region YMCA's, Los Angeles, 1969-71; nat. exec. dir. Nat. Council YMCA's, N.Y.C., 1971-80; exec. v.p. (Ind. Sector), Washington, 1980—; former lectr. Whittier Coll. Author: (with others) Thirty Days in the USSR. Past pres. Whittier Community Coordinating Council; trustee Whittier Coll., 1973-80, Am. Humanics Found. Bd. Recipient John R. Mott YMCA fellowship, 1967-68; Whittier Coll. Alumni Achievement award, 1972. Mem. Assn. Profl. YMCA Dirs. (pres. 1969-71), Am. Mgmt. Assn., Nat. Assembly of Nat. Vol. Health and Social Welfare Orgns. (pres. 1974-76), Non-Profit Mgmt. Assn. Home: 1662 Irving St NW Washington DC 20010 Office: 1828 L St NW Washington DC 20036 *In the final analysis it's the quality of relationships one has with his fellowman that is essential. When this is coupled with a high degree of competence, an ability to get action and results and a responsibility that keeps one to it, an optimism is produced for a better world in the future. A recognition that the Infinite is at work in the world, guiding the destinies of humankind gives us optimism and faith.*

HARLAN, ROMA CHRISTINE, portrait painter; b. Warsaw, Ind.; d. Charles William and Fern (McCormick) H. Student, Purdue U., Art Inst. Chgo. Art chmn. D.C. Fedn. Women's Clubs. One-man shows, Lake Shore Club, Chgo., Little Gallery of Esquire Theatre, Chgo., Purdue U., W. Lafayette, Ind., Hoosier Salon, Indpls., All.-Ill. Soc. Fine Arts, Chgo., Kaufmann's Galery, Chgo., Lafayette (Ind.) Art Assn., Arts Club, Washington, George Washington U., Washington; exhibited numerous group shows; represented in permanent collections at, U.S. Supreme Ct., D.C. Fed. Ct. House, SEC, U.S. Capitol, Nat. Presbyn. Ch., Va. Theol. Sem., Alexandria, Nat. Guard Bldg., St. Stephen's Sch. for Boys, Alexandria, Washington Nat. Fedn. Bus. and Profl. Women's Clubs, Washington, Children's Hosp. Nat. Med. Ctr., Alexandria, Lakeshore Club, Chgo. Dau. Ind. scholar. Mem. Ind. State Art Assn. Presbyterian. Club: Arts (Washington). Address: 1600 S Joyce St Arlington VA 22202 *A question frequently asked of me is, "What are you doing when you paint a portrait?" My answer has to be "Making this person, who is different from anyone else in the world, COME TO LIFE on the canvas."*

HARLAN, ROSS EDGAR, utility company executive; b. Poteau, Okla., July 11, 1919; s. Edgar Leslie and Leola (Carter) H.; m. Margaret Burns, May 31, 1942; children: Raymond Carter, Rosemary, Marvin Allen, Scott Lee. Student, Southeastern Okla. State U., 1937-38, Eastern Okla. State Coll., 1938-39; B.S.B.A., Okla. State U., 1941; postgrad., Harvard U., 1942. Mem. faculty, coach Poteau High Sch., 1945-46, Poteau Jr. Coll., 1945-46; with Okla. Gas & Electric Co., Oklahoma City, 1946—, mgr. rates and contracts dept., 1954-64, v.p., 1964-78, sr. v.p. div. mgmt., 1978-80, sr. v.p. adminstrn. and public affairs, 1980—. Author: Strikes, 1946. Pres. Okla. Council on Econ. Edn., 1977-79; bd. govs. Nat. Wrestling Hall of Fame, 1977—; pres. adv. bd. Okla. State U. Coll. Bus. Assos.; mem. adv. bd. Okla. State U. Tech. Inst.; bd. govs. Okla. State U. Found. Served with Army N.G., 1937-38; to lt. col. USAAF, 1941-46. Named to Okla. State U. Coll. Bus. Hall of Fame, 1980; recipient George Washington Honor medal Freedom Found. Am., 1970, Disting. Alumnus award Okla. State U., 1979; named Boss of Yr. Nat. Secs. Assn., 1977. Mem. Oklahoma City C. of C., Beta Gamma Sigma. Methodist. Home: 2639 Eagle Ln Oklahoma City OK 73127 Office: 321 N Harvey St Oklahoma City OK 73101

HARLAN, W. GLEN, lawyer; b. Stuart, Iowa, Oct. 14, 1912; s. Wilber George and Lillian (Russell) H.; m. Esther Wadleigh, Mar. 15, 1941; children: Michael Glen (dec.), Esther Elizabeth (Mrs. Richard Greb). A.B., Simpson Coll., 1936; J.D., State U. Iowa, 1939. Bar: Iowa 1939, Ga. 1942, N.Y. 1961. Law clk. to Wiley Rutledge; asso. justice U.S. Ct. Appeals D.C., 1939-41; asso. Gambrell & White, Atlanta, 1941-47; partner Gambrell, Harlan, Russell & Moye (and predecessors), 1948-67; v.p. legal affairs Eastern Air Lines, Inc., 1967-69, sr. v.p. legal affairs, 1969-77, mem. exec. com., dir., 1972-77; partner firm Gambrell, Russell & Mobley (and predecessors), Atlanta, 1978-81; of counsel Gambrell & Russell (and predecessors), 1981—. Former trustee Simpson Coll. Mem. ABA (ho. of dels. 1956-58), Fed. Bar Assn., Atlanta Bar Assn., N.Y. State Bar Assn., N.Y.C. Bar Assn., State Bar Ga., Am. Judicature Soc., Lawyers Club, Internat. Air Transport Assn. (chmn. legal com. 1975-76), Air Transport Assn. (chmn. law council 1976-77), Legal Aid Soc., Newcomen Soc. N.Am., Order of Coif, Pi Kappa Delta. Methodist. Clubs: Pinetree Country (Kennesaw, Ga.); Cherokee Town and Country (Atlanta); Waukewan Golf (Meredith, N.H.). Home: Wood Ridge RFD 2 Meredith NH 03253 Office: 4000 First Nat Bank Tower Atlanta GA 30383

HARLAN, WILLIAM ROBERT, JR., physician, educator; b. Richmond, Va., Nov. 1, 1930; s. William Robert and Helen J. (Weaver) H.; m. Linda Carol Mavencamp, Aug. 23, 1980; children: Elizabeth, William, Christopher, Nicole. B.A., U. Va., 1951; M.D. magna cum laude, Med. Coll. Va., 1955. Diplomate: Am. Bd. Internal Medicine, Am. Bd. Family Practice. Intern U. Wis., Madison, 1955-56; resident in medicine Duke U. Hosp., Durham, N.C., 1958-62; dir. Clin. Research Center, Med. Coll. Va., 1963-70; asso. dean U. Ala. Med. Sch., 1970-72; prof. medicine and community health scis. Duke U., 1972-74; prof. medicine and postgrad. medicine U. Mich., Ann Arbor, 1974—; cons. World Bank; mem. sci. adv. bd. U.S. Air Force; mem. Armed Forces Epidemiology Bd., NIH study sects. and adv. councils. Contbr. articles to med. jours. Served with M.C. USN, 1956-58. Mem. ACP, Am. Heart Assn., N.Y. Acad. Sci., Sigma Xi, Alpha Omega Alpha. Episcopalian. Club: Country (Va.). Office: Towsley Center U of Mich Med Sch Ann Arbor MI 48109

HARLEMAN, DONALD ROBERT FERGUSSON, civil engineering educator; b. Palmerton, Pa., Dec. 5, 1922; s. Robert Roy and Nora (Curry) H.; m. Martha Havens, Oct. 21, 1950; children: Kathleen T., Robert I.H., Anne C. B.S. in Civil Engring., Pa. State U., 1943; M.S., MIT, 1947, D.Sc., 1950. Design engr. Curtiss-Wright Corp., Columbus, O., 1944-45; research asst., research asso. Hydrodynamics Lab., Mass. Inst. Tech., 1945-50, asst. prof. hydraulics, 1950-56, asso. prof. hydraulics, 1956-62, prof. civil engring., 1963-75, Ford prof. engring., 1975—, head water resources and hydrodynamics div., 1971—, dir., 1973—; Vis. prof. Cal. Inst. Tech., 1962-63; del. U.S.-Japan Joint Sci. Seminar on Coastal Engring., 1964, 1974; sr. visitor applied math. and theoretical physics Cambridge (Eng.) U., 1968-69; vis. scientist Internat. Inst. Applied Systems Analysis, Vienna, 1977-78; Mem. Water Pollution Control Fedn.; mem. U.S. Nat. Com. Internat. Assn. Water Pollution Research. Bd. editors: Jour. Hydraulic Research. Recipient Desmond Fitzgerald medal Boston Soc. Civil Engrs., 1967; named Outstanding Alumnus Civil Engring., Pa. State U., 1979; Guggenheim fellow, 1968-69. Mem. ASCE (research prize 1960, Karl Hilgard Hydraulic prize 1971, 73, J.C. Stevens award 1973), Am. Geophys. Union, Internat. Assn. for Hydraulic Research, Am. Soc. Limnology and Oceanography. Research in fluid transport process and water quality control, waste heat disposal and power plant siting. Home: 100 Memorial Dr Cambridge MA 02142 Office: 48-335 Parsons Lab for Water Resources and Hydrodynamics Mass Inst Tech Cambridge MA 02139

HARLESS, BYRON BRITTINGHAM, newspaper exec.; b. Victoria, Va., May 15, 1916; s. Byron and Laura Belle H.; m. Betty Cabler Keefe, July 4, 1944; 1 dau., Bettina. B.A.E., U. Fla., 1938, M.A.E. (grad. fellow 1938), 1939; postgrad., Columbia U., 1939-41. Research asso. U. Fla., 1938-41, psychologist, 1945-46; pres. Byron Harless, Reid and Assos., Inc. (cons. psychologists), Tampa, Fla., 1946-70; sr. v.p. Knight-Ridder Newspapers, Inc., Miami, Fla., 1970—, also dir., mem. exec. and operating coms. Author: The Measurement of Behavior Problems in High School Students, 1941, also tests. Served with USAAF, 1941-46. Recipient Outstanding Exec. award Tampa chpt. Am. Soc. Sales Execs., 1960. Mem. Am. Psychol. Assn., Southeastern Psychol. Assn., Fla. Psychol. Assn. (Disting. Service award 1955). Episcopalian. Clubs: Riviera Country (Coral Gables); Tampa Yacht, University (Tampa); Bath (Miami Beach); Miami, Bankers (Miami). Home: 600 Biltmore Way Coral Gables FL 33134 Office: 1 Herald Plaza Miami FL 33101

HARLESTON, BERNARD WARREN, college president; b. N.Y.C., Jan. 22, 1930; s. Henry Mitchell and Anna (Tobin) H.; m. Marie Ann Lombard, June 19, 1954; children: David Warren, Jeffrey Stuart. B.S., Howard U., 1951; Ph.D., U. Rochester, 1955, D.Sc. (hon.), 1972. Instr. U. Rochester, 1954-55, asst. prof., 1955-56, research asso., 1956; asst. prof. psychology Tufts U., 1956-61, asso. prof., 1961-68, prof. psychology, dean, 1970-80, Moses Hunt prof. psychology, 1980-81; provost, prof. psychology Lincoln (Pa.) U., 1968-70; pres. City Coll., City U. N.Y., 1981—; research fellow Stanford U., 1963-64; vis. scholar Harvard U., 1980-81; vis. asst. prof. N.Y. U., summer 1959; mem. profl. adv. com. NIMH, 1966-68; dir. West Medford (Mass.) Community Center, 1966-68; chmn. Winchester (Mass.) Council Community Action, 1967-68; mem. grad. record exam. bd. Ednl. Testing Service, 1972-76; mem. vis. com. dept. Afro-Am. studies Harvard U.; mem. accrediting com. Commn. on Higher Edn.; field reader advanced instn. devel. program Office Edn., HEW.; Trustee Cambridge Friends Sch., Nat. Braille Press, 1973; mem. adv. council bd. trustees U. Rochester; mem. adv. council exptl. and spl. tng. rev. com. HEW, 1969—. Contbr. articles profl. jours.; Producer: TV series Principles of Behavior, Boston. Mem. minority higher edn. adv. council Commonwealth of Mass., 1976—; adv. council Danforth Adv. Council, 1977; corporator MIT, 1982—; mem. vis. com. Coll. Liberal Arts, U. Miami, 1983—; mem. community relations com. Lexington (Mass.) Bd. Selectmen; chmn. N.Y.C. Mayor's Commn. on Sci. and Tech. Fellow Mass. Psychol. Assn.; mem. Am. Psychol. Assn., AAUP, AAAS, Phi Beta Kappa, Sigma Xi. Office: City College 138th St and Convent Ave New York NY 10031

HARLEY, NAOMI HALLDEN, radiation specialist, environmental medicine educator; b. N.Y.C., Aug. 4, 1932; d. Carl Edward and Ida Wilson (Palmer) Hallden; m. John Henry Harley, Sept. 11, 1964. B.S., Cooper Union, N.Y.C., 1959; M.S., NYU, 1967, Ph.D., 1971, A.P.C., 1983. Phys. scientist U.S. Atomic Energy Commn., N.Y.C., 1961-65; research prof. environ. medicine NYU, 1965—; council mem., task group chmn. Nat. Council on Radiation Protection and Measurement, Washington, 1982—. Contbr. articles to profl. jours. USPHS fellow, 1965. Mem. Health Physics Soc., AAAS, N.Y. Acad. Sci. Democrat. Club: NYU Alumni. Office: NYU Sch of Medicine 550 1st Ave New York NY 10016

HARLEY, ROBISON DOOLING, physician, educator; b. Pleasantville, N.J., Feb. 27, 1911; s. Halvor L. and Alice (Robison) H.; children—Robison Dooling, Ardee R., Heather L., Halvor L. II, William W. B.Sc., Rutgers U., 1932; M.D., U. Pa., 1936; Ph.D., U. Minn., 1949. Diplomate: Am. Bd. Ophthalmology. Intern Phila. Gen. Hosp., 1936-38; fellowship Mayo Clinic, Rochester, Minn., 1938-41, jr. staff cons., 1941-42; pvt. practice as ophthalmologist and ophthalmic surgeon, Atlantic City and Phila., 1947—; attending surgeon, dir. ophthalmology St. Christopher's Hosp. for Children, Phila., 1958-70; chief surgeon Atlantic City Hosp., 1950-67; cons. Shore Meml. Hosp., Somers Point, 1958—; attending surgeon Temple U. Hosp., Phila., 1947—; also Wills Eye Hosp. and Research Inst.; cons. Betty Bacharach Home for Children and Children's Seashore Home, 1955—; attending surgeon, dir. dept. pediatrics and motility; formerly prof., chmn. ophthalmology, prof. pediatrics Temple U. Health Sci. Center, Phila.; now prof. emeritus; dir. Eye Program Project Hope; adj. prof. Thomas Jefferson U.; Morgan lectr., Toronto, Antonio Navas lectr., P.R., Frank Costenbader lectr., Washington. Author: (with Gibson) Visual Perception and Ocular Motility, 1966; contbg. author: Textbook of Pediatrics, 1975, 77, 79; contbr.: chpt. Pediatric Ophthalmological Surgery; Editor: Pediatric Ophthalmology, 1975; Contbr. numerous articles to profl. jours., chpts. to books; mem. editorial bd.: Jour. Pediatric Ophthalmology and Strabismus. Mem. exec. bd. Atlantic area council Boy Scouts Am., 1949—; bd. dirs. YMCA, 1957—; mem. med. adv. bd. Nevil Inst., Fight for Sight Inc., N.Y.C., Retinitis Pigmentosa Found. Served from lt. to lt. col. AUS, 1942-47. Decorated Legion of Merit from Panama (Vasco Nunez de Balboa). Fellow A.C.S. (gov. 1959-62), Am. Acad. Ophthalmology and Otolaryngology (asso. sec. continuing edn.); mem. Assn. Research Ophthalmology, Pan-Am. Congress Ophthalmology, Am. Ophthal. Soc., Phi Beta Kappa, Sigma Xi. Clubs: Explorers N.Y.C., Brigantine (N.J.) Yacht (commodore); Union League (Phila.)). Office: Wills Eye Hosp 9th and Walnut St Philadelphia PA 19107

HARLEY, WILLIAM GARDNER, communications consultant; b. Madison, Wis., Oct. 9, 1911; s. Joel Alva and Elizabeth (Gardner) H.; m. Jewell Bunnell, June 15, 1940; children: Cynthia Harley Foster, Linda Harley Cunningham, Gratia, Gail (dec.). B.A., U. Wis., 1935, M.A., 1940, LL.D. (hon.), 1972. Instr. dept. radio-TV edn. and staff Sta. WHA, U. Wis., 1936-42, asst. prof., 1942-53, asso. prof., 1953-57, prof., 1957-60; chief announcer Wis. Broadcasting System, 1935-40, program dir., 1940-44, acting dir., 1944-46; program coordinator Ford-Nat. Assn. Ednl. Broadcasters Adult Edn. Radio Project, 1950-52; pres. Nat. Assn. Ednl. Broadcasters, Washington, 1960-75; mem. nat. industry adv. com. FCC, 1960-72; del. Internat. Conf. on Schs. Broadcastings, Rome, 1961, Tokyo, 1964, Paris, 1967; bd. dirs. U.S.-Japan TV Program Exchange Center, 1964-68; dir. Joint Council Ednl. Telecommunications, 1960-75, pres., 1973-75, Ednl. Media Council, 1966-68; chmn. screening com. for radio-TV, Fulbright Scholarships, 1966-72; mem. U.S. Nat. Commn. UNESCO, 1962-68, 70-76; chmn. Mass Communications Com., 1967-68, 70-76; del. UNESCO Conf. Use Space Broadcasting, Paris, 1971, Internat. Broadcasting Unions Conf. Communications Satellites, 1972; mem. U.S. Nat. Commn. team, USSR, 1973, U.S. del. UNESCO Gen. Conf., 1974, 76, 78, 80; U.S. rep. Council of Internat. Program for Communications Devel., 1981, 82, 83; cons. Rothschild Found., AID, Com. for Econ. Devel., USPHS, U.S. Dept. State. Contbr. articles to profl. jours. Recipient Disting. Citizen award Creighton U., 1965, Disting. Alumnus award Wis. Alumni Assn. of Washington, 1966, Disting. Service in Journalism award U. Wis., 1973; Disting. Service award Nat. Assn. Ednl. Broadcasters, 1975; Thomas Jefferson Freedom of Info. award, 1983. Nat. Assn. Ednl. Broadcasters; Mem. Internat. Inst. Communications, Phi Kappa Phi, Phi Eta Sigma, Beta Theta Pi. Clubs: International, Cosmos (Washington). Home: 6323 Waterway Dr Falls Church VA 22044 Office: US Dept State IO/CU Washington DC 20520

HARLIN, VIVIAN KRAUSE, physician, educator; b. Seattle, Dec. 26, 1924; d. Louis Joseph and Julia (Rommel) Krause; m. Allan J. Harlin, June 26, 1948; children: Sandra Jeanne, Julie Ann, Andrew Edward. B.S. in Zoology, U. Wash., 1946, M.S. in Preventive Medicine, 1970; M.D., U. Oreg., 1950. Intern Swedish Hosp., Seattle, 1950-51, resident, 1951-52; practice medicine, Ballard, Seattle, 1952-53; clinic physician Snohomish County (Wash.) Health Dept., 1953; examining physician Seattle Pub. Schs., 1953-57, dir. health services, 1957-79; sr. fellow dept. preventive medicine U. Wash., 1968-69; clin. instr. Sch. Pub. Health and Community Medicine, 1969—; Cons. HEW. Contbr. articles to profl. jours. Recipient Sch. Bell award Physicians and Schs. Conf., 1969, Golden Acorn award Wash. Congress Parent-Tchr. Student Assn., 1973. Mem. Am. Med. Women's Assn. (past pres. br. 37, com. chmn., councilor for orgn. and mgmt., dir. jr. membership 1976-78, 1st v.p. 1978, 79, pres.-elect 1980, pres. 1981), Am. Sch. Health Assn. (pres. 1974—, mem. governing council 1978, editorial bd. 1978-79), AMA (Physicians Recognition award 1970-73, 79-82, 83), Wash. Med. Assn., King County Med. Soc. (chmn. sch. health com. 1964), Wash. Pub. Health Assn. (life), Wash. Tb. and Respiratory Disease Assn. (dir. 1972-73), Seattle-King County Tb. and Respiratory Disease Assn. (dir. 1970-73), Wash. Lung Assn. (dir., mem. King County regional council 1973-74), Wash. Soc. for Prevention Blindness (med. adv. com. 1969-74, dir. 1981-83), Eta Sigma Gamma (honor award 1975), Delta Kappa Gamma. Lutheran. Home: PO Box 340 Ravensdale WA 98051 Office: Old Capitol Bldg Olympia WA 98504

HARLLEE, JOHN, shipping management consultant, former naval officer; b. Washington, Jan. 2, 1914; s. William Curry and Ella Florence (Fulmore) H.; m. Jo-Beth Carden, Sept. 10, 1937; 1 son, John. B.S., U.S. Naval Acad., 1934; grad., Naval War Coll., 1950. Commd. ensign U.S. Navy, 1934, advanced through grades to rear adm.; comdr. motor torpedo squadron 12, 1943-44; mem. (Naval Congl. Liaison Unit), 1948-49, comdr. destroyer U.S.S. Dyess, 1949-50, comdr. destroyer div. 152, 1955-56, comdr. U.S.S. Rankin, 1958, ret., 1959; v.p. Edward I. Farley & Co., Inc. (investments), N.Y.C., 1960-61; mem. Fed. Maritime Commn. (and predecessor), 1961-69, chmn., 1963-69; exec. dir. San Francisco Twin Bicentennial, 1974-75; now mgmt. cons. shipping; dir. Orgn. Ams. for Energy Independence, 1975-77, 78. Contbr. articles to profl. jours. Chmn. Citizens for Kennedy and Johnson, No. Calif., 1960. Decorated Silver Star, Legion of Merit with combat V, Commendation ribbon with combat V, Presdl. Unit citation with bronze star. Mem. SAR, Sons Republic Tex., Tex. Soc. Washington. Clubs: Rotary, Tex. Breakfast (charter); Chevy Chase (Md.); Army Navy (Washington); N.Y. Yacht. Home: 135 Sherwood Ave Front Royal VA 22630 Office: 1776 K St NW Suite 605 Washington DC 20006

HARLOW, DONALD LINCOLN, association executive; b. Waterville, Maine, Sept. 22, 1920; s. Robert and Delaphine (Pearce) H.; m. Dorothy A. Hill, Sept. 4, 1943; children: Penny Lynn, Pamela Jo. B.S. in Bus. Adminstrn., Calif. Coll. Commerce, 1957. Exec. dir. Air Force Sgts. Assn., Suitland, Md., 1971—; advisor to bd. F&M Bank, No.Va. Contbr. articles to assn. publs. Served with USAF, 1969-71; Pentagon. Named USAF Outstanding Airman, 1976; named to Tactical Air Command, Order ot th Swort, 1980. Mem. Am. Soc. Assn. Execs. Club: NCO (hon.). Home: 310 Riley St Falls Church VA 22046 Office: Air Force Sergeants Assn 5211 Auth Rd Suitland MD 20746

HARLOW, HAROLD EUGENE, newspaper editor; b. Miami, Fla., Nov. 28, 1925; s. Eugene L. and Hattye (Tygrett) H.; m. Lela Mae Brenan, Sept. 1, 1950; children: Eugene Brenan, Mary Lee, Harold Alan, Carol Ann. Student, Western Ky. State U., 1946-47; B.S. in Journalism, U. Tenn., 1950. Copy editor Knoxville (Tenn.) News-Sentinel, 1949-59, asst. news editor, 1959-67, news editor, 1967-69, mng. editor, 1969-83, assoc. editor, 1983—. Served with USAAF, 1943-46. Mem. Tenn. Press Assn., Asso. Press Mng. Editors Assn., Sigma Delta Chi. Presbyn. (elder). Home: 11545 Nassau Dr Concord TN 37922 Office: 204 W Church Ave Knoxville TN 37901

HARLOW, JAMES GINDLING, JR., utility executive; b. Oklahoma City, May 29, 1934; s. James Gindling and Adalene (Rae) H.; m. Jane Marriott Bienfang, Jan. 30, 1957; children: James Gindling III, David Ralph. B.S., U. Okla., 1957, postgrad., 1959-61. Research analyst Okla. Gas and Electric Co., Oklahoma City, 1961-63, div. auditor, 1963-65, adminstrv. asst., 1965-66, asst. treas., 1966-68, treas., 1968-69, sec.-treas., 1969-70, v.p., treas., 1970-72, exec. v.p., treas., 1972-73, pres., 1973-76, pres., chief exec. officer, 1976-82, chmn. bd., pres., chief exec. officer, 1982—, also dir.; dir. Mass. Mut. Life Ins. Co., Fleming Cos., Inc., Oklahoma City. Pres. Missouri Valley Electric Assn., 1977-78; bd. dirs. Edison Electric Inst., 1983—; Bd. dirs. State Fair of Okla.; adv. bd. St. Anthony Hosp.; trustee Okla. Zool. Soc., Oklahoma City U., U. Okla. Found., Inc.; bd. govs. Okla. Center for Sci. and Arts, Inc.; pres. Allied Arts Found., 1982-84. Served with USNR, 1957-59. Mem. U.S. C. of C. (dir. 1978-84), Okla. C. of C. (dir. 1973—, pres. 1980), Oklahoma City C. of C. (pres. 1976), Okla. Soc. Security Analysts. Clubs: Petroleum, Oklahoma City Golf and Country, Economic of Okla., Men's Dinner, Beacon, Whitehall (Oklahoma City). Home: 1713 Pennington Way Oklahoma City OK 73116 Office: PO Box 321 Oklahoma City OK 73101

HARLOW, LEROY FRANCIS, organization and management educator emeritus, author; b. Seattle, Oct. 20, 1913; s. Milton N. and Ruby Blanche (Robinson) H.; m. Agda Sophie Gronbech, June 28, 1939; children: Steven G., John G., Christine G. Harlow Allie, Thomas G., David G., Peter G., Julia G. Harlow Doolittle. Student, Cameron Jr. Coll., 1931-32; B.S., Iowa State U., 1938; M.A. (Rockefeller Found. fellow), U. Minn., 1943. Assoc. engr. U.S. Pub. Works Adminstrn., Omaha, 1938-39; field asst. U.S. Social Security Bd., Des Moines and Lincoln, Nebr., 1939-42; assoc. budget examiner U.S. Bur. Budget, Washington, 1942-43; city mgr., City of Sweet Home, Oreg., 1943-45, City of Albert Lea, Minn., 1946-47, City of Fargo, N.D., 1947-49, City of Daytona Beach, Fla., 1952-55; staff cons. Public Adminstrn. Service, Chgo., 1945-46; dir. Minn. Efficiency in State Govt. Commn., St. Paul, 1949-51; village mgr., Village of Richfield, Minn., 1951-52; sr. assoc. Booz, Allen & Hamilton (mgmt. cons.), Chgo., Manila, San Francisco, 1955-61; dir. N.Mex. Revenue Structure Study Com., Santa Fe, 1961-63, Greater Cleve. Tax Policy Study Commn., 1963-64; exec. sec. Cuyahoga County Mayors and City Mgrs. Assn., Cleve., 1964-67; dir. Utah Local Govt. Modernization Study, Salt Lake City, 1968-73; prof. emeritus orgn. and mgmt. Brigham Young U., Provo, Utah, 1967—. Author: Handbook for the Study of State Government Administration, 1950, How to Achieve Greater Efficiency and Economy in Minnesota's Government, 1951, Opportunities for Improving the New Mexico Revenue System, 1962, Guides to Tax Policy Decisions in Greater Cleveland, 1964, Implementing the Metropolitan Desk Concept, 1966, Local Government Modernization Study, 5 vols, 1970, Utah Local Government Finance Study, 5 vols, 1973, Twelve Model Optional Plans of County Government, 12 vols, 1973, Helping Utah's Local Governments Help Themselves, 1973, Without Fear or Favor: Odyssey of a City Manager, 1977, Servants of All, 1981; contbr. articles to profl. jours. Served with U.S. Army, 1933-34. Recipient Disting. Faculty award Brigham Young U. Sch. Mgmt., 1978. Mem. Am. Soc. Public Adminstrn. (pres. N.E. Ohio chpt. 1966, Central Utah chpt. 1968, certificate of Merit 1967), Am. Polit. Sci. Assn., Internat. City Mgmt. Assn., Nat. Mcpl. League, Govtl. Research Assn. (nat. award for disting. research 1965, nat. award for effective presentation of govt. research 1970), Soc. Am. Mil. Engrs., Phi Kappa Phi. Mormon. Club: Commonwealth. Home: 1855 N Oak Ln Provo UT 84604

HARMAN, ALEXANDER M(ARRS), state justice; b. War, W.Va., Feb. 7, 1921; s. Alexander M. and Rose Sinclair (Brown) H. Student, Concord Coll., Athens, W.Va., 1938-41, LL.D. (hon.), 1970; LL.B., Washington and Lee U., 1944, LL.D. (hon.), 1974; grad., Nat. Coll. State Trial Judges, 1965. Bar: Va. 1943. Practice law, Pulaski, 1944-64; partner Gilmer, Harman & Sadler, 1952-64; judge 21st Jud. Circuit, 1964-69; justice Supreme Ct. Va., 1969-79, sr. justice, 1980—; town atty., Pulaski, 1944-46, substitute trial justice, 1945-47; Mem. Va. Com. Constl. Revision, 1968. Chmn. Pulaski County Devel. Authority, 1962-64; chmn. bd. zoning appeals, Pulaski, 1958-64; pres. N.R.V. Indsl. Found., 1963-82; chmn. Battle for Gov. Com. Pulaski County, 1949, Va. Bd. Elections, 1955-64, Pulaski County Democratic Com., 1960-64; mem. finance com. Va. Dem. Central Com., 1956-64, 19th Dist. Dem. Senatorial Com., 1956-64. Home: 1303 Prospect Ave Pulaski VA 24301 Office: Supreme Ct Bldg Richmond VA 23219 also Municipal Bldg Pulaski VA 24301

HARMAN, CHARLES MORGAN, mechanical engineer; b. Cannonsburg, Pa., July 25, 1929; s. Charles Nash and Mildred (Barker) H.; m. Althea Ann Ashton, June 12, 1956 (div.); children—Ruth Ann, Charles Morgan, Samuel Stuart. B.S., U. Md., 1954; M.S., U. N.D., 1957; Ph.D., U. Wis., 1961. Registered profl. engr., Wis., N.C. Asst. prof. mech. engring. Duke U., Durham, N.C., 1961-70, prof. mech. engring., 1970—, assoc. dean, 1970-80; pres. Synergy Research Corp., 1983—; engring. cons. Douglas Aircraft Co., 1961-64, Army Research Office, Durham, 1964—. Contbr. articles to profl. jours.; editor: Jour. Advanced Transp, 1976—. Served with USN, 1949-51. Ford Found. fellow, 1960-61; recipient Profl. Achievement citation Douglas Aircraft Co., 1964. Mem. ASME, ASHRAE, Advanced Transit Assn. Home: 2208 Elmwood Ave Durham NC 27707 Office: Dept Mech Engring Duke U Durham NC 27706

HARMAN, GEORGE GIBSON, physicist, consultant; b. Norfolk, Va., Dec. 7, 1924; s. George Gibson and Annie Wall (Baldwin) H.; m. Ann Worischek, Jan. 31, 1953; children: Joyce Catherine, Arthur Lawrence, Stewart Thomas. B.S. in Physics, Va. Poly. Inst., 1949, M.S., U. Md., 1959. With Nat. Bur. Standards, Washington, 1950—, sr. research scientist, 1976—; research fellow U. Reading, Eng., 1962-63. Contbr. articles to profl. jours.; patentee (4). Served with U.S. Army, 1943-46. Recipient Silver Medal U.S. Dept. Commerce, 1973, Gold medal U.S. Dept. Commerce, 1979. Fellow IEEE (Centennial medal 1984); mem. Am. Phys. Soc., Internat. Soc. Hybrid Microelectronics (chpt. pres. 1980-82, tech. achievement award 1981), ASTM. Home: 20226 Maple Leaf Ct Gaithersburg MD 20879 Office: Nat Bur Standards Div 726 Washington DC 20234

HARMAN, GILBERT HELMS, philosophy educator; b. East Orange, N.J., May 26, 1938; s. William Henry and Marguerite Variel (Page) H.; m. Lucy Newman, Aug. 14, 1970; children: Elizabeth, Olivia. B.A., Swarthmore Coll., 1960; Ph.D., Harvard U., 1964. With dept. philosophy Princeton U., 1963—, prof., 1971—; vis. prof. Rockefeller U., 1974-75; dir. Summer Inst. Philosophy and Linguistics, Irvine, Calif., 1971. Author: Thought, 1973, The Nature of Morality, 1977; Editor: On Noam Chomsky, 1974, (with Donald Davidson) Semantics of Natural Language, 1971, The Logic of Grammar, 1975. Am. Council Learned Socs. fellow, 1974-75; Guggenheim fellow, 1978-79; NEH fellow, 1983-84. Mem. Am. Philos. Assn., Philosophy of Sci. Assn. Home: 106 Broadmead St Princeton NJ 08540 Office: Dept of Philosophy Princeton Univ Princeton NJ 08540

HARMAN, JOHN ROBERT, JR., management consultant; b. Balt., Aug. 29, 1921; s. John Robert and Katherine Butterfield H.; m. Lois Chase, Aug. 28, 1948; children—Katherine, John, Douglas, James. Ph.B., Loyola Coll., Balt., 1942; B.S. in Engring, U.S. Mil. Acad., 1945; M.A. in Psychology, Vanderbilt U., 1950. Asst. mgr. manpower Fairchild Engine div., Deer Park, L.I., N.Y., 1956-59; asst. to personnel mgr. Grumman Aircraft Engring. Corp., Bethpage, L.I., N.Y., 1959-60; cons. Booz, Allen & Hamilton, Inc., N.Y.C., 1960-62, asso., 1962-65, mng. asso., 1965-67, v.p., 1967-72, sr. v.p., 1973-81, mem. operating council, 1973-80; v.p. Booz, Allen Acquisition Services, 1972-73; dir. Booz Allen Internat. Mergers, 1972-73, sr. v.p. and mng. officer exec. personnel services, 1972-81; pres. Harman & Co. (mgmt. cons.), New Canaan, Conn., 1981—, also dir. Contbr. articles profl. jours. Trustee Village of Branch, Smithtown, L.I., N.Y., 1959-63; bd. dirs., exec. com., treas. Am. Cancer Soc., N.Y.C., 1978—; trustee Assn. Grads. U.S. Mil. Acad., 1976—; bd. dirs. West Point Soc. N.Y.; bd. sponsors Sch. Bus. and Mgmt., Loyola Coll., Balt., 1981—. Served to lt. U.S. Army, 1945-63. Mem. Assn. Exec. Recruiting Cons. (dir. 1977-80), Inst. Mgmt. Cons., Newcomen Soc., Assn. Corp. Growth., NAM (corp. governance com.). Clubs: University (chmn. activities com. and council), Sky (N.Y.C.); Country (New Canaan); Landmark (Stamford, Conn.); Commerce (Atlanta); Amelia Island Plantation (Fla.). Home: 674 Silvermine Rd New Canaan CT 06840 also 2011 Beachwood Dr Amelia Island Plantation Amelia Island FL 32034 Office: Box 1231 New Canaan CT 06840

HARMAN, JOHN ROYDEN, lawyer; b. Elkhart, Ind., June 30, 1921; s. James Lewis and Bessie Bell (Mountjoy) H.; m. Elizabeth Rae Crosier, Dec. 12, 1943; 1 son, James Richard. B.S., U. Ill., 1943; J.D., Ind. U., 1949. Bar: Ind. 1949. Since practiced in, Elkhart; asso. firm Proctor & Proctor, 1949-52; partner firm Cawley & Harman, 1960-65, Thornburg, McGill, Deahl, Harman, Carey & Murray, 1965-72, Barnes & Thornburg, 1972—; atty., City of Elkhart, 1952-60. State del. Ind. Republican Com., 1962-70; Pres., bd. dirs. Crippled Childrens Soc.; bd. dirs. United Community Services Elkhart County. Served to 1st lt., F.A. AUS, 1943-46; PTO. Mem. ABA, Ind. Bar Assn. (council 3d dist. corp. counsel sect.), Elkhart County Bar Assn. (pres. 1977), Elkhart Bar Assn. (pres. 1970), Elkhart C. of C. (pres., dir. 1975—), Phi Kappa Psi, Alpha Kappa Psi, Phi Delta Phi. Presbyterian. Clubs: Rotary (pres. 1977-78), Elks, Elcona Country (Elkhart) (dir. 1981); Summit (South Bend, Ind.)). Home: 54905 Shorelane Elkhart IN 46514 Office: First Nat Bank Bldg Elkhart IN 46514 *Be honest and forthright—think positively—continually try to enhance the cause of mankind.*

HARMAN, WILLIAM BOYS, JR., lawyer; b. Newport News, Va., June 5, 1930; s. William Boys and Helen (Conner) H.; children: Susan Carol, Thomas Scott, Ann Carrington. A.B., Coll. William and Mary, 1951, J.D., 1956; LL.M., Georgetown U., 1960. Bar: Va. 1956, D.C. 1961. Tax atty. Gen. Motors Corp., Detroit, 1956-58; atty. Office Chief Counsel, IRS, Washington, 1958-59, Office of Tax Legis. Counsel, U.S. Treasury Dept., 1959-61; atty. firm Cummings & Sellers, Washington, 1961-62; asso. gen. counsel Am. Life Conv., Washington, 1962-67, gen. counsel, 1968-72; v.p. law Am. Life Ins. Assn., 1973-75; exec. v.p. Am. Council Life Ins., 1976-78; partner firm Sutherland, Asbill & Brennan, Washington, 1978—. Served with USCGR, 1952-54. Mem. Am. Bar Assn., Va. State Bar, D.C. Bar Assn., Assn. Life Ins. Counsel, Am. Law Inst., S.A.R., William and Mary Law Sch. Assn., Phi Beta Kappa, Phi Alpha Delta, Sigma Alpha Epsilon. Clubs: Washington Golf and Country, Met. Home: 1174 N Utah St Arlington VA 22201 Office: Sutherland Asbill & Brennan 1666 K St NW Washington DC 20006

HARMAN, WILLIAM RITTENHOUSE, lawyer; b. Dover, Del., Apr. 28, 1941; s. Jesse Archie and Maude Lattomus (Bramble) H.; m. Mary-Love Russell, July 23, 1966; 1 dau., Lisa Russell. A.B., Princeton U., 1963; J.D., U. Mich., 1966. Bar: N.Y. bar 1967. Asso. firm Mudge, Rose, Guthrie & Alexander, N.Y.C., 1966-72; v.p., sec., gen. counsel Morgan Stanley & Co., Inc., N.Y.C., 1972—, prin., 1981—. Mem. bd. deacons Brick Presbyterian Ch., N.Y.C., 1975-77; alumni class pres. Princeton U., 1978—; exec. com. Alumni Council, 1979—. Served with USMCR, 1966-72. Mem. Assn. Bar City N.Y., Am. Bar Assn., Securities Industry Assn., Nat. Assn. Securities Dealers. Clubs: Rockaway Hunting; Lawrence Beach (Lawrence, N.Y.). Home: 1 East End Ave New York NY 10021 Office: 1251 Ave of Americas New York NY 10020

HARMEL, MEREL HILBER, anesthesiologist, educator; b. Cleve., May 19, 1917; s. Louis and Hermine (Greenbaum) H.; m. Armide Chilcoat, July 2, 1944; children: Nancy Armide, Ruth Courtney, Priscilla Gover, Mary Louise. B.A., Johns Hopkins, 1938, M.D., 1943. Diplomate: Am. Bd. Anesthesiology. Practice medicine, specializing in anesthesiology, Albany, N.Y., 1948-52, Bklyn., 1952-68, Chgo., 1968-71; anesthesiologist-in-chief Albany Med. Center, 1948-52, State U. Kings County Med. Center, 1952-68, pres. med. bd., 1958-62, chmn. exec. com., 1964-65; cons. L.I. Jewish, St. Albans Naval, Maimonides, St. John's Episcopal, VA hosps.; prof., chmn. dept. anesthesiology State U. N.Y. Downstate Med. Center, 1952-68, Pritzker Sch. Medicine, U. Chgo., 1968-71; prof. anesthesiology Duke Med. Center, Durham, N.C., 1971—, chmn. dept. anesthesiology, 1971-83. Contbr. articles to profl. jours. Commonwealth fellow Oxford U., 1961-62. Fellow Am. Coll. Anesthesiology (gov.); mem. A.M.A., Am. Soc. Anesthesiologists, Assn. Univ. Anesthetists. Office: Dept Anesthesiology PO Box 3094 Duke U Med Center Durham NC 27710

HARMET, A(RNOLD) RICHARD, editor; b. Chgo., Nov. 13, 1932; s. Alfred Aloysius and Evelyn Amelia (Riesche) H.; m. Joan Harriet Morris, Dec. 28, 1957; children—Lynn Anne, Andrew Morris. B.A., Ripon Coll., 1954; M.S.J., Northwestern U., 1958. Mng. editor Popular Mechanics Press, Chgo., 1958-61; dir. publs. Ill. Inst. Tech., Chgo., 1961-63; dir. lit. counseling Am. Med. Assn., Chgo., 1963-65; mng. editor Sci. Yr., 1965; v.p., exec. editor World Book Yr. Book and Sci. Yr., 1966-69, World Book Ency., Chgo., 1969—. Served as lt., inf. AUS, 1954-56. Mem. Sigma Delta Chi. Home: 1530 N Dearborn Chicago IL 60610 Office: 546 Merchandise Mart Plaza Chicago IL 60654

HARMON, GARY LEE, educator; b. Aurora, Nebr., Aug. 16, 1935; s. Vyrle Martin and Esther (Koberstein) Uehling; m. Susanna Marie Pollock, Dec. 27, 1960; children: Thomas Thorburn, James Matthias, Nathan Martin. B.A., Hastings Coll., 1956; M.A. M.A.T., Ind. U., 1960, Ph.D., 1966; postgrad., U. Mich., 1962-63, Mich. State U., 1963-64. Instr. English, Flint (Mich.) Community Coll., 1960-64; asso prof., chmn. div. lang. and lit., dir. grad. English program Morehead (Ky.) State U., 1966-67; chmn. div. lang., lit., philosophy, chmn. English dept. Stephens Coll., Columbia, Mo., 1967-71; prof. lit. and English, chmn. dept. lang. and lit. U. North Fla., Jacksonville, 1971—. Author: (with R.F. Dickinson) Write Now, 1971, Write Now: Substance-Strategy-Style, 1972, Scholar's Market: An International Directory for Periodicals Publishing Literary Criticism, 1974, Fiction and Its Readers, 1980; also numerous articles on Am. lit. and popular culture. Ind. U. fellow, 1964-66; faculty research grantee Stephens Coll., 1971, U. North Fla., 1976, 79-80. Mem. MLA (exec. bd. popular culture div. 1978—), Popular Culture Assn. (v.p. 1980-81), Nat. Council Tchrs. of English, Am. Studies Assn., Popular Culture Assn. in South (pres. 1978, exec. sec. 1978—). Office: Dept Lang and Lit U North Fla Jacksonville FL 32216

HARMON, GEORGE MARION, college president; b. Memphis, Aug. 12, 1934; s. George M. and Madie P. (Foster) H.; m. Bessie W. Porter, Dec. 27, 1958; children: Nancy R., Mary K., Elizabeth T., George Marion. B.A., Southwestern U., 1956; M.B.A., Emory U., 1957; D.B.A., Harvard U., 1963. Market research analyst Continental Oil Co., Houston, 1957; research assoc. Harvard U., 1960-63; asst. prof. Coll. Bus. Adminstrn., dir. Salzberg Meml. Transp. Program Syracuse U., N.Y., 1963-66; sr. assoc. systems econs. div. Planning Research Corp., Washington, 1966-67; prof., chmn. dept econs. and bus. adminstrn., dir. continuing edn. program in econs. and bus. adminstrn. Southwestern U., Memphis, 1967-74; prof., dean div. bus. and mgmt. W.Va. Coll. Grad. Studies, Charleston, 1974-75; prof., dean Sch. Bus. and Mgmt. Saginaw Valley State Coll., University Center, Mich., 1975-78; pres. Millsaps Coll., Jackson, Miss., 1979—; mem. cons. staff Logistics Research, Inc., 1967—; dir. cons. staff Ramcon, Inc., 1968—; mem. faculty fin. Sch. Banking of the South, La. State U., 1968-72; dir. Audio Visual Systems, Inc., Tenn., 1970-72; v.p., treas. Allen Industries, Inc., Tenn., 1970-72; co-founder, v.p. Computer Survey Systems, Inc., Tenn., 1972-73; dir. McCarty Farms, Inc., Magee, Miss., Entex, Inc., Houston. Contbr. articles on bus. adminstrn. to profl. jours. Bd. dirs. Fayetteville-Manlius Central Sch. Dist., N.Y., 1961-63; trustee, chmn. personnel and labor relations com. Saginaw Osteo. Hosp., 1977-78; bd. dirs. Jackson Symphony Orch. Assn., 1981—, Miss. Opera Assn., 1981—; chmn. So. Colls. and Univs. Union, 1983—, Miss. Found. Ind. Colls., 1982. Served with U.S. Army, 1958-59. Mem. Jackson C. of C. (dir. 1981—), Phi Beta Kappa, Beta Sigma Gamma, Omicron Delta Kappa. Clubs: Scenic Hills Recreation (pres. 1971-74), Jackson Country, University, Petroleum. Lodge: Rotary. Home: 1837 Peachtree St Jackson MS 39202 Office: Millsaps Coll 1701 N State St Jackson MS 39210

HARMON, HARRY WILLIAM, architect, educator; b. San Francisco, Feb. 8, 1918; s. Harry A. and Isabel (Quagelli) A.; m. Lois Anna Holtin, July 28, 1953; children: Bruce Gregory, Mark Brian, Patricia Andree. B.Arch., U. So. Calif., 1941. Draftsman Kaufmann, Lippincott & Eggers (architects), Los Angeles, 1945-48; project architect UCLA, 1948-50, sr. architect, 1952-62; chief coll. facilities planning Calif. State Colls., Inglewood, Calif., 1962-67, asst. vice chancellor, Los Angeles, 1967-69, vice chancellor phys. planning, devel., 1969-75, exec. vice chancellor, 1975-83; Spl. cons. FAO.; Mem. Nat. Panel Arbitrators. Bd. dirs. Region III United Way. Served to lt. USNR, 1942-45; to lt. comdr., 1950-51; capt. Res.; ret.). Fellow AIA (nat. dir. 1977-80, sec. 1981-85); mem. Assn. Univ. Architects, Council Ednl. Facility Planners Internat., Soc. Coll. and U. Planners, Am. Arbitration Assn., U. So. Calif. Alumni Assn., Blue Key, Alpha Rho Chi. Home: 17477 Drayton Hall Way Rancho Bernardo CA 92128 Office: 400 Golden Shore Long Beach CA 90802

HARMON, JAMES ALLEN, investment banker; b. N.Y.C., Oct. 12, 1935; s. Bert and Belle (Kirschner) H.; m. Jane Elizabeth Theaman, Aug. 11, 1957; children—Deborah Lynn, Douglas Lee, Jennifer Ann. B.A., Brown U., 1957; M.B.A., Wharton Grad. Sch., U. Pa., 1959. With N.Y. Hanseatic Corp., N.Y.C., 1959-74, sr. v.p., 1969-74; gen. partner Wertheim & Co., Inc., 1975—, dir., vice chmn., 1980—; dir. Ames Dept. Stores, Inc., Hartford, Conn., Erbamont N.V., Augat, Inc., Attleboro, Mass., Lumex, Inc., Bay Shore, L.I., Mountain Fuel Supply Co., Salt Lake City, Compo Industries, Welded Tube Co. Am., Phila. Trustee Brown U.; bd. dirs. Cultural Assistance Center. Home: 43 Kettle Creek Rd Weston CT 06883 Office: 200 Park Ave New York NY 10166

HARMON, LEON C., banker; b. Lincoln, Kans., Sept. 17, 1925; s. Amos Earl and Aggie Olive (Shaefer) H.; m. Dorothy Lois Morrison, Aug. 18, 1967; children by previous marriage: Steve, Gail, Kent. Student, Sch. of Banking U. Colo., 1950-52. Cashier First Nat. Bank of Riverton, Wyo., 1952-55, v.p., 1955-56, pres., 1957-63; pres., chief exec. officer N.Mex. Bank & Trust Co., Hobbs, 1963-81, First Interstate Bank of Utah, Salt Lake City, 1981—; dir. Skaggs Cos., Inc., Salt Lake City. Bd. dirs. United Way, Salt Lake City, 1982—. Served with USN, 1943-46. Recipient Disting. Service award Jr. C. of C., Riverton, 1952. Mem. Am. Bankers Assn. (govt. relations council 1981), Utah Bankers Assn. (legis. com. 1981—). Republican. Methodist. Clubs: Country, Alta, Mason (Salt Lake City). Office: First Interstate Bank of Utah NA 175 S Main St Salt Lake City UT 84111

HARMON, LILY, artist, author; b. New Haven, Nov. 19, 1912; d. Benjamin and Bessie (Horowitz) Perelmutter; m. Joseph H. Hirshhorn, 1945 (div. 1956); children: Amy, JoAnn; m. Milton Schachter, Oct. 1972. Student, Yale Sch. Art, 1929-31, Academie Colarossi Paris, 1931-32, Art Students League, 1932-33. Illustrator: Pride and Prejudice (Jane Austen), 1950, Sounds of a Distant Drum (Bill Martin, Jr.), 1967; Japanese books Buddenbrooks (Thomas Mann), 1965, Symphonie Pastorale (André Gide), 1965, The Counterfeiters (André Gide), 1965, Dirty Hands (Jean Paul Sartre), 1965, The Castle (Franz Kafka), 1965, Metamorphosis (Franz Kafka), 1965, Lafcadio's Adventures (André Gide), 1972, Therese (Francois Mauriac), 1972, House of Mirth (Edith Wharton), 1975, Short Stories of Guy de Maupassant, 1976; author: autobiography Freehand, 1981; One-man shows, Asso. Am. Artists Galleries, N.Y.C., 1944, 50, 53, 56, 57, Silvermine Art Assn., 1954, Westchester County Arts & Crafts, 1950, Ann Ross Gallery, N.Y.C., 1959, Selected Artists Gallery, N.Y.C., 1960, HCE Gallery, Provincetown, Mass., 1961, Yamada Gallery, Kyoto, Japan, 1963, Scargo Lake Gallery, Dennis, Mass., 1964, Tirca Karlis Gallery, Provincetown, Krasner Gallery, N.Y.C., 1966, Provincetown Group Gallery, Internat. Salon Palace of Fine Arts, Mexico City, 1973, U. Richmond, Marsh Gallery, George M. Modlin Fine Arts Center, Krasner Gallery, N.Y.C., 1977, 81; One-man shows, Summit Gallery, N.Y.C., 1981; others, one-man retrospective show, Wichita Art Mus., Kans., 1982, Butler Inst. Am. Art, Youngstown, Ohio, 1983, Provincetown Art Assn. and Mus.; represented in permanent collections, Butler Art Inst., Youngstown, Ohio, Whitney Mus. Am. Art, N.Y.C., Newark Mus., Ein Harod and Tel Aviv (Israel) museums, U. Mass. at Amherst, Kalamazoo (Mich.) Art Inst., Smithsonian Art Inst., Washington, St. Lawrence U. Mem. Provincetown Art Assn., Artists Equity Assn., Nat. Acad. Design, Provincetown Art Assn., Fine Arts Work Ctr. Home: 151 Central Park West New York NY 10023 also 629 Commercial St Provincetown MA 02657

HARMON, MERLE REID, SR., sportscaster; b. Orchardville, Ill., June 21, 1927; s. Herschel and Oda Ethel (Holler) H.; m. Jeanette Kinner, Dec. 31, 1947; children: Reid, Keith, Kyle, Bruce, Kara. A.A., Graceland Coll., 1947; B.A., U. Denver, 1949. Pres. Merle Harmon Enterprises, Inc., Milw., 1967—, Fan Fair Corp., 1977—. Sportscaster, Topeka, Kans., 1949-52, Kansas. U. Network, Lawrence, 1952-54; baseball announcer, Kansas City A's, 1955-61, Milw. Braves, 1964-65, Minn. Twins, 1967-69, Milw. Brewers, 1970-79; sportscaster, ABC-TV, 1961-73; N.Y. Jets announcer, WABC Radio, N.Y., 1964-72; co-host, World Univ. Games from, Moscow, TVS Network, 1973, Big Ten Basketball, 1974-80; sportscaster, NBC Sports, N.Y.C., 1979—, Tex. Rangers, 1982—. Chmn. Easter Seal Campaign, Milwaukee County, Wis., 1981; bd. dirs. Easter Seal Soc., Milwaukee County, Wis., 1981—; trustee Park Coll., Parkville, Mo., 1979—. Served with USN, 1944-46. Recipient Outstanding Alumnus award Nat. Assn. Intercollegiate Athletics, 1972, Disting. Service award Graceland Coll., 1978. Mem. Nat. Assn. Sports Broadcasters, Brookfield Wis. C. of C., Wauwatosa Wis. C. of C. Mem. Ch. of Jesus Christ of Latter-day Saints. Office: care HSE Sports Entertainment PO Box 1111 Arlington TX 76010 *

HARMON, MONT JUDD, educator; b. Tremonton, Utah, Aug. 7, 1917; s. Mont and Alice (Judd) H.; m. Helen Gleave, Dec. 28, 1936; children—Judd Scott, Michael Mont. B.S., Utah State U., 1948; M.S., U. Wis., 1951, Ph.D., 1953. Instr. polit. sci. Utah State U., Logan, 1951-53, asst. prof., 1954-57, asso. prof., 1958-62, prof., 1962—, also Merrill prof. polit. sci., head dept. polit. sci., 1963-67, dean, 1967-69, 1970-76. Author: Political Thought: From Plato to the Present, 1964, Political Philosophy I, II, 1977; Contbg. editor: Dictionary of Political Science, 1964, Handbook of World History, 1967; editor: Essays on the Constitution of the United States, 1978. Served with USNR, 1944-46. Mem. Am., Western polit. sci. assns., Phi Kappa Phi, Pi Sigma Alpha. Home: 999 Sumac Dr Logan UT 84321

HARMON, MYRA RUTH FREED, accountant, tax cons.; b. Danville, Ind., June 7, 1917; d. John Elbert and Myra (Bartoo) Freed; m. Russell H. Harmon, Sept. 2, 1967 (div. dec. 1969); 1 stepdau., Mrs. Charles L. Vogt. Jr. B.A., De Pauw U., 1939. Asst. office and credit mgr. Firestone Stores, Lafeyette, Ind., 1939-41, office and credit mgr., 1942-68; sec.-treas. Monticello Tire Mart, Ind., 1963-74; now accountant and tax cons.; Mem. Fgn. Service Selection Bd., Dept. State, 1972; trustee Bus. and Profl. Women's Found., 1966-73. Mem. Internat. Fedn. Bus. and Profl. Women (finance chmn. 1971-77, hon. treas. 1977—), Nat. Bus. and Profl. Women's Club (pres. 1969-70), Ind. Bus. and Profl. Women's Club (pres. 1961-62), Lafayette Bus. and Profl. Women's Club (pres. 1944-45, Lady of Year award 1966), Pub. Mems. Assn. Fgn. Service, Lafayette Altrusa Club (dir. 1955-56, corr. sec. 1956-57), Delta Chi Sigma (pres. 1952-53). Home: 1964 W Acacia St Hemet CA 92343

HARMON, PATRICK, newspaperman; b. St. Louis, Sept. 2, 1916; s. Jack and Laura (Duchesne) H.; m. Anne M. Worland, Aug. 31, 1940; children—Michael, Timothy, Kathleen, Daniel, John, Sheila, Peggy, Brigid, Kevin, Teresa, Christopher. A.B., U. Ill., 1939. Sports editor News-Gazette, Champaign, Ill., 1942-47, Gazette, Cedar Rapids, Iowa, 1947-51, Post, Cin., 1951—; sports commentator Sta. WCPO-TV, Cin., 1953-56, Sta. WKRC, 1958, Sta. WLW-TV, 1958-68. Contbg. sports editor: World Book, 1959—; regional sports editor: Illustrated Ency. of Sports, 1960—. Recipient Fred Hutchinson Meml. award for community service, 1969; named Internat. Churchmen's Sports Writer of Year, 1973. Mem. Sigma Chi. Home: 19 Walnut St Wyoming OH 45215 Office: 125 East Ct Cincinnati OH 45202

HARMON, ROBERT LEE, business executive; b. St. Louis, Oct. 31, 1926; s. Jess G. and Lela E. H.; m. Carolyn Metzger, June 9, 1951; children: Robert Lee, Barbara C., Nancy K., Celia A., Julia G., Melinda M. B.S., B.A., Washington U., St. Louis, 1949. With IBM, 1949-60, exec. asst. to sales mgr., N.Y.C., then br. mgr., Chgo.; asst. v.p. McDonnell Aircraft Corp. (became McDonnell Aircraft Co. div. McDonnell Douglas Corp. 1968), St. Louis, 1960-66; gen. mgr. McDonnell Automation Center, 1960-66; v.p., gen. mgr. McDonnell Automation Co., St. Louis, 1966-70; exec. v.p. comml. McDonnell Douglas Automation Co., St. Louis, 1970-82; corp. v.p. McDonnell Douglas Corp., St. Louis, 1975—, corp. v.p. civic affairs, 1983—; dir. Bank Bldg. Corp. Pres. Mo. Bapt. Hosp. Pacesetters, 1973-75; mem. exec. com. bd. trustees Mo. Bapt. Hosp., St. Louis, 1978—; bd. dirs. St. Louis Regional Commerce and Growth Assn., 1983—; moderator Delmar Bapt. Ch., St. Louis, 1969-72, 76-78, mem. exec. council, 1969—, endowment fund dir., 1976—, pres. bd. trustees, 1979—, former deacon, Sunday sch. tchr.; chmn. New Frontiers dist. Boy Scouts Am., 1976-78, 80; trustee, chmn. long range planning com. Mo. Bapt. Hosp., St. Louis, 1978—; past pres. Century Club, Washington U. Served to lt. (j.g.) U.S. Mcht. Marines, 1944-47. Mem. Sales and Mktg. Execs., Washington U. Sch. Bus. Alumni Assn. (exec. com., chmn. bd. govs.), Omicron Delta Kappa, Delta Sigma Pi, Beta Gamma Sigma. Club: St. Louis Beta Theta Pi (past pres.). Home: 3 Portland St Saint Louis MO 63131 Office: PO Box 516 Saint Louis MO 63166

HARMONY, MARLIN DALE, chemistry educator, researcher; b. Lincoln, Nebr., Mar. 2, 1936; s. Philip and Helen Irene (Michael) H. A.A., Kansas City (Mo.) Jr. Coll., 1956; B.S. in Chem. Engring., U. Kans., 1958; Ph.D. in Chemistry, U. Calif.-Berkeley, 1961. Asst. prof. U. Kans., Lawrence, 1962-67, assoc. prof., 1967-72, prof., 1972—, chmn., 1980—; panel mem. NRC-Nat. Bur. Standards., 1969-78; mem.review panel NSF, 1977. Author: Introduction to Molecular Energies and Soectra, 1972; contbg. editor: Physics Vade Mecum, 1981; contbr. articles to profl. jours. Fellow NSF, 1961-62. Mem. Am. Chem. Soc., Am. Phys. Soc., AAAS, Alpha Chi Sigma, Phi Lambda Upsilon, Tau Beta Pi. Democrat. Home: 1033 Avalon Rd Lawrence KS 66044 Office: Dept Chemistry U Kans Lawrence KS 66045

HARMS, ELIZABETH LOUISE, artist; b. Milw., May 26, 1924; d. Frederick George and Veva (Sanderson) H.; m. Douglas Derwood Craft, Sept. 8, 1951. Diploma, Sch. Art Inst. Chgo., 1950, B.F.A., 1963, M.F.A., 1964. Instr. Ft. Wayne (Ind.) Art Mus. Sch., 1952-54; graphic designer Scott, Foresman Publs., Chgo., 1954-61; faculty Sch. Art Inst. Chgo., 1963-64, 65-66, Carnegie-Mellon U., Pitts., 1966-69, Fairleigh Dickenson U., Rutherford, N.J., 1969-71, Coll. New Rochelle, N.Y., 1979. One-man shows, 55 Mercer St., N.Y.C., 1980, Fisch- bach Gallery, N.Y.C., 1975, Carnegie Inst. Mus. Art, 1969, Condeso/ Lawler, N.Y.C., 1982, group shows include, Moravian Coll., Bethlehem, Pa., 1978, Jersey City Mus., 1980, North of New Brunswick, South of N.Y., Rutgers-Newark, 1981, Coll. of New Rochelle, 1982; rep. by, Condeso/Lawler, N.Y.C. Recipient hon. mention Pratt Graphic Center, N.Y.C., 1974, Armstrong prize Art Inst. Chgo., 1962; Tiffany Found grantee, 1977. Home: 240 Ogden Ave Jersey City NY 07307

HARMS, ROBERT THOMAS, linguist, educator; b. Peoria, Ill., Apr. 12, 1932; s. Wilbert Erwin and Mildred Matilda (Thomas) H.; m. Sirpa Helina Aaltonen, July 1, 1956; children: Kirsti Maria, Ritva Helena, Eerik Thomas, Timo Kalevi. A.B., U. Chgo., 1952, A.M. in Slavic Langs, 1956, Ph.D. in Linguistics, 1960; postgrad. (Fulbright scholar), U. Helsinki, Finland, 1954-56; U.S.-Soviet exchange, Leningrad State U., 1962-63. Instr. U. Tex., Austin, 1958-61, asst. prof. linguistics, 1961-64, asso. prof., 1965-67, prof., 1967—, chmn. dept. linguistics, 1973-77; Vis. asst. prof. Columbia U., 1960, vis. asso. prof., 1965, Ohio State U., 1964; U.S.-Hungary exchange prof. U. Szeged (Hungarian Acad. Scis.), Budapest, 1967-68. Author: Estonian Grammar, 1962, Finnish Structural Sketch, 1964, Introduction to Phonological Theory, 1968; Editor: (with Emmon Bach) Universals in Linguistic Theory, 1968. Fulbright research grantee, Finland, 1968; Nat. Acad. Scis. exchange prof. Acad. Scis. USSR and Estonian Acad. Scis. Mem. Linguistic Soc. Am., Finno-Ugrian Soc., Phi Beta Kappa. Lutheran. Home: 2609 Deerfoot Trail Austin TX 78704 Office: Dept of Linguistics U Tex Austin TX 78712

HARMSEN, TYRUS GEORGE, librarian; b. Pomona, Calif., July 24, 1924; s. Fred H. and Hazel (Weigle) H.; m. Lois Spaulding, Apr. 15, 1955; children—Mark Spaulding, Caroline Lora. A.B., Stanford, 1947, M.A., 1950; A.B. in L.S, U. Mich., 1948. Cataloguer dept. manuscripts Henry E. Huntington Library, San Marino, Calif., 1948-49, 50-59; librarian Occidental Coll., Los Angeles, 1959—; Vis. lectr. Sch. Library Sci., U. So. Calif., 1958, 68. Author: The Plantin Press of Saul and Lillian Marks, 1960. Served with AUS, 1943-46. Council on Library Resources fellow, 1969. Mem. ALA. Presbyterian. Clubs: Zamorano, Rounce and Coffin (Los Angeles) (treas. 1956—). Home: 1300 Medford Rd Pasadena CA 91107 Office: Occidental Coll Library 1600 Campus Rd Los Angeles CA 90041

HARNACK, MRS. CURTIS *See* **CALISHER, HORTENSE**

HARNACK, ROBERT SPENCER, educator; b. Milw., Oct. 22, 1918; s. Elmer Frank and Carolyn (Woppert) H.; m. Dorothy Helen Scherbarth, Sept. 5, 1942; children: Robert Spencer, William James. Ph.B., U. Wis., 1941, Ph.M., 1946, Ph.D., 1951. Curriculum coordinator pub. schs., Milw., 1951-54; mem. faculty State U. N.Y. at Buffalo, 1954—, prof. curriculum devel., 1954—, chmn. dept., 1965-75. Author: The Use of Electronic Computers to Improve the Individualization of Instruction Through Unit Teaching, 1965, Developing and Using Micro-computer-based Resource Units, 1983, The Grundtvig Culture, 1983. Served with USNR, 1941-45. Mem. Assn. Supervision and Curriculum Devel. (dir. N.Y. chpt. 1965-68), United Univ. Profs., N.Y. State United Tchrs. Home: 235 Siegfried Dr Buffalo NY 14221 *The education of children and adults will always be the most important task of civilization. To know, to think reflectively, and to initiate only actions which allow for further improvements of education and living is, to me, a combined goal and standard of conduct.*

HARNED, DAVID BAILY, college president; b. Allentown, Pa., June 5, 1932; s. William Biechele and Mary (Baily) H.; m. Elaine Paula Heydenreich, July 1, 1961; children: Christopher Baily, Timothy Heydenreich. B.A., Yale U., 1954, B.D., 1957, M.A., 1959, Ph.D., 1963; postgrad., New Coll. Edinburgh U., Scotland, 1954-55. Ordained to ministry Lutheran Ch., 1961; instr. Williams Coll., 1960-61, Yale U., 1962-63; asst. prof. religion Smith Coll., 1963-67, asso. prof., 1967; prof. religious studies U. Va., Charlottesville, 1967-80, chmn. dept., 1967-72, 75-80; pres. Allegheny Coll., Meadville, Pa., 1980—; vis. research prof. religious studies Punjabi U., Patiala, India, 1970, 78; chmn. bd. selection post-doctoral fellowships for Cross-Disciplinary Study, 1970-73; vis. prof. Christian dogmatics U. Edinburgh, Scotland, 1972-73, 76-77, 79-80; Westervelt lectr., 1979, Slover lectr., 1980. Author: Theology and the Arts, 1966, The Ambiguity of Religion, 1968, 69, Grace and Common Life, 1970 (Indian edit., 1970), rev., 1971, Faith and Virtue, 1973, Brit. edit., 1974, Images for Self-Recognition, 1977, Creed and Personal Identity, 1981, Brit. edit., 1981; Editor: (with J.F. Childress) Secularization and the Protestant Prospect, 1970, 71; mem. editorial bd.: Jour. Religious Studies, India, 1969—; others. Insight. Pres. League Winant Vols., 1951. Recipient Disting. Prof. award U. Va., 1978; Nat. Endowment for Humanities Jr. Humanist, 1970-71; fellow Soc. Religion in Higher Edn.; Kent fellow, 1957-60; Rockefeller doctoral fellow, 1959-60. Lutheran. Home: 286 Jefferson St Meadville PA 16335

HARNED, JOHN C., college administrator; b. Bronxville, NY, July 9, 1927; s. Samuel Albert and Elinor Clarke (Colwell) H.; m. Jill Fitz Randolph Walker, July 29, 1961; children: Peter Clarke, Wendy Linwood, Julie Colwell, James John. A.B., Dartmouth Coll., 1950; M.B.A., Harvard Univ., 1952. Fin. analyst Glore Forgan & Co., N.Y.C., 1953-65, ptnr., 1960-65; sr. v.p. Glore Forgan Staats Inc., N.Y.C., 1965-70, dir., 1965-70; pres. Bedford Advisers, Inc., N.Y.C., 1970-77; v.p. fin. St. Joe Minerals Corp., N.Y.C., 1977-82; exec. v.p., chief fin. officers Penn Central Corp., N.Y.C., 1982-83; v.p. Dartmouth Coll., Hanover, NH, 1984—. Bd. dirs. Caramoor, Katonah, N.Y., 1977-79; chmn. Lower Hudson chpt. Nature Conservancy, Mt. Kisco, N.Y., 1979-81, trustee, Mt. Kisco, N.Y., 1979-84; mem. Bedford Conservation Bd., N.Y., 1978-80. Served with USN, 1945-46; Sasebo, Japan. Mem. Bond Club N.Y., N.Y. Soc. Security Analysts. Presbyterian. Clubs: Wall St. (N.Y.C.); Bedford Golf and Tennis (gov. 1974-84, treas. 1978-81. Office: Dartmouth Coll 224 Blunt Alumni Ctr Hanover NH 03755

HARNEDY, EDMUND RICHARD, insurance executive; b. N.Y.C., June 11, 1930; s. Richard Joseph and Margaret (McSweeney) H.; m. Joan Catherine Holland, Dec. 29, 1962; children: Richard, Julia. B.S., U. Ill., 1952; J.D., Fordham U., 1957; LL.M., NYU, 1961. Bar: N.Y. 1957. Atty., New York Life Ins. Co., N.Y.C., 1957-63, asst. counsel, 1963-66, asso. counsel, 1966-69, asst. gen. counsel, 1969-72, 2d v.p., 1972-73, sec., 1973-82, v.p., sec., 1982—. Served to 1st lt. AUS, 1952-54. Mem. ABA, Am. Soc. Corp. Secs. Home: 611 Knollwood Rd White Plains NY 10603 Office: 51 Madison Ave New York NY 10010

HARNER, MICHAEL JAMES, anthropology educator; b. Washington, Apr. 27, 1929; s. Charles Emory and Virginia (Paxton) H.; m. June Knight Kocher, 1951; children: Teresa J., James E.; Sandra Ferial Dickey; 1966. A.B., U. Calif., Berkeley, 1953, Ph.D. (Social Sci. Research Council, Doherty Found., Am. Museum Natural History fellow and grantee), 1963. Asst. prof. Ariz. State U., 1958-61; from sr. mus. anthropologist to asso. research anthropologist, asst. dir. Lowie Mus. Anthropology, U. Calif., Berkeley, 1961-67; vis. asso. prof., then asso. prof. Columbia U., 1966-70; vis. asso. prof. Yale U., 1970, U. Calif., Berkeley, 1971, 72, vis. prof., 1975; asso. prof. to prof. grad. faculty New Sch. Social Research, N.Y.C., 1970—, chmn. dept. anthropology, 1973-77; research, Upper Amazon basin, 1956-57, 60-61, 64, 69, 73, Western N.Am., 1951-53, 59, 65, 76, 78; Mem. profl. and sci. advisory bd. on drug abuse Nat. Council on Drug Abuse; bd. dirs. Internat. Transpersonal Assn.; hon. mem. Synthesis Grad. Sch. Study of Man; founder and dir. Center for Shamanic Studies, Norwalk, Conn. Animist; author: The Jivaro: People of the Sacred Waterfalls, 1972, Music of the Jivaro of Ecuador, 1972, The Way of the Shaman, 1980; co-author: Cannibal, 1979; Editor: Hallucinogens and Shamanism, 1973; Contbg. editor: Jour. Calif. Anthropology. Fellow Am. Anthrop. Assn., Explorers Club, AAAS, N.Y. Acad. Scis. (co-chmn. anthropology sect. 1980-81); mem. Soc. Med. Anthropology, Am. Ethnol. Soc., Soc. Am. Archaeology, Soc. Ethnohistory, Assn. Transpersonal Anthropology, Soc. Econ. Anthropology, Latin Am. Anthropology Group, Assn. Transpersonal Psychology, Inst. Ecuatoriano de Anthropologia y Geografia. Address: Dept Anthropology Grad Faculty New Sch Social Research 65 Fifth Ave New York NY 10003

HARNER, PAUL B., gray iron foundry exec.; b. Kutztown, Pa., Oct. 30, 1909; s. John Z. and Katie (Breitensteine) H.; m. Flora A. Schoenley, Nov. 26, 1936; children—Carl J., Mary A. B.A., Franklin and Marshall Coll., 1931; M.B.A., U. Pa., 1932. With Union Mfg. Co., Inc., Boyertown, Pa., 1932-68, pres., 1963-68; with Fashion Hosiery Mills, Inc., Boyertown, 1936-68, pres., 1965-68; pres., dir. Berkmont Industries, Boyertown, 1968—, chmn. bd., 1974—; past dir. Farmers Nat. Bank & Trust Co., Boyertown. Bd. dirs., past chmn. indsl. com. United Chest Bovertown. Mem. Nat. Gray and Ductile Iron Soc. (dir., past sec., citation for service 1968), Am. Foundrymen's Soc. (dir. Phila. chpt. 1971-72, chmn. 1975-76), Gray and Ductile Iron Founders Soc. (dir. 1971-73, sec. 1967-68, treas. 1971-74). Club: Rotarian (past pres. Boyertown). Home: 600 Highland St Boyertown PA 19512 Office: Berkmont Industries 6th and Washington Sts Boyertown PA 19512

HARNESS, DON KENNETH, patent lawyer; b. Detroit, Apr. 24, 1921; s. J. King and Vera (Gregory) H.; m. Janice Smith, Nov. 23, 1974; children—Jay K., Linda J. Student, U. Mich. Engring. Coll., 1939-41; J.D., Wayne State U., 1947. Bar: Mich. bar 1947. With engring. dept. Chrysler Corp., 1941-44; with firm Harness, Dickey & Pierce, 1947—, partner, 1949—. Bd. dirs. Children's Center of Wayne County, 1953-60, 67-70, pres., 1957-59; bd. dirs. Cranbrook Sch., 1966-71, Mich. Assn. Emotionally Disturbed Children, Boys' Republic, 1954-69; pres. Boys' Republic, 1959-60; trustee Straith Meml. Hosp., 1953-78, pres., 1971-78. Served from pvt. to 1st lt., inf. AUS, 1944-46. Recipient Distinguished Service award U.S. Jr. C. of C., 1954. Mem. Am. Patent Law Assn., Am., Mich., Oakland County bar assns., Horsemen's Benevolent and Protective Assn. (pres. Mich. div. 1974-79, nat. v.p. 1977-79), Mich. Thoroughbred Breeders and Owners Assn. (dir. 1973-74), Delta Tau Delta, Delta Theta Phi. Lutheran. Clubs: Rotarian (pres. Detroit 1956-57), Orchard Lake Country (pres. 1966), Recess (pres. 1972—). Office: 1500 N Woodward Blvd Birmingham MI 48011

HARNESS, EDWARD GRANVILLE, soap products manufacturing company executive; b. Marietta, Ohio, Dec. 17, 1918; s. Lewis Nye and Mary (McKinney) H.; m. Mary McCrady Chaney, Aug. 7, 1943; children: Frances Ann (Mrs. Daniel J. Jones), Edward Granville, Robert R. A.B., Marietta Coll., 1940. With Procter & Gamble Co., Cin., 1940—, v.p. paper products div., 1963-66, v.p.-group exec., dir., 1966-70, exec. v.p., 1970-71, pres., 1971—, chmn. bd., chief exec. officer, 1974-81, chmn. exec. com., 1981—; dir. Caterpillar Tractor Co., Exxon Corp. Chmn. bd. trustees Marietta Coll.; trustee Ohio Found. Ind. Colls.; trustee, vice chmn. Conf. Bd. Served with USAAF, 1942-46. Mem. Bus. Council, Conf. Bd. Clubs: Commercial, Carmargo, Queen City, Commonwealth (Cin.). Office: Procter & Gamble Co 301 E 6th St Cincinnati OH 45202 *

HARNESS, WILLIAM EDWARD, tenor; b. Pendleton, Oreg., Nov. 26, 1940; s. Edward Cleo and Edna Margaret (Senn) H.; m. Anna Marie Ward, Jan. 11, 1964; children—Janine Kay, Heidi Maurine, William Edward, Shaana Marie, Shane Michael. Student pub. schs., Spokane, Wash. Gen. carpenter Rainway Mfg. Co., Spokane, 1958-61; with Wash. Water Power Co., Spokane, 1961-62; tech. service rep. Nat. Cash Register Co., Seattle, 1962-73. Concert and opera tenor various opera cos. and symphonies, 1973—; profl. debut, San Francisco Opera Co., 1973; debut with, N.Y.C. Opera, 1976, Met. Opera, N.Y.C., 1977, Hamberg (W.Ger.) Opera, 1978; maj. symphony debuts include, Vancouver (B.C., Can.), Seattle, Los Angeles Philharmonic, San Francisco, Minn., Milw. symphonies; sacred concert artist, 1978—; roles include; Edmondo in: Manon Lescaut; Tonio in: Daughter of the Regiment; Alfredo in: La Traviata; Rodolfo in: La Boheme; Count Almaviva in: The Barber of Seville; Tamino in: The Magic Flute; Faust in: Faust; Cauaradossi in: Tosca; Prince Calof in: Turandot. Recipient V.I.P. award Nat. Cash Register Co., 1970; Florence Bruce award San Francisco Opera, 1972; Enrico Caruso award, 1973; Cecilia Schultz award Seattle Opera, 1972; Distinguished Citizen award State of Wash., 1974; Nat. Opera Inst. fellow, 1973-74; Martha Baird Rockefeller grantee, 1974-76. Mem. Am. Guild Mus. Artists, Canadian Actors Equity. Address: 2132 W 235th Pl Torrance CA 90501 Office: care Columbia Artists Mgmt 165 W 57th St New York NY 10019 Office: William Harness Sacred Concert 1409 Marcelina Torrance CA 90501

HARNEST, GRANT HOPKINS, chemist, educator; b. Carthage, Ill., Nov. 23, 1916; s. Waldo Wright and Goldie (Hopkins) H.; m. Kathryn Irene Hampson, June 24, 1945. A.B., Knox Coll., 1939; M.S., Middlebury (Vt.) Coll., 1941; Ph.D., U. Va., 1945. Mem. faculty Middlebury Coll., 1943-45, 46—, prof. chemistry, 1956—, chmn. dept., 1953-70, John G. McCullough prof., 1964-75, Old Dominion prof., 1968-69, Irene Heinz and John LaPorte Given prof. in pre-med. scis., 1975-82, prof. emeritus, 1982—, chmn. div. natural scis., 1966-77; research asst. OSRD, U. Va., 1945-46. Contbr. articles to profl. jours. Recipient Bd. Visitors prize U. Va., 1947, James Flack Norris award for outstanding achievement in teaching chemistry, 1974, Knox Coll. Alumni Achievement award, 1982; Research Corp. grantee, 1948. Mem. Am. Chem. Soc. (pres. West Vt. sect. 1949-50, nat. councilor 1960-66), Sigma Xi, Alpha Chi Sigma (pres. U. Va. chpt. 1942-43). Home: 125 S Main St Middlebury VT 05753

HARNETT, DANIEL JOSEPH, diversified mfg. exec.; b. St. Paul, Aug. 1, 1930; s. Daniel Joseph and Catherine (Flynn) H.; m. Carolee Collins, Apr. 2, 1959; children—Lisa, Danny, Eric, Nicole. B.S., Marquette U., 1951, J.D., 1953; certificate exec. programs, U. Calif. at Los Angeles, 1967, Mass. Inst. Tech., 1968. Bar: Wis. bar 1953, Calif. bar 1959, U.S. Supreme Ct. bar 1962. With Northrop Corp., Beverly Hills, Calif., 1964-69; asst. adminstr. for industry affairs and tech. utilization NASA, Washington, 1969-72; now cons.; pres., chief operating officer, dir. Aeronca, Inc., Torrance, Calif., 1972-76; also dir. subsidiaries; chmn. bd., chief exec. officer Harnett and Assos., Los Angeles, 1975—. Mem. Sch. Bd., West Los Angeles, 1974; Pres. Nat. Contract Mgmt. Found.; bd. advisers Reliability and Maintainability Symposium, 1972; bd. cons. Marymount Schs., 1976—. Served with USNR, 1953-57; Hon. mem. faculty U.S. Army Logistics Mgmt. Center. Fellow Nat. Contract Mgmt. Assn. (bd. advisers); mem. Am., Fed., Calif., Wis. bar assns., Delta Theta Phi. Clubs: Jonathan, Brown's Run Country, Charlotte City. Home: 127 N Cliffwood Ave Los Angeles CA 90049

HARNETT, DAVID ARTHUR, univ. dean; b. Washington, Oct. 2, 1940; s. Arthur John and Anne Mary (Leonard) H. B.A., Georgetown U., 1962, M.A., Harvard U., 1962, Ph.D., 1969, diploma ednl. adminstrn., 1972. Dean Advanced Standing Harvard U., 1968-77, sec. faculty arts and scis., 1970-77; prof. social scis., dean Coll. Nova U., Ft. Lauderdale, Fla., 1977-79; prof. history, v.p., acad. dean Bradford (Mass.) Coll., 1979-80; prof. history, dean arts and scis. U. San Francisco, 1980—; trustee Mellen Found., United World Colls. Mem. Mayor of San Francisco Com. on San Francisco-Shanghai Relations, 1980—. Ekblom fellow, 1962-63; Danforth-Kent fellow, 1965-68. Mem. Soc. Values in Higher Edn. Democrat. Roman Catholic. Clubs: Harvard (San Francisco and N.Y.C.); Olympic (San Francisco). Office: Harney Center 240 U San Francisco CA 94117

HARNETT, DONALD LEE, business educator; b. Everett, Wash., Apr. 26, 1937; s. Arthur Lee and Anne (Kuchenreuther) H.; m. Janet Louise Hartman, June 22, 1963; children: Kendall Lee, Kristine Louise. B.A., Pa. State U., 1959, M.A., 1961; Ph.D., Cornell U., 1964. Asst. prof. Ind. U., Bloomington, 1964-68, assoc. prof., 1969-71, internat. research scholar, Brussels, Belguim, 1969-70, prof., chmn. qunatitative bus. analysis, Bloomington, 1971—; vis. assoc. prof. Harvard U., Boston, 1968-69; vis. prof. U. Hawaii, Honolulu, 1972. Author: An Introduction to Management Science, 1975, Introductory Statistical Analysis, 2d edit., 1980, Statistical Methods, 3d edit., 1982; contbr. articles to profl. jours. Recipient grant Ind. U., 1969-70, Teaching award Ind. U. Mem. Am. Inst. Decision Scis., Am. Statis Assn., Phi Kappa Phi, Pi Mu Epsilon. Presbyterian. Home: 2131 Meadowbluff Ct Bloomington IN 47401 Office: Ind U Sch Bus Bloomington IN 47401

HARNETT, JOSEPH DURHAM, oil company executive; b. Paterson, N.J., Aug. 23, 1917; s. James Harold and EMily (Steele) H.; m. Wilhelmina Nordstrom, June 21, 1941 (dec. July 1958); children: Gordon D., Linda C., Ralph H., David S.; m. Nancy Beam. B.S., Purdue U., 1939. With Consol. Edison Co., N.Y.C., 1939, Worthington Pump & Machinery Corp., 1940; with Standard Oil Co., Ohio, 1941-80, v.p., 1957-68, sr. v.p., 1968-70, exec. v.p., 1970-77, pres., 1977-80, also dir.; dir. Grace Geothermal Corp. Bd. dirs. Zaca Mesa Winery Cardiac Extension Inc. Mem. Am. Petroleum Inst. (dir.). Presbyterian. Clubs: Mentor Harbor Yacht, Country, Union, Pepper Pike (Cleve.); University (N.Y.C.). Home: 2799 Lander Rd Pepper Pike OH 44124 Office: Terminal Tower 1604 Terminal Tower Cleveland OH 44113

HARNETT, THOMAS AQUINAS, lawyer, insurance company executive; b. Bronx, N.Y., Mar. 22, 1924; s. William Joseph and Katherine Cecelia (Farrell) H.; m. Doris Mary Van Dien, Dec. 2, 1950; children: Dorisanne, Thomas A., William Arthur, Kathleen Anne. Tchrs. cert., Fordham U., 1943, LL.B., 1949; LL.D. (hon.), Coll. Ins., 1977. Bar: N.Y. 1949. With law dept. Nat. Surety Corp., N.Y.C., 1950-52; pvt. practice, N.Y.C., 1952-75; sr. partner firm Hart and Hume, 1969-75; supt. N.Y. State Ins. Dept., 1975-77; sr. v.p., counsel Travelers Corp., Hartford, Conn., 1977—; adv. Nat. Conf. Commrs. on Uniform State Laws, 1971-72. Contbr. articles to profl. publs. Bd. dirs. N.Y. State Urban Devel. Corp., 1975-77; bd. regents U. Hartford, 1980—; bd. dirs. Combined Health Appeal, 1980—, pres., 1983—; incorporator St. Francis Hosp., 1980—; pres. parish council Sacred Heart Roman Cath. Ch., Suffern, N.Y., 1966-70, also dir. religious edn.; chmn. Ramapo (N.Y.) Devel. Easement Acquisition Commn., 1968-75. Served with USAAF, World War II; PTO. Decorated Air medal. Fellow Internat. Acad. Trial Lawyers, Am. Bar Found.; mem. Internat. Assn. Ins. Counsel, Fed. Ins. Counsel, ABA (chmn. ins. sect. 1975-76), Am. Judicature Assn., N.Y. State Bar Assn. (ho. dels. 1974-75, chmn. ins. sect. 1974-75). Democrat. Clubs: Boca Raton (Fla.); University (Albany, N.Y.); Drug and Chemical, Manhattan (N.Y.C.); Nat. Lawyers (Washington); Glastonbury Hills. Home: 110 Millstone Rd Glastonbury CT 06033 also 875 E Camino Real Boca Raton FL Office: 1 Tower Sq (8PB) Hartford CT 06115

HARNEY, KENNETH ROBERT, editor, columnist; b. Jersey City, N.J., Mar. 25, 1944; s. Carroll John and Agnes Theresa (Flanagan) H.; m. Lynne Andrea Leon, Aug. 26, 1967; children: Alexandra Erin, Brendan Leon, Timothy Andrew. A.B. cum laude, Princeton U., 1966; postgrad. (grad. fellow), U. Pa., 1966-67. Progtam analyst U.S. Office Econ. Opportunity, 1970-72; exec. editor, partner The Housing & Devel. Reporter, Washington, 1972—; columnist Washington Post, 1974—; exec. dir. Inst. Profl. & Exec. Devel., Inc., Washington, 1977—; pres. Harney Corp., Bethesda, Md., 1980—; pub., editor Real Estate Rehab. Investor, 1983—; dir. BNA-Washington, Inc., Washington. Host radio show: Ken Harney on Real Estate, WASH-FM, Metromedia, 1980—; Author: Beating Inflation with Real Estate, 1979, Guide to Federal Housing Programs, 1982, Profits and Pitfalls: What Home Buyers and Investors Should Know About Equiting Sharing, 1983. Recipient First prize Nat. Journalism Achievement Competition Nat. Assn. Realtors, 1979, Golden Hammer award Nat. Assn. Home Builders, 1980. Mem. Nat. Assn. Real Estate Editors, AFTRA, Lambda Alpha. Republican. Clubs: Princeton, Nat. Press (Washington). Home: 3801 Bradley Ln Chevy Chase MD 20815 Office: 4853 Cordell Ave Penthouse Suite 5 Bethesda MD 20814

HARNICK, SHELDON MAYER, lyricist; b. Chgo., Apr. 30, 1924; s. Harry M. and Esther (Kanter) H.; m. Mary Boatner (annulled May 1957), Aug. 29, 1950; m. Elaine May, Mar. 25, 1962 (div. May 1963); m. Margery Gray, Oct. 8, 1965. Mus.B., Northwestern U., 1949. Writer light verse, songs; contbr. songs, Northwestern U.; ann. musical Waa-Mu Show, 1946-50; songs to Broadway, off-Broadway shows Two's Company, 1953, New Faces of 1952, John Murray Anderson's Almanac, 1954, The Shoestring Revue 1955, The Littlest Revue 1956, Shoestring '57, 1957; lyricist: (with composer Jerry Bock) Body Beautiful, 1958, Fiorello, 1959 (Tony awards, Pulitzer prize), Tenderloin, 1960, She Loves Me, 1963 (Grammy award), Fiddler on the Roof, 1964 (Tony award), Apple Tree, 1966, The Rothschilds, 1970, (with composer David Baker) Smiling the Boy Fell Dead, 1961, (with composer Richard Rodgers) Rex, 1976, (with composer Jack Beeson) Capt. Jinks of the Horse Marines, 1975, Dr. Heidegger's Fountain of Youth, 1978. Served with Signal Corps, AUS, 1943-46. Mem. Broadcast Music Inc., Am. Guild Authors and Composers, Dramatists Guild. Office: care David J Cogan 350 Fifth Ave New York NY 10001

HARNISCHFEGER, HENRY, building construction company; b. Milw., 1923. Pres., dir. Harnischfeger Homes, Inc., Milw.; chmn. bd. Harnischfeger Corp., Milw., 1970—, also chief exec. officer, former pres.; dir. First Wis. Corp., First Wis. Bancshares. *

HARNISH, JAY DEWEY, architect; b. Lancaster, Pa., May 21, 1898; s. Jacob Martin and Emma (Herr) H.; m. Jerene C. Reaver, Feb. 1, 1938 (dec. July 1980). B.Arch., U. Calif. at Berkeley, 1924. With art dept. MGM, 1936-37; sole practitioner, Ontario, Calif., 1940-60; pres. firm Harnish, Morgan & Causey (architects), Ontario, 1960-76, chmn. bd., 1976—; Sec., dir. Ontario Savs. & Loan Assn., 1960—; Mem. Calif. Bd. Archtl. Examiners, 1962-70, pres., 1964. Projects include San Antonio Community Hosp, Upland (recipient Hosp. of Month award Modern Hosp. 1966), HMC Bldg, Ontario (award for creative use concrete Portland Cement Assn. 1969), Ontario High Sch, (Merit award A.I.A. 1969), Lockheed Engring. Bldg, Ontario (Merit award A.I.A. 1970), Ontario Internat. Airport. Served with C.E. U.S. Army, 1916-17. Fellow AIA. Club: Red Hill Country (Cugamonga, Calif.). Home: 8060 Calle Carabe Ct Rancho Cucamonga CA 91730 Office: 500 East E St Ontario CA 91764

HARO, JOHN CALVIN, architect; b. East Chicago, Ind., June, 18, 1928; s. John Henry and Lydia (Lind) H.; m. Elizabeth Alison Smith, Dec. 26, 1954; children: John Stephen, Alexander James, Alison Margaret. Student, Mich. Technol. U., 1945-47; B.Arch., U. Mich., 1950; M.Arch., Harvard U., 1955. With firm Sanders & Malsin (Architects), Ann Arbor, Mich., 1950-51; firm Minoru Yamasaki & Assos., Detroit, 1952-54; with Albert Kahn Assos., Inc. (Architects & Engrs.), Detroit, 1955-73, asso., 1959-63, v.p., chief archtl. designer, 1963-73; also dir.; v.p., corporate dir. design Smith Hinchman & Grylls Assos., Inc. (Architects, Engrs., Planners), Detroit, 1973-77; v.p., dir. planning and design Albert Kahn Assos., 1977—; Instr. Boston Archtl. Center, 1954; adj. prof. Coll. Architecture and Design, U. Mich., 1972, 76, 77, Coll. Architecture and Urban Planning, U. Mich., 1976-78, chmn. alumni adv. bd., 1984—. Projects include physics and astronomy bldg., 1963, office and classroom bldg., 1971, both, U. Mich., Air Terminal Bldg, City Detroit, 1966; die and engring. facility, Gen. Motors Corp., Flint, Mich., 1968, also adminstrv. office bldg., Saginaw, Mich., 1969, southeastern br. facilities, Avon Products, Inc., Atlanta, 1970, Children's Hosp. of Mich, Detroit, 1971, office and pub. facilities, Washington Post, 1971, distbg. and mfg. facility, Eli Lilly Co., Indpls., 1974, Am. Motors Corp. office bldg, Southfield Mich., 1975, William Beaumont Hosp, Troy, Mich., 1975-77, Owens Corning Fiberglas Tech. Center, Granville, Ohio, 1976, John Deere Engring. Mfg. Bldg, Waterloo, Iowa, 1976, Detroit Free Press, 1977, Ford Motor Co. Mfg. Bldg, Batavia, Ohio, 1980. Mem. Detroit Inst. Arts, 1965—, Art. Assn. Birmingham, Mich., 1965—; mem. planning bd., City of Birmingham, 1971-76; trustee Founders Soc. Detroit Inst. Arts, 1974-80; bd. dirs. Birmingham Community House, 1976-79, New Center Area Council, 1978—, New Center Found., 1980—. Served to lt. (j.g.) USNR, 1951-52. Wheelwright Traveling fellow Harvard, 1960. Fellow A.I.A.; mem. Engring. Soc. Detroit. Unitarian. Home: 837 Shepardbush Rd Birmingham MI 48008 Office: New Center Bldg Detroit MI 48202

HARO, MICHAEL SAMUEL, psychologist, educator; b. East Chicago, Ind., Feb. 27, 1943; s. Alfonso Anthony and Angelina Tina (Mola) H.; m. Lynne Yungstrom, Sept. 1, 1973. B.S., Ball State U., 1965, M.S., 1967, Ed.S., 1974; Ph.D., Kent State U., 1976. Tchr. Concord High Sch., Elkhart, Ind., 1965-66; instr. U. Nebr., 1967-68; program specialist Am. Coll. Health Assn., Evanston, Ill., 1968-69; dir. Bur. Dental Health Edn., Am. Dental Assn., Chgo., 1970-71; asst. prof. State U. N.Y. at Cortland, 1972-74; grad. asst. Kent (Ohio) State U. Guidance Bur., 1974-75, instr. rehab. counseling, 1975-76; asso. prof. U. Houston at Clear Lake City, 1976-81; cons. and counseling psychologist, Houston, 1981—; cons. Nat. Dairy Council, Tenneco, NASA Johnson Space Center, Tompkins County (N.Y.) Mental Health Bd. Vol. Family Counseling, Cortland, 1973-74, Crisis Intervention Center, Muncie, Ind., 1972; sec. Nat. Interagy. Council on Smoking and Health; bd. dirs. Bay Area Com. on Drug Abuse, 1976-78, Clear Lake unit Am. Heart Assn., 1978-79. HEW fellow in health sci. Ball State U., 1971-72. Fellow Am. Sch. Health Assn. (Elizabeth A. Neilson scholar, pres. 1973-74, disting. service award 1977); mem. Am. Psychol. Assn., Tex. Psychol. Assn., Eta Sigma Gamma, Beta Theta Pi. Home: 16414 Havenhurst Houston TX 77059

HARPER, ASHBY TAYLOR, educator; b. Washington Crossing, N.J., Oct. 1, 1916; s. Frank Williamson and Roberta Ashby (Taylor) H.; m. Madge Lorene Palmer, Mar. 25, 1944; children: Frederick, Richard, David, Margery. A.B., Princeton U., 1939, postgrad., 1945-47; postgrad., Middlebury (Vt.) Coll., 1940. Asst. dir. athletics Princeton U., 1939-40; tchr., coach Mt. Hermon (Mass.) Sch., 1940-41; dir. Colegio Americano de Quito, Ecuador, 1947-51; headmaster Am. Sch., Lima, Peru, 1951-53, St. Louis Country Day Sch., 1953-62, Albuquerque Acad., 1964—; dir. Peace Corps program in Guatemala, 1962-64. Served to lt., aviator USNR, 1941-45; PTO. Decorated D.F.C., Air medal (4); oldest person to swim English Channel Aug. 28, 1982. Mem. Headmasters Assn., Country Day Sch. Headmasters Assn., Inter-Am. Edn. Assn. (founding dir.), Am. Assn. Tchrs. Spanish and Portuguese, Nat. Assn. Ind. Schs. (dir.). Club: Rotary. Home: 7816 Harwood Ave NE Albuquerque NM 87110 Office: 6400 N Wyoming Blvd Albuquerque NM 87109

HARPER, CHARLES LITTLE, steel company executive; b. Evanston, Ill., Mar. 23, 1930; s. H. Mitchell and Margaret (Little) H.; m. Alice Patterson Fall, Oct. 19, 1955; children: Charles, Margaret, Greta, Alice, Serena, Paisley. B.S., Princeton U., 1952. Successively metall. engr. process metallurgy, prodn. control, cost control The H.M. Harper Co., Morton Grove, Ill., 1954-68; with ITT Harper, Inc., Morton Grove, 1968—, pres., 1972-78; also dir.; v.p. Joslyn Mfg., 1979-80; v.p. ACF Industries, Houston, 1981—, gen. mgr. W-K-M div., 1981—. Served to lt. USN, 1952-54. Mem. Am. Soc. Metals, Am. Inst. Mining Engrs., Newcomen Soc. Clubs: Economic of Chgo.; Glen View (Golf) (Ill.). Office: PO Box 4334 Houston TX 77210

HARPER, CHARLES MICHEL, food company executive; b. Lansing, Mich., Sept. 26, 1927; s. Charles Frost and (Alma) Michel; s. Charles Frost and (Alma) H.; m. Joan Frances Bruggema, June 24, 1950; children: Kathleen, Carolyn, Charles Michel, Elizabeth. B.S. in Mech. Engring, Purdue U., 1949; M.B.A., U. Chgo., 1950. Supr. methods engring. Oldsmobile div. Gen. Motors Corp., Detroit, 1950-54; indsl. engr. Pillsbury Co., Mpls., 1954-55, dir. indsl. engring., 1955-60, dir. engring., 1961-66, v.p. research, devel. and new products, 1965-70, group v.p.-poultry, food service and venture businesses, 1970-74; exec. v.p., chief operating officer, dir. Conagra Inc., Omaha, 1974-76, pres., chief exec. officer, 1976-81, chmn. bd., chief exec. officer, 1981—; dir. Omaha Nat. Bank, Valmont Industries, Inc., Northwestern Bell Telephone Co., Internorth Inc. Mem. council Village of Excelsior (Minn.), 1965-70, mayor, 1974; trustee Bishop Clarkson Meml. Hosp.; bd. dirs. Creighton U.; pres. Mid Am. Council Boy Scouts Am. Served with AUS, 1946-48. Mem. Omaha C. of C. (chmn.), Bus. Roundtable, Ak-Sar-Ben (gov.), Beta Theta Pi. Home: 6105 Lamplighter Dr Omaha NE 68152 Office: Conagra Ctr One Central Park Plaza Omaha NE 68131

HARPER, CONRAD KENNETH, lawyer; b. Detroit, Dec. 2, 1940; s. Archibald Leonard and Georgia Florence (Hall) H.; m. Marsha Louise Wilson, July 17, 1965; children: Warren Wilson, Adam Woodburn. B.A., Howard U., 1962; LL.B., Harvard U., 1965. Bar: N.Y. 1966. Law clk. NAACP Legal Def. and Ednl. Fund, N.Y.C., 1965-66, staff lawyer, 1966-70; asso. firm Simpson Thacher & Bartlett, N.Y.C., 1971-74, ptnr., 1974—; lectr. law Rutgers U., 1969-70; vis. lectr. law Yale U., 1977-81; cons. HEW, 1977. Trustee N.Y. Pub. Library, Lawyers' Com. for Civil Rights under Law, Mus. City of N.Y.; vestryman Ch. of St. Barnabas, Irvington, N.Y. Fellow Am. Bar Found., Am. Coll. Trial Lawyers; mem. ABA (bd. editors Jour. 1980—), Nat. Bar Assn., N.Y. State Bar Assn., Assn. Bar City N.Y. (chmn. exec. com. 1979-80), Am. Law Inst., Council Fgn. Relations., Phi Beta Kappa. Democrat. Episcopalian. Clubs: Harvard of N.Y.C., India House (N.Y.C.). Home: Clifton Pl Irvington NY 10533 Office: 1 Battery Park Plaza New York NY 10004

HARPER, DEAN HARRISON, sociologist; b. Ames, Iowa, Jan. 5, 1929; s. Charles Asa and Frances Marie H.; m. Jeanne Barbara Facklam, July 5, 1958; children: Elizabeth, Anne, Carolyn, Mary Alice. B.S., Iowa State Coll., 1951, M.S., 1953; Ph.D., Columbia U., 1961. Asst. prof. sociology U. Rochester, 1958-64, assoc. prof., 1964-71, prof. sociology and psychiatry, 1971—; vis. scientist U. London, 1971-72. Editor: Living in Two Cultures, 1982. Served with U.S. Army, 1953-55. Lydia Roberts fellow, 1955-57; Ford Found. fellow, 1963; Social Sci. Research Council fellow, 1963; USPHS fellow, 1963-64, 71-72; Bridge fellow, 1979-80. Mem. AAAS, Am. Sociol. Assn., Am. Statis. Assn. Home: 296 Troy Rd Rochester NY 14618 Office: Harkness Hall 109 Univ of Rochester Rochester NY 14642

HARPER, DONALD JACK, manufacturing executive; b. Chgo., Mar. 10, 1928; s. John L. and Mabel A. (Best) H.; m. Barbara Lighthall, Apr. 14, 1951; children: Laura, Steven, Gregory, Peter. B.S. in Bus. and Mktg., U. Ill., 1950. Salesman, John I. Paulding Co., 1950-52; with Emerson Electric Co., 1952-72, exec. v.p., then pres. builder products div., 1965-69, pres. Fisher Radio div., 1970-72; with Insilco Corp., Meriden, Conn., 1973—, sr. v.p., 1978-80, pres., 1980—; chmn. bd., chief exec. officer Internat. Silver Co., Meriden, 1974-77; dir. Hartford Nat. Bank, Times Fiber Communications, Inc. Bd. dirs. Jr. Achievement S. Central Conn., 1978-80, Conn. Bus. and Industries Assn., 1981, New Eng. Council, Inc.; trustee Conn. Ednl. Telecommunications Corp., 1983—. Served with AUS, 1945-47. Mem. Electronics Industry Assn. (chmn. audio div. 1972), Home Ventilating Inst. (pres. 1965), Jewelry Industry Council (dir. 1977-80), Nat. Assn. Home Builders (dir. 1965-69), Chi Phi. Home: 10 Bridget Ln Cheshire CT 06410 Office: Insilco Corp 1000 Research Pkwy Meriden CT 06450

HARPER, DONALD VICTOR, transportation educator; b. Chgo., Mar. 27, 1927; s. Victor Rudolph and Mildred Victoria (Safbom) H.; m. Elizabeth Jane Wagner, May 17, 1952; children: Christine Ann, Diane Elizabeth, David Victor. Student, Wright Jr. Coll., 1945, 46-47; B.S. in Journalism, U. Ill., Urbana, 1950; Ph.D. in Econs., U. Ill., Urbana, 1957. Instr. Coll. Commerce and Bus. Adminstrn., U. Ill., Urbana, 1953-56; lectr. Sch. Mgmt., U. Minn., Mpls., 1956; asst. prof. Coll. and Grad. Sch. Bus. Adminstrn., U. Minn., 1956-59, asso. prof., 1959-65, prof. transp. and logistics, 1965—, chmn. dept. mgmt. and transp., 1967-70, dir. M.B.A. and Ph.D. programs, 1970-79, dir. Ph.D. program, 1979-80; cons. to bus. and govt. agys. Author: Economic Regulation of the Motor Trucking Industry by the States, 1959, Price Policy and Procedure, 1966, Transportation in America: Users, Carriers, Government, 2d edit. 1982; contbr. articles to profl. jours. Served with USNR, 1945-46. Mem. Am. Econ. Assn., Am. Mktg. Assn., Transp. Research Forum, Am. Soc. Traffic and Transp., Transp. Club Mpls. and St. Paul, Assn. ICC Practitioners. Home: 2451 Sheldon St Saint Paul MN 55113 Office: Sch Mgmt U Minn 271 19th Ave S Minneapolis MN 55455

HARPER, EDWARD J., clergyman; b. Bklyn., July 23, 1910; s. John Edward and Josephine (Realander) H. Student, St. Marys Coll., North East, Pa., 1928-33, St. Mary's Coll., Annapolis, 1933-34, Mt. St. Alphonsus Maj. Sem., 1934-40. Ordained priest Roman Catholic Ch., 1939; missionary, P.R., 1941-46, Dominican Republic, 1946-50; dean Mayaguez, P.R., 1950-56; superior Vice Province of San Juan Redemptorist Fathers, 1956-60; prelate, V.I., 1960, bishop, 1960—; 1st residential bishop Diocese of St. Thomas, 1977—. Pres. Citizens for Drug Edn., Inc., 1968—, Cath. Community Conscious Corp.; bd. dirs. V.I. Council on Alcoholism. Mem. bd. Econ. Devel. Council V.I. K.C. (charter). Address: Estate Elizabeth 9 Box 1825 St Thomas VI 00801

HARPER, EDWARD O'NEIL, psychiatrist, psychoanalyst; b. Bridgeville, Pa., Oct. 13, 1906; s. Edgar Perry and Hattie (Snyder) H.; m. Mary Louise Murray, Aug. 18, 1934; 1 dau., Susan Louis Harper Spring. A.B., Ohio Wesleyan U., 1928; M.D., U. Pa., 1932. Intern Mercy Hosp., Pitts., 1932-33; resident clin. chemistry, resident and Rockefeller fellow in psychiatry Pa. Hosp., Phils., 1933-34; instr. psychiatry U. Pa. Med. Sch., 1936-37; mem. faculty Case Western Res. U. Med. Sch. (and predecessor), 1946—, prof. psychiatry, 1970-73, prof. emeritus, 1973—, chmn. faculty senate, 1971; mem. hon. staff Univ. Hosp., Cleve.; lectr. U. Mich. Med. Sch., U. Iowa Med. Sch., U. Calif. Med. Sch., Los Angeles, Ohio State U. Med. Sch., U. Tex.; vis. prof. Ohio State U. Med. Sch., U. Ottawa; adv. commn. Ohio Dept. Mental Health, 1973; adv. bd. Planned Parenthood, Cleve., 1950-77; trustee Woodruff Hosp., Cleve., 1973-77; cons. in field, cons. to the surgeon gen. of U.S. Army; nat. cons. emeritus to surgeon gen. of U.S.A.F. Author papers gen. psychiatry.; Editorial bd.: Archives Gen. Psychiatry, 1962-72. Trustee Cleve. Goodwill Industries, 1963-77. Served as lt. col. M.C. AUS, World War II. Recipient William C. Porter award Assn. Military Surgeons of U.S., 1973. Founding fellow Am. Coll. Psychoanalysts, Am. Coll. Psychiatrists (Gold Medal award 1981); life fellow Am. Psychiat. Assn.; mem. ACP (life), AMA, AAAS, Am. Psychiat. Assn. (v.p. 1969-70, commendation 1973), Am. Psychoanalytic Assn., Am. Coll. Psychoanalysts (pres. 1973-74, commendation 1974, Laughlin Gold medal award 1982), Am. Coll. Psychiatrists (pres. 1977—, commendation), Cleve. Soc. Neurology and Psychiatry (pres. 1947), Group Advancement Psychiatry, Internat. Psychoanalytic Assn., Central Neuropsychiat. Assn. (pres. 1968), Ohio State Psychiat. Assn. (Meritorious award for Disting. Service 1981), Aesculapian Soc. Cleve. (pres. 1969-70, honored mem. 1977), Ohio State Med. Assn. (cert. of distinction 1982), Pasteur Club Cleve. (pres. 1961-62), Benjamin Rush Soc. (founder, 1st pres. 1979), Phi Beta Kappa. Methodist. Clubs: Skating (Cleve.); Cleve. Playhouse. Home: 16185 Cleviden Rd Cleveland OH 44112 Office: 11328 Euclid Ave Cleveland OH 44106

HARPER, EDWIN LELAND, manufacturing executive, former government official; b. Belleville, Ill., Nov. 13, 1941; s. Horace Edwin and Evelyn Ruth (Wright) H.; m. Lucy Davis, Aug. 21, 1965; children: Elizabeth Allen, Peter Edwin. B.A. with honors, Principia Coll., 1963; Ph.D., U. Va., 1968. Guest scholar Brookings Instn., Washington, 1965-66; lectr. Rutgers U., 1966-68; staff Bur. of Budget, Washington, 1968-69; sr. cons. Arthur D. Little, Inc., Washington, 1969; spl. asst. to pres. of U.S., 1969-72; asst. dir. Domestic Council, Washington, 1970-72; v.p. INA Corp., Phila., 1973-74; pres., chief exec. officer Air Balance, Inc., Chgo., 1975; sr. v.p. strategic planning, chief adminstrv. officer Certain Teed Corp., 1976-78; v.p. Emerson Electric Co., St. Louis, 1978-81; dep. dir. Office of Mgmt. and Budget; asst. to pres. of U.S., Washington, 1981-82, 82-83; chmn. Pres.'s Council on Integrity and Efficiency in Govt., 1982-83, Fed. Property Rev. Bd., 1982-83; exec. v.p. Overhead Door Corp., Dallas, 1983—; dep. exec. dir. platform com. Republican Conv., 1976; Mem. Pres.'s Commn. on Personnel Interchange, Washington, 1976-79, 81—; mem. Pres.'s Commn. on Indsl. Competitiveness, 1983—. Contbr. articles to profl. jours. Mem. nat. adv. bd. Goodwill Industries, 1977-81. Ford Found. grantee, 1965; Recipient Louis Brownlow award, 1969, Exec. Govt. award OICs of Am., 1982, Person of Yr. award Washington chpt. Inst. Internal Auditors, 1982, Spl. Commendation Assn. Spl. Investigators, 1983. Mem. Am. Soc. Public Adminstrn., Nat. Acad. Pub. Adminstrn., Am. Polit. Sci. Assn., Omicron Delta Kappa. Republican. Clubs: Raven, Northwood, Oakwood. Home: 7321 Oak Bluff Dallas TX 75240 Office: Overhead Door Corp PO Box 809046 Dallas TX 75380

HARPER, GEORGE MILLS, educator; b. Linn Creek, Mo., Nov. 5, 1914; s. Charles Avery and Grace (Shipman) H.; m. Mary Jane Hughes, June 15, 1944; children: Margaret Mills, Ann Christian. A.B., Culver-Stockton Coll., 1940; M.A., U. Fla., 1947; Ph.D., U. N.C., 1951; D.Litt. (hon.), Trinity Coll., Dublin, 1980. From instr. to prof. English, U. N.C., 1950-66, asso. dean arts and scis., 1955-60, chmn. English dept., 1962-66, chmn. faculty, 1961-64, chmn. humanities, 1962-65; prof., chmn. English dept. U. Fla., 1966-69; dean arts and scis., Univ. prof. Va. Poly. Inst., 1969-70; chmn. English dept. Fla. State U., Tallahassee, 1970-73, prof., 1970—, Disting. prof., 1978—; cons. U.S. Office Edn., 1967, 68, 69; lectr. Yeats Internat. Summer Sch., Ireland, 1964, 65, 68, 72, 74, 75, Internat. Congress Comparative Lit., Fribourg, Switzerland, 1964. Author: Neoplatonism of William Blake, 1961, Yeats's Quest for Eden, 1966, Yeats's Golden Dawn, 1974, Yeats's Theory of Theatre, 1975, W. B. Yeats and W. T. Horton, 1980; editor: (with Kathleen Raine) Thomas Taylor the Platonist, 1969; Editor: Yeats and the Occult, 1975, (with others) Letters to W.B. Yeats, 1977, (with W. K. Hood) A Critical Edition of Yeats's A Vision (1925), 1978; contbr. articles to profl. jours. Pres. Chapel Hill (N.C.) C. of C., 1965; bd. govs. Chapel Hill Pub. Library, 1959-65. Served to lt. comdr. USNR, 1942-46; comdr. Res. Mem. MLA (chmn. Celtic group 1967, 75), Coll. English Assn. (pres. 1975-76). Democrat. Methodist. Home: 407 Plantation Rd Tallahassee FL 32303

HARPER, HARLAN, JR., lawyer; b. San Antonio, Sept. 15, 1928; s. Harlan and Julia Viola (Kelley) H.; m. Linda A. Steere, July 16, 1960; children: Anne Elizabeth, David Harlan. B.A., So. Methodist U., J.D. Bar: Tex. bar. Asso. firm McNees & McNees, 1957; asso. John Harrison, 1958-61; partner firm Fanning, Harper, Wilson, Martinson & Fanning, Dallas, 1961—. Served with USAF, 1953-55. Mem. Am., Dallas bar assns., State Bar Tex., Tex. Def. Attys. Assn., Pi Kappa Alpha. Baptist. Home: 1705 Dakota Dr Garland TX 75043 Office: 4303 North Central Expressway Dallas TX 75205

HARPER, HEATHER MARY, soprano; b. Belfast, Ireland, May 8, 1930; d. Hugh Harper; m. Eduardo J. Benarroch, 1973. Student (Coll. fellow), Trinity Coll. Music, London; Mus.D. (hon.), Queen's U., Belfast, Frederic Husler, Helene Isepp, Frederic Jackson. Toured with, BBC Symphony Orch. in, U.S., 1965, BBC Symphony Orch. in, in USSR, 1967; recital tour, Australia, 1965; created: soprano role in world premier Britten's War Requiem in, Coventry Cathedral, 1962; soloist opening concerts at, Maltings at Snape, 1967, Queen Elizabeth Hall, ann. concert and opera tours in, U.S., 1967—, also concerts in, Asia, Middle East, Australia, S.Am., maj. European festivals; performed prin. roles at, Covent Garden, Deutsche Oper, Berlin, Netherlands Opera, Bayreuth Festival, Glyndebourne, Sadler's Wells, Teatro Colon, Buenos Aires, Argentina, Teatro Colon, Frankfort, Teatro Colon, Japan, Met., San Francisco, La Scala, Milan, Italy; performs regularly with main symphony orchs. in European Capitals: maj. roles include Arabella, Ariadne, Chrysothemis, Kaiserin, Marschallin in, Richard Strauss operas; appears regularly on, BBC-TV.; Recs. include Missa Solemnis. Decorated comdr. Brit. Empire; recipient Edison award, 1971; Grammy award, 1979. Mem. Royal Acad. Music (hon.). Office: care Harrison/Parrott Ltd 12 Penzance Pl London England W11 4PA

HARPER, JENE, oil producer, oil equipment supply company executive; b. Sapulpa, Okla., Dec. 27, 1910; s. Jacob P. and Myrtle (Ham) H.; m. June Aleff, Apr. 16, 1955; children: Paul, Ronald, Teresa, Debra. Student, U. Nev., 1929-30. Purchasing agt. Roosevelt Oil Co., Mt. Pleasant, Mich., 1933; founder, pres. Franklin Supply Co., Chgo. and Denver, 1933-74, chmn. bd., 1962-74; pres., dir. Lark Oil Co., Denver, Harper Internat. Ltd., Harper Petroleum Supply Ltd., Calgary, Alta., Can.; asst. regional adminstr. Region 6 support services Emergency Petroleum and Gas Adminstrn., Washington, 1966—; dir. Colo. Nat. Bank (both Denver), Red Top Valley Ditch Co., Granby, Colo., Mountain States Pipe & Supply Co., Colorado Springs, Colo., Mannesman-Export/Franklin Supply, London, Eng.; past pres., dir. Franklin Pipe & Supply. Bd. dirs. Nat. Western Stock Show, Denver, U. Colo. Found., Orme Sch., Mayer, Ariz.; past pres. bd. trustees Graland Country Day Sch. Mem. Rocky Mountain Oil and Gas Assn. (dir. 1968—), Petroleum Equipment Suppliers Assn. (dir. 1933-62), Ind. Petroleum Assn. Am. (dir. 1965—). Clubs: Denver (past dir.), Flatirons (dir.), Denver Country, Cherry Hills Country (Denver) (past dir., treas.); Chicago, Chicago Oil Men's; Castle Pines Golf (Castle Rock, Colo.). Home: 225 S Clermont St Denver CO 80222 Office: 1801 Broadway Suite 1203 Denver CO 80202

HARPER, JOHN DICKSON, aluminum manufacturing company executive; b. Louisville, Tenn., Apr. 6, 1910; s. Lafayette Rodgers and Mary Alice (Collier) H.; m. Samma Lucille McCrary, Oct. 21, 1937; children: Rodgers McCrary, John Dickson, Thomas William.; m. Mary Lee Lawson, May 27, 1982. B.S., U. Tenn., 1933; D.Eng., Maryville Coll., 1964, Lehigh U., Rensselaer Poly. Inst., Carnegie-Mellon U., 1982; LL.D., U. Evansville; Sc.D., Clarkson Coll. Tech.; D. Comml. Sci. (hon.), Widener Coll. With Aluminum Co. of Am., 1933—, successively elec. engr., Alcoa, Tenn., asst. dist. power mgr., works mgr., Rockdale, Tex., gen. mgr. smelting div., Pitts., asst. prodn. mgr., 1933-60, v.p., 1960, v.p. prodn., 1962, exec. v.p., 1962-63, pres., 1963—, chief exec. officer, 1965-75, chmn. bd., 1970-75, chmn. exec. com., 1965-78; chmn. bd. Communications Satellite Corp., 1979-83, chmn. fin. com., 1979-84, dir., 1973-84; chmn. bd. Coke Investors, Inc., 1979—; dir. Am. European Assocs., Inc., Crutcher Resources Corp. Mem. nat. council, nat. exec. com. Boy Scouts, past pres. N.E. region; trustee Com. Econ. Devel.; hon. mem. Bus. Council, Bus. Com. for Arts, Inc.; past chmn. Nat. Alliance Businessmen, Bus. Roundtable; councillor Conf. Bd.; mem. Pres.'s Export Council, Pres.'s Commn. on Personnel Interchange, Pub. Oversight Bd.; hon. trustee, past vice chmn. Carnegie-Mellon U.; mem. devel. bd. U. Tenn.; past chmn., hon. mem. Internat. Primary Aluminum Inst.; founding mem. Rockefeller U. Council. Recipient Silver Quill award Am. Bus. Press, Inc.; Gold medal Pa. Soc.; Invest in Am. Spokesman award; Nathan W. Dougherty award U. Tenn.; decorated knight's cross Order St. Olav (Norway). Fellow ASME (Gantt medal), IEEE (past v.p.); mem. Engrs. Soc. Western Pa. (Metcalf award), Newcomen Soc., Aluminum Assn. (hon. mem., past chmn.), Am. Soc. for Metals (life), Am. Soc.

Metals (Bryce Harlow award 1982), Nat. Acad. Engring., Tau Beta Pi, Eta Kappa Nu, Beta Gamma Sigma. Clubs: Duquesne, Harvard, Yale, Princeton, Allegheny, Fox Chapel, St. Clair Country (Pitts.); Rolling Rock (Ligonier, Pa.); Internat., F St., Met. (Washington); Links, Sky (N.Y.C.); Seminole Golf, Jonathan's Landing. Home: 880 Old Hickory Rd Pittsburgh PA 15243 Office: 1501 Alcoa Bldg Pittsburgh PA 15219 also Comsat Bldg Washington DC

HARPER, JOHN ROBB, mathematics educator; b. Evanston, Ill., July 28, 1941; s. Robert Anderson and Margaret (Johnston) H.; m. Doris Calton, Sept. 3, 1966; children: Jennifer Ann, Allison Nichole. B.S., Yale U., 1963; Ph.D., U. Chgo., 1967. Instr. MIT, Cambridge, 1967-69; prof. U. Rochester, N.Y., 1969—; vis. prof. Pontificia Universidade Catalica, Rio de Janeiro, 1971, UCLA, 1974-75, U. Calif.-San Diego, 1978-79. Author: (with M.J. Greenberg) Algebraic Topology, A First Course, 1981, N-Spaces with Torsion, 1979. Woodrow Wilson fellow, 1963; recipient grants NSF, 1970—, Binat. Sci. Found., 1981-83. Home: 106 N St Regis Dr Rochester NY 14618 Office: U Rochester Dept Math Rochester NY 14627

HARPER, JUDSON MORSE, university adminstrator, consultant, educator; b. Lincoln, Nebr., Aug. 25, 1936; s. Floyd Sprague and Eda Elizabeth (Kelley) H.; m. Patricia Ann Kennedy, June 15, 1958; children: Jayson K., Stuart H., Neal K. B.S., Iowa State U., 1958, M.S., 1960, Ph.D., 1963. Registered profl. engr., Minn. Instr. Iowa State U., Ames, 1958-63, asst. prof., 1963-64; dept. head Gen. Mills, Inc., Mpls., 1964-69, venture mgr., 1969-70; prof., dept. head agrl. and chem. engring. Colo. State U., Ft. Collins, 1970-82, v.p. for research, 1972-74; cons. USAID, Washington, 1972-74, various comml. firms., 1975—. Author: Extrusion of Foods, 1982; editor: newsletter Food, Pharmaceutical & Bioengineering News, 1979-83; contbr. articles to publs. in field; patentee. Mem. sch. bd. St. Louis Park, Minn., 1968-70. Recipient Food Engring. award Dairy and Food Industry Supply Assn. and Am. Soc. Agrl. Engrs., 1983, cert. of merit U.S. Dept. Agr.-Office Internat. Cooperation and Devel., 1983, service award CIATECH, Chihuahua, Mex., 1980, Disting. Service award Colo. State U., 1977. Mem. Am. Inst. Chem. Engring. (dir. 1981—), Am. Soc. Agrl. Engrs. (com. chmn. 1973-78, hon. engr. Rocky Mountain Region 1982), Inst. Food Technologists, AAAS, Am. Chem. Soc., Am. Soc. Engring. Edn. (com. chmn. 1976-77). Republican. Methodist. Home: 1908 Osage Fort Collins CO 80525 Office: Office Vice Pres for Research Colo State Univ Fort Collins CO 80523

HARPER, LAWRENCE AVERELL, lawyer, educator; b. Oakland, Calif., May 18, 1901; s. Fred Fogg Gale and Elizabeth Sarah (Averell) H.; m. Anna Virginia McCune, July 7, 1925; children: Lawrence Vernon, Virginia Ann, Robert Gale. A.B., U. Calif., 1922, A.M., 1924, J.D., 1925; student, King's Coll., U. London, 1925-26; Ph.D., Columbia, 1939. Bar: Calif. bar 1927. Mem. firm Harper & Harper (specializing in customs law), 1928-45, Lawrence, Tuttle & Harper, 1945-54; instr. history U. Calif. at Berkeley, 1928-39, asst. prof., 1939-43, asso. prof., 1943-47, prof., 1947-68, prof. emeritus, 1968—; Mem. council Inst. Early Am. History and Culture, 1969-71. Author: The English Navigation Laws, 1939, The Effect of the Navigation Acts on the Thirteen Colonies, In The Era of the American Revolution, 1939, Charts and Outlines for United States History (2 vols., syllabus series), 1943, 55, United We Stand; Divided We Fall in of Mother Country and Plantations, 1971, also contbr. to hist. and legal books and jours.; Editor: (with F.F.G. Harper) Harper's Customs Tariff, 1930; mem. editorial bd.: Am. Jour. Legal History; editorial adv. bd.: Am. History and Life, 1966—; prin. editorial cons. colonial statistics chpt.: Historic Statistics of U.S. 1960; cons. chpt. colonial statistics, rev. vol., 1975. Guggenheim fellow, 1944-45. Mem. Am. Hist. Assn., Am. Soc. Information Sci., Am. Econ. History Assn., Am. Soc. for Legal History (v.p. 1960, dir.), Phi Beta Kappa, Delta Theta Phi. Club: Berkeley Tennis. Co-investigator Earl Warren Oral History Project, 1968-71. Home: 52 Oakwood Rd Orinda CA 94563 Office: Dept History U Calif Berkeley CA 94720

HARPER, OWEN HOWE, banker; b. Lynchburg, Va., Sept. 27, 1937; s. Edwin Adams and Margaretta Smedley (Howe) H.; children—Hillary T., Eloise M., Charles P. B.A. in Econs, Washington and Lee U., Lexington, Va., 1959. Vice pres. First Nat. City Bank, N.Y.C., 1960-72; 1st v.p. Blyth Eastman Dillon & Co., N.Y.C., 1972-74; exec. v.p. Crocker Nat. Bank, Los Angeles, 1974—. Bd. dirs. Greater Los Angeles chpt. Am. Heart Assn., 1977-78, Met. YMCA, Los Angeles, 1977—; trustee Orthopaedic Hosp. of Los Angeles; mem. alumni bd. Washington and Lee U. Mem. Assn. Res. City Bankers, Calif. Bankers Assn. (dir.). Republican. Unitarian. Clubs: Burlingame Country (Hillsborough, Calif.); California, Los Angeles Country; Pacific Union, San Francisco Golf (San Francisco); Links (N.Y.C.). Home: 790 Pinehurst Dr Pasadena CA 91106 Office: 333 S Grand Ave Los Angeles CA 90071

HARPER, RALPH CHAMPLIN, ret. banker; b. Portland, Maine, Mar. 7, 1916; s. Ralph Champlin and Hulda Martha (Weise) H.; m. Nancy Peabody, Oct. 6, 1940; children—Susan (Mrs. Peter C. Naiden), Katharine (Mrs. Chandler G. Sinnett). Student, U. Wis., 1952. With Nat. Bank Commerce, Portland, 1933-58; with Maine Nat. Bank, Portland, 1958-81, exec. v.p. loans, 1970-81; dir. Devel. Credit Corp. of Maine, Augusta. Bd. dirs. Westbrook (Maine) Community Hosp. Mem. Robert Morris Assos. (bd. govs. New Eng. chpt. 1965-68). Clubs: Mason (32 deg., Shriner), Kiwanian (dir. Portland 1970-72), Portland Country, Woodfords (dir. 1969-73), Woodfords (Portland) (pres. 1977). Home: 7 Pine Ridge Rd Cumberland Foreside ME 04110

HARPER, RAMEY WILSON, railroad executive; b. Muskogee, Okla., Apr. 15, 1920; s. Edgar Batte and Eva (Stephens) H.; m. Elizabeth Martha Smith, July 9, 1966; children: Elizabeth Martha, Dorothea Louise. Student, Westminster Coll., 1938-40; B.S., U. Ariz., 1942. Sr. accountant Arthur Andersen & Co., Chgo., 1946-49; gen. auditor Midland Valley R.R. Co. (and affiliated cos.), Muskogee, 1949-64; spl. asst. staff studies A., T. & S.F. Ry. Co., Chgo., 1964-67, exec. asst. finance, 1967-70, v.p. finance, 1970-80; treas. Santa Fe Industries, Inc., Chgo., 1968-77, v.p. fin., treas., 1977-80, sr. v.p., 1981-84; v.p. exec. dept. Santa Fe So. Pacific Corp., 1984—; dir. Trailer Train Co., Railbox Co., Standard Office Bldg. Corp. Trustee Latin Sch. Chgo., 1981—. Served to comdr. USNR, 1942-46. Mem. Chgo. Athletic Assn, Chgo. Assn. Commerce and Industry, Phi Delta Theta. Presbyn. Home: 399 Fullerton Pkwy Chicago IL 60614 Office: 224 S Michigan Ave Chicago IL 60604

HARPER, ROBERT ALEXANDER, geography educator; b. Chgo., Apr. 16, 1924; s. Robert Haskell and May Isabelle (Wilsdon) H.; m. Sarah Ann Lofgren, Sept. 28, 1944; children: Carol Leslie, Judith Lynn, Robert Willard. Student, DePauw U., 1941-42; Ph.B., U. Chgo., 1946, S.B., 1947, S.M., 1948, Ph.D., 1950. Research asso. geography, then home study dept. U. Chgo., 1948-50; mem. faculty So. Ill. U., Carbondale, 1950-67, prof. geography, 1959-67, chmn. dept., 1959-66; vis. scientist Assn. Am. Geographers, 1965-66; chmn. dept. geography U. Md., 1967-79, prof., 1967—; exchange lectr. Sch. Geography, U. Manchester, Eng., 1961-62; vis. prof. U. Sydney, Australia, 1972, Hull (Eng.) U., 1975, U. Durban-Westville, South Africa, 1982; Mem. research tech. adv. com. Wabash Valley Bi-State Commn., 1961-65. Author: (with C.W.Sorensen) Europe and North America, 1955, Economic Geography, 1955, (with Sorensen and R.E. Crist) Learning About Latin America, 1961, Regions and Their Needs, 1972, (with T.H. Schmudde) Between Two Worlds, 1973, 2d edit., 1978, (with Joseph Stoltman) World Geography; Editor: (with Jean Gottmann) Metropolis on the Move, 1967, (with Charles Christian) Modern Metropolitan Systems. Served to 2d lt., navigator USAAF, 1943-45. Decorated Air medal with oak leaf cluster; recipient Profl. Achievement award U. Chgo. Alumni Assn., 1971. Mem. Assn. Am. Geographers (exec. council 1967-70), Nat. Council Geog. Edn. (pres. 1970-71), Nat. Council Soc. Scis., Sigma Xi, Phi Gamma Delta. Home: 13705 Creekside Dr Silver Spring MD 20904

HARPER, ROBERT ALLAN, consulting psychologist; b. Dayton, Ohio, Apr. 25, 1915; s. Earl Paull and Mary (Belden) H.; m. Flora Mie Bridges; children: Robert Belden, John Paull. Student, U. Dayton, 1934-36; B.A., Ohio State U., 1938, M.A., 1939, Ph.D., 1942. Instr. Kent State U., 1942-43; analyst War Manpower Commn., 1943; assoc. prof. Wagner Coll., 1943-45; psychiat. social worker U.S. Army, 1945-46; asst. prof. Ohio State U., 1946-50, dir. marriage counseling clinic, 1949-50; chmn. family life dept., dir. marriage counseling service Merrill-Palmer Inst., Detroit, 1950-53; pvt. practice psychotheraphy, Washington. Author: (with John F. Cuber) Problems of American Society, 1948, Marriage, 1949, Psychoanalysis and Psychotherapy: 36 Systems, 1959, (with Albert Ellis) Creative Marriage, 1961, A Guide to Rational Living, 1961, 75, (with Walter R. Stokes) 45 Levels to Sexual Understanding and Enjoyment, 1971, The New Psychotherapies, 1975; Cons. editor: Jour. Sex Edn. and Therapy. Fellow Am. Psychol. Assn. (pres. div. psychotherapy 1978-79, pres. div. cons. psychology 1980-81, pres. div. humanistic psychology 1983-84, exec. bd. div. ind. practice, council reps. 1978—), Am. Assn. Marriage Counselors (sec. 1954-58, pres. 1960-62), Nat. Council Family Relations (dir. 1951-55), Am. Acad. Psychotherapists (pres. 1961-63), Am. Group Psychotheraphy Assn., Eastern Psychol. Assn., D.C. Psychol. Assn. (dir. 1982—); mem. Am. Soc. Psychologists in Pvt. Practice (exec. com.), Soc. Sci. Study Sex, Interam. Soc. Psychologists, Am. Soc. Group Psychotherapy and Psychodrama, Internat. Council Psychologists (exec. bd. 1971-74), N.Y. Acad. Scis., Internat. Soc. Gen. Semantics, Inst. Rational Living (bd.), ACLU, Washington Soc. Clin. Psychologists (exec. com.), Phi Beta Kappa. Club: Cosmos. Home: 4903 Potomac Ave NW Washington DC 20007 Office: 4953 W St NW Washington DC 20007

HARPER, RONALD LEE, university official; b. Frankfort, Ohio, Jan. 8, 1938; s. Wilbur Edgar and Grace Elizabeth (Orr) H. B.S., Ohio State U., 1961, M.S., 1965, Ph.D., 1970. Adminstrv. asst. Office of Provost and v.p. acad. affairs Ohio State U., 1970-72; asst. prof., asso. dir. and sec. Sch. Allied Med. Professions, 1972-77; dean Sch. Allied Health, U. Kans., Kansas City, 1977-79; dir. Allied Health Programming U. Kans., Lawrence, 1977-79, dir. Gerontology Ctr., 1979—, prof. health services adminstrn., 1981—; Mem. adv. com. Am. Dietetics Assn., 1977-80; mem. research com. VA Med. Ctr., Leavenworth, Kans., 1978—. Mem. Am. Soc. Allied Health Professions, Mid-Am. Congress on Aging, Assn. Univ. Programs in Health Adminstrn. Office: 316 Strong Hall Univ of Kans Lawrence KS 66045

HARPER, ROY W., judge; b. Gibson, Mo., July 26, 1905; s. Marvin H. and Minnie (Brooks) H.; m. Ruth Butt, July 30, 1941; children: Katherine Brooks, Arthur Murray. A.B., U. Mo., 1929; L.L.B., 1929. Bar: Mo. bar 1929. Mem. tax ins. claims dep. dept. Shell Petroleum Corp., St. Louis, 1929-30; pvt. practice law, Steele, Mo., 1931-34; mem. firm Ward & Reeves, Caruthersville, 1934-47; U.S. dist. judge of Mo., Eastern and Western dists. of Mo., 1947—; chief judge Eastern Dist. Mo., 1959-70; sr. judge Eastern and Western Dists. Mo., 1971—; Mem. U.S. Judicial Conf., 1965-77, chmn. intercircuit assignment com., 1969-76; mem. Jud. Panel on Multidist. Litigation, 1977-83. Chmn. Mo. State Democratic Com., 1946-47; Bd. dirs. St. Louis unit Shriner's Crippled Children Hosp. Enlisted Air Corps U.S. Army, 1942; apptd. 2d lt., Sept. 1942; served with 35th Fighter Group, 1942—; Southwest Pacific; col. Air Corps Res., 1945. Recipient DeMolay Legion of Honor, 1957, Citation of Merit Mo. U. Law Sch., 1963; Partriots award Mo. soc. S.A.R., 1973; George Washington Honor medal Freedoms Found., 1975. Mem. Am., Mo., Pemiscot County bar assns., Order of Coif, Delta Theta Phi. Democrat. Club: Mason (33 deg., Shriner). Home: 1039 S Warson Rd St Louis MO 63124 Office: US Court House and Custom House St Louis MO 63101

HARPER, TERRELL RAY, architect; b. Ft. Worth, Oct. 30, 1908; s. John Thomas and Rachel (Evans) H.; m. Susie Mae Huckaba, June 13, 1931; children: Patricia Lois (Mrs. James Weaver Leftwich), Barbara Jeanne (Mrs. James Lowell McAlpin). Student, Tex. A. and M. Coll., 1925-27, Internat. Corr. Schs., 1940-42. Draftsman, constrn. inspector John M. Marriott (Architect), San Antonio, 1927-30; constrn. inspector, architect U.S. War Dept., C.Q.M., Tex. and Okla., 1930-34; constrn. inspector, office engr. PWA, Okla. and Tex., 1935-40; draftsman, specifications writer, asso. charge office George L. Dahl (architect-engr.), Dallas, 1940-54; propr. Terrell R. Harper (Architect), Dallas, 1954-55; partner Harper & Kemp (architects), Dallas, 1955-75, Harper, Kemp, Clutts and Parker (architects/planners), 1975—. Bd. dirs. Dallas County Community Chest, 1958-60, Dallas County United Fund., 1968-70. Fellow Constrn. Specifications Inst. (past pres. Dallas chpt., inst. pres. 1964-65), AIA (past pres., dir. Dallas chpt.); mem. Tex. Soc. Architects (past dir.). Methodist (chmn. adminstrv. bd. 1971-72). Club: Kiwanis. Home: 12234 Montego Plaza Dallas TX 75230 Office: 1201 Elm St Suite 5464 Dallas TX 75270

HARPER, THOMAS, lawyer, former member Democratic National Committee; b. Greenwood, Ark., Nov. 23, 1908; s. Robert Atlas and Merton (Othella) H.; m. Vivien W. Tatum, Jan. 16, 1939 (dec.); children: Thomas, Granville T., Blake, Kay Nelson. Student, U. Ill., 1927-28. Bar: Ark. 1930. Practiced in, Greenwood, 1930-39, Ft. Smith, Ark., 1939—; spl. assoc. justice Ark. Supreme Ct., 1975; gen. counsel City Nat. Bank.; mem. Ark. Statute Revision Commn., 1975-83; Chmn. Ark. Dem. Com., 1954-64; del. Dem. Nat. Conv., 1956, 60, 64, 68, chmn. del., 1960, 64; mem. Dem. Nat. Com. for Ark., 1964-72. Served to lt. (j.g.) USNR, 1944-46. Mem. Am. Coll. Trial Lawyers, Am., Ark., Sebastian County bar assns., Motor Carrier Lawyers Assn., Ft. Smith C. of C., Delta Upsilon, Phi Eta Sigma. Methodist. Clubs: Fianna Hills Country, Ft. Smith Town, Hardscrabble Country (past pres.). Home: 5001 S Cliff Dr Fort Smith AR 72903 Office: 510 N Greenwood Ave Fort Smith AR 72902

HARPER, VALERIE, actress; b. Suffern, N.Y., Aug. 22, 1940; d. Howard and Iva (McConnell) H.; m. Richard Schaal, 1964 (div. 1979). Student, Hunter Coll., New Sch. Social Research. Dancer corps de ballet, Radio City Music Hall, N.Y.C., 1956-57; actress, Second City, Chgo., 1964-69; appeared in: Broadway prodns. Lil Abner, 1958, Take Me Along, 1959, Wildcat, 1960, Subways Are For Sleeping, 1961, Something Different, 1968, Story Theatre, 1970-71, Metamorphoses, 1971; appeared on: Mary Tyler Moore Show, CBS-TV, 1970-74, Rhoda, CBS-TV, 1974-78; appeared in: films Freebie and the Bean, 1974, Chapter Two, 1979, Last Married Couple in America, 1979, Blame it on Rio, 1984; TV films Fun and Games, 1980, The Shadow Box, 1980, The Day the Loving Stopped, 1981. Recipient Emmy awards, Nat. Acad. TV Arts and Scis., 1971, 72, 73, 75; Golden Globe award for best actress, 1975; named Hasty Pudding Woman of Yr. Harvard Hasty Pudding Soc., 1975. Address: care Tony Cacciotti 9000 Sunset Blvd Suite 601 Los Angeles CA 90069 *

HARPER, WILLIAM HENRY, business consultant; b. Eatonia, Sask., Can., July 20, 1924; s. William Robertson and Susan Noretta (Tucker) H.; m. Isabel B. Daw, Aug. 18, 1947; children: Catherine Harper Estey, Joyce Harper Whidden, William R., Heather L. B.S. in Mech. Engring, U. Sask., 1946. Registered profl. engr., Ont. Dist. mgr. Carrier Air Conditioning Can. Ltd., 1947-53; chmn. bd., pres. Beaver Engring. Ltd., 1953-78, W.H. Harper, Inc., Toronto, 1978—; chmn. Lovell & Christmas (Can.) Ltd., 1977—, Winchester Cheese Inc., 1980—; vice chmn. KeepRite Inc., 1980—; dir. Trans Atlantic Gen. Devels. Ltd., Lowell & Christmas Holdings Ltd., London; dir. Can. bd. Liberty Mut. Ins. Co. Past bd. dirs. Jr. Achievement Met. Toronto, HARP House, Toronto. Served with Can. Army, 1945. Mem. Assn. Profl. Engrs. Ont., ASHRAE. Mem. United Ch. Can. Clubs: St. Georges Golf and Country, Muskoka Lakes Golf and Country, Good Fellowship, Riomar Golf and Beach, Riomar Bay Yacht, Bent Pine Golf and Country, Humber Valley Kiwanis (past pres.). Home: 2045 Lakeshore Blvd W Apt 4404 Toronto ON Canada M8V 2Z6 Office: 60 Harbour St World Trade Center Toronto ON Canada M5J 1B7

HARPER, WILLIAM LLOYD, lawyer; b. Atlanta, June 22, 1931; s. Lloyd Henry and Frances (Fleming) H.; m. Charlyn Bressler, June 16, 1953; children: Charles William, Nancy Ann. A.B., Emory U., 1954, LL.B., J.D., 1956. Bar: Ga. 1955. Assoc. firm Dorsey & Dorsey, Atlanta, 1958-61; asst. atty. gen. Ga. Dept. Law, 1961-71; exec. counsel to gov. Ga., 1971-77; U.S. atty. No. Dist. Ga., Atlanta, 1977-81; mem. law firm Hurt Richardson Garner Todd & Cadenhead, Atlanta, 1981—. Contbr. legal jours., encys. Served as asst. staff JAGC USAF, 1956-58; now brig. gen. USAFR; also moblzn. asst. JAG USAF. Mem. Am., Fed., Atlanta bar assns., Am. Judicature Soc., State Bar Ga., Am. Rhododendron Soc. Democrat. Club: Atlanta Lawyers. Office: 1100 Peachtree Center Harris Tower 233 Peachtree St NE Atlanta GA 30043

HARPHAM, VIRGINIA RUTH, violinist; b. Huntington, Ind., Dec. 10, 1917; d. Pyrl John and Nellie Grace (Whitaker) H.; m. Dale Lamar Harpham, Dec. 25, 1938; children—Evelyn, George. A.B., Morehead State U., 1939. Violinist, Nat. Symphony Orch., Washington, 1956—; prin. of second violin sect., 1964—; mem., Lywen String Quartet, 1960-69, Nat. Symphony String Quartet, 1973—. Episcopalian. Home: 3816 Military Rd NW Washington DC 20015

HARPOLE, MURRAY J., manufacturing company executive; b. Winterset, Iowa, 1921. Grad., Iowa State U., 1923. Chmn. Pentair, Inc., St. Paul. Office: Pentair Inc 1700 W Hwy 36 Saint Paul MN 55113 *

HARPSTEAD, DALE DOUGLAS, agronomist, educator; b. Sioux Falls, S.D., Sept. 10, 1926; s. Torkel O. and Ella Mae (Schultz) H.; m. Mary Lou Sorbel, Sept. 12, 1948; children—Daniel, Stanley, Philip, Thomas, Elizabeth. B.S., S.D. State U., 1950, M.S., 1954; Ph.D., U. Nebr., 1961. Mem. faculty S.D. State U., 1954-61, asso. prof., 1961; geneticist Rockefeller Found., N.Y.C., 1961-69; prof., chmn. crop and soil scis. Mich. State U., East Lansing, 1969—. Bd. dirs. World Service Commn., Luth. World Fedn., Geneva, Switzerland, 1978—. Served to 1st lt. U.S. Army, 1950-52. Fellow Am. Soc. Agronomy; mem. Crop Sci. Soc. Am. Office: 101 Soil Sci Bldg Mich State Univ East Lansing MI 48824

HARR, KARL GOTTLIEB, JR., lawyer, assn. exec.; b. South Orange, N.J., Aug. 3, 1922; s. Karl Gottlieb and Mildred (Reid) H.; m. Patricia Stratton Adams, Oct. 11, 1947; children—Timothy Adams, Karl Gottlieb III, Catherine Anne, Amy. A.B., Princeton, 1943; LL.B., Yale, 1948; D.Phil. (Rhodes scholar), Oxford U., 1950. Bar: N.Y. State bar 1951. Asso. firm Sullivan & Cromwell, N.Y.C., 1950-54; spl. asst. to under-sec. state for adminstrn., staff dir. sec. state's pub. com. on personnel, 1954-55; dir. spl. project Richardson Found., 1955; dep. asst. sec. def. for NSC affairs and plans, alternate def. mem. NSC Planning Bd., 1956-57; spl. asst. to Pres. U.S.; vice chmn. Ops. Coordinating Bd.; adviser Nat. Security Council Planning Bd., 1958-61; counsel to Rogers, Hoge, Hills, N.Y.C., 1961-63; pres. Aerospace Industries Assn. Am., Inc., Washington, 1963—; dir. First Am. Bank, Washington; mem. council Def. and Space Industry Assns.; chmn. Nat. Aero. Noise Abatement. Chmn. bd. dirs. Expt. in Internat. Living; alumni trustee Princeton, 1968-72. Served with AUS, 1943-46. Mem. Am. Bar Assn., Phi Beta Kappa, Phi Delta Phi. Home: 6 W Kirke St Chevy Chase MD 20015 Office: 1725 Desales St Washington DC 20036

HARR, LUTHER ARMSTRONG, computer cons.; b. Phila., Sept. 11, 1920; s. Luther Armstrong and Kathryn (Cressman) H.; m. Eileen Connor, Jan. 2, 1948. Grad., William Penn Charter Sch., Phila., 1937; B.S., Bowdoin Coll., 1941; M.B.A., Temple U., 1948. Sales mgr. Sperry Rand Corp., N.Y.C., 1948-56, br. mgr., 1957-61; mgr. Peat, Marwick Mitchell & Co. (C.P.A.'s), N.Y.C., 1956; dir. UNIVAC tabulating ops. Sperry Rand Internat. Corp., Lausanne, Switzerland, 1961-63; asst. to chmn. bd. Teleregister Corp., Stamford, Conn., 1963; (consol. with Bunker-Ramo Corp. 1964); v.p., gen. mgr. bus. and industry div. Bunker-Ramo Corp., 1964-66, exec. v.p., dir., 1966-68; sr. v.p., dir. Translux Corp., N.Y.C., 1968-69; pres. Luther Harr Assos., Inc., Lansdale, Pa., 1969—; br. mgr. Info. Scis. Inc., Phila., 1977—; lectr. Tech. Mem. Assn. Computing Machinery, Sigma Nu. Home and Office: 415 Hawthorne Ct Indian Harbour Beach FL 32937

HARRADENCE, JAMES HENRY CLYNE, lawyer; b. Blaine Lake, Sask., Can., July 29, 1925; s. Herbert and Cecilia Agnes (Horner) H.; m. Helen Louise Martin, Sept. 30, 1950; children: David, Keith, Hugh, James. Grad., U. Sask., 1949. Bar: Called to bar. Former mem. firm Diefenbaker, Cuelenare & Hall, Diefenbaker, Cuelenare, Hall & Harradence; now partner Harradence & Longworth, Prince Albert, Sask. Chmn. standing com. orgn. for nat. exec. Liberal Party Can., 1980—; chancellor Diocese Sask., Anglican Ch. Can., 1962—, prolocutor, 1979—. Served with RCAF, 1943-44. Mem. Can. Bar Assn., Sask. Law Soc. (bencher 1976-79), Law Soc. N.W. Terrs. Office: 1102 1st Ave W Prince Albert SK S6V 4Y6 Canada *

HARRAH, ROBERT EUGENE, manufacturing executive; b. Riverside, Washington, May 31, 1916; s. William Franklin and Irene Virginia (Clark) H.; m. Jayne Ann Knoblock, Aug. 10, 1937; children—Margie Lee, Bonnie Jean. Student, Taft Jr. Coll., 1934-36. Apprentice machinist Baash Ross Tool Co., 1936-41; with Mare Island Navy Yard, 1941-42, U.S. Engrs., Panama Canal, 1943; owner, operator co., 1943-52, owner co., 1952-68; founder, pres. Remco Hydraulics, Willits, Calif., 1957-68; owner, pres. Harrah Industries, Willits, 1968—; owner, chmn. bd. Microphor Inc., Willits, 1972-80; chmn., chief exec. officer Stanray Corp., Chgo., 1975—, also dir.; dir., asst. to pres. Abex Corp.; dir. IC Industries., Hussmann Corp. Mem. Willits Planning Commn., Willits City Council; chmn. bd. trustees Willits High Sch., 1949-59; pres. bd. trustees Howard Hosp., 1968—; governing bd. Ry. Progress Inst. Republican. Clubs: Rotary, Shriners, Masons. Inventor non-metallic cylinders, two-quart low flush toilet. Home: 451 E Hill Rd Willits CA 95490 Office: 42 Madrone St Willits CA 95490

HARRANGUE, RENEE LORRAINE, educator; b. Los Angeles, Mar. 19, 1934; d. William Barnaby and Lorraine (Torbett) H. B.A., Marymont Coll., 1957; M.A., Cath. U. Am., 1960, Ph.D., 1965. Tchr. Marymount Elem. Sch., Palos Verdes Estates, Calif., 1954-56, Sacred Heart May High Sch., Montebello, Calif., 1956-58; chmn. dept. psychology Marymount Coll., Rancho Palos Verdes, Calif., 1958-59,

1960-61, dean, 1968-73, acting pres., 1972-73; provost Loyola Marymount U., Los Angeles, 1973—, prof. psychology, 1976—. Bd. dirs. Upward Bound, 1965-66, United Way, 1969-71, St. John's Hosp., 1975-78. Recipient Emcalian award Marymount Palos Verdes Coll., 1978. Mem. Am. Assn. Higher Edn., AAUP, Am. Personnel and Guidance Assn., AAUW, Calif. Assn. Women Deans, Adminstrs. and Counselors, Nat. Assn. Women Deans, Adminstrs. and Counselors, Am. Psychol. Assn., Western Psychol. Assn., Calif. Psychol. Assn., Calif. Women in Higher Edn., Sigma Xi, Alpha Sigma Nu, Psi Chi. Democrat. Roman Catholic. Home: 8722 Delgany Ave 34 Play del Rey CA 90291 Office: 7101 W 80th St Los Angeles CA 90045

HARRAWOOD, PAUL, civil engineer, university dean; b. Akin, Ill., Aug. 28, 1928; s. Raymond E. and Verdie Alma (Galbraith) H.; m. June Anne Harris, Nov. 28, 1953; 1 dau., Laura Anne. B.S., U. Mo.-Rolla, 1951, M.S., 1956; Ph.D. (NSF fellow), N.C. State U., 1967. Instr. civil engring. U. Mo., Rolla, 1954-56; asst. prof. civil engring. Duke U., 1956-57, asst. dean engring., 1961-62; assoc. prof. civil engring. Vanderbilt U., Nashville, 1967-70, prof., 1970—, assoc. dean engring., 1962-79, acting dean engring., 1970-71, dean engring., 1979—; test engr. McDonnell Aircraft Corp., 1957; constrn. mgmt. engr. U.S. Army C.E., 1958. Served with USNR, 1951-54. Mem. ASCE, Soc. Am. Mil. Engrs., Am. Soc. Engring. Edn., Am. Assn. Higher Edn., AAAS, Sigma Xi, Tau Beta Pi, Chi Epsilon. Home: 5314 Camelot Ct Brentwood TN 37027 Office: Vanderbilt U Box 1607 Sta B Nashville TN 37235

HARRELL, BILLY EARL, utility, exploration and chemical comany executive; b. Birmingham, Ala., May 21, 1923; s. James Jackson and Lilla Louella (Green) H.; m. Juanita Foster, Mar. 4, 1944; children: Nita, Melanie, Stephanie. B.S., Auburn U., 1947. With Ark.-La. Gas Co., Shreveport, 1947—, v.p. gas supply, sales and v.p. LaT Dist. Oper. & Chem. Sales, 1964-72, sr. v.p. gas supply div. and expl. and prod. div. and Arkla Chem. Corp., beginning 1972, now exec. v.p. Ark.-La. Inc.; pres. Arkla Exploration Co. Chmn. United Fund Campaign, 1968; pres. bd. United Fund Campign, 1971; past pres. Metro YMCA, Central YMCA; pres. Demoiselle (Debutante) Club. Served with USAAF, World War II. Recipient Service award United Fund, Spl. Interest award YMCA. Mem. Am. Gas Assn., Mid-Continent Oil and Gas Assn., So. Gas Assn. (chmn. gas supply com.), Ind. Petroleum Producers Assn. (dir.), INGAA, Natural Gas Men of House, Natural Gas Men of Okla., C. of C. (dir.), Sigma Chi. Democrat. Baptist. Club: Shreveport Country (dir.). Office: Arkla Inc Arkla Bldg Shreveport LA 71151

HARRELL, DAVID EDWIN, JR., educator; b. Jacksonville, Fla., Feb. 22, 1930; s. David Edwin and Marilyn Mildred (Lee) H.; m. Adelia Francis Roberts, Sept. 6, 1955; children—Mildred Susan, David Edwin III, Elinor Elizabeth, Marilyn Lee, Harold Robert. B.A., David Lipscomb Coll., 1954; M.A., Vanderbilt U., 1958, Ph.D., 1962. Asst. prof. East Tenn. State U., 1961-64, asso. prof., 1964-66; assoc. prof. U. Okla., 1966-67, U. Ga., 1967-70; prof. U. Ala. at Birmingham, 1970-75, univ. scholar, 1975-81, chmn. dept. history, 1970-74; Disting. prof. U. Ark., 1981—. Author: Quest for a Christian America, 1966, White Sects and Black Men in the Recent South, 1971, The Social Sources of Division in the Disciples of Christ, 1973, All Things Are Possible: The Healing and Charismatic Revivals in Modern America, 1975; Editor: Varieties of Southern Evangelicalism, 1981; Contbr. articles to profl. jours. Sr. Fulbright scholar dept. history Allahabad (India) U., 1976-77; Recipient author's awards for best articles East Tenn. Hist. Soc., 1966, Mo. Hist. Soc., 1969. Fellow Inst. for Ecumenical and Cultural Research; mem. Am. Hist. Assn., Orgn. Am. Historians, So. Hist. Assn., Am. Soc. Church History, Disciples of Christ Hist. Soc. Home: 1125 Crossover Rd Fayetteville AR 72701

HARRELL, EVERETT RICHARD, JR., physician; b. Checotah, Okla., Apr. 5, 1922; s. Everett Richard and Golden (Duncan) H.; m. Ann McSwain, Oct. 17, 1947; children—Katherine R., Patricia A., Carolyn L., Nancy W. Student, Ohio Wesleyan U., summer 1942; M.D., Duke, 1946. Diplomate: Am. Bd. Dermatology (pres. 1976—). Intern Duke U. Hosp., 1946-47; resident dermatology U. Mich. Med. Center, 1949-52, instr. dermatology, 1952-53, asst. prof., 1953-56, asso. prof., 1956-60, prof., 1960-67, prof., chmn. dept. dermatology, 1967-75, clin. prof., 1975—; practice medicine, specializing in dermatology, Ann Arbor, Mich., 1952—. Contbr. articles profl. jours. Served to lt. USNR, 1947-49. Mem. Am. Acad. Dermatology (bd. dirs.), A.M.A. (chmn. sect. on dermatology 1973), Detroit Dermatol. Soc. (pres.), Sigma Xi, Alpha Omega Alpha, Sigma Alpha Epsilon, Phi Chi. Home: 3076 Geddes Ave Ann Arbor MI 48104

HARRELL, JAMES EARL, radiologist, educator; b. El Dorado, Ark., Dec. 25, 1931; s. Wilson M. and Edna Irene (Slater) H.; m. Betty Jacqueline (Rogers) Martin, Aug. 23, 1951 (div. 1977); children: James Earl, David Alan; m. Joan Marie Cordes, Oct. 20, 1977. B.A., Ouachita Baptist Coll., 1953, postgrad., 1956-57; M.D., U. Ark., 1962. Am. Bd. Radiology. Commd. 2d lt. U.S. Army, 1953, advanced through grades to lt. col., 1970; radiologist Walter Reed Gen. Hosp., 1963-71, Washington Hosp. Ctr., 1971-72, Methodist Hosp., Houston, 1972—, chief of radiology, 1976—; prof., chmn. dept. radiology Baylor Coll. Medicine, Houston, 1976—; physicist-in-charge dept. radiology Harris County Hosp. Dist., Houston, 1976—; pres. Houston Radiology Associated, 1976—; chief of radiology Jasper (Tex.) Meml. Hosp., 1981—, Lafayette (La.) Gen. Hosp., 1983—; resigned U.S. Army, 1971. Served to maj. gen. USAR; dep. surgeon gen. for mobzn. and res. affairs USAR, 1983—. Fellow Am. Coll. Radiology; mem. AMA, Harris County Med. Soc., Tex. Med. Assn., Am. Roentgen Ray Soc., Houston C. of C. Republican. Club: Westwood Country. Home: 2618 Glen Haven Blvd Houston TX 77025 Office: Baylor Coll Medicine 1200 Moursand Ave Houston TX 77030

HARRELL, LYNN MORRIS, cellist; b. N.Y.C., Jan. 30, 1944; s. Mack and Marjorie (Fulton) H.; m. Linda Blandford, Sept. 7, 1976. Student, Juilliard Sch. Music, Curtis Inst. Music. Tchr. cello Juilliard Sch. Music. Prin. cellist, Cleve. Orch., 1963-71, debut recital, Tully Hall, N.Y.C., 1971; cellist in premier: Donald Erb Cello Concerto, 1976; soloist with maj. orchs. U.S. and Europe; rec. artist, London/Decca Records; also appears on, EMI/Angel, RCA, CBS, Deutsche Gramaphon; rec. artist: recs. include Dvorak Concerto. Recipient 1st Piatigorsky award, Grammy award; co-recipient 1st Avery Fisher award, 1975. Office: care Columbia Artists Mgmt 165 W 57th St New York NY 10019

HARRELL, MORRIS, lawyer; b. Grandview, Tex., Apr. 16, 1920; s. Oscar H.; m. Rusty Baylor; children: James, Julia Boone, Rhoda Reynolds. B.B.A., Baylor U., 1942, LL.B., 1942. Bar: Tex. 1942, U.S. Supreme Ct. 1959, U.S. Ct. Claims 1965. Asst. U.S. atty. No. Dist. Tex., 1947-51; sole practice, 1956-55; assoc. Thompson, Knight, Wright & Simmons, Dallas, 1955-65; ptnr. Rain, Harrell, Emery, Young & Doke, Dallas, 1965—. Bd. trustees, chmn. exec. and planning com. Southwestern Legal Found., 1975-76, chmn. research fellow, 1975-76. Fellow Am. Coll. Trial Lawyers, Tex. Bar Found., Am. Bar Found.; mem. ABA (pres. 1982—, state del. ho. of dels. 1972-80, bd. govs. 1977-80), Dallas Bar Assn. (pres. 1962), State Bar Tex. (chmn. bd. dirs. 1968-69, pres. 1970-71), Nat. Conf. Bar Pres. (pres. 1976-77). Office: Am Bar Assn 1155 E 60th St Chicago IL 60637 *

HARRELL, SAMUEL MACY, grain company executive; b. Indpls., Jan. 4, 1931; s. Samuel Runnels and Mary (Evans) H.; m. Sally Bowers, Sept. 2, 1958; children: Samuel D., Holly Evans, Kevin Bowers, Karen Susan, Donald Runnels, Kenneth Macy. B.S. in Econs., Wharton Sch., U. Pa., 1953. Chmn. bd., chief exec. officer, chmn., exec. com. Early & Daniel Industries, Cin., 1971—; pres., chmn. bd., chmn. ecec. com. Early & Daniel Co., Cin., 1971—; chmn. bd., chief exec. officer, chmn. exec. com. Tidewater Grain Co., Phila., 1971—; dir. Wainwright Bank & Trust Co., Wainright Abstract Co., Nat. Grain Trade Council, U.S. Feed Grains Council; mem. Chgo. bd. Trade. Served with AUS, 1953-55. Mem. Young Pres.'s Orgn., U. Pa. Alumni Assn. (past pres.), Terminal Elevator Grain Mchts. Assn. (dir.), Millers Nat. Fedn. (dir.), Assn. Operative Millers, Am. Soc. Bakery Engrs., Am. Fin. Assn., Council on Fgn. Relations, Fin. Exec. Inst., N.Am. Grain Export Assn. (dir.), Mpls. Grain Exchange, St. Louis Mchts. Grain Exchange, Buffalo Corn Exchange, Delta Tau Delta (Past prs. Ind. alumni). Presbyterian. Clubs: Columbia, Indpls. Athletic, Woodstock, Traders Point Hunt, Dramatic, Players, Lambs (Indpls.); Racquet (Phila.); University (Washington). Lodges: Masons; Rotary. Home: 5858 Sunset Ln Indianapolis IN 46208 Office: 525 Carr St Cincinnati OH 45203

HARRELSON, WALTER JOSEPH, clergyman, educator; b. Winnabow, N.C., Nov. 28, 1919; s. Isham Danvis and Mae (Rich) H.; m. Idella Aydlett, Sept. 20, 1942; children: Marianne, David Aydlett, Robert Joseph. Student, Mars Hill (N.C.) Coll., 1940-41, Litt.D. (hon.), 1977; A.B., U. N.C., 1947; B.D., Union Theol. Sem., 1949, Th.D., 1953; postgrad., U. Basel, Switzerland, 1950-51, Harvard, 1951-53; D.D. (hon.), U. of South, 1974. Instr. philosophy U. N.C., 1947; ordained to ministry Baptist Ch., 1949; tutor asst., instr. Union Theol. Sem., 1949-50; prof. O.T. Andover Newton Theol. Sch., 1951-55; dean, asso. prof. O.T. U. Chgo. Div. Sch., 1955-60; prof. O.T. Div. Sch., Vanderbilt U., Nashville, 1960—, chmn. grad. dept. religion, 1962-67, dean, 1967-75, Disting. prof. O.T., 1975—; traveling fellow Union Theol. Sem., 1949; fellow Am. Council Learned Socs., 1950-51, 70; exchange fellow U. Basel, 1950-51; Fulbright research scholar, Rome, 1962-63; rector Ecumenical Inst. Advanced Theol. Studies, Jerusalem, 1977-78, 78-79; vice-chmn. transl. com. Rev. Standard Version of the Bible.; NEH Fellow, 1983-84. Author: Jeremiah, Prophet to the Nations, 1959, Interpreting the Old Testament, 1964, From Fertility Cult to Worship, 1969, 80, The Ten Commandments and Human Rights, 1980; co-author, editor: Teaching the Biblical Languages, 1967; Editor, contbr.: Israel's Prophetic Heritage, 1962. Mem. Soc. for Religion in Higher Edn. (pres. 1972-74), Soc. Bibl. Lit. (pres. 1971-72), Am. Schs. Oriental Research, Phi Beta Kappa. Home: 305 Bowling Ave Nashville TN 37205

HARRER, GUSTAVE ADOLPHUS, librarian; b. Durham, N.C., Dec. 30, 1924; s. Gustave Adolphus and Florence Caroline (Wagner) H.; m. Elizabeth Varnado, Sept. 3, 1948; children—Elizabeth Ida, Kathryn Florence, Hugh, Thomas. A.B., U. N.C., 1948, M.A., 1950, Ph.D. in Germanic Langs, 1953; M.S. in L.S. (Katherine L. Sharp fellow), U. Ill., 1954. Asst. prof. German and Latin Millsaps Coll., 1949-51; asst. order librarian U. Tenn. Libraries, 1954-55, asso. order librarian, 1955-57; chief acquisition librarian Stanford Libraries, 1957-58, asst. dir. for central services, 1958-60; dir. libraries Boston U., 1960-68, U. Fla., Gainesville, 1968—; bd. dirs. Southeastern Library Network, 1974-77, vice chmn., 1976-77; mem. OCLC Users Council, 1978-81. Contbr. articles to profl. jours. Served with AUS, 1943-45. Faculty fellow Fund for Advancement Edn., 1951-52; fellow Carnegie Project Advanced Library Adminstrn. Rutgers U., 1958. Mem. A.L.A. (life), Assn. Research Libraries (dir. 1973-76), Assn. Caribbean U. and Research Libraries (exec. council 1973-76, pres. 1977-78). Home: 2815 NW 29th St Gainesville FL 32605

HARRIGAN, ANTHONY HART, author; b. N.Y.C., Oct. 27, 1925; s. Anthony Hart and Elizabeth Elliott (Hutson) H.; m. Elizabeth McP. Ravenel, Aug. 16, 1950; children: Anthony Hart, Elizabeth Chardon, Elliott McP., Mary Ravenel. Student, Bard Coll., Kenyon Coll., Gambier, Ohio, U. Va. Reporter Virginian-Pilot, Norfolk, 1953-55; reporter Charleston (S.C.) News & Courier, asso. editor, 1957-70; exec. v.p. U.S. Indsl. Council, Nashville, 1970-78, pres., 1978—; pres. U.S. Indsl. Council Ednl. Found.; lectr. Harvard U., Nat. War Coll., Vanderbilt U., U. Colo.; Past mem. research com. S.C. Commn. Higher Edn. Author: Ten Poets Anthology, 1947, The Editor and the Republic, 1952, Red Star Over Africa, 1964, The New Republic, 1965, Defense Against Total Attack, 1966, A Guide to the War in Vietnam, 1965, American Perspectives, 1974, American Perspectives II, 1977; co-author: The Indian Ocean and the Threat to the West, 1976, The Southern Oceans and the Security of the Free World, 1978; co-author or editor: other works The Southern Oceans and the Security of the Free World, 1978; editorial adv. bd.: Modern Age, 1955—; author newspaper column, 1970—, also numerous articles in nat. jours. Served with USMCR, World War II. Recipient Mil Rev. award U.S. Army Command and Gen. Staff Coll., 1965; grantee Relm Found., 1966. Fellow Soc. Antiquaries of Scotland (dir.); Mem. Phila. Soc. (past 1st v.p.). Episcopalian. Clubs: Reform (London); Nat. Press (Washington); Carolina Yacht, EQB. Office: Realtors Bldg Nashville TN 37210

HARRIGAN, ARTHUR WASHINGTON, educator, former paper company executive; b. Bklyn., Mar. 18, 1919; s. Arthur Washington and Josephine (Ward) H.; m. Margaret Marrin, May 29, 1941; children: Arthur Washington, Patricia. B.S., N.Y. U., 1942, M.B.A., 1949, Ph.D., 1959. Editor Tel. & Tel. Age, N.Y.C., 1938-41; purchase analyst, buyer Western Electric Co., N.Y.C., 1946-53; purchasing agt., labor relations and personnel adminstr. Teletype Corp., Chgo., 1953-56; personnel and mfg. adminstr. Western Electric Co., Inc., N.Y.C., also Buffalo, 1956-60, purchasing controller, 1960-64, controller, 1964-65, dir. corporate analysis, 1966-68, v.p. finance, 1968-72; exec. v.p. Internat. Paper Co., N.Y.C., 1972-81, advisor to chmn., 1981-82, dir., 1973-81, ret., 1982; clin. prof. mgmt. NYU, 1982—. Served to lt. Supply Corps USNR, 1941-45. Recipient Madden Meml. award N.Y. U., 1980. Mem. Am. Econ. Assn., Fin. Execs. Inst., Am. Finance Assn. Home: 2 Woodmere Dr Summit NJ 07901 Office: Coll Bus and Pub Adminstrn 602 Tisch Hall NYU New York NY 10003

HARRIGAN, JOHN FREDERICK, banker; b. Eau Claire, Wis., June 22, 1925; s. Frederick H. and Marion F. (Farr) H.; m. Barbara Heald, July 1, 1950; children—Sarah H. Gruber, Peter Christopher. Student, U. Wis., 1946-49; grad., Rutgers U. Stonier Grad. Sch. Banking, 1965. With First Nat. Bank Oreg., Portland, 1949-71, exec. v.p., 1971; chmn. bd., chief exec. officer Pacific Nat. Bank Wash., Seattle, 1971-74, dir., 1971-80; vice chmn. bd. dirs. United Calif. Bank, Los Angeles, 1974-75; pres., dir. Western Bancorp., Los Angeles, 1975-80; chmn. bd., chief exec. officer, dir. Union Bank, Los Angeles, 1980—; dir. Nordstrom, Inc. Bd. dirs. Los Angeles Civic Light Opera Assn., So. Calif. chpt. Nat. Multiple Sclerosis Soc.; bd. visitors Grad. Sch. Mgmt., U. Calif., Los Angeles. Served with USMCR, 1943-45. Mem. Assn. Res. City Bankers, Smithsonian Assos. (dir.). Episcopalian. Clubs: Calif., Los Angeles Country., Eldorado Country. Address: 445 S Figueroa Los Angeles CA 90071

HARRIGAN, JOHN THOMAS, JR., physician, educator; b. Perth Amboy, N.J., Apr. 20, 1929; s. John T. and Mary E. (Czapp) H.; m. Marlene Lulka, Apr. 14, 1961 (div.); children: John, Alisa, Edmund. Student, U. Va., 1946-49; M.D., George Washington U., 1953. Diplomate: Am. Bd. Ob-Gyn. Intern Doctors Hosp., Washington, 1953-54; resident in ob-gyn Luth. Hosp., Balt., 1954-55, Providence Hosp., Washington, 1957-58, Free Hosp. for Women, Boston, 1958-59; practice medicine specializing in ob-gyn, sub specialist in maternal-fetal medicine, Jersey City, 1960-65, Colonia, N.J., 1962-70, Madison Twp., N.J., 1965-70; asst. attending in ob-gyn Margaret Hague Hosp., Jersey City, 1960-65; attending physician in ob-gyn Rahway (N.J.) Hosp., 1962-70, South Amboy (N.J.) Hosp., 1965-73, sec. to med. staff, 1970; attending in ob-gyn Martland Hosp. Unit, Newark, 1970-74; dir. dept. ob-gyn Monmouth Med. Center, Long Branch, N.J., 1974-76, dir. regional perinatal edn. program, 1975-78; dir. Monmouth Perinatal Center, Long Branch, 1975-78; sr. attending in ob-gyn St. Peters Med. Center, 1978—; assoc. prof. ob-gyn Hahnemann Med. Coll., Phila., 1975-78; prof. dir. div. maternal-fetal medicine Rutgers Med. Sch., Piscataway, N.J., 1978—; cons. in maternal-fetal medicine to physicians, Eastern N.J.; mem. maternal and infant care services com. N.J. Dept. Health, 1975—. Contbr. articles to med. jours. Served to capt. M.C. U.S. Army, 1955-57. Fellow Am. Coll. of Obstetricians and Gynecologists (vice chmn. N.J. sect. 1979-82, chmn. N.J. sect. 1982—); mem. AMA, N.J. Med. Soc., Am. Fertility Soc., N.J. Perinatal Assn. (v.p. 1980—), Baker Channing Soc., N.J. Ob-Gyn Soc. Democrat. Roman Catholic. Home: 919 Woodland Terr Bridgewater NJ 08805 Office: Dept Ob-Gyn St Peters Med Center 254 Easton Ave New Brunswick NJ 08903

HARRIGAN, KENNETH WILLIAM J., automotive products company executive; b. Chatham, Ont., Can., Sept. 27, 1927; s. Charles A. and Olga Jean (Wallace) H.; m. Margaret Jean Macpherson, June 18, 1955; children: Tara Lynne Harrigan Tomlinson, Stephen Charles. B.A. with honors, U. Western Ont., 1951. With Ford Motor Co. Can. Ltd., Oakville, Ont., 1951—, regional mgr. central region, 1965-68, gen. sales mgr., Oakville, 1968-71; dir. sales and mktg. Ford Asia Pacific Inc., Australia, 1971-73; group dir. So. Europe Ford Europe, Inc., 1973-76, v.p. truck sales and mktg., 1976-78; v.p., gen. mgr. sales Ford Motor Co. Can. Ltd., Oakville, 1978-81, pres., 1981—, chief exec. officer, 1982—; mem. policy com. (Bus. Council on Nat. Issues), mem. Bd. govs. Appleby Coll., Oakville. Mem. Conf. Bd. Can., Toronto Bd. Trade, Can. C. of C., Motor Vehicle Mfrs. Assn. (dir.). Clubs: Golf and Country (Mississauga, Ont.); (Canadian); (Empire). Home: 1 Maple Grove Dr Oakville ON Canada L6J 4T8 Office: The Canadian Rd Oakville ON Canada L6J 5E4

HARRIMAN, DAVID PARKER, publishing company executive; b. Balt., Oct. 23, 1948; s. Mark Weber and Carolyn (Potter) H.; m. Deborah Biemiller, Mar. 20, 1972; children: Andrew, Peter. B.A., U. Va., 1970; J.D., U. Md.-Balt., 1973. Bar: Va. 1975. Editor Michie Co., Charlottesville, Va., 1973, sr. editor, 1973-76; pvt. practice law, Charlottesville, 1976-77; exec. editor Michie Co., 1977-79, editor-in-chief, 1979-82, v.p., 1982—. Mem. Va. State Bar, Va. Bar Assn. Presbyterian. Home: 3700 Skyline Crest Dr Charlottesville VA 22901 Office: The Michie Co PO Box 7587 Charlottesville VA 22906

HARRIMAN, GERALD EUGENE, educator, univ. dean; b. Dell Rapids, S.D., May 30, 1924; s. Roy L. and Margaret (Schrantz) H.; m. Eileen Bernadine Bensman, June 10, 1950; children—G. Peter, Mary K., Margaret C., Elizabeth A. B.S., U. Notre Dame, 1947; A.M., U. S.D., 1949; Ph.D., U. Cin., 1957. Expediter Minn. Mining & Mfg. Co., 1947-48; from instr. to asst. dean, chmn. dept. bus. adminstrn. and finance Xavier U., 1949-66; prof. bus. adminstrn., chmn. div. bus. and econs. Ind. U. at South Bend, 1966-75, prof. bus. adminstrn. and econs., 1975—, dean faculties, 1975—, acting chancellor, 1979; vis. prof. fin. U. S.D., 1962; chmn. acad. deans Ind. Conf. Higher Edn., 1981-82; cons. in field. Mem. citizens adv. council long range financial planning Council of City Cin., 1963. Served with USNR, 1942-45. Mem. Am. Econs. Assn., Am. Finance Assn., Beta Gamma Sigma. Home: 16600 Gerald St Granger IN 46530 Office: 1700 Mishawaka Ave South Bend IN 46615

HARRIMAN, JOHN HOWLAND, lawyer; b. Buffalo, Apr. 14, 1920; s. Lewis Gildersleeve and Grace (Bastine) H.; m. Barbara Ann Brunmark, June 12, 1943; children—Walter Brunmark, Constance Bastine, John Howland. A.B. summa cum laude, Dartmouth, 1942; J.D., Stanford U., 1949. Bar: Calif. bar 1949. Asso. firm Lawler, Felix & Hall, Los Angeles, 1949-55; asst. v.p., then v.p. Security Pacific Nat. Bank, Los Angeles, 1955-72, sr. v.p., 1972—; sec. Security Pacific Corp., 1971—. Mem. Los Angeles adv. council Episcopal Ch. Found., 1977-79; mem. Republican Assos., 1951—, trustee, 1962-72; mem. Calif. Rep. Central Com., 1956-69, 81—, exec. com., 1960-62, 81—; mem. Los Angeles County Rep. Central Com., 1958-70, exec. com., 1960-62, vice chmn., 1962; chmn. Calif. 15th Congl. Dist. Rep. Central Com., 1960-62, Calif. 30th Congl. Dist. Rep. Central Com., 1962; treas. United Rep. Fin. Com. Los Angeles County, 1969-70; chmn. Commitment '80 Los Angeles County, Reagan-Bush campaign. Served with USAAF, 1943-46. Mem. Am. Bar Assn., Am. Soc. Corp. Secs. (pres. Los Angeles region 1970-71), State Bar Calif., Los Angeles Bar Assn., Town Hall Los Angeles, Phi Beta Kappa, Theta Delta Chi, Phi Alpha Delta. Clubs: Beach (Santa Monica, Calif.); California (Los Angeles); Lincoln, Breakfast Panel (pres. 1970-71). Office: 333 S Hope St Los Angeles CA 90071

HARRIMAN, WILLIAM AVERELL, former government official; b. Nov. 15, 1891; s. Edward Henry and Mary (Averell) H.; m. Kitty Lanier Lawrence, Sept. 21, 1915; children: Mary (Mrs. Shirley C. Fisk), Kathleen (Mrs. Stanley G. Mortimer, Jr.); m. Mrs. Marie Norton Whitney, Feb. 21, 1930 (dec. Sept. 1970); m. Pamela Digby Churchill Hayward, Sept. 27, 1971. B.A., Yale, 1913. Vice Pres. purchase and supplies Union Pacific R.R., 1915-17, chmn. bd., 1932-42, Mcht. Shipbldg. Corp., 1917-25, W.A. Harriman & Co., Inc., 1920-31; partner Brown Bros. Harriman & Co. (merger), 1931-46, ltd. partner, 1946—; chmn. exec. com. Ill. Central R.R. Co., 1931-42, dir., 1915-46; Adminstr. Div. II, N.R.A., 1934, spl. asst. adminstr., 1934, adminstrv. officer, 1934-35; mem. bus. adv. council Dept. Commerce, 1933, chmn., 1937-39; chief materials br. prodn. div. O.P.M., 1940-41; spl. rep. of Pres. in Gt. Britain with rank of minister, 1941, to USSR, chmn. mission), rank of ambassador, 1941; apptd. rep. in London of Combined Shipping Adjustment Bd., 1942; apptd. mem. London Combined Prodn. and Resources Bd., 1942; U.S. ambassador to, Russia, 1943-46, to Gt. Britain, 1946, sec. of commerce, 1946-48, U.S. rep. in Europe under ECA of 1948, rank of A.E. and P., 1948-50, spl. asst. to Pres., 1950-51; Am. rep. on com. to study Western def. plans NATO, 1951; dir. Mut. Security Agy., 1951-53; gov., N.Y., 1955-59, ambassador-at-large, 1961, 65-68, asst. sec. of state for Far Eastern affairs, 1961-63, under sec. of state polit. affairs, 1963-65, personal rep. of Pres. to conversations on Vietnam in, Paris, 1968-69. Author: Peace with Russia?, 1959, America and Russia in a Changing World, 1971, Special Envoy: To Churchill and Stalin, 1941-46, 1975. Chmn. fgn. policy task force adv. council Democratic Nat. Com., 1974—; del. Dem. Nat. Conv., 1976. Home: Willow Oaks Middleburg VA 22117 Office: 3032 N St NW Washington DC 20007

HARRINGER, OLAF CARL, architect, museum cons.; b. Hamburg, Germany, Apr. 29, 1919; came to U.S., 1927; s. Henry Theodore and Anke (Berger) H.; m. Helen Ehrat Hedges, Dec. 20, 1975; children—Carla, Brita, Eric. Student, Evanston Acad. Fine Arts, The New Bauhaus, 1937-38, Ill. Inst. Tech., 1942-45. Designer Raymond Loewy Assos., Chgo., 1946-49, H. Allan Majestic Assos., 1949-51, Dickens, Inc., 1951-52, Olaf Harringer and Assos. (architects/designers), 1952-

62; account exec. several exhibit firms, Chgo., 1962-68; dir. exhibits Mus. Sci. and Industry, Chgo., 1957-60, 68-80; prin. Olaf Harringer Assos., Chgo., 1981—. Mem. AIA, Am. Assn. Museums, ICOM. Home: 530 Hunter Rd Glenview IL 60025 Office: 53 W Jackson Blvd Chicago IL 60604

HARRINGTON, CONRAD FETHERSTONHAUGH, trust company director; b. Montreal, Que., Can., Aug. 8, 1912; s. Conrad Dawson and Muriel Theodora (Fetherstonhaugh) H.; m. Joan Roy Hastings, Aug. 6, 1940; children: Conrad, Jill, Susan. B.A., McGill U., 1933, B.C.L., 1936; postgrad., U. Besancon, France, 1936-37. Bar: Called to Que. bar 1936. With firm Phelan, Fleet, Robertson & Abbott, Montreal, 1937-39; with Royal Trust Co., Montreal, 1945—, mgr., supr. Ont. brs., Toronto, 1952-62, v.p., 1957-65, gen. mgr., 1963-65, pres., 1965-70, chmn. bd., chief exec. officer, 1970-73, chmn. bd., 1973-78, chmn. exec. com., 1973—, also dir.; chmn. bd. Glaxo Can. Ltd.; dir. Gerling Global Life Reins. & Gen. Ins. Cos., R.L. Crain Ltd., MPG Investment Corp. Chmn. campaign Toronto United Appeal, 1958; life gov. Trinity Coll. Sch., Port Hope, Ont.; gov. Montreal Children's Hosp., Montreal Gen. Hosp., Douglas Hosp.; emeritus gov., former chancellor McGill U., chancellor, 1976—; past chmn. McGill Fund Council; hon. bd. dirs. Quebec Council, St. John Ambulance; councillor Montreal Mus. Fine Arts; chmn. Montreal Citizens Adv. Bd., Salvation Army. Served from lt. to col. Royal Can. Arty., 1940-45. Mem. Trust Cos. Assn. Can. (pres. 1958-59, 70-71), Zeta Psi. Clubs: York, Toronto, Toronto Golf, University, St. James, Mount Bruno Golf, Mount Royal, Forest Stream. Home: 556 Lansdowne Ave Montreal PQ H3Y 2V6 Canada Office: 630 Dorchester Blvd W Montreal PQ Canada

HARRINGTON, (DANIEL) PATRICK, JR., actor; b. Astoria, N.Y., Aug. 13; s. Daniel Patrick and Anne Francis (Hunt) H.; m. Marjorie Gortner, Nov. 19, 1955; children: Patrick, Michael, Terry, Tresa Caitlin. B.A., Fordham U., 1950, M.A., 1952. Appearances TV include Jack Paar Show, 1958-60, Steve Allen Show, 1959-61, Danny Thomas Show, 1959-60; free-lance performer, 1961—; appeared in: Tattletales; co-star: TV series Mr. Deeds Goes to Town, 1969, Owen Marshall-Councilor at Law, 1971-72, One Day at a Time, 1975— (Golden Globe award 1981); appeared in: motion pictures The Wheeler Dealers, 1963, Move Over Darling, 1963, East Come, Easy Go, 1967, The President's Analyst, 1967, 2000 Years Later, 1969, The Candidate, 1970. Served to 1st lt. USAF, 1952-54. Mem. UCLA Chancellor's Assos. Democrat. Roman Catholic. Club: Riviera Country. *

HARRINGTON, DAVID VAN, educator; b. Plainview, Minn., Oct. 29, 1929; s. Glen Wesley and Gladys Beatrice (Cewe) H.; m. Aleda Mae Rehm, Aug. 25, 1957; children—Ann Kathryn, Linda Kay, Bruce David. B.A., Eastern Wash. State Coll., 1951; M.A., Wash. State U., 1956; Ph.D., U. Wis., Madison, 1960. Prof. English Gustavus Adolphus Coll., St. Peter, Minn., 1960—, chmn. dept. English, 1970—. Contbr. articles to profl. jours. Served with AUS, 1951-54. Mem. St. Peter Madrigal Singers. Republican. Presbyn. (elder). Home: 532 Capitol Dr St Peter MN 56082 Office: Gustavus Adolphus Coll St Peter MN 56082

HARRINGTON, FRED HARVEY, history educator; b. Watertown, N.Y., June 24, 1912; s. Arthur William and Elsie (Sutton) H.; m. Nancy Howes, Oct. 19, 1935; children: Heather Harrington Monroe, Holly, Hilary Harrington Mandel, Helise, Harvey. A.B. with honors, Cornell U., 1933; M.A. (Frederic Courtland Penfield fellow), NYU, 1934, Ph.D., 1937, LL.D., 1963; LL.D., U. Calif., 1965, Drake U., 1969, Loyola U., Chgo., 1970, U. Wis.-Milw., 1982; L.H.D., U. Maine, 1966, DePaul U., 1966, Miami U., 1967, Northland Coll., 1969; Litt.D., U. Ife, Nigeria, 1969. Instr. history Washington Square Coll., NYU, 1936-37; instr. history U. Wis., 1937-39, asst. prof., 1939-40; prof. history and polit. sci., chmn. dept. U. Ark., 1940-44; asso. prof. history U. Wis., 1944-47, prof., 1947-70, chmn. dept., 1952-55, spl. asst. to pres., 1956-58, v.p. acad. affairs, 1958-62, v.p. univ., 1962, pres., 1962-70, William F. Vilas research prof. history, 1970-82; program adviser in India, Sri Lanka and Nepal for Ford Found., 1971-77; vis. prof. U. W.Va., 1942, Cornell U., 1944, U. Pa., 1949, U. Colo., 1951, Oxford U., 1955; Am. studies seminar U. Kyoto, Japan, 1962; mem. Indo-Am. Subcommn. Edn. and Culture, 1975-80; dir. Carnegie study of role of univ. in adult edn., 1960-77; dir. study Internat. Linkages of Higher Edn., 1976-78; chmn. com. on instnl. coop. Big Ten and Chgo., 1960-62; bd. vis. Air Acad., 1961-64; Wis. chmn. Brotherhood Week NCCJ, 1965; pres. Nat. Assn. State Univs. and Land Grant Colls., 1968-69; mem. Army Adv. Panel on ROTC Affairs, 1963-68; mem. adv. panels AID, 1965-72; bd. dirs. U.S. Ednl. Found. in India, 1971-77, chmn., 1973-77. Author: God, Mammon and the Japanese: Dr. Horace N. Allen and Korean-American Relations (1884-1905), 1944, Fighting Politician: Major General N. P. Banks, 1948, (with M. Curti, R. H. Shryock, T.C. Cochran) An American History (2 vols.), 1950, Hanging Judge, 1951, History of American Civilization, The Future of Adult Education: New Responsibilities for Colleges and Universities, 1977. Guggenheim fellow, 1943-44; Ford Faculty fellow, 1955-56. Mem. Am. Hist. Assn., Am. Council Edn. (chmn. commn. acad. affairs 1962-65, bd. dirs. 1966-69), Fgn. Policy Assn. (bd. dirs. 1966-68), Nat. Commn. Accrediting (pres. 1966-68), Nat. Assn. Ednl. Broadcasters (bd. dirs. 1965-68), Orgn. Am. Historians (exec. com. 1944-48), Edn. Commn. of States (v.p. 1966-68), Fulbright Alumni Assocs. (dir. 1980-84), Phi Beta Kappa, Phi Kappa Phi. Home: 87 Oak Creek Trail Madison WI 53717 Office: 1840 Van Hise Hall U Wis Madison WI 53706

HARRINGTON, GEORGE WILLIAM, chemistry educator; b. N.Y.C., Nov. 13, 1929; s. George Washington and Hedwig Louise (Sommer) H.; m. Patricia Miller, June 4, 1955; children: Steven George, Cathy Louise. B.A., N.Y. U., 1954, Ph.D., 1959. Project engr. Philco Corp. (Lansdale Tube Co.), 1959; prof. chemistry Temple U., Phila., 1959—, asso. dean, 1968—, chmn. dept. chemistry, 1978-81; Research contractor AEC, 1959-62, Campbell Soup Co., 1963-65. Served with AUS, 1948-52; Korea. Recipient Founders Day award N.Y. U., 1969; grantee Nat. Cancer Inst., NIH, 1975—. Fellow Am. Inst. Chemists (sr. medal 1955); mem. Am. Chem. Soc. (chmn. phys. sect. Phila. 1969), AAUP, Sigma Xi. Research and publs. in electroanalytical chemistry, chem. carcinogens. Home: 1208 Duncan Dr Dresher PA 19025 Office: Dept Chemistry Temple Univ Philadelphia PA 19121

HARRINGTON, JEAN PATRICE, college president; b. Denver; d. James Michael and Katherine Ann (Holl) H. B.A., Coll. Mt. St. Joseph, 1953; M.A., Creighton U., 1958; Ph.D., U. Colo., 1967; L.H.D. (hon.), Xavier U., 1983. Joined Sisters of Charity of Cin., 1940; prin. St. Rose of Lima, Denver, 1953-56; tchr. Cathedral High Sch., Denver, 1956-58, prin., 1958-68; dir. instl. research Coll. Mt. St. Joseph, Cin., 1968-69, pres., 1977—; dir. 1st Nat. Bank., Cin. Bell. Bd. dirs. Penrose Hosp., Colorado Springs, Colo., 1976—, Cin. chpt. ARC, 1978—, Greater Cin. Center for Econ. Edn., 1980—, St. Mary Corwin Hosp., Pueblo, Colo., 1972-80, Good Samaritan Hosp and Health Center, Dayton, Ohio, 1978-80, Samaritan Health Resources, Inc., 1983—, St. Rita Sch. for Deaf, 1983, United Appeal Cabinet, 1983. Named Career Woman of Achievement YWCA, 1981, Disting. Bus. and Profl. Woman of Yr., 1982. Mem. Nat. Assn. Ind. Colls. and Univs., Assn. Cath. Colls. and Univs. (bd. dirs.), Ohio Coll. Assn. (pres. 1981-82), Council for Advancement of Small Colls. (bd. dirs. 1981—), Ohio Found. Ind. Colls., Greater Cin. Consortium Colls. and Univs. (vice chmn. 1980—), Council Ind. Colls. (bd. dirs. 1981—), Cin. C. of C. (trustee, sec. 1979—). Roman Catholic. Club: Cin. Women's. Home and Office: College of Mount St Joseph Mount Saint Joseph OH 45051

HARRINGTON, JEREMY THOMAS, clergyman; b. Lafayette, Ind., Oct. 7, 1932; s. William and Ellen (Cain) H. B.A., Duns Scotus Coll., 1955; postgrad., U. Detroit, 1955, Marquette U., 1961; M.A., Xavier U., Cin., 1965; M.S. in Journalism, Northwestern U., 1967. Joined Order Friars Minor, 1950; ordained priest Roman Catholic Ch., 1959; tchr. Roger Bacon High Sch., Cin., 1960-64; asso. editor St. Anthony Messenger, Cin., 1964-66, editor, 1966-81, pub., 1975-81; mem. bd. Franciscan Province Cin., 1969-72, 75-81, chief exec. bd., 1981—. Author: Your Wedding: Planning Your Own Ceremony, 1974; Editor: Conscience in Today's World, 1970, Jesus: Superstar or Savior?, 1972. Mem. Catholic Press Assn. (pres. 1975-77, dir.), Kappa Tau Alpha. Home and Office: 1615 Vine St Cincinnati OH 45210 *My success has been made by others. As a priest, as well as an editor and publisher, my challenge is to discover, recognize, encourage and make available to others the talents of authors and artists. To me, that's a parable of life. The more we can discover, appreciate and foster the good qualities and strengths of others, the more "successful" we are. Success in life is realizing how many gifts are made available to us by God and our fellow human beings.*

HARRINGTON, JOHN JOSEPH EDWARD, organization executive; b. Phila., Mar. 28, 1915; s. John Joseph and Agnes Veronica (O'Donnell) H.; m. Ruth L. Kelly, Sept. 2, 1939 (dec. 1971); children: Patricia M., Eileen F. Grad. high sch. Mem. Fraternal Order Police, 1940—, pres. Pa. lodge, 1958, 60, 62, pres. Phila. lodge No. 5, 1964, 66, 68, 70, nat. pres., 1965, 67, 69, 71, 73-83, life mem. nat. bd. Trustee Phila. Gen. Hosp., 1968-72. Recipient Gold medal Nat. Soc. SAR, 1975. Mem. Red Men Assn. Am. Home: 1 E Peace Valley Rd Chalfont PA 18914 Office: G3136 W Pasadena Ave Flint MI 48504

HARRINGTON, JOHN VINCENT, communications company executive, engineer, educator; b. N.Y.C., May 9, 1919; s. John Joseph and Dorothy (Neisel) H.; m. Frances Cullinane, Jan. 23, 1943; children: John F., Nancy Harrington Higgins, Jeffrey, Richard, Brian. B.E.E., Cooper Union, 1940; M.E.E., Poly. Inst. Bklyn., 1948; Sc.D., Mass. Inst. Tech., 1957. Research engr. U.S. Air Force Cambridge Research Lab., Mass., 1946-51; leader data transmission group Lincoln Lab., M.I.T., Cambridge, 1951-56, asso. div. head aircraft control and warning, 1956-58, head radio physics div., 1958-63; prof. aeros., astronautics and elec. engring., 1st dir. Center Space Research, M.I.T., 1963-73; v.p. research and engring. Communications Satellite Corp., Washington, 1973-79; sr. v.p. research and devel., dir. COMSAT Labs., Clarksburg, Md., 1979—; dir. Epsco, Inc., 1964-72, Shawmut County Bank, Cambridge, 1964-73, COMSAT Gen. Telesystems, Inc., Washington, 1973-81, Environ. Research and Tech., Inc., Concord, Mass., 1981-82; mem. Space Applications Bd., NRC, 1975-81. Contbr. articles to profl. jours. Served to lt. USN, 1942-46. Recipient Exceptional Civilian Service medal U.S. Air Force, 1952; Exceptional Profl. Achievement citation Cooper Union, 1965; Gano Dunn award Cooper Union, 1983. Fellow IEEE (dir. New Eng. regional meeting 1964-66), AAAS, AIAA; mem. Am. Phys. Soc., Am. Geophys. Union. Club: Univ. Home: 4425 Boxwood Rd Bethesda MD 20816 Office: 22300 COMSAT Dr Clarksburg MD 20871

HARRINGTON, JOSEPH JOHN, environmental engineering educator; b. N.Y.C., Jan. 17, 1937; s. Joseph John and Eileen Patricia (Cannon) H.; m. Maryalice Lawlor, Aug. 25, 1962; children: Karen, Beth. B.C.E., Manhattan Coll., 1958; A.M., Harvard U., 1959, Ph.D., 1963. Registered profl. engr., N.Y., Mass., N.H. Cons. engr. Thomas Crimmins Contracting Co., Malcolm Pirnie Engrs., N.Y.C., 1957-59; faculty Harvard U., Cambridge, Mass., 1963—, prof. environ. engring., 1964—, Gordon McKay prof., 1974—, acting dir. Center for Population Studies,, 1980-81, acting chmn. dept. population scis., 1980-81, dir. phys. scis. and engring. program, 1983—, chmn. dept. environ. sci. and physiology, 1983—; v.p., dir. Process Research, Inc., Cambridge, 1967-76; cons. Environ. Research and Tech., Inc., Concord, Mass., 1976-78, Metasystems, Inc., Cambridge, 1968-80, USPHS, NIH, other fed. agys., 1959—. Mem. water supply com. Town of Hingham (Mass.), 1973-82; mem. long-range solid waste disposal recycling com. Town of Hingham, 1975-82; mem. com. on coastal flooding from hurricanes Nat. Acad. Scis., 1981-83. Indo-Am. fellow U. Delhi, India, 1977. Fellow Am. Public Health Assn.; mem. ASCE, Am. Water Works Assn., Am. Public Works Assn., Water Pollution Control Fedn., AAAS, Air Pollution Control Assn., Chi Epsilon. Home: 18 Highland Ave Cambridge MA 02139 Office: Dept Environ Sci and Physiology Harvard U 665 Huntington Ave Boston MA 02115

HARRINGTON, LAMAR, curatorial consultant; b. Guthrie Center, Iowa, Nov. 2, 1917; d. Arthur Sylvester and Anna Mary (Landkamer) Hannes; m. Stanley John Harrington, 1938 (div. 1972); 1 dau., Linda Harrington Chace. B.A. in History of Art, U. Wash., 1979. Mem. staff Henry Art Gallery, U. Wash., Seattle, 1957-75, assoc. dir., 1969-75; curator, research asso. Archives Northwest Art, U. Wash. Libraries, 1975-77; cons. in arts, 1977—; mem. panel visual arts div. Nat. Endowment Arts, 1976-78; pres. Western Assn. Art Museums, 1973-75; trustee Pacific Northwest Arts Center, 1971-74; exec. com. Pacific Northwest Arts Council of Seattle Art Mus., 1976, mem. steering com. photography council, 1977-78; v.p. Pottery Northwest, 1977-78; participant 1st Symposium on Scholarship and Lang., Nat. Endowments for Humanities and Arts, 1981; mem. adv. com. N.W. Oral History Project, Archives Am. Art, 1981; trustee, chmn. archives Pilchuck Sch., 1981—; lectr. in field, organizer exhbns., leader seminars, mem. art juries, appearances on TV, 1963—. Author: Ceramics in the Pacific Northwest: A History, 1979, Washington Craft Forms: an Historical Perspective, 1981; founder: Archives of Northwest Art, U. Wash., 1969, Index of Art in Pacific Northwest, U. Wash. Press, 1970. Recipient Gov. Wash. Art award, 1971, 74, 80; Friends of Crafts award, Seattle, 1972; Woman of Achievement award Women in Communications, 1974. Mem. Am. Assn. Museums, Coll. Art Assn., Pacific Northwest Arts and Crafts Assn. (pres. 1957-59), Allied Arts Seattle (trustee 1962—). Address: 511 Galer St Seattle WA 98109

HARRINGTON, MARION RAY, ophthalmologist; b. Dallas, Sept. 20, 1924; s. Silas Fredrick and Mary Katherine (Ray) H.; m. Nan Puckhober, Oct. 1, 1942; 1 dau., Nan Katherine. Student, U. Tex., 1942, M.D., 1947. Diplomate: Am. Bd. Ophthalmology. Intern St. Paul Hosp., Dallas, 1941-48; chief ophthalmology Portsmouth (Va.) Naval Hosp., 1950-52; practice medicine specializing in ophthalmology, Dallas, 1952—; mem. faculty U. Tex., Southwestern Med. Sch., Dallas, 1952—, clin. prof., 1975—. Served with USN, 1947-48, 50-52. Fellow A.C.S., Internat. Coll. Surgeons; mem. Am., Tex. med. assns., Dallas County, So. med. socs., Am. Acad. Ophthalmology and Otolarlyngology, Am. Assn., Tex. Acad. Ophthalmology and Otolaryngology, Tex. Ophthalmologic Assn., Dallas Acad. Ophthalmologists, Royal Soc. Medicine, Internat. Lens Implant Soc., Contact Lens Soc. Episcopalian. Home: 4800 Lakeside Dr Dallas TX 75205 Office: 2811 Lemmon Ave E Dallas TX 75204

HARRINGTON, MICHAEL, author; b. St. Louis, Feb. 24, 1928; s. Edward Michael and Catherine (Fitzgibbon) H.; m. Stephanie Gervis, May 30, 1963. A.B., Holy Cross Coll., 1947; postgrad., Yale Law Sch., 1947-48; M.A., U. Chgo., 1949; D.H.L., Bard Coll., 1966. Asso. editor Catholic Worker, 1951-52; orgn. sec. Workers Def. League, 1953; cons. Fund for Republic, 1954—; editor New Am., 1961-62; organizer March on Convs. Movement, 1960; prof. polit. sci. Queens Coll., City U. N.Y., 1972—. Author: The Other America, 1963, The Retail Clerks, 1963, The Accidental Century, 1965, Toward a Democratic Left, 1968, Socialism, 1972, Fragments of The Century, 1974, Twilight of Capitalism, 1976, The Vast Majority: A Journey to the World's Poor, 1977, Decade of Decision: The Crisis of the American System, 1980, The Next America: The Decline and Rise of the U.S, 1981, The Politics at God's Funeral, 1983; Editor: Editor: (with Paul Jacobs) Labor in a Free Society, 1959; Editor: Newsletter Democratic Left, 1973—; editorial bd. jour.: Dissent. Mem. nat. exec. com. Socialist Party, 1960-72, nat. chmn., 1968-72; chmn. Democratic Socialist Organizing Com., 1973-82, Dem. Socialists of Am., 1982-83; co-chmn. Dem. Socialists of Am., 1983—; bd. dirs. Workers Def. League, ACLU. Recipient George Polk award, 1963, Sidney Hillman award, 1963, Riordan award D.C. Newspaper Guild, 1964; Eugene V. Debs award Eugene V. Debs Found., 1973. Office: 853 Broadway Room 617 New York NY 10003

HARRINGTON, PAUL FRANCIS, ins. co. exec.; b. Fall River, Mass., July 9, 1929; s. Michael F. and Margaret B. H.; m. Patricia M. Brewton, Aug. 26, 1961; 1 son, Matthew P. A.B. with honors, Nat. U. Ireland, 1950; M.Ed., Harvard U., 1952, M.B.A., 1956; LL.B., Boston Coll., 1965. Adminstrv. supr. John Hancock Mut. Life Ins. Co., Boston, 1956-69, 2d v.p., 1969, v.p., 1969-71, sr. v.p., 1971—; dir. Hanseco Ins. Co., Profesco Corp. Mem. Milton (Mass.) Town Meeting; past mem. Town Warrant Com.; past pres. Indian Cliff Assn., Milton; past chmn. Regional Vocat. Edn. Sch. Com.; past chmn. indsl. arts bldg. com. Milton High Sch. Mem. Nat. Assn. Life Underwriters. Roman Catholic. Home: 58 Indian Spring Rd Milton MA 02186 Office: John Hancock Pl PO Box 111 Boston MA 02117

HARRINGTON, ROBERT WARREN, educator; b. Morrison, Ill., May 21, 1923; s. Loyd Weaver and Anna (Mundt) H. B.S., Ill. State U., 1947; M.A., U. Iowa, 1948, Ph.D., 1952; postgrad., U. Wis., summer 1954, U. Cambridge, Eng., 1963. Instr. Central Coll., Pella, Iowa, 1948-50; from asst. to asso. prof. Wis. State Coll., Superior, 1951-56; prof. Ind. State U., Terre Haute, 1956-68; prof., dir. bus. and econs. Ill. Wesleyan U., Bloomington, 1968—. Served with USNR, 1943-46. Mem. Am., Midwest econs. assns., Pi Omega Pi, Alpha Kappa Psi, Phi Kappa Phi, Omicron Delta Kappa. Home: 401 E Phoenix Bloomington IL 61701

HARRINGTON, ROY VICTOR, chemist; b. Bklyn., Sept. 28, 1928; s. Victor Earl and Karen (Hanson) H.; m. Catherine Elisabeth Wiese, June 14, 1952; children—Bruce Allan, Karen Jane, Thomas Andrew. B.S. in Chemistry, Poly. Inst. Bklyn., 1952; Ph.D., U. Colo., 1955. Chemist Gen. Foods Corp., Hoboken, N.J., 1949-52, Corning Glass Works, N.Y., 1955-68; with Ferro Corp., Independence, Ohio, 1968—, asso. dir., then dir. research and devel., now v.p. research and devel.; pres. Cleve. Assn. Research Dirs., 1975; mem. panel radioactive waste disposal Nat. Acad. Scis., 1979-80. Author. Founder, pres. Corning Sci. Seminars Gifted High Sch. Students, 1960-67; Mem. steering com. Case Assos., Case Western Res. U. Mem. Am. Chem. Soc. (sect. chmn. 1978), Am. Ceramic Soc. Club: Lakeside Yacht (Cleve.). Patentee in field. Office: 7500 E Pleasant Valley Rd Independence OH 44131 *

HARRINGTON, RUSSELL DOYNE, JR., hospital administrator; b. Little Rock, Jan. 22, 1944; s. Russell Doyne and Willie Mae (Alford) H.; m. Donna Singer, Sept. 3, 1966; children: Stephanie, Brooks. B.S. in Edn., Ark. State U., 1966; M.S. in Health Service Mgmt., U. Mo., 1971. Adminstrv. asst. U. Ark. Med. Sch., 1971-73; asst. adminstr. Bapt. Med. Center, Little Rock, 1973-77; exec. dir. Bapt. Meml. Hosp., Kansas City, Mo., 1977-78; adminstr., asso. exec. dir. Bapt. Med. Center System, Little Rock, 1978—; bd. dirs. Central Ark. Radiation Therapy Inst., Little Rock, 1981—. Bd. dirs. United Way, Boy Scouts Am. Served to capt. Med. Service Corps, USAR, 1966-69. Decorated Army Commendation medal. Fellow Am. Coll. Hosp. Adminstrs.; Mem. Am. Hosp. Assn., Ark. Hosp. Assn. (com. chmn.), Met. Hosp. Council Little Rock (past pres.). Baptist. Club: Rotary. Office: 9601 Interstate 630 Little Rock AR 72201

HARRINGTON, WALTER JOEL, emeritus mathematics educator; b. Salamanca, N.Y., Nov. 9, 1916; s. Carl Ramon and Clara Frances (Bunce) H.; m. Hazel Irene Cheney, Aug. 23, 1941; children—Rachel (Mrs. LeRoy E. Doggett), James Edward. B.A., Cornell U., 1937, M.A., 1938, Ph.D., 1941. Instr. math. Pa. State Coll., 1941-44; research asso. Allegany Ballistics Lab., Md., 1944-46; vis. asst. prof. math. Cornell U., 1946-47; asst. prof. math. Pa. State Coll., 1947-51, asso. prof., 1951-57; prof. N.C. State U., Raleigh, 1957-82, prof. emeritus, 1982—; project dir. Office Sci. Research Grants, U.S. Air Force, 1967-72. Mem. Am. Math. Soc., Math. Assn. Am., Soc. for Indsl. and Applied Math., Phi Beta Kappa, Phi Kappa Phi, Sigma Xi, Pi Mu Epsilon. Home: 3010 Ruffin St Raleigh NC 27607

HARRINGTON, WILLIAM FIELDS, biochemist, educator; b. Seattle, Sept. 25, 1920; s. Ira Francis and Jessie Blanche (Fields) H.; m. Ingeborg Leuschner, Feb. 24, 1947; children: Susan, Eric, Peter, Robert, David. B.S., U. Calif. at Berkeley, 1948, Ph.D., 1952. Research chemist virus lab. U. Calif. at Berkeley, 1952-53; Nat. Found. Infantile Paralysis postdoctoral fellow Cambridge (Eng.) U., 1953-54: Nat. Cancer Inst. postdoctoral fellow Carlsberg Lab., Copenhagen, Denmark, 1954-55; asst. prof. chemistry Iowa State U., 1955-56; biochemist Nat. Heart Inst., 1956-60; prof. biology Johns Hopkins, Balt., 1960—, chmn. dept. biology, 1973-83, Henry Walters prof. biology, 1975—; dir. McCollum Pratt Inst., 1973-83; vis. scientist Wiezmann Inst., Rehovot, Israel, 1959, vis. prof., 1970, Oxford U., 1970; Mem. adv. panel physiol. chemistry NIH, 1962-66, adv. panel biophys. chemistry study sect., 1968-72; bd. sci. councillors Nat. Inst. Arthritis and Metabolic Diseases, 1968-72; mem. vis. com. for biology Brookhaven Nat. Lab., 1969-73; adv. bd. Fedn. Advanced Edn. in the Scis., 1975—. Co-editor: Monographs on Physical Biochemistry, 1970—; Bd. editors: Jour. Biol. Chemistry, 1963-68, Mechanochemistry and Motility, 1970-76, Biochemistry, 1971-77, Jour. Phys. Biochemistry, 1973—. Fellow Am. Acad. Arts and Sci.; mem. Biophysics Soc., Nat. Acad. Scis., Soc. Biol. Chemists, Phi Beta Kappa, Sigma Xi. Home: 2210 W Rogers Ave Baltimore MD 21209

HARRIOTT, PETER, educator; b. Ithaca, N.Y., July 21, 1927; s. John Frederick and Stella (Fahl) H.; m. Mary Louise White, Oct. 24, 1953; children—George, James, John, Paul, Douglas. B.Ch.E., Cornell U., 1949; Sc.D., Mass. Inst. Tech., 1952. Engr. Gen. Elec. Co., Waterford, N.Y., 1952-53; Mem. faculty Cornell U., 1953—, asst. prof., 1953-54, asso. prof., 1954-65, prof. chem. engring., 1965—, Fred Hoffman Rhodes prof. chem. engring., 1975—. Author: Process Control, 1964. NSF Postdoctoral fellow, 1966. Mem. Am. Chem. Soc., Am. Inst. Chem. Engrs., Sierra Club, Nature Conservancy, Sigma Xi, Tau Beta Pi, Phi Kappa Phi, Alpha Chi Sigma. Club: Adirondack Mountain. Home: 139 Ellis Hollow Creek Rd RD 2 Ithaca NY 14850

HARRIS, AARON, personnel executive, management consultant; b. Birmingham, Ala., Oct. 27, 1930; s. Moses and Fannie (Williams) H.; m. Edna Mabel Turner, May 13, 1954; children: Kevin Brian, Edwin Maurice. B.A., Talladega Coll., 1952; M.S., Columbia U., 1959; postgrad., Princeton U., 1961. Trainee Bklyn. Pub. Library, 1956-59;

asst. librarian Burroughs Wellcome Co., Tuckahoe, N.Y., 1959-64; asso. librarian IBM Corp., East Fishkill, N.Y., 1964-66; library mgr. IBM Research Lab., San Jose, Calif., 1966-73; personnel exec. IBM Corp., San Jose, 1973-77; data processing mgr. IBM, 1977-80, mgr. tng. and devel., 1980—; cons.; instr. Calif. State U., San Jose.; Vice pres., dir. Discovery Systems, Inc. Gen. chmn. Citizens Com. on Schs., San Jose, 1969-71; mem. San Jose CSC, 1974-78; foreman pro tem Santa Clara County Grand Jury, 1979-80; candidate San Jose Sch. Bd., 1969, 73; bd. dirs. Santa Clara chpt. ARC; Bd. dirs. Mus. Art, San Jose. Served with AUS, 1952-55. Recipient Citizen of Year award Omega Psi Phi, 1970. Mem. Omega Psi Phi. Mem. A.M.E. Zion Ch. Home: 1351 Box Canyon Rd San Jose CA 95120 Office: IBM Monterey and Cottle Rds San Jose CA 95193 *Those who have presented obstacles for failure have been overwhelmed by my confidence. Those who longed for my success have been supportive with encouragement and opportunity. The principles embodied in the golden rule are my constant aim.*

HARRIS, ALBERT EDWARD, consumer products manufacturing company executive; b. Trenton, N.J., July 2, 1932; s. Howard Irving and Miriam Anna (Weiss) H.; m. Sandra Stewart, Sept. 25, 1954; children: Susan, David, John, Emily. A.B., Harvard U., 1953, M.B.A., 1955. With Procter & Gamble Co., 1957—, v.p. packaged soap and detergent div., 1976-77, Cin., v.p. internat., Brussels, 1978-79, group v.p. worldwide indsl. divs., Cin., 1980-81, group v.p., packaged soap and detergent div., bar soap and household cleaning products div., beauty care div., also health and personal care div., 1981—. Trustee Knox Presbyn. Ch., Cin., Playhouse in the Park, Cin., Wilberforce (Ohio) U., Children's Psychiat. Center, Cin.; bd. dirs. Cin. Cancer Family Care; past vice chmn. Cin. United Fine Arts Campaign; gen. chmn. Cin. area United Negro Coll. Fund. Served with AUS, 1955-57. Clubs: Queen City, Harvard, Harvard Bus. Sch., Tennis (Cin.); Commonwealth. Office: 301 E 6th St Cincinnati OH 45202

HARRIS, ALFRED, social anthropologist educator; b. Abington, Pa., July 26, 1919; s. Henry S. and Margaret (Britton) H.; m. Grace Louise Gredys, Oct. 16, 1948. B.A., U. Chgo., 1941, M.A., 1952; postgrad., Oxford (Eng.) U., 1949-50; Ph.D., Cambridge (Eng.) U., 1958. Cartographer, 1942-47; teaching asst. U. Chgo., 1947-49; Colonial Social Sci. Research Council studentship and fellowship, 1949-53; instr., then lectr. Smith Coll., 1957-59, 59-60; vis. asst. prof. Brandeis U., 1960-61; mem. faculty U. Rochester, 1961—, asso. prof. anthropology, 1964-73, prof., 1973—, chmn. dept. anthropology, 1964-71; cons. in field, 1958—. Editorial staff: Am. Sociol. Rev, 1957-60; editor: Lewis Henry Morgan Lectures, 8 vols, 1963—. Fellow Am. Anthrop. Assn., African Studies Assn., Royal Anthrop. Inst., Assn. Social Anthropologists (U.K.); mem. Internat. African Inst., Northeastern Anthrop. Assn. (pres. 1973-74). Office: 334 Harkness Hall Univ Rochester Rochester NY 14627

HARRIS, ANN BIRGITTA SUTHERLAND, art historian; b. Cambridge, Eng., Nov. 4, 1937; came to U.S., 1965; d. Gordon B.B.M. and Gunborg Elizabeth (Wahlström) Sutherland; m. William Vernon Harris, July 13, 1965; 1 son, Neil William Orlando Sutherland. B.A. with 1st class honours, Courtauld Inst., U. London, 1961, Ph.D., 1965. Asst. lectr. U. Leeds, 1964-65; asst. prof. art history Columbia U., N.Y.C., 1965-71, Hunter Coll., 1971-73; asso. prof. SUNY, Albany, 1973-77; chmn. for acad. affairs Met. Mus. Art, N.Y.C., 1977-80; part-time faculty Juilliard Sch., N.Y.C., 1978—; a founder, 1st pres. Women's Caucus for Art, 1973-76; disting. vis. prof. U. Tex.-Arlington, fall 1982; Mellon prof. history of art U. Pitts., spring 1984. Author: Andrea Sacchi, 1977, Selected Drawings of Gian Lorenzo Bernini, 1977; co-author: Die Zeichnungen von Andrea Saachi und Carlo Maratta, 1967, Women Artists: 1550-1950; exhbn. catalogue, 1977. Fellow Guggenheim Found., 1971, Ford Found., 1975-76, Nat. Endowment Humanities, 1981-82. Mem. Coll. Art Assn. Address: 560 Riverside Dr Apt 17P New York NY 10027

HARRIS, ARTHUR BROOKS, physicist, educator; b. Boston, Mar. 25, 1935; s. Frank Ephraim and Wilhelmina (Sellers) H.; m. Margaret Marie Rees, Aug. 23, 1958; children: Katherine Margaret, William Brooks, Thomas Andrew. A.B., Harvard, 1956, M.A., 1959, Ph.D., 1962. Prof. physics U. Pa., Phila., 1965—; Program co-chmn. Magnetism and Magnetic Materials Conf., 1969; vis. scientist U.K. Atomic Energy Authority, 1965, Brookhaven Nat. Lab., 1972, Sandia Labs., 1974; Schlumberger-Doll researcher, 1983. Co-editor: Magnetic Material Digest, 1968. Alfred P. Sloan postdoctoral fellow, 1967-69; John Simon Guggenheim fellow, 1972-73. Club: Internat. Lawn Tennis. Home: 117 Bair Rd Berwyn PA 19312 Office: Dept Physics U Pa Philadelphia PA 19104

HARRIS, AURAND, playwright; b. Jamesport, Mo., July 4, 1915. A.B., U. Kansas City, 1936; M.A., Northwestern U., 1939; postgrad, Columbia U., 1945-47. Head drama dept. William Woods Coll., Fulton, Mo., 1942-45; drama tchr. Grace Ch. Sch., N.Y.C., 1946-77; tchr. Columbia U. Tchrs. Coll., N.Y.C., summers 1958-63; playright-in-residence U. Fla., Tallahassee, 1972, U. Tex., Austin, 1976-84, U. Kans, 1979, Calif. State U., Northridge, 1982, Young Audiences, Cleve., 1981-84; drama tchr. Western Conn. State Coll., Danbury, summer 1976; assoc. summer theater, Cape May, N.J., 1940, Bennington, Vt., 1947, Peaks Island, Maine, 1948, Harwich, Mass., 1963-75. Childrens plays include Pinocchio and the Fire-Eater, 1949, Once upon a Clothesline, 1944; The Doughnut Hole, 1947, The Moon Makes Three, 1947, Seven League Boots, 1947, Circus Days, 1948, rev. as Circus in the Wind, 1960, Pinocchio and the Indians, 1949, Simple Simon; or Simon Big-Ears, 1952, Buffalo Bill, 1953, We Were Young That Year, 1954, The Plain Princess, 1954, The Brave Little Tailor, 1960, Pocahontas, 1961, Androcles and the Lion, 1964, Rags to Riches, 1965, A Doctor in Spite of Himself, 1966, The Comical Tragedy or Tragical Comedy of Punch and Judy, 1969, Just So Stories, 1971, Ming Lee and the Magic Tree, 1971, Steal Away Home, 1972, Peck's Bad Boy, 1973, Robin Goodfellow, 1974, Yanke Doodle, 1975, Star Spangled Minstrel, Six Plays for Children, 1977, A Toby Show, 1978, Plays Children Love, 1980, The Arksansaw Bear, 1980, Treasure Island, 1983, The Magician's Nephew, 1984; adult plays Ladies of the Mop, 1945, Madam Ada, 1948. Recipient Chorpenning Cup Am. Theatre Assn., 1967; Nat. Endowment Arts grantee, 1976. Address: care Anchorage Press Box 8067 New Orleans LA 70182

HARRIS, BARBARA, actress; b. Evanston, Ill., 1935; d. Oscar and Natalie (Densmoor) H.; m. Paul Sills. Appeared with, Second City Co., Chgo., 1960-61; with, Second City Co. in, From the Second City, N.Y.C., 1961-62, Oh Dad, Poor Dad, Mama's Hung You in the Closet and I'm Feelin' So Sad, N.Y.C., 1962, Mother Courage and Her Children, N.Y.C., 1963, Dynamite Tonight (off-Broadway), On a Clear Day You Can See Forever, 1965, The Diary of Adam and Eve, The Lady or the Tiger?, Passionella, The Apple Tree, 1966, The Rise and Fall of the City of Mahagonny, 1970; appeared in: films Who is Harry Kellerman and Why Is He Saying Those Terrible Things About Me?, 1971, Oh Dad, Poor Dad, A Thousand Clowns, Plaza Suite, 1971, The War Between the Men and the Women, 1972, Mixed Company, 1974, Nashville, 1975, Freaky Friday, 1977, Movie, Movie, 1978, The North Ave. Irregulars, 1979, The Seduction of Joe Tynan, 1979, Second-Hand Hearts, 1980; also TV appearances. Recipient N.Y. Drama Critics award for most promising new actress Variety Poll, 1961, 62; Off-Broadway award Village Voice, 1962. Address: care Robinson & Assos Inc 132 S Rodeo Dr Beverly Hills CA 90212

HARRIS, BILL J., utilities executive; b. Mill Creek, Okla., Oct. 17, 1924; s. John M. and Irene W. (Penner) H.; m. Margarett Maxine Howard, July 25, 1947; children: Deborah, Gerald. B.S. in Biol. Sci. and Physics, East Central State Coll., 1947; M.S. in Secondary Edn, Okla. State U., 1952. With Pub. Service Co. of Okla., 1955-76, area mgr., McAlester, 1962-72, v.p. adminstrn., Tulsa, 1972-75, v.p. fuel, 1975-76; pres. Transok Pipe Line Co., 1975-76; pres., dir., chief operating officer Central & Southwest Corp., Dallas, 1976—. Served with USAAF, 1943-45. Mem. Edison Electric Inst. (dir., com. on research). Democrat. Methodist. Clubs: Masons (32 deg.); Bent Tree Country, Tower, Chaparral (Dallas). Office: PO Box 660164 Dallas TX 75266

HARRIS, BRUCE REED, army officer; b. Sullivan County, Ind., Aug. 13, 1934; s. Orville Reed and Cassie Myra (Cobb) H.; m. Claudia Jean Alley, Sept. 17, 1954; children: Bruce Reed, Mary Kathryn, Timothy, Bradley. B.S., Tenn. Technol. U., 1956; M.S., Auburn U., 1974; postgrad., U.S. Army Command and Gen. Staff Coll., 1967, Air Force War Coll., 1974. Commd. in U.S. Army, 1956, advanced through grades to brig. gen.; comdr. div. support command, Ft. Hood, Tex., 1978-79; chief of staff U.S. Army Signal Center, Ft. Gordon, Ga., 1980-81, dep. comdg. gen., 1981; dep. asst. sec. for legis. affairs Dept. Def., Washington, 1981—; service in, Vietnam. Decorated Legion of Merit, Bronze Star, Air medal (7), Meritorious Service medal, numerous others; named Ind. Sagamore of the Wabash, 1981. Mem. Assn. U.S. Army, Armed Forces Communications-Electronics Assn., Signal Corps Assn., VFW, 1st Cav. Div. Assn., 2d Armored Div. Assn., Army Aviation Assn. Methodist. Club: Kiwanis. Office: 9th Infantry Div Fort Lewis WA 98433 *

HARRIS, BRUCE S., publisher; b. Phila., Dec. 7, 1938; s. Louis Judah and Hannah Rose (Schwartz) H.; m. Susan Petersen, Aug. 5, 1974; children: Jonathan Louis, Andrew Ross, Petersen Nathaniel. A.B., NYU, 1960. Promotion writer Lothrop Lea & Shepard, N.Y.C., 1960-62; salesman, then sales mgr. Outlet Book Co., N.Y.C., 1962-71; publisher Harmony Books, N.Y.C., 1971—; v.p. mktg. Crown Publishers, 1975—; dir. publishing Crown Publishing Group, 1981—. Author: The Collected Drawings of Aubrey Beardsley, 1967, Complete Etchings of Rembrandt, 1968, Honore Daumier Selected Works, 1970, The Nothing Book, 1974, Mickey Mouse: 50 Happy Years, 1977. Served with USAR, 1960-66. Home: 118 Riverside Dr New York NY 10024 Office: 1 Park Ave New York NY 10016

HARRIS, BURT IRVING, communications company executive; b. St. Paul, Aug. 21, 1922; s. Nathaniel and Esther (Roberts) H.; m. Shirley Louise Kline, May 21, 1944; children—Janie Harris Rosenfeld, Burt Irving, Melissa Lou, Natalie Kim. Student, U. Minn., 1940-43. Gen. mgr. Lone Star Biscuit Co., Dallas, 1945-48; office mgr. Ashbach-Steenberg Constrn. Co., Exeter, Calif., 1948-51; gen. mgr. Sta. XELD-TV, Brownville, Tex., 1952; pres., chief exec. officer, dir. Harriscope Broadcasting Corp., Los Angeles, 1953—; pres., dir. Greentree Electronics Corp., Los Angeles, 1960-67, Metrolonics Corp., Burbank, Calif., 1960-65, Harriscope of Los Angeles, 1981—, Cable TV Co. of Greater San Juan (P.R.), 1974—; pres., chmn. bd., chief exec. officer, dir. Cypress Communications Corp., Los Angeles, 1970-72; vice chmn. Warner Cable Corp., N.Y.C., 1972-73; pres., chief exec. officer, dir. Harris Cable Corp., Los Angeles, 1973—; chmn. bd., chief exec. officer Premiere (Network), Los Angeles, 1980-81; dir. Telecor, Inc., Bank Hapolim, Women-in-Cable, Los Angeles, N.Mex. Broadcasting Co., Inc., Albuquerque, Electro Rents Corp., Burbank.; Bd. govs. Israel Inst. Tech.-Technion, 1972—; bd. dirs. Am. Technion Soc., 1970—. Served to 2d lt. AUS, 1942-45. Recipient Larry Boggs award Nat. Cable TV Assn., 1979. Mem. Nat. Acad. TV Arts and Scis., Nat. Acad. Rec. Arts and Scis., Nat. Assn. Broadcasters, Hollywood TV and Radio Assn. Democrat. Clubs: Regency, Hillcrest Country (Los Angeles). Home: 411 S Bristol Ave Los Angeles CA 90049 Office: 10889 Wilshire Blvd Suite 1240 Los Angeles CA 90024

HARRIS, CARL VERNON, educator; b. Morganton, N.C., Dec. 29, 1922; s. Asbury David and Laura (Clark) H.; m. Ida Lucille Sawyer, Aug. 6, 1955. A.A., Mars Hill (N.C.) Coll., 1942; A.B., Wake Forest U., 1944; B.D., Yale U., 1946, S.T.M., 1947; Ph.D., Duke, 1952. Tchr. Mars Hill Coll., 1947-50; with Va. Dept. Welfare and Instns., 1952-53; tchr. East Carolina U., Greenville, N.C., 1953-54; faculty U. Dubuque, Iowa, 1954-56, Wake Forest U., Winston-Salem, N.C., 1956—, now prof. classical langs. and lit. Author: Origen of Alexandria's Interpretation of the Teacher's Function in the Early Christian Hierarchy and Community, 1967. Mem. Am. Philol. Assn., Am. Acad. Religion, N.C. Council Human Relations, Am. Soc. Ch. History, Am. Classical League, Classical Assn. Middle West and South, N.C. Classical Assn., AAUP, Phi Beta Kappa, Eta Sigma Phi, Delta Kappa Alpha. Address: PO Box 7402 Reynolda Sta Winston Salem NC 27109

HARRIS, CARMON COLEMAN, judge; b. Boswell, Okla., Nov. 27, 1904; s. William Robberson and Lucy (Coleman) H.; m. Veryl Pauline Fox, Aug. 13, 1932; 1 son, Carmon Coleman. LL.B., U. Okla., 1929. Bar: Okla. bar 1929. Practice in, Oklahoma City, 1929-41, 46-49, dist. judge, Okla., 1967-84; instr. advocacy Oklahoma City U. Law Sch., 1970—, vis. lectr., 1971. Del. to Republican Nat. Conv., 1952: nominee for Congress, 1946, 48; active Rep. Com., 1934-66. Served with AUS, 1941-46; judge adv. staff Comdg. Gen. European Theater, 1944-45; prosecutor war crimes trials, 1945-46. Decorated Bronze Star medal. Mem. ABA, Oklahoma County Bar Assn., Nat. Conf. State Trial Judges, Okla. Bar Assn. (trustee), Sigma Phi Epsilon, Phi Delta Phi. Clubs: Mason, Lion. Home: 3132 NW 25th St Oklahoma City OK 73107 Office: County Courthouse Oklahoma City OK 73102

HARRIS, CHARLES EDGAR, wholesale distribution company executive; b. Englewood, Tenn., Nov. 6, 1915; s. Charles Leonard and Minnie Beatrice (Borin) H.; m. Dorothy Sarah Wilson, Dec. 27, 1916; children: Charles Edgar, William John. Office and credit mgr. H.T. Hackney Co., Knoxville, Greeneville and Athens, Tenn., 1948-66, v.p., 1966-71; treas. H.T. Hacney Co., Knoxville, Greeneville and Athens, Tenn., 1971-72; pres., treas. H.T. Hackney Co., Knoxville, Greeneville and Athens, Tenn., 1972, pres., chmn. bdm., chief exec. officer, 1972-82; cons. H. T. Hackney Co., Knoxville, Greeneville and Athens, Tenn., 1982—, hon. dir.; chmn. bd., chief exec. officer Central Oil Co., McMinnville, Tenn., 1971—; chmn. bd., dir., chief exec. officer Mid-State Investment Co., McMinnville, 1971—; v.p., dir. Hackney Carolina Co., Murphy, N.C., until 1972, chmn. bd., chief exec. officer, 1972-82; v.p., dir. Hackney Harlan Co., ky., until 1972, chmn. bd., dir, chief exec. officer, 1972-77; v.p., dir. Haywood Grocery Co., Waynesville, N.C., until 1972, chmn. bd., dir., chief exec. officer, 1972-82; v.p., dir. Park Oil Co., Alcoa, Tenn., until 1965, pres., dir., 1965-72, chmn. bd., dir., chief exec. officer, 1972-82; pres., dir. Knoxoil Co., Knoxville, until 1972, chmn. bd., dir. chief exec. officer, 1972-81; pres., dir. Valley Oil Co., Athens, Tenn., until 1972, chmn. bd., dir., chief exec. officer, Athens, 1972-81; v.p., dir. Testoil Co., Harlan, until 1972, chmn. bd., dir., chief exec. officer, 1972-82; pres., dir. Appalachian Realty Co., Knoxville, until 1972; chmn. bd., dir., chief exec. officer Appalanchian Realty Co., Knoxville, 1972-82; pres., dir., chmn. bd., chief exec. officer Pride Markets, Inc., Knoxville, until 1972; v.p., dir. Dale San Supply Co., Knoxville, until 1972, chmn. bd., chief exec. officer, dir., 1972-82; v.p., dir. Brink's Inc., Knoxville, until 1972, chmn. bd., dir., chief exec. officer, 1972-82, Jellico Grocery Co., Oneida and Elizabethton, Tenn., 1975-82, Corbin and Somerset, Ky., 1975-82, Tri-State Wholesale Co., Middlesboro, Ky., 1975-82, Hackney Jellico Co., Harlan, 1977-82, Foodservice Distbrs., Inc., Knoxville, 1977-82; dir. First Am. Nat. Bank, Knoxville, 1983—. Bd. dirs., v.p., mem. exec. com. Downtown Knoxville Assn., 1979-83; bd. dirs., mem. exec. bd. Greater Knoxville Smoky Mountain council Boy Scouts Am, 1956-57, 82—; bd. dirs., mem. exec. com. Met. YMCA, Knoxville, 1971-77, treas., Knoxville, 1975-76; mem. budget fin. com. United Way of Knoxville, 1974-80, bd. dirs., treas., chmn. fin. com., 1979-80; mem. budget com. 1982 World's Fair, Knoxville, 1980-82; bd. dirs. Vols. Am., Knoxville, 1981-83; deacon, trustee Central Baptist Ch., Knoxville, 1961—; active Knox County Assn. Baptists, Knoxville, 1964-77; mem. exec. bd. Tenn. Bapt. Conv., Nashville, 1976-82; asssoc. chmn. Layman's Nat. Bible Week, Washington, 1977-78; trustee Carson Newman Coll., Jefferson City, Tenn., 1983—. Recipient Outstanding Community Leadership award Religious Heritage Am., 1978, Red Triangle award and Silver Triangle award YMCA, 1979. Mem. Greater Knoxville C. of C. (bd. dirs. 1973-76, v.p. 1975-76, Outstanding Corp. Citizenship award 1982), Nat. Assn. Wholesalers-Distrbrs. (trustee 1977-82). Republican. Club: LeConte (Knoxville) (charter mem.). Lodge: Rotary (Knoxville). Home: 7914 Gleason Dr Unit 1071 Knoxville TN 37919 Office: H T Hackney Co 300 Fidelity Bldg Knoxville TN 37901 *All things in life, be it business, personal, spiritual, have a price. Success has a price, failure has a price. To me failure has a greater price to pay. Attained success has always been a result of researching what is the right thing to do under the circumstances and doing that, regardless of the consequences.*

HARRIS, CHARLES ELMER, lawyer; b. Williamsburg, Iowa, Nov. 26, 1922; s. Charles Elmer and Loretto (Judge) H.; m. Marjorie Clark, July 9, 1949 (div. June 1969); children: Martha Ann, Julie Ann, Charles Elmer III. Student, St. Ambrose Coll., 1940-42; B.S.C., U. Iowa, 1946, J.D., 1949. Bar: Iowa 1949. Mem. firm Brody, Parker, Roberts, Thoma & Harris, Des Moines, 1949-66, Herrick, Langdon, Belin Harris, Langdon & Helmick, 1966-78, Belin, Harris, Helmick, Heartney & Tesdell, 1978—; lectr. tax schs., meetings, 1951, 55, 67, 69, 77-84. Comments editor: Iowa Law Rev., 1948-49. Bd. dirs. NCCJ, 1964-67, Polk County Mental Health Center Bd., 1966-76, Iowa Bar Found., 1977—, Iowa Law Sch. Found., 1977—, United Way Found., 1981—. Served to lt. (j.g.) USNR, 1943-46. Fellow Am. Coll. Probate Counsel; mem. ABA, Iowa Bar Assn. (bd. govs. 1973-80, Merit award 1980), Polk County Bar Assn. (pres. 1972-73), Polk County Jr. Bar Assn. (pres. 1952-53), Order of Coif, Sigma Chi, Delta Theta Phi. Roman Catholic. Home: 5141 Robertson Dr Des Moines IA 50312 Office: 2000 Financial Center Des Moines IA 50309

HARRIS, CHARLES FREDERICK, univ. press dir.; b. Portsmouth, Va., Jan. 3, 1934; s. Ambrose Edward and Annie Eula (Lawson) H.; m. Sammie Lou Jackson, Dec. 8, 1956; children—Francis Charlton, Charles Frederick. Student, Norfolk (Va.) State Coll., 1951-53; B.A., Va. State Coll., 1955; postgrad., N.Y. U., 1957-63. Editor Doubleday & Co., Inc., N.Y.C., 1956-65; v.p., gen. mgr. subs. John Wiley & Sons, Inc., N.Y.C., 1965-67; sr. editor adult trade div. Random House, Inc., N.Y.C., 1967-71; exec. dir. Howard U. Press, Washington, 1971—; adj. prof. journalism Howard U. Co-editor: AMISTAD I and II, 1970. Served as 2d lt. inf. U.S. Army, 1956. Mem. Assn. Am. Pubs., Assn. Am. Univ. Presses, Reading is Fundamental (dir.), Nat. Press Club, Washington Area Book Pubs., Assn. Internat. Scholarly Pubs., Alpha Phi Alpha. Office: 2900 Van Ness St NW Notre Dame Hall Washington DC 20008

HARRIS, CHARLES UPCHURCH, clergyman, seminary president; b. Raleigh, N.C., May 2, 1914; s. Charles Upchurch and Saidee (Robbins) H.; m. Janet Jeffrey Carlile, June 17, 1940; children: John C., Diana Jeffrey (Mrs. Melvin). B.A., Wake Forest Coll., 1935, D.H.L. (hon.), 1979; B.D., Va. Theol. Sem., 1938, D.D. (hon.), 1958; postgrad., Union Theol. Sem., 1939-40; D.C.L. (hon.), Seabury-Western Sem., 1972. Ordained deacon P.E. Ch., 1938, priest, 1939; rector All Saints Ch., Roanoke Rapids, N.C., 1938-39; asst. rector St. Bartholomew's Ch., N.Y.C., 1939-40; rector Trinity Ch., Roslyn, L.I., 1940-46, Highland Park, Ill., 1946-57; pres., dean Seabury-Western Theol. Sem., Evanston, Ill., 1957-72, pres., dean emeritus, 1972—; dean Lake Shore Deanery; founder St. Gregory's Ch., Deerfield, Ill.; hon. canon St. James Cathedral, Chgo., 1975—; pres. Episc. Theol. Sch., Claremont, Calif., 1977-82; trustee Sch. Theology, Claremont, 1979—; chmn. exam. chaplains 5th and 6th provinces Episcopal Ch.; cons. nat. dept. Christian edn.; pres. Chgo. Theol. Inst., 1966-72; pres. Chgo. Inst. Advanced Theol. Studies, 1968-70; sec. Drafting Com. on Holy Eucharist, 1970-79; pres. Chgo. Inter-Sem. Faculties Union, 1971-72; vice chmn. N.Am. com. St. George's Coll., Jerusalem, 1981—; pres. Cyprus-Am. Archaeol. Inst., 1984—; mem. exec. com. Nat. Cathedral, Washington, 1978—; v.p. Chgo. Inst. Advanced Theol. Studies, 1967-72; Dir. Am. Consortium Joint Archaeol. Expdn., 1972-78. Author: (with A. LeCroy) Harris-LeCroy Report, 1975; Asst. editor, pres.: Anglican Theol. Rev, 1958—; Contbr.: Sermons on Death and Dying, 1975. Trustee Am. Schs. Oriental Research, 1976—; mem. bd. visitors Wake Forest U., 1979—, Div. Sch., U. Chgo. Mem. Am. Theol. Soc., Am. Acad. Sci. and Religion, Soc. Colonial Warriors, S.A.R. Clubs: University (Chgo.); Desert Forest Golf (Carefree, Ariz.); Glen View (Golf, Ill.). Home: Flint Hill Delaplane VA 22025

HARRIS, CHAUNCY DENNISON, geographer, educator; b. Logan, Utah, Jan. 31, 1914; s. Franklin Stewart and Estella (Spilsbury) H.; m. Edith Young, Sept. 5, 1940; 1 dau., Margaret. A.B., Brigham Young U., 1933; B.A. (Rhodes scholar), Oxford U., 1936, M.A., 1943, D.Litt., 1973; student, London Sch. Econs., 1936-37; Ph.D., U. Chgo., 1940; D.Econ. (honoris causa), Catholic U., Chile, 1956; LL.D. (h.c.), Ind. U., 1979. Instr. in geography Ind. U., 1939-41; asst. prof. geography U. Nebr., 1941-43, U. Chgo., 1943-46, asso. prof., 1946-47, prof., 1947-84, prof. emeritus, 1984—, dean social scis., 1955-60; dir. U. Chgo. Center for Internat. Studies, 1966-84; chmn. dept. geography U. Chgo., 1967-69, Samuel N. Harper Disting. Service prof., 1969-84, spl. asst. to pres., 1973-75, v.p. acad. resources, 1975-78; del. Internat. Geog. Congress, Lisbon, 1949, Washington, 1952, Rio de Janeiro, 1956, Stockholm, 1960, London, 1964, New Delhi, 1968, Montreal, 1972, Moscow, 1976, Tokyo, 1980; v.p. Internat. Geog. Union, 1956-64, sec.-treas., 1968-76; mem. adv. com. for internat. orgns. and programs Nat. Acad. Scis., 1969-73, mem. bd. internat. orgns. and programs, 1973-76; U.S. del. 17th Gen. Conf. UNESCO, Paris, 1972; exec. com. div. behavioral scis. NRC, 1967-70; mem. council of scholars Library of Congress, 1980-83. Author: Cities of the Soviet Union, 1970; editor: Economic Geography of the U.S.S.R, 1949, Internat. List of Geog. Serials, 1960, 71, 80, Annotated World List of Selected Current Geographical Serials, 1960, 64, 71, 80, Soviet Geography: Accomplishments and Tasks, 1962, Guide to Geog. Bibliographies and Reference Works in Russian or on the Soviet Union, 1975, Bibliography of Geography, Part I, Introduction to General Aids, 1976, Part 2, Regional, vol. 1, U.S., 1984; contbg. editor: The Geog. Rev., 1960-73; contbr. articles to profl. jours. Recipient Alexander Csoma de Kőrösi Meml. medal Hungarian Geog. Soc., 1971, Lauréat d'Honneur Internat. Geog. Union, 1976; Alexander von Humboldt gold medal Gesellschaft für Erkunde zu Berlin, 1978. Fellow Japan Soc. Promotion of Sci.; mem. Assn. Am. Geographers (sec. 1946-48, v.p. 1956, pres. 1957, Honors award 1976), Am. Geog. Soc. (council 1962-74, v.p. 1969-74), Am. Assn. Advancement Slavic Studies (pres. 1962, award for disting. contbns. 1978), Social Sci. Research Council (dir. 1959-70, vice chmn. 1963-65, exec. com. 1967-70), Internat. Council Sci. Unions (exec. com. 1969-72), Internat. Research and Exchanges Bd. (exec. com. 1968-71), Nat. Council Soviet and East European Research (dir. 1977-

83); hon. mem. Royal Geog. Soc., geog. socs. Berlin, Frankfurt, Rome, Florence, Paris, Warsaw, Belgrade, Japan, Chgo. (Disting. Service award 1965). Club: Quadrangle. Home: 5649 S Blackstone Ave Chicago IL 60637 Office: Dept Geography U Chgo 5828 University Ave Chicago IL 60637

HARRIS, CHRISTIE GUS, insurance company executive; b. Washington, Sept. 12, 1930; s. Gus and Nicoletopoulos H. B.A. in Econs., Duke U., 1952. Adminstrv. trainee Acacia Mut. Life Ins. Co., Washington, 1955-59, asst. mgr. premium acctg., 1959-60, adminstrv. asst., 1960-69, asst. v.p., 1969, 2d v.p. adminstrn., 1969-76, adminstrv. v.p., sec., 1977—, treas., 1982—; v.p., sec.-treas. Acacia Equity Sales Corp., Acacia Investment Mgmt. Corp.; sales edn. prodn. sec. Creative Bus. Concepts; sec.-treas. Acacia Fin. Corp. Mem. Vol. Services for Children, Duke U. Alumni Admissions Com., Duke Loyalty Fund, Washington Bd. Trade. Capt. U.S. Army, 1952-55. Mem. Life Office Mgmt. Assn., Washington Personnel Assn., Am. Soc. Personnel Adminstrs., Personnel Officers Round Table. Office: Acacia Mut life Ins Co 51 Luisiana Ave NW Washington DC 20001

HARRIS, CHRISTIE LUCY, author; b. Newark, Nov. 21, 1907; d. Edward and Matilda (Christie) Irwin; m. Thomas A. Harris, Feb. 13, 1932; children: Michael, Moira, Sheilagh, Brian, Gerald. Tchrs. cert., Provincial Normal Sch., Vancouver, B.C., Can., 1925. Tchr., B.C., 1925-32; free-lance scriptwriter Canadian Broadcasting Corp. radio, 1936-63; women's editor B.C. News Weekly, Abbotsford, 1951-57. Author: Raven's Cry, 1966, Mouse Woman books (3), 1976, 77, 79, The Trouble With Princesses, 1980, others. Decorated Order of Can.; recipient Can. Book of Yr. medal for Children's book, 1967, 77; Can. Council Children's Lit. prize, 1981. Mem. Writers' Union Can. Mem. Ch. of Eng. Address: care Writers Union of Can 24 Ryerson St Toronto ON Canada M5T 2P3 *I love my work and trust my subconscious.*

HARRIS, CHRISTOPHER, publisher, editor; b. Plainfield, N.J., June 7, 1933; s. Maynard Lawrence and Edith Johnson (Bushnell) H.; m. Linda Martin Robinson, Oct. 8, 1955 (dec. 1967); children—Katherine Hamilton, Stephen Christopher, Andrea Lawrence; m. Sarah Pickett Hargrove Sullivan, Aug. 18, 1977. B.A., Yale U., 1955. Book mfg. coordinator Rand McNally & Co., Hammond, Ind., and N.Y.C., 1955-60; mng. editor Studio Books div. Viking Press, N.Y.C., 1960-70; editor, pres. Chatham Press, Riverside and Old Greenwich, Conn., 1970-76; dir. design and prodn. Yale U. Press, New Haven, 1977—; editor Summer Hill Books, Madison, Conn., 1978—. Mem. Conn. Book Pubs. Assn. (pres. 1977-78). Democrat. Home: 659 Summer Hill Rd Madison CT 06443 Office: 302 Temple St New Haven CT 06520

HARRIS, COLIN CYRIL, educator, mineral engineer; b. Leeds, Eng., Jan. 9, 1928; came to U.S., 1960; s. Hyman Lewis and Sarah (Bloomenthall) H.; m. Sylvia Glonstein, Apr. 16, 1964 (dec. Oct. 1979). B.Sc. in Math. and Physics (Brit. Govt. scholar), London U., 1952; Ph.D. in Mineral Engring. and Coal Preparation, Leeds (Eng.) U., 1959. Chartered engr., Gt. Britain. Research asst. Leeds U., 1952-57; lectr. in coal preparation and mineral processing, 1957-60, 61-63; vis. asst. prof. mineral engring. Columbia U., 1960-61, asso. prof. mineral engring., 1963-70, prof., 1970—; adv. on faculty appointments, research and grad. programs to U.S. and fgn. univs.; external examiner fgn. univs.; adv. on research proposals to govt. funding agys.; adv., cons. to mining, research and mfg. cos.; mem. organizing coms. for several internat. confs. on mineral processing. Contbr. numerous articles on theory of mineral processing ops. to profl. publs.; editor: Symposium on Coal Preparation, 1957; asso. editor: Internat. Jour. Mineral Processing, 1973—; adv. to internat. jours. Served as sgt. Brit. Armed Forces, 1946-49. Recipient Nat. Coal Bd. research awards, 1959-60, 62-63; numerous research grants. Mem. Operational Research Soc. (London), Assn. Univ. Tchrs. (Gt. Brit.), Instn. Mining and Metallurgy (London), AIME (chmn. publs. com., mem. awards com.), Leeds Gramophone Soc., Wildlife Rescue. Club: Leeds U. Record (librarian 1954-59). Home: 392 Central Park W Apt 5N New York NY 10025 Office: School of Mines 907 Engring Center Columbia U New York NY 10027 *In the hierarchies of proof, the loftiest establishes that something is not merely so, but that it cannot be otherwise.*

HARRIS, CYRIL MANTON, electrical engineering and architecture educator, consulting acoustical engineer; b. Detroit, June 20, 1917; s. Bernard O. and Ida (Moss) H.; m. Ann Schakne, July 12, 1949; children: Nicholas Bennett, Katherine Anne. B.A., UCLA, 1938, M.A., 1940; Ph.D., MIT, 1945; Sc.D. (hon.), N.J. Inst. Tech., 1981. Teaching asst. UCLA, 1939-40; research fellow MIT, 1940; war research OSRD, 1941-44, teaching fellow, 1943-45; war research Carnegie Instn. Washington, 1941; mem. staff Bell Telephone Labs., 1945-51; cons. Office Naval Research, London, Eng., 1951; Fulbright lectr. Tech. U., Delft, Holland, 1951-52; now Charles Batchelor prof. elec. engring., prof. architecture and chmn. div. archtl. tech. Columbia U.; vis. Fulbright prof. U. Tokyo, 1960; acoustical cons. Met. Opera House, N.Y.C., John F. Kennedy Center for Performing Arts, Washington, Krannert Center for Performing Arts, U. Ill., Powell Symphony Hall, St. Louis, Nat. Acad. Scis. Auditorium, Washington, Minn. Orch. Hall, Mpls., Nat. Centre for Performing Arts, Bombay, India, new Avery Fisher Hall, State Theater reconstruction Lincoln Center, N.Y.C., Symphony Hall, Salt Lake City; past dir. U.S. Inst. Theatre Tech.; mem. noise control group, com. undersea warfare NRC, 1955-57; mem. council hearing and bio-acoustics Armed Forces-NRC, 1953-55; mem. NRC adv. panel 213 to Nat. Bur. Standards, 1966-69, chmn., 1969-71; mem. bldg. research adv. bd. NRC, 1977-79. Author: (with V.O. Knudsen) Acoustical Designing in Architecture, 1950, rev., 1980, Handbook of Noise Control, 1957, 2d edit., 1979, (with C.E. Crede) Shock and Vibration Handbook, 1961, 2d edit., 1976, Dictionary of Architecture and Construction, 1975; author: Historic Architecture Sourcebook, 1977, Illustrated Dictionary of Historic Architecture, 1983; Contbr. articles to profl. jours.; Editorial adv. bd.: Physics Today, 1955-66. Bd. dirs. Armstrong Meml. Research Found., 1976—; hon. v.p. St. Louis Symphony Soc., 1977—; mem. nat. adv. bd. Utah Symphony Orch., 1976—. Recipient Franklin medal, 1977, Emile Berliner award, 1977, Hon. award U.S. ITT, 1977, Wallace Clement Sabine medal, 1979, AIA medal, 1980, Gold Medal Audio Engring. Soc., 1984. Fellow Acoustical Soc. Am. (pres. 1964-65, asso. editor jour. 1959-70), IEEE (chmn. profl. group ultrasonic engring. 1957-58), I.E.E.E. (profl. group audio 1961-62), Audio Engring. Soc. (hon. mem.); mem. Am. Inst. Physics (governing bd. 1965-66), Nat. Acad. Scis., Nat. Acad. Engring., Sigma Xi, Tau Beta Pi. Office: Mudd Bldg Columbia U New York NY 10027

HARRIS, DALE BENNER, psychologist, educator; b. Elkhart, Ind., June 28, 1914; s. Ward Manning and Lillian (Benner) H.; m. Elizabeth Saltmarsh, July 17, 1935; children—Ruthann E., James S., David B., Geoffrey M. A.B. with high distinction (Rector scholar), DePauw U., 1935; M.A., U. Minn., 1937, Ph.D., 1941. Ednl. dir. Minn. Tng. Sch. for Boys, 1936-38; staff Inst. Child Welfare U. Minn., 1939-59, prof., 1948-59, dir., 1954-59; prof. psychology Pa. State U., 1959-79, prof. emeritus, 1979—, chmn. dept. psychology, 1962-67; Fulbright vis. prof. Ochanomizu U., Tokyo, 1968-69. Author: Children's Drawings as Measures of Intellectual Maturity, 1963; co-author: Child Care and Training, 8th edit, 1958; Editor: The Concept of Development, 1957, Child Development Abstracts, 1964-71; editorial com.: Ann. Rev. of Psychology, 1956-62; Contbr. articles to profl. jours. Mem. Mpls. Citizens Com. on Pub. Edn., 1946-59, Gov.'s Adv. Com. on Children and Youth, 1950-55, on Exceptional Children, 1956-59; mem. bd. Children's Home Soc. Minn., 1954-59; mem. adv. com. young workers Bur. Labor Standards, Dept. Labor, 1955-59; mem. adv. com. Clearing House for Research Relating to Children, U.S. Children's Bur., 1962-68; mem. exec. bd. Joint Commn. Correctional Manpower and Tng., 1965-69; mem. task force Joint Commn. Mental Health Children, 1966-69; research adv. com. Commonwealth Mental Health Research Found.; Mem. bd. Pa. Mental Health Assn., 1970-76. Fellow Am. Psychol. Assn. (past pres. div. developmental psychology), A.A.A.S. (governing council 1962-72, v.p., sect. I chmn. 1972), Soc. for Research in Child Devel. (sec., mem. governing council 1957-61, cons. editor monographs); mem. Nat. Soc. Study Edn., AAUP, Am. Edn. Research Assn. (v.p. 1964), Phi Beta Kappa, Sigma Xi, Psi Chi, Phi Sigma, Phi Delta Kappa. Home: 317 W Ridge Ave State College PA 16803

HARRIS, DARRYL WAYNE, publishing executive; b. Emmett, Idaho, July 29, 1941; s. Reed Ingval and Evelyn Faye (Wengreen) H.; m. Christine Sorenson, Sept. 10, 1965; children: Charles Reed, Michael Wayne, Jason Darryl, Stephanie, Ryan Joseph. B.A., Brigham Young U., 1966. Staff writer Deseret News, Salt Lake City, 1965, Post-Register, Idaho Falls, 1966-67; tech. editor Idaho Nuclear Corp., Idaho Falls, 1967-68; account exec. David W. Evans & Assos. Advt., Salt Lake City, 1968-71; pres. Harris Pub., Inc., Idaho Falls, 1971—; pub. Potato Grower of Idaho mag., 1972—, Snowmobile West mag., 1974—, Sugar Producer mag., 1974—. Campaign mgr. George Hansen for Congress Com., 1974, 76; 1st counselor to pres. Korean Mission, Ch. Jesus Christ of Latter-day Saints, Seoul, Korea, 1963, area public communications dir., Eastern Idaho, 1976—; holder Office of Seventy in Priesthood, 1980—. Mem. Agr. Editors Assn., Internat. Snowmobile Industry Assn. (Best Overall Reporting journalism award 1979, 80), World Champion Cutter and Chariot Racing Assn. (historian 1966-80), Kappa Tau Alpha. Clubs: Idaho Falls Kiwanis (pres. 1978, Disting. Club Pres. award 1978. Home: 3905 Brookfield Ln Idaho Falls ID 83401 Office: Harris Pub Inc 520 Park Ave Idaho Falls ID 83401

HARRIS, DAVID HENRY, life insurance company executive; b. N.Y.C., May 7, 1924; s. Julian A. and May L. (Wilenski) H.; 1 dau., Jean Harris Haig. Student, Sherborne (Eng.) Sch., 1937-40. With Prudential Ins. Co. Am., 1940-43; with Equitable Life Assurance Soc. U.S., N.Y.C., 1946—, exec. v.p., 1973-77, exec. v.p., chief adminstrv. officer, 1977-80, exec. v.p., chief staff, 1981—; chmn. bd. Equimatics, Inc., 1971-73, Informatics, Inc., 1974-75; vice chmn. Equitable Variable Life Ins. Co., 1975-76, chmn., 1976-77; dir. Equitable Life Holding Co., Equitable Life Assurance Soc. Served with AUS, 1943-46. Fellow Soc. Actuaries. Office: 1285 Ave of Americas New York NY 10019

HARRIS, DAVID WILLIAM, petroleum exec.; b. Machen, Ga., Sept. 7, 1891; s. Nathaniel Edwin (ex-gov. of Ga.) and Fannie (Burke) H.; m. Mildred Stoutenborough, July 2, 1914; children—Walter Alexander, Holton Edwin. B.S. in Elec. Engring, Ga. Inst. Tech., 1912. Engr. Denver Gas & Electric Co., 1912-13; dir. budget, asst. treas. Cities Service Co., 1913-23; treas. Empire Gas & Fuel Co., 1923-27; v.p. Ind. Ty. Ill. Oil Co., 1927-28; v.p., gen. mgr. Ark. Natural Gas Corp. (and subsidiary cos.), pres., 1944-45, Orange State Oil Co., 1939-45; v.p., dir. Cities Service Def. Corp., 1941-45; pres., chief exec. officer Universal Oil Products Co., 1945-60; chmn. David W. Harris & Assos. (cons.), 1962—; dir. Harrel, Inc. Recipient Alumni Distinguished Service award Ga. Inst. Tech., 1954. Mem. Mid-Continent Oil and Gas Assn. (exec. com., past pres. La.-Ark. div.), Am. Gas Assn. (dir. 1941-45), Bartlesville (Okla.) C. of C., Western Soc. Engrs., Newcomen Soc. N.Am., Chi Phi. Methodist. Clubs: Mason (32, K.T., Shriner), Chicago, Glen View, Westmoreland, McGraw Wildlife Found. Home: 2305 Central Park Ave Evanston IL 60201 Office: 2530 Crawford Ave Evanston IL 60201 *In life, the straight-shooter wins.*

HARRIS, DEL(MER) WILLIAM, basketball scout; b. Orleans, Ind., June 18, 1937; s. Elmer W. and Wilma (Whitten) H.; m. Joyce Crites, June 20, 1958; children: Larry, Alex, Stan, Carey Ann. A.B., Milligan Coll., Tenn., 1959; M.A. in History, Ind. U., 1965. Ordained minister Christian Ch., 1958; high sch. coach, 1959-64; basketball coach Earlham Coll. (Ind.), 1965-74; asst. coach ABA Utah Stars, 1974-75, U. Utah, 1975-76, Houston Rockets Profl. Basketball Team, 1976-79, head coach, 1979-83; scout, cons. Milw. Bucks, 1983—; speaker on motivation Intercontinental Tng. Systems, Inc. Author: Multiple Defenses, 1971; Zone Offense, 1975; juvenile novel Playing the Game, 1982. Mem. adv. bd. Gulf chpt. Leukemia Soc. Am., 1980—; active Muscular Dystrophy Assn., March of Dimes; mem. Spl. Olympics. Recipient Disting. Houstonian award, 1981; Eli Lilly fellow, 1965. Mem. Internat. Platform Assn. Address: 12103 Fawnview Dr Houston TX 77070 *Anyone who believes enough, works enough and pursues a course of positive action day after day will become sucessful in his endeavors in America.*

HARRIS, DIANE FEUILLAN, writer, editor; b. New Orleans, Feb. 3, 1932; d. William Adrian and Andree Marie (Cartier) Feuillan; m. Richard S. Harris, June 1957 (div. 1967). B.S., Northwestern U., 1953. Author: Women's Day Baking Book, 1976, No-Choice Diet, 1978, Women's Day Book of Great Sandwiches, 1982, Women's Day Guide to Organizing Your Life, 1984. Home: 404 E 66th St 12-J New York NY 10021 Office: E P Dutton 2 Park Aven New York NY 10021

HARRIS, DON VICTOR, JR., lawyer; b. Nottingham Twp., Ind., Jan. 16, 1921; s. Don Victor and Nellie Florence (Dukes) H.; m. Joan Elliott Haffler, Aug. 15, 1959; children: Leigh Elliott, Meghan St. Clair. A.B., DePauw U., 1943; J.D., Harvard U., 1945. Bar: D.C. 1947. Law clk. to judge U.S. Ct. Appeals 2d Circuit, 1945-46; assoc. firm Covington & Burling, Washington, 1946-57, partner, 1957—; lectr. in law George Washington U., 1963-64; lectr. tax insts.; mem. IRS Commr.'s Adv. Group, 1976. Contbr. articles to law jours.; Case editor: Harvard Law Rev. Bd. dirs. Carostead Found., Oak Hill Cemetery Co.; past bd. dirs. Nat. Eye Found. Fellow Am. Coll. Tax Counsel, Am. Bar Found.; Mem. Am. Law Inst. (life), ABA (chmn. sect. taxation 1976-77), D.C. Bar Assn., Fed. Bar Assn., Phi Beta Kappa, Beta Theta Pi, Am. Camellia Soc. (judge). Episcopalian. Clubs: Met., Chevy Chase, City Tavern. Home: 2803 P St NW Washington DC 20007 Office: 1201 Pennsylvania Ave NW Washington DC 20004

HARRIS, DONALD, composer; b. St. Paul, Apr. 7, 1931; s. Barney William and Hattie (Paper) H.; m. Marilyn Hackett, 1983; children: Daniel, Jeremy. Mus.B., U. Mich., 1952, Mus.M., 1954. Music cons. Am. Cultural Center, USIS, Paris, 1965-67; asst. to pres. for acad. affairs New Eng. Conservatory Music, Boston, 1967-71, v.p., 1971-74, exec. v.p., 1974-77, mem. teaching faculty depts. composition and music lit., 1967-77; composer-in-residence, prof. music, chmn. composition and theory Hartt Sch. of Music, U. Hartford, Conn., 1977-80, dean, 1981—; Lectr. Schoenberg Inst., 1974. Composer: Piano Sonata, 1956, Fantasy for Violin and Piano, 1957, Symphony in Two Movements, 1961, String Quartet, 1965, Ludus for 10 Instruments, 1966, Ludus II for 5 Instruments, 1973, Charmes for Voice and Orchestra, 1977, On Variations, 1976, For the Night to Wear, mezzo-soprano and 7 instruments, 1978, Balladen for solo piano, 1979, Of Hartford in a Purple Light (Wallace Stevens) for soprano and piano, 1979, Prelude to a Concert in Connecticut, 1981, On Vont les Morts (Marguerite Yourcenar) for mezzo-soprano and piano, 1983; Recs., CRI, Delos, Golden Crest Records. Mem. exec. com. Conn. Commn. on Arts, 1983—. Recipient commns. from Serge Koussevitzky Music Found., 1977, Elizabeth Sprague Coolidge Found., 1977, Goethe Inst., 1978, Conn. Commn. Arts, 1979, French Nat. Radio, 1972, Festival Contemporary Am. Music at Tanglewood, 1965, Boston Musica Viva, 1973, Cleve. Orch., 1975, Louisville Orch. award, 1954, Prince Rainier of Monaco Composition prize, 1960; Grantee-in-aid Rockefeller Found., 1969, Chapelbrook Found., 1970; Fellowship grantee Nat. Endowment for Arts, 1974; Fulbright scholar, 1956; Guggenheim fellow, 1965. Mem. League ISCM, Internat. Alban Berg Soc., Am. Soc. U. Composers, ASCAP (awards 1973—). Address: Hartt Sch Music U Hartford 200 Bloomfield Ave West Hartford CT 06117

HARRIS, DOUGLAS CLAY, newspaper exec.; b. Owensboro, Ky., Oct. 9, 1939; s. Marvin Dudley and Elizabeth (Adelman) H. B.S., Murray State U., 1961; M.S., Ind. U., 1964, Ed.D., 1968. Counselor, asst. to dean of students Ind. U., Bloomington, 1965-68; mgmt. appraisal specialist United Air Lines, Elk Grove Village, Ill., 1968-69; dir. manpower div. Computer Age Industries, Washington, 1969; area personnel dir. Peat Marwick Mitchell & Co., N.Y.C., 1969-72; v.p. personnel Knight-Ridder Newspapers, Inc., Miami, Fla., 1972—. Mem. editorial adv. bd.: Personnel Adminstr. Mem. adv. council Opportunities Industrialization Center of Dade County, 1980. Served to capt. U.S. Army, 1961-62. Mem. Am. Psychol. Assn., Fla. Psychol. Assn., Southeastern Psychol. Assn., Am. Soc. Personnel Adminstrs., Newspaper Personnel Relations Assn., Am. Compensation Assn. Democrat. Home: 1408 S Bayshore Dr Apt 1211 Miami FL 33131 Office: 1 Herald Plaza Miami FL 33101

HARRIS, E. EDWARD, business educator; b. West Burlington, Iowa, Nov. 15, 1931; s. Earl and Anne M. (Mollen) H.; m. Evonne L. Meier, May 29, 1954; children: Julie Anne, James Edward. B.A., U. No. Iowa, 1953; M.A., U. Minn., 1949; Ed.D., No. Ill. U., 1965. Tchr. Davenport (Iowa) Community Schs., 1955-63; head bus. edn. dept. West High Sch., 1960-63; asst. prof. edn. No. Ill. U., DeKalb, 1963-64, asso. prof., 1965-67, prof., 1968—, chmn. bus. edn. and adminstrv. services dept., 1973-81, dir. office of research Coll. of Bus., 1981-83; cons. in field; chmn. region V planning com. distributive end. U.S. Office Edn., 1966-69. Author: An Articulated Guide for Cooperative Occupational Education, 1971, 78, Marketing Research, 1971,78, Employer Preferences and Teacher Coordinator Practices, 1971, Methods of Teaching Business and Distributive Education, 3d edit, 1974, Retailing Principles and Practices, 7th edit, 1981, Handbook for Cooperative Vocational Education in Illinois, 1977, Annotated Bibliography of Instructional Materials in Cooperative Vocational Education, 1977, State of Illinois Marketing and Distributive Education curriculum Planning Guide, 1978, Curriculum Guide in Food Marketing, 1978, Curriculum Guide in Wholesaling, 1978, Curriculum Guide in General Retail Merchandising, 1978, Curriculum Guide in Finance and Credit, 1979 in Transportation and Warehousing, 1980, in Automotive and Petroleum, 1981, others; editor: Nat. Bus. Edn. Yearbook, 1976; editor mktg. and distbn. sect.: Nat. Bus. Forum, 1976-77; mng. editor: Mktg. and Distributive Educators' Digest, 1981-84; contbr. articles to profl. jours. Mem. DeKalb County Devel. Corp., 1974—; bd. dirs. Ill. Found. Distributive Edn., 1965—, Ill. Devel. Council, 1983—. Served with AUS, 1953-55. Recipient Outstanding Service award Distributive Clubs Am., 1963, Ill. chpt., 1967; Teaching Excellence award No. Ill. U., 1969; Man of Yr. award Distributive Edn. Clubs Ill., 1972; also Service award. Mem. Am. Vocat. Assn. (life chmn. distributive edn. publs. com. 1966-74, evaluation com. 1981-82), Ill. Bus. Tchr. Edn. Assn. (sec., pres. 1976-79, outstanding service award 1983), Nat. Bus. Edn. Assn., Mktg. and Distributive Edn. Assn. (life mem., chmn. coms.), Nat. Assn. Distributive Edn. Tchrs. (life), Council Distributive Tchr. Educators, Ill. Co-op. Vocat. Edn. Coordinators Assn. (dir.), Ill. Secondary Mktg. and Distributive Edn. Coordinators Assn. (dir.), Delta Pi Epsilon, Pi Omega Pi, Beta Gamma Sigma. Presbyterian (ruling elder). Home: 802 Sunnymeade Trail DeKalb IL 60115

HARRIS, EDWARD, lawyer; b. Rochester, N.Y., Sept. 24, 1912. A.B., Princeton, 1935; LL.B., Cornell U., 1938. Bar: N.Y. State bar 1939. Mem. firm Harris, Beach, Wilcox, Rubin & Levey, Rochester.; Trustee Rochester Savs. Bank; mem. adv. bd. Security Trust Co. Rochester, Security N.Y. State Corp., Sci. Calculations, Inc., Edmac Assos., Inc.; dir. Latex, Palo Alto, Calif., Dynecology, N.Y.C.; Mem. adv. bd. Cornell Law Sch., 1975-78. Trustee Columbia Sch., 1947-50, Allendale Sch., 1950-53, Auburn at Union Theol. Sem., 1959-62, Springfield Coll., 1964-77, U. Rochester; chmn. Morven Park Internat. Equestrian Inst., 1967-77; mem. exec. com. Center for Research on Instns. and Social Policy, N.Y.C. Mem. Am., Rochester, Monroe County bar assns., U.S. Combined Tng. Assn. (pres. 1966-68), Phi Delta Phi. Office: 2 State St Rochester NY 14614

HARRIS, ELLEN GANDY (MRS. J. RAMSAY HARRIS), civic worker; b. Spokane, Wash., Jan. 9, 1910; d. Lloyd Edward and Helen (George) Gandy; m. J. Ramsay Harris, Jan. 20, 1936; children—Sue Ellen, Hayden Henry. Student, U. Wash.; grad., Smith Coll., 1930. Mem. U.S. com. UNICEF, 1948-66; mem. Def. Adv. Com. Women in Service, 1951-54; nat. co-chmn. Citizens for Eisenhower, 1953-54; Republican candidate U.S. Congress from Denver, 1954; mem. Internat. Devel. Adv. Bd., 1955- 57; nat. co. chmn. Com. Internat. Econ. Growth, 1958-60; regional chmn. Met. Opera Council, 1958-66; mem. Gov. Colo.'s Local Affairs Commn., 1963-66; pres. Colo. Consumers Council, 1965-67; dir. Nat. Safety Council, 1958-60; mem. Nat. Adv. Council on Nurse Tng., HEW, 1969-73; pres. The Park People, 1975-79; Mem. Gov.'s Commn. on Status Women, 1970-75. Trustee Central City Opera, Inst. Internat. Edn., 4 Mile Historic Park. Mem. Assn. Jr. Leagues Am. (bd. dirs. 1947-50). Episcopalian. Home: 1077 Race St Denver CO 80206

HARRIS, ELLIOTT STANLEY, toxicologist; b. Bklyn., June 27, 1922; s. Edward Bernard and Bertha (Ruden) H.; m. Almeda Butler, Mar. 15, 1945; children: Jennifer Jo, Catherine Ann. B.A., U. Colo., 1948; M.S., U. So. Calif., 1950, Ph.D., 1954. Rosenstiehl postdoctoral fellow Roswell Park Meml. Inst., Buffalo, 1954-55, dir. clin. chemistry lab., 1955-56; research biochemist Wyeth Labs., Radnor, Pa., 1956-62; sr. research scientist Space Scis. Lab., Gen. Electric Co., Valley Forge, Pa., 1962-63; toxicologist, chief health services br. NASA, 1963-73; dir. div. biomed. and behavioral scis. Nat. Inst. Occupational Safety and Health, Cin., 1973-81, dep. inst. dir., 1981—; adj. asso. prof. U. Cin., 1974—; vis. prof. U. Ariz., 1980-81. Author numerous papers in field. Served with USAAF, 1943-45. Decorated D.F.C., Air medal with 3 oak leaf clusters. Fellow AAAS; mem. Am. Assn. Clin. Chemists, Am. Public Health Assn., Am. Indsl. Hygiene Soc., Soc. Toxicology, Am. Conf. Govt. Indsl. Hygienists, Soc. Ecotoxicology, Amateur Radio Relay League, Sigma Xi, Phi Lambda Upsilon, Alpha Epsilon Delta. Office: 1600 Clifton Rd Atlanta GA 30333

HARRIS, ELMER BESELER, electric utility executive; b. Chilton County, Ala., Apr. 8, 1939; s. Alton Curtis and Lero (Mitchell) H.; m. Glenda Steele, Sept. 15, 1962; children: Lera Lorraine, Thomas Alton. B.E. in Elec. Engring., Auburn U., 1962, M.S., 1968, M.B.A., 1970; student, U.S. Air Force Flight Sch., Tex., 1964, Air Command and Staff Coll., Maxwell AFB, Montgomery, Ala., 1970. With Ala. Power Co., Birmingham, Ala., 1975—, asst. v.p., 1975, asst. v.p., asst. treas., 1975-76, v.p. corp. fin. and planning, 1976, sr. v.p., 1978, exec. v.p., chief fin. officer, 1979, dir., 1980—; dir. So. Electric Gen. Co., Birmingham, 1979—. Fund solicitor Boy Scouts Am., Birmingham; funds solicitor Am. Heart Assn., Birmingham. Served to capt. USAF, 1964-65. Mem. Nat. Mgmt. Assn., Edison Elec. Inst. (corp. planning com.), Fin. Execs. Inst. Lodge: Kiwanis. Home: 3115 Club Dr Birminngham AL 35226 Office: Ala Power Co 600 N 18th St Birmingham AL 35291

HARRIS, EMMYLOU, singer; b. Birmingham, Ala., 1947; 1 dau., Hallie; m. Brian Ahern, Jan. 1977; 1 stepdau., Shannon; 1 dau., Megan Theresa. Student, U.N.C.-Greensboro, 1 yr. Country music performer, singer, 1967—; assisted, Gram Parsons; on albums GP and Grievous Angels; toured with, Him and Fallen Angel Band; performed across, Europe and U.S.; rec. artist on albums, Reprise Records; appeared in: rock documentary The Last Waltz, 1978; albums include Pieces of the Sky, Elite Hotel, Luxury Liner, Quarter Moon in a Ten-Cent Town, Roses in the Snow, A Light from the Stable, Evangeline, Blue Kentucky Girl, Cimarron, Last Date; appeared in: A Light from the Stable, Evangeline, 1981 (named Female Vocalist of Yr., Country Music Assn. 1980). Pres. Country Music Found., 1983—. Recipient Grammy awards, 1976, 77, 80, 81; named Female Vocalist of Yr., Country Music Assn., 1980. Office: care Mangler-Tickner Orgn PO Box 560 North Hollywood CA 91603 Office: care Monterey Peninsula Artists Box 7308 Carmel CA

HARRIS, EVERETTE BAGBY, exchange exec.; b. Norris City, Ill., Apr. 19, 1913; s. George N. and Maud (Bagby) H.; m. May June Smith, Sept. 6, 1970; children—Scott Walden, Dale Alan. A.B., U. Ill., 1935; M.B.A., U. Chgo., 1945. Staff soil conservation service Dept. Agr., 1935-38; economist Dept. Labor, 1938-46; tchr. econs. evening schs. De Paul U., U. Chgo., 1943-45; dir. personnel, supt. non-selling depts. Mandel Bros., Chgo., 1946-49; exec. sec. Chgo. Bd. Trade, 1949-53; pres. Chgo. Merc. Exchange, 1953-79, pres. emeritus, 1979—; pres. Internat. Monetary Market, 1972-79, pres. emeritus, 1979—; dir. Chgo. Regional Port Dist., Merc. Nat. Bank. Author: Earnings and Hours in Book and Job Printing, 1942; also chpt. Am. Peoples Ency. Mem. exec. and steering coms. Chgo. chpt. Nat. Found.; exec. bd. Chgo. council Boy Scouts Am.; Ill. chmn., mem. nat. council U.S.O., 1956-57; bd. dirs. Nat. Found., Chgo. Assn. Commerce and Industry, West Central Assn., Chgo. Internat. Port, 1979—; mem. exec. adv. bd. St. Joseph Hosp. Mem. Am. Statis. Assn., Am. Marketing Assn., Young Presidents Assn. Presbyn. Clubs: Mason (32 deg., Shriner), Elk, Lion., Metropolitan, Union League, Economic, Executives (Chgo.); Mattoon Country. Home: 505 N Lake Shore Dr Chicago IL 60611 Office: 444 W Jackson Blvd Chicago IL 60606 *Success in any field is 90 percent hard work. Success from luck is most often temporary. The greatest and most unusual successes come to courageous young men and women who "Don't know it can't be done!"*

HARRIS, FRANCO, football player; b. Ft. Dix, N.J., Mar. 7, 1950; s. Cadillac and Gina H. B.S., Pa. State U., 1972. Running back with Pitts. Steelers, 1972—; played in Pro Bowl, 1972-78. Named Sporting News AFC Rookie of Year, 1972, Sporting News AFC All-Star Team, 1972, 75, 77. Office: 400 W North ave Pittsburgh PA 15212 *

HARRIS, FRED EARL, coll. pres.; b. Washington, June 8, 1917; s. James Riley and Elizabeth Annette (Schoolfield) H.; m. Frances Bandy, Dec. 24, 1938; children—Susan, Nancy. B.S., Ind. State U., Terre Haute, 1940; M.S., 1942; Ed.D., Ind. U., 1950. Dir. grad. studies elementary edn., prof. edn. U. Ky., 1950-57; specialist fundamental edn. ICA, Egypt, 1954-55, cons. edn., Kabul, Afghanistan, 1959; dean coll. Baldwin-Wallace Coll., 1957-69, also vice pres. acad. affairs, 1964-69; v.p. acad. affairs U. Evansville, 1969-72; asso. gen. sec. for higher edn. United Meth. Ch., 1972-77; pres. W.Va. Wesleyan Coll., Buckhannon, 1977—; Mem. Nat. Edn. Study Team, Viet Nam, 1967, 70; cons. AID, Uganda, Tanzania, Kenya, 1969. Contbr. articles to profl. jours. Recipient Distinguished Alumni award Ind. State U., 1965. Mem. Comparative Edn. Soc., Phi Delta Kappa. Methodist. Office: WVa Wesleyan Coll Buckhannon WV 26201

HARRIS, FRED R., educator, former U.S. senator; b. Walters, Okla., Nov. 13, 1930; s. Fred Byron and Alene (Person) H.; m. LaDonna Crawford, Apr. 8, 1949 (div. 1981); children: Kathryn, Byron, Laura.; m. Margaret S. Elliston, Sept. 5, 1982. B.A. in Polit. Sci. U. Okla., 1952, J.D. with distinction, 1954. Bar: Okla. bar 1954. Founder, sr. partner firm Harris, Newcombe, Redman & Doolin, Lawton, Okla., 1954-64; mem. Okla Senate, 1956-64, U.S. Senate from Okla., 1964-73; prof. polit. sci. U. N.Mex., Albuquerque, 1976—. Author: Alarms and Hopes, 1969, Now Is The Time, 1971, The State of the Cities: Report of the Commission on Cities in the 70's, 1972, Social Science and National Policy; The New Populism, 1973, Potomoc Fever, 1977, America's Democracy, 1980, 2d edit., 1983; Co-author: America's Legislative Processes, 1983. Mem. Nat. Adv. Commn. Civil Disorders, 1967-68; Chmn. Democratic Nat. Com., 1969-70. Mem. Order of Coif, Phi Beta Kappa. Address: Dept Polit Sci U NMex Albuquerque NM 87131

HARRIS, FREDERICK GEORGE, publishing co. exec.; b. Niles, Ohio, Apr. 12, 1922; s. William H. and Nell H. (Zempkey) H.; m. Marjorie E. Bork, Sept. 10, 1950; children—Frederick, David, Joyce. B.S. in Bus. Adminstrn, Ohio State U., 1948. Staff accountant Lybrand, Ross Bros. & Montgomery, 1948-56; with Dow Jones & Co., Inc., 1956—, comptroller-asst. sec., 1970-76, mem. mgmt. com., 1972—, v.p., comptroller, 1976-77, v.p. fin., 1977—; v.p., treas. Dow Jones-Bunker Ramo News Retrieval Service, Inc., 1971-78. Trustee Trenton Lutheran Housing Corp., 1969-81, treas., 1974-80; Chmn. local troop Boy Scouts Am., 1965-67. Served with USAAF, 1942-45. Mem. Financial Execs. Inst. (chmn. orgn. planning com. N.Y. chpt. 1963-64), Nat. Assn. Accountants (asso. dir. N.Y. chpt. 1959-61), Inst. Newspaper Controllers and Finance Officers (dir. 1964-72, chmn. steering com. 1968-69, pres. 1970-71, Walter F. Carley award 1970, 73, 77), Delta Sigma Pi. Lutheran (v.p. ch. 1967-68, council 1965-71). Home: 113 Lewis Brook Rd Pennington NJ 08534 Office: PO Box 300 Princeton NJ 08540

HARRIS, GEORGE THOMAS, JR., lawyer; b. Henryetta, Okla., Sept. 12, 1922; s. George Thomas and Gertrude V. (Smith) H.; m. Martha J. Henry, Aug. 8, 1941; children: G. Thomas III, Ronald G., Debra Lyn. LL.B., U. N.Mex., 1950. Bar: N.Mex. 1950. Assoc. firm Simms and Modrall, Albuquerque, 1950-56; ptnr. firm Modrall, Sperling, Roehl, Harris & Sisk, 1956—. Served to 1st lt. USAAF, 1943-45; MTO. Fellow Am. Coll. Trial Lawyers; mem. Albuquerque Bar Assn. (past pres.), State Bar N.Mex. (past pres.), Am. Judicature Soc. Home: 1904 Apache Ct NE Albuquerque NM 87106 Office: Pub Service Bldg PO Box 2168 Albuquerque MN 87103

HARRIS, GRACE GREDYS, anthropology educator; b. Warren, Ohio, Feb. 5, 1926; d. Louis Abraham and Kunigunda Amalia (Mielke) G.; m. Alfred Harris, II, Oct. 16, 1948. Ph.B., U. Chgo., 1945, M.A., 1949; postgrad., Oxford (Eng.) U., 1949-50; Ph.D. (U.K.) Colonial Social Sci. Research Council fellow), Cambridge (Eng.) U., 1955. Instr., research asso. African studies program Boston U., 1956-57; asst. prof. anthropology, dept. sociology and anthropology U. Mass., Amherst, 1959-60; vis. asst. prof. dept. anthropology Brandeis U., Waltham, Mass., 1960-61; mem. faculty U. Rochester, N.Y., 1961—, prof. anthropology, 1977—, chmn. dept. anthropology, 1977-83, prof. religious studies, 1977—. Author: Casting Out Anger, 1978. Chmn. City of Rochester Museum Study Com., 1965-66; trustee Rochester Philharm. Orch., 1972-74. Mem. Am. Anthrop. Assn., AAAS, Assn. Social Anthropologists of Commonwealth. Greek Orthodox. Office: Harkness U Rochester Rochester NY 14627

HARRIS, GRANT ANDERSON, forester, educator; b. Logan, Utah, July 13, 1914; s. Joseph Smith and Hilda (Anderson) H.; m. Jennabee Ballif, Oct. 18, 1939; children: Judith (Mrs. Gaylon Sanford Campbell), Patricia Florence (Mrs. Harold Davis Oak), Joseph Ballif, Halli H. (Mrs. Mark Lee Stone). B.S., Utah State U., 1939, Ph.D., 1965; M.S., U. Idaho, 1941. Cert. Sr. ecologist, range mgmt. cons. Supt., Vigilante exptl. range U.S. Forest Service Research Br., Alder, Mont., 1941-48; project leader Upper Columbia Research Center, Spokane, Wash., 1948-51; asst. prof., extension forester, research Utah State U., 1951-56; assoc. prof., research forester Wash. State U., Pullman, 1956-67, prof., chmn. dept. forestry and range mgmt., 1967-80; cons., 1980—; chmn. bd. Decagon Devices Inc., 1983—; cons. West Pakistan Agrl. U. Editorial bd.: N.W. Sci; Contbr. articles to profl. jours. Active Boy Scouts Am. Served to lt. (j.g.) USNR, 1944-46. Recipient Silver Beaver award, 1977. Fellow AAAS; fellow Am. Soc. Range Mgmt. (Pacific N.W. sect. pres. 1964); mem. Soc. Am. Foresters (chmn. range ecology working group 1975-77), Am. Forestry Assn., N.W. Sci. Assn., Wash. Farm Forestry Assn., Wash. State Forestry Conf. (trustee, exec. com., Outstanding Service award 1980), Assn. State Colls. and Univs. Forestry Research Orgn. (chmn. Western region 1975—, exec. com. 1975—), Sigma Xi, Xi Sigma Pi. Mem. Ch. of Jesus Christ of Latter-day Saints (bishop Pullman ward 1965-73, stake patriarch 1980—). Home: NE 1615 Upper Dr Pullman WA 99163

HARRIS, GREGORY SCOTT, assn. exec.; b. Denver, June 5, 1955; s. Herbert E. and Marcia Jean (Raabe) H. B.S. in Journalism with honors, U. Colo., 1977; M.B.A., Loyola U., Chgo., 1981. Dir. public relations IMPACT Internat., Inc., Chgo., 1977-78; dir. edn. Nat. Home Furnishings Assn., Chgo., 1978-79; exec. dir. Interior Design Soc., Chgo., 1979—. Trustee Design Found., Chgo., 1980—. Mem. Am. Soc. Assn. Execs., Chgo. Soc. Assn. Execs. Club: Union League (Chgo.). Office: 405 Merchandise Mart Chicago IL 60654

HARRIS, HARWELL HAMILTON, architect, educator; b. Redlands, Calif., July 2, 1903; s. Frederick Thomas and May Julia (Hamilton) H.; m. Jean Murray Bangs, Feb. 23, 1937. Student, Pomona Coll., 1921-23, Otis Art Inst., 1923-25. Practice architecture with Richard Neutra, 1929-32; pvt. practice, Los Angeles, 1933-51, Austin, Tex., 1951-56, as Harris & Sherwood, Ft. Worth, 1956-57; architect with office in, Dallas, 1958-62, Raleigh, N.C., 1962—; lectr. U. So. Calif., 1945, 1946; vis. critic Columbia, 1943, Yale, 1950, 52; design cons. to Nat. Orange Show, 1950—; grad. design critic Columbia, 1960-61; prof. architecture N.C. State U., Raleigh, 1962-73; dir. Sch. Architecture, U. Tex., 1951-55; Internat. Exec., Service Corps, North Borneo, 1972, San Salvador, 1977, Singapore, 1978. Sculptor, 1926-29; Prin. works include Lowe House, 1934, Fellowship Park House, 1935, Havens House, 1941, Birtcher House, 1942, Johnson House, 1947, English House, 1950, Chadwick School, 1951, Texas State Fair House, 1954, J. Lee Johnson House, 1956, Am. Embassy, Helsinki, 1957, Havens Meml. Plaza, Berkeley, Calif., 1961, Greenwood Mausoleum, 1959, Dallas Unitarian Ch, 1964, St. Giles Presbyn. Ch, Raleigh, 1969, others; prin. projects include Segmental House for, Revere Cooper & Brass Co., 1942, Pottenger Hosp, 1946, Palos Verdes Coll, 1947, Homestyle Found. House for S.W, 1956. Recipient 1st prize Pitts. Glass Inst., 1937, 38. Fellow AIA, mem., Congrès Internationaux d'Architecture Moderne (sec. Am. chpt. 1932, chpt. for relief and postwar planning 1944), Tau Sigma Delta. Home: 122-A Cox Ave Raleigh NC Office: 122 Cox Ave Raleigh NC 27605

HARRIS, HENRY HITER, JR., banker; b. Richmond, Va., Aug. 16, 1922; s. Henry Hiter and Mary (Murdoch) H.; m. Elizabeth Spalding Trueheart, Apr. 16, 1955; children: Mary Lawrence and Elizabeth Robinson (twins), Henry Hiter III. Grad., Woodberry Forest Sch., 1941; A.B., Princeton U., 1945; postgrad., N.Y. U., 1946-47. Credit analyst Chem. Bank N.Y. Trust Co., N.Y.C., 1946-50; asst. treas., asst. v.p. Chase Manhattan Bank, N.Y.C., 1950-55; v.p. Colonial-Am. Nat. Bank, Roanoke, Va., 1955-59; v.p., dir. So. Bank, Richmond, 1959-61, pres., dir., 1961-72, 79—, chmn. bd., 1967—; chmn. bd., pres. So. Bankshares, Inc., Richmond, 1970-79; chmn. bd. Jefferson Bankshares, Inc., 1980—; dir. Bralley-Willett Tank Lines, Inc., Richmond, 1971-77, Bank of Lancaster, Kilmarnock, Va., 1977-79, Va. Indsl. Devel. Corp., 1961—, mem. exec. com., 1976—, chmn., 1978-79. Dir. Central Va. Ednl. TV Corp., 1964—, mem. exec. com., 1968—, pres., 1973-74, chmn. bd., 1974-75; Trustee U. Richmond, 1969-77; trustee, mem. exec. com. Mary Baldwin Coll., Staunton, Va., 1968-78, assoc. trustee, 1980—; trustee Va. Found. Ind. Colls., 1973—, Hampden-Sydney Coll., 1983—; bd. dirs. Crippled Childrens Hosp., 1962—, v.p., 1976—, mem. exec. com., 1967-70, 76—; bd. dirs. Richmond Meml. Hosp., 1961—, Richmond Eye Hosp., 1976-77, Richmond Eye and Ear Hosp. Authority, 1977—; vice chmn. Richmond Eye and Ear Hosp. Authority, 1978—; adv. trustee Greater Richmond Community Found., 1973—; trustee RPI Found., 1971-78, pres., 1976-78; bd. dirs. Richmond Symphony, Inc., 1963-66, hon. bd. dirs., 1966—; mem. Richmond City Sch. Bd., 1966-70; trustee, vice rector Richmond Profl. Inst. (name now Va. Commonwealth U.), 1962-68; mem. Va. State Commn. on Local Debt, 1962-73, chmn., 1970-73; bd. dirs. Retreat Hosp., 1961-68, Richmond C. of C., 1965-68, United Givers Fund, 1964-67, 70-73, Children's Home Soc. Va., 1960-76; pres. Children's Home Soc. Va., 1966-68; bd. dirs. Nat. Assn. Boys Clubs Am., 1972-75; bd. advisers Mus. Confederacy, 1977—; trustee Va.-Md. Bankers Sch., 1968-71; mem. fin. com. Historic Christ Ch. Fedn., 1981—; adv. trustee Greater Richmond Community Found., 1973—. Served to 1st lt. USAAF, 1943-45. Mem. Am. Bankers Assn. (mem. exec. com. state bank div. 1965-68), Soc. Colonial Wars, Va. Hist. Soc. Clubs: Forum, Richmond 100, Soixante Plus, Farmington Country, Commonwealth (past dir.), Country of Va. (past dir.); University (N.Y.C.)). Home: 72 Westham Green 300 Ridge Rd Richmond VA 23229 Office: PO Box 26363 Richmond VA 23260

HARRIS, HENRY UPHAM, JR., investment company executive. Vice chmn. Smith Barney, Harris, Upham and Co. Inc. Address: Smith Barney Harris Upham and Co Inc. 1345 Ave of Americas New York NY 10019 *

HARRIS, HENRY WILLIAM, physician; b. Catawba, N.C., Jan. 6, 1919; s. Henry William and Katie (Coulter) H.; m. Margaret Ann Roberts, Nov. 29, 1950; children: Henry William, John R., James P. B.A., U.N.C., 1940; M.D. cum laude, Harvard U., 1943. Diplomate: in pulmonary disease Am. Bd. Internal Medicine. Intern Harvard Med. Service, Boston City Hosp., 1944-45, asst. resident medicine, 1945-46; resident fellow Thorndike Meml. Lab., 1944, 46; resident chest service Bellevue Hosp., N.Y.C., 1947; staff physician Gunderson Clinic, LaCrosse, Wis., 1948-53; asst. prof. medicine U. Utah Coll. Medicine, 1955-59, asso. prof., 1959-60; chief pulmonary disease service VA Hosp., Salt Lake City, 1955-60; prof. chmn. dept. medicine Woman's Med. Coll. of Pa., 1960-67; chmn. dept. medicine Catholic Med. Center Bklyn. and Queens, 1967-70; asso. prof. clin. medicine N.Y.U. Sch. Medicine, 1969-70, prof., 1970—; acting dir. chest service Bellevue Hosp., N.Y.C., 1983—; attending Univ. Hosp., N.Y.C.; cons. VA Hosp., N.Y.C., Cath. Med. Center. Mem. editorial bd.: Annals of Internal Medicine, 1976-80; Contbr. articles to profl. publs. Bd. dirs. Am. Lung Assn., 1961-79, v.p., 1972-73; bd. dirs. N.Y. Lung Assn., v.p., 1983—; bd. dirs. Am. Bur. Med. Advancement in China., v.p., 1983—. Served to capt., M.C. AUS, 1953-55. Fellow A.C.P.; mem. Am. Thoracic Soc. (pres. 1962-63), N.Y. Acad. Sci., AAAS, N.Y. Acad. Medicine. Home: 14 Seabury Rd Garden City NY 11530 Office: Chest Service Bellevue Hosp 1st Ave and 27th St New York NY 10016

HARRIS, HENRY WOOD, cable TV executive; b. Raleigh, N.C., June 11, 1938; s. Henry W. and Charlotte Louise (Allen) H.; m. Mary Margaret Durham, June 10, 1960; children—Stephen Gregory, Charlotte Durham. B.S. in Bus. Adminstrn, U. N.C., 1960, M.B.A., 1964. Loan officer Trust Co. Bank, Atlanta, 1964-66; operating v.p. Cox Cable Communications Co., Atlanta, 1966-69, pres., 1969-79; exec. v.p. Cox Broadcasting Corp., Atlanta, 1977-79; pres. Metrovision, Inc., Atlanta, 1979—. Mem. lay adv. bd. Marist Sch.; deacon Peachtree Presbyterian Ch. Served with USMCR, 1960-63. Mem. Phi Beta Kappa, Phi Eta Sigma. Club: Capital City. Home: 1150 Angelo Ct Atlanta GA 30319 Office: 211 Perimeter Pkwy Suite 930 Atlanta GA 30346

HARRIS, HOLLIS LOYD, airline exec.; b. Carrollton, Ga., Nov. 25, 1931; s. Clarence L. and Nellie Ruth (Hardegree) H.; m. Joyce Entrekin, July 30, 1955; children—Patricia S., David L., Michael J. B.Aero. Engring., Ga. Inst. Tech., 1961. With Delta Air Lines, Inc., Atlanta, 1954—, asst. v.p. in-flight service dept., 1972-73, sr. v.p. passenger service, 1973—; trustee Delta Air Lines Found.; dir. Fayette State Bank, Fayette State Holding Co. Mem. exec. bd. Atlanta Area council Boy Scouts Am.; mem. nat. adv. council Nat. Multiple Sclerosis Soc. Served with AUS, 1951-54. Mem. AIAA, Ga. Archtl. and Engring. Soc. Presbyterian. Home: 405 Golf View Dr Peachtree City GA 30269 Office: Delta Air Lines Inc Hartsfield Atlanta Internat Airport Atlanta GA 30320

HARRIS, HOWARD HUNTER, oil company executive; b. Cushing, Okla., Dec. 7, 1924; s. Oscar Hunter and Gertie Lee (Stark) H.; m. Gwendolyne J. Moyers, Dec. 31, 1945; children: Howard Sidney, Rodney Craig. B.S. in Bus. Adminstrn., U. Okla., 1949, J.D., 1949; postgrad. in advt. mgmt., Stanford U., 1971. Atty. Emery & Harris, Cushing and Stillwater, Okla., 1949-50; staff atty. Sun Oil Co., Tusla, 1950-54; div. atty. Marathon Oil Co., Tusla, 1954-63; staff atty Marathon Internat. Oil Co., Findlay, Ohio, 1963-65; mgr. legal affairs Deutsche Marathon Petroleum Bnbh., Frankfurt and Munich, 1965-70; mktg. aty. and assoc. gen. counsel Marathon Oil Co., Findlay, Ohio, 1970-74, v.p. corp. external affairs, 1974—. Served with AUS, 1943-45. Decorated Bronze Star. Mem. Am. Petroleum Inst., ABA, Ohio Bar Assn., Okla. Bar Assn., Findlay Bar Assn., Order of Coif, Beta Gamma Sigma. Republican. Episcopalian. Lodges: Rotary (Findlay); Masons. Office: Marathon Oil Co 539 S Main St Findlay OH 45840

HARRIS, HUBERT LAMAR, association executive; b. Atlanta, July 15, 1943; s. Hubert Lmar and Jessie Marion (Ginn) H.; m. Joan Cole, Oct. 22, 1966; children: Hubert Lamar, III, Jonathan W., Christopher C. B.S. in Insdl. Mgmt, Ga. Inst. Tech., 1965; M.B.A., Ga. State U., 1973. Sales rep. Monsanto Co., St. Louis, 1965-69; v.p. Citizens & So. Nat. Bank, Atlanta, 1969-77; asst. dir. Office Mgmt. and Budget, Washington, 1977-80; exec. v.p. Associated Builders and Contractors, Washington, 1980—83; exec. dir. Internat. Assn. Fin. Planning, Inc., Atlanta, 1983—. Office: 5775 Peachtree Dunwoody Rd NE Suite 120-C Atlanta GA 30342

HARRIS, IRA WHITNEY, university dean, library educator; b. Ossining, N.Y., Apr. 14, 1924; s. Newton Willard and Aletha Emma (Comstock) H.; m. Alice May Dimon, Feb. 9, 1957; children: Deborah Lee, Alan Whitney. Student, U. Detroit, 1943-44, U. Pa. and Pa. Acad. Fine Arts, 1947-49; B.Indsl. Design, Pratt Inst., 1952; M.L.S., Rutgers U., 1957, Ph.D., 1966. Draftsman Otis Elevator Co., 1953-55; librarian trainee Newark Public Library, 1955-56, jr. librarian, 1957-58; asst. librarian N.J. Inst. Tech., 1958-62; instr. Grad. Sch. Library Service, Rutgers U., 1962-65; research asso. library U. Hawaii, 1965-66, dir. undergrad. library, 1966-69, asst. dean, 1969-75, acting dean, 1975-76, dean, 1976—; cons. library bldg. Contbr. articles to profl. publs. Mem. and conf. del. Citizen's Com. on Hawaii Constl. Conv., 1968. Served with U.S. Army, 1943-46. Council on Library Resources fellow, 1974. Mem. ALA (councilor 1972-77), Am. Soc. Info. Sci., Assn. Am. Library Schs., Hawaii Assn. Sch. Librarians, Hawaii Library Assn. (pres. 1970-71), Pacific Assn. Communications and Tech., Spl. Libraries Assn., Antique Automobile Club Am. Mem. United Ch. of Christ. Club: Elks. Research on patterns of library use and services, 1965-67, on computer-based reader services and ednl. requirements of librarians, 1974. Home: 3030 Felix St Honolulu HI 96816 Office: 2550 The Mall Honolulu HI 96822

HARRIS, IRVING, lawyer; b. Cin., May 23, 1927; s. Albert and Sadye H.; m. Selma Schottenstein, June 18, 1950; children: Jeffrey Philip, Jonathan Lindley, Lisa Ann. Undergrad. degree, U. Cin., 1948, LL.B., 1951. Partner firm Porter, Wright, Morris & Arthur, Cin.; spl. counsel to Atty. Gen. Ohio, 1963-71. Mem. Ohio Devel. Financing Commn., 1974—, vice chmn., 1978-79; trustee Skidmore Coll., 1976—. Served with USN, 1945-46. Mem. Am. Bar Assn. (Sherman Act com., sect. on antitrust), Ohio Bar Assn., Cin. Bar Assn., Am. Judicature Soc., Newcomen Soc. Democrat. Clubs: Bankers, Camargo Hunt. Home: 18 Grandin Ln Cincinnati OH 45208 Office: Porter Wright Morris & Arthur 201 E 4th St Cincinnati OH 45202

HARRIS, IRVING BROOKS, cosmetic company executive; b. St. Paul, Aug. 4, 1910; s. William and Mildred (Brooks) H.; m. Joan White; children—Roxanne, Virginia, William. A.B., Yale, 1931. Exec. in finance business, 1931-42, aircraft part bus., 1944-46; exec. Toni Home Permanent Co., 1946—; (sold stockholdings in Toni Co. to Gillette Safety Razor Co.), 1948; dir. Gillette Safety Razor Co., 1948-60; exec. v.p. Toni Co., 1946-52; chmn. bd. Sci. Research Assos., 1953-58; pres. Michael Reese Hosp. and Med. Center, Chgo., 1958-61, Harris Group, Inc., 1959-76; pres., dir. Standard Shares; chmn. bd. Pittway Corp.; dir. Brand Insulation, Inc. Trustee U. Chgo., Nat. Center Clin. Infant Programs, Chgo. Inst. Psychoanalysis, Chgo. Ednl. TV Assn.; chmn. Family Focus, Harris Found.; pres. Erikson Inst. Served with Bd. Econ. Warfare OPA, 1942-44. Clubs: Standard, Lake Shore Country, Midday, Saddle and Cycle (Chgo.). Office: Suite 1320 120 S LaSalle St Chicago IL 60603

HARRIS, ISAAC HENSON, university dean emeritus; b. Farmington, Ky., Dec. 12, 1912; s. Nat L. and Chiron (Hargrove) H.; m. Beatrice Larue Russell, Nov. 17, 1934; children: Janis Larue, Robert Lynn. B.S., Murray (Ky.) State Coll., 1934; M.A., Vanderbilt U., 1941; postgrad., U. Ill., 1946-47; Ed.D., U. Okla., 1953. Tchr. math. pub. schs., Okaloosa County, Fla., 1935-40; head math. dept. Campbell Coll., Buies Creek, N.C., 1941-42; instr. math. U. Tenn., 1946, U. Ill., 1946-47; prof. math., head dept. Okla. Baptist U., Shawnee, 1947-54; dean Wayland Coll., Plainview, Tex., 1954-57; adminstrv. v.p., dean Georgetown (Ky.) Coll., 1957-63; dean Slippery Rock (Pa.) State Coll., 1962-65; exec. v.p. Union U., Jackson, Tenn., 1965-66; v.p. acad. affairs Culver-Stockton Coll., Canton, Mo., 1966-80, dean emeritus, 1980—; acad. dean Midcontinent Bapt. Coll., 1981-83. Served to capt. USAAF, 1942-46. Mem. Am. Math Soc., Pi Mu Epsilon. Baptist. Clubs: Elk, Kiwanian. Home: Whispering Oaks Circle Route 1 Mayfield KY 42066

HARRIS, J(ACOB) GEORGE, health care company executive; b. Gastonia, N.C., Sept. 5, 1938; s. James A. and Carolyn (Hord) H.; m. Sondra Gilbert, Mar. 29, 1959; children: Cynthia, Susan, David. B.A. in Math, Duke U., 1960. With Am. Hosp. Supply Corp., 1960—, region mgr., South San Francisco, 1964-67, gen. mgr., Port Credit, Ont., Can., 1967-70, v.p. ops., Evanston, Ill., 1970-71, pres. dietary products div., McGaw Park, Ill., 1971-74, corp. v.p., Evanston, 1974-78, exec. v.p., 1978-84; chmn. chief exec. officer Health Group Inc., Nashville, 1984—; dir. Union Spl. Corp., Chgo. Bd. dirs. Highland Park (Ill.) Hosp., 1981—; trustee McCormick Sem., Chgo. Clubs: Tennaqua, Racquet. Home: 580 Standish Dr Deerfield IL 60015 Office: One American Plaza Evanston IL 60201

HARRIS, JAMES DEXTER, lawyer; b. Denver, Mar. 25, 1919; s. Rush O. and Mae (Smith) H.; m. Suzanne Parker Harris, Sept. 13, 1975; children by previous marriage: James Dexter, Jane, Laura, George Robert. B.S., U. Kans., 1940; LL.B., Stanford U., 1948. Bar: Calif. 1948. Since practiced in, Los Angeles; asso. firm Forster & Gemmill, Los Angeles, 1948-50, Meserve, Mumper & Hughes, 1950-54; chief counsel Fluor Corp., Ltd., 1954-56, v.p., gen. counsel, 1956-67; former ptnr. Voegelin, Barton, Harris & Callister, and Harris, Noble, Campbell & Uhler, Harris & Donovan; of counsel Witter & Harpole; Adv. bd. Internat. Comparative Law Center, Southwestern Legal Found. Served 2d lt. to maj. USMC, 1940-45; lt. col., Res. (ret.). Mem. Internat., Am., Los Angeles bar assns., State Bar Calif., Los Angeles World Affairs Council, Los Angeles County Mus. Assn., Am. Legion, S.A.R., Japan Am. Soc., Town Hall Calif., Phi Gamma Delta, Phi Delta Phi, Delta Sigma Pi. Republican. Congregationalist. Clubs: California, Valley Hunt, Los Caballeros, Flintridge Riding, Rancheros Visitadores.; Stock Exchange, Round Table (Los Angeles). Lodge: Masons. Home: 830 Hillside Terr Pasadena CA 91105 also 1363 Plaza Pacifica Montecito CA 93103 also 1277 Riverside Dr S Palm Springs CA 92262 Office: 350 S Figueroa St Suite 2707 Los Angeles CA 90071

HARRIS, JAMES FRANKLIN, educator; b. Nashville, June 30, 1941; s. James F. and Martha Belle (Elder) H.; m. Marged Griffith, Aug. 4, 1978; 1 son by previous marriage, James F. B.A., U. Ga., 1962, M.A., 1964; Ph.D., Vanderbilt U., 1966. Asst. prof. philosophy Transylvania Coll., Lexington, Ky., 1966-67, U. Ga., Athena, 1967-73; assoc. prof. philosopy Coll. William and Mary, Williamsburg, Va., 1973-78, prof., 1978—, Haserdt prof. of philosophy, 1984—; vis. instr. Inst. Higher Edn., U. Ga., Athens, 1967, 68; cons. Nat. Ctr. for State Cts., Williamsburg, 1978. Editor: Analyticity, 1970; author monographs in field. Fellow Am. Council Learned Soc. Mem. AAUP, Am. Philos. Assn., So. Soc. fro Philosophy and Psychology (Jr. award 1969), Soc. for Philosophy of Religion, Phi Beta Kappa. Democrat. Home: Star Route 449 Toano VA 23168 Office: Dept Philosophy Coll of William and Mary Williamsburg VA 23168

HARRIS, JEAN LOUISE, physician; b. Richmond, Va., Nov. 24, 1931; d. Vernon Joseph and Jean Louise (Pace) H.; m. Leslie John Ellis Jr., Sept. 25, 1955; children: Karen Denise, Pamela Diane, Cynthia Suzanne. B.S., Va. Union U., 1951; M.D., Med. Coll. Va., 1955; Sc.D. (hon.), U. Richmond, 1981. Intern Med. Coll. Va., Richmond, 1955-56; resident internal medicine, 1956-57, fellow, 1957-58; fellow, Strong Meml. Hosp.-U. Rochester (N.Y.) Sch. Medicine, 1958-60; research asso. Walter Reed Army Inst. Research, Washington, 1960-63; practice medicine specializing in internal medicine allergy, Washington, 1961-71; instr. medicine Howard U. Coll. Medicine, Washington, 1960-68, asst. prof. dept. community health practice, 1969-72; prof. family practice Med. Coll. Va., Va. Commonwealth U.; also dir. Center Community Health, 1972-77; sec. Human Resources, Commonwealth of Va., 1978-82; v.p. state mktg. programs Control Data Corp., 1982—; lectr. dept. med. care and hosps. Johns Hopkins, Balt., 1971-73; asst. clin. prof. dept. community medicine Charles R. Drew Postgrad. Med. Sch., Los Angeles, 1970-73; adj. asst. prof. dept. preventive and social medicine UCLA, 1970-72; chief bur. resources devel. D.C. Dept. Health, 1967-69; exec. dir. Nat. Med. Assn. Found., Washington, after 1970; Cons. div. health manpower intelligence HEW, 1969—; mem. recombinant DNA adv. com. HEW Public Health Service-NIH, 1979-82; vice chmn. Nat. Commn. on Alcoholism and Alcohol Related Diseases, 1980-82. Trustee U. Richmond. Recipient East End Civic Assn. award, 1955. Fellow Royal Soc. (Eng.); mem. Am. Pub. Health Assn., Richmond Med. Soc., Nat. Med. Assn., Am. Soc. Pub. Adminstrs., So. Inst. Human Resources (pres. 1980-81), Inst. Medicine/Nat. Acad. Scis., Beta Kappa Chi, Alpha Kappa Mu, Sigma Xi. Home: 3318 Chatham Rd Richmond VA 23237 Office: Control Data Corp 8100 34th Ave S Minneapolis MN 55440 *Life is an exciting continuum of choices. None of us is so fortunate as to always select the "best" among alternative options. Our true measure is taken by our ability to learn those lessons to be gained from each decision—whether "proper" or "improper"—and to push forward—always anticipating the next opportunity for choice as a welcome challenge upon which one builds the foundations of an interesting, exhilirating life.*

HARRIS, JEFFREY, lawyer, banker; b. Bklyn., Mar. 20, 1944; s. Herman and Pearl (Herman) H.; m. Joyce Rosa Meckler, June 22, 1975; 1 dau., Daniela Rose. B.S., NYU, 1965; J.D., Syracuse U., 1968. Bar: N.Y. 1969, U.S. Supreme Ct. 1976, D.C. 1977. Asst. U.S. atty. So. Dist. N.Y., U.S. Dept. Justice, N.Y.C., 1972-76, chief investigation rev. unit., 1976-77; dep. chief counsel U.S. Ho. of Reps., Korean Investigation, Washington, 1977-79; asst. dir. FTC, Washington, 1979-81; exec. dir. Atty. Gen.'s Task Force on Violent Crime, U.S. Dept. Justice, Washington, 1981; dep. assoc. atty. gen. U.S., Washington, 1981-83; sr. v.p. Capital Bank N.A., Washington, 1983—; sr. v.p., counsel Capital Bancorp, Miami, Fla., 1983—; instr. Advocacy Inst., U. Calif. Hastings Coll. Law, San Francisco, 1979-83; adj. asst. prof. George Washington U., Washington, 1980. Served to lt. (j.g.) USN, 1968-71. Named Meritorious Exec. Pres. of U.S.; recipient Spl. Commendation Atty. Gen. of U.S.; decorated Navy Commendation medal, Viet Nam Cross of Gallantry. Mem. ABA. Office: Captial Bank NA 815 Connecticut Ave NW Washington DC 20006

HARRIS, JEFFREY SHERMAN, medical management company executive; b. Boston, Aug. 18, 1944; s. Phillip Robert and Blanche Estell (Sherman) H.; m. Linda Braverman, Oct. 31, 1970; children: Penny, Samantha. B.S. in Bus. Adminstrn, Boston U., 1970. Field rep. ARC, Boston, 1970-72; emergency med. services project dir. Health Planning Council Greater Boston, 1972-75; office emergency med. services program mgr. Mass. Dept. Public Health, Boston, 1975-76; exec. dir. Nat. Assn. Emergency Med. Technicians, Waltham, Mass., 1977-81; pres., chief exec. officer, dir. ComSystems Technologies Inc., Hudson, Mass., 1980—. Assoc. editor: The EMT Jour, 1977-80; mem. editorial bd.: Emergency Med. Services Jour, 1978-81. Served with USN, 1967-70. Mem. Nat. Assn. EMTs (sec. 1975-77, Jeffrey S. Harris Nat. Leadership award 1980, A. Roger Fox Founders award 1981), Mass. Assn. EMTs (sec. 1973-75), Nat. Soc. EMT-Paramedics (founder), Nat. Soc. EMT Instructor/Coordinators (founder), Nat. Soc. Emergency Med. Service Adminstrs. (founder). Home: 79 Edgewater Dr Waltham MA 02154 Office: 176 Central St Hudson MA 01749

HARRIS, JEROME SYLVAN, physician, educator; b. N.Y.C., Feb. 27, 1909; s. Mark and Mary (Marcus) H.; m. Jacqueline Cato Hijmans, Oct. 23, 1958. A.B. summa cum laude, Dartmouth Coll., 1929; M.D. cum laude, Harvard U., 1933. Intern U. Chgo. Clinics, 1934; resident Boston Children's Hosp., 1935-36; mem. faculty Duke Sch. Medicine, Durham, N.C., 1937—, J. Buren Sidbury prof. pediatrics, also prof. biochemistry, 1950—; chmn. dept. pediatrics Duke Med. Center, 1954-68; Cons. Nat. Bd. Med. Examiners, 1956-60; mem. human embryology and devel. study sect. NIH, 1959-63. Contbr. articles to profl. jours. Bd. dirs. Durham Child Guidance Clinic, 1950-54. Served to lt. col. M.C. AUS, 1942-46. Mem. Am. Soc. Clin. Investigation, Soc. Pediatric Research, Am. Acad. Pediatrics, Am. Pediatrics Soc., So. Soc. Pediatric Research, Phi Beta Kappa, Sigma Xi, Alpha Omega Alpha. Office: Duke Hospital Durham NC 27710

HARRIS, JESSE GRAHAM, JR., psychologist, educator; b. Jacksonville, Fla., Jan. 5, 1926; s. Jesse Graham and Mona (Woods) H.; m. Julia Patricia McNamee, Sept. 5, 1953; children: Julia Kathleen, Cecilia Anne. B.A., Harvard U., 1946; Ph.D., Duke U., 1955. Diplomate: Am. Bd. Examiners Profl. Psychology. Asst. prof. psychology U. Conn., 1958-60; asso. prof., dir. psychology, dept. psychiatry U. Ky. Med. Center, 1960-63; prof. psychology U. Ky., 1963—, chmn. dept., 1963-67, 80—, dir. clin. tng., 1963-67, 69-75, chmn. faculty council Coll. Arts and Scis., 1978-79; vis. lectr. U. Hawaii, 1968; cons. USPHS Hosp., Lexington, 1961-72, VA hosps. in Ky., 1962—, Peace Corps, 1968-75; field selection officer, 1968-70, tng. devel. officer, 1970, cons. in research and placement, 1970-75; Chmn. Ky. Mental Health Manpower Commn., 1971-74; mem. Ky. Bd. Examiners of Psychologists, 1966-75, chmn. bd., 1970-75; chmn. adv. tng. council for psychology for Midwestern region VA, 1972. Adv. editor: Jour. Cons. and Clin. Psychology, 1970—; Contbr. articles to profl. jours., chpts. to books. Bd. dirs., v.p., mem. artists com. Central Ky. Concert and Lecture Series, 1960—; chmn. bd. dirs. Ky. Manpower Devel., Inc., 1974-78; leader forum, 1976; elder 2d Presbyn. Ch., Lexington. Served to lt. USNR, 1955-58; capt. Res. Sr. fellow Culture Learning Inst. East-West Center, Honolulu, 1975. Fellow Am. Psychol. Assn.; mem. Southeastern Psychol. Assn., Ky. Psychol. Assn. (pres. 1979-80, disting. service award 1983), Central Ky. Psychol. Assn. (pres. 1962), Western Fla. Psychol. Assn. (pres. 1957), Midwestern Psychol. Assn., Phi Beta Kappa (pres. U. Ky. chpt. 1972-73), Sigma Xi. Home: 3356 Bellefonte Dr Lexington KY 40502

HARRIS, JOE FRANK, governor Georgia; b. Cartersville, Ga., Feb. 16, 1936; s. Grove Franklin and Frances (Morrow) H.; m. Elizabeth Carlock Harris, June 25, 1961; 1 son. Joe Frank, Jr. B.B.A., U. Ga., 1958; LL.D. hon., Asbury Coll., 1983, Woodrow Wilson Coll. Law, 1981. Sec.-treas. Harris Cement Products, Inc., Cartersville, 1958-79; pres. Harris Georgia Corp., Cartersville, 1979-83; mem. Ga. Gen. Assembly, 1965-83; gov. State of Ga., 1983—. Served with U.S. Army, 1958. Democrat. Methodist. Home: 391 W Paces Ferry Rd NW Atlanta GA 30305 Office: State Capital Atlanta GA 30334

HARRIS, JOHN CHARLES, agriculturalist; b. Fresno, Calif., July 14, 1943; s. Jack A. and Theresa Elizabeth (McManus) H.; m. Carole Lynn Glotz, Dec. 28, 1965. B.S., U. Calif.-Davis, 1965. Exec. v.p. Harris Farms Inc., Coalinga, Calif., 1968-81, pres., 1981—; sec., dir. Calif. Thoroughbred Breeders Assn., Arcadia, Calif., 1975—, Calif. Westside Farmers, Fresno; vice chmn., dir. Calif. Beef Council, Foster City, 1981—; dir. Calif. Cattle Feeders Assn., Bakersfield. Bd. dirs. Valley Children's Hosp. Found., Fresno, 1982—, Calif. State U. Fresno Agrl. Found., 1982—, Friends of Channel 18 Sta. KMTF Pub. TV, Fresno, 1982—, Calif. Aggie Found., Davis, 1983—; state chmn. Pete Wilson for U.S. Senate, Calif., 1982. Served to 1st lt. U.S. Army, 1966-68. Mem. Young Pres.'s Orgn. Republican. Clubs: Lions (Five Points. Calif.); Chancellors (Davis, Calif.). Home: Route 1 Box 420 Coalinga CA 93210 Office: Harris Farms Inc Route 1 Box 420 Coalinga CA 93210

HARRIS, JOHN WILLIAM, physician, educator; b. Boston, Mar. 30, 1920; s. Ulysses Sylvester and Lillian (Dennett) H.; m. Stephanie Jean Bunting, Apr. 7, 1951; children: Wendy Alexandra, Alison Dennett, Stephen Bunting. B.S., Trinity Coll., Hartford, Conn., 1941; M.D., Harvard, 1944. Intern Boston City Hosp., 1944-45, resident, 1947-48; research fellow medicine Thorndike Meml. Lab., Harvard Med. Sch., 1948-51, research asso., 1951-52; sr. instr. medicine Western Res. U., Cleve., 1952-54, asst. prof., 1954-57, asso. prof., 1957-62, prof., 1962—; hematologist, vis. physician Cleve. Met. Gen. Hosp., 1952—, asso. dir. dept. medicine, 1967-81; attending physician VA Hosp., Cleve., 1953-58, sr. attending physician hematology, 1959—; cons. staff Lutheran Hosp., 1965—; mem. hematology study sect. NIH, 1962-66, mem. hematology tng. grants com., 1969-73; mem. com. blood and transfusion Nat. Acad. Scis.-NRC, 1963-65. Served to capt. U.S. Army, 1945-47. Recipient USPHS Research Career award, 1962, Martin Luther King, Jr. award for outstanding research in sickle cell anemia, 1972; Alfred Stengel Research fellow ACP, 1951-52; Markle scholar in medicine, 1955-60. Mem. Am. Fedn. Clin. Research, Am. Soc. Clin. Investigation (past v.p.), Central Soc. Clin. Research, Soc. Exptl. Biology and Medicine, Am. Soc. Hematology, A.C.P., Acad. Medicine Cleve., Assn. Am. Physicians, Phi Beta Kappa, Alpha Omega Alpha. Home: 3080 Coleridge Rd Cleveland Heights OH 44118 Office: 3395 Scranton Rd Cleveland OH 44109

HARRIS, JULIAN HOKE, sculptor; b. Carrollton, Ga., Aug. 22, 1906; s. Joseph H. and Margaret Myra (Kennedy) H.; m. Jean Sawyer Fambrough, Dec. 18, 1938; children—Jean Olivia Harris Wight, Judy Anne Harris Kirbow. B.S. in Architecture, Ga. Inst. Tech., 1928; studied sculpture, Pa. Acad. Fine Arts, 1930-33. Lic. architect, Ga. Draftsman Henz, Adler and Shutze, Atlanta, 1928-29; asst. designer Marye, Alger & Vinour, 1929; lectr., prof. of architecture Ga. Inst. Tech., 1936-70, prof. emeritus, 1970—; prof. Atlanta Art Inst., 1946-52. Free lance sculptor, Atlanta; art dir., Fed. Theatre, Atlanta, 1936-37; designed and executed: sculpture numerous pub. bldgs., including Commerce Bldg, Atlanta, Speech and Hearing Center, Nashville, also meml., portrait commns., including heroic bronze of, John Wesley, Buckhannon, W.Va., U. Va. Sesquicentennial, Sidney Lanier medallion for, Hall of Fame, N.Y. U., Joel C. Harris for, Soc. Medalists, 50th Anniversary medallion, Fox Theatre, Atlanta, 1980, one man shows, Atlanta Art Center, works exhibited, Jewish Mus., N.Y.C., Pa. Acad. Fine Arts, Mus. Modern Art, Rockefeller Center, N.Y. World's Fair, Nat. Sculpture Soc. Bas Relief Exhbn., medallions for, Monie A. Ferst award, 1976, campaign medal, inaugural medal for pres. elect, Jimmy Carter, 1976, portrait tablets, Pitts Meml. Library, Emory U., Atlanta, 1976, Fred B. Wenn, Georgia Inst. Tech., Atlanta. Served from 1st lt. to maj. USAAF, 1942-45. Recipient Edgar Tobin award So. States Art League, 1939; 1st prize sculpture Tri-County Exhbn., Atlanta, 1940; Nat. Art Week in Ga., 1951; Fine Arts medal AIA, 1954; Ivan Allen award Ga. chpt. AIA, 1961; Ga. Gov.'s award in arts, 1980; award of excellence in sculpture Atlanta Urban Design Commn., 1980; St. Paul medal Archbishop Greek Orthodox Ch. N. and S. Am., 1980; Henry Hering Meml. award Nat. Sculpture Soc., 1980; winner nat. competition for medallion to commemorate 40th Anniversary of Soc. Medalists, 1970. Fellow Nat. Sculpture Soc., AIA; mem. N.A.D. (academician), Atlanta Art Assn. (v.p. 1952-55), Studio Club Atlanta (pres. 1939-41), Assn. Ga. Artists (pres. 1935-36). Clubs: Piedmont Driving, Rotary. Home: 177 5th St NW Atlanta GA 30313

HARRIS, JULIE, actress; b. Grosse Pointe Park, Mich., Dec. 2, 1925; d. William Pickett and Elsie (Smith) H.; m. Jay I. Julien, Aug. 12, 1946; m. Manning Gurian, Oct. 21, 1954; 1 son, Peter; m. Erwin Carroll. Student, Perry Mansfield Theatre Work Shop, 1941-43, Yale Drama Sch., 1945. Appeared in: plays Sundown Beach, 1948, The Young and Fair, 1948-49, Magnolia Alley, 1949, Montserrat, 1949, The Member of the Wedding, 1950-51, I Am a Camera, 1951-52; film, 1956, The Lark, 1956, Little Moon of Alban, 1960, A Shot in the Dark, 1961, Marathon 33, 1964, Ready When You Are, C.B, 1964, Break a Leg, 1979; tour, Broadway The Warm Peninsula; appeared in: Skyscraper, 1965, Harper, 1966, And Miss Reardon Drinks A Little, 1971, Voices, 1972, The Last of Mrs. Lincoln, 1973, In Praise of Love, 1974, The Belle of Amherst, 1976; motion pictures Poacher's Daughter, 1960, The Haunting, The Moving Target, Voyage of the Damned, 1976, The Bell Jar, 1979; TV movie The Gift, 1979; (Grammy award for the Bells of Amherst 1977). Recipient Antoinette Perry award for East of Eden, 1956, best actress in Forty Carats, 1969, for The Last of Mrs. Lincoln, 1973. Address: care William Morris Agy 151 El Camino Blvd Beverly Hills CA 90212 *

HARRIS, K. DAVID, justice Iowa Supreme Ct.; b. Jefferson, Iowa, July 29, 1927; s. Orville W. and Jessie Heloise (Smart) H.; m. Madonna Theresa Coyne, Sept. 4, 1948; children—Jane Ann, Julia Heloise, Frederick Thomas. B.A., U. Iowa, 1949, J.D., 1951. Bar: Iowa bar 1951. Practiced in, Jefferson, Iowa, 1951-62, county atty., Greene County, Iowa, 1959-62; judge 16th Dist. Ct., Iowa, 1962-72; asso. justice Supreme Ct. Iowa, Des Moines, 1972—. Contbr. verse to mags. Served with AUS, 1944-46. Home: 507 W Harrison St Jefferson IA 50129 Office: Statehouse Des Moines IA 50319

HARRIS, LEONARD R., newspaper publishing company executive; b. N.Y.C., Oct. 16, 1922; m. Barbara Fox, 1949; 1 dau., Elizabeth V.A. Brown. Student, N.Y. U., Cornell, 1939-42; B.A., McGill U., 1947. Formerly dir. promotion, mem. editorial bd. Prentice Hall, Inc.; then dir. new products Bantam Books; officer Book Club Guild and Channel Press, Inc.; also cons. new publishing projects N.Y. Times; v.p. editorial Ency. Britannica, Chgo., 1967-69, v.p. corporate devel., 1967-69; exec. v.p., pub. World Pub. Co., 1969-73; dir. projects subsidiaries N.Y. Times, 1973-77, dir. corporate devel., 1977-80, dir. corp. relations and public affairs, 1980—. Contbr. to: numerous mags. Ency. Brit. Bd. dirs. N.Y. Conv. and Visitors Bur., Broadway Assn., Mayor's Midtown Com.; chmn. N.Y. State Newspapers Found. Served as sgt. AUS, 1943-46. Mem. N.Y. C. of C. Democrat. Clubs: Lotos, Players. Home: 300 Central Park West New York NY 10024

HARRIS, LOUIS, public opinion analyst, columnist; b. New Haven, Jan. 6, 1921; s. Harry and Frances (Smith) H.; m. Florence Yard, June 16, 1943; children: Susan, Peter, Richard. A.B. in Econs., U. N.C., 1942. With Elmo Roper and Assocs., 1946-56, partner, 1954-56; propr. Louis Harris and Assocs., Inc. (marketing and pub. opinion research), N.Y.C., 1956—; cons. CBS News, 1962-68, ABC News Nat. Polling Day, 1971—; columnist Washington Post, also Newsweek mag., 1963-68, Chgo. Tribune-N.Y. Daily News Syndicate, 1969—; dir. Time mag.-Harris Poll, 1969-72, Bus. Week-Harris Poll, 1982—; dir. Life Poll, 1969-71; faculty assoc. Columbia U., N.Y.C., 1953-64; adj. prof. polit. sci. U. N.C., 1964—; formerly v.p. Donaldson, Lufkin & Jenrette, N.Y.C., now dir. Author: Is There a Republican Majority?, 1954, (with William Brink) The Negro Revolution in America, 1964, Black and White, 1967, Black-Jewish Relations in New York City: The Anguish of Change, 1973, also numerous articles. Chmn. bd. dirs. Am. Councils for Arts, 1975-82; chmn. Nat. Research Center Arts, 1971—; vice chmn. bd. trustees Actors Studio, 1983—; bd. dirs. Eleanor Roosevelt Inst., 1983. Served as officer USNR, World War II. Mem. Am. Assn. Pub. Opinion (dir.), Am. Sociol. Assn., Am. Statis. Assn., Am. Mgmt. Assn., Am. Mktg. Assn., Am. Polit. Sci. Assn. Clubs: Century, Players. Office: Louis Harris & Assos 630 5th Ave New York NY 10020 *

HARRIS, MARK, educator, author; b. Mt. Vernon, N.Y., Nov. 19, 1922; s. Carlyle and Ruth (Klausner) Finkelstein; m. Josephine Horen, Mar. 17, 1946; children: Hester Jill, Anthony Wynn, Henry Adam. B.A., U. Denver, 1950, M.A., 1951; Ph.D., U. Minn., 1956; L.H.D., Ill. Wesleyan U., 1974. Reporter Port Chester (N.Y.) Item, 1944, PM, N.Y.C., 1945, I.N.S., St. Louis, 1945-46; prof. English San Francisco State Coll., 1954-68, Purdue U., 1967-70; mem. faculty Calif. Inst. Arts, Valencia, 1970-73, Immaculate Heart Coll., Los Angeles, 1973-74, U. So. Calif., 1973-75, U. Pitts., 1975—; Vis. prof. Brandeis U., 1963. Author: Trumpet to the World, 1946, City of Discontent, 1952, The Southpaw, 1953, Bang the Drum Slowly, 1956, Something About a Soldier, 1957, A Ticket for a Seamstitch, 1957, Wake Up, Stupid, 1959; play Friedman & Son, 1963, Mark the Glove Boy, 1964, Twentyone Twice: A Journal, 1966, The Goy, 1970, Killing Everybody, 1973, Best Father Ever Invented: Autobiography, 1976, It Looked Like For Ever, 1979, Saul Bellow: Drumlin Wdodchuck, 1980; also essays, articles, stories. Mem. San Francisco Art Commn., 1961-64. Served with AUS, 1943-44. Recipient award Nat. Inst. Arts and Letters, 1961; Fulbright prof., Japan, 1957; Ford grantee, 1960; Guggenheim Found. fellow, 1965, 74; numerous other invitations and awards. Home: 5801 Northumberland St Pittsburgh PA 15217 Office: Dept English Ariz State U Tempe AZ 85281 *I don't know if I have "present success." Success may lie in despising the usual ideas of success. I have been fortunate only. Success would mean enabling everyone else to be as fortunate. We must distribute the world's goods a great deal better than we do. We must focus not on gain, but on ending war. Only then can we even begin to think of such luxuries as success."*

HARRIS, MARKHAM, author, educator; b. N.Y.C., Jan. 2, 1907; s. Gibson William and Helen Taylor (Markham) H.; m. Phyllis Kathleen Pier, Aug. 29, 1959; children—Jeremy, Laurence, Timothy, Geoffrey. A.B., Williams Coll., 1929, M.A., 1931; postgrad., Columbia, 1934-35. Instr. pub. speaking and debate Whitman Coll., 1929-30, asst. prof., 1930-31; instr. English Williams Coll., 1931-34; editor, pres. Dingwall-Rock Ltd. (pub.), N.Y.C., 1935-36; editor, mgr., asst. v.p. Grolier Inc. (pub.), N.Y.C., 1936-43; instr. English U. Wash., 1946-47, asst. prof., 1947-57, asso. prof., 1957-70, prof., 1970—. Author: The Case for Tragedy, 1932, 2d edit., 1973, High Morning Fog, 1952; contbg. author: Story, 1939, Ency. Americana, 1937-56; translator: The Cornish Ordinalia, 1969, the Life of Meriasek, 1977; Contbr. articles and stories to lit. jours., popular mags. Served to lt. USNR, 1944-46. Mem. A.A.U.P., Zeta Psi, Delta Sigma Rho. Home: 3507 NE 43d St Seattle WA 98105

HARRIS, MARTIN HARVEY, aerospace company executive; b. N.Y.C., Mar. 14, 1932; s. Leo and Gertrude (Litt) H.; m. Patricia Ann Franklin, Apr. 27, 1970; children (by previous marriage): Lori Kathryn, Barbara Ann. B.Aero. Engring., N.Y. U., 1953; M.S. in Systems Mgmt, U. So. Calif., 1973. With Curtis-Wright Corp., Woodbridge, N.J., 1952-53; ops. analyst Martin Marietta Corp., Denver, 1957-58, dir. devel. programs, Orlando, Fla., 1958—. Contbr. articles to profl. publs. Trustee Aerospace Edn. Found. Served with USAF, 1953-57; col. Res. Mem. Air Force Assn. (nat. sec. 1971-76, dir. 1965—, named Nat. Man of Yr. 1972, Fla. Man of Yr. 1977, 79), Am. Ordnance Assn. (pres. Fla. Peninsula chpt. 1973-74, dir. 1968-80, nat. v.p. 1977-79), Orlando Area C. of C., AIAA, Am. Helicopter Soc., Am. Mgmt. Assn., Res. Officers Assn. Patentee in field. Home: 2845 Summerfield Rd Winter Park FL 32792 Office: PO Box 5837 MP-48 Orlando FL 32855

HARRIS, MARVIN, anthropology educator, author; b. Bklyn., Aug. 18, 1927; s. Irving and Sadie (Newman) H.; m. Madeline Grove, Jan. 25, 1953; children: Robert Eric (dec.), Susan Lynn. A.B., Columbia U., 1949, Ph.D., 1953. Mem. faculty Columbia U., 1952-81, prof.

anthropology, chmn. dept., 1963-66; grad. research prof. anthropology U. Fla., Gainesville, 1981—; tech. adviser Ministry Edn. Brazil, 1953; exec. sec. Columbia-Cornell-Harvard-Ill. summer field studies program, 1960-66. Author: Town and Country in Brazil, 1956, (with Charles Wagley) Minorities in the New World, 1958, Patterns of Race in the Americas, 1964, The Nature of Cultural Things, 1964, The Rise of Anthropological Theory, 1968, Culture, Man and Nature, 1971, Cows, Pigs, Wars and Witches: The Riddles of Culture, 1974, Culture, People, Nature, 1975, Cannibals and Kings: The Origin of Cultures, 1977, Cultural Materialism: The Struggle for a Science of Culture, 1979, Culture, People, Nature, 1980, America Now: Why Nothing Works, 1981, Cultural Anthropology, 1983. Served with AUS, 1945-47. Mem. Am. Anthrop. Assn., AAAS. Home: 1511 NW 38th St Gainesville FL 32605 Office: Dept Anthropology U Fla Gainesville FL 32611

HARRIS, MILTON, chemist; b. Los Angeles, Mar. 21, 1906; s. Louis and Naomi (Granish) H.; m. Carolyn Wolf, Mar. 30, 1934; children: Barney Dreyfuss (adopted), John. B.Sc., Oreg. State Coll., 1926; Ph.D., Yale, 1929; Dr. Textile Sci., Phila. Textile Inst., 1955. Research asso. Am. Assn. Textile Chemists and Colorists, Nat. Bur. Standards, 1931-39; dir. research Textile Found., 1939-45; pres. and founder Harris Research Labs., 1945-61; dir. research Gillette Co. (its subsidiaries), 1956-66, v.p. corp., 1957-66; dir., chmn. exec. com. Sealectro Corp.; dir. Warner Lambert Co.; adv. bd. Jour. Polymer Sci.; asso. editor Textile Research Jour.; cons. Exec. Office of Pres., Office Sci. and Technology, 1962-65; Adv. bd., cons. O.Q.M.G., World War II; chmn. com. on textiles and cordage, tropical deterioration project Nat. Def. Research Com.; sec. com. on clothing NRC, World War II; chmn. Wool Conservation Bd., World War II; mem. panel on clothing Research and Devel. Bd., World War II; mem. Yale Council, 1964-69, Yale Devel. Bd., 1964-67; exec. bd. Yale Grad. Sch. Assn., 1965—; mem. adv. com. Nat. Bur. Standards, 1971—, chmn. vis. com., 1973—; mem. sub-com. Food and Agrl. Orgn. UN; mem. Utilization research and devel. adv. com. U.S. Dept. Agr., 1966—; mem. adv. com. planning NSF, 1968—; mem. Pres.'s Sci. Adv. Com. Panel on Environment, 1968—; observer-cons. Task Group Nat. Systems Sci. and Tech. Information, Fed. Council Sci. and Tech., 1968—. Contbr. articles to tech. jours.; Editor: Chemistry in the U.S. Economy. Trustee Phila. Textile Inst., 1956-60; dir. Dermatology Found., Textile Research Inst.; bd. dirs. Sci. Service, Acorn Fund, Chgo. Recipient award Wash. Acad. Sci., 1943, Olney medal for textile chemistry research, 1945; honor award Am. Inst. Chemists, 1957; Harold DeWitt Smith Meml. medal, 1966; Distinguished Service award Oreg. State U., 1967; Perkin Medal award Soc. Chem. Industry, 1970; Wilbur Lucius Cross medal Yale, 1974; award for meritorious service Yale Sci. and Engring. Assn., 1983. Fellow Textile Inst., N.Y. Acad. Sci.; mem. Am. Assn. Textile Tech., Yale Chemists Assn. (past pres.), Am. Soc. Biol. Chemists, Nat. Acad. Engring., Am. Inst. Chemists (pres. 1960-61, Gold medal 1981), N.A.M., Textile Research Inst., Am. Assn. Textile Colorists and Chemists, Am. Oil Chemists Soc., Soc. Cosmetic Chemists, Fiber Soc. (hon.), Am. Chem. Soc. (chmn. bd. dirs. 1966-70, dir.-at-large, treas. 1973—, Priestley medal 1980), AAAS (editorial bd. publ. Sci. 1968-70), Soc. Chem. Industry, Wash. Acad. Sci., Sigma Xi, Tau Beta Pi, Phi Lambda Upsilon, Phi Kappa Phi, Gamma Alpha. Clubs: Cosmos (Washington); Chemists (N.Y.C.). Home: 4101 Linnean Ave Washington DC 20008 Office: 3300 Whitehaven St NW Washington DC 20007

HARRIS, MILTON M., distbg. co. exec.; b. San Francisco, Sept. 6, 1916; s. A.H. and Rebecca (Harris) H.; m. Lorraine D. Love, July 3, 1938; 1 son, Jerrold B. Ed. pub. schs. With Braun-Knecht-Heimann Co., San Francisco, 1933-60, v.p., 1951-60; (co. acquired by Van Waters & Rogers, Inc. (now Univar Corp.), San Francisco, 1960, sr. v.p., gen. mgr., 1960-61, pres., 1962-66, chmn., 1966-70, vice chmn., 1970—, also dir.; dir. Deep Water Chem. Co. Clubs: Cercle de l'Union, Olympic, Lakeside Country (San Francisco). Home: 50 Falkirk Ln Hillsborough CA 94010 Office: 1600 Norton Bldg Seattle WA 98104

HARRIS, MORGAN, educator; b. St. Anthony, Idaho, May 25, 1916; s. Archibald Overton and Augusta Pearl (Lewelling) H.; m. Marjorie Ruth Mason, Aug. 10, 1940; children—Roger Mason, Ronald Morgan. A.B. with highest honors, U. Calif. at Berkeley, 1938, Ph.D., 1941; George Leib Harrison postdoctoral research fellow, U. Pa., 1941-42; Merck sr. postdoctoral fellow, U. Paris, 1953-54. Teaching asst. dept. zoology U. Calif. at Berkeley, 1938-41, instr. zoology, 1945-46, asst. prof., 1946-50, asso. prof., 1950-56, prof., 1956—, vice chmn. zoology, 1952-57, chmn., 1957-63, Miller research prof., 1963-65; research asst. dept. biology Stanford, 1942-44; instr. zoology U. Wash., 1944-45; Research aviation physiology OSRD, 1942-44; mem. cell biology study sect., div. research grants NIH, 1958-60, 61-63, mem. nat. adv. gen. med. scis. council, 1963-65. Author: Cell Culture and Somatic Variation, 1964, also research papers. Guggenheim fellow, Cambridge, Eng., 1960-61. Mem. Tissue Culture Assn. (pres. 1958-60), Soc. Gen. Physiologists, Internat. Soc. Cell Biology (exec. com. 1964-72, treas. 1968-72), Am. Soc. Cell Biology (mem. exec. council 1964-68), Soc. for Growth and Devel., Internat. Fedn. for Cell Biology (exec. com. 1972-76), Am. Soc. Zoologists, Phi Beta Kappa, Sigma Xi, Phi Sigma (Scholarship medal 1937-38). Clubs: American Alpine (N.Y.C.); Sierra (Calif.). Home: 605 Plateau Dr Berkeley CA 94708

HARRIS, N. NEIL, editor; b. Lafayette, Ind., June 9, 1940; s. Cecil Worth and Ardis Jane (Davis) H.; m. Jennifer S. Helzberg; children—Nadine Ann, Nina Ann. Grad., high sch., Am. Sch. Photography. Asst. display mgr. Loeb's Inc., Lafayette, 1958-61; display asst. May Co., Redondo Beach, Calif., 1961-62; asst. historian Am. Numismatic Assn., Colorado Springs, Colo., 1969-70, historian, 1971-76, editor, 1974—. Artist, photographer, silkscreen, Nortronics Co., 1962; layout artist, profl. asst. med. illustrator, Purdue U., 1963-73; Author: Badges and Medals of the American Numismatic Association 1908-1969, 1969; co-author; illustrator: Fundamental Techniques in Veterinary Medicine, 1975; illustrator: Anatomy of the Dog, 1964; editor: Medals of the United States Mint, The First Century, 1792-1892, 1977, California Tokens, 1977, The Numismatist (recipient best writer award Numismatic Literary Guild 1973); Designer medals, Ind. State Numismatic Assn., 1965, 72; designer sculptor, 1973-76, 75th Anniversary medal, Med. Library Assn., 1975, Am. Numismatic Assn. Convention medal, 1977-78, 80. Mem. Token and Medal Soc. (dir. 1970-77, asso. book editor 1971-72, book editor 1972-77, 1st v.p. 1976-77, 77-78, 2d v.p. 1978-79, 79-80, pres. 1980-82), Ind. Numismatic Assn. (officer 1967-72, pres. 1973-74, hon. life mem., recipient 1st ann. founder's award 1971), Lafayette Numismatic Soc. (sec., dir. 1964-68, hon. life), Am. Numismatic Assn. (recipient Burton Saxton award 1969, medal of merit award 1980). Office: PO Box 2366 Colorado Springs CO 80901

HARRIS, NEISON, corp. exec.; b. St. Paul, Jan. 24, 1915; s. William and Mildred (Brooks) H.; m. Bette Deutsch, Jan. 25, 1939; children: Katherine, King, Toni. A.B., Yale U., 1936. Founder Toni Co.; pres. Toni div. Gillette Co.; pres. Paper Mate div.; dir. Gillette Co.; now chmn. bd., chief exec. officer, dir. Pittway Corp.; chmn. bd., chmn. exec. com., dir. Standard Shares, Inc. Named 1 of 10 outstanding young men U.S. Jr. C. of C., 1948. Clubs: Standard, Lake Shore Country (Chgo.); Boca Rio Country. Office: 333 Skokie Blvd Northbrook IL 60062

HARRIS, NELL, public relations executive, real estate executive; b. Palestine, Tex.; d. Thomas Jefferson and Nellie (Hester) H.; m. Charles Y. Swartz (div. Mar. 1947); children—Charles Harris, Mary Nell (Mrs. Charles E. Richards Jr.), Thomas Byrne; m. Bruce Stone, Jan. 12, 1952 (div. May 1963). A.B., Rice U.; student, Baylor U. Coll. Medicine, 1943-45; postgrad., Mayo Clinic, U. Minn., 1945; certificate phys. therapy, U. Tex., 1947; student hosp. adminstrn., U. Chgo., 1948, 50. Formerly engaged in rehab. handicapped children; established Hedgecroft Clinic for complete treatment handicapped, Houston, 1942, owner, 1942-48, 1948, chmn. bd., dir., 1948-51, exec. dir., trustee, 1951-58, dir., trustee, 1958-62; (center gen. rehab.), cons. orgn. and operation health and hosp. facilities, 1962-64, free-lance counselor pub. relations and advt., after 1964; pres. Hosp. Adv. Services, Inc., 1962—, Nell Harris Assos., Inc. (theatre and concert mgmt.); real estate broker investment and comml. properties. Contbr. articles to profl. publs., fiction to mags. Trustee Hedgecroft Hosp; sponsor Houston Pin Oaks Charity Horse Show Assn.; past pres. Houston Hosp. Council; trustee, mem. exec. com. Internat. Council Religions, 1979-80. Elected nominee Am. Coll. Hosp. Adminstrs. Mem. Advt. Fedn. Am., Am. Women in Radio and TV, Authors Unltd. Houston, Rice U. Women's Assn., Achievement Rewards for Coll. Scientists Found. Episcopalian. Club: Altrusa (past pres.). Address: 448 N Post Oak Ln Houston TX 77024

HARRIS, NICHOLAS GEORGE, pub.; b. Salisbury, Eng., Sept. 8, 1939; s. George Ivan and Phyllis Dorothy (Porter) H.; m. Margaret Jane Darling, Feb. 3, 1968; children—Nicola, Gregory. Sales rep. Collins Pubs., London, 1963-67, Montreal, 1967-72, sales dir., Toronto, 1972, exec. v.p., 1973; pres. William Collins Sons & Co., Can. Ltd., 1974—; dir. Pan Books, Can. Served to 1st lt. Brit. Army, 1958-63. Anglican. Office: 100 Lesmill Rd Don Mills ON M3B 2T5 Canada

HARRIS, OREN, federal judge; b. Belton, Ark., Dec. 20, 1903; s. Homer and Bettie Lee (Buloock) H.; m. Ruth Ross, May 9, 1934; children: Carolyn Marie, James Edward. B.A., Henderson State U., 1929; LL.B., Cumberland U., 1930. Bar: Ark. 1930, U.S. Supreme Ct. 1943. Dep. pros. atty. Union County, Ark., 1933-36; pros. atty. 13th Jud. Circuit, 1936-40; mem. 77th-89th congresses from 4th Dist. Ark.; chmn. com. on interstate and fgn. commerce, chmn. spl. investigatory com. on regulatory agys.; judge U.S. Dist. Ct. for Eastern and Western Dists. Ark., 1966—, sr. judge, 1976—; mem. budget com. Fed. Judiciary, 1973—; mem. Jud. Conf. U.S., 1971-74. Del. Democratic Nat. Conv., 1944, 52, 56, 60. Recipient Saturday Rev. award, 1960; Public Service award Air Freight Forwarders Assn., 1960; award of merit Air Traffic Control Assn., 1962; Disting. Public Service citation Western Ry. Club, 1962; Joint Chiefs of Staff Nat. Transp. award Nat. Def. Transp. Assn., 1962; Presdl. citation Pioneer Nat. Broadcasting Assn., 1963, Am. Public Health Assn., 1963; Albert Lasker Service award, 1964; George Washington award Good Govt. Soc., 1965; Oren Harris Chair of Transp. established at U. Ark., 1970. Mem. Am. Bar Assn., Ark. Bar Assn., Ark. Bar Found., Sigma Alpha Epsilon. Baptist. Clubs: Lions (Ark. dist. gov. 1939-40), Jaycees (life), Masons (33 deg.), Shriners, K.P. Home: 1110 W Main St El Dorado AR 71730 Office: 219 Fed Bldg El Dorado AR 71730

HARRIS, PATRICIA ROBERTS, former sec. HEW, lawyer, educator; b. Mattoon, Ill., May 31, 1924; d. Bert Fitzgerald and Hildren Brodie (Johnson) Roberts; m. William Beasley Harris, Sept. 1, 1955. A.B. summa cum laude, Howard U., 1945; J.D. (with honors), George Washington U., 1960; postgrad., U. Chgo., 1945-47, Am. U., 1949-50; LL.D., Lindenwood Coll., Morgan State Coll., 1967, Russell Sage Coll., Tufts U., Dartmouth Coll., 1970, Johns Hopkins, MacMurray Coll., U. Md., Williams Coll., Ripon Coll., 1972, Brown U., 1972, Wilburforce U., Aquinas Coll., Brandeis U., Colby Coll., No. Mich. U.; D.H.L., Miami U., 1967, Newton Coll. of the Sacred Heart, 1972, U. Mich., 1973, Smith Coll., Wittenberg U., 1974; D.C.L., Beaver Coll., 1968; P.Sc.D., Rollins Coll., 1974. Bar: D.C. 1960, U.S. Supreme Ct 1960. Program dir. YWCA, Chgo., 1946-49; asst. dir. Am. Council Human Rights, 1949-53; exec. dir. Delta Sigma Theta, 1953-59; research assoc. George Washington U. Sch. Law, 1959-60; trial atty. Dept. Justice, 1960-61; asso. dean students, lectr. law Howard U., 1961-63, prof. law, 1963-65, 67-69, dean, 1969; ptnr. Fried, Frank, Harris, Shriver & Kampelman, Washington, 1970-77; sec. HUD, Washington, 1977-79, HEW, 1979-81, HHS, 1980-81; prof. law George Washington U., Washington, 1981—; dir. Scott Paper Co., 1981—; mem. U.S.-P.R. Commn. Status P.R., 1964-66; U.S. ambassador to, Luxembourg, 1965-67; Alternate del. of U.S. to 21st-22d Gen. Assemblies of UN, 1966-67. Mem. exec. com. Nat. Citizens Com. Community Relations, 1964-65; co-chmn. Nat. Women's Com. Civil Rights, 1963-64; chmn. D.C. Law Revision Commn., 1975-77; vice chmn. Nat. Capitol Area Civil Liberties Union, 1962-65; exec. bd. D.C. chpt. NAACP, 1958-60; bd. dirs. Legal Def. Fund, 1967-77; chmn. welfare com. Urban League D.C., 1953-55; Del. Democratic Nat. Conv., 1964, chmn. credentials com., 1972; mem.-at-large Dem. Nat. Com., 1973-76, Dem. nat. committeewoman from D.C., 1976-77; presdl. elector, D.C., 1964; Bd. dirs. ACLU, 1964-65, YWCA of U.S., 1958-59, Am. Council Human Rights, 1953-55, Nat. Capitol area YWCA, 1963-65, Family and Child Services D.C., 1962-65, Home Rule Com. D.C., 1965-66, Com. on Admissions and Grievances U.S. Dist. Ct. for D.C., 1970-77; mem. Adminstrv. Conf. U.S., 1967-71; nat. adv. com. Reform Fed. Criminal Laws, 1967-70; mem. Nat. Com. on Causes and Prevention Violence, 1968-69, Carnegie Commn. on Future Higher Edn., 1969-73; Bd. dirs. Georgetown U., 1970-77, Nat. Merit Scholarship Found., 1975-76; trustee Twentieth Century Fund, 1969—; bd. govs. Atlantic Inst., 1967-77; adv. council Marshall Scholarship Program, 1973-77. Decorated Order of Oaken Crown, Luxembourg; recipient Distinguished Achievement award Women's Com., Yeshiva U., 1968; Distinguished Alumni award Howard U., 1966; Distinguished Service award Washington Alumnae chpt. Delta Sigma Theta, 1963; Aquinas award Aquinas Coll., 1972; One Nation award Phila. br. NAACP, 1972; named Woman of Year Women's Aux. Jewish War Vets., 1968, Woman of Year in Bus. and Professions Ladies Home Jour., 1974; Achievement award in professions Black Enterprise, 1976; award in honor women dirs. of corps. Catalyst, 1976. Mem. Council on Fgn. Relations, Fed. Bar Assn., ABA, Order of Coif, Phi Beta Kappa, Delta Sigma Theta, Kappa Beta Pi. Club: Cosmopolitan (N.Y.C.). Office: Nat Law Ctr George Washington U 720 20th St NW Washington DC 20052

HARRIS, PAUL, sculptor; b. Orlando, Fla., Nov. 5, 1925. Student, U. N.Mex., New Sch. Social Research, Hans Hofmann Sch. Fine Arts. Fulbright prof. sculpture Universidad Catolica de Chile, 1961-62; later faculty San Francisco Art Inst., Calif. Coll. Arts and Crafts, Oakland; artist-in-residence Rinehart Sch. Sculpture, Md. Inst. Art, 1981; Vis. critic, lectr. U.S.F.S. Centers, Valparaiso and Concepcion, Chile, 1962, Rinehart Sch. Sculpture, Md. Inst. Art, 1963, 66, 70, 73, 75, 77, 80, 84, U. Oreg., Eugene, 1968, Newark State U., N.J., 1970, Mont. State U. at Bozeman, 1970, 74, State U. N.Mex., Las Cruces, 1971, Montclair State U., 1973, Commonwealth U. Va., 1975, 76, Clemson U., 1975, Haverford Coll., 1977, Phila. Coll. Art, 1977, R.I. Sch. Design, 1977, Rinehart Grad. Sch. Sculpture, spring 1981. Exhibited group shows, Mus. Modern Art, N.Y.C., 1958, 63, N.Y. World's Fair, 1965, Art Inst. Chgo., Md. Inst. Art, 1966, Mus. Contemporary Crafts, 1966, 73, São Paulo Bienal, 1967, Smithsonian Instn. Traveling Exhbn., 1969, also Phila. Inst. Art, San Francisco Mus. Art, N.J. State Mus., Los Angeles County Mus., 1968, 73, Brandeis U., A.C.A. Gallery, 1972, Contemporary Art Center Cin., 1973, Coll. Marin Galleries, 1974, JPL Gallery, London, Eng., 1975, Yellowstone Art Center, Billings, Mont., 1976, Renwick Gallery, Nat. Coll. Fine Arts, Washington, 1976-77, Falkirk Center, San Rafael, Calif., 1980, Transam. Bldg. Gallery, San Francisco, 1982, San Francisco Mus. Modern Art, 1983, Otis Art Inst. Parsons Sch. Design, 1984, Fendrick Gallery, one-man show, Poindexter Gallery, N.Y.C., 1957, 60, 63, 67, 70, Lanyon Gallery, 1965, Berkeley Gallery, William Sawyer Gallery, San Francisco, 1969, 71, Galerie Thelen, Essen, 1970, San Francisco Mus. Art, 1972, U. Calif. at Santa Barbara, U. N.Mex., 1973, Ark. Arts Center, Loch Haven Art Ctr., Orlando, Fla., 1981, Stanford U. Art Mus. (Calif.), 1982, Greenville County Mus. Art (S.C.), Fuller Golden Gallery, San Francisco, 1983; collaborator (with Leni Alexander); on aspects of ballet A False Alarm on the Nightbell Once Answered—It Cannot Be Made Good, Not Ever; Contbr.: Art in Am. Illus. Torso (Dorothy Schmidt), 1974; drawings for Pas de Une, 1979. Recipient Longview Found. grant, 1960, Neallie Sullivan award, 1967; Tamarind fellow, 1969-70; named Miembro Academico de la Facultad de Bellas Artes Universidad Catolica de Chile, 1962; resident Macdowell Colony, 1977; grantee Lebovitz Fund, 1978; Guggenheim fellow, 1979. Address: Box 930 Bolinas CA 94924

HARRIS, PAUL STEWART, art historian; b. Orange, Mass., Mar. 7, 1906; s. Carl Chester and Elizabeth (Stewart) H.; m. Jean Lida Morrill, Jan. 28, 1944; children: Andrew Morrill, Alexandra Morrill. B.S., Antioch Coll., 1929; S.B. in Art History, Harvard, 1932; part-time student, Grad. Sch. of Fine Arts, N.Y. U., 1933-38; student art history in, Europe, 3 summers. Curatorial asst. and asst. curator decorative arts dept., dept. medieval art and the Cloisters Met. Mus. Art, N.Y.C., 1933-38; dir., sec. Des Moines Assn. of Fine Arts, 1938-40; sr. curator Mpls. Inst. Arts, 1941-42, 46; dir., curator J.B. Speed Art Mus., 1946-62; dep. dir. Winterthur Mus., 1962-67; dir. collections Henry Ford Mus., 1967-71; lectr. history Am. painting U. Minn., 1946; adviser to bldg. com. Satterwhite Wing, Louisville, 1953-54. Author: Fourteen Seasons of Art Accessions in Kentucky, 1947-60, 1960; also articles on art history and catalogues for mus. publs. Served from lt. to lt. comdr. USNR, World War II. Mem. Soc. Colonial Wars, Am. Assn. Museums, Coll. Art Assn. Conglist. Clubs: Mason, Rotarian., Harvard (N.Y.C. and Boston). Home: RFD Chesham Marlborough NH 03455

HARRIS, PHILIP JOHN, engineering educator; b. Montreal, Que., Can., Mar. 22, 1926; s. Thomas Percival and Gladys Marion (Gillett) H.; m. Norma Joyce Maynard, May 23, 1953; children: Elizabeth Joyce Harris Shwartz, Janet Constance. B.Sc., U. Man., 1948; M.Eng., McGill U., 1949, Ph.D., 1964. Structural designer Dominion Bridge Co. Ltd., Lachine, Que., 1949-51; chief civil engr. C.D. Howe Co., Ltd., Montreal, 1951-58; asst. prof. dept. civil engring. McGill U., Montreal, 1958-59, asso. prof., 1959-73, prof. dept. civil engring., 1973—, chmn. dept., 1977—, bd. govs., 1975-82; structural and found. engring. cons., 1958—. Contbr. articles to profl. jours. NRC Can. grantee, 1965-79; Natural Scis. and Engring. Research Council grantee, 1979—. Fellow Can. Soc. Civil Engring.; mem. Assn. Profl. Engrs. Ont., Order Engrs. Que.; Mem. ASCE, Am. Concrete Inst., Am. Soc. Engring. Edn. Anglican. Home: 4600 Mariette Ave Montreal PQ H4B 2G2 Canada Office: 817 Sherbrooke St W Montreal PQ H3A 2K6 Canada

HARRIS, PHILIP ROBERT, management and organizational psychologist; b. Bklyn., Jan. 22, 1926; s. Gorden Roger and Esther Elizabeth (Delahanty) H.; m. Dorothy Lipp, July 3, 1965. B.B.A., St. John's U., 1949; M.S. in Psychology, Fordham U., 1952, Ph.D., 1956; spl. student, NYU, 1948-49, Syracuse U., 1961. Lic. psychologist, N.Y. Dir. guidance St. Francis Prep. Sch., N.Y.C., 1952-56; dir. student personnel, v.p. St. Francis Coll., N.Y.C., 1956-63; exec. dir. Assn. Human Emergency-Thomas Murray Tng. Program, 1964-66; vis. prof. Pa. State U., 1965-66; vis. prof., cons. Temple U.; sr. assoc. Leadership Resources Inc., 1966-69; v.p. copley Internat. Corp., La Jolla, Calif., 1970-71; pres. Mgmt. and Orgn. Devel. Inc. (now Harris Internat. Ltd.), La Jolla, 1971—; adj. prof. U. Calif.-San Diego, 1982—, Pepperdine U., U. No. Colo., Calif. Space Inst. Author: Effective Management of Change, 1978, Improving Management Communication Skills, 1978, Managing Cultural Differences, 1979, New Worlds, New Ways, New Management, 1982, Improving Leadership Effectiveness, 1982, Managing Cultural Synergy, 1982; editor: Innovations in Global Consultation, 1980; author: Global Strategies in Human Resource Development, 1983; contbr. articles to jours. Vice-pres. Bklyn. Downtown Renewel Effort, 1957-59. Mem. Am. Psychol. Assn. Fulbright prof. to India U.S. State Dept., 1962. Mem. Internat. Cons. Found., Am. Soc. Tng. and Devel. (Torch award 1975), World Future Soc. Club: La Jolla Beach and Tennis. Home: 2702 Costebelle Dr La Jolla CA 92037 Office: Box 2321 La Jolla CA 92038

HARRIS, RANDY (ALAN HARRIS), lawyer, investment banking executive; b. Tulsa. B.A., Grinnell Coll., 1967; J.D. with honors, George Washington U., 1970. Bar: D.C. 1970, Ill. 1975, N.Y. 1982, U.S. Supreme Ct. 1976. Mem. staff U.S. Senate, Washington, 1967-70; with SEC, Washington, 1970-74, A.G. Becker Inc., Chgo., 1974—; gen. counsel A.G. Becker, Warburg Paribas Becker (and related cos.), 1977-82; mng. dir. A.G. Becker Paribas, 1983—; vice chmn. arbitration com. Chgo. Bd. Options Exchange, 1979-80. Mem. Securities Industry Assn. (fed. regulation com., tax policy and capital formation com.). Office: A G Becker Parabas Inc 55 Water St New York NY 10041

HARRIS, RICHARD HARVEY, broadcasting company executive; b. St. Louis, Sept. 8, 1929; s. Samuel Harvey and Marie Dorothy (Kiely) H.; m. Jessie Lynne Layman, Sept. 24, 1955; children: Randall, Cynthia, Brian, Kenneth, Leslie. B.A., U. Denver, 1950; postgrad., U. Mo. Sch. Journalism, 1953-54; grad. advanced mgmt. program, Harvard U., 1976. Ptnr. Dandy Broadcasting Co., 1958-61; gen. mgr. Sta.-WDGY, Mpls., 1961-64; with Group W Radio Sta. Group Westinghouse Broadcasting and Cable Inc., 1964—; pres. Group W radio sales Radio Advt. Reps., N.Y.C., 1973; pres. Group W Radio and Muzak Group W Radio and Muzak, N.Y.C., 1973—; pres. group Radio Advt. Reps. (Muzak), N.Y.C., 1982; also dir. Group W Radio and Muzak. Bd. dirs., chmn. exec. com. NAB Metro Market Com.; Bd. dirs. WNYC Found., Call for Action., WNYC Found. Served with U.S. Army, 1951-53. Mem. Nat. Assn. Broadcasters (bd. dirs. met. market com.), Omicron Delta Kappa. Roman Catholic. Club: Innis Arden Golf. Home: 6 Shadybrook Ln Old Greenwich CT 06870 Office: 888 7th Ave New York NY 10106

HARRIS, RICHARD LEE, retired army officer, engineering executive; b. Bellevue, Pa., Dec. 26, 1928; s. Everett Lee and Marjorie Anna (Messer) H.; m. Patricia Ann Walton, Dec. 12, 1953; children: Sandra Jo, Carole Jill, William Walton, Robert Lee. B.S., U.S. Mil. Acad., West Point, N.Y., 1951; student, Army Engr. Sch., 1951, 59; M.S., MIT, 1956; grad., Oak Ridge Sch. Reactor Tech., 1957, Command and Gen. Staff Coll., 1963, Nat. War Coll., 1967. Designated sr. parachutist, nuclear reactor comdr.; registered nuclear engr., Pa., Tex., Fla. Commd. 2d lt. U.S. Army, 1951, advanced through grades to maj. gen., 1973; with (32d Engrs. Combat Bn.), 1951, co-comdr., Korea, 1952-53, res. engr., 1953-54; engrs. supply officer Columbus Depot, 1954-55; tech. ops. officer AEC, N.Y.C., 1957-59; officer in charge (SM-1A Nuclear Power Plant), Alaska, 1960-62, with, 1963-65, bn. comdr., Vietnam, 1965-66; with Office Chief of Staff, U.S. Army, 1967-68, Hdqrs. U.S. Army Pacific, 1968-70; comdr. div. support command (1st Cav. Div.), Vietnam, 1970-71; asst. comdt. Army Engrs. Sch.,

1971-73; dir. mgmt. info. systems Office Chief Staff Army, Hdqrs. Dept. Army, 1973-76; comdr. U.S. Army Tng. Center-Engr. and Ft. Leonard Wood, Mo., 1976-78; div. engr. (North Central Engr. Div.), 1978-80, ret., 1980, engring. exec., Austin, 1980—. Decorated D.S.M., Legion of Merit with 4 oak leaf clusters, Bronze Star with 2 oak leaf clusters, Air medal with 4 numerals, Joint Services Commendation medal, Purple Heart. Mem. ASCE, Assn. Energy Engrs., Soc. Am. Mil. Engrs., Assn. U.S. Army, Comml. Devel. Assn., Ret. Officers Assn., Nat. Soc. Profl. Engrs., Phi Kappa Phi. Home: 8817 Balcones Club Dr Austin TX 78750 Office: PO Box 9948 Austin TX 78766

HARRIS, RICHARD MALLABY, business information company executive. Pres. Predicasts Inc., Cleve., 1981—. Office: Office of Pres Predicasts Inc 200 University Circle Research Ctr 11001 Cedar Ave Cleveland OH 44106§

HARRIS, RICHARD MAX, forest products company executive; b. San Jose, Ill., Mar. 13, 1935; s. James Elmer and Edith Catherine (Leipnick) H.; m. Carole June French, Dec. 22, 1957 (dec.); children: Tracy Lynn, Amy French, Richard Max II; m. Susan Rose Varrassi, May 31, 1975. B.S., U. Ill., 1959. Mgr. fin. Gen. Electric Co., Syracuse, N.Y., 1959-71; v.p. Warner Electric, South Beloit, Ill., 1971-73; controller Internat. Paper Co., N.Y.C., 1973-76, v.p., 1976-81, sr. v.p., 1981—. Active Pres.'s Council U. Ill., Urbana, 1983. Served with USAF, 1955-57. Republican. Presbyterian. Home: 300 E 40th St New York NY 10016 Office: Internat Paper Co 77 W 45th St New York NY 10036

HARRIS, RICHARD (ST. JOHN), actor; b. Limerick, Ireland, Oct. 1, 1933; s. Ivan and H.; m. (Joan) Elizabeth Rees-Williams, Feb. 9, 1957 (div.); m. Ann Turkel (div. 1981). Attended, London Acad. Music and Dramatic Arts, 1956. Producer, dir.: Winter Journey, London, 1956; joined, Joan Littlewood's Theatre Workshop, London, 1956; profl. acting debut in Littlewood's prodn. of The Quare Fellow at, Theatre Royal, Stratford, Eng., 1956; appeared on stage in: A View from the Bridge, London, 1956, Man, Beast and Virtue, London, 1958; toured, Russia and Eastern Europe in, MacBeth; and appeared in TV plays, 1956-58, first leading stage role in, London in, The Ginger Man, 1959; film debut in Alice and Kicking, 1958; other films include Shake Hands With the Devil, 1959, The Wreck of the Mary Deare, 1959, A Terrible Beauty, 1960, The Long and the Short and the Tall, 1961, The Guns of Navarone, 1961, Mutiny on the Bounty, 1962, This Sporting Life, 1963 (Cannes Film Festival Best Actor award 1963), The Red Desert, 1964, Major Dundee, 1965, The Heroes of Telemark, 1965, The Bible, 1966, Hawaii, 1966, Camelot, 1967, The Molly Maguires, 1969, A Man Called Horse, 1969, Cromwell, 1970, Man in the Wilderness, 1971, The Deadly Trackers, 1973, 99 44/100 Dead, 1974, Juggernaut, 1975, Robin and Marian, 1975, The Return of a Man Called Horse, 1976, The Cassandra Crossing, 1977, Orca, 1977, The Wild Geese, 1978, The Ravagers, 1979, The Last Word, 1979, Tarzan, the Ape Man, 1981; producer, music actor in: film Echoes of a Summer, 1976; songs recorded include McArthur Park, 1968, Didn't We, 1969, My Boy, 1971; albums include Great Performances. Recipient Golden Globe award for best actor for Camelot, 1968; Grammy award for best spoken work for Jonathan Livingston Seagull, 1973. Mem. Knights of Malta. Office: care Creative Artists Agy Inc 1888 Century Park E Suite 1400 Los Angeles CA 90067 *

HARRIS, ROBERT ALLEN, musician, condr., composer; b. Detroit, Jan. 9, 1938; s. Major Lee and Rusha Belle (Marshall) H.; m. Mary Louise Pickens, June 8, 1963; 1 dau., Shari Michelle. B.S., Wayne State U., Detroit, 1960, M.A., 1962; Ph.D., Mich. State U., 1971. Tchr. music Detroit public schs., 1960-64; asst. prof. Wayne State U., 1964-70; asso. prof., then prof. Mich. State U., 1970-77; prof. conducting, dir. choral orgns. Northwestern U., 1977—; past 2d v.p. Lansing (Mich.) Symphony Assn. Composer choral works, chamber music, solo voice pieces, others. Grantee Rockefeller Found., 1971, 72, Mich. State U. Mem. Am. Choral Condrs. Assn., Music Educators Nat. Conf., ASCAP, Pi Kappa Lambda, Phi Mu Alpha. Methodist. Home: 4550 Grove St Skokie IL 60076 Office: Music Adminstrn Bldg Sch Music Northwestern Univ Evanston IL 60201

HARRIS, ROBERT HARRY, environmental health scientist; b. Fairmont, W.Va., Oct. 16, 1941; s. Kenneth Leo and Nancy (Smith) H.; m. Stephanie Ann Gerbi, Aug. 30, 1969. B.S., W.Va. U., 1963; M.S., Cal. Inst. Tech., 1965; M.A., Ph.D., Harvard, 1971. Engr. James M. Montgomery Cons. Engrs., Pasadena, Calif., 1965; teaching fellow Harvard, 1969-71; dir. environ. engring. Process Research, Inc., Cambridge, Mass., 1971; asst. prof. U. Md., College Park, 1971-73; dir. toxic chems. program Environ. Def. Fund, Inc., Washington, 1973-79; assoc. Ralph Nader's Corporate Accountability Research Group, 1972-73; mem. Pres.'s Council on Environ. Quality, 1979-81; prin. Environ Corp., 1982—; Co-dir. Hazardous Waste Research Program, Princeton U., 1982—; mem. Potomac estuary com. NRC, 1975-79; mem. task force on research priorities in environ. health Nat. Insts. Environ. Health Scis., 1975-77; mem. panel on EPA 5-yr. research plan Office Tech. Assessment, U.S. Congress, 1976; vis. assoc. research biochemist U. Calif. at Berkeley, 1978-79. Contbr. articles to profl. jours. Vice pres. bd. dirs. Consumers Union of U.S., 1976-80; Bd. dirs. Acid Rain Found., 1982—. Recipient George Polk Meml. award for outstanding mag. reporting, 1974; Nat. Mag. award Am. Soc. Mag. editors, 1974; named Man of Yr. Nat. Water Supply Improvement Assn., 1975. Mem. A.A.A.S., Am. Chem. Soc., Sigma Xi. Democrat. Methodist. Home: 12915 Travilah Rd Potomac MD 20854 Office: 1525 18th St NW Washington DC 20036

HARRIS, ROBERT JENNINGS, polit. scientist, educator; b. Wilson County, Tenn., Oct. 25, 1907; s. Robert Jennings and Lucy (Talley) H.; m. Martha Dashiel Baxter, June 10, 1937. A.B. magna cum laude, Vanderbilt U., 1930; A.M. (polit. sci. scholar), U. Ill., 1931; Ph.D., Princeton, 1934. Asst. and fellow in politics Princeton, 1931-34; instr. polit. sci. U. Cin., 1934-36; asst. prof. govt. La. State U., 1936-38, asso. prof., 1938-43, prof., 1943-54, chmn. dept., 1941-54; prof. polit. sci. Vanderbilt U., 1954-63, chmn. dept., 1962-63; prof. polit. sci., dean faculty arts and sci. U. Va., 1963-68, James Hart prof. govt., prof. history, 1968-78, James Hart prof. emeritus, 1978—; vis. prof. Vanderbilt U., summer 1946, U. Minn., summer 1947, U. N.C., summer 1948, Columbia, 1957-58; Edward Douglass White lectr. La. State U., 1959; spl. staff Library of Congress, 1950. Author: The Judicial Power of the United States, 1940, The Quest for Equality: The Constitution, Congress and the Supreme Court, 1960, (with others) Continuing Crisis in American Politics, 1963; also articles, book reviews in profl. journals.; Bd. editors jour.: Politics, 1945-48; editor, 1939-45; asso. editor: Am. Polit. Sci. Rev, 1951-53; adv. bd. editors: Va. Quar. Rev, 1964-78; Collaborator: Constitution of the United States: Analysis and Interpretation, 1953. Mem. Am. Assn. U. Profs. (nat. council 1961-64), Am. Polit. Sci. Assn. (v.p. 1950), So. Polit. Sci. Assn. (pres. 1947), Phi Beta Kappa. Club: Colonnade. Home: 1311 Grove Rd Charlottesville VA 22901

HARRIS, ROBERT LAIRD, clergyman, educator; b. Brownsburg, Pa., Mar. 10, 1911; s. Walter William and Ella Pearl (Graves) H.; m. Elizabeth Kruger Nelson, Sept. 11, 1937 (dec. 1980); children: Grace, Alegra, Robert Laird; m. Anne Paxson Krauss, Aug. 1, 1981. B.S. in Chem. Engring, U. Del., Newark, 1931; postgrad, Washington U., 1931-32; Th.B., Westminster Theol. Sem., 1935, Th.M., 1937; M.A. in Oriental Studies, U. Pa., 1941; Ph.D., Dropsie Coll., 1947. Ordained to ministry Presbyterian Ch., 1936; instr. Faith Theol. Sem., Phila., 1937-43, asst. prof. Bibl. Exegesis, 1942-47, prof. Bibl. Exegesis, 1947-56; prof. Covenant Theol. Sem., St. Louis, 1956-81, dean, 1964-71, prof. emeritus, 1981—; vis. lectr. Wheaton Coll., Ill., 1957-61; prof. Winona Lake Summer Sch. of Theology, 1964, 66, 67, East Sch. Archaelogy and Bible, Jerusalem, 1962; lectr., Japan, Korea, 1965; vis. prof. China Grad. Sch. Theology, Hong Kong, 1981, Freie Theologische Akademie, Giessen, W.Ger., 1982-83. Author: Introductory Hebrew Grammar, 1950, Inspiration and Canonicity of the Bible, 1957, Man-God's Eternal Creation, 1971; editor: Theological Wordbook of the Old Testament, 2 vols., 1981; mem. editorial bd.: New Internat. Version of Bible, 1965—; chmn., 1970-74; contbg. author various books. DuPont fellow U. Del., 1930-31; recipient First Zondervan Textbook Contest, 1955; Foxwell Lecture lectureship Tokyo Christian Theol. Sem., 1981. Mem. Soc. Bibl. Lit. and Exegesis, Am. Sch. Oriental Research, Evang. Theol. Soc. (pres. 1961), Tau Beta Pi, Phi Kappa Phi. Republican. Home: 9 Homewood Rd Wilmington DE 19803 *I count it a privilege to have been a part of the movement of resurgence of evangelical Christianity and to have contributed in a small way to the exposition and defense of the Scriptures in the twentieth century.*

HARRIS, ROBERT MARTIN, educator; b. Atlantic City, N.J., Dec. 5, 1921; s. Martin Michaels and Grace (van Roth) H.; m. Lillian Marie Wells, Feb. 27, 1944; children—Richard, Robert, Steven, Lynne. Student, Phila. Coll. Pharmacy and Sci., 1940-42, 46-48; A.B., U. Calif. at Los Angeles, 1949, Ph.D., 1953. Teaching asst. U. Calif. at Los Angeles, 1949-51, research fellow, 1951-53; instr. U. Ariz., 1953-55, asst. prof., 1955-59, asso. prof., 1959-65, prof. botany, 1965—. Author: Survey of the Plant Kingdom, 1956, Survey and Uses of the Plant Kingdom, 1959, Experiments in Genetics, 1956, Plant Diversity, 1969; Editor: Jour. of The Ariz. Acad. Sci, 1958—. Served with AUS, 1942-46. Recipient Salgo-Noren Found. award teaching excellence, 1965. Fellow Ariz. Acad. Sci., A.A.A.S. (publs. bd. 1971-73, councillor 1971-73); mem. Genetics Soc. Am., Phi Lambda Upsilon, Beta Beta Beta, Alpha Epsilon Delta, Phi Delta Chi. Home: 841 E Alta Vista Tucson AZ 85719

HARRIS, ROBERT NORMAN, advertising and communications educator; b. St. Paul, Feb. 11, 1920; s. Nathan and Esther (Roberts) H.; m. Mildred Burton, June 21, 1941; children: Claudia, Robert Norman, Randolph B. B.A., U. Minn., 1940. A founder Toni Co., div. Gillette Co., 1940-55; exec. v.p. Lee King & Ptnrs., Chgo., 1955-60, Allen B. Wrisley Co., 1960-62, North Advt., 1962-72; pres. Westbrook/Harris, Inc., Chgo., 1973-77; exec. v.p., gen. mgr. Creamer Inc., Chgo., 1977-81; pres. The Harris Creative Group, Inc., 1981—; prof. advt. and mass communications San Jose State U. (Calif.), 1983—. Served with USNR, 1942-45. Mem. Nat. Acad. TV Arts and Scis., Am. Mktg. Assn., Am. Advt. Fedn., Am. Assn. Advt. Agys. Office: 7220 Via Sendero San Jose CA 95135

HARRIS, ROBERT S., university dean. Dean Sch. Architecture, U. Soc. Calif., University Park, 1980—. Office: Office of Dean U So Calif Sch Architecture University Park CA 90089§

HARRIS, ROBERT TAYLOR, philosophy educator; b. Joliet, Ill., Mar. 18, 1912; s. Eugene Nelson and Bess (Hutchinson) H.; m. Mary Margaret Simmons; children: Paul, Peter, Eugene, John. Ph.B. (Austin scholar), Northwestern U., 1937; M.A., Harvard, 1948, Ph.D., 1949. Mem. faculty U. Utah, 1949-52, So. Ill. U., 1952-55, Bradley U., 1955-58; prof. philosophy Miami U., Oxford, Ohio, 1958-70, chmn. dept., 1958-69; vis. prof. philosophy Simmons Coll., 1970-71, Northeastern U., 1971; prof. philosophy Framingham (Mass.) State Coll., 1972-82, prof. emeritus, 1982—. Author: (J. Jarrett) Language and Informal Logic, 1956, Social Ethics, 1962. Lt. col. ret. USMCR, 1942-45. Home: 107B Centre St Brookline MA 02146

HARRIS, RONALD DAVID, chemical engineer; b. Norman, Okla., Apr. 9, 1938; s. Loyd Ervin and Maurine Cora (Dill) H.; m. Judith Anne Wright, July 28, 1962; children: Todd David, Scott Howard, Susanna Katherine. B.Chem. Engring., Ohio State U., 1961, M.Sc., 1961; M.B.A., U. Cin., 1970; student, Chase Law Sch., Cin., 1970-71. Chem. engr. Procter & Gamble Co., Cin., 1961-62, process devel. group leader, 1964-71; mgr. food product devel. Clorox Co., Oakland, Calif., 1971-73, dir. research and devel., Pleasanton, Calif., 1973-77; v.p. research and devel. Anderson Clayton Foods, Dallas, 1977-81, v.p. tech. and productivity, 1981—. Trustee San Ramon Valley Unified Sch. Dist., 1977; mem. Richardson City Planning Commn., 1980-83, Richardson City Council, 1983—; mem. citizens adv. com. North Tex. Mcpl. Water Dist., 1980—; life mem. Julian C. Hyer Youth Camp. Served as officer AUS, 1962-64. Mem. Am. Chem. Soc., Inst. Food Technologists, Richardson C. of C. (1st v.p., dir., pres. 1982), Tau Beta Pi, Phi Eta Sigma (past chpt. pres.), Phi Lambda Upsilon, Delta Mu Delta, Kappa Sigma (past chpt. pres.). Lodges: Lions (dir., pres. 1982-83). Patentee process for adsorbent bleaching oils, dry prepared fluffy frosting mixes. Home: 2503 Springwood Ln Richardson TX 75081 Office: 3333 North Central Expressway Richardson TX 75080

HARRIS, ROSEMARY ANN, actress; b. Ashby, Eng., Sept. 19; d. Stafford Berkley and Enid (Campion) H.; m. Ellis Rabb, Dec. 4, 1959 (div. 1967); m. John Ehle, Oct. 21, 1967. Student, Royal Acad. Dramatic Art, Smith Coll., 1969, Wake Forest U., 1978, N.C. Sch. of Arts, 1980. Broadway debut in Climate of Eden, N.Y.C., 1952; other theatrical appearances include Seven Year Itch, London, 1953, Bristol Old Vic, 1954, London Old Vic, 1955-56, Interlock, N.Y.C., 1957, Group 20, Wellesley, Mass., 1958, 59, The Disenchanted, N.Y.C., 1958, The Tumbler, N.Y.C., 1960, Assn. Producing Artists Repertory Company, N.Y.C., 1960-67, Chichester (Eng.) Festival, 1963, 64, Brit. Nat. Theatre, 1964-65, Hamlet, Uncle Vanya, A Streetcar Named Desire, Merchant of Venice, N.Y.C., 1974, The Royal Family, N.Y.C., 1976, The Seagull, N.Y.C., 1980, All My Sons, London, 1981, Heartbreak House, London, 1983; appeared in: films Beau Brummell, 1954, The Shiralle, 1956, A Flea in Her Ear, 1967, The Boys from Brazil, 1978, The Ploughman's Lunch, 1983; TV series The Chisholms; films To the Lighthouse (Locarno Film Festival award 1983); other TV appearances include Hallmark Hall of Fame. Recipient Antoinette Perry award, 1966; Vernon Rice award, 1962; Theatre World award, 1953; Delia Austrian Drama League award, 1967; Obie award, 1961, 65; Whitbread award, 1965-67; London Evening Standard award, 1969; Outer Circle Critics award, 1972; Drama Desk award, 1971, 72, 76; Emmy award, 1976; Golden Globe award, 1978. Mem. Actors Equity Assn., AFTRA, Screen Actors Guild. Office: care Milton Goldman Internat Creative Mgmt 40 W 57th St New York NY 10019

HARRIS, ROY HARTLEY, electrical engineer; b. Madison, Ga., Dec. 17, 1928; s. Richard Paul and Florrie (Judd) H.; m. Margaret P. Pitman, Sept. 14, 1951; children: Kathryn, Audrey. B.S. in Elec. Engring., Ga. Inst. Tech., 1951; M.E.E., Poly. Inst. Bklyn., 1956. Sr. engr. Hazeltine Elec. Corp., Little Neck, L.I., N.Y., 1951-56; supr. Bell Telephone Labs., Burlington, N.C., 1956-64; guidance systems engring. mgr. Western Electric, Burlington, 1965-68, mgr. mil. systems engring., 1968-72, mgr. naval mil. engring., Winston-Salem, N.C., 1972-82, dir. govt. systems, Greensboro, N.C., 1982—. Mem. indsl. adv. com. N.C. A&T U., Greensboro, 1983—. Served with U.S. Army, 1946-47. Fellow IEEE (bd. dirs. 1978-79); mem. Anak Soc., Nat. Security Indsl. Assn. (mem. exec. com. 1983—), Omicron Delta Kappa, Phi Kappa Phi, Tau Beta Pi. Republican. Methodist. Club: Alamance Country (Burlington, N.C.). Office: Western Electric Inc Guilford Center PO Box 20046 Greensboro NC 27420

HARRIS, RUFUS CARROLLTON, university chancellor; b. Monroe, Ga., 1897; s. Virgil Vascar and Jessie (Green) H.; m. Mary Louise Walker, June 23, 1918; children: Rufus Carrollton, Joseph Henry Walker, Louie Kontz. Grad., Gordon Inst., Barnesville, Ga., 1915; A.B., Mercer U., 1917, LL.D., 1931; LL.B., Yale U., 1923, J.D., 1924; LL.D., U. Ala., 1941, William Jewell Coll., 1943, U. Maine, 1953, U. Chattanooga, 1953, Northwestern U., 1958, La. State U., 1960, Tulane U., 1965; Litt.D., Birmingham So. U., 1950, U. Miami, 1958; D.C.L., U. Hawaii, 1952; prof. honoris causa, U. Pueblo, 1956; L.H.D., Samford U., 1961, Stetson U., 1962, Jacksonville U., 1964, Flagler Coll., 1975. Prof. law Mercer U. Law Sch., 1923-27, dean, 1925-27; dean, prof. law Tulane U., 1927-37, pres., 1937-60, Mercer U., Macon, Ga., 1960-79, chancellor, 1979—; dir. U.S. Fed. Res. Bank, Atlanta, 1938-56, chmn. bd. dirs., 1954-56; Pres. So. Assn. Colls. and Secondary Schs., 1958; mem. Commn. on Colls., 1957-75; pres. Council So. Univs., 1956-57, So. U. Conf., 1941-43; mem. adv. com. VA, Washington, 1943-69, chmn., 1958-69; mem. U.S. Adv. Commn. on Internat. Ednl. and Cultural Affairs, 1965-69; chmn. So. Region Marshall Scholarship Com., 1956-73; mem. Ga. Higher Edn. Facilities Commn., 1964-74. Trustee Eisenhower Exchange Fellowships, Inc., 1953—, Inst. for Def. Analyses; mem. bd. Carnegie Found. for Advancement of Teaching, 1945-72, chmn., 1955. Served with inf. U.S. Army, 1917-19. Decorated chevalier French Legion of Honor, Confrerie des Chevaliers du Tastevin; Most Excellent Order Brit. Empire, 1970; Distinguished Civilian Service award Dept. Navy, World War II. Mem. Am., La., Ga., New Orleans bar assns., Nat. Planning Assn. (trustee, chmn. com. on So. devel.), Assn. Am. Law Schs. (sec. 1931-35, pres. 1935), Order of Coif, Phi Beta Kappa, Omicron Delta Kappa, Phi Delta Theta. Democrat. Baptist. Clubs: Mason., Boston, Round Table, Commerce (Atlanta); Century Assn. (N.Y.C.). Home: 1240 Elm Macon GA 31201 Office: Chancellor's Office Mercer U Macon GA 31207

HARRIS, RUTH BATES, government official; d. Harry B. and Florence (Graham) Delaney. B.S., Fla. A&M U.; M.B.A., NYU, 1957. Exec. dir. Washington Human Relations Commn. and; equal employment opportunity officer D.C., 1960-69; dir. human relations dept. Montgomery County (Md.) Pub. Schs., 1969-71; dep. asst. adminstr. NASA, 1971-76; human relations officer Dept. Interior, Washington, 1978—; lectr.; mem. Fed. Inter-agy. Minority Task Force, 1983. Author: Trigger Words. Recipient over 50 awards, including; Sojourner Truth award Nat. Assn. Negro Bus. and Profl. Womens' Clubs, 1966; Martin Luther King award D.C. chpt. NAACP, 1969; award Nat. Bus. League, 1974, space div. Rockwell Internat., 1975; Disting. Service award Federally Employed Women, 1976; award Cosmopolitan Bus. and Profl. Women's Club, 1978; keys to cities of Cocoa Beach and Jacksonville, Fla., 1980; award Omega Psi Phi, Sigma Gamma Rho, Alpha Phi Alpha. Mem. Delta Sigma Theta, Iota Phi Lambda (hon.), Cosmopolitan Bus. and Profl. Women's Club (pres.). Home: 901 6th St SW Washington DC 20024 Office: Office of Sec Human Relations Office Dept Interior Washington DC 20240 *I hope I never rise so high that I lose sight of the people who helped put me up there. True happiness is the reward we receive when we make others happy without reminding them.*

HARRIS, RUTH CAMERON, pediatrician, educator; b. Mt. Vernon, N.Y., Apr. 23, 1916; d. Robert Dimond and Jessie Van Wyck (Terwilliger) H.; m. A. Eugene Adams, Oct. 11, 1952; children: Lois H., Roberta H. A.B., Barnard Coll., 1937; M.D., Columbia Coll. Physicians and Surgeons, 1943. Asst. in pediatrics Coll. Physicians and Surgeons, Columbia U., N.Y.C., 1947, instr., 1948-51, assoc., 1951-55, asst. prof., 1955-72, assoc. prof., 1972-76; prof. and chmn. dept. pediatrics Marshall U. Sch. Medicine, Huntington, W.Va., 1976-81; emeritus prof. Marshall U., 1981—; asst. pediatrician Babies Hosp., and Vanderbilt Clinic, 1947-50; asst. attending pediatrician and cons. Babies Hosp., and Meddervilt Clinic, 1950-76; med. cons. Holt Adoption Program, Inc., 1972—; med. adv. chmn. Children's Liver Found., 1975—. Contbr. articles on pediatric liver problems to med. jours. Mem. Soc. Pediatric Research, Am. Pediatric Soc., Am. Assn. Study Liver Disease, Harvey Soc., N.Y. Acad. Sci., Am. Acad. Pediatrics, N.Am. Soc. Pediatric Gastroenterology, Am. Soc. Human Genetics, Am. Med. Women's Assn., AMA, Assn. Women in Sci. Home: 26 Keeneland Dr Huntington WV 25705

HARRIS, STANLEY GALE, JR., banker; b. Chgo., June 19, 1918; s. Stanley Gale and Muriel (Bent) H.; children: John Trumbull, Thomas Bartlett; m. Alice Harwood, Nov. 4, 1972. Student, Yale, 1936-38; certificate in indsl. adminstrn, Harvard Grad. Sch. Bus. Adminstrn., 1943. With Nat. Bank Commerce, Seattle, 1939-41, Carnegie-Ill. Steel Corp., 1943-44; with Harris Trust & Savs. Bank, Chgo., 1944—; formerly chmn. bd., now dir.; formerly chmn. bd. Harris Bankcorp Inc., now dir. Life trustee Rush-Presbyn.-St. Luke's Med. Center, Ill. Children's Home and Aid Soc.; trustee U. Chgo. Clubs: Chicago, Commercial, Casino, Little Wheels, Tavern, Yale (Chgo.); Skokie Country. Home: 180 E Pearson St Apt 4704 Chicago IL 60611 Office: Harris Trust & Savs Bank 111 W Monroe St Chicago IL 60603

HARRIS, SYDNEY JUSTIN, newspaper columnist; b. London, Sept. 14, 1917; m. Grace Miller (div. 1951); m. Patricia Roche, 1953; children: Carolyn (dec.), Michael, Barbara, David, Lindsay. Student, U. Chgo. and Central Coll., Chgo.; LL.D., Villa Maria Coll.; Litt.D., Schimer Coll.; D.H.L., Lenoir-Rhyne Coll. Employed in various positions Chgo. Herald and Examiner, 1934-35, Chgo. Daily Times, 1936; editor Beacon Mag., Chgo., 1937-38; with pub. relations dept. legal div., City of Chgo., 1939-41; with Chgo. Daily News, 1941-78; drama critic and writer column Strictly Personal (syndicated in U.S. and Can. by News Am. Syndicate), 1944—; mem. faculty Univ. Coll., U. Chgo., 1946—; vis. scholar Lenoir-Rhyne Coll., Hickory, N.C., 1980-82; dir. Hickory Humanities Forum, Wildacres, N.C., 1980—. Column appears in more than 200 newspapers; Author: Strictly Personal, 1953, A Majority of One, 1957, Last Things First, 1961, On the Contrary, 1964, Leaving the Surface, 1968, For the Time Being, 1972, The Authentic Person, 1972, Winners and Losers, 1973, The Best of Harris, 1975, Would You Believe?, 1979, Pieces of Eight, 1982; Mem. usage panel: Am. Heritage Dictionary. Trustee Francis W. Parker Sch., Chgo. Recipient Ferguson award Friends of Lit., 1958; Brotherhood award NCCJ, 1968; Press award ACLU, 1980. Mem. Sigma Delta Chi. Clubs: Arts, Headline, Press. Office: Chgo Sun-Times 401 N Wabash Ave Chicago IL 60611

HARRIS, SYDNEY MALCOLM, judge; b. Toronto, Ont., Can., June 23, 1917; s. Samuel Aaron and Rose (Geldzaeler) H.; m. Enid Harriet Perlman, Nov. 9, 1949; children—Mark, David. B.A., U. Toronto, 1939; Barrister-at-Law, Osgoode Hall Law Sch., Toronto, 1942. Bar: Called to Ont. bar 1942, created Queen's counsel 1962. Barrister, solicitor firm Harris & Rubenstein, Toronto, 1950-76; judge criminal div. Ont. Provincial Ct., Toronto, 1976—. Pres. Canadian Jewish Congress, 1974-77. Recipient Centennial medal, 1967, Queen's Jubilee medal, 1977. Mem. Canadian Bar Assn., Provincial Judges Assn., Can. Council on Corrections. Home: Apt 204 22 Shallmar Blvd Toronto ON M5N 2Z8 Canada Office: Old City Hall 60 Queen St W Toronto ON M5H 2M4 Canada

HARRIS, T. GEORGE, editor; b. Simpson County, Ky., Oct. 4, 1924; s. Garl and Luna (Byrum) H.; m. Sheila Hawkins, Oct. 31, 1953 (dec. Jan. 1977); children: Amos, Anne, Crane, Gardiner; m. Ann R. Roberts, Mar. 3, 1979; children: Clare, Joseph, Mary Louise and Rachel Pierson. Student, U. Ky., 1946; B.A., Yale U., 1949. Reporter Clarksville (Tenn.) Leaf-Chronicle, 1942; corr. Time Inc., 1949-55, Midwest bur. chief, 1955-58; contbg. editor Time, N.Y.C., 1958-60, N.W. bur. chief, 1960-62; sr. editor Look mag., 1962-68; editor-in-chief Psychology Today mag., 1969-76; cons. editor Next, Runner, Somatics, Industry Week mags. Addison-Wesley Pub. Co., 1976-81; founding editor American Health mag., 1981—; Vis. com. on humanities U. Chgo.; mem. scholar grants jury Nat. Endowment on Humanities. Bd. dirs. Ch. Soc. for Coll. Work. Served to 1st lt., F.A. AUS, World War II. Decorated Bronze Star, Air medal with cluster; named Outstanding Young Man of Chgo., 1955, Ky. col., to U. Ky. Hall of Fame; recipient prize mag. journalism U. Mo., Brotherhood award NCCJ. Mem. Phi Beta Kappa. Clubs: Yale, Nassau (N.Y.C.); Century. Home: 1125 Fifth Ave New York NY 10028 Office: American Health Mag 80 Fifth Ave New York NY 10011

HARRIS, THEODORE EDWARD, mathematician, educator; b. Phila., Jan. 11, 1919; s. Julius and Hazel (Rosenfield) H.; m. Constance Ruth Feder, June 29, 1947; children—Stephen Joel, Marcia Faye. Student, So. Meth. U., 1935-37; B.A., U. Tex., 1939; M.A., Princeton, 1946, Ph.D., 1947. With Rand Corp., 1947-66, chmn. dept. math., 1959-66; prof. math. U. So. Calif., 1966—; vis. asst. prof. U. Calif. at Los Angeles, 1949-50; vis. asso. prof. Columbia, 1953; vis. prof. Stanford, 1963. Author: The Theory of Branching Processes, 1963; Editor: Annals of Math. Statistics, 1955-58. Served to maj. USAAF, 1942-45. Fellow AAAS; mem. Am. Math. Soc., Inst. Math. Stats. (pres. 1966-67). Jewish. Home: 422 S Clark Dr Beverly Hills CA 90211 Office: Dept Math Univ Southern California Los Angeles CA 90089

HARRIS, THOMAS CUNNINGHAM, editor; b. Parrott, Va., July 28, 1908; s. Thomas Cunningham and Wilhelmina (Cassie) H.; m. Patricia Brock, May 19, 1929; children—Margaret Virginia and Shirley Patricia (Mrs. William T. Burgin) (twins), Sharon Anita. Grad. high sch. Reporter Times Pub. Co., St. Petersburg, Fla., 1923-26, city editor, 1927-30, mng. editor, 1931-41, exec. editor, 1941-62, gen. mgr., exec. v.p., 1962-67, asso. editor, 1967-68; exec. editor El Mundo (Spanish lang. newspaper), San Juan, P.R., 1968-75. Dir. Com. 100, Pinellas County, Fla., 1965-67. Mem. Inter Am. Press Assn. (dir. 1961-70, chmn. com. freedom of press 1967-70), AP Mng. Editors Assn. Fla. (past pres.), Nat. Press Club, St. Petersburg C. of C. (v.p. 1965), Sigma Delta Chi. Clubs: St. Petersburg Yacht; Bankers (San Juan, P.R.). Home: 1075 14th Ave N Saint Petersburg FL 33705 Office: 519 St Petersburg Times Bldg 440 1st Ave S Saint Petersburg FL 33701

HARRIS, THOMAS EVERETT, lawyer, government official; b. Little Rock, May 25, 1912; s. Marvin and Ina (Thomas) H.; m. Lucile Hassell, 1935 (div. 1944); children: Marvin Bryan, Ruffin Kirby; m. Margaret Samson, Aug. 14, 1944; 1 son, Thomas Everett. B.A., U. Ark., 1932; LL.B., Columbia U., 1935. Law clk. to Justice Stone, 1935-36; assoc. firm Covington & Burling, Washington, 1936-37; with Dept. Justice, 1937-41, Office Solicitor Gen., 1939-41; assoc. gen. counsel FCC, 1941-42, OPA, 1942-43; with Bd. Econ. Warfare, 1943; assoc. firm Cahill, Gordon, Zachry & Parlin, N.Y.C., 1943-45; with U.S. Mil. Govt. in, Germany, 1945-46; ptnr. firm Alvord & Alvord, Washington, 1946-47; spl. asst. to atty. gen., alien property div. Dept. Justice, 1947-48; assoc. gen. counsel CIO, 1948-55, AFL-CIO, 1955-75; Mem. Fed. Election Commn., 1975—. Democrat. Home: 1201 Key Dr Alexandria VA 22302 Office: 1325 K St NW Washington DC 20463

HARRIS, THOMAS L., public relations executive; b. Dayton, Ohio, Apr. 18, 1931; s. James and Leona (Blum) H.; m. JoAnn K. Karsh, Apr. 14, 1957; children: James Harris, Theodore Harris. B.A., U. Mich., 1953; M.A., U. Chgo., 1956. Exec. v.p. Daniel J. Edelman Inc., Chgo., 1957-67; v.p. pub. relations Neddham Harper & Steers, Chgo., 1967-72; pres. Foote Cone & Belding Pub. Relations, Chgo., 1973-78, Golin-Harris Communications Inc., 1978—. Served with U.S. Army, 1953-55. Mem. Public Relations Soc. Am. Home: 556 Cherokee St Highland Park IL 60035 Office: Golin-Harris Communications Inc 500 N Michigan Ave Chicago IL 60611

HARRIS, THOMAS RAYMOND, biomedical engineer, educator; b. San Angelo, Tex., Feb. 19, 1937; s. Loyd Franklin and Rubye (Mitchell) H.; m. Carol Ann Cox, June 1, 1963; children: Calvin Thomas, Andrew Mitchell. B.S., Tex. A&M U., 1958, M.S., 1962; Ph.D., Tulane U., 1964; M.D., Vanderbilt U., 1974. Design engr. Standard Oil Co. Calif., 1958-60; mem. faculty Vanderbilt U., Nashville, 1964—, prof. biomed. engring. and chem. engring., 1976—, asso. prof. medicine, 1980—, dir. biomed. engring. program, 1977—; cons. in field. Author articles in field; mem. editorial bds. profl. jours. Served as 2d lt. AUS, 1958-59. Nat. Heart, Lung and Blood Inst. grantee; NSF grantee; Martha Washington Straus-Harry H. Straus Found. grantee; Barbara Ingalls Shook Found. grantee. Mem. Am. Physiol. Soc., Am. Inst. Chem. Engrs., Am. Soc. Engring. Edn., Am. Heart Assn. (sci. councils), Biomed. Engring. Soc., Soc. Engring. in Medicine and Biology, Microcirculatory Soc. Baptist. Office: Box 1724 Sta B Vanderbilt U Nashville TN 37212

HARRIS, VINCENT CROCKETT, educator; b. Mpls., Jan. 26, 1913; s. Jesse Brownell and Virginia Case (Crockett) H.; m. Blanche Peterson Hanson, Jan. 3, 1945; children—Jacqueline Jones, Diane Harris Smith. B.A., Northwestern U., 1933, M.A., 1935, Ph.D., 1950; postgrad., U. Wis., 1935-38, U. Minn., summers 1932, 37, U. Kans., summer 1957. Acct. Wells Lamont Corp., 1938-41; instr. Northwestern U., 1946-50; asst. prof., asso. prof., prof. San Diego State U., 1950-76, prof. emeritus, 1976—; Summer faculty Ariz. State U., 1961, U. Mo., 1962, Northwestern U., 1963; vis. prof. U. Alta., spring 1976. Contbr. articles to profl. jours. Served to lt. USNR, 1942-46; PTO. Mem. Math. Assn. Am. (chmn. So. Calif. sect. 1966-67), Math. Assn. (Eng.), A.A.A.S., Fibonacci Assn., Phi Beta Kappa, Sigma Chi. Republican. Methodist. Home: 5054 55th St San Diego CA 92115

HARRIS, VINCENT MADELEY, bishop; b. Conroe, Tex., Oct. 14, 1913; s. George Malcolm and Margaret (Madeley) H. Student, St. Mary's Sem., La Porte, Tex., 1934; S.T.B., N.Am. Coll., Rome, 1936, J.C.B., 1939; J.C.L., Cath. U. Am., 1940; L.H.D., St. Edward's U., Austin, Tex., 1982. Ordained priest Roman Catholic Ch., 1938; prof. St. Mary's Sem., 1940-51; chancellor Diocese Galveston-Houston, 1948-66, diocesan consultor, 1951-66; domestic prelate, 1956, bishop of Beaumont (Tex.), 1966-71, coadjutor bishop of Austin (Tex.), 1971—, bishop, 1971. Decorated knight grand cross Equestrian Order Holy Sepulchre Jerusalem. Mem. Sons Republic of Tex. Club: K.C. (chaplain Tex. 1967-69). Home: 4007 Balcones Dr Austin TX 78731 Office: PO Box 13327 Capitol Sta Austin TX 78711

HARRIS, WALTER EDGAR, chemistry educator; b. Wetaskiwin, Alta., Can., June 9, 1915; s. William Ernest and Emma Louise (Humbke) H.; m. Phyllis Pangburn, June 14, 1942; children: Margaret Anne, William Edgar. B.S., U. Alta., 1938, M.S., 1939; Ph.D., U. Minn., 1944. Research fellow U. Minn., 1943-46; prof. analytical chemistry U. Alta., Edmonton, 1946—, chmn. dept. chemistry, 1974—, chmn. Pres.'s Adv. Com. on Campus Revs., 1980—. Author: (with H.W. Habgood) Programmed Temperature Gas Chromatography, 1965, (with B. Kratochvil) Chemical Separations and Measurements, 1974, Teaching Introductory Analytical Chemistry, 1974, (with H.A. Laitinen) Chemical Analysis, 1975, (with B. Kratochvil) An Introduction to Chemical Analysis, 1981; Contbr. numerous articles to profl. jours. Recipient Outstanding Achievement award U. Minn., 1973; Govt. Alta. Achievement award, 1974. Fellow AAAS, Royal Soc. Can.; mem. Chem. Inst. Can. (Fisher Sci. Lecture award 1969, Chem. Edn. award 1975), Am. Chem. Soc., Sigma Xi. Home: 9212 118th St Edmonton AB T6G 1T9 Canada Office: Department of Chemistry University of Alberta Edmonton AB T6G 2G2 Canada

HARRIS, WESLEY LAMAR, agricultural engineering educator; b. Taylorsville, Ga., Nov. 12, 1931; s. James Wesley and Etta (Womach) H.; m. Megaera Ausman, Nov. 19, 1982; children by previous marriage: James, William, Wesley, Gregory. B.S.A.E., U. Ga., 1953, M.S., 1958; Ph.D., Mich. State U., 1960. Agrl. engring. instr. U. Ga., Athens, 1956-58; grad. research asst. Mich. State U., East Lansing, 1958-60; asst. to assoc. prof. U. Md., College Park, 1960-69, prof. and acting chmn. dept. agrl. engring., 1969-74, chmn. dept. prof., 1974-76, dir. Md. Agrl. Expt. Sta., 1976—; mem. farm mechanization study Govt. Republic of Korea, 1971-72. Contbr. articles to profl. jours. Capt., C.E. U.S. Army, 1953-56. Mem. Am. Soc. Agrl. Engring., N.E. Expt. Sta. Dirs. Assn., AAAS, Sigma Xi, Phi Kappa Phi, Alpha Zeta, Omicron Delta Kappa. Office: Md Agrl Expt Sta 1326 Symonds Hall Univ Md College Park MD 20742

HARRIS, WHITNEY ROBSON, lawyer; b. Seattle, Aug. 12, 1912; s. Olin Whitney and Lily (Robson) H.; m. Jane Freund Foster, Feb. 14, 1964; 1 son, Eugene Whitney. A.B. magna cum laude, U. Wash., 1933; LL. B., J.D., U. Calif., 1936. Bar: Calif. 1936, U.S. Supreme Ct. 1945, Tex. 1953, U.S. Ct. Mil. Appeals 1955, Mo. 1964. Gen. law practice, Los Angeles, 1936-42; trial counsel U.S. Chief of Counsel, Nuremberg, 1945-46; chief legal advice br. U.S. Mil. Govt. for Germany, 1946-48; prof. law So. Meth. U., 1948-54; staff dir. legal service and proc. Com. Orgn. Exec. Br. Govt., 1954; exec. dir. ABA, 1954-55; solicitor for Tex. Southwestern Bell Telephone Co., Dallas, 1955-63, gen. solicitor, St. Louis, 1963-65; practice law, St. Louis, from 1965; now ptnr. Sumner, Harris, Sumner & Croft, Clayton, Mo. Author: Family Law, 1953, Tyranny On Trial, 1954, Legal Services and Procedure, 1955; Contbr. numerous articles to legal jours.; article on concentration camps Ency. Brit., 1954. Pres. St. Louis Civic Ballet, 1970-72; mem. pres.'s council Fontbonne Coll., 1971-73, Wellesley Coll., 1971-74; mem. St. Louis Center Holocaust Studies, 1980—; mem. adv. council, bd. govs. Winston Churchill Meml. and Library, 1980—; trustee Nat. Jewish Hosp. and Asthma Ctr., 1980—; chmn. pres.'s club St. Louis Children's Hosp., 1981—; bd. dirs. St. Louis Arthritis Found., 1982—, St. Louis Multiple Sclerosis Soc., 1983—, City Players of St. Louis, 1983—. Served from ensign to lt. comdr. USNR, 1942-46; capt. USN (ret.). Decorated Legion of Merit, other service medals; Churchill fellow Westminster Coll., 1979—; recipient Humanitarian award Nat. Jewish Hosp. and Research Ctr., 1980, Shalom award St. Louis Rabbinical Coll., 1982, Vol. of Yr. award St. Louis chpt. Nat. Soc. Fund Raising Execs., 1983, Nat. Outstanding Fund-Raising Vol. award Nat. Soc. Fund Raising Execs., 1983, Internat. Disting. Communal Service award B'nai B'rith, 1984. Mem. Internat. Bar Assn., Am. Bar Assn. (chmn. internat. law sect. 1953-54, chmn. adminstrv. law sect. 1960-61), Japan-Am. Soc. St. Louis (pres. 1978-80), Phi Beta Kappa, Order of Coif, Phi Kappa Psi, Delta Theta Phi. Jane and Whitney Harris Research Library established at Winston Churchill Meml. and Library, Fulton, Mo., 1980; Whitney Robson Harris collection on Third Reich dedicated at Washington U., 1980. Home: 2 Glen Creek Ln Saint Louis MO 63124 *Tyranny leads to inhumanity, and inhumanity is death. Let us resolve that tyranny shall not extend its sway, nor war become its game—placing our faith in the cause of justice, in the freedom of man, and in the mercy of God.*

HARRIS, WILLIAM CECIL, insurance company executive; b. Manchester, Lancs., Eng., Dec. 3, 1913; emigrated to U.S., 1954, naturalized, 1960; s. Richard C. and Florence (Fisher) H.; m. Florence Annie Tidswell, Mar. 21, 1940; 1 son, Timothy John. Matriculation, William Hulmes Sch. Chmn., pres. Phoenix of N.Y., N.Y.C., 1960-65; chief exec. Phoenix Group, London, 1969-79, dep. chmn., 1979—; pres. Chartered Ins. Inst., London, 1972-73; master Worshipful Co. of Insurers, London, 1979. Served to lt. RAF, 1940-45. Fellow Royal Soc. Arts, Chartered Ins. Inst. (pres. 1972-73), Brit. Ins. Assn. (chmn. 1976-77). Conservative. Mem. Ch. of Eng. Clubs: Pilgrims, City of London. Home: Hardbarrow Copse Ln West Chiltington West Sussex United Kingdom Office: 80 Maiden Ln New York NY 10038

HARRIS, WILLIAM GIBSON, lawyer; b. Greenville, S.C., Dec. 20, 1916; s. William Warren and Janie Cauble (Gibson) H.; m. Jane Hanway Hardy, Sept. 19, 1942; children: William Gibson II, Loring Hancock. A.B. summa cum laude, Princeton U., 1939; LL.B., U. Va., 1942. Bar: Va. 1941, D.C. 1963. Atty. WPB, 1942-43; asso. Covington & Burling, Washington, 1943-45; legal adviser Office Mil. Govt. Ger., Berlin, 1945-46; mem. McGuire, Woods & Battle (and predecessors), Richmond, Va., 1946-73, sr. ptnr., 1963—; pres. Church Schs. in the Diocese of Va., Richmond, 1972—; dir. So. Dept. Stores, Richmond, Tidewater Steel Co., Norfolk, Va., Truxmore Industries, Richmond, Camac Corp., Bristol, Va.; chmn. bd. Va. Capital Corp., Richmond, 1960-83, So. Industries, 1954—; Cologne Life Reins. Co., Ger. and Stamford, Conn., 1967—; trustee Va. Real Estate Investment Trust, Richmond, 1970-82; chmn. Gov.'s Adv. Bd. Indsl. Devel., 1982—. Editor: U. Va. Law Rev., 1942-43; contbr. legal jours. Mem. Gov.'s Adv. Com. on Taxation, 1965; chmn. com. finance and taxation Va. Code Commn., 1970; mem. Va. Commn. to Study Regulation Securities, 1973; pres. Princeton Class of 1939, 1970-71; chmn. Va. Vols. for Stevenson, 1952; fin. chmn. Senators Byrd and Spong, 1965; chmn. bd. govs. St. Christopher's Sch., Richmond, 1957-61; bd. dirs. Hardy-Harris Found., Richmond, 1960—, English Speaking Union U.S., N.Y.C., 1968-72; bd. dirs., v.p. Va. Mus. Fine Arts; trustee Richmond Meml Hosp. Mem. Va. Bar Assn. (pres. 1973-74), ABA, Phi Beta Kappa, Order of Coif, Raven Soc., Omicron Delta Kappa, Phi Delta Phi. Episcopalian. Clubs: Kiwanian.; Country of Virginia, Commonwealth, Downtown, Bull and Bear, Westwood Racquet (Richmond); Princess Anne Country (Virginia Beach, Va.); Farmington Country (Charlottesville, Va.); Gulf Stream Golf, Country of Florida, Bath and Tennis, Ocean, Little (Delray Beach, Fla.); Princeton, Racquet and Tennis (N.Y.C.); Buck's (London); Racing of France (Paris); Seminole Golf (Palm Beach, Fla.); Mid-Ocean (Bermuda). Home: 122 Tempsford Ln Richmond VA 23226

HARRIS, WILLIAM HAMILTON, orthopedic surgeon; b. Gt. Falls, Mont., Nov. 18, 1927; s. John H. and LaRue (Hamilton) H.; m. Johanna Alderfer, June 8, 1952; children: William Hamilton, Kristin, Jonathan, David. A.B. (Corp. scholar 1944-47, Clementine Cope fellow 1947), Haverford (Pa.) Coll., 1947; M.D., U. Pa., 1951. Intern U. Pa. Hosp., 1951-52; resident in orthopedic surgery Children's Med. Center, Boston, 1955, Mass. Gen. Hosp., 1957, Royal Nat. Orthopedic Hosp., London, 1959-60; mem. faculty Harvard U. Med. Sch., 1960—, clin. prof. orthopedic surgery, 1975—; orthopedic surgeon Mass. Gen. Hosp., 1960—, chief hip implant surgery unit, 1974—; sr. lectr. M.I.T., 1969—. Author articles in field, chpts. in books. Served to capt. M.C. USAF, 1952-54. Fellow Nat. Found., 1959-60, Sprague Found., 1960-61, Med. Found. Boston, 1961-64; traveling fellow Am. Orthopedic Assn., 1965; recipient Kappa Delta award for orthopedic research, 1970, 76. Mem. Internat. Hip Soc. (a founder), Hip Soc. (a founder, 1st pres. 1968), Am. Acad. Orthopedic Surgeons, Interurban Orthopedic Club, AMA, Mass. Med. Soc., Boston Orthopedic Club, Société Internationale de Chirurgie Orthopedique et de Tramatologie, Phi Beta Kappa, Alpha Omega Alpha. Home: 665 Concord Ave Belmont MA 02178 Office: 433 ACC Mass Gen Hospital Boston MA 02214

HARRIS, WILLIAM JAMES, JR., research administrator; b. South Bend, Ind., June 17, 1918; s. William James and Elizabeth M. (Scott) H.; m. Ruth Laubinger, Aug. 26, 1944 (dec. 1977); children: June Elizabeth Sherren, William James III, Debbie Shafer Hayden, Britta Shafer Kreuger, Barkley Shafer.; m. Elizabeth Dotten Shafer, June 24, 1978. B.S. in Chem. Engring; M.S. in Engring, Purdue U., 1940; D.Engring. (hon.), Purdue U., 1978; Sc.D., M.I.T., 1948. Head ferrous alloys br. metallurgy div. Naval Research Lab., 1947-51; exec. sec. materials adv. bd. Nat. Acad. Sci.-NRC, 1951-54, exec. dir., 1957-60, asst. sec., planning div. engring., 1960-62; asst. to dir. Battelle Meml. Inst., 1954-57, asst. to v.p., 1962-67; asst. dir. tech. Columbus Labs., 1967-69; v.p. research and test dept. Assn. Am. Railroads, 1970—; Pres., chmn. bd. Piscataway Co., Accokeek, Md., 1958-63; mem. Nat. Exec. Res. Dept. Transp., 1983—. Editor: (with others) Perspectives in Materials Research, 1963; Contbr. articles to tech. publs. Mem. nat. materials adv. bd. Nat. Acad. Sci., 1967—, chmn., 1969-70; sec. Pres.'s Com. on Hwy. Safety, 1969; mem. high speed ground transp. adv. com. U.S. Dept. Transp., 1972-74, Md. Gov.'s Sci. Adv. Com., 1972-76, Md. Gov.'s Energy Council, 1974-76; Pres. Moyoane Assn., 1951-53, 58; pres., chmn. bd. Alice Ferguson Found., 1966-68. Served to lt. comdr. USNR, 1941-45. Decorated Naval Letter of Commendation.; Recipient Distinguished Alumnus award Purdue U., 1965; Disting. Service award Transp. Research Bd.-NRC, 1977; named Railroad Man of Year, 1976. Fellow Am. Soc. Metals, Metall. Soc. (pres. 1970); mem. Am. Inst. Mining, Metall. and Petroleum Engrs. (dir. 1964-69, v.p. 1964—, chmn. inst. metals div. 1960, Mathewson medal 1950), Nat. Acad. Engring., Engrs. Joint Council (bd. dirs. 1965—, pres. 1968-70), Engring. Found. (chmn. research conf. com. 1964-67, bd. dir. 1968-70), Am. Ordnance Assn. (chmn. materials div. 1966-68), ASME (mem. transp. dir. 1973—), Nat. Security Indsl. Assn. (chmn. exec. planning com. 1965-67, chmn. research and devel. adv. com. 1967-69), Sigma Xi, Alpha Sigma Mu, Tau Beta Pi, Phi Lambda Upsilon, Sigma Delta Chi. Home: 1200 N Nash St Apt 1140 Arlington VA 22209 Office: 1920 L St NW Washington DC 20036

HARRIS, WILLIAM MERL, chemistry educator; b. Los Angeles, Feb. 23, 1931; s. Merl William Evans and Beatrice Theresa (Hawkins) H.; m. Ilse Anneliese Doebrich, Jan. 2, 1957. B.S., UCLA, 1956, Ph.D., 1965; postgrad., Loyola U. Law Sch., Los Angeles, 1982—. Registered patent agt. Mem. tech. staff Hughes Aircraft Co., Culver City, Calif., 1956-59; chemist FDA, Los Angeles, 1964-65; postdoctral research fellow in chemistry UCLA, 1965-66, instr., 1966-70; asst. prof. chemistry Los Angeles Valley Coll., Can Nuys, Calif., 1970-73, assoc. prof., 1973-77, coordinator instrn., 1976-77, prof., 1977—, chmn. dept., 1970—; lectr. chemistry U. Calif.-Santa Barbara., 1968; vis. prof. chemistry UCLA, 1979. Contbr. articles to profl. jours. Served with AUS, 1952-54. Named Outstanding Teaching Asst. UCLA, 1962; Hughes fellow, 1957-59. Mem. Am. Chem. Soc., Royal Soc. Chemistry (Eng.), State Bar Calif. (patent, trademark and copyright aect.), Los Angeles Patent Law Assn., Sigma Xi, Phi Lambda Upsilon. Lodge: Masons. Office: 5800 Fulton Ave Van Nuys CA 91401

HARRISBERGER, EDGAR LEE, engineering educator; b. Denver, Sept. 24, 1924; s. Ivan Albert and Gail Etta (Hinrichs) H.; m. Ruth Barbara Surgeson, Aug. 14, 1969; children: Russell, Ron, Dianne, Judy, David. Student, No. Okla. Jr. Coll., 1941-43; B.S., M.E., U. Okla., 1945; M.S., U. Colo., 1945; Ph.D., Purdue U., 1963. Registered profl. engr., Okla. Instr. Murray Coll., Tishomingo, Okla., 1946-49; asst. prof. mech. engring. U. Utah, Salt Lake City, 1950-54; asso. prof. mech. engring. N.C. State U., Raleigh, 1955-60; grad. asst. Purdue U., Lafayette, Ind., 1960-63; head Sch. Mech. and Aero. Engring., Okla. State U., Stillwater, 1966-71, prof. mech. engring., 1963-66; dean sci. and engring. U. Tex. Permian Basin at Odessa, 1971-75; Andrew Carnegie vis. prof. Cooper Union, N.Y.C., 1976-77; prof. mech. engring., dir. mech. engring. design clinic U. Ala., 1977—, head mech. engring., 1983—. Author: Mechanization of Motion, 1963, Enginermanship: A Philosophy of Design, 1966, Engineersmanship: The Doing of Engineering, 1982; Editor: Mech. Engring. News, 1964-70, ERMMag, 1968-71. Served with USNR, 1942-46. NSF research grantee, 1965-67; faculty fellow, 1960-62. Fellow Am. Soc. Engring. Edn. (v.p. 1970-73, pres. 1975-76); Mem. ASME, Nat. Soc. Profl. Engrs., Pi Tau Sigma, Sigma Xi, Tau Omega. Home: 4N Northwood Lake Northport AL 35476

HARRISON, ANNA JANE, chemist, educator; b. Benton City, Mo., Dec. 23, 1912; d. Albert S.J. and Mary (Jones) H. Student, Lindenwood Coll., 1929-31, L.H.D. (hon.), 1977; A.B., U. Mo., 1933, B.S., 1935, M.A., 1937, Ph.D., 1940, D.Sc. (hon.), 1983, Tulane U., 1975, Smith Coll., 1975, Williams Coll., 1978, Am. Internat. Coll., 1978, Vincennes U., 1978, Lehigh U., 1979, Hood Coll., 1979, Hartford U., 1979, Worcester Poly. Inst., 1979, Suffolk U., 1979, Eastern Mich. U., 1983, L.H.D., Emmanuel Coll., 1983. Instr. chemistry Newcomb Coll., 1940-42, asst. prof., 1942-45; asst. prof. chemistry Mt. Holyoke Coll., 1945-47, asso. prof., 1947-50, prof., 1950-79, prof. emeritus, 1979—, chmn. dept., 1960-66, William R. Kenan, Jr. prof., 1976-79; Mem. Nat. Sci. Bd., 1972-78. Contbr. articles to profl. jours. Recipient Frank Forrest award Am. Ceramic Soc., 1949; James Flack Norris award in chem. edn. Northeastern sect. Am. Chem. Soc., 1977; AAUW Sarah Berliner fellow Cambridge U., Eng., 1952-53; Am. Chem. Soc. Petroleum Research Fund Internat. fellow NRC Can., 1959-60; recipient Coll. Chemistry Tchr. award Mfg. Chemists Assn., 1969. Mem. AAAS (dir. 1979—, pres. 1983), Am. Chem. Soc. (chmn. div. chem. edn. 1971, pres. 1978, dir. 1976-79, award in chem. edn. 1982), Internat. Union Pure and Applied Chemistry (U.S. nat. com. 1978-81), Sigma Xi. Address: Dept Chemistry Mount Holyoke Coll South Hadley MA 01075

HARRISON, BARBARA GRIZZUTI, writer; b. Bklyn., Sept. 14, 1934; d. Dominick and Carmela (DiNardo) Grizzuti; children—Joshua Paul, Anna Edyth. Author: Unlearning the Lie: Sexism in School, 1971, Visions of Glory: A History and a Memory of Jehovah's Witnesses, 1975, Off-Center, 1980; contbr. writings to newspapers and mags. Mem. PEN (exec. bd.), Authors Guild, Nat. Book Critics Circle. Roman Catholic.

HARRISON, BENJAMIN LESLIE, retired army officer; b. Trumann, Ark., July 23, 1928; s. Benjamin Leslie and Ruth Venetta (Blackshane) H.; m. Carolyn Wright Algee, Sept. 29, 1951; children: Benjamin Leslie, III, Laura Louise. B.A., U. Miss., 1951; M.A., U. Mo., Kansas City, 1963; M.B.A., Auburn U., 1969; grad., Advanced Mgmt. Program, Harvard U., 1971. Enlisted U.S. Army, 1946, commd. 2d lt., 1951, advanced through grades to maj. gen., 1977; served as troop and staff officer, various locations, 1951-73; dep. comdt. U.S. Army Command and Gen. Staff Coll., Ft. Leavenworth, Kans., 1973-76; dep. comdg. gen. U.S. Army Aviation Center and Ft. Rucker, Ala., 1976-77; dir. rev. officers edn. and tng. U.S. Army, Washington, 1977-78; comdg. gen. U.S. Army Adminstrn. Center and Ft. Benjamin Harrison, Ind., 1978-79; ret., 1979. Decorated D.S.M., Silver Star with oak leaf cluster. Home: 221 E 21st Ave Belton TX 76513 Office: Tex Investments Corp Indsl Park Belton TX 76513 *My philosophy of life: Work and study as though you are going to live forever; enjoy life as though you are going to die tomorrow.*

HARRISON, BRIAN GRANVILLE, president Franklin Mint; b. Birmingham, Eng., Oct. 2, 1935; came to U.S., 1963, naturalized, 1972; s. Edwin Granville and LouiseDoris (Marks) H.; m. Maureen Sands, Oct. 12, 1959; children: Jacqueline, Stephanie. B.Sc. (hons.), U. Aston, Birmingham, 1959. Tech. officer Imperial Metal Industries, Eng., 1952-63; sr. metallurgist 3M Co., Mpls., 1963-66; with Franklin Mint, Phila., 1966—, pres., 1975, Franklin Mint Internat., London, 1971—. Trustee Internat. House. Fellow Royal Soc. Arts, Inst. Metallurgists, Am. Soc. Metals, Inst. Dirs. Clubs: Union League (Phila.); Aronomink Golf, Barnegat Yacht. Office: Franklin Mint Franklin Center PA 19091

HARRISON, CHARLES MAURICE, telephone company executive; b. Anderson, S.C., Aug. 30, 1927; s. Emmitte Smallwood and Jessie Maysel (Hawkins) H.; m. Lorna Jean Tomalty, June 27, 1970; children: Suzanne Elizabeth, Linda Jean. A.B., Marshall U., 1949; J.D., W.Va. U., 1952. Bar: W.Va. 1952, D.C. 1958, N.Y. 1965, N.J. 1972. Legal asst. W.Va. Dept. Ins., Charleston, 1952-54; hearing examiner Public Service Commn., Charleston, 1954-57; atty. Chesapeake and Potomac Telephone Co., Washington and Charleston, 1957-64, Western Electric Co., N.Y.C., 1964-69; gen. atty., sec., treas. Bellcomm, Inc., Washington, 1969-71; asst. gen. counsel, asst. sec. Bell Telephone Labs., Murray Hill, N.J., 1971-75, gen. atty., sec., 1975-76, sec., gen. counsel corporate matters, 1976—. Trustee Family Counseling Service Somerset County, N.J., pres., 1978-81; vice-chmn. govt. relations com. N.J. Research and Devel. Council; trustee Bridgewater (N.J.) United Methodist Ch. Served with AC U.S. Army, 1945-46. Mem. N.J. Assn. Corp. Counsel, Am. Bar Assn., W.Va. State Bar, D.C. Bar Assn., N.J. State Bar Assn. Republican. Office: Bell Telephone Labs 101 John F Kennedy Pkwy Short Hills NJ 07078

HARRISON, CLIFFORD JOY, JR., banker; b. Nashville, Feb. 21, 1925; s. Clifford Joy and Rosa Lee (Bennett) H.; m. Saralu Fondren, May 3, 1957; children—Julia Lee, Cliford Joy III, John Fondren. B.A., Vanderbilt U., 1949; postgrad., Law Sch., 1949-50, YMCA Law Sch., 1950-53; LL.B., Stonier Grad. Sch. Banking, Rutgers, 1963; student, Advanced Mgmt. Program, Harvard U., 1975. With 3d Nat. Bank, Nashville, 1950—, now vice chmn. in charge trust div., retail div. and mktg. Bd. dirs. Met YMCA. Served as 1st lt. USAAF, 1943-46. Decorated Air medal with oak leaf cluster. Mem. Tenn. Bankers Assn. (past pres. trust div.), Estate Planning Council (past pres.), Beta Theta Pi, Phi Alpha Delta. Episcopalian. Clubs: Exchange, City, Belle Meade Country (Nashville). Home: 207 Hillwood Dr Nashville TN 37205 Office: Nashville TN 37244

HARRISON, DONALD, editor; b. Phila., May 14, 1928; s. Martin and Diana (Feinstein) H.; m. Grace Wagner, Sept. 7, 1952; children—Eric Ethan, Lori Ann, Ellen Wendy. B.A., U. Pa., 1949. City editor Phila. Jewish Times, 1949-51; mng. editor News of Delaware County, 1954-63; asst. city editor Phila. Bull., 1963-69, city editor, 1969-72, editorial writer, 1972-73, editor arts and culture, 1973-79, regional editor, 1979-81, asst. mng. editor, 1981-82; assoc. editor editorial pages Phila. Daily News, 1982—; lectr. journalism U. Pa., 1960. Editor: From the Letters of Robert S. Gerdy (1942-45), 1969. Served with AUS, 1951-53. Mem. Phila. City Editors Assn. (past pres.), Sigma Delta Chi (past pres. Greater Phila. Profl. chpt.). Home: 1434 Westwood Ln Overbrook Hills PA 19151

HARRISON, DONALD CAREY, cardiologist; b. Blount County, Ala., Feb. 24, 1934; s. Walter Carey and Sovola (Thompson) H.; m. Laura Jane McAnnally, July 24, 1955; children—Douglas, Elizabeth, Donna Marie. B.S. in Chemistry, Birmingham So. Coll., 1954; M.D., U. Ala., 1958. Diplomate: Am. Bd. Internal Medicine (cardiovascular disease). Intern, asst. resident Peter Bent Brigham Hosp., 1958-60; fellow in cardiology Harvard U., 1961, NIH, 1961-63; mem. faculty Stanford U. Med. Sch., 1963—, chief div. cardiology, 1967—, prof. medicine, 1971—; chief cardiology Stanford U. Hosp., 1967—, William G. Irwin prof. cardiology, 1972—; cons. to local hosps., industry, govt. Editorial bd.: Am. Jour. Cardiology, 1970-78, Chest, Heart and Lung Jour, 1973-78, Drugs; Practical Cardiology, Clin. Cardiology; Contbr. articles to med. jours., chpts. to books. Served with USPHS, 1961-63. Fellow Interam. Soc. Cardiology (v.p. 1980—), Am. Coll. Cardiology (membership chmn., v.p. 1972-73, sec. 1969-70, trustee 1972-78), Am. Heart Assn. (fellow council circulation, clin. cardiology and basic sci., chmn. program com. 1972-76, chmn. publs. com. 1976-80, pres.-elect 1980-81, pres. 1981—); mem. Am. Soc. Clin. Investigation, Am. Fedn. Clin. Research, Am. Soc. Pharmacology and Exptl. Therapeutics, Am. Assn. Physicians, Am. Physiol. Soc., Calif. Acad. Medicine, A.C.P., Assn. U. Cardiologists. Home: 151 Mountain View Ave Los Altos CA 94022 Office: Room C-248 Stanford Univ Med Sch Stanford CA 94305

HARRISON, EARLE, former county ofcl.; b. Rainsville, Ala., May 20, 1905; s. Robert Lee and Sarepta Ophelia (Hansard) H.; m. Joan Mary Jackson, Jan. 24, 1942. A.B., Northwestern U., 1929, postgrad. in bus. adminstrn, 1942; LL.B., Chgo.-Kent Coll. Law, 1935. With Marshall Field & Co., Chgo., 1929-68, div. operating mgr., 1958-60, v.p. operations, 1960-64, v.p., treas., 1964-68; bd. dirs. Credit Bur. Cook County, 1949-69, pres., 1958-69; mem. bd. suprs., chmn. planning and zoning com., Lake County, Ill., 1970—; cons. finance and adminstrn. to hosps. and health care instns. Commr. Northeastern Ill. Planning Commn., 1970—; pres. Northeastern Ill. Plan Commn., 1973, now mem. exec. com.; Ret. pres., bd. dirs. Family Financial Counseling Service Greater Chgo.; bd. dirs. Condell Meml. Hosp., Libertyville, Ill., 1971—, adminstr., 1973—, pres., 1975-78; bus. cons., 1978—. Mem. Phi Delta Phi. Episcopalian. Club: Chgo. Athletic Assn. Home: 2712 Chrysler Dr Roswell NM 88201 *I feel that I owe whatever modest measure of success I have achieved primarily to the teachings of Aristotle, also to the encouragement of my late wife and my mother. Aristotle said that the chief goal in life is happiness; that to achieve happiness, one must do worthwhile things well. He also added that to accomplish this noble objective one must possess what he referred to as the four noble virtues; wisdom, which he defined as technical knowledge plus rationative ability; courage; temperance; justice or probity.*

HARRISON, EDWARD JAMES, lawyer, corporate executive; b. Streator, Ill., June 21, 1926; s. Frank J. and Nell (Webb) H.; m. Roberta I. Roberts, June 18, 1948; children: Victoria Beth, Cynthia Ann. B.S. in Law, U. Ill., 1950, J.D., 1952. Bar: Ill. 1951, Tex. 1974, D.C. 1982, U.S. Supreme Ct 1974. Trainee bus. program Gen. Electric Co., Bridgeport, Conn., 1952-54, asst. to trade regulation counsel legal dept., N.Y.C., 1954-55; sr. trial atty. anti-trust div. Dept. Justice, Washington, 1955-60; atty. law dept. Westinghouse Electric Corp., N.Y.C., 1960-66, chief counsel internat. sect., 1966, chief counsel N.Y. Office, 1966-69; v.p., sec., gen. counsel J.I. Case Co., Racine, Wis., 1969-74; sr. v.p., gen. counsel Tenneco Inc., Houston, 1974-76; v.p., gen. counsel Esmark, Inc., Chgo., 1976—. Bd. dirs. Chgo. Theatre Group Inc., Goodman Theatre. Served with USAAF, 1944-46. Mem. ABA; Mem. Chgo., Ill., D.C. bar assns., State Bar Tex., Assn. Gen. Counsel. Home: 1119 N Sheridan Rd Lake Forest IL 60045 Office: 55 E Monroe St Chicago IL 60603

HARRISON, EDWARD ROBERT, physicist, educator; b. London, Eng., Jan. 8, 1919; came to U.S., 1965; s. Robert and Daisy (White) H.; m. Photeni Marangas, June 23, 1945; children: John Peter, June Zoe. Student, Sir John Cass Coll., London U., 1937-40. With Atomic Energy Research Establishment, Harwell, Eng., 1948-64; vis. scientist CERN, Geneva, 1959-60; prin. scientist Rutherford High Energy Lab., Harwell, 1964-65; Nat. Acad. Sci. sr. research assoc., Washington., 1965-66; prof. dept. physics and astronomy U. Mass., Amherst, Amherst Coll., Mount Holyoke, Smith, Hampshire colls., 1966—, head five coll. astronomy dept., 1973-74; vis. prof. Astronomy Center, U. Sussex, Eng., 1974, U. Va., Charlottesville, 1976; staff mem. Nat. Radio Astronomy Obs., 1976; vis. astronomer Carter Obs., N.Z., 1981; lectr. various fgn. univs. Author: Cosmology: The Science of the Universe, 1981; Contbr. articles to profl. jours. Fellow Inst. Physics (Eng.), AAAS, Royal Astron. Soc., Am. Phys. Soc.; mem. Internat. Astron. Union, Am. Astron. Soc., Sigma Xi. Home: 73 Butterfield Terr Amherst MA 01002

HARRISON, E(RNEST) FRANK(LIN), university president; b. Seattle, July 1, 1929; s. Ernest and Ethel (Stutler) H.; m. Monique Adrienne Pelletier. B.A. magna cum laude, U. Wash., 1956, M.B.A., 1961, Ph.D., 1970. With Shell Oil Co., 1956-58; in mgmt. positions Boeing Co., 1958-70; lectr. Grad. Sch. Bus. Adminstrn., U. Wash., 1968-71, Seatle U., 1968-74; dir. Sch. Bus. Pub. Adminstrn. Seattle U.; dir. grad. programs, prof. mgmt. U. Puget Sound, 1970-74, dean Coll. Bus.; prof. mgmt. Ill. State U., 1974-78; chancellor, prof. mgmt. U. Alaska, Anchorage, 1978-81; pres., Disting. prof. So. Conn. State Coll., New Haven, 1981—. Author: The Managerial Decision Making Process, 1975, 81, Management and Organizations, 1978; contbr. articles to profl. jours. Served with USMC, 1946-49. Recipient Wall St. Jour. Student Achievement award, 1956. Mem. Acad. Mgmt., Am. Acad. Polit. Social Sci., Am. Inst. Decision Sci., Am. Social Assn., Phi Beta Kappa, Beta Gamma Sigma. Home: 85 Rimmon Rd Woodbridge CT 06525 Office: 501 Crescent St New Haven CT 06515

HARRISON, EVELYN BYRD, archaeologist, educator; b. Charlottesville, Va., June 5, 1920; d. William Byrd and Eva (Detamore) H. A.B., Barnard Coll., 1941; A.M., Columbia, 1943, Ph.D., 1952; postgrad., Bryn Mawr Coll., 1942-43. Instr. classics U. Cin., 1951-53; asst. prof. fine arts and archaeology Columbia, 1955-59, asso. prof., 1959-67, prof., 1967-70; prof. art and archaeology Princeton, 1970-74; prof. Inst. Fine Arts, N.Y. U., N.Y.C., 1974—; mem. Inst. for Advanced Study, 1961, 64. Author: The Athenian Agora, I, Portrait Sculpture, 1953, XI, Archaic and Archaistic Sculpture, 1965; Contbr. articles to profl. jours. Guggenheim fellow, 1954-55; Nat. Endowment for Humanities, 1968-69. Mem. Am. Acad. Arts and Scis., Am. Philos. Soc., Archaeol. Inst. Am., Soc. Promotion Hellenic Studies, German Archaeol. Inst. (corr. mem.). Home: 500 E 85th St New York NY 10028

HARRISON, FRANK, univ. pres.; b. Dallas, Nov. 21, 1913; s. Frank and Ruby (Davison) H.; m. Elsie Claire Redfearn, June 26, 1946; children—Frank, Susan Claire, James Redfearn. B.S., So. Methodist U., 1935; M.S., Northwestern U., 1936, Ph.D., 1938; M.D., U. Tex. Southwestern Med. Sch., 1956. Mem. faculty U. Tenn. med. units, Memphis, 1938-51, prof., 1946-51, chief div. anatomy, 1946-51; prof. anatomy U. Tex. Southwestern Med. Sch., Dallas, 1952-68, asso. dean, 1956-68; asso. dean grad. studies U. Tex. at Arlington, 1965-68, acting pres., 1968-69, pres., 1969-72, Health Sci. Center, San Antonio, 1972—. Named Distinguished Alumnus So. Meth. U., 1971. Mem. Am. Assn. Anatomists, Am. Physiol. Soc., Tex. Philos. Soc., Biophys. Soc., IEEE, Soc. Exptl. Biology and Medicine, Phi Beta Kappa, Alpha Omega Alpha, Kappa Sigma, Alpha Kappa Kappa. Office: U Tex Health Sci Center San Antonio TX 78284

HARRISON, FRANK, congressman; b. Washington, Feb. 2, 1940; s. Frank Gerard and Lillian Elizabeth (Clarke) H. A.B., King's Coll., 1961; LL.B., Harvard U., 1964. Bar: Pa. 1965, U.S. Ct. Mil. Appeals 1967. Of counsel firm Rosenn, Jenkins & Greenwald (Wilkes-Barre), Pa., 1969-82; lectr. dept. govt. and politics King's Coll., Wilkes-Barre, 1969-82; mem. 98th Congress from 11th Pa. Dist., Edn. and Labor com., Vet.'s Affairs com. Chmn. Downtown Devel. Authority, City of Wilkes-Barre, 1975-82; gen. chmn. Luzerne County Bicentennial Commn., Pa., 1975-76; bd. dirs. Osterhout Free Library, Wilkes-Barre, 1976—; mem. adv. bd. Catholic Social Serivces of Wyoming Valley, Wilkes-Barre, 1976—; mem. governing bd. Commn. Econ. Opportunity of Luzerne County, 1972-82. Served to capt. USAF, 1966-69. Recipient disting. service award Greater Wilkes-Barre Jaycees, 1976. Mem. VFW. Democrat. Roman Catholic. Club: Cath. War Vets. of Berwick (Pa.). Lodge: K.C. (Wilkes-Barre, Pa.). Home: 2 Irving Pl Wilkes-Barre PA 18702 Office: US Ho of Reps 1541 Longworth House Office Bldg Washington DC 20515

HARRISON, FRANK J., bishop; b. Syracuse, N.Y., Aug. 12, 1912. Ed., Notre Dame U., St. Bernard's Sem. Ordained priest Roman Catholic Ch., 1937; apptd. titular bishop of, Aquae in, Numidia, and aux. bishop of, Syracuse, 1971-76, appt. bishop of, 1976, installed, 1977—. Office: 4112 E Genessee St Dewitt NY 13214 *

HARRISON, FRANK RUSSELL, III, philosopher; b. Jacksonville, Fla., Mar. 11, 1935; s. Frank Russell, Jr. and Annye Mae (Blackwelder) H.; m. Dorothy Louise Gordy, Sept. 10, 1966. B.A., U. of South, 1957; M.A., U. Va., 1959, Ph.D., 1961. Instr. philosophy Roanoke Coll., Salem, Va., 1961-62; prof. philosophy U. Ga., Athens, 1962—; vis. prof. U. N.C., 1963, Emory U., 1965, Ga. Inst. Tech., 1966-67. Author: Deductive Logic and Descriptive Language, 1969; Mng. editor: Internat. Jour. for Philosophy of Religion, 1972—; Contbr.: chpts. to Religious Language and Knowledge, 1972, Theory Development and Educational Administration, 1973; also articles to profl. jours. Named Outstanding Educator of Am., 1973. Mem. Am. Guild Scholars, Am., Ga. philos. assns., Soc. for Philosophy Religion, So. Soc. for Philosophy and Psychology, Metaphys. Soc. Am., Phi Kappa Phi, Phi Sigma Tau. Episcopalian. Home: 310 Cedar Creek Dr Athens GA 30605

HARRISON, GEORGE, musician; b. Liverpool, Eng., Feb. 25, 1943; s. Harold and Louise H.; m. Patrician Ann Boyd, 1966 (div. 1977); m. Olivia Arias, 1978; 1 son, Dhani. Mem. The Rebels, 1956-58, The Quarrymen, 1958-60, The Beatles, 1960-70; solo performer, 1970—; organizer A Concert for Bangladesh, 1971. Numerous compositions, including While My Guitar Gently Weeps, Something, Here Comes the Sun, My Sweet Lord, Somewhere in England; films A Hard's Day's Night, 1964, Help!, 1965, Magical Mystery Tour, 1967, Let it Be, 1970 (Acad. award for soundtrack), A Concert for Bangladesh, 1972; albums include Wonderwall, Electronic Sounds, All Things Must Pass, Concert for Bangladesh, Living in the Material World, Dark Horse, Extra Texture, 33⅓, Best of George Harrison, George Harrison, Gone Troppo; author: I, Me, Mine, 1980. Recipient numerous Grammy awards with The Beatles.; Decorated Order Brit. Empire. Office: Dark Horse Records 3300 Warner Blvd Burbank CA 91505 *

HARRISON, GERALD, publisher; b. N.Y.C., Jan. 19, 1929; s. Harry and Beatrice (Levine) H.; m. Clarice Weisel, Feb. 14, 1953; children: Andrew, Robert, Steven. B.A., N.Y. U., 1949. Account exec. Benton & Bowles, Inc., N.Y.C., 1949-67; mktg. and sales dir. Graphics Internat., N.Y.C., 1967-70; exec. v.p., pub. juvenile books Random House, Inc., N.Y.C., 1970—. Served with Signal Corps AUS, 1950-52. Office: Juvenile Books Random House Inc 201 E 50th St New York NY 10022

HARRISON, GORDON RAY, research scientist; b. Wister, Okla., Dec. 14, 1931; s. Trannie Gordon and Isah Lee (Ray) H.; m. Barbara Ann Herndon, June 22, 1957; children: William Andrew, Melissa Leigh, Lori Jeanne, Amanda Ray. B.S. in Physics, U. Central Ark., 1952; M.S., Vanderbilt U., 1954, Ph.D., 1958. Sr. staff engr. and engrng. mgr. Sperry Microwave, Clearwater, Fla., 1957-71; prin. research scientist to lab. dir. Engrng. Expt. Sta., Ga. Inst. Tech., Atlanta, 1971-83; v.p. Electromagnetic Scis., Inc., Atlanta, 1983—. Contbr. chpt. to book, numerous articles to profl. jours. Fellow IEEE; mem. Soc. Microwave Theory and Techniques, Magnetics Soc., Mustang Club Am. (nat. dir.), Sigma Xi. Democrat. Methodist. Patentee microwave ferrimagnetic garnets. Office: Electromagnetic Scis Inc 125 Technology Park/Atlanta Norcross GA 30092

HARRISON, GREGORY, actor; b. Avalon, Calif., May 31, 1950. Studied at, Estelle Harman Actors Workshop and with Lee Strasberg and Stella Adler. Appeared in: movies Fraternity Row; star on: TV series Logan's Run, 1977-78, Trapper John, M.D, 1979—; role of Levi Zendt in: mini-series Centennial; appeared in: TV films include For Ladies Only, 1981, Trilogy in Terror, The Best Place To Be, The Gathering, Centennial, The Women's Room, Enola Gay, The Fighter; other TV appearances include Barnaby Jones; appeared on: stage in Festival, Los Angeles, San Francisco and Washington.; (Recipient Best New Actor award Dallas Film Festival 1976). Served with U.S. Army. Office: care Press Dept Twentieth Century-Fox TV PO Box 900 Beverly Hills CA 90213 *

HARRISON, HORACE HAWES, banker; b. Richmond, Va., Nov. 8, 1924; s. A.E. Willson and Anne Sterling (Hawes) H.; m. Sallie M. Labouisse, Feb. 18, 1949; children: Sally Cameron (Mrs. Thomas H. Lewis), Anne Hawes (Mrs. Alex S. Murchison). B.A., Yale U., 1948; grad., Stonier Grad. Sch. Banking, 1956, Mgmt. Program, U. Va. Grad. Sch. Bus., 1958. With United Va. Bank/State Planters (and predecessors), Richmond, 1948-72; pres. UVB Service Corp., 1971-72; exec. v.p. United Va. Bankshares, Inc., 1973-79; exec. v.p. adminstrn. United Va. Bank, 1980—. Mem. Richmond Tax Study Commn., 1971-72; Bd. dirs. Richmond Symphony, 1973-75, Hollywood Cemetary Co.; pres. Family and Children's Service Richmond, 1967-68; trustee Va. Council Health and Med. Care, 1969-71, Sch. for Bank Adminstrn at U. Wis., 1972-75. Served to 1st lt. AUS, 1942-46. Mem. Bank Adminstrn. Inst. (dir.-at-large 1969-71, nat. 1st v.p. 1973-74, nat. pres. 1974-75), Va. Bankers Assn., Soc. Colonial Wars (gov. 1982-84), Soc. of Cin., The Richmond German, The Richmond Hundred, Delta Kappa Epsilon, Berzelius. Clubs: Country of Va., Linville (N.C.) Golf. Home: 403 Harlan Circle Richmond VA 23226 Office: 919 E Main St Richmond VA 23219

HARRISON, JIM (JAMES THOMAS HARRISON), author; b. Grayling, Mich., Dec. 11, 1937; s. Winfield Sprague and Norma Olivia (Wahgren) H.; m. Linda May King, Oct. 10, 1959; children: Jamie Louise, Anna Severin. B.A. in Comparative Lit., Mich. State U., 1960, M.A., 1964. Instr. SUNY-Stony Brook, 1965-66. Author: Wolf: A False Memoir, 1971, A Good Day to Die, 1973, Farmer, 1976, Legends of the Fall, 1978, Warlock, 1981, Selected and New Poems, 1982; contbr. articles to Sports Illustrated. Nat. Endowment for Arts grantee; Guggenheim fellow, 1968-69. Mem. Trout Unltd., Grouse Soc. Office: EP Dutton Publishing 2 Park Ave New York NY 10016

HARRISON, JOEL PETER, advertising agency executive; b. Wilkes-Barre, Pa., Aug. 2, 1939; s. Frederick Martin and Celia (Landua) H.; m. Sally Golboro, Oct. 22, 1966; children: Jonathan David, Jeremy Andrew. B.A., Wilkes Coll., 1962. V.p., assoc. creative dir. Kenyon & Eckhardt, N.Y.C., 1971-77; sr. v.p., creative dir. Benton & Bowles, N.Y.C., 1977—. Author Clio award-winning works, 1971, 75, 77. Served to pfc. U.S. Army, 1962-68. Mem. The One Club, The Copy Club. Jewish. Club: Friars (N.Y.C.). Lodge: Indian Tr. Club. Office: Benton & Bowles Inc 909 Third Ave New York NY 10022

HARRISON, JOHN ALEXANDER, investment company executive, leasing company executive; b. Lakeland, Fla., Jan. 22, 1944; s. William Henry and Aileen Helen (Jarvi) H.; m. Susan Leigh Smart, May 9, 1970; children: Kathryn Leigh, Jane Elizabeth. B.I.E. with highest honors, Ga. Inst. Tech., 1966; M.B.A. (J. Spencer Love fellow 1966-68), Harvard U., 1968. With Baxter Travenol Labs., Inc., Deerfield, Ill., 1968-78, v.p. fin. and adminstrn. internat., 1977-78; v.p. fin. Tiger Leasing Group, 1980-82, N.Am. Car Corp. (subs. Tiger Internat., Inc.), Chgo., 1978-81; pres. Tiger Fin. Services, Inc., 1981-82; mng. dir. Merrill Lynch Capital Markets, N.Y.C., 1982—; exec. v.p. Merrill Lynch Leasing Inc., N.Y.C., 1982—. Bd. dirs. Youth Guidance, Chgo., 1979-80. Mem. Harvard Bus. Sch. Club Chgo. (dir. 1970-71), Tau Beta Pi, Phi Kappa Phi, Phi Eta Sigma, Tau Kappa Epsilon. Office: Merrill Lynch Leasing Inc 165 Broadway New York NY 10080

HARRISON, JOHN ARMSTRONG, univ. dean, historian; b. Johnstown, N.Y., July 4, 1915; s. Joseph Oliver and Rosalind (Rogers) H.; m. Clarice Troth, Jan. 18, 1943. B.A., Columbia, 1941; Ph.D., U. Calif. at Berkeley, 1949. Mem. faculty U. Fla., 1949-65, prof. history, 1956-65, chmn. dept., 1962-65, chmn. high honors studies, 1961-65; dean U. Miami Grad. Sch., Coral Gables, Fla., 1965-72, dean faculties, 1972-74, sr. acad. dean, 1974-81, disting. prof. history, 1974-81; mem. U.S. del. Internat. Congress Orientalists, Moscow, 1961, New Delhi, 1964; mem. com. lang. and area studies So. Regional Edn. Bd., 1963—; mem. Am. adv. bd. Japan Found., 1975—. Author books, articles history N.E. Asia.; Editor Jour.: Asian Studies, 1969-72. Served to lt. USNR, 1942-46; PTO. Decorated Order of Merit, Ecuador). Mem. Assn. Asian Studies (dir.). Home: 1500 NW 48 Terr Gainesville FL 32605

HARRISON, JOHN FRANCIS, educator; b. Liverpool, Eng., July 30, 1918; s. Thomas Walter and Alice Beatrice (Harrison) H.; m. Marjorie May Dysart, Nov. 25, 1959; children: Mary, Jean. B.A., Columbia U., 1938, M.A., 1940, Ph.D., 1952. Faculty English, Columbia Coll., Columbia Sch. Gen. Studies, Bethany Coll., also U. Newark, 1940-50; editorial staff Current Digest Soviet Press, 1950-52; cons. Fund for Advancement of Edn., 1952-54; chmn. dept. English, Transylvania U., Lexington, Ky., 1954-71, dean instrn., 1971-74, prof. English, 1974-80, adj. prof., 1980-83, prof. emeritus, 1983—. Served with AUS, 1942-46. Decorated Bronze Star, U.S.; Croix de Guerre (Belgium). Mem. AAUP. Home: 744 Reeder Rd Paramus NJ 07652

HARRISON, JOHN HARTWELL, surgeon, educator; b. Clarksville, Va., Feb. 16, 1909; s. Isaac Carrington and Rosalie (Smith) H.; m. Gertrude Chisholm, June 16, 1934 (dec. Feb. 1965); children: John Hartwell, Robert C. II, Cornelia, Jeffrey; m. Mary Louise Harding, July 16, 1965. B.S., U. Va., 1929, M.D., 1932; M.A. (hon.), Harvard, D.Sc., Roger Williams Coll., 1974. Diplomate: Am. Bd. Surgery, Am. Bd. Urology (examiner 1966—; pres. 1973). Intern Lakeside Hosp., Cleve., 1932-33; intern Peter Bent Brigham Hosp., Boston, also resident urology, asst. resident surgery, 1933-38, Harvey Cushing fellow surgery, 1939, sr. asso. urology, chief of service, 1940-45, urologic surgeon, chief of service, 1945-75, acting surgeon in chief, 1967, urologic surgeon emeritus, 1975—; asst. genito-urinary surgery Harvard Med. Sch., 1935-37, instr. surgery, 1938-39, instr. genito-urinary surgery, 1939-41, asso., 1941-46, asst. prof., 1946-48, asso. clin. prof., 1948-54, clin. prof., 1954-65, Elliott Carr Cutler prof. surgery, 1965-75, emeritus, 1975—; Edgar Burns vis. prof. urology Tulane U., 1961; Clyde Deming vis. prof. Yale Sch. Medicine, 1968; cons. urology Mass. Hosp. Sch. Crippled Children, Children's Med. Center, Boston Lying-In Hosp., VA Hosp., West Roxbury, Mass., Lemuel Shattuck

Hosp., Jamaica Plain, Mass.; vis. prof. Ohio State U., 1964, UCLA, 1966, 67, Duke U., 1967, 77, U. Mo., 1968, Johns Hopkins U., 1969, U. Va., 1970, U. Calif., San Francisco, 1972, Northwestern U., 1976, Med. Coll. S.C., 1977, Med. Coll. Va., 1973, Albany Med. Coll., 1981, La. State U. Med. Center, Shreveport, 1981; Louis McDonald Orr vis. prof. Emory U., 1981; Bishop John J. Russell Med. Coll. Va., 1981; lectr. St. Mary's Hosp.; mem. vis. faculty Mayo Clinic, 1965; cons. to surgeon gen. USAF. Author: Urology, 1970; Adv. bd.: Jour. Surgery; Editor: Campbell's Urology, 1978. Trustee Boston Med. Library; bd. visitors U. Va., 1966-74, chmn. med. com. Served to lt. col., M.C. AUS, 1942-45; PTO. Recipient Amory prize Am. Acad. Arts and Scis.; Ferdinand C. Valentine award N.Y. Acad. Medicine, 1970; Purkynje medal Czechoslovakian Med. Soc., 1971; Robert Cutler medal Peter Bent Brigham Trustees, 1973; Disting. Sci. Achievement award Mass. Kidney Found., 1979. Fellow ACS (gov. 1961-65); hon. fellow Royal Coll. Surgeons Ireland; mem. Am. Acad. Arts Scis., Am. Urol. Assn. (exec. com. 1961-62, Ramon Guiteras award 1965, pres. N.E. sect. 1953, hon. mem.), Boston Surgery Soc. (v.p. 1958, pres. 1972), N.E. Surgery Soc., Am. Surg. Assn. (1st v.p. 1970-71), Am. Assn. Genito-Urinary Surgeons (Barringer medal 1975, Edwin L. Keyes medal 1983, pres. 1976-77), Clin. Soc. Genito-Urinary Surgeons (pres. 1964-65), Urologic Forum Clin. Investigation, AMA, Roxbury Soc. for Med. Improvement, Phi Beta Kappa, Alpha Omega Alpha. Clubs: Tavern, Harvard, Brookline Country. Home: 25 Glenridge Rd Dedham MA 02026 Office: 319 Longwood Ave Boston MA 02115

HARRISON, JOHN RAYMOND, newspaper executive; b. Des Moines, June 8, 1933; s. Raymond Harrison and Dorothy (Stout) Harrison) Cohen; m. Lois Cowles, June 24, 1955 (dec. Apr. 1981); children: Gardner Mark, Kent Alfred (dec.), John Patrick, Lois Eleanor; m. Mary Gee MacQueen, Sept. 5, 1981. Grad., Phillips Exeter Acad., 1951; A.B., Harvard U., 1955; postgrad., Bus. Sch., 1955-56; D.H.L. (hon.), Fla. So. Coll. Vice pres. N.Y. Times Co.; dir. Internat. Herald Tribune, Paris; pres. Gainesville (Fla.) Sun Pub. Co., Lakeland (Fla.) Ledger Pub. Co., Ocala (Fla.) Star-Banner Pub. Co., Leesburg (Fla.) Comml. Pub. Co., Palatka (Fla.) Daily News Pub. Co., Avon Park (Fla.) Sun Pub. Co., Fernandina Beach (Fla.) News-Leader Pub. Co., Lake City (Fla.) Reporter Pub. Co., Sebring (Fla.) News Pub. Co., Marco Island (Fla.) Eagle Pub. Co., Zephyrhills (Fla.) News Pub. Co., Lexington (N.C.) Dispatch Pub. Co., Hendersonville (N.C.) Times-News Pub. Co., Wilmington (N.C.) Star News Pub. Co., Houma (La.) Newspapers, Inc., Comet-Press Newspapers, Inc., Thibadoux, La., Booneville Banner Ind. Pub. Co. (Miss.), Daily Corinthian Pub. Co., Corinth, Miss., Dyersburg State Gazette Pub. Co. (Tenn.), Sarasota Herald Tribune (Fla.), Florence Times Pub. Co. (Ala.), Harlan Daily Enterprise Pub. Co. (Ky.), York County Coast Pub. Co., Kenneburk, Maine, Lenoir News-Topic Pub. Co. (N.C.), Messenger Pub. Co., Madisonville, Ky., Middlesboro Daily News Pub. Co. (Ky.), Opelousas Daily World Pub. Co. (La.), New Tazewell Clarborne Progress Pub. Co. (Tenn.). Dir. Ft. Pierce (Fla.)-St. Lucie County Indsl. Devel. Council, 1959-62; Bd. dirs. Ft. Pierce Meml. Hosp., 1959-62, Lincoln Park Child Care Center, Ft. Pierce, 1959-62, Gainesville United Fund, 1965, Boys Club Gainesville, 1965, U. Fla. Found., 1967—, YMCA Greater Lakeland, 1967-69, Human Relations Council Lakeland, 1967-69, Boys Club Lakeland, A.R.C., 1967-69, Boys Club Lakeland, A.R.C., Lakeland; trustee Robert H. Anderson Found., Ridge Sch., Bartow, Fla.; mem. Pres.'s Resources Council Wellesley (Mass.) Coll.; bd. counsellors Fla. So. Coll., 1974; bd. visitors Emory U., 1984. Recipient Pulitzer prize editorial writing, 1965, Sigma Delta Chi Bronze medal, 1970, 73, Nat. Headliners award pub. service editorial writing, 1972, Walker Stone award for editorial writing Scripps-Howard Found., 1974, 76, Silver Gavel award for pub. service editorials Am. Bar Assn., 1977. Mem. Greater Lakeland C. of C. (dir. 1966-67), Associated Harvard Alumni (dir. 1979—), Spee Club, Hasty Pudding Inst. 1770. Clubs: Commerce (Atlanta); Surf (Wrightsville Beach, N.C.); Harvard of N.Y.C. Home: 2600 Peachtree Rd NW Unit 8 Atlanta GA 30305 Office: Monarch Plaza 3414 Peachtree Rd NE Suite 1560 Atlanta GA 30326

HARRISON, JOHN ROBERT, zoology educator; b. Washington, Oct. 11, 1923; s. William Henry and Edna Elizabeth (Rothery) H.; m. Muriel Ruth Adams, Sept. 26, 1946; children: William, Ellen. B.A., Am. U., 1948; M.A., Johns Hopkins, 1949; Ph.D., U. Minn., 1951. With dept. zoology Miami U., Oxford, Ohio, 1951-65, chmn. dept., 1958-61, research prof., 1961-65; chmn. dept. biology Washington and Jefferson Coll., 1965-68, State U. N.Y. at Oswego, 1968-70, chmn. dept. zoology, 1970-78, prof. zoology, radiation officer, 1978—; cons. in field. Contbr. articles to profl. jours. Served with USAAF, 1942-45. Mem. Am. Soc. Zoologists (mem. edn. com. 1961-69, chmn. 1964-67, 69), Soc. Developmental Biology, Nat. Assn. Biology Tchrs., Health Physics Soc., Sigma Xi. Home: RD 3 Box 113 Brown Dr Oswego NY 13126

HARRISON, LARRY DAVID, bank holding company executive, consultant; b. Wichita Falls, Tex., Sept. 12, 1939; s. V.C. and Kay B. (Brown) H.; m. Lynda W. Wolfe, Oct. 2, 1961 (div. Dec. 31, 1976); 1 son, Douglas. B.S.C., Tex. Christian U., 1962; postgrad., So. Meth. U., 1968-70. C.P.A., Tex. Acct. Ernst & Ernst, Ft. Worth, 1962-64; sr. v.p. fin. Tex. Am. Bacshares, Ft. Worth, 1964-74, Tex. Am. Bachshares, Mercantile, Tex., 1974-80, Tex. Am. Bancshares, Dallas, 1974-80; exec. v.p., treas. BancTex. Group, Dallas, 1980—. Mem. Fin. Execs. Inst. (pres. 1981-82), Am. Inst. C.P.A.s, Tex. Soc. C.P.A.s. Home: 2204 Golden Willow Richardson TX 75081 Office: BancTex Group Inc 1525 Elm St Dallas TX 75201

HARRISON, LOU, composer, educator; b. Portland, Oreg., May 14, 1917. Student, San Francisco State U., 1934-35, Henry Cowell and Arnold Schoenberg. Prof. music Black Mountain Coll., 1947-48, San Jose State Coll., Calif., 1967-80, Mills Coll., Oakland, Calif., 1980—; Am. rep. League of Asian Composers Conf., 1975. Composer Third Symphony, 1981-82; puppet opera Young Caesar, 1970-71; Four Strict Songs (commn. from Louisville Orch.), 1955, Suite for Piano, Violin and Small Orch., 1951. Recipient grant Guggenheim, 1952, Guggenheim, Rome, 1954, Rockefeller, Korea, 1962-63; Fulbright sr. scholar, N.Z., 1983. Mem. Charles Ives Soc. (dir.), Am. Acad. Arts and Letters (music mem.).

HARRISON, MARION EDWYN, lawyer; b. Phila., Sept. 17, 1931; s. Marion Edwyn and Jessye Beatrice (Cilles) H.; m. Carmelita Ruth Deimel, Sept. 6, 1952; children: Angelique Harrison Bounds, Marion Edwyn III, Henry Deimel. B.A., U. Va., 1951; LL.B., George Washington U., 1954, LL.M., 1959. Bar: Va. bar 1954, D.C. bar 1958, also Supreme Ct. bar 1958. Spl. asst. to gen. counsel Post Office Dept., 1958-60, asso. gen. counsel, 1960-61, mem. bd. contract appeals, 1958-61; partner firm Harrison, Lucey & Sagle (and predecessors), Washington, 1961-78, Barnett & Alagia, 1978—; Mem. council Adminstrv. Conf. U.S., 1971-78; mem. D.C. Law Revision Commn., 1975—; lectr. Nat. Jud. Coll., Reno, 1979. Author articles, manuals.; Editor-in-chief: Fed. Bar News, 1960-63; mem. editorial bd.: Adminstrv. Law Rev, 1976—. Pres. Young Republican Fedn. Va., 1954-55; mem. Va. Rep. Central Com., 1954-55; Bd. visitors Judge Advocate Gen. Sch., Charlottesville, Va., 1976-78. Served as officer AUS, 1955-58. Decorated Commendation medal. Fellow Am. Bar Found.; mem. ABA (chmn. sect. adminstrv. law 1974-75, ho. of dels. 1978—, bd. govs. 1982—), Fed. Bar Assn. (nat. council 1966-82), Inter-Am. Bar Assn., Bar Assn. D.C. (chmn. adminstrv. law sect. 1970-71, bd. dirs. 1971-72), George Washington U. Law Assn. (pres. 1974-77). Episcopalian (vestry). Clubs: Washington Golf and Country, Metropolitan, Nat. Lawyers (Washington); Farmington Country (Charlottesville, Va.). Home: 4111 N Ridgeview Rd Arlington VA 22207 Office: 1000 Thomas Jefferson St NW Washington DC 20007

HARRISON, MARK, newspaper editor; b. Aug. 10, 1924; s. Harry A. and Sonia (Doduck) H.; m. Isabel Clifton Hay-Roe, Feb. 24, 1950; children—Steven Paul, Timothy Jon, Judith Ann, Nancy Ellen. A.B., U. Toronto, 1948, postgrad., 1949. With Toronto Daily Star, 1949, exec. editor, 1969-77; editor Montreal Gazette, 1977—. Served with RCAF, 1943-46. Club: Royal Montreal Golf. Office: Montreal Gazette 250 Rue St Antoine Montreal PQ H2Y 3R7 Canada

HARRISON, MARK I., lawyer; b. Pitts., Oct. 17, 1934; s. Coleman and Myrtle (Seidenman) H.; m. Ellen R. Gier, June 15, 1958; children: Lisa, Jill. A.B., Antioch Coll., 1957; LL.B., Harvard U., 1960. Bar: Ariz. 1961. Law clk. to justices Ariz. Supreme Ct., 1960-61; since practiced in Phoenix; partner Harrison & Lerch, 1966—. Co-author: Arizona Appellate Practice, 1966; contbr. articles to legal jours. Bd. dirs. Careers for Youth, 1963-67, pres., 1966-67; vice chmn. Maricopa County Democratic Central Com., 1967-68, Ariz. Dem. Com., 1969-70; legal counsel Ariz. Dem. Com., 1970-72; del. Dem. Nat. Conv., 1968; chmn. Phoenix City Bond Adv. Commn., 1976-79; pres. Valley Commerce Assn., 1978. Fellow Am. Bar Found.; mem. ABA, Maricopa County Bar Assn. (pres. 1970), Am. Trial Lawyers Assn., Phoenix Assn. Def. Counsel, Am. Bd. Trial Advocates, State Bar Ariz. (bd. govs. 1971-77, pres. 1975-76), Nat. Conf. Bar Pres. (exec. council 1971-73, 75-79, pres. 1977-78), Western States Bar Conf. (pres. 1978-79), Am. Judicature Soc. (exec. com. 1983—), Ariz. Civil Liberties Union, Harvard Law Sch. Assn. (nat. exec. council 1980—). Home: 33 E State Ave Phoenix AZ 85020 Office: 650 N 2d Ave Phoenix AZ 85003

HARRISON, MAURICE R., JR., construction company executive; b. Des Moines, Iowa, Aug. 1, 1918; s. Maurice Rowlen and Helen (Cowles) H.; m. Mae McDonald; children: Maurice R., Michael J., Peter R. B.S. in Archtl. Engring., Civil Engring., Iowa State U., 1940. Registered profl. engr. Engr. M.R. Harrison Constrn. Corp., Miami, Fla., 1940-55, pres., 1955-72, chmn. bd., chief exec. officer, 1972—. Mem. Profl. Engrs. Assn. S.E. Fla. (pres. 1955-56), Young Pres.'s Orgn. (pres. 1960), Am. Auto. Assn. (chmn. 1977-78), Associated Gen. Contractors (pres. 1952-53), Execs. Assn. Democrat. Presbyterian. Clubs: Rotary (pres. 1959), Miami, Bath. Office: M R Harrison Constrn Corp PO Box 510215 Miami FL 33151

HARRISON, MICHAEL JAY, educator, physicist; b. Chgo., Aug. 20, 1932; s. Nathan J. and Mae (Nathan) H.; m. Ann Tukey, Sept. 1, 1970. A.B., Harvard, 1954; M.S., U. Chgo., 1956, Ph.D., 1960. Fulbright fellow and H. Van Loon fellow in theoretical physics U. Leiden, Netherlands, 1954-55; NSF fellow U. Chgo., 1957-59; research fellow math. physics U. Birmingham, Eng., 1959-61; asst. prof. Mich. State U., East Lansing, 1961-63, asso. prof., 1963-68, prof., 1968—, faculty grievance officer, 1972-73, dean, 1973—; vis. research physicist Inst. Theoretical Physics, U. Calif., Santa Barbara, 1980-81; with Air Force Cambridge Research Center, summer 1953, M.I.T. Lincoln Lab., summer 1954, RCA Sarnoff Lab., summers 1961-63; physicist Westinghouse Labs., summer 1956; cons. RCA Lab., 1961-64, United Aircraft Co., 1964-66, U.K. Atomic Energy Authority, Harwell Lab., summer 1960, Thailand project in Bangkok, Mich. State U.-AID, summer 1968. Contbr. articles to U.S., fgn. profl. jours. Am. Council on Edn. fellow U. Calif., Los Angeles, 1970-71; vis. research physicist Inst. Theoretical Physics, U. Calif., Santa Barbara, 1980-81. Fellow Am. Phys. Soc., Sigma Xi; mem. Phi Beta Kappa. Jewish. Clubs: Harvard of Central Michigan, Rotary. Office: Physics Dept Mich State U East Lansing MI 48824

HARRISON, REX CARY, actor; b. Huyton, Eng., Mar. 5, 1908; s. William Reginald and Edith (Carey) H.; m. Marjorie Noel Collette Thoma, 1934; 1 son; m. Lilli Palmer, 1943 (div. 1957); m. Kay Kendall, 1957 (div. dec. 1959); m. Rachel Roberts, 1962 (div. 1971); m. Elizabeth Rees Harris (div. 1976); m. Mercia Mildred Tinker. Ed., Liverpool Coll.; hon. degree, Boston U. Author: Rex, 1974, If Love Be Love; Stage debut, Liverpool (Eng.) Repertory Theatre, 1924, with theatre, 1924-27; played Jack: on tour with Charley's Aunt, 1927; London stage debut as Rankin in: The Ninth Man, Prince of Wales Theatre, 1931; N.Y.C. stage debut as Tubbs Barrow in: Sweet Aloes, Booth Theatre, 1936; appeared in: French Without Tears, at Criterion, 1936-38; in: Design For Living and No Time for Comedy, Haymarket Theatre, 1939-41, Anne of the Thousand Days, Schubert Theatre, N.Y.C., 1948-49 (Antoinette Perry award for best actor), The Cocktail Party, New Theatre, London, 1950, Venus Observed, Century Theatre, N.Y.C., 1952; as Henry Higgins in: My Fair Lady, Mark Hellinger Theatre, N.Y.C., 1956-57 (Antoinette Perry award for best actor), and at Drury Ln., London, 1958-59; in touring co., 1981; in: The Fighting Cock, Anta Theatre, N.Y.C., 1959, Platonov, Royal Ct., 1960 (Evening Standard award for best actor), August for the People, Edinburgh (Scotland) Festival, 1961 and, Royal Ct. Theatre; in the: Lionle Touch, Lyric, 1969, Henry IV, Her Majesty's, 1974; in: Perrichon's Travels, Chichester, 1976, Casar and Cleopatro, N.Y.C., 1977, and others; played in and produced: Bell, Book and Candle, Ethel Barrymore Theatre, N.Y.C., 1951, and Phoenix Theatre, London, 1954; dir. and appeared in: Love of Four Colonels, Schubert Theatre, N.Y.C., 1953; producer: Nina, Haymarket Theatre, London, 1955; appeared in: films including Storm in a Teacup, 1936, St. Martin's Lane, 1937, Over the Moon, 1938, Night Train to Munich, Major Barbara, 1940-41, Blithe Spirit, 1944, I Live in Grosvenor Square, 1944, The Rake's Progress, 1945, Anna and the King of Siam, 1946, The Ghost and Mrs. Muir, 1947, The Foxes of Harrow, 1947, Escape, 1948, Unfaithfully Yours, 1948, The Long Dark Hall, 1951, King Richard and the Crusaders, 1954, The Constant Husband, 1955, The Reluctant Debutante, 1958, Midnight Lace, 1960, The Happy Thieves, 1961, Cleopatra (as Julius Caesar), 1962, My Fair Lady, 1964 (Acad. award as best actor), The Yellow Rolls Royce, 1965, The Agony and the Ecstasy, 1965, The Honey Pot, 1967, Doctor Doolittel, 1967, A Flea in her Ear, 1967, Staircase, 1968, The Prince and the Pauper, 1976, Man in the Iron Mask, 1977, Ashanti, 1978; TV appearances: Don Quixote, 1972, The Kingfisher, 1982; author: Rex, 1974, If Love Be Love. Served with RAF Vol. Res., 1941-45. Decorated Order of Merit, Italy; recipient Golden Globe award, Film Critics award, Antoinette Perry award for David di Do'onattella award, Triomph award, Paris, 1957. Clubs: Players; Garrick, Beefstead, Green Room (London); Travelors (Paris). Office: La Renadière Carsinje 1252 Geneva Switzerland *

HARRISON, RICHARD DONALD, food company executive; b. Salt Lake City, May 19, 1923; s. William Z. and Mary Frances (Sappington) H.; m. Marian D. Fletcher, Feb., 1984; children: Amy Virginia, Leslie Lynn, Julie Fleming, Susan Elizabeth, Alyse Carrie, Richard Donald. B.A., Stanford U., 1946; LL.B., U. Mich., 1949. Bar: D.C., Mich., Utah 1950, Wash. 1952, also U.S. Supreme Ct., other fed. cts 1952. Spl. asst. to atty. tax div., appellate sect. Dept. Justice, 1950-52; pvt. practice, Seattle, 1952-54; with Fleming Cos., Inc., Topeka, 1954—, v.p., 1957-64, dir. planning, 1963-64, pres., 1964—, chief exec. officer, 1966—, chmn., 1981—, also dir.; dir. Fed. Res. Bank, Kansas City, Quaker Oats Co., Chgo., Coleman Co. Bd. dirs. United Way; chmn. Okla. Art Center; past pres. Okla. Sci. and Arts Found.; bd. dirs. Oklahoma City YMCA, Allied Arts Found., Oklahoma City Symphony, State Fair Okla., Oklahoma City Community Found., Food Mktg. Inst., Washington; bd. govs. Okla. Christian Coll.; trustee Oklahoma City U., Midwest Research Inst., Kansas City, Mo. Mem. Nat. Am. Wholesale Grocers (past pres.), Oklahoma City C. of C. (past pres.), Sigma Chi, Phi Delta Phi. Presbyn. Clubs: River (Kansas City); Beacon, Oklahoma City Golf and Country, Whitehall (Oklahoma City); Argyle (San Antonio).

HARRISON, RICHARD SWINTON, lawyer; b. Cranford, N.J., Dec. 7, 1932; s. Edgar E. and Ellen (Swinton) H.; children: Peter, Margaret. B.A., Bowdoin Coll., 1954; LL.B., Yale U., 1960. Bar: Ohio 1960. Atty. Squire, Sanders & Dempsey, Cleve., 1960-68, 71, ptnr., 1972—; asst. to pres. White Motor Co., Cleve., 1968-71; Tiffin Metal Products, Ohio. Trustee Big Bros., Cleve., 1978—. 1st lt. U.S. Army, 1955-57. Bowdoin scholar, 1954. Mem. ABA; me. Ohio Bar Assn.; mem. Phi Beta Kappa. Clubs: University, Cleve., Racquet. Office: 1800 Huntington Bank Bldg Cleveland OH 44115

HARRISON, ROBERT DREW, retail store executive; b. Des Moines, May 17, 1923; s. Roland T. and Grace M. (Drew) H.; m. Evelyn Colonna Berkley, June 5, 1948; children—Nancy Berkley, Evelyn Lee, Roberta Drew, Adrienne Tipp. S.B., Harvard, 1945, M.B.A., 1948. Mem. faculty Harvard Grad. Sch. Bus. Administrn., 1948-49; with John Wanamaker, Phila., 1949—, vice chmn., 1978—; dir. Provident Nat. Bank, Phila., Phila. Electric Co., Fidelity Mut. Life Ins. Co., Phila. Savs. Fund Soc., Bell Telephone of Pa., Mut. Assurance Soc. Bd. dirs. Phila. Urban Coalition, Old Phila. Devel. Corp., United Way Southeastern Pa., Pennjerdel. Served to lt (j.g.) USNR, 1943-46. Clubs: Union League (Phila); Merion (Pa.); Golf; Millrose Athletic Assn. (N.Y.C.) (bd. dirs.); Merior Cricket (Haverford)). Home: 326 Grays Ln Haverford PA 19041 Office: 1300 Market St Philadelphia PA 19101

HARRISON, ROBERT JOSEPH, utility company executive; b. St. Charles, Mo., June 21, 1931; s. Daniel Anthony and Marie Elizabeth (Riney) H.; m. Monique Gilbert, June 18, 1955; children: David, Gregory, Elizabeth, Thomas. B.B.A., U. Okla., 1957. With Public Service Co. N.H., Manchester, 1957—, fin. v.p., dir., until 1980, pres., 1980—, chief fin. officer, from 1980, now also chief exec. officer, dir.; trustee Mchts. Savs. Bank, Manchester. Bd. dirs. United Way, 1970-78, mem. exec. com., v.p., 1972—; pres. St. Catherine's Parish Council. Served with USAF, 1951-55. Mem. Fin. Execs. Inst., Atomic Indsl. Forum, Edison Electric Inst. (exec. com. fin. div.), Electric Council New Eng. Office: Pub Service Co NH PO Box 330 1000 Elm St Manchester NH 03105 *

HARRISON, RUSSELL EDWARD, banker; b. Grandview, Man., Can., May 31, 1921; s. Edward Smith and Annie L. H.; m. Nancy Doreen Bell, Oct. 18, 1944; 2 children. Ed., U. Man. With Canadian Imperial Bank of Commerce (formerly Canadian Bank of Commerce), 1945—, head of ops. in, Que., Montreal, 1956-69, exec. v.p., chief gen. mgr. head office, Toronto, Ont., 1969-73, pres., chief operating officer, 1973-76, chmn., chief exec. officer, 1976-84, chmn., 1984—, also dir.; dir. MacMillan Bloedel Ltd., Campbell Soup Co., Can. Life Assurance Co., Calif. Can. Bank, TransCan. PipeLines, Dominion Realty Co., Ltd., Royal Ins. Co. Can. Ltd., Falconbridge Ltd., ROINS Holding Ltd., Can. Eastern Fin. Co.; mem. Bd. Trade Met. Toronto. Mem. adv. bd. Bus. Sch., U. Western Ont., Bus. Sch., McMaster U. Served with Canadian Army, World War II. Clubs: Albany, Toronto, York (Toronto); Rosedale Golf.; Mt. Royal, St. James's (Montreal); Ranchmen's (Calgary). Office: Commerce Ct W Toronto ON Canada M5L 1A2

HARRISON, S. DAVID, lawyer; b. N.Y.C., Jan. 29, 1930; s. Louis and Molly (Ginsburg) H.; m. Joan S. Horowitz, Mar. 23, 1958; children: Andrew L., Rachel E. A.B., Harvard U., 1951, LL.B., 1954; LL.M., NYU, 1959. Bar: N.J. 1955, N.Y. 1968. Law sec. N.J. Supreme Ct. Justice William J. Brennan, Jr., 1954-55; asso., then partner firm Platoff, Platoff & Heftler, Union City, N.J., 1955-65; corp. counsel Beaunit Corp., N.Y.C., 1965-71, corp. sec., 1966-71; asst. sec. Tyrex, Inc., 1969-71; dir. Man-Made Fibers Producers Assn., 1970-71; pvt. practice law, N.Y.C., 1971-81; mem. firm McLaughlin Stern Ballen & Ballen; dir. various corps. Mem. Am., N.Y. State, Comml. Lawyers bar assns., Nat. Panel Arbitrators, Am. Arbitration Assn. Jewish. Club: Mason. Home: Two Oxford Rd Hastings-on-Hudson NY 10706 Office: 122 E 42d St New York NY 10168

HARRISON, SELIG SEIDENMAN, journalist; b. Wilkinsburg, Pa., Mar. 19, 1927; s. Coleman and Myrtle (Seidenman) H.; m. Barbara Johnston, Oct. 10, 1951; children—Coleman Peter, Kathreen Grosvenor. A.B., Harvard, 1948, 1954-55. With Detroit bur. A.P., 1949-50, fgn. desk, N.Y.C., 1951, 55, fgn. corr., New Delhi, India, 1951-54; research asso. Lang. and Communication Research Center, Columbia, 1955; cons. Center S. Asia Studies, U. Calif. at Berkeley, 1955-56; asso. editor New Republic, 1956-60, mng. editor, 1960-62; S. Asia corr. Washington Post, 1962-65, mem. editorial staff, 1966-67, nat. reporter, 1973-74; sr. fellow charge Asian studies Brookings Instn., 1967-68; chief N.E. Asia bur. Washington Post, Tokyo, 1968-72; sr. fellow East-West Center, Hawaii, 1972-73; sr. asso. Carnegie Endowment for Internat. Peace, 1974—. Author: India: The Most Dangerous Decades, 1960, The Widening Gulf: Asian Nationalism and American Policy, 1978, China, Oil and Asia: Conflict Ahead?, 1977, In Afghanistan's Shadow, 1981, also articles.; Editor: India and the United States, 1961. Mem. Am. Polit. Sci. Assn. Clubs: Overseas Writers, Nat. Press (Washington). Home: 400 E 54 St New York NY 10022 Office: Carnegie Endowment for Internat Peace 30 Rockefeller Plaza New York NY 10017

HARRISON, STEPHEN COPLAN, biochemist; b. New Haven, June 4, 1943; s. Harold E. and Helen Miriam (Coplan) H. A.B., Harvard U., 1963, Ph.D., 1968. Jr. fellow Harvard U. Soc. Fellows; also research fellow Children's Cancer Research Found., Boston, 1968-71; vis. scientist Max Planck Inst. Medizinische Forschung, Heidelberg, W.Ger., 1971-72; mem. faculty Harvard U., 1972—, prof. biochemistry, 1977—, chmn. bd. tutors in biochem. scis., 1972—. Mem. Am. Soc. Microbiology, Am. Crystallographic Assn., AAAS. Home: 240 Brattle St Cambridge MA 02138 Office: 7 Divinity Ave Cambridge MA 02138

HARRISON, THOMAS JAMES, electrical engineer; b. Wausau, Wis., May 13, 1935; s. Glenn M. and A. Laura (Barclay) H.; m. Carol H. Harrison; children: Nancy E., Kristine A. B.S. in Elec. Engring, Carnegie Inst. Tech., 1957, M.S., 1958; Ph.D., Stanford U., 1964. Registered profl. engr., Calif. Design engr. IBM, Poughkeepsie, N.Y., 1958-59, asso. engr., Peekskill, N.Y., 1960, staff engr., advisory engr., San Jose, Calif., 1960-68, sr. engr., Boca Raton, Fla., 1968-78, mem. corp. tech. com., Armonk, N.Y., 1979, program mgr., mgr. advanced software engring. tech., Boca Raton, 1980—; mem. U.S. Nat. Com. for Internat. Electrotech. Commn., 1972—; U.S. expert Internat. Orgn. Standardization Coms., 1975—; mem. engring. com. U. Fla., 1972—, Fla. Atlantic U., 1971—. Author, editor: Handbook of Industrial Control Computers, 1972, Minicomputers in Industrial Control, 1978; contbr. articles to tech. handbooks and jours. Served with AUS, 1959. Recipient Disting. Service award U. Fla., 1983. Fellow IEEE, Instrument Soc. Am. (dir. standards and practices bd. 1971—, v.p. 1980—), ASTM, Am. Nat. Standards Inst. (standard mgmt. bds.), Sigma Xi, Tau Beta Pi, Delta Upsilon, Omicron Delta Kappa, Eta Kappa Nu, Phi Kappa Phi. Club: Rotary. Patentee analog-to-digital converters, sampling filter. Home: 855 Alamanda St Boca Raton FL 33432 Office: IBM PO Box 1328 Boca Raton FL 33432

HARRISON, TIMOTHY STONE, physician; b. Kodaikanal, S. India, July 13, 1927; U.S., 1939; (parents U.S. citizens); s. Paul Wilberforce and Regina (Rabbe) H.; m. Eliza Middleton Cope, July 1, 1961; children—Abigail DeNormandie, Emily Cope. A.B., Hope Coll., Holland, Mich., 1949; M.D., Johns Hopkins U., 1953. Intern, then resident in surgery Johns Hopkins Hosp., Balt., 1953-56; resident in surgery Mass. Gen. Hosp., Boston, 1956-59; spl. research fellow in physiology Karolinska Inst., Stockholm, 1959-60; asst. prof., then assoc. prof. surgery U. Mich. Med. Sch., 1962-68, prof., 1971-75; prof. surgery, chmn. dept. Am. U., Beirut, 1968-71; prof. surgery and physiology Milton S. Hershey (Pa.) Med. Center, Pa. State U. Med. Sch., 1975—; cons. Kuwait Ministry Public Health, 1968—. Sr. author: Surgical Disorders of the Adrenal Gland: Physiologic Background and Treatment, 1975. Served with USNR and USMCR, 1945-47. Grantee NIH, 1963—. Mem. Endocrine Soc., Am. Surg. Assn., Soc. Clin. Surgery, Soc. U. Surgeons, Am. Physiol. Soc., Halsted Soc., James IV Assn. Surgeons. Episcopalian. Home: 137 Furnace St Lebanon PA 17042 Office: Hershey Med Center Hershey PA 17033

HARRISON, WALTER ASHLEY, physicist, educator; b. Flushing, N.Y., Apr. 26, 1930; s. Charles Allison and Gertrude (Ashley) H.; m. Lucille Prince Carley, July 17, 1954; children—Richard Knight, John Carley, William Ashley, Robert Walter. B. Engring. Physics, Cornell U., 1953; M.S., U. Ill., 1954, Ph.D., 1956. Physicist Gen. Elec. Research Labs., Schenectady, 1956-65; prof. applied physics Stanford, 1965—. Author: Pseudopotentials in the Theory of Metals, 1966, Solid State Theory, 1970, Electronic Structure and the Properties of Solids, 1980; editor: The Fermi Surface, 1960. Guggenheim fellow, 1970-71; recipient von Humboldt Sr. U.S. Scientist award, 1981; vis. fellow Clare Hall, Cambridge U., 1970-71. Fellow Am. Phys. Soc. Home: 817 San Francisco Ct Stanford CA 94305

HARRISON, WARD DUNCAN, paper mfr.; b. Blue Earth, Minn., Sept. 15, 1909; s. Charles H. and Grace (Putney) H.; m. Martha Jentz, Sept. 5, 1936; children—Frederick, Martha Ann, Lynn. B.S., Iowa State Coll., 1932; M.S., Inst. Paper Chemistry, Appleton, Wis., 1934, Ph.D., 1936. Registered engr., N.C. Chem. engr. Riegel Paper Corp., Milford, N.J., 1936-41, asst. to exec. v.p., N.Y.C., 1948-49; v.p., Milford, 1949-55, N.Y.C., 1955-58, dir., 1950-58; pres. Allied Paper Corp. (now Allied Paper Inc. div. SCM Corp.), 1958-64, chmn. bd., 1964-70, chief exec. officer, 1964-70; also dir.; v.p., dir. SCM Corp., 1968-70, asst. to exec. v.p., 1971; chmn. bd. Howard Paper Mills, Inc., Dayton, Ohio, 1971—, pres., 1972-73; also chief exec. officer; pres. Maxwell Paper Corp., 1972-73; also chief exec. officer; chmn. bd. Brazil Coal & Clay Corp., Ind., 1974—; pres. Harrison Enterprises, 1978—; chmn. bd. Watervliet Paper Co., Mich., 1981—; asst. gen. mgr. Ecusta Paper Corp., Psigah Forest, N.C., 1941-48. Contbr. articles to profl. publs. Mem. T.A.P.P.I. (pres. 1957-58), Paper Industry Mgmt. Assn. Presbyn. Club: Union League (N.Y.C.). Home: 2230 S Patterson Blvd Dayton OH 45409 Office: 115 Columbia St Dayton OH 45407

HARRISON, WILLIAM NEAL, author, educator; b. Dallas, Oct. 29, 1933; m. Merlee Portman, Feb. 1, 1959; children: Laurie, Sean, Quentin. B.A., Tex. Christian U., 1955; M.A., Vanderbilt U., 1960; postgrad., U. Ia., 1961-62. Prof. English U. Ark., 1968—. Author: The Theologian, 1965, In a Wild Sanctuary, 1969, Lessons in Paradise, 1971, Roller Ball Murder and Other Stories, 1975, Africana, 1976, Savannah Blue, 1981, Burton and Speke, 1982. Guggenheim Meml. fellow, 1973-74. Office: care Owen Laster William Morris Agy 1350 Ave of Americas New York NY 10019

HARRISON, WILLIAM WRIGHT, banker; b. Kingston, N.Y., Aug. 6, 1915; s. James Burwell and Isabella (Clarke) H.; m. Janet Phillips, Apr. 6, 1940; children—Janet P. (Mrs. Richard Rea Hinch), Susan F. (Mrs. Glassell Slaughter Fitz-Hugh, Jr.), William Wright. Student, U. Va., 1933-34. With Va. Nat. Bank (formerly Peoples Nat. Bank Charlottesville), 1942—, chmn., chief exec. officer, 1969-80, dir., cons., 1980—; former chmn. Allied Bank Internat.; dir. Shenandoah Life Ins. Co., Roanoke, Va., Royster Co., Norfolk; chmn. Minbanc Capital Corp., Washington. Former chmn. Municiple Bond Commn., Norfolk; chmn. Va. Found. Ind. Colls.; bd. dirs. Gen. Hosp. Virginia Beach, U. Va. Patent Found., Va. Opera, Old Dominion U. Research Found., Gov.'s Commn. on Indsl. Devel.; trustee Norfolk Found., Eastern Va. Med. Sch. Found., Chrysler Mus., Norfolk; former bd. visitors U. Va. Mem. Norfolk C. of C. (pres. 1971). Episcopalian. Clubs: Princess Anne Country, Harbor. Home: 1104 Wythe Ln Virginia Beach VA 23451 Office: 1 Commercial Pl Norfolk VA 23510

HARRISS, JULIUS WELCH, mfg. co. exec.; b. High Point, N.C., Oct. 26, 1905; s. Julius Ward and Florence (Welch) H. A.B., Duke U., 1927. Pres. Harriss & Covington Hosiery Mills, Inc., 1928-73, chmn. bd., 1974—; pres., dir. Harco, Inc. Mem. Edenton (N.C.) Hist. Commn.; past mem. interstate com. YMCA's of Carolinas; past mem. internat. com. YMCA's of U.S. and Can.; past mem. nat. council Met. Opera, N.Y.C.; Past bd. dirs. High Point Hist. Mus.; trustee Duke, 1947-73, trustee emeritus, 1973—; also mem. bldg. com. bd. visitors Duke Library; mem. Meth. Coll. Found. of N.C., Inc.; corporate mem. Research Triangle Inst.; past trustee, treas., mem. exec. com. High Point Meml. Hosp., now trustee emeritus; past bd. dirs. High Point Community Concert Assn., Carolina United Community Service; past bd. dirs., mem. exec. com. N.C. Symphony; former trustee N.C. Central U., High Point Pub. Library. Served to lt. comdr. USNR, World War II. Mem. N.C. Art Soc. (life, former dir.), N.C. Lit. and Hist. Assn. (life), Alpha Tau Omega. Methodist (steward). Clubs: High Point Rotary (past pres.), Emerywood Country (past sr. bd. dirs.), Quadrille, String and Splinter (High Point); Executives (past dir.). Office: 2525 E Green Dr High Point NC 27261

HARRITON, ABRAHAM, artist; b. Bucharest, Romania, Feb. 16, 1893; came to U.S., 1900, naturalized, 1906; s. Joseph and Ghizella (Scheiner) H.; m. Estelle Safron, Mar. 9, 1919; children: Charles Francis, Maria Louise. Student, N.A.D., (Hallgarten prize figure painting, 1911, compositon 1913, painting 1915, Suydam bronze medal still life, 2d Baldwin prize etching 1911, Baldwin prize etching 1913, 15), 1908-15. Exhbns. include, Panama-Pacific World's Fair, 1915, N.A.D., 1914-20, 41, 45, 47-48, 67, Whitney Mus., 1936, 37, 39, 40, 41, N.Y. World's Fair, 1939, Carnegie Inst., 1941, 43, 44, 45, 46, Corcoran Gallery, 1941, Met. Mus. Art, 1942, Goodwill Exhbn. Am. Art in, N.Y.C., London, Scotland, 1945, also Bklyn. Mus., St. Louis City Art Mus., Pa. Acad. Fine Arts, Art Inst. Chgo., Mus. Modern Art; represented in permanent collections, Whitney Mus. Am. Art, Hirshhorn Mus., Washington, Newark Mus., Montclair Art Mus., Oakland (Calif.) Art Mus., Addison Gallery Art, Ulrich Mus. Art, Wichita State U., Tel Aviv and Ain Harod mus., Israel, Living Arts Found., N.Y.C., Archives Am. Art of Smithsonian Instn., other pub. and pvt. collections. Served with U.S. Army, World War I. Recipient Patrons prize 2d ann. exhbn. Nat. Soc. Painters in Casein, 1956, Marine award 14th New Eng. Exhbn. Silvermine Guild of Artists, 1963; Marjorie Peabody Waite award Nat. Inst. Arts and Letters, 1968; Pauline Mintz Meml. award Audubon Artists, 1977; Alice G. Melrose Meml. award Audubon Artists 40th Anniversary Exhbn., 1982; Mark Rothko Found. grantee, 1974. Mem. Audubon Arts, Artists Equity Assn. Spl. work on theory and practice of underpainting and glazing. Abraham Harriton Manuscript Collection at Syracuse U. in Library Archives. Address: 66 W 9th St New York NY 10011 *I have always felt that my art should have elements of a lasting value, which means that it should bridge the gap from the great cultural past and extend in consonance to the future...*

HARRITT, NORMAN L., manufacturing company executive; b. Kansas City, Mo., Mar. 19, 1941; s. Gilbert Norman and Cladys Marie (Henderson) H.; m. Cynthia Marie Lanza, Aug. 4, 1965; children: Kevin, Mark. B.A. in Econs., Duke U., 1963; M.B.A. in Fin., U. Pitts., 1965. Group controller Rockwell Internat., Troy, Mich., 1976-77; v.p. and controller Consol. Foods Corp., Chgo., 1977-78; v.p. fin. and adminstrn. Truck Group Internat. Harvester Co., Chgo., 1978-80. Active Little League Baseball, Oak Brook, Ill. Served with USAR, 1964-69. Mem. Fin. Execs. Inst. Republican. Methodist. Clubs: Economic (Chgo.); Butterfield Country (Oak Brook, Ill.). Home: 8 Hampton Dr Oak Brook IL 60521 Office: Internat Harvester Co 401 N Michigan Ave Chicago IL 60611

HARROD, SCOTT, consulting manufacturing executive; b. Sandwich, Ill., Aug. 11, 1910; s. Fred and Hattie (Scott) H.; m. Doris Shearer, Sept. 10, 1938; children—Scott B., Frederick S. A.B. magna cum laude, Knox Coll., 1933. Tchr. math. Galva (Ill.) High Sch., 1933-36; investment analyst Lawrence Stern & Co., Chgo., 1936-38; asst. treas. Spiegel, Inc., Chgo., 1938-43, Bell & Howell Co., 1946-49, treas., 1949-50, sec.-treas., 1950-55; dir.; sec.-treas. Bell & Howell Can., 1954, Three Dimension Co., Chgo., 1954-55; sec. DeVry Corp., Chgo., 1955; v.p. DITTO, Inc., Chgo., 1955-57, exec. v.p., gen. mgr., 1957-58, pres., chief exec. officer, 1958-64; also dir.; exec. v.p., dir. H.M. Harper Co., 1965-66, pres., chief exec. officer, 1966-71; pres., dir. ITT Harper Inc., 1971-72; cons. ITT Tech. & Indsl. Products Group, 1972-74; cons. to mgmt. Anti Corrosive Metal Products Co., 1972—; treas., dir. Nat. Lecture Bur., Inc., 1950-55; dir., v.p. Bell & Howell Co., 1962-64. Contbr. articles to profl. publs. Pres. Park Ridge (Ill.) Sch. Bd., 1953-56; Trustee Knox Coll., 1961-64, 69—. Served with USNR, 1943-46. Recipient Sec. of Navy Forrestal commendation. Mem. Financial Execs. Inst., Phi Beta Kappa, Beta Theta Pi. Clubs: Univ., Econ. (Chgo.). Home: 21084 N Middleton Dr Kildeer IL 60047

HARROLD, BERNARD, lawyer; b. Wells County, Ind., Feb. 5, 1925; s. James Delmer and Marie (Mounsey) H.; m. Kathleen Walker, Nov. 26, 1952; children—Bernard James, Camilla Ruth, Renata Jane. Student, Biarritz Am. U., 1945; A.B., Ind. U., 1949, LL.B., 1951. Bar: Ill. 1951. Since practiced in, Chgo.; assoc., then mem. firm Kirkland, Ellis, Hodson, Chaffetz & Masters, 1951-67; sr. partner Wildman, Harrold, Allen & Dixon, 1967—. Note editor: Ind. Law Jour, 1950-51; contbr. articles to profl. jours. Mem. Winnetka Caucus Com., 1967-68. Served with AUS, 1944-46; ETO. Fellow Am. Coll. Trial Lawyers; mem. ABA, Ill. Bar Assn. (chmn. evidence program 1970), Chgo. Bar Assn., Law Club, Soc. Trial Lawyers, Order of Coif, Phi Beta Kappa, Phi Eta Sigma. Clubs: Chicago Curling, University; Executives (Chgo.). Home: 809 Locust St Winnetka IL 60093 Office: One IBM Plaza Chicago IL 60611 *I try to see people and events for what they really are, apply my talents, persevere, work hard, and pay attention to fairness.*

HARROLD, RONALD THOMAS, research scientist; b. Fulham, London, Eng., Apr. 4, 1933; came to U.S., 1963; s. John and Cicely Helen (Edenden) H.; m. Ann Marie Whitley, Dec. 3, 1955; children: Lesley Ann, Linda Jane. B.S., Chemford Coll. Tech., Eng., 1962, Twickenham Coll. Tech., Eng., 1955. Student apprentice Brit. Thomson-Houston Co., Willesden, London, Eng., 1950-55; lectr. radar tech. Army Sch. Electronics, Arborfield, Bershire, Eng., 1955-57; devel. engr. English Electric Valve Co., Chelmsford, Essex, Eng., 1957-61; research engr. Sylvania-Thorn Color TV Labs., Enfield, Middlesex, Eng., 1961-63; fellow research scientist Westinghouse Research and Devel., Pitts., 1963—. Contbr. articles to various publs.; patentee in field. Fellow IEE; mem. Instn. Electronics and Radio Engrs. Republican. Episcopalian. Club: Pittsburgh Racquet. Home: 4052 W Benden Dr Murrysville PA 15668 Office: Westinghouse Research and Devel Center 1310 Beulah Rd Pittsburgh PA 15235

HARROP, WILLIAM CALDWELL, ambassador, fgn. service officer; b. Balt., Feb. 19, 1929; s. George A. and Esther (Caldwell) H.; m. Ann G. Delavan, Aug. 22, 1953; children—Mark D., Caldwell, Scott N., George H. A.B., Harvard, 1950; postgrad., Grad. Sch. Journalism U. Mo., 1953-54; fellow, Woodrow Wilson Sch., Princeton, 1968-69. Fgn. service officer, 1954—, vice consul, Palermo, 1954-55, 2d sec., Rome, 1955-58; internat. relations officer Dept. State, 1958-63; 1st sec., Brussels, 1963-66, consul, Lubumbashi, Congo, 1966-68; dir. Office Research for Africa, Dept. State, Washington, 1969, mem. planning and coordination staff, 1972-73; dep. chief mission Am. embassy, Canberra, Australia, 1973-75; U.S. ambassador to Guinea, 1975-77, dep. asst. sec. of state for Africa, 1977-80, ambassador to Kenya and Seychelles, 1980—; Chmn. Am. Fgn. Service Assn., 1970-73. Served with USMCR, 1951-52. Recipient State Dept. Merit Service award, 1968. Mem. Am. Fgn. Service Assn. Clubs: Harvard Varsity, Fly (Cambridge Mass.); Metropolitan (Washington); Royal Leopold (Brussels); Royal Canberra, Nairobi. Address: State Dept 2201 C Street NW Washington DC 20520

HARROWER, GEORGE ALEXANDER, univ. pres.; b. Flesherton, Ont., Can., May 15, 1924; s. Joseph and Edith Winnifred (McCann) H.; m. Judith Lynne Bollman, Sept. 19, 1969; children—Timothy, Lisa, David, Kardi, Mark. B.Sc. in Physics, U. Western Ont., London, 1949, M.Sc., McGill U., Montreal, Que., Can., 1950, Ph.D., 1952. Prof. physics Queen's U., Kingston, Ont., Can., after 1955-78, dean, 1964-69, vice prin., 1969-76; pres. Lakehead U., Thunder Bay, Ont., 1978—. Contbr. articles on phys. electronics, radio astronomy to profl. jours. Served with RCAF, 1943-45. Mem. Internat. Astron. Union, Can. Astron. Soc. Mem. United Ch. of Canada. *

HARROWER, NORMAN, JR., foundation executive; b. Fitchburg, Mass., Sept. 23, 1921; s. Norman and Harriet (Greeley) H.; m. Leontine Lyle, Sept. 1, 1945; children: Harriet G., Norman, Mary Stuart. A.B., Harvard U., 1947, M.A., 1955. Asst. dean Harvard Coll., 1947-49; dir. admissions, chmn. history dept. Casady Sch., Oklahoma City, 1949-54; admissions and fin. aids dir. career adv. office Yale U., 1955-67; dir. New Haven (Conn.) Found., 1967—; commr. Office of Cultural Affairs New Haven, 1978—. Pres. Community Council New Haven; bd. dirs. United Way, 1959-64; trustee Conn. Ednl. Telecommunications Corp., 1979—. Served with USMC, 1942-45. Club: Rotary. Home: 184 Lawrence St New Haven CT 06511 Office: 1 State St New Haven CT 06510

HARRY, DEBORAH ANN, singer; b. Miami, Fla., July 11, 1945; d. Richard Smith and Catherine (Peters) H. A.A., Centenary Coll., 1965. Singer, songwriter rock group, Blondie; albums include Blondie, 1977, Plastic Letters, 1978, Parallel Lines, 1979, Eat to the Beat, 1979, Auto American, 1980; songs include Heart of Glass, Call Me, Tide is High; film appearances include Union City, Videodrome. Recipient Gold, Silver and Platinum records. Mem. ASCAP (Heart of Glass award), AFTRA, Screen Actors Guild. Address: care Press Relations Chrysalis Records 115 E 57th St New York NY 10022

HARSANYI, JANICE, soprano, educator; b. Arlington, Mass., July 15, 1929; d. Edward and Thelma (Jacobs) Morris; m. Nicholas Harsanyi, Apr. 19, 1952; 1 son, Peter Michael. B.Mus., Westminster Choir Coll., 1951; postgrad., Phila. Acad. Vocal Arts, 1952-54. Voice tchr. Westminster Choir Coll., Princeton, N.J., 1951-63, chmn. voice dept., 1963-65; lectr. music Princeton Theol. Sem., 1956-63; voice tchr. summer sessions U. Mich., 1965-70; artist-in-residence Interlochen Arts Acad., 1967-70; voice tchr. N.C. Sch. Arts, Winston-Salem, 1971-78; music faculty Salem Coll., 1973-76; condr. voice master classes, choral clinics various colls., 1954—; prof. voice Fla. State U., Tallahassee, 1978—, chmn. dept., 1979—. Concert singer, 1954—, debut, Phila. Orch., 1958; appearances with, Am., Detroit, Houston, Minn., Nat., Symphony of Air orchs., Bach Aria Group, 1967-68, maj. music festivals, U.S., 1960—; toured with, Piedmont Chamber Orch., 1971-78, concerts and recitals, in major U.S. cities, also in Belgium, Eng., Ger., Italy, Switzerland and Sweden; rec. artist, Columbia, Decca, CRI records. Mem. Nat. Assn. Tchrs. Singing, Music Tchrs. Nat. Assn., Coll. Music Soc., Riemenschneider Bach Inst., Sigma Alpha Iota. Home: 725 Duparc Circle Tallahassee FL 32312 Office: Sch Music Fla State U Tallahassee FL 32306

HARSCH, JOSEPH C., journalist, lectr.; b. Toledo, May 25, 1905; s. Paul Arthur and Leila Katherine (Close) H.; m. Anne Elizabeth Wood, Dec. 11, 1932; children—J. William Wood, Jonathan Hannum, Paul Arthur, III. A.B., Williams Coll., 1927, M.A. (hon.); B.A., Corpus Christi Coll., Cambridge (Eng.) U., 1929. With Christian Sci. Monitor, 1929—, corr., 1931-39, Rome, then Berlin, 1939-41, fgn. affairs columnist, 1952—, chief editorial writer, 1971-74, columnist, 1974—; asst. dir. Intergovtl. Com. (on leave from Monitor), 1939; news commentator CBS, 1943-49, NBC, 1953-67, sr. European corr., 1957-65, diplomatic corr., 1965-67; commentator ABC, 1967-71. Author: Pattern of Conquest, 1941, The Curtain Isn't Iron, 1950. Decorated comdr. Order Brit. Empire. Mem. Chi Psi. Christian Scientist. Clubs: Cosmos, Metropolitan (Washington); St. Botolph (Boston); Century (N.Y.C.); Garrick, St. James (London). Address: Highland Dr Jamestown RI 02835

HARSHAW, DAVID HARE, business executive; b. Phila., Mar. 6, 1904; s. Edward and Margaret Lyons (Jamison) H.; m. Frances Darlington Drewes, 1930; children: David Hare, Adele Drewes Smith; m. June Weaver French, 1974. B.S. in Econs, U. Pa., 1926; postgrad., Temple U. Law Sch., 1927-28; D.Sc., Stetson U., 1955. With U.G.I. Contracting Co., 1926-29, United Engrs. and Constrn. Co., 1929-35; with John B. Stetson Co., 1935—, sec., treas., 1942, v.p. and treas., 1945, pres., dir., 1947-66, vice chmn., 1966—; dir. Am. Mut. Ins. Co.; pres. John B. Stetson Co. of Can., Ltd. Bd. dirs. Greater Phila. Partnership; bd. dirs., v.p. Am. Missionary Fellowship; past pres. YMCA, Phila.; bd. dirs., past pres. West Park Hosp., Phila.; trustee Stetson U., Deland, Fla. Mem. Pa. C. of C. (past pres.), Phi Kappa Tau. Republican. Mem. Plymouth Brethren Meeting. Clubs: Union League, Philadelphia Country (Phila.). Home: 537 Brookfield Rd Drexel Hill PA 19026 Office: 595 Madison Ave New York NY 10022

HARSHBARGER, SAM ROSS, judge; b. Milton, W.Va., Sept. 9, 1928; s. Paul Scott and Emma Lene (Owens) H.; children—James Patrick, Samuel David. A.B., W.Va. U., 1949; LL.B., George Washington U., 1952. Bar: D.C. bar 1952, W.Va. bar 1956. Practiced in, Milton, W.Va., 1956-76, atty., Town of Milton, 1960-76; spl. judge Circuit Ct. of Cabell County, W.Va., 1974; justice W.Va. Supreme Ct. of Appeals, Charleston, 1976—. Past chmn. trustees sect. W.Va. Library Assn.; bd. dirs. Cabell County Pub. Library, 1956-77. Served with USAF, 1952-56. Mem. W.Va. Bar Assn., Cabell County Bar Assn. (past pres.), Am. Judicature Soc. Democrat. Methodist. Clubs: Lions, Masons, Shriners. Home: Trenol Heights Milton WV 25541 Office: Rm 307-E State Capitol Charleston WV 25305

HARSTON, ROBERT GORDON, Oil service company executive; b. Enid, Okla., Oct. 14, 1932; s. Gordon Cameron and Flora Dell (Baker) H.; m. Carol Ann Boggs, Aug. 15, 1953; children: Lynn, Lisa, Bryan. B.B.A., U. Okla., 1954. Mdse. mgr., gen. mgr. Pioneer Savs. Stamps, Lubbock, Tex., 1954-65, Kansas City, Mo., 1954-65, Denver, 1954-65; sales mgr. Petroleum Info. Corp., Denver, 1965-71, v.p., Houston, 1972-75, exec. v.p., 1975-78, pres., 1978-82, pres. and chief exec. officer, Denver, 1982—, also dir., 1975—. Assoc. U. Okla. Found., Norman, 1981—. Assoc. mem. Am. Assn. Petroleum Geologists, Am. Assn. Petroleum Landmen. Republican. Episcopalian. Clubs: Petroleum (Houston); (Denver); Metropolitan (Denver). Lodges: Masons; Shriners. Office: Petroleum Infor Corp PO Box 2612 Denver CO 80201

HART, ALEX WAY, banker; b. Meadville, Pa., June 4, 1940; s. Alex William and Rose Mary (Brown) H.; m. Fyanne Edwards, July 1, 1961; children: Alex, Michael, Gregory, Suzanne. A.B., Harvard U., 1962. Asst. v.p. Bank Ohio, Columbus, 1969-73; sr. v.p. First Chgo. Corp., Chgo., 1973-78; exec. v.p. First Interstate Bancorp, Los Angeles, 1978—; chmn. Cirrus Systems, Inc., Chgo., 1982—. Bd. dirs. Mus. Natural History, Los Angeles, 1983—. Mem. Bank Mktg. Assn. (dir. 1977-80). Republican. Roman Catholic. Club: Harvard (Los Angeles) (dir. 1982—). Office: First Interstate Bancorp 707 Wilshire Blvd Los Angeles CA 90017

HART, ALEX WILLIAM, glass company executive; b. Connellsville, Pa., May 22, 1927; s. G. Edward and Edith (Galagher) H.; m. Rosemary Brown, Aug. 18, 1939; children: Alex, Edward, Anne, Georgia, Miriam. B.A., Allegheny Coll., 1940. With Anchor Hocking Corp., Lancaster, Ohio, 1942—, asst. dir. package devel. labs., 1957-69, mgr. new products div., 1969-71, factories mgr. closure div., 1971, v.p., gen. mgr., 1972, group v.p. packaging, 1976, exec. v.p., 1977—. Active YMCA. Mem. Nat. Food Processors Assn., Glass Packaging Inst. Republican. Club: Lancaster Country. Home: 1414 Wheeling Rd Routel Lancaster OH 43130 Office: Anchor Hocking Corp 109 N Broad St Lancaster OH 43130

HART, ALVIN LEROY, electric manufacturing company executive; b. Oneida, N.Y., Sept. 22, 1925; s. Gould Leroy and Florence Mary (Dext) H.; m. Florence May Travers, Jan. 30, 1949; children: Susan Hart Clifton, Carol Hart Sumpter. Student, Sampson Coll., 1946-48; B.S. in Math. and Physics, U. Ill., 1950, B.E.E., 1951; postgrad., Cleve. Inst. Art, 1956. Illuminating engr. lamp div. Gen. Electric Co., Nela Park, Cleve., 1951-71, mgr. product evaluation and forecasts lamp bus. div., 1971-79, mgr. lighting tech. and services lighting bus. group, 1979-83, mgr. application engring. lighting bus. group, 1983—. Contbr. to: Illuminating Engring. Handbooks, 3d, 4th, 5th, 6th edits. Served with CWS and Signal Corps AUS, 1943-46. Fellow Illuminating Enging. Soc.; mem. Commn. Internationale de L'Eclairage (U.S. nat. com. 1960—, chmn. U.S. com. and U.S. expert on tech. com. exterior lighting practice 1960-71). Republican. Unitarian. Home: 3626 Langton Rd Cleveland Heights OH 44121 Office: Nela Park Cleveland OH 44112

HART, ARTHUR ALVIN, museum director; b. Tacoma, Feb. 13, 1921; s. Albert Arthur and Erma Lola (Maltby) H.; m. Novella D. Cochran, Feb. 26, 1944; children—Susanna, Robin, Catherine, Allison. B.A., U. Wash., Seattle, 1948, M.F.A., 1948; postgrad., Biarritz Am. U., Hans Hofman Sch. Fine Arts, U. Calif., Berkeley. Head art dept., chmn. div. fine arts Coll. Idaho, 1948-53; instr. art Colby Jr. Coll. Women, New London, N.H., 1953-54; head art dept., dir. adult edn. Bay Path Jr. Coll., Longmeadow, Mass., 1955-69; dir. Idaho Hist. Mus., Boise, 1969-75, Idaho Hist. Soc., 1975—; lectr. Am. architecture Boise State U., 1970—; mem. Boise Allied Arts Council,

1970-78, Idaho Historic Preservation Council, 1971—, Boise Bicentennial Commn., 1975-76; adv. bd. Snake River Regional Studies Center, 1969—. Author: Steam Trains in Idaho, 1971, Space, Style and Structure: Building in Northwest American, 1974, Fighting Fire on the Frontier, 1976, Historic Boise, 1979; also numerous articles. Served with USAAF, 1942-44; Served with AUS, 1944-46. Recipient Idaho Statesman Disting. Citizen award, 1973; Allied Arts Council award for hist. writing, 1972. Mem. AIA (hon.), AAUP, Coll. Art Assn., Soc. Archtl. Historians (pres. No. Pacific Coast chpt. 1974-76), Am. Assn. Museums (mem. council 1980—, pres. Western regional conf. 1979-81). Office: 610 N Julia Davis Dr Boise ID 83702

HART, AUGUSTIN SNOW, JR., retired food company executive; b. Bklyn., Aug. 5, 1915; s. Augustin Snow and Alice (O'Connor) H.; m. Margaret Stuart, Apr. 11, 1942; children: Augustin Snow III, Kathryn (Mrs. Robert Lansing), Douglas S., Harriet H., Robert D. B.A., Princeton U., 1937. With Quaker Oats Co., Chgo., from 1937—, now retired; hon. dir. U.S. Trust Co. of New York; dir. Banco di Roma, Chgo. Mem. adv. com. Chgo. Council Fgn. Relations.; Chmn. adv. council Inter-Am. Found.; bd. dirs. Lyric Opera of Chgo.; trustee Presbyn.-St. Lukes Hosp. Served with 82d Airborne Div., 1942-46. Clubs: Onwentsia, Old Elm (Lake Forest); Commercial, Chicago (Chgo.). Office: 345 Merchandise Mart Chicago IL 60654 *

HART, C. ALLAN, lawyer; b. St. Paul, Oct. 7, 1909. A.B., Stanford U., 1931; LL.B., Yale U., 1934. Bar: Oreg. bar 1934, U.S. Supreme Ct. bar 1939. Instr. Yale Law Sch., 1934-35; asst. U.S. atty., Oreg., 1936-38; spl. asst. to U.S. atty. gen. U.S. Dept. Justice, Washington, 1938-39; gen. counsel Bonneville Power Adminstrn., 1939-42; now mem. firm Lindsay, Hart, Neil & Weigler, Portland, Oreg. Mem. AMA, Multnomah County Bar Assn., Oreg. State Bar. Office: 700 Columbia Sq 111 SW Columbia St Portland OR 97201

HART, CRAIG C., savings and loan association executive; b. Streator, Ill., Jan. 11, 1934; s. Fred J. and Katherine (Crowl) H.; m. Alice B. Hart, Oct. 20, 1956; children: Bruce, Brian, Benjamin. B.S. in Acctg., M.B.A., U. Ill., 1956. Vice pres., dir. Heritage Enterprises, Bloomington, also Brittany Restaurants, Inc.; pres. Bloomington Fed. Savs. and Loan Assn., 1971—; Pres. Bloomington Unltd. Served to lt. (j.g.) USN, 1955. Mem. McLean County Assn. Commerce and Industry (pres. 1971-72). Clubs: Bloomington Country (treas. 1970-72, dir. 1970—. Home: 33 Country Club Pl Bloomington IL 61701 Office: 115 E Washington St Bloomington IL 61701

HART, DANIEL ANTHONY, bishop; b. Lawrence, Mass., Aug. 24, 1927; s. John J. and Susan T. (Tierney) H. B.S.B.A., Boston Coll., 1956; M.Ed., Boston State Coll., 1972; M.Div., St. John's Sem., Brighton, Mass., 1974. Ordained priest Roman Catholic Ch., 1953; asst. pastor, Lynnfield, 1953-54, Wellesley, 1954-56, Malden, 1956-64, all Mass., vice-chancellor, 1964-70, asst. pastor, Peabody, Mass., 1970-76, titular bishop of Tepelta, aux. bishop of Boston, 1976—, regional bishop Brockton Region, archdiocesan vicar for pastoral devel., 1976—; pres. Boston Senate of Priests, 1972-74; mem. exec. bd. Nat. Fedn. Priests' Councils, 1973-75. Address: 235 N Pearl St Brockton MA 02401

HART, DAVID WILLIAM, bank executive, lawyer; b. Albion, Pa., Feb. 6, 1921; s. William Lynn and Ruth Elizabeth (Lavely) H.; m. Jean Frances McCarthy, Apr. 4, 1942; children: Gordon William, Marilyn Jean. B.S. cum laude, Ohio State U., 1948, M.A., 1950, J.D., 1950. Bar: Ohio 1950, N.Y. 1957. Pvt. practice law, asso. law firm Fuller, Harrington & Seney, Toledo, 1950-51; atty. Gen. Electric Co., Schenectady, 1951-60; asst. sec., atty. White Motor Corp., Cleve., 1960-68; sec., dir. White Motor Credit Corp., 1962-68; pres. White Motor Internat. (S.A.), Cleve., 1970-71; v.p., gen. counsel Nat. City Bank, Cleve., 1971-80, sr. vice-pres., gen. counsel, 1980—; v.p., gen. counsel, sec. Nat. City Corp., Cleve., 1973-80, sr. v.p., gen. counsel, sec., 1980—. Served with AUS, 1942-46. Mem. Greater Cleve. Growth Assn., Phi Delta Phi, Beta Gamma Sigma, Beta Alpha Psi. Clubs: Canterbury Golf (past dir.), Union.). Office: 1900 E 9th St Cleveland OH 44114

HART, DONALD JOHN, management consultant, former business educator; b. Milw., Aug. 9, 1917; s. Edward William and Minnie Marie (Keller) H.; m. Margaret Ellen Thorpe, June 22, 1940; children: Roger, Susan (Mrs. Stephen R. Johnston), Charles, Mary (Mrs. Gregory L. Paul). A.B., Lake Forest (Ill.) Coll., 1938; M.A., U. Wis., 1941, Ph.D., 1951. Dir. publicity Lake Forest Coll., 1938-40; grad. asst. econs. U. Wis., 1940-41, 1946-47; chief priorities clk. purchasing dept. Allis-Chalmers Mfg. Co., Milw., 1941; asst. bus. mgr. Iowa State Coll., 1942-43; asso. prof. econs. Carroll Coll., 1947-50; dean Coll. Bus. Adminstrn. U. Idaho, 1950-56, U. Fla., 1956-68; prof. mgmt. Va. Poly. Inst., 1968-69; pres. St. Andrews Presbyn. Coll., Laurinburg, N.C., 1969-75; prof. mgmt. U. N.C. at Asheville, 1975-81, chmn. dept., 1975-81; mgmt. cons., 1981—; Vice pres. Idaho Inst. Christian Edn., 1952-56; Pub. mem., chmn. adv. council Employment Security Agy., Idaho, 1950-56. Author: Business in a Dynamic Society, 1963, Introduction to Business in a Dynamic Society, 1970; Contbr.: Ency. Britannica Book of Year, 1948-65. Trustee Fla. Presbyn. Coll., 1961-65; bd. dirs. Scotland United Fund, Internat. Ins. Seminars. Served as lt. supply corps USNR, 1943-46. Mem. Laurinburg C. of C. (bd. dirs.), Am. Assembly Collegiate Schs. Bus. (exec. com., sec.-treas. 1965-66, pres. 1967-68), Am. Acad. Mgmt. Presbyn. (ruling elder). Home: PO Box 1294 Black Mountain NC 28711

HART, DONALD MILTON, automotive and ranching exec., mayor; b. Terrabella, Cal., Oct. 22, 1915; s. Thomas Jefferson and Sara (L) H.; m. Margaret Willene, May 31, 1940; children—Donna Carol, Nancy Elizabeth, Donald Milton. B.A. in Edn, U. Calif. at Santa Barbara, 1938; M. Pub. Service, Calif. Poly. State U., San Luis Obispo, 1969. Vice pres. S.A. Camp Companies, San Joaquin Valley, Calif., 1946—, dir., 1947—; dir. mayor, City of Bakersfield, 1968-81. Trustee Calif. State Colls., 1960-68; chmn. bd. trustees Calif. State Univs. and Colls., 1967-68; alumni bd. dirs. U. Calif. at Santa Barbara, 1961—; mem. Calif. Citizen Adv. Com. Crime Prevention, 1955, Calif. Employment of Handicapped, 1956—, Calif. Bd. Edn., 1960-64, President's Com. Employment Handicapped, 1960-68, Bakersfield Police Commn., 1960-68. Served to capt. USAAF, 1942-46; CBI. Decorated by Govt. Republic of China; recipient Humanitarian award Kern County Lions Club, 1951, Outstanding Citizen award E. Bakersfield club, 1962; Named Man of Year Bakersfield chpt. Am. Legion, 1952; award of merit Kern County Office Civilian Def., 1953; Outstanding service award Bakersfield Assn. Retarded Children, 1958; award Kern County Com. Handicapped, 1959; Outstanding Service award Bakersfield Sr. Bowl, 1960; named to U. Calif. at Santa Barbara Athletic Hall Fame, 1961; Outstanding Alumni award U. Calif. at Santa Barbara, 1962; Silver Anniversary All-Am. Football award Sports Illus. mag., 1962; Outstanding Service to Mentally Retarded award Bakersfield Assn. Retarded Children, 1963; cited by Calif. Legislators for service to state in edn. and to handicapped, 1964; recognition service to community and children all races Chinese Ying On Assn., 1964; Benjamin Franklin award Sat. Eve. Post, 1962; Civil Service award Order of Eagles, 1972; Community Service award Bakersfield Advt. Club, 1972; medal of honor D.A.R., 1977; decorated commendatore Ordine al Merito della Repubblica Italiana. Home: 2308 Spruce St Bakersfield CA 93301 Office: PO Box 1556 Bakersfield CA 93301

HART, DWIGHT HOWARD, JR., hotel executive; b. Los Angeles, Sept. 10, 1921; s. Dwight Howard and Mable Sophie (Runge) H.; m. Patt Bailey Cox, Dec. 31, 1974; 1 dau., Rosslyn Diane (Mrs. Harry L. Whitaker, Jr.). Student, Harvard Mil. Sch., 1932-38; B.S., A.B., U. So. Calif., 1938-42. Former v.p. Allied Properties (owners Clift Hotels, San Francisco, Santa Barbara Biltmore Hotel); former v.p., mng. dir. Clift Hotel; supervising cons. Landmark Land Co.; dir. La Quinta Hotel, La Quinta, Calif. Mem. Am. Hotel Assn. (past dir.), Calif. Hotel Assn. (past pres.), Phi Kappa Alpha. Clubs: Mason (Shriner), Burlingame (Calif.) Country, La Quinta (Calif.) Country; Rancheros Vistadores (Santa Barbara, Calif.); Tavern (N.Y.C.). Home: PO Box 914 49-920 Lago Dr La Quinta CA 92253

HART, EDWARD LEROY, poet, educator; b. Bloomington, Idaho, Dec. 28, 1916; s. Alfred Augustus and Sarah Cecilia (Patterson) H.; m. Eleanor May Coleman, Dec. 15, 1944; children: Edward Richard, Paul LeRoy, Barbara, Patricia. B.S., U. Utah, 1939; M.A., U. Mich., 1941; D.Phil. (Rhodes scholar), Oxford (Eng.) U., 1950. Instr. U. Utah, Salt Lake City, 1946; asst. prof. U. Wash., Seattle, 1949-52, Brigham Young U., Provo, Utah, 1952-55, asso. prof., 1955-59, prof., 1959—; vis. prof. U. Calif., Berkeley, 1959-60, Ariz. State U., summer 1968; bd. dirs. Utah Arts Council. Author: Minor Lives, 1971, Instruction and Delight, 1976, Mormom in Motion, 1978; (poems) To Utah, 1979, Poems of Praise, 1980; More Than Nature Needs, 1982; contbr. articles to profl. jours. Served to lt. USNR, 1942-46. Am. Philos. Soc. grantee, 1964; First prize in poetry and biography Utah State Inst. Fine Arts, 1973,75; Fulbright-Hays sr. lectr., Pakistan, 1973-74; recipient Charles Redd award Utah Acad., 1976, Coll. Humanities Disting. Faculty award Brigham Young U., 1977. Fellow Am. Council Learned Socs., Found. Econ. Edn.; mem. MLA, Rocky Mountain MLA, Am. Soc. 18th Century Studies, Utah Acad. Sci., Arts and Letters, Phi Beta Kappa, Phi Kappa Phi. Democrat. Mormon. Home: 1401 Cherry Ln Provo UT 84604 Office: Dept English Brigham Young U Provo UT 84602 *As a young writer in graduate school, I made the shocking discovery one day that I had written some things I did not really believe. I wanted to be a writer, but I made a vow in my journal that I would not do so at the expense of my integrity: that I would never write anything again that I did not believe and accept with all my being. I have kept that promise, and at the same time have tried to be creative and resourceful. I do not believe that my writing has suffered from the attempt to be honest, but if it has, that is a small price to pay for self-respect.*

HART, EDWIN JAMES, chemist; b. Port Angeles, Wash., Feb. 7, 1910; s. Fitch James and Josie Anna Elizabeth (Blater) H.; m. Rozella Patricia Clark, June 17, 1939; children: Fitch J., Ann E., John P. B.S., M.S., Wash. State U., 1931; Ph.D., Brown U., 1934. With L.I. Biol. Lab., 1934-36, U.S. Rubber Co., 1936-48; sr. chemist Argonne Nat. Lab., 1948-75, cons., 1975—; Brit. Empire Cancer Campaign fellow Mt. Vernon Hosp., Eng., 1961-62; Mem. quartermaster dosimetry panel Nat. Acad. Sci., 1955-58, radiobiology com., 1958-64, food irradiation com., 1963-72; del. 2d UN Internat. Conf. on Peaceful Uses Atomic Energy, Geneva, 1958; mem. Internat. Com. on Radiol. Units, 1960-63; cons. Danish Atomic Energy Commn., 1967—; AEA cons. to Bhabha Atomic Research Centre, Trombay, India, winter 1970; mem. sci. staff U.S. Atoms in Action Program, Tehran, Iran, 1967; vis. prof. Hebrew U., Israel, fall 1967; cons. Lawrence Berkeley Lab., 1976—. Author: (with M. Anbar) The Hydrated Electron, 1970. Sr. U.S. scientist awardee Alexander von Humboldt Found., W. Ger., 1979-80; Recipient Weiss medal Assn. for Radiation Research, Eng., 1975, citation for disting. achievement Brown U., 1983. Mem. Am. Chem. Soc., AAAS, Soc. Free Radical Research (hon.), Radiation Research Soc., Phi Beta Kappa, Sigma Xi, Phi Kappa Phi, Phi Lambda Upsilon. Home: 2115 Hart Rd Port Angeles WA 98362

HART, ERIC MULLINS, corp. exec.; b. Clanton, Ala., May 6, 1925; s. Eric and Myrtle (Mullins) H.; m. Joy Porter, May 16, 1953; children—Anne Porter, Eric Mullins. B.S., U. Ala., 1946; grad., Harvard Advanced Mgmt. Program, 1970. With Internat. Paper Co., 1946-69, asst. to v.p.-treas., 1962-64, comptroller, 1964-69; treas. Red River Paper Mill, Inc., 1964-69; financial v.p., dir. Lever Bros. Co., 1969—; dir. Unilever U.S., Inc., MacMillan Inc. Trustee King Sch., Stamford, Conn., 1970-76. Mem. Sigma Alpha Epsilon. Home: PO Box 2999 Darien CT 06820 Office: 390 Park Ave New York NY 10022

HART, EVELYN, ballet dancer; b. Toronto, Apr. 4, 1956. Attended, Dorothy Carter Sch. Dance Arts, Nat. Ballet Sch., Royal Winnipeg Ballet, 1973-76. Debut with, Royal Winnipeg Ballet, 1976; soloist, 1978; prin. dancer, 1979—. Recipient Bronze medal World Ballet Concours, Japan, 1980, Gold medal 10th Internat. Ballet Competition, Varna, Bulgaria.; decorated Order of Can., 1983. Address: care Royal Winnipeg Ballet 289 Portage Ave Winnipeg MB R3B 2B4 Canada *

HART, FREDERICK DONALD, business executive; b. N.Y.C., May 12, 1915; s. Lewis T. and Charlotte (Hyde) H.; m. Ann Wright, Apr. 18, 1942; children: Anne, Charlotte, Jane. M.E., Cornell U., 1936, M.M.E., 1937. Mgmt. engr. E.I. duPont de Nemours Co., 1937-44; exec. v.p. Temco, Inc., Nashville, 1944-57, pres., 1957-64, Lear Siegler Internat., 1964-66; adminstrv. dir. Am. Gas Assn., Arlington, Va., 1966-68, mng. dir., 1968—, pres., 1971-76, sr. asso., 1976-80; pres. Hartland Corp., Franklin, Tenn., 1980—, Am. Nephaline Corp., Columbus, Ohio, 1977—; dir. Indusmin Ltd., First Am Bank of Va., Atlas Machine & Iron Works; pres. Lawson United Feldspar Corp.; Past pres. Inst. Appliance Mfrs., Gas Appliance Mfrs. Assn. Mem. Am. Ordnance Assn. (v.p. 1958-63), N.A.M. (v.p. 1960-65), Nashville C. of C. (past pres.), Cornell U. Council, Am. Nat. Standards Inst. Clubs: Belle Meade Country (Nashville); Union League (N.Y.C.); Internat. (Washington). Home: Route 7 Franklin TN 37064 Office: Farmington Dr Franklin TN 37064

HART, FREDERICK MICHAEL, law educator; b. Flushing, N.Y., Dec. 5, 1929; s. Frederick Joseph and Doria (Laurian) H.; m. Joan Marie Monaghan, Feb. 13, 1956; children—Joan Marie, Ellen, Christiane, F. Michael, Margaret, Andrew, Brigid, Patrick. B.S., Georgetown U., 1951, J.D., 1955; LL.M., N.Y. U., 1956; postgrad., U. Frankfurt, Germany, 1956-57. Lectr., dir. food law program N.Y. U., N.Y.C., 1957-58, asst. prof., 1958-59; prof. law Albany Law Sch., Union U., 1959-61, Boston Coll., 1961-66, Law Sch., U. N.Mex., Albuquerque, 1966—, dean, 1971-79, dir., 1967-69; vis. prof. U. Calif., Davis, spring 1981; pres., chmn. bd. trustees Law Sch. Admission Test Council, 1974-76. Author: Forms and Procedures Under the Uniform Commercial Code, 1963, Uniform Commercial Code Reporter-Digest, 1965, Handbook on Truth in Lending, 1969, Commercial Paper Under the U.C.C, 1972; editor: Am. Indian Law Newsletter, 1968-70. Served to lt. USAF, 1951-53. Mem. Order of Coif, Phi Delta Phi. Roman Catholic. Home: 1505 Cornell Dr NE Albuquerque NM 87106 Office: U NMex Sch Law 1117 Stanford Dr NE Albuquerque NM 87131

HART, GARY, Senator; b. Ottawa, Kans., Nov. 28, 1937; m. Lee Ludwig, 1958; children: Andrea, John. Grad., Bethany Nazarene Coll. (Okla.); LL.B., Yale, 1964. Began career as atty. U.S. Dept. Justice, Washington; then spl. asst. to sec. U.S. Dept. Interior; practiced in Denver, 1967-70, 72-74; nat. campaign dir. Senator George McGovern Democratic Presdl. Campaign, 1970-72; U.S. senator from Colo., 1975—; founder, 1st chmn. Environ. Study Conf., 1975; congl. adviser Salt II Talks, 1977; adviser UN Spl. Session on Disarmament, 1978; chmn. Nat. Commn. on Air Quality, 1978-81; founder Congl. Mil. Reform Caucus, 1981. Author: Right From the Start, 1973, A New Democracy, 1983. Student vol. John F. Kennedy Presdl. Campaign, 1960; vol. organizer Robert F. Kennedy Presdl. Campaign, 1968; bd. visitors U.S. Air Force Acad., 1975—, chmn., 1978-80; candidate for Democratic presdl. nomination, 1983-84. Office: SR-237 Russell Senate Office Bldg US Senate Washington DC 20510

HART, HUBERT J(OSEPH), bishop; b. Kansas City, Mo., Sept. 26, 1931; s. Hubert H. and Kathryn R. (Muser) H. Student, St. John's Sem., Kansas City, Mo., 1949-50; B.A., St. Meinrad Sem., 1952. Ordained priest Roman Catholic Ch., 1956; consecrated bishop, 1976, assoc. pastor in several parishes, Kansas City, 1956-69, pastor, 1969-76, aux. bishop Wyo., 1976-78, bishop of Wyo., 1978—. Office: PO Box 468 Cheyenne WY 82003

HART, JACK, lawyer; b. N.Y.C., Jan. 13, 1909; s. Harry and Clara (Mersack) H.; m. Rose Ratner, Aug. 15, 1937; children-William, Jane. B.A., Coll. City N.Y., 1930; LL.B., Columbia, 1933. Bar: N.Y. bar 1934. Practice in, N.Y.C., 1933—; asso. George Z. Medalie, 1933-38; pvt. practice, 1938- 50; partner Hart & Hume (and predecessor firms), 1950—. Mem. Am. Bar Assn., Internat. Assn. Ins. Counsel, N.Y. County Lawyers Assn. Club: Princeton (N.Y.C.). Home: 400 E 56th St New York City NY 10022 Office: 10 E 40th St New York City NY 10016

HART, JAMES DAVID, educator; b. San Francisco, Apr. 18, 1911; s. Julien and Helen Louise (Neustadter) H.; m. Ruth Arnstein, June 14, 1938 (dec. 1977); children: Carol Helen (Mrs. John L. Field), Peter David. A.B., Stanford, 1932; M.A., Harvard, 1933, Ph.D., 1936; L.H.D., Mills Coll., 1978. Instr. English U. Calif. at Berkeley, 1936-41, asst. prof., 1941-47, asso. prof., 1947-51, prof., 1951—, chmn. dept., 1955-57, 65-69, vice chancellor, 1957-60; acting dir. Bancroft Library, 1961-62, dir., 1969—; vis. prof. Harvard U., 1964; Phi Beta Kappa vis. scholar, 1980-81; chmn. Marshall Scholarship Com. Western U.S., 1959-63, 79—. Author: The Oxford Companion Am. Literature, 1941, rev. edits, The Popular Book, 1950, 61, America's Literature, (with C. Gohdes), 1955, American Images of Spanish California, 1960, The Private Press Ventures of Samuel Lloyd Osbourne and R.L.S, 1966, A Companion to California, 1978; Editor: My First Publication, 1961, The Oregon Trail (Francis Parkman), 1963, From Scotland to Silverado (Robert Louis Stevenson), 1966, A Novelist in the Making (Frank Norris), 1970; Contbr. articles to mags., revs. Trustee Mills Coll., 1970-78, 79—, pres. bd., 1973-76. Decorated comdr. Order Brit. Empire. Fellow Am. Antiquarian Soc., Am. Acad. Arts and Scis., Calif. Hist. Soc.; mem. Modern Lang. Assn., Philol. Assn. Pacific Coast, Book Club of Calif. (pres. 1956-60). Clubs: Bohemian, Century Assn., Grolier, Faculty (Berkeley). Home: 740 San Luis Rd Berkeley CA 94707

HART, JAMES WARREN, professional football player; b. Evanston, Ill., Apr. 29, 1944; s. George Ezrie and Marjorie Helen (Karsten) H.; m. Mary Elizabeth Mueller, June 17, 1967; children: Bradley James and Suzanne Elizabeth (twins), Kathryn Anne. B.S., So. Ill. U., 1967. Quarterback St. Louis Cardinals Profl. Football Team, 1966-83, Washington Redskins Profl. Football Team, 1984; radio sports personality Sta. KMOX, 1975—; co-owner Dierdorf & Hart's Steak House, St. Louis; head coach So. Ill. Spl. Olympics, 1973—, Mo. Spl. Olympics, 1976-78. Co-author: The Jim Hart Story, 1977. Gen. campaign chmn. St. Louis Heart Assn., 1974—; chmn. Multiple Sclerosis Read-a-thon; bd. dirs. Nat. Sports Com., 1977—. Named Most Valuable Player in Nat. Football Conf., 1974, Most Valuable Player with St. Louis Cardinals, 1973, 75, 78, Man of Year St. Louis Dodge Dealers, 1975, 76, Miller High Life, 1980; recipient Brian Piccolo Meml. Humanitarian award Nat. YMCA, 1981. Mem. Fellowship Christian Athletes (chpt. dir.), Nat. Football League Players Assn. (Byron White award 1976), AFTRA. Republican. Office: Dierdorf & Hart's Steak House 323 Westport Pl Saint Louis MO 63146

HART, JAMES WIRTH, manufacturing company executive; b. Trenton, N.J., July 31, 1933; s. Earle Russell and Mildred (Barnes) H.; m. N. Joanne Weber, Mar. 28, 1953; children: James Wirth, Steven Weber, Douglas Barnes, Jennifer Joanne Rife. B.S., Drexel U., 1955; M.B.A., U. Pitts., 1965; Ph.D., Harvard U., 1965. Sr. staff and operating positions Westinghouse Electric Corp., Pitts., 1955-66; exec. asst. to chmn. and chief exec. officer Bendix Corp., Detroit, 1966-67; asst. office pres. ITT, N.Y.C., 1967-69; pres. Laird Enterprises, N.Y.C., 1969-71; chief operating officer Weelabrator-Frye, Inc., N.Y.C., 1971-73; pres., chief exec. officer Mohawk Data Scis., 1974; chmn., pres. Schick Inc., Westport, Conn., 1975—. Clubs: Racquet and Tennis, Ox Ridge Hunt, Boardroom, Landmark. Home: 12 Sherry Ln Darien CT 06820 Office: Schick Inc 33 Riverside Ave Westport CT 06880

HART, JOHN, wholesale grocery distributing executive; b. 1928. With Thomas & Howard Co., 1950-59, Super Food Services, Inc., 1959-66; dir. distbn. locally Penn. Fruit Co., Inc., 1966-68; gen. mgr. Economy Stores, Inc., 1959-70; pres., chief exec. officer Associated Grocers Fla., Miami, 1970—, now pres., dir. Address: Associated Grocers Fla 6695 NW 36th Ave Miami FL 33147

HART, JOHN FRASER, geography educator; b. Staunton, Va., Apr. 5, 1924; s. Freeman H. and Jean. B. (Fraser) H.; m. Meredith A. Davis, Feb. 5, 1949; children: Richard L., Meredith A. A.B., Emory U., 1943; M.A., Northwestern U., 1949, Ph.D., 1950. Asst., then assoc. prof. U. Ga., 1949-55; from asst. prof. to prof. Ind. U., 1955-67; exec. sec. Assn. Am. Geographers, 1965-66; prof. geography U. Minn., Mpls., 1967—; vis. prof. Clansfield State Coll., 1976-77; Distinguished vis. prof. East Carolina U., 1977; Fulbright lectr. U. Lille (France), Durham U., 1960. Mem. editorial adv. bd.: Geog. Review, 61976—; Contbr. monographs, articles to profl. lit. Served with USNR, 1943-46. Recipient medaille de l'Université de Liège, 1960; Platinum Plow U. Minn. geography grad. students, 1971; named Friend of S.D. Geography, 1979. Fellow Am., Royal, Royal Scottish geog. socs.; mem. Assn. Am. Geographers (editor annals 1970-75, citation for meritorious contbns. 1969, councillor West Lakes div. 1976-79, pres. 1979-80, hon. life mem. Southeastern div.), Canadian Assn. Geographers (councillor 1974-77), Pierce County Geog. Soc., Inst. Brit. Geographers, Nat. Council Geog. Edn. (award for teaching geography 1971). Home: 4505 Drexel Ave S Edina MN 55424 Office: Geography Dept U Minn Minneapolis MN 55455

HART, JOHN LATHROP JEROME, lawyer; b. Denver, Aug. 15, 1904; s. Richard Huson and Elizabeth (Jerome) H.; m. Jane Kelsey, Oct. 19, 1935; children: Katherine Hart Zimmerman, Sally Hart Whiting, John. A.B., Harvard U., 1925; B.A. in Jurisprudence (Rhodes scholar), Oxford U., Eng., 1927, B.C.L., 1928, M.A., 1932. Bar: Colo. 1929. Trust dept. Colo. Nat. Bank, Denver, 1929-35; atty. RFC, Washington, 1935-37, IRS, 1937; asso. Henry McAllister in gen. practice of law, 1938-48; sr. partner Holland & Hart, Denver, 1948-79, of counsel, 1979—; various positions in reorganizing M.P. R.R., D. & R.G.W. R.R., others, 1942-61; gen. counsel Nat. Center Atmospheric Research, 1962-74, trustee emeritus, 1974—. Author: Fourteen Thousand Feet, 1925, rev. edit., 1931, 72, 73, 74. Hon. trustee Webb-Waring Lung Inst.; mem. Am. Coms. East-West Accord. Mem. Asso. Harvard Clubs (pres. 1960-61), Harvard Alumni Assn. (hon. dir.). Clubs: Harvard, Am. Alpine (pres. 1970-73), Century Assn. (N.Y.C.); Alpine (London); Colo. Arlberg (hon.), Colo. Mountain (hon.);

Bohemian (San Francisco); Cosmos (Washington). Address: 29396 Shell Cove Laguna Niguel CA 92677

HART, JOHN LEWIS, cartoonist; b. Endicott, N.Y., Feb. 18, 1931; s. Irwin James and Grace Ann (Brown) H.; m. Bobby Jane Hatcher, Apr. 26, 1952; children: Patti Sue, Perri Ann. Ed. pub. schs. Comic strip, B.C. nat. syndicated, 1958—, The Wizard of Id, 1964—. Served with USAF, 1950-53; Korea. Recipient award for best humor strip Nat. Cartoonists Soc., 1967; named Outstanding Cartoonist of Year, 1968; Yellow Kid award Internat. Congress Comics for best cartoonist, Lucca, Italy; France's highest award for best cartoonist of year, 1971. Mem. Nat. Comics Council, Nat. Cartoonists Soc. First nationally pub. cartoon appeared in Sat. Eve. Post, 1954. Address: care Field Newspaper Syndicate 1703 Kaiser Ave Irvine CA 92714

HART, JOHN RICHARD, journalist, TV news correspondent; b. Denver, Feb. 1, 1932; s. Edward Baldwin and Catherine (Richards) H.; m. Marlene Lula Watje (div.); children: Stephen, Kathryn; m. Karen Anne Dixon, 1975. B.A., Westmont Coll., 1953; M.S., UCLA, 1959. News dir. Sta. WSJV-TV, Elkhart, Ind., 1956-57; news dir. Sta. KPOL, Los Angeles, 1958-59; spl. assignment reporter Sta. KNXT-TV, Los Angeles, 1960-64; bur. mgr. CBS Stas., Washington, 1964-65; corr. CBS News, 1965-75, NBC News, N.Y.C., 1975—. Served with U.S. Army, 1954-56. Recipient award Overseas Press Club, Emmy award, Christopher award. Mem. AFTRA. Office: NBC News 30 Rockefeller Plaza New York NY 10020

HART, JOSEPH, bishop; b. Kansas City, Mo., Sept. 26, 1931. Ed., St. John Sem., Kansas City, St. Meinrad Sem., Indpls. Ordained priest Roman Catholic Ch., 1956; ordained titular bishop of Thimida Regia and aux. bishop Cheyenne, Wyo., 1976, apptd. bishop of Cheyenne, 1978. Office: Bishop's Residence Box 469 Cheyenne WY 83001 *

HART, KITTY CARLISLE, arts administrator; b. New Orleans, Sept. 3, 1917; d. Joseph and Hortence (Holtzman) Conn; m. Moss Hart, Aug. 10, 1946; children: Christopher, Cathy. Ed., London Sch. Econs., Royal Acad. Dramatic Arts; D.F.A. (hon.), Coll. New Rochelle, D.H.L., Hartwick Coll., Manhattan Coll. Chmn. N.Y. State Council on the Arts. Panelist: TV show To Tell the Truth; actress on stage and in films; singer, Met. Opera; TV moderator and interviewer.; Contbr. book revs. to jours. Asso. fellow Timothy Dwight Coll. of Yale U.; bd. dirs. Empire State Coll.; formerly spl. cons. to N.Y. Gov. on women's opportunities; mem. vis. com., bd. overseers Harvard U. Music Sch.; mem. vis. com. for the arts Mass. Inst. Tech. Office: 80 Centre St New York NY 10013 *

HART, LAWRENCE ELBERT, former univ. dean; b. Longmont, Colo., May 21, 1916; s. Burton O. and E. Margaret (Forsyth) H.; m. Alma Louise Knuckey, June 16, 1942; children—Jerri Linn Hart Phillips, Judith Elaine Hart Brunkow, Donald Wayne. B.Mus., U. Colo., 1938, M.Mus., 1941; D.Mus. Performance, Eastman Sch. Music, U. Rochester, 1958. Mem. faculty U. Colo., Boulder, 1941-61; prof. music, piano and theory, dir. grad. studies in music Iowa State U., Ames, 1961-66, chmn. dept. music, 1961-66; dean Sch. Music, U. N.C., Greensboro, 1966-81; chmn. commn. on undergrad. studies Nat. Assn. Schs. Music, 1978-81, cons., examiner, 1970-81; piano accompanist for performing artists.; Bd. dirs. Greensboro Symphony Orch., 1961-81; bd. dirs. Greensboro Chamber Music Assn., 1961-67. Served with USN, 1935-38. Recipient Alumni Achievement award in edn. U. Colo., 1981. Mem. Music Educators Nat. Conf., Music Tchrs. Nat. Assn., Coll Music Soc., AAUP, N.C. Music Educators Assn. (hon.). Republican. Presbyterian. Club: Kiwanis. Office: Sch Music U NC Greensboro NC 27412

HART, LORING EDWARD, university executive; b. Bath, Maine, Sept. 22, 1924; s. Joseph Edward and Elizabeth (Hayes) H.; m. Marilyn Louise Cummings, Jan. 7, 1950; children: Ellen Louise, Matthew Cummings. B.A., Bowdoin Coll., 1948; M.A., U. Miami, 1951; Ph.D., Harvard U., 1961. Teaching fellow Harvard U., 1954-56; instr. English U. Ky., 1956-57; from asst. prof. to prof. English Norwich U., Northfield, Vt., 1956—, head dept. English, 1961-68, dean of faculty, 1968-69, v.p., dean, 1969-72, pres., 1972-82; assoc. dir. devel. campaign Bowdoin Coll., Brunswick, Maine, 1983—. Mem. exec. com. New Eng. Bd. Higher Edn. Served with armored inf. AUS, World War II; ETO. Decorated Bronze Star, Combat Inf. badge; recipient Outstanding Serviceaward Air Force, Army ROTC. Mem. Phi Beta Kappa, Alpha Kappa Psi, Sigma Nu. Home: North Rd North Yarmouth ME 04096 Office: Cram House Bowdoin College Brunswick ME 04011

HART, MAURICE ARTHUR, lawyer; b. N.Y.C., Dec. 22, 1927; s. Larry and Irene (Levy) H.; m. Elynor Wayne, Nov. 12, 1950; children—Jana, Melissa. B.S., U. So. Calif., 1950, J.D., 1963. Bar: Calif. bar 1963. Vice-pres. Hollywood Plastics, Calif., 1955-63; practiced law, Los Angeles, 1963—; prin. firm Hart & Leonard, Los Angeles, 1968—; judge pro tem Los Angeles Mcpl. Ct.; spl. master State Bar Calif.; founding dir. Equity Savs. & Loan. Pres. Camp J.C.A., Los Angeles, 1971-74; bd. dirs. Com. on Children and TV.; pres. Leo Baeck Temple, 1979-81. Served with AUS, 1946-48. Address: 1888 Century Park E Los Angeles CA 90067

HART, N. BERNE, banker; b. Denver, Jan. 6, 1930; s. Horace H. and Eva (Saville) H.; m. Wilma Jean Shadley, Sept. 17, 1952; children: Linda Lea Hart Frederick, Patricia Sue Hart Sweeney, David Bruce. B.A., Colo. Coll., 1951; postgrad., Colo. Sch. Banking, 1958-60. Sales trainee U.S. Rubber Co., 1953; exec. trainee United Bank of Denver N.A., 1954-56, asst. operations mgr., 1956-58, asst. cashier, 1958-61, asst. v.p., 1961, cashier, 1961-65, v.p. operations, 1965-69, sr. v.p. personal banking div., 1969, sr. v.p., trust officer, 1969-73; v.p. United Banks Colo. Inc., 1974, exec. v.p., 1975-77, pres., 1977-78, chmn., pres., 1979—; mem. fed. adv. council Fed. Res. Bd., 1983—. Chmn. bd. dirs. St. Joseph Hosp., Denver; chmn. bd. trustees Colo. Sch. Banking. Served to capt. USMCR, 1951-53. Named Denver Met. Exec. of Year Denver chpt. Nat. Secs. Assn., 1968. Mem. Colo. Bankers Assn. (past pres.), Adminstrv. Mgmt. Soc. (past pres. Denver chpt.), Colo. Assn. Commerce and Industry (dir.), Bank Adminstrn. Inst. (chmn. 1980-81), Beta Theta Pi. Republican. Clubs: Rotary (pres. 1982-83), Lakewood Country, Univ. (Denver); Denver Country. Home: 2552 E Alameda Ave 99 Denver CO 80209 Office: 1700 Broadway Suite 3200 Denver CO 80274

HART, ORSON H., ins. co. exec.; b. Hartford, Conn., Feb. 22, 1913; s. Orson H. and Mabel (Evans) H.; m. Susan Moore, Feb. 14, 1942; children—Katherine, Sarah. B.A., Trinity Coll., 1935; Ph.D., Yale U., 1946. With Phoenix Mut. Life Ins. Co., Hartford, 1937-41, Office Price Adminstrn., Washington, 1941-43, Lionel D. Edie & Co., N.Y.C., 1943-48, Life Ins. Assn. Am., 1948-56; 2d v.p. N.Y. Life Ins. Co., N.Y.C., 1957-66, dir. econ. studies, 1964-66, v.p. econ. analysis, 1966-78, ret., 1978; econ. and fin. cons., 1978—; dir. Washington Nat. Life Ins. Co., N.Y. Contbr. articles to profl. jours. Mem. N.Y. C. of C. (vice chmn. fiscal and monetary com. 1975—), Nat. Assn. Bus. Economists, Am. Council Life Ins. (chmn. fiscal monetary policy com. 1969-72, chmn. investment research com. 1977). Clubs: Yale, Forecasters (N.Y.C.); Nat. Economists (Washington). Home and Office: Indian Waters Dr New Canaan CT 06840

HART, PATRICK JOSEPH, editor; b. Green Bay, Wis., June 14, 1925; s. Michael Joseph and Frances Marie (Fox) H. B.A. in Philosophy, U. Notre Dame, 1966. Joined Trappist Monks, Roman Cath. Ch., 1951; sec. to abbot Abbey of Gethsemani, Ky., 1957—; abbey rep. on Thomas Merton affairs, 1968—; mem. staff Abbot Gen.'s House Cistercian Monks, Rome, 1966-68; bd. dirs. Cistercian Publs., 1975—. Editor: Thomas Merton/Monk: A Monastic Tribute, 1974 (Religious Book award Cath. Press Assn. 1975), (Thomas Merton) The Monastic Journey, 1977, The Literary Essays of Thomas Merton, 1981, The Message of Thomas Merton, 1981; co-editor: The Asian Journal of Thomas Merton, 1973, (Thomas Merton) Love and Living, 1979; editor-in-chief: Cistercian Studies, 1981—. Address: Abbey of Gethsemani Trappist KY 40051 *This year, 1983, marks the 32rd anniversary of my life as a monk at the Abbey of Gethsemani in central Kentucky. It has been a wonderful life of prayer, work and study. A perfect setting for the kind of reflective editorial work in which I am involved.*

HART, PETER DAVID, opinion research firm executive; b. San Francisco, Jan. 3, 1942; s. James D. and Ruth (Arnstein) H.; m. Florence Rubenstein, Aug. 12, 1973; children: Elizabeth, Aaron. A.B., Colby Coll., 1964. Analyst, researcher Louis Harris & Assoc., N.Y.C., 1964-67, v.p., 1971-72; dir. field ops. J. Gilligan for Senator, Ohio, 1968-69; dir. research Democratic Nat. Com., Washington, 1969-70; v.p. Oliver Quayle & Co., Bronxville, N.Y., 1970-71; pres. Peter D. Hart Research Assoc., Inc., Washington, 1972—; spl. cons. CBS News, N.Y.C., 1974—; vis. fellow Woodrow Wilson Found., Princeton, N.J., 1975—. Mem. Nat. Council on Pub. Polls, Am. Assn. Pub. Opinion Research, Nat. Assn. Pvt. Pollsters. Democrat. Jewish. Office: Peter D Hart Research Assocs Inc 1724 Connecticut Ave NW Washington DC 20009

HART, RAY LEE, educator; b. Hereford, Tex., Mar. 22, 1929; s. Albert Mann and Ruby Douglas (Bracken) H.; m. Juanita Fern Morgan, Sept. 8, 1951; children: Douglas Morgan, Stuart Bracken. B.A., U. Tex., 1949; B.D., So. Methodist U., 1953; Ph.D., Yale U., 1959. Instr., then asst. prof. Drew U. Theol. Sch., 1956-63; asso. prof. philos. and systematic theology Vanderbilt U. Div. Sch., 1963-69; prof., chmn. dept. religious studies U. Mont., 1969—; Cons. on religious studies SUNY, 1972—. Author: Unfinished Man and the Imagination, 1968; trans. into Chinese, editor: Selections from Thomas Aquinas, 1966. Mayor, Polebridge, Mont., 1969-70. Mem. Am. Acad. Religion (editor jour. 1970-80, pres.-elect 1982-83, del. to Am. Council Learned Socs. 1980—, mem. exec. com., dir.), Metaphys. Soc. Am., Soc. Sci. Study Religion, Soc. Religion in Higher Edn. Home: 16 Carriage Way Missoula MT 59801

HART, RICHARD BANNER, life insurance company executive; b. Winston-Salem, N.C., Apr. 9, 1932; s. Samuel Bruce and Cordia M. (Lamb) H.; m. Jean Elizabeth Shinn, Apr. 28, 1956; 1 dau., Fabra. A.B. in Polit. Sci, U. N.C., Chapel Hill, 1957, J.D., 1959. Bar: N.C. bar 1959, Tenn. bar 1970; C.L.U., 1970. Asso. counsel Jefferson Standard Life Ins. Co., Greensboro, N.C., 1959-70; with Nat. Life and Accident Ins. Co., Nashville, 1970—, asst. v.p., counsel, 1973-75, sec., counsel, 1975—, NLT Corp., 1975—; sec., counsel, dir. Nat. Property Owners Ins. Co.; sec. NLT Mktg. Services Co., Guardsman Life Ins. Co.; lectr. in field. Bd. editors: U. N.C. Law Rev, 1958-59. Mem. budget com. Guilford County (N.C.) United Fund, 1968-69; mem. Guilford County Mental Health Assn., 1968-69; bd. dirs. Phi Kappa Sigma Found. Served with AUS, 1953-55. Mem. N.C., Nashville bar assns., N.C. State Bar, Assn. Life Ins. Counsel, Am. Soc. Corporate Secs. (exec. com., pres. S.E. region 1979—), Nashville Com. Fgn. Relations, Phi Delta Phi, Phi Kappa Sigma (nat. officer, exec. bd. 1971-77). Methodist. Clubs: Exchange (bd. dirs.), Maryland Farms Country, Nashville Athletic (Nashville). Home: 2815 Kenway Rd Nashville TN 37215 Office: Am Gen Center-Nashville: Nashville TN 37250

HART, RICHARD NEVEL, JR., food chain executive; b. Quincy, Mass., June 18, 1940; s. Richard N. and A. Carmel (Deady) H.; m. Monica Anne Rielly, July 22, 1967; children—Richard, Patricia, Michael, Daniel, John, Matthew. B.S. in Bus. Adminstrn, Boston Coll., 1962. With Peat, Marwick, Mitchell & Co. (C.P.A.'s), Boston, 1962-66; with Dunkin Donuts Inc., Randolph, Mass., 1966—, v.p., treas., 1978—; corporator Quincy Savs. Bank, Mass. Bd. corporators City Hosp. of Quincy.; bd. dirs. Carney Hosp. Found., South Shore Chpt. ARC of Mass. Bay; trustee Quincy Jr. Coll. Mem. Fin. Execs. Inst., Nat. Assn. Accountants, Nat. Inst. Investor Relations, Mass. Soc. C.P.A.s., South Shore C. of C. (bd. dirs.). Roman Catholic. Club: Wollaston Golf. Home: 5 Amber Rd Hingham MA 02043 Office: Box 317 Randolph MA 02368

HART, RICHARD WILLIAM, retail executive; b. Aug. 22, 1941; children: Trent, Dirk. B.S., Weber State U., 1966; M.B.A., Xavier U.; postgrad., Advanced Mgmt. Program, Harvard U., 1978, 79. V.p. Sanger Harris, Dallas, 1964-79; sr. v.p. I. Magnin, 1979-81; pres. Seligman & Latz, Inc., N.Y.C., 1981—; pres. chief exec. officer Fine Jewelry (div. Seligman & Latz, Inc.), N.Y.C., 1981—; Controller I. Magnin, San Francisco, 1972-74. Mem. Bus. Task Force, Ind. Sch. Dist., Com. for Performing Arts Center; bd. dirs. Dallas Civic Opera. Mem. Met. Opera Assn., Consumer Counseling Service. Office: Seligman & Latz 666 Fifth Ave New York NY 10019

HART, ROBERT CARMON, manufacturing company executive; b. Elizabethton, Tenn., Oct. 29, 1926; s. Samuel R. and Virginia E. (Snodgrass) H.; m. Hazel Campbell, Dec. 30, 1948; children—John Philip, Janet Hart Collins, James Robert, Joel Bruce, Julie Ellen. Student, Milligan Coll., 1944-45; B.M.E., U. Louisville, 1947; postgrad., U. Tenn., 1949-50. With Ky. Insp. Bur., 1947-48, N. Am. Rayon Corp., 1948-49; with Tenn. Eastman Co., Kingsport, 1950—, pres., 1979—; dir. First Tenn. Bank N.A., Kingsport/Bristol. Bd. dirs. Holston Valley Community Hosp., Kingsport, 1980—. Served with USNR, 1944-46. Fellow ASME; mem. Am. Inst. Chem. Engrs., Am. Assn. Textile Tech., Nat. Soc. Profl. Engrs., Soc. Chem. Industry, Rocky Mount Hist. Assn., Kingsport C. of C., Tau Beta Pi. Republican. Presbyterian. Office: PO Box 511 Kingsport TN 37662

HART, ROBERT GORDON, govt. ofcl.; b. San Francisco, Dec. 28, 1921; s. Edwin and Ruth Graves (Thompson) H. Student, Am. Inst. Banking, 1939-41. Br. mgr. Bank of Kodiak, Alaska, 1942-46; folk art cons. Indsl. Research Adv. Council, Honolulu, 1950-51; mgr. So. Highlanders, Inc., N.Y.C., 1946-52; Southwestern rep. Indian Arts and Crafts Bd., Santa Fe, 1954-57; treas. Westbury Music Fair, Inc., 1957; dir. public relations Constructive Research Found., N.Y.C., 1958-59; editor, dir. publs. Bklyn. Mus., 1959-61; gen. mgr. Indian Arts and Crafts Bd., Dept. Interior, Washington, 1961—; art and craft cons. Mus. Internat. Folk Art, Santa Fe, 1954-57; chmn. Fed. Inter-Departmental Agy. for Arts and Crafts, 1963—; U.S. del. OAS for Reunion Technica des Artesanias. Author: How to Sell Handicrafts, 1953, Alaska, 1959. Bd. dirs. Bur. Occupational Extension Services, N.Y.C., N.Y. Elder Crafts-Corp.; mem. nat. adv. bd. Foxfire Fund, Inc., 1981—. Served with AUS, 1943-45. Recipient N.Y. State Gov.'s award for outstanding service, 1951. Mem. Conseil Internat. des Musées, Am. Assn. Museums, Am. Craftsman's Council, World Crafts Council, Am. Polit. Sci. Assn. Home: 916 25th St NW Washington DC 20037 Office: Indian Arts and Crafts Bd Rm 4004 Interior Bldg Washington DC 20240

HART, ROBERT MAYES, oil executive, lawyer; b. Tulsa, Aug. 27, 1925; s. James Eben and Marthel (Mayes) H.; m. Joanne Krusen, Dec. 23, 1948; children: Robert Mayes, Nancy, Steven. A.B., Harvard U., 1946, M.B.A., 1947; LL.B., U. Okla., 1949; LL.M., NYU, 1957. Bar: Okla. 1949, N.Y. 1953; C.P.A., Okla. Clk. judge U.S. Dist. Ct., 1949-50; atty. Shell Oil Co., 1950-62, treas., 1962-63; gen. mgr. Shell Chem. Co., 1963-66; gen. mgr. transp. and supplies Shell Oil Co., 1966-67, v.p. transp. and supplies, 1967-68, exec. v.p., 1968-73; supply coordinator Shell Internat. Petroleum Co., 1973-81; mng. dir. Royal Dutch/Shell Group, 1976—; dir. Shell Transport and Trading Co. Ltd., 1976-79, mng. dir., 1979-82, Royal Dutch Petroleum Co., 1982—. Mem. Order of Coif, Phi Beta Kappa, Sigma Alpha Epsilon, Phi Delta Phi. Office: Shell Internat Petroleum Co Shell Centre London SE1 7NA England

HART, RONALD WILSON, radiobiologist, toxicologist, government research executive; b. Syracuse, N.Y., Mar. 23, 1942; s. Wilson and Annabell H.; m. Teresa Leigh Hoskins, Aug. 31, 1974. B.S., Syracuse U., 1967; M.S., U. Ill., 1969, Ph.D., 1971; postgrad. (Nat. Cancer Inst. trainee), Oak Ridge Nat. Lab., 1973. USPHS trainee, 1970-71; Asst. prof. Ohio State U., Columbus, 1971-75, dir. radiation biology research div., 1971-82, asso. prof. depts. biology, biophysics, 1975-78, asso. prof. depts. biology, biophysics dept. preventive medicine, 1976-78, asso. prof. pharmacology, medicinal chemistry dept. preventive medicine, 1977-78, dir. chem., biomed. environ. research group dept. preventive medicine, 1977-82, prof. depts. radiology, preventive medicine, pharmacology, medicinal chemistry, vet. pathobiology, 1978-82; dir. Nat. Center for Toxicological Research, Jefferson, Ark., 1980—; prof. U. Poona, India, 1978—, Cairo U., 1979—; cons. Oak Ridge Nat. Lab., 1971-75, Brookhaven Nat. Lab., 1975-78, Argonne Nat. Lab., 1975-78, EPA, 1976, 78, Am. Indsl. Health Council, 1978, PPG Industries, 1978, Informatics, 1978-80, FDA, 1980; mem. Nat. Scis./NRC Bd. on Toxicology and Environ. Health Hazards, 1976-82; mem. interagy. staff group Office Sci. and Tech. Policy Exec Office of Pres., 1982—, chmn., 1983—; bd. dirs. Ark. Sci. and Tech. Authority, 1983—. Contbr. chpts. to books, numerous articles to profl. jours. Recipient Hopkins award for grad. research, 1971, Japanese Med. Assn. award, 1978, Karl-August-Forester award, Germany, 1980, W. Ger., 1980, award of merit FDA, 1982, Sr. Exec. Service award, 1982, Superior Service award USPHS, 1983; named Syracuse U. Outstanding Alumnus, 1976. Mem. AAAS, Radiation Research Soc., Biophys. Soc., Photochem. and Photobiol. Soc., Gerontol. Soc., Am. Coll. Toxicology (pres. 1981), Sigma Xi. Office: Nat Center for Toxicological Research US Dept Health and Human Services Jefferson AR 72079

HART, SAMUEL FRIEDLANDER, foreign service officer, ambassador; b. Canton, Miss., Sept. 13, 1933; s. Clarence Jerome and Willie Beatrice (Erickson) H.; m. Lynne B. Kiene, May 4, 1959; children: Rebecca Lee, David Erickson. B.A. in Liberal Arts, U. Miss., 1955; M.A. in Internat. Relations, Fletcher Sch. Law and Diplomacy, 1958, Vanderbilt U., 1969. U.S. fgn. service officer Dept. State, Washington, 1958—, assignment in U.S. Uruguay, Indonesia, Malaysia, Costa Rica, Chile, Israel, ambassador to Ecuador, Quito, 1982—. Served to capt. U.S. Army, 1955-57. Recipient Meritorious Honor award U.S. Dept. State, 1971, Superior Honor award U.S. Dept. State, 1980. Mem. Am. Fgn. Service Assn. (dir. 1976-77, William Rivkin award 1971), Internat. Club, Ecuadorean (Am. C. of C., hon.). Clubs: Army Navy Country (Arlington, Va.); Internat. (Washington). Home and Office: APO US Embassy Quito Miami FL 34039

HART, STANLEY ROBERT, geochemist, educator; b. Swampscott, Mass., June 20, 1935; s. Robert Winfield and Ruth Mildred (Standley) H.; m. Joanna Smith, Sept. 1, 1956 (div. Dec. 1978); 1 dau., Jolene Kaweah; m. Pamela Coulouras Shepherd, Nov. 4, 1980; 1 dau., Elizabeth Ann Hart. B.S., Mass. Inst. Tech., 1956, Ph.D., 1960; M.S., Calif. Inst. Tech., 1957. Staff mem. Carnegie Instn., Washington, 1960-75; prof. dept. earth and planetary sci. Mass. Inst. Tech., Cambridge, 1975—; mem. U.S. Nat. Com. for Geochemistry, 1973-76, chmn., 1975; mem. ocean crust panel Internat. Phase of Ocean Drilling, 1974-76; mem. U.S. nat. com. Internat. Geol. Correlations Program, 1974-76. Assoc. editor: Jour. Geophys. Research, 1966-68, Reviews of Geophysics, 1970-72; Asso. editor: Geochimica et Cosmochimica Acta, 1970-76; adv. editorial bd.: Earth and Planetary Sci. Letters, 1977—; contbr. articles in field to profl. jours. Mem. Geol. Soc. Am., Am. Geophys. Union, Geochem. Soc. (councillor 1981-83), Nat. Acad. Scis. Home: 172 Mason Terr Brookline MA 02146 Office: Dept Earth and Planetary Sci Mass Inst Tech Cambridge MA 02139 *I view science, the search for truth and understanding, as an infinitely long road; therefore, getting to the end is not as important as how we get there.*

HART, THOMAS R., Romance languae educator; b. Raleigh, N.C., Jan. 10, 1925; s. Thomas Roy and Mary (Medlin) H.; m. Margaret Alice Fulton, June 30, 1945; children: John Fulton, Katherine Anne. B.A., Yale U., 1948, Ph.D., 1952. Instr. Amherst Coll., Mass., 1952-53, Harvard U., Cambridge, Mass., 1953-55; asst. prof. Johns Hopkins, Balt., 1955-60; assoc. prof. Emory U., Atlanta, 1960-64; prof. Romance langs. U. Oreg., Eugene, 1964—. Editor: Jour. Comparative Literature, Gil Vicente: Obras dramaticas castellanas, 1962, Gil Vincente: Farces and Festival Plays, 1972. Fulbright research grantee U.S. Govt., 1950-51, U.S. Govt., Madrid, Spain, 1966-67. Mem. Associacion Internacional de Hispanistas. Home: 2580 Spring Blvd Eugene OR 97403 Office: Dept Romance Langs U Oreg Eugene OR 97403

HART, WILLIAM LEVATA, police chief; b. Detroit, Jan. 17, 1924; s. Charles John and Gessener Mae (Brock) H.; m. Laura Elaine Johnson, Nov. 25, 1950; children: Cynthia Renee, Jennifer Lynn. B.S., Wayne State U., 1977, M.Ed., 1978, Ed.D. in Ednl. Sociology, 1981; grad., FBI Nat. Acad., 1972. Coal miner, Leechburg, Pa., 1940-43, 46-49; tool and die maker Ford Motor Co., 1950-52; with Detroit Police Dept., 1952—, insp., 1971-73, div. comdr., 1973-74, dep. chief hdqrs. bur., 1974-76, chief police, 1976—; instr. criminal justice Wayne State U.; bd. dirs. Criminal Law Revision Com., 1976—; chmn. bd. Detroit Met. Acad., 1978—; mem. U.S. Atty. Gen.'s Task Force on Violent Crime; witness juvenile justice subcom. of Senate Judiciary Com. on Juvenile Justice and Delinquency Prevention Program. Chmn. United Fund Drive, Detroit, 1978; mem. Mayor's Bus. and Labor Ad-Hoc Com.; bd. dirs. Boy Scouts Am., Boys Club of Met. Detroit. Served with USNR, 1943-46. Mem. Internat. Police Assn., Internat. Assn. Chiefs of Police, Nat. Exec. Inst., Police Found., Am. Acad. Profl. Law Enforcement, Mich. Assn. Chiefs of Police (crime prevention com., subcom. on use of deadly force), Wayne County Assn. Chiefs of Police, Major City Chiefs of Police Assn., Mich. Commn. Criminal Justice, Police Exec. Research Forum, Nat. Orgn. Black Law Enforcement Execs. (exec. bd.), Detroit Police Benefit and Protective Assn. (pres. trustees). Baptist. Clubs: Detroit Yacht, Masons. Office: 1300 Beaubien Detroit MI 48226 *Two standards or principles which I have maintained throughout my life are perseverance and integrity. Perseverance was a necessity during my work as a coal miner in Pennsylvania and while employed at the Ford Motor Company (in training and on the job as a tool and die maker). Integrity has been the one standard of conduct that I believe has carried me through the ranks of the Detroit Police Department up to my present assignment.* *

HART, WILLIAM MILTON, ophthalmologist, educator; b. St. Clair County, Mo., June 28, 1913; s. Ruben V. and Harriet (Hoskins) H.; m.

Ethelwyn Featherstun Stevens, Apr. 14, 1938; children—Juliet Katheryn, William Milton, Sarah Stevens, Ethelwyn Featherstun. A.B., S.E. Mo. State Tchrs. Coll., 1937; M.S., U. Iowa, 1939; Ph.D., U. Minn., 1941; M.D., Temple U., 1948. Diplomate: Am. Bd. Ophthalmology. Mayo Found. fellow physiology Mayo Clinic, 1939-41; research asso. ophthalmology U. Iowa, 1941-42; asso. physiology Jefferson Med. Coll., 1942-44, asst. prof. ophthalmology, 1952-53; asst. prof. biochemistry, clin. asst. ophthalmology Temple U., 1944-49, research asso. prof. ophthalmology, 1949-52; chief br. ophthalmology Nat. Inst. Neurol. Diseases and Blindness, 1953-54; clin. prof. neuro-ophthalmology U. Md.; chmn. Roy E. Mason Distinguished prof. ophthalmology, U. Mo., 1967-79; prof. ophthalmology U. Miss., Jackson, 1979—; chief ophthalmology VA Hosp., Jackson, 1979—; surgeon USPHS, 1953-57. Recipient prize ophthalmology Assn. for Research, 1941; Zentmayer award ophthalmology Coll. Physicians of Phila., 1946. Fellow A.C.S., Royal Soc. Medicine; mem. Am. Acad. Ophthalmology and Otolaryngology, Am. Physiol. Soc., Am. Chem. Soc., Sigma Xi, Alpha Omega Alpha. Republican. Methodist. Club: Kiwanian. Home: 1332 Linden Pl Jackson MS 39202

HART, WILLIAM SEBASTIAN, symphony orchestra conductor; b. Balt., Oct. 30, 1920; s. William Sebastian and Isabella Henrietta (Ornstein) H.; m. Regina Margaret Litsch, Apr. 10, 1950. Tchr.'s Certificate cum laude, Peabody Conservatory of Music, Balt., 1939; B.A., Johns Hopkins U., 1940; Ph.D., Golden State U., 1956; Mus.D., Allen U., Columbia, S.C., 1958; L.H.D., Mt. St. Mary's Coll., Emmitsburg, Md., 1962; LL.D., U. Tex., San Antonio, 1965. Mem. faculty Peabody Conservatory of Music, 1939-62; tchr. Balt. pub. schs., 1939-52; 1st chair musician Balt. Symph ony Orch., 1939-58; condr. Balt. Bur. Music, 1947-58; mem. faculty Morgan State Coll., 1962-65, Balt. Coll. Commerce, 1958-75; radio, then TV commentator, 1939-69, founder, 1958; since mus. dir. Gettysburg (Pa.) Symphony Orch.; guest condr. Royal Philharmonic Orch., 1965, 69, 78, 83, Nat. Symphony Orch., 1969, London Philharm. Orch., 1983, London Mozart Players, 1983; profl. lectr. Composer: Duet for Timpani, 1958. Mem. Am. Musicol. Soc., Baltimore County Hist. Soc. (pres. 1963-65, 68-70). Republican. Roman Catholic. Club: Johns Hopkins Faculty. Address: 1800 Cromwell Bridge Rd Baltimore MD 21234

HART, WILLIAM THOMAS, judge; b. Joliet, Ill., Feb. 4, 1929; s. William Michael and Geraldine (Archambeault) H.; m. Catherine Motta, Nov. 27, 1954; children: Catherine Hart Fornero, Susan Hart DeMario, Julie Hart Boesen, Sally, Nancy. J.D., Loyola U.-Chgo., 1951. Bar: Ill. 1951, U.S. Dist. Ct. 1957, U.S. Ct. Appeals 7th cir. 1954, U.S. Ct. Appeals D.C. 1977. Asst. U.S. atty. No. Dist. Ill., Chgo., 1954-56; spl. asst. atty. gen. State of Ill., 1957-58; spl. asst. state's Cook County, Ill., 1960; judge U.S. Dist. Ct., Chgo., 1982—; mem. firm Defrees & Fiske, 1956-59; ptnr. Schiff, Hardin & Waite, 1959-82. Pres. adv. bd. Mercy Med. Ctr., Aurora, Ill., 1980-81; v.p. Aurora Blood Bank, 1972-77; trustee Rosary High Sch., 1981-82; bd. dirs. Chgo. Legal Assistant Found., 1974-76. Served with U.S. Army, 1951-53. Decorated Bronze Star. Mem. 7th Cir. Bar Assn., Law Club, Legal Club. Office: US Courthouse 219 S Dearborn St Chgo. IL 60604

HARTE, EDWARD HOLMEAD, newspaper pub.; b. Pilot Grove, Mo., Dec. 5, 1922; s. Houston and Isabel (McCutcheon) H.; m. Janet Frey, Feb. 8, 1947; children—Christopher, Elizabeth, William, Julia. B.A., Dartmouth, 1947. With Kansas City Star, 1948-50; editor, co-owner Synder (Tex.) Daily News, 1950-52; pres. San Angelo (Tex.) Standard-Times, 1952-56; v.p. Corpus Christi Caller Times, 1956-62, pub., 1962—. Home: 222 Ohio St Corpus Christi TX 78404 Office: 820 Lower Broadway: Corpus Christi TX 78401

HARTE, HOUSTON HARRIMAN, newspaper-broadcasting exec.; b. San Angelo, Tex., Feb. 15, 1927; s. Houston and Caroline Isabel (McCutcheon) H.; m. Carolyn Esther Hardig, June 17, 1950; children—Houston Ritchie, David Harriman, Sarah Elizabeth. B.A., Washington and Lee U., 1950. Partner Snyder (Tex.) Daily News, 1950-52, editor, 1952-54; with Des Moines Register and Tribune, 1954-56; pres. San Angelo Standard, Inc., 1956-62; v.p. Express Pub. Co., San Antonio, 1962-66, pres., 1966-72; chmn. bd. Harte-Hanks Communications, Inc., 1971—. Pres. bd. dirs. San Angelo Symphony, 1960; v.p. Concho Valley council Boy Scouts Am., 1960-62; Bd. visitors USAF Acad., 1965-69; bd. regents East Tex. State U., 1970-81; trustee Stillman Coll., 1976—, Washington and Lee U., 1981—. Served with USNR, 1945-46. Democrat. Presbyterian. Office: PO Box 269 San Antonio TX 78291

HARTE, JOSEPH MEAKIN, bishop; b. Springfield, Ohio, July 28, 1914; s. Charles Edward and Ruth Elizabeth (Weisenstein) H.; m. Alice Eleanor Taylor, Oct. 14, 1941; children—Victoria Ruth, Joseph Meakin, Judith Alice. A.B., Washington and Jefferson Coll., 1936; D.D., U. South, 1955; S.T.B., Gen. Theol. Sem., 1939, S.T.D., 1955. Ordained deacon, priest Episcopal Ch., 1939; rector (All Saints Ch.), Miami, Okla., 1939-40; asst. Trinity Ch., Tulsa, 1940-42; rector (St. George's Ch.), Rochester, N.Y., 1942-43; chaplain Episcopal students U. Tex., Austin, 1943-51; dean St. Paul's Cathedral, Erie, Pa., 1951-54; suffragan bishop, Dallas, 1954-62, bishop of, Ariz., 1962-80; dir. Gt. Western Bank & Trust. Dep., Gen. Conv. Episcopal Ch., 1952; trustee Bloy Episcopal Sch. Theology.; pres. Pacific Province, 1967-68. Author: Some Sources of Common Prayer, 1944, The Language of the Book of Common Prayer, 1945, The Title Page of the Book of Common Prayer, 1946, The Church's Name, 1958, The Elizabethan Prayer Book, 1959, The 1662 Prayer Book, 1962. Mem. Am. Legion, Beta Theta Pi. Club: Mason. Office: 6300 N Central Phoenix AZ 85012

HARTER, DONALD HARRY, medical educator; b. Breslau, Germany, May 16, 1933; came to U.S., 1940, naturalized, 1945; s. Harry Morton and Leonor Evelyn (Goldmann) H.; m. Lee Grossman, Dec. 18, 1960 (div. 1976); children: Kathryne, Jennifer, Amy, David. A.B., U. Pa., 1953; M.D., Columbia U., 1957. Diplomate: Am. Bd. Psychiatry and Neurology. Intern in medicine Yale-New Haven Med. Center, 1957-58; asst. resident, then resident neurology N.Y. Neurol. Inst., 1958-61; guest investigator Rockefeller U., 1963-66; mem. faculty Columbia Coll. Physicians and Surgeons, 1960-75, prof. neurology and microbiology, 1973-75; vis. fellow Clare Hall, Cambridge, Eng., 1973-74; attending neurologist N.Y. Neurol. Inst., Presbyn. Hosp., 1973-75; Charles L. Mix prof., chmn. dept. neurology Northwestern U., 1975—; chmn. dept. neurology Northwestern Meml. Hosp., Chgo., 1975—; mem. adv. com. on fellowships Nat. Multiple Sclerosis Soc., 1976-79, chmn., 1977-79; mem. Nat. Commn. on Venereal Disease, HEW, 1970-72; mem. med. adv. bd. Am. Parkinsons' Disease Assn., 1976—, Myasthenia Gravis Found., 1980—; mem. sci. adv. council Nat. ALS Found., 1978—; mem. neurol. disorders program project rev. A com. Nat. Inst. Neurol. and Communicative Disorders and Stroke, NIH, HHS, 1981—. Editorial bd.: Neurology, 1976-82, Anns. of Neurology, 1983—; adv. bd.: Archives of Virology, 1975-81. USPHS spl. fellow, 1963-66; Am. Cancer Soc. scholar, 1973-74; Guggenheim fellow, 1973; recipient Joseph Mather Smith prize Columbia U., 1970, Lucy G. Moses award, 1970, 72. Mem. Am. Soc. Clin. Investigation, Am. Neurol. Assn. (membership adv. com. 1980-82), Am. Assn. Neuropathologists, Soc. Exptl. Biology and Medicine, Assn. Univ. Profs. Neurology, Infectious Disease Soc. Am., Soc. Neurosci., Am. Acad. Neurology (alt. rep. to Council of Med. Splty. Socs. 1979-82), Am. Assn. Immunologists, Am. Soc. Microbiology, Soc. Gen. Microbiology, Am. Epilepsy Soc., Am. Assn. for Study Headache, Am. Assn. for History Medicine, Pan Am Med. Assn., Phi Beta Kappa, Sigma Xi. Home: 900 Lake Shore Dr Chicago IL 60611 Office: Dept Neurology Northwestern U Med Sch 303 E Chicago Ave Chicago IL 60611

HARTER, HUGH ANTHONY, language educator; b. Columbus, Ohio, Dec. 13, 1922; s. Anthony Hugh and Georgiana (Hayes) H.; m. Driscilla Escher, Aug. 31, 1959 (div. 1961); m. Frances D. Reichman, Oct. 7, 1970; stepchildren: Ellen Berliner, Andrew Berliner, Nancy Berliner Rudolph. Student, Ohio Wesleyan U., 1940-41, Hamilton Coll., 1943, Ecole du Syndicat de la Haute Couture, Paris, 1947, NYU, 1975, New Sch. Social Research, 1975; B.A. cum laude, Ohio State U., 1947, Ph.D., 1959; M.A. cum laude, Mexico City Coll., U. Ams., 1951. Student teaching asst. Ohio State U., 1946-47, grad. teaching asst., 1951-53; asst. to prof. French Mexico City Coll., U. Ams., 1951; instr., asst. prof. Romance langs. Wesleyan U., Middletown, Conn., 1953-59; assoc. prof. Elmira Coll., 1959-60; Andrew Mellow postdoctoral fellow U. Pitts., 1960-61, spl. lectr., 1963-64, NDEA Insts. fellow, 1962, 63; assoc. prof. Chatham Coll., 1961-64, Loyola U., Chgo., 1964-66; prof. Ohio Westeyan U., Delaware, 1966—; chmn. dept. Romance langs. Ohio Wesleyan U., Delaware, 1966-80, Robert Hayward prof. modern fgn. langs., 1976—, dir. Internat. Inst. of Spain, 1984—; pres. Vitalicio, Fundacion Juan Ruiz, Segovia, Spain, 1971—, Horizons for Learning, Delaware, Ohio, 1974—; acct. Columbus Coated Fabrics Corp., Columbus, 1941-42; auditor European Post Exchange System, Bad Nauheim, Germany, 1948; co-owner John Anthony Studios, Columbus, 1954-64; v.p., dir. Von Mock Assocs., N.Y.C., 1969-70; spl. lectr. U. Catolica de Santa Maria, Arequipa, Peru, 1969; dir. Acad. Program in Segovia, 1969—. Author: (most recent) Gertrudis Gomez de Avellaneda, 1981; translator, author: Mother Comes of Age (Driss Chraibi), 1984, The Butts (Driss Chraibi), 1983; translator, editor: A History of Spanish Literature, 1971; co-editor: (with Willis Barnstone) Riconenete y Cortadillo, 1960; lyricist: More About the Pear Tree, 1976. Bd. dirs. Centro Segovia, 1971—; v.p. Delaware (Ohio) Heritage Inc., 1973-75, bd. dirs., 1975-78, pres., 1978-80; pres. Delaware Shakespeare Soc., 1980-81. Served with M.I. then Air Transport Command, U.S. Army; ETO. Named hon. citizen City of Segovia, 1976; grantee summer research Andrew Mellon Found., (Morocco), 1973; spl. grantee Govt. Morocco, 1975; spl. langs. grantee Mellon Mediterranean Studies, (Algeria and Tunisia), 1977. Mem. AAUP, MLA, Am. Assn. Tchrs. Spanish and Portuguese, Authors' Guild, Coll. Lang. Assn., ASCAP, La Academia de San Quirce (Segovia corr.). Episcopalian. Office: Ohio Wesleyan U Sandusky St Delaware OH 43015

HARTER, LAFAYETTE GEORGE, JR., educator; b. Des Moines, May 28, 1918; s. Lafayette George and Helen Elizabeth (Ives) H.; m. Charlotte Mary Toshach, Aug. 23, 1950; children—Lafayette George III, James Toshach, Charlotte Helen. B.A. in Bus. Adminstrn, Antioch Coll., 1941; M.A. in Econs, Stanford, 1948, Ph.D., 1960. Instr. Menlo Coll., Menlo Park, Cal., 1948-50; instr. Coll. of Marin, Kentfield, Calif., 1950-60; prof. econs. dept. Oreg. State U., 1960—, chmn. dept., 1967-71; mem. panel arbitrators Fed. Mediation and Conciliation Service, 1965—, Oreg. Conciliation Service, 1967—; mem. Univ. Centers for Rational Alternatives. Author: John R. Commons: His Assault on Laissez-faire, 1962, Labor in America, 1957, Economic Responses to a Changing World, 1972; editorial bd.: Jour. Econ. Issues, 1981—. Asso. campaign chmn. Benton United Good Neighbor Fund, 1970-72, campaign chmn., v.p., 1972-73, pres., 1973—; vice chmn.; pub. mem. Adv. Commn. on Unemployment Compensation, 1972, 73, chmn., 1974-78; Bd. dirs. Oreg. Council Econ. Edn., 1971—; Pub. mem. local profl. responsibilities Oreg. State Bar Assn. Served to lt. comdr. USNR, 1941-46. Mem. Am. Arbitration Assn. (mem. pub. employment disputes panel 1970—), Am., Western econ. assns., Indsl. Relations Research Assn., Am. Assn. for Evolutionary Econs., AAUP, Oreg. State Employees Assn. (v.p. faculty chpt. 1972, pres. 1973). Democrat. Mem. United Ch. of Christ (moderator 1972, 73; mem. fin. com. Oreg. conf. 1974-82, dir. 1978—, mem. personnel com. 1983—). Home: 3755 NW Van Buren St Corvallis OR 97330

HARTER, ROBERT HUGH, broadcasting company executive; b. Des Moines, Dec. 31, 1915; s. Hugh I. and Ila Louise (Mount) H.; m. Mary Louise Donegan, Apr. 13, 1941; children: Robert Michael, Martha Ann Harter Murphy. Student, Drake U.; B.S., U. Iowa, 1939; postgrad. in bus, Harvard U., 1942-43. Mem. sales staff Sta. WHO, Des Moines, 1939-42, 46; regional sales mgr. Sta. WHO, WHO-TV, KLYF-FM, 1947-56, gen. sales mgr., 1956-64; gen. mgr. WHO Broadcasting Co. div. Palmer Communications, Inc., 1964-66, v.p., dir., 1966-72, exec. v.p., dir., 1972-78, pres., 1978—, chmn., chief exec. officer, 1982—; Pres. Greater Des Moines Com.; mem. nat. bd. NCCJ. Served with USAAF, 1942-46. Mem. Nat. Assn. Broadcasters (chmn. radio code bd.), Iowa Broadcasters Assn. (pres. 1975-76), Greater Des Moines C. of C. (dir.), Better Bus. Bur. Des Moines, Nat. Cable TV Assn. Republican. Clubs: University (Chgo.); Des Moines, Wakonda Country, Embassy. Home: 3930 Grand Ave Suite 202 Des Moines IA 50312 Office: 1100 Walnut St Des Moines IA 50308

HARTER, ROBERT JACKSON, JR., lawyer; b. New Orleans, Nov. 6, 1944; s. Robert Jackson and Anne Marie (Carangelo) H.; m. Ann Eudean Peebles, Mar. 25, 1972; children: Ryan Scott, Ashley Ann. A.B., Stanford U., 1966; J.D., U. So. Calif., 1969. Bar: U.S. Dist. Ct., Calif. 1970. Law clk. to judge U.S. Ct. Appeals North Circuit, Los Angeles, 1969-70; assoc. Gibson, Dunn & Crutcher, Los Angeles, 1970-76, Shutan & Trost, 1976-78; assoc. gen. counsel Tiger Internat., Inc., Los Angeles, 1978-79, v.p.-law, 1979-82, v.p., gen. counsel, sec., 1982—. Mem. ABA, Los Angeles County Bar Assn., Order of Coif.

HARTER, ROBERT MICHAEL, financial executive; b. Ft. Worth, Tex., July 29, 1944; s. Robert Hugh and Mary Louise (Donegan) H.; m. Susan Mary Coult McKoin, Mar. 8, 1980; 1 dau., Megan Laura; 1 dau. (by previous marriage) Allison Erena. Student, Grinnell Coll., 1962-64; B.A. in Chemistry and Zoology, U. Iowa, 1966; J.D., 1969; Specialist in Accounting degree, Northwestern U., 1971. Tax cons. Arthur Young & Co., N.Y.C., 1969-74; controller White & Case, N.Y.C., 1974-77; fin. cons. William S. Paley, N.Y.C., 1977-78; v.p. finance, U.S. devel. and info., treas. The Conf. Bd., Inc., N.Y.C., 1978—. Mem. ABA, Iowa Bar Assn., N.Y. State Soc. C.P.A.s, Am. Inst. C.P.A.s, Arthur Young Businessmen's Assn. (pres., dir.). Roman Catholic. Home: 23 Chipmunk Ln Darien CT 06820 Office: The Conf Bd Inc 845 3d Ave New York NY 10022

HARTFIELD, DAVID, JR., lawyer; b. N.Y.C., May 25, 1919; s. David and Barbara Josie (Mayer) H.; m. Freda Lustick Burling, Nov. 21, 1964. B.A., U. Va., 1941, LL.B., 1943. Bar: N.Y. 1943, U.S. Supreme Ct. 1949. Asst. U.S. atty., So. Dist. N.Y., 1943-45; assoc. firm White & Case, N.Y.C., 1945-55, partner, 1955-82, of counsel, 1982—. Hon. bd. dirs. Kips Bay Boys Club, N.Y.C. Mem. Am. Bar Assn., Am. Law Inst., Fed. Bar Assn., N.Y. County Lawyers Assn., Am. Soc. Internat. Law, Am. Judicature Soc., Order of Coif. Republican. Clubs: Recess (N.Y.C.); Card Sound Golf (Key Largo, Fla.); Farmington Country (Charlottesville, Va.). Home: 39 Caro Sound Rd Key Largo FL 33037 Office: 14 Wall St New York NY 10005

HARTFORD, HUNTINGTON, financier, art patron; b. N.Y.C., Apr. 18, 1911; s. Edward Vassallo and Henrietta (Guerard) H.; m. Mary Lee Epling (div. 1939); m. Marjorie Steele, Sept. 10, 1949 (div. 1961); children: Catherine, John; m. Diane Brown, Oct. 6, 1962 (div. 1970); 1 dau., Cynara Juliet; m. Elaine Kay Hartford, May 21, 1974 (div. 1981). Grad., St. Paul's Sch., 1930; A.B., Harvard U., 1934. Hon. chmn. Tosco Corp. (formerly Oil Shale Corp.), Calif. Patron, Lincoln Center for Performing Arts; founder Gallery Modern Art, 1964, Huntington Hartford Found., 1949, Huntington Hartford Theatre, Calif., 1954; former owner, developer Paradise Island, Nassau, Bahamas.; Apptd. mem. Nat. Council on Arts, 1969. Author: play Jane Eyre, 1958, You Are What You Write, 1973. Served as lt. USCGR, 1942-45. Named Art Man of Year Nat. Art Materials Trade Assn., 1962; recipient Broadway Assn. Man of Year award; OAS award, 1966; Hon. fellow Nat. Sculpture Soc., 1960. Inventor Ten-Net, indoor-outdoor tennis game. Office: Care Townsend Rabinowitz Pantaleoni & Valente 535 Fifth Ave New York NY 10017 *

HARTFORD, JOHN COWAN, singer, songwriter; b. N.Y.C., Dec. 30, 1937. Student, Washington U., St. Louis, 1956-59. Watchman Green Line Steamers, 1952; deckhand Miss. Valley Barge Line, The Midwest Towing Co., 1953-54; radio announcer radio sta. KSTL, East St. Louis, 1962, WHOW, Clinton, Ill., KFAL, Fulton, Mo., KTCB, Maldin, Miss., 1963, WSIX and WWGM, Nashville, 1965. Studio musician, Nashville, 1965; songwriter, performer, 1965—; composer: song Gentle on My Mind (recorded by 330 artists and winner of 3 grammies); regular TV show Glen Campbell Goodtime Hour; guest appearances variety and talk shows; rec. artist, Flying Fish Records; albums include Earthwords and Music, 1967, Aero-Plain, Mark Twang (Grammy award for best ethnic or traditional rec. 1976), Down into the Mystery Below, 1978; Recipient (Grammy award for Song of Year 1966, as, Songwriter of Year 1966, Internat. Acad. Country and Western Music Splty. award for banjo 1969, 9 BMI awards for Gentle on My Mind.); Author: Word Movies, 1971. Hon. pres. John Edwards Meml. Found. Mem. Nat. Acad. Rec. Arts and Scis., AFTRA, Nashville Music Assn., Screen Actors Guild, Country Music Assn., Writers Guild Am., Acad. Country Music, BMI, Sons and Daus Pioneer Rivermen. Office: care Keith Case ICS 1201 Division St Washville TN 37203

HARTGEN, VINCENT ANDREW, educator, museum director, artist; b. Reading, Pa., Jan. 10, 1914; s. William J. and Jane (Hadfield) H.; m. Frances Caroline Lubanda, July 6, 1940; children: David Thomas, Stephen Anthony. B.F.A., U. Pa., 1940, M.F.A. (fellow), 1941. Traveling curator Anna Hyatt Huntington Exhbn. of Sculptures, 1937-39; dir. U. Maine Art Gallery; prof., head art dept. U. Maine, 1946-75, John H. Huddilston prof. art, 1962-82, John H. Huddilston prof. emeritus, 1983—, curator art collections, 1975-82; Art adviser Cultural Olympics, U. Pa., 1939-41; mem. Gov.'s Commn. Arts and Humanities, 1966-70. Works in collections including, Boston Mus. Fine Arts, Brooks Meml. Mus., Memphis, Howard U. Collection, John and Norma Marin Collection, Mus. Contemporary Arts, Houston, Wichita (Kans.) Art Mus., Butler Inst. Arts, Youngstown, Ohio, Everhart Mus., Scranton, Pa., U. Maine, Art Collection, Wadsworth Atheneum, Hartford, Smith, Colby colls., Reading (Pa.) Mus., Phoenix Art Mus., ITT Collection, Brandeis U., Elvejhem (Wis.) Mus., Kalamazoo Inst. Coll., Walker Art Inst., Mpls., Sheldon Swope Gallery, Terre Haute, Ind., one-man exhibits include, Binet Gallery, N.Y.C., one-man exhibits including, Md. Inst., Howard U., Everhart Mus., Claflin U., Coll. of Pacific, U. Idaho, Bermuda Art Assn., Chase Gallery N.Y., Farnsworth Mus., Rockland, Maine, State Dept. Art in the Embassies, also numerous others. Trustee Haystack Mountain Sch. of Crafts, Liberty, Maine, 1953-55. Recipient BAID award, 1935, Soldier Art award, 1945; Audubon Artists award, 1950; Audubon Artists medal for creative aquarelle, 1965; Silver medal Audubon Artists, 1974; Distinguished Faculty award, 1965; State Me. (Gov.'s) art award, 1967; Franklin Mint Bicentiennial Medal Design award, 1972; U. Maine Alumni Black Bear award, 1974. Mem. AAUP, Audubon Artists, Am. Watercolor Soc., Phi Kappa Phi. Home: 109 Forest Ave Orono ME 04473

HARTH, PHILLIP, English language educator; b. Sioux City, Iowa, Feb. 1, 1926; s. John Baptiste and Grace (Conlon) H.; m. Sydney Joan Jacobs, Dec. 19, 1953; children: David James, Margaret Rosalind, Rebecca Joan. A.B., Trinity Coll., 1946; postgrad., Univ. Coll., London (Eng.) U., 1954-56; M.A., U. Chgo., 1949, Ph.D., 1958. Instr. English Marquette U., 1949-50; from instr. to assoc. prof. English Northwestern U., 1953-54, 56-65; prof. English U. Wis., 1965—, Merritt Y. Hughes prof. English, 1977—, chmn. dept., 1974-77; mem. Inst. Research in Humanities, 1977—; vis. prof. U. Va., spring 1973. Author: Swift and Anglican Rationalism, 1961, Contexts of Dryden's Thought, 1968; Editor: The Fable of the Bees, 1970, New Approaches to Eighteenth Century Literature, 1974; Adv. editor: Eighteenth Century Studies, 1974-77; editorial bd.: Restoration, 1978—. Served with AUS, 1946-48. Fulbright grantee, 1954-55, 55-56; Guggenheim fellow, 1962-63; sr. fellow Humanities Research Center, Reed Coll., 1966-67; fellow Am. Council Learned Socs., 1977-78; sr. research fellow William Andrews Clark Meml. Library, 1982-83. Mem. Internat. Assn. Univ. Profs. English, Modern Lang. Assn., English Inst. (mem. supervising com. 1972-75), Internat. Soc. 18th Century Studies (exec. com. 1979-81), Am. Soc. 18th Century Studies (pres. 1978-79, exec. bd. 1976-81), Phi Beta Kappa (hon.). Home: 749 Miami Pass Madison WI 53711

HARTH, ROBERT JAMES, orchestra executive; b. Louisville, June 13, 1956; s. Sidney and Teresa O. H. B.A. in English, Northwestern U., 1977. Asso. mgr. Ravinia (Ill.) Festival Assn., 1977-79; gen. mgr. Los Angeles Philharm. Assn., 1979—. Office: 135 N Grand Ave Los Angeles CA 90012

HARTH, SIDNEY, musician, educator; b. Cleve., Oct. 5, 1929; s. Leonard and Anne (Dunnire) H.; m. Teresa Testa, July 7, 1949; children: Laura, Robert. Mus.B., Cleve. Inst. Music, 1947; studied with, Joseph Knitzer, Mishel Piastro, Georges Enesco. Asso. prof. U. Louisville, 1953-58; faculty DePaul U., 1959-62; chmn. dept. music, A.W. Mellon disting. prof. Carnegie-Mellon U., Pitts., 1963-73; mem. faculty Aspen (Colo.) Music Festival, 1963—; Exchange artist Les Jeungesses Musicales de France, 1952; Exchange artist internat. tours, France, Corsica, North Africa, State Dept. tour Germany, 1952; with Mrs. Harth nat. tour, 1952; concertmaster Louisville Orch., 1953-58, Chgo. Symphony, 1959, 62; condr. Evanston (Ill.) Orch., 1960-62; assoc. condr. Los Angeles Philharmonic, 1973—; chief guest condr. Jerusalem Symphony, 1977; music dir. Puerto Rican Symphony, 1977-79; condr. Can. Nat. Chamber Orch., 1979, 80; orch. dir. Mannes Coll. of Music, 1981—; prof. violin (laureate) SUNY-Stony Brook, 1981—, Yale U., 1982—; prof. violin Wieniawski competition Poland, 1957. Ann. internat. tours including, Yugoslavia, Poland, Belgium, Austria, Eng., USSR, Poland, Czechoslovakia, Romania, Switzerland, Holland.; Recs. for, Vanguard, Iramac, Concert Hall Soc.; Contbr. articles to nat. mags. Recipient Ysaye medal; Wieniawske medal. Home: 135 Westland Dr Pittsburgh PA 15217 Office: c/o Sheldon Soffer Mgmt 130 W 56th St New York NY 10019

HARTIG, ALBERT MORRIS, financial executive; b. N.Y.C., Apr. 25, 1921; s. Morris and Jeannette (Stern) H.; m. Joyce Elaine Beeman, Oct. 4, 1947 (dec. 1965); children: Terry Ann Hartig Gorzelany, David Albert, Steven Morris, Charles Michael (dec.); m. Betty May Harper, July 16, 1966 (dec. 1975); m. Linda J. Davidson, May 1, 1982. B.A., Hamilton Coll., 1942. Fin. ptnr. Gruntal & Co., N.Y.C., 1946—. Served to capt. AUS, 1942-46; served to maj. USAR. Mem. Res.

Officer's Assn. Republican. Office: Gruntal & Co 14 Wall St New York NY 10005

HARTIG, ELMER OTTO, aerospace co. exec.; b. Evansville, Ind., Jan. 23, 1923; s. Otto E. and Frieda K. (Sunderman) H.; m. Evelyn Ann Cameron, Aug. 21, 1949; children—Pamela Ann, Jeffery C., Gregory W., Bradley A. B.S.E.E., U. N.H., 1946, M.S. in Physics, 1947; Ph.D., Harvard U., 1950. With Goodyear Aerospace Corp., Akron, Ohio, 1950—, dir. research and engring., Litchfield Park, Ariz., 1976, v.p. research and engring., Akron, 1976-81, v.p. ops., def. and energy, 1981—; Mem. U.S. Army Sci. Bd., 1979—. Fellow IEEE; mem. AIAA. Office: 1210 Massillon Rd Akron OH 44315

HARTIGAN, GRACE, artist; b. Newark, Mar. 28, 1922; d. Matthew A. and Grace (Orvis) H.; m. Robert L. Jachens, May 1941 (div. 1948); 1 son, Jeffrey A.; m. Robert Keene, Dec. 14, 1959 (div. 1960); m. Winston H. Price, Dec. 24, 1960 (dec. 1981). Student pvt. art classes. Artist-in-residence Md. Inst. Grad. Sch. Painting, 1965—. One man shows, Tibor de Nagy Gallery, N.Y.C., 1951-55, 57-59, Vassar Coll. Art Gallery, 1954, Martha Jackson Gallery, N.Y.C., 1962, 64, 67, 70, U. Chgo., 1967, Gertrude Kasle Gallery, Detroit, 1968, 70, 72, 74, Robert Keene Gallery, Southampton, N.Y., 1957-59, Gres Gallery, Washington, 1960, U. Minn., 1963, William Zierler Gallery, N.Y.C., 1975—, Hamilton Gallery, N.Y.C., 1981, Gruenbaum Gallery, N.Y.C., 1984; exhibited in numerous group shows including, Modern Art in U.S., 1955-56, 3d Internat. Contemporary Art Exhbn., 1957, 4th Internat. Art Exhbn., Japan, IV Biennial, Sao Paulo, New Am. Painting Show, Europe, 1958-59, World's Fair, Brussels, 1958, The Figure Since Picasso, Mus. Ghent, Belgium, collections, Mus. Modern Art, N.Y.C., Walker Art Center, Whitney Mus. Am. Art, Art Inst. Chgo., Met. Mus., Raleigh Mus., Providence Mus., Bklyn. Mus., Mpls. Mus., Albright-Knox Gallery, Buffalo, numerous others. Recipient Merit award for art Mademoiselle Mag., 1957, Nat. Inst. Arts and Letters purchase award, 1974. Address: 1701 1/2 Eastern Ave Baltimore MD 21231

HARTIGAN, NEIL F., attorney general Illinois,, lawyer. former lieutenant governor Illinois; b. Chgo., May 4, 1938; S. David and Colletta (Dunne) H.; m. Marge Hartigan, June 9, 1962; children: John, Elizabeth, Laura, Bridget. Grad. social scis., Georgetown U., 1958; J.D., Loyola U., Chgo., 1961; LL.D. (hon.), Martin Luther King Coll., 1975. Bar: Ill. bar 1962. Formerly dep. adminstrv. officer, City of Chgo.; legis. counsel City of Chgo. in Ill. 75th Gen. Assembly; then chief legal counsel Chgo. Park Dist.; lt. gov., Ill., 1973-77; pres., chief exec. officer Real Estate Research Corp., Chgo., 1977-79, dir., 1977; sr. v.p. 1st Nat. Bank Chgo., 1977-83; sr. v.p., area head Western Hemisphere, 1979-83; atty. gen. State of Ill., 1983—; lectr. former mem. faculty John Marshall Law Sch. Active Am. Cancer Soc. drives; chmn. Nat. Conf. Lt. Govs., 1976; former mem. exec. com. Council State Govts.; bd. regents Georgetown U.; mem. vis. com. on public policy U. Chgo.; bd. dirs. Chgo. Conv. and Tourism Bur., TRUST, Inc., Lincoln Park Zool. Soc.; mem. exec. com. March of Dimes; chmn. Super-walk, 1978. Named One of 200 Hundred Young Ams. Most Likely To Provide New Generation of Leadership Time mag.; among Ten Outstanding Young Men of Yr. Chgo. Jr. C. of C., 1967; Man of Year Loyola U. Alumni Assn. and Chgo. Bar Assn., 1982; hon. pres. Spanish-speaking div. Jr. C. of C., Chgo. Mem. Am. Bar Assn., Ill. Bar Assn., Chgo. Bar Assn., Chgo. Assn. Commerce and Industry (v.p. urban affairs), Chgo. Council on Fgn. Relations, Young Presidents Orgn., Nat. Council on Aging, Irish Fellowship Club. Clubs: Economic, Executive, Rotary, K.C., Hundred of Cook County. Office: First Nat Bank Chgo One First Nat Plaza Chicago IL 60670

HARTIN, JOHN SYKES, educator, librarian; b. Columbus, Miss., Oct. 26, 1916; s. Jesse Sykes and Mattie Aura (Williams) H.; m. Rita Mae Miller, Oct. 26, 1943; children—Martha Elizabeth, John Sykes, Paul Francis. B.A., U. Miss., 1939; A.B. in L.S, U. Mich., 1940, A.M., 1942, 1953, Ph.D., 1956. Student asst. gen. library U. Miss., 1935-39; asst. gen. library U. Mich., 1940-42; librarian Sch. Music Library, 1942-45; chief pub. services Swarthmore Coll. Library, 1945-47; dir. libraries U. Miss., 1947-75, prof. library sci., 1975-82; Pres. U. Mich. Assn. Library Sci. Alumni, 1945-46; mem. exec. com. and planning com. Miss. Library Survey, 1949. Contbr. articles to profl. periodicals. Mem. Am., Miss., Southeastern library assns., Beta Phi Mu, Phi Eta Sigma, Phi Kappa Phi. Democrat. Methodist. Home: 205 Garner St Oxford MS 38655

HARTINGER, JAMES V., air force officer; b. Middleport, Ohio, Apr. 17, 1925; s. Lawrence C. and Violet M. H.; m. Mickey Christian, Oct. 7, 1979; children: Jimmer, Kris, Mike. B.S., U.S. Mil. Acad., 1949; postgrad., Basic and Advanced Flying Schs., Randolph AFB, Tex. and Williams AFB, Ariz., 1950, Squadron Officer Sch., 1955; M.B.A., George Washington U., 1963, Indsl. Coll. Armed Forces, Ft. McNair, Washington, 1966. Joined U.S. Army, 1943; commd. officer U.S. Air Force, 19—, advanced through grades to gen.; pilot tng., Randolph AFB, Tex., 1949; with 86th Fighter Bomber Wing, Furstenfeldbruck, Germany, 1950; pilot 474th Fighter Bomber Wing, Kunsan AB, Korea, 1953; gunnery instr. 3526th Pilot Tng. Squad, Williams AFB, Ariz., 1953; air ops. officer, Stewart AFB, N.Y., 1954; dir. requirements Hdqrs. USAF, 1958; stationed Hdqrs. PACAF, Hickam AFB, Hawaii, 1963, Ft. McNair, Washington, 1965, 43d tactical fighter squadron, MacDill AFB, Fla., 1966, Tan Son Nhut AB, 1966, Nellis AFB, Nev., 1968; comdr. 23d tactical fighter wing, McConnell AFB, Kans., 1968; with NORAD, Ent AFB, Colo., 1970; stationed, Maxwell AFB, Ala., 1973; comdr. Hdqrs. 9th Air Force, Shaw AFB, S.C., 1975, 12th Air Force, Bergstrom AFB, Tex., 1978; comdr. in chief N.Am. Aerospace Def. Command, Colorado Springs, Colo., 1980—. Decorated DSM with oak leaf cluster, Legion of Merit with oak leaf cluster, D.F.C., Air medal with one silver, three bronze oak leaf clusters. Mem. Ohio Commodores. Club: Rotary. Office: CINCNORAD Peterson AFB CO 80914 *

HARTJE, ROBERT GEORGE, educator; b. Conway, Ark., Aug. 8, 1922; s. Henry Cornelius and Perlin (Thayer) H.; m. Martha Elizabeth Feldkircher, June 20, 1946; children—John, Tom, James, Philip, Paul, Elizabeth Anne. Student, Ark. State Tchrs. Coll., 1940-42, Amherst Coll., 1943-44; B.A., Vanderbilt U., 1948, M.A., 1950, Ph.D., 1955; postgrad., Summer Nat. Endowment for Humanities Insts., Boston U., 1977, Northwestern U., 1980. Dir. U. Ga. Center, Augusta, 1952-53, Columbus, 1953-56; mem. faculty Wittenberg U., Springfield, Ohio, 1956—, prof. history, 1963—, chmn. dept., 1958-64, 66-70, dir. Am. studies, 1977—; dir. bicentennial project Am. Assn. For State and Local History, Nashville, 1970-72, bicentennial cons., 1974—; cons. self-study Ohio Hist. Soc., 1977-78, mus. cons., 1977-80; Harbison award, post-doctoral fellow Yale, 1964-65; mem. faculty U. Nebr., summer, 1965, Ohio State U., spring 1968, Middle Tenn. State U., summer 1972, Antioch Coll., winter 1974; mus. cons. Mo. Hist. Soc., 1977-80; dir. Lutheran Summer Camp, Gun Lake, Mich., summers 1957-61. Author: Van Dorn: The Life and Times of a Confederate General, 1967, Bicentennial, U.S.A.: Pathways to Celebration, 1973, also articles, speeches, book reviews. Served to 1st lt. AUS, 1942-46, 51-52. Mem. So. Hist. Assn., Ohio Acad. History (pres. 1979-80). Home: 2140 St Paris Pike Springfield OH 45504 *My goal in life has been to be a good teacher, whatever that is. Since Dexter Perkins' presdl. address at the 1956 annual meeting of the American Historical Association, I have pondered what it means to be a good teacher. The challenges of students, equipment, subject material, meaning—these boggle one's mind, yet they are the challenge and the excitement of the classroom. It is the teacher, finally who is the catylyst searching out meaning for and with the student. This seems to be what Jefferson meant in making public education the corner stone of American democracy.*

HARTL, ALBERT VICTOR, utility exec.; b. New Rockford, N.D., Oct. 21, 1911; s. William Robert and Frances (Dusek) H.; m. Ruth Alice Stenquist, June 25, 1935; children—Marlene, Claudeen, Kathleen, Mary Aldeen, Patricia Jean, Albert Vincent. B.S. in Commerce, U. N.D., 1932. Dep. tax commr. State of N.D., 1934-36; chief accountant N.D. Public Service Commn., 1936-41; with Otter Tail Power Co., 1946—, exec. v.p., then pres., 1958-75, chmn. bd., Bismarck, N.D., 1975—; dir. Pioneer Mut. Life Ins. Co., Security State Bank, Fergus Falls, Minn.; bd. dirs. Edison Electric Inst., Farm Electrification Council; instr. Mary Coll., Bismarck. Trustee Fergus Falls Public Library, 1960-69; dir. CD, Fergus Falls and Otter Tail County, 1949-58. Served with inf. AUS, 1941-46. Decorated Silver Star with oak leaf cluster, Bronze Star with 2 oak leaf clusters. Mem. Am. Mgmt. Assn. Republican. Roman Catholic. Clubs: Kiwanis, K.C., Elks. Home: 1111 N 1st St Bismarck ND 58501 Office: 215 S Cascade St Fergus Falls MN 56537

HARTL, RICHARD JAMES, chem. co. exec.; b. Milw., May 2, 1937; s. Lawrence J. and Greta Hartl; m. Joan Roy, June 10, 1961; children—Kathleen, Elizabeth. B.S., U. Wis., 1960; student, Am. Internat. Coll., 1961-63. With Monsanto Co., Springfield, Mass, 1960-68; with Wyomissing Corp., West Reading, Pa., 1968-71, Gen. Electric Co., Pittsfield, Mass., 1971-75, Avery Internat., Painesville, Ohio, and; San Marino, Calif., 1975—, now group v.p. tech. and ventures. Bd. dirs. San Marino Jr. Achievement, Boy Scouts Am., Cancer Family Services. Office: Avery International 150 N Orange Grove Blvd Pasadena CA 91103

HARTLAGE, LAWRENCE CLIFTON, neuropsychologist, educator; b. Portsmouth, Ohio, May 11, 1934; s. Clifton Paul and Mary Louise (Pierron) H.; m. Patricia Louise Hughes, Jan. 21, 1967; 1 dau., Mary Beth. B.S., Ohio State U., 1959; M.A., U. Louisville, 1962, Ph.D., 1968; postgrad., Ind. U. Med. Center, 1972. Dir. psychology Central State Hosp., Louisville, 1966-68; clin. dir. Asso. Psychol. Services, Louisville, 1968-70; head clin. psychology sect. pediatric neurology Ind. U. Med. Center, 1970-72; head neuropsychology sect., prof. neurology and pediatrics Med. Coll. Ga., Augusta, 1972—; cons. HEW, VA; vis. faculty Ind. and Ga. univs. Author: Mental Development Evaluation of the Pediatric Patient, 1973, Anthology of Theory, Practice and Research in Learning Disabilities, 1974; co-editor: Clin. Neuropsychology. Served with AUS, 1956-58. Rehab. Service Adminstrn. research grantee, 1970-72. Fellow Internat. Acad. Forensic Psychology, Am. Psychol. Assn., Nat. Acad. Neuropsychology (pres. 1978, 82-83); mem. Nat. Rehab. Tng. Inst. (pres. 1973-74), Nt. Rehab. Assn. (dir. 1972-73), Am. Soc. Human Genetics, Council for Exceptional Children, Sigma Xi. Home: Route 3 Box 395 Evans GA 30809 Office: Med Coll Ga Augusta GA 30902 *The concept of every right having a corresponding responsibility is one with application to all spheres of scientific endeavor. My right to publish scientific findings carries responsibility to be totally scientific about how the findings are achieved, interpreted, and presented; and my right of editorship carries responsibility for impartial and, even more important, humanitarian consideration of the work of my fellow scientists.*

HARTLE, RICHARD EASTHAM, physicist; b. Royal Oak, Mich., May 17, 1936; s. George Thomas and Mildred (Eastham) H.; m. Nancy Barbera Bales, Feb. 1, 1959; children: Thomas Eugene, Christopher Bales. B.S.E., U. Mich., 1959; Ph.D., Pa. State U., 1964. Research assoc. NRC, NASA Ames Research Center, Moffett Field, Calif., 1964-67; space scientist NASA Goddard Space Flight Center, Greenbelt, Md., 1967-76, head planetary aeronomy br., 1976—, acting head stratosphere physics and chemistry br., 1982—; mem. NASA Mgmt. Ops. Working Group for Planetary Atmospheres, 1981—; mem. space sci. bd., com. on solar and space physics Nat. Acad. Scis., 1977-80. Contbr. articles on atmospheres and ionospheres of Mercury, Venus, Mars and Titan, planetary exospheres and escape, solar wind theory, deuterium on Venus to profl. jours. Recipient Exceptional Performance award NASA, 1978. Mem. Am. Geophys. Union, Am. Phys. Soc. Home: 6325 Frostwork Row Columbia MD 21044 Office: Code 961 Planetary Aeronomy Br NASA Goddard Space Flight Center Greenbelt MD 20771

HARTLE, ROBERT WYMAN, foreign language educator; b. Kongmoon, China, Sept. 1, 1921; s. Jacob Everett and Margaret (Wyman) H.; m. Ann Dorothy Mordhorst, Jan. 5, 1980; 1 son, Robert Wyman; children by previous marriage: Shirley Ann (Mrs. Jan McDaniel), John Wyman. B.A., U. Tex., 1947, M.A., 1947; A.M., Princeton U., 1949, Ph.D., 1951. Instr. French Princeton U., 1950-53, asst. prof., 1953-60; asst. prof. Romance langs. Queens Coll., N.Y.C., 1960-61, prof., chmn. dept. Romance and Slavic langs., 1963-65, assoc. dean faculty, 1964-65, dean faculty, 1965-70, prof., 1972—; chmn. ad hoc legal affairs com., mem. univ. acad. senate, 1979-81; dir. Ph.D. program in France, CUNY, 1970-72; mem. senate CUNY. Author: Index du vocabulaire du théâtre classique, 8 vols, 1956-64; Translator: Tartuffe (Molière), 1963; Author articles on the iconography of Alexander the Great, 1955—. Bd. dirs. Am. Center for Students and Artists, 1970-78. Served with AUS, 1944-46; PTO. Decorated officier Ordre des Palmes Académiques; knight Order of Merit, Italy; officer's cross Order Merit, West Germany). Mem. MLA, AAUP (pres. chpt. 1975-80). Home: 405 Emory Dr Atlanta GA 30307 Office: Queens Coll Flushing NY 11367

HARTLEY, EARL EDWARD, state treasurer, lawyer; b. Curry County, N.Mex., May 29, 1913; s. Plumus B. and Martha (Potts) H.; m. Vora V. Lowe, July 31, 1938 (div. 1965); children: Teddy L., R. Thomas; m. Mary Elizabeth Lawrence, Jan. 27, 1965. B.A., U. N.Mex., 1941; LL.B., U. Colo., 1943. Bar: N.Mex. 1947. Tchr., Eunice, N.Mex., 1937-39; sec. to U.S. Senator, Washington, 1943-45; atty. gen. State of N.Mex., Santa Fe, 1961-65, treas., 1983—. Editor: Law Rev., 1942-43. City atty. Clovis (N.Mex.), 1948-52; mem. sch. bd. Clovis, 1955-60. Served with U.S. Army, 1945-46. Mem. Order of Coif. Democrat. Episcopalian. Lodges: Masons; Elks. Home: 165 Washington St #4 Santa Fe NM 87501 Office: State Treasurer La Villa Rivera Bldg Santa Fe NM 87504

HARTLEY, FRED LLOYD, oil company executive; b. Vancouver, B.C., Can., Jan. 16, 1917; came to U.S., 1939, naturalized, 1950; s. John William and Hannah (Mitchell) H.; m. Margaret Alice Murphy, Nov. 2; children: Margaret Ann, Fred Lloyd. B.Sc. in Applied Sci., U. B.C., 1939. Engring. supr. Union Oil Co. Calif., 1939-53; mgr. comml. devel. Union Oil Co. of Calif., 1953-55, gen. mgr. research dept., 1955-56, v.p. in charge research, 1956-60, sr. v.p., dir., 1960-63, exec. v.p., 1963-64, pres., chief exec. officer, 1964-73, chmn., pres., 1974—, also dir.; dir. Rockwell Internat. Corp., Daytona Internat. Speedway Corp., Union Bank. Bd. dirs. Los Angeles Philharm. Assn., U.S.-Korea Econ. Council; trustee Calif. Inst. Tech., Tax Found., Council Fgn. Relations, Inc., Com. Econ. Devel.; bd. dirs. Calif. C. of C. Mem. Nat. Petroleum Council, Am. Petroleum Inst. (dir., former chmn.). Office: Box 7600 Los Angeles CA 90051

HARTLEY, JOHN T., JR., corporate exec.; b. 1930; (married). B.S. in Elec. Engring, Auburn U., 1955. With Harris Corp., 1956—, v.p., gen. mgr., 1966-67, v.p., gen. mgr. electric systems div., 1967-71, v.p. systems group, 1971-73; corp. copr. v.p., group gen. exec., 1973-76, exec. v.p., 1976-78, pres., chief operating officer, 1978—, also dir. Office: Harris Corp Corporate Hdqrs Melbourne FL 32919

HARTLEY, JOSEPH WAYMAN, JR., food manufacturing executive; b. Indpls., Apr. 6, 1933; children: Joseph W. III, Jeffrey N.; m. 2d Carol J. McCready, June 7, 1975. B.S. in Mech. Engring, Purdue U., 1958. Design engr. Maui Pineapple Co. Ltd., Kahului, Hawaii, 1958-62, budget dir., 1962-66, cannery mgr., 1966-67, v.p., ops. mgr., 1967-77, pres., 1977—, also dir. Pres. Maui United Way, 1982-83, bd. dirs., 1982-83. Served with U.S. Army, 1953-55. Office: Maui Pineapple Co Ltd 120 Kane St PO Box 187 Kahului HI 96732

HARTLEY, MARIETTE (MARIETTE HARTLEY BOYRIVEN), actress; b. N.Y.C., June 21; d. Paul Hembree and Mary Ickes (Watson) H.; m. Patrick Francois Boyriven, Aug. 13, 1976; children: Sean Paul, Justine Emilia. Student, Carnegie Tech. Inst., 1956-57; studied with, Eva Le Gallienne. Co-host (Today Show), June 9-27, 1980. Appeared with, Shakespeare Festival, Stratford, Conn., 1957-60; appeared in: nat. tours of Winter's Tale; films Ride the High Country, 1961, Marooned, 1968, Improper Channels, 1981, O'Hara's Wife, 1982; TV appearances include Incredible Hulk (Emmy award for best actress 1979), Mash, Star Trek; TV series include: The Hero, Goodnight, Beantown; TV films include: Last Hurrah, African Queen, No Place to Hide, Calloway's Climb, The Halloween that Almost Wasn't, The Second Time Around, The Secret War of Jackie's Girls. Recipient Clio award, 1979, 80, 81, Golden Apple award Hollywood Women's Press Club, 1979. Mem. Acad. Motion Picture Arts and Scis. *

HARTLEY, RICHARD GLENDALE, assn. exec.; b. Bennet, Nebr., Feb. 16, 1926; s. Charles Lynn and Hazel Myra (Williams) H.; m. Wynona Elaine Smutz, Oct. 27, 1962; 1 dau., Patricia Ann (Mrs. Thomas H. Young). Student, U. Nebr., 1945-46, Hastings (Nebr.) Coll., 1947-48. Mgr. Mt. Pleasant (Iowa) C. of C., 1959-62; mgr. Kearney (Nebr.) C. of C., 1962-67; mgr. membership Greater Kansas City (Mo.) C. of C., 1967-68; exec. v.p. Kansas City (Kans.) Area C. of C., 1968-72; mng. dir. Missouri Valley Electric Assn., 1972—. Revised, edited jour.: Evaluating Chamber Mgmt. Opportunities, 1966. Served with AUS, 1944-45, 53-56. Mem. Am. Soc. Assn. Execs. Home: 8704 Lafayette Ct Kansas City KS 66109 Office: 3435 Broadway Kansas City MO 64111

HARTLEY, ROBERT FRANK, business educator; b. Beaver Falls, Pa., Dec. 15, 1927; s. Frank Howell and Marie Eleanor (Thies) H.; m. Dorothy Mayou, June 30, 1962; children: Constance Ann, Matthew. B.B.A., Drake U., 1949; M.B.A., U. Minn., 1962, Ph.D., 1967. Store mgmt. staff S.S. Kresge Co., 1949-54; J.C. Penney Co., 1954-59; mdse. staff Dayton's, Mpls., 1959-61; central buyer subs. Dayton Target, 1961-63; asst. prof. George Washington U., Washington, 1965-69, asso. prof., 1969-72; prof. mktg. Cleve. State U., 1972—. Author: Marketing: Management and Social Change, 1972, Retailing—Challenge and Opportunity, 1975, 2d edit., 1980, 3d edit., 1984, Marketing Fundamentals for Responsive Management, 1976, Marketing Mistakes, 1976, 2d edit., 1981, Japanese translation, Sales Management, 1979, Spanish translation, Management Mistakes, 1983, Marketing Fundamentals, 1983; co-author: Essentials of Marketing Research, 1983; Author: Marketing Successes, 1985. Mem. Am. Mktg. Assn., So. Mktg. Assn., So. Case Research Assn. Home: 17405 S Woodland Rd Shaker Heights OH 44120 Office: Dept Mktg Cleveland State U Cleveland OH 44115 *The ability to write should be zealously cultivated. It can be an intriguing and rewarding lifetime endeavor. Good writing in my opinion is concise, clear, interesting, unpretentious—all this, hopefully, with a modicum of inspiration. This I have sought and will continue to seek.*

HARTLEY, STUART LESLIE, diversified company executive, accountant; b. Luton, Eng., Apr. 3, 1938; emigrated to Can., 1960; s. Leslie and Isobel (Buchan) H.; m. Patricia Holmers, Dec.27, 1960; children: Stephen, Caroline, Susan. Gen. cert., edn. Royal Liberty Sch., London, 1955. Controller IBM Can. Ltd., Toronto, Ont., 1971-73; dir. fin. for Latin Am. IBM Am.'s Far East Corp., Rio de Janeiro, Brazil, 1973-74; v.p. fin. and planning Gen. Bus. Group, IBM Can. Ltd., Toronto, Ont., 1975-79; sr. v.p. fin. Moslon Cos. Ltd., Toronto, Ont., Can., 1979—; mem. Fin. Execs. Council, Conf. Bd. Can., Ottawa, Ont., 1981—. Fellow Inst. Chartered Accts. (Eng. and Wales); mem. Inst. Chartered Accts. (Ont.), Fin. Execs. Inst. (bd. dirs. Toronto chpt. 1983—). Office: Molson Cos Ltd 2 International Blvd Rexdale ON Canada M9W 1A2

HARTLIEB, GORDON WESLEY, banker; b. Ravenna, Ohio, July 4, 1920; s. George Wesley and Mildred (Arteno) H.; children—Raymond Meyer, George Wesley, Lynda Mae. B.A., Kent (Ohio) State U., 1949; J.D., Ohio State U., 1953. Bar: Ohio bar 1953, Alaska bar 1953. U.S. commr., Anchorage, 1954-55; partner firm Hartlieb, Groh & Rader, Anchorage, 1955-63; founder First Fed. Savs. & Loan Assn., Anchorage, 1956, pres., chmn. bd., atty., 1968-74, chmn. bd., 1974—, also dir.; founder Security Title & Trust Co. Alaska, 1965; dir., mem. exec. com. Nat. Bank Alaska, 1961—; instr. bus. law U. Alaska, 1954-70. Councilman, Anchorage, 1968-75, mayor pro-tem, 1970; Chmn. adv. com. to bd. regents U. Alaska. Served with USNR, 1943-46. Mem. Am., Ohio, Alaska, Anchorage bar assns., Am. Trial Lawyers Assn., A.I.M. (pres. council), U.S. Savs. and Loan League, Alaskan League Insured Savs. and Loan Assns. (charter), Ohio State U. Alumni Assn., Model A Restorers Club Am. Republican. Methodist. Club: Elks. Home: 1331 W 7th Ave Anchorage AK 99501 Office: 813 W Northern Lights Blvd Anchorage AK 99503 also PO Box 4-2200 Anchorage AK 99509

HARTMAN, ARTHUR A., ambassador to Soviet Union; b. N.Y.C., Mar. 12, 1926. A.B., Harvard U., 1944; postgrad., Law Sch., 1947-48. Econ. officer ECA, Paris, 1948-52; mem. U.S. del. European Army Conf., Paris, 1952-54; polit.-mil. officer Paris/USRO, 1954-55, Saigon, 1956-58; internat. affairs officer Econ. Orgn. Affairs Sect., Bur. European Affairs, Dept. State, 1958-61, staff asst. to undersec. for econ. affairs, 1961-62, spl. asst., 1962-63; chief econ. sect. Am. Embassy, London, 1963-67; spl. asst. and staff dir. to undersec. Dept. State, 1967-69, dep. dir. for coordination, 1969-72; dep. chief of mission and minister counselor to USEC, Brussels, 1972-74; asst. sec. for European affairs Dept. State, Washington, 1974-77; U.S. ambassador to France, Paris, 1977-81, U.S. ambassador to Soviet Union, Moscow, 1981—. Office: US Embassy Ulitsa Chaykovskogo 19/21/23 Moscow USSR *

HARTMAN, ASHLEY POWELL, training systems company executive; b. St. Paul, Feb. 26, 1922; s. Thomas and Mollie (Powell) H.; m. Tracy Robertson, Nov. 19, 1971; children: Timothy, Sabrina, Scott, William. B.A., U. Minn., 1948. Vice pres. Ridder Johns Co. (advt. sales), Los Angeles; v.p. Miller Freeman Pub. Co.; pub. Sea Mag., Newport Beach, Calif.; now Western mgr. Yachting mag., Newport Beach; now pres. Creative Tng. Systems, El Toro, Calif.; instr. Maximize Course; lectr. on sales tng. mgmt., stress mgmt., communications, pub. speaking. Author: How to Maximize Your Life; producer: cassette album Stress Management System; Contbr. numerous travel and marine-oriented articles to profl. jours., popular mags. Served with USAAF, 1942-46. Mem. So. Calif. Marine Assn.

(dir., pres. 1984-85), Am. Assn. Newspaper Reps. (pres. 1954). Republican. Mem. Reformed Ch. Am. Office: 23331 El Toro Rd Suite 107 El Toro CA 92630 *What we are, compared to what we could be, is like the pinpoint of a star compared to the roaring inferno of its surface. Our Creator gave us immeasurably more in mental and physical abilities than we will ever use, but I feel the greatest happiness of reasoning men is to recognize this vast, untapped ability, and to explore its depths.*

HARTMAN, CHARLES HENRY, association executive; b. Red Lion, Pa., Feb. 1, 1933; s. Earl Eugene and Jeannette (Kline) H.; m. Patricia A. Cooper, Aug. 3, 1956 (div. May 1974); children: Elizabeth Jean, Amy Joan; m. 2d Catherine M. Wheeler, June 7, 1975; children: Eric Michael, Jennifer Leigh, David Wheeler, Scott Andrew. B.S., Millersville U., 1954; M.A., Mich. State U., 1958, D. Edn., 1962. Cert assn. exec. Tchr. Hollidaysburg Pub. Schs., Pa., 1956-57; assoc. prof. Ill. State U., Normal, 1959-62; vis. lectr. edn. U. Wis., Madison, 1962-63, U. Wis.-Milw., 1963-64; dir. edn. Automobile Safety Fedn./Hwy. Users Fedn., Washington, 1964-70; dep. adminstr. Nat. Hwy. Traffic Safety Adminstrn., Washington, 1970-73; pres. Motorcycle Safety Found., Chadds Ford, Pa., 1973—; dir. Nat. Safety Council, Chgo., 1976-79, vice chmn. traffic conf., 1976-78; presdl. appointee Nat. Hwy. Safety Adv. Commn., Washington, 1977-80; gov.'s appointee Pa. Task Force on Alcohol and Hwy Safety, 1981-82; vice chmn. Alliance for Traffic Safety, 1981-83, chmn., 1983—; mem. policy commn. Hwy. Users Fedn.; cons. Nat. Assn. Women Hwy. Safety Leaders, Md. State Edn. Dept., 1969-70; trustee Nat. Motorcycle Safety Fund; speaker pub. meetings, U.S. and abroad. Served with AUS, 1954-56; ETO. Recipient Wis. Traffice Edn. Assn. Traffic Safety Educator of Yr. award, 1972, U.S. Dept. Transp. Sec.'s award, 1973. Fellow Am. Acad. Safety Edn. (pres. 1975-76); mem. Am. Soc. Assn. Execs., Soc. Automotive Engrs., Pres. Assn./Am. Mgmt. Assn., Am. Driver and Traffic Safety Edn. Assn., Phi Delta Kappa. Republican. Home: 49 Blue Stone Dr Chadds Ford PA 19317 Office: Motorcycle Safety Foundation PO Box 120 Chadds Ford PA 19317

HARTMAN, DAVID DOWNS, TV host; b. Pawtucket, R.I., May 19, 1935; s. Cyril Baldwin and Fannie Rodman (Downs) H.; m. Maureen Downey, June 1974; children: Sean, Brian, Bridget, Conor. B.A. in Econs, Duke U., 1956; grad., Am. Acad. Dramatic Arts, 1961. Actor: appearing in My Fair Lady, 1962-63; original cast of: Hello Dolly, Broadway, 1963-65; films include Miracle on 34th St; appeared on: NBC-TV in regular running roles in The Virginian, 1968-69; appearing on: The Bold Ones, 1969-73, Lucas Tanner, 1974-75; producer: Birth and Babies, ABC-TV; host: Good Morning Am., ABC-TV network news and info. program, 1975—; exec. producer and host: ABC-TV spl. on photojournalists. Vice pres. Muscular Dystrophy Assns. Am., 1970—; nat. bd. dirs. UNICEF, 1980; bd. dirs. Found. Jr. Blind. Served with USAF, 1956-59. Address: care Trascott Alyson & Craig Inc 222 Cedar Ln Teaneck NJ 07666

HARTMAN, EDWARD JAMES, public utility executive; b. Guthrie Center, Iowa, Nov. 16, 1924; s. Walter Ray and Verdie May (Tickner) H.; m. Janet Hulmes Keppen, Sept. 15, 1951 (div.); children: Roger K., Timothy E.; m. Marilyn Jean Swanson, Nov. 20, 1982. B.A., U. Iowa, 1948, J.D., 1950. Bar: Iowa 1950, Ill. 1965, U.S. Supreme Ct. 1955, U.S. Dist. Ct. (no. dist.) Iowa 1952, U.S. Dist. Ct. (so. dist.) Iowa 1956, U.S. Ct. Mil. Appeals 1955. Spl. agt. U.S. Dept. Justice, FBI, Washington, 1950-51; assoc. Simmons, Perrine, Albright & Neff, Cedar Rapids, Iowa, 1951-55; v.p., gen. counsel Iowa-Ill. Gas and Electric Co., Davenport, Iowa, 1955—; instr. M.B.A. program St. Ambrose Coll., Davenport, 1982—. Served to lt. USNR, 1943-46. Mem. ABA, Iowa Bar Assn., Ill. Bar Assn., Order of the Coif. Clubs: Crow Valley Country, Davenport, Des Moines; Army and Navy (Washington); Moose. Home: 4301 Christie Ct Davenport IA 52807 Office: Iowa-Ill Gas and Electric Co 206 E 2d St PO Box 4350 Davenport IA 52808

HARTMAN, GEOFFREY H., educator; b. Germany, Aug. 11, 1929; came to U.S., 1946, naturalized, 1946; s. Albert and Agnes (Heumann) H.; m. Renee Gross, Oct. 21, 1956; children: David, Elizabeth. B.A., Queens Coll., 1949; Ph.D., Yale, 1953, U. Dijon, France, 1951-52. Mem. faculty Yale, 1955-62, prof. English and comparative lit., 1967—, Karl Young Prof., 1974—; prof. U. Iowa, 1962-65, Cornell U., Ithaca, N.Y., 1965-67; Vis. lectr. and/or prof. U. Chgo., U. Wash., Hebrew U., Jerusalem, U. Zürich, Switzerland, Princeton; Clark lectr. Trinity Coll., Cambridge, 1983; Tamblyn lectr. U. Western Ont., 1983; dir., sr. fellow Sch. Theory and Criticism, Northwestern U. Author: The Unmediated Vision, 1954, Andre Malraux, 1960, Wordsworth's Poetry, 1964, Beyond Formalism, 1970, The Fate of Reading, 1975, Akiba's Children; poetry, 1978, Criticism in the Wilderness, 1980, Saving the Text, 1981. Trustee English Inst. Served with AUS, 1953-55. Recipient Christian Gauss prize, 1965; Distinguished Alumnus award Queens Coll., U. City N.Y., 1971; study fellow Am. Council Learned Socs., 1963, 79; Gauss seminarist Princeton, 1968; Guggenheim fellow, 1969; fellow Humanities Center, Wesleyan U., 1972; Nat. Endowment for Humanities fellow, 1975. Mem. Modern Lang. Assn. (exec. council 1977-80), Am. Acad. Arts and Scis. Home: 260 Everit St New Haven CT 06511

HARTMAN, GEORGE EDWARD, mktg. scientist, lawyer, educator; b. Newton, Kans., Oct. 20, 1926; s. Albert J. and Ellen (Pawlick) H. B.S., Kans. U., 1950; M.B.A., Ind. U., 1951; Ph.D., U. Ill., 1958; J.D., U. Cin., 1964. Bar: Ohio bar 1964. Instr. in mktg. Tex. A. and M. U., 1951-52; asst. prof. U. N.D., Grand Forks, 1952-55; instr. U. Ill., Urbana, 1955-58; prof. U. Cin., 1958—; practice law, Cin., 1964—; cons. mktg. Contbg. author: Handbook of Modern Marketing, 1970, Business and Its Environment 1984, 1974, Fundamentals of Management Finance, 1981; bd. editors legal devel. sect.: Jour. Mktg, 1965—; columnist: Mktg. News, 1965—. Mem. regional export council Dept. Commerce, 1969-74; mem. bd. mgrs. U. Cin. YMCA; bd. dirs. U. Cin., 1978-80, S.W. Ohio Consumer Assn. Served with Adj.-Gen.'s Office AUS, 1945-46. Mem. World Trade Club (chmn. edn. com. 1974-75), Cin. C. of C., Am. Mktg. Assn., Am., Ohio bar assns., Acad. Internat. Bus., Am. Council Consumer Interests, AAUP, Beta Gamma Sigma, Delta Sigma Pi, Phi Delta Phi, Lambda Chi Alpha. Democrat. Presbyterian. Club: Masons. Home: 310 Bryant St Cincinnati OH 45220

HARTMAN, GEORGE EITEL, architect; b. Ft. Hancock, N.J., May 7, 1936; s. George Eitel and Evelyn (Ritchie) H.; m. Ann Burdick, May 22, 1965; children—Sarah, Joshua. B.A., Princeton, 1957, M.F.A., 1960. Pvt. practice architecture, 1964-65; ptnr. Hartman-Cox Architects, Washington, 1965—; Design critic Cath. U. Am., 1964-69, U. Md., 1972, 79, Kea Disting. prof. architecture, 1973-74, N.C. State U., 1977. Works include EURAM office bldg, Washington, Dodge Center Coml. Complex, Washington; Brewer residence, Chevy Chase, Md., Conant residence, Potomac, Md., Nat. Humanities Center, Raleigh, N.C., Nat. Permanent Bldg, Washington, 1001 Pennsylvania Ave; Folger Shakespeare Library, Washington, Immanuel Presbyn. Ch., McLean, Va. Served to 2d Lt., F.A. AUS, 1957. Recipient nat. honor awards AIA, 1970, 71, 81, 83, Biennial award Potomac Valley chpt., 1968, 70, 72, 74, 76; Washington Met. chpt. design award, 1979, 81, 83; preservation awards, 1977, 78, 80, 81; AIA House and Home award, 1976, 81; AIA-A.A.J.C. award, 1970, 71, 75; award for architecture Met. Washington Bd. of Trade, 1967, 69, 71; Louis Sullivan award for architecture, 1972; fellow Am. Acad. in Rome, 1977-78. Fellow A.I.A. (dir. at large Washington met. chpt. 1969-71, treas. 1972, sec. 1973, pres. 1975, chmn. nat. capitol com. 1976, chmn. nat. com. on design 1977). Club: Cosmos (Washington). Home: 47 West Lenox St Chevy Chase MD 20815 Office: 1071 Thomas Jefferson St NW Washington DC 20007

HARTMAN, GLEN WALTER, radiologist; b. Pepin, Wis., Nov. 14, 1936; s. Walter Edward and Marie Emma (Castleberg) H.; m. Dorothy Fredrickson, June 23, 1957; children: Thomas, Laura, Robert. B.S., U. Wis., Madison, 1958, M.D., 1961. Intern USPHS Hosp., Balt., 1961-62; physician Indian Health Service, USPHS, Browning, Mont., 1962-64; resident in radiology Mayo Grad. Sch. Medicine, Rochester, Minn., 1964-67; hon. clin. fellow X-ray diagnosis Univ. Coll. Hosp., London, 1967-68; cons. diagnostic radiology Mayo Clinic, 1967—; prof. radiology Mayo Med. Sch., 1981—; asso. dir. Sch. Health Related Scis., Mayo Found., 1981—. Bd. dirs. Ability Bldg. Center, 1971—. Recipient Disting. Alumnus award U. Wis.-River Falls, 1983. Mem. Uroradiology Soc. (pres. 1980), Am. Roentgen Ray Soc. (exec. com. 1979—, chmn. adv. com. edn. and research 1979—), Am. Coll. Radiology, Radiol. Soc. N. Am., AMA, Minn. Med. Assn., Minn. Radiol. Soc. (pres. 1983), Sigma Xi. Office: 200 1st St SW Rochester MN 55905

HARTMAN, HOWARD CARL, newspaperman; b. Morris Twp., N.J., Jan. 9, 1917; s. Dennis and Ruth (Shavelson) H.; m. Josephine M. Troxell, Aug. 25, 1942; 1 dau., Jessica A. Student, George Washington U., 1932-33; A.B., Princeton, 1936; M.A. in Journalism, Columbia, 1942. Engaged in gold mining, Calif., 1936-37, translator, publicity, copy boy, reporter various newspapers, 1937-40; fgn. editor Puerto Rico World-Jour., San Juan, P.R., 1940-41; reporter, rewrite man N.Y.C. News Assn., 1941; Washington corr. Jewish Telegraphic Agy., also Overseas News Agy., 1942-44; city editor Puerto Rico World-Jour., 1944; with Asso. Press, 1944—, assigned, N.Y.C., Madrid, Paris, Washington, Vienna, 1944-57, corr., Budapest, Hungary, 1957-59, staff mem., Frankfurt, 1959, corr., Berlin, 1959-63, Bonn and European Econ. Affairs, 1963-67, Common Market and NATO, Brussels, 1967-78; European editor, N.Y.C., 1978; reporter internat. econ. affairs AP World Services, Washington, 1978—. Alternate Pulitzer travelling fellow, 1942. Mem. Berlin Fgn. Press Assn. (pres. 1960-61), Anglo-Am. Press Assn. Paris (dir. 1951, 56), Overseas Writers Club, Nat. Press Club, Phi Beta Kappa. Home: 1066 Thomas Jefferson St NW Washington DC 20007 Office: Associated Press 2021 K St NW Washington DC 20036

HARTMAN, JAMES THEODORE, physician, educator; b. De Ridder, La., June 13, 1925; s. George Bernhardt and Mary Gertrude (Moore) H.; m. Jean Ann Rinehart, Dec. 29, 1954; children: James Theodore, Thomas Moore, Martha Susan. B.S., Iowa State U., 1949; B.S.M., Northwestern U., 1949, M.D., 1952. Intern Charity Hosp. La., New Orleans, 1952-53; resident U. Mich. Hosp., Ann Arbor, 1953-57; registrar Nuffield Orthopedic Centre, Oxford (Eng.) U., 1957-58; instr. orthopedic surgery U. Mich., Ann Arbor, 1958-61; mem. staff Cleve. Clinic, 1961-68; chmn. dept. orthopedic surgery Cook County Hosp., Chgo., 1968-71; asso. prof. Northwestern U., Chgo., 1968-71; prof. Tex. Tech. U. Sch. Medicine, Lubbock, 1971—, chmn. dept. orthopedic surgery, 1971-81, dean, 1981—; mem. Am. Bd. Orthopaedic Surgery, 1978—. Author: Fracture Management: A Practical Approach, 1977; contbr. articles to profl. jours. Served in AUS, 1943-46. Fellow A.C.S.; mem. Assn. Orthopaedic Chairmen (pres. 1979-80), Tex. Med. Assn., Am. Orthopaedic Assn., Assn. Bone and Joint Surgeons, Clin. Orthopaedic Soc., Am. Acad. Orthopedic Surgeons, Sigma Xi, Phi Delta Theta, Nu Sigma Nu. Home: 4910 21st St Lubbock TX 79407 Office: Office of the Dean Texas Tech Univ Lubbock TX 79430

HARTMAN, JOHN WHEELER, publisher; b. Detroit, June 3, 1922; s. Hubert Ezra and Margaret Mary (Martin) H.; m. Esther Kelly Bill, Nov. 8, 1947; children: Kelly Bill, Raymond Bill. Student, Colgate U., 1939; B.A., Duke U., 1944. Pub. U.S. Navy News, 1945-46; area corr. United Press., 1946; partner, founder Bacon, Hartman & Vollbrecht, Inc. (advt. agy.), Jacksonville, Fla., 1946-69; dir. sales Sales Mgmt. Mag., N.Y.C., 1951-57; exec. v.p. Bill Communications, Inc., N.Y.C., 1955-57, pres., 1957-65, chmn. bd., 1966—; chmn. bd. Hartman Communications, Inc., Restaurant Bus., Inc. Bd. dirs. Duke U., People-to-People Sports Com. Inc. Served to lt., j.g. USNR, 1943-45; ETO. Mem. Young Pres's. Orgn. (internat. pres. 1963-64), Chief Execs. Orgn. (dir.), Advt. Research Found., Mag. Pubs. Assn. (dir.), Am. Bus. Press and Nat. Bus. Publs. (vice chmn.), World Bus. Council. Clubs: Wee Burn Country (Darien, Conn.) (dir); Sky, Pinnacle, Univ. (N.Y.C.); Old Lyme (Conn.); Country; Card Sound Golf, Ocean Reef Yacht, Racquet (Ocean Reef, Fla.). Home: 29 E Snapper Point Dr Ocean Reef Club Key Largo FL 33037 Office: 633 3d Ave Bill Communications Inc New York NY 10017

HARTMAN, MARGARET JANE, biologist, educator, university official; b. Columbus, Ohio, Nov. 10, 1943; d. Herbert Joyce and Amabelle Bailey (Haller) H. B.S., Calif. Poly. State U., 1966; M.S., Oreg. State U., 1968, Ph.D., 1970. Mem. faculty Calif. State U., Los Angeles, 1970—, prof. biology, 1980—, chmn. dept., 1977-83, asst. v.p. for acad. affairs, 1981—. Author insect pests of rangeland. Grantee Calif. State U., Boston Land Co., Gill Cattle Co. Mem. Entomol. Soc. Am., AAAS, Sigma Xi, Phi Beta Phi, Beta Beta Beta.

HARTMAN, PAUL ARTHUR, microbiology educator, consultant; b. Blat., Nov. 23, 1926; s. Carl G. and Eva M. (Rettenmeyer) H.; m. Marjorie Ann Stewart, Aug. 19, 1950; children: Philip S., Helen A., Mark A. B.S., U. Ill., 1949; M.S., U. Ala., 1951; Ph.D., Purdue U., 1954. Faculty mem. Iowa State U., Ames, 1954—, prof. microbiology, 1962—, Disting. prof., 1972—, chmn. dept., 1976-81; U.S. Dept. Agr. collaborator Nat. Animal Disease Ctr., Ames, 1973—; cons. Hach Co., Loveland, Colo., 1977—. Author: Miniaturized Microbiological Methods, 1968; patentee antibiotic bloat control. Organizer, chmn bd. dirs. Ames PreSch. Ctr., 1968—; rep. Ames Child Caring Council, 1981-83. Served with USAAF, 1945-46; ETO. Fellow Mid-Am. State Univs. Assn., 1974, 75; NSF grantee, 1960-70, 72-75; NIH grantee, 1960-69; U.S. Dept. Agr. grantee, 1966-70; EPA grantee, 1977-79. Fellow Am. Acad. Microbiology, Sigma Xi; mem. AAAS, Am. Soc. Microbiology, Internat. Assn. Milk, Food and Evniron. Sanitarians, Inst. Food Technologists, Soc. Indsl. Microbiology, Soc. Gen. Microbiology, Soc. Applied Bacteriology, Chi Beta Chi, Alpha Delta Phi. Mem. Christian Ch. Home: 2300 Timberland Rd Ames IA 50010 Office: Dept Microbiology Iowa State U 205 Sci I Ames IA 50011

HARTMAN, PAUL THEODORE, educator; b. Toledo, Dec. 8, 1930; s. Paul and Helen (Hostetter) H.; m. Shirley Joan Herreid, Sept. 12, 1950; children—Janette, Paul Leonard, Barbara. B.A., Claremont Men's Coll., 1956; M.A., U. Calif., Berkeley, 1960, Ph.D., 1966. Grad. research economist U. Calif., Berkeley, 1956-60; asst. prof. Stanford U., 1961-64; acting asst. prof. U. Calif., Berkeley, 1964-66; asst. prof. U. Ill., Urbana-Champaign, 1966-68, asso. prof., 1968-72, prof. econs., labor, indsl. relations, 1972—. Author: Changing Patterns of Industrial Conflict, 1960, Collective Bargaining and Productivity, 1969. Served with U.S. Army, 1948-52. Mem. Am. Econs. Assn. Lutheran. Home: 2032 Burlison Dr Urbana IL 61801 Office: 461 Commerce W 1206 S 6th St Champaign IL 61820

HARTMAN, RICHARD LEON, physicist; b. Pitts., July 5, 1937; s. Leon Jones and Jane Louise (Hayes) H.; m. Cynthia Marie Park, Oct. 31, 1964; children—Keith, Susan. B.S., Carnegie Inst. Tech., 1958, M.S., 1961, Ph.D., 1965; S.M., M.I.T., 1973. Research physicist U.S. Army Missile Command, Redstone Arsenal, Ala., 1965-73, group leader, 1973-74, acting dir. aeroballistics, 1974-75, dir. phys. scis., 1977-78, dir. research, 1978—. Contbr. articles to profl. jours. Served with U.S. Army, 1958-60. NSF fellow, 1960-61; Alfred P. Sloan fellow, 1972-73. Mem. Am. Phys. Soc., Am. Inst. Physics, AAAS, Optical Soc. Am., Soc. Photo-Optical Instrumentation Engrs., Ala. Acad. Sci. Patentee in field. Office: Research Directorate Army Missile Lab US Army Missile Command Redstone Arsenal AL 35898

HARTMAN, RICHARD RUSSELL, financial executive; b. Schuylkill Haven, Pa., May 19, 1926; s. Elvyn and Ethel (Shingle) H.; m. Rebecca Mae MacKenzie, Dec. 13, 1925; children: Laura, Robert, James, Jean. A.B., Dartmouth Coll., 1946, M.B.A., 1948. Vice-pres., treas. Mass. Mut. Mortgage & Realty, Springfield, 1971—; v.p. Mass. Mut. Life Ins. co., Springfield, 1978—; bd. govs. Nat. Assn. Real Estate Investment Trusts, Washington, 1975-81. Mem. sch. com. Wilbraham Regional Com., 1964-68. Republican. Presbyterian. Office: Mass Mut Mortgage & Realty 1295 State St Springfield MA 01111

HARTMAN, ROBERT LEROY, artist, educator; b. Sharon, Pa., Dec. 17, 1926; s. George Otto and Grace Arvada (Radabaugh) H.; m. Charlotte Ann Johnson, Dec. 30, 1951; children: Mark Allen, James Robert. B.F.A., U. Ariz., 1951, M.A., 1952; postgrad., Colo. Springs Fine Arts Center, 1947, 51, Bklyn. Mus. Art Sch., 1953-54. Instr. architecture, allied arts Tex. Tech. Coll., 1955-58; asst. prof. art U. Nev., Reno, 1958-61; mem. faculty dept. art U. Calif., Berkeley, 1961—, prof., 1972—, chmn. dept., 1974-76; mem. Inst. for Creative Arts, U. Calif., 1967-68. One man exhbns. include, Bertha Schafer Gallery, N.Y.C., 1966, 69, 74, Santa Barbara Mus. Art, 1973, Cin. Art Acad., 1975, Hank Baum Gallery, San Francisco, 1973, 75, 78, San Jose Mus. Art, 1983, group exhbns. include, Richmond Mus., 1966, Whitney Mus. Biennial, 1973, Oakland Mus., 1976; represented in permanent collections, Nat. Collections Fine Arts, Colorado Springs Fine Arts Center, Corcoran Gallery, San Francisco Art Inst., Roswell Mus. U. Calif. humanities research fellow, 1980. Office: Dept Art Univ of Calif Berkeley CA 94720

HARTMAN, ROBERT S., paper co. exec.; b. Chgo., Oct. 7, 1914; s. Edward A. and Blanche S. (Straus) H.; m. Betty Regenstein, Oct. 25, 1941; children—Ann (Mrs. Charles H. Arrington III), Ruth (Mrs. Christopher LaTour). Student, Northwestern U., 1933-34. Br. mgr. Draper & Kramer, Inc., 1937-41; pres. Arvey Corp., Chgo., 1941—. Vice pres., bd. dirs. Chgo. Boys Clubs. Served with AUS, 1943-46. Mem. Chgo. Envelope Mfg. Assn. (pres. 1949-51), Envelope Mfg. Assn. Am. (dir. 1950-54). Clubs: Mid-America (Chgo.); Lake Shore Country (Glencoe, Ill.). Home: 220 Woodley Rd Winnetka IL 60093 Office: 3450 N Kimball St Chicago IL 60618

HARTMAN, RONALD LEE, lawyer, transportation company executive; b. Chgo., June 29, 1934; s. Henry Howard and Jean (Marks) H.; m. Phyllis Lerner, June 13, 1959; children: Susan, Wendy, Douglas. B.S. in Fgn. Trade, U. So. Calif., 1958, LL.B., 1961. Bar: Calif. 1962, U.S. Ct. Appeals (5th cir.) 1976, U.S. Ct. Appeals (9th cir.) 1962, U.S. Ct. Appeals (10th cir.) 1977, U.S. Supreme Ct. 1974. Assoc. Hill, Farrer & Burrill, Los Angeles, 1961-65; ptnr. Hindin, McKittrick & Powsner, Los Angeles, 1965-70, Hartman, Haile & Hughes, 1970-79; sr. v.p., gen. counsel, dir. Bekins Co., Glendale, Calif., 1979—; judge pro tem Los Angeles Mcpl. Ct., 1977—; arbitrator Superior Ct., Los Angeles, 1978—; lectr. Calif. Continuing Edn. of Bar, 1977—, ICC Practitioners Assn., 1983. Pres. Lake Encino Homeowners Assn., Calif., 1973-74; bd. dirs. Inglewood Gen. Hosp., Legion Lex., Los Angeles, 1978-79. Served with U.S. Army, 1953-55; Korea. Recipient Service award Am. Arbitration Assn., 1976. Mem. ABA, Am. Soc. Corp. Secs. (dir. 1981), Los Angeles County Bar Assn., Am. Movers Conf. (dir. 1980—, author arbitration plan 1981). Office: The Bekins Co 777 Flower St Glendale CA 91201

HARTMAN, WILLIAM VERNON, coal company executive; b. Pittsburg, Kans., Aug. 15, 1922; s. William Vernon and Rose Marie (Kelce) H.; m. Junko Yamada, May 1965; children: Linda E., William Vernon, Douglas F., Tami Marie. B.S. in Mining Engring, Mo. Sch. Mines, 1948, E.M., 1971. Registered profl. engr., Ohio, Ind., Ill., Mo., Okla., W.Va., Ky. Engr. Sinclair Coal Co., Kansas City, Mo., 1937-41; with Raymond Concrete Pile, Honolulu, 1942-43, Princess Elkorn Coal Co., David, Ky., 1948-49, Paul Weir Co., Chgo., 1949-50, Sinclair Coal Co., St. Louis, 1950-55; gen. supt. Peabody Coal Co., St. Louis, 1955-60, v.p. overseas, 1960-67, v.p. spl. projects, 1967-75, v.p. ops., 1975-77, sr. v.p., 1977-79, exec. v.p., 1979-82; pres., chief exec. officer Peabody Devel. Co., 1983—; chmn. bd. Rail to Water Transfer Corp.; Pres. Mined Land Conservation Conf., 1966-67; vice chmn. Nat. Coal Policy Conf., 1966-69; mem. Mo. Land Reclamation Commn., 1971-75. Served with USAAF, 1943-46. Clubs: Mo. Athletic, St. Louis, Port Royal, Ocean Reef, Noonday, Naples B and T, Wings of St. Albans. Lodge: Masons. Office: Peabody Coal Co 301 N Memorial Dr Saint Louis MO 63102

HARTMAN-GOLDSMITH, JOAN, art historian; b. Malden, Mass., June 3, 1933; d. Hyman and Ruth (Hadler) Lederman; m. Alan Hartman, Jan. 10, 1952 (div.); 1 dau., Hedy Hartman; m. 2d Robert Goldsmith, Aug. 12, 1976. Instr., coordinator, initiator art history program China Inst. in Am., N.Y.C., 1967-77; lectr. Sch. Continuing Edn. NYU, 1967-77; exec. officer, dir. pub. info. Jewish Mus., N.Y.C., 1977-80; dir. Inst. for Asian Studies, INc., N.Y.C., 1981—; lectr. Cooper-Hewitt Mus. of Design (Smithsonian Inst.), 1976, 83; lectr. museums, Los Angeles, St. Louis, Pitts., Indpls., Buffalo, Rochester, N.Y., Toronto, Can., Denver Art Mus., Seattle Art Mus., Asian Art Mus. San Francisco; spl. lectr. tour Archaeol. Inst. Am., 1977; condr. seminars on Chinese jade Met. Mus. Art, N.Y.C., 1977, 81, 83, fellow in perpetuity, mem. vis. com. slide and photograph library; trustee Indpls. Mus. Art; mem. art com. China House Gallery, N.Y.C.; program chmn. ann. conf. MAR-Assn. Asian Studies, Buchnel U., 1974. Am. corr.: Oriental Art mag., London, 1963—; contbr. feature articles to profl. publs.; guest curator, author catalogs; author: slide survey Introduction to Chinese Art, 1973; contbr. book revs. to learned jours. Nat. Endowment grantee, vis. specialist Buffalo Mus. Sci., 1972, Indpls. Mus. Art, 1971; reviewer NEH div. pub. programs, 1978—. Mem. Am. Oriental Soc., Assn. for Asian Studies (founding mem. Mid-Atlantic Region 1972, sec.-treas. 1973, adv. council 1974-75), Oriental Club of N.Y. Treas., Upper Eastside Jewish Community Council, N.Y.C. Office: Inst for Asian Studies PO Box 1603 FDR Station New York NY 10022 *Challenge has always spurred my motivation, along with the desire to know the satisfaction of a job well done. Then again, one hopes to make some contribution, leave some small measure of innovation and/or understanding, when one's term of life is done. Integrity and a conscious effort to help others have guided my personal and professional life. There are times when one's principles dictate the lone stand. And it is not easy to stand alone against the tide. In the final analysis, however, we have the comfort of a few good friends; hopefully, many more who do not think badly of us; and the respect of our peers is the ultimate goal.*

HARTMANIS, JURIS, computer scientist, educator; b. Riga, Latvia, July 5, 1928; came to U.S., 1950, naturalized, 1956; s. Martins and Irma (Liepins) H.; m. Ellymaria Rehwald, May 16, 1959; children—Reneta, Martin, Audrey. Student, U. Marburg, 1947-49; M.A., U.

Kansas City, 1951; Ph.D., Calif. Inst. Tech., 1955. Instr. Cornell U., Ithaca, N.Y., 1955-57, prof., 1965—, Walter R. Read prof. engring., 1980—, chmn. dept. computer sci., 1965-71, 77—; asst. prof. Ohio State U., 1957-58; research mathematician Gen. Electric Research & Devel. Center, Schenectady, 1957-65. Author: (with R.E. Stearns) Algebraic Structure Theory For Sequential Machines, 1966, Feasible Computations and Provable Complexity Properties, 1978; Editor: SIAM Jour. Computing; asso. editor: Jour. Computer and Systems Scis, 1966—, Jour. Math. Systems Theory, 1966—; co-editor: Springer-Verlag Lecture Notes in Computer Sci, 1973—. Mem. Am. Math. Soc., Math. Assn. Am., Assn. Computing Machinery, Sigma Xi. Home: 324 Brookfield Rd Ithaca NY 14850

HARTMANN, EDWARD GEORGE, historian, educator; b. Wilkes-Barre, Pa., May 3, 1912; s. Louis and Catherine (Jones-Davis) H. A.B., Bucknell U., 1937, A.M., 1938; Ph.D., Columbia, 1947, B.S. in L.S, 1948. Instr. history Ann-Reno Inst., N.Y.C., 1942-43; asst. prof. Wilkes Coll., 1946-47; fellow in library, lectr. history City Coll. N.Y., 1947-48; dir. libraries, mem. faculty Suffolk U., Boston, 1948-58, prof. history, 1956—. Author: The Movement to Americanize the Immigrant, 1948, A History of American Immigration, 1967, Americans from Wales, 1967, History of the Welsh Congregational Church of the City of New York, 1801-1951, 1969, American Immigration, 1979, The Welsh Society of Philadelphia, 1729-1979, 1980; also articles.; Editor: Tough 'Ombres, The Story of the 90th Infantry Division, 1944, A Short History of the 357th Infantry Regiment, 1945, Centennial History of the Welsh Baptist Association of Pennsylvania, 1955. Bd. dirs. Nat. Welsh-Am. Found., 1980—. Served with AUS, 1943-46; ETO; maj. USAF Ret. Mem. Am. Hist. Assn., Soc. Am. Historians, Hon. Soc. of Cymmrodorion (London, Eng.) (hon. v.p. 1983—), Welsh Soc. Phila. (gold medallion 1966), St. David's Soc. N.Y. State (Hopkins medal 1970), Nat. Gymanfa Ganu Assn., Wyo. Hist. and Geol. Soc., German Soc. Pa., 90th Div. Assn., St. David's Soc. Wyoming Valley, Soc. King's Chapel (Boston), Immigration History Soc., Boston Athenaeum, Order Lafayette, Phi Beta Kappa. Clubs: Columbia University (N.Y.C.); United Oxford and Cambridge University (London). Home: 69 Hancock St Boston MA 02114 Office: Suffolk U Beacon Hill Boston MA 02114

HARTMANN, FREDERICK HOWARD, political science educator; b. N.Y.C., July 6, 1922; s. Frederick Herman and Grace (MacNamara) H.; m. Regina Lou Kiracofe, Dec. 26, 1943; children—Lynne Merry, Vicky Carol, Peter Howard. A.B., U. Calif. at Berkeley, 1943; M.A., Princeton, 1948, Ph.D., 1949; student, Grad. Inst. Internat. Studies, U. Geneva, Switzerland, 1947. Instr. politics Princeton, 1947; from asst. prof. to prof. polit. sci. U. Fla., 1948-66; dir. Inst. Internat. Relations, 1963-66; Alfred Thayer Mahan prof. maritime strategy and spl. acad. adviser to pres. U.S. Naval War Coll., 1966—; Vis. prof. Wheaton (Mass.) Coll., part-time, 1966-69, Brown U., 1968-69; vis. prof. U. R.I., part-time, 1970-71; vis. Univ. prof. Tex. Tech U., 1974-75; vis. scholar Hoover Instn., Stanford (Calif.) U. and vis. prof. polit. sci. U. Calif., Berkeley, 1979-80; lectr., cons. in field, 1955—. Author: The Relations of Nations, 4th edit, 1973, 5th edit., 1978, 6th edit., 1983, The Swiss Press and Swiss Foreign Affairs, 1960, Germany Between East and West, 1965, The New Age of American Foreign Policy, 1970; Editor: Basic Documents of International Relations, 1951, Readings in International Relations, 1952, World in Crisis, 4th edit, 1973; contbr. to the: System for Educating Military Officers in the U.S, 1976, The Conservation of Enemies, 1981. U. Fla. rep. Fla. Bd. Control Com. Acad. Freedom, 1961-62; mem. Fulbright Nat. Selection Com., 1954-56; U.S. del. 4th Conf. Naval War Colls. Am., 1966, 6th Conf., 1970, 10th Conf., 1980. Served to lt. (j.g.) USNR, 1943-46; capt. Res. Fulbright research prof. U. Bonn, Germany, 1953-54; Rockefeller grantee, 1959; Exxon Corp. grantee, 1973. Mem. AAUP (pres. U. Fla. chpt. 1959-60, mem. nat. council 1963-66), Am. Polit. Sci. Assn., Internat. Studies Assn. (pres. New Eng. div. 1971-72), New Eng. Polit. Sci. Assn. (exec. com. 1982-84), Internat. Inst. Strategic Studies (London), Blue Key, Pi Sigma Alpha, Delta Phi Epsilon. Home: 22 Chartier Circle Newport RI 02840 Office: US Naval War Coll Newport RI 02840

HARTMANN, FREDERICK WILLIAM, editor; b. Wilmington, Del., Feb. 3, 1928; s. William and Louise (Askani) H.; m. Mary Lucille Nelson, Oct. 16, 1954; children: Michele Mary, Randi Lucille, Frederick Andrew, Eric William, Adam Nelson. B.A., U. Del., 1951; postgrad., Am. U., 1952; M.S., Columbia U. Grad. Sch. Journalism, 1953. Reporter A.P., N.Y.C., 1954; dir. news and sports WDEL Radio, Wilmington, 1954-56; reporter Morning News, News-Jour. Co., Wilmington, 1956-60, asst. city editor, 1961-62, city editor, 1962-64, Morning and Evening Jour., 1964-67, met. editor, 1967-72, asst. to pres., 1972-74, dir. corp. mktg., 1974-75, exec. editor, 1975-80, v.p., 1977-80; mng. editor Fla. Times-Union, Jacksonville, 1980-83; exec. editor Times-Union/Jacksonville Jour., Jacksonville, 1983—; lectr. U. Del., 1971, 72. Mem. budget com. United Way of Del., 1973, 74; v.p. Brandywine Little League, 1973; bd. dirs. United Cerebral Palsy Assn. of Del., 1970-72. Served with AUS, 1946-48. Mem. Theta Chi. Home: 1847 Montgomery Pl Jacksonville FL 32205 Office: PO Box 1949-F Jacksonville FL 32231

HARTMANN, GEORGE HERMAN, mfg. co. exec.; b. N.Y.C., Nov. 6, 1927; s. Herman Dietrich and Margaret Bertha (Winkler) H.; m. Anne Katharine Martin, July 9, 1960; children—Michael George, Steven Herman, Katharine Margaret, Elizabeth Anne. A.B., Dartmouth Coll., 1949, M.S. in Mech. Engring, 1950. With Gen. Electric Co., 1950-70; v.p. mfg. Gen. Signal Corp., 1970-71; exec. v.p., then pres. GE Espanola, 1971-74; pres. Davol Co. (subs. Internat. Paper Co.), 1975-78, corp. v.p. human resources, then v.p. materials, 1979-80; pvt. investor, 1980-81; group v.p. Textron Inc., Providence, 1981—; dir. Indsl. Nat. Bank, Providence. Trustee R.I. Council Econ. Edn., 1977; trustee Am. Sch., Bilbao, Spain, 1972-74, chmn., 1973-74. Served to lt. (j.g.) USNR, 1955-58. Mem. NAM (dir. 1977-80), R.I. C. of C. (dir. 1977-78), Greater Providence C. of C. (dir. 1976-78). Republican. Unitarian. Club: N.Y. Yacht. Office: 40 Westminster St Providence RI 02903

HARTMANN, ROBERT CARL, physician, educator; b. Everett, Wash., July 23, 1919; s. Rudolf and Eugene (Kaiser) H.; m. Margaretta O'Sullivan, Mar. 16, 1946 (div. Aug. 1975); children—Kathleen, Robert Carl, David, Richard, Margaret, Ellen; m. Joyce S. Anton, Sept. 4, 1977. A.B., Johns Hopkins U., 1941, M.D., 1944. Rotating intern Pa. Hosp., 1944-45, resident medicine, 1945-46; fellow medicine Johns Hopkins Sch. Medicine, 1948-49, 50-52, resident in medicine, 1949-50; faculty Vanderbilt U. Sch. Medicine, Nashville, 1952-74, prof. medicine, 1963-74, dir. div. hematology, 1952-74; prof. medicine U. South Fla. Coll. Medicine, 1974—; chief sect. hematology/oncology, 1974-79, mem. staff div. hematology, 1979—; Cons. nat. nutrition survey USPHS; anemia and nutrition survey Inst. Nutrition for Central Am. and Panama, Guatemala, 1965-68; mem. hematology study sect., sub-com. platelet-glass-adhesion Internat. Commn. Haemostasis and Thrombosis, 1967-71; adv. com. blood disease and blood resources NIH, 1980—. Contbr. papers to profl. jours. Served with AUS, 1946-48. Mem. So. Soc. Clin. Research, Am. Soc. Clin. Investigation, Am. Soc. Clin. Oncology, Am., Internat. socs. hematology, Am. Fedn. Clin. Research, Am. Assn. Physicians, Johns Hopkins Alumni Assn. (pres. Tenn. chpt. 1967). Home: 3630 Little Rd Lutz FL 33549 Office: 13000 Bruce Downs Blvd Tampa FL 33612

HARTMANN, ROBERT ELLIOTT, mfg. co. exec.; b. Bklyn., Apr. 10, 1926; s. James and Edna Mae (Schroeder) H.; m. Anne Marie Mongiello, Feb. 15, 1948; children—Barbara (Mrs. Peter Kaszor), Donna (Mrs. Ronald G. Garber). B.S., Miami U., Oxford, Ohio, 1946. C.P.A., N.Y. Accountant Price, Waterhouse & Co., N.Y.C., 1948-57; mgr. financial accounting Air Products & Chemicals, Allentown, Pa., 1957-58; v.p. Alpha Portland Cement Co. div. Alpha Portland Industries, Inc., Easton, Pa., 1958—; sec. Alpha Portland Industries, Inc., Easton; sec., treas. Energy & Resource Recovery Corp.; sec., treas., dir. H.O.H. Corp. Served to lt. Supply Corps USNR, World War II. Mem. Nat. Assn. Accountants (pres. Lehigh Valley chpt. 1973-74), Financial Execs. Inst. (treas. N.E. Pa. chpt. 1972-74), Am. Inst. C.P.A.'s, Am. Soc. Corp. Secs. Mem. Moravian Ch. Am. (trustee). Clubs: Pomfret (Easton); Marco Polo (N.Y.C.). Home: 285 Bridle Path Rd Bethlehem PA 18017 Office: 15 S 3d St Easton PA 18042

HARTMANN, ROBERT TROWBRIDGE, author, consultant; b. Rapid City, S.D., Apr. 8, 1917; s. Miner Louis and Elizabeth (Trowbridge) H.; m. Roberta Sankey, Jan. 17, 1943; children: Roberta T. (Mrs. Charles F. Brake), Robert S. A.B., Stanford U., 1938. Reporter Los Angeles Times, 1939-41, 45-48, editorial and spl. writer, 1948-54, chief Washington bur., 1954-63; chief (Mediterranean and Middle East Bur.), 1963-64, FAO info. adviser, Washington, 1964-65; editor Republican Conf. U.S. Ho. Reps., 1966-69; minority sgt.-at-arms U.S. Ho. Reps., 1969-73; chief staff to the Vice Pres., 1973-74; counsellor (with cabinet rank) to Pres. Gerald R. Ford, 1974-77; sr. research fellow Hoover Instn., Stanford U., 1977—; trustee Gerald R. Ford Found., 1981—; mem. staff 1st U.S. Ho. of Reps. Mission to Peoples' Republic of China, 1972; dir. Fedco, Inc. Author: Palace Politics, An Inside Account of the Ford Years, 1980. Asst. to permanent chmn. Rep. Nat. Conv., 1968, 72; bd. visitors U.S. Naval Acad., 1977-80. Served from ensign to lt. comdr. USNR, 1941-45; PTO; now capt. Res.; ret. Recipient Sigma Delta Chi Distinguished Service award for Washington Corrs., 1957; Better Understanding citation English Speaking Union of U.S., 1958; Overseas Press Club citation for best articles on Latin Am., 1961; Freedoms Found. citation, 1963; Distinguished Eagle Scout award Boy Scouts Am., 1975; Reid Found. fellow, Middle East, 1951. Mem. Navy League, Oceanic Ednl. Found., Hammer and Coffin Soc., Delta Chi, Sigma Delta Chi, Delta Sigma Rho. Mem. Ch. of Christ. Clubs: Nat. Press, Internat., Nat. Aviation, Capitol Hill (Washington); Mil. Order of the Carabao, Chevaliers du Tastevin. Home: 5001 Baltimore Ave Bethesda MD 20816 *I'm not sure I have "achieved success" but I have had a very good life so far. The greatest evil in life is a lie, and the greatest blessings are love and laughter.*

HARTMANN, SVEN RICHARD, physicist; b. N.Y.C., Feb. 22, 1932; s. Fred Valdemar and Hertha Ingeborge (Palme) H.; m. Helen C. Gellhorn, Dec. 24, 1954 (div. 1979). B.S., Union Coll., 1954; postgrad., U. Minn.-Mpls., 1954-55; Ph.D., U. Calif.-Berkeley, 1961. Jr. research asst. U. Calif., Berkeley, 1961-62; asst. prof. physics Columbia U., N.Y.C., 1962-65, assoc. prof., 1965-68, prof. physics, 1968—; adv. editorial bd. Optics Communictions, 1972-82; dir. Columbia Radiation Lab., 1968-70, co-dir., 1971-75. Inventor spin locked double Resonance, 1961. Served to 1st lt. USAF, 1955-57. A.P. Sloan research fellow, 1963-67; Guggenheim fellow, 1977-78; recipient R.W. Wood Prize Am. Optical Soc. Fellow Am. Phys. Soc.; mem. Am. Optical Soc., Sigma Xi. Home: 404 Riverside Dr New York NY 10025 Office: Columbia Univ Dept Physics New York NY 10027

HARTMANN, WILLIAM HERMAN, pathologist, educator; b. N.Y.C., Mar. 13, 1931; m. Loreen Moyer, Feb. 27, 1954; children: Daniel M., William Geoffrey, Lindsey M. B.A. in Chemistry, Syracuse U., 1951; M.D., SUNY, 1955. Diplomate: Am. Bd. Pathology (Anatomic Pathology, Clin. Pathology). Intern Detroit Receiving Hosp., 1955-56; resident Henry Ford Hosp., Detroit, 1956-58, Meml. Hosp. for Cancer and Allied Disease, N.Y.C., 1958-60; trainee Nat. Cancer Inst., 1958-60; practice medicine specializing in pathology, Nashville, 1971—; asst. prof. pathology Johns Hopkins U. Sch. of Medicine, Balt., 1962-66, assoc. prof., 1966-67; exchange prof. pathology Cayetano-Heredia Sch. Medicine, Lima, Peru, 1965; assoc. pathologist El Camino Hosp., Mountain View, Calif., 1968-71; prof. pathology Vanderbilt U. Sch. Medicine, Nashville, 1971—, dir. surg. pathology, 1971-73, chmn. dept. pathology, 1973—, pathologist-in-chief, 1973—, 1973—; chmn. pathology quality control program, breast cancer detection demonstration projects Nat. Cancer Inst., 1975—. Contbr. articles to med. jours.; editor: Atlas of Tumor Pathology Series, 1976. Served with M.C. U.S. Army, 1960-62. Fellow Am. Soc. Clin. Pathologists, Coll. Am. Pathologists; mem. Internat. Acad. Pathology (pres. U.S.-Can. div. 1979—), Tenn. Soc. Pathologists (pres. 1976-78), Assn. Pathology Chairmen (pres. 1980—), Nashville Acad. Medicine (dir. 1978—), Am. Cancer Soc. (dir.-at-large), Tenn. Med. Assn., Arthur Purdy Stout Soc. Surg. Pathologists, Sociedad Latino Americana De Patologia. Office: Vanderbilt Univ School of Medicine Nashville TN 37232

HARTNACK, CARL EDWARD, banker; b. Los Angeles, Apr. 9, 1916; s. Johannes C. and Kate (Schoneman) H.; m. Roberta DeLuce, Sept. 6, 1939; children—Richard, Robert, Gretchen. Grad., Pacific Coast Banking Sch., Seattle, 1950, Am. Inst. Banking, 1949. With Security Pacific Nat. Bank, Los Angeles, 1934—, sr. v.p., 1961-69, pres., 1969—, chmn. bd., 1978-80, chmn. internat. bd., 1981—, also dir.; chmn. bd. Security Pacific Corp., 1978-80, dir., 1981—; dir. Hughes Aircraft Co., Smith Internat., Inc., J.G. Boswell Co., Whittaker Corp. Clubs: Stock Exchange, Los Angeles Country, California (Los Angeles); La Jolla Country, Bankers of San Francisco. Office: 333 S Hope St Los Angeles CA 90071

HARTNETT, JAMES PATRICK, engineering educator; b. Lynn, Mass., Mar. 19, 1924; s. James Patrick and Anna Elizabeth (Ryan) H.; m. Shirley Germaine Carlson, July 14, 1945 (div. 1969); children: James, David, Paul, Carla, Dennis; m. Edith Zubrin, Sept. 10, 1971. B.S. in Mech. Engring, Ill. Inst. Tech., 1947; M.S., Mass. Inst. Tech., 1948; Ph.D., U. Calif. at Berkeley, 1954. Engr. gas turbine div. Gen. Electric Co., 1948-49; research engr. U. Calif. at Berkeley, 1949-54; from asst. prof. to prof. mech. engring. U. Minn., 1954-61; Guggenheim fellow, vis. prof. U. Tokyo, Japan, 1960; cons. ICA, Seoul, Korea, 1960; Fulbright lectr., cons. mech. engring. U. Alexandria, Egypt, 1961; H. Fletcher Brown prof. mech. engring., chmn. dept. U. Del., 1961-65; engring. cons., 1954-74; prof., head dept. energy engring. U. Ill., Chgo., 1965-74; dir. Energy Resources Center, 1974—; Sci. exchange visitor, Romania, 1969; vis. prof. Israel Inst. Tech., 1971; cons. Asian Inst. Tech., Bangkok, 1977. Editor: Recent Advances in Heat and Mass Transfer, 1961; co-editor: Internat. Jour. Heat and Mass Transfer, 1960—, (with T.F. Irvine, Jr.) Advances in Heat Transfer, 1963—, Heat Transfer-Japanese Research, Soviet Research, 1971, Fluid Mechanics-Soviet Research, 1971, (with W.M. Rohsenow) Handbook of Heat Transfer, 1973; Contbr. articles on heat transfer, fluid mechanics, energy to tech. jours. Mem. organizing com. and sci. council Internat. Centre Heat and Mass Transfer, Belgrade, Yugoslavia, 1969—, Ill. Energy Resources Commn., 1974—; mem. sci. council Regional Center for Energy, Heat and Mass Transfer for Asia and Pacific, 1976—. Recipient Profl. Achievement award Ill. Inst. Tech. Alumni Assn., 1977, Luikov medal Internat. Ctr. Heat and Mass Transfer, 1981. Fellow ASME (Meml. award Heat Transfer div. 1969); mem. AIAA, Am. Inst. Chem. Engring., Am. Soc. Engring. Edn., AAUP, AAAS, Sigma Xi, Tau Beta Pi, Pi Tau Sigma. Home: 200 E Delaware Chicago IL 60611

HARTNETT, RAYMOND MAURICE, refrigeration and air conditioning executive; b. N.Y.C., May 14, 1935; s. Maurice T. and Laura (Kent) H.; m. Catherine Spencer, Mar. 3, 1957; children: Christopher, Elizabeth, Colin, Caroline, Raymond. B.S., Fordham U., 1956; M.B.A., Duquesne U., 1963. Cons. Booz, Allen & Hamilton, N.Y.C., 1966-69; group controller Singer Co., N.Y.C., 1969-71; v.p. controller Wheelabrator-Frye, N.Y.C., 1971-72; v.p. brass div. Anaconda Co., Waterbury, Conn., 1973-79; v.p. fin. Copeland Corp., Sidney, Ohio, 1979—. Mem. Monmouth County Bd. Edn., Freehold N.J., 1972. Served to capt. USAF, 1956-60; Korea. Mem. Fin. Execs. Inst. Clubs: Troy Country (Ohio); Racquet (Dayton). Office: Copeland Corp 1675 Campbell Rd Sidney OH 45365

HARTNETT, THOMAS FORBES, Congressman; b. Charleston, S.C., Aug. 7, 1941; s. Thomas C. and Catherine (Forbes) H.; m. Bonnie Lee Kennerly, 1965; children: Thomas Forbes, Lee Anne. Student, Coll. Charleston, 1960-62, U. S.C., 1978; cert. real estate appraisal, U. Ga., 1978. Sr. cert. appraiser Am. Assn. Cert. Appraisers; pres. Hartnett Realty Co.; mem. S.C. Ho. of Reps., 1965-73, S.C. Senate, 1973-80, 97th-98th Congresses from 1st Dist. S.C. Served with USAF, 1963. Mem. S.C. Realtors Assn., Greater Charleston Bd. Realtors, Nat. Assn. Realtors, Hibernian Soc. Charleston. Republican. Roman Catholic. Clubs: K.C., Elks. Office: Room 228 Cannon House Office Bldg Washington DC 20515 *

HARTON, JOHN JAMES, utility executive; b. Del Rio, Tex., Dec. 26, 1941; s. John Teague and Ara Velva (Boggs) H.; m. Dianne Voss, May 30, 1968; children: Angela Deanne, John Jay. B.S. in Elec. Engring, U. Ark., 1964, M.S., 1965. With Ark. Power & Light Co., 1965—, dir. corp. planning, Little Rock, 1974-79, treas., asst. sec., 1979—, v.p., chief fin. officer, 1981—; instr. Pines Vocat.-Tech. Sch., Pine Bluff, Ark., 1966-68. Mem. bd. Wesley United Meth. Ch., Pine Bluff, 1971; mem. bldg. com. St. Johns United Meth. Ch., Little Rock, 1980-81. Mem. IEEE, Nat. Soc. Profl. Engrs. Club: Shriners. Office: PO Box 551 Little Rock AR 72203

HARTRANFT, JOSEPH BECKWITH, JR., association executive; b. Buffalo, May 24, 1915; s. Joseph Beckwith and Leila Cooledge (Sherman) H.; m. Dorothy May DuQuoin, Dec. 31, 1937; m. Evelyn Lapariere Melby, July 3, 1948 (dec. Feb. 1964); 1 dau., Diane Lynn. B.A., Wharton Sch. of U. Pa., 1937; D. Aero. Sci, Embry Riddle Aero. U., 1976. Mem. staff Aircraft Owners and Pilots Assn., 1939—, pres., 1952—, chmn. bd., chief exec. officer, 1977—; pres. Aircraft Owners and Pilots Found., 1951—, chmn. bd., chief exec. officer, 1977—; pres. Aircraft Owners and Pilots Service Corp., 1953—, chmn. bd., chief exec. officer, 1977—; pres. Internat. Council Aircraft Owners and Pilots Assns., 1961—, Aircraft Owners and Pilots Assn. Ins. Internat.; dir. Avemco Corp.; Sec. Interdeptl. Air Traffic Control Bd., War Aviation Com.; mem. bd. Aviation Devel. Adv. Com., Joint Mil.-Civilian Air Def. Com.; founder U.S. Air Guard, 1940; adv. bd. Nat. Intercollegiate Flying Assn.; mem. Radio Tech. Commn. for Aero. Trustee Bates Found. Aero. Edn. Served to lt. col. USAAF, World War II. Mem. S.R., Royal Aero Club (hon.), Washington Air Derby Assn. (hon.), Nat. Citizens Commn. Internat. Coop., Nat. Aviation Club, Aero Club Washington. Clubs: Rotary (Chevy Chase, Md.); Pacific; U. Pa. (Washington); Nantucket (Mass.); Yacht; Executives (Chgo.); Columbia Country (Chevy Chase, Md.); Annapolis Yacht (Md.). Home: The Tecumseh Eastport MD 21403 Office: Aircraft Owners and Pilots Assn 421 Aviation Way Frederick MD 21701 PO Box 7550 Schiphol-Central Netherlands also 44 Washington St Nantucket MA 02554 also Tecumseh Port Eastport Box 3347 Annapolis MD 21403

HARTSAW, WILLIAM O., mechanical engineering educator; b. Tell City, Ind., Oct. 17, 1921; s. William A. and Hazel (Barr) H.; m. Delma Stuckey, June 30, 1946; 1 son, Mark Alan. B.S. in Mech. Engring., Purdue U., 1946, M.S. in Engring., 1953; Ph.D., U. Ill., 1966. Instr. engring. U. Evansville, Ind., 1946-52, asst. prof., 1952-54, assoc. prof., 1954-63, prof. engring., 1963—, dir. engring., 1958-68, dean engring., 1968-76, chmn. dept. mech. engring., 1977—; vice chmn. Evansville Environ. Protection Agy., 1980—. Author: The Peltier Effect, 1958, Low Cycle Fatigue Strength Investigation of a High Strength Steel, 1966. Mem. exec. bd. Buffalo Trace council Boy Scouts Am., 1969—, chmn. service com., 1975-76; mem. Evansville Urban Transp. Advisory, 1975—. Served with USAAF, 1942-43. Recipient Alumnus Certificate of Excellence U. Evansville, 1972, Tech. Achievement award Tri-State Council for Sci. and Engring., 1979; NSF fellow, 1961-62. Mem. ASME (faculty adviser student chpt. 1968—, nat. com. div. solar energy com. on components 1975—, vice chmn. faculty advisers region VI 1975-76, chmn. faculty advisors region VI 1976-78, vice pres.-elect 1981-82, vice pres. region VI, vice chmn. Evansville sect. 1980-81, chmn. Evansville sect. 1981-82, v.p. elect Region VI 1982-83, v.p. Region VI 1983—, Centennial Service award 1980, Centennial medal 1980), Am. Soc. Engring. Edn., ASHRAE (pres. Evansville chpt. 1966-67), ASTM, AAUP, AAAS, Am. Soc. Metals, Phi Kappa Phi, Phi Beta Chi. Methodist. Home: 1407 Green Meadow Rd Evansville IN 47715 *I have attempted to maintain a healthy attitude toward life. I maintain that my wife and respectable son, church and position are the best in the world. I am pleased to extend a helping hand when needed and desired. It goes without saying that I have dedicated my life to God, my home, and position. I measure the success of my life by the success of those who have studied and worked under me.*

HARTSFIELD, HENRY WARREN, JR., astronaut; b. Birmingham, Ala., Nov. 21, 1933; s. Henry Warren and Alice Norma (Sorrell) H.; m. Judy Frances Massey, June 30, 1957; children: Judy Lynn, Keely Warren. B.S., Auburn U., 1954; postgrad., Duke U., 1954-55, Air Force Inst. Tech., 1960-61; M.S., U. Tenn., 1970. Commd. 2d lt. U.S. Air Force, 1955, advanced through grades to col., 1974, assigned to tour with 53d Tactical Fighter Squadron, Bitburg, W.Germany, 1961-64; instr. USAF Test Pilot Sch., Edwards AFB, Calif., 1965-66; assigned to Manned Orbiting Lab. USAF, 1966-69; astronaut, NASA Lyndon B. Johnson Space Ctr., 1969—, mem. support crew Apollo 16, Skylabs 2, 3, 4 missions, pilot STS-4; ret. USFA, 1977; civilian astronaut NASA. In space: 169 hours, 11 minutes. Decorated Meritorious Service medal, D.S.M. NASA, 1982; recipient Nat. Geog. White Space Trophy, 1973. Mem. Soc. Exptl. Test Pilots, Air Force Assn., Sigma Pi Sigma. Office: Astronaut Office Code CB NASA Lyndon B Johnson Space Ctr Houston TX 77058

HARTSHORN, JOSEPH HAROLD, geologist, educator; b. Cleve., June 23, 1922; s. Humphrey and Ella (Krise) H.; m. Eleanor Clover Johnson, Dec. 13, 1942 (dec. Jan. 1978); children: John Edward, Jo Ann Hartshorn Morrisson; m. Sheila Dean Garvey, Oct. 30, 1980. S.B., Harvard U., 1947, M.A., 1950, Ph.D., 1955. With U.S. Geol. Survey, 1950-67, asst. to br. chief, 1961-67; part-time geologist, 1967—; vis. prof. U. Mich., Ann Arbor, 1963; asso. prof. geology U. Mass., Amherst, 1967-70, prof., 1970—, head dept., 1970-77; Mem. sch. com. Town of Boxborough, Mass., 1954-68, Acton-Boxborough Regional Sch. Com., 1955-68. Mem. Gov.'s Commn. Preservation Commonwealth Heritages, 1960. Served with RCAF, 1941-44; to maj. USAAF, 1944-46; ETO; col. Res.; ret. Decorated D.F.C., Air medal with four oak leaf clusters; D.F.C.(Great Britain); recipient Tchr. of Yr. award U. Mass., 1973. Fellow AAAS, Geol. Soc. Am. (vice chmn.,

chmn. N.E. sect. 1977-78), Arctic Inst. N.Am., Sigma Xi; mem. Am. Polar Soc., Nat. Assn. Geology Tchrs., Internat. Glaciol. Soc., Am. Quaternary Assn. Home: 1150 Bay Rd Amherst MA 01002

HARTSHORNE, CHARLES, philosopher, retired educator; b. Kittanning, Pa., June 5, 1897; s. Francis Cope and Marguerite (Haughton) H.; m. Dorothy Eleanore Cooper, Dec. 22, 1928; 1 dau., Emily Lawrence (Mrs. Nicolas D. Goodman). Student, Haverford Coll., 1915-17; A.B., Harvard U., 1921, A.M., 1922, Ph.D., 1923; postgrad., U. Freiburg, Germany, 1923-25, U. Marburg, 1925; L.H.D., Haverford Coll., 1967, Episcopal Theol. Sem. of Southwest, 1977; Litt. D., Emory U., 1969; Ph.D. (hon.), U. Louvain, Belgium, 1978. Sheldon travelling fellow Harvard, 1923-25, instr., research fellow, 1925-28; mem. faculty U. Chgo., 1928-55, mem. federated theol. faculty, 1943-55, prof. philosophy, 1949-55, Emory U., Atlanta, 1955-62, U. Tex., Austin, 1962-63, Ashbel Smith prof. philosophy, 1963-76, prof. emeritus, 1976—; Vis. prof. Stanford, 1937, New Sch. Social Research, 1941-42, Johann Wolfgang Goethe U., Frankfurt, Germany, 1948-49, U. Wash., 1958, Banaras Hindu U., Varanasi, India, 1966, Colo. Coll., 1977, 79, U. Louvain, 1978; Terry lectr. Yale, 1947; Fulbright lectr., Melbourne, 1952, Kyoto, Japan, 1958, 66; Dudleian lectr. Harvard, 1963; Morse lectr. Union Theol. Sem., 1964; Lowell lectr. Harvard U., 1979, 81; others. Author: The Philosophy and Psychology of Sensation, 1934, Beyond Humanism, 1937, Man's Vision of God, 1941, The Divine Relativity, 1948, Reality as Social Process, 1953, (with Wm. Reese) Philosophers Speak of God, 1953, The Logic of Perfection, 1962 (Lecomte du Noüy award 1963), Anselm's Discovery, 1965, A Natural Theology for Our Time, 1967, Creative Synthesis and Philosophic Method, 1970, Whitehead's Philosophy, 1972, Born to Sing: An Interpretation and World Survey of Bird Song, 1973, Aquinas to Whitehead: Seven Centuries of Metaphysics of Religion, 1976, (with Creighton Peden) Whitehead's View of Reality, 1981, Insights and Oversights of Great Thinkers, 1983, Omnipotence and Other Theological Mistakes, 1983, Creativity in American Philosophy, 1984; also numerous articles in profl. jours.; Editor: (with Paul Weiss) The Collected Papers of Charles S. Peirce, 1931-35. Served with U.S. Army, 1917-19. Fellow Am. Acad. Arts and Scis.; mem. Am. Philos. Assn. (pres. western div. 1948-49), Internat. Phenomenological Soc., Metaphys. Soc. Am. (pres. 1954-55), Charles Peirce Soc. (pres. 1950-51), Am. Ornithol. Union, Soc. Philosophy Religion (pres. 1963-64), So. Soc. Philosophy and Psychology (pres. 1964-65), European Soc. for Process Thought (hon. pres. 1978—), Phi Beta Kappa. Home: 724 Sparks Ave Austin TX 78705 Office: Waggener Hall Univ Tex Austin TX 78712

HARTSOCK, LINDA SUE, educational and management development executive; b. St. Joseph, Mo., Feb. 20, 1940; d. Waldo Emerson and Martha (Skelkop) H. B.S., Central Meth. Coll., Fayette, Mo., 1962; M.Ed., Pa. State U., 1965; Ed.D., 1971. Cert. assn. exec. Am. Soc. Assn. Execs. Tchr. Jr. High Sch. (North Kansas City (Mo.) Public Sch. System), 1962-63; sr. resident Pa. State U., 1963-64, asst. coordinator residence halls, 1964-65, residence hall coordinator, 1965-66, asst. dean women, 1966-68, asst. dean students, 1968-71; researcher Center for Study Higher Edn., 1971, dir. new student programs, 1971-72; nat. dir. program AAUW, 1972-76; exec. dir. Adult Edn. Assn., Washington, from 1976; now pres. Hartsock Assocs., assn., edn. and mgmt. devel., Alexandria, Va.; designer tng. and ednl. programs for various orgns. and firms; speaker in field; adj. faculty George Washington U.; mem. Conf. Planning Com. on Adult Human Rights Edn., 1979; v.p. fin. Com. for Full Finding Edn., 1979; mem. first adv. panel convened future directions of a learning soc. project Coll. Entrance Exam. Bd., 1978, mem. planning group for course-by-newspaper exam. project, 1979; bd. dirs. Coalition Adult Edn. Orgns., 1976; mem. White House Conf. on Aging Planning, 1979; mem. nat. adv. bd. Nat. Center Higher Edn. Mgmt. System Project to Develop a Taxonomy for the Field of Adult Edn., 1978; bd. dirs. Nat. Joint Steering Com. on Community Edn., 1978; nat. adv. council on adult edn. Futures and Amendments Project, 1977; adv. Collection of Census Data, Nat. Center Ednl. Stats., 1977; mem. public policy com., program com. chmn. Adv. Council Nat. Orgns. to Corp. for Public Broadcasting, 1976; adv. devel. New Mediated Programs, Office Instructional Resources, Miami Dade Community Coll., 1976; mem. innovative awards com. Nat. Univ. Extension Assn., 1977; field reader U.S. Dept. Edn., 1981-83. Editorial bd.: Off to Coll. mag, 1972—; contbr. articles to profl. jours. Asst. sec. HEW Conf. Women's Issues; mem. White House Conf. Human Resources and World of Work. Recipient Disting. Alumni award Central Meth. Coll., 1978. Mem. Am. Soc. Assn. Execs. (individual membership council 1979—), Washington Women's Forum (budget, program and exec. com. 1978—), Am. Assn. Higher Edn. (nat. conf. program screening com. 1979), Adult Edn. Assn. U.S.A., Am. Acad. Polit. and Social Scis., AAUW, Washington Soc. Assn. Execs., Pi Lambda Theta. Office: PO Box 10201 Alexandria VA 22310

HARTSOUGH, WALTER DOUGLAS, physicist; b. Merced, Calif., Sept. 17, 1924; s. Douglas John and Josephine Mary (Oneto) H.; m. Patricia Meta Fain, June 24, 1945; children—Linda Anne, Marian Jane, Joan Marie, Michael David. A.B. in Physics, U. Calif., Berkeley, 1944, postgrad., 1946-48. Mem. staff U. Calif. Lawrence Berkeley Lab., 1946—, physicist, bevatron group leader, 1958-73, asso. dir., staff sr. scientist, div. head engring. and tech. services, 1973—; mem. U.S.-People's Republic China Joint Com. High Energy Physics, 1979—. Author papers, reports in field. Served with USNR, 1942-46. Democrat. Roman Catholic. Club: U. Calif. at Berkeley Faculty. Home: 649 Ironbark Circle Orinda CA 94563 Office: 1 Cyclotron Rd Berkeley CA 94720

HARTSTEIN, JACOB I., educator; b. Stary Sambor, Austria, Sept. 10, 1912; came to U.S., 1920, naturalized, 1922; s. Nathan B. and Lea (Harris) H.; m. Florence Waldman, Aug. 16, 1942; children: Kalman, Norman Bernard. Ed., Talmudical Acad.; A.B., Yeshiva Coll., 1932, L.H.D., 1962; M.S., N.Y. City Coll., 1933; M.A., Columbia, 1936; Ph.D., N.Y. U., 1945. Sec. Rabbi Elchanan Theol. Sem. Tchrs. Inst., 1929-37; instr. social scis. Talmudical Acad., 1932-36; acting registrar Yeshiva Coll., 1935-36, registrar, 1936-44, sec. faculty, 1938-43, instr. edn., 1939-41, asst. prof. edn., 1941-44; dir., asst. prof. edn. Bernard Revel Grad. Sch., 1944-45; prof. edn., dir. Grad. Schs., Yeshiva U., 1945-50, dean, 1950-53; also dean Sch. Edn. and Community Adminstrn., Yeshiva U., 1948-53; lectr. edn. L.I. U., 1938-41, also psychology, 1939-41, asst. prof. edn. and psychology, 1941-45, prof., 1945-64, acting head dept., 1944-45, head dept., 1945-60, chmn. grad. div., 1949-51, dir., 1951-52, dean, 1953-60, dean sch. edn., 1960-64; pres. Kingsborough Community Coll., 1964-69; prof. City U. N.Y., 1964—; Supt. of schs., bd. secular edn. The United Yeshivos, 1945-48; research cons. Human Engring. div. U.S. Navy; cons. U.S. Office Edn.; dir. ednl. survey Jewish Community, Portland, Me.; vice chmn. Mayor's Com. on Scholastic Achievement, N.Y.C., 1954-66, Gov.'s Com. on Scholastic Achievement, 1966—; on state, city, regional edn. coms.; mem., presiding officer Nat. Adv. Com. on Supplementary Ednl. Centers and Services, U.S. office Edn., 1965-68; bd. dirs., pres. Council Higher Ednl. Instns. in, N.Y.C. Author: State Regulatory and Supervisory Control of Higher Education in New York, Jewish Education in New York City; Co-author: A Model Program for the Talmud Torah; Editor: Jews in America: Heritage and History, Edn. Abstracts, The Jews in America, History: A Resource Book for Teachers, 2 edits., Psychology, 3 edits.; bd. editors: Presdl. Studies Quar; Contbr. on ednl. history and problems and psychology of learning to tech. and trade jours. Bd. govs. Jewish Acad. Arts and Scis.; mem. acad. adv. council; trustee Bar-Ilan U., Israel; mem. Met. N.Y. Commn. Tchr. Edn. and Profl. Standards, Community Planning Bd. 4, Borough Bklyn.; Bklyn. citizens adv. bd. N.Y. State Constl. Conv.; mem. acad. adv. council Ferkauf Grad. Sch. Edn., Yeshiva U.; bd. educators Center for Study of Presidency; bd. dirs. Bd. Jewish Edn. N.Y.C.; trustee Fifth Ave. Synagogue; chmn. presdl. planning com. Yeshiva U. Recipient Abraham Freeda award; Yeshiva Flatbush award Yeshiva Coll. Alumni Assn.; Bernard Revel Meml. award in arts and scis.; Chief Rabbi Isaac Halevi Herzog Fellowship Gold Medal award, 1965; Yeshiva U. Distinguished Service award, 1970; N.Y. Gov.'s citation for ednl. leadership, 1972, 76; Alumni Service award CCNY, 1978. Fellow AAAS, Nat. Assn. Jewish Day Sch. Prins. (pres.); mem. N.Y. Acad. Pub. Edn., Am. Ednl. Research Assn., Am. Assn. Sch. Adminstrs., AAUP, N.Y. Psychol. Assn., Am. Psychol. Assn., Eastern Psychol. Assn., Bklyn Psychol. Assn. (chmn. com. profl. ethics; exec. com.), Eastern Assn. Coll. Deans (exec. com., dir.), Nat. Council Jewish Edn., NEA, Nat. Soc. Coll. Tchrs. Edn., N.Y. Counsellors Assn., Religious Edn. Assn. U.S., Soc. Advancement Edn., CCNY Edn. Alumni Assn. (pres.), Phi Delta Kappa, Phi Alpha Theta, Kappa Delta Pi. Jewish Orthodox. Club: Mason. Home: 165 E 72d St New York NY 10021 Office: City Coll City Univ NY Convent Ave at 136th St New York NY 10031 *The satisfaction derived from contributing to human development and the advancement of society and the joy of creation are their own greatest reward.*

HARTT, FREDERICK, art history educator; b. Boston, May 22, 1914; s. Rollin Lynde and Jessie Clark (Knight) H.; m. Margaret DeWitt Veeder, Mar. 11, 1943 (div. July 1960). B.A., Columbia, 1935; postgrad., Princeton, 1935-36; M.A., N.Y. U., 1937, Ph.D., 1949. Asst. Yale Art Gallery, 1941-42; vis. lectr. art, acting dir. art mus. Smith Coll., 1946-47; lectr. fine arts N.Y. U., 1948-49; from asst. prof. history art to prof. Washington U., St. Louis, 1949-60; prof. history art U. Pa., 1960-67, chmn. dept. art, 1960-65; McIntire prof. history art U. Va., Charlottesville, 1967—, chmn. dept. art, 1967-76; dir. U. Art Mus., 1971-76; vis. prof. history Harvard U., summer 1961, Franklin and Marshall Coll., 1966-67; Vis. art historian Harvard Renaissance Center, Florence, Italy, 1965-66. Author: Florentine Art Under Fire, 1949, Botticelli, 1952, Giulio Romano, 2 vols, 1958, (with Kennedy and Corti) The Chapel of the Cardinal of Portugal, 1964, Love in Baroque Art, 1964, The Paintings of Michelangelo, 1964, Michelangelo, the Complete Sculpture, 1969, History of Italian Renaissance Art, 1969, 2d rev. edit., 1979, Michelangelo's Drawings, 1971, Donatello, Prophet of Modern Vision, 1973, Art, A History of Painting, Sculpture and Architecture, 2 vols, 1976, Michelangelo's Three Pietàs, 1976, also numerous articles. Mem. exec. com. Com. to Rescue Italian Art, 1966—; Bd. dirs. Am. Com. Restoration Italian Monuments, 1946-49. Served to 1st lt. USAAF, 1942-46. Decorated Bronze Star medal; knight of Crown of Italy; knight officer Order Merit Italian Republic; hon. academician Acad. Arts Design, Florence, 1970; hon. alumnus Baylor U., 1981; named hon. citizen, Florence, 1946; Guggenheim fellow, 1948-49, 54-55; Fulbright research grantee, 1954-55, 65-66; Am. Council Learned Socs. fellow, 1965-66. Mem. Coll. Art Assn. Am. (dir. 1959-62), Am. Assn. U. Profs., Renaissance Soc. Am. (council 1970), Soc. Archtl. Historians, Nat. Trust Hist. Preservation. Roman Catholic. Home: 1007 Rugby Rd Charlottesville VA 22903

HARTT, JULIAN NORRIS, religion educator; b. Selby, S.D., June 13, 1911; s. Albert and Laura (Beals) H.; m. Neva Beverly Leonard, June 16, 1935; children: Beverly Ann, Susan Laura, Julian Norris. A.B., Dakota Wesleyan, 1932, D.Litt., 1959; B.D., Garrett Bibl. Inst., 1937, Litt.D., 1961, D.D., 1973; M.A., Northwestern U., 1938; Ph.D., Yale U., 1940; D.D., St. Olaf Coll., 1982, Garrett Evang. Theol. Sem., 1983. Asso. prof. philosophy and religion Berea Coll., 1940-43; Noah Porter prof. philos. theology Yale U., 1943-72, chmn. dept. religion, 1956-64, dir. grad. studies, dept. religious studies, 1964-67, chmn. dept. religious studies, 1967-72; William Kenan Jr. prof. religious studies U. Va., Charlottesville, 1972-81, emeritus, 1981—. Co-author: The Lost Image of Man, 1963, A Christian Criticism of American Culture; Author: Theology and the Church in the University, 1969, The Restless Quest, 1975, Theological Method and Imagination, 1977. Fulbright fellow, 1963-64; Guggenheim fellow, 1963-64. Mem. Am. Philos. Assn., Am. Acad. Polit. Sci. Home: 1939 Thomson Rd Charlottesville VA 22903

HARTUNG, ERNEST WILLIAM, JR., university president; b. N.Y.C., Jan. 20, 1917; s. Ernest W. and Marie (Drescher) H.; m. Mary W. Dennen, June 17, 1944; children: John W., Katharine D., Ernest D. A.B., Dartmouth Coll., 1938; A.M., Harvard U., 1940, Ph.D., 1942. Teaching fellow Harvard U., also Radcliffe Coll., 1940-42; instr. to asst. prof. U. Vt., 1946-48; vis. lectr. Harvard U., 1947, asst. prof., summers 1948-52; asst. prof., then v.p. U. R.I., 1948—, chmn. dept. zoology, 1953-60, dean Grad. Sch., coordinator research Grad. Sch., 1960-65; pres. U. Idaho, Moscow, 1965-77, pres. emeritus, 1977—; exec. dir. U. Idaho Found., 1977-82. Trustee Knox Sch., 1949-53. Served from 2d lt. to capt. USAAF, 1942-45. Cramer fellow, Dartmouth, 1938-39; grantee cancer research USPHS; Am. Cancer Soc. Fellow N.Y. Acad. Scis. Mem. R.I. Heart Assn., Am. Soc. Zoologists, Soc. Study Devel. and Growth, Am. Inst. Biol. Scis., Am. Assn. U. Profs., Am. Genetic Assn., N.E.A., Sigma Xi, Phi Kappa Phi, Phi Sigma, Sigma Alpha Epsilon. Unitarian (chmn. bd. trustees). Home: 5050 Old Pullman Rd Moscow ID 83843

HARTUNG, WALTER MAGNUS, aeronautical academy president; b. N.Y.C., Aug. 10, 1907; s. Magnus and Amelia (Bradtke) H.; m. Emily L. M. Stasse, Oct. 19, 1935; 1 dau., Gale Anne (Mrs. James G. Baldwin). B.S. in Mech. Engring, N.Y. U., 1928, 1936; M.A., 1957; Ph.D., 1960. Registered profl. engr., N.Y. Airplane designer Aeromarine-Klemm Corp., 1928-29; asst. chief engr. Aircraft Improvement Corp., 1929-30; dean aero. engring. Beckley Coll., Pa., 1931-32; aero engr. Granville Aircraft Corp., 1932-33; chief engring. instrn. Casey Jones Sch. Aeros., 1933-43; exec. v.p., dean Acad. Aeros., Flushing, N.Y., 1946-63, pres., 1964—; mem. Queens adv. bd. Mfrs. Hanover Trust Co., 1970-79; chmn. U.S. Tech. Edn. Del. to USSR, 1961; mem. audit and rev. com. Accreditation Bd. Engring. and Tech.; Chmn. planning bd., Tenafly, N.J., 1961-63; mem. adv. com. on accreditation and instnl. eligibility Office Edn., HEW, 1969-71; mem. aviation adv. com. Dowling Coll., 1973-75; mem. Nat. Com. for Aviation Exploring, 1974-76. Mayor Borough Tenafly, N.J., 1970-75; trustee Bergen Community Coll., 1970-78, chmn. bd. trustees, 1976-77; trustee Aviation Hall of Fame of N.J., 1974—, pres., 1983—; trustee N.Y. Inst. Tech., 1976—. Served from capt. to col. USAF, 1943-46. Decorated Bronze Star medal with oak leaf cluster. Fellow AIAA, Am. Soc. Engring. Edn. (charter fellow; hon.; v.p., chmn. tech. inst. council 1964-66, mem., ethics and legal phases com. 1968-71), N.Y. U. Alumni Fedn. (pres. 1963-65), Air Force Assn., Engrs. Council Profl. Devel. (chmn. engring. tech. com. 1966-68, engring. edn. and engring. accreditation and engring. tech. joint com. 1969-71, bd. dirs. 1968-70), Nat. Indsl. Conf. Bd. (exec. com. 1968-71), Nat. Soc. Profl. Engrs. (chmn. engring. tech. com. 1969-70), Queens C. of C. (chmn. aviation com. 1981-82), Delta Chi. Presbyterian. Clubs: Knickerbocker Country (Tenafly) (pres. 1979-80); Englewood, Englewood Field (N.J.); Nat. Aviation, Army and Navy (Washington); Wings (N.Y.C.) (council 1965—, pres. 1967-68); Kiwanis, N.Y. Univ. (N.Y.C.) (gov. 1965-68). Home: 1 Byrne Ln Tenafly NJ 07670 Office: LaGuardia Airport Flushing NY 11371

HARTWELL, STEPHEN, investment company executive; b. Phila., Apr. 10, 1916; s. Stephen Warren and Elizabeth (Thompson) H.; m. Elizabeth van Laer Speer, Feb. 21, 1946 (div. 1973); children: Stephen Warren II, Robert van Laer; m. Norma Bostick, Dec. 9, 1978. B.S. in Adminstrv. Engring., Lafayette Coll., 1936. Investment analyst Pa. Co. Banking & Trusts, 1936-41; procurement officer electronic equipment CAA, 1947-48; indsl. specialist AEC, 1948-49, chief progress and stats. sect., prodn. div., 1949-51, chief constr. engring. reports br., 1951-54; exec. v.p. Steadman Security Corp. (and predecessor cos.), 1954-68; v.p. Washington Mut. Investors Fund, Inc., 1968-81, pres., 1981—; chmn. adv. bd. Woodlawn Nat. Bank, Alexandria, Va., 1966-73; pres., dir. Colchester Corp., Woodbridge, Va., 1971—, WMIF Mgmt. Corp., Washington; dir. First Am. Bank of Va., Wentz Corp., Wilmington, Del., Precious Metals Holdings Inc., Boston. Mem. Fairfax County (Va.) Planning Commn., 1961-67, chmn., 1964-66; mem. No. Va. Regional Planning and Econ. Devel. Commn., 1963-64, Fairfax County Republican Com., 1955-61, 66-70, 79-81; bd. govs. Gunston Hall Sch., Va.; bd. visitors Coll. Bus. Adminstrn., Am. U.; trustee Am. U., 1983—, Fairfax Hosp. Assn., 1983—, Woodlawn Found., 1983—. Served to maj. AUS, 1941-46. Mem. Washington Soc. Investment Analysts, SAR, Nat. Assn. Securities Dealers (dist. 10 com. 1968-71), Zeta Psi. Clubs: Met., Nat. Economists (Washington). Home: Riversedge Mount Vernon VA 22121 Office: Southern Bldg 1101 Vermont Ave NW Washington DC 20005

HARTWICK, ELBERT STUART, investor; b. Fargo, N.D., Dec. 7, 1903; s. Louis B. and Roberta Frances (Stuart) H.; m. Margaret Smith, Dec. 29, 1930 (dec. Jan. 1980); m. Joy Iverson, Sept. 26, 1981; 1 son, Ronald Stuart. A.B., U. Minn., 1930, J.D., 1930. Bar: Ill. bar 1931, Minn. bar 1931. Atty. Theodore, Gary & Co., Chgo., 1930-33; atty., sec. Carnation Co., Los Angeles, 1933-44, v.p., dir., 1944-67, sr. v.p., 1967-70; past pres., dir. Dairy Foods, Inc., Carnaco Equipment Co.; dir. Olson Farms, Inc.; pres., dir. Bus. Investments Co., Rialto Center Co., Citrus Village, Inc. Formerly mem. Calif. Republican State Central Com.; hon. trustee Republican Assn.; Trustee emeritus U. Redlands. Recipient Outstanding Achievement award U. Minn., 1974. Mem. Am., Ill., Minn. bar assns., Acacia, Gray Friar, Alpha Delta Sigma, Pi Delta Epsilon, Phi Alpha Delta. Republican. Episcopalian. Clubs: Mason (Shriner), Rotarian., Los Angeles Country, Thunderbird Country. Home: 875 Comstock Ave Apt 12B-East Bldg Los Angeles CA 90024

HARTWIG, CLEO, sculptor; b. Webberville, Mich., Oct. 20, 1911; d. Albert and Julia (Klunzinger) H.; m. Vincent Glinsky, 1951 (dec. Mar. 1975); 1 son, Albert. A.B., Western Mich. U., 1932, D.F.A. (hon.), 1973; student, Internat. Sch. Art, Europe, 1935. Tchr. pvt. schs., N.Y.C., 1935-42; instr. Cooper Union, 1945-46; sculpture instr. Montclair (N.J.) Art Mus., 1945-71. First one man show, 1943; one-man show, Sculpture Ctr., N.Y.C., 1981; included group exhbns., Nat. Acad., Pa. Acad., Detroit Inst. Arts, Art Inst. Chgo., Met. Mus., Phila. Mus., Whitney Mus., Newark Mus., Phila. Art Alliance, Denver Art Mus., Boston Mus. Sci., N.Y. Zool. Soc., Nebr. Art Assn., State U. Iowa, U. Ark., Des Moines Art Center, So. Vt. Art Center, U. Conn., Smithsonian Instn. Natural History, USIA in Europe, Nat. Inst. Arts and Letters, U. Minn., Canton Art Inst., N.Y. Bot. Garden, others, traveling one-man show, Can., U.S.; represented in permanent collections, Brookgreen Gardens Mus., S.C., Newark Mus., Detroit Inst. Arts, Pa. Acad., Montclair Art Mus., Mt. Holyoke Coll., Western Mich. U., Oswego (N.Y.) Univ., Nat. Mus. Am. Art, Smithsonian Instn., Chrysler Mus., Norfolk, Va., NAD, So. Vt. Art Center. Recipient Kamperman Haass prize Mich. Artists Annual, 1943; Anna Hyatt Huntington prize for sculpture, 1945; L. Reusch & Co. prize N.Y. Soc. Ceramic Arts, 1946; Nat. Assn. Women Artists 1st prize for sculpture, 1951; medal of honor, 1967; Audubon Artists prize for sculpture, 1952; Pres.'s award, 1972; Today's Art award and medal of merit, 1975; award mural and sculpture competition Munson-Williams-Proctor Inst., 1958; Feist Meml. prize, 1968; Salomone prize, 1972; Jeffrey Childs Willis Meml. prize, 1975; Amelia Peabody award, 1976; Silver medal Nat. Sculpture Soc., 1969; C. Percival Dietsch prize, 1976; Ellin P. Speyer prize NAD, 1979; L. J. Liskin Purchase prize Nat. Sculpture Soc., 1980. Fellow Nat. Sculpture Soc. (Leonard Meiselman prize 1978); mem. Audubon Artists, Sculptors Guild, Nat. Assn. Women Artists, Soc. Animal Artists, Nat. Acad. Design (academician). Home: 9 Patchin Pl New York City NY 10011 Studio: 5 W 16th St: New York NY 10011 *I prefer carving to modeling, and the color, veining and density of the stone or wood often influence the choice of subject matter, usually nature forms. Instead of adhering strictly to realism, I try to "interpret" the subject, and to design a satisfying sculpture using very simplified forms and contours.*

HARTY, JAMES D., manufacturing company executive; b. Bridgeport, Conn., Oct. 5, 1929; s. John S. and Catherine (Lee) H.; m. Margaret O'Connor, June 4, 1955; children—Shaun, Kevin, Maura, Megan. Degree in indsl. engring, U. Bridgeport, 1962. Analyst E.I. DuPont, 1947-51; prodn. control mgr. Sikorsky Aircraft, 1954-62; plant mgr. Stanley Works, 1962-68; corp. mgr. prodn. and inventory control ITT, 1968-70; corp. dir. mfg. projects Singer Co., N.Y.C., 1970-74; pres., chief operating officer Raymond Corp., Greene, N.Y., 1974—, also dir.; dir. G.N. Johnston Equipment Co. Ltd., Ont., Can., C.J. Ellis Corp., Ala. Handling Co., Endicott Trust Bank, N.Y., Brauer Material Handling Co., Harris Equipment, Nebr. Material Handling, Raymond Handling, Storage Concepts. Bd. dirs. Our Lady of Lourdes Hosp., Binghamton, N.Y.; mem. engring. tech. adv. com. and M.B.A. adv. bd. SUNY—, Binghamton. Served with U.S. Army, 1951-53. Mem. Am. Mgmt. Assn., Am. Prodn. and Inventory Control Soc. (past internat. v.p. edn. and research), Material Handling Inst., Indsl. Truck Assn. Clubs: Binghamton Country, Binghamton City. Home: 308 Ridgefield Rd Endicott NY 13760 Office: Raymond Corp Greene NY 13778

HARTZELL, ANDREW CORNELIUS, JR., lawyer; b. Balt., Nov. 5, 1927; s. Andrew Cornelius and Mary Frances (Milholland) H.; m. Mary Leontine McPhillips, July 31, 1954; children: Andrew Cornelius, Stephen Carroll, James Francis, Mary Leontine, John Michael, Peter Milholland. B.A., Yale U., 1950, LL.B., 1953. Bar: N.Y. 1953, Ohio 1955, U.S. Supreme Ct. Law clk. Fed. Judge Irving R. Kaufman, N.Y.C., 1953-54; assoc. firm Thompson, Hine & Flory, Cleve., 1954-63, Debevoise, Plimpton, Lyons & Gates, N.Y.C., 1963-65; partner Debevoise and Plimpton and predecessor firms, 1966—. Contbr.: articles to legal jours. and to Antitrust Advisor, McGraw-Hill Pub. Co., 1971, 78; Note and Comment editor: Yale Law Jour, 1952-53. Mem. bd. archtl. rev. Village of Scarsdale, N.Y., 1965-67. Served with U.S. Army, 1946-48; Japan. Fellow Am. Coll. Trial Lawyers; mem. Assn. Bar City N.Y., N.Y. State Bar Assn., Am. Bar Assn., Am. Law Inst. Roman Catholic. Clubs: Yale of N.Y.; Town (Scarsdale, N.Y.). Home: 7 Eastwoods Ln Scarsdale NY 10583 Office: 875 3d Ave New York NY 10022

HARVANEK, ROBERT FRANCIS, philosophy educator, clergyman; b. Chgo., Nov. 26, 1916; s. Frank George and Bures H. B.A., Loyola U. of Chgo., 1939, M.A., 1941; Ph.D., Fordham U., 1944. Prof. philosophy West Baden Coll., West Baden Springs, Ind., 1951-64, Bellarmine Sch. Theology, North Aurora, Ill., 1964-67; provincial superior Chgo. Province S.J., Oak Park, Ill., 1967-73; prof. philosophy Loyola U. of Chgo., 1974—, chmn. dept., 1979—. Mem. Am. Philos. Assn. (pres. 1982-83), Medieval and Renaissance Philos. Assn. Home:

6525 N Sheridan Rd Chicago IL 60626 Office: Loyola U of Chgo 6525 N Sheridan Rd Chicago IL 60626

HARVEY, ABNER MCGEHEE, physician, educator; b. Little Rock, July 30, 1911; s. George S. and Jenette (McGehee) H.; m. Elizabeth Baker Treide, June 21, 1941; children: Jenette, Elizabeth, Joan, George. A.B., Washington and Lee U., 1930, D.Sc., 1949; M.D., Johns Hopkins U., 1934; Sc.D., U. Ark., 1951, Med. Coll. Ohio, 1976. Intern Johns Hopkins Hosp., 1934-35, asst. resident, 1935-37; research fellow Nat. Inst. Med. Research, London, 1937-39; Johnson Found. for Biophysics fellow U. Pa., 1939-40; resident physician Johns Hopkins Hosp., 1940-41; asst. prof. medicine Vanderbilt U. Med. Sch., 1941-42; Disting. Service prof. medicine Johns Hopkins Med. Sch.; physician-in-chief emeritus Johns Hopkins Hosp.; archivist Johns Hopkins Med. Instns., 1983—. Author: (with J. Bordley III and Jeremiah Baronders) Differential Diagnosis, 1979, Two Centuries of American Medicine 1776-1976, 1976, Adventures in Medical Research, 1976, History of the Interurban Clinical Club, 1978, History of the American Clinical and Climatological Association, History of Clinical Research in American Medicine, 1981; editor: The Principles and Practice of Medicine, 1984. Served from capt. to lt. col. M.C., AUS, 1942-45; PTO. Recipient R.H. Williams award, 1975. Fellow Royal Soc. Medicine (hon.), Am. Acad. Arts and Scis., Am. Philos. Soc.; mem. Am. Rheumatism Assn., Assn. Am. Physicians (pres. 1968, George M. Kober medal 1981), Am. Soc. Clin. Investigation (pres. 1956), Physiol. Soc. Gt. Britain, Interurban Clin. Club, Am. Physiol. Soc., Am. Clin. and Climatol. Assn. (pres. 1971), A.C.P. (master 1971, Distinguished Tchr. award 1977), Med. and Chirurg. Faculty Md., Balt. City Med. Soc., Am. Soc. Pharmacology and Exptl. Therapeutics, Assn. Profs. Medicine (pres. 1960), Am. Osler Soc. (pres. 1976), Phi Beta Kappa, Alpha Omega Alpha, Nu Sigma Nu, Sigma Chi. Home: 4201 Saint Paul St Baltimore MD 21218 Office: Johns Hopkins Hosp Baltimore MD 21205

HARVEY, ALEXANDER, II, judge; b. Balt., May 3, 1923; s. Fred B. and Rose (Hopkins) H.; m. Mary E. Williams, Feb. 24, 1951; children—Elizabeth H., Alexander IV. B.A., Yale, 1947; LL.B., Columbia, 1950. Bar: Md. bar 1950. Asso. firm Ober, William, Grimes & Stinson, Balt., 1950-66, partner, 1953-66; asst. atty. gen., Md., 1957-58; judge U.S. Dist. Ct. for Md., 1966—; Mem. Gov. Md. Com. to Study Blue Sky Law of Md., 1961; mem. character com. Ct. Appeals Md. 8th Jud. Circuit. Bd. dirs. Balt. Symphony Assn., 1966-68; pres., dir. Balt. Opera Guild, 1960; bd. dirs. Balt. Council Social Agys., 1957-63; trustee Ch. Home and Hosp., Balt., 1952-71. Served to 1st lt. AUS, World War II; ETO. Mem. Am., Md., Balt. bar assns., Phi Beta Kappa. Episcopalian (vestry 1967-70). Home: 7300 Brightside Rd Baltimore MD 21212 Office: 101 W Lombard St Baltimore MD 21201

HARVEY, ANTHONY KESTEVEN, film director; b. London, June 3, 1931; s. Geoff and Dorothy (Leon) Harrison. Student, Royal Acad. Dramatic Art. Film actor; editor: films including The Whisperers, Lolita, Dr. Strangelove; Editor (films including) The Spy Who Came in from the Cold; films including The L-Shaped Room; dir.: The Dutchman, 1966 (Best New Dir. award Cannes Film Festival), The Lion in Winter, 1968 (Dirs. Guild award), They Might Be Giants, 1970, The Abdication, 1973, The Ultimate Solution of Grace Quigley, 1983; TV drama The Glass Menagerie (1st prize London Film Festival), 1973 (2 Emmy awards), Eagles Wing, 1978, Players, 1979, Richard's Things, 1980, Gipsy House, 1981, The Disappearance of Aimee, Svengali. Mem. Acad. Motion Pictures, Dirs. Guild Am. Office: care Arthur Greene 666 Fifth Ave New York NY 10019

HARVEY, BERNARD GEORGE, nuclear physicist; b. England, Oct. 5, 1919; came to U.S., 1953, naturalized, 1960; s. Ernest Arthur and Clarice Maria (Bull) H.; m. Margaret Mary Brooker, Dec. 23, 1941; children—Richard A., Christopher J., Michael J., Alison M., Philip R. B.A., Oxford U., 1940, B.Sc., 1941, M.A., D.Sc., 1958; hon. doctorate, U. Grenoble, France, 1979. Physicist Imperial Chem. Industries, Ltd., 1941-43, Brit.-Can. Atomic Energy Project, Montreal, Que., Can., 1943-45, Can. Atomic Energy Project, Chalk River, Ont., 1946-53; mem. staff U. Calif. Lawrence Berkeley Lab., 1953—, head nuclear sci. div., asso. lab. dir., 1975-79, dir. cyclotron lab., univ. lectr. chemistry, 1979—; mem. nuclear sci. adv. com. Dept. Energy-NSF, 1977-79; vis. prof. U. Grenoble, 1981-82. Author textbooks, research papers in field. Guggenheim fellow, 1961. Fellow Am. Phys. Soc. (chmn. div. nuclear physics 1980-81); mem. European Phys. Soc., Soc. Française Physique. Democrat. Home: 2650 Hilgard Ave Berkeley CA 94709 Office: Lawrence Berkeley Lab Berkeley CA 94720

HARVEY, CURRAN WHITTHORNE, JR., investment management executive; b. Balt., Dec. 23, 1928; s. Curran Whitthorne and Charlotte C. (Cromwell) H.; m. Marjorie Jo Simons, Apr. 23, 1955; children: Charlotte B., Curran Whitthorne III, Marjorie M., Roland S. B.Engring., Yale U., 1951; postgrad., Columbia U., 1951-52, Johns Hopkins U., 1959-61. Project mgr. Belock Instrument Co., College Point, N.Y., 1954-55; sr. sales engr. Ford Instrument Co. div. Sperry Rand Corp., 1955-59; sales mgr. aerospace div. Aeronca Mfg. Co., 1959-61; security analyst T. Rowe Price Assos., Inc., Balt., 1961-70, vice chmn. bd., 1974-80, dir. counsel div., 1976-79, chief operating officer, 1978-81, pres., 1980—, chief exec. officer, 1981—, dir., 1970—; v.p., dir. T. Rowe Price New Horizons Fund, Inc., Balt., 1965-69, pres., dir., 1969-78, chmn. bd., 1978—; pres., dir. T. Rowe Price Growth Stock Fund, 1982—; dir. T. Rowe Price Growth & Income Fund, 1982—; bd. govs. Investment Co. Inst., 1980—. Trustee Boys' Latin Sch., 1980, Walters Art Gallery, Balt., 1983—. Served with USNR, 1951-54. Mem. Balt. Security Analysts Soc. Roman Catholic. Clubs: Yale (N.Y.C.); Elkridge, Center (Balt.). Home: 1866 Circle Rd Baltimore MD 21204 Office: 100 E Pratt St Baltimore MD 21202

HARVEY, CYNTHIA, principal ballet dancer; b. San Rafael, Calif. Studied with, Christine Waltone, The Novato Sch. Ballet; student, San Francisco Ballet Sch., Marin Ballet Sch., Sch. Am. Ballet, N.Y.C., Am. Ballet Theatre Sch., N.Y.C., Nat. Ballet Sch. Can., Toronto. With Am. Ballet Theatre, N.Y.C., 1974—, soloist, 1978—, prin. dancer, 1982—. Creator: role of Gamzatti in La Bayadere; appeared in: Apollo, Billy the Kid, Fancy Free, Giselle, Raymonda. Office: Am Ballet Theatre 890 Broadway New York NY 10003 *

HARVEY, DAVID EUGENE, constrn. co. exec.; b. Wilmette, Ill., Feb. 6, 1922; s. Frank William and Helen Geraldine (McJunkin) H.; m. Patricia Meany, Sept. 2, 1950; children—Jerome, Michael, David Eugene, Barbara, Donna, Janice, Brian, Mary Ann, Frank, Eileen, Patricia. B.S. in Archtl. Engring, U. Ill., 1951. Architect Ragnar Benson Constrn. Co., Chgo., 1951-52; engr., estimator W.S. Bellow Constrn. Co., Houston, 1952-53, Benson Co. Builders, 1953-58; founder, 1958; since chmn. bd., chief exec. officer Harvey Constrn. Co., Houston; dir. Galleria Bank, Houston. Served with USAAF, 1943-46. Recipient award excellence Urban Land Inst., 1979. Mem. Asso. Gen. Contractors (sec. Houston chpt. 1981), Houston C. of C. Republican. Roman Catholic. Club: K.C. (3 deg.). Office: PO Box 864 Houston TX 77001

HARVEY, DONALD, artist, educator; b. Walthamston, Eng., June 14, 1930; s. Henry and Annie Dorothy (Sawell) H.; m. Elizabeth Clark, Aug. 9, 1952; children—Shan Mary, David Jonathan. Art tchrs. diploma, Brighton Coll. Art, 1951. Art master Ardwyn Grammar Sch., Wales, 1952-56; mem. faculty dept. art U. Victoria, B.C., Can., 1961—, now prof. painting. One man exhbns. include, Albert White Gallery, Toronto, 1968, retrospective, Art Gallery of Victoria, 1968; represented in permanent collections, Nat. Gallery Can., Montreal Mus., Albright-Knox Mus., Seattle Art Mus. Bd. dirs. Norfolk House Sch. Bd., 1974-76; mem. accessions com. Art Gallery of Victoria, 1969-72. Can. Council fellow, 1966. Asso. Can. Acad. Can.; mem. Can. Group Painters, Can. Painters and Etchers. Home: 1025 Joan Crescent Victoria BC V8S 3L3 Canada Office: Univ of Victoria Victoria BC Canada

HARVEY, DONALD JOSEPH, history educator; b. N.Y.C., Oct. 4, 1922; s. William Harold and Helen (Chiampou) H.; m. Jacqueline Rozendaal, June 11, 1955; 1 dau., Nanette. B.A. cum laude, Princeton U., 1943; M.A., Columbia U., 1948, Ph.D., 1953; postgrad., U. Paris, 1950-51. Instr. Hunter Coll., City U. N.Y., 1951-56, asst. prof., 1956-60, asso. prof., 1960-67, prof. history, 1967—, chmn. dept. history, 1968-71; Reader/cons. univ. presses Yale, Cornell, State U. N.Y.; cons. Rockefeller Found. humanities fellowship program, 1974-78, Nat. Endowment for Humanities, 1977-83. Author: (with E.M. Earle) Modern France, 1951, France Since the Revolution, 1968, (with W.O. Shanahan) Nationalism: Essays in Honor of Louis Snyder, 1981; assoc. editor: (with H. Rowen) Reviews in European History, 1973-79; contbr. articles to profl. jours. Served to capt., arty. AUS, 1943-46; ETO. Ford Found. fellow, 1954-55; Fulbright alternate, 1959-60. Mem. Am. Hist. Assn., Soc. for French Hist. Studies, AAUP, Phi Alpha Theta. Home: 279 Park Ave Manhasset NY 11030 Office: 695 Park Ave New York NY 10021

HARVEY, DONALD PHILLIPS, retired naval officer; b. Geddes, S.D., Jan. 24, 1924; s. Ernest Lyle and Beryl (Phillips) H.; m. Deborah Stults, Dec. 13, 1952; children—Craig, Lynn, Reid, Anne. B.S., U.S. Naval Acad., 1947; M.A., Fletcher Sch. Law and Diplomacy, 1961. Commd. ensign U.S. Navy, 1947, advanced through grades to rear adm., 1973; service in, Pacific, Atlantic, Bahrain, France and Japan; dir. Naval Intelligence, Washington, 1976-78; sr. staff TRW, Washington, 1978—. Decorated DSM, Legion of Merit, Meritorious Service medal, Joint Commendation medal (2), Navy Commendation medal (2). Mem. U.S. Naval Inst., Nat. Mil. Intelligence Assn. (chmn. adv. bd.). Republican. Episcopalian. Club: Army-Navy Country. Home: 8203 Jeb Stuart Rd Potomac MD 20854 Office: TRW 7600 Coleshire Dr McLean VA 22102

HARVEY, DOROTHY MAY, newspaper editor; b. Bartlesville, Okla., Apr. 3, 1922; d. Paul and Vila May (Ray) H. B.S. in Commerce, Okla. A. and M. Coll., 1950. Tech. asst. research dept. Phillips Petroleum Co., 1942-48; program dir., pub. relations dir. Topeka YWCA, 1950-55; asso. editor Capper's Weekly, Topeka, 1955-73, editor, 1974—. Mem. Women in Communications. Republican. Methodist. Home: 2311 Hazelton Ct Topeka KS 66606 Office: 616 Jefferson St Topeka KS 66607

HARVEY, DOUGLASS COATE, retired photographic company executive; b. Batavia, N.Y., Aug. 28, 1917; s. Homer A. and Della S. H.; m. Elizabeth Kellas, June 27, 1942; children: Robert, Anne, Katharine, Douglass Coate. B.S.M.E. with highest distinction, Purdue U., 1939, Dr. Engring. h.c., 1982. With Eastman Kodak Co., Rochester, N.Y., 1939-82, dir. corporate product devel., 1970-73, v.p., gen. mgr. apparatus div., 1973-77, exec. v.p., gen. mgr., 1977-82, also dir.; pres. Kodak Employees Assn., 1976. Trustee Alfred (N.Y.) U., Eastman Dental Center; former exec. bd. Otetiana council Boy Scouts Am.; former chmn. bd. dirs. Rochester and Monroe County YMCA, also mem. nat. bd. dirs.; chmn. engring. adv. council Clarkson Coll.; former bd. mgrs. Meml. Art Gallery. Mem. Nat. Acad. Engring., Indsl. Mgmt. Council, Optical Soc. Am., Photog. Soc. Am., Soc. Profl. Scientists and Engrs., Rochester Engring. Soc., Rochester C. of C., Nat. Security Indsl. Assn. (trustee 1973-78). Republican. Clubs: Rochester Country (bd. stewards), Ausable, Lake George, Rotary, Genesee Valley (Rochester). Home: 3155 East Ave Rochester NY 14618

HARVEY, EDMUND HUXLEY, JR. (TAD HARVEY), editor; b. Wilmington, Del., Oct. 27, 1934; s. Edmund Huxley and Margaret Howland Silliman H.; m. Nancy Day Brill, June 11, 1955 (div. 1970); children—Christopher LeRoy, Edmund Fenn, Abigail Day, Jonathan Easton; m. Gail Stephenson Dravneek, Oct. 10, 1970; children—Hannah Stephenson, Caroline Fletcher. A.B. in English, Harvard, 1956. Writer Street & Smith, N.Y.C., 1956-58; asso. J.F. McCrindle Lit. Agy., N.Y.C., 1958-59; writer Doubleday & Co., N.Y.C., 1959-61; asso. editor Western Publs., N.Y.C., 1961-62, Sci. World, Scholastic Mags., 1962-65, mng. editor, 1971, editor, 1972-76; asso. editorial dir. social studies and sci. Scholastic Mags., 1976-77, editorial dir., 1977—; acting editor Update, 1983—; freelance writer, N.Y.C., 1965-67; sr. editor Reader's Digest Gen. Books, N.Y.C., 1967-71. Author: Quest of Michael Faraday, 1961, Quest of Archimedes, 1962, Exploring Biology, 1963, Television, 1968, Mission to the Moon, 1969; Contbr. sci., med. articles to popular mags.; contbr. to books. Spl. asst. to U.S. Senator John V. Tunney of Calif., 1972. Mem. Nat. Assn. Sci. Writers. Episcopalian. Clubs: Harvard (N.Y.C.); Montauk (Bklyn.). Home: 438 7th St Brooklyn NY 11215 Office: Scholastic Inc 730 Broadway New York NY 10003

HARVEY, EDWIN MALCOLM, manufacturing company executive; b. Hattiesburg, Miss., July 23, 1928; s. Clarence C. and Ezilda (Pegues) H.; m. Charlotte Trewolla, July 7, 1951; children—Sylvia Jane, Sharon Ann, Rebecca Lynn. B.S. in Chem. Engring, La. State U., 1950. With Ethyl Corp., Richmond, Va., 1950-66, mgr. econ. research, dir. econ. evaluation, 1963-66; pres., treas. William L. Bonnell Co., Inc. (subs. Ethyl Corp.), Newnan, Ga., 1966—; also dir.; v.p. Aluminum div. Ethyl Corp., 1975—; pres. Capitol Products Corp. (subs.), 1975—; dir. First Nat. Bank, Newnan. Bd. dirs. Newnan Hosp. Mem. Ga., Newnan-Coweta chambers commerce., Aluminum Assn. (dir.). Episcopalian. Club: Newnan Country. Home: 246 Jackson St Newnan GA 30264 Office: 25 Bonnell St Newnan GA 30264

HARVEY, ELAINE BUTLER, university dean; b. Milan, Tenn., Sept. 3, 1924; d. Wallace Marion and Maggie Pearl (Gwaltney) Butler; m. Bernard Charles Harvey, Nov. 13, 1943; children: Bernard Charles, William Wallace, Lisa Elaine, Christine Marie. R.N., U. Tenn., Memphis, 1946; B.S. in Biology and Nursing, Murray (Ky.) State U., 1962; M.S. in Maternity Nursing, Ind. U., 1969; M.S.N. in Pediatrics, Ind. U., 1971; Ed.D. in Adminstrn, Higher Edn., 1976. Various nursing and supervisory positions hosps. in, Tenn. and Ky., 1943-69; mem. pediatric nursing faculty Ind. U. Sch. Nursing, Indpls., 1969-73, assoc. prof., coordinator undergrad. jr. year, 1973-76, acting chmn. dept. grad. pediatric nursing, 1976-77; prof., dean Sch. Nursing, Ft. Hays State U., Hays, Kans., 1977—; mem. Kans. State Bd. Nursing, 1979—, pres., 1980; Bd. dirs. Community Day Care Center, 1978-83, v.p., 1980-81; mem. nursing edn. dept. Colby Coll., 1978-79. Mem. adv. and exec. bd. Adult Restorative Service/Day Treatment Project, 1978—. Nurse Tng. Act stipend, 1943; grantee HEW, 1976, Allied Health Inst., 1977, Delta Project, 1977; March of Dimes grantee for Perinatal/Neonatal Conf. Mem. Am. Nurses Assn., Kans. Nurses Assn., Nat. League Nursing, Ind. U. Alumni Assn. (life), Phi Delta Kappa, Sigma Theta Tau. Baptist. Office: School of Nursing Fort Hays State University Hays KS 67601-4099

HARVEY, F. BARTON, JR., investment banker; b. June 22, 1921; s. F. Barton and Rose (Hopkins) H.; m. Grace Locke, Jan. 25, 1946; children—F. Barton, Grace Locke, John Locke, Rose Hopkins. A.B., Harvard U., 1942. Instr. Johns Hopkins McCoy Coll. (now Johns Hopkins Evening Sch.), 1946-50; with Alex, Brown & Sons (investment bankers), Balt., 1946—, partner, 1953-66, mng. partner, 1966—; dir. Republic Airways, Inc., Canton Co., Savs. Bank of Balt., Balt. & Annapolis R.R., Comml. Credit Co., C & P Telephone Co. Mem. overseers' com. on univ. resources, mem. fund council Harvard U.; bd. dirs. United Fund of Central Md., Greater Balt. Med. Center, Home for Incurables of Balt. City, Family and Children's Soc. Balt., The Friendly Inn Assn.; trustee Hill Sch., Pottstown, Pa. Served wtih USMC, 1942-45. Decorated Purple Heart, Navy Cross. Mem. N.Y. Stock Exchange (bd. govs. 1969-71), Investment Bankers Assn. Am. (past v.p.). Home: 2 Lindsay Ln Baltimore MD 21212 Office: 135 E Baltimore St Baltimore MD 21202

HARVEY, FRANK W., retail company executive; b. Knoxville, Tenn., Apr. 13, 1931; s. Frank R. and Mildred (Noe) H.; m. Patricia Johnson, Mar. 3, 1963; children: Heather Lea, Frank Whitney. B.S. in Econ., Vanderbilt U., 1957. With Cain Sloan Co., 1958, 66-76, sr. v.p., gen. mdse. mgr., Nashville, 1966-70, pres., 1970-76; divisional mdse. mgr. The Fashion, Columbus, Ohio, pres., mng. dir., 1965-66, Maas Bros. of Fla., Tampa, 1976—; dir. Exchange Nat. Bank, Tampa. Bd. dirs. U. South Fla. Found.; trustee chmn. bd. fellows U. Tampa. Served with USMC, 1950-52. Mem. Greater Tampa C. of C. (sec.-treas.). Methodist. Clubs: Palma Geia Golf and Country, Tampa Yacht, Univ. Home: 4901 New Providence St Tampa FL 33609 Office: Maas Bros PO Box 311 Tampa FL 33601

HARVEY, FREDERICK PARKER, advertising agency executive; b. Syracuse, N.Y., Feb. 8, 1920; s. Fred Davey and Grace Aileen (Parker) H.; m. Ann Crowthers, July 20, 1946; children: Ellen Parker, Frederick Crowthers, John Berry. A.B.-B.J., Syracuse U., 1942, B.S. in Physics, 1943; postgrad., Harvard U., 1944, M.I.T., 1945. Advt. mgr. Sylvania Electric Co., Boston, 1947-52; account exec. Fuller & Smith & Ross, N.Y.C., 1952-59; v.p., account supr. Donahue & Coe Inc., N.Y.C., 1959-63; sr. v.p., corp. sec. West, Weir & Bartel, N.Y.C., 1963-68; sr. v.p., mgmt. supr. D'Arcy-MacManus & Masius, N.Y.C., 1968-83; dir. Keene Corp. Elder Larchmont Avenue Ch., Larchmont, N.Y., 1982—. Served to capt. Signal Corps, U.S. Army, 1943-46. Mem. Air Force Assn. (exec. council Iron Gate chpt. 1980—), Phi Beta Kappa, Sigma Pi Sigma, Sigma Delta Chi. Republican. Mem. United Ch. of Christ. Home: 146 Baker Dr Tryon NC 28782

HARVEY, GEORGE BURTON, office equipment company executive; b. New Haven, Apr. 7, 1931; m. Elizabeth Mary Viola, June 30, 1962; children: Paul, George, David. B.S., U. Pa., 1954. V.p. fin. Pitney Bowes, Stamford, Conn., 1973-76, group v.p. bus. equipment, 1976-78, pres. bus. systems, 1978-81, pres., chief operating officer, 1981-83, chmn., pres., chief exec. officer, 1983—; dir. Norton Co., Worcester, Mass., CT Bank & Trust Co., Hartford, Conn., Bus. Equipment Mfrs. Assn., Washington; trustee Northeast Utilities, Hartford, Conn. Bd. dirs St. Joseph Hosp., Stamford, New Neighborhoods Inc., Stamford; trustee King Sch., Stamford, Conn. Coll., New London. Served with U.S. Army, 1954-56. Mem. Southwestern Area Commerce and Industry Assn. (dir.), Conn. Bus. Industry Assn. (dir.). Home: 313 Wahackme Rd New Canaan CT 06840 Office: Pitney Bowes Inc Walter H Wheeler Jr Dr Stamford CT 06926

HARVEY, GLENN F., association executive; b. Tarentum, Pa., May 10, 1940; s. Howard F. and Evelyn H.; m. Linda M. Herr, Mar. 19, 1960; children: Jeffrey Howard, Lisa Anne. B.S.Ed., Slippery Rock State Coll., 1961; M.Ed., Duquesne U., 1964; M.B.A., U. Pitts., 1975. Tchr. Fox Chapel Area Schs., Pitts., 1961-67; exec. dir. Instruments Soc. Am., Pitts., 1967—; dir. Sta. WQED-TV, Pitts. Mem. Council Engring. and Sci. Soc. Execs. (bd. dirs.). Republican. Office: Instrument Soc Am 67 Alexander Dr Box 12277 Research Triangle Park NC 27709

HARVEY, IRWIN M., carpet mill executive; b. Chgo., Apr. 24, 1931; s. Herman and Clara (Pomerantz) Harvey S.; m. Marilyn G. Greenspahn, June 7, 1952; children: Beth I. Dorfman, Jill F., Gail L. B.S., Roosevelt U., 1952. Sales rep. Pinksy Floor Covering Co., Chgo., 1954-58; sales agt. Hyams & Harvey, Chgo., 1958-63; v.p., regional mgr. Evans & Black Carpet Mills, Elk Grove Village, Ill., 1963-67, v.p., dir. mktg., Dallas, 1967-68; chmn.-pres. Galaxy Carpet Mills Inc., Elk Grove Village, Ill., and Chatsworth, Ga., 1968-83, chmn., chief exec. officer, 1984—; bd. dirs., exec. com. Floor Covering Industry Found., Chgo., 1980-83; mem. adv. bd. Acad. Design Sch., Chgo., 1978-83, Dallas Trade Mart, 1983—. Served with U.S. Army, 1952-54. Named Man of Year Floor Covering Industry Found., 1983. Mem. Carpet and Rug Inst. (dir. 1971-82, exec. com. 1973-82, 1978-80), Chgo. Floor Covering Assn. Jewish. Home: 868 Thackeray Dr Highland Park IL 60035 Office: Galaxy Carpet Mills Inc 850 Arthur Ave Elk Grove Village IL 60007

HARVEY, JAMES NEAL, advertising agency executive; b. Derby, Conn., Dec. 21, 1925; s. Edward John and Eunice Johnson (Neal) H.; m. Anne Bottomley, July 15, 1950 (div. 1968); children: Neal, Craig, Dean, Grant, Claudia; m. Ursula Menzel, Nov. 1, 1969. B.A., Syracuse U., 1951. Copywriter Young & Rubicam, N.Y.C. and Hollywood, Calif., 1951-55; creative group head McCann Erickson, N.Y.C., 1956-59; pres., creative dir. Richard K. Mannoff, N.Y.C., 1959-65; pres. James Neal Harvey, Inc., N.Y.C., 1965—, Harvey Travel, Inc., Rowayton, Conn., Harvey & Ptnrs., Inc., N.Y.C., Gemini Electronics, Inc., Amherst, N.H. Author: Star Power (pseudonym Leslie Deane), 1978, also numerous TV scripts, mag. articles. Served with U.S. Merchant Marine, 1943-46. Mem. ASCAP. Home: 9 Cameron Dr Greenwich CT 06830 Office: 477 Madison Ave New York City NY 10022

HARVEY, JAMES ROSS, diversified service company executive; b. Los Angeles, Aug. 20, 1934; s. James Ernest and Loretta Berniece (Ross) H.; m. Charlene Coakley, July 22, 1971; children: Kjersten Ann, Kristina Ross. B.S. in Engring., Princeton U., 1956; M.B.A., U. Calif.-Berkeley, 1963. Engr. Standard Oil Co. (Calif.), San Francisco, 1956-61; acct. Touche, Ross, San Francisco, 1963-64; chmn. bd., pres., chief exec. officer, dir. Transamerica Corp., San Francisco, 1965—; dir. Transam. Delaval Inc., Transam. Occidental Life Ins. Co., Transam. Fin. Corp., Transam. Airlines, Transam. Ins. Co., Transam. Interway Inc., Transam. Title Ins. Co., Safeway Stores, Inc., Pacific Telesis Group. Trustee West Coast Cancer Found.; bd. regents St. Mary's Coll.; bd. dirs. U. Calif. Bus. Sch., Nat. Park Found., Calif. State Parks Found., Fine Arts Museums of San Francisco, Bay Area Council. Served with AUS, 1958-59. Mem. San Francisco C. of C. (dir., pres.). Clubs: Bohemian, Pacific-Union (San Francisco); Union League (N.Y.C.). Office: 600 Montgomery St San Francisco CA 94111

HARVEY, JOHN COLLINS, physician, educator; b. Youngstown, Ohio, Sept. 11, 1923; s. J. Paul and Mary J. (Collins) H.; m. Adele Dillon, Nov. 26, 1949; children—Elizabeth V.R. (Mrs. Charles Yon), John Collins Jr., William Charles II, Amy L.R. (Mrs. L. F. Reese), Margaret J.B. Grad., Phillips Exeter Acad., 1941; B.S., Yale, 1944; M.D., Johns Hopkins, 1947, M.L.A., 1968, M.A.S., 1974; M.A., St. Mary's U., 1975. Diplomate: Am. Bd. Internal Medicine. Successively house officer, asst. resident, resident Osler Med. Service, Johns

Hopkins Hosp., 1947-53, physician, 1953-73; successively instr., asst. prof., asso. prof., prof. medicine Johns Hopkins, 1953-73; prof. medicine Georgetown U., Washington, 1973—; Vis. prof. medicine U. Ibadan, Nigeria, 1964; hon. asso. prof. medicine Guy's Hosp., London, 1973. Contbr. articles to profl. publs. Mem. various local, state and nat. govt. med. adv. coms.; trustee Hosp. for Sick Children, Washington, Washington Home for Incurables, M.C., USAR. A. Blaine Brower Traveling fellow A.C.P. to Guy's Hosp., London, 1956. Fellow A.C.P., Am. Pub. Health Assn.; mem. A.A.A.S., A.M.A., Am. Clin. and Climatol. Assn., Biophys. Soc., So. Med. Assn., Phi Beta Kappa, Sigma Xi, Alpha Omega Alpha. Republican. Roman Catholic. Knight St. Gregory, Knight of Malta. Clubs: Peripatetic, Tudor and Stuart (Balt.); Yale (N.Y.C.); Chevy Chase (Md.); Cosmos (Washington). Research in muscle disease. Home: 8629 Fenway Rd Bethesda MD 20034 Office: Georgetown U Hosp Washington DC 20007

HARVEY, JOHN GROVER, mathematics educator, computer science educator; b. Waco, Tex., Aug. 10, 1934; s. John Grover and Mary Inez (Davidson) H. A.A., Navarro Jr. Coll., Corsicana, Tex., 1953; B.S., Baylor U., 1955; M.S., Fla. State U., 1957; Ph.D., Tulane U., 1961. Instr. math. U. Ill., Urbana, 1961-63, asst. prof., 1963-66; assoc. prof. math. U. Wis., Madison, 1966-75, prof., 1975—; prin. investigator Wis. Research and Devel. Ctr. for Congnitive learning, Madison, 1968-78. Editor: (with T.A. Romberg) Problem Solving in Mathematics, 1980. Mem. Math. Assn. Am. (assoc. editor 1969-74), Am. Ednl. Research Assn., Nat. Council Tchrs. Math., Wis. Math. Council, Phi Delta Kappa. Democrat. Lutheran. Home: 5606 Stadium Dr Madison WI 53705 Office: Dept Mathematics Univ Wis 480 Lincoln Dr Madison WI 53706

HARVEY, JOSEPH PAUL, JR., medical educator; b. Youngstown, Ohio, Feb. 28, 1922; s. Joseph Paul and Mary Justinian (Collins) H.; m. Martha Elizabeth Toole, Apr. 12, 1958; children—Mary Alice, Martha Jane, Frances Elizabeth, Helen Lucy, Laura Andre. Student, Dartmouth, 1939-42; M.D., Harvard, 1945. Diplomate: Nat. Bd. Med. Examiners. Intern Peter Bent Brigham Hosp., Boston, 1945-46; resident Univ. Hosp., Cleve., 1951-53, Hosp. Spl. Surgery, N.Y.C., 1953-54; instr. orthopedics Cornell Med. Coll., N.Y.C., 1954-62; mem. faculty Sch. Medicine, U. So. Calif., Los Angeles, 1962—, prof. orthopedic surgery, 1966—, chmn. sect. orthopedics, 1964-78; dir. dept. orthopedics U. So. Calif.-Los Angeles County Med. Center, 1964-79, mem. staff, 1979—. Editor-in-chief: Contemporary Orthopedics. Served to capt. AUS, 1946-48. Exchange orthopedic fellow Royal Acad. Hosp., Upsala, Sweden, 1957. Fellow Western Orthopedic Assn., Am. Acad. Orthopedic Surgery, A.C.S.; mem. Los Angeles County, Calif. med. assns., Am. Rheumatism Assn., Am. Orthopedic Assn., Am. Soc. Testing Materials, Internat. Soc. Orthopedics and Truamatology. Club: Boston Harvard. Home: 2050 Lorain Rd San Marino CA 91108 Office: Dept Orthopedic Surgery Univ Southern Calif Los Angeles County Med Center 1200 N State St Los Angeles CA 90033

HARVEY, LEONARD A., chem. co. exec.; b. St. Catharines, Ont., Can., Aug. 20, 1925; came to U.S., 1952, naturalized, 1960; m. Shirley Williams, Oct. 7, 1950; children—Brian, Bruce, Christopher. B.Sc. with honors, Queens U., 1950. With Borg Warner Chems. Inc., 1952—, pres., Parkersburg, W.Va., 1976—; dir. McGean Chem. Co., Parkersburg Nat. Bank. Served with RCAF, World War II. Mem. Soc. Plastics Industry, Chem. Mfrs. Assn., Parkersburg C. of C. (pres. 1981-82). Address: Box 1868 Parkersburg WV 26101

HARVEY, NORMAN RONALD, financial executive; b. Rahway, N.J., Aug. 17, 1933; s. George Henry and Jennie Louise (Proudfoot) H.; m. Gail Molitor, May 26, 1962; 1 dau., Anne. B.A. in Econs., Cornell U., 1955; M.B.A., NYU, 1962. Security analyst Bankers Trust Co., N.Y.C., 1958-61, Anchor Corp., Elizabeth, N.J., 1961-64; dir. research Auerbach, Pollak & Richardson, N.Y.C., 1964-75; chief investment officer E.W. Axe & Co., Inc., Tarrytown, N.Y., 1975-82; sr. v.p., sr. equity funds investment officer Merrill Lynch Asset Mgmt., Inc., N.Y.C., 1982—. Served to 1st lt. USAR, 1957-58. Corson Meml. scholar, 1951. Mem. N.Y. Soc. Security Analysts, N.Y. Assn. Bus. Economists. Republican. Club: Darlington Racquet. Home: 27 Carlough Rd Upper Saddle River NJ 07458 Office: Merrill Lynch Asset Mgmt Inc 633 Third Ace New York NY 10017

HARVEY, PAUL, news commentator, author, columnist; b. Tulsa, Sept. 4, 1918; s. Harry Harrison and Anna Dagmar (Christiansen) Aurandt; m. Lynne Cooper, June 4, 1940; 1 son, Paul Harvey. Litt.D. (hon.), Culver-Stockton Coll., 1952, St. Bonaventure U., 1953; LL.D., John Brown U., Ark., 1959, Mont. Sch. Mines, 1961, Trinity Coll. Fla., 1963, Parsons Coll., 1968; H.H.D., Wayland Bapt. Coll., 1960, Union Coll., 1962, Samford U., 1970, Howard Payne U., Tex., 1978. Announcer radio sta. KVOO, Tulsa; sta. mgr., Salina, Kans.; spl. events dir. radio sta. KXOK, St. Louis; program dir. radio sta. WKZO, 1941-43; dir. news and information OWI, Mich., Ind., 1941-43; news commentator, analyst ABC, 1944—; syndicated columnist Los Angeles Times Syndicate (formerly Gen. Features Corp.), 1954—; TV commentator, 1968. Author: Remember These Things, 1952, Autumn of Liberty, 1954, The Rest of the Story, 1956, You Said It, Paul Harvey, 1969, Our Lives, Our Fortunes, Our Sacred Honor; Album rec. Yesterday's Voices, 1959, Testing Time, 1960, Uncommon Man, 1962. Recipient citation D.A.V., 1949; Freedoms Found. award, 1952, 53, 61, 62, 64, 65, 67, 68, 74, 75, 76; radio award Am. Legion, 1952; citation of merit, 1955, 57; certificate of merit V.F.W., 1953; Bronze Christopher's award, 1953; award of honor Sumter Guards, 1955; elected to Okla. Hall of Fame, 1955; nat. pub. welfare services trophy Colo. Am. Legion, 1957; named Top Commentator of Year Radio-TV Daily, 1962; Great Am. KSEL award, 1962; Spl. ABC award, 1973; Ill. Broadcaster award, 1974; John Peter Zenger Freedom award Eagles, 1975; Am. of Year award Lions Internat., 1975; named to Nat. Assn. Broadcasters Hall of Fame, 1979; recipient Father of Yr. award Father's Day Council, 1980; Outstanding Broadcast Journalism award, 1980; Gen. Omar N. Bradley Spirit of Independence trophy, 1980; Man of Yr. award Chgo. Broadcast Advt. Club, 1981; Horatio Alger award, 1983. Mem. Washington Radio and Television Corrs. Assn., Aircraft Owners and Pilots Assn. Club: Chicago Press. Broadcasts and columns reprinted in Congressional Record 102 times. Office: 360 N Michigan Ave Chicago IL 60601

HARVEY, PAUL HENRY, crop scientist, educator; b. St. Paul, Nebr., Aug. 2, 1911; s. William and Ella Mae (Roe) H.; m. Ethel Marie Larson, June 8, 1938; children: Ann (Mrs. Herbert P. Scott), Lois Kay (Mrs. Robert Morin), David Paul. B.S. in Agr, U. Nebr., 1934, D.Sc. (hon.), 1983; Ph.D. in Genetics, Iowa State U., 1938. Grad. asst. in genetics Iowa State U., 1934-38; mem. faculty N.C. State U. at Raleigh, 1938—, prof. agronomy, 1945-56, William Neal Reynolds prof., 1955-80, prof. emeritus, 1980—, head dept. crop sci., 1956-74; on leave as agrl. adminstr. Coop. State Research Service, U.S. Dept. Agr., Washington, 1970-71, agronomist, 1974-75; staff scientist corn, sorghum and millets Agrl. Research, Beltsville, Md., 1975-80; part time cons., coordinator Nat. Corn Research Study dept. crop sci. N.C. State U., 1981—. Mem. Am. Soc. Agronomy, Crop Sci. Soc. Am. (pres. 1965), Sigma Xi, Phi Kappa Phi, Gamma Sigma Delta (nat. award distinguished service agr. 1956), Farm House Frat. Club: Kiwanian (pres. 1969). Home: 1311 Mayfair Rd Raleigh NC 27608

HARVEY, PETER ROBERT, manufacturing executive; b. Chgo., Dec. 11, 1934; s. John E. and Dolores H. (Goss) H.; m. Jean Marie Schroeder, Aug. 24, 1968; children: Robert Alan, Lisa Jean. B.A., U. Fla., 1961. Pres., Artra Group Inc. (formerly Dutch Boy, Inc.), Northfield, Ill., 1969—, also dir.; chmn. bd., dir. Technical Tape, Inc.; chmn. bd. Matrix Corp.; dir. Tensor Corp., Kroehler Mfg. Co. Mem. Kappa Sigma. Home: 25 Bridlewood Rd Northbrook IL 60062 Office: 500 Central Ave Northfield IL 60093

HARVEY, ROBERT DUNCAN, librarian; b. Bklyn., Feb. 9, 1919; s. John L. and Edith L. (Bligh) H.; m. Mary Jane Hatfield, May 14, 1945; 1 son, Spencer Gordon. B.A., Wesleyan U., Middletown, Conn., 1941; M.S. in L.S, Columbia, 1950. Head pub. services U. Vt. library, 1950-56; chief reference and spl. services Northwestern U. Library, 1956-59; head librarian, prof. library sci. S.W. Mo. State U., Springfield, 1959—. Mem. S.W. Mo. Library Network Adv. Council, v.p., 1977-78. Served to 1st lt. USAAF, 1942-45. Mem. Am., Mo. library assns., Am. Assn. U. Profs., Mo. Assn. Coll. and Research Libraries (pres. 1968-69). Home: 821 E Delmar St Springfield MO 65807

HARVEY, ROBERT WILSON, editor; b. Washington, Mar. 18, 1920; s. Robert Porter and Margaret (Posey) W.; m. Barbara Ann Landon, Sept. 3, 1941; children: Michael L., Martha E., Sara M. B.A., Dartmouth Coll., 1941; postgrad., U. Stockholm, 1946-47. Reporter Washington Post, 1941-43; asst. mng. editor The Nation, N.Y.C., 1945-46; free-lance corr., Stockholm, 1946-47; asst. mng. editor The Reporter, Washington, 1948; staff editor Changing Times, Washington, 1948-51, asst. mng. editor, 1951-58, mng. editor, 1958-64, editor, 1964-74, asso. publisher, 1975-79; dir. Kiplinger Washington Editors, Inc., 1965-80. Bd. dirs. D.C. Heart Assn., 1964-68, Council for Family Financial Edn., 1969-72; gov. D.C. Amateur Athletic Assn., 1962-64; trustee Conn. River Found. Served with USMCR, 1943-45. Episcopalian. Clubs: Black Hall (Old Lyme, Conn.); Dartmouth of Southeastern Conn. Home: PO Box 331 Essex CT 06426

HARVEY, RONALD GILBERT, research chemist; b. Ottawa, Ont., Can., Sept. 9, 1927; came to U.S., 1948; s. Gilbert and Adeline (LeClair) H.; m. Helene H. Szpara, May 18, 1952; 1 son, Ronald Edward. B.S. in Biology, UCLA, 1952; M.S. in Chemistry, U. Chgo., 1956, Ph.D., 1960. Project leader Sinclair Research Labs., Harvey, Ill., 1956-58; instr. U. Chgo., 1960-63, asst.prof., 1964-68, assoc. prof., 1968-75, prof., 1975—; postdoctoral fellow Inperial Coll., London, Eng., 1963-64; cons. Nat. Cancer Inst., Washington, Farmacon Corp., Oakbrook, Ill., CIDAC, Palo Alto, Calif., 1978-80; OMNI Research Mayaguex, P.R., 1973-74. Patentee Synthesis of a-olefine, 1959; contbr. articles to profl. jours. Fellow Royal Chem. Soc., Am. Inst. Chemists; mem. Am. Chem. Soc., Am. Assn. Cancer Research, AAAS, Sigma Xi. Home: 7350 Choctaw Rd Palos Heights IL 60463 Office: U chgo Ben May Lab Cancer Research 950 E 59th St Chicago IL 60637

HARVEY, VAN AUSTIN, educator; b. Hankow, China, Apr. 23, 1926; s. Earle Ralston and Mary Lee (Mullis) H.; m. Margaret Jean Lynn, Aug. 31, 1950; children: Jonathan Lynn, Christopher Earle. B.A., Occidental Coll., 1948, H.H.D. (hon.), 1964; B.D. (Day fellow, Kent fellow), Yale, 1951, Ph.D., 1957; postgrad., Marburg (Germany) U., 1960-61, Oxford (Eng.) U., 1966-67. Asst. prof. religion dept. Princeton (N.J.) U., 1954-58; assoc. prof. Perkins Sch. Theology, So. Meth. U., Dallas, 1958-62, prof., 1962-68, dir. grad. studies, 1965-68; prof. religious thought U. Pa., Phila., 1968-77, chmn. dept., 1971-76, dir. grad. studies, 1969-71; prof. religious studies Stanford U., Calif., 1977—, chmn. dept., 1980—. Author: A Handbook of Theological Terms, 1964, The Historian and the Believer, 1966; Contbr. articles to religious and theol. jours. Served with USNR, 1943-46. Guggenheim fellow, 1966, 71; NEH sr. fellow, 1979. Mem. Am. Acad. Religion, Am. Theol. Soc., Phi Beta Kappa. Office: Dept Religious Studies Stanford U Stanford CA 94305

HARVEY, WATKINS PROCTOR, physician, educator; b. Lynchburg, Va., Apr. 19, 1918; s. William Cochran and Caroline (Proctor) H.; m. Irma M. Burns, Apr. 30, 1949; children: Watkins Proctor, Janet Carolyn, Blair Burns (dec.). A.B., Lynchburg Coll., 1939; M.D., Duke, 1943; Sc.D. (hon.), Georgetown U., 1979. Intern medicine Peter Bent Brigham Hosp., Boston, 1943-44, sr. asst. resident medicine, 1948-49, chief resident medicine, 1949-50; fellow medicine Harvard Med. Sch., 1946-48; faculty Georgetown U. Sch. Medicine, 1950—, prof. medicine, 1960—; staff div. cardiology Georgetown U. Hosp., 1950—; cons. Walter Reed Army, VA, U.S. Naval, hosps., Dept. State, NIH. Co-author: Clinical Auscultation of the Heart, rev. edit, 1959; Co-editor: Year Book Series on Cardiology, 1962—; editor-in-chief: Current Problems in Cardiology. Master A.C.P., Am. Coll. Cardiology (Distinguished Tchr. award 1972); mem. Am. Heart Assn. (pres. 1969-70, fellow council clin. cardiology, chmn. 1969-70, Gold Heart award 1972, James Herrick award 1978), Washington Heart Assn. (pres. 1962-64), Assn. U. Cardiologists (sec.-treas. 1967-69, v.p. 1969-70, pres. 1970-71), Assn. Am. Physicians, Clin. and Climatol. Assn., Am. Fedn. Clin. Research, AMA, D.C. Med. Soc., So. Soc. Clin. Research, Clinico-Path. Soc. D.C., Alpha Omega Alpha. Office: care Georgetown U Hosp 3800 Reservoir Rd NW Washington DC 20007

HARVEY, WILLIAM BRANTLEY, JR., lawyer, former state lieutenant governor; b. Walterboro, S.C., Aug. 14, 1930; s. William Brantley and Thelma (Lightsey) H.; m. Helen Coggeshall, Dec. 30, 1952; children: Eileen L., William Brantley, III, Helen C., Margaret D., Warren C. A.B. in Polit. Sci, The Citadel, 1951, LL.D. (hon.), 1978; J.D. magna cum laude, U. S.C., 1955. Bar: S.C. 1955. Since practiced in, Beaufort; sr. partner firm Harvey & Battey; mem. S.C. Ho. of Reps. from Beaufort County, 1958-74, chmn. rules com., mem. constl. revision com.; lt. gov., S.C., 1974-78; local dir. C & S Nat. Bank of S.C.; dir. Tidewater Investment and Devel. Corp.; bd. govs. S.C. Bar. Commr. S.C. Parks, Recreation and Tourism Commn.; Trustee Allen U.; chmn. Beaufort County Democratic Party.; vice chmn. Citadel Devel. Found. Served to lt. AUS, 1952-54. Mem. Am., S.C., Beaufort County bar assns., Phi Beta Kappa, Kappa Alpha, Phi Delta Phi. Presbyterian (elder). Home: 501 Pinckney St Beaufort SC 29902 Office: 1001 Craven St PO Box 1107 Beaufort SC 29902

HARVEY, WILLIAM BURNETT, educator, lawyer; b. Greenville, S.C., Sept. 4, 1922; s. Charles Hugh and Emma (Ballenger) H.; m. Mary Louise Geleide, Mar. 28, 1945; children: Anne Constance, David Kent. A.B., Wake Forest Coll., 1943; J.D., U. Mich., 1948; postgrad., U. Heidelberg, Germany, 1955-56. Bar: D.C. 1949, Mass. With firm Hogan & Hartson, Washington, 1949-51; prof. law U. Mich., 1951-66; prof. law, dean faculty law U. Ghana, 1962-64; prof. law, polit. sci. Ind. U., Bloomington, 1966-73, dean faculty law, 1966-71; on leave as vis. prof. law U. Nairobi, Kenya, 1971, Duke U., 1972, Harvard U., 1977; prof. law and polit. sci. Boston U., 1973—, gen. counsel, 1982—. Contbr. articles to profl. jours. Served to lt. USNR, 1943-46. Mem. Mass. Bar Assn. Democrat. Episcopalian. Home: 137 Marlborough St Boston MA 02116

HARVEY, WILLIAM FRANKLIN, legal educator; b. Eldon, Mo., Oct. 20, 1932; s. Harold Franklin and Marion Jeannette (Carroll) H.; m. Geralene L. Lawrence, Feb. 19, 1956; children: Carolyn J., William L.F. A.B., U. Mo., 1954; J.D., Georgetown U., 1959, LL.M., 1961. Bar: Ind. 1968, Va. 1959, D.C. 1960, U.S. Supreme Ct. 1964. Law clk. Hon. John A. Danaher, U.S. Ct. Appeals, D.C. Circuit, 1960-61, Hon. Thomas D. Quinn D.C. Ct. Appeals, 1959-60; prof. law Washburn U., 1961-68, Ind. U., 1968—, Carl M. Gray prof., 1979—, dean, 1973-79. Contbr. articles in field to profl. jours. Served to lt. U.S. Navy, 1954-56. Fellow Am. Bar Found.; mem. Am. Law Inst., Adminstrv. Conf. U.S., Ind. Bar Assn., Va. Bar Assn., D.C. Bar Assn., ABA, Indpls. Bar Assn. Methodist. Club: Indpls. Athletic. Home: 8949 Sassafras Ct Indianapolis IN 46260 Office: 735 W New York St Indianapolis IN 46202

HARVEY, WILLIAM ROBERT, university president; b. Brewton, Ala., Jan. 29, 1941; s. Willie D. C. and Mamie Claudis (Parker) H.; m. Norma Baker, Aug. 13, 1966; children: Kelly Renee, William Christopher, Leslie Denise. B.A., Talladega Coll., 1961; D.Ed., Harvard U., 1971. Asst. to dean Harvard U. Grad. Sch. Edn., 1969-70; adminstrv. asst. to pres. Fisk U., Nashville, 1970-72; v.p. student affairs/dir. planning Tuskegee (Ala.) Inst., 1972-75, v.p. adminstrv. services, 1976-78; pres. Hampton (Va.) Inst., 1978—; dir. United Va. Bank, Hampton, Newport News Savs. & Loan, Va. Contbr. articles to profl. jours. Bd. dirs. Nat. Merit Scholarship Corp.; bd. dirs. United Way, Peninsula Econ. Devel. Council, Presdl. Scholars Commn.; mem., vice-chmn. President's nat. adv. council ESEA; mem. Harvard U. Alumni Council.; trustee U. Va. Served with U.S. Army, 1962-65. Woodrow Wilson Martin Luther King fellow, 1968-70; Woodrow Wilson Found. intern fellow, 1970-72; Harvard U. Higher Edn. Adminstrv. fellow, 1968-70. Mem. Am. Council Edn., Am. Assn. Higher Edn., Nat. Assn. Equal Opportunity in Higher Edn., Va. Assn. Higher Edn., Peninsula C. of C. (dir.), Omega Psi Phi. Baptist. Office: Hampton Inst Hampton VA 23668 *It is very important today for people to have the opportunity to do some thinking about ethics and morals. It is my firm belief that decency is as important as degrees and this means not only being good doctors, lawyers, professors, engineers and nurses, but good moral leaders who have a sense of community and service as well.*

HARVIE, ERIC A., securities industry educator; b. Edmonton, Atla., Can., 1931; s. Alan D. and Marjorie (Stocks) H.; m. Judith Aykroyd, Jan. 9, 1965; children: Marjorie, Jennnifer. B.A., U. Alta., Edmonton, 1954; M.A., Trinity Coll. Oxford U., Eng., 1956. Editor Maclean Hunter Pub., Toronto, Ont., 1956-61; educator Investment Dealers Assn., Toronto, 1961-70, Can. Securities Inst., 1970—. Author: play Family Property, 1981; editor: Canadian Securities Course, 1964, How to Invest in Canadian Securities, 1961. Home: 25 Hi Mount Dr Willowdale ON Canada M2K 1X3 Office: Can Securities Inst 360 33 Yonge St Toronto ON Canada M5E 1G4

HARVIN, ROGER AUGUST, fast food company executive; b. Joliet, Ill., July 17, 1933; s. Irving and Ruth H.; m. Marsha Roslyn Rosenblum, May 29, 1965; children: Jeri Teresa, Howard Jonathan. B.S., San Diego U., 1960; M.S., UCLA, 1961. Exec. v.p. Church's Fried Chicken, San Antonio, 1968-75, asst. store mgr., 1968-75, pres., chief operating officer, 1975-80, chmn., pres., chief exec. officer, 1980—. Office: 355A Spencer Ln San Antonio TX 78201

HARVIN, WILLIAM CHARLES, lawyer; b. San Francisco, Feb. 15, 1919; s. William Charles and Irma Beth (Hawkins) H.; m. Ruth Helen Beck, Nov. 30, 1942; children: David Tarleton, Susan Elizabeth Harvin Lawhon, Andrew Richard. B.A., U. Tex., 1940, LL.B., 1947. Bar: Tex. 1946. With firm Baker & Botts, Houston, 1947—, partner, 1956—, mng. partner, chmn. exec. com., 1972-84; dir. Tex. Commerce Bancshares, Inc., 1975—; chmn. bd. dirs. Houston C. of C.; chmn. U.S. Circuit Judge Nominating Commn. 5th Circuit; lectr. legal insts. and law schs. Contbr. articles to legal periodicals. Bd. dirs. Tex. Med. Center, Inc., St. Luke's Episcopal Hosp., U. Tex. Health Scis. Center, Houston, San Jacinto History Mus.; trustee St. John's Sch., Houston, Episc. Theol. Sem. of S.W., Austin. Served with USN, 1941-45. Fellow Am. Coll. Trial Lawyers, Am., Tex. bar founds.; mem. Council on Fgn. Relations, Philos. Soc. Tex., Am. Law Inst., Am. Bar Assn., Fedn. Ins. Counsel (pres. 1969-70), Def. Research Inst. (dir. 1969-72), Phi Delta Theta, Phi Delta Phi. Episcopalian (vestry). Clubs: Houston Country, Ramada. Office: Baker & Botts One Shell Plaza Houston TX 77002

HARVIN-WELCH, VIRGINIA RAINES, mathematics educator; b. Louisville, May 14, 1919; d. Verner V. and Clara P. (Rosenberger) Raines; m. W. Scott Harvin, Apr. 21, 1939 (dec. 1960); 1 dau., Ellen Harvin Miller; m. Ronald C. Welch, Aug. 15, 1975. B.S., Limestone Coll., Gaffney, S.C., 1938; M.Ed., U. Louisville, 1955; Ed.D., Ind. U., 1964. Tchr., prin. S.C. Pub. Schs., 1938-52; tchr. Louisville Pub. Schs., 1952-58, counselor, 1958-61; asst. prof. Ky. State U., Bowling Green, 1961-62; assoc. prof. SUNY-Buffalo, 1964-66; prof. Ind. U., Indpls., 1966—; cons. Commonwealth of Ky., 1961-62, Ky. Sch. Corp., Ind. Sch. Corp.; assoc. dir. Metric Fedn. Ind. Contbr. articles to profl. jours. Active Am. Cancer Soc., Multiple Sclerosis. Mem. Nat. Council Tchrs. Math., Diagnostic Math. Tchrs., Ind. Math. Council, Ind. Computer Tchrs., Pi Lambda Theta, Phi Delta Kappa, Kappa Delta Pi. Clubs: Profl. Women, Order Eastern Star. Home: 6315 Brokenhurst Rd Indianapolis IN 46220 Office: Ind U 902 W New York St Indianapolis IN 46223

HARWELL, DAVID WALKER, state justice; b. Florence, S.C., Jan. 8, 1932; s. Baxter Hicks and Lacy (Rankin) Il.; (div.)children—Robert Bryan, William Baxter. LL.B., J.D., U. S.C., 1958. Bar: S.C. bar. Partner firm Harwell & Harwell; circuit judge, S.C., 1973-80; justice S.C. Supreme Ct., 1980—. Mem. S.C. Ho. of Reps., 1962-73. Served with USNR, 1952-54. Mem. Am. Bar Assn., Am. Trial Lawyers Assn., S.C. Bar Assn., S.C. Trial Lawyers Assn. Democrat. Presbyterian. Address: City-County Complex Florence SC 29501

HARWELL, EDWIN WHITLEY, judge; b. Ashland, Ala., June 4, 1929; s. William Thomas and Effie Belle (Whitley) H.; m. Olma Lillian Motes, Nov. 27, 1957. Student, Jacksonville State U., 1948-49; B.S., J.D., U. Ala., 1952. Bar: Ala. bar 1952. Practicing atty., 1954-71, circuit judge, Anniston, Ala., 1971-77, city judge, City of Oxford, 1977—, individual practice law, 1977—. Served with AUS, 1952-54. Mem. Ala. Bar Assn., Calhoun County Bar Assn. (past pres.), V.F.W., Ala. Municipal Judges Assn. (past pres.), United Comml. Travelers. Baptist. Clubs: Elk, Moose., Anniston Exchange (past pres.). Home: 813 Blue Ridge Dr Anniston AL 36201 Office: Anniston AL 36201

HARWELL, RICHARD BARKSDALE, retired librarian; b. Washington, Ga., June 6, 1915; s. Davis Gray and Helen (Barksdale) H. A.B., Emory U., 1937, B.L.S., 1938; D.Litt., New Eng. Coll., 1966. Asst., Flowers collection Duke Library, 1938-40; staff Emory U. Library, 1940-54, asst. librarian, 1948-54; dir. Southeastern Interlibrary Research Facility, 1954-56; dir. publs. Va. State Library, 1956-57; exec. sec. Assn. Coll. and Research Libraries, 1957-61; asso. exec. dir. A.L.A., 1958-61; librarian Bowdoin Coll., Brunswick, Maine, 1961-68, Smith Coll., Northampton, Mass., 1968-70; dir. libraries Ga. So. Coll., Statesboro, 1970-75; curator of rare books and manuscripts U. Ga. Library, 1975-80; bibliog. cons. U. Va. Library, 1953, Boston Athenaeum, 1953; adv. bd. Civil War Centennial Commn.; cons. U. Jordan library, 1966. Author: Confederate Belles-Lettres, 1941, Confederate Music, 1950, Songs of the Confederacy, 1951, Cornerstones of Confederate Collecting, 1953, The Confederate Reader, 1957, More Confederate Imprints, 1957, The Union Reader, 1958, The Alma College Library, (with R.L. Talmadge), 1957, The Arizona State University Library, (with E.T. Moore), 1959, The War They Fought, 1960, Confederate Imprints in the University of Georgia Libraries, 1964, The Confederate Hundred, 1964, Hawthorne and

Longfellow, 1966, Brief Candle, The Confederate Theatre, 1973, The Mint Julep, 1975, (with R. M. Willingham) Georgiana; Editor: Stonewall Jackson and the Old Stonewall Brigade (J.E. Cooke), 1954, Destruction and Reconstruction (Richard Taylor), 1955, The Committees of Safety of Westmoreland and Fincastle, 1956, Cities and Camps of the Confederate States (FitzGerald Ross), 1958, Kate: The Journal of a Confederate Nurse (Kate Cumming), 1959, Outlines from the Outpost (J.E. Cooke), 1961, Lee (1 vol. abridgement of D.S. Freeman's R.E. Lee), 1961, The Colorado Volunteers in New Mexico, 1862 (O.J. Hollister), 1962, A Confederate Marine, 1963, The Uniform and Dress of the Army and Navy of the Conferate States, 1960, Hardtack and Coffee (John D. Billings), 1960, Two Views of Gettysburg (Sir A.J.L. Fremantle, Frank Haskell), 1964, Washington (1 vol. abridgement D.S. Freeman's George Washington), 1969, Georgia Scenes (A.B. Longstreet), 1975, Margaret Mitchell's Gone with the Wind Letters, 1936-49, 1976, GWTW The Screenplay (Sidney Howard), 1980, Gone With the Wind as Book and Film, 1983, The South to Prosperity, 3d edit., 1983; Asso. editor: Emory Sources and Reprints series, 1948-54; editor: College & Research Libraries, 1962-63; Editorial bd.: Emory U. Quar, 1946-54, Civil War History, 1954-69, Jefferson Davis Papers; Contbr.: Conf. Imprints, 1955, The Lasting South, 1957, Lincoln for the Ages, 1960, The Idea of the South, 1964, Vintage Tales, 1984; articles, revs. to gen. and profl. publs. Bd. dirs. Kittredge Found. Served to lt. USNR, 1943-46. Recipient Award of Distinction Atlanta Civil War Round Table, 1983, Nevins-Freeman award Chgo chpt., 1984; Fellow Henry E. Huntington Library, 1951, 67. Mem. Ga. Hist. Soc. (curator 1954-56), Atlanta Hist. Soc. (dir. 1955-56), So. Hist. Soc., ALA, Southeastern Library Assn. (exec. sec. 1952-54), Ga. Library Assn., Am. Antiquarian Soc., Hereward the Wake Soc., Phi Beta Kappa, Sigma Alpha Epsilon. Clubs: Grolier (N.Y.C.); Kiwanis, Symposium (Atlanta). Home: PO Box 607 Washington GA 30673

HARWELL, WILLIAM EARNEST (ERNIE HARWELL), broadcaster; b. Washington, Ga., Jan. 25, 1918; s. Davis Gray H.; m. Lula Tankersley, Aug. 30, 1941; children: William Earnest, Gray Neville, Julie, Carolyn. A.B., Emory U., 1940. Sports dir. Sta. WSB, Atlanta, 1940-43; announcer Atlanta Crackers, 1946-48, Bklyn. Dodgers, 1948-49, N.Y. Giants, 1950-53, Balt. Orioles, 1954-59, Detroit Tigers, 1960—; announcer All-Star games, World Series, NBC, CBS Radio, pro football Balt. Colts, N.Y. Giants. Served with USMC, 1942-46. Inducted into Baseball Hall of Fame, 1981. Mem. ASCAP, Sigma Alpha Epsilon. Presbyterian. Home: 25387 Witherspoon Rd Farmington Hills MI 48018 Office: Tiger Stadium Detroit MI 48216

HARWIT, MARTIN OTTO, astrophysicist, educator; b. Prague, Czechoslovakia, Mar. 9, 1931; came to U.S., 1946, naturalized, 1953; s. Felix Michael and Regina Hedwig (Perutz) Haurowitz; m. Marianne Mark, Feb. 1, 1957; children: Alexander, Eric, Emily. B.A. in Physics, Oberlin Coll., 1951, M.A., U. Mich., Ann Arbor, 1953, postgrad., 1953-54; Ph.D. in Physics, Mass. Inst. Tech., 1960. NATO postdoctoral fellow Cambridge (Eng.) U., 1960-61; NSF fellow Cornell U., Ithaca, N.Y., 1961-62, asst. prof. astronomy, 1962-64, asso. prof., 1964-68, prof., 1968—, chmn. dept. astronomy, 1971-76; E.O. Hulburt fellow Naval Research Lab., Washington, 1963-64; Nat. Acad. Sci. exchange visitor Czechoslovak Acad. Sci., Prague, 1969-70; v.p., dir. Spectral Imaging Inc., Concord, Mass., 1971-77; external mem. Max Planck Inst. Radioastronomy, Bonn., W. Ger., 1979—; cons. NASA.; chmn. space history Nat. Air and Space Mus., Smithsonian Instn., 1983. Author: Astrophysical Concepts, 1973 (transl. into Chinese 1981), (with N.J.A. Sloane) Hadamard Transform Optics, 1979, Cosmic Discovery-The Search, Scope and Heritage of Astronomy, 1981 (transl. into German and French 1982). Served with AUS, 1955-57. Recipient Alexander von Humboldt Found. sr. U.S. scientist award Max Planck Inst. Radioastronomy, 1976-77; NSF grantee, 1963-68; Research Corp. grantee, 1970-75; NASA grantee, 1965—; Air Force Cambridge (Mass.) Research Labs. grantee, 1969—. Mem. Am. Astron. Soc., Am. Phys. Soc., Royal Astron. Soc., AAAS. Research on infrared astron. observations from rockets and aircraft; theoretical astrophysics; cryogenic optics; Hadamard transform optics; history of astron. discoveries. Home: 1105 Taughannock Blvd Ithaca NY 14850 Office: Space Sci Bldg Cornell U Ithaca NY 14853

HARWOOD, DOUGLAS AMEND, marketing consultant; b. N.Y.C., June 17, 1912; s. Brunn and Elsie Amelia (Amend) H.; m. Laura Lucille Turner, Apr. 16, 1952; 1 son, Douglas Turner. B.A., Yale, 1932; postgrad., Columbia, 1934. Welding industry sales engr., 1935-41; exec. asst., liaison officer to Maritime Commn., WPB, 1941-42; regional mgr., asst. dir. devel. N.A.M., 1946-51; cons. Office Civilian Requirements; dir. program planning staff NPA, 1951-52; dir. sales promotion, fleet div. Chrysler Corp., 1952-54; with Mut. Security Program and Fgn. Aid Program, 1955-64, dir. in, East Pakistan, 1958-60, in Mali, Guinea and Equatorial Africa, 1961-64; sr. market devel. officer, dir. mktg. activities Bur. Internat. Commerce, Dept. Commerce, 1964-68, nat. export sales mgr., dir. global mktg. campaigns, dir. program coordination staff, export devel. activities program, 1968-72; dir. U.S. exhbns., 1972-79; cons. to govt. and pvt. industry in field of internat. trade, 1980—. Served to 1st lt. AUS, 1942-46; PTO. Club: Yale (N.Y.C. Washington and Sarasota). Home: Bar H Ranch Rout 2 Box 342-H Sarasota FL 33582

HARWOOD, JERRY, market research executive; b. Jersey City, June 19, 1926; s. Louis and Dorothy (Cohen) Horowitz; m. Ruthella Zimmerman, June 25, 1950; children: Robin Jill, Dean Brook. B.A. cum laude, L.I. U., 1949; M.A., N.Y. U., 1953. Tech. instr. U.S. Bur. Census, 1950-51; account exec. Martin E. Segal (pension and welfare cons.), N.Y.C., 1958-60; v.p., asso. research dir. Kenyon & Eckhardt Advt., N.Y.C., 1962-66; sr. v.p., dir. research Needham, Harper & Steers Advt., N.Y.C., 1966-73; v.p., asso. research dir. Benton & Bowles Advt., N.Y.C., 1975—; mem. Census Adv. Com., 1976—; Mem. research com. Am. Assn. Advt. Agys., Consumer Research Inst., Grocery Mfrs. Am.; mem. bd. N.Y. Inst. Consumer Edn. Bd. dirs. Mus. Black History and Culture, Jewish Counseling Service Agy., Jewish News; mem. Millburn Commn. on Crime, Alcoholism and Drug Abuse, 1972—; chmn. market research div. United Jewish Appeal Greater N.Y., co-chmn., Short Hills, N.J. Served with USAAF, 1944-46. Mem. Am. Mktg. Assn. (founder EFFIE awards, Advt. Effectiveness Awards Program, pres. N.Y.C. chpt. 1970-71, v.p. public policy and issues 1973, nat. v.p. mktg. research 1981-82, nat. v.p., sec.-treas. 1983—), Am. Sociol. Assn., Am. Acad. Polit. and Social Sci., Am. Assn. Pub. Opinion Research, Am. Psychol. Assn., B'nai B'rith. Jewish (pres. temple 1980-82). Home: 22 Athens Rd Short Hills NJ 07078 Office: 909 3d Ave New York NY 10022 *The individual who respects the rights, opinions and needs of others is the individual who manages his own life most productively and successfully.*

HARWOOD, JOHN HENRY, corp. exec.; b. Milw., Apr. 3, 1919; s. Paisley B. and Sylvia (Rehm) H.; m. Betty Ann Cattell, Feb. 10, 1942; children—John C., Nevin R., James C., Christopher R. B.S., U. Mich., 1941, M.B.A., 1942. Sales rep. Metal Goods Corp., St. Louis, 1947-51, personnel dir., 1951-59, sec.-treas., 1959-68, v.p. finance, 1968-69, dir., 1960-69; asst. to pres. Debron Corp. (formerly Mississippi Valley Structural Steel Co.), Chgo., 1969-70, v.p. finance and adminstrn, 1970-74, also dir., 1973-77; pres. John H. Harwood & Co., cons. to mgmt., 1974-78; corp. valuations officer A.G. Edwards & Sons, Inc., 1978-80, v.p., 1980—; dir. Intertherm, Inc., 1975-78. Mem. Am. Soc. Corp. Secs., Financial Execs. Inst. Home: 9 Willow Oak Ln Saint Louis MO 63122 Office: 1 N Jefferson Ave Saint Louis MO 63103

HARWOOD, RICHARD LEE, journalist, newspaper editor; b. Chilton, Wis., Mar. 29, 1925; s. Luther Milton and Ruby (Heath) H.; m. Beatrice Bottrell Mosby, Dec. 18, 1950; children: Helen, John, Richard, David. A.B., Vanderbilt U., 1950. Reporter Nashville Tennessean, 1947-52, Louisville Courier-Jour. and Times, 1952-61, Washington corr., 1961-65; nat. corr. Washington Post, 1966-68, nat. editor, 1968-70, asst. mng. editor, 1970-74, dep. mng. editor, 1976—; v.p. Trenton Times Newspapers, 1974-76. Author: Lyndon, a Biography of L.B. Johnson; Contbr. articles to nat. mags. Served with USMCR, 1942-46; PTO. Recipient citation Nat. Edn. Writers Assn., 1957; George Polk Meml. award L.I. U., 1967, 71; Distinguished Service medal Sigma Delta Chi, 1967, 71; Nieman fellow in Journalism Harvard U., 1955-56; Carnegie fellow in journalism Columbia U., 1965-66. Mem. Soc. Nieman Fellows (dir. So. chpt. 1959-61), A.C.L.U. (dir. Ky. 1959-61), Am. Polit. Sci. Assn. (citation 1960). Democrat. Clubs: Nat. Press, Fed. City (Washington). Office: care Washington Post 1150 15th St NW Washington DC 20071 *

HARWOOD, RICHARD ROBERTS, JR., mfg. co. exec.; b. Balt., May 1, 1921; s. Richard Roberts and Willyhyde (Hart) H.; m. Marion Virginia Smith, Feb. 23, 1946; children—Richard Roberts III, Edward Smith, William Whittingham. A.B., Princeton, 1948. With Mfrs. Record Pub. Co., Balt., 1947-55; v.p. Fleet McGinley Balt., 1955-56; asst. to pres. Young & Selden Co., Balt., 1956-57, exec. v.p., 1957-58, pres., dir., 1958-62, Master Power Corp., Solon, Ohio, 1962-64, chmn. bd., dir., 1964-66; v.p. adminstrn. Black & Decker Mfg. Co., Towson, Md., 1963-66; adminstrv. v.p. Arundel Corp., 1966-69; pres., chief exec. officer Barton-Cotton, Inc., Balt., 1969-75; owner, operator Purnell Art Co., Inc., Balt., 1975—. Trustee Commn. Govt. Efficiency and Economy Inc., Balt., 1954-57, 63—, mem. exec. com., 1963—, chmn., 1970—; chmn. downtown div. A.R.C. campaign, 1954; Bd. dirs. Keswick Home; trustee St. Paul's Sch. for Boys; founding trustee St. Paul's Sch. for Girls, treas., 1958-63. Served with USAAF, 1942-43. Mem. Balt. Jr. Assn. Commerce (pres. 1953-54). Republican. Episcopalian (vestryman, diocesan treas. 1964-72). Home: 303 Club Rd Baltimore MD 21210 Office: 407 N Charles St Baltimore MD 21202

HARWOOD, THOMAS FREDERICK, retail company executive; b. Elgin, Ill., June 24, 1937; m. Fred C. and Catherine (Wolf) H.; m. Carol J. Black, Aug. 16, 1958; children: John, William. B.S., U. Ill.-Chgo., 1959; M.B.A., U. Wis.-Madison, 1964. V.p. growth and devel. Chgo. Osco Drug Stores, 1967-69, v.p. pharmacy, 1969-71; exec. v.p. Mass Feeding Inc., div. Jewel Cos., Inc., Schaumburg, Ill., 1971-73, pres., 1973-81; pres. franchise group Jewel Cos., Inc., Chgo., 1981-83, sr. v.p., 1983—. Home: 1300 Larkin Ave Elgin IL 60120 Office: Jewel Cos Inc 5725 N East River Rd Chicago IL 60631

HARWOOD, VANESSA CLARE, ballet dancer; b. Cheltenham, Eng., 1947; emigrated to Can., 1951, naturalized, 1961; d. Peter G. and Hazel M. (Smith) H.; m. Hugh E. Scully, June 14, 1980. Grad., Nat. Ballet Sch. Can., 1964. Mem. corps Nat. Ballet Can., Toronto, 1965—, soloist, 1967—, prin. dancer, 1970—; tchr. master class U. So. Fla., 1977; tchr. Dance Centre Toronto, 1981; guest artist Australian Ballet, Sydney, 1977, Detroit Symphony, 1977, Chgo. Ballet, 1978, Dominion U., Norfolk, Va., 1978, Dutch Nat. Ballet, Amsterdam, 1979, Munich (Germany) Opera, 1981. Appearances in TV ballet specials. Grantee Can. Council, 1969. Mem. Canadian Actors Equity, Assn. Canadian TV and Radio Artists. Address: 157 King St E Toronto ON M5C 1G9 Canada *If something is meant to be it will be, but achieved by work and perserverance.*

HARZA, RICHARD DAVIDSON, civil engineer; b. Chgo., Oct. 7, 1923; s. Leroy F. and Zelma D. H.; m. Dorothy Goettsch, Apr. 23, 1953; children: Laura A., John D. B.S. in Mech. Engring, Northwestern U., 1944, M.S. in Civil Engring, 1947. Registered profl. engr., Ill. Instr. civil engring. dept. Northwestern U., 1946-47; with Harza Engring. Co., Chgo., 1947—; v.p., dir., dir. U.S. Water and Land Resources Mgmt. Group, 1962-76, v.p., dir., dir. adminstrv., financial and corporate ops., 1976-77; pres., dir., 1977—; dir. Harza Engring. Co. Internat., Harza Overseas Engring. Co., Harza Agrl. Services. Contbr. tech. articles to profl. jours. Served to ensign USNR, 1943-46. Mem. Am. Inst. Cons. Engrs., ASCE, Am. Water Resources Assn. (past pres.), Cons. Engrs. Assn. Ill., Cons. Engrs. Council, Nat., Ill. socs. profl. engrs., U.S. Commn. on Large Dams (past chmn.). Clubs: Metropolitan; Union League, Chicago (Chgo.); Tower. Office: 150 S Wacker Dr Chicago IL 60606 *

HASCHEMEYER, AUDREY ELIZABETH VEAZIE, molecular biologist; b. Chgo., Oct. 31, 1936; d. Waldemar H. and Elizabeth (Gibson) Veazie. B.S. in Chemistry, U. Ill., 1957; Ph.D., U. Calif., 1961. Research assoc. MIT, 1961-64, Harvard U. Med. Sch., 1965-67; assoc. in biol. chemistry Mass. Gen. Hosp., Boston, 1967-69; mem. faculty Hunter Coll., CUNY, 1969—, prof. biology and biochemistry, 1974—, chmn. dept. biol. scis., 1980—; chief scientist R-V Alpha Helix, 1978, USCG Polar Star, 1981; project leader McMurdo Sta., Antarctica, summers 1978-80; sta. sci. leader Palmer Sta., Antarctica, summer 1982. Author numerous papers in field. Recipient Bronze tablet U. Ill., 1957; named Outstanding Woman Scientist N.Y. chpt. Am. Women in Sci., 1981; fellow NSF, 1957-59, Procter & Gamble, 1959-60, UPSHS, 1962-64, Helen Hay Whitney Found., 1964-67; research scholar Am. Cancer Soc., 1976; grantee NIH, NSF, Am. Cancer Soc., CUNY, NATO. Mem Am. Soc. Biol. Chemists; mem. Am. Physiol. Soc., Biophys. Soc.Soc. (council 1976-79, exec. com. 1978-79), Am. Soc. Zoologists, Soc. de Chimie Biologique, Am. Inst. Biol. Scis., Marine Biol. Lab., Sigma Xi. Office: Hunter Coll CUNY 695 Park Ave New York NY 10021

HASELDEN, CLYDE LEROY, librarian; b. Latta, S.C., Aug. 26, 1914; s. Hampton Berry and Mary Beulah (Allen) H.; m. Erva Lee Buchanan, Dec. 3, 1940 (dec. Apr. 15, 1982); 1 dau., Janice Charlotte. B.A., Furman U., 1938; B.S. in L.S, Columbia, 1939; M.A., U. Chgo., 1948. Fellow reference dept. City Coll. N.Y., 1938-39; reference asst. U. Ark., 1939-43; assignee Civilian Pub. Service, 1943-46; librarian Parsons Coll., Fairfield, Iowa, 1947-50, Baldwin-Wallace Coll., 1950-59, Lafayette Coll., 1959-80; coll. and univ. library bldg. cons. Fellow Council on Library Resources, 1972. Contbr. articles to profl. jours. Mem. A.L.A., Ohio Coll. Assn. (pres. 1954-56), Pa. Library Assn., Assn. Coll. and Research Libraries (pres. Phila. 1965-67), AAUP, Phi Kappa Phi. Home: 1921 Washington Blvd Easton PA 18042

HASELHORST, DONALD DUANE, manufacturing company executive; b. Northville, S.D., May 21, 1930; m. Nancy G. Wilz, Aug. 29, 1953; children: Stephen, Linda, Lynn. B.S. in Elec. Engring, S.D. State U., Brookings, 1956. Engr. Univac div. Sperry Rand Corp., St. Paul, 1956-59; v.p. Fabri-Tek Inc., Amery, Wis., 1959-67; chmn., chief exec. officer Nicolet Instrument Corp., Madison, Wis., 1967—; dir. M & I Bank of Madison, Demco Inc., Viking Ins. Co., Realist Inc., Sigma-Aldrich Chem. Co., Union State Bank, Central Life Assurance Co. Pres. Madison Service Clubs Council, 1976-77; bd. dirs. Oakwood Luth. Homes, Madison, 1976—, Madison Gen. Hosp. Served with USAF, 1948-52. Recipient Disting. Engr. award S.D. State U., 1981, Disting. Alumni award S.D. State U., 1982. Mem. IEEE, Am. Mgmt. Assn. (president's council), Sales and Mktg. Assn. (Exec. of Yr. award 1981). Lutheran. Clubs: West Kiwanis (past pres.), Nakoma Golf, Madison. Office: 5225 Verona Rd Madison WI 53711

HASELKORN, ROBERT, virology educator; b. Bklyn., Nov. 7, 1934; s. Barney and Mildred (Seplowin) H.; m. Margot Block, June 23, 1957; children: Deborah, David. A.B., Princeton U., 1956; Ph.D., Harvard U., 1959. Asst. prof. biophysics U. Chgo., 1961-64, asso. prof., 1964-69, prof., chmn. dept., 1969—, F.L. Pritzker prof. biol. scis., 1973—; Cons. virology and rickettsiology study sect. USPHS, 1969-73; mem. sci. adv. bd. Sloan-Kettering Inst., 1972—; chmn. virology study sect. NIH, 1978-80; chmn. sci. adv. bd. Sloan Kettering Inst., 1978-79; mem. nitrogen fixation panel U.S. Dept. Agr., 1978-79. Editor: Virology, 1973—; contbr. to sci. jours. Am. Cancer Soc. postdoctoral research fellow ARC Virus Research Unit, Cambridge, Eng., 1959-61; Guggenheim fellow Institut Pasteur, Paris, 1975; recipient USPHS Research Career Devel. award, 1963-69, Interstate Postgrad. Med. Assn. Research award, 1967. Mem. Am. Soc. Virology (founding; council), Internat. Soc. Plant Molecular Biology (founding; council), Bot. Soc. Am. (Darbaker prize 1982). Home: 5834 S Stony Island Ave Chicago IL 60637

HASELMAYER, LOUIS AUGUST, college president emeritus; b. Newark, June 4, 1911; s. Louis A. and Helen (Kaufhold) H. B.A., Williams Coll., 1933, LL.D. (hon.), 1978; Ph.D., Yale, 1937; M.Div., Gen. Theol. Sem., 1941, D.D., 1974; postgrad., Oxford U., 1952, U. Paris, 1955, Goethe Inst., Munich, 1956, U. Florence, 1960, U. Salzburg, 1961, 65; L.H.D., Iowa Wesleyan Coll., 1980. Instr. U. Minn., 1936-38, Gen. Theol. Sem., N.Y.C., 1938-41; ch. work, 1941-49; dean Cathedral Sch., Dallas, 1949-50; prof. Daniel Baker Coll., Tex., 1950-51; head dept. English Iowa Wesleyan Coll., Mt. Pleasant, 1952—, chmn. div. humanities, 1954, pres., 1970-82, also dir.; Archives. Lit. critic Burlington Hawk-Eye. Author: Lambeth and Unity, 1948, Christmas Past and Christmas Present; poem, 1965, The 125th Anniversary History of Iowa Wesleyan College 1842-1967, 1967; Founder, editor: Design mag, 1954; editor: Iowa Wesleyan Faculty Lecture Series, 1959-69; asso. editor: Anglican Theol. Rev, 1948—, Lyrical Iowa, 1959- 69, Iowa English Yearbook, 1959-63; Contbr. articles and poems to profl. jours. Pres. Community Concert Assn., 1959-64. Mem. Modern. Lang. Assn., Nat. Council Tchrs. English, Coll. English Assn., Ch. Hist. Soc., Phi Beta Kappa, Alpha Psi Omega, Sigma Tau Delta, Lambda Chi Alpha. Club: Rotarian. Home: PO Box 1 Mount Pleasant IA 52641

HASELTON, WILLIAM RAYMOND, paper company executive; b. Glens Falls, N.Y., Jan. 11, 1925; s. Raymond R. and Mary (Vanderwerker) H.; m. Frances C. Crooks, July 10, 1948; children: Susan, Judith, June. B.S. in Chem. Engring, Rensselaer Poly. Inst., 1949; M.S. in Chemistry, Lawrence U., 1951, Ph.D., 1953. With Rhinelander Paper Co. div. St. Regis Paper Co., Rhinelander, Wis., 1953-61, v.p., gen. mgr., 1958-1961; v.p. St. Regis Paper Co., Tacoma, 1961-69, sr. v.p., 1969-71, exec. v.p., 1971-73, pres., 1973-81, chief exec. officer, 1979—, chmn. bd., 1981—, also dir.; dir. Allendale Ins. Co., Johnston, R.I., Allied Inc., Morristown, N.J. Served with USNR, 1943-46. Recipient Westbrook Steele award Inst. Paper Chemistry, 1953. Home: 16 Shagbark Rd Darien CT 06820 Office: St Regis Paper Co 237 park ave New York NY 10017 *

HASEN, BURTON STANLY, artist; b. N.Y.C., Dec. 19, 1921; s. Herman Harold and Mina (Leibowitz) H.; m. Mary Hasen, Nov. 28, 1983. Student, Art Students League, 1940-42, 46, H. Hoffmann Sch. Fine Arts, 1947-48, Acad. dela Grande-Chaumiere, Paris, 1948-50, Acad. delle Belle-Arti, 1959-60. Tchr. Sch. Visual Arts, N.Y.C., 1953—, Mpls. Sch. Art and Design, 1966. One-man shows include, T'Pandje Gallerie, Belgium, 1981, group shows include, Mus. Modern Art, Paris, 1951, Whitney Mus. Am. Art, N.Y.C., 1964, Corcoran Gallery Art, Washington, 1959, Kresge Art Center, U. So. Ill., 1961, Am. Acad. Arts and Letters, N.Y.C., 1965, Berlin Acad. Arts, 1956, W.G. Picker Gallery, 1969, Colgate U., Hamilton, N.Y., Mus. Modern Art, N.Y.C., 1966, Met. Mus. Art, N.Y.C., 1952, Worcester (Mass.) Art Mus., 1968, Walker Art Center, Mpls., 1966, Bklyn. Mus., 1954; represented in permanent collections, Walker Art Center, Worcester Art Mus., Hampton Inst.; illustrator books, 1959-62. Served with AUS, 1942-46. Recipient Emily Lowe Found. Purchase prize, 1955. Office: 209 E 23d St New York NY 10010 *The motivating force of my life has been the desire to paint meaningful paintings that express my deepest inner feelings. Art for me is the exhilerating experience of discovering new worlds. Each work is a projection of myself into the universe. This compulsion to paint my fantasy has never faultered, and has never deceived me.*

HASEN, IRWIN HANAN, cartoonist; b. N.Y.C., July 8, 1918; s. Jack and Serena (Weinberg) H. Student, NAD, 1938-40, Art Student League, N.Y.C., 1939-40. Creator: comic cartoon strip The Goldbergs; co-creator: cartoon strip Dondi, 1955—. Served with AUS, 1944-46. Mem. Nat. Cartoonist Soc., Comics Council. Jewish. Office: care Chgo Tribune-NY News Syndicate Inc News Bldg 220 E 42d St New York NY 10017 *

HASERICK, JOHN ROGER, dermatologist; b. Mpls., Sept. 23, 1915; s. Ernest B. and Addie (Swanson) H.; m. Jane Margaret Fleckenstein, May 10, 1941; children—John Roger, Jane. B.A., Macalester Coll., 1937; M.D., U. Minn., 1941, M.S. in Dermatology, 1946. Diplomate: Am. Bd. Dermatology (pres. 1975). Intern Ancker Hosp., St. Paul, 1940-41; resident in medicine Univ. Hosps., Mpls., 1941-42, resident in dermatology, 1945-46; practice medicine specializing in dermatology, Pinehurst, N.C., 1970—; head dept. dermatology Cleve. Clinic, 1948-67; prof. Case Western Res. U., Cleve., 1967-70; clin. prof. medicine and dermatology Duke U., Durham, N.C., 1970—; with Pinehurst Dermatology Clinic, 1970—. Contbr. articles to med. jours.; Author: LE Primer, 1972. Served with U.S. Army, 1942-46. Fellow ACP; mem. AMA (Hektoen Silver award 1952), Am. Acad. Dermatology (pres. 1974), Am. Soc. Dermatopathology (pres. 1975), N.C. Med. Assn., Am. Soc. Investigative Dermatology, Am. Dermatol. Assn. Republican. Clubs: Country of N.C., Wolves (Pinehurst). Discovered LE factor in blood of patients with lupus erythematosus. Home: PO Box 669 Pinehurst NC 28374 Office: Pinehurst Dermatology PA Pinehurst Med Center Pinehurst NC 28374

HASKAYNE, RICHARD FRANCIS, petroleum company executive; b. Calgary, Alta., Can., Dec. 18, 1934; s. Robert Stanley and Bertha (Hesketh) H.; m. Lee Mary Murray, June 25, 1958. B.Comm., U. Alta., 1956; postgrad., U. Western Ont., 1968. Chartered acct., Alta. With Riddell, Stead & Co., chartered accts., Calgary, 1956-60; with Hudson's Bay Oil & Gas Co., Ltd., Calgary, 1960-81, v.p., treas., controller, 1970-73, sr. v.p., 1975-77, exec. v.p., dir., 1977-80, pres., dir., 1980-81; pres., chief exec. officer Home Oil Co., Calgary, 1982—; controller Can. Arctic Gas Pipeline Ltd., Calgary, 1973-75. Bd. dirs. Alta. Children's Hosp. Found., Alta. Pediatric Research Center, 1977—. Mem. Alta. Inst. Chartered Accts., Can. Petroleum Assn. (bd. govs.), Kappa Sigma. Club: Calgary Petroleum (dir. 1983—). Home: 6942 Leaside Dr SW Calgary AB T3E 6H5 Canada Office: 324 8th Ave SW Calgary AB T2P 2Z5 Canada

HASKELL, ALBERT RUSSELL, coll. adminstr.; b. Waterville, Maine, July 6, 1925; s. Kennard Gordon and Florence Maude (Kilton) H.; m. Mary M. Gerth, July 18, 1946; children—Daniel Lee, Alene Venn. B.S. in Pharmacy, U. Kans., 1950, M.S., 1951; Ph.D., U. Fla.,

1956. Head dept. pharmacology-toxicology Jensen-Salsbury Lab., Kansas City, Mo., 1956-59; research dir. Marion Labs., Inc., Kansas City, Mo., 1959-63; sci. dir., 1963-65; faculty pharmacy, dental research U. Tenn. Med. Center, Memphis, 1965-67, 71-72, exec. asst. to chancellor, acting vice chancellor, 1967-71; dean, prof. Coll. Pharmacy, U. Nebr. Med. Center, Omaha, 1972—. Mem. adv. council Nat. Inst. Environ. Health Scis., 1976-80. Served with USNR, 1942-46. Named Tenn. Pharmacist of Yr., 1967. Mem. Am. Pharm. Assn., Nebr. Pharm. Assn., N.Y. Acad. Scis., AAAS. Republican. Methodist. Clubs: Masons, Shriners. Home: 9633 Parker St Omaha NE 68114 Office: Coll Pharmacy U Nebr Med Center 42d and Dewey Ave Omaha NE 68105

HASKELL, ARTHUR JACOB, steamship company executive; b. Newark, Apr. 16, 1926; s. Isidore David and Elena (Greenbaum) H.; m. Amparo Serrano, Dec. 31, 1958 (div.); children: Aparo Rocio, Vincent Isidore, Joaquin Arthur. B.S., U.S. Naval Acad., 1947; postgrad., MIT, 1950-53. Sr. procurement engr. Nat. Bulk Carriers, N.Y.C., 1956-62; asst. plant mgr. Western Gear Corp., Belmont, Calif., 1962-64; project engr. Matson Nav. Co., San Francisco., 1964-70, v.p., 1970-73, sr. v.p., 1973. Bd. dirs. San Francisco Marine Exchange, 1975-78, v.p., 1976-77, pres., 1977-78. Served to comd. USN, 1947-56. Mem. Soc. Naval Architects and Marine Engrs. (chmn. No. Calif. sect. 1971-72, v.p. 1973-83, exec. com. 1977-80, hon. v.p. for life 1983—), Nat. Reserch Council (Marine bd. 1981—). Home: 24 Via Cheparro Greenbrae CA 94904 Office: Matson Navigation Co 333 Market St San Francisco CA 94105

HASKELL, BARBARA, curator; b. San Diego, Nov. 13, 1946; d. John N. and Barbara (Freeman) H. B.A., UCLA, 1969. Dir. Exptl. Arts Festival U. Calif., Los Angeles, 1966; asst. registrar Pasadena (Calif.) Art Mus., 1969, curatorial asst., 1970, asst. curator, 1970, assoc. curator, 1970-72, curator painting and sculpture, 1972-74, dir. exhbns. and collections, 1974; curator Whitney Mus. Am. Art, N.Y.C., 1975—. Office: Whitney Museum American Art New York NY 10021

HASKELL, BLANTON WINSHIP, wood pulp co. exec.; b. Savannah, Ga., Mar. 28, 1920; s. George Owens and Frances Ralls (Winship) H.; m. Myrtice Harris Draughon, July 7, 1943; children—Robert Winship, Sally Gordon. B.S. in Mech. Engring, Ga. Sch. Tech., 1942. With Gen. Electric Co., Schenectady, 1946-47; resident engr. Rayonier, Inc., Fernandina, Fla., 1947-53, resident mgr., 1957, Jesup, Ga., 1958-66, asst. gen. mfg. mgr., 1967; dir. planning ITT-Rayonier, Inc., N.Y.C., 1968-69, v.p. planning, 1971-73, sr. v.p. operations, planning research, devel. and engring., 1973-75, sr. engring. and environ., 1976—; also dir.; acting pres. Rayonier Quebec, 1972-75, pres., 1975-76; also dir., mem. exec. com.; dir., mem. exec. com. Rayonier Can., 75; dir. spl. projects natural resources ITT, 1976; mgmt. cons. to pulp and paper industry, 1977—. Served to capt. AUS, World War II; ETO. Decorated Purple Heart. Mem. TAPPI, Can. Pulp and Paper Assn., Tau Beta Pi. Home: 740 Wilmington Island Rd Savannah GA 31410

HASKELL, JOHN HENRY FARRELL, JR., investment banking company executive; b. N.Y.C., Jan. 24, 1932; s. John Henry Farrell and Paulette (Heger) H.; m. Francine G. Le Roux, June 30, 1955; children: Michael J., Christopher E., Diana F. T. B.S., U.S. Mil. Acad., 1953; M.B.A. with distinction, Harvard U., 1958. Assoc. Dillon, Read & Co., N.Y.C., 1958-61, mgr. European office, Paris, 1961-66, v.p., N.Y.C., 1964-75, mng. dir., 1975—; pres., dir. Scandinavian Securities Corp., Moet-Hennessy U.S. Corp., ASA Ltd., Dynalectron Corp.; dir. Dillon Read Ltd.; mem. adv. council Overseas Pvt. Investment Co., 1972-75. Served with U.S. Army, 1953-56. Decorated croix de chavalier Ordre National du Merite, France. Mem. Securities Industry Assn. (internat. fin. com.), Council Fgn. Relations, French-Am. C. of C. (dir.). Clubs: Links (N.Y.C.); Piping Rock (Locust Valley, N.Y.). Home: 120 East End Ave New York NY 10028 Office: Dillon & Read & Co 535 Madison Ave New York NY 10022

HASKELL, JOSEPH FARRELL, management consultant; b. Ft. Omaha, Nebr., July 1, 1908; s. Gen. William Nafew and Winifred (Farrell) H.; m. Elizabeth Weld Brett, 1962; children by former marriage—William N., Julia (Mrs. Hugh E. Paine, Jr.), Janet (Mrs. Charles Spalding). B.S., U.S. Mil. Acad., 1930; grad., Command and Gen. Staff Sch., 1940. Commd. 2d lt. U.S. Army, 1930, advanced through grades to col., 1946; assigned posts in, U.S., Philippines, 1930-41, asst. chief of staff for intelligence, 1941-42, staff, London, Eng., 1943, chief secret ops., London, 1943, comdr., 1944-45, asst. chief of staff, 1945-46, assigned, 1946, ret., 1946; with Nat. Distillers & Chem. Corp., N.Y.C., 1946-63, v.p. indsl. relations, 1957-63; v.p. Rogers Slade & Hill, N.Y.C., 1964-69; chmn. Haskell & Stern Assocs., Inc., N.Y.C., 1969-82. Decorated Silver Star, Legion of Merit, Bronze Star medal with cluster, U.S.; Legion of Honor; Croix de Guerre with palm, France; King Christian X's Medal of Liberation, Denmark). Roman Catholic. Club: Union (N.Y.C.). Home: 136 E 64th St New York NY 10021 Office: 529 Fifth Ave New York NY 10017

HASKELL, PETER ABRAHAM, actor; b. Boston, Oct. 15, 1934; s. Norman Abraham and Rose Veronica (Golden) H.; m. Ann Compton, Feb. 27, 1960 (div. 1974); m. Dianne Tolmich, Oct. 26, 1974; children: Audra Rosmary, Jason Abraham. B.A., Harvard U., 1962. Appeared in: off-Broadway play The Love Nest, 1963; films include Finnegans Wake, 1965, Legend of Earl Durand, 1972, Christina, 1974; Appeared in: TV series Bracken's World, NBC, 1968-70, Rich Man Poor Man, Book II, ABC, 1976-77, Ryan's Hope, ABC, 1982-83, Search for Tomorrow, NBC, 1983—. Served with U.S. Army, 1954-56. Mem. Screen Actors Guild (dir.), Actors Equity, AFTRA, Am. Film Inst. Democrat. Office: care Jack Fields & Assos 9255 Sunset Blvd Suite 1105 Los Angeles CA 90069

HASKELL, ROBERT NELSON, bus. exec.; b. Bangor, Maine, Aug. 24, 1903; s. Hiram S. and Maude M. (Gulliver) H. B.S. in Elec. Engring, U. Maine, 1925. Design engr. Bangor Hydro-Electric Co., Maine, 1925, field engr., 1926-27, v.p., comml. mgr., 1928-34, v.p., gen. mgr., 1935-58, pres., 1958-77, chmn. bd., chief exec. officer, 1977—; dir. Maine Electric Power Co.; pres. East Br. Improvement Co. Mem. Maine Ho. of Reps., 1945-46; mem. Maine Senate, 1947-53, pres. senate, 1955-59; gov. State of Maine, Jan. 2-Jan. 8, 1959; Pres., dir. Bangor Humane Soc. Mem. NAM, Phi Gamma Delta. Republican. Club: Mason. Home: 645 Hammond St Bangor ME 04401 Office: 33 State St Bangor ME 04401

HASKETT, MARY ELLEN, journalist; b. Fond du Lac, Wis., Oct. 8, 1952; d. Gerald Michael and Eleanore Katherine (Konen) H. Student, U. Iowa, 1971-72; B.A., U. Wis., 1975. With UPI, Cheyenne, Wyo., 1975—, bur. mgr., Annapolis, Md., 1977-78, state editor for Md. and Del., Balt., 1978-81, for Pa., Phila., 1981-82, regional exec. Md., Del., N.J., 1982-83, N.E. sales mgr., Boston, 1983—. Office: One Herald Sq 300 Harrison Ave Boston MA 02118

HASKIN, LARRY ALLEN, scientist, educator; b. Olathe, Kans., Aug. 17, 1934; s. Harvard Glenn and Mary Virginia (Callaway) H.; m. Mary Anita Gehl, Dec. 21, 1963; children: Dierk Allen, Rachel Lee, Jean Marie. B.A., Baker U., 1955; Ph.D., U. Kans., 1960. Asst. prof. Ga. Inst. Tech., 1959-60; instr. U. Wis., Madison, 1960-61, asst. prof., 1961-65, asso. prof., 1965-68, prof. chemistry, 1968-73; cons. NASA, 1970-73, Argonne Nat. Lab., 1960-68; chief planetary and earth scis. div. NASA-JSC, 1973-76; prof. earth and planetary scis. Washington U., St. Louis, 1976—, chmn. dept., 1976—; mem. mercury rev. panel Nat. Acad. Scis., 1970-71; mem. U.S. Nat. Com. on Geochemistry, 1975-78, NASA Solar System Exploration Com., 1983—. Recipient Exceptional Sci. Achievement award NASA, 1971; Guggenheim fellow Max Planck Inst. for Nuclear Physics, Heidelberg, Germany, 1966-67. Mem. Am. Chem. Soc., Geochem. Soc., Am. Geophys. Union, A.A.A.S., Phi Beta Kappa, Sigma Xi. Research on trace inorganic elements in meteoritic, lunar and terrestrial matter.

HASKIN, MARVIN EDWARD, radiologist, educator; b. Ardmore, Pa., May 28, 1930; m. Pamela Herr. B.A., Temple U., Phila., 1951, M.D., 1955. Diplomate: Am. Bd. Radiology. Intern Phila. Gen. Hosp., 1955-56, resident, 1956-57, 59-61; instr. radiology Temple U., 1961-63; chief diagnostic radiology Phila. Gen. Hosp., 1961-63; assoc. radiologist Hahnemann Hosp., Phila., 1964-66, clin. asst. prof., 1967-70, research asst. prof., 1969; prof. radiology, chmn. dept. Hahnemann U., Phila., 1970—; secretariat-chmn. Ansi N-44, N.Y.C., 1982—; rep. Ansi PH-2, N.Y.C., 1984—; cons. Internat. Electrotechnical Commn., 1984—. Author: Roentgenologic Diagnosis, 1979, Surgical Radiology, 1981; editor: The Radiologic Clinics of North America, 1972, 83. Mem. Gov.'s Task Force on Nutrition, Chgo., 1974. Served with USAF, 1957-59. Fellow Am. Coll. Radiology, ACP, Phila. Coll. Physicians, Soc. Advanced Med. Systems; mem. Phila. Roentgen Ray Soc. (sec. 1974-77, Blue Ribbon 1982), Radiol. Soc. N.Am. Office: Dept Diagnostic Radiology Hahnemann U Broad St and Vine St Philadelphia PA 19102

HASKINS, CARYL PARKER, research scientist, educator; b. Schenectady, Aug. 12, 1908; s. Caryl Davis and Frances Julia (Parker) H.; m. Edna Ferrell, July 12, 1940. Ph.B., Yale U., 1930; Ph.D., Harvard U., 1935; D.Sc., Tufts Coll., 1951, Union Coll., 1955, Northeastern U., 1955, Yale U., 1958, Hamilton Coll., 1959, George Washington U., 1963; LL.D., Carnegie Inst. Tech., 1960, U. Cin., 1960, Boston Coll., 1960, Washington and Jefferson Coll., 1961, U. Del., 1965, Pace U., 1974. Staff mem. research lab. Gen. Electric Co., Schenectady, 1931-35; research asso. Mass. Inst. Tech., 1935-45; pres., research dir. Haskins Labs., Inc., 1935-55, dir., 1935—, chmn. bd., 1969—; research prof. Union Coll., 1937-55; pres. Carnegie Instn. of Washington, 1956-71, also trustee, 1949—; Asst. liaison officer OSRD, 1941-42, sr. liaison officer, 1942-43; exec. asst. to chmn. NDRC, 1943-44, dep. exec. officer, 1944-45; sci. adv. bd. Policy Council, Research and Devel. Bd. of Army and Navy, 1947-48; cons. Research and Develop. Bd., 1947-51, to sec. def., 1950-60, to sec. state, 1950-60; mem. Pres.'s Sci. Adv. Com., 1955-58, cons., 1959-70; mem. Pres.'s Nat. Adv. Commn. on Libraries, 1966-67, Joint U.S.-Japan Com. on Sci. Coop., 1961-67, Internat. Conf. Insect Physiology and Ecology, 1971-73; panel advisers Bur. East Asian and Pacific Affairs, Dept. State, 1966-68; mem. Sec. Navy Adv. Com. on Naval History, 1971-83, vice chmn., 1975-83. Author: Of Ants and Men, 1939, The Amazon, 1943, Of Societies and Men, 1950, The Scientific Revolution and World Politics, 1964; contbr. to anthologies and tech. papers.; Editor: The Search for Understanding, 1967; Chmn. bd. editors: Am. Scientist, 1971—; chmn. publs. com., 1971—. Trustee Carnegie Corp. N.Y., 1955-80, hon. trustee, 1980—, chmn. bd., 1975-80; trustee Rand Corp., 1955-65, 66-75; fellow Yale Corp., 1962-77; regent Smithsonian Instn., 1956-80, regent emeritus, 1980—, mem. exec. com., 1958-80; bd. dirs. Council Fgn. Relations, 1961-75, Population Council, 1955-80, Ednl. Testing Service, 1958-61, 67-71; chmn. bd. Ednl. Testing Service, 1969-71, Center for Advanced Study in Behavioral Scis., 1960-75, Thomas Jefferson Meml. Found., 1972-78, Council on Library Resources, 1965—, Pacific Sci. Center Found., 1962-72, Asia Found., 1960—, Marlboro Coll., 1962-77, Wildlife Preservation Trust Internat., Inc., 1976—, Nat. Humanities Center, 1977—; trustee Woods Hole Oceanographic Instn., 1964-73, mem. council, 1973—; bd. dirs. Franklin Book Programs, 1953-58; mem. Save-The-Redwoods League, 1943—, mem. council, 1955—; Mem. vis. coms. Harvard, Johns Hopkins; bd. visitors Tulane U. Recipient Presdl. Certificate of Merit, U.S., 1948, King's medal for Service in Cause of Freedom, Gt. Britain, 1948. Fellow Am. Phys. Soc., A.A.A.S. (dir. 1971-75), Am. Acad. Arts and Scis., Royal Entomol. Soc., Entomol. Soc. Am., Pierpont Morgan Library; mem. N.Y. Zool. Soc., Washington Acad. Scis., Nat. Geog. Soc. (trustee 1964—, finance com. 1972—, com. on research and exploration 1972—, exec. com. 1972—), Royal Soc. Arts (Benjamin Franklin fellow), Faraday Soc., Met. Mus. Art, Am. Mus. Natural History (trustee 1973—, bd. mgmt. 1973—), Am. Philos. Soc. (councillor 1976-78, 81-83), Brit. Assn. Advancement Sci., Linnean Soc. London, Internat. Inst. Strategic Studies, Asia Soc., Japan Soc., Biophys. Soc., Nat. Acad. Sci., N.Y. Acad. Scis., Audubon Soc., N.Y. Bot. Garden, P.E.N., Pilgrims, Phi Beta Kappa, Sigma Xi (nat. pres. 1966-68, dir. 1966—), Delta Sigma Rho, Omicron Delta Kappa. Episcopalian. Clubs: Somerset, St. Botolph (Boston); Century, Yale, Coffee House (N.Y.C.); Mohawk (Schenectady); Metropolitan, Cosmos (Washington) (bd. mgmt. 1973-76); Lawn (New Haven)). 22 Green Acre Ln Westport CT 06880 Home: 1545 18th St NW Washington DC 20036 Office: 2100 M St NW Washington DC 20037

HASKINS, GEORGE LEE, lawyer, educator; b. Cambridge, Mass., Feb. 13, 1915; s. Charles Homer and Clare (Allen) H.; m. Anstiss Crowninshield Boyden, July 15, 1944 (dec. 1978). Classical diploma, Phillips Exeter Acad., 1931; A.B. summa cum laude, Harvard U., 1935, J.D., 1942; M.A. (hon.), U. Pa., 1971. Bar: Mass. 1943, ICC 1951, Pa. 1952, Maine 1968, U.S. Supreme Ct. 1952, various fed. cts. in 1st and 3d circuits. Jr. fellow Soc. of Fellows, Harvard U., 1936-42, lectr. dept. sociology, 1937-38; Lowell lectr., Boston, 1938; assoc. Herrick, Smith, Donald & Farley, Boston, 1942; with office of spl. asst. to sec. of state, 1946; asst. prof. law U. Pa., 1946-48, assoc. prof., 1948-49, prof., 1949—, Algernon Sydney Biddle prof., 1974—, mem. faculty arts and scis., 1976—; ofcl. observer War Dept.; rep. U.S. delegation to UN Conf., San Francisco, 1945; spl. atty. legal dept. Pa. R.R., 1951-54, cons. counsel, 1954-70; apptd. by Pres. Eisenhower to Permanent Com. on Oliver Wendell Holmes Devise, 1956; asst. reporter for Supreme and Superior Cts. Pa., 1970-72; Univ. seminar assoc. Columbia, 1971-73, 77—; U.S. Supreme Ct. Hist. Soc. lectr., 1981; Permanent mem. Jud. Conf. U.S. Third Circuit; vice chmn. com. on legal history fellowships Am. Bar Found., 1978—; dir., v.p. Pa. Mut. Fund, N.Y.C., 1961-68. Author: The Statute of York and the Interest of the Commons, 1935, The Growth of English Representative Government, 1948, (with others) American Law of Property, 1952, (with M.P. Smith) Pennsylvania Fiduciary Guide, 1957, 2d edit., 1962, Law and Authority in Early Massachusetts, 1960, 2d edit., 1977, A History of the Town of Hancock, Maine, 1978, (with others) A History of the U.S. Supreme Court, vol. 2, part 1: John Marshall Foundations of Power, 1981; also numerous articles in U.S., fgn. periodicals; contbr.: Ency. Britannica; mem. panel of authors preparing: History of U.S. Supreme Ct. (authorized by Congress), 1958; Editor: Death of a Republic (John Dickinson), 1963, Phi Beta Kappa series, 1934-37; Adv. bd. editors: Speculum, 1949-69; bd. editors: William and Mary Quar., 1969-70, Papers of John Marshall, Williamsburg, Va., (with others) Justice Bradley papers, Studies in Legal History. Mem. Hancock (Maine) 1976 Bicentennial Commn., 1978, Sesquicentennial History Commn., Internat. Commn. for History of Rep. Instns.; mem. humanities council Sta. WHYY-TV, Phila., Wilmington, Del., 1976—. Served with CAC AUS, 1942-43; from 1st lt. to capt. War Dept. Gen. Staff, 1943-46; from 1st lt. to capt. Gen. Staff Corps, 1945; maj. Res., 1946-54. Decorated Army Commendation medal with oak leaf clusters, various merit citations U.S. Army and sec. of state, 1946; Demoblzn. award Social Sci. Research Council, 1946; elected Consejero del Instituto Internacional para Unificacion Derecho Publico, 1956; John Simon Guggenheim fellow, 1957. Fellow Royal Hist. Soc., Am. Soc. for Legal History (hon.); mem. Am., Mass., Maine, Pa., Phila. bar assns., Assn. Bar City of N.Y., Hancock County Bar Assn., Swedish Colonial Soc., Am. Judicature Soc., Am. Arbitration Assn. (nat. panel arbitrators 1968—), Société Internationale pour l'Histoire du Droit (council 1970, 75—), Am. Soc. for Legal History (pres. 1970-74, dir. 1977-80), Am. Antiquarian Soc., Internat. Law Soc., Soc. Colonial Wars, Am. Acad. Polit. Sci., Am. Hist. Assn., Am. Law Inst. (hon. life mem.), Assn. ICC Practitioners, Juristic Soc., Brit. Records Assn., Mediaeval Acad. Am. (council 1958-60), Soc. Comparative Legis., Colonial Soc. Mass., Mass. Hist. Soc. (corr. mem.), Maine Hist. Soc., Va. Hist. Soc., Colonial Soc. Pa. (gov.'s council 1977), Art Alliance Phila., Selden Soc., Am. Geneal. Soc., Geneal. Soc. Pa., Inst. Early Am. History and Culture (council, editorial bd.), Société Jean Bodin Pour l' Histoire Comparative des Institutions, Société Internationale pour l'Etude de Philosophie Medievale (membre titulaire), Academie d'Histoire Européenne (hon. corr.), S.R., Mayflower Descs., Boston Athenaeum, Library Co. Phila., U.S. Ct. Tennis Assn., Order of Coif (award for scholarly writing Pa. chpt. 1982), Am. Soc. Ancient Instruments, Am. Soc. 18th Century Studies, Internat. Soc. St. Thomas Aquinas, Mil. Order Fgn. Wars U.S. (companion), Soc. War 1812, New. Eng. Land Title Assn., Hancock Hist. Soc. (dir. 1979-80), Phi Beta Kappa. Clubs: Somerset (Boston); Legal, Racquet, Harvard (Phila.); Met. (Washington); Brit. Schs. and Univs., Pilgrims of U.S., Century (N.Y.C.); Royal Automobile (London). Home: PO Box 760 Paoli PA 19301 Office: 3400 Chestnut St Philadelphia PA 19104 Office: PO Box 97 Hancock ME 04640

HASKINS, JACK BURTON, communications educator; b. Macon, Ga., Mar. 20, 1922; s. DeForest Algood and Fleeta (Ward) H.; m. Tommie Spann, Nov. 7, 1976; 1 son, Casey Reed. A.B., U. Ga., 1949; M.A., Emory U., 1951; Ph.D., U. Minn., 1959. News editor Gainesville (Ga.) News, 1949-50; instr., asst. research dir. Sch. Journalism, U. Minn., 1951-56; sr. research exec. Curtis Pub. Co., Phila., 1956-61; advt. research mgr. (Ford div.), Dearborn, Mich., 1961-63; prof., chmn. mass communications Ind. U., 1963-66; John Ben Snow research prof. Syracuse (N.Y.) U., 1966-71, also dir.; dir. (Communications Research Center); prof. Coll. Communications, U. Tenn., Knoxville, 1971—; Gannett Disting. vis. prof. U. Fla., 1978-79; chmn. bd. So. Opinion, Mktg. and Advt. Research, Inc., Knoxville. Author: How to Evaluate Mass Communication, 1968, Advertising Research and Testing, 1969, Introduction to Advertising Research, 1976; Contbr. articles profl. jours. Served with USNR, 1943-46, 52-54. Fellow Am. Psychol. Assn.; mem. Am. Assn. Pub. Opinion Research, Assn. for Edn. in Journalism, Internat. Communications Assn., Phi Beta Kappa, Phi Kappa Phi. Office: Coll Communications U Tenn Knoxville TN 37916

HASLER, ARTHUR DAVIS, educator; b. Lehi, Utah, Jan. 5, 1908; s. Walter Thalmann and Ada (Broomhead) H.; m. Hanna Prusse, Sept. 6, 1932 (dec.); children: Sylvia (Mrs. Gilbert Thatcher), A. Frederick, Mark, Bruce, Galen, Karl; m. Hatheway Minton, July 24, 1971. B.A., Brigham Young U., 1932; Ph.D., U. Wis., 1937; D.Sc., U. Nfld., 1967. Aquatic biologist U.S. Fish and Wildlife Service, 1935-37; instr., prof. U. Wis., Madison, 1937-78, prof. emeritus, 1979—, chmn. dept. zoology, 1953, 55-57, dir. Lab. Limnology, 1963-79; chmn. com. freshwater productivity internat. biol. program, 1964-74, Nat. Acad. Sci.-NRC, 1963-70; chmn. nat. com. Internat. Union Biol. Scis., 1965-69, chmn. com. ecology, 1966-69; pres. Internat. Congress Limnology, 1962, Internat. Assn. Ecology, 1962-74; dir. The Inst. Ecology, 1971-74; Disting. prof. U. Va., 1981, Tex. A & M U., 1979. Author: Underwater Guideposts, 1966; Contbr. articles to profl. jours. French horn player, mem. exec. com. Madison Civic Music Assn., 1937-65; chmn. Lake Mendota Problems Com., 1965-72. Fulbright research scholar, Germany, 1955, Finland, 1963; recipient Disting. Service award Am. Inst. Biol. Scis., 1980, Soil Sci. Soc. Am., 1980, Nat. Sea Grant Assn., 1980. Fellow Societas Zoologica Botanica Fennica Finland, Phila. Acad. Sci., Am. Acad. Arts and Sci., Royal Netherlands Acad. Sci.; mem. Am. Behavioral Soc., A.A.A.S. (past v.p. div. F), Am. Soc. Limnology and Oceanography (past pres.), Ecol. Soc. Am. (past pres.), Am. Fisheries Soc. (award of excellence 1977), Am. Soc. Naturalists (past v.p.), Am. Soc. Zoologists (pres. 1971), Nat. Acad. Scis. U.S., Internat. Assn. Limnology, Phi Kappa Phi (hon.). Mem. Ch. of Jesus Christ of Latter-day Saints. Home: 1233 Sweet Briar Rd Madison WI 53705

HASPEL, STANLEY JOEL, advt. agy. exec.; b. N.Y.C., Nov. 6, 1931; s. Irving Max and Lillian H.; m. Elaine Rita Tabin, Sept. 19, 1959; children—Marc, Scott, Samantha. B.B.A., Baruch Sch., CCNY, 1953; LL.B., Bklyn. Law Sch., 1959. Bar: N.Y. bar 1959. Gen. practice law, N.Y.C., 1959-69; with Wells, Rich, Greene, Inc., N.Y.C., 1970—, sr. v.p. legal, 1979—; dir. A.A.A.A. Ins. Co. Pres., Lindenwood Civic Assn., 1965-67. Served with AUS, 1953-55. Mem. N.Y. County Lawyers Assn. Office: 767 Fifth Ave New York NY 10022

HASS, ANTHONY, food co. exec.; b. Vienna, Austria, Dec. 15, 1923; m. Patricia Cary Cecil, July 20, 1957; children—Anthony, Elizabeth, John. B.S.E. in Chem. Engring, Princeton U., 1944. Research chemist Hercules Powder Co., Wilmington, Del., 1944-46; Del., sci. cons. U.S. Army Intelligence, 1946-47; dir., gen. mgr. Kilgore Chems., Inc., Washington, 1947-49; div. mgr. Atlantic Research Corp., Alexandria, Va., 1949-54; pres. Dryomatic Corp., Alexandria, 1954-62; v.p. LogEtronics, Inc., Alexandria, 1962-65; dir. adminstrn. internat. div. Schering Corp., Bloomfield, N.J., 1965-68; v.p. Mergers & Acquisition, Inc., Washington, 1968-69; v.p. external devel. Gen. Foods Corp., White Plains, N.Y., 1969—. Mem. Newcomen Soc. N.Am., Am. Chem. Soc., Assn. Corp. Growth (dir., past pres.). Clubs: Met. (Washington); Princeton (N.Y.C.). Home: 391 Round Hill Rd Greenwich CT 06830 Office: 250 North St White Plains NY 10625

HASSAN, FAROOQ AZIM, lawyer, educator; b. Lahore, Pakistan, Oct. 17, 1941; came to U.S., 1978; s. Peroze and Daisy Dilara (Admad Shuja) H.; m. Salma, Mar. 7, 1969; children: Mehreen, Amber, Uzma. B.A. with honors, Panjab U., 1961, Oxford U., 1964, M.A., 1968; B.Litt., 1972; D.Phil., Oxford U., 1973; diploma, Acad. Am. and Internat. Law, 1972, Hague Acad. Internat. Law, 1973, 74, Internat. Inst. Human Rights, 1974, East-West Ctr., Honolulu, 1977. Called to bar Lincoln's Inn, London, Pakistan, Oreg. 1982. Internat. legal cons. Govt. of Pakiston UN, Geneva, 1965-66; advocate Supreme Ct. of Pakistan, 1970, sr. advocate, 1975; advocate gen., Panjab, Pakistan, 1975; vis. prof. Law Sch. Am. U., Washington, 1978-79; dir., vis. prof. University Coll., London, 1979; prof. law Willamette U. Coll. Law, Salem, Oreg., 1979—; prof. humanities West Pakistan Engring. U., 1966-72; prof. law Punjab U., Lahore, 1966-75; internat. legal cons. to embassies, govts., univs., corps.; sec. gen. Bar Assn. Pakistan, 1977. Author: Principles of Public International Law, 1972, Introduction to the Study of Diplomacy, 1973, The Right to be Different, 1980, The Concept of State and Law in Islam, 1981; contbr. articles to profl. jours. Pres. Pakistan Human Rights Soc., 1978—; patron Islamic Learning Inst. Pakistan, 1980—. Home: 6122 Liberty Rd Salem OR 97302 Office: Willamette Univ 250 Winter St SE Salem OR 97302

HASSAN, IHAB HABIB, author, comparative literature educator; b. Cairo, Egypt, Oct. 17, 1925; came to U.S., 1946, naturalized, 1956; s. Habib and Faika (Hamdi) H.; m. Sarah Margaret Greene, 1966; 1 son by previous marriage, Geoffrey. B.Sc. with highest honors, U. Cairo, 1946; M.S., U. Pa., 1948, M.A., 1950, Ph.D., 1953. Instr. English Rensselaer Poly. Inst., 1952-54; mem. faculty Wesleyan U., Middletown, Conn., 1954-70, Benjamin L. Waite prof. English, 1962-70, chmn. dept. English, 1963-64, 68-69; dir. Coll. Letters, 1964-66, Center for Humanities, 1969-70; Vilas Research prof. English and comparative lit. U. Wis., Milw., 1970—; vis. fellow Woodrow Wilson Internat. Center for Scholars, 1972; mem. editorial bd. Am. Quar., 1965-67, Wesleyan U. Press, 1963-66; mem. PMLA adv. bd., 1979-83; lectr. Salzburg Seminars Am. Studies, summers 1965, 75; Fulbright lectr. to, France, 1966-67, 74-75; Distinguished Fulbright lectr. Kyoto Seminars in Am. Studies, summer 1974; dir. NEH summer seminars for coll. tchrs., 1982, 84. Author: Radical Innocence: Studies in Contemporary Affairs, Novel, 1961, Crise du Heros Americain Contemporain, 1963, The Literature of Silence: Henry Miller and Samuel Becket, 1967, The Dismemberment of Orpheus: Toward a Postmodern Literature, 1971, 82, Contemporary American Literature: 1945-72, 1973, Paracriticisms, 1975, The Right Promethean Fire, 1980; editor: Liberations: New Essays on the Humanities in Revolution, 1971; co-editor: Innovation/Renovation: New Perspectives on the Humanities, 1983. Guggenheim fellow, 1958-59, 62-63; fellow Ind. U. Sch. Letters, 1964; sr. fellow Camargo Found., 1974-75; vis. scholar Rockefeller Bellagio Study and Conf. Center, 1978; Japan Found. grantee, 1979. Mem. Sigma Xi. Home: 2137 N Terrace Ave Milwaukee WI 53202

HASSAN, WILLIAM EPHRIAM, JR., hospital executive; b. Brockton, Mass., Oct. 13, 1923; s. William Ephriam and Matilda (Salemey) H.; m. Rosetta Theresa Amodeo, June 30, 1951; children: William Anthony, Thomas Edward. B.S., Mass. Coll. Pharmacy, 1945, M.S., 1947, Ph.D., 1951; LL.B., Suffolk U., Boston, 1965. Bar: Mass. 1965. Dir. Peter Bent Brigham Hosp., Boston, 1967-78; adj. prof. jurisprudence and hosp. pharmacy Mass. Coll. Pharmacy, 1967-69; v.p. ops., asso. gen. counsel Nat. Med. Care Co., 1968-71; exec. v.p. Brigham and Women's Hosp., Boston, 1978-83, v.p., gen. counsel, 1983—; mem. faculty Harvard U. Med. Sch., 1968—; dir. Controlled Risk Ins. Co., Health Providers Ins. Co. Author: Hospital Pharmacy, 4th edit, 1981, Law For the Pharmacy Student, 1971. Trustee Mass. Coll. Pharmacy; bd. dirs. St. Jude's Children's Research Hosp.; hosp. chmn. United Way Mass., 1979; mem. Joint Legis. Commn. Hosp. Charges, 1980—; Trustee Emanuel Coll., Boston, Am. U., Beirut. Recipient Disting. Alumni award Mass. Coll. Pharmacy, 1973, Cutler medal Peter Bent Brigham Hosp., 1975. Mem. Am. Coll. Hosp. Adminstrs., Am. Hosp. Assn., Am. Pharm. Assn., Am. Coll. Apothecaries, Am. Soc. Hosp. Pharmacists, Am. Soc. Pharmacy Law, Am. Soc. Law and Medicine, Nat. League Nursing, Mass. Hosp. Assn., Mass. Bar Assn., Boston Bar Assn., Kappa Psi. Office: 10 Vining St Boston MA 02115

HASSARD, HOWARD, lawyer; b. Oakland, Calif., Mar. 10, 1910; s. Henry Houston and Amalia (Duchrau) H.; m. Dorothy Jones, Nov. 7, 1931; children—James Cushing, Elizabeth B., Kathryn A. A.B., U. Calif., 1931, LL.B., 1934. Bar: Calif. bar 1934. Atty. office Hartley F. Peart, 1934-42; partner Hassard, Bonnington, Rogers & Huber, San Francisco; v.p., sec. Swinerton & Walberg Co., 1958—, sec., treas., 1960—; exec. dir. Calif. Med. Assn., 1958-67, gen. counsel, 1945—, Blue Shield Med. Care Plans, Blue Shield of Calif., Calif. Physicians Service. Editor: Medical Malpractice, 1967. Fellow ACLM (hon.); mem. Am., Calif., San Francisco bar assns. Clubs: Bohemian, Commonwealth, Olympic. Home: 135 Fernwood Dr San Francisco CA 94127 Office: 44 Montgomery St San Francisco CA 94104

HASSE, WILLIAM FREDERICK, former banker; b. New Haven, May 10, 1906; s. William Frederick and Lillie (Ammann) H.; m. Helen Scholz, Sept. 20, 1930; children—William Frederick III, Robert G. Grad., Am. Inst. Banking, 1930, Stonier Sch. Banking, Rutgers U., 1944. Auditor New Haven Bank, 1945-57, comptroller, 1951-57, 1st New Haven Nat. Bank, 1957-69, v.p., 1964-70, ret.; instr. Am. Inst. Banking, 1945-67, 1946-49, Quinnipiack Coll., 1945-57, Stone's Coll., 1950-67; mem. Conn. State Bank Examining Com., 1964—. Author: History of Banking in New Haven, 1946, History of Money and Banking in Connecticut, 1957. Treas., Town of East Haven, 1946-48; asst. treas. USO, 1942-46; Dir., sec., treas. New Haven Safety Council, 1959-62; chmn. Housing Authority East Haven, 1969; auditor Old Stone Ch.; Pres., bd. dirs. East Lawn Cemetery; bd. dirs. Stone Coll., 1960-67. Mem. Am. Inst. Banking (past pres. local chpt.), Bank Auditors and Comptrollers (past pres. local chpt.), Conn. Bankers Assn., Financial Execs. Inst. Home: 350 Mansfield Grove Rd East Haven CT 06512

HASSELMAN, RICHARD B., railroad executive; b. Jersey City, Nov. 28, 1926; s. Benjamin R. and Clara A. (Borchert) H.; m. Mildred E. Schaber, May 29, 1954; children: Richard Dwight, James Christopher. B.E. in Mech. Engring., Yale U., 1947; M.B.A., NYU, 1949. Student engr. N.Y. Central R.R., 1947-49, trainee, 1949-52, brakeman, 1952-53, signalman, freight agt., 1953; transp. insp. Eastern Region-N.Y. Central R.R., Syracuse, N.Y., 1953-55; trainmaster Mohawk div. N.Y. Central R.R., Albany, N.Y., 1955-57; div. trainmaster Syracuse div. N.Y. Central R.R., 1957; div. supt. Boston & Albany div. N.Y. Central R.R., Springfield, Mass, 1957-59; dist. transp. supt. Western Region-N.Y. Central R.R., Cleve., 1959-60; gen. supt. yards and terminals N.Y. Central System, N.Y.C., 1960-63; gen. mgr. Ind. Harbor Belt and Chicago River & Ind. R.R., Hammond, Ind., 1963, No. Region-ind. Harbor Belt and Chicago River & Ind. R.R., Detroit, 1964, So. Regionl-Inc. Harbor Belt and Chicago River & Ind. R.R., Indpls., 1965-67, Western Regional-Ind. harbor Belt and Chicago River & Ind. R.R., Cleve., 1967; asst. v.p. transp. N.Y. Central System, N.Y.C., 1967-68, Penn. Central, Phila., 1968-73, 74-76; sr. v.p. ops. Consol. Rail Corp. (Conrail), Phila., 1976—; pres., dir. Ind. harbor Belt R.R. Co.; dir. Detroit River Tunnel Co., Niagara River Bridge Co., St. Lawrence & Adirondack Rwy. Co., Terminal R.R. Co. of, St. Louis, Toledo Terminal R.R. Home: 669 Dodds Ln Gladwyne PA 19035 Office: Consolidated Rail Corp 1740 Six Penn Center Philadelphia PA 19104

HASSELMEYER, EILEEN GRACE, med. research adminstr.; b. Bklyn., May 23, 1924; d. Edwin Allen and Margaret Grace (Cody) H. R.N., Bellevue Sch. Nursing, 1946; B.S., N.Y. U., 1954, M.A., 1956, Ph.D., 1963. Staff Pediatric Metabolic & Nutritional Research Service, N.Y. U. Children's Med. Service, Bellevue Hosp., N.Y.C., 1946-56, study coordinator, 1951-56; research nursing supr. Met. Hosp., N.Y.C., 1951; lectr. pediatric nutrition research U. Tex. Sch. Nursing, 1952-53; nursing dir. nutritional research studies Children's Hosp. of John Seely Hosp. (U. Tex. Med. Br.), Galveston, 1952-53; lectr. and nursing research asso. nutritional service Dept. Pediatrics, Hosp. Infantile, Mexico City, 1953; nursing dir. research unit Willowbrook State Sch., S.I., 1953-54; nurse cons. Div. Nursing Resources, Bur. Med. Services, USPHS, Washington, 1956-59; prin. investigator Handling & Premature Infant Behavior project, N.Y. U., N.Y.C., 1961-63; sr. nurse cons. Div. Nursing, Bur. State Services, USPHS, Washington, 1963; spl. asst. for prematurity Office of Dir., Nat. Inst. Child Health and Human Devel., Bethesda, Md., 1963-66, acting dir. perinatal biology and infant mortality program, extramural programs, 1967-68, dir., 1969-74, asst. to dir. for perinatology, 1974-80; chief pregnancy and infancy br. Center for Research for Mothers and Children, 1974-79, acting chief clin. nutrition and early devel. br., 1979-80; asso. dir. for sci. rev. Office of Dir., 1979—; Annie W. Goodrich vis. prof. Yale U. Sch. Nursing, New Haven, 1968-69; asst. surgeon gen. USPHS, Dept. Health & Human Services, 1981—; chmn. Dept. Health & Human Services Interagy. Panel on Sudden Infant Death Syndrone, 1974—, others; commd. USPHS, 1956, advanced through grades to asst. surgeon gen. Contbr. articles to profl. jours. Recipient NICHD Recognition of Outstanding Performance, 1973; HEW-USPHS Commendation medal, 1975; named Bellevue Sch. Nursing Disting. Alumna, 1976; recipient Perinatal Research Soc. award, 1979; N.Y. U. Sch. Edn., Health, Nursing and Arts Professions Creative Leadership award, 1980; Nat. League for Nursing Commonwealth fellow, 1959-62; NIH fellow, 1962-63; Am. Nurses Found. grantee, 1962-63; State of Conn. Maternal and Infant Program grantee, 1969; Sigma Theta Tau research grantee, 1969-71; Yale U. Sch. Nursing developmental grantee, 1969. Mem. Am. Nurses Assn., Nat. League Nursing, AAAS, Am. Public Health Assn., Perinatal Research Soc., Am. Pediatric Soc., PHS Commd. Officers Assn., Bellevue Alumnae Assn. Office: 7910 Woodmont Ave Rm C608 Bethesda MD 20205

HASSELMO, NILS, university official, linguistics educator; b. Kola, Sweden, July, 2, 1931; came to U.S., 1958; s. A. Wilner and Anna Helena (Backlund) H.; m. Patricia June Tillberg, Oct. 25, 1958; children: Nils Peter, Michael Erik, Anna Patricia. Fil. mag., Uppsala U., 1956, Fil. lic., 1962, Philosfie Doktor h.c., 1979; B.A., Augustana Coll., 1957; Ph.D., Harvard U., 1961. Asst. prof. Swedish Augustana Coll., Rock Island, Ill., 1958-59, 61-63; assoc. prof. Scandinavian langs. and lit. U. Minn., Mpls., 1965-70, prof., chmn. Scandinavian langs. and lit., 1970-73, dir. Ctr. for Northwest European Langs. and Area Studies, 1970-73, assoc. dean Coll. Liberal Arts, 1973-78, v.p. for adminstrn. and planning, 1980-83; sr. v.p. acad. affairs, provost U. Ariz., Tucson, 1983—, prof. English and linguistics, 1983—; 1st v.p. Swedish Am. Hist. Soc., 1981—; mem. vis. com. dept. Germanic langs. and lit. Harvard U., Cambridge, Mass., 1981—. Author: Amerikasvenska, 1974, Swedish America: An Introduction, 1976; editor: Perspectives on Swedish Immigration, 1978. Bd. dirs. Swedish Council Am., 1978—; mem. Gov.'s Task Force on Technology and Improvement of Employment, Minn., 1982-83; mem. bd. overseers Mpls. Coll. Art & Design, 1982-83. Served to sgt. Signal Corps Royal Swedish Army, 1951-54. Fulbright-Hays fellow, 1968; decorated Royal Order of North Star, Sweden, 1973; recipient King Carl XVI Gustaf's Bicentennial medal in Gold, Sweden, 1976. Mem. Soc. for Advancement Scandinavian Study, MLA, Linguistic Soc. Am., Vetenskaps-Societeten, Royal Gustavus Adolphus Acad.

HASSENFELD, ALAN GEOFFREY, toy co. exec.; b. Providence, Nov. 16, 1948; s. Merrill Lloyd and Sylvia (Kay) H. B.A., U. Pa., 1970. Asst. to pres. Hasbro Industries, Inc., Pawtucket, R.I., 1969-72, v.p. internat. ops., 1972-78, v.p. mktg. and sales, 1978-80, exec. v.p. ops., 1980—, dir., 1976—; dir., chmn. bd. Hasbro Canada, 1979—; dir. Hasbro Internat., Hong Kong. Bd. dirs. Internat. House R.I., Providence, 1975—; mem. Pan Am.-New Eng. Adv. Coml. Bd., R.I. Air Adv. Task Force. Served with Air Force N.G., 1967-73. Mem. Toy Mfrs. Assn. (dir.). Office: 1027 Newport Ave Pawtucket RI 02861

HASSENFELD, STEPHEN DAVID, manufacturing company executive; b. Providence, R.I., Jan. 19, 1942; s. Merrill Lloyd and Sylvia Grace (Kay) H. Student, Johns Hopkins U., 1959-62; D. Pub. Service, R.I. Coll., 1984. With Hasbro Industries, Inc., Pawtucket, R.I., 1963—, v.p. mktg., 1967-68, exec. v.p., 1968-74, pres., 1974—, chmn. bd., 1980—, also dir. Fellow Brandeis U., Waltham, Mass., 1977—; trustee Temple Emanu-El, Providence, R.I., 1981—, R.I. Pub. Expenditures Council, 1982—, Found. for Repertory Theatre of R.I., 1978—; bd. dirs. Jewish Fedn. R.I., 1976—, Southeastern region NCCJ, 1976—, John H. Chaffee Steering Com., 1975-82, Am. Jewish Joint Distbn. Com., N.Y.C., 1982—; mem. R.I. Council of Nat. Jewish Hosp.-Nat. Asthma Center, 1980—, Corp. of R.I. Philharmonic Orch., 1981; mem. bus. adv. council U. R.I., 1976-78; bd. dirs. Children's Friend and Service, Providence, 1974-77, Fed. Hill House, Providence, 1973-76; mem. adv. com. R.I. Strategic Devel. Commn., 1982—; mem. adv. council Sch. Continuing Studies, Johns Hopkins U., 1983—. Mem. Toy Mfrs. Assn. (dir. 1974-76). Home: 100 Sunrise Ave Apt 602E Palm Beach FL 33480 Office: 1027 Newport Ave Pawtucket RI 02862

HASSIALIS, MENELAOS DIMITRI, engineering educator; b. N.Y.C., Dec. 25, 1909; s. Dimitri A. and Marie (Mantsalis) H.; m. Ruth Elizabeth Arnold, June 17, 1931; children: Joan Ileane, Peter John. A.B., Columbia U., 1931; D.Sc. (hon.), Bard Coll., Annandale-on-Hudson, N.Y., 1953. Engaged research Columbia U., 1934-37; faculty Columbia Sch. Mines, 1937—; prof. Krumb Sch. Mines, 1937-49, prof. mineral engring., 1949-59, Henry Krumb chair in mining, 1959—, emeritus, 1978—, exec. officer, 1951-67, mem. exec. com. senate, 1969—, chmn. investment policy com., 1969—; pres. Pacific Uranium Mines Co., 1959-61; v.p. Tech. Investors Corp., 1961-62, Tech. Investors Mgmt. Co., 1961-63; pres., dir. T.I.C. Mining Co., 1969—; chmn. bd. dirs. Sandvik Steel Inc., 1973—, Disston Corp., 1976—, Strata Bit Corp., 1983—; co-chmn. Breton Corp.; v.p. Sanmine Exploration Co., Toronto, Ont., Can.; dir. Ambrosia Lakes Uranium Corp., Sandvik Conveyor Co., Tudor Industries Corp., Kermac Nuclear Fuels Corp.; Cons. fields ore dressing, petroleum engring., surface chemistry, mining, mineral econs.; dir. Columbia Mineral Benefication Lab. operated for AEC, 1951-58; mem. adminstrv. bd. Lamont Geol. Obs., 1965-78; mem. and vice chmn. adminstrv. board Inst. for Study of Sci. in Human Affairs, 1967-70; mem. Council for Atomic Age Studies; chmn. phosphate slimes panel, minerals and metals adv. bd. Nat. Acad. Scis., NRC. Contbg. author: (by A.F. Taggart) Handbook of Mineral Dressing; contbr.: articles to pubs. Am. Inst. Mining Engrs, 1936—. Am. del. to Geneva Conf. on Peaceful Uses of Atomic Energy, 1955, 58; Am. rep. to Paris meeting on atomic energy UNESCO; ad-hoc adv. com. to Bur. Mines, 1972—; head UN spl. fund mission, Turkey, 1964 head UN spl. fund mission, Spain, 1965; Vice pres., trustee Valley Hosp., Ridgewood, N.J. Recipient Great Tchrs. award, 1957; 1st encumbent of Henry Krumb chair in mining, Columbia, 1959; Lion award Columbia Alumni Assn., 1960; Bicentennial medal Freiberg Bergakadamie, E.Ger., 1965; Bicentennial award Tech. U. West Berlin, 1966; citation Govt. of Turkey, 1964, Govt. of Pakistan, 1956. Fellow Explorers Club; mem. AIME (regional vice chmn., beneficiation div.), Am. Chem. Soc., AAAS, Sigma Xi, Tau Beta Pi. Clubs: Century Assn., Marshall Chess (N.Y.C.); Ridgewood (N.J.); Bridge, Ridgewood Country. Home: 122 Phelps Rd Ridgewood NJ 07450 Office: Columbia Sch Mines New York NY 10027

HASSID, SAMI, architect, educator; b. Cairo, Egypt, Apr. 19, 1912; came to U.S., 1957, naturalized, 1962; s. Joseph S. and Isabelle (Israel) H.; m. Juliette Mizrahi, June 29, 1941; children: Fred, Muriel. Diploma in architecture with distinction, Sch. Engring., Giza, Egypt, 1932; B.A. in Architecture with honors, U. London, Eng., 1935; M.Arch., U. Cairo, 1943; Ph.D. in Architecture, Harvard U., 1956. Tchr. Alexandria (Egypt) Tech. Sch., 1932-34; successively tchr., lectr., asst. prof. U. Cairo, 1934-56; prof. architectural theory and design U. Ein-Shams, Cairo, 1957; mem. faculty U. Calif., Berkeley, 1957—, prof. architecture, 1964-79, prof. emeritus, 1979—, also assoc. dean, 1977-83, faculty asst. to vice-chancellor for campus planning, 1980—; archtl. practice, Cairo, 1932-57, Berkeley, 1957—; from draftsman to sr. designer office Ali Labib Gabr (architect), Cairo, 1935-47; ptnr. Sami Hassid and Youssef Shafik, Cairo, 1947-57, Hassid and Kelemen, Berkeley, 1963-65. Author: The Sultan's Turrets, 1939, Architectural Construction Details, 1954, Development and Application of a System for Recording Critical Evaluations of Architectural Works, 1964, Architectural Education U.S.A, 1967, (with others) Innovations in Housing Design and Construction Techniques as Applied to Low-Cost Housing, 1969, Surface Materials in Architecture, 1970, Doctoral Studies in Architecture, 1971, Methods for the Development of Shipboard Habitability Design Criteria, 1974, Fire Safety in Buildings, A Course Offering Package, 1976; prin. works include Hill House; student hostel, Am. U. Cairo, 1952. Commr. Calif. Bd. Archtl. Examiners, 1961—. Fulbright grantee, 1954-56; recipient First prize Al-Chams Competition, Cairo, 1947, San Francisco AIA Hdqrs. Competition, 1963. Mem. AIA, Bldg. Research Inst., Assn. Collegiate Schs. Architecture. Democrat. Jewish (trustee temple; v.p. East Bay synagogue council 1970-71). Office: U Calif Office Campus Planning 300 A & E Bldg Berkeley CA 94720

HASSLEIN, GEORGE JOHANN, architectural engineering educator; b. Los Angeles, Aug. 31, 1917; s. August Theodore and Lena (Matranga) H.; m. Neva B. Henderson, Oct. 13, 1945 (dec. Dec. 1963); children: Vaughn, Tracey; m. Marilyn L. Collins, Sept. 10, 1966 (dec. Dec. 1967). B.Arch., U. So. Calif., 1945. Registered architect, Calif. With Army Engrs., 1942-44; archtl. designer firm Welton Becket (architect), Los Angeles, 1948-50; mem. faculty Calif. State Poly. Coll., San Luis Obispo, 1949—, prof., head dept. archtl. engring., 1952-68, founding dean Sch. Architecture and Environ. Design, 1968-84; Archtl. adviser bd. trustees Calif. State Univs. and Colls., 1961—; regent Roofing Industry Ednl. Inst., 1979—. Chmn. Indsl. Survey Com. San Luis Obispo, 1955, Traffic Survey Com., 1956; chmn. Bldg. Appeals Bd. San Luis Obispo, 1963-65. Recipient Achievement award Los Angeles C. of C., 1981. Fellow AIA (Distinguished service award edn. 1971, Excellence in Edn. award 1977); mem. Am. Arbitration Assn., Scarab, Delta Phi Delta, Tau Sigma., Alpha Rho Chi. Address: Calif Polytechnic State U San Luis Obispo CA 93407

HASSLER, DONALD MACKEY, II, educator, writer; b. Akron, Ohio, Jan. 3, 1937; s. Donald Mackey and Frances Elizabeth (Parsons) H.; m. Diana Cain, Oct. 8, 1960 (dec. Sept. 1976); children: Donald, David; m. Sue Smith, Sept. 13, 1977; children: Shelly, Heather. B.A. (Sloan fellow), Williams Coll., 1959; M.A. (Woodrow Wilson fellow), Columbia U., 1960, Ph.D., 1967. Instr. U. Montreal, 1961-65; instr. English Kent (Ohio) State U., 1965-67, asst. prof., 1967-71, assoc. prof., 1971-76, prof., 1977—, acting dean honors and exptl. coll., 1979-81, dir., 1973-82. Author: Erasmus Darwin, 1974, The Comedian as the Letter D: Erasmus Darwin's Comic Materialism, 1973, Asimov's Golden Age: The Ordering of an Art, 1977, Hal Clement, 1983, Comic Tones in Science Fiction, 1982, Patterns of the Fantastic, 1983. Co chmn. Kent Am. Revolution Bicentennial Commn., 1974-77; deacon Presbyterian Ch., 1971-74, elder, 1974-77. Mem. Sci. Fiction Research Assn. (treas. 1983—), Phi Beta Kappa. Lodges: Kiwanis (dir. 1974-76, pres. 1983-84). Home: 1226 Woodhill Dr Kent OH 44240

HASSLER, FRANCIS JEFFERSON, agricultural engineer, educator; b. Cooper Hill, Mo., Aug. 2, 1921; s. Millard Franklin and Etta (Jett) H.; m. Oneta Marceline Miller, Aug. 5, 1942; children—Olivia Ann, Reginald Robert, Gregory, Rodney, Melanie. B.S. in Agrl. Engring, U. Mo., 1946; M.S., Mich. State U., 1948, Ph.D., 1950. Mem. faculty N.C. State U. at Raleigh, 1950—, prof. agrl. engring., 1954—, head dept. agrl. engring., 1961-65, head dept. biol. and agrl. engring., 1965—, William Neal Reynolds prof., 1961—, charge tobacco curing research, 1952-61. Served to 1st lt. AUS, 1943-46. Named Tarheel of Week News and Observer, Raleigh, 1960. Fellow Am. Soc. Agrl. Engrs., AAAS; mem. Am. Soc. Engring. Edn., N.C. Soc. Engrs. (Outstanding Engring. achievement award 1982), Sigma Xi, Tau Beta Pi, Pi Mu Epsilon, Sigma Pi Sigma, Phi Kappa Phi, Gamma Sigma Delta, Alpha Zeta (assoc.). Club: Rotarian. Patentee in field. Home: 1404 Eden Ln Raleigh NC 27608

HASSO, SIGNE ELEONORA CECILIA, actress; b. Stockholm, Sweden, Aug. 15, 1915; d. Kefas Johannes and Helfrid Elisabet (Lindstrom) Larsson; (div.) 1 son, Henry (dec.). Ed., Royal Acad. Dramatic Arts. Actress, Royal Dramatic Theatre of Sweden, 1927—; now adj. prof. drama dept., U. Miami; appeared in plays in, Scandinavia, Eng., Scotland, U.S., Can., films, Europe and U.S.; films including House on 92nd Street, Double Life, Crisis; appeared on television, Europe and U.S.; writer, corr., lyricist, composer; performed in: A Little Night Music, Folkan Theatre, Stockholm, 1978-79; recorded Where the Sun Meets the Moon; songs of her own lyrics and music.; Recipient (Swedish Oscar 1937, Gösta Ekman Scandinavian theatrical award 1939, Le Grand Prix Edison award for English lyrics of album Scandinavian Folksongs with Alice and Svend 1965); Author: prize winning novel Momo, 1977, Kom Slott, 1978; poetry Verbal Lace; co-author: (with Helena Davis) Your Life in Numbers. Decorated knight 1st class Royal Order Vasa, 1972. Home: 215 W 90th St Apt 7F New York NY 10024 *Success (in anything) is not a Destination—it is a Journey.*

HAST, ADELE, editor, historian; b. N.Y.C., Dec. 6, 1931; d. Louis and Kate (Miller) Krongelb; m. Malcolm Howard Hast, Feb. 1, 1953; children—David Jay, Howard Arthur. B.A. magna cum laude, Bklyn. Coll., 1953; M.A., U. Iowa, 1969, Ph.D., 1979. Research asso. Atlas Early Am. History Project, Newberry Library, Chgo., 1971-75; asso. dir. Atlas Great Lakes Indian History Project, 1976-79, Hist. Boundary Data File Project, 1979-81; editor-in-chief Marquis Who's Who, Inc., Chgo., 1981—; mem. faculty Newberry Library Summer Inst. Cartography, 1980. Author: Loyalism in Revolutionary Virginia, 1982; asso. editor: Atlas of Great Lakes Indian History, 1985; contbr. articles to profl. jours. Sec.-treas., bd. dirs. Chgo. Map Soc., 1980-81; mem. New Trier Twp. High Sch. Bd. Caucus, 1972-74. Colonial Williamsburg Found. grantee-in-aid, 1975; Brit. Acad. research fellow, 1979; Am. Council Learned Socs. grantee-in-aid, 1980. Fellow Royal Historical Society, Phi Beta Kappa, Kappa Delta Pi; mem. Am. Hist. Assn., ALA, Am. Soc. Legal History, Orgn. Am. Historians, Soc. Scholarly Pub. (pub. affairs com. 1983—) Office: 200 E Ohio St Chicago IL 60611

HAST, MALCOLM HOWARD, medical educator; b. N.Y.C., May 28, 1931; s. Irving William and Rose Lillian (Berlin) H.; m. Adele Krongelb, Feb. 1, 1953; children: David Jay, Howard Arthur. B.A., Bklyn. Coll., 1953; postgrad., U. So. Calif., 1955-57; M.A., Ohio State U., 1958, Ph.D. (NIH fellow), 1961. Instr. U. Iowa, 1961-63, NIH spl. fellow, 1963-65, asst. prof., 1965-69; asso. prof. otolaryngology Med. Sch., Northwestern U., 1969-74, prof., 1974—, dir. research otolaryngology, 1969—; prof. anatomy med. and dental schs. Northwestern U., 1977—; asso. staff Northwestern Meml. Hosp., 1969—; guest scientist Max Planck Inst. für Psychiatrie, 1976; vis. prof. Royal Coll. Surgeons Eng., 1980—; mem. task force on new materials Am. Bd. Otolaryngology, 1969-72; dir. Ill. Soc. Med. Research, 1973-77. Contbr. articles to profl. jours.; chpts. to books. Mem. adv. bd. Center on Deafness, 1977-80; bd. dirs. Cliff Dwellers Arts Found., 1979-82; trustee Wilmette Library Bd., 1982-83. Served with AUS, 1953-55. Recipient Gould Internat. award, 1971; Alumnus award of honor Bklyn. Coll., 1977; NIH research grantee, 1964-84; NSF research grantee, 1975-77; NATO sr. fellow in Sci. Oxford (Eng.) U., 1978. Fellow Linnean Soc. (London), Am. Speech and Hearing Assn., Royal Soc. Medicine, AAAS, Am. Acad. Otolaryngology—Head and Neck Surgery; mem. Am. Physiol. Soc. (animal care and experimentation com. 1976-82), N.Y. Acad. Scis., Am. Soc.

Mammalogists, AAUP (chpt. pres. 1977-82), Anat. Soc. Gt. Britain and Ireland, Am. Assn. Anatomists, Am. Assn. History of Medicine, Sigma Xi (pres. chpt. 1971-72), Sigma Alpha Eta. Club: Cliff Dwellers. Research on neuromuscular physiology, embryology and comparative anatomy of the larynx. Office: 303 E Chicago Ave Chicago IL 60611

HASTIE, REID WILLIAM, art educator; b. Donora, Pa., Feb. 14, 1916; s. William and Ellen (Reid) H.; m. Olivia Kendrick, Aug. 8, 1941; children—Reid K., Bruce C. B.S., State Tchrs. Coll., Edinboro, Pa., 1936; M.A., U. W.Va., 1940; Ph.D., U. Pitts., 1953; student, Carnegie Inst. Tech., Harvard U., U. Minn. Art supr. Monongalie County Schs., W.Va., 1936-38; art tchr. Pitts. pub. schs., 1938-40; instr. dept. fine arts U. Pitts., 1940-41, 46-49; asst. prof., asso. prof., then prof. dept. art edn. U. Minn., 1949—; mem. fine arts staff Carnegie Inst., Pitts., 1939-40, 46-49; prof. Tex. Tech U., Lubbock, 1969—; Cons. Central Midwestern Regional Ednl. Lab., Inc. Exhibited paintings, Carnegie Inst., St. Paul Gallery, Mpls., Inst. Arts, Walker Art Center, U. Minn., water color exhibit, Minn. State Fair.; Author: (with Christian Schmidt) Encounter with Art, 1969; Editor: Art Education, 1965. Served to lt. USNR, 1941-46. Mem. Nat. Art Edn. Assn. (pres.), Western Arts Assn., Asso. Artists, St. Paul Painters and Sculpture Assn., NEA, Nat. Soc. Study Edn., Phi Delta Kappa, Delta Phi Delta, Omicron Delta Kappa. Home: 3021 21st St Lubbock TX 79410 Office: Tex Tech U Lubbock TX 79409

HASTIE, ROBERT BENJAMIN, oil pipeline company executive; b. Lead, S.D., Apr. 24, 1924. B.S., Northwestern U., 1948. Sr. v.p. ARCO Pipe Line Co., Los Angeles, 1979—. Office: ARC Pipe Line Co Alaska Div 300 Oceangate Long Beach CA 90802

HASTINGS, ALBERT BAIRD, researcher; b. Dayton, Ky., Nov. 20, 1895; s. Otis Luther and Elizabeth (Henry) H.; m. Margaret Anne Johnson, 1918 (dec. 1979); 1 son, Alan Baird. B.S., U. Mich., 1917; Ph.D., Columbia U., 1921; Sc.D., U. Mich., 1941, Oxford, 1952, Boston U., 1956; M.A., Harvard, 1942, Sc.D., 1945, St. Louis U., 1965, Columbia, 1967, Ind. U., 1972. Chemist USPHS, 1917-21, Rockefeller Inst., 1921-26; prof. physiol. chemistry U. Chgo., 1926-28; prof. biochemistry Lasker Found. for Med. Research, 1928-35; Hamilton Kuhn prof. biol. chem. Harvard Med. Sch., 1935-59, emeritus, 1959—; head lab. metabolic research Scripps Clinic and Research Found., La Jolla, Calif., 1959-66, mem. emeritus, 1966—; hon. prof. U. San Marcos, 1957; research asso. U. Calif. at San Diego, 1960—; Vis. prof. Pahlavi Univ., Shiraz, Iran, 1967; syndic Harvard Univ. Press; Fulbright lectr. Oxford U., 1952; mem. sr. common room Trinity Coll., 1953—. Writer various articles; editor: Jour. Biol. Chemistry, 1941-54, 55-59, Am. Jour. Physiology, 1956-63, Endocrinology, 1963-67. Trustee Brookhaven Nat. Lab., Asso. Univs., 1948-51; cons. Com. on Biology and Medicine, U.S. AEC, 1947-63; mem. Nat. Adv. Health Council, 1947-48, USPHS Nat. Adv. Arthritis and Metabolic Diseases Council, 1956-60, Heart Council, 1960-64; cons. sci. adv. bd. Walter Reed Army Inst. Research, 1956-62; mem. vis. com. Brookhaven Nat. Lab., 1956—, chmn., 1962-63; nat. sci. adv. com. Okla. Med. Research Found. and Inst.; Mem. Com. on Med. Research, OSRD, 1941-46, Nat. Adv. Cancer Council, 1943-46; Research Bd. for Nat. Security, 1945; Mem. Sci. Adv. Com. The Nutrition Found., 1947-61; adv. bd. Biochem. Preparations, 1945-68; adv. council Life Ins. Med. Research Fund, 1946-50; nat. adv. com. to White House Conf. on Aging, 1970-72. Recipient President's medal for Merit, 1948, Distinguished Service award Med. Alumni Assn. U. Chgo., 1961; Banting medal Am. Diabetes Assn., 1962; A.C.P. award, 1964; USPHS citation, 1964; Modern Medicine Distinguished Achievement award, 1965. Mem. Assn. Am. Physicians, Nat. Acad. Scis., AAAS, Royal Danish Acad. Sci. and Letters, Am. Acad. Arts and Scis., Am. Chem. Soc., Am. Soc. Biol. Chemists (pres. 1945-46), Am. Philos. Soc., Am. Physiol. Soc., Soc. Exptl. Biol. Medicine (pres. 1945-46), Assn. Clin. Chemists (hon.), Harvey Soc., Sinfonia (Phi Mu Alpha), Alpha Chi Sigma, Sigma Xi, Alpha Omega Alpha. Clubs: Century Assn., Harvard (N.Y.C.); Cosmos (Washington); Chicago Literary. Home: 233 Prospect La Jolla CA 92037 *At 85, to have been able to serve my fellow men and women through medical research is a privilege for which I am their debtor.*

HASTINGS, ALCEE LAMAR, judge; b. Altomonte Springs, Fla., Sept. 5, 1936; s. Julius C. and Mildred L. H.; 1 child. B.A., Fisk U., 1958; postgrad., Howard U. Sch. Law, 1958-60; J.D., Fla. A&M U., 1963. Bar: Fla. 1963. Mem. firm Allen and Hastings, Ft. Lauderdale, 1963-66; sole practice, Ft. Lauderdale, 1966-77, judge, Circuit Ct. Broward County, Fla., 1977-79, judge U.S. Dist. Ct. So. Dist. Fla., 1979—; adj. prof. criminal justice dept. Nova U.; lectr. So. Regional Council on Black Am. Affairs; lectr., cons. Internat. Juvenile Officers Assn., Peace Corps Vols. in Avon Park, Fla., 1966; legal counsel Community Action Migrant Program, Broward County Classroom Tchrs.; mem. Gov.'s Conf. on Criminal Justice, State of Fla.; lectr., cons. to elem. and secondary public and pvt. schs., chs., synagogues, social orgns., civic orgns., colls. and univs. in U.S.; co-propr. Tri-City News. Host TV program: Pride, Sta. WPLG; columnist: West Side Gazette. Atty. various civic assns., Broward County and State of Fla.; mem. Bi-Racial Adv. Commn., Broward County Personnel Adv. Commn.; sec. Fla. Council on Aging; chmn. Broward Youth Services Task Force; mem. State of Fla. Edn. Commn., Task Force on Crime, Democratic Exec. Com; candidate for Fla. Ho. of Reps., Fla. Senate, U.S. Senate, Fla. Public Service Commn.; bd. dirs. Urban League of Broward County, Child Advocacy, Inc., The Starting Place, Broward County Sickle Cell Anemia Found., Fla. Voters League, Broward County Council on Human Relations; trustee Mt. Hermon A.M.E. Ch., Ft. Lauderdale, Broward Community Coll., Bethune Cookman Coll. Recipient numerous awards and honors including; Humanitarian award Broward County Young Democarts, 1978; Citizen of Year award Zeta Phi Beta, 1978; Sam Delevoe Human Rights award Community Relations Bd. of Broward County, 1978; Glades Festival of Afro Arts award Zeta Phi Beta, 1981; named Man of Year, Com. Italian Am. Affairs, 1979-80. Mem. ABA (standing com. profl. discipline), Nat. Bar Assn. (Chmn.'s award 1981), Am. Trial Lawyers Assn., Fla. Bar Assn., U.S. Dist. Judges Council., A.M.E. Ch. Clubs: Elks, KP. Judge Alcee Hastings Day proclaimed for City of Daytona Beach in his honor on Dec. 14, 1980. Office: 300 NE 1 Ave US Courthouse Rm B-29 Miami FL 33101 *

HASTINGS, DONALD FRANCIS, actor, writer; b. Bklyn., Apr. 1, 1934; s. Charles Benedict and Hazel May (Kirk) H.; m. Noretta Kennedy, Dec. 29, 1956 (div. Feb. 1980); children: Jennifer, Julie Ann, Matthew.; m. Leslie Denniston, June 7, 1980; 1 dau., Katharine Scott. Student pvt., pub. schs., N.Y. State. Appeared on network radio shows, 1940-53; including Cavalcade of Am; appeared in: plays Life With Father, 1941-43, I Remember Mama, 1944-45, On Whitman Avenue, 1946, Young Man's Fancy, 1947, Summer and Smoke, 1948; various TV shows, 1947—; including Captain Video, 1949-55, Studio One, 1955, Big Story, 1959, Chevrolet on Broadway, 1948, Edge of Night, 1956-60, As The World Turns, 1960—; author: scripts for As The World Turns, 1972-73, Guiding Light, 1974, 77; film Prisoner At Gilbert House, 1976. Mem. AFTRA, Screen Actors Guild, Actors Equity, Writers Guild-East. Roman Catholic. Office: care Pub Relations Dept CBS 51 W 52d St New York NY 10019

HASTINGS, EDWARD WALTON, theater director; b. New Haven, Apr. 14, 1931; s. Edward Walton and Madeline (Cassidy) H. B.A., Yale, 1952; postgrad., Royal Acad. Dramatic Art, London, 1953, Columbia U., 1955-56. Cons. Nat. Endowment for Arts/Rockefeller Found., 1976; bd. dirs. Asian/Am. Theater Co., 1977. Dir.: Australian premiere Hot L Baltimore, 1975, Shakespeare's People, nat. tour, 1977; Yugoslavian premiere Buried Child, 1980; Macbeth, Guthrie Theatre, Mpls., 1981, 84 Charing Cross Road, nat. tour, 1983, others; exec. dir., Am. Conservatory Theatre, San Francisco, 1965-80; free-lance dir., 1980—. Served with U.S. Army, 1953-55. Club: Elizabethan (New Haven). Office: American Conservatory Theatre 450 Geary St San Francisco CA 94102

HASTINGS, ELIZABETH THOMSON, univ. dean; b. Providence, Sept. 27, 1913; d. William Thomson and Hester Jane (Mercer) H. A.B., Pembroke Coll., Brown U., 1934, A.M., 1935; Ph.D., Yale U., 1939. Instr. Ill. Coll., 1939-42, asst. prof., 1942-44, prof., co-chmn. dept. English, 1944-51; prof. English, dean Flora Stone Mather Coll. of Case-Western Res. U., 1951-72, dean spl. assignments, 1972-79, prof. English, 1972-79, prof. emeritus, 1979—. Mem. Modern Lang. Assn., Am. Studies Assn., AAUP, AAUW, League Women Voters, ACLU, Common Cause, Sierra Club, Wilderness Soc., Soc. Hist. Preservation, Phi Beta Kappa. Unitarian. Home: 2419 Queenston Rd Cleveland OH 44118

HASTINGS, GORDON HENRY, broadcasting executive; b. Worcester, Mass., Oct. 17, 1941; s. Calvin R. and Elsa (Brandt) H.; m. Lynn Ann Daly, Apr. 8, 1978; children: Dwight Sanford, Gordon Calvin, Brandt Daly. Talent news Sta. WAAB/WAAF, Worcester, 1955-63, salesman, 1963-68, v.p., gen. mgr., 1968-70, RKO-FM Reps., N.Y.C., 1970-72; v.p. radio Katz Radio, N.Y.C., 1972-76; sr. v.p. Katz Communications, N.Y.C., 1976—. Elder Brick Presbyterian Ch., N.Y.C., 1983—; treas. Town of Boylston, Mass., 1964-66; v.p. Internat. Radio and TV Found., 1983—; bd. dirs. TV-Radio Polit. Action Com., 1981—. Home: 1155 Park Ave New York NY 10028 Office: Katz Communications One Dag Hammarskjold Plaza New York NY 10017

HASTINGS, JOHN WOODLAND, educator, biologist; b. Salisbury, Md., Mar. 24, 1927; s. Vaughan Archelaus and Kathrine (Stevens) H.; m. Hanna Machlup, June 6, 1953; children—Jennifer, David, Laura, Karen. B.A., Swarthmore Coll., 1947; M.A., Princeton, 1950, Ph.D., 1951; M.A., Harvard, 1966. AEC postdoctoral fellow Johns Hopkins, 1951-53; instr. to asst. prof. biol. scis. Northwestern U., 1953-57; from asst. prof. to prof. biochemistry U. Ill. at Urbana, 1957-66; prof. biology Harvard, 1966—; master North House, 1976—; summer research participant Oak Ridge Nat. Lab., 1958; vis. lectr. biochemistry Sheffield (Eng.) U., 1961-62; instr. physiology Marine Biol. Lab., Woods Hole, Mass., 1961-66, dir., 1962-66, mem. corp., 1961, trustee, 1966-74, exec. com., 1968-74; guest investigator Rockefeller U., 1965-66, Inst. Biol. Phys. Chemistry Paris, 1972-73; guest prof. U. Konstanz, Ger., 1979-80; mem. panel molecular biology NSF, 1963-66, mem. adv. com. biology and medicine, 1968-71; com. postdoctoral fellowships chemistry Nat. Acad. Scis., 1965-67, com. photobiology, 1965-71, com. on phototherapy, 1971-73, com. on low frequency radiation, 1975-77; mem. Commn. Undergrad. Edn. in Biol. Scis., 1965-66; space biology com. NASA, 1966-71; biochemistry tng. com. Nat. Inst. Gen. Med. Scis., 1968-72; a founding mem., mem. internat. adv. bd. Marine Biol. Lab., Eilat, Israel, 1968—. Contbr. profl. jours. Served with USNR, 1944-45. Guggenheim fellow, 1965-66; NIH fellow, 1972-73; recipient Alexander von Humboldt prize, 1979. Mem. AAAS, Am. Soc. Biol. Chemists, Biophys. Soc., Soc. Am. Microbiologists, Soc. Gen. Physiology (pres. 1963-65), Am. Acad. Arts and Scis., Johns Hopkins Soc. Scholars. Home: 46 Linnaean St Cambridge MA 02138 Office: 16 Divinity Ave Cambridge MA 02138

HASTINGS, LAWRENCE VAETH, physician, lawyer; b. Flushing, N.Y., Nov. 23, 1919; s. Henry Luftman and Lillian (Vaeth) H.; m. Doris Lorraine Erickson, Dec. 11, 1971; children: Lance Clifford, Wilhelmina Streeton and Laura Thynne (twins). Student, Columbia U., 1939-40, student Law Sch., 1949-50; student, U. Mich. Engring. Sch., 1942-43, Washington U., 1943-44, U. Vt., 1943; M.D., Johns Hopkins U., 1948; J.D., U. Miami, 1953. Bar: Fla. 1954, U.S. Supreme Ct. 1960, D.C. 1976; cert. Am. Bd. Legal Medicine. Intern, U.S. Marine Hosp., S.I., N.Y., 1948-49; asst. surgeon, sr. asst. surgeon USPHS, 1949-52; asst. resident surgery Bellevue Hosp. Med. Center, 1951; med. legal cons., trial atty., Miami, Fla., 1953—; sr. partner Hastings & Goldman; asst. prof. medicine U. Miami, 1964—, lectr. law, 1966; adj. prof. St. Thomas of Villanova Law Sch., Biscayne Coll., Miami, Fla. Contbr. articles to profl. publs. Bd. dirs. Miami Heart Inst.; trustee Barry Coll., Miami, 1976—, Fla. Internat. U., Miami, 1979—. Served with AUS, 1943-46. Fellow Acad. Fla. Trial Lawyers, Am. Coll. Legal Medicine, Law-Sci. Acad. Found. Am.; mem. Am. Acad. Forensic Scis., Assn. Trial Lawyers Am., Fla. Bar (vice chmn. med. legal com. 1957, vice chmn. trial tactics com. 1963-65, chmn. steering com. trial tactics and basic anatomy seminars), Pitts. Inst. Legal Medicine, AMA, Fla., Dade County med. assns., Johns Hopkins Med. and Surg. Assn., Pithotomy Club, Assn. Mil. Surgeons, U. Miami Law Alumni Assn. (pres. 1967), ABA, Fla., Dade County bar assns., Acad. Psychosomatic Medicine, Com. of 100 Miami Beach, Alpha Delta Phi, Phi Eta Sigma, Phi Alpha Delta. Roman Catholic. Clubs: Two Hundred, Bankers, Jockey, Palm Bay, Miami; Bal Harbour (Fla.); LaGorce Country, Bath, Surf (bd. govs. 1976—, chmn. bd. 1978-82, pres. 1978-80), Com. 100, Indian Creek Country, Miami Beach, River of Jacksonville; N.Y. Athletic, Metropolitan, Princeton (N.Y.C.); Balt. Home: 229 Bal Cross Dr Bal Harbour FL 33154 Office: 530 City National Bank Bldg 300 71st St Miami Beach FL 33141

HASTINGS, L(OIS) JANE, architect, educator; b. Seattle, Mar. 3, 1928; d. Harry and Camille (Pugh) H.; m. Norman John Johnston, Nov. 22, 1969. B.Arch., U. Wash., Seattle, 1952, postgrad. in Urban Planning, 1958. Architect Boeing Airplane Co., Seattle, 1951-54; recreational dir., Germany, 1954-56, architect, Seattle, 1956-59, pvt. practice architecture, 1959-74; instr. archtl. drafting Seattle Community Coll., part-time 1969-80; owner/founder The Hastings Group Architects, Seattle, 1974—; lectr. design Coll. Architecture, U. Wash., 1975; incorporating mem. Architecta (P.S.), Seattle, 1980, pres., from 1980; Mem. adv. bd. U. Wash. YWCA, 1967-69; mem. Mayor's Com. on Archtl. Barriers for Handicapped, 1974-75; chmn. regional public adv. panel on archtl. and engring. services GSA, 1976; mem. citizens adv. com. Seattle Land Use Adminstrn. Task Force, from 1979; mem. Seattle Landmarks Preservation Bd., from 1981. Design juror for nat. and local competitions, including red cedar shingle/AIA awards, 1977, current use honor awards, AIA, 1980, exhibit of sch. architecture award, 1981; Contbr. to: also spl. features newspapers, articles in profl. jours. Sunset mag. Mem. bd. Am. Women for Internat. Understanding, del. to, Egypt, Israel, USSR, 1971, del. to, Japan and Korea, 1979. Recipient AIA/The Seattle Times Home of Month Ann. award, 1968; Exhbn. award Seattle chpt. AIA, 1970; Environ. award Seattle-King County Bd. Realtors, 1970, 77; AIA/House and Home/The American Home Merit award, 1971; Honor award Seattle chpt. AIA, 1977; Nat. Endowment for Arts grantee, 1977; others. Fellow AIA (pres. Seattle chpt. 1975, pres. sr. council 1980, state exec. bd. 1975, NW regional dir. from 1982), Internat. Union Women Architects (v.p. 1969-79), Council of Design Professions, Asso. Woman Contractors, Suppliers and Design Cons.'s, Allied Arts Seattle, Fashion Group, Tau Sigma Delta, Alpha Rho Chi. Office: 1516 E Olive Way Seattle WA 98122 *It is not the quantity but the quality of space that is important.* *

HASTINGS, PHILIP KAY, psychology educator; b. Worcester, Mass., Aug. 27, 1922; s. Rowl and Eunice (Leach) H.; m. Elizabeth Frances Hann, Mar. 11, 1950; children: Pamela Dillenback, Elizabeth Leach, Ann Upton, Mary Florence. B.A., Williams Coll., 1943; M.A., Princeton U., 1949, Ph.D., 1950. Instr. psychology Williams Coll., 1946-48, lectr., asst. prof., asso. prof., 1951-61, prof. psychology and polit. sci., 1961—; instr. psychology Princeton U., 1950-51; chmn. Survey Research Consultants Internat., 1977—; research asso. Psychol. Corp. N.Y.; cons. AT&T, 1944-58, Gen. Electric Co., 1975—. Contbr. articles to profl. jours.; editor: Index to International Public Opinion, 1979—. Served to lt. (j.g.) USNR, 1944-46. Fellow Am. Psychol. Assn., Am. Sociol. Assn.; mem. World Assn. Pub. Opinion Research (pres. 1971-72), Am. Assn. Pub. Opinion Research, Sigma Xi. Home: Bulkley St Williamstown MA 01267

HASTINGS, ROBERT HAVEN, publisher; b. Watertown, N.Y., Mar. 11, 1917; s. Eugene Morenus and Carolyn Mae (Haven) H.; m. Helen Elizabeth Prescott, Mar. 4, 1944; children—Joel Prescott, Mark Haven, Patricia Carolyn. Student, U.Y. State Coll. Forestry, 1936-38. Realtor Hastings Realty Agy., Pulaski, N.Y., 1939-40, 46; editor N.Y. Holstein News, 1947-57, Pa. Holstein News, 1956-57; asso. editor Holstein-Friesian World, Lacona, N.Y., 1949-59, exec. editor, 1960-76, editor, 1976—; v.p., dir. Holstein-Friesian World, Inc., Lacona, 1956-76, pres., 1976-80; v.p. Corse Press, Inc., Sandy Creek, N.Y., 1956-71. Editor: Holstein-Friesian World Annual, 1975. Village trustee, Sandy Creek, 1956-72; Trustee Ainsworth Meml. Library, Sandy Creek, 1955-80, chmn. bd., 1963-70; trustee N. Country Library System, Watertown, N.Y., 1973-78. Served with AUS, 1940-46. Named Ky. col., 1970. Mem. Council Agrl. Sci. and Tech., Holstein-Friesian Assn. Am., N.Y. Holstein Assn., Oswego Holstein Club (sec. 1948-50), V.F.W. (post quartermaster 1948-50). Republican. Methodist (chmn. bd. 1953-54). Club: Dairy Shrine (life). Home: P O Box 288 Sandy Creek NY 13145 Office: 10 Lake St Sandy Creek NY 13145

HASTINGS, ROBERT PUSEY, lawyer; b. Los Angeles, May 23, 1910; s. Hill and Mary Garvin (Brown) H.; m. Susan S. Schriber, July 9, 1938; 1 dau., Susan Hastings Mallory. B.A., Yale U., 1933; LL.B., Harvard U., 1936. Bar: Calif. 1936. Since practiced, Los Angeles; counsel Motion Picture div. Office Coordinator Inter-Am. Affairs, 1942-43; partner firm Paul, Hastings, Janofsky & Walker, 1946-81, of counsel, 1981—. Chmn. Calif. campaign USO, 1956-57; pres., chmn. bd. Los Angeles Civic Light Opera Assn., 1959-65, trustee, 1939-79; trustee Calif. Light Opera Assn., 1979; sec., trustee Music Center Operating Co., 1961-65; trustee Harvey Mudd Coll. Sci. and Engring., 1956—, vice chmn. bd., 1956-80; chmn. Thacher Sch., 1965-70, trustee, 1938-73; trustee Friends of Claremont Colls., 1970—, pres., 1973-75; trustee Friends Huntington Library and Art Gallery; bd. overseers Huntington Library and Art Gallery; trustee Winston Churchill Found. U.S., Miss Porter's Sch., 1969-73. Served to lt. USNR, 1943-45. Decorated Bronze Star medal; Hon. Order British Empire. Mem. Am., CAlif., Los Angeles County bar assns., So. Calif. Harvard Law Sch. Assn. (trustee, chmn. 1967-69), Delta Kappa Epsilon. Republican. Episcopalian (vestryman 1968-69, 72-73). Clubs: Chancery, California, Sunset (past sec., pres. 1970-71), Zamorano, Lincoln, Brit. United Services (Los Angeles); Grolier (N.Y.C.). Home: 855 Rosalind Rd Pasadena CA 91108 Office: 555 S Flower St Los Angeles CA 90071

HASTINGS, WILLIAM CHARLES, state supreme ct. judge; b. Newman Grove, Nebr., Jan. 31, 1921; s. William C. and Margaret (Hansen) H.; m. Julie Ann Simonson, Dec. 29, 1946; children—Pamela, Charles, Steven. B.Sc., U. Nebr., 1942, J.D., 1948. Bar: Nebr. bar 1948. With FBI, 1942-43; mem. firm Chambers, Holland, Dudgeon & Hastings, Lincoln, 1948-65; judge 3d jud. dist. Nebr., Lincoln, 1965-79, Supreme Ct. Nebr., 1979—. Pres. Child Guidance Center, Lincoln, 1962, 63; v.p. Lincoln Community Council, 1968, 69; vice chmn. Antelope Valley council Boy Scouts Am., 1968, 69; pres. 1st Presbyn. Ch. Found., 1968—. Served with AUS, 1943-46. Mem. Am. Bar Assn., Nebr. Bar Assn., Lincoln Bar Assn., Nebr. Dist. Judges Assn., Phi Delta Phi. Republican. Presbyterian (deacon, elder, trustee). Club: East Hills Country (pres. 1959-60). Home: 1544 S 58th St Lincoln NE 68506 Office: Nebr Supreme Ct State House Lincoln NE 68509

HASTINGS, WILMOT REED, lawyer; b. Salem, Mass., May 29, 1935; s. Abner Horace and Florence (Hylan) H.; m. Joan Amory Loomis, Aug. 30, 1958; children: W. Reed, Jr., Melissa H., Claire A. A.B. magna cum laude, Harvard U., 1957, LL.B., 1961; postgrad., U. Paris, 1957-58. Bar: Mass. 1961. Law clk. Chief Justice Raymond S. Wilkins, Boston, 1961-62; asso. firm Bingham, Dana & Gould, Boston, 1962-68; 1st asst. and dep. atty. gen., Mass., 1968-69, spl. asst. and exec. asst. to undersec. state, 1969-70; gen. counsel HEW, 1970-73; partner firm Bingham, Dana & Gould, Boston and London, 1973—. Republican. Home: 660 Concord Ave Belmont MA 02178 Office: 100 Federal St Boston MA 02100

HASTORF, ALBERT HERMAN, psychologist, ednl. adminstr.; b. N.Y.C., Nov. 26, 1920; s. Albert Herman and Hilda (Menke) H.; m. Barbara E. Reck, Oct. 4, 1943; children—Elizabeth C., Christine A. A.B., Amherst Coll., 1942; Ph.D., Princeton, 1949, Amherst College, 1967. Instr. psychology Princeton, 1947-48; with dept. psychology, Dartmouth, 1948-61, successively instr., asst. prof., 1948-55, prof., chmn. dept., 1955-61; prof. dept. psychology and Grad. Sch. Bus., Stanford, Calif., 1961—, exec. head dept. psychology, dean humanities and scis., 1970-73, v.p., provost, 1980—; bd. examiners of psychologists State of N.H., 1956-60; Trustee Mills Coll., 1967-77. Contbr. articles to profl. publs. Served from pvt. to sgt. USAAF, 1942-46. Recipient fellowship Center for Advanced Study in Behavioral Scis., Palo Alto, Calif. Fellow Am. Psychol. Assn. Address: 571 Foothill Rd Stanford CA 94305

HASTRICH, JEROME JOSEPH, clergyman; b. Milw., Nov. 13, 1914; s. George Philip and Clara (Dettlaff) H. Student, Marquette U., 1933-35; B.A., St. Francis Sem., Milw., 1940, M.A., 1941, Cath. U. Am., 1947. Ordained priest Roman Cath. Ch., 1941; assigned to Milw. Chancery, 1941; curate St. Ann's Ch., Milw., St. Bernard's Ch., Madison, Wis.; asst. chaplain St. Paul U. Chapel, U. Wis., sec. to bishop of, Madison, 1946-52; chancellor Diocese Madison, Wis., 1952-53, apptd. vicar gen., 1953, domestic prelate, 1954, protonotary apos., 1960; aux. bishop, 1963-67, titular bishop of Gurza and aux. of Madison, 1963; pastor St. Raphael Cathedral, Madison, 1967-69; bishop, Gallup, N.Mex., 1969—; Diocesan dir. Confraternity Christian Doctorine, 1946—, St. Martin Guild, 1947—; aux. chaplain U.S. Air Force, 1947-67; pres. Latin Am. Mission Program; sec. Am. Bd. Cath. Missions; vice chmn. Bishop's Com. for Spanish Speaking; mem. subcom. on allocations U.S. Bishops Com. for Latin Am.; pres. Queen of Americas Guild, 1979, The Blue Army of Our Lady of Fatima, 1980. Mem. Gov. Wis. Commn. Migratory Labor, 1964—. Club: K.C. (hon. life mem.; chaplain N.Mex.). Address: PO Box 1338 Gallup NM 87301

HASWELL, FRANK IRVIN, chief state justice; b. Gt. Falls, Mont., Apr. 6, 1918; s. Irvin Archibald and Laura (Cool) H.; m. June Elizabeth Arnold, May 5, 1951; children—Frank, Bruce, Jack. B.A., U. Wash., 1941; J.D., U. Mont., 1947. Bar: Mont. bar 1947. Asso. Jardine, Chase & Stephenson, Gt. Falls, 1947-48; pvt. practice, Whitefish, 1948-51; partner Haswell & Ryan, Whitefish, 1951-54, Haswell & Heckathorn, 1954-58; dist. judge 11th Judicial Dist. Mont., Kalispell, 1958-67; justice Mont. Supreme Ct., Helena, 1967—, chief justice, 1978—; Chmn. Mont. Probate Commn., 1972—, Gov.'s Juvenile Justice Adv. Council, 1972—. Served with USMCR, 1943-46.

Mem. Mont. Judges Assn. (past pres.). Clubs: Elk, Eagle, Rotarian. Home: 1370 Mill Rd Helena MT 59601 Office: State Capitol Bldg Helena MT 59601

HATALA, ROBERT JOHN, chemist, educator, ednl. adminstr.; b. Duquesne, Pa., Apr. 10, 1931; s. John George and Mary Martha (Bavolar) H.; m. Rodameir Gale Duncan, June 15, 1957; children—Gradette, Jason Brandt, Duncan John. B.S., Juniata Coll., 1952; Ph.D., Yale U., 1957. Research chemist DuPont, Wilmington, Del., 1957-63; asst. prof. U. Del., 1960-63; prof. chemistry Eckerd Coll., St. Petersburg, Fla., 1963-75; dean Univ. Coll., Memphis State U., 1975-80; dean arts and scis. U. So. Maine, Portland, 1980—; vis. prof. Harvard U., Tunghai U.; cons. in field. Contbr. articles to profl. jours. Vestryman Episcopal Ch.; active cub scouts Pinellas County council Boy Scouts Am., Danforth Asso., 1968—. Fellow in acad. adminstrn. Am. Council on Edn., 1974-75; NSF grantee, 1965-69; NIH grantee, 1965-67; Danforth Found. grantee, 1973-79; Kellogg Found. grantee, 1977-80; HEW grantee, 1976-80. Mem. Am. Assn. for Higher Edn., Am. Chem. Soc., AAUP, Council for Advancement of Experiential Learning, Sigma Xi, Alpha Chi Sigma. Democrat. Patentee polymer latex. Office: U Southern Maine Portland ME 04103

HATCH, CALVIN SHIPLEY, home products executive; b. Heber City, Utah, Feb. 23, 1921; s. Edwin D. and Vernico B. (Burton) H.; m. JeNeal Nebeker, Dec. 23, 1945; children: Marcia Ann, Julie Lynne. B.S. in Fin., U. Utah, 1943. Salesman, N.Y. Life Ins. Co., Salt Lake City, 1946-47; with Procter & Gamble Co., 1947-71, sales merchandising mgr., Cin., 1966-68, mgr. central div., 1968-71; v.p. sales Clorox Co., Oakland, Calif., 1971-73, group v.p., 1973-76, exec. v.p., 1977-81, pres., chief exec. officer, 1981-82, chmn., chief exec. officer, 1982—, also dir.; dir. Interstate Bank Calif. Active fund raising Salvation Army, Better Bus. Bur. Served to capt. F.A., AUS, 1942-45. Mem. Oakland, Orinda chambers commerce, Am. Advt. Fedn. (dir. 1977—), Assn. Nat. Advertisers (dir. 1976—). Home: 3853 Palo Alto Dr Lafayette CA 94549 Office: 1221 Broadway Oakland CA 94612

HATCH, DAVID LINCOLN, educator; b. Belmont, Mass., Oct. 2, 1910; s. Roy Winthrop and Bertha May (Roper) H.; m. Mary Alice Gies, Aug. 24, 1940; children—Charles Winthrop, Abby (Mrs. Joel S. Cleland), Faith Winslow (Mrs. William R. Mann), Elizabeth Ann (Mrs. Terry R. Dimmery). A.B., Darmouth Coll., 1933; M.A., Montclair State Coll., 1934, Harvard U., 1948, Ph.D., 1949. Tchr. history and social studies pub. high schs., Madison, N.J., 1934-36, Summit, N.J., 1936-37, Montclair, N.J., 1937-40; instr. sociology Conn. Coll. for Women, New London, 1942-43; vis. lectr. sociology Clark U., Worcester, Mass., 1945-46; asst. prof. sociology U. Ky., Lexington, 1946-48; asso. prof. Syracuse (N.Y.) U., 1948-54; prof., head dept. history and sociology, dir. div. social sci. Madison Coll., Harrisonburg, Va., 1954-57; prof. U. S.C., Columbia, 1957—, acting chmn. dept. anthropology and sociology, 1969-70, chmn. dept., 1970-73; vis. prof. Benedict Coll., Columbia.; Research cons. S.C. State Hosp., Columbia, 1962-64. Author: (with R. W. Hatch) The Story of New England, 1938, (with Mary G. Hatch) Under the Elms: Yesterday and Today, 1949; Contbr. numerous articles to profl. jours., popular mags. Mem. adv. bd. Le Domain Humain, London, Eng., 1964-76; mem. adv. council S.C. Sch. Desegregation Cons. Center, Columbia, 1968; mem. regional aging adv. com. Central Midlands Regional Planning Council, S.C. Fellow Am. Sociol. Assn. (chmn. com. on recruitment for S.C. 1964-67); mem. Soc. Sci. Study Religion, Nat. Council on Family Relations, Eastern Sociol. Soc., So. Sociol. Soc. (chmn. com. on teaching sociology 1958-60), S.C. Sociol. Assn. (pres. 1977-78). Home: 2420 Terrace Way Columbia SC 29205

HATCH, EASTMAN NIBLEY, physics educator; b. Salt Lake City, June 14, 1927; s. Joseph Eastman and Florence (Nibley) H.; m. Anne Clawson, June 21, 1952; children: Joseph Eastman II, Richard Clawson, Anne Florence. Student, U. Utah, 1946-48, 51-52; B.S., Stanford, 1950; Ph.D., Calif. Inst. Tech., 1956. Postdoctoral fellow in physics Calif. Inst. Tech., 1956-57; research asso. physics Brookhaven Nat. Lab., Upton, N.Y., 1957-58; sci. liaison with USN in Frankfurt/Main, Germany, 1958-60; guest physicist Heidelberg U., Germany, 1960-61; assoc. prof. physics Iowa State U., 1961-66, prof. physics, 1966-69; asst. dean Grad. Coll., 1967-69; physicist Ames Lab., 1961-66, sr. physicist, 1966-69; prof. physics Utah State U., Logan, 1969—, head dept. physics, 1972-74, dean sch. grad. studies, 1974-79; vis. prof. physics Freiburg U., W. Ger., 1979-80; vis. research assoc. Los Alamos Sci. Lab., 1971-83. Served with USNR, 1945-46. Fellow Am. Phys. Soc., Phi Beta Kappa, Sigma Xi. Home: 1795 Country Club Dr Logan UT 84321

HATCH, GEORGE CLINTON, TV executive; b. Erie, Pa., Dec. 16, 1919; s. Charles Milton and Blanche (Beecher) H.; m. Wilda Gene Glasmann, Dec. 24, 1940; children: Michael Gene Zbar Arnow, Diane Glasmann Orr, Jeffrey Beecher, Randall Clinton, Deborah Lynne Winslow Hatch. B.A., Occidental Coll., 1940; M.A., Claremont Coll., 1941. Chmn. Intermountain Network, Inc., Salt Lake City, 1941—, Telemation, Inc., 1969, Nat. Telefilm Assos., Inc., Los Angeles, 1971—; chmn. Kans. State Network, Wichita, 1981—; pres. Communications Investment Corp., Salt Lake City, 1945—, KUTV-TV, Inc., 1956—, Gem State Broadcasting Corp., Boise, Idaho, 1962—, Copper Broadcasting Co., Billings, Utah, Idaho Broadcasting Corp., Idaho Falls, KVEL, Inc., 1978, Garden City Broadcasting Corp., 1979—, CJC Cable Inc., Hardin, Mont.; chmn. KSN Cable Inc., Wichita; v.p. Ill. Community Cablevision Inc.; treas. Standard Corp., Ogden; pres. KUTV Community Services Inc., Salt Lake City; mem. Salt Lake adv. bd. First Security Bank Utah; past chmn. Rocky Mountain Pub. Broadcasting Corp.; pres. Sun Progress, Inc.; Past chmn. bd. govs. Am. Information Radio Network; past bd. govs. NBC-TV Affiliates. Past pres. Salt Lake Com. on Fgn. Relations; mem., past chmn. Utah State Bd. Regents, 1964—. Recipient Service to Journalism award U. Utah, 1966, Silver Medal award Salt Lake Advt. Club, 1969, Disting. award Utah Tech. Coll., 1984. Mem. Nat. Assn. Broadcasters (past pres. radio bd. dirs.), Utah Broadcasters Assn. (past pres., Mgmt. award 1964, Hall of Fame award 1981), Phi Beta Kappa, Phi Rho Pi (life). Clubs: Rotarian., Ft. Douglas. Home: 1537 Chandler Dr Salt Lake City UT 84103 Office: 2185 S 3600 W Salt Lake City UT 84119

HATCH, HAROLD ARTHUR, marine corps officer; b. Avon, Ill., Dec. 29, 1924; s. Walter Samuel and Marie (Fennessy) H.; m. Mildred Jean Gehrig, Aug. 18, 1950; children—Sue, Sara, Sallie. B.S., Coll. William and Mary, 1962. Commd. 2d lt. U.S. Marine Corps, 1949, advanced through grades to lt. gen., 1981; div. asst. chief staff for logistics (3d Marine Div.), Okinawa, 1970-71; dep. chief staff Fleet Marine Force Pacific, Hawaii, 1971-74; dep. chief staff for installations and logistics Hdqrs. U.S. Marine Corps, Washington, 1977—; bd. dirs. Navy Mut. Aid Ins. Co. Decorated Legion of Merit, Bronze Star, Air Medal, Meritorious Service Medal. Mem. Nat. Def. Preparedness Assn., Am. Logistics Assn., Nat. Def. Transp. Assn., Nat. Security Indsl. Assn. Republican. Presbyterian. Home: 82 Westover Ave Bolling AFB Washington DC 20336 Office: DC/S I&L Code L HQMC Washington DC 20380

HATCH, HENRY CLIFFORD, beverage company executive; b. Toronto, Ont., Can., Apr. 30, 1916; s. Harry C. and Elizabeth (Carr) H.; m. Joan Ferriss, May 1, 1940; children: Henry Clifford, Gail Elizabeth Todgham, Sheila Mary Stephens, Richard Ferriss. Student, St. Michael's Coll. Sch., Toronto. Salesman T.G. Bright & Co., Ltd., Niagara Falls, Ont., 1933-37; now dir.; merchandising staff Hiram Walker, Inc., Walkerville, Ont., 1937; asst. to v.p. in charge sales, 1946—, v.p., 1946—; v.p., dir. Hiram Walker-Gooderham & Worts, Ltd., Walkerville, 1955-61, exec. v.p., 1961-64, pres., 1964-78, chmn. bd., chief exec. officer, 1978-81; chmn. bd., dir. Hiram Walker Resources Ltd., 1981-82, chmn. bd., pres., chief exec. officer, 1982—; dir. Toronto-Dominion Bank, Bell Canada, T.G. Bright & Co. Ltd., R. Angus Atla. Ltd., Edmonton, Can. Served as comdr. Royal Canadian Navy, 1940-45; in command HMCS; Drummondville, Ville de Que. Clubs: Rosedale Golf, York (Toronto); Essex Golf, Detroit Athletic.; Lost Tree (North Palm Beach, Fla.). Home: 7130 Riverside Dr E Windsor ON N8S 1C3 Canada Office: 1 First Canadian Pl Suite 4200 PO Box 90 Toronto ON M5X 1C5 Canada

HATCH, JAMES ALFRED, newspaper photographer; b. Lakewood, Ohio, June 30, 1939; s. Leon A. and Adia A. (Builder) H.; m. Marianne Kovacs, Sept. 10, 1961; children—Sharon, Charlene. Student, Western Res. U., 1958-59, Kent State U., 1959-60. Copyboy The Plain Dealer, Cleve., 1958-61, staff photographer, 1961-81, chief photographer, 1981—. Mem. Ohio News Photographers Assn. (past chmn. bd.), Nat. Press Photographers Assn. Home: 3595 Hunter Dr North Olmsted OH 44070 Office: 1801 Superior Ave Cleveland OH 44114

HATCH, JOHN DAVIS, museum cons., historian; b. Oakland, Calif., June 14, 1907; s. John Davis and Gethel (Gregg) H.; m. Olivia Phelps Stokes, Oct. 14, 1939; children—John Davis III, Daniel Lindley, James Stokes, Sarah Stokes. Student, U. Calif., 1926-28, Harvard U., 1932, Princeton U., 1938, Yale U., 1940. Landscape architect, Santa Barbara, Calif., 1925, Seattle, 1928; exec. sec. Seattle Art Inst., 1928-29, dir., 1929-31; v.p. Western Assn. Art Museums, 1930-31; surveyed facilities and materials for Far Eastern studies in U.S. and Can., 1932-35, Am. studies in U.S. colls. and univs. for Am. Council Learned Socs., 1938-39; dir. U.S. art projects in, New Eng., 1933-34; mem. McDowell Colony, 1938; asst. dir. Isabella Stewart Gardner Mus., Boston, 1932-35; founder, adviser So. Negro Colls. Coop. Exhibits Group, 1936-41; founder Am. Artist Depository, 1938, Am. Drawing Ann., 1940, Commn. on Art Studies, 1941; Dir. Albany Inst. History and Art, 1940-48; vis. prof. U. Oreg., 1948-49, U. Calif., summer 1949, U. Mass., summer 1971; dir. Norfolk Mus. Arts and Scis., 1950-59; pres. Phelps Stokes Corp., 1959-62; coordinating adviser, acting chmn. fine arts div. Spelman Coll., Ga., 1964-70; v.p. Nevada Co.; Chmn., founder Old Curtisville, 1965, pres. emeritus, 1981—; former trustee Lenox Sch., Hoosac Sch. Author: American sect. Great Drawings of All Times, 1962, Historic Survey of Painting in Canada, 1946, Historic Church Silver in the Southern Diocese of Virginia, 1952; Editor: Parnassus, 1937-39, Albany County Hist. Assn. Record, 1941-48, Early Am. Industries Chronicle, 1942-49; traveling exhibits for, Carnegie Corp., 1935-37, 100 Am. drawings, Dublin, London, Paris, 1976-77; had pioneer exhibit The Negro Artist Comes of Age, 1945, Outdoor Sculptors of Berkshires, 1978. Mem. Master Drawing Assn. (trustee, founder 1962), Am. Drawing Soc. (adv. bd.), Berkshire County Hist. Soc. (past treas., trustee), Stockbridge Bowl Assn. (past pres.), Stockbridge Hist. Com. (chmn.), Am. Assn. Mus. (founder N. Eastern conf. 1941, S.E. conf. 1951). Episcopalian. Clubs: Rotary (past pres.), Grolier (N.Y.C.)). Address: Lenox MA 01240

HATCH, ORRIN GRANT, U.S. Senator; b. Homestead Park, Pa., Mar. 22, 1934; s. Jesse and Helen (Kamm) H.; m. Elaine Hansen, Aug. 28, 1957; children: Brent, Marcia, Scott, Kimberly, Alysa, Jesse. B.S., Brigham Young U., 1959; J.D., U. Pitts., 1962. Bar: Pa. 1962, Utah 1962. Ptnr. firm Thomson, Rhodes & Grigsby, Pitts., 1962-69, Hatch & Plumb, Salt Lake City, 1976; mem. U.S. Senate from Utah, 1977—. Contbr. articles to newspapers and profl. jours. Mem. Am., Nat., Utah, Pa. bar assns., Am. Judicature Soc. Republican. Mormon. Office: 135 Hart Senate Office Bldg Washington DC 20510

HATCH, RICHARD, actor; b. Santa Monica, Calif., May 21. Ed., Harbor Coll. Appeared: off-Broadway in Love Me, Love My Children; regular on: TV series Battlestar Galactica; other TV appearances include Addie and the King of Hearts; appeared in: TV films The Third Cry; participant: Circus of the Stars; appeared in: feature film Charlie Chan and the Curse of the Dragon; movie Battlestar Galactica; theater performances include P.S., Your Cat is Dead, Chgo. Office: care Elsboy Inc 1604 Courtney Ave Los Angeles CA 90046

HATCH, ROBERT NORRIS, banker; b. Disputanta, Va., Sept. 8, 1914; s. John Henry and Hettie (Neblett) H.; m. Helen Elizabeth Tierney, Jan. 6, 1945; 1 son, Robert Norris. Student, U. Richmond, 1936-37, 39-40. Clk. Life Ins. Co. Va., Richmond, 1932-37; cashier Gen. Motors Acceptance Corp., Richmond, 1937-40; v.p. Bank of Va., Norfolk, 1940-69; chmn. bd., chief exec. officer Bank of Va.-Peninsula, Newport News, 1969-72; also dir.; vice chmn. Bank Va. Co., Richmond, 1972-78, pres. chief adminstrv. officer, 1978-80, also dir. Bd. govs. United Givers Fund, Richmond; past dir. Hampton Roads Maritime Assn., Norfolk YMCA. Served with USNR, 1942-46, 51-52. Mem. Am. Inst. Banking. Methodist. Clubs: Norfolk Yacht Country (past pres.), Norfolk Kiwanis, Country of Va., Commonwealth. Home: 8922 Ginger Way Dr Richmond VA 23229

HATCH, ROBERT WINSLOW, consumer products corporation executive; b. Hanover, N.H., Sept. 8, 1938; s. Winslow Roper and Dita Meiggs (Keith) H.; m. Nancy Packard Murphy, June 30, 1962; children: Kristin, Robert Winslow. B.A., Dartmouth Coll., 1960, M.B.A., 1962. Sales rep. Libby Glass Co., N.Y.C., 1961-62; research asst. Amos Tuck Sch., Hanover, 1962-63; with Gen. Mills, Inc., Mpls., 1963-84, product mgr., 1965-68, mktg. dir., 1968-71; exec. v.p. Gorton Corp., 1971-73, gen. mgr. protein div., 1973-75, gen. mgr., 1976, 1976-78, group v.p. splty. retailing, 1978-80, exec. v.p. splty retailing, collectibles and furniture, 1980-84, asst. to vice chmn. consumer non-foods, 1983; pres., chief exec. officer Interstate Bakeries Corp., Kansas City, Mo., 1984—; dir. Leslie Paper Co.; Pres. bd. East Side Neighborhood Services (Settlement House), from 1980. Exec. com. Mpls. Boys Club, 1978-83. Recipient Mpls. City Council's Com. on Urban Environment award, 1980. Republican. Presbyterian. Club: Calhoun Beach (pres. bd. govs. 1981-83). Office: Interstate Bakeries Corp PO Box 1627 Kansas City MO 64141

HATCHER, CHARLES, Congressman; b. Doerun, Ga., July 1, 1939. Student, Ga. So. Coll., U. Ga. Sch. Law. Bar: Ga. bar 1969. Practice law, Albany, Ga.; mem. Ga. Ho. of Reps., 1973; asst. adminstrn. floor leader for Gov. George Busbee; mem. 97th Congress from 2d Ga. Dist. Served with USAF. Office: Rm 1726 Longworth House Office Bldg Washington DC 20515 *

HATCHER, GORDON MERRELL, coll. dean; b. Sonora, Calif., Nov. 22, 1934; s. Gordon Andrew Merrell and Hazel Virginia H. Student, Northeastern Okla. A. and M. Jr. Coll., 1952-53; B.A., Okla. Bapt. U., 1956; M.R.E., Central Bapt. Theol. Sem., Kansas City, Kans., 1957; postgrad., Golden Gate Bapt. Theol. Sem., Strawberry Point, Calif., 1959, Pacific Sch. Religion, Berkeley, 1959; S.Ed., New Orleans Bapt. Theol. Sem., 1966, Okla. State U., 1966-70; M.A. in Religious Edn, U. Pacific, Stockton, Calif., 1968; Ph.D. in Counseling and Guidance in Higher Edn, Western Colo. U., 1974. Childhood edn. and family life edn. fellow New Orleans Bapt. Theol. Sem., 1960-62, group leader pastoral counseling, 1960-63, cons. religious vocation, counselor, 1961-64; dir. counseling and guidance, instr. gen. and ednl. psychology Norman Coll., 1964-66; instr. Okla. Bapt. U., 1966-67, dir. field services, 1966-70; cons. high sch. relations, instr. psychology and sociology Oklahoma City Southwestern Jr. Coll., 1970-71, St. Gregory's Coll., Shawnee, Okla., 1970; dean student services, instr. psychology, sociology and philosophy Crowder Coll., 1971—; Instr. speech and pastoral ministries Union Bapt. Theol. Sem., New Orleans, 1960-61. Contbr.: articles to Care mag. and; other jours.; Lesson writer: Bapt. Sunday Sch. Bd, 1974—. Counselor Goodwill Industries New Orleans, 1961-64; group and individual counselor Sellers Home for Unwed Mothers, New Orleans, 1962-63; counselor clin. pastoral edn. East La. State Hosp., Jackson, 1963; Bd. dirs. St. Charles Parish Guidance Center, Norco, La., 1962-64. Mem. Am., Mo., Mo.-Ozark personnel and guidance assns., Am. Coll. Personnel Assn., Mo. Assn. Jr. Colls., Mo. State Tchrs. Assn., Mo. Assn. Deans Student Devel., Newton-McDonald Counselor's Assn. Club: Lion. Home: Crowder Coll Neosho MO 64850

HATCHER, JAMES DONALD, medical educator; b. St. Thomas, Ont., Can., June 22, 1923; s. Fred Thomas and Cora (Rooke) H.; m. Helen Edith Roberts, June 15, 1946; children: Janet Louise, Carolyn Elizabeth. M.D., U. Western Ont., London, Can., 1946, Ph.D., 1951. Intern Hamilton Gen. Hosp., Ont., Can., 1946-47; instr. medicine Sch. Medicine, Boston U., 1950-52; mem. faculty dept. physiology Queen's U. Med. Sch., Kingston, Ont., Can., 1952-75, asso. prof., 1955-59, prof., chmn. dept., 1959-75; asso. dean Faculty Medicine, 1968-71; prof. physiology, dean Faculty Medicine, Dalhousie U., Halifax, N.S., Can., 1976—; attending physician Hypertensive and Cardiac Clinic, Mass. Meml. Hosp., Boston, 1950-52; research fellow Robert Dawson Evans Meml. Hosp., Boston, 1950-52; Mem. arctic panel Def. Research Bd. Can., 1957-67, mem. adv. com. bd., 1962-67; mem. adv. com. Surgeon Gen., Dept. Nat. Def., 1964-66; mem. grant panel Med. Research Council Can., 1964-74, 76-81, mem. council, 1967-70; dir. Connaught Labs. Contbr. profl. jours. Mem. adv. com. Ont. Heart Found., 1966-71, bd. dirs., 1969-71; bd. dirs. Dalhousie Med. Research Found. Served to lt. M.C. Royal Canadian Army, 1944-50. Nat. Research Council grad. med. research fellow, 1947-50; Markle scholar, 1952-57; Nuffield traveling fellow, 1956; Ont. Heart Found. fellow, 1957-59; Nat. Heart Found. Can. sr. research fellow, 1959-60; recipient Med. Research Council sabbatical award U. Calif. Med. Center, San Francisco, 1971-72. Fellow Royal Coll. Physicians and Surgeons (Can.); mem. Canadian Physiol. Soc. (pres. 1970-71), Exec. Assn. Can. Med. Schs., Alpha Omega Alpha. Home: 24 Rockwood Armdale Halifax NS Canada

HATCHER, JOHN HENRY, archivist; b. Prestonburg, Ky., Dec. 10, 1924; s. William Boone and Dora (Meador) H.; m. Hildegard Ostemeier, Feb. 19, 1961; children: Eva-Marie Elizabeth, John Henry. Student, U. Ky., 1942-43; B.G.E., U. Md., 1962; M.A., Hardin Simmons U., 1963; Ph.D., U. Cin., 1967. Enlisted U.S. Army, 1943; served as command sgt. USAF, 1971; ret., 1971, combat crew men., communications staff officer, adminstr., Stuttgart, Ger., 1967-72; prof. U. Md., 1967-72; archivist U.S. Army, Washington, 1974—; vis. prof. Kultus Ministerium, Baden-Wurttember State Govt., 1968-69; adj. prof. Am. U., Washington, 1977-81; German and mil. specialist Nat. Archives, Washington. Author: Users' Guide to Sources on the War in Viet Nam, 1975, Select Bibliography, The War in Vietnam, 1977, U.S. Army Combat Units of the War in Vietnam, 1979. Decorated Legion of Merit, Air medal, knight of grace Order St. John of Jerusalem; recipient Meritorious Civilian Service medal Dept. Army, 1979. Mem. Assn. Records Mgrs. and Adminstrs., Nat. Classifications Mgmt. Soc., Orgn. Am. Historians, Am. History Assn., W. Tex. Hist. Assn., Filson Club, Ky. Hist. Soc., Order Ky. Cols., Air Force History Found., AAUP, Am. Cath. Fedn. Austrian, German and Swiss Univ. Profs., ACLU, Air Force Sgts. Assn., Air Force Assn., U.S. Army Assn., Soc. Am. Archivists, Ky. Soc. of Washington, Wolf Trap Assn., Smithsonian Assn., Nebraska of Washington, Acad. Polit. Sci, Am. Acad. Polit. and Social Sci., Phi Alpha Theta. Republican. Lutheran. Home: 5251 Rolling Rd Springfield VA 22151 Office: Dept Army Records Mgmt Div Adj Gen Ctr Washington DC 20310

HATCHER, RICHARD G., mayor; b. Michigan City, Ind., July 10, 1933; s. Carlton and Catherine H. B.A., Ind. U.; J.D., Valparaiso U. Bar: Ind. bar. Practiced in, East Chicago, formerly dep. prosecutor, Lake County, Ind.; councilman-at-large Gary City Council, 1963-66; mayor of, Gary, 1967—; co-chmn. legis. action com., trustee, mem. human resources com., mem. exec. bd., chmn. adv. bd. U.S. Conf. Mayors, pres., 1980-81. Co-author commn. report on del. selection. Mem. steering com. on human resources devel. Nat. League Cities, now chmn. com., also bd. dirs.; a founder Muigwithania, social and civic club, now v.p.; mem. Nat. Com. of Inquiry; mem. task force on presdl. TV debates 20th Century Fund; chmn. edn. subcom. Ind. adv. com. to U.S. Commn. Civil Rights; nat. chmn. bd. dirs. Operation PUSH, 1979—; mem. exec. com. Nat. Urban Coalition; founder Nat. Black Caucus of Locally Elected Ofcls.; convenor Nat. Black Polit. Conv., Nat. Conf. on a Black Agenda for the 80's, 1980; pres. Nat. Conf. Democratic Mayors, Nat. Conf. Black Mayors; mem. steering com. Nat. Black Assembly; chmn. Ind. State Black Caucus; mem. Ind. exec. bd. NAACP, legal adviser, Gary chpt.; bd. dirs. Greater Gary United Fund; trustee, mem. adv. com. Gary Urban League; chmn. bd. Transafrica; mem. adv. bd. Ind. U. N.W., Robert Woods Johnson Meml. Found.; chmn. Gary City Dem. Com.; mem. Ind. Dem. State Central Com., Nat. Dem. Com. on Del. Selection, Dem. Nat. Com.; vice chmn. Dem. Nat. Com., 1980—; mem. U.S. intergovtl. adv. commn. on edn. to Sec. of Edn.; chmn. bd. Trans-Africa. Mem. ABA, Ind. Bar Assn., Gary Bar Assn. (exec. com.), Gary Jaycees. Address: City Hall 401 Broadway Gary IN 46402 *The central principle of my political life has been simply this: the richest nation in the world cannot long afford to continue to oppress its Black people, its poor and its disadvantaged. All other considerations are secondary to this moral requirement - that there must be opportunity for all Americans, regardless of race, regardless of status. To this end I have dedicated my public and private life.*

HATCHER, ROBERT DOUGLAS, educator, physicist; b. St. John's, Nfld., Can., June 26, 1924; came to U.S., 1947, naturalized, 1952; s. Charles W. and Lillian (Nichols) H.; m. Helen Charlotte Schober, June 16, 1951; children—Robert, Brian, Peter, Christopher. B.Sc., Dalhousie U., Halifax, N.S., Can., 1945, M.Sc., 1947; M.S., Yale, 1948, Ph.D., 1949. From instr. to asso. prof. N.Y.U., 1949-62; mem. faculty Queens Coll., City U. N.Y., 1962—, prof. physics, 1962—, chmn. dept. physics, 1965-67; Cons. Brookhaven Nat. Lab., 1958—. Fellow N.Y. Acad. Scis., Am. Phys. Soc.; mem. Am. Assn. Physics Tchrs., Am. Assn. U. Profs. Spl. Research radiation defects in ionic crystals, defects in metals, phys. properties pure ionic crystals. Home: 8 Winchester Ln Halesite NY 11743 Office: Physics Dept Queens Coll Flushing NY 11367 *I have always tried to understand, as much as possible, the material I was studying or the enterprise I was engaged in; and to try to empathize or put myself in the position of the other person in human relations.*

HATCHER, WILLIAM C., distributing company executive; b. Bleeker, Ala., 1922; married. With Genuine Parts Co. Inc., Atlanta, 1940—; sales mgr. Birmingham br. Genuine Parts Co. Inc., Atlanta, 1949-52, mgr. New Orleans ops., 1952-61, in charge ops. Atlanta, 1962-65, exec. v.p. ops., 1965-73, pres., 1973, dir., Am. Reassurance Co., Nat. Service Industries. Office: Genuine Parts Co Inc 2999 Circle 75 Pkwy Atlanta GA 30339 *

HATCHER, WILLIAM HAMILTON, educator; b. Carthage, Mo., Mar. 14, 1922; s. James Walter and Emilie (Hamilton) H.; m. Dorothy Maxine Hedrick, Oct. 9, 1943 (dec. 1978); children—Judith (Mrs. David Thomas Jenkins), Suzanne (Mrs. Elton Van Elkins); m. Janet A. Hughes, May 18, 1980. B.A., U. Ark., 1949, M.A., 1950; Ph.D., Duke, 1961. Prof. polit. sci. Va. Poly. Inst., 1949-59, N.E. Mo. State Coll., 1959-62; prof. polit. sci. U. So. Miss., 1962—, dir. univ. honors program, 1965-74; chmn. dept. polit. sci., 1967—. Editor: So. Quar, 1965-73. Served with AUS, 1942-45. Duke fellow, 1954-56. Mem. Miss. Polit. Sci. Assn. (pres. 1972-73), So. Polit. Sci. Assn., Pi Gamma Mu, Phi Alpha Theta, Alpha Kappa Psi, Phi Kappa Phi, Omicron Delta Kappa. Democrat. Methodist. Club: Kiwanian (chmn. Circle K com. Hattiesburg 1965-70). Home: Box 5108 So Sta Hattiesburg MS 39401

HATCHER, WILLIAM JULIAN, JR., engineering educator; b. Augusta, Ga., July 21, 1935; s. William Julian and Norvell (Kelley) H.; m. Sharon Lynn Hancock, Jan. 18, 1958; children: Jeffrey Craig, Rebecca Lynn, Michael William. B.Ch.E. with honors, Ga. Inst. Tech., 1957; M.Ch.E., La. State U., 1964, Ph.D., 1968. Research engr. Esso Research Labs., Baton Rouge, La., 1960-66; research asso. La. State U., 1966-68; sr. research engr. Esso Research Labs., Baton Rouge, 1968-69; asso. prof. chem. engring. U. Ala., 1969-76, prof., 1976—, dept. head, 1973-82; acting dean Sch. Engring., 1981-82; cons. U.S. Bur. Mines, 1972—; mem. adj. faculty USMC Command and Staff Coll., 1978—; Mem. Ala. Hazardous Wastes Adv. Com., 1978—. Contbg. author: Environmental Engineering Handbook, 1973, Computer Programs for Chemical Engineering Education, Vols. II and IV, 1972. Served to lt. USMC, 1957-60. NSF research grantee, 1970-72, 77-80. Mem. Am. Inst. Chem. Engrs., Am. Soc. Engring. Edn., Phi Kappa Phi, Tau Beta Pi, Phi Eta Sigma, Omega Chi Epsilon, Phi Lambda Upsilon. Methodist. Research in petroleum processes, 1960-66; air pollution control, 1968-69; catalysis, 1970. Home: 30 Woodland Hills Tuscaloosa AL 35405 Office: PO Box G University AL 35486

HATCHER, WILLIAM SPOTTSWOOD, mathematician, educator; b. Charlotte, N.C., Sept. 20, 1935; emigrated to Can., 1968; s. Albert Spottswood and Helen (Hardman) H.; m. Judith Ann Bernstein, June 6, 1959; children—Sharon Nur, Carmel Lynne, Benjamin Faizi. B.A. cum laude, Vanderbilt U., 1957; M.A. in Teaching (duPont fellow), 1958; Docteur ès Sciences (scholar Fonds national suisse pour la recherche scientifique 1962-64), U. Neuchâtel, Switzerland, 1963. Teaching asst. in math. Vanderbilt U., 1958-60; research asso. U. Neuchâtel, 1962-64, prof. in charge of course, 1965; asso. prof. math. U. Toledo, 1965-68; asso. prof. U. Laval, Que., Can., 1968-72, prof., 1972—; guest prof. Ecole Polytechnique Fédérale, Lausanne, Switzerland, 1972-73; guest lectr. various univs., Europe, N.Am.; Mem. Nat. Spiritual Assembly of Baha'is of Switzerland, 1962-65; founding mem. exec. com. Assn. for Baha'i Studies, 1975—. Author: books including Foundations of Mathematics, 1968, The Science of Religion, 1977, (with S. Whitney) Absolute Algebra, 1978; The Logical Foundations of Mathematics, 1982; contbr. articles to profl. jours. Can. NRC grantee, 1969—; Que. Ministry Edn. grantee, 1970-74, 82—; IBM grantee, 1973-74. Mem. Am. Math. Soc., Math. Assn. Am., Assn. Symbolic Logic (council 1979-82). Office: Dept Math Faculty Scis and Engring U Laval Quebec PQ G1K 7P4 Canada *I feel that individual achievement has meaning only in the larger context of human society and the social goal of establishing a just and progressive social order. It is such a spirit of humility and mutual cooperation alone that allows individual gifts or talents to assume genuine significance.*

HATCHETT, EDWARD EARL, aerospace manufacturing company executive; b. Amarillo, Tex., Aug. 18, 1923; s. Edward Lockett and Cora (Graham) H.; m. Kathryn Farwell, Apr. 27, 1943; 1 dau., Diane Hatchett Sanford. B.S. in Mgmt. Engring, Tex. A&M Coll., 1947, Stanford U., 1968. Registered profl. engr., Tex. Timestudy engr. Montgomery Ward & Co., Ft. Worth, 1947-49; with Ft. Worth div. Gen. Dynamics Corp., 1949—, v.p. fin., 1970—. Div. sec., chmn. Ft. Worth United Way, 1974-80; bd. dirs., adv. council Ft. Worth Salvation Army, 1978-83; bd. dirs. Casa Mãnana Musicals, Ft. Worth, 1980—; chmn. Ft. Worth Area Com. for Employer Support of the Guard and Res.; exec. bd. Longhorn council Boy Scouts Am., 1981—; mem. North Tex. Commn. Strategic Issues Adv. Council. Served to maj. USAAF, 1943-46, 51-53. Recipient Presdl. citation Am. Soc. Value Engrs., 1974, Exec. of yr. award Exec. Women Internat., 1976. Mem. Am. Def. Preparedness Assn. (pres. Lone Star chpt. 1976-78, exec. com., dir. 1979—, Outstanding Leadership award Lone Star chpt. 1977), Fin. Execs. Inst., Air Force Assn., Gen. Dynamics Mgmt. Assn., Ft. Worth Air Power Council, Ft. Worth C. of C. (dir. 1976, 81-82, mem. mil. affairs com.). Methodist. Club: Ridglea Country. Office: PO Box 748 MZ 1230 Fort Worth TX 76101

HATCHETT, JOSEPH WOODROW, judge; b. Clearwater, Fla., Sept. 17, 1932; s. John Arthur and Lula Gertrude (Thomas) H.; m. Betty Lue Davis, Aug. 20, 1956; children—Cheryl Nadine, Brenda Audrey. A.B., Fla. A. and M. U., 1954; J.D., Howard U., 1959, U.S. Naval Justice Sch., Newport, R.I., 1973. Bar: Fla. bar 1959. Practice in, Daytona Beach, 1959-66; asst. U.S. atty. Dept. Justice, Jacksonville, Fla., 1966-70; U.S. magistrate U.S. Cts., Jacksonville, 1971-75; justice Supreme Ct. Fla., Tallahassee, 1975-79; judge U.S. Ct. of Appeals, Fifth Circuit, 1979—; Cooperating atty. N.A.A.C.P. Legal Def. Fund, 1960-66; gen. counsel Masons of Fla., 1963-66; cons., mem. staff dept. urban renewal, Daytona Beach, 1963-66, spl. asst. to city atty., 1964; Mem. com. selection for Jacksonville Naval Res. Officer Tng. Corps, 1971. Contbr. articles to profl. jours. Mem. John T. Stocking Meml. Trust, med. sch. scholarships, 1961-66; Co-chmn. United Negro Coll. Fund of Volusia County, Fla., 1962; bd. dirs. Jacksonville Opportunities Industrialization Center, 1972-75. Served to 1st lt. AUS, 1954-56; Germany. Recipient Mary McCloud Bethune medallion for community service Bethune-Cookman Coll., 1965, medallion for human relations, 1975. Mem. Am., Nat., Fla., Jacksonville, D. W. Perkins, Fed. bar assns., Am. Judicature Soc., Nat. Council Fed. Magistrates, V.F.W., Omega Psi Phi. Baptist (trustee). Club: Fla-Jax (Jacksonville) (Man of Year 1974). Home: PO Box 981 Tallahassee FL 32302 Office: Suite 810 Lewis State Bank Bldg PO Box 10429 Tallahassee FL 32302

HATFIELD, DAVID UNDERHILL, artist; b. Plainfield, N.J., July 16, 1940; s. Richard Pearson and Margaret (Weldon) H. B.F.A., Miami U., Oxford, Ohio, 1962; postgrad., Art Students League, 1964, Sch. Visual Arts, 1963. One-man exhbns. include, Nat. Arts Club, N.Y.C., 1976, Christopher Gallery, 1981; two-man, Christopher Gallery, N.Y.C., 1979; group exhbns. include, Nat. Acad. Galleries, N.Y.C., 1968, 70, 71, 72, 73, 74, 75, 76, 77, 84, Nat. Arts Club, 1970, 71, 72, 75, 76, 77, work appeared on cover, Am. Artist mag., Dec. 1981, Prevention mag., Jan. 1982. John F. and Anna Lee Stacy grantee, 1975; Elizabeth T. Greenshields Meml. Found. grantee, 1973, 74; Recipient Julius Hallgarten prize Nat. Acad. Design, 1970; Margaret Dole meml. award Am. Artists Profl. League, 1972; Carl Matson Meml. award Rockport Art Assn., 1979; Best in show award Westfield Art Assn., 1982; Figure award Rockport Art Assn., 1982. Mem. Grand Central Art Galleries, Am. Artists Profl. League, Allied Artists Am., Hudson Valley Art Assn., Rockport Art Assn., Westfield Art Assn., North Shore Art Assn. Club: Salmagundi (Arthur T. Hill Meml. award 1980) (N.Y.C.). Address: 9 River St Hoosick Falls NY 12090 *Fortunately, from my early training through college, the concern was with "what looked good," not "what would sell."*

HATFIELD, ELAINE CATHERINE, psychology educator; b. Detroit, Oct. 22, 1937; d. Charles E. and Eileen (Kalahar) H. B.A., U. Mich., 1959; Ph.D., Stanford U., 1963. Asst. prof. U. Minn., 1963-64; asso. prof. U. Rochester, 1966-68, U. Wis., Madison, 1968-69, prof., 1969-81; chmn. dept. U. Hawaii of Manoa, 1981—. Author: Interpersonal Attraction, 1969, 2d edit., 1978, Equity: Theory and Research, 1978, A New Look at Love, 1978, Psychology of Sexual Behavior, 1983; Contbr. articles to profl. jours. Fellow Am. Psychol. Assn., Am. Sociol. Assn. Home: 3334 Ano'ai Pl Honolulu HI 96822 Office: 2430 Campus Rd Honolulu HI 96822

HATFIELD, HENRY CARAWAY, German educator, author; b. Evanston, Ill., June 3, 1912; s. James Taft and Estelle (Caraway) H.; m. Jane Stauff, Mar. 15, 1937; children: Robert Allan, Barbara. A.B., Harvard U., 1933; A.M., Columbia U., 1938, Ph.D., 1942. Instr. Williams Coll., 1938-42, asst. prof., 1942-46, Columbia U., 1946-48, asso. prof., 1948-54, Harvard U., 1954-56, prof. German, 1956-70, Kuno Francke prof. German lit., 1967-78, sr. research prof., 1978-82, chmn. dept. Germanic lang. and lit., 1957-59; vis. prof. Free U. Berlin, 1961; With O.W.I., London, 1944-45. Author: Winckelmann and His German Critics, 1943, Thomas Mann, 1951, rev. 1962, (with J.M. Stein) Schnitzler, Kafka, Mann, 1953, (with F.H. Mautner) The Lichtenberg Reader, 1959, Goethe: A Critical Introduction, 1963, Aesthetic Paganism in German Literature, 1964, Thomas Mann, A Critical Anthology, 1964, Modern German Literature, 1967, Crisis and Continuity in Modern German Fiction, 1969, Clashing Myths in German Literature, 1974, From the Magic Mountain: Mann's Later Masterpieces, 1979; gen. editor: Germanic Rev, 1947-53; editorial bd.: PMLA, 1951-56. Recipient Guggenheim and Fulbright fellowships, 1952-53; Am. Council Learned Socs. awards, 1962, 67, 75; Nat. Endowment for Humanities grantee, 1975. Mem. Modern Lang. Assn. Am. (exec. com. 1956-59), Am. Acad. of Arts and Scis., Am. Assn. Tchrs. German, ACLU. Home: 40 Fernald Dr Cambridge MA 02138 Home: Groton VT 05046 Office: 747 Widener Library Harvard Univ Cambridge MA 02138

HATFIELD, JAMES E., labor union official. Pres. Glass, Pottery, Plastics & Allied Workers Internat. Union. Office: 608 E Baltimore Pike PO Box 608 Media PA 19063§

HATFIELD, LEONARD FRASER, bishop; b. Port Greville, N.S., Can., Oct. 1, 1919; s. Otto Albert and Ada (Tower) H. B.A., King's-Dalhousie U., Halifax, N.S., 1940, M.A., 1943; D.D. hon., King's-Dalhousie SU., 1956. Ordained deacon Anglican Ch. of Can., 1942, ordained priest, 1943; priest asst. All Sts. Cathedral, Halifax, 1942-46; rector Antigonish, N.S., 1946-51; asst. sec. council social service Anglican Ch. of Can., 1951-54, gen. sec., 1955-61; rector Christ Ch., Dartmouth, N.S., 1961-71, St. John's Ch., Truro, N.S., 1971-76; cannon All Sts. Cathedral, Halifax, 1969; suffragen bishop of Nova Scotia, 1976-80, bishop of N.S., Halifax, 1980-84; chmn. Diocesan Counsil of N.S. Synod, corp. Anglican Diocesan Ctr.; chmn. Dean and Chpt. All Sts. Cathedral; organizing sec. primate's World Relief and Devel. Fund; mem. Council of Chs. on Justice and Corrections; founding mem. Vanier Inst. Family, Ottawa; mem. Anglican Consultative Council; various coms. World Council Chs. 2d Gen. Synod; convenor Primate's Task Force on Ordination of Women to Priesthood; Anglican Chamber of Can. rep. Internat. Bishops' Seminar, Rome, 1980. Author: He Cares, 1958. Chmn. bd. govs. King's Coll.; former bd. dirs. Inst. Pastoral Tng. Atlantic Sch. Theology. Office: Synod Office Diocese of Nova Scotia 5732 College St Halifax NS Canada B3H 1X3

HATFIELD, MARK, U.S. senator; b. Dallas, Oreg., July 12, 1922; s. Charles Dolen and Dovie (Odom) H.; m. Antoinette Kuzmanich, July 8, 1958; children: Mark, Elizabeth, Theresa, Charles. A.B., Willamette U., 1943; A.M., Stanford U., 1948. Instr. Willamette U., 1949, dean students, asso. prof. polit. sci., 1950-56; mem. Oreg. Ho. of Reps., 1951-55, Oreg. Senate, 1955-57; sec. State of Oreg., 1957-59, gov., 1959-67; U.S. senator from Oreg., 1967—, chmn. appropriations com.; mem. energy and natural resources com., rules and adminstrn. com. Author: Not Quite So Simple, 1967, Conflict and Conscience, 1971, Between A Rock and A Hard Place; co-author: Amnesty: The Unsettled Question of Vietnam, 1973, Freeze!, 1982, The Causes of World Hunger, 1982. Served to lt. j.g. USN, 1943-45. Recipient numerous hon. degrees. Baptist. Office: Room SH-711 US Senate Washington DC 20510

HATFIELD, PAUL GERHART, lawyer, judge; b. Great Falls, Mont., Apr. 29, 1928; s. Trueman LeRoy and Grace Lenore (Gerhart) H.; m. Dorothy Ann Allen, Feb. 1, 1958; children—Kathleen Helen, Susan Ann, Paul Allen. Student, Coll. of Great Falls, 1947-50; LL.B., U. Mont., 1955. Bar: Mont. bar 1955. Asso. firm Hoffman & Cure, Gt. Falls, Mont., 1955-56, Jardine, Stephenson, Blewett & Weaver, Gt. Falls, 1956-58, Hatfield & Hatfield, 1959-60; chief dep. county atty., Cascade County, Mont., 1959-60; dist. ct. judge 8th Jud. Dist., Mont., 1961-76; chief justice Supreme Ct. Mont., Helena, 1977-78; U.S. Senator from Mont., 1978-79; U.S. dist. judge for Dist. of Mont., Gt. Falls, 1979—; Vice chmn. Pres.'s Council Coll. of Great Falls. Author: standards for criminal justice, Mont. cts. Served with U.S. Army, 1953-55; Korea. Mem. Am., Mont. bar assns. Roman Catholic. Home: 2919 4th Ave N Great Falls MT 59401 Office: PO Box 1529 Great Falls MT 59403

HATFIELD, RICHARD BENNETT, Canadian provincial official; b. Hartland, N.B., Can., Apr. 9, 1931; s. Heber Harold and Dora Fern (Robinson) H. B.A., Acadia U., 1952; LL.B., Dalhousie U., 1956; LL.D., U. Moncton, 1971, U. N.B., 1972, St. Thomas U., 1973, Mt. Allison Coll., 1975; Dr. in Polit. Sci. (hon.), U. Ste. Anne, 1983. Bar: N.S. 1956. With firm Patterson, Smith, Matthews & Grant, Truro, N.S., 1957; exec. asst. to minister trade and commerce, Ottawa, Ont., Can., 1957-58; mem. N.B. Legislative Assembly, 1961—; elected leader Progressive-Conservative party, 1969—; elected premier of, N.B., 1970—. Bd. dirs. Canadian Council of Christians and Jews. Hon. Micmac-Màliseet chiefton, 1970; Recipient Can.-Israel Friendship award, 1973; mem. Queen's Privy Council. Office: PO Box 6000 Fredericton NB Canada E3B 5H1

HATFIELD, ROBERT SHERMAN, former packaging company executive; b. Utica, N.Y., Jan. 16, 1916; s. Albert R. and Mary (Sherman) H.; m. Roberta Sullivan, May 8, 1937; children: Roberta A. Hatfield Williamson, Suzanne S. Hatfield Miele, Molly J. Hatfield DuPre, Robert Sherman. Student, Cornell U., 1937; LL.B., Fordham U., 1945; postgrad., Advanced Mgmt. Program, Harvard U., 1954. With Continental Group, Inc. (name formerly Continental Can Co.), Stamford, Conn., 1936-81, chmn., chief exec. officer, 1971-81; pres. Soc. of N.Y. Hosp., N.Y.C., 1981—; dir. Johnson & Johnson, N.Y. Stock Exchange, Inc., Citicorp/Citibank, N.A., Gen. Motors Corp., Eastman Kodak Co., Nabisco Brands Inc., Marsh & McLennan. Mem. Bus. Council; dir. N.Y.C. Partnership; trustee Cornell U., Conf. Bd.; chmn. exec. com. Internat. Exec. Service Corps. Clubs: Chicago; Pinnacle, Links, River, Cornell (N.Y.C.); Blind Brook (Port Chester, N.Y.); Pine Valley (N.J.) Golf, Augusta (Ga.) Nat. Golf. Home: Greenwich CT 06830 Office: 633 3d Ave New York NY 10017

HATFIELD, W.C., banking consultant; b. Denison, Tex., Aug. 18, 1926; s. Roy E. and Henretta (Biggerstaff) H.; m. Wilma L. Nichols, July 5, 1953; children: David L., Sharon, Amy Dawn. B.S., Austin Coll., Sherman, Tex., 1950; M.B.A., Tex. A&M U., 1951; postgrad., Southwestern Grad. Sch. Banking, So. Methodist U., 1962. C.P.A., Tex. With Peat, Marwick, Mitchell & Co., Dallas, 1951-57; trust tax adminstr. to exec. v.p. Republic Nat. Bank of Dallas, 1957—; exec. v.p. Republic of Tex. Corp., Dallas, 1974-78, vice-chmn., 1978—, also dir.; chmn. Republic Bank Trust Co., 1981—; dir. Halliburton Oil Producing Co., Blue Cross/Blue Shield of Tex., Allied Lakewood Bank; Mem. Dallas Estate Planning Council, 1972—; mem. accounting faculty adv. bd. North Tex. State U.; Trustee Abilene Christian U., Harding Coll., LIFE Found. Am. Bd. dirs. devel. council Coll. Bus. Adminstrn., Tex. A&M U. Served with AUS, 1944-46; PTO. Mem. Am. Inst. C.P.A.s, Tex. Soc. C.P.A.s (treas. 1972-73, past pres. Dallas chpt.), Tex. Assn. Bank Holding Cos. (treas.). Mem. Ch. of Christ. Office: 230 North Tower Plaza of Ams Dallas TX 75201

HATFIELD, WILLIAM EMERSON, chemist, educator; b. Ransom, Ky., May 31, 1937; s. Emerson B. and Pricy Gardner (Hatfield) H.; m. Peggy Ranson, Dec. 17, 1955 (div. 1967); children: Timothy Edward, Robert Bruce, Maryan, Julia, Ellen; m. Jane Alice Cheek, Nov. 22, 1967 (div. 1973). B.S., Marshall U., 1958, M.S., 1959; Ph.D., U. Ariz., 1962. Postdoctoral research asso. U. Ill., Urbana, 1962-63; asst. prof. chemistry U. N.C., Chapel Hill, 1963-67, asso. prof., 1967-72, prof., 1972—; vis. scholar Cambridge U., 1978; vis. prof. U. Petroleum and Minerals, Dhahran, Saudi Arabia, 1980, Tata Inst., Bombay, India, 1981; guest prof. Johannes Gutenberg U., Mainz, W. Ger.; mem. acad. adv. council GTE Labs, Inc., 1980-81; Am. specialist U.S. Dept. State, 1977; external examiner U. Sierra Leone, 1976-78; cons. in field; dir. NATO Advanced Research Inst., 1978. Author: (with R.A. Palmer) Problems in Structural Inorganic Chemistry, 1971, (with W.E. Parker) Symmetry in Chemical Bonding and Structure, 1974; Editor: Molecular Metals, 1979; Mem. editorial adv. bd.: Jour. Inorganic and Nuclear Chemistry, 1977—. Recipient Disting. Alumnus award Marshall U., 1976. Mem. AAAS, Am. Chem. Soc. (chmn. inorganic exam. subcom. 1974—), U. Ariz. Alumni Assn. (pres. N.C. chpt. 1977—), Sigma Xi. Democrat. Methodist. Home: 400 Wesley Dr Chapel Hill NC 27514 Office: Kenan Lab U NC Chapel Hill NC 27514

HATHAWAY, ALDEN MOINET, bishop; b. St. Louis, Aug. 13, 1933; s. Earl Burton and Margaret (Moinet) H.; m. Anna Harrison Cox, Dec. 29, 1956; children: Alden Moinet II, Christopher L., Melissa A. B.S., Cornell U., 1955; B.D., Episcopal Theol. Sch., Cambridge,Mass., 1962. Ordained priest Episcopal Ch., 1962. Rector Trinity Ch., Bellefontaine, Ohio, 1962-65; assoc. rector Christ Ch. Cranbrook, Bloomfield Hills, Mich., 1965-71; rector St. Christopher's Ch., Springfield, Va., 1972-81; bishop Diocese of Pitts., 1981—. Served to lt. USNR, 1956-59. Home: 617 S Linden Ave Pittsburgh PA 15208 Office: Episcopal Diocese of Pitts 325 Oliver Ave Pittsburgh PA 15222

HATHAWAY, CARL EMIL, investment management company executive; b. Boston, Aug. 12, 1933; s. Carl Barbour and Tekla (Neumaier) H.; m. Gail Humphries Oglee, Dec. 6, 1958; children: Brian Kent, Carl Nichols, Andrew Oglee. B.A., Harvard U., 1955; M.B.A., Cornell U., 1959. With Morgan Guaranty Trust Co. N.Y., 1959-81, sr. v.p. pension investments, vice chmn. trust and investments dept., 1969-81; pres. Hathaway & Assos. Ltd. (instl. investment mgmt.), Rowayton, Conn., 1981—. Mem. Conn. Adv. Council on Career and Vocat. Guidance, Darien Town Retirement Com. Served to lt. (j.g.) USNR, 1955-57. Clubs: Links (N.Y.C.); Tokeneke (Darien, Conn.); Chequesset Yacht (Wellfleet, Mass.); Harvard (Fairfield County, Conn.); Eastward Ho Country (Chatham, Mass.). Home: Homewood Ln Darien CT 06820 Office: Hathaway & Assos Ltd Rowayton Ave Rowaton CT 06853

HATHAWAY, HAROLD GRANT, bank holding company executive; b. N.Y.C., 1927; s. Harold Grant and Louise (Phillips) H.; m. Mary Elizabeth Mundy, June 1963. With Equitable Bank, Balt., 1955—, v.p., 1963-69, sr. v.p., 1969-71, exec. v.p., 1971-73, pres., 1973-79, chmn. bd., chief exec. officer, 1979—; with Equitable Bancorp., Balt., 1958—, pres., 1975—, also chief exec. officer, dir. Mem. Am. Bankers Assn., Assn. Reserve City Bankers, Md. Bankers Assn. Office: Equitable Bank 100 S Charles St Baltimore MD 21201

HATHAWAY, RICHARD DEAN, educator; b. Chillicothe, Ohio, Aug. 8, 1927; s. Dale and Edith (Hart) H.; m. Viola Hale, Apr. 16, 1978; children by previous marriage: Linda Hathaway Ellis, Bruce. A.B. summa cum laude, Oberlin Coll., 1949; A.M., Harvard U., 1952; Ph.D., Western Res. U., 1964. Exec. sec. New Eng. Fellowship of Reconciliation, Boston, 1953-55; instr. in English, Rensselaer Poly. Inst., Troy, N.Y., 1957-62; asst. prof. SUNY, New Paltz, 1962-65, asso. prof., 1966-69, prof., 1970—; asso. prof. Millsaps Coll., Jackson, Miss., 1965-66. Author: Sylvester Judd's New England, 1981; contbr. poems to mags. and revs. Chair legis. com. SCLC Poor People's Campaign, 1968. Served with USNR, 1945-46. Mem. MLA, Am. Studies Assn., Phi Beta Kappa. Mem. Religious Soc. of Friends. Home: 11 Crescent Ln New Paltz NY 12561 Office: SUNY New Paltz NY 12561 *

HATHAWAY, RICHARD LEE, lawyer; b. Topeka, Apr. 12, 1948; s. William Daniel and Katherine E. (Repper) H.; m. Beverly B. Brown, Aug. 23, 1969; children: Brett, Blair. B.S., Washburn U., 1970, J.D., 1973. Bar: U.S. Ct. Appeals (10th cir.) 1975, Kans. 1973, Mo. 1978. Sole practice, Kansas City, Mo.; corp. atty., sec. Far-Mar Co., Hutchinson, Kans., 1982—. Home: 3604 Basswood St Lee's Summit MO 64063 *The true qualities for success are integrity, tenacity, pragmatism, a grand sense of humor and a realization that true success results from accumulating a wealth of appreaciation for the simple things in life.*

HATHAWAY, WALTER MURPHY, museum exec.; b. Norfolk, Va., Feb. 25, 1939; s. Alvin Earl and Minneta Seybolt (Kerton) H.; m. Anna Elizabeth Burton, Nov. 26, 1960; children—Anna Elizabeth, Michael Burton, John Carter. B.F.A., Va. Commonwealth U., 1961; M.S., Fla. State U., 1964. Tchr. art Norfolk Public Schs., 1961-63; instr. Lake City Jr. Coll., 1964-67; asst. prof. art Longwood Coll., 1967-70; cons. in art N.C. Dept. Public Instrn., Raleigh, 1970-72; dir. Roanoke (Va.) Fine Arts Center, 1972-77, Columbia (S.C.) Museums Art and Sci., 1977—. Mem. Am. Assn. Museums, Assn. Art Mus. Dirs., Southeastern Museums Conf., S.C. Fedn. Museums. Roman Catholic. Club: Rotary (Columbia). Office: 1112 Bull St Columbia SC 29201

HATHEWAY, JOHN HARRIS, advertising agency executive; b. Waterbury, Conn., Aug. 9, 1926; s. Fred Whipple and Louise (Wood) H.; m. Patricia Mary Flaherty, Sept. 24, 1955; children: John Harris, Geoffrey Mills, Sara Wood. A.B., Dartmouth Coll., 1948, M.B.A., 1950. With Young and Rubicam Inc., N.Y.C., 1950—, sr. v.p., mgmt. supr., 1968-74, sr. v.p., group dir., 1974-83, exec. v.p., group dir., 1983—, also dir.; bd. overseers Hanover Inn, N.H., 1968—. Mem. Council of Alumni Dartmouth, 1968—; Bd. dirs. Chappaqua Summer Sch. Program, Horace Greeley Ednl. Fund, 1978—; mem. Diocesan Mission Com. Served with AUS, 1945-46. Recipient Alumni award Dartmouth Coll., 1980. Mem. Phi Beta Kappa. Episcopalian (vestryman, warden). Clubs: New Castle Town (Chappaqua, N.Y.); Dartmouth Coll. of New York (pres. 1965-66, bd. dirs. 1958-64, 67-70, 72—), Waccabuc Country, Manchester (Vt.) Country, Houston

Center. Home: Hoffman Rd RFD 1 Mount Kisco NY 10549 Office: 285 Madison Ave New York NY 10017

HATHORN, RICHMOND YANCEY, educator; b. Alexandria, La., July 31, 1917; s. John Wesley and Aimee Aileen (Sleet) H.; m. Isabel Voelker, May 23, 1947; children—Isabel Voelker, Richmond Yancey, Emily Montgomery. B.A., La. Coll., 1937; M.A., La. State U., 1940; Ph.D., Columbia, 1950. Lectr. classics Columbia, 1947-53; prof. Northwestern State Coll. La., 1953-61; asso. prof. La. State U., 1961-62; prof. classics, chmn. dept. U. Ky., 1962-66; prof. European langs. and lit. Am. U. Beirut, 1966-69; prof., chmn. dept. classics State U. N.Y., Stony Brook, 1969—; vis. prof. U. Mich., 1959. Author: Tragedy, Myth and Mystery, 1962, Handbook of Classical Drama, 1967, Greek Mythology, 1977. Mem. Am. Philol. Assn. Address: Dept Classics State U NY Stony Brook NY 11794

HATIE, GEORGE DANIEL, lawyer; b. Detroit, Mar. 11, 1910; s. George Leon and Mildred Belle (Edwards) H. J.D., U. Detroit, 1933. Bar: Mich. bar 1933. Since practiced in, Detroit; mem. firm Cross, Wrock, Miller & Vieson, 1936—, partner, 1945—; Bd. govs. Am. Numis. Assn., 1967-75, 77-81, legal counsel, 1965-69, 81—, v.p., 1973-75, 77-79, pres., 1979-81; bd. dirs. Mich. Humane Soc., 1953—, pres., 1957-63; mem. U.S. Assay Commn., 1975. Contbr. articles to numis. jours.; lectr. in field. Bd. dirs. Mich. Kidney Found., 1969-80, Girl Scouts Met. Detroit, 1970-73; trustee Nat. Kidney Found., 1973-80, mem. exec. com., 1975-77. Mem. Am. Numis. Soc., Mich. Numis. Soc. (pres. 1964), Detroit Numis Soc. (pres. 1964), Grosse Pointe Numis Soc. (pres. 1960), Central States Numis Soc. (pres. 1970-72), Token and Medal Soc. (pres. 1970-72), Soc. Paper Money Collectors (gov. 1964-66), Am. Humane Soc. (hon. v.p. 1959-63), ABA, Detroit Bar Assn., State Bar Mich. Republican. Roman Catholic. Home: 1126 Whittier Rd Grosse Pointe Park MI 48230 Office: 400 Renaissance Center Suite 1900 Detroit MI 48243

HATSOPOULOS, GEORGE NICHOLAS, mechanical engineer, thermodynamicist, educator; b. Athens, Greece, Jan. 7, 1927; came to U.S., 1948, naturalized, 1954; s. Nicholas and Maria (Platsis) Hatzopoulos; m. Daphne Phylactopoulos, June 14, 1959; children: Nicholas, Marina. Student, Nat. Tech. U., Athens, 1945-47; B.S., M.S., M.I.T., 1950, M.E., 1954, Sc.D., 1956; Sc.D. (hon.), N.J. Inst. Tech., 1982. Instr. M.I.T., 1954-56, asst. prof. mech. engring., 1956-58, assoc. prof., 1959-62, sr. lectr. in mech. engring., 1962—; founder, pres., chief exec. officer Thermo Electron Corp., developer, mfr. and marketer of products based on thermodynamic technologies of heat transfer and energy conversion, Waltham, Mass., 1956—; chmn. bd. Coll. Yr. in Athens; mem. adv. bd. Energy Productivity Center, Carnegie-Mellon Inst., 1978-81; tech. witness numerous Senate and Congl. hearings; mem. engring. edn. com. M.I.T. Center for Policy Alternatives, 1973; mem. policy com. for innovation program NSF at M.I.T., 1973-74; mem. ad hoc com. on air quality and power plant emissions NRC, 1974-75; mem. environ. ad. com. FEA, Washington, 1974-75; dir. Fed. Res. Bank of Boston. Author: Principles of General Thermodynamics, 1965, Thermionic Energy Conversion, vol. 1, 1973, vol. 2, 1979; contbr. numerous articles to profl. jours. Recipient Corp. Leadership award M.I.T., 1980. Fellow IEEE, Am. Acad. Arts and Scis., Nat. Acad. Engring., ASME (chmn. exec. com. div. energetics 1968-69); mem. Am. Acad. Achievement (Golden Plate award 1961), AIAA, Sigma Xi, Pi Tau Sigma (Gold Medal award 1960). Greek Orthodox. Home: Tower Rd Lincoln MA 01773 Office: PO Box 459 101 First Ave Waltham MA 02254

HATT, GUNTHER JOSEF, hotel exec.; b. Krun, W. Ger., Dec. 7, 1939; came to U.S., 1964, naturalized, 1971; s. Wilhelm and Maria Kramer H.; m. Marie Anne von Malottke, Aug. 31, 1961. Diploma, Hotel and Commerce Sch. W. Kermess, Munich, W. Ger., 1957; student various mgmt. seminars, Sonesta Internat. Hotels, 1964-72. In various hotel mgmt. positions, Germany, 1958-63, Switzerland, 1962-64, France, 1963-64; in various mgmt. positions Sonesta Internat. Hotels, Houston, 1964-69; mem. exec. mgmt. team Royal Sonesta, New Orleans, 1969-71, Sonesta Beach Hotel and Golf Club, Nassau, Bahamas, 1971-72; in charge rehab. Parker House Dunfey Hotels, Boston, 1972-75; gen. mgr. Baystate West Hotel, Springfield, Mass., 1975, Dunfey's Royal Coach, Houston, 1975-77, Ala Moana Americana, Honolulu, 1977—; bd. dirs. Council Hawaiian Hotels. Exhibited paintings at, Gallery Hawaii, Honolulu, 1978. Recipient Sales and Mktg. Planning award Americana Hotels, 1978. Mem. Hawaii Hotel Assn., Am. Hotel and Motel Assn., Hawaii Visitors Bur., Epicurean Assn. of the Pacific, Pacific Area Travel Agts., Am. Soc. Travel Agts. Office: 410 Atkinson Dr Honolulu HI 96814

HATTEBERG, LARRY MERLE, photojournalist; b. Winfield, Kans., June 30, 1944; s. Merle Lawrence and Mary Dorothy (Early) H.; m. Judy Beth Keller, June 6, 1965; children: Sherry Renee, Susan Michelle. Student, Kans. State Tchrs. Coll., 1962-63, Emporia-Wichita State U., 1963-66. Photographer Sta. KAKE-TV, Wichita, Kans., 1963, photojournalist, 1966-67, chief photographer, 1967-81, asso. news dir., chief photographer, 1981—; Mem. faculty Nat. Press Photographers TV Workshop, U. Okla., 1975-84. Served with USAR, 1966-72. Mem. Nat. Press Photographers Assn. (Nat. TV News Photographer of Yr. award 1975, 77). Mennonite. Office: 1500 N West St Wichita KS 67212

HATTEN, WILLIAM SEWARD, manufacturing company executive; b. Chgo., Apr. 7, 1917; s. William Seward and Margaret (Ahearn) H.; m. Marjorie Popp, Dec. 29, 1939; 1 dau., Patricia Marie (Mrs. Dudley D. Pendleton III). B.A., Lawrence Coll., 1939; M.B.A., Northwestern U., 1944. Indsl. engr. Sears, Roebuck & Co., 1940-43; mgr. control div. Chgo. Ordnance Dist., 1943-45; owner Eskimo Ice Cream Co., Tucson, 1945-50; gen. mgr. Utica Knitting Co., N.Y., 1950-54; cons. Worden & Risberg, Phila., 1954-64; pres., chief exec. officer, dir. Clayton Mark & Co., Evanston, Ill., 1964-67; chmn. bd. Ken-Ray Brass Products, Inc., Vermont, Ill., 1964-67; pres., chief exec. officer, dir. Harper-Wyman Co., Hinsdale, Ill., 1967-69; exec. v.p. Warner Electric Brake & Clutch Co., Beloit, Wis., 1969-72; group v.p. engines and generators, dir. Kohler Co., Wis., 1973-80; pres. Hatten & Assocs., Plymouth, Wis., 1980—. Mem. Ill. C. of C., Chgo. Assn. Commerce and Industry, Am. Ordance Assn., N.A.M., Northwestern U. Grad. Bus. Alumni Assn., Am. Inst. Mgmt., Phi Delta Theta. Episcopalian. Clubs: Golf, University (Evanston); Union League, Executives (Chgo.); Sheboygan Country. Home: Route 2 Plymouth WI 53073 Office: Plymouth WI 53073

HATTER, TERRY JULIUS, JR., judge; b. Chgo., Mar. 11, 1933. A.B., Wesleyan U., 1954; J.D., U. Chgo., 1960. Bar: Ill. 1960, Calif. 1965, U.S. Dist. Ct. 1960, U.S. Ct. Appeals 1960. Adjudicator, VA, Chgo., 1960-61; asso. Harold M. Calhoun, Chgo., 1961-62; asst. public defender Cook County, Chgo., 1961-62; asst. U.S. atty. No. Dist. Calif., San Francisco, 1962-66; chief counsel San Francisco Neighborhood Legal Assistance Found., 1966-67; regional legal services dir. Exec. Office Pres. OEO, San Francisco, 1967-70; exec. dir. Western Center Law and Poverty, Los Angeles, 1970-73; exec. asst. to mayor, dir. criminal justice planning, City of Los Angeles, 1974-75, spl. asst. to mayor, dir. urban devel., 1975-77; judge Superior Ct. Calif., Los Angeles, 1977-80, U.S. Dist. Ct. Central Dist. Calif., 1980—; asso. clin. prof. law U. So. Calif. Law Center, 1970-74; prof. law Loyola U. Sch. Law, Los Angeles, 1973-75; mem. faculty Nat. Coll. State Judiciary, Reno, 1974; lectr. Police Acad., San Francisco Police Dept., 1963-66, U. Calif., San Diego, 1970-71, Colo. Jud. Conf., 1973. Vice pres. Northbay Halfway House, 1964-65; vice chmn. Los Angeles Regional Criminal Justice Planning Bd., 1975-76; mem. Los Angeles Mayor's Cabinet Com. Econ. Devel., 1976-77, Mayor's Policy Com., 1973-77; chmn. housing econ. and community devel. com., City Los Angeles, 1975-77, chmn. housing and community devel. tech. com., 1975-77; vice chmn. Young Democrats Cook County, 1961-62; chmn. bd. Real Estate Coop; bd. dirs. Bay Area Social Planning Council, Contra Costa, Black Law Center Los Angeles, Nat. Fedn. Settlements and Neighborhood Centers, Edn. Fin. and Governance Reform Project, Mexican Am. Legal Def. and Ednl. Fund, Nat. Health Law Program, Nat. Sr. Citizens Law Center, Calif. Law Center, Los Angeles Regional Criminal Justice Planning Bd.; mem. exec. com. bd. dirs. Richmond chpt. NAACP, Constl. Rights Found.; trustee Wesleyan United Meth. Ch. Mem. Nat. Legal Aid and Defender Assn. (dir., vice chmn.), Los Angeles County Bar Assn. (exec. com.), Am. Judicature Soc., Charles Houston Law Club, Order of Coif, Phi Delta Phi. Office: US Courthouse 312 N Spring St Los Angeles CA 90012 *

HATTERY, ROBERT R., radiologist, educator; b. Phoenix, Dec. 15, 1939; s. Robert Ralph and Goldie M. (Secor) H.; m. D. Diane Sittler, June 18, 1961; children: Angela, Michael. A.B., Ind. U., 1961, M.D., 1964; cert. in diagnostic radiology, Mayo Grad. Sch. Medicine, 1970. Diplomate: Am. Bd. Radiology. Intern Parkland Meml. Hosp.-Southwestern Med. Sch., Dallas, 1964-65; fellow Mayo Clinic, Rochester, Minn., 1967-70, cons., 1970-81, chmn. dept. diagnostic radiology, 1981—; instr. radiology Mayo Med. Sch., 1973-75, asst. prof. radiology, 1975-78, assoc. prof. radiology, 1978-82, prof. radiology, 1982—. Author numerous jour. articles and abstracts, book chpts. Served to capt. USAF, 1965-67; Willford Hall Hosp., San Antonio. Mem. Radiol. Soc. N.Am., Am. Coll. Radiology, Am. Roentgen Ray Soc., Soc. Computed Body Tomography (pres. 1982-83), Soc. Genitourinary Radiography. Office: Mayo Clinic 200 First St SW Rochester MN 55905

HATTIN, DONALD EDWARD, geologist, educator; b. Cohasset, Mass., Nov. 16, 1928; s. Edward Arthur and Una Vestella (Whipple) H.; m. Marjorie Elizabeth Macy, July 15, 1950; children: Sandra Jane, Ronald Scott, Donna Jean. B.S., U. Mass., 1950; M.S., U. Kans., 1952, Ph.D. (Shell fellow), 1954. Asst. instr. geology U. Kans., 1950-52, instr., 1953-54; asst. prof. geology Ind. U., Bloomington, 1954-60, assoc. prof., 1960-67, prof., 1967—; asst. geologist Kans. Geol. Survey, 1952, research assoc., 1959-68, 70-74, 77-82; geologist Ind. Geol. Survey, 1957-58; cons. in field. Author: Stratigraphy of the Wreford Limestone, 1957, Stratigraphy of the Carlile Shale, 1962, Stratigraphy of the Graneros Shale in Central Kansas, 1965, Stratigraphy and Depositional Environment of Greenhorn Limestone of Kansas, 1975, Upper Cretaceous Stratigraphy and Depositional Environments of Western Kansas, 1978; author: Stratigraphy and Depositional Environment of Smokey Hill Chalk, Niobrara Chalk, Western Kansas. Served to capt. USAF, 1955-57. Recipient Erasmus Haworth Distinguished Alumni Honors in Geology, 1976; NSF grantee, 1975-77; fellow, 1969; Geol. Soc. Am. grantee, 1975; Am. Chem. Soc. grantee, 1978-80. Fellow Geol. Soc. Am.; mem. Am. Assn. Petroleum Geologists, Soc. Econ. Paleontologists Mineralogists, Paleontol. Soc. Republican. Office: Dept Geology Ind U Bloomington IN 47405

HATTON, EDWARD HENRY, lawyer; b. Chgo., July 25, 1916; s. Edward Howard and Elizabeth (Sprague) H.; m. Marian Gertrude Sollitt, Feb. 27, 1943; children: Kathleen, Edward, Spencer. B.S., Amherst Coll., 1939; J.D., Northwestern U., 1942. Bar: Ill. 1942. Atty. Dept. Justice, Washington, 1942-46; ptnr. Jenner & Block, Chgo., 1946—; dir. George Sollitt Constrn. Co., Chgo. Active Northbrook Village Bd., 1964-68, Northbrook High Sch. Bd., 1966-69. Mem. ABA, Ill. State Bar Assn. Presbyterian. Clubs: Law, Legal (Chgo.). Home: 1344 Ridgewood Dr Northbrook IL 60062 Office: 1 IBM Plaza Chicago IL 60611

HAUBERG, ROBERT ENGELBRECHT, former U.S. dist. atty.; b. Brookhaven, Miss., Nov. 20, 1910; s. Frederick and Wilhelmina (Mortensen) H.; m. Robbie Mae Bowen, Dec. 11, 1940; 1 son, Robert Engelbrecht. Student, Millsaps Coll., 1928-30; LL.B., Jackson (Miss.) Sch. Law, 1932. Bar: Miss. bar 1932. Since practiced in, Jackson; prof. law Jackson Sch. Law, 1933-64, registrar, 1933-44, vice-dean, 1938-44, dean, 1944-64; asst. city pros. atty., Jackson, 1932-37, asst. U.S. atty., 1944-54; U.S. dist. atty. for So. Dist. Miss., 1954-80, ret., 1980. Mem. Miss. Senate from 12th senatorial dist., 1940-44; Treas. Hinds County chpt. A.R.C., 1937-46; bd. dirs. Miss. Assn. on Crime and Delinquency, 1941; mem. Jackson Juvenile Council, Council Social Agys., 1939-43. Mem. Fed., Am., Miss., Hinds County bar assns., Jackson Jr. C. of C. (charter mem., pres. 1935), Alpha Omega, Sigma Delta Kappa. Methodist. Club: Knife and Fork. Home: 1045 Claiborne St Jackson MS 39209

HAUCK, CHARLES FRANCIS, manufacturing and engineering consultant; b. Cleve., Sept. 26, 1912; s. William C. and Nell (Terwoord) H.; m. Lillian B. Nocar, Aug. 19, 1940; children: Nancy, Judy. B.S., John Carroll U., 1940. Plant engr. Atlas Powder Co., 1940-45; sr. staff design engr. Hagan Chem. & Control Co., 1946-51; mgr., v.p. sales chem. plants div. Blaw-Knox Co., Pitts., 1952-64, v.p., gen. mgr. chem. plants div., 1964-67, sr. v.p., 1967, pres., 1967-81, chief exec. officer, 1968-81; cons., 1981—; dir. White Consol. Industries, Inc., Cleve., Pitts.-Des Moines Steel Corp., Fudición Nodular S.A. Vice pres. Pa. area Boy Scouts Am.; trustee La Roche Coll. Mem. Pitts. C. of C., Am. Inst. Chem. Engrs. (exec. council past chmn. Pitts.), Am. Iron and Steel Inst., Nat. Soc. Profl. Engrs., Engring. Soc. Western Pa. (dir.). Clubs: Duquesne, Allegheny Country (Pitts.); Laurel Valley Golf, Rolling Rock (Ligonier, Pa.). Office: 202 Pitts Nat Bank Bldg Sewickley PA 15143

HAUCK, FREDERICK HAMILTON, naval officer, atronaut; b. Long Beach, Calif., Apr. 11, 1941; s. Phillip Bowman and Virginia (Hustvedt) H.; m. Dolly Bowman, Aug. 27, 1962; children: Whitney Irene, Stephen Christopher. B.S., Tufts U., 1962; M.S., MIT, 1966. Commd. ensign U.S. Navy, 1962, advanced through grades to capt., 1983; instr. pilot Attack Squadron 42, Oceana, Va., 1970-71; test pilot Naval Air Test Ctr., Patuxent River, Mass., 1971-74; ops. officer Carrier Air Wing 14, Miramar, Calif., 1974-76; exec. officer Attack Squadron 145, Whitney Island NAS, Wash., 1976-78; astronaut NASA, Houston, 1978—, space shuttle pilot, 1982-83, space shuttle comdr., 1983—. Decorated Navy Commendation medal (2), Air medal (9), NASA Flight medal. Assoc. fellow AIAA; mem. Soc. Exptl. Test Pilots. Office: Lyndon B Johnson Space Center NASA Houston TX 77058

HAUCK, MARGUERITE HALL, broadcasting executive; b. Bayside, N.Y., June 30, 1948; d. Carlyle Washington and Anzonette Marguerite (Asmussen) Hall. Student, Syracuse U., 1966-67; B.A. summa cum laude, Queens Coll., CUNY, 1974. Assoc. producer Animatic Prodns., Ltd., N.Y.C., 1968-72; mktg. analyst BBDO, Inc., N.Y.C., 1974-75, CBS, Inc., 1975-76, dir. mktg. and research FM nat. sales, Radio div., 1976—. Author: The $321 Billion Dollar Market, 1981, The Mid-Day Myth Exploded, 1982; columnist, TV-Radio Age mag., 1982. Bd. dirs. Queens Coll. Student Services Corp., 1973-74. Recipient Queens Coll. Disting. Service award, 1974. Mem. Nat. Assn. Female Execs. Home: 20 Continental Ave Forest Hills NY 11375 Office: CBS 51 W 52d St New York NY 10019

HAUER, JOHN LONGAN, lawyer; b. Chgo., Sept. 20, 1918; s. Royal Andrew and Agnes Scott (Longan) H.; m. Mary Lee Humlong, Apr. 19, 1941; children: John, Margaret Lee, William Hervey. B.A., Yale U., 1940; LL.B., Stanford U., 1948. Bar: Tex. 1948, U.S. Supreme Ct. 1957, D.C. bar 1971. Asso. firm Leachman, Matthews and Gardere, 1948-50, Carrington, Gowan, 1950-56, Turner, White, Dallas, 1956-63; partner firm Akin, Gump, Strauss, Hauer & Feld (and predecessor firms), Dallas, Washington, 1963—, mng. partner, 1963—; gen. counsel Dallas Transit Co., 1958-63. Bd. dirs. Dallas Community Chest; trustee Dallas Bar Found. Served to lt. USN, 1942-45. Fellow Am. Coll. Trial Lawyers; mem. Am. Bar Assn., State Bar of Tex. (dir. 1982—), Dallas Bar Assn. (pres. 1981). Clubs: Dallas Country, City, Tower, Chaparral. Home: 3553 Marquette Dallas TX 75225 Office: 2800 Republic Bank Bldg Dallas TX 75201

HAUGAARD, NIELS, pharmacologist; b. Copenhagen, Denmark, Feb. 25, 1920; U.S., 1940, naturalized, 1952; s. Gotfred C. and Karen L. (Pedersen) H.; m. Ella Elizabeth Shwartzman, June 22, 1947 (dec. Feb. 1980); children: David Gregory, Lisa Karen. Student, U. Copenhagen, 1938-40; A.B. with honors, Swarthmore Coll., 1942; Ph.D. in Biochemistry, U. Pa., 1949. Instr. U. Pa. at Phila., 1949-52, asst. prof. research medicine, 1952-54, asst. prof. pharmacology, 1954-60, asso. prof., 1960-65, prof., 1965—; mem. Med. Council, 1972-75; mem. cardiovascular scis. study sect. NIH, 1978-82. Sect. editor: Chem. Abstracts, 1960-65; editorial bd.: Circulation Research, 1964-69; contbr. articles to profl. jours. Mem. Bristol Twp. (Pa.) Sch. Bd., 1957-60. Guggenheim Found. fellow, 1952; Commonwealth Found. fellow, 1965. Mem. Am. Soc. Biol. Chemists, Am. Soc. Pharmacology and Exptl. Therapeutics (editorial bd. jour. 1965-68), ACLU, AAUP. Research on mechanism of hormone action, oxygen toxicity, mitochondrial metabolism. Home: 129 Maple Ave Bala Cynwyd PA 19004 Office: Dept Pharmacology Sch Medicine U Pa Philadelphia PA 19104

HAUGAN, ROBERT ELLSWORTH, printing and publishing company executive; b. New Richland, Minn., Mar. 21, 1917; s. Henry Albert and Ella Pauline (Gardson) H.; m. Clyde Johnson, Jan. 2, 1946; children: Eric A., Robert R., Caryl C. B.B.A., U. Minn., 1942. C.P.A. With Ernst & Ernst (C.P.A.s), Mpls., 1942, 46-51; controller Corn Belt Hatcheries, Joliet, Ill., 1951-54, Webb Co., St. Paul, 1954-69, pres., 1969-82, chmn. bd., 1982—; dir. J.L. Shiely Co., Minn. Mut. Life Ins. Co. Served to lt. USNR. Mem. Graphic Arts Tech. Found., St. Paul C. of C. (pres. 1981). Lutheran. Clubs: Minn., Town and Country, St. Paul Athletic, St. Paul Rotary, Masons, Shriners. Home: 2 Shelby Pl Saint Paul MN 55116 Office: Webb Pub Co 1999 Shepard Rd Saint Paul MN 55116

HAUGEN, EINAR INGVALD, emeritus language educator, author; b. Sioux City, Iowa, Apr. 19, 1906; s. John and Kristine (Gorset) H.; m. Eva Lund, June 18, 1932; children: Anne Margaret, Camilla Christine. Student, Morningside Coll., Sioux City, 1924-27, Litt.D. (hon.), 1978; B.A., St. Olaf Coll., 1928, D.H.L. (hon.), 1958, Litt.D., 1983; M.A., U. Ill., 1929, Ph.D., 1931; Litt.D. (hon.), U. Mich., 1953, M.A., Harvard U., 1960; Ph.D. honoris causa, U. Oslo, Norway, 1961, U. Reykjavik, 1971, U. Trondheim, 1972, U. Uppsala, 1976; H.H.D., U. Wis., 1969, Luther Coll., 1975. Asst. prof. Scandinavian Langs. U. Wis., 1931-36, asso. prof., 1936-38, Thompson prof. Scandinavian langs., 1938-62, Vilas research prof. Scandinavian lang. and linguistics, 1962-64; Victor S. Thomas prof. Harvard U., 1964-75, prof. emeritus, 1975—; dir. Linguistic Inst., 1943-1944; tchr. army specialized tng. program, 1943-44; cultural relations officer (attaché) Am. embassy, Oslo, 1945-46; guest lectr. U. Oslo, 1938, Fulbright research prof., 1951-52; Fulbright lectr. U. Uppsala, 1976-77; instr. summers U. Minn., 1948, 58, 81, U. Mich., 1949, Georgetown U., 1954, Ind. U., 1964, U. Kiel, 1968; cons. English Lang. Exploratory Com., Tokyo, summer 1958, 1st sem., 1959-60; Guggenheim fellow, 1942-43; spl. State Dept. lectr. U. Iceland, Reykjavik, other Scandinavian univs., 1955-56; pres. IX Internat. Congress Linguists, 1962; mem. Permanent Internat. Com. Linguistics, pres., 1966-72. Author: Beginning Norwegian, 1937, 61, Norsk i Amerika (Oslo), 1939, 75, Reading Norwegian, 1940, Norwegian Word Studies, 2 vols, 1941, Voyages to Vinland, 1941, 42, Spoken Norwegian, 1946, (with K.G. Chapman) Spoken Norwegian, rev. edits., 1964, 82, First Grammatical Treatise, 1950, rev. edit., 1972, Norwegian Language in America: A Study in Bilingual Behavior, 1953, rev. edit., 1969, Bilingualism in the Americas: A Guide to Research, 1957, 2d edit., 1964, Norwegian-English Dictionary, 1965, 3d edit., 1983, Language Conflict and Language Planning: The Case of Modern Norwegian, 1966, The Norwegians in America, 1967, 75, Riksspraak og folkemaal, 1969, Ecology of Language, 1972, Studies, 1972, (with T.L. Markey) The Scandinavian Languages: 50 yrs. Ling Res, 1972, Bibliography of Scandinavian Languages and Linguistics, 1974, The Scandinavian Languages: An Introduction to their History, 1976, (with Eva L. Haugen) Land of the Free, 1978, Björnsön's Vocabulary, 1978, Ibsen's Drama: Author to Audience, 1979, Scandinavian Language Structures, 1982, Oppdalsmaalat, 1982; Editor: Dumézil's Gods of the Ancient Northmen, 1973, (with M. Bloomfield) Language as a Human Problem, 1974, Translated Beyer's History of Norwegian Lit, 1956, Fire and Ice, Three Icelandic Plays, 1967, Kamban's We Murderers, 1970, Koht's Life of Ibsen, 1971; Contbr. to publs. Decorated Order of St. Olaf, 1st class, Norway; comdr. Order of North Star, Sweden).; Fellow Center Advanced Study Behavioral Studies, 1963-64; sr. fellow Nat. Endowment for Humanities, 1967-68; Nansen award, Oslo, 1970; Jancke prize, Uppsala, 1976. Mem. Am. Acad. Arts and Scis., Danish, Icelandic, Norwegian, Swedish acads. sci., Royal Norwegian Sci. Soc., Am. Dialect Soc. (pres. 1965), Modern Lang. Assn., Linguistic Soc. Am. (pres. 1950), Norwegian-Am. Hist. Assn. (bd. editors), others. Home: 45 Larch Circle Belmont MA 02178 Office: 146 Widener Library Harvard U Cambridge MA 02138

HAUGEN, ROLF EUGENE, food company executive; b. Mpls., July 2, 1936; s. Roy Arnold and Geneva (Willette) H.; 6 children. B.B.A., U. Minn., 1958. Pub. accountant firm Peat, Marwick, Mitchell & Co., Mpls., 1958-62; asst. controller Gamble-Skogmo, Inc., Mpls., 1962-71; group v.p., chief fin. officer Land O'Lakes, Inc., Mpls., 1971—; chmn. Bank Coops. Nat. Com., Farm Credit Adminstrn., 1976-80. Treas., councilman Eden Prairie Village, Minn., 1962-71; treas., bd. dirs. Eden Prairie Athletic Assn., 1972-77; bd. dirs. ATO Found., U. Minn. Mem. Am. Inst. C.P.A.'s, Minn. Soc. C.P.A.'s, Nat. Council Farmer Cooperatives, Fin. Execs. Inst. (pres.). Home: 1241 Nursery Hill Rd Arden Hills MN 55112 Office: 4001 Lexington Ave N Arden Hills MN 55112

HAUGERUD, HOWARD EDWARD, business executive; b. Harmony, Minn., Aug. 22, 1924; s. Sherman Allen and Anna (Armstrong) H.; m. Mary E. Stafford, Apr. 2, 1946; children: Mark, James Sherman, Kent, Lisa. B.A., U. Minn., 1955; grad., Advanced Mgmt. Program, Harvard U., 1968. Asst. to U.S. Senator Humphrey, 1956-59; profl. staff mem., subcom. nat. policy machinery U.S. Senate Com. Govt. Operations, 1959-61; dep. undersec. army for internat. affairs, 1961-63, asst. sec. state, dep. insp. gen. fgn. assistance, 1963-69; chmn. Nat. Interdepartmental Seminar, 1969-76; chmn. Fgn. Affairs Exec. Seminar, 1972-76; v.p. fed. relations Dana Corp., Toledo, 1976-83; chmn. bd. Controlled Environ. Systems Inc. Pres. U.S. Senate staff, 1956-58; pres. bd. McClellan Aviation Safety Found., 1958—, Capitol Hill Symphony Soc., 1964-66. Served as pilot USAAF, 1942- 45, 48-53. Recipient Exceptional Civilian Service medal Army Dept., 1963;

award for saving a life ARC. Mem. Army Aviation Asso. (v.p. 1957-61), Sigma Delta Chi. Clubs: Harvard Bus. Sch. (dir.), International (Washington)). Home: 1201 Eads Apt 1908 Arlington VA 22202 Office: PO Box 1190-B Rockville MD 20850

HAUGH, ROBERT JAMES, insurance company executive; b. Milw., Jan. 19, 1926; s. John J. and Adeline (Bolmes) H.; m. Mary Jane Botsch, Oct. 15, 1949; children: Jane, William, Nancy. Ph.B., Marquette U., 1946, J.D., 1948. With St. Paul Fire & Marine Ins. Co., 1948—, sr. v.p. ops., 1976-78, pres., chief exec. officer, 1978—; pres., chief operating officer St. Paul Cos., Inc., 1982—; trustee Underwriters Labs. Bd. dirs. ARC, St. Paul, Minn. Public Radio. Mem. Ins. Inst. Am. (dir.), Am. Fgn. Ins. Assn. (trustee), Ins. Services Office (dir.). Republican. Roman Catholic. Clubs: Minnesota, St. Paul Athletic. Office: 385 Washington St Saint Paul MN 55102

HAUGHEY, JAMES MCCREA, lawyer, artist; b. Courtland, Kans., July 8, 1914; s. Leo Eugene and Elizabeth (Stephens) H.; m. Katherine Hurd, Sept. 8, 1938; children: Katherine (Mrs. Lester B. Loo), Bruce Stephens, John Caldwell. LL.B., U. Kans., 1939. Bar: Kans. 1939, Mont. 1943. Landman Carter Oil Co., 1939-43; practice in, Billings, Mont., 1943—; partner firm Crowley, Haughey, Hanson, Toole & Dietrich, 1950—; dir. Mont.-Dakota Utilities Co. One-man shows include, U. Kans., U. Mont., Mont. State U., Concordia Coll., C.M. Russell Gallery, Great Falls, Mont., Boise Mus. Art, Mont. State Mus., Helena, also numerous group shows. Pres. Rocky Mountain Mineral Law Found., 1957-58, trustee, 1955—; pres. Mont. Inst. Arts Found., 1965-67, Yellowstone Art Center Found., 1969-71; trustee Yellowstone Art Center Found., 1964-81; Mem. Mont. Ho. of Reps., 1960-64, Mont. Senate, 1966-70; senate minority leader, 1969-70. Recipient Gov.'s award for Arts, 1981. Fellow Mont. Inst. Arts (Permanent Collection award 1960); mem. ABA, Yellowstone County Bar Assn. (pres. 1960-61), Am. Watercolor Soc. (Midwest v.p. 1978-82), N.W. Watercolor Soc., Midwest Watercolor Soc., Kans. Watercolor Soc. (hon. mem.), Mont. Watercolor Soc. (hon. mem.), Am. Judicature Soc., Am. Artists Profl. League, Phi Delta Theta, Phi Delta Phi. Republican. Episcopalian. Home: 2205 Tree Ln Billings MT 59102 Office: TransWestern Plaza II 490 N 31st St Billings MT 59101

HAUGHT, JAMES ALBERT, JR., journalist; b. Reader, W.Va., Feb. 20, 1932; s. James Albert and Beulah (Fish) H.; m. Nancy Carolyn Brady, Apr. 22, 1958; children: Joel, Jacob, Jeb, Cassie. Student, Morris Harvey Coll.; part-time, W.Va. State Coll., 1950-52, 1960-63. Apprentice printer Charleston Daily Mail, 1951-53; reporter Charleston Gazette, 1953—, serving at various times as night and weekend city editor, music and film critic, police, city hall, cts., schs., suburbs and religion reporter, becoming full-time investigator, 1970-82, assoc. editor, 1983—. Recipient Nat. Headliner award for expose of $3 million pyramid sales promotion Nat. Headliners Club, 1971; 1st Ann. Consumer Writing prize Nat. Press Club, 1973; Nat. Hwy. Safety Writing award Uniroyal Tire Co., 1975; First Amendment award Sigma Delta Chi, 1977; Merit award Am. Bar Assn., 1977; Consumer Writing prize Nat. Press Club, 1979, 83; Spl. award Religion Newswriters Assn., 1980; Health Journalism award Am. Chiropractic Assn., 1981, 83. Mem. Investigative Reporters and Editors. Democrat. Unitarian. Home: 6-KH Lake Shore Dr Charleston WV 25313 Office: 1001 Virginia St E Charleston WV 25301

HAUGHT, WILLIAM DIXON, lawyer; b. Kansas City, Kans., June 12, 1939; s. Walter Dixon and Florence Louise (Rhoads) H.; m. Julia Jane Headstream, July 22, 1967; 1 dau., Stephanie Jane. B.S., U. Kans., 1961; LL.B., U Kans., 1964; LL.M., Georgetown U., 1968. Bar: Kans. 1964, Ark. 1971. Assoc. Stanley, Scroeder, Weeks, Thomas & Lysaught, Kansas City, Kans., 1968-70; ptnr. Wright, Lindsey & Jennings, Little Rock, 1970—. Author: Arkansas Probate System, 1977, (3d edit.) Arkansas Probate System, 1981, (with others) Probate and Estate Administration: The Law in Arkansas, 1983. Served to capt. USAR, 1964-68; Korea, Washington. Mem. ABA (council, co-chmn. coms.), Am. Coll. Probate Counsel (regent, editor studies program), Internat. Acad. Estate and Trust Law, Am. Agrl. Law Assn., Ark. Bar Assn. (chmn. probate law sect. 1981-82, chmn. econs. and law practice com. 1982-84), Central Ark. Estate Council, Pulaski County Bar Assn. Presbyterian. Clubs: Country of Little Rock, Capital, Little Rock. Office: Wright Lindsey & Jennings 2200 Worthen Bank Bldg Little Rock AR 72201

HAUGHTON, KENNETH ELWOOD, university dean; b. Myrtle Point, Oreg., Jan. 8, 1928; s. Herbert Richard and Bernice Helene (Davenport) H.; m. Beverly Mae Bacon, June 15, 1950; children: Kelly Lynn, Kevin Mark, Brian Allen. B.S. in Mech. Engring, U. Calif., Berkeley, 1952, Ph.D., 1964; M.S., Iowa State Coll., 1955. Design engr. Gen. Electric Co., Hanford, Wash., 1952-53; instr. engring. graphics Iowa State Coll., 1953-56; instr. engring. mechanics Cornell U., 1956-57; research engr., then product devel. engr. IBM Corp., San Jose, Calif., 1957-77, dir. engring. lab., Lexington, Ky., 1977-80, San Jose, 1980-82; dean engring. U. Santa Clara, 1982—; former mem. faculty San Jose State Coll.; industry co-chmn. Coll. Cluster-Ky. State U. Author papers in field. Served with USMC, 1946-48. Fellow ASME; mem. Am. Soc. Engring. Edn. Republican. Episcopalian.

HAUGHTON, RONALD WARING, government official, arbitrator; b. Toronto, Can., July 20, 1916; came to U.S., 1927, naturalized, 1927; s. Herbert J. and Lilian J. (Strachan) H.; m. Anne Fletcher, Feb. 23, 1952; children—Jan, Patricia, Leslie, John. B.A., U. Wash., 1937; M.A., U. Wis., 1938. Assembly worker Gen. Electric Co., 1936-37; chief contested claims Wash. State Unemployment Compensation Div., 1938-40; Rockefeller research grant, 1940; tech. adviser U.S. Social Security Bd., 1941-42; successively disputes dir. Detroit Regional War Labor Bd.; dir. strike div. Nat. War Labor Bd., 1942-45; asst. to dir. U.S. Conciliation Service, 1945-47; asst. dir. Inst. Indsl. Relations, U. Calif. at Berkeley, 1947-50; impartial arbitrator Ford Motor Co. and United Automobile Workers, 1950-55; prof. mgmt., co-dir. Inst. Labor and Indsl. Relations, U. Mich., Wayne State U., 1956-79, v.p. urban affairs, 1972-79; chmn. Fed. Labor Relations Authority, Washington, 1979-83, mem., 1983—, Fgn. Service Labor Relations Bd., 1981-83; pres. Bd. Mediation for community disputes, N.Y.C., 1970-71; permanent arbitrator labor disputes bus. firms and unions, 1948-78; chmn. Ford Motor Co.-United Auto Workers Joint Pension Bd., 1950-78; cons. to Sec. of Labor, 1960, 63, to USAF, 1961, to govt. agys, 1960-62, to UN, Minsk, Russia, 1964, to Mayors of Detroit, Boston, Newark, Phila., San Francisco, 1967, 71, 73, 74; Mem. adv. com. on Pres.'s Com. Equal Employment Opportunity; chmn. Presdl. Fact Finding Bds. in maritime, r.r. and airline industries, 1962-64; 64; fact finder for govs., Mich., Calif., 1966—; lectr. U. Stockholm, Sweden, 1966. Cons. Cost of Living Council, Washington, 1973. Mem. Am. Arbitration Assn. (dir.), Nat. Acad. Arbitrators (past sec.), Soc. Fed. Labor Relations Profls. Mem. Soc. of Friends. Home: 4305 Embassy Park Dr Bethesda MD 20016 Office: Fed Labor Relations Authority Washington DC 20424

HAUGLAND, JOHN CLARENCE, univ. vice chancellor; b. Superior, Wis., Nov. 29, 1929; s. Christ R. and Molla (Haugen) H.; m. Joan C. Palm, Sept. 23, 1950; children—Debra Ann, Gregg John. B.S., Wis. State U., Superior, 1954; postgrad., U. Wis., 1955; M.A., U. Minn., 1958, Ph.D., 1961. Tchr. pub. schs., Manitowoc, Wis., 1954-56; with J.C. Penney Co., Sioux City, Ia., 1956-57; adminstrv. fellow, faculty U. Minn., 1957-61, tchr., asst. grad. dean, 1963-65; faculty Wis. State U., Superior, 1961-63, 66—, dean letters and sci., 1966-67, vice chancellor acad. affairs, dean of faculty, 1967—; postdoctoral acad. adminstrn. internship Am. Council Edn., U. Md., 1965-66. Contbr. articles profl. jours. Mem. Douglas County Overall Econ. Devel. Plan Com., 1968—; Alderman Superior City Council, 1971—; Bd. dirs. Wis. Community Devel. Inst., Superior YMCA, Catholic Charities Bur. Served with U.S. Army, 1948-50, 50-51. Recipient U. Minn. Grad. Sch. grant, 1960, Wis. State U.-Superior research grant, 1962. Mem. Superior C. of C. Club: Rotarian. Home: 1717 Ogden Ave Superior WI 54880

HAUK, A. ANDREW, U.S. district judge; b. Denver, Dec. 29, 1912; s. A.A. and Pearl (Woods) H.; m. Jean Nicolay, Aug. 30, 1941; 1 dau., Susan. A.B. magna cum laude, Regis Coll., 1935; LL.B., Catholic U. Am., 1938; J.S.D. (Sterling fellow), Yale U., 1942. Bar: Calif. 1942, Colo. 1939, D.C. 1938, U.S. Supreme Ct. 1953. Spl. asst. to atty. gen., counsel for govt. antitrust div. U.S. Dept Justice, Los Angeles, Pacific Coast, Denver, 1939-41; asst. U.S. atty., Los Angeles, 1941-42; with firm Adams, Duque & Hazeltine, Los Angeles, 1946-52; individual practice law, Los Angeles, 1952-64; asst. counsel Union Oil Co., Los Angeles, 1952-64; judge Superior Ct., Los Angeles County, 1964-66; U.S. dist. judge Central Dist. Calif., 1966—, chief judge, 1980, now sr. judge, chief judge emeritus; instr. Southwestern U. Law Sch., 1939-41; lectr. U. So. Calif. Law Sch., 1947-56; Vice chmn. Calif. Olympic Com., 1954-61; ofcl. VIII Olympic Winter Games, Squaw Valley, 1960; Gov. Calif.'s del. IX Olympic Games, Innsbruck, Austria, 1964. Bd. dirs. So. Calif. Com. for Olympic Games. Served from lt. to lt. comdr., Naval Intelligence USNR, 1942-46. Recipient scroll Los Angeles County Bd. Suprs., 1965, 66, 75; Alumnus of Yr. Regis Coll., 1967; named to Nat. Ski Hall of Fame, 1975. Mem. Los Angeles Town Hall, World Affairs Council, Los Angeles County Bar Assn. (chmn. pleading and practice com. 1963-64, chmn. Law Day com. 1965-66), State Bar Calif. (corps. com., war work com. past vice-chmn.), ABA (com. criminal law sect.), Fed. Bar Assn., Lawyers Club Los Angeles, Am. Judicature Soc., Am. Legion, Navy League, U.S. Lawn Tennis Assn., So. Calif. Tennis Assn. (dir., bd. govs. 1972—), So. Calif. Tennis Patrons Assn. (bd. govs.), Far West Ski Assn. (Nat. Sr. Giant Slalom champion 1954), Yale Law Sch. Assn. So. Calif. (dir., past pres.), Town Hall. Clubs: Yale of So. Calif. (dir. 1964-67), Newman; Valley Hunt (Pasadena); Jonathan (Los Angeles). Office: US Court House 312 N Spring St Los Angeles CA 90012

HAUN, JAMES WILLIAM, chemical engineer, food co. exec.; b. Birmingham, Ala., Sept. 8, 1924; s. James Cecil and Eva (Walker) H.; m. Lucia Land, Sept. 6, 1946; children: James William, Lucy Margaret, Daniel Victor, Robert Paul. B.S. in Chem. Engring, U. Tex., 1946, M.S., 1948, Ph.D. (Humble Oil & Refining Co. fellow 1949-51), 1950; grad. Advanced Mgmt. Program, Harvard, 1961. Registered profl. engr. Instr. chem. engring. U. Tex., 1948-49; successively research engr., sr. research engr. and research group leader plastics div. Monsanto Chem. Co., 1950-56; with Gen. Mills, Inc., Mpls., 1956—, dir. corp. engring., 1960—, v.p., 1963-75, v.p. engring. policy, 1975—; mem. environ. engring. com. Sci. Adv. Bd. EPA; dir. Gold Medal Ins. Corp.; mem. food industry adv. com. U.S. Dept. Energy, 1978-81; mem. indsl. adv. council U. Minn. Inst. Tech.; dept. chem. engring. U. Calif. at, Berkeley, 1971-77; chmn. Internat. Centre for Industry and Environ., Paris and Nairobi, 1977-80; bd. dirs. World Environ. Center, N.Y.C., Environ. Law Inst., Washington. Chmn. bd. dirs. Center for Parish Devel., Naperville, Ill. Served with USMCR, 1942-46. Named Engr. of Year Minn. Soc. Profl. Engrs., 1974. Mem. Am. Inst. Chem. Engrs., Nat. Soc. Profl. Engrs., NAM (dir., chmn. environ. quality com. 1973-79), C. of C. U.S. (com. on environ.), Sigma Xi, Omega Chi Epsilon, Phi Lambda Upsilon. Home: 6912 E Fish Lake Rd Maple Grove MN 55369 Office: Gen Mills Inc Minneapolis MN 55440

HAUN, JOHN DANIEL, petroleum geologist, educator; b. Old Hickory, Tenn., Mar. 7, 1921; s. Charles C. and Lydia (Rhodes) H.; m. Lois Culbertson, June 30, 1942. B.A., Berea Coll., 1948; M.A., U. Wyo., 1949, Ph.D., 1953. Registered profl. engr., Colo. Geologist Stanolind, Amoco, Vernal, Utah, 1951-52; v.p. Petroleum Research Corp., Denver, 1952-57; mem. faculty dept. geology Colo. Sch. Mines, Golden, 1955—, prof., 1963—; pres. Barlow & Haun, Inc., Evergreen, Colo., 1957—; cons. Potential Gas Agy., 1966-78; mem. exec. adv. com. Nat. Petroleum Council, 1968-70; mem. adv. com. Colo. Water Pollution Control Commn., 1969-70; mem. adv. council,Kans. Geol. Survey, 1971-76; del. Internat. Geol. Congress, Sydney, Australia, 1976; U.S. rep. Internat. Com. on Petroleum Res. Classification UN, N.Y.C., 1976-77; mem. oil shale adv. com. Office of Tech. Assessment, Washington, 1976-79, mem. U.S. natural gas availability adv. panel, 1983; mem. Colo. Oil and Gas Conservation Commn., 1977—; mem. energy resources com. Interstate Oil Compact Commn., 1978—; mem. Nat. Petroleum Council, 1979—, mem. com. on unconventional gas sources, 1978-80; com. on Arctic oil and gas resources, 1980-81; mem. U.S. Nat. Com. on Geology Dept. Interior and Nat. Acad. Scis., 1982—. Editor: The Mountain Geologist, 1963-65, Future Energy Outlook, 1969, Methods of Estimating the Volume of Undiscovered Oil and Gas Resources, 1975; asst. editor: Geologic Atlas of the Rocky Mountain Region, 1972; co-editor: Subsurface Geology in Petroleum Exploration, 1958, Symposium on Cretaceous Rocks of Colorado and Adjacent Areas, 1959, Guide to the Geology of Colorado, 1960; contbr. articles to profl. jours. Served with USCG, 1942-46. Recipient Disting. Service award Am. Assn. Petroleum Geologists, 1973; Outstanding prof. award Colo. Sch. Mines, 1973. Fellow Geol. Soc. Am., AAAS; mem. Am. Assn. Petroleum Geologists (editor 1967-71, pres. 1979-80), Am. Inst. Profl. Geologists (v.p. 1974, pres. 1976, exec. com. 1981-82), Am. Geol. Inst. (governing bd. 1976, 79-82, sec.-treas. 1977-78, v.p. 1980-81, pres. 1981-82), Rocky Mountain Assn. Geologists (sec. 1961, 1st v.p. 1964, pres. 1968, hon. mem. 1974—), Soc. Econ. Paleontologists and Mineralogists, Am. Petroleum Inst. (com. exploration 1971-73, 78—), Geochem. Soc., Nat. Assn. Geology Tchrs., Wyo. Geol. Assn. (hon. life), Colo. Sci. Soc., Sigma Xi, Sigma Gamma Epsilon, Phi Kappa Phi. Home: 1238 County Rd 23 Evergreen CO 80439 Office: Colo Sch of Mines Golden CO 80401

HAUNZ, EDGAR ALFRED, physician, emeritus educator; b. London, Eng., Dec. 12, 1910; came to U.S., 1916, naturalized, 1921; s. Charles F. and Caroline (Weissenberger) H.; m. Millicent Arnold, Mar. 19, 1948; children: Barbara Jane, William Edgar. M.D., U. Buffalo, 1943; M.S. in Medicine (Mayo fellow), U. Minn., 1947; D.Sc. (hon.), U. N.D., 1978. Intern Buffalo Gen. Hosp., 1943-44; resident fellow medicine Mayo Found., Mayo Clinic and (Affiliated Hosps.), Rochester, Minn., 1944-47; practice medicine, specializing in internal medicine and diabetology, Grand Forks, N.D., 1947—; mem. staff United Hosp., Grand Forks, Deaconess Hosp., chief of staff, 1968-69; prof., chmn. dept. medicine U. N.D. Sch. Medicine, 1960-74, emeritus prof., 1974—; spl. cons. in diabetes USPHS, 1952-60; founder Diabetic Children's Camp Sioux, 1952—; lectr. on diabetes and endrocrinology, U.S. and abroad, 1947—. Author diabetes sect.: Emergency Medicine, 1984; Editorial bd.: Jour. Clin. Medicine, 1950—, Jour. Lancet, 1955-68, Jour. Cardiovascular Diseases; Author: diabetes sect. Current Therapy, 1981; Contbr. articles to med. jours. and textbooks. Chmn. Greater Grand Forks chpt. A.R.C., 1956-57; mem. Grand Forks Bd. Edn., 1955-64, pres., 1962-64; mem. Grand Forks Symphony Orch., Nat. Med. Adv. Bd. on Ednl. Film Prodn.; Bd. dirs. Medic-Alert, 1963. Recipient N.D. Gov.'s award for service to handicapped, 1966, Service to Mankind award Sertoma Club, 1963. Fellow A.C.P. (life); mem. Am. Diabetes Assn. (dir., past chmn. bd. govs,, asst. treas. 1968-70, 1st Pfizer award as outstanding physician in diabetes in U.S. 1975, mem. nat. fund raising com. 1976, mem. nat. nominating com. 1977-78), N.D. Diabetes Assn. (exec. sec.-treas.), Pan Am. Med. Assn., N.D. Med. Assn., Grand Forks Dist. Med. Soc. (past pres.), Am. Soc. Internal Medicine, Alpha Omega Alpha, Sigma Xi. Clubs: Kiwanian (hon. life, Distinguished Service award 1962), Rotarian (past dir. Grand Forks). Home: 1029 Lincoln Dr Grand Forks ND 58201 Office: Grand Forks Clinic Medical Park Grand Forks ND 58201 *As the early years hopefully season us with circumspection, irresistable compulsion emerges—the unquenchable desire to achieve beyond our capabilities, love beyond our dreams, play with complete abandon, and surfeit our ego with the self-gratification derived from service to others...*

HAUPTFLEISCH, LOUIS ALOIS, investment co. exec.; b. Waterloo, Ill., July 17, 1918; s. Herman E. and Amanda L. (Koenigsmark) H.; m. Margaret Jane Hall, Oct. 31, 1942; 1 son, David L.; m. Pamela Wilson Mitchell, Sept. 6, 1974; children—Melinda, Gayle, Lauren, Hillary. B.S., U. Ill., 1940. Vice pres. Halsey, Stuart & Co., Inc., N.Y.C., 1946-60, exec. v.p., dir., 1968-72; 1st v.p. Smith Barney, Harris Upham & Co. Inc., N.Y.C., 1973—; v.p. Goldman, Sachs & Co., N.Y.C., 1961-68. Served with AUS, 1942-45. Decorated Bronze Star medal, Purple Heart. Mem. Municipal Bond Club N.Y. (pres. 1976-77). Clubs: Univ. (N.Y.C.); Morris County Golf (Convent, N.J.). Home: 10 Sherman Ave Summit NJ 07901 Office: 1345 Ave of Americas New York NY 10019

HAUPTFUHRER, GEORGE JOST, JR., lawyer; b. Abington, Pa., Aug. 1, 1926; s. George Jost and Emilie (Schoenhut) H.; m. Barbara Barnes, Sept. 9, 1950; children: George Jost, William Barnes. A.B., Harvard U. 1948; J.D., U. Pa., 1951. Bar: Pa. 1951. Assoc. Dechert Price & Rhoads, and predecessor, Phila., 1951-59; ptnr. Dechert Price & Rhoads, and predesessor, Phila., 1951-59; dir. The West Co., Inc., Ransome Airlines, Inc. Assoc. editor: How to Live and Die with Pennsylvania Probate, 1970; contbr. articles to profl. jours. Trustee Princess Grace Found., Abington Meml. Hosp.; trustee, sec. Am. Coll.; chmn. adv. com. Joint State Govt. Commn. Commonwealth of Pa., 1982—; former com. mem. Phila. Orch. Pension Fund; former trustee and pres. S.E. Pa. chpt. Multiple Sclerosis Soc. Fellow Am. Bar Found.; mem. Am. Coll. Probate Counsel (regent), ABA (past chmn. real property, probate and trust law sect.), Order of Coif. Clubs: Philadelphia, Pine Valley Golf, Union League, Racquet, Roaring Gap, Huntingdon Valley Golf, Harvard of Philadelphia. Home: 1700 Old Welsh Rd Huntingdon Valley PA 19006 Office: 3400 Centre Sq W 1500 Market St Philadelphia PA 19102

HAUPTFUHRER, ROBERT PAUL, oil company executive; b. Phila., Dec. 31, 1931; s. George J. and Emilie M. (Schoenhut) H.; m. Barbara Ellen Dunlop, May 11, 1963; children—Brenda Lynn, Bruce Andrew, Bryan Dunlop. A.B., Princeton U., 1953; M.B.A., Harvard U., 1957. With Sun Co., Inc., Radnor, Pa., 1957—, gen. mgr. corp. adminstrv. ops., 1971-73; v.p. Sun Ventures, 1973-75; pres. Sun Enterprises Group, 1975-79; sr. v.p. Sun Co., Inc., 1979—; dir. Quaker Chem. Corp. Trustee Lankenau Hosp.; dir. Curtis Inst. Music. Served with USN, 1953-55. Mem. Am. Petroleum Inst. Republican. Presbyterian. Clubs: Union League, Phila. Country, Pine Valley Golf, Merion Cricket. Office: 100 Matsonford Rd Radnor PA 19087

HAUPTMAN, MICHAEL, broadcasting company executive; b. Bklyn., Jan. 6, 1933; s. Hyman A. and Toba L. (Hershman) H.; m. Betty Holzman, Nov. 28, 1957; children—James, William. B.A., U. Vt., 1954. Program dir. WSTC Radio, Stamford, Conn.; 960-61; prodn. mgr. WABC Radio, N.Y.C., 1961-62, advt., promotion mgr., 1962-63; with WINS Radio, N.Y.C., 1963-67, KYW-TV, Phila., 1967-68; mgr. mktg. services Westinghouse Broadcasting Co., N.Y.C., 1968-69; dir. retail mktg. ABC owned radio stas., N.Y.C., 1969-72, dir. planning, 1972-73; v.p. ABC Radio, 1973-76, sr. v.p., 1976—; v.p.-in-charge ABC Radio Enterprises, Inc., 1981—. Mem. Representative Town Meeting, Greenwich, Conn.; pres. Commuters Action Com. of Fairfield County. Mem. Internat. Radio and TV Soc., Phi Sigma Delta. Home: Carriage Rd Cos Cob CT 06807 Office: 1330 Ave of Americas New York NY 10019

HAUROWITZ, FELIX, biochemist, educator; b. Prague, Czechoslovakia, Mar. 1, 1896; came to U.S., 1948, naturalized, 1952; s. Rudolf and Emilie (Russ) H.; m. Gina Perutz, June 23, 1925. M.D., German U., Prague, 1922, Sc.D., 1923; M.D. (hon.), U. Istanbul, Turkey, 1973, Ph.D., Ind. U., 1974. Asst. prof. physiol. chemistry Med. Sch. German U., Prague, 1952-30, asso. prof., 1930-39; head dept. biol. chemistry, also prof. Med. Sch. U. Istanbul, Turkey, 1939-48; prof. chemistry Ind. U., 1948—, Distinguished prof., 1958—. Author: Biochemistry, 1955, Progress in Biochemistry, since 1949, 1959, Chemistry and Function of Proteins, 1963; Immunochemistry and the Biosynthesis of Antibodies, 1968. Recipient Paul Ehrlich prize and gold plaquette Paul Ehrlich Fund, Frankfurt, Germany, 1960. Fellow Am. Acad. Arts and Sci.; mem. Am. Chem. Soc. (chmn. div. biol. chemistry 1962-63), Leopoldina Acad. Scis., Am. Soc. Biol. Chemists, Am. Assn. Immunologists, Nat. Acad. Scis., Am. Soc. Microbiology (hon.), Societe de Chimie Biologique (hon.), Societe Immunologique (hon.). Spl. research protein chemistry and immunochemistry. Home: 910 Juniper Pl Bloomington IN 47401

HAURWITZ, BERNHARD, educator; b. Glogau, Germany, Aug. 14, 1905; came to the U.S., 1941, naturalized, 1946; s. Paul and Betty (Cohn) H.; m. Eva Schick, May 11, 1934 (div. Nov. 1946); 1 son, Frank David; m. Marion B. Wood, Jan. 16, 1961. Ph.D., U. of Leipzig, 1927. Privatdozent U. of Leipzig; 1931-32; research asso. Harvard, 1932-35; lectr. U. Toronto, 1935-37; meteorologist, Dominion, Can., 1937-41; asso. prof. meteorology Mass. Inst. Tech., 1941-47; asso. Woods Hole Oceanographic Inst., 1947- 59; prof., chmn. dept. meteorology and oceanography N.Y.U., 1947-59; prof. astrogeophysics U. Colo., 1959-64, prof. geophysics, 1960; with Nat. Center Atmospheric Research, Boulder, Colo., 1964—, dir. advanced study program, 1968-69; prof. atmospheric scis. U. Tex., 1966-68, also Colo. State U.; prof. U. Alaska, 1970—. Contbr. tech. articles to numerous publs. Decorated Cross of Merit 1st class Fed. Republic of Germany; recipient Recipient Rossby award Am. Meteorol. Soc., 1962. Mem. Nat. Acad. Sci., Deutsche Akademie der Naturforscher Leopoldina, Royal Meteorol. Soc., Am. Meteorol. Soc. (hon. mem.), Am. Geophys. Union (Bowie award 1970), ACLU, Sigma Xi. Home: 2523 Constitution Ave Fort Collins CO 80526 Office: Dept Atmospheric Sci Colo State Univ Fort Collins CO 80523

HAURY, EMIL WALTER, emeritus anthropology educator; b. Newton, Kans., May 2, 1904; s. Gustav A. and Clara K. (Ruth) H.; m. Hulda E. Penner, June 7, 1928; children: Allan Gene, Loren Richard. Student, Bethel Coll., Newton, Kans., 1923-25; A.B., U. Ariz., 1927, M.A., 1928; Ph.D., Harvard U., 1934; LL.D., U. N.Mex., 1959. Instr. U. Ariz., 1928-29, research asst. in dendrochronology, 1929-30; asst. dir. Gila Pueblo, Globe, Ariz., 1930-37; prof. anthropology U. Ariz., 1937-70, Fred A. Riecker Disting. prof. anthropology, 1970-80, emeritus, 1980—, head dept., 1937-64; dir. Ariz. State Mus., 1938-64; Chmn. div. anthropology and psychology Nat. Acad. Scis.-NRC, 1960-62; mem. Adv. Bd. Nat. Parks, Historic Sites, Bldgs. and Monuments, 1964-70, chmn., 1968-70. Author: publs. including The Excavations of Los Muertos and Neighboring Ruins in the Salt River Valley, Southern Arizona, Peabody Museum Papers, Vol. XXIV. No. 1, 1945, (with others) The Stratigraphy and Archaeology of Ventana Cave,

1950, The Hohokam: Desert Farmers and Craftsmen, Excavations at Snaketown, 1964-65, 1976. Guggenheim fellow, 1949-50; Viking Fund medalist in anthropology, 1950; recipient Alumni Achievement award U. Ariz., 1957; Salgo-Noren Found. award for teaching excellence, 1967; Conservation Service award Dept. Interior, 1976; Alfred V. Kidder award for Am. archeology, 1977; Disting. Citizen award U. Ariz. Alumni Assn., 1980; award Am. Soc. Conservation, 1980; Merit award Ariz. Hist. Soc., 1981; Disting. Scholar award Southwestern Anthrop. Assn., 1982. Mem. Nat. Council Humanities, Am. Philos. Soc., Am. Acad. Arts and Scis., Nat. Speleological Soc. (hon. life mem.), Soc. for Am. Archaeology, Am. Anthrop. Assn. (pres. 1956), Nat. Acad. Scis., Tree-Ring Soc., AAAS, Sigma Xi, Phi Beta Kappa, Phi Kappa Phi. Home: 2749 E 4th St Box 40543 Tucson AZ 85717

HAUS, HERMANN ANTON, electrical engineering educator; b. Ljubljana, Yugoslavia, Aug. 8, 1925; came to U.S., 1948, naturalized, 1956; s. Otto Maxmilian and Helene (Hynek) H.; m. Eleanor Laggis, Jan. 24, 1953; children: William Peter, Stephen Christopher, Cristina Ann, Mary Ellen. Student, Technische Hochschule, Graz, 1946-48, 1948; B.S., Union Coll., 1949; M.S., Rensselaer Poly. Inst., 1951; Sc.D., Mass. Inst. Tech., 1954. Asst. prof. Mass. Inst. Tech., Cambridge, 1954-58, asso. prof., 1958-62, prof. elec. engring., 1962-73, Elihu Thomson prof. elec. engring., 1973—; vis. prof. Technische Hochschule, Vienna, 1959-60, Tokyo Inst. Tech., 1980; vis. MacKay prof. U. Calif. at Berkeley, summer 1968; cons. Raytheon Co., 1956—, Lincoln Labs., 1963—; mem. Nat. Acad. Scis. adv. panel, Radio Propagation Lab. Nat. Bur. Standards, 1965-67. Author: (with R.B. Adler) Circuit Theory of Linear Noisy Networks, 1959, (with L.D. Smullin) Noise in Electron Devices, 1959, (with P. Penfield, Jr.) Electrodynamics of Moving Media, 1967; Mem. editorial bd.: Jour. Applied Physics, 1960-63, (with P. Penfield, Jr.) Electronics Letters, 1965-73, Internat. Jour. Electronics, 1975—. Guggenheim fellow, 1959-60. Fellow IEEE, Am. Acad. Arts and Scis.; mem. Nat. Acad. Engring., Am. Phys. Soc., Sigma Xi, Eta Kappa Nu, Tau Beta Pi, Phi Delta Theta. Home: 3 Jeffrey Terr Lexington MA 02173 Office: 77 Massachusetts Ave Cambridge MA 02139

HAUSCHKA, STEPHEN DENISON, developmental biologist, educator; b. Phila., Apr. 18, 1940; s. Theodore Spaeth and Elsa (Voorhees) H.; m. Sarah Cheney, June 12, 1964; children: Peter Jameson, Alice Denison. B.A., Amherst Coll., 1962; Ph.D., Johns Hopkins U., 1966. Research assoc. biochemistry U. Wash., Seattle, 1966-67, asst. prof., 1967-74, assoc. prof. biochemistry and zoology, 1974-80, prof., 1980—; mem. devel. biology study sect. NSF, 1977-79; mem. preclin. drug testing task force Muscular Dystrophy Assn., 1979—. Contbr. articles to profl. jours. Recipient Outstanding Tchr. award Mortar Bd. U. Wash., 1981. Mem. Am. Soc. Devel. Biology, Am. Soc. Cell Biology, Am. Soc. Biochemistry, Am. Soc. Zoology, Soc. Neurosci. Home: 1821 E McGraw St Seattle WA 98112 Office: Sch Medicine U Wash Dept Biochemistry Seattle WA 98195

HAUSCHKA, THEODORE SPAETH, biologist; b. Reichenau, Austria, July 31, 1908; came to U.S., 1928, naturalized, 1937; s. Hugo and Carola (Spaeth) H.; m. Elsa Voorhees, Mar. 29, 1938; children—Stephen Denison, Peter Voorhees, Margaret Spaeth. A.B., Princeton, 1930; M.S. (Harrison fellow), U. Pa., 1941, Ph.D., 1943. Tchr. biology Chestnut Hill Acad., Phila., 1935-39; instr. U. Pa., 1942-43, Army specialist tng. program, 1943-44; biologist Lankenau Hosp. Research Inst., Phila., 1943-48, sr. mem., 1949-54; asso. dir. Marine Exptl. Sta., Truro, Mass., 1945-47; sr. mem. Inst. Cancer Research, Phila., 1949-54; cons. cancer research Lederle Lab., Am. Cyanamid Co., 1953-65; dir. biol. research Roswell Park Meml. Inst., Buffalo, 1954-75, cons., 1975—; research prof. biology State U. N.Y. at Buffalo Grad. Sch., 1954—; Mem. carcinogenesis adv. panel, cons. Nat. Cancer Inst., 1972-74. Contbr. articles to profl. jours. Trustee Med. Found. Buffalo, 1965-69. Fellow AAAS, 3N.Y. Acad. Sci.; mem. Am. Assn. Tissue Banks, Am. Genetic Assn., Soc. for Developmental Biology, Am. Naturalists, Soc. Exptl. Biology and Medicine, Transplantation Soc., Am. Assn. Cancer Research (v.p. 1958, pres. 1959), Sigma Xi. Home: RFD 1 Box 228 Damariscotta ME 04543

HAUSE, JESSE GILBERT, coll. pres.; b. Ft. Lupton, Colo., July 26, 1929; s. Jesse William and Evelyn Hattie (Frye) H.; m. Gertrude Virginia Kuntz, June 15, 1952; children—J. David, Douglas C., Patrick D. B.A., U. No. Colo., 1951, M.A., 1952; Ed.D., U. Colo., 1962. Chief of Party, prof. U.S. AID Project, Inst. Edn. and Research, U. Dacca, Bangladesh, 1960-66; sec. bd. trustees, v.p., prof. U. No. Colo., 1966-77; pres. Black Hills State Coll., Spearfish, S.D., 1977—; bd. dirs. Estes Park (Colo.) Center for Research and Edn. Pres. Dist. VII, Colo. Mcpl. League, 1972-74; city councilman, Greeley, Colo., 1969-74. Served with USNR, 1952-55. Recipient Disting. Alumnus award U. No. Colo., 1979. Mem. Nat. Assn. Univ. Research Adminstrs., Am. Assn. State Colls. and Univs., North Central Assn. Acad. Deans (pres. 1970-71), Spearfish C. of C. (v.p. 1980-81), Phi Delta Kappa, Kappa Delta Pi. Republican. Roman Catholic. Club: Kiwanis. Home: 815 State St Spearfish SD 57783 Office: 1200 University Black Hills State Coll Spearfish SD 57783

HAUSER, CHARLES NEWLAND MCCORKLE, newspaper editor; b. Newton, N.C., Feb. 3, 1929; s. John Nathaniel and Charlotte (McCorkle) H.; m. Jane Ann Edwards, Dec. 29, 1956; children—David McCorkle, Susan Jane. A.B., U. N.C., 1954; postgrad., Harvard, 1968. Washington corr. Charlotte (N.C.) Observer, 1961-62, Carolinas editor, 1962-65; fgn. corr. U.P.I., London, Eng., 1958-59, Paris, France, 1959-60; mng. editor Greensboro (N.C.) Daily News, 1965-66, exec. news editor, 1967-68; v.p., gen. mgr. Virginian-Pilot & Ledger Star, Norfolk, Va., 1969-73; v.p., exec. editor Providence (R.I.) Jour. and Eve. Bull., 1973—; lectr. Am. Press Inst., Reston, Va., 1969—; adj. asso. prof. Brown U., Providence, 1981—; Ordained as ruling elder United Presbyn. Ch. in, U.S.A., 1977. Served with AUS, 1951-54. Decorated Bronze Star medal, Purple Heart. Mem. Am. Soc. Newspaper Editors, Alpha Tau Omega. Club: Nat. Press (Washington). Home: 55 Appian Way Barrington RI 02806 Office: 75 Fountain St Providence RI 02902

HAUSER, CRANE CHESHIRE, lawyer; b. Newark, Jan. 8, 1923; s. Simeon Floyd and Jessie Walrath (Crane) H.; m. Mary Corliss Kosovinc, May 29, 1949; 1 son, Stephen Crane. A.B., Franklin and Marshall Coll., 1946; J.D., Northwestern U., 1950; C.P.A., U. Ill., 1953. Bar: Ill. bar 1950. Asso. firm Winston, Strawn, Black & Towner, Chgo., 1950-54; partner firm Winston & Strawn, Chgo., 1954-61, 63—; chief counsel Internal Revenue Service; also asst. gen. counsel Treasury Dept., 1961-63; dir. Stanadyne, Inc.; Mem. Ill. Bd. Examiners Accountancy, 1966-69. Bd. visitors Franklin and Marshall Coll. Served with AUS, 1943-46. Mem. Am., Fed., Ill., Chgo. bar assns., Am. Law Inst., Ill. Soc. C.P.A.s (Gold medal 1953), Chgo. Fed. Tax Forum, Northwestern U. Law Sch. Alumni Assn. (bd. dirs. 1961—). Presbyn. (elder). Clubs: National Lawyers (Washington); Mid-Day, Racquet (Chgo.). Home: 1515 Astor St Chicago IL 60610 Office: One First National Plaza Chicago IL 60603

HAUSER, GUSTAVE M., cable and electronic communications company executive; b. Cleve., Sept. 3, 1929; s. Abraham and Stella H.; m. Rita Abrams, June 10, 1956; children: Glenvil A., Patricia A. A.B., Western Res. U., 1950; J.D., Harvard U., 1953; LL.M., NYU, 1957; diplome in law, U. Paris, 1958. Bar: Ohio bar 1953, N.Y. State bar 1957. Instr. Harvard U. Law Sch., 1955-56; counsel internat. affairs Office Sec. Def., 1958-60; v.p. Gen. Telephone & Electronics Internat., 1960-71; exec. v.p. Western Union Internat., 1971-73; pres. Warner Cable Corp., 1973-75, chmn., chief exec. officer, 1975-79, Warner Amex Cable Communications, Inc., N.Y.C., 1979-83, Hauser Communications, Inc., 1983—; dir.-at-large U.S. Overseas Pvt. Investment Corp., 1969-77. Author: A Guide to Doing Business in the European Common Market, 1960. Served with AUS, 1953-55. Mem. Nat. Cable TV Assn. (dir. 1976—, exec. com. 1978—, vice chmn. 1983—). Office: Hauser Communications Inc 437 Madison Ave New York NY 10022

HAUSER, HARRY RAYMOND, lawyer; b. N.Y.C., July 12, 1931; s. Milton I. and Lillian (Perlman) H.; m. Deborah Marlowe, Aug. 6, 1954; children: Mark Jeffrey, Joshua Brook, Bradford John, Matthew Milton. A.B., Brown U., 1953; J.D., Columbia U., 1959. Bar: N.Y. 1959, Mass. 1963, Washington 1972. Practice in, N.Y.C., 1959-61, Boston, 1962—; atty. Sperry Rand Corp., 1959-61, Hotel Corp. Am., N.Y.C., 1961-62, v.p., sec., gen. counsel, 1962-70; mem. firm Gadsby & Hannah, 1971—. Trustee, mem. bd. of property mgrs. Temple Israel, Boston. Served to lt. comdr. USNR, 1954-57. Mem. Am., N.Y., Mass., Washington bar assns. Club: Brown U. (N.Y.C.). Home: 37 Claremont St Newton MA 02158

HAUSER, JON WILLIAM, industrial designer; b. Sault Ste. Marie, Mich., June 8, 1916; s. Kenneth and Arlie (Hershey) H.; m. Jean MacCallum, Aug. 30, 1939; 1 son, Jon William II. Designer Gen. Motors Corp., 1936-41, Chrysler Corp., 1941-43; dir. design Sears, Roebuck & Co., 1943-45; designer with Dave Chapman, Chgo., 1945-46, Barnes & Reinecke, 1946-49; asso. Reinecke Assos., Chgo., 1949-52; pres. Jon W. Hauser, Inc., St. Charles, Ill., 1952—; vis. prof. U. Ill., 1978-79; Del. Internat. Council Socs. Indsl. Design, Paris, 1963, Vienna, 1965, Montreal, 1967. Vice pres. bd. trustees Delnor Hosp., 1973-77, pres., 1977-82, past chmn. bd., 1982—. Fellow indsl. Designers Inst. (Design award 1956, exec. v.p. 1961-62, pres. 1962-64, chmn. bd. 1964), Indsl. Designers Soc. Am. (chmn. bd. 1967-68, dir.). Clubs: Mason (Shriner), St. Charles Country; Quiet Birdmen (Chgo.). Two designs included in Best 100 Designs in History, 1959. Home: 3N981 Route 31 Saint Charles IL 60174 Office: 10 E State Ave Saint Charles IL 60174

HAUSER, MICHAEL GEORGE, astrophysicist; b. Chgo., Dec. 3, 1939; s. Julius and Sylvia Ann (Gross) H.; m. Miriam Freedman, Sept. 11, 1960 (div. May 1977); children—Karen Celia, Gerald Paul; m. Deanna Grove, May 8, 1981. B.Engring. Physics with distinction, Cornell U., 1962; Ph.D. (NSF fellow), Calif. Inst. Tech., 1967. Instr. Princeton U., 1967-70, asst. prof. physics, 1970-72; sr. research fellow in physics Calif. Inst. Tech., 1972-74; head infrared astronomy group lab. for high energy astrophysics Goddard Space Flight Center, Greenbelt, Md., 1974-77, head sect. infrared astrophysics, lab. for extraterrestrial physics, 1977—. Vice pres. PTA, Kensington (Md.) Jr. High, 1977-78, mem. exec. bd., 1978-79. Hon. Woodrow Wilson fellow, 1962. Mem. Am. Astron. Soc., Am. Phys. Soc., AAAS, Sigma Xi. Research, numerous publs. on elementary particle physics and astronomy, 1967. Office: Code 693 2 Goddard Space Flight Center Greenbelt MD 20771

HAUSER, NANCY MCKNIGHT, dance teacher, choreographer; b. Bayside, L.I., N.Y., Nov. 20, 1909; d. Edgar Scott and Adelaide Burton McKnight; m. Rudolph Alonzo Hauser, Jan. 1, 1934; children: Michael Scott, Heidi Hauser Jasmin, Anthony Paul. Dance tng. with, Louise Revere Morris, Doris Humphrey, Charles Weidman, Hanya Holm, 1926-36. Mem. Hanya Holm Dance Co., 1932-36; instr. Finch Jr. Coll., 1933-37, Milw. Dept. Recreation, 1938-43, Carleton Coll., 1944-47, asst. prof., 1950-60; instr. Macalester Coll., 1946-49; founder Dance Guild Theatre and Sch., 1961; artistic dir. Guild Peforming Arts and Nancy Hauser Dance Co., Mpls., 1968—; instr. Hanya Holm Sch. Dance, Colo. Coll., Colorado Springs, 1978—, U. Minn., 1981—; cons. artists-in-schs. Nat. Endowment for Arts. Mem. Mpls. Arts Commn., 1976-79, Minn. Alliance Arts in Edn., 1978-80; vis. artist U. Wis., Madison, spring 1983. Dancer in: Lysistrata, 1930; Choreographer: Visions, 1966, Saeta, 1967, Everyman Sonata, 1966, Counterpoint, 1970, Lyric Suite, 1970, No Comment, 1971, Parta Partita, 1970, Abstract Beginnings, 1972, Back to Back, 1979, Getting Along, Getting Together, 1978, Recherche, 1976, Dream Cycle, 1977, Everness, 1978, Circle of the Sun, 1980, U.S., Inc, 1981, Wheeling, 1981, Romanza, 1981, Requiem, 1983. Twin City Met. Arts Alliance. Minn. State Arts Bd. grantee, 1976, 77, 80; YWCA Outstanding Achievement in Arts award. Home: 233 Bedford St SE Minneapolis MN 55414

HAUSER, NORBERT, industrial engineering educator; b. Poland, Aug. 13, 1924; came to U.S. 1940, naturalized, 1945; s. Morris and Debora (Griminger) H. B.Mech.Engring., Cooper Union, 1950; M.I.E., N.Y. U., 1955, Engr. Sci.D., 1962. Quality Control engr. Gen. Electric Co., 1950-55; from instr. to assoc. prof. indsl. engring. and ops. research N.Y. U., 1955-65; vis. assoc. prof., mem. NSF project on use of computers in engring. edn. U. Mich., 1965; prof. indsl. engring. and mgmt. sci. Poly. Inst. N.Y., 1966—, head dept. ops. research and system analysis, 1966-73, chmn. faculty senate, 1975-76, acting head dept. mgmt., 1976-77, dean div. mgmt., 1980-83; cons. in field, 1955—. Contbr. profl. jours. Served with AUS, 1943-46. Mem. Inst. Indsl. Engrs. (sr.), Inst. Mgmt. Scis., Am. Soc. Engring. Edn., AAUP, Sigma Xi, Tau Beta Pi, Alpha Pi Mu, Pi Tau Sigma. Home: 21 Pomander Walk New York NY 10025 Office: 333 Jay St Brooklyn NY 11201

HAUSER, PHILIP MORRIS, educator; b. Chgo., Sept. 27, 1909; s. Morris and Ann (Diamond) H.; m. Zelda B. Abrams, Nov. 27, 1935; children—William Barry, Martha Ann. Ph.B., U. Chgo., 1929, M.A., 1933, Ph.D., 1938; L.H.D., Roosevelt U., Chgo., 1967; LL.D., Loyola U., Chgo., 1969. Instr. sociology U. Chgo., 1932-37; now Lucy Flower prof. emeritus urban sociology, dir. emeritus Population Research Center; sr. fellow East West Population Inst., chmn. dept. sociology, 1956-65; chief labor inventory sect. F.E.R.A. and W.P.A., 1935-37; asst. to dir. Study of Social Aspects of Depression, Social Sci. Research Council, 1937; asst. chief statistician Nat. Unemployment Census, 1937-38; asst. chief statistician for population Bur. of Census, 1938-42, asst. dir., 1942-46, dep. dir., 1946-47; acting dir. of U.S. Census, 1950; asst. to sec. Dept. of Commerce, 1945-47; U.S. rep. Population Commn. UN, 1947-51; statis. adviser to Govt. Union of Burma, UN Tech. Assistance, 1951-52; expert cons. to sec. of nat. def. Research and Devel. Bd.; statis. adviser to govt., Thailand, 1955-56; Walker-Ames prof. U. Wash., 1958; vis. Ford prof. Ind. U., 1960, U. Wash., 1961, 62; asso. Leo J. Shapiro and Assos., Inc., 1977-81; Dir. Family of Selected Funds.; Former mem. bd. govs. Met. Planning and Housing Council, Chgo.; cons., or mem. various comns. re population and vital statistics reporting. Former dir. Social Sci. Research Council. Author: Workers on Relief in U.S., 2 vols, 1939, Movies, Delinquency and Crime, (with Herbert Blumer), 1933, Population Perspectives, 1960, (with Beverly Duncan) Housing A Metropolis- Chicago, 1960, The Challenge of America's Metropolitan Population Outlook—1960-1985, 1968, (with Patricia Leavey Hodge) Social Statistics in Use, 1975, World Population and Development: Challenges and Prospects, 1979; assoc. editor: Jour. Am. Statis. Assn, 1945-49, Am. Jour. Sociology; editor: (with W.R. Leonard) Government Statistics for Business Use, 1946, rev., 1956, Population and World Politics, 1958, Urbanization in Asia and the Far East, 1958, The Study of Population; An Inventory and Appraisal, 1959, (with O.D. Duncan) Urbanization in Latin America, 1961, The Population Dilemma, 1963, 2d edit., 1969, The Study of Urbanization, 1965, (with Leo F. Schnore) Handbook for Social Research in Urban Areas, 1965, (with Judah Matras) Differential Mortality in the United States: A Study in Socioeconomic Epidemiology, 1973; Contbr. articles to profl. jours. Chmn. Adv. Panel on Integration Chgo. Pub. Schs., 1963-64; mem. Ill. Am. Negro Emancipation Commn., 1963-65; dir. Task Force on Edn., White House Conf. to Fulfill These Rights, 1966; bd. dirs. Nat. Assembly for Soc. Policy and Devel.; pres. Nat. Conf. Social Welfare, 1973-74; mem. exec. com. S.E. Asia Devel. Adv. Group. Fellow Am. Statis. Assn. (pres. 1962—), AAAS (sect. v.p. 1959), Am. Assn. for Pub. Opinion Research (chmn. standards com. 1948); mem. AAUP, Population Assn. Am. (pres. 1951), Am. Sociol. Assn. (pres. 1967-68), Internat. Statis. Inst., Inst. Math. Statistics, Sociol. Research Assn. (pres. 1961), Nat. Acad. Scis., Am. Acad. Arts and Scis., Am. Philos. Soc., Internat. Union for Sci. Study Population, Phi Beta Kappa, Lambda Alpha, Pi Gamma Mu. Home: 1440 N State Pkwy Chicago IL 60610

HAUSER, RITA ELEANORE ABRAMS, lawyer; b. N.Y.C., July 12, 1934; d. Nathan and Frieda (Litt) Abrams; m. Gustave M. Hauser, June 10, 1956; children—Glenvil Aubrey, Ana Patricia. A.B. magna cum laude, Hunter Coll., 1954; Dr. Polit. Economy with highest honors (Fulbright grantee), U. Strasbourg, France, 1955; Licence en Droit, U. Paris, 1958; LL.B., Harvard and N.Y. U., 1959; LL.D., Seton Hall U., 1969, Finch Coll., 1969, U. Miami, Fla., 1971. Bar: D.C. 1959, N.Y. 1961, U.S. Supreme Ct. 1967. Practiced in, N.Y.C., 1961—; partner firm Moldover, Hauser, Strauss & Volin, 1968-72, Stroock & Stroock & Lavan, 1972—; mem. exec. com. Lawyers Commn. for Civil Rights Under Law, 1969-78; dir. ARA Services, Inc., Wickes Cos., Inc., Aristar, Inc. Contbr. articles on internat. law to profl. jours. U.S. rep. to UN Commn. on Human Rights, 1969-72; mem. U.S. del. to Gen. Assembly UN, 1969; vice chmn. U.S. Adv. Com. on Internat. and Cultural Affairs, 1973-77; mem. N.Y.C. Bd. Higher Edn., 1974-76, Bd. Internat. Broadcasting, 1978-80; co-chmn. Com. for Re-election Pres., 1972, Presdl. Debates, 1976; Bd. dirs. Legal Aid Soc. N.Y., 1973-76, March of Dimes of N.Y.; trustee Internat. Legal Center, N.Y., 1974-77; trustee, co-chmn. Philharm. Soc.; trustee co-chmn., Coalition for Reagan/Bush; bd. govs., chmn. exec. com. Am. Jewish Com. Mem. Assn. Bar City N.Y., Am. Bar Assn. (world order under law standing com. 1969-78, adv. bd. jour. 1973-78), Am. Soc. Internat. Law (exec. com. 1971-76), Am. Fgn. Law Assn. (dir.), Am. Arbitration Assn. (panel arbitrators), World Order Under Law (standing com.), 1969-78). Republican. Home: 700 Park Ave New York NY 10021 Office: 7 Hanover Sq New York NY 10004

HAUSER, WALTER, educator; b. Berlin, Germany, June 9, 1924; came to U.S., 1936, naturalized, 1944; s. Louis and Lieba (Stumler) H.; m. Betty Wolkenfeld, Mar. 29, 1949; children—Neal, David, Sharon, Eli M. B.S., Bklyn. Coll., 1947; Ph.D., Mass. Inst. Tech., 1950. Asst. prof. Boston U., 1950-55; mem. staff Mass. Inst. Tech. Lincoln Lab., Lexington, Mass., 1955-60; prof. physics Northeastern U., Boston, 1960—. Author: Introduction to the Principles of Mechanics, 1965, Introduction to the Principles of Electromagnetism, 1971. Served with AUS, 1944-46. Home: 99 Marion St Brookline MA 02146 Office: Department of Physics Northeastern University Boston MA 02115

HAUSERMAN, WILLIAM FOLEY, manufacturing company executive; b. Cleve., Nov. 2, 1919; s. Earl Frederic and Mary (Martin) H.; m. Diane DuBois, Jan. 26, 1946. B.S., Lehigh U., 1941. With The E.F. Hauserman Co., Cleve., The E.F. Hauserman Co. subsidiary Hauserman, Inc., 1946—; pres. The E.F. Hauserman Co., 1969—, chmn. bd., 1972—; pres., dir. Hauserman, Inc., Cleve., 1970-83, chmn., dir., 1983—. Home: 33200 Fairmount Blvd Pepper Pike OH 44121 Office: 5711 Grant Ave Cleveland OH 44105

HAUSMAN, ARTHUR HERBERT, electronics company executive; b. Chgo., Nov. 24, 1923; s. Samuel Louis and Sarah (Elin) H.; m. Helen Mandelowitz, May 19, 1946; children: Susan Lois, Kenneth Louis, Catherine Ellen. B.S. in Elec. Engring, U. Tex., 1944; S.M., Harvard U., 1948. Electronics engr. Engring. Research Assos., St. Paul, 1946-47; supervisory electronics scientist U.S. Dept. Def., Washington, 1948-60; now cons.; v.p., dir. research Ampex Corp., Redwood City, Calif., 1960-63, v.p. operations, 1963-65, group v.p., 1965-67, exec. v.p., 1967-71, exec. v.p., pres., chief exec. officer, from 1971-83, now chmn. bd.; dir. Drexler Tech. Inc., T.C.I. Inc., Synthetic Vision Systems Inc.; Chmn. tech. adv. com. computer peripherals Dept. Commerce, 1973-75; mem. subcom. on export adminstrn. President's Export Council. Trustee United Bay Area Crusade.; mem. vis. com. dept. math. MIT; Bd. dirs. Bay Area Council. Served with USNR, 1944-54. Recipient Meritorious Civilian Service award Dept. Def. Mem. IEEE, Army Ordnance Assn. (dir. chpt. 1969-71), Am. Electronics Assn. (dir.). Club: Commonwealth of Calif. Office: 401 Broadway Redwood City CA 94063

HAUSMAN, BRUCE, corporation executive; b. N.Y.C., Mar. 4, 1930; s. Samuel and Vera (Kuttler) H.; m. Jeanne Epstein, June 8, 1952; children: Robert Lloyd, Arlene. B.A., Brown U., 1951; M.S., Columbia U., 1952; postgrad., N.Y. Law Sch., 1979. Bar: N.Y. 1980. Dir. Belding Real Estate Corp., Corticelli Real Estate Corp., 1960-63; pres., dir. Va. Dyeing Corp., 1962-64; div. mgr. M. Hausman & Sons, Inc. (named changed to Belding Hausman Fabrics Inc.) 1952-64; partner Kastex Corp., Los Angeles, 1964; regional sales mgr. Belding Heminway Co., Inc., 1965; pres., dir. Mozzil Knits Inc., contract knitting div. Belding Heminway Co., Inc., 1969-73, exec., adminstrv. officer apparel fabric div., N.Y.C., 1966-73; exec. asst. to chmn. bd. Belding Heminway Co., Inc., 1973-74, group pres. home furnishings div., 1975-79, corp. v.p., 1979, corp. counsel, sr. vice chmn., 1980, chmn. exec. com., 1981—, also dir.; of counsel Hershcopf, Stevenson, Backenroth & McConnell, N.Y.C.; exec. adminstrv. head Belding Hausman Fabrics Inc., 1975-79; adminstrv. officer Va. Dyeing Corp., Belding Corticelli Fiberglass Fabrics Inc.; pres., dir. M.K. Leasing Corp., 1974; dir. Vornado, Inc.; Bd. dirs. NCCJ, 1974—; bd. overseers Parsons Sch. Design, 1975—. Trustee, mem. exec. com. Beth Israel Med. Center, N.Y.C., 1976—. Named Man of Yr. Fabric Salesmens Guild, Inc., 1972. Mem. Textile Salesmen's Assn. (bd. govs., Man of Yr. award 1982), Textile Distbrs. Assn. (gov. 1979, v.p. 1982, sec. 1983), Am. Arbitration Assn. Office: Belding Hemingway Co Inc 1430 Broadway New York NY 10018

HAUSMAN, CARL R., philosophy educator; b. St. Louis, Dec. 7, 1924; s. Carl and Estelle (Ransdell) H.; m. Carolyn Hancock, June 17, 1951; children—Lynn, Callie. A.B., U. Louisville, 1949; M.A., Duke U., 1952; Ph.D., Northwestern U., 1960. Former mem. faculty Kans. State U., U. Colo.; former mem. faculty dept. philosophy Northwestern U.; also chmn. dept. philosophy; prof. philosophy Pa. State U., University Park; also chmn. dept.; mem. faculty summer symposia U. Pacific; exec. dir. Found. for Philosophy of Creativity. Author: A Discourse on Novelty and Creation, 1975; editor: (with A. Rothenberg) The Creativity Question, 1976; contbr. articles to profl. jours. Served with USAAF, 1943-46. Am. Philos. Soc. research grantee, 2 summers, 1960's. Mem. Am. Philos. Assn., Am. Soc. Aesthetics, Peirce Soc., Soc. Philosophy Creativity. Office: 246 Sparks University Park PA 16802 *

HAUSMAN, JEROME JOSEPH, college official; b. N.Y.C., May 4, 1925; s. Benjamin and Etta (Kobak) H.; m. Flora Siman, June 20, 1948; children: Sandra Ellen, Madelynn, Leah Ann. Student, Pratt Inst., 1942-43; A.B., Cornell U., 1946, Columbia U., 1947-48, Art

Students League, 1948; M.A., N.Y. U., 1951, Ed.D., 1954. Free-lance artist, N.Y.C., 1946-47; analytical chemist Lederle Labs., Pearl River, N.Y., 1947; art tchr. pub. schs., Elizabeth, N.J., 1949- 53; vis. lectr. Sch. Art, Syracuse U., 1957; vis. prof. art edn. dept. Pa. State U., 1958; asso. prof. Sch. Fine and Applied Arts, Ohio State U., 1953-68; acting dir. Sch. Fine and Applied Arts, 1958-59, dir., 1959-68; prof. div. creative arts N.Y. U., 1968-75; pres., prof. Mpls. Coll. Art and Design, 1975-82; v.p. acad. affairs Mass. Coll. Art, Boston, 1982—; Mem. arts and humanities panel U.S. Office Edn., 1964-70; cons. John D. Rockefeller III Fund, 1969-75; pres. Minn. Pvt. Coll. Council, 1980-81; Vice pres. Mpls. Soc. Fine Arts, 1975—; bd. dirs. Arts, Edn. and Ams., 1978—. Editor: yearbook Research in Art Edn, Nat. Art Edn. Assn., 1959, Studies in Art Edn, Jour. Issues and Research; editorial bd.: Jour. Aesthetic Edn, 1968—; Contbr. articles to profl. jours. Served USNR, 1943-46. Mem. Nat. Art Edn. Assn. (life, past chmn. research com., adv. research bd.), Nat. Commn. Art Edn. (chmn.), Art Students League (life), Am. Soc. Aesthetics, Western Arts Assn., Inst. for Study Art in Edn. (past (pres.), Minn. Alliance for Arts Edn. (pres. 1977-78). Home: 10 Elena Rd Lexington MA Office: Mass Coll Art Boston MA 02215

HAUSMAN, JERRY ALLEN, economics educator, consultant; b. Weirton, W.Va., May 5, 1946; s. Harold H. and Rose (Hausman); m. Margaretta Stone, Dec. 21, 1968; children: Nicholas, Claire. A.B., Brown U., 1968; B.Phil., Oxford U., 1972, D.Phil., 1973. Mem. faculty MIT, Cambridge, 1973—, prof. econs., 1979—. Contbr. articles to profl. jours. Office: MIT Dept Econs Cambridge MA 02139

HAUSMAN, SAMUEL, textiles exec.; b. Austria, Nov. 14, 1897; s. Morris and Bertha (Hoffman) H.; m. Vera Kuttler, May 4, 1924; children—Bruce Alan, Merna (Mrs. Richard Miller), Alice (Mrs. Morton I. Davidson). Vice chmn. bd. and dir. Belding Hemingway Co., Inc. Hon. chmn. United Jewish Appeal; 1st v.p. bd. Beth Israel Hosp.; trustee Fedn. Jewish Philanthropies; bd. dirs. Am. Jewish Com.; former trustee N.Y. State U.; bd. sponsors Met. Adv. Council Internat. Recreation, Culture and Lifelong Edn.; former mem. Commn. to Establish Human Rights N.Y., N.Y. State Manpower Advt. Council; chmn. legis. adv. com. N.Y. Bd. Rabbis; past mem. adv. council Urban Devel.; past mem. fin. agy. N.Y. State Med. Care Facilities; past chmn. N.Y. State Health and Hosp. Commn.; treas. Am. Jewish Conf. on Soviet Jewry. Mem. Am. Arbitration Assn. Clubs: City Athletic (N.Y.C.); Fresh Meadow Country (Great Neck, N.Y.); Capitol Hill (Washington); Palm Beach Country. Home: 930 Fifth Ave New York NY 10021 Office: 10 E 32d St New City NY 10016 also 1430 Broadway New York NY 10018

HAUSMAN, WILLIAM RAY, college president; b. Bradford, Pa., Apr. 22, 1941; s. Raymond Harvey and Eleanor Janet (Freeman) H.; m. Rosalyn Schmidt, Aug. 16, 1963; children: Valerie Noelle, Stephanie Carol. A.B., Wheaton Coll., 1963; Ed.M., Harvard U., 1977; D.D., Trinity Evang. Div. Sch., 1981; M.A., North Park Theol. Sem., 1969. Ordained to ministry Evang. Covenant Ch., 1971. Minister Christian edn. Glen Ellyn (Ill.) Covenant Ch., 1966-69; registrar, dir. admissions Trinity Evang. Div. Sch., Deerfield, Ill., 1969-72, dean admissions and records, 1972-75, v.p. student affairs, 1975-77, assoc. dean, 1977-80; pres. North Park Coll. and Theol. Sem., Chgo., 1980—. Trustee Swedish Covenant Hosp., Lincoln Acad.; mem. exec. bd. Evang. Covenant Ch.; mem. exec. com. Associated Colls. Ill.; bd. dirs. North River Commn., Chgo., 1980—; mem. Bd. Edn. Dist. 109, Deerfield, Ill, 1978-80. Mem. Am. Assn. Theol. Edn., Fedn. Ind. Ill. Colls. and Univs., Fellowship of Evang. Sem. Pres. Home: 108 17th St Wilmette IL 60091 Office: North Park Coll and Theol Sem 3225 W Foster Ave Chicago IL 60625

HAUSMANN, FRANK WILLIAM, JR., banker; b. Chgo., May 18, 1914; s. Frank William and Laurette I. (Bresnen) H.; m. Mary Frances Sullivan, Nov. 26, 1938; children: John Francis, Regina Denise, Mary Loretta. A.B., Loyola U., Chgo., 1936, J.D., 1940; postgrad. in bus. adminstrn., Northwestern U., 1941. Bar: Ill. 1940; Chartered fin. analyst. Ins. broker, 1934-37; asst. sec. No. Trust Co., Chgo., 1937-53; with Nat. Bank of Detroit, 1953-79, sr. v.p., sr. trust investment officer, 1967-79; investment adviser, fin. cons., expert witness, 1982—; mem. Investment Adv. Com., State of Mich. Pension Funds, 1979—; chmn., dir. Grosse Pointe Farms Econ. Devel. Corp., 1979—; dir. Nat. Casualty Co., Mich. Life Ins. Co. Assoc. editor: Financial Analysts Jour, 1964-71. Chmn. bd., mem. exec. com. Mich. Diabetes Assn., 1972-74; bd. dirs. Am. Diabetes Assn., 1976-79. Served to 1st lt. USAAF, 1943-46. Cited for disting. service Loyola U., Chgo., 1969. Mem. Fin. Analysts Soc. Detroit (past pres.), Fin. Analysts Fedn. (v.p. dir. chmn. corp. info. com. 1969-71), Inst. Chartered Fin. Analysts (charter, chmn. profl. grievances com. 1972-74), Delta Theta Phi. Clubs: Athletic, Detroit (Detroit).

HAUSNER, HENRY H., consulting engineer, editor, educator; b. Vienna, Austria, June 1, 1901; came to U.S., 1940, naturalized, 1946; s. Hans and Helene (Tritsch) H.; m. Elizabeth Wallner, July 30, 1927 (dec.); m. Hedda M. John, Nov., 1962 (dec.); m. Ada Berger, May, 1970. E.E., Technische Hochschule, Vienna, 1925; D.Eng., U. Vienna, 1938. Registered profl. engr., N.Y. Supervising engr. Elin A.G., Vienna, 1925-38; dir. research Elix Gluehlampenfabrik, Vienna, 1938-40; research engr. Am. Electro Metal Corp., Yonkers, N.Y.; chief research engr. Gen. Ceramics & Steatite Corp., Keasbey, N.J., 1940-45; cons. engr.; research assoc. NYU, 1946-48; adj. prof. N.Y. U., 1947-48; research cons. Rutgers U., 1946; sect. head metall. research lab. Sylvania Electric Products, Inc., Bayside, L.I., 1948-51, mgr. engring., atomic energy div., 1951-55; adj. prof. Bklyn. Poly. Inst., 1951—; mgr. sci. information services Franklin Inst. Research Labs., 1970—; v.p. Penn-Texas Corp., N.Y.C., 1956-58; research scientist Rensselaer Poly. Inst.; vis. prof. UCLA, 1962—; prof. Olivetti Technol. Inst., Ivrea, Italy, 1967—; hon. prof. Poly. Inst. N.Y., 1977—; guest prof. Max-Planck Inst., Germany, 1971—; lectr. NYU, 1973—. Author: Powder Metallurgy, 1947, (with W.E. Kingston, others) The Physics of Powder Metallurgy, 1951, (with others) Human Engineering, 1951, (with S.B. Roboff) Materials for Nuclear Power Reactors, 1955, (with others) Metal Beryllium, 1955, Metallurgy of Zirconium, 1955, Powder Metallurgy in Nuclear Engineering, 1957, Vacuum Metallurgy, 1958, Metals for Supersonic Aircraft and Missiles, 1958, (with C.R. Tipton, Jr., others) Materials, 2d edit, 1960, Powder Metallurgy in Nuclear Reactor Construction, 1961, also Polish edit., (with others) New Types of Metal Powders, 1964, Modern Developments in Powder Metallurgy, 1966, Fundamentals of Refractory Compounds, vol. 1-4, 1968-71, Handbook of Powder Metallurgy, 1973, 2d edit., 1982 (also Chinese transl. 1982); also edits. of sci. books.; Editor: Internat. Jour. Powder Metallurgy and Powder Tech, 1965—, Powder Metallurgy Science and Technology, 1969—; Contbr. articles to sci. jours. Recipient Powder Metall. Achievement award Stevens Inst. Tech., 1956, Powder Metall. Pioneer award Stevens Inst. Tech., 1984; ann. Henry H. Hausner Achievement award established by Fine Particle Soc., 1980; achievement award Am. Powder Metallurgy Inst., 1981. Mem. Am. Inst. Mining and Metall. Engrs. (chmn. powder metall. com. 1954-55, 62-63), Internat. Plansee Soc. Powder Metall., Am. Soc. Metals, Inst. Metals London (life), German Soc. Metals, Internat. Inst. Sci. of Sintering (hon.), Soc. Applied Spectroscopy (treas. 1945), Powder Metall. Assn. India (hon.), Sigma Xi. Club: Metal Science (N.Y.C.). Home and office: 67 Red Brook Rd Kings Point NY 11024

HAUSPURG, ARTHUR, utilities company executive; b. N.Y.C., Aug. 27, 1925; s. Otto and Charlotte (Braul) H.; m. Catherine Dunning Mackay, July 26, 1947; children: Peter R., David A., Daniel L. B.S.E.E., Columbia U., 1945, M.S.E.E., 1947. Asst. v.p. Am. Electric Power Corp., 1968; v.p. Consol. Edison Co. N.Y., Inc., 1969-73, sr. v.p., 1973-75, exec. v.p., chief operating officer, 1975, pres., chief operating officer, 1975-81, chief exec. officer, 1981—, chmn., 1982—, also dir.; dir. Prudential-Bache High Yield Fund, Inc., Prudential-Bache High Yield Mcpls., Inc., Prudential-Bache Tax-Free Money Fund, Inc., Prudential-Bache New Decade Growth Fund, Inc., Prudential-Bache Govt. Securities Trust; Bd. dirs. Com. for Econ. Devel., Regional Plan Assn., N.Y.C. Partnership, Econ. Devel. Council N.Y.C. Contbr. articles to profl. jours. Bd. dirs. N.Y. Zool. Soc. Served with USNR, 1943-46. Fellow IEEE; mem. Nat. Acad. Engring., Council Fgn. Relations (dir.), Chamber Commerce and Industry (bd. dirs.). Patentee in field. Home: 5 John Jay Pl Rye NY 10580 Office: 4 Irving Pl New York NY 10003

HAUSSER, ROBERT LOUIS, lawyer; b. Cin., Apr. 3, 1914; s. Oscar and Alma J. (Ebel) H.; m. Dorothy Ann Oakes, Aug. 17, 1940; children—George Louis, Robert Oakes, Julia Janet Guffey and Joel Severin (twins). A.B., DePauw U., Greencastle, Ind., 1936; LL.B., Columbia U., 1939. Bar: Ohio bar 1939, N.Y. bar 1940. Practice in, N.Y.C., 1939-41, Marietta, Ohio, 1941—; assoc. Baldwin, Todd & Young, 1939-41; pvt. practice, 1941—; v.p., dir. Ohio Bar Title Ins. Co., Dayton; dir. Dime Bank, Marietta.; Instr. Wash. Tech. Coll., 1973. Author: Ohio Real Property, 5 vols, 1952-58, (with William R. Van Aken) Ohio Real Estate Transactions, 3 vols, 1964, (with Allen B. Diefenbach) Ohio Estate Planning and Probate Administration, 2 vols, 1969; Editor: Title Topics, monthly jour. Ohio Land Title Assn, 1967—, Newsletter; Quar. bull. of real property sect., Ohio Bar Assn., 1973-76. Pres. Washington County Hist. Soc., 1964; Judge Marietta Police Ct., 1946-57; pres. Marietta Bd. Edn., 1963; mem. Marietta Civil Service Commn., 1967—. Served with AUS, 1944-45. Decorated Purple Heart with oak leaf cluster. Fellow Am. Coll. Probate Counsel; mem. Ohio Bar Assn. (past sect. chmn., past mem. exec. com.), Am. Legion, Phi Beta Kappa. Democrat. Presbyn. (past elder, clk. of session). Clubs: Lion. (pres. 1948), Marietta Country, Marietta Senior Reading (pres. 1961-62). Home: 507 8th St Marietta OH 45750 Office: New Dime Bank Bldg Marietta OH 45750

HAVAS, PETER, physicist, educator; b. Budapest, Hungary, Mar. 29, 1916; came to U.S., 1941, naturalized, 1948; s. George G. and Irene (Harmos) H.; m. Helga Francis Höllering; children: Eva Catherine, Stephen Walter. Absolutorium, Technische Hochschule, Vienna, Austria, 1938; Ph.D., Columbia U., 1944. Research asst. in mass spectroscopy U. Vienna, 1937-38; research fellow Institut de Physique Atomique, Lyon, France, 1938-41; lectr. in physics Columbia U., N.Y.C., 1941-45; instr. physics Cornell U., 1945-46; asst. prof. physics Lehigh U., Bethlehem, Pa., 1946-49, asso. prof., 1949-54, prof., 1954-65; mem. Inst. for Advanced Study, Princeton, N.J., 1953-54; prof. physics Temple U., Phila., 1965—; Vis. prof. U. Göttingen, Germany, 1973. Mem. editorial bd.: Acta Phys. Austriaca, 1968-76, Jour. Math. Physics, 1975-77, KINAM (Mex.), 1979—. Guggenheim fellow, 1953-54. Fellow AAAS, Am. Phys. Soc. Research on classical and quantum theories of radiation, theory of relativity, especially equations of motion, foundation problems, math. physics, history and philosophy of physics. Office: Dept Physics Temple U Philadelphia PA 19122

HAVDALA, HENRI SALOMON, physician, educator; b. Minia, Egypt, Apr. 12, 1931; came to U.S., 1957, naturalized, 1963; s. Jacques S. and Regine (Levy) H.; m. Sandra Abrams, Aug. 27, 1961; children—Jack, Debra, Ellen, Michael. B.S. in Sci, St. Mark Coll., 1948; M.B., B.Ch., U. Alexandria, Egypt, 1956. Diplomate: Am. Bd. Anesthesiology. Practice medicine, specializing in anesthesiology Mt. Sinai Hosp., Chgo., 1961—; now chmn. dept. anesthesiology; mem. faculty Chgo. Med. Sch., 1961-74, asst. prof. anesthesiology, 1971-72, asso. prof., 1972, prof., 1972-74, chmn. dept., 1965-74, acting dean Sch., 1973-74; prof. anesthesiology Rush Med. Coll., 1975—; Bd. govs. Ill. State Med. Ins. Exchange, 1977; trustee Mt. Sinai Hosp. Anesthesiologists (dir.), 1977. Fellow Am. Soc. Anesthesiologists, Inst. Med., Philippine Coll. Anesthesiologists; mem. Ill. Soc. Anesthesiologists (sec. 1971-73, pres. 1976-77), Chgo., Ill. med. socs., AMA, Chgo. Anesthesiology Soc., Internat. Anesthesia Research Soc., Am. Soc. Anesthesiologists (dir.), Am. Soc. Respiratory Therapy, N.Y.C. Acad. Scis., Am. Coll. Chest Physicians, Ill. Council Continuing Med. Edn., Council for Jewish Elderly (dir.), Sigma Xi, Alpha Omega Alpha.; Mem. B'nai B'rith. Home: 4408 Morse St Lincolnwood IL 60646 Office: 2750 W 15th Pl Chicago IL 60608

HAVEL, JEAN EUGENE MARTIAL, author, educator; b. Le Havre, France, June 16, 1928; emigrated to Can., 1959, naturalized, 1966; m. Anne Marie Luhr, Aug. 22, 1955 (dec. Jan. 1977); children—Jean Guillaume, Frederik, Sophie Mathilde, Ingrid Lucie. Licencé en Droit, Université de Paris, 1950; diploma, Institut des Etudes Politiques, 1952; postgrad., Institut des Etudes Scandinaves, 1952-53, Doctorat es Lettres, 1956. Part-time tchr. extension div. U. Stockholm, 1956-59; asst. prof. polit. sci. U. Montreal (Can.), Sudbury, Ont., Can., 1959-69, Laurentian U., 1962-66, asso. prof., 1966-69, prof., 1969—; guest speaker U. N.B., 1968, U. London, 1969, U. Helsinki/Helsingfors (Finland), 1969, U. Padova (Italy), 1969, U. Rouen (France), 1969, U. Caen (France), 1969, U. Liège (Belgium), 1981, U. Stockholm, 1983, U. Helsinki, 1983; learned jours. grant assessor Can. Council Arts, 1976, 77; mem. exec. council Social Sci. Research Council Can., 1968-69. Author: Cours de Journalisme: La Rédaction, 1956, La Fabrication du Journal, 1957, Cent soixante-quinze ans de peinture et de sculpture en France, 1957, La Politique Suédoise du Logement de, 1940, à, 1957, 1957, Le Mouvement Socialiste Norvégien, 1958, Le Socialisme Danois, 1958, Le Socialisme Réformiste Modéré en Suède, 2 vols, 1958, La Condition de la Femme, 1961; also Italian, Spanish, Japanese transl.; Politics in Sudbury: A Survey of Mass Communications, Political Behavior, and Political Parties in Sudbury, 1966, Les Citoyens de Sudbury et la Politique, 1966, also English transl., Les Etats Scandinaves et l'Intégration Europeenne, 2d edit, 1970; Spanish transl. Habitat et Logement, 4th edit, 1974, La Finlande et la Suède, 1978; contbr. articles to profl. jours. Recipient Centennial medal Govt. Can., 1967, award European Center Carnegie Endowment for Internat. Peace, 1958, French Acad. Moral and Polit. Sci., 1962; Norwegian govt. scholar, 1953-54, 82; Swedish Inst. Cultural Relations with Fgn. Countries scholar, 1954-55, 83; Council Europe research scholar, 1957-58; Can. Council Leave fellow, 1968-69, 75-76; Finnish govt. scholar, 1983. Mem. Can. Polit. Sci. Assn. Home: 175 Boland Ave Sudbury ON P3E 1X1 Canada *I write because I feel an inner urge to do it. I dream of a world of men and women who are both free and responsible. And I try to contribute, small steps by small steps, to build such a world. To be successful, I try to set up my contributions on the findings of the observers of human nature.*

HAVEL, RICHARD JOSEPH, physician; b. Seattle, Feb. 20, 1925; s. Joseph and Anna (Fritz) H.; m. Virginia Johnson, June 28, 1947; children: Christopher, Timothy, Peter, Julianne. B.A., Reed Coll., 1946; M.S., M.D., U. Oreg., 1949. Intern Cornell U. Med. Coll., N.Y.C., 1949-50, resident in medicine, 1950-53; clin. asso. Nat. Heart Inst., NIH, 1953-54, research asso., 1954-56; faculty Sch. Medicine, U. Calif., San Francisco, 1956—, prof. medicine, 1964—; asso. dir. Cardiovascular Research Inst., 1961-73, dir., 1973—; chief metabolism sect., dept. medicine, 1967—; dir. Arteriosclerosis Specialized Center of Research, 1970—; mem. bd. sci. counselors Nat. Heart, Lung and Blood Inst., 1976-80. Contbr. chpts. to books, numerous articles to profl. jours.; Editor: Jour. Lipid Research, 1972-75; mem. editorial bd.: Jour. Biol. Chemistry, 1981—, Jour. Arteriosclerosis, 1980—; mem. bd. cons. editors: Am. Jour. Medicine, 1981—. Served with USPHS, 1951-52. Recipient Theobald Smith award AAAS, 1960. Mem. Am. Fedn. for Clin. Research (pres. 1965-66), Am. Heart Assn. (established investigator 1956-61, chmn. Council on Arteriosclerosis 1977-79), Assn. Am. Physicians, Western Soc. for Clin. Research (v.p. 1964), Am. Physiol. Soc., Am. Soc. for Clin. Investigation, Western Assn. Physicians, Nat. Acad. Scis., Phi Beta Kappa, Alpha Omega Alpha. Office: Cardiovascular Research Inst Sch Medicine U Calif - San Francisco San Francisco CA 94143

HAVELIWALA, YOOSUF ABDULKAIYUM, psychiatrist, health facility administrator; b. Surat, India, Nov. 15, 1934; came to U.S., 1964, naturalized, 1976; s. Abdulkaiyum Y. and Sarah A. H.; m. Purviz Motiwala, Dec. 1, 1973; 1 son, Hozefa Y. M.B.B.S., U. Bombay, India, 1957; diploma in psychol. medicine, U. London, Eng.; cert. in community mental health services adminstrn.; M.S. in Pub. Health and Epidemiology, State U. N.Y., Buffalo, 1976. Diplomate: Am. Bd. Psychiatry and Neurology. Intern St. Vincent Hosp., S.I., N.Y., 1964-65; resident Norwich (Conn.) Hosp.; psychiatrist Buffalo Psychiat. Center, 1968-72; dep. dir. clin. South Beach Psychiat. Center, S.I., 1972-74; dir. Harlem Valley Psychiat. Center, Wingdale, N.Y., 1974-79, Creedmoor Psychiat. Center, Queens Village, N.Y., 1979—; assoc. clin. prof. psychiatry Columbia U. Coll. Phys. and Surgs., N.Y.C., 1983—; adj. prof. psychiatry N.Y. Med. Coll.; clin. asst. prof. psychiatry Downstate Med. Center, Bklyn, 1973—; clin. asso. prof. psychiatry Cornell U. Med. Coll., N.Y.C., 1979—; attending prof. psychiatry N.Y. Hosp., N.Y.C., 1979—. Author: Common Sense in Therapy, 1979; contbr. articles to sci. jours. Bd. dirs. United Way of Dutchess County (N.Y.). Fellow Internat. Assn. Social Psychiatry, Am. Psychiat. Assn. (cert. in adminstrv. psychiatry, sec. Mid-Hudson Dist. br.); mem. Am. Assn. Psychiat. Adminstrs. (pres. N.Y. State chpt. 1982-83), N.Y. Acad. Scis., Royal Coll. Psychiatrists, Assn. Facility Dirs. of N.Y. State Office Mental Health (pres. 1982-83), AMA, Dutchess County Med. Soc., Am. Assn. Psychiatrists from India (founder, pres. 1980—). Home: 80-45 Winchester Blvd Queens Village NY 11427 *Make a sincere effort and do not worry about results.*

HAVELOCK, CHRISTINE MITCHELL, art historian; b. Cochrane, Ont., Can., June 2, 1924; d. William Waterson and Annie Margaret (Graham) Mitchell; m. Eric A. Havelock, Nov. 21, 1962. B.A., U. Toronto, 1946; Ph.D. (Charles Eliot Norton fellow), Harvard U., 1958. Mem. faculty Vassar Coll., 1953—, prof. art history, 1967—, chmn. art dept., 1968-71, asst. to pres., 1972-73. Author: Hellenistic Art, 2d edit, 1981. Mem. mng. com. Am. Sch. Classical Studies, Athens, Greece. Mem. Am. Inst. Archeology, Coll. Art Assn., AAUW. Address: Vassar Coll Poughkeepsie NY 12601

HAVEN, THOMAS KENNETH, business executive, educator; b. Muskegon, Mich., June 27, 1906; s. Ole B. and Minnie B. (Larson) H.; m. Marion L. Reading, Dec. 11, 1935; children: Carl, Donna Jean, Madge, Daniel. A.B., U. Mich., 1928, M.B.A., 1929, Ph.D., 1940. Research asso. Bus. Adminstrn. Sch., U. Mich., 1929-36, grad. teaching staff, summer 1940; with Watling, Lerchen & Co., investment bankers, Detroit, 1936-42; rep. bd. dirs. Wabash Portland Cement Co., Dayton, Ohio, 1940-44; v.p. charge finance Reichhold Chems., Inc., Detroit, 1942-47, dir., 1946-54, exec. v.p., 1947-54; v.p., dir. Detrex Corp., 1954; pres., dir. Pioneer Finance Co., Mobile Homes Life Ins. Co., 1958-66; v.p., dir. Beaver Precision Products, Inc., 1957-65; founding dir., v.p. Detroit Med. Center Devel. Corp., 1961-65; founding dir. Ferndale Nat. Bank, 1948-58; adv. dir. Detroit Bank and Trust Co., Ferndale br., 1958-66; dir. Seibert Oxidermo Co., Vac-Hyd Co., Detrex Chem. Industries, Inc.; prof. finance Sch. Bus. Adminstrn. U. Mich., 1970-74, prof. finance for exec. devel. program, 1973; financial and econ. cons. to DuPont Corp., 1974-79; fin. adviser, Malaya, 1966-67, Financiera Dominicana (S.A.), Dominican Republic, 1968—; cons. Levi Strauss, 1981.; lectr. fin., Australia, 1964. Author: Investment Banking Under the Securities and Exchange Commission, 1940. Past pres., trustee Grace Hosp.; trustee Harper-Grace Detroit; treas., vice chmn., chmn. Cranbrook Ednl. Community, 1963-76. Mem. Delta Sigma Pi. Clubs: Circumnavigators, Bloomfield Hills Country, Detroit, Pres.'s U. Mich., Century (Oakland U.). Home: 3675 Ward Point Dr Orchard Lake MI 48033 *Basic principle: Integrity, education, family, and a willingness to share both time and money if good fortune shines on one.*

HAVENS, A. EUGENE, rural sociology educator, consultant; b. Brooks, Iowa, Dec. 22, 1936; s. Glade Elbert and Louis Edna (Odell) H.; m. Marilyn Joyce Jentz, June 11, 1960 (div. Dec. 1974); children: Julia Liana, Maria Teresa; m. Susana E. Lastarria Cornhill, Jan. 17, 1975; 1 dau. Daniela. B.S., Iowa State U., 1959; M.S., Ohio State U., 1960, Ph.D., 1962. Asst. dean men Ohio State U., Columbus, 1962-62; Fulbright prof. Nat. U. Colombia, Bogota, 1962-63; asst. prof. to prof. rural sociology U. Wis., Madison, 1962—, dir. Ctr. for Developing Nations, 1968-70, chmn. dept. rural sociology, 1981—; vis. prof. Cath. U. Peru, Lima, 1974-77; cons. Ford Found., N.Y.C., 1975-80, Nat. Planning Com., Damacus, Syria, 1979, Agrarian Reform Inst., Managua, Nicaragua, 1979—; dir. Ct. for Comparative Study, Soc. Agr., Madison, Wis., 1982—. Author: (with W. L. Flinn) Internal Colonialism and Structure Change in Columbia, 1970, (with James Petras) Class, State and Power in the Third World, 1980, (with E. Baumesiter) Problemas Laborales en el Sector Agro-Exportador in Nicaragua Libre, 1983, Tamesis: Estructura y Cambio, 1966. Served to capt. U.S. Army, 1966-68. Named Fulbright research prof. U.S. Edn. Exchange, 1962; recipient grant Ford Found., 1969-72, Best Article in Rural Soc. award Cornell U., 1966. Fellow Am. Sociol. Assn.; mem. Rural Sociol. Soc. (council 1981-83), Latin Am. Rural Sociol. Assn. Home: 6 Vista Rd Mdison WI 53705 Office: Dept Rural Sociology 1450 Linden Dr Madison WI 53706

HAVENS, JOHN FRANKLIN, banker; b. Marietta, Ohio, May 14, 1927; s. William F. and Nola F. (Dysle) H.; m. Sally Luethi, June 19, 1950; children: John C., Thomas F., Ellen Havens Hardymon, Suzanne. B.S., Ohio State U., 1949. Owner, operator real estate, constrn. and brokerage co., Columbus, Ohio, 1950-54; pres. Equitable Investment, Columbus, 1954-63; chmn. bd. U.S. Land Inc., Columbus, 1964-67, Homewood Co., 1966-70; chmn. Franklin Bank, Columbus, 1970-80, Banc One Corp., 1980—; dir. W.W. Williams Co., Columbus, T.R.I., San Francisco, Evans Adhesive, Sanderville, Ga.; chmn. Muirfield Ltd., Dublin, Ohio. Trustee Marietta Coll., Ohio State U. Served with USCG, 1945. Named Outstanding Citizen Citizen Jour., Columbus, 1964, Outstanding Exec. Fin. Analyst Citizen Jour., Columbus, 1969, Nat. Developer Am. Builders Council, 1970; recipient Outstanding Achievement award Nat. Assn. Real Estate, 1966. Mem. Phi Gamma Delta. Methodist. Clubs: Varsity O (Columbus); Firestone Country (Akron) (gov.); Muirfield Village Golf (Dublin) (gov.). Office: Banc One Corp 100 E Broad St Columbus OH 43271

HAVENS, LESTON LAYCOCK, psychiatrist, educator; b. Bklyn., July 31, 1924; s. Valentine Britton and Nellie Falk (Laycock) H.; m. Susan Elizabeth Miller, May 19, 1973; 1 dau., Emily E.; children by previous marriage—Christopher W., Jeffrey B., Jennifer F., Sarah B. B.A., Williams Coll., 1947; M.D., Cornell U., 1952. Intern N.Y. Hosp.,

1952-53, asst. resident internal medicine, 1953-54; resident, chief of service Mass. Mental Health Center, Boston Psychopathic Hosp., 1954-58, staff visit and asst. clin. dir., 1958-62, prin. investigator studies in visual word perception, 1960-66; program dir. Psychiat. Rehab. Internship Program, 1962-68; asst. prof. psychiatry Harvard Med. Sch., Boston, 1963-64, asso. clin. prof. psychiatry, 1965-71, psychoanalyst, 1967—, prof. psychiatry, 1971—; Carnegie vis. prof. humanities M.I.T., 1968; H.B. Williams travelling prof. Australian and N.Z. Coll. of Psychiatrists.; Chief psychiat. cons. Mass. Rehab. Commn., 1959-65; mental health adminstr. Region VI, Mass. Dept. Mental Health, 1968-69. Author: Approaches to the Mind: Movement of the Psychiatric Schools from Sects toward Science, 1973, Participant Observation, 1976; Contbr. articles to profl. jours. Served to 2d lt. AUS, 1944-46. Recipient H.C. Solomon award, 1977. Mem. Am. Psychiat. Assn., Boston Psychoanalytic Soc. and Inst., Soc. Biol. Psychiatry (A.E. Bennett award 1958), Mass. Soc. for Research in Psyciatry (McCurdy prize 1962), Phi Beta Kappa, Alpha Omega Alpha. Club: Harvard (Boston). Home: 151 Brattle St Cambridge MA 02138 Office: Cambridge Hosp Cambridge MA 02138

HAVENS, MURRAY CLARK, political scientist, educator; b. Council Grove, Kans., Aug. 21, 1932; s. Ralph Murray and Catherine Clara (Clark) H.; m. Agnes Marie Scharpf, July 5, 1958 (dec. 1969); children—Colin Scott, Theresa Agnes. B.A., U. Ala., 1953; M.A. (Woodrow Wilson fellow 1953-54), Johns Hopkins U., 1954, Ph.D., 1958. Postdoctoral fellow Brookings Instn., Washington, 1958-59; asst. prof. polit. sci. Duke U., 1959-61; from asst. prof. to prof. U. Tex., Austin, 1961-73; vis. lectr. U. Sydney (Australia), 1966; prof. polit. sci. Tex. Tech. U., Lubbock, 1973—, chmn. dept., 1975—. Author: City Versus Farm?, 1957, The Challenges to Democracy, 1965, The Politics of Assassination, 1970, Assassination and Terrorism, 1975; book rev. editor: Jour. Politics, 1971—. Served with AUS, 1954-56. Mem. Am. Polit. Sci. Assn., So. Polit. Sci. Assn., Midwest Polit. Sci. Assn., Southwestern Polit. Sci. Assn. (pres. 1983-84), AAUP, Phi Beta Kappa. Home: 7408 Topeka Ave Lubbock TX 79424 Office: Dept Polit Sci Tex Tech Univ Lubbock TX 79409

HAVENS, OLIVER HERSHMAN, lawyer, consultant; b. Bradley Beach, N.J., July 19, 1917; s. Abram Vaugn and Sara Mildred (Atkinson) H.; m. Ervanna Josephine Cummings, Aug. 16, 1941 (div. 1976); children: Janice Patricia Havens Greer, Judity Ann Havens Sherman; m. 2d Elizabeth Lewis Lykes, Nov. 13, 1976. B.A., Princeton U., 1939; J.D., Yale U., 1942. Bar: N.Y. 1947; conseil juridique, France, 1978. Assoc. Cahill Gordon & Reindel, N.Y.C., 1946-54, ptnr., 1955-82, ret., 1982; cons. Mehdi Corp. and Basa Corp., Princeton, N.J., 1983—. Served to capt. U.S. Army, 1942-46. Mem. ABA, N.Y. State Bar Assn., Assn. Bar City of N.Y. Republican. Episcopalian. Clubs: Baltusrol Golf (Springfield, N.J.); Island (Hobe Sound, Fla.); Travellers (Paris). Home: 14 Kenilworth Dr Short Hills NJ 07078

HAVENS, WILLIAM WESTERFIELD, JR., physicist; b. N.Y.C., Mar. 31, 1920; s. William Westerfield and Elsie (Medl) H.; m. Aldine V. Morris, Oct. 22, 1944; children—Nancy E., Cynthia (Mrs. John H. Gosline). B.S., City Coll. N.Y., 1939; M.A., Columbia U., 1941, Ph.D., 1946. Asst. in physics Columbia U., 1940; research scientist Manhattan Project, 1941-45, instr. physics, 1945-47, asst. prof., 1947-50, asso. prof., 1950-55, prof., 1955—, dir. div. nuclear sci. and engring., 1961-78; dir. Energy Research Center, 1979—; Chmn. European Am. Nuclear Data Com., 1970-72; mem. nuclear cross sect. adv. com. AEC; mem. adv. com. I.A.E.A. Anglo-Am. Hellenic Bur. Edn. Contbr. numerous articles neutron spectroscopy to sci. jours. Recipient Townsend Harris medal City Coll. N.Y., 1975. Fellow Am. Phys. Soc. (exec. sec. 1966—); mem. AAAS (v.p. 1967-68), Am. Inst. Physics (exec. com., gov. bd.). Home: 219 Palisade Ave Dobbs Ferry NY 10522 Office: 520 W 120th St New York NY 10027

HAVERTY, JOHN RHODES, physician, university dean; b. Atlanta, Apr. 4, 1926; s. John Rhodes and Mary Frances (Cooledge) H.; children: Kathleen Amanda, Lisa Frances, John Rhodes III. A.B., Princeton U., 1948; M.D., Med. Coll. Ga., 1953. Intern Jackson Meml. Hosp., Miami, Fla., 1953-54; resident St. Christopher's Hosp. Children, Phila., 1954-56, Grady Meml. Hosp., Atlanta, 1956-57; practice medicine, specializing in pediatrics, Atlanta, 1957-68; dean Coll. Health Scis., Ga. State U., Atlanta, 1968—; assoc. chmn. dept. pediatrics Crawford W. Long Hosp., Atlanta, 1960—; mem. staff Henrietta Egleston Hosp. Children, Piedmont Hosp., Northside Hosp., St. Joseph's Infirmary; assoc. pediatrics Sch. Medicine, Emory U., Atlanta, 1960—; pres. Nat. Commn. on Certification Physicians' Assts., 1976; dir. Haverty Furniture Cos., Inc.; mem. Nat. Bd. Med. Examiners, 1980—, mem. com. allied health edn. and accreditation, 1979—, vice chmn. com., 1980-82, chmn. com., 1982-83; bd. dirs. Council on Postsecondary Accreditation, 1984. Bd. dirs. Atlanta chpt. ARC, 1980—. Served with USNR, 1944-46. Fellow Am. Acad. Pediatrics; mem. AMA, Am. Soc. Allied Health Professions (pres. 1975), Med. Assn. Ga. (pres. 1974), Med. Assn. Atlanta, So. Assn. Colls. and Schs. (bd. dirs. 1980—). Presbyterian (elder). Club: Piedmont Driving (Atlanta). Home: 3720 Paces Valley Rd Atlanta GA 30327

HAVERTY, RAWSON, retail furniture company executive; b. Atlanta, Nov. 26, 1920; s. Clarence and Elizabeth (Rawson) H.; m. Margaret Middleton Munnerlyn, Aug. 25, 1951; children: Margaret Elizabeth, Jane Middleton, James Rawson, Mary Elizabeth, Ben Munnerlyn. B.A., U. Ga., 1941. With Haverty Furniture Co., 1941-42, Haverty Furniture Cos., Inc., Atlanta, 1946—, pres., 1955—, chmn. bd., chief exec. officer, 1984—, also dir.; dir. J.M. Tull Industries, Inc., Barclays Am.; instr. credit and collection So. Retail Furniture Assn. Sch. for Execs., U. N.C., 1950, instr. credits, collections, market analyses, 1951; instr. br. stores Nat. Retail Furniture Sch. for Execs., U. Chgo., 1957—; chmn. bd., dir. Bank of the South, N.A./Bank South Corp.; dir. Piedmont Aviation, Inc., Winston-Salem, N.C., Central Atlanta Progress. Former chmn. Met. Atlanta Rapid Transit Authority; chmn. bd. trustees St. Joseph's Hosp.; pres. U. Ga. Alumni Soc., 1973-75, mem. exec. com., 1975—, chmn. loyalty fund, 1969-70, 70-71; past pres. bd. trustees St. Joseph's Village; trustee Atlanta Arts Alliance, Westminster Sch., Atlanta, U. Ga. Found.; past pres. bd. sponsors Atlanta Art Sch.; bd. sponsors High Mus. Art; former mem. Fulton Indsl. Authority. Served as maj. AUS, 1942-46. Decorated Bronze Star medal; Order of Leopold; Croix de Guerre with palms (Belgium); named All Am. Mcht. in retail furniture industry, 1958. Mem. Atlanta Retail Mchts. Assn. (past pres., dir.), Nat. Home Furnishings Assn. (past v.p., dir., Retailer of Year 1979-80), Am. Retail Fedn., Atlanta Jr. C. of C. (hon. life), Assn. U.S. Army (past pres., adv. bd.), Atlanta C. of C. (dir., past pres.), Sigma Alpha Epsilon. Roman Catholic. Clubs: Kiwanian., Piedmont Driving, Capital City (Atlanta); Ponte Vedra (Fla.). Home: 3740 Paces Valley Rd NW Atlanta GA 30327 Office: 866 W Peachtree St NW Atlanta GA 30308

HAVIGHURST, CLARK CANFIELD, legal educator; b. Evanston, Ill., May 25, 1933; s. Harold Canfield and Marion Clay (Perryman) H.; m. Karen Waldron, Aug. 28, 1965; children: Craig Perryman, Marjorie Clark. B.A., Princeton U., 1955; J.D., Northwestern U., 1958. Bar: Ill. 1958, N.Y. 1961. Assoc. Debevoise Plimpton Lyons & Gates, N.Y.C., 1958, 61-64; assoc. prof. law Duke U., Durham, N.C., 1964-68, prof., 1968—; dir. Program on Legal Issues in Health Care Duke U., Durham, N.C., 1969—; adj. scholar Am. Enterprise Inst. Pub. Policy Research, 1976—; resident cons. FTC, Washington, 1979-79; scholar in residence Inst. Medicine of Nat. Acad. Sci., Washington, 1972-73. Author: Deregulating the Health Care Industry, 1982; editor: Deferred Compensation for Key Employees, 1964, Regulating Health Facilities Construction, 1974, Law an Contemporary Problems jour., 1965-70. Mem. sec.'s task force on competition HHS, 1981-82. Served with U.S. Army, 1958-61. Mem. Inst. Medicine of Nat. Acad. Sci., Nat. Health Lawyers Assn., Order of Coif. Home: 3610 Dover Rd Durham NC 27707 Office: Duke University School of Law Durham NC 27706

HAVIGHURST, ROBERT J., chemistry educator; b. DePere, Wis., June 5, 1900; s. Freeman Alfred and Winifred (Weter) H.; m. Edythe McNeely, June 21, 1930; children—Helen S., Ruth L., Dorothy C., James P., Walter M. A.B., Ohio Wesleyan Univ., 1921; Ph.D., Ohio State U., 1924. NRC fellow in physics Harvard, 1924-26; asst. prof. chemistry Miami U., Oxford, Ohio, 1927-28; asst. prof. physics, adviser in exptl. coll. U. Wis., 1928-32; asso. prof. sci. edn. Ohio State U., Columbus, 1932-34; asst. dir. for gen. edn. Gen. Edn. Bd. (Rockefeller Found.), 1934-37; dir. for gen. edn., 1937-41; prof. edn. U. Chgo., 1941—; Co-dir. Brazil Govt. Center Ednl. Research, 1956-58. Co-author: Who Shall be Educated, 1944, Father of the Man, 1947, Adolescent Character and Personality, 1949, Personal Adjustment in Old Age, 1949, Social History of a War Boom Community, 1951, The American Veteran Back Home, 1951, Intelligence and Cultural Differences, 1951, Older People, 1953, The Meaning of Work and Retirement, 1954, American Indian and White Children, 1954, Educating Gifted Children, 1957, Society and Education, 1979, Psychology of Moral Character, 1960, Growing Up in River City, 1962, Society and Education in Brazil, 1965, Brazilian Secondary Education and Socioeconomic Development, 1969, 400 Losers, 1971, Adjustment to Retirement, 1970, Farewell to Schools???, 1971, Cross-National Research: Social Psychological Methods and Problems, 1972, To Live on This Earth: American Indian Education, 1972, Character y Personalidad del Adolescente, 1962, Social Scientists and Educators: Lives After Sixty, 1976; author: Developmental Tasks and Education, 1972, Human Development and Education, 1953, American Higher Education in the 1960's, 1960, Sociedad y Educacion en America Latina, 1962, The Public Schools of Chicago, 1964, The Educational Mission of the Church, 1965, Education in Metropolitan Areas, 1971, Comparative Perspectives on Education, 1968, Optometry: Education for the Profession, 1973; Contbr. articles to profl. jours. Mem. Soc. Research in Child Devel., AAAS, Am. Psychol. Assn., Am. Sociol. Assn., Am. Ednl. Research Assn., AAUP, Nat. Acad. Edn., Gerontol. Soc. (Kleemeier award for research 1967, Brookdale award 1979), Nat. Soc. Study Edn., Phi Beta Kappa, Sigma Xi, Phi Delta Theta. Address: Judd Hall U Chgo Chicago IL 60637

HAVILAND, FRED RUSS, JR., marketing and corp. planning cons., nurseryman; b. Tampa, Fla., Mar. 24, 1915; s. Fred Russ and Louise M. (Kerns) H.; m. Barbara Roland Moses, May 20, 1943; children—Sarah Keith Haviland Brewer, Susan Holmes Haviland Bendfelt, Fred Russ III. B.A., Carleton Coll., 1938; M.B.A., Northwestern U., 1941. Sr. asso., part owner Stewart, Dougall & Assos., N.Y.C., 1946-51; dir. market devel., chmn. long range planning com. Mpls.-Honeywell Regulator Co., 1951-56; dir. bus. planning Anheuser-Busch, Inc., 1956-59; with Jos. Schlitz Brewing Co., 1959-77, v.p. marketing and corp. planning, 1963-64, exec. v.p., 1964-74, gen. marketing cons., 1974-77; marketing and corp. planning cons. to various firms, 1974—; owner Haviland Nurseries; prof. mktg. U. Central Fla., Orlando, 1976—; Mem. exec. devel. program adv. com. Mgmt. Inst., U. Wis., 1964—. Author: Changing Perspectives in Marketing, 1951. Served to maj. USAAF, 1941-45. Mem. Inst. Mgmt. Scis., Am. Mgmt. Assn. (Outstanding Contbn. to Marketing award 1948), AAAS, Assn. Nat. Advertisers. Home: 1506 Williams Dr Winter Park FL 32789 Office: Route 1 Box 612-H Apopka FL 32703

HAVILAND, JAMES WEST, physician; b. Glens Falls, N.Y., July 18, 1911; s. Morrison LeRoy and Mabel Eva (West) H.; m. Marion Cranston Bertram, Oct. 23, 1943; children—James Marshall, Elizabeth Bullard, Donald Sherman, Martha Adams. A.B., Union Coll., Schenectady, 1932; M.D., Johns Hopkins, 1936. Intern medicine Johns Hopkins Hosp., 1936-37, intern, asst. resident, chief outpatient dept. pediatrics, 1937-38, asst. resident medicine, 1939-40, New Haven Hosp., 1938-39; instr. medicine Yale Med. Sch., 1938-39, Johns Hopkins Sch. Medicine, 1939-40; chief services crippled children Wash. Dept. Social Security, also Dept. Health, 1940- 42; lectr. medicine U. Wash. Sch. Nursing, 1946-60; practice medicine, Seattle, 1946—; clin. asst. prof., to clin. prof. U. Wash. Sch. Medicine, 1947—, asst. dean, 1949-53, 1954-59, acting dean, 1953-54, asso. dean, 1972-76. Trustee Seattle Artificial Kidney Center, Seattle Symphony Orch. Served as lt. comdr., M.C. USNR, 1942-46. Fellow Am. Geog. Soc. N.Y., Am. Heart Assn.; mem. Wash. State Med. Assn. (sec.-treas. 1948-51), Seattle Acad. Internal Medicine (pres. 1952-53), King County Med. Soc. (pres. 1962), AMA (council med. edn. 1966-76, chmn. 1974-76), Pacific Interurban Clin. Club, AAAS, Am. Fed. Med. Research, Western Soc. Clin. Research, North Pacific Soc. Internal Medicine, A.C.P. (pres. 1970), Am. Clin. and Climatol. Assn. (pres. 1981), Am. Assn. History Medicine, Nat. Acad. Scis. (Inst. Medicine), Phi Beta Kappa, Sigma Xi, Alpha Omega Alpha, Kappa Alpha. Home: 8208 SE 30th St Mercer Island WA 98040 Office: 721 Minor Ave Seattle WA 98104

HAVOC, JUNE, actress; b. Vancouver, B.C., Can., Nov. 8, 1916; came to U.S., 1916; d. John Olaf and Rose (Thompson) Hovick; m. William Spier, Dec. 22 (div. 1973). Artistic dir. New Orleans Repertory Theatre, 1969-71. Film appearances: Baby June, 1918; vaudeville appearances, (as Dainty June) the Darling of Vaudeville, registered U.S. Patent Office; headliner, Keith-Orpheum Circuit, 1923-25; actress: 22 Broadway shows including Pal Joey, 1941, To Annie, 1982; Sweeney Todd on tour, 1982; 43 films including Gentlemen's Agreement, Hello, Frisco, Hello, The Iron Curtain, Chicago Deadline, Can't Stop the Music; creator, dir.: one-woman show An Unexpected Evening with June Havoc -or- Baby June remembers, 1983; radio, TV, person appearances, Las Vegas, 1950-60; author: Early Havoc, 1959, More Havoc, 1980; play Marathon '33, 1963. Active restoration pre-Civil War village, animal welfare. Home: 30 Cannon Rd Wilton CT 06897

HAWES, ALEXANDER BOYD, JR., journalist; b. Washington, May 5, 1947; s. Alexander Boyd and Elizabeth (Armstrong) H.; m. Jane Ann Gepfert, Dec. 27, 1969; children: Alexander Boyd, III, Ellen Booth. Student, U. Denver, 1965-69. Gen. Assignment reporter Berkshire Eagle, Pittsfield, Mass., 1970-72; gen. assignment reporter, city hall reporter Colorado Springs (Colo.) Sun, 1973-76; gen. assignment reporter, mem. Spotlight team investigative reporters, city hall bur., asst. treas., human resources dir., asst. mng. editor Boston Globe, 1976—; bd. dirs. Colorado Springs Press Assn., 1975-76. Recipient Pulitzer prize for spl. local reporting, 1980, New Eng. Community Service award UPI, 1980, Sevellon Brown award New Eng. AP Press News Execs. Assn., 1980.

HAWES, DOUGLAS WESSON, lawyer; b. West Orange, N.J., Nov. 17, 1932. B.A., Principia Coll., 1954; J.D., Columbia U., 1957; M.B.A., N.Y. U., 1961. Bar: N.Y. 1958, U.S. Supreme Ct. 1961. Assoc., then ptnr. LeBoeuf, Lamb, Leiby & MacRae, N.Y.C., 1958—; adj. prof. law Vanderbilt U., 1972—, N.Y. U., 1976—; dir. New Holographic Design Ltd., Everfast, Inc., Hackensack Water Co. Contbr. articles to legal publs. Trustee Principia Coll. Mem. ABA (fed. securities law com.), N.Y. State Bar Assn., Bar Assn. City N.Y. (corp. law com.), Am. Law Inst., Internat. Faculty for Corp. and Capital Market Law. Home: 755 Park Ave New York NY 10021 Office: 520 Madison Ave New York NY 10022

HAWK, CARL CURTIS, transp. co. exec.; b. New Philadelphia, Ohio, Sept. 29, 1931; s. Raymond Carl and Freda Emily (Walters) H.; m. Nan Campbell Kernohan, Aug. 21, 1954; children—Barbara Ann, Beverly Sue, Cynthia Lynn, Jeffrey Carl. B.S., Bowling Green State U., 1953; M.B.A., Case-Western Res. U., 1959. Tax acct. Nat. City Bank Cleve., 1954-56; budget and internal audit supr. Ferro Corp., Cleve., 1956-60; with Chessie System/CSX Corp., Richmond, Va., 1960—, sec., sr. asst. v.p., 1977-80, v.p., sec., 1980—. Mem. Am. Soc. Corp. Secs., Alpha Tau Omega, Beta Mu Epsilon, Kappa Mu Epsilon. Republican. Presbyterian. Office: 1500 Federal Reserve Bldg Richmond VA 23219

HAWK, GEORGE WAYNE, aerospace consultant; b. Warren, Ohio, Feb. 21, 1928; s. Oscar W. and Morda Irene (Klingensmith) H.; m. Charline Bond, Feb. 12, 1955; children—George Wayne, David James, John Robert. B.S. in Aero. Engring, Purdue U., 1951; M.S. in Mech. Engring, U. So. Calif., 1955. Asst. research and devel. officer gas dynamics facility Arnold Engring. Devel. Center, Tullahoma, Tenn., 1951-53; project engr. Hughes Research and Devel. Lab., Culver City, Calif., 1953-56; sr. research engr. Goodyear Aircraft Corp., Akron, Ohio, 1956-57; with Moog Inc., East Aurora, N.Y., 1957-81, v.p. aerospace div., 1968-69, exec. v.p., dir., gen. mgr. controls div., 1969-76, exec. v.p., dir. pres. controls group, 1976-81; pres. G.W. Hawk Inc., 1981—; chmn. bd. Comptek Research Inc., 1983—; dir. Acme Electric Corp., Comptex Research Inc., Conax Corp., Sierra Research Corp., Mfrs. Hanover Trust Co., Gordon Instruments. Contbr. articles profl. jours. Past chmn. bd. dirs. Buffalo Philharm. Orch.; bd. dirs. Buffalo chpt. ARC; past pres. Greater Niagara Frontier council Boy Scouts Am.; pres. Greater Buffalo Devel. Found. Served with AUS, 1946-48; Served with USAF, 1951-53. Fellow AIAA (assoc.); Mem. Air Force Assn., Navy League, Nat. Fluid Power Assn. (chmn. bd.), Buffalo C. of C. (past vice chmn.). Lutheran. Clubs: Buffalo Country, Grag Burn, Buffalo, Aero (dir.). Home: 280 Greenwood Ct East Aurora NY 14052 Office: GW Hawk Inc Box 446 East Aurora NY 14052

HAWK, ROBERT STEVEN, library administrator; b. Athens, Ohio, June 6, 1949; s. John Paul and Mary Lois (Briggs) H.; m. Constance Lynne Jodoin, June 16, 1979. B.S., Wright State U., 1971; M.S. in L.S., U. Ky., 1974. Library asst. Dayton and Montgomery County Pub. Library, Dayton, Ohio, 1972-73; project dir. Miami Valley Library Orgn., Dayton, 1974-76; library devel. cons. State Library of Ohio, Columbus, 1976-77; librarian, asst. dir. main library Akron Summit County Pub. Library, 1977-79, librarian, asst. dir. brs., 1979-80, librarian, dir., 1980—. Host, writer: cable TV program INFOCUS, 1982. Mem. Gov's Pub. Library Fin and Support Com., Columbus, Ohio, 1983—, Ohio Multiple Interlibrary Coop. Com., 1980-81, Library and Info. Services to Citizens of Ohio Implementation Adv. Com., Columbus, 1983—; mem. adv. com. Kent State U. Sch. Library Sci., 1980—, U. Akron Continuing Edn. and Pub. Services, 1981—. Mem. ALA, Ohio Library Assn., Beta Phi Mu. Methodist. Clubs: Akron Torch (sec.), U. Akron Hilltoppers). Lodge: Kiwanis. Home: 1643 Tanglewood Dr Akron OH 44313 Office: 55 S Main St Akron OH 44326

HAWKE, BERNARD RAY, planetary scientist; b. Louisville, Oct. 28, 1946; s. Arvil Abner and Elizabeth Ellen (Brown) H. B.S. in Geology, U. Ky., 1970, M.S., 1974; M.S., Brown U., 1977, Ph.D. in Planetary Geology, 1978. Geologist U.S. Geol. Survey, 1967-68; researcher U. Ky., 1972-74, Brown U., 1974-78; planetary scientist Hawaiian Inst. Geophysics, U. Hawaii, Honolulu, 1978—; prin. investigator NASA grants. Author papers in field. Served with USAR, 1970-72. Decorated Bronze Star. Mem. Geochem. Soc., Meteoritcal Soc., Am. Geophys. Union, Sigma Xi, Sigma Gamma Epsilon, Alpha Tau Omega. Republican. Office: HIG University of Hawaii Honolulu HI 96822

HAWKE, SHARON LYNNE, lawyer; b. Terre Haute, Ind., June 14, 1945; d. Harold and Dorothy L. (Tygret) H. Student, U. So. Calif., 1963-65, Millikin U., 1965-66; B.A., Am. U., 1968; J.D. cum laude, Baylor U., 1971. Bar: Tex. bar 1971, Colo. bar 1978. Atty. Butler, Binion, Rice, Cook & Knapp, Houston, 1972-76; corporate counsel, corporate sec. Crystal Oil Co., Shreveport, La., 1976-78; officer, dir., shareholder Cohen Brame & Smith (P.C.), Denver, 1978—. Mem. Am., Tex., Colo., Denver bar assns. Home: 7430 S Harrison Way Littleton CO 80122 Office: 3500 Amoco Bldg 1670 Broadway Denver CO 80202

HAWKES, CAROL A., college president; b. N.Y.C.; d. Howard N. and Lavinia M. (Lally) H. B.A., Barnard Coll., 1943; M.A., Columbia U., 1944, Ph.D., 1949. Dir. acad. English liberal arts div. Katharine Gibbs Sch., N.Y.C., 1950-57; prof. English, chmn. dept. English and comparative lit. Finch Coll., N.Y.C., 1957-75; v.p. for ednl. affairs, dean of coll. Hartwick Coll., Oneonta, N.Y., 1975-80; pres. Endicott Coll., Beverly, Mass., 1980—; dir. Bank of Boston Essex; Trustee Endicott Coll.; dir. grad. faculties alumni Columbia U.; chmn. bd. dirs. NECCUM Consortium. Author: Master's Degree Programs and the Liberal Arts College, 1968. Mem. MLA, Modern Humanities Research Assn., Am. Assn. Higher Edn., AAUP, LWV, Phi Beta Kappa. Clubs: Cornell, Princeton (N.Y.C.). Office: Endicott Coll Beverly MA 01915

HAWKES, JOHN, author, humanities educator; b. Stamford, Conn., Aug. 17, 1925; s. John C. B. and Helen (Ziefle) H.; m. Sophie Goode Tazewell, Sept. 5, 1947; children: John Clendennin Burne III, Sophie Tazewell, Calvert Tazewell, Richard Urquhart. A.B., Harvard, 1949; A.M. (hon.), Brown U., 1962. Asst. to prodn. mgr. Harvard U. Press, 1949-55; vis. lectr. English Harvard, 1955-56, instr. English, 1956-58; asst. prof. Brown U., 1958-62, assoc. prof. English, 1962-67, prof. English, 1967—, univ. prof., 1973—; spl. guest Aspen (Colo.) Inst. Humanistic Studies, summer 1962; mem. staff Utah Writers Conf., summer 1962, Bread Loaf Writers Conf., summer 1963; vis. lectr. Stanford, 1966-67; vis. distinguished prof. City Coll. N.Y., 1971-72. Author: novels The Cannibal, 1949, The Beetle Leg, 1951, The Goose on the Grave and The Owl (one vol.), 1954, The Lime Twig, 1961, Second Skin, 1964, The Blood Oranges, 1971, Death, Sleep and the Traveler, 1974, Travesty, 1976, The Passion Artist, 1979, Virginie: Her Two Lives, 1981; 4 short plays The Innocent Party, 1966; shorter fiction Lunar Landscapes, 1969. Served with Am. Field Service, 1944-45; Italy and Germany. Recipient Prix du Meilleur Livre Etranger, 1973; Grantee in lit. Nat. Inst. Arts and Letters, 1962; Guggenheim fellow, 1962-63; Ford Found. fellow poets and fiction writers, 1964; Rockefeller Found. grantee, 1966. Mem. Am. Acad. Arts and Sci., Am. Acad. and Inst. of Arts and Letters. Home: 18 Everett Ave Providence RI 02906

HAWKES, ROBERT HOWIE, manufacturing company executive; b. Toronto, Ont., Can., Mar. 9, 1930; s. Robert Kelvin and Agnes (Howie) H.; m. Joan May Lepard, May 6, 1960; 1 son, Robert Scott. B.A., Victoria Coll., U. Toronto, 1951; LL.B., Osgoode Hall Law Sch., 1955. Bar: Called to Ont. bar 1955, created Queen's Counsel 1969. Asst. to gen. counsel Swift Can. Co., 1955-58; with Rothmans of Pall Mall Can. Ltd. (tobacco products), Dons Mills, Ont., 1958—, v.p., gen. counsel, 1970-72, pres., chief exec. officer, 1972—; pres. House of

Craven, Rock City Tobacco Co. Ltd., Alfred Dunhill of London, Ltd.; dir. Rothmans Investments Ltd., Am. Express Can. Inc.; exec. com. Rothmans Internat.; mem. Bus. Council Nat. Issues, Ont. Bus. Adv. Council, Can. Tobacco Mfrs. Council. Pres. Craven Found.; bd. govs. N. York Gen. Hosp. Mem. Can. Bar Assn., Patent and Trademark Inst. Can., Law Soc. Upper Can. Progressive Conservative. Mem. United Ch. Clubs: Empire; Lawyers (Toronto); Granite, National, Hidden Valley Highlands Ski, Port Sydney Yacht.

HAWKES, THOMAS FREDERICK, bankholding co. exec.; b. London, Jan. 8, 1903; s. William Thomas and Emily Janet (Norman) H.; m. Virginia Taylor Romney, June 5, 1929; children—Barbara, Julie, Robert. With First Security Corp., Salt Lake City, 1923—, now v.p., treas. Mem. Fin. Execs. Inst. Republican. Clubs: Alta, Hidden Valley Country. Office: PO Box 30006 Salt Lake City UT 84125

HAWKEY, PENELOPE JEAN, advt. agy. exec.; b. Morristown, N.J., Sept. 17, 1942; d. William R. and Jeanne Elizabeth (Haas) Sharp; m. William Stevenson Hawkey, May 26, 1968; children—Adam Stewart, Robin Davidge, Renn McDonnell, Timothy Schuyler, Molly Driscoll; stepchildren—Elizabeth Martin, William Stevenson. B.A., Ohio U., Athens, 1964; M.A., N.Y. U., 1973. Jr. writer Grey Advt., N.Y.C., 1966; jr. writer, then v.p. J. Walter Thompson Co., N.Y.C., 1966-73; v.p., asso. creative dir. McCann-Erickson, N.Y.C., 1973-74; partner, exec. v.p. Dillon, Gordon, Hawkey, Shortt, N.Y.C., 1974-75; sr. v.p., asso. creative dir. McCann-Erickson, 1975—. Recipient Cannes Film Festival Gold Lion, 1972; Clio award, 1980; Healey award, 80; Art Dir.'s Show award, 1980, 81; Ceba award, 1980. Mem. Screen Actors' Guild, AFTRA, Am. Nurseyman's Assn., N.Y. State Cert. Nurserymen, N.Y. State Nurseymen's Assn. Office: McCann-Erickson 485 Lexington Ave New York NY 10017

HAWKINS, ARMIS EUGENE, judge; b. Natchez, Miss., Nov. 11, 1920; s. Charles Mayfield and Lela (Hill) H.; m. Patricia Burrow, Aug. 20, 1948; children: Janice Hawkins Shrewsbury, Jean Ann, James Charles. Student, Wood Jr. Coll., 1938-39, Millsaps Coll., 1943; LL.B., U. Miss., 1947. Bar: Miss. Individual practice law, Houston, Miss., 1947; dist. atty. 3d Circuit Ct. Dist. Miss., 1951-59; assoc. justice Miss. Supreme Ct., 1980—. Served with USMC, 1942-46; PTO. Mem. ABA, Am. Judicature Soc., Miss. Trial Lawyers Assn., Miss. State Bar. Baptist. Office: Gartin Bldg Jackson MS 39205 *

HAWKINS, ARTHUR HANSON, III, publishing executive; b. N.Y.C., Mar. 11, 1930; s. Arthur Hanson, Jr. and Patricia (Laporte) H.; m. Kathleen Hogan Walsh, Jan. 3, 1966; children: Jesse, Linda, Matthew, Arthur, Sally, Andrew. Student, U. Va., 1951. With McCann-Erickson Inc., N.Y.C., 1953-57, J. Walter Thompson Ltd., London, 1957-59, Young & Rubicam, Inc., N.Y.C., 1959-60; v.p., co-creative dir. Marschalk Inc., N.Y.C., 1960-64; v.p., asso. creative dir. Grey Advt., N.Y.C., 1964-66; sr. v.p., creative dir., dir. West, Weir & Bartel, N.Y.C., 1966-68; sr. v.p., corp. creative dir. Ketcham MacLeod & Grove, N.Y.C., 1968-72; pres. Hawkins Co., N.Y.C., 1972-75; founding partner Hawkins, McCain & Blumenthal, N.Y.C., 1975-80; sr. v.p. Benton & Bowles, Inc., N.Y.C., 1980-81; pres. Hawkins House Pub. Co., Rye, N.Y., 1981—; pub. Credits Mag.; tchr. Parsons Sch. Design, 1961-62; Bd. dirs. Point O'Woods Assn., 1980—. Served to 1st lt. AUS, 1951-53. Recipient numerous nat. advt. awards. Clubs: Union League (N.Y.C.); Point O'Woods (gov.). Home: 770 Boston Post Rd Rye NY 10580 also Point O'Woods NY 11706

HAWKINS, ASHTON, mus. adminstr.; b. N.Y.C., May 11, 1937; s. Ashton W. and Kyra S. H. Grad., Phillips Exeter Acad., 1955; B.A. cum laude, Harvard U., 1959, J.D., 1962. Bar: N.Y. bar 1963, U.S. Supreme Ct. bar 1968. Asso. firm Cadwalader, Wickersham & Taft, N.Y.C., 1962-65; asst. atty. gen. State of N.Y., 1965-68; asst. sec. Met. Mus. Art, N.Y.C., 1968, sec., 1969-74, sec., counsel, 1974-77, v.p., sec., counsel, 1977—; co-founder Mus. Law Conf., 1973. Trustee Goodwill Industries Greater N.Y., 1967—; trustee, sec. George Pompidou Art and Culture Found., 1980. Mem. Assn. Bar City N.Y., Council on Fgn. Relations. Clubs: Brook, Century, Coffee House, Knickerbocker. Office: Met Mus of Art Fifth Ave and 82d St New York NY 10028

HAWKINS, AUGUSTUS FREEMAN, congressman; b. Shreveport, La., Aug. 31, 1907; s. Nyanza and Hattie H. (Freeman) H.; m. Pegga A. Smith, Aug. 28, 1945 (dec. Aug. 1966); m. Elsie Taylor, June 30, 1977. A.B. in Econs, U. Cal. at, Los Angeles, 1931. Engaged in real estate and retail bus., Los Angeles, from 1945—; mem. Calif. Assembly from, Los Angeles County, 1935-62, chmn. rules com., 1961-62; mem. 88th to 93d congresses from 21st dist. Calif., 94th-96th Congresses from 29th Calif. dist.; chmn. employment opportunities subcom. House Edn. and Labor Com.; chmn. House Adminstrn. Com. Democrat. Methodist. Club: Masons. Office: 2371 Rayburn House Office Bldg Washington DC 20515 *

HAWKINS, BRETT WILLIAM, social scientist; b. Buffalo, Sept. 15, 1937; s. Ralph C. and Irma A. (Rowley) H.; m. Linda L. Knuth, Oct. 31, 1974; 1 son, Brett William. A.B., U. Rochester, 1959; M.A., Vanderbilt U., 1962, Ph.D., 1964. Instr. polit. sci. Vanderbilt U., 1963; instr. in polit. sci. Washington and Lee U., 1963-64, asst. prof., 1964-65, U. Ga., Athens, 1965-68, asso. prof., 1968-70, U. Wis., Milw., 1970-71, prof., 1971—. Author: Nashville Metro, 1964, The Ethnic Factor in American Politics, 1970, Politics in the Metropolis, 2d edit, 1971, Politics and Urban Policies, 1971, The Politics of Raising State and Local Revenue, 1978, Professional Associations and Municipal Innovation, 1981; contbr. articles to profl. jours. Mem. Phi Beta Kappa, Iota of N.Y. Home: 3730 N Morris Blvd Shorewood WI 53211 Office: Dept Polit Sci U Wis Milwaukee WI 53201

HAWKINS, DAVID FREDERICK, educator; b. Sydney, Australia, Dec. 13, 1933; s. Gordon Frederick and Heather R. (Baird) H.; m. Barbara A. Brown; children—Phillip, John, Peter, Andrew, Katharine, Richard, Matthew, Thomas. A.B. cum laude, Harvard U., 1956, M.B.A. with distinction, 1958, D.B.A., 1962. Research asst. Harvard U. Bus. Sch., Cambridge, Mass., 1961-62, asst. prof., 1962-67, assoc. prof., 1967-69, prof., 1970—; exec. asst. to mng. dir. and corp. sec. Australian Carbon Black Pty. Ltd., Melbourne, 1958-60; dir. Hadco Printed Circuits, Cambridge. Author: (with Brandt Allen) Computer Models for Business Case Analysis, 1968, Corporate Financial Reporting: Text and Cases, rev. edit, 1977, (with others) Controlling Foreign Operations, (1971) Financial Reporting Practices of Corporations, 1972, (with Mary Wehle) Accounting for Leases by Lessees, 1973, (with Walter Campbell) Equity Valuation: Models, Analysis and Implications, 1978, (with Barbara A. Brown) Rating Industrial Debt; contbg. author: Contemporary Studies in the Evolution of Accounting Thought, 1968, The History of American Management, 1969, Financial Accounting Theory II, 1969, Management Accounting, 1970, Motivation and Control in Organizations, 1971, Investment Environment, Analysis and Alternatives, 1977; contbr. articles to profl. jours. Recipient Newcomen Soc. award Bus. History Rev., 1963; McKinsey award Calif. Mgmt. Rev., 1970; Graham & Dodd scroll Fin. ANalysts Jour., 1977; named to All Am. Research Team Instl. Investor, 1976, 77, 78, 79, 80, 81. Mem. Am. Acctg. Assn., Newcomen Soc. Clubs: Country, Porcellian, Harvard, Harvard Varsity. Home: 285 Dudley St Brookline MA 02146 Office: Harvard Bus Sch Allston MA 02163

HAWKINS, DAVID ROLLO, psychiatrist, educator; b. Springfield, Mass., Sept. 22, 1923; s. James Alexander and Janet (Rollo) H.; m. Elizabeth G. Wilson, June 8, 1946; children: David Rollo, Robert Wilson, John Bruce, William Alexander. B.A., Amherst Coll., 1945; M.D., U. Rochester, N.Y., 1946. Intern Strong Meml. Hosp., Rochester, 1946-48; Commonwealth Fund fellow in psychiatry and medicine U. Rochester, 1950-52; instr. psychiatry U. N.C. Sch. Medicine, 1952-53, asst. prof., 1953-57, asso. prof. psychiatry, 1957-62, prof., 1962-67, dir. curriculum rev. and revision, 1965-67; prof., chmn. dept. psychiatry U. Va. Sch. Medicine, 1967-77, Alumni prof. psychiatry, 1977-79, asso. dean, 1969-70; psychiatrist-in-chief U. Va. Hosp., 1967-77; prof. psychiatry Pritzker Sch. Medicine, U. Chgo., 1979—; dir. liaison and consultation services dept. psychiatry Michael Reese Hosp., Chgo., 1979—; asso. attending physician N.C. Meml. Hosp., Chapel Hill, 1952-62, attending physician, 1962-67; cons. Watts Hosp., Durham, 1952-67, VA Hosp., Fayetteville, N.C., 1956-67, Eastern State Hosp., Williamsburg, Va., 1971—; spl. research fellow Inst. Psychiatry, U. London, 1963-64, Fogarty internat. research fellow, 1976-77; U.S.-USSR and Romania health exchange fellow, 1978; cons. VA Hosp., Salem, Va., 1969—, mem. deans com., 1971-77. Review editor: Psychosomatic Medicine, 1958-70; asso. editor, 1970—, Psychiatry. Mem. small grants com. NIMH, 1958-62; mem. nursing research study sect. NIH, 1965-67; mem. Gov.'s Commn. Mental, Indigent and Geriatric Patients, 1968-72; mem. research evaluation com. Va. Dept. Mental Hygiene and Hosps., 1971-73, chmn., 1972-73; mem. behavioral sci. test com. Nat. Bd. Med. Examiners, 1970-74. Served as capt. MC Aus, 1948-50. Fellow Am. Coll. Psychoanalysts (charter, bd. regents 1979-81), Am. Psychiat. Assn.; mem. Am. Psychosomatic Soc. (mem. council 1959), AMA, Group for Advancement Psychiatry (chmn. com. med. edn.), Royal Soc. Medicine (London), Assn. Am. Med. Colls. (council acad. socs. 1973-78), Am. Psychoanalytic Assn., Am. Coll. Psychiatrists, AAAS, Va. Psychoanalytic Soc., Washington Psychoanalytic Soc., Chgo. Psychoanalytic Soc., Ill. Psychiat. Soc. (council 1981-82), AAUP, Soc. Neurosci., Am. Assn. Chmn. Depts. Psychiatry (sec.-treas. 1971-73, pres. 1974-75), Assn. Psychophysiol. Study Sleep, Nat. Bd. Med. Examiners (exam. com. 1983—), Phi Beta Kappa, Sigma Xi, Alpha Omega Alpha. Office: Dept Psychiatry Michael Reese Hosp 29th St and Ellis Ave Chicago IL 60616

HAWKINS, DONALD MERTON, lawyer; b. Manhattan, Kans., June 19, 1921; s. Floyd and Madge (Thompson) H.; m. Lucille Bilsborough, Dec. 25, 1942; children: Frances Elizabeth Hawkins Lossing, Shirley Lorraine Hawkins Lowe, Richard Henry, Rebecca Susan. Student, U. Mich., 1943; A.B., U. Chgo., 1946, J.D., 1947. Bar: Ill. 1947, Ohio 1948. Ptnr. Fuller & Henry (and predecessors), Toledo, 1952—. Pres. Toledo Area Council Chs., 1968-69, Toledo Dist. Methodist Union, 1966-70; del. Gen. Conf. United Meth. Ch., 1972; pres. council fin. and adminstrn. W. Ohio Conf. United Meth. Ch., 1972-76, trustee, 1978—, chmn. bd. trustees, 1979—; trustee Goodwill Industries Toledo, 1957-81, sec., 1963-68, v.p., 1968-72, pres., 1972-75. Served to 1st lt. USAAF, 1943-46. Fellow Am. Bar Found., Ohio State Bar Found.; mem. Am., Ohio, Toledo bar assns., Am. Judicature Soc., Order of Coif, Kappa Sigma. Club: Toledo. Home: 2227 Innisbrook Rd Toledo OH 43606 Office: 300 Madison Ave PO Box 2088 Toledo OH 43603

HAWKINS, ELIOT DEXTER, lawyer; b. N.Y.C., May 6, 1932; s. Dexter Clarkson and Evelyn Byrd (Eliot) H.; m. Margaret O. Childers, Jan. 13, 1962 (div. 1976); children: Robert E.D., Ruthanna C. B.A., Harvard U., 1954, J.S., 1960; B.A., Oxford U., Eng., 1956, M.A., 1960. Bar: N.Y. 1960. Assoc. Winthrop, Stimson, Putnam & Roberts, N.Y.C., 1960-69, Milbank, Tweed, Hadley & McCloy, 1969-73, ptrn., 1974—. Mem., trustee Community Service Soc. of N.Y., 1962-78, 80—. 1st lt. U.S. Army, 1956-58. Mem. Assn. Bar CityN.Y., N.Y. State Bar Assn., ABA. Club: Harvard (N.Y.C.). Office: Milbank Tweed Hadley & McCloy 1 Chase Manhattan Plaza New York NY 10005

HAWKINS, EUGENE PALMER, corp. exec.; b. St. Louis, Mar. 18, 1904; s. Eugene Palmer and Sarah F. (Anderson) H.; m. Rachel E. Heppenstall, July 18, 1935 (dec. June 1970); 1 dau., Eleanor Forman (Mrs. John D. Durno); m. Jean McKiggan, Jan. 2, 1971. B.S. in Mech. Engring, Washington U., 1925. Account exec. Goldman Sachs & Co., 1928-42; gen. mgr. subsidiary cos., Callaway Mills, 1945-50; asst. to v.p. Revere Copper & Brass, Inc., Detroit, 1950-52, asst. gen. mgr., 1952-55, v.p., exec. head, 1955-69; v.p. Revere Jamica Alumina Ltd., 1969—; dir. Itusco Realty Co., Indsl. Towel & Uniform Co. (both Houston), Frank Bancroft Co., Inc., Dearborn, Mich. Bd. dirs. Jr. Achievement, Employer's Assn. Detroit, Traffic Safety Assn. Council of Detroit. Served to lt. comdr. USNR, 1942-45. Mem. Detroit Bd. Trade, Newcomen Soc. N. Am., Tau Beta Pi. Clubs: Country of Detroit, Witenagamote (Detroit); Gulf Stream Bath and Tennis, Little (Gulfstream, Fla.). Home: 91 Touraine Rd Grosse Pointe Farms MI 48236 also 2103 S Ocean Blvd Delray Beach FL 33444

HAWKINS, FALCON BLACK, judge; b. Charleston, S.C., Mar. 16, 1927; s. Falcon Black and Mae Elizabeth (Infinger) H.; m. Jean Elizabeth Timmerman, May 28, 1949; children—Richard Keith, Daryl Gene, Mary Elizabeth Hawkins Eddy, Steely Odell II. B.S., The Citadel, 1958; LL.B., U. S.C., 1963, J.D., 1970. Bar: S.C. bar 1963. Leadingman electronics Charleston (S.C.) Naval Shipyard, 1948-60; salesman ACH Brokers, Columbia, S.C., 1960-63; asso. to sr. partner firm Morris, Duffy & Boone (and predecessor firms), Charleston, 1963-79; U.S. dist. judge Dist. of S.C., Charleston, 1979—. Served with Mcht. Marines, 1944-45; Served with AUS, 1945-46. Mem. Jud. Conf. 4th Jud. Circuit, Am. Bar Assn., S.C. Bar Assn., Charleston County Bar Assn., Am. Trial Lawyers Assn., S.C. Trial Lawyers Assn. Democrat. Methodist. Clubs: Hibernian Soc. Charleston, Masons. Office: US Courthouse Charleston SC 29402

HAWKINS, FRANCIS GLENN, banker; b. Jamesville, Mo., May 31, 1917; s. Ottas G. and Mary (Uhrig) H.; m. Virginia Mavis Saker, Jan. 18, 1947; children: Glenn Joseph, Russell Brian. A.B., S.W. Mo. U., 1938; M.A., Okla. State U., 1941; J.D., U. Tulsa, 1955. Reporter Monahans (Tex.) Express, 1938-39; trainee Montgomery Ward, Springfield, Mo., 1941-42; research asst. Fed. Res. Bank, Kansas City, 1945-46; with Bank of Okla., Tulsa, 1946—, sr. v.p., sr. trust officer, sr. v.p. charge bank ops., 1970-73, sr. v.p. charge adminstrv. services, 1973-77, sr. v.p., sr. trust officer, trust div., from 1977, sr. v.p. and trust counsel, now trust counsel; of counsel Robinson, Boese and Davidson. Mem. men's adv. bd. Assistance League Tulsa. Served to capt. USAAF, 1942-45; ETO; lt. col. Res., ret. Decorated Air medal with oak leaf cluster, Bronze Star medal. Mem. Am. Inst. Banking (past chpt. pres.), Tulsa Estate Planning Forum (past pres.), Okla. Bankers Assn. (past pres. trust div.), Okla., Tulsa County bar assns., Tulsa C. of C., Pi Gamma Mu, Phi Alpha Delta. Home: 4410 S Louisville St Tulsa OK 74135 Office: PO Box 2300 Tulsa OK 74192

HAWKINS, GEORGE ELLIOTT, JR., animal scientist; b. Caldwell County, Ky., July 26, 1919; s. George Elliott and Mary Elizabeth (Rodgers) H.; m. Mary Elizabeth Cline, Apr. 6, 1946; 1 dau., Mary Anne Hawkins Murray. B.S., Western Ky. U., 1941; M.S., U. Ga., 1947; Ph.D., N.C. State U., 1952. Teaching asst. U. Ga., Athens, 1946-47, instr., 1948, asst. prof., 1948-49; grad. research asst. N.C. State U., Raleigh, 1949-51; asst. prof dept. animal and dairy scis. Auburn (Ala.) U., 1952-54, assoc. prof., 1954-59, prof., 1959-82, prof. emeritus, 1982—. Contbr. articles to profl. jours. Served to capt. AUS, 1942-46. Decorated Bronze Star, Purple Heart.; Recipient honors award So. div. Am. Dairy Sci. Assn., 1981. Mem. Am. Dairy Sci. Assn. (pres. So. div. 1975-76), Am. Soc. Animal Sci., Am. Inst. Nutrition, Ala. Farm Bur. Fedn., Gamma Sigma Delta. Roman Catholic. Clubs: Dairy Shrine, University, Saugahatchee Country. Home: 601 Auburn Dr Auburn AL 36830 Office: Animal and Dairy Sci Depts Auburn U Auburn AL 36849

HAWKINS, GEORGE OLIVER, animal feed co. exec.; b. Antioch, Ill., Apr. 13, 1920; s. Arthur McKinley and Harriet Gertrude (Miller) H.; m. Virginia Mae Ames, Nov. 23, 1942 (dec. 1946); 1 son, Arthur; m. Sally Elizabeth Welch, June 28, 1948; children—Lark, Scott. Student, U. Ill., 1938-39. Owner, operator Mt. Hatcheries, Antioch, 1947-57; sales mgr. FS Services, Inc., Bloomington, Ill., 1952-65; v.p., gen. mgr. feed div. Hales & Hunter, Inc., 1965-69; pres. Pioneer Pellets, 1967-69; gen. mgr. Nixon Feed div. ConAgra, Inc., Omaha, 1969-74; pres. Honeggers & Co., Fairbury, Ill., 1974—, also pres. several sub.'s; dir. Honegger Feeds.; Auditor Township of Antioch, 1960-64; bd. dirs. Immigrant Service League, Chgo., 1966-70, Travelers Aid Soc., 1968-70; past bd. mem. Contbr. articles to profl. publs. Mem. sch. bd.; mem. ch. Vestry Episcopal Ch.; pres. Assn. of Commerce, Fairbury, 1980. Served with USAAF, 1942-46. Mem. Am. Feed Mfrs. Assn. (dir.). Republican. Clubs: Lions (Antioch) (pres. 1959); Moose (life), Masons.). Office: 201 W Locust St Fairbury IL 61739

HAWKINS, GEORGE TERRY, company executive; b. Bedford, Ind., Mar. 8, 1948; s. George Curtis and Betty Regina (Anderson) H.; m. Jennifer Nichols; children: Nicholas, Brooke, Tara. Student, Purdue U., 1966-67; B.S. in Gen. Sci., Ind. U.-Bloomington, 1970, M.B.A., 1971; J.D., U. Louisville, 1975. Gen. mgr. Monroe All-Channel Cablevision, Bloomington, 1971-72, Tri-County Cable TV, Seymoure, Ind., 1972-73; dir. Instructional Communications Ctr. U. Louisville, 1974-77; v.p. Coaliquid, Inc., Louisville, 1977-80; pres. CoaLiquid, Inc., Louisville, 1980—; instr. bus. law, adminstrv. law and communications law U. Louisville, 1975-80. Assoc. producer, host 4 radio series, Louisville. Named Outstanding Young Man in Am Jaycees, 1978. Mem. Ky. Bar Assn. Home: 1305 Glenbrook Rd Anchorage KY 40223 Office: CoaLiquid Inc 737 Executive Park Louisville KY 40207

HAWKINS, HARVEY KYLE, utility executive; b. Hazelhurst, Miss., Mar. 12, 1934; s. Harvey Delanore and Ruth (Kyle) H.; m. Cecile Laurie, Sept. 28, 1957; children: Craig, Christy, Wayne.; m. Beverly deLeaumont, May 12, 1983. B.C.S., Loyola U., New Orleans, 1964, M.B.A., 1968. With New Orleans Public Service Co., 1956—, asst. to treas., 1971, asst. sec., 1972-76, treas., 1972—, exec. dir. customer services, 1981—; bd. dirs. Consumer Credit Counseling Service New Orleans, 1975—. Mem. fin. com. New Orleans Bd. Trade, 1981; Bd. dirs. New Orleans Met. Area Com., 1974—. Served with USN, 1952-56. Mem. Nat. Inst. Credit, Internat. Consumer Credit Assn., Consumer Credit Assn. New Orleans (pres. 1972), Am. Gas Assn., Postal Customers Council, New Orleans Assn. Credit and Fin. Mgmt., New Orleans C. of C., Cross Keys, Beta Gamma Sigma. Roman Catholic. Club: Internat. House. Address: PO Box 60340 New Orleans LA 70160

HAWKINS, HOWARD GRESHAM, JR., corporate executive, lawyer; b. Terre Haute, Ind., June 6, 1916; s. Howard Gresham and Margaret Josephine (Smith) H.; m. Gloria Althea Olson, July 22, 1950 (dec. Apr. 1966); children—Howard Gresham III, Susan Alison, Lawrence Arthur. Student, Mich. State U., 1934-37; A.B., U. Chgo., 1939, J.D., 1941, M.B.A., 1953. Bar: Ill. 1941, N.Y. 1942, Calif. 1954. Practiced in, N.Y.C., 1941-42, Chgo., 1946-52, San Francisco, 1952—; sec. Kern County Land Co., 1955-68; sr. v.p., sec., gen. counsel Dean Witter Reynolds Orgn. Inc., San Francisco, 1968-82; asst. counsel Diasonics, Inc., Milpitas, Calif., 1983—. Served to 2d lt., CIC, also OSRD AUS, 1942-46. Mem. Am. Bar Assn., Am. Soc. Corp. Secs. Republican. Episcopalian. Club: Stock Exchange (San Francisco). Home: 70 Country Club Dr Hillsborough CA 94010 Office: 1708 McCarthy Blvd Milpitas CA 95035

HAWKINS, HUGH DODGE, history educator; b. Topeka, Sept. 3, 1929; s. James Adam and Rena Augusta (Eddy) H. A.B., DePauw U., 1950; Ph.D., Johns Hopkins U., 1954; M.A. (hon.), Amherst Coll., 1969. Instr. history U. N.C., Chapel Hill, 1956-57; instr. history and Am. studies Amherst (Mass.) Coll., 1957-59, asst. prof., 1959-64, asso. prof., 1964-69, prof., 1969-75; Anson D. Morse prof. history and Am. Studies, 1975—; Fulbright lectr., Goettingen, W. Ger., 1973-74; vis. asso. Center for Studies in Higher Edn., U. Calif., Berkeley, 1978-79, 82-83. Author: Pioneer: A History of the Johns Hopkins University, 1874-1889, 1960, Between Harvard and America: The Educational Leadership of Charles W. Eliot, 1972, (with others) Education at Amherst Reconsidered: The Liberal Studies Program, 1978; editor: Booker T. Washington and His Critics, 1962, rev. edit., 1974, The Abolitionists: Immediatism and the Question of Means, 1964, rev. edit., 1972, The Emerging University and Industrial America, 1970. Served with U.S. Army, 1954-56. John Simon Guggenheim fellow, 1961-62. Mem. AAUP, Am. Hist. Assn. (Moses Coit Tyler prize 1959), Orgn. Am. Historians, History of Edn. Soc., So. Hist. Assn., Conf. on Peace Research in History, Phi Beta Kappa. Home: RFD 2 Amherst MA 01002 Office: Dept Am Studies Amherst Coll Amherst MA 01002

HAWKINS, JAMES VICTOR, auto supply co. exec.; b. Coeur d'Alene, Idaho, Sept. 28, 1936; s. William Stark and Agnes M. (Ramstedt) H.; m. Gail Ruth Guernsey, June 19, 1959; children—John William, Nancy Clare. B.S., U. Idaho, 1959; postgrad., Am. Savs. and Loan Inst., 1960-67, Pacific Coast Banking Sch., 1970—. Mgmt. trainee Gen. Telephone Co. of N.W., Coeur d'Alene, 1959-60; asst. mgr. First Fed. Savs. & Loan Assn., Coeur d'Alene, 1960-67; v.p., gen. mgr. Idaho S.W. Devel. Co., Boise, 1967-68; v.p., trust officer First Security Bank of Idaho, N.A., Boise, 1968-72; pres. Statewide Stores Inc., Boise, 1972—; dir. United 1st Fed. Savs. & Loan Assn., Boise, Chandler Corp.; Chmn. adv. bd. Coll. Bus. and Econs., U. Idaho. Bd. dirs. St. Alphonsus Hosp. Found., Idaho Council Econ. Edn., Boise United Fund, Boise Art Assn.; pres., mem. U. Idaho Found. Named Outstanding Young Idahoan Idaho Jr. C. of C., 1967; Eagle Scout. Mem. Am. Inst. Banking, Boise C. of C., U. Idaho Alumni Assn. (mem. exec. bd.), Phi Gamma Delta. Episcopalian. Clubs: Elk, Rotarian., Crane Creek Country, Arid. (Boise). Home: 1900 Harrison Blvd Boise ID 83702 Office: PO Box 8477 Boise ID 83707

HAWKINS, JASPER STILLWELL, JR., architect; b. Orange, N.J., Nov. 10, 1932; s. Jasper Stillwell and Bernice (Ake) H.; m. Patricia A. Mordigan, Mar. 22, 1980; children: William Raymond, John Stillwell, Karen Ann, Jasper Stillwell. B.Arch., U. So. Calif., 1955. Founder, prin. Hawkins & Lindsey & Assocs., Los Angeles, 1958-78, Hawkins Lindsey Wilson Assocs., Los Angeles and Phoenix, 1978-81; pres. Fletcher-Thompson Assocs., 1981—; bd. visitors Nat. Fire Acad., 1978-80; bd. dirs. Nat. Inst. Bldg. Scis., 1976—, chmn. bd. dirs., 1981—, consultative council, 1978—; mem. com. protection of archives and records centers GSA, 1975-77; mem. archtl. adv. panel Calif. State Bldg. Standards Commn., 1964-70; mem. com. standards and evaluation Nat. Conf. States on Bldg. Codes and Standards, 1971—; participant and speaker confs. Contbr. articles to profl. jours.; maj. works include Valley Music Theatre, Los Angeles, Houston Music Theatre, Sundome Theatre and R.H. Johnson Center, Sun City

West, Ariz., U. Calif. at Irvine Student Housing, Oxnard (Calif.) Fin. Center, condominium devels. Mem. Nev. Gov.'s Commn. Fire Safety Codes, 1980-81; mem. fire research panel Nat. Bur. Standards, 1978-81; mem. Pres.'s Commn. on Housing, 1981. Recipient design awards from Ariz. Rock Products Assn. Theatre Assn. Am., Nat. Food Facilities, House and Home Mag., Practical Builders Mag., Am. Builders Mag., others. Fellow AIA (nat. codes and standards com. 1970—, chmn. 1970-73, nat. liaison commn. with Asso. Gen. Contractors 1969-70, chmn. nat. fire safety task force 1972-74, chmn. Calif. council of AIA state code com. 1964-68, chmn. nat. conf. industrialized constrn. 1969-70, nat. com. bldg. industry coordination 1969-70, nat. rep. to Internat. Conf. Bldg. Ofcls. 1969); mem. Nat. Fire Protection Assn. (com. bldg. heights and areas 1965—, chmn. 1968-72, fire prevention code com. 1974—), ASCE (task force bldg. codes 1971-74), Phoenix C. of C. (Water task force 1982-83), Ariz. C. of C. (policy com. 1983—), Ariz. Biltmore Village Estates Homeowners Assn. (pres. 1981—). Office: 111 E Camelback Rd Phoenix AZ 85012

HAWKINS, JOSEPH ELMER, JR., acoustic physiologist; b. Waco, Tex., Mar. 4, 1914; s. Joseph Elmer and Maude Burke (Schlenker) H.; m. Jane Elizabeth Daddow, Aug. 24, 1939; children: Richard Spencer Daddow, Peter Douglas Huntington, James Marion Davis, William Alexander Parmley, Priscilla Ann (Mrs. Philip Leach). Student, Altes Realgymnasium, Munich, 1929-30; A.B., Baylor U., 1933; postgrad., Brown U., 1933-34; B.A. in Physiology (Rhodes scholar Tex. and Worcester), U. Oxford, 1937, M.A., 1966, D.Sc., 1979; Ph.D. in Med. Scis, Harvard U., 1941. Teaching fellow physiology Harvard U. Med. Sch., 1937-41, instr., 1941-45; asst. investigator NDRC-OSRD, 1941-43; spl. research asso. Harvard Psycho-Acoustic Lab., 1943-45; asst. prof. physiology Bowman Gray Sch. Medicine, Wake Forest Coll., 1945-46; research asso., head neurophysiology Merck Inst. for Therapeutic Research, Rahway, N.J., 1946-56; asso. prof. otolaryngology N.Y.U. Sch. Medicine, 1956-63; prof. otorhinolaryngology U. Mich., Ann Arbor, 1963—, chmn. grad. program in physiol. acoustics, 1969-81; asso. dir. Kresge Hearing Research Inst., 1979—; mem. NIH sensory diseases study sect., 1958-61, communicative disorders research tng. com., 1965-69, communicative scis. study sect., 1975-79; mem. Nat. Library Medicine Communicative Disorders Task Force, 1977—; lectr. Armed Forces Inst. Pathology, 1969-74; cons. various pharm. cos. Contbr. to: Ency. Brit, 1974; Editor: (with M. Lawrence and W.P. Work) Otophysiology, 1973, (with S.A. Lerner and G.T. Matz) Aminoglycoside Ototoxicity, 1981; Contbr. sci. articles to profl. jours. Pres. Fleming Creek Neighborhood Assn., Washtenaw County, Mich., 1973-74; mem. Bd. Edn., Cranford, N.J., 1958-61. USPHS spl. fellow Öronkliniken Sahlgrenska sjukhuset U. Goteborg, Sweden, 1961-63; Nat. Acad. Scis. exchange lectr. to, Yugoslavia and Bulgaria, 1977; Chercheur etranger de l'INSERM Lab. d'Audiologie Experimentale, U. Bordeaux II, 1978; Recipient Disting. Achievement award Baylor U., 1982. Fellow Acoustical Soc. Am.; mem. Am. Physiol. Soc., Assn. for Research in Otolaryngology, Gerontol. Soc., Collegium Oto-rhino-laryngologicum Amicitiae Sacrum, Bárány Soc., European Workshop for Inner Ear Biology, Am. Otol. Soc. (asso.), Societe Francaise d'Oto-Rhino-Laryngologie (corr.), Pacific Coast Oto-ophthalmol. Soc. (hon.), Phi Beta Kappa, Sigma Xi. Anglican. Club: Connetablie de Guyenne (Bordeaux) (asso.). Home: 4004 E Joy Rd Ann Arbor MI 48105 Office: Kresge Hearing Research Inst U Mich Med Sch Ann Arbor MI 48109 *Intellectual honesty, by virtue of its extreme scarcity, has become more precious than diamonds. No monopoly labors to restrict its supply, but hardly any institution seeks to foster its development or to assure its survival. As rare things will, it threatens to vanish from the American scene.*

HAWKINS, K(ENNETH) COURTENAY, JR., banker; b. Pensacola, Fla., Oct. 6, 1923; s. Kenneth Courtenay and Atlanta V. (Day) H.; m. Charlotrte Virginia Uhlik, June 28, 1947; children—Sharon Hawkins Cockroft, Vickie Hawkins Dominick. Student, Pasadena (Calif.) Jr. Coll., 1940-41, U. So. Calif., 1946-47, U. Wis. Grad. Sch., 1967. With Security Pacific Nat. Bank, Los Angeles, 1947—, v.p. charge nat. banking dept., then sr. v.p., 1968-76, sr. v.p. charge European div., 1976-79, exec. v.p. charge No. Calif., San Francisco, 1979—, also mem. mgmt. and sr. loan coms., fin. and strategic planning coms.; dir. Security Pacific Leasing Corp., SEPAC Lease Systems, Inc. Bd. dirs. Bay Area Council, San Francisco Boys Club, San Francisco Planning and Urban Research Assn.; adv. council San Francisco Jr. Achievement. Served with USNR, 1942-46. Mem. Calif. Bankers Assn. (dir.), San Francisco C. of C. (dir.), Newcomen Soc. Republican. Clubs: Commonwealth, St. Francis Yacht, Family, California. Office: Security Pacific Nat Bank 1 Embarcadero Center San Francisco CA 94111

HAWKINS, MERRILL MORRIS, college administrator; b. Maben, Miss., Mar. 19, 1914; s. Edgar Preston and Viola (Monts) H.; m. Carrie Lee Brabham, Dec. 22, 1946; children: Jane (Mrs. William L. Smith), Merrill Morris. Student, Wood Jr. Coll., 1934-36; B.S., Miss. State U., 1944, M.S., 1950; Ed.D., U. Miss., 1960. Supt. schs., Centreville, Miss., 1953-56; critic tchr. Univ. High Sch., U. Miss., 1956-57; instr. edn. U. Miss., 1956-57; prof. dept. elementary and secondary edn. Miss. State U., State College, 1965-66; asst. dean Coll. Edn., 1966-68, asso. dean, 1968-70; dean Coll. Edn., dir. tchr. edn., 1970-79, dean emeritus, 1979—; v.p. devel. Wood Jr. Coll., 1979—; asst. supt. schs., Vicksburg, Miss., 1957-60, supt., 1960-65. Served with AUS, 1941-43. Mem. Miss. Assn. Sch. Adminstrs. (past pres.), Starkville C. of C., Phi Delta Kappa, Kappa Delta Pi, Phi Kappa Phi, Omicron Delta Kappa, Blue Key.; mem. Order Eastern Star (dist. gov.). Methodist. Club: Mason. Home: Tally-ho Dr Starkville MS 39759 Office: Miss State U PO Box 771 Mississippi State MS 39762

HAWKINS, MICHAEL DALY, lawyer; b. Winslow, Ariz., Feb. 12, 1945; s. William Bert and Patricia Agnes (Daly) H.; m. Phyllis A. Lewis, June 4, 1966; children—Aaron, Adam. B.A., Ariz. State U., 1967, J.D. cum laude, 1970. Bar: Ariz. bar 1970, U.S. Ct. Mil. Appeals 1971, U.S. Supreme Ct. bar 1974. Individual practice law, Phoenix, 1973-77, 80—; chief legal counsel Dem. Party of Ariz., 1976-77; U.S. atty. Dist. Ariz., Phoenix, 1977-80. Staff editor: Ariz. State U. Law Jour, 1968-70. Mem. Ariz. Lottery Commn. Served to capt. USMC, 1970-73. Mem. Maricopa County Bar Assn. (bd. dirs. 1975-77, 81—), State Bar of Ariz., Am. Bar Assn., Ariz. Trial Lawyers Assn. (bd. dirs. 1976-77, state sec. 1976-77), Phoenix Trial Lawyers Assn. Democrat. Lutheran. Home: 105 E Northern Ave Phoenix AZ 85020 Office: United Bank Tower 20th Floor 3300 N Central Ave Phoenix AZ 85012

HAWKINS, NEIL MIDDLETON, educator, civil engineer; b. Sydney, Australia, Jan. 31, 1935; s. Cecil Alfred and Sybil Mabel (Ralph) H.; m. Saundra Ann Youmans, Sept. 15, 1961; children: Susan Elizabeth, David Clark. B.Sc., U. Sydney, 1955, B.E., 1957; M.S., U. Ill., 1959, Ph.D., 1961. Cons. engr., Sydney, 1958; lectr. U. Sydney, 1962-65, sr. lectr., 1966-68; devel. engr. Portland Cement Assn., Chgo., 1965-66; asso. prof. U. Wash., Seattle, 1968-72, prof., 1972—, chmn. dept. civil engring., 1978—; prin. investigator NSF projects on seismic resistance of structures, 1973—. Contbr. articles to profl. jours. Served to 2d lt. Australian Citizen Mil. Forces, 1953-62. Fellow Am. Concrete Inst. (dir. 1982—, Wason medal 1970, Raymond C. Reese award 1978); mem. Australian Instn. Engrs. (Edward Noyes prize 1967), ASCE (State of the Art award 1974, Raymond C. Reese award 1976), Earthquake Engring. Research Inst., Post-Tensioning Inst. Home: 18204 NE 28th St Redmond WA 98502 Office: U Wash Seattle WA 98195

HAWKINS, OSIE PENMAN, JR., opera and concert singer; b. Phenix City, Ala., Aug. 16, 1913; s. Osie Penman and Eula Myrtle (Brown) H. Pvt. vocal studies with, Margaret Hecht, Frederich Schorr, Renato Cellini, Samuel Margolis. Choir soloist First Presbyn. Ch., also Temple Israel, Columbus, Ga., 1930-42; Wagnerian bartione Met. Opera Co., N.Y.C., 1941—, exec. stage mgr., 1963-78, spl. cons., 1978—. Leading baritone appearing roles, Central City (Colo.) Opera House Assn.; singer, with Cin. Zoo Summer Opera; concert, radio, TV and oratorio singer European tour, summer and fall 1954; Appearances on, Ed Sullivan Show, Omnibus and, 1st closed circuit theater, TV-Carmen., Opera recordings, RCA Victor, Met. Opera Book-of-the-Month Recordings. Recipient Verdi Meml. award for Achievement Met. Opera Nat. Council, 1978; Met. Opera scholar. Mem. Am. Guild Mus. Artists (gov.), AFTRA, Ala. Fedn. Music Clubs (hon. mem.), Ga. Fedn. Music Clubs (hon. mem.), Phenix City Jr. C. of C. Baptist. Club: Orpheus (Columbus). Home: 904 19th St Phenix City AL 36867 also 500 E 77th St New York NY 10162

HAWKINS, PAULA (MRS. WALTER E. HAWKINS), Senator; b. Salt Lake City; d. Paul B. and Leoan (Staley) Fickes; m. Walter Eugene Hawkins, Sept. 5, 1947; children: Genean, Kevin Brent, Kelley Ann. Student, Utah State U., 1944-47, H.H.D. (hon.), 1982. Dir. Southeast 1st Nat. Bank, Maitland, Fla., 1963-74; mem. Fla. Republican Nat. Conv., 1968, 72; mem. rules com. Fla. Rep. Nat. Conv., 1972; mem. Nat. Fedn. Rep. Women, 1965—; bd. dirs. Fla. Fedn. Rep. Women, 1968—; mem. Rep. Nat. Com. for Fla., 1968—, mem. rule 29 com., 1973-75; mem. U. S. Senate from Fla., 1980—. Mem. Maitland Civic Center, 1965—; charter mem. bd. dirs. Fla. Americans Constl. Action Com. of 100, 1966-68, sec.-treas., 1966-68; mem. Central Fla. Museum Speakers Bur., 1967-68, Fla. Gov.'s Commn. Status Women, 1968-71; Mem. Fla. Pub. Service Commn., Tallahassee, 1973-76, commr., Tallahassee, 1977-79; mem. Pres.'s Commn. White House Fellowships, 1975. Recipient citation for service Fla. Rep. Party, 1966-67, award for legis. work Child Fund Inc, 1982; named Guardian of Small Bus. Nat. Fedn. Ind. Bus., 1982, Rep. Woman of Yr. Women's Nat. Rep. Club, 1981, Outstanding Woman of Yr. in Govt. Orlando C. of C., 1977, Good Govt. award Maitland Jaycees, 1976, Woman of Yr., KC, 1973. Mem. Maitland C. of C. (chmn. congl. action com. 1967). Mem. Ch. Jesus Christ of Latter-day Saints (pres. Relief Soc., Orlando Stake 1964-64, Sunday sch. tchr. 1964—). Club: Capitol Hill (Washington). Office: 313 Hart Senate Office Bldg Washington DC 20510

HAWKINS, ROBERT L(EWIS), JR., lawyer; b. Quincy, Ill., Feb. 23, 1922; s. Robert L. and Katherine Bailey (Cleek) H.; m. Elizabeth Bell Hunter, May 23, 1942; children: Katherine Hawkins Clarke, Barbara Hawkins Martin, Robert Lewis III. Student, Westminster Coll., Fulton, Mo., 1939-43, Mich. State U., 1943; LL.B., U. Mo., Columbia, 1948. Bar: Mo. 1948. Assoc. Hunter, Chamier and Motley, Moberly, Mo., 1948-51; individual practice, Monroe City, Mo., 1951-56; gen. atty. Mo. Power & Light Co., Jefferson City, Mo., 1956-61; sr. partner Graham and Hawkins, Jefferson City, 1961-75; pres. Hawkins, Brydon & Swearengen, P.C., Jefferson City, 1975—; dir. United Mo. Bank of Jefferson City, Mo. Telephone Co. Mem. staff: U. Mo. at Columbia Law Sch. Law Rev., 1946-48. Trustee Mel. Community Hosp., Jefferson City, 1963-66, 67-70, 71-74, pres. bd., 1968. Served with AC, U.S. Army, 1943-46; to col. JAGC, USAR, 1950-62; with USNG, 1962-79. Recipient Alumni Achievement award Westminster Coll., 1968, Alumni Service award U. Mo. at Columbia Law Sch., 1974. Fellow Am. Bar Found. (state chmn. 1977—); mem. Mo. Bar (bd. govs. 1964-75, v.p. 1971-72, pres. 1973-74), ABA (ho. of dels. 1976—, state del. 1980—), Order of Coif. Club: Rotary (Jefferson City) (pres. local club 1967-68). Home: Route 1 Lohman MO 65053 Office: 312 E Capital Ave Jefferson City MO 65101

HAWKINS, WALTER LINCOLN, engineer; b. Washington, Mar. 21, 1911; s. William Langston and Catherine Elizabeth (Johnson) H.; m. Lilyan Varina Bobo, Aug. 19, 1939; children: W. Gordon, Philip L. Chem.E., Rensselaer Poly. Inst., Troy, N.Y., 1932; M.S., Howard U., Washington, 1934; Ph.D., McGill U., Montreal, Que., 1938; LL.D., Montclair State Coll., 1974, Kean State Coll., 1983; D.Eng., Stevens Inst. Tech., 1979. Sessional lectr. McGill U., 1938-41; NRC fellow Columbia, 1941-42; with Bell Telephone Labs., Inc., Murray Hill, N.J., 1942—. Editor: Polymer Stabilization; Contbr. articles to profl. jours., chpts. to books. Trustee Montclair State Coll. Recipient Honor scroll Am. Inst. Chemists, 1970. Mem. Nat. Acad. Engring. Patentee in field. Home: 26 High St Montclair NJ 07042 Office: Bell Telephone Labs Murray Hill NJ 07971 *There are many measures of success, but none to be more cherished than the role one may have played in encouraging others to follow in your footsteps.*

HAWKINS, WILLIAM LYCETT, retired association executive; b. Bridgeport, Conn., May 12, 1915; s. William Joseph and Irene (Burns) H.; m. Marion G. Sullivan, Sept. 27, 1947; children: Sally, Elizabeth, William, Jane. A.B., Tufts U., 1937; postgrad., U. Va.; hon. doctorate, Fairfield U., 1980. With Census Bur. of U.S. Dept. Commerce, 1949-50; exec. v.p. Bridgeport Area C. of C., 1950-76, pres., 1976-80, ret., 1980. Trustee Mech. & Farmers Savs. Bank; chmn. Trumbull Indsl. Devel. Commn., 1957-59; Treas. Greater Bridgeport Symphony Soc.; bd. assos. U. Bridgeport, 1960—; trustee Bridgeport Engring. Inst. Served to col. USMC, 1940-46. Decorated Legion of Merit, Silver Star. Mem. New Eng. Assn. C. of C. Execs. (pres. 1965), Conn. Assn. C. of C. Execs. (pres. 1963-64). Club: Algonquin (Bridgeport). Home: 21 Woodcrest Ave Trumbull CT 06611

HAWKINS, WILLIS MOORE, JR., aircraft company executive; b. Kansas City, Mo., Dec. 1, 1913; s. Willis Moore and Elizabeth (Daniels) H.; m. Anita E. Stanfil, June 22, 1940 (dec. Nov. 5, 192); children—Nancy Gay, Willis Moore, James Walter. Student, Ill. Coll., 1932-34, D.Sc., 1966; B.S. in Aero. Engring, U. Mich., 1937, D.Eng., 1964. Engr. trainee Grumman Aircraft Co., 1936-37; with Lockheed Aircraft Co., 1937-54, dir. advanced design, 1942-54; with Lockheed Missiles and Space Div., Sunnyvale, Calif., 1954-63, asst. gen. mgr., 1957-61, v.p., gen. mgr. space systems, 1961-62, corporate v.p. engring., 1962-63; lectr. aerospace scis. and mgmt. U. Calif. at, Los Angeles, 1954-55; asst. sec. army for research and devel., 1963-66; v.p. sci. and engring. Lockheed Aircraft Corp., Burbank, Calif., 1966-70, sr. v.p., 1970-74, sr. adviser, 1974-76, dir, 1972-80; pres. Lockheed Calif. Co., 1976-79, sr. v.p. (aircraft), 1979-80, sr. advisor, 1980—; dir. Wackenhut Corp., Billings Corp., AVEMCO; mem. Army Sci. Adv. Panel, 1957-74; adviser NACA, 1952-54; mem. adv. council NASA, 1978-83, chmn. safety adv. panel, 1981—. Recipient Disting. Pub. Service medal for contbns. to Polaris fleet ballistic missile system Navy Dept., 1961; Disting. Civilian Service medal Dept. Army, 1965; with laurel, 1966; Disting. Civilian Service medal NASA, 1975; Wright Bros. Meml. Trophy, 1982. Fellow AIAA, Royal Aero. Soc.; mem. Nat. Acad. Engring., Tau Beta Pi. Home: 4249 Empress Ave Encino CA 91436 Office: Lockheed Corp Burbank CA 91520

HAWKINSON, JOHN, investment mgmt. co. exec.; b. Walker, Iowa, May 26, 1912; s. Theodore W. and Gertrude (Nietert) H.; m. Florence Mallaire, Oct. 12, 1946; children—Diane, Judith. A.B., U. Iowa, 1936. With investments dept. Halsey, Stuart & Co., Inc., Chgo., 1936-41, v.p., 1946-49; v.p. finance, dir. Central Life Assurance Co., Des Moines, 1950-62; dir. Kemper Fin. Services, Inc., Chgo., 1962—, Tech. Fund, Inc., 1963—, Kemper Total Return Fund, Inc., Kemper Growth Fund, Inc., Kemper Income & Capital Preservation Fund, Kemper Money Market Fund, Inc., Kemper Summit Fund, Kemper Municipal Bond Fund Inc.; pres., dir. Kemper Option Income Fund, Inc., Kemper High Yield Fund, Kemper Fund for Govt. Guaranteed Securities, Kemper Internat. Fund, Inc., Kemper Cash Equivalent Fund; dir. Am. Fed. Savs. & Loan Assn. of Des Moines, Iowa-Kemper Ins. Co., Mapco, Inc., Berkley & Co., Kansas City So. Industries, Kansas City So. Ry., La. & Ark. Ry., UMC Industries; trustee Gen. Growth Properties.; Bd. dirs., mem. divisional com., investment adviser div. Investment Co. Inst., bd. govs.; bd. dirs. U. Iowa Found.; Mem. Ill. Securities Adv. Commn. Served to col., intelligence AUS, 1942-46; ETO. Mem. Nat. Fedn. Financial Analysts. Clubs: Des Moines, Wakonda (Des Moines); Chicago, Attic, Economic (Chgo.); Winnetka (Ill.). Home: PO Box 220 McGregor IA 52157 Office: 120 S LaSalle St Chicago IL 60603

HAWKINSON, ROBERT WAYNE, retired manufacturing company executive; b. Chgo., Jan. 12, 1920; s. Frank W. and Esther (Hallgren) H.; m. Janet Ristow, Dec. 16, 1944; children: Robert Wayne, John A., Barbara J. Student, Wright City Coll., 1941-42, Ill. Inst. Tech., 1949-50, U. Chgo., 1954. With Belden Corp., Chgo., 1945—82, asst. to the pres., 1962-63, pres., 1963—82, chief exec. officer, 1965—82, dir., 1964-80; dir. Union Spl. Corp., Nat. Can Corp. (both Chgo.), Crouse-Hinds Co., Syracuse, N.Y., Nat.-Standard Co., Niles, Mich. Mem. Chgo. Crime Commn., Glen Ellyn (Ill.) Dist. 41 Sch. Bd., 1964-70; Bd. dirs. Central DuPage Hosp., Winfield, Ill., 1964-74, v.p. bd. govs., 1974-76, pres., 1976-78; vice chmn. Central DuPage Health Care Fedn., Wheaton, Ill. Served to capt. USAAF, 1942-45. Decorated D.F.C., Air medal, Purple Heart; recipient Horatio Alger award, 1966. Mem. Ill. C. of C., Nat. Elec. Mfrs. Assn. (bd. govs., vice-chmn. 1978-80, chmn. 1980-81), Am. Assn. Indsl. Mgmt. (dir. Midwest div.), Elec. Mfrs. Club, Ill. Mfrs. Assn. (vice chmn. 1979, chmn. 1980-81), Am. Mgmt. Assn., Am. Soc. Testing and Materials, Armed Forces Communications and Electronics Assn. Lutheran. Club: Glen Oak Country. Home: 284 Maple St Glen Ellyn IL 60137

HAWLEY, ALEXANDER, banker; b. Bridgeport, Conn., Sept. 29, 1917; s. Samuel M. and Cornelia (Hincks) H.; m. Barbara King, Nov. 15, 1940; children—James M., Alexandra, Bronson K. B.A., Yale U., 1940. With Conn. Nat. Bank, Bridgeport, 1940—, exec. v.p., 1964-68, pres., from 1968, chmn., 1974—, chief exec. officer, 1976-79, also dir.; dir. Acme United Co. Mem. Pomperaug council Boy Scouts Am.; hon. mem. Jr. Achievement; mem. adv. bd. Goodwill Industries; bd. govs. Fairfield Found., Diocese of Bridgeport; trustee Sacred Heart U., Conn. Pub. Expenditure Council; bd. dirs. Goodwill Industries Western Conn., St. Vincent's Hosp., Bridgeport, Bridgeport Econ. Devel. Corp. Served as officer USNR, World War II. Mem. Bridgeport C. of C., Conn. Bus. and Industry Assn. (dir.), Am. Bankers Assn. (chmn. U.S. savs. bonds vol. com. Conn.), Conn. Bankers Assn. (past pres.), U.S., C. of C., Newcomen Soc. Clubs: Algonquin, Rotary (Bridgeport); Country (Fairfield); Potatuck (Newtown, Conn.); Landmark (Stamford, Conn.); Aspetuck Fish and Game, Ekwanok, Links; Yale (N.Y.C.). Office: Conn Nat Bank 888 Main St Bridgeport CT 06602 *

HAWLEY, DONALD THOMAS, author; b. St. Paul, Mar. 13, 1923; s. Donald Dewey and Ruth Lucille (Thomas) H.; m. Helen Weston Beasley, July 9, 1946; children: Casandra June, Craig Scott, Shareen Renee; m. Anita Mae Broder, Jan. 1, 1981. B.A., Union Coll., Lincoln, Nebr., 1950. Ordained to ministry Seventh-day Adventist Ch., 1955; asst. mgr. Nebr. Book and Bible House, Lincoln, 1950-51; dist. pastor, Nebr., 1951-56; chaplain Seventh-day Adventist Hosp., Karachi, Pakistan, 1956-61; dir. pub. relations Hinsdale (Ill.) Sanitarium and Hosp., 1961-63, Mich. Conf. Seventh-day Adventists, Lansing, 1963-66; dir. communications Greater N.Y. Conf. Seventh-day Adventists, 1966-71; mng. editor Life and Health mag., Washington, 1971-75, editor, 1975-77; dir. devel. It Is Written telecast, Thousand Oaks, Calif., 1977-80; freelance writer, 1980—; cons. med. recruitment Atlantic Union conf. Seventh-day Adventists, S. Lancaster, Mass., 1966-71; mem. exec. com. Protestant Council, N.Y.C., 1966-71; mem. nat. mass media com. Religion in Am. Life, 1966-71; chmn. nat. communication awards com. Religious Public Relations Council, 1970; pres. N.Y. chpt. 1971; rep. Fedn. Protestant Welfare Agys., N.Y.C., 1966-71; chmn. bd. Americans United in Northeastern U.S., 1969, temp. exec. sec. Ams. United in Greater N.Y., 1970; v.p. N.Y. State, 1970; dir. radio and TV interviews World Congress Seventh-day Adventists, 1971, 79. Author: Pakistan Zindabad!, 1961, From Gangs to God, 1973, Getting It All Together, 1974, Come Alive!, 1975, (under pseudonym Robert McDermott) Hypnosis; Is It for You?; also articles. Served with USNR, 1943-46. Clubs: Rotary, Kiwanis. Address: Box 904 Loma Linda CA 92354 *It has been my observation that the world is continually in short supply of individuals who will accept responsibility and carry a steady work load. Any such person, with a modicum of talent, can hardly avoid rising to a position of leadership.*

HAWLEY, PHILIP METSCHAN, retail executive; b. Portland, Oreg., July 29, 1925; s. Willard P. and Dorothy (Metschan) H.; m. Mary Catherine Follen, May 31, 1947; children: Diane (Mrs. Robert Bruce Johnson), Willard, Philip Metschan Jr., John, Victor, Edward, Erin, George. B.S., U. Calif., Berkeley, 1946; grad., Advanced Mgmt. Program, Harvard U., 1967. With Carter Hawley Hale Stores, Inc., Los Angeles, 1958—, pres., 1972-83, chief exec. officer, 1977—, chmn., 1983—, also dir.; dir. Atlantic Richfield Co., BankAm. Corp., Pacific Tel. & Tel. Co., Walt Disney Productions. Trustee Huntington Library and Art Gallery, Conf. Bd., Com. for Econ. Devel., Aspen Inst., Calif. Inst. Tech.; mem. vis. com. Harvard U. Grad. Sch. Bus. Adminstrn., UCLA Grad. Sch. Mgmt.; mem. Bus. Council, Bus. Roundtable; chmn. Los Angeles Energy Conservation Com., 1973-74. Served to ensign USNR, 1944-46. Decorated hon. comdr. Order Brit. Empire; knight comdr. Star Solidarity Republic Italy; recipient award of merit Los Angeles Jr. C. of C., 1974; Coro Pub. Affairs award, 1978; named Calif. Industrialist of Year Calif. Mus. Sci. and Industry, 1975. Mem. Phi Beta Kappa, Beta Alpha Psi, Beta Gamma Sigma. Clubs: California, Los Angeles Country (Los Angeles); Bohemian, Pacific-Union (San Francisco); Newport Harbor Yacht (Newport Beach, Calif.); Multnomah (Portland). Office: 550 S Flower St Los Angeles CA 90071

HAWLEY, SAMUEL WALLER, banker; b. Bridgeport, Conn., Feb. 24, 1910; s. Samuel M. and Cornelia B. (Hincks) H.; m. Florence I. Roberts, 1937; children: Bruce B., Carolyn Hawley Davis, Samuel Waller. B.A., Yale U., 1931; M.B.A., Harvard U., 1933; D.Pub.Service (hon.), Fairfield (Conn.) U., 1976, LL.D., Sacred Heart U., 1979. With People's Savs. Bank, Bridgeport, 1933-80, pres., 1956-71, chmn. bd., 1971-80, also dir.; dir. Middlesex Mut. Assurance Co., East Group Properties. Bd. dirs. Bridgeport Hosp. Address: Peoples Savs Bank Main and State Sts Bridgeport CT 06602

HAWLEY, WILLIS D., college dean political science educator. Dean, prof. polit. sci. George Peabody Coll. for Tchrs., Vanderbilt U., Nashville. Office: Office of Dean George Peabody Coll for Tchrs Vanderbilt U Nashville TN 37240§

HAWN, GOLDIE, actress; b. Washington, Nov. 21, 1945; d. Edward Rutledge and Laura (Steinhoff) H.; m. Gus Trinkonis, May 16, 1969 (div.); m. Bill Hudson; children: Oliver, Kate Garry. Student, Am. U. Profl. dancer, 1965; 1st profl. acting in: Good Morning, World, 1967-68; mem. company: Laugh-In, 1968-70; appeared in: TV spl. Pure Goldie, 1971; films Cactus Flower, 1969 (Acad. award best supporting actress), There's A Girl In My Soup, 1970, Dollars, 1971, Butterflies Are Free, 1971, The Sugarland Express, 1974, The Girl from Petrovka, 1974, Shampoo, 1975, The Duchess and the Dirtwater Fox, 1976, Foul Play, 1978, Seems Like Old Times, 1980, Best Friends, 1982; exec. producer and star: Private Benjamin, 1980; host: TV spl. Goldie and Kids—Listen to Us!, 1982. Office: care William Morris Agy 151 El Camino Dr Beverly Hills CA 90212 *

HAWORTH, DONALD ROBERT, educator, association executive; b. Steubenville, Ohio, Jan. 26, 1928; s. Henry L. and Mary Etta (Morton) H.; m. Amelia B. Speciale, Mar. 8, 1977; children: Jared, Maria. B.S. in Mech. Engring, Purdue U., 1952, M.S., 1955; Ph.D., Okla. State U., 1961. Registered profl. engr., Okla. Designer-draftsman Bell Helicopter Corp., Ft. Worth, 1952-54; instr. Purdue U., 1954-56; propulsion engr. Chance Vought Aircraft Co., Dallas, 1956-58; asst. prof. Okla. State U., 1958-61, asso. prof., 1962-66; sr. scientist LTV Research, Dallas, 1961-62; prof. mech. engring., chmn. dept. U. Nebr., Lincoln, 1966-75; mng. dir. edn. ASME, 1976—; engring. cons., 1962—. Contbr. articles in field to profl. jours. Served with AUS, 1946-48. Fellow ASME (mech. engring. dept. heads chmn. region VII 1968-70, nat. vice chmn. 1968-69, chmn. 1969-70, mem. policy bd. edn. 1969-75); mem. Profl. Engrs. Nebr. (sec. 1970-71, dir. 1971-72, v.p. 1972-73), N.Y. State Soc. Profl. Engrs., Am. Soc. Engring. Edn. (ME div. sec. 1971-72, vice chmn. 1972-73, chmn. 1973-74), Nat. Soc. Profl. Engrs., Engring. Council Profl. Devel. (dir. 1971-74), Sigma Xi, Pi Tau Sigma (nat. v.p. 1963-68, nat. pres. 1968-71), Tau Beta Pi, Phi Kappa Phi, Sigma Tau. Club: University Flying (U. Nebr.) (pres. 1968). Home: 9 Hunt St Rowayton CT 06853

HAWORTH, GERRARD WENDELL, office systems manufacturing company executive; b. Alliance, Nebr., Oct. 9, 1911; s. Elmer R. and Lulu (Jones) H.; m. Dorcas A. Snyder, June 22, 1938 (dec.); children: Lois, Richard, Joan, Mary; m. 2d Edna Mae Van Tatenhove, Feb. 5, 1979. A.B., Western Mich. U., 1937; M.A., U. Mich., 1940. Tchr. Holland High Sch., Mich., 1937-48; chmn. bd. Haworth Inc., Holland, Mich., 1965—. Home: 50 W 27th St Holland MI 49423 Office: Haworth Inc One Haworth Ctr Holland MI 49423

HAWORTH, HOWARD HARRISON, furniture manufacturing company executive; b. Buffalo, Nov. 25, 1934; s. Cecil Elwood and Esta Ruth (Bedford) H.; m. Patricia Ellen Garrison, Nov. 28, 1958; children: Elizabeth Ellen, Lucy Bedford. B.A., Guilford Coll., 1957. Prodn. trainee, sales asst. Heritage Furniture Co., High Point, N.C., 1958, sales asst., 1959-62, sales rep., 1962-63, adminstrv. asst. sales, 1963, asst. sales mgr., 1963-67, v.p., upholstered product mgr., 1967-68, v.p., merchandise mgr., 1968-69; v.p., gen merchandise mgr. Drexel Enterprises Inc., (N.C.), 1969-73; pres. Drexel Heritage Furnishings, Inc., (N.C.), 1969-73, chmn., bd., pres., chief exec. officer, 1982-83, chmn. bd., 1983—; dir. Myrtle Desk Co., High Point, N.C., Northwestern Fin. Corp., North Wilkesboro, N.C. Vice-chmn. bd. trustees Guilford Coll., GreensboroN.C.; mem. exec. bd. Piedmont council Boy Scouts Am.; pres. bd. dirs. Grace Hosp., Morganton N.C.; bd. dirs. Western Piedmont Community Coll. Found., Morganton N.C., Children's Home Inc., Winston-Salem N.C.; bd. trustees Crossnore Sch., (N.C.). Clubs: Mimosa Hills Golf and Country (Morganton, N.C.); Grandfather Golf and Country (Linville, N.C.); Linville Golf and Country; Emerywood-Willow Creek Golf and Country (High Point, N.C.). Home: 216 Riverside Dr Morganton NC 28655 Office: Drexel Heritage Furnishings Inc Drexel NC 28619

HAWORTH, JAMES CHILTON, educator; b. Gosforth, Eng., May 29, 1923; emigrated to Can., 1957, naturalized, 1972; s. Walter Norman and Violet Chilton (Dobbie) H.; m. Eleanor Marian Bowser, Oct. 18, 1951; children—Elizabeth Marian, Peter Norman James, Margaret Jean, Anne Ruth. M.B., Ch.B, U. Birmingham, Eng., 1945, M.D., 1960. House physician Birmingham Gen. and Children's Hosps., 1946-47; fellow Cin. Children's Hosp., 1949-50; house physician Hosp. for Sick Children, London, 1951; pediatric registrar Alder Hey Children's Hosp., Liverpool, Eng., 1951-52; sr. registrar Sheffield Children's Hosp., 1953-57; pediatrician Winnipeg (Man., Can.) Clinic, 1957-65; asst. prof. dept. pediatrics U. Man., 1965-67, asso. prof., 1967-70, prof., 1970—, head dept., 1979—; mem. active staff Health Scis. Centre-Children's, 1957—; cons. staff St. Boniface Hosp. Contbr. numerous articles to profl. jours. Served with Royal Naval Vol. Res., 1947-49. Fellow Royal Coll. Physicians (Can.) (London); mem. Canadian Med. Assn., Am. Acad. Pediatrics, Am. Pediatric Soc., Soc. Pediatric Research, Canadian Pediatric Soc., Midwest Soc. Pediatric Research. Home: 301 Victoria Crescent Winnipeg MB R2M 1X8 Canada Office: Department of Pediatrics Childrens Hospital 678 William Ave Winnipeg MB R3E 0W1 Canada

HAWORTH, LAWRENCE LINDLEY, philosophy educator; b. Chgo., Dec. 14, 1926; s. Lawrence Lindley and Ruth Ethyl (Johnson) H.; children: Lawrence Lindley III, Ruth Ellis. B.A. with highest distinction, Rollins Coll., 1949; M.A., U. Ill. at Urbana, 1950, Ph.D. (Univ. fellow), 1952. Asst. prof. U. Ala., 1952-54, asst. dean, 1953-54; asst. prof. Purdue U., 1954-59, assoc. prof., 1959-65; prof. philosophy U. Waterloo, Ont., Can., 1965—, chmn. dept. philosophy, asso. dean grad. studies, research cons., 1967-70; Cons. Inst. Pub. Affairs, Washington, 19—. Author: The Good City, 1963, Decadence and Objectivity, 1977; Contbr. articles to profl. jours. Served with AUS, 1945-46. Purdue U. research fellow, 1956, 59, 64; U. Waterloo research fellow, 1967, 68, 69, 70; Can. Council leave fellow, 1971-72; Can. Council research grantee, 1973-75, 81—. Mem. Am., Canadian philos. assns., Phi Beta Kappa. Office: Dept Philosophy Univ Waterloo Waterloo ON Canada

HAWORTH, LESLIE WILLIAM, transportation company executive; b. Birkenhead, Merseyside, Eng., Apr. 18, 1943; emigrated to Can., 1965; s. John James and Catherine (Dutton) H.; m. Beryl Ann Williams, Jan. 9, 1962; children: Michael Robert, Melani Jane. Ed., pub. schs. Staff acct. McEwan, Wallace, Howell & Co. (Birkenhead), 1959-65; mgr. Coopers & Lybrand, Hamilton, Ont., Can., 1965-68; treas. Abbey Can., Hamilton, 1968-72; v.p. fin. Laidlaw Transp. Ltd., Hamilton, 1972—. Mem. Can. Inst. Chartered Accts., Ont. Inst. Chartered Accts., Inst. Chartered Accts. Eng. and Wales (13th cert of merit 1961, 8th cert. of merit 1964, Plender prize for taxation 1964). Club: Royal Hamilton Yacht (Hamilton). Office: 110 King St W Suite 490 Hamilton ON Canada L8P 4S6

HAWORTH, MICHAEL ELLIOTT, JR., aerospace company executive; b. Pitts., Dec. 18, 1928; s. Michael E. and Margarett (Thomas) H.; m. Elizabeth Jean Evans, Dec. 20, 1949; children: Michael Elliott III, Jean Evans. Student, U. Ala., 1946-50; B.S., Samford U., 1958. Certified profl. contracts mgr. Gen. mgr. Haworth Engring. & Mfg. Co., Birmingham, Ala., 1954-56; chief contract negotiator U.S. Army Ordnance, Birmingham, 1956-61; dir. procurement Kennedy Space Center NASA, 1961-67; v.p., sec. Hayes Internat. Corp., Birmingham, 1967—, also dir., mem. mgmt. com. Served with Quartermaster Corps AUS, 1952-54. Mem. Nat. Contract Mgmt. Assn. (dir. Birmingham Area chpt. 1976-78, pres. 1978-79), Am. Def. Preparedness Assn. (life, chpt. pres. 1969-71, 82-84), Nat. Aerospace Services Assn. (dir. 1971-74, chmn. 1972-73), Council Def. and Space Industry Assns. (vice chmn. 1973-74, chmn. 1974-75), Birmingham Urban League (dir. 1971-75), Phi Gamma Delta. Presbyterian (elder). Clubs: Birmingham Country, The Club, Relay House, Downtown (Birmingham). Home: 3724 Rockhill Rd Birmingham AL 35223 Office: PO Box 2287 Birmingham AL 35201

HAWPE, DAVID VAUGN, journalist; b. Pikeville, Ky., Feb. 4, 1943; s. Chester and Betty Frances (Fletcher) H.; m. Linda Shadoin, Aug. 13, 1966; children: Christopher Fidler, Joanthan Bragdon. A.B. in Journalism, U. Ky., 1965; postgrad. (Nieman fellow), Harvard U., 1974-75. Reporter, editor A.P., Lexington and Louisville, 1965-67; editorial writer St. Petersburg Times, Fla., 1967-69; various positions Courier-Jour., Louisville, 1969-78, mng. editor, 1979—; city editor Louisville Times, 1978-79; tchr. Appalachian studies Harvard U., spring 1975; tchr. Appalachian studies and journalism U. Louisville. Served with USAR, 1956-73. Mem. Am. Soc. Newspaper Editors, A.P. Mng. Editors. Democrat. Presbyterian. Home: 430 Oxford Pl Louisville KY 40207 Office: The Courier-Journal 525 W Broadway Louisville KY 40202

HAWTHORNE, EDWARD WILLIAM, university dean, physiology educator; b. Port Gibson, Miss., Nov. 30, 1921; s. Edward William and Charlotte Bernice (Killian) H.; m. Eula Roberts, June 19, 1948; children: Coral, Dayle, Hilary, Leigh, Edward. B.S., Howard U., 1941, M.D., 1946; M.S., U. Ill., 1949, Ph.D., 1951. Asst. in physiology Howard U. Coll. Medicine, 1942-44; intern Freedmen's Hosp., Washington, 1946-47, asst. resident, 1947-48; asst. in physiology U. Ill., Chgo., 1948-49; Life Ins. Med. Research fellow in physiology Howard U. Coll. Medicine, Washington, 1949-51, asso. prof., head dept. physiology, 1951-58, prof., head dept., 1958-69, asst. dean, 1962-67, asso. dean, 1967-70, research prof., chmn. dept. physiology and biophysics, 1969-74, research prof., 1969—; dean Grad. Sch. Arts and Scis., Howard U., 1974—; vis. prof. Sch. Vet. Medicine, Tuskegee (Ala.) Inst., 1966; vis. prof. dept. physiology U. Ala. Med. Center, Birmingham, 1968; med. advisor U.S. SSS, 1960-70; mem. medicine and osteopathy spl. improvement grants rev. com. Bur. Health Professions Edn. and Manpower, HEW, 1968-69; mem. cardiovascular rev. panel Space Sci. Bd., Nat. Acad. Sci., 1968-74; chmn. adv. com. for SCOR Hypertension, Nat. Heart, Lung and Blood Inst., 1972-75; mem. hypertension detection and follow up program policy adv. bd. NIH, 1972-73; mem. clin. applications and prevention adv. com. Nat. Heart, Lung and Blood Inst., 1975-78, mem. hypertension task force, 1975-78; mem.-at-large Space Programs Adv. Council, NASA, 1976-77; mem. NASA Adv. Com., Ames Research Center, Moffett Field, Calif., 1976; del.-at-large White House Conf. on Handicapped Individuals, 1977; cons. minority hypertension research devel. program Bowman Gray Sch. Medicine, Wake Forest U., 1977; mem. Md. State Planning Council on Devel. Disabilities, 1977, mem. council developmental disabilities tech. assistance system, 1977—; mem. planning and adv. com. developmental disabilities councils consumer's tng. sessions Developmental Disabilities Tng. and Tech. Assiance Center, HEW, 1978; mem. Nat. Acad. Scis., 1980-81. Mem. editorial bd.: Am. Physiol. Soc, 1966-72, Jour. Med. Edn, 1969-72, New Directions, Howard U., from 1977; contbr. articles to profl. jours. Recipient Helen B. Taussig award Central Md. chpt. Am. Heart Assn., 1975; Percy L. Julian award Sigma Xi, 1980; numerous other awards, citations. Mem. Am. Heart Assn. (exec. com. council on basic sci. 1962-74, dir. 1964-73, policy com. from 1965, chmn. council on basic sci. 1966-68, mem. exec. com. 1966-73, v.p. 1969-72), Washington Heart Assn. (research com. 1963-67, dir. 1966-71), Assn. Former Interns and Residents Freedmen's Hosp. (exec. sec. 1957-69, pres. 1971-72), Am. Physiol. Soc. (co-chmn. Porter physiology devel. program from 1971), John Andrew Clin. Soc. (pres. 1965-66), Fedn. Am. Socs. Exptl. Biology, Am. Coll. Cardiology, Soc. Exptl. Biology and Medicine, Nat. Med. Assn., AMA, N.Y. Acad. Scis., Md. Acad. Scis., Physiol. Soc. Phila., Cardiac Muscle Soc., D.C. Med. Soc., AAUP, Medico-Chirurg. Soc., AAAS, Washington Soc. Pathologists, Am. Assn. Higher Edn., Orgn. Black Scientists, Sigma Xi, Alpha Omega Alpha, Alpha Phi Alpha. Office: 2419 6th St NW Washington DC 20009 *

HAWTHORNE, FRANK HOWARD, lawyer; b. Hope Hull, Ala., Sept. 16, 1923; s. William Blackwell and Bessie Louise (Greene) H.; m. Esther Rae Wille, Feb. 26, 1952; children: Frank Howard, Raymond James, Mary Jule. Student, Vanderbilt U., 1943-44; B.S., Auburn U., 1946; LL.B., U. Ala., 1949. Bar: Ala. 1949. Instr. Auburn U., 1946, U. Ala., 1946-49; partner firm Balch, Bingham, Baker, Hawthorne, Williams & Ward, Birmingham and Montgomery, Ala., head, 1955—; Dir., mem. exec. com. New Southland Nat. Ins. Co. Chmn. adv. bd. Salvation Army, 1968-70; mem. adv. council, sch. bus. Auburn U., 1973, 78, 81, chmn., 1977—; past chpt. chmn. Nat. Found. Served to 2d lt. USAAF, 1943-45; 1st lt. USAF, 1951-52. Mem. ABA (mem. resolutions com. 1959-60), Ala. Bar Assn. (grievance com. 1961-62, chmn. legis. com. 1972—), Montgomery County Bar Assn., Auburn U. Alumni Assn. (exec. com. 1957-59), Newcomen Soc. N.Am., Pioneers of Montgomery (pres. 1972), The Thirteen, Montgomery C of C (treas. 1973, v.p. 1974, pres. 1975, dir.), Omicron Delta Kappa, Pi Tau Chi, Pi Kappa Phi (nat. historian 1954-56, nat. chancellor, mem. nat. council 1954-64, bd. dirs., pres. Pi Kappa Phi Properties 1966-70), Phi Alpha Delta. Episcopalian. Clubs: Capital City Kiwanis (charter member), Men of Montgomery (bd. of control 1968-71), Montgomery Country, Montgomery Auburn (past pres.). Home: 3382 Thomas Ave Montgomery AL 36111 Office: 600 N 18th St Birmingham AL 35203 also 2 Dexter Ave Montgomery AL 36104 PO Box 751 Montgomery AL 36102

HAWTHORNE, JOSEPH CAMPBELL, conductor, music director, violist; b. Provincetown, Mass., June 25, 1908; s. Charles Webster and Marion (Campbell) H.; m. Hazel Russel Wragg, Nov. 11, 1949; 1 dau., Caro Campbell. Studied violin with, Melzar Chaffee and Edouard Dethier, beginning at age 6; attended, Friends Sem., N.Y.C.; student in Conducting (Walter Damrosch scholar), Fontainebleau, Conservatoire Americaine, 1927; B.A., Princeton, 1930; regular and grad. diplomas (sch. scholar), Inst. Musical Art Julliard Sch. Music, 1930-36; studied viola with, William Primrose, 1938-40; diploma (Assn. scholar), Nat. Orchestral Assn., N.Y.C., 1938; hon. doctorate, Coll. St. Scholastica, Duluth, 1977. Tchr. Columbia, U. Chattanooga, U. Wis.-Superior, Juilliard Prep. Centers. Condr., Mozart Festival Orch. and Cape Cod Summer Symphony, 1941; condr. various groups in, N.Y.C., Hartford, Conn., Trenton, N.J., until 1942; asst.-asso. condr., prin. violist, Dallas Symphony Orch., 1945-49; condr., music dir., Chattanooga Symphony Orch., 1949-55, Toledo Orch., 1955-64, Provincetown (Mass.) Symphony, 1955-69, Duluth (Minn.) Symphony Orch., 1967-77; Laureate condr., 1977—; Guest condr., N.Y.C., 1951, Radio Beromunster Orch., Zurich, Switzerland, 1957, Composers' Showcase, N.Y.C., 1961, Haifa (Israel) Orch., 1964, Mpls. Symphony Orch., 1967, Cabrillo Festival, 1979; also in, Detroit, Austin, Tex., Providence (selected as one of four guest grad. condrs. Nat. Orchestral Assn., N.Y.C. 1957); Author books of notes, catalogues of retrospectives and; contbg. author prefaces to several books on Charles Webster Hawthorne's paintings.; Condr. numerous contemporary works, premiere, U.S. premiere, and first local performances; recs. include Sammartini Concerto Grosso Opus 3, 3, Listening Records; viola soloist in: (with Gregor Piatigorsky) Strauss' Don Quixote, 1948, (and with Yehudi Menuhin in) Mozart Symphony Concertante, 1961. Served with USNR, 1942-46. Recipient citation Bruckner-Mahler Soc., 1954, Alice M. Ditson award, 1961. Club: Century Assn. (N.Y.C.). Home: 5830 London Rd Duluth MN 55804 Office: care Duluth Symphony 506 W Michigan St Duluth MN 55802

HAWTHORNE, MARION FREDERICK, chemistry educator; b. Ft. Scott, Kans., Aug. 24, 1928; s. Fred Elmer and Colleen (Webb) H.; m. Beverly Dawn Rempe, Oct. 30, 1951 (div. 1976); children: Cynthia Lee, Candace Lee; m. Diana Baker Razzaia, Aug. 14, 1977. B.A., Pomona Coll., 1949; Ph.D. (AEC fellow), U. Calif. at Los Angeles, 1953; D.Sc. (hon.), Pomona Coll., 1974. Research asso. Iowa State Coll., 1953-54; research chemist Rohm & Haas Co., Huntsville, Ala., 1954-56, group leader, 1956-60, lab. head, Phila., 1961; vis. lectr. Harvard, 1960, Queen Mary Coll., U. London, 1963; vis. prof. Harvard U., 1968; prof. chemistry U. Calif. at Riverside, 1962-68, U. Calif. at Los Angeles, 1968—; vis. prof. U. Tex., Austin, 1974; Mem. sci. adv. bd., USAF, 1980—. Editor: Inorganic Chemistry, 1969—; Editorial bd.: Progress in Solid State Chemistry, 1971—, Inorganic Syntheses, 1966—, Organometallics in Chemical Synthesis, 1969—, Synthesis in Inorganic and Metalorganic Chemistry, 1970—. Recipient Chancelors Research award, 1968; Herbert Newby McCoy award, 1972; Am. Chem. Soc. award in inorganic chemistry, 1973; Nebr. sect. award, 1979; Sloan Found. fellow, 1963-65; named Col. Confederate Air Force, 1984. Fellow AAAS, Am. Acad. Arts and Scis.; mem. Aircraft Owners and Pilots Assn., Nat. Acad. Scis., Sigma Xi, Alpha Chi Sigma, Sigma Nu. Club: Cosmos. Home: 3415 Green Vista Dr Encino CA 91316

HAXO, FRANCIS THEODORE, biology educator; b. Grand Forks, N.D., Mar. 9, 1921; s. Henry Emile and Florence (Shull) H.; m. Judith Morgan McLaughlin, Apr. 15, 1961; children: John Frederick, Barbara, Philip, Francis Theodore, Aileen. B.A., U. N.D., 1941; Ph.D., Stanford U., 1947. Teaching, research asst. Stanford U., 1941-44, acting instr., 1943; research asst. Calif. Inst. Tech., 1946; research asso. Hopkins Marine Sta., Pacific Grove, Calif., 1946-47; from instr. to asst. prof. plant physiology Johns Hopkins U., 1947-52; mem. faculty U. Calif. Scripps Inst. Oceanography, La Jolla, 1952—, prof. biology, 1963—, chmn. marine biology dept., 1960-65, chmn. marine biology research div., 1971-77; instr. marine botany Marine Biol. Lab., Woods Hole, Mass., 1949-52, 70; vis. faculty botany U. Calif. at Berkeley, 1957, U. Wash. Marine Lab., Friday Harbor, 1963. Abraham Rosenberg fellow Stanford, 1945. Fellow A.A.A.S., San Diego Zool. Soc.; mem. Am. Soc. Photobiology, Am. Soc. Plant Physiologists, Phycological Soc. Am., Western Soc. Naturalists, Internat. Phycological Soc., Phi Beta Kappa, Sigma Xi. Spl. research photosynthesis, plant pigments, physiology of algae. Home: 6381 Castejon Dr La Jolla CA 92037

HAXTON, DAVID, photographer, filmmaker, art educator; b. Indpls., Jan. 6, 1943; s. John Laird and Dorothy Margaret (Peters) H.; m. Kay Elizabeth Keller, Feb. 8, 1969. B.A., U. South Fla., 1965; M.F.A., U. Mich., 1967. Asst. prof. art William Paterson Coll., N.Y.C., 1974—. One-man shows include, Sonnabend Gallery, N.Y.C., 1979, 80, 81, 83, Sonnabend Gallery, Paris, 1978, Mus. Modern Art, N.Y.C., group shows include, Whitney Mus. Am. Art, N.Y.C., 1979, 81, 83, U. Calif., Irvine, 1980; represented in permanent collections, Mus. Modern Art, N.Y.C., Whitney Mus. Am. Art, N.Y.C., Denver Art Mus., Australian Mus. Art. N.Y. Council on Arts grantee, 1977-78; Nat. Endowment for Arts grantee, 1978-79; Individual Artist fellow, 1979-80. Office: care Sonnabend Gallery 420 W Broadway New York NY 10012

HAY, DAVID WILLIAM, clergyman, educator; b. South Africa, Aug. 18, 1905; emigrated to Can., 1944, naturalized, 1955; s. David and Elizabeth (Hendry) H.; m. Christina C. Reid, Apr. 26, 1936; children: Olive Allen, David Alastair. M.A. (Vans Dunlop scholar, Ferguson scholar), Edinburgh U., 1929; postgrad., New Coll., Edinburgh, 1929-32; D.D. (hon.), Queen's U., 1949, Trinity U., 1973, King's Coll. U., 1977, St. Michael's Coll. U. Ordained to ministry Ch. of Scotland, 1933, Presbyn. Ch. in Can., 1944; minister St. Margaret's Ch. of Scotland, Dunfermline, 1933-40; prof. Knox Coll., Toronto, Ont., Can., 1944-75; Pollok lectr. Pinehill Div. Hall, Halifax, N.S., Can., 1939; Birks Meml. lect. McGill U., Montreal, Que., Can., 1973; lect. liturgics Knox Coll., 1945-75; pres. Student Christian Movement Can., 1960, Canadian Council of Chs., 1962-63; mem. faith and order commn. World Council Chs., 1954-63; moderator Presbyn. Ch. in, Can., 1975; minister Knox and Claude Presbyn. chs., Town of Caledon, Ont., 1976-79, Presbyn. ch., St. David's, Ont., 1979-83. Asso. editor: Canadian Jour. Theology, 1965-70; Contbr. articles to profl. jours., chpts. to books. Served as chaplain Her Majesty's Scots Guards, 1941-44. Mem. Canadian Soc. Bibl. Lit. (pres. 1951), Canadian Theol Soc. (1960).

HAY, FREDERICK DALE, automotive supply company executive; b. Balt., Nov. 7, 1944; s. David Edward and Dorothy Hune (Weisbach) H.; m. Kathleen Vera Brown, June 17, 1967; children: Jordan, Maureen, Owen David. B.A. in Econs., Union Coll., Schenectady, N.Y., 1966; M.B.A., Ind. State U., 1970. Fin. mgr. Ford Motor Co., Dearborn, 1974-81; v.p. bus. planning United Techs. Automotive Group, Dearborn, 1981—. Served to 1st lt. U.S. Army, 1966-69. Club: Economic of Detroit. Home: 28467 Wellinton Farmington Hills MI 48018 Office: United Techs Automaotive Group 5200 Auto Club Dr Dearborn MI 48126

HAY, GEORGE AUSTIN, motion picture producer, director, artist, actor; b. Johnstown, Pa., Dec. 25, 1915; s. George and Mary Louise (Austin) H. B.S., U. Pitts., 1938; postgrad., U. Rochester, 1939; M.Litt., U. Pitts., 1948; M.A., Columbia U., 1948. Dir. Jr. League hosp. shows, N.Y.C., 1948-53. Motion picture casting dir. for, Dept. Def. films, 1955-70; motion picture producer-dir., U.S. Dept. Transp., Washington, 1973—; group exhbns. of paintings and sculpture include, Lincoln Center, N.Y.C., 1965, Parrish Art Mus., Southampton, N.Y., 1969, Carnegie Inst., 1972, Duncan Galleries, N.Y.C., 1973, Bicentennial Exhbn. Am. Painters, Paris, 1976, Chevy Chase Gallery, 1979, Watergate Gallery, 1981, Le Salon des Nations a Paris, 1983; rep. permanent collections, Met. Mus. Art, N.Y.C., Library Congress, also, pvt. collections; Author, illustrator: Seven Hops to Australia, 1945; Dir.: Bicentennial documentary Highways of History, 1976; dir.: film World Painting in Museum of Modern Art, 1972; Composer: Rhapsody in E Flat for piano and strings, 1950; writer: TV program Nat. Council Chs., 1965; Broadway appearances include: What Every Woman Knows, 1954; appearances include: Inherit the Wind, 1955-57; feature films include Pretty Boy Floyd, 1960, The Landlord, 1970, Child's Play, 1971, Being There, 1980; TV appearances include Am. Heritage, 1961, U.S. Steel Hour, 1963, Another World, 1965, Edge of Night, 1968, As the World Turns, 1969, Love Is a Many-Splendored Thing, 1972, The Adams Chronicles, 1976; piano soloist in concerts and recitals, 1937. Served with AUS, 1942-46. Recipient Loyal Service award Jr. League, 1953, St. Bartholomew's Silver Leadership award, 1966, Gold medal Accademia Italia, 1980, Smithsonian Instn. Pictorial award, 1982. Mem. Nat. Acad. TV Arts and Scis., Screen Actors Guild, Am. Artists Profl. League, Allied Artists Am., Internat. Bach Soc., Music Library Assn., AFTRA, Actors Equity, Nat. Trust Hist. Preservation, SAR, Nat. Parks and Conservation Assn., Washington Film Council, Pres.'s Council Coll. William and Mary, Shakespeare Oxford Soc., St. Andrew's Soc., Cambria County Hist. Soc., Am. Philatelic Soc., Fed. Design Council, Sigma Chi, Phi Mu Alpha. Clubs: Nat. Press, Nat. Arts, Players, Arts (Washington) (gov., trustee). Home: 2022 Columbia

Rd NW Washington DC 20009 also Hay Ave Johnstown PA 15902 Office: Dept Transp 400 7th St SW Washington DC 20590

HAY, JAMES MILLER, chemical company executive; b. Regina, Sask., Can., July 9, 1929; s. Charles Cecil and Florence (Miller) H.; m. Mary Susanne Cantlon, Oct. 28, 1950. B.E., U. Sask., 1950; M.P.E., U. Tulsa, 1954; Ph.D., U. Toronto, 1957. With Dow Chem. Co. Can. Ltd., 1957-68, 73—, v.p. ops., Sarnia, Ont., 1973-80, pres., chief exec. officer, 1980-83, chmn., 1983—, also dir. Fellow Chem. Inst. Can.; mem. Can. Chem. Producers Assn. (chmn.), Assn. Profl. Engrs. Ont. Address: Dow Chemical Canada Inc PO Box 1012 Sarnia ON Canada

HAY, JESS THOMAS, financial company executive; b. Forney, Tex., Jan. 22, 1931; s. George and Myrtle H.; m. Betty Jo Peacock, 1951; children: Deborah Hay Werner, Patricia Hay Mauro. B.B.A., So. Meth. U., 1953, J.D. magna cum laude, 1955. Bar: Tex. Asso. firm Locke, Purnell, Boren, Laney & Neely, 1955-61, partner firm, 1961-65; pres., chief exec. officer Lomas & Nettleton Fin. Corp., Dallas, 1965-69, chmn. bd., chief exec. officer, 1969—, also dir.; chmn. bd., chief exec. officer Lomas & Nettleton Mortgage Investors, 1969—, also dir.; chmn. bd., chief exec. officer, dir. Lomas & Nettleton Co., L & N Housing Corp.; dir. Trinity Industries, Inc., Merc. Tex. Corp., Verex Corp., Republic Fin. Services, Inc., Allied Fin. Co., Exxon Corp., Greyhound Corp. Former mem. Democratic Nat. Com.; former nat. fin. chmn. Dem. Nat. Com.; trustee, bd. govs. So. Meth. U.; bd. regents U. Tex. System; mem. Dallas Citizens Council; former mem. Dallas Assembly; mem. Dallas Council on World Affairs; mem. governing bd. Tex. Arts Alliance; treas. Greater Dallas Planning Council; mem. adv. council Dallas Community Chest Fund, 1981—; bd. dirs. Tex. Research League. Mem. Dallas Bar Assn., Tex. Bar Assn., Am. Bar Assn., Am. Judicature Soc., Newcomen Soc. N.Am. (vice chmn. Dallas com.). Methodist. Home: 7236 Lupton Circle Dallas TX 75225 Office: PO Box 225644 Dallas TX 75265

HAY, JOHN THOMAS, chamber of commerce executive; b. Lincoln, Nebr., Jan. 30, 1921; s. Ronald Harding and Luella (Sands) H.; m. Mable Margaret Secund, May 26, 1942; children: Susan Diane, Sally Lynn, John Thomas. Grad., U. Nebr., 1942; postgrad., Harvard, 1943. Sec. Colby (Kans.) C. of C., 1946; mgr. Columbus (Nebr.) C. of C., 1947-51; asst. mgr. Greater Muskegon (Mich.) C. of C., 1951-52, mgr., 1952-59; exec. v.p. St. Paul Area C. of C., 1959-67, Calif. C. of C., Sacramento, 1967—; Organizer Mich. C. of C., 1958-59; v.p. for Mich.-Gt. Lakes States Indsl. Devel. Council, 1958-59; chmn. Calif. Gov.'s Blue Ribbon Com., Summer Youth Job Campaign, 1968-69, Inst. for C. of C. Execs., U. Colo., 1965, bd. regents, 1960-66, instr., 1960-67; bd. regents U. Santa Clara, 1973-75. Co-author: Raising Money. Served to capt. Q.M.C. AUS, 1942-46. Recipient Distinguished Service award as Greater Muskegon's Outstanding Young Man of Year, 1954, F.O.Y.M. award as one of five outstanding young men of Mich., 1955, Outstanding U.S. Chamber Program of Work award, Muskegon, 1958, St. Paul, 1960, 62; Accreditation award St. Paul C. of C., 1962. Mem. Am. C. of C. Execs. (past dir.), Minn. C. of C. Execs. (past pres.), Calif. Chamber of Commerce Execs. (dir.). Home: 1316 San Augustine Way Sacramento CA 95831 Office: 1027 10th St Sacramento CA 95814

HAY, PETER HEINRICH, college dean, lawyer; b. Berlin, Sept. 17, 1935; U.S., 1953, naturalized, 1969; s. Edward Arthur and Margot Hedwig (Tull) H.; m. Norma M. Gossman, 1958 (div. 1973); m. Grazina O. Parokas, Jan. 26, 1974; children: Cedric, Tomas, Tadas. B.A., U. Mich., 1958, J.D., 1958; postgrad., univs. Göttingen and Heidelberg, Ger., 1959-60. Asst. prof. law U. Pitts., 1961-63; asst. prof. law U. Ill., Urbana, 1963-64, asso. prof., 1964-66, prof., 1966—, asso. dean, 1974-80, dean, 1980—; hon. prof. U. Freiburg, Ger., 1975—; cons. U.S. Dept. State, 1974-77. Editorial bd.: Am. Jour. Comparative Law, 1961, Cahiers de Droit Européen, Brussels, 1969—; Author: (with Stein) Law and Institutions of the Atlantic Area, 1963, 67, Federalism and Supranational Organizations, 1966, International Trade, Investment and Organizations, 1967, Symposium on International Unification of Law, 1968, Einführung in das amerikanische Recht, 1975, An Introduction to U.S. Law, 1976, European Community Law in Perspective, 1976, Ungerechtfertigte Bereicherung im internationalen Privatrecht, 1976, (with Roxunda) The American Federal System, 1982, (with Scoles) Conflict of Laws, 1982, 84; also numerous articles. Mem. Internat. Acad. Comparative Law (asso.), AAUP, Société de Legislation Comparée (Paris), Am. Fgn. Law Assn., Am. Bar Assn. (asso.), Am. Soc. Internat. Law. Roman Catholic. Club: Rotary. Home: 2302 Shurts Circle Urbana IL 61801 Office: 209 Law Bldg 504 E Pennsylvania Ave Champaign IL 61820

HAY, ROBERT DEAN, business educator; b. LaPorte, Ind., Nov. 17, 1921; s. Carl Roy and Almetta (Diedrich) H.; m. Margaret B. Appelman, 1944; children—Sue Ann, Carol Lynn. B.S., U. Okla., 1949, M.B.A., 1950; Ph.D., Ohio State U., 1954. C.P.A., Okla. Mem. faculty U. Ark., Fayetteville, 1949—, prof. mgmt., 1959—. Author: (with F. Broyles) Athletic Administration, 1979, (with Ed Gray) Business and Society, 1980; also 4 other books. Served with USAAF, 1942-47. Mem. Am. Bus. Communications Assn., Acad. Mgmt., Case Research Assn. Office: University of Arkansas Fayetteville AR 72701

HAYAKAWA, KAN-ICHI, food science educator; b. Shibukawa, Gumma, Japan, Aug. 12, 1931; came to U.S., 1961, naturalized, 1974; s. Chyogoro and Kin (Hayakawa) H.; m. Setsuko Maekawa, Feb. 18, 1967. B.S., Tokyo U. Fisheries, 1955; Ph.D., Rutgers U., 1964. Research fellow Canners' Assn. Japan, 1955-60; asst. prof. food sci. Rutgers U., New Brunswick, N.J., 1964-70, assoc. prof. food sci., 1970-77, prof. food engrng. and physics, 1977-82, Disting. prof. food engrng. and physics, 1982—; OAS vis. prof. U. Campinas, Brazil, summers 1972, 73; cons. to food processing cos. Organizer, chmn., participant NSF sponsored U.S.-Japan Coop. Conf., Tokyo, 1979; lectr. Industry Research and Devel. Inst. and Nat. Taiwan U., both Taiwan, June 1982. Contbr. articles to books, profl. jours. and encys. USPHS research grantee, 1966-73; NSF travel grantee, 1972; NABISCO Research Found. grantee, 1975-76; Rutgers Research Found. travel grantee, 1977; NSF research grantee, 1981-82. Mem. AAAS, Am. Inst. Chem. Engrs., ASHRAE (chmn. tech. com. on thermophys. property values of food), Am. Soc. Agrl. Engrs., Can. Inst. Food Sci. and Tech., Inst. Food Technologists, Sigma Xi. Developer new math. methods for predicting safety of food processes; found theoretical and exptl. theorems on heat and mass transfer in biol. material. Home: 631 Lake Dr Princeton NJ 08540 Office: Food Sci Dept Rutgers U PO Box 231 New Brunswick NJ 08903 *When I chose the field of my study in my youth, I determined to become the foremost learned person in this chosen area. To attain an achievement in life, I considered it important to work steadily and for longer hours each day than anyone else. Throughout my life, I concentrated on the fixed goal without sidestepping. The sense of fulfillment was the reward for the work. Mrs. Hayakawa's consistent and unselfish support and encouragement made it possible for me to concentrate my efforts on the scientific and academic work.*

HAYAKAWA, SAMUEL ICHIYE, former U.S. senator, former college president, writer; b. Vancouver, C., Can., July 18, 1906; s. Ichiro and Tora (Isono) H.; m. Margedant Peters, May 27, 1937; children: Alan Romer, Mark, Wynne. B.A., U. Man., 1927; M.A., McGill U., 1928; Ph.D., U. Wis., 1935; D.F.A. (hon.), Calif. Coll. Arts and Crafts, 1956; D.Litt. (honoris causa), Grinnell Coll., 1967; L.H.D., Pepperdine U., 1972; LL.D., The Citadel, 1972. Instr. English extension div. U. Wis., 1936-39; asst. prof. English Ill. Inst. Tech., 1940-42, asso. prof., 1942-47; lectr. univ. coll. U. Chgo., 1950-55; prof. English San Francisco State Coll., 1955-68, acting pres., 1968-69, pres., 1969-73, pres. emeritus, 1973—; U.S. senator from, Calif., 1977-81; Alfred P. Sloan vis. prof. Menninger Sch. Psychiatry, 1961. Author: (with Howard M. Jones) Oliver Wendell Holmes, 1939, Language in Action, 1941 (Book-of- the-Month Club selection), Language in Thought and Action, 1949, Language, Meaning and Maturity, 1954, Our Language and Our World, 1959, Symbol, Status and Personality, 1963, Through the Communication Barrier, 1979; Columnist: Chgo. Defender, 1942-47, Register and Tribune Syndicate, 1970-76; Editor: A Review of General Semantics, 1943-70, Funk & Wagnalls Modern Guide to Synonyms, 1968; supr. editorial bd.: Funk & Wagnalls Standard Dicts; Contbr. to: Middle English Dict, U. Mich., 1933-38. Fellow AAAS, Am. Psychol. Assn., Am. Sociol. Assn.; mem. Modern Lang. Assn., Internat. Soc. for Gen. Semantics (pres. 1949-50), Consumers Union U.S. (dir. 1953-55), Inst. Jazz Studies (dir.). Clubs: Press San Francisco, Pannonia Athletic, Bohemian. *

HAYASHI, TERU, educator, zoologist; b. Atlantic City, Feb. 12, 1914; s. Andrew Tetsuji and Shizuka H.; m. Sarah Darlington Rexon, Sept. 22, 1943; children: Curt, Tesa, Tomi, Tuck; m. Sarah Dixon Browne, May 15, 1970. B.S., Ursinus Coll., 1938; student, U. Pa., 1939; Ph.D., U. Mo., 1943. Instr. physics USAAF-ASTP program, 1943- 44; instr. zoology U. Mo., 1944-45, research asso. zoology, 1945-46; mem. faculty Columbia, 1946-67, prof. zoology, 1958-67, chmn. dept. zoology, 1963-67; prof., chmn. dept. biology Ill. Inst. Tech., Chgo., 1967-79; sr. scientist Papanicolaou Cancer Research Inst., Miami, Fla., 1980—; vis. prof. Japan Soc. Promotion Sci., 1974; Mem. NRC. Author articles in field.; Editor: Subcellular Particles; co-editor: Molecular Architecture in Cell Physiology. Trustee Marine Biol. Lab., Woods Hole, Mass., 1968—. Recipient award Ill. Acad. Sci., 1978, Alexander von Humboldt award, 1979; Fulbright and Guggenheim fellow, Denmark, 1954-55; Fulbright fellow, Germany, 1975. Mem. Soc. Gen. Physiologists (pres. 1962-63), Am. Inst. Biol. Scis., Am. Physiol. Soc., Harvey Soc., Am. Soc. Cell Biology, AAAS, Biophys. Soc., Japan Soc. Cell Biology. Address: 7105 SW 112 Pl Miami FL 33173

HAYASHI, TERUO TERRY, physician, educator; b. Sacramento, July 23, 1921; s. Jinnosuke and Koto (Watanabe) H.; m. Ursula M. Promann, Nov. 29, 1953; children: William Promann, Peter John, James Douglas, Ann Koto, Robert Terry. Student, U. Calif.-Berkeley, 1939-42, Temple U., 1943-44, M.D., 1948. Diplomate: Am. Bd. Ob-Gyn (dir. 1976—). Intern Temple U. Hosp., 1949, resident, 1951-54; instr. Temple U. Med. Sch., 1954-59, asst. prof., 1960-62, asso. prof., 1963-65; prof. ob-gyn U. Pitts., 1965—, chmn. ob-gyn, 1974—; study sect. human embryology and devel. NIH, 1964-68, mem. com. perinatal biology and infant mortality br., 1970-73; chmn. maternal and child health research com. Nat. Inst. Child Health and Human Devel., 1979-83. Served with AUS, 1949-51. Mem. Am. Coll. Ob-Gyn, Soc. Gynecol. Investigation, Am. Soc. Biol. Chemists, Am. Gynecol. and Obstet. Soc. (sec. 1981-84), Sigma Xi. Home: 146 Woodshire Dr Pittsburgh PA 15215

HAYASHI, TETSUMARO, English language educator, author, editor; b. Sakaide City, Japan, Mar. 22, 1929; came to U.S., 1954, naturalized, 1969; s. Tetsuro and Shieko (Honjyo) H.; m. Akiko Sakuratani, Apr. 14, 1960; 1 son, Richard Hideki. B.A., Okayama (Japan) U., 1953; M.A. (Rotary Internat. Jr. fellow), U. Fla., 1957, Kent State U., 1959, Ph.D., 1968. Asso. dir. Culver-Stockton Coll. Library, Canton, Mo., 1959-63; also asst. prof. English; instr. Kent (Ohio) State U., 1965-68; prof. English Ball State U., Muncie, Ind., 1968—, mem. doctoral faculty, 1969—. Author: Sketches of American Culture, 1960, John Steinbeck- A Concise Bibliography, 1967, Arthur Miller Criticism, 1969, Robert Greene Criticism, 1971, Shakespeare's Sonnets: A Record of 20th Century Criticism, 1972, Index to Arthur Miller-Criticism, 1976; Editor: A Looking Glass for London and England (Thomas Lodge, Robert Greene), an Elizabethan Text, 1970, (with Richard Astro) Steinbeck-The Man and His Work, 1971, Steinbeck's Literary Dimension, 1973, A Study Guide to Steinbeck: A Handbook of His Major Works, 1974, (with Richard Astro) John Steinbeck: A Dictionary of His Fictional Characters, 1976; also 7 monographs; founder, editor-in-chief: Steinbeck Quar, 1968—; gen. editor: Steinbeck Monograph Series, 1970—. Editorial research grantee, 1970; summer research grantee, 1971, 75, 78, 80; Folger fellow, 1972; Am. Philos. Soc. fellow, 1975, 81; Am. Council Learned Socs. fellow, 1976. Mem. Modern Lang. Assn. Am., Midwest Modern Lang. Assn., Am. Studies Assn., Shakespeare Assn. Am., Internat. John Steinbeck Soc. (founder, pres.). Home: 1405 N Kimberly Ln Muncie IN 47304

HAYASHI, TOSHINORI, trading co. exec.; b. Gifu, Japan, Nov. 15, 1926; s. Shunjiro and Kazue (Kunieda) H.; m. Michiko Arima, Nov. 7, 1959; children—Misuzu, Miharu. B.S., Hitotsubashi U., 1950. With C. Itoh & Co., Ltd., Japan, 1950—, mng. dir., 1977—; pres. C. Itoh & Co. (Am.), Inc., N.Y.C., 1980—. Served with Japanese Army, 1945. Buddhist. Clubs: Bd. Rm. (N.Y.C.); Cykagyle Country. Office: 270 Park Ave New York NY 10017

HAYASHI, YOSHIMI, justice state supreme court; b. Honolulu, Nov. 2, 1922; s. Shigeo and Yuki H.; m. Eleanor Hayashi, Aug. 8, 1953; 1 son, Scott K. B.A., U. Hawaii, 1950; LL.B., George Washington U., 1958. Bar: Hawaii 1958. Practice of law, Lihue, Kauai, Hawaii, 1958-61, asst. U.S. atty., 1961-67, U.S. atty. for Hawaii, 1967-69; judge Hawaii Dist. Ct. 1st Circuit, 1972-74, 74-82; assoc. justice Hawaii Supreme Ct., Honolulu, 1982—. Served to sgt. U.S. Army, 1943-46. Democrat. Buddhist. Office: Hawaii Supreme Court 417 S King St Honolulu HI 96813 *

HAYCRAFT, ALAN FINCH, paper company executive; b. Renfrew, Ont., Can., May 7, 1925; s. Cyril Charles and Violet Ethel (Finch) H.; m. Joyce Maxwell, June 4, 1949; children—Janice, Paul, Barbara. B.Sc., Queen's U., Kingston, Ont., 1946; S.M. in Mgmt. (Sloan fellow 1967), M.I.T., 1968. Registered profl. engr., Ont. With Kimberly-Clark Can. Ltd., 1960—, pres., Toronto, 1971-73, chmn. bd., gen. mgr. consumer and service products div., 1974-82, chmn. bd., 1983—. Mem. Canadian Pulp and Paper Assn. (exec. bd.). Anglican. Clubs: National, Port Credit Yacht. Office: 365 Bloor St E Toronto ON M4W 3L9 Canada

HAYDE, JOAN CORA, journalist; b. N.Y.C., Jan. 5, 1929; d. Patrick and Elizabeth (Fitzgerald) Mayfield; m. Donald Hayde, May 29, 1950; children—Donald, Brian, Keith, Carol, Michael, Margaret. Student, N.Y. U., 1948-49. Reporter, women's page editor Newsletter, Netcong, N.J., 1963-64; reporter Daily Advance, Dover, N.J., 1964-74, N.J. Herald, Newton, 1974—. Recipient Investigative Reporting award N.J. Press Assn., 1974, George Polk Meml. award, 1974. Mem. N.J. Presswomen Assn., Hopatcong Heights Civic Assn., V.F.W. Aux. Democrat. Roman Catholic. Home: 105 Francis Ave Hopatcong Heights Rural Delivery 1 Stanhope NJ 07874

HAYDEN, DONALD EUGENE, educator; b. Blairstown, Mo., Aug. 28, 1915; s. Frank Langston and Georgia May (Jefferson) H.; m. Mary Frances Dick, Sept. 12, 1939; children— Donald Eugene, Elizabeth Ann. B.A., U. Mo., 1936, M.A., 1937; Ph.D., Syracuse U., 1946. Instr. English Syracuse U., 1937-42; head English dept. Westbrook Jr. Coll., Portland, Maine, 1942-47; asst. prof. English U. Tulsa, 1947-51, asso. prof., 1951-56, prof. English, 1956, asst. dean liberal arts, 1956-57, dean, 1957-70. Author: After Conflict, Quiet-A Study of Wordsworth, 1951, (with E. Paul Alworth) A Semantics Workbook, 1956, Classics in Semantics, 1964, His Firm Estate, 1967, (with E. Paul Alworth and Gary Tate) Classics in Linguistics, 1967, Classics in Composition, 1969, The Creative Process: Introspection, 1971, Literary Studies: The Poetic Process, 1978, Wordsworth's Walking Tour of 1790, 1983. Chmn. Tulsa Com. for UN, 1956-58; chmn. Tulsa Community Relations Commn., 1961-64; Tulsa v.p. Nat. Conf. of Christians and Jews, 1968-70; Pres. Tulsa Psychiat. Found., 1959-64. Mem. Okla. Univ. and Coll. Deans Assn. (pres. 1965-66), South Central Modern Lang. Assn., Phi Beta Kappa, Phi Gamma Kappa, Phi Eta Sigma, Omicron Delta Kappa. Mem. Christian Ch. (Disciples of Christ) (elder; pres. ofcl. bd. 1954-57). Home: 3626 S Birmingham Ave Tulsa OK 74105

HAYDEN, JOHN MICHAEL, insurance agent, state representative; b. Colby, Kans., Mar. 16, 1944; s. Irven Wesley and Ruth (Kelly) H.; m. Patti Ann Rooney, Aug. 26, 1968; children: Chelsi, Anne. B.S., Kans. State U., 1966; M.S., Ft. Hays State U., 1974. Exec. mgr. Rawlins County Promotional Council, Atwood, Kans., 1973-77; agt. E.C. Mellick Agy., Atwood, 1977—; speaker Kansas Ho. of Reps. Pres. U.S. Hwy. 36 Assn. Served to 1st lt. AUS, 1967-70; Vietnam. Mem. Am. Legion, VFW. Republican. Methodist. Club: Ducks Unltd. (Atwood). Lodge: Rotary (Atwood). Home: 107 Page St Atwood KS 67730 Office: E C Mellick Agency 406 State St Atwood KS 67730

HAYDEN, JOSEPH PAGE, JR., finance company executive; b. Cin., Oct. 8, 1929; s. Joseph Page and Amy Dorothy (Weber) H.; m. Lois Taylor, Dec. 29, 1951; children: Joseph Page III, William Taylor, John Weber, Thomas Richard. B.S. in Bus, Miami U., Oxford, Ohio, 1951; student, U. Cin. Law Sch., 1952. With mobile home div. Midland-Guardian Co., Cin., 1952-61, v.p., 1954-60; pres., chief exec. officer, dir. Midland Co., Cin., 1961-80, chmn. bd., chief exec. officer, dir., 1980—; dir. Fed. Nat. Mortgage Assn., First Nat. Cin. Corp., First Nat. Bank Cin. Mem. bus. adv. com. Miami U., Oxford, Ohio; mem. pres.'s council Xavier U., Cin. Mem. Bankers Club, Sigma Chi. Clubs: Queens City, Hyde Park Golf and Country, University (Cin.). Home: 775 Watch Point Dr Cincinnati OH 45230 Office: 111 E 4th St Cincinnati OH 45202

HAYDEN, JULIUS JOHN, JR., coll. pres.; b. Pass Christian, Miss., May 19, 1920; s. Julius John and Forrest (Spring) H.; m. Lillian R. Aschbacher, Apr. 23, 1943; children—Julius John, III, Glover Richard, Susie Stafford. B.S., Miss. State U., 1949, M.S., 1950; Ed.D., U. So. Miss., 1966. Tchr., coach Lee Rd. Sch., St. Tammy Parish, La., 1949-50; instr. history, then dean Perkinston (Miss.) Jr. Coll., 1950-53, pres., 1953-62, Miss. Gulf Coast Jr. Coll., Perkinston, 1962—; mem. edn. com. Miss. Econ. Council. Served with USAAF, 1940-41; Served with USCGR, 1941-45. Named Boss of Yr. Gulfport (Miss.) Jaycees, 1976; Ednl. Adminstr. of Yr. Miss. Assn. Ednl. Secs., 1981. Mem. Navy League, Phi Theta Kappa (oir. 1967-78), Kappa Delta Pi, Phi Alpha Theta. Clubs: Wiggins Rotary, Biloxi Cavaliers, Miss. Coast Power Boat Squadron. Address: Miss Gulf Coast Jr Coll Perkinston MS 39573

HAYDEN, LARRY DUANE, investment banker; b. Paonia, Colo., June 30, 1936; s. George B. and Alma Estell (Dodge) H.; m. Russann L. Kingsley, Dec. 21, 1963; children: Heather Marie, Erin Elizabeth. A.S., Garden City Coll., 1959; B.A., Western State Coll., 1961; cert. achievement, Securities Industry Assn., Phila., 1982. Cert. fin. planner, Pa. Asst. dir. Nat. Assn. Securities Dealers, Denver, 1968-73; dir. compliance Barton & Co., Denver, 1973-74; pres. REHL Assocs., Arvada, Colo., 1974-81; v.p., treas., dir. Westamerica Fin. Corp., Denver, 1975-77; pres. Hayden Fin. Mgmt. Group, Arvada, 1981—; exec. v.p., dir. Hanifen, Imhoff Inc., Denver, 1977—. Served to cpl. USMC, 1954-57. Mem. Inst. Cert. Fin. Planners, Nat. Assn. Securities Dealers (vice chmn. dist. 3 1982, chmn. 1983, gov.-elect 1984). Republican. Presbyterian. Clubs: Denver Club; Sunset Beach and Racquet (Golden, Colo.). Lodges: Elks; Lions. Office: Hanifen Imhoff Inc 1125 17th St Suite 1700 Denver CO 80202

HAYDEN, MARTIN SCHOLL, newspaperman; b. Detroit, May 21, 1912; s. Jay G. and Marguerite (Scholl) H.; m. Elizabeth Dodds, July 26, 1938; children: Jay G. II, John D., Martin Scholl. Grad., Culver Mil. Acad., 1929; A.B., U. Mich., 1934; L.H.D., Detroit Coll. Law, 1967. Reporter Kansas City (Mo.) Star, 1929-30; mem. staff Detroit News, 1930-77, Ann Arbor (Mich.) corr., 1930-34, gen. reporter, 1934-37, city and state polit. writer, 1938-47, Washington corr., 1948-58; fgn. assignments include, Japan, China, Philippines, 1936, 1954, Poland, 1955, 1956, 1957; asso. editor Detroit News, 1958, editor-in-chief, 1959-77; pub. relations cons. Ford Motor Co., 1977—; v.p. A.P., 1971, vice chmn., 1973, also dir. Trustee Cranbrook Sch., bd. pres., 1963-67; trustee Harper-Grace Hosp.; pres. Leader Dogs for Blind; bd. dirs. Detroit Med. Center; mem. Mich. Jud. Tenure Com., 1977—, vice chmn., 1982. Served from 2d lt. to lt. col. AUS, 1942-45; ETO; Served from 2d lt. to lt. col. AUS, D-Day; ETO. Decorated Normandy Beach arrowhead. Newspaper Editors, Sigma Chi. Clubs: Chevy Chase, Gridiron, Nat. Press, Overseas Writers (Washington); Detroit, Country of Detroit; York Golf and Tennis (Maine). Home: 218 Merriweather Rd Grosse Pointe Farms MI 48236

HAYDEN, NEIL STEVEN, newspaper publisher; b. Bronx, N.Y., May 23, 1937; s. Aaron Alvin and Selma (Turtletaub) H.; m. Elaine Charlotte Lawson, July 3, 1960 (div. 1975); children—Stephanie, Jennifer, Aaron Alexander II; m. Carolyn Sue Smith, May 8, 1975; 1 stepson, Michael Sean. Student, U. Fla., 1955-58, U. Miami, Coral Gables, Fla., 1958. Mem. copy staff Miami Herald, 1958; reporter Albany (Ga.) Herald, 1959, Hickory (N.C.) Daily Record, 1959-60; editor Jackson Herald, Jefferson, Ga., 1960-62; editor, pub. Hartwell (Ga.) Sun; also pres. Sun, Inc., 1962-67; pub. Athens (Ga.) Banner-Herald, also Daily News, 1967-72; pres., pub. Huntington (W.Va.) Herald-Dispatch and Huntington Advertiser, 1972-76, Salem (Oreg.) Statesman and Capital Jour., 1976-79, Courier-Post, Cherry Hill, N.J., 1979-80, The Bulletin, Phila., 1980—; Mem. bus. adv. com. Nat. Alliance Businessmen, 1972—. Bd. dirs. Huntington-Cabell County chpt. ARC, 1972-74; bd. dirs. Huntington Galleries, 1973-76, Cammack Children's Center, 1973-76, Stella Fuller Settlement, 1973-76, Marion-Polk (Salem) United Way, 1976—, Mission Mill Mus., 1976—, Salem Boys Club, 1976—, Salem Symphony Soc., 1976—, Salem YMCA, 1978—, Oreg. Symphony, 1978—, World Affairs Council, Phila., 1980—, Police Athletic League, 1980—, Phila. Orch. Council, 1979—, United Way Camden County, 1979—; exec. bd. Tri-State area council Boy Scouts Am., 1972-76, pres., 1975-76; exec. bd. Camden County Council, 1979; mem. adv. com. Huntington YWCA, 1975-76; adv. bd. Haddonfield Symphony Soc., 1979—. Recipient numerous nat. and state journalism awards, 1961—; Outstanding Young Man of Yr. award Huntington Jaycees, 1972. Mem. Am. Newspaper Pubs. Assn. (prodn. mgmt. com. 1975—), Oreg. Newspaper Pubs. Assn., Pa. Newspaper Pubs. Assn., N.J. Press Assn. (prodn. com. 1980), Nat. Newspaper Assn. (rep. to Am. Council Edn. for Journalism, edn. com. 1977-78), Am. Soc. Newspaper Editors (bull. com. 1976-77, freedom of info. com. 1977-78), South Jersey C. of C. (dir. 1979—), Women in Communications, Inc., Cherry Hill C. of C.

(dir. 1980—), N.J. State C. of C., N.J. Press Assn., Sigma Delta Chi (mem. undergrad. liaison com. Atlanta chpt. 1968-69, pres. N.E. Ga. chpt. 1969-70, regional dep. dir. 1970). Office: The Herald Examiner 1111 S Broad Way Los Angeles CA 90015

HAYDEN, RALPH FREDERICK, accountant, corporation executive; b. N.Y.C., Jan. 15, 1922; s. Fred T. and Thrya (Ohlson) H.; m. Gloria McCormick, Feb. 27, 1943; children—Craig O., Glen R. B.B.A., Pace U., 1951. Sr. ptnr. Hayden & Hayden (accountants and auditors), Huntington, N.Y., 1941—; sr. v.p., sec., dir. King Kullen Grocery Co., Inc., Westbury, N.Y., 1948—. Contbr. articles to profl. jours. Pres. Old Chester Hills Civic Assn., 1962-64, Goose Bay Civic Assn., 1975-76; v.p. Bi-County Devel. Corp., 1972—; pres. L.I. YMCA, 1976-81; dir. at large, chmn. Suffolk County Co-op. Extension, 1968-76; bd. dirs. L.I. Com. for Crime Control, 1972—; mem. Suffolk County Republican Com., 1958-77; vice-chmn. Suffolk County Airport Adv. Com., 1976—; trustee, chmn., mem. exec. com. L.I. Ednl. TV, Channel 21. Served with USCGR, 1942-45. Mem. Empire State Assn. Pub. Accountants, Nat. Soc. Pub. Accountants, Aviation Council L.I. (treas. 1971—), USCG Aux., N.Y. Soc. Ind. Accts., C.W. Post Tax Inst., Real Estate Inst., Huntington C. of C., Suffolk County Gem and Mineral Club. Clubs: Kiwanis (past pres. local chpt.), Met. Office: 43 Prospect St Huntington NY 11743

HAYDEN, RICHARD MICHAEL, investment banker; b. Balt., July 31, 1945; s. Richard Taylor and Cecelia (Hense) H.; m. Susan Frances Margolies, June 4, 1978. A.B., Georgetown U., 1967; M.B.A., U. Pa., 1969. Assoc. Goldman, Sachs & Co., N.Y.C., 1969-73, v.p., 1974-80, gen. ptnr., 1980—. Served with USNG, 1968-73. Mem. Phi Beta Kappa. Republican. Roman Catholic. Club: Downtown Assn. (N.Y.C.). Office: Goldman Sachs & Co 85 Broad St New York NY 10004

HAYDEN, STERLING, actor, author; b. Montclair, N.J., Mar. 26, 1916; s. George and Frances Walter; m. Madeleine Caroll, 1942 (div. 1946); m. Betty Ann DeNoon, 1947 (div. 1955); children: Gretchen, Matthew, Christian, Thor; m. Catherine McConnell, 1960; 2 children. Seaman sailing ships and fishing boats, became first mate, then capt. Author: Wanderer, 1963; novel Voyage, 1976; film debut in Virginia, 1941; other films include Asphalt Jungle, 1950, The Star, 1953, Johnny Guitar, 1954, Prince Valiant, 1954, The Killing, 1956, Dr. Strangelove, 1964, Loving, 1970, The Godfather, 1972, The Long Goodbye, 1973, 1900, 1977, Winter Kills, 1979, Nine to Five, 1980, Gas, 1981, Venom, 1982; also appeared: TV plays including A Sound of Different Drummers, 1957, The Last Man, 1958, Old Man, 1958, Ethan Frome, 1960; TV miniseries The Blue and the Gray, 1982. Served to capt. USMC, World War II. Decorated Silver Star. Address: care GP Putnam's & Sons 200 Madison Ave New York NY 10016 *

HAYDEN, TOM, state legislator, author; b. Royal Oak, Mich., Dec. 11, 1939; m. Jane Fonda; children: Troy, Vanessa. Grad., U. Mich. Co-founder Students for a Democratic Soc., 1961, pres., 1962, 63; Staff Student Non-violent Coordinating Com., 1963; co-founder Econ. Research and Action Project, 1964; leader Newark Community Union Project, 1964-67; founder Indochina Peace Campaign; Candidate for U.S. Senate in Calif. Democratic Primary, 1976; founder, chmn. Calif. Campaign for Econ. Democracy, 1977—; chmn. SolarCal Council, State of Calif., 1978-82; mem. Calif. State Assembly, 1982—. Author: Port Huron Statement, 1962; Author: Rebellion in Newark, 1967, Rebellion and Repression, 1969, Trial, 1970, The Love of Possession is a Disease with Them, 1972, The American Future, 1980; co-author: The Other Side, 1967; contbr.: articles to periodicals including Washington Post, Los Angeles Times, N.Y. Times. Office: 1337 Santa Monica Mall #313 Santa Monica CA 90401 Office: State Capitol Sacramento CA 95814

HAYDEN, VIRGIL O., life insurance company executive; b. Marcola, Oreg., Oct. 17, 1921; s. Albert O. and Bessie (Mortimore) H.; m. Norma F. Colby, May 12, 1946; children: Susan, Sally Ann, Robert. B.S., Boston U., 1947. With Mut. Benefit Life Ins. Co., Newark, 1947—, v.p., mathematician, then sr. v.p., mathematician, 1966-73, sr. v.p., chief actuary, 1973—; dir. Mut. Benefit Fin. Service Co., 1969-76; dir., sec.-treas. Retirement Plans, Inc.; v.p. MBL Holding Co., 1981—. Trustee Heart Research Inst., St. Michael's Med. Center, Newark, 1980—. Served to lt. (j.g.) USNR, 1942-46. Fellow Soc. Actuaries; charter mem. Am. Acad. Actuaries; mem. Internat. Actuarial Assn. Club: Canoe Brook Country (Summit, N.J.). Office: Mut Benefit Life Ins Co 520 Broad St Newark NJ 07101

HAYDEN, WILLIAM JOSEPH, automobile co. exec.; b. West Ham, London, Jan. 19, 1929; s. George and Mary Ann (Overhead) H.; m. Mavis Ballard, Feb. 20, 1954; children—Christopher, Andrew, Elisabeth, Tracey. Student, Romford Tech. Coll., 1939-45. With Ford Motor Co., Briggs Motor Bodies Ltd., Dagenham, Eng., 1950-57; fin. staff Ford Britain, Dagenham, 1957-63; div. controller (Ford Chassis, Transmission and Engine Div.), Dagenham, 1963-67, gen. ops. mgr. transmission and chassis ops., 1967, gen. ops. mgr. truck mfg. ops., 1968, v.p. truck mfg. ops., 1971, v.p. power train ops., 1972; corporate v.p. and v.p. mfg. Ford of Europe Inc., Essex, Eng., 1974—. Served with Brit. Army, 1947-49. Decorated comdr. Brit. Empire. Home: Park House 259 Brentwood Rd Herongate Brentwood Essex England Office: Ford of Europe Inc Warley Brentwood Essex England

HAYDON, HAROLD EMERSON, educator, artist; b. Ft. William, Ont., Can., Apr. 22, 1909; came to U.S., 1918, naturalized, 1942; s. Albert Eustace and Edith Elizabeth (Jones) H.; m. Virginia Elnore Sherwood, July 4, 1937. Ph.B., U. Chgo., 1930, M.A. in Philosophy, 1931; student, Sch. Art Inst., Chgo., 1932-33. Artist in residence Pickering Coll., Newmarket, Ont., 1933-34; from instr. to asst. prof. arts George Williams Coll., Chgo., 1934-44; asst. to prof. art U. Chgo., 1944-75, prof. emeritus, 1975—, dean students in coll., 1957-59, marshal of univ., 1962-67; dir. Midway Studios, 1963-75; art critic Chgo. Sun-Times, 1963—; adj. prof. fine arts Ind. U. N.W., 1976-82; vis. lectr. Sch. of Art Inst. Chgo., 1976-81. Exhibited paintings, U.S. and Can., 1933—, mobile sculpture, 1948—, murals and paintings permanent collections, Pickering Coll., tapestry ark cover, Temple Sholom, Chgo., 1958, mosaic mural, 1968, mosaic murals, Congregation Beth Israel, Hammond, Ind., 1959-60, ceramic murals, Sonia Shankman Orthogenic Sch., Chgo., 1961, 66, porcelain enamel murals, 1977, 81, mosaic, St. Francis Assisi in St. Cletus Roman Cath. Ch., La Grange, Ill., 1963, stained glass windows, Rockefeller Chapel U. Chgo., 1972, 79, tapestry ark veil, needlepoint ark interior, Niles Twp. Jewish Congregation, Skokie, Ill., 1976, 80; Author: Great Art Treasures in America's Smaller Museum, 1967. Recipient prize for excellence in teaching U. Chgo., 1945. Mem. Artists League Midwest (pres. 1947-50), Artists Equity Assn. (pres. Chgo. 1950-52, 55-57), Chgo. Soc. Artists (pres. 1959-61), Renaissance Soc. U. Chgo. (pres. 1956-67, 74-75), Nat. Soc. Mural Painters, AAUP, Artists Guild Chgo. (hon. life), Alumni Assn. Sch. Art Inst. Chgo. (hon. life), Phi Beta Kappa, Psi Upsilon, Order of C. Home: 5009 Greenwood Ave Chicago IL 60615

HAYES, ALFRED, banker; b. Ithaca, N.Y., July 4, 1910; s. Alfred and Christine Grace (Robertson) H.; m. Vilma F. Chalmers, Dec. 30, 1937; children: Anita Robertson (Mrs. Henry Weare Gratwick), Thomas Chalmers. Grad., Milton (Mass.) Acad., 1926; student, Harvard, 1926-27, Harvard Grad. Sch. Bus. Adminstrn., 1930-31; B.A., Yale, 1930; B.Litt. (Rhodes scholar), New Coll., Oxford, Eng., 1933. Investment analyst City Bank Farmers Trust Co., N.Y.C., 1933-40; bond dept. Nat. City Bank of N.Y., N.Y.C., 1940-42; asst. sec. investment div. N.Y. Trust Co., 1942-47, asst. v.p. fgn. div., 1947-49, v.p. charge fgn. div., 1949-56; pres. Fed. Res. Bank of N.Y., 1956-75; vice-chmn. Fed. Open Market Com., 1956-75; chmn. Morgan Stanley Internat. Inc., 1975-81; adv. dir. Morgan Stanley Inc., 1975—. Pres. bd. trustees Lingnan U., Canton, China, 1947-54; mem. council Yale U., 1961-68; pres. Howard Florey Biomed. Found., 1973—. Served from lt. (j.g.) to lt. USNR, 1944-46. Decorated Order of Merit of Italian Republic; recipient C. Walter Nichols award N.Y. U., 1967; Distinguished Service award U.S. Treasury, 1969; Hon. fellow New Coll., 1975. Mem. Council Fgn. Relations, Pilgrims U.S., Can. Soc., Phi Beta Kappa, Sigma Xi, Phi Alpha Kappa, Beta Gamma Sigma, Alpha Delta Phi. Clubs: Economic (pres. 1965-66), Century Assn., River (N.Y.C.). Home: 401 Brushy Ridge Rd New Canaan CT 06840

HAYES, ALICE BOURKE, biologist, educator, university official; b. Chgo., Dec. 31, 1937; d. William Joseph and Mary Alice (Cawley) Bourke; m. John J. Hayes, Sept. 2, 1961 (dec. July 1981). B.S., Mundelein Coll., Chgo., 1959; M.S., U. Ill., 1960; Ph.D., Northwestern U., 1972. Researcher Mcpl. Tb San., Chgo., 1960-62; mem. faculty Loyola U., Chgo., 1962—, chmn. dept. natural sci., 1968-77, dean natural scis. div., 1977-80, prof., 1979—, asso. acad. v.p., 1980—. Contbr. articles to profl. publs. Trustee Chgo.-No. Ill. div. Nat. Multiple Sclerosis Soc. Fellow in botany U. Ill., 1959-60, NSF, 1969-71; grantee Am. Orchid Soc., 1967, HEW, 1969, 76, NSF, 1975, NASA, 1980-83. Mem. Am. Soc. Plant Physiology, Bot. Soc. Am., Soc. Ill. Microbiologists, AAAS, Am. Inst. Biol. Scis. Roman Catholic. Office: 810 N Michigan Ave Chicago IL 60611

HAYES, ARTHUR HULL, JR., physician, clinical pharmacology educator, medical school dean; b. Highland Park, Mich., July 18, 1933; s. Arthur Hull and Florence Margaret (Gruber) H.; m. Barbara Anne Carey, July 16, 1960; children: Arthur Hull III, Elizabeth, Katherine. A.B. magna cum laude, U. Santa Clara, 1955, D.Public Service (hon.), 1980; M.A., Oxford U., 1957; postgrad., Georgetown U., 1957-60; M.D., Cornell U., 1964; LL.D. (hon.), St. John's U., 1983, D.Sc., N.Y. Med. Coll., 1983. Intern in medicine N.Y. Hosp., N.Y.C., 1964-65, resident in cardiology, 1967-68; assoc. prof. pharmacology, asst. prof. medicine, assoc. dean Cornell U. Med. Coll., N.Y.C., 1968-72; prof. pharmacology and medicine, chief div. clin. pharmacology Pa. State Coll. Medicine, Hershey (Pa.) Med. Center, 1972-81; U.S. commr. food and drugs, asst. surgeon gen. USPHS, Rockville, Md., 1981-83; provost, dean, prof. medicine and pharmacology N.Y. Med. Coll., 1983—; dir. Cadbury-Schweppes, Stamford, Conn., Westchester Artificial Kidney Center, Valhalla, N.Y. Contbr. articles to profl. jours. Trustee U.S. Pharmacopeial Conv., 1980-81; Bd. dirs. Peace Found., N.Y.C., Food and Drug Law Inst., Washington. Served as capt. M.C. U.S. Army, 1965-67. Decorated Knight of Holy Sepulchre; recipient Foch medal Govt. of France, 1953; Recipient Nobili medal U. Santa Clara, 1955, Good Physician award Cornell Med. Coll., 1964, Faculty Devel. award Pharm. Mfrs. Assn. Found., 1968, Bronze medallion seal award Dept. Health and Human Services, 1982, Disting. Pub. Service award, 1983; Rhodes scholar, 1955; Danforth fellow, 1955; NIH fellow, 1960-62. Fellow N.Y. Acad. Medicine, Am. Coll. Clin. Pharmacology, Am. Coll. Cardiology, ACP, Royal Soc. Medicine, Coll. Physicians Phila., Am. Coll. Chest Physicians, Acad. Pharm. Scis.; mem. Am. Soc. Pharmacology and Exptl. Therapeutics, Am. Soc. Clin. Pharmacology and Therapeutics (pres. 1980-81), Am. Fedn. Clin. Research, N.Y. Acad. Sci., Harvey Soc. (nat. council on drugs), Pa. Med. Soc., AMA, Assn. Am. Med. Colls. (council of deans, council acad. socs.), Phi Beta Kappa, Sigma Xi, Alpha Sigma Nu, Alpha Omega Alpha. Roman Catholic (permanent deacon). Office: New York Medical College Elmwood Hall Valhalla NY 10595

HAYES, ARTHUR MICHAEL, lawyer; b. New Orleans, July 3, 1915; s. Dennis J. and Aline (Vivien) H.; m. Hilda Mae Sciortino, June 13, 1939; children: Arthur M., Dennis Lee, Patrick J. B.S. in Econs. cum laude, Loyola U., New Orleans, 1936, LL.B. cum laude, 1941. Bar: La. 1941, N.Y. State 1950. Practiced in, La., 1941-46, N.Y.C., 1950—; sr. accountant J.Y. Fauntleroy & Co., New Orleans, 1936-41; sr. tax Accountant Esso Standard Oil Co., Baton Rouge, 1941-46, chief tax accountant, N.Y.C., 1946-54; head legal div. tax dept. Standard Oil Co., N.J., 1954-55, dep. mgr. tax dept., 1955-69; gen. tax counsel Exxon Corp., N.Y.C., 1969-80, corp. v.p., 1980; counsel Satterlee & Stephens, N.Y.C., 1980—; pres. Nat. Tax Assn.-Tax Inst. Am., 1974-75. Mem. pres.'s council Loyola U., New Orleans. Mem. ABA (chmn. gen. income tax com. sect. taxation 1974-75). Clubs: Manhasset Bay Yacht, Westhampton Country, North Hempstead Country, Jupiter Hills, University. Home: 5 Knolls Ln Manhasset NY 11030 Office: 400 Beach Rd Apt 501 Tequesta FL 33458

HAYES, CHARLES A., mill company executive; b. Gloversville, Ky., 1935; married. With Lee Dyeing Co., Inc., to 1961, Guilford Mills, Inc., Greensboro, N.C., 1961—, exec. v.p., 1961-68, pres., chief exec. officer, 1968-76, chmn. bd., 1976—, also dir. Office: Guilford Mills Inc 2925 W Market St Box U-4 Greensboro NC 27402 *

HAYES, CHARLES A., Congressman; b. Cairo, Ill., Feb. 17, 1918; widower; children: Barbara Delaney, Charlene Smith. Internat. v.p., dir. Region #12 United Food & Comml. Workers Internat. Union, AFL-CIO & CLC, 1968-83; mem. 98th Congress from Ill., 1983—; dist. dir. Dist. #1 UPWA, 1954-68; field rep., exec. v.p. Coalition Black Trade Unionists; v.p. Ill. State AFL-CIO, Operation PUSH, Chgo.; exec. bd. Chgo. Urban League; mem. Ill. State Commn. Labor Laws. Office: Room 1631 Longworth House Office Bldg Washington DC 20515 *

HAYES, CHARLES LAWTON, insurance company executive; b. Cherryville, N.C., Nov. 8, 1927; s. Charles Lafayette and Alma H.; m. Joyce Williams, Oct. 7, 1950; children: Charles Gregory, Joy and Hill (twins). B.S.B.A., U. N.C., 1949. C.P.A., Md. With Monumental Life Ins. Co. (subs. Monumental Corp.), Balt., 1949-68, sr. v.p., until 1968, sec.-treas. parent co., 1968—. Bd. dirs. Jr. Achievement Met. Balt.; trustee Western Md. Coll. Served with USNR, 1945-46. Fellow Life Office Mgmt. Assn.; mem. Am. Soc. Corp. Secs., Phi Beta Kappa, Beta Gamma Sigma. Office: 2 E Chase St Baltimore MD 21202 *

HAYES, DAVID MICHAEL, lawyer; b. Syracuse, N.Y., Dec. 2, 1943; s. James P. and Lillie Anna (Wood) H.; m. Elizabeth S. Tracy, Aug. 26, 1972; children: Timothy T., Ann Elizabeth S. A.B., U. Va., 1968. Bar: N.Y. 1969, Va. 1968. Assoc. Hiscock, Lee, Rogers, Henley & Barclay, Syracuse, 1968-72; asst. gen. counsel Agway Inc., Syracuse, 1972-81, gen. counsel, 1981—; sec. counsel to bd. dirs. Texas City City Refining Inc., 1978—. Bd. dirs. Syracuse Boys Club, 1980. Served with U.S. Army N.G., 1968-74. Mem. ABA, Onondaga County Bar assn., N.Y. State Bar Assn., Va. State Bar Assn. Democrat. Club: University (Syracuse). Office: Agway Inc 333 Butternut Dr Dewitt NY 13214

HAYES, DAVID VINCENT, sculptor; b. Hartford, Conn., Mar. 15, 1931; s. David Vincent and Adelaide (Brown) H.; m. Julia Moriarty, June 22, 1957; children—David Matthew, Brian James, Mary Judith, John Mark. A.B., U. Notre Dame, 1953; M.F.A., Ind. U., 1955. Vis. lectr. visual and environmental studies Harvard, 1972-73. One man shows include, U. Ind., 1955, Wesleyan U., Middletown, Conn., 1958, Mus. Modern Art, 1959, Willard Gallery, N.Y.C., 1961-64, 66, 69, 71, U. Notre Dame-Ind. U., 1963, Root Art Center, Clinton, N.Y., Galerie David Anderson, Paris, France, 1966, Columbus (Ohio) Mus., 1974, Martha Jackson Gallery, N.Y.C., Everson Mus., Syracuse, N.Y., 1975, DeCordova Mus., Lincoln, Mass., 1977, Springfield (Mass.) Mus., 1978, SUNY, Albany, Dartmouth Coll., 1979, Amherst Coll., Nassau County (N.Y.) Mus., Saratoga Performing Arts Center, Sarasota Springs, N.Y., 1980, Old State House, Hartford, 1981, numerous group shows, 1959—; represented in permanent collections, Mus. Modern Art, Guggenheim Mus., Carnegie Inst., Joseph Hirshhorn Found., N.Y.C., U. Notre Dame, Mus. Fine Arts, Houston, Wadsworth Atheneum, Hartford, Addison Gallery Am. Art, Andover, Mass., Currier Gallery Art, Manchester, N.H., Williams Coll., Dartmouth Coll., Harvard U., others. Recipient Logan medal Art Inst. Chgo., 1960; Fulbright research grantee, 1961; Guggenheim fellow, 1961; grantee Nat. Inst. Arts and Letters, 1965.

HAYES, DENIS ALLEN, educator; b. Wisconsin Rapids, Wis., Aug. 29, 1944; s. Archibald John and Antoinette Jacqueline H.; m. Gail Boyer, June 14, 1971; 1 dau., Lisa Antoinette. A.A., Clark Coll., 1964; B.A., Stanford U., 1969. Founder, coordinator Environ. Action, Inc., Washington, 1969-71; vis. scholar Smithsonian Instn., 1971-72; dir. Ill. State Energy Office, 1974-75; sr. researcher Worldwatch Inst., Washington, 1975-79; dir. Solar Energy Research Inst., Golden, Colo., 1979-81; Regents' prof. U. Calif.-Santa Cruz, 1981—. Author: Rays of Hope, 1977. Trustee Stanford U., 1971-72; chmn. bd. Solar Lobby, 1978-79, Center for Renewable Resources, 1978-79; bd. dirs. Environ. Action Found., 1977-79, Urban Environ. Found., 1977-79, Environmentalists for Full Employment, 1978-79; mem. energy adv. research bd. U.S. Dept. Energy.; mem. Renewable Energy Inst., 1982—, Solary Lobby, 1983—. Recipient Jefferson medal Am. Inst. for Public Service, 1979; award for outstanding public service U.S. Dept. Energy, 1978. Mem. Fedn. Am. Scientists (dir.), Aspen Inst. Energy Group, Internat. Solar Energy Soc., Am. Solar Energy Soc. Office:: Center Innovation and Entreprenurial Devel U Calif Santa Cruz CA 95066

HAYES, DENNIS EDWARD, geophysicist; b. St. Joseph, Mo., Oct. 3, 1938; s. William Franklin and Gertrude Margaret (Lorson) H.; m. Leslie Eve Price, May 17, 1978; children—Jennifer, Katharine, Elizabeth, Elan. B.S.E. summa cum laude, Kans. U., 1961; Ph.D., Columbia U., 1966. Research asso. Columbia U., 1966-71, sr. research asso., 1971-74, asso. prof., 1974-77, prof. geophysics, 1977—; asso. dir. Lamont-Doherty Geol. Obs., 1978—; mem. Nat. Acad. Scis. ocean scis. bd.; mem. adv. panel to earth scis. div. NSF. Contbr. articles to profl. jours.; editor: books, including Antarctic Oceanology II, 1972, Marine Geophysics of SE Asia, I and II, 1978, 83. Recipient Haworth Disting. Alumni Honors in Geology Kans. U., 1977; NSF fellow, 1961-65; John Simon Guggenheim fellow, 1980-81. Fellow Am. Geophys. Union, Geol. Soc. Am.; Mem. Soc. Exploration Geophysicists, Tau Beta Pi. Home: 6 Century Rd Palisades NY 10964 Office: Lamont-Doherty Geol Obs Palisades NY 10964 *I believe maintaining one's personal integrity may be the single most important ingredient in a successful and satisfying career.*

HAYES, DEREK CUMBERLAND, manufacturing company executive, lawyer; b. Toronto, Ont., Can., Sept. 27, 1936; s. Charles Walter and Phyllis (Cumberl) H.; m. Susan Howard Bennett, July 13, 1963; children—Sean, Kate, Stewart. B.A., U. Toronto, 1958; LL.B., 1961; LL.M., U. London, 1965. Bar: Called to Ont. bar 1963. Solicitor firm McCarthy & McCarthy, Toronto, 1963-67; lawyer Massey-Ferguson Ltd., Toronto, 1967-71, sec., 1977-80; v.p., gen. counsel, sec. Shell Can. Ltd., Toronto, 1980—; sr. solicitor T. Eaton Co. Ltd., Toronto, 1971-73; legal adviser Govt. of Tanzania, 1973-74. Bd. dirs. John Howard Soc. Met. Toronto, 1975—, pres., 1977-79; bd. dirs. Toronto Arts Prodns., 1975-79, v.p., 1976-79; mem. exec. com. Trinity Coll., 1977-83. Mem. Law Soc. Upper Can., Can. Bar Assn. Club: Univ. (Toronto). Home: 47 Oriole Pkwy Toronto ON M4V 2E2 Canada Office: 505 University Ave Toronto ON M5W 1E1 Canada

HAYES, DOUGLAS ANDERSON, educator; b. b Highland Park, Mich., Feb. 27, 1918; s. Edward N. and Lillian (Anderson) H.; m. Anne Martin, Dec. 7, 1940; children—Douglas M., Randall B., Susan A. A.B., U. Mich., 1939, M.B.A., 1940, Ph.D., 1949. Research asso. Investment Council, Inc., Detroit, 1940-42; faculty U. Mich., 1946—, prof. finance, 1955—, dir., 1952—; cons. economist Treasury Dept., 1951-53; ednl. cons. Mich. Bankers Assn., 1952—; Chmn. bd. Security Bancorp Inc. Author: Appraisal and Management of Securities, 1956, Investments, Analysis and Management, 1961, 3d edit., 1976, Bank Lending Policies, Domestic and International, 1977, Bank Funds Management: Issues and Practices, 1980. Mem. bd. pensions United Presbyn. Ch. U.S. Served with USNR, 1943-45. Mem. Financial Analysts Soc. Detroit., Am. Finance Assn. (v.p. 1966—), Am. Econs. Assn., Inst. Chartered Fin. Analysts (trustee 1968-70), Phi Beta Kappa, Sigma Phi, Beta Gamma Sigma. Presbyterian (past trustee). Home: 2200 Belmont Ann Arbor MI 48104

HAYES, EDWIN JUNIUS, JR., leisure goods manufacturing company executive; b. Brockton, Mass., July 20, 1932; s. Edwin Junius and Edith Franklin (Miller) H.; m. Brenda Storrs, Apr. 19, 1958; children: Bradford, Jonathan, Christopher. A.B., Dartmouth Coll., 1954, M.B.A., 1955; cert., U. Manchester (Eng.) Inst. Sci. and Tech., 1972. Various positions Gen. Mills, 1955-67; product group mgr. Quaker Oats Co., Chgo., 1967-69; dir. mktg. Quaker Oats Ltd. (U.K.), London, 1969-72, v.p. internat., mng. dir., 1972-76; v.p. internat. William Underwood Co., Boston, 1976-77, exec. v.p., 1977-79; pres., chief exec. officer M. Grumbacher, Inc., N.Y.C., 1979—, also dir.; dir. Chartpak, Pickett Industries, Norfra Shipping Co., M. Engel Co. Served with U.S. Army, 1956-58. Fellow Inst. Dirs. (London); mem. Am. Mgmt. Assn., Nat. Art Materials Trade Assn., Art and Craft Material Inst., Mus. Fine Arts of Boston, Nat. Maritime Mus. of Greenwich (Eng.), Mus. Modern Art (N.Y.C.), Delta Upsilon. Office: 460 W 34th St New York NY 10001

HAYES, ELVIN, basketball player; b. Rayville, La., Nov. 17, 1945; m. Erna H. Hayes; children: Elvin, Erna, Erica, Ethan. Grad., U. Houston, 1968. With San Diego Rockets, 1968-71, Houston Rockets, 1971-72, 81—, Balt. Bullets, 1972-73, Capital Bullets, 1973-74, Washington Bullets, 1974-81; mem. NBA All-Star First Team, 1975, 77, 79; led NBA in scoring, 1969, led NBA in rebounding, 1970, 74; mem. NBA championship team, 1978; all-time leader in minutes played NBA. Named Coll. Player of Yr. Sporting News, 1968. Office: care Houston Rockets The Summit Ten Greenway Plaza E Houston TX 77046 *

HAYES, FRANK N., salt products company financial executive; b. Detroit, Jan. 14, 1938; s. Frank N. and Blanche C. (McDermott) H.; m. Gilda McGill, Mar. 26, 1977; children by previous marriage: William, Michael, Christopher, Kathleen. B.S. in Accounting, U. Detroit, 1960; M.B.A., Wayne State U., 1970. C.P.A., Mich. Auditor, accountant Price Waterhouse & Co., Detroit, 1959-63; gen. accounting mgr. Diamond Crystal Salt Co., St. Clair, Mich., 1963-68, asst. treas., 1968-71, treas., 1971-81, treas., chief fin. officer, 1981—. Mem. Am. Inst. C.P.A.s, Mich. Assn. C.P.A.s, Fin. Execs. Inst., Beta Alpha Psi, Sigma Phi Epsilon. Home: 2932 Woodstock Circle Port Huron MI 48060 Office: 916 S Riverside Ave St Clair MI 48079

HAYES, HAROLD THOMAS PACE, broadcasting executive; b. Elkin, N.C., Apr. 18, 1926; s. James M. and Aline (Pace) H.; m. Susan Meredith, Apr. 7, 1955 (div. 1983); children: Thomas Pace, Carrie Meredith.; m. Judy Kessler, Mar. 4, 1983. B.S., Wake Forest Coll., 1948. With So. Bell Telephone Co., Atlanta, 1948-49; with U.P.I., Atlanta, 1949-50; asst. editor Pageant mag., N.Y.C., 1952, asso. editor, 1953, Tempo mag., 1953; editor Picture Week mag., 1954; asst. to pub. Esquire mag., N.Y.C., 1955-59, articles editor, 1959-62, mng. editor, 1962-63, editor, 1963-73, asst. pub., 1973; free lance journalist, cons. editor, 1973—; instr. mag. journalism New Sch. for Social Research, N.Y.C., 1961-63; mem. exec. com., dir. Sat. Review, 1977—; Chmn. bd. visitors Wake Forest U., 1972-76. Host: nightly discussion show Roundtable, Channel 13, N.Y.C., 1974—; exec. producer: TV spl. The Late Great, 1968; sr. editorial producer: 20-20, ABC News, 1978; v.p. editorial planning, CBS, 1980—; Author: The Last Place on Earth, 1977, Three Levels of Time, 1981; Editor: Smiling Through the Apocalypse, 1970. Served with USNR, 1943-45; to 1st lt. USMCR, 1950-52. Nieman fellow Harvard U., 1958-59; Recipient Distinguished Alumni award Wake Forest U., 1968. Mem. Am. Soc. Mag. Editors (chmn. exec. com. 1969). Office: CBS 1515 Broadway New York NY 10036

HAYES, HELEN, actress; b. Washington, Oct. 10, 1900; d. Francis Van Arnum and Catherine Estell (Hayes) Brown; m. Charles MacArthur, Aug. 17, 1928 (dec. Apr. 1956); 1 son, James. Grad., Sacred Heart Acad., Washington, 1917; L.H.D., Hamilton Coll., Clinton, N.Y., 1939, Smith Coll., 1940, Elmira (N.Y.) Coll.; Litt.D., Columbia U., 1949, U. Denver, 1952; D.F.A., Princeton U., St. Mary's Coll. First appeared on stage, age six; mem. Columbia Players, Washington, 4 seasons; toured with Lew Fields and John Drew; mem. A.P.A. Phoenix Repertory Co., from 1966. Played in: Old Dutch, Prodigal Husband, Pollyanna, Penrod; appeared with: (William Gillette in) Dear Brutus; appeared in: Clarence, Bab, To The Ladies, We Moderns, Dancing Mothers, Caesar and Cleopatra, What Every Woman Knows, Coquette, Mr. Gilhooley, Mary of Scotland, 1934, Victoria Regina, 1937-38, Ladies and Gentlemen, 1939-40, Twelfth Night, 1940-41, Candle in the Wind, 1941-42, Harriet, 1943-45, Happy Birthday, 1948, The Glass Menagerie, London, 1948, Farewell to Arms, 1950, Vanessa, 1950, The Wisteria Trees, 1950, Mrs. McThing, 1952, Mainstreet to Broadway, 1953, Skin of Our Teeth, Europe and U.S., 1955, Harvey, Long Days Journey Into Night, 1971; motion pictures The Sin of Madelon, Claudet (Acad. award 1932), Arrowsmith, My Son John, 1951, Anastasia, 1956, Airport, 1970 (Acad. award Best Supporting Actress 1971), Herbie Rides Again, 1974, Helen Hayes: Portrait of an American Actress, 1974, One of Our Dinosaurs is Missing, 1975, Candleshoe, 1978, Hopper's Silence, 1981; TV shows The Snoop Sisters, 1972-74; other TV appearances; played Mrs. Derth in: TV revival Barrie's Dear Brutus, 1956. Pres. Am. Nat. Theatre and Acad.; hon. pres. Am. Theatre Wing; 2d v.p. Actors Fund, from 1975—; chmn. women's activities Nat. Found. for Infantile Paralysis. Recipient best actressaward Motion Pictures Acad. Arts and Scis., 1932, Emmyaward, 1954, Antoinette Perry award for best actress in Time Remembered, 1958, Medal of City of N.Y., Medal of Arts, Finland, Am. Exemplar medal Freedoms Found., 1978, Laetare medal U. Notre Dame, 1979. Republican. Roman Catholic. *

HAYES, ISAAC, composer, singer; b. Covington, Tenn., Aug. 20, 1942. Formerly singer rhythm and blues recs., Stax Records; known for home-play psychodramas; albums recorded included Black Moses, Hot Buttered Soul, Enterprise: His Greatest Hits, Hotbed, Isaac Hayes Movement, . . . To Be Continued, Greatest Hit Singles, (with Dionne Warwick) A Man and A Woman; composer: musical score film Shaft; appeared: on TV show Rockford Files (Recipient Grammy, Oscar for score Shaft.). Address: care Poly Gram Records Inc 810 7th Ave New York NY 10019 *

HAYES, JAMES EDWARD, retired insurance executive; b. Mound City, Mo., June 7, 1928; s. Edward Perry and Gladys Marie (Plummer) H.; m. Edith Louise Beckett, June 15, 1951. B.S., U. Mo., 1951. Vice pres. mortgage and real estate Equitable Life Assurance Soc., N.Y.C., 1970-74, v.p. bond investments, 1974-76, sr. v.p. investment affairs, 1976-79, sr. v.p. fin. ops. area, 1979-80; exec. v.p. Equitable Life Assurance Soc. of U.S.; exec. v.p. and chief ops. officer Equitable Life Holding Corp., 1980-83. Chmn. bd., chief exec. officer Equico Lessors, Inc., 1982-83; chmn. bd., dir. Equico Capital Corp., Inc., to 1983, Equico Securities, Inc., to 1983. Served with U.S. Army, 1946-47, 51-53. Mem. Am. Mgmt. Assn., Am. Inst. Real Estate Appraisers, N.Y. Real Estate Bd. Club: North Shore Yacht. Home: 306 Quail Hollow Saint Michaels MD 21663

HAYES, JAMES MARTIN, archbishop; b. Halifax, N.S., Can., May 27, 1924; s. Leonard J. and Rita (Bates) H. Student, St. Mary's U., Halifax, 1939-43; B.A., Holy Heart Sem., Halifax, 1947; J.C.D., Angelicum, Rome, 1957; Litt. D. (hon.), St. Anne's U., Church Pt., N.S., 1966, S.T.D., Kings Coll., Halifax, 1967. Ordained priest Roman Cath. Ch., 1947; chancellor Archdiocese of Halifax, 1957-63; rector St. Mary's Basilica, Halifax, 1963-66; aux. bishop, Halifax, 1965-67, archbishop, 1967—. Address: 6541 Coburg Rd PO Box 1527 Halifax NS 2Y3 Canada B3J *

HAYES, JANET GRAY, former mayor; b. Rushville, Ind., July 12, 1926; d. John Paul and Lucile (Gray) Frazee; m. Kenneth Hayes, Mar. 20, 1950; children: Lindy, John, Katherine, Megan. A.B., Ind. U., 1948; M.A., U. Chgo., 1950. Psychiat. caseworker Jewish Family Service Agy., Chgo., 1950-52; vol. Denver Crippled Children's Service, 1954-55, Adult and Child Guidance Clinic, San Jose, 1958-59; mem. San Jose City Council, 1971—, mem. regional housing subcom., 1973-74, mem. personnel com., 1973-74, vice mayor, 1973-74, mayor, 1975-82; client/community relations dir. Q Tech, 1983—; trustee U.S. Conf. Mayors, 1979—; co-chmn. Task Force on Aging, 1976—, co-chmn. com. urban econs., 1976—, mem. task force income security, 1975—, sci. and tech. task force, 1976—, mem. spl. com. on growth, 1976—, mem. energy and environ. com., 1979-80, chmn. affirmative action subcom., 1980—, housing and community devel. com., 1980; bd. dirs. League Calif. Cities, 1977-82, mem. property tax task force, 1979—, mem. housing task force, 1979—, mem. organizational com., 1980; mem. natural resources policy com. Nat League of Cities, 1979-82, chmn. energy, environ. quality and natural resources steering com., 1980-82; chmn. State of Calif. Urban Devel. Adv. Com., 1976-77; mem. Calif. Commn. Fair Jud. Practices, 1976—, Democratic nat. campaign com., 1976, Calif. Dem. Commn. Nat. Platform and Policy, 1976; bd. dirs. South San Francisco Bay Dischargers Authority; chmn. Santa Clara County Sanitation Dist.; mem. San Jose/Santa Clara Treatment Plant Adv. Bd.; chmn. Santa Clara Valley Employment and Tng. Bd., 1976-78; pres. Inter-Govtl. Council of Santa Clara County, 1981-82; mem. Sci. and Innovation Task Force, 1980-82, Calif. Solid Waste Mgmt. Bd., 1980-82, Guadalupe Corridor Study Analysis Com.; past mem. EPA Aircraft/Airport Noise Task Group; bd. dirs. Calif. Center Research and Edn. in Govt., AAUW Edn. Found., 1980, Public Technology Inc. Mem. Assn. Bay Area Govts. (exec. com. 1971-78, regional housing subcom. 1973-74), Inst. for Local Self Govt., LWV (pres. San Francisco Bay Area chpt. 1968-70, pres. local 1966-67). Democrat. Club: Century. Home: 1155 Emory St San Jose CA 95126 Office: Q Tech 4701 Patrick Henry Dr Santa Clara CA 95050

HAYES, JEREMIAH FRANCIS, electrical engineering educator; b. N.Y.C., July 8, 1934; s. James Joseph and Mary Margaret (Sheehan) H.; m. Florence Marie Perrella, Sept. 1, 1962; children: Mary, Ann, Jeremiah, Martin. B.E.E., Manhattan Coll., N.Y.C., 1956; M.S., NYU, 1961; Ph.D., U. Calif.-Berkeley, 1966. Mem. tech. staff Bell Labs., Murray Hill, N.J., 1956-60; research engr. Electronics Research Labs. Columbia U., N.Y.C., 1960-62; research engr. U. Calif., Berkeley, 1962-66; asst. prof. elec. engring. Purdue U., Lafayette, Ind., 1966-69; mem. tech. staff Bell Labs., Holmdel, N.J., 1969-78; prof. elec. engring. McGill U., Montreal, 1978—. Fellow IEEE (editor transactions 1981—, bd. govs. Communications Soc. 1983—). Home: 3429 Belmore Ave Montreal PQ Canada H4B 2B8 Office: McGill Univ 3480 Univ St Montreal PQ Canada H3A 2A7

HAYES, JOE LYNN, civil engineer, state legislator; b. Bakersfield, Mo., Feb. 18, 1930; s. Norman and Dicy Mace (Cotter) H.; m. Patricia Marsette Anderson, Sept. 1, 1951; children: Debra C. Hayes Gravo, Karin L., Laura B. Hayes Kolbeck; m. 2d Diane Marie Kroesing, Dec. 30, 1977. B.S. in Civil Engring., U. Wash., 1955; M.S. in Engring. Mgmt., U. Alaska, 1966. Registered profl. civil engr., Alaska, Hawaii, Ariz.; land surveyor, Alaska, Ariz. Assoc., ptnr. Tryck, Nyman & Hayes, Anchorage, 1959-74; v.p., co-owner Borough-City Devel. Inc., Anchorage, 1974-79; personal investigator, Anchorage, 1979—; mem. ALaska Ho. of Reps., 1977—, Republican minority leader, 1978-81, speaker of house, 1981—; chmn. bd. Alaska Continental Bank, Anchorage, 1983—, Pacific Rim Title Agy., 1983—; dir., officer Interior Energy Corp., Fairbanks, Alaska, 1979—; dir. Northcorp., Anchorage, 1983—. Mem. ASCE, Nat. Soc. Profl. Engrs. Lutheran. Club: Pioneers of Alaska. Lodges: Rotary; Elks. Home: 9710 Arlene Dr Anchorage AK 99502 Office: Alaska Ho of Reps 515 D St Suite 201 Anchorage AK 99501

HAYES, JOHN FRANCIS, lawyer; b. Salina, Kans., Dec. 11, 1919; s. John Francis and Helen (Dye) H.; m. Elizabeth Ann Ireton, Aug. 10, 1950; children: Carl Ireton, Ann Chandler. A.B., Washburn Coll., 1941; LL.B., 1946. Bar: Kans. 1946. Practice law, Hutchinson, Kans., 1946—; dir. Gilliland, Hayes & Green, P.A. (and predecessors), 1946—; mem. Commn. Uniform State Laws, 1975—; dir. Central State Bank, Hutchinson. Mem. Kans. Ho. of Reps., 1953-55, 67-79, majority leader, 1975-77. Served as capt. AUS, 1942-46. Fellow Am. Coll. Trial Lawyers; mem. Hutchinson C. of C. (pres. 1961), Kans. Assn. Def. Counsel (pres. 1972-73), Internat. Assn. Ins. Counsel. Republican. Home: 2607B Nottingham Dr Hutchinson KS 67501 Office: 330 W 1st St Hutchinson KS 67501

HAYES, JOHN FREEMAN, architect; b. Media, Pa., June 16, 1926; s. James Alfred and Katharine Stoddard (Williams) H.; m. Anne Gitt Fox, Apr. 5, 1952; children—John Fox, Thomas Freeman, Anne Clarke. Grad., Haverford Sch., 1944; B.Arch., U. Pa., 1950. With various cos., 1954-60; partner Hayes & Hough (Architects), Phila., 1960—. Served with USNR, 1944-46; Served with USAF, 1951-53. Fellow Am. Inst. Architects. Episcopalian. Clubs: Martins Dam, Phila. Curling. Office: 1218 Chestnut St Philadelphia PA 19107

HAYES, JOHN PATRICK, manufacturing company executive; b. Manistee, Mich., May 9, 1921; s. John David and Daisy (Davis) H.; m. Margaret Barbara Butler, Apr. 12, 1947; children—John Patrick, Timothy Michael. Student, U. Detroit, 1939-42, 46-47. With Nat. Gypsum Co., 1947—, group v.p., 1970-75, pres., 1975—, chmn. bd., chief exec. officer, 1983—, also dir.; dir. Republic Bank Dallas. Served to 1st lt. AUS, 1942-45. Clubs: Brookhollow Golf, Petroleum (Dallas). Office: 4100 1st Internat Bldg Dallas TX 75270

HAYES, JOSEPH, author; b. Indpls., Aug. 2, 1918; s. Harold J. and Pearl (Arnold) H.; m. Marrijane Johnston, Feb. 18, 1938; children—Gregory J., Jason H., Daniel D. Student, Ind. U., 1941, D.H.L., 1970. Asst. editor: Samuel French Plays, 1941-43; free-lance writer, 1943—; Co-producer-dir.: play The Happiest Millionaire, 1956; Author: Leaf and Bough, 1949; book, play, motion picture The Desperate Hours (Lit. Guild, Readers Digest book clubs) selection), 1954 (Antoinette Perry award 1954-55); play The Midnight Sun, 1959; novel The Hours After Midnight, 1959; play Calculated Risk, 1962; novel Don't Go Away Mad, 1963, The Third Day, 1964, The Deep End, 1967, Like Any Other Fugitive, 1971, The Long Dark Night, 1974, Island on Fire, 1979, Winner's Circle, 1980, No Escape, 1982; numerous screen plays.; Co-author (with wife) 18 pub. plays; also (novel) Bon Voyage, 1956; novel Missing and Presumed Dead, 1977; play Impolite Comedy, 1976; Contbr. short stories to nat. mags. Chmn. Sarasota (Fla.) Theatre Performing Arts, 1962—; Chmn. Sarasota chpt. ACLU, 1963—. Home: 1168 Westway Dr Sarasota FL 33577

HAYES, LARRY GENE, association executive; b. Batesville, Ind., Nov. 16, 1939; s. Faye E. and Edna Pearl (DeLay) H.; 1 dau., Kimberly Ann. B.A., Asbury Coll., 1965; postgrad., U. Ky., 1968. Tchr. Woodford County Jr. High Sch., Versailles, Ky., 1965-67; prin. Nonesuch Elem.-Jr. High Sch., Versailles, 1967-69; dir. Moser Sch., Chgo., 1969-74; dir. admissions Am. Inst. Real Estate Appraisers, Chgo., 1974-79, exec. v.p., 1979—. Mem. Am. Soc. Assn. Execs., Chgo. Soc. Assn. Execs., Execs. Club Chgo. Office: Am Inst Real Estate Appraisers 430 N Michigan Ave Chicago IL 60611

HAYES, MARK ALLAN, educator, surgeon; b. Bay City, Mich., Oct. 19, 1914; s. Howard Mark and Mildred Marian (Anderson) H.; m. Margaret Mary Rupff, June 23, 1948; 1 son, Mark Allan. A.B., U. Mich., 1937, M.D. cum laude, 1940, Ph.D., 1948, M.S., 1951; M.A. (hon.), Yale, 1961. Diplomate: Am. Bd. Surgery. Intern U. Mich. Hosp., 1940-41, asst. resident surgery, 1941-42, resident surgery, 1942-43, 48-49, demonstrator anatomy, 1942-43, Kellogg fellow anatomy, 1946-47; mem. faculty U. Mich. Med. Sch., 1947-52, asst. prof. sugery, 1951-52; mem. faculty Yale Med. Sch., 1952—, dir., 1952-54, asso. prof. surgery, 1952-61, prof. surgery, 1961-79, prof. emeritus, 1979—. Served to lt. comdr., M.C. USNR, 1942-46. Fellow A.C.S.; mem. Am. Surg. Assn., Am. Gastroenterol. Assn., Frederick A. Coller, New Eng. surg. socs., Soc. Univ. Surgeons, Soc. Surgery Alimentary Tract (a founder), Sigma Xi, Alpha Omega Alpha. Home: 163 Ridgewood Ave Hamden CT 06517

HAYES, MRS. PETER LIND *See* **HEALY, MARY**

HAYES, NATHANIEL PERKINSON, steel fabricator; b. Wise, N.C., Sept. 29, 1901; s. Malvern Hill and Olivia (Perkinson) H.; m. Louise Elizabeth Hull, Nov. 24, 1927; 1 son, Nathaniel Perkinson. A.B., U. N.C., 1921, B.S., 1922. Engr. McClintic-Marshall Co., Pitts., 1922-26; engr. Carolina Steel Corp., Greensboro, 1926-30, sales mgr., 1930—, dir., 1941-81, pres., 1951-67, chmn. bd., 1967-79, hon. chmn. bd., 1979—, ret., 1981; past dir., mem. exec. com. Home Fed. Savs. & Loan Assn.; dir. emeritus N.C. Nat. Bank, Pomona Corp.; Pres. Greensboro Industries, Inc., 1953, Greensboro Tb Assn., 1949; Dir. Am. Inst. Steel Constrn., Inc., 1946-69, 2d v.p., 1952, 1st v.p., 1954-56, pres., 1956-58; Pres. Bus. Found. of N.C., Inc., 1958-60. Former trustee Moses H. Cone Meml. Hosp., Inc.; trustee Oak Ridge Found., Inc. (Oak Ridge Mil. Inst.), 1965—, N.C. Found. Ch.-Related Colls., Bennett Coll., Greensboro; N.C. bd. visitors St. Andrews Presbyn. Coll., Campbell Coll., Guiford Coll.; bd. dirs. N.C. Engring. Found.; mem. adv. bd. U. N.C. Press, Chapel Hill, N.C. Recipient Disting. Alumnus award U. N.C., Chapel Hill, 1977; Disting. Citizen award Greensboro C. of C., 1978. Fellow Am. Soc. C.E.; mem. C. of C. (pres. 1951), N.A.M. (dir. 1969, v.p. So. div. 1972). Presbyterian (ruling elder). Clubs: Greensboro City (dir., exec. com.), Kiwanis.). Home: 2109 Lafayette Ave Greensboro NC 27408

HAYES, NEVIN WILLIAM, clergyman; b. Chgo., Feb. 17, 1922; s. James Timothy and Ella Mary (Williams) H. Ph.B., Mt. Carmel Coll., 1943; postgrad., Whitefriars Hall, Washington, 1943-47, Cath. U., 1944-50. Joined Carmelite Order, 1939; ordained priest Roman Catholic Ch., 1946; instr. Romance langs. Carmelite Sem., Hamilton, Mass., 1947-51; pastor, Lima, Peru, 1951-59, prelate nullius, Sicuani, Peru, 1959-70, bishop, Sicuani, 1965-70, aux. bishop, Chgo., 1971—; Episcopal vicar Hispanic Apostolate, Diocese of Chgo., 1979-83, vicar for sr. priests, 1983—; Episcopal vicar Western suburbs; Co-founder Instituto Pastoral Andino, Cuzco, Peru, 1969, bd. dirs., 1969-71; pres. Comité Episcopal de Religiosos, Lima, 1967-70, Comité Episcopal para Laicos, 1970-71; chmn. com. for ch. in Latin Am. Nat. Council Bishops, 1976-79. Home: 6949 W Addison Chicago IL 60634 Office: 155 E Superior St PO Box 1979 Chicago IL 60690

HAYES, PAUL GORDON, writer; b. Springfield, Ill., Aug. 24, 1934; s. Dale Arthur and Pauline Esther (Holcomb) H.; m. Philia Geotes, May 17, 1961; children—Nicholas Dale, John Edward. B.J., U. Ill., 1957. Copy editor, picture editor Des Moines Register, 1959-61; transp. reporter Milw. Jour., 1962-68, environ. reporter, 1969-77, sci. writer, 1978—. Author: (with Foell, Holden, MacDonald, Potter and Vansina) Resources and Decisions, 1975. Served with U.S. Army, 1957-59. Am. POlit. Sci. Assn. Congl. fellow, 1968-69; Leonardo scholar, 1973; recipient Westinghouse Sci. Writing award, 1977. Unitarian. Office: 333 W State St Milwaukee WI 53201

HAYES, PETER LIND, actor; b. San Francisco, June 25, 1915; s. Joseph Conrad and Grace Dolores (Hayes) L.; m. Mary Healy, Dec. 19, 1940; children: Peter Michael, Cathy Lind. Student parochial schs., Cairo, Ill. Author: Twenty-five Minutes from Broadway, 1961; Debut, Palace Theatre, N.Y.C., 1932; worked (with mother, Grace Hayes), 1932-42, (with wife, Mary Healy), 1946—; writer, producer, host: When Television Was Live, 1975; The 5000 Fingers of Dr. T; producer movies, from 1939; Movies Million Dollar Legs, All Women Have Secrets, These Glamour Girls, 1940, Seventeen, Dancing on a Dime, Playmates, Seven Days Leave; appeared: in TV series Star of the Family; Arthur Godfreys replacment on, CBS radio and TV; writer, producer: Columbia Discovers America; columnist: Valley Times. Served as tech. sgt. USAAF, 1942-46; PTO. Decorated 2 Battle and 1 Bronze Star. Roman Catholic. Club: Pelham Country. Home: 3538 Pueblo Way Las Vegas NV 89109

HAYES, RICHARD JOHNSON, association executive, lawyer; b. Chgo., May 25, 1933; s. David John Arthur and Lucille Margaret (Johnson) H.; m. Mary R. Lynch, Dec. 2, 1961; children: Susan, Richard, John, Edward. B.A., Colo. Coll., 1955; J.D., Georgetown U., 1961. Bar: Ill. 1961. Assoc. firm Barnabas F. Sears, Chgo., 1961-63, Peterson, Lowry, Rall, Barber and Ross, 1963-65; staff dir. Am. Bar Assn., Chgo., 1965-70; exec. dir. Internat. Assn. Ins. Counsel, Chgo., 1970—; instr. various legal programs, 1966—, Ins. Counsel Trial Acad., 1973—. Editor: Antitrust Law Jour, 1969—. Served to 1st lt. AUS, 1955-57. Mem. Am., Chgo. socs. assn. execs., ABA (chmn. prepaid legal services 1977-78), Ill. Bar Assn., Chgo. Bar Assn., Jr. Bar (chmn. 1965), Nat. Conf. Lawyers and Ins. Cos. (bd. dirs. 1983—), Phi Alpha Delta, Beta Theta Pi. Clubs: Rotary/One, Tower (Chgo.); Mich. Shores (Wilmette, Ill.). Home: 1920 Thornwood St Wilmette IL 60091 Office: 20 N Wacker Dr Chicago IL 60606

HAYES, ROBERT BRUCE, educator; b. Clarksburg, W.Va., Nov. 15, 1925; s. Bruce and Ruby (Hitt) H.; m. Ruth Harrison, July 19, 1947 (dec.); children: Steven, Ruthann, Mark; m. Kathleen Peters. Student, Fairmont (W.Va.) State Coll.; B.A., Asbury Coll., Wilmore, Ky., 1950; M. Ed., U. Kans., 1956, Ed. D., 1960. Tchr., prin. elem. and secondary schs., Kans., 1951-57; chmn. dept. edn. and psychology Asbury Coll., Wilmore, Ky., 1957-59; dir. tchr. edn. Taylor U., Upland, Ind., 1959-65; dean Coll. Edn. Marshall U., Huntington, W.Va., 1965-74, pres., 1974-83; prof. ednl. adminstrn. Coll. Edn., Marshall U., 1983—; mem. W.Va. Adv. Com. Tchr. Edn., 1965-74; dir. Twentieth St. Bank. Editor, contbr.: 1966 Yearbook of Assn. Student Teaching. Bd. dirs. Cabell-Wayne United Way, 1981; chmn. bd. Green Acres, 1983—; commr. Cabell County (W.Va.), 1983—. Served with USMCR, 1944-46. Recipient Green Acres award for contbn. to mentally retarded, 1972, Golden Knight award Nat. Mgmt. Assn., 1981. Mem. Huntington Area C. of C. (dir. 1974—), Phi Delta Kappa. Methodist. Club: Kiwanis. Home: 180 S Edgemont Rd Huntington WV 25701

HAYES, ROBERT EMMET, insurance company executive; b. Los Angeles, Nov. 21, 1920; s. Robert and Marion Verbeck (Weatherwax) H.; m. Alice McCarthy, June 26, 1943; children: Kathleen Byers, Joanne, Marianne Frank, Robert Emmet, Janet Gheer, Philip. A.B., Loyola U., Los Angeles, 1941. Group ins. rep. Aetna Life Ins. Co., N.Y., Conn., Calif., Oreg., 1941-46; co-pilot Matson Nav. Co., San Francisco, 1946-47; employee benefit cons. Cosgrove & Co., Los Angeles, 1947-57; v.p. Marsh & McLennan, Inc., Los Angeles, 1957-62, Equitable Life Assurance Soc., N.Y.C., 1962-67; sr. v.p., group nat. accounts Met. Life Ins. Co., N.Y.C., 1967—; Bd. dirs. Hwy. Users Fedn. Served with USN, 1941-45. Clubs: Calif. (Los Angeles); Union League (N.Y.C.); Stanwich (Greenwich, Conn.); Duquesne (Pitts.). Home: 73 Locust Hill Rd Darien CT 06820 Office: 1 Madison Ave New York NY 10010

HAYES, ROBERT MAYO, educator; b. N.Y.C., Dec. 3, 1926; s. Dudley Lyman and Myra Wilhelmina (Lane) H.; m. Alice Peters, Sept. 2, 1952; 1 son, Robert Dendrou. B.A., U. Calif. at Los Angeles, 1947, M.A., 1949, Ph.D., 1952. Mathematician Nat. Bur. Standards, Washington and Los Angeles, 1949-52; mem. tech. staff Hughes Aircraft Co., 1952-54; head applications group Nat. Cash Register Co., 1954-55; head bus. systems group Magnavox Co., 1955- 60; pres. Advanced Information Systems, Inc., Los Angeles, 1960-64; v.p., sci. dir. Electrada Corp., Los Angeles, 1960-64; lectr. dept. math. U. Calif. at Los Angeles, 1952-64, prof. library and info. sci., 1964—, dean, 1974—, dir., 1965-70; vis. lectr. Am. U., 1959, U. Wash., 1960-62; Windsor lectr. U. Ill., 1970; mem. adv. com. White House Conf. Library and Info. Services, 1979; v.p. Becker & Hayes, Inc., 1969-73. Co-author: Introduction to Information Storage and Retrieval: Tools, Elements, Theory, 1963, Handbook of Data Processing for Libraries, 2d edit, 1974, U.S. regional editor Problems in Information Storage and Retrieval, 1959-63; editor: Info. Scis. Series, 1963—; editorial bd.: Library Research, 1978—. Mem. A.L.A. (pres. information sci. and automation div. 1969), Am. Soc. Information Sci. (pres. 1962-63, nat. lectr. 1968), Am. Math. Soc., Assn. Computing Machinery (asso. editor jour. 1959-69, nat. lectr. 1969), Phi Beta Kappa, Sigma Xi. Home: 3943 Woodfield Dr Sherman Oaks CA 91403 Office: U Calif Westwood CA 90024

HAYES, SAMUEL PERKINS, social scientist, educator; b. South Hadley, Mass., Jan. 28, 1910; s. Samuel Perkins and Agnes Hayes (Stone) H.; m. Alice Mary Cable, Mar. 25, 1937; children—Susan, Jonathan. A.B., Amherst Coll., 1931, L.H.D., 1966; Ph.D., Yale, 1934; postgrad. (fellow Social Sci. Research Council), U. Chgo., 1937-38. Asst. psychology Yale U. Inst. Human Relations, 1931-34; instr. psychology Mt. Holyoke Coll., 1934-37; faculty dept. econs. Sarah Lawrence Coll., 1938-40; market research Young & Rubicam, Inc., N.Y.C., 1940-42; various positions U.S. govt. in, Washington, Algiers,

London, Scandinavia, 1942-45, 48-51; asso. dir. mktg. and research div. Dun & Bradstreet, Inc., N.Y.C., 1945-48; chief Spl. Tech. and Econ. Mission, Indonesia, 1951-52; asst. dir. Mut. Security Agy., Far East, 1952-53; dir. Found. for Research on Human Behavior, 1953-60; lectr. econs. U. Mich., 1955-57, prof. econs., 1959-62; dir. Center for Research on Econ. Devel., 1961-62; pres. Fgn. Policy Assn., 1962-74; now bd. dirs.; dir. N.Y. regional office Campaign for Yale, 1974-76; asso. Devel. Alternatives Inc., 1981—; cons. UNESCO, 1954-58, President's Task Force on Fgn. Econ. Assistance, 1961, Peace Corps, 1961-62, World Bank, 1976-82, U.S. AID, 1978—, U.S. Ho. of Reps. Com. on Agr., 1979-81; sr. specialist East-West Center, Honolulu, 1968; resident scholar Villa Serbelloni, Italy, 1971. Author: Measuring the Results of Development Projects, 1959, An International Peace Corps, 1961, Evaluating Development Projects, 1966, The Beginning of American Aid to Southeast Asia, 1971; Editor: (with others) Some Applications of Behavioral Research, 1957; Contbr. articles to profl. publs., also chpts. to books. Fellow AAAS; mem. Washington Inst. Fgn. Affairs, Soc. Internat. Devel., Am. Econ. Assn., Council Fgn. Relations, Amateur Chamber Music Players (treas.), Phi Beta Kappa, Sigma Xi, Chi Phi. Democrat. Clubs: Cosmos, St. Alban's Tennis. Home: 2122 California St NW Apt 652 Washington DC 20008 Office: 624 9th St NW Washington DC 20001

HAYES, SARAH HALL, mag. editor; b. Anderson, S.C., Dec. 3, 1934; d. Wilton Earle and Mary Elizabeth (Lightsey) Hall; m. John Haralson Hayes, Sept. 6, 1958; children—Heather Ruth, John Alexander, Megan Elizabeth. B.A., Agnes Scott Coll., 1956; postgrad., Candler Sch. Theology, Emory U., 1957, So. Baptist Sem., 1958, Princeton Sem., 1959-60. Instr. Trinity U., San Antonio, 1968-69; sr. book editor Droke House Publs., Anderson, S.C., 1968-69; asso. editor Quote mag., Anderson and Atlanta, 1971-73, editor, 1973—. Editor: The Quotable Lyndon Johnson, 1968. Democrat. Baptist. Address: 976 Swathmore Dr NW Atlanta GA 30327

HAYES, SUSAN SEAFORTH, actress; b. San Francisco; d. Harry Charles and Elizabeth (Harrower) Seabold; m. Bill Hayes, Oct. 12, 1974. A.A., Los Angeles City Coll., 1969. Appeared in theatre, film, radio and TV prodns., 1948—; appeared: in series General Hospital, ABC-TV, The Young Marrieds; appearing: Days of Our Lives, NBC-TV, 1968— (named Most Popular Actress, Daytime TV Mag. 1976, 77), NBC-TV (recipient Most Popular Daytime Actress award Photoplay Mag. 1977), NBC-TV (Emmy nominee 1975, 76). Mem. AFTRA, Actors Equity. Mem. Christian Ch. (Disciples of Christ). Address: care NBC Press Dept 30 Rockefeller Plaza New York NY 10020 *

HAYES, VERTIS CLEMON, painter, sculptor, educator; b. Atlanta, May 20, 1911; s. Lather Thomas and Willie Josie (Williams) H.; m. Florence Alexander, June 1, 1949; children—Vertis Clemon, Gregory William. Student, Nat. Acad. Design, 1934, Florence Kane Sch. Art, 1934, Art Students' League, 1943, Art Inst. Boston, 1971. Dir. LeMoyne Fed. Art Gallery, Memphis, 1938-39; tchr. LeMoyne Coll., 1939-50; founder, dir. Hayes Acad. Art, Memphis, 1947-52; product designer Sierra Columbia Inc., 1935-66. Mural painter, W.P.A., 1936-38; (Recipient Creative Communications award Art Inst. Boston 1971), one-man exhbns include, Rabouin Gallery, N.Y.C., Family Savs. & Loan, Los Angeles, Brentwood Gallery, Los Angeles, group exhbns. include, Artists Union, 1934, Harlem Artists Guild, 1937, Caz-Delbo, N.Y.C., Atlanta U., 1962-65, sculpture commns., Family Savs. and Loan Assn., Los Angeles, 1963, Harrison-Ross Mortuary, Los Angeles, 1971, 72, Home Savs. and Loan Assn., Los Angeles, 1965—. Carter Found. grantee, 1965. Fellow Black Acad. Arts and Letters (founder). Club: Mason (Shriner). Address: 5767 Bowcroft St Los Angeles CA 90016

HAYES, WALTER (LEOPOLD ARTHUR HAYES), automobile mfg. co. exec.; b. Eng., Apr. 12, 1924; s. Walter and Hilda H.; m. Elizabeth Holland, 1949; 3 children. Student Brit. schs. Editor Sunday Dispatch, 1956-59; asso. editor Daily Mail, 1959-65; dir. Ford of Britain, 1965-68; v.p. Ford of Europe Inc., 1968; dir. Ford Advanced Vehicles Ltd., 1963, Ford Switzerland, Ford Belgium and Ford Werke A.G., 1970-80; v.p. public affairs Ford Motor Co. U.S., Detroit, 1980—. Author: Angelica: A Story for Children, 1968, The Afternoon Cat and Other Poems, 1976. Clubs: Detroit; Marylebone Cricket, Royal Automobile (London). *

HAYES, WAYLAND JACKSON, JR., toxicologist, educator; b. Charlottesville, Va., Apr. 29, 1917; s. Wayland Jackson and Mary Lula (Turner) H.; m. Barnita Donkle, Feb. 1, 1942; children: Marie Hayes Sarneski, Maryetta Hayes Hacskaylo, Lula Hayes McCoy, Wayland, Roche del Hayes Moser. B.S., U. Va., 1938, M.D., 1946; M.A., U. Wis., 1940, Ph.D., 1942. Chief vector-transmission investigations USPHS, Savannah, Ga., 1947-48, chief toxicology sect., 1949-60, Atlanta, 1960-67, chief toxicologist, 1967-68; prof. biochemistry Vanderbilt U. Sch. Medicine, Nashville, 1968—; Vol. asso. prof. pharmacology Emory U., Atlanta, 1962-68; cons. WHO, 1950—, Nat. Acad. Scis.-NRC, 1964—. Author: Clinical Handbook on Economic Poisons, 1963, Toxicology of Pesticides, 1975, Pesticides Studied in Man, 1982; Mem. editorial bds.: Jour. Pharmacology and Exptl. Therapeutics, 1962-64, Archives Environmental Health, 1965-72, 76—, Food and Cosmetics Toxicology, 1967-78, Essays in Toxicology, 1972-76; Contbr. sci. papers to profl. lit. Served with AUS, 1943-46. Recipient Meritorious Service medal USPHS, 1964. Mem. Soc. Toxicology (charter, pres. 1971-72), Am. Soc. Pharmacology and Exptl. Therapeutics, Am. Soc. Tropical Medicine and Hygiene, Am. Conf. Govtl. Indsl. Hygienists. Home: 2317 Golf Club Ln Nashville TN 37215

HAYES, WEBB COOK, III, lawyer; b. Toledo, Ohio, Sept. 25, 1920; s. Webb Cook and Martha (Wilder) H.; m. Betty Frost, May 14, 1945; children: Webb Cook, Burke Frost, Stephen Austin, Jeffrey Kent. B.A., Yale U., 1942; LL.B., George Washington U., 1948. Bar: D.C. 1948, U.S. Ct. Claims 1951, U.S. Ct. Mil. Appeals 1951, U.S. Supreme Ct. 1951. Ptnr. Frost & Towers, Washington, 1948-73, Baker & Hostetler, 1973—; dir. Textron Inc., Providence, mem. exec., audit, nominating coms. Pres. trustee Rutherford B. Hayes Presdl. Ctr., Fremont Ohio, 1952—; trustee Washington Hosp. Ctr., Bethesda,Md., 1962-72, James Johnston Trust, 1970-78. Served to lt. USN, 1942-46. Mem. ABA, D.C. Bar Assn., Bar Assn. D.C., Barristers, Lawyers Club D.C. Republican. Clubs: Chevy Chase, Burning Tree, Met., Johns Island. Home: 4401 Boxwood Rd Bethesda MD 20816 Office: 818 Connecticut Ave NW Washington DC 20006

HAYES, WILLIAM ALOYSIUS, educator; b. Chgo., June 25, 1920; s. John and Stella (Ahern) H.; m. Joan Leahy, Aug. 22, 1953; children—Mary, Joseph, William, Anne, Patrick, Margaret, John, Teresa. A.B., DePaul U., 1942; M.A., Cath. U. Am., 1948, Ph.D., 1952. Instr. econs., asst. prof., asso. prof. DePaul U., Chgo., 1950-60, prof. econs., 1960—, chmn. dept., 1959-67. Exec. bd. Nat. Cath. Social Action Conf., pres., 1962; bd. dirs. Adult Edn. Centers, Chgo. Mem. Am. Econ. Assn., Cath. Econ. Assn. (exec. council, pres. 1968), AAUP, Blue Key, Beta Gamma Sigma, Pi Gamma Mu. Home: 10600 S Leavitt St Chicago IL 60643 *I try to be the type of person that I would like each one of my children to be as they develop into and through their adult years.*

HAYES, WILLIAM FOSTER (BILL HAYES), actor; b. Harvey, Ill., June 5, 1925; s. William Foster and Betty (Mitchell) H.; m. Mary L. Hobbs, Feb. 1, 1947 (div. Aug. 1969); children: Carolyn (Mrs. L. Dean Samuel), William, Catherine, Thomas, Margaret; m. Susan Seaforth, Oct. 12, 1974. B.A., DePauw U., 1947; M.Mus., Northwestern U., 1949. Appeared with, Olsen & Johnson, 1949, Your Show of Shows, 1950-53, Me and Juliet, 1953-54, The Ballad of Davy Crockett, 1955 (Gold Record), Oldsmobile shows, 1956-60, Bye-Bye Birdie, 1961-62, The Cardinal, 1963; club and theatre appearances, 1964-66, Sta. WFLD-TV, Chgo., 1967-69; star TV series: Days of Our Lives, 1970—; artist-in-residence, Millikin U., 1966. Served with USNR, 1943-45. Mem. Lambda Chi Alpha, Pi Kappa Lambda. Address: care International Creative Mgmt 40 W 57th St New York NY 10019 *

HAYES, WILLIAM NORMAN, brokerage firm executive; b. Charlotte, N.C., Oct. 3, 1929; s. Charles T. and Inez (Gregory) H.; m. Betty Walker, Mar. 30, 1950 (div. Apr. 1969); children: Terry Lee, T. Wesley, James Allen; m. Sherryl A. McNeil, Oct. 17, 1979; 1 son, William Scott. A.A., U. N.C.-Charlotte, 1951. Account exec. Goodbody & Co., Charlotte, 1950-61; br. mgr. Bache & Co., Charlotte, 1961-68; sr. v.p., regional dir., dir. Prudential-Bache Securities, Dallas, 1969—; mem. bus. research adv. council Dept. of Labor, Washington, 1977—. Clubs: Charlotte Exchange (pres. 1959 Man of Yr. 1959, dist. gov. 1960), Charlotte Athletic (pres. 1968). Office: Prudential Bache Securities Inc 3 North Park E Suite 100 Dallas TX 75231

HAYFLICK, LEONARD, microbiologist, gerontologist, educator; b. Phila., May 20, 1928; s. Nathan Albert and Edna (Wilbert) H.; m. Ruth Louise Heckler, Oct. 3, 1954; children: Joel, Deborah, Susan, Rachel, Anne. B.A., U. Pa., 1951, M.S., 1953, Ph.D., 1956. Research fellow U. Tex.-Galveston, 1956-58; assoc. mem. Wistar Inst., Phila., 1958-68; asst. prof. U. Pa., Phila., 1966-68; prof. microbiology Stanford U. Med. Sch., Calif., 1968-76; sr. research cell biologist Children's Hosp., Oakland, Calif., 1976-81; prof. zoology U. Fla., Gainesville, 1981—, dir. Ctr. for Gerontol. Studies, Coll. Liberal Arts and Scis., prof. immunology and med. microbiology dept. immunology and med. microbiology Sch. Medicine, prof. microbiology and cell sci. Inst. Food and Agrl. Scis., affiliate prof. Ctr. for Climacteric Studies Sch. Medicine; founding mem. Nat. Adv. Council on Aging, NIH, Bethesda, Md., 1975; exec. com. mem. Internat. Orgn. Gerontology, Jerusalem, 1972-75; mem. cell biology study sect. Am. Cancer Soc., N.Y.C., 1974-78; cons. Officer of Dir. Nat. Cancer Inst., Bethesda, 1963-74; vis. scientist Weizmann Inst. Sci., Ctr. for Aging, Rehovoth, Israel, 1980; lectr. in field. Editor: Biology of the Mycoplasmas, 1969, Handbook of the Biology of Aging, 1977; contbr. numerous articles on gerontology, cell biology and med. microbiology to profl. jours.; mem. ediotrial bd.: Exec. Health Report, 1970—; mem. editorial bd.: Mechanisms of Aging and Devel., 1972—, Gerontology and Geriatrics Edn., 1980—; bd. dirs., mem. editorial bd.: Bollettino Dell Instituto Sieroterapico Milanese, Archivo de Microbiologia ed Immunologia, Milan, Italy, 1968—. Rep. from Calif. White House Conf. on Aging, Washington, 1972, observer, Washington, 1981. Recipient Karl-Forster lectureship award Acad. Sci. and Lit., Mainz, Germany, 1983, Leadership award Am. Fedn. Aging Research, 1983, numerous other lectureships, Career Devel. award Nat. Cancer Inst., NIH, 1962-70. Fellow Gerontol Soc. Am. (program and awards com. 1972-77, com. on internat. relations 1980-82, pub. policy com. 1980-82, pres. 1982-83, ann. Robert W. Kleemeier award 1972, Brookdale award 1980); mem. Am. Soc. for Microbiology, AAAS, Tissue Culture Assn. (v.p. 1974-76, mem. council 1972-74, pres. Calif. chpt. 1971-73, trustee 1966-68, program com. 1970), Soc. for Exptl. Biology and Medicine, Assn. for Advancement of Aging Research (adv. council 1970-71), Am. Aging Assn., Am. Cancer Soc., Internat. Assn. of Microbiol. Standardization, Internat. Orgn. for Mycoplasmology, Western Gerontol. Soc. (council 1972-74, 81-83), Western Gerontol Soc. (program com. 1977-79), Western Gerontol. Soc. (bd. dirs. 1981-83), Am. Fedn. Aging Research (bd. dirs., sci. adv. bd., exec. com.), Fedn. Am. Socs. for Exptl. Biology, Aging Prevention Research Found. (sci. adv. bd. dirs.), Am. Assn. for Cancer Research, Am. Assn. Pathologists, Calif. Found. for Biomed. Research, Am. Longevity Assn. (sci. adv. bd. dirs. 1981—), Internat. Assn. Gerontology (exec. com. 1972-75). Office: U Fla 3357 GPA Gainesville FL 32611

HAYFORD, WARREN J., manufacturing company executive; b. 1929; married. B.S., U.S. Mil. Acad., 1952. With The Continental Group, Inc., 1955—, asst. to gen. mgr. sales metal ops., 1955-57, salesman Eastern Metal div., 1957-60, dist. sales mgr., 1960-63, gen. mgr. new container metal ops., 1963-66, gen. mgr. mktg. and product planning, 1966-67, gen. mgr. mktg., 1967-68, v.p. mktg., 1968-69, v.p. and gen. mgr. paperboard and Kraft Paper div., 1969-71, v.p. and gen. mgr. paper sales and converting ops., 1971-73, sr. v.p. and dir. corporate staff, 1973-74, chief fin. and adminstrv. officer, 1974-75, exec. v.p., 1974-81; pres. Continental Can Co., 1975-79; pres., chief operating officer Internat. Harvester Co., Chgo., 1979-82, Gen. Tire & Rubber Co., Akron, Ohio, 1982—, also dir.; dir. Burlington No. Corp. Served as 1st lt. U.S. Army, 1946-55. Office: Gen Tire and Rubber Co. One General St Akron OH 44329 *

HAYGREEN, JOHN GRANT, educator; b. Champaign, Ill., Oct. 10, 1930; s. Glenn Allen and Lucile Paula (Nicolet) H.; m. Elizabeth Jean Reager, June 21, 1952; children—James Grant, Mark William, Lisa Jean. B.S., Iowa State U., 1952; M.S., Mich. State U., 1958, Ph.D., 1961. With Long Bell Lumber Co., DeRidder, La., 1954, Frank Paxton Lumber Co., Kansas City, Mo., 1955-56; mem. faculty Mich. State U., 1956-61, Colo. State U., Ft. Collins, 1961-63, U. Minn., St. Paul, 1963—, prof. wood sci., 1965—, head forest products dept., 1970—; cons., partner Wood Sci. Service, 1963—. Author book on wood sci., also 60 articles. Served to 1st lt. AUS, 1952-54; Korea. Fellow Internat. Acad. Wood Sci.; mem. Soc. Wood Sci. and Tech. (pres. 1970), Forest Products Research Soc. (pres. 1977), Soc. Am. Foresters, ASTM. Patentee in field. Home: 2232 S Rosewood St Roseville MN 55113 Office: Forest Products Dept Univ Minn Saint Paul MN 55108

HAYHURST, JAMES FREDERICK PALMER, communications holding company executive; b. Toronto, Ont., Can., May 24, 1941; s. W. Palmer and Jean E. (Hunnisett) H.; m. Susan Ebbs, Oct. 17, 1964; children: Cindy, Jim, Barbara. H.B.A., U. Western Ont., 1963. Brand man Procter & Gamble, Toronto, 1963-66, exec. v.p., 1975-82; pres. Hedwyn Communications Inc., Toronto, 1983-84; chmn. Hayhurst Advt. Ltd., Toronto, 1984—. Clubs: Tornoto Golf; Badminton and Racquet (Toronto). Office: Hayhurst Advt Ltd 55 Eglinton Ave E Toronto ON Canada M4P 1G9

HAYMAN, HARRY, association executive, electrical engineer; b. Lewistown, Pa., Mar. 20, 1917; s. Sidney and Nettie (Hirsch) H.; m. Edith Harriet Levitz, Mar. 18, 1946; children: Gail A., Beth (Mrs. Malcolm Basil Miller), Sidney F., Stuart A. B.S., NYU, 1938; postgrad., George Washington U., 1947-50. Engr. FCC, Washington, 1940-54; pres., gen. mgr. radio sta. WPGC, Morningside, Md., 1954-55; project mgr. U.S. Navy and FAA, Washington, 1956-60; program mgr. NASA project Apollo, Washington, 1960-71; exec. sec. IEEE Computer Soc., N.Y.C., 1971-82, dir. confs. and tutorials, Silver Spring, Md., 1982—, chmn. Washington chpt., 1965. Vice pres. Nat. Childrens Center, 1960; pres. Henryton State Hosp. Assn., 1970, 74; bd. dirs. D.C. Assn. Retarded Children, 1956-70, pres. Washington chpt., 1953-55; pres. Gt. Oaks Aux., 1975-78. Served with USNR, 1944-46. Recipient Apollo Achievement award, 1969. Mem. IEEE (treas. computer soc. internat. conf. 1970, treas. internat. conf. on computer communications 1972, spl. asst. to chmn. conf. on computer communications 1974). Home: 738 Whitaker Terr Silver Spring MD 20901 Office: PO Box 639 Silver Spring MD 20901

HAYMAN, JAMES HENRY, advertising executive; b. N.Y.C., Nov. 2, 1940; s. Robert Theodore and Mary (Eaton) H.; m. Jeanne Mary O'Tolle, Mar. 21, 1970; children: Katherine Louise, Benjamin John. B.A., Brown U., 1963; postgrad., NYU, 1965. Copywriter Ted Bates, Inc., N.Y.C., 1966-68; v.p. Compton Advt., N.Y.C., 1968-75; sr. v.p. Young & Rubicam, Inc., N.Y.C., 1976—. Office: 285 Madison Ave New York NY 10017

HAYMAN, RICHARD WARREN JOSEPH, conductor; b. Cambridge, Mass., Mar. 27, 1920; x. Fred Albert and Gladys Marie (Learned) H.; m. Maryellen Daly, June 25, 1960; children: Suzanne Marie, Olivia Kathryn. D.Hum. (hon.), Detroit Coll. Bus., 1980. Free-lance composer, arranger 20th Century Fox, Warner Bros., MGM, Universal Film Studios; music arranger, dir. Vaughn Monroe Orch. records and TV show, N.Y.C., 1945-50; chief arranger Arthur Fiedler and Boston Pops Orchestra, 1950-80; mus. dir. Mercury Record Corp., N.Y.C., 1950-65, Time-Mainstream Records, 1960-70; prin. pops condr. Detroit Symphony Orchs., St. Louis, Birmingham (Ala.), Hartford (Conn.), Calgary (Can.). Composer: No String Attached, Skipping Along, Carriage Trade, Serenade to a Lost Love, Olivia, Suzanne, Freddie the Football. Recipient Best Instrumental Record award WERE, (Cleve.), 1963, Best TV Comm. Jingle award Nat. Acad. Rec. Arts and Scis., (N.Y.C.), 1960. Mem. Nat. Acad. Rec. Arts and Scis., ASCAP, Am. Fedn. Musicians. Roman Catholic. Home: 1020 Park Ave New York NY 10028 Office: Sheldon Soffer Mgmt 130 W 56th St New York NY 10019

HAYMAN, SEYMOUR, food company executive; b. N.Y.C., Sept. 24, 1914; s. Louis and Ettie (Friedman) H.; m. Dorothy Silverman, Aug. 7, 1951; children: Jonathan F., Valerie A. B.S., NYU, 1934. Officer Hayman & Lindenberg, Inc., 1934-40; v.p., dir. Dellwood Foods, Inc. (and predecessor cos.), Yonkers, N.Y., 1940-78, sr. v.p., dir., 1978-80, vice-chmn., 1980-82. Trustee Local 680 Internat. Brotherhood Teamsters Pension and Welfare Fund, 1961—, also locals 584 and 338, Milk Industry Office Employees Pension Fund, Joint Council 16 Welfare Fund.; treas., bd. dirs. Westchester Student Advocacy Coalition; Former pres., dir. Ft. Hill Civic Assn.; former v.p., dir. Greenville Community Council. Mem. Milk Industry Assn. N.J. (dir., past pres.), Tau Epsilon Phi. Home: 315 Evandale Rd Scarsdale NY 10583 Office: 177 Lake St White Plains NY 10604

HAYMES, HARMON HAYDEN, economist, educator; b. Lynchburg, Va., June 8, 1927; s. Joseph Albert and Reba (Hayden) H.; m. Beatrice Ann Mason, Nov. 26, 1952; children—Ann Elizabeth, William Hayden. B.A. magna cum laude, Lynchburg Coll., 1954; M.A., U. Va., 1956, Ph.D., 1959. Acting asst. prof. Lynchburg Coll., 1956-57; instr. U. Va., 1957-59; asst. prof. Smith Coll., 1959-61, Washington and Lee U., 1961-64; asst. v.p. Fed. Res. Bank of Richmond, 1964-68; prof. econs., 1968-77; chmn. dept. econs. Va. Commonwealth U., 1968-73, also acting dir.; prof. econs. St. Mary's Coll. Md., 1977—, provost, dean of faculty, 1978—; Mem. Gov.'s Adv. Com. for Urban Incentive Fund, 1970—, Gov.'s Revenue Resources and Econ. Study Commn., 1972-75. Editor: Va. Social Sci. Jour, 1970-73; asso. editor: Atlantic Econ. Jour, 1973—; Contbr. articles to profl. jours. Served with AUS, 1950-52. Recipient McKinsey award Bus. Horizons, 1962; duPont fellow, 1954; John Y. Mason fellow, 1955; Virginia Mason Davidge fellow, 1955. Mem. Am. Econ. Assn., So. Econ. Assn., Omicron Delta Epsilon. Home: PO Box 154 St Mary's City MD 20686

HAYMES, ROBERT C., physicist, educator; b. N.Y.C., July 3, 1931; s. Michael and Winifred (Koenig) H.; m. Jamie Buswell, Jan. 22, 1965; children—Douglas Fletcher, Lisa Melanie, Nancy Shannon. B.A., N.Y. U., 1952, M.S., 1953, Ph.D., 1959. Research asso. N.Y. U., 1955-59, asst. prof. physics, 1959-62; resident research fellow Jet Propulsion Lab., Calif. Inst. Tech., 1962-64; asst. prof. space sci. Rice U., Houston, 1964-66, asso. prof., 1966-71, prof. space physics and astronomy, 1972—, chmn. dept. space physics and astronomy, 1982—, Master Will Rice Coll., 1982—; cons. in field. Recipient sr. award Alexander von Humboldt Found., 1976. Mem. AAUP, Am. Geophys. Union, Internat. Astron. Union, Am. Astron. Soc., Sigma Xi, Sigma Pi Sigma. Research gamma-ray astronomy, cosmic rays, atmospheric electricity. Space scientist who calculated Gemini 7's time slowdown; 1st to detect nuclear gamma rays from sources beyond the sun. Home: Will Rice Master's House PO Box 3312 Houston TX 77253 *One of the purposes of life is to reduce ignorance; it is this that distinguishes humankind.*

HAYMON, MONTE ROY, packaging manufacturing company executive; b. Bklyn., Sept. 23, 1937; s. Jack and Ann H.; m. Jane Ellen Kraft, June 26, 1960; children: Karen, Debra, Jacqueline. B.S.Ch.E., Tufts U., 1959; postgrad., Am. Internat. Coll., 1960-61; grad. advanced mgmt. program, Harvard U., 1980. Process engr. Monsanto Co., Springfield, Mass., 1960-62; mktg. mgr., then dir. mktg. Tenneco Plastics, Piscataway, N.J., 1962-68; v.p. mktg. Rexene Polymers Co., Paramus, N.J., 1968-73, v.p. mfg., 1973-76; v.p., gen. mgr. Tenneco Chems., Inc., Piscataway, 1976-80, group v.p., 1980-81; pres., chief operating officer Packaging Corp. Am., Evanston, Ill., 1981-82, pres., chief exec. officer, 1982—; dir. Electric Audio Dynamics, Inc. Bd. dirs. Evanston Econ. Devel. Corp. Served with USAR, 1959-60. Mem. Soc. Chem. Engrs., Am. Chem. Soc., Am. Paper Inst. (bd. dirs.), Fourdrinier Kraft Bd. Group (bd. dirs.), Inst. Paper Chemistry (trustee). Club: Harvard. Office: Packaging Corp Am 1603 Orrington Ave Evanston IL 60204

HAYNE, DAVID MACKNESS, educator; b. Toronto, Ont., Can., Aug. 12, 1921; s. Herbert George and Elizabeth (Mackness) H.; m. Madge Hood Robertson, Dec. 20, 1955; children—Heather, Fred, Bruce. B.A., U. Toronto, 1942; M.A., U. Ottawa, Ont., 1944, Ph.D., 1945. Lectr. in French U. Toronto, 1945-50, asst. prof. French, 1950-56, asso. prof., 1956-61, prof., 1961—. Co-author: Bibliographie critique du roman canadien-français, 1968; contbr. numerous articles, revs. on French or Que. subjects to profl. publs.; editor: Papers of the Bibliographical Soc. of Can. Vols I-XI, 1962-72, Dictionary of Can. Biography Vol. 2, 1969. Recipient Centennial medal Govt. Can., 1967, Queen Elizabeth II Silver Jubilee medal, 1977. Fellow Royal Soc. Can.; mem. Assn. Can. Univ. Tchrs. French, Assn. Can. and Que. Lits., Bibliographical Soc. Can. (pres. 1978), Can. Comparative Lit. Assn. Anglican. Home: Rural Route 2 Claremont ON L0H 1E0 Canada Office: Univ Coll U Toronto ON M5S 1A1 Canada

HAYNES, ARDEN, oil company executive; b. Sask., Can. B.Commerce, U. Man., Winnipeg, 1951. With Imperial Oil Ltd., 1951-68, 72—, gen. mgr. mktg. dept., Toronto, 1973-74, sr. v.p., 1974-82, pres., 1982—; pres., chief exec. officer subs. Esso Resources Can. Ltd., Calgary, Ont., 1978-81, chmn. bd., chief exec. officer, 1981—, dir.; with Standard Oil Co. (N.J.), N.Y.C., 1968-72. Chmn. fund-rasing campaign Diabetes Can.; bd. dirs. Ont. Trillium Found. Office: Imperial Oil Ltd 111 Saint Clair Ave W Toronto ON Canada M5W 1K3

HAYNES, BOYD WITHERS, JR., surgeon; b. Brandenburg, Ky., July 5, 1917; s. Boyd Withers and Sallie Katherine (Allen) H.; m. Peggy Jane Harrison, May 21, 1955. A.B., U. Louisville, 1939, M.D., 1941. Diplomate: Am. Bd. Surgery. Intern Med. Coll. Va., Richmond, 1941-42, resident fellow in surgery, 1944-45, research surgeon, 1945-48, asso. in surgery, 1948-49, asst. prof., 1953-59, asso. prof., 1960-66, prof., 1966, prof., chmn. div. trauma surgery, 1972-82, attending surgeon in charge burn service and gen. surgery service, 1954; asso. in surgery Baylor U. Coll. Medicine, Houston, 1949-50, asst. prof., 1951-53; cons. gen. surgery McGuire VA Hosp., Richmond, Va., 1966—; Mem. Task Force Health Sers. Adminstrn. NIH, 1976; mem. Va. Gov.'s Com. Emergency Med. Sers., 1976-78. Asso. editor: Yearbook Plastic and Reconstructive Surgery, 1970—; Contbr. articles on shock, trauma and burns to profl. jours. Served as maj. M.C. AUS, 1953-55. Recipient Harvey Stuart Allen Disting. Ser. award Am. Burn Assn., 1979, commendation for contbn. to burn care Standards, 1977; cert. of recognition NASA, 1978; Disting. Service to Medicine award Med. Coll. Va., 1983. Fellow ACS (Va. pres. 1969-70, gov. 1971-77, chmn. subcom. functions and purposes 1975-77); mem. Am. Burn Assn. (pres. 1969-70, chmn. ad hoc com. care standards 1976-78, chmn. adhoc com. to trustees on membership 1981-82), Soc. Univ. Surgeons, Med. Soc. Va., Am. Assn. Surgery of Trauma, Internat. Soc. Burn Injury (U.S. rep. 1965-70), Am. Surg. Assn., So. Surg. Assn., Richmond Acad. Medicine, Surg. Biology Club, Va. Surg. Soc., Univ. Assn. Emergency Med. Sers. (regional dir. 1976-78), Surg. Infection Soc. (founder 1980), Société Internationale de Chirurgie, Halsted Soc., Alpha Omega Alpha. Home: 5105 Cary St Rd Richmond VA 23226 Office: Box 661 MCV Sta Med Coll Va Richmond VA 23298

HAYNES, BRUCE GRIFFITH, professional baseball executive; b. Washington, May 26, 1947; s. Joseph Walton and Thelma (Griffith) H.; m. Deborah Lee, Nov. 2, 1974; children: Joseph A., Andrew Lee. Grad., Ariz. State U. Profl. baseball player Minn. Twins, Mpls., 1971-75, v.p., 1976-78, exec. v.p., dir., 1979—. Office: Minnesota Twins Baseball Inc 801 Chicago Ave S Minneapolis MN 55415

HAYNES, DONALD, librarian; b. Fieldale, Va., Oct. 8, 1934; s. Thomas Bernard and Laura Jeannette (Richardson) H. B.A., U. Va., 1960; M.L.S., U. N.C., 1966. Tchr. Va. pub. schs., 1960-62; manuscripts and reference asst. U. Va. Library, Charlottesville, 1963-65; librarian, asst. prof. Eastern Shore br., U. Va., Wallops Island, 1966-69; dir. library services Va. State Library, Richmond, 1969-72, state librarian, 1972—. Editor: Virginiana in the Printed Book Collections of the Virginia State Library, 1975. Mem. Va. Historic Landmarks Commn., 1973—; chmn. Va. Hist. Records Adv. Bd., 1976—, Va. State Rev. Bd. for Landmarks, 1980—; Statewide coordinator Va. United Way, 1976; bd. dirs. Central Va. Ednl. TV, 1972—; mem. exec. bd. Edgar Allan Poe Found., 1982—. Served with AUS, 1954-56. Mem. Am., Southeastern, Va. library assns., Chief Officers Stat Library Agys., Soc. Am. Archivists, Beta Phi Mu. Home: 300 W Franklin St Richmond VA 23220 Office: Virginia State Library Richmond VA 23219

HAYNES, DOUGLAS MARTIN, physician, educator; b. N.Y.C., Jan. 25, 1922; s. Daniel Hagood and Courtenay (Collins) H.; m. Elizabeth B. Johnson, June 17, 1961; children: Douglas Marshall, Lewis Daniel. B.A., B.S., So. Meth. U., 1943; M.D., Southwestern Med. Coll., 1946. Diplomate: Am. Bd. Obstetrics and Gynecology (assoc. examiner). Intern in pathology Parkland Meml. Hosp., Dallas, 1946-47, resident obstetrics and gynecology, 1949-52; asst. prof. obstetrics and gynecology U. Tex. Southwestern Med Sch., 1952-55; asso. prof. obstetrics and gynecology U. Louisville Sch. Medicine, 1955-57, prof., 1957—, chmn. dept., 1957-69, interim dean, 1969-70, dean, 1970-72. Author: Medical Complications During Pregnancy, 1969; Contbr. articles to med. jours. Served to capt., M. C. AUS, 1947-49. Fellow AMA, Am. Gynec. and Obstet. Soc.; mem. Am. Coll. Obstetricians and Gynecologists, A.C.S., Central Assn. Obstetricians and Gynecologists (v.p. 1977-78), So. Med. Assn., Phi Beta Kappa, Phi Chi, Delta Chi, Alpha Omega Alpha, Phi Kappa Phi. Democrat. Presbyterian. Home: 5204 Tomahawk Rd Louisville KY 40207 Office: 550 S Jackson St Louisville KY 40292

HAYNES, EUGENE, JR., pianist, composer; b. East St. Louis, Ill.; s. Eugene and Claudia (Hampton) H. Undergrad. diploma, Juilliard Sch. Music, 1947, Postgrad. diploma, 1949; studied with, Nadia Boulanger, Paris, 1951-54, Isador Philipp, 1954, Isabella Vengeroua, N.Y.C., 1955. Prof. music Lincoln U., Jefferson City, Mo., 1973—; dir. Performing Arts Tng. Center, So. Ill. U., East St. Louis, 1980—; music dir. Radio Sta. KSCFM, Florissant, Mo., to 1982. Composer: String Quartet, 1951, Song Cycle, 1952, Fantasy for Piano and Orchestra, 1956, Symphony, 1960, Rhapsody on a Gospel Song, 1978; European concert tour for, USIS, 1956, Carnegie Hall debut, 1958, Carnegie concerts, 1962, 69, 71, European concert tour, 1964, South Am. tour, 1959, incidental music for, Riddersalen Teater, Copenhagen, 1954; host: Wonderful World of Music with Eugene Haynes, KSD Radio, St. Louis, 1965-73. Moton fellow Moton Center for Ind. Studies, Phila., 1976-77, 77-78; Recipient Maurice Loeb prize for overall excellence in grad. studies Juilliard, 1949; honored by Nat. Assn. Negro Musicians, San Francisco, 1974. Mem. A.F.T.R.A., Am. Fedn. Musicians, Am. Music Center for Composers. Home: 710 Lafayette St Jefferson City MO 65101

HAYNES, GARY ALLEN, journalist; b. Beloit, Kans., Jan. 25, 1936; s. Blair W. and Evelyn H. (Allen) H.; m. Paulette Riley, Nov. 9, 1968; children by previous marriage—Stephanie L., Philip. B.S. in Journalism, Kans. State U., Manhattan, 1957. Picture bur. mgr. UPI, Detroit, Phila., 1959-62, Atlanta, 1962-64, photographer, N.Y.C., 1965, picture bur. mgr., Los Angeles, 1965-68, div. newspictures mgr., 1968-70, asst. to mng. editor newspictures, N.Y.C., 1970-71; asst. picture editor N.Y. Times, N.Y.C., 1971-74; photo editor San Francisco Examiner, 1974; graphic arts dir. Phila. Inquirer, from 1974, now asst. mng. editor. Picture editor: Assignment America, 1972. Served to capt. Adj. Gen. Corps U.S. Army, 1957-58. Recipient 1st pl. award Look Mag. Sports Photo Contest, 1962; 1st and 3d pl. awards Gen. News Pictures of Yr. Competition, 1969. Mem. Nat. Press Photographer's Assn. Home: 234 Pine St Philadelphia PA 19106 Office: 400 N Broad St Philadelphia PA 19101

HAYNES, HAROLD WALTER, aircraft manufacturer; b. Snoqualmie, Wash., Jan. 23, 1923; s. Ralph and Bertha (Sewell) H.; m. Barbara J. Tatham, Oct. 11, 1943; children—Christine, Steven, Kevin. B.A., U. Wash., 1948. C.P.A., Wash. With Touche, Ross, Bailey & Smart (C.P.A.'s), Seattle, 1948-54, Boeing Co., 1954—, v.p. finance, 1960-70, sr. v.p. finance, 1970-75, exec. v.p., chief finance officer, 1975—, also dir.; dir. First Interstate Bank of Wash., Safeco, Itel Corp. Served as pilot USMCR, 1942-45. Mem. Financial Execs. Inst. Home: Highlands Seattle WA 98177 Office: PO Box 3707 10-14 Seattle WA 98124

HAYNES, HILDA MOCILE LASHLEY, actress; b. N.Y.C.; d. Charles C. and Leonora (Alkins) Lashley; (dec. Jan. 24, 1984); 1 son, Christopher C. Diploma, Braithwaite Bus. Sch., 1934; postgrad., Am. Negro Theatre, 1941, Am. Theatre Wing, 1950, Am. Shakespeare Festival Acad., 1959. Appearances on Broadway include Deep Are the Roots, 1946, Anna Lucasta, 1947, A Streetcar Named Desire, 1948, King of Hearts, 1954, Wisteria Trees, 1954, Lost in the Stars, 1956, The Long Dream, 1959, The Irregular Verb To Love, 1963, Blues for Mr. Charlie, 1964, The Great White Hope, 1968; appeared in off-Broadway prodns., summer stock; Blues for Mr. Charlie, World Theatre Festival, London, 1965, The Great White Hope, Washington, 1967, Golden Boy, Chgo., 1968, London, Seattle Repertory Theatre, 1971, Mourning in a Funny Hat; summer stock tour, 1972, Wedding Band, N.Y.C., 1972, The River Niger; nat. tour, 1973; numerous appearances on TV, including: The Rookies, Gimme a Break, Trapper John, M.D., Dynasty, Miracle Worker, Executive Suite, Sanford & Son, Starsky & Hutch, The Jeffersons, Good Times; lead on: on TV, including Frontiers of Faith episode Light in the Southern Sky, 1958; appeared in: motion pictures including Purlie Victorious; co-star, 1963, Home from the Hill, Keywitness, Taxie, A Face in the Crowd, Stage Struck, The Pawnbroker, Across 110th St, Diary of a Mad Housewife, River Niger, Let's Do It Again. Supr. Title II cultural enrichment program, Virgin Islands, 1966. Mem. NAACP, Negro Actors Guild, Actors Equity Assn. (councillor), Screen Actors Guild, AFTRA. Mem. Ch. Religious Sci. *In spite of a lifetime of discrimination, I believe that I have an active faith in God and myself. I believe with courage and perserverance I can succeed. I have a sense of humor and a positive and creative outlook on life. I believe life is to be lived fully, victoriously, joyously. I am a survivor and shall continue to thank God for life and exciting days!*

HAYNES, JAMES EARL, JR., association executive; b. Bakersfield, Calif., Oct. 11, 1943; s. James E. and Ruth M. (Campbell) H.; m. Norma Beth Jordan, Feb. 10, 1978; 1 son, Andrew Jordan. B.A. in Journalism, Los Angeles State Coll., 1967. Asst. mgr. West Covina C. of C., Calif., 1966-68; mgr. Monterey Park C. of C., Calif., 1968-72; gen. mgr. ops. San Francisco C. of C., 1972-76; exec. v.p. Phoenix C. of C., 1976—; mem. bd. regents Insts. for Orgn. Mgmt. U.S. C. of C. Mem. Am. C. of C. Execs., Ariz. C. of C. Mgrs. Assn. Office: Phoenix C of C 34 W Monroe St Phoenix AZ 85003

HAYNES, JOHN JACKSON, civil engr., educator; b. Dallas, Sept. 13, 1925; s. Frank Hooker and Annie Laurie (Richardson) H.; m. Louise Elizabeth Vaughn, June 5, 1948. B.S. in Civil Engring, Tex. Tech. Coll., 1949; M.S., Tex. A. and M. U., 1959, Ph.D., 1964. Registered profl. engr., Tex. Asst. resident engr. Tex. Hwy. Dept., 1949-51; city engr., Arlington, Tex., 1952; design engr. tex. Hwy. Dept., 1953- 55; asso. prof. Arlington State Coll., 1955-58; prof. civil engr., chmn. dept. U. Tex. at Arlington, 1959-72, dir. pub. transp. center, 1972-77, prof., 1977—. Chmn. regional codes com. N. Central Tex. Council Govts., 1967-70. Served with USNR, 1943-46. Mem. ASCE (pres. Tex. sect. 1979-80), Am. Soc. Engring. Edn., Inst. Transp. Engrs., Nat. Soc. Profl. Engrs., Tex. Soc. Profl. Engrs. (chpt. Engr. of Yr. 1980), Sigma Xi, Tau Beta Pi, Chi Epsilon. Home: 1200 Windmill Ct Arlington TX 76013

HAYNES, JOHN MABIN, utilities executive; b. Albany, N.Y., Apr. 22, 1928; s. John Mabin and Gladys Elizabeth (Phillips) H.; m. Marion Enola Hamilton, Apr. 7, 1956; children: John David, Douglas Hamilton, Robert Paul. B.S., Utica Coll., Syracuse U., 1952. Accountant Price Waterhouse & Co., N.Y.C., Syracuse, N.Y., 1953-61; successively auditor, adminstrv. asst., asst. treas., treas., treas. and v.p., sr. v.p. Niagara Mohawk Power Corp., Syracuse, 1961—; dir. N.Y. Bus. Devel. Corp.; dir., treas. N M Uranium, Inc., Canadian Niagara Power Co. Ltd.; past treas. Moreau Mfg. Co., St. Lawrence Power Co.; treas. Empire State Power Resources, Inc.; past dir. and treas. Beebee Island Corp.; dir., v.p., treas. Caagh Investments, Ltd.; dir., treas. Opinac Investments Ltd.; dir., v.p. Opinac Energy Ltd.; mng. dir. Niagara Mohawk Fin. N.V. Mem. Westhill Central Sch. Bd. Edn., 1968-73, pres., 1969-71; dir., 1st v.p. N.Y. Bus. Devel. Corp. Served with AUS, 1945-47. Mem. Nat. Assn. Accountants (past dir.), Fin. Execs. Inst., Am. Gas Assn. (fin. com.), Fin. Execs. Inst. Clubs: Bond of Syracuse (dir.), Masons). Home: 100 Lathrop Rd Syracuse NY 13219 Office: 300 Erie Blvd W Syracuse NY 13202

HAYNES, JUDITH WALTON, editor; b. New Haven, Nov. 21, 1942; d. Charles Guthrie and Jessie Irene (Smith) H. B.A. in Journalism, Kent State U., 1973. With The Plain Dealer, Cleve., 1973-78, 79-82, asst. city editor, 1977-78, editor mag., 1979-82; editor Va. mag., Virginian-Pilot, Ledger-Star, 1982—; asst. news editor San Diego Union, 1978-79. Recipient Clarion award Women in Communications Inc., 1977. Mem. Sigma Delta Chi. Home: 409 Botetourt Norfolk VA 23510 Office: 150 W Brambleton Norfolk VA 23510

HAYNES, KENNETH GEORGE, former naval officer, business executive; b. McKinney, Tex., Nov. 30, 1925; s. Fletcher Johnson and Vyola Mae (Young) H.; m. Margaret Jane Conroy, Aug. 8, 1948; children: Kenneth George, Melinda, Christopher. B.S., U. Tex., 1947; postgrad., Naval Postgrad. Sch., 1951, Naval War Coll., 1962; M.A., George Washington U., 1964. Commd. ensign U.S. Navy, 1947, advanced through grades to rear adm., 1974; comdg. officer in U.S.S. Edson, 1964, U.S.S. Preble, 1966, U.S.S. R.K. Turner, 1970, U.S.S. Providence, 1971; head modern langs. dept. U.S. Naval Acad., Annapolis, Md., 1967-68; mem. staff chief naval ops. Navy Dept., Washington, 1972-74; dep. dir. ops. Def. Communications Agy., Washington, 1974-76; dir. naval communications, 1976; joint staff Orgn. Joint Chiefs Staff, 1976-78, ret., 1978; supt. Tex. Maritime Acad., 1978-79, dean, 1978-82, also prof. marine transp.; v.p. ops. Am. Satellite Co., Rockville, Md., 1982—. Decorated Legion of Merit, Bronze Star, Meritorious Service medal, Def. Superior Service medal. Mem. Armed Forces Communications-Electronics Assn., Navy League (life). Methodist (past chmn. bd.). Lodge: Rotary. Home: 15759 Buenavista Dr Derwood MD 20855 Office: Am Satellite Co Rockville MD 20850

HAYNES, LEONARD L., philosophy educator, clergyman; b. Austin, Tex., Mar. 13, 1923; s. Leonard L. and Thelma Z. (Watkins) H.; m. Leila Louise Davenport, Nov. 28, 1947; children: Leonard L., Walter Lafayette, Angeline Thelma, Leila Anne. A.B., Houston Tilliston Coll., 1942; M.Div., Interdenominational Theol. Center, 1945; Th.D., Boston U. Sch. Theology, 1948; postgrad., Yale U., 1964. Dean of students Philander Smith Coll., 1948; dir. humanities Ark. A & M U., Pine Bluff, 1952-54; dean of instrn. Claflin Coll., Orangeburg, S.C., 1954; pres. Morris Jr. Coll., Morristown, Tenn., 1957-59; prof. Wiley Coll., Marshall, Tex., 1960-61; ordained to ministry Meth Ch., 1948; pastor Wesley United Meth. Ch., Baton Rouge, 1961—; prof. philosophy So. U., Baton Rouge, 1963—, co-dir., 1978-79, dir. student internship program, 1980-81; exec. dir. Opportunities Industrialization Center, Baton Rouge, 1980—. Author: The Negro Community Within American Protestantism 1619-1844, 1952, The Religion of Struggle and Survival, 1972; contbr. articles to profl. jours. Bd. discipleship La. Conf., United Meth. Ch., 1972-76; Pres. Commn. on Civil Rights, 1981—; bd. dirs. Community Assn. for Welfare of Sch. Children, 1980—, Region VI, Republican Party, 1981—; gov.'s appointee La. Engrs. Selection Bd., 1983; mem. various religious coms. United Meth. Crusade scholar, 1945. Mem. Am. Acad. Religion, Am. Acad. Liturgical Scholars, AAUP, Omega Psi Phi, Alpha Kappa Mu. Republican. Methodist. Club: Masons (33 deg.). Address: 1798 77th St Baton Rouge LA 70821

HAYNES, MICHAEL JAMES HEFLIN, professional football player; b. Dennison, Tex., July 1, 1953; s. Hutson James and Barbara Helen (Belt) Heflin; m. Julie Ann Imdieke; children: Aaron James, Jared Daniel. B.S., Ariz. State U., 1981. Defensive back New Eng. Patriots, 1976—. Named Defensive Rookie of Yr. Nat. Football League, 1976; named Am. Football Conf. All-pro, 1976, 77, 78, 79, 80, 82. Mem. Nat. Football League Players Assn. Nat. coll. leader in number of interceptions, 1974. Home: 10 Lantern Ln Norfolk MA 02056 Office: care New England Patriots Schaefer Stadium Foxboro MA 02035

HAYNES, MOSES ALFRED, physician; b. Guyana, Nov. 11, 1921; came to U.S., 1947, naturalized, 1955; s. Milton Alphonso and Charlotte Mildred (Alleyne) H.; m. Hazel Louise Edgecombe, July 1, 1951; 1 dau., Theresa Sue (Mrs. Larry Watkins). B.S., Columbia, 1951; M.D., State U. N.Y., 1954; M.P.H., Harvard, 1963. Intern St. John's Episcopal Hosp., Bklyn., 1954-55; physician USPHS Indian Hosp., Cheyenne Agy., S.D., 1955-59; asst. prof. community medicine U. Vt., 1959-64; asso. prof. Sch. Pub. Health, Johns Hopkins, 1966-69; prof. preventive and social medicine and pub. health U. Calif. at Los Angeles, 1969-77; asso. dean Drew Postgrad. Med. Sch., Los Angeles, 1969-77, chmn. dept. community medicine, 1969-74, acting dean, 1975-76, dean, 1977—; pres. SECON Inc., 1977-79; vis. prof. Med. Coll., Trivandrum, Kerala, India, 1964-66. Chmn. health task force Urban Coalition, 1968-69; mem. Pres.'s Com. Health Edn., 1972; exec. dir. Nat. Med. Assn. Found., 1968-69; mem. adv. com. Nat. Center Health Statistics, 1974-76. Served with USPHS, 1955-59. Fellow Am. Coll. Preventive Medicine, Am. Pub. Health Assn.; mem. Inst. Medicine of Nat. Acad. Sci., AAAS, Alpha Omega Alpha. Home: 4964 Delacroix Rd Rancho Palos Verdes CA 90274 Office: 1621 E 120 St Los Angeles CA 90059 *Being is more important than doing.*

HAYNES, NORMAN RAY, aerospace engr.; b. Kalamazoo, June 14, 1936; s. George Hudson and Kathryn Lucille (DeVlieg) H.; m. Susan Caroline Howes, Aug. 23, 1958; children—Kristine, Julie, David, Carolyn. B.S. in Aerospace Engring, Purdue U., 1959, M.S., U. So. Calif., 1961. Engr. jet propulsion lab. Calif. Inst. Tech., Pasadena, 1959-68; mgr. mission analysis and engring. Mariner 9 project, 1968-73, mgr. sect. mission design, 1973-76, mgr. space program devel., 1976-78; mgr. sci. and mission design Project Galileo, 1978-80, mgr. systems div., 1980—. Recipient Distinguished Service medal NASA. Republican. Presbyterian. Home: 1220 Tropical Ave Pasadena CA 91107 Office: 4800 Oak Grove Dr Pasadena CA 91130

HAYNES, R. MICHAEL, lawyer; b. Safford, Ariz., Oct. 3, 1940; s. Rodman Mulvehill and Angeline Edna H.; m. Anne Marie de Almeida, Aug. 15, 1972; 1 dau., Michelle Chloe. B.A., Rutgers U., 1963, J.D. with honors, 1968. Bar: N.Y. bar 1969, N.J. bar 1977, U.S. Supreme ct. bar 1973. Asso. firm Cooper, Ostrin, DeVargo & Ackerman, N.Y.C., 1968-69; asst. dist. atty., dep. chief rackets bur. N.Y. County Dist. Atty.'s Office, N.Y.C., 1969-74; exec. asst. dist. atty. spl. narcotics Prosecutor's Office, N.Y.C., 1974-76; asst. U.S. atty. Dist. N.J., Newark, 1976-79; minority counsel Com. on Small Bus., U.S. Senate, Washington, 1979-81, chief counsel, 1981—; adj. prof. L.I. U., 1975-76; instr. N.Y. State Commn. Investigation, 1974-75, Atty. Gen.'s Adv. Inst., Dept. Justice, 1978-79; counsel White House Conf. on Small Bus., 1980. Recipient Atty. Gen.'s Spl. Achievement award, 1977. Republican. Home: 6898 Deer Run Dr Alexandria VA 22306 Office: 428A Russell Senate Office Bldg Washington DC 20510 *The law holds everyone equally accountable, but imposes upon the lawyer a higher duty both to honor the principles that the law prescribes and to serve the people whom it governs. To that end, the lawyer must ensure that the law itself remains just and fair and that those who make, administer and enforce the law do so with integrity and conviction.*

HAYNES, ROBERT VAUGHN, historian, university administrator; b. Nashville, Nov. 28, 1929; m. Martha Farr, Dec. 25, 1952; children: Catherine Anne, Carolyn Alice, Charles Allen. B.A., Millsaps Coll., 1952; M.A., Peabody Coll., 1953; Ph.D., Rice U., 1959. Mem. faculty U. Houston, 1956-84, prof. history, 1967-84, acting dir. Afro-Am. studies, 1969-71, interim dir. libraries, 1976-78; dir. libraries U. Houston central campus, 1978-80, assoc. provost, 1980-81, dep. provost, 1981-84; v.p. acad. affairs Western Ky. U., Bowling Green, 1984—; vis. prof., Black studies cons. U. Ala., 1970; dir. Inst. Cultural Understanding, 1971; mem. adv. planning com. Tex. Conf. on Library and Info. Services, 1978-79. Author: A Night of Violence: The Houston Riot of 1917, 1976, The Natchez District and the American Revolution, 1976; editor: The Houston Rev., 1981-84; Contbr. articles to profl. jours. Mem. Houston United Campus Christian Life com., 1973—; chmn. ch. and soc. com. Synod of Tex., Presbyn. Ch. U.S.A., 1970-73; treas. Houston Com. on the Humanities, 1978-79. Served with USAF, 1950-51. Danforth asso., 1969; Carnegie fellow, 1952-53; Nat. Endowment Humanities fellow, 1973. Mem. Am. Hist. Assn., Orgn. Am. Historians, ALA, So. Hist. Assn., Am. Studies Assn., Miss. Hist. Soc., Tex. Hist. Assn., Inst. Early Am. History and Culture, Tex. Library Assn., Phi Kappa Phi (past chpt. pres.), Tex. Assn. Coll. Tchrs. (past chpt. pres.). Democrat. Office: Office of VP Acad Affairs Western Ky U Bowling Green KY 42101

HAYNES, SHERWOOD KIMBALL, educator; b. Boston, Apr. 7, 1910; s. John and Jessie M. (Bailey) H.; m. Pauline J. McBride, 1943; children—Charles M., Margaret E., Sherwood K. II, J. Marie. A.B., Williams Coll., 1932; Ph.D., Calif. Inst. Tech., 1936. Instr. Williams Coll., 1936-39; asst. prof. Brown U., 1940-42; instr. elec. communications Radar Sch., Mass. Inst. Tech., 1942-44, asst. dir., 1944-45; asso. prof. Vanderbilt U., 1945-51, prof., 1951-58; head dept. physics and astronomy Mich. State U., 1957-66, chmn. dept. physics, 1966-69, prof. physics, 1969-80, prof. emeritus, 1980—; vis. scientist Am. Inst. Physics, 1963-72, mem. placement service adv. com., 1970-73, mem. manpower adv. com., 1973-79, bd. govs., 1974-77; Cons.-examiner North Central Assn. Colls. and Secondary Schs., 1964—; vis. physicist IKO, Amsterdam, 1965; cons. Fulbright selection com., 1955, Midwest planning com., 1959. French sci. fellow Inst. Internat. Edn., 1939-40; Fulbright lectr., Paris, France, 1954-55; Recipient Disting. faculty award Mich. State U., 1977. Am. Phys. Soc. (v.p. Southeastern sect. 1953-54), AAAS; mem. Am. Assn. Physics Tchrs. (v.p. 1972, pres. 1974). Home: 2821 E Mt Hope Rd Okemos MI 48864 Office: Michigan State U East Lansing MI 48824

HAYNES, THOMAS MORRIS, philosophy educator; b. Waukesha, Wis., Oct. 24, 1918; s. George Albert and Lois (Morris) H.; m. Jane Louise Riggs, Sept. 12, 1942; children: Christopher Thomas, Jonathan Marshall, Carolyn Martha. A.B., Butler U., 1941; Ph.D., U. Ill., 1949. Indsl. engr. RCA, Indpls., 1942-44; research and devel. engr. P.R. Mallory, Indpls., 1944-46; postdoctoral fellow Faculty Law U. Paris, Indpls., 1949-50; instr. philosophy U. Ill., 1950-51, research asst., 1950-51; instr. philosophy Lehigh U., 1952-54, asst. prof., 1954-61, asso. prof., 1961-69, prof., 1969—. Mem. Am. Philos. Assn., AAUP, Phi Beta Kappa. Home: 640 High St Bethlehem PA 18018 Office: Dept Philosophy Lehigh U Bethlehem PA 18015

HAYNES, ULRIC ST. CLAIR, JR., business executive; b. Bklyn., June 8, 1931; s. Ulric St. Clair and Ellaline (Gay) H.; m. Yolande Toussaint, Sept. 20, 1969; children: Alexandra, Gregory. B.A., Amherst Coll., 1952; LL.B., Yale U., 1956; LL.B. (hon.), Ind. U., 1981, John Jay Coll., 1981, Fisk U., 1982, Ala. State Coll., 1982. Exec. asst. N.Y. State Dept. Commerce, Albany, 1956-57; adminstrv. officer UN European Office, Geneva, 1959-60; asst. to rep. Ford Found., Lagos, Nigeria, Tunis, Tunisia, 1960-63; asst. officer in charge Moroccan affairs Dept. State, Washington, 1963, officer in charge, 1963-64; mem. NSC staff White House, 1965-66; pres. Mgmt. Formation Inc., N.Y.C., 1966-70; sr. v.p. Spencer Stuart and Assocs. Mgmt. Consultants, N.Y.C., 1970-72; v.p. for mgmt. devel. Cummins Engine Co.,

Columbus, Ind., 1972-74, v.p. for, Mid East and Africa, 1974-77; ambassador to Algeria, Am. Embassy, Algiers, 1977-81; v.p. internat. bus. planning Cummins Engine Co., 1981-83; dir. Marine Midland Banks; cons., 1984—. Contbr. articles to profl. publs. Bd. dirs. Inst. Study of Diplomacy, Pratt Inst.; bd. govs. UN Assn. USA. Root-Tilden scholar; John Hay Whitney scholar. Mem. Council Fgn. Relations., Assn. Black Am. Ambassadors, Council Am. Ambassadors. Democrat. Episcopalian. Club: Yale (N.Y.C.). Home: 361 S Sussex Pl Columbus IN 47201

HAYNIE, HOWARD EDWARD, lawyer; b. Chgo., May 30, 1928; s. Howard Edward and Jean Potter (Faller) H.; m. Charlotte Ruth Monson, Sept. 25, 1954; children: Roy, Robin, Guy. B.S.B.A. with highest distinction, Northwestern U., 1951; J.D. cum laude, Loyola U., Chgo., 1959-69. Bar: Ill. 1959. Loan supr. Northwestern Mut. Life Ins. Co., Chgo., 1954-59; assoc. Sidley & Austin, Chgo., 1959-69, ptnr., 1969—. Bd. dirs. Chgo. Assn. Retarded Citizens, 1970—, Wilmette Camp Property, Inc., 1970—, Wilmette Forum; mem. Wilmette Zoning Bd., 1970-80; chmn. Willmett Zoning Bd., 1975-80; bd. dirs. New Trier Twp. Citizens League, 1980—. Served to 1st lt. USMCR, 1951-54. Mem. Law Club Chgo., Legal Club Chgo., Phi Alpha Delta, Beta Gamma Sigma, Sigma Chi. Republican. Clubs: Union League (Chgo.); Sheridan Shore Yacht, Westmoreland (Wilmette). Lodges: Masons; Shriners. Home: 2347 Pomona Ln Wilmette IL 60091 Office: Sidley & Austin One 1st National Plaza Chicago IL 60603

HAYNIE, HUGH, editorial cartoonist; b. Reedville, Va., Feb. 6, 1927; s. Raymond Lee and Margaret Virginia (Smith) H.; m. Oleta Joanne Stevens; children: Hugh Smith, Tiffany Dawn. A.B., Coll. William and Mary, 1950; L.H.D., U. Louisville, 1968. Cartoonist Richmond (Va.) Times-Dispatch, 1950-53; Cartoonist, Greensboro (N.C.) Daily News, 1953-55, 56-58, Atlanta Jour., 1955-56; with Louisville Courier Jour., 1958—, now editorial cartoonist. Author: Hugh Haynie: Perspective, 1974. Served to lt. USCGR, 1944-46, 51-52; PTO. Recipient Headliner award, 1966; Freedoms Found. award, 1966-70; Disting. Service award and bronze medallion Sigma Delta Chi, 1971; Alumni medal for service and loyalty Coll. William and Mary, 1977; Civil Libertarian of Yr. award Ky. Civil Liberties Union, 1978. Mem. Soc. Alumni Coll. William and Mary (past dir.), Phi Beta Kappa, Omicron Delta Kappa, Pi Kappa Alpha. Democrat. Episcopalian. Clubs: Windmill Point (Weems, Va.); Yacht (Windmill Point, Va.); Filson (life mem.). Home: Prospect Farms Rose Island Rd Prospect KY Office: Courier-Jour 525 W Broadway Louisville KY 40202

HAYNIE, THOMAS POWELL, III, physician; b. Hearne, Tex., Aug. 9, 1932; s. Thomas Powell, Jr. and Sue Cummings (Gibson) H.; m. Bette Floessel, Mar. 10, 1956; children: David Powell, Amy Cummings, Sue Cummings. Student, U. South, Sewanee, Tenn., 1949-51, U. Tex., Austin, 1951-52; M.D., Baylor U., 1956. Diplomate: Am. Bd. Internal Medicine, also Sub-Bd. Med. Oncology, Am. Bd. Nuclear Medicine. Intern, then resident in internal medicine U. Mich. Med. Center, Ann Arbor, 1956-60, instr., 1960-62; asst. prof. medicine, dir. nuclear med. service U. Tex. Med. Br., Galveston, 1962-65; asso. prof. medicine U. Tex.-M.D. Anderson Hosp. and Tumor Inst., Houston, 1965-75, prof., 1975—, chief sect. nuclear medicine, 1967—, head dept. internal medicine, 1977—; cons. in field. Author articles in field, chpt. in books; mem. editorial bds. profl. jours. Mem. AAAS, Am. Coll. Nuclear Physicians, ACP, Am. Fedn. Clin. Research, AMA, Am. Soc. Internal Medicine, Am. Thyroid Assn., Soc. Nuclear Medicine, Tex. Acad. Internal Medicine, Tex. Med. Assn., Tex. Assn. Physicians' in Nuclear Medicine, Harris County Med. Soc., Houston Soc. Internal Medicine, Sigma Xi. Episcopalian. Club: Doctor's (Houston). Office: 6723 Bertner Ave Houston TX 77030

HAYNSWORTH, CLEMENT FURMAN, JR., judge; b. Greenville, S.C., Oct. 30, 1912; s. Clement Furman and Elsie (Hall) H.; m. Dorothy Merry Barkley, 1946. Ed., Darlington Sch., Rome, Ga.; A.B., Furman U., 1933; LL.B., Harvard, 1936; LL.D., Furman U., 1964. Bar: S.C. 1936. Mem. firm Haynsworth, Perry, Bryant, Marion & Jonstone, Greenville, until 1957; judge U.S. Ct. Appeals 4th Circuit, 1957-64, chief judge, 1964-81, now sr. judge. Adv. council Furman U. Served as officer USNR, 1942-45. Mem. Am., S.C., Greenville bar assns., Am. Law Inst. (council, life mem.), Am. Judicature Soc. (dir. 1970-74), Inst. Ct. Mgmt. (dir.), Greenville County Hist. Soc. (dir.). Episcopalian. Home: 111 Boxwood Ln Greenville SC 29605 Office: Fed Bldg Greenville SC 29603

HAYNSWORTH, HARRY J., IV, lawyer, educator; b. Greensboro, N.C., Apr. 9, 1938; s. Harry J. and Ruth (Eberhardt) H., Jr. A.B., Duke U., 1961, J.D., 1964; postgrad., U. Denver Law Center, 1972. Bar: S.C. 1965. Assoc. firm Haynsworth, Perry, Bryant, Marion & Johnstone, Greenville, S.C., 1964-69, ptnr. firm, 69-71; asso. prof. law U. of S.C., 1971-74, prof., 1974—, asso. dean, 1975-76, acting dean, 1976-77; vis. prof. U. Leeds, Eng., 1978-79; mem. S.C. Legis. Consumer Law Com., 1975-80. Author: Proposed Uniform Consumer Credit Code, 1969, Comments, S.C. Consumer Protection Code, 1983; contbr. articles to profl. jours.; mem. editorial bd.: Am. Bar Assn. Jour, 1977-83; chmn. editorial bd., 1982-83. Chmn. bd. S.C. Commn. for Blind, 1973-75; bd. dirs. Greenville County (S.C.) Housing Commn., 1970-71; v.p., dir. United Speech and Hearing Center, Greenville, 1970-71; trustee Heathwood Hall, 1976—, Randolph-Macon Women's Coll., Lynchburg, Va., 1970-75; co-chmn. regulatory flexibility task force SBA, 1980—. Mem. ABA (small bus. com., spl. cons. corporate laws com. 1978-82), S.C. Bar Assn. (vice chmn. consumer and comml. law com. 1975-78, bd. govs. 1976-77, sec., mem. exec. com. 1972-75, exec. dir. 1971-72), Richland County Bar Assn., Am. Law Inst., 4th Circuit Jud. Conf. Home: 1781 Roslyn Dr Columbia SC 29206 Office: Univ SC Sch Law Main & Green Sts Columbia SC 29208

HAYON, ELIE M., chemist, educator; b. Cairo, Egypt, May 15, 1932; came to U.S., 1965; s. Mayer E. and Regina (Cohen). B.Sc., U. Strathclyde, Glasgow, Scotland, 1954; Ph.D., Durham U., Newcastle-upon Tyne, Eng., 1957. Brit. Empire Cancer Research fellow Kings Coll., Newcastle-upon Tyne, 1957-58, Brookhaven Nat. Lab., Upton, N.Y., 1958-60, Cambridge (Eng.) U., 1960-62, Centre Nuclear Studies, Saclay, France, 1963-65; head phys. chemistry Natick (Mass.) Labs., 1966-75, Gen. Foods Corp., Tarrytown, N.Y., 1976-78; dean grad. studies and research, prof. chemistry Queens Coll., City U.N.Y., 1978—. Contbr. articles to profl. jours. Mem. numerous profl. assns. in U.S. and U.K. Home: 240 E 82d St New York NY 10028 Office: Queens Coll Flushing NY 11367

HAYREH, SOHAN SINGH, ophthalmologist; b. Kandole Kilan, Punjab, India, Nov. 6, 1927; came to U.S., 1973; s. Surjit Singh and Balwant Kaur (Kandola) H.; m. Shelagh Bell Henderson, Sept. 18, 1971; children: Davinder J.S., Ravinder G.S. B.Medicine and Surgery, Med. Coll., Amritsar, India, 1951; M.Surgery, Panjab U., Chandigarh, India, 1959; Ph.D., London U., 1965. Lectr. Med. Coll. Patiala, India, 1955-59, asst. prof., 1959-61; Beit Meml. research fellow Inst. Ophthalmology, London, 1961-64; lectr. ophthalmology U. London, 1965-69; sr. lectr. U. Edinburgh, Scotland, 1969-72, reader in ophthalmology, 1972-73; prof. ophthalmology U. Iowa, 1973—; cons. in field; mem. vision research program com. NIH; mem. ophthal. adv. com. FDA; Arris & Gale lectr. Royal Coll. Surgeons Eng., 1963. Author: Anterior Ischemic Optic Neuropathy, 1975; research numerous publs. on optic nerve and blood circulation of eye in health and disease; editorial bd.: Internat. Ophthalmology, 1977—, Ophthalmologica, Afro-Asian Jour. Ophthalmology. Served as capt. Indian Army, 1952-55. Recipient Shakuntala Amir Chand prize Indian Council Med. Research, 1961; Instituto Barraquer prize, Barcelona, Spain, 1963; Watumull Found. prize and Gold medal, Honolulu, 1964; Norman McAllister Gregg prize and medal Ophthal. Soc. New South Wales, Australia, 1964; Middlemore prize Brit. Med. Assn., 1966. Fellow Royal Coll. Surgeons Eng., Royal Coll. Surgeons Edinburgh; mem. AMA, AAAS, Am. Assn. Research in Vision and Ophthalmology, Am. Acad. Ophthalmology, European Assn. Eye Research, Brit. and European Microcirculation Soc., Gonin Club, Internat. Glaucoma Com., Ophtalmol. Soc. U.K. (Nettleship prize 1971), French Ophthalmol. Soc., Oxford Ophthalmol. Soc., Soc. Clin. Trials, Internat. Soc. Eye Research, Soc. Exptl. Biology and Medicine, Retina Soc., Macula Soc. Sikh. Home: 600 River St Iowa City IA 52240 Office: Dept Ophthalmology U Hosp Iowa City IA 52242

HAYS, DAVID ARTHUR, theater producer, stage designer; b. N.Y.C., June 2, 1930; s. Mortimer and Sarah (Reich) H.; m. Lenore Landau, Dec. 28, 1954; children: Julia Carrie, Daniel Edward. A.B. magna cum laude, Harvard U., 1952; M.A. (teaching fellow), Boston U., 1955; student, Yale Drama Sch., 1953-54; L.H.D., Gallaudet Coll., 1975. Tchr. stage designing NYU, 1961-62, Boston U., 1963; asst. prof. Columbia U., 1964-65, Conn. Coll., 1971—; guest lectr. English Harvard U., 1977, 79; v.p., trustee Eugene O'Neill Meml. Theatre Center, Waterford, Conn., 1970-80; tech. adviser Kabuki tour U.S., Japan, 1960; vis. com. on performing arts Harvard bd. overseers. Apprentice Brattle Theatre, Cambridge, Mass., 1949-52; designer stock theatres, Green Mansions, N.Y., 1954, Tanglewood, Mass., 1955; off-Broadway prodns. The Iceman Cometh, 1956, Cradle Song, 1955, Children of Darkness, 1958, Endgame, 1958, The Quare Fellow, 1958, Our Town, 1959, The Balcony, 1960, Desire Under the Elms, 1963; Broadway prodns. including Night Circus, 1957, The Innkeepers, 1956, Long Day's Journey into Night, 1956, Tenth Man, 1959, Roman Candle, 1960, All the Way Home, 1960, Love and Libel, 1960, Sunday in New York, 1961, Gideon, 1961, Strange Interlude, 1963, A Family Affair, 1962, Look, We've Come Through, 1961, No Strings, 1962, In the Counting House, 1962, Lorenzo, 1963, A Murderer Among Us, 1964, Marco Millions, 1964, The Last Analysis, 1964, The Changeling, 1964, Tartuffe, 1964, Peterpat, 1964, Hughie, 1964, The Diamond Orchid, 1965, Drat the Cat, 1965, Mrs. Dally, 1965, UTBU, 1966, Dinner at Eight, 1966, We Have Always Lived in the Castle, 1966, Yerma, 1966, The Goodbye People, 1968, The Miser, 1969, Two By Two, 1970, The Gingerbread Lady, 1970, Platinum, 1978, Bring Back Birdie, 1981, Kingdoms, 1981, Scarlett, Tokyo, 1970, Gone With the Wind, London, 1972, N.Y.C. Opera prodns., St. Joan, 1959, The Cradle Will Rock, 1960, Met. Opera prodns., Susannah, 1965, La Boheme, 1966; tech. supr.: Wozzeck, 1959; co-designer, Mummers Theatre, Oklahoma City; designer, Shakespeare Festival prodns., Hamlet, Stratford, Conn., 1958, A Mid-Summer Night's Dream, 1958, Romeo and Juliet, 1959, A Winter's Tale, 1958, Murder in the Cathedral, 1965, N.Y.C. Ballet; prodns. Pastorale, 1958, The Masquers, 1957, Stars and Stripes, 1959, Native Dancers, 1959, Episodes, 1959, Panamerica, 1960, Liebeslieder Waltzer, 1960, Electronics, 1961, Midsummer Night's Dream, 1962, Bugaku, 1963, The Chase, 1963, Irish Fantasy, 1964, Divertimento No. 15, 1966; staff designer, Vivian Beaumont Theatre, Lincoln Center, The Miser, Lincoln Center, 1968, A Cry of Players, 1969; designer: Harlem prodns. Dance Theatre of, Bugaku, 1974, Spiritual Suite, 1976; dir.: Four Saints in Three Acts, Nat. Theatre of Deaf, 1976; playwright: The Wooden Boy, Nat. Theatre of Deaf, 1979. Fulbright grantee to Old Vic, London, Eng., 1952-53; Ford Found. grantee to design an ideal theatre, 1959-61; recipient Obie awards for The Quare Fellow, 1958, Obie awards for The Balcony, 1960; Critic's poll best designer award for No Strings, 1962; ann. award New Eng. Theater Conf., 1967. Mem. Phi Beta Kappa, Société Nautique de Casablanca. Club: Ocean Cruising. Holder passage record for small boat sailing from Africa to N.Y., 1963; 1st ocean passage catboat, 1980; Feller trophy for ocean dinghy passage, 1980. Address: Nat Theatre of Deaf Hazel E Stark Ctr Chester CT 06412

HAYS, DONALD OSBORNE, retired government official; b. New Braintree, Mass., June 5, 1907; s. Edward Christopher and Grace Theresa (Osborne) H.; m. Mary Katherine Jackson Oliver, Aug. 30, 1937. Student, Middlebury Coll., 1925-27; B.A., U. Colo., 1929; M.A., Columbia U., 1937, postgrad., 1942; postgrad., Am. U., 1951. Tchr. English, head dept. English, pub. schs. of, Colo., Pa., 1929-38; head English dept., sr. master Woodmere (L.I.) Acad., 1938-42; mgmt. analyst, asst. dir., mgmt. and planning staff Spl. Services, VA, 1946-51; asst. dir. budget and mgmt. div. NPA, 1951-53; asst. dist. commr. for adminstrn. IRS, Balt., 1953, asst. regional commr. for adminstrn., Boston, 1953-54, Phila., 1954-57; asst. to dir. Bur. Fgn. Commerce, Dept. Commerce, Washington, 1957-61, Bur. Internat. Commerce, 1961-63; dir. overseas personnel div. Office Fgn. Comml. Services, 1963-68, dir. performance evaluation div., 1968-70; dir. performance evaluation Fgn. Comml. Services Staff, 1970-75; asst. to dir. support services Office of Internat. Mktg., Bur. Internat. Commerce, 1975; Dept. Commerce mem. 13th and 16th Fgn. Service Officer Selection Bd. Dept. State, 1959, 62; dep. examiner Bd. Fgn. Service Examiners, 1960-74. Active numerous civic orgns. Served from lt. (j.g.) to lt. comdr. USNR, 1942-46; staff Comdr. Fourth Fleet, 1943-44; Recife, Brazil; contact negotiator, electronics div. Bur. Ships, also staff Navy Manpower Survey Bd., 1944-46. Mem. Cum Laude Soc., SAR (past pres. D.C. chpt.), Alpha Sigma Phi, Kappa Phi Kappa. Episcopalian (jr. warden 1968-73). Club: Met. (Washington). Home: 4000 Massachusetts Ave Washington DC 20016

HAYS, HOWARD H (TIM HAYS), editor, publisher; b. Chgo., June 2, 1917; s. Howard H. and Margaret (Mauger) H.; m. Helen Cunningham, May 27, 1947; children—William, Thomas. B.A., Stanford U., 1939; LL.B., Harvard, 1942. Bar: Calif. 1946. Spl. agt. FBI, 1942-45; reporter San Bernardino (Calif.) Sun, 1945-46; asst. editor Riverside (Calif.) Daily Press, 1946-49, editor, 1949-65, editor, co-pub., 1965-83, editor, pub., chief exec. officer, 1983—; Mem. Pulitzer Prize Bd., 1976—, AP Bd., 1980—. Recipient Dist. award Calif. Jr. C. of C., 1951; named Pub. of Year Calif. Press Assn., 1968. Mem. Calif. Bar Assn., Am. Soc. Newspaper Editors (dir. 1969-76, pres. 1974-75), Stanford Alumni Assn. (dir. 1970-74), Internat. Press Inst. (chmn. Am. com. 1971-72, mem. exec. bd. 1977—), Am. Press Inst. (chmn. 1978-83), Kappa Tau Alpha. Home: 2750 Rumsey Dr Riverside CA 92506 Office: 3512 14th St Riverside CA 92501

HAYS, JACK D.H., state supreme court justice; b. Lund, Nev., Feb. 17, 1917; s. Charles Harold and Thelma (Savage) H.; children (by previous marriage)—Eugene Harrington, Rory Cochrane, Bruce Harvey, Victoria Wakeling. Grad., So. Meth. U., 1941. Bar: Ariz. bar 1946. Since practiced in, Phoenix, asst. city atty., 1949-52; U.S. atty. Dist. Ariz., 1953-60; superior ct. judge, Maricopa County, 1960-69; justice Ariz. Supreme Ct., 1969—, chief justice, 1972-74; Mem. 21st Ariz. Legislature, 1952; mem. Young Republican Exec. Com., 1948-50, Rep. State Central Com., 1948-53; vice chmn. Maricopa Rep. Com., 1949-53; Ariz. chmn. Eisenhower for Pres., 1952. Mem. State Justice Planning Governing Bd., 1969-74; mem. adv. bd. Roosevelt council Boy Scouts Am., also, Salvation Army; awards juror Freedoms Found., Valley Forge, 1973; Bd. dirs. Maricopa Legal Aid Soc.; pres. bd. Phoenix Jr. Coll. Found. Served as maj. F.A. AUS, 1941-46. Recipient Big Brother of Year award, 1966. Mem. Am. Judicature Soc. (Herbert Lincoln Harley award 1974), Am. Law Inst., Fed., Am., Inter-Am. bar assns., Ariz. Judges Assn. (pres. 1965-66), Inst. Jud. Adminstrn., Ariz. Acad., Lambda Chi Alpha, Phi Alpha Delta. Episcopalian. Club: Rotary. Home: 207 W Clarendon # 2-D Phoenix AZ 85013 Office: 221 West Wing State Capitol Phoenix AZ 85007

HAYS, JAMES DOUGLAS, geologist; b. Johnstown, N.Y., Dec. 26, 1933; m. Joyce Blakeslee, June 12, 1965; children—Vanessa, Alexander. A.B., Harvard U., 1956; M.S., Ohio State U., 1960; Ph.D., Columbia U., 1964. Asst. prof. geology Columbia U., 1967-70, asso. prof., 1970-74, prof., 1975—; dir. deep-sea sediments core lab. Lamont-Doherty Geol. Obs., 1967—; research asso. Am. Mus. Natural History, 1970—; acting dir. CLIMAP Project, 1971-74, 77; pres. DOBEX Internat. Ltd., 1974—. Asso. editor: Am. Geophys. Union, 1976—. Served with USNR, 1956-58. Fellow Geol. Soc. Am. (editor Memoir 126 1970, co-editor Memoir 145 1976); mem. Petroleum Exploration Soc. N.Y., Sigma Xi. Club: Century of N.Y. Home: 88 Van Houten Fields West Nyack NY 10994 Office: Lamont-Doherty Geol Obs Palisades NY 10964

HAYS, JAMES FRED, geologist, educator; b. Little Rock, July 10, 1933; s. Orren Lee and Virginia (Russell) H.; m. Diane Lee Huntoon, Dec. 22, 1956; 1 dau., Lee Anne. A.B., Columbia U., 1954; M.S. (NSF fellow), Calif. Inst. Tech., 1961; Ph.D., Harvard U., 1966. Geologist U.S. Geol. Survey, 1961; guest investigator Geophys. Lab., Carnegie Instn. of Washington, 1965; Soc. Fellows jr. fellow Harvard U., 1963-66, asst. prof. geology, 1966-69, asso. prof., 1969-72, prof., 1972-84, chmn. dept. geol. scis., 1981-82; dir. div. earth scis. NSF, 1982—; cons. NASA Astronaut Tng. Program, 1969-73; mem. NASA Lunar Sample Analysis Planning Team, 1973-76; chmn. Lunar and Planetary Rev. Panel, 1978-81; prin. investigator Apollo Lunar Sample Program; vis. prof. chemistry and geology Ariz. State U., 1978-79; mem. Harvard Center for Earth and Planetary Physics., 1970-84; mem. sci. adv. bd. Mt. St. Helens National Volcanic Monument; mem. adv. com. on mining and minerals research Dept. Interior; mem. Working Group for U.S.-Peoples' Republic of China Agreement for Cooperation in Earth Scis. Asso. editor: Nature of the Solid Earth, 1970, Jour. Geophys. Research, 1978-80, 83—. Served to capt. USNR, 1954-59. NSF grantee, 1974-82; NASA grantee, 1971-82. Fellow Geol. Soc. Am., Mineral. Soc. Am.; mem. Am. Geophys. Union, Geol. Soc. Washington, Geochem. Soc., Potomac Geophys. Soc., Meteoritical Soc., Am. Ornithologists Union, Naval Res. Assn., Phi Beta Kappa, Sigma Xi. Club: North Medford. Research and publs. on exptl. petrology and geochemistry. Home: 1022 N Cleveland St Arlington VA 22201 Office: Div Earth Scis NSF Washington DC 20550

HAYS, KATHRYN, actress; b. Princeton, Ill., July 26; d. Roger and Daisy Muriel (Hays) Piper; m. Glenn Ford (div.); 1 dau., Sherri Naomi.; m. Wolfgang G. Lieschke, Jan. 14, 1984. Student, Northwestern U. Fashion photographer's model, Chgo. and N.Y.C., 1953-62. Actress on Broadway, 1962-66, also TV shows, on tour, also on TV, 1969-72; daily appearance: on TV show As The World Turns, 1971—. Nat. chmn. Eye Dog Found., 1968. Christian Scientist. Office: 211 E 70th St New York NY 10021

HAYS, LEWIS W., amateur baseball executive; b. Butler, Pa., Nov. 22, 1914; s. William Edwin and Mina (Berger) H.; m. Margaret Lois Goe, June 24, 1939; children: Peggy Lou, Edward Bateman, Robert Goe. A.B., Muskingum Coll., 1938; L.H.D., Washington and Jefferson Coll., 1976. Sports editor Brownsville (Pa.) Telegraph, 1938-46, Washington (Pa.) Observer and Reporter, 1946-53; founder Pony Baseball, Inc., commr., 1951-65, pres., 1965-81; chmn. U.S. Baseball Fedn., 1976—. Author: Pony Tales and Diamond Dust, 1981, (with wife) Poems and Pictures, 1983. Moderator Washington Presbytery, United Presbyn. Ch., 1968; moderator Synod of the Trinity, 1974, chmn. gen. council, 1975, chmn. budget and finance, 1974—; chmn. dept. ch. and community Pa. Synod; mem. bd. nat. missions Gen. Assembly; mem. nat. council, v.p. synod council U.P. Men; mem. gen. assembly Council Adminstrv. Services; mem. U.S. Olympic Games Com.; mem. ho. of dels., exec. bd. U.S. Olympic Com. Recipient Christian Bus. Man of Year award, Optimist Man of Year award, Citizen citation Washington and Jefferson Coll., 1962, Disting. Alumni award Muskingum Coll., 1972; Disting. Citizen award County of Washington, Pa., 1981; Spl. award K.C., 1981; Disting. Service award Jr. C. of C., 1982. Mem. Order Ky. Cols., Dukes of Paducah, Fellowship Christian Athletes, Pa. Soc., Theta Gamma Epsilon, Sigma Tau Delta, Alpha Phi Gamma. Presbyn. (elder). Club: Kiwanian (pres. 1961). Home: 25 Sherwood Pl Washington PA 15301 Office: 300 Clare Dr Washington PA 15301 *Young people don't do what you tell them to; young people will do what you do!*

HAYS, MARGUERITE THOMPSON, physician; b. Bloomington, Ind., Apr. 15, 1930; d. Stith and Louise (Faust) Thompson; m. David G. Hays, Feb. 4, 1950 (div. 1975); children: Dorothy Adele, Warren Stith Thompson, Thomas Glenn. A.B. cum laude, Radcliffe Coll., 1951; postgrad., Harvard U. Med. Sch., 1954; M.D., UCLA, 1957; Sc.D. (hon.), Ind. U., 1979. Diplomate: Am. Bd. Internal Medicine, Am. Bd. Nuclear Medicine. Intern UCLA Sch. Medicine, 1957-58, resident, 1958-59, 61-62, USPHS postdoctoral trainee, 1959-61, USPHS postdoctoral fellow, 1963-64, asst. prof. medicine, 1964-68, SUNY, Buffalo, 1968-70, asst. prof. biophys. sci., 1968-74, assoc. prof. medicine, 1970-76, clin. assoc. prof. nuclear medicine, 1973-77; asst. chief nuclear medicine VA Med. Center, Wadsworth, Calif., 1967-68; chief nuclear medicine Buffalo VA Med. Center, 1968-74, assoc. chief of staff for research, 1971-74; dir. med. research service VA Central Office, Washington, 1974-79, asst. chief med. dir. for research and devel., 1979-81; chief of staff Martinez (Calif.) VA Med. Center, 1981—; prof. radiology Sch. Medicine, U. Calif., Davis, 1981—, assoc. dean, 1981; vis. research scientist, Euratom, Italy, 1962-63; chmn. radiopharm. adv. com. FDA, 1974-77; co-chmn. biomedicine com. Pres.'s Fed. Council on Sci., Engring. and Tech., 1979-81. NIH grantee, 1964-71; VA research Funds recipient, 1968—. Fellow ACP; mem. Soc. Nuclear Medicine (chmn. publs. com., trustee, v.p. 1983-84), Am. Thyroid Assn., Endocrine Soc., Am. Fedn. Clin. Research. Research, publs. in field. Home: 270 Campesino Avenue Palo Alto CA 94306 Office: 3801 Miranda Ave Palo Alto CA 94304

HAYS, PATRICK GREGORY, hospital administrator; b. Kansas City, Kans., Sept. 9, 1942; s. Vance Samuel and Mary Ellen (Crabbe) H.; m. Penelope Ann Hall, July 3, 1976; children—Julia L., Jennifer M. Meyer, Emily J. Meyer, Drew D. Meyer. B.S. in Bus. Adminstrn, U. Tulsa, 1964; M.H.A., U. Minn., 1971; postgrad., U. Mich. Grad. Sch. Bus. Adminstrn., 1977. Mfg. analyst N.Am. Rockwell Corp., Tulsa, 1964-66; asst. adminstr., adminstr. for ops. Henry Ford Hosp., Detroit, 1971-75; exec. v.p. Methodist Med. Center of Ill., Peoria, 1975-77; adminstr. Kaiser Found. Hosp., Los Angeles, 1977-80; pres. Sutter Community Hosps. and Sutter Health System, Sacramento, 1980—; trustee Central Area Teaching Hosps., Inc., Los Angeles, 1977-79; clin. preceptor U. Minn., Xavier U., Tulane U., Ariz. State U.; Bd. dirs. New Center Area Council, Detroit, 1973-75, Arthritis Found. Central Ill., 1976-77; Vice chmn. bd. Arthritis Found. No. Calif., 1980-82; Bd. dirs. Calif. Hosps. Polit. Action Com.; mem. exec. com. St. Jude Children's Research Hosp. Midwest Affilate, Peoria, 1975-77; adv. bd. Grad. Program in Health Services Adminstrn. U. So. Calif.-Sacramento. Contbr. articles on health services to publs. Mem. Pvt. Industry Council, Sacramento Employment and Tng. Agy. Served with U.S. Army, 1966-69. Decorated Army Commendation medal, cert. of appreciation Dept. Army; USPHS fellow, 1969-71; recipient Commendation resolution Calif. Senate, 1979; Recipient Whitney M. Young award Sacramento Urban League, 1983. Mem. Am. Coll. Hosp. Adminstrs., Calif. Hosp. Assn. (legis. com.), Sacramento-Sierra Hosp. Assn. (exec. com., pres.), Hosp. Council No. Calif. (nominating, pub. affairs and long-range planning coms.), Royal Soc. Health (U.K.), Am. Mgmt. Assn. (pres.' club), Hollywood C. of C. (Hollywood revitalization com. 1979), Sacramento C. of C. (bd. dirs. 1982-85), Kappa Sigma, Sigma Iota Epsilon. Presbyterian. Office: 1111 Howe Ave Sacramento CA 95816

HAYS, PETER L., educator; b. Bremerhaven, Germany, Apr. 18, 1938; came to U.S., 1938, naturalized, 1945; s. Eric and Elsa (Nussbaum) H.; m. Myrna Grace Mantel, Sept. 14, 1963; children—Melissa, Eric, Jeffrey. A.B., U. Rochester, 1959; M.A., N.Y. U., 1961; Ph.D., Ohio State U., 1965. Instr. Ohio State U., English, 1965-66; asst. prof. U. Calif., Davis, 1966-72, asso. prof., 1972-77, prof., 1977—, coordinator undergrad. studies, 1973-74, chmn. dept. English, 1974-77; chmn. U. Calif. English Council, 1975-77. Author: The Limping Hero, 1971; contbr. articles to profl. jours. Served with U.S. Army, 1959-60. Danforth Found. fellow, 1976; Fulbright lectr. Am. lit. Johannes-Gutenberg-Universitat, Mainz, W. Ger., 1977-78. Mem. MLA, Philol. Assn. Pacific Coast. Office: Dept English U Calif Davis CA 95616

HAYS, ROBERT L., corp. exec.; b. Cleve., June 28, 1903; s. Louis Henry and Jessie (Feiss) H.; m. Lois Mendelson, Feb. 1, 1938; children—Michael Louis, Mary. A.B., Cornell U., 1924. Pres., treas. Kaynee Co., Cleve., 1937-54; with McDonald & Co., Cleve., 1955—, partner, 1958—; dir. Myers Industries, Akron, J. M. Smucker Co., Orrville, Ohio. Clubs: Cornell, Union (Cleve.). Home: 18975 Van Aken Blvd Apt 308 Shaker Heights OH 44122 Office: Central Nat Bank Bldg Cleveland OH 44114

HAYS, RONALD JACKSON, naval officer; b. Urania, La., Aug. 19, 1928; s. George Henry and Fannie Elizabeth (McCartney) H.; m. Jane M. Hughes, Jan. 29, 1951; children: Dennis, Michael, Jacquelyn. Student, Northwestern U., 1945-46; B.S., U.S. Naval Acad., 1950. Commd. ensign U.S. Navy, 1950, advanced through grades to adm., 1983; destroyer officer Atlantic Fleet, 1950-51; attack pilot Pacific Fleet, 1953-56; exptl. test pilot, Patuxent River, Md., 1956-59; comdr. All Weather Attack Squadron, Atlantic Fleet, 1965-67; comdg. officer Naval Sta., Roosevelt Roads, P.R., 1971-72; dir. Navy Planning and Programming, 1973-74; comdr. Carrier Group Four, Norfolk, Va., 1974-75; dir. Office of Program Appraisal, Sec. of Navy, Washington, 1975-78; dep. and chief staff, comdr. in chief U.S. Atlantic Fleet, Norfolk, Va., 1978-80; comdr.-in-chief U.S. Naval Force Europe, London, 1980-83; vice chief naval ops. Dept. Navy, Washington, 1983—. Decorated Legion of Merit, Silver Star with 2 gold stars, D.F.C. with 6 silver and gold stars, Disting. Service medal with 2 gold stars, Air Medal with numeral 14 and gold stars. Baptist. Home: Qtrs AA 2300 E St NW Washington DC 20037 Office: Vice Chief Naval Ops Dept Navy Washington DC 20350

HAYS, STEELE, judge; b. Little Rock, Mar. 25, 1925; s. L. Brooks and Marion (Prather) H.; m. Peggy Wall, July 12, 1980; children: Andrew Steele, Melissa Louise, Sarah Anne. B.A., U. Ark., 1948; J.D., George Washington U., 1951. Bar: Ark. 1951. Adminstrv. asst. to Congressman Brooks Hays, 1951-53; practice in Little Rock, 1953-79; mem. firm Spitzberg, Mitchell & Hays, 1954-70, 71-79; circuit judge 6th Jud. Circuit Ark., Little Rock, 1970-71; judge Ark. Ct. Appeals, 1979-81; assoc. justice Ark. Supreme Ct., 1981—; chmn. Bd. Law Examiners, 1968-70. Mem. Ark. com. U.S. Civil Rights Commn.; Del. Presbyn. Ch. Consultation on Ch. Union, 1968-70; Trustee Presbyn. Found. Mem. ABA, Ark. Bar Assn. (past sec.-treas.), Sigma Chi, Delta Theta Phi. Home: 3515 Hill Rd #4 Little Rock AR 72205 Office: Justice Bldg Little Rock AR 72201

HAYS, THOMAS CHANDLER, tobacco company executive; b. Chgo., Apr. 21, 1935; s. Marion C. and Carolyn (Reid) H.; m. Mary Ann Jergens, June 8, 1958; children—Thomas, Michael, Paul, Jennifer. B.S., Calif. Inst. Tech., 1957, M.S., 1958; M.B.A. with high distinction (Baker scholar), Harvard U., 1963. Ops. research analyst Lockheed Corp., Los Angeles, 1963-64; product mgr. Andrew Jergens Co. (subs. Am. Brands), Cin., 1964-70, v.p. mktg., 1970-78, exec. v.p., 1978, pres., chief exec. officer, 1979-80; v.p. mktg. Am. Tobacco Co. div. Am. Brands, 1980-81, exec. v.p., 1981—; dir. Am. Brands. Trustee, treas. Cin. Country Day Sch., 1978—; bd. dirs., treas. Meml. Community Center, 1965-75. Served to 1st lt. USAF, 1958-61. Republican. Presbyterian. Clubs: Cin. Country, Bel Air Bay., Tokeneke. *

HAYSLETT, JOHN PAUL, physician, medical educator, researcher; b. Greenwich, Conn., Jan. 6, 1935; s. Paul and Evelyn (Drago) H.; m. Roseanne Ann Borchetta, June 11, 1960; children: Francesca, Paul. A.B., Holy Cross Coll., Worcester, Mass., 1956; M.D., Cornell U., 1960, Yale U., 1978. Instr. medicine Yale U., 1967-68, asst. prof., 1968-72, assoc. prof., 1972-78, prof., 1978—, chief. sect. nephrology, New Haven, Conn., 1972—. Author: (with others) Advances in Systemic Lupus Erythematosus, 1983; contbr. articles in field to profl. jours.; assoc. editor: Am. Jour. Kidney Diseases, 1980—. Served to capt. USAF, 1961-63. Fellow ACP; mem. Am. Heart Assn. (established investigator 1971-76, chmn. Council on Kidney 1979-81), Nat. Kidney Found. (chmn. sci. adv. bd. 1981-83), Alpha Sigma Nu, Delta Epsilon Sigma, Alpha Omega Alpha. Democrat. Roman Catholic. Home: 11 Prospect Rd Woodbridge CT 06512 Office: Yale Univ Sch of Medicine 333 Cedar St New Haven CT 06520

HAYTER, JOHN SAMUEL, advertising agency executive; b. Toronto, Ont., Can., Sept. 20, 1940; came to U.S., 1980; s. Evan William and Geraldine Nellie (Acres) H.; m. Gillian Sally Brown, Sept. 22, 1962; children: Geoffrey William, Sara Jane. Student, U. N.B., 1959-61. Account supr. J. Walter Thompson, Toronto, 1967-68; gen. mgr. Alberto-Culver Co., London, 1971-80, gen. mgr., v.p., Chgo., 1980-81; sr. v.p., gen. mgr. Young & Rubicam Inc., Chgo., 1981—. Office: Young & Rubicam 111 E Wacker Dr Chicago IL 60601

HAYTHORNE, ROBERT E., lawyer; b. Moose Jaw, Sask., Can., Oct. 24, 1915; came to U.S., 1915, naturalized, 1948; s. Percy B. and Catherine (Eckles) H.; m. Alice Hudelson, Nov. 8, 1947; children—Robert E., Catherine Elizabeth. A.B., U. Chgo., 1936, J.D., 1938. Bar: Ill. bar 1938, N.Y. bar 1940. Practice in, Chgo., 1938; mem. legal staff SEC, Washington, 1938-40; practice in, N.Y.C., 1940-41; grad. U.S. Army Command and Gen. Staff Sch., 1944; atty. U.S. Chief of Counsel, Nuremburg War Crime Trials, 1945; asst. gen. counsel Fgn. Liquidation Commn., U.S. Dept. of State, 1946; with firm Seyfarth, Shaw & Fairweather, Chgo., 1946-53, Milliken, Vollers & Parsons, 1955-57; v.p., gen. counsel Am.-Maritetta Co., Chgo., 1957-61; partner Kirkland & Ellis (and predecessor firm), Chgo., 1963-80; individual practice law, Geneva, Ill., 1980—. Served to maj. AUS, 1941-46; lt. col. Res. Mem. Am., Ill., Kane County bar assns., S.A.R., Phi Alpha Delta. Home and Office: 207 S 5th St Geneva IL 60134

HAYTHORNTHWAITE, ROBERT MORPHET, civil engineer, educator; b. Whitley Bay, Eng., May 5, 1922; came to U.S., 1953, naturalized, 1964; s. William and Doris (Morphet) H.; m. Beatrice Mary Swift, Mar. 29, 1952; children: Richard Swift, Jennifer Anne, Susan Mary, Sheila Margaret. B.Sc., Durham U., 1942, London U., 1945, Ph.D., 1952; M.S., Brown U., 1953, M.A., 1957. Registered profl. civil engr., Pa. Sci. officer Bldg. Research Sta., Watford, Eng., 1942-47; lectr. Sheffield U., 1947-53; instr. to asso. prof. Brown U., 1953-59; prof. engring. sci. U. Mich., 1959-67; prof. engring. mechanics Pa. State U., 1967-79, head dept., 1967-74; dean Coll. Engring. Tech., Temple U., Phila., 1979-81, prof. engring. sci., 1979—; vis. prof. Cambridge U., 1961, Manchester U., 1965-66, Lehigh U., 1974-75; cons. to Council Grad. Schs. U.S., Detroit Tank Arsenal, Engrs. Council for Profl. Devel., NASA, NSF. Editor: Proceedings of the Third U.S. Nat. Congress Applied Mechanics, 1958, Mechanics, 1972, 73; contbr. articles to profl. jours. Commonwealth Fund fellow, 1950. Fellow ASCE (research prize 1963, tech. editor Jour. Engring. Mechanics div. 1967-70, chmn. engring. mechanics div. 1966-67), Am. Acad. Mechanics (pres. 1969-71, endowment chmn. 1976—); mem. Am. Soc. M.E., Am. Soc. Engring. Edn. (chmn. mechanics div. 1966-67), Sigma Xi, Tau Beta Pi (faculty adviser Pa. Beta chpt. 1968-79). Home: 313 Wellington Terr Jenkintown PA 19046

HAYTIN, HAROLD ALEXANDER, venture capital company executive; b. Denver, Aug. 17, 1918; s. Alexander and Bess H.; m. Lois A. Lasker, Sept. 4, 1940; children: Daniel, Jane. B.A., UCLA, 1940, grad. exec. program, 1961. Exec. v.p. Telecor, Inc., Beverly Hills, Calif., 1970-72, chmn. bd., pres., chief exec. officer, 1972-80; pres. Newcraft, Inc., 1966-72; cons. Matsushita Electric Corp. Am., 1980; chmn. Calif. Capital Investors Co., Los Angeles, 1980—; dir. Photo and Sound Co.; moderator, lectr. Grad. Sch. Mgmt., UCLA extension. Pres. Los Angeles Bd. CSC, 1979—; trustee City of Hope, 1972—; pres. bd. trustees UCLA Found., 1976—; bd. advs. UCLA Hosp. and Clinics, 1978—; mem. chancellors assos. UCLA, 1966—; patron Los Angeles County Mus. Art, 1965—. Clubs: Riviera Country, Braemar Country. Office: 11812 San Vicente Blvd Los Angeles CA 90049

HAYTON, BEN CHARLES, chem. co. exec.; b. Brenham, Tex., Aug. 22, 1925; s. Ben T. and Nora Lee (Loyd) H.; m. Joan Dickens, Sept. 21, 1958; 1 son, Loyd Conyers. B.S. in Chem. Engring, Rice U., 1945. With Jefferson Chem. Co., 1946-66, asst. sales mgr., until 1966; with Texaco Inc., 1966—, v.p. petrochem. dept., 1972-80; pres. Texaco Chem. Co., Houston, 1980—. Trustee Houston United Way, 1980-82; chmn. gen. ann. fund drive Rice U., 1981-82. Served as ensign USNR, 1945-46. Mem. Chem. Mfrs. Assn., Nat. Petroleum Refiners Assn., Am. Chem. Soc., Am. Inst. Chem. Engrs., Tex. Chem. Council. Republican. Baptist. Clubs: Houston, University (Houston); Metropolitan (N.Y.C.); Wee Burn Country. Office: 4800 Fournace Pl Bellaire TX 77401 *

HAYTON, JACOB WILLIAM, lawyer; b. Carterville, Ill., Mar. 17, 1926; s. James Wesley and Zella (West) H.; m. Beata Mueller, Mar. 17, 1962; 1 son, James Wesley. B.A., U. Chgo., 1946, J.D., 1950. Bar: Ill. bar 1950. Since practiced in, Chgo.; partner firm Bell, Boyd & Lloyd, 1965—. Treas. Beacon Neighborhood House, 1952-64, Chgo. Fedn. Settlements, 1959- 62. Mem. Chgo. Am., bar assns., Phi Beta Kappa., Order of Coif. Unitarian. Clubs: Univ., Legal. Home: 1133 Hinman Ave Evanston IL 60201 Office: 3 First National Plaza Chicago IL 60603

HAYWARD, JOHN TUCKER, mgmt. cons.; b. N.Y.C., Nov. 15, 1910; s. Charles Brian and Rosa (Valdetaro) H.; m. Leila Marion Hyer, Oct. 14, 1932; children—Mary Shelley, Leila Marion, Victoria, Jenny, John T. B.S., U.S. Naval Acad., 1930; student, U. Pa., U. N.Mex., U. Calif., Stanford U., Calif. Inst. Tech.; D.Sc., U. Portland, 1965; LL.D., Providence Coll., 1968. Commd. ensign USN, 1930, advanced through grades to vice adm., 1959, designated naval aviator, 1931; various assignments ships and naval stas., 1931-40; with RAF, Eng., 1940-41; comdg. officer Bombin 106, Pacific, 1942-44; assigned Manhattan Project, Los Alamos Sci. Lab., exptl. officer rocket ordnance and weaponry, Inyokern, 1944-47; plans and operations for atomic weapons and warfare Armed Forces Spl. Weapons Base, Sandia, 1947-51; head weapons research, div. mil. applications AEC, 1951-53; with Task Group 95, Yellow Sea, 1953-54; dir. Naval Ordnance Lab., 1954-56; comdg. officer U.S.S. Franklin Roosevelt, 1956-57; spl. asst. to dir. strategic plans div. DCNO, Navy Dept., 1957-59, DCNO, 1959-62; comdr. Carrier div. 2, 1962-63; comdr. anti-submarine warfare force, Honolulu, 1963-66; pres. Naval War Coll., Newport, R.I., 1966-68; v.p. Gen. Dynamics Corp., Pierre La Clede, Mo., 1968-75; mgmt. cons. Hayward Assos., Newport, R.I., 1975—. Bd. dirs. John Hertz Found., Charles Stark Draper Lab. Decorated Silver Star, D.F.C. with three oak leaf clusters, Air medal (5), Bronze Star, Legion of Merit, D.S.M. with oak leaf cluster, Congressional medal for life saving, U.S., Order Brit. Empire; Order So. Cross, Brazil; Order Taegu, Korea; Legion of Honor, France; knight comdr. Order Merit, Italy; Knight of Malta.; Benjamin Franklin fellow Royal Soc. Arts. Fellow Am. Inst. Aeros. and Astronautics, Royal Aero Soc. Gt. Britain; mem. Am. Phys. Soc., Am. Inst. Physics, AAAS, Newcomen Soc. Home and office: 3 Barclay Sq Newport RI 02840

HAYWARD, RONALD HAMILTON, surgeon; b. Wellington, N.Z., Nov. 7, 1927; s. Frederick Howard and Emma Mathilde (Hannibal) H.; m. Elizabeth Ruth Wells, Sept. 16, 1961; children—Maureen, John, Gregory, Jennifer. Ed., Wellington Coll., 1941-45; M.B., Ch.B., U. Otago, 1951; Ph.D. in Surgery, U. Minn., 1961. Resident Mayo Clinic, Rochester, Minn., 1956-62; practice medicine specializing in thoracic and cardiovascular surgery, Ft. Worth, 1962-65, Scott & White Clinic, Temple, Tex., 1965—; prof., chmn. dept. surgery Tex. A&M Med. Sch., 1979—. Recipient Alumni award Mayo Clinic, 1959. Mem. AMA, Tex. Med. Assn., Tex. Surg. Soc., So. Thoracic Surg. Assn., Soc. Thoracic Surgeons, Sigma Xi. Republican. Episcopalian. Patentee in field. Office: Scott & White Clinic Temple TX 76508 *

HAYWOOD, BRUCE, coll. pres.; b. York, Eng., Sept. 30, 1925; came to U.S., 1951, naturalized, 1957; s. Joseph Edgar and Eva (Street) H.; m. Isona Gretchen Shelley, June 21, 1947; children—Anne Margaret, Elizabeth Shelley. Student, U. Leeds, Eng., 1947-48; B.A., McGill U., 1950, M.A., 1951; Ph.D., Harvard, 1956. Mem. faculty Kenyon Coll., 1954, prof. German lit., 1960-63, dean coll., 1963-67, provost, 1967-80; pres. Monmouth (Ill.) Coll., 1980—. Author: The Veil of Imagery, 1959. Served with Brit. Army, 1943-47. Mem. Am. Assn. Tchrs. of German. Home: 605 N 6th St Monmouth IL 61462

HAYWOOD, CHARLES, musicologist, retired educator; b. Grodno, Russia, Dec. 20, 1904; came to U.S., 1916, naturalized, 1922; s. Nathan and Dora (Blume) H.; m. Frances Dillon, May 24, 1928 (dec.); 1 son, John. B.S., City Coll. N.Y., 1926; artist diploma, Inst. Mus. Art, 1930; diploma, Juilliard Grad. Sch. Music, 1935; M.A., Columbia, 1940, Ph.D., 1949. Lectr. Juilliard Sch. Music, 1939-52; prof. music Queens Coll., CUNY, 1939-73, ret., 1973; now bd. dirs. Acad. for Humanities and Sci.; vis. prof. Hunter Coll., 1958-59, U. Minn., 1959, Ind. U., 1960, U. Calif. at Los Angeles, 1961; lectr. Harvard, Columbia; founder, co-dir. Dici Sch. Performing Arts, L.I., 1930-38. Opera singer, concert artist, soloist symphony orchs.; also radio and TV appearances, 1930—; Author: James A. Bland: His Life and Songs, 1946, Modern Russian Art Songs, 1947, Cervantes and Music, 1948, Masterpieces of Sacred Songs, 1958, A Bibliography of North American Folklore and Folksong, rev. and enlarged edit., 2 vols, 1961, Folk Songs of the World, 1966, Negro Minstrelsy and Shakespearean Burlesque, 1966, Latin American Music in the College Curriculum: Problems and Prospects, 1966, Maretzek's Revelations of an Opera Manager, 1968, George Bernard Shaw on Incidental Music in the Shakespearean Theater, 1969, Ralph Vaughan-Williams and Maud Karpeles: A Correspondence, 1973, Pablo Casals and Catalan Folk Music, 1974, Charles Dickens and Shakespeare; or The Irish Moor of Venice, O'Thello, 1977; also numerous articles.; Editor: Yearbook Internat. Folk Music Council, 1970-74; exec. bd., 1971-81. Pres. U.S. nat. com. Internat. Folk Music Council, 1962-82; ednl. coordinator, program dir. U.S.O., 1940-45. Juilliard grad. fellow, 1930-35; Folger Shakespeare fellow, 1951; Henry F. Huntington fellow, 1952-53; Fulbright Research grantee, Austria, 1961-62, 67-68. Mem. Nat. Folk Festival Assn. (mem. exec. bd.), Am. Musicol. Soc., Am. Folklore Soc., Ethnomusicol. Soc. (mem. council), Am. Shakespeare Soc., N.Y. Folklore Soc., Friends of Bodleian Library, Phi Beta Kappa. Home: 145 E 92d St New York NY 10028

HAYWOOD, CHARLES FOSTER, educator; b. Ludlow, Ky., Apr. 7, 1927; s. Charles Adam and Julia (Strode) H.; m. Josephine Richards, June 15, 1948 (div. July 1981); children—Julia Elizabeth, Mary Josephine, Charles Ransome, John Watson. A.B., Berea Coll., 1949; A.M., Duke U., 1950; Ph.D., U. Calif.-Berkeley, 1955. Econ. analyst Am. Bankers Assn., 1954-55; asst. prof. Tulane U., 1955-57; economist Bank of Am., 1957-58, dir. econ. research, 1963-65; prof. banking U. Miss., 1958-60, provost, 1960-63; dean Coll. Bus. and Econs., U. Ky., Lexington, 1965-75, prof. econs. and fin., 1975—; on leave with Am. Bankers Assn., 1969-70; with Ky. Dept. Finance, also state sec. for devel., 1973-74; chmn. bd. Carter H. Golembe Assos., Inc., Washington, 1967-71; vice-chmn. Bank Lexington; dir. Conna Corp., Jerrico Inc., Pittston Co.; cons. economist Am. Bankers Assn., 1978—. Author: The Regulation of Deposit Interest Rates, 1968, The Pledging of Bank Assets, 1967, The Expansion of Bank Funds in the 1970's, 1969, Regulation Q and Monetary Policy, 1971, The Potential Competition Doctrine, 1972, A Perspective for Energy Planning in Kentucky, 1976, Commercial Banking, A Guide for Auditors and Accountants, 1980. Mem. Ky. Econ. Devel. Commn., 1965-79; chmn. Ky. Council Econ. Advisers, 1971-76; chmn. state adv. bd. Econ. Stablzn. Program, 1972-74; Ky. rep. Appalachian Regional Commn., 1973-75; trustee Berea Coll. Served with U.S. Mcht. Marine, 1945; Served with AUS, 1946-48. Mem. Am., So. econ. assns. Democrat. Mem. Christian Ch. Home: 231 Chenault Rd Lexington KY 40502

HAYWOOD, CLARENCE ROBERT, history educator; b. Fowler, Kans., Aug. 27, 1921; s. C.O. and Elsie (Long) H.; m. Louise Marie Stephenson, Jan. 2, 1943; children: Sandra Jarvis, Robert Alan, Ray. A.B., U. Kans., 1947, M.A., 1948; Ph.D., U. N.C., 1956; B.A. (hon.), Southwestern Coll., 1983. Mem. faculty Southwestern Coll., Winfield, Kans., 1948-66, dean coll., 1956-66; dean Coll. Arts and Scis., Millikin U., 1966-69; v.p. acad. affairs, provost Washburn U., Topeka, 1969-82, disting. prof. history, 1982—. Author: The Doing of History, 1978; Contbr. articles to profl. jours. Served with USNR, 1942-45. Mem. So. Hist. Soc., Orgn. Am. Historians, Am. Conf. Acad. Deans. Democrat. Methodist. Home: 2001 Oakley Ave Topeka KS 66604

HAYWOOD, EGBERT LYNCH, lawyer; b. Durham, N.C., June 4, 1911; s. Charles Lewis and Zoa Lee (Rigsbee) H.; m. Margaret Davis, June 21, 1938; children—Egbert Lynch, John Davis. A.B., U. N.C., 1931; LL.B., Harvard, 1934. Bar: N.C. bar 1934. Since practiced in, Durham; sr. partner firm Haywood, Denny and Miller; asst. city atty., Durham, 1946-56; Dir. Citizens Nat. Bank, 1946-59; chmn. bd. N.C. Nat. Bank, 1974-76, dir., 1959—; pres. Arden Properties, Inc., 1956—; dir. Research Triangle Service Bd., 1976—. Served to lt. comdr. USNR, 1942-45. Mem. ABA (mem. ho. of dels. 1953-73, gov. 1959-62, adv. bd. jour. 1962-66), N.C. Bar Assn., Durham County Bar Assn., Internat. Assn. Ins. Counsel (exec. com., pres. 1967-68), Am. Judicature Soc. (dir.), N.C. Harvard Law Assn. (pres.), Harvard Law Sch. Assn., Am. Legion (past post comdr.), Durham Jr. C. of C. (past pres.), Jud. Conf. U.S. (com. on evidence), Soc. Cincinnati, Chi Phi. Baptist (deacon). Clubs: Kiwanis (past pres.), Torch, Cotillion (Durham); Hope Valley Country. Home: 28 Oak Dr Durham NC 27707 Office: 200 Wachovia Bldg Durham NC 27701

HAYWOOD, HARRIS HURLEY, race car driver; b. Chgo., May 4, 1948; s. Harris and Jeannette (Hurley) H. B.A., Jacksonville (Fla.) U., 1971. Profl. race car driver, 1969—; champion Internat. Motor Sports Assn., 1971, 72. Republican. Roman Catholic. Winner Daytona (Fla.) Race, 10 times, Daytona 24 Hours Race, 4 times, Le Mans (France) Race, 1978, Indy 500, 1980. Address: 7653 Los Palmas Way Jacksonville FL 32216

HAYWOOD, H(ERBERT) CARL(TON), psychologist; b. Taylor County, Ga., July 2, 1931; s. Howard Chapman and Rosebud (Smith) H.; m. Nancy Patricia Roberts, Oct. 5, 1951 (div. Mar. 1971); children: Carlton, Terence, Elizabeth, Kristin. A.B., San Diego State Coll., 1956, M.A., 1957; Ph.D., U. Ill., 1961. Mem. faculty George Peabody Coll. (merged with Vanderbilt U. 1979), Nashville, 1962—, prof. psychology, 1969—, prof. spl. edn., 1975-79, dir. mental retardation research tng. program, 1968-70; dir. Inst. Mental Retardation and Intellectual Devel., 1970-73, Office Research Adminstrn., 1974-76, John F. Kennedy Center Research Edn. and Human Devel., 1971-83; prof. neurology Vanderbilt U. Sch. Medicine, 1971—; vis. prof. U. Toronto, 1965-66; sr. fellow Vanderbilt Inst. Pub. Policy Studies, 1983—; chmn. Nat Mental Retardation Research Center Dirs., 1979-82; adv. bd. Ill. Inst. Developmental Disabilities, Chgo., 1970-78, Eunice Kennedy Shriver Center Mental Retardation, Waltham, Mass., 1973—, Tenn. Dept. Mental Health, 1964—; cons. President's Com. on Mental Retardation, 1968-73; mem. sci. rev. com., health research facilities br., div. edn. and research facilities NIH, 1967-71. Editor: Brain Damage in School Age Children, 1968, Social Cultural Aspects of Mental Retardation, 1970, (with Begab and Garber) Prevention of Retarded Development in Psychosocially Disadvantaged Children, 1981, (with J.R. Newbrough) Living Environments for Developmentally Retarded Persons, 1981; editor: Am. Jour. Mental Deficiency, 1969-79; editorial bd.: Jour. Abnormal Child Psychology, 1973—, Contemporary Psychology, 1982—; Contbr. articles on child devel., motivation and mental retardation to profl. jours. Served with USN, 1950-54. Fellow Am. Assn. Mental Deficiency (v.p. psychology 1975-77, 1st v.p. 1978-79, pres. 1980-81), Am. Psychol. Assn. (pres. Div. 33 1978-79, mem. Council of Reps. 1980-82); mem. Soc. Research Child Devel., Inst. Medicine, Psychonomic Soc. Democrat. Episcopalian. Club: Cosmos (Washington). Office: Inst for Public Policy Studies Peabody Coll Vanderbilt U Nashville TN 37203 *Dominant values include enthusiasm for scholarship, equal parts of dedication to science for its own sake and concern for social progress, and the conviction that self-concern and self-seeking constitute the most dangerous threat to the collective goals of humanity. The future lies in education designed to stretch minds and develop processes of critical thought rather than to impart job-oriented skills.*

HAYWOOD, L. JULIAN, educator, physician; b. Reidsville, N.C., Apr. 13, 1927; s. Thomas Woodly and Louise Viola (Hayley) H.; m. Virginia Elizabeth Paige, Dec. 3, 1953; 1 son, Julian Anthony. B.S., Hampton Inst., 1948; M.D., Howard U., 1952. Intern St. Mary's Hosp., Rochester, N.Y., 1952-53; resident Los Angeles County Hosp., 1956-58; fellow cardiology White Meml. Hosp., 1959-61; traveling fellow U. Oxford, Eng., 1963; instr. medicine Loma Linda (Calif.) U., 1960-61, asst. prof., 1961-72, asso. clin. prof., 1973—; asst. prof. medicine U. So. Calif., 1963-68, asso. prof., 1968-76, prof., 1976—; dir. comprehensive sickle cell ctr. Los Angeles County-U. So. Calif. Med. Center, dir. coronary care unit; past dir. physicians tng. program (Regional Med. Programs), 1970-75; cons. Los Angeles County

Coroner, Indsl. Accident Bd. Calif., Health Care Tech. Div., USPHS, Nat. Heart and Lung Inst.; past mem. cardiology adv. com. div. heart and vascular diseases. Bd. dirs., pres. Sickle Cell Disease Research Found. Contbr. articles profl. jours.; Mem. editorial bds.: Jour. Nat. Med. Assn. Served with M.C. USNR, 1954-56. Recipient award of merit Los Angeles County Heart Assn., 1968, 69, 73, 75. Fellow Los Angeles Acad. Medicine, A.C.P., Am. Coll. Cardiology, Am. Heart Assn. (fellow council on clin. cardiology; mem. council on other osclerosis; mem. exec. com. council on epidemiology; mem. long-range planning com., dir., past sec., v.p. Greater Los Angeles affiliate, now pres.); mem. Am. Fedn. Clin. Research, AAAS, Soc. Clin. Investigation, Western Soc. Clin. Research, Assn. Advancement Med. Instrumentation, AMA, Nat. Med. Assn. (Charles Drew Med. Soc.), N.Y. Acad. Scis., Hampton Inst. Alumni Assn. (past pres. Los Angeles chpt.), Med. Faculty Assn. U. So. Calif. Sch. Medicine (past pres.), Los Angeles Soc. Internal Medicine (past pres.), Western Assn. Physicians, AAUP, Fedn. Am. Scientists, Alpha Omega Alpha. Home: 3551 Lowry Rd Los Angeles CA 90027 Office: 1200 N State St Los Angeles CA 90033

HAYWOOD, OLIVER GARFIELD, engineer; b. Highland Mills, N.Y., Nov. 29, 1911; s. Oliver Garfield and A. Olive (Wiggins) H.; m. Helen Elizabeth Salisbury, June 12, 1936; children: Barbara Ann, Betty Jean, Richard William, Robert Carroll. B.S., U.S. Mil. Acad., 1936; M.S., Harvard U., 1940; D.Sc., Mass. Inst. Tech., 1940; grad., Air War Coll., 1950. Commd. 2d lt., C.E. U.S. Army, 1936, advanced through grades to col., 1947; served to col. USAF, 1947-53, resigned, 1953, brig. gen. Res., 1954-67, ret., 1967; mgr. missile systems lab. Sylvania Electrics Products, Inc., Whitestone, N.Y., 1953-54, lab. mgr. electronic systems div., Waltham, Mass., 1955-56; v.p. Emerson Electric Mfg. Co., St. Louis, 1957-58, Huyck Corp., Wake Forest, N.C., 1958-65, pres., chief exec. officer, 1966-73, chmn., 1973-80, also dir.; dir. Dynalectron Corp., Harris Corp.; trustee MITRE Corp., 1960-70; Vice chmn. sci. adv. group Office Aerospace Research, 1963-67. Trustee Hudson Inst., 1972-81, chmn. bd., 1973-77; Bd. dirs. Univ. Maine Pulp and Paper Found., 1971-74. Decorated Legion of Merit with oak leaf cluster. Mem. Council on Fgn. Relations. Clubs: Army-Navy Country (Arlington, Va.); Board Room (N.Y.C.); Johns Island, Bent Pine Golf (Vero Beach, Fla.). Home and Office: 800 Beach Rd Apt 374 Vero Beach FL 32963

HAYWOOD, THEODORE JOSEPH, physician, educator; b. Monroe, N.C., Feb. 33, 1929; s. Jesse Beman and Mary (McDonald) H.; m. Nancy Hume Ferguson, Dec. 21, 1959; children: Elizabeth Linscott, Keene McDonald, Mark Shepard. B.S., The Citadel, 1948; M.D., Vanderbilt U., 1952. Diplomate: Am. Bd. Pediatrics, Am. Bd. Allergy and Immunology. Pvt. practice allergy, Houston, 1958—; mem. staff Tex. Children's Hosp., 1958—, attending allergist, 1977—; mem. faculty Baylor U. Coll. Medicine, 1958—, clin. asst. prof. microbiology and pediatrics, 1967-75, clin. asso. prof. microbiology and pediatrics, 1975—; mem. faculty U. Tex. Grad. Sch. Biomed. Scis., 1960—, asso. prof. allergy, 1969—. Served with M.C. AUS, 1955-57. Fellow Am. Coll. Allergists, Am. Acad. Allergy, Am. Acad. Pediatrics, Am. Acad. Psychoanalytic Medicine; mem. Sigma Xi. Republican. Episcopalian. Club: River Oaks Country (Houston). Home: 3257 Reba Dr Houston TX 77019 Office: 6969 Brompton Rd Houston TX 77025

HAZAN, MARCELLA MADDALENA, cookbook author, educator, consultant; b. Cesenatico, Italy, Apr. 15, 1924; d. Giuseppe and Maria (Leonelli) Polini; m. Victor Hazan, Feb. 24, 1955; 1 son, Giuliano. Dr. in Natural Scis., U. Ferrara, 1952, Dr. in Biology, 1954. Researcher Guggenheim Inst., 1955-58; prof. math. and biology Italian State schs., 1963-66; founder Sch. of Italian Cooking, N.Y.C., 1969—, Marcella Hazan Sch. of Classic Italian Cooking, Bologna, Italy, 1976—; v.p. Hazan Classic Enterprises, Inc., 1978—. Author: The Classic Italian Cookbook, 1973, More Classic Italian Cooking, 1978. Mem. Am. Inst. Food and Wine (bd. advisers), Accademia Della Cucina Italiana. Roman Catholic. Address: 155 E 76th St New York NY 10021

HAZARD, CYRIL, physics and astronomy educator. Richard K. Mellon prof. physics and astronomy U. Pitts. Office: U Pitts Dept Physics and Astronomy Pittsburgh PA 15260§

HAZARD, FREDERICK ROWLAND, dredging and marine construction company executive; b. N.Y., June 11, 1923; s. Frederick Rowl and Rozelia (Beldon) H.; m. Fredericka Wilhelmina Aldred, Sept. 18, 1948; children: Susan, Frederick, Caroline, Elizabeth. B.S. in Civil Engring, Brown U., 1948. Engr. Fitzsimmons & Connell Dredge & Dock div. Dunbar & Sullivan, 1948, v.p., to 1967; gen. supt. Gt. Lakes Dredge & Dock Co., Oak Brook, Ill., 1967-71, v.p., 1971-78, v.p., gen. mgr., from 1978, now exec. v.p., dir., 1980—; exec. v.p., dir. parent co. Gt. Lakes Internat. Served with Army Engrs., 1942-46. Mem. ASCE, Nat. Assn. Dredging Contractors (v.p., dir.), River and Harbor Improvement Assn. (pres.). Home: 411 E 3d St Hinsdale IL 60521 Office: Gt Lakes Dredge & Dock Co 2122 York Rd Oak Brook IL 60521

HAZARD, GEOFFREY CORNELL, JR., educator; b. Cleve., Sept. 18, 1929; s. Geoffrey Cornell and Virginia (Perry) H.; m. Elizabeth O'Hara; children—James G., Katherine W., Robin P., Geoffrey Cornell III. B.A., Swarthmore Coll., 1953; LL.B., Columbia U., 1954. Bar: Oreg. bar 1954, Calif. bar 1960. Asso. firm Hart, Spencer, McCulloch, Rockwood & Davies, Portland, Oreg., 1954-57; exec. sec. Oreg. Legis. Interim Com. Jud. Adminstrn., 1957-58; asso. prof. law, then prof. U. Calif. at Berkeley, 1958-64; prof. law U. Chgo., 1964-71, Yale U., 1971—, prof. mgmt., 1979—, Garver prof., 1976-81, Baker Prof., 1981—, dep. dean, 1981—; Exec. dir. Am. Bar Found., Chgo., 1964-70; reporter Am. Bar Assn. Commn. on Standards of Jud. Adminstrn., 1971-77, Am. Law Inst. Restatement of Judgments, 1974—; mem. Adminstrv. Conf. U.S., 1971-78. Author: (with David W. Louisell) Pleading and Procedure, 1962, 4th edit., 1979, Research in Civil Procedure, 1963, (with Fleming James) Civil Procedure, 2d edit, 1977, Ethics in the Practice of Law, 1978, also articles.; Editor: Law in a Changing America, 1968. Served with USAF, 1948-49. Mem. ABA (Commn. to Evaluate Profl. Standards 1978—), Calif. Bar Assn., Assn. Bar City N.Y., Phi Beta Kappa. Episcopalian. Home: 207 Armory St New Haven CT 06511

HAZARD, JOHN BEACH, physician; b. White Horse, Pa., Jan. 7, 1905; s. Frank Birdsall and Blanche Darrah (Stong) H.; m. Etta Mae Holly, Sept. 3, 1931. B.S., U. Fla., 1924, M.S., 1925; M.D., Harvard U., 1930. Intern, resident, asst. in pathology Mallory Inst. Pathology, Boston City Hosp., 1930-34; practice medicine, specializing in pathology, Boston, 1934-46, Cleve., 1946-70; dir. pathology Faulkner Hosp., 1935-46; cons. pathology Robert B. Brigham Hosp., 1937-46; head dept. tissue pathology Cleve. Clinic Found., 1946-70, chmn. div. pathology, 1957-70, emeritus cons., 1970—; acting dir. div. research, 1966-67, vice chmn., 1967-70; instr. pathology Sch. Medicine, Boston U., 1931-32; instr., asst. prof. pathology Med. Sch. Tufts Coll., 1932-46; asso. pathology to clin. prof. pathology Sch. Medicine, Case Western Res. U., 1952-70, emeritus clin. prof., 1970—; mem. pathology study sect. NIH, 1962-65. Editor, author: chpt. The Thyroid, 1964; endocrine pathology sects. Concepts of Disease, 1971; editorial bd.: Am. Jour. Pathology, 1965-82. Bd. dirs. Cleve. chpt. A.R.C., Blue Cross N.E. Ohio. Served from maj. to col., M.C. AUS, 1942-46. Mem. A.M.A. (past chmn. sect. pathology), Am. Assn. Pathologists and Bacteriologists, Am. Soc. Clin. Pathologists (past dir.), Am. Thyroid Assn. (past v.p.), Coll. Am. Pathologists, Internat. Acad. Pathology (past pres.), N.Y. Acad. Sci., A.A.A.S., Am. Soc. Cytology, Royal Soc. Medicine. Home: 200 Ocean Lane Dr Key Biscayne FL 33149

HAZARD, JOHN NEWBOLD, retired public law educator; b. Syracuse, N.Y., Jan. 5, 1909; s. John Gibson and Ada Bosarte (DeKalb) H.; m. Susan Lawrence, March 8, 1941; children: John Gibson, William Lawrence, Nancy, Barbara Peace. Ed., The Hill Sch., 1926; A.B., Yale U., 1930; LL.B., Harvard U., 1934; certificate, Moscow Juridical Inst., 1937; J.S.D., U. Chgo., 1939; LL.D., U. Freiburg, 1969, Lehigh U., 1970, Leiden U., 1975, U. Paris, 1977, U. Louvain, 1979. Bar: N.Y. bar, U.S. Supreme Ct. bar. Fellow Inst. of Current World Affairs (student of Soviet law), 1934-39; asso. with law firm Baldwin, Todd & Young, N.Y.C., 1939-41; dep. dir. U.S.S.R. br. Fgn. Econ. Adminstrn. (and predecessor agys.), 1941-45; adv. on state trading Dept. State, 1945-46; prof. public law Columbia, 1946-77, Nash prof. law, 1976-77, Nash prof. law emeritus, 1977—; adviser on Soviet law to U.S. chief of counsel for prosecution of Axis criminality, 1945; lectr. Soviet law U. Chgo., 1938-39; lectr. Soviet polit. instns. Columbia U., 1940-41; lectr. internat. politics Fgn. Service Ednl. Found., 1944-46; vis. prof. law Yale U., spring 1949, 50, 52, 54, 56; vis. Fulbright prof. U. Cambridge, London Sch. Econs., 1952-53, U. Louvain, Belgium, 1979; vis. prof. U. Tokyo, summer 1956, Geneva, 1959-60; prof. Luxembourg Comparative Law Faculty, summers 1958-60, Strasbourg Comparative Law Faculty, summers 1962-82; vis. prof. U. Teheran, fall 1966, U. Sydney, 1978; Goodhart prof. Cambridge U., 1981-82; prof. European U. Inst., 1984-85; sr. specialist East-West Center Hawaii, spring 1967; fellow Center for Advanced Study in the Behavioral Scis., 1961-62. Author: Soviet Housing Law, 1939, Law and Social Change in the USSR, 1953, The Soviet System of Government, 1957, Settling Disputes in Soviet Society, 1960, (with I. Shapiro) The Soviet Legal System, 1962, Communists and Their Law, 1969, Managing Change in the USSR, 1983; Recollections of a Pioneer Sovietologist, 1983; Editor: Soviet Legal Philosophy, 1951; Bd. editors: Am. Slavic and East European Rev; mng. editor, 1951-59; bd. editors: Am. Polit. Sci. Rev, 1950, Am. Jour. Internat. Law, 1956-72; hon. editor, 1974—; bd. editors: Am. Jour. Comparative Law, 1952—. Dir. and sec. Am. Assn. for the Advancement of Slavic Studies, 1948-60, treas., 1961-65. Recipient Pres.'s Certificate of Merit, 1947. Mem. Am. Bar Assn. (vice chmn. internat. and comparative law 1951-58), Assn. Bar City N.Y. (chmn. com. fgn. law 1947-50), Am. Polit. Sci. Assn., Am. Soc. Internat. Law (exec. council 1946-49, 51-54, v.p. 1971-73, hon. v.p. 1973-84, hon. pres. 1984-85), Am. br. of Internat. Law Assn. (chmn. exec. com. 1958-59, v.p. 1957-73, pres. 1973-79), Internat. Acad. Comparative Law (pres. 1984—), Internat. Assn. Legal Sci. (pres. 1968-70), Am. Philos. Soc., Am. Acad. Arts and Scis., World Assn. Law Profs. (co-chmn. 1975—), Am. Fgn. Law Assn. (pres. 1973-76), Brit. Acad. (corr.), Phi Alpha Delta, Alpha Delta Phi. Democrat. Episcopalian. Clubs: Century (N.Y.); University (Washington); Wolf's Head. Home: 20 E 94th St New York NY 10028 Office: 435 W 116th St New York NY 10027

HAZARD, JOHN WHARTON, columnist; b. Washington, June 15, 1912; s. Elmont Bibb and Lillian (Wooldridge) H.; m. Celima Roi Leonard, Aug. 31, 1935 (div. 1950); 1 dau., Celima (Mrs. Robert Eugene Richardson); m. Helen Latham Kerr, Nov. 11, 1950; children: Anne Latham, John Wharton, Amanda Agney, Thomas Bibb, Charlotte Wooldridge, Charles Allen Kerr. A.B., Haverford (Pa.) Coll., 1933. Reporter Wall St. Jour., Washington, 1934-37; reporter King Features Syndicate, Washington, 1937-42; asso. editor Changing Times, Kiplinger Washington Editors Inc., 1946-53, sr. editor, 1953-65, exec. editor, 1965-74, spl. asst. to pres., dir., 1974-78, ret., 1978; editorial cons., 1978—; columnist U.S. News & World Report; chmn. bd., dir. Colchester Corp. Author: Success With Your Money, 1956, (with Lew G. Coit) The Kiplinger Book on Investing for the Years Ahead, 1962, (with Milton Christie) The Investment Business, 1964, Choosing Tomorrow's Growth Stocks Today, 1968, Success With Your Investments, 1973. Pres. Gunston Hall Sch. Served to lt. comdr. USNR, 1942-46. Mem. Sigma Delta Chi. Clubs: Army-Navy, Nat. Press; Sandy Bay Yacht (Rockport, (Mass.); Masons. Home and Office: 5809 River Dr Lorton VA 22079

HAZARD, ROBERT CULVER, JR., hotel executive; b. Balt., Oct. 23, 1934; s. Robert Culver and Catherine B. H.; m. Mary Victoria Cranor, Jan. 2, 1981; children by previous marriage: Alicia W., Letitia A., Robert Culver, III, Thomas E.J., Anne. B.A. cum laude, Woodrow Wilson Sch., Princeton U., 1956; postgrad., Johns Hopkins U., U. Denver. Mktg. rep. IBM Corp., Denver, 1959-68; with Am. Express Co., 1968-74, v.p. exec. accounts reservations, 1973-74; chief exec. officer Best Western Internat., 1974-80; pres., chief exec. officer Quality Inns Internat., Silver Spring, Md., 1980—. Served to capt. USAF, 1956-59. Recipient Man of Yr. award Motel Brokers Assn. Am., 1976, Silver Plate award Hospitality mag., 1979. Mem. Am. Hotel and Motel Assn., Discover Am. Travel Orgn. Office: 10750 Columbia Pike Silver Spring MD 20901

HAZARD, WILLIS GILPIN, indsl. hygienist; b. West Chester, Pa., Apr. 27, 1907; s. Willis Hatfield and Mary D. (Creigh) H.; m. Elizabeth Anne Ericson, Sept. 20, 1941; children—Willis Gilpin, Samuel Garth, David Creigh, Barbara Anne. A.B., Harvard U., 1929, M.A., 1930. Registered profl. engr., Ohio. Instr. indsl. hygiene Harvard U. Sch. Pub. Health, 1930-34; with personnel relations dept. Owens-Ill. Glass Co. (name later changed to Owens-Ill. Inc.), Toledo, 1934-72, dir. indsl. hygiene, 1942-72; cons. indsl. hygiene, Toledo, 1972—; mem. indsl. hygiene fellowship bd. Oak Ridge Inst. Nuclear Studies, 1960-63; trustee Indsl. Health Found., Pitts. Contbr. articles to profl. jours. Served as maj. USPHS, 1941-46. Mem. Am. Indsl. Hygiene Assn. (pres. 1961-62, Cummings award 1968), Am. Bd. Indsl. Hygiene (diplomate, dir. 1964—, pres. 1966—), Acoustical Soc. Am., Am. Soc. Heating, Refrigeration and Air Conditioning Engrs., Am. Pub. Health Assn. Episcopalian. Patentee in field. Home and office: 3609 Mapleway Dr Toledo OH 43614

HAZEL, DAVID WILLIAM, coll. dean; b. Boston, May 15, 1920; s. Francis Putnam and Bessie (Coleman) H.; m. Ruth Naomi Rivers, Dec. 26, 1946; children—Cheryl (Mrs. Russell Roberts), Daryl, David, Kim. A.B., Tufts U., 1943; M.Ed., Boston U., 1946; Ph.D., U. Mich., 1957. Asst. prof. sociology and polit. sci. Tuskegee (Ala.) Inst., 1946-47, 49-52; asst prof. econ. Prairie View (Tex.) A. and M. Coll., 1953-57; asso. prof. polit. sci. So. Univ., Baton Rouge, 1957-58; prof. polit. sci. Central State U., Wilberforce, Ohio, 1958-65, chmn. dept., 1966-71, dean, 1971—; vis. prof. Miami U. Ohio, Central Mich. U. Treas. Mental Health Assn. Greene County, 1971-72; mem. sub-com. community planning, comdg. gen.'s com. Wright-Patterson AFB, 1971; Bd. dirs. Faith Community Methodist Housing Authority, Xenia, Ohio. Served with USAAF, 1942-43. Gen. Edn. Bd. fellow, 1947-49; So. Fellowship Fund fellow, 1956-57. Mem. Am. Polit Sci. Assn. (ethics com.). Democrat. Episcopalian. Home: PO Box 127 Wilberforce OH 45384 *There are many opportunities in the life of each of us: it is up to us to convert them to our advantage. In my professional life I have always tried to understand the problems facing me, to deal with my associates diplomatically and, after having weighed the merits of each case, have never failed to take a very definite stand.*

HAZEL, KURT DONALD, company executive; b. Detroit, Feb. 10, 1938; s. Carl Joseph and Rosa (Himmel) H.; m. Christine Dodd; children: Jason, Jennifer. B.S. in Engring, Princeton U., 1959, M.S., 1961. With Touche Ross & Co. (C.P.A.s), N.Y.C., 1961-72, partner, 1968-72; asst. treas. E.I. dupont de Nemours & Co., Inc., Wilmington, Del., 1972-75, product mgr., mktg. mgr., 1975-78, sr. v.p., 1978—; dir. Emhart Corp., Hartford, Conn.; mem. internat. adv. bd. Am. Security Bank, Washington. Bd. dir. Del. Art Mus.; Bd. dirs. Grand Opera House, Wilmington, 1973-75. Clubs: Bohemian (San Francisco); Burning Tree, Metropolitan (Washington). Office: Werik Bldg 251 Essex St Milburn NJ 07041

HAZELRIGG, CHARLES TABB, educator; b. Mt. Sterling, Ky., Aug. 18, 1915; s. Charles Tibbs and Mattie Elrod (Tabb) H.; m. Margie Louise Hedrick, Nov. 1, 1942; children—Charles Tabb, Anne Hedrick. B.A., Centre Coll., 1937; M.A., Yale, 1942, Ph.D., 1947. Instr. English and Am. lit. Centre Coll. of Ky., Danville, 1941-42, asst. prof., 1947-49, asso. prof., 1949-50, prof., 1950—, chmn. English dept., 1949-72, chmn. humanities div., 1972—. Author: American Literary Pioneer, 1953; Co-editor: Principles and Standards in Composition, 1957; Mem. editorial bd.: Univ. Press of Ky; contbr. article to profl. jour. Served with USNR, 1942-45. Recipient Outstanding Citizen award, Danville, 1954. Mem. Modern Lang. Assn., Nat. Council Tchrs. English, Phi Beta Kappa Found. Mem. Christian Ch. (chmn. bd.). Club: Rotarian. Home: 332 McDowell Dr Danville KY 40422

HAZELTINE, BARRETT, elec. engr., educator; b. Paris, France, Nov. 7, 1931; came to U.S., 1932; s. L. Alan and Elizabeth (Barrett) H.; m. Mary Frances Fenn, Aug. 25, 1956; children—Michael B., Alice W., Patricia F. B.S.E., Princeton U., 1953, M.S.E., 1956; Ph.D., U. Mich., 1962. Registered profl. engr., R.I. Asst. prof. engring. Brown U., 1959-66, asso. prof., 1966-72, prof., 1972—, asst. to dean, 1962-63, asst. dean, 1968-74, asso. dean, 1974—; lectr., vis. prof. U. Zambia, Lusaka, 1970-71; -76-77; vis. prof. U. Malawi-Poly., Blantyre, 1980-81; asst. to mgr. research labs., space and info. systems div. Raytheon Co., 1964-65, cons., 1965-67, R.I. Utilities Commn., 1977-80. Author: Introduction to Electronic Circuits and Applications, 1980. Recipient award for excellence in instrn. Western Electric, 1968; grantee NSF, Dept. Edn., Met. Life Ins. Ednl. Found. Mem. IEEE (chmn. Providence sect. 1971-72), Providence Engring. Soc. (pres. 1977-78), Am. Soc. Engring. Edn., Sigma Xi, Tau Beta Pi. Congregationalist (deacon). Clubs: Providence Art, Providence Review. Patentee color recognition system. Home: 60 Barnes St Providence RI 02906 Office: Div Engring Brown U Providence RI 02912

HAZELTINE, HERBERT SAMUEL, JR., lawyer; b. Huntington Beach, Calif., Dec. 12, 1908; s. Herbert S. and Emma (Phelps) H.; m. Frances Sue Coffin, July 5, 1936; children: Susan, Ann, Lynn. A.B., Stanford U., 1931; LL.D., Harvard U., 1934, U. So. Calif., 1979. Bar: Calif. 1935. Partner Adams, Duque & Hazeltine, Los Angeles, 1945—. Sec., gen. counsel Boys' Club Found. So. Calif.; bd. dirs. Los Angeles chpt. A.R.C.; Trustee U. So. Calif. Served as lt. comdr. USNR, 1942-45. Mem. ABA, Am. Soc. Corp. Secs. Clubs: California; Valley (Montecito, Calif.); Cypress Point, Annandale Golf. Home: 495 Orange Grove Circle Pasadena CA 91105 Office: 523 W 6th St Los Angeles CA 90014

HAZELTON, PAUL VERNON, teacher educator; b. Biddeford, Maine, July 22, 1919; s. Charles Bernard and Jessie (Sands) H.; m. Jane O'Connell Desaulniers, Nov. 14, 1942; children: Stephen, Mary, Anne. B.S., Bowdoin Coll., 1942; postgrad., Yale U., 1947-48; M.Ed., Harvard U., 1958. Tchr., English pub. and pvt. schs., Maine, Va., Conn., 1944-48; admissions officer, instr. English Bowdoin Coll., Brunswick, Maine, 1948-57, prof. edn., 1957—; tchr. Colby Coll., 1963, U. Maine, 1964, 70. Mem. Maine State Bd. Edn., 1968-72; chmn. Maine Adv. Council on Vocat. Edn., 1972-75; mem. Maine Humanities Council. Served with AUS, 1942-43. Mem. Am. Ednl. Research Assn., AAUP. Democrat. Home: 33 Elm St Topsham ME 04086 Office: Sills Hall Bowdoin Coll Brunswick ME 04011

HAZEN, DAVID COMSTOCK, aerospace and mechanical engineering educator; b. Greenburg, N.Y., July 3, 1927; m. Mary Ann Shipherd, Nov. 27, 1948; children: George Shipherd, Thomas Coe, Anne Scott. Grad. cum laude, Choate Sch., 1944; B.S. magna cum laude in Engring, Princeton U., 1948, M.S., 1949. Instr. Princeton U., 1949-51, research asso., 1951-53, asst. prof. aerospace and mech. engring., 1953-56, asso. prof., 1956-63, prof., 1963-83, prof. emeritus, 1983—, asso. dean faculty, 1966-69, asso. chmn. dept. aerospace and mech. Scis., 1969-74; mem. various engring. sch. coms. and univ. coms. coms.; exec. dir. Assembly of Engring. NRC, 1980-82—, exec. dir. Commn. on Engring. and Tech. Systems, 1982—; cons. in field; mem. Research Adv. Com. Lab. Adv. Bd. for Naval Ships, 1968-78; mem. (Naval Research Adv. Com. Marine Corps Panel), 1969-78, chmn., 1970-78, mem., 1971-74, 1971-78, vice chmn., 1972-75, chmn., 1975-77; mem. naval studies bd. NRC, 1978—. Trustee Sterling Sch., Craftsbury Common, Vt. (chmn. 1965-70, vice chmn. 1970-72), Robert Coll. Istanbul, Turkey, 1969-81, Univ. Petroleum and Minerals, Saudi Arabia, 1973—; mem. Princeton-in-Asia Found., 1964-80, v.p., 1968-80. Recipient Dept. Navy Distinguished Service award, 1977, certificate of commendation USMC, 1978. Fellow AIAA (chmn. edn. com. 1965-68, v.p. edn. 1971-73); mem. Aero. Soc. India (governing bd. Kanpur br. 1964-65), Wingfoot Lake Lighter Than Air Soc. (hon.), Am. Ordnance Assn., Engrs. Council for Profl. Devel. (mem. bd. 1971-77), Am. Soc. Engring. Edn. (exec. com. aerospace div. 1971), Sigma Xi, Phi Beta Kappa. Address: 1657 B S Hayes St Arlington VA 22202

HAZEN, EDWARD GATES, ret. banker; b. Thomaston, Conn., June 8, 1906; s. Robert and Helen (Gates) H.; m. Virginia May Robert, Sept. 10, 1938; children—Edward Gates, Robert Dana. Student, Lawrence Acad., 1922-24; A.B., Amherst Coll., 1928; LL.B., U. Conn., 1938. Clk. Waterbury Savs. Bank, Conn., 1929; trainee Scovill Mfg. Co., 1930-32; clk. Colonial Bank & Trust Co., 1933-46, trust officer, 1946-55, v.p., trust officer, 1955-65, sr. v.p., 1965-67, exec. v.p., 1967-69; exec. v.p., chmn. trust com., 1969-71; vice chmn. Thomaston Savs. Bank, 1971-80, chmn., 1980-81, also dir., corporator, ret., 1981; dir. Hallden Machine Co.; Mem. Conn. Bankers Trust Com., 1966-71. Mem. bd. finance, Town of Thomaston, 1946-48; trustee Waterbury Found., Inc., 1970-78, treas., 1968-80; mem. Watertown Sch. Bldg. Com., 1956-59, chmn., 1958-59; Trustee Waterbury chpt. A.R.C., 1961-63. Served with USAAF, 1943-45. Clubs: Litchfield County University (Watertown) (treas. 1975—); Waterbury. Home: 99 North St Watertown CT 06795

HAZEN, RICHARD, engineer; b. Dobbs Ferry, N.Y., Aug. 5, 1911; s. Allen and Elizabeth (McConway) H.; m. Elizabeth Shute, June 19, 1937; children: Richard (dec.), Annah Putnam Hazen Gorman, Mary Vanderlyn Hazen Gillam. A.B., Dartmouth Coll., 1932; B.C.E., Columbia U., 1934; M.S. in San. Engring, Harvard U., 1937. Asst. engr. Westvaco Corp., 1934-36; asst. engr. Malcolm Pirnie (Engrs.), 1937-40, asso. engr., 1940-42, partner, 1946-51, Hazen and Sawyer, N.Y.C., 1951-81; vis. prof. U. N.C., Chapel Hill, 1968; cons. planning and design of water supply and waste disposal to govt. and industry. Contbr. articles to profl. jours., also chpts. on water supply to encys. and engring. handbooks. Bd. dirs. Children's Village, Dobbs Ferry, N.Y., 1952; bd. dirs. Dobbs Ferry Bd. Edn., 1946-52, pres., 1948-51. Served with USNR, 1942-46. Mem. Nat. Acad. Engring., Am. Inst. Cons. Engrs. (pres. 1968), ASCE (dir. 1966-69, hon. mem. 1983), Am.

Water Works Assn. (hon. mem., dir. 1951-56), Am. Acad. Environ. Engring., Water Pollution Control Fedn., TAPPI, New Eng. Water Works Assn., Phi Beta Kappa, Tau Beta Pi. Club: Harvard (N.Y.C.). Home: 76 Oliphant Ave Dobbs Ferry NY 10522

HAZEN, SALLY SUE, oil and gas company executive; b. Monroe, La., Aug. 10, 1929; d. Charles Addison and Helen Louise (Gass) H. B.S. in Bus. Adminstrn, La. State U., 1950. Stenographer-sec. United Gas Corp., Shreveport, 1950-70; asst. corp. sec. Pennzoil Co., Houston, 1970-76, corp. sec., 1976—. Mem. Am. Soc. Corp. Secs. Republican. Presbyterian. Club: Plaza. Office: Pennzoil Pl 700 Milam St Houston TX 77002

HAZEN, STANLEY PHILLIP, periodontology educator, university dean; b. Alexandria, Minn., Aug. 29, 1924; s. Ray and Edith (Packard) H.; m. Evelyn Joyce Edwards, Aug. 21, 1948; children: Jean, Elizabeth, Robert, Patricia, James, Anne, Suzanne. B.A., Macalester Coll., 1949; D.D.S., U. Minn., 1953; M.S., U. Rochester, 1960; certificate, Eastman Dental Center, 1960. Asso., dept. periodontology Eastman Dental Center, Rochester, N.Y., 1960-63; asso. prof., chmn. dept. periodontology State U. N.Y. at Buffalo, 1963-67; prof., dir. grad. and postgrad. studies Temple U. Dental Sch., Phila., 1967-70; prof., head dept. periodontology U. Conn. Dental Sch., Hartford, 1970-73; dean sch. dental medicine So. Ill. U., Edwardsville, 1973-77; prof., chmn. dept. periodontology U. Detroit Dental Sch., 1977-80, asso. dean acad. affairs, 1980-82; prof. periodontology Georgetown U. Sch. Dentistry, Washington, 1982—, dean, 1982—. Served with USNR, 1942-46, 53-57. Postdoctoral research fellow NIH, 1957-60. Mem. ADA, Am. Acad. Periodontology, Am. Assn. Dental Schs., Internat. Assn. Dental Research, Am. Coll. Dentists, D.C. Dist. Dental Soc., Omicron Kappa Upsilon. Home: 4617 4th Rd N Arlington VA 22203

HAZEN, WILLIAM HARRIS, finance executive; b. Salem, Mass., Jan. 6, 1931; s. Julius Elijah and Dorothy (Harris) H.; m. Judith Ettl, Feb. 22, 1959; children: Cordelia, Alexes. A.B., Bowdoin Coll., 1952; J.D., Harvard U., 1958. Bar: N.Y. 1959. With firm Pell, Butler, Hatch, Curtis & LeViness, N.Y.C., 1959-61; exec. asst. to N.Y. supt. banks, 1962-64; with J.W. Seligman & Co., N.Y.C., 1964-68, partner, 1969-80; pres., chief exec. officer Seligman Securities, Inc., N.Y.C., 1981-83, J. & W. Seligman Trust Co., 1983—; v.p. Union Capital Fund, Inc., 1969-81, Tri-Continental Corp., N.Y.C., 1969-81, Broad St. Investing Corp., 1969-81, Nat. Investors Corp., 1969-81, Union Income Fund, Inc., 1969-81. Adv. mem. Joint Legislative Com. Revise Banking Laws, N.Y. State, 1964; Pres. Bklyn. Heights Landmarks Conservancy, Inc., 1979—. Served to lt. USNR, 1952-55; Korea. Mem. Zeta Psi. Congregationalist (trustee). Club: Heights Casino (Bklyn.). Home: 55 Remsen St Brooklyn Heights NY 11201 Office: One Bankers Trust Plaza New York NY 10006

HAZLEHURST, FRANKLIN HAMILTON, fine arts educator; b. Spartanburg, S.C., Nov. 6, 1925; s. Robert Purviance and Lottie Lee (Nicholls) H.; m. Carol Foord, Aug. 26, 1950; children: Franklin Hamilton, Robert Purviance II, Mary Hadley, Abigail Norris. B.A., Princeton, 1949, M.F.A., 1952, Ph.D. (Charlotte Elizabeth Proctor fellow), 1956. Instr. Princeton, 1954-56; lectr. Frick Collection, Princeton Theol. Sem., 1956-57; asst. prof., asso. prof. U. Ga., 1957-63; prof., chmn. dept. fine arts Vanderbilt U., Nashville, 1963—. Author: Jacques Boyceau and the French Formal Garden, 1966, Gardens of Illusion: The Genius of André Le Nostre, 1980 (Alice Davis Hitchcock award 1982); Contbr. articles to profl. jours. Served with AUS, 1944-46. Fulbright fellow, 1953-54; Sarah H. Moss fellow U. Ga., 1961-62; summer grantee Am. Council Learned Socs., 1967, Am. Philos. Soc., 1967-68, 83; recipient Madison Sarratt prize for excellence in undergrad. teaching, 1970. Mem. Coll. Art Assn. Am., Soc. Archtl. Historians (Alice Davis Hitchcock award 1982), La Société de l'histoire de l'art francais. Home: 4430 Shepard Pl Nashville TN 37205

HAZLEHURST, ROBERT PURVIANCE, JR., lawyer; b. Spartanburg, S.C., Jan. 7, 1919; s. Robert Purviance and Lottie Lee (Nicholls) H.; m. Mary Kieruff, Feb. 20, 1947 (dec. July 1971); children: Ellen Hazlehurst Ojeda, Charlotte, Anne Hazlehurst Goldberg; m. Dorothy Wilson Deemer, Jan. 7, 1972. A.B., Princeton U., 1940; LL.B., Yale U., 1947. Bar: N.J. 1947. Since practiced in Newark and Morristown; partner Pitney, Hardin, Kipp & Szuch, 1952—; Bd. dirs. Princeton Fund, 1966-71, chmn. ann. giving campaign, 1967-68. Sec., trustee Greater Newark Hosp. Devel. Fund; trustee Kent Pl. Sch., Summit, N.J., 1960-70; trustee, v.p. Silver Hill Found., New Canaan, Conn.; trustee United Hosps. Newark, 1958-73, pres., 1970-73. Served to capt. USAAF, 1942-45. Mem. Am., N.J., Essex County, Morris County bar assns. Clubs: Essex (Newark); Morristown, Short Hills, Nassau, Princeton (N.J.). Home: 38 Sinclair Terr Short Hills NJ 07078 Office: 163 Madison Ave Morristown NJ 07960

HAZLETT, JAMES ARTHUR, ins. adminstr.; b. Kansas City, Mo., May 26, 1917; s. Arthur J. and Clara E. (Quackenbush) H.; m. Mary Quinn Pope, July 3, 1937; 1 son, Stephen. B.S., Kansas City Tchrs. Coll., 1937; M.A., U. Kansas City, 1943; postgrad., U. Mo.; Ed.D., U. Kan., 1974; LL.D., Park Coll., 1958. Tchr. Kansas City Pub. Schs., 1938-45, elementary sch. prin., 1945-51, dir. research, 1951-55, supt. schs., 1955-69; adminstrv. dir. Nat. Assessment Program Edn. Commn. States, Denver, 1969-74; v.p. Forrest T. Jones Ins. Co., Kansas City, Mo., 1974—; lectr. edn., prin. Summer Demonstration Sch., U. Mo. at Kansas City, 1950-55, 76—. Mem. bd. Kansas City Mus., Philharmonic Assn., area council Boy Scouts; treas. Mid-Continent Regional Edn. Lab., 1966-68; Chmn. Pres.'s Nat. Adv. Council Supplementary Centers and Services, 1968-70. Recipient of Nat. Human Relations award from the Nat. Conf. Christians and Jews, 1962. Mem. Am. Assn. Sch. Adminstrs. (chmn. resolutions com. 1967), Mo. Tchrs. Assn. (past pres.), Nat. Congress Parents and Tchrs. (bd. mgrs. 1968-71), N.E.A., Native Sons Kansas City, Phi Delta Kappa. Methodist (bd.). Home: 631 E 115th Terr Kansas City MO 64131 Office: 3130 Broadway Kansas City MO 64111

HAZLETT, JAMES STEPHEN, university dean; b. Kansas City, Mo., Feb. 27, 1940; (m), 1961; 2 children. Student, Inst. Polit. Studies, Paris, 1960-61; B.A., Yale U., 1962; M.A., Harvard U., 1963; Ph.D., U. Chgo., 1968. Instr. edn. U. Chgo., 1967-68, asst. prof., 1968-71; asst. prof. cultural founds. edn. U. Tex., Austin, 1971-74, asso. prof., 1975-80; prof. ednl. adminstrn., supervision and founds., asso. dean Coll. Edn., U. Nebr., Omaha, 1980-83; dean Sch. Edn., Ind. State U., Terre Haute, 1983—. Sch Edn Ind State U Terre Haute IN 47809

HAZLETT, ROBERT CUMMINS, banker; b. Wheeling, W.Va., June 7, 1910; s. Robert and Anne (Cummins) H.; m. Susan Arbenz, Oct. 17, 1936; children: Robert Cummins, John A., James B., George S., Thomas McK. Grad., Linsly Mil. Inst., Wheeling, 1927; C.E., Cornell U., 1931. With Wheeling Dollar Savs. & Trust Co., 1931—, v.p. charge trusts, 1931-58, pres., 1958—, chmn. bd., 1978—; dir. Wheeling Stamping Co. Mem. Ohio County Bd. Ed., 1952-68; past pres. Community Chest.; Pres., dir. Greenwood Cemetery Assn., Wheeling; trustee emeritus Linsly Mil. Inst., Ohio Valley General Hosp., Wheeling; trustee Reynolds Meml. Hosp., Glendale, W.Va. Named Citizen of Year, Wheeling, 1952. Mem. W.Va. Bankers Assn. (pres. 1968-69), Symposhiarchs, Phi Kappa Sigma. Presbyterian (trustee). Clubs: Elks, Fort Henry, Why Country (Wheeling); Statler (Cornell U.). Home: 6 Echo Point Circle Wheeling WV 26003 Office: Bank Plaza Wheeling WV 26003

HAZLITT, HENRY, editor, author; b. Phila., Nov. 28, 1894; s. Stuart Clark and Bertha (Zauner) H.; m. Frances S. Kanes, 1936. Student, CCNY, 1912; Litt. D., Grove City Coll., Pa., 1958; LL.D., Bethany Coll., 1961; S.Sc.D., Universidad Francisco Marroquin, Guatemala, 1976. Mem. staff Wall St. Jour., 1913-16; fin. staff N.Y. Evening Post, 1916-18; monthly fin. Letter of Mechanics and Metals, Nat. Bank, N.Y.C., 1919-20; fin. editor N.Y. Evening Mail, 1921-23; editorial writer N.Y. Herald, 1923-24, The Sun, 1924-25, lit. editor, 1925-29, The Nation, 1930-33; editor Am. Mercury, 1933-34; editorial staff N.Y. Times, 1934-46; asso. Newsweek; writer column Bus. Tides, 1946-66; internationally syndicated columnist, 1966-69; co-editor The Freeman, 1950-52, editor-in-chief, 1953. Author: Thinking as a Science, 1916, 69, The Anatomy of Criticism, 1933, A New Constitution Now, 1942, rev. edit., 1974, Economics in One Lesson, 1946, rev. edit., 1979 (10 translations), Will Dollars Save The World?, 1947, Condensed in Reader's Digest, 1948, The Great Idea, 1951, rev. as Time Will Run Back, 1966, The Free Man's Library, 1956, The Failure of the New Economics; An Analysis of the Keynesian Fallacies, 1959, 73, What You Should Know About Inflation, 1960, 65, The Foundations of Morality, 1964, 73, Man vs. The Welfare State, 1969, The Conquest of Poverty, 1973, The Inflation Crisis and How to Resolve It, 1978, From Bretton Woods to World Inflation, 1983; editor: A Practical Program for America, 1932, The Critics of Keynesian Economics, 1960, new edit., 1977. Served in A.S., U.S. Army, World War I. Recipient Honor medal Freedoms Found., 1950, 60, 62. Mem. Mont Pelerin Soc. Clubs: Authors (London, Eng.); Century, Dutch Treat, Overseas Press (N.Y.C.). Home: 59 Courtland Ave Stamford CT 06902

HAZZARD, SHIRLEY, author; b. Sydney, Australia, Jan. 30, 1931; d. Reginald and Catherine (Stein) H.; m. Francis Steegmuller, Dec. 22, 1963. Ed., Queenwood Sch., Sydney, to 1946. With Combined Services Intelligence, Hong Kong, 1947-48, U.K. High Commr.'s Office, Wellington, N.Z., 1949-51, UN (Gen. Service Category), N.Y.C., 1952-62; Boyer lectr., Australia, 1984. Author: Cliffs of Fall and Other Stories, 1963; novel The Evening of the Holiday, 1966; fiction People in Glass Houses, 1967; novel The Bay of Noon, 1970; social history Defeat of an Ideal: A Study of the Self-Destruction of the United Nations, 1973; novel The Transit of Venus, 1980; contbr.: short stories to New Yorker mag. Trustee N.Y. Soc. Library. Recipient 1st prize O. Henry Short Story Awards, 1976; grantee in lit. Nat. Inst. Arts and Letters, 1966; Guggenheim fellow, 1974; Nat. Book Critics Circle award for Fiction, 1981; Christian Gauss lectureship award Princeton U., 1982. Mem. Nat. Inst. Arts and Letters. Address: 200 E 66th St New York NY 10021

HEACOCK, RAYMOND LEROY, space exploration and research executive; b. Santa Ana, Calif., Jan. 9, 1928; s. George Leslie and Mildred Marie (Saylor) H.; m. Yvonne Ann, Mar. 31, 1962; children: Lisa Ann, David Raymond, Michele Lynn; children by previous marriage: John Alan, Gale Susan. Student, Santa Ana Coll., 1948-49; B.S. in Elec. Engring, Calif. Inst. Tech., 1952, M.S., 1953. With Jet Propulsion Lab., Pasadena, Calif., 1953—, spacecraft systems mgr. Voyager Project, 1970-77, dep. project mgr. Voyager Project, 1977-79, project mgr. Voyager Project, 1979-81, advance space missions project mgr., 1981-82, acting project mgr. widefield/planetary camera for space telescope, 1982—. Served with USN, 1946-48. Recipient James Watt Internat. Gold medal Instn. Mech. Engrs., London, 1980, Astronautics Engr. award Nat. Space Club, 1981, Disting. Service medal NASA, 1981. Mem. AIAA, Alumni Assn., Calif. Inst. Tech. (sec., treas., v.p., pres. bd. dirs.). Republican. Presbyterian. Selected as experimenter Ranger missions VII thru IX, NASA, 1964-65. Office: Jet Propulsion Lab 4800 Oak Grove Dr Pasadena CA 91109

HEACOCK, WALTER JUDSON, museum director; b. Talladega, Ala., May 5, 1921; s. Walter Judson and Minnielou (Kelley) H. Student, Harvard U. Bus. Sch., 1943-44; B.A., Furman U., 1943, Litt.D., 1960; M.A., U. Wis., 1947, Ph.D., 1951. Asst. prof. history Furman U., 1949-51; dir. exhbn. bldgs. Colonial Williamsburg (Va.), 1951; lectr. Coll. William and Mary, 1951-52; dir. Hagley Mus., Wilmington, Del., 1954—; gen. dir. Eleutherian Mills-Hagley Found., Inc., Greenville and Wilmington, 1966—; bd. dirs., v.p. Old Brandywine Vill., Inc., Wilmington, 1962—; cons., hon. trustee Kenmore Assos., Fredericksburg, Va.; cons. Shakertown at Pleasant Hill, Ky. Served to lt. USNR, 1943-46. Named Distinguished Delawarean, 1976. Mem. Am. Assn. Museums, Nat. Trust Hist. Preservation, Assn. State, Local History, Hist. Soc. Del. (dir. 1964—, pres. 1972-80), Del. Art Mus. (exec. com. 1972—), Phi Beta Kappa. Clubs: Wilmington; Cosmos (Washington). Home: PO Box 3866 Greenville DE 19807 Office: Eleutherian Mills-Hagley Found Greenville PO Box 3630 Greenville DE 19807

HEAD, DANIEL GEORGE, construction company executive; b. N.Y.C., Sept. 10, 1924; s. Charles William and Nellie (O'Donoghue) H.; m. Mary Joyce Head, Aug. 24, 1957; children—Patricia, Moira, Daniel, Charles, Eileen. B.C.E., Manhattan Coll., 1949; LL.D. (hon.), St. John's U., Jamaica, N.Y., 1981. Registered profl. engr., N.Y.C. Structural engr. James P. O'Donnell, N.Y.C., 1950-52; constrn. supt. John A. Johnson Co., N.Y.C., 1954-57; gen. supt. constrn. Terminal Constrn. Co., N.Y.C., 1957-59; project mgr., v.p. estimating George A. Fuller Co., N.Y.C., 1959-79, pres., 1979—; v.p. ops. Joseph L. Muscarello, Inc., N.J., 1982—; v.p. Northrop Corp., 1979—; cons. com. engring. Manhattan Coll.; adv. com. N.Y. Real Estate Bd.; Mem. Norwood (N.J.) Bd. Adjustment, 1960-62. Pres. Norwood Bd. Edn., 1965-68. Served with USNR, 1943-45. Mem. ASCE, Nat. Soc. Profl. Engrs. Roman Catholic. Club: N.Y. Athletic. Office: 595 Madison Ave New York NY 10022 *

HEAD, EDWARD DENNIS, bishop; b. White Plains, N.Y., Aug. 5, 1919; s. Charles W. and Nellie (O'Donahue) H. Student, Cathedral Coll., Columbia, St. Joseph's Sem., Dunwoodie, Yonkers, N.Y.; M.A., N.Y. Sch. Social Work, 1948. Ordained priest Roman Catholic Ch., 1945; tchr. Notre Dame Coll., S.I.; asst. pastor Sacred Heart Ch., Bronx, St. Roch's Ch., S.I.; with Cath. Charities Office, Archdiocese of New York, 1947-66; exec. dir. Cath. Charities, 1966-70; aux. bishop of New York, 1970-73, bishop of Buffalo, 1973—; Chmn. health affairs com. U.S. Cath. Conf. Office: 35 Lincoln Pkwy Buffalo NY 14222 *

HEAD, FLOYD NEWTON, food manufacturing company executive; b. San Mateo, Calif., June 14, 1920; m. Betty Lou Ackeman, Sept. 26, 1921; children: Daniel, Ronald, Gary, Susan. A.A., San Mateo Coll., 1940. Eastern region sales mgr. Gerber Products Co., Fremont, Mich., 1959-66, gen. sales mgr., 1966-67, v.p. sales, 1967-72, v.p. mktg., 1972-74, exec. v.p., 1974—, dir.; dir. Gerber Life Ins. Co. Served with USAAF, 1942-45. Mem. Calif. Grocers Assn., Def. Supply Assn. Republican. Episcopalian. Clubs: Ramshorn Contry (membership chmn. 1978—), Asparagus (Fremont)). Office: Gerber Products Co 445 State St Fremont MI 49412

HEAD, HOLMAN, association executive; b. Mineola, N.Y., Jan. 13, 1926; s. Middleton Edward and Fannie Marie (Holman) H.; m. Harriet Fuller, Nov. 7, 1953; children: Hallie Head Rawls, Robert Holman, Martin Edward. Student, Dartmouth Coll.; A.B., U. Ala., 1947, M.B.A., 1955. Asst. dir. U. Ala. Montgomery Center and Mobile Center, 1950-53; dir. U. Ala. Montgomery Center, 1953-58; dir. personnel and adminstrn. Blount Bros. Corp., Montgomery, 1958-68, exec. asst. to pres., 1968-69, v.p. adminstrn., 1969; exec. asst. to Postmaster Gen. U.S. Postal Service, Washington, 1969-71; exec. v.p. Birmingham Area C. of C., 1971-74; v.p. adminstrn. Blount, Inc., Montgomery, 1974-79; exec. v.p. Ala. C. of C., 1980—. Bd. dirs. Montgomery Area United Way, campaign chmn., 1976, pres., 1979; bd. dirs. Met. YMCA, Birmingham, 1972-74, Birmingham Festival of Arts Assn., 1972-74, Ala. Council Econ. Edn., 1960-65, S.E. Ala. Regional Sci. Fair, 1959-64, Montgomery Mental Health Assn., 1956-60, Montgomery Spastic Sch., 1955-58; founding trustee Montgomery Acad.; mem. Art Inc. Com., Montgomery Mus. Fine Arts. Served with USNR, 1943-46. Mem. Ala. Assn. Ind. Colls. and Univs. (bd. govs.), Asso. Industries Ala. (dir.), Montgomery Area C. of C. (dir.), U.S. C. of C., U. Ala. Nat. Alumni Assn. (past v.p.), U. Ala. Alumni Assn., Montgomery County (past pres.). Republican. Episcopalian. Clubs: Mountain Brook, Montgomery Country, Capital City (bd. govs.). Home: 2442 Midfield Dr Montgomery AL 36111 Office: 468 S Perry St Montgomery AL 36195

HEAD, HOWARD, mfr. and designer skis; b. Phila., July 31, 1914; s. Joseph and Annie (Wilkinson) H.; 1 dau., Nancy Stratton Head Thode. Grad., William Penn Charter Sch., Phila., 1928-32; A.B. in Engring. Scis, Harvard U., 1936. Journalist, writer, motion picture editor, 1937-38; mem. engring. dept. Glenn L. Martin Co., Balt., 1939-47; cons., designer engring. and physics research depts. Johns Hopkins U., Balt., 1948-51; organizer, 1952-70; pres., chmn. bd., treas. Head Ski Co., Inc., Timonium, Md., 1950-70; chmn. bd. Prince Mfg., Inc., Princeton, N.J., 1971—; Chmn. industry fund raising U.S. Olympic Ski Team, 1961-62. Mem. Ski Industries Am. (founding mem., pres., dir. 1958-59). Democrat. Clubs: Harvard, Baltimore County, Ski (Balt.). Conceived, designed and developed ski derived from metal sandwich aircraft constrn.; conceived, invented, developed Prince Tennis racket. Address: 100 W Cold Spring Ln Baltimore MD 21210

HEAD, IVAN LEIGH, research institute executive; b. Calgary, Alta., Can., July 28, 1930; s. Arthur Cecil and Birdie Hazel (Crockett) H.; m. Barbara Spence Eagle, June 23, 1952; children: Laurence Allan, Bryan Cameron, Catherine Spence, Cynthia Leigh; m. Ann Marie Price, Dec. 1, 1979. B.A., U. Alta., 1951, LL.B., 1952, LL.M., Harvard U., 1960. Bar: Called to Alta. bar, Queen's Counsel, Can. Practiced in, Calgary, 1953-59; partner firm Helman, Barron & Head, 1955-59; fgn. service officer Dept. External Affairs, Ottawa, Kuala Lumpur, 1960-63; prof. law U. Alta., 1963-67; asso. counsel to Minister of Justice, Govt. of Can., 1967-68; spl. asst. to prime minister of Can., 1968-78; pres. Internat. Devel. Research Centre, Ottawa, 1978—. Author: International Law, National Tribunals and the Rights of Aliens, 1971; editor: This Fire Proof House, 1967, Conversation with Canadians, 1972; contbr. articles to profl. jours. Trustee Internat. Food Policy Research Inst.; mem. Ind. Commn. on Internat. Humanitarian Issues. Chief Justice's medallist U. Alta. Law Sch.; Frank Knox Meml. fellow Harvard Law Sch., 1959-60; Ford Found. fellow, 1966-69. Mem. Internat. Law Assn., Can. Council Internat. Law, Can. Inst. Internat. Affairs, Am. Soc. Internat. Law, Law Soc. Alta. Anglican. Home: 2095 Chalmers Rd Ottawa ON Canada K1H 6K4 Office: 60 Queen St Ottawa ON Canada K1G 3H9

HEAD, JAMES DEAN, newspaper and magazine editor; b. Independence, Kans., Mar. 11, 1926; s. James Edward and Ruby (Brown) E.; m. Gladys Corel Dunkley, Aug. 28, 1948; children: Laura, Lynn, Kathleen, Michael. Student, Washburn U., 1944-45; B.S., Kans. U., 1949. Staff Lawrence (Kans.) Jour.-World, 1949-54, Miami (Fla.) Herald, 1954-59, Miami News, 1959-62, N.Y. Herald Tribune, 1962-63; exec. sports editor Detroit Free Press, 1963-66; exec. editor Today (newspaper), Cape Kennedy, Fla., 1966-68, Hartford (Conn.) Times, 1969-70; exec. editor, v.p. Westchester-Rockland Newspapers, White Plains, N.Y., 1970-75; asst. publisher Parade Mag., 1975-78, editor, 1978-80; pub., pres. 3 to Get Ready, 1980-81; exec. editor King Features Syndicate, 1981—. Served with USNR, 1944-46. Mem. Overseas Press Club, Sigma Delta Chi. Home: River Rd Cold Spring NY 10516 Office: 235 E 45th St New York NY 10017

HEAD, JOHN DOUGLAS, glass company executive; b. Detroit, Nov. 28, 1927; s. Herbert and Alice (Hewitt) H.; m. Carol Edythe Seidel, Oct. 14, 1960; children: Cynthia Carol, Jeffrey David. B.A. in Bus. Adminstrn., Wittenberg U., 1950. Fin. mgr. Ford of Italy, Rome, 1966-69, Ford of Europe, Warley, Brentwood, Eng., 1969-71; pres., chief exec. officer Ford Ghia Ops., Turin, Italy, 1971-76; div. controller Ford Glass Div., Detroit, 1976-81; pres., chief exec. officer Ford Glass ltd., Toronto, Ont., Can., 1981—; dir. Lamilite Inc., Saratoga Springs, N.Y. Bd. dirs. Franklin Wright Settlements, Detroit, 1977-80; dir. sch. bd. Internat. Sch., Turin, 1972-76; pres. Internat. Bus. Men's Group, Lisbon, Portugal, 1965-66. Served with U.S. Army, 1946-47. Clubs: National (Toronto); Country of Detroit. Home: 61 St Clair Ave W Suite 1207 Toronto ON Canada M4V 2Y8 Home: 59 Stonehurst Rd Grosse Pointe Shores MI 48236 Office: Ford Glass Ltd 101 Richmond St 20th Floor Toronto ON Canada M5H 1V9

HEAD, PATRICK JAMES, lawyer; b. Randolph, Nebr., July 13, 1932; s. Clarence Martin and Ellen Cecelia (Magirl) H.; m. Eleanor Hickey, Nov. 24, 1960; children: Adrienne, Ellen, Damian, Maria, Brendan, Martin, Sarah, Daniel, Brian. A.B. summa cum laude, Georgetown U., 1953, LL.B., 1956, LL.M. in Internat. Law, 1957. Bar: D.C. bar 1956, Ill. bar 1966. Asso. firm John L. Ingolsby (and predecessor firm), Washington, 1956-64; gen. counsel internat. ops. Sears, Roebuck & Co., Oakbrook, Ill., 1964-70, counsel midwest ter., Skokie, Ill., 1970-72; v.p. Montgomery Ward & Co., Inc., Washington, 1972-76, v.p., gen. counsel, sec., Chgo., 1976-81; v.p., gen. counsel FMC Corp., Chgo., 1981—. Mem. Chgo. Crime Commn.; bd. dirs. Constl. Rights Found., Provident Hosp., Chgo.; bd. regents Georgetown U., Washington. Mem. D.C. Bar Assn., Chgo. Bar Assn., ABA. Democrat. Roman Catholic. Clubs: Met. (Washington); Chgo., Internat. Office: FMC Corp 200 E Randolph St Chicago IL 60601

HEADINGTON, JOHN TERENCE, physician; b. Grand Rapids, Mich., June 15, 1930; m. Jill Loubser, June 20, 1957; children—Lisa, Peter. B.S., U. Mich., 1952, M.D., 1957. Intern Virginia Mason Hosp., Seattle, 1957-58; resident U. Mich. Hosp., Ann Arbor, 1958-62; practice medicine, specializing in dermatology and pathology, Ann Arbor, Mich., 1964—; chief, clin. pathology Letterman Gen. Hosp., 1962-64; instr. dermatology and pathology U. Calif., San Francisco, 1963-64; asst. prof. pathology, U. Mich., 1964-68, asso. prof., 1968-71, prof. pathology and dermatology, 1971—; asst. prof. pathology U. Ill. (Chiang Mai Project), 1966-68. Recipient Bronze medal Gougerot Soc., 1974. Mem. AAAS, Am. Assn. Pathologists, Internat. Acad. Pathologists, Am. Acad. Dermatologists, Soc. for Investigative Dermatology, St. Johns Hosp. Dermatol. Soc. Club: Dowling. Home: 2812 Colony Rd Ann Arbor MI 48104 Office: 1335 E Catherine St Ann Arbor MI 48109

HEADLEE, RAYMOND, psychoanalyst, educator; b. Shelby County, Ind., July 27, 1917; s. Ortis Verl and Mary Mae (Wright) H.; m. Eleanor Case Benton, Aug. 24, 1941; children—Sue, Mark, Ann. A.B. in Psychology, Ind. U., 1939, A.M. in Exptl. Psychology, 1941, M.D., 1944; grad., Chgo. Inst. Psychoanalysis, 1959. Diplomate: Am. Bd. Psychiatry and Neurology (examiner 1964—). Intern St. Elizabeth's

Hosp., Washington, 1944-45, resident in psychiatry, 1945-46, Milw. Psychiat. Hosp., 1947-48, pres. staff, 1965-70; practice medicine specializing in psychiatry and psychoanalysis, Elm Grove, Wis., 1949—; clin. asst. prof. psychiatry Med. Coll. Wis., 1958-59, clin. asso. prof., 1959-62, clin. prof., 1962—, chmn. dept. psychiatry, 1963-70; prof. psychology Marquette U., 1966-76; Bd. dirs. Elm Brook (Wis.) Meml. Hosp., 1969-71. Author: (with Bonnie Corey) Psychiatry in Nursing, 1949; contbr. numerous articles to profl. jours. Served to 1st lt. Ft. Knox Armored Med. Research Lab. AUS, 1945; to maj. at NIH, USPHS, 1953; Bethesda, Md. Fellow Am. Psychiat. Assn. (life), Am. Coll. Psychiatry; mem. State Med. Soc. Wis. (editorial dir. 1971-77), Wis. Psychiat. Assn. (pres. 1971-72). Clubs: Beefeater (London) (upper warder 1972—); Milw., Confrerie des Chevaliers du Tastevin. Home: 12505 Gremoor St Elm Grove WI 53122 Office: 1055 Legion St Box 207 Elm Grove WI 53122 *My life story represents a gradual and often difficult transition from the puritan ethic, which got me into this book, to a lighter style of living. This is what the Germans call Lebenskünstler.*

HEADLEE, RICHARD HAROLD, insurance company executive; b. Ft. Dodge, Iowa, May 16, 1930; s. William Clarke and Violet Rebecca (Lunn) H.; m. Mary E. Mendenhall, Oct. 21, 1948; children: Mike, Douglas, Kathy, Bruce, Natalie, Carolyn, Laura, Howard, Elaine. B.A., Utah State U., 1953; hon. doctorate, Coll. So. Utah, 1983. Account exec. Burroughs Corp., Detroit, 1957-66; engaged as cons. and field dir. Romney Assos., 1967; pres. Morbark Industries, Winn, Mich., 1968-69, Hamilton Internat. Devel. Co., 1970-72; pres., chief exec. officer Alexander Hamilton Life Ins. Co. Am., 1972—; pres., chief exec. officer, Hamilton Internat. Corp., 1972—; dir. Household Fin. Corp.; Chmn. S. Davis United Fund, 1960; mem. steering com. Am. Landmarks Com., 1963-66. Bd. editors: Outstanding Young Men of America, 1964-66. A founder S. Davis Welfare Com., 1960, Bountiful Community Concerts Assn., 1961; mem. Nat. Mental Health Adv. Bd., Project Concern Internat., 1963—; adv. bd. Small Bus. Adminstrn.; del. White House Conf. on Inflation.; Pres. Bountiful (Utah) Jr. C. of C., 1960, Utah Jr. C. of C., 1962; bd. dirs. U.S. Jr. C. of C., 1961-65, v.p., 1962-63, pres., 1963-64, chmn. bd., 1964-65; life mem., senator; chmn. Mich. C. of C., 1980; bd. dirs. Citizen's Choice, Washington, Nat. Multiple Sclerosis Soc., 1963-65; vice chmn. bd. trustees Oakland U., from 1975, chmn., 1980-81; chmn. Taxpayers Research Inst., 1978; Taxpayers United for Tax Limitation, 1978; Asst. campaign chmn. gov. of Mich., 1966; chmn. Citizens for Romney; nat. chmn. Young Civic Leaders for Nixon-Agnew, 1968; mem. exec. com. United Rep. Fund.; nat. co-chmn., chmn. Citizens for Am., Washington, 1983—; mem. exec. com. Voter's Choice, Mich.; mem. president's round table Utah State U., 1974—; Rep. candidate for gov. of Mich., 1982. Served to 1st lt. AUS, 1953-56. Recipient Outstanding Alumnus award Utah State U., 1964; Distinguished Service award Bountiful, 1960, Golden Key Oakland U., 1983; named Citizen of Yr., Mich., 1980. Mem. Presidents' Assn., Am. Mgmt. Assn., Nat. Assn. Life Underwriters, Am. Council Life Ins. (exec. round table 1972—); mem. U.S. C. of C. (dir. 1964-65); Mem. Blue Key, Sigma Nu, Beta Gamma Sigma (hon.). Mem. Ch. Jesus Christ Latter-Day Saints (bishop 1969, pres. stake 1974, regional rep. 1983). Club: Economic (Detroit). Office: Alexander Hamilton Life Ins Co Am 33045 Hamilton Blvd Farmington Hills MI 48018

HEADLEE, ROLLAND DOCKERAY, association executive; b. Los Angeles, Aug. 27, 1916; s. Jesse W. and Cleora (Dockeray) H.; m. Alzora D. Burgett, May 13, 1939; 1 dau., Linda Ann (Mrs. Walter Pohl). Student, UCLA, 1939. Asst. mgr. Par Assos., Los Angeles, 1935-43, Finance Assos., 1946-58; financial cons., lectr., 1958-63; account exec. Walter E. Heller & Co., Los Angeles, 1963-66; exec. dir. Town Hall Calif., Los Angeles, 1966—; Dir. Am. Internat. Bank, Mfrs. Assos., R.H. Investment Corp. Served to 1st lt. AUS, 1943-46. Mem. Mensa, Los Angeles World Affairs Council, Newcomen Soc. Methodist. Clubs: Commonwealth of Calif., Economic of Detroit, Los Angeles Stock Exchange. Home: 8064 El Manor Ave Los Angeles CA 90045 Office: 523 W 6th St Los Angeles CA 90014

HEADLEY, SHERMAN KNIGHT, broadcasting consultant; b. St. Paul, Oct. 10, 1922; s. Louis Sherman and Sylvia (Knight) H.; m. Alta McDonald, June 5, 1943; children: Sherman (dec.), Timothy, James, Susan. Student, Carleton Coll., 1939-41, U. Wis., 1941-42; B.S., U. Minn., 1948. Tech. dir. Belfry Theatre, Lake Geneva, Wis., summer 1942, Youngstown (Ohio) Playhouse, 1942-43, Cleve. Play House, 1943-45, Chautauqua Theatre, summers 1944-45; dir. Kanawha Players, Charleston, W.Va., 1946-47, Belfry Theatre, summer 1947, Tuscon Little Theatre, 1947-48; prodn. mgr. Sta. WCCO-TV, Mpls., 1948-52, asst. mgr., 1952-69, v.p., gen. mgr., 1969-77, cons., 1977—; exec. v.p., exec. dir. Minn. Mus. Art, St. Paul, 1977-78, ret., 1978; Mem. journalism adv. bd. U. Minn. Pres. Guild of Performing Arts, 1962; bd. dirs. Mpls. Downtown Council, 1958-62, Minn. Ednl. TV, 1966—, Minn. affiliate Am. Heart Assn., 1978; pres. Mpls. Aquatennial, 1964-65. Mem. Minn. Broadcasters Assn. (pres. 1960-63), Mpls. Advt Club (pres. 1965-66), Am. Fedn. Advt. (past lt. gov., Silver Medal award 1977), Mpls. Better Bus. Bur., Mpls. C. of C. Home: 18194 Verano Dr San Diego CA 92128 *Some do much; others do nothing at all, but each of us in our lifetime has the opportunity to help move civilization forward.*

HEADRICK, ROGER LEWIS, food company executive; b. West Orange, N.J., May 13, 1936; s. Lewis B. and Marian E. (Rogers) H.; m. C. Lynn Cowell, Sept. 29, 1962; children: Hilary R., Mark C., Christopher C., Heather R. A.B., William Coll., 1958; M.B.A., Columbia U., 1960. Fin. analyst Standard Oil (N.J.), Esso Eastern, Inc., N.Y.C., 1960-65, treas., Tokyo, 1965-70, v.p., Manila, 1970-73, treas., mgr. fin. and planning, Houston, 1973-78; dep. controller Exxon Corp., N.Y.C., 1978-82; exec. v.p., chief fin. officer The Pillsbury Co., Mpls., 1982—; adv. Fin. Acctg. Standards Bd. Trustee Dunwoody Indsl. Inst., Mpls., 1982—, The Blake Schs., 1983—. Served with Air Force Res.-N.G., 1960-66. Mem. Fin. Execs. Inst. Office: Pillsbury Co 200 S 6th St Minneapolis MN 55402

HEADRICK, THOMAS EDWARD, lawyer, univ. adminstr., educator; b. East Orange, N.J., June 28, 1933; s. Lewis Barnard and Marian Elizabeth (Rogers) H.; m. Mary Margaret Shontz, June 27, 1957; children—Trevor, Todd. B.A., Franklin and Marshall Coll., 1955; B.Litt., Oxford (Eng.) U., 1958; LL.B., Yale U., 1960; Ph.D., Stanford U., 1975. Bar: Conn. bar 1960, Calif. bar 1962. Asst. dir. Ansonia (Conn.) Redevel. Agy., 1959-60; law clk. to justice Wash. State Supreme Ct., Olympia, 1960-61; asso. firm Pillsbury, Madison & Sutro, San Francisco, 1961-64; mgmt. cons. Emerson Cons., London, 1964-66, Baxter, McDonald & Co., Berkeley, Calif., 1966-67; asst. dean Stanford U. Law Sch., 1967-70; v.p. acad. affairs Lawrence U., 1970-76; dean SUNY at Buffalo Law Sch., 1976—, prof. law, 1976—; cons. Nat. Endowment for Humanities, NSF; legal commentator Sta. WKBW-TV, 1978-80. Author: The Town Clerk in English Local Government, 1962. Mem. Am. Polit. Sci. Assn., Law and Soc. Assn., N.Y. State Bar Assn., Erie County Bar Assn., Phi Beta Kappa. Office: SUNY at Buffalo Law Sch 319 O'Brian Hall Buffalo NY 14260

HEADY, EARL OREL, economics educator; b. Chase County, Nebr., Jan. 25, 1916; s. Orel C. and Jessie (Banks) H.; m. Marian R. Hoppert, Mar. 1, 1941; children: Marilyn Heady Kling, Stephen, Barbara Heady Erickson. B.S., U. Nebr., 1939, M.S., 1940, D.Sc. (hon.), 1960; Ph.D., Iowa State U., 1945; postgrad., U. Chgo., 1941; D.Sc. (honoris causa), U. Uppsala (Sweden), 1965, Warsaw Agrl. U., 1979, Debrecen U. (Hungary), 1979. Faculty Iowa State U., Ames, 1940—, prof. econs., 1949—, Curtis Distinguished prof., 1956—; dir. Center for Agrl. and Econ. Devel., 1958—; vis. prof. U. Ill., 1950, N.C. State U., 1952, U. Calif.-Berkeley, 1954, Harvard, 1956; Cons. TVA, 1950—, Dept. Agr., 1953—, Ministry Food and Agr. Govt. India, 1959, 81, OECD, AID, Dept. State, 1971—, Ministry Agr. Kingdom Thailand, 1971—, Ministry Agr. in Romania, 1970—, Research Inst. Agrl. Econs., Hungary, 1970-73, Ministry Agr. and Water of Kingdom Saudi Arabia, 1970, Ford Found., Rockefeller Found.; chief cons. to Govt. of Greece (on nat. research program), 1963, 64, Egyptian Ministry Agr. and Food Security, 1982—, Ministry Agr. and Fisheries, Portugal, 1977, 82, Indonesia, 1979—, Mex. Ministry Agr., 1964-73, Internat. Inst. Applied Systems Analysis, Vienna, 1978—; cons. Office of Tech. Assessment, U.S. Ho. of Reps., 1980—, FAO-UN, 1981—; dir. sector planning programs, Mexico and Thailand, 1970—; permanent chmn. East-West Conf. Agrl. Economists; mem. White House Com. on Domestic Affairs; mem. research and adv. com. AID U.S. Dept. State, 1971—; mem. Commn. on Human Settlements, 1969-70; adv. panel to Nat. Water Commn., 1970-71; mem. adv. com. State Univs. and Land Grant Colls. and Univs. Office for Advancement Negro Colls.; Mem. adv. bd., bd. dirs. Econs. Inst. Author: Economics of Agricultural Production and Resource Use, 1952, Linear Programming Methods, 1958, Agricultural Production Functions, 1960, Resource Demand and Industry Structure: Farm Management Economics, Records and Accounting; Agricultural Policy Under Economic Development, Economics of Agricultural Production and Resource Use: Roots of the Farm Problem, Problems and Policies of Agriculture in Developed Countries, Food, Agriculture and Economic Policy, Economic Models and Quantitative Methods for Decisions and Planning of Agriculture, 1971, Studies in Farm Policies, 1971, Operations Research Methods, 1973, World Food Production, Demand and Trade, 1973, Spatial Models of Agricultural Development, 1975, Economics of Cooperative Farming, 1976, World Food Aid, 1975, Water Production Functions in Irrigated Agriculture, 1977, 82, Quadratic Programming Models of Agricultural Policies, 1978, Agricultural Production Ecomonics, 1983, Models of Agricultural Technology, Conservation and Environmental Improvement, 1984; Contbr. numerous papers and bulls. to profl. jours. Recipient Social Sci. Research Council Faculty award, 1951-53; fellow Center Advanced Studies Behavioral Scis., 1960-61; recipient Distinguished Service award Am. Agrl. Editors Assn.; Internat. award for Outstanding Service to World Agr. Gamma Sigma Delta, 1975; World Citizenship award Des Moines C. of C., 1975; A.W. Browning medal Am. Soc. Agronomy, 1977; citation Iowa State U. Alumni, 1977; Wilton Park award, 1977; Henry A. Wallace award, 1978; Rockefeller Study and Conf. Ctr. resident scholar, 1983. Fellow Am. Acad. Arts and Scis., Am. Statis. Assn., Center Advanced Studies in Behavioral Scis., AAAS, Econometric Soc., Am. Agrl. Econs., Assn. (Spl. award 1978), Am. Acad. Arts and Scis.; mem. Soviet All-Union Acad. Agrl. Sci., Can. Agrl. Econ. Soc. (v.p.), Am., Western econ. assns., Econometrica, Am. Farm Econs. Assn. (v.p., editorial council, research and publ. award 1949, 53, 56, 59, 73, 74, 75, 76, 80), Canadian Agr. Econs. Assn. (v.p.), Internat. Agr. Econs. Assn., Hungarian Acad. Sci. (hon.), Royal Swedish Acad. Sci. (hon.), Sigma Xi, Phi Beta Kappa, Phi Kappa Phi, Alpha Zeta, Gamma Sigma Delta (Iowa Distinguished Service award). Club: Kiwanis. Home: 919 Gaskill Dr Ames IA 50010

HEADY, FERREL, emeritus educator; b. Ferrelview, Mo., Feb. 14, 1916; s. Chester Ferrel and Loren (Wightman) H.; m. Charlotte Audrey McDougall, Feb. 12, 1942; children—Judith Lillian, Richard Ferrel, Margaret Loren, Thomas McDougall. A.B., Washington U., St. Louis, 1937, A.M., 1938, Ph.D., 1940; hon. degrees, Park Coll., 1973, John F. Kennedy U., 1974. Jr. adminstrv. technician, also adminstrv. asst. Office Dir. Personnel, Dept. Agr., 1941-42; vis. lectr. polit. sci. U. Kansas City, 1946; faculty U. Mich., 1946-67, prof. polit. sci., 1957-67; dir. Inst. Pub. Adminstrn., 1960-67; acad. v.p. U. N.Mex., Albuquerque, 1967-68, pres., 1968-75, prof. pub. adminstrn. and polit. sci., 1975-81, prof. emeritus, 1981—; Asst. to commr. Com. Orgn. Exec. Br. of Govt., 1947-49; dir., chief adviser Inst. Pub. Adminstrn. U. Philippines, 1953-54; mem. U.S. del. Internat. Congress Adminstrn. Scis., Spain, 1956, Germany, 1959, Austria, 1962, Poland, 1964, Mexico, 1974, Spain, 1980; exec. bd. Inter-Univ. Case Program, 1956-67; sr. specialist in residence East-West Center, U. Hawaii, 1965; mem. Conf. on Pub. Service, 1965-70; chmn. bd. Asso. Western Univs., 1970-71; commr. Western Interstate Commn. Higher Edn., 1972-77; mem. commns. on bus. professions and water resources, mem. exec. com. Nat. Assn. State Univs. and Land Grant Colls., 1968-75. Author: Administrative Procedure Legislation in the States, 1952, (with Robert H. Pealy) The Michigan Department of Administration, 1956, (with Sybil L. Stokes) Comparative Public Administration: A Selective Annotated Bibliography, 1960, Papers in Comparative Public Administration, 1962, State Constitutions: The Structure of Administration, 1961, Public Administration: A Comparative Perspective, 1966, rev. edit., 1979; Contbr. profl. jours. Chmn. state affairs com. Ann Arbor (Mich.) Citizens Council, 1949-52; mem. exec. com. Mich. Meml.-Phoenix Project and Inst. Social Research, 1960-66; mem. Gov. Mich. Constl. Revision Study Commn., 1960-62; schs. and univs. adv. bd. Citizens Com. for Hoover Report, 1949-52, 54-58; cons. to Ford Found., 1962; chmn. Council on Grad. Edn. in Pub. Adminstrn., 1966; mem., vice chmn. N.Mex. Gov.'s Com. on Reorgn. of State Govt., 1967-70; mem. N.Mex. Am. Revolution Bicentennial Commn., 1970-73, N.Mex. Gov.'s Com on Tech. Excellence, 1969-75, Nat. Acad. Pub. Adminstrn. Served to lt. USNR, 1942-46. Recipient Faculty Disting. Achievement award U. Mich., 1964; N.Mex. Disting. Pub. service award, 1973; award of distinction U. N.Mex. Alumni Assn., 1975; Outstanding Grad. Tchr. award U. N.Mex., 1981-82. Mem. Am. Polit. Sci. Assn., Am. Soc. Pub. Adminstrn. (pres. 1969-70), AAUP (chmn. com. T 1957-61), Am. Council Edn. (mem. commn. on fed. relations 1969-72), Phi Beta Kappa, Phi Kappa Phi. Presbyterian. Home: 2901 Cutler Ave NE Albuquerque NM 87106

HEADY, HAROLD FRANKLIN, ecologist; b. Buhl, Idaho, Mar. 29, 1916; s. Orah E. and Edith A. (Philbrick) H.; m. E. Eleanor Butler, June 12, 1940; children—Carol Marie, Kent Arthur. B.S., U. Idaho, 1938; M.S., N.Y. State Coll. Forestry, 1940; postgrad., U. Minn., 1940-41; Ph.D., U. Nebr., 1949. Range conservationist U.S. Soil Conservation Service, White Salmon, Wash., 1941; asst. prof. N.Y. State Coll. Forestry, Syracuse, 1942, Mont. State U., Bozeman, 1942-47; asso. prof. Tex. A. and M. U., College Station, 1947-51; faculty U. Calif. at Berkeley, 1951—, prof. forestry, 1962—, asso. dean, 1974-77, asst. v.p. agr. and univ. services, asso. dir., 1977-80; Pasture cons. FAO, Saudi Arabia, 1962-63. Illustrator 4 books. Fulbright Research scholar, East Africa, 1958-59, Australia, 1966; Guggenheim fellow, 1958-59. Mem. Ecol. Soc. Am., Soc. for Range Mgmt. Research and numerous publs. on ecol. relationships and methods sampling grasslands and deserts, influence of domestic and wild animals on vegetation, range mgmt. Home: 1864 Capistrano Ave Berkeley CA 94707

HEAFEY, EDWIN AUSTIN, JR., lawyer; b. Nov. 1, 1930; s. Edwin Austin and Florence M. H.; (div.)children—Ryan, Matthew, Alison. A.B., U. Santa Clara, Calif., 1952; LL.B., Stanford U., 1955. Bar: Calif. bar 1955. Sr. partner firm Crosby, Heafey, Roach & May, Oakland, 1955—; mem. faculty Boalt Hall Law Sch., U. Calif., Berkeley, 1963-78; 9th circuit atty. rep. Jud. Conf. Com., 1972, 81; Bd. regents U. Santa Clara; bd. dirs. Holy Names Coll. Fellow Am. Coll. Trial Lawyers; mem. Am. Bd. Trial Advocates (past nat. and chpt. pres.), Am. Assn. R.R. Trial Counsel, Am. Trial Lawyers Assn., Am. Bar Found., Internat. Soc. Barristers. Republican. Roman Catholic. Club: Claremont Country (Oakland). Home: 5710 Margarido Dr Oakland CA 94618 Office: 1939 Harrison St Oakland CA 94612

HEAGARTY, MARGARET CAROLINE, pediatric physician; b. Charleston, W.Va., Sept. 8, 1934; d. John Patrick and Margaret Caroline (Walsh) H. B.A., Seton Hill Coll., 1957; B.S., W.Va. Sch. Medicine, 1959; M.D., U. Pa., 1961. Diplomate: Am. Bd. Pediatrics. Intern Phila. Gen. Hosp., 1961-62; resident in pediatrics St. Christopher's Hosp. for Children, Phila., 1962-64; dir. pediatric ambulatory care services N.Y. Hosp.-Cornell Med. Ctr., N.Y.C., 1969-78; dir. pediatrics Columbia U.-Harlem Hosp. Ctr., N.Y.C., 1978—; cons. Dept. HEW Promotion of Child Health, Washington; mem. Com. Community Oriented Primary Care Inst. Medicine, Washington. Author: Changing the Medical Car System-Report of an Experiment, 1974, Medical Sociology: A Systems Approach, 1975, Child Health: Basics for Primary Care, 1980. Robert Wood Johnson, Inst. Medicine fellow, 1975; recipient grant Commonwealth Fund, 1981, Robert Wood Johnson Found., 1983. Mem. Inst. Medicine, Amblatory Pediatric Assn. (pres. 1976-77), Soc. Pediatric Research, Am. Pediatric Soc., Nat. Bd. Med. Examiners. Home: 2520 Kingsland Ave Bronx NY 10469 Office: Columbia U-Harlem Hosp Ctr 506 Lenox Ave New York NY 10037

HEAGY, HENRY CYRUS, clergyman, religious adminstr.; b. Lebanon, Pa., Sept. 27, 1921; s. Forney and Emma Mabel (Smith) H.; m. Dorothy Ann Wenger, June 26, 1943; children—David, Della, Ruth, Elva, Glenn, Edward, Thelma, Lynwood, Nelson, Luke, Samuel, Alice. Ed. high sch. Ordained to ministry United Christian Ch., 1953; minister, Lebanon County, Pa., 1947—; chmn. ch. conf., 1956, presiding elder, 1965—, mem. mission bd., 1952—. Address: Route 4 Box 110 Lebanon PA 17042

HEALD, DARREL VERNER, Canadian Federal judge; b. Regina, Sask., Can., Aug. 27, 1919; s. Herbert Verner and Lottie (Knudson) H.; m. Doris Rose Hessey, June 30, 1951; children: Lynn, Brian. B.A., U. Sask., 1938, LL.B., 1940. Bar: Called to Sask. bar 1941. Partner firm Noonan, Embury, Heald, Molisky and Gritzfeld, Regina, until 1964; atty. gen. and provincial sec., Province Sask., 1964-71, mem., 1964-71; judge trial div. Fed. Ct. of Can., Ottawa, Ont., 1971-75; judge Fed. Ct. of Appeal, Ottawa, 1975—. Served with RCAF, 1941-45. Home: 44 Aleutian Rd Ottawa ON K2H 7C8 Canada Office: Suite 71 Supreme Ct Bldg Ottawa ON K1A 0H9 Canada

HEALD, JAMES EUDEAN, educator; b. Moscow Station, Mo., Jan. 3, 1929; s. James Wilfred and Elsie Clare (Smith) H.; m. Phyllis Anita Kosir, Sept. 9, 1951; children—Paul Justin, Laura Kay. B.S., Ill. State U., 1951, M.S., 1952; Ph.D. (Univ. fellow), Northwestern U., 1957. Tchr. Evanston (Ill.) Twp. High Sch., 1954-59; asst. prin. Shorewood (Wis.) High Sch., 1959-61; asst. to supt. Ladue (Mo.) Pub. Schs., 1961-63; prof. ednl. adminstrn. Mich. State U., 1963-70; dean Coll. Edn., No. Ill. U., DeKalb, 1970-79, prof. ednl. adminstrn., 1979—; mem. faculty U. Wis., 1960-61, Northwestern U., 1958; cons. Nat. Insts. Mental Health, U.S. Dept. Def., U.S. Dept. State. Author: (with Samuel A. Moore III) The Teacher and Administrative Relationships in School Systems, 1968, (with Louis Romano and Nicholas Georgiady) Selected Readings on General Supervision, 1970, The Middle School, 1973. Served with U.S. Army, 1952-54. Recipient U.S. Office Edn. grants, 1969, 70. Mem. Am. Ednl. Research Assn., Am. Assn. Sch. Adminstrs., Nat. Soc. for Study Edn., Am. Assn. Colls. Tchr. Edn. (dir. 1979—), Ill. Assn. Colls. Tchr. Edn. (v.p. 1976-77), Phi Delta Kappa. Conglist. (deacon). Home: 6 Greenwood Ct De Kalb IL 60115

HEALD, MARK AIKEN, educator, physicist; b. Princeton, N.J., Jan. 27, 1929; s. Mark Mortimer and June (Kilts) H.; m. Jane Dewey, June 9, 1952; children—Kathryn, John S., Charles K. B.A., Oberlin Coll., 1950; M.S., Yale, 1951, Ph.D., 1954. Mem. research staff Project Matterhorn, Princeton, 1954-59; mem. faculty Swarthmore Coll., 1959—, prof. physics, 1970—; U.S. tech. del. UN Conf. Peaceful Uses Atomic Energy, 1958; NSF sci. faculty fellow Culham Lab., U.K. AEA, 1963-64, Plasma Physics Lab., Princeton, 1969-70, vis. staff, 1974-75; vis. scientist Plasma Fusion Center, MIT, 1978-79. Author: (with C.B. Wharton) Plasma Diagnostics with Microwaves, 1965, (with W.C. Elmore) Physics of Waves, 1969, (with J.B. Marion) Classical Electromagnetic Radiation, 1980. Mem. Phi Beta Kappa, Sigma Xi. Home: 420 Rutgers Ave Swarthmore PA 19081

HEALD, MILTON TIDD, educator, geologist; b. Woburn, Mass., Feb. 19, 1919; s. Walter Milton and Susan Edgell (Tidd) H.; m. Doris Shirley Ethier, June 15, 1941; children—Sandra (Mrs. Robert G. Simmons), Cynthia (Mrs. Stephen B. Patton), Marcia (Mrs. Michael M. McGlothlin). B.A., Wesleyan U., Middletown, Conn., 1940; M.A., Harvard, 1947, Ph.D., 1949. Mem. faculty W.Va. U., Morgantown, 1948—, asso. prof. geology, 1955-60, prof., 1960—; cons. to industry. Cooperating geologist W.Va. Geol. Survey, 1970—. Contbr. articles to profl. jours. Served to lt. (j.g.) USNR, 1943-46. Fellow Geol. Soc. Am.; mem. Am. Assn. Petroleum Geologists, Soc. Econ. Paleontologists and Mineralogists, Nat. Assn. Geology Tchrs. (v.p. 1958), W.Va. Acad. Scis., Sigma Xi, Phi Beta Kappa. Home: 672 Colonial Dr Morgantown WV 26505

HEALD, MORRELL, educator; b. Oak Park, Ill., July 16, 1922; s. Howard Leslie and Helen (Morrell) H.; m. Barbara Legg, June 25, 1949; children—David M., Seth G., Sarah H. A.B., Yale U., 1946, A.M., 1947, Ph.D., 1951. Instr. history Yale, 1950-53; mem. faculty Case Inst. Tech., 1953-68, asso. prof. history, 1958-68, chmn. dept. humanities and social studies, 1959-62; prof. Am. studies Case Western Res. U., 1968-82, Samuel B. and Virginia C. Knight prof. humanities, 1982—, chmn. div. spl. interdisciplinary studies, 1971-78, 79-82; vis. prof. Am. history Indian Inst. Tech., Kanpur, 1966-67; dir. Armington Research Program on Values in Children, 1978-80, chmn. adv. com., 1978-82. Author: The Social Responsibilities of Business: Company and Community, 1900-1960, 1970, (with Lawrence S. Kaplan) Culture and Diplomacy: The American Experience, 1977; Co-editor: The Aims and Organization of Liberal Studies, 1966. Vice pres. Cleveland Heights Your Schools Com., 1962, pres., 1965; Pres. of the First Ward Democratic Club, Cleveland Heights, 1962. Served with AUS, 1943-45; ETO. Mem. Soc. History Tech., Am. Soc. Engring. Edn. (v.p. humanities and Social sci. sect. 1962-63), Am. Hist. Assn., Am. Studies Assn., Ohio Acad. History, Phi Beta Kappa. Episcopalian. Home: 2219 Demington Dr Cleveland Heights OH 44106 Office: 10900 Euclid Cleveland OH 44106

HEALEY, ARTHUR H., state supreme court justice; b. New Haven, May 5, 1920; s. Arthur and Agnes (Hannon) H.; m. Fances T. Murphy, Apr. 24, 1954; children: Theresa A., Monica F., Moira A., Arthur T., Alicia M., Francis J., Michael K., Matthew M., Anne E. B.A., Trinity Coll., 1944; LL.B., Harvard U., 1947. Bar: Conn. 1948. Mem. Conn. Senate, 1955-61, minority leader, 1957-59, majority leader, chmn. state legis. council, 1959-61; judge Ct. Common Pleas, 1961-65, Superior Ct., Hartford, Conn., 1965-79, chief judge, 1977-78, presiding judge appellate session, 1977-79; assoc. justice Conn. Supreme Ct., Hartford, 1979—; mem. Jud. Rev. Council, 1978-79; co-chmn. Conn. Justice Commn., 1978-79. Mem. State Library Bd., 1979. Served with AUS, World War II. Mem. Conn. Bar Assn., New Haven

County Bar Assn. Office: Conn Supreme Ct Supreme Ct Bldg Hartford CT 06106

HEALEY, DEREK EDWARD, composer; b. Wargrave, Eng., May 2, 1936; s. Clement Percival and Helen Gladys (Rose) H.; m. Olive May Smith, Apr. 9, 1960; 1 dau., Jacqueline. A.R.C.M. in Organ and Piano Teaching, Royal Coll. Music, London, 1957; F.R.C.O., Royal Coll. Organists, London, 1957; B.Mus., U. Durham, Eng., 1961; student in composition under, Boris Porena, Rome, 1962-63; postgrad., Accademia Chigiana, Siena, Italy, summers 1961-63, 66; D.Mus., U. Toronto, Ont., Can., 1974. Dir. music various schs., pub. and pvt., Eng., 1957-69; lectr. U. Victoria, B.C., Can., 1969-71; vis. lectr. U. Toronto, 1971-72; assoc. prof. composition and ethno music U. Guelph, Ont., 1972-78; assoc. prof. composition U. Oreg., Eugene, 1979—; lectr., adjudicator in field. Compositions include Twelve Preludes; piano, 1960, The Shepherd Boy's Song; choir and organ, 1965, Three Quiet Pieces; organ, 1974, Primrose in Paradise; orch., 1975, Arctic Images, 1971, Seabird Island; opera, 1977, A Shape-Note Symphony; orch., 1979, Numerous works commd. by Canadian orgns. Recipient Cobbett prize Royal Coll. Music, 1956, Sullivan prize, 1956, Farrar prize, 1957; F. M. Napolitano prize Accademia Chigiana, 1962; winner U. Louisville Second Internat. Composition Contest, 1980, Delius Composition Contest Delius Festival, 1981. Fellow Royal Coll. Organists; mem. Performing Rights Orgn. Can., Am. Soc. Univ. Composers, Composers Guild Gt. Brit., Coll. Music Soc. Episcopalian. Home: 2877 Timberline Dr Eugene OR 97405 Office: Sch Music U Oreg Eugene OR 97403 *A creative artist should always have the utmost confidence in his own judgement since he is almost invariably right; think twice before following somebody elses advice. I have found that artistic progress is unpredictable-there are times when one moves forward as though riding on a hurricane, whilst at others nothing seems to avail. Regarding music, all can be changed or destroyed with the exception of the harmonic series which is God-given and indestructable.*

HEALEY, FRANK HENRY, research executive; b. Worcester, Mass., Oct. 5, 1924; s. Frank H. and Elizabeth (MacGillivray) H.; m. Loretta Mrguerite Finnigan, June 5, 1948; children: Steven Allen, Elaine Elizabeth, Frank Healey. A.B., Clark U., 1947, Ph.D., 1949. Asst. prof. chemistry Lehigh U., Bethlehem, Pa., 1949-56; with Lever Bros. Co., Edgewater, N.J., 1956—, v.p. research and devel, 1964-73, research v.p., 1973-78, v.p. research and engring., 1978-80, research v.p., dir., 1980—. Served to lt. (j.g.) USN, 1943-46. Mem. Indsl. Research Inst. (pres. 1977-78, dir. 1972-79), Assn. Research Dirs., Am. Chem. Soc., Dirs. Indsl. Research, Am. Oil Chemists Soc., Soap and Detergent Assn. (steering com. and materials div.). Club: Ridgewood Country (sec.) (1981-82). Home: 255 W Ridgewood Ave Ridgewood NJ 07450 Office: 45 River Rd Edgewater NJ 07020

HEALEY, JAMES FRANCIS, mfg. co. exec.; b. Cambridge, Mass., Jan. 13, 1920; s. Hugh Henry and Mary Elizabeth (Seifen) H.; m. Madelon Kathryn O'Brien, Oct. 11, 1942; children—James J., John M. B.S., Mass. Inst. Tech., 1941, M.S., 1948. Commd. 2d lt. USAAF, 1941; advanced through grades to col. USAF, 1955; various research and devel. assignments in field aircraft and missiles; ret., 1955; dir. research and planning Mpls.-Honeywell, St. Petersburg, Fla., 1957-61, v.p., gen. mgr. aero. div., 1961-66; group exec. def. space group Internat. Tel. & Tel. Co., N.Y.C., 1966-67; pres., dir., chief operating officer KMS Industries, Inc., 1967-72; v.p. Singer Co., N.Y.C., 1972-75; chmn., pres., chief exec. officer Milton Roy Co., St. Petersburg, 1975—; dir. Fla. Fed. Savs. and Loan Assn., St. Petersburg.; Mem. USAF Sci. Adv. Bd., 1958—. Trustee All Childrens Hosp., St. Anthony's Hosp., both St. Petersburg; pres. Salvador Dali Inst., St. Petersburg. Asso. fellow Am. Inst. Aeros. and Astronautics; mem. Fla. Council of 100, Air Force Assn., Navy League. Clubs: Feathersound Country, Marco Polo, St. Petersburg Yacht. Home: 1361 Snell Harbor Dr Saint Petersburg FL 33704 Office: Suite 900 One Plaza Pl NE Saint Petersburg FL 33701

HEALEY, ROBERT JOSEPH, paper company executive; b. Phila., Dec. 23, 1925; s. Joseph Aloysius and Mary Elizabeth (Mackey) H.; m. Nancy Williams, July 1, 1950; children: Annette Marie, Peter Warren, Christopher Hughes. A.B., Haverford Coll., 1950. With Scott Paper Co., 1950—; v.p. fin. Scott Paper Ltd., Vancouver, B.C., Can., 1961-68; v.p., treas. Scott Paper Co., Phila., 1971-81; mng. dir. Bowater-Scott Corp. Ltd., U.K., 1981—, also dir. Served with USAAF, 1944-45. Clubs: Waynesborough Country (Paoli, Pa.); Merion Cricket (Haverford, Pa.); RAC (London). Home: Fairstowe Warren Rd Crowborough East Sussex TN6 1TU England Office: Bowater-Scott House East Grinstead West Sussex RH19 1UR England

HEALEY, THOMAS J., government official; b. Balt., Sept. 14, 1942; 2 children. A.B., Georgetown U., 1964; M.B.A., Harvard U., 1966. Mng. ptnr. Camargo Assocs., 1967-71; v.p. fin. Instrumentation Engring., Inc., 1971-75; mgr. project fin. group Dean Witter, 1975-82; mng. dir., mgr. corp. fin. Dean Witter Reynolds Capital Markets, 1982-83; asst. sec. domestic fin. Dept. of Treasury, Washington, 1983—. Office: Dept of Treasury 15th and Pennsylvania Ave NW Washington DC 20220

HEALY, EDWARD LELAND, mining company executive, consulting engineer; b. Kennecott, Alaska, Feb. 9, 1919; s. Ralph L. and Eva (Cole) H.; m. Jean Elizabeth Muir, Nov. 15, 1947; children: Martha Jean, Ruth Ellen, Kathryn Eva. B.A.Sc. in Mining Engring, U. Toronto, 1941. Registered cons. engr., Ont. With Falconbridge Nickel Mines Ltd., Toronto, Ont., 1948-81, mgr., 1961-64, dir. mining engring. and research, 1964-68, v.p. nickel div., 1965-67, dir., 1967-79, exec. v.p. ops., 1968-76; pres., chief exec. officer Mine-Met Cons. Can. Ltd., Toronto, 1976-81, also dir.; dir. VAT Petroleum Ltd.; pres., dir. Lakefield Research of Can. Ltd., until 1981; cons. mining engr., 1981—. Served to 1st lt. Royal Canadian Engrs., 1942-45. Decorated Mil. Cross. Mem. Can. Inst. Mining and Metallurgy, AIME, Assn. Profl. Engrs. Ont. Home and office: 17 Scenic Millway Willowdale ON M2L 1S4 Canada

HEALY, FRANK ALBERT, III, investment banker; b. Bridgeport, Conn., Jan. 16, 1942; s. Frank Albert, Jr. and Eleanor (MacKenzie) H.; m. Pamela Hobson, Oct. 1, 1966; children: Frank Albert IV, Jason, Rebecca, Sarah. B.A., Brown U., 1964. Asst. treas. City Trust Co., Bridgeport, 1964-69; sr. v.p. Blyth Eastman Dillon, N.Y.C., 1969-79, E.F. Hutton & Co., 1979—. Republican. Episcopalian. Club: Brooklawn Country (Bridgeport). Home: 81 N Park Ave Easton CT 06612 Office: EF Hutton & Co 1 Battery Park Plaza New York NY 10004

HEALY, GEORGE ROBERT, college provost; b. Milw., May 31, 1923; s. Russell Kerfoot and Elmina (Hodgson) H.; m. Dorothy Ann Kohli, Aug. 14, 1948; children: David George, Thomas Robert, Roger Knowles. B.A., Oberlin Coll., 1948; M.A., U. Minn., 1950, Ph.D., 1956. Instr. history U. Minn., 1951-52; instr., then asst. prof. history MIT, 1952-57; assoc. prof. cultural heritage and history Bates Coll., 1957-62, chmn. dept. cultural heritage, 1958-62, dean faculty, 1962-71, provost, 1970-71; v.p. for acad. affairs Coll. William and Mary, 1971-82, provost, 1982—, vis. prof., summer 1960. Contbr. profl. jours.; Editor, translator: (Montesquieu): Lettres persanes, 1964. Served with USAAF, 1943-45. Mem. Am. Hist. Assn., Soc. French Hist. Studies, Conf. Acad. Deans. Home: The Archibald Blair House Williamsburg VA 23185

HEALY, GEORGE WILLIAM, III, lawyer; b. New Orleans, Mar. 8, 1930; s. George William and Margaret Alford H.; m. Sharon Saunders, Oct. 26, 1974; children: George W. IV, John Carmichael, Floyd Alford, Hyde Dunbar, Mary Margaret. B.A., Tulane U., 1950, J.D., 1955. Bar: La. bar 1955, U.S. Supreme Ct. bar 1969. Asso. firm Phelps, Dunbar, Marks, Claverie & Sims, New Orleans, 1955-58, partner, 1958—; mem. U.S. del. Comite Maritime Internat., Tokyo, 1969; lectr. in field. Served with USN, 1951-53. Fellow Am. Coll. Trial Lawyers, Maritime Law Assn. U.S. (exec. com.), Am. Bar Assn.; mem. La. State Bar Assn., La. Assn. Def. Counsel, New Orleans Assn. Def. Counsel. Republican. Episcopalian. Clubs: Boston, La., Stratford, Plimsoll, Whitehall, Yale, Recess (pres. 1978), Pinfeathers Hunting, New Orleans Lawn Tennis, Propeller, Mariners. Home: 6020 Camp St New Orleans LA 70118 Office: 30th Floor Texaco Bldg 400 Poydras St New Orleans LA 70130

HEALY, HAROLD HARRIS, JR., lawyer; b. Denver, Aug. 27, 1921; s. Harold Harris and Lorena (Isom) H.; m. Elizabeth A. Debevoise, May 24, 1952; 1 son, Harold Harris III. A.B., Yale, 1943, LL.B., 1949. Bar: N.Y. bar 1949. Now mem. firm Debevoise & Plimpton, N.Y.C., resident partner, Paris, 1964-66; exec. asst. to U.S. atty. gen., 1957-58; Mem. Am. adv. council Ditchley Found., 1972—; Bd. dirs. Legal Aid Soc., 1968—, chmn., 1975-79. Bd. dirs. Met. Opera Guild, 1975—; trustee Vassar Coll., 1977—. Served from 2d lt. to capt. F.A. AUS, 1943-46; ETO. Decorated Bronze Star medal. Mem. Am., N.Y. State bar assns., Assn. Bar City N.Y. (sec. 1959-61), Am. Law Inst., Order of Coif, Am. Soc. Internat. Law (mem. exec. council 1977-80), Internat. Law Assn., Internat. Bar Assn., Union Internationale des Avocats (pres. 1979—), Council Fgn. Relations, France-Am. Soc., Pilgrims U.S., Phi Beta Kappa, Zeta Psi, Phi Delta Phi. Republican. Episcopalian. Clubs: University, Century Assn. (N.Y.C.); Travellers, Cercle de l'Union Interalliée (Paris); Metropolitan (Washington). Home: 1170 Fifth Ave New York NY 10029 Office: 299 Park Ave New York NY 10171

HEALY, JOSEPH FRANCIS, JR., lawyer; b. N.Y.C., Aug. 11, 1930; s. Joseph Francis and Agnes (Kett) H.; m. Patricia A. Casey, Apr. 23, 1955; children: James C., Timothy, Kevin, Cathleen M., Mary, Terence. B.S., Fordham U., 1952; J.D., Georgetown U., 1959. Bar: D.C. 1959. With gen. traffic dept. Eastman-Kodak Co., Rochester, N.Y., 1954-55; air transp. examiner CAB, Washington, 1955-59; practiced in, Washington, 1959-70, 80-81; asst. gen. counsel Air Transport Assn. Am., 1966-70; v.p. legal Eastern Air Lines, Inc., N.Y.C. and Miami, Fla., 1970-80; ptnr. Ford, Farquhar, Kornblut & O'Neill, Washington, 1980-81; v.p. legal affairs Piedmont Aviation, Inc., Winston Salem, N.C., 1981-84, sr. v.p. legal affairs, 1984—. Served to 1st lt. USAF, 1952-54. Mem. ABA, Fed. Bar Assn., Internat. Bar Assn., Am. Soc. Corp. Secs., Am. Irish Hist. Soc., Nat. Aero. Assn., Beta Gamma Sigma, Phi Delta Phi. Clubs: Univ., Internat. Aviation (Washington); Wings (N.Y.C.); Twin City (Winston-Salem). Home: 236 Heatherton Way Winston Salem NC 27104 Office: Piedmont Aviation Inc Smith Reynolds Airport Winston Salem NC 27156

HEALY, KENT ALLEN, engineering educator; b. New Haven, Sept. 30, 1932; s. Kent Tenney and Ruth Emily (Allen) H.; m. Maureen Therese Flanders, Nov. 9, 1967; children: William, Elizabeth, Jonathan, Sameul, Allen. B.S.C.E., Worcester Poly. Inst., 1959; Sc.D., M.I.T., 1963. Registered profl. engr., Conn., Mass., R.I. Foundation engr. LeMessurier & Assos., Boston, 1963-64; prof. civil engring. and geotech. engring. U. Conn., Storrs, 1964-83; cons. geotech. engring. Treas. Parish Hill High Sch., Chaplin, Conn., 1976-83. Served with USCG, 1952-56. Mem. ASCE, Sigma Xi. Patentee in field. Home and Office: RFD Box 556A Vineyard Haven MA 02568

HEALY, MARY (MRS. PETER LIND HAYES), singer, actress; b. New Orleans, Apr. 14, 1918; d. John Joseph and Viola (Armbruster) H.; m. Peter Lind Hayes, Dec. 19, 1940; children—Peter Michael, Cathy Lind. Student parochial schs., New Orleans, St. Bonaventure U. With 20th Century Fox, Hollywood, Cal. Author: Twenty-five Minutes from Broadway, 1961; pictures and others, 1937-40; Broadway prodns. Around the World, 1943-46; (with husband) TV series Inside U.S.A, 1949, Peter and Mary Show, Star of the Family, 1952, Peter Lind Hayes Radio show, CBS, 1954-57; Broadway prodn. Who Was That Lady, 1957-58, Peter Lind Hayes show, ABC-TV, 1958-59, Peter and Mary, ABC-Radio, 1959—, Peter and Mary in Las Vegas; TV-film; Star WOR radio show, 6 yrs; TV film series Fin. Planning for Women; lectr. with husband.: Film The 5000 Fingers of Dr. T, 1953; Appeared in: Peter Loves Mary, 1960, When Television Was Live, 1975. Roman Catholic. Club: Pelham Country. Home: 3538 Pueblo Way Las Vegas NV 89109

HEALY, NICHOLAS JOSEPH, lawyer, educator; b. N.Y.C., Jan. 4, 1910; s. Nicholas Joseph and Frances Cecilia (McCarthy) H.; m. Margaret Marie Ferry, Mar. 29, 1937; children: Nicholas, Margaret Healy Parker, Rosemary Healy Bell, Mary Louise Healy White, Donall, Kathleen Healy Hamon. A.B., Holy Cross Coll., 1931; J.D., Harvard U., 1934. Bar: N.Y. 1935. Pvt. practice, N.Y.C., 1935-42, 48; mem. Healy & Baillie (and predecessor law firms), 1948—; pres., dir. Victory Carriers, Inc. (and affiliated cos.); spl. asst. to atty. gen. U.S., 1945-48; tchr. admiralty law NYU Sch. Law, 1947—, adj. prof., 1960—. Contbr.: chpts. on admiralty to Annual Survey Am. Law, 1948—; author: (with Sprague) Cases on Admiralty, 1950, (with Currie) Cases and Materials on Admiralty, 1965, (with Sharpe) Cases and Materials on Admiralty, 1974; editor: Jour. Maritime Law and Commerce; assoc. editor: American Maritime Cases; mem. bd. editors: Il Dirittimo Marittimo; contbr. to Ency. Brit. Chmn. USCG adv. panel on Rules of the Road, 1966-72; mem. permanent adv. bd. Tulane Admiralty Inst. Served to lt. (s.g.) USNR, 1942-45. Mem. Maritime Law Assn. U.S. (pres. 1964-66), Assn. Average Adjusters U.S. (chmn. 1959-60), ABA (ho. dels. 1964-66), N.Y. State Bar Assn., Comité Maritime Internat. (exec. council 1972-79), Assn. Bar City N.Y., Soc. Friendly Sons St. Patrick. Democrat. Roman Catholic. Clubs: Harvard, India House, Downtown Athletic (N.Y.C.). Home: 132 Tullamore Rd Garden City NY 11530 Office: 29 Broadway New York NY 10006

HEALY, PAUL FRANCIS, newspaperman; b. Chgo., Mar. 1, 1915; s. Waldo and Julia (Henzie) H.; m. Constance Maas, Jan. 2, 1943 (div.); children: Kevin, Julie, Monica, Jane, Kathleen. Ph.B., Loyola U., Chgo., 1938. Reporter Chgo. Tribune, 1938-43; asso. editor Popular Mechanics mag., 1943-45; mem. Chgo. bur. Time, Inc., 1945; civilian info. officer War Dept., 1945; Washington corr. N.Y. Daily News, 1945—. Author: (with B. K. Wheeler) Yankee From The West, 1962, Cissy, A Biography of Eleanor M. Patterson, 1966; Contbr. to nat. periodicals. Mem. White House Corrs. Assn. (pres. 1977-78). Roman Catholic. Clubs: Washington Press, Gridiron (Washington). Office: 2101 L St NW Washington DC 20037

HEALY, ROBERT EDWARD, business executive; b. Bklyn., Aug. 15, 1904; s. Walter F. and Florence D. (Davis) H.; m. Lilie Rose, Aug. 3, 1927 (div. Jan. 1957); children: Lilie Jane, Patricia Anne, Robert Edward (dec.); m. Wayne Clark, Jan. 11, 1957; 2 sons, Edward Walter, James Davis. Grad., Dwight Prep. Sch., N.Y.C., Pace Inst., N.Y.C.; D.C.S (hon.), Pace Coll. Asst. to v.p. in charge sales promotion Johns-Manville Co., 1928-33; brand advt. mgr. Colgate-Palmolive Co., 1939-42, gen. advt. mgr., 1942-46, became v.p. in charge advt., 1946; dir., v.p., treas. McCann-Erickson, Inc., 1952-53, gen. mgr., 1954, exec. v.p. charge, 1955-58, mem. finance com., 1956-62, vice chmn. bd., 1958-61; chmn. McCann Erickson Corp. (Internat.), 1956-58; pres. Inter-public (S.A.), Geneva, Switzerland, 1962-65; exec. v.p. Interpub. Group of Cos., Inc., 1965-67, pres., chief exec., 1967-72, mem. exec. com., 1967-77, chmn. bd., 1968-73, hon. chmn., 1973-83. Clubs: N.Y. Athletic, Paris Am., Chaine Des Rotisseurs (N.Y.C.); Ocean Reef (Key Largo, Fla.). Home: Penthouse C-1202 1111 Crandon Blvd Key Biscayne FL 33149

HEALY, THERESA ANN, former ambassador; b. Bklyn., July 14, 1932; d. Anthony and Mary Catherine (Kennedy) H. B.A., St. John's U., 1954. Tchr. elem. and secondary schs., N.Y.C., 1951-55; with U.S. Fgn. Service, 1955—, ambassador to Sierra Leone, 1980-83; with Ctr. for Internat. Affairs, U. South Fla., Tampa, 1983—. Mem. Am. Fgn. Service Assn. Roman Catholic. Club: Fgn. Service. Office: Ctr for Internat Affairs U South Fla Tampa FL

HEALY, TIMOTHY STAFFORD, university president; b. N.Y.C., Apr. 25, 1923; s. Reginald Stafford and Margaret Dean (Vaeth) H. B.A., Woodstock Coll., Md., 1946, M.A., 1947; S.T.L., Facultes St. Albert, Louvain, Belgium, 1954; M.A., Fordham U., N.Y.C., 1959; D.Phil., Oxford U., 1965; M.A., 1979; M.A. hon. degrees, Nazareth Coll., Pace U., Syracuse U., Marymount Coll., U. Notre Dame. Joined S.J., 1940; ordained priest Roman Catholic Ch., 1953; instr. Latin and English Fordham Prep. Sch., N.Y.C., 1947-50; instr. English, asst. prof., asso. prof., prof. Fordham U., 1955-69, exec. v.p., 1965-69; prof. English, vice chancellor for academic affairs City U. N.Y., 1969-76; prof. English, pres. Georgetown U., Washington, 1976—; mem. Pres.'s Commn. on Fgn. Lang. and Internat. Studies, 1978-79; mem. exec. com. Nat. Council Ednl. Research, 1980—; cons. Pres.'s Commn. on Campus Unrest (Scranton Commn.), 1970; mem. Middle States Assn. Commn. on Higher Edn., 1976-79, D.C. Commn. on Crime and Justice, 1982—; mem. Nat. Adv. Com. on Accreditation and Instl. Eligibility U.S. Dept. Edn., 1981—; bd. dirs. Council for Fin. Aid to Higher Edn., 1977—, Nat. Assn. Ind. Colls. and Univs., 1977-80, chmn., 1980-81; bd. dirs. Am. Council on Edn., 1979—, chmn., 1983-84; bd. dirs. Pan Am. Devel. Found., 1979—; exec. com. Consortium of Univ. of Washington, 1976—, chmn., 1978-79, 84—. Author: John Donne: Ignatius His Conclave, 1969; editor: (with Dame Helen Gardner) John Donne: Selected Prose, 1967; bd. dirs.: Jour. History of Ideas, 1975—; contbr. articles to profl. publs. Mem. Folger Com., Folger Shakespeare Library, 1980—; Mem. Fed. City Council, Washington, 1976—. Kent fellow, 1962-65; Am. Council Learned Socs. grantee, 1971. Fellow Soc. for Values in Higher Edn.; mem. Am. Oxonians, Phi Beta Kappa. Democrat. Address: Georgetown U Washington DC 20057

HEAMAN, WILLIAM MCPHERSON, engineer, former naval officer; b. White Salmon, Wash., Apr. 2, 1910; s. Bertram M. and Harriet (McPherson) H.; m. Mildred Coe, Oct. 8, 1937; children: Patricia Louise Heaman Murphy, Richard Coe. B.S. in Civil Engring., U. Wash., 1935; grad., Armed Forces Staff Coll., 1947; postgrad., George Washington U., 1961. Registered profl. engr., Oreg., Fla., Hawaii. Engr. with Nat. Tank and Pipe Co., Portland, Oreg., 1935-41; commd. lt. (j.g.) Civil Engr. Corps, U.S. Navy, 1941, advanced through grades to rear adm., 1965; assigned Pearl Harbor, 1941-44, assigned Newport, R.I., 1944-47, mem. staff Fleet Marine Force, Pacific, 1947-50, assigned Seabee Center, Pt. Hueneme, Calif., 1950-51, assigned Bur. Yards and Docks, Washington, 1951-55, pub. works officer Naval Air Sta., Alameda, Calif., 1955-59, officer charge constrn., Philippines, 1959-60, asst. chief Bur. Yards and Docks, 1960-61, comdr. Seabees, Atlantic Fleet, 1962-63, dir. S.E. div. Bur. Yards and Docks, 1963-65, officer charge constrn., Vietnam, 1965, comdr. Pacific div. Naval Facilities Engring. Command, 1965-69; pres. W.M. Heaman & Assocs., 1970—. Mem. Soc. Am. Mil. Engrs., Nat. Soc. Profl. Engrs., Nat. Rifle Assn., Sigma Chi. Office: 981401 Kaonohi St Aiea HI 96701

HEANEY, GERALD WILLIAM, U.S. judge; b. Goodhue, Minn., Jan. 29, 1918; s. William J. and Johanna (Ryan) H.; m. Eleanor R. Schmitt, Dec. 1, 1945; children—William M., Carol J. Student, St. Thomas Coll., 1935-37; B.S.L., U. Minn., 1939, LL.B., 1941. Bar: Minn. bar 1941. Lawyer securities div. Dept. of Commerce Minn., 1941-42; mem. firm Lewis, Hammer, Heaney, Weyl & Halverson, Duluth, 1946-66; judge 8th Jud. Circuit, U.S. Court Appeals, 1966—. Mem. Dem. Nat. Com. from Minn., 1955; Bd. regents U. Minn., 1964-65. Served from pvt. to capt. AUS, 1942-46. Mem. Am., Minn. bar assns. Roman Catholic. Office: US Court of Appeals Duluth MN 55802 *

HEANEY, ROBERT PROULX, physician, educator; b. Omaha, Nov. 10, 1927; s. Clarence Earl and Lorraine (Proulx) H.; m. Barbara Rose Reardon, July 12, 1952; children—Robert Michael, Marian Ghislaine, Barbara Lorraine, Rachel Ann, Margaret Reardon, Christopher Joseph, Elizabeth Joan. B.S., Creighton U., 1947, M.D., 1951. Intern St. Louis City Hosp., 1951-52, asst. resident internal medicine, 1952-53; clin. fellow Okla. Med. Research Hosp., Oklahoma City, 1953-55; clin. asso. NIH, 1955-57; mem. faculty Creighton U. Sch. Medicine, 1957—, prof. medicine, chmn. dept., 1961-69, v.p. health scis., 1971-84, John A. Creighton univ. prof., 1984—; mem. dental tng. com. NIH, 1962-66, gen. medicine B study sect., 1966-71, orthopedic tng. com., 1971-73; mem. spl. rev. com. Council on Dental Edn., ADA, 1978-79; mem. arthritis, bone and skin project rev. group NIAMDD, 1977-78; mem. Am. Inst. Biol. Scis. (med. scis. adv. panel to NASA), 1976-80; chmn. ad hoc com. rev. mineralization research effort Nat. Inst. Dental Research, 1973, chmn. spl. grants rev. com., 1982—; chmn. Gordon Research Conf. Bones and Teeth, 1966; Bd. dirs. Health Planning Council of the Midlands, 1971-81. Mem.editorial bd.: Calcified Tissue Internat., 1967-77, 78—, Jour. Clin. Endocrinology and Metabolism, 1968-70, Jour. Lab. and Clin. Medicine, 1976—; Mem. editorial bd.: Metabolic Bone Disease and Related Research, 1981—. Pres. parish council St. John's Ch., also mem. archdiocesan commn. on sacred liturgy, music and art, 1968-81; trustee Loyola U.-Chg., 1981—. Served with USPHS, 1955-57. Recipient Lederle Faculty award, 1960-63; Kappa Delta award Am. Acad. Orthopedic Surgeons, 1970; Ohio State award, 1979; Creighton Disting. Staff award, 1974. Fellow ACP; mem. Am. Soc. Clin. Investigation, Central Soc. Clin. Research (council 1966-69), Endocrine Soc., Assn. Academic Health Centers (dir. 1975-81, pres.-elect 1979, chmn. bd. 1979-80), Am. Fedn. Clin. Research., Physicians for Social Responsibility. Roman Catholic. Home: 5210 Burt St Omaha NE 68132

HEAPHY, JOHN MERRILL, lawyer; b. Escanaba, Mich., Apr. 27, 1927; s. John Merrill and Catherine R. (Feeney) H.; m. Martha Jean Knowles, Nov. 16, 1951; children—John Merrill III, Catherine Jean, Barbara Ann. B.A., U. Mich., 1950; J.D., Wayne State U., 1953. Bar: Mich. bar 1954. Atty. office of gen. counsel HEW, Washington, 1954-57; practiced in, Detroit, 1957—; mem. firm Vandeveer, Garzia, Tonkin Kerr & Heaphy, Detroit, 1958—. Served with USNR, 1945-46. Mem. Internat. Assn. Ins. Counsel, Mich., Am., Fed. bar assns., Delta Theta Phi, Alpha Sigma Phi. Republican. Presbyn. Home: 5561 Tequesta Dr West Bloomfield MI 48033 Office: 333 W Fort St Suite 1600 Detroit MI 48226

HEAPS, ALVIN EUGENE, labor union executive; b. Royalton, Ill., Dec. 4, 1919; s. John and Susie (Sprouse) H.; m. Evelyn M. Lassa, May 22, 1941 (div. Feb. 1968); 1 dau., Melody M.; m. Jo Anne C. Gibilaro, Mar. 10, 1968. Mem. Retail, Wholesale and Dept. Store

Union, 1941—, pres., 1946-48, internat. sec.-treas., 1948-76, internat. pres., 1976—, also chmn. bd. trustees union industry pension fund and union industry health and welfare fund; mem. exec. bd., indsl. union dept., until 1980; mem. exec. council AFL-CIO, 1977—; Mem. Ill. Retail Industry Minimum Wage Bd., 1946-47; labor mem. Dept. Labor (com. fair labor standards to P.R.), 1963; mem. Labor Dept. (exchange program to Japan), 1964; mem. exec. com. Internat. Fedn. Comml., Clerical and Tech. Employees, Internat. Union Food and Allied Workers.; mem. Adv. Council on Social Security, 1982—. Served with inf. AUS, 1943-45; ETO. Decorated Silver Star with oak leaf cluster, Purple Heart. Office: 30 E 29th St New York NY 10016

HEAPS, MARVIN DALE, food services company executive; b. Boone, Iowa, June 26, 1932; s. Donald and Mary Isabel (Robson) H.; m. Martha Coleman Davis, July 4, 1957; children—Mitchell, Matthew, Martha. B.A. in Econs, Whitworth Coll., 1953; postgrad., George Washington U., 1957; M.B.A. (Achievement scholar), U. Pa., 1959. Asso. McKinsey & Co. (mgmt. cons.), Washington, Geneva and N.Y.C., 1960-66; dir. service systems engring. Automatic Retailers of Am., Phila., 1967, v.p., 1968; sr. v.p. ARA Services, Inc., Phila., 1969-71, exec. v.p. ops., 1975-77, pres., chief operational officer, 1977-81; also dir.; pres. Marvin D. Heaps Assos., Inc., 1981—; pres. ARA Food Services Co., 1971-75; dir. Morse/Diesel, Inc., Jerricho, Inc., J.H. Chapman Group, Inc., Provident Am. Co.; cons. to Office Edn., HEW; mem. food service industry adv. com. Exec. Office of Pres., 1969—. Bd. dirs., chmn. Young Life Campaign; bd. dirs. Whitworth Coll., Phila. Coll. Art, Greater Phila. YMCA, Acad. Natural Scis., Salvation Army. Served to lt. USNR, 1955-59. Mem. Conf. Bd., Am. Mgmt. Assn., Soc. Personnel Adminstrn., Assn. Internat. Devel., Nat. Automatic Mdse. Assn. (dir.), Wharton MBA Alumni Club. Republican. Presbyterian (elder). Clubs: Metropolitan (Washington); Union League (Phila.). Home: 301 Elm Ave Swarthmore PA 19081 Office: 301 Elm Ave Swarthmore PA 19106

HEARD, ARTHUR BERNARD, lawyer; b. Cleve., Oct. 26, 1924; s. Gus and Henri (Chambliss) H.; m. Marion Elizabeth Dennis, Mar. 3, 1945; 1 son, Martin Bernard. Cert. in acctg., Fenn Coll., Cleve. State U., 1959; J.D., Cleve. Marshall Coll. Law, 1963. Bar: Ohio 1963. Teller, bookkeeper Quincy Savs. & Loan Co., Cleve., 1953-60, corporate sec., mng. officer, 1960-75, pres., mng. officer, 1975-76; practice in Cleve., 1976—. Mem. Cleve. Zoning Bd. Appeals, 1974—; dir. Office Equal Opportunity, Bd. Commrs. Cuyahoga County; v.p. Cleve. CSC, 1970-74; treas. Greater Cleve. Growth Corp., 1972—; pres. bd. trustees Cleve. Pub. Library; trustee Cath. Charities. Served with USMCR, 1943-46. Recipient Outstanding Alumnus award Cleve. Marshall Law Coll., 1964, Interracial Justice award Cath. Interracial Council, 1975. Mem. Cuyahoga County Bar Assn., Savs. and Loan Accounting Soc., Cath. Lawyers Guild (treas. 1975—). Republican. Roman Catholic (eucharistic minister). Club: KC (4 deg.). Home: 3751 E 154th St Cleveland OH 44128 Office: 17017 Miles Ave Cleveland OH 44128

HEARD, EDWIN ANTHONY, banker; b. N.Y.C., Oct. 31, 1926; s. Edwin Anthony and Frances Weaver (Taylor) H.; m. Phyllis Marie Gregory, Dec. 18, 1948; children: Elizabeth Gregory, Edwin Anthony. A.B., Princeton U., 1948; grad., Advanced Mgmt. Program, Harvard U., 1966. Ill. Vice pres. Irving Trust Co., N.Y.C., 1960-71; treas. U.S. Trust Co., N.Y.C., 1971-73, exec. v.p., 1973-76, vice chmn., 1976—; dir. U.S. Trust Corp. Trustee Collegiate Sch. Served with USNR, 1944-46. Clubs: Links, Down Town Assn., Bond (N.Y.C.). Home: 1133 Park Ave New York NY 10028 Office: 45 Wall St New York NY 10005

HEARD, (GEORGE) ALEXANDER, political science educator; b. Savannah, Ga., Mar. 14, 1917; s. Richard Willis and Virginia Lord (Nisbet) H.; m. Laura Jean Keller, June 17, 1949; children: Stephen Keller, Christopher Cadek, Francis Muir, Cornelia Lord. A.B., U. N.C., 1938, LL.D., 1968; M.A., Columbia U., 1948, Ph.D., 1951, LL.D., 1965. U.S. Govt. service in depts. Interior, War and State, 1939-43; research asso. bur. pub. adminstrn. U. Ala., 1946-49; research asso. Inst. Research in Social Sci., U. N.C., 1950-51, research prof., 1952-58; asso. prof. polit. sci. U. N.C., 1950-51, prof. polit. sci., 1952-63, dean Grad. Sch., 1958-63; prof. polit. sci. Vanderbilt U., 1963—, chancellor, 1963-82; dir. Time Inc., 1968—. Author: (asst. to V. O. Key, Jr.) Southern Politics in State and Nation, 1949, (with Donald S. Strong) Southern Primaries and Elections, 1950, A Two-Party South?, 1952, The Costs of Democracy, 1960, rev. edit., 1962, The Lost Years in Graduate Education, 1963; editor and contbr.: State Legislatures in American Politics, 1966. Chmn. Pres.'s Commn. on Campaign Costs, 1961-62; spl. adviser to Pres. U.S. on campus affairs, 1970; Pres., bd. dirs. Citizens' Research Found., 1958-71; mem. U.S. Adv. Commn. Intergovtl. Relations, 1967-69; Trustee Ford Found., 1967—, chmn., 1972—; trustee Robert A. Taft Inst. Govt., 1973-76; public trustee Nutrition Found., 1976-82; mem. council Rockefeller U., 1977-82; mem. Commn. on U.S. Policy Toward So. Africa, Fgn. Policy Study Found., 1979—. Served from ensign to lt. USNR, 1943-46. Mem. Internat. Polit. Sci. Assn., Am. Polit. Sci. Assn. (v.p. 1962-63), So. Polit. Sci. Assn. (pres. 1961-62), Assn. Am. Univs. (dir. council fed. relations 1969-70, v.p. 1973-74, pres. 1974-75), Am. Acad. Arts and Scis., Council on Fgn. Relations, Center for Inter-Am. Relations, Phi Beta Kappa (senator united chpts. 1964-70), Sigma Alpha Epsilon. Episcopalian. Clubs: Cosmos (Washington); Belle Meade Country (Nashville); Century Assn. (N.Y.C.). Home: 2100 Golf Club Ln Nashville TN 37215 Office: 1801 Edgehill Ave Vanderbilt U Nashville TN 37212

HEARD, WILBUR WRIGHT, lawyer; b. New Orleans, Jan. 29, 1905; s. William Wright and Isabelle (Manning) H.; m. Agnes Peyton Marshall, June 22, 1931; children—Ann Marshall, Courtenay (Mrs. Charles B. Tetrick), William Wright, Agnes Elizabeth. LL.B., Tulane U., 1926; postgrad., Harvard, 1952. Bar: La. bar 1926, Okla. bar 1941. Practice in, New Orleans, 1926-36, Tulsa, 1936—; atty. Pan. Am. Petroleum Corp., Tulsa, 1936-50, gen. atty., 1950-61, gen. counsel, 1961-70; also dir.; regional counsel Office Emergency Petroleum and Gas Adminstrn., Dept. Interior, to 1970; ret., 1970. Mem. Am., La., Okla. bar assns. Episcopalian. Home: 1325 E 31st St Tulsa OK 74105

HEARIN, WILLIAM JEFFERSON, publishing company executive; b. Mobile, Ala., Aug. 27, 1909; s. William Jefferson and Mary Lou (Ludington) H.; m. Emily Staples Van Antwerp, July 2, 1981; 1 dau., Ann Bartlett. Classified and retail advt. solicitor Mobile News-Item, 1927-32; retail advt., solicitor, retail advt. mgr., nat. advt. mgr., circulation mgr., advt. dir., bus. mgr. Mobile Press Register, 1932-44, gen. mgr., exec. v.p., 1944-65, co-pub., 1965-70, pub. pres., 1970—, also dir; pub., pres. Miss. Press Register, Pascagoula; dir. Mobile Gas Service Corp., First Nat. Bank Mobile. Bd. dirs. United Fund, YMCA; mem. nat. adv. bd. Salvation Army, Jr. Achievement; regent Spring Hill Coll. Named Hon. Col. Salvation Army, 1974, Lion of Yr., 1975, Mobilian of Yr., 1977. Mem. Am. Newspaper Pubs. Assn., So. Pubs. Assn., Ala. Press Assn., Mobile C. of C. (pres.), Sigma Delta Chi. Office: 304 Government St Mobile AL 36630

HEARLE, DOUGLAS GEOFFREY, public relations consultant; b. N.Y.C., Apr. 7, 1933; s. Douglas G. and Regina Irene (Booth) H.; m. Mary Elizabeth Hogan, July 13, 1957; children: Douglas, Christopher, Matthew. B.A., Iona Coll., 1954, M.B.A., 1970. Reporter-editor N.Y. Jour.-Am., N.Y.C., 1954-63; pub. relations mgr. Borden Inc., N.Y.C., 1963-66; account exec. Hill & Knowlton, N.Y.C., 1966-70, v.p., 1970-73, sr. v.p., 1973-80, exec. v.p., 1980—, dir., 1980—; pres. John W. Hill Found., N.Y.C., 1980—; adj. prof. Iona Coll., 1982-84; disting. lectr. Ball State U., 1981, U. Tex., 1984. V.p. Bd. Edn., Pelham, N.Y., 1972-78, N.Y. Newspaper Reporters Assn., 1961-63; mem. exec. council Boy Scouts Am., 1957-59. Recipient Disting. Service award Asean P.R. Congress, Jakarta, Indonesia, 1981, Citizen of Yr. award Pelham Men's Club, 1978. Mem. Silurians, N.Y. Newspaper Reporters Assn., Asia Soc., U.S.-Australian C. of C., Internat. C. of C. Republican. Roman Catholic. Clubs: Pelham Country, Pelham Men's; N.Y. Athletic (N.Y.C.). Home: 254 Cliff Ave Pelham NY 10803 Office: Hill & Knowlton Inc 420 Lexington Ave New York NY 10017

HEARN, EDELL MIDGETT, university dean, teacher educator; b. Watertown, Tenn., Oct. 3, 1929; s. Will Ray and Verna Tillie (Midgett) H.; m. Jeanette Weaver, Apr. 19, 1952; children: Janna, Valerie Elizabeth, Kaydell. A.A., Tenn. Wesleyan Coll.; B.S., Middle Tenn. State Coll., 1952, M.A., 1953; Ed.D., U. Tenn., 1959. Tchr. Central High Sch., Murfreesboro, Tenn., 1952-53, South High Sch., Knoxville, Tenn., 1955- 57, Knoxville Adult High Sch., 1956-57; instr. U. Tenn., 1958-59, assoc. prof., dir. student teaching, 1958-61; vis. prof. Tenn. Technol. U., Cookeville, summer 1958; prof. edn. Tenn. Tech. U., 1961—, chmn. dept., 1961-62, dean Coll. Edn., 1963—; Mem. State Adv. Com. on Certification and Tchr. Edn.; mem. Nat. Council for Accreditation of Tchr. Edn., 1976—, mem. council, 1979—, mem. coordinating bd, 1981—. Author: Test in Tennessee History and Government, Forms A and B, 1957, Public Educational Changes in Tennessee Through Legislation, 1959, Planning Effective Meetings, 1964, Simulated Behavioral Teaching Situations, 1971, also articles and papers for nat. socs. Served with AUS, 1953-55. Mem. NEA, Tenn. Edn. Assn., Assn. Supervision and Curriculum Devel., Nat. PTA, Phi Delta Kappa, Kappa Delta Pi, Phi Kappa Phi, Theta Sigma Chi. Methodist. Clubs: Mason (32 deg.), Lion (pres. 1973). Home: Route 5 Box 26 Hillwood Estates Cookeville TN 38501

HEARN, GEORGE HENRY, lawyer, steamship corporate executive; b. Bklyn., July 4, 1927; s. Henry G. and Grace A. (Flaherty) H.; m. Cecelia Anne Philbin, June 28, 1952; children—Annemarie Jude, Margaret Mary, George Henry. B.A., St. Francis Coll., 1950; student, Fordham U. Sch. Bus. Adminstrn., 1948; LL.B., St. John's U., 1954. Bar: N.Y. bar 1955, also D.C. bar 1955, U.S. Supreme Ct. bar 1955. With firm Haight, Gardner, Poor and Havens (specializing admiralty matters), N.Y.C., 1954-61; mem. CAB, 1961-64; commr. Fed. Maritime Commn., 1964-75; maritime adminstr. Govt. Sultanate of Oman, 1975—; counsel to firm Hill, Rivkins, Carey, Loesberg & O'Brien (specializing in maritime and transp. law), N.Y.C., 1977-82; sr. v.p. Waterman Steamship Corp., N.Y.C., 1982—; lectr. transp. Georgetown U., Am. U., Tulane U., St. Francis Coll. Contbr. articles to profl. jours. Dist. commr. Boy Scouts Am., 1958—; Mem. N.Y.C. Council, 1958-61; chmn. Kings County speakers com. for 1960 presdl. election; vice chmn. com. nationalists and intergroup relations N.Y. State Democratic Com., 1960—. Served with USNR, World War II; PTO. Recipient Distinguished Service award U.S. Jr. C. of C., 1958; Man of Year awards N.Y. Freight Forwarders and Brokers Assn., 1968, Cathedral Club of Bklyn., 1974. Mem. Maritime Law Assn. U.S., Maritime Adminstrv. Bar Assn., D.C., Fed. bar assns., Adminstrv. Conv. U.S., St. Patrick's Soc. Bklyn. (past pres.), Am. Com. Italian Migration (recording sec. Bklyn. div.). Club: K.C. Home: 78 Roxbury Rd Garden City NY 11530 also 110 Baldwin Ave Point Lookout NY 11569 Office: 120 Wall St New York NY 10005

HEARN, RUBY PURYEAR, foundation executive; b. Winston-Salem, N.C., Apr. 13, 1940; c. Mahlon Tasher H. and Ruby Mae (Hamilton) Puryear; m. Robert W. Hearn, Dec. 30, 1961; children: Janna E., Jennifer L. B.A., Skidmore Coll., 1960; M.S., Yale U., 1964, Ph.D., 1969. Postdoctoral research assoc. Yale U., New Haven, 1968-69; dir. content devel. Children's TV Workshop, 1972-76; program officer Robert Wood Johnson Found., Princeton, N.J., 1976-80, sr. program officer, 1980-82, v.p., 1983. Trustee Meharry Med. Coll., 1981—. Recipient Outstanding Alumnae award Skidmore Coll., 1972. Mem. Inst. Medicine, Ambulatory Pediatric Assn., AAAS, ABA (pub. mem. accreditation com. 1980-82), Periclean Honor Soc. Democrat. Home: 7 Saint Johns Rd Baltimore MD 21210 Office: Robert Wood Johnson Found PO Box 2316 Princeton NJ 08540

HEARN, THOMAS K., JR., university president; b. Opp, Ala., July 5, 1937; s. Thomas K. H.; m. Barbara Neely, Dec. 24, 1959; children: Thomas K., William Neely, Lindsay. B.A. summa cum laude, Birmingham-So. Coll., 1959; B.D., Baptist Theol. Sem., 1963; Ph.D. (NDEA fellow), Vanderbilt U., 1965. Instr. Birmingham-So. Coll., summers 1964-65; asst. prof. Coll. William and Mary, 1965-68, assoc. prof., 1968-74; prof. philosophy U. Ala., Birmingham, 1974-83, chmn. dept. philosophy, 1974-76, dean Sch. Humanities, 1976-78, v.p. Univ. Coll., 1978-83; pres. Wake Forest U., Wiston-Salem, N.C., 1983—. Contbr. articles to profl. jours. Recipient Thomas Jefferson Teaching award, 1970; summer grantee Nat. Found. Humanities, 1967; summer fellow Council Philos. Studies, 1968; fellow Coop. Program in Humanities, 1969-70; faculty summer grantee Coll. William and Mary, 1970, 72, 73. Mem. So. Soc. Philosophy, Psychology (exec. council 1974-77, Jr. award 1968), Soc. Philosophy Religion (pres. 1974-75), Am. Philos. Assn., AAUP, David Hume Soc., Newcomen Soc. N.Am., Phi Beta Kappa, Omicron Delta Kappa, Phi Kappa Phi. Home: 2601 Wake Forest Dr Winston-Salem NC 27106 office: Wake Forest Univ Office of the President Winston-Salem NC 27109

HEARNE, JOSEPH FREDERIC, musician; b. Lorain, Ohio, Aug. 20, 1942; s. Wayne and Meta (Loose) H.; m. Myra Ruzsits, Mar. 29, 1965 (div. June 1978); children: Michelle, Sean, Lia; m. Jan Brett, Aug. 18, 1980. Student, Juilliard Sch. Music, 1960-62, New Eng. Conservatory Music, 1962-64. Mem., Portland (Oreg.) Symphony Orch., 1959-60, Aspen (Colo.) Festival Orch., 1961, Boston Symphony Orch., 1962—; asst. prin. double-bass, Boston Pops Orch.; prin. double-bass, Boston Opera Co., 1967; artist-in-residence, Boston Conservatory Music, 1968-69; mem., Incredible String Quartet, 1975-80. Recipient award Oreg. Com. Mus. Arts, 1960; Am. Fedn. Musicians Internat. Congress of Strings fellow, 1960; Eleanor Morgan Satterlee Meml. scholar Juilliard, 1961-62. Home: 132 Pleasant St Norwell MA 02061 Office: Symphony Hall Boston MA 02090

HEARNES, WARREN EASTMAN, lawyer, former state governor; b. Moline, Ill., July 23, 1923; s. Earle B. and Edna May (Eastman) H.; m. Betty Sue Cooper, July 2, 1948; children: Lynn, Leigh, Julia B. B.S., U.S. Mil. Acad., 1946; A.B., U. Mo., 1952, LL.B., 1952. Bar: Mo. 1952. Served as enlisted man, inf. AUS, World War II; commd. 2d lt. U.S. Army, 1946, advanced through grades to 1st lt., 1947; ret., 1949; mem. Mo. Ho. of Reps. from Mississippi County, 1951-61, majority floor leader, 1957, 59; sec. of State Mo., 1961-65; gov. Mo., 1965-73; exec. dir. South Mo. Legal Services, Inc., Charleston. Mem. Am., Mo. bar assns., VFW, Am. Legion, Phi Delta Theta, Phi Delta Phi. Democrat. Baptist. Lodges: Masons; Shriners. Home: PO Box 349 Charleston MO 63834 Office: 118 N Main St Charleston MO 63834

HEARNS, THOMAS, professional boxer; b. Grand Juction, Teen., Oct. 18, 1958. Turned profl. in, 1977; won World Boxing Assn. welterweight championship, 1980; lost World Boxing Assn. welterweight championship, 1981; won World Boxing Assn. super-welterwieght championship, 1982; World Boxing Assn. super-welterweight champion, 1982—. Winner Nat. AAU title, 1977, Golden Gloves championship, 1977. Office: care Emanuel Steward 19600 W McNichol St Detroit MI 48219

HEARON, JAMES HAMILTON, III, banker; b. Tucson, Feb. 22, 1934; s. James Hamilton H. and Ulah Sinter; m. Hanet C. Boss, Nov. 25, 1961; children: James H., Jennifer. B.S., U. Ariz., 1955; M.B.A., Golden Gate U., 1972. V.p. nat. div. United Calif. Bank, San Francisco, 1970-73, v.p., group head U.S., Claif., Can. group internat. div., 1973-74, sr. v.p. consumer banking for br. system, 1974-75; pres., chief adminstrv. officer, dir. United Calif. Bank Internat., N.Y.C., 1975-78; pres., chief operating officer, dir. Nat. City Bank, Mpls., 1978-81, pres., chief exec. officer, dir., 1982—; dir. Nat. City Bancorp., Mpls. Bd. dirs. Minn. Orch., Mpls., 1981—, St. Paul-Ramsey Arts and Sci. Council, 1980—, Courage Ctr., Mpls., 1980—; chmn. bd. dirs. Met. Econ. Devel. Assn., Mpls., 1979—. Served to 1st lt. U.S. Army, 1955-57. Recipient Dean Edward J. Kelly award, 1972. Mem. Fin. Execs. Inst., Robert Morris Assn. Republican. Presbyterian. Clubs: Minneapolis Interlachen, Minneapolis Country. Home: 6204 Loch Moor Dr Edina MN 55435 Office: PO Box E-1919 Minneapolis MN 55480

HEARON, WILLIAM RAY, community college president; b. Pontotoc, Okla., Jan. 8, 1933; s. Jess Ballard and Lucille Myrtle (Duty) H.; m. Barbara Ann Gardiner, Oct. 28, 1966; children: Mark, Marjorie, Rhonda. B.A., U. Calif., Berkeley, 1956, M.A., 1957; Ed.D., UCLA, 1970. Tchr., counselor, asst. prin. McFarland (Calif.) High Sch., 1957-61; dean students Shafter (Calif.) High Sch., 1961-65, West High Sch., Bakersfield, Calif., 1965-67; dean student personnel Moorpark (Calif.) Coll., 1967-74, pres., 1974—; adv. com. Pedderdine U., Los Angeles, Lutheran Coll., Thousand Oaks, Calif. Chmn. bd. Ventura chpt. Am. Heart Assn., 1979-80, bd. dirs. Calif. affiliate, 1980—; bd. dirs. KVPB Public Radio; chmn. fund raising adv. com. Calif. Heart Assn., 1982—. Recipient Service award Am. Heart Assn., 1978-79; fellow NDEA Counseling Inst., 1965. Mem. So. Calif. Community Coll., Chief Adminstrs. Assn. (pres. 1979-80), Calif. Community Coll. Adminstrs. Assn., Phi Delta Kappa. Democrat. Clubs: Rotary, Lions, Kiwanis. Home: 5577 LaCumbre Rd Camarillo CA 93010 Office: 7075 Campus Rd Moorpark CA 93021

HEARST, AUSTINE MCDONNELL, newspaper reporter, freelance feature writer, columnist; b. Warrenton, Va., Nov. 22, 1928; d. Austin and Mary (Belt) McDonnell; m. William Randolph Hearst, Jr., 1948; children—William Randolph III, John Augustine Chilton. Ed. Warrenton County schs., Convent Notre Dame, Md., King-Smith Jr. Coll. Columnist Washington Times-Herald, 1946-56; syndicated columnist King Features Syndicate; radio commentator CBS, 1946-56. Clubs: Nat. Press, Sulgrave (Washington); Cosmopolitan. Office: Hearst Corp 959 8th Ave New York NY 10019

HEARST, BELLA RACHAEL, physician, researcher, artist; b. Pitts.; d. Aba and Bertha (Alpern) H. B.M., Chgo. Med. Sch., 1949, M.D., 1950; postgrad., Johns Hopkins U., 1952-53, Art Inst. Chgo., 1958-68. Rotating intern Norwegian Am. Hosp., Chgo., 1949-50; jr. asst. pathologist Cook County Hosp, Chgo., 1950-52; fellow med. legal pathology U. Md., 1953-54; sr. pathology resident Charity Hosp., New Orleans, 1955-56; spl. cardiac researcher Armed Forces Inst. Pathology, Washington, 1956-57; dir., coordinator pathology dept Hosp. O'Horan Menda Yucatan, Mexico, 1957-58; founder Bertha Hearts Found., Inc., 1958, exec. dir., 1958-63; founder Diabetic Inst. Am., Inc., Chgo., 1959, exec. dir., 1959-63; founder Internat. Diabetic Inst., Inc., Chgo., 1963, exec. dir, 1963—; dist. med. dir. compensation U.S. Dept. Labor, Chgo., 1968—; with Chgo. Dept. Health, 1977—, Uptown Neighborhood Health Ctr., 1977-78, Copernicus Multipurpose Ctr., 1978-79, Lakeview Neighborhood Health Ctr., Chgo., 1979—; research dir. Fed. Safety and Fire Council, Chgo.; research assoc. microbiology Stritch Sch. Medicine, Loyola U., Chgo.; staff physician Western Ill. U., 1971-72, assoc. prof., 1971-72. Author: Diabetes and Juvenile Delinquency, 1964, Diabetes and Fitness, 1964, Diabetic Statistical Research Survey, 1961-65, Diabetes and Blood Groups, 1965, Diabetes and Aging, 1965, Diabetes and Newborns; contbr. articles to various publs., art exhibit, Shuster Art Gallery, N.Y., 1966, Internat. Dermatology Congress, Munich, 1967. Recipient 3d prize AMA Conv., Chgo., 1962, testimonial plaque for work sr. citizens Chelsea House, Chgo. Fellow Am. Coll. Angiology, Internat. Coll. Angiology, Am. Geriatric Soc., Royal Soc. Pub. Health; mem. Internat. Acad. Pathology, Am. Women's Med. Assn., Am. Soc. Microbiology, Am. Assn. for Study Neoplastic Diseases, Reticuloendothelial Soc. Office: 8 S Michigan Blvd Chicago IL 60603 Office: PO Box A3579 Chicago IL 60690

HEARST, GEORGE RANDOLPH, JR., diversified ranching, real estate executive; b. San Francisco, July 13, 1927; s. George and Blanche (Wilbur) H.; m. Mary Thompson, Apr. 23, 1951 (dec. Dec. 1969); children: Mary, George Randolph III, Stephen T., Erin; m. Patricia Ann Bell, Nov. 30, 1969. Pvt. bus., 1946-48; staff Los Angeles Examiner, 1948-50, San Francisco Examiner, 1954-56; with Los Angeles Evening Herald-Express, from 1956, bus. mgr., 1957, pub., from 1960, Los Angeles Herald-Examiner, from 1962; v.p. Hearst Corp., 1977—; also dir. Trustee Hearst Found. Served with USNR, 1945-46; with AUS, 1950-54. Mem. V.F.W. Clubs: Burlingame Country, Jonathan, California, Riviera. Office: Hearst Corp 1150 S Olive St Suite 2620 Los Angeles CA 90015 *

HEARST, JOSEPH ALBERT, JR., educator, arbitrator; b. Leavenworth, Wash., Apr. 16, 1917; s. Joseph Albert and Lou (Risk) H.; m. Priscilla D. Fox, June 23, 1949; children—Jonena M., Alice L., Joseph Albert III, Melissa A. B.S., U. Wash., 1940, M.A., 1948; Ph.D., Columbia, 1959. Grad. asst. dept. history U. Wash., 1946; research fellow Bur. Govtl. Research and Services, 1947, Univ. fellow dept. polit. sci., 1947; spl. research asso. Inst. Pub. Affairs, 1948; tutor Columbia, 1948-50; instr. dept. polit. sci. Whitman Coll, Walla Walla, Wash., 1950-53; lectr. govt. Barnard Coll., also Columbia, 1952-56; prof. govt. Idaho State U., Pocatello, 1956-65, 75—, asst. dean, 1965-67, dean, 1967-74. Contbr. articles to profl. jours. Mem. Law Enforcement Planning Commn. Served to capt., inf. AUS, 1940-45. Decorated Bronze Star. Mem. Am. Polit. Sci. Assn., Western Polit. Sci. Assn. (past mem. exec. bd.), Am. Soc. Internat. Law, Am. Arbitration Assn., Pi Sigma Alpha, Phi Kappa Phi. Home: 1230 College Rd Pocatello ID 83201

HEARST, RANDOLPH APPERSON, publishing executive; b. N.Y.C., Dec. 2, 1915; s. William Randolph and Millicent (Willson) H.; m. Catherine Campbell, Jan. 12, 1938 (div. Apr. 1982); children: Catherine, Virginia, Patricia, Anne, Victoria.; m. Maria C. Scruggs, May 2, 1982. Student, Harvard U., 1933-34. Asst. to editor Atlanta Georgian, 1934-38; asst. to pub. San Francisco Call-Bull., 1940-44, exec. editor, 1947-49, pub., 1950-53; asso. pub. Oakland Post-Enquirer, 1946-47; pres., dir., chief exec. officer Hearst Consol. Publs., Inc. and Hearst Pub. Co., Inc., 1961-64; pres. San Francisco Examiner, 1972—; dir. The Hearst Corp., 1965—, chmn. exec. com., 1965-73, chmn., 1973—; Dir. Hearst Found., 1945—, pres., 1972—; dir. Wm. Randolph Hearst Found., 1950—. Served as capt., Air Transport Command USAAF, 1942-45. Roman Catholic. Clubs: Piedmont Driving (Atlanta); Burlingame Country, Pacific Union; Press (San Francisco). Office: 110 5th St San Francisco CA 94103

HEARST, WILLIAM RANDOLPH, JR., editor; b. N.Y.C., Jan. 27, 1908; s. William Randolph and Millicent Veronica (Willson) H.; m. Austine McDonnell, July 29, 1948; children—W.R. Hearst III, John Augustine Chilton. Student, U. Calif., 1925-27; LL.D., U. Alaska. Began career with N.Y. Am., N.Y.C., 1928, as reporter, asst. to city editor, pub., 1936-37; pub. N.Y. Jour.-Am., N.Y.C., 1937-56; served as war corr., 1943-45; now chmn. exec. com., dir. Hearst Corp. Bd. dirs. Hearst Found., William Randolph Hearst Found., USO of Met. N.Y., Research to Prevent Blindness, Ear Research Inst. Recipient Pulitzer prize, 1956; Overseas Press Club award, 1958. Mem. UPI Inter-Am. Press Assn. (dir.), Sigma Delta Chi, Phi Delta Theta. Clubs: Brook, Madison Square Garden, Marco Polo (N.Y.C.); Met., Nat. Press, F St., Burning Tree (Washington); Pacific Union, Bohemian (San Francisco). Office: 959 8th Ave New York NY 10019

HEARTH, DONALD PAYNE, aero. engr., NASA ofcl.; b. Fall River, Mass., Aug. 13, 1928; s. Alvin George and Hildreth (Fogwell) H.; m. Joan Hall Smith, Dec. 30, 1950; children—Susan Hall, Douglas Payne, Anne Hall, Janet Hall. B.S. in Mech. Engring, Northeastern U., Boston, 1951; postgrad., U. Calif., Los Angeles, U. So. Calif.; grad., Fed. Exec. Inst., 1973. With NASA, 1951-57, mgr. advanced programs, 1962-67, dir. planetary programs, Washington, 1967-70; dep. dir. Goddard Space Flight Center, Greenbelt, Md., 1970-75; dir. Langley Research Center, Hampton, Va., 1975—; project mgr., dept. mgr. Marquardt Corp., Van Nuys, Calif., 1957-62. Author articles. Recipient Exceptional Service medal NASA, 1969; Exec. Performance award, 1975; Distinguished Service award, 1975. Fellow Am. Inst. Aeros. and Astronautics, Am. Astronautical Soc.; mem. Am. Soc. Pub. Adminstrn. Office: Langley Research Center NASA Hampton VA 23665

HEARTNEY, MATTHEW JOSEPH, JR., lawyer; b. Des Moines, June 29, 1916; s. Matthew Joseph and Elizabeth (Skahill) H.; m. Marjorie Parker, Aug. 5, 1950 (div. Sept. 1968); children: John P., Matthew T., Eleanor T., Francis J., James P., Edward P. B.A., State U. Iowa, 1936, J.D., 1940; postgrad. (Sterling fellow), Yale U., 1940-41. Bar: Iowa 1940. Practiced in Des Moines, 1941—; mem. Heartney Harvey Butters & Ottoson (and predecessors), 1941-80, Belin, Harris, Helmick, Heartney & Tesdell, Des Moines, 1980—; dir. First Fed. State Bank, Des Moines. Chmn. Council Social Agys., 1963-66; pres. Polk County Mental Health Assn., 1966-68; mem. consumers adv. council Health Planning Assembly, 1971—; bd. dirs., mem. exec. com. Iowa Assn. Mental Health, Nat. Assn. Mental Health; bd. dirs. Bd. Internat. Students, 1962-68, United Community Services, 1960-66, Polk County Health Services, 1983—. Fellow Am. Bar Found.; mem. Iowa Bar Assn. (com. taxation 1953-61, probate trust com. 1961-82), Polk County Bar Assn. (pres. 1956-57), Phi Beta Kappa, Delta Theta Phi, Delta Sigma Rho. Clubs: Rotary, Pioneer (pres. 1980-81). Home: 3333 Grand Apt 263 Des Moines IA 50312 Office: 2000 Financial Center Des Moines IA 50309

HEARTZ, DANIEL LEONARD, music educator; b. Exeter, N.H., Oct. 5, 1928; s. Harold Francis and Katherine (McEnhill) H. A.B., U. N.H., 1950; A.M., Harvard U., 1951, Ph.D. (Sheldon fellow), 1957. Instr. U. Chgo., 1957-58, asst. prof., 1958-60, U. Calif. at Berkeley, 1960-65, asso. prof., 1965-67, prof., 1967—, chmn. music dept., 1969-73. Author: Pierre Attaingnant, Royal Printer of Music, 1969; Editor: Preludes, Chansons and Dances for Lute, 1964, (with Alfred Mann) Theorie-und Kompositionsstudien bei Mozart (Thomas Attwood), 1964-1969, Idomeneo (Mozart), 1972, (with Bonnie Wade) Report of the 12th Congress I.M.S., 1977. Humanities Research fellow Princeton U., 1963-64; Guggenheim fellow, 1967-68, 78-79. Mem. Am. Musicological Soc. (council 1960-62, 66-68, v.p. 1974-76, Kinkeldy award 1971), Royal Mus. Assn. (Dent medal 1970), Société Française de Musicologie. Home: 1098 Keith Ave Berkeley CA 94708

HEASLIP, WILLIAM A., sportswear company executive. Former pres., now chmn., chief exec. officer Grafton-Fraser, Inc., Toronto, Ont., Can. Office: Grafton-Fraser Inc 9 Sunlight Park Rd Toronto ON Canada

HEATH, DOUGLAS HAMILTON, educator; b. Woodbury, N.J., Oct. 1, 1925; s. Russell M. and Eleanor H. (Conrow) H.; m. Harriet Elizabeth Frye, June 15, 1952; children—Russell, Wendilee, Anne Marie. Student, Swarthmore Coll., 1941-42; A.B. summa cum laude, Amherst Coll., 1949; A.M., Harvard, 1952, Ph.D., 1954. Instr. grad. sch. edn. Harvard, 1953-54; asst. Haverford (Pa.) Coll., 1954-59, asso. prof., chmn. psychology dept., 1959-65, 67-68, 78-79, prof., 1965—; Nat. Sci. Faculty fellow U. Mich., 1957. Author: Explorations of Maturity, 1965, Growing Up In College: Liberal Education and Maturity, 1968, Humanizing Schools: New Directions, New Decisions, 1971, Maturity and Competence: A Transcultural View, 1977. Served with AUS, 1942-44. Fulbright Research scholar, 1965-66. Fellow Am. Psychol. Assn. Mem. Soc. of Friends. Home and Office: 223 Buck Ln Haverford PA 19041

HEATH, DWIGHT BRALEY, educator, anthropologist; b. Hartford, Conn., Nov. 19, 1930; s. Percy Leonard and Luise (Hosp) H.; 1 son, David Braley. A.B. in Social Relations, Harvard, 1952; Ph.D. in Anthropology, Yale, 1959. Mem. faculty Brown U., 1959—, prof. anthropology, 1970—; vis. prof., U.S. and abroad, cons. in field. Author: A Journal of the Pilgrims at Plymouth, 1963, Land Reform and Social Revolution in Bolivia, 1969, Historical Dictionary of Bolivia, 1972, Contemporary Cultures and Societies of Latin America, 2d edit, 1974, Cross-Cultural Approaches to the Study of Alcohol, 1976, Alcohol Use and World Cultures, 1980, Cultural Factors in Alcohol Research and Treatment of Drinking Problems, 1981, also articles. Served with AUS, 1952-54. Grantee Nat. Acad. Scis., 1974, Am. Philos. Soc., 1972, Social Sci. Research Council, 1958, Doherty Found., 1956-57. Mem. Am. Anthrop. Assn., Am. Ethnol. Soc., A.A.A.S., Am. Soc. Ethnohistory, Royal Anthrop. Inst., Latin Am. Studies Assn. Office: Dept Anthropology Brown U Box 1921 Providence RI 02912

HEATH, EDWARD CHARLES, biochemist, educator; b. St. Louis, Mar. 29, 1926; s. Glenn Garrison and Edna M. (Fluchel) H.; m. Patricia L. Nolan, Jan. 29, 1947; children—Justin P. (dec.), Paula J., Dana J. B.S., St. Louis U., 1949; A.M., U. Mo., 1951; Ph.D., Purdue U., 1955. Instr. to asso. prof. microbiology U. Mich., 1957-63; asso. prof. physiol. chemistry Sch. Medicine Johns Hopkins U., Balt., 1963-66, prof., 1966-71; prof., chmn. dept. biochemistry U. Pitts. Sch. Medicine, 1971-76; prof., head dept. biochemistry U. Iowa Coll. Medicine, 1976—; cons. USPHS, NRC, Cystic Fibrosis Research Found., Nat. Bd. Med. Examiners; mem. biochemistry tng. com. NIH. Exec. editor: Archives Biochemistry and Biophysics; Editorial bd.: Analytical Biochemistry, Jour. Biol. Chemistry, Biochemistry; Contbr. articles sci. jours. Served with USNR, 1944-46. Mem. Am. Soc. Biol. Chemists, Am. Chem. Soc., Am. Soc. Microbiology, Sigma Xi, Phi Lambda Upsilon. Home: Rural Route 2 Box 321 F North Liberty IA 52317

HEATH, GEORGE ROSS, oceanographer, university dean; b. Adelaide, Australia, Mar. 10, 1939; s. Frederick John and Eleanora (Blackmore) H.; m. Lorna Margaret Sommerville, Oct. 5, 1972; children: Amanda Jo, Alisa Jeanne. B.Sc., Adelaide U., 1960, 1961; Ph.D., Scripps Instn. Oceanography, 1968. Geologist S. Australian Geol. Survey, Adelaide, 1961-63; asst. prof. oceanography Oreg. State U., Corvallis, 1969-72, assoc. prof., 1972-75, prof., dean, 1978—; chmn. bd. govs. Joint Oceanographic Instns. Inc., 1982-84; prof. U. R.I., Narragansett, 1974-78. Contbr. articles to profl. jours. Fellow Geol. Soc. Am., Am. Geophys. Union; mem. Clay Mineral Soc. Office: Coll Oceanography Oreg State Univ Corvallis OR 97331

HEATH, GLORIA WHITTON, aerospace cons.; b. N.Y.C., May 7, 1922; d. Royal Vale and Lillian (Hart) H. Grad., The Putney Sch., 1939; A.B., Smith Coll., 1943. Ops. analyst engring. dept. Am. Export Airlines, N.Y.C., 1943; air force service pilot WASP, 1943-44; dir. summer aviation program Conn. Coll., 1945; spl. asst. to chief engr. loss prevention Aero Ins. Underwriters, N.Y.C., 1945-48; with Flight Safety Found., N.Y.C., 1948-65; as spl. asst. to managing dir., dir. pvt. flying, dir. spl. affairs; asst. dir. Cornell-Guggenheim Aviation Safety Center, N.Y.C., 1965-68; prin. dir. SAR-ASSIST, Inc., 1968—; Civilian adv. com. to FAA, 1967-70; Bd. govs., mem. exec. com. Flight Safety Found., 1970—; mem. Barbour Internat. Air Safety Award Bd., 1966—, chmn., 1978-81. Recipient Lady Hay Drummond-Hay trophy, 1955; Amelia Earhart award, 1957; Hon. Mem. award Wives Wing Aerospace Med. Assn., 1962; Laura Taber Barbour Internat. Air Safety award, 1965; Smith Coll. medal, 1971. Asso. fellow Am. Inst. Aeros and Astronautics; mem. Nat. Pilots Assn. (nat. sec. 1966), Am. Astronaut Soc. (nat. sec. 1962-65, chmn. safety tech. com. 1969-77), Aviation Space Writers Assn., Ninety-Nines, Internat. Acad. Astronautics (corr. mem.; mem. internat. space rescue and safety studies com. 1968—, chmn. 1978—). Home: One Island Ln Greenwich CT 06830 *To the extent that a person can free himself from a sense of self, one experiences a falling aside of seeming terminuses in one's path (self-limitation)—a sense of self is bound to stand between oneself and clearer outward perception (and consequently inward as well).*

HEATH, JAMES LEE, educator, researcher; b. Monroe, La., Dec. 6, 1939; s. James Lee and Alodi (Blank) H.; m. Mary Alice Noble, Dec. 25, 1960. B.S., La. State U., 1963, M.S., 1968, Ph.D., 1970. Asst. prof. food sci. U. Md., 1970-74, asso. prof., 1974-79, prof., 1979—. Editor: Md. Poultryman, 1976-78; asso. editor: Poultry Sci. Jour, 1980—; contbr. articles to profl. publs. Served as officer U.S. Army, 1963-65. Recipient research and service awards, 1979, alumni award for research, 1981. Mem. Poultry Sci. Assn., Am. Inst. Biol. Scis., Inst. Food Tech., World's Poultry Congress, Sigma Xi (sec. Md. chpt. 1976-77, pres. chpt. 1977-78), Gamma Sigma Delta, Alpha Zeta. Home: 6224 86th Ave New Carrollton MD 20784 Office: Dept Poultry Science U Maryland College Park MD 20742

HEATH, JESSE BOYD, JR., lawyer; b. Madisonville, Tex., May 25, 1940; s. Jesse Boyd and Bernice (Davis) H.; m. Helen Hughetta Shell, Sept. 8, 1962; children: Heather, Jesse Boyd III. Student, U. Tex. at Austin, 1958-61; B.B.A., So. Meth. U., 1963, LL.B., 1966. Bar: Tex. 1966. Law clk. to U.S. dist. judge, 1966-68; practiced in, Dallas, 1968-70, Houston, 1970—; asso. firm Carrington, Coleman, Sloman & Blumenthal, 1968-70; mem. firm Heath & Knippa, 1973-83, Jenkens, Gilchrist & Heath, Houston, 1983—; Bd. visitors So. Meth. U. Law Sch., 1977-80; bd. govs., mem. exec. com. Am. Coll. Real Estate Lawyers, 1980-83, treas., 1983—. Mng. editor: Southwestern Law Jour, 1965-66; Contbr. articles to profl. publs. Mem. Houston Bar Assn. (chmn. real estate law sect. 1980-81), ABA (council mem. real property, probate and trust law sect., joint editorial bd. uniform real property acts), State Bar Tex. (sec.-treas. sect. on corp., banking and bus. law 1969-70, mem. sect. council 1978—, real property, probate and trust law), Anglo-Am. Real Estate Inst., So. Meth. U. Law Sch. Alumni Assn. (dir., vice chmn. 1974-75), Phi Delta Theta (pres. Houston Alumni Assn. 1974, pres. Rho South province 1975-77), Phi Delta Phi. Methodist. Club: River Oaks Country. Home: 3434 Del Monte Dr Houston TX 77019 Office: 2800 Tex Commerce Tower Houston TX 77002

HEATH, JOHN LAWRENCE, candy company executive; b. Robinson, Ill., Dec. 30, 1935; s. Vernon Lawrence and Beatrice (Kane) H.; m. Sheila Carole Owens, June 8, 1958; children: Lawrence A., Kerry L., April J., David O. Student, U. Ill., 1953-55; B.S. in Social Sci., Eastern Ill. U., 1958. Program dir., sta. mgr. Sta. WEIC, Charleston, Ill., 1960-62; with L.S. Heath & Sons Inc., Robinson, Ill., 1962—, advt. merchandising and promotions mgr., 1962-64, gen. mgr. fund raising div., 1964-69, sr. v.p., 1969-71, chmn., pres., chief exec. officer, 1971—; dir. 1st Nat. Bank Robinson, 1970—, vice chmn., 1976—; dir. Central Ill. Pub. Service Co., Springfield. Mem. adminstrv. bd. 1st United Meth. Ch., Robinson, 1968—, chmn. adminstrv. bd., Robinson, 1982, lay leader, Robinson, 1972-75; trustee Wesley Found., So. Ill. U., Carbondale, 1980—; mem. Ill. Bldg. Authority, 1971-74; county fund raising chmn. Blackhawk dist. Wabash Valley Council Boy Scouts Am., 1970-71; bd. dirs. Embarras Regional Health Planning Council, Olney, Ill., 1975—, 1st v.p., 1970-71; trustee U. Ill. YMCA, Champaign, 1970-75; bd. dirs. Ill. 4-H Found. Campaign, 1973-75, Eastern Ill. U. Found., Charleston, 1980—, Crawford County Hosp. Dist., 1974—; 1st vice chmn. Crawford County Hosp. Dist., 1975-76, 79, chmn., 1977-78, 80. Served with AUS, 1958-60. Mem. Nat. Confectioners Assn. (dir. 1974-79, v.p. 1981—, co-chmn. nat. conv. 1974, chmn. 1980), Nat. Candy Wholesalers Assn. (hon. dean), Chocolate Mfrs. Assn. U.S. (dir. 1977-80), Robinson C. of C. (dir. 1968-71), U.S. C. of C., Ill. C. of C. (dir. 1976—, v.p. 1978-80), Eastern Ill. U. Alumni Assn. (dir. 1980—, v.p. 1981-82, chmn. alumni giving campaign 1981-82), Alpha Tau Omega. Clubs: Quail Creek County (Robinson) (trustee 1974-78); Union League (Chgo.)). Office: L S Heath & Sons Inc 206 S Jackson St Robinson IL 62454

HEATH, MICHAEL H., newspaper executive; b. N.Y.C., July 12, 1941; s. Frederick K. and Mary H. H.; m. Mary Louise Agemian, June 27, 1964; children: Christine Cordell, Jacqueline Ann, Carolyn Louise. B.A., William Coll., 1963; M.B.A., Harvard U., 1967. Mfg. engr. Westinghouse Electric Co., Pitts., 1963-65; with Chem. Bank, 1967-78, v.p., Bronx, N.Y., 1975-77, Brussels, 1977-78; pres. Bergen Record Corp., Macromedia, Inc., Hackensack, N.J., 1978—, also dir.; dir. Gremac, Inc., United Jersey Bank, Hackensack, Gateway Communications, Inc., Monmouth News, Inc., Toms River Pub. Co., Inc., Passaic Eve. Record Corp., News Carriers, Inc. Pres. bd. trustees Dwight-Englewood (N.J.) Sch., 1979-85. Mem. N.J. Press Assn., Commerce and Industry Assn. No. N.J., Choate Sch. Alumni Assn., Ind. Sch. Chmn.'s Assn. (bd. dirs.). Clubs: Englewood Field; University (N.Y.C.); Spring Lake (N.J.) Bath and Tennis; Knickerbocker Country (Tenafly, N.J.). Office: 150 River St Hackensack NJ 07602

HEATH, PERCY, jazz bassist; b. Wilmington, N.C., Apr. 30, 1923; s. Percy Leroy and Arlethia (Wall) H.; m. June Ellen Jones, Mar. 31, 1950; children: Percy Leroy, Jason, Stewart. Mem. faculty Sch. Jazz, Lenox, Mass. Founder mem., Modern Jazz Quartet, 1955—; string bass player, 1951—; bass player, 2d Internat. Jazz Festival, ensemble of Howard McGhee, 1948; played at, Maggio Musicale, Florence, Italy, 1959, Contemporary Music Festival, Donaueschingen, W. Ger., 1957; appeared with, Sarah Vaughn, Newport Jazz Festival; played with, Miles Davis, J.J. Johnson, Dizzy Gillespie; formed, Heath Bros. group with Jimmy, Tootie and Stanley Cowell. Served with AUS, 1943-45. Office: care Ted Kurland Assocs 46 Ashford St Boston MA 02134 *

HEATH, RICHARD MURRAY, hosp. adminstr.; b. Amanda, Ohio, Sept. 24, 1927; s. Cecil E. and Mary Eva (Murray) H.; m. Charlene Wilson, June 4, 1948; children—Jenifer Sue, Janet Lynn. B.S. in Edn, Wilmington (Ohio) Coll., 1949; M.S. in Social Adminstrn, Western Res. U., 1953, Northwestern U., 1958. Adminstr. Orient (Ohio) State Hosp., 1956-61; asst. supt. Colo. State Hosp., 1961-72; dir. instl. services N.Y. State Dept. Mental Hygiene, 1972-77; dir. Utica (N.Y.)-Marcy Psychiat. Centers, 1977—; project dir. NIMH grants; survey cons. Author articles in field. Served with USNR, World War II. Recipient Kleber award N.Y. State Assn. for Blind, 1976. Mem. (Nat. Assn. Social Workers, charter), Assn. Mental Health Adminstrs. (pres. 1970). Club: Masons. Office: 1213 Court St Utica NY 13502

HEATH, RICHARD RAYMOND, business executive; b. La Junta, Colo., June 22, 1929; s. Perry Stanford and Genevieve Anabelle (Whitney) H.; m. Arlene Newbrow, Nov. 3, 1961. B.A. in Econs, U. Colo., 1951, LL.B., 1954. Bar: Colo. 1954, Calif. 1957, Ark. 1973. Mem. firm Neyhart & Grodin, San Francisco, 1957-66; dep. Peace Corps dir., Ivory Coast, 1966-68, dir., 1968-69, Peace Corps dir., Mali, 1969-72; dir. Ark. Dept. Fin. and Adminstrn.; also chief fiscal officer, commr. revenues State of Ark., mem. gov.'s cabinet, 1972-77; dir. San Francisco Internat. Airport, 1977-81; v.p., dir. mktg. AIS, Inc., 1981-84; exec. v.p., chief fin. officer United Bank, San Francisco, 1984—; Vice chmn. Multi-State Tax Commn., 1973-74, chmn., 1976—, mem. exec. com., 1974—; del. Conf. State Bar Dels. Mem. nat. bd. dirs. Coalition for a Dem. Majority, 1973-1976; chmn. bd. dirs. FORUM; mem. conservative caucus Nat. Tax Limitation Com., 1980—; mem. Republican Presdl. task force Rep. Nat. Com., 1980—. Served to 1st lt. USAF, 1955-57. Mem. State Bar Calif., San Francisco Bar Assn. (past chmn. indsl. accident com.), San Francisco Lawyers Club, Am., Calif. trial lawyers assns., San Francisco Planning and Urban Renewal Assn., Nat. Parks Assn., Calif. Applicants Attys. Assn. (v.p.). Clubs: Little Rock Racquet; San Francisco Tennis (San Francisco) (gov.); Rotary Internat.). Home: 26 Woodhaven Ct San Francisco CA 94131 office: 130 Montgomery St San Francisco CA 94104

HEATH, ROBERT GALBRAITH, neurologist, educator; b. Pitts., May 9, 1915; s. Robert Malcolm and Minnie Coleman (Galbraith) H.; m. Eleanor Bugher Wright, Sept. 7, 1940; children: Anne, Shari, Barbara, Carol, Robert Galbraith. B.S., U. Pitts., 1937, M.D., 1938; D.M.Sc., Columbia U., 1949. Intern Mercy Hosp., Pitts., 1939; instr. medicine U. Pitts., 1939-40; asst., chief resident neurology Neurol. Inst., N.Y., 1940-42, asst. attending neurologist, 1946-49; psychiatrist Pa. Hosp. Nervous and Mental Diseases; also demonstrator neurology Jefferson Med. Coll., 1942-43; instr. neurology Columbia, 1946-49, attending psychoanalyst, 1951-56; prof. Tulane U., 1949—, chmn. dept. psychiatry and neurology, 1949-80; sr. vis. physician Charity Hosp.; cons. VA Hosp., New Orleans, Southeast La. State Hosp., East La. State Hosp.; med. staff DePaul Hosp.; chief med. officer Mcht. Marine Rest Center, U.S. Marine Hosp.; chief psychiatrist U.S. Penitentiary, Lewisburg, Pa., 1943-46; Pres. Inst. Mental Hygiene of New Orleans, med. dirs., 1965—; Med. adviser to La. dir. SSS; USPHS (coms. psychosurgery and tng. grants); com. med. edn. Am. Psychiat. Assn.; U.S. rep. Internat. Symposium on Biol. and Clin. Aspects Central Nervous Systems, Basle, Switzerland; mem. sci. adv. bd. Am. Council on Marijuana, 1980—. Author: Selective Partial Ablation of the Frontal Cortex (ed. F. A. Mettler), 1949; editor: Studies in Schizophrenia, 1954; Editor: Serological Fractions in Schizophrenia, 1963, The Role of Pleasure in Behavior, 1964; adv. bd.: Jour. Nervous and Mental Disease, 1978—; author: 350 sci. papers. Recipient Mental Health award Mental Health Assn. La., 1978. Fellow Am. Coll. Neuropsychopharmacology (charter), Am. Acad. Neurology, N.Y. Acad. Medicine, ACP; mem. Am. Neurol. Assn., Am. Assn. Psychonalytic Medicine, AMA, Soc. Research Psychosomatic Problems, Soc. Biol. Psychiatry (v.p. 1967-68, pres. 1968-69, Gold Medal award for pioneer research in field 1972, Disting. Service award 1983), Assn. Research in Nervous and Mental Disease, AAAS, Am. Acad. Psychonanalysis (trustee, Frieda Fromm-Reichman award 1974), La. Psychiat. Assn. (pres. 1960-61, award 1977), Sigma Xi. Address: 1430 Tulane Ave New Orleans LA 70112

HEATH, WILLIAM WEBSTER, educator; b. Buffalo, July 1, 1929; s. William Russell and Elizabeth (Webster) H.; m. Mary Louise Townsend, June 21, 1952; children: Elizabeth Townsend, Emily Byron. B.A., Amherst Coll., 1951; M.A., Columbia, 1952; Ph.D., U. Wis., 1956. Teaching asst. English U. Wis., 1952-56; instr. English Amherst Coll., 1956-59, asst. prof., 1959-64, asso. prof., 1964-69, prof., 1969—; vis. prof. English U. Mass., summers 1962, 64, 65, 66, 67, 68, 70. Author: Elizabeth Bowen: An Introduction to Her Novels, 1961, Wordsworth and Coleridge: A Study of Their Literary Relations, 1801-02, 1970; Editor: Major British Poets of the Romantic Period, 1972. Mem. Modern Lang. Assn. Democrat. Home: 36 Snell St Amherst MA 01002

HEATHCOCK, CLAYTON HOWELL, chemistry educator, researcher; b. San Antonio, Tex., July 21, 1936; s. Clayton H. and Frances E. (Lay) H.; m. Mable Ruth Sims, Sept. 6, 1957 (div. 1972); children: Cheryl Lynn, Barbara Sue, Steven Wayne, Rebecca Ann; m. Cheryl R. Hadley, Nov. 28, 1980. B.Sc., Abilene Christian Coll., Tex., 1958; Ph.D., U. Colo., 1963. Supr. chem. analysis group Champion Paper and Fiber Co., Pasadena, Tex., 1958-60; asst. prof. chemistry U. Calif.-Berkeley, 1964-70, assoc. prof., 1970-75, prof., 1975—; chmn. Medicinal Chemistry Study Sect., NIH, Washington, 1981-83. Author: Introduction to Organic Chemistry, 1976; contbr. numerous articles to profl. jours. Recipient Alexander von Humboldt U.S. Scientist, 1978. Mem. Am. Chem. Soc. (Chmn. organic div. 1984), Chem. Soc. London, AAAS. Home: 20 Highgate Ct Kensington CA 94720 Office: Dept Chemistry U. Calif Berkeley CA 94707

HEATHERINGTON, J. SCOTT, osteopathic physician and surgeon; b. Athol, Kan., Apr. 22, 1919; s. Clarence Linder and Nora B. (Scott) H.; m. Geraldine Virginia Greene, Feb. 20, 1942; children: Jeffrey Scott, Douglas Linder, Marc Gilbert. B.S., York Coll., 1943; D.O., Still Coll. Osteopathy and Surgery, 1944; L.H.D., Westmar Coll., 1971, Coll. Osteo. Medicine and Surgery, 1969; LL.D., Phia. Coll. Osteo. Medicine, 1970. Intern Detroit Osteo. Hosp., 1944-45; pvt. practice, Medford, Oreg., 1945-57, Gladstone, Oreg., 1957-76; guest lectr. Coll. Osteo. Medicine and Surgery, Des Moines, Phila. Coll. Osteo. Medicine; pres. staff Portland (Oreg.) Osteo. Hosp., 1963-64, 73-74, v.p. staff, 1972-73, bd. dirs., 1971-76, Eastmoreland Gen. Hosp., 1972-76, treas., 1973-74, v.p., 1974-75, pres. bd., 1975-76; dean, prof. osteo. medicine Okla. Coll. Osteo. Medicine and Surgery, 1976-78; med. dir., dir. med. edn. Okla. Osteo. Hosp., 1978-80; dir. osteo. services Eastmoreland Gen. Hosp., 1980—. Editorial cons.: Adult and Child Med. Challenge, 1970-78, Northwest Medicine, 1976-77; editor: Osteo. Medicine Jour, 1976-81. Mem. Oreg. Meth. Conf. Fin. Commn., 1956-60; mem. Okla. State Anat. Bd., 1976-78; trustee Coll. Osteo. Medicine and Surgery, 1967-71, Medford Salvation Army, 1954-57, Rogue River Valley Manor, 1951-57, Nat. Osteo. Found., 1960-69; adv. com. Okla. Physician Manpower Tng. Commn., 1976-78. Named Oreg. Osteo. Gen. Practicioner of Year, 1974; Conv. Man of Year Conv. Bur. Portland-Oreg. C. of C., 1974. Mem. Am. Osteo. Assn. (ho. dels. 1954-63, trustee 1959-68, exec. com. 1964-71, pres. elect 1968-69, pres. 1969-70), Oreg. Osteo. Assn. (trustee 1949-63, pres. 1952-53, 60-61), So. Oreg. Osteo. Soc. (pres. 1949), Am. Acad. Osteopathy (trustee 1974-81, chmn. finance com., chmn. membership com., pres. 1979-80), N.W. Acad. Osteopathy (v.p. 1972-74, pres. 1974-76), Oreg. Tri-City C. of C. (dir. 1960-62), Am. Assn. Colls. Osteo. Medicine (council deans, bd. govs.), Am. Coll. Gen. Practitioners in Osteo. Medicine and Surgery (editor ofcl. jour. 1976-81), Oreg. Acad. Cranio-mandibular Disorders (dir. 1981-82), Sigma Sigma Phi (hon.). Republican. Clubs: Rotarian (pres. Oregon City 1961-62), Oswego Lake (Oreg.) Country; Clackamas County Knife and Fork (Milwaukie, Oreg.) (pres. 1962-63). Home: 20 Hotspur Lake Oswego OR 97034 Office: Eastmoreland Gen Hosp 2900 SE Steel St Portland OR 97202

HEATON, CULVER, architect; b. Los Angeles, Jan. 3, 1912. B.Arch., U. So. Calif., 1936. With Culver Heaton & Assos., Pasadena, Calif., 1941—. Prin. works include Muir High Sch, Pasadena; 300 ch. projects, including Covenant Presbyn. Ch, Long Beach, St. Peter's By The Sea Presbyn. Ch, Portuguese Bend, Anaheim United Meth. Ch; comml. projects include Ralph C. Sutro Co. Hdqrs, Los Angeles, Allianz Ins. Co, Los Angeles and N.Y.C. Fellow AIA (pres. Pasadena 1951, dir. 1952, treas. Calif. council 1952, dir. 1958); mem. Guild Religious Architecture (western regional dir. 1969-70). Address: 774 N Lake Ave Pasadena CA 91104

HEAVENRICH, ROBERT MAURICE, pediatrician; b. Saginaw, Mich., Sept. 21, 1913; s. Max Philip and Minna (Enggass) H.; m. Emily Schweizer, Apr. 14, 1946; children: Robert Maurice, James L., Polly Ann. Grad., Phillips Acad., Andover, Mass., 1932; A.B., Yale, 1936; M.D., Columbia, 1940. Diplomate: Am. Bd. Pediatrics. Intern pediatrics, then resident Mt. Sinai Hosp., N.Y.C., 1940-42, 46-48; practice medicine specializing in pediatrics, Saginaw, 1948—; mem. staff Saginaw Gen., St. Mary's hosps.; mem. cons. staff St. Luke's, Saginaw Community hosps.; non-resident lectr. U. Mich. Sch. Pub. Health, 1966-69; clin. prof. human devel. Mich. State U. Sch. Human Medicine, 1969—. Assoc. editor: Pediatric Annals, 1982—. Pres. Saginaw Valley Child Guidance Clinic, 1961-64, bd. dirs., 1950—; cons. Mich. Health Dept., 1954—; mem. Mich. Youth Commn., 1960-70, Nat. Health Council, 1969-72; mem. council Med. Specialty Soc., 1971-73; joint council Nat. Pediatric Soc., 1971-73. Served to maj. USAAF, 1942-46. Mem. Am. Acad. Pediatrics (life; pres. 1972-73), Am. Med. Soc., Mich. Med. Soc. (citation 1964), Saginaw County Med. Soc., Detroit, N.E. Mich., Bela Shick ped. socs. Clubs: Rotarian (pres. 1966-67), Torch (pres. 1970-71), Saginaw, Germania (Saginaw). Home: 460 Canterbury St Saginaw MI 48603 Office: 1107 Gratiot St Saginaw MI 48602

HEBALD, MILTON ELTING, sculptor; b. N.Y.C., May 24, 1917; s. Nathan and Eva (Elting) H.; m. Cecile Rosner, June 10, 1938; 1 dau., Margo. Student, Art Students League, 1927-28, Nat. Acad. Design, 1931-32, Beaux Arts Inst. Design, 1932-35. Tchr. Am. Artist Sch., 1940-41, Cooper Union, 1945-53, Bklyn. Mus. Art Sch., 1946-52, Skowhegan Art Sch., summers 1950-52, U. Minn., 1949, Long Beach (Calif.) State, summer 1968. (Recipient 2d prize Social Security Competition, U.S. Govt. relief in Post Office, Toms River, N.J. 1940, 2d prize Wings for Victory 1942, 1st prize Bklyn. Mus. 1950, 2d prize Pa. Acad. 1951, 1st prize N.Y.C. Dept. Pub. Works for East Bronx Tb Hosp. 1953, Prix de Rome in Sculpture 1955-58); Commns. include facade Equador Pavilion, N.Y. World's Fair, 1939; trophy, Rep. Aviation Co., 1942, Turtle Tent; play sculpture, Phila., 1954, Isla Verdi Aeroport, San Juan, P.R., 1954, 16 foot bronze group, East Bronx (N.Y.), Tb Hosp, 1954; portrait bust of Archibald MacLeish, Am. Acad. Arts and Letters, 1957; bronze relief Zodiac, Pan Am. Terminal, Kennedy Airport, 1957-58, Ackland Meml, U. N.C., 1961, James Joyce Monument, Zurich, Switzerland, 1966, Marshall Field Meml, Sun-Times Bldg., Chgo., 1966, Shakespeare Group, Central Park, N.Y.C., 1973; heroic head C.V. Starr, Tokyo, 1974; Shakespeare relief, Oslo, Norway, 1975, Joyce Portrait, Tower Mus., Dublin, 1975, Starr Portrait, Tokyo and Hong Kong, 1975, Heroic Romeo and Juliet, Central Park, N.Y.C., 1979, Richard Tucker Monument, N.Y.C., 1980, Romeo and Juliet bronze, Wilshire Blvd, Los Angeles, 1981, others, one-man exhbns. include, ACA Gallery, N.Y.C., 1937, 40, Grand Central Moderns, N.Y.C., 1950, 54, Schneider Gallery, Rome, Italy, 1957, Nordness Gallery, N.Y.C., 1959-71, Cheekwood Center, Nashville, 1968, 78, Mickelson Gallery, Washington, 1972, 78, Aschehoug Gallery, Oslo, 1975, Sestiere Gallery, Rome, Yares Gallery, Scottsdale, Ariz., 1975, 78, Heritage Gallery, Los Angeles, 1978, Gilman Gallery, Chgo., Harmon Gallery, Naples, Fla., 1978, 81, Randall Gallery, N.Y.C., 1978, Foster Harmon Gallery Am. Art, Sarasota, Fla., 1981, group shows include, Arte Figurativo, Rome, Italy, 1964, 67, Carnegie Inst., Pitts., 1967, Va. Mus. Fine Arts; represented permanent collections, N.Y. Acad. Arts and Letters, Notre Dame U., N.J., Phila. Mus., Whitney Mus. Am. Art, Yale, U. Ariz., U. N.C., Brandeis U., Columbia (S.C.) Mus. Art, Ackland Meml., Tel Aviv Mus., Israel, Joyce Mus., Dublin, Oslo U., Bergan, Norway, Privatbank, others. Fellow Am. Acad. in Rome; mem. Annual Am. Group. Subject of monograph by Frank Getlein, 1970. Office: Studio Via Orti D'Alibert 7A Rome Italy

HEBARD, EMORY A., state treasurer, real estate broker, appraiser; b. Carmel, Maine, Sept. 28, 1917; s. William E. and Viola (Conant) H.; m. Irma Maginnis Mills, Mar. 30, 1941; 1 child. A.B., Middlebury Coll., 1938. Mem. Vt. Ho. of Reps., 1961-76, chmn. ways and means com., 1967-68, chmn. appropriations com., 1973-74, 75-76; mem. State Emergency Bd., 1967-68, 73-74, 75-76; treas. State of Vt., 1977—. Mem. joint fiscal com. Gov.'s Commn. on Med. Care; mem. Ad. Hoc com. on Alcohol Legis.; past moderator Town of Glover, Vt., Lake Region Union High Sch. Dist.; past lister Town of Glover. Served with USCGR; World War II; Korea. Republican. Congregationalist. Home: PO Box 286 Barton VT 05822

HEBB, CHRISTOPHER HARVEY, technology company executive; b. Halifax, N.S., Can., June 18, 1942; s. Harvey D. and Eirene M. (Walker) H.; m. Dorothy A. Wettstein, Oct. 1, 1977. B.A. in History, U. Alta., 1962; LL.B., U. Toronto, 1966. Bar: Called to Alta. bar 1967. V.p., gen. counsel, sec. Kaiser Resources Ltd., Vancouver, B.C., 1976-79, exec. v.p. adminstrn. and legal services, 1979-80, sr. v.p., gen. counsel, sec., 1980-81; sr. v.p. Kaiser Steel Corp., Oakland, Calif., 1979-80; pres. Cavell Investments Ltd., Vancouver, 1981-83, CMG Technologies, 1983—. Mem. Alta. Law Soc., B.C. Law Soc., Can. Bar Assn. Office: 1285 W Pender St Vancouver BC V6E 4B1 Canada

HEBB, DONALD BRUCE, JR, investment banker; b. Balt. B.A., Kenyon Coll., 1964; LL.B., Harvard U., 1967, M.B.A., 1970. Assoc. Alexander Brown & Sons, Balt., 1970-75, gen. ptnr., 1976—. Office: Alex Brown & Sons 135 E Baltimore Baltimore MD 21202

HEBB, MALCOLM HAYDEN, physicist; b. Marquette, Mich., July 21, 1910; s. Thomas Carlyle and Evelyn Shewell (Hayden) H.; m. Marion Elizabeth Evers, May 8, 1943. B.A., U. B.C., 1931, D.Sc. (hon.), 1963; postgrad., U. Wis., 1931-34; Ph.D., Harvard, 1936. Instr. physics Harvard, 1936-37; Harvard Sheldon travelling fellow to U. Utrecht, 1937-38; instr. physics Duke, 1938-42; anti-submarine devices Harvard Underwater Sound Lab., Nat. Def. Research Com., 1942-45; physicist research lab. Sharples Corp., 1945-49; research asso. Gen. Electric Co., 1949-51, mgr. gen. physics research dept., 1951-68, physicist, 1968-75; Vis. com. physics Tufts U., 1967; mem. council Harvard Found., 1958-63; vis. com. elec. engring. Princeton, 1959-71. Recipient Gov. Gen. Medal, B.C., 1931. Fellow Am. Phys. Soc.; mem. Netherlands Phys. Soc., Sigma Xi. Clubs: Mohawk, Mohawk Golf. Home: 1600 E Crooked Lake Dr Eustis FL 32726 Office: Research Lab Gen Electric Co Schenectady NY 12345

HEBBLE, WILLIAM JOSEPH, utility executive; b. Indpls., Oct. 18, 1931; s. Edmond O. and Rose (French) H.; m. Virginia L. Reese, Aug. 11, 1950; 1 dau., Sharon L. Student coll. night courses. With Public Service Co. of Ind., Inc., Plainfield, 1949—, treas., 1977—. Mem. Danville (Ind.) Town Bd., 1966-71. Mem. Nat. Corp. Cash Mgmt. Assn., Nat. Assn. Corp. Treas., Phi Delta Kappa. Republican. Roman Catholic. Club: Elks. Office: 1000 E Main St Plainfield IN 46168

HEBEBRAND, KARL WERNER, manufacturing company executive; b. Frankfurt, Germany, Aug. 16, 1930; s. Werner and Margarete (Leistikow) H.; m. Agathe Lexis, June 1, 1956; children: John, Ann, Andrew, Benjamin, Charlotte, Carol. Student, Philipps U., Marburg, W. Ger., 1951, 52-55, Grinnell Coll., 1951-52; Ph.D. in Econs, U. Marburg, 1957. With Siemens AG, Erlangen, W. Ger., 1956-63; adminstr. Siemens Med. Am., Inc., Union, N.J., 1963-68; mgmt. positions Siemens AG, Munich, W. Ger., 1968-77; exec. v.p., chief fin. officer, treas. Siemens-Allis, Inc., Atlanta, 1979—. Bd. dirs., treas. Arbor Acad., sch. handicapped children. Mem. Fin. Execs. Inst. Office: PO Box 89000 Atlanta GA 30338

HEBEL, ANTHONY JEROME, advertising agency executive; b. LaSalle, Ill., Mar. 2, 1928; s. Anthony Joseph and Minerva (Maher) H.; m. Lynn DeBiasio, June 16, 1951; children: Thomas, Richard and William (twins). B.A., U. Ill., 1951. Account supr. McCann-Erickson, Inc., Chgo., 1951-59; v.p. Post & Morr. Inc., Chgo., 1959-61; sr. v.p. Post & Moor, Inc., Chgo., 1959-61, Post, Moor & Gardner, Inc., 1961-63; exec. v.p., treas., dir., chmn. operations com., chmn. profit sharing trust fund com. Post-Keyes-Gardner, Inc., Chgo., 1963-79; exec. v.p. Cunningham & Welsh, Inc., 1979-80; pres. AJH & Assos., Deerfield, 1980—; chmn. exec. com. Nutrition Dynamics, Inc. Active Chgo. Crusade of Mercy and United Settlement Appeal campaign drives, 1964-71; co-chmn. Pro-Am. Golf Tournament, Lake County Cancer Soc., 1981, 82, 83. Served with USNR, 1946-48. Mem. Chgo. Assn. Commerce and Industry, John Henry Newman Honor Soc., Wilderness Soc., Isaac Walton League, Nat. Parks Assn., Lincoln Park Zool. Soc., Am. Field Service Art Inst., Alpha Delta Sigma. Club: Knollwood Country (Lake Forest, Ill.) (bd. govs.). Home and Office: 1037 Warrington Rd Deerfield IL 60015

HEBELER, HENRY KOESTER, aerospace company executive; b. St. Louis, Aug. 12, 1933; s. Henry and Viola O. (Koester) H.; m. Mirriam Robb, Aug. 12, 1978; children by previous marriage: Linda Ruth, Laura Ann. B.S. in Aero. Engring., MIT, 1956, M.S., 1956. Gen. mgr. research/engring. Boeing Aerospace Co., Seattle, 1970-72; v.p. bus. devel. The Boeing Co., Seattle, 1973-74; pres. Boeing Engring. & Constrn. Co., Seattle, 1975-79, Boeing Aerospace Co., 1980—; Mem. fusion panel Ho. of Reps., 1979-81; mem. energy research adv. bd. Dept. Energy, 1980-81; mem. task force on internat. industry Def. Sci. Bd. Bd. govs. Sloan Sch., MIT, 1981—; bd. visitors Def. Systems Mgmt. Coll., Ft. Belvoir, Va. Recipient Mead prize for aero. engrs., 1956; Kuljian humanities award, 1954; Sperry Gyroscope fellow, 1956; Sloan fellow M.I.T., 1970. Mem. Am. Def. Preparedness Assn., Nat. Aeros. Assn., Assn. of U.S. Army, Armed Forces Communications and Electronics Assn., Aviation Hall of Fame, AIAA. Mormon. Clubs: Meridian Valley Country, Ala. Space & Rocket Center (sci. and adv. com. 1980—), Nat. Space (bd. govs. 1980—), Burning Tree). Patentee in field. Home: 13335 SE 243rd Pl Kent WA 98042 Office: PO Box 3999 Seattle WA 98124

HEBERLEIN, GARRETT THOMAS, university administrator; b. Milw., Apr. 11, 1939; s. Edward Garrett and Ruth (Andrus) H.; m. Donna Lee Frohm, Jan. 12, 1966; children: Wendy Ann, Edward Garrett. A.B., Ohio Wesleyan U., 1961; M.S., Northwestern U., 1963, Ph.D. (NIH fellow 1963-66), 1966; postgrad., U. Gent, Netherlands, 1966-67. Asst. prof., then asso. prof. biology N.Y. U., 1967-73, chmn. dept., 1970-73; asso. prof., chmn. dept. U. Mo., St. Louis, 1973-76; prof. biology, chmn. dept. biol. scis. Bowling Green (Ohio) State U., 1976-80, dean Grad. Coll., vice provost for research, 1980—; mem. adv. com. on grad. study Ohio Bd. Regents, 1980, chmn.-elect adv. com. on grad. study, 1983. Contbr. articles to profl. jours. Trustee Univ. Heights Presbyn. Ch., N.Y.C., 1969-72, univ. Heights Day Care Center, N.Y.C., 1970-72; elder 1st Presbyn. Ch., Bowling Green, 1979—; mem. Met. St. Louis Planning Bd., 1973-76. Grantee NIH, 1963—, NSF, 1967-81; others. Mem. N.Y. Acad. Scis., AAAS, Am. Soc. Microbiology, Am. Inst. Biol. Scis., Am. Soc. Plant Physiologists, Nat. Sci. Tchrs. Assn., Nat. Assn. Biology Tchrs., Am. Assn. Univ. Adminstrs., Ohio Acad. Sci., Plant Growth Regulator Working Group, People to People, Sigma Xi, Phi Gamma Delta. Clubs: Kiwanis, Junto (pres. 1982-83). Home: 1111 Bourgogne St Bowling Green OH 43402 Office: Graduate College Bowling Green State U Bowling Green OH 43403 *My accomplishments as a citizen, teacher, scientist, scholar, and academic adminstrator are an outcome of my faith in the capacity and integrity of people from all backgrounds, as well as my decication to quality, open-mindedness, and the work ethic. Self confidence is a critical factor in achieving success and happiness. The key to achieving self-respect is in respecting others.*

HEBERT, A. HERVE, businessman, university chancellor; b. Montreal, Que., Can., Apr. 3, 1929; s. Calixte and Yvonne H.; children: Giles, Jean-Charles, Johanne, Jocelyne, Nathalie. B.Sc., U. Montreal, Que., Can. Actuarial asst. Sun Life Assurance, Montreal, Que., Can., 1951-55; actuary Desjardins Mut., Levis, Que., Can., 1955-65; cons. actuary Hebert, LeHouillier & Assocs., Inc., Quebec, Montreal, Que., Can., 1965-77; pres. Fiducie du Que., Can., 1977—; chancellor U. Montreal, Que., Can.; dir. various cos. Fellow Soc. Actuaries; mem. Montreal Bd. Trade, Chambre de Commerce de Montreal. Office: Office of Chancellor U Montreal CP 6128 Succursale A Montreal PQCanada H3C 3J7 *

HEBERT, BLISS EDMUND, opera director; b. Faust, N.Y., Nov. 30, 1930; s. Wilfrid Joseph and Merle Addasah (Bliss) H. B.A., Syracuse U., 1951, M.Mus., 1952; piano pupil of, Robert Goldsand, Simone Barrere, Lelia Gousseau. Gen. mgr. Washington Opera Soc., 1960-63; guest dir. Juilliard Sch., 1975-76; mem. faculty Boston U., 1952-53, U. Wash., 1969. Stage dir., Met. Opera, N.Y.C., 1973-75, N.Y. City Opera, 1963-75, Sante Fe Opera, 1957—; dir. opera companies of, San Francisco, 1963, Houston, 1964, Toronto, 1972, San Diego, 1970, Vancouver, B.C., 1969, Ft. Worth, 1966, Washington, 1959, Cin., 1968, Chgo., 1983, Montreal, 1984, Portland, Oreg., 1969, Caramoor Festival, Katonah, N.Y., 1966, La Gune Festival, 1968—, La Gune Festival, New Orleans, 1970, La Gune Festival, Balt., 1972, La Gune Festival, Tulsa, 1975, La Gune Festival, Miami, Fla., La Gune Festival, Charlotte, N.C., La Gune Festival, Dallas, 1977, La Gune Festival, Shreveport, La.; rec. artist, Columbia records; as stage dir. for Igor Stravinsky's major operas under his conducting. Served AUS, 1954-56. Mem. Lambda Chi Alpha, Phi Mu Alpha. Office: care Robert Lombardo 30 W 60th St Suite 3A New York NY 10023 *

HEBERT, JOSEPH FLOYD, hotel executive; b. Edmundston, N.B., Can., Feb. 18, 1931; s. Adrian and Martina (McCluskey) H.; m. Doreen Merle Astle, June 14, 1958; children: Michael, Stephen, Patricia, Jeffrey. B.S.B.A., Denver U., 1959. With The Sheraton Corp., formerly in Phila., Pitts., Syracuse, Columbus, Chgo., and Toronto, 1959—; v.p., gen. mgr. Royal Hawaiian Hotel, Honolulu, 1974—. Bd. dirs. Honolulu Boys Choir. Served with USAF, 1951-54. Mem. Hawaii Hotel Assn. (past pres.), Air Force Assn. Hawaii (dir.), Japan-Am. Soc., Honolulu C. of C. (dir.). Roman Catholic. Clubs: Skal of Hawaii (past pres.), Honolulu Rotary (pres.), Waialae Country.

HEBERTSON, VAL M., oil company executive; b. Provo, Utah, Jan. 7, 1935; s. Thorit Charles and Susan (Madsen) H.; m. Suzanne Elizabeth Fife, June 2, 1962; children: Valerie Suzanne, Gregory Fife, Christopher Fife. B.S., Brigham Young U., 1957. Cert. petroleum geologist, Tex. Geologist El Paso Natural Gas Co., (Tex.), 1957-62; with econs. and planning depts. Mobile Oil Co., N.Y.C., 1964-70; asst. treas. Amerada Hess Corp., N.Y.C., 1970-72, v.p. offshore ops., Houston, 1973-79, v.p. U.S. exploration and offshore ops., Tulsa, 1979-83, v.p. exploration planning and tech., 1983—. Dist. fin. chmn. Boy Scouts Am., Houston, 1974-78, chmn. troop com., Tulsa, 1980-82. Served with U.S. Army, 1958-60. Mem. Am. Assn. Petroleum Geologists, Tulsa Geol. Soc. Republican. Mormon. Home: 3258 S Delaware Pl Tulsa OK 74105

HEBNER, PAUL CHESTER, oil co. exec.; b. Warren, Pa., Dec. 29, 1919; s. Henry G. and Mabel (Gross) H.; m. Dorothy Farrell, Feb. 16, 1943; children—Richard P., Kathleen D., Susan M., Christine L., Elizabeth A., Jeannie M. Accountant, adminstrv. asst. Altman-Coady Co., Columbus, Ohio, 1940-41; mgr. accounting, exec. adminstr. T & T Oil Co. (and asso. cos.), Los Angeles, 1954-57; with Occidental Petroleum Corp., Los Angeles, 1957—, sec.-treas., 1958-68, v.p., sec., 1968-80, exec. v.p., sec., 1980—, dir., 1960—; officer, dir. subs. cos. Mem. Los Angeles Beautiful. Served to maj. USAAF, 1942-45. L.S.B. Leakey Found. fellow. Mem. Am. Soc. Corp. Secs. Home: 12 Amber Sky Dr Rancho Palos Verdes CA 90274 Office: 10889 Wilshire Blvd Los Angeles CA 90024

HECHINGER, FRED MICHAEL, newspaper editor, found. executive; b. Nuremberg, Germany, July 7, 1920; came to U.S., 1937, naturalized, 1943; s. Dr. Julius and Lilly (Niedermaier) H.; m. Grace Bernstein; children: Paul David, John Edward. A.B., CCNY, 1943; student, NYU, 1937-38; postgrad., U. London, 1945; LL.D., Kenyon Coll., 1955, Bates Coll., 1963, U. Notre Dame, 1963, Knox Coll., 1966; L.H.D., Bard Coll., 1956, Wash. Coll., 1965, Wilkes Coll., 1968, St. Joseph's Coll., 1970, Rider Coll., 1972, Paine Coll., 1972, Trinity Coll., 1973, City Coll. N.Y., 1977. Corr. for the London Times Ednl. Supplement, 1946-47; ednl. columnist Washington Post, 1947-50; edn. editor, fgn. corr., cons. to pub. Sunday Herald, Bridgeport, Conn., 1947-50; fgn. corr. Overseas News Agy., 1948-50; spl. writer This Week mag., 1946-59; edn. editor N.Y. Herald Tribune, 1950-56; asso. pub. The Sunday Herald, Bridgeport, Conn., 1956-59; edn. editor The N.Y. Times, N.Y.C., 1959-69, mem. editorial bd., 1969-77, asst. editorial page editor, 1976, edn. columnist, 1978—; pres. N.Y. Times Co. Found., 1977—; also bd. dirs.; contbg. editor Saturday Rev., 1977-78; adj. prof. City U. N.Y., 1974-78; cons. edn. and cultural relations div. U.S. Mil. Govt., summers 1948, 49; Served with Office Mil. Attache Am. Embassy, London; also with Brit. War Office, 1944-46; Bd. dirs. Am.-Scandinavian Found. Author: An Adventure in Education, 1956, New Approaches, 1955, Worrying About College, 1958, The Big Red Schoolhouse, 1959, (with Grace Hechinger) Teen-age Tyranny, 1963, The New York Times Guide to N.Y.C. Pvt. Schools, 1968, Pre-School Education Today, 1966, Growing Up In America, 1975; Education editor: Parents' Mag, 1957-59; Contbr. to: Change mag. Pres. N.Y. Times Neediest Cases; Fund, 1977—; bd. dirs. Acad. Ednl. Devel.; mem. Pres.'s Commn. on Fgn. Langs. and Internat. Studies, 1978-79. Recipient Brit. Empire Medal, George Polk Meml. Award, 1950, 51, Fairbanks Award, 1952, Townsend Harris medal, 1968, Soc. Silurians editorial writing award, 1971, 76; Disting. Alumni medal, 1973; Disting. Service award Council Chief State Sch. Officers; Carnegie Found. Advancement of Teaching fellow, 1980-82; Horace Mann Guardian award, 1983. Mem. Edn. Writers Assn. (pres. 1956, awards 1948, 49, 52, 64, 68, 73, 74, 76), Phi Beta Kappa. Clubs: Coffee House, Century Assn. Office: 229 W 43d St New York NY 10036

HECHINGER, JOHN WALTER, hardware chain exec.; b. Washington, Jan. 18, 1920; s. Sidney Lawrence and Sylvia (Frank) H.; m. June Ross, May 26, 1946; children—Nancy, John Walter, S. Ross, Sally. B.S., Yale U., 1941. With Hechinger Co., Landover, Md., pres., 1958—, also chief exec. officer. Mem. D.C. City Council, chmn., 1967-69; commnr. D.C. Jud. Nominating Com., 1980—; mem. Democratic Nat. Com.; rep. UN, from 1978; bd. dirs. Eugene and Agnes Meyer Found., Nat. Urban Coalition, Handgun Control, Inc. Served with USAAF, World War II. Decorated Air medal. Jewish. Office: 3500 Pennsy Dr Landover MD 20785 *

HECHLER, KEN, former congressman, political science educator, author; b. Roslyn, N.Y., Sept. 20, 1914; s. Charles Henry and Catherine Elizabeth (Hauhart) H. A.B., Swarthmore Coll., 1935; A.M., Columbia U., 1936, Ph.D., 1940. Lectr. govt. Barnard Coll.-Columbia Coll., N.Y.C., 1937-41; research asst. to Judge Samuel I. Rosenman, 1939-50; research asst. on Pres. Roosevelt's pub. papers, 1939-50; sect. chief Bur. Census, 1940; personnel technician Office Emergency Mgmt., 1941; adminstrv. analyst Bur. of Budget, 1941-42, 46-47; spl. asst. to Pres. Harry S. Truman, 1949-53; research dir. Stevenson-Kefauver campaign, 1956; adminstrv. aide Senator Carroll of Colo., 1957; mem. 86th to 94th Congresses from 4th W.Va. Dist.; mem. Sci. and Tech. Com. 86th to 94th Congresses from 4th W.Va. Dist., chmn. Energy (Fossil Fuels) Subcom.; mem. Joint Com. on Orgn. of Congress, 1965-66, NASA Oversight Subcom. (U.S. Congress); asst. prof. politics Princeton U., 1947-49; prof. polit. sci. Marshall U., Huntington, W.Va., 1957, 82—; sci. cons. U.S. House Com. on Sci. and Tech., 1978-80; radio, TV commentator Sta. WHTN, Huntington, 1957-58, Sta. WWHY, 1978; adj. prof. polit. sci. U. Charleston (W.Va.), 1981. Author: Insurgency: Personalities and Politics of the Taft Era, 1940, The Bridge at Remagen, 1957, West Virginia Memories of President Kennedy, 1965, Toward the Endless Frontier, 1980, The Endless Space Frontier, 1982, Working with Truman, 1982. Bd. dirs. W.Va. Humanities Found., 1982—; del. Democratic Nat. Conv., 1964, 68, 72, 80. Served to maj. AUS, 1942-46; served to col. Res. Decorated Bronze Star. Mem. Am. Polit. Sci. Assn. (assoc. dir. 1953-56), Civitan, Am. Legion, VFW, DAV. Democrat. Episcopalian. Lodge: Elks. Home: 917 5th Ave Huntington WV 25701 *Early in my Congressional career, I brought a group of West Virginia students to the White House lawn where President Kennedy was speaking. He remarked that the Greek definition of happiness was the development of your fullest powers and resources along the lines of excellence in order to serve other people. This prescription articulated for me the surest route to personal happiness.*

HECHT, ALAN DANNENBERG, insurance executive; b. Balt., Aug. 31, 1918; s. Lee I. and Miriam (Dannenberg) H.; m. Margaret R. Moses, June 27, 1943; children: Stephen Lee, Nancy H., Elizabeth Ann. B.S., Johns Hopkins U., 1940, M. Liberal Arts, 1976. C.L.U. Solicitor Travelers Ins. Co., 1945-60; partner Hecht-Schoenfeld Ins. Agy., 1960-62; merged and formed Wolman-Hecht-Schoenfeld, Inc., 1962, v.p., 1962-64, Wolman-Hecht, Inc., 1964-70, pres., 1971—; formed Alan D. Hecht & Co., Inc., 1964, 1966, now pres., 1966; gen. agt. Sun Life Ins. Co. Am. and other cos., Balt., 1960—; pres. Balt. Estate Planning Council; tchr. C.L.U. econs. and fin. Johns Hopkins U., 1954-81; mem. faculty dept. econs. St. Mary's Coll., Emmitsburg, Pa., 1981—; past bd. graders Am. Coll. Life Underwriters. Pres. Balt. Jewish Council, 1971-73; life and qualifying mem. Million Dollar Round Table, 1981, mem. resolutions com., 1976—; Bd. dirs. Balt. chpt. Am. Jewish Com., pres., 1958-60, now mem. nat. exec. com.;

trustee Sinai Hosp. of Balt., 1959-68. Served to 1st lt. AUS, 1941-45. Recipient Nat. Quality award Nat. Assn. Life Underwriters; Nat. Sales Achievement award; Szold award Temple Oheb Shalom Brotherhood, 1980; George S. Robertson award Balt. Life Underwriters Assn., 1981. Mem. Am. Soc. C.L.U.'s (dir. 1957—, nat. sec. 1962-63, pres. 1964-65), Omicron Delta Kappa, Pi Delta Epsilon. Jewish (pres. congregation 1968-70, past dir.). Home: 9 Skylark Trail SW Fairfield PA 17320 Office: 330 N Charles St Baltimore MD 21201 *With some background in economics, I believe that we can improve our life and environment only by greater productivity. Each person should accept responsibility for finishing assigned tasks at every level, no matter how menial or important that task may seem.*

HECHT, ANTHONY EVAN, poet; b. N.Y.C., Jan. 16, 1923; s. Melvyn Hahlo and Dorothea (Holzman) H.; m. Patricia Harris, Feb. 27, 1954 (div. 1961); children: Jason, Adam; m. Helen D'Alessandro, June 12, 1971; 1 son, Evan Alexander. B.A., Bard Coll., 1944, D.Litt. (hon.), 1970; M.A., Columbia U., 1950; L.H.D. (hon.), Georgetown U., 1981, Towson State U., 1983. Tchr. Kenyon Coll., 1947, State U. Iowa, 1948, N.Y. U., 1949, Smith Coll., 1956-59; assoc. prof. English Bard Coll., 1961; faculty U. Rochester, 1967; Hurst prof. Washington U., fall 1971; vis. prof. Harvard U., 1973, Yale U., 1977; faculty Salzburg Seminar in Am. Studies, 1977; cons. in poetry Library of Congress, 1982-84; trustee Am. Acad. in Rome, 1983—. Author: A Summoning of Stones, 1954, The Seven Deadly Sins, 1958, A Bestiary, 1960, The Hard Hours (Brit. Poetry Book Soc. choice 1967, Miles Poetry award Wayne U., Pultizer Prize 1968), 1968 (Russell Loines award Nat. Inst. Arts and Letters), Millions of Strange Shadows, 1977, The Venetian Vespers, 1979; co-author, co-editor: Jiggery Pokery, 1967; translator: (with Helen Bacon) Seven Against Thebes (Aeschylus), 1973. Recipient Prix de Rome, 1950, Brandeis U. Creative Arts award, 1965; Guggenheim fellow, 1954, 59; Hudson Rev. fellow, 1958; Ford Found. fellow, 1960; Rockefeller Found. fellow, 1967; Fulbright prof., Brazil, 1971; recipient Bolligen prize, 1983. Fellow Acad. Am. Poets (chancellor 1971); mem. Nat. Inst. Arts and Letters, Am. Acad. Arts and Scis. Home: 19 East Blvd Rochester NY 14610

HECHT, CHIC, U.S. Senator; b. Cape Giradeau, Mo., Nov. 30, 1928; m. Gail Hecht; children: Lori, Leslie. B.S., Washington U., St. Louis, 1949; postgrad., Mil. Intelligence Sch., Ft. Holibird, Mo., 1951. Mem. Nev. State Senate, 1966-74, Republican minority leader, 1968-72; mem. U.S. Senate from Nev., 1982—, mem. Banking, Housing and Urban Affairs Com., chmn. Ins. Com.; mem. Energy and Natural Resources Com. Served with U.S. Army, 1951-53. Mem. Nat. Counter Intelligence Corps. (past pres.), Nat. Mil. Intelligence Assn. Address: Room 302 Hart Senate Office Bldg Washington DC 20510

HECHT, HENRY ROLF, financial writer and editor; b. Fuerth, Germany, Feb. 13, 1923; came to U.S., 1934, naturalized, 1940; s. Julius R. and May (Miller) H.; m. Alice Offord, Mar. 12, 1955; children: Andrew, Neil, Peter. B.A., Columbia U., 1944. With Merrill Lynch & Co. (and predecessors), N.Y.C., 1946-77; editor Investor's Reader, 1971-74, mgr. editorial projects, corp. relations dept., 1974-77; sr. editorial officer Bank of America, 1977-80; editorial mgr. Merrill Lynch & Co., N.Y.C., 1980—; v.p. Merrill Lynch, Pierce Fenner & Smith, N.Y.C., 1983—. Served with AUS, 1943-46. Home: 487 Beatrice St. Teaneck NJ 07666 Office: Corporate Relations Merrill Lynch & Co One Liberty Plaza 165 Broadway New York NY 10080

HECHT, JAIME SELIG, utility exec.; b. N.Y.C., Apr. 23, 1929; s. Samuel T. and Kate (Reisman) H.; m. Suzanne Goldemberg, June 8, 1952; children—Rachel, Joseph, David. B.A., Columbia U., 1950; LL.B., 1953. Bar: N.Y. State bar 1954. Labor relations specialist Gen. Electric Co., Conneaut, Ohio, Louisville, 1953-61; atty. N.Y. State Electric & Gas Corp., Binghamton, 1961-63, Ithaca, 1963-67, asst. sec., 1967-70, sec., 1970—. 1em. Tompkins County Bar Assn., Am. Soc. Corp. Secs. Home: 1446 Hanshaw Rd Ithaca NY 14850 Office: PO Box 287 Ithaca NY 14850

HECHT, LEE MARTIN, artificial intelligence company executive; b. Phila., May 11, 1942; s. Hymen Nathan and Anne Rosalee (Brodsky) H.; m. Kenney Jean Schowalter, June 17, 1967; 1 dau., Kimberley Kenney. M.S. in Physics, U. Chgo., 1965, M.B.A. (NDEA fellow), 1969. Teaching asst. physics, research asst. U. Chgo., lectr. physics, 1966-67, applied maths., 1967-69, policy studies, 1973-80; pres., chief exec. officer Phoenix-Hecht Inc. (computer services co.), Chgo., 1968-75, dir., 1968-76; pres., chief exec. officer Phoenix-Hecht Cash Mgmt. Services Inc., Chgo., 1973-75, dir., 1973-76; pres., chief exec. officer Kenwood-Pacific Corp., San Francisco, 1973—; dir. Holloway Health Mgmt. Group, Ltd., Chgo., 1973-82, chmn., 1976-82; pres., chief exec. officer Electron Storage Ring Corp., San Francisco, 1977—; chmn., chief exec. officer Teknowledge, Inc., Palo Alto, Calif., 1981—; pres. Middlefield Group Inc., Middlefield Capital Corp., 1981—; dir. Digital Pathways Inc., Palo Alto, Calif.; chmn. Kenwood Group Inc., 1978-82; lectr. bus. adminstrn. U. Calif.-Berkeley, 1975-77; vis. lectr. mgmt. Stanford U., 1976; v.p. Nat. Vidiograph Inc. (motion picture prodn.), Berkeley, 1975-77. Trustee Anne R. Hecht Trust. Mem. Am. Phys. Soc. Clubs: Economic, Tavern (Chgo.). Address: 37 Irving Ave Atherton CA 94025

HECHT, LOUIS ALAN, elec. component co. exec.; b. Chgo., July 20, 1944; s. Bernard T. and Dorthe E. (Callen) H.; m. Joanne Lebow, Aug. 16, 1967; children—Jonathan D., Peter A. B.S., U. Ill., J.D., 1969. Bar: Ill. bar 1969. Mem. firm Hofgren, Wegner, Allen, Stellman & McCord, Chgo., 1969-71, Coffee & Sweeney, 1971-74; patent counsel Molex, Inc., Lisle, Ill., 1974-76, sec., gen. counsel, 1976—. Mem. Am. Bar Assn., Ill. State Bar Assn., Chgo. Bar Assn., Am. Patent Lawyers Assn., Patent Lawyers Assn. Chgo. Office: 2222 Wellington Ct Lisle IL 60532

HECHT, ROBERT EARL, SR., savings and loan executive; b. Chgo., Jan. 27, 1925; s. Frank C. and Katherine V. (Headrick) H.; m. Marion Ann Stout, Sept. 4, 1950; children: Marion A. Hecht West, Robert E., Jr., Catherine A. Hecht Young, Frances A. Hecht Becker, Patricia A., Susan A. Hecht Maggio, Thomas A., Teresa A., Margaret A., William Y. Ph.B., Loyola U., Chgo., 1948; LL.B., Marquette U., 1950. Bar: Wis. 1950, U.S. Supreme Ct. 1954, Md. 1964. Spl. agt. FBI, 1954-59; with Balt. Fed. Savs. and Loan Assn., 1959—, chmn. bd., pres., 1975—; chmn. bd., dir. Gen. Service Corp., Protective Ins. Agy., Inc.; chmn. Fin. Mgmt. Services, Inc.; dir. Arundel Corp. Pres. bd. dirs. Assoc. Cath. Charities; mem. steering com. Econ. Devel. Council of Greater Balt.; bd. dirs. Washington/Balt. Regional Assn.; chmn. Md. Housing Policy Commn.; mem. law rev. Community Devel. Assn. Served to lt. comdr. USNR, 1943-46, 50-54. Mem. U.S. League of Savs. Assns. (polit. liaison com.), Md. League Fin. Instns. (chmn. bd.). Roman Catholic. Clubs: Baltimore Country, Merchants, Center, Automobile of Md. (bd. govs.). Home: 713 Cooks Ln Baltimore MD Office: Balt Fed Fin 300 E Lombard St Baltimore MD 21202

HECHT, SIDNEY MICHAEL, chemistry educator, pharmaceutical company executive; b. N.Y.C., July 27, 1944; m., 1966. A.B., U. Rochester, 1966; Ph.D., U. Ill., 1970. USPHS fellow U. Wis., 1970-71; from asst. prof. to assoc. prof. MIT, Cambridge, 1971-79; John W. Mallet prof. chemistry U. Va., Charlottesville, 1978—; v.p. preclin. research and devel. Smith Kline & French Labs., 1981-83, v.p. chem. research and devel., 1983—. Alfred P. Sloan research fellow, 1975-79; John Simon Guggenheim fellow, 1977-78; NIH research career devel. grantee, 1975-80. Mem. AAAS, Am. Chem. Soc., Royal Soc. Chemistry, Am. Soc. Biol. Chemists, Sigma Xi. Office: Dept Chemistry U Va Charlottesville VA 22901

HECHTER, OSCAR MILTON, physiology educator; b. Chgo., Sept. 29, 1916; s. Charles and Bertha (Buchman) H.; m. Gertrude Horowitz, Oct. 8, 1940; 1 son, Michael. B.S., U. Chgo., 1938; Ph.D., U. So. Calif., 1943. Research asso. dept. metabolism and endocrinology Michael Reese Hosp., Chgo., 1937-40; Research Labs. Cedars of Lebanon Hosp., Los Angeles, 1940-44; scientist Worcester Found. Exptl. Biology, Shrewsbury, Mass., 1944-50, sr. scientist, 1950-66; asso. prof. physiology Boston U. Sch. Medicine, 1951-58; vis. prof. biology Brandeis U., Waltham, Mass., 1961-62; dir. dept. regulatory biology, mem. Inst. for Biomed. Research, Edn. and Research Found., AMA, Chgo., 1966-70; prof. physiology Northwestern U. Sch. Medicine, Chgo., 1970—, Nathan Smith Davis chmn. dept., 1970-78; professorial lectr. dept. physiology U. Chgo., 1966-70; cons. Syntex (S.A.), Mexico, 1954, Schenley Pharms., 1956-58, Ayerst Labs., 1958-66; Mem. sci. adv. com. Worcester Found. for Exptl. Biology, 1968-73; mem. panel on regulatory biology NSF, 1969-71; mem. sci. adv. com. Lab. for Reproductive Biology, U. N.C., 1969-78; with Elan Pharm. Research Corp., 1981—. Contbr. numerous articles on biochemistry and physiology especially hormone action to tech. jours. Recipient Ciba award in endocrinology Endocrine Soc. Am., 1950; Gold medal of Milan Internat. Conf. on Cyclic AMP, 1971. Fellow N.Y. Acad. Scis., Am. Acad. Arts and Scis.; mem. Am. Physiol. Soc., Endocrine Soc., AAAS. Home: 3730 N Lake Shore Dr Chicago IL 60613

HECK, ALBERT FRANK, neurologist; b. Balt., Oct. 9, 1932; s. Albert Franklin and Dorothy Mary (Jirsa) H.; m. Carole Ann Blomeier, Aug. 25, 1956; children—Albert William, Karl Andrew, Robert Conrad, Paul Christopher. A.B., Johns Hopkins U., 1954; M.D., U. Md., 1958. Diplomate: Am. Bd. Psychiatry and Neurology. Intern Mercy Hosp., 1958-59; NIH fellow in neurology U. Md., Balt., 1959-62, faculty, instr. to prof., 1964-77; prof., chmn. dept. neurology U. Tenn. Center for Health Scis., Memphis, 1977-82, dir. neurosci. program, 1978-82; prof. neurology W. Va. U., 1982—; vis. prof. Medezinische Hochschule Hannover, W. Ger., 1973-74. Contbr. writings to profl. publs. Served with M.C. U.S. Army, 1962-64. Recipient jr. investigator award NIH, 1965, U.S. sr. scientist award, 1973; Humboldt Found. prize Fed. Republic Germany, 1973-74. Fellow Am. Acad. Neurology; mem. Am. Neurol. Assn., Stroke Council of Am. Heart Assn., Internat. Coll. Angiology, Microcirculatory Soc., European Soc. Microcirculation, Internat. Soc. Biorrheology, Alpha Omega Alpha. Condr. research in field. Home: 1122 Highland Rd Charleston WV 25302 Office: Doctors Park Charleston WV 25302

HECK, CHARLES VOISIN, orthopaedic surgeon, association executive; b. Collinsville, Ill., Aug. 17, 1918; s. Charles John and Ada (Voisin) H.; m. Susan Virginia Jones, July 4, 1948; children: Charles Chandler and Helen Kay (twins). A.B., U. Ill., 1939, B.S., M.D., 1943. Diplomate: Am. Bd. Orthopaedic Surgery. Intern Ill. Research and Ednl. Hosps., Chgo., 1943-44; resident St. Luke's Hosp., Chgo., 1945-46, preceptor, 1948-50; practice medicine specializing in orthopaedic surgery, Chgo., 1948-68; dir. Am. Acad. Orthopaedic Surgeons, Chgo., 1968-71, exec. dir., 1976-84, cons., 1984—; research asst. U. Ill. Coll. Medicine, Chgo., 1948-50, asst. prof. orthopaedic surgery, 1950-58, asso. prof., 1958-71, Rush Med. Center, 1971-72, prof., 1972—; mem. staff Rush Presbyn.-St. Luke's Med. Center; dir. Services By Satellite, Inc., Washington.; Bd. dirs. Pub. Service Satellite Consortium, Washington, 1975—. Author: Fifty Years of Progress; Contbr. articles on spine and hip to med. publs. Co-trustee Hulbert Fund, Chgo. Served with M.C. AUS, 1946-48, 50-51. Mem. ACS, Am. Acad. Orthopaedic Surgeons, Internat. Soc. Orthopaedics and Trauma, Clin. Orthopaedic Soc., Inst. Medicine Chgo., Am. Orthopaedic Assn., Mid-Am. Orthopaedic Assn., Assn. Ret. Physicians Am. (dir. 1975-77). Presbyterian. Club: Oak Park (Ill.) Country. Home: 906 Fair Oaks St Oak Park IL 60302 Office: 444 N Michigan Ave Chicago IL 60611

HECK, JAMES BAKER, university administrator; b. Columbus, Ohio, Aug. 26, 1930; s. Arch O. and Frances (Agnew) H.; m. Jo Ann Gatton, Nov. 18, 1950; children—Janice M., Judith L., J. Jeffrey. B.S., Ohio State U., 1953, M.A. (Nat. Def. Edn. Act fellow), 1961, Ph.D., 1967. Comml. sales engr. Ohio Bell Telephone Co., Dayton, 1955-57; tchr. Ohio Pub. Schs., Dayton, 1957-59, sch. counselor, 1959-60; instr. Ohio State U., 1960-63, asst. to dean, 1963-66, asst. dean faculties, research asso., 1966-67, asso. dean faculties, asst. prof. edn., 1967-68, prof., dean, dir., 1971-78; dean regional campus affairs U. South Fla., 1978-81, asso. v.p. for acad. affairs, dean regional campus affairs, 1981—; asst. state supr. for guidance service Ohio Dept. Edn., 1962-63; Am. Council on Edn. fellow in academic adminstrn. U. Ill., 1965-66; prof., dean Coll. Edn., U. Del., Newark, 1968-71; evaluator Nat. Council for Accreditation Tchr. Edn., 1972—; mem. planning com. Nat. Conf. Br. and Regional Campus Adminstrs., 1973-82, chmn., 1972, 80; chmn. planning com. Am. Council Edn. Acad. Fellows Working Reunion; vice chmn. Am. Council Edn. Council Fellows, 1980-81, chmn., 1981-82, exec. con., 1980-83; cons., lectr. in field. Co-author: Counseling; Selected Readings, 1962, Educational Administration: Selected Readings, 1965, 2d edit., 1971, Analysis of Educational Change in Ohio Public Schools, 1968; also numerous articles, monographs, papers, book revs., abstracts in field. Gen. chmn. Mansfield Area United Way campaign, 1975, bd. dirs., 1976-78, v.p., 1977, 78; bd. dirs. Mansfield Symphony Orch., 1972-78, pres., 1978; bd. dirs. Research for Better Schs., Inc., 1968-71, pres., 1970-71; mem. citizens adv. com. Richland County Regional Planning Commn., 1973-74, bd. dirs., 1975-78, v.p., 1977, 78; mem. Manpower Adv. Council Richland and Morrow Counties; trustee Hillsbrough County Hosp. Authority, Tampa, Fla., 1980—. Served with USAF, 1953-55; Res., ret., 1973. Mem. Am. Assn. Higher Edn. (life), Mansfield-Richland Area C. of C. (dir. 1972-78, v.p. 1974, 75, 76, 77, 78), Ohio State U. Assn. (life), Greater Tampa C. of C., Phi Delta Kappa (life), Kappa Delta Pi, Phi Kappa Phi. Club: Univ. Area Civitan (founding pres. 1980-81). Address: U South Fla Tampa FL 33620

HECK, L. DOUGLAS, diplomat; b. Bern, Switzerland, Dec. 14, 1918; s. Lewis and Dorothy (Tompkins) H.; m. Ernestine Harriet Sherman, Mar. 27, 1972; children: Elizabeth Tompkins, Judith Kingsbury. Grad., Phillips Acad., Andover, Mass., 1937; B.A., Yale U., 1941. With Dept. State, Washington, 1943-53; joined Fgn. Service, 1952; polit. officer Am. consulate gen., Calcutta, India, 1953-56, Am. embassy, New Delhi, India, 1956-69, polit. counselor, New Delhi, 1962-65, chargé d'affaires, Kathmandu, Nepal, 1959, dep. chief mission, Nicosia, Cyprus, 1959-62; assigned to Nat. War Coll., 1965-66; country dir. for India, Nepal, Ceylon, and Maldive Islands Dept. State, Washington, 1966-68; consul gen. Am. consulate gen., Istanbul, Turkey, 1968-70; minister-counselor, dep. chief mission Am. embassy, Tehran, Iran, 1970-74; ambassador to Niger, Niamey, 1974-76; dir. Office Combat Terrorism, Dept. State, 1976-77; ambassador to Nepal, Kathmandu, 1977-80; Mem. Am. del. to coronation of King Birendra of Nepal, 1975. Mem. Diplomatic and Consular Officers Ret. (asso.), Zeta Psi. Clubs: Himalaya, Delhi Golf. Office: New Delhi Dept State Washington DC 20520

HECK, MARTIN HENRY, banker; b. Amsterdam, N.Y., June 24, 1918; s. Albert Frederick and Emma Cornelia (Herzberger) H.; m. Alison Irene Rausch, Feb. 14, 1942; children—Martin H., Deborah H. (Mrs. Russell Puppe), Barbara H. (Mrs. Albert L. Bartoletti). B.A., Union Coll., 1940. Cashier Farmers Bank, Amsterdam, 1940-53; exec. v.p. State Bank of Albany, N.Y., 1953—. Bd. dirs., mem. endowment and exec. coms. Albany Boys' Club, 1968—; bd. dirs. Workshop, Inc., 1958—, Camp Thacher; bd. dirs., treas. State U. N.Y. at Albany Found. Served with AUS, 1940-45. Decorated Bronze Star. Mem. Reformed Ch. Clubs: Mason., Fort Orange, Wolferts Roost (Albany). Home: 16 Point View Dr East Greenbush NY 12061 Office: 69 State St Albany NY 12201

HECK, ROBERT WARREN, architecture educator, consultant; b. Des Moines, Iowa, Oct. 14, 1924; s. Edward James and Florence (Langmade) H.; m. Evelyn Louise McKinley, Sept. 1, 1952; children: Robert Gregory, Paul Anthony, Catherine Fleming. B.Arch., U. Notre Dame, 1949; M.Arch., Columbia U., 1962. Instr. archtl. design U. Fla., Gainesville, 1949-51; asst. prof. Auburn U., 1951-54; asst. prof. archtl. design and theory La. State U., Baton Rouge, 1955-59, assoc. prof., 1959-65, prof., 1965-79, alumni prof., 1979—; archtl. hist. consultant R.W. Heck, Baton Rouge, 1970—; dir. La. State U. London-Florence, 1975-83. Author: Historic Baton Rouge, 1970, Historic Alexandria, 1973; contbg. author: The Cajuns: Essays on Their History and Culture, 1978. Mem. Hist. Preservation and Cultural Commn. State of La., 1968-71; pres. Found. for Hist. La., Baton Rouge, 1968-72; mem. rev. com. Nat. Register for Historic Places, Baton Rouge, 1972-80. Served with U.S. Army, 1943-44. Recipient Preservation award for edn. Found. for Hist. La., 1975; grantee in field. Mem. Soc. Archtl. Historians, Assn. Collegiate Schs. of Architecture. Democrat. Roman Catholic. Home: 321 Magnolia Woods Ave Baton Rouge LA 70808 Office: Sch A'chitecture La State Univ Baton Rouge LA 70803

HECKART, EILEEN, actress; b. Columbus, Ohio, Mar. 29, 1919; d. Leo Herbert and Esther (Stark) Purcell; m. John Harrison Yankee, Jr., June 26, 1943; children: Mark Kelly, Philip Craig, Luke Brian. B.A., Ohio State U., 1942, L.H.D. (hon.), 1981; student, Am. Theatre Wing, 1944-48; LL.D., Sacred Heart U., Bridgeport, Conn., 1973; D.F.A. (hon.), Niagara U., 1981. Actress: Broadway plays Voice of the Turtle, 1944, Brighten the Corner, 1946, They Knew What They Wanted, 1948, Stars Weep, 1949, The Traitor, 1950, Hilda Crane, 1951, In Any Language, 1953, Picnic, 1953, Bad Seed, 1955, A View From the Bridge, 1956, Dark at the Top of the Stairs, 1958, Invitation to a March, 1960, Everybody Loves Opal, 1961, Family Affair, 1962, Too True To Be Good, 1963, And Things That Go Bump in the Night, 1965, Barefoot in the Park, 1965-66, You Know I Can't Hear You When the Water's Running, 1967, The Mother Lover, 1968, Butterflies Are Free, 1969, Veronica's Room, 1973, The Effect of Gamma Rays on Man-in-the-Moon Marigolds, 1971, Remember Me, 1975, Mother Courage and Her Children, 1975, Mrs. Gibbs in Our Town, 1976; one-woman show Eleanor, 1976, Ladies at the Alamo, 1977; movies My Six Loves, 1962, Up the Down Staircase, 1966, No Way To Treat A Lady, 1968, Butterflies Are Free, 1972, Zandy's Bride, 1974, The Hiding Place, 1975, Burnt Offerings, 1975, Wedding Band, 1975; TV actress, 1947—; TV series: Trauma Center; (Oscar nomination 1956, Film Daily citation 1956, Variety Poll of N.Y. Drama Critics award 1958, N.Y. Emmy for Save Me A Place at Forest Lawn 1967, Acad. award for Butterflies Are Free 1973, Straw Hat award 1973, 75, 77). Recipient Outer Circle award, 1953, Daniel Blum award, 1953, Sylvania TV award, 1954, Donaldson award, 1955; Hollywood Fgn. Press award, 1956; March Dimes award, 1970; Aegis award, 1970; Ohio State U. Centennial award, 1970; Gov.'s award of Ohio, 1977; Ohiana Library award, 1978. Mem. Pi Beta Phi. Home: 135 Comstock Hill Rd New Canaan CT 06840 Office: care Internat Creative Mgmt 1301 Ave of Americas New York NY 10019

HECKEL, INGE, zoo director, former college president; b. N.Y.C., Jan. 2, 1940. A.A., Bradford Jr. Coll., 1959; A.B. in English, U. N.C., 1961. With Architects and Engrs. Service, N.Y.C., 1961-62; exec. sec., jr. council Mus. Modern Art, N.Y.C., 1962-66; assoc. dir. devel. Channel 13/WNET, N.Y.C., 1966-67; mgr. devel. and promotion Met. Mus. Art, N.Y.C., 1967-79; pres. Bradford (Mass.) Coll., 1979-82; exec. dir. Met. Boston Zoo, 1982—; dir. BayBank/Merrimack Valley N.A.; Mem. art adv. com. Mt. Holyoke Coll. Art Mus., 1980—; bd. dirs. Internat. Council Museums Com. for Public Relations, 1978—. Author: (with Diana Goldin) A Tale of Two Williams, 1977. Decorated Order of Isabel La Católica, Spain). Club: Cosmopolitan (N.Y.C.). Office: Met Boston Zoos Franklin Park Boston MA 02121

HECKEL, JOHN (JACK) LOUIS, aerospace company executive; b. Columbus, Ohio, July 12, 1931; s. Russel Criblez and Ruth Selma (Heid) H.; m. Jacqueline Ann Alexander, Nov. 21, 1959; children: Heidi, Holly, John. B.S., U. Ill. Div. mgr. Aerojet Divs., Azusa, Calif., 1956-70, Seattle and Washington, 1956-70; pres. Aerojet-Space Gen. Co., El Monte, Calif., 1970-72, Aerojet Liquid Rocket Co., Sacramento, 1972-77; group v.p. Aerojet Sacramento Cos., 1977-81; pres. Aerojet Gen., La Jolla, Calif., 1981—. Chancellor's assoc. U. Calif.-San Diego, 1981—; mem. cabinet United Way Campaign, San Diego, 1982-83; bd. dirs. San Diego Econ. Devel. Corp., 1983. Recipient Disting. Alumni award U. Ill. Ann. Alumni Conv., 1979. Fellow AIAA (assoc.); mem. Aerospace Industries Assn. Am. (gov. 1981), Navy League U.S., Am. Def. Preparedness Assn., San Diego C. of C. (bd. dirs.). Republican. Club: Lomas Santa Fe Country (Solana Beach, Calif.). Office: Aerojet Gen 10300 N Torrey Pines Rd La Jolla CA 92037

HECKEL, JOHN LOUIS, diversified company executive; b. Columbus, Ohio, July 12, 1931; s. Russel Criblez and Ruth Selma (Heid) H.; m. Jacqueline Ann Alexander, Nov. 21, 1959; children: Heidi Ann, Holly Christine, John Andrew. B.S., U. Ill., 1954. With Aerojet-Gen. Corp., La Jolla, Calif., 1953—, mgr., 1956-70; pres. Space Gen. Co., 1970-72, Aerojet Liquid Rocket Co., 1972-77; group v.p. Aerojet-Gen. Corp., 1977-81, pres., 1981—. Served with USAF, 1954-56. Recipient Disting. Alumni award U. Ill., 1979. Mem. Am. Def. Preparedness Assn., AIAA, Navy League U.S., NAACP, Sacramento Urban League, Aerospace Industries Assn. Am. Democrat. Clubs: Rio Del Oro Swim and Tennis, U.S. Tennis Assn., Cuyamaga. Office: Aerojet-Gen Corp 10300 N Torrey Pines Rd La Jolla CA 92037 *

HECKEL, RICHARD WAYNE, educator; b. Pitts., Jan. 25, 1934; s. Ralph Clyde and Esther Vera (Zoerb) H.; m. Peggy Ann Simmons, Jan. 3, 1959; children—Scott Alan, Laura Ann. B.S. Met.E., Carnegie-Mellon U., 1955, M.S., 1958, Ph.D., 1959. Sr. research metallurgist E.I. duPont de Nemours & Co., Wilmington, Del., 1959-63; prof. metall. engring. Drexel U., Phila., 1963-71; head dept. metallurgy and materials sci. Carnegie-Mellon U., Pitts., 1971-76; pres., prof. metall. engring. Mich. Technol. U., Houghton, 1976—. Contbr. articles to profl. jours. Served to 1st lt., Ordnance Corps U.S. Army, 1959-60. Recipient Lindback Teaching award Drexel U., 1968. Fellow Am. Soc. Metals (Bradley Stoughton Young Tchr. of Metallurgy award 1969, Phila. Ednl. Achievement award 1967); Mem. AIME, Am. Welding Soc. (Adams Meml. mem. 1966), Am. Soc. Engring. Edn., Am. Powder Metallurgy Inst., Inst. of Metals (Eng.), AAAS, Sigma Xi, Omicron Delta Kappa, Tau Beta Pi, Phi Kappa Phi, Alpha Sigma Mu. Home: 1281 Hickory Ln Houghton MI 49931 Office: Dept Metallurgical Engring Mich Technol U Houghton MI 49931

HECKELMANN, CHARLES NEWMAN (PEN NAME CHARLES LAWTON), author, publishing consultant; b. Bklyn., Oct. 24, 1913; s. Edward and Sophia (Hodum) H.; m. Anna M. Auer, Apr. 17, 1937;

children: Lorraine Heckelmann Kane, Thomas Edward. B.A. maxima cum laude, U. Notre Dame, 1934. Sports feature writer Bklyn. Eagle, 1934-37; editor-in-chief Cupples & Leon, N.Y.C., 1937-41, Popular Library, 1941-58, v.p., 1953-58; pres., editor-in-chief Monarch Books, Inc., N.Y.C., 1958-65; mng. editor, rights dir. David McKay, N.Y.C., 1965-68; sr. editor Cowles Book Co., N.Y.C., 1968-71; sr. editor, rights dir. Hawthorn Books, N.Y.C., 1971-72, editor-in-chief, 1972-75, v.p., 1972-75; book editor Nat. Enquirer, 1975-78. Author: Vengeance Trail, 1944, Lawless Range, 1945, Six-Gun Outcast, 1946, Deputy Marshal, 1947, Guns of Arizona, 1949, Let The Guns Roar, 1950, Two-Bit Rancher, 1950, Outlaw Valley, 1950, Danger Rides the Range, 1950, Fighting Ramrod, 1951, Hell In His Holsters, 1952, The Rawhider, 1952, Hard Man With A Gun, 1954, Bullet Law, 1955, Trumpets in the Dawn, 1958, The Big Valley, 1966, The Glory Riders, 1967, Writing Fiction for Profit, 1968, Stranger from Durango, 1971, Return to Arapahoe, 1980, Wagons to Wind River, 1982; books and stories adapted for motion pictures Deputy Marshal, 1949; Stranger from Santa Fe, 1947, Frontier Feud, 1948; author (pen name Charles Lawton): Clarkville's Battery, 1937, Ros. Hackney, Halfback, 1937, The Winning Forward Pass, 1940, Home Run Hennessey, 1941, Touchdown to Victory, 1942, Jungle Menace, 1937. Mem. Cath. Writers Guild of Am. (pres. 1949-52), Western Writers of Am. (v.p. 1955-57, pres. 1964-65). Home: 10634 Green Trail Dr S Boynton Beach FL 33436

HECKER, GUY LEONARD, JR., consultant, retired air force officer; b. Louisville, Mar. 6, 1932; s. Guy Leonard and Mary Lee (Pugh) H.; m. Frances Louise Kea, Dec. 28, 1956; children: Scott, Michael, Karen. B.A., The Citadel, 1954; M.S., George Washington U., 1972; postgrad., Indsl. Coll. Armed Forces, 1966, Royal Air Force Command and Staff Coll., 1967, Harvard U. Grad. Sch. Bus., 1971, Nat. War Coll., 1972. Commd. 2d lt. USAF, 1954, advanced through grades to maj. gen., 1980; service in, Vietnam, 1967; comdr. 509th Bombardment Wing, Pease AFB, N.H., 1976-78, 45th Air Aiv., 1978; spl. asst. for MX matters DCS/RD&A, Hdqrs. USAF, Washington, 1978-80; dir., legis. liaison Office Sec. Air Force, Washington, 1980-82, ret., 1982; pres. Stafford, Burke & Hecker, Inc., Alexandria, Va., 1983—; Mem. adv. bd. Marion Mil. Inst. Decorated Silver Star, D.S.M., Legion of Merit, D.F.C., Bronze Star medal, Air medal with nine oak leaf clusters. Mem. Air Force Assn. (dir.), Marion Mil. Inst. Alumni Assn. Clubs: Greater Washington Area, Citadel (pres.). Home: 1314 Gatewood Dr Alexandria VA 22307 Office: Stafford Burke & Hecker Inc 1006 Cameron St Alexandria VA 22314

HECKER, LEWIS J., corporation executive; b. N.Y.C., Feb. 2, 1934; s. Charles E. and Fannie (Goldfinger) H.; m. Miriam Panich, Feb. 8, 1959; children: Charles Eli, Judith Bryna. B.A., CCNY, 1957; M.A., NYU, 1959, LL.B., 1963. Bar: N.Y. 1963. Pvt. practice, N.Y.C., 1963-68; v.p., gen. counsel Bangor Punta Ops., Inc., 1968-69, group v.p. leisure time group, dir., 1969-77; pres., dir. Starcraft Co., Goshen, Ind., 1977-80; pres. Armored Vehicle Builders, Pittsfield, Mass., 1980-82, Consolidated Refining Co., Mamaroneck, N.Y., 1982—. Served with AUS, 1954-56. Mem. Queens County Bar Assn., Nat. Assn. Engine and Boat Mfrs. (dir.), Order of Coif. Home: Stamford CT Office: Consolidated Refining Co 115 Hoyt Ave Mamaroneck NY 10543

HECKERT, RICHARD EDWIN, chemical company executive, chemist; b. Oxford, Ohio, Jan. 13, 1924; s. John W. and Winifred E. (Yahn) H.; m. Barbara Kennedy, Jan. 13, 1945; children: Alex Y., Andra Heckert Rudershausen. B.A., Miami U., Ohio, 1944; M.S. in Organic Chemistry, U. Ill., 1947, Ph.D., 1949. Chem. asst. Miami U., Oxford, Ohio, 1942-44; gen. foreman Eastman Kodak Co., Oak Ridge, 1946; teaching asst. dept. chemistry U. Ill., Urbana, 1946-49; research chemist Du Pont Co., Wilmington, Del., 1949-54, supr. film dept., Richmond, Va., 1954-58, tech. supt. film dept., Clinton, Iowa, 1958-59, plant mgr., Circleville, Ohio, 1959-63, dir. supporting research and devel., asst. gen. mgr., Wilmington, 1963-69, gen. mgr., 1969-71, v.p., 1972-73, sr. v.p., 1973-81, pres., 1981; vice chmn., chief operating officer Du Pont Ops., 1981—; mem. Adv. Com. for Trade Negotiations. Contbr. articles on cyanocarbon chemistry to sci. jours.; patentee in field. Pres. Longwood Gardens, Inc.; dean's assoc. bus. adv. council Miami U. Sch. Bus. Adminstrn.; Trustee Carnegie Instn. of Washington, Joint Council on Econ. Edn.; bd. dirs. U. Ill. Found. Served with U.S. Army, 1944-46. Mem. Am. Chem. Soc., NAM (bd. dirs.), Soc. of Chem. Industry, AAAS. Clubs: Pine Valley Golf, Rodney Sq., Wilmington., Vicmead Hunt/Bidermann Golf. Office: 9000 Du Pont Bldg 1007 Market St Wilmington DE 19898

HECKLER, GEORGE EARL, educator, chemist; b. Marietta, Ohio, Dec. 20, 1920; s. Charles Davis and Georgia (Hendershott) H.; m. Hilde Unterleitner, Aug. 11, 1945; children: Mary, William, Jane, John. B.A., Marietta Coll., 1947; Ph.D., U. Wis., 1952. Research chemist E.I. duPont de Nemours & Co., 1952-56; mem. faculty Idaho State U., 1956—, prof. chemistry, 1964—, chmn. dept., 1961-83. Contbr. profl. jours. Served with USAAF, 1942-45. Decorated Air medal with 4 oak leaf clusters. Mem. Am. Chem. Soc., AAAS, ACLU, AAUP (nat. council 1967-70), Phi Beta Kappa, Sigma Xi. Home: 529 S 7th Ave Pocatello ID 83201

HECKLER, MARGARET MARY, secretary HHS; b. Flushing, N.Y., June 21, 1931; d. John and Bridget (McKeon) O'Shaughnessy; m. John M. Heckler, Aug. 29, 1953; children—Belinda West, Alison Anne, John M. B.A., Albertus Magnus Coll., 1953; LL.B., Boston Coll., 1956; student, U. Leiden, Holland, 1952, Northeastern U., Stonehill Coll., Emmanuel Coll., Regis Coll., Albertus Magnus Coll., Wheaton Coll., St. Bonaventure U., Assumption Coll., Boston Coll. Bar: Mass. bar 1956, also U.S. Supreme Ct 1956. Practice in, Boston, 1956-66; mem. 90th to 97th Congresses, 10th Dist. Mass., Joint Econ. Com., Sci. and Tech. Com., Vets. Affairs Com., Nat. Republican Congl. Com.; co-chmn. Congl. Women's Caucus; sec. HHS, 1983—; mem. Mass. Gov.'s Council, 1962-66; Alternate del. Republican Nat. Conv., 1964, del., 1968, 72, 80; speaker Nat. Rep. Womens Fedn. Conv., 1967. Named Outstanding Young Woman Am., 1965. Mem. Mass. Womens Rep. Clubs: Cath. Womens Coll. Alumnae Assn. (past pres.), 90th Club U.S. Congress, Bus. and Profl. Womans Club.

HECKMAN, JAMES JOSEPH, economist, econometrician; b. Chgo., Apr. 19, 1944; s. John Jacob and Bernice Irene (Medley) H.; m. Lynne Pettler, 1979; 1 son, Jonathan Jacob. A.B. in Math. summa cum laude (Woodrow Wilson fellow), Colo. Coll., 1965; M.A. in Econs, Princeton U., 1968; Ph.D. in Econs. (Harold Willis Dodds fellow), Princeton U., 1971. Lectr. Columbia U., 1970-71, asst. prof. econs., 1971-73, assoc. prof., 1973-74; assoc. prof. econs. U. Chgo., 1974-76, prof., 1976—; research assoc. Nat. Bur. Econs. Research, 1970-77, sr. research assoc., 1977—; treas. Chgo. Econ. Research Assos.; research assoc. Econs. Research Center/NORC, 1979—; cons. in field; fellow Center for Advanced Study in Behavioral Scis., Palo Alto, Calif., 1978-79; cons. Chgo. Urban League, 1978—. Contbr. numerous articles on labor supply, income distbn. theory, duration and survival analysis, analysis of discrete data, edn. and affirmative action, econometric theory; assoc. editor: Jour. Econometrics, 1977-83; editor: (with B. Singer) The Analysis of Longitudinal Labor Market Data, 1984, Labor Economics; Am. editor: Rev. Econ. Studies, 1982—; editor: Jour. Polit. Economy, 1981—. Recipient John Bates Clark medal Am. Econ. Assn., 1983; J.S. Guggenheim fellow, 1978-79; Social Sci. Research Council fellow, 1977-78. Fellow Econometric Soc.; mem. Am. Econ. Assn., Am. Statis. Assn., Indsl. Relations Research Assn., Phi Beta Kappa. Home: 2100 Lincoln Park W Chicago IL 60614 Office: 1126 E 59th St Chicago IL 60637

HECKMANN, IRVIN LEE, coll. dean; b. Omaha, Apr. 25, 1925; s. Irvin Lee and Kathryn Pauline H.; m. Phyllis Marie Calabrese, June 20, 1953; children—Kathryn Anne, Peter James. B.S. in Commerce, Creighton U., 1950; M.B.A., U. Wis., 1951, Ph.D. (fellow econ. edn. 1954), 1955. From instr. to asso. prof. mgmt. U. Ill., 1954-63, acting head dept. mgmt., 1961-63; prof. mgmt., dean Coll. Bus. Adminstrn., Creighton U., 1963-68; prof. mgmt. U. Ill., Chgo., 1968—, dean, 1968-75; cons. exec. devel., labor arbitrator; pres. TLD Sers. Inc.; dir. T/D Systems, Inc., Tng. and Devel. Corp. Am. Co-author: Human Relations in Management, 1972, Management of the Personnel Function, 1962; Contbr.: Ency. Mgmt, 1972, Critical Incidents in Management, 1963. Mem. U.S. Postal Service Manpower Selection Bd., 1969—; mem. State Ill. Gov.'s Grievance Panel, 1972—, State of Ill. Unit Sch. Dist. 220.; Trustee Ill. Council Econ. Edn. Served with AUS, 1942-46. Mem. Acad. Mgmt., Am. Soc. Tng. and Devel., Am. Mgmt. Assn., Am. Soc. Personnel Adminstrn. (accredited personnel diplomate), Beta Gamma Sigma. Club: Economic (Chgo.). Home: 92 Old Mill Ct Barrington IL 60010 Office: Coll Bus Adminstrn U Ill at Chgo Circle Chicago IL 60680

HECKSCHER, MORRISON HARRIS, museum curator, architectural historian; b. Harrisburg, Pa., Dec. 12, 1940; s. Gustave Adolph H. and Anna (Harris) Hechscher; m. Fenella Greig, May 18, 1974. B.A., Wesleyan U., 1962; M.A., U. Del., 1964; postgrad., Columbia U., 1964-66. Asst. curator am. Wing, Met. Mus. Art, N.Y.C., 1968-72; assoc. curator Am. Wing, Met. Mus. Art, N.Y.C., 1973, curator, 1973-78, Am. Decorative Arts, Met. Mus. Art, 1978—; pres. Am. Friends Attingham, 1982—. Grantee Samuel H. Kress Found., 1966; Chester Dale fellow Met. Mus. Art, 1966-68. Mem. Soc. Archtl. Historians (dir. 1973-76, pres. local chpt. 1973-75), Furniture History Soc., Strawberry Banke (overseer 1973-79). Episcopalian. Club: Century Assn. (N.Y.C.). Home: 176 W 87th St New York NY 10024 Office: Met Mus Art Fifth Ave at 82d St New York NY 10028

HECTOR, LOUIS JULIUS, lawyer; b. Fort Lauderdale, Fla., Dec. 11, 1915; s. Harry Howard and Grace Elizabeth (Kellerstrass) H.; m. Dorothy Anne Dooley, Aug. 12, 1950 (dec. 1973); children: Denis Howard, Dorothy Anne, William Frederic, Louis Julius; m. Nancy Bean Hilles, Dec. 11, 1976. B.A., Williams Coll., 1938; postgrad., Christ Church Oxford (Eng.) U., 1939; LL.B., Yale U., 1942. Atty. Dept. Justice, Washington, 1942-43; asst. to under sec. Dept. State, 1944; practice law, Miami, 1946-47; pres. Hector Supply Co., Miami, 1948-56; mem. CAB, 1957-59; partner firm Steel, Hector & Davis, Miami, 196—; dir. Pan Am Airlines, S.E. Banking Corp. Trustee emeritus U. Miami; trustee Rockefeller U., 1978—; mem. council Nat. Endowment for Humanities, 1978—. Served with OSS. Home: 3507 Saint Gaudens Rd Coconut Grove FL 33133 Office: Steel Hector & Davis Southeast First National Bank Bldg 100 S Biscayne Blvd Miami FL 33131

HEDBERG, HOLLIS DOW, geologist, educator; b. Falun, Kans., May 29, 1903; s. Carl A. and Zada M. (Dow) H.; m. Helen F. Murray, Nov. 8, 1932; children: Ronald M., James D., William H., Franklin A., Mary F. A.B., U. Kans., 1925; M.S., Cornell U., 1926; Ph.D., Stanford, 1937; Hon. Doctorate, U. Uppsala, Sweden, 1977. Asst. Kans. Geol. Survey, 1924-25; petrographer Lago Petroleum Corp., Venezuela, 1926-28; stratigrapher, dir. geol. lab. Mene Grande Oil Co., Venezuela, 1928-39, asst. chief geologist, 1939-46; chief geologist fgn. prodn. div. Gulf Oil Corp., 1946-51, exploration mgr., 1951-52, chief geologist, Pitts., 1952-53, exploration coordinator, 1953-57, v.p., 1957-64, exploration adviser, 1964—; prof. geology Princeton, 1959-72, emeritus, 1972—; Mem. Am. Com. Stratigraphic Nomenclature, 946-60, chmn., 1950-52; pres. Iunternat. Com. Stratigraphic Terminologyy, 1952-76; v.p. Internat. Commn. Stratigraphy, 1968-76; chmn. Consortium Exploration Adv. Group, Iran, 1965-72; chmn. tech. subcom. petroleum resources of ocean floor Nat. Petroleum Council, 1968-73; chmn. coordinating panel Internat. Geol. Correl. Program, 1969-72; chmn. JOIDES Panel Pollution Prevention and Safety, 1970-77; Bd. dirs. Cushman Found. Foraminiferal Research, 1951-63; mem. corp. Woods Hole Oceanographic Inst., 1972—. Editor: Internat. Stratigraphy Guide, 1975—; Contbr. articles profl. jours. Decorated Medalla de Honor de la Instruccion Publica, Venezuela).; Recipient Sidney Powers medal Am. Assn. Petroleum Geologists, 1963; Distinguished Service award U. Kans., 1963; Wollaston medal Geol. Soc. London, 1975; Distinguished Achievement award Offshore Tech. Conf., 1975. Fellow Geol. Soc. Am. (pres. 1959-60, asso. editor bull. 1962-68, Penrose medal 1980); mem. Nat. Acad. Sci. (Mary Clark Thompson award 1973), Am. Assn. Petroleum Geologists (asso. editor bull. 1937—, pres. Eastern sect. 1948-49, Human Needs award 1973), A.A.A.S., Am. Petroleum Inst., Am. Geophys. Union, Paleontol. Soc. Am. (v.p. 1952), Soc. Econ. Paleontology and Minerology, Swiss Geol. Soc., Soc. Exptl. Geophys., Am. Inst. Mining, Metall. and Petroleum Engrs., Am. Geol. Inst. (pres. 1962-63, Ian Campbell medal 1983), Internat. Union Geol. Scis. (chmn. U.S. nat. com. on geology 1965-66), Am. Inst. Profl. Geologists, Geol. Soc. Stockholm (hon. corr.), Assn. Venezolana Geol. Mining Petroleum (hon.), U.S. Nat. Com. World Petroleum Congresses, Geol. Soc. London (hon.), Danish Royal Acad. Sci., Phi Beta Kappa, Sigma Xi, Phi Kappa Phi, Sigma Gamma Epsilon. Clubs: Cosmos (Washington); Duquesne (Pitts.); Princeton, Mining (N.Y.C.). Home: 118 Library Pl Princeton NJ 08540

HEDBERG, PAUL CLIFFORD, broadcasting executive; b. Cokato, Minn., May 28, 1939; s. Clifford L. and Florence (Erenberg) H.; m. Juliet Ann Schubert, Dec. 30, 1962; children: Mark, Ann. Student, Hamline U., 1959-60, U. Minn., 1960-62. Program dir. Sta. KRIB, Mason City, Iowa, 1957-58, Sta. WMIN, Mpls., 1959; staff announcer Time-Life broadcast Sta. WTCN-AM-TV, Mpls., 1959-61, Crowell Collier broadcast Sta. KDWB, St. Paul, 1961-62; founder, pres. Sta. KBEW Radio Blue Earth, Minn., 1963—, Sta. KQAD and KLQL-FM, LuVerne, Minn., 1971—; pres. stas. KMRS-AM and KKOK-FM, Morris, Minn., 1971—; founder, pres. Blue Earth Cablevision, Inc., 1973-82, Courtney Clifford Inc. (advt. rep.), Mpls., 1977—; founder, owner Market Quoters Inc., Blue Earth, 1974—; pres., owner Sta. KEEZ-FM, Mankato, Minn., 1977—; founder The Motion Graphics Group, 1983, Sta. KUOO-FM, Spirit Lake, Iowa, 1984—; owner Stas. KSMN and KLSS-FM, Mason City, Iowa, 1984—; dir. First Nat. Bank, Blue Earth.; Bd. dirs. Minn. Good Roads, v.p., 1976-79, pres., 1979-81; bd. dirs. Blue Blue Earth Indsl. Service Corp., pres., 1970-76. Served with USCGR, 1962-70. Recipient Disting. Service award Blue Earth Jaycees, 1971. Mem. Minn. A.P. Broadcasters (pres. 1966, dir. 1976—), Blue Earth C. of C. (Leadership Recognition award 1967, pres. 1967), Nat. Assn. Broadcasters, Minn. Assn. Broadcasters (dir. 1975—, v.p. 1980-81, pres. 1983-84), Minn. Press Council. Lutheran. Clubs: Mason, Shriner, Kiwanis. Home: W Okoboji Rural Route Box 9379 Spirit Lake IA 51360 Office: Hedberg Bldg Blue Earth MN 56013

HEDBERG, ROBERT DANIEL, investment counselor; b. Portland, Oreg., Mar. 14, 1922; s. John and Emma Sophia (Gronberg) H.; m. Martha Jane Carr, Oct. 27, 1945; children—Hanna, John, Sarah. A.B. in Math, U. Pa., 1946, M.S. in Banking and Finance, 1947. Mng. gen. partner Hedberg Assos., Ltd., Paoli, Pa., 1970—; chmn., dir. Patrician Paper Co., N.Y.C., 1963-79; trustee Patrician Paper Liquidating Trust, 1979—; dir. Betz Labs., Inc., Kappe Assos., Inc., Tamaqua Cable Products; cons. corp. fin. planning, 1948—; lectr. investments Wharton Grad. div. U. Pa., 1960. Mem. Fin. Analysts Fedn. (chmn. 1974-75). Clubs: Racquet (Phila.); Metropolitan (N.Y.C.); Adirondack League (Old Forge, N.Y.); Whitford (Exton, Pa.). Home: 208 N Ship Rd Exton PA 19341 Office: 14 Paoli Ct Paoli PA 19301

HEDDEN, ALFRED JOHN, savings and loan executive; b. Stirling, N.J., Jan. 8, 1924; s. Alfred J. and Florence (Hearn) H.; m. Catherine E. Egan, Nov. 4, 1950; children: Thomas, Kathleen. Student spl. courses in banking and mgmt., Ind. U., Rutgers and Seton Hall univs., 1965, Dartmouth Coll., 1975, Harvard U., 1980. With City Fed. Savs. & Loan Assn., Elizabeth, N.J., 1952, asst. loan officer, v.p. and mortgage officer, sr. v.p., chief loan officer, exec. v.p. investments, exec. v.p. adminstrn., 1952-79; pres., chief operating officer, dir. Fed. Savs. & Loan Assn., Elizabeth, N.J., 1979—; dir. Interstate Service Corp. PAMICO, Blue Bell, Pa. Vice-chmn. N.J. Higher Edn. Assistance Authority. Served with AUS, 1943-46. Mem. Garden State Savs. and Loan Inst. Republican. Roman Catholic.

HEDDEN, RUSSELL ALFRED, manufacturing company executive; b. Kearny, N.J., May 1, 1918; s. George Arthur and Anna (Meyer) H.; m. Dorothy Williams, June 15, 1939; children: Russell Alfred, Susanne (Mrs. John Moaradian), Linda Jean (Mrs. Charles B. Centivany), Nancy Ellen, Richard Earl. B.S. in Mech. Engring., Newark Coll. Engring., 1941; postgrad., Gen. Motors Inst., 1939-40, NYU, 1944-45. Research asso. Nat. Indsl. Conf. Bd., N.Y.C., 1946-48; asst. to pres., budget dir. Carrier Corp., Syracuse, N.Y., 1948-51; controller, dir. mfg. S. Morgan Smith Corp., York, Pa., 1951-59; work mgr. Allis Chalmers Mfg. Co., West Allis, Wis., 1959-62; with Bendix Corp., 1962-72, pres. indsl. group, Southfield, Mich., 1970-72; pres., chief operating officer Kearney & Trecker Corp., 1972-73, pres., chief exec. officer, 1973—, also dir.; pres., chief exec. officer Cross & Trecker Corp., from 1978, now chmn. bd.; dir. Marine Exchange Bank, Milw. Bd. regents Milw. Sch. Engring. Mem. Financial Execs. Inst., Nat. Machine Tool Builders Assn. (dir. 1970-72, chmn. 1978-79), Allied Products Inst. (trustee council technol. advancement). Republican. Episcopalian (vestryman, sr. warden). Clubs: Quayl Creek Country, Oakland Hills Country. Office: 505 N Woodward Ave Bloomfield Hills MI 48013

HEDDESHEIMER, WALTER JACOB, lawyer; b. Akron, Ohio, Nov. 11, 1910; s. Jacob and Anna (Mueller) H.; m. Grace Gilpin, Dec. 31, 1937; children: Walter Jon, Don James, Philip David, Ann Marie Heddesheimer Geldis. A.B. magna cum laude, Ohio Wesleyan U., 1932; LL.B., Harvard, 1935. Bar: Ohio 1935. Practiced with Musser, Kimber & Huffman, Akron, 1935-42; regional enforcement atty. OPA, Cleve., 1942-47; atty. Central Nat. Bank, Cleve., 1947-56, gen. counsel, 1956-72, v.p., sec., 1962-72; counsel Baker, Hostetler & Patterson, 1972-80; practice law, Cleve., 1980—; village solicitor, Rochester (Ohio), 1940-45. Trustee Union Coll., Lutheran Home, Westlake, Ohio. Recipient award appreciation for service on tech. adv. com. Comptroller's Manual for Nat. Banks, U.S. Treasury, 1963. Mem. Am., Ohio, Cleve. bar assns., Phi Beta Kappa, Alpha Tau Omega. Republican. Lutheran. Club: Mason. Home: 17668 Ridge Creek Dr Strongsville OH 44136 Office: 1248 Engineers Bldg Cleveland OH 44114

HEDERMAN, THOMAS MARTIN, JR., retired newspaper editor; b. Jackson, Miss., May 23, 1911; s. Thomas Martin and Pearl (Smith) H.; m. Bernice Flowers, May 11, 1938; children: Thomas Martin III (dec. USAF), Bernice Hederman Hussey. B.A., Miss. Coll., 1932, LL.D. (hon.), 1967; postgrad., Columbia U., 1932-33. Assoc. editor Clarion-Ledger, Jackson, Miss., 1948, editor, co-pub., from 1948; pres. Miss. Publs. Corp., Capitol Broadcasting Co.; owners KNAZ, Flagstaff, Ariz.; former dir. First Magnolia Fed. Savs. & Loan Assn., Jackson. Contbr. to: World Book ency. Trustee, chmn. bd. Miss. Coll.; past mem. exec. com. Miss. Research and Devel. Commn.; past pres., now bd. dirs. Central Growth Found. Named Outstanding Alumnus of Year Miss. Coll.; recipient Silver EM award Miss. Scholastic Press Assn. and Miss. Journalism Assn., 1970. Mem. Miss. Press Assn. (past pres.), Am. Soc. Newspaper Editors, Am. Newspaper Pubs. Assn., So. Newspaper Pubs. Assn. (dir. 1947-49), Am. Press Inst., Internat. Press Inst., C. of C. (v.p., pres.). Office: 311 E Pearl St Jackson MS 39201

HEDGE, GEORGE ALBERT, physiologist; b. St. Louis, June 7, 1939; s. George Calvin and Elsie Margaret (Metz) H.; m. Jacqueline Stake McMillan, Aug. 31, 1963; children—Naomi C., David T. B.S. in Biology, U. Mo., 1961, M.A. in Pharmacology, 1963; Ph.D. in Physiology, Stanford U., 1966. Research fellow dept. pharmacology U. Utrecht, Netherlands, 1966-68; asst. prof. dept. physiology Coll. Medicine, U. Ariz., Tucson, 1968-72, asso. prof., 1972-77; prof., chmn. dept. physiology Sch. Medicine, W.Va. U., Morgantown, 1977—; ad hoc cons. NIH; mem. physiology commn. Nat. Bd. Med. Examiners. Reviewer manuscripts for profl. jours.; Author numerous abstracts and sci. papers. Served with U.S. Army, 1957. NIH research grantee. Mem. Am. Physiology Soc., Endocrine Soc., Internat. Soc. Neuroendocrinology, Assn. Chmn. Depts. Physiology, Am. Thyroid Assn. Home: 677 Nueva Morgantown WV 26505 Office: Dept Physiology WVa Univ Med Center Morgantown WV 26506

HEDGECOCK, ROGER ALLAN, mayor, lawyer; b. Compton, Calif., May 2, 1946; s. Lester and Carmel (Pean) H.; m. Cynthia Cloverdale, Oct. 18, 1975; children: James, Christopher. A.B., U. Calif.-Santa Barbara, 1968; J.D., U. Calif.-Hastings, 1971. Bar: Calif. 1972. Atty. Higgs, Fletcher, Mack, San Diego, 1972-76; city atty. City of Del Mar, Calif., 1974-75; mem. San Diego County Bd. Suprs., San Diego County, Calif., 1976-83; mayor City of San Diego, 1983—; vice chmn. Met. Transit Dist. Bd., City of San Diego, 1983—; chmn. Regional Employment Tng. Consortium, 1981—. Chmn. San Diego Festival of Arts, 1983. Mem. U.S. Conf. Mayors. Republican. Roman Catholic. Office: 202 C St San Diego CA 92101

HEDGES, DANIEL KULDELL, lawyer; b. Houston, Sept. 18, 1946; s. David Talmadge and Ethelyn May (Kuldell) H.; m. Adele Oglesbee, May 22, 1976; 1 son. Clinton Kuldell. B.A., Dartmouth Coll., 1968; J.D., U. Tex.-Austin, 1974. Bar: Tex. 1974, U.S. Supreme Ct. 1977. Assoc. litigation dept. Fulbright & Jaworski, Houston, 1974-81; U.S. atty. so dist. Tex. U.S. Dept. Justice, 1981—; bd. advisors Fed. Civil Practice Inst., Houston, 1983—. Bd. dirs. Met. YMCA Camps Bd., Houston, 1980—, Downtown YMCA, Houston, 1982—, Rice Design Alliance, Houston, 1982—; patron Stehlin Found. for Cancer Research, Houston, 1981—. Served to lt. USNR, 1968-71. Named Outstanding Young Lawyer of Tex. Tex. Young Lawyers Assn., 1982-83, Outstanding Young Lawyer of Houston Houston Young Lawyers Assn., 1983. Fellow Tex. Bar Found., Houston Bar Found.; mem. ABA, Tex. Young Lawyers Assn., Houston Young Lawyers Assn. Republican. Episcopalian. Office: US Atty 515 Rusk St 12th Floor Houston TX 77002

HEDGES, DONALD W., lawyer; b. Kansas City, Mo., May 24, 1921; s. Byron C. and Irma (McCleary) H.; m. Mary Elizabeth Mancill, Jan. 29, 1944 (div.); children: Judith Elizabeth, Donna Louise, Byron C. III, Steven M.; m. Diane Scheid, Jan. 15, 1965; children: Scott Andrew, Hillary Carson. Student, Principia Coll., 1939-40; B.S.,

Wharton Sch., U. Pa., 1943; LL.B., U. Pa., 1947; D. Bus. Sci. (hon.), Webber Coll., 1947. Bar: Pa. 1948, U.S. Circuit Ct. Appeals 1949, U.S. Dist. Ct. (ea. dist.) Pa. 1949. Law clk. Chief Justice Pa. Supreme Ct., 1948-49; mem. firm Mancill, Cooney, Semans & Hedges, 1949-64; partner Wolf, Block, Schorr & Solis Cohen, Phila., 1965-78; dir. Servotronics, Inc., Christiana Metals Corp., Sonobond Ultrasonics, Inc. Served as lt. (j.g.) Air Force, USNR, 1943-46. Decorated Distinguished Flying Cross, Air medal. Mem. Am., Pa., Phila. bar assns., Juristic Soc. Phila., Beta Theta Pi. Episcopalian. Clubs: Union League (Phila.); Sharswood Law (U. Pa.), Merion Cricket. Home: 1026 Rock Creek Rd Bryn Mawr PA 19010

HEDGES, HARRY GEORGE, educator; b. Lansing, Mich., Oct. 7, 1923; s. Charles William and Elsie (Frost) H.; m. Mary J. Corbishley, June 14, 1944 (dec.); children—Susan, Martha. B.S., Mich. State U., 1949, Ph.D., 1960; M.S., U. Mich., 1954. Electronics engr. USAF Wright Air Devel. Center, Dayton, Ohio, 1949-51; research asso. U. Mich., 1951-54; instr. Mich. State U., East Lansing, 1954-60, asst. prof., 1960-63, asso. prof., 1963-69, prof., chmn. dept. computer sci., 1969—; Dir. Nat. Electronics Conf., Inc., 1968—. Tech. editor: Analysis of Discrete Physical Systems, 1967; mem.: Computer Sci. Bd, 1973—; chmn., 1974-75. Chmn. Selective Service Bd. 264, Lansing, 1970-76. Served with AUS, 1943-46; PTO. NSF sci. faculty fellow, 1960. Mem. Am. Soc. Engring. Edn. (chmn. N.Central sect. 1968-69), IEEE (dir. 1967-69, treas. 1969, vice chmn. 1973, chmn. 1974, Southeastern Mich. sect.). Home: 1623 Woodside Dr East Lansing MI 48823

HEDGES, JOHN LELAND, foreign service officer; b. Chgo., Feb. 5, 1927; s. Leland Gillel and Ethelyn Blanche (MacMillan) H.; m. Margaret Houser, Aug. 20, 1946; children: Jeffrey Leland, John Arthur. A.B., Harvard U., 1948; M.S., George Washington U., 1967; postgrad., Air War Coll., 1967. Adminstrv. officer info. div. Marshall Plan European Hdqrs., Paris, 1949-50; asst. info. officer Spl. and Tech. Mission to Indochina, Saigon, 1950-51; overseas ops. officer info. div. ECA/Mut. Security Agy., Washington, 1951-53; gen. mgr. Congressional Quar. Newsfeatures, Washington, 1953-54; public affairs officer for Western France, Tours, 1954-56; labor info. officer, Paris, 1956-57, public affairs officer So. France, Marseille, 1957-59; press attache Am. embassy, Paris, 1959-62; country public affairs officer, Brazzaville, Congo, 1962-63, dep. country public affairs officer, Rabat, Morocco, 1963-66; policy officer for Africa USIA, 1967-69; country public affairs officer, 1st sec., Beirut, 1969-71, counselor embassy for public affairs, Bangkok, Thailand, 1971-75, Lagos, Nigeria, 1975-77; asst. dir. for Africa USIA, Washington, 1977-78; dir. for African affairs U.S. Internat. Communications Agy., Washington, 1978-79; counselor for public affairs Am. embassy, Paris, 1979-83; career minister Dept. State, 1982; counselor USIA, Washington, 1983—. Free-lance writer, Paris, 1948. Served with USNR, 1945-46. Recipient Edward R. Murrow award, 1980. Mem. Am. Fgn. Service Assn. Clubs: Nat. Press (Washington); Harvard (N.Y.C.); Cercle Suedois, Jeu de Paume (Paris). Home: 139 Grafton St Chevy Chase MD 20015 Office: USIA Washington DC

HEDGES, RALPH RICHARD, naval officer; b. Chgo., Oct. 26, 1927; s. Ralph Earl and Carrie Helen (Symons) H.; m. Phyllis Isabel Bacon, Dec. 25, 1952; children: Jean Laurie, Scott Richard. B.S., U.S. Naval Acad., 1952, Navy Postgrad. Sch., 1958; M.S. in Nuclear Engring, Iowa State U., 1959; grad., Army Command and Staff Coll., 1965. Enlisted in U.S. Navy, 1945, commd. ensign, 1952, advanced through grades to rear adm., 1976; mem. staff COMPATWINGSPAC; comdg. officer Naval Air Sta., Moffett Field, Calif., 1973-75; head nat. policy and command orgn. br. Office Chief Naval Ops., Washington, 1975-76; comdr. patrol wings U.S. Atlantic Fleet, Brunswick, Maine, 1976-79; dep. chief of staff ops. CINCLANTFLT, Norfolk, Va., 1979-81; comdr. Naval Forces Caribbean, P.R., 1981-82, U.S. Forces Caribbean, Key West, Fla., 1982. Decorated Legion of Merit with 1 gold star, Meritorious Service medal with 1 gold star, Air medal, Navy Commendation medal. Methodist. Home: Quarters A Trumbo Point Key West FL 33040 Office: Comdr US Forces Caribbean NAS Key West FL 33040

HEDGES, WILLIAM LEONARD, humanities educator; b. Arlington, Mass., Feb. 16, 1923; s. James B. and Nina (Leonard) H.; m. Elaine Catherine Ryan, June 28, 1956; children—Marietta, James Leonard. B.A., Haverford Coll., 1946; Ph.D., Harvard, 1954. Teaching fellow Harvard, 1950-53; instr. U. Wis., 1953-56; mem. faculty Goucher Coll., 1956-57, 58—, prof. English, 1967, chmn. dept. English, 1968-71, 77-81, chmn. Am. studies, 1972—, Elizabeth Todd Research prof., 1975-80; vis. asst. prof. U. Calif. at Berkeley, 1957-58. Author: Washington Irving: An American Study, 1965; contbg. author and editor: Major Writers of America, 1962; co-author and co-editor: (with Elaine Hedges) Land and Imagination: The Rural Dream in Am, 1980; contbg. author: Landmarks of American Writing, 1970, The Chief Glory, 1973, The Oldest Revolutionary, 1976; Mem. editorial bd.: Early American Lit, 1971-74. Served with AUS, 1943-45. Decorated Purple Heart.; Fulbright fellow, France, 1949-50; fellow Am. Council Learned Socs., 1963-64. Mem. Modern Lang. Assn., Phi Beta Kappa. Home: 317 Hawthorne Rd Baltimore MD 21210

HEDIEN, WAYNE EVANS, insurance company executive; b. Evanston, Ill., Feb. 15, 1934; s. George L. and Edith P. (Chalstrom) H.; m. Colette Johnston, Aug. 24, 1963; children: Mark, Jason, Georgiana. B.S. in Mech. Engring, Northwestern U., 1956, M.B.A., 1957. Engr. Cook Electric Co., Skokie, Ill., 1957-64; bus. mgr. Preston Sci., Inc., Anaheim, Calif., 1964-66; security analyst Allstate Ins. Co., Northbrook, Ill., 1966-70, portfolio mgr., 1970-73, asst. treas., 1973-78, v.p., treas., 1978-80, sr. v.p., treas., 1980-83, exec. v.p., chief fin. officer, 1983—. Bd. dirs. North Suburban YMCA, 1978—. Mem. Inst. Chartered Fin. Analysts (chartered fin. analyst), Newcomen Soc. Club: Economic (Chgo.). Office: Allstate Ins Co Allstate Plaza Northbrook IL 60062

HEDISON, DAVID ALBERT, actor; b. Providence, May 20, 1930; s. Albert David and Rose (Boghosian) H.; m. Bridget Mori, June 29, 1968; children: Alexandra Mary, Serena Rose. Student, Brown U., 1949-51; grad., Neighborhood Playhouse Sch. of Theatre, N.Y.C., 1953. Played Beliaev in: A Month in the Country, Phoenix Theatre, 1956 (Theatre World award as most promising newcomer); with, 20th Century Fox, 1957—; films include The Enemy Below, 1957, The Fly, 1958, Son of Robin Hood, 1958, The Lost World, 1959, Marines, Let's Go, 1960, The Greatest Story Ever Told, Live and Let Die, Esther, Ruth and Jennifer, The Naked Face; off-Broadway appearances Clash by Night; appeared in: Bad Bad Jo Jo, London; appeared on tour in: Chapter II; starred in: TV series Five Fingers, 1960, Voyage To The Bottom of The Sea, 1964-68; TV mini series A.D., NBC, 1985; numerous guest appearances on TV shows; frequent Brit. TV appearances, including Summer and Smoke, BBC; (Recipient Barter Theatre award.). Mem. Actors Studio. Office: care Nanas Stern Biers & Co 9454 Wilshire Blvd Beverly Hills CA 90212

HEDLEY-WHYTE, JOHN, physician, educator; b. Newcastle-upon-Tyne, Eng., Nov. 25, 1933; came to U.S., 1960, naturalized, 1965; s. Angus and Nancy (Nettleton) H.-W.; m. Elizabeth Tessa Waller, Sept. 19, 1959. Student, Harrow Sch., 1947-52; B.A. (Rothschild scholar Clare Coll.), Cambridge U., 1955, M.B., 1958, M.A., 1959, M.D., 1972; A.M. (hon.), Harvard U., 1967. House surgeon St. Bartholomew's Hosp., London, 1958-59; resident in anesthesia Mass. Gen. Hosp., 1960-62, hon. anesthetist, 1977—; clin. asst. anesthesia Harvard U., 1961-63, instr., 1963-65, clin. asso., 1965-67, asso. prof., 1967-69, prof., 1969-76, 1st David S. Sheridan prof. anaesthesia and respiratory therapy, 1976—, chmn. faculty seminar in health and medicine, 1975-76; anesthetist-in-chief Beth Israel Hosp., Boston, 1967—, chmn. com. on research, 1976-82; cons. in field; mem. tech. adv. bd. on med. devices tech. Am. Nat. Standards Inst., 1973—; leader U.S. del. Internat. Orgn. Standardisation, Geneva, 1973—. Author: Respiratory Care, 1965, Applied Physiology of Respiratory Care, 1976; Contbr. articles to profl. jours. Mem. Am. Physiol. Soc., Abernethian Soc. (past pres.), Am. Soc. Anesthesiologists (chmn. com. mech. equipment 1977-82, chmn. com. on equipment and standards 1982—), Mass. Soc. Anesthesiologists (pres. 1973-74), Am. Soc. Pharmacology and Exptl. Therapeutics, Roxbury Soc. Med. Improvement (librarian 1970—), Mass. Med. Soc. (council 1975-78). Democrat. Episcopalian. Clubs: Boodle's, The Country, Somerset, Harvard of Boston, Vicarage. Home: 231 Pond Ave Brookline MA 02146 Office: 330 Brookline Ave Boston MA 02215

HEDLUND, CHARLES JOHN, oil executive; b. Appleton, Minn., Nov. 3, 1917; s. William M. and Sophia (Stickney) H.; m. Helen Marie Thorstenson, Aug. 30, 1940; children: Susan Louise Hedlund Vicinelli, Patricia Jo Hedlund Oxman, Ann Elizabeth Hedlund Domandi, Christopher Charles. B.Chem. Engring., U. Minn., 1940, B.B.A., 1940. Process engr. Standard Oil Co., N.J., Baton Rouge, 1940-47, mgr. dept. coordination and petroleum econs., 1954-60, with dept., 1947-52; dir. program div. Petroleum Adminstrn. for Def., Washington, 1952-53; chmn. petroleum working group NATO, Paris, 1952-53; exec. v.p. Esso Standard Italiana, Genoa, 1960-62; pres. Svenska Esso AB, Stockholm, 1962-66; v.p. mktg. Esso Europe Inc., London, 1966-67; v.p. Middle East, Exxon Corp., N.Y.C., 1968-80; pres. Esso Middle East, 1969-80. Trustee Am. Mus. Natural History, N.Y.C; chmn. bd. trustees Am. U., Cairo. Mem. Nature Conservancy (chmn. bd. govs.), Tau Beta Pi, Phi Lambda Upsilon, Beta Gamma Sigma. Clubs: Century Assn. (N.Y.C.); Queen's and Lansdowne (London); Baltusrol (Springfield, N.J.). Office: American Univ in Cairo 866 United Nations Plaza New York NY 10017

HEDLUND, RONALD, bass-baritone; b. Mpls., May 12, 1939; s. Cyril and Mildred H.; m. Barbara Smith, Nov. 12, 1974. B.A., Hamline U.; M.Mus., Ind. U. Mem. faculty dept. music U. Ill., 1970-74. Appeared throughout U.S. including opera cos. of, San Francisco, Chgo., Houston, Miami, Seattle, Dallas, Ft. Worth, Phila., Washington, Omaha, Santa Fe, Lake George, Boston, N.Y.C. Opera, Met. Opera Nat. Co., New Orleans. Served with USNR, 1958-63. Office: care Dorothy Cone Artists Reps 250 W 57th St Suite 2316 New York NY 10019

HEDMEG, ANDREW, state ofcl.; b. Bratislava, Czechoslovakia; came to U.S., 1912, naturalized, 1922; s. John and Susan (Hutnik) H.; m. Jennie Katonak, May 21, 1932; 1 dau., Andra (Mrs. Francis Ledet). A.B., Ohio State U., 1931, M.D., 1936; M.P.H., Johns Hopkins, 1941. Diplomate: Am. Bd. Preventive Medicine. County health officer Miss. Bd. Health, 1937-52; dir. preventive medicine div., local health services div. La. Bd. Health, 1952-66; pres. La. Bd. Health, state health officer, 1966-72; dir. div. health La. Health and Human Resources Adminstrn., 1973-74; ret., 1974; Clin. prof. pub. health adminstrn. La. State U. Med. Center, 1953—, acting head dept. pub. health and preventive medicine, 1975—; adj. prof. Tulane U. Sch. Tropical Medicine and Pub. Health, New Orleans, 1953—. Served with AUS, 1942-46. Recipient C.B. White Meml. award La. Pub. Health Assn., 1964, Outstanding Service award So. br. Am. Pub. Health Assn., 1966; Outstanding Service award Am. Assn. Pub. Health Physicians, 1974; Gov.'s Outstanding Service award to citizen La., 1974. Life fellow Am. Pub. Health Assn.; mem. Am. Coll. Preventive Medicine, La. State, Orleans Parish med. socs. Home: 900 Robert E Lee Blvd New Orleans LA 70124 Office: PO Box 60630 New Orleans LA 70160

HEDRICH, WILLIAM CLIFFORD, photographer; b. Chgo., June 21, 1912; s. Theodore Louis and Anna Sophia (Knudsen) H.; m. Te'a Dora Kre'mer, June 3, 1942; children—Ronald Ted, Paul Scott, Sandi Ann. Student, U. Ill., 1930-31, Inst. Design, Chgo., 1945-46, U.S. Army Motion Picture Sch., London, 1943. Partner Hedrich-Blessing Studio, Chgo., 1931-46; chmn. bd. Hedrich-Blessing Ltd., Chgo., 1946—, also dir.; owner Hedrich Island Homes, St. Maarten, N.A., 1970—; dir. Oyster Pond Devel. Corp., St. Maarten, N.A. Photographer architecture and interiors, 1931—, group shows with, Hedrich-Blessing, Mich. Sq. Rotunda, Chgo., 1935, Offices Perkins & Will, Chgo., 1967, Archtl. Photographers Am. exhibits, 1946-62, AIA Exhibit, 1978-79; also represented in permanent collections; photographs include Falling Water, a widely pub. archtl. photograph. Bd. dirs. Golden Sect. Soc., Boy Scouts Am., 1922-25. Served with U.S. Army, 1942-45. Decorated Bronze Star; recipient Gold medal award AIA, 1967, Archtl. Photographers Invitational award Pitts. Plate Glass, 1973, also other awards; named to Photography Hall of Fame, Santa Barbara, Calif., 1978. Mem. Profl. Photographers Am., Chgo. Photog. Guild. Lutheran. Club: South End Gun (Granville, Ill.). Office: 11 W Illinois St Chicago IL 60610

HEDRICK, BASIL CALVIN, museum director, ethnohistorian, educator; b. Lewistown, Mo., Mar. 17, 1932; s. Truman Bloice and M. LaVeta (Stice) H.; m. Susan Kehoe, Jan. 19, 1957 (div. 1979); 1 dau., Anne Lanier Hedrick Caraker; m. Susan Elizabeth Pickel, Oct. 2, 1980. A.B., Augustana Coll., Rock Island, Ill., 1956; M.A., U. Fla., 1957; Ph.D., Inter-Am. U., Saltulla, Mex., 1965; cert., U. Vienna, Strobl, Austria, 1956. Asst. prof., assoc. prof., prof. So. Ill. U., Carbondale, 1967-74, asst. dir. Univ. Mus., 1967-70, dir. Univ. Mus. and Art Galleries, 1970-74, dean internat. edn., 1972-74; asst. dir. Ill. Div. Mus., Springfield, 1977-80; prof. history U. Alaska, Fairbanks, 1980—, dir. U. Alaska Mus., 1980—, dir. inter. affairs, 1980—; Fulbright sr. lectr., Brazil, 1972, mem. nat. register adv. panel, Ill., 1977-80; mem. Alaska Council on Arts, Anchorage, 1983—; chmn. Fairbanks Hist. Preservation Commn., 1982—. Author: (with others) A Bibliography of Nepal, 1973, (with Carroll L. Riley) The Journey of the Vaca Party, 1974, Document Ancillry to the Vaca Journey, 1976, (with C.A. Letson) Once Was A Time, a Wery Good Time: An Inquiry into the Folklore of the Bahamas, 1975, (with J.E. Stephens) In the Days of Yesterday and in the Days of Today: An Overview of bahamian Folkmusic, 1976, It's Natural Fact: Obeah in the Bahamas, 1977, Contemporary Practices in Obeah in the Bahamas, 1981; compilations and collections, 1959-69; editor: (with J. Charles Kelley and Riley) The Classic Southwest: Readings in Archaeology, Ethnohistory and Ethnography, 1973, (with J. Charles Kelley and Riley) The Mesoamerican Southwest: Readings in Archaelogy, Ethnohistory and Ethnology, 1974, (with Riley) Across the Chichimec Sea, 1978, New Frontiers in the Archaeology and Ethnohistory of the Greater Southwest, 1980, Trans. of Ill. Acad. Sci., 1979-81; contbr. articles to profl. jours. Chmn. Goals for Carbondale, 1972; active various local state, nat. polit. campaigns. Mem Am. Assn. Mus. (mem., leader accredidation teams 1977—); mem. Ill. Archaeol. Soc. (pres. 1973-74), Mus. Alaska, Assn. Sci. Mus. Dirs., Midwest Mus. Conf. (treas. 1977-80, merit 1981), Phi Kappa Phi, Phi Alpha Theat, Sigma Delta Pi. Home: 1601 Central St Fairbanks AK 99701 Office: U Alaska Mus U Alaska Fairbanks AR 99701 *Pragmatism has been the ruling factor in both my personal and professional life. I have never assumed that anything is immutable and, therefore, I have rarely been overly surprised or disappointed in changes which have occured. In our rush to succed and excel, we often forego the realities of daily life in order to attempt the literally impossible. The better rule is, I feel, to adapt to reality without losing ethical and moral principle. Relax and learn.*

HEDRICK, DONALD WARD, agronomist, college dean emeritus; b. Willapa, Wash., July 20, 1917; s. Henry Ward and Bertha (Fisch) H.; m. Pauline E. Gray, May 14, 1944; children: Donine, Ronald, David, Lora. B.S., Wash. State U., 1939; M.S., U. Calif.-Berkeley, 1949; Ph.D., Texas A&M U., 1951. Jr. range conservationist Soil Conservation Service, Spur, Tex., 1939-40, Pleasanton, Tex., 1941-47; asst. range conservationist U. Calif., Berkeley, 1947-49, assoc. specialist, 1949-51; asst. prof. range mgmt. Oreg. State U., Corvallis, 1951-54, assoc. prof., 1954-62, prof., 1962-69; dean Sch. Natural Resources, Humbolt State U., Arcata, Calif., 1969-81, emeritus, 1981—; pasture agronomist Ministry Agr. and Natural Resources, Western Nigeria, 1959-61, forage agronomist, The Gambia, 1981-83; Vice chmn., commr. N. Coast region Calif. Coastal Zone Conservation Commn., 1972-75, chmn., 1975-77. Served with USAAF, 1942-45. Decorated Silver Star, Purple Heart. Mem. Soc. Range Mgmt., Sigma Xi. Home: PO Box 111A Arcata CA 95521

HEDRICK, FLOYD DUDLEY, government official, author; b. Lynchburg, Va., Jan. 19, 1927; s. Silas Dudley and Alice (Stowe) H.; m. Rachel Conelia Childress, May 27, 1950; children: Susan Kaye, Alice Rae. Grad., Va. Comml. Coll., 1948; grad., Advanced Mgmt. Program, Harvard, 1971; Ph.D., U. Central Calif., 1981. Purchasing agt., supt. stores Trailways, Inc., 1947-65; v.p. purchasing Macke Co., Washington, 1966-72; pres. subsidiary Atlantic Supply Co., Hyattsville, Md., 1967-72; chief procurement and supply div. Library of Congress, Washington, 1973—; mem. Inter-Agy. Procurement Policy Com., 1973—, Inter-Agy. Metrecation Com., 1976—; Pres. Lynchburg chpt. Fed. and State Credit Unions, 1956-57. Author: Purchasing Management in the Smaller Company, 1971, Purchasing for Owners of Small Plants, 1976, 79; asso. editor: Purchasing Handbook, 1973, 81, Am. Mgmt. Assn. Management Handbook, 1981. Served with USNR, 1944-46, 50-52. Mem. Am. Mgmt. Assn. (mem. purchasing planning council 1969—), Nat. Assn. Purchasing Mgmt. (v.p. 1972-73, chmn. orgn. and planning com., Disting. Service award 1976), Purchasing Mgmt. Assn. Washington (pres. 1969-70), Izaak Walton League (v.p. Lynchburg 1957). Club: Mason (32 deg.). Home: 3824 King Arthur Rd Annandale VA 22003 Office: 10 1st St SE Washington DC 20540

HEDRICK, FREDERIC CLEVELAND, JR., lawyer; b. Jacksonville, Fla., July 18, 1911; s. Frederic Cleveland and Edith (Warrington) H.; m. Rosalie Sutton, May 10, 1939; children: Frederic Cleveland III, Meredith, Charles Warrington. B.S., U. Fla., 1936, LL.B., 1938. Bar: Fla. 1938, D.C. 1944. Practice in, Washington, 1945—; spl. asst. antitrust div. U.S. Atty. Gen., 1938-41; mem. firm Pierson & Ball, 1946-52; pvt. practice, 1952-55; sr. partner Hedrick & Lane, 1955-82; mem. firm Wilkes, Artis, Hedrick & Lane, Chartered, 1982—. Past trustee Fauquier Ednl. Found. Served from lst lt. to lt. col. AUS, 1941-45. Recipient Legion of Merit award for work with SSS, 1945. Fellow Am. Bar Found.; mem. ABA (mem. ho. dels. 1970-78), D.C. Bar Assn. (past sect. chmn., dir.), Nat. Tax Assn.-Tax Inst. Am. (past pres.), Am. Law Inst., Am. Judicature Soc., U. Fla. Alumni Assn. (past pres. Washington chpt.), Blue Key, Alpha Tau Omega, Phi Delta Phi. Episcopalian (past vestry). Clubs: Army and Navy, Metropolitan (Washington); Chevy Chase (Md.). Home: 5215 Cammack Dr Bethesda MD 20816 Office: 1666 K St NW Washington DC 20006

HEDRICK, JERRY LEO, biochemistry and biophysics educator; b. Knoxville, Iowa, Mar. 11, 1936; s. Harvard L. and Dorothy E. (Hardin) H.; m. Karel J. Harper, June 22, 1957; children: Michael L., Kerry L., Benjamin A., Kimberly L. B.S., Iowa State U., 1958; Ph.D., U. Wis., 1961, postgrad., 1961-62; postgrad., U. Wash., 1962-65. Asst. prof. U. Calif.-Davis, 1965-68, assoc. prof., 1968-74, prof. biochemistry, 1974—, chmn. dept., 1982—. Recipient Guggenheim award John Simon Guggenheim Found., 1971; numerous research grants NIH, NSF, 1966—; John Simon Guggenheim fellow Cambridge, Eng., 1971-72. Mem. AAAS, Am. Soc. Biol. Chemists, Am. Chem. Soc., Soc. Study Reprodn., Am. Soc. Cell Biology, Sigma Xi. Home: 14 Carlsbad Ave RFD 2 Davis CA 95616 Office: U Calif Dept Biochemistry and Biophysics Davis CA 95616

HEDRICK, WALLY BILL, artist; b. Pasadena, Calif., 1928; s. Walter Thomas and Velma Laurel (Thurman) H.; m. Jay Defeo, 1956. Student, Otis Art Inst., Los Angeles, 1947; B.F.A., Calif. Coll. Arts and Crafts, Calif. Sch. Fine Arts, 1952-55. Instr. San Francisco Art Inst., 1959-69, San Jose U., 1971-73, Indian Valley Colls., 1974—. One-man shows include, M.H. de Young Meml. Mus., San Francisco, 1955, Calif. Sch. Fine Arts, San Francisco, 1956, Isaacs Gallery, Toronto, Can., 1961, New Mission Gallery, San Francisco, 1963, San Francisco Art Inst., 1967, Sonoma Satte Coll., Calif., 1968, 63 Bluxome St., San Francisco, 1975, group exhbns. include, Mus. Modern Art, N.Y.C., 1959, San Francisco Mus. Art, 1962, 66, Norton Simon Mus. Art, Pasadena, 1962, Dallas Mus. Fine Arts, 1974, San Francisco Mus. Modern Art, 1977, Gallery Paula Anglim, San Francisco, 1981; represented in permanent collections, Aldrich Mus. Contemporary Art, Ridgefield, Conn., Mus. Modern Art, N.Y.C., Smithsonian Instn., San Francisco Mus. Modern Art, City and County San Francisco. Served with AUS, 1950-52. Nat. Endowment Arts grantee, 1968, 82.

HEDRICK, WALTER RUSSELL, JR., real estate cons., ret. air force officer; b. Hawley, Tex., Aug. 2, 1921; s. Walter Russell and Mary (James) H.; m. Betty Ben Sanford, Jan. 17, 1941; children—Walter Russell III, Robert Douglas. B.S. in Physics, U. Md., 1941, M.S., 1952. Commd. 2d lt. USAAF, 1941; advanced through grades to brig. gen. USAF, 1966; with (86th Fighter-Bomber Group), World War II, assigned, Brooks Field, Tex., 1947-48, Orlando AFB, Fla., 1948-49, project officer sec. air force, 1949-51, with test br., 195255, chief tech. ops. div., Kirtland AFB, N.Mex., 1955-57, comdr., Eniwetok, 1957-58, asst. to group comdr., later air comdr., Kirtland AFB, 1958-60, assigned, Los Angeles, 1960-65, dep. comdr. for space, 1966-67, dir. space, dep. chief staff research and devel., 1967-70, ret., 1970; became v.p. Itek Corp., 1970; now with Hedrick Co. Decorated Legion of Merit, Air medal with 4 oak leaf clusters, Air Force Commendation medal. Home: 112 Camino Escondido Santa Fe NM 87501 Office: Hedrick Co PO Box 2185 Santa Fe NM 87501

HEEBE, FREDERICK JACOB REGAN, U.S. district judge; b. Gretna, La., Aug. 25, 1922; s. Bernhardt and Marguerite (Reagan) H.; m. Betty Mae Rowden, Dec. 25, 1976; children: Frederick Riley, Adrea Dee. B.A., Tulane U., 1943, LL.B., 1949. Bar: La. 1949. Practice in, Gretna, 1949-60; dist. judge div. B, 24th Jud. Dist. Ct., Jefferson Parish, La., 1961-66; U.S. dist. judge Eastern Dist. La., 1966—, now chief judge. Charter mem. Community Welfare Council Jefferson Parish, 1957—; chmn. Jefferson Parish Bd. Pub. Welfare, 1953-55; Mem. Jefferson Parish Council, 1958-60, vice chmn., 1958-60; Bd. dirs. Social Welfare Planning Council New Orleans, New Orleans Regional Mental Center and Clinic, W. Bank Assn. for Retarded. Served to capt., inf. AUS, World War II. Decorated Purple Heart, Bronze Star. Mem. Am., La., New Orleans, Fed. bar assns., Am. Judicature Soc., Phi Beta Kappa. Office: Chambers C-525 US Courthouse 500 Camp St New Orleans LA 70130 *

HEEBNER, ALBERT GILBERT, economist, banker; b. Phila., Mar. 7, 1927; s. Albert and Julia (Zwada) H.; m. Dorothy Mae Kiler, Aug. 16, 1952. A.B., U. Denver, 1948; A.M., U. Pa., 1950, Ph.D., 1967. Instr. econs. Coll. of Wooster, Ohio, 1950-52; with Phila. Nat. Bank (now subs. CoreStates Fin. Corp.), 1952—; economist Phila. Nat. Bank, 1960—, asst. v.p., 1961-64, v.p., 1964-70, sr. v.p., 1970-73, exec. v.p., 1973-83, exec. v.p., economist, 1983, CoreStates Fin. Corp., 1983—; spl. asst. to chmn. Council Econ. Advisers, Washington, 1971-72; vis. prof. econs. Swarthmore (Pa.) Coll., 1976; adj. prof. econs. Eastern Coll., St. Davids, Pa., 1982; chmn. econ. adv. com. Am. Bankers Assn., 1978-80; bd. dirs. Nat. Bur. Econ. Research, 1983—. Author: Negotiable Certificates of Deposit: The Development of a Money Market Instrument, 1969. Served with USNR, 1945-46. Mem. Am. Econ. Assn., Am. Finance Assn., Nat. Assn. Bus. Economists (pres. 1975-76), Conf. Bus. Economists. Baptist. Clubs: Union League, Sunday Breakfast (Phila.). Home: 7 Blackwell Pl Philadelphia PA 19147 Office: Broad and Chestnut Sts Philadelphia PA 19101

HEEFNER, WILLIAM FREDERICK, lawyer; b. Perkasie, Pa., July 8, 1922; s. Russell Edgar and Lydia Victoria (Spielman) H. B.A., Ursinus Coll., 1942, LL.D., 1975; LL.B., Temple U., 1949. Bar: Pa. bar 1951. Assoc. Curtin & Heefner, Morrisville, 1951—, sr. partner, 1966—; Dir. Bucks County Bank & Trust Co., William Penn Savs. & Loan Assn. Sec. Bedminster Twp. Planning Commn., 1961—; Treas. Bucks County Democratic Com., 1966—; Bd. dirs., v.p. Ursinus Coll.; pres., trustee Mercer Mus. and Library, Fonthill Trust and Mus. Served to 1st lt., inf. AUS, 1942-46. Decorated Purple Heart. Fellow Am. Bar Found.; mem. ABA, Pa. Bar Assn. (ho. of dels. 1971-79, bd. govs. 1976-79, chmn. law office econs. and mgmt. com. 1972-73), Bucks County Bar Assn. (pres. 1965-66), Symposium (Trenton, N.J.), Phi Alpha Delta. Lutheran. Clubs: Metropolitan (N.Y.C.); Trenton, Trenton Country. Home: Old Bethlehem Rd Perkasie PA 18944 Office: 250 N Pennsylvania Ave Morrisville PA 19067

HEEGER, ALAN JAY, physicist; b. Sioux City, Iowa, Jan. 22, 1936; s. Peter J. and Alice (Minkin) H.; m. Ruthann Chudacoff, Aug. 11, 1957; children: Peter S., David J. B.A., U. Nebr., 1957; Ph.D., U. Calif., Berkeley, 1961. Asst. prof. U. Pa., Phila., 1962-64, asso. prof., 1964-66, prof. physics, 1966-82, U. Calif.-Santa Barbara, 1982—; dir. Lab. for Research on Structure of Matter, 1974-81, acting vice provost for research, 1981-82; Morris Loeb lectr. Harvard U., 1973; cons. various sci. labs. Contbr. sci. articles to profl. jours. Recipient Oliver E. Backley prize in solid state physics, 1983; Alfred P. Sloan fellow; Guggenheim fellow; Govt. grantee; Internat. Exchange scholar, USSR, 1976, Japan, 1978. Mem. Am. Phys. Soc. Patentee in field. Office: Dept Physics U Calif Santa Barbara CA 93103

HEELAN, PATRICK AIDAN, philosophy educator; b. Dublin, Ireland, Mar. 17, 1926; s. Matthew Henry and Pauline (Beirens) H. Student, Belvedere Coll., 1938-42; B.A., Univ. Coll., Dublin, 1947, M.A., 1948; Ph.D., St. Louis U., 1952; S.T.L., Jesuit Theol. Faculty, Dublin, 1959, Princeton U., 1960-62; Ph.D., U. Louvain, 1964. Ordained priest Soc. Jesus, Roman Catholic Ch., 1958; lectr. math. physics Univ. Coll., Dublin, 1964-65; research asso. Dublin Inst. Advanced Studies, 1952-54, 64-65; asst. prof. philosophy Fordham U., 1965-67, asso. prof., 1967-70; prof. philosophy, chmn. dept. SUNY at Stony Brook, 1970-74, acting v.p. liberal studies, 1975-77, v.p. liberal studies, 1977-79, prof. philosophy, 1979—; external appraiser philosophy and arts and scis. programs U. Western Ont., Lowell U., John Carroll U. Author: Quantum Mechanics and Objectivity, 1965, Space-Perception and Philosophy of Science, 1983; mem. editorial bd.: Jour. Sci. and Bio Structures; Contbr. articles profl. jours. Fulbright fellow, 1960-62. Mem. Am. Catholic Philos. Assn. (council 1973-75), Center for Integrative Edn. (council 1972-74), Am. Philos. Assn. (program com. Eastern sect. 1975), Philosophy Sci. Assn., Brit. Soc. Philosophy Sci., AAAS, Soc. Phenomenology and Existential Philosophy, N.Y. Acad. Scis., Phi Beta Kappa, Sigma Xi. Home: 6 Park St Setauket NY 11733 Office: Office Dept Philosophy State U NY Stony Brook NY 11794

HEER, DAVID MACALPINE, educator; b. Chapel Hill, N.C., Apr. 15, 1930; s. Clarence and Jean Douglas (MacAlpine) H.; m. Nancy Whittier, June 29, 1957 (div. 1980); m. Kaye S. Heymann, Dec. 11, 1980; children—Douglas (dec.), Laura, Catherine. A.B. magna cum laude, Harvard U., 1950, M.A., 1954, Ph.D., 1958. Statistician population div. U.S. Bur. Census, Washington, 1957-61; lectr., asst. research sociologist U. Calif., Berkeley, 1961-64; asst. prof. demography Harvard U. Sch. Public Health, Boston, 1964-68, asso. prof., 1968-72; prof. sociology U. So. Calif., Los Angeles, 1972—; mem. population research study sect. NIH, 1971-73. Author: After Nuclear Attack: A Demographic Inquiry, 1965, Society and Population, 1968; editor: Readings on Population, 1968, Social Statistics and the City, 1968. Mem. Population Assn. Am. (dir. 1970-73), Am. Sociol. Assn., Internat. Union Sci. Study Population, Nat. Council Family Relations. Home: 10251 Monte Mar Dr Los Angeles CA 90064

HEER, NICHOLAS LAWSON, near Eastern languages and literature educator; b. Chapel Hill, N.C., Feb. 8, 1928; s. Clarence and Jean Douglas (MacAlpine) H. B.A., Yale U., 1949; Ph.D., Princeton U., 1955. Transl. analyst Arabian Am. Oil Co., Saudi Arabia, 1955-57; asst. prof. Stanford U., Calif., 1959-62; vis. lectr. Yale U., New Haven, 1962-63; asst. prof. Harvard U., Cambridge, Mass., 1963-65; assoc. prof. U. Wash., Seattle, 1965-76, prof. Near Eastern langs. and lit., 1976—; acting chmn. dept. Near East langs. and lit. U. Wash, 1982—; middle east curator Hoover Instn., Stanford, Calif., 1958-62. Editor: Tirmidhi: Bayan al-Farq, 1958, Jami: Al-Durrah al-Fakhirah, 1981; translator: Jami: The Precious Pearl, 1979. Mem. Am. Oriental Soc., Middle East Studies Assn., Am. Assn. Tchrs. of Arabic (treas. 1964-76, pres. 1981, dir. 1982—). Home: 1821 10th Ave E Seattle WA 98102 Office: Dept Near Eastern Langs and Lit DH-20 U Wash Seattle WA 98195

HEESCHEN, DAVID SUTPHIN, astronomer, educator; b. Davenport, Iowa, Mar. 12, 1926; s. Richard George and Emily (Sutphin) H.; m. Eloise St. Clair, June 11, 1950; children: Lisa Clair, David William, Richard Mark. B.S., U. Ill., 1949, M.S., 1951; Ph.D., Harvard U., 1954; Sc.D. (hon.), W.Va. Inst. Tech., 1974. Instr. Wesleyan U., Middletown, Conn., 1954-55; lectr., research assoc. Harvard U., 1955-56; scientist Nat. Radio Astronomy Obs., 1956-77, sr. scientist, 1977—, dir., 1962-78; research prof. astronomy U. Va., 1980—; Cons. NASA, 1960-61, 68-72. Contbr. sci. jours. G.R. Agassiz fellow Harvard Obs., 1953-54; Recipient Disting. Public Service award NSF, 1980. Fellow AAAS; mem. Am. Astron. Soc. (v.p. 1969-71, pres. 1980-82), Internat. Astron. Union (v.p. 1976-82), Internat Sci. Radio Union, Nat. Acad. Sci., Am. Acad. Arts and Sci., Am. Philos. Soc.

HEESE, MARTHA OSSIAN, government official; b. Hattiesburg, Miss., Aug. 14, 1942; d. John William and Geraldine (Ossian) Hesse. B.S., U. Iowa, 1964; postgrad., Northwestern U., 1976-77; M.B.A., U. Chgo., 1979. Dir., chief operating officer SEI Info. Tech., Chgo., 1969-80; assoc. dep. sec. U.S. Dept. Commerce, Washington, 1981-82; exec. dir. Pres.'s Task Force on Mgmt. Reform, 1982; asst. sec. U.S. Dept. Energy, 1982—. Republican. Home: 2700 Virginia Ave NW Washington DC 20037 Office: US Dept Energy 1000 Independence Ave NW Washington DC 20585

HEFFELBOWER, DWIGHT EARL, engineering services company executive; b. Newton, Kans., Aug. 28, 1925; s. Fred Clifford and Ruby Esther (Garrison) H.; m. Darlene Dorey, Feb. 1, 1948; children: Darl Jay, Kent Lewis, Gail Marie. B.S. in Chem. Engring., Kans. State U., 1949; student, Presbyn. Coll. of S.C., 1943. Engr. Burlington AEC plant Mason & Hanger-Silas Mason Co., Inc., Burlington, Iowa, 1949-56, chief engr., 1956-63, plant mgr. Iowa Army Ammunition plant, 1963-73, v.p., Lexington, Ky., 1973-80, exec. v.p. ops., Lexington, 1980—, also dir., 1975—; dir. Mason Chamberlain Inc., Picayune, Miss., 1976—, pres., 1976—; chmn. bd. DWC Computer Solutions Inc., Lexington, 1982—; mem. Dept Energy Weapons Intelligence Panel, 1983, Indsl. Com. of Ammunition Producers, 1983. Named hon. Ky. Col. 2d lt. USAAF, 1943-45. Mem. Am. Def. Preparedness Assn. (adv. bd. dirs. 1978—), Lexington C. of C. Home: 1894 Parkers Mill Rd Lexington KY 40504 Office: Mason & Hanger-Silas Mason Co Inc 200 W Vine St Lexington KY 40507

HEFFELFINGER, WILLIAM STEWART, government official; b. Effingham, Kans., Jan. 31, 1925; s. William Stewart and Nora (Estell) H.; m. Dorothy M. Shockley, Sept. 24, 1944; children: William Stewart III, Sharon A., Lee S. With Sweet Hotel System, 1942-43; bus. mgr. Eleemosynary Instns., Kans., 1946-53; sec., trustee A. J. Rice Estates, 1948—; dir. Olney facility FCDA, 1953-54, dir. adminstrv. operations office, 1955-56, asst. adminstr. for gen. adminstrn., 1956-58; mem. adv. com. GSA, 1956-62; dir. adminstrn. Exec. Office of Pres. U.S., 1958-62; reviewing officer Bd. of Surveys, 1956-62; chmn. bd. U.S. Civil Service Examiners, 1955-62; dir. program rev. Martin-Marietta Corp., 1962-69; spl. asst. to asst. sec. water and power devel. Dept. Interior, 1969; dep. asst. sec. Dept. Transp., Washington, 1969-70, asst. sec., 1970-77; asst. adminstr. for mgmt. and adminstrn. Fed. Energy Adminstrn., 1977; dir. adminstrn. Dept. Energy, 1977-81, asst. sec. energy for mgmt. and adminstrn., 1981-82, dir. adminstrn., 1982—; mem. Joint Task Force Seven in Operation Redwing, 1956; vice chmn. ex-personnel bd. Dept. Transp.; vice chmn. Transp. System Acquisition Council; treas. U.S. Ry. Assn., 1974; mem. Fed. Adv. Council on Occupational Safety and Health, 1971-77. Served with AUS, 1943-46. Recipient Wm. A. Jump Meml. Found. Meritorious award, 1960. Mem. Am. Soc. Pub. Adminstrn., Am. Legion. Club: Mason. Office: Dept Energy 1000 Independence Ave Washington DC 20585

HEFFERN, GORDON EMORY, banker; b. Utica, Pa., Feb. 19, 1924; s. Claude E. and Lillian A (McKay) H.; m. Neva Lepley, Sept. 19, 1946; children: Mary Heffern Maddex, John, Robert, Richard. Student, Stevens Inst. Tech., 1944, U. Va., 1949. Asst. to pres., security analyst Peoples Nat. Bank of Charlottesville, Va., 1949-51; v.p. Nat. City Bank of Cleve., 1951-62, First Nat. City Bank of Alliance, Ohio, 1962-63; pres., chief exec. officer Goodyear Bank, Akron, 1963-74; pres., dir. Society Nat. Bank, Cleve., 1974—, Society Corp., 1975—. Bd. dirs., chmn. fin. com. Mt. Union Coll.; mem. exec. bd., pres. Greater Cleve. council Boy Scouts Am.; bd. dirs. Univs. Hosps., Cleve., Bill Glass Evangelistic Assn.; mem. exec. com., treas. Downtown Cleve. Corp.; mem. session Fairmount Presbyterian Ch.; trustee John Carroll U. Served with USNR, 1942-46. Mem. Assn. Res. City Bankers, Bluecoats, Inc. (asst. treas.), Musical Arts Assn., Am. Def. Preparedness Assn., Univ. Circle. Republican. Clubs: Akron City, The Country, Pepper Pike, Portage Country, Union, Canterbury Golf; 50 (Cleve.). Home: 22450 Canterbury Ln Shaker Heights OH 44122 Office: Society Corp 127 Public Square Cleveland OH 44144

HEFFERNAN, JAMES PATRICK, lawyer, business executive; b. N.Y.C., Nov. 27, 1933; s. James and Nora (Mannion) H.; m. Elaine Kirschner, July 29, 1955; children: Stephen, Stacey, Barbara, Audrey, Elizabeth, Jonathan. B.S., Fordham Coll., 1955; postgrad. (Fulbright scholar), Helsinki U., 1955-56; LL.B., J.D., Cornell U., 1959. Bar: N.Y. bar 1959. Asso. firm Davies, Hardy & Schenck, N.Y.C., 1959-65; labor counsel, sr. div. counsel Sylvania Electric Products, N.Y.C., 1965-72; sec., counsel N.Y. Racing Assn., Jamaica, 1972-77, v.p., 1976-77, pres., 1977-82, Am. Totalisator Inc., Sparks, Md., 1982—; bd. dirs. Thoroughbred Racing Assn., Thoroughbred Racing Protective Bur. Mem. Byram Hills Sch. Bd., Armonk, N.Y., 1973-76. Mem. ABA, Bar Assn. City N.Y. Roman Catholic. Office: 7 Loveton Circle Sparks MD 21152

HEFFERNAN, JOHN, actor; b. N.Y.C., May 30, 1934. Student, CCNY, Columbia U.; B.F.A., Boston U. Co-founder, Charles Street Playhouse, Boston; appearing in: numerous plays including The Crucible, The Grass Harp, A View from the Bridge, Blood Wedding, The Iceman Cometh, Hotel Paradiso, Shadow of a Gunman; N.Y. debut at the, Masque, 1958; appeared in: Julius Caesar, N.Y. Shakespeare Festival, 1959, The Great God Brown, 1959, Lysistrata, 1960, Peer Gynt, 1960, Henry IV, The Taming of the Shrew, 1960, She Stoops to Conquer, 1960, The Plough and the Stars, 1960, The Octoroon, 1961, Hamlet, 1961, Androcles and the Lion, 1961, A Man's a Man, 1962, The Winter's Tale, As You Like It, 1963, Luther, 1963; toured in role of Luther, 1964; other stage appearances include The Alchemist, 1964, Arms and the Man, 1967, Saint Joan, 1968, The Memorandum, 1968, Woman Is My Ideal, 1968, Invitation to a Beheading, 1969, Purlie, 1970; co-producer, appeared in: The Shadow of a Gunman, Syracuse, N.Y., 1973; films include The Time of the Heathen, The Sting, 1973; also numerous TV appearances. (Recipient Obie award 1960, Variety Critics poll award for Tiny Alice 1964-65). Office: 20 Fifth Ave New York NY 10011 *

HEFFERNAN, NATHAN STEWART, chief justice Wisconsin Supreme Court; b. Frederic, Wis., Aug. 6, 1920; s. Jesse Eugene and Pearl Eva (Kaump) H.; m. Dorothy Hillemann, Apr. 27, 1946; children: Katie (Mrs. Howard Thomas), Michael, Thomas. B.A., U. Wis., 1942, LL.B., 1948; student, Harvard U. Bus. Sch., 1943-44. Bar: Wis. 1948. Assoc. firm Schubring, Ryan, Peterson & Sutherland, Madison, Wis., 1948-49; practice in, Sheboygan, Wis., 1949-59; partner firm Buchen & Heffernan, 1951-59; counsel Wis. League Municipalities, 1949; research asst. to gov. Wis., 1949; asst. dist. atty. Sheboygan County, 1951-53; city atty. City of Sheboygan, 1953-59; dep. atty. gen. State of Wis., 1959-62; U.S. atty. Western Dist. Wis., 1962-64; justice Wis. Supreme Ct., 1964—, chief justice, 1983—; lectr. mepl. corps., 1961-64; lectr. appellate procedure and practice U. Wis. Law Sch., 1971—; faculty Appellate Judges Seminar, NYU, 1972—; former mem. Nat. Council State Ct. Reps., chmn., 1976-77; dir. Nat. Center State Cts., 1976-77, mem. adv. bd. appellate justice project; former mem. Wis. Jud. Planning Com.; chmn. Wis. Appellate Practice and Procedure Com., 1975-76; mem. exec. com. Wis. Jud. Conf., 1978—, chmn., 1983; pres. City Attys. Assn., 1958-59. Wis. chmn. NCCJ, 1966-67; past exec. bd. Four Lakes Council Boy Scouts Am.; gen. chmn. Wis. Democratic Conv., 1960, 61; mem. Wis. Found.; bd. visitors U. Wis. Law Sch., 1970—, chmn., 1973-76; past mem. corp. bd. Meth. Hosp.; curator Wis. Hist. Soc.; trustee Wis. Meml. Union, Wis. State Library. Served to lt. (s.g.) USNR, 1942-46; ETO, PTO. Recipient distinguished service award NCCJ, 1968. Fellow Am. Bar Found. Mem. Am. Law Inst., Inst. Jud. Adminstrn. (mem. faculty seminar), ABA (past mem. spl. com. on adminstrn. criminal justice, mem. com. fed.-state delineation of jurisdiction), Wis. Bar Assn., Dane County Bar Assn., Sheboygan County Bar Assn., Am. Judicature Soc. (dir. 1977-80, chmn. program com. 1979-81), Wis. Law Alumni Assn. (bd. dirs.), Order of Coif, Iron Cross, Phi Kappa Phi, Phi Delta Phi. Congregationalist (former deacon). Clubs: Milwaukee, Madison Lit. (pres. 1979-80), Harvard, Harvard Bus. Sch. Home: 17 Thorstein Veblen Pl Madison WI 53705 Office: State Capitol Madison WI 53702

HEFFERNAN, PAUL MALCOLM, architect, educator; b. Decorah, Iowa, Jan. 23, 1909; s. Walter A. and Laura D. (Bethuram) H. B.S. in Archtl. Engring, Iowa State U., 1929, M.S. Archtl. Engring, 1931; M. Arch., Harvard, 1935; student, Ecole des Beaux Arts, Paris, France, 1935-38. Instr. Iowa State U., 1931-33; mem. faculty Coll. Architecture, Ga. Inst. Tech., Atlanta, 1938—, Prof, 1944-76, dir. coll., 1956-76, dir. and prof. emeritus, 1976—, adj. prof. study abroad program, Paris, 1976-77; designer Bush-Brown, Gailey and Heffernan (which conducted master plan and bldg. plans for Ga. Inst. Tech.), 1944-54; cons. archtl. edn. So. Regional Edn. Bd., 1953; cons. architect Ga. Inst. Tech., 1956-64, local firms; cons. design PHA, Washington; mem. archtl. award juries. Mem. Ga. Bd. Exam. and Registration of Architects, 1961-71, pres., 1967-69. Summer fellow Found. Architecture and Landscape Architecture, Lake Forest, Ill., 1929; Condé-Nast fellow Am. architecture, 1929-30; Sheldon fellow; also Appleton fellow Harvard, 1935; recipient Eugene Dodd medal Harvard, 1934; 28th Paris prize Soc. Beaux-Arts Architects, N.Y.C.; also certificate Beaux-Arts Inst. Design, N.Y.C., 1935; citation for effective teaching archtl. design Coll. Fellows AIA, 1955; hon. mention for West Stands Ga. Inst. Tech., Progressive Architecture mag., 1948; award for Price Gilbert Library AIA, 1952; citation Atlanta chpt. AIA, 1965; citation for profl. achievement Iowa State U., 1973; Bronze medal award Ga. Assn. AIA, 1982. Fellow AIA (com. scholarships and awards 1956-58), Royal Soc. Arts (London); life fellow Internat. Inst. Arts and Letters, Lindau, Germany; mem. Theta Delta Chi, Tau Beta Pi, Phi Kappa Phi, Tau Sigma Delta, Sigma Upsilon. Home: 166 5th St NW Atlanta GA 30313

HEFFERNAN, PHILLIP THOMAS, JR., publisher; b. Natick, Mass., July 2, 1922; s. Phillip Thomas and Hazel (Toner) H.; m. Mildred Brock Lippitt, Aug. 27, 1949; children—Phillip Thomas III, John, Lisa, Caroline. B.S., Northeastern U., 1947. With Gage Pub. Co., N.Y.C. and Chgo., 1947-58, bus. mgr., 1956-58; sales mgr. Conover Mast Publs., N.Y.C., 1958-60; v.p., pub., dir. Ziff Davis Pub. Co.; pubs. of Popular Electronics, Stereo Rev., Electronics World mags., 1960—. Pres. Park Forest (Ill.) Playhouse, 1952-53. Served to capt. USMCR, 1942-45. Decorated D.F.C., Air medal, Silver Star, Bronze Star. Mem. Sigma Soc. Clubs: Princeton (N.Y.C.); Siwanoy Country (Bronxville, N.Y.). Home: 12 Meadow Ave Bronxville NY 10708 Office: 1 Park Ave New York City NY 10016

HEFFERNAN, WILBERT JOSEPH, social worker, educator; b. Pontiac, Mich., Aug. 18, 1932; s. Wilbert Joseph and Theresa Martina (Dannehl) H.; m. Charlene Pellowe, Dec. 20, 1958; children: Katy, Kristi, Amy. B.S., Va. Polytech. Inst., 1953; M.A., Duke U., 1955; M.S.W., U. Mich., 1959; Ph.D., U. N.C., 1964. Sr. research staff Inst. for Research on Poverty, U. Wis., 1967-75; prof. Sch. Social work, 1972-78; sr. staff Center for Study of Public Policy, 1975-78; dean Sch. of Social Work U. Tex., Austin, 1978-80, prof. public affairs, 1980—. Author: Power, Scarcity and Common Human Needs, 1979. Mem. exec. com. Dan County (Wis.) Democratic Party, 1974-78. Mem. Council on Social Work Edn. (exec. com.), Am. Polit. Sci. Assn., Sierra Club. Democrat. Congregationalist. Office: LBJ Sch of Public Affairs Univ of Tex Austin TX 78712

HEFFNER, GROVER CHESTER, research institute executive, retired naval officer; b. Seattle, Mar. 25, 1919; s. Grover C. and Ida (Bevan) H.; m. Jane Ellen Bender, Apr. 18, 1942; children: Jann Kathryn, Grayson Chester. B.S., U. Wash., 1940; M.B.A., Stanford U., 1950; grad., Nat. War Coll., 1964. Commd. ensign USN, 1940; advanced through grades to rear adm., 1967; assigned U.S.S. Altair, 1941, Naval Supply Depot, Brisbane, Australia, 1942-44, U.S.S. Euryale, 1945-46; with Office Sec. of Navy, 1950-53; comdg. officer Naval Supply Facility, C.Z., 1953-55; force supply officer Cruiser/Destroyer Pacific Fleet, 1955-57; dir. Supply Corps personnel, 1957-60; dir. supply Puget Sound Naval Shipyard, 1960-63; comdg. officer Naval Supply Center, Long Beach, Calif., 1964-66; insp. Gen. Def. Supply Agy., 1966-67; comdr. Def. Indsl. Supply Center, Phila., 1967-70, Def. Constrn. Supply Center, Columbus, Ohio, 1970-75; ret. U.S. Navy, 1975; asst. to chief exec. officer, corp. div. Battelle Meml. Inst., Columbus, 1975—; mem. bd. Battelle Meml. Inst. Found.; chmn. bd. Ohio Center. Pres. United Way, Columbus, 1975; v.p. Central Ohio Transit Authority.; trustee Otterbein Coll., Westerville, Ohio. Decorated Joint Commendation medal, Navy Distinguished Service medal, Legion of Merit. Mem. C. of C. (chmn. mil. affairs com., Downtown Action com.), Navy League U.S. (nat. v.p.), Sigma Alpha Epsilon. Presbyterian. Clubs: Stanford, Columbus Athletic, Columbus Country. Lodges: Masons; Shriners; Rotary. Home: 5199 Doral Ave Columbus OH 43213 *Persistency in driving toward your career aspirations is vital, however, integrity of your principles must never be marred to achieve your desires.*

HEFFNER, RICHARD DOUGLAS, communications educator and consultant, television producer; b. N.Y.C., Aug. 5, 1925; s. Albert Simon and Cely (Bender) H.; m. Anne de la Vergne, Dec. 14, 1946; m. Elaine Segal, July 30, 1950; children: Daniel Jason, Charles Andrew. A.B., Columbia U., 1946, M.A. (Mitchell fellow), 1947. Teaching asst. history U. Calif. at Berkeley, 1947-48; instr. Am. history Rutgers U., 1948-50, Univ. prof. communications, pub. policy, 1964—; lectr. history Columbia, 1950-52; prof. history Sarah Lawrence Coll., 1952-53; dir. pub. affairs WNBC-TV, N.Y.C., 1955-57; dir. programs Met. Ednl. TV Assn., N.Y.C., 1957-59; editorial cons. CBS, Inc.; mem. editorial bd., dir. spl. projects CBS-TV Network, 1959-61; v.p., gen. mgr. ednl. TV Channel 13 WNET, N.Y.C., 1961-63; pres. Richard Heffner Assocs., Inc., N.Y.C., 1964—; mem. program adv. bd. Teleprompter Corp.; Dir. commn. on campaign costs Twentieth Century Fund, 1968-69; dir. Ford Found. study of TV's environ. messages, 1970-72; chmn. bd. classification and rating adminstrn. Motion Picture Assn. Am., 1974—. Producer-moderator: The Open Mind, NBC-TV, 1956-59, WPIX-TV, N.Y.C., 1973—; moderator-host: Nat. Ednl. TV series People and Politics, 1964; exec. editor-host: KPIX-TV From the Editor's Door, 1981—; Author: A Documentary History of the United States, 1952; Editor: Democracy in America, 1956. Mem. exec. com., bd. dirs. N.Y.C. Police Found. Mem. AAAS, Acad. Motion Picture Arts and Scis., Am. Hist. Assn., Nat. Assn. Ednl. Broadcasters, Phi Beta Kappa. Club: Century. Home: 90 Riverside Dr New York NY 10024 Office: 522 Fifth Ave New York NY 10036

HEFFRON, HOWARD A., lawyer; b. N.Y.C., Oct. 3, 1927; s. Jack and Sophie (Malkin) H.; m. Stella Meller, July 4, 1946; children: James, Robert, Nancy. A.B., Columbia U., 1948; LL.B., Harvard U., 1951. Bar: N.Y. State 1953, D.C. 1953. Practiced law, N.Y.C. and Washington, 1953-58, 61-66, 69-77; asst. U.S. atty. So. Dist. N.Y., 1953-57; first asst. tax div. and asst. dep. atty. gen. Dept. Justice, Washington, 1958-61; chief counsel Fed. Hwy. Adminstrn., Dept. Transp., Washington, 1967-69; partner firm Jones, Day, Reavis & Pogue, Washington, 1979—; dir. Office Rail Public Counsel, Washington, 1977-79; prof. law U. Wash., Seattle, 1965-67; cons. Pres.'s Commn. on Law Enforcement and Adminstrn. of Justice, Washington, 1965-66, Nat. Commn. on Product Safety, 1969-70. Author: Federal Consumer Safety Legislation, 1970. Served with U.S. Army, 1946-47. Mem. Assn. Bar City N.Y., D.C. Bar Assn., Am. Bar

Assn. Club: Harvard of N.Y.C. Office: 1735 Eye St NW Washington DC 20006

HEFLIN, HOWELL THOMAS, lawyer, U.S. Senator, former chief justice Supreme Ct. Ala.; b. Poulan, Ga., June 19, 1921; s. Marvin Rutledge and Louise D. (Strudwick) H.; m. Elizabeth Ann Carmichael, Feb. 23, 1952; 1 son, Howell Thomas. A.B., Birmingham So. Coll., 1942; J.D., U. Ala., 1948, LL.D. (hon.); LL.D. (hon.), U. No. Ala., Samford U., Del. Law Sch., Widener Coll., Troy State U., Ala. Christian Coll.; D.H.H., Birmingham So. Coll., 1980. Bar: Ala. 1948. Practiced in, Tuscumbia; sr. partner firm Heflin, Rosser and Munsey; chief justice Supreme Ct. Ala., 1971-77; chmn. Nat. Conf. Chief Justices, 1976-77; U.S. Senator, 1979—; chmn. Ethics Com.; mem. Judiciary Com., Commerce, Sci. and Transp. Com., Agr. Com.; Bd. dirs. Meth. Pub. House, 1952-64; lectr. U. Ala., 1946-48, U. North Ala., 1948-52; Tazewell Taylor vis. prof. law Coll. William and Mary, 1977. Mem. Ala. Edn. Commn., 1957-58; chmn. Colbert County A.R.C., 1950; Ala. field dir. Crusade for Children, 1948; pres. Ala. Com. Better Schs., 1958-59; chmn. Tuscumbia Bd. Edn., 1954-64, Ala. Tenure Commn., 1959-64; pres. U. Ala. Law Sch. Found., 1964-66; co-chmn. NCCJ, Tri-Cities area, 1949-70; chmn. Brotherhood Week; bd. dirs., v.p. Nat. Center for State Cts., 1975-77; trustee Birmingham So. Coll.; hon. pres. Troy State U. Served to maj. USMC, 1942-46. Decorated Silver Star, Purple Heart; recipient Ala. Citizen of Yr. award Ala. Cable TV Assn., 1973, 82; Outstanding Alumnus award U. Ala. and Birmingham So. Coll., 1973; Herbert Lincoln Harley award Am. Judicature Soc., 1973; Justice award, 1981; Ala. Citizen of Year award Ala. Broadcasters Assn., 1975; mem. Ala. Acad. Honor; named Outstanding Appellate Judge in U.S. Assn. Trial Lawyers Am., 1976; recipient Highest award Am. Judges Assn., 1975, Thomas Jefferson award Ala. Press Assn., 1979; Inst. Human Relations award, 1980; Silver Chalice award Am. Council on Alcoholism, 1980; Disting. Am. award Nat. Football Found. and Hall of Fame; Warren E. Burger award Inst. Ct. Mgmt.; others. Fellow Internat. Acad. of Law and Scis., Internat. Acad. Trial Lawyers, Internat. Soc. Barristers, Am. Coll. Trial Lawyers; mem. Ala. Law Inst. (v.p.), ABA, Ala. Bar Assn. (pres. 1965-66), Colbert County Bar Assn. (past pres.), Ala. Bar Found. (past pres.), Am. Judicature Soc. (v.p. 1977-79), Ala. Law Sch. Alumni Assn. (past pres.), Ala. Trial Lawyers Assn. (pres.), V.F.W., Am. Legion, 40 and 8, D.A.V., Third Marine Div. Assn., Omicron Delta Kappa, Phi Delta Phi, Tau Kappa Alpha, Lambda Chi Alpha. Methodist. Office: 725 Hart Senate Office Bldg Washington DC 20510

HEFNER, HUGH MARSTON, magazine publisher; b. Chgo., Apr. 9, 1926; s. Glenn L. and Grace (Swanson) H.; m. Mildred M. Williams, June 25, 1949 (div.); children: Christie A., David P. B.S., U. Ill., 1949. Subscription promotion writer Esquire mag., 1951; promotion mgr. Pubs. Devel. Corp., 1952; circulation mgr. Children's Activities mag., 1953; chmn. bd. HMH Pub. Co. Inc. (now Playboy Enterprises, Inc.), 1953—, also chief exec. officer; editor, pub. Playboy mag., from 1953; pres. Playboy Clubs Internat., Inc., from 1959; editor, pub. VIP mag., 1963-75, Oui mag., 1972-81. Served with AUS, 1944-46. Named Mag. Man of Yr. Mag. Industry Newsletter, 1967; recipient 1st Amendment Freedom award B'nai B'rith Anti-Defamation League, Los Angeles, 1980. Office: 919 N Michigan Ave Chicago IL 60611 *

HEFNER, ROBERT ALAN, judge; b. Los Angeles, May 24, 1929; s. Earl C. and Igerna Nellie (Ferguson) H.; m. Elizabeth Sykes, Dec. 17, 1955; children—Coral E., Robert Alan. B.A., U. Calif., Los Angeles, 1955, LL.D., 1958. Bar: U.S. Dist. Ct. bar, So. Dist. Calif 1959, Calif. bar 1959, U.S. Supreme Ct. bar 1964. Practiced law, Escondido, Calif., 1959-68, 71-74; asst. atty. gen. Saipan (Mariana Islands) Trust Terr., Pacific Islands, 1968-69, dep. atty. gen., 1969-70, atty. gen., 1970-71; asso. justice High Ct. Trust Terr., Pacific Islands, Palau, Western Caroline Islands, Saipan, Mariana Islands, 1974-79; chief judge Commonwealth Ct., Saipan, 1979—; instr. in real estate law and gen. law Palomar Jr. Coll., 1965-66. Pres. Escondido Republican Club, 1962-63; campaign mgr. Republican Congl. Candidate, N. San Diego County, 1972; chmn. Escondido Planning Commn., 1963-68. Served with USN, 1950-54; Korea. Recipient Man of Yr. award Jr. C. of C. of Escondido, 1963. Mem. ABA, Calif. Bar Assn., No. San Diego County Bar Assn. (pres. 1962-63), San Diego County Bar Assn. (v.p. 1963-64), Trust Terr. Bar Assn., Escondido C. of C. (pres. 1963-64). Home: Saipan Mariana Islands 96950 Office: Courthouse Saipan Mariana Islands 96950

HEFNER, THOMAS REEDER, insurance company executive, consultant; b. Akron, Ohio, Nov. 7, 1925; s. Paul Reeder and Opal (McPherson) H.; m. Jean Constance Kendle, Feb. 11, 1950; 1 dau., Constance Sheridan. B.S., Marshall U., Huntington, W.Va., 1950. Agent Life Ins. Co. Va., 1950-51; with Govt. Employees Life Ins. Co., 1951-81, exec. v.p., 1974-75, pres., 1975-81, chief exec. officer, 1976-81, vice chmn. bd., 1981-82; ins. cons., 1982—; v.p. Govt. Employees Ins. Co., 1975-76, Govt. Employees Fin. Corp., 1975-76, Criterion Ins. Co., 1975-76. Trustee Asbury Meth. Village, Gaithersburg, Md., 1981—; mem. exec. bd. Nat. Capital Area council Boy Scouts Am., 1981—. Served with USAAF, 1944-46. Club: Argyle Country. Home: 8415 Galveston Rd Silver Spring MD 20910 Office: 1701 Research Blvd Rockville MD 20850

HEFNER, W. G. (BILL HEFNER), congressman; b. Elora, Tenn., Apr. 11, 1930; s. Emory James and Icie Jewel (Holderfield) H.; m. Nancy Louise Hill, Mar. 23, 1952; children: Stacye Hugh, Shelly Gay. Grad. high sch. Mem. 94th-98th Congresses from 8th N.C. Dist.; mem. Dem. steering and policy com., appropriations com., budget com. Former profl. entertainer with, Harvesters Quartet; former performer weekly gospel show, WXII-TV, Winston-Salem, N.C.; also appeared on, WBTV, Charlotte, N.C., WRAL-TV, Raleigh, N.C., WGHP-TV, High Point, N.C., WBTW-TV, Florence, S.C. Bd. dirs. Piedmont Residential Redevel. Center, Concord, N.C. Democrat. Home: Concord NC Office: 2161 Rayburn House Office Bldg Washington DC 20515

HEFTEL, CECIL, Congressman; b. Cook County, Ill., Sept. 30, 1924; m. Joyce Glasmann; children—Cathi, Lani, Peggy, Susan, Christopher, Terry, Richard. B.S., Ariz. State U., 1951; postgrad., U. Utah, N.Y. U. Pres. Heftel Broadcasting Co.; mem. 95th-98th Congresses from 1st Hawaii Dist.; mem. Ways and Means com. Active March of Dimes. Mem. Am. Legion. Democrat. Clubs: Elks, Eagles, Shriners. Office: 1030 Longworth House Office Bldg Washington DC 20515

HEFTI, NEAL PAUL, composer, music publisher; b. Hastings, Nebr., Oct. 29, 1922; s. John Henry and Norma (Conway) H.; m. Chiarina Francesca Bertocci, Nov. 3, 1945; children: Marguerita Christina, Paul Anthony. Grad. high sch. Operator music pub. cos., 1950—; pres. Neal Hefti Music, Inc., Marguerita Music Corp., Encino Music Co. Trumpet player with, Woody Herman, Harry James orchs., 1942-50; leader own orch., 1950-60; condr.: Arthur Godfrey Show, CBS-TV, 1954, Kate Smith Show, CBS-TV, 1960, ABC Network, 1957, NBC Bandstand, 1957; composer scores for motion pictures, 1964—, including, Sex and the Single Girl, 1964, How to Murder Your Wife, 1964, Synanon, 1965, Harlow, 1965, Boeing-Boeing, 1965, Lord Love A Duck, 1965, Batman TV Theme, 1966 (Grammy award), Duel at Diablo, 1966, Oh Dad Poor Dad, 1966, Barefoot in the Park, 1967, P.J, 1967, The Odd Couple, 1967; musical dir.: The Fred Astaire Show, NBC-TV Spl, 1968 (recipient Emmy award), The Odd Couple TV series, 1970; Composer: Coral Reef, 1951, Lil Darlin, Don't Dream of Anybody But Me, 1958, Cute, 1958, I Must Know, 1964, Lonely Girl, 1965, Girl Talk, 1965, Batman Theme, 1966, Barefoot in the Park, 1967, Fred, 1968, The Odd Couple, theme, 19680, Gotham City Municipal Swing Band, 1966. Mem. A.S.C.A.P., Nat. Acad. Recording Arts and Scis. (past bd. govs.), Composers and Lyricists Guild Am. Roman Catholic. Office: care ABC 1995 Broadway Room 501 New York NY 10023 *

HEGARTY, THOMAS JOSEPH, university executive; b. Boston, Dec. 6, 1935; s. Thomas John and Abigail Barbara (Dunlap) H.; s. Louisa Ivanova, May, 1959; children: Alton Dunlap, Allison McAndrew. A.B., Harvard U., 1957, A.M., 1958, Ph.D., 1965; cert., Inst. Ednl. Mgmt. Harvard U., 1973. Asst. prof. history and history of ideas Brandeis U., 1962-67; assoc. prof. history, chmn. Soviet and East European studies program Boston U., 1961-71; assoc. prof. history, dean grad. studies Boston State Coll., 1971-78; prof. history, v.p. provost SUNY-Potsdam, 1978-82; v.p. aacad. affairs Butler U., Indpls., 1982—; assoc. Russian Research Ctr., Harvard U., 1968-72. Bd. dirs. Internat. Ctr., Indpls., 1983—, Park-Tudor Sch., Indpls., 1983—. Fellow Ford Found., 1957-61. Mem. Indpls. Council World Affairs, Am. Assn. State Colls. and Univs., Resource Ctr. for Planned Change. Episcopalian. Office: Office Acad Affairs 600 Sunset Ave Indianapolis IN 46208

HEGARTY, WILLIAM EDWARD, lawyer; b. N.Y.C., Nov. 18, 1926; s. William Alfred and Mary Johanna (Condon) H.; m. Barbara Meade Fischer, Oct. 26, 1950; children—Katharine Hegarty Bouman, Mary Hegarty Colombo, William, Amanda. A.B., Princeton U., 1947; LL.B., Yale U., 1950. Bar: N.Y. 1951, U.S. Supreme Ct. 1962, D.C. 1973. With firm Cahill, Gordon & Reindel (and predecessors), N.Y.C., 1950—, ptnr., 1962—, sr. ptnr., 1969—. Served with USNR, 1944-46. Mem. Am. Bar Assn., Assn. Bar City N.Y., Am. Law Inst., Am. Coll. Trial Lawyers., Am. Bar Found., N.Y.C. Legal Aid Soc. (dir.). Clubs: Indian Harbor Yacht, India House. Home: Mead's Point Greenwich CT 06830 Office: 80 Pine St New York NY 10005

HEGARTY, WILLIAM KEVIN, med. center exec.; b. Sask., Can., Feb. 14, 1926; came to U.S., 1951; s. William Alexander and Lila (Taylor) H.; m. Doreen Alice Symon, Sept. 8, 1951; children—Kelley, Kerry, Michael. B. Commerce, U. Man., 1949; M.H.A., Northwestern U., 1953. Exec. dir. Calif. Hosp., Los Angeles, 1966-69; v.p. Lutheran Hosp. Soc., Los Angeles, 1969-74; pres. Huntington Meml. Hosp., Pasadena, Calif., 1974—; Bd. dirs. Blue Cross of So. Calif. Contbr. articles to profl. jours. Mem. Am. Hosp. Assn., Calif. Hosp. Assn. (pres. 1977, Outstanding Service award), Hosp. Council So. Calif. (pres. 1973), Assn. Am. Med. Colls. Congregationalist. Club: Rotary Internat. Home: 1745 Chelsea Rd San Marino CA 91108 Office: 100 Congress St Pasadena CA 91105

HEGELMANN, JULIUS, pharmacy educator; b. N.Y.C., Oct. 19, 1921; s. Julius and Augusta (Schubert) H.; m. Marjorie Scallon, May 30, 1943; children: Marjorie Ann (Mrs. Gerome Thompson), Jill Marie (Mrs. F. Menshel). B.S. in Pharmacy, Rutgers U., 1943. Prodn. mgr. Ebbilhuber Inc., 1939-50; v.p., sales mgr., dir. Knoll Pharm. Co., 1950-62; with Hegelmann & Bartolone Inc., N.Y.C., 1962-70, chmn. bd., 1962-70; pres. J. Hegelmann Assos., Inc., Franklin Lakes, N.J., 1970-73; asst. prof., dir. pharm. extension services Rutgers U., New Brunswick, N.J., 1973-78, asso. prof., 1978—; exec. sec. Rutgers Nat. Pharm. Conf. Author: The Evolution of Knoll Pharmaceutical Company 1904-1975, The 75th Anniversary. Pres. Orange (N.J.) C. of C., 1956; trustee Franklin Lakes Library; mem. Franklin Lakes Bd. Adjustment. Served with AUS, 1943-46; ETO; 1st lt. Res. Fellow Am. Soc. Cons. Pharm.; mem. Am. Mgmt. Assn., Am. Pharm. Assn., Pharm. Advt. Club, Am. Assn. Colls. Pharmacy, Am. Inst. History of Pharmacy, N.J. Acad. Cons. Pharm., Delta Sigma Theta, Rho Chi. Club: Rotarian (pres. Orange 1956). Home: 263 Arbor Rd Franklin Lakes NJ 07417 Office: Rutgers U New Brunswick NJ

HEGENER, MARK PAUL, publisher, clergyman; b. Petoskey, Mich., Apr. 6, 1919; s. John and Anna Marie (Mayer) H. A.B., St. Joseph Sem., Teutopolis, Ill., 1938; postgrad., 1942-46; postgrad., St. Joseph Sem., Cleve., 1939-42; B.J., Marquette U., 1948. Joined Order of Friars Minor, Roman Catholic Ch., 1938; ordained priest Order of Friars Minor Roman Catholic Ch., 1945; mng. dir. Franciscan Herald Press, Chgo., 1949—; pub. Franciscan Herald mag., 1955—; provincial dir. Lay Franciscans, 1949-79. Author: Poverello: St. Francis of Assissi, 1958, Short History of the Third Order of St. Francis, 1963. Pres., founder Mayslake Village Retirement Complex, Oak Brook, Ill., 1962—, Chariton Apts. Retirement Complex, St. Louis, 1968—; v.p. Back of the Yards Community Council, Chgo.; founder, trustee Cath. Theol. Union at Chgo., 1968-76; trustee Quincy Coll., 1972-76. Mem. Am. Home Builders Assn., Cath. Press Assn. Home: 5045 S Laflin St Chicago IL 60609 Office: 1434 W 51st St Chicago IL 60609

HEGG, GEORGE LENNART, diversified manufacturing company executive; b. Mpls., Oct. 5, 1930; s. Gunnar S. and Ruth S. (Hellberg) H.; m. Joan C. McLaughlin, Jan. 10, 1953; children: Deborah, Jeffrey. B.S. in Chem. Engring. and Bus. Adminstrn., U. Minn., 1952. With 3M Co., St. Paul, 1950—, v.p., 1975-79, mem. corp. mgmt. com., 1979—, group v.p. memory techs., 1983—; dir. Century Boat Co., Manistee, Mich., Southwall Technologies Corp., Palo Alto, Calif. Served with USNR. Republican. Clubs: White Bear Yacht (White Bear Lake, Minn.); St. Paul Athletic, Minneapolis; Desert Highlands Country (Scottsdale, Ariz.). Office: 3M Co Bldg 220/3M Center St Paul MN 55144

HEGGERS, JOHN PAUL, educator, microbiologist, retired army officer; b. Bklyn., Feb. 8, 1933; s. John and May (Hass) H.; m. Rosemarie Niklas, July 30, 1977; children: Arn M., Ronald R., Laurel M., Gary R., Renee L., Annette M. B.A. in Bacteriology, Mont. State U., 1958; M.S. in Microbiology, U. Md., 1965; Ph.D. in Bacteriology and Pub. Health, Wash. State U., 1972. Diplomate: Am. Bd. Bioanalysis. Med. technologist U.S. Naval Hosp., St. Albans, N.Y., 1951-53; bacteriologist Hahnemann Hosp., Worcester, Mass., 1958-59; commd. 2d lt. U.S. Army, 1959, advanced through grades to lt. col., 1975; mem. staff dept. bacteriology 1st U.S. Army Med. Lab., N.Y.C., 1959-60; chief clin. lab. U.S. Army Hosp., Verdun, France, 1960-63; chief virology and rickettsiology div. dept. microbiology 3d U.S. Army Med. Lab., Ft. McPherson, Ga., 1965-66; chief diagnostic bacteriology 9th Med. Lab., Saigon, Vietnam, 1966-67; chief microbiology div. dept. pathology Brooke Gen. Hosp., Ft. Sam Houston, Tex., 1967-69; lab. scis. officer Office Surgeon Gen., Washington, 1972-74; microbiologist spl. mycobacterial disease br. div. geog. pathology Armed Forces Inst. Pathology, Washington, 1973, spl. asst. to dir., 1973-74; chief clin. research lab. clin. research service Madigan Army Med. Center, Tacoma, 1974-76, asst. chief clin. investigation service, 1976-77; ret., 1977; asso. prof. dept. surgery U. Chgo., 1977-80, prof., 1980—; instr. bacteriology Basic Lab. Sch., Ft. McPherson, 1965-66; chmn. dept. microbiology U.S. Army Sch. Med. Tech., Ft. Sam Houston, 1967-69; instr. bacteriology eve. div. San Antonio Jr. Coll., 1969; instr. immunology, parasitology and mycology Clover Park Vocat. Tech. Inst., 1976-77. Author: Current Problems in Surgery, 1973; Contbr. articles to profl. jours.; Contbg. editor: Jour. Am. Med. Tech, 1972—. Decorated Bronze Star; Legion of Merit; recipient certificate of appreciation A.C.S., 1969, Armed Forces Inst. Pathology, 1974; Valley Forge Honor certificate Freedoms Found., 1974; Fisher award in med. tech. Am. Med. Technologists, 1968, 82; Gerard B. Lambert award, 1973; Ednl. Found. Research award Am. Soc. Plastic and Reconstructive Surgery, 1978. Fellow N.Y. Acad. Sci., Am. Acad. Microbiology, Royal Soc. Tropical Medicine and Hygiene, Am. Geriatrics Soc.; mem. Nat. Registry Microbiologists (chmn. exec. council 1976-79), Am. Soc. Microbiology (chmn. com. tellers 1974-75), Wash. Soc. Am. Med. Technologists (pres. 1975-77), Wash. Soc. Med. Tech. (chmn. sect. microbiology sci. assembly, dir. 1975-77), Assn. Mil. Surgeons U.S., Am. Soc. Clin. Pathologists (asso.), Am. Med. Technologists (disting. service award 1975, exceptional merit award 1976, nat. dir. 1979-80, nat. sec. 1980-82, nat. v.p. 1982—, Technologist of Yr. 1983), Am. Burn Assn. (President's continuing edn. award 1981), Plastic Surgery Research Council, Surg. Infection Soc. (charter), Ill. State Soc., Med. Technologists (v.p. 1979), AVMA, Internat. Soc. for Burn Injuries, Sigma Xi. Club: Elks. Home: 10S-082 Lakewood Dr Hinsdale IL 60521 Office: Box 269 Dept Surgery U Chgo 950 E 59th St Chicago IL 60637 *The difficulties of life are only surmounted with compassion, consistency, and by painful study and preparation.*

HEGGIE, ROBERT JAMES, steel company executive; b. Gary, Ind., Dec. 27, 1913; s. Robert Bruce and Persis (Hart) H.; m. Maxine Dixon, Apr. 30, 1959; children: Frank Anderson, Robert Heggie (dec.), Karen Armstrong, Jane Major, Janet Anderson. Student, U. Ill., 1931-33. With A.M. Castle & Co., Franklin Park, Ill., 1934—, pres., 1961-80, now dir.; dir. Employers Mut. Ins. Co. of Wausau, 1st State Bank & Trust Co. of Franklin Bank. Mem. Am. Iron and Steel Inst., Steel Service Center Inst. (pres. 1961—, dir. 1953-70), Copper and Brass Wholesale Assn. (dir. 1965-70). Republican. Presbyterian. 12112 Caminito Campana San Diego CA 92128

HEGGLAND, RADOY WITT, energy company executive; b. Chgo., July 15, 1928; s. Thurlow Martin and Alice Marie (Witt) H.; m. Nancy Elizabeth Redd, June 12, 1949; children—Sherry, Sally. B.S., Calif. Inst. Tech., 1949; M.S. (Sloan fellow), Mass. Inst. Tech., 1965. Mem. geol. dept. staff Continental Oil co. (now Conoco Inc.), Wichita Falls, Tex., Roswell, N.Mex., New Orleans, Houston, 1949-62, divs. exploration mgr., Lafayette, La., 1962-64, chief geologist internat., N.Y.C., 1965-67, mgr. exploration for N. Am., Houston, 1967-69, v.p., 1970-76, exec. v.p. minerals, Denver, 1976—. Mem. Am. Assn. Petroleum Geologists, Am. Mining Congress., Soc. Mining Engrs. Clubs: Hiwan Golf, Denver Petroleum. Home: 31615 Canyon Circle Evergreen CO 80439 Office: 555 17th St Denver CO 80202

HEGINBOTHAM, ERLAND HOWARD, government official, economist; b. Salt Lake City, Oct. 29, 1931; s. Joseph Howard and Lois (White) H.; m. Eleanor Frances Elson, July 30, 1960; children: Robin Carol, Eric Erland. Student, Institut des Etudes Politiques, Paris, 1952-53; B.A. magna cum laude, Stanford U., 1954, postgrad., 1955, M.I.T., 1962-63. Research asst. Stanford Research Inst., 1953-55; research specialist Dept. State, Washington, 1955-58; asst. program officer ICA, Seoul, Korea, 1959-60; econ. officer Am. Embassy, Monrovia, 1960-62; chief program economist AID, Saigon, Viet Nam, 1963-66; dir. internat. monetary affairs Dept. State, Washington, 1967-70; econ. comml. counselor Am. Embassy, Jakarta, Indonesia, 1971-75; asso. asst. adminstr. for devel. coordination AID, 1975; v.p. for devel. and planning Overseas Pvt. Investment Corp., Washington, 1976; dep. asst. sec. econ. and comml. Bur. East Asian and Pacific Affairs, Dept. State, Washington, 1977-80; dir. gen. U.S. Fgn. Comml. Service, Dept. Commerce, 1980-82; sr. profl. staff mem. U.S. Senate Fgn. Relations Com., 1983—. Elder Nat. Presbyn. Ch., 1968-70. Fed. Exec. fellow Brookings Inst., 1970-71. Mem. Am. Fgn. Service Assn. (treas., mem. governing bd.), Asia Soc., Phi Beta Kappa. Home: 8502 Wilkesboro Ln Potomac MD 20854 Office: Dept Commerce 14th and Constitution Ave Washington DC 20230

HEGRE, THEODORE A., clergyman; b. Woodville, Wis., Mar. 17, 1908; s. Adolph and Maria (Bodsberg) H.; m. Lucile Alta Conley, Oct. 1, 1935; children: Jean Marie Hegre Mikkelson, Joane Carol Hegre Brooks. Ordained to ministry, 1944; pastor Bethany Missionary Ch., Mpls., 1943—; pres. Bethany Fellowship Inc., Mpls., 1945-83; prin. Bethany Fellowship Missionary Tng. Center, Mpls., 1948-80; internat. sec. Bethany Fellowship Missions, 1962—. Author: The Cross and Sanctification, 1960, How to Find Freedom from the Power of Sin, 1961, Creative Faith, 1980; contbr. articles to numerous jours. Home and office: 6820 Auto Club Rd Minneapolis MN 55438

HEGSTAD, ROLAND REX, mag. editor; b. Stayton, Oreg., Apr.7, 1926; s. Phillip Rol and Lydia Bertha (Prospal) H.; m. Stella M. Radke, Aug. 22, 1949; children—Douglas Roland, Sheryl Marie, Kimberly Marie. B.Th., Walla Walla Coll., 1949; M.A., Andrews U., Berrien Springs, Mich., 1954. Ordained to ministry Seventh-day Adventist Ch., 1955; pastor Upper Columbia Conf. Seventh-day Adventists, 1949-55; asst. editor, asso. editor These Times, mag., Nashville, 1955-58; book editor So. Pub. Assn., Nashville, 1958-59; acting editor Insight mag., Washington, 1971-72; editor Liberty mag., Washington, 1959—; Mem. Seventh-day Adventist Bd. Higher Edn., 1973-80; mem. exec. com. Gen. Conf. Seventh-day Adventists. Author: Who Causes Man's Suffering, 1965, Spirits, Man and Magic, 1973, As the Spirit Speaks, 1973, Rattling the Gates, 1974, Baseball Popcorn, Apple Pie and Liberty, 1979. Mem. Acad. Adventist Ministers, Walla Walla Alumni Assn., Andrews U. Alumni Assn. Club: Rotary. Home: 2121 Sondra Ct Silver Spring MD 20904 Office: 6840 Eastern Ave NW Washington DC 20012

HEGSTED, DAVID MARK, biochemistry educator, research administrator; b. Rexburg, Idaho, Mar. 25, 1914; s. John and Edna Margaret (Porter) H.; m. Maxine Scow, May 26, 1941; children: Christina, Eric John. B.S., U. Idaho, 1936; M.S., U. Wis., 1938, Ph.D., 1940; A.M. (hon.), Harvard U., 1962. Research asst. U. Wis., 1936-41; research chemist Abbott Labs., 1941-42; assoc. nutrition Harvard Schs. of Medicine and Pub. Health, 1942-43, asst. prof., 1943-48, assoc. prof., 1948-62, prof., 1962-80, prof. nutritron emeritus, 1980—; assoc. dir. research New Eng. Regional Primate Research Ctr. Harvard Sch. Medicine, 1982—; adminstr. Human Nutrition Center, U.S. Dept. Agr., Washington, 1978-82; Cons. nutrition to Colombian Govt., 1946; nutritionist Inst. Inter-Am. Affairs, Peru, 1950-51; cons. UN FAO, Chile, 1956, Rome, 1961, 69, WHO, 1962, 70, NIH, 1958—; mem. food and nutrition bd. NRC, 1955-72, chmn. food and nutrition bd., 1968-72. Editor: Nutrition Revs, 1968-78; contbr. articles, chpts. profl. jours. and books. Named to U. Idaho Hall of Fame, 1976. Mem. Am. Inst. Nutrition (Osborne Mendel award 1965, Conrad A. Elvehjem award 1979, pres. 1972-73), Am. Chem. Soc., Am. Pub. Health Assn., N.Y. Acad. Scis., Peruvian Pub. Health Soc., A.M.A. (council foods and nutrition 1960-68), Nat. Acad. Scis., Am. Dietetic Assn. (hon.), Sigma Xi, Alpha Chi Sigma, Sigma Alpha Epsilon. Clubs: Harvard, Cosmos. Home: 58 Boulder Rd Wellesley Hills MA 02115

HEGYI, ALBERT PAUL, association executive; b. Reading, Pa., Dec. 31, 1944; s. Frank and Adeline (Mazzolla) H.; m. Ceil A. Tompkins, Apr. 29, 1972; children: James Lawrence, Andrew Clark. A.B., Dartmouth Coll., 1965; M.B.A., 1966; J.D., U. Pa., 1969. With Assn. of M.B.A. Execs., Inc., N.Y.C., 1970—; pres. Assn. of M.B.A. Execs. Inc, 1970—.

HEGYI, JULIUS, conductor, musician; b. N.Y.C., Feb. 2, 1923; s. Francois and Rose (Konye) H.; m. Charlotte Ann Barrier, Aug. 27,

1953; 1 dau., Lisa. B.A., Juilliard Sch. Music, 1943; pupil violin, Sascha Jacobsen, Jacques Gordon, Eddy Brown; pupil composition, Vittorio Giannini; pupil conducting, Dimitri Mitropoulos. With music faculty Williams Coll., 1965—, lectr. music, condr. and violinist in residence, 1971—; spl. cons. Nat. Endowment for Arts, Washington, 1979—. Condr., Wagner Coll. Symphony, 1941-43; asso. condr., San Antonio Symphony, 1948-51; condr., San Antonio Little Orch., 1949-51, Abilene (Tex.) Symphony, 1952-55, Southwestern Symphony Center, 1951-56, Chattanooga Symphony, 1955-65; founder-dir., Sewanee Summer Music Center, 1958; founder-condr., Carlatti Orch., 1964; debut violinist, Town Hall, N.Y., 1945, chamber music concerts, solo recitals, U.S., Mexico; founder, Hegyi and Amati string quartets, 1941, Music in the Round series, 1951; mem., Gordon, Am. string quartets, N.Y. Philharmonic, City Center Ballet, RCA Victor Symphony, N.Y. Little Orch. Soc.; performer: complete Beethoven String Quartet cycle Music in the Round series, Bershire Quartet, 1970; mem., Williams Trio; dir. chamber music activities; music dir., condr., Albany (N.Y.) Symphony, 1966—, Berkshire Symphony. Recipient Frank Damrosch Scholarship, 1941, Alice Ditson award for service, 1957, nat. condr. recognition award Am. Symphony League, 1959; award for artistic excellence Albany League Arts, 1977; Alice M. Ditson Condrs. award Columbia U., 1983. Home: Northwest Hill Rd Williamstown MA 01267

HEH, JACK CHIEN-KUO, chemical engineer; b. China, Sept. 3, 1944; s. Chia-Heng and Yen-Kuer (Shih) Ho; m. Sheau-Yen Kuo, June 28, 1969; children: Ca-May, Karen. Ph.D., Kent State U., 1978. Chmn. engr. Chung Tai Rubber Goods Mfg. Co., Ltd., Taipei, Taiwan, 1970-73; instr. Central Police Coll., Taipei, 1972-73; postdoctoral fellow Marquette U., Milw., 1978-79; scientist Magnetic Peripherals, Inc., Mpls., 1979—. Mem. Am. Chem. Soc., Soc. Rheology. Home: 9485 Garrison Way Eden Prairie MN 55344 Office: Magnetic Peripheralss Inc 7801 Computer Ave Minneapolis MN 55435

HEHEMANN, ROBERT FREDERICK, educator; b. Cin., Feb. 10, 1921; s. Fred H. and Edna (Timberman) H.; m. Ruth Louise Graham, Sept. 8, 1945; children—David G., Elizabeth A. B.S. in Engring, U. Mich., 1943; M.S., Case Inst. Tech., 1949, Ph.D., 1953. Mem. faculty Case Western Res. U., 1946—, prof. metall. engring., 1959—, acting head dept. of metallurgy, 1967-69; research asso. Argonne Nat. Lab., summer 1965. Contbr. profl. jours. Served to capt. AUS, 1943-46. Fellow Am. Soc. Metals (Bradley Stoughton award 1958); mem. Am. Inst. M.E., Sigma Xi, Tau Beta Pi, Iota Alpha, Phi Eta Sigma, Sigma Alpha Epsilon, Scabbard and Blade. Home: 7280 Shadowbrook Dr Kirtland OH 44094 Office: Case Western Res U Univ Circle Cleveland OH 44106

HEHMEYER, ALEXANDER, lawyer; b. N.Y.C., Oct. 20, 1910; s. Frederick William and Catherine Enole (Schrader) H.; m. Florence Isobel Millar, Oct. 10, 1936 (dec. 1967); children: Alexander Millar, Christine McKesson; m. Sheila Mary Vought, 1968. B.S., Yale U., 1932; LL.B., Columbia U., 1935. Bar: N.Y. 1936, Ill. 1968. Asso. firm Cravath, Swaine and Moore, N.Y.C., 1935-40, 44-46; asst. to chmn. Time, Inc., 1940-43; legal-econ. cons. Fgn. Econ. Adminstrn., 1943-44; partner firm Paul, Weiss, Rifkind, Wharton & Garrison, N.Y.C., 1946-67; exec. v.p., gen. counsel, dir., mem. exec. com. Field Enterprises, Inc., Chgo., 1967-75; counsel firm Isham, Lincoln & Beale, Chgo., 1976-82; v.p., dir. Gahagan Dredging Corp., 1953-70; dir., mem. exec. com. Am. Heritage Pub. Co., Inc., 1954-69; dir. AM. Research Bur., 1965-69, Field Creations, Inc., Field Communications Corp., Field Enterprises Endl. Corp., Field Enterprises Realty Corp., FSC Paper Corp., Manistique Pulp & Paper Co., Met. Printing Co., P.H.S. Finance Corp., World Book Life Ins. Co., Field Enterprises Charitable Corp.; mem. mgmt. bd. Kaiser Broadcasting Co., Field Newspaper Syndicate, 1967-75. Author: Time for Change, 1943. Vice chmn., counsel U.S. Econ. Missions to West Berlin, 1952, Gold Coast, 1954; trustee, chmn. Midwest adv. bd. Inst. Internat. Edn.; trustee Kent (Conn.) Sch.; mem. adv. council Peace Corps; pres. N.Y. Young Republican Club, 1944-46. Fellow ABA; mem. Ill., N.Y. State, Chgo. bar assns., Assn. Bar City N.Y., Chgo. Council Fgn. Relations (past vice chmn., mem. exec. com.), Phi Gamma Delta. Clubs: University (N.Y.C.); Commercial, Chicago, Racquet, Saddle and Cycle (Chgo.). Home: 1332 Sandburg terr Chicago IL 60610 also 57 Owenoke Park Westport CT 06880

HEIBERG, ELVIN RAGNVALD, III, civil engineer, army officer; b. Schofield Barracks, Hawaii, Mar. 2, 1932; s. Elvin R. and Evelyn (Lytle) H.; m. Kathryn Louise Schrimpf, June 16, 1953; children: Kathryn Anna Heiberg Young, Walter Dodge, Elvin Ragnvald IV, Kay Louise. B.S., U.S. Mil. Acad., 1953; M.S.C.E., MIT, 1958; M.A. in Govt, George Washington U., 1961; M.S. in Adminstrn, George Washington U., 1971. Registered profl. engr., La. Commd. 2d lt. U.S. Army, 1953, advanced through grades to maj. gen., 1978; service in, Korea, 1954-55, co. comdr., Germany, 1961-62; faculty U.S. Mil. Acad., 1965-68; bn. comdr., Vietnam, 1968-69, detailed to Exec. Office of Pres., 1969-70, staff positions in Pentagon, 1971-74, dist. engr. C.E., New Orleans, 1974-75, div. engr. C.E., Ohio River, 1975-78; engr. U.S. Army-Europe, 1978-79; dir. civil works, Washington, 1979-82, dep. chief of engrs., 1982-83; program mgr. Army Ballistic Missile Dep. Orgn., Washington, 1983—; v.p. Permanent Internat. Assn. Nav. Congresses., 1983—. Pres. Stratford-on-the-Potomac Citizens Assn., 1972-73; mem. Mississippi River Commn., 1975-78, Ohio River Commn., 1975-78. Decorated Silver Star, Legion of Merit (3), D.F.C.; recipient Meritorious Service award Office Emergency Preparedness, 1970. Mem. ASCE, Soc. Am. Mil. Engrs., Assn. U.S. Army, Assn. Grads. U.S. Mil. Acad., Res. Officers Assn., Ret. Officers Assn. Methodist. Office: Program Mgr Army Ballistic Missile Dep Orgn Washington DC 20314 *Engineering is a profession which demands much but gives much, and does not tolerate major errors. An Army officer's calling also demands much but gives much, and the contribution to a strong United States defense helps insure peace. Both these professions require a deep understanding of people, and my twin careers are built on insuring top performance.*

HEIDEL, CHARLES MACLEISH, electric company executive; b. Detroit, July 19, 1925; s. Charles Richard and Anna Laura (MacLeish) H.; m. Barbara Cele, Aug. 7, 1948; children: Kerry, Kathy Heidel Okla, Kenneth, Keith, Karol. B.S. in Mech. Engring, Iowa State U., 1947. Registered profl. engr., Mich. With Detroit Edison Co., 1947—, mgr. engring., 1970-71, mgr. ops., 1971-73, v.p. engring. and constrn., 1973-75, exec. v.p. divs., 1975-77, exec. v.p. ops., 1977-81, pres., chief operating officer, 1981—; dir. 1st Fed. Savs. & Loan. Bd. dirs. Children's Hosp. Served in USNR, 1943-46. Mem. ASME, Engring. Soc. Detroit, Soc. Am. Mil. Engrs., Edison Electric Inst. Clubs: Detroit Athletic, Econ. (Detroit). Office: Detroit Edison Co 2000 2d Ave Detroit MI 48226 *

HEIDELBERGER, KATHLEEN PATRICIA, physician; b. Bklyn., Apr. 13, 1939; d. William Cyprian and Margaret Bernadette (Hughes) H.; m. Charles William Davenport, Oct. 8, 1977. B.S. cum laude, Coll. Misericordia, 1961, M.D., Woman's Med. Coll. Pa., 1965. Intern Mary Hitchcock Hosp., Hanover, N.H., 1965-66, resident in pathology, 1966-70; mem. faculty U. Mich., Ann Arbor, 1970—, assoc. prof. pathology, 1976-79, prof., 1979—. Mem. Am. Soc. Clin. Pathologists, Internat. Acad. Pathology, Pediatric Pathology Club, Coll. Am. Pathologists. Office: Dept Pathology Box 045 U Mich Ann Arbor MI 48109

HEIDEMANN, ROBERT ALBERT, chemical engineering educator, researcher; b. St. Louis, Aug. 31, 1936; emigrated to Can., 1968; s. William Joseph and Gladys Emilie (Digma) H.; m. Linda Bea Szold, June 9, 1968; children: David, Douglas. B.Sc. in Chem. Engring., Washington U., St. Louis, 1958, Sc.D., 1966. Asst. prof. chem. engring. Drexel Inst. Tech., Phila., 1963-68; assoc. prof. U. Calgary (Alta.), 1968-77, prof., 1977—, head dept. chem. and petroleum engring., 1981—; cons., 1982—. Co-author: (with M.F. Mohtadi) Properties of Gases and Liquid, 1973; author: Three Phases of Matter, 1978; contbr. articles to profl. jours. Fellow Chem. Inst. Can.; mem. Canadian Soc. Chem. Engrs., Am. Inst. Chem. Engrs., Am. Chem. Soc., Am. Soc. Engring. Edn., Assn. Profl. Engrs., Geologists and Geophysicists of Alta., Tau Beta Pi. Home: 6212 Dalmarnock Crescent NW Calgary AB Canada T3A 1H2 Office: U Calgary 2500 University Dr NW Calgary AB Canada T3N 1N4, consumer finance company executive

HEIDEN, CHARLES KENNETH, former army officer, metals company executive; b. Detroit, July7, 1925; s. Carl William and Elsie Mae (Langley) H.; m. Nancy Earle Gray, June 7, 1949; 1 son, Charles Gray. B.S., U.S. Mil. Acad., 1949; M.S. in Mech. Engring, U. Mich., 1957; grad. mgmt. execs. program, U. Pitts., 1971. Registered profl. engr., Ky. Commd. 2d lt. U.S. Army, 1949, advanced through grades to maj. gen., 1977; services in, France, Korea and Vietnam; dep. dir. ops. Nat. Mil. Command Center, Joint Chiefs of Staff, 1973-74; dir. enlisted personnel U.S. Mil. Personnel Center, Washington, 1974-76; comdr. U.S. Army Mil. Personnel Center, 1977-80; comdg. gen. U.S. Army Tng. Command, Ft. Dix, N.J., 1980-81; pres. Montel Metals Inc., 1981—. Bd. dirs. Park Glen Heights Assn., Annandale, Va., 1974-76, Cedar Lake Lodge Inc., La Grange, Ky.; pres. Our Saviour Luth. Ch., Arlington, Va., 1974-76. Decorated D.S.M., D.F.C., Legion of Merit with 3 oak leaf clusters, Air medal with 10 oak leaf clusters, Joint Services Commendation medal, Army Commendation medal with 2 oak leaf clusters, Meritorious Service medal with oak leaf cluster; Cross of Gallantry with silver star, Vietnam; recipient Pace award Office Sec. Army, 1963. Mem. Nat. Soc. Profl. Engrs., Armed Forces Relief and Benefit Assn. (dir. 1977-81), West Point Alumni Assn., U.S. Armour Assn., U.S. Army War Coll. Alumni Assn., 4th Inf. Div. Assn. Home: 10500 Brookhill Ct Louisville KY 40223

HEIDEN, HEINO, choreographer, dir., balletmaster; b. Barmen, Germany, Oct. 6, 1923; s. Gerhard and Madeleine (Devreker) H. Grad. high sch. Soloist with State Opera, Berlin, 1946-48; soloist, balletmaster, State Opera Dresden, 1948-49; soloist, Komische Opera Berlin, 1949; balletmaster, Hamburg Ballet Theater Co., 1950; soloist, Ballet de France, Paris, 1951; soloist, balletmaster, States Operetta, Munich; tchr., choreographer, B.C. Sch. of Dancing, B.C. Ballet, Vancouver, 1952-54; choreographer, Can. Broadcasting Co., Montreal, 1954-60; free lance choreographer, Royal Winnipeg Ballet, 1959, Washington Ballet, 1957-65; dir., choreographer, Royal Opera, Antwerp, Belgium, 1966, choreographies for, Scapino Ballet, Amsterdam, 1968, Nat. Theatre, Mannheim, Germany, 1960-63; dir., Ballet of Lubeck and Kiel, Germany, 1967-69, State Opera Munich, 1969, others; choreographer, Can. Nat. Ballet La Prima Ballerina, Expo-Montreal, 1967; founder, dir., Galerie Heino Heiden, 1971—; founder Lübecker Kinder-Tanz-Theater Heino Heiden, 1977. Recipient 1st prize Daphnis and Chloe B.C. Ballet. Can. Ballet Festival Assn., 1953. Home: 1280 St Marc St Apt 1410 Montreal PQ Canada Office: Die Schule fur Ballett 24 Lübeck Dr Julius-Leber St Str 23 West Germany

HEIDENHEIM, ROGER STEWART, automotive and electronic consultant; b. Phila., Oct. 5, 1909; s. Samuel and Rose (Sadler) H.; m. Edna June Heidenheim; 1 son, Taylor. Ed., U. Calif. Mem. staff sales dept. McQuay Norris Mfg. Co., St. Louis, 1929-42, dist. sales mgr., 1946-54, nat. sales mgr., 1954-59, exec. v.p., 1960-68, pres., 1968—, also dir.; cons. automotive and electronic industries, 1979—; pres. Am. Automotive Products Co., Advt. Distributors, Inc., McQuay Norris, Inc., 1977; v.p., dir. Dura Bond Bearing Co., Palo Alto, Calif.; v.p. Eaton Corp., Cleve., 1971-79; pres. McQuay Norris Mfg. Co., Toronto, Can., 1976-79, also dir.; cons. SKF Industries, Phila., 1978-79; dir. Permancer Corp., St. Louis, MCR Tech. Inc., Goleta, Calif.; Bd. dirs. Nat. Standard Parts Assn., Chgo., 1957-58, Automotive Service Industry Assn., 1961-64; chmn. Automotive Engine Rebuilders Assn. Affiliate Council, 1964-66; pres. Piston and Pin Mfg. Group, 1965-66, Piston Ring Mfg. Group, 1967-68, Engine Bearing Mfg. Group, 1972-73. Mem. President's Council St. Louis U. Served as maj. AUS, 1942-46. Mem. Nat. Engine Parts Mfg. Assn. (dir., pres. 1972-73). Club: Montecito (Calif.) Country. Home and office: 1500 E Mountain Dr Santa Barbara CA 93108

HEIDENREICH, DOUGLAS ROBERT, lawyer; b. St. Paul, Feb. 29, 1932; s. Raymond F. and Pearl E. (Duncanson) H.; children—Lisa, Beth, John. A.B., U. Minn., 1953; J.D., William Mitchell Coll. Law, 1961. Bar: Minn. bar 1961. Asso. firm Erickson, Popham, Haik & Schnobrich, Mpls., 1961-63; asst. prof. law, asst. dean William Mitchell Coll. Law, 1963-64, prof., dean, 1964-75, prof., 1975—; spl. master in antibiotics anti-trust litigation U.S. Dist. Ct. for Dist. Minn., 1971-77; exec. dir. Minn. Bd. Continuing Legal Edn., 1975—; lectr. continuing edn. Mem. Minn. Gov.'s Commn. on Crime Prevention and Control, 1972-75; mem. Minn. Bd. Human Rights, 1972-75. Contbg. author: Mich. Inst. Continuing Legal Edn. Mem. Am., Minn. bar assns., Am. Law Inst., Selden Soc. Home: 11 Summit Ct 16 Saint Paul MN 55102 Office: 875 Summit Ave Saint Paul MN 55105

HEIDER, JON VINTON, lawyer, corporate executive; b. Moline, Ill., Mar. 1, 1934; s. Raymond and Doris (Hinch) H.; Dec. 27, 1960 (div.); children: Loren P., John C., Lindsay L. A.B., U. Wis., 1956; J.D., Harvard U., 1961; grad., Advanced Mgmt. Program, 1974. Bar: Pa. 1962, U.S. Dist. Ct. for Eastern Dist. Pa 1962, U.S. 3d Circuit Ct 1962. Assoc. Morgan Lewis & Bockius, Phila., 1961-66; counsel Catalytic, Inc., Phila., 1966-68, Houdry Process & Chem. Co., 1968-70; counsel chems. group Air Products & Chems., Inc., Valley Forge, Pa., 1970-75, asst. gen. counsel, 1975-76, assoc. gen. counsel, 1976-78, gen. counsel, Allentown, Pa., 1978-80, v.p. corp. devel., 1983—; v.p.-corp. affairs and sr. adminstrv. officer-Europe Air Products Europe, Inc., London, 1980-83. Served to lt. USNR, 1956-58. Office: PO Box 538 Allentown PA 18108

HEIDER, KAR GUSTAV, anthropology educator; b. Northampton, Mass., Jan. 21, 1935; s. Fritz and Grace (Moore) H.; m. Eleanor Rosch, Jan. 1967 (div. 1973); m. 2d Mary Elizabeth Bruton, Nov. 27, 1976; children: Mary Winn, John Bruton, Paul Moore. Student, Williams Coll., 1952-54; B.A., Harvard U., 1956; postgrad., U. Vienna, Austria, 1957-58; M.A., Harvard U., Ph.D., 1965. Instr. Harvard U., Cambridge, Mass., 1965-66; asst. prof., then assoc. prof. Brown U., Providence, 1966-71; vis. assoc. prof. U. Calif.-Berkeley, 1971-73; lectr. Stanford U., Calif., 1972-74, UCLA, 1973-74; prof. anthropology, chmn. dept. U. S.C., Columbia, 1975—. Co-author: Gardens of War, 1969; author: Ethnographic Film, 1976, Grand Valley Dani, 1979; producer: film Dani Sweet Potatoes, 1974. Sheldon Traveling fellow in Asia Harvard U., 1956-57; Ctr. for Advanced Study fellow Stanford U., 1974-75. Fellow Am. Anthrop. Assn. (chmn. ethics com. 1978-79), Royal Anthrop. Inst.; mem. Am. Ethnol. Soc., Assn. Social Anthropology in Oceania, Polynesian Soc. (life). Presbyterian. Club: Kosmos (Columbia). Home: 211 Southwood Dr Columbia SC 29205 Office: Dept Anthropology U SC Columbia SC 29208

HEIDRICK, GARDNER WILSON, management consultant; b. Clarion, Pa., Oct. 7, 1911; s. R. Emmet and Helen (Wilson) H.; m. Marian Eileen Lindsay, Feb. 19, 1937; children: Gardner Wilson, Robert L. B.S. in Banking and Fin, U. Ill., 1935. Indsl. dist. sales mgr. Scott Paper Co., Phila., 1935-42; dir. personnel Farmland Industries, Kansas City, Mo., 1942-51; assoc. Booz, Allen & Hamilton, Chgo., 1951-53; co-founder partner, chmn. Heidrick & Struggles, Inc., Chgo., 1953-82; co-founder, chmn. Heidrick Ptnrs., Inc., Chgo., 1982—; dir. Internat. Exec. Service Corp., Keller-Taylor Corp. Vice pres., bd. dirs. U. Ill. Found.; bd. dirs. Keller Grad. Sch. Mgmt. Served with USNR, 1945-46. Recipient Pres.'s award U. Ill. Found., 1979. Mem. U. Ill. Alumni Assn. (past pres.,, Achievement award 1980), Phi Kappa Sigma. Clubs: Chicago, Tower (Chgo.); Hinsdale (Ill.) Golf (past pres.); University (N.Y.); Country of Fla., Ocean (Delray Beach). Office: Heidrick Ptnrs Inc 20 N Wacker Dr Chicago IL 60606

HEIDT, JOHN MURRAY, banker; b. Oceanside, N.Y., Dec. 25, 1931; s. Horace and Adaline (Sohns) H.; m. Mary Ann Kerans, June 18, 1953; children: John, Ann. A.B., Stanford U., 1954; grad., Pacific Coast Banking Sch., 1965; M.B.A., U. So. Calif., 1969. With Union Bank, Los Angeles, 1959—, exec. v.p., 1971-75, pres., dir., 1975—; dir. Union Bank, Union Venture Corp. Trustee St. John's Hosp., Marlborough Sch. Served as spl. agt. OSI USAF, 1954-57. Recipient Man of Hope award City of Hope, 1978. Mem. Calif., Am. bankers assns., Assn. Res. City Bankers, Phi Gamma Delta. Clubs: Los Angeles Country, California (Los Angeles); Vintage (Palm Springs, Calif.). Office: 445 S Figueroa St Los Angeles CA 90071

HEIDT, WALTER DANIEL, manufacturing company executive; b. Savannah, Ga., Nov. 28, 1940; s. George Walter and Helen (Gay) H.; m. Julia Braxton, Dec. 30, 1982. B.S. Indsl. Mgmt., Ga. Inst. Tech., 1963; M.B.A., Ind. U., 1966. Mgmt. trainee Firestone Tire & Rubber, Akron, Ohio, 1963-64; mfg. engr. Lockheed-Ga., Marietta, 1966-68; dir. mfg. Lockheed-Calif., Burbank, 1968-79; pres. Fairchild Swearingen, San Antonio, 1979-82, Murdock Engring. Co., Irving, Tex., 1982—; dir. First Bank, Irving; indsl. adviser UCLA Sch. Engring., 1977-78. Pres. 100 Men-Boys Club, Hollywood, Calif., 1975-77; bd. dirs. Valley Presbyn. Hosp., Los Angeles, 1978-79. Recipient Tech. Mgmt. award Soc. Mfg. Engrs., 1975; named Industrialist of Yr. Soc. Mfg. Engrs., 1976; recipient Engring. Merit award Engr.'s Council, 1979. Mem. Soc. Automotive Engrs. (vice chmn. mfg. com. 1978-79). Club: Rotary. Office: Murdock Engring Co 5100 Airport Freeway West Irving TX 75061

HEIFETZ, ALAN WILLIAM, judge; b. Portland, Maine, Jan. 15, 1943; s. Ralph and Bernice (Diamon) H.; m. Nancy Butler Stone, Aug. 11, 1968; children: Andrew Stone, Peter Stone. A.B., Syracuse U., 1965; J.D., Boston U., 1968. Bar: Maine 1968, Mass. 1968, U.S. Dist. Ct. Mass. 1969, U.S. Supreme Ct. 1972. Assoc. Chayet and Flash, Boston, 1968-70; trial atty. ICC, Washington, 1970-72, counsel to chmn., 1972-78, adminstrv. law judge, 1978-80, Fed. Labor Relations Authority, 1980-82; cheif adminstrv. law judge Dept. HUD, Washington, 1982—; mem. forum faculty Am. Arbitration Assn., Washington, 1983—. Mem. Fallsmead Civic Assn. (Md.). Mem. ABA, Fed. Adminstrv. Law Judges Conf. (mem. exec. com. 1982—). Club: Potomac Tennis (Md.). Home: 23 Infield Ct N Potomac MD 20854 Office: US Dept HUD 451 7th St SW Washington DC 20410

HEIFETZ, JASCHA, violinist; b. Vilna, Russia, Feb. 2, 1901 (Jan. 20, Russian calendar); m. Florence Vidor, Aug. 20, 1928; children—Josepha, Robert; m. Frances Spiegelberg, Jan. 1947 (div.); 1 son, Joseph. Student at age 5, Royal Sch. of Music, Vilna, grad. at 9; pupil of Prof. Leopold Auer, St. Petersburg; Mus.D. (hon.), Northwestern U., 1949. Staff dept. music U. So. Calif. Appeared in: films They Shall Have Music, Carnegie Hall, Of Mice and Men; New York debut, Carnegie Hall, Oct. 27, 1917. Donor of concert hall at, Tel-Aviv, Palestine, 1926. Decorated comdr. Legion of Honor, France, 1957; recipient Grammy award. Mem. Am. Guild Mus. Artists (1st v.p.). Began learning violin at age of 3; made first pub. appearance at 5 years; played Mendelssohn Concerto at 7, first recital in St. Petersburg at 9, engaged for solo with Symphony Orch., Pavlovsk, playing before audience of 5,000; later appeared in leading cities of the world. Home: Beverly Crest Beverly Hills CA 90210 *

HEIGES, DONALD RUSSEL, clergyman, educator; b. Biglerville, Pa., June 25, 1910; s. Edmund Dale and Elsie (Slaybaugh) H.; m. Mary Susannah Kump, June 1, 1935; children—Carol Sue (Mrs. Kenneth Reinhardt), Joan Christina (Mrs. David Blythe). B.A., Gettysburg Coll., 1931, D.D., 1955; B.D., Luth. Theol. Sem., Gettysburg, 1934; M.A., Union Theol. Sem. and Columbia, 1941; D.D., Concordia Coll., Moorhead, Minn., 1954. Ordained to ministry Luth. Ch., 1935; mem. faculty, chaplain Gettysburg Coll., 1934-44; Luth. pastor to students, counselor Columbia, 1944-50; exec. sec. div. coll. and univ. work Nat. Luth. Council, 1950-58; dean Chgo. Luth. Theol. Sem., 1958-62; pres. Luth. Theol. Sem. at Gettysburg, 1962-76, Luth. Theol. Sem. at Phila., 1964-70; exec. dir. Council for Luth. Theol. Edn. in NE, 1976—; Bd. dirs. Nat. Luth. Campus Ministry; mem. directing com., div. ednl. services Luth. Council U.S. Author: The Christian's Calling, 1958. Mem. Phi Beta Kappa, Eta Sigma Phi, Phi Sigma Kappa. Republican. Address: 35 N Hay St Gettysburg PA 17325

HEIGES, JESSE GIBSON, lawyer; b. nr. Shippensburg, Pa., Sept. 19, 1914; s. Jesse Shearer and Susan (Fickes) H.; m. Virginia M. Rodgers, Apr. 20, 1957. A.B., Ursinus Coll., 1935, LL.D., 1974; LL.B., U. Pa., 1938. Bar: N.Y. bar 1939. Atty. Mudge, Stern, Williams & Tucker, N.Y.C., 1939-43, 46-50, Pfizer Inc., 1950-56, sec., 1956-69, gen. counsel, 1956-79, v.p., 1967-79, dir., 1960-79, corp. adv. council, 1983—; dir. USLIFE Corp.; Bd. dirs. Nat. Legal Center for the Public Interest; chmn. Mid-Atlantic Legal Found. Served as lt. USNR, 1943-46. Mem. Am., N.Y. bar assns., Assn. Bar City N.Y. Clubs: River of New York, West Side Tennis of Forest Hills (gov. 1955-62); Maidstone (East Hampton); Bath and Tennis, Everglades (Palm Beach, Fla.). Home: Middle Ln Box J East Hampton NY 11937

HEIGES, RICHARD FICKES, political science educator; b. Findlay, Ohio, Jan. 22, 1931; s. Ralph Eby and Ruth (Bretz) H.; m. Betty Ann Kummer, June 12, 1955; children: Susan Heiges, Nancy, Linda, Richard. Student, Swarthmore Coll., 1949-50; B.S., Indiana (Pa.) U., 1953; M.A., Ohio State U., 1955, Ph.D., 1959. Faculty polit. sci. dept. Ohio State U., 1956, 58-60; tchr. South High Sch., Columbus, Ohio, 1956-58; research asso. Ohio Legis. Service Commn., 1960-61; prof. Indiana (Pa.) U., 1961—, chmn. polit. sci. dept., 1966—. Served with AUS, 1953-55. Presbyterian (elder). Home: 660 Diamond Ave Indiana PA 15701

HEIKOFF, JOSEPH MEYER, educator public administration; b. Bklyn., Nov. 18, 1917; s. Reuben and Rose (Dubin) H.; m. Helen Ethel Gilman, May 9, 1948 (dec. 1983); children: Sara Elizabeth, Barbara Michelle. B.S., CCNY, 1938; B.Landscape Arch., Harvard U., 1943, M.P.A., 1957; M.A., U. Chgo., 1953, Ph.D., 1959. Vis. prof. U. P.R., 1949-51; chief planning dept. P.R. Indsl. Devel. Co., San Juan, 1953-55; city planner U.S. Urban Renewal Adminstrn., San Juan, P.R., 1955-56; exec. dir. City Planning Commn., Syracuse, N.Y., 1957-59; prof. urban planning, dir. bur. community planning U. Ill. at Urbana, 1959-69; prof. pub. adminstrn. Grad. Sch. Pub. Affairs, State U. N.Y. at Albany, 1969—; now sr. fellow Inst. Humanistic Studies.

Author: Management of Industrial Particulates, 1974, Politics of Shore Erosion: Westhampton Beach, 1976, Coastal Resources Management: Programs and Institutions, 1977, Marine and Shoreland Resources Management, 1980; Contbr. articles to profl. jours. and procs. Served with USAAF, 1942-46. Univ. fellow U. Chgo., 1952-53; Littauer fellow Harvard, 1956-57; Fulbright research fellow, Madrid, Spain, 1965-66. Office: State U New York Grad Sch Pub Affairs Albany NY 12222

HEILBRON, JOHN L., historian; b. San Francisco, Mar. 17, 1934; s. Louis Henry and Delphine A. (Rosenblatt) H.; m. Patricia Ann Lucero, Mar. 25, 1959. A.B., U. Calif., Berkeley, 1955, M.A., 1958, Ph.D., 1964. Asst. dir. Sources for History of Quantum Physics, Berkeley and Copenhagen, 1961-64; asst. prof. history, philosophy of sci. U. Pa., Phila., 1964-67; asst. prof. history U. Calif., Berkeley, 1967-71, asso. prof., 1971-73, prof., 1973—; dir. Office for History of Sci. and Tech., 1973—. Author: H.G.J. Moseley, The Life and Letters of an English Physicist, 1887-1915, 1974, (with P. Forman and S. Weart) Personnel, Funding and Productivity of the Academic Establishments, 1975, (with W. Shumaker) John Dee on Astronomy, 1978, Electricity in the 17th and 18th Centuries: A Study of Early Modern Physics, 1979, Historical Studies in the Theory of Atomic Structure, 1981, Elements of Early Modern Physics, 1981; editor: Historical Studies in the Physical Sciences, (with B.R. Wheaton) Literature on the History of Physics in the 20th Century, 1981, An Inventory of Published Letters to and from Physicists, 1982. Mem. History of Sci. Soc., Brit. Soc. History of Sci., Soc. for History of Tech. Home: 689 Alvarado Rd Berkeley CA 94705 Office: 470 Stephens Hall U Calif Berkeley CA 94720

HEILBRON, LOUIS HENRY, lawyer; b. Newark, May 12, 1907; s. Simon L. and Flora (Karp) H.; m. Delphine Rosenblatt, Oct. 30, 1929; children: John L., David M. A.B., U. Calif., Berkeley, 1928, LL.B., 1931, LL.D., 1961; LL.D., Golden Gate Coll., 1970. Bar: Calif. 1931. With firm Heller, Ehrman, White & McAuliffe, 1934—, mem., 1948—; prin. atty. Bd. Econ. Warfare, 1942-43; asst. to dean of men U. Calif. at Berkeley, 1928-31; sec. Calif. Dept. Social Welfare, 1932; asst. relief adminstr., Calif., 1933; spl. cons. Calif. Relief Adminstrn., also Calif. Dept. Social Welfare, 1934-41. Mem. Calif. Bd. Edn., 1959-61, pres., 1960-61; mem. Calif. Coordinating Council Higher Edn., 1961-69; chmn. trustees Calif. State Colls., 1960-63, chmn. ednl. policy com. and faculty staff com., 1963-69; mem. Nat. Commn. on Acad. Tenure, 1971-73, Select Com. to Rev. Calif. Master Higher Edn. Plan, 1971-72, Fedn. Regional Accrediting Commns. Higher Edn., 1972—, also, Council Post Secondary Edn.; Pres. San Francisco Jewish Community Center, 1949-52, San Francisco Pub. Edn. Soc., 1950-52; chmn. San Francisco Com. Fgn. Relations, 1977-79; trustee, exec. com. World Affairs Council No. Calif., 1951—, pres., 1965-67; trustee Sta. KQED, 1966-72, v.p., 1971-72; trustee Golden Gate U., 1969—, chmn., 1979-81; trustee Newhouse Found., 1956-76, U. Calif. Internat. House, 1953-77, U.C. Found., 1973-79, Calif. Hist. Soc., 1978—; v.p. Calif. Hist. Soc., 1981-83, pres., 1983—; mem. San Francisco Human Rights Commn., 1969-75; Chmn. adv. San Francisco State Coll., 1970-76. Served to maj. AUS, 1944-46; ETO. Decorated Bronze Star. Mem. ABA, Internat. Law Com., Phi Beta Kappa (pres. No. Calif. 1972-73), Zeta Beta Tau. Jewish (pres. congregation 1954-57). Home: 2164 Hyde Ave San Francisco CA 94109 Office: 44 Montgomery St San Francisco CA 94104

HEILBRONER, ROBERT L., economist, author. B.A., Harvard U.; Ph.D., New Sch. Social Research; LL.D., LaSalle Coll., Ripon Coll., L.I. U., Wagner Coll. Norman Thomas prof. New Sch. for Social Research, 1972—; lectr. univ., bus. and labor groups. Author: Future as History, 1960, Great Ascent, 1963, Limits of American Capitalism, 1966, Between Capitalism and Socialism, 1970, The Making of Economic Society, rev. edit., 1979, (with Lester Thurow) The Economic Problem, rev. edit, 1983, The Worldly Philosophers, rev. edit, 1980, Between Capitalism and Socialism, 1970, An Inquiry into the Human Prospect, rev. edit., 1980, Business Civilation in Decline, 1976, Beyond Boom and Crash, 1978, Marxism: For and Against, 1980, (with Lester Thurow) Five Economic Challenges, 1981, Economics Explained, 1982; also many articles and brochures in field. Chmn. bd. Town Sch., N.Y.C., 1963-73, Council Econ. Priorities, 1973-79. Guggenheim fellow, 1983. Fellow AAAS; Mem. Am. Econ. Assn. (exec. com. 1972). Club: Century Association (N.Y.C.). Address: care New Sch Social Research 66 W 12th St New York NY 10011

HEILBRUN, CAROLYN GOLD, English literature educator; b. East Orange, N.J., Jan. 13, 1926; d. Archibald and Estelle (Roemer) Gold; m. James Heilbrun, Feb. 20, 1945; children: Emily, Margaret, Robert. B.A., Wellesley Coll., 1947; M.A., Columbia U., 1951, Ph.D., 1959. Instr. Bklyn. Coll., 1959-60, Columbia U., N.Y.C., 1960-62, asst. prof., 1962-67, assoc. prof., 1967-72, prof. English lit., 1972—; vis. prof. U. Calif., Santa Cruz, 1979, Princeton U., N.J., 1981. Author: The Garnett Family, 1961, Towards Androgyny, 1973, Reinventing Womanhood, 1979; 7 novels as Amanda Cross, 1964— (recipient Nero Wolfe award 1981). Guggenheim fellow, 1966; Rockefeller fellow, 1976; recipient Alumnae Achievement award Wellesley Coll., 1984. Mem. MLA (pres. 1983), Mystery Writers Am. (exec. bd. 1982-84), Phi Beta Kappa. Club: Cosmopolitan (N.Y.C.). Office: Grad Dept English Columbia U 613 Philosophy Hall New York NY 10027

HEILBRUN, JAMES, economist, educator; b. N.Y.C., Dec. 13, 1924; s. Maurice L. and Hortense (Unger) H.; m. Carolyn Gold, Feb. 20, 1945; children: Emily, Margaret, Robert. B.S., Harvard Coll., 1945; M.A., Harvard U., 1947; PH.D., Columbia U., 1964. Asst. economist Prentice Hall Inc., N.Y.C., 1947-50; econ. analyst Chase Manhattan Bank, N.Y.C., 1951-55; instr. Columbua U., N.Y.C., 1961-65; asst, prof. econs. Columbia U., N.Y.C., 1965-70; assoc prof. econs. Fordham U., Bronx, 1970-74, prof., 1974—; research dir. Harlem Devel. Project, Columbia U., 1967-68. Author: Real Estate Taxes and Urban Housing, 1966, Urban Economics and Public Policy, 1973, (2d edit.) Urban Economics and Public Policy, 1981. Served with USN, 1944-46. Fellow Com. on Urban Econs., 1960-61, Ford Found., 1969-70; UCLA resident scholar, 1978. Mem. Am. Econ. Assn., Nat. Tax Assn., Regional Sci. Assn., Am. Real Estate Urban Econs. Assn., Assn. Cultural Econs., Lambda Alpha. Home: Dept Econs Fordham U Bronx NY 10458

HEILIG, WILLIAM WRIGHT, coal and mfg. co. exec.; b. Phila., Jan. 24, 1940; s. Alois Bube and Anna Marguerite (Wright) H.; m. Louise Fay Hamon, July 31, 1971; 1 dau., Elizabeth Anne. A.B. with dept. honors in econs, Hamilton Coll., 1962; M.B.A., U. Pa., 1964. C.P.A., Pa. Auditor, mgmt. cons. Coopers & Lybrand, Phila. and Bermuda, 1964-70; asst. treas. Berwind Corp., Phila., 1970-75, treas., 1975-80, v.p., treas., 1981—. Republican. Presbyterian. Clubs: Phila. Treasurers, Union League (Phila.). Home: 924 Winding Ln Media PA 19063 Office: 3000 Centre Sq W Philadelphia PA 19102

HEILMAN, EARL BRUCE, univ. pres.; b. La Grange, Ky., July 16, 1926; s. Earl Bernard and Nellie (Sanders) H.; m. Betty June Dobbins, Aug. 27, 1948; children—Bobbie Lynn, Nancy Jo, Terry Lee, Sandra June, Timothy Bruce. B.S., Peabody Coll., 1950, M.A., 1951, Ph.D., 1961; postgrad., U. Tenn., U. Omaha, U. Ky.; LL.D., Wake Forest U., 1967, Ky. Wesleyan Coll., 1980; L.H.D., Campbell Coll., 1971. Instr. bus. Peabody Coll., 1950-51, bursar, 1957-60, adminstrv. v.p., 1963-66; instr. accounting Belmont Coll., Nashville, 1951-52; auditor Albert Maloney Co., Nashville, 1951-52; asst. prof. accounting, bus. mgr. Ky. Wesleyan Coll., 1952-54; treas. Georgetown (Ky.) Coll., 1954-57, 1954-57; coordinator higher edn. and spl. schs., Tenn., 1960-61; v.p., dean Ky. So. Coll., Louisville, 1961-63; prof. ednl. adminstrn. George Peabody Coll. Tchrs., Nashville, 1963-66; pres. Meredith Coll., Raleigh, N.C., 1966-71, U. Richmond, Va., 1971—; bd. dirs. Cooperating Raleigh Colls., 1967-71; cons. indsl. studies in edn. and adminstrn., 1954—; Dir., cons. long range planning confs. Fund Advancement Edn., 1960—; cons. Acad. Ednl. Devel., 1966—; mem. steering com. Baptist Ednl. Study Task, 1964-65; mem. Wake County-Raleigh City Sch. Merger Study Com., 1969; adv. com. N.C. Dept. Pub. Instrn., 1970; dir. Central Fidelity Bank, Fidelity Bankers Life Ins. Co., A.H. Robins Co., all Richmond; adv. bd. WLEE Radio-TV. Author: (with others) Sixty College Study, 1954; also booklets and articles. Chmn. blood com. for edn. ARC, 1971; mem. Nashville Urban Renewal Coordinating Com., 1965-66; ann. giving chmn. for N.C. Peabody Coll., 1970-72; mem. Friends of HOME, 1974—; chmn. trustee orientation com N.C. Baptist Conv., 1961; mem. edn. commn. So. Baptist Conv.; mem. bd. advisers Bapt. Hosp. Sch. Nursing, Nashville, 1956-60, 64—; mem. com. Met. Gen. Hosp. Sch. Nursing, 1965-68; mem. Federated Arts Council Richmond, 1975—, Robert Lee council Boy Scouts Am., 1975—; mem. devel. adv. bd. Va. Center Performing Arts, 1980; bd. dirs. Bill Wilkerson Speech and Hearing Center, Nashville, 1963-64, N.C. Symphony, United Fund Wake County, 1968-71, N.C. Mental Health Assn., 1969-71, Wake County Mental Health Assn., 1969-71, Va. Thanksgiving Festival, 1972, Richmond Pub. Library, Richmond chpt. NCCJ, Va. Inst. Sci. Research, 1971—, Leadership Metro Richmond, 1980—; hon. dir. Richmond Ballet, 1971; bd. govs. United Givers Fund Richmond, 1971; trustee Inst. Mediterranean Studies, 1972—, E.R. Patterson Ednl. Found., 1972—, U. Richmond, 1973—, Marine Mil. Acad., 1979—. Served with USMCR, 1944-47. Recipient award Owensboro (Ky.) Jr. C. of C., 1953; Agrl. and Industry Service award U. Nashville, 1961; Outstanding Civic and Ednl. award, Raleigh, 1970; Distinguished Salesman award, Richmond, 1972; Paul Harris Rotary fellow, 1970; named Ky. col., 1969; Distinguished Citizen of Oldham County (Ky.); award Va. assn. Future Farmers Am., 1976; Meredith Coll., 1977. Mem. Internat. Assn. Univ. Pres.'s (N. Am. council 1976—), Nat. Fedn. Bus. Officers, Nat. Fedn. Bus. Officers Cons. Service, So. Assn. Colls. Women (pres. 1969), Nat. Soc. Lit. and the Arts, So. Univ. Conf., Am. Council Edn., Tenn. Edn. Assn., Ky. Ednl. Buyers Assn., Am. Assn. Pres.'s Ind. Colls. and Univs., Ky. Assn. Acad. Deans, Peabody Alumni Assn. (exec. com), Nat., So. assns. coll. and univ. bus. officers, Assn. Governing Bds. Univs. and Colls., Coll. and Univ. Personnel Assn., Internat. Platform Assn., Nashville, Raleigh, Richmond, Va. chambers commerce, Nat. Assn. Ind. Colls. and Univs., Navy League U.S., Marine Corps League, Council Ind. Colls. in Va. (pres. 1974-76), Va. Found. Ind. Colls., Assn. Va. Colls., Assn. So. Bapt. Colls. and Schs. (pres. 1976), N.C. Found. Ch.-Related Colls., Assn. Am. Colls., So. Assn. Colls. and Schs. (trustee 1977), Phi Beta Kappa, Pi Omega Pi, Kappa Phi Kappa, Kappa Delta Pi, Delta Pi Epsilon, Omicron Delta Kappa, Beta Gamma Sigma, Lambda Chi Alpha, Va. Bapt. Hist. Soc., English-Speaking Union, Newcomen Soc. N. Am. Democrat. Baptist (deacon). Clubs: Rotary (bd. advisers Raleigh 1966-71), Execs. (v.p., dir. 1971), City (Raleigh); Downtown (Richmond); The Club, Forum. Home: 7000 River Rd Richmond VA 23229

HEILMAN, ROBERT BECHTOLD, English educator; b. Phila., July 18, 1906; s. Rev. Edgar James and Mary Alice (Bechtold) H.; m. Ruth Delavan Champlin, July 31, 1935; 1 son, Champlin Bechtold. A.B., Lafayette Coll., 1927; teaching fellow in English, Tufts Coll., 1927-28; A.M., Ohio State U., 1930, Harvard U., 1931, Ph.D., 1935; Litt.D. (hon.), Lafayette Coll., 1967, U. of South, 1978, LL.D., Grinnell Coll., 1971, L.H.D., Kenyon Coll., 1973, H.H.D., Whitman Coll., 1977. Instr. in English Ohio U., 1928-30, U. Maine, 1931-33, 1934-35; instr. English La. State U., 1935-36, asst. prof., 1936-42, asso. prof., 1942-46, prof., 1946-48, U. Wash., 1948-76, chmn. dept. English, 1948-71; Arnold prof. Whitman Coll., 1977. Author: America in English Fiction, 1760-1800, 1937, This Great Stage: Image and Structure in King Lear, 1948, Magic in the Web: Action and Language in Othello, 1956 (Explicator award), Tragedy and Melodrama: Versions of Experience, 1968, The Iceman, the Arsonist, and the Troubled Agent: Tragedy and Melodrama on the Modern Stage, 1973, The Charliad, 1973, The Ghost on the Ramparts and Other Essays in the Humanities, 1974, The Ways of the World: Comedy and Society, 1978 (Christian Gauss prize Phi Beta Kappa 1979); Editor: (with Cleanth Brooks) Understanding Drama: Twelve Plays, 1948, Modern Short Stories: A Critical Anthology, 1950, Swift's Gulliver's Travels, 1950, rev. edit., 1969, An Anthology of Pre-Shakespearian Drama, 1952, Conrad's Lord Jim, 1957, Hardy's Mayor of Casterbridge, 1962, Eliot's Silas Marner, 1962, Shakespeare's Cymbeline, 1964, Euripides' Alcestis, 1965, Hardy's Jude the Obscure, 1966, Shakespeare's Taming of the Shrew, 1966, Hardy's Tess of the Durbervilles, 1971; editorial adviser: Coll. English, 1951-53, 56-61, Shakespeare Studies, 1965, Studies in the Novel, 1966—, Modern Lang. Quar, 1972-76, Sewanee Rev, 1974—, Miss. Studies in Lit., 1980—. Trustee Seattle Repertory Theatre, 1979-82. Recipient Ariz. Quar. essay prize, 1956; Longview Found. essay award, 1960; George Washington Kidd award for career distinction Lafayette Coll., 1983; Huntington Library grantee, 1959; Guggenheim fellow, 1964-65, 76; NEH sr. fellow, 1971-72. Mem. Internat. Assn. Univ. Profs. English, MLA (mem. nat. exec. council 1966-69), Nat. Council Tchrs. English (Distinguished lectr. 1968), Philol. Assn. Pacific Coast (pres. 1959), AAUP (mem. nat. council 1962-65), Shakespeare Assn. Am. (ann. lectr. 1973, trustee 1977-80), Phi Beta Kappa (senator 1967—, exec. com. 1973—). Home: 4554-45th Ave NE Seattle WA 98105

HEILMANN, CHRISTIAN FLEMMING, multi-industry company executive; b. Penang, Malaysia, Apr. 26, 1936; came to U.S., 1977; s. Poul Bent and Hedvig (Buchwald) H.; m. Marilyn Mildred Harter, July 9, 1959 (div. 1973); children: Christian, Nicholas, Claire; m. 2d Judith Lucy Tucker, Sept. 15, 1973; children: Per, Niels. B.A. in Econs. and Law, Downing Coll.-Cambridge (Eng.) U., 1957, M.A. in Law, 1960. Mng. dir. Metal Box South Africa Ltd., Johannesburg, 1970-76; v.p. comml. Continental Can Co., Stamford, Conn., 1977-78; exec. v.p., dep. gen. mgr. Continental Group of Europe, Brussels, 1978, pres., 1978-81, Continental Diversified Industries, Stamford, 1981; exec. v.p., chief adminstrv. officer Continental Group, Stamford, 1982—. Bd. dirs., trustees Nat. Devel. and Mgmt. Found., South Africa, 1971-75. Clubs: Greenwich (Conn.) Country, Stamford Yacht. Office: The Continental Group Inc One Harbor Plaza Box 10129 Stamford CT 06904-2129

HEILMEIER, GEORGE HARRY, research electrical engineer; b. Phila., May 22, 1936; s. George C. and Anna I. (Heineman) H.; m. Janet S. Faunce, June 24, 1961; 1 dau., Elizabeth. B.S. in Elec. Engring., U. Pa., 1958; M.S. in Engring., Princeton U., 1960, A.M., 1961, Ph.D., 1962. With RCA Labs., Princeton, N.J., 1958-70, dir. solid state device research, 1965-68, dir. device concepts, 1968-70; White House fellow, spl. asst. to sec. def., Washington, 1970-71; asst. dir. def. research and engring. Office Sec. Def., 1971-75; dir. Def. Advanced Projects Agy., 1975-77; v.p. research, devel. and engring. Tex. Instruments Inc., 1978-83, sr. v.p., chief tech. officer, 1983—; mem. vis. com. Moore Sch., U. Pa., Stanford U.; also elec. engring. dept. Princeton U.; mem. Def. Sci. Bd., Air Force Sci. Adv. Bd.; mem. adv. group on electron devices Dept. Def. Author. Recipient IEEE David Sarnoff award RCA, 1969; IR-100 New Product award Indsl. Research Assn., 1968, 69; Sec. Def. Disting. Civilian Service award, 1975, 77; Arthur Flemming award U.S. Jaycees, 1974. Fellow IEEE (Sarnoff Field award 1976, Outstanding Achievement award Dallas chpt. 1984); mem. U. Pa., Princeton U. Grad. alumni assns., Nat. Acad. Engring., Sigma Xi, Tau Beta Pi, Eta Kappa Nu (Outstanding Young Engr. in U.S. award 1969). Methodist. Patentee in field. Office: Tex Instruments 13500 North Central Expy Box 225474 MS 400 Dallas TX 75265

HEILOMS, MAY (MRS. SAMUEL HELLOMS), painter; b. Russia; came to naturalized, 1932; d. Mark A. and Eugenie (Mogilensky) Levinson; m. Samuel Heiloms, June 12, 1938. Student, Hunter Coll., 1929, Art Students League. Adviser Ford Found. Program in Humanities, 1958, 59; invited juror exhbn. Am. Acad. Arts and Letters. Exhibited paintings, Pa. Acad., Bklyn. Mus., Cleve. Mus., Denver Mus., Silvermine Guild, Butler Inst. Am. Art, Nat. Acad., Nat. Arts Gallery, Mexico Mus. Fine Arts, Okla. City Mus., others, one-man shows, Monmouth Guild, 1960, Bennett Coll., 1961, Silvermine Guild Conn., Jeanette Nessler Gallery, N.Y.C., East Central State Mus., Okla., Cortland Art Center, N.Y., Paducah Art Guild, Ky., Warder Pub. Library, Springfield, Ohio, Five Corners Library, Hudson Gallery, N.Y.C., Muhlemberg Library, N.Y., Mus. Fine Arts, Mexico City, Nat. Mus. Sports, N.Y.C., Loeb Center, N.Y. U., 1979, 80, Custom House Twin Towers Gallery, N.Y.C., 1980, 81, others, also univs. and colls., traveling shows, Cleve. Mus. Art, Allbright Art Gallery, Buffalo, Dallas Mus. Art, Corcoran Gallery, Rochester Meml. Art Gallery, Columbia Mus. Art, also Lisbon, Portugal, Naples, Italy, Athens, Greece, Brussels, Belgium, also, Museo De Bellas Artes, Buenos Aires, Argentina, paintings permanent collections, Phila. Mus. Art, Samuel S. Fleisher Meml. Art Found., Ludwig Bowman Collection, Collectors of Am. Art, Norfolk Mus. Art, Safed State Mus., Israel, Bat Yam Museum, Israel, Okla. City Mus., Denny Collection, Kenny Internat. Found., also pvt. collections. Recipient prize for oil Jersey City Mus., 1950, 51, 59, 63, 1st prize, medal, 1956; prize Painters and Sculptors N.J., 1952, 55, 75; Bocour prize, 1958; prize for oil, 1960, 62, Bklyn. Soc. Artists, 1957; Atwood Klinger prize for abstract oil Nat. Assn. Women Artists, 1954; Patricia Murphy prize, 1958; E. Morse Genius prize for watercolor, 1960; M. Grumbacher prize oil, 1961; Sarah E. Good prize oil, 1962; Bainbridge prize watercolor, 1963; prize watercolor Bklyn. Soc. Artists, 1958; Nat. Soc. Painters in Casein, prize casein, 1962; prize, 1967, 70, 73; prize for oil Painters and Sculptors N.J., 1964; prize for watercolor Nat. Assn. Women Artists, 1966; M.H. Steiglitz prize Nat. Soc. Painters in Casein, 1966; prize (oil) Am. Soc. Contemporary Artists, 1967, 68, 71, 80; Windsor Newton prize, 1980; prize for acrylic Nat. Soc. Painters in Casein and Acrylic, 1974; memorabilia on microfilm Archives Am. Art, Smithsonian Instn.; prize for oil Painters and sculptors N.J., 1975, Nat. Arts, 1975, 76; Bocour prize for oil Bergen County Mus., 1982; Emily Lowe award for oil Allied Artists, 1983. Fellow Royal Acad. Arts (Eng.); mem. Am. Painters and Sculptors (dir.), Painters and Sculptors N.J. (hon. life pres.), Audubon Artists (v.p.), Painters in Casein (dir.), Artists Equity, Nat. Assn. Women Artists, Bklyn. Soc. Artists, Casein Soc., Allied Artists (officer exec. bd.), Watercolor Soc. Ala., Am. Soc. Contemporary Artists (1st v.p.), Knickerbocker Artists, Silvermine Guild, N.Y. Soc. Women Artists (chmn. membership com.), Art Students League, Manhattan Gallery Group, Am. Soc. Contemporary Artists (prize for oil). Studio: 340 W 28th St New York NY 10001 *My aim, my goal, is to bring beauty, joy, a kindly understanding by sharing my observations, my philosophy, by painting with my heart and mind.*

HEILPRIN, LAURENCE BEDFORD, physicist, educator; b. N.Y.C., May 26, 1906; s. William Albert and Jessie Emma (Heine) H.; m. Marilyn Joyce Heyman, Sept. 3, 1953; children: Jean Frances, John Michael. B.S. in Econs, U. Pa., 1928, M.A. in Physics, 1931, Ph.D., Harvard U., 1941. Instr. physics and math. Northeastern U., 1935-40; asst. thermodynamics Harvard U., 1941; with Nat. Bur. Standards, 1941-51; research ordnance electronics patents Diamond Ordnance Lab., 1945-51, tchr. in grad. sch., 1949-51; physicist Taub Engring. Co., 1952-54; analyst ops. evaluation group U.S. Navy, Mass. Inst. Tech., 1954-56; physicist info. systems Documentation Inc., 1956-57; staff physicist Council on Library Resources, Inc., Ford Found., 1958-67; prof. info. sci. Library Sch. and Computer Center, U. Md., 1967-76, prof. emeritus, 1976—; professorial lectr. George Washington U. Grad. Sch. Engring., 1959-62, Am. U. Center Tech. and Adminstrn., 1965-66; Founding mem., dir. Com. Investigate Copyright Problems Affecting Communican in Sci. and Edn., 1959—. Author works on info. sci. and cybernetics, 1951—. Mem. Am. Soc. Info. Sci. (pres. 1965, founding mem., chmn. Spl. Interest Group on Founds. of Info. Sci. 1972-74), Am. Phys. Soc., Optical Soc. Am., Am. Assn. Physics Tchrs., IEEE, Philos. Soc. Washington, Washington Assn. Scientists (founding mem.), AAAS, Am. Soc. Cybernetics. Club: Harvard (Washington). Home: 4800 Berwyn House Rd College Park MD 20740 Office: Coll Library and Information Sci U Md College Park MD 20742

HEIM, LEO EDWARD, musician, conservatory administrator; b. Chandler, Ind., Sept. 22, 1913; s. Raymond Earl and Emily J. H.; m. Margaret Bregetta Borchers, Feb. 14, 1942. Student, Northwestern U., 1931-32; B.M., Am. Conservatory Music, 1935, M.M., 1946. Mem. piano faculty Am. Conservatory Music, Chgo., 1935—, asst. dean, 1956-57, dean, 1957-71, pres., 1971-81, pres. emeritus, 1981—; pianist, accompanist, ensemble player; former examiner, mem. ind. schs. com. Nat. Assn. Schs. Music. Trustee Am. Conservatory Music.; pres. Cliff Dwellers Arts Found., 1980-82. Served with USAAF, 1942-45. Decorated Bronze Star. Mem. Soc. Am. Musicians, Musicians Union, Phi Mu Alpha Sinfonia. Christian Scientist (organist). Clubs: Cliff Dwellers (pres. 1978-80), University (Chgo.)). Home: 515 Vine Ave Park Ridge IL 60068 Office: Am Conservatory Music 116 S Michigan Ave Chicago IL 60603

HEIMAN, GROVER GEORGE, editor; b. Galveston, Tex., July 26, 1920; s. Grover George and Rose Mary (Ulch) H.; m. Virginia Deene Williamson, Feb. 14, 1942; children: Virginia, Grover, Deborah, Richard. Student, Lee Coll., 1937-40, U. Tex., 1940-41; B.S. in Office Mgmt. cum laude, U. So. Calif., 1959. News reporter Corsicana (Tex.) Daily Sun, 1945-47; commd. 2d lt. USAAC, 1942; advanced through grades to col. U.S. Air Force, 1963; spl. asst. to USAF Chief of Staff, Pentagon, Washington, 1959-63; chief of info. Allied Air Forces So. Europe, Naples, Italy, 1963-66; chief mags. and books Dept. Def., Pentagon, 1966-68; ret., 1968; mng. editor Armed Forces Mgmt. mag., Washington, 1968—; assoc. editor Nation's Business mag., Washington, 1970-82, industry editor, 1976-82, mng. editor, 1978-82, editor, 1980-82, editor emeritus, 1982—; Chmn. Naples Dependent Schs. bd., 1964-65. Author: (with Rutherford Montgomery) Jet Navigator, 1959, Jet Tanker, 1961, Jet Pioneers, 1963, (with Virginia Myers) [Careers For Women In Uniform, 1971, Aerial Photography, 1973. Served with USAAF, 1941-45. Decorated Legion of Merit. Mem. Authors League, Authors Guild, Jet Pioneers Am., Beta Gamma Sigma, Alpha Tau Omega. Roman Catholic. Clubs: Cedar Crest Country, National Press. Home: 2881 Glenvale Dr Fairfax VA 22031 Office: 1615 H St NW Washington DC 20062

HEIMANN, JOHN GAINES, investment banker; b. N.Y.C., Apr. 1, 1929; s. Sidney M. and Dorothy V.B. (Gainesburg) H.; m. Margaret E. Fechheimer, Dec. 2, 1956; children: Joshua Gaines, Eliza Faith. A.B., Syracuse (N.Y.) U., 1950. Vice pres. Smith, Barney & Co., N.Y.C.,

1955-66; sr. v.p., dir. E.M. Warburg, Pincus & Co., Inc., N.Y.C., 1967-75; N.Y. State supt. banks, 1975-76, N.Y. State commr. housing and community renewal, 1976-77, comptroller of the currency, Washington, 1977-81; co-chmn. exec. com. Harburg, Paribas, Becker, N.Y.C., 1981-83; dep. chmn. A.G. Becker Paribas Inc., Paribas Internat.; dir. FDIC, 1977-81, Fed. Nat. Mortgage Assn., 1977-80, Neighborhood Reinvestment Corp., 1978-81, Australis Securities Ltd., Colonial Penn Group Inc.; chmn. Fed. Fin. Instns. Exam. Council, 1979-81, Comml. Reinvestment Taskforce, 1978-81; mem. Depository Instns. Deregulation Com., 1980-81; spl. adviser to Gov. on Temporary Commn. Banking, Ins. and Fin. Reform; lectr. Harvard U., Yale U., Columbia U., U. Calif., N.Y. U. Named Housing Man of Yr. Nat. Housing Conf., 1976; recipient Chancellor medal Syracuse U., 1978, Bank Adminstrn. Key for Disting. Service, 1980, Alexander Hamilton award Treasury Dept., 1981. Mem. Fgn. Relations Council. Democrat. Club: F Street (Washington). Office: 55 Water St New York NY

HEIMANN, WILLIAM EMIL, lawyer; b. New Braunfels, Tex., Oct. 5, 1928; s. Emil Erno and Gladys Lorene (Cook) H.; m. Mary Elizabeth Welch, May 21, 1960; children—Martin Emil, David Phillips. LL.B., Okla. U., 1951. Bar: Okla. bar 1951. Partner Kerr-Davis-Roberts-Heimann-Irvine & Burbage, Oklahoma City, 1956-60; atty. Kerr-Conn & Davis, Oklahoma City, 1954-60; gen. atty., asst. sec. Kerr-McGee Corp., Oklahoma City, 1965-73, v.p., gen. counsel, asst. sec., 1973-75, v.p., gen. counsel, sec., 1975—. Bd. editors: Okla. Law Rev, 1949-50. Served with U.S. Army, 1951-53. Mem. Am. Bar Assn., Am. Soc. Corp. Secs., Okla. Bar Assn., Okla. County Bar Assn., Order of Coif, Phi Delta Phi, Lambda Chi Alpha. Presbyterian. Home: 836 NW 39th St Oklahoma City OK 73118 Office: PO Box 25861 Oklahoma City OK 73125

HEIMBAUGH, JAMES ROSS, hotel executive; b. Monett, Mo., Jan. 27, 1918; s. James Ross and Sarah Jeanette (Hayes) H.; m. Ruby Virginia Murphy, Aug. 17, 1946; children: Judy Rae, David Ross. Grad., U. Ill., 1941; summer hotel course, Cornell U., 1952. With Hilton Hotels, 1938-56; sales mgr. Palmer House, Chgo., 1952-55; officer, v.p. sales Tisch Hotels Co., 1956-61; officer, v.p. mktg. and sales Loews Hotels Co., 1961-71, officer, exec. v.p. charge sales, mktg. and advt., 1971-72; pres., dir. Americana Hotels, N.Y.C., 1972-79; owner, pres. James R. Heimbaugh's Assocs. Inc., 1979—. Served with USNR, 1941-46. Decorated Silver Star, Bronze Star. Mem. Am. Hotel and Motel Assn. (chmn. conv. liaison com. 1977—), Hotel Sales Mgmt. Internat., Am. Soc. Assn. Execs., Am. Soc. Travel Agts., Sales Execs. Club N.Y.C. (dir., Man of Year award 1975). Presbyterian. Clubs: Skeeters (N.Y.C.); Seaview (N.J.) Country, Masons. Home: 1600 Parker Ave Fort Lee NJ 07024 Office: 2175 Lemoine Ave Suite 426 Fort Lee NJ 07024

HEIMBERG, MURRAY, pharmacologist, physician, educator; b. Bklyn., Jan. 5, 1925; s. Gustav and Fannie (Geller) H.; children by previous marriage: Richard G., Steven A.; m. Anna Frances Langlois Knox, July 12, 1964; stepchildren: Larry M. Knox, David S. Knox. B.S., Cornell U., Ithaca, N.Y., 1948, M.N.S., 1949; Ph.D. (NIH fellow), Duke, 1952; M.D., Vanderbilt U., 1959. NIH Postdoctoral fellow in biochemistry Med. Sch. Washington U., St. Louis, 1952-54; research asso. physiology Med. Sch. Vanderbilt U., 1954-59, asst. prof. to prof. pharmacology, and asst. prof. medicine, 1959-74; prof., chmn. dept. pharmacology, prof. medicine U. Mo., 1974-81; prof. and chmn. dept. pharmacology, prof. medicine U. Tenn., Center for the Health Scis., Memphis, 1981—; Cons. NSF, NIH; cons., established investigator Am. Heart Assn. Contbr. numerous articles to profl. jours. Served with AUS, 1943-45; ETO. Decorated Purple Heart; recipient Lederle Med. Faculty award; research grantee. Fellow AAAS; Mem. Am. Soc. Biol. Chemists, Am. Soc. Pharmacology and Exptl. Therapeutics, Endocrine Soc. Home: 105 Devon Way Memphis TN 38111 Office: Dept Pharmacology 100 Crowe Bldg Coll Medicine U Tenn 874 Union Ave Memphis TN 38163

HEIMBOLD, CHARLES ANDREAS, JR., manufacturing company executive; b. Newark, May 27, 1933; s. Charles Andreas and Mary Joseph (Corrigan) H.; m. Monika Astrid Barkvall, Sept. 22, 1962; children: Joanna, Eric, Leif, Peter. B.A. cum Laude, Villanova U., 1954; LL.B. cum laude, U. Pa., 1960; LL.M., NYU, 1966; postgrad., Hague Acad. Internat. Law, 1959. Bar: N.Y. 1962. Assoc. Milbank, Tweed, Hadley & Mc Cloy, 1960-63; with Bristol Myers, N.Y.C., 1963—, dir. corp. devel., 1970-73, v.p. planning and devel., 1973—. Bd. dirs. Sheltering Arms Children's Service, Putnam-Indian Field Sch. Service with USN, 1957-60. Mem. Assn. Bar City N.Y. Clubs: The Board Room (N.Y.C.); Riverside Yacht (Conn.). Home: Leeward Ln Riverside CT 06878 Office: 345 Park Ave New York NY 10022

HEIMLICH, HENRY JAY, physician, surgeon; b. Wilmington, Del., Feb. 3, 1920; s. Philip and Mary (Epstein) H.; m. Jane Murray, June 3, 1951; children: Philip, Peter, Janet and Elizabeth (twins). B.A., Cornell U., 1941, M.D., 1943; D.Sc. (hon.), Wilmington Coll., 1981, Adelphi U., 1982, Rider Coll., 1983. Diplomate: Am. Bd. Surgery, Am. Bd. Thoracic Surgery. Intern Boston City Hosp., 1944; resident VA Hosp., Bronx, 1946-47, Mt. Sinai Hosp., N.Y.C., 1947-48, Bellevue Hosp., 1948-49, Triboro Hosp., Jamaica, N.Y., 1949-50; attending surgeon div. surgery Montefiore Hosp., N.Y.C., 1950-69; dir. surgery Jewish Hosp., Cin., 969-77; prof. advanced clin. scis. Xavier U., Cin., 1977—; asso. clin. prof. surgery U. Cin. Coll. Medicine, 1969—; mem. Pres. Commn. on Heart Disease, Cancer and Stroke, 1965; Pres. Nat. Cancer Found., 1963-68, bd. dirs., 1960-70; founder, pres. Dysphagia Found. Author: Postoperative Care in Thoracic Surgery, 1962, (with M.O. Cantor, C.H. Lupton) Surgery of the Stomach, Duodenum and Diaphragm, Questions and Answers, 1965; also; contbr. chpts. to books; numerous articles to med. jours.; Producer: films Esophageal Replacement with a Reversed Gastric Tube (awarded Medaglione Di Bronzo Minerva 1961), Reversed Gastric Tube Esophagoplasty Using Stapling Technique, How to Save a Choking Victim: The Heimlich Maneuver, 1976, 2d edit., 1982, How To Save a Drowning Victim: The Heimlich Maneuver, 1981, Stress Relief: The Heimlich Method, 1983; mem. editorial bd.: Reporte's Medicos. Bd. dirs. Community Devel. Found., 1967-70, Save the Children Fedn., 1967-68, United Cancer Council, 1967-70. Served to lt. (s.g.) USNR, 1944-46. Fellow A.C.S. (chpt. pres. 1964), Am. Coll. Chest Physicians, Am. Coll. Gastroenterology; mem. Soc. Thoracic Surgeons (founding mem.), AMA (cons. to jour.), Cin. Soc. Thoracic Surgery, N.Y. Soc. Thoracic Surgery, Soc. Surgery Alimentary Tract, Am. Gastroent. Assn., Pan Am. Med. Assn., Collegium Internat. Chirurgiae Digestive, Central Surg. Assn. Developer Heimlich Operation reversed gastric tube esophagoplasty) for replacement of esophagus; inventor Heimlich chest drain valve; developer Heimlich Maneuver to save lives of victims of food choking (listed in Random House, Oxford Am. and Webster dictionaries); developer Computers for Peace, a program to maintain peace throughout world. Office: Xavier U Cincinnati OH 45207 *I have never been satisfied with existing methods and seek to simplify and improve them. After devising an operation for replacement of the esophagus, I became aware that with one such discovery I could help more people in a few weeks than in my entire lifetime as a surgeon in the operating room. The Heimlich Maneuver, which saves thousands of choking victims annually, confirmed this realization. My ultimate goal is to avoid needless death and promote well-being for the largest number of people by establishing a philosophy that will eliminate war.*

HEIMLICH, RICHARD ALLEN, geologist; b. Elizabeth., N.J., Aug. 8, 1932; s. Simon William and Sidnie W. (Simon) H.; m. Charlee Marcus, July 23, 1961; children: Steven A., John P. B.S., Rutgers U., 1954; M.S., Yale U., 1955, Ph.D. (J.D. Dana scholar 1956), 1959. Mem. faculty Kent (Ohio) State U., 1961—, prof. geology, 1970—, chmn. dept., 1976—. Author: Field Guide: Southern Great Lakes, 1977, Field Guide: The Black Hills, 1980; also papers and articles. Served with Ordnance Corps AUS, 1959-60. Grantee NSF, 1969-71, Los Alamos Sci. Lab., 1979, 80, U.S. Office Edn., 1979, 80, 81, 82, 83. Fellow Geol. Soc. Am.; mem. Soc. Econ. Geologists, Am. Inst. Profl. Geologists, No. Ohio Geol. Soc., Sigma Xi. Home: 1596 Woodway St Kent OH 44240 Office: Dept Geology Kent State U Kent OH 44242

HEIMSCH, CHARLES, retired botany educator; b. Dayton, Ohio, May 4, 1914; s. Charles and Martha Louise (Sawesky) H.; m. Dorothy Hogue Johnson, Sept. 17, 1938 (dec. Feb. 1973); children: Richard Charles, Carolyn Marie, Alan; m. Evah Jo Johnson, Mar. 17, 1974; stepchildren: Steven Eric, Nanci Lynne, Douglas Allen (dec.), Donald Scott. A.B., Miami U., 1936; M.A., Harvard U., 1939, Ph.D., 1941. Teaching asst. biology Harvard U., 1936-37, research asst., 1939-40, Austin teaching fellow, 1940-41, Sheldon traveling fellow, 1941-42; teaching asst. biology Radcliffe Coll., 1937-39; instr. botany Swarthmore Coll., 1942-46; asst. prof. biology Amherst Coll., 1946-47; asst. prof. botany U. Tex., 1947-50, assoc. prof., 1950-54, prof., 1954-59; prof. botany Miami U., 1959-81, prof. emeritus, 1981—, chmn. dept., 1959-77; State exec. com. U. Interscholastic League, 1956-59; Tech. aide tropical deterioration OSRD-NDRC. Author: (with others) Principles of Biology, 1954, rev. 1964, (with A.E. Lee) Development and Structure of Plants, 1962; research papers on systematic and developmental plant anatomy.; Editor: Am. Jour. Botany, 1964-69. NATO sr. fellow in sci., 1972-73; recipient Benjamin Harrison award Miami U., 1981. Fellow AAAS, Ohio Acad. Scis. (v.p. plant scis. sect. 1963-64); mem. Bot. Soc. Am. (chmn. membership com. 1952-55, treas. 1962-63, v.p. 1971, pres. 1972, program dir. 1979-82), Internat. Assn. Wood Anatomists, Phi Beta Kappa, Sigma Xi, Omicron Delta Kappa, Phi Kappa Phi, Phi Sigma, Phi Eta Sigma, Phi Delta Theta, Explorers Club. Address: Miami U Oxford OH 45056

HEIN, JOHN WILLIAM, dentist, educator; b. Chester, Mass., Sept. 29, 1920; s. Rudolf Jacob and Mercedes Viola H.; m. Jeanette Marie BeVier, Dec. 16, 1944. B.S., Am. Internat. Coll., 1941; D.M.D., Tufts U., 1944; Ph.D., U. Rochester, 1952; A.M. (hon.), Harvard, 1962, D.Sc., Am. Internat. Coll., 1979. Student instr. oral pathology Tufts Coll. Dental Sch., 1943-44; head div. dental research U. Rochester, 1948-52, sr. fellow dental research, 1949-52, instr. pharmacology, 1951-53, asst. prof. dental research, 1952-55, asst. prof. pharmacology, 1954-55, chmn. dept. dentistry and dental research, 1952-55; instr. anatomy and physiology Eastman Sch. Dental Hygiene, 1950-55, lectr. dental research, 1953-55; research specialist Bur. Biol. Research, Rutgers U., 1955-59; dental dir. Colgate Palmolive Co., 1955-59; prof. preventive dentistry, dean Sch. Dental Medicine, Tufts U., 1959-62; dir. Forsyth Dental Center, 1962—; prof. dentistry Harvard Dental Sch., 1962-67. Trustee Am. Internat. Coll., 1960-76. Served to capt. AUS, 1942-47. Fellow AAAS, Internat. Coll. Dentists (regent 1967-72, pres. U.S. 1975-76, internat. pres. 1983-84); mem. ADA, Mass. Dental Soc. (pres. 1964-65), Internat. Assn. Dental Research (treas. 1978-82), Am. Acad. Dental Sci., New Eng. Dental Soc. (hon. pres. 1978), Am. Soc. Dentistry for Children, Assn. Ind. Research Insts. (1st v.p. 1980, pres. 1981-83), Sigma Xi, Omicron Kappa Upsilon, Delta Sigma Delta. Club: Harvard (Boston). Home: Bridge St Medfield MA 02052 Office: 140 The Fenway Boston MA 02115

HEIN, LEONARD WILLIAM, educator; b. Forest Park, Ill., Feb. 17, 1916; s. Harry Christian and Clara Antoinette (Klein) H.; m. Akemi Kishi, Feb. 28, 1981. B.S.C., Loyola U., Chgo., 1952; M.B.A., U. Chgo., 1954; Ph.D. (U. Calif. at Los Angeles Bus. Sch. Alumni Assn. fellow, Univ. fellow, Ford Found. fellow), U. Calif. at Los Angeles, 1962. C.P.A., Ill. With San. Dist. Chgo., 1941-56; asst. prof. accounting Calif. State U. at Los Angeles, 1956-59, asso. prof. accounting, 1959-65, prof. accounting, 1965—, coordinator program bus. info. systems, 1956-73, asst. dean grad. studies, 1963-72; Mem. nat. panel arbitrators Am. Arbitration Assn., 1972—. Author: Introduction to Electronic Data Processing for Business, 1961, Quantitative Approach to Managerial Decisions, 1967, Contemporary Accounting and the Computer, 1969, The British Companies Acts and the Practice of Accountancy, 1844-1962, 1978; Contbr. articles to profl. jours. Served with USNR, 1942-45. Mem. Am. Inst. C.P.A.'s, Am. Accounting Assn., Calif. Soc. C.P.A.'s, Beta Gamma Sigma, Beta Alpha Psi, Alpha Kappa Psi, Phi Kappa Phi. Home: 1225 N Granada Ave Alhambra CA 91801 Office: Cal State Univ 5151 State University Dr Los Angeles CA 90032

HEINDEL, NED DUANE, chemistry educator; b. Red Lion, Pa., Sept. 4, 1937; s. Penrose Horace and Dorothy May (Strayer) H.; m. Linda Clarelle Heefner, Aug. 26, 1959. B.S., Lebanon Valley Coll., Annville, Pa., 1959; M.S., U. Del., 1961, Ph.D., 1963; postdoctoral studies, Princeton U., 1964. Instr. chemistry U. Del., 1962-63; asst. prof. chemistry Ohio U., Ironton, 1964-65, Marshall U., Huntington, W. Va., 1964-66; asst. prof. to assoc. prof. chemistry Lehigh U., Bethlehem, Pa., 1966-73, H.S. Bunn prof., 1973—, dir. Ctr. Health Scis., 1980—; prof. nuclear medicine Hahnemann Med. U., Phila., 1971—; cons. Pa. State Police Crim Lab., Bethlehem, 1975—; cons. safety program J.T. Baker Chem. Co., Phillipsburh, N.J., 1978—; regional lectr. Middle Atlantic region Sigma Xi. Author: Iron, Armor and Adolescents, 1982; editor: Chemistry of Radiopharmaceuticals, 1978; contbr. numerous articles to profl. jours. Trustee keystone Jr. Coll, LaPlume, Pa., 1975—, Ctr. for History of Chemistry, Phila., 1982—. Recipient Alumni Assn. award Lebanon Valley Coll., 1971; fellow NSF, 1963-64; recipient numerous research grants. Mem. Am. Chem. Soc. (councilor), Royal Soc., Soc. Nuclear Medicine, Sigma Xi. Republican. Mehtodist. Home: Box 510 Hexenkofp Rd Easton PA 18042 Office: Ctr for Health Science Bldg 17 Lehigh U Bethlehem PA 18015

HEINDL, CLIFFORD JOSEPH, physicist; b. Chgo., Feb. 4, 1926; s. Anton Thomas and Louise (Fiala) H. B.S., Northwestern U., 1947, M.S., 1948; A.M., Columbia U., 1950, Ph.D., 1959. Sr. physicist Bendix Aviation Corp., Detroit, 1953-54; orsort student Oak Ridge Nat. Lab., 1954-55; asst. sect. chief Babcock & Wilcox Co., Lynchburg, Va., 1956-58; research group supr. Jet Propulsion Lab., Pasadena, Calif., 1959-65, mgr. research and space sci., 1965—. Served with AUS, 1944-46. Mem. AIAA, Am. Nuclear Soc., Health Physics Soc., Planetary Soc. Home: 179 Mockingbird Ln South Pasadena CA 91030 Office: 4800 Oak Grove Dr Pasadena CA 91109

HEINDL, WARREN ANTON, educator; b. Chgo., Dec. 2, 1922; s. Anton T. and Louise (Fiala) H.; m. Margaret Carriger, July 11, 1958. Student, Morton Jr. Coll., 1941-43; LL.B., Chgo.-Kent Coll. Law, 1947, LL.M., 1948; B.S., Northwestern U., 1949. Bar: Ill. bar 1947. Practiced in, Chgo., 1951-65; mem. faculty Chgo.-Kent Coll. Law, 1948-69, asst. prof., 1951-65, asso. prof., 1965-69; prof. law Ill. Inst. Tech., Chgo., 1969—. Fellow Chgo.-Kent Honor Council; mem. Am., Ill. bar assns., Soc. Kent Honor Men, Delta Mu Delta. Home: 508 Selborne Rd Riverside IL 60546 Office: Ill Inst Tech Sch Law Chicago IL 60616

HEINE, AALBERT, museum director; b. The Hague, Netherlands, Oct. 1, 1920; came to U.S., 1951, naturalized, 1956; m. Willem Jacobus and Johanna (Pronk) H.; m. Cornelia Sluiter, Sept. 26, 1946; children—Marianne, Peggy Ann. M.S., Poly. Sch., The Hague, 1942, ingenieur, 1942. Vol., then lectr. Mus. for Edn., The Hague, 1940-51; instr. Am. Mus. Natural History, N.Y.C., 1951-57; dir. Corpus Christi (Tex.) Mus., 1957—; adj. prof. Corpus Christi State U. Author papers in field. Recipient Americanism award DAR, 1974; named Citizen of Yr. Corpus Christi Bd. Realtors, 1975. Mem. Am. Assn. Youth Museums, Am. Assn. Museums, Internat. Council Museums, Mountain Plains Museums Assn., Tex. Assn. Museums. Home: 1110 Clare Dr Corpus Christi TX 78412 Office: 1900 N Chaparral Corpus Christi TX 78401 *During my experience as a political prisoner in Germany, which lasted from 1943 to my liberation in 1945, my views on life were shaped. They basically are: "to consider the preciousness of all living things, and our duty to pay close attention to the welfare and education of our youth."*

HEINE, EDWARD JOSEPH, JR., lawyer; b. Orange, N.J., Sept. 2, 1925; s. Edward Joseph and Jane E. (Regan) H.; m. Mary Jane Day, Apr. 11, 1953; children: Edward J., Timothy J., Christopher J., Kevin J., Brian J. B.S., U.S. Mcht. Marine Acad., 1946, Seton Hall U., 1948; LL.B., Fordham U., 1953; postgrad., N.Y. U., 1956-58. Bar: N.Y. bar 1954. Asst. mgr. dept. mem. firms N.Y. Stock Exchange, 1948-50, 52-53; atty., sr. partner firm Kirlin, Campbell & Keating, N.Y.C., 1953-67; exec. v.p. U.S. Lines Inc., N.Y.C., 1967-70, pres., chief exec. officer, 1970-79, vice chmn., 1979-80; partner firm Gilmartin, Poster & Shafto, N.Y.C., 1980-82; pres., chief exec. officer, chmn. bd. Vinnell Corp., Fairfax, Va., 1982—; dir. Atlantic Transport Co. Ltd., U.S. Lines, Inc., 1969-80, U.K. Mut. S.S. Assurance Asso. (Bermuda) Ltd., 1970-81, Through Transport Mut. Ins. Assn. Ltd.; Pres., dir. Maritime Services Com., 1971-80; mem. Law of Sea Adv. Com., 1973-76; Bd. govs. Nat. Maritime Council, 1971-80, India House; bd. dirs. N.Y. Shipping Assn., 68-71, 73-80, Nat. Def. Transp. Assn., 1969—, Nat. Fgn. Trade Council, 1971-80; mem. council Fordham U.; chmn. adv. bd. U.S. Mcht. Marine Acad., Kings Point, N.Y., 1974-78. Served with U.S. Mcht. Marine, 1944-46; Served with USN, 1950-51. Named Profl. Man of Year U.S. Mcht. Marine Acad., 1966. Propeller Club Port N.Y., Maritime Adminstrn. Bar Assn., Maritime Assos., Maritime Assn. Port N.Y., Am. Bur. Shipping, Newcomen Soc. N.Am. Clubs: Economic, Union League, Downtown Athletic Assn., Whitehall (N.Y.C.); Spring Lake (N.J.) Golf and Country. Office: 10530 Rosehaven St Fairfax VA 22030

HEINE, RICHARD WALTER, metallurgical engineer; b. Detroit, July 22, 1918; s. Walter G. R. and Lisette H.; m. Mary Arlene Conklin, Mar. 30, 1940; children: Sally Lee, Robert Walter. B.S.Ch.E., Wayne State U., 1940; M.S. in Metall. Engring, U. Wis., 1948. Instr. Gen. Motors Inst., Flint, Mich., 1940-43, 46-47; instr. U. Wis., Madison, 1947-48, asst. prof. metall. engring., 1948-54, asso. prof., 1955-62, prof., 1962—, chmn. dept. metall. engring., 1964-74; asso. dir. Engring. Expt. Sta., 1974-76; cons. to industry. Author: Principles of Metal Casting, 1965; contbr. numerous articles on metal casting processes to profl. publs. Served to lt. Ordnance Corps USN, 1943-46; PTO. Recipient C.H. Jennings award Am. Welding Soc., 1976, Ragnar E. Ohnstad award Coll. Engring., U. Wis., 1979. Mem. AIME (C.W. Briggs award 1975), Am. Soc. Metals, Am. Soc. Engring. Edn., Am. Inst. Chem. Engrs., Am. Foundrymen's Soc. (Mac Fadden Gold medal 1966, Silver Anniversary Best Paper award 1983), Inst. Metals, Nat. Soc. Profl. Engrs., YMCA, Sigma Xi. Lutheran. Club: Masons (Madison). Home: 6407 Bridge Rd Apt 203 Madison WI 53713 Office: U Wis 1509 University Ave Madison WI 53706

HEINE, WILLIAM COLBOURNE, newspaper editor; b. St. John, N.B., Can., Nov. 21, 1919; s. Roland W. and Winnifred B. (Trider) H.; m. Vivian Scribner, May 17, 1944. B.A., U. Western Ont., 1949. Mem. staff London, Ont., Can., 1949—, editor, 1967—; adj. prof. U. Western Ont., 1965; chmn. bd. Ryerson Press, Toronto, 1970-75. Author: Historic Ships of the World, 1978, Journalism Case Book, 1973, Shunpiker's Choice, 1974; novels The Last Canadian, 1974, The Swordsman, 1979. Pres. London Family Services Bur., 1965-67, United Community Services London, 1967-69, London Art Gallery, 1973-74. Served with Canadian Army, 1939-42; Served with RCAF, 1942-45. Mem. Internat. Press Inst., Canadian Press Assn., Canadian Daily Newspaper Pubs. Assn., World Press Freedom Com., Commonwealth Press Union, Am. Soc. Newspaper Editors. Mem. United Ch. Can. Clubs: London, London Hunt. Home: 647 Hillcrest Dr London ON N6K 1A8 Canada Office: London Free Press Box 2280 London ON Canada

HEINECKEN, ROBERT FRIEDLI, educator, artist; b. Denver, Oct. 29, 1931; s. Friedli Wilhelm and Mathilda Louise (Moehl) H.; m. Janet Marion Storey, Jan. 7, 1955 (div. 1980); children—Geoffrey Robert, Kathé Marie, Karol Leslie. A.A., Riverside Coll., 1951; B.A., U. Calif. at Los Angeles, 1959, M.A., 1960. Vis. faculty Harvard, 1972, San Francisco Art Inst., 1970, Art Inst. Chgo., 1970, Internat. Museum Photography, Rochester, N.Y., 1967, State U. N.Y. at Buffalo, 1969; prof. art U. Calif. at Los Angeles, 1960—. One-man shows at, Light Gallery, N.Y.C., Witkin Gallery, N.Y.C., Pasadena Art Mus., Focus Gallery, San Francisco, Madison (Wis.) Art Center, Friends of Photography Gallery, Carmel, Calif., Internat. Mus. Photography, 1976; exhibited in group shows at, Mus. Modern Art, N.Y.C., Whitney Mus., N.Y.C., Nat. Gallery Can., Ottawa, Camden Arts Center, London, Eng.; represented in permanent collections, Internat. Mus. Photography, Rochester, Mus. Modern Art, N.Y.C., Fogg Art Mus., Cambridge, Mass., San Francisco Mus. Art, Oakland (Calif.)Mus. Art, Library of Congress, Washington, Pasadena Mus. Art, U. Ariz., Tucson. Trustee Friends of Photography, Carmel, 1974-75. Served with USMCR, 1953-57. Guggenheim fellow, 1975; Nat. Endowment for Arts grantee, 1977, 81. Mem. Soc. for Photog. Edn. (chmn. bd. dirs. 1970-72). Office: Dept Art U Calif 405 Hilgard Ave Los Angeles CA 90024

HEINEKEN, ALFRED HENRY, brewery exec.; b. Amsterdam, Netherlands, Nov. 4, 1923; s. H.P. and C. (Breitenstein) H.; m. L. Cummins, 1948. Ed. Kennemer lyceum. Adviser to mgr. Heineken Breweries, Inc., U.S., 1945-48; now pres. bd. mng. dirs. Heineken N.V., Netherlands; pres. Heineken Holding N.V.; mem. supervisory bd. Gen. Bank Netherlands, N.V., Thyssen Bornemisza Group N.V. Address: Heineken NV Postbox 28 1000 AA Amsterdam Netherlands

HEINEMAN, ANDREW DAVID, lawyer; b. N.Y.C., Nov. 5, 1928; s. Bernard and Lucy Rose (Morgenthau) H. B.A., Williams Coll., 1950; LL.B., Yale U., 1953. Bar: N.Y. 1953. Mem. firm Proskauer Rose Goetz & Mendelsohn, N.Y.C., 1953—, ptrn., 1963—; dir. M.H. Lamston, Inc., N.Y.C. Pres., bd. dirs. Ernest and Mary Hayward Weir Found., N.Y.C., 1969—; trustee Williams Coll., 1980—, Mt. Sinai Med. Sch., 1976—, Jewish Home and Hosp. for Aged, 1967—, Abelard Found., 1976—; exec. asst. Citizens for Kennedy and Johnson, N.Y.C., 1960; mem. Gov.'s Commn. on Minorities in Med. Schs., N.Y.C., 1982. Mem. Yale Law Sch. Assn. N.Y. (pres. 1970-73), Yale Law Sch. Alumni Assn. (v.p. 1973-76). Club: Yale. Office: Proskauer Rose Goetz & Mendelsohn 300 Park Ave New York NY 10022

HEINEMAN, BEN WALTER, corporation executive; b. Wausau, Wis., Feb. 10, 1914; s. Walter Ben and Elsie Brunswick (Deutsch) H.; m. Natalie Goldstein, Apr. 17, 1935; children: Martha Heineman

Pieper, Ben Walter. Student, U. Mich., 1930-33; LL.B., Northwestern U., 1936; LL.D. (hon.), Lawrence Coll., 1959, Lake Forest Coll., 1966, Northwestern U., 1967. Bar: Ill. 1936. Pvt. practice law and govt. service, Chgo., Washington, Algiers, 1936-56; chmn. bd. dirs. Four Wheel Drive Auto Co., 1954-57; now chmn. N.W. Industries, Inc.; chmn. C. & N.W. Ry. Co., 1956-72; dir., mem. exec. com. 1st Nat. Bank, Chgo.; chmn. orgn. com. First Chgo. Corp.; Chmn. White House Conf. to Fulfill These Rights, 1966, Pres.'s Task Force on Govt. Orgn., 1966-67, Pres.'s Commn. Income Maintenance Programs, 1967-69. Life trustee U. Chgo.; chmn. Ill. Bd. Higher Edn., 1962-69; trustee, mem. investment com. Savs. and Profit Sharing Fund of Sears Roebuck Employees, 1966-71; vis. com. dept. econs. Harvard, 1965-71; trustee, mem. exec. com., chmn. audit com. Rockefeller Found., 1972-78; life bd. dirs. Lyric Opera, Chgo.; trustee Orchestral Assn., Chgo.; sustaining fellow Art Inst. Chgo. Fellow Am. Bar Found. (life), Am. Bar Assn., Am. Acad. Arts and Scis.; mem. Am. Law Inst. (life), Ill., Chgo. bar assns., Order of Coif, Phi Delta Phi (hon.). Clubs: Ephraim (Wis.) Yacht; Mid-America, Chicago, Casino, Commonwealth, Wayfarers, Economic, Standard, Quadrangle, Executives, Commercial, Chicago Yacht (Chgo.); Metropolitan, Carlton. Home: 180 E Pearson St Chicago IL 60611 Office: 6300 Sears Tower Chicago IL 60606

HEINEMAN, BENJAMIN WALTER, JR., lawyer; b. Chgo., Jan. 25, 1944; s. Benjamin Walter and Natalie (Goldstein) H.; m. Jeanne Cristine Russell, June 7, 1975; children: Matthew R., Zachary R. B.A. magna cum laude, Harvard U., 1965; B.Letters, Balliol Coll., Oxford U., Eng., 1967; J.D., Yale U., 1971. Bar: D.C. bar 1973, U.S. Supreme Ct. bar 1973. Reporter Chgo. Sun Times, 1968; law clk. Asso. Justice Potter Stewart, U.S. Supreme Ct., 1971-72; staff atty. Center for Law and Social Policy, 1973-75; with Williams Connolly and Califano, Washington, 1975-76; exec. asst. to Sec. Joseph A. Califano, Jr., HEW, Washington, 1977-78; asst. sec. for planning and evaluation HEW, 1978-79; partner Califano, Ross & Heineman, Washington, 1979-82, Sidley & Austin, 1982—. Author: The Politics of the Powerless: A Study of the Campaign Against Racial Discrimination, 1972, Memorandum for the President: A Strategic Approach to Domestic Affairs in the 1980's, 1981; editor-in-chief: Yale Law Jour., 1970-71. Rhodes scholar, 1965-67. Mem. Phi Beta Kappa. Home: 4914 30th Pl NW Washington DC 20008 Office: 1722 Eye St NW Washington DC 20006

HEINEMAN, HEINZ, scientist, consultant; b. Berlin, Aug. 21, 1913; U.S., 1938; s. Felix and Edith (Boehm) H.; m. Elaine P. Silverman, Feb. 12, 1948; children: Susan C., Peter M. Ph.D., U. Basel, 1937. Lab. supr. Attapulgus Clay Co., Phila., 1941-48; sect. chief Houdry Process Corp., Marcus Hook, Pa., 1948-57; dir. chem. and engring. research M.W. Kellogg Co., N.Y.C., 1957-69; mgr. catalysis research Mobil Research and Devel. Corp., Princeton, N.J., 1969-78; staff sr. scientist Lawrence Berkeley Lab., U. Calif., Berkeley, 1978—, lectr. chem. engring. dept., 1979—; cons. in field; cons. editor Marcel Dekker, Inc., N.Y.C., 1977—. Contbr. numerous articles to profl. jours.; patentee in field. Bd. dirs. Phila. Chamber Music Soc., 1946-47, N.J. Council for Research, Trenton, 1975-78; mem. Flood Control Commn., Princeton, 1972-75. Recipient Houdry Catalysis Soc. N.Am., 1975. Fellow AAAS, Am. Inst. Chemists; mem. Am. Chem. Soc. (E.V. Muryhree 1972), Internat. Congress on Catalysis (pres. 1956-60), Catalysis Soc. Phila. (pres. 1949-50), Am. Inst. Chem. Engrs. Club: Chemists (N.Y.C.). Home: 1588 Campus Dr Berkeley CA 94708 Office: Univ California Lawrence Berkeley Lab Berkeley CA 94720

HEINEMAN, NATALIE (MRS. BEN W. HEINEMAN), civic worker. Formerly med. social worker, Chgo.; pres. Child Welfare League Am., 1971-74; now bd. dirs. Chmn. citizens com. Ill. Adoption Service, 1959-71; pres. Chgo. Child Care Soc., 1967-71, now bd. dirs.; bd. dirs. United Way Met. Chgo., United Way Am., 1973-79, Erickson Inst. for Advanced Study in Child Devel., Chgo. Fedn. Settlements, 1957-68; mem. women's bd. Field Mus. Natural History, U. Chgo., Northwestern U.; vis. com. U. Chgo. Sch. Social Service Service. Address: 180 E Pearson St Chicago IL 60611

HEINEMAN, PAUL LOWE, consulting civil engineer; b. Omaha, Oct. 24, 1924; s. Paul George and Annie L. (Lowe) H.; children—Karen E., John F., Ellen F. Student, U. Omaha, 1942-43; B.S.C.E., Iowa State U., 1945, M.S., 1948. Registered profl. engr. Mo., Calif., N.Y., Kans., 25 other states and Republic of Colombia. Instr. Iowa State U., 1946-48; designer Howard, Needles, Tammen & Bergendoff (Cons. Engrs.), Kansas City, Mo., 1948-64, partner, 1965—; exec. v.p. Howard, Needles, Tammen & Bergendoff Internat., Inc., Kansas City, 1967—; pres., v.p. subs. Served with C.E. USNR, 1945-46. Fellow Am. Cons. Engrs. Council, ASCE; mem. Am. Ry. Engring. Assn., Am. Concrete Inst., Nat. Soc. Profl. Engrs. Presbyterian (elder 1958—, trustee 1960—). Clubs: Kansas City, Rotary, Engrs. (Kansas City). Office: 9200 Ward Pkwy Kansas City MO 64114

HEINEMAN, WARNER, banker; b. Hannover, Germany, July 19, 1922; came to U.S., 1937, naturalized, 1945; s. Hugo and Charlotte (Guthmann) H.; m. Anne Fisher, Sept. 3, 1949; children—Lawrence Jeffrey, Carol Anne. B.A., U. Mich., 1943; M.B.A., U. So. Calif., 1952. Lic. pub. acct. Calif. With Union Bank, Los Angeles, 1943-81, v.p., 1958-62, sr. v.p., 1962-64, regional v.p., Beverly Hills, 1964-67, exec. v.p., 1967-76, vice chmn., 1976-81; ret., 1981; mem. exec. com., sr. v.p. City Nat. Bank, Beverly Hills, Calif., 1981—; mem. editorial bd. State Bar Calif. Chmn. Mayor's Sister Cities Com.; Bd. dirs. Music Guild; bd. dirs., treas. Music Center Opera Assos., both Los Angeles; trustee Southwestern U. Sch. Law; pres. Bel Air Assn. Served with AUS, 1945-46. Mem. Am. Bankers Assn. (past mem. exec. com. internat. div.), Robert Morris Assos. (past dir.), Los Angeles Area C. of C. (past dir.), Zeta Beta Tau. Clubs: Brentwood Country, Jonathan. Home: 457 St Pierre Rd Los Angeles CA 90077 Office: City Nat Bank 400 N Roxbury Dr Beverly Hills CA 90210

HEINEMAN, WILLIAM ARTHUR, chain store executive; b. Bklyn., Jan. 8, 1924; s. William C. and Vera (Irwin) H.; m. Jean E. Bonvicino, June 25, 1950; children—Deborah Ann, Geoffrey W. B.S., NYU, 1952, LL.B., 1956, LL.M., 1982. Bar: N.Y. 1957, U.S. Supreme Ct. 1964. With Merc. Stores Co., Inc., N.Y.C., 1941—, treas., 1967—, v.p., 1972—. Served with USNR, 1943-46. Mem. Beta Gamma Sigma. Home: 588 Madison Ave Baldwin NY 11510 Office: Mercantile Stores Co Inc 128 W 31st St New York NY 10001

HEINEMANN, GEORGE ALFRED, television company executive; b. Chgo., Dec. 9, 1918; s. George Gross and Mamie Agnes (Dall) H.; m. Jacqueline Holsinger, 1945 (div. 1952); 1 dau., Michael Ann; m. Jacqueline Ann Pashley, 1953 (div. 1964); children: Robin Anne, Kim Louise; m. Helen Leach English, Dec. 19, 1967; stepchildren: Helen Elizabeth, David S., Frederick G. B.A., Northwestern U., 1941. With NBC, N.Y.C., 1956—, dir. pub. affairs, 1967-70, v.p. children's programs, 1970-73, v.p. spl. children's programs, 1973-78, v.p., gen. program exec., 1978-81; pres. Showmakers, Inc., N.Y.C., 1982—; instr. TV creative thinking and prodn. Northwestern U., 1952-56, Columbia U., 1958-60, NYU, 1964-68, adj. prof. TV Sch. of Arts, 1982; instr. TV creative thinking and prodn. St. John's U., N.Y.C., 1972-77; Newhouse chair Syracuse U. (Emmy nomination or award 1952, 62, 64, 68, 76, 77, 78, 79, Christopher award 1966, 68, 70, 77, 78, Best Children's Program in World award Prix Jeunesse Internat. 1966, ACT Achievement award 1976, 77). Mem. White House Conf. Children, 1970; Mem. nat. adv. com. Boy Scouts Am., 1966-77, YMCA, 1968-75, Girl Scouts, 1969-71, Nat. Council Chs., 1970-77; bd. dirs. N.Y.C. YMCA, 1968-73. Served to comdr. USNR, World War II. Recipient Alumni award Northwestern U., 1965, Peabody award, 1953, 66, 67, 68, 72, 74, 78. Mem. Nat. Acad. TV Arts and Scis. (nat. trustee), Internat. Radio and TV Soc., Navy League Am. (bd. dirs. 1958-73), Acacia, Sigma Delta Chi. Clubs: Moose., Overseas Press (N.Y.C.). Home: 11 W 81st St New York NY 10024 Office: 454 W 46th St New York NY 10036 *1. Decisions are the easiest after we make them. 2. Hearing only what we want to hear is the real communication dilemma. 3. Change is constant and success without imperfection is fatal. 4. Creativity is two parts organization, one part concept and one part unending hope. Mix well.*

HEINEN, ERWIN, accountant; b. Comfort, Tex., Mar. 17, 1906; s. Hubert and Else (Strohacker) H.; m. Emily Blanton Plummer, June 25, 1929; children—Nancy Blanton (Mrs. Arnold Earl Luetge), Hubert Plummer. B.B.A., U. Tex., 1927. With Ernst & Whinney (C.P.A.'s), Houston, 1927—, partner, 1948-69, cons., 1969—; former chmn. accounting faculty assos. U. Tex. Sch. Bus. Adminstrn. Vice pres. Houston Grand Opera Assn., 1958-69; treas. Music Guild, 1963-68; bd. mgrs. Harris County Hosp. Dist., 1971-73; Past bd. dirs. Houston Symphony Soc.; trustee Bd. Edn. Houston Ind. Sch. Dist., 1973-77, pres., 1977; former treas. Houston Mus. Fine Arts; chmn. Cultural Arts Council of Houston. Mem. Am. Inst. C.P.A.'s, Tex. Soc. C.P.A.'s, So. States Conf. C.P.A.'s (past pres.), Nat. Accountants Assn., Houston C. of C. (vice chmn. cultural arts com.). Episcopalian. Clubs: River Oaks Country, Houston, Houston Rotary (past pres., (dist. gov.) 1970-71), Harvard Business School (dir.). Home: 5406 Huckleberry St Houston TX 77056 Office: 333 Clay St Suite 3100 Houston TX 77002

HEINER, CLYDE MONT, energy company executive; b. Wendell, Idaho, Apr. 4, 1938; s. Mont A. and Margaret (Alexander) H.; m. Gail Tanner, Dec. 28, 1966; children: Jeremy, Emily, Sean, Forrest, Joshua, Jenny Lee, Mandy, Marci. B.A., Columbia U., 1960, B.S. in Structural Engring., 1961; M.B.A., Stanford U., 1966. Registered profl. engr., Utah, Wyo., Idaho, D.C. Budget dir. Mountain Fuel Supply Co., Salt Lake City, 1968-69, dir. rates and planning, 1974-76, mgr. engring., 1976-77, v.p. engring., 1977-80, sr. v.p. corp. devel., 1980—; asst. adminstr. U. Utah Hosp., Salt Lake City, 1969-74. Mem. adv. council U. Utah Coll. Engring., Salt Lake City, 1980-83; chmn. bd. Salt Lake chpt. ARC, 1982—; mem. Clearfield City Council, Utah, 1973-74. Mem. Nat. Soc. Profl. Engrs., Am. Gas Assn., Pacific Coast Gas Assn., Am. Inst. Indsl. Engrs. (past pres.). Mormon. Home: 1462 Alta Circle Salt Lake City UT 84103 Office: 180 E 1st South St Salt Lake City UT 84139

HEINEY, JOHN WEITZEL, former utility executive; b. Lancaster, Pa., Nov. 9, 1913; s. George and Gertrude G. (Weitzel) H.; m. Betty M. Horn, Apr. 12, 1941. B.S. in Bus. Adminstrn, Lehigh U., 1935. With various subsidiaries Am. Water Works Co., 1935-41, 46-60; pres., chief exec. officer, dir. Indiana Gas Co., Inc., Indpls., 1960-73, chmn. bd., chief exec. officer, 1973-78, chmn. bd., 1978-84; pres., dir. Ohio River Pipe Line Corp., 1964-73, chmn. bd., 1973-78; pres., chmn. Gen. Assurance Services, Ltd., 1975-84; dir. Mchts. Nat. Bank & Trust Co. Indpls., Mchts. Nat. Corp., Indpls. Bd. dirs. United Fund Greater Indpls., 1960-77; bd. dirs. Community Hosp. Indpls., 1968-73, 75-81, chmn., 1972-73; bd. dirs., chmn. Community Health Services Found., 1983—. Served to lt. col., inf. AUS, 1941-46. Decorated Bronze Star medal. Mem. Am. Gas Assn. (past chmn. spl. com. on consumer affairs, 1st vice chmn. 1968, chmn. 1969, dir., Distinguished Service award 1975), Ind. Gas Assn. (past pres. and dir.), Inst. Gas Tech. (trustee 1965, chmn. bd. trustees 1968), Internat. Gas Union (mem. council and bur. 1973-75), Ind. C. of C. (dir. 1973-80), Newcomen Soc. N.Am., Beta Theta Pi. Club: Meridian Hills Country.

HEININGER, ERWIN CARL, lawyer; b. Ann Arbor, Mich., Apr. 9, 1921. A.B., U. Mich., 1943, J.D., 1952. Bar: Mich. 1953, Ill. 1953, U.S. Dist. Ct. (no. dist.) Ill. 1954, U.S. Ct. Claims 1957, U.S. Ct. Appeals (7th cir.) 1962, U.S. Ct. Appeals (3d cir.) 1981, U.S. Ct. Appeals (2d cir.) 1983, U.S. Supreme Ct. 1960. Trial atty. antitrust div. Dept. Justice, Chgo., 1953-55; assoc. Mayer, Friedlich, Spies, Tierney, Brown & Platt, Chgo., 1955-60; ptnr. Mayer, Brown & Platt, Chgo., 1960—. Contbr. articles to profl. jours. Fellow Am. Coll. Trial Lawyers; mem. ABA, Fed. Bar Assn., Ill. Bar Assn., Chgo. Bar Assn., Bar Assn. 7th Fed. Cir., Chgo. Council Lawyers, Law Club Chgo., Legal Club Chgo., Assn. Trial Lawyers Am., Maritime Law Assn. U.S., Phi Delta Phi, Lambda Chi Alpha. Clubs: University, Metropolitan, Executive; Columbia Yacht (Chgo.); National Lawyers (Washington). Office: Mayer Brown & Platt 231 S LaSalle St Chicago IL 60604

HEININGER, S(AMUEL) ALLEN, chemical company executive; b. New Britain, Conn., June 13, 1925; s. Alfred D. and Erma Geraldine (Kline) H.; m. Barbara Ashenfelter Griffith, June 16, 1948; children: Janet, Kathryn, Kenneth, Keith. A.B., Oberlin Coll., 1948; M.S., Carnegie Inst. Tech., 1951; D.Sc., 1952. Research chemist Monsanto Chem. Co., Dayton, Ohio, 1952-56, group leader, 1956-58, project mgr. devel. dept. Organic Chems. div., St. Louis, 1958-59, mgr. fine chems. intermediates and market exploration sect., 1959-65, dir. comml. devel., 1965-67, dir. food and fine chems., 1967-71, dir. corp. plans and devel., 1971-74, dir. corp. research and devel., 1976-77, v.p. research and devel., 1977-79, v.p. tech. devel., 1979-80, v.p. corp. plans and bus. devel., 1980—; gen. mgr. plasticizers div. Monsanto Indsl. Chems. Co., St. Louis, 1974-76. Contbr. articles to profl. jours. Alderman, City of Warson Woods (Mo.), 1961-65, police commr., 1967-71. Served to lt. USNR, 1943-46. Mem. Am. Chem. Soc., Indsl. Research Inst., Soc. Chem. Industry, N.Y. Acad. Scis. Republican. Episcopalian. Clubs: Old Warson Country, Creve Coeur Racquet. U.S., fgn. patentee in field. Office: 800 N Lindbergh Saint Louis MO 63167

HEINLEIN, ROBERT ANSON, author; b. Butler, Mo., July 7, 1907; s. Rex Ivar and Bam (Lyle) H.; m. Virginia Doris Gerstenfeld, Oct. 21, 1948. Grad., U.S. Naval Acad., 1929; postgrad. physics and math., UCLA, 1934; L.H.D. (hon.), Eastern Mich. U., 1977. Commd. ensign U.S. Navy, 1929, advanced to lt. (j.g.), 1932; assignments at sea; disabled, retired, 1934; aviation engr. U.S. Navy, 1942-45; owner silver mine Shively & Sophie Lodes, Silver Plume, Colo., 1934-35; James V. Forrestal Meml. lectr. U.S. Naval Acad., 1973. Author: 45 books including Beyond This Horizon, 1948, The Green Hills of Earth, 1951, Puppet Masters, 1951, Double Star, 1956 (Hugo award), The Door Into Summer, 1957, Citizen of the Galaxy, 1957, Methuselah's Children, 1958, Have Space Suit-Will Travel, 1958, Starship Troopers, 1959 (Hugo award), Stranger in a Strange Land, 1961 (Hugo award), Glory Road, 1963, The Moon is a Harsh Mistress, 1966 (Hugo award), I Will Fear No Evil, 1970, Time Enough for Love, 1973, others; films Destination Moon, 1950, Project Moonbase, 1954; works included in numerous anthologies and collections, stories have been sold or leased to TV and radio for various space series; guest commentator Apollo-11 1st lunar landing, 1969; author: tech. books including Test Procedures for Plastic Materials Intended for Structural and Semi-Structural Aircraft Uses, 1944; also tech. and popular novels and lectures. Recipient Best Sci. Fiction Novel award World Sci. Fiction Conv., 1956, 59, 61, 66; Sequoyah award, 1961; Best Liked Book award Boys Clubs Am., 1959; Humanitarian of Year award Asso. Health Found. and Nat. Rare Blood Club, 1974; Nebula award Sci. Fiction Writers Am., 1975; also named Grand Master; Inkpot award, 1977; Humanitarian award Nat. Rare Blood Club, 1974; award Am. Assn. Blood Banks, 1977, Council Community Blood Centers, 1977; Tomorrow Starts Here award Delta Vee Soc. Mem. Am. Inst. Aero. and Astronautics, Authors Guild Am., U.S. Naval Acad. Alumni Assn., Retired Officers Assn., Navy League, Assn. U.S. Army, Air Force Assn., World Future Soc., Nat. Rare Blood (donors) Club, U.S. Naval Inst., Calif. Arts Soc., Minutemen of U.S.S. Lexington, Am. Assn. Blood Banks. Home: care Spectrum Literary Agency 432 Park Ave S #1205 New York NY 10016

HEINLY, DAVID REED, editor; b. Allentown, Pa., Feb. 23, 1931; s. David Maguire and Alma Reed (Ressler) H.; m. Louise J. Ringrose, Apr. 28, 1962; children: Robert R., Elizabeth D. B.S. in Journalism, U. Md., 1958. Pub. info. officer U.S. Weather Bur., 1958-60; assoc. editor Washington bur. Chilton Publs., 1960-64, Bur. Nat. Affairs, 1964-65; leigs. aide, press sec. to mem. Congress, 1965-67; assoc. editor Traffic World Mag., 1967-72; Washington editor and bur. chief Cahners Pub. Co., 1972—. Served with USAF, 1951-55. Mem. Nat. Assn. Real Estate Editors, Nat. Press Club. Home: 5910 Grayson St Springfield VA 22150 Office: 1435 G St NW Room 639 Washington DC 20005

HEINRICH, BERND, biologist; b. Bad Polzin, Germany, Apr. 619, 1940; came to U.S., 1950, naturalized, 1958; s. Gerd Hermann and Hildegard Maria (Bury) H. B.A., U. Maine, 1964, M.S., 1966; Ph.D. in Zoology, UCLA, 1970. Teaching and research asst. UCLA, 1966-70; asst. prof. entomology U. Calif., Berkeley, 1971-78, prof., 1978—. Author: Bumblebee Economics, 1979, Insect Thermoregulation, 1981, In a Patch of Fireweed, 1984; co-author also 80 articles. Grantee NSF, 1971—. Fellow AAAS; mem. Am. Soc. Zoologists, Ecol. Soc. Am. Office: Dept Zoology U Vt Burlington VT 05405

HEINRICH, ROSS RAYMOND, geophysicist, educator; b. St. Louis, Dec. 12, 1915; s. Edward Ernst and Mary R. (Busch) H.; m. Marie Frances McKinnon, June 3, 1948; children: Ross Thaddeus, Christopher Edward, Anita Marie, Victoria Margaret. A.B., U. Mo., 1936; M.S., St. Louis U., 1938, Ph.D., 1944. With St. Louis U., 1936—, successively grad. fellow geophysics, instr., asst. prof., asso. prof., 1936-51, prof., 1951-80, prof. emeritus, 1981—, dir. dept. geophysics and geophys. engring., 1956-63, acting dean Inst. of Tech., 1968-71, chmn. dept. earth and atmospheric scis., 1975-80; cons. ground vibration problems, 1938—; Mem. St. Louis County Explosives Control Adv. Bd., 1964-75; trustee Univ. Corp. Atmospheric Research, 1960-71. Mem. Am. Inst. Mining and Metall. and Petroleum Engrs., Am. Meteorol. Soc., Nat. Soc. Profl. Engrs., Air Pollution Control Assn., Am. Geophys. Union, A.A.A.S., Geol. Soc. Am., Am. Soc. Engring. Edn., Seismol. Soc. Am., Phi Beta Kappa, Sigma Xi. Home: 21 Larkin Ln Saint Louis MO 63128

HEINRICHS, WILLIAM LEROY, obstetrician, gynecologist, educator; b. Collinsville, Okla., Aug. 14, 1932; s. Daniel J. and Ruby (Just) H.; m. Phyllis M. Smith, May 28, 1954; children—Stephen C., Lynn K. B.S., Southwestern State Coll., 1954; M.D., U. Okla., 1958; Ph.D., M.Sc., U. Oreg., 1967. Diplomate: Am. Bd. Obstetrics Gynecology. Rotating intern St. Anthony Hosp., Oklahoma City, 1958-59; resident in obstetrics and gynecology Harper Hosp., Detroit, 1959-62; USPHS post-residency fellow depts. obstetrics gynecology biochemistry U. Oreg., Portland, 1962-67, clin. instr., 1965-67; asst. prof. dept. obstetrics gynecology U. Wash., Seattle, 1967-69, asso. prof., 1969-72, prof., 1972-76; prof., chmn. dept. gynecology obstetrics Stanford (Calif.) U., 1976—; vis. fellow Battelle Meml. Inst., Seattle Research Center, 1973; attending staff U. Hosp. and Harborview Med. Center, Seattle, 1967-76, Stanford U. Med. Center, 1976—, Santa Clara Valley Med. Center, San Jose, Calif., 1976—; cons. USPHS Hosp., Seattle, 1971-76, Madigan Army Med. Center, Tacoma, Wash., 1971-76, Oakland Naval Hosp., 1979—; mem. Study Sect. Human Embryo and Devel., NIH, 1974-78, chmn., 1979-81; del. Sister City Affiliation, Seattle and Tashkent, Uzbekistan, USSR, 1974, 13th Annual Japan-U.S. Congress of Mayor and C. of C. Pres.'s, Sapporo, Japan, 1975. Asso. editor gynecologic obstet. investigation: Internat. Jour. Sci. of Reproduction, 1970; Contbr. numerous articles to med. jours. Recipient Pres.'s First award for research Am. Coll. Obstetricians and Gynecologists, 1970. Fellow Am. Coll. Obstetricians and Gynecologists; mem. AAAS, Endocrine Soc., Soc. for Gynecologic Investigation, Western Soc. for Clin. Research, Am. Soc. Biol. Chemists, Shufelt Soc., Peninsula Obstet. and Gynecol. Soc., San Francisco Obstet. and Gynecol. Soc., Am. Assn. Obstetrics and Gynecology, Am. Gynecol. Soc., Alpha Phi Sigma, Beta Beta Beta. Presbyterian. Home: 8 Campbell Ln Menlo Park CA 94025 Office: Stanford U Med Center Rm A332 Stanford CA 94305

HEINRIKSON, ROBERT LEROY, biochemistry educator, researcher; b. Sioux City, Iowa, Dec. 31, 1935; s. William Frederick and Norma Margaret (Johnson) H.; m. Jane Mary Randi, Aug. 18, 1963; children: Elise Anne, John William. B.A., Augustana Coll., Rock Island, Ill., 1958; Ph.D., U. Chgo., 1963. Research assoc. Rockefeller U., N.Y.C., 1963-65; NATO research fellow MRC Lab. of Molecular Biology, Cambridge, Eng., 1965-66; asst. prof. biochemistry U. Chgo., 1966-72, assoc. prof., 1972-79, prof., 1979; panel mem. Bioinstrumentation NSF, 1979—. Editor: Proteins in Biology and Medicine, 1983; mem. editorial bd.: Jour. Biol. Chemistry, 1978-83, Jour. Protein Chemistry, 1982—; contbr. numerous articles to profl. jours. Recipient grant NSF, USPHS, 1968—. Mem. Am. Soc. Biol. Chemists, Phi Beta Kappa, Sigma Xi. Democrat. Home: 9216 S Pleasant St Chicago IL 60620 Office: Dept Biochemistry U Chgo 920 E 58th St Chicago IL 60637

HEINS, ALBERT EDWARD, mathematician; b. Boston, Sept. 7, 1912; s. Samuel and Rose Lily H.; m. Miriam Yaskin, Aug. 15, 1939; 1 dau., Ellen Ruth. B.S., M.I.T., 1934, M.S., 1935, Ph.D., 1936. Instr. math. Purdue U., 1935-40, asst. prof., 1940-42, 46; research asso. Radiation Lab. (N.D.R.C. Project), M.I.T., 1942-46; asso. prof. math. Carnegie Inst. Tech., 1946-51, prof., 1951-59; prof. math. U. Mich., Ann Arbor, 1959—; guest prof. Technische Hochschule, Darmstadt, W. Ger., 1980. Purdue Research Found. fellow, 1941; John Simon Guggenheim Found. fellow, 1953-54; Horace Rackham grantee U. Mich., 1960. Mem. Am. Math Soc., AAUP. Home: 1618 Shadford Rd Ann Arbor MI 48104 Office: U Mich Dept Math Ann Arbor MI 48109

HEINS, ALLISON EDWARD, journalist, educator; b. Marquette, Mich., May 4, 1931; s. Arthur Edward and Ululla (Prothero) H.; m. Audrey Louise Noring, Aug. 4, 1957; children: Alan, John, Susan. B.S., U. Wis., 1953. Weekly editor Crawford County Press, Prairie du Chien, Wis., 1953; legis. reporter, bur. mgr. U.P.I., Des Moines, 1956-60; weekly editor Waverly (Iowa) Newspapers, 1960-63; reporter, asst. mng. editor, mng. editor Des Moines Register & Tribune Co., 1963-74; publisher, exec. v.p. Concord Pub. House, Inc., Cape Girardeau, Mo., 1974-79; vis. prof., then assoc. prof. Sch. Journalism, U. Mo., Columbia, 1979—. Served with AUS, 1954-56. Recipient Am. Polit. Sci. Soc. nat. award for distinguished govtl. reporting, 1967. Methodist. Office: 100 Neff Hall U Mo Columbia MO 65201

HEINS, ARTHUR JAMES, educator, economist; b. Tigerton, Wis., May 30, 1931; s. Rufus Carl and Emelyn (Murphy) H.; m. Nancy Lee Woltman, Feb. 18, 1952; children: Michael James, Robert Todd, Barbara Lynn (dec.), Mary Margaret. B.S., U. Wis., 1953, M.S., 1957, Ph.D., 1961; student, U. Calif. at Los Angeles, 1957-58. Mem. faculty U. Ill. at Urbana, 1960—, prof. econs., 1969—; vis. staff mem. Inst. Research on Poverty, U. Wis., 1968-69; cons. to govt. and bus. Author:

Constitutional Restrictions Against State Debt, 1963, Illinois Economic Growth Study, 1976, The Illinois Economy: An Analysis of Economic Growth Since 1947, 2 vols., 1983; also articles. Served with USN, 1953-56. Recipient award outstanding contbn. undergrad. edn. Zeta Beta Tau, 1965. Mem. Am., Midwest econs. assns. Home: 2507 S Cottage Grove Urbana IL 61801

HEINS, ETHEL L., magazine editor; b. N.Y.C., Apr. 9, 1918; d. H. H. and Rose (M.) Yaskin; m. Paul Heins, June 27, 1943; children: Peter S., Margery E. B.A., Douglass Coll., 1938; postgrad., Harvard Grad. Sch. Edn., 1964. Children's librarian N.Y.C. Public Library, 1938-43, Boston Public Library, 1955-62; instructional materials specialist Lexington (Mass.) Public Schs., 1962-74; editor The Horn Book Mag., Boston, 1974—; adj. prof. Simmons Coll. Center for the Study of Children's Lit. Contbr. chpt. to book; articles to publs. including Education Today. Recipient citation Rutgers U. Grad. Sch. Library and Info. Sci., 1979. Mem. Douglass Soc. for Alumnae of Disting. Achievement.; Mem. ALA, New Eng. Library Assn., New Eng. Round Table of Children's Librarians, Children's Lit. Assn., Internat. Research Soc. for Children's Lit., Nat. Council Tchrs. of English, Sch. Library Assn. (Eng.). Home: 29 Hope St Auburndale MA 02166 Office: Park Square Bldg Boston MA 02166 *I have worked nearly all my life to instill and to increase in young people a love of reading for its own sake. Now, in an increasingly technological world, many people fear that literacy will decline still further, along with the humanities in American life. Those of us who can convey the power of literature need to work with passionate conviction to convince the young that books too, are supremely "user-friendly"—in order to keep alive reading and the living word.*

HEINS, MAURICE HASKELL, mathematics educator; b. Boston, Nov. 19, 1915; s. Samuel and Rose (Golbert) H.; m. Hadassah Wagman, Aug. 25, 1940; children: Sulamith Hannah, Samuel David. A.B. summa cum laude, Harvard U., 1937, Henry Russell Shaw travelling fellow, 1937-38, M.A., 1939, Ph.D., 1940. Asst. Inst. for Advanced Study, 1940-42; asst. prof. Ill. Inst. Tech., 1942- 44; mathematician Office Chief of Ordnance War Dept., 1944-45; asso. prof. Brown U., 1946-47, prof., 1947-58; prof. math. U. Ill., Urbana, 1958-74; also distinguished prof., chair complex analysis U. Md., College Park, 1974—; vis. prof. U. Calif., Berkeley, 1963-64; exchange prof. Paris IV, 1979; President's fellow, 1952-53; Fulbright Research scholar attached to the Faculté des Sciences, U. Paris, 1952-53; mem. Inst. for Advanced Study, 1956-57. Author: Hardy Classes on Riemann Surfaces. Recipient Bowdoin prize, 1940. Fellow Am. Acad. Arts and Scis.; mem. Am. Math. Soc. (mem. council, editor Proc. 1962-68), London Math. Soc., Phi Beta Kappa, Sigma Xi. Home: 3304 Winnett Rd Chevy Chase MD 20815

HEINSELMAN, JAMES L., coll. pres.; b. Floyd County, Iowa, Apr. 25, 1935; s. James L. and Alpha L. (Behne) H.; m. Shirley Ann Kleinschmidt, June 8, 1956; children—Criag, Lisa, Brian, Lori. B.A., U. No. Iowa, 1956, M.A., 1960; postgrad., Am. U., 1959, U. Denver, 1960, Mich. State U., 1965, Ill. State U., No. Ill. U., Tex. A&M U. Tchr. physics and math. public schs., Denison, Iowa, 1957-59; mem. faculty depts. math. and physics Port Huron Jr. Coll., 1960-67; also depts.; chmn. dept. phys. sci. Coll. of DuPage, Ill., 1967-68, asst. dean, then asso. dean instrn., 1968-73; dean instrn. Los Angeles City Coll., 1973-78, Los Angeles Trade Tech. Coll., 1978-80; pres. Los Angeles Harbor Coll., 1980—. Mem. Am. Assn. Higher Edn., Am. Assn. Jr. and Community Colls., Calif. Community and Jr. Coll. Assn. Home: 3701 Fuchsia St Seal Beach CA 90740 Office: 1111 Figueroa Pl Wilmington CA 90744

HEINSELMAN, MIRON LEE, forest ecologist; b. Duluth, Minn., Feb. 7,1920; s. Everett Millard and Helena Alvina (Kruger) H.; m. Frances Ruth Brown, Sept. 18, 1942; children: Russell Craig, Ann Louise Heinselman Stolee. B.A., U. Minn., 1942, B.S., 1948, M.F., 1951, Ph.D., 1961. Research forester North Central Forest Expt. Sta., U.S. Forest Service, Rhinelander, Wis., 1948-50, Grand Rapids, Minn., 1951-66, prin. plant ecologist, St. Paul, with summer field office in, Ely, Minn., 1966-74, ret., 1974; now adj. prof. ecology and behavioral biology U. Minn., Mpls.; chmn Friends of the Boundary Waters Wilderness, 1976-78. Contbr. articles on forest ecology, peatlands ecology and ecol. role of fire in No. conifer forests to profl. jours. on preservation of boundary waters Canoe Area Wilderness to popular mags. Served with U.S. Army, 1942-43, 45-46. Recipient Cottrell award Nat. Acad. Sci., 1977, Conservation award Am. Motors Co., 1977, Dr. Robert Green award Mpls. Jaycees, 1978. Mem. Ecol. Soc. Am., AAAS, Am. Inst. Biol. Scis., Soc. Am. Foresters, Sierra Club (Minn. Environmentalist-Citizen award 1978), Izaak Walton League Am., Wilderness Soc., Nat. Audubon Soc., Nat. Wildlife Fedn., Algonquin Wildlands League. Democrat. Home: 1783 Lindig St Saint Paul MN 55113

HEINTZ, JACK, publishing company executive; b. Chenoa, Ill., Jan. 19, 1907; s. Michael Matthew and Ida Luella (Thayer) H.; m. Mary Louise Keller, June 4, 1927; 1 son, Michael. Student, Ill. Wesleyan U. Dept. store mgr., 1928-33, dist. mgr. ins. firm, 1933-36, radio sales mgr., 1936-37; radio sta. mgr. WCBS, 1937-43; radio cons. The Copley Press, Inc., 1946-47, v.p., dir., 1958—, Hawaii resident mgr., officer, rep., 1964-74; v.p., gen. mgr. KSDO radio sta., 1946-54, KCOP-TV, 1954-58, radio and TV gen. cons., 1957; pub. Ill. State Jour., Ill. State Register, 1958-64; dir. Radio Sta. KGU, Honolulu. Profl. e'glomisé artist; exhibited works in several one-man shows. Trustee Lincoln Coll., Lincoln Library; bd. dirs. Cerebral Palsy Found., Ill. Arts Council. Served as lt. USNR, 1943- 46. Mem. Navy League, Assn. Honolulu Artists, Tau Kappa Epsilon. Republican. Episcopalian. Clubs: Mason (33 deg., Shriner), Rotary, Nat. Press (Washington); Pacific; Sangamon, Illini Country (Springfield, Ill.); Island Bay Yacht. Home: Town House 718 S 7th St Springfield IL 62703

HEINTZBERGER, HENRY JOHN, life ins. co. exec.; b. South Bend, Ind., Dec. 24, 1915; s. Henry John and Catherine (von Amersvoort) H.; m. Victoria S. Shelley, Aug. 6, 1943; children—Emily C., Edward H., Henry John, Victor C. A.B., DePauw U., 1938; M.S., U. Notre Dame, 1940; student, U. Mich., 1945-46. Actuarial asst. Monumental Life Ins. Co., 1946-52; group actuary Am. United Life Ins. Co., 1952-59; with Phila. Life Ins. Co., 1959-69, exec. v.p., 1967-69, pres., 1975-76, vice chmn. bd., chief exec. officers, 1976—, dir., 1971—; pres., dir. San Francisco Life Ins. Co., from 1969; v.p, dir. III Mgmt. Co., 1968-69; v.p., dir., prin. mem. III Distbg. Co. Served to lt. USNR, 1941-45. Mem. Asso. Soc. Actuaries. Clubs: Comml., Engrs. (San Francisco). Office: Phila Life Ins Co 1700 Montgomery St San Francisco CA 94111 *

HEINZ, ELISE BROOKFIELD, lawyer, state legislator; b. Plainfield, N.J., Jan. 14, 1935; d. Winfield Bernard and Rachel Edwards (Clarke) H.; m. James Edwin Clayton, 1961; children: Jonathan Brown Clayton, David Lake Clayton. B.A., Wellesley Coll., 1955; LL.B. cum laude, Harvard U., 1961. Bar: D.C. 1961, Va. 1969. Atty. firm Fowler, Leva, Hawes & Symington, Washington, 1961-64; individual practice law, Washington, 1968-69, Arlington, Va., 1968—; mem. Va. Ho. of Dels., 1978-82; adj. prof. Georgetown U. Law Center, 1971-72. Trustee Va. Found. Prepaid Legal Services. Mem. Am. Bar Assn., Arlington County Bar Assn., Va. State Bar, Am. Law Inst. Home and Office: 2728 N Fillmore St Arlington VA 22207

HEINZ, HENRY JOHN, II, food products manufacturing company executive; b. Sewickley, Pa., July 10, 1908; s. Howard and Elizabeth (Rust) H.; m. Joan Diehl, June 18, 1935 (div.); 1 son, Henry John III; m. Drue Maher, Aug. 22, 1953. Grad., Shadyside Acad., 1927; A.B., Yale, 1931; student, Trinity Coll., Cambridge, 1931-32. With H.J. Heinz Co., 1932, asst. to pres., 1937-41, pres., 1941-59, chmn., 1959—. Pres. Sarah Heinz House, Pitts.; mem. exec. com. Allegheny Conf. on Community Devel.; chmn. Agribus. Council, Inc., Yale Art Gallery; trustee U.S. council Internat. C. of C., Com. Econ. Devel.; v.p., dir. Pitts. Symphony Soc.; Bd. dirs. Bus. Com. for Arts, Inc., Pitts. Regional Planning Assn., Nat. Assos. Smithsonian Instn.; mem. Conservation Found.; trustee Carnegie Inst., Carnegie-Mellon U., Nutrition Found., World Affairs Council Pitts. Decorated cross of comdrs. Royal Order of Phoenix, Greece; chevalier Legion of Honor, France; Knight comdr. Brit. Empire; comdr. Order of Merit, Italy). Mem. Council on Fgn. Relations, Am. Ditchley Found., Brit. N.Am. Com. Republican. Presbyn. Clubs: Duquesne, Allegheny Country (Pitts); Buck's and White's (London); River (N.Y.C.); Rolling Rock and Laurel Valley (Ligonier, Pa.); The Brook. Office: HJ Heinz Co 600 Grant St Pittsburgh PA 15230 *

HEINZ, HENRY JOHN, III, U.S. senator; b. Pitts., Oct. 23, 1938; s. Henry John II and Joan (Diehl) H.; m. Teresa Simoes-Ferreira, 1966; children: Henry John IV, Andre, Christopher Drake. Grad., Phillips Exeter Acad., 1956; B.A., Yale U., 1960; M.B.A., Harvard U., 1963. Gen. product mgr. marketing H.J. Heinz Co., Pitts., 1965-70; lectr. Carnegie-Mellon U. Grad. Sch. Indsl. Adminstrn., 1970-71; mem. 92d-94th congresses from 18th Dist. Pa.; U.S. senator from, Pa., 1977—; Del. Republican Nat. Conv., 1968, 72, 76, 80; chmn. Pa. Rep. Platform Com., 1970. Trustee Howard Heinz Endowment, Childrens Hosp., Pitts., U. Pitts.; bd. overseers Grad. Sch. Bus., Harvard U.; chmn. H.J. Heinz II Charitable and Family Trust. Served with USAF, 1963. Mem. Am. Inst. Pub. Service. Office: 277 Russell Senate Office Bldg Washington DC 20510 *

HEINZ, WALTER ERNST EDWARD, chemical company executive; b. Milw., Jan. 3, 1920; s. Paulina and William (Krueger) H.; m. Gayle Virginia Hillegeist, Mar. 29, 1946; children: Richard Lee, Jenny Lee, Paula Stel. B.S., U. Wis., 1942, M.S., 1948. Chemist, then sect. leader Celanese Chem. Co., Corpus Christi, Tex., 1948-62; tech. mgr. Tilona Polymerwerke, Celanese/Hoechst Joint Venture, Kelsterbach, W. Ger., 1962-64; market devel. mgt. Celanese Plastics Co., Newark, 1964-65, mgr. formed plastic products, Clark, N.J., 1965-66, tech. and prodn. mgr., Greer, S.C., 1966-69; dir. devel. Celanese Chem. Co., Inc., Corpus Christi, 1969—; tchr. organic chemistry Del Mar Coll. Served as aviator USN, 1942-46. Mem. Am. Chem. Soc., Am. Inst. Chem. Engrs., Alpha Chi Sigma. Republican. Presbyterian. Patentee in field (30). Office: PO Box 9077 Corpus Christi TX 78408

HEIPLE, LOREN RAY, civil engineer, educator; b. Oakwood, Ill., Apr. 19, 1918; s. Eldridge Winfield and Mary Lucile (Oliphant) H.; m. Bonnie E. Tillman, Apr. 20, 1944; children: Tim Alan, Lynne Alice (Mrs. Cope). B.C.E., Iowa State Coll., 1939, C.E., 1950; M.S., Harvard, 1940; Ph.D., Stanford, 1967. Registered profl. engr., Ark., Iowa. Service, devel. engr. Infilco, Chgo., 1940-41; jr. san. engr. Iowa Ordnance Plant, 1941; instr. civil engrng. dept. Iowa State Coll., 1941-42, asst. prof., 1946-48; city engr., Boone, Iowa, 1948-49; cons. engr. Pub. Adminstrn. Service, Chgo., 1949-50; prof., head civil engring. dept. U. Ark., Fayetteville, 1950-71, dean engring., 1971-79, prof. civil engring., 1979—. Served as capt. San. Corps U.S. Army, 1942-46; col. Res. Mem. ASCE, Nat. Soc. Profl. Engrs., Am. Soc. Engring. Edn., Sigma Xi, Theta Tau, Tau Beta Pi. Presbyn. Club: Rotarian. Home: 1492 Century Dr Fayetteville AR 72701

HEIRES, JOHN HOPKINS, international banker, lawyer; b. Sioux City, Iowa, Sept. 19, 1918; s. Arthur Francis and Frances (Hopkins) H.; m. Alice Rea Chamberlin, May 14, 1955; children: John Hopkins, David Chamberlin, Gregory Norris. B.A. magna cum laude, Yankton Coll., 1939; J.D., Yale, 1946; M.Litt (Rhodes scholar), Oxford (Eng.) U., 1948. Bar: D.C. bar 1950, also U.S. Supreme Ct. bar 1950. With Dept. Justice, 1941; legal asst. Pillsbury, Madison & Sutro, San Francisco, 1949-50; asso. Covington & Burling, Washington, 1950-53; asst. to chief estimates staff and estimates officer Bd. Nat. Estimates, 1953-57; sec. intelligence adv. com. Nat. Security Council, 1957-58; exec. sec. U.S. Intelligence Bd., 1958-62; dep. legis. programs coordinator AID, 1962, officer charge Pakistan affairs, 1962-64; moderator Naval Acad. Fgn. Affairs Conf., 1964; regional legal counsel, attache for embassy and U.S. AID missions to, India, Nepal and Ceylon, New Delhi, 1964-69; v.p., sec. Pvt. Investment Co. for Asia (PICA), S.A., Tokyo, 1969-72, Singapore, 1972-73; v.p., internat. sec. Marine Midland Bank, N.Y.C.; corporate sec. Marine Midland Internat. Corp., Marine Midland Overseas Corp., Marine Midland, Inc., 1973-76; adviser Fed. Res. Bank N.Y., 1976—. Note editor: Yale Law Jour, 1942; case editor, 1946. Served to lt. USNR, 1942-46. Mem. Internat. Am., D.C. bar assns., Am. Soc. Internat. Law, Assn. Am. Rhodes Scholars, Fgn. Policy Assn., Bankers Assn. for Fgn. Trade, Council of Americas, Asia Soc., Far East-Am. Council Commerce and Industry, Japan Soc., Am.-Arab Assn., Yale Law Assn., English Speaking Union, Pi Kappa Delta, Phi Delta Phi. Clubs: Chevy Chase, Internat. (Washington); Yale, Economic (N.Y.C.); Milbrook (Greenwich, Conn.); Delhi Gymkhana (New Delhi); Fgn. Corrs., American (Tokyo); Tokyo Lawn and Tennis; American (Singapore). Home: 8 Wildwood Dr Greenwich CT 06830 Office: 33 Liberty St New York NY 10045

HEISE, GEORGE ARMSTRONG, educator, psychologist; b. N.Y.C., Dec. 8, 1924; s. George William and Margaret (Armstrong) H.; m. Barbara Fry, Dec. 27, 1951; children—Laura, Kenneth, Anne, John, Thomas. B.A., Swarthmore Coll., 1944; M.A., Harvard, 1950, Ph.D., 1952. Instr., then asst. prof. Oberlin (O.) Coll., 1951-56; sr. scientist Hoffman LaRoche, Inc. (pharms.), Nutley, N.J., 1956-62; asso. prof. Haverford (Pa.) Coll., 1962-64; mem. faculty Ind. U., Bloomington, 1964—, prof. psychology, 1968—; adj. asso. prof. Rutgers U., 1958-61; Mem. com. behavorial pharmacology Psychopharmacology Service Center, NIMH, 1962-66. Mem. adv. bd. Bloomington Twp., 1970-74; commr. Bloomington Environ. Quality and Conservation Commn., 1976—, chmn., 1979—. Served as ensign USNR, 1944-46. Fellow Am. Psychol. Assn. (council reps. 1970-72, pres. div. 28 1973-74), AAAS; mem. Sigma Xi. Home: 2369 Browncliff St Bloomington IN 47401 Office: Dept Psychology Ind Univ Bloomington IN 47401

HEISER, ARNOLD MELVIN, astronomer; b. Bklyn., Feb. 9, 1933; s. Hyman Samuel and Sadie (Kretchmer) H.; m. Vivian Carol Jacobs, June 6, 1964; children—Naomi Elizabeth, David Alan. A.B., Ind. U., 1954, M.A., 1956; Ph.D., U. Chgo., 1961. Research asst. Ind. U., 1954-56; research fellow U. Chgo., 1956-61; asst. prof. physics and astronomy Vanderbilt U., Nashville, 1961-66, asso. prof., 1966—; dir. A.J. Dyer Obs., 1972—; H. Shapley vis. prof. Am. Astron. Soc., 1969—. Contbr. articles to astron. jours. Mem. Am. Astron. Soc., Internat. Astron. Union, Royal Astron. Soc., Tenn. Acad. Sci., AAAS, Sigma Xi. Home: 6132 Gardendale Dr Nashville TN 37215 Office: A J Dyer Observatory Vanderbilt University Nashville TN 37235

HEISER, CHARLES BIXLER, JR., educator; b. Cynthiana, Ind., Oct. 5, 1920; s. Charles Bixler and Inez (Metcalf) H.; m. Dorothy Gaebler, Aug. 19, 1944; children—Lynn Marie, Cynthia Ann, Charles Bixler III. A.B., Washington U., St. Louis, 1943, M.A., 1944; Ph.D., U. Calif. at Berkeley, 1947. Instr. Washington U., St. Louis, 1944-45; asso. botany U. Calif. at Davis, 1946-47; mem. faculty Ind. U., Bloomington, 1947—, prof. botany, 1957—, Disting. prof., 1979—. Author: Nightshades, The Paradoxical Plants, 1969, Seed to Civilization, The Story of Man's Food, 1973, The Sunflower, 1976, The Gourd Book, 1979. Guggenheim fellow, 1953; NSF Sr. Postdoctoral fellow, 1962. Mem. Am. Soc. Plant Taxonomists (pres. 1967, Disting. Econ. Botanist 1984), Bot. Soc. Am. (Merit award 1972, pres. 1980), Soc. Study Evolution (pres. 1974), Am. Soc. Naturalists, AAAS, Internat. Assn. Plant Taxonomy, Soc. Econ. Botany (pres. 1978), Phi Beta Kappa, Sigma Xi. Research, numerous publs. on systematics flowering plants, natural and artificial hybridization, origin cultivated plants. Home: 1018 Southdowns St Bloomington IN 47401

HEISER, JOSEPH MILLER, JR., retired army officer, business executive; b. Charleston, S.C., Jan. 22, 1914; s. Joseph Miller and Alma (Maetze) H.; m. Edith Cox, Sept. 24, 1937; children: Annette Heiser Ficker, Joel M., Joan Heiser Weizel. Student, Providence Coll., 1932-34, The Citadel, 1939-41, Command and Gen. Staff Coll., 1949; M.B.A., U. Chgo., 1956; postgrad., Nat. War Coll., Washington, 1960-61. Enlisted as pvt. U.S. Army, 1942, 1st sgt., 1942-43, commd. 2d lt., 1943, advanced through grades to lt. gen., 1969; asst. exec. officer Office Chief of Ordnance, 1946-49, exec. officer, 1956-60; ammunition supply officer, asst. ordnance officer Pusan Base Command, 1950; exec. officer, dir. tng. Ordnance Sch., CONUS, Aberdeen Proving Ground, Md., 1951-54; asst. chief of staff G-4, 4th Logistical Command, Verdun, France, 1961-62, chief of staff and dep. comdr., 1962-63; chief of staff U.S. Army Communications Zone, Europe, Orleans, France, 1963-65, comdg. gen., 1965; spl. asst. CINCUSAREUR, 1965; asst. dep. chief of staff for logistics Dept. Army, Washington, 1966-68; comdg. gen. 1st Logistical Command, U.S. Army, Vietnam, 1968-69; dep. chief of staff Dept. Army, 1969-73; v.p. Wilbur Smith and Assos., Columbia, S.C., 1973—; dir. 1st Citizens Bank & Trust Co.; cons., lectr. Comptroller Gen. GAO, Sec. Def., Washington, Hdqrs. NATO, Brussells; U.S. Presdl. adviser; adj. prof. U. S.C., Appalachian State U.; bd. advisers Soc. Logistics Engrs. Contbr. articles to profl. publs. Dist. chmn. Fleur-de-Lis (France) council Boy Scouts Am., 1963-65; mem. nat. bd. Boy Scouts Am.; bd. dirs., camp and athletic dir. Boys Clubs Am., 1928-34. Decorated D.S.M. with 2 oak leaf clusters, Legion of Merit with oak leaf cluster, Bronze Star, Air medal with eight oak leaf clusters, Army Commendation medal, French Legion of Honor, numerous others; recipient Bunker award Armed Forces Mgmt. Assn.; award pub. service U.S. Comptroller Gen., 1977; Price medal U. Pa.; named to Hall of Fame, U.S. Army Ordnance Corps; Heiser award established U.S. Army Ordnance Ctr. and Sch., 1982. Mem. Am. Def. Preparedness Assn. (officer, bd. advisers), Assn. U.S. Army, Nat. Security Indsl. Assn. (hon. life mem., cert. of merit, award of Logistics Emeritus 1980), Am. Mgmt. Assn., Soc. Logistics Engrs. (pres. logistical edn. fund, Founders award 1982), Ret. Officers Assn. (dir.). Roman Catholic. Club: Alumni U. Chicago. Home: 3486 North Shore Rd Columbia SC 29206 *Any secret of "success" must begin with "The Golden Rule." Only in America could an ordinary citizen, "who knew no one," enter the army as a private and advance through all the ranks to lieutenant general in 26 years (with the help of "great ordinary" Americans every step of the way). One gains success, however measured, through the reflections of the good done by associates. So kindness to others is really good for all. People are nice to nice people*

HEISERMAN, RICHARD DEAN, financial executive; b. Portland, Oreg., May 29, 1938; s. Ord J. and Lillian Irene (Poyser) H.; m. Patricia Ann Boyd, Mar. 19, 1960; children—Richard Scott, James Todd, Judith Ann, Pamela Sue. B.S. in Bus. Adminstrn, U. Denver, 1960; grad. diploma, Savs. & Loan Inst., 1966; postgrad., U. Ind., 1976. Mgmt. trainee Capitol Fed. Savs. & Loan Assn., Denver, 1960, sr. v.p., 1976-78, 1978, chmn. bd., pres., dir., 1978—; pres., chmn. bd. 1st Capitol Corp., 1971—, Columbine Title Co., 1974-80, C & H Investment Co., 1975-80; chmn. bd. First Capitol Mortgage, 1978-80. Mem. Denver U. adv. bd. real estate and constrn. mgmt., 1981; bd. dirs. Schlessman br. YMCA, 1962-64, Colo. Apt. Assn., 1972-75, Home Builders of Met. Denver, 1975. Mem. Denver C. of C. (chmn. econ. devel. council 1980-81), Mountain States Alumni Assn. of SAE (pres. 1966), U.S. League Savs. Assn. (mem. legis. com. 1979-80), Savs. & Loan League of Colo. (legis. steering com. 1980, pres., dir. 1980-81). Republican. Methodist. Clubs: Masons (Shriner), Rotary (program chmn.). Home: 5651 S Hanover Way Englewood CO 80111 Office: 2625 S Colorado Blvd Denver CO 80222

HEISKELL, ANDREW, publishing executive; b. Naples, Italy, Sept. 13, 1915; s. Morgan and Ann (Hubbard) H.; m. Cornelia Scott, Nov. 12, 1937 (div.); children: Diane, Peter; m. Madeleine Carroll (div.); 1 dau., Anne M.; m. Marian Sulzberger Dryfoos, 1965. Ed. in, France; student, Harvard Bus. Sch., 1935-36; LL.D., Shaw U., 1968, Lake Erie Coll., 1969, Hofstra U., 1972, Hobart and William Smith Colls., 1973; D.Litt., Lafayette Coll., 1969. Reporter N.Y. Herald-Tribune, 1936-37; assoc. editor Life mag., 1937-39, asst. gen. mgr., 1939-42, gen. mgr., 1942-46, pub., 1946-60; v.p. Time, Inc., 1949-60, chmn. bd., 1960-69, chmn. bd., chief exec. officer, 1969-80; dir. Am. TV & Communications Corp., Book-of-Month Club, Inc., Inland Container Corp., Temple-Eastex, Inc. Bd. dirs. Independent sector, Enterprise Found., People for the Am. Way, Internat. Exec. Service Corps; chmn. bd. trustees N.Y. Public Library, 1981—; vice chmn. Brookings Instn., chmn. exec. com.; trustee Trust for Cultural Resources of N.Y.C.; bd. advisors Dumbarton Oaks Research Library and Collection; chmn. Bryant Park Restoration Corp., Pres.'s Com. on Arts and Humanities. Fellow Harvard Coll. 10020

HEISKELL, JAMES NETHERLAND, insuracne company executive; b. Houston, Aug. 6, 1923; s. Clarence Luther and Lela Maude (Ward) H.; m. Alice Louise Williams, Nov. 27, 1946; children: James Douglas, William Randall, Rebecca Ann, Christie Lynn. Student, pub. schs. Sec. Republic Fin. Services, Inc., Dallas, 1956-60, v.p., 1960-73, sr. v.p., 1973—. Republican. Presbyterian. Home: 623 Green Hills Rd Duncanville TX 75237 Office: Republic Fin Services Inc 2727 Turtle Creek Blvd Dallas TX 75219

HEISKELL, MARIAN SULZBERGER (MRS. ANDREW HEISKELL), newspaper executive, civic worker; b. N.Y.C., Dec. 31, 1918; d. Arthur Hays and Iphigene (Ochs) Sulzberger; m. Orvil Eugene Dryfoos, July 8, 1941 (dec. May 1963); children: Jacqueline Hays, Robert Ochs, Susan Warms; m. Andrew Heiskell, Jan. 30, 1965. Grad., Frobeleague Kindergarten Tng. Sch., N.Y.C., 1941; LL.D. (hon.), Poly. Inst. N.Y., 1974, Dartmouth Coll., 1975. Dir. N.Y. Times Co., 1963—; Bd. dirs. N.Y.C. Partnership; chmn. Council on Environment N.Y.C.; bd. dirs. Regional Plan Assn., Inc.; chmn. Gateway Nat. Recreation Area Adv. Commn.; bd. mgrs., exec. com. N.Y. Bot. Garden; mem. council Nat. Parks System Adv. Bd.; mem. State Park and Recreation Commn. for City N.Y.; bd. dirs. Nat. Audubon Soc., N.Y. Citizens for Balanced Transp.; chmn. Citizens Westway Park Adv. Com.; trustee Parks Council, Consol. Edison Co. N.Y., Inc.; co-chmn. We Care About N.Y., Inc.; dir. Ford Motor Co., Merck & Co., Inc. Recipient Mrs. Lyndon B. Johnson ann. award Keep Am. Beautiful, 1974; with husband) Disting. Service award Citizens Union, 1975. Mem. Inter Am. Press Assn. (dir.). Home: 870 UN Plaza New York NY 10017 also 237 Long Neck Point Rd Darien CT 06820 Office: Room 1031 NY Times 229 W 43d St New York NY 10036

HEISLER, JOHN COLUMBUS, investment banker; b. Evanston, Ill., Mar. 19, 1926; s. John Columbus and Dolly Ruth (Ramsey) Hardin; m. Mary Anne Foley, Jan. 6, 1951; children—John, Peter, Tod, Anne. A.B., Harvard, 1948, M.B.A., 1950. With Eagle-Picher Industries, Cin., 1950-74, fin. v.p., 1965-74, dir., 1965-74; fin. v.p. Gardner-Denver Co., Dallas, 1974-77, dir., 1975-77; gen. partner Edward D. Jones & Co., St. Louis, 1977—; dir. Hilltop Concrete Corp., Cin., Carthage Marble Corp., Mo. Served with USNR, 1944-46. Presbyn. (elder). Home: 7 Little Ln Saint Louis MO 63124 Office: Edward D Jones & Co 201 Progress Pkwy Maryland Heights MO 63043

HEISS, RICHARD WALTER, banker; b. Monroe, Mich., July 8, 1930; s. Walter and Lillian (Harpst) H.; m. Nancy J. Blum, June 21, 1952; children: Kurt Frederick, Karl Richard. B.A., Mich. State U., 1952; LL.B., Detroit Coll. Law, 1963; LL.M., Wayne State U., 1969. Asst. trust officer Mfrs. Nat. Bank of Detroit, 1960-62, trust officer, 1962-66, v.p., trust officer, 1966-68, v.p., sr. trust officer, 1968-75, 1st v.p., sr. trust officer, 1975-77, sr. v.p., 1977—; lectr. Pa. Bankers Assn., Inst. Continuing Legal Edn., U. Detroit Bus. Sch., Procknow Grad. Sch. Banking, U. Wis., Southwestern Grad. Sch. Banking, Am. Bankers Assn., Banking Sch. of South; mem. exec. com. Trust Mgmt. Seminar, chmn., 1980. Trustee Detroit Coll. Law, pres., 1983—; mem. Mich. State U. Devel. Council and Bus. Sch. Alumni Bd. Served to 1st lt. Q.M.C. AUS, 1952-57. Mem. Am., Mich., Detroit bar assns., Am. Bankers Assn. (pres. 1981, exec. com. trust div.), Mich. Bankers Assn. (chmn. trust div. exec. com. 1975), Mich. State U. Bus. Alumni Assn. (dir., pres. 1983), Delta Chi, Sigma Nu Phi. Republican. Lutheran. Clubs: Economic, Detroit, Detroit Golf (dir.), Detroit Golf (pres. 1983). Home: 30684 Sudbury Ct Farmington Hills MI 48018 Office: 100 Renaissance Center Detroit MI 48243

HEIST, LEWIS CLARK, forest products company executive; b. Bridgeport, Conn., June 6, 1931; s. Floyd L. and Gladys M. (Hall) H.; m. Mary E. Lyman, Feb. 5, 1954; children: Jane, William Peter, Matthew. B.A. in Econs., Yale U., 1953, M.F., 1957. With U.S. Plywood, Hartford, Conn., 1957-61, sales Mgr., Pitts., 1961-64; v.p. bus. planning U.S. Plywood-Champion Paper, N.Y.C., 1970-75; exec. v.p. Timberlands div. Champion Internat. Corp., Stamford, Conn., 1976-82, exec. v.p. pulp, paper and paperbd. mfg., 1982—; v.p., dir. Lyman Farm Inc., Middlefield, Conn., 1975—. Bd. dirs. United Way, Greenwich, Conn., 1977—, Old Greenwich Community Ctr., 1973-77. Served to 1st lt. USMC, 1953-55. Mem. Soc. Am. Foresters, Am. Forestry Assn., Nat. Forest Products Assn. Presbyterian. Club: Rocky Point. Home: 187 Shore Rd Old Greenwich CT 16870 Office: Champion Internat Corp One Champion Plaza Stamford CT 96921

HEITLER, GEORGE, lawyer; b. N.Y.C., Sept. 3, 1915; s. John J. and Celia (Zeichner) H.; m. Florence A. Posner, Apr. 21, 1940; children—James B., Richard S. B.S., Columbia, 1936, J.D., 1938. Bar: N.Y. bar 1938, Ill. bar 1962. Asso. firm Cutler, Wilson & McMahon, N.Y.C., 1938-40; spl. asst. to David L. Podell; counsel to Hays, Podell & Schulman, N.Y.C., 1940; asso. atty. firm Coughlan & Russell; also mng. agt. and asst. sec. Central Manhattan Properties, Inc., N.Y.C., 1940-43; chief clk., legal adviser rents and claims bd. 4th Service Command, U.S. Army, 1943-45; engaged as bus. exec., also house counsel various comml. orgns., 1946-57; asst. sec., staff counsel Blue Cross Assn., N.Y.C., 1957-60, corporate sec., staff counsel, 1960-61; v.p., sec. Legal counsel, Chgo., 1961-71, sr. v.p., corporate sec., gen. counsel, 1971—; sr. v.p., legal counsel Nat. Blue Shield Assn., 1978-81; counsel to Kaye, Scholer, Fierman, Hays & Handler, N.Y.C., 1981—; spl. adviser Dept. Labor, also speaker and panelist. Author articles. Mem. Am., Chgo. bar assns., Assn. Bar City N.Y., Am. Ethical Union, Chgo. Ethical Humanist Soc. (trustee). Home: 20 Waterside Plaza New York NY 10010 Office: 425 Park Ave New York NY 10022

HEITMAN, BETTY GREEN, polit. party exec.; b. Malvern, Ark., Nov. 27, 1929; d. George Anderson and Inell Green (Cooper) Green; m. Henry Schrader Heitman, Apr. 3, 1951; children—Donna, Thomas, Perry, Paul. B.S., Tex. Women's U. Adminstrv. dietitician Hotel Dieu Hosp., New Orleans, 1950-51, Clarkson Meml. Hosp., Omaha, 1951-52; pediatric dietician Charity Hosp., New Orleans, 1952-53; pres. La. dn. Republican Women, 1967-71; treas. Nat. Fedn. Republican Women, 1971-76, 1st v.p., 1976-78; mem. from La. Nat. Republican Com., 1974-77, now co-chmn.; Trustee Public Affairs Research Council La.; mem. adv. bd. Internat. Mgmt. and Devel. Inst. Washington. Recipient Disting. Alumna award Tex. Women's U. Episcopalian. Home: 655 Waverly Dr Baton Rouge LA 70806 Office: 310 1st St SE Washington DC 20003

HEITMAN, HUBERT, JR., animal science educator; b. Berkeley, Calif., June 2, 1917; s. Hubert and Blanche (Peart) H.; m. Helen Margaret McCaughna, Aug. 7, 1941; children: James Hubert, William Robert. B.S., U. Calif.-Davis, 1939; A.M., U. Mo., 1940, Ph.D., 1943. Asst. instr. animal husbandry U. Mo., 1939-43; mem. faculty U. Calif. at Davis, 1946—, prof. animal sci., 1961—, chmn. dept., 1963-68, 81-82, acad. asst. to vice chancellor acad. affairs, 1971-78; livestock supt. Calif. State Fair, 1948-59; v.p. at large Nat. Collegiate Athletic Assn., 1975-77; pres. Far Western Intercollegiate Athletic Conf., 1971-72, 77-78, Golden State Conf., 1979-80. Pres. Yolo County Soc. Crippled Children, 1954-56; Bd. dirs. Calif. Soc. Crippled Children and Adults, 1954-56. Served to capt., San. Corps AUS, 1943-46. Mem. AAAS, Am. Soc. Animal Sci. (pres. Western sect. 1953), Animal Behavior Soc., Internat. Soc. Biometeorologists, Calif., N.Y. acads. scis., Nutrition Soc. (Gt. Britain), Brit. Soc. Animal Prodn., Sigma Xi, Alpha Zeta, Gamma Sigma Delta, Gamma Alpha, Sigma Chi. Home: 518 Miller Dr Davis CA 95616

HEITMAN, RICHARD EDGAR, cons. co. exec.; b. N.Y.C., Mar. 30, 1930; s. Harry and Rose H.; m. Ann Reeves, May 29, 1968; 1 son, Andrew. B.S. in Chem. Engring, M.I.T., 1952, M.S., Princeton U., 1953, Ph.D. in Chem. Engring. (Textile Research Inst. fellow), 1961. Staff cons. Arthur D. Little, Inc., Cambridge, Mass., 1958-65, mgr. mgmt. scis., London, 1965-69, sr. staff mem., Cambridge, 1969-73, sr. v.p. corp. services, 1973—; dir. Multibank Fin. Corp. Served with Chem. Corps, 1953-55. Mem. Assn. Princeton Grad. Alumni (governing bd.). Office: 25 Acorn Park Cambridge MA 02140

HEITMANN, FREDERICK WILLIAM, bank executive, lecturer; b. Chgo., Apr. 14, 1922; s. Frederick William and Louise (Snyder) H.; m. Peggy A. Smith, Sept. 6, 1947; children: Daryl Jean Riley, Scott Keith; m. 2d Deborah Lee Drinan, Oct. 1, 1980. B.S., Northwestern U., 1943; M. in Banking, U. Wis., 1953. Vice-pres. Northwest Nat. Bank, Chgo., 1952-57, exec. v.p., 1957-63, pres., chief exec. officer, 1963—; dir. Northbrook Trust & Savs. Bank, Ill., W.N. Lanne Interfinancial Inc., Northbrook; faculty mem. various univs. Chmn. State Ill. Commn. Higher Edn., 1960-65, vice-chmn., 1965-75; chmn. banking and fin. div. Ill. Crusade of Mercy, 1976. Recipient Silver Anniversary All-Am. award Sports Illus. Mag., 1967, Disting. Alumnus Merit award Northwestern U., 1968; F.H.A. Pub. Housing citation, Washington, 1970. Clubs: Mid-Am. (Chgo.); North Shore Country (Glenview, Ill.) (treas., dir.); Bankers; Chikaming Country (Lakeside, Mich.). Home: 3761 N Mission Hills Rd Northbrook IL 60062 Office: Northwest National Bank of Chicago 3985 Milwaukee Ave Chicago IL 60641

HEITNER, ROBERT RICHARD, educator; b. St. Louis, Feb. 1, 1920; s. Henry John and Anna (Waltke) H.; m. Pauline M. Spitz, Dec. 26, 1949; children—David H., Laura (Mrs. D.F. Greeley). A.B., Washington U., St. Louis, 1941, M.A., 1942; Ph.D., Harvard U., 1949. Asst. prof. German Washington U., 1949-55; German faculty U. Calif. at Los Angeles, 1955-64, chmn. dept., 1961-64; prof. German U. Tex., 1964-66, U. Ill. at Chgo. Circle, 1966—, chmn. dept., 1966-76. Author: German Tragedy in the Age of Enlightenment, 1963; Editor: German Quar, 1967-70, Maria Stuarda (1683), by A.A. von Haugwitz, 1974; Contbr. articles to profl. jours. Served with AUS, 1942-45. Mem. Modern Lang. Assn. Am., Lessing Soc. (v.p. 1974-76, pres. 1977-78), Phi Beta Kappa, Phi Kappa Phi. Home: 1555 Astor St Apt 32W Chicago IL 60610 Office: Dept German Univ Ill at Chicago Circle Chicago IL 60680

HEITZ, GLENN EDWARD, banker; b. Madison, Ind., Jan. 3, 1924; s. Edward Joseph and Dora (Wilkins) H.; m. Lucille Poteete, Dec. 29, 1946; children—William Edward, Michael Glenn, Joseph Andrew. Student, Davis and Elkins Coll., 1943-44; B.S., Purdue U., 1948, M.S., 1950. Teaching asst., research asst. agrl. econs. dept. Purdue U., 1948-50; asst. sec.-treas. Greenscastle (Ind.) Prodn. Credit Assn., 1950; asst. sec.-treas., then sec.-treas. LaFayette (Ind.) Prodn. Credit Assn., 1950-58; cons. FCA, Washington, 1958—, dep. gov., dir. coop. bank service, 1959-69; pres. Fed. Land Bank St. Louis, 1970-; dir. Am. Inst. Cooperation, 1975—. Bd. dirs. Mo. Bapt. Hosp. Served with USAAF, 1943-46. Recipient Ind. 4-H and Sears Agrl. scholarships, 1942-43. Mem. Ind. Fedn. Prodn. Credit Assns. (sec.- treas. 1955-58), Soc. Farm Mgrs. and Rural Appraisers (chmn. 1956-57), Ceres, Alpha Zeta. Baptist (deacon). Club: Rotary. Home: Route 5 Box 108-B Pacific MO 63069 Office: Fed Land Bank St Louis MO 63103 *Most people can achieve whatever they genuinely strive to do through sufficient dedication, sacrifice, hard work and faith in God.*

HEITZMAN, ROBERT EDWARD, materials handling equipment manufacturing company executive; b. Covington, Ky., May 7, 1927; s. Edward John and Philomena (Tegeder) H.; m. Mary Ellen Grom, Aug. 28, 1948; children: Robert Edward, Barbara E., William F. B.S.M.E., U. Cin., 1951. Registered profl. engr., Ohio. Internat. engring. mgr. Procter & Gamble Corp., 1951-66; internat. bus. mgr. Allied Chem. Corp., 1966-69; v.p. mfg. Whitehall div. Am. Home Products Corp., 1969-74; sr. v.p. internat. Englehard Industries div. Engelhard Minerals & Chems. Corp., Iselin, N.J., 1975-82; exec. v.p., co-owner Buck-El Inc., Murray Hill, N.J., 1983—. Served with USNR, 1945-46; with AUS, 1947-48. Mem. Greater Newark C. of C. (dir., exec. com. 1978-79), Delta Tau Delta. Home: 34 Wyndmoor Dr Convent Station NJ 07961 Office: 564 Central Ave Murray Hill NJ 07974

HEITZMANN, ALFRED OTTO, lawyer; b. St. Louis, Aug. 20, 1913; s. Alfred O. and Susanna (Herget) H.; m. Mary Jane Mattox, June 19, 1948; children: James A., Thomas W., Catherine Ann, John M. A.B., Washington U., 1938; LL.B., Columbia, 1941; postgrad., Stanford U., 1943-44. Bar: N.Y. 1941, Mo. 1946. With Hines, Rearick Dorr & Hammond, N.Y.C., 1941-42; partner Lowenhaupt, Waite, Chasnoff & Stolar, St. Louis, 1946-56, Stolar, Heitzmann Eder, Seigel & Harris (and predecessor firm), 1956—. Active St. Louis United Fund, 1969-82. Served as sgt. AUS, 1942-46. Mem. Phi Beta Kappa, Omicron Delta Gamma. Presbyn. Home: 430 Webster Forest Dr Webster Groves MO 63119 Office: 515 Olive St St Louis MO 63101

HEIZER, EDGAR FRANCIS, JR., business development company executive; b. Detroit, Sept. 23, 1929; s. Edgar Francis and Grace Adelia (Smith) H.; m. Molly Bradley Hunt, June 17, 1952; children: Linda Bradley Seaman, Molly Hunt, Edgar Francis. B.S., Northwestern U., 1951; J.D., Yale U., 1954. Mem. audit and tex staff Arthur Andersen & Co., Chgo., 1954-56; fin. analyst Kidder, Peabody & Co., Chgo., 1956-58; mgmt. cons. Booz, Allen & Hamilton, Chgo., 1958-62; asst. treas. Allstate Ins. Co., Northbrook, Ill., 1952-69; chmn., pres. Heizer Corp., Chgo., 1969—; dir. Amdahl Corp., Sunnyvale, Calif., Fotomat Corp., St. Petersburg, Fla., Computer Consoles, Inc., Rochester, N.Y., Omex, Santa Clara, Calif., IDC Services, Inc., Chgo., Internat. Capital Equipment Inc., Vacation Resorts Inc., Aspen, Colo., Material Scis. Corp., Elk Grove Village, Ill., Am. Bus. Conf., Washington. Bd. dirs. Northwestern U., 1982-83; chmn. White House Conf. for Capital Formation Task Force, 1978-80. Republican. Presbyterian. Clubs: Chicago Curling, Shoreacres, Mid-Ocean. Office: Heizer Corp 20 N Wacker Dr Chicago IL 60606

HEJDUK, JOHN QUENTIN, architect; b. N.Y.C., July 19, 1929; s. John Quentin and Mary (Renzler) H.; m. Gloria-Maria Fiorentino, Sept. 8, 1951; children—Rafael, Renata. Student, Cooper Union Sch. Arch., 1950; B.S., U. Cin., 1952; M.A., Harvard Grad. Sch. Design, 1953. Chmn. dept. arch. Cooper Union, 1964-75, dean, 1975—; pvt. practice architecture, N.Y.C., 1966—. Fellow Royal Soc., AIA. Home and office: 5721 Huxley Ave Riverdale NY 10471

HEJNA, WILLIAM FRANK, surgeon, college administrator; b. Chgo., May 13, 1932; s. William H.; m. Eva Lee Goodale, June 11, 1955; children: William, David, Michael, Susan. B.A., Grinnell Coll., 1954, D.Sc., 1974; M.D., Washington U., St. Louis, 1958. Diplomate: Am. Bd. Orthopedic Surgery (examiner 1969-74). Intern Presbyn.-St. Luke's Hosp., Chgo., 1958-59, coordinator orthopedic clinics and med. sch. tng., 1963-70, dir. electromyography lab., 1963-70, asst. chmn. dept. orthopedic surgery, 1965-70, asso. attending surgeon, 1967-70, sr. attending surgeon, 1971—; resident in orthopedic surgery U. Ill. Research and Ednl. Hosps., Chgo., 1959-63; asso. dean Office Surg. Scis. and Services, Rush-Presbyn.-St. Luke's Med. Center, 1970-73; v.p. med. affairs, dean Rush Med. Coll., 1973-76; sr. v.p. Rush U., 1976—, also prof. orthopedic surgery; prof. health systems mgmt. Ripon Coll., 1982—; pres. BioService Corp., 1977-80, Bus. Cons., Inc., 1970—, Biotech. Maintenance and Repair Corp., 1978—; cons. Whittaker Corp., 1978—; chmn. physician adv. bd. Smith Labs., 1980—. Contbr. articles to profl. jours.; editorial bd. Health Care Mgmt. Rev., 1982—. Trustee MacNeal Meml. Hosp., 1982—, Ripon Coll., 1982—. Fellow ACS, Am. Acad. Orthopedic Surgeons; mem. AMA, Ill., Chgo. med. socs., Chgo. Surg. Soc., Inst. Medicine, Orthopedic Research Soc., Clin. Orthopedic Soc. Clubs: Econs., Execs. (Chgo.). Home: 321 N Delaplaine Rd Riverside IL 60546 Office: 1725 W Harrison St Chicago IL 60612

HEKIMIAN, NORRIS CARROLL, instrumentation and systems executive; b. Washington, Jan. 14, 1926; s. Nejib and Louise Marie (Von Andrian) H.; m. Joan Elizabeth Scovall, June 15, 1955; 1 stepson, Allen Mark Knechtel; children: Joan Allison, Christopher David, Catherine Louise. B.S.E.E., George Washington U., 1949; M.S., U. Md., 1951, Ph.D., 1969. Registered profl. engr., Md. Radio engr. Nat. Bur. Standards, Washington, 1949-54; br. chief Nat. Security Agy., Ft. Meade, Md., 1954-61; asst. dir. research and devel. Page Communications Engrs., Inc., Washington, 1961-68; founder, pres. Hekimian Labs., Inc., Rockville, Md., 1969-81, chief exec. officer, Gaithersburg, Md., 1981-82, v.p. research and devel., 1983—; cons. Boggs & Hekimian, Kensington, Md., 1953-60. Contbr. articles to mags., chpts. in books; holder 24 patents. Dir. Corp. for Tech. Tng., Montgomery County, Md., 1983—; engring. alumni bd. dirs. George Washington Enging. Alumni Assn., 1969-79. Served to pvt. USAAF, 1944-45. Recipient Alumni Achievement award George Washington U., 1976. Fellow IEEE (Patron award 1979, mem. exec. com. Washington sect. 1968-78); mem. Sigma Tau, Eta Kappa Nu. Republican. Unitarian. Club: Lakewood Country (Rockville). Home: 11004 Homeplace Ln Potomac MD 20854 Office: Hekimian Laboratories Inc 9298 Gaither Rd Gaithersburg MD 20877

HELBERT, CLIFFORD L., graphic designer, journalism educator; b. Miles City, Mont., May 3, 1920; s. L. Roy and M. Mae (Stevenson) H.; 1944; children: Susan M., Thomas F., David P., Louise M., Anne R. Ph.B., Marquette U., 1948, A.M., 1955. Supt. Marquette U. Press, 1947-51, asst. bus. mgr., 1951-55, bus. mgr., 1955-61; mem. faculty Coll. Journalism, Marquette U., 1947—, prof., 1964—, dean coll., 1965-71; newspaper designer, 1951—, mag. designer, 1951—, book designer, 1947—, cons. in field, 1951—. Editor: Printing Progress a Mid-Century Report, 1959; also contbr.: Harpers Ency. Sci. Served to 1st lt. AUS, 1942-46. Named Internat. Craftsman of Year, 1961; recipient Andrew Hamilton award Marquette U., 1962; Benjamin Franklin award Graphic Arts Assn. Wis., 1966, Milw.-Racine Club of Printing House Craftsmen, 1981; fellow Internat. Newspaper Advt. Exec. Assn., 1963. Fellow Royal Soc. Art (London); mem. AAUP, Internat. Assn. Printing House Craftsman, Soc. Typog. Arts, Graphic Designer Can., Printing Hist. Soc. (London, Eng.), Internat. Center Typog. Arts, Am. Printing History Assn., Soc. Newspaper Design, Alpha Sigma Nu, Kappa Tau Alpha, Sigma Delta Chi, Alpha Delta Sigma. Home: PO Box 97 Milwaukee WI 53201 Office: 1131 W Wisconsin Ave Milwaukee WI 53233 *Three things distinguish the legacy of each man: his search for truth, chimerical and elusive as it is; his search for artistic integrity and the beauty and utility he achieves in the things he makes; his search and repose in love for his fellowman. To excel in one is amazing; to excel in two is astounding; to excel in all is the mark of genius. But to strive in all is to live life to the fullest.*

HELBLING, ROBERT EUGENE, educator; b. Lucerne, Switzerland, May 6, 1923; came to U.S., 1948, naturalized, 1954; s. Emil and Senta (Lamm) H.; m. Suzanne Ottinger, June 9, 1956. Diplom, Handelsschule Lucerne, 1943; M.A., U. Utah, 1949; postgrad., Columbia U., 1951; Ph.D., Stanford U., 1958, U. Calif., Berkeley, summer 1961. Jr. exec. R.I. Geigy, Inc. Chem. Works, Basle, Switzerland, 1945-47; instr. dept. langs. U. Utah, Salt Lake City, 1950-57, asst. prof. French, German and comparative lit., 1958-61, asso. prof., 1962-65, prof., 1966—, honors dir., 1964-66, coordinator humanities program, 1958-76, chmn. dept. langs., 1965-77, Reynolds lectr. and Disting. Honors prof., 1983—; vis. asso. prof. L.I. U., summer 1962; Guest Fgn. Ministry German Fed. Republic, 1970. Author: (with Andrée M.L. Barnett) Le Langage de la France Moderne, 1961, L'Actualite Française, 1967, Introduction au français actuel, 1973; Author, editor: Dürrenmatt's Die Physiker, 1965, Kleist, Novellen und Aesthetische Schriften, 1968, Kleist, 1975, Heinrich von Kleist, Erzahlurger, 1983; Editor: Les Carnets du Major Thompson, 1959, (with others) The Intellectual Tradition of the West, 1967, 68, First Year German, 1974, 3d edit., 1983, Dürrenmatt: Groteskes und Absurdes, 1976. Served with Swiss Army, 1943-45. Named 1 of Outstanding Educators Am., 1971. Mem. AAUP (past chpt. pres.), Modern Lang. Assn., Am. Assn. Tchrs. German, Am. Assn. French Tchrs., Assn. Depts. Fgn. Langs. (exec. com. 1973-75, pres. 1974), Joint Nat. Council for Langs. (chmn. 1975), Phi Kappa Phi, Pi Delta Phi, Phi Sigma Iota, Sigma Delta Pi, Delta Phi Alpha. Home: 3018 St Mary's Circle Salt Lake City UT 84108

HELBURN, NICHOLAS, educator; b. Salem, Mass., Dec. 20, 1918; s. Willard and Margaret (Mason) H.; m. Tess Loth (dec.); m. Suzanne E. Williams, Aug. 2, 1969; children—Stephen, Peter. B.A., U. Chgo., 1940; M.S., Mont. State U., 1941; Ph.D., U. Wis., 1950. Asst. prof., then asso. prof. Mont. State U., Bozeman, from 1947, prof., chmn. dept. geography and geology, until 1964; dir. high sch. geography project Assn. Am. Geographers, Boulder, Colo., 1964-69; prof. geography Western Mich. Univ., Kalamazoo, 1969-70; dir. ERIC Clearinghouse, Social Sci. Edn. Consortium, Boulder, 1970-72; prof. geography, grad. adminstr. U. Colo., Boulder, 1971—; cons. Ford Found., 1952-53, NSF, 1965-71, U. Phoenix, 1978—. Author: Some Trends in Turkish Agriculture, 1953, Montana in Maps, 1962; Editor: Challenge and Change in College Geography. Mem. AAAS, Assn. Am. Geographers, Nat. Council Geog. Edn., Social Sci. Edn. Consortium. Democrat. Mem. Soc. of Friends. Home: 3743 Nelson Rd Longmont CO 80501 Office: Geography Dept Box 260 U Colo Boulder CO 80309

HELCK, CLARENCE PETER, artist; b. N.Y.C., June 17, 1893; s. Henry Philip and Clara (Br) H.; m. Priscilla Smith, Sept. 30, 1922; 1 son, Jerry Peter. Ed. public sch. and, DeWitt Clinton High Sch., N.Y.C.; studied under, George Bridgeman, 1915, Sir Frank Brangwyn, 1920-23, Harry Wickey, 1923-28, Lewis Daniel, 1940-45; student, Art Students League, 1912, 23. Founding faculty mem. Famous Artists Schs., Westport, Conn., 1948—. Advt. artist for maj. indsl. and transp. corps., 1918—; illustrator leading publs., 1925-60; represented in permanent collections of, Met. Mus. Art, N.Y.C., Congl. Library, Washington, Mus. of Fine Arts, Phila., Detroit Pub. Library, Harrah's Auto Collection, Reno, Nev., Montagu Motor Mus., Beaulieu, Eng., Cunningham Automotive Mus., Costa Mesa, Cal., L.I. Auto Mus., Southampton, N.Y., Indpls. Speedway Mus., others, also pvt. collections; Author, illustrator: The Checkered Flag, 1961 (winner gold medals Salmagundi Club 1961, Soc. Illustrators 1962, Thomas McKean Meml. trophy 1962, Byron Hull cup 1962, 77), Great Auto Races, 1976 (winner Thomas McKean Meml. trophy 1977); Editorial staff: Bulb Horn, 1945—, Antique Automobile, 1946—, Automobile Quar, 1964—, Road & Track, 1980—. Recipient Harvard award, 1929; N.Y. Art Directors medal, 1931, 36, 41, 44, 51; Phila. Art Dirs. 1st awards, 1939, 40; Chgo. Art Dirs. medal, 1947; Detroit Art Dirs. 1st awards, 1950-52; medals, 1954, 56; Cleve. Art Dirs. medal, 1951; Distinguished Service citation Automotive Old Timers, 1966. Mem. NAD, Allied Artists, Am. Watercolor Soc., Audubon Artists, Soc. Illustrators (Hall Fame 1968); hon. mem. Vet. Motor Car Club Am., Antique Automobile Club Am., Automobilists Upper Hudson Valley, Conn. Automobile Hist. Soc., H.H. Franklin Club, Vintage Sports Car Club Am., Horseless Carriage Club. Presbyn. Home and Studio: Boston Corners RD 2 Millerton NY 12546

HELD, JOE ROGER, veterinarian, government official; b. Los Angeles, June 23, 1931; s. Edward Samuel and Carmen Antoinette (Planas) H.; m. Carolyn Ann Friderich, May 26, 1956; children: Lisa Lynn, Robert Joseph, Leslie Ann, Teresa Jeanne. B.S., U. Calif., Davis, 1953, D.V.M., 1955; M.P.H., Tulane U., 1959. Commd. officer USPHS, 1955, asst. surgeon gen. (rear adm.), 1978; various assignments in communicable diseases and epidemiology; grant adminstr. primate centers, animal resources br. NIH, Bethesda, Md., 1962-64; research parasitologist Nat. Inst. Allergy and Infectious Diseases, Chamblee, Ga., 1964-67; epidemiologist Pan Am. Health Orgn., Buenos Aires, 1967-69; chief vet. resources br., div. research service NIH, Bethesda, 1969-72, div. dir., 1972—; cons. WHO; mem. sci. authority endangered species Dept. Interior; mem. biol. research rev. com. Nat. Bur. Standards, 1976; mem. engring. tech. community adv. com. Montgomery Coll., Rockville, Md., 1976. Contbr. to profl. jours. Recipient Meritorious Service medal USPHS, 1972, Disting. Service medal USPHS, 1982; Outstanding Alumnus award Sch. Public Health and Tropical Medicine, Tulane U., 1977. Mem. AAAS, AVMA, D.C. Vet. Med. Assn. (pres. 1975), Conf. Pub. Health Vets. (sec.-treas. 1960-62), USPHS Commd. Officers Assn. (dir. 1973—), Am. Assn. Lab. Animal Sci., Nat. Capital Assn. Lab. Animal Sci. (pres. 1972-73), Am. Soc. Tropical Medicine and Hygiene, Found. Advanced Edn. in the Scis., Assn. Mil. Surgeons U.S. (exec. bd. 1976), Delta Omega. Home: 16305 Grande Vista Dr Rockville MD 20855

Office: Div Research Services NIH Bldg 12A Room 4007 9000 Wisconsin Ave Bethesda MD 20205

HELD, PHILIP, artist; b. N.Y.C., June 2, 1920; s. Conrad Christopher and Charlotte (Ditchett) H.; m. Ann Caine, Sept. 12, 1950; 1 son, Andrew Christopher. Student, Art Students League of N.Y., 1938-42, 46, Sch. for Art Studies, N.Y.C., 1947-48, Tchrs. Coll., Columbia U., summer 1949. Tchr. Fieldston Sch., N.Y., 1952-71, chmn. art dept., 1962-71; art edn. coordinator Booker-Bay Haven Sch., Sarasota, 1971-79; instr. painting, photography, calligraphy Visual and Performing Arts Center of Sarasota County, 1980—. One-man shows at, Eggleston Gallery, N.Y.C., 1948, Berkshire Mus., Mass., 1949, 67, Camino Gallery, N.Y.C., 1960, 62, Phoenix Gallery, N.Y.C., 1965, 67, Fontana Gallery, Phila., 1965, 67, 72, Gladstone Gallery, Woodstock, N.Y., 1965, Polari Gallery, Woodstock, 1970, Brevard Coll., Fla., 1973, Lighthouse Gallery, Tequesta, Fla., 1980; exhibited in group shows, Mus. Modern Art, N.Y.C., 1958, Pa. Acad. Fine Arts, 1962, U. Mass., 1966, Albany Inst. Arts and History, 1960, 63, L.I. U., 1960, Brown U., 1963, Phila. Mus., 1968, St. Johns U., 1970, Winthrop Coll., S.C., 1963, St. Paul Art Center, Drew U., 1966, Ringling Mus., Sarasota, Fla., 1973, Riverside Mus., N.Y.C., 1959, 60, Gallery Contemporary Art, Winston Salem, N.C., 1972, Fontana Gallery, Phila., 1975-76, Gallery of Sarasota, 1976, Hilton Leech Gallery, 1977, Pleiades Gallery, N.Y.C., Harmon Gallery, Naples and Sarasota, Fla., 1978, 80, 83, N.Y. State Council on Arts Exhbn., 1977-80, Fla. Artists Group XXXI Ann., Sarasota, 1980, St. Petersburg Pub. Library, 1982, Lighthouse Gallery, Tequestar, Fla.; represented in permanent collections, U. Mass., Berkshire Mus., Pittsfield, Mass., Art Students League of N.Y., Ringling Mus. Tchr., Scarborough Sch., N.Y., 1947-52; represented by, 302 Gallery, Phila., Editorial Photocolor Archives, N.Y.C. Mem. Sarasota Concert Band, Sarasota Brass Quintet., Suncoast Symphony; Chmn. Woodstock Artists Assn., 1959-60, bd. dirs., 1957-61. Served with AUS, 1942-46; ETO. Kleinert Found. grantee, 1966. Mem. Art Students League of New York (life), Sarasota Art Assn., Fla. Artists Group, Art League Manatee County, Am. Fedn. Musicians. Address: 3035 Wood St Sarasota FL 33577 *It is merely a commonplace to observe that all ages have had their problems and difficulties; but I am glad to be a part of my time and place... and to have the chance in a quiet way to contribute to its arts, and hence its life.*

HELD, RICHARD MARX, educator, psychologist; b. N.Y.C., Oct. 10, 1922; s. Lawrence W. and Tessie (Klein) H.; m. Doris F. Bernays, June 29, 1951; children: Lucas D.B., Julia B., Andrew L.B. B.A., Columbia U., 1943, B.S., 1944; M.A., Swarthmore Coll., 1948; Ph.D., Harvard U., 1952. Research asst. Swarthmore Coll., 1946-48; research fellow Jackson Hole Wildlife Park, summer 1948; research asst. psycho-acoustic lab. Harvard U., 1949-52, teaching fellow, 1950-51; NIH postdoctoral fellow, 1952-53; instr., then asst. prof. psychology Brandeis U., 1953-58, asso. prof., then prof., chmn. dept. psychology, 1958-62; mem. Inst. Advanced Study, Princeton, 1955-56; sr. research fellow NSF, 1962-63; vis. prof. Mass. Inst. Tech., Cambridge, 1962-63, prof. psychology, 1963—, chmn. dept., 1977—; dir. Sinauer Assocs., Transkinetics Inc.; Mem. com. vision Armed Forces-NRC; exec. com. mem.; assoc. Neuroscis. Research Program.; mem. vision research program com. Nat. Eye Inst. Editorial bd.: Psychol. Research, Perception. Bd. dirs. Founds.' Fund for Research in Psychiatry. Recipient Glenn A. Fry award, 1978. Fellow Am. Acad. Arts and Scis., Am. Acad. Optometry, AAAS, Am. Psychol. Assn.; mem. Nat. Acad. Sci., Eastern Psychol. Assn., Assn. for Research in Vision and Ophthalmology, Internat. Brain Research Orgn., Soc. Neuroscis., Soc. Exptl. Psychologists, Psychonomic Soc., Old Cambridge Shakespeare Assn., Sigma Xi. Home: 102 Appleton St Cambridge MA 02138

HELD, VIRGINIA, philosophy educator; b Mendham, N.J., Oct. 28, 1929; d. John Howard Nott and Margaretta (Wood) Potter; divorced; children: Julia, Philip. A.B., Barnard Coll., 1950; Ph.D., Columbia U., 1968. Mem. staff Reporter mag., 1954-65; lectr. philosophy Barnard Coll., 1964-66; mem. faculty Hunter Coll., CUNY, 1965—, prof. philosophy CUNY Grad. Sch., 1977—; vis. lectr. Yale U., 1972; dir. NEH Summer seminar, Stanford U. Law Sch., 1981; vis. scholar Harvard U. Law Sch., 1981-82. Author: The Public Interest and Individual Interests, 1970, Rights and Goods Justifying Social Action, 1984; also articles; editor: Property, Profits and Economic Justice, 1980; co-editor: Philosophy and Political Action, 1972, Philosophy, Morality and International Affairs, 1974; mem. editorial bd.: Ethics, Hypatia, Polit. Theory, Social Theory and Practice. Fulbright fellow, 1950; Rockefeller Found. fellow, 1975-76; fellow Ctr. for Advanced Study in Behavioral Scis., 1984—. Mem. Am. Philos. Assn. (exec. com. Eastern div. 1979-81), Columbia U. Seminars (Assoc.), Conf. Methods (exec. com. 1971—), Internat. Assn. Philosophy Law and Social Philospohy (pres. Am. sect. 1981-83), Soc. Philosophy and Pub. Affairs (chmn. 1972), Soc. Women in Philosophy. Democrat. Office: Dept Philosophy City U NY Grad Sch 33 W 42d St New York NY 10038

HELD, WALTER GEORGE, business and public policy educator; b. Willow Grove, Pa., Oct. 11, 1920; s. Ezra and May Theresa (Leahy) H.; m. Eleanor Parry, Sept. 23, 1943; children: Gale Ann, Suzanne Lee, Barbara Jeanne. A.B., Bucknell U., Lewisburg, Pa., 1943; M.A. (teaching fellow 1948-50), Am. U., 1949, Ph.D., 1951. Instr. polit. sci. Bucknell U., 1946-48; asst. prof. public adminstrn. Am. U., 1950-52; supervisory auditor, orgn. and methods examiner Office Chief Ordnance, Dept. Army, 1952-54; dep. comptroller Aberdeen (Md.) Proving Ground, 1954-56; dir. govt. ops. and expenditures program U.S. C. of C., 1956-60; dir. bus. programs advanced study program Brookings Instn., 1960-70, dir. adminstrn., then dir. advanced study program, 1971-79; dir. Washington affairs Standard Oil Co. N.J., 1970-71; prof. bus. and public policy, dir. Center Bus. and Public Policy, Am. U., Washington, 1979-81, adj. prof. bus. and public policy, 1981—; vis. prof. Coll. William and Mary, Williamsburg, Va., 1968; disting. vis. prof. public adminstrn. Nat. Def. U. Indsl. Coll. Armed Forces, 1981-82; cons. on bus. and pub. policy, 1982—; professorial lectr. George Washington U., 1953-54, 57-70; Nat. lectr. Nova U.; trustee Public Affairs Council Found., 1978-82; acad. adviser Bryce Harlow Found., 1982—; mem. Washington policy council Internat. Mgmt. and Devel. Inst., 1975—; bd. advisers for Center for Study Adminstrn., Nova U., 1978—; mgr. task force President's Personnel Mgmt. Project, 1978; resource leader President's Mgmt. Intern Program, 1978-79. Author: Decisionmaking in the Federal Government: The Wallace S. Sayre Model, 1979, Management Study Course on Government and Business, 1967—, rev. edits., 1968-77, also articles. Trustee Bucknell U., 1969-74. Served with USNR, 1943-46. Recipient Meritorious Service award Aberdeen Proving Ground, 1956, Disting. Service award CSC, 1978. Mem. Nat. Acad. Public Adminstrn., Am. Soc. Public Adminstrn., Am. Assembly Collegiate Schs. Bus. (vice chmn. com. govt. relations 1977-79), Bus.-Govt. Relations Council, Washington Reps. Research Group, Gen. Alumni Assn. Bucknell U. (pres. 1966-67), Phi Beta Kappa, Pi Sigma Alpha. Presbyterian. Club: Cosmos (Washington). Lodge: Masons. Home and Office: 2042 Rockingham St McLean VA 22101

HELD, WARREN HOWARD, JR., educator; b. Allentown, Pa., Oct. 9, 1928; s. Warren H. and Evelyn (Muschlitz) H.; m. Gerardina Vuyk, Sept. 1, 1951; children: Amy Ellen, Warren H. III. B.A., Princeton U., 1950; M.A., Yale U., 1952, Ph.D., 1955. Instr. Fairleigh Dickinson U., 1956-58, asst. prof. classics, 1958-61, asso. prof., 1961-67; prof. U. N.H., 1967—, also chmn. Spanish-classics dept., former assoc. dean liberal arts. Served with AUS, 1954-56; comdr. Portsmouth Power Squadron, 1971—. Mem. Classical Assn. N.H. (hon.), Linguistic Soc. Am., Am. Oriental Soc., Classical Assn. New Eng., Am. Sch. Oriental Research. Home: 1 Woodridge Rd Durham NH 03824

HELDENFELS, FREDERICK WILLIAM, JR., contractor; b. Beeville, Tex., Sept. 5, 1911; s. Frederick William and Alice (Cullen) H.; m. Rae Orms, Mar. 4, 1934 (dec. Feb. 1967); children: Frederick William III, John Orms; m. Paula Jackson Gierhart, Sept. 20, 1969. B.S. in Civil Engring., Tex. A&M Coll., 1933. Partner, Heldenfels Bros. (contractors), Corpus Christi, 1936-75, chmn. bd., 1975—; partner Heldenfels Farms, 1951—; v.p. Harris Concrete Co., Inc., 1941-66, pres., 1966-75; v.p. Counts Concrete Co., to 1975; pres. Heldenfels Constrn. Materials, Inc., 1975—; sec.-treas. Heldenfels Properties, Inc.; dir. 1st Nat. Bank, Rockport, Tex. Corpus Christi State Nat. Bank; pres. Constructor Mag., 1958-59; mem. constrn. industry adv. com. OPA, 1951-53; dir. Inter-Am. Fedn. Constrn. Industry, 1960-66; del. Inter-Am. Constrn. Congress, Mexico City, 1960, Rio de Janeiro, Brazil, 1962, Lima, Peru, 1964. Pres. bd. govs. United Community Services of Corpus Christi, 1963; bd. regents Del Mar Coll., chmn., 1963-73; bd. govs. Corpus Christie Art Found., Inc., 1976—; councilor Tex. A&M U. Research Found., 1974—. Cited by Tex. Ho. of Reps. for outstanding service, 1957. Mem. Asso. Gen. Contractors Am. (pres. Tex. hwy.-heavy br. 1949-51, nat. chmn. hwy. div. 1952-53, nat. pres. 1958, co-chmn. joint coop. com. with Am. Assn. State Hwy. Ofcls. 1954-56), Cons. Constructors Council Am., U.S. C. of C., Corpus Christi C. of C. (dir., Big Thinker award 1958, chmn. indsl. com. 1963-66), Tex. Employers Ins. Assn. (dir.), Tau Beta Pi. Episcopalian. Home: 5015 Ocean Dr Corpus Christi TX 78412 Office: PO Box 4957 Corpus Christi TX 78408

HELDMAN, ALAN WOHL, lawyer; b. Birmingham, Ala., Mar. 12, 1936; s. Max and Josephine (Wohl) H.; m. Ann Huntington, Jan. 28, 1961; children: Alan Wohl, Samuel H., Katherine Ann. A.B. cum laude, Vanderbilt, 1957; J.D., Harvard, 1961. Bar: Ala. bar 1961, U.S. Supreme Ct. bar 1976. Practiced in, Birmingham, 1961—; asso. Deramus & Johnston, 1961-65; partner Johnston, Barton, Proctor, Swedlaw & Naff, 1965—; Spl. asst. atty. gen., Ala., 1971. Dir. at large Ala. Clean Air Com., 1970—; Chmn. Conservation Com. Ala. Conservancy Birmingham Group, 1972—; dir. Ala. Com. to Reclaim the Earth from Strip Mining. Served to capt. U.S. Army, 1958-65. Mem. Am., Ala., Birmingham bar assns., Sierra Club (vice chmn. Birmingham Group 1972—), Explorers Club. Democrat. Jewish. Clubs: Explorers, Young Mens Business (Birmingham) (past pres.). Home: 3857 Cromwell Dr Birmingham AL 35243 Office: 1100 Park Pl Tower Birmingham AL 35203

HELDMAN, DENNIS RAY, agrl., food engr.; b. Hancock County, Ohio, June 12, 1938; s. Merritt L. and Lavon M. H.; m. Joyce M. Anspach, Dec. 21, 1956; children—Cynthia, Candace, Craig. B.S., Ohio State U., 1960, M.S., 1962; Ph.D., Mich. State U., 1965. Asst. instr. Ohio State U., 1960-62; faculty agrl. engring., food scis. depts. Mich. State U., East Lansing, 1965—, prof., 1971-75, prof., chmn. agrl. engring. dept., 1975-79, prof. food engring., 1979—; intern Am. Council on Ednl. Adminstrn., 1974; vis. asso. prof. U. Calif., Davis, 1970, vis. prof., 1980. Author: Food Process Engineering, 1975, 2d edit. (with R. Paul Singh), 1981; Editorial bd., AVI Pub. Co., Food and Nutrition Press, 1977—; cons. editor, McGraw-Hill Co., 1980—. Recipient Disting. Alumni award Ohio State U., 1978. Mem. Am. Soc. Agrl. Engrs. (Young Researcher award 1974, Food Engring. award 1981), Inst. Food Technologists, Am. Soc. Engring. Edn., Sigma Xi, Phi Kappa Phi, Alpha Epsilon, Phi Tau Sigma. Home: 1950 Wembley Way East Lansing MI 48823 Office: Dept Food Sci and Human Nutrition Mich State U East Lansing MI 48824

HELDRING, FREDERICK, banker; b. Amsterdam, Netherlands, Mar. 25, 1924. Student, Free U., Amsterdam, 2 years; grad., Wharton Sch., U. Pa., 1951. With internat. div. Phila. Nat. Bank, 1951—, v.p., 1962-63, head internat. div., 1963-66, vice chmn., 1970-74, pres., 1974-80, dep. chmn., 1980—; chmn. bd. Phila. Internat. Bank, 1970—; ptnr. Greater Phila. Partnership.; dir. Core States Fin. Corp., Quaker Chem. Corp. Mem. Phila. Clearing House. Mem. Phila. Com. Fgn. Relations, Internat. C. of C. (U.S. council). Home: Wayne PA Office: Phila Nat Bank Broad and Chestnut Sts Philadelphia PA 19101

HELFER, HERMAN LAWRENCE, astronomy educator; b. N.Y.C., Nov. 11, 1929; s. Paul Walter and Alice Mildred (Ross) H.; m. Joanne L. Salomon, Dec. 22, 1956; children: Adam Daniel, Elizabeth Laura, Martha Blanche, Tamara Toby. Ph.B., U. Chgo., 1948, Ph.D., 1953. Research fellow radioastronomy Carnegie Instn., Washington, 1953-54, 56-57, Calif. Inst. Tech., 1957-58; asst. prof. physics and astronomy U. Rochester, N.Y., 1958-63, asso. prof., 1963-70, prof. astronomy, 1970—. Served with AUS, 1954-56. NSF Predoctoral fellow, 1952-53; Guggenheim Meml. Found. fellow, 1965-66. Fellow Royal Astron. Soc.; mem. Am. Astron. Soc., AAAS, Phi Beta Kappa. Research in galactic structure, radio and infrared astronomy, astron. spectroscopy, theoretical astrophysics. Home: 30 Bradford Rd Rochester NY 14618

HELFFERICH, FRIEDRICH G., chemical engineer, educator; b. Berlin, Germany, Aug. 1, 1922; s. Karl and Anna Clara Johanna (Siemens) H.; m. Barbara Schlubach, July, 1947; children: Christiane, Cornelia.; m. Hana M. Konecna, Feb., 1961; 1 dau., Stefanie. B.S., U. Hamburg, 1949, M.S., 1952; Ph.D., U. Goettingen, 1955. Research asst. Max Planck Inst., 1951-56, MIT, 1954, Calif. Inst. Tech., 1956-58; vis. scientist Max-Planck Inst., 1958; sr. research asso. Shell Devel. Co., 1958-79; lectr. U. Calif., Berkeley, 1962-63; vis. prof., lectr. U. Houston, Rice U., U. Tex., 1980; prof. chem. engring. Pa. State U., 1980—; chmn. Gordon Research Conf. on Ion Exchange. Author: 3 books in field, including Multicomponent Chromatography, 1970; Editor: Fire and Movement mag., 1978—, Reactive Polymers, 1981—; Contbr. articles to profl. jours. Fulbright scholar, 1954. Fellow Am. Inst. Chemists; mem. Am. Inst. Chem. Engrs., Soc. Petroleum Engrs. Club: Commonwealth of Calif. Home: 1845 Woodledge State College PA 16801 Office: Pa State Univ University Park PA 16802

HELFGOTT, ROY B., economist, educator; b. Bklyn., Oct. 27, 1925; s. Moses N. and Dorothy A. (Levine) H.; m. Gloria Wolff, July 4, 1948; 1 son, Daniel Andrew. B.S. in Social Sci, City Coll., N.Y., 1948; M.A., Columbia U., 1949; Ph.D., New Sch., 1957. Research dir. N.Y. coat bd. Internat. Ladies Garment Workers Union, 1949-57; indsl. relations analyst Wage Stblzn. Bd., 1952; economist N.Y. Met. Regional Study, 1957-58; asst. prof. Pa. State U., 1958-60; research dir. Indsl. Relations Counselors, N.Y.C., 1960-66, 67-68; cons. Orgn. Resources Counselors, Inc., N.Y.C., 1968—; indsl. devel. officer UN, 1966-67; distinguished prof. econs. N.J. Inst. Tech., Newark, 1968—; adj. asso. prof. Baruch Coll., 1961-68; head UN mission, Lower Mekong Basin, 1967. Author: Labor Economics, 1974, 2d edit., 1980; co-author: Industrial Planning, 1969, Management, Automation and People, 1964, Made in New York, 1959. Served with AUS, 1944-46. Decorated Bronze Star, Combat Inf. badge; fellow Inter-Univ. Inst. Social Gerotology, Berkeley, Calif., 1959; sr. Fulbright research scholar, U.K., 1955-56. Mem. Am. Econ. Assn., Indsl. Relations Research Assn., Phi Beta Kappa. Home: Route 341 Warren CT 06754 Office: 323 High St Newark NJ 07102

HELFRECHT, DONALD JOHN, utility company executive; b. Madison, Wis., Feb. 22, 1922; s. Aaron J. and Lillian (Miller) H.; m. Carol E. Hoveland, June 25, 1949; 1 dau., Karen. B.S.E.E., U. Wis., 1944. Registered profl. engr., Wis. Various engring. assignments Madison Gas and Electric Co., 1946—, v.p. elec. system operation, 1970-74, exec. v.p., 1974-76, pres., chief exec. officer, 1976—, dir.; dir. 1st Nat. Bank, Wis., Meth. Hosp. Corp., Madison United Hosp. Laundry. Bd. dirs. U. Wis. Found.; chmn. gold medal div. United Way of Dane County, Madison, 1979; mem. Dane County Exec. Commn. on Mgmt., 1981—, Mayor's Arson Task Force, Madison, 1981-82; mem. fin. com. Jim Johnson for Congress campaign, 1982. Served to 1st lt. Signal Corps, U.S. Army, 1943-46. Recipient disting. service citation U. Wis., 1981. Mem. Edison Electric Inst., Am. Gas Assn., Wis. Utilities Assn. (chmn. bd. 1980-81), Wis. Elec. Utilities Found. (pres. 1980), Wis. Soc. Profl. Engrs. (Engr. of Yr. 1977, 81), Nat. Soc. Profl. Engrs., IEEE (chmn. Madison sect.), Madison Tech. Club, Dane County Pub. Affairs Council. Lutheran. Clubs: Kilowatt Klub, Madison, Maple Bluff Country. Lodge: Rotary (dir. 1981-83). Home: 913 Mohican Pass Madison WI 53711 Office: Madison Gas and Electric Co PO Box 1231 Madison WI 53701

HELGELAND, GLENN BERNARD, publisher, magazine editor; b. Barron, Wis., Mar. 15, 1943; s. Adolph Bernard and Gladys Iola (Hammann) H.; m. Judith Ellen Voland, Nov. 26, 1966; children: Jody Lynn, Bryant Bernard, Amanda Kay. B.S., U. Wis., Madison, 1965. Reporter Daily News, Winona, Minn., 1965-66; info. specialist Bur. Comml. Fisheries Dept. Interior, Chgo., 1966-68; asso. editor Nat. Wildlife mag., Milw., 1968-70; mng. editor WaterSport Mag., Milw., 1968-70, editor, 1970-75, Archery World mag., Milw., 1970-80, Archery Retailer mag., 1976-80, Archery World's Complete Guide to Bowhunting, 1975; editor/pub. Wis. Master Plumber mag., 1979—; pres. Target Communications Corp., Grafton, Wis., 1980—. Contbr. articles, photographs to major outdoor mags. Recipient Certificate of Merit Nat. Archery Assn. U.S., 1977; Outstanding Conservation Writing award Safari Club Internat., 1977. Mem. Am. Outdoor Writers Assn. (dir.). Home: 10459 N Wauwatosa Rd Mequon WI 53092 Office: 7626 W Donges Bay Rd Mequon WI 53092

HELIKER, JOHN, artist; b. Yonkers, N.Y., Jan. 17, 1909; s. John Edward and Jane (MacLaughlin) H. Student, Art Students League, N.Y.C.; studied with, Kimon Nicolaides, Kenneth Hayes Miller, Boardman Robinson; A.F.D. (hon.), Colby Coll., 1966. Ret. asso. prof. Columbia U. Paintings exhibited, Whitney Mus., Corcoran Gallery Art, Toledo Mus. Art, Va. Mus. Fine Arts, Richmond, Art Inst. Chgo., Met. Mus. Art, Carnegie Inst., Pa. Acad. Fine Arts, Worcester (Mass.) Mus. Art, Cleve. Mus. Art, Fine Arts Club, Chgo., Mus. Modern Art, N.Y.C., one man shows, Maynard Walker Gallery, 1938, 41, Kraushaar Gallery, 1945, 51, 54, 68, 71, 74, 80; represented permanent collections, Mus. Modern Art, N.Y.C., Met. Mus., N.Y.C., Phila. Mus., Pa. Acad., New Britain Mus., Telfair Acad., Walker Art Center, U. Neb., Fogg Mus. Art, Addison Gallery Am. Art, Andover, Mass., Corcoran Gallery, Whitney Mus., San Francisco Mus. of Art, in Brussels World Fair, 1958, Worlds Fair, Osaka, 1970, retrospective, Whitney Mus. Am. Art, 1968. Recipient Nat. Inst. Arts and Letters award, 1957; Am. Acad. Arts and Letters award, 1967; Ford Found. purchase award, 1960; fellow in the Am. Acad., Rome, 1948; Guggenheim fellow., 1951. Mem. Nat. Inst. Arts and Letters.

HELINSKI, DONALD RAYMOND, biologist; b. Balt., July 7, 1933; s. George L. and Marie M. (Naparstek) H.; m. Patricia G. Doherty, Mar. 4, 1962; children—Matthew T., Maureen G. B.S., U. Md., 1954; Ph.D. in Biochemistry, Western Res. U., 1960; postdoctoral fellow, Stanford U., 1960-63. Asst. prof. Princeton (N.J.) U., 1963-65; mem. faculty U. Calif., San Diego, 1965—, prof. biology, 1970—, chmn. dept., 1979-81; mem. com. guidelines for recombinant DNA research NIH, 1975-78. Author papers in field. Mem. Am. Soc. Biol. Chemistry, Am. Soc. Microbiology, AAAS, Nat. Acad. Scis., Genetics Soc. Office: 4222 Bonner Hall U Calif La Jolla CA 92093

HELLAND, GEORGE ARCHIBALD, JR., equipment manufacturing company executive; b. San Antonio, Nov. 28, 1937; s. George Archibald and Ruth (Gorman) H.; m. Josephine Howell, June 9, 1962; children—Jane Elizabeth, Thomas Gorman. B.S.M.E., U. Tex., 1959; M.B.A. with distinction, Harvard U., 1961. Registered profl. engr., Tex. With Cameron Iron Works, Inc., Houston, 1961-77, asst. sales mgr., 1963, dist. sales mgr., Houston, 1964, U.K., Africa, 1965, product mgr., 1966, plant mgr., Leeds, Eng., 1967, mgr. oil tool products, Houston, 1968, v.p., 1969-75, exec. v.p., 1975-77; v.p. Weatherford Internat., Inc., Houston, 1977, pres., 1977-79, chief exec. officer, dir., 1978-79; pres. McEvoy Oilfield Equipment Co. (name Sii McEvoy div. Smith Internat., Inc. 1980), Houston, 1979—. Bd. dirs. Briarwood Sch., Houston.; Trustee SW Research Inst.; mem. exec. com. Jr. Achievement of SE Tex. Recipient Five Outstanding Young Texans award Tex. Jr. C. of C., 1972; named Outstanding Young Houstonian Houston Jr. C. of C., 1972; Disting. Grad. Sch. Engring., U. Tex., 1977. Mem. Am. Inst. Mining, Metall. and Petroleum Engrs., ASME, Am. Petroleum Inst. (dir.), Inst. Gas Engrs. (U.K.), Tex. Soc. Profl. Engrs., Am. Wellhead Equipment Assn. (pres. 1967), Petroleum Equipment Suppliers Assn. (pres. 1976-77), Houston C. of C., Brit. Am. Bus. Assn. (dir.), Tau Beta Pi, Phi Eta Sigma, Pi Tau Sigma, Sigma Nu, Frairs Soc. Presbyterian. Home: 5385 Sugar Hill Houston TX 77056 Office: Sii McEvoy Div Smith Internat Inc PO Box 3127 Houston TX 77001

HELLAWELL, ROBERT, legal educator; b. Long Island, N.Y., Jan. 24, 1928; s. Edwin V. and Nora D. (Mahoney) H.; m. Jane Buck, June 16, 1951; 1 dau., Kathleen Abbott. A.B., Williams Coll., 1950; LL.B., Columbia U., 1953. Bar: N.Y. 1954, Ohio 1955. Law clk. U.S. Circuit Ct. judge, 1953-54; with firm Jones, Day, Cockley & Reavis, Cleve., 1954-61, partner, 1961; atty., adviser formation Peace Corps, 1961, dir. projects in, Tanganyika, 1961-63, dep. assoc. dir. corps, 1963-64; assoc. prof. law Columbia Law Sch., N.Y.C., 1964-67, prof. law, 1967—, vice dean, 1973-76, acting dean, 1976-77, dir. African Law Center, 1971-77, co-dir. Investment Negotiation Center, 1973-82, dir. Center for Law and Econs., 1978-79; vis. prof. U. Ghana, 1969; cons. admiralty law UN Commn. Internat. Trade Law, 1971. Co-author: The Study of Federal Tax Law, Business Enterprises, 1980, Transnational Transactions, 1981; editor: United States Taxation and Developing Countries, 1980; co-editor: Competition in International Business, 1981, Negotiating Foreign Investments, 1982; Notes editor: Columbia Law Rev, 1952-53. Bd. dirs. Internat. Law Inst., Georgetown U., 1973—. Served with AUS, 1946-48; Korea. Mem. Delta Kappa Epsilon, Phi Delta Phi. Office: Columbia Law Sch New York NY 10027

HELLEINER, GERALD KARL, educator; b. St. Pölten, Austria, Oct. 9, 1936; s. Karl Ferdinand and Grethe (Deutsch) H.; m. Georgia Stirrett, Aug. 16, 1958; children—Jane Leslie, Eric Noel, Peter David. B.A., U. Toronto, 1958; Ph.D., Yale U., 1962. Asst. prof. Yale U., 1961-65; asso., then prof. U. Toronto, 1965—; dir. Econ. Research Bur., Dar es Salaam, Tanzania, 1966-68; vis. fellow Inst. Devel. Studies, 1971-72, 75, Queen Elizabeth House, Oxford, 1979. Author: Peasant Agriculture, Government and Economic Growth in Nigeria, 1966, Agricultural Planning in East Africa, 1968, International Trade and Economic Development, 1972, A World Divided, 1976, International Economic Disorder, 1981, Intrafirm Trade and the Developing Countries, 1981, For Good or Evil: Economic Theory and North-South Relations, 1982. Gugenheim fellow, 1971-72. Fellow Royal Soc. Can.; mem. Royal Econs. Assn., Can. Econs. Assn., Am. Econs. Assn., Soc. Internat. Devel., North-South Roundtable, Can.

African Studies Assn. Office: 150 St George St Toronto ON M5S 1A1 Canada

HELLEMS, HARPER KEITH, physician; b. Sinks Grove, W.Va., Mar. 16, 1920; s. Harvey Kem and Nilah Irene (Epling) H.; m. Martha Cooper. Student, U. Va., 1938-40, M.D., 1943. Diplomate: Am. Bd. Internal Medicine. Intern Montreal (Que., Can.) Gen. Hosp., 1944-45; research fellow medicine Peter Bent Brigham Hosp., also Harvard U. Med. Sch., Boston, 1946-48; teaching fellow Harvard U. Med. Sch., 1949-50; from asst. prof. to prof. medicine Wayne State U. Med. Sch., Detroit, 1950-60; prof. medicine, dir. div. cardiovascular diseases N.J. Coll. Medicine, 1960-65; prof. medicine, chmn. dept. U. Miss. Med. Center, Jackson, 1965—; cons. Jackson VA Hosp. Author research papers. Served to lt., M.C. USNR, 1944-46. Fellow Am. Coll. Cardiology (Theodore and Susan Anthony award 1964, 67), A.C.P.; mem. Central Soc. Clin. Research, Am. Soc. Clin. Investigations, Assn. Am. Physicians, Am. Physiol. Soc., Assn. Univ. Cardiologists, So. Soc. Clin. Investigation, Am. Clin. and Climatol. Assn., Assn. Profs. Medicine, Assn. Program Dirs. Internal Medicine. Office: Dept Medicine UMC 2500 N State St Jackson MS 39216 *

HELLENBRAND, SAMUEL HENRY, diversified industry executive, lawyer; b. N.Y.C., Nov. 11, 1916; s. Louis H. and Fannie (Cohen) H.; married; children: Kathy Noreen, Linda Caryn. LL.B., Bklyn. Law Sch. St. Lawrence U., 1941, LL.M., 1942. Bar: N.Y. 1942. With N.Y. Central R.R., 1942-68, atty., asst. to gen. atty., tax atty., 1942-52, gen. tax atty., 1952-56, dir. taxes finance dept., 1956-63, v.p. planning and devel., 1963-64, v.p. real estate, 1964-68; v.p. indsl. devel. and real estate Penn Central Co., 1968-70, v.p. real estate and taxes, 1970-71; pres. Pa. Co., 1970-71; v.p. exec. asst. to pres., dir. real estate affairs ITT, 1971-81; chmn. fin. com., vice-chmn. AMTRAK, 1982—. Mem. Am., N.Y. State bar assns., Assn. Bar City N.Y. Home: 177 E 75th St New York NY 10021 Office: 320 Park Ave New York NY 10022

HELLENDALE, ROBERT, paper co. exec.; b. N.Y.C., Nov. 19, 1917; m. Jill Hibben, Aug. 29, 1945; children—William C., Rufus P., Sheila. B.A., Wesleyan U., Middletown, Conn., 1939; LL.B., Harvard, 1942. Bar: N.Y. bar 1946, Me. bar 1954. Practice in, N.Y.C., 1946-54, atty., paper co. exec., 1954—; v.p. Gt. No. Paper Co., 1964-74, pres., 1974-78; exec. v.p. Gt. No. Nekoosa Corp., 1970-78, pres., 1978—, chmn., 1980—; dir. Irving Trust Co. Served with AUS, 1941-45. Home: 21 Shoal Point Ln Riverside CT 06878 Office: 75 Prospect St Stamford CT 06901

HELLER, ALFRED, pharmacologist, educator; b. Chicago, July 23, 1930; s. Selig and Lena (Rochelle) H.; m. Barbara Ruth Steigman, July 22, 1956; 1 son, Daniel Jacob. B.S. with Honors, U. Ill., 1952; Ph.D. (NSF fellow), U. Chgo., 1956; M.D. with honors (Laverne Noyes fellow), U. Chgo., 1960. Intern U. Chgo.-Billings Hosp.; asst. prof. pharmacology U. Chgo., 1960-65, asso. prof., 1965-72, prof., 1972—, acting chmn. dept. pharm. and physiol. scis., 1973, chmn., 1973—. Grantee USPHS, 1962-81. Mem. AAAS, Am. Soc. for Pharmacology and Exptl. Therapeutics, Am. Soc. for Neurochemistry, Internat. Soc. for Neurochemistry, Soc. for Neurosci., NIH Gen. Med. Scis. Council. Home: 1455 E Park Pl Chicago IL 60637 Office: 947 E 58th St Chicago IL 60637

HELLER, ANN WILLIAMS, nutritionist, writer; b. Vienna, Austria, Aug. 25, 1904; came to U.S., 1938, naturalized, 1944; d. Friedrich C. and Elsa (Spitzer) Wilhelm; m. Walter L. Heller, Dec. 27, 1933 (dec. Sept. 1966). Student, U. Vienna, 1933-34, Columbia U., 1938-39. Food and equipment editor Everywomans Mag., N.Y.C., 1955-57. Writer: feature articles mags. including Womans Day; contbr.: articles to newspapers, trade jours. and syndicate features, including all major syndicates; writer consumer product books; books include Soybeans from Soup to Nuts, 1944, Cooked to Your Taste, 1945, Its a Sin to Be Fat, 1947, Reducers Cookbook, 1948, The Busy Woman's Cookbook, 1948, Thrifty Gourmet's Meat Cookbook, 1971, Eat and Get Slim Cookbook, 1973, Nature's Own Vegetables Cookbook, 1973. Mem. Greater N.Y. Dietetic Assn., Am. Soc. Journalists and Authors, Food and Nutrition Council Greater N.Y. Address: 1100 Madison Ave New York NY 10028

HELLER, ARTHUR, advertising executive; b. Bklyn., Mar. 14, 1930; s. Max and Tecla (Jacobs) H.; m. Phyllis Olarsch, Dec. 25, 1954; children: Todd, Tracy. B.A., Bklyn. Coll., 1951, M.A., 1952. Speech and speech correction tchr. N.Y.C. Bd. Edn., 1951-55; v.p., assoc. media dir., media analysis and planning Benton & Bowles, Inc., 1955-66; with Ted Bates & Co., N.Y.C., 1966—, v.p., media dir., 1966-69, v.p., asso. dir. media-program dept., 1969-71, sr. v.p., 1971—, also account dir., 1974-78; sr. v.p., dir. media-programming-mktg. services Griffin Bacal Inc., N.Y.C., 1978-82, exec. v.p., 1982—; also dir. Served with AUS, 1952-54. Mem. Radio and TV Research Council, Actors Equity Assn. Home: 2251 Legion St Bellmore NY 11710 Office: 380 Lexington Ave New York NY 10168

HELLER, CHARLES ANDREW, JR., electric utilities co. exec.; b. Teaneck, N.J., Mar. 18, 1929; s. Charles Andrew and Lillian Laura (Reuter) H.; m. Helen Johansen, July 19, 1952; children—Charles Andrew, Janice Maria, Richard Craig. B.A., Rutgers U., 1951; M.B.A., U. Pa., 1956; M.S. (Alfred P. Sloan fellow), M.I.T., 1966. With Am. Electric Power Service Corp., N.Y.C., 1956-63; with Ohio Power Co., Canton, 1963-68, 70—, v.p., 1974-76, exec. v.p., 1976-81, chief operating officer, 1976—, pres., 1981—; exec. asst. Wheeling Electric Co., W.Va., 1968-70; exec. v.p., dir. Ohio Electric Co.; v.p., dir. Cardinal Operating Co., Central Coal Co., Central Ohio Coal Co., Central Operating Co., So. Ohio Coal Co., Windsor Power House Coal Co., 1976—; v.p. Beech Bottom Power Co., Inc., Franklin Real Estate Co., 1976—, Ind. Franklin Realty, Inc., 1979—; dir. Ohio Electric Utility Inst., 1976—, pres., 1978—; dir. Central Trust Co. Northeastern Ohio, 1975—. Mem. Council for Reorganization of Ohio State Govt., 1967; dir. Canton Welfare Found., 1975-78; mem. Malone Coll. Adv. Bd., 1976—. Served to capt. USAF, 1951-53. Republican. Lutheran. Clubs: Rotary, Canton, Brookside Country, Columbus Athletic, Elks. Office: 301 Cleveland Ave SW Canton OH 44701

HELLER, EDWIN, lawyer; b. N.Y.C., Dec. 8, 1929; s. Joseph and Gizela H.; m. Dorothy L. Killgrew, Mar. 5, 1958; children: Dana, William. B.A., Cornell U., 1950; LL.B., Harvard U., 1954. Bar: N.Y. 1955. Teaching fellow Harvard U. Law Sch., 1956-57; ptnr. firm Fried, Frank, Harris, Shriver & Jacobson, N.Y.C., 1957—. Office: Fried Frank Harris Shriver & Jacobson One New York Plaza New York NY 10004

HELLER, ERICH, educator, author; b. Komotau, Bohemia, Mar. 27, 1911; came to the U.S., 1959; s. Alfred and Else (Hoenig) H. Doctorate in Law and German Lit, Charles U., Prague, Czechoslovakia, 1935; Ph.D., Cambridge (Eng.) U., 1948; Litt.D. (hon.), Emory U., 1965. Asst. lectr. German London Sch. Econs., 1943-45; lectr. German, dir. studies modern langs. Peterhouse Coll., Cambridge U., 1945-48; prof. German U. Wales, 1948-60; vis. prof. U. Hamburg, 1947, U. Göttingen, 1948, U. Bonn, 1948, Harvard, 1953-54, Brandeis U., 1957-58; prof. German Northwestern U., 1960-67, Avalon prof. emeritus humanities, 1968—; vis. prof. German U. Heidelberg, summer 1963; Carnegie vis. prof. humanities Mass. Inst. Tech., fall 1963. Author: The Disinherited Mind, Essays in Modern German Literature and Thought, 1952, The Ironic German, a Study of Thomas Mann, 1958, The Artist's Journey into the Interior and Other Essays, 1965, Essays über Goethe, 1970, Franz Kafka, 1974-75, Versuche über Rilke, 1975, The Poet's Self and the Poem, 1976, Die Wiederkehr der Unschuld, 1977, In the Age of Prose, 1983; Editor: Studies in Modern European Lit. and Thought, 1950-68, Kafka's Letter to Felice, 1967, 73; Contbr. profl. and lit. jours. Recipient Kulturkreis lit. prize German industry, 1958; Johann-Heinnich-Merck prize for essay and lit. criticism German Acad. Lang. and Lit., 1969; decorated Great Cross of Merit, W. Ger.). Fellow Am. Acad. Arts and Letters; mem. Bayerische Akademie der Schönen Künste, Deutsche Akademie für Sprache und Dichtung, P.E.N. Club (Germany and Austria). Address: Dept German Northwestern U Evanston IL 60201

HELLER, FRANCIS HOWARD, political science educator; b. Vienna, Austria, Aug. 24, 1917; came to U.S., 1938, naturalized, 1943; s. Charles A. and Lily (Grunwald) H.; m. Donna Munn, Sept. 3, 1949; 1 son, Denis Wayne. Student, U. Vienna, 1935-37; J.D., U. Va., 1941, M.A., 1941, Ph.D., 1948. Asst. prof. govt. Coll. William and Mary, 1947; asst. prof. polit. sci. U. Kans., Lawrence, 1948-51, asso. prof., 1951-56, prof., 1956—, Roy A. Roberts prof. law and polit. sci., 1972—, asso. dean Coll. Liberal Arts and Scis., 1957-66, asso. dean of faculties, 1966-67, dean, 1967-70, vice chancellor for acad. affairs, 1970-72; vis. prof. Inst. Advanced Studies, Vienna, 1965, U. Vienna Law Sch., 1985. Author: Introduction to American Constitutional Law, 1952, The Presidency: A Modern Perspective, 1960, The Korean War: a 25-Year Perspective, 1977, The Truman White House, 1980, Economics and the Truman Administration, 1981. Mem. Kans. Commn. on Constl. Revision, 1957-61; mem. Lawrence City Plan Commn., 1957-63; ednl. adv. commn. U.S. Army Command and Gen. Staff Coll., 1969-72; bd. dirs. Harry S. Truman Library Inst. (vice chmn.), Benedictine Coll. (chmn. 1971-79). Served from pvt. to 1st lt., arty. AUS, 1942-47; to capt., 1951-52; maj. Res. ret. Decorated Silver Star, Bronze Star with cluster. Mem. Am. Polit. Sci. Assn. (exec. council 1958-60), Order of Coif, Phi Beta Kappa, Pi Sigma Alpha (mem. nat. council 1958-60). Office: Sch Law U Kans Lawrence KS 66045

HELLER, FRED, illumination mfg. co. exec.; b. N.Y.C., Sept. 4, 1924; s. William and Rae H.; m. Erna Davis, June 10, 1948; children—Jeffrey, William. B.Mech.Engring., Rensselaer Poly. Inst., 1947; M.Adminstrv.Engring., N.Y. U., 1949. Gen. mgr. Omaton div. Burndy Corp., 1959-64; sr. v.p. ops. Lightolier Inc., Jersey City, 1964-72, vice chmn., chief exec. officer, 1972—, also dir.; dir. Energy Clinic Corp. Served with USNR, 1943-46, 50-51. Sr. mem. IEEE. Office: 346 Claremont Ave Jersey City NJ 07305

HELLER, FREDERICK, mining company executive; b. Detroit, May 6, 1932; s. Robert and Lois (Mouch) H.; m. Barbara Ann McGreevy, Nov. 22, 1979; children: Thomas M., John G., Cynthia R. B.A., Harvard U., 1954. With Hanna Mining Co., 1957—, v.p. sales, 1973-76, sr. v.p. sales and transp., Cleve., 1976-81, sr. v.p. mktg., 1981—. Trustee, mem. exec. com. Cleve. Inst. Art, 1977—; trustee, mem. fin. com. McGregor Home, 1978—; trustee, mem. adv. bd. Lake Carriers Assn., 1976-81. Served with U.S. Army, 1954-56. Mem. Ferroalloys Assn. (dir.), Am. Iron and Steel Inst., Am. Mining Congress, Am. Iron Ore Assn., Soc. Mining Engrs. Republican. Episcopalian. Clubs: Union, Kirtland Country, Pepper Pike, Tavern, Duquesne. Home: 2942 Fontenay Rd Shaker Heights OH 44120 Office: Hanna Mining Co 100 Erieview Plaza Cleveland OH 44114

HELLER, GERALD SILAS, electrical engineering educator; b. Detroit, Sept. 5, 1920; s. Joseph and Augusta (Galper) H.; m. Betty Steinhardt, Jan. 9, 1943; children: Allen Harvey, Wendy Beth. Sc.B., Wayne U., 1942; Sc.M. in Applied Math., Brown U., 1946; Ph.D. in Physics, Brown U., 1948. Staff mem. Radiation Lab. MIT, 1942-45, group leader Lincoln Lab., 1954-62, vis. prof. elec. engring, 1962-63; asst. prof. physics Brown U., Providence, 1948-54, prof. engring., 1963—, dir. Materials Research Lab., 1969—; cons. magnetic materials. Contbr. articles to profl. jours.; patentee in field. Fellow IEEE; mem. Am. Phys. Soc., Am. Math. Soc., Sigma Xi, Sigma Pi Sigma. Home: 450 Brook St Providence RI 02906 Office: Box M Brown U. Providence RI 02912

HELLER, JACK ISAAC, lawyer; b. Passaic, N.J., July 12, 1932; s. Aaron and Ruth (Brown) H.; m. Naomi Birnbaum, Mar. 8, 1959; children—Michael Adam, Daniel Noah, Rafael Gustav. A.B., U. Chgo., 1952; LL.B., Columbia, 1958. Teaching fellow, research asst. internat. program in taxation Harvard Law Sch., 1958-61; sr. tax adviser OAS, Washington, 1961-62; tax economist Latin Am. Bur., U.S. AID, 1962-65; with Office Gen. Counsel, AID, 1965-66; legal adviser AID, Brazil, 1966-67, asst. dir., 1967-68; dir. Office of Devel. Programs, Latin Am. Bur., AID, 1969-72; atty., mgr. spl. projects Office Gen. Counsel, Gen. Electric Co., 1972-74; practice law, Washington, 1974—; partner firm Heller & Lloyd, 1979—. Author: Tax Incentives for Industry in Less Developed Countries, 1963. Served with AUS, 1953-55. Fellow Inst. Policy Studies, Washington, 1963-65. Home: 3431 Porter St NW Washington DC 20016 Office: 1776 K St NW Washington DC 20006

HELLER, JAMES JOHN, college administrator, clergyman; b. Utica, N.Y., May 5, 1921; s. John Frederick and Madeline (Forgy) H.; m. Alice Mackey Wallace, Sept. 2, 1944; children—Janet Ann, Stephen James, Mark Jonathan, Elizabeth Grace. B.A. in Philosophy, Tex. Christian U., 1944; B.D., Princeton Theol Sem., 1947, Ph.D. in N.T. Theology, 1955; H.H.D., Allentown Coll. Ordained minister Moravian Ch., 1952; prof. bibl. theology Moravian Theol. Sem., 1950-61; v.p. for acad. affairs, dean of coll. Moravian Coll., Bethlehem, Pa., 1961—; ednl. cons., evaluation team chmn. Middle States Assn. Schs. and Colls., 1968—. Author: A Faith for Life, 1961, Our Victorious Lamb, 1982—; Contbr. to profl. jours. Trustee Moravian Preparatory Sch., Bethlehem, 1958-61; bd. dirs. Muhlenberg Med. Center, Bethlehem, 1978—. N.T. Theology fellow Princeton Theol. Sem., 1948-49. Mem. Am. Conf. Acad. Deans, Eastern Assn. Academic Deans and Advisers of Students. Home: 1331 Bonnie Ave Bethlehem PA 18017

HELLER, JOHN HERBERT, research scientist; b. Wilton, Conn., Nov. 28, 1921; s. Herbert Charles and Helen (Breschel) H.; m. Maria Stokes Vecchio; children: Adrian, Yvette, John C., Maurice, Kathleen, Susan, Julian, Sandra. B.A., Yale U., 1942; M.D., Case Western Res. U., 1945. Resident, Cornell Bellevue Hosp., N.Y.C., 1945-46; instr. pathology Yale U., New Haven, Conn., 1947-49, Am. Heart Assn. research fellow, 1949-51, attending physician, 1950-54, radio physics health officer, 1950-54, asst. prof. internal medicine, 1951-52, chmn. sect. med. physics, 1952-54, asst. prof. physiology, 1952-53; asst. physician Yale-New Haven Hosp., 1948-49; asso. physician Grace-New Haven Community Hosp., 1949-54; investigator Am. Heart Assn., 1951-54; project dir. AEC, 1951-55; exec. dir., pres. New Eng. Inst., Ridgefield, Conn., 1954—, prof. interdisciplinary studies, 1966, chmn. bd., 1976-78, prof. emeritus, 1981—; pres. Heller Assocs., 1982—; mem. panel atmospheric scis. NRC-Nat. Acad. Scis., 1961; mem. panel Space Sci. Bd., 1962; mem. Shroud of Turin Research Project, 1978-83; mem. panel instrumentation and mechanization in sci. research Office Spl. Studies, NSF, 1961; mem. panel experts sci. rev. br. NIH; Wilhelmina Key lectr. Am. U., 1969; cons., lectr. in field; chmn. Yale-New Eng. Inst. Task Force on Biol. Parameters in Human Behavior, 1972-75. Author: Of Mice, Men and Molecules, 1960, Report on the Shroud of Turin, 1983; contbr. to: Reticuloendothelial Structure and Function, 1960, Yearbook of the American Philosophical Society, 1959, The Biological Basis of Medicine, 1969, Science Looks at Itself, 1970; also 90 articles. Served with M.C. USNR, 1942-45. Decorated Silver medal, Belgium; recipient Bronze medal Squibb; Silver medal Pasteur Inst.; Internat. Gold medal for outstanding achievement in reticuloendothelial system research; Woods Hole Marine Biology Lab. fellow. Fellow N.Y. Acad. Scis., Oceanographic Inst., Royal Soc. Health, Oceanic Inst. Alliance; mem. Am. Astron. Soc. (sr.), Biophys. Soc., Soc. Exptl. Biology and Medicine, Am. Physiol. Soc., World Population Soc., Am. Chem. Soc., AAAS, Soc. Nuclear Medicine, Am. Geophys. Union, Am. Fedn. Clin. Research, Am. Coll. Emergency Physicians, Internat. Soc. Research on Reticuloendothelial System, Epigraphic Soc., Navy League U.S., U.S. Naval Inst., Bioelectromagnetic Soc., Sigma Xi. Office: 228 Danbury Rd Wilton CT 06897

HELLER, JOSEPH, writer; b. Bklyn., May 1, 1923; m. Shirley Held, Sept. 3, 1945; children—Erica Jill, Theodore Michael. B.A., N.Y. U., 1948; M.A., Columbia, 1949, Oxford U., 1949-50. Instr. Pa. State U., 1950-52; advt. writer Time mag., 1952-56, Look mag., 1956-58; promotion mgr. McCall's, 1958-61; formerly tchr. writing Yale U., U. Pa., City U. N.Y. Author: novel Catch-22, 1961; play We Bombed in New Haven, 1968, Something Happened, 1974, Clevinger's Trial, 1974; novel Good as Gold, 1979. Served to lt. USAF, World War II. Nat. Inst. Arts and Letters grantee in lit., 1963. Address: care Press Relations Simon & Schuster 630 Fifth Ave New York NY 10020 *

HELLER, JULES, university dean; b. N.Y.C., Nov. 16, 1919; s. Jacob Kenneth and Goldie (Lassar) H.; m. Gloria Spiegel, June 11, 1947; children—Nancy Gale, Jill Kay. A.B., Ariz. State Coll., 1939; A.M., Columbia U., 1940; Ph.D., U. So. Calif., 1948. Spl. art instr. 8th St. Sch., Tempe, Ariz., 1938-39; dir. art and music Union Neighborhood House, Auburn, N.Y., 1940-41; prof. fine arts, head dept. U. So. Calif., 1946-61; vis. asso. prof. fine arts Pa. State U., summers 1955, 57, dir., 1961-63, founding dean, 1963-68, Faculty of Fine Arts, York U., Toronto, 1968-73, prof. fine arts, 1973-76; dean Coll. Fine Arts, Ariz. State U., Tempe, 1976—; vis. prof. Silpakorn U., Bangkok, Thailand, 1974, Coll. Fine Arts, Colombo, Sri Lanka, 1974; lectr., art juror; Cons. Open Studio, 1975-76; mem. vis. com. on fine arts Fisk U., Nashville, 1974. Printmaker; exhibited one man shows, Gallery Pascal, Toronto, U. Alaska, Fairbanks, Alaskaland Bear Gallery, Visual Arts Center, Anchorage, group shows, Canadian Printmaker's Showcase, Pollack Gallery, Toronto, Mazelow Gallery, Toronto, Santa Monica Art Gallery, Los Angeles County Mus., Phila. Print Club, Seattle Art Mus., Landau Gallery, Kennedy & Co. Gallery, Bklyn. Mus., Cin. Art Mus., Dallas Mus. Fine Arts, Butler Art Inst., Oakland Art Mus., Pa. Acad. Fine Arts, Santa Barbara Mus. Art, San Diego Gallery Fine Arts, Martha Jackson Gallery, N.Y.C., Yuma (Ariz.) Fine Arts Assn., Toronto Dominion Centre; represented in permanent collections, Long Beach Mus. Art, Library of Congress, York U., Allan R. Hite Inst. of U. Louisville, Ariz. State U., Tamarind Inst., U. N.Mex., Can. Council Visual Arts Bank, also pvt. collections.; Author: Problems in Art Judgment, 1946, Printmaking Today, 1958, revised, 1972, Papermaking, 1978, 79; Contbg. artist: Prints by California Artists, 1954, Estampas de la Revolucion Mexicana, 1948; Illustrator: Canciones de Mexico, 1948; Author numerous articles. Adv. bd. Con. affairs com. Americas Soc. Served with USAAF, 1941-45. Can. Council grantee.; Landsdowne scholar U. Victoria. Mem. Coll. Art Assn., Authors Guild, Ariz. Alliance for Art Edn. (dir.), Am. Color Print Soc., Print Club, Internat. Assn. Paper Historians, Internat. Council Fine Arts Deans (pres. 1968-69), Nat. Soc. Arts and Letters (dir. Ariz. chpt.). Home: Scottsdale AZ Office: Coll Fine Arts Ariz State U Tempe AZ 85287

HELLER, PAUL, medical educator; b. Komotau, Czechoslovakia, Aug. 8, 1914; came to U.S., 1946, naturalized, 1948; s. Alfred and Elsa (Hoenig) H.; m. Alice H. Florsheim, Aug. 3, 1946; children—Thomas Allen, Carol Elizabeth. M.D., Charles U., Prague, Czechoslovakia, 1938. Instr. biochemistry, Prague, 1935-37; intern, then resident Beth Israel and Montefiore hosps., N.Y.C., 1946-48; physician, Washington, 1948-51, VA Hosp., Omaha, 1952-54; dir. research West Side VA Hosp., Chgo., 1954-67, chief med. service, 1967-69; prof. medicine U. Ill. Coll. Medicine, 1963—, chief hematology sect., 1966—; sr. med. investigator VA, 1969—; cons. hematologist Presbyn.-St. Luke's Hosp., MacNeal Meml. Hosp.; Mem. adv. bd. Am. Cancer Soc., Chgo. Leukemia Research Found.; cons. USPHS. Author research papers, chpts. in books.; Editorial bd.: Yearbook of Medicine, Jour. Lab. Clin. Medicine, Blood. Recipient Middleton award for med. research, 1975; Esther Langer award for cancer research, 1980. Fellow ACP, AAAS; mem. Central Soc. Clin. Research, Am. Assn. Immunologists, Assn. Am. Physicians, Am., Internat. socs. hematology. Imprisoned in German concentration camps, 1939-45. Home: 1522 Dobson Evanston IL 60202 Office: 820 S Damen St Chicago IL 60612

HELLER, PAUL MICHAEL, film producer; b. N.Y.C., Sept. 25, 1927; s. Alex Gordon and Anna (Rappaport) H.; 1 son, Michael Peter. Student, Drexel Inst. Tech., 1944-45; B.A., Hunter Coll., 1950. Prodn. exec. Warner Bros., 1970-71; pres. Paul Heller Prodns. Inc.; instr. N.Y. U., 1964-66. Scenic designer, N.Y.C., 1952-61; film producer, 1961—; films include David and Lisa, First Monday in October. Chmn. bd. Plumstead Theatre Soc.; chmn. bd. dirs. Community Film Workshop Council; founding mem. Com. 100, Am. Film Inst. Served with U.S. Army. Recipient spl. award Nat. Assn. Mental Health. Mem. United Scenic Artists, Dirs. Guild Am., Screen Actors Guild, Actors Equity Assn. Club: Lotos. Home and Office: 1666 N Beverly Dr Beverly Hills CA 90210 Office:

HELLER, REINHOLD AUGUST, art educator, consultant; b. Fulda, Hesse, Germany, July 22, 1940; came to U.S., 1949; s. Griedrich Leonhard and Brigitte Hermine (Schuler) H.; m. Vivian Faye Hall, June 11, 1966; children: Frederick Andreas, Erik Reinhold. Student, George Washington U., 1958-59; B.S., St. Joseph's Coll., 1963; M.A., Ind. U., 1966, Ph.D., 1968. Asst. prof., prof. U. Pitts., 1968-78; prof. U. Chgo., 1978—; cons., guest curator Nat. Gallery of Art, Washington, 1972,78. Author: Edvard Munch: The Scream, 1973, The Art of Wilhelm Lehmbruck (Catalogue), 1972. Am. Council Learned Socs. and Social Sci. Research Council fellow, 1966-68; Fulbright fellow, 1966; Guggenheim fellow, 1975-76. Mem. Coll. Art Assn. Home: 1325 Linden Rd Homewood IL 60430 Office: Art Dept U Chgo 5540 S Greenwood Ave Chicago IL 60637

HELLER, RICHARD H., author, editor, book critic, publisher; b. Yonkers, N.Y.; s. Otto and Mary (Cohen) H.; m. Sonja Mentikov; 1 son, Matthew. A.B. cum laude, Syracuse U. Editor, also editorial dir. Sterling Group, N.Y.C., 1954-62; editor Dell Pub. Co.; also editorial dir. Dell Mags., N.Y.C., 1962-68; v.p., editor-in-chief Pyramid Books, N.Y.C., 1968-72; pres., editor, pub. Heller & Son, Inc., New Rochelle, N.Y., 1972—; columnist and book reviewer Gannett Westchester Newspapers, 1976—. Author: Who's Who in TV, 1967, The Adventure Book, 1976; Editor: The President Speaks, 1964, The Life and Death of Robert F. Kennedy, 1968. Served with USMC. Mem. Am. Soc. Mag. Editors, Nat. Book Critics Circle, Mystery Writers Am., Sigma Delta Chi, Sigma Alpha Mu. Club: Dutch Treat.

HELLER, ROBERT CLARENCE, retail company executive; b. Lakewood, Ohio, Dec. 23, 1920; s. Paul William and Virginia Margaret (Thompson) H.; m. Ruth Anne Rouch, Aug. 1, 1945;

children—Robert, Patricia, Thomas. B.B.A., U. Mich., 1947. With F.W. Woolworth Co., N.Y.C., 1947—, asst. sec.-treas., 1965-71, sec., 1972—. Served to capt. USAF, 1941-45. Mem. Am. Soc. Corp. Secs., Chatham Fish and Game Protective Assn. Home: 110 Huron Dr Chatham NJ 07928 Office: 233 Broadway New York NY 10279

HELLER, ROBERT LEO, university provost, geology educator; b. Dubuque, Iowa, Apr. 10, 1919; s. Edward W. and May Olive (Bauck) H.; m. Geraldine Hanson, Sept. 26, 1946; children: Roberta, Katherine, Nancy. B.S., Iowa State U., 1942; M.S., U. Mo., 1943, Ph.D., 1950. Geologist U.S. Geol. Survey, 1943-44; mem. faculty U. Minn., Duluth, 1950—, prof. geology, chmn. dept., 1960-67, from asst. to provost to asso. provost, 1965-76, provost, 1977—, also prof. geology; dir. NSF earth sci. curriculum project U. Colo., 1963-65; mem. U.S. Nat. Com. Geology, 1977-81; editor Environment Times, 1976-80. Contbr. numerous articles to profl. publs. Vice pres. St. Louis County Heritage and Arts Center, 1974-77. Served to 2d lt. C.E. AUS, 1944-47. Recipient Neil Miner award Nat. Assn. Geology Tchrs., 1965; citation of merit Coll. Scis. and Humanities, Iowa State U., 1976. Mem. Nat. Assn. Geology Tchrs. (pres. 1976-77), Am. Geol. Inst. (v.p. 1977-78, pres. 1978-79), Council Sci. Soc. Presidents (vice chmn. 1980-81, chmn. 1981-82), Geol. Soc. Am., Paleontol. Soc., AAAS, Am. Assn. Petroleum Geologists, Council of Sci. Soc. Presidents (vice chmn. 1981), U. Minn. Alumni Assn. (Disting. Service award 1972). Office: 515 Oarland Administration Bldg U Minn Duluth MN 55812

HELLER, WALTER WOLFGANG, economist, educator; b. Buffalo, Aug. 27, 1915; s. Ernst and Gertrude (Warmburg) H.; m. Emily K. Johnson, Sept. 16, 1938; children: Walter P., Eric J., Kaaren Louise. A.B., Oberlin Coll., 1935, LL.D., 1964; M.A., U. Wis., 1938, Ph.D., 1941, LL.D., 1969; Litt. D., Kenyon Coll., 1965; LL.D., Ripon Coll., 1967, L.I. U., 1968; L.H.D., Coe Coll., 1967, Loyola U., 1970, Roosevelt U., 1976. Fiscal economist U.S. Treasury, 1942-46, cons., 1946-53; asso. prof. econs. U. Minn., Mpls., 1946-50, prof., 1950-66, Regents prof. econs., 1966—, chmn. dept. econs., 1957-61; vis. lectr. U. Wis., 1947, U. Wash., 1950, Harvard, 1951; mem. internat. adv. bd. Banca de Nazionale del Lavoro, Rome; dir. Internat. Multifoods, Inc., Comml. Credit Corp., Nat. City Bank, Mpls., Comprehensive Care Corp., Newport Beach, Calif., Gen. Growth Properties; Chief internal finance U.S. Mil. Govt., Germany, 1947-48; chmn. Council Econ. Advisers to the Pres., 1961-64; cons. UN, 1952-60, Minn. Dept. Taxation, 1955-60, NEA, 1958, Exec. Office of Pres., 1965-69, 74-77; tax adviser Gov. of Minn., 1955-60; mem. OECD Group of Fiscal Experts, 1964-68, chmn., 1966-68; cons. Congl. Budget Office, 1975—; mem. Trilateral Commn., 1978—; mem. econ. adv. bd. Time mag.; mem. bd. contbrs. Wall St. Jour.; chmn. econ. study group Ctr. Nat. Policy. Author: (with Clara Penniman) State Income Tax Administration, 1959, New Dimensions of Political Economy, 1966, (with Richard Ruggles and others) Revenue Sharing and the City, 1968, (with Milton Friedman) Economic Growth and Environmental Quality: Collision or Coexistence?, 1973, What's Right with Economics, 1975, The Economy: Old Myths and New Realities, 1976, Economic Policy for Inflation (in Reflections of America), 1981. Mem. Carnegie Commn. on the Future of Pub. Broadcasting, 1977-78; trustee Oberlin Coll., 1966-78, German Marshall Fund, Coll. Retirement Equities Fund, 1968-72; hon. chmn. Lupus Found. Am., Inc., chmn. nat. campaign com. Distinguished fellow Am. Econ. Assn. (v.p. 1967-68, pres. 1974); fellow Am. Philos. Soc., Am. Acad. Arts and Scis.; mem. Internat. Mgmt. and Devel. Inst. (asso.), Nat. Bur. Econ. Research (dir., chmn. 1971-74, 82-83), Phi Beta Kappa, Beta Gamma Sigma, Alpha Kappa Psi. Clubs: Federal City (Washington); Skylight (Mpls.). Office: Dept Econs U Minn Minneapolis MN 55455

HELLERMAN, FRED, folksinger, composer; b. Bklyn., May 13, 1927; s. Harry and Clara (Robinson) H.; m. Susan Lardner, Aug. 8, 1970; children—Caleb H., Simeon J. B.A., Bklyn. Coll., 1949; student, N.Y. U., 1943, Columbia, 1950. Mus. dir. Elektra Records, 1954-58; mem. faculty Met. Sch. Music, N.Y.C., 1955-56; v.p. Sanga Music, Inc., 1957—, Fall River Music, Inc., 1961—, Appleseed Music, Inc., 1961—. Co-founder, 1948, mem. the, Weavers; concert and recording artists, 1948-64; Author: (with others) Weavers Songbook, 1960, Kisses Sweeter Than Wine, 1951, (with M. Barer) I'm Just a Country Boy, 1954, I Never Will Marry, 1958, (with F. Minkoff) Come Away Melinda, 1962, The Honey Wind Blows, 1964, Travelin' On With the Weavers, 1966, (with F. Minkoff) Quiet Room, 1966; Composer: incidental music Broadway prodn. The Moon Besieged, 1962, (with James Thurber, Haila Stoddard and Fran Minkoff) Out On A Limb, 1978; film score Lovin' Molly, 1973; contbr.: Broadway prodn. New Faces of 1968; producer: Alice's Restaurant. Served with USCGR, 1944-45. Mem. ASCAP, Am. Guild Authors and Composers, Nat. Acad. Recording Arts and Scis. Home: 83 Goodhill Rd Weston CT 06883 Office: 250 W 57th St New York NY 10019

HELLERSON, CHARLES BENEDICT, former accounting firm executive; b. N.Y.C., Oct. 1, 1912; s. Charles E. W. and Helen (Lumley) H.; m. Hildegard M. Pietzsch, June 22, 1940; children: Robert K., Douglas C. A.B., Princeton U., 1933. Exec. partner Main Hurdman (C.P.A.s), N.Y.C., 1953-81; ret., 1981; dir. Century Sports, Inc., N.J. Trustee emeritus, treas. Wardlaw-Hartridge (N.J.) Sch. Served to lt. comdr. USNR, 1940-45. Mem. Am. Inst. C.P.A.s, N.Y. State, N.J. socs. C.P.A.s, Nat. Assn. Accts., Am. Acctg. Assn. Clubs: Princeton (N.Y.C.); Nassau of Princeton (N.J.). Home: 101 Carter Rd Princeton NJ 08540

HELLERSTEIN, WILLIAM EMANUEL, lawyer; b. N.Y.C., Apr. 8, 1939; s. Martin and Rose (Cohen) H.; m. Michael Gage, Jan. 9, 1977. A.B. cum laude, Bklyn. Coll., 1959; J.D., Harvard U., 1962. Bar: D.C. bar 1962, N.Y. bar 1964. Staff counsel U.S. Commn. on Civil Rights, Washington, 1962-63; asso. firm Brennan, London & Buttenwieser, N.Y.C., 1963-64; appellate counsel Legal Aid Soc., N.Y.C., 1964-69; atty. in charge Criminal Appeals Bur., 1969—; adj. asso. prof. law N.Y. U., 1978—. Mem. Am. Law Inst., Assn. Bar City N.Y., Am. Bar Assn., N.Y. State Bar Assn., Nat. Legal Aid and Defender Assn. Democrat. Office: 15 Park Row New York NY 10038

HELLIE, RICHARD, Russian history educator, researcher; b. Waterloo, Iowa, May 8, 1937; s. Ole Ingeman and Mary Elizabeth (Larsen) H.; m. Jean Laves, Dec. 23, 1961; 1 son, Benjamin. B.A., U. Chgo., 1958, M.A., 1960, Ph.D., 1965; postgrad., U. Moscow, 1963-64. Vis. asst. prof. Rutgers U., 1965-66; asst. prof. Russian history U. Chgo., 1966-71, assoc. prof., 1971-80, prof., 1980—. Author: Muscovite Society, 1967, Enserfment and Military Change in Muscovy, 1971 (Am. Hist. Assn. Adams prize 1972), Slavery in Russia 1450-1725, 1982. Ford Found. Fgn. Area Tng. fellow, 1962-65; Guggenheim Found. fellow, 1973-74; NEH fellow, 1978-79; NEH grantee, 1982-83. Mem. Am. Hist. Assn., Am. Soc. Legal History, Am. Assn. Advancement Slavic Studies, PEN. Home: 4917 S Greenwood Ave Chicago IL 60615-1582 Office: Dept History U Chgo 1126 E 59th St Box 78 Chicago IL 60637-1587

HELLIWELL, DAVID LEEDOM, investment company executive; b. Vancouver, C., Can., July 26, 1935; s. John Leedom and Kathleen B. (Kerby) H.; m. Margaret Jeanette Adam, June 2, 1961; children: Kerby C., Wendy J., Catherine J., Marnie L., John A. B.A., U. B.C., 1957. With Thorne Riddell & Co., 1962-65; div. mgr. Steel Bros. Can. Ltd., 1965, v.p., gen. mgr., for B.C., 1967, for Alta., 1969, exec. v.p., 1971-73, pres., 1973-78; pres., chief exec. officer B.C. Resources Investment Corp., Vancouver, 1978-80, chmn., 1980-81; pres. Marin Investments Ltd., Vancouver, 1981—; dir. Barbecon, Inc., Concord Devel. Ltd., Fidelity Life Assurance Co., Gt. West Steel Industries Ltd., Steel Bros. Can. Ltd., Seaboard Life Ins. Co., Whistler Mountain Ski Corp., Westcoast Transmission Co. Ltd., Swiss Bank Corp., Can. Fellow Inst. Chartered Accts. of B.C.; mem. Can. Inst. Chartered Accts. Anglican. Clubs: Vancouver, Vancouver Law, Tennis and Badminton. Office: 2950 700 W Georgia St PO Box 10130 Vancouver BC Canada V7Y 1C6

HELLIWELL, JOHN FORBES, economist; b. Vancouver, B.C., Can., Aug. 15, 1937; s. John Leedom and Kathleen Birnie (Kerby) H.; m. Judith Isobel Millsap, Oct. 24, 1969; children: David Forbes, James Allen. B.Comm., U. B.C., Vancouver, 1959; B.A. (Rhodes scholar), Oxford (Eng.) U., 1961, D.Phil., 1966. Mem. research staff Can. Royal Commn. on Banking and Fin., Toronto, Ont., 1962-63, Can. Royal Commn. on Taxation, Ottawa, Ont., 1963-64; research fellow Nuffield Coll., Oxford U., 1965-67; assoc. prof. econs. U. B.C., 1967-71, prof., 1971—; econometric adv. to research dept. Bank of Can., Ottawa, 1965-81; vis. economist Res. Bank Australia, Sydney, 1971; mem. Fed. Adv. Com. on Taxation of Personal Investment Income, 1982; chmn. Econ. Adv. Panel to Fed. Ministry of Fin., 1982-83. Author: Public Policies and Private Investment, 1968, (with others) The Structure of RDX2, 1971, Aggregate Investment, 1976; author: (with others) Energy and the National Economy: An Overview of the MACE Model, 1983; mng. editor: Can. Jour. Econs, 1979-82. Vice pres. Consumers' Assn. Can., B.C., 1973-77; trustee Inst. for Research on Public Policy, Montreal, 1974-79. Fellow Royal Soc. Can.; mem. Can. Econs. Assn. (v.p. 1983-84). Anglican. Office: Dept Econs U BC 997-1873 East Mall Vancouver BC Canada V6T 1Y2

HELLIWELL, ROBERT ARTHUR, electrical engineering educator; b. Red Wing, Minn., Sept. 2, 1920; s. Harold Harlowe and Grace (Robson) H.; m. Jean Perham, Apr. 5, 1942; children: Bradley Athearn, David Robson, Richard Perham, Donna Marie. B.E.E., Stanford U., 1942, M.A., 1943, E.E., 1944, Ph.D. in Elec. Engring, 1948. Mem. faculty Stanford U., 1946—, prof. elec. engring., 1958—, dir. Ctr. for Space Sci. and Astrophysics, 1983—. Author: Whistlers and Related Ionospheric Phenomena, 1965, also articles. Recipient Antarctica Service medal Royal Soc., London, Appleton prize, 1972. Fellow IEEE, Internat. Sci. Radio Union; mem. Am. Geophys. Union, AAAS, AAUP, Nat. Acad. Scis., Phi Beta Kappa, Sigma Xi, Tau Beta Pi. Home: 2240 Page Mill Rd Palo Alto CA 94304 Office: Star Lab Stanford CA 94305

HELLMAN, F(REDERICK) WARREN, investment company executive; b. N.Y.C., July 25, 1934; s. Marco F. and Ruth (Koshl) H.; m. Patricia Christina Sander, Oct. 5, 1955; children: Frances, Patricia H., Marco Warren, Judith. B.A., U. Calif.-Berkeley, 1955; M.B.A., Harvard U., 1959. With Lehman Brothers, N.Y.C., 1959—, ptnr., 1963—; exec. mng. dir. Lehman Bros., Inc., 1970-73, pres., 1973-75; ptnr., trustee Hellman Ferri Investment Assocs., 1981—, Matrix Ptnrs., 1981—; dir. Crown Zellerbach Corp., DN & E Walter, Alamitos Land Co., Shaughnessy Holdings Inc., Midway Airlines, Inc., Chgo., Il Fornaio Inc., ITEL Corp. Served to 1st lt. AUS, 1955-57. Mem. Explorers Club. Clubs: Bond, Piping Rock, Century Country, Family, Pacific Union. Home: 3415 Pacific Ave San Francisco CA 94118 Office: Hellman Ferri & Co Inc One Federal St Boston MA 02110

HELLMAN, HENRY MARTIN, educator; b. Norrfors, Sweden, July 4, 1920; came to U.S., 1927, naturalized, 1942; s. Karl Johan and Mathilda (Karlsson) H.; m. Isabel Julia Paul, Dec. 21, 1951. B.S., Ind. U., 1943; M.S., Purdue U., 1945, Ph.D., 1947. Instr. N.Y.U., 1947-50, asst. prof. chemistry, 1950-55, asso prof., 1955-69, prof. organic chemistry, 1969—, chmn. chemistry dept., 1964-70. Contbr. articles profl. jours. Hon. fellow Am.-Scandinavian Found.; mem. Am. Chem. Soc., Chem. Soc. London, Sigma Xi, Phi Lambda Upsilon. Home: 200 Cabrini Blvd New York NY 10033 Office: Dept Chemistry NY U Washington Sq New York NY 10003

HELLMAN, JOSEPH S., lawyer; b. N.Y.C., Sept. 12, 1930; s. Irving and Anna (Handelman) H.; m. Roberta Langbaum, July 4, 1954; 1 son, James S. A.B., Queens Coll., 1952; J.D., Columbia U., 1954. Bar: N.Y. 1954. Since practiced in, N.Y.C.; asso. firm Botein, Hays, Sklar & Herzberg, 1954-62; now mem. firm Kronish, Lieb, Shainswit, Weiner & Hellman; adj. prof. law N.Y. U. Law Sch., 1972—. Mem. bd. editors: Columbia Law Rev, 1953-54. Mem. Am., N.Y. State bar assns., Bar City N.Y., N.Y. Securities Law Inst. Office: 1345 Ave of Americas New York NY 10105

HELLMAN, LEON, physician; b. N.Y.C., May 23, 1921; s. Isaac and Cecile (Rosen) H.; children: Robert, Lara. A.B., Columbia U., 1941, Med. Sc.D., 1951; M.D., Downstate Med. Ctr.-SUNY, 1945. Diplomate: Am. Bd. Internal Medicine. Intern L.I. Coll. Hosp., 1945-46; med. resident Montefiore Hosp., N.Y.C., 1946-48; AEC-NRC fellow Sloan-Kettering Inst. for Cancer Research, N.Y.C., 1948-50, asst., 1950-52, assoc., 1952-59; mem. staff Sloan-Kettering Inst. Cancer Research, N.Y.C., 1959-62, 73-76; adj. mem. staff Sloan-Kettering Inst. for Cancer Research, N.Y.C., 1976—; attending physician Montefiore Med. Ctr., N.Y.C., 1961—, chmn. dept. oncology, 1961-76; program dir. NIH Clin. Research Ctr.; co-dir. Inst. Steroid Research, 1963-76; attending physician Meml. Hosp. Cancer and Allied Diseases, 1973-76, cons. physician, 1976—; attending surgeon Hosp. Einstein Coll. Medicine, 1977—, Bronx Mcpl. Hosp. Ctr., 1977—; asst. prof. Cornell Med. Coll., N.Y.C., 1952-58, assoc. prof., 1958-62, prof. medicine, 1963—, prof. surgery, 1977—, Gutman prof. oncology, 1975-76; dir. div. surg. immunoendocrionology Einstein Coll. Medicine, Bronx, N.Y., 1981—; mem. oncology drug panel U.S.F.D.A., 1979-81. Researcher human steroid hormones, cancer biology and therapy; contbr. articles to sci. papers, books. Served to capt. AUS, 1953. Fellow ACP; mem. Assn. Am. Physicians, Am. Soc. Clin. Investigation, Endocrine Soc., Am. Fedn. Clin. Research, Am. Assn. Cancer Research, Am. Heart Assn., Soc. Exptl. Biology and Medicine, Assn. for Psychophysiol. Study Sleep, Bronx County Med. Soc., Harvey Soc., Alpha Omega Alpha. Office: Albert Einstein Coll Medicine 1300 Morris Park Ave Bronx NY 10461

HELLMAN, LOUIS M., government official, physician, educator; b. St. Louis, Mar. 22, 1908; s. Max and Helen (Schwab) H.; m. Ernestine Crummel, Jan. 26, 1934; children: Michael Moore, Ann Harper. Ph.B., Yale U., 1930; M.D., Johns Hopkins U., 1934. Instr., then asst. prof. Sch. Medicine, Johns Hopkins U., 1938-42, asso. prof. obstetrics, 1945-51; asso. obstetrician Johns Hopkins Hosp.; prof., chmn. dept. obstetrics and gynecology State U. N.Y. Coll. Medicine, N.Y.C., and Kings County Hosp., 1950-70; dep. asst. sec. population affairs HEW, 1970-77; adminstr. Health Services Adminstrn., 1976-77; dir. med. info. Population Reference Bur., 1977-78; Chmn. adv. com. obstetrics and gynecology FDA, 1965-69. Author: (with R.A. Hingson) Anesthesia for Obstetrics, (with J.A. Pritchard) Williams Obstetrics, 14th edit, (with M. Kobayashi) Sonographic Atlas of Obstetrics and Gynecology; Contbr. to med. jours. Served to lt. comdr. M.C. USNR, World War II. Mem. N.Y. Obstet. Soc. (pres. 1969), Assn. Profs. Gynecology and Obstet., Am. Assn. Obstetricians and Gynecologists, Am. Assn. Pathologists and Bacteriologists, Soc. Gynecologic Investigation (pres.), ACS, N.Y. Acad. Medicine (trustee), Am. Gynecol. Soc. (pres. 1974), Royal Coll. Obstetricians and Gynecologists, Phi Beta Kappa, Alpha Omega Alpha. Home: 2475 Virginia Ave NW Washington DC 20037

HELLMAN, SAMUEL, physician, educator; b. N.Y.C., July 23, 1934; s. Henry Sidney and Anna (Egar) H.; m. Marcia Sherman, June 30, 1957; children: Jeffrey Richard, Deborah Susan. B.S. magna cum laude, Allegheny Coll., 1955; M.D. cum laude, SUNY, Syracuse, 1959; M.S. (hon), Harvard U., 1968. Med. intern Beth Israel Hosp., Boston, 1959-60; asst. resident radiology Yale Sch. Medicine and Grace-New Haven Hosp., 1960-62, postdoctoral fellow radiotherapy and cancer research, 1962-64; postdoctoral fellow Inst. Cancer Research and Royal Marsden Hosp., London, Eng., 1965-66; asst. prof. radiology Yale Sch. Medicine, 1966-68; asso. prof. radiology Harvard Med. Sch., 1968-70; dir. Joint Center for Radiation Therapy, 1968—, asso. prof., chmn. dept. radiation therapy, 1970, prof., chmn. dept., 1970-83, also Alvan T. and Viola D.-Am. Cancer Soc. prof.; physician-in-chief, chief med. officer Meml. Sloan Kettering Cancer Ctr., 1983—; chmn. bd. sci. counselors div. cancer treatment Nat. Cancer Inst. Contbr. numerous articles to med. jours. Trustee Allegheny Coll. Recipient Rosenthal award for cancer research, 1980. Mem. Am. Radium Soc., New Haven County Med. Assn., Radiation Research Soc., Am. Soc. Therapeutic Radiologists (pres. 1983), Am. Coll. Radiology, Assn. Univ. Radiologists, Soc. Chairmen Acad. Radiology Depts., N.Y. Acad. Scis., Phi Beta Kappa, Sigma Xi, Alpha Omega Alpha. Home: 40 E 61st St New York NY Office: 1275 York Ave New York NY 10021

HELLMAN, YEHUDA, organization administrator; b. Riga, Latvia, Feb. 10, 1920; came to U.S., 1946, naturalized, 1951; s. Jacob and Sulamith H.; m. Aviva Weinberg, Sept. 26, 1948; children—Dorlee, Jonathan. B.A., Am. U., Beirut, 1945. Fgn. corr. Jerusalem Post, 1942-46; head Jewish Telegraphic Agy. and Overseas News Agy., Paris, 1949; exec. vice chmn. Conf. Presidents of Maj. Am. Jewish Orgns., N.Y.C., 1959—; lectr. Middle Eastern affairs, cons. to orgns. dealing with Middle East, 1946—; mem. internat. steering com. World Conf. Jewish Communities on Soviet Jewry, 1971—. Office: Conf of Presidents Maj Am Jewish Orgns 515 Park Ave New York NY 10022

HELLMANN, DONALD CHARLES, political science educator; b. Rochester, N.Y., June 24, 1933; s. Charles F. and Agnes A. (Genrich) H.; m. Margery Holburne Saunders, July 6, 1960; children: Jane A., Thomas M., John C. A.B., Princeton U., 1955; M.A., U. Calif. at Berkeley, 1960, Ph.D., 1964. Instr. polit. sci. Vanderbilt U., Nashville, 1963-64; asst. prof. polit. sci. Swarthmore Coll., Swarthmore, Pa., 1964-67; asso. prof. U. Wash., Seattle, 1967-72, prof. polit. sci. and internat. studies, 1972—, acting dir., 1971-72, dir., 1967-72, acting chmn., 1975-76, 80-81; dir. for Asia Commn. on Critical Choices for Ams., 1974-76; adj. scholar Am. Enterprise Inst., 1973—, mem. acad. adv. bd., 1975—; cons. Dept. of State, Nat. Security Council, Brookings Inst., others. Author: Japanese Domestic Politics and Foreign Policy, 1969, Japan and East Asia: The New International Order, 1972; Editorial bds.: Asian Survey, 1969—, Jour. of Japanese Studies, 1974—; editor, contbr.: China and Japan: A New Balance of Power, 1976, Southern Asia: The Politics of Poverty and Peace, 1976; contbr. articles to profl. jours. Served with U.S. Army, 1955-57. U. Calif. at Berkeley Center for Japanese Studies fellow, 1959-61; Ford Found. Fgn. Area tng. fellow, 1961-63; Council on Fgn. Relations Internat. Affairs fellow, 1970-71; Fulbright-Hays fellow, 1970-71. Mem. Am. Polit. Sci. Assn., Assn. for Asian Studies. Club: Cosmos. Home: 4154 42d Ave NE Seattle WA 98105 Office: Sch Internat Studies U Wash Seattle WA 98195

HELLMUTH, GEORGE FRANCIS, architect; b. St. Louis, Oct. 5, 1907; s. George W. and Harriet M. (Fowler) H.; m. Mildred Lee Henning, May 24, 1941; children: George William, Nicholas Matthew, Mary Cleveland, Theodore Henning, Daniel Fox. B.Arch., Washington U., 1928, M.Arch., 1930; diploma, Ecole des Beaux Arts, Fontainebleau, France. With Hellmuth, Yamasaki & Leinweber, 1949-55; prin. Hellmuth, Obata & Kassabaum, 1955-78; chmn. bd. HOK Internat., Inc., 1977—, St. Louis, N.Y.C., San Francisco, Dallas, Washington, Houston, San Diego, Denver, Los Angeles, Riyadh, Saudi Arabia, Cairo, Egypt, Stuttgart, Germany; pres. Bald Eagle Co., Gladden, Mo., Roaring Springs Corp. (mfrs. charcoal); Chmn. St. Louis Landmarks and Urban Design Commn., 1950-70. Prin. archtl. works include: (outside U.S.) King Saud U., Riyadh, Saudi Arabia; King Khaled Internat. Airport, Riyadh; prin. archtl. works include: (outside U.S.) Nile Tower, Cairo, Egypt, U. West Indies, Trinidad, Spanish Honduras secondary sch. system, Am. Embassy, El Salvador, Am. embassy housing, Cairo, Canadian medium and maximum prisons, Taipei World Trade Ctr., Taiwan, Housing for Royal Saudi Naval Forces, Saudi Arabia, Military Secondary Schools, Saudi Arabia, Air Def. Command Hdqtrs. Complex, Saudi Arabia, Burgan Bank Hdtrs., Kuwait; prin. archtl. works include: (U.S.) Nat. Air and Space Mus., Washington, Marion Fed. Maximum Security Prison, (Ill.), IBM Advanced systems Lab, Los Gatos, Calif., Dallas/Ft. Worth Regional Airport, U. Wis. Med. Center, Madison; Internat. Rivercenter, New Orleans; prin. archtl. works include: (U.S.) SUNY Health Scis. Complex, Buffalo, The Galleria/Post Oak Center, Houston, E.R. Squibb Co, Lawrenceville, N.J., McDonnell Planetarium, St. Louis, Dow Research and Devel. Facility, Indpls.; Commonwealth P.R. Penal System; Duke U. Med. Center, Durham, N.C.; prin. archtl. works include: (U.S.) Lubbock Regional Airport, (Tex.), Lambert-St. Louis Internat. Airport, St. Louis, D.C. Courthouse, St. Louis U. Sch. Nursing, No. Ill. U. Library, Mobil Oil Hdqtrs., Fairfax, Va., Cities Service Research Ctr., Tulsa, Marriott Corp. Hdqtrs., Bethesda, Md., McDonnell Douglas Automation Ctr., St. Louis, Moscone Conv. Ctr., San Francisco, Piers 1, 2, 3., Boston, Clark County Dentention Ctr., Las Vegas, Nev., Pillsbury Research and Devel. Facility, Mpls., Exxon Research and Egrning. Ctr., Clinton, N.J., Incarnate Word Hosp., St. Louis; many other indsl. and bus. corporate hdqrs., research centers. Recipient First Honor award AIA, 1956; knight Sovereign Mil. Order Malta in U.S.A. Fellow AIA. Clubs: Racquet, Strathalbyn, Noonday (St. Louis); Sky (N.Y.C.). Home: 5 Conway Lane St Louis MO 63124 Office: 100 N Broadway St Louis MO 63102 *My aims and objectives focused on a single thought that persisted over a lifetime, i.e., to make a significant contribution to man's environment, using the skills best suited to my talents, and coordinating and directing the abilities of other professionals.*

HELLMUTH, PAUL FRANCIS, lawyer; b. Springfield, Ohio, Dec. 7, 1918; s. Andrew Alfred and Clara Elizabeth (Link) H. A.B., U. Notre Dame, 1940; LL.B., Harvard U., 1947; spl. courses, MIT, Harvard Grad. Sch. Public Adminstrn. Bar: Ohio 1947, Mass. 1952. Dir. Bessemer Securities Corp., United Screw & Bolt Corp., Robbins & Myers, Inc., W.R. Grace & Co., Pioneer Western Corp.; chmn., chief exec. officer, dir. Maynard H. Murch Co., Cleve., Computer Systems Am., Inc., Figgie Internat.; chmn. bd., dir. Am. Energy Services, Inc. Overseer Boys' Club of Boston, Inc.; trustee Univ. Hosp., Boston Ballet, Mus. of Science, Boston, Boston Mus. Fine Arts; trustee, vice chmn. Boston U. Med. Center; trustee, fellow U. Notre Dame; bd. govs. New Eng. Aquarium; bd. overseers Children's Hosp., Med. Center; mem. law sch. council U. Notre Dame; trustee, corporate mem. Retina Found.; fellow Brandeis U. Served from pvt. to 2d lt. AUS, 1941-42; advanced to lt. col. USAAF, 1945. Decorated Legion of Merit, Bronze Star medal; French Croix de Guerre. Mem. Harvard Law Sch. Assn. (treas.). Clubs: Union, Harvard, Comml., Somerset (Boston); Country (Springfield). Home: 100 Memorial Dr Cambridge MA 02142

HELLMUTH, WILLIAM FREDERICK, JR., economics educator; b. Washington, Jan. 8, 1920; s. William Frederick and Sybel (Grant) H.; m. Jean A. Dieffenbach, Feb. 14, 1943; children: James (dec.), Suzanne, William L., Peter G. B.A., Yale U., 1940, Ph.D., 1948. Instr. econs. Yale U., 1945-48; mem. faculty Oberlin Coll., 1948-68, prof. econs., 1958-68, dean, 1960-67; dep. asst. sec. treasury for tax policy, 1968-69; v.p. arts, prof. econs. McMaster U., Hamilton, 1969-73, also bd. govs., 1969-73; prof. econs. Va. Commonwealth U., 1973—, chmn. dept. econs., 1973-82; economist Fed. Res. Bd., 1954-56; prof. U. Wis., 1959, Univ. Coll., Dar es Salaam, Tanzania, 1965, 66. Mem. Nat. Com. Taxation with Representation; mem. Oberlin City Council, 1957-63, 67-68; pres. 1st Unitarian Ch., Richmond, 1976-78; mem. Welfare Adv. Bd., City of Richmond, 1976-83; staff dir. Capital City Govt. Commn., 1980-81. Served to maj. F.A. AUS, World War II. Decorated Air medal, Bronze Star. Mem. Am. Econ. Assn. (com. on status of women in econs. profession 1977-79), Nat. Tax Assn., Va. Assn. Economists (pres. 1978-79), AAUP, So. Econ. Assn., Nat. Economists Club, Phi Beta Kappa. Home: 3117 Bute Ln Richmond VA 23221

HELLUMS, JESSE DAVID, univ. dean; b. Stamford, Tex., Aug. 19, 1929; s. John V. and Fannie May (Beauchamp) H.; m. Marilyn Biel, July 13, 1957; children—Mark William, Jay David, Robert James. B.S., U. Tex., 1950, M.S., 1957; Ph.D., U. Mich., 1960. Registered profl. engr., Tex. Process engr. Mobil Oil Co., Beaumont, Tex., 1950-54; mem. faculty Rice U., Houston, 1960—, prof. chem. engring., 1968—, dir. biomed. engring. lab., 1968-80, chmn. dept., 1969-75, dean engring., 1980—; adj. prof. Baylor U. Coll. Medicine, 1960—, U. Tex. Med. Sch., 1977—; NSF sci. faculty fellow Cambridge (Eng.) U., 1967-68; vis. prof. Imperial Coll., London, 1973-74. Author papers in field. Served to 1st lt. USAF, 1954-56. Mem. Am. Inst. Chem. Engrs., Am. Chem. Soc., AAAS, AAUP, Am. Soc. Artificial Internal Organs, Microcirculation Soc., Soc. Rheology, Bioelectromagnetics Soc. Home: 2202 Albans Rd Houston TX 77005 Office: PO Box 1892 Houston TX 77001

HELLWARTH, ROBERT WILLIS, physicist, educator; b. Ann Arbor, Mich., Dec. 10, 1930; s. Arlen Roosevelt and Sarah Matilda (Townsend) H.; m. Abigail Gurfein, Sept. 20, 1957 (div. 1979); children: Benjamin John, Margaret Eve, Thomas Abraham. B.S., Princeton U., 1952; D.Phil. (Rhodes scholar), St. John's Coll., Oxford (Eng.) U., 1955. Sr. scientist, mgr. Hughes Research Labs., Malibu, Calif., 1956-70; vis. asso. prof. elec. engring. and physics U. Ill., Urbana, 1964-65; research asso., sr. research fellow Calif. Inst. Tech., Pasadena, 1966-70; NSF sr. postdoctoral fellow Clarendon Lab.-St. Peter's Coll., Oxford (Eng.) U., 1970-71; George Pfleger prof. physics and elec. engring. U. So. Calif., 1970—. Author monograph, articles in field; asso. editor: IEEE Jour. Quantum Electronics, 1964-76. Grantee NSF, Dept. Energy, Air Force Office Sci. Research, U.S. Army Research Office. Fellow IEEE, Am. Phys. Soc., AAAS; mem. Nat. Acad. Engring., AAUP, Phi Beta Kappa, Sigma Xi, Eta Kappa Nu. Patentee Q-switched laser, nonlinear optical microscope, phase conjugate mirror. Home: 921 12th St Santa Monica CA 90403 Office: SSC 303 Physics Dept U So Calif Los Angeles CA 90089

HELLWIG, LANGLEY ROBERTS, petroleum and chem. co. exec.; b. Beaumont, Tex., May 21, 1928; s. Alban Clifford and Theresa Catherine (Langley) H.; m. Sula Katherine Carlisle, Sept. 8, 1951; 1 son, Austin. B.S. in Chem. Enging, U. Tex., Austin, 1949, M.S., 1951, Ph.D., 1955. Tech. service engr. Ethyl Corp., Baton Rouge, La., 1954-58; with Cities Service Co., 1958—, dir. chems. research, Princeton, N.J., 1963-69, v.p. planning, N.Y.C., 1972-76, exec. v.p. chems. group, Tulsa, 1976-79; pres., chief exec. officer Columbian Chems. Co., Tulsa, 1980—, also dir. Mem. Am. Inst. Chem. Engrs., Am. Chem. Soc., Am. Petroleum Inst. Home: 2747 E 68th St Tulsa OK 74136 Office: PO Box 37 Tulsa OK 74102

HELLY, WALTER SIGMUND, educator; b. Vienna, Austria, Aug. 22, 1930; came to U.S., 1938, naturalized, 1944; s. Edward and Elizabeth (Bloch) H.; m. Dorothy Oxman, Mar. 4, 1956; 1 dau., Miranda. B.A., Cornell U., 1950; M.S., U. Ill., 1954; Ph.D., Mass. Inst. Tech., 1959. With Sylvania Electric Co., Waltham, Mass., 1954-56; sr. engr. Melpar Co., Boston, 1956-59; mem. tech. staff Bell Telephone Labs., N.Y.C., 1959-62; sr. engr. Port of N.Y. Authority, 1962-65; prof. ops. research Poly. Inst. N.Y., 1966—; cons. on traffic flow. Author: Urban Systems Models, 1975; Book rev. editor: Jour. Ops. Research, 1970—; Contbr. articles to profl. jours. Mem. Ops. Research Soc. Am. (past chmn. transp. sci. sect.). Home: 91 Central Park W New York City NY 10023 Office: 333 Jay St Brooklyn NY 11201

HELLYER, CLEMENT DAVID, writer; b. Glendale, Calif., Aug. 15, 1914; s. Clement David and Frances Edna (Dodge) H.; m. Gertrude Gloria Phillips, Sept. 8, 1939; children: Gloria Penrose, David Phillips, John Christian. A.B., Principia Coll., 1936; M.S., Columbia, 1938, U. Fla., 1950-52. Newspaper reporter San Diego Union-Tribune, 1939-41; pub. relations dir. San Diego C. of C., 1941-43; civilian aerial navigator USN, 1943-45; prof.journalism San Diego State Coll., 1947-49; dir. Centro Cultural Costarricense-Norteamericano, San Jose, Costa Rica, 1949-50; asst. dir. Sch. Inter-Am. Studies, U. Fla., 1950-52; vis. lectr. U.S. journalism Dept. State program leaders and specialists exchange, Latin Am. countries, 1952; Latin-Am. editor San Diego Union, 1953-60; freelance writer, Sao Paulo and Rio de Janeiro, Brazil, 1960-62, writer, lectr. Latin Am. affairs, 1950—; U.S. del. Jose Toribio Medina Centenary, Santiago, Chile, 1952; editor, pub. South Pacific Mail, Santiago, 1964-66; editorial dir. radio-TV sta. KOGO, San Diego, 1966-69; univ. editor, pub. affairs officer U. Calif., San Diego, 1969-74, lectr., 1969—; owner Five Quail Books, 1978—. Author: (with Charles Mattingly) American Air Navigator, 1946, Story of the U.S. Border Patrol, 1963, Making Money with Words, 1981; Contbr. articles to prin. newspapers, periodicals U.S. Recipient Maria Moors Cabot award Columbia, 1959; 1st prize editorial competition Radio and TV News Dirs. Assn., 1968. Mem. Sigma Delta Chi. Home: PO Box 7 Dorchester IA 42150

HELLYER, GEORGE MACLEAN, consultant; b. Riverside, Ill., Feb. 28, 1912; s. Harold J. and Dorothy A. (Maclean) H.; m. Margaret H. Dawson, July 2, 1953; children by previous marriage: Marion M. Hellyer King, J., Robert T., David R. Cert., U. Lausanne, Switzerland, 1935. Tea mfr. Hellyer and Co., Shizouka, Japan, 1932-34; lectr. Com. to Defend Am. by Aiding Allies, 1939; Western dir. Fed. Union, Inc., 1940-41; mgr. Robert Anderson and Co. (tea mfrs.), Hong Kong, 1946, Taipei, 1947-48, partner, 1949-52; with USIA (and predecessors), 1952-70, pub. affairs officer and attache, Saigon, Phnom Penh and Vientiane, 1952-54, dep. asst. dir., Washington, 1954-55, asst. dir. charge Far Eastern programs, 1955-58; counsellor for pub. affairs Am. embassy, Tokyo, 1958-60, U.S. Mission to European Communities, Brussels, 1961-67, Am. embassy, Kinshasa, Dem. Republic of Congo, 1967-69; mem. U.S. del. NATO, Brussels, 1969-70; ret., 1970, cons., 1970—. Served from pvt. to capt. AUS, 1942-45. Decorated Bronze Star, Air medal; Mil. Cross, U.K. Clubs: Hong Kong, Royal Hong Kong Yacht, Orcas Island Yacht. Home: Route 1 Box 850 Eastsound WA 98245

HELLYER, PAUL THEODORE, journalist, Canadian government official; b. Waterford, Ont., Can., Aug. 6, 1923; s. Audrey S. and Lulla M. (Anderson) H.; m. Ellen Jean Ralph, June 1, 1945; children: Mary Elizabeth, Peter Lawrence, David Ralph. Diploma aero. engring., Curtiss-Wright Tech. Inst., 1941; B.A., U. Toronto, 1949. With Fleet Aircraft Mfg. Co., Ft. Erie, Ont., 1942-44; propr. Mari-Jane Fashions, Toronto, 1945-56; treas. Curran Hall Ltd., Toronto, 1950, pres., 1951-62, Trepil Ltd., Toronto, 1951-62, Hendon Estates Ltd., 1959-63; mem. Ho. of Commons from Davenport Dist., 1949-57, from Trinity Dist., 1958-74; joined Parliamentary Press Gallery, 1974; now syndicated columnist for Toronto Sun; parliamentary asst. to minister nat. def., 1956; mem. Privy Council, 1957—; asso. minister def., 1957, minister nat. def., 1963-67, minister transport, 1967-69, minister responsible for housing, 1968-69; distinguished visitor environ. studies York U., 1969-70; founding chmn. Action Canada, 1971; Chmn. Task Force on Housing and Urban Devel., 1968-69. Author: Agenda: A Plan for Action, 1971, Exit Inflation, 1981. Served Royal Can. Air Force; Served Canadian Army, World War II. Fellow Royal Soc. for Encouragement Arts, Manufactures and Commerce. Club: Ontario. Home: 65 Harbour Sq Suite 506 Toronto ON M5J 2L4 Canada

HELM, DONALD CAIRNEY, hydrogeologist; b. Yokohama, Japan, Mar. 26, 1937; s. Nathan Teal and Rebecca Forsyth (Cairney) H.; m. Karen Gertrude Reed; 1 dau., Rebecca Bernice Vera. B.A. cum laude, Amherst Coll., 1959; M. Div., Hartford Sem. Found., 1962; postgrad., Colo. Sch. Mines, 1962-63, 64-65; M.S., U. Calif.- Berkeley, 1970, Ph.D, 1974. Vol. in rural devel. Mitraniketan Project, Kerala State, India, 1963-64; hydraulic engr. U.S. Geol. Survey, Portland, Oregon, 1965-68, research hydrologist, Sacramento, 1969-78; research physicist Lawrence Livermore Nat. Lab., U. Calif., 1978—, group leader, geohydrology and environ. studies group, 1981—; instr. U.S. Geol. Survey Advanced Groundwater Sch., Denver, 1972-78, UNESCO Internat. Workshop on Land Subsidence, Mexico City, 1979, Pacific Sch. Religion, Berkeley, Calif., 1982; adviser Geothermal Subsidence Research Program, Dept. Energy, 1976—; vis. sr. research scientist State Elec. Commn. Victoria, Australia, 1982-83. Contbr. articles to sci. jours., chpts. to books. Co-chmn. New Eng. Student Christian Movement, 1958-59; mem. high sch. com. Am. Friends Service Com., Salem Oreg., 1966-68; bd. dirs. Ctr. Theology and Natural Scis. grad. Theol. Union, Berkeley, Calif., 1981—. Recipient Bennet-Tyler award in systematic theology, 1962; scholar, Amherst Coll.; Merit fellow, Hartford Sem. Found.; Phillips Petroleum fellow, Col. Sch. Mines; Pan Am. Petroleum fellow, Colo. Sch. Mines; U.S. Geol. Survey fellow, U. Calif.- Berkeley. Mem. AM. Geophys. Union, ASCE, Assn. Engring. Geologists, Assn. Geoscientists for Internat. Devel., ASTM (com. solid waste disposal), Nat. Water Well Assn. Unitarian. Club: Outlook. Office: PO Box 808 Livermore CA 94550

HELM, LEWIS MARSHALL, public affairs executive; b. Riverdale, Md., Sept. 9, 1931; s. William P. and Selma S. (Snyder) H.; m. Alice L. Kupferman, Sept. 12, 1953. A.A. in Communications, Am. U., 1957, M.S. in Public Relations, 1979; grad., U.S. Army War Coll., 1977. Newspaper reporter Wichita (Kans.) Eagle, 1950-51, Washington Times-Herald, 1951-54; press asst. Republican Nat. Com., 1954-55; pub. relations dir. Plumbing Fixture Mfrs. Assn., Washington, 1956-59, Home Mfrs. Assn., 1961-63; pub. relations cons., 1959-60, 64-68; info. dir. Citizens for Nixon, 1968; asst. to sec. U.S. Dept. Interior, Washington, 1969, dep. asst. sec. mineral resources, 1969-72; asst. sec. for pub. affairs HEW, Washington, 1973-76; pres. Capital Counselors, Inc., Washington, 1976—; Instr. econs. Catholic U. Am., 1974; assoc. lecturing prof. polit. sci. George Washington U., 1980; Pub. relations dir. Citizens for Presdl. Vote for D.C., 1961. Co-author: Informing the People: A Public Affairs Handbook, 1981. Col. U.S. Army Res.; cons. faculty mem. U.S. Command and Gen. Staff Coll.; Ft. Leavenworth, Kans. Recipient Meritorious Service medal Dept. Interior and Dept. Army, Spl. citation for distinguished service Sec. HEW, 1975. Presbyterian. Home: 7000 Millwood Rd Bethesda MD 20817 Office: Suite 503 1700 K St NW Washington DC 20006

HELM, P. RALPH, manufacturing company executive; b. Phoenix, Dec. 25, 1926; s. Percy Ralph and Maria (Hardy) H.; Nov. 24, 1951; children—Robert William, Jane Louise, Percy Ralph, III, John. Student, Ariz. State U., 1947-50. Crane operator Ariz. Sand and Rock Co.; from sales trainee to Can. sales mgr. Marion Power Shovel Co., Ind., 1952-57; partner, v.p. Depco Equipment Co., Detroit, 1957-61; dir. mktg., then exec. v.p. Manitowoc Engring. Co., Wis., from 1961; dir. Manitowoc Co., 1965—, v.p., 1967-82, pres., chief operating officer, 1982—, also pres. sales subsidiaries; bd. dirs., past v.p. N.E. Wis. Indsl. Assn. Bd. dirs. Silver Lake Coll. Served with A.C. USNR, 1944-46. Mem. Manitowoc C. of C. (past dir.). Clubs: St. Stephen's (London); Milw. Athletic; Branch River Country (Manitowoc); Masons. Home: 1732 Blue Heron Rd Manitowoc WI 54220 Office: 500 S 16th St Manitowoc WI 54220

HELM, ROBERT MEREDITH, philosophy educator; b. Winston-Salem, N.C., Feb. 19, 1917; s. Robert Meredith and Mary Alma (Jones) H. B.A., Wake Forest Coll., 1939; M.A., Duke U., 1940, Ph.D., 1950. Mem. faculty Wake Forest U., 1940—, prof. philosophy, 1962—, Worrell prof. philosophy, 1983; asso. prof. Salem Coll., 1958-60; mem. faculty N.C. Sch. Arts, 1967-69. Author: The Gloomy Dean: The Thought of William Ralph Inge, 1962; Co-editor, contbr.: Studies in Nietzsche and the Classical Tradition, 1976; Co-author: Meaning and Value in Western Thought, Vol. I, The Ancient Foundations, 1981. Bd. dirs. pres. James W. Denmark Loan Fund. Served to maj. AUS, 1941-46; ETO. Decorated Army Commendation medal.; Recipient Patriotic Civilian Service citation Dept. Army, 1979. Mem. Am. Philos. Assn., Am. Acad. Religion, AAUP, N.C. Philos. Soc., Internat. Soc. Neoplatonic Studies, Phi Beta Kappa, Omicron Delta Kappa, Delta Sigma Rho-Tau Kappa Alpha, Sigma Pi. Democrat. Mem. Moravian Ch. Home: PO Box 7243 Reynolda Station Winston-Salem NC 27109

HELMAN, ALFRED BLAIR, college president; b. Windber, Pa., Dec. 25, 1920; s. Henry E. and Luie (Pritt) H.; m. Patricia Ann Kennedy, June 22, 1947; children: Harriet Ann Helman Hill, Patricia Dawn Helman Magaro. A.B. magna cum laude, McPherson Coll., 1946, D.D., 1956; M.A., U. Kans., 1947, postgrad., 1948-51; LL.D., Juniata Coll., 1976; L.H.D., Bridgewater Coll., 1977, Ind. U., 1981. Ordained to ministry Ch. of Brethren, 1942; pastor, Newton, Kans., 1944-46, Ottawa, Kans., 1946-54, First Ch. of Brethren, Wichita, Kans., 1954-56; faculty Ottawa U., 1947- 48, 51-54, chmn. div. social scis., 1952-54; faculty U. Kans., 1951-54, Friends U., 1955-56; pres. Manchester (Ind.) Coll., 1956—; Chmn. com. higher edn. Ch. of Brethren, 1965-67, 76-78, nat. moderator, 1975-76, mem. rev. and evaluation com., 1983-85; Trustee McPherson Coll., 1951-56, chmn., 1955-56; trustee Kans. Found. Pvt. Colls. and Univs., 1955-56; pres. Ind. Conf. Higher Edn., 1960-61; mem. policy bd. dept. higher edn. Nat. Council Chs. of Christ Am., 1960-71; pres.'s adv. com. Nat. Assn. Intercollegiate Athletics, 1966-70; dir., mem. exec. com. Ind. Council Chs., 1960-62; pres. Independent Colls. and Univs. of Ind., 1966-67, bd. dirs., 1977-83, 84—, chmn., 1978—; chmn., interim pres. Council Protestant Colls. and Univs., 1967, bd. dirs., 1961-69; chmn. bd. dirs. Central States Coll. Assn., 1968; pres. Asso. Colls. of Ind., 1970-72; mem. commn. on religion in higher edn. Assn. Am. Colls., 1968-71; bd. dirs. CTB, Inc., 1977—. Author articles religion and higher edn. Named Sagamore of Wabash Gov. of Ind., 1980; Ky. Col. Gov. of Ky., 1964; recipient Outstanding Local Citizen award, 1972, Alumni Honor award Manchester Coll., 1981. Mem. Am. Hist. Assn., Soc. Historians of Am. Fgn. Relations, Internat. Assn. Univ. Presidents (steering com. N.Am. Council 1982-84), Ind. Assn. Ch.-Related and Ind. Colls. (pres. 1966-67), Am. Assn. for Higher Edn., Am. Acad. Polit. and Social Sci., Nat. Assn. Ind. Colls. and Univs. (bd. dirs. 1983-84), C. of C., Phi Beta Kappa, Phi Alpha Theta, Pi Sigma Alpha, Pi Kappa Delta. Clubs: Kiwanian., Columbia (Indpls.); University (Chgo.); Wabash Country (Ind.); University (N.Y.C.).

HELMAN, GERALD BERNARD, government official; b. Detroit, Nov. 4, 1932; s. Leo and Ann (Glassman) H.; m. Dolores Hammel, May, 1953; children: Ruth Leea, Deborah Gayle, David Robert. A.B., U. Mich., 1953, LL.B., 1956. Bar: Mich. 1956. Research asst. U. Mich., 1955; intelligence research specialist Dept. State, 1957, econ. consular officer, Milan, Italy, 1958, polit. officer, Vienna, Austria, 1960-62, econ. officer, Barbados, 1962-63, fgn. affairs officer, Washington, 1963-68; polit. mil. affairs officer, counselor U.S. Mission to NATO, Brussels, Belgium, 1968-73, dep. dir. NATO-Atlantic polit. mil. affairs, Washington, 1974-76, dir. UN polit. affairs, 1976-77; dep. asst. sec. Bur. Internat. Orgn. Affairs, 1977-79; U.S. ambassador to UN Orgns. in Europe, 1979-81; dep. to undersec. for polit. affairs Dept. State, Washington, 1982—. Woodrow Wilson fellow Princeton U., 1973. Jewish. Home: 2900 Maplewood Pl Alexandria VA 22302 Office: Dept State Washington DC 20520

HELMAN, JOSEPH ARTHUR, art dealer; b. St. Louis, Mar. 19, 1937; s. David Wroy and Pauline Jean (Manlin) H.; m. Barbara Lee Kaufman, Apr. 2, 1960 (div.); children: Robin, Elizabeth, Jody; m. Ursula Fey, Dec. 22, 1981. Student, Washington U., St. Louis, 1958-61. Pres. Green Trails Devel. Co., St. Louis, 1961-69; gallery owner, art dealer Helman Gallery, St. Louis, 1970-72; pres. Blum Helman Gallery, N.Y.C., 1974—. Served with U.S. Army, 1957-59. Mem. Art Dealers Assn. Represented, exhibited, and sold works by various artists including Ralston Crawford, Bryan Hunt, Ellsworth Kelly, Roy Lichtenstein, Richard Serra, Donald Sultan, Robert Moskowitz. Office: Blum Helman Gallery 20 W 57th St New York NY 10019

HELMAN, ROBERT ALAN, lawyer; b. Chgo., Jan. 27, 1934; s. Nathan W. and Esther (Weiss) H.; m. Janet R. Williams, Sept. 13, 1958; children—Marcus E., Adam J., Sarah E. Student, U. Ill., 1951-53; B.S.L., Northwestern U., 1954, LL.B., 1956. Bar: Ill. 1956. Asso. firm Isham, Lincoln & Beale, Chgo., 1956-64, partner, 1965-66; partner firm Mayer, Brown & Platt, Chgo., 1967—; dir. Goldblatt Bros., Inc. Co-author: Commentaries on 1970 Illinois Constitution, 1971; contbr. articles to legal jours. Mem. Chgo. Crime Commn.; chmn. Citizens Com. on Juvenile Ct. Cook County, 1969-81; mem. Adminstrv. Rules Commn., State of Ill., 1978—; pres. Hyde Park Neighborhood Club, 1966-67, Legal Assistance Found., Chgo., 1973-76; bd. dirs. United Charities Chgo., 1967-73, Ill. Neighborhood Devel. Corp., 1973—. Served with AUS, 1956-58. Mem. Chgo., Am., Fed. Energy bar assns., Am. Law Inst., Chgo. Council Lawyers, Legal Club Chgo., Law Club Chgo., Order of Coif. Clubs: Comml., Chgo., Mid-Day, Economics, Union League (Chgo.); Point-O-Woods Country (Mich.). Home: 4940 S Kimbark Ave Chicago IL 60615 Office: 231 S LaSalle St Chicago IL 60604

HELMBOLD, F. WILBUR, librarian, clergyman; b. Fowlerville, Pa., May 13, 1917; s. Andrew K. and Emma L. (Hildebr) H.; m. Neola E. Wood, June 10, 1942; children—Neola J. (Mrs. Robert N. Trapnell), Arthur J. (dec.), Martha W. (Mrs. James F. Evans), Dale Marjorie (Mrs. Terry H. Cutrer). A.B. with honors, Samford U., 1949; M.A., Duke, 1954. Newspaper reporter Wilkes-Barre (Pa.) Record, 1934-36; printer Dallas (Pa.) Post, also owner printing bus., 1936-42; ordained to ministry Baptist Ch., 1947; pastor, Selma, Ala., 1947-49, Springville, Ala., 1949-50, Durham, N.C., 1951-54, supply pastor, 1954—; librarian Barrington (R.I.) Coll., 1954-57, Samford U., Birmingham, Ala., 1957—; dir. Inst. Genealogy and Hist. Research, 1965—; curator Ala. Bapt. Hist. Commn., 1957—; Library cons., 1958-; founding chmn., adv. cons. Bapt. Info. Retrieval System, 1972—. Author: Born of the Needs of the People, 1967, Tracing Your Ancestry and Logbook, 1976; Editor: Ala. Bapt. Historian, 1967—; gen. editor: pubs. Banner Press, 1961-66; pres., 1966—; Contbr. to religious and hist. jours. Served with USAAF, 1942-46; ETO. Mem. S.E., Ala. library assns., Ala. Hist. Assn., So. Bapt., Ala. Bapt., hist. socs., Nat. Geneal. Soc., Assn. Gen. Edn. (founding pres.). Home: 2305 Harmony Ln Birmingham AL 35226

HELMER, GEORGE ALFRED, chemical company executive, lawyer; b. Berkeley, Calif., Aug. 7, 1915; s. George A. and Nell (Hodnett) H.; m. Nancy Noel Hoguet, Jan. 22, 1946. A.B., U. San Francisco, 1936, LL.B., 1940. Bar: Calif. bar 1940. Practice in, San Francisco, 1940-61, dep. city atty., 1946-47; mem. firm Cooper, White & Cooper, 1947-61; sr. v.p., gen. counsel Engelhard Minerals and Chems. Corp., Murray Hill, N.J., 1961-72; also dir.; pres., gen. counsel Engelhard Hanovia, Inc.; with Cullinan Brown & Helmer, San Francisco, 1973-82. Served as lt. USNR, 1942-46. Mem. Am. Bar Assn., Assn. Bar City N.Y., State Bar Calif. Home: 2795 Vallejo St San Francisco CA 94123 Office: 712 Sansome St San Francisco CA 94111

HELMERICH, WALTER HUGO, III, oil company executive; b. Tulsa, Jan. 12, 1923; s. Walter Hugo, Jr. and Cadijah (Colcord) H.; m. Peggy Varnadow, Nov. 24, 1951; children: Walter Hugo IV, Dow Zachary, Matthew Galloway, Hans Christian, Jonathan David. B.A., U. Okla., 1948; M.B.A., Harvard, 1950. With Helmerich & Payne, Inc., Tulsa, 1950—, pres., 1960—, also dir.; dir. Natural Gas Odorizing, Inc., Rikwell Co., Caterpillar Tractor Co., Atwood Oceanics, Inc., Combustion Engring., Inc., First Tulsa Bancorp., Inc., 1st Nat. Bank & Trust Co. Tulsa, I.C. Industries; trustee Northwestern Mut. Life Ins. Co. Chmn. Okla. World's Fair Commn., 1964-65; bd. dirs. Salvation Army, Okla. Acad. for State Goals, Okla. Health Scis. Found., Okla. Med. Research Found., Holland Hall Sch., 1962-71; trustee Tulsa Psychiat. Center, Inc., Retina Research Found., Houston, Hillcrest Med. Center. Mem. Ind. Petroleum Assn. Am. (dir.), Chief Execs. Forum, World Bus Council, Tulsa C. of C. (dir.), Sigma Nu. Methodist (bd. stewards, chmn. 1967-70). Home: 2121 S Yorktown St Tulsa OK 74114 Office: Utica at 21st Tulsa OK 74114

HELMERICKS, HARMON, author, explorer; b. Gibson City, Ill., Jan. 18, 1917; s. Clarence James and Abbie (Cornelius) H.; m. Constance Chittenden, Apr. 27, 1941; children—Constance Jean, Carol Ann; m. Martha M. Paxton; children—James Woodrow, Mark Harmon, Jeffrey Todd. Student, U. Ariz., 1940-41. Sheet metal worker Army Engrs., Seaward, Alaska, 1941- 44; assoc. with Constance Helmericks in study of Arctic, 1944-46; writer, lectr. on Arctic Am., 1946—, organizer expdn. by air north of Arctic Circle, Alaska and Can., 1947; founder (with Martha M. Helmericks) Arctic Tern Fish-Freight Co., 1952; asst. curator Kansas City Mus.; cons. Arctic oil operation Gulf Oil Co., Sohio Oil Co., Union Oil Co.; founder (with Martha M. Helmericks) Arctic Sch. for Boys, 1974; Arctic cons. to Eastman Kodak Co.; chmn. bd. Colville Environ. Services; dir. Alaska Interior Resources; master guide Alaskan Game Commn.; active in conservation in Africa, India, Europe Arctic Inst. N. Am., Airplane Owners and Pilots Assn. Author: Oolak's Brother, 1952, Arctic Hunters, 1955, (with Constance Helmericks) We Live in the Arctic, 1947, Our Summer With the Eskimos, 1948, Our Alaskan Winter, 1949, Flight of the Arctic Tern, 1952, Arctic Bush Pilot, 1968, The Last of the Bush Pilots, 1968; also mag. articles.; films for, Am. Motors Corp., TV shows on Arctic research. Clubs: Circumnavigators, Explorers. Originated (with Fred Duthweilder and James Callender) arctic ice island oil drilling concept. Address: 930 9th Ave Fairbanks AK 99701 *My principles of conduct are simply, to treat others as I would have them treat me; and that you can't do a kindness too soon, since you* *never know how soon it will be too late. This about sums up my way of meeting the situations of life.*

HELMETAG, CARL, JR., lawyer; b. Phila., Dec. 2, 1913; s. Carl and Gertrude R. (Whitty) H.; m. Marjorie Dearnley, May 17, 1947; children: Carl, Peter Eric, Roger Keith. B.S., U. Pa., 1936, LL.B., 1939. Bar: Pa. 1939. Since practiced in, Phila.; with Pa. R.R. Co., 1939-68, asst. gen. counsel, 1953-65, gen. atty., 1965-68; with Pa. Central Transp. Co., 1968—, sr. gen. atty., 1971-72, gen. counsel reorgn., 1972-76, v.p., gen. counsel, 1976-78; gen. counsel litigation Penn Central Corp., 1978—; dir. Lehigh Valley R.R. Co., 1982—; lectr. in law U. Pa., 1967-73; mem. drafting com. Pa. Criminal Code, 1947-49, 66-71. Contbr. articles to profl. publs. Bd. dirs. Met. YMCA, Phila., 1958-64, Phila. Lyric Opera Co., 1965-70, Chesnut Hill Community Assn., 1970, Community Chest Phila., 1952-60; bd. dirs. Meml. Hosp., Roxborough, Pa., 1960-80, vice chmn. bd., 1977; chmn. bd. Woodmere Art Gallery, Phila., 1972-77. Served to capt. C.E. AUS, 1940-45; ETO. Mem. Phila. Bar Assn., ABA, First Troop Phila. City Cav. Clubs: Phila. Cricket, U. Pa. Varsity, Rittenhouse (Phila.); University (N.Y.C.). Home: 701 Saint Georges Rd Philadelphia PA 19119 Office: 3100 IVB Bldg 1700 Market St Philadelphia PA 19103

HELMETAG, CHARLES HUGH, foreign language educator; b. Camden, N.J., Apr. 7, 1935; s. Charles Henry and Agnes Beatrice (Gibb) H.; m. Ruth Judith Crispin, Aug. 22, 1959; children: Steven, Diana. B.A., U. Pa., 1957; M.A., U. Ky., 1959; Ph.D., Princeton U., 1968. Instr. German Purdue U., West Lafayette, Ind., 1960-62; asst. prof. German Villanova U., Pa., 1964-75, assoc. prof., 1975-80, prof., 1980—, chmn. dept. modern langs. and lits., 1973—. Contbr. articles, revs. to profl. jours. Pres. Rosemont elem. Sch. PTA, 1973-74, bd. dirs., 1974-75. Fulbright scholar, U. Goettingen (W. Ger.), 1959-60; Germanistic Soc. Am. grantee, summer 1968; German Acad. Exchange Service grantee, summer 1978. Mem. Am. Assn. Tchrs. German, MLA, N.E. MLA, AAUP (pres. local chpt. 1972-73), Phi Kappa Phi (pres. Villanova chpt. 1984). Office: Villanova U Villanova PA 19085

HELMHOLZ, AUGUST CARL, physicist, educator; b. Evanston, Ill., May 24, 1915; s. Henry F. and Isabel G. (Lindsay) H.; m. Elizabeth J. Little, July 30, 1938; children—Charlotte Chaffee King, George L., Frederic V., Edith L. A.B., Harvard U., 1936; student, Cambridge U., 1936-37; Ph.D., U. Calif., Berkeley, 1940; Sc.D. (hon.), U. Strathclyde, 1979. Instr. physics U. Calif. at Berkeley, 1940-43, asst. prof., 1943-48, asso. prof., 1948-51, prof., 1951-80, emeritus, 1980—, chmn. dept., 1955-62; research physicist Lawrence Berkeley Lab., 1940—; Guggenheim fellow, 1962-63; Vis. Scientist Program, 1966-71; Dir. Conwed Corp., 1963—. Recipient Citation U. Calif., Berkeley, 1980. Fellow Am. Phys. Soc.; mem. Am. Inst. Physics (governing bd. 1964-67), AAAS, Am. Assn. Physics Tchrs., AAUP, Phi Beta Kappa, Sigma Xi. Home: 28 Crest Rd Lafayette CA 94549 Office: Dept Physics Univ California Berkeley CA 94720

HELMOND, KATHERINE, actress; b. Galveston, Tex., July 5, 1934; d. Patrick Joseph and Thelma Louise (Malone) H.; m. David Christian, June, 1971. Pres. Taur Can Prodns., Hollywood, Calif., 1979—. Appears as Jessica Tate in: TV series Soap, 1978—; numerous guest star appearances in TV series and movies including Pearl, Diary of a Teenage Hitchhiker; film appearances include Time Bandits; appeared in numerous summer stock prodns. and reporetory theatres including, Asso. Producing Artists, N.Y.C., Trinity Sq. Repertory Co., R.I., Hartford Stage, Phoenix Repertory, N.Y.C.; (Recipient N.Y. Drama Critics Variety award 1971, Clarence Derwent award, 1971 for role of Bananas in House of Blue Leaves, Los Angeles Drama Critics award 1972, Golden Globe award 1980). Mem. Screen Actors Guild, AFTRA. Roman Catholic. Address: PO Box 4016 Hollywood CA 90028

HELMREICH, JONATHAN ERNST, history educator; b. Brunswick, Maine, Dec. 21, 1936; s. Ernst Christian and Louise Bertha (Roberts) H.; m. Martha Anne Schaff, Aug. 22, 1959 (div. 1978); children—Anne Linden, Dana Louise, Douglas Ernst Folger; m. Nancy L. Ross, Feb. 21, 1979. B.A. magna cum laude, Amherst Coll., 1958; M.A., Princeton, 1959, Ph.D., 1961; postgrad. (Fulbright grantee), Free U. of Brussels, 1961-62. Teaching asst. Princeton, 1961; asst. prof. Allegheny Coll., Meadville, Pa., 1962-66, asso. prof., 1966-72, prof., 1972—, dean of instrn., 1966-81. Author: Belgium and Europe: A Study in Small Power Diplomacy, 1976; Contbr. articles to profl. pubIs. Mem. Pa. Trial Judge Nominating Commn. for Crawford County, 1973-75; Pres., bd. dirs. United Housing Corp. of Meadville, Fairview Housing Corp. of Meadville. Mem. Am. Hist. Assn., Phi Beta Kappa, Pi Gamma Mu. Democrat. Methodist. Club: Rotarian. Home: 370 Jefferson St Meadville PA 16335

HELMREICH, ROBERT LOUIS, psychologist, educator; b. Kansas City, Kans., Apr. 29, 1937; s. Ralph Louis and Caroline (Sheetz) H. B.A., Yale U., 1959, M.S., 1965, Ph.D., 1966. Mem. faculty U. Tex., Austin, 1966—, prof. psychology, 1972—, chmn. grad. program social psychology, 1973—; pres. Robert Helmreich, Inc., 1973—. Co-author: Groups Under Stress, 1968, Social Psychology, 1973, Masculinity and Femininity, 1978; editor: Jour. Personality and Social Psychology, 1984-85; contbr. articles to profl. pubs. Served to lt. USNR, 1959-63. Hoveland fellow, 1962; grantee Office Naval Research, 1966-69, NASA, 1971—, NIMH, 1973—, NSF, 1978—. Mem. Soc. Exptl. Social Psychology (pres. 1978-79), AAAS, Am. Psychol. Assn., Human Factors Soc., Southwestern Psychol. Assn. Clubs: Yacht; Yale (Austin) (pres. 1979—). Home: 3811 W Lake Dr Austin TX 78746 Office: Dept Psychology U Tex Austin TX 78712

HELMS, CHARLES BRUMM, JR., manufacturing company executive; b. Phila., Nov. 5, 1922; s. Charles Brumm and Eva (Jagger) H.; m. Sarajane Fink, Dec. 20, 1947 (dec. June 1981); children: Jeffrey Charles, Janet Leslie.; m. Mary-Anne Hehir, Dec. 11, 1982. Certificate of proficiency, Lafayette Coll., 1944; B.S., U. Pa., 1950. C.P.A., Pa. Mem. audit staff Arthur Young & Co., Phila., 1950-52; asst. dir. fin. City of Phila., 1952-56; group controller Warner Lambert Pharm. Co., Morris Plains, N.J., 1956-61; v.p. fin., dir. Warner Co., Phila., 1961-64, Ultronic Systems Corp., Morrestown, N.J., N.Y.C., 1964-67, Crompton & Knowles Corp., 1967—; dir. Crompton & Knowles Overseas Corp., Crompton & Knowles Can. Ltd., Kem Mfg. Corp., So. Mill Creek Products Corp. Bd. dirs. Crompton & Knowles Found. Served with U.S. Army, 1942-46; ETO. Mem. Fin. Execs. Inst. Republican. Presbyterian. Club: University (N.Y.C.). Home: 39 Cameron Ct Princeton NJ 08540 Office: 345 Park Ave New York City NY 10154

HELMS, FRED BRYAN, lawyer; b. Union County, N.C., Apr. 12, 1896; s. Emanuel M. and Frances P. (Austin) H.; m. Margaret V. Harrelson, July 14, 1927 (dec.); children: Margaret Harrelson (Mrs. Joseph B. Tyson), Frances (Mrs. Frances H. Abernethy); m. Susan Erwin Williamson, Mar. 3, 1978. Student, U. Ga., 1919-20; J.D., Wake Forest Coll., 1922; postgrad., Columbia U., 1922. Bar: N.C. 1922. Tchr. pub. schs., Union County, 1914-15, mgr. chain clothing stores, Athens, Ga., East Moline, Ill., Muscatine, Iowa, 1919-22, since practiced in, Charlotte, pros. atty., City of Charlotte, 1925-27, county judge, Mecklenburg County, N.C., 1927-31, pvt. practice, specializing in civil law, 1931—. Organizer, 1st pres. Charlotte Community Chest, 1932-33; chmn. Citizens Com., 1941-45; mem. Commn. to Study and Revise Ins. Laws N.C., 1945-47, Commn. for Improvement Adminstrn. of Justice in N.C., 1947-49, N.C. Jud. Council, N.C. Gov.'s adv. commn. on segregation, Nat. Commn. Reform Fed. Criminal Laws.; Past trustee Wingate Coll. Presdl. elector N.C., 1956; Organizer, atty., commr. Charlotte Meml. Hosp. Authority. Served as 2d lt., F.A. U.S. Army, 1918-19. Recipient Silver medallion NCCJ, 1958; Distinguished Service Citation in law Wake Forest U., 1971. Fellow Am. Coll. Trial Lawyers; mem. Am. Soc. Internat. Law, Am. Legion, Am., Mecklenburg County bar assns., N.C. State Bar, Inc. (v.p. 1944-46, pres. 1946-47), Am. Judicature Soc., Am. Law Inst. Democrat. Clubs: Kiwanis, City, Charlotte Country (Charlotte). Home: 1571 Queens Rd W Charlotte NC 28207 Office: 2800 NCNB Plaza Charlotte NC 28280 *My ambition from childhood, has been and is, to be a qualified, worthy, loyal and active member of and leader in the profession of the law (one of the three great professions), my church, my city, my state and my country; and at all times to be devoted to my family, my home and my God.*

HELMS, J. LYNN, former government agency administrator; b. DeQueen, Ark., Mar. 1, 1925; s. Frank and Mamie (Johnson) H.; m. Lorraine Bisgard, Mar. 16, 1947; children: Loralyn, Jon, Carole, Zack. Dir. mktg. and sales N. Am. Aviation Co., Columbus, Ohio, 1956-62; group v.p. Bendix Corp., Ann Arbor, Mich., 1962-70; pres. Norden div. United Technologies Corp., Norwalk, Conn., 1970-74, Piper Aircraft Corp., Lock Haven, Pa., 1974-81, chmn. bd., 1978-81; adminstr. FAA, Washington, 1981-83; dir. Birchminster Industries. Served to lt. col. USMC, 1944-56. Decorated Air medal with oak leaf cluster. Fellow AIAA; mem. Soc. Exptl. Test Pilots.

HELMS, JESSE, U.S. senator; b. Monroe, N.C., Oct. 18, 1921; s. Jesse Alexander and Ethel Mae (Helms) H.; m. Dorothy Jane Coble, Oct. 31, 1942; children: Jane (Mrs. Charles R. Knox), Nancy (Mrs. John C. Stuart), Charles. Student, Wingate (N.C.) Jr. Coll., Wake Forest Coll. City editor Raleigh (N.C.) Times, 1941-42; news and program dir. Sta. WRAL, Raleigh, 1948-51; adminstrv. asst. to U.S. senators Willis Smith and Alton Lennon, 1951-53; exec. dir. N.C. Bankers Assn., 1953-60; exec. v.p., vice chmn. Capitol Broadcasting Co., Raleigh, 1960-72; U.S. senator from, N.C., 1973—; chmn. Com. on Agr., Nutrition and Forestry, Com. on Fgn. Relations, Select Com. on Ethics, Rules Com., also asst. minority whip.; Chmn. bd. Specialized Agrl. Publs., Inc., Raleigh, 1964-72; Mem. Raleigh City Council, 1957-61, chmn. law and finance com. Bd. dirs. N.C. Cerebral Palsy Hosp., Durham, United Cerebral Palsy N.C., Wake County Cerebral Palsy and Rehab. Center, Raleigh, Camp Willow Run, Littleton, N.C.; former trustee Campbell Coll., Wingate Coll., Meredith Coll., John F. Kennedy Coll. Served with USNR, 1942-45. Recipient Freedoms Found. award for best TV editorial, 1962, for newspaper article, 1973, So. Bapt. Nat. award for Service to mankind, 1972; Gold medal VFW; Conservative Congressional award, 1976; Liberty award Am. Econ. Council, 1978; Disting. Public Service award Public Service Research Council, 1978; Watchdog of Treasury award; Guardian of Small Bus. award; named Man of Yr. Women for Constl. Govt., 1978; Legislator of Yr. award Nat. Rifle Assn., 1978; other awards. Republican. Baptist (deacon). Clubs: Rotary (past pres. Raleigh), Raleigh Executives (past pres.), Masons (32 deg.). Home: 1513 Caswell St Raleigh NC 27608 Office: 409 Dirksen Senate Office Bldg Washington DC 20510 *

HELMS, RICHARD MCGARRAH, internat. cons.; b. St. Davids, Pa., Mar. 30, 1913; s. Herman H. and Marion (McGarrah) H.; m. Julia Bretzman Shields, Sept. 8, 1939 (div. 1968); 1 son, Dennis J.; m. Cynthia McKelvie, 1968. B.A., Williams Coll., 1935. Staff corr. UP, Europe, 1935-37; mem. staff Indpls. Times Pub. Co., 1937-42; with CIA, 1947-73, dep. dir., then dir., 1965-73; ambassador to, Iran, 1973-76, internat. cons., 1977—; pres. Safeer Co., Washington, 1977—. Served with OSS USNR, 1942-46; ETO. Recipient Career Service award Nat. Civil Service League, 1965. Mem. Phi Beta Kappa. Clubs: Chevy Chase (Md.); Rolling Rock (Ligonier, Pa.); Alibi, Alfalfa (Washington). Home: 4649 Garfield St NW Washington DC 20007 Office: Safeer Co Suite 402 1627 K St Washington DC 20006

HELMS, W. RICHARD, lawyer; b. Wilmington, Del., Mar. 4, 1929; s. Emile and Agnes Mary (Ringland) H.; m. Carole J. Cohn, May 3, 1958; children: Catherine E., Leah J., Carolyn G. Student, U. Pa., 1948-50; B.S., Northwestern U., 1952, J.D., 1956; postgrad., U. Paris, 1952-53. Bar: Ill. 1956. Ptnr. Jenner & Block, Chgo., 1965—. Chmn. Western Springs (Ill.) Zoning Bd. Appeals, 1978—. Served with USAF, 1946-48. Mem. Chgo. Bar Assn., Ill. State Bar Assn., ABA. Club: Law Club (Chgo.).

HELMSLEY, HARRY B., real estate company executive; b. N.Y.C., 1909; m. Leona M. Pres. Helmsley-Spear, Inc., N.Y.C. Office: Helmsley-Spear Inc 60 E 42d St New York NY 10165

HELMSLEY, LEONA MINDY, hotel executive; b. N.Y.C.; m. Harry B. Helmsley, Apr. 8, 1972. Vice pres. Pease & Elliman, N.Y.C., 1962-69; pres. Sutton & Towne Residential, N.Y.C., 1967-70; sr. v.p. Helmsley Spear, N.Y.C., 1970-72, Brown, Harris, Stevens, 1970-72; pres. Helmsley Hotels, Inc., N.Y.C., 1980—. Named Woman of Yr. N.Y. Council Civic Affairs, 1970, Town & Country Condos & Coops., 1981; recipient Service award Ort Sch. Engring., 1981, Profl. Excellence award Les Dames d'Escoffier, 1981, Spl. Achievement award Sales Execs. Club N.Y., 1981, Woman of Yr. award Internat. Hotel Industry, 1982. Home: 36 Central Park S New York NY 10019 Office: Helmsley Hotels The Helmsley Palace Hotel 455 Madison Ave New York NY 10022

HELMSTETTER, CHARLES EDWARD, microbiologist; b. Newark, Oct. 18, 1933; s. Charles Edward and Elsa Simpson (Taylorson) H.; m. Carol Ann Krajewski, Sept. 26, 1975; children—Charles Edward, Michael Frederick. B.A., Johns Hopkins U., 1955; M.S., U. Mich., 1956, U. Chgo., 1957, Ph.D., 1961. Scientist NIH, Bethesda, Md., 1961-63; USPHS fellow U. Copenhagen, 1963-64; scientist Roswell Park Meml. Inst., Buffalo, 1964—, dir. dept. exptl. biology, 1974—. Contbr. articles to sci. jours.; mem. editorial bd.: Jour. Bacteriology, 1970-76, 80—. Recipient Selman A Waksman award Theobald Smith Soc., 1970; yearly NIH grantee, 1965—. Mem. AAAS, Am. Soc. Microbiology, Am. Soc. Biol. Chemists, Biophys. Soc., Sigma Xi. Home: 34 Park St Buffalo NY 14201 Office: 666 Elm St Buffalo NY 14263

HELOISE, columnist, lecturer, broadcaster; b. Waco, Tex., Apr. 15, 1951; d. Marshal H. and Heloise K. (Bowles) C.; m. David L. Evans, Feb. 13, 1981. B.S. in Math. and Bus, S.W. Tex. State U., 1974. Owner, pres. Heloise, Inc. Asst. to columnist mother, Heloise, 1974-77; upon her death took over column, 1977; author: internat. syndicated column Hints from Heloise; Hints From Heloise, 1980, Help From Heloise, 1981; contbg. editor: Good Housekeeping Mag., 1981; Co-founder, 1st co-pilot: Mile High Pie in the Sky Balloon Club. Mem. Women in Communication, Tex. Press Women, Screen Actors Guild, AFTRA, Women in Radio and TV, Confrerie de la Chaine des Rotisseurs (bailli San Antonio chpt.); mem. Ordre Mondial des Gourmets De'Gustateurd de U.S.A.; Mem. Good Neighbor Council Tex.-Mex. Club: Death Valley Yacht and Racket. Home: PO Box 32000 San Antonio TX 78216 Office: care King Features Syndicate 235 E 45th St New York NY 10017

HELPERN, DAVID MOSES, shoe corporation executive; b. Boston, Nov. 14, 1917; s. Myron Earl and Rose H.; m. Charlotte Cooper, May 2, 1943 (dec. 1948); children: David Moses, Elizabeth; m. Joan Marshall Gruen, Aug. 14, 1960. A.B., Harvard U., 1938, postgrad. Sch. Edn., 1940. Chmn. bd. Joan & David Helpern, Inc., N.Y.C., 1948—; chmn. Suburban Shoe Stores, Inc., Cambridge, Mass., 1948—; cons. Melville Shoe Corp., N.Y.C., 1966-67. Served with AUS, 1943-46. Recipient Coty award, 1978. Mem. Nat. Shoe Retailers Assn. (dir. 1966-69). Democrat. Jewish. Club: Harvard. Home: 1010 Memorial Dr Cambridge MA 02138 Office: Joan & David Helpern Inc 4 W 58th St New York NY 10019

HELPERN, JOAN MARSHALL, designer; b. N.Y.C., Oct. 10, 1926; d. Edward and Ethel (Tilzer) Marshall; m. David M. Helpern, Aug. 14, 1960; children—David M., Elizabeth Joan. B.A., Hunter Coll., N.Y.C., 1947; M.A. (grantee 1947-48), Columbia U., 1948; postgrad., Harvard U., 1960-67. With personnel services depts. N.Y.C. Bd. Edn., Yeshiva U., also Hunter Coll., 1948-60, Lexington (Mass.) public schs., Lesley Coll., Cambridge, Mass., also Harvard U., 1960-68; cons. child devel. and pupil personnel programs U.S. Dept. Edn. (state univs. and state depts. edn.), 1948-69; pres. Joan and David Helpern, Inc. (shoe design and mfg.), N.Y.C., 1968—. Fashion cons., Melville Shoe Co., 1968-70 (Recipient Coty award Am. design 1978); Author: Guidance of Children in the Elementary Schools, 1950; past mem. editorial bds.: Am. Sch. Counselors Assn. Club: Harvard (Boston). Office: 4 W 58th St New York NY 10019

HELPHAND, BEN J., ins. co. exec.; b. Columbus, Nebr., Feb. 2, 1915; s. David and Bessie (Krupinsky) H.; m. Bessie H. Stine, Sept. 16, 1937; 1 dau., Cathy Dee. Student, U. Nebr., 1932-35; B.A., U. Iowa, 1936, M.A., 1937. Actuarial asst. Pacific Mut. Life Ins. Co., Newport Beach, Calif., 1937-42, v.p., actuary, 1947-80; cons. actuary, 1980—; actuary Dept. Ins. State S.C., Columbia, 1946-47. Served to maj. USAAF, 1942-46. Fellow Soc. Actuaries (bd. govs.); mem. actuarial clubs Pacific States (past pres.), Los Angeles (past pres.), Am. Acad. Actuaries, Sigma Xi. Home: 1321 Keel Dr Newport Beach CA 92625 Office: 4201 Birch St Newport Beach CA 92660

HELPRIN, MARK, author; b. N.Y.C., June 28, 1947; s. Morris A. and Eleanor (Lynn) H.; m. Lisa Kennedy, June 28, 1980. A.B., Harvard U., 1969, A.M., 1972; postgrad., Magdalen Coll., Oxford (Eng.) U., 1976-77. Author: A Dove of the East and Other Stories, 1975, Refiner's Fire, 1977, Ellis Island and Other Stories, 1980, Winter's Tale, 1983. Served with Israeli Army and Air Force, 1972-73. Recipient Prix de Rome Am. Acad. and Inst. Arts and Letters, 1982, Nat. Jewish Book award, 1982.

HELRICH, MARTIN, educator, physician; b. N.Y.C., Mar. 31, 1922; s. Abraham and Anna (Kornblau) H.; m. Ina Brunstein, Aug. 13, 1950; children: Carol Lisa, Karen Lee. B.S., Dickinson Coll., 1946; M.D., U. Pa., 1946. Diplomate: Am. Bd. Anesthesiology (dir., sec., treas.). Intern Atlantic City Hosp., 1946-47; resident N.Y.U.-Bellevue Hosp., 1948-50; postdoctorate research fellow U. Pa. Med. Sch., 1953-54, asst. prof. anesthesiology, 1954-56; prof. anesthesiology, chmn. dept. U. Md. Sch. Medicine, 1956—; head dept. anesthesiology U. Med. Hosp., 1956—, chmn. residency rev. com. for anesthesiology, 1979—; cons. in field. Chmn. anesthesia adv. com. to FDA, 1970-74. Served to capt., M.C. AUS, 1947, 51-53. Fellow Am. Coll. Anesthesiologists (gov. 1970-74); mem. Am. Soc. Pharmacology and Exptl. Therapeutics, Assn. Univ. Anesthetists, Am. Soc. Anesthesiologists (dir. 1968-71), Internat. Anesthesia Research Soc., Md. Soc. for Med. Research, Soc. Acad. Anesthesia Chmn., Md. Thoracic Soc., Md. Soc. Anesthesiologists (pres., sec.), Phi Beta Kappa, Sigma Xi. Home: 3507 Old Post Dr Baltimore MD 21208

HELSEL, MARGIE LOUISE, banker; b. Roaring Spring, Pa., Sept. 14, 1924; d. George Blair and Bertha Marie (Ayers) Hess; m. Merrill P. Helsel, May 4, 1946. Bookkeeper, teller Roaring Spring Bank, 1943-51; teller, corp. sec. Suburban Bank (Suburban Bancorp.), Bethesda, Md., 1951—; corp. sec. Suburban Funding Corp., Bethesda, 1980—, Suburban Mortgage Assn., 1980—, Suburban Capital Corp., 1980—, Suburban Bank, Del., Dover, 1982—. Mem. Nat. Assn. Bank Women. Republican. Baptist. Home: 14603 Kelmscot Dr Silver Spring MD 20906 Office: Suburban Bancorp 6610 Rockledge Dr Bethesda MD 20817

HELSING, JOHN ERIC, life insurance executive, lawyer; b. Jersey City, N.J., Nov. 6, 1933; s. John and Martha M. (Johanson) H.; m. Lorraine Esther Hoover, Sept. 16, 1961; children: Dawn, Deborah, Karen. A.B., Muhlenberg Coll., Allentown, Pa., 1955; LL.B., Rutgers U., 1960. Bar: N.J. 1960; C.L.U., 1966. With firm Hein, Smith & Mooney, Hackensack, N.J., 1960-61; with Mut. Benefit Life Ins. Co., Newark, 1961—, asso. counsel, 1971-75, v.p., gen. counsel, 1975-79, sr. v.p., gen. counsel, 1979—. Served with AUS, 1957-58. Mem. ABA, Soc. C.L.U.s, Assn. Life Ins. Counsel. Republican. Presbyterian. Home: 5850 Pembroke Ct Shawnee Mission KS 66208 Office: 2345 Grand Ave Kansas City MO 64108

HELSLEY, GROVER CLEVELAND, pharm. co. exec.; b. Strasburg, Va., Sept. 26, 1926; s. Grover Clevel and Vallie Mae (Putnam) H.; m. Betty Jean Midkiff, Oct. 30, 1949; children—Grover Cleveland, Linda Suzanne, Robert Christopher. B.S. with honors, Shepherd Coll., 1954; M.S., U. Va., 1956, Ph.D. (Philip Francis duPont fellow), 1958. Research chemist E.I. duPont de Nemours & Co., Inc., Richmond, Va., 1958-62; research chemist A.H. Robins Co., Richmond, 1962-64, group leader, 1964-68, asso. dir. chem. research, 1968-70; dir. research Hoechst-Roussel Pharms. Inc., Somerville, N.J., 1970-72, v.p. pharm. research, 1972—. Contbr. sci. articles to profl. jours. Served with USAAF, 1945-47. Mem. Am. Chem. Soc., Pharm. Mfrs. Assn. (editorial adv. bd. drug devel. research 1980), Indsl. Research Inst. Mem. Disciples of Christ Ch. Patentee in field. Home: PO Box 117 Pottersville NJ 07979 Office: Hoechst-Roussel Pharms Inc Route 202-206 N Somerville NJ 08876

HELSON, HENRY BERGE, educator; b. Lawrence, Kan., June 2, 1927; s. Harry and Lida G. (Anderson) H.; m. Ravenna W. Mathews, June 12, 1954; children—David M., Ravenna A., Harold E. A.B., Harvard, 1947, Ph.D., 1950; Sheldon travelling fellow, Warsaw and Wroclaw (Poland), 1947-48. Lectr. U. Uppsala, Sweden, 1950-51; instr., then asst. prof. math. Yale, 1951-55; mem. faculty U. Calif. at Berkeley, 1955—, now prof. math.; vis. prof. Swedish univs., spring 1962, U. Paris, Orsay, France, 1966-67, U. Sci. and Tech., Kumasi, Ghana, spring 1969, U. du Languedoc, Montpellier, France, 1971-72, Marseille, France, fall 1976, Indian Statis. Inst., Calcutta, spring 1980. Mem. Soc. Friends. Home: 15 The Crescent Berkeley CA 94708

HELSTAD, ORRIN LAVERNE, lawyer, legal educator; b. Ettrick, Wis., Feb. 9, 1922; s. Albert J. and Martha H. (Gimse) H.; m. Charlotte Dart Ankeney, June 26, 1954. Student, U. Wis., La Crosse, 1940-42, B.S., 1948, LL.B., 1950. Bar: Wis. 1950. Research assoc. Wis. Legis. Council, 1950-61; assoc. prof. law U. Wis., Madison, 1961-65, prof., 1965—, assoc. dean, 1972-75, acting dean, 1975-76, dean, 1976-83; mem. consumer advisory council Wis. Dept. Agr., 1970-72; vice chmn. Wis. Supreme Ct. com. on the State bar, 1977; mem. Fed. Jud. Nominating Commn. Western Dist. Wis., 1979-83. Contbr. articles to law revs.; co-author, editor: Wisconsin Uniform Comml. Code Handbook, 1965, 1971. Fellow Am. Bar Found.; mem. State Bar Wis.,

ABA (council sect. on local govt. law 1975-79), Wis. Bar Assn., Dane County Bar Assn., Am. Judicature Soc. Unitarian. Home: 4134 Mandan Crescent Madison WI 53711 Office: U Wis Law Sch Madison WI 53706

HELTON, DANNY ORVILLE, chemist; b. Booneville, Miss., Oct. 5, 1944; s. Orville and Thelma Yvlette (Green) H.; m. Sarah Frances Cole, Aug. 22, 1966; children: Raymond, Orville. B.S., U. Louisville, 1966, Ph.D., 1972. Assoc. chemist Midwest Research Inst., Kansas City, Mo., 1973-75, sr. chemist, 1975—; lectr. U. Mo., Kansas City. Mem. Republican Nat. Com., 1980—. NDEA fellow, 1968-69. Mem. Am. Chem. Soc., Mid. Am. Cancer Ctr. Program, Phi Lambda Upsilon. Baptist. Club: Chung's Karate Sch. Pioneer in rapid assay method for N 5 rocket propellant. Home: 9626 Overhill Rd Kansas City MO 64134 Office: Midwest Research Inst 425 Volker Blvd Kansas City MO 64110

HELVESTON, EUGENE MCGILLIS, pediatric ophtalmologist, educator; b. Detroit, Dec. 28, 1934; d. Eugene McGillis and Ann (Fay) H.; m. Barbara Hiss, June 15, 1959; children: Martha Hiss, Lisa Hiss. B.A., U. Mich., 1956, M.D., 1960. Intern St. Joseph Hosp., Ann Arbor, Mich., 1960-61; resident Ind. U. Hosps., Indpls., 1961-66; dir. pediatric opthalmology Ind. U. Sch. Medicine, Indpls., 1967—, asst. prof., 1967-72, assoc. prof., 1972-76, prof., 1976—, chmn., 1981—; dir. ophthalmology Wishard Meml. hosp., Indpls., 1975-79; med. dir. Ind. Lions Eye Bank; fellow in opthalmology Wilmer Inst., Balt., 1966-67. Author: Atlas of Strabismus Surgery, 1973, Pediatric Ophthalmology Practice, 1980; chief editor: Am. Orthoptic Jour., 1976-82; contbr. articles to profl. jours. Bd. dirs. Ind. Soc. Prevention of Blindnes, Indpls., 1968-83; mem. celebrity host com. 500 Festival Assn., Indpls., 1975-76, mem. queen selection com., Indpls., 1982-83. Kellogg scholar, 1959; grantee Heed scholar Heed Found., Chgo., 1966; recipient Outstanding Heed Fellow award, 1975. Fellow ACS, Am. Orthoptic Council (pres. 1976-80). Office: Ind U Sch Medicine 702 Rotary Circle Indianapolis IN 46223

HELVEY, JULIUS LOUIS II, financial executive; b. Boise, Idaho, May 21, 1931; s. Julius Louis H. and Adeline (Jonasson) Turpin; m. Barbara June Ellis, Aug. 29, 1959; children: Janet E., Julius Louis III, Jennifer S., Mary A., Rebecca E. B.S., U.S. Naval Acad., 1953; M.B., Stanford U., 1959. C.P.A., Calif. Auditor, audit supr. Touche, Ross & Co., San Francisco, 1959-65; fin. v.p. Golden West Fin. Corp., Oakland, Calif., 1965-67, sr. v.p., 1973—; audit mgr. Touche Ross & Co., San Francisco, 1967-73. Scoutmaster Boy Scouts Am., Lafayette,Calif., 1975-77. Served to lt. USN, 1953-57. Mem. Am. Inst. C.P.A.s, Calif. Soc. C.P.A.s, U.S. Naval Acad. Alumni. Republican. Men. Ch. of Jesus Christ of Latter-day Saints. Club: Stanford Bus Sch. Office: Golden West Fin Corp 1970 Broadway Oakland CA 94612

HELWIG, ELSON BOWMAN, physician; b. Pierceton, Ind., Mar. 5, 1907; s. Llewellyn and Grace (Bowman) H.; m. Mildred Stoelting, Apr. 20, 1933; children—Alan S., Warren B., Ann (Mrs. Thomas Gordon). B.S., Ind. U., 1930, M.D., 1932. Diplomate: Am. Bd. Pathology. Rotating intern Indpls. City Hosp., 1932-33, resident pathology, 1933- 34; asst. resident pathology Inst. Pathology, Western Res. U., 1934-35; resident pathology Cleve. City Hosp., 1935-36; asst. pathologist New Eng. Deaconess Hosp., Boston, 1936-39; mem. faculty Washington U. Sch. Medicine, St. Louis, 1939-46, asst. prof. pathology, 1946; sr. pathologist, chief skin and gastro-intestinal pathology br. Armed Forces Inst. Pathology, 1946—, chief dept. pathology, 1955-74, 1955-74, asso. dir. for consultation, 1967—; profl. lectr. George Washington U. Sch. Medicine, 1947-64, clin. prof., 1964—; clin. prof. pathology Sch. Medicine, Uniformed Services U. Health Scis., 1976—; vis. profl. dermatol. pathology Temple U. Sch. Medicine, 1958—, cons. skin and cancer hosp. of univ., 1959—; cons. Walter Reed Army Hosp., 1953—, WHO, 1965—; Mem. Armed Forces Epidemiol. Bd., 1968—; chmn. Center Advanced Pathology, Armed Forces Inst. Pathology, 1974—. Co-author: International Histopathological Classification of Tumors, 1975; Editor: The Skin, 1971, (with others) Dermal Pathology, 1972; editorial bd.: Jour. Cancer; Author numerous articles in field. Served to col., M.C. AUS, 1942-45; PTO. Recipient Meritorious Civilian Service award Dept. Army, Exceptional Civilian Service award, 1964; Distinguished Civilian Service award Dept. Def., 1965; President's award for Distinguished Fed. Civilian Service, 1966; Heath Meml. award, 1975. Mem. Coll. Am. Pathologists, Am. Soc. Clin. Pathologists, Internat. Assn. Pathologists, Am. Assn. Pathologists and Bacteriologists, AMA, Mass. Med. Soc., Washington Pathology Soc., Washington Dermatol. Soc., Am. Acad. Dermatology, Washington Acad. Medicine, Assn. Mil. Dermatologists, Am. Soc. Dermatopathology (pres. 1964-65), Assn. Mil. Surgeons, Histochem. Soc., Stout-Pathology Soc., Am. Dermatol. Assn., Pacific Dermatol. Assn., Soc. Columbiana de Patologica, French Soc. Dermatology and Syphiology (fgn. corr.). Identified and classified adnexal tumors of skin; established relationship between Bowen's disease and internal cancer; identified cloacagenic carcinoma of anus, anatomic and histochem. changes in skin after laser irradiation. Home: 14 W Maple St Alexandria VA 22301 Office: Armed Forces Inst Pathology Washington DC 20305

HELWIG, GILBERT JOHN, lawyer; b. Connellsville, Pa., June 5, 1918; s. August Henry and Germaine (Laurent) H.; m. Diane Ketchum, Nov. 27, 1948; children: David, Lisa, Erika, Anne. A.B., Duquesne U., 1938, LL.B. (now J.D.), 1948. Bar: Pa. 1948. Teaching fellow Duquesne U., 1938-40, adj. prof. law, 1949-70; vol. Defenders Office, Allegheny County, 1948-49; asst. dist. atty., Allegheny County, 1949-51; mem. firm Stone, Silvestri & Helwig, Pitts., 1949-51; partner firm Reed, Smith, Shaw & McClay, Pitts., 1951—; mem. jud. council Supreme Ct. Pa., 1970-75; Chmn. hearing com. Pa. Disciplinary Bd., 1973-78, mem., 1982—. Served with USAAF, 1942-46. Fellow Am. Bar Found., Am. Coll. Trial Lawyers, Internat. Acad. Trial Lawyers; mem. Am. Law Inst., Third Circuit Jud. Conf., Am. Bar Assn., Pa. Bar Assn., Fla. Bar Assn. Office: Union Trust Bldg PO Box 2009 Pittsburgh PA 15230

HELZER, JAMES DENNIS, hospital executive; b. Fresno, Calif., Apr. 27, 1938; s. Alexander and Katherine (Scheidt) H.; m. Joan Elaine Alinder, Feb. 25, 1967; children: Amy, Rebecca. B.S., Fresno State Coll., 1960; M.Hosp. Adminstrn., U. Iowa, 1965. Adminstrv. asst. Twilight Haven, Fresno, Calif., 1960-61; asst. adminstr. U. Calif. Hosps. and Clinics, San Francisco, 1965-68, Fresno Community Hosp., 1968-71, exec. adminstr., 1971-82, pres., chief exec. officer, 1982—. Served with U.S. Army, 1961-63. Mem. Am., Calif. hosp. assns., Am. Coll. Hosp. Adminstrs. Presbyterian. Club: Rotary. Home: 5909 E Hamilton Fresno CA 93727 Office: PO Box 1232 Fresno CA 93715

HEMBREE, GEORGE HUNT, chem. mfg. co. lab. exec.; b. Richmond, Ky., Sept. 2, 1930; s. George Nelson and Mirian Grace (Tuttle) H.; m. Betty Jo Williams, June 7, 1952; children—George Hunt, Elizabeth Ann, Susan Grace. B.S., Eastern Ky. U., 1952; Ph.D., Ohio State U., 1958. With E.I. du Pont de Nemours & Co., 1958—, research mgr., Rochester, N.Y., 1969-71, Parlin, N.J., 1971-73, mktg. mgr., Wilmington, Del., 1973-74, lab. dir., Wilmington, 1974-75, Brevard, N.C., 1975—. Served with AUS, 1953-55. Mem. Am. Chem. Soc., Soc. Photg. Scientists and Engrs., Ky. Acad. Scis., Sigma Xi, Phi Lambda Upsilon. Baptist. Office: PO Box 267 Brevard NC 28712 *

HEMBREE, HUGH LAWSON, III, diversified holding co. exec.; b. Fort Smith, Ark., Nov. 16, 1931; s. Raymond N. and Gladys (Newman) H.; m. Sara Janelle Young, Sept. 1, 1956; children—Hugh Lawson IV, Raymond Scott. B.S. in Bus. Adminstrn, U. Ark., 1953, J.D., 1958. In middle mgmt. Ark.-Best Freight Inc., Fort Smith, 1958-61, dir. finance, 1961-65, v.p., 1965-67; pres., dir. Ark.-Best Corp., Fort Smith, 1967-73, chmn. bd., chief exec. officer, 1973—; pres. Sugar Hill Farms, Inc.; dir. Nat. Bank of Commerce, Dallas, 1967—, Mchts. Nat. Bank Fort Smith, 1st Fed. Savs. & Loan Assn., Fort Smith, Mid-Am. Industries, Scheduled Skyways Airline, Fayetteville, Ark.; nat. adv. bd. Comml. Nat. Bank, Little Rock. Mem. Ark. Bd. Higher Edn., 1975—; Sec. Fort Smith/Sebastian County Joint Planning Commn., 1959-72; Ark. chmn. Radio Free Europe Program, 1968-69; chmn. devel. council, mem. dean's adv. com. Sch. Bus., U. Ark., chmn. exec. com. univ. devel. assn., 1975—; mem. Sebastian County Regional Park Commn., 1968—, Democratic Central Com. Ark., 1968—; pres. Westark area council Boy Scouts Am., 1966-67, now area pres., mem. exec. com. South Central region; Chmn. Ark.-Okla. Livestock and Ednl. Found., 1975—; chmn. bd. trustees St. Edward Hosp., 1972—; chmn. fund raising program U. Ark., 1973-74; trustee John Brown U., Siloam Springs, Ark., U. Ark. Found., 1975—. Served to capt. USAF, 1953-55. Recipient Silver Antelope award, 1974; Recipient Silver Beaver award Boy Scouts Am., 1967, 69, Ark. Leadership and Community Service award, 1970, 75; named Ark. Outstanding Young Man of Year Ark. Jaycees, 1967. Mem. Nat. Assn. of Devel. Orgns. (chmn. adv. com. 1969-72), Ark. C. of C. (1st v.p. 1970-73, pres. 1973, dir. 1972—), Ft. Smith C. of C. (pres. 1970-73), Nat. Young Presidents Orgn., U. Ark. Alumni Assn. (dir., mem. bldg. com.), Am. Trucking Assn., Nat. Assn. Mfrs. (dir. 1976, regional v.p. 1973-75, regional dir. 1976—), Ark. Arts Center, Scabbard and Blade, Sigma Alpha Epsilon, Beta Gamma Sigma, Phi Eta Sigma, Delta Theta Phi, Alpha Kappa Psi. Episcopalian (vestryman). Clubs: Mason (32 deg., Shriner), Chaparral, Lancers, Economics (Dallas); Ft. Smith Hardscabble Country and Town, Fianna Hills Country (Ft. Smith); Capitol (Little Rock); N.Y. Athletic. Home: 3220 Park Ave Fort Smith AR 72903 Office: 1000 S 21st St Fort Smith AR 72901

HEMBREE, JAMES D., chemical company executive; b. Morris, Okla., Feb. 27, 1929; s. James D. and Mary Eleanor (Hacker) H.; m. Joyce Pickrell, Aug. 25, 1951; Victoria Lee Stilwell, Alex James, Kent Douglas. B.S.Ch.E., Okla. State U., 1951; M.S.Ch.E., U. Mich., 1952. Dir. mktg. inorganic chems. Dow chem U.S.A., Midland, Mich., 1968-78; gen. mgr. designed products dept. Dow Chem U.S.A., Midland, Mich., 1976-78, v.p., 1978-80, group v.p., 1980-83; pres., chief exec. officer Dow Chem. Can., Sarnia, Ont., 1983—; dir. Dow Chem Can., Sarnia, Ont. Office: Dow Chem Can Inc Modeland Rd PO Box 1012 Sarnia ON Canada N7T 7K7

HEMENS, HENRY JOHN, lawyer; b. Montreal, Que., Can., June 16, 1913; s. Sidney John and Margaret Ann (O'Brien) H.; m. Sarah Ann Wright, Nov. 4, 1939; children: Mary-Margaret, John, Paul, Eileen. B.A., Loyola Coll., Montreal, 1932; B.C.L., McGill U., Montreal, 1935; postgrad., U. Paris, 1935-36; LL.D., Concordia U., 1982. Bar: Called to Que. bar 1935, created Queen's counsel 1956. Mem. legal dept. DuPont Can. Inc., Montreal, 1939-54, gen. counsel, 1954-62, sec., 1962-69, v.p. and sec., 1969-77, dir., 1971-78, cons., 1977—; counsel firm Hemens, Harris, Thomas, Mason, Schweitzer & McNeill, Montreal, 1977—; dir. Dennison Mfg. Can. Inc., Que. Distillers Corp.; mcpl. judge Town of Rosemere, Que., 1965-76. Chancellor, bd. govs. Concordia U.; mayor Town of Rosemere, 1955-59. Mem. Assn. Can. Gen. Counsel, Can. Mfrs. Assn., Can. C. of C. Roman Catholic. Clubs: Order of Malta, St. James, Lorraine Golf. Home: 214 Rose Alma St Rosemere PQ Canada J7A 386 Office: 505 Dorchester Blvd W Montreal Canada H2Z 1A8

HEMINGWAY, RICHARD KEITH, banker; b. Salt Lake City, Oct. 18, 1920; s. Harold E. and Isabelle (Whitlam) H.; m. Shirley V. Stranquist, Oct. 4, 1948; children: Harold, Ann, Henry, Helen, Jane. Student, U. Wash., 1938-42, Pacific Coast Sch. Banking-No. Western U., 1948, Sch. Financial Relations, 1955, Sch. Bus., Weber State Coll., Ogden, Utah, 1975. With Comml. Security Bank, Ogden, Utah, 1937—, v.p., 1950-60, exec. v.p., 1960-66, pres., 1966—, chmn. bd., 1966—, Idaho Bank & Trust Co., Pocatello; dir. Box Elder County Bank, Brigham City, Utah. Mem. Utah Bankers Assn. (pres. 1975), Ogden C. of C. (pres. 1970), Sigma Chi. Club: Alta (Salt Lake City). Home: 908 East S Temple Salt Lake City UT 84102 Office: 50 S Main St Salt Lake City UT 84144

HEMINGWAY, RICHARD WILLIAM, lawyer, educator; b. Detroit, Nov. 24, 1927; s. William Oswald and Iva Catherine (Wildfang) H.; m. Vera Cecilia Eck, Sept. 12, 1947; children: Margaret Catherine, Carol Elizabeth, Richard Albert. B.S. in Bus, U. Colo., 1950; J.D. magna cum laude (J. Woodall Sr. Gold medal 1955), So. Meth. U., 1955; LL.M. (William S. Cook fellow 1968), U. Mich., 1969. Bar: Tex. 1955, Okla. 1981. Assoc. firm Fulbright, Crooker, Freeman, Bates & Jaworski, Houston, 1955-60; lectr. Bates Sch. Law, U. Houston, 1960; assoc. prof. law Baylor U. Law Sch., Waco, Tex., 1960-65; vis. asso. prof. So. Meth. U. Law Sch., 1965-68; prof. law Tex. Tech U. Law Sch., Lubbock, 1968-71; Paul W. Horn prof. Tex. Tech. U Law Sch., 1972-81; acting dean Tex. Tech U. Law Sch., 1974-75, dean ad interim, 1980-81; prof. law U. Okla., Norman, 1981-83, Eugene Kuntz prof. oil, gas and natural resources law, 1983—. Author: The Law of Oil and Gas, 1971, 2d edit., 1983, lawyer's edit., 1983, West's Texas Forms (Mines and Minerals), 1977; contbg. editor various law reports, cases and materials. Served with USAAF, 1945-47. Mem. Am. Bar Assn., Okla. Bar Assn., Tex. Bar Assn., Cleveland County Bar Assn., Lubbock Bar Assn., Scribes, Order of Coif (faculty), Beta Gamma Sigma. Lutheran. Home: 1411 Greenbriar Dr Norman OK 73069 Office: Sch Law U Okla Norman OK 73019

HEMION, DWIGHT ARLINGTON, TV producer, director; b. New Haven, Mar. 14, 1926; s. Dwight Arlington and Bernice Ruby (Berquist) H.; m. Katherine Bridget Morrissy, Sept. 1, 1973; children—Katherine, Dwight Gustav. Student pub. schs., Verona, N.J. Asso. dir. ABC-TV, N.Y.C., 1946-49; TV dir. Tonight Show, NBC-TV, N.Y.C., 1950-60; dir. Perry Como TV show, N.Y.C., 1960-67; producer/dir. Yorkshire Prodns., N.Y.C., 1967-70; producer/dir. TV spls. in assn. with ATV, London; producer/dir. Smith-Hemion Prodns., Los Angeles, 1975—. Dir.: Frank Sinatra: A Man and His Music, 1965 (Emmy award TV Acad. Arts and Scis.); The Sound of Burt Bacharach, 1969, Singer Presents Burt Bacharach, 1970, Barbra Streisand and Other Musical Instruments, 1973, Steve and Eydie-Our Love is Here to Stay, 1975, America Salutes Richard Rodgers: The Sound of His Music, 1976, Bette Midler-Ol' Red Hair is Back, 1977, Ben Vereen . . . His Roots, 1977, Steve and Eydie Celebrate Irving Berlin, 1978, IBM Presents Baryshinikov on Broadway, 1979 (Emmy award), Goldie and Kids . . . Listen to Us!, 1982 (Emmy award). Served in AC U.S. Army, 1944-46. Named Dir. of Year in TV Dirs. Guild Am., 1965. Club: Bel-Air Country. Office: 1438 N Gower St Box 15 Los Angeles CA 90028

HEMKE, FREDERICK, saxophonist; b. Milw., July 11, 1935; s. Fred and May Harriet (Rowell) H.; m. Junita C.A. Borg, Dec. 26, 1959; children—Elizabeth Anne, Frederic John Borg. Premier Prix, Paris Conservatory Music, 1956; B.S., U. Wis.-Milw., 1958; Mus.M., Eastman Sch., U. Rochester, 1962; D.Mus. Arts, U. Wis., 1975. Dir. bands West Allis (Wis.) public schs., 1958-60; mem. faculty Northwestern U., Evanston, Ill., 1962—, prof. music, 1963—, chmn. dept. wind and percussion instruments, 1963—; vis. prof. music U. Wis., Madison, 1970-75; Morton vis. prof. Ohio U., Athens, 1977; vis. prof. music Interlochen (Mich.) Arts Acad., 1975—; clinician Selmer Co. Elkhart, Ind., 1957—, ednl. dir., 1978-81. Dir.: Chamber Ensemble; saxophonist, Chgo. Symphony Orch., 1962-81; N.Y. Town Hall debut, 1962; Author: The Early History of the Saxophone, 1975, A Comprehensive Listing of Saxophone Literature, 1964, The Orchestral Saxophone, 1973; Recs. The American Saxophone, 1971, Music for Tenor Saxophone, 1971, Contest Music for Saxophone, 1961, Finney Concerto for Saxophone and Winds, 1976, Benson Quintet for Saxophone and String Quartet, 1978. Bd. dirs. Evanston Symphony Orch., 1968-71; host 6th World Saxophone Congress, 1979. Research grantee Northwestern U., 1972, 78. Mem. N.Am. Saxophone Alliance (pres. 1976-78), Phi Mu Alpha Sinfonia (province gov. 1975), Pi Kappa Lambda, Kappa Kappa Psi. Lutheran. Office: Regenstein Hall Sch Music Northwestern U Evanston IL 60201

HEMLOW, JOYCE, educator, author; b. Liscomb, N.S., Can., July 30, 1906; d. William and Rosalinda (Redmond) H. B.A., Queen's Coll., Kingston, Can., 1941, M.A., 1942; A.M., Radcliffe Coll., 1944, Ph.D., 1948; LL.D., Queen's, 1967, Dalhousie U., 1972. Mem. faculty McGill U., 1945—, Greenshields prof. English lit. and lang., 1965—, prof. emerita, 1975—. (Recipient James Tait Black Meml. book prize for best biography in U.K., The History of Fanny Burney 1958, also Gov. Gen. Can. medal for academic non-fiction 1958, Rose Mary Crawshay prize Brit. Acad. 1960); Editor: Journals and Letters Fanny Burney (Madame d'Arblay). Guggenheim fellow, 1951-52, 66-67; Distinguished Achievement medal Radcliffe Coll., 1969. Fellow Royal Soc. Can.; mem. Johnsonians, Phi Beta Kappa. Home: 3555 Atwater Ave Montreal PQ H3H 1Y3 Canada also Liscomb NS Canada

HEMMER, PAUL EDWARD, broadcasting executive, musician; b. Dubuque, Iowa, Oct. 12, 1944; s. Andrew Charles and Elizabeth Marie (Goerdt) H.; m. Janet T. Demmer, Feb. 7, 1970; children: Michelle, Steven. B.S., U. Wis.-Platteville, 1966. Program dir. Sta. WDBQ, Dubuque, 1967-75; ops. mgr. Sta. WDBQ-KIWI-FM, Dubuque, 1975-83; pub. affairs dir. Sta. WDBQ-KLYV, Dubuque, 1983—. Composer music and lyrics for musical comedy. Chmn. Ret. Sr. Vol. Program Adv. Bd., 1976-79; local adminstr. Music Performance Trust Fund of Rec. Industry. Named Citizen of Yr. Dubuque Telegraph-Herald, 1976. Mem. Am. Fedn. Musicians (mem. internat. public relations com., state legis. affairs div.). Republican. Roman Catholic. Club: Kiwanis. Home: 1030 Boyer Dubuque IA 52001 Office: 1170 Iowa St Dubuque IA 52001

HEMMING, ROY G., writer, magazine editor; b. Hamden, Conn., May 27, 1928; s. Benjamin Whitney and Anna (Sexton) H. B.A., Yale U., 1949; M.A., Stanford U., 1951; grad. cert., U. Geneva, 1950. News editor, program dir. Sta. WAVZ-AM-FM, New Haven, 1948-50; writer Voice of Am., 1951-52; with news dept. NBC, N.Y.C., 1953-54; writer-editor Scholastic Mags., Inc., N.Y.C., 1954-74; publs. dir. Scholastic Internat., 1972-74; editor-in-chief Retirement Living, also 50 Plus, Whitney Communications Corp., N.Y.C., 1975-80; contbg. editor Stereo Rev., 1973-80, Ovation mag., 1980—; revs. editor Video Rev., 1980—; bd. advisers Eastern Music Festival, Greensboro, N.C., 1970—; mem. Montreux (Switzerland) Internat. Record Award Com., 1971-76. Program producer, scriptwriter N.Y. Philharm. weekly nat. radio broadcasts, 1979—; Author: Discovering Music: Where to Start on Records and Tapes, 71974, Movies on Video, 1981. Mem. Young Republican Club, New Haven, 1949-51 Mem. Young Republican Club, N.Y.C., 1951-58. Served with USNR, 1945-46. Recipient All-Am. award Ednl. Pubs. Assn., 1965, 67. Clubs: Overseas Press; Deadline, Yale (N.Y.C.); Stanford of N.Y., N.J., Conn. Home: 106 E 60th St New York NY 10022 Office: 350 E 81st St New York NY 10028

HEMMINGHAUS, ROGER ROY, energy company executive, chemical engineer; b. St. Louis, Aug. 27, 1936; s. Roy Geroge and Henrietta E.M. (Knacht) H.; m. Delores de la Rua, June 7, 1958 (div. 1974); children: Sheryl, Ann, Susan Lynn, Sally Ann; m. Dorotyh O'Kelly, Aug. 18, 1979; children: R. Patrick, Kelley Elizabeth Roger Christian. Student, Purdue U., 1954-56; B.S. in Chem. Engring., Auburn U., 1958; grad. cert., Bettis Reactor Engring., Pitts., 1959; postgrad., La. State U., 1963-66. Various tech. and mgmt. positions Exxon Co. U.S.A., Baton Rouge, 1962-70, Benicia, Calif., 1962-70, Houston, 1962-70; refinery gen. mgr. C.F. Industries, East Chicago, Ind., 1976-77; pres. Petro United Inc., Houston, 1977-80; v.p. planning United Gas Pipe Line, Houston, 1980-82, United Energy Resources, 1982—; adv. dir. Osiris Fin. Ventures, Ltd., 1983; mem. Council Sr. Execs., Houston, 1982-83. Adviser Jr. Achievement, Baton Rouge, 1956-66; pres. congregation Lutheran Ch., Baton Rouge, 1965 pres. congregation Lutheran Ch., Moraga, Calif., 1969; chmn. indsl. div. United Crusade, Solano County, Calif., 1970; assoc. gen. chmn. United Way, Tex. Gulf Coast, 1983-84, gen. chmn.-elect, Tex. Gulf Coast, 1985. Served to lt. USN, 1958-62. Mem. Am. Chem. Soc., Am. Inst. Chem. Engrs., Soc. Naval Architects and Marine Engrs., So. Gas Assn., Soc. N.Am. Planners, Tau Beta Pi, Phi Lambda Upsilon, Phi Kappa Phi, Kappa Alpha. Clubs: Met. Racquet, Houston (Houston). Home: 725-1 Route 1 Willis TX 77378 Office: United Energy Resources Inc PO Box 1478 Houston TX 77001

HEMOND, ROLAND, baseball executive; b. Central Falls, R.I., Oct. 26, 1929; m. Margaret Quinn. Past dir. player personnel Chgo. White Sox, now exec. v.p., gen. mgr.; formerly with Boston/Milw. Braves, Calif. Angels. Served in USCG. Named The Sporting News Major League Exec. of Year, 1972, 83. Office: Comiskey Park Chicago IL 60616 *

HEMPEL, CARL GUSTAV, educator; b. Oranienburg, Germany, Jan. 8, 1905; came to U.S., 1937, naturalized, 1944; s. Carl Friedrich and Charlotte (Kessler) H.; m. Eva Beate Ahrends, 1935 (dec. 1944); 1 son, Peter Andrew; m. Diane Perlow, 1947; 1 dau., Toby Anne. Student, U. Goettingen, 1923-24, U. Heidelberg, 1924, U. Berlin, 1924-28, U. Vienna, 1929-30; Ph.D., U. Berlin, 1934; Dr. Sc., Washington U., St. Louis, 1975; D. Litt., Northwestern U., 1975; L.H.D., Princeton U., 1979, Carleton Coll., 1981. Pvt. research and writing, Brussels, Belgium, 1934-37; research asso. philosophy U. Chgo., 1937-38; mem. dept. philosophy Coll. City N.Y., 1939-40, Queens Coll., Flushing, N.Y., 1940-48, Yale, 1948-55; prof. philosophy Princeton, 1955, Stuart prof. philosophy, 1956-73, prof. emeritus, lectr., 1973—; vis. prof. philosophy Columbia, 1950; Hibben research fellow Princeton, 1952; Fulbright Sr. Research fellow Oxford U., 1959-60; vis. lectr. Harvard U., 1953-54; Guggenheim fellow, 1947-48; fellow Center Advanced Study Behavioral Scis., Stanford, 1963-64; hon. research fellow dept. philosophy U. Coll. London, 1971-72; vis. prof. Hebrew U., Jerusalem, 1974, U. Calif. at Berkeley, 1975, 77, Carleton Coll., 1976; U. Calif., Irvine, 1978; Gavin David Young lectr. U. Adelaide, Australia, 1979; vis. prof. U. Pitts., 1976, Univ. prof. philosophy, 1977—. Author: (with P. Oppenheim) Der Typusbegriff im Lichte der neuen Logik, 1936, Fundamentals of Concept Formation in Empirical Science, 1952, La formazione dei concetti e delle teorie nella scienza empirica, 1961, Aspects of Scientific Explanation and other Essays in the Philosophy of Science, 1965, Philosophy of Natural Science, 1966; Editorial bd.: Am. Philos. Quar, 1962-76; cons. editor: Jour. Symbolic Logic, 1940-62; co-editor: Erkenntnis, 1974—; Contbr. articles to profl. jours. Fellow Am. Acad.

Arts and Scis., Brit. Acad.; mem. Am. Philos. Assn. (pres. Eastern div. 1961), Académie internationale de philosophie des sciences, Am. Philos. Soc., Philosophy of Sci. Assn., Brit. Soc. for Philosophy of Sci. Office: Dept Philosophy U Pitts Pittsburgh PA 15260

HEMPEL, VALDEMAR, communications consultant; b. Kolding, Denmark, Dec. 8, 1919; came to U.S., 1947, naturalized, 1951; s. Soren Christian and Ingeborg (Knipschildt) H.; m. Helen Elizabeth Benthen; 1 dau. by previous marriage, Johanna. N.B., Niels Brock Sch., Copenhagen, Denmark, 1942; M.A., San Francisco State U., 1961. Div. dir. Def. Lang. Inst., Monterey, Calif., 1947-66; chief editor L.W. Singer Co., N.Y.C., 1966-68; exec. editor D.C. Heath & Co., Lexington, Mass., 1968-74; pub. Val Hempel Co., Lexington, 1974-80; pres. Hempel & Hempel, communications cons., Carmel Valley, Calif., 1980—; Cons. fgn. lang. edn. and fgn. lang. pub.; hon. faculty U.S. Army Command and Gen. Staff Coll., 1961. Author: Danish Reader II. Exec. trustee Am.-Scandinavian Found., 1972—; mem. adv. council State of Calif., 1981—. Decorated knight cross Order of Dannebrog, Denmark; recipient medal for meritorious civilian service Dept. Army, 1960. Mem. Modern Lang. Assn. Am., Rebild Nat. Park Soc. Address: 179 E Caminito Carmel Valley CA 93924

HEMPHILL, BERNICE MONAHAN (MRS. CHARLES D. HEMPHILL), association executive, civic leader; b. San Francisco; d. Thomas E. and Anne J. (McGinerty) Monahan; m. Charles D. Hemphill, June 30, 1939. Bioanalyst, U. Calif. Supervising technologist Honolulu Blood Plasma Bank, 1941- 43; exec. dir., sec. Irwin Meml. Blood Bank, San Francisco Med. Soc., 1944-82, dir. emeritus, 1983—; sec. Calif. Blood Bank System, 1951-57; charter mem., treas. Am. Assn. Blood Banks, 1949-74, pres. elect, 1975, pres., 1976-77, emeritus dir., 1978—, originator bloodbank clearinghouse concept, 1951, chmn. nat. clearing house program, 1953—, mem. com. on external affairs, com. on internat. relations, 1978; mem. Pres.'s exec., fin., personnel coms. Am. Blood Commn., 1978-80, bd. dirs., 1981-83; cons. blood bank projects AMA, Am. Hosp. Assn., other nat. health orgns., other countries; Mem. adv. com. blood and blood derivatives Calif. Dept. Pub. Health, 1964—; mem. Nat. Adv. Council for Disease Control, 1969-72; exec. sec. Zone 1 Federacion Pan Americana Pro Donacion Voluntaria de Sangre, 1980—; bd. dirs. Health Care Found. of San Francisco, 1983, Nat. Center for Voluntary Action, 1976-77; bd. dirs. San Francisco unit Am. Cancer Soc., 1978-83, sec. San Francisco unit, 1981-83; mem. steering com. Learn Through Internat. Vol. Effort Conf., 1975-76; mem. adv. bd. U. Santa Clara Bus. Sch., 1980-83; active San Francisco United Way Bay Area, mem. health council, mem. joint budget study com. program for hosps. and health agys., 1966-75, mem. casework services com. program for aging, 1961-62, Hispanic affairs com., 1981-82; mem. Cath. Social Service San Francisco, Mayor San Francisco Citizens Com. Centennial Golden Gate Park, 1969-70; also mem. hosp. aux. U. Calif.; aux. St. Francis Hosp., Calif., Laguna (Calif.) Honda Home; women's aux. San Francisco Dental Soc.; aux. Little Children's Aid, St. Francis Yacht Club, St. Anthony's Dining Room, Guide Dogs for Blind., S.F. Opera Guild, S.F. Symphony Assn. Mem. Women for Nixon-Agnew Com., 1968; co-chmn. Women's Adv. Com. for Re-election Pres., 1972; mem. nat. adv. com. Women for Pres. Ford, 1976; mem. adv. com. on fiscal affairs Republican Nat. Com., 1977-80; mem. Manila-San Francisco Sister City Com., 1981-82; bd. dirs. San Francisco Convention and Visitors Bureau, 1982—; bd. dirs., chmn. vol. com. Hearing Soc. for Bay Area, Inc., 1983; bd. dirs. Green Hills Towers, 1983; mem. San Francisco-Osaka Sister City Com., 1983. Named Distinguished Woman San Francisco Examiner, 1960, U.S. Lady of Month U.S. Lady mag., 1963; recipient John Elliot award contbns. blood banking Am. Assn. Blood Banks, 1960, Award of Merit for Cath. charities services Archdiocese San Francisco, 1962, commendation exceptional services to patients Ft. Miley VA Hosp., San Francisco, 1961, 80, citation for vol. community services Lane Bryant, 1965, 66, 67, 68, Cert. of Honor City and County of San Francisco Bd. of Supervisors, 1971, 82, diploma 2000 Women of Achievement, 1972, Award of Honor Pan Am. Fedn. for Voluntary Blood Donations, 1972, Award of Merit Nat. Orgn. of Voluntary Blood Donors of Venezuela, 1973, Key of Guild award Medico Dental Study Guild, Calif., 1973; 1st. Ann. Lecture award S. Central Assn. of Blood Banks, 1975; KABL Citizen of the Day award, 1975, 82; cert. of appreciation Kiwanis Club of Benicia, 1977; Owen Thomas Meml. award Calif. Blood Bank System, 1978; Woman of Achievement award Bus. and Profl. Women's Club of San Francisco, 1981; commendation Calif. State Senate, 1982, VA, 1982; Resolution of Recognition Calif. Med. Assn., 1983; Hon. Life Mem. Calif. Blood Bank System, 1983. Mem. Women's Forum West (v.p. 1980-81), San Francisco Assn. Mental Health, Med. Dental Study Club San Francisco (life mem.), Internat. Soc. Blood Transfusion, Ambassador League of San Francisco, Am. Women for Internat. Understanding (pres. 1973—), World Affairs Council No. Calif., Host Com. San Francisco, Nat. Conf. Social Welfare (chmn. sponsoring com. 1975), San Francisco C. of C. (dir., exec. com. 1980-82, chmn. health care com. 1983, award for Lifetime Dedication to People and to a City 1981), UN Assn. San Francisco (steering com. for internat. women's com. 1975, coordinating com. Calif. Internat. Women's Year 1977), UN Assn. of U.S., Nat. Com. on U.S.-China Relations; hon. mem. Pan Am. Fedn. Voluntary Blood Donations. Republican. Clubs: Doctors' Wives, Francisca; Commonwealth (San Francisco) (membership com. 1983); Capitol Hill (Washington)). Home: 1070 Green St San Francisco CA 94133 Office: 270 Masonic Ave San Francisco CA 94118 *In my profession of blood banking, a people-service, I have seen millions of volunteer blood donors give of themselves to help patients in need of blood transfusions. The selflessness of these men and women have been a continual inspiration to me. As a result, in my professional career and in my volunteer efforts to help people at community, national and international levels, I have always attempted to foster this spirit of volunteerism and the concept of people sharing and caring.*

HEMPLER, ORVAL FREDERICK, artist; b. Almena, Kans., Jan. 9, 1915; s. Otto and Margaret Em (Schurz) H. B.F.A., U. Colo., 1938; student (Frank Alva Parsons Meml. fellow) of, Van Day Truex, Paris, 1938-39; M.A. (Univ. scholar), U. Iowa, 1941; student of, Grant Wood, 1939-40. Instr. art U. N.H., 1941-42; tchr. art Los Angeles Unified Schs., 1965-73; guest artist for adult edn. classes; tchr. workshops. Head window designer, Carson, Perie Scott & Co., Chgo., 1942-45; artist-designer, Lamps of Calif., Santa Monica, 1945-65; exhibited watercolors and serigraphs in one-man shows, Mandell Gallery, Chgo., 1945, St. John's, Santa Monica, 1965; exhibited in group shows, Chapell House, Denver, 1938, Etats Unis, Paris, 1939, Los Angeles County Art Mus., 1973; represented in permanent collections, U. Kans., Manhattan, Layton Mus. Visual Arts, Hollywood, Calif., Los Angeles County Mus.; designer for mfrs. Capt. Democratic Precinct, Santa Monica. Recipient Sweepstakes award Kans. State Fair, 1937; named to Denver Post Gallery Fame, 1938; Italian traveling scholar, 1939-40. Mem. UCLA Art Council, Los Angeles County Mus. Art, Norton (Kans.) Art Council, Delta Phi Delta., Phi Mu Alpha. Roman Catholic. Home: 2302 2d St Santa Monica CA 90405 *Set your goals early in life; knock them down one by one, and you will find that you are at the top. Not over the hill.*

HEMPSTONE, SMITH, JR., journalist; b. Washington, Feb. 1, 1929; s. Smith and Elizabeth (Noyes) H.; m. Kathaleen Fishback, Jan. 30, 1954; 1 dau. Student, George Washington U., 1946-47; B.A. with honors, U. of South, 1950; Litt.D. (hon.), U. of South, 1969; Nieman fellow, Harvard, 1964-65. Rewrite man AP, Charlotte, N.C., 1952; with Nat. Geog. mag., Washington, 1954; reporter Louisville Times, 1953, Evening Star, Washington, 1955-56; fgn. corr., Africa, Asia, Europe and Latin Am. for Chgo. Daily News, 1960-66, Washington Evening Star, 1966-69, asso. editor, 1970-75; exec. editor Washington Times, 1982—; Fellow Inst. Current World Affairs, 1956-60. Author: Africa, Angry Young Giant, 1961, Rebels, Mercenaries and Dividends-The Katanga Story, 1962; (novel) A Tract of Time, 1966, In the Midst of Lions, 1968; editorial bd.: Nieman Reports, 1965-73. Alumni trustee U. South, 1974-78; bd. govs. Inst. Current World Affairs, 1974-78. Recipient Fgn. Corr. award Sigma Delta Chi and Overseas Press Club. Episcopalian. Clubs: Chevy Chase (Md.); Metropolitan (Washington); Explorers (N.Y.C.). Address: 7611 Fairfax Rd Bethesda MD 20814

HEMRY, JEROME ELDON, lawyer; b. Kirksville, Mo., July 22, 1905; s. U.S.G. and Rose M. (Plumb) H.; m. Martha L. Langston, Aug. 1, 1934; children: Jerome Louis, Kenneth Marshall. A.B., Oklahoma City U., 1926; J.D., U. Okla., 1928; LL.M., Harvard U., 1929. Bar: Okla. 1928. Partner Hemry & Hemry, Oklahoma City, 1931-82, of counsel, 1983—; prof. law Central Okla. Sch. Law, 1931-41; dean, prof. law Langston U., 1948-49; dir., counsel Am. Gen. Life Ins. Co. Okla., 1959-79; pres., gen. counsel Gen. Constrn. Corp., 1941-45; legislative counsel Okla. Chain Store Assn., 1941-44; Mem. Bd. Conf. Claimant's Okla. Ann. Conf.; treas. Oklahoma City S. Dist. Contbr. articles legal jours. Bd. dirs. Family and Children's Service, 1939-56. Mem. Okla. Assn. Mcpl. Attys. (pres. 1956-57), Am., Okla. bar assns., Order of Coif, Phi Delta Phi, Lambda Chi Alpha. Methodist (pres., counsel trustees). Clubs: Lions, Men's Dinner (Oklahoma City). Home: 2255 NW 55th St Oklahoma City OK 73112 Office: 420 NW 6th St Oklahoma City OK 73101

HEMRY, LESLIE PLUMB, ret. assn. exec., lawyer; b. Oklahoma City, Oct. 18, 1911; s. Ulysses Sidney Grant and Rose May (Plumb) H.; m. Mary Jane Carson, Oct. 28, 1933; 1 dau., Mary Ann (Mrs. John Edward Sheridan). B.A., Oklahoma City U., 1931; LL.B., Okla. U., 1934; LL.M., Harvard, 1935; grad., Advanced Mgmt. Program, 1952. Bar: Mass. bar 1935, also Okla. bar 1935. Atty. Am. Mut. Liability Ins. Co., Wakefield, Mass., 1935-55, sr. v.p., 1955-68; pres. Health Ins. Assn. Am., Washington, 1968-76; cons., 1976—. Served to lt. USNR, 1944-46. Mem. Okla., Mass., Am. bar assns., Internat. Assn. Ins. Counsel (v.p. 1944). Clubs: University (Washington); Metropolitan (N.Y.C.). Home: 2300 Riverside Dr Apt 126 Tulsa OK 74114 Office: 1750 K St NW Washington DC 20006

HEMSING, ALBERT E., public affairs adviser; b. Barmen, Germany, Feb. 27, 1921; s. Paul and Josephine (Ferder) H.; m. Esther Davidson, Dec. 27, 1944; 1 dau., Josephine Claudia. B.S.S., CCNY, 1942; M.A., NYU, 1947. With East and West Assn., 1942-43, OWI, 1943-46, State Dept., 1946-47; ind. documentary film producer, 1947-51; with ECA, Paris, 1951-55; chief overseas operations div. USIA, Washington, 1955-58; press officer then pub. affairs officer U.S. mission, Berlin, 1958-64, counselor of embassy pub. affairs, Bonn, Germany, 1964-67; dep., then asst. dir. USIA, in charge of Western Europe, 1969-71, insp. gen., 1971-73; minister-counselor pub. affairs Am. embassy, New Delhi, 1973-76; mem. Bd. Internat. Broadcasting, 1976-77; dir. Am. Inst., Freiburg, Germany, 1978-83; mem. State Dept. Sr. Seminar Fgn. Policy, 1967—; mem. bd. examiners Fgn. Service, 1970-73; lectr. CCNY, 1946-51, Am. U., 1956-58. Co-author: (with Esther Hemsing) and dir.) documentary The Yellow Star (Acad. award nomination 1981); writer, producer: Top Secret—The July 20, 1944 Revolt Against Hitler, 1980. Bd. dirs. Carl Schurz House, Freiburg, 1978-83. Recipient Meritorious Honor award USIA. Mem. Am. Fgn. Service Assn., Phi Beta Kappa. Home: 215 E 79th St New York NY 10021

HEMSLEY, SHERMAN, comedian, actor; b. Phila., Feb. 1. Student, Phila. Acad. Dramatic Arts; student acting, Lloyd Richards. Postal worker; active advance workshop Negro Ensemble Co., N.Y.C. Joined, Theatre XIV, Phila., children's theater with, Phoenix Prodns.; co-star: local Phila. TV comedy series Black Book; mem., Society Hill Playhouse, Vinnette Carroll's Urban Art Corps; off-Broadway debut in: The People vs. Ranchman, 1968; Broadway debut in: Purlie, 1970; appeared with, Toronto and San Francisco cos., Don't Bother Me, I Can't Cope; on stage in The Odd Couple, Dallas and Chgo.; TV series The Jeffersons, 1975—; other TV appearances. Mem. AFTRA. Office: care Kenny Johnston 6920 Sunset Blvd. Suite 1002 Los Angeles CA 90028 *

HENAHAN, DONAL, music critic; b. Cleve., Feb. 28, 1921; s. William Anthony and Mildred (Doyle) H. Student, Kent U., 1939-40, Ohio U., 1940-42; B.A., Northwestern U., 1948; postgrad., U. Chgo., 1949, Chgo. Sch. Music, 1950-57. With Chgo. Daily News, 1947-67, music critic, 1957-67; with N.Y. Times, 1967—, chief music critic, 1980—. Served to 1st lt. USAF, 1942-45. Decorated Air medal with 3 oak leaf clusters. Club: Century (N.Y.C.). Office: 229 W 43d St New York NY 10036

HENDEE, JOHN H., JR., banker; b. 1926; married. B.A., Williams Coll., 1949; M.B.A., U. Wis., 1956. With 1st Wis. Nat. Bank of Milw., 1949—, sr. v.p., 1970-72, exec. v.p., 1972-76, pres., 1976—, dir. Office: First Wisconsin Nat Bank Milwaukee 777 E Wisconsin Ave Milwaukee WI 53202 *

HENDEE, WILLIAM RICHARD, medical physicist, educator; b. Owosso, Mich., Jan. 1, 1938; s. C.L. and Alvina M. H.; m. Jeannie Wesley, June 16, 1960; children: Mikal, Shonn, Eric, Gareth and Gregory (twins), Lara and Karel (twins). B.S., Millsaps Coll., Jackson, Miss., 1959; Ph.D., U. Tex., 1962. Diplomate: Am. Bd. Radiology, Am. Bd. Health Physics. AEC fellow Nat. Reactor Testing Sta., Idaho Falls, Idaho, 1960; asst. prof., then assoc. prof. physics Millsaps Coll., 1962-65, chmn. dept., 1964-65; instr. Miss. State U. (extension), 1963; asst. prof., then assoc. prof. radiology (med. physics) U. Colo. Med. Center, 1965-73, prof., 1974—, chmn. dept., 1978—; mem. staff VA Hosp., Denver, 1970—, Mercy Hosp., 1971—, Denver Gen. Hosp., 1971—, Beth Israel Hosp., 1974—; vis. lectr. Oak Ridge Associated Univs., 1964. Contbr. articles to profl. jours. Served with USMC, 1957-62. Recipient Theta Nu Sigma award, 1955; Disting. Alumnus award Millsaps Coll., 1967; Robert S. Landauer Meml. award, Chgo., 1977; Gilbert-X-Ray fellow, 1960-62; summer fellow NSF, AEC; campus asso. Danforth Found. Fellow Am. Coll. Radiology; mem. Health Physics Soc. (chmn. coms., Elda E. Anderson award 1972), Am. Assn. Physics Tchrs., AAAS, Am. Phys. Soc., Am. Assn. Physicists in Medicine (pres. 1976-77), Soc. Nuclear Medicine (pres. 1980-81), Omicron Delta Kappa. Home: 4248 N 109th Rd Lafayette CO 80026 Office: 4200 E 9th Ave A031 Denver CO 80262

HENDEL, FRANK JOSEPH, chemical engineer, educator, technical consultant; b. Sambor, Poland, Dec. 2, 1918; came to U.S., 1950, naturalized, 1955; s. Emil and Henrietta (Sprecher) H.; children: Anna H. (Mrs. Gary Carrillo), Emily E. (Mrs. Rudy Lacoe), Erica F. Ph.D., Tech. U. Lwow, 1941. Chief chem. engr. Wigton-Abbott Corp. (engrs. and constructors), Plainfield, N.J., 1950-56; head chem. engring. Aerojet Gen. Corp., Azusa, Calif., 1956-61; staff scientist, space div. N.Am. Aviation, Downey, Calif., 1961-64; mem. tech. staff Jet Propulsion Lab., Calif. Inst. Tech., Pasadena, 1964-67; prof. aerospace sci. and aero. engring., dept. aero. and mech. engring. Calif. Poly. State U., San Luis Obispo, 1967—; also tchr. courses on energy; cons. Nat. Acad. sci., 1961-63, Vandenberg AFB (Western Test Range and Space Missile Test Center), 1968-75; mem. faculty Inst. Aerospace Safety and Mgmt., U. So. Calif., 1970-73; lectr. aerospace propulsion and ordnance systems UCLA Extension, 1964-67; researcher Laramie (Wyo.) Energy Tech. Center, U.S. Dept. Energy, 1977-78; aero. engr. Flight Test Center, Edwards AFB, summer 1980; research specialist Lockheed Missile & Space Co., Sunnyvale, Calif., summers 1981-82; research specialist in ordnance/propulsion Lockheed Missile & Space Co., Sunnyvale, Calif., summers 1981, 82; gen. engr. U.S. Navy Pacific Missile & Test Ctr., Port Mugu, summer 1983. Edn. Abstractor: Chem. Abstracts, 1952—; Contbr. articles to profl. jours. and books. Fellow Am. Inst. Chemists and Chem. Engrs.; asso. fellow AIAA (chmn. edn. sect. com. on symposium on alt. fuel resources 1976); mem. Am. Soc. Engring. Designer, engr. several chem., indsl. petroleum, other fossil energy plants, pyrotechnics and ordnance for space vehicles and missiles, and facilities to protect environment. Home: 721 Johnson Ave San Luis Obispo CA 93401

HENDEL, SAMUEL, educator; b. N.Y.C., July 6, 1909; s. Jodah and Leah (Gerber) H.; m. Clara Hoch, May 14, 1932; children—Linda Susan, Steven. LL.B. cum laude, Bklyn. Law Sch., 1930, B.S.S., Coll. City N.Y., 1936; Ph.D., Columbia U., 1948. Bar: N.Y. bar 1931. Practice in, N.Y.C., 1931-41, legal cons., 1941—; mem. faculty Coll. City N.Y., 1941-70, prof. polit. sci., 1957-70, chmn. dept., 1957-62, chmn., 1960-70, ombudsman, 1969-70; prof., polit. sci. Trinity Coll., Hartford, Conn., 1970-78, chmn. dept., 1970-73; vis. prof. govt. grad. faculty Columbia U., 1958-60, summer 1962; vis. prof. comparative govt. and internat. relations (Claremont Grad. Sch.), spring 1962; vis. prof. Grad. Center, U. City N.Y., spring 1975, Law Sch. U. Conn., fall 1975; adj. prof. N.Y. U., spring 1979, 80; vis. prof. Barnard Coll., spring 1980, 81, fall 1982, spring 1983. Author: Charles Evans Hughes and The Supreme Court, 1951; co-author, co-editor: The U.S.S.R. After 50 Years; Promise and Reality, 1967; Editor: The Soviet Crucible, 5th edit, 1980, The Politics of Confrontation, 1971; co-editor: Basic Issues of American Democracy, 6th edit, 1970; editor 7th edit., 1973, 8th edit., 1976. Chmn. acad. freedom com. ACLU, 1959-60, 66-73, bd. dirs., 1967-77, vice chmn., 1974-76; chmn. commn. on internat. affairs Am. Jewish Congress, 1959-61. Ford Faculty fellow, 1953-54; grantee to visit USSR Inter-University Com. Travel Grants, 1957. Mem. Am. Polit. Sci. Assn. (council 1965-67), Am. Assn. Advancement Slavic Studies, Phi Beta Kappa (pres. Gamma chpt. 1960-61). Home: 180 West End Ave New York NY 10023

HENDERSHOT, JAMES CALVIN, chemical company executive; b. Louisville, Dec. 30, 1917; s. Calvin Leroy and Ruth Vern (Kenady) H.; m. Elaine Dishion, Nov. 14, 1942; children: Kenady Lynn, James Calvin, Thomas Keith. Student, U. Louisville, 1935-38. With Reliance Universal, Inc., Louisville, 1938—, exec. v.p., 1962-63, pres., 1963—, chmn. bd., 1977—, also dir.; dir., mem. exec. com. Ky. Blue Cross; chmn. bd. Louisville br. Fed. Res. Bank St. Louis.; dir. emeritus 1st Ky. Nat. Corp. Bd. dirs. Internat. Center, U. Louisville, 1971—; chmn. bd. overseers U. Louisville. Served with AUS, 1943-45, ETO. Mem. Ky. C. of C., Louisville C. of C. (bd. dirs. 1971—), Am. Presidents Assn., Associated Industries Ky., NAM (dir.), Conf. Bd., UN Assn. U.S.A., Nat. Kitchen Cabinet Mfg. Assn., Nat. Paint and Coatings Assn. (dir., mem. exec. com. 1971—). Republican. Mem. Christian Ch. (deacon, trustee). Clubs: Flight, Pendennis, Rotary, Louisville Country, Jefferson, Juniper (Louisville). Office: 1930 Bishop Ln 1600 Watterson Towers Box 21413 Louisville KY 40218 *

HENDERSHOTT, PHILLIP LEROY, banker; b. Ithaca, Mich., June 6, 1937; s. William L. and Elizabeth R. (Klumpp) H.; m. Barbara J. Jurgens, Aug. 13, 1960; children: Gregory W., Karen J. B.B.A., U. Mich., 1963. V.p. Chase Manhattan Bank, N.Y.C., 1963-72; sr. v.p. R.H. Lapin & Co., N.Y.C., 1972; exec. v.p. J.I. Kislak Mortgage Corp., Newark, 1972-74; sr. v.p. Citicorp, Detroit, 1974-76; exec. v.p. First Bank System, Mpls., 1976—; chmn. FBS Fin. Corp., Mpls., 1977—, FBS Mortgage Corp., 1980—, FBS Bus. Fin. Corp., 1982—, FBS Venture Capital Corp., 1983—, FBS Ins., 1981—. Served with U.S. Army, 1955-58. Mem. Mortgage Bankers Assn. Am., Minn. Mortgage Bankers Assn. (gov. 1981-82). Republican. Episcopalian. Club: Decathalon (Bloomington, Minn.). Home: 6900 Gleason Rd Edina MN 55435 Office: First Bank System Inc 1200 First Bank Pl E Minneapolis MN 55402

HENDERSON, ALBERT, publishing company and dairy executive; b. Phila., July 9, 1938; s. Harry Brinton, Jr. and Beatrice (Conford) H.; m. Tamara Ann McCormick, Feb. 14, 1968; children—Christopher Findley, Theodore Leon. Mus.B., Ithaca Coll., 1960; postgrad., N.Y. U. Editorial asst. Hearst Headline, 1960-62; asst. sales mgr. Royal McBee, 1960-64; editor Johnson Reprint Corp., 1964-69; gen. mgr., v.p., treas. Brit. Book Centre, Inc., N.Y.C., 1969-77; dir. Pergamon Press, Inc., v.p., treas., 1971-77; exec. v.p., dir. Newman Grove Creamery Co., Nebr., 1977-81; dir. publs. Am. Solar Energy Soc., N.Y.C., 1981—; dir. Meadowlark Farms. Mem. Nebr. Dairy Industries Assn. (dir.), Bookman's League N.Y., Spl. Libraries Assn., Am. Soc. Info. Sci., St. George Soc., AAAS, Nat. Micrographics Assn., Soc. Scholarly Publs., Council Biology Editors. Home: 2423 Noble Sta Bridgeport CT 06608 *Never say no to an opportunity.*

HENDERSON, ALBERT JOHN, judge; b. Canton, Ga., Dec. 12, 1920; s. Albert Jefferson and Cliffie Mae (Cook) H.; m. Jenny Lee Medford, Feb. 24, 1951; children—Michael John, Jenny Lee. LL.B., Mercer U., 1947. Bar: Ga. bar 1947. Practiced law, Marietta, Ga., 1948-60; judge Juvenile Ct. Cobb County, Ga., 1953-60, Superior Ct. Cobb County, 1961-68, U.S. Dist. Ct. for No. Dist. Ga., Atlanta, 1968-76, chief judge, 1976-79; judge U.S. Circuit Ct. of Appeals for 5th Circuit, 1979—; asst. solicitor gen. Blue Ridge Jud. Circuit, 1948-52. Chmn. Cobb dist. Atlanta council Boy Scouts Am., 1964. Served with AUS, 1943-46. Fellow Am. Bar Found.; mem. State Bar Ga., Am., Atlanta, Cobb Jud. bar assns., Lawyers Club Atlanta, Am. Judicature Soc. Office: US Ct Appeals PO Box 1638 Atlanta GA 30301

HENDERSON, ALICE ELIZABETH, broadcasting company executive; b. Freeport, N.Y., Dec. 12, 1947; d. Harry G.A. and Alice L. (Modin) McManus; m. Robert B. Henderson, Jan. 3, 1973 (div.). Student, Wood Secretarial Sch., N.Y.C., 1966. Editor program practices CBS, Inc., N.Y.C., 1966-71, dir. program practices, 1975-77, v.p., N.Y.C., 1977—; asst. to v.p. Bloomingdale's, N.Y.C., 1972. Trustee AWRT Edn. Found., 1979-80. Mem. Am. Film Inst., Acad. TV Arts and Scis., Hollywood Radio and TV Soc., Am. Advt. Fedn., Am. Women in Radio and TV. Office: CBS Inc 51 W 52d St New York NY 10019

HENDERSON, ARNOLD GLENN, architect, educator; b. Shawnee, Okla., Nov. 10, 1934; s. Henry Glenn and Pearlalee H.; children—Eric Neal, Alex Jon. B.Arch., U. Okla., 1961, B.S. in Archtl. Engring, 1961; M.S. in Architecture, Columbia U., 1964. Asst. prof. architecture U. Ill., Urbana, 1964-68; asso. prof. U. Okla., 1968-73, prof., 1973—; pvt. practice architecture, Norman, Okla., 1975—. Author: Document for an Anonymous Indian, 1974, The Surgeon General's Collection, 1976, (with others) Architecture in Oklahoma, 1978; co-editor: Point Riders Press, 1974—. Chmn. Norman Housing Authority, 1972-77; co-chmn. Norman Community Devel. Steering Com., 1974; mem. Hist. Preservation and Landmark Commn., Guthrie, Okla., 1979-81. Served with U.S. Army, 1953-55. Recipient grants NSF, Nat. Endowment Arts, AIA, Okla. Arts Council, Okla. Humanities Com. Mem. AIA (award of excellence 1976), Soc. Archtl. Historians, Nat. Trust Hist. Preservation, Okla. Hist. Soc., Sigma Tau. Democrat. Presbyterian. Home: 1208 Barkley Ave Norman OK 73071 Office: Sch Architecture U Okla Norman OK 73019

HENDERSON, BRUCE DOOLIN, management executive, educator; b. Nashville, Apr. 30, 1915; s. John B. and Ceacy (Doolin) H.; m. Frances Fleming, Sept. 5, 1949; children: Asta, Bruce Balfour, Ceacy, Bruce Alexander.; m. Bess L. Wilson, Oct. 22, 1983. B.E., Vanderbilt U., 1937; postgrad., Harvard U. Bus. Sch., 1940-41; L.L.D. (hon.), Babson Coll., 1983. Trainee Frigidaire div. Gen. Motors Corp., 1937-38; sales Leland Electric Co., 1938-39; buyer Westinghouse Electric Corp., 1941, asst. purchasing agt., Lima, Ohio, 1942, purchasing agt., Newark, 1943-46, mgr. purchases, stores, Sharon, Pa., 1946-49; asst. to v.p. Westinghouse Electric Co., Pitts., 1950, gen. purchasing agt., 1951, gen. mgr. purchases and traffic, 1952, v.p. purchasing and traffic, 1953-55, v.p., mem. corp. mgmt. com., gen. mgr. air conditioning div., 1955-59; v.p. in charge mgmt. services div. Arthur D. Little, Inc., 1959-60, sr. v.p. charge mgmt. cons. div., 1960-63; sr. v.p. Boston Safe Deposit & Trust Co., 1963-68; founder Boston Cons. Group, Inc., 1963, pres., 1968-80, chmn. bd., 1980—; prof. mgmt. Vanderbilt U. Owen Grad. Sch. Mgmt. Author: Henderson on Corporate Strategy. Clubs: Bellemeade Country, University (Nashville); Duquesne (Pitts.); Union League (Chgo.); (N.Y.C.); Harvard (Boston); St. Croix (V.I.) Country. Home: 110 Christopher Pl Nashville TN Office: One Boston Pl Boston MA 02106 Owen Grad Sch Mgmt Vanderbilt U 21st Ave S Nashville TN Boston Cons Group 200 S Wacker Dr Chicago IL 60606 *It may be that it is better to be born lucky rather than born smart. Whatever I was born with, it was better for me to set goals that tested my ability, even though high hurdles could not always be cleared. When I failed, the most important thing of all was to be able to pick myself up, keep my self-respect, keep my energy, and then to set new goals and try again.*

HENDERSON, CHARLES BROOKE, research company executive; b. Washington, Mar. 13, 1929; s. Robert Neel and Dorothy (Brooke) H.; m. Elizabeth Ann Carter, June 6, 1954; children: Katherine, Roger, Sally. B.S., Purdue U., 1950; S.M. in Chem. Engring, M.I.T., 1952. With Atlantic Research Corp., Alexandria, Va., 1954—, dir. research and tech., 1971-76, v.p., 1976-80, sr. v.p., 1980—, also dir. Active Boy Scouts Am., 1965-69, Girl Scouts U.S.A., 1969-71. Fellow AIAA (asso.); mem. Am. Inst. Chem. Engring., Sigma Xi. Patentee in field. Office: 5390 Cherokee Ave Alexandria VA 22312 *

HENDERSON, CHARLES, JR., educator; b. Lynchburg, Va., Aug. 22, 1923; s. Charles and Rosalie (Florance) H.; m. Ethel Ann Bolton, Aug. 16, 1944 (div.); children: Elizabeth Ann, Charles III, William Abbot, Rosalie Nathan, John Quintus. A.B., Davidson Coll., 1942; M.A., U. N.C., 1947, Ph.D., 1955. Teaching fellow U. N.C., 1942, 46-49; instr. classics N.Y. U., 1950-55; mem. faculty U. N.C., 1955-64; asso. prof. classics, 1958-64, dean student affairs, 1960-63; prof. classics Smith Coll., 1964—, chmn. dept., 1967-74, asst. to pres., 1972-77. Author: (with B.L. Ullman) Latin for Americans, 2 vols, 1968; also articles; Editor: Studies in Honor of B.L. Ullman, 1963. Served to capt. USNR, 1942-46. Mem. Am. Philol. Assn. (sec.-treas. 1962-65), Classical Assn. New Eng., Phi Beta Kappa, Delta Phi Alpha, Sigma Delta Psi, Eta Sigma Phi, Phi Mu Alpha, Sigma Phi Epsilon. Democrat. Episcopalian. Home: York Harbor ME 03911 Office: 76 Elm St Smith Coll Northampton MA 01060

HENDERSON, DAN FENNO, lawyer, educator; b. Chelan, Wash., May 24, 1921; s. Joe and Edna (Fenno) H.; m. Carol Drake Hardin, Sept. 14, 1957; children—Louis, Karen, Gail, Fenno. A.B., Whitman Coll., 1944, LL.D., 1983; A.B., U. Mich., 1945; J.D., Harvard U., 1949; Ph.D. in Polit. Sci, U. Calif., Berkeley, 1955. Bar: bar Wash 1949, Korea 1955, Japan 1955, Calif 1956. Movie, radio censor Dept. Def., Japan, 1946-47; teaching asst. polit. sci. dept. U. Calif., Berkeley, 1949-51; atty. firm Little, LeSourd, Palmer & Scott, Seattle, 1951-52; instr. ext. div. U. Calif., Berkeley, 1952-54; atty. firm Graham James & Rolph, San Francisco, 1955-57, ptnr., Tokyo, 1957-62; ptnr. firm Adachi, Henderson, Miyatake and Fujita, Tokyo, 1973—; Prof. law, dir. Asian law program U. Wash. Sch. Law, 1962—; vis. prof. law Harvard U., 1968-69, Monash U., Melbourne, Australia, 1979, Cambridge (Eng.) U., 1980; cons. Asia Found., 1967—, Battelle Inst., 1969—. Author: Conciliation and Japanese Law, 1965, The Constitution of Japan, It's First Twenty Years, 1969, Foreign Enterprise in Japan, 1973, Village Contracts in Tokugawa, Japan, 1975, Civil Procedure in Japan, 1981; Bd. editors: Jour. Japanese Studies; Contbr. articles in field to profl. jours. Trustee Seattle Art Mus. Served to lt. AUS, 1943-46. Investment fellow Am. Soc. Internat. Law, 1962-64. Mem. Assn. Asian Studies, Am. C. of C. Japan (past sec., dir.), Japanese-Am. Soc. Legal Studies (dir.), Am. Assn. Comparative Study of Law (dir.). Clubs: University (Seattle); Tokyo Lawn Tennis. Home: 632 36th Ave E Seattle WA 98112 Office: U Wash Seattle WA 98105 also CPO Box 96 Tokyo 100 Japan

HENDERSON, DONALD AINSLIE, university dean; b. Cleve., Sept. 7, 1928; s. David Alexander and Grace Eleanor (McMillan) H.; m. Nana Irene Bragg, Sept. 1, 1951; children: Leigh Ainslie, David Alexander, Douglas Bruce. B.A., Oberlin (Ohio) Coll., 1950, D.Sc. (hon.), 1979; M.D., U. Rochester (N.Y.), 1954, D.Sc. (hon.), 1977; M.P.H., Johns Hopkins U., 1960; LL.D. (hon.), Marietta (Ohio) Coll., 1978, D.Sc., U. Ill., 1979, U. Md., 1980, M.D., U. Geneva, 1980, L.H.D., SUNY, 1981. Diplomate: Am. Bd. Preventive Medicine. Intern, then resident Mary Imogene Bassett Hosp., Cooperstown, N.Y., 1954-55, 57-59; chief epidemic intelligence service Center Disease Control, USPHS, Atlanta, 1955-57, chief surveillance sect., 1960-66; chief med. officer smallpox edn. WHO, Geneva, 1966-77; dean Johns Hopkins U. Sch. Hygiene and Pub. Health, 1977—. Contbr. articles to med. jours. Recipient Commendation medal USPHS, 1962, Disting. Service medal, 1976; Ernst Jung prize, 1976; award Govt. India-Indian Soc. Malaria and Other Communicable Diseases, 1975; Rosenthal internat. award for excellence, 1975; George MacDonald medal London Sch. Hygiene and Tropical Medicine, Royal Soc. Tropical Medicine and Hygiene, 1976; Health medal Govt. Afghanistan, 1976; Spl. Albert Lasker Pub. Health Service award for WHO, 1976; Public Welfare medal Nat. Acad. Scis., 1978; Joseph C. Wilson award in internat. affairs, 1978; James D. Bruce Meml. award, 1978; 50th Anniversary Disting. Service award Blue Cross-Blue Shield, 1979; medal for contbns. to health Govt. of Ethiopia, 1979; Outstanding Alumnus award Delta Omega, 1980; Disting. Alumnus award Johns Hopkins U., 1982; Internat. Merit award Gairdner Found., 1983. Hon. fellow Am. Acad. Pediatrics, Royal Coll. Physicians (U.K.); mem. Inst. Medicine (Nat. Acad. Scis.), Am. Public Health Assn., Internat. Epidemiol. Assn., Royal Soc. Tropical Medicine and Hygiene, Indian Soc. Malaria and Other Communicable Diseases. Home: 3802 Greenway Baltimore MD Office: 615 N Wolfe St Baltimore MD 21205

HENDERSON, DONALD MUNRO, geology educator; b. Boston, Nov. 8, 1920; s. William Davis and Margaret (Fessenden) H.; m. Margaret R. Foster, 1948; children: Donald M., Robert W., Peter F., Margaret A., Alexander M. A.B., Brown U., 1943; Ph.D., Harvard U., 1950. Faculty U. Ill., Urbana-Champaign, 1948—, prof. geology specializing in mineralogy, 1969—. Home: 301 W Michigan Ave Urbana IL 61801 Office: 245 NHB Geology 1301 W Green St IL Urbana 61801

HENDERSON, DOUGLAS BOYD, lawyer; b. Pitts., Sept. 21, 1935; s. Arthur G. and Mildred E. (Rickenbach) H.; m. Olivia Lauer, July 6, 1957; children: Scotland Weaver, Keith Arthur, Heather Alice. B.S. in Indsl. Engring., Pa. State U., 1957; J.D. with honors, George Washington U., 1963. Bar: Va. 1962, D.C. 1963. Mfs. agt. firm Arthur G. Henderson & Assos., Pitts., 1957-59; patent agt. Swift & Co., Washington, 1959-62; law clk. to Hon. Donald E. Lane U.S. Ct. Claims, Washington, 1962-63; asso. firm Irons, Birch, Swindler & McKie, Washington, 1963-65; founding partner firm Finnegan, Henderson, Farabow, Garrett & Dunner (and predecessors), Washington, 1965—; chmn. Ct. Appeals for Fed. Cir. Com., 1982-83. Author: Recent Developments in United States Licensing Law; contbr. articles to legal jours. Mem. Internat. Bar Assn.; Mem. Fed. Bar Assn., Va. Bar Assn., ABA (asst. sec. patent, trademark and copyright law sect. 1975-79), D.C. Bar Assn. (chmn. patent, trademark and copyright law sect. 1974-75, mem-council 1981—, chmn. ct. of claims com. 1973-74, dir. 1975-76, trustee, sec. research found 1980-82), U.S. C. of C. (chmn. patent, trademark and copyright council 1980-82), Am. Patent Law Assn., U.S. Trademark Assn., Patent and Trademark Inst. Can., Patent Office Soc., Patent Lawyers Club, Am. Judicature Soc., Am. Arbitration Assn., Licensing Execs. Soc., Christian Legal Soc., Supreme Ct. Hist. Soc., Tech. Transfer Soc., Phi Gamma Delta, Delta Theta Phi. Presbyterian (elder 1980—). Clubs: Touchdown, University, International (Washington). Home: 6715 Wemberly Way McLean VA 22101 Office: 1775 K St Washington DC 20006 *I have sought to keep my life and my daily efforts in proper perspective by remembering that we are admonished to seek first the kingdom of God and his righteousness.*

HENDERSON, DWIGHT FRANKLIN, university dean, educator; b. Austin, Tex., Aug. 14, 1937; s. Ottis Franklin and Leona (Bady) H.; m. Connie Chorlton, Dec. 24, 1966; 1 dau., Patricia Ross. B.A., U. Tex., 1959, M.A., 1961, Ph.D., 1966. Asso. prof. Ind. U., Ft. Wayne, 1966-68, chmn. dept. history, 1968-71, asso. prof. history, 1971-80, chmn. arts and scis., 1971-76, dean arts and letters, 1976-80, acting chancellor, 1978-79; prof. history, dean Coll. Social and Behavioral Scis. U. Tex., San Antonio, 1980—. Author: Private Journals of Georgiana Gholson Walker, 1963, Courts for a New Nation, 1971. Bd. dirs. Ft. Wayne Philharmonic Orch., 1973-74, Public Transp. Corp. Ft. Wayne, 1975-77. Served with AUS, 1962-64. Tex. Soc. Colonial Dames fellow, 1964-65, 65-66; Ind. U. fellow, 1968, 70, 72. Mem. Orgn. Am. Historians, So. Hist. Assn., Delta Sigma Rho, Phi Alpha Theta. Home: 2410 Shadow Cliff San Antonio TX 78232 Office: U Tex San Antonio TX 78285

HENDERSON, EDWARD NEIL, gas co. exec.; b. Andalusia, Ala., Dec. 10, 1920; s. J. V. and Maude (McNair) H.; m. Virginia Estelle Whatley, Apr. 3, 1948; children—Robert E., Bruce C. B.S. in Mech. Engring, Auburn U., 1943, 1947. Jr. engr. Ark. La. Gas Co., Shreveport, 1947-48, engr. gen. engring. dept., 1948-52, asst. supt. natural gas div., 1952-53, spl. assignment ops., 1953, acting chief engr., 1953-57, v.p., chief engr., from 1957; now exec. v.p.; v.p., dir. Arla Air Conditioning, 1957—; pres., dir. Ark. Cement Corp., 1958—; dir. Ark. Exploration Co., Ark. La. Fin. Corp., Arkla Chem. Corp., Arkla Industries Inc. Pres., bd. mem. English Speaking Union; co-chmn. United Fund campaign; chmn. indsl. div. United Fund; mem. City Charter Study Task Force, Task Force on Planning and Zoning; bd. dirs. Lyric Ball, Parents League, Shreveport Opera; mem.; Met. Planning Commn. Mayor's Adv. Fiscal Policy Com.; bd. dirs., exec. v.p. Shreveport Symphony; pres. Shreveport Opera. Served with C.E. U.S. Army, World War II. Mem. Am. Gas Assn., Ind. Petroleum Assn. Am., Air Force Assn., Am. Legion, Mid-Continent Oil and Gas Assn., So. Gas Assn. C. of C. (govt. affairs com.). Republican. Presbyterian. Clubs: Shreveport Country (dir., treas.), Shreveport, Cotillion (dir., pres.), Ambassadors (dir.), Pierremont Oaks Tennis, Racket, Rotary. Office: PO Box 21734 Shreveport LA 71151 *

HENDERSON, EDWARD SHELTON, oncologist; b. Ventura, Calif., July 19, 1932; s. Edward and Leigh Claiborn (Shelton) H.; m. Barbara Wunschmann, Oct. 1, 1970; children: Peter, Emilie, Jacqueline, John. B.A., Stanford U., 1953, M.D., 1956. Intern, then resident in internal medicine Los Angeles County Gen. Hosp., 1956-59; fellow hematology, instr. medicine U. So. Calif. Med. Sch., 1959-61; clin. asso. Nat. Cancer Inst., NIH, Bethesda, Md., 1961-63, sr. investigator, lab. chem. pharmacology, 1963-65, head leukemia service, medicine br., 1965-72; chief dept. med. oncology Roswell Park Meml. Inst., Buffalo, 1973—; prof. medicine, chief div. med. oncology SUNY Med. Sch., Buffalo; also co-chmn. cancer edn. com.; bd. dirs., chmn. chemotherapy com. Cancer and Leukemia Group B; med. adv. panel Leukemia Soc. Am., 1976-81, 84—; prin. investigator (Clin. Cancer Research Center), 1973—; sci. adv. bd. Am. Cancer Soc., 1978—. Author articles, chpts. in books.; Co-editor: (with Fred Gunz) Leukemia; asso. editor: Med. and Pediatric Oncology; editorial bd.: Leukemia Research. Served with USPHS, 1961-64. Mem. Am. Fedn. Clin. Research, Am. Soc. Clin. Investigation, Am. Soc. Hematology, Am. Soc. Clin. Oncology, Am. Assn. Cancer Research, Internat. Soc. Exptl. Hematology, Assn. Gnotobiology, Transplanation Soc. Address: Dept Med Oncology Roswell Park Meml Inst Buffalo NY 14263

HENDERSON, EDWIN HAROLD, clergyman; b. Pittsburgh, Tex., Sept. 17, 1927; s. Ether Chaney and Myrtle (Davis) H.; m. Velma Jean Smith, June 2, 1948; children—Steve Edwin, Cherilyn Cheree, Sharon Leigh. B.A. cum laude, Tex. Christian U., 1954; B.D., Southwestern Baptist Theol. Sem., 1957, Th.D., 1963. Ordained to ministry Baptist Ch., 1945; pastor First Bapt. Ch., Hydro, Okla., 1947-51, Parker St. Bapt. Ch., Mineral Wells, Tex., 1951- 53, First Bapt. Ch. Trinity Heights, Dallas, 1953-60; chmn. dept. Bible Jacksonville (Tex.) Bapt. Coll., 1960-61; pastor Central Bapt. Ch., Lubbock, Tex., 1961-75, Bethel Bapt. Ch., Dallas, 1975-77; founder Inst. Bautista Biblico de Lubbock, 1971; founder, dir. Upreach Ministries, Dallas. Author: Now Abideth Faith, 1962, Roman Dogma and Bible Doctrine, 1964, Bible Doctrines Baptists Believe, 1964, The Triumph of Trust; Contbr. articles to profl. jours. Mem. Bapt. Missionary Assn. Tex. (pres.), Bapt. Missionary Assn. Am. (pres. 1966-68, writer Adult Sunday Sch. Quar. 1957—), Plains Bapt. Assn. (pres. 1965-70). Home: 4838 Chilton Dr Dallas TX 75227

HENDERSON, ERNEST, III, business exec.; b. Boston, Oct. 25, 1924; s. Ernest and Mary G. (Stephens) H.; m. Mary Louise Campbell, Dec. 31, 1953; children—Ernest Flagg IV, Roberta Campbell. S.B., Harvard, 1944, M.B.A., 1949; L.H.D. (hon.), Bard Coll., 1976. With Sheraton Corp. Am., 1946-69, dir., 1953-69, treas., 1956-63, pres., 1963-69, chief exec. officer, 1967-69; pres. Henderson Houses Am., Inc. (and affiliates), Wellesley Hills, Mass., Sudbury Pines Nursing Home; pres., dir. Vaqueria Ranch (S.A.), Paraguay; treas., dir. Kyoto Restaurants, Inc.; dir. Pan Am. Financiera (S.A.), Asuncion, Paraguay, Hotels del Bahia, Paraguay; vice chmn. bd. Solid State Tech., Inc. Mem. permanent com. Harvard Class, 1946; permanent sec. Harvard U. Bus. Sch. Class, 1949; Republican jr. nat. committeeman, 1956-57; mem. Wellesley Town Meeting, 1970—; grand marshal Wellesley Vets. Day Parade, 1978; Trustee Northeastern U., Edmunds Trust, Henderson Estate, Henderson Found., George B. Henderson Found., Boston Biomed. Research Inst.; trustee, mem. exec. com., vice chmn. bd. Bard Coll.; trustee, vice chmn. bd. Simon's Rock Early Coll.; bd. dirs. Wellesley Community Center, Inc. Served as lt. (j.g.) USNR, World War II. Named hon. Big Chief Many Tepees and blood brother Creek Indian Nation. Mem. Chief Exec.'s Forum, Marlowe-Shakespeare Soc. (dir.), Mensa. Clubs: Wellesley Country; Harvard Business School Assn. (Boston) (past pres.); Circumnavigators.). Home: 171 Edmunds Rd Wellesley Hills MA 02181 Office: 892 Worcester St Wellesley MA 02181

HENDERSON, FLORENCE (FLORENCE HENDERSON BERNSTEIN), actress, singer; b. Dale, Ind., Feb. 14, 1934; d. Joseph and Elizabeth Elder H.; m. Ira Bernstein, Jan. 9, 1956; 4 children. Attended, St. Francis Acad., Owensboro, Ky; studied at, Am. Acad. Dramatic Arts. Broadway and stage debut in: Wish You Were Here, 1952; appeared in: on tour Oklahoma!, 1952-53 and at, N.Y.C. Center, 1953; The Great Waltz, Los Angeles Civic Light Opera Assn., 1953; played title role in: Fanny at, Majestic, N.Y.C., 1954; appeared in Oldsmobile indsl. shows, 1958-61; toured in: The Sound of Music, 1961; appeared on Broadway in: The Girl Who Came to Supper, 1963; appeared in: revival of South Pacific, 1967; toured in: Annie Get Your Gun, 1974; appeared in: Sound of Music with, Los Angeles Civic Light Opera Assn., 1978; movie Song of Norway, 1970; appeared: on TV in Sing Along, 1958, The Today Show, 1959-60, The Brady Bunch, 1969-75, The Brady Bunch Hour, 1977; numerous other TV appearances include Brady Brides, 1981, Hart to Hart, 1981, Fantasy Island, 1981, 83, Alice, 1983; appeared in: TV film & series The Love Boat, 1976, 83. Recipient Sarah Siddons award. Office: care Katz-Gallin-Morey Enterprises Inc 9255 Sunset Blvd Suite 1115 Los Angeles CA 90069

HENDERSON, FRANK ELLIS, state supreme court justice; b. Miller, S.D., Apr. 2, 1928; s. Frank Ellis and Hilda (Bogstad) H.; m. Norma Jean Johnson, Dec. 27, 1956; children: Frank Ellis, III, Kimberly, Patrick, Andrea, Eric, John, Anastasia, Matthew. LL.B., U. S.D., 1951. Bar: Fed. Dist. Ct. bar for Dist. S.D 1954. Practiced law, Pennington County, S.D., 1953-74; judge 7th Jud. Circuit, State of S.D., 1975-78; justice S.D. Supreme Ct., 1979—; mem. S.D. Senate, 1965-66, 69-70. Served to 1st lt. inf. U.S. Army, 1951-53; Korea. Decorated Bronze Star. Mem. Pennington County Bar Assn., S.D. State Bar Assn., Am. Legion, VFW (nat. legal staff 1960-61), DAV (state staff judge adv. 1963-64, post comdr. 1962), Phi Delta Theta. Republican. Roman Catholic. Office: State Capitol Bldg Pierre SD 57501 *

HENDERSON, FREDERICK BISHOP, office equipment manufacturer executive; b. Atlantic Beach, Fla., May 11, 1941; s. Martin Madden and Martha (Dollison) H.; m. Emily Marie Danford, Nov. 21, 1970; children: Mary H., Matthew B., Liane G., Julie M., Frederick B. B.S., Jacksonville U., 1964. Vice pres., regional gen. mgr. Bus. Systems Group Xerox Corp., Santa Ana, Calif., 1977-79, v.p. mktg. bus. systems, Rochester, N.Y., 1979-80, sr. v.p. field ops. Bus. Systems Group, 1980-81, sr. v.p. customer services Bus. Systems Group, 1981-83, v.p. quality office, Stamford, Conn., 1983—. Vice chmn. United Way Orange County, Calif., 1978; mem. Hillside Children's Center Com., Rochester, 1982-83. Presbyterian (trustee 1983). Office: Xerox Corp PO Box 1600 Stamford CT 06904

HENDERSON, GEORGE, educational sociologist, educator; b. Hurtsboro, Ala., June 18, 1932; s. Kidd Large and Lula Mae (Crawford) H.; m. Barbara Ann Beard, Aug. 9, 1952; children: George, Michele, Faith, Lea, Joy, Lisa, Dawn. Student, Mich. State U., 1950-52; B.A., Wayne State U., 1957, M.A., 1959, Ph.D. in Ednl. Sociology, 1965. Social casework Ch. Youth Service, Detroit, 1957-59; social economist Detroit Housing Commn., 1960-61; community services dir. Detroit Urban League, 1961-63; program dir. Mayor's Com. for Detroit Youth, 1963-64; asst. dir. delinquency control tng. center Wayne State U., 1964-65; asst. dir. intercultural relations Detroit Public Schs., 1965-66, asst. to supt., 1966-67; asso. prof. sociology and edn. U. Okla., 1967-69, Sylvan N. Goldman prof. human relations, prof. edn., asso. prof. sociology, chmn. dept. human relations, 1969—; vis. prof. sociology Langston U., 1969-70; disting. vis. prof. U.S. Air Force Acad., 1980-81; cons. in field. Author: Foundations of American Education, 1970, Teachers Should Care, 1970, America's Other Children, 1971, To Live in Freedom, 1972, Education for Peace, 1973, Human Relations, 1974, Human Relations in the Military, 1975, A Religious Foundation of Human Relations, 1977, Introduction to American Education, 1978, Understanding and Counseling Ethnic Minorities, 1979, Police Human Relations, 1981, Transcultural Health Care, 1981, Physician-Patient Communication, 1981, The Human Rights of Professional Helpers, 1983, The State of Black Oklahoma. Recipient Outstanding Achievement award Human Relations Assn., 1975, Human Relations award Met. Human Relations Commn. Nashville, 1979. Mem. Am. Sociol. Assn., Nat. Assn. Human Rights Workers, Assn. Black Sociologists, AAUP, Assn. Supervision and Curriculum Devel., Inter-Univ. Seminar on Armed Forces and Soc., Internat. Soc. Law Enforcement and Criminal Justice Instrs., Omicron Delta Kappa, Delta Tau Kappa, Kappa Alpha Psi. Democrat. Baptist. Home: 2616 Osborne Dr Norman OK 73069 Office: 601 Elm Norman OK 73019

HENDERSON, GERALD GORDON LEWIS, oil company executive; b. Vernon, C., Can., June 10, 1926; s. John Alexander and Marion Colles (Brehon) H.; m. Beverley May Godwin, Oct. 16, 1954; children: Patrica Lynn, Gail Karen, Tara Anne. B.Sc., McGill U., 1948, M.Sc., 1950; Ph.D., Princeton U., 1953. Geologist dept. mines, Province of B.C., 1950-53; with Chevron Can. Resources Ltd., Calgary, Alta., Can., 1953—, chief geologist, 1963-67, v.p., 1967-78, sr. v.p., 1978-81, pres., 1981—, also dir. Recipient Alta. Soc. Petroleum Geologists Medal of Merit, 1954. Fellow Royal Soc. Can., Geol. Assn. Can.; mem. Can. Soc. Petroleum Geologists, Am. Assn. Petroleum Geologists, Assn. Profl. Engrs., Geologists and Geophysicists of Alta. Home: 1111 Beverley Blvd Calgary AB Canada T2V 2C4 Office: 500 5th Ave SW Calgary AB Canada T2P 0L6

HENDERSON, GIRARD BROWN, corp. exec.; b. Bklyn., Feb. 25, 1905; s. Alexander D. and Ella (Brown) H.; m. Theodore Huntington, Jan. 28, 1927 (div. Aug. 1960); children—Theodora Ives, Dariel Henderson; m. Mary Hollingsworth, 1965. Grad., Storn King Sch., Cornwall-on-Hudson, N.Y., 1923. Comml. transp. pilot, 1931—; founder, chmn. bd. Alexander Dawson, Inc., 1946—; chmn. Dawson Corp., 1959—, Blue Channel Corp., 1961—. Founder, chmn. Alexander Dawson Sch., Lafayette, Colo.; chmn. bd. trustees Alexander Dawson Found. Clubs: U Mont. Grizzly Riders (Missoula); Roundup Riders of the Rockies (Denver). Address: PO Box 19720 Las Vegas NV 89132

HENDERSON, GORDON DESMOND, lawyer; b. Oakland, Calif., May 25, 1930. A.B. magna cum laude, Harvard U., 1951, J.D. magna cum laude, 1957. Bar: D.C. 1957, N.Y. 1965. Partner Barrett, Smith, Schapiro, Simon & Armstrong, N.Y.C., 1965-79, Weil, Gotshal & Manges, 1979—; spl. counsel to SEC, 1962-64; chmn. policy adv. group. N.Y. Joint Legis. Commn. to Study N.Y. State Tax Law, 1982—. Mem.: Harvard Law Rev, 1955-57. Mem. Scarsdale Planning Commn., 1975-77; pres. Civic Assn. Hollin Hills, Alexandria, Va., 1962. Mem. Assn. Bar City N.Y. (chmn. com. on corp. law 1969-72), N.Y. State Bar Assn. (chmn. tax sect. 1979), ABA, Am. Coll. Tax Counsel, Am. Law Inst., Phi Beta Kappa. Home: Sunset Ln Rye NY 10580 Office: 767 Fifth Ave New York NY 10153

HENDERSON, HAROLD LAWRENCE, tire and rubber company executive; b. Wayne County, Iowa, Nov. 11, 1935; s. Clell Dallas H. and Martha Mason Henderson; m. JoAnn Wyoma Garber, June 27, 1958; 1 son, Donald Paul. B.A., U. Chgo., 1962, J.D., 1964. Bar: Ill. 1966. Exec. v.p., gen. counsel Firestone Co., Akron, Ohio, 1982—; assoc. Cravath, Swaine & Moore, N.Y.C., 1964-66, Isham, Lincoln & Beale, Chgo., 1966-67, Mayer, Brown & Platt, 1967-68; resource group counsel Gen. Dynamics, Chog., 1968-70; asst. counsel Firestone Co., Akron, Ohio, 1970-78, asst. gen. counsel, 1978-80, v.p., gen. counsel, 1980-82; DIR. Akron Priority Corp. Mem. Akron area Salvation Army, 1978—. Served with USAF, 1954-57; ETO. Clubs: Firestone Country (Akron); Union (Cleve.); Silver Lake Country (Ohio). Home: 370 Wyoga Lake Blvd Stow OH 44224 Office: Firestone Tire & Rubber Co 1200 Firestone Pkwy Akron OH 44317

HENDERSON, HARRY BRINTON, JR., author, editor; b. Kittanning, Pa., Sept. 9, 1914; s. Harry Brinton and Sallie Campbell (Findley) H.; m. Beatrice Conford, 1937; children—Albert K., Harry Brinton III (dec.), Joseph P. B.S., Pa. State Coll., 1936. Reporter various Pa. newspapers, 1936-40; contbr. to Argosy, Collier's, Cosmopolitan, Redbook, Harper's, Readers Digest, others, 1956—; with World Wide Med. Press, also Med. Tribune and Hosp. Tribune, N.Y.C., 1956—, editor-in-chief, 1971-79. Author: (with Sam Shaw and H.C. Morris) War in Our Time, 1942, (with Romare Bearden) Six Black Masters of American Art, 1972, History of America's Black Artists, 1984-85. Mem. Author's Guild. Home: 18 Franklin Ave Croton-on-Hudson NY 10520

HENDERSON, HERSCHEL BRADFORD, publishing executive; b. Waltham, Mass., July 10, 1929; s. Herschel Clifford and Lucy E. (Sturtevant) H. B.A., New Sch. for Social Research, 1959. Reporter Am. Banker, N.Y.C., 1959-62, reporter, news editor, asso. editor, 1963-64, mng. editor, 1964-73, v.p., 1973-76, editor, 1976-82, dir. product devel., 1982—; reporter N.Y. Post, 1962-63. Served with USN, 1951-54. Mem. N.Y. Fin. Writers Assn. Democrat. Office: Am Banker One State St Plaza New York NY 10004

HENDERSON, HORACE EDWARD, real estate and management consultant; b. Henderson, N.C.; s. T. Brantley and Maude (Duke) H.; m. Vera S. Schubert; children by previous marriage: Terri Kelley, Elizabeth Smith. Student, Coll. William and Mary, 1934-37, Yale U., 1941-42. Owner Henderson Real Estate & Ins., Williamsburg, Va., 1947-52; coordinator Nat. Automobile Dealers Assn., Washington, 1954-56; dir. gen. World Peace Through Law Center, Geneva, 1964-69; exec. dir. World Assn. Judges, 1968-69; pres. Community Methods, Inc., 1969-76; chmn. Congl. Speaker Reform Com., Washington, 1976; exec. v.p. Am. Lawmakers Assn., Washington, 1977; chmn. bd. Henderson Real Estate, McLean, Va., 1964-66; pres. Williamsburg Vacation Resort, Inc., 1983—; Adv. bd. Mut. Security Agy., 1952-53; mem. Pres.'s Conf. on Indsl. Safety, 1952-53; exec. com. U.S. Com for UN, 1954; dir. Nat. Citizens Com. for Hoover Report, 1954; indsl. adv. com. Fed. Civil Def. Adminstrn., 1952-53; cons. to dir. ICA, 1956; dir. spl. liaison, spl. asst. dep. under sec. state, Washington, 1958, dep. asst. sec. state internat. orgn. affairs, 1959-60; dir. Exile Orgns. Free Europe Com., 1962; U.S. del. to ILO, UNESCO, FAO, WHO, ECOSOC, UN. Mem. Republican Nat. Com., 1962-64; chmn. Va. Rep. party, 1962-64, Americans for Asian Security and Freedom, 1961; campaign dir. Am. Nationalities for Nixon-Lodge, 1960; Rep. candidate for Congress, 1956, for lt. gov. Va., 1957; permanent chmn. Va. Rep. Conv., 1957; asst. nat. dir. Rockefeller for Pres. Campaign, 1964, Scranton for Pres. Campaign, 1964; ind. Candidate for U.S. Senator, 1972; mem. Williamsburg (Va.) City Council, 1948-50; chmn. Com. Against Recognition Red Hungary, 1963; World vice chmn. Operation Brotherhood, 1954-55; owner Powhatan Hist. Co., Williamsburg, Va., 1957; chmn. Conv. for Peaceful Settlement Internat. Disputes, 1975-77; pres. Internat. Domestic Devel. Corps, 1975; chmn. Assn. for Devel. Edn., Washington, 1978-80; Trustee Valley Forge Found., 1952-55, Jr. C. of C. War Meml. Hdqrs. Served from pvt. to capt., C.E. AUS, 1942-46. Recipient spl. citizenship award Am. Heritage Found., 1953; named outstanding jaycee of World, 1954. Mem. Nat. Acad. Disting. Ams. (chmn. 1979—), Jaycees (internat. v.p. 1951), Jr. C. of C. (nat. pres. 1952-53), U.S. C. of C. (dir. 1954), Sigma Alpha Epsilon. Presbyn. Club: Yale. Visited 47 countries organizing young men's civic groups, 1953-54. Home: 1136 York Ln Virginia Beach VA 23451 Office: 210 Laskin Rd Suite 5 Virginia Beach VA 23451 *As my father always told me, "Life is not getting what you want, but making the best of what you get."*

HENDERSON, HOWARD DEWEESE, oil and gas consultant; b. Eminence, Mo., June 7, 1907; s. William Nathan and Fidelia Frances (DeWeese) H.; m. Marie Chloe Tackett, Aug. 19, 1930; children: Elizabeth Dee Babcock. Student, Draughton's Bus. Coll., 1926, Harvard U. Bus. Sch., 1951. With Sands Petroleum Co., 1926, White Eagle Oil & Refining Co., 1926-27, Skelly Oil Co., 1927-30, Continental Oil Co., 1930-46; with Sohio Petroleum Co., 1946-56, coordinator fgn. exploration, 1955-56; with Trunkline Gas Co., 1956—, sr. v.p., 1971-72; pres. Pan Eastern Exploration Co., 1971-72; sr. v.p. Panhandle Eastern Pipe Line Co., 1971-72; oil and gas cons., 1972—. Mem. Harris County Grand Jury Assn. Mem. Houston Landmen's Assn. (past pres.), Tex. Mid-Continent Oil and Assn., Interstate Oil Compact Commn., 25 Year Club Petroleum Industry, Am. Petroleum Inst. Presbyterian. Clubs: Lakeside Country (past pres.), Houston, Petroleum, Harvard Bus. Sch. Home: 3825 Overbrook Ln Houston TX 77027 Office: PO Box 27553 Houston TX 77227

HENDERSON, HUBERT PLATT, educator; b. Milford, Conn., Aug. 24, 1918; s. Archibald Forbes and Harriet A. (Platt) H.; m. Georgia Bryan Logan, Aug. 30, 1947; children: Douglas Scott, Gordon Lyon, David Brooks. A.B., U. N.C., 1941, M.A., 1950, Ph.D., 1962. Instr. music U. N.C., 1946-51; dir. bands U. Mont., 1954-55; asso. prof., dir. instrumental music U. Md., 1955-65; chmn. dept. music U. Ky., Lexington, 1965-66, dir. Sch. Fine Arts, also assoc. dean. Coll. Arts and Scis., 1966-72; Dir. Office Fine Arts Extension, 1972—; music cons. Ky. Arts commn., 1967-76; dir. Am. Bandmasters Assn. Research Center, U. Md., 1964-65. Founding editor: Jour. Band Research, 1964-66; Contbr. articles and revs. to periodicals, also material to music edn. source books. Served with USAAF, 1941-46; Served with USAF, 1951-53. Mem. Am. Bandmasters Assn. (dir. 1964-66), Am. Musical. Soc. (editor newsletter 1974-76), Coll. Music Soc., Phi Mu Alpha, Kappa Kappa Psi. Episcopalian. Home: 925 Albany Circle Lexington KY 40502

HENDERSON, JACK (WAYNE HENDERSON), artist, art educator; b. Kenosha, Wis., Mar. 12, 1931; s. Linton Oliver and Dorothy Ellen (Howery) H. B.F.A., Kansas City Art Inst. and Sch. Design, U. Mo., 1951, M.F.A., 1952; postgrad., Ecole des Beaux Arts, Paris, 1952-53, Art Students League, N.Y.C., 1955-58. Assoc. prof. Moore Coll. Art, Phila., 1967—; instr. Art Students League, N.Y.C., 1975—; mem. Edwin Austin Abbey Mural Fellowship Bd., NAD. (Recipient Goldsmith prize Am. Watercolor Soc. 1959, Clarke prize NAD 1967), One-man shows include, NAD, 1968, Ranger Fund Exhbn., 1974, group shows include, Pa. Acad. Fine Arts, 1959, 61, Am. Watercolor Soc. Ann., N.Y.C., 1969-70; represented in permanent collections, NAD, N.Y.C., Nat. Portrait Gallery, London, Am. Acad. Rome, Nat. Portrait Gallery, Smithsonian Instn., Washington, Curtis Inst. Music, Phila. Fulbright scholar, 1952-53; Pulitzer fellow, 1955; Abbey fellow Am. Acad. Rome, 1963-65. Mem. NAD, Am. Watercolor Soc., Nat. Soc. Mural Painters, Art Students League. Home: 118 Remsen St Brooklyn NY 11201

HENDERSON, JAMES ALAN, engine company executive; b. South Bend, Ind., July 26, 1934; s. John William and Norma (Wilson) H.; m. Mary Evelyn Kriner, June 20, 1959; children: James Alan, John Stuart, Jeffrey Todd, Amy Brenton. A.B., Princeton U., 1956; Baker scholar, Harvard U., 1961-63. With Scott Foresman & Co., Chgo., 1962; staff mem. Am. Research & Devel. Corp., Boston, 1963; faculty Harvard Bus. Sch., 1963; asst. to chmn. Cummins Engine Co., Inc., Columbus, Ind., 1964-65, v.p. mgmt. devel., 1965-69, v.p. personnel, 1969-70, v.p. ops., 1970-71, exec. v.p., 1971-75, exec. v.p., chief operating officer, 1975-77, pres., 1977—, also dir.; dir. Cummins Engine Found., Ind. Bell Telephone Co., Indpls., Inland Steel Co., Chgo., Hayes-Albion Corp., Jackson, Mich., Ameritech, Chgo. Author: Creative Collective Bargaining, 1965. Pres. Jr. Achievement, Columbus, 1967-69; gen. chmn. Bartholomew County United Fund Campaign, 1970; trustee Princeton U.; bd. dirs. Culver Ednl. Found., Heritage Fund of Bartholomew County, Inc. Served to lt. USNR, 1956-61. Mem. Columbus Area C. of C. (pres. 1973, adv. com. 1974). Presbyn. (elder). Home: 4228 Riverside Dr Columbus IN 47201 Office: Cummins Engine Co Inc Box 3005 Columbus IN 47201

HENDERSON, JAMES ALEXANDER, financial and banking executive; b. N.Y.C., Feb 6, 1921; s. James A. and Charlotte (Fisher) H.; m. Jean Conway, June 16, 1951; children: Elizabeth Barrera, Hilary Anne, James Alexander III, John Geoffrey. A.B., Hamilton Coll., 1941; postgrad., Columbia, 1946-47. With Gen. Electric Co., 1941-42; with Am. Express Co., 1947-82, asst. v.p., 1954-57, v.p., 1958-63, sr. v.p., 1964-66, treas., 1966—, exec. v.p., 1968-82; chmn. bd., dir. Am. Express Pub. Corp., 1968-80; pres., dir. Am. Express Can., Inc., 1975-82; affiliate mem. World Tourism Orgn. Bd. mgrs. Madison Sq. Boys Club; trustee Knox Sch.; former trustee Hamilton Coll. Served with AUS, 1942-46; ETO. Decorated Bronze Star. Mem. Internat. Golf Assn. Democrat. Episcopalian. Clubs: River, University (N.Y.C.); Nissequogue Golf (gov.), Turf and Field). Office: American Express Plaza New York NY 10004

HENDERSON, JAMES BROOKE, oil company executive; b. Washington, Feb. 26, 1926; s. Robert Neel and Dorothy (Brooke) H.; m. Joan Yvonne Niksch, Feb. 3, 1948; children: Janet, Robert. B.S., Purdue U., 1946, Ph.D., 1949. With Shell Chem. Co., 1949-72, gen. mgr. indsl. chems. div., 1966-69, v.p., 1969-72; with Shell Oil Co., 1972-77, v.p. mktg., 1974-75, v.p. oil products, 1975-77; with Shell Internat. Petroleum Co., Lt., London, 1977-79, dir., 1978-79; exec. v.p., dir. Shell Oil Co., Houston, 1979—; pres. Shell Chem. Co., 1979-83; dir. Nat. Gypsum Co.; Chmn., bd. dirs. Am. Indsl. Health Council; bd. dirs. Am. Petroleum Inst.; bd. govs. Purdue Found. Mem. NAM (vice-chmn., dir.), Chem. Mfrs. Assn. (dir., exec. com.), Am. Chem. Soc., Am. Inst. Chem. Engrs. Clubs: Lakeside Country, Lochinvar Golf, Heritage; Sunningdale Golf (Eng.). *

HENDERSON, JAMES HENRY MERIWETHER, educator; b. Falls Church, Va., Aug. 10, 1917; s. Edwin Bancroft and Mary (Meriwether) H.; m. Betty Alice Francis, Mar. 28, 1948; children—Edith Ellen, Dena R., James F., Edwin B. II. B.S., Howard U., 1939; M.Ph., U. Wis., 1941, Ph.D., 1943. Jr. chemist Badger Ordnance Works, Baraboo, Wis., 1942-43; research asst. U. Chgo., 1943-45; research asso. Carver Found., Tuskegee (Ala.) Inst., 1945-48, asst. prof., 1950-54, assoc. prof., 1954-57, prof., 1957—, chmn. dept. biology, 1957-68, chmn. div. natural scis., 1968—; dir. Carver Research Found., 1968-75, sr. research prof. biology, chmn. div. natural sci., 1975—; research fellow Calif. Inst. Tech., 1948-50; NSF fellow Le Phytotron-Gif-sur-Yvette, France, 1961-62; commr. CUEBS, 1967-70. Contbr. articles to profl. jours. Vice-chmn. Macon County (Ala.) Bd. Edn., 1968-74; Trustee Stillman Coll. Recipient Alumni Achievement award Howard U., 1975. Fellow AAAS; mem. Am. Soc. Plant Physiologists (chmn. So. sect. 1970), Nat. Inst. Sci., N.Y. Acad. Sci., Soc. for Freedom in Sci., Soc. Devel. Biology, Tissue Culture Assn., Phi Beta Kappa, Sigma Xi, Phi Sigma, Gamma Alpha, Beta Kappa Chi. Presbyn. (clk. session, moderator). Home: PO Box 247 Tuskegee Institute AL 36088 *One of the soundest precepts of nature is the constant change in function and form in living organisms by which ALL species eventually do one of two things: evolve into new forms or become extinct. Man is no exception to this rule, unless by his own undoing he prevents the laws of nature and God from prevailing. Is this in itself a part of the plan of the laws of nature and God?*

HENDERSON, JAMES MARVIN, advertising agency executive; b. Atlanta, Mar. 28, 1921; s. Isaac Harmon and Ruth (Ashley) H.; m. Donna Fern Baade, Apr. 28, 1945; children: Linda Dee, James Marvin, Deborah Fanchon. Student, Furman U., 1939-40, Clemson Coll., 1940-42; also night classes, N.Y.U., 1943-44; B.S., U. Denver, 1946; grad., Advanced Mgmt. Program, Harvard, 1956. Sales supr. Gen. Foods Corp., N.Y.C., 1942-44; account exec. Curt Freiberger Advt. Agy., Denver, 1944-46; pres. Henderson Advt., Inc., Greenville, S.C., 1946—; now chmn. bd., chief exec. officer; pres. Henderson-Saussy Advt., New Orleans, 1966-69; dir. Citizens & So. Nat. Bank, First Fed. Savs. and Loan Assn., Greenville., 1st Fed. of S.C.; Spl. asst. to postmaster gen., 1969-70; adj. prof. Clemson U. and Furman U. Mem. Greenville Youth Commn., 1953-54; chmn. Leadership Greenville Com., 1975, Eisenhower campaign Greenville County, 1952; Republican candidate for lt. gov. S.C., 1970; S.C. state chmn. com. to Re-elect Pres., 1972; adv. bd. Campaign '76 for Pres. Ford, 1976; pres. Greenville Heart Assn.; pres., bd. dirs. Greenville Mental Hygiene Clinic, United Fund.; bd. dirs. Clemson Found.; trustee Converse Coll. Served with AUS, World War II. Named Young Man of Year, Greenville, 1954. Mem. S.C. Jr. C. of C. (past dir.), Greenville Jr. C. of C. (past pres.), Greater Greenville C. of C. (past pres.), Young President's Orgn. (chmn. S.E. chpt.), Greenville Advt. Council (past pres.), Am. Assn. Advt. Agys. (vice chmn. SE region 1954, chmn. SE council 1955, client service com. 1963, nat. dir. 1964, gov. Eastern region 1965, sec.-treas. 1971). Methodist. Lodge: Kiwanis (past pres.). Home: Route 7 Hickory Ln Greenville SC 29609 Office: 60 Pelham Pointe Greenville SC 29615

HENDERSON, JAMES MICHAEL, electric utility executive; b. Detroit, Sept. 4, 1922; m. Joan Kuhns; children: Michael, Kathleen, John, Jan, Timothy. B.S. in Elec. Engring., U. Ill. System studies engr. Detroit Edison Co., 1947-53; electric utility application engr. Gen. Electric Co., 1953-63; v.p. Middle West Services Co., 1963-68; dir. systems engring. div. Commonwealth Assocs., 1968-70; v.p. San Diego Gas & Electric Co., 1970-78; pres., chief exec. officer Central La. Electric Co. Inc., Pineville, 1978—; dir. Guaranty Bank & Trust Co., Alexandria, La., Southeastern Electric Exchange. Author numerous tech. publs. Bd. dirs. St. Frances Cabrini Hosp., Alexandria; pres. Atakapas council Boy Scouts Am., Alexandria. Served as ensign USN, 1943-46; PTO. Home: 4002 Wellington Blvd Alexandria LA 71301 Office: Central Louisiana Electric Co Inc 415 Main St Pineville LA 71360

HENDERSON, JOHN B., bus. exec.; b. Sydney, Australia, Apr. 6, 1925; s. Sydney Woodburn and Rosalind (Funch) Batty; children—Anita, Susan, Sophie. A.B., Brown U., 1946; LL.B., Harvard U., 1949. Bar: D.C., Va., Pa., R.I. bars. With Office Gen. Counsel, Dept. Def., 1950-55; with legal dept. Aluminum Co. Am., 1956-62; with Textron Inc., 1962—, sec., 1966-67, v.p., gen. counsel, sec., 1968-70, sr. v.p., 1972—. Served as ensign USNR, World War II. Mem. Phi Beta Kappa, Delta Phi. Clubs: Georgetown, Capitol Hill (Washington); Art (Providence). Home: Watergate East Washington DC Office: 1090 Vermont Ave NW Suite 1100 Washington DC 20005

HENDERSON, JOHN BROWN, govt. ofcl., economist; b. Glasgow, Scotland, Jan. 3, 1918; came to U.S., 1950, naturalized, 1956; s. John Brown and Mary (Kerr) H.; m. Joanna Baxter, Sept. 10, 1954; children—Mary Joanna, Margaret Brown, Elizabeth Campbell, John Stalker Kerr. M.A., U. St. Andrews, Scotland, 1939; student, King's Coll., Cambridge (Eng.) U., 1939-40; Ph.D., Harvard, 1956. Lectr. polit. economy U. St. Andrews, 1946-52; vis. prof. Union Coll., Schenectady, 1950-51; tutor econs. Harvard, 1954-56; economist Fed. Res. Bank N.Y., 1956-60; Andrew Wells Robertson prof. econs. Allegheny Coll., Meadville, Pa., 1960-66; internat. economist Joint Econ. Com., U.S. Congress, 1966-68; dep. asst. sec. for econ. affairs Dept. Commerce, 1968-70; dir. econ. studies div. Bur. Labor Statistics, Dept. Labor, 1970-72; chief econs. div. Congl. Research Service, Library of Congress, 1972-75, sr. specialist in price econs., 1975—. Mem. Meadville Charter Commn., 1965. Served to flight lt. RAF, 1941-46. Mem. Am. Econ. Assn. Home: 4119 N 27th Rd Arlington VA 22207 Office: Library of Congress Washington DC 20540

HENDERSON, JOHN WARREN, physician, educator; b. Sidney, Nebr., Sept. 11, 1912; s. Edgar Forrest and Lillian (Sending) H.; m. Nadine Evelyn Downing, June 25, 1933; children: Sally, Holly. B.S., U. Nebr., 1934, M.A., 1936, M.D., 1937; M.S., U. Minn., 1943; D.Sc. (hon.), No. Mich. U., 1973, 1973. Intern Cin. Gen. Hosp., 1937-38; fellow in ophthalmology Mayo Grad. Sch., U. Minn., 1938-41; 1st asst. dept. ophthalmology Mayo Clinic, Rochester, Minn., 1941-43, cons. dept. ophthalmology, 1946-61, chmn. dept., 1961-74; prof. ophthalmology U. Minn. Grad. Sch., 1962-81, Mayo Med. Sch., 1972-77, emeritus, 1977—; prof. ophthalmology La. State U. Med. Sch., 1981—; chief sect. ophthalmology VA Med. Sch., Shreveport, La., 1981—. Author: Orbital Tumors, 1973, 2d edit., 1980; Contbr. numerous articles on ophthalmology and ophthalmic surgery to med. jours. Served with M.C. AUS, 1943-46. Mem. Am. Ophthal. Soc., Am. Acad. Ophthalmology, AMA, Phi Beta Kappa, Sigma Xi, Alpha Omega Alpha, Chi Phi. Office: VA Med Ctr 510 E Stoner Shreveport LA 71130

HENDERSON, JOHN WOODWORTH, ophthalmologist, educator; b. Clarinda, Iowa, Mar. 8, 1916; s. Frank Arthur and Bertha (Woodworth) H.; m. Joyce Hildebrandt, June 27, 1942; children: John H., Louise W. A.B., Occidental Coll., 1937; M.S., M.D., Northwestern U., 1942; Ph.D., U. Mich., 1948. Intern U. Mich. Hosp., 1942, resident ophthalmology, 1943-48; mem. faculty U. Mich. Med. Sch., 1948—, prof. opthalmology, 1962—, chmn. dept. ophthalmology, 1968-78; cons. VA Hosp., USPHS Milan Prison, Mich. Eye Bank. Mem. Am. Ophthal. Soc. (pres. 1980), Am. Acad. Ophthalmology, Assn. Univ. Profs. Ophthalmology (pres. 1976), AMA, Sigma Xi, Phi Beta Kappa, Alpha Omega Alpha, Phi Gamma Delta. Home: 6360 Lower Shore Dr Harbor Springs MI 49740

HENDERSON, J(OSEPH) WELLES, lawyer; b. Phila., Aug. 29, 1920; s. Joseph Welles and Anne K. (Dreisbach) H.; m. Helen R. Lipscomb, 1943 (div. 1947); 1 son, Joseph Welles III; m. Hannah Lowell Bradley, Aug. 27, 1949; children—G.L. Cabot, David R., Elizabeth M., T. Handasyd P. Grad., St. George's Sch., 1939; A.B. cum laude, Princeton U., 1943; J.D., Harvard U., 1949. Bar: Pa. bar 1950, D.C. bar 1962, also U.S. Supreme Ct. bar 1962. Practiced in, Phila., 1950—; mem. firm Rawle & Henderson, 1949-79, partner firm, 1956-79, Palmer Biezup & Henderson, 1979—; hon. consul gen. of Japan, Phila., 1978—; U.S. commr. gen. for Internat. Exposition on Environ. (Expo '74), Spokane; U.S. del. Internat. Conf. on Marine Pollution, Inter-Govtl. Maritime Consultative Orgn., London, 1973. Author: catalogue Port of Philadelphia, 1957; co-editor: The Challenger Sketch Book, 1972; asso. editor: Am. Maritime Cases, 1954—. Founder, chmn. and/or pres. Phila. Maritime Mus., 1960—; bd. dirs. Phila. Mus. Art, 1975—, World Affairs Council Phila., 1960-64, 79-83, Independence Hall Assn., 1978—, Fairmount Park Art Assn., 1969—; trustee Erdman Trust Wildlife Sanctuaries, 1960—; mem. Pa. Humanities Council, 1978—. Served to 1st lt. AUS, World War II. Recipient tribute City of Phila., 1961, award of merit Colonial Phila. Hist. Soc., 1969; medal of honor DAR, 1981. Fellow Am. Bar Found. (life); mem. Am. Bar Assn., Pa. Bar Assn., Phila. Bar Assn. (past sec., vice chmn. corp. banking and bus. law com.), Maritime Law Assn., Juristic Soc. (past pres.), Port of Phila. Maritime Soc. (pres. 1965-66, ann. award 1970), St. Andrew's Soc. Phila. (pres., also pres. found. 1969-71), Hist. Soc. Pa. (dir. 1959-68), Pa. Acad. Fine Arts (dir. 1959-67), Navy League. Republican. Presbyterian (deacon 1956-58, elder 1958-64). Clubs: Philadelphia, Merion Cricket, Union League, Courts, Downtown. Home: 1830 Rittenhouse Sq Philadelphia PA 19103 Office: Palmer Biezup and Henderson Public Ledger Bldg Suite 956 Independence Square Philadelphia PA 19106

HENDERSON, KATHRYN SILVERTHORNE, editor; b. Buffalo, 1916; d. Frederick William and Florence (Krause) Silverthorne; m. Edward Henderson, 1944; children: Edward Bell, Susan Lee. Student, Northwestern U. Sch. Journalism, 1934-35, Irvine Studio of Drama, N.Y.C., 1938, Feagin Sch. Acting, N.Y.C., 1939. Sec. to advt. mgr. Esquire mag., Chgo.; sec. to pub. Radio Guide mag., Chgo. and N.Y.C., Miami (Fla.) Tribune; publicity dir., account exec. Posner Advt. Agy., N.Y.C.; nat. advt. time sales person North Central Broadcasting System, N.Y.C.; asst. to exec. dir. Am. Geriatrics Soc., N.Y.C., 1962-73, exec. dir., 1973-83, editor monthly newsletter, 1979-84. Actress, Mae Desmond Players, radio shows and summer stock; staff commentator, Sta. WBAB, Atlantic City; traveling fashion show commentator, Lever Bros. Co. Mem. Gerontol. Soc. Am. Presbyterian. Home: 220 Central Park S New York NY 10019

HENDERSON, LAVELL MERL, educator, biochemist; b. Swan Lake, Ida., Sept. 9, 1917; s. George Merl and Nellie Marie (Gambles) H.; m. Jennie Maurine Criddle, Aug. 16, 1939; children—Janet Louise, Jeanne, Linda Marie. B.S. in Chemistry, Utah State U., 1939, D.Sc. (hon.), 1974; M.S. in Biochemistry, U. Wis., 1941, Ph.D., 1947. Research asst. U. Wis., 1939-41, 46-47, instr., 1947-48; asst. prof. biochemistry U. Ill., 1948-57; prof. biochemistry, head dept. Okla. State U., 1957-63; prof. biochemistry U. Minn., 1963—, head dept., 1963-74, asso. dean, 1978—; Collaborator Brookhaven Nat. Lab. and Lalor Found. award, summer 1955; mem. food and nutrition bd. NRC, 1968-74; Mem. bd. Hormel Inst., 1963-75. Author articles in field. Served with AUS, 1941-46; lt. col. Res. Mem. Am. Soc. Biol. Chemists, Am. Inst. Nutrition (councilor 1973-76, pres. 1977-78), Am. Bd. Clin. Nutrition, Am. Chem. Soc., Am. Soc. Microbiologists, AAAS, Sigma Xi, Phi Lambda Upsilon, Alpha Chi Sigma, Phi Kappa Phi. Home: 2154 Folwell St Saint Paul MN 55108

HENDERSON, LENNEAL JOSEPH, JR., political science educator; b. New Orleans, Oct. 27, 1946; s. Lenneal Joseph and Marcelle (Heno) H. A.B., U. Calif. at Berkeley, 1968, M.A., 1969, Ph.D., 1976; postgrad. in Sci., tech. and pub. policy, George Washington U. Asst. dean students, asst. prof. govt. St. Mary's Coll., Calif., 1969-71; vis. prof. polit. sci. Xavier U., New Orleans, 1970, Howard U., Washington, 1971; dir. ethnic studies, asst. prof. govt. U. San Francisco, 1971—; prof. Morgan State U., Balt., 1975—; asst. dean

Sch. of Mgmt. John F. Kennedy U., Martinez, 1974-75; vis. faculty city and regional planning dept. U. Calif. at Berkeley, 1974-75; vis. prof. Howard U., Washington, 1975-76; also lectr. polit. sci. Morgan State U., Balt.; asso. dir. research Joint Center Polit. Studies, Washington, 1977-78; pub. adminstrn. fellow U.S. Dept. Energy, 1979—; lectr. urban studies Inst. Urban Studies U. Md., College Park; for U.S. State Dept. in, Somalia, Tanzania and Nigeria, S. Africa, Swaziland, India; prof. Sch. Bus. and Public Adminstrn., Howard U., 1979—; Cons. Booz-Allen Pub. Adminstrn. Services, Inc., 1973-74, Shepard Assos., 1973-74, Morrison & Rowe, Inc., 1974, Dukes, Dukes & Assos., 1974-75; mem. U.S. del. Energy and Human Habitat Conf., EEC, Ottawa, Can., 1977. Editor: Black Political Life in the U.S, 1970; Book review editor: Jour. on Political Repression; mem. editorial bd.: Bureaucrat; Contbr. articles to profl. jours. Pres., bd. dirs. Children and Youth Service Agy. of San Francisco, 1974-75; chmn. local reviewing com. San Francisco County Campaign for Human Devel., 1973-74; pres. San Francisco Youth Assn., 1964-65; mem. regional task force on open space Assn. of Bay Area Govt., 1973-75; pres., bd. dirs. African Am. Hist. and Cultural Soc., Inc., 1975-76; chmn. Mayor's Citizen Adv. Com. for Washington, 1981, Mayor's Budget Adv. Com., Washington, 1983. Calif. State fellow, 1969-71; Urban Affairs fellow, 1969-70; fellow Moton Center Ind. Studies, summer 1978; Nat. Assn. Schs. Public Affairs and Public Adminstrn. fellow U.S. Dept. Energy, 1978-79; research fellow Rockefeller Found.; research asso. Harvard U.; NRC postdoctoral fellow Johns Hopkins U. Sch. Advanced Internat. Studies, 1983-84. Mem. Am. Polit. Sci. Assn., Am. Soc. Pub. Adminstrn., AAAS, Western Govtl. Research Assn., Internat. Personnel Mgmt. Assn., Am. Social and Behavioral Sci. Assn. Democrat. Roman Catholic. Office: Sch Bus and Public Adminstrn 1003 K St NW Suite 408 Washington DC 20001 *Service is the heart of my life. Its demands hold me to the highest humanitarian ideals. Its standards teach me the value of mistakes made right. Without service, humanity falls below the lowest of life forms; for all animals serve God's purpose. So service will continue to lead me to others; to their needs, hopes, desires. And, as I fulfill these needs, hopes, desires, I fulfill my own.*

HENDERSON, LOWELL LAWRENCE, physician; b. Kokomo, Ind., Apr. 22, 1916; s. Lawrence Roy and Alzada Gladys (Baker) H.; m. Anna Margaret Shaffer, Oct. 28, 1939; children—Margaret Ann (Mrs. R.J. Smalling), Beverly Jean (Mrs. R.L. Nelson), Marilyn Kay (Mrs. T.M. Parker), Sue Ellen (Mrs. Steven Delaney), Patricia Marie. A.B., Ind. U., 1938, M.D., 1941; M.S. in Medicine, U. Minn., 1948. Diplomate: Am. Bd. Internal Medicine, 1948, in Allergy, 1957. Intern Indpls. City Hosp., 1941-42; fellow internal medicine Mayo Clinic, 1942-44, 47-48; cons. internal medicine and allergy Carle Hosp. Clinic, Urbana, Ill., 1948-52, Mayo Clinic, 1953—; asst. prof. medicine Mayo Grad. Sch., U. Minn., 1962-67, asso. prof. clin. medicine, 1967-70, prof. clin. medicine, 1970-72; prof. medicine Mayo Med. Sch., 1972—; mem. bd. med. dirs. Allergy Found. Am., 1965—; mem. bd. subcertification Allergy in Internal Medicine, 1961-66. Author articles in field. Served to capt., M.C. AUS, 1944-46. Fellow Am. Coll. Allergists (pres. 1966); mem. AMA (sec. sect. allergy 1965—), Am. Acad. Allergy, N. Central Allergy Soc. (pres. 1960-62), AAAS, Internat. Soc. Allergology (treas. 1967-70, sec. gen. 1973—), Midwest Forum on Allergy (exec. com. 1966-69), Am. Assn. Certified Allergists (pres. 1972-73), Phi Beta Kappa, Sigma Xi, Delta Upsilon, Nu Sigma Nu, Alpha Omega Alpha. Episcopalian (warden). Home: 1102 10th St SW Rochester MN 55901 Office: 200 1st St SW Rochester MN 55901

HENDERSON, LOY WESLEY, retired educator, foreign service officer; b. Rogers, Ark., June 28, 1892; s. George Milton and Mary May (Davis) H.; m. Elise Marie Heinrichson, Dec. 3, 1930. A.B., Northwestern U., 1915, LL.D., 1953; student, Denver U. Law Sch., 1917-18, D.Pub. Service, 1953; LL.D., U. Ark. Bates Coll., 1957, Wayne U., 1962; D.Pub. Adminstrn., Southwestern Coll., 1959. Mem. Inter-Allied Commn. to Germany for repatriation of prisoners of war, 1919, ARC Commn. to Western Russia and Baltic States, 1919-20; in charge ARC in Germany, 1920-21; vice consul, Dublin, 1922, Queenstown, 1923; with Div. Eastern European Affairs, Dept. State, 1925; 3d sec. of legation, Riga, Kovno and Tallinn, 1927, 2d sec., 1929; with Div. Eastern European Affairs, Dept. State, 1930; 2d sec. of embassy, Moscow, 1934, 1st sec., 1935, 1st sec. and intermittently charge d'affaires, 1935-38; ast. chief Div. of European Affairs, Dept. State, 1938; insp. diplomatic missions and consulate offices, 1942-43, counselor of embassy and charge d'affaires, Moscow and Kuibyshev, 1942, E.E. and M.P. to Iraq, 1943-45; dir. Near Eastern and African Affairs, Dept. State, 1945-48; A.E. and P. to India also E.E. and M.P. to Nepal, 1948, became A.E. and P. to Iran, 1951, dep. under sec. of state for adminstrn., 1955; bd. cons. Nat. War Coll., 1957-60; chief of mission to arrange for opening new diplomatic and consular establishments in newly emerging countries in Africa, 1960, ret.; prof. internat. relations, dir. Ctr. for Diplomacy and Fgn. Policy Am. U., 1961-68; apptd. U.S. career ambassador, 1956; del. 17th Internat. Geol. Congress, Moscow, 1937, Baghdad Pact Conf., Iran, 1956; Am. mem. Suez Com., Cairo; mem. U.S. del. 2d Suez Canal Conf., London, 1956; Am. observer Baghdad Pact Meeting, 1957. Bd. govs. Nat. ARC, 1957. Recipient award of Merit Northwestern Alumni Assn., 1952, Disting. Service award Dept. State, 1954, Pres.'s award for Disting. Fed. Civilian Service, 1958; decorated Insignia of Imperial Order Homayoun, 1st class, Iran, Grand Cross Royal Order George I, Greece, comdr. de l'Ordere de la Republic of Tunisia. Mem. Am. Fgn. Service Assn. (pres. 1956), Washington Inst. Fgn. Affairs (pres. 1961-73, chmn. bd. 1973—), Council on Fgn. Affairs, Delta Tau Delta, Phi Delta Phi. Clubs: Metropolitan, International, Cosmos. Home: 2727 29th St NW Apt 732 Washington DC 20008

HENDERSON, MAUREEN MCGRATH, medical educator; b. Tynemouth, Eng., May 11, 1926; came to U.S., 1960; d. Leo E. and Helen (McGrath) H. M.B. B.S, U. Durham, Eng., 1949, D.P.H., 1956. Prof. preventive medicine U. Md. Med. Sch., 1968-75, chmn. dept. social and preventive medicine, 1971-75; asso. epidemiology Johns Hopkins U. Sch. Hygiene and Pub. Health, 1970-75; asso. v.p. health scis., prof. medicine, prof. health services U. Wash. Med. Sch., 1975-81, prof. epidemiology and medicine, 1981—; chmn. epidemiology and disease control study sect. NIH, 1969-72; chmn. clin. trials rev. com. Nat. Heart, Lung and Blood Inst., 1975-79; mem. Nat. Cancer Adv. Bd., 1979-84. Contbr. med. publs. Luke-Armstrong scholar epidemiology, 1956-57; John and Mary Markle scholar acad. medicine, 1963-68. Mem. Inst. Medicine (council 1981-85), Assn. Tchrs. Preventive Medicine (pres. 1972-73), Soc. Epidemiol. Research (chmn. 1969-70), Internat. Assn. Epidemiol. Assn. (exec. officer 1971-76), Am. Epidemiol. Assn., Royal Soc. Medicine. Home: 5309 NE 85th St Seattle WA 98115 Office: School of Public Health and Community MED SC-30 Univ Wash Seattle WA 98195

HENDERSON, MILTON ARNOLD, association executive; b. Chattanooga, June 22, 1922; s. Milton Arnold and Margaret (Rawlings) H.; m. Joyce Crowder (dec.); children: George, Linda, Philip.; m. Betty Ann Harnage, Aug. 20, 1982. B.S., Northwestern U., 1938. Asst. sales mgr. Coca-Cola Bottling Co., Savannah and Macon, Ga., 1948-54; field rep. Gideons Internat., Nashville, 1954-55, promotion mgr., 1955-56, exec. dir., 1956—. Editor: Gideon Info. Bull, 1956—. Served to capt. USAAF, 1942-46; Served to capt. USAF, 1951-52. Recipient numerous awards. Mem. Am. Mgmt. Assn. Republican. Presbyterian (elder). Clubs: Ravenwood (Nashville); Nashville City. Home: 2524 Stones River Ct Nashville TN 37214 Office: 2900 Lebanon Rd Nashville TN 37214

HENDERSON, PAUL AUDINE, banker, consultant; b. Canton, Ohio, May 21, 1925; s. Allen and Bobye Ruth (Marshall) H.; m. Betty Jean Arnett, July 7, 1951; children: Martha Lee, Laura Jean, Paul Marshall, Bruce Douglas, Allen William. A.B., Hiram Coll., 1949; M.B.A., Wharton Sch. U. Pa., 1951. Sr. v.p. Huntington Nat. Bank, Columbus, Ohio, 1960-74; pres., chief exec. officer Nat. Bank & Trust Co. South Bend, Ind., 1974-83; pres. Paul A. Henderson & Assocs. Inc., South Bend, 1983—. Active various community affairs; bd. dirs. South Bend Symphony Orch., Meml. Hosp. Served with Armed Forces, 1943-46. Unitarian. Clubs: Summit, Pickwick, Signal Point, South Bend Country. Home: 1604 E Jefferson Blvd South Bend IN 46617

HENDERSON, RALPH B., department store chain executive; b. Chgo., 1926; s. Ralph B. and Francis A. (Wedd) H.; m. Mildred A. Morgan, Feb. 20, 1946 (dec.); m. Grace E. Richardson, Mar. 3, 1979; children: Susan, Ralph B., Meryl, Beth. B.A., Yale U., 1946. With Montgomery Ward & Co., 1947-63; with J.C. Penney Co., Inc., 1963—, now exec. v.p., dir. distbn., planning and research, real estate, constrn., corp. devel., N.Y.C. Served with USN, 1944-47. Office: 1301 Ave of Americas New York NY 10019

HENDERSON, RALPH HALE, physician; b. N.Y.C., Mar. 5, 1937; s. Ralph Ernest and Clifford West (Sellers) H.; m. Ilze Sarma, May 21, 1966. A.B., Harvard U., 1959, M.D., 1963, M.P.H., 1970, M.Pub. Policy, 1972. Intern, then resident in internal medicine Boston City Hosp., 1963-65; joined USPHS, 1965, capt., 1973-81, asst. surgeon gen., 1981—, service in, U.S. and West Africa, 1965-69; asst. chief venereal disease br., state and community services div. Centers Disease Control, Atlanta, 1972-73; dir. venereal disease control div. Bur. State Services, 1973-76; program mgr. expanded program on immunization WHO, Geneva, 1977-78, dir. expanded program immunization, 1979—. Contbr. to med. publs. Trustee Dermatology Found., 1975-77. Recipient Commendation medal USPHS, 1969. Mem. U.S.-Mex. Border Health Assn., Am. Coll. Preventive Medicine, Am. Venereal Disease Assn. Home: 31 Chemin Moise Duboule 1209 Geneva Switzerland Office: care Expanded Program on Immunization WHO 1211 Geneva 27 Switzerland

HENDERSON, ROBERT ARTHUR, educator; b. Oakland, Calif., Apr. 3, 1925; s. Harold Eugene and Charlotte (Peregrine) H.; m. June Virginia Crawford, Sept. 15, 1945; children: Barbara Ann, Kerrie Lee, Lawrence A. A.B., U. Calif. at Berkeley, 1947; M.A., San Francisco State Coll., 1950; Ed.D., U. Ill., 1957. High sch. tchr., elementary prin., Sonoma County, Calif., 1947-49, tchr. mentally retarded, Stockton, Calif., 1952-54; asst. prof. U. Conn., 1957-58; cons. bur. spl. edn. Calif. Dept. Edn., 1958-62; tchr., research asst. Inst. Research Exceptional Children, U. Ill., 1954-56, prof. spl. edn. and ednl. adminstrn., 1962—; mem. Inst. Research Exceptional Children, 1962-74, chmn. dept. spl. edn. univ., 1962-72, 81—; mem. adj. faculty Marine Corps Command and Staff Coll., 1968-73; Research fellow Nat. Inst. Mental Health, 1956-57; mem. adv. council div. tng. programs, bur. edn. handicapped. U.S. Office Edn., 1967-71; Exceptional Child chmn. Ill. Congress Parents and Tchrs., 1983—. Contbr. articles to profl. jours.; Cons. editor: Jour. Edn. Research, 1964-67; asso. editor: Exceptional Children, 1966—, Tchr. Edn. and Spl. Edn., 1980—; cons. editor: Edn. and Tng. of the Mentally Retarded, 1981—. Active local Boy Scouts Am. Served to col. USMCR, World War II and; Korea. Decorated Purple Heart. Fellow Am. Assn. Mental Deficiency, Royal Soc. Health; life mem. Council Exceptional Children, NEA; mem. Nat. Soc. Study Edn., Phi Delta Kappa. Address: 807 S Maple St Urbana IL 61801

HENDERSON, ROBERT DEAN, educator, business consultant; b. Pitts., Sept. 22, 1916; s. William James and Margaret (Shaw) H.; m. Grace Waters, Sept. 3, 1941; children: Robert Dean, Carol Lynne. B.B.A., Westminster Coll., 1938; M.B.A., Ohio State U., 1941; Ph.D., U. Pitts., 1949. Prof. econs. Bucknell U., 1946-54; prof. mgmt. Bowling Green (Ohio) U., 1954-73, chmn. dept. bus. adminstrn., 1954-66; Dana prof. mgmt. U. Tampa, Fla., 1973-80, dir. grad. studies in bus. adminstrn., 1973-76, dir. grad. programs, 1974-76; adj. prof. Coll. Bus., U. South Fla., Tampa, 1980—, disting. lectr., 1981—. Asso. editor: Jour. Purchasing, 1965—; Contbr. articles to profl. jours. Fellow Acad. Mgmt. (pres. Midwest div. 1964-65, nat. sec.-treas. 1965-68); mem. Nat. Assn. Purchasing Mgmt. (v.p. dist. six 1968-69, mem. cert. bd. 1976-79, chmn. 1978-79), Purchasing Mgmt. Assn. Toledo (pres. 1967-68), Fla. West Coast Purchasing Mgmt. Assn. (dir. 1975—), Indsl. Relations Research Assn. (pres. N.W. Ohio chpt. 1960), Alpha Sigma Phi, Tau Kappa Alpha, Pi Gamma Mu, Pi Delta Upsilon, Beta Gamma Sigma, Delta Sigma Pi. Home: 11801 Lipsey Rd Tampa FL 33618

HENDERSON, ROBERT JULES, food service executive; b. Seaforth, Ont., Can., Aug. 24, 1943; children: Derek, Kim. B.Commerce with honors in Bus. Adminstrn., U. Windsor, 1966. Chartered acct., London, 1969. Vice pres. Beaver Foods Ltd., London, Ont., Can., Arvak Mgmt. Inc., London, Ont.; pres. Cal Van Canus Camp Services, Vancouver, B.C., Can. Mem. Fin. Execs. Inst., Inst. Chartered Accts. Ont. Club: London (Ont.). Home: 56 Hillsmount Rd London ON Canada N6K 1W2 Office: Arvak Mgmt Inc 1925 Dundas St E London ON Canda N5V 1P7

HENDERSON, ROBERT WAUGH, religion educator; b. Evanston, Ill., May 21, 1920; s. Robert Houston and Eunice (Swain) H.; m. June Elizabeth Whamond, Dec. 15, 1945 (dec. Jan. 1978); children: Robert James, Judith Lynn; m. Belva Lou Pascoe Dickman, Nov. 21, 1978. A.B., Princeton U., 1941; B.D., McCormick Theol. Sem., 1949; Ph.D., Harvard U., 1959. Ordained to ministry Presbyn. Ch., 1949; pastor First Ch. (Congl.), East Derry, N.H., 1950-57; asst. prof. U. Tulsa, 1958-65, asso. prof., 1965-70, prof. religion, 1970—, dir. Center for Humanities, 1969-74, chmn. faculty religion and humanities, 1980—; research asso. dept. theology Reformed Alliance, Geneva, 1967—. Author: Teaching Office in the Reformed Tradition: History of the Doctoral Ministry, 1962—, Profile of the Eldership, 1974, 1975; also articles and revs. Served from 2d lt. to capt. F.A. AUS, 1941-45. Postdoctoral fellow, summer 1969. Mem. Am. Assn. U. Profs. (pres. Okla. 1970-71, exec. com. 1968—), Am. Hist. Assn., Am. Soc. Ch. History, Am. Soc. for Reformation Research, Sixteenth Century Studies Conf. Address: U Tulsa Tulsa OK 74104

HENDERSON, SKITCH CEDRIC, pianist, conductor; b. Halstad, Minn., Jan. 27, 1918; m. Ruth Einsiedl; children: Heidi, Hans Christian. Studied piano with, Malcolm Frost, Roger Aubert; conducting with, Albert Coates, Fritz Reiner; harmony with, Schoenberg. Performed with area bands, theater orchs., with film and radio studios, West Coast, 1939-40; piano soloist: Crosby, Sinatra radio shows, 1946; on tour with own dance band, 1947-49, radio work, 1949-51; pianist, condr., NBC, N.Y.C., from 1951; leader, comedian: Steve Allen TV Tonight Show, 1955-56; guest condr., N.Y. Philharmonic, Mpls. Symphony, others, frequent TV appearances. Served with USAAF, 1941-45. Address: care Gurtman & Murtha Assocs Inc 162 W 56th St New York NY 10019 *

HENDERSON, STANLEY DALE, lawyer, educator; b. Monona, Iowa, June 17, 1935; s. Leon Gilbert and Iva Elizabeth H.; m. DeArliss Garretson, June 15, 1957; children: Lesli Kara, Heidi Elizabeth, Holly Ann. A.B., Coe Coll., 1957; postgrad., Cornell U., 1957-58, U. Chgo. Law Sch., 1958-59; J.D., U. Colo., 1961. Bar: Colo. 1961, Va. 1973. Law clk. U.S. Dist. Ct., Denver, 1961-62; mem. firm Williams and Zook, Boulder, Colo., 1962-64; mem. faculty U. Wyo. Coll. Law, 1964-69; prof. law U. Va. Law Sch., Charlottesville, 1970-79, F.D.G. Ribble prof. law, 1979—; vis. prof. law Ind. U., 1974, Harvard Law Sch., 1978-79. Contbr. articles to profl. jours. Mem. Colo. Bar Assn., Va. State Bar, Am. Law Inst., Am. Arbitration Assn., Order of Coif, Phi Beta Kappa, Phi Kappa Phi. Democrat. Presbyterian. Home: 1615 King Mountain Rd Charlottesville VA 22901 Office: Sch of Law Univ of Va Charlottesville VA 22901

HENDERSON, THELTON EUGENE, federal judge; b. Shreveport, La., Nov. 28, 1933; s. Eugene M. and Wanzie (Roberts) H.; m. Kare Anderson, Jan. 28, 1979; 1 son, Geoffrey A. B.A., U. Calif.-, Berkeley, 1956, J.D., 1962. Bar: Calif. 1962. Atty. U.S. Dept. Justice, 1962-63; assoc. firm FitzSimmons & Petris, 1964, assoc., 1964-66; directing atty. San Mateo County (Calif.) Legal Aid Soc., 1966-69; asst. dean Stanford (Calif.) U. Law Sch., 1968-76; ptnr. firm Rosen, Remcho & Henderson, San Francisco, 1977-80; judge U.S. Dist. Ct. No. Dist. Calif., San Francisco, 1980—; asso. prof. Sch. Law, Golden Gate U., San Francisco, 1978-80. Served with U.S. Army, 1956-58. Mem. Nat. Bar Assn., Charles Houston Law Assn. Office: 450 Golden Gate Ave Room 19042 San Francisco CA 94102 *

HENDERSON, WALTER G., utility company executive; b. Edgemont, S.D., Dec. 19, 1930; s. Andrew M. and Agnes (Galbraith) H.; m. Pamela J. Naeve, Oct. 26, 1974; children: Kevin, Jennifer. B.A. in Bus, U. Nebr., 1953; LL.B., U. Colo., 1957. With El Paso (Tex.) Natural Gas Co., 1957—, asst. v.p., 1974-77, v.p., 1977-79, sr. v.p., 1979-80, exec. v.p., 1980—; dir. various subsidiaries and affiliates of El Paso Natural Gas Co. Served with USMC, 1953-55. Mem. Pacific Coast Gas Assn., So. Gas Assn. Episcopalian. Office: PO Box 1492 El Paso TX 79978 *

HENDERSON, WILLIAM BOYD, corporation engineering executive; b. Greenock, Scottland, Feb. 13, 1936; emigrated to Can., 1958; s. William Nisbet and Margaret Wilson (Austin) H.; m. Elizabeth Hill White, July 9, 1957; children: Carol Anne, Elizabeth Janet, William Nisbet, Steven John. B.S. with honors in Mining Engring., Glasgow U., 1957; diploma in Geology, U. Strathclyde, 1958. Project engr. Can. Bechtel Ltd., Montreal, Que., 1964-73; mgr. indsl. dept. SNC Ltd., Montreal, 1973-76; project mgr. Patrick Harrison & Co., Toronto, Ont., Can., 1976-77; mgr. engring. and constrn. Internat. Nickel, Toronto, 1977-79, Cofremmi, Paris, 1979-81; v.p. engring. Domtar Inc., Montreal, 1981—; dir. Ormiston Mining, Sask., Can., 1982—; mem. Can. Adv. bd. Arkwright-Boston, Waltham, Mass., 1982—. Mem. Ordre des Ingenieures du Que., Assn. Profl. Engrs. Ont., Project Mgmt. Inst. (adv. bd. Montreal br. 1981—). Home: 60 Rue de Bresoles Montreal PQ Canada H2Y 1V5 Office: Domtar Inc 395 de Maisonneuve W Montreal PQ Canada H3A 1L6

HENDERSON, WILLIAM CHARLES, editor; b. Phila., Apr. 5, 1941; s. Francis Louis and Dorothy Price (Galloway) H. B.A., Hamilton Coll., 1963; postgrad., Harvard U., 1963, U. Pa., 1965-66. Asso. editor Doubleday & Co., N.Y.C., 1972-73; pub. Pushcart Press, Yonkers, N.Y., 1972—; sr. editor Coward, McCann & Geohagan, Inc., N.Y.C., 1973-75; cons. editor Harper & Row Inc., 1976—; guest lectr. Harvard U., summer 1974, Sarah Lawrence Coll., U. Rochester, summer 1978; lectr. Columbia U., 1978—; mem. nat. advisory bd. Center for the Book Library of Congress, 1979. Author: The Galapagos Kid, 1971, His Son: A Child of the Fifties, 1981; editor, pub.: The Publish It Yourself Handbook, 1973, The Pushcart Prize: Best of the Small Presses, 1976—; editor: The Art of Literary Publishing, 1980. Recipient Author award N.J. English Tchrs. Assn., 1972; Newsboy award Horatio Alger Soc., 1973; Carey-Thomas award, 1978. Mem. P.E.N. (exec. bd.), Com. of Small Mag. Editors. Home: PO Box 380 Wainscott NY 11975

HENDERSON, WILLIAM L., ednl. adminstr. B.S., A.M., Ph.D., Ohio State U. John E. Harris prof. econs. Denison U., 1960-63, 65-73, asst. to pres., 1970-73; dir. devel. and planning Wabash Coll., 1973-75; John E. Harris prof. econs. Denison U., 1975—. Address: Denison U Granville OH 43023

HENDIN, DAVID BRUCE, journalist; b. St. Louis, Dec. 16, 1945; s. Aaron and Lillian (Karsh) H.; children: Sarah Tsvia, Benjamin Judah. B.S. in Biology Edn, U. Mo., 1967, M.A. in Journalism, 1970. Sr. v.p., editorial dir. United Media Enterprises Inc., N.Y.C., 1971—; clin. prof. off campus U. Mo. Sch. Journalism, 1971—; adj. lectr. Columbia U. Sch. Journalism, 1974-76. Author: Everything You Need to Know About Abortion, 1971, The Doctor's Save-Your-Heart Diet, 1972, Death As a Fact of Life, 1973, rev. edit., 1984, Save Your Child's Life, 1973, The Life Givers, 1975, Guide to Ancient Jewish Coins, 1975, The World Almanac Whole Health Guide, 1977, The Genetic Connection, 1978, Collecting Coins, 1979. Bd. dirs. Holyland Conservation Fund, 1973—; v.p. Council Advancement Sci. Writing, 1975—; trustee Scripps-Howard Found., 1978—; chmn. numis. com. The Jewish Mus., 1980—. Recipient award merit Am. Assn. Blood Banks, 1972; Claude Bernard Sci. Journalism award, 1972; certificate commendation Am. Acad. Family Physicians, 1973; Med. Journalism award AMA, 1973; Blakeslee award Am. Heart Assn., 1973; Book of Yr. award Am. Med. Writers Assn., 1977. Mem. Council for Advancement Sci. Writing, Am.-Israel Numismatic Assn. (v.p. 1979—), Kappa Tau Alpha, Sigma Alpha Mu. Home: PO Box 661 Bardonia NY 10954 Office: 200 Park Ave New York NY 10166

HENDL, WALTER, conductor, pianist, composer; b. West New York, N.J., Jan. 12, 1917; s. William and Ella (Wittig) H.; m. Barbara Heisley; 1 dau by previous marriage, Susan. Pvt. study piano with, David Saperton; with, Clarence Adler, 1934-37; pvt. study conducting with, Fritz Reiner, Curtis Inst. Music, 1937-41. Dir. Eastman Sch. Music, Rochester, N.Y., 1964-72. Active as condr. and pianist, Berkshire Music Center, 1941-42; asst. condr., pianist, N.Y. Philharmonic Symphony Orch., 1945-49; mus. dir., Dallas Symphony, 1949-58, Chautauqua (N.Y.) Symphony Orch., 1953-72; asso. condr., Chgo. Symphony Orch., 1958-64; mus. dir., Ravinia (Ill.) Festival, 1959-63; orchestral dir., Erie (Pa.) Philharm., 1976—; guest condr. in, Europe, USSR, S. Am.; Composer: Broadway prodn. Dark of the Moon, 1945, A Village Where They Ring No Bells, Loneliness (Recipient Alice M. Ditson award, Columbia 1953). Office: Erie Philharmonic 409 Baldwin Bldg Erie PA 16501

HENDLEY, DAN LUNSFORD, banker; b. Nashville, Apr. 26, 1938; s. Frank E. and Mattie (Lunsford) H.; m. Patricia Fariss, June 18, 1960; children: Dan Lunsford, Laura Kathleen. B.A., Vanderbilt U., 1960; grad., Stonier Grad. Sch. Banking, Rutgers U., 1969; student, Advanced Mgmt. Program, Harvard, 1972. With N.Y. Life Ins. Co., 1960-62; with Fed. Res. Bank Atlanta, 1962-73, v.p., officer in charge Birmingham br., 1969-73; formerly exec. v.p. Ala. Bancorp., Birmingham, 1973-77; exec. v.p. First Nat. Bank Birmingham, 1976-77, pres., 1977-79, chmn. bd., chief exec. officer, 1979-83; pres., chief operating officer Am South Bank, N.A., 1983—, also dir.; dir., vice chmn. Am. South Bancorp.; dir. Engel Mortgage Co., Inc. Trustee

Children's Hosp., Samford U.; bd. visitors U. Ala.; mem. president's council U. Ala.-Birmingham; membership chmn. Boy Scouts Am. Mem. Tenn. Air N.G., 1961-67. Mem. Vanderbilt U. Alumni Assn., Kappa Sigma. Baptist. Clubs: Kiwanis, Mountain Brook, Vestavia Country, Riverchase Country, Shoal Creek.; The Club (bd. govs.). Home: 3258 Dell Rd Birmingham AL 35223 Office: PO Box 11007 Birmingham AL 35288

HENDON, ROBERT CARAWAY, cons., former transportation and manufacturing company executive; b. Shelbyville, Tenn., Jan. 13, 1912; s. William Oscar and Anna Bertha (Caraway) H.; m. Ruth Perham, Apr. 23, 1936; children: Robert Caraway, Elizabeth Anne (Mrs. MacDonald Dunbar, Jr.). B.A. in Journalism, U. Mont., 1931, J.D., 1934. Bar: Mont. and Tenn. 1934. Gen. practice law, Monterey, Tenn., 1934-35; spl. agt., spl. agt. in charge FBI, 1935-39, insp., adminstrv. asst. to dir., mem. exec. com., 1939-47; exec. rep. to pres. Ry. Express Agy. (later REA Express), N.Y.C., 1947, various exec. positions, 1947-50; asst. to pres., dir. personnel Mathieson Chem. Corp., 1950-52; v.p. personnel and indsl. relations REA Express, 1953-55, v.p. operations, 1955-64, v.p. exec. dept., 1964-68; dir. REA Leasing Corp., 1961-68, pres., 1964-67, vice chmn. bd., 1967-68; pres., dir. TOFC Leasing Corp., 1965-68, REA Express-Seven Arts Transvision, Inc., 1965-68; dir., chmn. exec. com. Fast Service Shipping Terminals, Inc., 1961-68; v.p. Consol. Freightways Inc., 1968-77; dir., mem. exec. com., chmn. nominating, exam. and auditing, mgmt. devel. and compensation coms. Manhattan Life Ins. Co.; dir., mem. exec. com., chmn. auditing, nominating, mgmt. devel. and exec. compensation coms. Manhattan Life Corp.; dir., chmn. exec. com., chmn. auditing com. Manhattan Nat. Life Ins. Co. (name formerly No. Nat. Life Ins. Co.). Author: Frontiers in Labor-Management Problems, 1956, Seniority. First In, Last Out, 1958; also articles. Del. Atty. Gen.'s Conf. on Juvenile Delinquency, 1936; mem. U.S. Com. for Security of War Info., 1942; mem. prevention com. Assn. Am. Railroads, 1947-50; mem. manpower com. Mfg. Chem. Assn., 1950-53; trustee, mem. exec. com., past pres. U. Mont. Found., Center for Environ. and Resource Analysis; bd. dirs., chmn. awards com. Nat. Safety Council, 1963-68. Recipient Distinguished Service award U. Mont., 1967. Mem. Soc. Former Spl. Agts. FBI, Transp. Assn. Am. (policy implementation and facilitation coms. 1969-77), Internat. Assn. Chiefs of Police (life mem.), Nat. Def. Transp. Assn., Phi Sigma Kappa, Sigma Delta Chi. Episcopalian (former vestryman, warden). Clubs: University (Larchmont, N.Y.) (past pres.); Grizzly Riders Internat. (Mont.) (dir.). Home: 134 Harpeth Trace Dr Nashville TN 37221

HENDON, ROBERT RANDALL, lawyer; b. Earlsboro, Okla., Mar. 20, 1894; s. Robert Randall and Mary Belle (Neabors) H.; m. Kathlene Marie Grubaugh, Dec. 21, 1921 (dec. Oct. 6, 1956); children—Robert Randall, Owen William; m. Muriel Louise Mackenzie, Mar. 29, 1958. LL.B., U. Okla., 1916; grad., Command and Gen. Staff Sch., 1935, War Dept. Indsl. Coll., 1945. Bar: Okla. bar 1916, U.S. Supreme Ct. bar 1920, D.C. bar 1933, U.S. Ct. Hawaii 1944, Md. bar 1954, ICC bar 1954, U.S. Ct. Claims 1956. Gen. law practice, Wewoka, Okla., 1916-17, mem. law firm, Shawnee, Okla., 1921-25; atty. Bd. Contract Adjustment, War Dept., 1919, asso. mem., legal advisor to sec. war, 1920-21; atty., sr. atty., adminstrv. law judge ICC, 1925-50; asso. counsel U.S. Senate Com. Investigating R.R. Financing, 1934-36; dir. tax ammortization and def. loan div. Def. Transport Adminstrn., 1950-54; gen. law practice, 1954—; chief contract termination div. Office Chief Engrs., Washington, 1945-46; spl. asst. to adminstr. War Assets Adminstrn., 1946-47, dir. property mgmt. div., Mar.-Dec. 1947, mem. gen. bd., Jan.-May 1948; chief spl. projects div. Munitions Bd., Office Sec. Def., 1948-49; pres. Army Phys. Review Council, Office Sec., Dept. Army, Jan.-Nov. 1950; dir. C. & G.S., Dept. Army (O.R.C. School), Washington, 1950-54. Served as 1st lt. A.E.F., 1918-19; France; col. Arty. A.U.S., 1940-50; comdr. 98th Anti-Aircraft Regt. and Searchlight-Radar Groupment, 1942-45; P.T.O. Decorated Purple Heart, Bronze Star citation, Legion of Merit, Commendation from Sec. of War, Nat. Mil. Establishment badge. Mem. ICC Practitioners Assn., Internat. Platform Assn., Res. Officer Assn. of U.S., Nat. Assn. Ret. Civil Employees, Am. Legion, DAV, Am. Security Council (nat. adv. bd.), Ret. Mil. Officers Assn., Order of Lafayette. Democrat. Baptist (chmn. finance com., trustee 1970—). Clubs: Mason (Shriner; life), Army and Navy, Nat. Lawyers (founder, life mem.). Address: 4000 Massachusetts Ave NW Washington DC 20016 *My entire life has been conducted with a complete faith in God, patriotism to my country, faith in its democratic principles, fairness and honesty toward my fellowman, and with a goal to serve as a lawyer and soldier with distinction and honor to myself and country.*

HENDRICK, CLYDE, psychology educator, adminstrator; b. Reed, Okla., July 13, 1936; s. Allen Boyd and Fannie Mae (Martin) H.; m. Wyota Sue Crawford, Oct. 24, 1956 (div. June 1977); children: David, Scott; m. Susan Singer, Sept. 18, 1977; stepchildren: Mark Stephan, Rachel Stephan. B.A., Humboldt State Coll., Arcata, Calif., 1963; M.A., U. Mo., 1965, Ph.D., 1967. Asst. prof. psychology Humboldt State U., 1967-68; assoc. prof. psychology Kent State U., 1968-75, prof., 1975-77; prof., chmn. dept. psychology U. Miami, Coral Gables, Fla., 1977—. Author: (with others) Introduction to Social Psychology, 1979; Liking, Loving and Relating, 1983; editor: Perspectives on Social Psychology, 1977, Personality and Social Psychology Bull., 1975-78; acting editor: Jour. Personality and Social Psychology, 1979-80; contbr. articles to profl. jours. Fellow Am. Psychol. Assn.; mem. Soc. Exptl. Social Psychology. Democrat. Lutheran. Office: Dept Psychology U Miami Coral Gables FL 33124

HENDRICK, GEORGE, educator; b. Stephenville, Tex., Mar. 30, 1929; s. Hoyt and Bessie Lea (Sears) H.; m. Willene Lowery, Jan. 21, 1955; 1 dau., Sarah. B.A., Tex. Christian U., 1948, M.A., 1950; Ph.D., U. Tex., 1954. Mem. English faculty S.W. Tex. State U., 1954-56, U. Colo., 1956-60; prof. Am. studies J.W. Goethe U., Frankfurt, Germany, 1960-65; prof. U. Ill., Chgo., 1965-67, Urbana, 1967—. Author: Katherine Anne Porter, 1965, Henry Salt: Humanitarian Reformer and Man of Letters, 1977, Remembrances of Concord and the Thoreaus, 1977, (with Fritz Oehlschlaeger) Toward the making of Thoreau's Modern Reputation, 1980, (with Willene Hendrick) On the Frontier: Dr. Hiram Rutherford, 1981, Thoreau Amongst Friends and Philistines, 1982, (with Margaret Sandburg) Ever the Winds of Chance, 1983. Grantee Am. Council Learned Socs., Ford Found. Mem. MLA. Office: English Dept U Ill Urbana IL 61801

HENDRICK, JAMES POMEROY, lawyer; b. Wainscott, N.Y., July 31, 1901; s. Ellwood and Josephine (Pomeroy) H.; m. Elinor Sullivan, Nov. 21, 1927; children: Arthur Pomeroy, Alice (Mrs. James Hardigg), Robert. B.A., Yale, 1923; student, Corpus Christi Coll., Cambridge, Eng., 1924; LL.B., Yale, 1927. Bar: N.Y. bar 1929. Atty. Winthrop, Stimson, Putnam & Roberts, N.Y.C., 1928-41; asst. to under sec. war, later sec. war, 1941-46; adviser to U.S. rep. UN Commn. on Human Rights, 1946-48; asst. to adminstr. ECA, 1948-53; asst. to sec. Treasury Dept., dep. asst. sec., 1953-67, spl. asst. to sec. (for enforcement), 1967-69; Vice pres. INTERPOL, 1968-69; counselor St. Croix Prison Rehab. Com., 1971—; mem. U.S. Dist. Ct. Commn. to investigate V.I. Prison System, 1976, V.I. Parole Bd., 1976-83, chmn., 1981-83; mem. U.S. Dept. Justice Task Force to Study Corrections in V.I., 1976; V.I. rep. Nat. Parole Symposium, 1980. Contbr. articles to profl. publs. Served to col. AUS, 1942-46. Decorated Legion of Merit, 1945; Ordre Nationale de Viet Nam, 1953. Mem. Wolf's Head Soc., Alpha Delta Phi, Phi Delta Phi. Democrat. Episcopalian. Clubs: Century Assn., Dutch Treat, The Players, River, Metropolitan, Chevy Chase. Home: PO Box 2931 Christiansted Saint Croix VI 00820

HENDRICKS, BARBARA, opera singer; b. Stephens, Ark., Nov. 20, 1948. Studied with, Jennie Tourel. Debut with, San Francisco Spring Opera in, Ormindo, 1974; since has performed with maj. opera companies in, U.S. and Europe, including, Boston Opera, St. Paul Opera, Santa Fe Opera, Deutsche Oper, Berlin, Aix-en-Provence Festival, Houston Opera, De Nederlandse Operastichting, Glyndebourne Festival Opera, also recitals, appearances with symphony orchs., including, Boston Symphony Orch., N.Y. Philharm., Los Angeles Philharm., Cleve. Symphony Orch., Phila. Orch., Chgo. Symphony, Berlin Philharm., Vienna Philharm., London Symphony Orch., Orchestre de Paris, Orchestre Nationale de France. (Recipient Grand Prix due Disque 1976) *

HENDRICKS, CALVIN, retail company executive; b. Centerville, Utah, Mar. 6, 1933; s. Mile Calvin and Linda Randall (Watkins) H.; m. Lona Clair Jones, Nov. 24, 1956; children—Dixie, Jana, Kent, Denise, Craig, Jill. Student, Boise Jr. Coll., 1954-55; B.S., Brigham Young U., 1956-57. Staff accountant Price Waterhouse and Co., Seattle, 1957-62; vice chmn. bd. Pay'n Save Corp., Seattle, 1962—, also dir. Served with USAF, 1951-54. Home: 19455 Marine View Dr SW Seattle WA 98166 Office: 1511 6th Ave Seattle WA 98101

HENDRICKS, CHARLES DURRELL, JR., educator, physicist; b. Lewiston, Utah, Dec. 5, 1926; s. Charles Durrell and Louise (McAlister) H.; m. Leah Funk, Mar. 4, 1948; children—Katherine, Martha Jane. B.S., Utah State U., 1949; M.S., U. Wis., 1951; Ph.D., U. Utah, 1955. Research asst. U. Utah, 1953-55; staff mem. Lincoln Lab., Mass. Inst. Tech., 1955-56; faculty U. Ill. at Urbana, 1956—, prof. dept. elec. engring., 1961—, prof. nuclear engring., 1965—, also dir. charged particle research lab., 1964—; now asso. program leader for fusion target fabrication U. Calif. Lawrence Livermore Nat. Lab.; vis. prof. Mass. Inst. Tech., 1967-68; sr. research fellow U. Southampton, Eng., 1971-72; editor Blaisdell Pub. Co.; cons. indsl. firms. Fellow AAAS, Am. Phys. Soc., Am. Inst. Aeros. and Astronautics (asso.), IEEE; mem. Am. Assn. Physics Tchrs., Electrostatics Soc. Am. (exec. council 1970—), Phi Beta Kappa, Sigma Xi, Tau Beta Pi, Phi Kappa Phi, Eta Kappa Nu. Mormon. Home: 2817 Pardee Pl Livermore CA 94550

HENDRICKS, CHARLES HENNING, physician; b. Traverse City, Mich., Oct. 26, 1917; s. Henning Vitalis and Jennie (Burnett) H.; m. Geraldine Ruth Chisholm, Sept. 27, 1942; children: William Allen, Charles Henning, Mary Beth, Judith Ann, Cynthia Ruth. A.B., U. Mich., 1941, M.D., 1943; M.D. (hon.), U. Uruguay, 1980. Diplomate: Am. Bd. Obstetrics and Gynecology (examiner 1961-80, dir. 1977-80). Intern Univ. Hosp., Ann Arbor, Mich., 1943-44, resident, 1944-46, Columbus, Ohio, 1948-49; practice medicine, specializing in obstetrics, and gynecology, Columbus, 1949-54, Cleve., 1954-68; instr. Coll. Medicine, Ohio State U., 1949-51, asst. prof., 1951-54; asso. prof. obstetrics and gynecology Sch. Medicine, Case Western Res. U., 1954-62, prof., 1962-68, U. N.C. Sch. Medicine, Chapel Hill, 1968—, chmn. dept. obstetrics and gynecology, 1968-80, Robert A. Ross distinguished prof., 1971—. Asso. editor: Jour. Ob-Gyn, 1980—. Served to capt. AUS, 1946-48. Recipient Ann. Prize award Central Assn. Obstetricians and Gynecologists, 1955; Found. prize Am. Assn. Obstetricians and Gynecologists, 1956; Macy fellow U. Uruguay, 1957. Mem. AMA, Soc. Gynecol. Investigation (pres.), Am. Gynecol. Soc. (v.p.), Norman F. Miller Gynecol. Soc., Allan C. Barnes Gynecol. Soc., Am. Assn. Obstetricians and Gynecologists, Central Assn. Obstetricians and Gynecologists, S. Atlantic Assn. Obstetricians and Gynecologists, Cleve. Soc. Obstetrics and Gynecology (past pres.), Edmonton Soc. Obstetrics and Gynecology, hon. mem.), Pacific N.W. Soc. Obstetrics and Gynecology (hon. mem.), N.D. Soc. Obstetrics and Gynecology (hon. mem.), Soc. Perinatal Obstetricians (hon. mem.), Piedmont Soc. Obstetrics and Gynecology, Assn. Profs. Gynecology and Obstetrics, Am. Coll. Obstetricians and Gynecologists, AAAS, AAUP, Biol. Soc. Montevideo (hon.), Sociedad Ginecotologica del Uruguay (hon.), Va. Obstet. and Gynecol. Soc. (hon.), Durham-Orange County Med. Soc., Wash. Obstet. Assn. (hon.), Royal Coll. Ob-Gyn (ad eundem), N.C. Obstetric-Gynecologic Soc., South Atlantic Assn. Obstetricians and Gynecologists, Robert A. Ross Obstet. and Gynecol. Soc., Med. Soc. N.C., Am. Assn. Planned Parenthood Physicians, So. Perinatal Assn., Human Betterment League (pres.), Sociedad Paraguaya de Ginecologia y obstetricia (hon.), Sigma Xi. Club: Central Travel. Home: 102 Boulder Ln Chapel Hill NC 27514

HENDRICKS, DONALD DUANE, librarian, university dean; b. Flint, Mich., Nov. 3, 1931; s. Edgar F. and Grace L. (Roska) H.; m. Mary Jean Elrich, Feb. 17, 1951; children—Phillip, Scott, Randall. A.B., U. Mich., A.M. in L.S, 1955; Ph.D., U. Ill., 1966. With Detroit Pub. Library, 1955-57; head librarian Owosso (Mich.) Pub. Library, 1957-60, Millikin U., 1960-63; dir. libraries Sam Houston State Univ., 1966-70; dir. S. Central Regional Med. Library Program, Dallas, 1970-78, U. Tex. Health Sci. Center Library, 1971-78, Earl K. Long Library, U. New Orleans, 1978—, dean library services, 1981—; cons. in field. Author: Centralized Processing and Regional Library Development, 1970, also monographs, articles.; Co-Author: Resources of Texas Libraries, 1968, Centralized Processing and Regional Library Development—The Midwestern Regional Library System, 1970, The Louisiana State Library Processing Center: An Evaluation, 1971, Medical Libraries, Needs and Services, 1972. Grantee U.S. Office Edn., 1965. Mem. ALA, Bibliog. Soc. (London, Eng.), Bibliog. Soc. Am. Club: Grolier (N.Y.C.). Home: Route 2 Box 51 Brittany Dr LaCombe LA 70445 Office: Lake Front New Orleans LA 70122

HENDRICKS, ED JERALD, pathologist; b. Temple, Tex., Aug. 26, 1935; s. John and Lucille (Withers) H.; m. Susan Meredith Brown, Sept. 2, 1959; children: David Wesley, Deborah Kay, John Michael, James Gregory. B.A., Rice U., 1957; M.D., Columbia U., 1961. Diplomate: Am. Bd. Pathology, Nat. Bd. Med. Examiners. Intern Parkland Meml. Hosp., Dallas, 1961-62; resident U. Minn., 1962-66; assoc. pathologist St. Joseph Hosp., Houston, 1969-72; dir. clin. labs.-dept. pathology Fresno Community Hosp., Calif., 1972—, Clovis Community Hosp., 1981—. Contbr. articles to profl. jours. Served to capt. USAF, 1966-69. Fellow Am. Soc. Clin. Pathology, Coll. Am. Pathologists; mem. Fresno County Med. Assn., Calif. Med. Assn., AMA, Calif. Soc. Pathologists (dir. 1982, 83, v.p. 1984), Fresno Pathology Soc. (pres. 1978-79), Pathology Practice Assn. (dir. 1984), Phi Beta Kappa, Sigma Xi. Clubs: pres. (Fresno); Fresno Yacht. Home: 5680 E Alluvial Clovis CA 93612 Office: PO Box 1232 Fresno and R Sts Fresno CA 93715

HENDRICKS, GEOFFREY, artist; b. Littleton, N.H., July 30, 1931; s. Walter and Flora (Bishop) H.; m. Beatrice Cobb Forbes, June 24, 1961 (div. 1973); children—Tyche, Bracken. B.A. cum laude, Amherst Coll., 1953; postgrad. (Sch. fellow), Yale-Norfolk Art Sch., summer 1953, Cooper Union Art Sch., 1953-56; M.A., Columbia U., 1962. Asst. instr. art Douglass Coll., Rutgers-The State U., New Brunswick, N.J., 1956-58, isntr., 1958-61, asst. prof. art, 1961-67, asso. prof., 1967-80, prof., 1980—, grad. dir., 1981—; instr. Earlham Coll./N.Y. Music Art and Drama Program, 1965-69; panelist-juror Creative Arts Public Service Program, 1980; fellow MacDowell Colony, 1955; founder (with Brian Buczak), pres. Money for Food Press, 1977—. Exhibited in one-man shows, Bianchini Gallery, N.Y.C., 1966, Tokyo Gallery, 1968, Apple Gallery, N.Y.C., 1970, Galerie Baecker, Bochum, W. Ger., 1972, 74, 78, Rene Block Gallery, N.Y.C., 1976-77, Studio Morra, Naples, Italy, 1980, numerous group shows, including, Nelson Gallery, Kansas City, Mo., 1965, Kunstverein, Cologne, W. Ger., 1970, Galleria d'Arte Moderna, Turin, Italy, 1973, Henie-Onstad Mus., Oslo, 1978, Kunstverein für die Rheinlande, Düsseldorf, W. Ger., 1980; represented in permanent collections, Hopkins Art Center, Hanover, N.H., Modern Art Museum, Vienna, Austria, Rose Art Mus., Waltham, Mass., Lehmbruck Mus., Duisburg, W. Ger., Met. Mus. Art, N.Y.C., Mus. Modern Art, N.Y.C., N.J. State Mus., Trenton, and pvt. collections; works include Sky Wall; mural at, Aral Hdqrs., Bochum, 1978; Author: Ring Piece, 1973, Between Two Points/Fra Due Poli, 1976, Five Found Photos, 1979, La Capra, 1979. Served alt. mil. duty as occupational therapy artist St. Barnabas Hosp., 1953-56; Bronx, N.Y. Nat. Endowment for Arts grantee, 1977. Mem. AAUP, Coll. Art Assn., Fluxus. Quaker. Office: Visual Art Dept Mason Gross Sch of Arts Douglass Coll Campus Rutgers-The State U New Brunswick NJ 08903 *I've turned corners, dug roots, tasted silence, listened to sounds within rocks, smelled the arrival of spring, and watched the sky change. Sitting in the present the arms of the chair become yesterday and tomorrow.*

HENDRICKS, JAMES POWELL, artist; b. Little Rock, Aug. 7, 1938; s. Leland Fuller and Christia Beatrice (Powell) H.; m. Marcia Reed-Hendricks, May 27, 1978. B.A., U. Ark., 1962; M.F.A., U. Iowa, 1964. Instr. art State U. Iowa, 1962-64, Mt. Holyoke Coll., 1964-65; mem. faculty U. Mass., Amherst, 1965—, prof. art, 1977—, dir. undergrad. programs in art, 1968-71, dir. grad. programs art, 1974-77. One-man exhbn., Nat. Air and Space Mus., Smithsonian Instn., fall 1969, group exhbns. include, Nat. Gallery Art, 1970, Nat. Air and Space Mus., 1976, 4th Internat. Biennial, Medellin, Colombia, 1981. Named Ark. Traveler, 1971. Office: Art Dept U Mass Amherst MA 01003

HENDRICKS, JOHN CARL, singer, songwriter; b. Newark, Ohio, Sept. 16, 1921; m. Judith Hendricks. Student, U. Toledo. Drummer with own group, Rochester N.Y., after World War II; sang, played drums with own quartet, Toledo, until 1952; songwriter, 1957—; teamed (with Dave Lambert); to produce new version of Four Brothers for, Decca, 1957; joined (with Annie Ross), to produce multi-tape rec. of old Count Basie recs.; first album produced Sing a Song of Basie, 1958; 2d album Sing Along with Basie, 1958; trio played theatre dates with, Basie, 1959; moved to London, 1968; touring throughout, Europe and Africa; composer: I Want You To Be My Baby, 1957; also instrumental Minor Catastrophe; author: musical revue performed Evolution of the Blues, Monterey Jazz Festival, 1960; revised version performed, Broadway Theatre, San Francisco, 1974-75 (Recipient Down Beat Critics poll as new vocal star 1959), Broadway Theatre, San Francisco (trio won Down Beat Readers poll as number 1 vocal group 1959) *

HENDRICKS, WILLIAMS HULIN, banker; b. Youngstown, Ohio, Oct. 17, 1932; s. Oscar W. and Gertrude E. (Potter) H.; m. Phylles J. Weimer, June 17, 1954; children: Scott, Stephen. B.S., Ohio State U., 1954, M.S., 1958. Fed. Res. Bank, Cleve., 1958—, v.p., 1967-72, sr. v.p., 1972-82, 1st. v.p., 1982—. Served to 1st lt. U.S. Army, 1955-57. Office: Fed Res Bank Cleve 1455 E 6th St Cleveland OH 44101

HENDRICKSEN, HOLMES, hotel exec.; b. Holyoke, Colo., Apr. 22, 1933; s. Fred Willard and Esther Irene H.; m. Christine Lee Dishman, May 26, 1979. B.S., U. Utah, 1956. With Harrah's, Tahoe, Nev., 1957—; gen. mgr. Harrah's Tahoe, 1968-71; v.p. entertainment Harrah's Reno/Tahoe, 1971-76, exec. v.p. entertainment and public relations, 1977—; pres. AIR Corp. Clubs: Hidden Valley Country, Friars. Office: PO Box 10 Reno NV 89504

HENDRICKSON, BRUCE CARL, life insurance company executive; b. Holdrege, Nebr., Apr. 4, 1930; s. Carl R. and Ruth E. (Bosserman) H.; m. Carol Schepman, June 12, 1952; children: Julie, Mark Bruce. B.A., U. Nebr., 1952. C.L.U.; chartered fin. cons. Life underwriter Bankers Life Co., Holdrege, 1950—. Bd. govs. Central Nebr. Tech. Community Coll.; mem. Nebr. Edn. Commn. of States, Nat. Hwy. Safety Advisors Com.; elder United Presbyterian Ch., Holdrege; pres. Holdrege City Council, 1979. Served with USNR, 1953-56. Bruce Hendrickson Week declared by Gov. of Nebr., 1975; recipient Distinguished Alumni Achievement award U. Nebr., 1977. Mem. Nat. Assn. Life Underwriters (pres. 1975-76), Assn. Advanced Life Underwriting, Am. Soc. C.L.U.s, Life Underwriters Polit. Action Com. (vice chmn. 1978—), Life Underwriters Tng. Council (trustee 1979—), Million Dollar Round Table, Phi Kappa Psi. Republican. Clubs: Rotary, Holdrege Country (Holdrege); Am. Legion, Elks. Home: 305 11th Ave Holdrege NE 68949 Office: 415 East Ave Holdrege NE 68949

HENDRICKSON, JAMES BRIGGS, educator, chemist; b. Toledo, Jan. 3, 1928; s. Philip and Dorothy (Briggs) H.; m. Sybil Pardee, May 30, 1953; children—Jared Jeffrey Raymond, Sonia Catherine Angell. B.S., Calif. Inst. Tech., 1950; M.A., Harvard, 1951, Ph.D., 1955. NRC postdoctoral fellow U. London, Eng., 1954-55; asst. prof. U. Calif. at Los Angeles, 1957-63; asso. prof. Brandeis U., 1963-66, prof. chemistry, 1966—; cons. Sandoz Pharms., Inc., Hanover, N.J. Author: Biosynthesis of Steroids, Terpenes and Acetogenins, 1963, The Molecules of Nature, 1965, (with others) Organic Chemistry, 1970; also research papers. Served with AUS, 1946-48; Korea. Sloan fellow, 1962-66; Guggenheim fellow, 1964; Fulbright prof. U. Cape Coast, Ghana, 1974-76. Mem. Am. Chem. Soc., Chem. Soc. (London). Home: 9 Acacia St Cambridge MA 02138 Office: Dept Chemistry Brandeis Univ Waltham MA 02254

HENDRICKSON, ROBERT FREDERICK, pharmaceutical company executive; b. Cambridge, Mass., Jan. 5, 1933; s. Charles H. and Ruth E. (Bjorklund) H.; m. Virginia H. Emery, Apr. 27, 1963; children: Karen, Susan, Douglas. A.B. in Econs. magna cum laude, Harvard U., 1954, M.B.A., 1958. Engaged in prodn. planning, internat. div. Internat. Latex Corp., Dover, Del., 1958-61; mgr. prodn. planning and control Merck Sharp & Dohme, West Point, Pa., 1961-66, dir. long-range planning, 1966-68, exec. sec. new products com., 1968-69, dir. prodn. planning and control, 1969-71, dir. ops., 1971-72, v.p. ops., 1972-80; sr. v.p. Merck & Co., Inc., Rahway, N.J., 1981—. Bd. dirs. Lenape Valley Mental Health Found., 1972-80, pres., 1976-77; trustee N.J. State Safety Council, 1980—. Served with AUS, 1954-56. Mem. North Penn C. of C. (dir. 1974-77), Pharm. Mfg. Assn. (chmn. prodn. and engring. sect. 1980-81). Presbyn. (elder). Home: 204 Gallup Rd Princeton NJ 08540 Office: Merck & Co Inc PO Box 2000 Rahway NJ 07065

HENDRICKSON, ROBERT MELAND, insurance company executive; b. Fargo, N.D., Aug. 23, 1929; s. Reinhard Oscar and Beatrice Harriet (Mel) H.; m. Kathleen McCauley, 1950 (div. 1979); children: David, Nancy; m. Patricia Kruk, 1981. B.S., N.D. State U., 1950. With Equitable Life Assurance Soc., N.Y.C., 1950—, exec. v.p., chief investment officer, dir., 1975-80, exec. v.p., chief ins. officer, dir., 1980-81, sr. exec. v.p., asst. to chief exec. officer, dir., 1981—; dir. Equitable Life Holding Corp., Crown Zellerbach. Mem. Am. Econs. Assn., Am. Fin. Assn., Econ. Club N.Y.

HENDRIE, JOSEPH MALLAM, physicist, nuclear engineer, government official; b. Janesville, Wis., Mar. 18, 1925; s. Joseph Munier and Margaret Prudence (Hocking) H.; m. Elaine Kostell, July 9, 1949; children: Susan Debra, Barbara Ellen. B.S., Case Inst. Tech., 1950; Ph.D., Columbia U., 1957. Registered profl. engr., N.Y., Calif. Asst. physicist Brookhaven Nat. Lab., Upton, N.Y., 1955-57, asso. physicist, 1957-60, physicist, 1960-71, sr. physicist, 1971—, chmn. steering com., project chief engr. high flux beam reactor design and constrn., 1958-65, acting head exptl. reactor physics div., 1965-66, project mgr. pulsed fast reactor project, 1967-70, asso. head engring. div., dept. applied sci., 1967-71, head, 1971-72, chmn. dept. applied sci., 1975-77, spl. asst. to dir., 1981—; dep. dir. licensing for tech. rev. U.S. AEC, 1972-74; chmn. U.S. Nuclear Regulatory Commn., Washington, 1977-79, 81, commr., 1980; lectr. nuclear power plant safety MIT, Ga. Inst. Tech., Northwestern U., summers 1970-77; cons. radiation safety com. Columbia U., 1964-72; mem. adv. com. reactor safeguards AEC, 1966-72, chmn., 1970; U.S. mem. sr. adv. group on reactor safety standards IAEA, 1974-78. Mem. editorial adv. bd.: Nuclear Tech, 1967-77. Served with AUS, 1943-45. Recipient E.O. Lawrence award, 1970; decorated comdr. Order of Leopold II (Belgium), 1982. Fellow Am. Nuclear Soc. (dir. 1976-77, v.p. 1983-84, pres. 1984-85), ASME; mem. Nat. Acad. Engring., Am. Phys. Soc., Am. Concrete Inst., IEEE, Nat. Soc. Profl. Engrs., Sigma Xi, Tau Beta Pi. Research, publs. on physics nuclear reactors, nuclear power plant safety, engring. design reactors, elec. power transmission, chem. physics nitrogen dissociation process, structure oxygen molecule. Co-inventor high flux beam reactor. Office: Brookhaven Nat Lab Upton NY 11973

HENDRIX, DENNIS RALPH, gas transmission company executive; b. Selmer, Tenn., Jan. 8, 1940; s. Forrest Ralph and Mary Lee (Tull) H.; m. Jennie L. Moore, Dec. 28, 1960; children—Alisa Lee, Natalie Moore, Amy Louise. B.S., U. Tenn., 1962; M.B.A., Ga. State U., 1967. C.P.A., Ga. Staff accountant, cons. Arthur Andersen & Co., Atlanta, 1962-65; faculty Ga. Inst. Tech., 1965-67; sr. cons. Touche, Ross & Co., Memphis, 1967-68; pres. United Foods, Inc., Memphis, 1968-73; asst. to pres. Tex. Gas Transmission Corp., Owensboro, Ky., 1973-75, pres., 1976—, chief exec. officer, 1978—, chmn., 1982—; dir. First City Bancorp. of Tex., Inc., Provident Life and Accident Ins. Co.; Bd. dirs. Am. Petroleum Inst., Coal Policy Council, Commonwealth of Ky. Bd. dirs. Ky. Center for Energy Research; vice pres., dir. Jr. Achievement, Owensboro; bd. dirs. Nat. Jr. Achievement, Ky. Econ. Devel. Corp., U. Tenn. Devel. Council; trustee Brescia Coll., Owensboro. Mem. NAM (dir.), Interstate Natural Gas Assn. Am. (dir.), Nat. Ocean Industries Assn. (dir.); mem. Ky. Council Higher Edn. (dir.). Presbyterian. Clubs: Owensboro Country; River Oaks Country, Ramada (Houston). Home: 23 Stone Creek Park Owensboro KY 42301 Office: 3800 Frederica St Owensboro KY 42301

HENDRIX, JAMES HARVEY, plastic surgeon; b. Newbern, Tenn., Jan. 22, 1920; s. James Harvey and Zola (Burkett) H.; m. Barbara Corcoran, Feb. 26, 1944; children—Susan (Mrs. Robert Cronin), Jane, Sarah. B.S., U. Tenn., Knoxville, 1942, M.D., 1943. Diplomate: Am. Bd. Plastic Surgery (dir.). Rotating intern Methodist Hosp., Memphis, 1943-44; resident gen. surgery, plastic surgery U. Tex. Med. Br., Galveston, 1944-47, Baptist Meml. Hosp., Memphis, 1947-51; pvt. practice medicine specializing in plastic surgery, Memphis, 1951-52, 72—, Jackson, Miss., 1952-72; asst. dept. surgery U. Tenn., Memphis, 1951-52; chief plastic surgery U. Miss., Jackson, 1955-72; prof. surgery, chief plastic surgery U. Tenn., Memphis, 1972-78, clin. prof., 1978—; cons. in field. Served with AUS, 1944-46. Fellow ACS (chmn. adv. council plastic and maxillofacial surgery); mem. Am. Soc. Plastic and Reconstructive Surgeons (pres. 1973-74), Southeastern Soc. Plastic and Reconstructive Surgeons (pres. 1969), Am. Assn. Plastic Surgeons (historian 1966-69), AMA (chmn. residency rev. com. plastic surgery 1971-72), Am. Cleft Palate Assn., Am. Trauma Soc., Memphis, Singleton surg. socs., Plastic Surgery Research Council (chmn. 1956). Home: 4657 Hemlock Ln Memphis TN 38117 Office: 910 Madison Ave Suite 525 Memphis TN 38103

HENDRY, IAIN WILSON MENZIES, lawyer; b. Glasgow, Scotland, June 14, 1927; emigrated to came to Can., 1954; s. James Robertson and May Gold (Bryce) H.; m. Elizabeth Alice Robertson, Apr. 2, 1954; children: Neil Robertson, James Cowan, Ian Douglas, Jill Elizabeth. B.A. with honors, Cambridge U., 1950; LL.B., Glasgow U., 1952. Bar: B.C. 1955, Ont. 1957. Barrister, solicitor Davis & Co., Vancouver, B.C., Can., 1954-56, Norris & Cumming, Vancouver, 1956-57, Westinghouse Can., Hamilton, Ont., Canada, 1957-61, asst. gen. counsel, 1962-81, v.p., sec. gen. counsel, 1981—; solicitor Wilson Chalmers & Hendry, Glasgow, 1961-62. Served to lt. Brit. Army, 1945-48. Mem. Assn. Can. Gen. Counsel, Can. Mfrs. Assn., Upper Can. Law Soc., Can. Bar Assn., Hamilton Law Assn. Progressive Conservative. Presbyterian. Clubs: Hamilton Golf and Country (bd. dirs.); Hamilton. Home: 146 Crestview Ave Ancaster ON Canada L9G 1E1 Office: Westinghouse Can Inc 120 King St West Hamilton ON Canada L8P 4V2

HENDRY, THOMAS BEST, playwright, lyricist; b. Winnipeg, Man., Can., June 7, 1929; s. Donald and Martha (Best) H.; m. Judith Carr, Nov. 22, 1963; children: Thomas John, Christopher Stefan, Ashleigh Elizabeth Jane. Student, U. Man., First Year U.-Arts, 1947. Partner Hendry & Evans (Chartered Accountants), Winnipeg, 1955-59; partner Theatre 77, 1957-58; founder, adminstr. Man. Theatre Centre, Winnipeg, 1958-63; sec. gen. Canadian Centre of Internat. Theatre Inst., Toronto, 1964-69; lit. mgr. Stratford (Can.) Festival, 1969-70; founder, pres., pres. bd. Toronto Free Theatre, 1971-82, producer, 1980-82; dir., co-founder Advanced Playwriting Workshop, Banff (Alta.) Sch. Fine Arts, 1974-76; co-founder, chmn. bd. Playwrights Co-op., Toronto, 1971-79, Playwrights Can., 1979-82; fellow Bethune Coll., York U., Downsview, Ont.; organizer Colloquium, 1967. Sr. writer: TV series King of Kensington; Author: plays Fifteen Miles of Broken Glass, 1968, How Are Things With the Walking Wounded, 1972, You Smell Good to Me, 1972, (with Steven Jack) Gravediggers of 1942, 1973, (with Stanley Silverman) Satyricon!, 1969, (with Stanley Silverman and Richard Foreman) Dr. Selavy's Magic Theatre, 1972, Aces Wild, 1974, Naked at the Opera, 1974, A Memory of Eden, 1975, Byron, 1975, (with Walter Buczynski) Naked at the Opera, 1977; Hogtown, Farr Away; Recorded: Dr. Selavy's Magic Theatre, 1974. Chmn. Ont. Performing Arts Touring Program Centennial, 1966-67; mem. Pres.'s Com., UNESCO-Can., 1966-69; Bd. dirs. Canadian Forum mag., 1971-79; mem. Toronto Arts Council, 1983—; audit officer Dept. Nat. Rev.-Customs and Excise. Recipient Sr. Arts awards Can. Council, 1963-64, 71, 74—, Centennial medal Ont.; Lt. Gov.'s medal for playwriting, 1970; Queen Elizabeth Jubilee medal, 1977. Mem. Inst. Chartered Accountants of Man. and Ont., Canadian Inst. Chartered Accountants, Actors Equity Assn. (Canadian exec. com.), Winnipeg Press Club. Address: 34 Elgin Ave Toronto ON Canada *One's views are generally best stated, sometimes only by implication, in one's work. I have tried to be receptive to the small voice inside me which tends to give good and truthful advice about the way ahead. Following its urgings has, at times, meant turning my back on people and places for whom I feel great affection. Fortunately I have a family prepared to trust my instinct and to put up with the consequences of decisions.*

HENDSEY, SUSANNE BRENNAN, librarian; b. Providence, Mar. 19, 1936; d. Laurence J. and Harriet E. (Delaplane) Brennan. B.A., U. Conn., 1960; M.L.S., U. Mich., 1967. Head M.B.A. Library, Univ. Conn., Hartford, 1964-66; asst. librarian Cornell Univ. Grad. Sch. Bus., Ithaca, N.Y., 1967-72; head reader's services FTC Library, Washington, 1972-79, library dir., 1979—. Mem. Law Librarians Soc. (dir. 1980-81), Spl. Libraries Assn., Am. Assn. Law Libraries, D.C. Library Assn. Office: Fed Trade Commission 6th and Pennsylvania Ave NW Washington DC 20580

HENEBERRY, DAVID ARTHUR, direct marketing agency executive; b. Decatur, Ill., Feb. 7, 1931; s. Will and Mary Alice (Bresnan) H.; m. Elizabeth C. Heckman, Aug. 8, 1953; children: Michael, Susan, Paula, Anne, Amy, Thomas. B.S. in Journalism, U. Ill., 1953. Asst. subscription mgr. Better Homes and Gardens, Des Moines, 1955-60; asst. advt. dir. Bankers Life and Casualty, Chgo., 1960-62; v.p. account service Marshall John Advt., Chgo., 1962-65; v.p. mktg. LaSalle Extension U., N.Y.C., 1965-68; pres. RCA Music Service, N.Y.C., 1968-78; v.p. mktg. RCA Videodiscs, N.Y.C., 1978-81; mng. dir., sr. ptnr. Tatham Laird & Kudner, N.Y.C., 1981—; dir. Loo Art Press, Colorado Springs, Colo., 1977—. Served to 1st lt. Security Agy. U.S. Army, 1953-55. Named Mktg. Man of Yr. 100 Million Club, N.Y.C., 1980. Mem. Direct Mktg. Assn. (chmn. 1978-80). Democrat. Roman Catholic. Club: Country of Darien (Conn.). Home: 66 Summit Ridge Rd New Canaan CT 06840 Office: Tatham Laird & Kudner Direct Mktg 605 3d Ave New York NY 10016

HENEMAN, HARLOW JAMES, management consultant; b. Minn.; s. Herman and Alice (Burfield) H.; m. Avis Louise Dayton; children: Joyce, Burfield. A.B., U. Minn.; M.A., U. Calif.; Ph.D., U. London. Asso. prof. polit. sci. U. Mich.; editorial adviser Oxford U. Press; mgmt. analyst U.S. Bur. Budget; U.S. Mil Govt., Berlin; cons. U.S. rep. on U.N.A.E.C., Dept. State (and pvt. firms), spl. asst. to asst. sec. for occupied areas, dir. mgmt. staff; formerly gen. partner firm Cresap, McCormick & Paget; pvt. cons.; mem. bus. and arts com. N.Y. Bd. Trade, 1966-69; Pres. faculty rev. bd. U.S. Mil. Acad., 1967-68; pres. Cresap, McCormick and Paget Found., 1967-68; chmn. commn. on policies and operations Nat. Endowment for Arts, 1972-73; dir. Sci. Am., Inc.; cons. Mayo Clinic-Found., 1969—. Author: (with others) Financing Higher Education, 1960-70, 1959, Professional Practices in Management Consulting, 1959, The Arts; A Central Element of a Good Society, 1965, The Arts: Planning for Change, 1966, Readings in Financial Analysis, 1970; Bd. editors: Financial Analysts Jour, 1964-67; Contbr. to profl. jours. in law, finance, health and edn. Bd. dirs. Salk Inst. Biology, 1960-61, Am. Symphony Orch. League, 1967-69; trustee Nat. Planning Assn., 1963-70, New Coll., 1966-69, Ringling State Mus. Art, 1971-80, Sarasota Meml. Hosp. Found., 1976—, Mote Marine Lab., 1978—, Selby Bot. Gardens. Served with M.I. Service War Dept. Gen. Staff. Recipient Outstanding Citizen of Year award Fla. Library Assn., 1977, Disting. Layman of Yr. Fla. Med. Assn., 1982. Club: Field (Sarasota, Fla.). Home: 4822 Ocean Blvd Siesta Key Sarasota FL 33581

HENEMAN, HERBERT GERHARD, JR., educator; b. Lester Prairie, Minn., Dec. 2, 1916; s. Herbert Gerhard and Alta (Beise) H.; m. Jane Lloyd Roberts, Oct. 14, 1940; children—Alta (Mrs. John A. Fossum), Herbert Gerhard III, Robert Lloyd. B.B.A., U. Minn., 1938, M.A., 1943, Ph.D., 1948. Chief accountant Midland Coop. Wholesale, Mpls., 1938-40; faculty U. Minn., Mpls., 1940—, prof., 1954-80, prof. emeritus, 1981—, chmn. dept. indsl. relations, 1960-73; asst. dir. Indsl. Relations Center, 1947-59, dir., 1959-73, chmn. grad. faculty indsl. relations, 1959-73; Vis. prof. Stanford, 1959, U. Richmond, 1952, U.S. Naval Postgrad. Sch., 1962, U. Western Australia, 1973, 79; cons. U.S. Civil Service Dept., U.S. Dept. Labor, HEW, U.S. Postal Service; arbitrator, chmn. fact-finding commns. Author: Labor Economics and Industrial Relations, 1959, Labor Economics, 1965, Employer Manpower Planning and Forecasting, 1971; Editor: Local Labor Market Research, 1948, Personnel Administration and Labor Relations, 1952, Employment Relations Research, 1960, Handbook of Personnel Management and Industrial Relations, 1958, Personnel and Industrial Relations Handbook, 1979; Contbr. bulls., articles to profl. jours. Chmn. Minn. Gov.'s Manpower Adv. Council, 1954-72, St. Paul Fair Employment Practices Commn., 1956-61, Minn. Gov.'s Task Force Labor Relations, 1961-62, Minn. Gov.'s Task Force Unemployment Compensation-Workmen's Compensation, 1956. Served to lt. USNR, 1944-46. Recipient Outstanding Service award U. Minn., 1980. Fellow Social Sci. Research Council; mem. AAUP (pres. Minn. 1960, mem. com. N 1969-71), Indsl. Relations Research Assn., Am. Econ. Assn., Am. Soc. Personnel Adminstrn. (accredited personnel diplomate; hon. life, dir. Personnel Accreditation Inst.), Iota Rho Chi. Home: 92 Norma St Belen NM 87002

HENEY, JOSEPH EDWARD, environmental engineer; b. Brockton, Mass., Feb. 22, 1927; s. John J. and Nellie A. (Byrnes) H.; m. Frances McElroy, Feb. 22, 1955; children: Mary, John, Edward, Stephen. B.S., Northeastern U., 1952; M.S. in San. Engring, Harvard U., 1954. Diplomate: Am. Acad. Environ. Engrs. With Camp, Dresser & McKee, Inc., Boston, 1950—, now pres., chmn. bd.; dir. Camp Scott Furphy Pty. Ltd., Melbourne, Australia; Mem. Northeastern U. Corp. Fellow Am. Cons. Engrs. Council, ASCE, Instn. Engrs. (Australia); mem. Boston Soc. Civil Engrs., Am. Water Works Assn., New Eng. Water Works Assn., New Eng. Water Pollution Control Assn., Inter-Am. Assn. San. Engrs. Home: 26 Winthrop Rd Hingham MA 02043 Office: Camp Dresser & McKee Inc 1 Center Plaza Boston MA 02108

HENEY, THOMAS TRACY, institute director; b. N.Y.C., Nov. 26, 1910; s. Thomas and Ellen (Farley) H.; m. Helen Cronin, Apr. 15, 1939; children: Tracy (dec.), Marcia, Mary Ellen, William, John, Kevin, Timothy. B.A., Middlebury Coll., 1930; LL.B., Union U., Albany, N.Y., 1936. Bar: N.Y. 1936, Fed. 1936, U.S. Supreme Ct. 1939. With firm Staley, Tobin & Manley, Albany, 1936-39, Blake, Voorhees & Stewart, N.Y.C., 1939-44; with Nat. Sugar Refining Co., N.Y.C., 1944-71, exec. v.p., 1957-68, pres., 1968-71; exec. dir. Practising Law Inst., N.Y.C., 1971-82, cons., 1983—; lectr., adj. asst. prof. law N.Y. U. Sch. Law, 1951-66. Office: 810 7th Ave New York NY 10019

HENGEN, WILLIAM LINCOLN, journalist; b. Mpls., Feb. 12, 1914; s. William Henry and Florence (Melchisedech) H.; m. Florence Eleanor Bott, Sept. 12, 1940; children: Patricia (Mrs. Larry Wayne Whittlef), Mary (Mrs. William Robert McCleary), William Michael, Catherine (Mrs. Randall Curtis Koyonen), Stephen, Elizabeth. B.A., St. Thomas Coll., St. Paul, 1935. Writer Mpls. Jour., 1936-39; Sunday sports editor Mpls. Star-Jour. and Star Tribune, 1941-58; asst. sports editor Mpls. Star, 1958-67, sports editor, 1967-69, columnist, 1969—. Served with USMCR, 1944-46. Recipient Merit award Nat. Bowling Writers, 1959, Flowers for Living bowling award, 1973. Mem. Nat. Bowling Writers (past pres.). Home: 6844 Wentworth Ave S Richfield MN 55423 Office: 425 Portland Ave Minneapolis MN 55488

HENICAN, CASWELL ELLS, lawyer; b. New Orleans, Feb. 10, 1905; s. Joseph Patrick and Alice (Boning) H.; m. Elizabeth Cleveland, June 18, 1930; children: Alice (Mrs. Claude V. Perrier, Jr.), Caswell Ellis, Margaret (Mrs. F. Gordon Wilson, Jr.), Dorothy (Mrs. Charles E. Heidingsfelder), Joseph Patrick III. LL.B., Tulane U., 1926. Bar: La. 1926. Since practiced in, New Orleans; assoc. Lemle, Moreno & Lemle, 1926-33; sr. partner Henican, Carriere & Cleveland, 1933-40, Henican, James & Cleveland, 1940—. Chmn. La. State Bd. Pub. Welfare, 1940-47; pres. New Orleans Community Chest, 1940, Council Social Agencies, 1939, Assoc. Cath. Charities New Orleans, 1938; chmn. bd. Mercy Hosp.; mem. exec. com., pres. Magnolia Sch. Bd. Named Most Outstanding Young Man New Orleans Jr. C. of C., 1940; Most Outstanding Alumnus Jesuit High Sch., 1960; named to Tulane U. Hall of Fame, 1978, Greater New Orleans Hall of Fame, 1980; decorated Knight St. Gregory, Knight St. Louis. Mem. New Orleans Bar Assn., La. Bar Assn., ABA, Soc. Hosp. Attys. of Am., Hosp. Assn. (charter), Nat. Assn. Honest Lawyers. Home: 1831 Octavia St New Orleans LA 70115 Office: Heritage Plaza Veterans Meml Dr Metairie LA 70005 *Throughout my life, I have conducted my personal and professional affairs by following the simple principle of doing the best that I could with what I had at the moment that I had to do it, and I have always tried to have clearly in mind a hierarchy of values.*

HENINGTON, DAVID MEAD, city library ofcl.; b. El Dorado, Ark., Aug. 16, 1929; s. Bud Henry and Lucile Check (Scranton) H.; m. Barbara Jean Gibson, June 2, 1956; children—Mark David, Gibson Mead, Paul Billins. B.A., U. Houston, 1951; M.S. in L.S, Columbia U., 1956. Young adult librarian Bklyn. Public Library, 1956-58; head lit. and history dept. Dallas Public Library, 1958, asst. dir., 1962-67; dir. Waco (Tex.) Public Library, 1958-62, Houston Public Library, 1967—; pres. HBW Assos. (Library Planners & Cons.), Houston, 1979—. Served with USAF, 1951-55. Council on Library Resources fellow, 1970-71; recipient Liberty Bell award Houston Bar Assn., 1976. Mem. ALA, Southwestern Library Assn., Tex. Library Assn. (Librarian of Year 1976), Am. Mgmt. Assn., Tex. Mcpl. Librarian Assn. Methodist. Club: Rotary. Home: 6225 San Felipe Rd Houston TX 77057 Office: Houston Public Library 500 McKinney Ave Houston TX 77002

HENIZE, KARL GORDON, astronomer, astronaut; b. Cin., Oct. 17, 1926; s. Fred R. and Mabel (Redmon) H.; m. Caroline Rose Weber, June 27, 1953; children: Kurt Gordon, Marcia Lynn, Skye Karen, Vance Karl. Student, Denison U., 1944-45; B.A., U. Va., 1947, M.A., 1948; Ph.D., U. Mich., 1954. Observer U. Mich. Lamont-Hussey Obs., Bloemfontein, Union S. Africa, 1948-51; Carnegie postdoctoral fellow Mt. Wilson Obs., Pasadena, Calif., 1954-56; sr. astronomer charge Photog. Satellite Tracking Stas., Smithsonian Astrophys. Obs., Cambridge, 1956-59; asso. prof. dept. astronomy Northwestern U., 1959-64, prof., 1964-72; adj. prof. dept. astronomy U. Tex., 1972—; Scientist-astronaut NASA, 1967—, mem. astronomy subcom. NASA Space Sci. Steering Com., 1965-68, AAS vis. prof., 1958-61; guest observer Mt. Stromlo Obs., Canberra, Australia, 1961-62; jet pilot tng., Vance AFB, Enid, Okla., 1968-69; mem. support crew Apollo 15 mission and Skylab mission, 1970-73; mission specialist for ASSESS 2 Spacelab simulation, 1977, mission specialist Spacelab 2, 1985; prin. investigator NASA expts. for Gemini 10, 11 and 12 and Skylab 1, 2 and 3, 1964-78; team leader NASA Facility Definition Team for Starlab Telescope, 1974-78; chmn. NASA working group for Spacelab Wide-Angle Telescope, 1978-79. Served with USNR, 1944-46; lt. comdr. Res., ret. Recipient Robert Gordon Meml. award, 1968; NASA medal for exceptional sci. achievement, 1974. Mem. Am., Royal, Pacific astron. socs., Internat. Astron. Union, Phi Beta Kappa. Research on planetary nebulae, emission-line stars, ultraviolet stellar spectra. Home: 18630 Point Lookout Dr Houston TX 77058 Office: Astronaut Office NASA Johnson Space Center Houston TX 77058 *Is there purpose to human existence; does mankind have a destiny? If so, (and I am sure we all hope it is so) then the very existence of human intelligence and human curiosity make it clear that this destiny is to explore and to understand Nature and the Universe from the realm of sub-nuclear processes to the regions of the farthest galaxies. It is unthinkable that the end all of human intelligence is simply to ensure the creature comfort of our own species.*

HENKE, EMERSON OVERBECK, accountant, educator; b. Stendal, Ind., Feb. 20, 1916; s. George A. and Sarah (Overbeck) H.; m. Beatrice Arney, June 6, 1939; children: Michael, Pamela Henke Bailes. B.S., Evansville Coll., 1937; M.S., Ind. U., 1939; D.B.A., 1953. Clk. Gen. Foods Corp., Evansville, Ind., 1937-38; cost acct. Hoosier Lamp & Stamping Corp., Evansville, 1939-40; instr. to prof. Evansville Coll., 1940-48; prof., chmn. acctg. dept. Baylor U., Waco, Tex., 1948-67, dean, 1967-77, disting. prof. acctg., 1977—; vis. prof. U. Miami, Coral Gables, Fla., 1946, U. Tex., Austin, 1966; Disting. vis. prof. U. Denver, 1971-72; Disting. prof. HanKamer Sch. Bus., 1977-78; research cons. Am. Inst. C.P.A.s, 1959-62. Author: Accounting for Non-Profit Organization: An Exploratory Study, 1965, Accounting for Non-Profit Organizations, 1966, 2d edit., 1977, 3d edit., 1983, (with W. Smith) CPA Review Outline, 1969, (with others) Handbook of Modern Accounting, 1970, Introduction to Accounting: A Conceptual Approach, 1974, CPA Review Outline for Theory, Auditing and Practice, 1977, (with Roderick L. Holmes and Lucian Conway) Managerial Use of Accounting Data, 1978, Introduction to Nonprofit Organization Accounting, 1980, (with others) Handbook of Accounting and Auditing, 1981, (with C. William Thomas) Auditing Theory and Practice, 1983. Named Most Popular Bus. Prof. Baylor U., 1965, Most Outstanding Prof., 1980; U. Evansville Alumni Cert. of Excellence, 1978; named to Athletic Hall of Fame, U. Evansville, 1983. Mem. Am. Inst. C.P.A.s, Am. Acctg. Assn., Central Tex. Chpt. C.P.A.s (pres.), S.W. Bus. Adminstrn. Assn. (pres.), Tex. Soc. C.P.A.s, Beta Alpha Psi (nat. sec.-treas., council mem., pres.), Beta Gamma Sigma. Presbyterian (deacon, elder). Home: 3317 Lake Shore Dr Waco TX 76708

HENKEL, JOHN HARMON, educator; b. Kentwood, La., Aug. 14, 1924; s. William Hatton and Margaret Gwendolyn (Watson) H.; m. Sara Ernestine Saucier, Apr. 23, 1948; children—Wendolyn Elizabeth, Sally Lee Henkel Bone (dec.), Jenny Saucier, Margaret Loraine, Pamela Ann. Student, Southeastern La. Coll., 1941-43; B.S., Tulane U., 1947, M.S., 1948; Ph.D., Brown U., 1954. Jr. research technologist Magnolia Petroleum Co., Dallas, 1948-51, sr. research technologist, 1954-55; research asst. Brown U., Providence, 1951-54; asst. prof. physics U. Ga., Athens, 1955-58, asso. prof., 1958-64, prof., 1964—. Served with USNR, 1943-46. NSF fellow, 1959-60; grantee, 1962-69. Fellow AAAS; mem. Am. Phys. Soc., Ga. Acad. Sci., Sigma Xi, Sigma Chi. Methodist. Clubs: Kiwanis, Green Hills Country. Office: U Ga Physics Dept Athens GA 30602 *

HENKELMAN, FRANK W., fiberglass manufacturing company executive. Pres., chief exec. officer Fiberglass Can., Inc., Toronto, Ont. Office: Fiberglass Can Inc 3080 Yonge St Toronto ON Canada M4N 3N1§

HENKELMAN, WILLARD MAX, lawyer; b. Scranton, Pa., June 7, 1914; s. Max Frederick and Emilie (Neuls) H.; m. Elizabeth Tweedle, Feb. 21, 1943; children—Elizabeth L., Steven W. Grad., Phillips Exeter Acad., Exeter, N.H., 1932; A.B., Princeton U., 1936; J.D., Harvard U., 1939. Bar: Pa. bar 1940. Practiced in, Scranton, 1940-41; asso. Henkelman, Kreder, O'Connell & Brooks (and predecessor firms), Scranton, 1946-52, partner, 1952—; Gen. counsel, advisory dir. Citizens Savs. Assn. Mem. Exeter Grad. Council, Princeton Alumni Council. Served from pvt. to maj. AUS, 1942-46; PTO; col. Res. ret. Decorated Bronze Star. Mem. ABA, Pa. Bar Assn., Lackawanna Bar Assn. (exec. com. 1974-79), Waynewood Assn. (pres. 1969-70), Lackawanna Hist. Soc. (v.p. 1969-72), N.E. Pa. Princeton Alumni Assn. (pres. 1952-55, chmn. alumni schs. com. 1960-70), Northeast Pa. Exeter Assn. (pres. 1953-55). Presbyn. Clubs: Kiwanian (pres. 1961), Scranton, Princeton Tower. Home: 1741 N Washington Ave Scranton PA 18509 Office: 200 Bank Towers PO Box 956 Scranton PA 18501

HENKELS, PAUL MACALLISTER, engring. and constrn. co. exec.; b. Phila., Oct. 7, 1924; s. John Bernard, Jr. and Anne (McCloskey) H.; m. Barbara Brass, Jan. 4, 1958; children—Mary, Paul MacAllister, Christopher B., Andrew M., T. Roderick, Amy, Timothy W., Angela, Carol, Barbara. B.A. in Engring, Haverford (Pa.) Coll., 1947. With Henkels & McCoy, 1947—, v.p., then exec. v.p., Blue Bell, Pa., 1958-72, pres., 1972—; bd. mgrs. Beneficial Mut. Savs. Bank, 1978—; Mem. adv. council Coll. Arts and Letters, U. Notre Dame, 1964—, chmn., 1968-70. Mem. Phila. com. United Negro Coll. Fund; chmn. Montgomery County United Way, 1977; vice chmn. Cath. Charities Appeal, Archdiocese of Phila., 1980-81; trustee Temple U., Phila., 1968-72, 79—, exec. com., 1969-72; bd. govs. Temple U. Hosp., 1975—, vice chmn., 1975-79; trustee Ind. Colls. Pa., 1976—, exec. com., 1977—, chmn. bd., 1980—; trustee Chestnut Hill Coll., 1978—. Served with AUS, 1944-46. Decorated Purple Heart; recipient Disting. Service award United Vets. Council, Phila., 1967; Man of Yr. award Notre Dame Club, Phila., 1980. Mem. Am. Nat. Standards Inst., Nat. Elec. Contractors Assn. (gov. 1963-67, Coggeshall award 1971), Atlantic Contractors Assn. (1st pres. 1965), Greater Phila. Utility Contractors Assn. (1st pres. 1972-74), Soc. Gas Lighters, Acad. Applied Elec. Sci. (dir. 1980—). Republican. Roman Catholic. Clubs: Pine Valley Golf, Whitemarsh Valley Country, Seaview Country. Home: 345 Stenton Ave Plymouth Meeting PA 19462 Office: Henkels & McCoy Jolly Rd Blue Bell PA 19422

HENKEN, WILLARD JOHN, university dean; b. Waupun, Wis., Aug. 15, 1927; s. John Gerrit and Emma Amelia (Korth) H.; m. Dolores Ebert, Aug. 26, 1949; children—Thomas, Susan, Richard. B.S., U. Wis. at Oshkosh, 1951; M.S., U. Wis. at Madison, 1958, Ph.D., 1966. Tchr. Cedarburg (Wis.) High Sch., 1951-56, prin., 1956-62; supt. Am. Internat. Sch., New Delhi, India, 1962-64; adminstrv. asst. Sch. Edn., U. Wis. at Madison, 1964-66; dean U. Wis. Center, Fond du Lac, 1966—. Mem. U. Wis. Oshkosh Found., 1966—; Bd. dirs. Fond du Lac Conv. and Visitors Bur., 1982—; mem. Fond du Lac County Bd. Suprs., 1977—, vice chmn., 1980. Served with USN, 1945. Mem. Am. Assn. Sch. Adminstrs., U. Wis. at Madison Alumni Assn., U. Wis. at Oshkosh Alumni Assn., Fond du Lac Area Assn. Commerce (dir. 1982—), Phi Delta Kappa. Home: 736 Nakoma Ave Fond du Lac WI 54935 *My mother and father recognized the value of an education, even though economic conditions forced them to terminate their formal schooling after completing the eighth grade. They encouraged me to pursue my education to the limit of my ability, and provided financial support to the extent they could. Because of their efforts, I developed a love for learning that will last a lifetime. I try to instill that same love in my students.*

HENKIN, DANIEL ZWIE, association executive; b. Washington, May 10, 1923; s. Zalmen and Sadie (Weinberg) H.; m. Hannah Ronen, May 19, 1957; children—Doron, Leora, Tamar. B.A., U. Calif. at Berkeley, 1948. Asst. editor, then editor Jour. Armed Forces, 1948-65; dir. ops. Office Asst. Sec. Def. Pub. Affairs, 1965-67; dep. asst. sec. def., 1967-69, asst. sec. def. for pub. affairs, 1969-73; v.p. for pub. information Air Transport Assn., Washington, 1973—; lectr. Nat. War Coll., Indsl. Coll. Armed Forces. Served with USCGR, 1942-45. Recipient Meritorious Civilian Service medal sec. def.; Distinguished Pub. Service award Dept. Def. Club: Nat. Press (Washington). Home: 2306 Washington Ave Chevy Chase MD 20815 Office: Air Transport Assn 1709 New York Ave NW Washington DC 20006

HENKIN, LEON ALBERT, educator, mathematician; b. Bklyn., Apr. 19, 1921; s. Ascher and Rose (Goldberg) H.; m. Ginette Potvin, Sept. 8, 1950; children: Paul Jacques, Julian David. A.B., Columbia U., 1941; M.A., Princeton U., 1942, Ph.D., 1947. Mathematician, Manhattan Dist. Project, 1942-46; Henry B. Fine instr., Frank Jewett postdoctoral fellow Princeton, 1947-49; from asst. prof. to asso. prof. math. U. So. Calif., 1949-53; faculty U. Calif.-Berkeley, 1953—, prof. math., 1958—, chmn. dept., 1966-68, 83—; vis. prof. Dartmouth Coll., 1960-61; Fulbright research scholar, Amsterdam, Netherlands, 1954-55, Technion, Haifa, Israel, spring 1979; Guggenheim fellow, mem. Inst. Advanced Study, Princeton, 1961-62; vis. fellow All Souls Coll., Oxford (Eng.) U., 1968-69; vis. scholar U. Colo., 1975. Author: La Structure Algebrique des theories Mathématique, 1955, (with others) Retracing Elementary Mathematics, 1962, Cylindric Algebras, 1971; also articles. Mem. U.S. Commn. on Math. Instrn., 1978—, chmn., 1981-82. Fellow AAAS (council del. for math. sect.); mem. Nat. Council Tchrs. Math., Assn. Symbolic Logic (pres. 1962-64), Am. Math. Soc. (council 1962-64), Math. Assn. Am. (Chauvenet prize 1964), ACLU (bd. dirs. Berkeley 1964-66), Phi Beta Kappa, Sigma Xi. Home: 9 Maybeck Twin Dr Berkeley CA 94708

HENKIN, LOUIS, educator, lawyer; b. Russia, Nov. 11, 1917; came to U.S., 1923, naturalized, 1930; s. Yoseph Elia and Frieda Rebecca (Kreindel) H.; m. Alice Barbara Hartman, June 19, 1960; children: Joshua, David, Daniel. A.B., Yeshiva Coll., 1937, L.H.D., 1963; LL.B., Harvard U., 1940. Bar: N.Y. 1941, U.S. Supreme Ct 1947. Law clk. to Judge Learned Hand, 1940-41, Justice Frankfurter, 1946-47; cons. legal dept. UN, 1947-48; with State Dept., 1945-46, 48-57; U.S. rep. UN Com. Refugees and Stateless Persons, 1950; adviser U.S. del. UN Econ. and Social Council, 1950, UN Gen. Assembly, 1950-53, Geneva Conf. on Korea, 1954; asso. dir. Legis. Drafting Research Fund; lectr. law Columbia U., 1956-57; vis. prof. law U. Pa., 1957-58, prof. law, 1958-62; prof. internat. law and diplomacy, prof. law Columbia U., 1962, mem. Inst. War and Peace Studies, 1962—, Hamilton Fish prof. internat. law and diplomacy, 1963-78, Harlan Fiske Stone prof. constl. law, 1978-79, Univ. prof., 1979—, co-dir. Center for Study of Human Rights, 1978—; U.S. mem. Permanent Ct. Arbitration, 1963-69; Carnegie lectr. Hague Acad. Internat. Law, 1965; Gottesman lectr. Yeshiva U., 1975; Lockhart lectr. U. Minn. Law Sch., 1976; Francis Biddle lectr. Harvard Law Sch., 1978; Univ. lectr. Columbia U., 1979; Sherrill lectr. Yale U. Law Sch., 1981; Jefferson lectr. U. Pa. Law Sch., 1983; cons. to govt. Pres., U.S. Inst. Human Rights, 1970—; chief reporter Am. Law Inst. Restatement of Fgn. Relations Law of U.S., 1979—; adviser, U.S. del. UN Conf. on Law of Sea, 1972-81. Author: Arms Control and Inspection in American law, 1958, The Berlin Crisis and the United Nations, 1959, Disarmament: The Lawyer's Interests, 1964, How Nations Behave: Law and Foreign Policy, 2d edit., 1979, Law for the Sea's Mineral Resources, 1968, Foreign Affairs and the Constitution, 1972, The Rights of Man Today, 1978; Editor: Arms Control: Issues for the Public, 1961, (with others) Transnational Law in a Changing Society, 1972, World Politics and the Jewish Condition, 1973, (with others) International Law, Cases and Materials, 1980, The International Bill of Rights: The International Covenant of Civil and Political Rights, 1981; bd. editors: Am. Jour. Internat. Law, 1967—; co-editor-in-chief, 1978—; Contbr. (with others) articles to profl. jours. Served with AUS, 1941-45. Decorated Silver Star; Guggenheim fellow, 1979-80; recipient Alumni medal of Excellence, Columbia U., 1982. Fellow Am. Acad. Arts and Scis.; mem. Council Fgn. Relations, Am. Soc. Internat. Law (v.p. 1974-75), Internat. Law Assn. (v.p. Am. br. 1973—), Am. Soc. Polit. and Legal Philosophy, Am. Polit. Sci. Assn. Home: 460 Riverside Dr New York NY 10027

HENKIND, PAUL, ophthalmologist, educator; b. N.Y.C., Dec. 12, 1932; s. Samuel Joseph and Sadie (Weitzen) H.; m. Ellen G. Bogen, June 9, 1956; children: Steven Joseph, Karen Grace, Jennifer Faith; m. Janice V. Benjamin, May 22, 1977; 1 son, Aaron Samuel. B.A., Columbia U., 1955; M.D. (Fight for Sight student fellow), N.Y. U., 1959; M.S. in Ophthalmology, N.Y. U., 1964; Ph.D. in Pathology, U. London, Eng., 1965. Diplomate: Am. Bd. Ophthalmology. Intern Henry Ford Hosp., Detroit, 1959-60; resident N.Y. U. (Bellevue Hosp.), N.Y.C., 1960-63; NIH spl. fellow Inst. Ophthalmology, London, 1963-65; asst. prof. ophthalmology N.Y. U., 1965-68, asso. prof., 1968-70; prof., chmn. dept. ophthalmology Albert Einstein Coll. Medicine, Bronx, N.Y., 1970—, Frances De Jur prof.; dir. ophthalmology Montefiore Hosp. and Med. Center, Bronx, 1970—; pres. Med. Dialogues, Inc., 1977—; cons. N.Y. Zool. Soc., New Rochelle Hosp., Peninsula Gen. Hosp., Hackensack Hosp. Assn.; mem. sci. adv. bd. Fight for Sight, 1975—; mem. vision research and tng. com. Nat. Eye Inst., NIH, 1972-76; cons., 1972—, Harvey Breslin Meml. lectr., 1975, Seymour Roberts Meml. lectr., 1975, G. Victor Simpson lectr., 1975, Royal Coll. Physicians and Surgeons (Can.) lectr., 1977, Alan Firman lectr., 1979; Paul Chandler lectr. Harvard U., 1979; A.A. Ticho lectr., Israel, 1979; Alex Krill lectr. Chgo Opthal. Soc., 1980; Mark Schoenberg lectr. N.Y. Soc. Clin. Ophthalmolo, 1983; R. Stein lectr. Tel Aviv U., 1983; other named Lectureships; vis. prof. Royal Soc. Medicine, London, 1981. Author: (with others) The Retinal Circulation, 1971, Manual for Eye Examination and Diagnosis, 1975, 2d edit., 1981, Diagnosis and Management of Open Angle Glaucoma, 1977, Compendium of Ophthalmology, 1983; editor: Physicians Desk Reference for Ophthalmology, 1972—, Ophthalmic Seminars, 1976-77, Ophthalmology; mem. editorial bd.: Investigative Ophthalmology, 1968-72, Survey Ophthalmology, 1970—, Am. Jour. Ophthalmology, 1974-79, Neuroradiology, 1976—, AMA Archives of Ophthalmology, 1976-79, Perspectives in Ophthalmology, 1978-81, Jour. Dermatol. Surgery and Oncology, 1978—, Ophthalmologica, 1983—; sect. editor systemic ophthalmology: Duane's Clin. Ophthalmology, 1976—; ophthalmic editor: Marcel Dekker, Inc, 1976-79; contbr. articles to profl. jours. USPHS grantee, 1968-80. Fellow A.C.S., N.Y. Acad. Sci.; mem. Assn. Research Vision and Ophthalmology (chmn. sect. pathology 1968, chmn. sect. anatomy and pathology 1969, sec.-treas. 1976-81), Am. Acad. Ophthalmology (asso. sec. continuing edn. 1974-79, chmn. com. ophthalmic pathology 1976-80, editor 1980—), N.Y. Soc. Clin. Ophthalmology (chmn. program 1972-73, v.p. 1974-75, pres. 1975-76), Manhattan Ophthalmology Soc. (sec.-treas. 1972-74), AAAS, N.Y. Acad. Medicine, Ophthal. Soc. U.K., French Ophthal. Soc., Peruvian Ophthal. Soc. (hon.), Can. Ophthal Soc. (hon.), Colombian Ophthalmology Soc., Opthal Soc. N.Z. (hon.). Address: Montefiore Hosp and Med Center Bronx NY 10467 *I do not wish to be in a different time or a different place, nor wish a different mind or a different face. The challenge within is simply to be the man in me.*

HENKLE, ROGER BLACK, English language educator; b. Lincoln, Nebr., Dec. 15, 1935; s. Elmer E. and Helen (Black) H.; m. Carol Thompson, June 28, 1960; children: Timothy R., Jennifer K. B.A., U. Nebr., 1956; LL.B., Harvard U., 1959; Ph.D., Stanford U., 1968. Bar: Okla. 1961. Assoc. Kerr, Conn & Davis, Oklahoma City, 1960-64; mng. editor San Francisco Bay Guardian, 1966-68; asst. prof. Brown U., Providence, 1968-74, assoc. prof., 1974-80, prof., 1980—, chmn. dept. English, 1981—, Nicholas Brown prof. oratory and belles lettres, 1981—; cons. U. Tulsa, 1982; mem. NEH rev. panel, 1972-76, 79-80. Author: Reading the Novel, 1977, Comedy and Culture, 1980 (named an Outstanding Book of 1980-81 Assn. Coll. and Research Libraries); mng. editor: Novel: A Forum on Fiction, 1970—. Brown U. Henry Merrit Wriston grantee, 1978; NEH grantee, 1982-83. Mem. MLA (del. gen. assembly 1977-79). Democrat. Home: 73 Everett Ave Providence RI 02912 Office: Brown U Dept English Providence RI 02912

HENLE, GERTRUDE, virologist; b. Mannheim, Germany, Apr. 3, 1912; came to U.S., 1937, naturalized, 1943; d. Theophil and Eleneore (Baumgart) Szpingler; m. Werner Henle, Mar. 13, 1937. M.D., U. Heidelberg, Germany, 1936; D.M.S. (hon.), Med. Coll. Pa., 1975. Intern Inst. Hygiene, U. Heidelberg, 1936-37; mem. faculty U. Pa., 1937—, instr. to prof. bacteriology, 1940—, asst. to prof. virology in pediatrics, 1940—; mem. research staff Children's Hosp. of Phila., 1940—. Contbr. numerous articles on influenza, mumps, hepatitis, infectious mononucleosis and tumor viruses to sci. jour. Recipient Mead-Johnson award Am. Acad. Pediatrics, 1950, Variety of Heart award City of Phila., 1970, Smith, Kline and French award for excellence in research, 1971, Robert-Koch medaille and Robert-Koch preis Robert-Koch-Stiftung, 1971; Robert de Villiers award Leukemia Soc. Am., Inc., 1975; Virus Cancer Program award Nat. Cancer Inst., 1975; Sci. award Phila. chpt. Am. Cancer Soc., 1977; Disting. Achievement in Cancer Research award Bristol Myers Co., 1979. Mem. Am. Acad. Microbiology, Nat. Acad. Scis., Tissue Culture Assn. Home: 533 Ott Rd Bala-Cynwyd PA 19004 Office: 34th St and Civic Center Blvd Philadelphia PA 19104

HENLE, GUY, mag. editor; b. N.Y.C., Dec. 22, 1920; s. James and Marjorie (Jacobson) H.; m. Mary Ellen Bowlby, Jan. 5, 1947; children—Richard Flexner, Peter Bradley (dec. June 1973). A.B., Swarthmore Coll., 1941; M.S. in Journalism, Columbia, 1942. With Vanguard Press, Inc., N.Y.C., 1946-53, asso. editor, 1949-51, sales mgr., 1951-53; workshop editor Woman's Home Companion mag., 1953-56; exec. editor House Beautiful mag., N.Y.C., 1957-72; bldg. architecture editor Am. Home mag., N.Y.C., 1973; mng. editor Consumer Reports, 1974-79, exec. editor, 1979—. Author: How to Plan Your Attic and Basement, 1955. Served to 1st lt. AUS, 1942-46; capt. Res. Home: 21 Round Hill Rd Scarsdale NY 10583 Office: 256 Washington St Mount Vernon NY 10550

HENLE, PETER, economic consultant, arbitrator; b. N.Y.C., Feb. 12, 1919; s. James and Marjorie (Jacobson) H.; m. Theda W. Ostrander, Aug. 25, 1941; children: Michael G., James M., Paul J. B.A., Swarthmore Coll., 1940; M.A., Am. U., 1947. Asst. dir. research Am. Fedn. Labor and AFL-CIO, Washington, 1955-61; chief economist Bur. Labor Stats., U.S. Dept. Labor, Washington, 1961-71, dept. dep. asst. sec., 1977-79; sr. specialist Labor Congl. Research Service, Library of Congress, Washington, 1972-77; econ. cons., arbitrator, Arlington, Va., 1979—. Contbr. articles to profl. jours. Chmn. Arlington County (Va.) Manpower Planning Council, 1975-77. Served with AUS, 1941-42; Served with USAAF, 1942-45. Recipient Disting. Achievement award U.S. Dept. Labor, 1968; Brookings Instn. fed. exec. fellow, 1971-72. Mem. Am. Econ. Assn., Indsl. Relations Research Assn., Am. Arbitration Assn. Office: 3219 N Wakefield St Arlington VA 22207

HENLE, ROBERT JOHN, former univ. pres.; b. Muscatine, Iowa, Sept. 12, 1909; s. Edward M. and Mary Ann (Hauber) H. Student, Creighton U., 1926-27; A.B., St. Louis U., 1931, A.M., 1932, Licentiate in Philosophy, 1935, S.T.L., 1941; Saint Stanislaus Novitiate, Cleve., 1941-42, U. Toronto, 1942-43, 44-45, Ph.D., 1954. Entered Soc. of Jesus, 1927; instr. classics St. Louis U. High Sch., 1935-37; ordained priest, 1940; instr. Latin Summer Sch., St. Louis U., 1938-41, asst. prof. philosophy, 1947-54, asso. prof., 1954-58, prof., 1958-69, dean, 1943-51, 1951-52, 1950-64, mem. univ. council, 1947-51, trustee, 1949-69; pres. Georgetown U., Washington, 1969-76; McDonnell prof. justice in Am. soc. St. Louis U., 1976—. Author: numerous books and articles, including Fourth Year Latin, 1941, Method in Metaphysics, 1950, Saint Thomas and Platonism, 1956; Editor: The Modern Schoolman, 1945-50. Mem. Am. Cath. Philos. Assn., Nat. Cath. Edn. Assn., AAAS, Philosophy of Edn. Soc., Am. Philos. Soc., Midwest Conf. Grad. Study and Research. Address: St Louis Univ St Louis MO 63103 *My life has been based on a profound and practical conviction that an almighty and all-loving God exists and is active in all our lives; that he sent Christ as our Saviour. I have tried to maintain a direct personal relationship with Christ in God. I have expressed these convictions in a concern for students and their full development. I have found freedom to dedicate myself fully through my vows as a Jesuit priest. In my 68th year my only regret is that I have never been able to keep up with God's Grace and inspiration.*

HENLEY, ARTHUR, author, editor, TV consultant; b. Rockaway Beach, N.Y., Sept. 9, 1921; s. Nathan Siegel and Theresa (Hohauser) H.; m. Janet Radskin, June 3, 1950; children: Eric, Kenneth. Engr. Assoc., Pratt Inst., 1944; B.A., CCNY, 1969. Tech. writer Fairchild Camera Co., 1944-45; TV program cons., 1960—; mem. faculty N.Y. U., 1969-70; mental health cons., Nat. Assn. Mental Health Keynoter, coll. lectr. Radio writer, producer: shows Bob & Ray, Make Up Your Mind, 13 by Henley; others; also writer advt. jingles; TV producer Kate Smith Show, Make Up Your Mind, Broadway Open House; TV writer, producer: also indsl. films others; mag. contbr.: Ladies Home Jour., McCalls, Family Health, Public Affairs Com., N.Y. Times, Sat. Eve Post, others, 1961—; Author: The Mathematics of Humor, 1948, Demon In My View, 1966, Make Up Your Mind, 1967, Yes Power, 1969, The Right to Lie, 1970, Schizophrenia, 1971, The Montanari Book: What Other Child-Care Books Don't Tell You, 1972, The Complete Alibi Handbook, 1972, The Difficult Child, 1973, How to Be a Perfect Liar, 1978, Don't Be Afraid of Cataracts, 1978, Don't be Afraid of Cataracts, rev. edit., 1983; Contbr.: anthologies How to Write for Pleasure and Profit, You and Your Mind, Treasury of Tips for Writers; editor: Interdisciplinary Communications Program, Smithsonian Inst., 1975; Cons. med. editor: Globe Communications, 1976-79; Columnist: Brides Mag, 1970. Recipient Russell Sage Found. award., TV-Radio Mirror Gold medals (2).; Work included in U. Wyo. div. spl. collections. Mem. Am. Soc. Journalists and Authors, Nat. Assn. Sci. Writers, AFTRA. Club: Nat. Press. Home: 73-37 Austin St Forest Hills NY 11375 Office: A H Productions 234 Fifth Ave New York NY 10001 *If I have learned anything from living it is that a static life is no life at all while a life of change without direction is only half a life.*

HENLEY, EARLE BURR, JR., manufacturing company executive; b. Oakland, Calif., Apr. 16, 1915; s. Earle Burr and Pauline (Matthews) H.; m. Grace H. Jones, 1940; children: Matthew O., Peter J. B.S., Cornell U., 1937, LL.B., 1940. Bar: N.Y. 1940, also U.S. Supreme Ct. 1946. With firm Mudge, Stern, Williams & Tucker, N.Y.C., 1940-43, Mudge, Stern, Baldwin & Todd, 1946-55; sec. Gen. Equipment Precision Corp., Tarrytown, N.Y., 1955-68; asst. sec. Singer Co., N.Y.C., 1968—. Mem., chmn. New Castle (N.Y.) Town Planning Bd., 1958-80. Served to 1st lt. AUS, 1943-46. Republican. Club: Church (N.Y.C.). Home: 192 N Bedford Rd Chappaqua NY 10514 Office: 8 Stamford Forum Stamford CT 06904

HENLEY, ELIZABETH BECKER, writer; b. Jackson, Miss., May 8, 1952; d. Charles Boyce and Elizabeth Josephen (Becker) H. (Caldwell). B.F.A. with honors, So. Methodist U., 1974; postgrad., U. Ill., 1975-76. Playwright: Am I Blue, 1972, Crimes of the Heart, 1978 (Pulitzer prize 1981), The Mis Firecracker Contest, 1979, The Wake of Jamey Foster, 1981, The Debutante Ball, 1983; writer: screenplay The Moonwatcher, 1980. Office: Gilbert Parker care William Morris Agy 1350 Ave of Americas New York NY 10019

HENLEY, ERNEST JUSTUS, educator; b. Frankfort am Main, Germany, Sept. 30, 1926; came to U.S., 1935, naturalized, 1939; s. Clemens Isidore and Martha (Henle) H.; m. Barbara Mayfield Miller, Jan. 17, 1957; children—Davis Clemens, Alan Miller. S.B., U. Del., 1950; M.S., Columbia, 1951, D.Engring. Sci., 1953; M.E., Stevens Inst. Tech., 1963. Asst. prof. chem. engring. Columbia, 1953-58; prof. chemistry, chem. engring. Stevens Inst. Tech., 1958-66; prof. chemistry, asso. dean engring. U. Houston, 1966—; Dir. RAI Research Inc., Procedyne Corp., Houston Glass Fabricating Co., Cache Corp., Fluidotherapy Corp., Continuous Learning Corp.; dir. Coade Corp., Inacom Corp. Author: Chemical Engineering Calculations, 1959, Stagewise Process Calculations, 1963, Material and Energy Balance Computations, 1969, The Physics and Chemistry of High Energy Reaction, 1969, Graph Theory in Modern Engineering, 1973, Generic Techniques in Reliability Assessment, 1974, Reliability Engineering and Risk Assessment, 1981, Equilibrium-Stage Separation Operations in Chemical Engineering, 1981; Co-editor: Advances in Nuclear Science and Technology, 12 vols, 1961—; Contbr. articles to profl. jours. Served to 1st lt. AUS, 1944-46; ETO. NSF Am. Chem. Soc.; AEC grantee. Fellow Am. Inst. Chemistry, N.Y. Acad. Sci.; mem. Sigma Xi, Tau Beta Pi, Phi Kappa Phi, Phi Lambda Upsilon. Club: Houston Racquet. Home: 359 Westminster St Houston TX 77024

HENLEY, ERNEST MARK, physics educator; b. Frankfurt, Germany, June 10, 1924; came to U.S., 1939, naturalized, 1944; s. Fred S. and Josy (Dreyfuss) H.; m. Elaine Dimitman, Aug. 21, 1948; children: M. Bradford, Karen M. B.E.E., Coll. City N.Y., 1944; Ph.D., U. Calif. at Berkeley, 1952. Physicist Lawrence Radiation Lab., U. Calif. at Berkeley, 1950-51; research asso. physics dept. Stanford, 1951-52; lectr. physics Columbia, 1952-54; mem. faculty U. Wash., Seattle, 1954—, prof. physics, 1961—, chmn. dept., 1973-76, dean, 1979—. Author: (with W. Thirring) Elementary Quantum Field Theory, 1962, (with H. Frauenfelder) Subatomic Physics, 1974, Nuclear and Particle Physics, 1975. F.B. Jewett fellow, 1952-53; NSF sr. fellow, 1958-59; Guggenheim fellow, 1967-68; NATO sr. fellow, 1976-77. Mem. Am. Phys. Soc. (chmn. div. nuclear physics 1979-80), Nat. Acad. Scis., Sigma Xi. Research and numerous publs. on symmetries, nuclear reactions and high energy particle interactions. Office: Physics Dept FM 15 U Wash Seattle WA 98195

HENLEY, FRED LOUIS, state justice; b. Caruthersville, Mo., Oct. 25, 1911; s. Louis Moreau and Dottye Gray (Call) H.; m. Bernice Chilton, Aug. 3, 1939; children: Sally Kate (Mrs. Gerald W. Sisson), Lynda Wayne (Mrs. James C. Walters), Karen Janet (Mrs. Michael E. Kettler), Joseph Oliver Chilton. LL.B., Cumberland U., 1934. Bar: Mo. 1935, U.S. Supreme Ct 1945. Gen. practice, Caruthersville, 1936-64; judge 38th Jud. Circuit Mo., 1955-60, Supreme Ct. Mo., 1964-78, sr. judge, 1979—. Chmn. Mo. Hwy. Commn., 1961-64. Served with USAAF, 1942-46; mem. Res. Mem. Am. Bar Assn., Mo. Bar. Club: Mason (Shriner). Home: 1301 Dixon Dr Jefferson City MO 65101

HENLEY, HENRY HOWARD, JR., manufacturing company executive; b. Helena, Ark., Aug. 16, 1921; s. Henry Howard and Harriet Louise (Gibbs) H.; m. Dorothy Ray Hutcheson, Aug. 23, 1943; children: Charles Ray, Philip Howard, Henry Howard III. B.A., Hendrix Coll., 1943. With McKesson & Robbins, 1939-67, successively staff, Memphis, San Antonio, dist. operations mgr., dist. sales mgr., dist. v.p. S.W. dist., 1939-56, v.p. drug merchandising, 1956-59, exec. v.p. co., 1959-62, pres., 1962-67, dir., mem. exec. com., 1962-67; chmn. Cluett-Peabody & Co., Inc., N.Y.C., 1967—; chief exec. officer Cluett-Peabody Co., 1970—, chmn. bd., 1979, also dir.; dir. Home Life Ins. Co., Bristol-Myers Co., Clupak Co., Mfrs. Hanover Trust Co., Gen. Electric Co., Olin Corp. Trustee Presbyn. Hosp., N.Y.C. Served to lt. USNR, 1943-46. Clubs: Economic, Links (N.Y.C.); Blind Brook, Siwanoy, Augusta (Ga.) Nat. Golf, Presidents. Office: 510 Fifth Ave New York NY 10036

HENLEY, VERNARD WILLIAM, banker; b. Richmond, Va., Aug. 11, 1929; s. Walter Abraham and Mary Ellen (Crump) H.; m. Pheriby Christine Gibson, June 14, 1958; children: Vernard William, Wade Gibson, Adrienne Christine. B.S., Va. State Coll., 1951. Teller, cashier Mechanics & Farmers Bank, Durham, N.C., 1951-52, 54-58; v.p. Consol. Bank & Trust Co., Richmond, 1958-71, pres., trust officer, from 1971, chmn. bd., chief exec. officer, trust officer, 1984—; bd. govs. Consumer Adv. Council, Fed. Res. Bd., 1979-83; mem. Deferred Compensation Bd., 1982. Mem. Downtown Devel. Commn., City of Richmond; mem. gen. vocat. edn. adv. council Richmond Pub. Schs., 1975-78; dist. commr. Robert E. Lee council Boy Scouts Am., 1964-69; vice chmn. adv. com. Vol. Service Bur., 1964-69; asst. treas. Richmond chpt. ARC, 1968-69; bd. mgmt. North br. YMCA Met. Richmond, 1975-79; commr. Va. Housing Devel. Authority, 1972-83, chmn., 1980-83; bd. dirs. Richmond Community Hosp., 1970-83, Inst. Bus. and Community Devel., 1966-69, Richmond Met. Authority, 1966-69, Human Services Planning div. United Way Greater Richmond, 1970-72, Church Hill Econ. Devel. Corp., 1971-75, Central Va. Ednl. TV, 1971—, Children's Hosp., 1975—, Richmond Met. Blood Services, 1975-83, Atlantic Rural Exposition, 1976, Pvt. Industry Council Richmond, 1983—, Federated Arts Council Richmond, 1979, Richmond Meml. Hosp. Found., 1980—, Project AID-SIR, 1979-80, Maymont Found., 1973—, Richmond Renaissance, Inc., 1982—; pres. Maymont Found., 1983—; mem. Gov's Econ. Adv. Council, 1982; adv. council Salvation Army Boys Club, 1970—; trustee Richmond Meml. Hosp., 1970—, Va. Mus. Fine Arts, 1983—, St. Paul's Coll., Lawrenceville, Va., 1976; mem. nat. corp. com. United Negro Coll. Fund, 1975—; vice chmn. audit com. City of Richmond, 1983. Served to 1st lt. AUS, 1952-54. Decorated Bronze Star; recipient Order of Merit Boy Scouts Am., 1967; Man and Boy award Boys Club, 1969; Citizenship award NAACP, 1974, Astoria Beneficial Club, 1976; Brotherhood award Richmond chpt. NCCJ, 1979. Mem. Am. Inst. Banking, Bank Adminstrn. Inst., Am. Banking Assn. (minority lending com. comml. lending div. 1976-79), Central Richmond Assn. (dir. 1971-72), Ind. Order St. Luke (trustee 1970), Alpha Phi Alpha, Alpha Eta Boule, Sigma Phi. Lodge: Kiwanis (Richmond). Home: 1728 Hungary Rd Richmond VA 23228 Office: 320 N 1st St PO Box 10046 Richmond VA 23240

HENLEY, WILLIAM BALLENTINE, rancher, lawyer, lectr.; b. Cin., Sept. 19, 1905; s. William Herbert and May G. (Richards) Ballentine (later assumed name of stepfather, Charles E. Henley); m. Helen McTaggart, 1942. A.B., U. So. Calif., 1928; postgrad., Sch. Religion, 1928-29, Yale, 1929-30; M.A., U. So. Calif., 1930, J.D., 1933, M.S. in P.A, 1935; LL.D., Willamette U., 1937; Sc.D., Kansas City Coll. Osteopathy and Surgery, 1949; R.Sc.D., Inst. Religious Sci. and Philosophy, 1949; L.H.D. Los Angeles Coll. Optometry, 1958; Sc.D., Pepperdine Coll., 1966. Lectr. pub. adminstrn., asst. to co-ordination officer U. So. Calif., 1928-29; dir. religious edn. First Methodist Ch., New Haven, 1929-30; lectr. in pub. adminstrn. U. So. Calif., 1930-33, exec. sec., 1930-40, acting dean, 1937-38, dir., 1937-38, asst. to dean, 1934-36, asst. prof. pub. adminstrn., 1935-39, asso. prof., 1939-40, dir. co-ordination, 1938-40; pub. speaking instr. and debate coach Am. Inst. Banking, 1928-40; pres. Calif. Coll. Medicine, Los Angeles, 1940-66, Coll. Osteopathic Surgeons, 1940-66; provost U. Calif. at Irvine-Calif. Coll. Medicine, 1966-69; pres., chmn. bd. trustees United Ch. Religious Sci., 1969—, prof., 1972—; exec., speakers' panel Gen. Motors Corp., 1956-75. Author: The History of the University of Southern California, 1940, Man's Great Awakening, or Beautiful Mud, 1974, also mag. articles. Bd. dirs. Glendale Community Hosp., Glendale Adventist Med. Center, 1978—; mem. Bd. Water and Power Commrs., Los Angeles, 1944-62, pres., 1946, v.p., 57-58; mem. Employees' Pension and Retirement Bd. Mgmt, 1946; mem. adv. bd. Los Angeles County Gen. Hosp., 1940-65; v.p. Los Angeles County Safety Council, 1971—; mem. Los Angeles Def. Council, 1941-44, War Council, 1944-45, Calif. Civil Def. Com.; guest observer UN Conf., San Francisco, 1945; A.T. Still Meml. lectr., Washington, 1958. Mem. Am., Calif., Los Angeles bar assns., NEA, Am. Pub. Health Assn., AAAS, Am. Saddle Horse Breeding Futurity Assn. (dir.), Am. Aberdeen Angus Breeders Assn., Sigma Alpha Epsilon, Phi Delta Phi, Phi Kappa Phi, Phi Sigma Gamma, Sigma Sigma Phi, Delta Sigma Rho, Phi Delta Kappa, Pi Sigma Alpha, Alpha Delta Sigma, Phi Eta Sigma, Sigma Sigma, Skull and Dagger. Republican. Clubs: Mason (32 deg.), Los Angeles Rotary (pres. 1955-56), Los Angeles Rotary (chmn. conf. dist. 160-A, gov. dist. 528 1959-60), Los Angeles Rotary (mem. internat. community service consultative group), Los Angeles Rotary (chmn. host club exec. com. for 1962 internat. conv.), Los Angeles Rotary (mem. world community service com.). Home and office: Creston Circle Ranch Paso Robles CA 93446 *Never allow yourself to get discouraged. Put your faith and confidence in God (creative cosmic consciousness). Get behind a cause—a cause that is bigger than you are—and work.*

HENN, CATHERINE EMILY CAMPBELL, lawyer; b. St. Louis, May 13, 1942; d. Robert A. and Rachel (Davis) Campbell; m. John H. Henn, Nov. 1, 1969. B.A., Wellesley Coll., 1964; J.D., Harvard U., 1969. Bar: Mass. 1969. Assoc. Bingham, Dana & Gould, Boston, 1970-80; corp. counsel, clk. Affiliated Publs., Inc. and subs., Boston, 1980—. Chmn. Oxfam Am., Inc., Boston, 1982—, bd. dirs., Boston, 1980—; pres. Women's Tech. Inst., Boston, 1979-83, bd. dirs., Boston, 1979—; bd. dirs. The Boston Globe Found., Inc., 1981—; mem. Boston Com. on Fgn. Relations exec. com., 1980-83. Mem. ABA, Mass. Bar Assn., Boston Bar Assn. Office: Affiliated Publs Inc 135 Morrissey Blvd Boston MA 02107

HENN, HARRY GEORGE, legal educator; b. New Rochelle, N.Y., Oct. 8, 1919; s. Harry Christian and Mollie (Malsch) H. B.A. summa cum laude, N.Y.U., 1941; LL.B. with distinction, Cornell U., 1943; J.S.D., N.Y.U., 1952. Bar: N.Y. bar 1944. Asso. firm Whitman, Ransom & Coulson, N.Y.C., 1943-53; mem. faculty Cornell U. Law Sch., 1953—, prof. law, 1957—, Edward Cornell prof. law, 1970—, Donald C. Brace Meml. lectr., 1978; vis. prof. law Hastings Coll. Law, 1979, NYU, 1983; spl. counsel Cornell U., 1953-56; pres., dir. Cornell Daily Sun, 1966-73; guest lectr. N.Y. U., 1953-78; acting village justice, Cayuga Heights, Ithaca, N.Y., 1965-74; Trustee Copyright Soc. U.S., 1953—, pres., 1961-63; mem. UNESCO panel internat. copyright; also panel cons. gen. revision copyright law; cons. corp. law annotated project Am. Bar Found., 1959-60, 63-64, 68; research cons. N.Y. State Joint Legislative Com. to Study Revision Corp. Law; also Library of Congress. Author: Copyright Primer, 1979, Agency, Partnership and Other Unincorporated Business Enterprises, 1972, Cases and Materials on the Laws of Corporations, 1974, supplement, 1980; co-author: Laws of Corporations and Other Business Enterprises, 3d edit., 1983; Author also articles.; Contbr. to: Ency. Brit; Editor-in-chief: Cornell Law Quar, 1943. Pres. Ithaca Opera Assn., 1968-73, 79-81; trustee S. Central Research Library, 1967-74. Mem. ABA (past chmn. copyright div.), N.Y. State Bar Assn., Tompkins County Bar Assn., N.Y. County Lawyers Assn., Internat. Assn. Advancement of Teaching and Research in Intellectual Property, Assn. Litteraire et Artistique Internationale, AAUP (chpt. pres. 1968-70), N.Y. State Assn. Magistrates, Internat. Gesellschaft für Urheberrecht E.V., Phi Beta Kappa, Order of Coif, Delta Upsilon, Phi Kappa Phi (chpt. pres. 1964-65), Phi Delta Phi. Clubs: Ithaca Yacht; Statler (Cornell U.); Tower (Ithaca Coll.). Home: 130 Sunset Dr Ithaca NY 14850

HENNE, FRANCES ELIZABETH, library science educator; b. Springfield, Ill., Oct. 11, 1906; d. J.Z. and Laura (Taylor) H. A.B., U. Ill., 1929, M.A., 1934; B.S., Columbia, 1935; Ph.D., U. Chgo., 1949. Mem. library staff Springfield (Ill.) Pub. Library, 1930-34, N.Y. Pub. Library, 1935, N.Y. State Tchrs. Coll., Albany, 1935-38; librarian U. High Sch., U. Chgo., 1939-42; instr. N.Y. State Coll. for Tchrs., 1937-38, 39, U. Chgo. Grad. Library Sch., 1939-46; asst. prof. Grad. Library Sch., U. Chgo., 1946-49, asso. prof., 1949-54, asso. dean, dean of students, 1947-50, acting dean, 1951-52; asso. prof. Sch. Library Service, Columbia, N.Y.C., prof., now prof. emerita; vis. prof. U. Minn., summer 1950, Rutgers U., summer 1954; Mem. N.Y. State Regents Adv. Council on Libraries, 1964-74; mem. com. on library devel. N.Y. State Commr. Edn., 1967-70. Author: Youth Communication and Libraries, 1949, Planning Guide for the High School Library Program, 1951; also numerous articles in field. Recipient Carnegie fellowship, 1938; Lippincott award, 1963; Beta Phi Mu award, 1978. Mem. ALA (spl. centennial citation 1976, Pres.'s award 1979), Am. Assn. Sch. Librarians (nat. pres. 1948-49). Home: 345 E 50th St New York NY 10022

HENNEBACH, RALPH L., non-ferrous metal company executive; b. Garfield, Utah, May 2, 1920; s. Leo and Consuelo (Herrerias) H.; m. Mary Louise Johnston, Sept. 14, 1946; children: Mark Leo, Anne Louise, Margo Lynnne. Metall. Engr., Colo. Sch. Mines, 1941; M.S. in Indsl. Mgmt. (Sloan fellow), MIT, 1953. With ASARCO Inc., 1941—, asst. to v.p. smelting and refining, 1958-63, v.p. smelting and refining, 1963-66, exec. v.p., 1966-71, pres., 1971-82, chmn., 1982—, also dir.; dir. Crompton & Knowles, So. Peru Copper Co., Mex. Desarollo Indsl. Minero, Capco Pipe Co., Federated Metals, Enthone, Sunworks, Lac D'Amiante du Quebec, Neptune Mining, Bolivia Lead Co.; trustee Com. for Econ. Devel.; mem. Bus. Roundtable. Served to lt. (j.g.) USNR, 1944-46. Recipient Disting. Achievement medal Colo. Sch. Mines, 1965. Mem. AIME (Charles Rand Gold medal 1983), Mining and Metall. Soc., Colo. Sch. Mines Alumni Assn., Sigma Alpha Epsilon, Theta Tau. Clubs: Mining, Wall St., Metropolitan, Downtown Assn. (N.Y.C.); Canoe Brook Country (Summit, N.J.); Baltusrol Golf (Springfield, N.J.); Economic. Home: 33 Tennyson Dr Short Hills NJ 07078 Office: 180 Maiden Ln New York NY 10038

HENNELLY, MARK M., railroad company executive, lawyer. Bar: Mo. Individual practice law, St. Louis, judge; with Mo. Pacific R.R. Co. subs. Mo. Pacific Corp., St. Louis, 1957—, gen. solicitor, 1960-62, v.p., gen. counsel, 1962-77, sr. v.p., gen. counsel, 1977—, dir., exec. v.p. parent co.; v.p. law Tex. & Pacific Ry. Co.; dir. Chgo. & Eastern R.R. Co. Contbr. writings to various publs. in field; patentee. Recipient various awards Dept. Interior. Mem. Am. Inst. Mining, AIME (past chmn. Extractive Metallurgy, past v.p.), Metall. Soc. Am. (past pres.), AAAS, Soc. Mining Engrs., Sigma Xi. Mormon. Office: Mo Pacific RR subs Mo Pacific Corp Missouri Pacific Bldg Saint Louis MO 63103

HENNEMAN, DOROTHY HUGHES, physician; b. Sao Paulo, Brazil, Sept. 3, 1923; d. Reynold King and Edna Margaret (Geyer) Hughes (parents Am. citizens); m. Philip H. Henneman, Aug. 25, 1945 (div. 1963); children—Carolyn Hughes, Sally Edna Henneman Linder, Philip Lee, Diane Gail Henneman Smith; m. John M. Clark, June 27, 1976 (dec. Aug. 1977); m. David H. Conklin, May 12, 1979. B.A. (scholar), Wellesley Coll., 1945; postgrad., Radcliffe Coll., 1945-46; M.D., Johns Hopkins U., 1949. Intern McClean Hosp., Waltham, Mass., 1949-51; resident in endocrinology Mass. Gen. Hosp., 1951-53, fellow in anesthesia, 1954-55, research asso. in anesthesia, 1955-56; research asst. McLean Hosp., Waverly, Mass., 1950-54; research asso. anesthesia, asst. surgery Peter Bent Brigham Hosp., Boston, 1956-58; cons. bone metabolism; asst. attending physician Jersey City Med. Center, 1958-66; spl. isotope trainee Columbia U., N.Y.C., 1961; instr. medicine Seton Hall Coll., Jersey City, 1958-62; instr. bacteriology Rutgers U., New Brunswick, N.J., 1963; sr. scientist Inst. for Med. Research, E.R. Squibb, New Brunswick, 1963-66, Ortho Research Found., Raritan, N.J., 1966-67, research fellow, 1967-71; asso. cons. in medicine, sr. research asso. Cancer Research Inst. New Eng., Deaconess Hosp., Boston, 1971-73; research fellow anesthesia Harvard U., 1954-55, research asso., 1955-58, asst. in surgery, 1956-58, asst. prof. medicine, 1971-73; asso. prof. health sci. and chem. engring., coordinator clin. studies U. Del., Newark, 1973-76; prof. medicine Downstate Med. Center, SUNY, Bklyn., 1976-81; adj. prof. chem. engring. U. Del., 1976—; spl. asst. to dean in edn., asso. chief staff edn. VA Hosp., Bklyn., 1976-80; cons. Nat. Heart and Lung Inst., NIH, Bethesda, Md., 1969—; mem. research panel Nat. Inst. Child Health and Devel., 1972—; mem. team to reorganize Med. Sch. Nat. U. Iran, 1974. Acad. Arts and Sci. fellow, 1949-50; USPHS postdoctoral fellow, 1950-54; NIH sr. research fellow, 1961-63; recipient Distinguished Medal AMA, 1970. Fellow Neurosci. Inst. U. Del., N.Y. Acad. Medicine; mem. Endocrine Soc., New Eng. Diabetes Assn., Am. Fedn. for Clin. Research, Am. Physiol. Soc., Nat. Am. Diabetes Assn., AAAS, N.Y. Acad. Scis., Phi Beta Kappa, Alpha Omega Alpha. Home and office: 1141 Calvert Rd Rising Sun MD 21911 *The opportunity for self-expression within the structure and protection of my family, the economic establishment, and the academic environment nurtured my development as a woman, a mother, a physician, and a scientist. All guide my ultimate concern in medical ethics.*

HENNEMAN, ELWOOD, educator, neurophysiologist; b. Washington, Dec. 22, 1915; s. Harry Edwin and Rubina (Raihle) H.; m. Karel Van Syckel Toll, Dec. 30, 1950; children—Cyrena Van Syckel (dec.), Abby Hastings. A.B., Harvard, 1937; M.D., McGill U., 1943. Intern Royal Victoria Hosp., Montreal, 1943-44; house officer Montreal Neurol. Inst., 1944; fellow physiology Johns Hopkins Sch. Medicine, 1946-47; research asst. Ill. Neuropsychiat. Inst., Chgo., 1947-49; vis. investigator Rockefeller Inst. Med. Research, N.Y.C., 1949-51; asst. prof. physiology Johns Hopkins Sch. Medicine, 1951-55; mem. faculty Harvard Med. Sch., 1960—, prof. physiology, 1969—, chmn. dept. physiology, 1971-74, 78-79; neurophysiologist Mass. Gen. Hosp., Boston, 1960—; mem. radiobiology panel Pres.'s Space Sci. Bd., 1971—. Mem. editorial bd.: Am. Jour. Physiology, 1960-63, Jour. Neurophysiology, 1964-70, Physiol. Rev, 1965-66; sect. editor neurophysiology: Am. Jour. Physiology, 1962-63; asso. editor: Exptl. Neurology, 1979—. Served to lt. USNR, 1944-46. Recipient medal College de France, 1976; Guggenheim fellow, 1949-50. Mem. Am. Acad. Arts and Scis., Am. Physiol. Soc., Internat. Brain Research Orgn., Soc. for Neuroscis., AAAS, Belgian Soc. Electromyography and Clin. Neurophysiology (hon.), Sigma Xi. Clubs: Longwood Cricket (Chestnut Hill, Mass.); Badminton and Tennis (Boston). Home: 15 Snake Hill Rd Belmont MA 02178 Office: 25 Shattuck St Boston MA 02115

HENNEMAN, JOHN BELL, JR., university library bibliographer; b. N.Y.C., Nov. 1, 1935; s. John Bell and Esther Gracie (Ogden) H.; m. Margery Meigs Clifford, Sept. 17, 1960; children: John, Charles, Margery. A.B., Princeton U., 1957; A.M., Harvard U., 1961, Ph.D, 1966; M.A. in L.S., U. Iowa, 1982. Lectr. McMaster U., Hamilton, Ont., Can., 1965-66, asst. prof. history, 1966-69; assoc. prof. U. Iowa, Iowa City, 1969-73, prof. history, 1973-83, chmn. dept. history, 1980-83; history bibliographer Princeton U. Library, N.J., 1983—; N. Am. sec.-treas. Internat. Commn. for History of Rep. and Parliamentary Instns., 1975-81. Author: Royal Taxation in 14th Century France: 1322-1356, 1971, Royal Taxation in 14th Century Frances: 1356-1370, 1976; editor: The Medieval French Monarchy, 1973. Served to lt. (j.g.) USNR, 1957-60. Woodrow Wilson fellow, 1960; fellow J.S. Guggenheim Found., 1976. Mem. Am. Hist. Assn., ALA, Medieval Acad. Am., Soc. for French Hist. Studies, AAUP (pres. Iowa Conf. 1977-79, exec. sec. conf. 1979-80), Phi Beta Kappa. Republican. Episcopalian. Home: 78 Shady Brook Ln Princeton NJ 08540 Office: University Library Princeton U Princeton NJ 08544

HENNES, ROBERT TAFT, management consultant; b. Jamestown, N.Y., Mar. 8, 1930; s. Theodore Preston and Lucille (Kane) H.; m. Frances Walker Pratt, May 9, 1953 (div. 1962); children: Robert Taft, Duncan Pratt, Margaret Nickerson, Theodore Preston II; m. Grace Margaret Bruton, Oct. 9, 1971. A.B., Harvard U., 1951; M.B.A., U. Pa., 1952. With Lummus Co., N.Y.C., 1952-62; exec. v.p., dir. Conahay & Lyon, Inc. (advt.), N.Y.C., 1962-70; sr. v.p. Cole & Assos., Boston, 1970-72; chmn., dir. Hennes & Cox Inc., N.Y.C., 1972-77; v.p., prin. Spencer Stuart & Assos., N.Y.C., 1977—; dir. Oldwyck Industries, Inc., N.Y.C. Mem. Harvard Soc. Scientists and Engrs. Club: Harvard (N.Y.C.). Home: 40 E 84th St New York NY 10028 Office: 55 E 52d St New York NY 10055

HENNESSEY, EDWARD FRANCIS, state supreme ct. justice; b. Boston, Apr. 20, 1919; s. Thomas M. and Winifred C. (Tracey) H.; m. Elizabeth Ann O'Toole, Oct. 15, 1945; 1 dau., Beth Ann. B.S. cum laude, Northeastern U., 1941, LL.D., 1976; LL.B. cum laude, Boston U., 1949, LL.D., 1976, Suffolk U., 1974, New Eng. Sch. Law, 1974. Bar: Mass. bar 1949. Partner firm Martin, Magnuson & Hennessey, Boston, 1950-66; judge Mass. Superior Ct., 1967-71; asso. justice Supreme Jud. Ct. of Mass., 1971-76, chief justice, 1976—; lectr. on trial practice Boston U., 1956-64. Author: (with Martin) Trial Practice, 2 vols, 1954. Served to capt. U.S. Army, 1941-45. Decorated Bronze Star; recipient Distinguished Pub. Service award Boston U., 1975, St. Thomas More Pub. Service award Diocese of Worcester, 1975. Fellow Am. Bar Assn.; mem. Boston, Mass. bar assns. Home: 29 Rosalie Rd Needham MA 02192 Office: Supreme Judicial Ct Courthouse Boston MA 02108

HENNESSEY, FRANK M., audio products company executive; b. 1938; married. Ptnr. Coopers & Lybrand, 1964-81; pres. Handleman Co., Inc., Clawson, Mich., 1981—, also dir. Office: Handleman Co Inc 1055 W Maple Rd Clawson MI 48017 *

HENNESSEY, JOHN WILLIAM, JR., business management educator; b. Danville, Pa., Mar. 25, 1925; s. John William and Martha Scott (Braun) H.; m. Jean Marie Lande, June 26, 1948; children: John William III, Martha Scott. A.B., Princeton, 1948; M.B.A., Harvard, 1950; Ph.D., U. Wash., 1956; M.A. (hon.), Dartmouth, 1959, L.H.D., York Coll. of Pa., 1978, U. N.H., 1981. From instr. to asso. prof. orgn. and adminstrn. Coll. Bus. Adminstrn., U. Wash., 1950-57; prof. Amos Tuck Sch. Bus. Adminstrn., Dartmouth, 1957—, asso. dean, 1962-68, dean, 1968-76, Charles H. Jones 3d Century prof. mgmt., 1976—; prof. Institut pour l'Etude des Méthodes de Direction de l'Enterprise, Lausanne, Switzerland, 1959; Dir. H.P. Hood, Inc., 1976-80, Zayre Corp., Conn. Mut. Life Ins. Co. Author: (with Austin Grimshaw) Organizational Behavior, 1960, (with others) Hospital Policy Decisions, 1966. Trustee Mary Hitchcock Meml. Hosp., Hanover, chmn. bd., 1977-83; trustee Ednl. Testing Service, chmn. bd., 1978-80; chmn. governing council Dartmouth Hitchcock Med. Center, 1977-83; bd. visitors Grad. Sch. Bus., U. Pitts., 1970-76, 79—; mem. Pres.'s Council on Bus. Sch. U. Vt., 1982—. Served to 1st lt. AUS, 1943-46. Mem. Am. Assembly Collegiate Schs. Bus. (dir. 1970-77, pres. 1975-76), Phi Beta Kappa. Home: 4 Webster Terr Hanover NH 03755

HENNESSY, DANIEL KRAFT, lawyer; b. Summit, N.J., Jan. 4, 1941; s. Robert Emmett and Agnes Lyons (Lindle) H.; m. Susan Elizabeth (Bettina) Ware, June 17, 1972; children—Mary Elise, Daniel Joseph, Michael Ware, Catherine Anne. B.S. with highest honors, U.S. Naval Acad., 1963; J.D. cum laude, Harvard, 1970. Bar: Tex. bar 1970. Commd. ensign U.S. Navy, 1963, advanced through grades to lt., 1966; service in, Vietnam, resigned, 1967, since practiced in, Dallas; partner firm Hughes & Hill, 1973—. Editor: Harvard Law Rev, 1969-70. Bd. advisers Jesuit Coll. Prep. Sch., Dallas, 1975—; bd. dirs. Dallas-North Tex. region NCCJ, 1976—, Morality in Media in Tex., 1981—. Mem. ABA, Dallas Bar Assn., State Bar Tex. Roman Catholic. Home: 4405 Beverly St Dallas TX 75205 Office: 1000 Mercantile Dallas Bldg Dallas TX 75201

HENNESSY, EDWARD LAWRENCE, JR., diversified manufacturing, chemical and energy company executive; b. Boston, Mar. 22, 1928; s. Edward Lawrence and Celina Mary (Doucette) H.; m. Ruth Frances Schilling, Aug. 18, 1951; children: Michael E., Elizabeth R. B.S., Fairleigh Dickinson U., 1955; student, NYU Law Sch. With Heublein, Inc., Hartford, Conn., 1965-72, v.p. finance, 1965-68, sr. v.p. adminstrn., finance, 1969-72; sr. v.p. fin. and adminstrn. United Techs. Corp., Hartford, 1972-77, chief fin. officer, group v.p., 1977, exec. v.p., 1978-79; chmn., pres., chief exec. officer Allied Corp., Morris Township, N.J., 1979—; dir. Fed. Res. Bank N.Y., Martin Marietta Corp., DNA Plant Tech. Trustee Cath. U. Am., Fairleigh Dickinson U., USCG Acad. Found. Served with USNR, 1949-55. Mem. Fin. Execs. Inst., Econ. Club N.Y. Roman Catholic. Clubs: Cat Cay (Bahamas); N.Y. Yacht; Ocean Reef (Key Largo, Fla.). Office: Morristown NJ 07960

HENNESSY, JOHN FRANCIS, consulting engineer; b. N.Y.C., July 18, 1928; s. John F. and Dorothy (O'Grady) H.; m. Barbara McDonnell, Oct. 24, 1953; children—John, Kathleen, James, Kevin, Peter, David; m. Bruce Rial, Dec. 30, 1971. B.S. in Physics, Georgetown U., 1949, Mass. Inst. Tech., 1951. Registered profl. engr., N.Y., Calif., Colo., Conn., Va., D.C., Ga., N.J., Ill., Ind., others. With Syska & Hennessy, Inc., N.Y.C., 1951—, exec. v.p., 1955-66, pres., 1967—, chmn., 1973—, chief exec. officer, 1976—; dir. Franklin Soc. Fed. Savs. & Loan. Mem. exec. bd. Greater N.Y. council Boy Scouts Am., 1958—; chmn. com. architects and engrs. Cardinal's Com. on Laity; former trustee Whitby Sch., New Canaan, Conn., Clark Coll.; former mem. bd. dirs. Catholic Interracial Council; bd. dirs. N.Y. Heart Assn., Battery Park City Authority. Served with USAF, 1951-52. Fellow Am. Cons. Engrs. Council; mem. Nat., N.Y. State, Conn. socs. profl. engrs., N.Y. Assn. Cons. Engrs. (past pres.), N.Y. Bldg. Congress, Soc. Am. Mil. Engrs., ASME. Clubs: River, Links, Univ. (N.Y.C.); Capitol Hill, Fed. City, Met. (Washington); Lyford Cay (Nassau); Shinnecock Golf, Nat. Golf Links, Seaview Country; Marks (London); Travellers (Paris). Office: 11 W 42 St New York NY 10036

HENNESSY, THOMAS CHRISTOPHER, university dean, educator; b. N.Y.C., Nov. 3, 1916; s. Thomas C. and Anna E. (Regan) H. A.B., Woodstock Coll., 1940; M.A. in Latin and Greek Classics, Fordham U., 1947; M.S. in Edn., Fordham U., 1957, Ph.D., 1962. Joined S. J., ordained priest Roman Catholic Ch., 1947; tchr. Fordham Prep. sch., N.Y.C., 1940-43, 49-52; high sch. counselor Fordham Prep. Sch., 1952-61; counselor educator Fordham U., N.Y.C., 1961-81; dean, prof. counselor edn., Sch. Edn. Marquette U., Milw., 1981—; dir. W.A. Kelly Counseling Lab. Foreham U. at Lincoln Ctr., 1969-81. Editor: The Inner Crusade: The Closed Retreat in the U.S., 1965, The High School Counselor Today, 1966, The Interdisciplinary of Guidance, 1966, Values and Moral Development, 1976, Value-Moral Education: The Schools and the Teachers, 1979; cons. editor: Personnel and Guidance Jour., 1978-81; contbr. numerous articles to profl. jours. Bd. dirs. Alfred Adler Mental Hygiene Clinic, N.Y.C., 1978-81. Mem. Am. Psychol. Assn., Am. Assn. for Counseling and

Devel., Fordham Personnel and Guidance Assn. (founder, prin. faculty adviser 1965-81). Home: 1404 W Wisconsin Ave Milwaukee WI 53233 Office: Sch Edn Schroeder Comples R 176-G Marquette U Milwaukee WI 53233

HENNESSY, WESLEY JOSEPH, management consultant; b. Queens, N.Y., Aug. 17, 1914; s. Charles A. and Lydia (Schneider) H.; m. Virginia Pershing MacArthur, June 20, 1942 (dec. Aug. 1955); children: Heather Michele, David Charles, Holly MacArthur; m. Virginia Ann Campbell, Apr. 4, 1959; children: Mark Campbell, Kevin, Karen, Anne. Student, Syracuse U., 1934-37; B.S. cum laude, Columbia, 1951; LL.D., Phila. Coll. Osteopathy, 1966; D.Sc., Bethany (W.Va.) Coll., 1966. Pres. World's Fair Employees Assn., 1939; dir. tng. Grumman Aircraft Engring. Corp., Bethpage, L.I., 1940-44; asst. to dean Columbia U., N.Y.C., 1944-48, asst. dean, 1948-53, asso. dean, 1953-64, exec. dean, 1964-69, dean, 1969-75, dean emeritus, 1975—, adv. council, 1975—; resident dir. Summer Sch. Engring., Lakeside, Conn., 1946-64; spl. lectr. world econ. geography; condr. seminar on human relations ICA, Guatemala, 1959; pres. Polychrome Corp., Yonkers, N.Y., 1975-77, also dir.; dir. Hazeltine Corp., Greenlawn, N.Y., 1973-77, Megadiamond Industries, N.Y.C., Combustion Equipment Assos.; bd. advisers Gulf & Western Invention Devel. Corp.; Mgmt. cons. research and devel. div. Am. Machine & Foundry, Reflectone Electronics, Unidynamics div. Universal Match Corp., 1960-64; dir. refugee scientists program Nat. Acad. Scis., 1961-64; cons. Pres. of Korea on Indsl. and Higher Edn. Programs, 1968-80; Mem. N.Y. Gov.'s Adv. Commn. Higher Edn., 1958, Pres.'s Adv. Panel Aid to Edn. for Latin Am., 1961, N.Y. State Bd. Regents Task Force on Profl. Edn., 1971—. Bd. dirs. Am. Council for Emigres in Professions, 1962-80; trustee St. Hilda's Sch., N.Y.C., 1952-55, Hudson River Mus., Yonkers, 1975-78; bd. dirs. Armstrong Meml. Research Found., 1970—, pres., 1973-80; mem. bd. Anglo-Am. Hellenic Bur. Edn., 1971-76; adv. council Manhattan Coll., 1976; mem. N.Y. State Task Force on Hudson River, 1980—. Recipient Distinguished Pub. Service award Columbia U. Sch. Gen. Studies, 1967, Gt. Tchr. award Columbia U., 1975. Mem. Am. Soc. Engring. Edn., Columbia U. Engring. Sch. Alumni Assn. (asso.), Assn. Deans Engring. Colls. N.Y. State (v.p. 1972—), Am. Geog. Soc. (council 1973, dir. 1973—, v.p. 1978—), Am. Arbitration Assn., Am. Birding Assn. (charter), Linnaean Soc. Clubs: Columbia, Men's Faculty, Faculty House (Columbia); Princeton (N.Y.C.). Home and office: West Shore Towers 101 Gedney St Nyack NY 10960

HENNESSY, WILLIAM JOSEPH, II, publisher; b. Joliet, Ill., June 29, 1936; s. William Joseph and Helen T. (Scheidt) H.; m. Mary Francis Cassidy, Jan. 20, 1973. A.B., Northwestern U., 1958; student, Law Sch., 1958-61. With B.F. Bills Mgmt. Consultants, Chgo., 1958-60, Haywood Pub. Co., 1961-62; with Indsl. Pub. Co., Cleve., 1962—; pub. Material Handling Engring., 1962—; cons. to material handling cos., 1962—. Served with U.S. Army, 1960-61. Mem. Bus. Profl. Advt. Assn., Internat. Material Mgmt. Assn., Assn. Indsl. Advertisers, Sigma Chi. Roman Catholic. Club: Chgo. Athletic Assn. Home: 12700 Lake Ave Lakewood OH 44117 Office: Penton/IPC 1111 Chester Ave Cleveland OH 44114

HENNEY, JANE ELLEN, public health administrator; b. Kendallville, Ind., Mar. 26, 1947; d. Harry H. and Jeanette (Parkes) H.; m. J. Robert Graham, June 6, 1975. B.S., Manchester Coll., North Manchester, Ind., 1969; M.D., Ind. U.-Indpls., 1973. Intern St. Vincent's Hosp., Indpls., 1973-74; with Nat. Cancer Inst., Bethesda, Md., 1976—, drug monitor cancer therapy evaluation program, sr. investigator, spl. asst. clin. affairs div. cancer treatment, acting dep. dir., acting dir., 1976-81, dep. dir., 1982—. Served with USPHS, 1976—. Recipient commendation USPHS, 1979, 81. Mem. Am. Soc. Clin. Oncology. Home: 9413 Locust Hill Rd Bethesda MD 20014 Office: Nat Cancer Inst 9000 Rockville Pike Bethesda MD 20205

HENNIGAN, JOHN V., securities company executive; b. Yonkers, N.Y., Feb. 3, 1942; s. Thomas A. and Catherine (Nannery) H.; m. Sherryl A. Allison, Dec. 19, 1970; children: Sean Thomas, Brian Perry. B.A. in Econs., U. Notre Dame, 1963. Vice pres., br. mgr. Walston & Co., Inc., N.Y.C., 1969-73; sr. v.p., regional dir. Prudential Bache Securities Co., N.Y.C., 1973-83; pres., chief exec. officer Jesup & Lamont Securities Co., Inc., N.Y.C., 1983—. Served to lt. USN, 1963-68. Republican. Roman Catholic. Clubs: Manursing Island (Rye, N.Y.) (gov. 1982-83); Campfire Am. (Chappaqua, N.Y.)). Office: Jesup & Lamont Securities Co Inc 360 Madison Ave New York NY 10017

HENNING, CHARLES NATHANIEL, finance educator; b. Pitts., June 20, 1915; s. William P. and Eleanor (Hill) H.; m. Virginia Marie Doerr, June 30, 1945. A.B., UCLA, 1938, A.M., 1940, Ph.D., 1953. Teaching asst., lectr. econs. UCLA, 1939-42; economist Far Eastern div. U.S. Dept. Commerce, 1942-48; asst. prof. fin. U. Wash., 1948-53, asso. prof., 1953-55, prof. fin., 1955—, dir. bus. adminstrn. faculty publs., 1961-72, coordinator bus. adminstrn. faculty research, 1971-72, acting chmn. dept. fin., bus. econs. and quantitative methods, 1974; mem. extension faculty Pacific Coast Banking Sch., 1954—, ednl. adviser, 1960—, Pacific Rim Bankers Program, 1977—; dir. Korean Bankers Program, 1980—; cons. various investment firms, banks; The Boeing Co., Fgn. Transp. Inst., Am. U., 1946, 48; cons. Ops. Research Office, Johns Hopkins, 1952-61, Research Analysis Corp., 1962-67; mem. Central Banking Seminar, Fed. Res. Bank of San Francisco, 1951; mem. U.S. del. Internat. Conf. on World Trade and Employment, Geneva, 1947. Author: International Finance, 1958, (with William Pigott and R.H. Scott) Financial Markets and the Economy, 1975, 2d edit., 1978, 3d edit., 1981, 4th edit., 1984, International Financial Management, 1978; contbr.: Ency. Brit; editor: (with James A. Crutchfield and William Pigott) Money, Financial Institutions and the Economy, 1965, U. Wash. Bus. Rev, 1954-71. Mem. Am. Econ. Assn., Am. Fin. Assn., Seattle C. of C., World Trade Club Seattle, World Affairs Council Seattle, Am. Acad. Polit. and Social Sci., Artus, Pan Xenia, Phi Beta Kappa, Pi Gamma Mu, Alpha Kappa Psi, Beta Gamma Sigma. Address: 12714 42d Ave NE Seattle WA 98125

HENNING, DANIEL E., professional football coach; b. Bronx, N.Y., June 21, 1942. Student, Coll. William and Mary. Player San Diego Chargers, AFL, 1964-66; asst. coach Homer L. Ferguson High Sch., Newport News, Va., 1967, Fla. State U., 1968-70, 74, Va. Tech. U., Blacksburg, 1971, 73, Houston Oilers, NFL, 1972, N.Y. Jets, NFL, 1976-78, Miami Dolphins, NFL, 1979-80, Washington Redskins, NFL, 1981-82; head coach Atlanta Falcons, NFL, 1983—. Office: Atlanta Falcons 1-85 and Suwanee Rd Suwanee 30174

HENNING, DOUG, illusionist; b. Ft. Garry, Man., Can., 1947; m. Barbara De Angelis, Dec. 1977. Grad. in Physiol. Psychology, McMaster U., Hamilton, Ont. Created, starred in: rock magic musical Spellbound, Toronto, 1973-74; co-creator: star rock magic musical The Magic Show, N.Y.C., 1974-75; TV spls. Doug Henning's World of Magic, 1975, 76, 77, 78; lecture tour on magic and consciousness expansion, univs., U.S. and Can., 1977-78; appeared casino shows, Las Vegas and Lake Tahoe. (Recipient Las Vegas best spl. attraction of year award 1978); Author: (with Charles Reynolds) Houdini, His Legend and His Magic, 1977. Office: care The Goldstein Co 10100 Santa Monica Blvd Suite 348 Los Angeles CA 90067 *What has helped me the most in my career and personal life has been Transcendental Meditation. After learning T.M., my creativity just blossomed. I actually began to experience many qualities of enlightenment, including heightened sensory awareness, intuition and creative energy. I realized that magic can create the same feeling of wonder that I was beginning to feel for the world as my consciousness continued to expand. This inner growth is what has really made me a top magician.*

HENNING, EDWARD BURK, museum curator; b. Cleve., Oct. 23, 1922; s. Harold and Marguerite (Burk) Wagner; m. Margaret Revacko, Dec. 31, 1942; children: Eric M., Lisa A. Henning Puzder, Geoffrey A. B.S. magna cum laude, Western Res. U., 1949; cert., Cleve. Inst. Art, 1949; postgrad., Acad. Julian, Paris, 1949-50; M.A., Western Res. U., 1952. Instr. Cleve. Mus. Art, 1951-53, asst. curator edn., 1953-56, asso. curator edn., 1956-58, asst. to dir., 1958-70, curator contemporary art, 1970-72, curator modern art, 1972-78, chief curator modern art, 1978—; adj. prof. art history Case Western Res. U., Cleve., 1967—; cons. in field. Author: Paths of Abstract Art, 1960, Fifty Years of Modern Art, 1966, The Spirit of Surrealism, 1979; contbr. articles to profl. jours. Served with U.S. Army, 1942-46. Mem. Soc. Aesthetics, Coll. Art Assn., Am. Assn. Museums, New Orgn. Visual Arts. Office: 11150 E Boulevard Cleveland OH 44106

HENNING, GEORGE THOMAS, JR., steel company executive; b. West Reading, Pa., Sept. 26, 1941; s. George Thomas and Helen Virginia (Spangler) H.; m. Susan Young, July 21, 1962; children: George Thomas III, Michael Kevin. B.A., Pa. State U., 1963; M.B.A., Harvard, 1965. Mgr. econ. analysis Eastern Gas & Fuel, Boston, 1967; mgr. gen. accounting Ohio River Co., Cin., 1968; asst. to controller Eastern Gas & Fuel Assos., Boston, 1969; dir. corporate planning Boston Gas Co., 1970; controller Eastern Asso. Coal Corp., Pitts., 1971-74; v.p., controller Lykes Resources, Inc., 1974-78; asst. controller Jones & Laughlin Steel Corp., 1979—. Mem. World Affairs Council, Pitts. Mem. Am. Inst. Corp. Controllers, Assn. Computing Machinery, Soc. Mining Engrs., Omicron Delta Kappa, Pi Gamma Mu. Presbyn. Club: Pa. State University Alumni (Allegheny County, Pa.). Home: 680 Fruithurst Dr Pittsburgh PA 15228 Office: 3 Gateway Center Pittsburgh PA 15263

HENNING, HAROLD WALTER, dentist, athletic association executive; b. Lockport, N.Y., Feb. 25, 1919; s. Harold Walter and Erna (Kandt) H. B.A., N. Central Coll., 1941; D.D.S. cum laude, Chgo. Coll. Dental Surgery, 1949; postgrad., U. Ill., Ohio State U. Sci. tchr., Roseville, Ill., 1941-42, gen. practice dentistry, Naperville, Ill., 1949—; Amateur coach N. Central Coll., Naperville, 1948-62; bd. govs. Nat. Amateur Athletic Union, 1954—, mem. fgn. relations com., 1954—; pres. Central Assn., 1965-66; chmn. U.S. men's swimming com., 1959-65; bd. dirs. U.S. Olympic Com., 1969—, exec. com., 1972-81, chmn. swimming com., 1959-65; mem. organizing com. Pan Am. Games, Chgo., 1959, dir. aquatic competition, 1959; sec.-treas. Amateur Swimming Union Ams., 1963-71, pres., 1971-75; del. Fedn. Internationale Natation Amateur, 1964—, hon. sec., 1968-72, pres., 1972-76; chmn. exec. com. Olympic Men's and Women's Swimming Trials, 1972, 76; dir. Olympic Games, charge swimming, diving and water polo events, 1972; mgr. U.S. Olympic Swimming Team, Tokyo, 1964, U.S. Pan Am. Team, Mex., 1955; coach mgr. U.S. Teams to, Guatemala and Japan, 1954-62; ofcl., referee various internat. games, 1952-68; pres. World Swimming Championships, 1973, 75; pres. Internat. Swimming Hall of Fame, 1983. Mem. Naperville Bd. Edn., 1954-59. Served with USNR, 1942-45. Decorated 1st Order Sports, Egypt; recipient award Internat. Amateur Athlete, 1964, Ill. Gov. Athletic medallion, 1968; R. Max Ritter medallion, 1976; Prize Eminence award Fedn. Internationale Natation Amateur, 1976; Gold medal for distinguished services in sports, Republic of China, 1976; Silver Medal Order Internat. Olympic Com.; named to Helms Hall of Fame, 1964, Internat. Swimming Hall of Fame, 1979. Fellow Internat. Coll. Dentists; mem. Am., Ill. dental assns., W. Suburban, Far W. study clubs, Fedn. Dentaire Internationale, Acad. Gen. Dentistry. Clubs: Masons, Rotary. Home: Walnut Woods S Julian St Naperville IL 60540 Office: 555 N Washington St Naperville IL 60540

HENNING, JOEL FRANK, lawyer, author, publisher, consultant; b. Chgo., Sept. 15, 1939; s. Alexander M. and Henrietta (Frank) H.; m. Grace Weiner, May 24, 1964; children: Justine, Sarah-Anne, Dara. A.B., Harvard U., 1961, J.D., 1964. Bar: Ill. 1965. Assoc. firm Sonnenschein, Levinson, Carlin, Nath & Rosenthal, Chgo., 1965-70; fellow, dir. program Adlai Stevenson Inst. Internat. Affairs, Chgo., 1970-73; nat. dir. Youth Edn. for Citizenship, 1972-75; dir. profl. edn. Am. Bar Assn., Chgo., 1975-78, asst. exec. dir. communications and edn., 1978-80; sr. ptnr. Joel Henning & Assocs., 1980—; pres., pub. LawLetters, Inc., 1980—; pub. Lawyer Hiring and Training Report, 1980—, Corp. Legal Strategist, 1984—, Almanac of Fed. Judiciary, 1984—; editor Bus. Law Memo, 1980—; mem. faculty Inst. on Law and Ethics, Council Philos. Studies; chmn. Fund for Justice, Chgo., 1979—. Author: Law-Related Education in America: Guidelines for the Future, 1975, Holistic Running: Beyond the Threshhold of Fitness, 1978, Mandate for Change: The Impact of Law on Educational Innovation, 1979; contbr. articles and criticism to nat. mags. and legal publs. Chmn. Gov.'s Commn. on Financing Arts in Ill., 1970-71; bd. dirs. Ill. Arts Council, 1971-81, Columbia Coll., Chgo.; bd. dirs., mem. exec. com. ACLU of Ill.; trustee S.E. Chgo. Commn.; mem. Joseph Jefferson Theatrical Awards Com. Fellow Am. Bar Found.; mem. Am. Law Inst., ABA, Chgo. Bar Assn., Chgo. Council Lawyers (co-founder), Social Sci. Edn. Consortium. Office: 116 S Michigan Ave Suite 300 Chicago IL 60603 *The hardest question for me to answer is, "What do you do?" I do a lot. Some of it returns money and satisfaction. Some returns more of one than the other. And, I do some things that make me feel fit. The best of what I do helps integrate my various selves and improves my relations with the world. But I have no facile way to say all of this at cocktail parties when, invariably, that question is popped.*

HENNING, JOHN FREDERICK, JR., publishing company executive; b. San Francisco, Nov. 28, 1923; s. John Frederick and Mary Ellen (Bashore) H.; m. Frances R. Sorensen, Jan. 4, 1947; children: John Frederick III, Robert Turner. B.A. with distinction, Stanford U., 1947. In promotion and gen. assignment positions San Francisco Examiner, 1947-51; with Lane Pub. Co., Menlo Park, Calif., 1951—, v.p., 1963-82, asst. pub., 1967-72, assoc. pub., 1972-74, v.p., gen. mgr., 1974-82, pres., assoc. pub., 1982—. Served to lt. (j.g.) USNR, 1943-45. Mem. Am. Soc. Travel Agts., Advt. Club San Francisco, Mag. Pubs. Assn., Wine and Food Soc. San Francisco. Presbyterian. Clubs: The Family, World Trade, Stanford Golf. Office: 80 Willow Rd Menlo Park CA 94025

HENNING, WILLIAM ANDREW, educational administrator; b. Blantyre, Ont., Can., July 1, 1935; came to U.S., 1935; s. Ralph McClure and Sara Lina (Sewell) H.; m. Rose Marie Hesselgrave, Aug. 7, 1957; children: Beverly, Paul. B.A., Wheaton Coll., 1955; M.A., Ind. U., 1961, Ph.D., 1964. Vis. asst. prof. Fla. State U., Talahassee, 1962; lectr. French Ind. U., Bloomington, 1963-64; prof. French Concordia Coll., Moorhead, Minn., 1964-66, Wheaton Coll., Ill., 1966-80, dean Arts and Scis., 1980—. Co-author French lang. course, 1979. Am. Council Learned Soc. fellow, 1963. Mem. Am. Assn. Tchrs. of French, Am. Assn. Higher Edn. Baptist. Home: 323 E Madison St Wheaton IL 60187 Office: Wheaton Coll Wheaton IL 60187

HENNINGER, JOHN GEORGE, banker; b. Cleve., Oct. 24, 1916; s. John and Antoinette (Heideman) H.; m. Emily Stochmal, Nov. 29, 1941; children: Thomas P., Mary Ann, Rita M., Marcia A. B.B.A., Fenn Coll., 1939; J.D., Cleve. Marshall Law Sch., 1947. Bar: Ohio bar 1947. With White Motor Co., 1939-40, Household Finance Corp., 1940-41, Gen. Motors Acceptance Corp., 1941-42, Thompson Products, 1942-45; asst. treas., br. mgr. Bank of Ohio, Cleve., 1945-54; with Society Nat. Bank., Cleve., 1954—, sr. v.p., 1970—; pres. Euclid Nat. Bank, Cleve., 1971—, now also chmn., chief exec. officer; dir. Kimsafe, Inc., Troy Mfg. Co., Process Industries Equipment Corp., Elmar Corp., Bank One Cleve. N.A.; lectr. Center for Family Owned Businesses. Pres. bd., treas. Van Aken Center Assn.; councilman local United Appeal, Health Fund, ARC, Holy Name Soc.; vis. com. Cleve. State U.; trustee Fenn Coll., Cornelia Schnurmann Found., Fenn Ednl. Found., Madonna Hall; mem. nat. bd. Adrian Generalate. Named Man of Year Fenn Coll., 1965, Alumnus of Yr. John Nance Coll., Cleve. State U., 1982. Mem. Cuyahoga Bar Assn., Greater Cleve. Bar Assn., Delta Theta Phi. Roman Catholic. Clubs: Mid-Day, Canterbury Golf, Commerce, Union (Cleve.). Home: 21900 Shelburne Rd Shaker Heights OH 44122 Office: 1255 Euclid Ave Cleveland OH 44115

HENNINGS, JOSEPHINE SILVA (HALPIN HENNINGS), retired government official; b. St. Louis; d. Francois P. and Mary Josephine (Barrick) Silva; m. Breen Halpin (dec.); children: Breen, Joan; m. Thomas C. Hennings, Jr. (dec.). B.A., Washington U.; postgrad. in polit. sci, George Washington U. News reporter-editor Sta. KMOX, St. Louis; later STA. KGU, Honolulu; news analyst, dir. radio Civil Def., P.R., Virgin Islands; fgn. corr. St. Louis Globe-Democrat, C.B.S., Caribbean, Pacific; columnist, feature writer Honolulu Advertiser; feature editor St. Louis Star Times; editor Inter-Am. Affairs, USIA, State Dept.; sr. radio officer UN; news reporter-editor Sta. WINS, N.Y.C.; news reporter-editor, TV panelist ABC; dir. pub. relations V.I. Hotel, St. Thomas; editor U.S. Comptrollers Office, St. Thomas; later fed. govt. liaison officer Dept. Def., Washington, now ret. Named Top Am. Woman Broadcaster in internat. field UN, U.S. Dept. Labor. Mem. Am. Women in Radio and TV. Clubs: Washington Press, Nat. Press (Washington); Overseas Press (N.Y.C.). Home: 2501 Calvert St NW Washington DC 20008 also La Jolla CA

HENNINGS, ROBERT EDWARD, historian; b. Evanston, Ill., Aug. 4, 1925; s. Abraham James and Mervyna Barbara (Dolsen) H.; m. Nancy Harriet Wensley, July 21, 1949; children—Deirdre Ellen, Robert Edward, Joseph Turner. A.B., Oberlin (Ohio) Coll., 1950; M.A., U. Calif., Berkeley, 1957, Ph.D., 1961. Tchr. social studies and English, public high schs., Calif., Ohio, 1953-56; instr. Am. history U. Ky., Lexington, 1961-62; mem. faculty Eastern Ill. U., Charleston, 1962—, prof. history, 1973—, chmn. dept., 1974—; chmn. council faculties to bd. govs. State Colls. and Univs. Ill., 1970-72. Contbr. articles to profl. jours. Pres. bd. dirs. Charleston Community Theatre, 1972-75. Served with AUS, 1944-46. Mem. AAUP (past chpt. pres.), Am. Assn. State and Local History, Am. Hist. Assn., Coles County Hist. Soc., Ill. Hist. Soc., So. Hist. Soc., Nat. Trust Historic Preservation, Orgn. Am. Historians. Democrat. Home: Bird Hill Rte 4 Charleston IL 61920 Office: Dept History Eastern Ill U Charleston IL 61920

HENNINGSEN, PETER, JR., diversified industry exec.; b. Mpls., Oct. 6, 1926; s. Peter and Anna O. (Kjelstrup) H.; m. Donna J. Buresh, June 19, 1948; children—Deborah, Pamela, James. B.B.A., U. Minn., 1950. Packaging engr. govt. and aero. products div. Honeywell, Inc., Mpls., 1950-72; mgr. packaging Internat. Tel. & Tel., N.Y.C., 1972-80; v.p. Raymond Eisenhardt & Son, Inc., 1980—; Mem. Soc. Packaging and Handling Engrs., 1951—, fellow, 1970, pres., 1970-71, chmn. bd., 1972-73. Editorial cons. mags. in field. Served with USNR, 1944-46. Named Man of Year, 1968. Mem. Am. Soc. Testing Materials, Aerospace Industries Assn. (chmn. packaging com. 1967). Methodist. Club: Mason (Shriner). Home: 6 Littlejohn Pl White Plains NY 10605 Office: 95 Bauer Dr Oakland NJ 07436

HENNION, REEVE LAWRENCE, news agency executive; b. Ventura, Calif., Dec. 7, 1941; s. Tom Reeve and Evelyn Edna (Henry) H.; m. Carolyn Laird, Sept. 12, 1964; children: Jeffrey Reeve, Douglas Laird. B.A., Stanford U., 1963, M.A., 1965. Reporter Tulare (Calif.) Advance-Register, 1960-62; reporter UPI, San Francisco, 1963-66, mgr., Fresno, Calif., 1966-68, regional exec., Los Angeles, 1968-69, mgr., Honolulu, 1969-72, San Francisco, 1972-75, Calif. editor, 1975-77, gen. news editor, 1977-81, bus. mgr., 1981-83, v.p., gen. mgr. Pacific div., 1983—. Editor: The Modoc Country, 1971. Treas. Calif. Freedom of Info. Com., chmn., 1983—. Mem. Delta Kappa Epsilon, Sigma Delta Chi. Home: 105 W Santa Inez Hillsborough CA 94010 Office: UPI 1212 Fox Plaza San Francisco CA 94102

HENREID, PAUL (PAUL GEORG JULIUS VON HERNRIED RITTER VON WASEL-WALDINGAU), actor, director; b. Trieste, Austria; came to U.S., 1940; s. Carl Alphons and Maria Louise (Lendecke) von Hernreid; m. Elizabeth Glueck, 1936; children: Mimi, Monika. Grad., Academie Graphic Arts, Vienna; also, Konservatorium Dramatic Arts, Vienna. Mem. Max Reinhardt's Vienna Theatre and others. Also appeared in: Austrian films Hohe Schule, Nur Ein Komoediant; appeared in: London plays The Jersey Lilly; also films Night Train, 1935-40 (best fgn. actor in film N.Y.C. critics); N.Y.C. stage appearances in Flight to the West, 1941, Festival, 1955; motion pictures include: Casablanca, Now Voyager, Of Human Bondage, Spanish Main, Deception, Song of Love, others; producer: film Hollow Triumph (The Scar); co-producer, star: So Young So Bad; producer, dir., star: For Men Only; dir.: Dead-Ringer (Dead Image) (outstanding award merit Motion Picture Council Cal.), Ballade in Blue; actor: The Heretic; actor, dir. numerous TV films; starred as Comdr. in: Nat. tour and Don Juan in Hell, N.Y.C., 1972-73. Recipient Cross of Honor for scis. and arts, 1st class Republic of Austria, 1980; Artistry in Cinema award Am. Classic Screen Awards, 1980; Yellow Rose award Tex. Film Soc., 1983; Eagle award Dept. Army, 1983. Mem. Screen Actors Guild, AFTRA, Dirs. Guild Am., Actors Equity, Acad. Motion Picture Arts and Scis. Club: Vereinigung Ehemaliger Theresianisten (Vienna). Home: 18068 Bluesail Dr Pacific Palisades CA 90272

HENRICHS, ALBERT MAXIMINUS, philologist; b. Cologne, Germany, Dec. 29, 1942; came to U.S., 1971; s. Johannes and Berti H.; m. Ingrid Ursula Schaadt, June 4, 1965; children: Markus, Helen Felicitas. Student, U. Cologne, 1962-66, U. Bonn, 1962-63; Dr.phil., U. Cologne, 1966, habilitation, 1969; M.A. (hon.), Harvard U., 1972. Vis. lectr. U. Mich., 1967-69; prof. U. Cologne, 1970-71; asso. prof. Classics U. Calif., Berkeley, 1971-73; prof. Greek and Latin. Harvard U., Cambridge, Mass., 1973—, chmn. dept. classics, summer 1982—, mem. affiliated faculty Div. Sch., 1982—. Author: Didymos der Blinde. Kommentar zu Hiob (Tura-Papyrus), 2 vols, 1968, Die Phoinikika des Lollianos, 1972; Editor: Harvard Studies in Classical Philology, 1975-79; mem. adv. bd.: Harvard Library Bull., 1981—, Greek, Roman and Byzantine Studies, 1984—; Contbr. articles on ancient Greek lit., papyrology, mythology and religion to profl. jours. Mem. Am. Philol. Assn., Assn. Internationale de Papyrologues., Egypt Exploration Soc. Home: 144 Longwood Ave Brookline MA 02146 Office: Dept Classics 319 Boylston Hall Harvard U Cambridge MA 02138

HENRIE, THOMAS A., chief scientist; b. Sutherland, Utah, Feb. 6, 1923; s. Francis and Emily (Judd) H.; m. Faye Davis, June, 1943; children: Dale, Robert, David, Joy, Janice, Jane. B.S. in Chemistry and

Math., Brigham Young U., 1952; Ph.D. in Metallurgy, U. Utah, 1955. Lab instr. Brigham Young U., Provo, Utah, 1950-55; research asst. U. Utah, Salt Lake City, 1952-55; research chemist Electormetallurgical Co., Niagara Falls, N.Y., 1955-58; supervisory metallurgist Reno Research Ctr. and Boulder City, Nev., N.Y., 1958-61; supervisory research metallurgist Reno Research Ctr., 1961-66, research dir., 1966-70; dep. dir. mineral resource and environ. devel. Bur. Mines, Washington, 1970-75, assoc. dir., 1975-79, chief scientist, 1979—. Contbr. writings to various publs. in field; patentee. Recipient various awards Dept. Interior. Mem. Am. Inst. Mining, AIME (past chmn. Extractive Metallurgy, past v.p.), Metall. Soc. Am. (past pres.), AAAS, Soc. Mining Engrs., Sigma Xi. Mormon. Home: 1304 Winding Waye Ln Silver Spring MD 20902 Office: Bureau of Mines 2401 E St NW Washington DC 20240

HENRIKSEN, MELVIN, educator, mathematician; b. N.Y.C., Feb. 23, 1927; s. Kaj and Helen (Kahn) H.; m. Lillian Viola Hill, July 23, 1946 (div. 1964); children—Susan, Richard, Thomas; m. Louise Levitas, June 12, 1964. B.S., Coll. City N.Y., 1948; M.S., U. Wis., 1949, Ph.D. in Math, 1951. Asst. math., then instr. extension div. U. Wis., 1948-51; asst. prof. U. Ala., 1951-52; from instr. to prof. math. Purdue U., 1952-65; prof. math., head dept. Case Inst. Tech., 1965-68; research asso. U. Calif. at Berkeley, 1968-69; prof., chmn. math. dept. Harvey Mudd Coll., 1969-72, prof., 1972—; mem. Inst. Advanced Study, Princeton, 1956-57, 63-64; vis. prof. Wayne State U., 1960-61; research asso. U. Man., Winnipeg, Can., 1975-76; vis. prof. Wesleyan U., Middletown, Conn., 1978-79, 82-83. Author: (with Milton Lees) Single Variable Calculus, 1970; Contbr. articles profl. jours. on algebra, rings of functions, gen. topology. Sloan fellow, 1956-58. Mem. Am. Math. Soc., Math. Assn. Am. Home: 504 Bowling Green Dr Claremont CA 91711

HENRION, MARC, distilled beverage company executive. Exec. v.p. The Seagram Co. Ltd., Montreal, Que., Can. Office: The Seagram Co Ltd 1430 Peel St Montreal PQ Canada H3A 1S9§

HENRY, ANTHONY RAY, community organizer; b. Houston, Aug. 14, 1938; s. Lawrence G. and Autry B. (Thomas) H. B.A., U. Tex.-Austin, 1960; M.Ed., Springfield Coll., 1961. Community devel. vol. Am. Friends Service Com., Tanzania, East Africa, 1961-63, dir. preadolescent enrichment program, Chgo., 1963-66, dir. housing program, 1966-69, dir. nationwide tenants rights program, Washington, 1969; dir. Nat. Tenants Orgn., Inc., Washington, 1969-71, 74-75, Nat. Tenants Info. Service, Inc., 1971-74; spl. asst. Newark Tenants Council, Inc., 1975-76; nat. rep. criminal justice programs Am. Friends Service Com., Phila., 1976-78; affirmative action sec. AFSC, Phila., 1978-81; exec. sec. AFSC No. Calif. Regional Office, San Francisco, 1981—; Mem. rent adv. bd. to Price Commn., Phase II Econ. Stblzn. Program, 1972-73; mem. community relations com. Am. Friends Service Com., 1972-76, mem. internat. affairs div. com., 1974-76; dep. nat. coordinator So. Christian Leadership Conf.'s Poor People Campaign, 1968; mem. Quaker UN Com., 1975-76; bd. dirs. Nat. Housing Conf., 1971-76, Rural Housing Coalition, 1971-73, Nonprofit Housing Center, 1972-73, Met. Washington Planning and Housing Assn., 1971-74, Tenant Resources Center, Washington, 1976-77, Nat. Coalition Against Death Penalty, 1976-78; incorporator, bd. dirs. Nat. Center for Housing Mgmt., 1972-81, vice chmn., 1974-81; bd. dirs. Tenant Action Group, Phila., 1976-81, sec., 1977-78, co-chairperson, 1978-81; bd. dirs., chmn. Low Income Housing Info. Center, Washington, 1977-82; bd. dirs. Nat. Coalition Against Grand Jury Abuse, 1977-78, Nat. Tenants Union, 1980-81. Mem. Interreligious Task Force on Criminal Justice, 1977-78, Pa. Council for Sexual Minorities, 1978-81. Home: 1860 Turk St San Francisco CA 94115 Office: 2160 Lake St San Francisco CA 94121

HENRY, BUCK, writer; b. N.Y.C. Student, Dartmouth Coll. Film appearances include Catch 22, 1970, Taking Off, 1971, The Man Who Fell to Earth, 1977, Heaven Can Wait, 1978, Old Boyfriends, 1979, First Family, 1980, Gloria, 1980; dir.: film Heaven Can Wait, 1978, First Family, 1980; film writing credits include The Troublemaker, 1964, The Graduate, 1967, Candy, 1968, Catch 22, 1970, The Owl and the Pussycat, 1970, What's Up Doc?, 1972, The Day of the Dolphin, 1973, First Family, 1980; co-creator: television series Get Smart; writer, performer: The Steve Allen Show, That Was the Week That Was; stage appearances include The Premise. Served with U.S. Army. Mem. Writers Guild Am., Dirs. Guild. *

HENRY, CARL FERDINAND HOWARD, theologian; b. N.Y.C., Jan. 22, 1913; s. Karl F. and Johanna (Vaethroeder) H.; m. Helga Bender, Aug. 17, 1940; children: Paul Brentwood, Carol Jennifer. B.A., Wheaton (Ill.) Coll., 1938, M.A., 1940; B.D., No. Baptist Theol. Sem., Chgo., 1941, Th.D., 1942; Ph.D., Boston U., 1949; Litt.D. (hon.), Seattle-Pacific Coll., 1963, Wheaton Coll., 1968, L.H.D., Houghton Coll., 1973, D.D., Northwestern Coll., 1979, Gordon-Conwell Theol. Sem., 1984. Ordained to ministry Bapt. Ch., 1941; asst. prof., then prof. theology No. Bapt. Theol. Sem., 1942-47; acting dean Fuller Theol. Sem., Pasadena, Calif., 1947, prof., 1947-56, Peyton lectr., 1963, vis. prof., 1980; vis. prof. theology Wheaton Coll., Gordon Div. Sch., Columbia Bible Coll., 1977, 80, Japan Sch. Theology, Trinity Evang. Div. Sch., Denver Conservative Bapt. Sem., 1981, 83; vis. prof. Eastern Bapt. Theol. Sem., 1969-70, prof.-at-large, 1970-74; lectr.-at-large World Vision, 1974—; Disting. vis. prof. Christian studies Hillsdale Coll., 1983-84; faculty mem. flying seminar to Europe and Nr. East Winona Lake (Ind.) Sch. Theology, 1952; daily radio commentator Let the Chips Fall, Los Angeles, 1952-53; chmn. World Congress Evangelism, Berlin, 1966, Consultation Scholars, Washington, 1967; program chmn. Jerusalem Conf. Bibl. Prophecy, Israel, 1971; Latin Am. Theol. Frat. lectr., 1973; lectr. Evangelism Internat., Singapore, 1976, 78, All-India Evang. Conf. on Social Action, Madras, 1979, Liberia Bapt. Theol. Sem., Monrovia, 1982, Cameroun Bapt. Theol. Coll., Ndu, 1982; vis. lectr. Asian Center Theol. Studies and Mission, Seoul, Korea, 1974, 74, 76, 78, 80, Teoloski Facultet, Matija Vlacic Illrik, Zagreb, Yugoslavia, 1977, Asian Theol. Sem., Manila, 1980; bd. dirs. Inst. Advanced Christian Studies, 1976-79, 81—, pres., 1971-74; bd. dirs. Ethics and Public Policy Center, 1979—, Inst. Religion and Democracy, 1981—, Prison Fellowship, 1981—; trustee Gordon Cowell Theol. Sem., 1965-68; bd. dirs. Ministers Life and Casualty Union, 1968-77; co-chmn. Rose Bowl Easter Sunrise Service, 1950-56. Author: A Doorway to Heaven, 1941, Successful Church Publicity, 1942, Remaking the Modern Mind, 1948, The Uneasy Conscience of Modern Fundamentalism, 1948, Giving a Reason for Our Hope, 1949, The Protestant Dilemma, 1949, Notes on the Doctrine of God, 1949, Fifty Years of Proestant Theology, 1950, The Drift of Western Thought, 1951, Personal Idealism and Strong's Theology, 1951, Glimpses of a Sacred Land, 1953, Christian Personal Ethics, 1957, Evangelical Responsibility in Contemporary Theology, 1957, Aspects of Christian Social Ethics, 1964, Frontiers in Modern Theology, 1966, The God Who Shows Himself, 1966, Evangelicals at the Brink of Crisis, 1967, Faith at the Frontiers, 1969, A Plea for Evangelism Demonstration, 1971, New Strides of Faith, 1972, Evangelicals in Search of Identity, 1976, God, Revelation and Authority, vols. 1 and 2, 1976, vols. 3 and 4, 1979, vol. 5, 1982, vol. 6,, 1983; editor: Contemporary Evangelical Thought, 1957; Editor: Revelation and the Bible, 1959, The Biblical Expositor, 1960, Basic Christian Doctrines, 1962, Christian Faith and Modern Theology, 1964, Jesus of Nazareth: Saviour and Lord, 1966, Fundamentals of the Faith, 1969, Horizons of Science, 1978, The Christian Mindset in a Secular Society, 1984; editor-in-chief: Baker's Dictionary of Christian Ethics, 1973; cons. editor: Baker's Dictionary of Theology, 1964; editor: Christianity Today, 1956-68; editor-at-large, 1968-77; contbg. editor: World Vision Mag., 1976—. Recipient Freedoms Found. award, 1954, 66, Religious Heritage Am. award, 1975. Mem. Soc. Sci. Study Religion, AAAS, Am. Soc. Christian Ethics, Am. Acad. Religion, Am. Theol. Soc. (v.p. 1974-75, pres. 1979-80), Evang. Theol. Soc. (pres. 1969-70), Conf. Faith and History, Nat. Assn. Evangelicals (bd. administrn. 1956-70), Am. Philos. Assn., Am. Soc. Ch. History, Soc. Oriental Research, Soc. Christian Philosophers, Nat. Assn. Bapt. Profs. of Religion, Evang. Press Assn. (hon. life), Soc. Bibl. Lit. Club: Cosmos (Washington). Address: 3824 N 37th St Arlington VA 22207

HENRY, DAVID HOWE, II, former diplomat and international organization official; b. Geneva, N.Y., May 19, 1918; s. David Max and Dorothy (Buley) H.; m. Margaret Beard, Nov. 16, 1946; children: David Beard, Peter York, Michael Max, Susan. Student, Hobart Coll., 1935-37, Sorbonne, 1937-38; A.B., Columbia U., 1939, Russian Inst., 1948-49, Harvard U., 1944-45, Nat. War Coll., 1957-58. Ins. agt., 1939-41; mem. fgn. service Dept. State, 1941-71, assigned, Montreal, 1941-42, Beirut, 1942-44, Washington, 1944-45, 48-52, 57-66, 70, Moscow, 1945-48, 52-54, Vladivostok, 1945-46, Berlin, 1955-57; acting dir. Office Research and Intelligence Sino-Soviet bloc, 1958-59; dir. dept. polit. affairs Nat. War Coll., 1959-61; dep. dir. Office Soviet Affairs, 1961-64, dir., 1964-65; mem. Policy Planning Council, 1965-66; dep. chief of mission Am. embassy, Reykjavik, Iceland, 1966-69; information systems specialist, 1970; polit. and security council affairs UN, N.Y.C., 1971-78. Mem. Kappa Alpha. Presbyterian. Club: Rotarian. Home: Seaside Apt 20 3541 NE Ocean Blvd Jensen Beach FL 33457

HENRY, DEWITT PAWLING, II, creative writing educator, writer, arts administrator; b. Wayne, Pa., June 30, 1941; s. Jonh and Kathryn (Thralls) Heary; m. Constance Joy Sherbill, Aug. 25, 1973; 1 dau., Ruth Kathryn. A.B., Amherst Coll., 1963; A.M., Harvard U., 1965, Ph.D., 1971; postgrad., U. Iowa-Iowa City, 1964-66. Editor Ploughshares, dir. Ploughshares, Inc., Watertown, Mass., 1971—; dir. Book Affairs; Inc., Watertown, 1975—; adj. prof. Emerson Coll., Boston, 1982-83, asst. prof. creative writing and lig., 1983—; mem. adv. panel Mass. Council on the Arts, Boston, 1981—; literature panelist Nat. Endowment fot the Arts, Washington, 1982—; mem. adv. bd. New England Found. for Arts, 1983—. Columnist: Wilson Library Bull., 1979; staff editor: The Pushcart Prize, 1978—. Fellow Woodrow Wilson found., 1963, Coordinating Council of Literary Mags., 1979, Nat. Endowment for Arts, 1979. Mem. Associated Writing Programs, Phi Beta Kappa. Presbyterian. Home: 72 Westminster Ave Watertown MA 02172 Office: Ploughshares Inc 214A Waverley Ave Watertown MA 02172

HENRY, DONALD LEE, retired banker; b. Evansville, Ind., Jan. 25, 1918; s. Robert D. and Mary A. (Swope) H.; m. Mary Lou Hess, Dec. 24, 1941; children: Judith Ann, Don Richard. B.S., Purdue U., 1939, M.S., 1941, Ph.D., 1947; postgrad., U. Chgo., U. Chgo., 1946. Agrl. economist Fed. Res. Bank St. Louis, 1947-54, asst. cashier, 1954-56, cashier, 1957, mgr., 1957, v.p., 1957-68, sr. v.p., 1969-83. Past pres. Old Ky. Home council Boy Scouts Am., past pres. Ky.-Tenn. area, also mem. nat. exploring com. Served to lt. col. USAR. Mem. Sigma Xi, Alpha Zeta. Club: Rotarian. Home: 520 Leicester Circle Louisville KY 40222

HENRY, EDWARD LEROY, college president; b. St. Cloud, Minn., Mar. 30, 1921; s. John A. and Rose C. (Kraker) H.; m. Elizabeth Anne Reiten, Aug. 11, 1947; children: Anne, Paula, Susan, Stephan, Michael, Mary, Rebecca, Peter, John. Student, St. John's U., 1943, Harvard U., 1943-44; M.A., U. Chgo., 1947, M.B.A., 1948, Ph.D. in Polit. Sci, 1955. Prof. polit. sci. Mount St. Scholastica Coll., Atchison, Kans., 1948-54; mem. faculty St. Johns' U., Collegeville, Minn., 1954-72, prof. polit. sci., 1957-72, v.p. devel., 1962-64, dir., 1967-72, prof. govt., 1974, disting. service prof., 1975; pres. St. Mary's Coll., Notre Dame, Ind., 1972-74, St. Michael's Coll., Winooski, Vt., 1976—; cons. edn., govt., 1967—; pres. Vt. Higher Edn. Council, 1978-79, Assn. Vt. Ind. Colls., 1980-83. Author: Micropolis in Transition: A Story of A Small City, 1971; Editor: Metropolis, 1968. Mem. Minn. Boundaries Commn., 1965-67; chmn. Minn. Tech. Rev. Panel, 1969-71, Minn. Adv. Commn. Community Service and Continuing Edn., 1971-72; Mem. bd. St. Cloud Pub. Sch. Dist., 1958-64; mayor, St. Cloud, 1964-70. Served with USNR, 1943-46. Recipient Pres.'s medal Coll. St. Benedict, St. Joseph, Minn., 1970, Community Leadership award City St. Cloud, 1970, Tri-Cap award OEO, 1970; Distinguished Service award Gov. Minn., 1976. Mem. AAUP, Am. Polit. Sci. Assn., League Minn. Municipalities (pres. 1968-69). Roman Catholic. Home: 104 S Cove Rd Burlington VT 05401

HENRY, HAROLD ROBERT, engineering educator, consultant; b. Stockridge, Ga., June 2, 1928; s. Walter Raleigh and Annie Lou (Flake) H.; m. Sue Groome, Dec. 26, 1950; children: Jonathan, Martha Sue, Rebecca, Sarah, Rachel. B.C.E., Ga. Inst. Tech., 1947; M.S., Iowa State U., 1950; Ph.D., Columbia U., 1960. Registered profl. engr., N.Y., Mich., Ala. Instr. civil engring. Ga. Inst. Tech., Atlanta, 1949-50; lectr. engring. Columbia U., N.Y.C., 1950-54; civil engr. Ebasco Services, N.Y.C., 1953-54; asst. prof. Mich. State U., East Lansing, 1954-61, assoc. prof., 1961-64; prof. engring. U. Ala., Tuscaloosa, 1964—, head dept. civil engring., 1969—; cons. hydrology U.S. Geol. Survey, Washington, 1958-64; cons. fluid mechanics U.S. Army Missile Command, Huntsville, Ala., 1964-69; cons. hydrology U.S. Army Corps Engrs., Mobile, Ala., 1978—; nat. adviser Environ. Health Sci. Council, Washington, 1974-78; mem. tech. adv. bd. Inst. Creation Research. Author profl. papers. Mem. ASCE, Am. Geophys. Union, Am. Soc. Engring. Edn., Am. Soc. Profl. Engrs. Baptist. Home: 9 Lenora Dr Tuscaloosa AL 35401 Office: Dept Civil Engring U Ala PO Box 1468 University AL 35486

HENRY, HERMAN LUTHER, JR., university dean, industrial engineer; b. Arcadia, La., Mar. 6, 1918; s. Herman Luther and Louannie (Rogers) H.; m. Eva Grissom, Dec. 23, 1941; children: Krista Ann, David Michael. B.S. in Mech. and Elec. Engring., La. Poly. Inst., 1940; M.S. in Mech. Engring., Ill. Inst. Tech., 1946. Registered profl engr., La., Tex. Instr. tech. drawing Ill. Inst. Tech., 1942-46; faculty La. Tech. U., 1946-51, 55—, prof., head indsl. engring. and computer sci. dept., 1964-76; asso. dean Coll. Engring., 1976—; project engr. Dow Chem. Co., 1951-55. Mem. Inst. Indsl. Engrs., Am. Soc. Engring. Edn., Nat. Soc. Profl. Engrs., Nat. Council Engring. Examiners. Home: 910 Dogwood St Ruston LA 71270

HENRY, HUGH FORT, physicist, educator; b. Emory, Va., Apr. 25, 1916; s. Howell Meadors and Addie Amanda (Fort) H.; m. Emmaline Rust, Aug. 22, 1942; children—Hugh Littell, Margaret Henry Rati, Howell George, Harold William. B.A., B.S., Emory and Henry Coll., 1936; M.S. in Physics, U. Va., 1938, Ph.D., 194O. Head dept. physics and math. Coll. of Ozarks, Clarksville, Ark., 1940-41; asso. prof. physics U. Ga., 1941-49; head safety fire and radiation control dept. Oak Ridge gaseous diffusion plant Union Carbide Nuclear Co., 1949-61; prof. physics, head dept. DePauw U., Greencastle, Ind., 1961—; Pres. bd. dirs. Central States Univs., 1967; Vice chmn. com. N-13, radiation protection U.S.A. Standards Inst., 1956—, chmn. subcom. N-7.3, 1956—, mem. subcoms. N-7.2 and N-6.8, 1956—; organizer dirs. course nuclear safety fissionable materials users AEC, 1957, 59; U.S. del. tech. com. 85 Internat. Standards Orgn., 1958, 60, 65; research with Nat. Radiol. Protection Bd., Harwell, Eng., 1975-76, Atomic Energy Research Establishment, Harwell, 1975-76. Author: Fundamentals of Radiation Protection, 1969; Author, editor tech. manuals. Recipient Silver Beaver award Boy Scouts Am. Mem. Am. Phys. Soc. (treas. Southeastern sect. 1947-50), Am. Assn. Physics Tchrs. (pres. Ind. sect. 1972-73), Am. Nuclear Soc., Health Physics Soc., Optical Soc. Am., A.A.A.S., Sigma Xi. Clubs: Elk, Rotarian (pres. 1967-68). Home: 404 Linwood Dr Greencastle IN 46135

HENRY, JAMES B., college dean. Dean Kent State U. Coll. Bus., Ohio. Office: Office of Dean of Bus Kent State U. Kent OH 44242§

HENRY, JOHN BERNARD, pathologist, university dean; b. Elmira, N.Y., Apr. 26, 1928; m. Georgette Boughton, June 10, 1953; children: Maureen Anne, Julie Patricia, William Bernard, Paul Bernard, John Bernard, Thomas David. A.B., Cornell U., 1951; M.D., U. Rochester, 1955. Diplomate: Am. Bd. Pathology (v.p. 1974-75, pres. 1976-78, trustee). Intern ward med. service Barnes Hosp., St. Louis, 1955-56; resident pathology Presbyn. Hosp., N.Y.C., 1956-58, New Eng. Deaconess Hosp., Boston, 1958-60; trainee Nat. Cancer Inst., NIH, 1958-60; clin. pathologist, chmn. clin. lab. com., dir. Blood Bank and Clin. Labs. Teaching Hosp. and Clinic, U. Fla., 1960-64; asst. medicine Washington U. Sch. Medicine, St. Louis, 1955-56; asst. pathology, then instr. pathology Columbia Coll. Phys. and Surg., 1956-58; teaching fellow pathology Harvard U. Med. Sch., 1959-60; asst. prof., then asso. prof. pathology U. Fla. Coll. Medicine, 1960-64; prof. pathology Coll. Medicine; dir. clin. pathology SUNY, Upstate, Syracuse, 1964-79; dean Coll. Health Related Professions SUNY Upstate Med Ctr., 1971-77; dean Georgetown U. Sch. Medicine, Washington, 1979—. Author numerous articles on chemistry, med. edn. and immunopathology field. Served with U.S. Navy, 1946-48; as lt. comdr. USNR, 1958-66; capt. USNR, 1974—. Fellow Coll. Am. Pathologist, Am. Soc. Clin. Pathologists (bd. dirs. 1974-82, pres. 1980-81, S.C. Dyke Founder award 1979); mem. Am. Acad. Clin. Toxicology, AAAS, Am. Blood Commn. (pres. 1978-80), Am. Assn. Blood Banks (pres. 1970-71), Am. Assn. Clin. Chemists, Am. Assn. History Medicine, Am. Assn. Med. Writers, Am. Chem. Soc., Am. Mgmt. Assn., AMA, Assn. Am. Med. Colls., Internat. Acad. Pathology, Soc. Advanced Med. Systems, Transplantation Soc., Royal Soc. Health, Internat. Soc. Blood Transfusion, Pan Am. Med. Assn., Soc. Med. Consultants to Armed Forces, World Assn. Socs. Pathology, Med. Soc. D.C. (exec. bd. 1983—), Alpha Omega Alpha. Address: Georgetown U Sch Medicine 3900 Reservoir Rd NW Washington DC 20007

HENRY, JOHN FREDERICK, educator; b. Anniston, Ala., Mar. 2, 1931; s. Leonard Groves and Margret Albertine (Nonnenmacher) H.; m. Julia Ann Hubbard, June 6, 1954; children—Melanie Ann, Deborah Jean, John Frederick. B.S. in Indsl. Mgmt, Auburn U., 1954, M.S., Ga. Inst. Tech., 1957; Ph.D. in Bus. Adminstrn, U. Ala., 1964. Grad. instr. Ga. Inst. Tech., 1956-57; asst. prof. indsl. mgmt. Auburn (Ala.) U., 1957-58, asst. prof. indsl. mgmt., indsl. engring., 1959-64, asso. prof. econs. and bus. adminstrn., 1964-69, asso. prof., head mgmt. dept., 1969-70, prof., head mgmt. dept., 1970—; grad. instr. mgmt. U. Ala., 1958-59; cons. for municipal employee tng. program Small Bus. Adminstrn. and pvt. industry. Author: Investment Decisions In Wood Product Firms, 1968, What Cost Comparisons Show, 1969, Management Practices In Alabama Industries, 1970, How to Set Up Your Own Market Research, 1972. Served with USNR, 1954-56. Mem. Ala. Acad. Sci., So. Econ. Assn., So. Mgmt. Assn. (dir. 1969—), Soc. Advancement Mgmt., Acad. Mgmt., Beta Gamma Sigma, Omicron Delta Epsilon. Methodist (trustee ofcl. bd., commn. chmn.). Club: Kiwanian (treas., dir. 1965—). Home: PO Box 185 Auburn AL 36830 *One must work with and through people rather than by directing or ordering performance; one must recognize each individual's capability and encourage him to that level.*

HENRY, J(OHN) PORTER, JR., sales consultant; b. Webster Groves, Mo., Oct. 25, 1911; s. J(ohn) Porter and Imogen Edith (Adams) H.; m. Mary Lee Harney, Mar. 5, 1941 (dec. Dec. 1977); children: Barbara Henry Drews, Richard Adams; m. Martha Rush Philley, Mar. 10, 1978. A.B., Washington U., St. Louis, 1932. With St. Louis Star-Times, 1933-35, Thomas W. Parry Corp., St. Louis, 1935-37, Cin. Post, 1937; asst. sec. Optimist Internat., 1936-39; mem. staff St. Louis Post-Dispatch, 1939-41, N.Y. Daily News, 1941-43; founder, since pres. Porter Henry & Co., N.Y.C., 1945. Author: Handbook of Outboard Motors, 1948; co-author: Effective Sales Incentive Compensation, 1980, Greater Efficiency in the Small Office, 1983; Contbr. to mags., jours. Served with USAAF, 1943-45; ETO. Decorated Medal of Freedom. Mem. Phi Beta Kappa, Sigma Chi. Mem. Community Ch. Clubs: N.Y. Sales Execs., Overseas Press, Huguenot Yacht (N.Y.C.). Home: 1124 Hunter Ave Pelham NY 10803 Office: 370 Lexington Ave New York NY 10017

HENRY, JOHN THOMAS, newspaper executive; b. St. Paul, May 30, 1933; s. Harlan A. and Roxane (Thomas) H.; m. Carla Joyce Lechthaler, Jan. 2, 1982; children: Alexandra, Elizabeth, John, Catherine. B.B.A., U. Minn., 1955. With St. Paul Dispatch and Pioneer Press, 1955—, asst. to publisher, then bus. mgr., 1971-76, gen. mgr., 1976—. Vice pres. St. Paul Jr. C. of C., 1965-66; bd. dirs. St. Paul Jr. Achievement, 1979—, Better Bus. Bur. of Minn., 1980—. Served with USAF, 1956-59. Recipient Disting. Service award Classified Advt. Mgrs. Assn., 1971. Home: 4436 Oakmede Ln White Bear MN 55110 Office: 55 E 4th St Saint Paul MN 55101

HENRY, JOSEPH LOUIS, university dean; b. New Orleans, May 2, 1924; s. Varice S. and Mabel (Mansion) H.; m. Dorothy L. Whittle, July 28, 1954; children: Joseph Louis, Ronald Maurice, Joan Alison, Leilani Cecile (Mrs. P. Smith), Peter Donald. D.D.S., Howard U., 1946; B.S., Xavier U., 1948, Sc.D., 1975; M.S., Ill. U., 1949, Ph.D., 1951; D.H.L., Ill. Coll. Optometry, 1973; M.A. (hon.), Harvard U., 1975. Diplomate: Am. Bd. Oral Medicine. Instr. oral medicine Coll. Dentistry, Howard U., Washington, 1946-48, asso. prof. oral medicine, 1951-53, supt. clinics, 1953-65, prof. oral medicine, 1958-66, dir. clinics, 1965-66, dean, 1966-75; chmn., prof. oral diagnosis and radiology Sch. Dental Medicine, Harvard U., 1975—, assoc. dean, 1978—; research fellow U. Ill.; extern U. Ill. Research and Ednl. Hosp., Chgo., 1948-51; cons. Freedmen's Hosp., 1951—, Tuskegee VA Hosp., 1951—, Crownsville (Md.) State Hosp., 1960—, Ill. Coll. Optometry, 1972, trustee, 1982; cons. Essex Community Coll., 1972, Roxbury Med.-Tech. Inst., 1969—, Bakers Dozen Youth Center, Project Headstart, Peace Corps, Mt. Altoe Vets. Hosp.; bd. govs. D.C. Gen. Hosp., 1971-72; mem. dental editorial award com. William J. Gies Found. Advancement Dentistry. Contbr. to: Optometry: Education for the Profession, 1973, Optometric Education, A Summary Report, 1973, also articles in profl. jours. Mem. White House Conf. Internat. Relations, 1965; cons. White House Conf. Employment Handicapped, 1967, Nat. Urban Coalition, 1971, Nat. Commn. on Optometry, 1971-72; sponsor Boys Town, 1955—; life mem. NAACP; sponsor Urban League, 1953—; program dir. YMCA, 1950-51; mem. St. Gabriel's PTA, 1960—; trustee D.C. div. Am. Cancer Soc., Ill. Coll. Optometry; bd. dirs. Inst. Myofunctional Therapy, 1973, Symposia and Seminars, Inc., 1974; mem. Commn. Ednl. Credit Am. Council Edn., 1974; trustee Roxbury Latin Sch.; bd. dirs. W.E.B. DuBois Inst. Harvard U. Afro-Am. Research, 1976. Served to 2d lt. ASTP, 1942-43. Recipient Student Body and Student

Council Faculty award, 1964; Chi Delta Mu Achievement award, 1967; Achievement award Howard U. Dental Coll., 1967; Wisdom award Honor, 1970; Dental Alumni award, 1971; Inter-Alumni award United Negro Coll. Fund, 197O; Pub. Service award Urban League, 1970; awards Nat. Dental Assts., 1970, Nat. Naval Dental Sch., 1971, Roxbury Med.-Tech. Inst., 1972; Founders award Nat. Optometric Assn., 1973; Triennial award Nat. Dental Assn., 1973; award services D.C. govt., 1975; named Dentist of Year D.C. Dental Soc., 1973. Fellow AAAS (v.p., chmn. sect. on dentistry, mem.-at-large sect. dentistry), Internat., Am. coll. dentists, Royal Soc. Health; mem. Nat. Dental Assn. (Achievement award 1967, dentist of year award 1972, Presdl. award 1976), ADA (Quiz bowl champion trophy 1970, chmn. sect. periodontics ann. meeting 1976), Am. Acad. Oral Medicine (Robert T. Freeman award 1972), Inst. Medicine, D.C. Dental Soc., Maimonides Dental Soc., Internat. Assn. Dental Research, Nat. Acad. Scis., Washington Acad. Sci., N.Y. Acad. Scis., Am. Acad. Polit. and Social Scis., Am. Assn. Tchrs. Practice Adminstrn. (pres., v.p., mem. exec. com.), Greater Washington Periodontal Soc. (pres. 197O), Am. Acad. Periodontology, AAUP, Am. Assn. Dental Schs., Acad. Dental Practice Adminstrn. (chmn. profl. liaison com. 1972), Acad. History of Dentistry, Am. Coll. Health Orgn., Howard U., U. Ill., Xavier U. alumni clubs, Sigma Xi, Alpha Eta Epsilon, Alpha Kappa Mu, Chi Delta Mu, Chi Lambda Kappa, Omicron Kappa Upsilon. Roman Catholic. Home: 342 Dudley Rd Newton Centre MA 02159 Office: 188 Longwood Av Boston MA 02115 *My success is primarily attributable to "the way the twig was bent" by my parents. They provided a home in which love for God, each other and our fellowman prevailed.*

HENRY, LAURIN LUTHER, university dean; b. Kankakee, Ill., May 23, 1921; s. Laurimer Luther and Jeanette Belle (Wagner) H.; m. Kathleen Jane Stephan, May 18, 1946; children—Stephanie Jane, Robin Leigh. B.A., DePauw U., 1942; M.A., U. Chgo., 1948, Ph.D., 1960. Staff asst. Public Adminstrn. Clearing House, Chgo. and Washington, 1950-55; research asso., sr. staff mem. Brookings Instn., Washington, 1955-64; prof. govt. and fgn. affairs U. Va., 1964-78; dean Sch. Community and Public Affairs, Va. Commonwealth U., Richmond, 1978—; vis. prof. Johns Hopkins U.; cons. to govt. Author: Presidential Transitions, 1960, The NASA-University Memorandum of Understanding, 1967; co-author: Presidential Election and Transition of 1960-61, 1961; contbr. articles profl. publns. Served with USNR, 1942-46. Recipient L.D. White prize Am. Polit. Sci. Assn., 1961. Mem. Nat. Acad. Public Adminstrn., Nat. Assn. Schs. Public Affairs and Adminstrn. (pres. 1971-72), Am. Soc. Public Adminstrn., Policy Studies Assn., So. Polit. Sci. Assn., Phi Beta Kappa. Home: 1905 Stuart Ave Richmond VA 23220 Office: 901 W Franklin St Richmond VA 23284

HENRY, MARGUERITE, author; b. Milw.; d. Louis and Anna (Kaurup) Breithaupt; m. Sidney Crocker Henry. Author: Auno and Tauno, 1940, Dilly Dally Sally, 1940, Eight Pictured Geographies, Mexico, Canada, Alaska, Brazil, Argentina, Chile, West Indies, Panama, 1941, Geraldine Belinda, 1942, Birds at Home, 1942, rev. edit., 1972, Their First Igloo, (with Barbara True), 1943, A Boy and A Dog, 1944, Justin Morgan Had a Horse, 1945, rev. edit., 1954, film, 1971; Robert Fulton, Boy Craftsman, 1945, The Little Fellow, 1945, rev. edit., 1975, Eight Pictured Geographies, Australia, New Zealand, Bahama Islands, Bermuda, Brit., Honduras, Dominican Republic, Hawaii, Virgin Islands, 1946, Benjamin West and His Cat Grimalkin, 1947, Always Reddy, 1947, Misty of Chincoteague, 1947, King of the Wind, 1948 (John Newbery award), Little or Nothing from Nottingham, 1949, Sea Star: Orphan of Chincoteague, 1949, Born to Trot, 1950, Album of Horses, 1951, Portfolio of Horses, 1952, Brighty of the Grand Canyon, 1953 (William Allen White award 1956), Wagging Tails, 1955, Cinnabar, the One O'clock Fox, 1956, Black Gold, 1957 (Sequoyah Children's Book award 1959), Muley-Ears, Nobody's Dog, 1959, Gaudenzia, Pride of the Palio, 1960 (Clara Ingram Judson award Soc. Midland Authors 1961), Misty, 1961, Five O'clock Charlie, 1962, All About Horses, 1962, rev. edit., 1967, Stormy, Misty's Foal, 1963, White Stallion of Lipizza, 1964, Mustang, Wild Spirit of the West (Western Heritage award Nat. Cowboy Hall of Fame 1967), 1966 (Sequoyah children's Book award 1970), Brighty; film, 1967; Dear Readers and Riders, 1969, Album of Dogs, 1970, San Domingo, the Medicine Hat Stallion, 1972 (Soc. Midland Authors award 1973), Stories from Around the World, 1974, Peter Lundy and the Medicine Hat Stallion; film, 1977; One Man's Horse, 1977, The Illustrated Marguerite Henry, 1980 (Recipient So. Calif. Council Lit. for Children award 1973, Kerlan award U. Minn. 1975), A Pictorial Life Story of Misty, 1976, The Story of a Book; 19-minute documentary, 1979; Marguerite Henry's Treasury, 1982. Office: care Rand McNally & Co 8255 Central Park Ave Skokie IL 60076

HENRY, MARION LUCAS, public health consultant; b. Canandaigua, N.Y., Aug. 8, 1907; s. John William and Nellie Viola (LaDue) H.; m. Dorothy Theresa Bottum, July 17, 1944; children: Carol Janet, Linda Ruth, Robert Marion. Cert., Albany (N.Y.) Sch. Accounting, 1934. With N.Y. State Dept. Health, Albany, 1925-70, asst. commr. adminstrn. and mgmt., 1958-65, asst. commr. health planning and adminstrn., 1966-70; exec. dir. Am. Pub. Health Assn., Washington, 1973; mng. editor Am. Jour. Pub. Health, 1973; cons. health budgeting and mgmt., Port Richey, Fla., 1973—; lectr. schs. pub. health Columbia, 1960-69, Johns Hopkins, 1961-66, Harvard, 1962-67; Mem. N.Y. State Mgmt. Improvement Council, 1964-70; adv. com. govtl. services State U. N.Y. Grad. Sch. Pub. Affairs, 1966-70; treas., dir. Health Research, Inc., Albany and Buffalo, 1956-70, Health Edn. Service, Inc., 1952-70. Co-author: A Guide to Public Health Program Accounting, 1959, N.Y. State's Performance Budget Experiment, 1960; Contbr. articles to profl. jours. Sec., bd. dirs. Albany Jr. C. of C., 1936-39; pres. McKownville (N.Y.) Improvement Assn., 1951-52; mem. investment adv. com. Bethlehem Sch. Bd., Delmar, 1960-61. Fellow Am. Pub. Health Assn. (treas., exec. bd., gov. council 1967-75), Am. Soc. Public Adminstrn. (pres. Albany chpt. 1958-59, nat. council 1960-62), N.Y. State Acad. Pub. Adminstrn.; hon. life mem. N.Y. State Pub. Health Assn. (pres. 1961-62); mem. Am. Acad. Health Adminstrn. (Nat. Honor award 1973, pres. 1962-63). Episcopalian (past warden, vestryman). Clubs: Timber Oaks (Port Richey, Fla.); Timber Oaks Golf, Live Oaks. Home: 2115 Los Alamos Dr Port Richey FL 33568

HENRY, NICHOLAS LLEWELLYN, political science educator, university administration; b. Seattle, May 22, 1943; s. Samuel Houston and Ann (Connor) H.; m. Muriel Bunney, June 3, 1967; children: Adrienne Richardson, Miles Houston. B.A., Centre Coll. Ky., 1965; M.A., Pa. State U., 1967; M.P.A., Ind. U., 1970, Ph.D., 1971. Asst. to dean Coll. Arts and Scis.; instr. Ind. State U., 1967-69; vis. asst. prof. U. N.Mex., 1971-72; asst. prof. polit. sci. U. Ga., 1972-75; dir. Center Public Affairs; asso. prof. Ariz. State U., 1975—, dean Coll. Public Programs, 1980—. Author 12 books; contbr. numerous articles to profl. jours. Mem. Ariz. Mgmt. Devel. Bd., 1980. Recipient Author of Yr. award Assn. Sci. Jours. Home: 701 E Alameda Dr Tempe AZ 85282 Office: Ariz State U Tempe AZ 85287

HENRY, RAGAN AUGUSTUS, broadcasting executive; b. Sadiesville, Ky., Feb. 2, 1934; s. Augustus William and Ruby H.; m. Regina A. Henry, Mar. 20, 1980; children: Vincent, Joseph, Richard, Leah. A.B. cum laude, Harvard U., 1956, LL.B. (Whitney Found. Opportunity fellow, Noyes and Whitney Found. fellow), 1961; postgrad., Temple U., Phila. Bar: Pa. bar. Law clk. Office Gen. Counsel, Dept. Air Force, 1960-61; asso. firm Narin, Garfinkel & Mann, Phila., 1961-64; gen. counsel Phila. Housing Devel. Corp., 1966-69; partner firm Goodis, Greenfield, Henry & Edelstein, Phila., 1964-77; lectr. Temple U. Law Sch., 1968-72, La Salle Coll., Phila., 1971-73; pres. Broadcast Enterprises Nat., Inc. (and subsidiaries), Phila., 1973—; partner firm Wolf, Blcok, Schorr & Solis-Cohen, Phila., 1977—; vis. prof. S.I. Newhouse Sch. Communications, Syracuse (N.Y.) U., 1979-81; dir. Continental Bank, Phila., Abt Assos., Boston. Bd. dirs. La Salle Coll., Hosp. U. Pa.; chmn. John McKee Scholarship Com.; bd. dirs., exec. com. Greater Phila. Partnership; mem. overseers com. Harvard U.-Radcliffe Coll.; bd. dirs., treas. Elderhostel, Boston; trustee Syracuse U. Served with AUS, 1957-59. Noyes Found. fellow, 1956-57. Fellow Am. Bar Assn., Pa. Bar Assn., Phila. Bar Assn.; mem. Nat. Assn. Black Owned Broadcasters (pres., dir.), Nat. Black Network Adv. Bd. (dir.), Nat. Radio Broadcasters Assn., Nat. Assn. Broadcasters. Clubs: Sunday Breakfast (Phila.); University (Rochester, N.Y.). Office: 1422 Chestnut St 8th Floor Philadelphia PA 19102 *

HENRY, RALPH SETH, investment company executive; b. East Palestine, Ohio, Nov. 14, 1921; s. Cecil Charles and Mary Eleanor (Charlton) H.; m. Hazel Marie Haddox, Dec. 17, 1944; children: Sandra Sue, Stephenie Jo, Jessica Ann, Ralph Seth. A.B., Oberlin Coll., 1943. Salesman Stone & Webster Securities Corp., Boston, 1945-54; v.p., dir. Wall St. Investing Corp., N.Y.C., 1955-57; ptnr. John H.G. Pell, N.Y.C.; also Wall St. Planning Corp., N.Y.C., 1956-57; chmn. bd., pres., dir. ITB Distbrs. Inc., Boston, 1970—; pres., treas., dir. Devonshire St. Fund, Inc., Boston, 1960-83; sr. v.p., dir. Moseley Capital Corp.; pres. Investment Trust Boston, 1957; dir. ITB High Income, ITB Mass. Taxfree Fund.; Bd. govs. Investment Co. Inst. Served with USNR, World War II; lt. comdr. Res. Mem. Newcomen Soc. N.Am. Clubs: Union, Harvard (Boston) (asso. mem.); Dedham Country and Polo, Laurel Brook. Home: 49 Elm St Medfield MA 02052 Office: 60 State St Boston MA 02109

HENRY, RENE ARTHUR, JR., management and sports marketing consultant; b. Charleston, W.Va., June 13, 1933; s. Rene A. and Lillian E. (Reveal) H.; children: Deborah Marie, Bruce Rexford. A.B., Coll. William and Mary, 1954; postgrad., W.Va. U., 1954-56. Account exec. Flournoy & Gibbs, Toledo, 1956-59; publicity dir. Lennen & Newell, Inc., San Francisco, 1959-67; sr. v.p., dir. Daniel J. Edelman, Inc., Los Angeles, 1967-70; pres. Rene A. Henry, Jr., Inc., Los Angeles, 1970-74; partner Allen, Ingersoll, Segal & Henry, Inc., Los Angeles, 1974-75; prin. ICPR, Los Angeles, 1975-81; exec. sec. to bd. dirs. Council Housing Producers, 1968-78. Author: How to Profitably Buy and Sell Land, 1977. Served with U.S. Army, 1956-58. Named San Francisco Bay Area Pub. Relations Man of Year, 1963; recipient Clarion award for human rights Women in Communication, 1980. Mem. Pub. Relations Soc. Am. (Disting. Citizen award Los Angeles chpt. 1979), Acad. Motion Picture Arts and Scis., Acad. TV Arts and Scis., Football Writers Assn. Am., U.S. Basketball Writers Assn., Nat. Assn. Real Estate Editors, Assn. Internationale de la Presse Sportive, Sigma Nu. Republican. Episcopalian. Club: South Bay Yacht Racing. Home: 809 S Bundy Dr Los Angeles CA 90049

HENRY, RICHARD CHARLES, retired air force officer; b. Streator, Ill., Dec. 17, 1925; s. Richard Harley and Mary Sarah (Weber) H.; m. Cheryl Dee Barton, Dec. 27, 1949; children—Nanette (Mrs. Gunther Doerr), Richard B., Pamela D. B.S., U.S. Mil. Acad., 1949; M.S., U. Mich., 1954; certificate, Nat. War Coll., 1967; LL.D. hon., Northrup U. Commd. 2d lt. USAF, 1949, advanced through grades to lt. gen., 1978; Gemini program control mgr. (Manned Space Program NASA), 1964-66, operational comdr. tactical fighter ops., U.S. and Vietnam, 1967-72, command insp. gen., 1972-73, 1973-74, vice comdr., 1974-76; dir. devel. and acquisitions Hdqrs. USAF, Washington, 1976-78; comdr. (Air Force Space div.), 1978-83, ret., 1983. Decorated Legion Merit, D.S.M. with oak leaf cluster, D.F.C., NASA D.SM., Air medal with 9 oak leaf clusters; recipient Sustained Superior Performance award NASA, 1966. Address: 81 Angelo Walk Long Beach CA 90803

HENRY, RICHARD CONN, astrophysicist, educator; b. Toronto, Ont., Can., Mar. 7, 1940; came to U.S., 1962, naturalized, 1973; m. Edwin Mackie and Jean Bonar (Conn) H.; m. Rita Mahon, May 10, 1975. B.Sc., U. Toronto, 1961, M.A., 1962; Ph.D., Princeton U., 1967. Research asso. Inst. Advanced Study, 1967; research appointee E.O. Hulburt Center Space Research, Naval Research Lab., Washington, 1967-69, research physicist, 1969-76; asst. prof. Johns Hopkins U., Balt., 1968-74, asso. prof., 1974-77, prof., 1977—; vis. staff Los Alamos Sci. Lab.; dep. dir. astrophysics div. NASA, 1976-78. Editor-in-chief: Astrophys. Letter. Recipient Gold medal Royal Astron. Soc. Can., 1961; Alfred P. Sloan fellow, 1971-75. Mem. AAAS, Am. Phys. Soc., Am. Astron. Soc., Internat. Astron. Union. Club: Princeton (N.Y.C.). Office: Physics Dept Johns Hopkins Baltimore MD 21218

HENRY, RYDER, lawyer; b. East Quoque, N.Y., July 27, 1909; s. Clement S. and Adelaide R. (Jackson) H.; m. Frederica Poor, Oct. 18, 1955. Grad. cum laude, Hotchkiss Sch., 1926; A.B. with honors, Princeton U., 1930; J.D., Columbia U., 1941. Bar: N.Y. 1941. With Bankers Trust Co., N.Y.C., 1930-37; since practiced in, N.Y.C.; asso. White & Case, 1941-42, 46-52; partner Casey, Lane & Mittendorf, 1952-73, Bache & Co., 1954-66. Former pres., trustee Allen-Stevenson Sch. Served from 2d lt. to lt. col. USAAF, 1942-46. Decorated Bronze Star. Mem. Am., N.Y. State, N.Y.C. bar assns., Huguenot Soc. (past v.p.), Assn. Ex-Mems. Squadron A (gov.), Soc. Cin., St. Nicholas Soc., Phi Delta Phi. Episcopalian. Clubs: Union, Leash (N.Y.C.); Piping Rock (Locust Valley, N.Y.); Maidstone (East Hampton); Everglades (Palm Beach, Fla.). Home and office: 153 Egypt Ln East Hampton NY 11937

HENRY, WAIGHTS GIBBS, JR., college chancellor, clergyman; b. Tuscaloosa, Ala., Feb. 13, 1910; s. Waights Gibbs and Mary Eliza (Davis) H.; m. Mamie Lark Brown, Feb. 16, 1935; children: George Madison, Waights Gibbs III, Mary Ann (Mrs. Ed P. Kirven). Student, Emory U., 1927-28; A.B., Birmingham-So. Coll., 1930, D.D., 1947; B.D., Yale U., 1934. Asst. pastor Bunker Hill Congl. Ch., Waterbury, Conn., 1932-36; joined N. Ga. Conf. Meth. Ch., 1936; ordained to ministry Meth. Ch., 1938; pastor, Hoschton, 1937-38, Clayton, 1939-42, Epworth Ch., Atlanta, 1943-44; exec. sec. Bd. Edn., No. Ga. Conf., 1945-48; pres. LaGrange (Ga.) Coll., 1948-78, chancellor, 1978—; mem. Pacific Rim. Seminar in, Clina, Korea, Japan, 1980; preacher Meth. Series of Protestant Hour (radio), 1960; Sunday columnist Columbus (Ga.) Ledger-Enquirer, 1950—. Contbr. ch. publs. Del. to Gen. Confs., 1948-56, Jurisdictional Confs., 1948-64; Chmn. bd. Protestant Radio and TV Center, 1970-71; chmn. Meth. Joint Radio Com., 1952-56, Gen. Bd. Edn., 1948-52; pres. Ga. Found. Ind. Colls., 1959-60, 70-71, Ga. Meth. Colls. Assn., 1950-62, Ga. Assn. Colls., 1959-60; mem. Ga. Higher Edn. Facilities Commn.; mem. pres.'s adv. com. Med. Coll. Ga., chmn. admissions policies com.; commr. Roosevelt Little White House; bd. dirs. East-West Found., Pitts Found., 1948-78, Meth. Found. Ret. Ministers, 1960-78; former bd. mgrs. Camp Glisson. Recipient award Assn. Pvt. Colls. and Univs. in Ga., 1981; Paul Harris fellow. Mem. Chattahoochee Valley Art Assn., Newcomen Soc. N.Am., Lafayette Groupe French Resistance Movement(Le Puy, France) (hon.), Omicron Delta Kappa, Pi Kappa Alpha, Pi Gamma Mu. Clubs: Mason, Rotarian (dist. gov. 1974-75), Highland Country (LaGrange)). Judge Miss America Pageant, 1952. Address: LaGrange Coll LaGrange GA 30240 *Greatness lies in the quality of private living and public service. All else is periferal.*

HENRY, WALTER LESTER, JR., educator, physician; b. Phila., Nov. 19, 1915; s. Walter Lester and Vera (Robinson) H.; m. Ada Clarice Palmer, Sept. 7, 1942. A.B., Temple U., 1936; M.D., Howard U., 1941; student, U. Pa. Grad. Sch. Medicine, 1948-49. Diplomate: Am. Bd. Internal Medicine (mem. bd. 1970-77, mem. residency rev. com. 1970-77). Intern Freedmen's Hosp., Washington, 1941-42, resident, 1949-51; fellow endocrinology Michael Reese Hosp., Chgo., 1951-53; mem. faculty Howard U., 1953—, prof. medicine, 1963—, chmn. dept., 1962-73, William B. Allen prof. medicine, 1972-73, John B. Johnson prof. medicine, 1973—; Mem. Washington Med. Care and Hosp. Com. Faculty trustee Howard U., 1970-75. Served to maj. M.C. AUS, 1942-46; Italy. Decorated Bronze Star with cluster; Markle scholar med. scis., 1953-58. Mem. Am., Nat. med. assns., A.C.P. (regent 1974-80), Am. Fedn. Clin. Research, NAACP, D.C. Med. Soc. (1st v.p.), Alpha Phi Alpha. Presbyn. (elder). Home: 1780 Redwood Terr NW Washington DC 20012

HENRY, WILLIAM ALFRED, III, journalist, critic, author; b. South Orange, N.J., Jan. 24, 1950; s. William Alfred and Catherine Anne (Elliott) H.; m. Gail Louisa Manyan, Oct. 3, 1981. B.A. (Scholar of the House), Yale U., 1971; postgrad. in History, Boston U., 1973-74. Edn. writer Boston Globe, 1971-72, arts critic, 1972-74, state house polit. reporter, 1974-75, editorial writer, 1975-77; TV editor and columnist Boston Globe, syndicated Field New Service, 1977-80; also weekly book reviewer and occasional nat. and fgn. polit. reporter; critic-at-large N.Y. Daily News, 1980-81; assoc. editor Time mag., N.Y.C., 1981—, press critic, 1982—; lectr. Harvard U., MIT, Columbia U. and other schs.; mem. faculty Tufts U., 1979, Yale U., 1980; Young Am. Leader traveling fellow EEC, 1977; Poynter fellow in journalism Yale U., 1980; mem. theater panel Mass. Council on Arts, 1977-80. Prin. author: The Insiders Guide to the Colleges, 1970, 2d edit., 1971; author: (with C. Vizas) The Blue Football Book, 1971; contbg. author: Great Voices, Small Trumpets—The Media and Minorities, 1980, What's News—The Media in American Society, 1981, Fast Forward, 1983, Pro and Con, 1983; contbr. articles to newspapers, mags.; numerous radio, TV appearances. Mem. task force Mass. Commn. Edn., 1972; bd. dirs. Stone Trust Corp., N.Y.C., 1971—, Proposition Workshop Inc., Cambridge, 1974—, Cambridge Ensemble, 1976—, Leukemia Soc. Greater Boston, 1978-80; active in fund raising for Yale U., various humane socs., arts groups. Recipient Story of Yr. award New Eng. AP, 1976, Best Feature of Yr. award New Eng. UPI, 1976; co-recipient UPI New Eng. editorial prize, 1977; Pulitzer prize in criticism, 1980; co-finalist Nat. Mag. award, 1982. Mem. TV Critics Assn. (founding treas. 1978-79, chmn. speakers bur. and profl. edn. 1979-80, dir. 1980-81), ACLU. Clubs: Yale, St. Botolph (Boston); Book and Snake, Elizabethan (New Haven); Yale (N.Y.C.). Home: 960 Woodland Ave Plainfield NJ 07060 Office: Time Mag Time Life Bldg Rockefeller Center New York NY 10020

HENRY, WILLIAM EARL, educator, psychologist; b. Holyoke, Mass., Nov. 14, 1917; s. Jesse Earl and Ellen (Elliott) H. B.A., U. Utah, 1939; student, U. Calif. at Berkeley, 1940; Ph.D., U. Chgo., 1944. Mem. faculty U. Chgo., 1944-78, prof. psychology and human devel., 1958-78, emeritus, 1978—, chmn. com. human devel., 1953-58, 65-68, 72-76; Ford distinguished vis. prof. Mich. State U., 1960-61, U. Wis., 1962; cons. Nat. Inst. Mental Health, 1964-77; chmn. editorial com. Jossey-Bass Pubs., Inc., San Francisco, 1965-78; v.p., editor Social and Behavioral Scis., 1978—; editorial cons. Atherton Press, 1963-66. Author: The Analysis of Fantasy, 1956, (with E. Cumming) Growing Old, 1961, (with others) The Fifth Profession: Becoming a Psychotherapist, 1971, Public and Private Lives of Psychotherapists, 1973; Cons. editor: Jour. Profl. Psychology, 1972-76. Fellow Am. Psychol. Assn., Gerontological Soc., Am. Sociol. Assn., Soc. Projective Techniques (pres. 1958-59); mem. Sigma Xi, Phi Kappa Phi. Home: 2400 Great Highway San Francisco CA 94116

HENRY, WILLIAM RAY, educator; b. Russellville, Ark., Dec. 30, 1925; s. Mace Leon and Violet May (Shinn) H.; m. Norma Talmadge Wright, Nov. 27, 1954; children—William Ray, Lisa Carolyn, Linda Carol, Lara Carleen. B.S., U. Ark., 1948, M.S., 1953; Ph.D., N.C. State U., 1957. Asst. prof., then asso. prof., prof. N.C. State U., Raleigh, 1956-70; prof. bus. adminstrn. Ga. State U., Atlanta, 1970—. Author: (with others) Managerial Economics, 1978; contbr. articles to profl. jours. Served with USAAF, 1944-45. Recipient award of merit Am. Agrl. Econs. Assn., 1957, 61. Mem. Am. Econs. Assn., AAUP. Office: University Plaza Atlanta GA 30303 *

HENSEL, H. STRUVE, retired lawyer; b. Hoboken, N.J., Aug. 22, 1901; s. Herman D. and Eliza (Struve) H.; m. Edith T. Wyckoff, Oct. 3, 1929 (div. 1948); m. Isabel S. Bower, June 9, 1948. A.B., Princeton U., 1922; LL.B., Columbia U., 1925. Bar: N.Y. 1925, D.C. 1943. Asso. Cravath, deGersdorff, Swaine & Wood, N.Y.C., 1925-33; mem. Milbank, Tweed & Hope, N.Y.C., 1933-41; organizer and 1st chief procurement legal div. U.S. Navy Dept., 1941-44; gen. counsel Navy Dept., 1944-45; asst. sec. Navy, 1945-46; mem. Carter, Ledyard & Milburn, N.Y.C., 1946-53; cons., spl. adviser to sec. def., 1952; gen. counsel Dept. Def., 1952-54; asst. sec. def. for internat. security affairs, 1954-55, returned to pvt. practice law, Washington, 1955; partner Coudert Bros., N.Y.C., Washington, Paris, London, Hong Kong, Tokyo, Singapore, Brussels, 1966-76; pres., mng. dir. Maritime Fruit Carriers Co. Inc., London, 1976; of counsel Vorys, Sater, Seymour & Pease, Washington, 1983—; dir. EDO Corp., A.A.I. Corp., Integrated Resources, Inc., Internat. Controls Corp.; cons. Commn. on Orgn. Exec., 1948. Decorated D.S.M. Navy; medal of Freedom, 1953. Republican. Clubs: City Tavern Assn., Chevy Chase, Metropolitan (Washington); University, Princeton, Pinnacle (N.Y.C.); Union Interalliee (Paris, France). Home: 5020 Overlook Rd NW Washington DC 20016 Office: 1828 L St NW Washington DC 20036

HENSHALL, JAMES ARTHUR, JR., oil company executive, lawyer; b. Denver, Dec. 6, 1941; s. James Arthur and Mary Elizabeth (Eagleson) H.; m. Barbara Ann Fisher, June 12, 1982; children by previous marriage: Robbyn Elizabeth, David James, Kathryn Suzanne; stepchildren: Kathryn Ellen Deuter, David Arthur Deuter, Douglas Taylor Deuter, Daniel Adam Deuter. B.S. in Fin, U. Colo., 1963, LL.B., 1966. Bar: Colo. 1966, Ill. 1975. Pvt. practice law, Boulder, Colo., 1966-74; prin. firm Martin, Riggs & Henshall (P.C.), Boulder, 1969-74; v.p., gen. counsel Martin Oil Service, Inc., Chgo., 1974—, officer, dir. affiliated corps. Served with USNR, 1966-69. Mem. Am., Colo., Ill., Lawyer-Pilots bar assns. Unitarian. Club: Torch (Chgo.). Office: 4501 W 127th St Alsip IL 60658

HENSHAW, JONATHAN COOK, manufacturing company executive; b. Dobbs Ferry, N.Y., Jan. 29, 1922; s. Elmer Ellsworth and Leonora Agnes (Scott) H.; m. Martha Emily Stock, July 14, 1948; children: William, Jane, Mary, Thomas, Daniel, Anne. B.S., Fordham U., 1950; M.B.A., N.Y. U., 1952. C.P.A., N.Y. Staff accountant Coopers & Lybrand, N.Y.C., 1951-55, 68-69; v.p., treas. J.A. Ewing & McDonald, Inc., N.Y.C., 1955-62; asst. treas. Block Drug Co., Jersey City, 1962-64; controller, asst. treas. Turner Jones Co., Inc., N.Y.C., 1964-68; treas. Visual Electronics, N.Y.C., 1969—, Crane Co., 1970-80; sales agt. Fox & Lazo Realtors, Phila., 1980-83; assoc. broker John T. Henderson, Inc., 1983—. Served as sgt. AUS, 1943-46. Decorated Purple Heart. Roman Catholic. Home: 48 Falcon Rd Levittown PA 19056 Office: John T Henderson Inc 1 S Main St Yardley PA 19067

HENSHAW, PAUL CARRINGTON, mining company executive; b. Rye, N.Y., Nov. 15, 1913; s. R. Townsend and Clara (Venable) H.; m. Helen Elizabeth Runals, May 25, 1939; children: Sydney Parker (Mrs. Paul W. Nordt III), Guy Runals, Paul Carrington. A.B. magna cum laude, Harvard, 1936; grad. Advanced Mgmt. Program, Harvard U., 1958; M.S., Calif. Inst. Tech., 1938, Ph.D., 1940. Head geologist Cerro Corp., Morococha, Peru, 1940-43; geologist Consorcio Minero del Peru, Mina Calpa, 1943-45, Compania Peruana de Cemento Portland, Lima, 1945, Day Mines, Inc., Wallace, Idaho, 1945-46; asso. prof., acting head dept. geology U. Idaho, Moscow, 1946-47; chief geologist San Luis Mining Co., Tayoltita, Dgo, Mexico, 1947-53, Homestake Mining Co., San Francisco, 1953-60, v.p., 1961-70, pres., 1970-71, pres., chief exec. officer, 1971-79, chmn., chief exec. officer, 1977-79, chmn. bd., 1979-82, dir., 1982—. Mem. AIME (Rand medal 1981, Rand medal 1981), Canadian Inst. Mining and Metallurgy, Geol. Soc. Am., Soc. Econ. Geologists (past pres., councilor), World Affairs Council No. Calif., Mining and Metall. Soc., Am. Geol. Inst., Societe de Geologie Appliquee, Phi Beta Kappa, Sigma Xi. Clubs: Pacific Union, Commonwealth of Calif., Bankers, World Trade, Harvard, Engineers (San Francisco); Mining (N.Y.C.). Office: 650 California St San Francisco CA 94108 *

HENSHEL, HARRY BULOVA, watch manufacturer; b. N.Y.C., Feb. 5, 1919; s. Harry D. and Emily (Bulova) H.; m. Joy Altman, Nov. 4, 1948; children—Dale, Patti, Diane, Judith. A.B., Brown U., 1940; grad., U.S. Army Command and Gen. Staff Sch., 1945; M.B.A., Harvard U., 1951. With Bulova Watch Co., Inc., Flushing, N.Y., 1938—, asst. sec., 1950, sec., 1951, v.p. finance, 1957, exec. v.p., 1958, pres., 1959—, chmn., 1973—; dir. Bulova Watch Co., Ltd., Toronto, Can., 1953-81; chmn., dir. Bulova Internat., Ltd., 1961-81; chmn. Atlantic Time Products Corp. Vice chmn. and trustee Adelphi U., Brown U. Fund; bd. overseers Parsons Sch. Design; bd. dirs. U.S. Com. for UNICEF, 1979—; mem. policy study com. Heller Inst., 1979; bd. dirs. Fedn. Employment and Guidance Services. Mem. Am. Assembly, Amateur Athletic Union U.S. (timing com.), N.Y. C. of C. (dir.), Am. Ordnance Assn (life), Newcomen Soc. N.Am., UN Assn. U.S. (dir.), Thoroughbred Owners and Breeders Assn., Sigma Chi (Significant Sig medal). Republican. Clubs: Harvard Business School, Sales Executives, New York (dir.), Brown Univ., Harmonie, Economic; Army and Navy (Washington); Old Oaks Country (Purchase, N.Y.); Turf and Field; Town (Scarsdale). Home: 24 Murray Hill Rd Scarsdale NY 10583 Office: Bulova Park Flushing NY 11370

HENSKE, JOHN M., corporate executive; b. Omaha, 1923. B.S. in Chem. Engring. and Indsl. Adminstrn, Yale U., 1948. Vice-pres., dir. Dow Chem. Co., 1948-69; group v.p.-chems. Olin Corp., Stamford, Conn., 1969-71, sr. v.p. and pres.-chems group, 1971-73, pres., dir., 1973-78, chmn., chief exec. officer, 1978—; dir. Am. Precision Industries, Inc., N.E. Bancorp, Inc., Scovill Mfg. Co., Sun Co. Served with U.S. Army, 1943-46. Mem. Chem. Mfg. Assn. (chmn., dir.). Home: 104 Beachside Ave Greens Farms CT 06436 Office: Olin Corp 120 Long Ridge Rd Stamford CT 06904

HENSLER, GUENTER M., record company executive; b. Lindau, Feb. 4, 1939; s. Hugo and Hilde (Spengler) H.; m. Maren Homann, Nov. 7, 1964; 1 child, Astrid. Diplom-Kaufmann, U. Cologne, W. Ger., 1964. Trainee EMI-Electrola, Cologne, W. Ger., 1958-63; asst. to pres. Vox Prodns., Inc., N.Y.C., 1966-68; with Polygram Records, Inc., N.Y.C., 1968—, pres., 1981—. Mem. Am. Mgmt. Assn. Office: 810 7th Ave New York NY 10019

HENSLEY, ELIZABETH CATHERINE, nutritionist, educator; b. Mpls., Feb. 27, 1921; d. Erich Christian and Lulu Mabel (Elliott) Selke; m. Eugene B. Hensley, June 10, 1954. B.S. in Edn., Cornell U., 1942, M.S., 1944, postgrad., 1950-51. Instr. food and nutrition U. Del., 1944-47; asst. prof. Okla. A&M U., 1947-50; mem. faculty U. Mo., Columbia, 1951—, prof. food and nutrition, 1954—, chmn. dept. home econs., 1954-55, head dept. food and nutrition, 1955-65, co-chmn. dept. human nutrition, 1973-76. Author: Basic Concepts of World Nutrition, 1981. Mem. Am. Home Econs. Assn., Nutrition Today Soc., mo. Home Econs. Assn., PEO, Pi Lambda Theta, Omicron Nu, Phi Upsilon Omicron, Gamma Sigma Delta, Kappa Alpha Theta. Mem. Christian Ch. (Disciples of Christ). Home: 802 Greenwood Ct Columbia MO 65201 Office: 217 Gwynn Hall U Mo Columbia MO 65211

HENSLEY, EUGENE BENJAMIN, physicist, educator, researcher; b. Augusta, W.Va., Jan. 6, 1918; s. Elbert B. and Anna Francis (Milhoan) H.; m. Elizabeth Selke, June 6, 1954. A.B., Central Meth. Coll., Fayette, Mo., 1947; M.A., U. Mo.-Columbia, 1948, Ph.D., 1951. Mem. staff Research Lab. Electronics, MIT, 1951-53; asst. prof. physics U. Mo., Columbia, 1953-57, assoc. prof. physics, 1957-63, prof., 1963—, acting chmn. dept. physics, 1977-78, assoc. chmn., 1981—. Contbr. articles to profl. jours. Served with USNR, 1942-46. Recipient research contracts Office of Naval Research, 1953-66, NSF, 1965-76. Mem. Am. Phys. Soc., AAAS, Sigma Xi. Mem. Disciples of Christ. Home: 802 Greenwood Ct Columbia MO 65201 Office: Dept Physics Univ Mo Columbia MO 65211

HENSLEY, GEORGE HUGHES, coal sales co. exec.; b. Corbin, Ky., July 10, 1920; s. William KcKinley and Bessie (Hughes) H.; m. Iris Loretta Hundley; children—Patricia, William. Student, Bowling Green Bus. U., 1937-38. Acct. U.S. Steel Corp., Harlan-Wallins Coal Corp.; with Pittston Co., Clinchfield Coal Corp., Pittston Coal Sales Corp., 1949—; now pres., dir. Pittston Coal Sales Corp. Mem. N.Y. Coal Trade Assn. (past pres.). Republican. Congregationalist. Clubs: Stanwich, Masons. Office: 1 Pickwick Plaza Greenwich CT 06830

HENSON, ALBERT LEE, furniture mfg. exec., lawyer; b. Chgo., Aug. 30, 1910; s. A. Lee and Nelle (Smith) H.; m. Margaret Elizabeth Spray, Oct. 16, 1937; children—Albert Lee III, Judd W. B.A., Grinnell Coll., 1931; J.D. with distinction, U. Mich., 1934. Bar: Mich. bar 1934, Ill. bar 1946. Practice in, Detroit, 1934-46; mem. firm Yerkes, Goddard & McClintock, 1934-42; individual practice, 1942-46; indsl. relations mgr. Kroehler Mfg. Co., Naperville, 1946-74, v.p. legal, indsl. relations dir., 1951-74, sec., 1970—, v.p., gen. counsel, 1974-76, also dir.; Mem. Ill. Personnel Adv. Bd., 1960-64, Ill. Commn. on Labor Laws, 1969—. Bd. dirs., sec. Kroehler Found.; bd. dirs. Family Service Assn., Dupage County, Ill. Mem. Am., Ill. bar assns., State Bar Mich. Home: 33 W Birchwood Dr Hinsdale IL 60521 Office: Kroehler Mfg. Co 222 Fifth Ave Naperville IL 60540

HENSON, ARNOLD, lawyer; b. White Plains, N.Y., Oct. 28, 1931; s. Philip Truman and Gwendolen (Bossi) H.; m. Cynthia Madsen, Feb. 27, 1954; children: Philip, Palmer, Drusilla. A.B., Colgate U., 1953; J.D., U. Mich., 1959. Asso. firm Chadbourne, Parke, Whiteside & Wolff, N.Y.C., 1959-66, partner, 1967-81; sr. v.p., gen. counsel, dir. Am. Brands, Inc., N.Y.C., 1981—. Chmn. Conservation Adv. Bd., New Castle, N.Y., 1972-75; mem. New Castle Planning Bd., 1975-81, chmn., 1981. Served to lt. (j.g.) USNR, 1953-56. Mgm. Am. Bar Assn., Assn. Bar City N.Y., Namequoit Sailing Assn. (commodore 1979-81). Republican. Clubs: N.Y. Yacht, Camp Fire of Am. Home: 60 Wildwood Rd Chappaqua NY 10514 Office: Am Brands Inc 245 Park Ave New York NY 10167

HENSON, JAMES MAURY, puppeteer, television producer; b. Greenville, Miss., Sept. 24, 1936; s. Paul Ransom and Elizabeth Marcella (Brown) H.; m. Jane Anne Nebel, May 28, 1959; children: Lisa Marie, Cheryl Lee, Brian David, John Paul, Heather Beth. B.A., U. Md., 1960. Pres. Henson Assos.; Pres., bd. dirs. Am. Center of Union Internationale de la Marionnette, 1974—. Creator: The Muppets, 1954; producer: Sam and Friends, Washington, 1955-61; puppeteer: Rowlf on Jimmy Dean Show, N.Y.C., 1963-66, numerous TV guest appearances; creator numerous TV commls.; Sesame Street Muppets, 1969—, Muppet Show, from 1976; producer: The Muppet Movie, 1979; dir.: film The Great Muppet Caper, 1981; co-dir.: The Dark Crystal, 1981; producer, dir. TV shows. Recipient Emmy award for best entertainment program, 1958; Emmy award for outstanding individual achievement in children's programming, 1973—74, 75—76; Entertainer of yr. award AGVA; TV Acad. award for outstanding comedy, variety or music series, 1978; citation for The Muppet Movie Film Adv. Bd., 1979; Peabody award for excellence in TV programming, 1979; Grammy award for The Muppet Show album, 1979; Best TV Script of Yr. award for The Muppet Show Writers Guild Am., 1979, 80, Grammy award for best children's record, 1981, President's Fellow award R.I. Sch. Design, 1982. Mem. Puppeteers of Am. (pres. 1962-63), AFTRA, Dirs. Guild Am., Writers Guild, Nat. Acad. TV Arts and Scis., Screen Actors Guild. Office: 117 E 69th St New York NY 10021 *

HENSON, JOSEPH M., computer company executive; b. Ft. Smith, Ark., 1933. Student, U. Ark., 1954. Vice-pres. mfg. services IBM, to 1981; pres., chief exec. officer Prime Computer Inc., Natick, Mass., 1981—. Address: Prime Computer Inc Prime Park Natick MA 01760

HENSON, PAUL HARRY, communications company executive; b. Bennet, Nebr., July 22, 1925; s. Harry H. and Mae (Schoenthal) H.; m. Betty L. Roeder, Aug. 2, 1946; children: Susan Irene Flury, Lizbeth Henson Barelli. B.S. in Elec. Engring, U. Nebr., 1948, M.S., 1950. Registered profl. engr., Nebr. Engr. Lincoln (Nebr.) Tel. & Tel. Co., 1941-42, 45-48, div. mgr., 1948-54, chief engr., 1954-59; v.p. United Telecommunications, Inc., Kansas City, Mo., 1959-60, exec. v.p., 1960-64, pres., 1964-73, chmn., 1966—, also dir.; dir. Armco, Duke Power, The Williams Cos.; Hon. consul for, Sweden. Trustee Midwest Research Inst., Tax Found., U. Nebr. Found., U. Mo. at Kansas City. Served with USAAF, 1942-45. Mem. Nat. Soc. Profl. Engrs., IEEE, Armed Forces Communications Electronics Assn., U.S. Ind. Telephone Assn. (dir. 1960-76, pres. 1964-65), Sigma Xi, Eta Kappa Nu, Sigma Tau, Kappa Sigma. Clubs: Mason (Shriner), Kansas City, Kansas City Country, Mission Hills Country, River, Burning Tree, Chicago, Surf, Castle Pines. Office: Box 11315 Kansas City MO 64112

HENSON, RAY DAVID, lawyer, educator; b. Johnston City, Ill., July 24, 1924; s. Ray David and Lucile (Bell) H. B.S., U. Ill., 1947, J.D., 1949. Bar: Ill. 1950, U.S. Supreme Ct. 1960. Counsel Continental Assurance and Continental Casualty Cos., Chgo., 1952-70; prof. law Wayne State U., 1970-75, Hastings Sch. Law, U. Calif., San Francisco, 1975—; mem. adv. com. on legal matters N.Y. Stock Exchange, 1972-75. Author: Landmarks of Law, 1960, Secured Transactions, 1973, 2d edit., 1979, Documents of Title, 1983; also various other books and numerous articles.; editor: The Business Lawyer, 1967-68. Served with USAAF, 1943-46. Mem. Am. Law Inst., Am. Bar Assn. (chmn. corp., banking and bus. law sect. 1969-70, adv. bd. jour. 1974-80), Ill. Bar Assn. (chmn. comml. banking and bankruptcy law sect. 1963-65), Chgo. Bar Assn., Selden Soc. Club: Univ. (San Francisco). Home: 2298 Pacific Ave San Francisco CA 94115 Office: 200 McAllister St San Francisco CA 94102

HENSON, ROBERT FRANK, lawyer; b. Jenny Lind, Ark., Apr. 10, 1925; s. Newton and Nell Edith (Kessinger) H.; m. Jean Peterson Henson, Sept. 14, 1946; children—Robert F., Sandra Henson Curfman, Laura, Thomas, David, Steven. B.S., U. Minn., 1948, J.D., 1950. Atty. Soo Line R.R., 1950-52; ptnr. firm Cant, Haverstock, Beardsley, Gray & Plant, Mpls., 1952-66; sr. ptnr. firm Henson & Efron, Mpls., 1966—; chmn. Minn. Lawyers Profl. Responsibility Bd., 1981. Trustee Mpls. Found., 1974—; chmn. Hennepin County Mental Health and Mental Retardation Bd., 1968-70. Served with USN, 1943-46. Fellow Am. Bar Found.; Mem. ABA, Hennepin County Bar Assn. (pres. 1968-69), Minn. Bar Assn., Order of Coif. Unitarian. Office: 1200 Title Ins Bldg Minneapolis MN 55401 *

HENSON, WALTER EUGENE, manufacturing company executive; b. St. Louis, Nov. 18, 1931; s. Walter and Alice Marie (Walters) H.; m. Carleen May Schott, Aug. 18, 1956; children—Caryla Jean, Brian Alan. B.S.B.A., U. Mo., Columbia, 1953; postgrad., Washington U., St. Louis, 1956-59. Controller A.G. Edwards & Sons, Inc., St. Louis, 1967-70; v.p. ops., chief fin. officer Rexall Drug Co., St. Louis, 1970-75; exec. v.p. fin. West Bend Co., Wis., 1975-78, exec. v.p. mfg. ops., 1978-81; sr. v.p. fin. ops. Hobart Corp. div. Dart & Kraft, Troy, Ohio, 1981-83; pres. Hobart Internat. for Western Hemisphere and Far East div. Dart & Kraft, Troy, Ohio, 1983—. Bd. dirs. St. Joseph's Community Hosp., West Bend, 1976—, Kettle Moraine YMCA. Served with M.I. U.S. Army, 1953-55. Mem. Nat. Assn. Accountants, Am. Mgmt. Assn., Alpha Tau Omega. Club: Rotary. Office: Hobart Corp Troy OH 45374

HENSTOCK, BARRY ANTHONY, publishing company executive; b. Barrow, Eng., Nov. 26, 1939; m. Winifred Turner; children: Mike, Nicky, Chris, Sarah. Vice pres. fin. Bell Thread Co., On., Can., 1969-74; dir. fin. Tootal Co., Eng., 1974-76; dir. No. Telecom, Ont., 1976-78; controller Brascan Ltd., Ont., 1978-80; v.p. fin. Harlequin Enterprises, Don Mills, Ont., 1980-82, Torstar Corp., Toronto, 1982—. Fellow Inst. Chartered Accts. Eng. and Wales (prizes). Home: 1190 Botany Hill Oakville ON Canada L6J 6J5 Office: Torstar Corp 1 Yonge St Toronto ON Canada

HENTHORN, GEORGE LESLIE, communications executive; b. Montreal, Que., Canada, Jan. 22, 1923. B.Commerce, McGill U., 1949. Treasury dept. Bell Can., 1941-42; AT&T, N.Y.C., 1958-60; treasury dept. Bell Can., Montreal, 1960, gen. supr. fin. studies, 1964, regional acctg. supr., 1966, regional acctg. mgr., 1967, comptroller, 1969, v.p., comptroller, treas., 1973—; vice chmn. FEI Can.; dir. Nfld. Telephone Co. Ltd., Tele-Direct Publs., Bell Investment Mgmt. Corp. Served with Royal Can. Navy, 1942. Mem. Montreal Soc. Fin. Analysts, Telephone Pioneers of Am., Fin. Execs. Inst. Address: Bell Canada 1050 Beaver Hall Hill Montreal PQ Canada H2Z 1S4

HENTOFF, MARGOT, columnist; b. N.Y.C., July 5, 1930; d. David B. and Theresa (Lazarus) Goodman; m. Devi Wolynski (div. July 1959); children: Mara Wolynski, Lisa Wolynski; m. Nat Hentoff, Aug. 15, 1959; children: Nicholas, Thomas. Student, Syracuse U., 1947-50, New Sch. for Social Research, 1950-53. Columnist: Village Voice, 1966-69, 74—; contbr.: movie and book revs. Vogue, 1969-70; TV and book revs. N.Y. Rev. of Books, 1968—; contbg. editor: Am. Jour, 1972—; author: essays, revs. and short stories others. Address: 25 Fifth Ave New York NY 10003

HENTOFF, NATHAN IRVING, writer; b. Boston, June 10, 1925; s. Simon and Lena (Katzenberg) H.; m. Miriam Sargent, 1950 (div. 1950); m. Trudi Bernstein, Sept. 2, 1954 (div. Aug. 1959); children—Jessica, Miranda; m. Margot Goodman, Aug. 15, 1959; children—Nicholas, Thomas. B.A. with highest honors, Northeastern U., 1945; postgrad., Harvard U., 1946; Fulbright fellow, Sorbonne, Paris, 1950. Writer, producer, announcer radio sta. WMEX, 1944-53; asso. editor Down Beat mag., 1953-57; co-founder, co-editor The Jazz Review, 1958-60; staff writer The New Yorker, N.Y.C., 1960—; columnist and staff writer Village Voice, 1957—; faculty New Sch. Social Research; adj. asso. prof. N.Y. U. Mus. adviser: The Sound of Jazz, The Sound of Miles Davis, CBS-TV; Editor: (with Nat Shapiro) Hear Me Talkin' to Ya, 1955, The Jazz Makers, 1957, (with Albert McCarthy) Jazz, 1959, The Collected Essays of A.J. Muste, 1966; Author: The Jazz Life, 1961, Peace Agitator: The Story of A.J. Muste, 1963, The New Equality, 1964, Jazz Country, 1965, Call the Keeper, 1966, Our Children Are Dying, 1966, Onwards, 1967, A Doctor Among the Addicts, 1967, I'm Really Dragged but Nothing Gets Me Down, 1967, Journey into Jazz, 1968, A Political Life: The Education of John V. Lindsay, 1969, In The Country of Ourselves, 1971, State Secrets: Police Surveillance in America, 1973, This School Is Driving Me Crazy, 1975, Jazz Is, 1976, Does Anybody Give a Damn? Nat Hentoff on Education, 1977, The First Freedom: The Tumultuous History of Free Speech in America, 1980, Does This School Have Capital Punishment?, Blues for Charles Darwin, 1982, The Day They Came to Arrest the Book, 1982; contbr. to: (with others) others. Mem. steering com. Reporters Com. for Freedom of Press. Mem. Authors League Am., ACLU (dir.), N.Y. Civil Liberties Union (dir.), AFTRA. Office: 25 Fifth Ave New York NY 10003 *There is a probably apocryphal Talmudic saying that has helped: If you don't know where you're going, any road will take you there.*

HENTON, WILLIS RYAN, bishop; b. McCook, Nebr., July 5, 1925; s. Burr Milton and Clara Vaire (Godown) H.; m. Martha Somerville Bishop, June 7, 1952; 1 son, David Vasser. B.A., Kearney (Nebr.) State Coll., 1949; S.T.B., Gen. Theol. Sem., N.Y.C., 1952, D.S.T., 1972; D.D., U. of South, Sewanee, Tenn., 1972. Ordained priest Episcopal Ch., 1953; missionary St. Benedicts Mission, Besao, Mountain Province, Philippines, 1952-57; mem. staff St. Lukes Chapel, N.Y.C., 1957-58; rector Christ Ch., Mansfield, La., 1958-61, St. Augustine's Ch., Baton Rouge, 1961-64; archdeacon Diocese of La., 1964-71; bishop coadjutor Diocese N.W. Tex., 1971-72; bishop N.W. Tex., Lubbock, 1972-80, Western La., 1980—; vice chmn. faith and order div. La. Conf. Chs., 1969-71. Regent U. of South; trustee Episcopal Sem. S.W., Austin, Tex.; pres. Tex. Conf. Chs., 1978-80. Served with inf. AUS, 1944-46. Decorated Bronze Star. Office: PO Box 4046 Alexandria LA 71301

HENTSCHEL, DAVID A., oil company executive; b. 1934; married. B.S. in Phys. edn., La. State U., Okla. State U. Reservoir engr. Ark. Fuel Corp., 1957-61; with Cities Service Co., Tulsa, 1961—, prodn. engr., 1961-64, gas. ops. engr., 1964-65, buyer purchasing div., 1965-68, auto services mgr., 1968-70; gen. mgr. purchasing Cities Services mgr., Tulsa, 1970-74; gen. mgr. so. region Cities Service Co., 1974-77; v.p. Western area energy resources group Cities Service co., Tulsa, 1977-79; v.p. Western internat. area energy resources group Cities Service Co., Tulsa, 1979-80, exec. v.p. planning, tech. and services, 1980-82, corp. exec. v.p., pres. PPG group, 1982—. Served with USAF, 1957-59. Office: Cities Service Co 7th and Boulder Sts Tulsa OK 74101

HENWOOD, DEREK EDWIN, natural gas transmission company executive; b. St. John, N.B., Can. Project dir., co. dir. Sable Gas Systems Ltd., Halifax, N.S., Can.; v.p. Trans Can. PipeLines Ltd., Toronto, Ont.; dir. Welding Inst., Toronto. Mem. Profl. Engrs. N.S., Profl. Engrs. N.B. Office: Sable Gas Systems Ltd PO Box 462 Sta M Halifax NS Canada B3J 2P8

HENYAN, DON D., insurance company executive; b. Manchester, Iowa, Nov. 18, 1926; s. Austin A. and Opha A. (Smith) H.; m. Shirley Lou Henyan, June 4, 1950; children: Melissa Ann Henyan Radler, Molly Sue. B.S., Coe Coll. With Northwestern Nat. Life Ins. Co., Mpls., now exec. v.p., group; pres., chief exec. officer Northwestern Nat. Life Gen. Co., Mpls., 1981, also dir.; dir. North Atlantic Life Ins. Co., Jericho, N.Y., Nicolet-Eitel Corp., Mpls. Bd. dirs. Minn. Coalitio on Health Care, Mpls. Mem. Health Ins. Assn. Am. (vice chmn. group com. 1981—), Am. Council on Life Ins. (group com. 1981—). Republican. Club: Edina Country (Minn.). Home: 6344 Red Fox Ln Edina MN 55436 Office: Northwestern Nat Life Ins Co 20 Washington Ave S Minneapolis MN 55440

HENZE, CALVIN RUDOLPH, utility executive; b. Seguin, Tex., Jan. 28, 1924; s. Martin A. and Alice (Nolte) H.; m. Irene Daum, Feb. 14, 1947; children: Sandra (Mrs. Kimsey Cress), Patricia Ann. A.A., Tex. Lutheran Coll., 1948; B.B.A., S.W. Tex. State Coll., 1949. C.P.A., Tex. Internal auditor City Pub. Service Bd., San Antonio, 1949-56; comptroller City Water Bd., 1957-61; asst. controller Sweeney & Co., Inc., San Antonio, 1956-57; with Memphis Light, Gas & Water Div., 1961-78, pres., 1969-78; gen. mgr. Fla. Mcpl. Power Agy., Orlando, 1978—. Bd. dirs. Jr. Achievement Club, Memphis. Served with USAAF, 1943-46. Mem. Gas Research Inst. (dir. 1977), Am. Pub. Power Assn. (chmn. acctg. and fin. com. 1966-67, pres. 1978-79), Am. Gas Assn., Tex. Soc. C.P.A.s, Gas Research Inst. (dir.). Lodge: Rotary. Home: 8218 Tansy Dr Orlando FL 32819 Office: 7200 Lake Ellenor Dr Suite 154 Orlando FL 32809

HENZE, PAUL BERNARD, author, former government official; b. Redwood Falls, Minn., Aug. 29, 1924; s. Paul Henry and Elizabeth Ann (Rush) H.; m. Martha Elaine Heck, Sept. 15, 1951; children: John, Elizabeth, Martin, Mary, Alexander, Samuel. A.B., St. Olaf Coll., 1948; A.M., Harvard U., 1950; postgrad., U. Nebr., 1943-44, U. Maine, 1947, U. Minn., 1948. Fgn. affairs officer Dept. Def., 1950-51; policy adviser Radio Free Europe, Munich, West Germany, 1952-58; communications adviser, Turkey, 1958-59; mem. sr. research staff Ops. Research Office, Johns Hopkins, 1960-61; exec. Dept. Def., 1961-68; 1st sec. Am. embassy, Addis Ababa, Ethiopia, 1969-72; assigned Dept. State, Washington, 1973; 1st sec. Am. embassy, Ankara, Turkey, 1974-77; mem. staff NSC, Washington, 1977-80; resident cons. RAND Corp., Washington, 1982—. Author: Ethiopian Journeys, 1977, The Plot To Kill the Pope, 1983; contbg. author: The Middle East in Transition, 1958, Advances in Writing Systems, 1976; contbr. articles to profl. jours. Served with AUS, World War II; ETO. Fellow Wilson Center at Smithsonian Instn., 1982. Mem. Brit. Inst. Archaeology at Ankara, Archeol. Inst. Am., Assn. for Field Archaeology, Inst. Ethiopian Studies, Nat. Parks Assn., Royal Soc. for Asian Affairs (London), AAAS, Appalachian Trail Conf., Textile Mus. (Washington), Piedmont Environ. Council, Rappahannock League Environ. Protection, Com. for Free World, Am.-Turkish Soc., Greek Heritage Soc., East African Wildlife Soc., Soc. for Central Asian Studies, Brit. Inst. in Eastern Africa, Internat. Haji Baba Soc. Club: Federal City (Washington). Home: 6014 Namakagan Rd Washington DC 20816

HEPBURN, AUDREY, actress; b. Brussels, Belgium, May 4, 1929; d. Joseph Anthony and Baroness Ella (van Heemstra) H.; m. Melchor Gaston Ferrer, Sept. 25, 1954; 1 son, Sean; m. Andrea Dotti, 1969; 1 son, Luca. Ed., Day Sch., Arnhem, Netherlands, Conservatory of Music, Arnhem; student ballet with, Sonia Gaskel, Amsterdam, Marie Rambert, London. Mem., Corps de Ballet; appeared: with Sauce Tartare, also Sauce Piquante, West End, London; appeared in: Cabaret; appeared on TV; actress in: small parts in motion pictures Nous irons à Monte Carlo; leading roles in: Am. motion pictures Roman Holiday, 1953 (Acad. award as best actress 1954), Sabrina

Fair, 1954, War and Peace, 1955, Funny Face, 1956, Love in the Afternoon, 1956; first legitimate play Gigi, N.Y.C., 1951; appeared in: Ondine, N.Y.C., 1954, Producers Showcase; TV, 1957; films Green Mansions, 1958, The Nun's Story, 1959, The Unforgiven, 1960, Breakfast at Tiffany's, 1960, The Children's Hour, 1962, Charade, 1962, My Fair Lady, 1963, Paris When it Sizzles, 1964, How to Steal a Million, 1965, Two for the Road, 1966, Wait Until Dark, 1967, Robin and Marian, 1976, Bloodline, 1979, They All Laughed, 1981. Recipient spl. Tony award, 1968. Office: care Kurt Frings 415 N Crescent Dr Suite 320 Beverly Hills CA 90210 *

HEPBURN, KATHARINE, actress; b. Hartford, Conn., 1909; m. Ogden Ludlow. (Awarded first honors 1934, by vote of Acad. of Motion Picture Arts and Scis. for performance in Morning Glory 1933); appeared in: play The Philadelphia Story, Woman of the Year, 1942, Without Love, 1942, Keeper of the Flame, 1943, Dragon Seed, 1944, Undercurrent, 1946, Sea of Grass, 1946, Song of Love, 1947, State of the Union, 1948, Adam's Rib, 1949, As You Like It; Rosalind, 1950, African Queen, 1951, Pat & Mike, 1952, The Millionairess; play, Eng. and U.S.A., 1952, Summertime, 1955 (award Acad. Motion Picture Arts and Scis. 1955), Iron Petticoat, The Rainmaker, The Desk Set, 1957; plays Taming of the Shrew, Merchant of Venice, Measure for Measure, Eng. and Australia, 1955, Much Ado About Nothing, 1957; play Suddenly Last Summer, 1959; film Long Days Journey into Night; motion picture, 1962, Guess Who's Coming to Dinner, 1967 (Acad. award for best performance by actress 1968), Lion in Winter, (Acad. award best actress 1969), Mad Woman of Chaillot, 1969, Trojan Women, 1971; appeared on: stage in CoCo; musical, N.Y., 1970, on tour, 1971, A Delicate Balance; movie, 1973, Glass Menagerie; TV movie, 1973, Rooster Cogburn; movie, 1975, Love Among the Ruins; TV movie, 1975, A Matter of Gravity; play, 1976-78, The Corn is Green; TV movie, 1979 (Recipient gold medal as world's best motion picture actress, Internat. Motion Picture Expn., Venice, Italy 1934, N.Y. Critic's award for performance in picture The Philadelphia Story 1940, Annual award Shakespeare Club N.Y.C. 1950, Whistler Soc. award 1957, Hasty Pudding Club's annual woman of year award 1958, Outstanding Achievement award for fostering the finest ideals of the acting profession 1980).

HEPFER, JOHN WILLIAM, JR., consultant, retired air force officer; b. Waynesboro, Pa., Feb. 9, 1924; s. John William and Alice Holtzman H.; m. Janet Larue Miller, Apr. 19, 1946; children—John W., Stephen J. B.A., Bridgewater Coll., 1950; B.S.E., Air Force Inst., 1953; M.A., U. Md., 1971. Commd. 2d lt. USAF, 1943, advanced through grades to maj. gen., 1977; project mgr. (Navaho Guidance Systems), Wright-Patterson AFB, Ohio, 1953-57; mgr. Air Force Bombing and Nav. System, Andrews AFB, Md., 1958-62; chief missile guidance minuteman, Norton AFB, Calif., 1967-70, comdr., 1970-73, Norton AFB, Calif., 1974-81, ret., 1981; now cons. USAF. Decorated Legion of Merit, Air medal, Def. Disting. Service medal, others.; Recipient Norman P. Hays award Inst. Nav., 1977; Bernard A. Schriever award Air Force Assn., 1977. Mem. AIAA, IEEE, Inst. Nav., Ret. Officers Assn., Air Force Assn. Club: Elks. Address: 2619 Parisian Ct Punta Gorda FL 33950

HEPLER, ROBERT SIDNEY, ophthalmologist; b. Indianapolis, Ind., Dec. 27, 1934; s. Russell Lamar and Lela Pearl (Fowler) H.; m. Marilyn Marie Spaan, Aug. 17, 1957; children—Daniel, Elizabeth, Jeanne, David. B.A., Occidental Coll., Los Angeles, 1957; M.D., UCLA, 1961. Mem. faculty UCLA Med. Sch., 1967—, prof. ophthalmology, 1975—, chief neuro-ophthalmology, 1978—. Address: 800 Westwood Plaza UCLA Med Center Los Angeles CA 90024

HEPP, K. KEVIN, glass co. exec.; b. Buffalo, Mar. 2, 1917; s. Harold H. and Frances W. (Keogh) H.; m. Betty A. Smith, June 2, 1943; children—K. Kevin, Christopher, Ryan, Constance. B.A., U. Mich., 1939. With Owens-Ill. Glass Co., 1939—, sales mgr. Central region, 1961-64, v.p., gen. mgr. Central region, glass container div., Skokie, Ill., 1964-72, v.p., gen. mgr. closure and metal container div., Toledo, 1972-79, v.p., gen. mgr. worldwide bus. devel., 1979-80, sr. v.p., 1980—; dir. Guardsman Chems., Inc. Served to lt. USNR, 1942-45. Mem. Delta Upsilon. Club: Belmont (Perrysburg, Ohio). Home: 521 E Front St Perrysburg OH 43551 Office: PO Box 1035 Toledo OH 43666

HEPPEL, LEON ALMA, biochemist; b. Granger, Utah, Oct. 20, 1912; s. Leon George and Rosa (Zimmer) H.; m. Adelaide Keller, June 6, 1944; children: David E., Alan B. B.S. in Chemistry, U. Calif. at Berkeley, 1933, Ph.D. in Biochemistry, 1937; M.D., U. Rochester, 1941. Intern Strong Meml. Hosp., Rochester, N.Y., 1941-42; officer USPHS, 1942—, med. dir., 1956; research indsl. toxicology, 1942-47, enzymology, 1948—; now specializing in membrane transport and energy transduction; specialist in studies membrane structure and function NIH, 1958-67; prof. biochemistry Cornell U., Ithaca, N.Y., 1967—. Recipient 3M award in life scis. FASEB, 1977; Guggenheim fellow, Cambridge, Eng., 1953, Imperial Cancer Research Fund, London, 1975; Fogarty scholar NIH, 1982-83. Mem. Am. Soc. Biol. Chemists, Am. Chem. Soc. (Hillebrand award Washington sect. 1959), Nat. Acad. Scis. Office: Dept Biochemistry Cornell U Ithaca NY 14850

HEPPNER, JAMES PAUL, physicist; b. Winona, Minn., Aug. 9, 1927; s. Diedrick John and Alice (Gengnagel) H.; m. Edith Summa, July 21, 1955; children: Alex, Annet, Peter. Student, U. Nebr., 1945; B.Physics, U. Minn., 1948; M.S., Calif. Inst. Tech., 1950, Ph.D., 1954. Project leader Geophys. Inst., U. Alaska, 1950-52; head electromagnetic fields sect. Naval Research Lab., Washington, 1954-58; head fields and particles br. NASA, Goddard Space Flight Center, Greenbelt, Md., 1959-69, asso. chief lab. for space physics, 1970-73, head electrodynamics br., 1973—; discipline chmn. Inter-Union Commn. on Solar-Terrestrial Physics; tech. advisor Bilateral U.S.-USSR Cooperation in Space. Contbr. articles to profl. jours. Recipient medal for exceptional sci. achievement NASA, 1972, John C. Lindsay Meml. award Goddard Space Flight Center, 1983. Fellow Am. Geophys. Union; mem. AAAS, Internat. Union Geodesy and Geophysics, Union Radio Sci. Internat. Home: 536 Ednor Silver Spring MD 20904 Office: Code 696 Goddard Space Flight Center Greenbelt MD 20771

HERBERG, ROLAND LEO, real estate devel. co. exec.; b. Gascoyne, N.D., July 29, 1927; s. Albert A. and Helen Magdelen (Kaczmarek) H.; m. Margaret Eleanor Rudolph, June 21, 1952; children—David, Catherine, James. B.S., San Diego State Coll., 1950; M.B.A., Stanford U., 1952. With constrn. industry, San Francisco, 1952-54; indsl. and mgmt. engr. Ryan Aero. Co., San Diego, 1954-63; v.p. Janss Corp. (real estate devel.), Los Angeles and Aspen, Colo., 1963-69; pres. Snowmass Am. Corp., Aspen and Honolulu, 1969-70; chmn., pres. Real Estate Affiliates, Inc., Aspen Denver, 1970—; pres. Brewer, Inc., Aspen, Denver and Honolulu, 1973—; sr. v.p. C. Brewer & Co., Ltd. (agribus. conglomerate), Honolulu, 1974—; pres. Hawaiiana Investment Co. (real estate, hotel and resort ops.), Honolulu, 1974—; broker Brewer Realty Co., Honolulu, 1977—; dir. Aspen Broadcasting Co., 1968-75. Pres. West Village Assn., Aspen, 1967-69; Mem. Hawaii State Citizen's Adv. Com. Coastal Zone Mgmt., 1975—; pres. Aspen Grand Devel. Co., non-profit community devel. corp., 1967-74; Trustee Aspen Valley Hosp., 1969-73, Pacific and Asian Affairs Council, 1979—; mem. recreational devel. council Urban Land Inst., 1979—. Served with USNR, 1945-46. Home: 1627 Kamole St Honolulu HI 96821 Office: 827 Fort St Honolulu HI 96813

HERBERGER, G. ROBERT, business executive; b. Osakis, Minn., Sept. 12, 1904; s. George and Emily (Curry) H.; m. Katherine Kierland, Aug. 25, 1934; children: Gail Roberta (dec.), Gary Kierland, Judd Robert. Student, Hibbing Jr. Coll., U. Minn. Founder, pres. Herberger-Hart Co., St. Cloud, Minn., 1927; pres., gen. mgr. G.R. Herberger's Inc., 1942-47, chmn. bd., 1950-72, hon. chmn. bd., 1972—; pres. So. Land and Cattle Co., 1937-47, dir., 1937-52, St. Cloud Guaranty State Bank & Trust Co., 1947; v.p., dir. Keller Drug Co., Mpls., 1946-47; pres. Butler Bros., Chgo., 1947-49, dir., 1948-57, chmn. bd., 1949-50, Tigrett Enterprises, Inc., 1950-51; pres., dir. Desert Springs Water Co., Scottsdale, Ariz, 1955-71, chmn. bd., 1971-73; pres., dir. Paradise Valley Devel., Inc., 1956-71, chmn. bd., 1971—; sec., dir. Herberger-Cruse Co., Osakis; v.p., dir. Gainey Water Co., Scottsdale, 1956—; pres. Herberger Enterprises, Scottsdale, 1952-71, chmn. bd., 1971—; pres. Chandler Heights Land Co., 1960-74; dir. Channel 8, 1975-77. Chmn. ARC, Stearns County, Minn.; mem. Minn. State Vets. Service Bldg. Commn., 1946-47, UN Bd. State Minn., 1946-47; trustee Phoenix Fine Arts Assn., 1951-70; v.p., dir. Paradise Valley Improvement Assn., 1952-55; bd. dirs. Am. Grad. Sch. Internat. Mgmt., 1952-81, exec. com., 1960-77; mem. pres.'s adv. com. for John F. Kennedy Center for Performing Arts, 1970-77; mem. adv. council Small Bus. Adminstrn., 1970—; chmn. adv. com., mem. exec. com. Fiesta Bowl, 1971-81; bd. dirs. Phoenix Symphony Assn., v.p., exec. com., 1962-79; founding mem. Phoenix Chamber Music Soc., 1953-78, bd. dirs., 1960-77; del. Nat. Republican Conv., 1956, alt. del., 1968; mem. Rep. Nat. Fin. Com., 1959-70; trustee Ariz. Sunset Home, Phoenix; founder, bd. dirs. Herberger Found., 1961—; trustee Cradle Soc., Evanston, Ill., 1947-53; founder, mem. fin. com. Valley Presbyterian Ch.; bd. dirs. U. Minn. Found., 1977-80; mem. dean's adv. council Ariz. State U., 1977—; trustee, dir. numerous civic orgns.; founder, mem. fin. com. Valley Presbyn. Ch. Mem. Newcomen Soc., Jr. Assn. Commerce (co-founder, 1st v.p. St. Cloud, Minn. chpt. 1931). Clubs: Elk., Chicago (Chgo.); Phoenix Executives (pres. 1967-67, dir. 1961-68), Alexandria (Minn.) Country.). Home: 6439 E Luke Paradise Valley AZ 85253 Office: 7045 E Camelback Rd Scottsdale AZ 85251

HERBERS, TOD ARTHUR, publisher; b. Cin., Sept. 11, 1948; s. Walter Fred and Jeanette Ruth (Dalton) H.; m. Suzanne Jeannine Daly, Sept. 7, 1974. B.A., Catholic U. Am., 1970. With Nation's Bus. mag., Washington, 1972-75, promotion dir., 1974-75, Washingtonian mag., Washington, 1975-76, circulation and promotion dir., asso. pub., 1976-77; pub. Am. Film mag., Washington, 1977-82; mng. pub. Science 83 Mag., Washington, 1982—. Home: 8428 Holly Leaf Dr McLean VA 22102 Office: 1101 Vermont Ave NW Washington DC 20005

HERBERT, ALBERT EDWARD, JR., interior and industrial designer; b. Detroit, June 12, 1928; s. Albert Edward and Gladys Mae (Speechley) H. Student, Pratt Inst., 1947-50. With Knoll Internat. Planning Unit, 1950-52, SLS Envionetics Co., 1956-57; owner, operator Albert Herbert Designs, East Hampton, N.Y., 1957—; designer for V'Soske, Inc., Baker. Author: (with Roger P. Myers) The Last Survivor, 1976, Killer Pack, 1976; Contbr. articles on design to mags. Served with USAF, 1952-56. Fellow Am. Soc. Interior Designers (past pres. N.Y. chpt.); mem. Am. Inst. Interior Designers (past pres. N.Y. chpt.). Home: Box 824 East Hampton NY 11937

HERBERT, CHARLES JEROME, distilling executive; b. Balt., Oct. 4, 1926; s. Phillip Benjamin and Ann (Loughran) H.; m. Annalee Wells, Nov. 12, 1955; children—Charles, John, Robert, Elizabeth. B.S., U. Md., 1951; grad. Advanced Mgmt. Program, Harvard, 1971. With Heublein Co., various locations, 1958—, v.p., gen. sales mgr., Hartford, Conn., 1971-72, pres. Theodore Hamm Co. div., St. Paul, 1972-74; pres. Arrow Liquor Co. div. Heublein Inc., Hartford, 1974—, Heublein Spirit Sales Cos., 1975—. Served as sgt. AUS, 1945-46. Roman Catholic. Clubs: Wampanoag Country., Hartford Golf. Home: 30 Norwood Rd West Hartford CT 06117 Office: 330 New Park Ave Hartford CT 06101

HERBERT, DONALD JEFFREY (MR. WIZARD), film and TV producer-performer; b. Wauconia, Minn., July 10, 1917; s. Herbert Geoffrey and Lydia (Peopple) Kemske; m. Norma Kasell, 1972. B.S., LaCrosse State Tchrs. Coll., 1940. Pres. Prism Prodns. Inc., Canoga Park, Calif. Actor stage mgr., Minn. Stock Co., Mpls., 1940- 41, Minn. Stock Co., N.Y.C., 1941-42; radio actor, writer, Chgo., 1945-47; radio dir., Community Fund, Chgo., 1948-49; co-producer, interviewer: radio show It's Your Life, Cong. Indsl. Health Assn., 1949-50; creator and star of: Mr. Wizard TV show, NBC Network, 1951-65; television progress reporter: Gen. Electric Co, CBS Network, 1954-62; exec. producer: Experiment: The Story of a Scientific Search, 1963-66, Science Close Up; ednl. film series, 1964—; producer: video series for schools Assignment: Science; star: Mr. Wizard TV Show, 1970-71; producer, host: film Nuclear Power Questions—and Answers, 1974; producer, star: Mr. Wizard Close-Ups, 1976; exec. producer, on-camera reporter: sci. and engring. oriented TV news reports How About, 1979-83; creator, star: Mr. Wizard's World for Nickleodean Cable Network, 1983; Author: Mr. Wizard's Science Secrets, 1952, Mr. Wizard's Experiments for Young Scientists, 1959, Beginning Science with Mr. Wizard, 1960, (with Fulvio Bardossi) Kilauea, Case History of a Volcano, 1968, Secret in the White Cell, 1969; sci. kits Mr. Wizard's Experiments in Chemistry, 1970, Ecology, Crystal Growing, Mr. Wizard's Mystery Garden; Mr. Wizard's Supermarket Science. Served from pvt. to capt. USAAF, 1942-45. Recipient D.F.C., Air Medal with 3 oak leaf clusters, Sch. Broadcast award, 1951, N.J. Sci. Tchrs. award, 1951, Chgo. Federated Advt. Club award, 1951, Peabody award, 1953, 1st award Inst. Radio and TV Broadcasting, Ohio State U., 1952-53; 1st award Inst. for Edn. by Radio-TV, Ohio State U., 1953, 54, 55, 57; Spl. award Mfg. Chemists Assn., 1957, 58; Thomas Alva Edison Found. Nat. Mass Media awards, 1955, 63. Mem. Nat. Acad. Television Arts and Scis. (gov. 1963-64). Office: Prism Prodns Inc PO Box 83 Canoga Park CA 91305

HERBERT, DONALD ROY, lawyer, business exec.; b. Mpls., Nov. 4, 1935; s. Roy Patrick and Bertha Lydia (Mathre) H.; m. Carol A. Elofson, June 12, 1958; children—Karen, James, Phillip. B.S.L., U. Minn., 1957, LL.B. cum laude, 1959. Mem. firm Dorsey, Owen, Barker, Scott & Barber, Mpls., 1959-62; corp. lawyer Peavey Co., Mpls., 1962-77, v.p., gen. counsel, sec., 1977—. Mem. Am. Bar Assn., Minn. State Bar Assn. (bd. govs. 1976-77), Corp. Counsel Assn. Minn. (pres. 1975-76). Republican. Lutheran. Club: Mpls. Athletic. Home: 1500 16A St NW New Brighton MN 55112 Office: 730 2d Ave S Minneapolis MN 55402

HERBERT, EDWARD, molecular biologist, educator; b. Hartford, Conn., Jan. 28, 1926; s. Nathan and Celia (Katz) H.; m. Phyllis Sydney Torgan, June 8, 1948; 1 son, Edward A. B.S., U. Conn., 1949; Ph.D., U. Pa., 1953. Instr. biology MIT, Cambridge, 1955-57, asst. prof. biology, 1957-61, assoc. prof., 1961-63; assoc. prof. chemistry U. Oreg., Eugene, 1963-66, prof., 1966—, dir. cell biology program, 1982-83; dir. Inst. Advanced Biomed. Research Oreg. Health Scis., Portland, 1983—; mem. NIH study sect USPHS, Washington, 1981—; mem. NIH adv. panel for tng. grant programs; mem. editorial bd. Addison Wesley Pub. Co., Reading, Mass., 1961—. Contbr. over 80 articles in field to profl. jours.; author 25 book chpts. in field of neurobiology. Mem. adv. bd. State Legislative Com. on Trade and Econ. Devel., Salem, Oreg., 1982—. Served with USN, 1943-45. Recipient Career Devel. award USPHS, 1964-74, Pfizer award and lectureship Clin. Research Inst., Montreal, 1978, Rosetta Briegal award U. Okla., 1981, Leslie Bennett award U. Calif., San Francisco, 1982, First Mark O. Hatfield award Oreg. Health Scis. U., 1983; grantee NSF, NIH, Am. Heart Assn., Oreg. Heart Assn. Mem. Internat. Soc. Biochem. Endocrinology (v.p. 1980—), Am. Soc. Biol. Chemists, Endocrine Soc. Home: 2750 Onyx St Eurgen OR 97403 Office: Dept Chemistry U Oregon Eugene OR 97403

HERBERT, FRANK PATRICK, author; b. Tacoma, Oct. 8, 1920; s. Frank and Eileen M. (McCarthy) H.; m. Beverly Ann Stuart, June 23, 1946; children: Penny (Mrs. D.R. Merritt), Brian, Bruce. Student, U. Wash., 1946-47. Lectr. gen. and interdisciplinary studies U. Wash., Seattle, 1970-72; cons. social and ecol. studies, Far East affairs Lincoln Found., Vietnam and Pakistan, 1971. Author: Under Pressure, 1955, Dune, 1965, Green Brain, 1966, Destination Void, 1965, Eyes of Heisenberg, 1966, Heaven Makers, 1967, Santaroga Barrier, 1968, Dune Messiah, 1969, Whipping Star, 1970, New World or No World, 1970, Worlds of Frank Herbert, 1970, Soul Catcher, 1971, God Makers, 1971, Book of Frank Herbert, 1972, Project 40, 1972, Threshold, 1973, Best of Frank Herbert, 1973, Children of Dune, 1976, The Dosadi Experiment, 1977, (with B. Ransom) The Jesus Incident, 1979, Priests of Psi, 1979, Direct Descent, 1980, God Emperor of Dune, 1981, (with M. Barnard) Without Me You're Nothing: The Essential Guide to Home Computers, 1981, The White Plague, 1982, (with B. Ransom) Lazarus Effect, 1983; dir. writer, photographer: TV show The Tillers, 1973. Mem. collegeum World Without War Council, 1970-73; bd. dirs. Seattle World Without War Council, 1972—. Home: Port Townsend WA

HERBERT, GAVIN SHEARER, pharmaceutical company executive; b. Los Angeles, Mar. 26, 1932; s. Gavin and Josephine (D'Vitha) H.; m. Dorrine Winter, Oct. 16, 1954; children: Cynthia, Lauri, Gavin, Pam. B.S., U. So. Calif., 1954. With Allergan Pharms., Inc., Irvine, Calif., 1950—, v.p., 1956-61, exec. v.p., pres., 1961-77, chmn. bd., chief exec. officer, 1977—, pres., from 1977, pres. eye and skin care products group, from 1981; v.p. Smith Kline Corp., 1980—, also dir. Trustee U. So. Calif., Scripps Med. Clinic and Research Found. Served with USN, 1954-56. Mem. Beta Theta Pi. Republican. Clubs: Big Canyon Country, Balboa Bay, Newport Harbor Yacht. Office: Allergan Pharms Inc 2525 DuPont Irvine CA 92713 *

HERBERT, GEORGE RICHARD, research executive; b. Grand Rapids, Mich., Oct. 3, 1922; s. George Richard and Violet (Wilton) H.; m. Lois Anne Watkins, Aug. 11, 1945; children: Gordon, Patricia, Alison, Douglas, Margaret. Student, Mich. State U., 1940-42; B.S., U.S. Naval Acad., 1945; D.Sc. (hon.), N.C. State U., 1967; LL.D. (hon.), Duke U., 1978, U. N.C.-Chapel Hill, 1984. Line officer USN, 1945-47; instr. elec. engring. Mich. State U., 1947-48; asst. to dir. Stanford Research Inst., 1948-50, mgr. bus. ops., 1950-55, exec. asso. dir., 1955-56, asst. sec., 1950-56; treas. Am. & Fgn. Power Co., Inc., N.Y.C., 1956-59; pres. Research Triangle Inst., 1959—; chmn., dir. Microelectronics Center N.C.; dir. Central Carolina Bank & Trust Co., Duke Power Co.; mem. N.C. Sci. and Tech., 1963-79; mem. tech. adv. bd. U.S. Dept. Commerce, 1964-69, N.C. Atomic Energy Adv. Com., 1964-71; mem. Korea-U.S. joint com. for sci. cooperation Nat. Acad. Scis., 1973-78; mem. bd. sci. and tech. for internat. devel. Nat. Acad. Sci., 1978-83. Bd. dirs. Oak Ridge Assoc. Univs., 1971-74, 78—. Mem. Sigma Alpha Epsilon. Clubs: Cosmos (Washington); Hope Valley Country. Home: 46 Beverly Dr Durham NC 27707 Office: Box 12194 Research Triangle Park NC 27709

HERBERT, IRA C., food processing company executive; b. Chgo., Oct. 5, 1927; s. Solomon David and Helen (Burstyn) Chizever; m. Lila Faye Eilman, Jan. 6, 1951; children: Carrie Jo, Jeffrey, Fred. B.A., Mich. State U., 1950. Account exec. McFarland Aveyard, Chgo., 1951-56; account supr. Edward H. Weiss, Chgo., 1956-63; v.p. McCann Erickson, Los Angeles and Atlanta, 1963-65; sr. v.p. Coca-Cola U.S.A., 1965-74; exec. v.p. Coca-Cola Co., pres. food div., from 1975, exec. v.p., 1979—; dir. Pabst Brewing Co., Tex. Commerce Bank. Served with USAAF, 1945-47; with U.S. Army, 1951-52. Mem. Advt. Council (dir.). Jewish. Clubs: Westwood Country, Univ. (Houston); Standard, Commerce (Atlanta). *

HERBERT, JAMES ARTHUR, painter, film maker; b. Boston, Feb. 13, 1938; s. James Arthur and Bernice Frances (Burns) H. A.B. magna cum laude, Dartmouth Coll., 1960; M.F.A., U. Colo., 1962. Instr. U. Colo., 1962; artist-in-residence Yale Summer Sch. Art and Music, 1965; mem. faculty dept. art U. Ga., Athens, 1962—, prof., 1973—. One-man shows, Babcock Galleries, N.Y.C., 1967, U. Colo., Boulder, 1972, Poindexter Gallery, N.Y.C., 1972, 73, 74, 76, Mus. Modern Art, N.Y.C., 1970, 72, 74, 77, 81, Walker Art Center, Mpls., 1973, 82, Harvard U., 1973, High Mus. Art, Atlanta, 1979, Kennedy Center, Washington, 1981, Library of Congress, Washington, 1983—, group shows include, Krannert Art Mus., Urbana, Ill., 1974, New Orleans Mus. Art, 1975, 80, Whitney Mus. Am. Art, 1969, 73, 74, 83, Westdeutsche Kurzfilmtage, Oberhausen, W. Ger., 1970, 72, La Cinémathèque Royale de Belgique, Knokke-Heist, Belgium, 1974-75, Mus. Modern Art, 1979, P.S. 1, N.Y.C., Stedelijk Mus., Amsterdam, 1982, Kennedy Center, Washington, 1983, Monique Knowlton Gallery, N.Y.C., Monique Knowlton Gallery, N.Y.C.; represented in permanent collections, N.Y. U., Am. Fedn. Arts, Royal Film Archives Belgium, Centre Beaubourg, Paris, Mus. Modern Art, Whitney Mus. Am. Art, Cornell U., Am. Film Inst. Woodrow Wilson fellow, 1960-62; Am. Film Inst. grantee, 1969; Guggenheim Found. fellow, 1971-72; Nat. Endowment Arts grantee, 1975, 78, 81, 82; Louis Comfort Tiffany Found., 1980; commn. Library of Congress, 1983. Mem. Phi Beta Kappa. Office: Art Dept Univ of Ga Athens GA 30602

HERBERT, JAMES HALL, retired equipment leasing company consultant; b. East Liverpool, Ohio, Oct. 5, 1915; s. Josiah T. and Elizabeth (Hall) H.; m. Joanne E. Moore, Mar. 30, 1940; children: James Hall II, Jennifer E. B.A., Ohio State U., 1936; grad., Sch. Banking, U. Wis., 1950; now student, Scottsdale Community Coll. (Ariz.). With Universal Credit Co., 1936-43; from installment loan mgr. to v.p. Coshocton Nat. Bank, Ohio, 1946-56; v.p. Harter Bank & Trust Co., Canton, Ohio, 1956-59; with Lorain Nat. Bank, Ohio, 1959-75, pres., 1962-75, chmn. bd., 1975; cons. Res. Fin. Services, Cleve., from 1975; former pres. James H. Herbert Fin. Cons. Services Inc., Scottsdale, Ariz.; mem. interview staff Greenwich (Conn.) Research Assocs.; dir. Grant-Holladay Constrn. Corp., Washington; former mem. faculty Ohio Sch. Banking; former dir. seminars Lorain County Community Coll.; instr. adult courses Scottsdale Community Coll. Past pres. Lorain County United Community Services; former mem. exec. com., nat. budget and cons. com. United Fund Am.; Trustee; former mem. adv. bd., chmn. fin. com. St. Joseph Hosp., Lorain; former chmn. bd. dirs. Lorain Community Coll. Found. Served as pilot USAAF, World War II. Decorated Air medal with 6 clusters. Mem. Am. Bankers Assn., Ohio Bankers Assn. (pres. 1972-73), Phi Delta Theta. Home: 5540 N 77 Pl Scottsdale AZ 88253

HERBERT, JAMES KELLER, lawyer; b. Titusville, Pa., Feb. 16, 1938; s. James Keller and Mary Louise (Carey) H.; m. Carol Sellers, Nov. 13, 1980; children—Michael Brendan, Mary Frances. B.S., Stanford U., 1959; LL.B., U. Calif., Berkeley, 1962. Bar: Calif. bar

1963. Asso. McCutchen, Black, Verleger & Shea, Los Angeles, 1962-64; asst. prof. Loyola U. Law Sch., Los Angeles, 1964-68; partner firm Richards, Watson, Dreyfuss & Gershon, Los Angeles, 1968—; exec. dir. Harcourt, Brace, Jovanovich Legal, Inc., Los Angeles, 1966—; adj. prof. McGeorge Sch. Law, UCLA, 1973-74. Served with Calif. Army N.G., 1956-62. Mem. Calif. Bar Assn., Los Angeles County Bar Assn. Club: Jonathan (Los Angeles). Home: 4412 N Wilson St Fresno CA 93704 Office: 11801 W Olympic St Suite 7 Los Angeles CA 90064

HERBERT, JAMES PAUL, advertising executive; b. Pitts., Nov. 12, 1941; s. Lewis Brown and Clare Alice (Morehead) H.; m. Delfina Elvira Acuto, Nov. 28, 1964. B.S., Fordham U., 1964. C.P.A., N.Y. Sr. auditor Arthur Andersen & Co., N.Y.C., 1964-69; corp. controller, v.p. Norman, Craig & Kummel, N.Y.C., 1969-71; exec. v.p., treas., dir., mem. exec. com. Van Brunt & Co., N.Y.C., 1971-76; founder Advt. Agy. Fin. Cons., N.Y.C., 1976—; v.p. fin. B. Hodes Advt., Inc., N.Y.C., from 1978, now chief fin. officer and mem. exec. com. Trustee BHA Profit Sharing Plan, N.Y.C., 1978—; Mem. Friends of Library, 1974—. Mem. Am. Assn. Advt. Agys., Am. Inst. C.P.A.s, N.Y. State Soc. C.P.A.s, Nat. Assn. Accountants, Financial Execs. Inst., Beta Gamma Sigma, Beta Alpha Psi. Home: 1706 Sandalwood Dr Sarasota FL 33581 Office: 711 Fifth Ave New York NY 10022

HERBERT, JOHN RUGGLES, banker, editor; b. Boston, Nov. 30, 1908; s. Charles J. and Evelyn E. (Harvey) H.; m. Elsa O. Johnson, Dec. 15, 1934 (dec. Oct. 20, 1980); children: John A., Robert M.; m. Margot S. Robinson, Aug. 1, 1981. B.S., Boston U., 1931, L.H.D., 1969; D. Journalism, Suffolk U., 1958. Mng. editor Patriot Ledger, Quincy, Mass., 1936-52, editor, 1952—, Boston Herald, 1967-74; exec. editor Boston Herald Traveler, 1970-72; exec. dir. Mass. Newspaper Pubs. Assn., Quincy, 1973-75; chmn. bd., pres. Quincy Coop. Bank, 1975-83; chief operating officer Boston Bank of Commerce, 1983—; Hon. pres. Inter-Am. Press Assn. Tech. Center N.Y.; dir., mem. exec. com. Inter-Am. Press Assn. N.Y. Editorial adv. bd.: Am. Neptune mag. Mem. Carribean Conservation Corp.; Trustee New Eng. Aquarium; bd. dirs. Bostonian Soc., World Peace Found., Internat. Center New Eng. Recipient Tom Wallace award for assistance to Latin Am. press Inter-Am. Press Assn., 1961; Maria Moors Cabot prize for promotion Inter-Am. relations Columbia, 1962; Yankee Quill award and citation Sigma Delta Chi, 1964; Order Merit Duarte, Sanchez and Mella, Grand Ofcl. Grade Dominican Republic Latin Am., 1964. Mem. Am. Soc. Newspaper Editors, Internat. Press Inst. (chmn. joint com. fgn. journalist exchanges), Brotherhood of Green Turtle, Acad. New Eng. Journalists, Pan Am. Soc. New Eng. (pres.), Sigma Delta Chi (mem. CBA Alumni Hall of Fame 1969). Clubs: Rotary (past pres.), Neighborhood (Quincy); Union (Boston); Overseas Press (N.Y.). Lodge: Rotary (past pres.). Home: 181 Bellevue Rd Quincy MA 02171 Office: 1259 Hancock St Quincy MA 02169

HERBERT, JOHN WARREN, forest products executive; b. Columbus, Ohio, June 20, 1924; s. Logan R. and Ruth (Warren) H.; m. Elizabeth Knapp, Oct. 15, 1949; children: Kathryn, Steve, Lisa, David, Laura. B.S., U. Pa., 1948; A.M.P., Harvard U., 1966. Salesman Mead Corp., Dayton, Ohio, 1948-54, regional mgr., 1954-63, v.p., 1963-66, v.p., gen. sales mgr., 1967-70, pres. Mead Paper and exec. v.p. Paper Group, pres. Mead Printing and Writing, 1970-71, group v.p., 1981—; dir. First Nat. Bank, Dayton, 1977—. Served with U.S. Army, 1943-46. Republican. Presbyterian. Clubs: Moraine Country (bd. govs.), Dayton Racquet). Office: The Mead Corp World Hdqrs Courthouse Plaza NE Dayton OH 45463

HERBERT, KEVIN BARRY JOHN, classics educator; b. Chgo., Nov. 18, 1921; s. William Patrick and Margaret (Lomasney) H.; m. Margaret Frances Lambin, Dec. 28, 1946; children: John Barry, Catherine Ann (Mrs. John Reilly). B.A., Loyola U., Chgo., 1946; M.A., Harvard U., 1949, Ph.D., 1954. Instr. classics Marquette U., Milw., 1948-52; instr. Ind. U., 1952-54; master St. Paul's Sch., Concord, N.H., 1954-55; asst. prof. Bowdoin Coll., Maine, 1955-62; asso. prof., prof. Washington U., St. Louis, 1962—, chmn. dept., 1982—, curator Wulfing collection classical coins, 1968—; reader Advanced Placement Latin, 1962-68, chief reader, 1969-73; mem. Latin test com. Coll. Entrance Exam. Bd., 1968-73; dir. tours to Europe and Middle East, 1973—. Author: Hugh of St. Victor: Soliloquy on the Earnest Money of the Soul, 1956, Ancient Art in Bowdoin College, 1964, Greek and Latin Inscriptions in the Brooklyn Museum, 1972; co-editor: Ancient Collections in Washington University, 1973; Contbr. to: Great Events from History, 2 vols., 1972, Greek Coins in the Wulfing Collection of Washington University, 1979, Maximum Effort: The B-29s Against Japan, 1983; also articles and revs. to profl. jours. Served to staff sgt. USAAF, 1942-45. Decorated D.F.C., Air medal with two silver oak leaf clusters, others; Wilbour fellow Bklyn. Mus., 1967; grantee Nat. Endowment Humanities, 1972—. Mem. Am. Philol. Assn., Archeol. Inst. Am., Am. Schs. Oriental Research, Classical Assn. Middle West and South, Am. Numismatic Soc. Home: 1124 Basswood Ln Saint Louis MO 63132

HERBERT, MICHAEL KINZLY, magazine editor; b. Battle Creek, Mich., Dec. 1, 1942; s. Walter N. and Elaine F. (Hamblet) H.; m. Lana Ann Viereg Stanton, May 7, 1966; children: Nancy Ann, Susan Elaine. Student, Kenyon Coll., 1961-62, Kellogg Community Coll., 1962-63; B.A., Western Mich. U., 1966. Tchr. English Orchard View High Sch., Muskegon, Mich., 1966-67; counselor, dormitory dir. Western Mich. U., Kalamazoo, 1967-68; sports reporter Chgo. Tribune, 1968-71; mng. editor Letterman Mag., Wheaton, Ill., 1971-72; editor Century Pub. Co. (publishing Auto Racing Digest, Baseball Digest, Basketball Digest, Bowling Digest, Football Digest, Hockey Digest, Soccer Digest, Sports Gift Digest, Inside Sports), Evanston, Ill., 1972—. Author: The Riddell Guide to Physical Fitness, 1977, Mike Schmidt, The Human Vacuum, 1983. Mem. Profl. Football Writers Am., Football Writers Assn. Am., Profl. Basketball Writers Assn. Am., U.S. Basketball Writers Assn., Profl. Soccer Reporters Assn. Am., Am. Auto Racing Writers and Broadcasters Assn., Midwest Bowling Writers, Bowling Writers Assn. Am. Office: 1020 Church St Evanston IL 60201

HERBERT, ROBERT LOUIS, art history educator; b. Worcester, Mass., Apr. 21, 1929; s. John Newman and Rose (Harr) H.; m. Eugenia Warren, June 6, 1953; children: Timothy, Rosemary, Catherine. B.A., Wesleyan U., Middletown, Conn., 1951; student, U. Paris, France, 1951-52; M.A., Yale, 1954, Ph.D., 1957. Mem. faculty Yale, 1956—, prof. history of art, 1967—, chmn. dept., 1965-68, Robert Lehman prof. history of art, 1974—; Slade prof. Oxford U., 1978. Organized exhbns., author catalogues for, Mus. Fine Arts, Boston, Barbizon Revisited, 1962-63, Neo-Impressionism, Guggenheim Mus., 1968, J.F. Millet, Louvre, Paris and Arts Council, London, 1975, Millet's Gleaners, Mpls. Inst. Arts, 1978, Léger's Le Grand Déjeuner, Mpls. Inst. of Arts and Detroit Inst. Arts, 1980; Author: Barbizon Revisited, 1962, Seurat's Drawings, 1962, The Art Criticism of John Ruskin, 1964, Modern Artists on Art, 1964, Neo-Impressionism, 1968, David's Brutus, 1972; co-editor: The Société Anonyme and the Dreier Collection at Yale University, 1984; Author also articles. Home: PO Box 3894 Yale Station New Haven CT 06520 Office: 56 High St Yale New Haven CT 06520

HERBERT, THOMAS M., lawyer; b. Columbus, Ohio, 1927. B.S., Ohio State U., then LL.B. and J.D.; grad., Nat. Coll. State Trial Judges, Sr. Appellate Judges Seminar, N.Y. U. Sch. Law. Bar: Ohio; Lic. pvt. pilot, amateur radio operator. Former judge 10th jud. dist. Ohio Ct. Appeals; former sr. assoc. justice Ohio Supreme Ct.; U.S. bankruptcy judge, Columbus. Former mem. Ohio Gen. Assembly. Served with USAF, 1951-55; Korea. Mem. Am., Ohio, Columbus bar assns., Am. Judicature Soc., Nat. Inst. Jud. Adminstrn. Lodges: Masons (33 deg.); Shriners. Office: U.S. Bankruptcy Ct 85 Marconi Blvd Columbus OH 43215

HERBERT, VICTOR JAMES, assn. exec.; b. Follansbee, W.Va., Aug. 6, 1917; s. Oliver James and Gertrude Mae (Lazear) H.; m. Dorothy Clara Johnson, Sept. 2, 1942; children—Victor J., Dorothy Constance. A.B., Bethany (W.Va.) Coll., 1940. Adminstr., negotiator, airline employee orgns.; a founder Air Line Stewards and Stewardesses Assn., Internat., 1946, acting pres., 1946-51, asst. to pres., 1951-59; in charge edn. and orgn. dept. Air Line Pilots Assn. A.F.L., 1946-62; pres. Airline Employees Assn. Editor: Air Line Employee. Pres. bd. dirs. Bus. Indsl. Ministry. Mem. Beta Theta Pi. Presbyn. Club: Mason. Home: 5401 Central Ave Western Springs IL 60558 Office: 5600 S Central Ave Chicago IL 60638

HERBERTT, STANLEY, performing arts adminstr., choreographer, lectr.; b. Chgo., Apr. 11, 1919; s. Samuel W. and Anna (Sturt) H. Grad., Herzl Jr. Coll., Chgo., 1938; B.Ed., Chgo. Tchrs. Coll., 1942; M.A., Nat. Acad. Ballet, N.Y.C., 1960. With Chgo. Civic Opera Ballet, 1940-43, San Carlo Opera Ballet, Chgo., 1940-43, Littlefield Ballet Co., 1941-42; soloist Ballet Theater of N.Y., N.Y.C., 1943-47; soloist, choreographer Cain Park Summer Theater, Cleve., 1950-51; propr., dir. Ballet Arts Acad., St. Louis, 1951—; founder, dir. St. Louis Civic Ballet, 1959—; lectr. St. Louis U., 1965—; Nat. Soc. Arts and Letters, St. Louis, 1961—, Copper Coin Civic Ballet, Springfield, Ill., 1975—; mem. dance faculty Webster Coll., Webster Groves, Mo., 1976-77; participant Internat. Festival Youth Orchs. and Performing Arts, Aberdeen, Scotland, also London, 1976. Soloist: Broadway musical Carousel, 1947-49, Inside U.S.A, 1947-49; choreographer, Columbus (Ohio) Ballet Theatre, TV commls.; dir. musical fashion shows for, Stix Baer and Fuller Dept. Stores; dir., choreographer: ednl. program The History of Dance from Jig to Jet, 1967-81, Dance—Our American Heritage; Contbr. articles on dance and choreography to profl. jours. Mem. dance com. Mo. Council on athe Arts, 1968—. Recipient Edn. for Arts award Stix Baer and Fuller, 1963; Plaque award St. Louis Civic Ballet, 1965; Merit award Fontbonne Coll., 1972; Maharishi award, 1977; commendations Mayor of St. Louis, 1976, 79, Gov. of Mo., 1977. Mem. Dance Masters of Am. Home: 7548 Parkdale Saint Louis MO 63105 Office: 7620 Wydown Blvd St Louis MO 63105

HERBICH, JOHN BRONISLAW, engineering educator; b. Warsaw, Poland, Sept. 1, 1922; came to U.S., 1953, naturalized, 1962; s. Henry Pawel and Jadwiga Eleonora (Lopienski) H.; m. Margaret Pauline Boylan, Jan. 27, 1951; children: Ann (dec.), Barbara K., Gregory J., Patricia J. B.Sc., U. Edinburgh, Scotland, 1949; M.S. in C.E, U. Minn., 1957; Ph.D., Pa. State U., 1973; postgrad., U. Calif., Berkeley, 1964, Utah State U., 1966. Registered profl. engr., Tex. Field engr. John Laing & Son, London, Eng., 1948; research engr. U. Delft, Netherlands, 1949-50; research fellow, intermediate engr. Aluminum Co. Can., Ltd., 1950-53; research fellow U. Minn., 1953-57; asst. prof. Lehigh U., 1957-60, asso. prof., 1960-65, prof., 1965-67; prof. civil engring., head ocean and hydraulic engring. group, head ocean engring. program, dir. Center for Dredging Studies, Tex. A. and M. U. College Station, 1967—; on leave as UN project mgr. Central Water and Power Research Sta., Govt. of India, Khadakwasla, Poona, 1972-73; lectr. in, Venezuela, India, China, other countries; dir. Ocean Pollution Control, Inc., Dallas; v.p. Cons. and Research Services, Inc., Bryan, Tex. Author: Coastal and Deep Ocean Dredging, 1975, Offshore Pipelines: Design Elements, 1981, Scour Around Offshore Structures, 1983; also numerous articles and reports; contbr.: chpts. to Studies in Marine Environmental Pollution, 1980. Pres. PTA Hamilton Sch., Bethlehem, Pa., 1965-66. Served with Brit. Army, 1940-45. Recipient Karl Emil Hilgard Hydraulic Prize Am. Soc. C.E., 1965-66; NSF Faculty-Sci. fellow, 1963-64. Mem. Internat. Assn. Hydraulic Research, World Dredging Assn., Am. Soc. Engring. Edn., ASCE, Marine Tech. Soc., Permanent Internat. Assn. Nav. Congresses, Sigma Xi, Phi Kappa Phi, Chi Epsilon. Patentee in field. Home: 764 S Rosemary Dr Bryan TX 77802 Office: Ocean Engring Program Tex A and M U College Station TX 77843

HERBRANDSON, HARRY FRED, educator, chemist; b. Watertown, S.D., July 25, 1921; s. Harry Oscar and Alice (Smith) H.; m. Doris May Hamilton, Oct. 27, 1946; children—Patricia J., Karen A., Carl H.R. B.Chemistry, U. Minn., 1942; Ph.D., U. Ill., 1945. Research chemist Nat. Aniline Co., 1945-46; research fellow Harvard, 1946-47; asst. prof. Union Coll., Schenectady, 1947-49; faculty Rensselaer Poly. Inst., 1949—, prof. chemistry, 1957—; cons. to industry, 1953—. Contbg. author: Determination of Organic Structures by Physical Methods, Vol. 1, 1955. Fellow Chem. Soc. London, AAAS; mem. Am. Chem. Soc., N.Y. Acad. Scis., Phi Beta Kappa, Sigma Xi. Home: 214 Forts Ferry Rd Latham NY 12110 Office: Rensselaer Poly Inst Troy NY 12181

HERBRANSON, KAI WOLD, hotel executive; b. Bagley, Minn., Apr. 27, 1935; s. Joseph H. and Kari (Wold) H.; m. Donna Lou Stamos, Sept. 2, 1961; children: Shawn, Adam, Jill. B.A., St. Olaf Coll., Northfield, Minn., 1957, Mich. State U., 1960, M.A., 1961. With Sheraton Hotel Corp., 1961—; v.p., gen. mgr. Lord Baltimore Hotel, Balt., 1969-71, Royal Hawaiian Hotel, Honolulu, 1971-73; sr. v.p. Sheraton Hotels Ltd.; gen. mgr. Sheraton Centre, Toronto, Ont., Can., 1973—; v.p. Met. Toronto Conv. Bur., 1976—; dir. ITT Industries Can. Past pres. Met. Toronto Boy Scouts. Served with AUS, 1958. Recipient Medal of Merit Boy Scouts Can. Mem. Am. Hotel and Motel Assn., Ont. Hotel and Motel Assn. (v.p. 1977-78), Met. Toronto Hotel and Motel Assn. (chmn. bd. 1978, hon. pres. 1979), Hotel Sales Mgrs. Assn. Clubs: Treasure, Skal. Address: 123 Queens St W Toronto ON Canada M5H 2M9

HERBST, ARTHUR LEE, obstetrician-gynecologist; b. N.Y.C., Sept. 14, 1931; s. Jerome Richard and Blanche (Vatz) H.; m. Lee Ginsburg, Aug. 10, 1958. A.B. magna cum laude, Harvard Coll., 1953, M.D. cum laude, 1959. Intern Mass. Gen. Hosp., Boston, 1959-60, resident, 1960-62; resident in obstetrics and gynecology Boston Hosp. for Women, 1962-65; instr., assoc. prof. obstetrics-gynecology Mass. Gen. Hosp. and Harvard U. Med. Sch., Boston, 1965-76; Joseph B. DeLee prof. obstetrics and gynecology U. Chgo., 1976—; chmn. dept. obstetrics-gynecology Chgo. Lying In Hosp., 1976—; chmn. exec. com. U. Chgo. Hosps. and Clinics, 1980—. Contbr. articles to med. jours. Served with USN, 1953-55. Mem. AMA, Am. Coll. Obstetricians and Gynecologists, Am. Gynecol. and Obstet. Soc., Am. Assn. Profs. Obstetrics and Gynecology, Central Assn. Obstetricians and Gynecologists, A.C.S., Soc. Pelvic Surgeons, Endocrine Soc., Infertility Soc., Soc. Gynecologic Oncologists. Home: 1234 N State Pkwy Chicago IL 60610 Office: 5841 S Maryland Ave Chicago IL 60637

HERBST, JURGEN, educator; b. Braunschweig, Germany, Feb. 22, 1928; came to U.S., 1954, naturalized, 1957; s. Hermann and Annemarie (Otto) H.; m. Susan Lou Allen, Sept. 16, 1951; children—Christian, Annemarie, Stephanie. Student, U. Gottingen, 1947-48; B.A., U. Nebr., 1950; M.A., U. Minn., 1952; Ph.D., Harvard U., 1958. Instr. edn. and history Wesleyan U., Middletown, Conn., 1958-59, asst. prof., 1959-65, asso. prof., 1965-66; asso. prof. ednl. policy studies and history U. Wis., 1966-69, prof., 1969—. Author: The German Historical School in American Scholarship, 1965, The History of American Education, 1973, From Crisis to Crisis: American College Government, 1636-1819, 1982; editor: Our Country, 1963. Am.Council Learned Socs. grantee, 1960; Fulbright Commn. grantee, 1963, 81; Nat. Endowment for Humanities grantee, 1972-73; Nat. Inst. Edn. grantee, 1973-76; Internat. Research and Exchanges Bd. grantee, 1977; Guggenheim Found. grantee, 1978-79; Wis. Inst. Research in Humanities grantee, 1978-79. Mem. Am. Hist. Assn., Orgn. Am. Historians, History of Edn. Soc. Historische Kommission der Deutschen Gesellschaft für Erziehungswissenschaft. Democrat. Congregationalist. Office: Dept Educational Policy Studies University of Wisconsin Madison WI 53706

HERBST, ROBERT LEROY, orgn. exec.; b. Mpls., Oct. 5, 1935; s. Walter Peter and Bernice Mickey (Mikkelson) H.; m. Evelyn Clarice Elford, Sept. 22, 1956; children—Eric Elford, Peter Robert, Amy Jo. B.S. in Forest Mgmt, U. Minn., St. Paul, 1957. Dep. commnr. Minn. Conservation Dept., 1966-69; nat. exec. dir. Izaak Walton League Am., 1969-70; commr. natural resources State of Minn., 1971-77; asst. sec. fish, wildlife and parks Dept. Interior, Washington, 1977-81, sec., Jan. 20-26, 1981; exec. dir. Trout Unltd., 1981—; instr. U. Minn., 1954; mem. adv. faculty N. Am. Sch. Conservation, 1969-77; vice chmn. Gt. Lakes Fisheries Commn., 1978-79, chmn., 1979-80; mem. U.S. Commn. UNESCO, 1978-79, Pres. Carter's Interagency Council, 1978-80. Author: Careers in Environment, 1973, also articles. Mem. nat. bd. Boy Scouts Am., 1969-77; exec. bd. Viking council, 1975-76; mem. bd. House of Prayer Lutheran Ch., Richfield, Minn., 1969-77; bd. govs. African Inst. Econ. Edn. and Devel., 1980. Recipient Nat. Service award Izaak Walton League Am., 1971; Silver Beaver award Boy Scouts Am., 1977; Distinguished Service award U. Minn., 1969; named Pub. Adminstr. of Year in Minn. Am. Soc. Pub. Adminstrn., 1976. Mem. numerous conservation orgns. Democrat.

HERCULES, DAVID MICHAEL, chemistry educator, consultant; b. Somerset, Pa., Aug. 10, 1932; s. Michael George and Kathryn (Saylor) H.; m. Nancy Catherine Miller, Sept. 23, 1957 (div. 1968); 1 dau., Kimberly Ann; m. Shirley Ann Hoover, Dec. 14, 1970; children: Sherri Kathryn, Kevin Michael. B.S., Juniata Coll., 1954; Ph.D., MIT, 1957. Asst. prof. Lehigh U., 1957-60; assoc. prof. Juniata Coll., Huntington, Pa., 1960-63; asst. prof. MIT, 1963-68, assoc. prof., 1968-69, U. Ga., Athens, 1969-74, prof., 1974-76; prof. dept. chemistry U. Pitts., 1976—, chmn., 1980—; mem. vis. com. for chemistry Lehigh U., 1980—; vis. prof. Mich. State U., 1972; chmn. Gordon Research Conf. on Electron Spectroscopy, 1974, Gordon Research Conf. on Analytical Chemistry, 1966; co-chmn. Internat. Conf. Chemiluminescence, 1972; univ. rep. Council on Chem. Research, 1980—; mem. program com. Pitts. Conf. on Analytical Chemistry and Applied Spectroscopy, 1977—; mem. vis. scientist program NSF, 1964-76. Mem. editorial bds.: Applied Spectroscopy, 1963-65, Analytical Chemistry, 1964-67, Jour. Electron Spectroscopy, 1971-77, Environ. Analytical Chemistry, 1973—, Spectrochimica Acta, 1973—, Talanta, 1974-80, Spectroscopy Letters, 1975—, The Scis., 1979—, Trends in Analytical Chemistry, 1980—, Jour. Trace and Microprobe Techniques, 1980—; patentee (in field). Mem. Am. Chem. Soc. (Petroleum Research Fund adv. bd. 1978-80, chmn. div. analytical chemistry 1977-78), Soc. Applied Spectroscopy (Lester W. Strock medal New Eng. sect. 1981), Am. Vacuum Soc., Photoelectric Spectrometry Group, Pa. Acad. Scis., Spectroscopy Soc. Pitts., Soc. Analytical Chemists Pitts., Sigma Xi. Home: 4245 Parkman Ave Pittsburgh PA 15213 Office: Dept Chemistry U Pitts Pittsburgh PA 15260

HERD, HAROLD SHIELDS, state supreme ct. justice; b. Coldwater, Kans., June 3, 1918. B.A., Washburn U., 1941, J.D., 1942. Bar: Kans. bar 1943. Partner firm Rich and Herd, Coldwater, 1946-53; individual practice law, Coldwater, 1953-81; asso. justice Kans. Supreme Ct., 1981—; mayor, Coldwater, 1949-53, county atty., Comanche County, Kans., 1954-58; mem. Kans. Senate, 1965-73. Bd. govs. Washburn Law Sch.; mem. exec. com. Kans. Com. for Humanities, 1975—. Mem. S.W. Bar Assn. (pres. 1977), Kans. Bar Assn. (exec. council 1973—). Office: Kans Jud Center 10th and Harrison Sts Topeka KS 66612 *

HERDER, STEPHEN RENDELL, newspaper publisher; b. St. John's, Nfld., Can., July 15, 1928; s. Ralph Barnes and Mary (Rendell) H.; m. Joan Bursey, Sept. 9, 1949; children: A. Daniel, Stephanie L. Grad., Mt. Allison Acad., Sackville, N.B., Can., 1945. Reporter St. John's Evening Telegram, 1945-49, news editor, mng. editor, 1950-66, gen. mgr., 1966-70, pub., 1970—; reporter Ont. dailies, 1949-50. Mem. Canadian Press, Canadian Daily Newspaper Pubs. Assn., Salmon Assn. Eastern Nfld., Atlantic Salmon Assn., Can. Wildlife Fedn., Nfld. Wilderness Soc.; hon. mem. Canadian Univ. Press. Mem. United Ch. Can. Club: St. John's Curling. Office: 400 Topsail Rd St John's NF A1C 5X7 Canada

HERDRICH, NORMAN WESLEY, editor; b. Spokane, Wash., July 17, 1942; s. Fred N. and Florice J. (Birchill) H.; m. Mary Susan Webb, Aug. 16, 1975; children: Megan Marie, Heidi Susan. B.S., Wash. State U., 1969. Field editor Washington-Farmer-Stockman, Northwest Unit Farm mags., Spokane, 1969-78, prodn. editor, 1978—. Served with USNR, 1963-65. Mem. Wash. State Grange, Soc. Profl. Journalists, Nat. Rifle Assn., Spokane Editorial Soc. (sec.-treas. 1974-77, 1st v.p. 1977-78, pres. 1978-79), Wash. Wool Growers Assn., Sigma Delta Chi. Methodist. Clubs: Spokane Press (dir. 1978, treas. 1979. Home: E 12711 Saltese Rd Spokane WA 99216 Office: Room 212 Review Tower W 999 Riverside Spokane WA 99210

HEREFORD, FRANK LOUCKS, JR., university president; b. Lake Charles, La., July 18, 1923; s. Frank L. and Marguerite (Roussel) H.; m. Ann Lane, Jan. 3, 1948; children—Frank, Sarah, Robert. B.A., U. Va., 1943, Ph.D. in Physics, 1947; D.Sc., Fla. Inst. Tech., 1974; LL.D., Hampden-Sydney Coll., 1974. Physicist Bartol Research Found., Swarthmore, Pa., 1947-49; mem. faculty U. Va., 1949—, prof. physics, 1952—, dean, 1962-66, Robert C. Taylor prof. physics, 1966—, provost, v.p., 1966-71, pres., 1974—; Fulbright scholar U. Birmingham, Eng., 1957-58; vis. prof. U. St. Andrews, Scotland, 1971-72; dir. Gould, Inc., Rolling Meadows, Ill. Contbr. profl. jours. Bd. govs. Belfield Sch., Charlottesville, 1959-62, 63-65, chmn. bd., 1962; bd. dirs. St. Anne's Sch., Charlottesville, 1966-70; trustee Woodberry Forest Sch., 1968-74, Mariner's Mus., Newport News, Va., 1975—. Recipient Devel. award U.S. Navy Ordnance Dept., 1945; Horsley Research prize Va. Acad. Sci., 1953. Fellow Am. Phys. Soc. (chmn. Southeastern sect. 1961-62), Phi Beta Kappa, Sigma Xi, Omicron Delta Kappa, Alpha Tau Omega. Home: Carr's Hill Charlottesville VA 22901

HERFINDAHL, LLOYD MANFORD, painter; b. Emmons, Minn., June 15, 1922; s. Albert and Betsy (Singlestad) H. Student, Mpls. Coll. Art and Design, 1952; pupil of, Adolph Dehn, also student in. Co-pres. Internat. Grand Prix Painting Palm D'Or Des Beaux Arts, Palais de la Scala, Monte Carlo, Monaco, 1968; internat. cultural counselor Internat. Arts Guild, Monte Carlo, 1968; fgn. corr. Internat. Arts Bull., Monte Carlo, 1970-75; art dir. Lutheran Sentinel, 1966-69; fgn. corr. Minn. Arts Assn., 1974-77; chief dir. U.S.A. N.Y. exhbn. Festival Internat. de St-Germain-des-Pres, 1978; art cons. Boy Scouts Am., 1964. Exhbns. include, Salon des Independents, Grand Palais, Paris, 1972, Soc. Acad. Des Arts Liberaux, Paris, Bertrand Russell Peace

Found. Centenary, London, Festival Internat. St. Germain, Burssels, 1973, Festival Internat. St. Germain, Paris, 1974-75, Mus. Modern Art, Paris, 1974, Holyland Mus., Los Angeles, Salon de l'Ecole de Thouet, Thovars, France, 1973, Luxembourg Palace, 1978, Ukrainian Inst. Am.; rep. permanent collection, Montbard (France) Mus. Fine Art, 1974. Chmn. ARC disaster com., Freeborn County and Albert Lea, Minn., 1966. Named Hon. Citizen of Mpls. for mural Guardians of Our Freedoms, 1976; commd. portrait King Olave V of Norway for Norse Heritage Series, 1968; decorated Order du Chevalier Belgio-Hispanica, Paris, 1974; named personal délèqué Vallobra de Grandry and Ehvoye Extra-ordinair, Belgium, 1978; recipient Queen Fabiola Gold medal Belgio-Hispanica, Belgium, 1973; Silver medal Soc. d'Encoyragement au Proges, Paris, 1974; Grand Prix de Humanitaire de France, 1975; Paris Critique Palm of Gold Acad. des Arts, Paris, 1975; Raymond and Isadora Duncan medal, 1978. Hon. mem. Minn. Artists Assn.; mem. Assn. Belgio-Hispanique, Soc. d'Encouragement au Progres, Internat. Arts Guild, Grand Prix Humanitair, Sons of Norway. Lutheran. Club: Kiwanis Day-Breakers (Albert Lea) (hon.). Address: 809 John Farry Pl Albert Lea MN 56007

HERGE, HENRY CURTIS, SR., retired educator; b. Bklyn., June 29, 1905; s. Rev. Henry John and Theresa (Maaz) H.; m. Josephine E. Breen, July 2, 1931 (dec. Oct. 8, 1975); children: Joel Curtis, Henry Curtis; m. Alice V. Wolfram, Apr. 21, 1976. B.S., NYU, 1929, M.A., 1931, Ed.D., 1942; M.A. (hon.), Wesleyan U., 1946; Ph.D., Yale U., 1956. Instr. English, Sr. High Sch., Port Washington, N.Y., 1928-38; dist. prin., Bayville, N.Y., 1938-41, Bellmore, N.Y., 1941-45; asst. dir. study on Armed Services edn. programs Am. Council Edn., Washington., 1945-46; dir. higher edn., tchr. edn. cert. Conn. Dept. Edn., 1946-53; dean, prof. edn. Rutgers U., 1953-64, prof. edn., 1964-75, asso. dir. Center for Internat. Programs, 1968-75; vis. prof. Hartford U., 1950-52, Fairfield U., 1950-53, U. So. Calif., summer 1964, NYU, 1964-65; del. White House Conf. Edn., 1957; edn. cons. USOM Asuncion and ICA dir. ednl. priorities study for ministry of edn., Paraguay, 1961; team leader Rutgers-U.S. AID field survey, Zambia and Malawi, 1961-62; chief human resource devel. officer U.S. AID, Jamaica, 1966-68; Fulbright rapporteur Seminar in Univ. Adminstrn., U.S. and Italy, 1970; OAS sr. research fellow, Paraguay and Jamaica, 1972-73. Author: Wartime College Training Programs of Armed Services, 1948, The College Teacher, 1966; editor: Disarmament in the Western World, 1968, Common Concerns in Higher Education: An Italian-American Universities Project, Phase I, 1970; contbr. numerous articles to profl. publs. Past pres. troop com. Boy Scouts; v.p. Parents Assn. Rutgers Coll.; pres. Shadow Lake Assn., Vt., 1976-78; sec. Fed. Lake Assns., No. Vt., 1980—; project dir. Hilton Head Plantation Public Forum for Humanities, 1980-81; chmn. bd. trustees Coll. Hilton Head (S.C.), 1984—. Served as comdg. officer Wesleyan U. Navy V-12 unit, 1943-45; lt. comdr. USNR (Ret.). Recipient certificate of recognition NCCJ, 1958. Mem. Nat. Assn. State Dirs. Tchr. Edn. and Certification (past pres.), Nat. Soc. for Study Edn., N.J. Congress Parents and Tchrs. (hon. life), N.J. Secondary Sch. Tchrs. Assn. (trustee 1954-66, merit award 1966), Am. Assn. Higher Edn., N.J. Council on Edn., N.J. Schoolmasters Club, AAUP, Naval Res. Assn. (life), Phi Delta Kappa (emeritus), Epsilon Pi Tau (laureate trustee), Kappa Delta Pi (Compatriot in Edn. award 1976). Republican. Presbyterian. Home: 39 Pineland Rd Hilton Head Island SC 29928 *"Educators must be optimistic because they have cast their lot with the rising generation—the generation of hope and expectation, the generation which will transform the problems of the present into the opportunities and accomplishments of the future."*

HERGE, J. CURTIS, lawyer; b. Flushing, N.Y., June 14, 1938; s. Henry Curtis and Josephine E. (Breen) H.; m. Joyce Dorean Humbert, Aug. 20, 1960; children: Cynthia Lynda, Christopher Curtis. Student, Cornell U., 1956-58; B.A., Rutgers U., 1961, J.D. (Sebastian Gaeta scholar), 1963. Bar: N.Y. 1964, U.S. Supreme Ct. 1970, U.S. Ct. Claims 1974, D.C. 1974, Va. 1976. Assoc. firm Mudge Rose Guthrie & Alexander, N.Y.C., 1963-71; spl. asst. to atty. gen. U.S. Dept. Justice, Washington, 1973; asso. solicitor conservation and wildlife U.S. Dept. Interior, Washington, 1973-74, asst. to sec. and chief staff, 1974-76; partner Sedam & Herge, McLean, Va., 1976—; dir. Diversified Labs., Inc., Ann E.W. Stone & Assocs., Inc., Job Sharers, Inc.; dir., sec. Conservative Computer Services, Inc., 1981—; dir. Villaggio Italia, Inc., 1967-74, pres., 1971-74; sec., dir. David Rhodes Co., Inc., 1967-73, Artists Workshop, Inc., 1965-69, Am. Mgmt. and Devel. Corp., 1978-82; dir. Palmer Tech. Services, Inc., Eaton Design Group, Inc., Savant Press, Inc.; mem. adv. bd. The Palmer Nat. Bank. Contbr. articles to profl. jours. Asst. sec., asst. treas. Royal Soc. Medicine Found., 1969-73; asst. sec. Accion Internat., 1969-72; co-chmn. N.Y. Honor Am. Day Com., 1970; chmn. Council for Nat. Def., Inc., 1977-79; asst. sec. Found. for Def. Analysis, 1978-83; sec. Nat. Conservative Polit. Action Com., 1978—, Nat. Pvt. Bus. Polit. Fund, 1980—; bd. dirs., sec.-treas. Nat. Coalition for Less Govt., 1978-80; mem. adv. bd. Washington Legal Found., 1978—, Western Legal Found., Nat. Taxpayers Legal Fund, 1978—, Lozanov Ednl. Research Found., 1979—; bd. dirs., sec., treas. Citizens United Found., 1980—; bd. dirs., sec. Am. Lobby Econ. Recovery Task Force, 1982—; Va. Commonwealth escheator Loudoun County City of Fairfax, 1979-83; co-dir. Presdl. Inaugural Com., 1973; dep. dir. spokesmen resources Com. for Reelection of Pres., 1971-72; mem. natural resources council Republican Nat. Com.; mem. Fairfax County Rep. Com.; bd. dirs. Citizens United for Am., 1979—; mem. Office Pres.-Elect Fed. Election Commn. Transition Team, 1980. Mem. Am., N.Y. State, Va., D.C. bar assns., Phi Kappa Sigma. Club: Capitol Hill. Home: 1102 Waynewood Blvd Alexandria VA 22308 Office: Sedam & Herge 8300 Greensboro Dr McLean VA 22102

HERGENHAN, JOYCE, utilities executive; b. Mt. Kisco, N.Y., Dec. 30, 1941; d. John Christopher and Goldie (Wago) H. B.A., Syracuse U., 1963; M.B.A., Columbia U., 1978. Reporter White Plains Reporter Dispatch, 1963-64; asst. to Rep. Ogden R. Reid, Washington, 1964-68; reporter Westchester Rockland Newspapers, 1968-72; with Consol. Edison Co. of N.Y., Inc., N.Y.C., 1972—, v.p., 1977—, exec. asst. to chmn. bd., 1978, sr. v.p. pub. affairs, 1979—. Home: 201 E 79th St New York NY 10021 Office: Consolidated Edison Co of New York Inc 4 Irving Pl New York NY 10003

HERGENRATHER, EDMUND RICHARD, exec. recruiting cons.; b. Troy, Ohio, Aug. 20, 1917; s. Harry F. and Mellie S. (Gillespie) H.; m. Kathryn Monson, Dec. 7, 1941; children—John M., Jeffrey Y., Richard A., Holly Kay. B.S. in Econs, Iowa State U., 1940; postgrad., U. Chgo., 1940-42. Asst. mgr. Chgo. YMCA Hotel, 1940-42; cons. Booz, Allen & Hamilton, 1942-46; mfrs. rep. Leekley-Hergenrather, Los Angeles, 1946-49; asso. prof. alumni devel. Iowa State U., 1949-53; sales mgr. Miller Desk & Safe Co., Los Angeles, 1953-54; founder, pres. Hergenrather & Co. (exec. recruiting cons.), Los Angeles, 1954—; dir. Direction Sports. Trustee San Francisco Theol. Sem.; bd. govs. Iowa State U. Found.; mem. exec. com. Los Angeles Area council Boy Scouts Am. Mem. Sigma Chi. Presbyterian (elder). Clubs: Los Angeles, Rotary, Alisal Golf. Office: 3435 Wilshire Blvd Los Angeles CA 90010

HERING, ANTHONY JOSEPH, beverage company executive; b. Phila., Oct. 27, 1931; s. Anthony Joseph and Beatrice (Finnegan) H.; m. Ann Miller, Jan. 14, 1956; children: Anthony Joseph III, William, Daniel. B.S. in Acctg., La Salle Coll., Phila., 1953. C.P.A. Staff acct. Lybrands, Columbus, Ohio, 1955-62; controller BMI, Columbus, 1962-70; sr. v.p., treas. Allegheny Beverage Corp., Cheverly, Md., 1970—. Served with U.S. Army, 1953-55. Republican. Roman Catholic. Home: 514 Heavitree Garth Severna Park MD 21146 Office: Allegheny Beverage Corp Macke Circle Cheverly MD 21146

HERING, ANTHONY JOSEPH, JR., beverage company executive; b. Phila., Oct. 27, 1931; s. Anthony Joseph and Beatrice Elizabeth (Finnegan) H.; m. Ann Miller, Jan. 14, 1956; children: Anthony Joseph III, William, Daniel. B.S., LaSalle Coll., 1953. Staff accountant Cooper's Lybrand (C.P.A.s), Columbus, Ohio, 1955-62; comptroller Beverage Mgmt. Inc., Columbus, 1962-69; sr. v.p., treas. Allegheny Beverage Corp., Balt., 1970—. Served with AUS, 1953-55. Mem. Ohio Soc. C.P.A.s, Am. Inst. C.P.A.s, Nat. Acctg. Assn. Club: KC. Home: Severna Park MD 21146 Office: Macke Circle Cheverly MD 20781

HERING, DORIS MINNIE, arts adminstr., critic; b. N.Y.C., Apr. 11, 1920; d. Harry and Anna Elizabeth (Schwenk) H. B.A. cum laude, Hunter Coll., 1941; M.A., Fordham U. Free-lance dance writer, 1946-52; asso. editor, prin. critic Dance mag., N.Y.C., 1952-72; exec. dir. Nat. Assn. for Regional Ballet, N.Y.C., 1972—; adj. asso. prof. dance history N.Y. U., 1968-78; Mem. dance panel Nat. Endowment for Arts, 1972-75; mem. adv. panel Riverside Dance Festival, N.Y.C., 1981—; bd. dirs. Walnut Hill Sch., 1975—, Internat. Ballet Competition, 1981—; hon. bd. dirs. Phila. Dance Alliance, 1980—. Author: 25 Years of American Dance, 1950, Dance in America, 1951, Wild Grass, 1965, Giselle and Albrecht, 1981. Mem. Nat. Assn. for Regional Ballet, Dance Critics Assn., Phi Beta Kappa, Chi Tau Epsilon (hon.). Home: 140 W 79th St New York NY 10024 Office: 1860 Broadway New York NY 10023

HERING, GUNTHER ERWIN, international engineering, construction and natural resources company executive; b. Munich, Germany, Sept. 22, 1936; came to U.S., 1962; s. Erwin and Wera (Binder) H.; m. Jan T. Turner, Dec. 2, 1978; 1 son, John Gunther. M.B.A., U. Hamburg, Germany, 1959. Mgr. mktg. Dexter Co., Pearl River, N.Y., 1962-67; dir. mktg. Europe Hull Corp., Hatboro, Pa., 1967-68; v.p., gen. mgr. Schuler Bros., Bergenfield, N.J., 1968-71; sr. cons. McKinsey & Co., N.Y.C., 1971-75; v.p. corp. devel. Fluor Corp., Irvine, Calif., 1975—. Knight Johanniter Orden, Bonn, Germany, 1978—; mem. Ven. Order of St. John, London, 1982; dir. Orange County Health Planning Council, Tustin, Calif., 1979-82; com. mem. 552 Club Hoag Meml. Hosp., Newport Beach, Calif., 1983. Mem. Planning Execs. Council, Conf. Bd., Assn. Corp. Growth. Clubs: Lahaina Yacht, Big Canyon Country. Home: 62 Royal St George Rd Newport Beach CA 92660 Office: Fluor Corp 3333 Michelson Dr Irvine CA 92730

HERING, ROBERT GUSTAVE, mech. engr., educator, univ. adminstr.; b. Chgo., Feb. 18, 1934; s. Gustave and Mathilda (Horn) H.; m. Joan Myrna Basil, June 2, 1956; children—Deborah Joan, Cynthia Jean, Kathleen Jane, Robert William. B.S.M.E., U. Ill., 1956; M.S.M.E., U. So. Calif., 1958; Ph.D. in Mech. Engring, Purdue U., 1961. Research asst. Armour Research Found., 1956; mem. tech. staff Hughes Research and Devel. Lab., 1956-59; supr. heat transfer group Allison div. Gen. Motors Corp., 1960-61; asst. prof. mech. engring. U. Ill., 1961-64, asso. prof., 1964-68, prof., 1968-71; prof., chmn. dept. mech. engring. U. Iowa, Iowa City, 1971-72; acting dean Coll. Engring., 1972-73, dean, 1973—; cons. Hughes Research and Devel. Lab., Jet Propulsion Lab., Caterpillar Tractor Co.; mem. Iowa Hwy. Research Bd., 1972—, chmn., 1978; vis. prof. Hokkaido U., Japan, 1978. Contbr. articles to profl. jours. Fulbright-Hayes research scholar U. Stuttgart, W. Ger., 1980-81. Mem. ASME, AIAA, Am. Soc. Engring. Edn., Optical Soc. Am., Iowa Engring. Soc., Sigma Xi, Tau Beta Pi, Pi Tau Sigma. Lutheran. Home: 1415 Cedar Iowa City IA 52240 Office: 3102 Engring Bldg Iowa City IA 52242

HERINGER, LESTER S., food company executive. Chmn. Calif. Canners & Growers, San Francisco. Office: Calif. Canners & Growers 3100 Ferry Bldg San Francisco CA 94106§

HERKNESS, LINDSAY COATES, III, securities broker; b. N.Y.C., Feb. 8, 1943; s. Lindsay C. and Harriett (Richard) H. B.A., Trinity Coll., Hartford, Conn., 1965. With Reynolds Securities, Inc. (merged with Dean Witter & Co. 1978), N.Y.C., 1965-78; sr. v.p. investments Dean Witter Reynolds, Inc., N.Y.C., 1978—. Bd. dirs. Manhattan Eye, Ear and Throat Hosp. Clubs: Union, Downtown Assn. (N.Y.C.); Rockaway Hunting; Piping Rock (Locust Valley, N.Y.); Bath and Tennis (Palm Beach, Fla.). Office: Dean Witter Reynolds Inc Five World Trade Center New York NY 10048

HERLEMAN, WILLIAM NICHOLAS, ret. mfr. mus. instruments and vending machines; b. Quincy, Ill., Jan. 29, 1924; s. Russell D. and Ruth (Kiem) H.; m. Terry Fey, Aug. 20, 1950; children—Christine, Cynthia, Charles William. B.S. with honors, U. Ill., 1948. Asst. to gen. mgr. W.W. Kimball Co., 1948-52; sales mgr. electronics div. Central Comml. Co., 1952-56; with Wurlitzer Co., Chgo., 1956-81, v.p., mgr., 1960-61, exec. v.p., 1961-67, pres., 1967-78, chmn. bd., pres., 1978-81; dir. 1st Savs. & Loan Sycamore, Ill. Trustee Sigma Chi Found.; mem. exec. adv. bd. Sch. Bus., No. Ill. U., DeKalb. Mem. U. Ill. Alumni Assn. (dir.), Internat. Platform Assn., Beta Gamma Sigma, Phi Kappa Phi, Sigma Chi (Significant Sig award 1973). Home: 116 W Lincoln St Sycamore IL 60178 Office: Wurlitzer Co 403 E Gurler Rd Dekalb IL 60115

HERLIHY, DAVID JOSEPH, history educator; b. San Francisco, May 8, 1930; s. Maurice Peter and Irene (O'Connor) H.; m. Patricia McGahey, June 4, 1952; children: Maurice, Christopher, David, Felix, Gregory, Irene. B.A., U. San Francisco, 1952; M.A., Cath. U. Am., 1953; Ph.D., Yale U., 1956. Asst. prof., then asso. prof. history Bryn Mawr Coll., 1955-64; prof. history U. Wis., 1964-72, Harvard U., 1972—, Henry Charles Lea prof., 1979—, master Mather House, 1976—; lectr. other univs. Author: Medieval and Renaissance Pistoia, 1967, Pisa in the Early Renaissance, 1957, (with Christiane Klapisch) Les Toscans et leurs familles, 1978; also articles. Fulbright fellow, 1954-55; Guggenheim fellow, 1961-62; fellow Am. Council Learned Socs., 1966-67, Center for Advanced Study in Behavorial Scis., 1972-73, NEH, 1977. Fellow Mediaeval Acad. Am. (pres. 1981-82); mem. Am. Hist. Assn., Am. Cath. Hist. Assn. (pres. 1971-72), Midwest Mediaeval Conf. (pres. 1971-72), Soc. Italian Hist. Studies (pres. 1981-83). Home: Master's Residence Mather House Harvard Univ Cambridge MA 02138

HERLIHY, FRANCIS BOND, indsl. exec.; b. Methuen, Mass., Nov. 20, 1921; s. Frank Joseph and Anne C. (Cronin) H.; m. Marion von Burchard Herlihy, 1972; children—David Michael, Patricia Anne, Mark Francis. Grad., Boston Latin Sch.; B.S. in Metallurgy, Mass. Inst. Tech., 1942. Metallurgist ABEX Corp., Mahwah, N.J., 1945-57, dir. research, 1957-65, v.p., N.Y.C., 1965—, also dir.; dir. Lloyds-Burton, Ltd., Lloyds-Abex Ltd., Burton, Eng. Served to maj. AUS, 1942-46. Mem. Am., Brit. iron and steel insts., Inst. Metals (London). Home: 150 E 69th St Apt 17P New York NY 10021 Office: ABEX Corp 530 Fifth Ave New York NY 10036

HERLIHY, HORACE MURRAY, educator; b. Coleman, P.E.I., Can., Feb. 1, 1917; s. James Alexander and Minnie (MacPhee) H.; m. Doreen Alice Hosford, Aug. 5, 1942. B.A., U. Alta., 1948; M.A. in Econs, U. Chgo., 1950, Ph.D., 1954. Staff economist Joint Congl. Commn. on R.R. Retirement, Washington, 1952-53; lectr. St. Xavier Coll., 1953; asst. prof. Valparaiso U., 1954-55, Mich. State U., 1955-57; asso. prof. Lake Forest (Ill.) Coll., 1957-61, prof., 1961—, chmn. econs. dept., 1960-77, acting dir., 1978; Chmn. Gov.'s Commn. on Manpower Utilization, 1965-67; impartial chmn. pension commn. Fansteel Metall. Corp., 1958-61; ednl. TV lectr. Channels 11, 2, 7, Chgo., 1962-64; mem. faculty adv. com. Ill. Bd. Higher Edn., 1972-75. Contbg. author: Am. Educator Ency, 1963—. Mem. Internat. Relations Library, 1965—; mem. pres.'s council Rosary Coll., River Forest, Ill., 1970—; pres., chmn. bd. mgrs. Malibu Condominium Assn., 1972-73; cons. nursing resource needs to nursing div. HEW, 1977. Served with Royal Canadian Corps of Signals, 1940-45. Mem. Am. Econ. Assn., Indsl. Relations Research Assn., Am. Assn. U. Profs. (chpt. pres. 1962-63, 79-80), Phi Delta Theta. Democrat. Club: Quadrangle (Chgo.). Home: 6007 Sheridan Rd Chicago IL 60660 Office: Econs Dept Lake Forest Coll Lake Forest IL 60045

HERLIHY, JAMES EDWARD, retail food company executive; b. Englewood, N.J., Dec. 29, 1942; s. James Edward and Agnes Cecilia (McNeil) H.; m. Sidonia Lewnicka, Dec. 8, 1973; 1 dau., Courtney; 1 dau. by previous marriage, Kimberly Ann. B.S. in Acctg., Fairleigh Dickinson U., 1965. Sr. mgr. Allied Suppliers Ltd., London, 1979-80; v.p., controller Grand Union Co., Paramus, N.J., 1980-83, sr. v.p. and chief fin. officer, 1983—; dir. Grand Union, Paramus, N.J., Cavenham Inc, USA. Mem. Am. Inst. C.P.A.s, N.J. State Soc. C.P.A.s, Fin. Execs. Inst., N.J. Food Council. Home: 1600 Parker Ave Apt 22C Fort Lee NJ 07024 Office: Grand Union Co 100 Broadway Elmwood Park NJ 07407

HERLIHY, JAMES LEO, playwright, novelist; b. Detroit, Feb. 27, 1927; s. William Francis and Grace (Oberer) H. Student, Black Mountain Coll., 1947-48, Pasadena Playhouse, 1948-50; RCA fellow, Yale Drama Sch., 1956-57. Author: (with William Noble) play Blue Denim, 1957; motion picture, 1959; play Crazy October, 1958, The Sleep of Baby Filbertson and other stories, 1959; novel All Fall Down, 1960; motion picture, 1961, Midnight Cowboy, 1965, 1969, A Story That Ends With a Scream, and Eight Others, 1967; play Stop, You're Killing Me, 1970; novel The Season of the Witch, 1971; starred in: prodn. of The Zoo Story, Paris, 1963; actor in: film Four Friends, 1982. Served with USNR, 1945-46. Address: care Jay Garon 415 Central Park W New York NY 10025 *

HERLING, JOHN, newspaperman; b. N.Y.C., Apr. 16, 1907; s. Morris and Mollie (Konrad) H.; m. Mary Fox, Sept. 16, 1937 (dec. Nov. 1978); 1 stepson, David Fox Stolberg.; m. Alice Dodge Wolfson, Jan. 24, 1982; 3 stepsons. A.B., Harvard, 1928. Publ. sec., also exec. sec. Emergency Com. Strikers Relief of League Indsl. Democracy, 1930-34; asst. editor United Features Syndicate, 1935; Washington corr. Milw. Leader, also other papers, 1936-37; mem. Washington staff Time Inc., 1937; publicity dir. March of Time, 1937-38; dir. Childrens Crusade for Children, 1939-40; asst. sec. New Sch. Social Research, 1940-41; dir. labor and social relations div. Office Inter-Am. Affairs, 1941-46; spl. corr. in Europe for Newspapers, 1946; editor, pub. John Herling's Labor Letter, 1947—; syndicated columnist labor and gen. affairs; lectr. abroad labor affairs for State Dept., 1956, 60, 63, 65. Author: Great Price Conspiracy, 1962, Labor Unions in America, 1964, Right to Challenge, 1972; Contbr. magazines. Recipient Journalist award Wash. Newspaper Guild, 1962, 64; Norman Thomas-Eugene V. Debs award, 1978. Mem. Am. Polit. Sci. Assn., Am. Hist. Soc., Council Fgn. Relations, Authors Guild, Indsl. Relations Research Assn. (pres. Washington chpt. 1955), White House and Congl. Corrs. Assn., Sigma Delta Chi. Clubs: Nat. Press, Overseas Writers, Federal City, Harvard (Washington); Silurians (N.Y.C.). Home: 6504 E Halbert Rd Bethesda MD 20817 Office: 1411 K St NW Washington DC 20005

HERMACH, FRANCIS LEWIS, cons. engr.; b. Bridgeport, Conn., Jan. 8, 1917; s. Frank and Barbara (Dauenheimer) H.; m. Frances M. Roberts, June 22, 1940; children—George, William (dec.). B.E.E., George Washington U., 1943. Sci. aid Nat. Bur. Standards, Washington, 1939-42; elec. engr., 1942-63, chief elec. instruments sect., 1963-72, dep. chief electricity div., 1970-72, cons., 1972-76; cons. engr. Elec. Measurements, Silver Spring, Md., 1976—. Contbr. articles on elec. measurements to profl. jours. Served with USNR, 1945-46. Recipient Distinguished service award Dept. Commerce, 1954; Morris E. Leeds award IEEE, 1976. Fellow IEEE, Instrument Soc. Am., Washington Acad. Scis.; mem. Precision Measurements Soc., Philos. Soc. Washington. Methodist. Patentee in field. Home: 2415 Eccleston St Silver Spring MD 20902

HERMAN, ABE MITCHELL, lawyer; b. Ft. Worth, July 14, 1905; s. David Sam and Rose (Waxman) H.; m. Sarah Foreman, Oct. 29, 1933; children—Donald Sidney, Morton Lee. J.D., U. Tex., Austin, 1927. Bar: Tex. bar 1927. Since practiced in, Ft. Worth; sr. mem. firm Brown, Herman, Scott, Dean & Miles, 1927—; participant Duolopy hearings FCC, 1940-45; lectr. Southwestern Legal Found., Bur. Nat. Affairs; former dir. 1st Nat. Bank Ft. Worth. Treas. Clear Channel Broadcasting Service, 1965—; Gen. counsel Amon G. Carter Found., Joseph R. White Lecture Found., Carter Blood Center; adv. dir. Tex. Coll. Osteo. Hosp.; bd. dirs. Harris Hosp., St. Joseph Hosp., Ft. Worth Osteo. Hosp., United Fund and Goodwill of Am.; pres. Ft. Worth Childrens Hosp. Recipient Wisdow award of Honor, Distinguished Service to Journalism award Soc. Profl. Journalists. Mem. ABA (chmn. radio sect.), FCC Bar Assn., Tex. Bar Assn. (co-chmn. pub. relations com.), Ft. Worth-Tarrant County Bar Assn., Assn. Maximum Service Telecasters, Ft. Worth Squadron Assn., Tau Delta Phi. Clubs: Mason (Shriner), Fort Worth, Ridglea Country, Admirals (Ft. Worth). Home: 3308 Tanglewood Trail Fort Worth TX 76109 Office: Ft Worth Club Bldg Fort Worth TX 76102

HERMAN, CHARLES ROBERT, opera association executive; b. Glendale, Calif., Feb. 24, 1925; s. Floyd Caves and Anna (Merriken) H. A.B. in German summa cum laude, U. So. Calif., 1949. Asst. to head opera dept. U. So. Calif., Los Angeles, 1949-53; asst. mgr., artistic adminstr. Met. Opera, N.Y.C., 1953-72; gen. mgr. Greater Miami (Fla.) Opera Assn., 1973—; exec. dir. New World Festival, Inc., Miami, 1980-82. Served with U.S. Army, 1944-46; lt. col. Res. ret. Decorated Army Commendation medal; cavaliere Order of Merit, Italy; officers cross Order of Merit, W.Ger.; Austrian Honor Cross for Sci. and Art 1st class. Mem. Dade County Cultural Execs. Council, OPERA Am. (pres.). Home: 3441 Poinciana Ave Coconut Grove FL 33133 Office: 1200 Coral Way Miami FL 33145

HERMAN, DAVID THEODORE, educator; b. Chgo., Apr. 1, 1916; s. William and Cecelia (Cohen) H.; m. Evelyn A. Swartz, Jan. 29, 1967; 1 dau. (by previous marriage), Deborah Ann. B.A. with honors, Ind. U., 1940; M.A. in Speech Pathology, 1942; Ph.D. in Psychology, 1947. Instr. psychology Ind. U., 1945-47; asst. prof. La. State U., 1947-49; faculty Wichita State U., 1949—, prof. psychology, 1957—. Mem. Am. Psychol. Assn. Home: 2523 N Roosevelt Ct Wichita KS 67220

HERMAN, EDITH CAROL, public relations manager; b. Edgewood, Md., July 1, 1944; d. Herbert R. and Thirza E. (Simmons) H.; m. Leonard Wiener. B.A., Purdue U., 1966. Reporter Hollister Newspaper Chain, Wilmette, Ill., 1966-68; reporter Chgo. Tribune Newspaper, 1968-79, edn. editor, 1971-74, state reporter, 1974-75, feature writer, 1976-79; sr. editor TV Digest Inc., 1980-83; pub. relations mgr. Am.

Tel. & Tel., 1983—. Recipient Journalism award Ill. Edn. Assn., 1969-70; Editorial award Ill. Automatic Merchandising Council, 1977. Mem. Sigma Delta Chi. Home: 5501 Burling Ct Bethesda MD 20817 Office: 1000 Connecticut Ave NW Washington DC 20036

HERMAN, GEORGE EDWARD, radio-TV correspondent; b. N.Y.C., Jan. 14, 1920; s. Sydney H. and Tessie Samuels (Dryfoos) H.; m. Patricia Kerwin, Feb. 19, 1955; children—Charles, Scott, R. Douglas. A.B. cum laude, Dartmouth Coll., 1941; M.S., Columbia U., 1942. Night news editor radio sta. WQXR, N.Y.C., 1942-44; joined CBS, 1944, bur. mgr., Tokyo, Japan, 1950-53, Washington corr., 1954—; moderator Face the Nation, 1969-84; also lectr. Contbr. articles to mags. Mem. Overseas Writers Assn., Am. Automobile Assn., AAAS, AFTRA (v.p. 1970-78). Clubs: Overseas Press, Press (Tokyo); Washington Press. Address: 3115 O St NW Washington DC 20007

HERMAN, HAROLD WILCOX, mgmt. cons.; b. Kodaikanal, India, May 22, 1913; s. Harold C. and Winifred (Wilcox) H.; m. Georga Fern Burk, July 6, 1939; 1 dau., Haleen Louise. A.B., Carleton Coll., 1935. Asst. membership sec. Dayton (Ohio) YMCA, 1935, publicity dir., 1936-41; publs. sec. U.S. Jr. C. of C., 1941-44, exec. v.p., 1944-45; mng. editor Coll. and Univ. Bus., 1945-51, editor, 1952-68; v.p. Corco, Inc., Chgo., 1969, Vector Co., 1970; sr. editor Field Enterprises Ednl. Corp., Chgo., 1971-72; asst. to adminstr. Plymouth Place, Inc., La Grange Park, Ill., 1973; v.p. mktg. Exertia, Inc., mgmt. cons. for phys. plant ops. sch. dists., colls., univs. and hosps., Park Ridge, Ill., 1973—; Faculty mem. coll. bus. mgmt. workshop U. Omaha, U. Cal. Contbr. coll. mags. Mem. family welfare rev. com. Community Fund Chgo.; pres. Oak Park Community Lectures, 1973-79; Trustee Village of Oak Park, Ill., 1969-73; bd. assos. Chgo. Theol. Sem.; bd. dirs. Med. Center YMCA, Bensenville (Ill.) Home Soc. Served with USCGR, 1943-45. Recipient Jesse H. Neal editorial achievement award Am. Bus. Press, Inc., 1965. Fellow A.I.M.; mem. Irving Soc. (past pres.), Carleton Coll. Alumni Assn. Ill. (past pres.), Sigma Delta Chi. Conglist. (former chmn. Bd. World Service; chmn. bd. trustees). Club: Headline, Chicago Press (Chgo.). Home: 641 N Grove Ave Oak Park IL 60302 Office: 819 Busse Hwy Park Ridge IL 60068

HERMAN, HERBERT, materials science educator; b. N.Y.C., June 15, 1934; s. Samuel and Frances (Friedman) H.; m. Barbara R. Budin, July 1, 1963; 1 son, Daniel. B.S., DePaul U., 1956; M.S., Northwestern U., 1958, Ph.D., 1961. Fulbright scholar U. Paris, 1961-62, Argonne Nat. Lab., 1962-63; asst. prof. U. Pa., 1963-68, Ford Found. prof. in industry, 1967-68; prof., chmn. dept. materials sci. SUNY, Stony Brook, 1968—; liaison scientist U.S. Office Naval Research, London, 1975-76; mem. and chmn. NRC panels, 1978-81; indsl. cons. Editor-in-chief: Treatise on Materials Science and Technology, 1972—, (Materials Sci. and Engring., internat. jour.); co-editor: series Ocean Technology, 1976—; contbr. articles to profl. jours. NSF grantee, 1964-69, 78—; AEC grantee, 1968-74; Office Naval Research grantee, 1974—; NASA grantee, 1980—; also others. Mem. AIME, Am. Soc. Metals, Am. Phys. Soc., Am. Ceramic Soc., Am. Crystallogrphic Soc., Marine Tech. Soc. (chmn. marine materials com.), Am. Soc. Engring. Edn., AAAS, Sigma Xi. Office: Dept Materials Sci State U NY Stony Brook NY 11794

HERMAN, JAMES RICHARD, union executive; b. Newark, Aug. 21, 1924; s. Milton Matthew and Larraine Catherine (Kelly) H. Student public schs., N.J. Pres. Internat. Longshoremen's and Warehousemen's Union, San Francisco, 1977—. Bd. dirs. Delancey St. Found., St. Anthony's Dining Rm., Columbia Pk. Boys Club; mem. Dem. State Central Com., Calif. Named Labor Man of Yr. Alameda County Central Labor Council, 1973. Mem. Maritime Inst. for Research and Indusl. Devel. (dir.). Democrat. Roman Catholic. Club: Concordia. Office: 1188 Franklin St San Francisco CA 94109 *

HERMAN, JERRY, composer-lyricist; b. N.Y.C., July 10; s. Harry and Ruth (Sachs) H. B.A., U. Miami, 1953. Composer-lyricist: I Feel Wonderful, 1955, Nightcap, 1958, Parade, 1960, Milk and Honey, 1961, Hello Dolly, 1964, La Cage aux Folles (Tony award for Best Score 1984); also film Hello Dolly, 1970; Mame, 1966, also film, 1974; Dear World, 1969, Mack and Mabel, 1974, The Grand Tour, 1979; play La Cage aux Folles, 1983; wrote: Pres. Lyndon B. Johnson's campaign song Hello, Lyndon, 1964. Recipient Tony award for Hello, Dolly, 1965, Variety Poll award for best music and lyrics, 1965, Grammy award for best song, 1964, WPAT award for best song, Shalom, 1961, Radio-TV All Am. award best song of year, Hello, Dolly, 1964, Variety poll award for best lyrics, Mame, 1966, Grammy award, 1967; Order Merit U. Miami, 1971. Address: care ASCAP One Lincoln Plaza New York NY 10023 *

HERMAN, KENNETH, psychologist; b. Englewood, N.J., Mar. 4, 1927; s. Joseph and Rose (Sattenstein) H.; m. Benita Saievetz, June 7, 1959; children: Michael Robert, Deborah Lynn, Joseph Todd, Rebecca Jane. A.B., Fla. So. Coll., 1950; M.Ed., Boston U., 1952; Ed.D., Columbia U., 1955, N.Y. U., 1956. Diplomate: Am. Bd. Clin. Psychology; cert. sex therapist. Research Bergen County Dept. Probation, Hackensack, N.J., 1948; investigator Child Welfare Home, Hackensack, 1948; psychometrist Student Clinic, Fla. So. Coll., Lakeland, 1948-50; clin. psychologist Mass. Gen. Hosp., Boston, 1951-54; research psychologist Med. Sch., Harvard, 1952-53; psychologist Speech Clinic, Boston U., 1952-53; research asst. State U. Iowa, 1954; founder Psychol. Service Center, Teaneck, N.J., 1955, dir., 1955—; dir. Reading Clinic, Child Study Center, 1965-66; chmn. bd., pres. Child Growth and Devel. Corp., 1969. Contbr. articles to profl. jours. Dir. Antipoverty Program, Garfield, N.J., 1965-66; bd. examiners Internat. Assn. Counseling Services, 1973-80; dir. Center Sexual and Relationship Enrichment, 1978—, Psycom Corp., 1980, 2d Self Discovery Program, 1980; cons. Hackensack Juvenile Counseling Program, 1974-76, N.Y. and N.J. Council of Chs., 1979—; participant radio and TV programs. Served with AUS, 1945-46. Mem. Am. Soc. Clin. Hypnosis, Soc. Clin. Exptl. Hypnosis, N.J. Personnel and Guidance Assn., Eastern Psychol. Assn., N.J. Clin. Psychologists, Nat. Council on Family Relations, Bergen County Sch. Psychologists Assn., Psychologists Interested in Advancement Psychotherapy, Am. Group Psychotherapy Assn., Psychologists Interested in Pvt. Practice, Am. Assn. Sex Educators, Counselors and Therapists, Nat. Vocat. Guidance Assn., Acad. Psychologist Marital Counseling, Am. Personnel and Guidance Assn., Am. Speech and Hearing Assn., N.J. Speech Assn., Tau Epsilon Phi, Kappa Delta Pi, Pi Gamma Mu, Omicron Delta Kappa. Home: 342 Orchard Rd Wyckoff NJ 07481 Office: 175 Cedar Lane Teaneck NJ 07666 *I am truly happiest when I am doing things for others—when presented with the chance to make the world better. In order to justify one's existence a thinking person must assume the responsibility for helping fellow human beings. I am thrilled that I can utilize my intellect and personality to achieve this aim. I cannot tolerate wasting time. A poor book, movie, or companion can only lead to boredom. I try to live each moment with the realization that time is truly a precious gift.*

HERMAN, KENNETH NEIL, journalist; b. Bklyn., May 20, 1954; s. David and Doris H.; m. Sharon Jayson.; 1 dau., Tracey Elise. A.A., Miami-Dade Community Coll., 1973; B.A., Fla. Atlantic U., 1975. Reporter Lufkin (Tex.) News, 1975-77; newsman Dallas bur. AP, 1977-78; AP corr., Harlingen, Tex., 1978-79, AP newsman, Austin, Tex., 1979—. Recipient Pulitzer Prize for Meritorious Pub. Service, 1977; Outstanding News Reporting award Nat. Headliners Club, 1977. Jewish. Home: 8104 Furness Cove Austin TX 78753 Office: PO Box 12247 Austin TX 78711

HERMAN, LAWRENCE, scientist, educator; b. N.Y.C., May 22, 1924; s. Bernard and Pauline (Gross) H.; m. Janice Helmer, Jan. 21, 1961; children—Glenn Eric, Bernard Peter. A.B., N.Y. U., 1947; M.A., Columbia U. Tchrs. Coll., 1948; Ph.D., U. Chgo., 1956. Instr. biology Olivet (Mich.) Coll., 1948-49; instr. Allegheny Coll., Meadville, Pa., 1949-51, Wilson Jr. Coll., Chgo., 1952-53, Wright Jr. Coll., 1953-55; teaching asst. zoology U. Chgo., 1955-56; research asso. electron microscopy, pathology dept. Cornell U., 1956-57; asst. prof. pathology SUNY, Downstate Med. Center, N.Y.C., 1957-62, asso. prof., 1962-68, prof., 1968-76; prof., chmn. dept. anatomy N.Y. Med. Coll., Valhalla, 1976—. USPHS fellow, 1968-69; Fulbright fellow, 1975-76; Fogarty Internat. scholar, 1978. Office: Dept Anatomy NY Med Coll Basic Science Bldg Valhalla NY 10595

HERMAN, MICHAEL EDWARD, pharm. co. exec.; b. N.Y.C., May 31, 1941; s. Harris Abraham and Sally (Ruzga) H.; m. Karen May Kuivinen, May 29, 1966; children—Jolyan Blake, Hamilton Brooks. B.Metall. Engring., Renaselaer Poly. Inst., Troy, N.Y., 1962; M.B.A., U. Chgo., 1964. Sr. bus. analyst W.R. Grace & Co., N.Y.C., 1964-66; asst. to pres., v.p. corp. devel. subs. Nuclear Fuel Service, Washington, 1966-68; v.p. Laird, Inc., N.Y.C., 1968-70; founding gen. partner Dryden & Co., N.Y.C., 1970-74; sr. v.p., chief fin. officer, mem. Office of Pres.; dir. Marion Labs., Inc., Kansas City, Mo., 1974—; dir. Janus Fund, Boatmen's Bank, Kansas City, Mo.; vis. lectr. Kansas U. Grad. Sch. Bus.; asso. prof. Rockhurst Coll. Grad. Sch. Bus. Mem. fin. steering com., trustee Kansas City Royals Baseball Club Profit Sharing Trust; mem. pension com. Maj. League Baseball Players Relations Com.; chmn. fund raising Sunset Hill Lower Sch., Kansas City, 1978. Mem. Assn. Corp. Growth, Pharm. Mfrs. Assn. (dir., mem. fin. steering com.), Fin. Analysts Fedn. Jewish. Clubs: Kansas City, N.Y. Athletic, Lake Quivira Country. Home: 310 Lake Shore E Lake Quivira KS 66106 Office: 9221 Bunker Ridge Rd Kansas City MO 64114

HERMAN, MORRIS, physician; b. N.Y.C., Oct. 3, 1906; s. Jacob and Bertha (Faber) H.; m. June O'Brien, Apr. 19, 1932 (div. May 1972); children: Joan (Mrs. John Lepik), Henry; m. Lucille P. Lake, June 1972 (div. July 1973). B.S., CCNY, 1926; M.D., N.Y. U., 1930. Diplomate: Am. Bd. Psychiatry and Neurology. Interne Bellevue Hosp., N.Y.C., 1930-32, psychiatrist, 1932- 40, asst. dir. psychiatry, 1941-48, vis. neurologist and psychiatrist, 1949—; instr. psychiatry N.Y. U., 1935-37; asst. clin. prof., 1938- 41, asst. prof., 1942-47, asso. prof., 1947-49, prof. clin. psychiatry, 1949-51, prof. psychiatry, 1951—, acting chmn. dept. psychiatry, 1969-76, prof. emeritus, 1979—; vis. psychiatrist U. Hosp., N.Y. U., 1950-69, asso. dir. psychiatry and neurology, 1969—, acting dir. psychiat. service, 1969-76; chmn. adv. com. to divs. psychiatry, psychology and neurology VA, Washington; cons. in psychiatry Cabrini Health Center, 1975—, Bellevue Hosp., 1976—; Mem. joint legis. com. to study narcotics problems N.Y. State; mem. adv. com. on alcoholism N.Y. State Interdepartmental Health Resources Bd.; mem. N.Y. State Mental Hygiene Med. Rev. Bd. Contbr. to med. publs. Chmn. internat. adv. bd. Kittay Sci. Found., 1972. Fellow N.Y. Acad. Medicine; mem. N.Y. Soc. Clin. Psychiatry (pres.), Am. Psychiat. Assn., Am. Neurol. Assn. Home: 10 Park Ave Apt 3D New York NY 10016 Office: 530 First Ave New York NY 10016

HERMAN, ROBERT, physicist, educator; b. N.Y.C., Aug. 29, 1914; s. Louis and Marie (Lozinsky) H.; m. Helen Pearl Keller, Nov. 24, 1939; children—Jane Barbara, Lois Ellen, Roberta Marie. B.S. cum laude, CCNY, 1935; M.A., Princeton U., 1940, Ph.D., 1940. Fellow physics dept. CCNY, 1935-36; research asst. Moore Sch. Elec. Engring., U. Pa., 1940-41; instr. physics CCNY, 1941-42; supr. chem. physics group, physicist, asst. to dir. Applied Physics Lab., John Hopkins U., 1942-55; vis. prof. physics U. Md., 1955-56; cons. physicist Gen. Motors Research Labs., Warren, Mich., 1956, asst. chmn. basic sci. group, 1956-59, dept. head theoretical physics dept., 1959-72, traffic sci. dept., 1972-79; prof. physics Center for Studies in Statis. Mechanics; L.P. Gilvin prof. civil engring. U. Tex., Austin, 1979—; Regents lectr. U. Calif., Santa Barbara, 1975; mem. Assembly Math. and Phys. Scis. NRC, 1977-80, mem. Commn. on Engring. and Tech. Systems, 1980—, mem. Com. on Resources for Math. Scis., 1981—; Smeed Meml. lectr. Univ. Coll. London, 1983; cons. in field. Assoc. editor: Revs. of Modern Physics, 1953-55, Ops. Research Soc. Am, 1960-74; founding editor: Transp. Sci, 1967-73; Author: (with Robert Hofstadter) High Energy Electron Scattering Tables, (with Ilya Prigogine) Kinetic Theory of Vehicular Traffic; Contbr. articles to profl. jours. Recipient numerous awards including Naval Ordnance Devel. award, 1945, Lanchester prize Johns Hopkins U. and Ops. Research Soc. Am., 1959, medal Université Libre de Bruxelles, 1963, Townsend Harris medal City Coll. N.Y., 1963, Magellanic Premium Am. Philos. Soc., 1975, Prix Georges Vanderlinden Belgian Royal Acad., 1975. Fellow Am. Phys. Soc., Washington Acad. Sci., Franklin Inst. (John Price Wetherill gold medal 1980); mem. Ops. Research Soc. Am. (George E. Kimball medal 1976, pres. 1980-81), Washington Philos. Soc., Assembly Math. and Phys. Sci., NRC, Nat. Acad. Engring., Am. Acad. Arts and Scis., Phi Beta Kappa, Sigma Xi. Research in vibration-rotation spectra and molecular structure, infrared spectroscopy, solid state physics, astrophysics and cosmology, theory of traffic flow, high energy electron scattering. Office: Dept Civil Engring U Tex Austin TX 78712

HERMAN, ROBERT DIXON, judge; b. Northumberland, Pa., Sept. 24, 1911; s. Chester B. and Esther (Maurer) H.; m. Lou C. Witmer (dec. Nov. 1959); m. Elizabeth Dunn DeWitt, Apr. 4, 1963; 4 children. A.B., Bucknell U., 1935; LL.B., Cornell U., 1938. Bar: Pa. bar 1938. Practiced law, 1938-58, asst. dist. atty., Dauphin County, Pa., 1942-44; mem. Pa. Gen. Assembly, 1948-50; Dauphin County solicitor, 1950-57; judge Dauphin County Cts. Common Pleas, 1958-70, Juvenile Ct., 1965-70, U.S. Dist. Ct. for Middle Pa., Harrisburg, 1970-81, sr. judge, 1981—. Former bd. mgrs. Harrisburg Area YMCA, Harrisburg Hosp.; former bd. dirs. Am. Cancer Soc. Served to lt. USNR, World War II. Mem. Am. Legion, VFW, Navy League (pres. Harrisburg council 1967-68, dir.), Harrisburg C. of C., Pa., Dauphin County bar assns., Nat. Lawyers Club (hon.). Mem. United Ch. Christ (trustee). Club: Mason (33 deg.). Office: Box 829 Federal Bldg Harrisburg PA 17108

HERMAN, ROBERT DUNTON, sociologist; b. Champaign, Ill., May 17, 1928; s. Abbott Phillip and Marjorie (Dunton) H.; m. Carol Baber, Sept. 10, 1951; children—David R., Molly E., Paul A. B.A., Pomona Coll., 1951; M.A., U. Wis., 1954, Ph.D., 1959. Instr. Iowa State U., 1955-58, asst. prof. sociology, 1958-60; asst. prof. Pomona Coll., 1960-65, asso. prof., 1965-74, prof., 1974—; cons. Nat. Endowment for Humanities. Author: Gamblers and Gambling, 1976; contbr. numerous articles to profl. jours.; editor: Gambling, 1967. Served with USN, 1946-48. Mem. Am. Sociol. Assn. Home: 357 W 10th St Claremont CA 91711 Office: Pomona Coll Claremont CA 91711

HERMAN, ROBERT S., former state official, educator; b. Newburgh, N.Y., Dec. 18, 1919; s. Bernard O. and Leona (Gottlieb) H.; m. Beatrice Hirsch, June 20, 1942; children: Gerald W., Arthur P. A.B., Union Coll., 1941; M.A., U. Cin., 1942; Ph.D., N.Y. U., 1950. Lectr. Syracuse U., 1947-60; vis. prof. Russell Sage Coll., 1948-57, State U. N.Y., 1960-62; vis. lectr. Econ. Devel. Inst., Washington, 1958-69; dir. research and fiscal policy div. budget N.Y. State Exec. Dept., Albany, 1950-63, dir. budget planning and devel., 1963, asst. budget dir., 1963-66; exec. dir. Commn. on Constl. Conv., 1966-67; exec. asst. to pres. N.Y. State Constl. Conv., 1967; dir. N.Y. Senate Com. on Higher Edn., 1968-72; prof. CUNY, 1968, SUNY, Albany, 1968-69, vis. prof., 1970—; prof. econs. and pub. adminstrn., chmn. dept. Union Coll., Schenectady, 1969-74; adviser N.Y. State Assembly, 1974—; chmn. Kennerman Assos., 1979—; cons. UN; former U.S. adviser to, Venezuela, Peru, India, Greece, Ecuador, Nigeria, Turkey, Iran, Guatemala, Iran, U.S. State Dept. lectr., India, Nepal, Iran, 1972. Contbr. articles to profl. jours. Mem. adv. com. Nat. Planning Assn., Center for Econ. Projections, Rand Corp., Ford Found.; adviser Asso. Arts Councils, Inst. Man and Sci.; staff v.p. Nat. Conf. State Legislatures, 1974—; dir. Traffic Safety Inst. Mem. Phi Beta Kappa. Home: 9 Southwood Dr Slingerlands NY 12159 Office: G-SPA SUNYA 411 State St Albany NY 12203

HERMAN, RUSSEL HAROLD, JR., oil company executive; b. Woodbury, N.J., Oct. 6, 1930; s. Russel Harold and Madlyn (Beck) H.; m. Sandra J. Ross, Jan. 5, 1973; 1 son, Douglas; children by previous marriage—Mary Cynthia, Melissa Lou, Christina Lee, Russel Harold III, Tammy Ann. B.S. in Chem. Engring, Pa. State U., 1951. With Exxon Corp. (and affiliates), 1951-81, v.p. internat. sales, 1967-69, dep. coordinator corp. planning, 1969-70, exec. v.p., dir. internat. affiliate, 1970-72, sr. v.p. domestic affiliate, 1972-73, corp. v.p. logistics and mktg., 1973-79; pres., chief exec. officer Esso Eastern, Inc., Houston, 1979-83; exec. vp. Esso Europa, Inc.,, London, 1983—. Clubs: American (London); Lakeside (Houston); Stanwich Country (Conn.). Office: Esso Europe Inc 50 Stratton St London England SW1

HERMAN, STEPHEN MARK, lawyer; b. Evanston, Ill., Mar. 9, 1932; s. Edward Martin and Bernice Jane (Kitzelman) H.; m. Lail Lewis, Aug. 26, 1956; children—Ellen, William, Thomas, Jane. B.A., Northwestern U., 1954; J.D., Harvard, 1957. Bar: Ill. bar 1957. Since practiced in, Chgo.; Sec., counsel Wurlitzer Co., Chgo., 1969-73, v.p., gen. counsel, 1973-77; sr. atty. Household Finance Corp., Chgo., 1977-78, asst. dir. law dept., Prospect Heights, Ill., 1978-81, v.p., dir. law dept., 1981—. Home: 1051 Cherry St Winnetka IL 60093 Office: Household Finance Corp Prospect Heights IL 60070

HERMAN, THEODORE LEE, ins. co. exec.; b. Boston, Dec. 21, 1936; s. Harry and Celia H.; m. Brenda Herman, May 20, 1962; children—Lynda, Carole. B.S., Boston U., 1958; M.A., George Washington U., 1960. With Am. Life Ins. Co. of N.Y., N.Y.C., 1962—, mgr., 1970-75, pres., 1975—, chief exec. officer, also dir. Served with USMC, 1958-60. Office: 810 7th Ave New York NY 10019

HERMAN, WILLIAM SPARKES, zoology educator; b. Seattle, Oct. 12, 1931; s. William Sparkes and Jane Ione (Ardery) Weidel; m. Charlotte Katherine Meyer, Oct. 5, 1962; children: Alexandria, Max, Carter. B.S., Portland State Coll., 1958; M.S., Northwestern U., 1960, Ph.D., 1964. NIH postdoctoral fellow U. Calif., Berkeley, 1964-66; asst. prof. U. Minn., Mpls., 1966-70, asso. prof., 1970-75, prof. zoology, 1976—, head genetics and cell biology dept., 1981—; cons. in field. Contbr. articles to profl. jours. Served with USAF, 1954-58. Mem. AAAS, Am. Soc. Zoologists. Home: 79 Clarence Ave SE Minneapolis MN 55414 Office: Genetics and Cell Biology Dept Univ of Minn Saint Paul MN 55455

HERMAN, WOODROW CHARLES (WOODY HERMAN), orchestra leader; b. Milw., May 16, 1913; s. Otto C. and Myrtle (Barth) H.; m. Charlotte Neste, Sept. 27, 1936; 1 dau., Ingrid. Grad., St. John's Cathedral Prep. Sch., Milw., 1930; student, Marquette U., 1930-31. Appeared: vaudeville as Boy Wonder of the Clarinet, 1919; with, Tom Gerun Orch., 1931, Gus Arnheim, 1933, Harry Sesnick, Isham Jones, 1934-36; organized orch., Band t at Plays the Blues, 1936, later named First Herd, also Third Herd; now known as, Woody Herman and the Young Thundering Herd; toured, Europe for, State Dept., 1960, 67; appeared at, Newport, Monterey and Concord festivals; performer, Woody Herman's, New Orleans, 1981—; Composer: songs including Goosey Gander, Apple Honey, Northwest Passage, Woocroppers Ball, Blowin' Up a Storm, Blues on Parade. Founder Woody Herman-Sister Fabian Scholarship Fund, 1975. Winner popularity poll Down Beat mag., 1945, Metronome mag., 1946, 53; recipient Billboard award, 1946; Silver award Esquire mag., 1946-47; Grammy award, 1963, 73, 74; named to Down Beat Mag. Hall of Fame. Mem. Am. Fedn. Musicians, ASCAP. Address: care Willard Alexander 660 Madison Ave New York NY 10021 *

HERMANIUK, MAXIM, archbishop; b. Nowe Selo, Ukraine, Oct. 30, 1911; emigrated to Can., 1948, naturalized, 1954; s. Mykyta and Anna (Monczuk) H. Student philosophy and theology, Louvain, Belgium, 1933-35; Dr. Theol., Maitre Agrege Theol., 1947; student, Orient. Philol. and History, 1943. Joined Redemptorist Congregation, 1933, ordained priest, 1938; supr. vice provincial, Can. and U.S., 1948-51, aux. bishop, Winnipeg, Man., Can., 1951, apostolic adminstr., 1956, archbishop met., 1956—; First editor Logos, Ukraine Theol. Rev., 1950-51; mem. Vatican II Council, 1962-65, Secretariat for Promoting Christian Unity, Rome, 1963; prof. moral theology, sociology and Hebrew, Beauplateau, Belgium, 1943-45; prof. moral theology and holy scripture Redemptor Sem. Waterford, Ont., Can., 1949-51; mem. Pontifical Commn. for Revision of Kodex of Oriental Canon Law. Author: La Parabole Evangelique, 1957, Our Duty, 1960. Co-founder, mem. Ukrainian Relief Com., Belgium, 1942-48; co-founder 1st pres. Ukrainian Cultural Soc., Belgium, 1947; organizer Ukrainian univ. students orgn., Obnova, Belgium, 1946-48 organizer Ukrainian univ. students orgn., Can., 1953; mem. joint working group Cath. Ch. and World Council Chs., 1969; mem. council to Secretariat Synod of Bishops, Rome, 1977, 83. Decorated Order of Can., 1982. Mem. World Congress Free Ukrainians, Taras Shevchenko Sci. Soc., Ukrainian Hist. Assn. Address: 235 Scotia St Winnipeg MB Canada RV2 1V7

HERMANN, DONALD HAROLD JAMES, lawyer, educator; b. Southgate, Ky., Apr. 6, 1943; s. Albert Joseph and Helen Marie (Snow) H. A.B. (George E. Gamble Honors scholar), Stanford U., 1965; J.D. (John Noble fellow), Columbia U., 1968; LL.M. Harvard fellow in the humanities, Harvard U., 1974; M.A., Northwestern U., 1979, Ph.D., 1981. Bar: Ariz. 1968, Wash. 1969, Ky. 1971, Ill. 1972, U.S. Supreme Ct. 1974. Mem. staff, directorate devel. plans Dept. Def., 1964-65; With Legis. Drafting Research Fund, Columbia U., 1966-68; asst. dean Columbia Coll., 1967-68; mem. faculty U. Wash., Seattle, 1968-71, U. Ky., Lexington, 1971-72, DePaul U., 1972—, prof. law and philosophy, 1973—, dir. acad. programs and interdisciplinary study, 1975-76, asso. dean, 1975-78; lectr. dept. philosophy Northwestern U., 1979-81; vis. prof. Washington U., St. Louis, 1974, U. Brazilia, 1976; lectr. law Am. Soc. Found., 1975-78, Sch. Edn. Northwestern U., 1974-76, Christ Coll. Cambridge (Eng.) U., 1977, U. Athens, 1980; Judicial fellow U.S. Supreme Ct., 1983-84; mem. Nat. Endowment for Humanities seminar on property and rights Stanford U., 1981; participant law and econs. program U. Rochester, 1974; fellow in law and econs. U. Chgo., 1975-76; fellow in law and humanities Harvard U., 1973-74; grad. fellow Northwestern U., 1978-81; mem. faculty summer seminar in law and humanities UCLA, 1978; fellow Sch. Criticism and Theory, Northwestern U., 1981-82; NEH fellow Cornell U., 1982; bd. dirs. Council Legal Edn. Opportunity, Ohio Valley Consortium, 1972, Ill. Bar Automated Research Corp., 1975—,

Criminal Law Consortium Cook County, Ill., 1977-80; cons. Adminstrv. Office Ill. Cts., 1975—; reporter cons. Ill. Jud. Conf., 1972—; mem. Am. Law Inst., 1975—, Center for Law Focused Edn., Chgo., 1977—; faculty Instituto Superiore Internazionale Di Science Criminali, Siracusa, Italy, 1978—; bd. dirs. Ctr. for Ch.-State Studies, 1982—; cons. Commerce Fedn., State of São Paulo, Brazil, 1975. Mem. Am., Ill., Chgo. bar assns., Am. Acad. Polit. and Social Sci., Am. Econ. Assn., Am. Soc. Polit. and Legal Philosophy, Am. Judicature Soc., Am. Philos. Assn., Soc. for Bus. Ethics, Soc. for Phenomenology and Existential Philosophy, Internat. Assn. Philosophy of Law and Soc., Soc. Writers on Legal Subjects, Internat. Penal Law Soc., Soc. Am. Law Tchrs., Am. Assn. Law Schs. (del., sect. chmn., chmn. sect. on jurisprudence), Chgo. Hist. Preservation Soc., Evanston Hist. Soc., Northwestern U. Alumni Assn. (bd. dirs.), Signet Soc. of Harvard. Episcopalian. Clubs: Hasty Pudding (Harvard); University, Quadrangle (Chgo.); Univ. (Evanston). Home: 1243 Forest Ave Evanston IL 60202 Office: DePaul U Coll Law 25 E Jackson St Chicago IL 60604 *The application of reason and the acceptance of responsibility are the two guiding rules which I attempt to bring to bear upon the problems which I face as an educator, a professional and citizen. The goals for which I aim in my work are mastery, understanding and creativity. Clarity, insight and soundness are the qualities which I aim to infuse into my work.*

HERMANN, ERNEST THEODORE, indsl. developer; b. Pasadena, Calif., Nov. 3, 1918; s. Ernest Theodore and Maiza Lillieth (Atwater) H.; m. Gwendolyn Jane Dahlman, Feb. 8, 1952; children—Randall, Gail, James, Rand, Karen. B.A., George Pepperdine Coll., Los Angeles, 1942; M.B.A., Harvard U., 1956. Registered profl. engr., Calif. Asst. to pres. J.M. Montgomery & Co., Los Angeles, 1942-46; pres. Hermann Co. (gen. contractors), Los Angeles, 1946-52, Pacific Mill & Elevator Co., San Rafael, Calif., 1951-63, Pacific Freeport Group, Sparks, Nev., 1963—, Trans Western Leasing Corp., Sparks, 1967—; dir. Nev. State Bank, Las Vegas. Pres., dir. Nev. Taxpayers Assn., 1979—; vice chmn. Reno Airport Commn., 1972-74; mem. Nev. Legis. Airport Study Com., 1975-76; a founder chmn. Mountain States Legal Found., Denver, 1977—. Mem. ASCE, Am. Warehousemen's Assn., Nat. Council Phys. Distbn. Mgmt., Nev. C. of C. Assn. (pres. 1975-79), Harvard Bus. Sch. Assn. (dir.), Advanced Mgmt. Assn. No. Calif. (past pres.), Beta Gamma Sigma. Republican. Presbyterian. Clubs: St. Francis Yacht, Commonwealth, World Trade (San Francisco); Traffic (N.Y.C.); Hidden Valley Country, Prospectors (Reno); Thunderbird Country (Palm Springs, Calif.). Inventor collapsible concrete form. Home: 1236 Riverside Dr Reno NV 89503 Office: 901 E Glendale Ave Sparks NV 89431

HERMANN, PAUL DAVID, association executive; b. Chgo., Feb. 1, 1925; s. Edgar Paul and Marjory (Alexander) H.; m. Joan Louise Mullin, Nov. 10, 1948; children: Bruce Phillip, Susan Marie. Student, Lawrence U., 1942-45; B.S. in Bus. Adminstrn, Northwestern U., 1948. Cert. assn. exec. Asst. dir. news bur. Ill. Inst. Tech., Chgo., 1945-48; editor Constrn. Equipment News, Chgo., 1948-49; exec. v.p. Asso. Equipment Distbrs., Oak Brook, Ill., 1950—; pres. AED Research & Services Corp., 1974—. Contbr. articles on assn. mgmt. to various jours. Mem. Am. Soc. Assn. Execs. (pres. 1974), Chgo. Soc. Assn. Execs. (pres. 1969), U.S. C. of C. (dir. 1980-82, chmn. assn. com. 1981—, small bus. council 1976-82), Nat. Chamber Alliance for Politics (adv. council 1978-82), Inst. Orgn. Mgmt. (mem. bd. regents 1969-72), Oak Brook (Ill.) Assn. Commerce Industry, Delta Tau Delta. (Alumni Achivement award 1982). Club: Chambord Bath Tennis (Oak Brook). Home: 2 S 751 Cherbourg Ave Oak Brook IL 60521 Office: 615 W 22d St Oak Brook IL 60521

HERMANN, PHILIP J., lawyer; b. Cleve., Sept. 17, 1916; s. Isadore and Gazella (Gross) H.; m. Cecilia Alexander, Dec. 28, 1945; children: Gary, Ann. Student, Hiram Coll., 1935-37; B.A., Ohio State U., 1939; J.D., Western Res. U., 1942. Bar: Ohio 1942. Partner firm Hermann Cahn & Schnieder (and predecessors), Cleve., 1946—; pres., then chmn. bd. Jury Verdict Research, Cleve.; chmn. bd. Lawyer Consultation Panel. Author: Better Settlements Through Leverage, 1965, Do You Need a Lawyer?, 1980; contbr. legal articles to various publs. Served to lt. comdr. USNR, 1942-46; PTO. Mem. ABA (past vice chmn. casualty law com., past chmn. use of modern tech. com.), Ohio Bar Assn. (past chmn. ins. com., past chmn. fed. ct. com., past mem. ho. of dels.), Cleve. Bar Assn. (past chmn. membership com.), Am. Law Firm Assn. (past chmn. bd.), Fedn. Ins. Counsel. Club: Walden Golf and Tennis. Home: 615 Acadia St Apt P7 Aurora OH 44202 Office: Hermann Cahn & Schnieder 1070 Huntington Bank Bldg Cleveland OH 44115 *Being what some people label "a perfectionist" is not easy and certainly not popular. It takes time and effort to collect information, to analyze it, to apply these to decisions and to insist upon careful work, but in the long run it is rewarding.*

HERMANN, ROBERT JAY, manufacturing company engineering executive, consultant; b. Sheldahl, Iowa, Apr. 6, 1933; s. John and Ellen Melinda (Ericson) H.; m. Darlene Velda Lowman, Mar. 20, 1954; children: Scott Alan, Sherie Lynn. B.S.E.E., Iowa State U., 1954, M.S.E.E., 1959, Ph.D., 1963. Dep. dir. research and engring. Nat. Security Agy., Ft. Meade, Md., 1973-75; spl. asst. to supreme alleid comr. Europe SHAPE, Casteau, Belgium, 1975-77; dep. under sec. of def. for research and engring. Dept. Def., Washington, 1977-79, asst. sec. of Air Force for research, devel. and logistics, 1979-81, spl. asst. for intelligence to under sec. of def. for research engring., 1981-82; v.p. systems tech., electonics sector United Techs., Hartford, Conn., 1982—; dir. Ultra Systems, Inc., Irving, Calif.; cons. Dept. Def., 1982—. Served to 1st lt. USAF, 1955-57. Recipient Arthur Fleming Washington Jaycees, 1972, Nat. Capital Nat. Capital Area Architects and Engrs., Washington, 1967, Air Force Disting. Service medal USAF, Washington, 1980. Mem. Armed Forces Communications and Electronics Assn. (bd. dirs. 1979-83), Security Activities Support Assn. (pres. 1983—). Home: 5 Stonepost Rd Simsbury CT 06070 Office: United Techs Corp 1 Financial Plaza Hartford CT 60101

HERMANN, ROBERT RINGEN, diversified manufacturing and commercial company executive; b. St. Louis, Jan. 3, 1923; s. Frederick A. and Evelyn (Ringen) H.; (married); children: Carlotta Hermann Holton, Robert Ringen; stepchildren: Robert Scherer, Steve Scherer, Mark Scherer, Lesley Scherer. B.S., Princeton U., 1944. Pres., chmn. bd. of Hermann Corp., Inc.; with divs. Hermann Properties, St. Louis, 1952—, (also subsidiaries Anchor Industries, Inc., Anchor Mktg., Inc.), 1960—; pres., gen. chmn. V.P. Fair Inc.; dir. Hermann Oak Leather Co., Link, C.A. Div. vice chmn. United Fund, 1960—; chmn. Muscular Dystrophy of Mo., 1960—; bd. dirs. N.Am. Soccer League, 1968-80, chmn. exec. com., 1970-80; bd. dirs. Barnes Med. Center, 1962—, St. Louis Sports Hall of Fame, 1970—; trustee Mo. Bot. Garden, 1965—; bd. dirs. St. Louis Symphony, Jefferson Nat. Expansion Meml.; trustee St. Louis Mcpl. Opera, 1968—, pres., 1979—; v.p. Fair, Inc., pres., 1980, chmn. bd., 1981-83; chmn. bd. Arts and Edn. Council St. Louis. Served to lt. USN, 1943-46. Mem. Nat. Council for Arts and Edn. (mem. exec. com. 1974—), Princeton Alumni Council. Clubs: Princeton of St. Louis (pres. 1960-62), St. Louis Country, Log Cabin, Yacht Club of St. Louis (commodore), Stadium (dir.). An ann. trophy award to most valuable coll. soccer player in the U.S. is named in his honor by U.S. Soccer Fedn. Office: 1400 N Price Rd Saint Louis MO 63132

HERMANN, THEODORE STEVEN, research institute executive; b. Chgo., Jan. 11, 1934; s. Steven John and Margaret H.; children: John-David, Beth Ann. A.B. in Chemistry, Ind. Central U., 1956, Ph.D., U. Mo.-Columbia. Prin. chemist MRI, Kansas City, Mo., 1963-69; chief scientist Litton Industries, Mpls., 1969-71; dept. head Gen. Mills., Mpls., 1969-72; sr. scientist, mem. exec. com. North Star Research and Devel. Inst., Mpls., 1971-72; exec. v.p. Langston Labs., Inc., Leawood, Kans., 1972-75; pres. Mellon Inst., Pitts., 1975—; dir. MPC Corp.; bd. dirs. Indsl. Health Found.; mem. adv. bd. Army Sci. Bd., EPA; mem. SBA. Contbr. articles to profl. jours. Served with U.S. Army, 1956-58. Monsanto fellow, 1960-61; named an Outstanding Young Man of Am. U.S. Jaycees, 1965. Mem. Am. Chem. Soc., Optical Soc. Am., Soc. Applied Spectroscopy, Research Soc. Am., AAAS, N.Y. Acad. Sci. Home: 100 Oxford Rd Apt 422 Monroeville PA 15146 Office: Mellon Inst 4400 5th Ave Pittsburgh PA 15213

HERMANN, WILLIAM HENRY, hospital administrator; b. Hillsboro, Ill., Apr. 6, 1924; s. Fred William and Mearle Hermann (Reinecke) H.; m. Loretta Pfister, July 28, 1956; children—Karen Elise, Diane Ellen. B.A., U. Mo., 1951; M.S., Yale U., 1953. With Arabian-Am. Oil Co., Dhahran, Saudi Arabia, 1953-58; adminstr. Dhahran Health Center, 1956-58; mem. staff Touro Infirmary, New Orleans, 1958-67, dir., 1962-64, exec. dir., 1965-66; coordinator program in hosp. adminstrn. Tulane U. Med. Sch., 1965-68; adminstr. Mary I. Bassett Hosp. and Clinics, Cooperstown, N.Y., 1968—; adj. asst. prof. pub. health and adminstrv. medicine Columbia U. Sch. Medicine. Mem. adv. com. State U. Coll., Utica, N.Y.; bd. dirs. Clara Welch Thanksgiving Home, Cooperstown, 1975—. Served with M.C. USNR, 1945-47. Mem. Am. Coll. Hosp. Adminstrs., N.Y. Hosp. Assn., U.S. Pony Club, Pi Kappa Alpha (life). Episcopalian (vestryman). Clubs: Internat. House (New Orleans); Yale (N.Y.C.). Office: Atwell Rd Cooperstown NY 13326

HERMANOVSKI, EGILS P., designer, artist; b. Latvia; the U.S., 1947, naturalized, 1952; s. Theodor H.; m. Ibolya. Ed., U. Latvia, Tech. U., Stuttgart, Germany. Owner Studio H Gallery, N.Y.C.; chmn. bd. Internat. Bus. Designs, N.Y.C. Artist, designer one man shows include, Studio H Gallery, Bayville, N.Y., 1981, Studio H Gallery, Manhasset, N.Y.; exhbn. series The Endless Space; archtl. designs for residences, restaurants, offices, motels, clubs; designer furniture, built-ins, fabrics, lighting, also indsl. designs; Books include Compact and Vacation Homes; Contbr. articles to popular mags., trade papers, U.S. and Europe. Recipient numerous awards including Nat. Award for best house of the year Am. Home mag.; Nat. Award for best design and use of materials U.S. Plywood Corp.; Design award for residences Today's Home mag.; 1st prize Bronze Plaque for excellence in design C. of C., Borough of Queens; prize for community center, hosp., chapel, theater, sr. citizen homes, Toronto. Mem. A.I.D., Latvian Inst. Architects. Imprisoned by Nazis, 1944. Office: 77 Pershing Ave Locust Valley NY 11560

HERMANOWICZ, HENRY JOSEPH, college dean; b. Chgo., Jan. 6, 1928; s. William Joseph and Sophie (Reile) H.; children—Kenneth, Neal, Glenn, Carol, Kay, Bruce, Joseph. B.S. Ed., No. Ill. U., 1949, M.S.Ed., 1954; Ed.D., Columbia U., 1959. Pub. sch. tchr., DeKalb, Ill., 1949-56; instr. Columbia U. Tchrs. Coll., 1956-58; asst. dir. research Field Enterprises Ednl. Corp., Chgo., 1958-59; from asst. prof. edn. to prof. edn. Ill. State U., Normal, 1959-65, dean, 1966-74, Coll. Edn., Pa. State U., 1974—; chmn. coordinating bd. Nat. Council Accreditation Tchr. Edn., 1977-78; pres. Ill. Assn. Colls. Tchrs. Edn., 1973-74; trustee Joint Council Econ. Edn., 1979-85. Co-author: The Real World of the Beginning Teacher, 1966, Teacher Education in Thailand: Problems and Prospects, 1971; cons. editor: Ency. Ednl. Research, 1982. Served with USNR, 1945-46. World Book Ency. fellow, 1957-58. Mem. Am. Ednl. Research Assn., Am. Assn. Colls. Tchr. Edn. (pres. 1977-78), Sigma Zeta, Kappa Delta Pi, Phi Delta Kappa. Democrat. Home: 543 Britanny Dr State College PA 16801 Office: 275 Chambers Bldg Pa State Univ University Park PA 16802 *Being constantly intrigued by controversies and problems as puzzles to be solved, I have always been willing to learn from others and from reflecting upon my experience. Furthermore, I try to exercise my convictions without cultivating a sense of self-rightious arrogance.*

HERNADI, PAUL, comparative literature and English educator; b. Budapest, Hungary, Nov. 9, 1936; s. Lajos and Zsuzsanna (Furedi) H.; m. Virginia Tucker, Aug. 18, 1964; children: Charles, Christopher. Ph.D., U. Vienna, 1963, Yale U., 1967. Asst. prof. German Colo. Coll., Colorado Springs, 1967-69; assoc. prof. German and comparative lit. U. Rochester, N.Y., 1969-75; prof. English and comparative lit. U. Iowa, Iowa city, 1975-84; resident fellow Wesleyan U., Middletown, Conn., 1974; summer seminar dir. NEH, Iowa City, 1978-80; prof. English and comparative lit. U. Calif.-Santa Barbara, 1982; vis. prof. English U. Calif.-Santa Barbara, 1982. Author: Beyond Genre-New Directions in Literary Classification, 1972; editor: What is Literature, 1978, What is Criticism, 1981, The Horizon of Literature, 1982. NEH fellow for ind. study and research, 1982-83. Mem. MLA (exec. council 1983—), Midwest MLA (exec. sec. 1977-81), Am. Compartive Lit. Assn. (adv. bd. 1983—). Office: Dept English U Calif Santa Barbara CA 93106

HERNANDEZ, GONZALEZ JOSE MARIA, Roman Catholic Bishop; b. Penjamo, Mexico, Jan. 17, 1927. Ordained priest, Roman Catholic Ch., 1950. Priest Roman Catholic Ch., 1950—, consecrated bishop, Chilapa, Mexico. Address: Obispado Am Revolucion 500-A Cilapa Mexico

HERNANDEZ, KEITH, professional baseball player; b. San Francisco, Oct. 20, 1953. Student, Coll. San Mateo. With St. Louis Cardinals (Nat. League), 1974-83, N.Y. Mets (Nat. League), N.Y.C., 1983—; mem. Nat. League All-Star Team, 1979, 80. Named to Sporting News Nat. League All-Star Fielding Team, 1978-80; named Most Valuable Player Nat. League, 1979; winner Nat. League batting title, 1979. Office: care NY Mets Shea Stadium Roosevelt Ave and 126th St Flushing Meadow NY 11368 *

HERNDON, CHARLES HARBISON, orthopaedic surgeon; b. Dublin, Tex., Dec. 12, 1915; s. G. Perkins and May (Williams) H.; m. Kathryn Blair, Apr. 14, 1944; children: Charles Laylin, David Newcomb. B.A., U. Tex., 1937; M.D., Harvard, 1940. Diplomate: Am. Bd. Orthopaedic Surgery (mem. bd. 1960-66, chmn. exam. com. 1961-64, pres. 1964-66). Rotating surg. intern Univ. Hosps., Cleve., 1940-41; jr. orthopaedic surgeon Am. Hosp., Oxford, Eng., 1942; Gerard Beekman fellow orthopaedic surgery Hosp. Spl. Surgery, N.Y.C., 1945-46, resident in orthopaedic surgery, 1946-47; mem. faculty Case-Western Res. U. Sch. Medicine, 1947—, Rainbow prof. orthopaedic surgery, 1961-82, emeritus prof. orthopaedic surgery, 1982—; dir. dept. orthopaedic surgery Univ. Hosps., Cleve., 1953-82, Rainbow Hosp., 1952-82; sr. cons. orthopaedic surgery Cleve. VA Hosp., 1956—; asso. orthopaedic surgeon Highland View Hosp., 1953—. Contbr. numerous articles to profl. jours., chpts. in books. Mem. profl. adv. bd. Ohio Services Crippled Children, 1959—; skeletal system com. NRC-Nat. Acad. Scis., 1958-67, chmn., 1962-67; Trustee Jour. Bone and Joint Surgery, 1969-74, treas., 1971-74. Served to maj. M.C. AUS, 1942-45; ETO. Mem. AMA, Am. Surg. Assn., A.C.S. (2d v.p. 1973-74), Am. Acad. Orthopaedic Surgeons (pres. 1968, exec. com. 1967-71), Orthopaedic Research Soc. (pres. 1957, exec. com. 1954-60), Am. Orthopaedic Assn., Internat. Soc. Orthopaedic Surgery and Traumatology, Am. Rheumatism Soc., Cleve. Orthopaedic Club (pres. 1963-64), Ohio Orthopaedic Soc. (sec.-treas. 1956-57), Clin. Orthopaedic Soc., Assn. Orthopaedic Chmn. (pres. 1974-75), Council Med. Spltys. Soc. (pres. 1976). Home: 2380 Edgehill Rd Cleveland Heights OH 44106 Office: 2065 Adelbert Rd Cleveland OH 44106

HERNDON, CLAUDE NASH, educator, physician; b. Greensboro, N.C., Feb. 23, 1916; s. Claude Nash and Annie Lee (Mann) H.; m. Margaret Forester Caldwell, Oct. 10, 1942; children: Anne Herndon, Claude Nash III. A.B., Duke U., 1935; M.D., Jefferson Med. Coll., 1939; postgrad., U. Mich., 1941-42. Intern Charity Hosp., New Orleans, 1939-40; Carnegie fellow med. genetics Bowman Gray Sch. Medicine, Winston-Salem, N.C., 1940-41; research asso. U. Mich., 1941-42; instr. Bowman Gray Sch. Med., Wake Forest U., 1942-45, asst. prof., 1945-51, asso. prof., 1951-54, prof. med. genetics, 1954—; chmn. dept. preventive medicine and genetics, 1957-70, asso. dean research devel., 1966-79, sr. asso. dean, 1979—; Mem. genetics research adv. com. AEC, 1955-58; mem. adv. coms. on research career awards and health research facilities NIH, 1957-69; mem. population com. Nat. Inst. Child Health and Human Devel., 1970-74. Editor: Am. Jour. Human Genetics, 1961-64; Mem. editorial bd.: Stedman's Medical Dictionary, 1970-83; Contbr. articles profl. jours. Bd. dirs. Children's Home Soc. N.C. Mem. Am. Soc. Human Genetics (dir. 1951-58, pres. 1955), Am. Eugenics Soc. (pres. 1952-55). Home: 1600 Lynwood Ave Winston-Salem NC 27104

HERNDON, JAMES FRANCIS, educator; b. Indpls., Aug. 11, 1929; s. Francis Earl and Agnes (Demmer) H.; m. Doris Arlene Beall, Dec. 24, 1952; 1 son, David Lyle. Student, John Herron Sch. Fine Arts, 1949; B.A., Ind. U., 1952; M.A., Wayne State U., 1956; Ph.D., U. Mich., 1963. Instr. Drake U., Des Moines, 1959-60; asst. prof. U. N.D., 1960-63, asso. prof., 1963-67, coordinator, 1965-66, asso. dean arts and scis., 1967; asso. prof. Va. Poly. Inst., Blacksburg, 1967-70, prof., chmn. dept. polit. sci., 1970-74, also dir. summer course math. models in polit. sci., 1973; dir. Summer Inst. in Math. Applications in Polit. Sci., 1969-73. Co-editor: Selected Bibliography of Materials in State and Local Government, 1963, Mathematical Applications in Political Science, Vols. V-VII, 1971-74; editorial bd.: Jour. Politics, 1973-75. Served with CIC U.S. Army, 1952-54. Recipient Faculty-Student Teaching award U. N.D., 1965; Faculty lectr., 1966. Mem. Am., Midwest, So. polit. sci. assns., Va. Social Sci. Assn. (v.p. 1979-80, pres. 1980-81), Ams. for Democratic Action, ACLU (vice chmn. Va.), Omicron Delta Kappa, Pi Sigma Alpha. Unitarian. Home: 1110 E Roanoke St Blacksburg VA 24060

HERNDON, JOHN JOYCE CARTER, diversified company executive; b. N.Y.C., Nov. 19, 1931; s. John Joyce Carter H. and Catherine Monroe (Converse) Treat; s. Joanne Hearst, May 10, 1959 (div. 1963); children: 1 son, John H.; m. Matilde Baroni, May 19, 1971. B.A., Yale U., 1953. Mng. dir. Rheem Chilena, Santiago, Chile, 1959-62, Rheem N.Z., Wellington, 1962-67; pres. Rheem-Safim, Milan, Italy, 1967-76; sr. v.p. City Investing Co., N.Y.C., 1976—. Trustee Friends of N.Y. Fire Dept. Collection Inc., 1982-83. Served to 1st lt. U.S. Army, 1954-57. Republican. Roman Catholic. Clubs: Brook, Racquet & Tennis (N.Y.C.); Stanwich (Greenwich, Conn.). Home: 839 Lake Ave Greenwich CT 06830 Office: City Investing Company 59 Maiden Ln New York NY 10038

HERNDON, ROBERT MCCULLOCH, experimental neurologist; b. Richmond, Va., May 29, 1935; s. Lee Roy and Lois Ruth (McCulloch) H.; m. Kathryn Lucille Stearns, June 11, 1955; children: Robert McCulloch, William, Cynthia. B.A., U. Chgo., 1955; M.D., U. Tenn., 1958. Diplomate: Am. Bd. Psychiatry and Neurology. Intern, then resident in neurology Wayne State U. Hosp., Detroit, 1959-61; fellow in neuropathology Montreal (Que., Can.) Neurol. Inst., 1962-63; fellow in anatomy Harvard U. Med. Sch., 1955-66; asst. prof. neurology Stanford U. Med. Sch., 1966-69; neurologist, then chief neurology Palo Alto (Calif.) VA Hosp., 1966-69; asso. prof. Johns Hopkins U. Med. Sch., 1969-77; prof. neurology, chmn. Center Brain Research, U. Rochester (N.Y.) Med. Center, 1977—; dir. Multiple Sclerosis Soc. Clinic, Rochester, 1978—. Served with USAF, 1963-65. Recipient Arthur Weil award Am. Assn. Neuropathologists, 1969, 72. Fellow Am. Acad. Neurology; mem. Am. Neurol. Assn., Am. Acad. Sci., Am. Assn. Neuropathologists (Moore award 1983), Soc. Neurosci., Sigma Xi, Alpha Omega Alpha. Office: 601 Elmwood Ave Box 605 Rochester NY 14642

HERNDON, TERRY EUGENE, assn. exec.; b. Russellville, Ky., Feb. 24, 1939; s. Chester and Wilma (Camp) H.; m. Mary Jeanne Gandolfi, 1962; children—Julie, Holly. B.S., Wayne State U., Detroit, 1961, M.A., 1964; H.H.D., Morehead (Ky.) State U., 1974. Tchr. Warren (Mich.) Consol. Schs., 1962-67; urban rep. N.E.A., Washington, 1967-68, specialist negotiations, 1968; exec. dir. Mich. Edn. Assn., 1969-73, N.E.A., 1973—. Chmn. Nat. Found. Improvement Edn.; bd. dirs. Nat. Council Children and Television, Coalition Am. Pub. Employees; pres. Warren Edn. Assn., 1966-67; bd. dirs. Mich. Assn. Professions, 1969-73; mem. Council on Hemispheric Affairs; trustee Nat. Planning Assn.; bd. dirs. UN Assn. Named Outstanding Citizen, Lansing, Mich., 1974. Mem. Phi Delta Kappa, Delta Chi. Office: 1201 16th St NW Washington DC 20036

HERNDON, WILLIAM CECIL, university dean, chemistry educator; b. El Paso, Tex., Aug. 12, 1932; s. Robert and Elizabeth (Masten) H.; m. Nancy R. Fairbanks, Dec. 27, 1956; children: William Robert, Matthew Fairbanks. B.S., Tex. Western Coll., 1954; Ph.D., Rice U., 1959. Research chemist Am. Cyanamid Co., 1958-61; asst. prof. U. Miss., 1961-64; assoc. prof. Fla. Atlantic U., 1964-66; prof. chemistry Tex. Tech U., Lubbock, 1966-72; chmn. dept. chemistry U. Tex. at El Paso, 1972—, dean Coll. of Sci., 1982—, on leave, 1975-76; program dir. chem. dynamics NSF, 1975-76.; Vis. prof. Bell Telephone Labs., 1966, 68. Contbr. articles to profl. jours. NSF fellow, 1954. Fellow A.A.A.S., N.Y. Acad. Scis.; mem. Am. Chem. Soc., Sigma Xi. Address: Chemistry Dept U Tex at El Paso El Paso TX 79968

HERNDON, WILSON WARREN, lawyer; b. Cameron, Tex., Mar. 3, 1933; s. Hugh Warren and MaAida (Wilson) H.; m. Betty Webster, May 13, 1955. Student, Va. Mil. Inst.; B.S., S.W. Tex. State U., 1954; J.D. with honors (asso. editor law rev.), U. Tex., 1961. Bar: Tex. bar 1961. Tchr. high sch. English and journalism, Gregory, Tex., 1954-55, since practiced in, Dallas; as partner firm Strasburger & Price; faculty mem., speaker, panelist numerous law assns. and schs. Contbr. numerous articles to legal publs. Served to capt. USAF, 1955-58. Fellow Internat. Acad. Trial Lawyers, Tex. Bar Found.; mem. Am. Law Inst., Am. Bar Assn. (chmn. subcom. on multidist. litigation antitrust sect. 1975-79, chmn. civil practice and procedure com. antitrust sect. 1979—), State Bar Tex. (chmn. substantive laws com. antitrust sect. 1977-79), Tex. Law Rev. Assn. (life), Phi Delta Phi. Episcopalian. Clubs: Dallas Country, City, T Bar M Racquet (Dallas); Garden of the Gods (Colorado Springs, Colo.). Home: 4520 Bordeaux Ave Dallas TX 75205 Office: One Main Pl Dallas TX 75250

HERNON, JOSEPH MARTIN, JR., history educator; b. Washington, June 30, 1936; s. Joseph Martin and Lucille (Mearns) H. A.B. magna cum laude, Cath. U. Am., 1959; Ph.D., Trinity Coll., Dublin U., 1963. Instr., Ohio State U., 1963-65; asst. prof. Cath. U. Am., 1965-67; asst. prof. history U. Md., 1967-68; asst. prof. U. Mass., Amherst, 1968-69, asso. prof., 1969-77, prof., 1978—; vis. prof. Dublin

U., 1970, U. Stirling, 1976; lectr. Amherst Coll., Bentley Coll., Georgetown U.; cons. NEH, World Book Ency. Author: Celts, Catholics and Copperheads: Ireland Views the American Civil War, 1968; contbr. numerous articles and poems to profl. jours. Mem. exec. com. Coll. Young Dems., 1959; U.S. del. NATO Conf. Young Polit. Leaders, 1960. Am. Philos. Soc. grantee, 1970; U. Mass. Faculty grantee, 1970; 3d pl. winner Brigadoon 1st ann. poetry contest, 1980. Fellow Royal Hist. Soc.; mem. Am. Hist. Assn., Am. Cath. Hist. Assn., Am. Com. Irish Studies (treas. 1966-71), Phi Beta Kappa, Delta Epsilon Sigma, Pi Gamma Mu, Blue Key. Democrat. Roman Catholic. Home: 26 Cosby Ave Amherst MA 01002 Office: Dept History U Mass Amherst MA 01003

HERNSTADT, JUDITH FILENBAUM, city planner, real estate executive, broadcasting executive; b. N.Y.C., Nov. 18, 1942; d. Alex and Ruth Selena (Silberman) Filenbaum. B.A., NYU, 1964, M.Urban and Regional Planning and Housing, 1966; certificate, Harvard Bus. Sch., 1977. With Office Planning Coordination, State of N.Y., 1966-68; partner Devel. Planning Assos., N.Y.C., 1967-68; with engring. scis. dept. Service Bur. Corp., N.Y.C., 1968-69; planning cons. Llewelyn-Davies Assos., N.Y.C., 1969-71, Arlen Realty & Devel. Corp., 1971-73; partner Planning & Devel. Team, N.Y.C. and Las Vegas, 1974—; v.p. Nev. Ind. Broadcasting Corp. (KVVU/TV), Las Vegas, 1974-75, pres., 1976-77, Hernstadt Broadcasting Corp., 1978-81. Condr. TV interview programs. Del. Fine Arts Fedn. N.Y., 1970—; mem. Hudson Inst., 1980—; mem. fine arts com. U.S. Dept. State; mem. Pres.'s Council Tulane U., 1976—; bd. dirs. Hebrew Immigrant Aid Soc.; co-chmn. Latin-Am. Ops. Com.; bd. dirs. Decorative Arts Trust. Mem. Am. Inst. Planners (assoc.), Am. Soc. Planning Ofcls., South Fla. Econ. Soc. (dir.). Club: Bankers (Miami, Fla.). Home: 927 Fifth Ave New York NY 10021 also 3111 Bel Air Dr Las Vegas NV 89109

HERNSTADT, WILLIAM H., broadcasting company executive, state senator; b. N.Y.C., Nov. 21, 1935; s. William L. and Alma (Cunningham) H.; m. Judith Filenbaum, Oct. 1973; children by previous marriages—Ruth Ellen, Edward William, Liane Winifred, Stephanie Elizabeth. B.S. in Physics, Rensselaer Poly. Inst., 1957. With Globus, Inc., 1960, M.A. Lomasney & Co., 1961; staff security analyst Alleghany Corp., N.Y.C., 1962-67, asst. treas., 1965-67; registered rep. Bruns, Nordeman, Rea & Co., N.Y.C., 1967-70; owner-mgr. Alvernie Apts., 1970-71; chmn. bd., gen. mgr. Nev. Ind. Broadcasting Corp.; operator TV sta. KVVU-TV, Henderson-Las Vegas, 1971-79; treas. Hernstadt Broadcasting Corp., WKAT, Miami, Fl. Rep. Town Meeting, Greenwich, Conn., 1965-69; mem. Nev. State Senate, 1976—; Bd. dirs. Clark County Apt. Owners Assn., treas., 1972, pres., 1973; bd. dirs. Nev. Apt. Assn., 1977—, Clark County chpt. Am. Cancer Soc., 1970-72, Jewish Fedn. of Las Vegas, 1974—; v.p. Jewish Fedn. of Las Vegas, 1979-82, pres., 1982—; bd. dirs. Nev. Kidney Found., 1979—, v.p., 1980—. Clubs: Las Vegas Country; Sleepy Hollow Country (Tarrytown, N.Y.); Harmonie of N.Y. Home: 3111 Bel Air Dr Apt 25G Las Vegas NV 89109

HERO, ALFRED OLIVIER, JR., foundation executive; b. New Orleans, Feb. 7, 1924; s. Alfred Olivier and Effel Anita (Pearson) H.; m. Barbara Ann Ferrell, May 22, 1954 (div. 1972); children—Alfred Olivier III, Barbara Ann Hero Ruyle, Michelle Claire, David E. Student, Va. Mil. Inst., 1941-42; B.S., U.S. Mil. Acad., 1945; M.A., Vanderbilt U., 1950; postgrad., Georgetown U., 1950-51; Ph.D., George Washington U., 1957; student, Inf. Sch., 1952-53. Commd. 2d lt. U.S. Army, 1945, advanced through grades to capt., 1950; mem. occupation forces (Office Mil. Govt. U.S.), Germany, 1945-48; staff Office Chief Personnel G-1, Dept. Army, 1950-52; faculty (Inf. Sch.), Fort Benning, Ga., 1953; exec. sec. World Peace Found., 1954-70, dir., sec., 1970—; mng. editor Internat. Orgn., 1954-71, bd. editors, 1972-82; sec. Greater Boston Fund for Internat. Affairs, 1973-82; Vis. scholar Harvard U. Center for Internat. Affairs, 1982-83; Bissell prof. Can.-Am. Relations U. Toronto, 1983—. Author: The Southerner and World Affairs, 1965, The Reuther-Meany Foreign Policy Dispute, 1971, American Religious Groups View Foreign Policy, (with Carl E. Beigie) Natural Resources in U.S.-Canadian Relations, 3 vols, 1980-82, The American People and South Africa, 1981. Mem. Am. Polit. Sci. Assn. Home: 8 St Thomas St Toronto ON Canada 7552B8 Office: 22 Batterymarch St Boston MA 02109

HEROLD, DONALD GEORGE, museum director; b. Bklyn., June 8, 1927; s. Charles George and Emmy (Partheymuller) H.; m. Elaine A. Bluhm, Jan. 15, 1964; children: Jennifer Ann, Katherine Elaine Patricia. B.A., SUNY-Albany, 1948. Dir. Miami Jr. Mus., Fla., 1950-51; asst. dir. Mus. Village, Monroe, N.Y., 1953-56; dir. exhibits and interpretation Va. 350th Anniversary, Jamestown, 1956-57; dir. Davenport Pub. Mus., Iowa, 1958-68, Polk Pub. Mus., Lakeland, Fla., 1968-69, Mus. Arts and Scis., Daytona Beach, Fla., 1969-70, Charleston Mus., S.C., 1971-82, Buffalo Mus. Sci., N.Y., 1982—. Trustee Cypress Gardens of Charleston. Served with USMC, 1951-53. Recipient Elsie M.B. Naumburg award Natural Sci. for Youth Found., 1978. Mem. Am. Assn. Museums, S.E. Mus. Conf., Midwest Mus. Conf., Am. Assn. State and Local History, Sci. Museums Dirs. Assn., Assn. Systematics Collections, S.C. Fedn. Museums Collections (v.p.), N.Y. State Assn. Museums (pres. 1983—), N.E. Museums Conf., Am. Assn. for State and Local History. Office: Buffalo Mus of Sci Humboldt Pkwy Buffalo NY 14211

HEROLD, EDWARD WILLIAM, elec. engr.; b. N.Y.C., Oct. 15, 1907; s. Carl Frederick and Marie (Wollersheim) H.; m. Alexandra Dacis, Aug. 4, 1931; 1 dau., Linda Marlene Herold Johnson. B.S., U. Va., 1930; M.S., Poly. Inst. Bklyn., 1942, D.Sc. (hon.), 1961. Registered profl. engr., N.J. Research asst. Bell Telephone Labs., N.Y.C., 1924-26; engr. E.T. Cunningham Co., N.Y.C., 1927-29, RCA, Harrison, N.J., 1930-42; successively mem. tech. staff, dir. tube lab., dir. electronic research lab. RCA Labs., Princeton, N.J., 1942-59; v.p. research Varian Assos., Palo Alto, Calif., 1959-64; dir. tech. RCA Corp., Princeton, 1965-72; cons. electronics, mgmt. and patents, 1972—; bd. dirs. Inst. Radio Engrs., 1956-58, Engring. Found., 1975-78; chmn. bd. Palisades Inst., 1969—; adv. council elec. engring. dept. Princeton U., 1957-71; cons. Dept. Def., 1950-76. Co-author: Color Television Picture Tubes, 1974; Author 50 tech. articles in field. Fellow IEEE (Founder's medal 1976); mem. Phi Beta Kappa, Sigma Xi. Dir. devel. 1st color TV picture tube, 1949-50; holder 47 patents. Address: 332 Riverside Dr E Princeton NJ 08540 *In the 1930's, when accolades and emoluments were scant, we learned to be content with the old maxim, virtue is its own reward. This still is the best credo for a happy life: do what is morally right, don't expect much in return, and those rewards which do come are like icing on the cake.*

HEROLD, JOHN WILLIAM, JR., hotel exec.; b. Savannah, Ga., Sept. 26, 1944; s. John William and Margaret Theresa (Southwood) H.; m. Caroline Ina Liscoe, Jan. 8, 1972. A.S. in Applied Sci, Paul Smith Coll., 1965. Service supr. Sky Chefs Inc. (restaurant), N.Y.C., 1965-67; ops. analyst Loews Hotels, N.Y.C., 1967-68, San Juan, P.R., 1968-70; resident mgr. Airport Marina Hotel, Los Angeles, 1970; v.p., gen. mgr. Fred Harvey Hotels, Los Angeles and San Francisco, 1971-72; gen. mgr. Marriott's Essex House, N.Y.C., 1972-80; v.p. Marriott Hotels, Washington, 1980—. Trustee Paul Smith Coll.; bd. dirs. N.Y.C. Conv. and Tourist Bur. Mem. Hotel Assn. N.Y.C. (pres.), Hotel Sales Mgrs. Assn., Central Park South Assn. Address: 160 Central Park S New York NY 10019

HERON, DAVID WINSTON, librarian; b. Los Angeles, Mar. 29, 1920; s. Charles Morton and Elizabeth (Atsatt) H.; m. Winifred Ann Wright, Aug. 24, 1946; children—Holly Winston, James, Charles. A.B., Pomona Coll., 1942; B.L.S., U. Calif. at Berkeley, 1948; M.A., U. Calif. at Los Angeles, 1951. Reference asst. U. Calif. at Los Angeles Library, 1948-52; librarian Am. embassy, Tokyo, Japan, 1952-53; staff asst. to librarian, librarian Grad. Reading Room U. Calif. at Los Angeles, 1953-55; asst. to dir. Stanford Libraries, 1955-57, asst. dir., 1959-61; asst. librarian Hoover Instn., Stanford, 1957-59; dir. libraries U. Nev., Reno, 1961-68, U. Kans., Lawrence, 1968-74; univ. librarian U. Calif. at Santa Cruz, 1974-78, emeritus librarian, 1979—; sr. lectr. Sch. Library and Info. Studies, 1978-79; head reader services Hoover Instn., 1980—; library adviser U. Ryukyus, Naha, Okinawa, 1960-61; mem. Kans. Library Adv. Commn., 1973-74. Editor: A Unifying Influence, 1981; Editorial bd.: Coll. and Research Libraries; Contbr. articles to gen. and profl. jours. Served as 1st lt. AUS, 1942-46; ETO. Mem. ALA (exec. bd.), Kans. Library Assn., Nev. Library Assn. (pres. 1963-65), Assn. Research Libraries (bd. dirs. 1974), ACLU, Assn. Coll. and Research Libraries (editor monographs; chmn. U. libraries sect. 1970-71), Am. Inst. Conservation Historic and Artistic Works, Book Club Calif. Democrat. Club: Roxburghe (San Francisco).

HERON, (STEPHEN) DUNCAN, JR., educator; b. Jackson, Miss., Sept. 18, 1926; s. Stephen Duncan and Laura Belle (Wilson) H.; m. Rebecca Ann Melton, Apr. 3, 1948; children—Stephani Ann (Mrs. Morton Arnold Emmons), Stephen Duncan III. Student, Millsaps Coll., 1944-45; B.S., U. S.C., 1948, M.S., 1950; Ph.D., U. N.C., 1958. Mem. faculty Duke U., 1950—, asst. prof. geology, 1954-58, asso. prof., 1958-70, prof., 1970—, chmn. dept., 1968-77. Contbr. articles to profl. jours.; Editor-in-chief: Southeastern Geology, 1959—. Recipient Oak Leaf award Nature Conservancy, 1976; Gov.'s award for environ. quality N.C. Wildlife Fedn., 1975. Fellow Geol. Soc. Am. (chmn. S.E. sect. 1981-82); mem. Am. Assn. Petroleum Geologists, Carolina Geol. Soc. (permanent sec.-treas.), Sigma Xi. Home: 4425 Kerley Rd Durham NC 27705

HEROY, WILLIAM BAYARD, JR., educator; b. Washington, Aug. 13, 1915; s. William Bayard and Jessie Minerva (Page) H.; m. Dorothy M. Meincke, June 16, 1937; children: Bayard Page, David Bassett, June Catherine, Barbara Ann. A.B., Dartmouth Coll., 1938; Ph.D., Princeton U., 1941. Geologist Texaco, 1941-45; geologist Geotech. Corp., Garland, Tex., 1945-47, supr., 1947-52, v.p., dir., 1952-65, pres., 1960-65; group exec. Teledyne, 1965-68, asst. to pres., 1968-70; v.p., treas. So. Meth. U., 1970-77, prof. geol. sci., 1977-81, prof. emeritus, 1981—; pres. Inst. Study Earth and Man. Trustee Hockaday Sch., 1981, Ft. Burgwin Research Ctr.; bd. dirs. Meml. Hosp. Garland, Circle 10 council Boy Scouts Am., Space Applications Bd. NASA, 1971-77. Fellow Geol. Soc. Am. (councilor 1967-70, treas. 1976-82), AAAS; mem. Am. Assn. Petroleum Geologists, Am. Geol. Inst. (fin. v.p. 1966-69, pres. 1969), Am. Inst. Profl. Geologists (cert.), Soc. Exploration Geophysicists, Dallas Geophys. Soc. (hon., life), Dallas Geog. Soc. Republican. Unitarian. Club: Cosmos (Washington). Home: 3901 Montecito St Apt 610 Denton TX 76201 Office: 131 Heroy Bldg So Meth U Box 274 Dallas TX 75275

HERPEL, GEORGE LLOYD, marketing educator; b. St. Louis, Aug. 31, 1921; s. George Martin and Irene (Lloyd) H.; m. June L. Stamm, Nov. 22, 1944; children: John, Mark. B.A., Vanderbilt U., 1943, M.A., 1943, M.B.A., 1955; Ph.D., St. Louis U., 1958. Gen. sales mgr., dir. pub. relations C.V. Mosby Pub. Co., St. Louis, 1947-54; dir. mgmt. devel. Internat. Shoe Co., St. Louis, 1954-62; sr. prof. mktg. Temple U., 1962-83; prof. bus. adminstrn. Villanova U., 1983—; pres. Hedgerow Theatre Corp., 1971-73; dir. W.A. Krueger Co., 1972—, J. Deeter Corp., 1977—, Ensco, Inc., 1978—; Chmn. bd. trustees Sales Mktg. Execs. Grad. Sch. Sales and Mktg. Mgmt., Syracuse U., 1962-64, dean faculty, 1964; nat. ednl. cons. Splty. Advt. Assn., Dallas, 1972—. Author: Specialty Advertising in Marketing, 1972, New Dimensions in Creative Marketing, 1983. Mem. Regional Export Expansion Com., 1966-74; chmn. Export Planning Com., Phila. Served with USNR, 1943-46. Mem. Sales Execs. Assn. St. Louis (pres. 1954-56), Am. Mktg. Assn. (pres. St. Louis 1957-58, nat. v.p. 1963-65), Am. Soc. Internat. Execs. (dir., sec. 1975—), Sales Mktg. Execs. Internat. (dir., v.p., exec. com. 1954-64), Nat. Speakers Assn. (charter), Vanderbilt U. Alumni Assn. (pres. St. Louis 1950), Pi Sigma Epsilon (dir. 1960-69), Beta Theta Pi (pres. St. Louis 1949). Home: 9 Single Ln Wallingford PA 19086 Office: Sch Commerce and Fin Villanova U Villanova PA 19085

HERR, DAN, association executive; b. Huron, Ohio, Feb. 11, 1917; s. William Patrick and Wilhelmina Margaret (Slyker) H. B.A., Fordham U., 1938; postgrad., McGill U., 1938, Columbia U., 1939; LL.D. (hon.), Rosary Coll., 1967. Asst. to editor Inf. Jour., Washington, 1945-46; free lance writer, 1946-48; pres. Thomas More Assn., Chgo., 1948-82, chmn. bd., 1982—; pub. The Critic, 1948-81; editor Overview, 1967-73. Author: Stop Pushing, 1961, Start Digging, 1985; co-editor six anthologies. Pres. Nat. Catholic Reporter, 1968-71; trustee Rosary Coll., 1969-73, chmn. bd. trustees, 1970-72. Served to maj. inf. AUS, 1941-45. Decorated Purple Heart, Silver Star; recipient Pere Marquette award Marquette U., 1957; Assn. Chgo. Priests award, 1978. Home: 111 E Chestnut StApt 37F Chicago IL 60611 Office: 223 W Erie St Chicago IL 60610

HERR, KENNETH JULIAN, charitable foundation executive; b. Millersville, Pa., Aug. 29, 1927; s. G. Norman H. and Elva Esther (Bucher); m. Helena Jean DiMeglio, July 13, 1957; 1 son, Brian K. B.S. in Econs., Franklin and Marshall Coll., 1952. Staff acct. Price Waterhouse & Co., N.Y.C., 1954-60; asst. to treas. A.P, N.Y.C., 1954-60; controller Am. Nat. Standards Inst., N.Y.C., 1964-68; treas. Andrew W. Mellon Found., N.Y.C., 1968—. Served with Mcht. Marine, 1944-48; served with AUS, 1952-54. Mem. Am. Inst. C.P.A.s. Home: 121 Fox Dr Allendale NJ 07401 Office: Mellon Found 140 E 62d St New York NY 10112

HERR, RICHARD, history educator; b. Guanajuato, Mexico, Apr. 7, 1922; s. Irving and Luella (Winship) H.; m. Elene Fernandez Mel, Mar. 2, 1946 (div. 1967); children: Charles Fernandez, Winship Richard; m. Valerie J. Jackson, Aug. 29, 1968; children: Sarah, Jane. A.B., Harvard U., 1943; Ph.D., U. Chgo., 1954. Instr. Yale U., 1952-57, asst. prof., 1957-59; assoc. prof. U. Calif., Berkeley, 1960-63, prof. history, 1963—; directeur d'études associé, sixième sect. Ecole Pratique des Hautes Etudes, Paris, 1973; dir. Madrid Study Center, 1975-77; bd. dirs. Inst. Hist. Study. Author: The Eighteenth Century Revolution in Spain, 1958, Tocqueville and the Old Regime, 1962, Spain, 1971; Co-editor, contbr.: Ideas in History, 1965; Asst. editor: Jour. Modern History, 1949-50; Mem. editorial bd.: French Historical Studies, 1966-69. Served with AUS, 1943-45. Social Sci. Research Council grantee, 1963-64; Guggenheim fellow, 1959-60; sr. fellow Nat. Endowment for Humanities, 1968-69. Mem. Am. Hist. Assn., Soc. For French Hist. Studies, Soc. for Spanish and Portuguese Hist. Studies, Real Academia de la Historia Madrid. Office: Dept of History Univ California Berkeley CA 94720

HERRELL, WALLACE EDGAR, physician, editor; b. Marshall, Va., Oct. 1, 1909; s. Bennett Frost and Bessie (Ballard) H.; m. Margaret Harwick, Jan. 18, 1936; children: Stephen, John, Sarah (Mrs. J. Brady Foust). M.D., U. Va., 1933; M.S., U. Minn., 1937. Intern Virginia Mason Hosp., Seattle, 1933-34; resident Mayo Found., Rochester, Minn., 1934-37; instr. medicine Mayo Found. Grad. Sch. U. Minn., 1938-43, asst. prof. medicine, 1943-47, asso. prof., 1947-52, prof., 1952-53; cons. in medicine Mayo Clinic, 1938-53, head sect. in medicine, 1946-53; cons. medicine Lexington (Ky.) Clinic, 1953-67; clin. prof. medicine U. Ky., 1961—; editor-in-chief Clin. Medicine and Med. Digest publs., Northfield, Ill., 1967-74; Instr. U.S. Army Med. Center, Washington, 1948-49. Author: Penicillin and Other Antibiotic Agents, 1945, Erythromycin, 1955, Lincomycin, 1969; Contbr. chpts. to textbooks, over 200 articles to med. jours.; Editorial bd.: Am. Review of Microbiology, 1947-52, MD Med. mag, 1956—. Mayo Found. fellow, 1934-37; Recipient Distinguished Service award U.S. Jr. C. of C., 1943. Mem. AMA, ACP (life), AAAS, Am. Soc. Clin. Investigation, Central Soc. Clin. Research, Am. Fedn. Clin. Research, Am. Med. Writers Assn., Alumni Assn. Mayo Found., U. Va. Alumni Assn. (life), Minn. Soc. Internal Medicine (hon.), Omaha Mid-West Clin. Soc. (hon.), Am. Soc. Clin. Pharmacology and Therapeutics, Zumbro Valley Med. Soc., Minn. State Med. Assn., Am. Soc. Microbiology, Sigma Xi, Alpha Omega Alpha, Phi Chi. Episcopalian. Clubs: Rochester Golf and Country, University (Rochester); Thoroughbred Am. (Lexington). Home: 1305 9th St SW Rochester MN 55902

HERRICK, JOHN DENNIS, food products corporation executive; b. St. Paul, Oct. 8, 1932; s. Willard R. and Gertrude (O'Connor) H. B.A., Coll. St. Thomas, 1954. Field auditor Gen. Mills, Inc., Mpls., 1954-59, acctg. supr., Kankakee, Ill., 1959-61, adminstrv. mgr., Chgo., 1961-62, mgr. auditing, Mpls., 1962-65, mgr. new bus. devel., 1965-66, dir. adminstrn. and controller Smiths Food Group (subs.), London, 1966-68; pres. Gen. Mills Cereals Ltd., Toronto, Ont., Can., 1968-71; chmn. bd., pres., chief exec. officer Gen. Mills Canada, Inc., Toronto, 1971—; dir. Grocert Products Mgrs. of Can., Toronto, CP Express & Transport; 2d v.p. Nat. Pasta Assn., Arlington, Va. Pres. Jr. Achievement of Can., Toronto, 1971-72, Jr. Achievement of Toronto, 1970-71; mem. World Bus. Council, N.Y.C.; gov. Jr. Achievement of Can., Queensway Gen. Hosp., Toronto; past pres. Toronto Area Indsl. Devel. Bd.; past pres., mem. council Bd. Trade Met. Toronto; dir. Emmanuel Convalescent Found., Toronto; past pres. American Club, Toronto; dir. Centre Stage Co., Toronto; gov. Nat. Theatre Sch. of Can., Montreal. Capt. USAF. Recipient Queen's Silver Jubilee Medal, 1977. Republican. Roman Catholic. Clubs: Beefeater (N.Y.C.); Empire Club, Canadian, Royal Can. Yacht, Lambton Golf and Country (Toronto); Accademia Italiana Della Cucina; Bd. of Trade (Toronto). Lodges: KC; Rotary. Home: 33 Harbour Sq Apt 3409 Toronto ON Canada M5J 2G2 Office: General Mills Canada Inc 1330 Martin Grove Rd Rexdale ON Canada M9W 4X4

HERRICK, KENNETH GILBERT, business executive; b. Jackson, Mich., Apr. 2, 1921; s. Ray Wesley and Hazel Marie (Forney) H.; m. Shirley J. Todd, Mar. 2, 1942; children: Todd Wesley, Toni Lynn. Student public and pvt. schs., Howe, Ind.; L.H.D. (hon.), Siena Heights Coll., 1974, H.H.D., Adrian Coll., 1975, Detroit Inst. Tech., 1980; LL.D., Judson Coll., 1975; D. Engring. (hon.), Albion Coll., 1981. With Tecumseh Products Co., Mich., 1940-42, 45—, v.p., 1961-66, vice chmn. bd., 1964-70, pres., 1966-70, chmn. bd., chief exec. officer, 1970—; dir. United Savs. Bank, Tecumseh, Mfrs. Nat. Bank Detroit, Gen. Telephone Co., Muskegon, Mich. Bd. dirs. Howe Mil. Sch.; pres. Herrick Meml. Hosp. Bd., 1970-81, Herrick Found., 1970—; mem. exec. adv. bd. St. Jude Children's Hosp., 1978—. Served with USAAC, 1942-45. Recipient Hon. Alumni award Mich. State U., 1975; Disting. Service award Albion Coll., 1975. Presbyterian. Clubs: Lenawee Country, Elks (Adrian, Mich.); Tecumseh Country, Masons (Tecumseh). Office: Tecumseh Products Co 100 E Patterson Tecumseh MI 49286

HERRICK, PETER, banker; b. White Plains, N.Y., Nov. 10, 1926; s. Harold and Alta (Lake) H.; m. Beatricia Bierau, Oct. 7, 1950; children: David, Wendy. A.B., Williams Coll., 1950. With The Bank of N.Y., N.Y.C., 1951—, v.p., 1967-72, sr. v.p., 1973-79, exec. v.p., chief comml. banking officer, 1979-82, pres., chief operating officer, dir., 1982—; pres., dir. N.Y. Bus. Devel. Corp., N.Y. Bus. Devel. Capital Corp.; dir. The Bank of N.Y. Internat. Inc., The Bank of N.Y. Co., Inc., BNY Internat. Investments, Inc., BNY Leasing Inc., BNY Fin. Corp., BNY Holdings Corp. (Del.), ARCS Mortgage Inc., Beacon Capital Mgmt., Inc., Bank of N.Y. Life Ins. Co. Inc., Bank of N.Y. Trust Co., Ennia Reins. Co. Am. Vice chmn. mem. exec. com. Better Bus. Bur. Met. N.Y.; bd. assocs. Hood Coll.; trustee N.Y. Community Trust; bd. govs. Hundred Yr. Assn. N.Y. Served with U.S. Army Air Corps, 1944-46; with USAF, 1950-51. Mem. Assn. Res. City Bankers., N.Y. State Bankers Assn. (v.p., dir.). Clubs: India House, Shenorock Shore., Siwanoy Country, Econ. of N.Y., Pilgrims of U.S. Office: 48 Wall St New York NY 10015

HERRICK, ROBERT FORD, college trained personnel consultant; b. Youngstown, Ohio, Oct. 2, 1912; s. George Franklin and Evelyn L. (Spear) H.; m. Elizabeth June Myers, June 30, 1938; 1 son, Robert Frank. B.A., Lehigh U., 1934. Editor alumni bull. Lehigh U., 1936-40; exec. sec. Alumni Assn., 1940-44, dir. univ. pub. relations, 1946-56; exec. dir. Coll. Placement Council, Inc., Bethlehem, Pa., 1956-77, sec.-treas., dir., 1968-77; sec. bd. Coll. Placement Services, Inc., 1965-77; sec.-treas. CPC Found., 1966-77; cons. coll. trained personnel, 1977—. Author: Career Planning and Placement in the Mid-Seventies, 1976; Editor: (with Everett A. Teal) Fundamentals of College Placement, 1962, Jour. Coll. Placement, 1956-62, Coll. Placement Ann, 1956-62. Del. White House Conf. on Youth, 1971; Nat. bd. dirs. Council Student Personnel Assn. in Higher Edn.; bd. dirs. Ctr. Health Edn., 1982—. Served with AUS, 1944-46. Recipient Disting. Service award Middle Atlantic Placement Officers Assn., 1968, So. Coll. Placement Assn., 1969. Mem. Pi Delta Epsilon, Omicron Delta Kappa., Alpha Sigma Phi. Episcopalian. Clubs: Bethlehem, Rotary. Home and office: 208 Langhorne Ave Bethlehem PA 18017

HERRIFORD, ROBERT LEVI, SR., army officer; b. Lewistown, Ill., May 4, 1931; s. John and Lola (Braden) H.; m. Muriel Jean Davis, July 10, 1949; children: Robert Levi, Thomas Merle, David William, Deborah S., Traci Ann. B.S., U. Ariz., 1966, M.B.A., 1968. Enlisted in U.S. Army, 1948, commd. 2d lt., 1952, advanced through grades to maj. gen., 1979; service in, Vietnam, 1966-67, comdr., Ft. Bragg, N.C., 1969-71, chief spl. items mgmt., Detroit, 1971-72, comdr., Seoul, 1973-74, dir. procurement, Rock Island, Ill., 1974-76, comdr., N.Y., 1976-78, asst. dep. chief of staff logistics, 1978-80, dir. procurement and prodn., Alexandria, Va., 1980—. Chmn. Minority Bus. Opportunity Council, N.Y.C., 1976-78. Decorated Legion of Merit, D.S.M., Def. Superior Service medal, Bronze Star, Airmedal, numerous others. Mem. Am. Def. Preparedness Assn., Assn. U.S. Army, Am. Legion, Nat. Contracts Mgmt. Assn. (chpt. pres. 1975-76). Office: 9700 S Cass Ave Argonne IL 60439 *There is no substitute in any career, but particularly in an Army officer's career, for hard work, dedication and absolute integrity. Subordinates, peers, and superiors can sense it in training, in garrison, and in battle. Many people, in all pursuits and professions, are created equal in talent. Only a very few are willing to give to that talent all the care and dedication that is required to bring it to the top of their chosen field. It is often easier to explain why you didn't make it than to devote all that is required to develop this talent.*

HERRIN, MORELAND, educator, engring. cons.; b. Morris, Okla., Nov. 14, 1922; s. Birney D. and Lucille (Morel) H.; m. Nancy M. Jameson, Dec. 24, 1946; children—Jeannie N., Stanley M., Gwen M. B.S. in Civil Engring, Okla. State U., 1947, M.S., 1949; Ph.D., Purdue

U., 1954. Instr. Okla. State U., 1947-49, asso. prof., 1954-58; prof. civil engrng. U. Ill. at Urbana, 1958—; dir. Ill. Coop. Transp. Program; design engr. Hudgins, Thompson & Ball (engrs.), Oklahoma City, 1949-50; materials engr. Garnett, Fleming, Cordray and Carpenter, Belvidere, Ill., 1957; asst. materials engr., road test Am. Assn. State Hwy. Ofcls., Ottawa, Ill., 1958; cons. hwy. materials, pavement design, 1955—. Contbr. articles to profl. jours. Served to capt. USAAF, 1943-46. Recipient Epstein award U. Ill., 1962. Mem. Transp. Research Bd., Assn. Asphalt Paving Technology (pres. 1978), ASCE, Am. Soc. Engrng. Edn., Am. Soc. Testing Materials, Chi Epsilon, Tau Beta Pi. Mem. Disciples of Christ Ch. Home: 1414 W William St Champaign IL 61820 Office: Talbot Lab Urbana IL 61801

HERRING, JACK HERMAN, oil company executive; b. Coal County, Okla., Jan. 18, 1922; s. James Simmons and Susie (Hamilton) H.; m. Hazel Marie Jackson, Feb. 5, 1943; children. Judith Ann, David Robert. B.S. in Petroleum Engrng., U. Tex., 1950; postgrad. advanced mgmt. program, Harvard U. Bus. Sch., 1967. Various position in engrirng. and mgmt. Marathon Oil Co., Houston and Findlay, Ohio, 1950-69; v.p. employee relations Marathon Oil Co., Findlay, 1969-70, v.p. prodn. ops., 1970-72, v.p. mktg., 1972-77, sr. v.p. exploration and prodn., 1977—, dir., mem. exec. com.; mem. Southwestern Legal Found., Richardson, Tex., 1982—, Engrng. found. Adv. Council, Austin, Tex., 1983—. Past pres. United Way, Findlay, 1973. Served with USAAF, 1942-46; ETO. Named Disting. Grad. coll. Engrng. U. Tex., 1981. Mem. Soc. Petreum Engrs. (AIME), Am. Petrleum Inst., Ind. Petroleum Producers Assn. Am. Presbyterian. Findlay Country. Clubs: Muirfield Country (Columbus, Ohio); Houston Petroleum; Onion Creek country, Headliners (Austin). Office: Marathon Oil Co 539 S Main St Findlay OH 45840

HERRING, JACK WILLIAM, educator; b. Waco, Tex., Aug. 28, 1925; s. Benjamin Oscar and Bertha (Shiplet) H.; m. Daphne L. Norred, June 10, 1944; children—Penny Elizabeth, Paul William. B.A., Baylor U., 1947, M.A., 1948; Ph.D., U. Pa., 1958. English instr. Howard Coll., Birmingham, Ala., 1948-50; asso. prof., acting chmn. dept. English Grand Canyon Coll., Phoenix, 1951-55; asst. prof. English Ariz. State U., Tempe, 1955-59; dir. Armstrong Browning Library, Baylor U., 1959—, asso. prof. English, 1959-62, prof. English, 1962-73, Margaret Root Brown prof. Robert Browning studies, 1973—. Author: Browning's Old School Fellow, 1972; Editor: Studies in Browning and His Circle. Mem. Modern Lang. Assn., Am. Assn. U. Profs. Club: Kiwanis (pres. Waco club 1976-77). Home: 200 Guittard Ave Waco TX 76706 *There is no substitute for tested truth.*

HERRING, JERONE CARSON, banker, lawyer; b. Kinston, N.C., Sept. 27, 1938; s. James and Isabel (Knight) H.; m. Patricia Ann Hardy, Aug. 6, 1961; children—Bradley Jerone, Ansley Carole. A.B., Davidson Coll., 1960; LL.B., Duke U., 1963. Bar: N.C. bar 1963. Asso. firm McElwee & Hall, North Wilkesboro, N.C., 1965-69; partner firm McElwee, Hall & Herring, North Wilkesboro, 1969-71; v.p., sec. Br. Banking & Trust Co., Wilson, N.C., 1971—. Served to capt. U.S. Army, 1963-65. Mem. Am. Bar Assn., N.C. State Bar, N.C. Bar Assn., Wilson County Bar Assn. Democrat. Presbyterian. Home: 1309 Lakeside Dr Wilson NC 27893 Office: 223 W Nash St Wilson NC 27893

HERRING, LEONARD GRAY, marketing company executive; b. nr. Snow Hill, N.C., June 18, 1927; s. Albert Lee and Josie (Sugg) H.; m. Rozelia Sullivan, June 18, 1950; children: Sandra Grey, Albert Lee II. B.S., U. N.C., 1948. With Dun & Bradstreet, Inc., Raleigh, N.C., 1948-49; with H. Weil & Co., Goldsboro, N.C., 1949-55; pres., chief exec. officer Lowe's Cos., Inc., North Wilkesboro, N.C., 1955—; dir. Northwestern Financial Corp., Lowe's Cos. Profit Sharing Plan and Trust.; mem. listed co. adv. com. N.Y. Stock Exchange, N.Y.C. Trustee Pfeiffer Coll., Misenheimer, N.C.; mem. adv. bd. Duke U. Hosp., Durham, N.C. Mem. Chi Psi. Democrat. Methodist. Home: 310 Coffey St North Wilkesboro NC 28659 Office: Lowe's Cos Inc Hwy 268 East North Wilkesboro NC 28656

HERRING, WILLIAM CONYERS, physicist; b. Scotia, N.Y., Nov. 15, 1914; s. William Conyers and Mary (Joy) H.; m. Louise C. Preusch, Nov. 30, 1946; children—Lois Mary, Alan John, Brian Charles, Gordon Robert. A.B., U. Kans., 1933; Ph.D., Princeton, 1937. NRC fellow Mass. Inst. Tech., 1937-39; instr. Princeton, 1939-40, U. Mo., 1940-41; mem. sci. staff Div. War Research, Columbia, 1941-45; prof. applied math. U. Tex., 1946; research physicist Bell Telephone Labs., Murray Hill, N.J., 1946-78; prof. applied physics Stanford (Calif.) U., 1978—; mem. Inst. Advanced Study, 1952-53. Recipient Army-Navy Cert. of Appreciation, 1947; Distinguished Service citation U. Kans., 1973; J. Murray Luck award for excellence in sci. reviewing Nat. Acad. Scis., 1980; von Hippel award Materials Research Soc., 1980. Fellow Am. Phys. Soc. (Oliver E. Buckley solid state physics prize 1959), Am. Acad. Arts and Scis.; mem. AAAS, Nat. Acad. Scis. Home: 3945 Nelson Dr Palo Alto CA 94306 Office: Dept Applied Physics Stanford U Stanford CA 94305

HERRINGER, FRANK CASPER, business executive; b. N.Y.C., Nov. 12, 1942; s. Casper Frank and Alice Virginia (McMullen) H.; m. Nancy Lynn Blair, Dec. 21, 1968; 1 son, William Laurence. A.B. magna cum laude, Dartmouth, 1964, M.B.A. with highest distinction, 1965. Prin. Cresap, McCormick & Paget, Inc. (mgmt. cons.), N.Y.C., 1965-71; staff asst. to Pres., Washington, 1971-73; adminstr. U.S. Urban Mass Transp. Adminstrn., Washington, 1973-75; gen. mgr., chief exec. officer San Francisco Bay Area Rapid Transit Dist., 1975-78; sr. group v.p. Transamerica Corp., San Francisco, 1979—; dir. Occidental Life Ins. Co., Transam. Ins. Co., Fred S. James Corp., Budget-Rent-A-Car Corp., Transam. Fin. Corp., Transam. Interway, Transam. Delaval Co. Trustee Pacific Med. Center, San Francisco Zool. Trust. Mem. Phi Beta Kappa. Republican. Clubs: Olympic, Bankers, Commonwealth, Contra Costa Country. Home: 4175 Canyon Rd Lafayette CA 94549 Office: 600 Montgomery St San Francisco CA 94111

HERRINGTON, JOHN DAVID, III, law firm executive; b. Warren, Ohio, Nov. 19, 1934; s. John David, Jr. and Gertrude Francis (Herlinger) H.; m. Phoebe Jane Henderson, Mar. 16, 1957; children: Gay Annette, Joy Ann, Jennifer John. B.Sc. in Bus. Adminstrn, Ohio State U., 1956. C.P.A., Pa. With Price Waterhouse & Co., Pitts., 1956-63; asst. to sec.-treas. Fisher Sci. Co., Pitts., 1963-65, controller, 1965-71, v.p. fin., treas., 1971-78, sr. v.p. fin., treas., 1979-82; exec. dir. Reed Smith Shaw & McClay, law firm, Pitts., 1982—; dir. Hi Pure, Inc., Rochester Sci., Pfeiffer Glass, E & A Bldg. Corp., F.S. de Mexico, Conco Inc. Served with AUS, 1957-58. Mem. Fin. Execs. Inst., Tax Execs. Inst., Planning Execs. Inst., Am. Inst. C.P.A.s, Pa. Soc. C.P.A.s, Assn. Legal Adminstrs. Home: 9402 Babcock Blvd Allison Park PA 15101 Office: 747 Union Trust Bldg PO Box 2009 Pittsburgh PA 15230

HERRINGTON, JOHN S., government administrator, lawyer; b. Los Angeles, May 31, 1939. A.B., Stanford U., 1961; J.D., U. Calif., 1964. Bar: Calif. Dep. asst. atty., Ventura, Calif., 1967-81; ptnr. Herrington & Herrington, 1967-81; founder Quail Hill Ranch Co., 1967-81; dep. asst. for personnel Office of Pres., 1981; asst. sec. Dept. Navy, 1981; spl. cons. manpower and res. affairs Office Chief of Stall, 1983—. Served to lt. USMC. Office: Office Manpower and Res Affairs Dept Nvy The Pentagon Washington DC 20350 *

HERRINGTON, LOIS HAIGHT, government official, lawyer; b. Seattle, Dec. 6, 1939; d. Herbert Schuler and Marie Yvonne (Young) H.; m. John Stewart Herrington, Apr. 10, 1965; children: Lisa Marie, Victoria Jean. B.A., U. Calif.-Davis, 1961; LL.B., Hastings Coll. Law, 1965. Probation officer San Joaquin County, Calif., 1962; counselor Juvenile Hall, Calif., 1963-65; mem. firm Herrington & Herrington, Calif., 1967-76; dep. dist. atty. Alameda County, Oakland, Calif., 1976-81; asst. atty. gen. Dept. Justice, Washington, 1983—; chmn. Pres.' Task Force on Victims of Crime, Washington, 1982; ex-officio mem. adv. bd. Nat. Inst. for Judiciary, Washington, 1983—; mem. Fed. Coordinating Council, Washington, 1983—. Vic-pres. Diablo Scholarships, Calif., 1973-76; sr. advisor USO, Calif., 1972-75; vol. high sch. vocat. counselor, 1974-76; coordinator Drug Diversion Program, Calif., 1975-76; mem. Contra Costa Child Devel. Council, Calif., 1973-76; hon. mem. Calif. Sexual Assault Investigations; mem. Alemeda County Women's Coalition on Domestic Violence, Calif., 1979-81. Recipient Outstanding Community Service Commendation Concord Police Dept, Crime Victims Rights award Family and Friends of Missing Persons and Violent Crime Victims, 1983, Outstanding Pub. Policy Leadership in Service to Victims award Nat. Orgn. Victims Assistance, 1983, Highest Quality Profl. Service to Criminal Justice and Law Enforcement award Nat. Law Enforcement Council, 1983. Mem. ABA, Calif. Bar Assn., Calif. Dist. Attys. Assn., Queen's Bench Assn., Hastings Law Sch. Alumni Assn. Republican. Episcopalian. Home: 1104 Waverley Way McLean VA 22101 Office: Dept Justice OJARS 633 Indiana Ave NW Washington DC 20531

HERRINTON, JOHN PETER, lawyer; b. Detroit, Feb. 8, 1943; s. Wilbur C. and Virginia B. (Briskey) H.; m. Rosanne G. Moran, May 14, 1966; children: Kathleen Ann, Christine Ann. B.S., U. Detroit, 1965, J.D., 1969. Bar: Mich. 1969; C.P.A., Mich. Mgr. Perrin, Fordree, Davidson & Co., Troy, Mich., 1966-70; since practiced in, Detroit; partner firm Chirco, Herrinton, Runstadler & Thomas, Troy, 1970—; instr. bus. adminstrn. U. Detroit, 1971—. Mem. Exchange Club Detroit (pres. 1973-74), Am., Detroit bar assns., State Bar Mich. (mem. council tax sect. 1975-78), Am. Inst. C.P.A.s, Mich. Assn. C.P.A.s, Am. Assn. Atty. C.P.A.s. Home: 225 Beaupre Ave Grosse Pointe Farms MI 48236 Office: Chirco Herrinton Runstadler & Thomas 2833 Crooks Rd PO Box 2501 Troy MI 48007-2501

HERRMANN, ARTHUR DOMINEY, banker; b. Louisville, Sept. 29, 1926; s. Arthur Chester and Mattie Belle (Dominey) H.; m. Lucy Kindred, Apr. 7, 1951; children: Lucy Wharton, Anne Dominey, Martha Kindred. B.A., Ohio State U., 1947, J.D., 1949; postgrad., Rutgers U., 1956. Bar: Ohio 1950. Practiced in, Columbus, 1950; asst. trust officer Huntington Nat. Bank, Columbus, 1951-56, trust officer, 1956-63, v.p., 1963-67, sr. v.p., 1967-69, exec. v.p., 1969-72, pres., chief exec. officer, 1972-75, also dir.; exec. v.p., sec. Huntington Bancshares, Inc., 1966-70, pres., 1974-81, chief exec. officer, 1975-81, vice chmn., 1974-79, chmn., 1980-81, also dir.; chmn., pres., chief exec. officer, dir. BancOhio Corp., Columbus, 1981—; chmn., chief exec. officer, dir. BancOhio Nat. Bank, 1981—; dir. N.Am. Broadcasting Co. Treas., bd. dirs. Columbus Retail Mchts. Assn., 1966—; pres., trustee Mt. Carmel Hosps., 1974-76; trustee Columbus Mus. Fine Art, 1974—, v.p., 1979-82, pres., 1982—; trustee Ohio Dominican Coll., 1978—; bd. dirs. Columbus Conv. Bur. Mem. Ohio Bankers Assn., Columbus Bar Assn., Columbus Area C. of C. (bd. dirs., vice chmn. exec. com. 1983—), Sigma Chi, Phi Delta Phi. Clubs: Mason., Columbus, Scioto Country, City (Columbus). Office: 155 E Broad St Columbus OH 43265 *

HERRMANN, BENJAMIN EDWARD, insurance executive; b. Bensonhurst, N.Y., May 9, 1919; s. Benjamin Edward and Ethel (Cuff) H.; m. Jean Clare Yancey, Oct. 19, 1946; children—Benjamin E., Elizabeth M. B.S., Columbia, 1941. C.L.U. With Home Life Ins. Co. N.Y., N.Y.C., 1941-68; regional v.p. Northeastern U.S., P.R., 1960-68; agy. v.p. Acacia Mut. Life Ins. Co., Washington, 1968-75; exec. com., dir. Acacia Nat. Life Ins. Co.; Acacia Equity Sales Corp. regional v.p. Met. N.Y., Home Life Ins. Co., N.Y.C., 1975-78, v.p. sales adminstrn., 1978-80, v.p. mktg., 1980—. Mem. Planning Bd., Madison, N.J., 1963-68, chmn., 1967-68; mem. Zoning Bd. Adjustment, 1964-68, chmn., 1966. Served to 1st lt. USAAF, 1943-46; PTO. Fellow Life Mgmt. Inst.; mem. Life Ins. Mgmt. and Research Assn. (exec. devel. com., chmn. agy. officers round table com. 1968-76, chmn. 1976, chmn. tng. dirs. subcom. 1974-76, grad. sch. agy. mgmt., agy. officer sch., sr. marketing officers' seminar), Soc. C.L.U.s, N.Y.C. Life Underwriters Assn., N.Y.C. Gen. Agts. and Mgrs. Assn., Golden Key Soc., Intertel. Republican. Presbyn. Clubs: Twin Oaks Tennis, Park Pl. Squash, No. N.J. Squash Racquets Assn., Chatham Squash and Racquet, Met. N.Y. Squash Racquets Assn.; Mchts., Fifth Ave. Raquet Club (N.Y.C.). Home: 159 Woodland Rd Madison NJ 07940 Office: 253 Broadway New York NY 10007

HERRMANN, CHRISTIAN, JR., med. educator; b. Lansing, Mich., 1921; s. Christian and Agnes (Bauch) H. A.B., U. Mich., 1942, M.D., 1944. Diplomate: neurology Am. Bd. Psychiatry and Neurology. Intern Harper Hosp., Detroit, 1944-45; asst. resident medicine Henry Ford Hosp., Detroit, 1945-46; resident neurology Neurol. Inst., N.Y.C., 1948-50, research asst. neurology, 1950-51, chief resident neurology, 1951-52, asst. neurology, 1950-51, 51-52, asst. attending, 1953-54; mem. faculty U. Calif. at Los Angeles Med. Sch., 1954—, prof. neurology, 1969—, vice chmn. dept. Neurology, 1970—. Vice chmn. Calif. chpt. Myasthenia Gravis Found., 1966—; chmn. med. adv. bd. Calif. Chpt., 1968-72, pres. Cal. chpt., 1972-74. Served as lt. (j.g.) M.C. USNR, 1946-48. USPHS research fellow neurology Columbia Coll. Phys. and Surg., 1952-54. Office: Dept Neurology Reed Neurol Research Center Univ Calif Los Angeles CA 90024

HERRMANN, DANIEL ALFRED, retail drug store chain executive; b. Rochester, N.Y., Sept. 10, 1930; s. Alfred Joseph and Josephine J. (Wecker) H.; children: Michael, Susan. B.S. in Pharmacy, U. Buffalo, 1952. Registered pharmacist, N.Y., Mich. Pharmacist, store mgr. Miller Drug Co., Buffalo, 1952-61; v.p. Fay's Drug Co., Syracuse, N.Y., 1961-76, pres., 1976—. Bd. dirs. Syracuse Chiefs Baseball Team, 1979—; vice chmn. Hiawatha council boy Scouts Am., Syracuse, 1982-83. Mem. Affiliated Drug Stores Inc. (chmn. 1982-83), Nat. Assn. Chain Drug Stores, Better Bus. Bur. Central N.Y. (chmn. 1978-81). Republican. Presbyterian. Club: Cavalry Country. Office: Fay's Drug Co Inc 7245 Henry Clay Blvd Liverpool NY 13088

HERRMANN, DANIEL LIONEL, state chief justice; b. N.Y.C., June 10, 1913; s. Philip and Rose (Schendelman) H.; m. Zelda W. Kluger, Apr. 14, 1940; children: Stephen Eric, Richard Kurt. A.B., U. Del., 1935, LL.D. (hon.), 1976; LL.B., Georgetown U., 1939, LL.D. (hon.), 1981, Del. Law Sch., 1978. Bar: D.C. 1938, Del. 1940. Practiced in, Wilmington, 1940-51, asst. U.S. atty., 1948-51; asso. judge Superior Ct., Orphans Ct. Del., 1951-58; asso. justice Del. Supreme Ct., 1965—, chief justice, 1973—; sr. partner Herrmann, Bayard, Brill & Russell, 1958-65; Dir., mem. exec. com. Del. Power & Light Co., 1962-65. Chmn. State Goals Commn., 1960-64; mem. Wilmington Bd. Pub. Edn., 1961-65; chmn. State Planning Commn., 1962-64; Pres. Legal Aid Soc. Del.; pres., chmn. bd. Jewish Fedn. Del., 1956-58; former mem. bd. dirs., exec. com. United Community Fund, Children's Bur. Del., Welfare Council Del., Del-Mar-Va council Boy Scouts Am., Jewish Community Center, Kutz Home for Aging; trustee, v.p. U. Del.; trustee Wilmington Med. Center; bd. mgrs. Wilmington Inst. Free Library. Served to maj. AUS, 1942-46. Recipient Public Service award Del. C. of C., 1981, First Disting. Service award. Fellow Inst. Jud. Adminstrn.; mem. Am., Del. bar assns., Am. Judicature Soc. (dir., Herbert Harley award 1976). Clubs: Rotarian (Pub. Service award 1979), Wilmington, University. Office: State Office Bldg Wilmington DE 19801

HERRMANN, DONALD JOSEPH, educator; b. Lee, Ill., Nov. 8, 1915; s. Fred and Agnes (O'Donnell) H.; m. Marcella Bastian, Aug. 27, 1955; children—Bernice Agnes, Mark Edward. B.Ed., No. Ill. U., 1941; M.A., Mich. State U., 1949, Ph.D., 1952. Counselor No. Ill. U., 1947-48, Mich. State U., 1948-51; mem. faculty Coll. William and Mary, Williamsburg, Va., 1951-81, prof. edn., 1961-81, emeritus, 1981—; dir. summer session, coordinator branches, 1961-65, dir. summer session and extension, 1965-68; dean Sch. Continuing Studies, 1968-72, dir. instl. research, 1972-76, dir. grad. study, 1976-81; cons. in field, 1952—. Contbr. profl. jours. Served with USAAF, 1941-46. Mem. Assn. for Instl. Research, Nat. Soc. Study Edn., Assn. Higher Edn., Omicron Delta Kappa, Phi Delta Kappa, Kappa Delta Pi. Home: 206 Matoaka Ct Williamsburg VA 23185

HERRMANN, EDWARD KIRK, actor; b. Washington, July 21, 1943; s. John Anthony and Jean Eleanor (O'Connor) H. B.A., Bucknell U., 1965; postgrad. (Fulbright scholar), London Acad. Music and Dramatic Art, 1968-69. With Dallas Theater Center, 4 years. Appeared in: numerous Broadway plays, including Moonchildren, Mrs. Warren's Profession (Tony award for Best Supporting actor 1976), Journey's End, 1978, The Beach House, 1979-80; films include The Paper Chase, 1972, The Great Gatsby, 1973, Day of the Dolphin, 1973, The Great Waldo Pepper, 1974, The Betsy, 1977, The North Avenue Irregulars, 1977, The Brass Target, 1978, Take Down, 1978, Harry's war, 1979, Reds, 1981, Death Valley, 1982, A Little Sex, 1982, Annie, 1982; TV appearances include Eleanor and Franklin: The White House Years (TV Critics Circle award as Best Actor 1977), A Love Affair: The Eleanor and Lou Gehrig Story, 1978, Freedom Road, 1978, Portrait of a Stripper, 1979, Sorrows of Gin, 1979, M.A.S.H, 1979, The Private History of a Campaign that Failed, 1980; theater appearances include Hedda Gabler; TV movies include Dear Liar, The Electric Grandmother, The Gift of Life. Lantz Agency 115 E 55th St New York NY 10022

HERRMANN, GEORGE, educator; b. USSR, Apr. 19, 1921. Dipl. C.E., Swiss Fed. Inst. Tech., 1945, Ph.D. in Mechanics, 1949. Asst., then asso. prof. civil engring. Columbia, 1950-62; prof. civil engring. Northwestern U., 1962-69; prof. applied mechanics Stanford, 1969—; cons. SRI Internat., 1970-80. Contbr. 200 articles to profl. jours; editorial bd. numerous jours. Fellow ASME (Centennial medal 1980); mem. ASCE (Th. v. Karman medal 1981), Nat. Acad. Engring., AIAA. Address: Div Applied Mechanics Durand Bldg Stanford U Stanford CA 94305

HERRNSTEIN, RICHARD JULIUS, psychology educator; b. N.Y.C., May 20, 1930; s. Rezso and Flora Irene (Friedman) H.; m. Barbara Brodo, May 28, 1951 (div. Feb. 1961); 1 dau., Julia; m. Susan Chalk Gouinlock, Nov. 11, 1961; children: Max Gouinlock, James Rezso. B.A., CCNY, 1952; Ph.D., Harvard U., 1955. Research psychologist Walter Reed Army Med. Center, Washington, 1956-58; lectr. U. Md., 1957-58; faculty Harvard U., 1958—, dir. psychol. labs., 1965-67, prof., chmn. dept. psychology, 1967-71. Author: (with E.G. Boring) A Source Book in the History of Psychology, 1965, (with J.C. Stevens and G.S. Reynolds) Laboratory Experiments in Psychology, 1965, I.Q. in the Meritocracy, 1973, (with R. Brown) Psychology, 1975; editor: Psychol. Bull., 1975-81; contbr. articles to profl. jours. Served to 1st lt. AUS, 1956-58. Guggenheim Found. fellow, 1977-78. Mem. Am., Eastern psychol. assns., Am. Acad. Arts and Scis., AAAS, Phi Beta Kappa, Sigma Xi. Home: 126 Brook St Wellesley MA 02181 Office: William James Hall Harvard Cambridge MA 02138

HERROLD, KENNETH FREDERICK, educator, psychologist; b. Lewisburg, Pa., Aug. 23, 1913; s. Benton Elijah and Millie (Else) H.; m. Elizabeth McMahan, June 21, 1941; children—Carolann, Edmund, William, John. A.B., Bucknell U., 1936; M.P.H. (fellow), U. Mich., 1940; Ed.D., Columbia U., 1948. Instr. biology Bucknell U., 1936-39, asst. prof. physiology, 1940-42; research asst. Mich. Med. Coll., 1939-40; mem. faculty dept. psychology and edn. Tchrs. Coll., Columbia U., 1947-78, prof., 1956—; pres. Herrold Assos., 1956—; research asso. Inst. Psychol. Research, 1950-54; profl. asso. Human Interaction Research Inst., Edward Glaser Assos., 1963-73; cons. in field. Mem. editorial bd.: Jour. of Social Issues; Contbr. articles to profl. jours., chpts. to books. Bd. elders Madison Ave. Presbyn. Ch., N.Y.C., West Side Presbyn. Ch., Ridgewood, N.J. Served with USN, 1941-44. Recipient award Phi Sigma-AAAS, 1935; Leader's award Harlem Prep, 1971; grantee U.S. Air Force Human Factors Operation Research Lab., 1953, 54, Hogg Found., 1956, USPHS, 1956, NIH, 1958, NDEA, 1962, Dept. Labor, 1965, 66, 67, AID, 1966, N.J. Edn. Commn., 1972, 73. Fellow Am. Psychol. Assn., Am. Sociol. Assn.; mem. AAAS, N.Y. Acad. Sci., AAUP, Am. Personnel and Guidance Assn. (chmn. membership com.). Home: 369 Godwin Ridgewood NJ 07451

HERRON, JAMES DUDLEY, chemist, educator; b. Providence, Ky., June 15, 1936; s. Clarence James and Willie Marie (Cates) H.; m. Joyce Faith Kincer, July 6, 1956; children: James Dudley, David Keith, Benjamin Alan. A.B. in Edn, U. Ky., 1958; M.S., U. N.C., 1960; Ph.D., Fla. State U., 1965. Tchr. sci., supr. Woodford County (Ky.) Schs., 1958-59, 60-62; tchr. chemistry Kaiserslautern Am. High Sch., Germany, 1962-63; asst. prof. Purdue U., West Lafayette, Ind., 1965-70, asso. prof., 1970-77, prof. sci. edn., 1977—; tng. adv. Regional Edn. Centre for Sci. and Math., Penang, Malaysia, 1972-73; program coordinator AAAS Elem. Tchr. Edn. Project, 1968. Author: New UNESCO Sourcebook for Science Teachers, 1973, (with others) Summary of Research in Science Education, 1974, Understanding Chemistry: A Preparatory Course, 1981. Recipient Jour. of Research in Sci. Teaching award for outstanding research article, 1977, 80, Catalyst of Yr. award Chem. Mfrs. Assn., 1983; NSF grantee, 1968-74; Lilly Endowment Open fellow, 1982-83. Fellow AAAS; mem. Nat. Sci. Tchrs. Assn., Am. Chem. Soc., Nat. Assn. for Research in Sci. Teaching, Phi Beta Kappa, Kappa Delta Pi (Outstanding Tchr. award 1971), Phi Delta Kappa. Home: 1770 N River Rd West Lafayette IN 47906 Office: Dept Chemistry Purdue U West Lafayette IN 47907

HERRON, JAMES M., lawyer; b. Chgo., May 4, 1934; s. J. Leonard and Sylvia H.; m. Janet Ross, June 12, 1955; children: Kathy Lynn, Tracy Ellen, Andrew Ross. A.B., U. Mo., Columbia, 1955; postgrad., Northwestern U., 1958-59; J.D., Washington U., 1961. Bar: Mo. 1961, Ohio 1971, Fla. 1975. Asst. gen. counsel, asst. sec. May Dept. Stores Co., St. Louis, 1961-70; asso. counsel Federated Dept. Stores, Inc., Cin., 1970-71; v.p., sec., gen. counsel Kenton Corp., N.Y.C., 1971-73; gen. counsel Ryder System, Inc., Miami, Fla., 1973-74, v.p., sec., gen. counsel, 1974-78, sr. v.p., sec., gen. counsel, 1978-79, exec. v.p., gen. counsel, 1979—, sec., 1983—. Trustee, bd. dirs. Greater Miami Opera Assn., 1980-81, chmn. corp. devel. com., 1981-82. Served with USMC, 1955-58. Mem. Am. Bar Assn., Mo. Bar Assn., Bar Assn. Met. St. Louis, Assn. Bar City of N.Y., Am. Soc. Corp. Secs., Fla. Bar Assn., Dade County Bar Assn. Club: Royal Palm Tennis (dir.). Home: 5945 SW 113th St Miami FL 33156 Office: 3600 NW 82d Ave Miami FL 33166

HERRON, LOWELL WILLIAM, ednl. adminstr.; b. Salem, Ohio, Feb. 2O, 1916; s. James and Susan (Sell) H.; m. Mary Lucile Shriver, July 29, 1950; children—James Hoopes, Virginia Carolyn. B.S. in Bus Adminstrn. summa cum laude, Kent State U., 1938, LL.D., 1963; M.A., U. Iowa, 1939; postgrad., Ohio State U., 1939-4O; Sc.D., Clarkson Coll. Tech., 1963; D.H.L., Inter Am. U. of P.R., 1969. With Clarkson Coll. Tech., Potsdam, N.Y., 1940-66, prof. bus. adminstrn., 1944-66, chmn. dept., 1944-48, asst. to pres., 1948-50; dean Sch. Arts, Scis. and Bus. Adminstrn., 1950-58, dean coll., 1958-63, v.p., 1963-66; v.p. acad. affairs Inter Am. U. of P.R., San German, 1966-69, prof. bus. adminstrn., 1966-69; v.p. for fin. affairs, prof. bus. adminstrn. Fairleigh Dickinson U., 1969—; treas., dir. N.J. Assn. Colls. and Univs., 1978—; indsl. cons. Aluminum Co. Am., Racquette River Paper Co., U.S. Hoffman Machinery Corp., Gen. Electric Co., Procter & Gamble Co., Goodyear Tire and Rubber Co., others; dir. Univ. Plaza Corp., Montross Corp., Harbinger Corp., Two Univ. Plaza Corp.; Lectr. Canadian Mgmt. Confs., 1952-64. Contbr. to publs. Mem. Middle States Assn. Colls. Bus. Adminstrn. (pres. 1954-55), Am. Mgmt. Assn., Sigma Tau Iota, Beta Gamma Sigma, Pi Delta Epsilon, Delta Upsilon, Order of Artus. Republican. Methodist. Club: Pennington (bd. dirs.). Address: 1031 East Saddle River Rd Ho-Ho-Kus NJ 07423

HERRON, ORLEY R., college president; b. Olive Hill, Ky., Nov. 16, 1933; s. Orley R. and Hyllie W. (Weaver) H.; m. Donna Jean Morgan, Aug. 24, 1956; children: Jill Donette, Morgan Niles, Mark Weaver. B.A., Wheaton Coll., 1955; M.A., Mich. State U., 1959, Ph.D., 1965; Litt. D. (hon.), Houghton Coll., 1972, L.H.D., Leslie Coll., 1983. Dean of students Westmont Coll., Santa Barbara, Calif., 1961-67; dir. doctoral program/student personnel U. Miss., 1967-68; asst. to pres. Ind. State U., 1968-70; pres. Greenville (Ill.) Coll., 1970-77, Nat. Coll. Edn., Evanston, Ill., 1977—; mem. Ill. Commn. for Improvement Elem. and Secondary Edn., 1983-1985. Author: Role of the Trustee, 1969, Input-Output, 1970, New Dimensions in Student Personnel Administration, 1970, A Christian Executive in a Secular World, 1979, Who Controls Your Child?, 1980; author: cassette tape Governing Higher Education in the 70's, 1970. Rep. of Pres. U.S. 25th Anniversary UNESCO, 1971; mem. adv. bd. Expt. on Internat. Living, Santa Barbara.; Bd. dirs. Ch. Centered Evangelism. Recipient Crusader Christian Contbn. award Wheaton Coll., 1955, 74, Outstanding Citizen award Greenville Jaycees, 1971. Mem. Am. Assn. Higher Edn., AAUP, Council on Inter-Instnl. Cooperation (pres.), Council Advancement Small Colls. (sec.), Christian Coll. Consortium (exec. com.), Fedn. Ind. Ill. Colls. (exec. bd. 1971—), Nat. Assn. Evangelicals (exec. com. 1974—), Assn. Free Meth. Ednl. Instns. (pres. 1973-75). Club: Kiwanian (hon.). Office: Nat Coll Edn 2840 Sheridan Rd Evanston IL 60201

HERRON, STEPHEN HOUSE, securities investment and counseling executive; b. Seattle, Oct. 27, 1925; s. Willard George and Osceola (House) H.; m. Elsbeth Ann Mauk, Sept. 1, 1951; children: Stephen Christopher, Timothy House, Todd Scrafford, Elsbeth Young. B.S., UCLA, 1948; LL.B., U. Wash., 1952. Rep. Dean Witter & Co., Seattle, 1955-64; chief exec. officer, chmn. bd. Herron Northwest, Inc., Seattle, 1964-69, Herron, Hooper & Co., Inc., 1970-75; chief officer Northwest Group of Companies, Herron Holdings Corp., 1976—. Trustee U. Calif. at Los Angeles Found. Served as ensign USNR, 1944-46. Mem. Phi Gamma Delta, Phi Delta Phi. Episcopalian. Clubs: Seattle Tennis; Overlake Golf and Country (Medina, Wash.). Home: 1935 91st Pl NE Bellevue WA 98004 Office: PO Box 69 Medina WA 98039

HERSCHBACH, DUDLEY ROBERT, educator, chemist; b. San Jose, Calif., June 18, 1932; s. Robert Dudley and Dorothy Edith (Beer) H.; m. Georgene Botyos, Dec. 26, 1964; children—Lisa Marie and Brenda Michele. B.S. in Math, Stanford U., 1954, M.S. in Chemistry, 1955; A.M. in Physics, Harvard U., 1956; Ph.D. in Chem. Physics, Harvard U., 1958; D.Sc. (h.c.), U. Toronto, 1977. Jr. fellow Harvard U., 1957-59; faculty U. Calif.-, Berkeley, 1959-63; prof. chemistry Harvard U., 1963-76, Frank B. Baird prof. sci., 1976—, chmn. chemistry dept., 1977-80, mem. faculty council, 1980-83, master Currier House, 1981—; cons. editor W.H. Freeman; lectr. Haverford Coll., 1962; Falk-Plaut lectr. Columbia, 1963; vis. prof. Göttingen (Germany) U., summer 1963, U. Calif. at Santa Cruz, 1972; Harvard lectr. Yale, 1964; Debye lectr. Cornell U., 1966; Rollefson lectr. U. Calif. at Berkeley, 1969; Guggenheim fellow U. Freiburg, Germany, 1968; vis. fellow Joint Inst. for Lab. Astrophysics U. Colo., 1969; Reilly lectr. U. Notre Dame, 1969; Phillips lectr. U. Pitts., 1971; Distinguished vis. prof. U. Ariz., 1971, U. Tex., 1977, U. Utah, 1978; Gordon lectr. U. Toronto, 1971; Clark lectr. San Jose State U., 1979; Fairchild Distinguished scholar Calif. Inst. Tech., 1976; Sloan fellow., 1959-63, Exxon Faculty fellow, 1980—. Asso. editor: Jour. Phys. Chemistry. Recipient pure chemistry award Am. Chem. Soc., 1965, Centenary medal, 1977, Pauling medal, 1978; Spiers medal Faraday Soc., 1976; Polanyi medal, 1981; Langmuir prize, 1983. Fellow Am. Phys. Soc. (chmn. chem. physics div. 1971-72), Am. Acad. Arts and Scis; mem. Am. Chem. Soc., AAAS, Nat. Acad. Scis., Phi Beta Kappa, Sigma Xi. Office: 12 Oxford St Cambridge MA 02138

HERSCHENSOHN, BRUCE, film director, writer; b. Milw., Sept. 10, 1932. Ed., Los Angeles. With art dept. RKO Pictures, 1953-55; dir., editor Gen. Dynamics Corp., 1955-56; dir., writer, editor Karma for Internat. Communications Found.; editor, co-dir. Friendship Seven for NASA; dir., editor Tall Man Five-Five for Gen. Dynamics Corp. and SAC; dir. motion picture and TV Service USIA, 1968-72, spl. cons. to dir., 1972—; staff asst. to Pres. U.S., 1972; dep. spl. asst. to Pres., 1973-74, mem. transition team, 1981; tchr. U. Md., 1972; spl. cons. to Rep. Nat. Conv., 1972; polit. analyst KABC-TV. Directed and wrote films for, USIA including, Bridges of the Barrios, The Five Cities of June, The President, John F. Kennedy: Years of Lightning, Day of Drums, Eulogy to 5:02; (Acad. award for Czechoslovakia 1968 as best documentary short 1969); Author: The Gods of Antenna, 1976; Contbg. editor: Conservative Digest. Bd. govs. Charles Edison Meml. Youth Fund. Served with USAF, 1951-52. Recipient Arthur S. Flemming award as 1 of 10 outstanding young mem in fed. govt., 1969; Distinguished Service medal USIA, 1972; Ann. award Council Against Communist Aggression, 1972. Office: KABC-TV 4151 Prospect Ave Hollywood CA 90027

HERSCHLER, ED, governor of Wyoming; b. Kemmerer, Wyo., Oct. 27, 1918; s. Edgar F. and Charlotte (Jenkins) H.; m. Kathleen Sue Colter, 1944; children: Kathleen Sue (Mrs. Jerry Hunt), James C. Student, U. Colo., 1936-41; LL.B., U. Wyo., 1949. Bar: Wyo. 1949. Gov. Wyo. County and pros. atty., Lincoln County, Wyo., 1951-59; mem. Wyo. Ho. of Reps., 1961-71, Parole Bd., State of Wyo., 1971-73; gov., Wyo., 1975—. Bd. dirs. Wyo. Heart Assn. Served with USMCR. Decorated Silver Star medal, Purple Heart. Mem. Wyo. State Bar (pres. 1968-69). Democrat. Office: Office of Gov Capitol Bldg Cheyenne WY 82001 *

HERSCHLER, ROBERT JOHN, biological chemist, company executive; b. Portland, Oreg., Mar. 10, 1923; s. William H. and Mildred (Haynes) H.; m. Janet L. Kelly, Apr. 2, 1953; children: Rebecca Sue, Cynthia Lou, Jennifer Lee. B.S., Washington U., St. Louis, 1948. With research dept. Crown Zellerbach Corp., 1948-70; cons. dept. surgery U. Oreg. Med. Sch., 1970—; Exec. v.p. Wildlife Vaccines Inc., 1974-75; pres. Bio-Delivery Systems Inc., 1977—; chmn. bd. DUSA Corp.; dir. DMSO Research Inst. Served to lt. (j.g.) USNR, 1943-46. Recipient Gov. Oreg. N.W. Scientist award, 1965. Mem. N.Y. Acad. Scis., AAAS, Am. Chem. Soc. Research and patents in field anti-pollution chems. Discoverer DMSO biological usefulness in agriculture, biological usefulness of methylsulfonylmethane (MSM); co-discoverer therapeutic usefulness DMSO. Home: 3080 NW 8th Ave Camas WA 98607

HERSCHORN, MICHAEL JULIUS, mathematics educator; b. Montreal, Que., Apr. 21, 1933; s. Sheea and Molly (Surkes) H.; m. Shirley Sand, June 20, 1954; children: Sally Deborah, Madelyn Grace. B.A., McGill U., 1953, M.A., 1956, Ph.D., 1958. Asst. prof. math. McGill U., Montreal, Que., 1959-67, assoc. prof. math., 1967-79, assoc. dean faculty of sci., 1969-78, dean students, 1978-82, prof. math., 1979—, chmn. dept. math. and stats., 1982—. Chmn. bd. edn. Solomon Schechter Acad., Montreal, 1969-78; pres. Jewish Edn. Council Greater Montreal, 1977-79; v.p. Assn. Jewish Day Schs., Montreal, 1979—, Allied Jewish Community Services, Montreal, 1980—. Recipient Anne Molson Gold medal in math. and natural philosophy McGill U., 1953. Mem. Am. Math. Soc., Can. Math. Soc., Am. Schs. Oriental Research, AAAS, Sigma Xi. Home: 5235 Saranac Ave Montreal PQ Canada H3W 2G5 Office: Dept Math and Stats McGill U 805 Sherbrooke St W Montreal PQ Canada H3A 2K6

HERSEY, DAVID FLOYD, information resources management consultant; b. Balboa, C.Z., Jan. 7, 1928; s. Ralph George and Marie M. (Ortiz) H.; m. Phyllis May Peterson, Aug. 26, 1961; children: David Floyd, Ruth Ellen, Thomas Owen. B.S., Trinity U., 1948; M.S., U. Ill., 1949; Ph.D., Washington U., St. Louis, 1952. Diplomate: Am. Acad. Microbiology. Asso. dir. Sci. Info. Exchange, Smithsonian Instn., Washington, 1961-63, dep. dir., 1964-71, pres., 1972—; mem. virus and rickettsial study sect. USPHS, 1957-61; cons. Microbiol. Assos., Inc., 1960-70, Cooke Engring. Co., Arlington, Va., 1969-72. Contbr. articles on microbiology and info. sci. to profl. jours. Commd. 1st lt. U.S. Air Force, 1952; advanced through grades to col. Res., 1973; chief clin. lab. 3700th USAF Hosp., 1952-54; Lackland AFB, Tex.; established 1st USAF Epidemiol. Lab., 1957-58; asst. chief virology br. Armed Forces Inst. Pathology, 1960-61; Washington; resigned, 1961. Decorated Air Force Commendation medal. Mem. Acad. Medicine, Am. Soc. Microbiology, Am. Soc. Info. Sci. Club: Cosmos (Washington). Home and Office: 11602 Gilson St Silver Spring MD 20902

HERSEY, DAVID KENNETH, theatrical lighting designer; b. Rochester, N.Y., Nov. 30, 1939; s. Charles Kenneth and Ella Morgan (Decker) H.; m. Demetra Maraslis; children: Demitri, Ellen; 1 dau. by previous marriage, Miranda. Lighting cons. Nat. Theater, Eng., 1975-81; founder David Hersey Assos. Ltd., London, Eng., 1975, chmn., 1975—; free-lance lighting designer, 1968—. Lighting designer 150 prodns. Brit. theater cos. including, Nat. Theatre, Royal Shakespeare Co., Royal Opera House, English Nat. Opera, various London theatres; active, various European cities, Japan, Australia; designer: lighting for Evita, Los Angeles, 1979 (Los Angeles Drama Critics award 1979, Tony award 1980), The Crucifier of Blood (Dramalogue award 1980), Los Angeles, 1980, The Life and Adventures of Nicholas Nickleby, N.Y.C., 1981, Merrily We Roll Along, N.Y.C., 1981. Mem. Soc. Brit. Theatre Designers (exec.), United Scenic Artists. Developer various lighting effects including light curtains and gobos; completed 3 month trip on own boat Eng. to Greece, 1977. Office: 162 Anyards Rd Cobham Surrey KT 11 1AA England *

HERSEY, GEORGE LEONARD, art history educator; b. Cambridge, Mass., Aug. 30, 1927; s. Milton Leonard and Katherine (Page) H.; m. Jane Maddox Lancefield, Sept. 2, 1953; children: Donald, James. B.A., Harvard U., 1951; M.F.A., Yale U., 1954, M.A., 1961, Ph.D., 1964. Instr. art Bucknell U., Lewisburg, Pa., 1954-55, asst. prof., 1955-59, acting chmn., 1958-59; instr. Yale U., New Haven, Conn., 1963-65; asst. prof. Yale, 1965-68; assoc. prof. Yale U., 1968-74, prof., 1974—; Mem. adv. bd. Conn. Preservation Trust; mem. Conn. State Commn. Capitol Restoration, 1977-79. Author: Alfonso II and the Artistic Renewal of Naples, 1969, The Aragonese Arch at Naples, 1443-1475, 1973, High Victorian Gothic, 1972, Pythagorean Palaces: Magic and Architecture in the Italian Renaissance, 1975, Architecture, Poetry and Number in the Royal Palace at Caserta, 1983; author articles and revs.; Co-editor: Architectura, 1971—; editor: Yale Publs. in History of Art, 1974—; mem. adv. bd.: Pre-Raphaelite Rev. Served with U.S. Army, 1946-47. Fulbright scholar, Italy, 1962; Am. Philos. Soc. fellow, Italy, 1962; Morse fellow, 1966; Schepp fellow, Florence, Italy, 1972. Mem. Soc. Archtl. Historians (dir. 1971-73), Renaissance Soc. Am., Coll. Art Assn., Victorian Soc. (U.S. and Great Britain) (dir. chpt.). Democrat. Home: 167 Linden St New Haven CT 06511 Office: Dept of History of Art Yale University New Haven CT 06520

HERSEY, JOHN, writer; b. Tientsin, China, June 17, 1914; s. Roscoe Monroe and Grace (Baird) H.; m. Frances Ann Cannon, Apr. 27, 1940 (div. Feb. 1958); children: Martin, John, Ann, Baird; m. Barbara Day Kaufman, June 2, 1958; 1 dau., Brook. Student, Hotchkiss Sch., 1927-32, Clare Coll., Cambridge (Eng.) U., 1936-37; B.A., Yale U., 1936; M.A. (hon.), Yale U., 1947; LL.D., Washington and Jefferson Coll., 1950; D.H.L., Dropsie Coll., 1950; L.H.D., New Sch. for Social Research, 1950; Litt.D., Wesleyan U., 1954, Bridgeport U., 1964, U. New Haven, 1970, Clarkson Coll. Tech., 1972, Syracuse U., 1983, Yale U., 1984. Pvt. sec. to Sinclair Lewis, summer 1937; writer for Time mag., editor, 1937-44; sr. editor Life mag., 1944-45; war and fgn. corr. Time, Life, New Yorker, 1942-46; fellow Berkeley Coll., Yale U., 1950-65; master Pierson Coll., Yale, 1965-70, fellow, 1965—; writer in residence Am. Acad. in Rome, 1970-71; lectr. Yale U., 1971-76, vis. prof., 1976-77, prof., 1977-84; mem. faculty Salzburg Seminar in Am. Studies, 1975; vis. prof. Mass. Inst. Tech., 1975. Author: Men on Bataan, 1942, Into the Valley, 1943, A Bell for Adano, 1944, Hiroshima, 1946, The Wall, 195O, The Marmot Drive, 1953, A Single Pebble, 1956, The War Lover, 1959, The Child Buyer, 1960, Here To Stay, 1963, White Lotus, 1965, Too Far To Walk, 1966, Under the Eye of the Storm, 1967, The Algiers Motel Incident, 1968, Letter to the Alumni, 1970, The Conspiracy, 1972, The Writer's Craft, 1974, My Petition for More Space, 1974, The President, 1975, The Walnut Door, 1977, Aspects of the Presidency, 1980. Chmn. Conn. Com. for Gifted, 1954-57; mem. vis. com. Harvard Grad. Sch. Edn., 1960-65, Loeb Drama Center, Harvard, 1980—; trustee Putney Sch., 1953-56, Nat. Citizens' Council for Pub. Schs., 1956-58, Nat. Com. for Support Pub. Schs., 1962-68; del. White House Conf. on Edn., 1955, PEN Congress, Tokyo, 1958; commr. Nat. Commn. on New Tech. Uses of Copyrighted Works, 1975-78. Recipient Pulitzer prize for fiction, 1945; Sidney Hillman Found. award, 1951; Howland medal Yale, 1952; Hon. fellow Clare Coll., Cambridge, 1967. Mem. Authors League Am. (council 1946-70, 75—, v.p. 1948-54, pres. 1975-80), Am. Acad. and Inst. Arts and Letters (sec. 1962-77, chancellor 1981—), Am. Acad. Arts and Scis., Authors Guild (council 1946—, chmn. contract com. 1963—). Home: 420 Humphrey St New Haven CT 06511

HERSH, SEYMOUR M., journalist; b. Chgo., Apr. 8, 1937; s. Isadore and Dorothy (Margolis) H.; m. Elizabeth Sarah Klein, May 30, 1964; children: Matthew, Melissa, Joshua. B.A. in History, U. Chgo., 1958. Police reporter City News Bur., 1959-60; UPI Corr., Pierre, S.D., 1962-63, A.P. corr., Chgo. and Washington, 1963-67; with staff N.Y. Times (Washington bur.), 1972-75, N.Y.C., 1975-78, Washington, 1979; nat. corr. Atlantic Monthly, 1983—; press sec. Senator Eugene J. McCarthy of Minn. (in N.H. primary), 1968. Offered stories on My Lai through, Dispatch News Service.; Author: Chemical and Biological Warfare: America's Hidden Arsenal, 1968, My Lai 4: A Report on the Massacre and Its Aftermath, 1970, Cover-Up: The Army's Secret Investigation of the Massacre of My Lai 4, 1972, The Price of Power: Kissinger in the Nixon White House, 1983; Contbr. articles to mags. Recipient Worth Bingham prize, Sigma Delta Chi Disting. Service award, Pulitzer prize for internat. reporting, 1970; George Polk Meml. award, 1970; Scripps-Howard Pub. Service award and 2d Polk award for stories on B-52 bombing in Cambodia, 1973; Sidney Hillman and 3d Polk awards for stories on domestic CIA spying, 1974; John Peter Zenger Freedom of The Press award, 1975; Drew Pearson prize for stories on CIA involvement in Chile.; 2d Sigma Delta Chi Disting. Service award, 1981; 4th Polk prize, 1981. Office: Nat Press Bldg Washington DC 20045

HERSHBERGER, ERVIN N., clergyman, editor; b. Grantsville, Md., Apr. 17, 1914; s. Noah E. and Savilla S. (Yoder) H.; m. Barbara Beachy, May 12, 1940; 1 dau., Mildred Elizabeth Hershberger Yoder. Student pub. schs. Editor Herold der Wahrheit, 1955-69, Calvary Messenger, Meyersdale, Pa., 1970—; ordained deacon Mennonite Ch., 1964; Dairy farmer, Meyersdale. Mem. Mennonite Mission Bd., mem. com. mission interests, 1963-74; chmn. bd., asst. prin. Calvary Bible Sch., 1971-80, prin., 1980—. Address: RD 1 Box 176 Meyersdale PA 15552

HERSHENOV, BERNARD ZION, electronics research and development company executive; b. N.Y.C., Sept. 22, 1927; s. Joseph and Rebecca (Landes) H.; m. Miriam Leah Gold, Oct. 27, 1950; 1 dau., Ruth Lois. B.S., U. Mich., 1950, M.S., 1952, Ph.D., 1959. Asso. research engr. U. Mich., Ann Arbor, 1951-59; devel. engr. Gen. Electric Co., Schenectady, 1959-60; mem. tech. staff, head microwave integrated circuits RCA Research Labs., Princeton, N.J., 1960-72; dir. Research Labs., Tokyo, 1972-75, head energy systems, Princeton, 1976-79, dir. Solid State Devices Lab., 1979-83, dir. Optical Systems and Display Materials Lab., 1983—. Contbr. articles in field. Vice pres. Jewish Community Center, Princeton, 1970-71, pres., 1971-72, trustee, 1977-79. Served with USN, 1946-47. Recipient RCA Outstanding Achievement awards, 1963, 66. Fellow IEEE; mem. Am. Phys. Soc., Sigma Xi, Phi Kappa Phi. Jewish. Home: 22 Raleigh Rd Kendall Park NJ 08824 Office: PO Box 432 Princeton NJ 08540

HERSHENSON, HAROLD, medical device company executive; b. Chgo., Sept. 28, 1927; s. Peter and Anna (Frischer) H.; m. Eugenia Julia Aberson, Aug. 17, 1947 (div. 1969); children: Neal Steven, Janet Louise Hershenson Hinckley, Karen Joyce; m. Paula Westrope Murray, Dec. 28, 1970. B.S., UCLA, 1947; M.S., U. So. Calif., 1962. Jr. profl. asst. chemist U.S. Navy, San Francisco, 1947-48; dir. chem. research and devel. McGraw Labs., Los Angeles, 1948-70; from staff chemist to exec. v.p. Cordis Corp., Miami, Fla., 1970—; dir. Cordis-Dow Corp., Miami, 1982—. Patent container syringe; co-patentee (fat emulsion, starch pasma expander). Bd. dirs. Chopin Found. Council, South Fla., 1980—. Mem. Am. Chem. Soc., Soc. Plastics Engrs., Am. Soc. Quality Control, Assn. for Advancement of Med. (Instrumentation), Health Industry Mfrs. Assn., Sigma Xi, Phi Lambda Upsilon, Alpha Sigma Lambda, Ephebian Soc. Club: Coral Gables Country. Home: 1020 Castile Ave Coral Gables FL 33134 Office: Cordis Corp 10555 W Flagler St Miami FL 33152

HERSHEY, ALFRED DAY, geneticist; b. Owosso, Mich., Dec. 4, 1908; s. Robert Day and Alma (Wilbur) H.; m. Harriet Davidson, Nov. 15, 1946; 1 son, Peter. B.S., Mich. State U., 1930, Ph.D. in Chemistry, 1934, D.M.S., 1970; D.Sc. (hon.), U. Chgo., 1967. Asst. bacteriologist Washington U. Sch. Medicine, St. Louis, 1934-36, instr., 1936-38, asst. prof., 1938-42, asso. prof., 1942-50; mem. staff, genetics research unit Carnegie Inst. of Washington, Cold Spring Harbor, N.Y., 1950-62, dir., 1962-74; ret., 1974. Contbr. articles to profl. jours. Recipient Nobel prize in Medicine (joint), 1969; Albert Lasker award Am. Pub. Health Assn., 1958; Kimber Genetics award Nat. Acad. Scis., 1965. Mem. Nat. Acad. Scis. Address: Genetics Research Unit Carnegie Instn Washington PO Box 200 Cold Spring Harbor NY 11724 *

HERSHEY, BARBARA, actress; b. Hollywood, Calif.; 1 son, Tom. Student public schs., Hollywood. Appeared in: TV series The Monroes, 1966-67, From Here to Eternity, 1979; mini-series A Man Called Intrepid, 1979; other TV appearances include Gidget, 1965; The Invaders, 1967, Daniel Boone, 1967, Love Story, 1973, Bob Hope Chrysler Theatre, 1967, High Chaparral, 1967, Kung Fu, 1973, CBS Playhouse, 1967; TV films include In the Glitter Palace, 1977; Just a Little Inconvenience, 1977, Sunshine Christmas, 1977, Angel on My Shoulder, 1980; movies include With Six You Get Egg Roll, 1968; Last Summer, 1968, Heaven with a Gun, 1968, The Liberation of L.B. Jones, 1969, The Baby Maker, 1969, The Pursuit of Happiness, 1969, Dealing, 1970, Boxcar Bertha, 1971, Angela-Love Comes Quietly, 1972, The Crazy World of Julius Vrooder, 1973, The Last Hard Men, 1975, Diamonds, 1975, A Choice of Weapons, 1975, The Stuntman, 1978, The Entity, 1983, The Right Stuff, 1983, The Natural, 1984. Office: care Creative Artists Agy 1888 Century Park East Los Angeles CA 90067 *

HERSHEY, DANIEL, chemical engineering educator; b. N.Y.C., Feb. 12, 1931; s. Frank and Anna (Scharf) H.; m. Barbara Fay Drury, Sept. 5, 1965; children—Michael David, Andrea Lynn. B.S., Cooper Union, 1953; M.S., U. Tenn., 1959, Ph.D., 1961. Chem. engr. Merck, Sharp & Dohme, 1961-62; faculty U. Cin., 1962—, prof. chem. engring., 1969—, asst. to pres., 1973-75, dir. gerontology council, 1975-80; v.p. Basal-Tech, Inc., 1982—; convenor Greater Cin. Gerontology Consortium, 1975-83. Author: My University, My God, 1970, Everyday Science, 1971, Transport Analysis, 1973, Lifespan and Factors Affecting It, 1974, A New Age-Scale for Humans, 1980, Must We Grow Old (From Pauling to Prigogine to Toynbee), 1983; editor: Chemical Engineering in Medicine and Biology, 1967, Blood Oxygenation, 1970; patentee whole-body calorimeter, 1983. Mem. Cin. adv. bd. Univ. Without Walls, 1977—. Served with AUS, 1955-57. Recipient Outstanding Tchr. award Tau Beta Pi, 1970, 72; NIH grantee, 1964-69; Fulbright fellow, 1975. Mem. A.A.U.P. (pres. U. Cin. chpt. 1971-72), Sigma Xi (pres. U. Cin. chpt. 1973-75). Home: 726 Lafayette Ave Cincinnati OH 45220

HERSHEY, FALLS BACON, educator, surgeon; b. Chgo., Aug. 16, 1918; s. Charles O. and Emma L. (Eby) H.; m. Julia K. Elder, Oct. 15, 1955; children—Charles O., Laura V., James E., Julian. Student, Goshen (Ind.) Coll., 1935-37; B.S., U. Ill., 1939; M.D., Harvard, 1943. Diplomate: Am. Bd. Surgery. Med. intern Peter Bent Brigham Hosp., Boston, 1943; surg. intern, asst. resident surgery Mass. Gen. Hosp., 1946-48, 1st asst. resident surgery, 1948-51; research asso. biology Mass. Inst. Tech., 1948-50; teaching fellow surgery Harvard Med. Sch., 1952; chief resident surgery Mass. Gen. Hosp., Boston, 1952; from instr. to asso. prof. surgery Washington U. Sch. Medicine, St. Louis, 1953-64, asso. prof. clin. surgery, 1966—; chief surgery VA Hosp., St. Louis, 1955-60; acting chief Hartford Burn Unit, Washington U., 1966-67; prof. surgery Chgo. Med. Schs.; also chmn. dept. surgery Michael Reese Hosp. and Med. Center, Chgo., 1964-66; dir. vascular surgery, dir. blood flow lab. St. John's Mercy Med. Center, 1974. Author: (with C.H. Calman) Atlas of Vascular Surgery, 1963; also articles. Vice pres. Eastern Mo. Exptl. Health Services, Inc., Eastern Mo. Profl. Rev. Orgn.; mem. bd. Mo. Blue Cross Inc.; Bd. dirs. St.

Louis Heart Assn.; councillor Mo. chpt. Am. Cancer Soc. Served as med. officer USPHS, 1944-46; med. officer U.S.S. Charlottesville. Mem. Internat. Cardiovascular Soc., St. Louis County Med. Soc. (pres. 1971), Western Surg. Assn., Soc. for Cryobiology, Alpha Omega Alpha. Home: 11 Wydown Terr Clayton MO 63105 Office: 621 S New Ballas Rd Saint Louis MO 63141

HERSHEY, GERALD LEE, psychologist; b. Detroit, Mar. 7, 1931; s Von Waltz and Clementine H.; m. Shirley Gauld, Oct. 2, 1954; children: Bruce, Dale, James. Student, UCLA, 1949-54; B.A. with honors, Mich. State U., 1957, M.A., 1958, Ph.D., 1961. Asst. instr., research assoc. Mich. State U., East Lansing, 1958-61; mem. faculty dept. psychology Fullerton Coll., Calif., 1961—, prof., 1965—, chmn. dept., 1980—; vis. prof. Chapman Coll., Calif., 1962-69. Co-author: Human Development (2d edit.), 1978, Living Psychology (3d edit.), 1981. Served to 1st lt. AUS, 1954-56. Mem. Am. Psychol. Assn., Assn. Humanistic Psychology, NEA. Lodge: Lions. Office: Fullerton College 321 E Chapman Ave Fullerton CA 92634

HERSHEY, NATHAN, lawyer, educator; b. N.Y.C., Apr. 28, 1930; s. Harry and Hannah (Horwitz) H.; m. Carol Fine, July 13, 1958; children—Suzanne, Madeleine. A.B., N.Y. U., 1950; LL.B., Harvard, 1953. Bar: D.C. bar 1953, N.Y. bar 1955, Pa. bar 1977. Individual practice law, N.Y.C., 1955-56; research asso. in health law U. Pitts., 1956-58, asst. prof., 1958-63, asso. prof., 1963-68, prof., 1968—; mem. Pa. Bd. Med. Edn., 1974-80; of counsel firm Markel, Schafer & Means, Pitts., 1977—; cons. Pa. State Com. on Public Health and Welfare, 1973-80. Author: (with others) Hospital Law Manual, 1959, (with Robert D. Miller) Human Experimentation and the Law, 1976, Hospital-Physician Relations, 1982; contbr. articles to profl. jours. Bd. dirs. Women's Health Services, 1976—, Bd. v.p., 1982—; Bd. dirs. Hill House Assn., Pitts., 1964-71. Served with U.S. Army, 1953-55. Mem. Inst. Medicine-Nat. Acad. Scis., Am. Soc. Hosp. Attys. (past pres.), Soc. Hosp. Attys. Western Pa. (dir. 1974—, past pres.), Am. Pub. Health Assn., Am. Bar Assn. Democrat. Jewish. Home: 5423 Northumberland St Pittsburgh PA 15217 Office: 1120 Grant Bldg Pittsburgh PA 15219

HERSHMAN, JACOB EARL, govt. ofcl.; b. Mechanicsburg, Pa., Nov. 7, 1913; s. John R. and Fairy (Pfaltzgraff) H.; m. Alberta Garns, Jan. 2, 1942; children—Joan Elaine, John Garns, Lucie Ann. B.S., Elizabethtown (Pa.) Coll., 1936; M.Ed., U. Md., 1949, D.Ed., 1956. Regional display supr. Montgomery Ward Co., 1939-42; high sch. tchr., Washington, Md., 1945-56; curriculum specialist South Hagerstown (Md.) High Sch., 1956-57; prin. Hancock (Md.) High Sch., 1957-61; dean Elizabethtown Coll., 1961-66; program specialist Bur. Higher Edn., Office of Edn., HEW, Washington, 1966-67, higher edn. specialist, div. coll. facilities, 1967, chief instl. eligibility unit colls. and univs., accreditation and instl. eligibility staff, until 1981, ret., 1981; now cons. higher edn. instns. Active Boy Scouts, Community Chest, A.R.C. fund drives.; Bd. dirs. Hancock Free Library. Served as sgt. AUS, 1942-45. Mem. N.E.A., Md., Washington County tchrs. assns., Nat., Md. assns. secondary sch. prins., Nat. Biology Tchrs. Assn., Md. History Tchrs. Assn., Eastern Assn. Coll. Deans, Pa. Assn. Acad. Deans, Phi Delta Kappa. Club: Rotarian. Home: 1217 Gaskins Rd Apt D Richmond VA 23233

HERSHMAN, LYNN LESTER, artist; 1 dau., Dawn. B.S., Case-Western Res. U., 1963; M.A., San Francisco State U., 1972. Vis. prof. art U. Calif., Berkeley, Calif. Coll. Arts and Crafts, San Jose State U., 1974-78; asso. project dir. Christo's Running Fence, 1973-76; founder, dir. Floating Mus., 1975-79; ind. film producer and cons., 1979—. Author works in field.; one-man shows include, Santa Barbara Mus. Art, 1970, Univ. Art Mus., Berkeley, Calif., 1972, Mills Coll., Oakland, Calif., 1973, William Sawyer Gallery, 1974, Nat. Galleries, Melbourne, Australia, 1976, Mandeville Art Gallery, U. Calif., San Diego, M.H. de Young Art Mus., 1978, Pallazo dei Diamonte, Ferrara, Italy, San Francisco Art Acad., 1980, Portland Center Visual Arts, New Mus., New Sch., N.Y.C., 1981, Inst. Contemporary Art, Phila., Anina Nosai Gallery, N.Y.C., Contemporary Art Center, Cin., 1982, group exhbns. include, Calif. Coll. Arts and Crafts, 1981, San Francisco Mus. Modern Art, 1980, Art-Beaubourg, Paris. Bd. dirs. San Francisco Art Acad., Spectrum Found., Goodman Bldg., Motion a Performance Collective. Mem. Assn. Art Pubs. (dir.) *

HERSHMAN, MENDES, lawyer; b. Northampton, Pa., May 20, 1911; s. Joel and Rose (Grossman) H.; m. Frances Sybil Stackell, June 2, 1935; children: Jane, Martha. A.B., N.Y.U., 1929; LL.B., Harvard U., 1932. Bar: N.Y. 1933. Spl. counsel for housing N.Y. Life Ins. Co., N.Y.C., 1946-62, asst. gen. counsel, 1962-64, assoc. gen. counsel, 1964-69, v.p., gen. counsel, 1969-72, sr. v.p., gen. counsel, 1972-77; sr. partner firm Rosenman Colin Freund Lewis & Cohen, N.Y.C., 1977—; lectr. joint com. on continuing legal edn. Am. Law Inst.-Am. Bar Assn., Practising Law Inst.; chmn. legal adv. com. to bd. dirs. N.Y. Stock Exchange, 1978—; vis. prof. Marshall-Wythe Law Sch., Coll. William and Mary, 1978-79; chmn. Mayor's Com. on Judiciary, 1972-77, N.Y. State Commn. on Jud. Nominations, N.Y. State Commn. on Uniform State Laws. Bd. editors: N.Y. Law Jour, 1969—; Contbr. articles profl. jours. Bd. dirs. N.Y. Landmarks Conservancy, N.Y.C. Pub. Devel. Corp.; bd. dirs. council governing bds. Ind. Colls. and Univs. N.Y. State; vice chmn. Citizens Union. Recipient N.Y. State award, certificate of Outstanding Pub. Service, 1960. Fellow Am. Bar Found.; mem. Assn. Bar City N.Y. (com. chmn., past v.p., chmn. exec. com.), Am. Bar Assn. (mem. council, sect. officer), Am. Law Inst. (chmn. com. on continuing legal edn.), Harvard Law Sch. Assn. N.Y.C. (trustee, pres.), Phi Beta Kappa. Home: 200 E 66th St New York NY 10021 Office: 575 Madison Ave New York NY 10022

HERSMAN, MARION FRANK, city manager, lawyer; b. Huntington, W.Va., Nov. 12, 1932; s. Marion Rockefeller and Frances Mae (Peabody) H.; m. Carole Anne Birthright, Oct. 1960 (div.); 1 son, Frank Eric Birthright; m. Nina Claire Mohay, Dec. 24, 1976 (div.); 1 dau., Alicia Claire. B.S. in Chemistry, Physics and Math, Ohio State U., 1953; Ph.D. in Chemistry (Victor Chem. fellow, Colgate Palmolive-Peet fellow, Univ. fellow), U. Ill., 1956; J.D., George Washington U., 1958, LL.M., 1960; M.A., New Sch. for Social Research, 1964. Bar: N.Y. State bar, U.S. Supreme Ct. bar, Dist. Ct. for D.C. bar. Teaching fellow U. Ill.; patent examiner U.S. Patent Office, Washington, 1956-57; assoc. firm Burns Doane, Benedict & Irons, Washington, 1957-59, Arthur, Dry & Dole, N.Y.C., 1959-60, Fish, Richardson & Neave, 1960-64; staff assoc. office sci. resources planning NSF, Washington, 1964-67, office of planning and policy studies, 1967-69, head office intergovtl. sci. programs, 1969-72, dir. office intergovtl. sci. and research utilization, 1972-75; exec. dir. Colo. Planning Coordinating Council, 1976; spl. asst., sci. and tech. advisor to Gov. Colo., 1976; sci. and tech. advisor Fedn. Rocky Mountain States, Denver, 1977; dir. Rocky Mountain Tech. Sharing Task Force, 1977, Div. Water Resources, 1977; dir. Div. Pub. Utilities Hillsborough County (Fla.), Tampa, 1977-78; dir. Office of Planning and Intergovtl. Relations Hillsborough County, Tampa, 1978-79; asst. county adminstr. Hillsborough County (Fla.) Div. Pub. Utilities, 1978-79; vice chmn. Hillsborough Intergovtl. Resource Recovery Mgmt. Com.; mem. Fla. Community Conservation Com., 1978-80, Urban Consortium, 1978-80; spl. asst. to pres. U. South Fla., 1979-80; atty. NSF, 1980-82; dir. com. on hazardous materials Fed. Emergency Mgmt. Agy., 1981—; vis. disting. prof. Nova U., 1982, spl. asst. to pres. for program devel., 1982; asst. city mgr. for health and human services, City of Austin, (Tex.), 1982—; speaker in field. Teaching asso. George Washington U., 1957-59; chmn., exec. dir. com. on intergovtl. sci. relations Fed. Council Sci. and Tech., Exec. Office of Pres., 1969-73; mem. Agrl. Yearbook adv. bd. U.S. Dept. Agr., 1969, mem. tech. adv. bd. nat. rural communities facilities assessment, 1978; chmn. com. on policy mgmt. and assistance U.S. Office Mgmt. and Budget, Washington, 1974-75; mem. com. on tech. sharing President's Office Sci. and Tech., 1972-74; prof. urban engring. Nat. U. Mex., Mexico City, 1975; vis. faculty CSC, Kings Point, N.Y., 1975, Fed. Exec. Inst., Charlottesville, Va., 1977, Golden Gate U., 1979-80; vis. prof. U. Colo. Grad. Sch. Pub. Affairs, 1976-77, U. South Fla., 1978; spl. asst. to dir. NSF, 1976-80; cons. Office Sci. and Tech., Exec. Office of Pres., 1976-80, Western Govs.' Task Force on Regional Policy Mgmt., 1976-77; mem. Subcom. on Research Utilization Transp. Research Bd.-NRC-Nat. Acad. Scis., 1981-82. Contbg. author: Science and Technology Policies, 1973; bd. editors and consultants: Scholar and Educator, 1977; mem. editorial bd.: Jour. Edn. and Scholar, 1977—; contbr. articles to profl. jours. Bd. dirs. Warwick Assn., 1980-81; chmn. consumers and bus. affairs com. D.C. Area Neighborhood Council. Recipient Pub. Service award states of Ga., La., Ala., Pa., Okla., N.C., So. Interstate Nuclear Bd., Nat. Conf. State Legislatures; Picatinny Arsenal grantee; U.S. Govt. grantee. Mem. Va., D.C., Fed. bar assns., Am. Chem. Soc., Am. Soc. Pub. Adminstrn. (chmn. sect. on intergovtl. adminstrn. and mgmt. 1977-79, Public Service award), AAAS, Sigma Xi, Phi Lambda Upsilon, Delta Theta Phi (chmn. scholarships), Alpha Chi Sigma, Kappa Sigma. Home: 1319 North Carolina Ave NE Washington DC 20002 Office: City Hall PO Box 1088 Austin TX 78767

HERST, HERMAN, JR., writer; b. N.Y.C., Mar. 17, 1909; s. Herman and Lillian (Myers) H.; m. Ida Busch, June 24, 1957; children: Patricia Herst Held, Kenneth Reed; stepchildren: Gary K. Busch, Gail Busch. B.A., Reed Coll., 1931; M.A., U. Oreg., 1932; D.Litt. (hon.), William Penn Coll., 1982. Profl. philatelist and cons. Herman Herst Jr. Inc., N.Y.C., 1933-73; free-lance writer, Boca Raton, Fla., 1973—. Author: Nassau Street, 1960, Fun and Profit in Stamp Collecting, 1964, Stories to Collect Stamps By, 1968, More Stories to Collect Stamps By, 1982; numerous tech. books on philatelic subjects; staff columnist: Hobbies, Stamps, Stamp Collector, Linns Stamp News, Stamp Wholesaler, Stamp Rev. Mem. Boca Raton Bicentennial Com., 1975. Recipient Merit medal New Haven Philatelic Soc., 1955, disting. service award Soc. Philatelic Ams., 1974, Good Citizen's medal Fla. State SAR. Mem. Internat. Philatelic Press Club, Am. Philatelic Soc. Writers' Unit, Association Internationale de Journalistes Philateliques, Mayflower Soc. (hon. life), Mayflower award 1964), Am. Philatelic Soc. (life), John A. Luff award 1961), Collectors' Club. Democrat. Jewish. Clubs: Boca Raton, Boca Pointe. Lodges: Masons; Shriners. Home: 1098 Spanish River Rd Boca Raton FL 33432 *I have been most fortunate in enjoying every activity in which I have participated, and doubly so, when in performance of my tasks adding to the happiness of others by assisting them with their hobby of philately.*

HERSTAND, THEODORE, theatre artist, educator; b. N.Y.C., May 14, 1930; s. Max Arthur and Rose (Shyatt) H.; m. Jo Ellen Gillette, Aug. 23, 1957; children: Sarah Ellen, Michael Simpson. Certificate Advanced Studies, U. Birmingham (Eng.), 1951; B.A., U. Iowa, 1953, M.A., 1957; Ph.D., U. Ill., 1963. Instr. theatre Parsons Coll., Fairfield, Iowa, 1953-54, Eastern Ill. U., Charleston, 1957-59; asst. prof. State U. N.Y. at Plattsburgh, 1960-64, asso. prof., 1963-64; asst. prof. U. Ill., 1964-66; asso. prof. U. Minn., Mpls., 1966-70; prof., chmn. dept. theatre, drama and dance Case Western Res. U., Cleve., 1970-77, chmn. faculty senate, 1975-76; dir. Sch. Drama, U. Okla., Norman, 1977-79, prof., 1979—; artistic dir., actor Okla. Profl. Theatre, 1978; vis. prof. Mpls. Coll. Art and Design, 1969; vis. dir. Colo. Shakespeare Festival, Boulder, 1968, 82; theatre bldg. cons. Eastern Ill. U., Charleston, Ill. State U., Bloomington, Jewish Community Center Theater, Mpls.; ednl. cons. in arts; spl. contbr. Silver Burdett Music Series. Profl. actor, dir. over 50 plays; Author: plays Sugar and Lemon, 1968; new version of Oedipus, 1978; Dov, 1982; others.; Asso. editor: Drama Survey, 1967-70; Contbr. revs., articles to profl. jours.; founder: Klein Nat. Playwriting award, 1974, Bliss Nat. Playwriting award, 1980. Bd. dirs. Theater-in-the-Round, Mpls., 1968, v.p. bd., 1969; bd. dirs. Great Lakes Shakespeare Festival, 1970-71; trustee Karamu House, 1975-77; chmn. bd. dirs. Okla. Hillel Found., 1981-82. Served to 1st lt. USAF, 1954-56. Mem. Nat. Theatre Conf., Dramatists Guild, S.W. Theatre Conf., Am. Theatre Assn., Am. Community Theatre Assn., Omicron Delta Kappa. Home: 4418 Manchester Ct Norman OK 73069 Office: Sch Drama U Oklahoma Norman OK 73019

HERSTEIN, ISRAEL NATHAN, mathematician, educator; b. Lublin, Poland, Mar. 28, 1923; came to U.S., 1946, naturalized, 1955; s. Jacob and Mary (Lichtenstein) H.; m. Marianne Deson, June 16, 1946 (div. Mar. 1973); m. Barbara, Mar. 20, 1980. B.Sc. with honors, U. Man., 1945; M.A., U. Toronto, 1946; Ph.D., Ind. U., 1948. Instr. U. Kans., 1948-50; lectr. Ohio State U., 1951; asst. prof. math. U. Chgo., 1951-53, prof., 1962—; asst. prof. U. Pa., 1953-56, asso. prof., 1956-57; asso. prof. math. Cornell U., Ithaca, N.Y., 1957-58, prof., 1958-62; vis. prof. U. Rome, 1961-62, 63, 65, 66, 68, Stanford U., 1960, 64, U. Calif.-, San Diego, 1979-80; Fulbright lectr., Rio de Janeiro, Brazil, 1967; joint prof. Weizmann Inst., 1971-73; vis. prof. U. Auckland, New Zealand, summer 1976; Fulbright lectr. Laguna U., 1976; vis. prof. Hebrew U., 1977-78; cons. Ramo Woodridge Co., 1956, Gen. Electric Co., 1958-60, Lincoln Labs., 1958-59; editor Harper & Row, 1962—. Author: Topics in Algebra, 1964, Non-Commutative Rings, 1967, Topics in Ring Theory, 1968, (with Sandler) Introduction To The Calculus, 1971, (with Kaplansky) Matters Mathematical, 1974, Rings with Involution, 1976; Contbr. numerous articles to profl. jours. Dir. Comitato Internat. Matematico Estivo, Varenna, Italy, 1965. Guggenheim fellow, 1961-62, 68-69. Mem. Am. Math. Soc., Math. Assn. Am. Home: 3530 N Lake Shore Dr Chicago IL 60657

HERTEL, DENNIS MARK, congressman, lawyer; b. Detroit, Dec. 7, 1948; s. John and Marie (Kaufmann) H.; m. Cynthia S. Grosscup, Sept. 2, 1971; children: Heather, Heidi, Katie. H.S. cum laude, Eastern Mich. U., 1971; J.D., Wayne State U., 1974. Bar: Mich. 1975. Tchr. public schs., Detroit, 1972-74; mem. Mich. Ho. of Reps., 1974-80, 97th-98th congresses from 14th Dist. Mich. Mem. Am. Bar Assn., State Bar Mich., Wayne State U. Alumni Assn., East Warren Businessmen's Assn., Eastern Mich. U. Alumni, Grosse Pointe Jaycees, Steuben Soc. Am. Democrat. Clubs: St. Matthew's Mens., Lions. Office: 218 Cannon House Office Bldg Washington DC 20515 *

HERTIG, ARTHUR TREMAIN, physician; b. Mpls., May 12, 1904; s. Charles Marshall and Florence (Long) H.; m. Linda Woodworth, Dec. 22, 1932; children: Helen (Mrs. T.G. Craig) (dec.) Andrew. B.S., U. Minn., 1928; M.D., Harvard, 1930. Diplomate: Am. Bd. Obstetrics and Gynecology, Am. Bd. Pathology (trustee 1959-70, pres. 1969-70). Entomol. asst. Kala Azar Field Studies, Rockefeller Found., Peking, China, 1925-26; pathol. tng. Peter Bent Brigham Hosp., Boston, Lying-in-Hosp. and Children's Hosp., 1930-33; NRC fellow in embryology Carnegie Instn. of Washington, 1933-34; with Boston Lying-in Hosp. (now Brigham and Women's Hosp), 1934—, obstet. trainee, 1936-38, asst. pathologist, 1934-39, pathologist, 1939-52, cons. pathology, 1952—; pathologist Free Hosp. for Women, Brookline, Mass., 1938-52, cons. pathologist, 1952—; with Harvard Med. Sch., 1931—, prof. pathology, 1948-52, 70-74, Shattuck prof. path. anatomy, 1952-70, Shattuck prof. path. anatomy emeritus, 1974—, chmn. dept. pathology, 1950-68; chief div. pathobiology New Eng. Regional Primate Research Center, Southboro, Mass., 1968-74, assoc. dir. for research, 1972-74; cons. in pathology Armed Forces Inst. Pathology, Washington, 1948-78, mem. sci. adv. bd. cons., 1970-74; cons. in obstet. and gynecol. pathology USN, Chelsea, Mass., 1947-67; former sr. cons. adminstrn., edn. pathology Lemuel Shattuck Hosp.; cons. pathologist Peter Bent Brigham, Beth Israel, Children's hosps., all Boston. Contbr.: articles (with John Rock) on early development of normal and abnormal human embryos to Contributions to Embryology, 1941-58; Ultrastructure of mammalian oocytes and human corpus luteum, 1960-68, anatomy and pathology female reprodn. in subhuman primates, 1968—, also numerous articles in field. Trustee Boston Med. Library, 1945-48. Recipient Am. Gynecol. Soc. award (with John Rock) for fundamental research on human reprodn., 1949; Outstanding Achievement award Centennial Celebration U. Minn., 1951; Ward Burdick award Am. Soc. Clin. Pathologists, 1966; Disting. Service award Coll. Am. Pathologists-Am. Soc. Clin. Pathologists, 1972, Am. Coll. Obstetricians and Gynecologists, 1975; Gold-Headed Cane Am. Soc. Pathology, 1979; named a Leader in Medicine Boston U. Sch. Medicine, 1980. Fellow Royal Coll. Obstetricians and Gynecologists (London); mem. Am. Soc. Clin. Pathologists (hon.), Soc. Exptl. Pathologists, Coll. Am. Pathologists (gov. 1959-62), Am. Coll. Obstetricians and Gynecologists (Hall of Fame 1983), Internat. Acad. Pathology, Am. Assn. Pathology and Bacteriology, Am. Gynecology Soc., AAAS, Am. Acad. Arts and Sci., Am. Assn. Anatomists, N.E. Obstet. and Gynecol. Soc. (pres. 1950-51), N.E. Soc. Pathology (past pres.), Mass. and Middlesex East med. socs., Obstet. Soc. of Boston (past pres.), Sigma Xi, Alpha Omega Alpha, Nu Sigma Nu (past exec. councilor). Clubs: Harvard (Boston); Country (Winchester). Home: 21 Everett Ave Winchester MA 01890 Office: New Eng Regional Primate Research Center Southborough MA 01772

HERTING, ROBERT LESLIE, pharmaceutical executive; b. Aurora, Ill., Jan. 26, 1929; s. Herold Edward and Marie Christine (Parr) H.; m. Claireen LaVern Molzan, June 5, 1954; 1 son, Robert Leslie. B.S., U. Ill., 1950, M.D., 1954; M.S. in Biochemistry, Ill. Inst. Tech., 1961; Ph.D. in Biology, Ill. Inst. Tech., 1970. Diplomate: Am. Bd. Internal Medicine. Intern Ill. Central Hosp., Chgo., 1954-55; asso. dir. clin. research Abbott Labs., North Chicago, Ill., 1957-63, mgr. clin. pharmacology, 1963-68, med. dir., 1968-71, divisional v.p., 1971-76; v.p. med. research Schering-Plough Corp., Bloomfield, N.J., 1977-80; v.p. internat. clin. research and med. affairs G.D. Searle & Co., Skokie, Ill., 1980—; clin. asso. prof. medicine U. Ill., 1957-77. Mem. editorial bd.: Antimicrobial Agents and Chemotherapy, 1963-65. Served with U.S. Army, 1955-57. Fellow ACP; mem. AMA, Am. Soc. Internal Medicine, Chgo. Soc. Internal Medicine, Am. Soc. Microbiology, Am. Soc. Clin. Pharmacology and Therapeutics, Sigma Xi. Home: 1281 N Northwest Hwy Park Ridge IL 60068 Office: 4901 Searle Pkwy Skokie IL 60077

HERTZ, ARTHUR HERMAN, business company executive; b. Bklyn., Sept. 10, 1933; s. Edwin Carl and Blanche H.; Stephen R., Andrew P. B.B.A., U. Miami, Fla., 1955, postgrad., 1955-56. Acct. Aetna Mortgage Co., Miami, Fla., 1955, Wometco Enterprises, Inc., Miami, 1955-60, controller, v.p., 1960-72, exec. v.p., chief fin. officer, 1971—, also treas., dir.; treas. Wometco Cable TV Inc.; mem. regional cons. bd. SE 1st Nat. Bank of Miami. Mem. Orange Bowl Com.; pres. U. Miami Alumni Assn., 1979, trustee. Mem. Am. Inst. C.P.A.'s, Broadcasting Fin. Mgmt. Assn., Greater Miami C. of C. (gov. 1975-78), Phi Kappa Phi, Omicron Delta Kappa, Beta Gamma Sigma. Lodge: Kiwanis. Home: 610 Fluvia Ave Coral Gables FL 33134 Office: Wometco Enterprises Inc 316 N Miami Ave Miami FL 33128

HERTZ, BARBARA VALENTINE (MRS. DAVID BENDEL HERTZ), publisher; b. N.Y.C., Mar. 1, 1921; d. Herbert I. and Helen (Lachman) Valentine; m. David Bendel Hertz, Dec. 20, 1941; children: Barbara Bendel (Mrs. Winthrop A. Burr), Valentine (Mrs. Robert Kass). Student, Swarthmore Coll., 1939-40; B.A., Barnard Coll., 1943. Comml. continuity radio sta. WQXR, 1945-46; free lance writing and publicity, 1947-51; assoc. editor Parents mag., 1951-56, mng. editor, 1956-68; dir. devel. Barnard Coll., N.Y.C., 1968-77; pub. Prime Time mag.; pres. Prime Time Publs., N.Y.C., 1978-82, Midlife Markets, Inc., Miami, Fla., 1982-83; dir. devel. Rosenstiel Sch. Marine and Atmospheric Sci., U. Miami, Fla., 1983—. Mem. Friends Sem. Sch. Com., 1971-77; pres. Class of 1943, Barnard Coll., 1953-58. Mem. AAAS (investment and fin. com. 1978-82), Alumni Assn. Friends Sem. (pres. 1954-56), Woman's Conf. Group N.Y.C. (exec. com.). Club: Cosmopolitan. Home:: 5909 SW 96th St Miami FL 33156

HERTZ, DAVID BENDEL, management consultant, educator, lawyer; b. Yoakum, Tex., Mar. 25, 1919; s. Emanuel and Wilhelmina (Schmulen) H.; m. Barbara Hope Valentine, Dec. 20, 1941; children: Barbara Hertz Burr, Valentine Hertz Kass. B.A., Columbia U., 1939, B.S., 1940, Ph.D., 1949; M.S., U.S. Navy Postgrad. Sch., 1944; J.D., NYU, 1980. Prodn. engr. RCA, 1940-41; asst. chief devel. engr. Celanese Corp. Am., 1945-49; asst. prof. Sch. Engring., Columbia U., 1949-52, assoc. prof., 1952-54; dir. engring. Celanese Corp. Am., 1953-54; asst. to pres. Popular Mdse. Co., Fairlawn, N.J., 1954-55; pres. David B. Hertz Co. (cons.), N.Y.C., 1955-57; prin. Arthur Andersen & Co. (C.P.A.'s), N.Y.C., 1957-62; dir. McKinsey & Co. (mgmt. cons.), N.Y.C., 1962-80; chmn. Prime Time Communications, Inc., 1979-82; disting. prof. Sch. Bus. Adminstrn. U. Miami, Coral Gables, Fla., 1983—; Disting. prof. Sch. Bus. Adminstrn. U. Miami (Fla.), 1983—; adj. prof. Sch. Law U. Miami, Fla., 1983—; chmn. Media Commentary Council, Inc., N.Y.C.; pub. Channels mag., 1980—; dir. Intelligent Computer Systems Research Inst., Coral Gables, Fla., 1983—; prof. Sch. Law U. Miami, Coral Gables, Fla., 1983—; dir. Intelligent Computer Systems Research Inst., Coral Gables, 1983—; counsel Leva, Hawes, Symington, Martin & Oppenheimer, Washington, 1983—; vis. prof. London (Eng.) Grad. Sch. Bus. Studies, 1971-72; adj. prof. Grad. Sch. Bus., Columbia U, 1972, chmn. adv. council faculty engring. and applied sci., 1972; dir. Syncom, Inc. Author several books; contbr. numerous articles to mgmt., tech. jours. Trustee Columbia U., 1977-83, Columbia U. Press, 1972—; bd. govs. Opportunity Funding Corp., 1970—, chmn. bd. govs., 1970-76; Mem. Pres.'s Adv. Council for Minority Enterprise Exec. Commn., 1969-74; mem. sci. adv. council Picatinny Arsenal, 1950-55; mem. sec. navy's shipbldg. study group, 1965, vice chmn. mayor's ops. research council, N.Y.C., 1966-70; mem. adv. panel to tech. analysis div. Inst. Applied Tech., Nat. Bur. Standards, 1969-74, chmn. adv. panel, 1975-78; mem. adv. com. behavioral sci. research Dept. Def., Nat. Acad. Scis., 1970-71; bd. dirs. Council Governing Bds. Pvt. Univs. Served with USNR, 1941-45; Comdr. Res. ret. USNR. Fellow AAAS, ASME; Mem. Inst. Mgmt. Scis. (mem. council 1964-65, pres. 1963-64), Ops. Research Soc. Am. (pres. 1974-75, George S. Kimball medal 1981), Internat. Fedn. Operational Research Socs. (pres. 1977-80), Beta Gamma Sigma. (hon.). Clubs: Athenaeum, Reform (London); Columbia U., Board Room (N.Y.C.). Patentee plastic, electronic and textile machinery. Home: 5909 SW 96th St Miami FL 33156 Office: U Miami PO Box 248237 Coral Gables FL 33124 *You have to earn your intellectual freedom by consistently coming up with ideas. I am aware constantly of this pressure to perform. I cannot say I always enjoy it, but I am sure life would be less interesting if I were free of it.*

HERTZ, KENNETH THEODORE, ballet company executive; b. Jackson Heights, N.Y., Aug. 19, 1951; s. Irwin R. and Dorothy S. H.

B.A. in Spl. Studies, SUNY, Fredonia, 1974. Gen. mgr. Cape Cod Symphony, West Barnstable, Mass., 1974-75; mng. dir. Tulsa Philharm., 1975-78; pres., gen. mgr. Atlanta Ballet, 1979—; instr. continuing edn. Oglethorpe U.; speaker at profl. workshops, art adminstrn. programs; dir. Dance/USA; mem. dance panel Ga. Council for Arts, City of Atlanta, NEA. Chmn. Ga. Profl. Arts Caucus. Mem. Midtown Bus. Assn. (dir.), Ga. Citizens for Arts, Am. Symphony Orch. League, Alpha Phi Omega. Lodge: Rotary (Atlanta). Office: 477 Peachtree St NE Atlanta GA 30308

HERTZ, RICHARD CORNELL, rabbi; b. St. Paul, Oct. 7, 1916; s. Abram J. and Nadine (Rosenberg) H.; m. Mary Louise Mann, Nov. 25, 1943 (div. July 1971); children: Nadine (Mrs. Michael Wertheimer), Ruth Mann (Mrs. Alain Joyaux); m. Renda Gottfürcht Ebner, Dec. 3, 1972. A.B., U. Cin., 1938; M.H.L., Hebrew Union Coll., 1942, D.D. (hon.), 1967; Ph.D., Northwestern U., 1948. Ordained rabbi, 1942; asst. rabbi N. Shore Congregation Israel, Glencoe, Ill., 1942-47; asso. rabbi Chgo. Sinai Congregation, 1947-53; sr. rabbi Temple Beth El, Detroit, 1953-82, rabbi emeritus, 1982—; adj. prof. Jewish thought U. Detroit, 1970—, disting. prof. Jewish studies, 1980—; spl. cons. to pres. Cranbrook Ednl. Community, 1983—; del. to internat. conf. World Union for Progressive Judaism, London, 1959, 61, Amsterdam, 1978, bd. dirs. union, 1973—; Lectr. Jewish Chautauqua Soc.; former mem. plan bd. Synagogue Council Am.; mem. chaplaincy commn., former bd. dirs. Nat. Jewish Welfare Bd.; former mem. exec. com., vice chmn. Citizen's Com. for Equal Opportunity; mem. Mich. Gov.'s Com. on Ethics and Morals, 1963-69; mem. Mich. adv. council U.S. Commn. on Civil Rights, 1979—; mem. nat. bd. dirs. Religious Edn. Assn.; adv. bd. Joint Distbn. Com.; former mem. nat. rabbinical council United Jewish Appeal; mem. rabbinic cabinet Israel Bonds, 1972—; pres. Hyde Park and Kenwood Council Chs. and Synagogues, Chgo., 1952. Author: Rabbi Yesterday and Today, 1943, This I Believe, 1952, Education of the Jewish Child, 1953, Our Religion Above All, 1953, Inner Peace for You, 1954, Positive Judaism, 1955, Wings of the Morning, 1956, Impressions of Israel, 1956, Prescription for Heartache, 1958, Faith in Jewish Survival, 1961, The American Jew in Search of Himself, 1962, What Counts Most in Life, 1963, What Can A Man Believe, 1967, Reflections for the Modern Jew, 1974, Israel and the Palestinians, 1974, Roots of My Faith, 1980, also articles in sci., popular publs. Dir. Am. Jewish Com., mem. nat. exec. bd., former hon. vice-chmn. Detroit chpt.; past dir. Mich. Soc. Mental Health, Jewish Family and Children's Services, United Community Services, Jewish Welfare Fedn. Detroit, Jewish Community Council Detroit; dir. United Found., Boys Clubs, Mich. region Anti-Defamation League; chmn. bd. overseers Hebrew Union Coll.-Jewish Inst. Religion, 1968-72; bd. govs. Detroit Inst. Tech., 1955-70. Served as chaplain AUS, 1943-46. Fellow Am. Sociol. Soc.; mem. Detroit Hist. Soc., Central Conf. Am. Rabbis (former nat. chmn. com. on Jews in Soviet orbit), Am. Jewish Hist. Soc., Am. Legion (dept. chaplain 1956-57), Jewish War Vets. (dept. chaplain 1958-59, 72—), Alumni Assn. Hebrew Union Coll.-Jewish Inst. Religion (past dir.). Clubs: Rotary, Economic (Detroit) (dir.); Wranglers (past pres.), Great Lakes, Standard, Franklin Hills, Knollwood, Tam O'Shanter. Went on spl. mission for White House to investigate status Jews and Judaism in USSR 1959, mission for chief chaplains Def. Dept. to conduct retreats for Jewish chaplains and laymen, Berchtesgaden, Germany, 1973; mem. mission to Arab countries and Israel, Nat. Council Chs.-Am. Jewish Com., 1974; 1st Am. rabbi received in pvt. audience at Papal Palace by Pope Paul VI, 1963. Home: 4324 Knightsbridge Ln West Bloomfield MI 48033 Office: Temple Beth El 7400 Telegraph Rd at 14 Mile Birmingham MI 48010

HERTZBERG, ABRAHAM, university research scientist and official, educator; b. N.Y.C., July 8, 1922; s. Rubin and Paulien (Kalif) H.; m. Ruth Cohen, Sept. 3, 1950; children: Eleanor Ruth, Paul Elliot, Jean R. B.S. in Aero. Engring, Va. Poly Inst., 1943, M.S., Cornell U., 1949; postgrad., U. Buffalo, 1949-53. Engr. Cornell Aero. Lab., 1949-57, asst. head aerodynamics research, 1957-59, head aerodynamics research, 1959-65; prof. aeros. and astronautics, dir. aerospace research lab. U. Wash., 1966—; Cons. Aerospace Corp.; cons., mem. bd. Math. Scis. N.W. Inc., Lockheed Missiles & Space Co.; past mem. sci. adv. bd. USAF; past mem. electro-optics panel SAB, mem. various ad hoc coms.; past mem. research and tech. adv. council NASA; mem. plasma dynamics rev. panel NSF, U.S. Army.; honored speaker Laser Inst. Am., 1975; mem. theory adv. com. Los Alamos Nat. Lab.; vis. lectr. Chinese Acad. Scis., Beijing, 1983. Editor: Physics of Fluids, 1968-70; Contbr. numerous articles on modern high energy engring., high powered lasers, controlled thermonuclear fusions processes, space laser and solar energy concepts to profl. jours. Served with AUS, 1944-46. Prin. investigator on numerous fed. research grants. Fellow AIAA (Dryden lectr. 1977, Agard lectr. 1978); mem. Am. Phys. Soc., Nat. Acad. Engrs., Sigma Xi. Patentee in field. Home: 10317 SE 28th Pl Bellevue WA 98004 Office: Aerospace & Engring Research Bldg F1-10 U of Wash Seattle WA 98195

HERTZBERG, ARTHUR, rabbi; b. Lubaczow, Poland, June 9, 1921; s. Zvi Elimelech and Nehamah (Alstadt) H.; m. Phyllis Cannon, Mar. 19, 1950; children: Linda, Susan. A.B., Johns Hopkins U., 1940; M.H.L., Jewish Theol. Sem., 1943; Ph.D., Columbia U., 1966; D.D., Lafayette Coll., 1970; D.H.L., Balt. Hebrew Coll., 1974. Rabbi, 1943; Hillel dir. Mass. State and Amherst Coll., 1943-44; rabbi Congregation Ahavath Israel of Oak Lane, Phila., 1944-47, West End Synagogue, Nashville, 1947-56, Temple Emanu El, Englewood, N.J., 1956—; lectr., adj. prof. history Columbia U., 1959-61; vis. asso. prof. Jewish studies Rutgers U., 1966-68; lectr. religion Princeton U., 1968-69; vis. prof. history Hebrew U., Jerusalem, 1970-71; pres. Conf. Jewish Social Studies, 1967-72; mem. exec. com. World Zionist Orgn., 1969-78, Jewish Agy. for Israel, 1969-71, bd. govs., 1971-78; pres. Am. Jewish Congress, 1972-78, Am. Jewish Policy Found., 1978—; v.p. World Jewish Congress, 1975—. Author: The Zionist Idea, 1959, (with Martin Marty and Joseph Moody) The Outbursts that Await Us, 1963, The French Enlightenment and the Jews, 1968, Being Jewish in America, 1979; editor: Judaism, 1961; sr. editor: Ency. Judaica, 1972; contbr.: Ency. Brit., 1975. Vice pres. bd. dirs. Meml. Found. for Jewish Culture; bd. dirs. Jewish Home and Hosp., Jersey City. Served 1st lt., chaplain USAF, 1951-53. Recipient Amram award, 1967. Home: 83 Glenwood Rd Englewood NJ 07631 Office: 147 Tenafly Rd Englewood NJ 07631

HERTZBERG, HAZEL WHITMAN, history educator; b. Bklyn., Sept. 16, 1918; d. Charles Theodore and Grace Manross (Wood) Whitman; m. Sidney Hertzberg, Aug. 25, 1941; children: Hendrik, Katrina. A.B., U. Chgo., 1958; M.A., Tchrs. Coll., Columbia U., 1961; Ph.D., Columbia U., 1968. Cert. tchr., N.Y. Exec. sec. Nat. Sharecroppers Fund, N.Y.C., 1947-49; social studies and English tchr. Ramapo Central Sch. Dist., Suffern, N.Y., 1957-62; instr. Tchrs. Coll., Columbia U., N.Y.C., 1963-68, asst. prof. history and edn., 1968-69, assoc. prof. history and edn., 1970-78, prof. history and edn., 1978—; cons. numerous sch. dists., 1974-84, Am. Indian Ctr., Newberry Library, Chgo., 1977-78, Nat. Inst. Edn., Washington, 1977. Author: The Great Tree and the Longhouse: The Culture of the Iroquois, 1966, The Search for an American Indian Identity: Modern Pan Indian Movements, 1970, Social Studies Reform, 1880-1980, 1981. Exec. sec. India Famine Emergency Corp., N.Y.C., 1946; co-founder Ramapo LWV, 1952. Guggenheim fellow, 1983-84; NEH fellow, 1974-75; Woodrow Wilson Internat. Ctr. for Scholars fellow, 1975, 84. Mem. Social Sci. Edn. Consortium (bd. dirs. 1974-77), Conf. on Iroquois Research (planning com. 1978), Orgn. Am. Historians (planning com. 1981), Am. Hist. Assn. Democrat. Home: 35 Iroquois Ave Palisades NY 10964 Office: Tchrs Coll Columbia U 525 W 120th St New York NY 10027

HERTZBERG, HENDRIK, magazine editor, writer; b. N.Y.C., July 23, 1943; s. Sidney and Hazel Manross (Whitman) H.; m. Helen Christian Rogan, Aug. 27, 1975 (div. Apr. 1978); m. Michele Slung, Jan. 30, 1982. A.B., Harvard U., 1965. Editorial dir. U.S. Nat. Student Assn., Washington, 1965-66; corr. Newsweek, San Francisco, 1966-67; staff writer The New Yorker, N.Y.C., 1969-77; speechwriter to pres. The White House, Washington, 1981—. Author: One Million, 1970. Served to lt. (j.g.) U.S. Navy, 1967-69. Democrat. Clubs: Harvard (N.Y.C.); Nat. Press (Washington). Home: 1808 Kilbourne Pl NW Washington DC 20010 Office: The New Republic 1220 19th St NW Washington DC 20036

HERTZBERG, PAUL STUART, producer, publisher, writer; b. Chgo., Dec. 7, 1949; s. Irving Raymond and Syril H.; m. Sandy Weingart, June 20, 1971 (div. July 14, 1983); children: Lauren Michelle, Jordan Edward. B.S., U. Ill., 1971. Advt. sales mgr. Publishers Devel. Corp., 1971-72; pres. Hertzberg & Kramer, Inc. (pubs.), Niles, Ill., 1972-79; pub. snowmobile Travel Guide, 1974; author weekly column Chgo. Daily News, Chgo. Sun-Times; freelance travel editor; pres. Multi-Media Publs., Inc., Chgo., 1975-81; pres., exec. producer Chgo. Teleprodns., Inc., 1980; v.p., mgmt. supr. Stratford, Somerset & Greenwood, Inc., Chgo., 1980; snowmobile and camping writer Chgo. Sun-Times; writer, producer, announcer daily Snowmobile News, Radio Sta. WJJD, Chgo., 1978. Recipient awards Internat. Snowmobile Industry Assn., 1975, 76, 77, 78. Mem. AFTRA. Home: 900 Skokie Blvd Suite 103 Northbrook IL 60062 Office: 547 W Jackson St Chicago IL 60606 *Always be willing to take a chance. Anticipate the future and learn from the past.*

HERTZBERG, RICHARD WARREN, metallurgy educator, researcher; b. N.Y.C., Aug. 17, 1937; s. Nelson Bert and Alice (Sobin) H.; m. Linda Judith Wishnow, June 18, 1961; children: Michelle, Ilyce, Jason Lyle. B.S.M.E., CCNY, 1960; M.S. in Metallurgy, MIT, 1961, Ph.D., Lehigh U., 1965. Research asst. MIT, 1960-61; research scientist United Aircraft Corp., East Hartford, Conn., 1961-64; dir. mech. behavior Lehigh U., Bethlehem, Pa., 1964—, N.J. Zinc prof. metallurgy, 1978—, short course organizer, 1977—; vis. prof. Ecole Polytechnique Federale de Lausanne (Switerland), 1976; v.p. Del Research Corp., Hellertown, Pa., 1969-74. Author: Deformation and Fracture Mechanics of Engineering Materials, 1976, 83, (with John A. Manson) Fatigue of Engineering Plastics, 1980; co-editor: Conference on In Situ Composites II, 1980. Bd. dirs. Temple Beth El, Allentown, Pa., 1973-76; sec. Temple Beth El Endowment Found., 1979—; bd. dirs. Temple Am Haskalah, Allentown, 1982—. Recipient award for outstanding research Alcoa Found., Bethlehem, 1972, 73; co-recipient Eleanor and Joseph Libsch award for outstanding achievement and distinction in research Lehigh U., 1983. Mem. Am. Soc. Metals (chmn. nat. young mems. com. 1969-72, Phila. chpt. Notable Achievement award 1982); Outstanding Young Men Lehigh Valley William Woodside Meml. lectr. (1978, George Burgess Meml. lectr., 1982); mem. ASTM, AIME. Democrat. Jewish. Office: Lehigh U Dept Metallurgy and Materials Engring Bldg 5 Bethlehem PA 18015

HERTZFELD, KURT MAXIMILIAN, univ. adminstr.; b. Austria, Oct. 9, 1918; U.S., 1935, naturalized, 1939; s. Joseph Pierre and Elsa (Fishel) H.; m. Nora Elizabeth Alfs, July 4, 1942; children—Kurt Maximilian, Elizabeth Nora, Anne Morely, Susan Laurene. B.A., Harvard U., 1941, M.B.A., 1942. With Calvert Distilling Co., 1942-43, Ford Motor Co., 1946-47, Fasco Industries, 1947-49; bus. mgr. U. Rochester, 1949-59; v.p. adminstrv. affairs Boston U., 1959-67, v.p., treas., 1967-68; treas. Amherst (Mass.) Coll., 1968—; chmn. bd. Permatach Diamond Tool Co., Milford, N.H., Exolon Co., Tonawanda, N.Y., dir., O'Rourke Diamond Co., North Hollywood, Calif.; v.p. Amherst Savs. Bank, Mass. Author articles. Mem. Health and Ednl. Facilities Authority; trustee Ednl. Testing Service, Princeton, N.J. Served with AUS, 1943-46. Mem. Nat. Fedn. Coll. and Univ. Bus. Officers (v.p. 1957-59, dir. 1955-65), Eastern Assn. Coll. and Univ. Bus. Officers (sec.-treas. 1955-65, pres. 1966). Home: 43 Sunset Ave Amherst MA 01002

HERVEY, FREDERICK TAYLOR, multiple company executive; b. El Paso, Tex., June 28, 1909; s. Taylor Master and Sarah Gertrude (Crossett) H.; children: Helen Shirleen, Evelyn Diane Herbery Ruby, Frederick Taylor. Pres., chmn. bd. Sun World Corp., 1976—; chmn. bd. Circle K Corp., 1951-83, vice chmn. bd., 1983—; chmn. bd. Bank of Scottsdale, (Ariz.), 1974—, Am. Bank of Commerce, 1970-82, Coaches of Am., Inc., 1971-74; dir. Circle K Corp. Met. chmn. Nat. Alliance of Businessmen, 1969-70; Democratic candidate U.S. Congress, 1950; del. Dem. Nat. Conv., 1956, Rep. Nat. Conv., 1968; mayor City of El Paso, 1951-54, 71-74; mem. Tex. Rep. Exec. Com., 1971-72, El Paso County Rep. Adv. Com., 1965-75, El Paso Republican Fin. Com., 1965-75. Served with USNR, 1943-45. Office: Circle K Convenience Stores Inc 4500 S 40th St Phoenix AZ 85040

HERVIEUX-PAYETTE, CELINE, canadian government official; married; 3 children. J.D., U. Montreal, 1973. Various adminstrv. posts in Que. provincial govt., 1973-78; head of policy com. Liberal Party of Can., 1978; Minister of State for Fitness and Amateur Sport Can. Cabinet, 1983; head Dept. of Youth, Can. Ministry, Ottawa, Ont., 1984—. Office: Dept Youth Can Ministry Parliament Bldgs Ottawa ON Canada K1A 0A2

HERZ, CARL SAMUEL, mathematician; b. N.Y.C., Apr. 10, 1930; s. Michael M. and Natalie (Hyman) H.; m. Judith Scherer, Feb. 28, 1960; children—Rachel, Nathaniel. B.A., Cornell U., 1950; Ph.D., Princeton U., 1953. Instr. Cornell U., 1953-56, asst. prof. math., 1956-58, asso. prof., 1958-63, prof., 1963-70, McGill U., Montreal, Que., Can., 1970—; mem. Inst. Advanced Study, Princeton, N.J., 1957-58; vis. prof. U. Paris, 1962, 64, 68, Brandeis U., 1969-70. Alfred P. Sloan fellow, 1962-63. Mem. Am. Math. Soc., Can. Math. Soc., Royal Soc. Can. Home: 228 Simcoe Ave Montreal PQ H3P 1W9 Canada Office: 805 Sherbrooke St W Montreal PQ H3A 2K6 Canada

HERZ, LEONARD, service industry consultant; b. Bronx, N.Y., June 25, 1931; s. Emanuel and Henrietta (Morris) H.; m. Sally Jampolsky, May 2, 1954; children: Michael, Hildee, Larry. B.B.A., CCNY, 1952. C.P.A., N.Y. Auditor Lybrand Ross Bros. (C.P.A.s), N.Y.C., 1954-60; asst. controller Merritt Chapman Scott, N.Y.C., 1960-66; treas. Baker Industries Inc., Parsippany, N.J., 1966-73; v.p. finance Del Labs. Inc., Farmingdale, N.Y., 1973-74; exec. v.p. Holmes Protection, Inc., N.Y.C., 1974-82; cons. to service industries, Dix, N.Y., 1982—; Bd. dirs. Central Sta. Electric Protective Assn. Served with AUS, 1952-54. Mem. N.Y. State Soc. C.P.A.s, Am. Inst. C.P.A.s. Jewish (treas. 1972—). Home: 22 Durham Dr Dix Hills NY 11746 Office: 22 Durham Dr Dix NY 11746

HERZ, MARVIN I., psychoanalyst; b. N.Y.C., Dec. 24, 1927; s. Jules Edward and Vivian M. (Becker) H.; m. Beatrice Leslie Mittelman, Sept. 13, 1952; 3 children. B.A., U. Mich., 1949; M.S. in Psychology, Yale U., 1950; M.D., Chgo. Med. Sch., 1955. Diplomate: Am. Bd. Psychiatry and Neurology (asso. examiner). Intern U. Ill. Research and Ednl. Hosps., 1955-56; resident in psychiatry Michael Reese Hosp., Chgo., 1956-59; dir. inpatient service div. psychiatry Montefiore Hosp., N.Y.C., 1961-63; dir. Westchester Sq. Day Hosps., N.Y.C., 1963-65; asst. prof. psychiatry Albert Einstein Coll. Medicine, N.Y.C., 1963-65; asso. in psychiatry Columbia U., 1965-68, asst. prof. clin. psychiatry, 1968-72, asso. prof., 1972-77; ward adminstr. Washington Heights Community Service, N.Y. State Psychiat. Inst., 1965-68; asst. attending psychiatrist Vanderbilt Clinic, Presbyn. Hosp., N.Y.C., 1965-68; dir. Washington Hts. Community Service, 1968-72; dir. community services N.Y. State Psychiat. Inst., 1972-77, acting clin. dir., 1975-76; med. dir. Ga. Mental Health Inst., Atlanta, 1977-78; dir. ops. research, 1977-78; prof. psychiatry Emory U., 1977-78; prof., chmn. dept. psychiatry SUNY Sch. Medicine, Buffalo, 1978—; dir. psychiatry Erie County Med. Center, Buffalo, 1978—; head dept. psychiatry Buffalo Gen. Hosp., 1978—; cons. in psychiatry VA Hosp., Buffalo, 1978—; ednl. cons. Nat. Heart and Lung Inst.; cons. Task Panel of Pres.' Commn. on Research in Mental Illness, 1977; cons. psychiatry edn. br. NIMH, 1978; chmn. psychiat. adv. com. N.Y. State Office Mental Health. Contbr. articles to med. jours. Served to lt. comdr. USNR, 1959-61. Fellow Am. Psychiat. Assn., Am. Acad. Psychoanalysis (trustee 1978—), Am. Coll. Psychiatrists, Am. Coll. Psychoanalysts; mem. Assn. Psychoanalytic Medicine (chmn. com. on community psychiatry 1975-76), AAAS, Am. Psychopathological Assn., Alpha Omega Alpha. Home: 91 Rolling Meadow East Amherst NY 14051 Office: Dept Psychiatry Sch Medicine SUNY Buffalo 462 Grider St Buffalo NY 14215

HERZ, WERNER, educator, chemist; b. Stuttgart, Germany, Feb. 12, 1921; came to U.S., 1937, naturalized, 1944; s. Alfred and Hedwig (Loewenstein) H.; m. Marcia Lucile King, Feb. 22, 1945; children—Michael John, Patrick Werner, Monica Lucile, Andrea Lauren. B.A., U. Colo., 1943, M.A., 1945, Ph.D., 1947. Instr. math. U. Colo., 1946-47; Am. Cyanamid fellow U. Ill., 1947-49; with Fla. State U., Tallahassee, 1949—, prof. chemistry, 1959—; mem. chemistry panel Cancer Chemotherapy Nat. Service Center, 1959-62, NSF, 1961-64; cons. Nat. Cancer Inst., 1962-65; mem. cancer chemotherapy study sect. NIH, 1962-66, mem. medicinal chemistry study sect., 1970-74. Author: The Shape of Molecules, 1963; Editorial bd.: Jour. Organic Chemistry, 1962-63; sr. editor, 1963—; editor: Fortschritte der Chemie Organischer Naturstoffe, 1969—; bd. editors: Planta Medica, 1978—, Phytochemistry, 1981—. Mem. Am. Chem. Soc. (councilor Fla. sect. 1960-79, adv. bd. Petroleum Research Fund 1970-72), Chem. Soc. London, Phi Beta Kappa, Sigma Xi, Sigma Pi Sigma, Alpha Chi Sigma, Pi Mu Epsilon, Phi Lambda Upsilon. Research and numerous publs. on isolation and structure determination of plant products with emphasis on possible applications to chemotaxonomy and cancer chemotherapy, structure synthesis and transformations of terpenoid substances; studies of molecular rearrangements in chemistry. Home: 314 Saratoga Dr Tallahassee FL 32312

HERZBERG, FREDERICK, educator, psychologist; b. Lynn, Mass., Apr. 18, 1923; s. Lewis and Gertrude Ann (Copleman) H.; m. Shirley Bedell, June 1, 1944; 1 son, Mark Allen. B.S.S., CCNY, 1946; M.S., U. Pitts., 1949, Ph.D., 1950, M.P.H., 1951. Lectr. U. Pitts., 1946-48, instr., 1949-51; prin. personnel adminstr., City Richmond, Va., 1948-49; research dir. Psychol. Service Pitts., 1953-57; prof. psychology, chmn. dept., dir. indsl. mental health program, Douglas McGregor distinguished prof. Western Res. U., Cleve., 1957-72; Univ. Disting. prof. mgmt. U. Utah, Salt Lake City, 1972—; cons. to govtl., indsl., ednl. and social orgns. throughout world. Author: Job Attitudes: Research and Opinion, 1957, The Motivation to Work, 1959, Work and the Nature of Man, 1966, The Managerial Choice: To Be Efficient and To Be Human, 1976, 2d rev. edit., 1982 (James A. Hamilton Book of Yr. award Am. Coll. Hosp. Adminstrs.); also films on motivation; contbg. editor: Industry Week Mag. Served with AUS, 1943-46; res. scientist USPHS, 1953. Recipient Exceptional Contbn. citation Comdg. Gen. Air Force Logistics Command; W.M. McFeely award Internat. Mgmt. Council; award Dow Jones/Am. Assembly Collegiate Schs., 1982; Fulbright research fellow, Finland, 1963-64; named 1 of Top 10 Contbrs. to Mgmt. Internat. Mgmt. mag., 1982. Mem. Am. Psychol. Assn. (Cattel Research award), AAUP, Sigma Xi, Psi Chi. Home: 905 Little Valley Rd Salt Lake City UT 84103 *The central core of my work stems from World War II experiences in Dachau Concentration Camp where I realized that a society goes insane when the sane are driven insane. As a psychologist, I believe that sanity requires as much professional attention to nourishment of the humanistic content of character and ethics as to compassion for differences in personality. The insane also require care and compassion but their insane actions should never be reinforced by ethically neutral strategies. My theories have tended to emphasize strategies for keeping the sane sane.*

HERZBERG, GERHARD, physicist; b. Hamburg, Ger., Dec. 25, 1904; emigrated to Can., 1935, naturalized, 1945; s. Albin and Ella (Biber) H.; m. Luise H. Oettinger, Dec. 29, 1929 (dec.); children: Paul Albin, Agnes Margaret; m. Monika Tenthoff, Mar. 21, 1972. Dr. Ing., Darmstadt Inst. Tech., 1928; postgrad., U. Goettingen, U. Bristol, 1928-30; D.Sc. hon causa, Oxford U., 1960, U. Chgo., 1967, Drexel U., 1972, U. Montreal, 1972, U. Sherbrooke, 1972, McGill U., 1972, Cambridge U., 1972, U. Man., 1973, Andhra U., 1975, Osmania U., 1976, U. Delhi, 1976, U. Bristol, 1975, U. Western Ont., 1976; Fil. Hed. Dr., U. Stockholm, 1966; Ph.D., Weizmann Inst. Sci., 1976; LL.D., St. Francis Xavier U., 1972, Simon Fraser U., 1972, others. Lectr., chief asst. physics Darmstadt Inst. Tech., 1930-35; research prof. physics U. Sask., Saskatoon, 1935-45; prof. spectroscopy Yerkes Obs., U. Chgo., 1945-48; prin. research officer NRC Can., Ottawa, 1948, dir. div. pure physics, 1949-69, disting. research scientist, 1969—; Bakerian lectr. Royal Soc. London, 1960; holder Francqui chair U. Liege, 1960. Author books including: Spectra of Diatomic Molecules, 1950; Electronic Spectra and Electronic Structure of Polyatomic Molecules, 1966, The Spectra and Structures of Simple Free Radicals, 1971, (with K.P. Huber) Constants of Diatomic Molecules, 1979. Recipient Faraday medal Chem. Soc. London, 1970, Nobel prize in Chemistry, 1971; named companion Order of Can., 1968, academician Pontifical Acad. Scis., 1964. Fellow Royal Soc. London (Royal medal 1971), Royal Soc. Can. (pres. 1966, Henry Marshall Tory medal 1953), Hungarian Acad. Sci. (hon.), Indian Acad. Scis. (hon.), Am. Phys. Soc., Chem. Inst. Can.; mem. Internat. Union Pure and Applied Physics (past v.p.), Am. Acad. Arts and Scis. (hon. fgn. mem.), Am. Chem. Soc. (Willard Gibbs medal 1969, Centennial fgn. fellow 1976), Nat. Acad. Sci. India, Indian Phys. Soc. (hon.), Japan Acad. (hon.), Chem. Soc. Japan (hon.), Royal Swedish Acad. Scis. (fgn., physics sect.), Nat. Acad. Sci. (fgn. asso.), Faraday Soc., Am. Astron. Soc., Can. Assn. Physicists (past pres., Achievement award 1957), Optical Soc. Am. (hon., Frederic Ives medal 1964). Home: 190 Lakeway Dr Rockcliffe Park Ottawa ON Canada Office: Nat Research Council Ottawa ON K1A 0R6 Canada

HERZBRUN, HELENE MCKINSEY, artist, educator; b. Chgo.; d. Edward E. and Lillian (Smith) Eichenbaum; m. Philip Herzbrun, Nov. 11, 1961. B.A., U. Chgo., 1945; postgrad., Am. U., 1951-55. Staff, then partner Charles Elwyn Hayes Advt., Chgo., 1945-50; prof. art Am. U., Washington, 1958—, chmn. dept., 1964-66, 70-72, 76-78. One-woman shows, 1958—, work represented in permanent collections including, Watkins Collection, Am. U., U. Va., Phillips Collection, Nat. Mus. Am. Art. Mem. Phi Beta Kappa. Office: Dept Art Am U Washington DC 20016 *

HERZEG, LADD KEITH, football club executive; b. Jan. 31, 1946; s. Steve Herczeg and Agnes (Stolz) H.; m. Kathleen M. Vinson, Aug. 31, 1968. Student, U. Hawaii, 1964-65; B.S., Ohio State U., 1968. Audit mgr. Arthur Andersen & Co., Cleve., 1968-76; v.p. fin. Houston Oilers, Inc., 1976-79, sr. v.p., 1979-81, exec. v.p., gen. mgr., 1981—; mem. Nat. Football League pension com.; dir. KSA Industries, Adams Resources. Served with U.S. Army, 1969-70. Office: 6910 Fannin Suite 318-S Houston TX 77030

HERZEL, LEO, lawyer; b. N.Y.C., Sept. 10, 1923; s. Salomon and Rose (Kalt) H.; m. Eileen Louise Engel, Feb. 2, 1946; children: David Franklin, Sarah Elizabeth. A.B., U. Iowa, 1947; postgrad., London Sch. Econs., 1947-48; M.A., U. Ill., 1949; J.D., U. Chgo., 1952. Bar: Ill. 1952. Assoc. Mayer, Brown & Platt, Chgo., 1952-61, ptnr., 1962—; dir. Brunswick Corp., Skokie, Ill. Contbr. articles to legal jours.; editor-in-chief: U. Chgo. Law Rev., 1951-52. Mem. ABA, Ill. Bar Assn., Chgo. Bar Assn., Chgo. Council of Lawyers, Phi Beta Kappa. Clubs: Chicago; Attic (Chgo.). Home: 344 South Ave Glencoe IL 60022 Office: Mayer Brown & Platt 231 S LaSalle St Chicago IL 60604

HERZENBERG, ARVID, physicist, educator; b. Vienna, Austria, Apr. 16, 1925; s. Harry and Wilhelmine (Pfeiffer) H.; m. Marjorie Swift, Nov. 30, 1949; children: Catherine, Anne, Stephen. B.S., U. Manchester, Eng., 1949, D.Sc., 1964. Mem. faculty U. Manchester, 1952-69; prof. applied physics Yale, 1969—. Contbr. articles to profl. jours. Fellow Brit., Am. phys. socs. Home: 6 Le Grand Rd North Haven CT 06473 Office: 403 Becton Center Yale University New Haven CT 06520

HERZFELD, CHARLES MARIA, physicist; b. Vienna, Austria, June 29, 1925; came to U.S., 1942, naturalized, 1949; s. August Alfred and Frieda Auguste (Poehlman) H.; m. Norma Ann Krause, May 15, 1954 (div. 1979); children: Charles Christopher, Thomas Augustine, Paul Vincent; m. Zofia E. Dziewanowska, Aug. 1, 1981. B.S. in Chem. Engring. cum laude, Cath. U. Am., 1945; Ph.D. (Carnegie Found. fellow), U. Chgo., 1951. Lectr. chemistry Cath. U. Am., 1946; lectr. gen. sci. Coll. U. Chgo., 1946-47; lectr. physics DePaul U., Chgo., 1948-50; physicist Ballistic Research Lab., Aberdeen, Md., 1951-53, Naval Research Lab., Washington, 1953-55; lectr. physics U. Md., 1953-57, prof. physics, 1957-61; cons. chief heat and power div. Nat. Bur. Standards, 1955-56, acting asst. chief, 1956-57, chief heat div., 1957-61, asso. dir. bur., 1961; asst. dir. Advanced Research Project Agy., Dept. Def., 1961-63, dir. ballistic missile def., 1963; dep. dir. Advanced Research Projects Agy., 1963-65, dir., 1965-67; tech. dir. def. space group ITT, Nutley, N.J., 1967-74, tech. dir. aerospace-electronics-components-energy group, 1974-76, tech. dir. telecommunications and electronics group N.Am., 1978-79; v.p., dir. research ITT Corp., 1979-83, v.p., dir. research and tech., 1983—; Mem. Def. Sci. Bd.; cons. USN, Nat. Security Council; fellow mem. Hudson Inst.; mem. Brookings Inst. Fifth Conf. for Career Execs. in Fed. Govt., 1958. Editor: Temperature, Its Control in Science and Industry, vol. III, 1962; contbr. articles to profl. jours. Recipient Flemming award, 1963; Meritorious Civilian Service medal Dept. Def., 1967. Fellow Phys. Soc., Council Fgn. Relations, AAAS, Conf. on Sci., Philosophy and Religion; mem. Am. Ordnance Assn., N.Y. Acad. Scis., Inst. for Strategic Studies (London), Cath. Assn. Internat. Peace (pres. 1959-61), Sigma Xi. Clubs: Cosmos (Washington); Explorers (N.Y.C.); Raritan Yacht (Perth Amboy, N.J.). Home: 509 Woodland Ave Westfield NJ 07090 Office: ITT Corp New York NY 10022

HERZOG, ARTHUR, III, author; b. N.Y.C., Apr. 6, 1927; s. Arthur, Jr. and Elizabeth Lindsay (Dayton) H.; 1 son by previous marriage, Matthew Lennox. Student, U. Ariz., 1945-46; B.A., Stanford U., 1950; M.A., Columbia U., 1956. Editor Fawcett Publs., 1957-59; Cons. Peace Corps, 1967-68; polit. cons., 1969-71. Author: (with others) Smoking and the Public Interest, 1963, The War-Peace Establishment, 1965, The Church Trap, 1968, McCarthy for President, 1969, The B.S. Factor, 1973, The Swarm, 1974, Earthsound, 1975, Orca, 1977, Heat, 1977, IQ 83, 1978, Make Us Happy, 1978, Glad To Be Here, 1979, Aries Rising, 1980, The Craving, 1982, L.S.I.T.T., 1983; Contbr. articles to leading Am. publs. Campaign mgr. Oreg., nat. pub. relations dir. Eugene McCarthy Presdl. Campaign, 1968; founder New Democratic Coalition, N.Y. and nationally, 1968-69; mem. Lexington Dem. Club, 1974. Served with USNR, 1944-45. Mem. Authors Guild, Authors League, P.E.N. Address: 400 W 43d St Suite 39G New York NY 10036 *I do not believe that success should figure as strongly as it does in our estimate of what is a good life. Since it often does, though, I would point to perseverance as a major element of success. Another, mostly overlooked, is a lack of dogmatism and a belief in skepticism and personal happiness as ends in themselves.*

HERZOG, BERTRAM, computer scientist; b. Offenburg, Baden, Germany, Feb. 28, 1929; came to U.S., 1945, naturalized, 1951; s. Rudolf and Irma (Wolff) H.; m. Alice Kathryn Yeager, Jan. 16, 1971; children: Linda Ruth, Janice Kaye, Alice Marla. B.S. in Physics, Case Inst. Tech., 1949, M.S. in Engring. Mechanics, 1955, Ph.D., U. Mich., 1961. Registered profl. engr., Ohio. With Ohio Inspection Bur., Cleve., 1950-51, Osborn Engring. Co., 1951-52, Dalton-Dalton Assocs., 1952-53, Barber-Magee, 1953; instr. Case Inst. Tech., 1953-55; instr. (NSF faculty fellow 1958-59) U. Mich., Ann Arbor, 1955-61, asst. prof. engring. mechanics, 1961, assoc. prof., 1962-63, assoc. prof. indsl. engring., 1965-68, prof., 1968-75; dir. MERIT Computer Network, 1968-74; mgr. engring. methods dept. Ford Motor Co., Dearborn, Mich., 1963-65; dynamics analyst Minuteman missile system Boeing Aircraft Corp., Seattle, 1962; dir. computer center, prof. elec. engring. and computer sci. U. Colo., Boulder, 1976-81; prin. Herzog Assos. Inc., Boulder, 1981—; cons. to sci. and industry; IBM, lectr. courses and confs. in, U.S., Can., Italy, France, Germany, Sweden, Eng., P.R., Japan. Asso. editor: Computer Graphics, IEEE Computer Graphics and Applications, 1972-75; contbr. articles to publs. Mem. Assn. Computing Machinery, ASME, AAAS, AAUP, Am. Soc. Engring. Edn., Sigma Xi. Home: 335 Inca Pkwy Boulder CO 80303 Office: Herzog Assos Inc PO Box 3169 Boulder CO 80307

HERZOG, DONALD ROSWELL, educator; b. Warsaw, Ill., Sept. 2, 1924; s. John Henry and Anna Elizabeth (Jingst) H.; m. Elaine Lydia Lawson, Sept. 3, 1949; children: Daryl R., Marla A., Darwin R. B.S., U.S. Mcht. Marine Acad., 1945, Bradley U., 1948; M.A., U. Iowa, 1954, Ph.D., 1955; A.A., Prairie State Coll., 1977. Registered profl. engr., Calif., Fla. Cryptographer AUS, Washington, 1942-43; market analyst W. A. Sheaffer Pen Co., Ft. Madison, Iowa, 1948-51; mgr. market research ARO Corp., Bryan, Ohio, 1955-58; mktg. specialist Solar Aircraft Co., San Diego, 1958-60; mgr. market research Tex. Instruments Inc., Dallas, 1960-62; sr. program research adminstr. N. Am. Aviation, Los Angeles, 1962-65; cons. mgmt. engr. Herzog & Assos., Torrance, Calif., also Chgo., 1965—; prof. bus. Calif. State U. at Chico, 1968-71; prof. Gov.'s State U., Park Forest South, Ill., 1971-82; mem. faculty Fla. Internat. U., Miami, 1982—; vis. scientist Argonne (Ill.) Nat. Lab., 1977-78. Contbr. numerous articles to profl. jours. Served to lt. USNR, 1943-46, 51-52; col. USAF Res.; ret. Mem. Am. Inst. Indsl. Engrs. (sr.), Assn. Energy Engrs., Soc. Logistics Engrs., Am. Soc. Engring. Edn., Ret. Officers Assn., Bradley Fedn. Scholars, Zeta Phi. Home: 8860 Fontainebleau Blvd Apt 104 Miami FL 33172 Office: Ind Systems Coll Tech Fla Internat U Miami FL 33199

HERZOG, DORREL NORMAN ELVERT (WHITEY HERZOG), baseball manager; b. New Athens, Ill., Nov. 9, 1931. Infielder, outfielder Washington Senators, 1956-58, Kansas City Athletics, 1958-60, Balt. Orioles, 1961-62, Detroit Tigers, 1963; scout Kansas City Athletics, 1964, coach, 1965, N.Y. Mets, 1966, dir. player devel., 1967-72; mgr. Tex. Rangers, 1973; coach Calif. Angels, 1974-75, interim mgr., 1974; mgr. Kansas City Royals, 1975-79; mgr., gen. mgr. St. Louis Cardinals, 1980—. Named Sporting News Man of Year, 1982. Office: care St Louis Cardinals Busch Meml Stadium 250 Stadium Plaza Saint Louis MO 63102 *

HERZOG, FRED F., lawyer; b. Austria. Ed. univs., Grenoble, Paris, Vienna and Graz; D.Laws, U. Graz, 1931; J.D. (Am. Com. for Guidance of Profl. Personnel fellow), U. Iowa, 1942. Fed. judge in, Austria, to 1938; prof. law Chgo.-Kent Coll. of Law, 1947-70, dean, 1970-73; 1st asst. atty. gen., state of Ill., 1973-76; prof. John Marshall Law Sch., Chgo., 1974—, dean, 1976—; spl. counsel Met. San. Dist. Greater Chgo., 1963-73; spl. asst. atty. gen., Ill., 1976—. Contbr. articles to profl. jours. Address: 315 S Plymouth Ct Chicago IL 60604

HERZOG, HAROLD KENNETH, insurance company executive; b. N.Y.C., Feb. 13, 1924; s. Phillip and Lillian (Kronick) H.; m. Elizabeth Ann Huffaker, Dec. 15, 1944. B.S., N.Y. U., 1953, M.B.A., 1959. Accountant N.Y. Life Ins. Co., N.Y.C., 1941-51, fin. analyst, 1952-62, asst. v.p., 1962-66, 2d v.p., 1966-72, v.p. investment dept., 1972-80, sr. v.p. in charge investments, 1980-83, sr. v.p. in charge real estate, 1983—; dir. Holly Hill Fruit Products, Davenport, Fla. Served with U.S. Army, 1943-46. Home: 72 Clapboard Hill Rd New Canaan CT 06840 Office: 51 Madison Ave New York NY 10010

HERZOG, PETER EMILIUS, legal educator; b. Vienna, Austria, Dec. 25, 1925; came to U.S., 1950, naturalized, 1955; s. Paul and Leopodine (Mannhart) H.; m. Brigitte Ecolivet, June 29, 1970; children: Paul, Elizabeth Ann. Student, U. Vienna, 1949-50; B.A., Hobart Coll., 1952; LL.B. summa cum laude, Syracuse U., 1955; LL.M. (Jervey fellow), Columbia U., 1956. Bar: N.Y. 1957. Dep. asst. atty. gen. N.Y. State Dept. Law, Albany, 1955-57, asst. atty. gen., 1957-58; asst. prof. law Syracuse U. Coll. Law, 1958-62, assoc. prof., 1962-66, prof., 1966-83, Crandall Melvin prof., 1983—, law librarian, 1960-68; staff mem. Columbia U. Project on Inter Procedure, 1960-63; asso. dir. Project on European Legal Instns., 1968—; staff mem. UN Commn. on Internat. Trade Law, 1968-69; research fellow Procedural Aspects of Internat. Law, Inst., 1968-71; dir. studies Hague (Netherlands) Acad. Internat. Law, 1969; cons. N.Y. State Eminent Domain Commn., 1971; vis. prof. U. Paris, 1976-77. Author: (with Martha Weser) Civil Procedure in France, 1967, (with Ivan Head and Frank Dawson) International Law, National Tribunals and the Rights of Aliens, 1971, (with Hans Smit) The Law of the European Economic Community, A Commentary, 1976; contbr. articles to legal publs.; mem. bd. editors: Am. Jour. Comparative Law, 1977—. Mem. Am. Soc. Internat. Law, Société de Législation Comparée, Internat. Law Assn., Wissenschaftiche Gesellschaft für Verfahrensrecht, Order of Coif, Phi Beta Kappa. Roman Catholic. Home: 112 Erregger Rd Syracuse NY 13224

HERZOG, RICHARD BARNARD, lawyer; b. N.Y.C., Sept. 6, 1939; s. Sol Alexander and Grace (Fedir) H.; m. Barbara Kinsley, Apr. 12, 1970; children: Kari, Jeffrey. B.A., Williams Coll., 1960; LL.B., Harvard U., 1963. Bar: D.C. 1965. Assoc. Covington and Burling, Washington, 1963-72; dep. asst. dir. for gen. litigation, asst. dir. for nat. advt. Bur. Consumer Protection, FTC, Washington, 1972-77; asst. adminstr. for enforcement, dep. adminstr. for policy Econ. Regulatory Adminstrn., Dept. Energy, Washington, 1977-79; ptnr. Pepper, Hamilton & Scheetz, Washington, 1979—. Contbr. articles to legal jours. Recipient various govt. awards. Mem. ABA, D.C. Bar Assn., Phi Beta Kappa. Office: 1777 F St NW Washington DC 20006

HERZOG, WHITEY *See* **HERZOG, DORREL NORMAN ELVERT**

HESBURGH, THEODORE MARTIN, clergyman, university president; b. Syracuse, N.Y., May 25, 1917; s. Theodore Bernard and Anne Marie (Murphy) H. Student, U. Notre Dame, 1934-37; Ph.B., Gregorian U., 1939; postgrad., Holy Cross Coll., Washington, 1940-43; S.T.D., Cath. U. Am., 1945, Bradley U., LeMoyne Coll., U. R.I., Cath. U. of Santiago, Chile, Dartmouth, Villanova U., St. Benedict's Coll., Columbia, Princeton, Ind. U., Brandeis U., Gonzaga U., U. Calif. at Los Angeles, Temple U., Northwestern U., U. Ill., Fordham U., Manchester Coll., Atlanta U., Wabash Coll., Valparaiso U., Providence Coll., U. So. Calif., Mich. State U., St. Louis U., Cath. U. Am., Loyola U. at Chgo., Anderson Coll., State U. N.Y. at Albany, Utah State U., Lehigh U., Yale, Lafayette Coll., King's Coll., Stonehill Coll., Alma Coll., Syracuse U., Marymount Coll., Hobart and William Smith Coll., Hebrew Union Coll., Cin., Harvard. Entered Order of Congregation of Holy Cross, 1934; ordained priest Roman Catholic Ch., U. Notre Dame, 1943; chaplain Nat. Tng. Sch. for Boys, Washington, 1943-44; vets. chaplain U. Notre Dame, 1945-47, asst. prof. religion, head dept., 1948-49, exec. v.p., 1949-52, pres., 1952—; trustee Chase Manhattan Bank. Author: Theology of Catholic Action, 1945, God and the World of Man, 1950, Patterns for Educational Growth, 1958, Thoughts for Our Times, 1962, More Thoughts for Our Times, 1965, Still More Thoughts for Our Times, 1966, Thoughts IV, 1968, Thoughts V, 1969, The Humane Imperative: A Challenge for the Year 2000, 1974, The Hesburgh Papers: Higher Values in Higher Education, 1979. Former dir. Woodrow Wilson Nat. Fellowship Corp.; mem. Civil Rights Commn., 1957-72; mem. of Carnegie Commn. on Future of Higher Edn.; chmn. U.S. Commn. on Civil Rights, 1969-72; mem. Commn. on an All-Volunteer Armed Force, 1970; chmn. with rank of ambassador U.S. delegation UN Conf. Sci. and Tech. for Devel., 1977—; Bd. dirs. Am. Council Edn., Freedoms Found. Valley Forge, Adlai Stevenson Inst. Internat. Affairs; past trustee, chmn. Rockefeller Found.; trustee Carnegie Found. for Advancement Teaching, Woodrow Wilson Nat. Fellowship Found., Inst. Internat. Edn., Nutrition Found., United Negro Coll. Fund, others; chmn. Overseas Devel. Council; chmn. acad. council Ecumenical Inst. for Advanced Theol. Studies, Jerusalem. Recipient U.S. Navy's Disting. Pub. Service award, 1959; Presdl. Medal of Freedom, 1964; Gold medal Nat. Inst. Social Scis., 1969; Cardinal Gibbons medal Cath. U. Am., 1969; Bellarmine medal Bellarmine-Ursuline Coll., 1970; Meiklejohn award A.A.U.P., 1970; Charles Evans Hughes award Nat. Conf. Christians and Jews, 1970; Merit award Nat. Cath. Ednl. Assn., 1971; Pres.' Cabinet award U. Detroit, 1971; Am. Liberties medallion Am. Jewish Com., 1971; Liberty Bell award Ind. State Bar Assn., 1971; others. Fellow Am. Acad. Arts and Scis.; mem. Internat. Fedn. Cath. Univs., Freedoms Found. (dir., mem. exec. com.), Nutrition Found., Commn. on Humanities, Inst. Internat. Edn. (pres., dir.), Cath. Theol. Soc., Chief Execs. Forum, Am. Philos. Soc., Nat. Acad. Edn., Council on Fgn. Relations (trustee). Office: Office of Pres U Notre Dame Notre Dame IN 46656 *

HESKETT, JAMES LEE, educator; b. Cedar Falls, Iowa, May 8, 1933; s. Gail Stewart and Leone (Stein) H.; m. Marilyn Louise Taylor, July 13, 1955; children: Sarah Louise, Charles Taylor, Benjamin. A.B., Iowa State Tchrs. Coll., 1954; M.B.A., Stanford U., 1958, Ph.D., 1960; M.A. (hon.), Harvard U., 1970. Asst. prof. Ohio State U., 1960-63, asso. prof., 1963-65, Harvard Grad. Sch. Bus. Adminstrn., 1965-69, 1907 prof. bus. logistics, 1969—, sr. asso. dean for ednl. programs, 1980-83; pres. Logistics Systems, Inc., 1968-69; dir. Des Moines Register & Tribune, Cardinal Foods, Inc., Distek, Inc., Community Music Center Boston, The Window Shop, Inc., ISTUD, Italy, IPADE, Mex. Author: (with Glaskowsky and Ivie) Business Logistics, 1964, 2d edit., 1973, (with Germane and Glaskowsky) Highway Transportation Management, 1963, (with Schneider, Ivie and Glaskowsky) Case Problems in Business Logistics, 1973, Marketing, 1976; Bd. editors: Transp. Jour., Jour. Bus. Logistics. Served with AUS, 1954-56; ETO. Recipient Alumni Achievement award Iowa State Tchrs. Coll., 1971. Mem. Soc. Logistics Engrs. (dir.), Am. Mktg. Assn., Transp. Research Forum, Nat. Council Phys. Distbn. Mgmt. (John Drury Sheahan award 1974), Am. Soc. Traffic and Transp. Home: 233 Prospect St Belmont MA 02178

HESLIN, JAMES J., association executive; b. Cambridge, Mass., June 25, 1916; s. James Joseph and Helen (Burns) H.; m. Phyllis Stacy Brissette, July 13, 1940. B.S., Boston Coll., 1949; M.A., Boston U., 1949, Ph.D., 1952; M.S., Columbia U., 1954. Fellow history Boston U., 1950-52; 1st asst. Am. history div. N.Y. Pub. Library, 1953-54; asst. dir. univ. libraries U. Buffalo, 1955-56; asst. dir., librarian N.Y. Hist. Soc., 1956-58, assoc. dir., 1958-60, dir., 1960-82, dir. emeritus, 1982—; lectr. Columbia U., 1957-68; mem. adv. com. Archives Am. Art, N.Y.C., 1972—, Abigail Adams Smith Mus., 1972—, Eleutherian Mills-Hagley Found., Greenville, Del., 1975-78; cons. Winterthur Mus., Wilmington, Del., N.Y. State Council on Arts, N.J. Hist. Soc. Contbr. to books and periodicals. Mem. Landmarks Preservation Commn., N.Y.C., 1971-74, N.Y.C. Bicentennial History Com., 1975-76; trustee Sleepy Hollow Restorations, Inc. Served with AUS, 1943-46. Fellow Rochester Mus. and Sci. Ctr.; mem. Am. Hist. Assn., Am. Assn. State and Local History (mem. council 1962-64), N.Y. State Hist. Assn. (trustee, Gold medal 1982), Mass. Hist. Soc., Am. Assn. Mus. (accreditation com.), Am. Antiquarian Soc., Bibliog. Soc. Am. (pres. 1972-73), Colonial Soc. Mass. Clubs: Century Assn., Grolier, Coffee House (N.Y.C.). Home: 25 Central Park W New York NY 10023

HESLING, DONALD MILLS, consulting engineer; b. Dubuque, Iowa, Nov. 3, 1914; s. Francis J. and Mae L. (Mills) H.; m. Rheata E. Peterson, Apr. 2, 1945; children: Donald, Christine, Mary, Carol, Joanne, Terry, Judy, David, Debra, Patrice, Daniel, Dennis, Thomas. Student, Muskegon (Mich.) Community Coll., 1934-36, U. Mich., 1936-37. With Sealed Power Corp., Muskegon, 1946—, mgr. mfg. engring., then v.p. mfg. engring., 1952-57, v.p. research engring., 1957-80; cons. engr., 1980—. Contbr. articles to profl. jours. Mem. IEEE, AIM, Am. Mgmt. Assn., Am. Ordnance Assn., Nat. Bus. Aircraft Assn., Soc. Automotive Engrs., Serra Internat. Roman Catholic. Home and Office: 1419 Chapel Rd Muskegon MI 49441

HESPOS, RICHARD FRANKLIN, insurance company executive; b. North Bergen, N.J., Aug. 26, 1934; s. Franklin D. and Margaret E. (Merkel) H.; m. Arlene A. Merkl, June 7, 1958; children: Sheryl, Michael, Susan. B.S.E., Princeton U., 1955; M.B.A., Harvard U., 1959; Eng. Sc.D., Columbia U., 1966. Cons. McKinsey & Co., N.Y.C., 1962-69; v.p. Dun & Bradstreet Cos., N.Y.C., 1970-77; sr. v.p. Continental Corp., N.Y.C., 1977—; dir. Continental Reins. Co., N.Y.C., 1977—, Quotron Systems Inc., Los Angeles, 1970—, Am. Title Ins. Co., Miami, Fla., 1977—. Mem. adv. council Princeton U. Computer Ctr., 1970—, Princeton U. Computer, N.Y.C., 1967—. Home: 84 Partrick Rd Westport CT 06880 Office: Continental Corp 80 Maiden Ln New York NY 10038

HESS, ARTHUR, anatomist; b. N.Y.C., Feb. 19, 1927; s. David and Anna (Kruger) H.; m. Gloria Joy Tomsen, Dec. 25, 1953; children—Douglas Thomas, Elisa Tilda. B.S., U. Ark., 1946, M.S., 1947; Ph.D., Univ. Coll. London, 1949; D.Sc., U. London, 1959. Faculty Wash. U. Sch. Medicine, 1951-61, asst. prof. anatomy, 1954-61; asso. prof. physiology U. Utah Coll. Medicine, 1961-67; prof., chmn. dept. anatomy Rutgers Med. Sch., 1967—. Mem. Am. Assn. Anatomists, Soc. for Neurosci. Research and publs. on fine structure of nerve and muscle-electron microscopy, histochemistry, histology. Home: 211 Lincoln Ave Highland Park NJ 08904 Office: Dept Anatomy Rutgers Med Sch Piscataway NJ 08854

HESS, BERNARD ANDES, JR., chemistry educator; b. Wilmington, Del., Apr. 20, 1940; s. Bernard Andes and Camille (Robinson) H.; m. Betty Bray Gardner, Aug. 24, 1963; children: Elizabeth Robinson, John Garder. B.A., Williams Coll., 1962; M.S., Yale U., 1966, Ph.D., 1963. Postdoctoral fellow U. Oreg., Eugene, 1966-68; asst. prof. Vanderbilt U., Nashville, 1968-72, assoc. prof., 1972-80, prof. chemistry, 1980—, chmn. dept., 1982—. NIH fellow, 1963-66, 66-88; exchange scientist Nat. Acad. Scis., 1973-74. Mem. Am. Chem. Soc. Home: 219 Bowling Ave Nashville TN 37205 Office: Vanderbilt U PO Box 6220 Nashville TN 37235

HESS, CHARLES EDWARD, college dean; b. Paterson, N.J., Dec. 20, 1931; s. Cornelius W. M. and Alice (Debruyn) H.; m. Marie Grace Casella, June 28, 1953; children: Mary, Carol, Nancy, John. B.S., Rutgers U., 1953; M.S., Cornell U., 1954, Ph.D., 1957. Asst. prof. Purdue U., West Lafayette, Ind., 1958-61, assoc. prof., 1962-64, prof., 1965; research prof., dept. chmn. Rutgers U., West Brunswick, N.J., 1966; assoc. dean, dir. N.J. Agrl. Exptl. Sta., Rutgers U., West Brunswick, 1970; acting dean Coll. Agrl. and Environ. Sci., Rutgers U., West Brunswick, N.J., 1971; dean Cook Coll., Rutgers U., West Brunswick, N.J., 1972-75, Coll. Agr. and Environ. Scis., U. Calif.-Davis, 1975—; assoc. dir. Calif. Agrl. Exptl. Sta., 1975—; cons. AID, 1965, Office Tech. Assessment, U.S. Congress, 1976—; chmn. study team world food and nutrition study Nat. Acad. Scis., 1976. Mem. West Lafayette Sch. Bd., Ind., 1963-65, sec., Ind., 1963, pres., Ind., 1964; mem. N.J. Pesticide Adv. Council, Dept. Environ Protection, 1972—, Gov.'s Commn. Blueprint for Agr., 1971-73. Served with AUS, 1956-58. Mem. AAAS, Am. Soc. Hort. Sci. (pres. 1973), Internat. Plant Propagators Soc. (pres. 1973), Agrl. Research Inst., Phi Beta Kappa, Sigma Xi, Alpha Zeta. Home: 2949 Portage Bay Apt 163 Davis CA 95616 Office: Coll Agr and Environ Scis U Calif Davis CA 95616

HESS, DENNIS JOHN, investment banker; b. Manila, July 7, 1940; s. Carl and Anna (Harris) H.; m. Marilyn Goldchert, July 7, 1977; children: Whitney, Christine, Craig. B.S., U. Calif., Berkeley, 1962. With Merrill Lynch & Co., Inc., 1969—, v.p., 1977-80; chmn. bd., chief exec. officer Merrill Lynch, Hubbard, Inc., N.Y.C., 1980—; pres., chief operating officer ML Realty, 1983—; dir. United First Mortgage Corp., M.L. Huntoon Paige Inc., MLH Puerto, S.A. Served to 1st lt. USAF, 1962-66. Republican. Roman Catholic. Club: Waccabuc Country. Home: 321 Main St Ridgefield CT 06877 Office: 2 Broadway New York NY 10006

HESS, DONALD K., university administrator; b. Lititz, Pa., Nov. 18, 1930; s. Charles S. and Anna Mae (Kready) H.; m. Nancy Gordon, June 9, 1951; 1 dau., Jennifer Lynn. B.A., Franklin and Marshall Coll., 1952; M.P.A., Syracuse U., 1953. With AEC, Washington, 1953-58; asso. dir. Advanced Research Projects Agy., Dept. Def., Washington, 1958-66, OEO, 1966-70; dir. Peace Corps, Korea, 1970-72; asso. dir. for internat. ops. ACTION; dir. Peace Corps, Washington, 1972-74; v.p. campus affairs U. Rochester (N.Y.), 1974-83, v.p. adminstrn., 1983—; dir. EDMAC Assocs., Inc. Trustee Associated Univs., Inc.; past pres. Norman Howard Sch. Bd.; bd. overseers Center for Naval Analyses; mem. bd., past chmn. and pres. Rochester Assn. UN; bd. dirs. Rochester United Community Chest; pres. alumni exec. bd.

Franklin and Marshall Coll. Home: 215 Danbury Circle N Rochester NY 14618

HESS, ECKHARD HEINRICH, psychologist, educator; b. Bochum, Germany, Sept. 27, 1916; came to U.S., 1927, naturalized, 1943; s. Heinrich Peter and Wilhelmina (Salewski) H.; m. Dorothea Burghard-Nawiasky, Sept. 29, 1942. A.B., Blue Ridge Coll., New Windsor, Md., 1941; M.A., Johns Hopkins U., 1947, Ph.D., 1948. Jr. instr. Johns Hopkins U., 1946-47; faculty U. Chgo., 1948—, prof. psychology, 1959—, chmn. dept., 1963-68; dir. W.C. Allee Lab. Animal Behavior, 1960-70; spring vis. asso. prof. Swarthmore Coll., 1957, U. Calif. at Berkeley, 1958; vis. prof. U. Md.-Balt. County, 1975; Cons.-dir. Perception Lab., Interpublic, Inc., N.Y.C., 1960-67; mem. com. comparative devel. Social Sci. Research Council, 1961-67. Author: The Tell-Tale Eye: How Your Eyes Reveal Hidden Thoughts and Emotions; Co-editor: Psychologische Forschung, 1967-74, Brain, Behavior, and Evolution, 1968—; asso. editor: Animal Learning and Behavior, 1971-77; contbr. articles to sci. jours. Served with AUS, 1943-44. Fellow Center Advanced Studies Behavioral Scis., 1955-56. Fellow AAAS (life), Soc. Exptl. Psychologists, Am. Psychol. Assn., Animal Behavior Soc.; mem. Internat. Brain Research Orgn., Am. Mus. Natural History, Nat. Geog. Soc., Psychonomic Soc., Soc. Neurosci., Behavior Genetics Soc., Internat. Ethology Congress (internat. exec. com.), Sigma Xi. Club: Quadrangle (Chgo.). Home: PO Box 431 Cambridge MO 21613

HESS, EDWIN JOHN, oil company executive; b. Newark, Nov. 9, 1933; s. Harry E. and Victoria (Bienkowski) H.; m. Barbara Claire Gernert, June 29, 1957; children: Susan Lynn, Cheryl Lee, Nancy Jean, Cynthia Ann, Edwin John. Mech. engr., Stevens Inst. Tech., 1955; M.B.A., Harvard U., 1957. Engr. Exxon Co., U.S.A., Linden, N.J., 1957-60, supply mktg., Houston, Midland, Tex. and Los Angeles, 1960-72, retail bus. mgr., 1972-74, dep. dept. mgr., N.Y.C., 1974-78, v.p. mktg., 1978-81, sr. v.p., 1981—. Bd. dirs. St. Joseph's Hosp. Found., Houston, 1981—; co-pres. exec. council Harvard Bus. Sch. Assn., Boston, 1982-83; bd. dirs. council Better Bus. Bur., Arlington, Va., 1980—, Hwy. Users Fedn., 1978-81. Served with U.S. Army, 1959. Recipient Alumni Achievement award Stevens Inst. Tech., 1980. Republican. Presbyterian. Clubs: Lakeside Country; Petroleum (Houston). Office: Exxon Co USA 800 Bell Ave Houston TX 77001

HESS, EUGENE LYLE, ret. assn. exec., biologist; b. Superior, Wis., May 14, 1914; s. Lyle Sidney and Olga (Otteson) H.; m. Lila A. Huhtala, Dec. 20, 1941; children—Gretchen, Jennifer. B.Ch., U. Minn., 1938; M.S., U. Wis., 1942, Ph.D., 1947. Research asso. Rheumatic Fever Research Inst., Northwestern U., Chgo., 1948-57; sr. scientist Worcester Found. for Exptl. Biology, Shrewsbury, Mass., 1957-66; affiliate prof. chemistry Clark U., Worcester, Mass., 1962-65; program dir. metabolic biology NSF, Washington, 1965-66, sect. head molecular biology, 1966-69, sr. staff asso. to asst. dir. research, 1969-71; exec. dir. Fedn. Am. Socs. for Exptl. Biology, Bethesda, Md., 1971-79; trustee Biosis, 1976—, treas., 1978—; cons. NSF, 1977-80, NRC, 1974-80. Contbr. articles to profl. jours. Served to lt. col. AUS, 1940-46. Fellow AAAS; mem. Am. Chem. Soc., Am. Soc. Biol. Chemists, Am. Inst. Biol. Scis., N.Y. Acad. Sci., Biophys. Soc., Sigma Xi. Club: Cosmos (Washington). Address: 8706 Yarmouth Ct Potomac MD 20854

HESS, EVELYN VICTORINE (MRS. MICHAEL HOWETT), medical educator; b. Dublin, Ireland, Nov. 8, 1926; U.S., 1960, naturalized, 1965; d. Ernest Joseph and Mary (Hawkins) H.; m. Michael Howett, Apr. 27, 1954. M.B., B.Ch., B.A.O., U. Coll., Dublin, 1949; M.D., 1980. Intern West Middlesex Hosp., London, Eng., 1950; resident Clare Hall Hosp., London, 1951-53, Royal Free Hosp. and Med. Sch., 1954-57; asst. prof. internal medicine U. Tex. Southwestern Med. Sch., 1960-64; asso. prof. dept. medicine U. Cin. Coll. Medicine, 1964-69, McDonald prof. medicine, 1969—, dir. div. immunology, 1964—; sr. investigator Arthritis and Rheumatism Found., 1963-68; attending physician Cin. Gen. Hosp., VA Hosp., Holmes Hosp.; chief clinician Arthritis Clinic, Cin. Gen. Hosp., 1965—; cons. Children's Hosp., Cin., 1967—, Children's Convalescent Hosp., Jewish Hosp., 1968—; mem. various coms. NIH, mem. nat. adv. council; mem. various coms. FDA and profl. socs. Contbr. articles on immunology, rheumatic diseases to jours., chpts. to books. Active Nat. Parks Assn., Smithsonian Instn., others. Research fellow in epidemiology of Tb, 1955; Royal Free Med. Sch. Traveling fellow to, Scandinavia, 1956; Traveling fellow Empire Rheumatism Council, 1958-59. Fellow A.C.P., Am. Acad. Allergy; mem. Heberden Soc., Am. Rheumatism Assn., Central Soc. for Clin. Research, Am. Fedn. for Clin. Research, Am. Assn. Immunologists, Am. Soc. Nephrology, Am. Soc. Clin. Pharmacology and Therapeutics, Transplantation Soc., Reticuloendothelial Soc., N.Y. Acad. Scis., Alpha Omega Alpha. Home: 2916 Grandin Rd Cincinnati OH 45208 Office: U Cin Med Center Cincinnati OH 45267

HESS, GEORGE KELLOGG, JR., engineer; b. Orange, N.J., Aug. 27, 1922; s. George Kellogg and Henrietta (Spruhan) H.; m. Ruth Agnes Kelly, Nov. 3, 1945; children: Kathleen Janeth, James Douglas, Andrew Martin, Anne Elizabeth. B.S. in Enging. Mechanics, U. Mich., 1945; M.S. in Enging. Mechanics, U. Mich., 1947, Ph.D., 1954. Instr. U. Mich., 1946-49; mem. staff Los Alamos Sci. Lab., 1949-52; group leader, 1955-59; project engr. A.D. Little & Co., Cambridge, Mass., 1952-54; project leader Bendix Corp., Detroit, 1954-55, asst. to gen. mgr., Southfield, Mich., 1959-62; chief scientist USAF, Patrick AFB, Fla., 1962-67, dep. for engring. to asst. sec., 1967-69; dir. Advanced Materiel Concepts Agy., U.S. Army, Alexandria, Va., 1970-74; sr. sci. adviser magnetic fusion energy div. Dept. Energy, Germantown, Md., 1974-81; program mgr. Martin-Marietta, Orlando, Fla., 1981—; Cons. Los Alamos Sci. Lab., 1959-60. Mem. troop com. Central Brevard council Boy Scouts Am., 1963-65; Trustee Fla. Inst. Tech., Melbourne, 1962-68. Served as ensign USNR, 1945-46. Recipient Miller award in math. U. Mich., 1945; Outstanding Performance award USAF, 1964, 65, 66, 68, U.S. Army, 1972, 73; Exceptional Civilian Performance award, 1966. Mem. Am. Inst. Aeros. and Astronautics (dir. Canaveral chpt. 1963-64), Am. Rocket Soc., ASME, IEEE, Sigma Xi, Tau Beta Pi, Phi Eta Sigma. Episcopalian. Spl. research ship vibration, nuclear rocket engine controls, missile range instrumentation. Home: 1212 Pawnee Terr Indian Harbour Beach FL 32937 Office: Martin Marietta PO Box 5837 Orlando FL 32855

HESS, HANS OBER, lawyer; b. Royersford, Pa., Nov. 8, 1912; s. Samuel Harley and Annamae (Wenger) H.; m. Dolores Groke, May 18, 1940; children: Antonine (Mrs. Joseph J. Gal), Roberta (Mrs. Edward S. Trippe), Liese (Mrs. Arleigh P. Helfer, Jr.), Kristina (Mrs. Charles H. Bonner). A.B., Ursinus Coll., 1933, LL.D., 1979; LL.B., Harvard U., 1936; LL.D., Muhlenberg Coll., 1964. Sr. partner firm Ballard, Spahr, Andrews & Ingersoll, Phila.; dir. Paper Mfrs. Co., Ferag Corp., Bergen Evening Record Corp., Gateway Communications, Inc. Editor: Fiduciary Rev, monthly, The Nature of a Humane Society, 1976. Former mem. exec. council Lutheran Ch. in Am.; trustee Lankenau Hosp., Phila. Coll. Art; pres. Mary J. Drexel Home; trustee Marie M. Barclay Endowment; bd. dirs., sec. Phila. Orch. Assn., Acad. Music Phila.; former mem. Harvard Overseers Com. to Visit Law Sch.; former nat. chmn. Harvard Law Sch. Fund. Mem. Am., Pa., Phila., Montgomery County bar assns., Harvard Law Sch. Assn. Clubs: Philadelphia, Union League, Philadelphia Country (Phila.); Cotton Bay (Bahamas). Home: 1235 Conshohocken State Rd Gladwyne PA 19035 Office: 30 S 17th St Philadelphia PA 19103

HESS, KARSTEN, trading company executive; b. Vejle, Denmark, May 20, 1930; came to U.S., 1963; s. Harald Ejnar and Inger Marie (Karster) H.; m. Lillian Becker-Christensen, May 14, 1960; children: Regitze Marianne, Jannike Julie, Peter Martin. Diploma, Copenhagen Comml. Coll., 1951. Registered indsl. acct., Can. Mgmt. trainee East Asiatic Co., Ltd., Copenhagen, 1948-51; jr. exec., then chief accountant/budget controller East Asiatic Co. (Can.) Ltd., Vancouver, B.C., 1952-63; div. controller East Asiatic Co., Inc., San Francisco, 1963-71, corp. v.p., sec.-treas., N.Y.C., 1971—. Bd. dirs., chmn. fin. com. Day Care Center Tarrytowns, N.Y., 1978—; deacon Second Reformed Ch., Tarrytown, 1978—. Served with Danish Army, 1951-52. Mem. Danish Am. C. of C. (dir., treas. 1980—), Soc. Mgmt. Accountants Can., Am. Acctg. Assn., Nat. Cash Mgmt. Assn., Danish Am. Soc. Clubs: Royal Vancouver Yacht, World Trade Center. Office: 65 Springfield Ave PO Box 639 Springfield NJ 07081

HESS, LEON, oil company executive; b. 1914; (married). With Hess Oil & Chem. Corp. (and predecessor), 1946-69, pres., 1962-65, chmn. bd., chief exec. officer, 1965-69, also dir.; chmn. bd., chief exec. officer Amerada Hess Corp. (merger Hess Oil & Chem. Corp. and Amerada Petroleum Corp.), N.Y.C., 1971—, also dir.; co-owner, chmn. bd. N.Y. Jets Football Team, N.Y.C., 1963—. Served with AUS, 1942-45. Office: Amerada Hess Corp 1185 Ave of Americas New York NY 10036 *

HESS, OLEEN, agricultural economic development consultant, retired Fgn. Service officer; b. Plymouth, Utah, Oct. 25, 1923; s. George Albert and Elizabeth (Stokes) H.; m. Neva C. Moon, May 19, 1944; children: Kathryn (Mrs. Jonathan Vaughan), Dwight, Marsha (Mrs. Nicholas Lopez), Theresa (Mrs. Douglas V. Wright), Jeffery. B.S. in Agronomy, Utah State U., 1948; M.S. in Agrl. Edn, Oreg. State U., 1958; Ed.D., U. Utah, 1964; postdoctoral study internat. agr. and relations, Cornell U., 1974-75. Tchr. vocat. agr. Union High Sch., Molalla, Oreg., 1949-56; agrl. edn. adviser AID, PI.I., 1956-59, agrl. tng. adviser, Liberia, 1960-62, tng. officer, Sudan, 1964-65, agrl. officer for, East S.Africa, Washington, 1965-68, agrl. officer, Tanzania, 1968-74, Ghana, 1975-81, ret., 1981; v.p. agrl. and rural devel. Urban Resources Cons. Inc., Washington, 1981—; cons. in internat. econ. devel., 1981—. Author: Approved Poultry Production Practice, 1957, 68, 71, Vocational Guide in Coffee Production, 1958, Vocation Guide in Cacao Production, 1959, Agriculture Education and Agriculture Extension in Developing Nations, 1970, Tanzania: Ujamaa and Development, 1976, The Establishment of Cattle Ranching Associations among the Masai in Tanzania, 1976. Served with USNR, 1942-44. Decorated Air Medal. Mem. Phi Delta Kappa. Republican. Mem. Ch. of Jesus Christ of Latter-day Saints (br. pres., ward clk.). Home: 622 Winchester Dr Henderson NV 89015

HESS, PATRICK HENRY, chemist; b. Albia, Iowa, Aug. 6, 1931; s. John Henry and Mary Ellen (Judge) H.; m. Ann Marie Malone, June 6, 1959; children: Michelle, Maria, Margaret, Catherine, John. B.S. in Chemistry, U. Iowa, 1953; M.S. in Organic Chemistry, U. Nebr., 1958, Ph.D., 1960. Chemist Iowa State Hygienic Labs., 1953-54; teaching asst. U. Nebr., 1956-57, research asst., 1957-58, research fellow, 1958-60; research chemist Chevron Research Co., Richmond, Calif., 1960-64, Oil Field Research Co.-Chevron, La Habra, Calif., 1964-65, sr. research chemist, 1965-69, sr. research assoc., 1969—; research group supr., cons. Stanford Oil Calif. Contbr. articles to profl. jours.; patentee crude oil recovery. Active youth sports PTA. Served with USAF, 1954-55. Research fellow 3-M, 1958-59, Monsanto, 1959-60. Mem. Am. Chem. Soc., Soc. Petroleum Engrs., Sigma Xi, Alpha Chi Sigma, Alpha Tau Omega. Republican. Roman Catholic. Home: 23615 Sunset Crossing Diamond Bar CA 91765 Office: PO Box 446 La Habra CA 90631 *I am muli-blessed, especially in my career. I am working; I truly enjoy my work and feel that I am making meaningful contributions; I work among fellow scientists, young and old, who are capable, creative, invigorating. I have developed and maintained my enthusiasm by seeking out new challenges and learning experiences. I have always considered work to be a priviledge rather than a requirement.*

HESS, ROBERT DANIEL, education and psychology educator; b. Shambaugh, Iowa, Mar. 10, 1920; s. John Henry and Allilian (Weavers) H.; m. Betsy N. Muelke, June 18, 1949 (div. June 1969); children—Jared A., Alyssa N., Devin A., Bradley B. A.B. in Psychology, U. Calif. at Berkeley, 1947; Ph.D. in Human Devel, U. Chgo., 1950. Mem. faculty Com. on Human Devel., U. Chgo., 1949-67, chmn., 1959-64; dir. Urban Child Center, 1964-67; fellow Center Advanced Study Behavioral Scis., Stanford, Calif., 1966-67; Lee L. Jacks prof. child edn., prof. psychology Stanford, 1967—; ednl. cons. Author: (with Gerald Handel) Family Worlds: A Psychosocial Approach to Family Life, 1959, (with Judith V. Torney) The Development of Political Attitudes in Children, 1967, (with Virginia Shipman, Jere Brophy, Roberta Bear) The Cognitive Environments of Urban Preschool Child, 1968, (with Decker Walker) Instructional Software: Principles for Design and Use; Editor: (with Roberta M. Bear) Early Education: Current Theory, Research and Practice, 1968. Served with USMCR, 1942-46. Fellow AAAS, Am. Psychol. Assn., Am. Sociol. Assn.; mem. Am. Ednl. Research Assn., Soc. Research Child Devel. Home: 116 Lois Ln Palo Alto CA 94303 Office: Sch Edn Stanford U Stanford CA 94305

HESS, ROBERT LEE, college president; b. Asbury Park, N.J., Dec. 18, 1932; s. Henry and Ada (Davis) H.; m. Frances H. Aaron, Apr. 9, 1960; children: Carl, Laura, Jonathan, Roger. B.A., Yale U., 1954, M.A., 1955, Ph.D., 1960; D.H.L. (hon.), Spertus Coll. Judaica, 1978. Instr., then asst. prof. Carnegie Inst. Tech., 1958-61; asst. prof. Mt. Holyoke Coll., 1961-64, Northwestern U., 1964-65; asso. prof., then prof. U. Ill., Chgo. Circle, 1966-79, asso. dean liberal arts and scis., 1970-72, asso. vice chancellor acad. affairs, 1972-79; pres. Bklyn. Coll., 1979—, Coll. Community Services, Inc., 1979—. Author: Italian Colonialism in Somalia, 1966, Ethiopia: The Modernization of Autocracy, 1970, Bibliography of Primary Sources for 19th Century Tropical Africa, 1972, Dictionary of African Biography: Ethiopia, 1977; editor proc.: 5th Internat. Conf. Ethiopian Studies, 1979. Mem. Glencoe (Ill.) Planning Commn., 1975-76; bd. dirs. Jewish Council Urban Affairs, Chgo., 1972-79, Bklyn. Econ. Devel. Corp., 1980—, Maimonides Hosp. Research and Devel. Found.; mem. exec. bd. Bklyn. Jewish Hospice; bd. dirs. N.Y.C. Holocaust Meml. Commn.; mem. exec. bd. Jr. League Bklyn.; mem. exec. com. Greater N.Y. Conf. on Soviet Jewry. Decorated Officer de l'Ordre des Palmes Academiques (France); Fulbright fellow, 1956-58; summer travel grantee Ford Found., 1964; Guggenheim fellow, 1968-69. Mem. Am. Hist. Assn., African Studies Assn., Middle Eastern Studies Assn. N.Am., Am. Profs. for Peace in Middle East. Jewish. Clubs: Mory's, Elizabethan (New Haven); Brooklyn; Yale, University (N.Y.C.). Office: Office of President Brooklyn Coll Brooklyn NY 11210

HESS, SIDNEY J., JR., lawyer; b. Chgo., June 26, 1910; s. Sidney J. and Alma (Katz) H.; m. Jacqueline Engelhardt, Aug. 28, 1948; children—Karen E., Lori Ann. Ph.B., U. Chgo., 1930, J.D., 1932. Bar: Ill. 1932. Practiced in, Chgo., 1932—; mem. firm Aaron, Schimberg, Hess, Rusnak, Deutsh & Gilbert, Chgo., 1933—; dir., legal counsel Jewish Fedn. of Met. Chgo., 1968-77, v.p., 1972-74, pres., 1974-76; dir., legal counsel Jewish United Fund Met. Chgo., 1971-77, pres., 1974-76; legal counsel Jewish Welfare Fund Met. Chgo., 1969-73; dir. S. Silberman & Sons, Walston Aviation Inc., Chgo. Metallic Products, Inc., Erman Corp., Vienna Sausage Mfg. Co. Mem. exec. com. Anti-Defamation League, 1954-57, HIAS, 1974—; mem. nat. devel. council, aims com., citizens bd. U. Chgo.; bd. dirs. Schwab Rehab. Hosp., 1954—, pres., 1959-64. Recipient Judge Learned Hand Human Relations award Am. Jewish Com. Mem. Am., Ill. State, Chgo. bar assns., Am. Judicature Soc., U. Chgo. Law Sch. Assn. (dir.), Phi Beta Kappa., Pi Lambda Phi. Clubs: Standard (past pres., dir.), Mid-Day (Chgo.); Northmoor Country (Highland Park, Ill.). Home: 1040 N Lake Shore Dr Chicago IL 60611 Office: Xerox Center 55 W Monroe St Chicago IL 60603 *In my judgment the principles and standard of conduct which one must observe in daily life include a clear recognition of the rights and privileges of others, coupled with a desire to provide assistance to those who are less fortunate and unable to provide for themselves. No conduct of one's affairs can be adequate and fulfilling without recognition and observance of relationships with family. In all dealings, one must act with the highest degree of integrity and conscientious application.*

HESS, SIDNEY WAYNE, chemical company executive; b. Ames, Iowa, Oct. 21, 1932; s. Edwin M. and Mina Larson H.; m. Grayce Ann Medici, Oct. 9, 1954; children: Debra, Peter, Diana. B.S., M.I.T., 1953; postgrad., Delft Technische Hogeschool, 1953-54; Ph.D., Case Inst. Tech., 1960; M.A. (hon.), U. Pa., 1971. Mgr. ops. research Atlas Chem. Industries, Inc., Wilmington, Del., 1959-66; assoc. prof., dir. Mgmt. and Behavioral Sci. Center, U. Pa., 1966-75; dir. pharm. program devel. ICI Americas, 1974-76, v.p. planning and research, Wilmington, Del., 1976-80, v.p., gen. mgr. aerospace div., 1980—; dir. Ketron, Inc.; prin. Becknell, Frank, Gross & Hess, Inc., 1968-71. Contbr. articles to profl. jours. Mem. adv. com. Drexel Inst. Tech., 1979—; bd. dirs. Girls Clubs of Del., 1980—; trustee Concord Presbyn. Ch., 1978-80; mem. Adv. Com. on Indsl. Innovation, Dept. Commerce, 1978-79. Served to 1st lt. U.S. Army, 1954-56. Fulbright fellow, 1953. Mem. Inst. Mgmt. Sci. (past internat. sec. and pres.), Ops. Research Soc. Am. (past pres. Delaware Valley sect.), Ops. Research Soc. (U.K.), IEEE, Am. Def. Preparedness Assn., Soc. Chem. Industry (U.K.), Sigma Xi, Tau Beta Pi, Theta Chi. Club: Greenville Country. Office: PO Box 819 Valley Forge PA 19482

HESS, STEPHEN, political scientist, author; b. N.Y.C., Apr. 20, 1933; s. Charles and Florence (Morse) H.; m. Elena Shayne, Aug. 23, 1959 (div. 1979); children: Charles P., James R.; m. Beth Amster, Aug. 22, 1982. Student, U. Chgo., 1950-52; B.A., Johns Hopkins U., 1953. Jr. instr. polit. sci. Johns Hopkins U., 1953-55; staff asst. to U.S. Pres., 1959-61; asst. to minority whip U.S. Senate, 1961; asso. fellow Inst. for Policy Studies, 1964-65; fellow Inst. Politics J.F. Kennedy Sch. Govt., Harvard, 1967-68; dep. asst. to U.S. Pres. for urban affairs, 1969; nat. chmn. White House Conf. on Children and Youth, 1969-71; sr. fellow Brookings Instn., Washington, 1972—; Mem. Washington regional selection panel Pres.'s Commn. on White House Fellows, 1973; asso, Acad. for [Contemporary Problems, 1973-76; cons. Ford Found., 1974-76; mem. D.C. Bd. Higher Edn., 1973-76; chmn. D.C. Council Home Rule Transition Commn., 1974; U.S. alt. rep. UNESCO Gen. Conf., 1974; alumni fellows adv. com. Inst. Politics, J.F. Kennedy Sch. Govt., Harvard U., 1974—; adv. com. Smithsonian Instn.-Am. U. Project Family History, 1974-77; mem. 20th Century Fund task forces, 1975, 78, U.S. Nat. Commn. for UNESCO, 1975-77; editor-in-chief Nat. Republican Platform, 1976; mem. adv. council on gen. govt. Rep. Nat. Com., 1978-81; U.S. alt. rep., UN Gen. Assembly, 1976; cons. USIA, 1976, U.S. Office Mgmt. and Budget, 1977, German Marshall Fund of U.S., 1978; mem. bd. Internat. Writers Service, 1978—; vis. com. Gerald R. Ford Inst. for Public Services, Albion Coll., 1979-82; fellow faculty govt. Harvard U., 1979—; cons. Russell Sage Found., 1980; adv. com. Fund for Investigative Journalism, 1981—. Author: (with Malcolm Moos) Hats in the Ring: The Making of Presidential Candidates, 1960, America's Political Dynasties, 1966, (with David S. Broder) The Republican Establishment, 1968, (with Milton Kaplan) The Ungentlemanly Art: A History of American Political Cartoons, 1968, rev. edit., 1975, (with Earl Mazo) Nixon: A Political Portrait, 1968, rev. edit., 1969, The Presidential Campaign: The Leadership Selection Process after Watergate, 1974, rev. edit., 1978, Organizing The Presidency, 1976, The Washington Reporters, 1981; contbr. (with Earl Mazo) articles to profl. jours.; syndicated newspaper columnist. Served with AUS, 1956-58. Mem. Nat. Acad. Pub. Adminstrn. Home: 3705 Porter St NW Washington DC 20016 Office: Brookings Instn 1775 Massachusetts Ave NW Washington DC 20036

HESS, WHEELER HERDMAN, insurance executive; b. Shavertown, Pa., Nov. 8, 1931; s. Wheeler H. and Mary (Thomas) H.; m. Lorraine Sickler, June 5, 1954; children: Linda, David, Brenda. A.B., Gettysburg Coll., 1953; M.B.A., U. Conn., 1963; A.M.P., Harvard U., 1979. Asst. sec. Travelers Ins. Co., Hartford, Conn., 1966-67, sec., 1967-69, 2d v.p., 1969-71, v.p., 1971-76, sr. v.p., 1976—; dir. Ins. Services Office, N.Y.C., 1979—, Nat. Council Compensation Ins., 1979—. Capt. USAF, 1954-56. Republican. Congregationalist. Club: Hartford. Home: 422 Lake Rd Andover CT 06232 Office: Travelers Insurance Co 1 Tower Sq Hartford CT 06115

HESS, WILFORD MOSER, botanist, educator; b. Clifton, Idaho, Feb. 18, 1934; s. Lewis William and Arville (Moser) H.; m. Carlene Bess Falkenburg, July 2, 1954; children—Carl Zane, Carla Ann. B.S., Brigham Young U., 1957; M.S., Oreg. State U., 1960, Ph.D., 1962. Research asst. expt. sta. Dept. Agr., Salinas, Calif., 1958; research asst. depts. horticulture, botany and plant pathology Oreg. State U., 1959-62; mem. faculty Brigham Young U., Provo, Utah, 1962—, prof. botany, 1971—, dir. electron optics lab., 1976—; postdoctoral research Cell Research Inst., U. Tex., 1964-65, Swiss Fed. Inst. Tech., Zurich, 1966-67. Co-author lab. manuals; contbr. profl. jours.; co-editor: The Fungal Spore, Form and Function, 1976; sr. editor: Science and Religion: Toward a More Useful Dialogue, vols. I and II, 1979. Served to 1st lt. AUS, 1957. Recipient Career Devel. award NIH, 1969-74; Karl G. Maeser Research award Brigham Young U., 1972; Faculty Coll. Achievement award, 1979. Mem. Internat. Soc. Plant Pathology, Am. Phytopath. Soc., Bot. Soc. Am., Mycol. Soc., Electron Microscopy Soc. Am., Am. Soc. Cell Biology, AAAS, Sigma Xi (ann. lectr. 1974-75), Phi Kappa Phi (pres. chpt. 1979—). Republican. Mormon. Home: 670 E 2780 N Provo UT 84601 Office: 129 WIDB Dept Botany Brigham Young U Provo UT 84602 *Establish priorities; then proceed with prudence and perseverance.*

HESS, WILMOT NORTON, sci. adminstr.; b. Oberlin, Ohio, Oct. 16, 1926; s. Walter Norton and Rachel Victoria (Metcalf) H.; m. Winifred Esther Lowdermilk, June 16, 1950; children—Walter Craig, Alison Lee, Carl Ernest. B.S. in Elec. Engring, Columbia, 1946; M.A. in Physics, Oberlin Coll, 1949; D.Sc., 1970; Ph.D., U. Calif., Berkeley, 1954. Staff Lawrence Radiation Lab., U. Calif., Berkeley and Livermore, 1954-59, head plowshare div., Livermore, 1959-61; dir. theoretical div. Goddard Spaceflight Center (NASA), Greenbelt, Md., 1961-67; dir. sci. and applications Manned Spacecraft Center, Houston, 1967-69; dir. NOAA Research Labs. (Commerce Dept.), Boulder, Colo., 1969-80, Nat. Center for Atmospheric Research, 1980—; adj. prof. U. Colo., 1970-78. Contbr. articles to profl. jours.; editor: Introduction to Space Science, 1965; author: Radiation Belt and Magnetosphere, 1968, (with others) Weather and Climate Modification, 1974; asso. editor: Jour. Geophys. Research, 1961-67, Jour. Atmospheric Sci, 1961-67, Jour. Am. Inst. Aeros. and

Astronautics, 1967-69. Served with USN, 1944-46. Fellow Am. Geophys. Union, Am. Phys. Soc.; mem. Nat. Acad. Engring. Club: Cosmos (Washington). Home: 4927 Idylwild Trail Boulder CO 80301 Office: Nat Center Atmospheric Research Boulder CO 80307

HESSE, MARTHA O., government official; b. Hattiesburg, Miss., Aug. 14, 1942; d. John and Jerry (Ossian) H. B.S., U. Iowa, 1964; postgrad., Northwestern U., 1972-76; M.B.A., U. Chgo., 1979. Research analyst Blue Shield, 1964-66; dir. div. data mgmt. Am. Hosp. Assn., 1966-69; v.p., chief operating officer SEI Info. Tech., 1969-81; assoc. dep. sec. Dept. of Commerce, 1982; exec. dir. Pres.' Task Force on Mgmt. Reform, 1982; asst. sec. mgmt. and adminstrn. Dept. of Energy, Washington, 1982—; vice chmn. dean's fund U. Chgo. Grad. Sch. Bus., 1981—. Office: Dept of Energy Management and Administration 1000 Independence Ave SW Washington DC 20585 *

HESSE, WILLIAM R., association executive; b. Dayton, Ohio, Jan. 19, 1914; s. Julius R. and Margaret (Reid) H.; m. Anne E., Vandervort, July 3, 1941; children: William R., Carol Anne, Mark Vandervort. A.B., U. Cin., 1938. Supr. employment for men Procter & Gamble, Cin., then asst. to sales mgr., 1937-46; v.p. Batten, Barton, Durstine & Osborn, Inc., Pitts. and N.Y.C., 1946-56; sr. v.p. Benton & Bowles, Inc., N.Y.C., 1956-58, exec. v.p., 1958-61, pres., 1961-68, chief exec. officer, 1965-68; also dir.; pres., chief exec. officer William R. Hesse Assos., N.Y.C. and Greenwich, Conn., 1968-75; sr. v.p. Am. Assn. Advt. Agys., Washington, 1975-78, pres., chief exec. officer, 1978; chmn. Fahlgren & Ferriss Advt. Agy., 1979; sec., dir. Advt. Council; dir. Nat. Advt. Rev. Com., Advt. Research Found., Traffic Audit Bur.; partner Pacifica Park, Seattle. Mem. mgmt. com. YMCA; mem. adv. bd. Nat. Coffee Assn. Bd.; dirs. Urban League of N.Y. Served as lt. col. Inf. AUS, 1941-45. Recipient Putnam award Nat. Indsl. Advertisers Assn., 1949. Mem. Am. Mgmt. Assn., Am. Assn. Advt. Agys. (dir.-at-large), Royal Soc. Arts. (hon. corr.). Clubs: N.Y. Athletic, Athletic, Cummaquid Golf.; Imperial Golf (Naples, Fla.). Home: 177 Mid Pine Rd Yarmouth Port MA 02675

HESSELS, JAN-MICHIEL, chemical company executive; b. The Hague, Netherlands, Dec. 21, 1942; came to U.S., 1982; s. Johan H. and Emmy H.P. (Boots) H.; s. Liesbeth W.M. Hillen, Nov. 12, 1970; children: Maartje, Laurien, Pieter. LL.M., Ryks U., Leiden, Holland, 1966; postgrad., London Sch. Econs., 1966-67; M.B.A., U. Pa., 1969. Trainee S.G. Warburg & Co., London, 1967; asst. to gen mgr. Overseas Devel. Bank, Geneva, 1969-70; assoc. McKinsey & Co., N.Y.C., 1968, engagement mgr., Amsterdam, 1971-73; corp. treas. Akzo N.V., Arnhem, Holland, 1973-77; pres. Akzo Ltda., Sao Paulo, Brazil, 1977-82; exec. v.p., dir. Akzona Corp., Asheville, N.C., 1982—; dir. Robrasco A.A., Rio de Janeiro, 1980-82; pres. Fontanus Argentina S.A., Buenos Aires, 1977-82. Pres. Escolha Rainha Juliana, Sao Paulo, 1981-82. Home: 3 Valley springs Rd Asheville NC 28803 Office: Akzona Inc 1 N Pack Sq PO Box 2930 Asheville NC 28802

HESSEMAN, HOWARD, actor; b. Lebanon, Oreg., Feb. 27, 1940; s. George Henry and Edna (Forster) H. Student, U. Oreg. Mem. The Com. (improvisational theatre co.), 1965-75. Appeared in: numerous films including The Jerk; appears in: TV series as Dr. Johnny Fever, WKRP in Cin; appeared in: numerous films including Petulia, Billy Jack, Steelyard Blues, Shampoo, The Sunshine Boys, Jackson County Jail, The Big Bus, The Other Side of Midnight, Silent Movie, Honky Tonk Freeway, Doctor Detroit; TV movies Hustling, The Life and Times of Senator Joe McCarthy, The Amazing Howard Hughes, The TV TV Show, Tarantulas: The Deadly Cargo, The Comedy Company, The Ghost of Flight 401, You Can't Take It with You, Skyward, The Victim, In Our Hands; appears in: TV series as Dr. Johnny Fever, WKRP in Cincinnati; TV series One Day At A Time, numerous others. Office: care Baumann Hiller & Assocs 9220 Sunset Blvd Los Angeles CA 90069

HESSER, LEON FRANCIS, agricultural economist; b. Winchester, Ind., July 27, 1925; s. George and Frances Madonna (Bolinger) H.; m. Florence Ellen Life, Aug. 11, 1946; children: Gwendolyn, George. B.S., Purdue U., 1958, M.S., 1960, Ph.D., 1962. Agr. economist U.S. Dept. Agr., Lafayette, Ind., 1958-62; agrl. economist Fed. Res. Bank of Kansas City, Mo., 1962-66; asst. dir. for agrl. policy AID State Dept., Islamabad, Pakistan, 1966-73; agrl. economist (AID), Washington, 1973-74; dir. Office Agr., Tech. Assistance Bur., 1974-78; pres. Randiana Farms, Inc., Winchester, Ind., 1978-79; dir. office agr. Pacific Consultants, Washington, 1978-79; program officer Internat. Agrl. Devel. Service, N.Y.C., 1980-82, Arlington,, Va., 1982—. Served with AUS, 1944-46. Vis. scholar Harvard, 1970-71. Mem. Internat. Assn. Agrl. Economists, Am. Econ. Assn., Am. Agrl. Econ. Assn. Methodist. Home: 104 S 1600 Eads St Arlington VA 22202 Office: Internat Agrl Devel Service 1611 N Kent St Arlington VA 22209

HESSIAN, PATRICK JOHN, army officer, clergyman; b. Belle Plaine, Minn., May 20, 1928; s. Emmett William and Oleta Ann (Schuler) H. B.A., St. Paul Sem., 1949; M.A., U. Kans., 1978; postgrad., Command and Gen. Staff Coll., 1974, Army War Coll., 1978. Ordained priest Roman Cath. Ch., 1953; asst. pastor St. James Ch., St. Paul; commd. 1st lt. U.S. Army, 1963, advanced through grades to maj. gen.; post chaplain, Ft. Leonard Wood, Mo., 1971-73, Ft. Campbell, Ky., 1975; command chaplain XVIII Airborne Corps, Ft. Bragg, N.C., 1975-77; dep. chief chaplains, Washington, 1979—. Decorated Bronze Star with 3 oak leaf clusters, Air medal, Purple Heart, others. Mem. Mil. Chaplains Assn. Club: K.C. Home: 3705 S George Mason Dr Falls Church VA 22401 Office: DACH-ZA Dept Army Washington DC 20310

HESSION, RAYMOND VINCENT, Canadian government official; b. Regina, Sask., Can., June 27, 1940; s. Edmund Gilbert and Marion Elizabeth (Lawlor) H.; m. Louis Richard, Apr. 20, 1963; children: Natalie, Brian, Raymond, Adele. Student, Coll. Militaire Royal de Saint-Jean, Que., 1957-60; B.A., Royal Mil. Coll., 1962. Mgr. IBM Can. Ltd., Ottawa, Montreal and Toronto, 1965-74, Multiple Access Ltd., Ottawa, Montreal and Toronto, 1965-74; exec. dir. Can. Mortgage & Housing Corp., Ottawa, 1974, v.p., 1975, pres., 1976; dep. minister Supply Adminstrn., Supply and Services Can., Hull, Que., 1982—; chmn. bd. dirs. Royal Can. Mint., Ottawa, 1982; dir. Can. Comml. Corp., Ottawa, 1982. Clubs: Royal Mil. Coll., Royal Ottawa Golf; Le Cercle (Ottawa). Home: 308 Cathcart St Ottawa ON Canada K1N 0S5 Office: Supply and Services Can Phase 111 Place du Portage Hull PQ Canada KIA OS5

HESSLER, CURTIS ALAN, lawyer; b. Berwyn, Ill., Dec. 27, 1943; s. Robert A. and Ruth T. (Teeter) H.; m. Christine Mary Cocker, Dec. 14, 1968; children: Alexander, Francesca. B.A., Harvard U., 1966; postgrad. (Rhodes scholar), Oxford U., 1966-69; J.D., Yale U., 1973; M.A. in Econs, U. Calif., Berkeley, 1976. Exec. asst. to Sec. Treasury, Dept. Treasury, Washington, 1977-79, asst. sec. for econ. policy, 1980; asso. dir. Office Budget and Mgmt., Washington, 1979-81; ptnr. Paul Weiss Rifkind Wharton & Garrison, 1981-82; sr. v.p. Sears World Trade, Inc., 1982—. Home: 3113 Dogwood St NW Washington DC 20015

HESSLER, DAVID WILLIAM, library educator, media consultant; b. Oak Park, Ill., May 9, 1932; s. William Wigney and Gwendolyn Eileen (Butler) H.; m. Helen Montgomery, Aug. 27, 1955; children: Leslie Susan, Laura Lynn. B.A., U. Mich., 1955, M.A., 1961; Ph.D., Mich. State U., 1972. Comml. photographer Oscar & Assos., Chgo., 1950; equipment engr. Western Electric Co., Chgo., 1958-59; cons. and asst. dir. U. Mich. Audio-Visual Edn. Center, 1960-66; dir. libraries and media Ann Arbor (Mich.) Public Schs., 1966-67; asst. prof. edn. Western Mich. U., 1967-72, assoc. prof., 1974-77; dir. instructional services U. S.C., 1973-74; prof. library sci. U. Mich., 1977—, dir. instructional strategy services for schs., 1979-81; cons. Presdl. Commn. on World Hunger; cons. media and tech.; instructional designer and evaluator. Author: (with others) Student Production Guide, 1975, Technology for Communication and Instruction, 1983; producer, dir. numerous films, filmstrips, TV programs and sound/slide programs for various ednl. levels. Served to lt. USAF, 1955-58; capt. Res. ret. Decorated Air Force Commendation medal; named Most Valuable Tchr. Chrysler Corp., 1965; Ednl. Profl. Devel. Act fellow, 1968-69. Mem. Mich. Audio Visual Assn. (sec.-treas. 1960-65), ALA, Assn. Ednl. Communications and Tech., Mich. Assn. Media in Edn., Assn. for Library and Info. Sci. Edn., Assn. Coll. and Research Libraries, Am. Soc. Tng. and Devel., Am. Assn. Sch. Librarians, Mich. Alumni Soc., Mich. State U. Alumni Assn., Phi Delta Kappa, Phi Kappa Phi. Club: U. Mich. M. Home: 3677 Frederick Dr Ann Arbor MI 48105 Office: U Mich Sch Library Sci Ann Arbor MI 48109

HESSLER, ROBERT ROAMIE, company executive; b. Toledo, Aug. 23, 1918; s. Roamie C. and Lily (Zenthoefer) H.; m. Winifred J. Graves, Aug. 3, 1940; 1 son, Robert Roamie. B.B.A., U. Toledo, 1940. Dir. taxes and ins. Willys Overland Motors, Inc., Toledo, 1946-54; gen. mgr. Buggie div. (Burndy Corp.), Toledo, 1955-60; v.p. Questor Corp., Toledo, 1961-82; ptnr. R & R Cons., Ltd., Toledo, 1983—; lectr. U. Toledo, 1946-48. Mem. adv. com. George C. Beinke Scholarship Trust, Goerlich Found.; bus. adv. council U. Toledo; bd. dirs. Toledo Zool. Soc. Served to 1st lt. Q.M.C. AUS, 1944-46. Mem. Nat. Assn. Accountants (pres. Toledo chpt. 1953-54), Fin. Execs. Inst. Club: Toledo. Lodges: Masons; Shriners; Jesters. Home: 2620 Pemberton Dr Toledo OH 43606 Office: PO Box 2789 Toledo OH 43606

HESSON, JAMES MARSH, army officer; b. St. Paul, Nov. 28, 1931; s. Floyd Edward and Hulda (Rasmussen) H.; m. Joyce Lorraine Martin, Aug. 1, 1952; children—Leslie Ann Hesson Whitaker, James Marsh, Jeffrey W., Laurie Jo. B.S., St. Benedict's Coll., 1967; M.S., George Washington U., 1973; grad., Command and Gen. Staff Coll., 1966, Indsl. Coll. Armed Forces, 1973. Commd. 2d lt. U.S. Army, 1952; advanced through grades to brig. gen., study dir., Washington, 1973-75; project mgr. CH-47 Modernization Program, St. Louis, 1975-79; dep. comdr. U.S. Army Troop Support and Aviation Materiel Readiness Comd., DARCOM, St. Louis, 1979-82; dir. plans and ops. Dep. Chief Staff for Logistics, Washington, 1982—. Decorated Legion of Merit with oak leaf cluster, D.F.C., Bronze Star medal, Air medal with two oak leaf clusters. Mem. Assn. U.S. Army, Army Aviation Assn. Methodist. Home: 7814 Cliffside Ct Springfield VA 22153 Office: The Pentagon Washington DC 20310

HESTER, DOUGLAS BENJAMIN, lawyer, legislative counsel; b. McKenzie, Ala., Sept. 18, 1927; s. Mack Ellis and Carrie Lottie (Taylor) H.; m. Melissa Hood Fuller, Apr. 16, 1960; children: Carlotta Marie, Benjamin Alexander. B.S., U. Ala., 1950, LL.B., 1952. Bar: Ala. 1952, D.C. 1960. Law asst. Office Legis. Counsel-U.S. Senate, Washington, 1952-54, asst. counsel, 1954-69, sr. counsel, 1969—. Trustee Centro Anglo-Espanol, Washignton. Served with AUS, 1945-47. Mem. D.C. Bar Assn., Ala. Bar Assn. Home: 218 Maryland Ave Ne Washington DC 20002 Office: Room SD 668 Dirksen Senate Office Bldg Washington DC 20510

HESTER, JAMES J., anthropology educator, archaeological consultant; b. Anthony, Kans., Sept. 21, 1931; s. Simon Fredric and Ada Belle (Smith) H.; m. Adrienne Arlene Davis, Oct. 1, 1955; children: Michael Allen, Frederick Randall, John David. B.A., U. N.Mex.-Albuquerque, 1953; Ph.D., U. Ariz.-Tucson, 1961. Asst. curator Mus. N.Mex., Santa Fe, 1959-64; exec. sec. grants com. NIH, Washington, 1965-67; state archeologist Colo. Hist. Soc., Denver, 1974-76; chief archeologist Adv. Council on Historic Preservation, Washington, 1978-79; prof. antrhopology U. Colo., Boulder, 1967—. Author: Introduction to Archaeology, 1976, (with J. Grady) Introduction to Archaeology, 2d edit., 1982. Bd. dirs. Unitarian Ch., Boulder, Colo., 1978. Served to 1st lt. USAF, 1954-56. Mem. Am. Soc. Conservation Archaeology (pres. 1975-76), Soc. Profl. Archaeologists (treas. 1976-77, pres. 1980-81), Colo. Hist. Soc. (trustee 1982—, recipient Sr. archaeologist award 1980), Colo. Archaeol. Soc. (editor 1972-76). Democrat. Club: Explorers (chmn. 1972-73). Home: Jamestown Star Route Boulder CO 80302 Office: Dept Anthropology Univ Colo Boulder CO 80309

HESTER, JAMES LYNN, educator; b. Vicksburg, Miss., Aug. 8, 1939; s. James Hosie and Rena (Maners) H.; m. Ouida Blackmon, May 15, 1965; children—Jennifer Paige, Allyson Susanne. B.S., Miss. State U., 1961, M.B.A., 1961; Ph.D., U. Ark., 1965. Part-time instr. U. Ark., 1961-64; asst. prof. La. State U., New Orleans, 1964-66; dir., div. bus. and econ. research La. Tech. U., Ruston, 1966-69, prof. mgmt., 1966—; dean Grad. Sch., dir. sponsored programs, 1969-76, chmn. dept. bus., 1977—; mgmt. cons. Mem. Acad. Mgmt., Nat. Council Research Adminstrs., Ozark Econ. Assn., Am. Soc. Personnel Adminstrn., Beta Gamma Sigma (pres. 1969), Blue Key, Phi Kappa Phi, Omicron Delta Epsilon, Alpha Kappa Psi. Episcopalian (vestryman). Home: 315 Neal St Ruston LA 71270

HESTER, JAMES MCNAUGHTON, botanical garden administrator; b. Chester, Pa., Apr. 19, 1924; s. James Montgomery and Margaret (McNaughton) H.; m. Janet Rodes, May 23, 1953; children: Janet McN., Margaret, Martha. B.A., Princeton U., 1945, LL.D. (honoris causa), 1962; B.A. (Rhodes scholar 1947-50), Oxford (Eng.) U., 1950, D.Phil., 1955; LL.D., Lafayette Coll., 1964, Morehouse Coll., 1967; L.H.D., Hartwick Coll., 1964, Pace U., 1971, U. Pitts., 1971, Colgate U., 1974, N.Y. U., 1977; D.C.L., Alfred U., 1965; LL.D., Hofstra U., 1967, Hahnemann Med. Coll., 1967, Fordham U., 1971, Amherst Coll., 1975, New Sch. for Social Research, 1975, Union Coll., 1983. Civil information officer Fukuoka Mil. Govt. Team, Japan, 1946-47; asst. to Am. sec. to Rhodes Trustees, 1950; asst. to pres. Handy Assos., Inc. (mgmt. cons.), N.Y.C., 1953-54; account supr. Gallup and Robinson, Inc., Princeton, N.J., 1954-57; provost Bklyn. center L.I. U., 1957-60, v.p., 1958-60; prof. history, exec. dean arts and sci., dean Grad. Sch. Arts and Sci. N.Y.U., 1960-61, pres., 1962-75; rector UN U., Tokyo, 1975-80; pres. N.Y. Bot. Garden, 1980—; Dir. Union Carbide Corp. Trustee Met. Mus. Art, 1963-75, Lehman Found., Global Tomorrow Edn., United Bd. for Christian Higher Edn. in Asia. Served with USMCR, 1943-46, 51-52. Mem. Pilgrims U.S., Council Fgn. Relations, Assn. Am. Rhodes Scholars, Phi Beta Kappa. Clubs: Cosmos (Washington); Century Assn., University, Knickerbocker, Pretty Brook Tennis. Office: NY Botanical Garden Bronx NY 10458

HESTER, LAWRENCE LAMAR, JR., medical educator; b. Anderson, S.C., May 23, 1920; s. Lawrence Lamar and Carrie Rose (McCelvey) H.; m. Ruth Elizabeth Catling, July 12, 1947; children: Barrie, Lawrence Lamar, Elizabeth Porcher, Frances Stuart. B.S., The Citadel, 1941, D.Sc., 1980; M.D., Med. U. S.C., 1944. Intern Roper Hosp., Charleston, S.C., 1944-45, resident, 1945-46, 48-50; instr. Med U. S.C., Charleston, 1950-52, asst. prof., 1954-56, prof., chmn. dept. obstetrics and gynecology, 1956—. Served to capt. USAF, 1946-48. Fellow South Atlantic Assn. Obstetricians and Gynecologists, Am. Coll. Obstetricians and Gynecologists, Am. Gnecol. and Obstet. Soc.; mem. S.C. Obstet. and Gynecol. Soc. (pres. 1959), Am. Gynecol. Club (pres. 1980-81). Episcopalian. Home: 615 Pitt St PO Box 553 Mount Pleasant SC 29464 Office: Med Univ SC 171 Ashley Ave Charleston SC 29425

HESTER, THOMAS PATRICK, lawyer, utility company executive; b. Tulsa, Nov. 20, 1937; s. Elmo P. and Mary J. (Layton) H.; m. Nancy B. Scofield, Aug. 20, 1960; children: Thomas Patrick, Ann S., John L. Student, Colo. Sch. Mines, 1955; B.A., U. Okla., 1961, LL.B., 1963. Bar: Okla. 1963, Mo. 1963, N.Y. 1970, D.C. 1973, Ill. 1975. Assoc. McAfee, Taft, Cates, Kuntz & Mark, Oklahoma City, 1963-66; atty. Southwestern Bell Telephone Co., Oklahoma City, 1966-67, St. Louis, 1967-69, AT&T, N.Y.C., 1969-72, exec. asst. atty., Washington, 1972-75, gen. atty., Springfield, Ill., 1975-77, gen. solicitor, Chgo., 1977-83; v.p., gen. counsel Ill. Bell Telephone Co., Chgo., 1983—. Served to capt. JAGC U.S. Army, 1959-68. Mem. Order of Coif. Home: 33 S County Line Rd Hinsdale IL 60521 Office: Ill Bell Telephone Co 225 W Randolph Chicago IL 60606

HESTER, THOMAS RAYMOND, JR., business executive; b. Louisville, Feb. 19, 1948; s. Thomas Raymond and Alma Jane (Thompson) H.; m. Sharon R. Weber, Nov. 26, 1966; children: Thomas Raymond, III, Amy Rose. B.A. in Acctg., Bellarmine Coll., 1970. C.P.A., Ky. Sr. acct. Coopers & Lybrand (C.P.A.s), Louisville, 1970-73; asst. controller, then controller Jerrico, Inc., Lexington, Ky., 1973-77, treas., 1977—, v.p. fin., 1983—. Bd. dirs. Jr. Achievement Blue Grass, 1977—, pres., 1980. Mem. Ky. Air N.G., 1970-76. Mem. Am. Inst. C.P.A.s, Nat. Assn. Accts., Nat. Restaurant Assn., Ky. Soc. C.P.A.s, Lexington C. of C. Roman Catholic. *

HESTER, THOMAS ROY, anthropologist; b. Crystal City, Tex., Apr. 28, 1946; s. Jim Tom and Mattie Laura (Umphres) H.; m. Lynda Sue Broadway, July 2, 1966; children: Lesley Elise, Amy Lynne. B.A. with honors, U. Tex., Austin, 1969; Ph.D., U. Calif., Berkeley, 1972. Acting asst. prof. anthropology U. Calif., Berkeley, 1972-73; asst. prof. anthropology U. Tex., San Antonio, 1973-75, asso. prof., 1975-77, prof., 1977—; dir. Center for Archaeol. Research, 1974—; vis. asso. prof. U. Calif., Berkeley, 1976; cons. Southwest Research Inst., San Antonio, 1975—. Author: (with R. Heizer and J. Graham) Field Methods in Archaeology, 1975, Digging into South Texas Prehistory, 1980, (with R. Heizer and C. Graves) Archaeology: A Bibliographical Guide to the Basic Literature, 1980, (with G. Ligabue, S. Salvatori, M. Sartor) Colha e I Maya Dei Bassipiani, 1983; Contbr. articles to profl. jours. Woodrow Wilson fellow, 1969-70. Fellow Tex. Archeol. Soc.; mem. Soc. Am. Archaeology (exec. com. 1984-86), Assn. Field Archaeology (mem. exec. com. 1979-82), AAAS, Soc. Archaeol. Sci., Sigma Xi (pres. Alamo chpt. 1979). Democrat. Methodist. Home: 105 Country Club Ln San Antonio TX 78232 Office: Center for Archaeological Research U Tex San Antonio TX 78285

HESTON, CHARLTON, actor; b. Evanston, Ill., Oct. 4, 1924; s. Russell Whitford and Lilla (Charlton) Carter; m. Lydia Marie Clarke, Mar. 17, 1944; children—Fraser Clarke, Holly Ann. Student, Northwestern U., 1941-43. Mem. Nat. Council on the Arts, 1967-72. Stage appearances in Antony and Cleopatra, 1947, Leaf and Bough, 1948, Design for a Stained Glass Window, 1949, The Tumbler, 1960; TV appearances in Wuthering Heights, Macbeth, Taming of the Shrew, Of Human Bondage, Jane Eyre; motion picture star appearing in: Gray Lady Down, 1950—, Dark City, Greatest Show on Earth, Ruby Gentry, Naked Jungle, The Ten Commandments, The Big Country, Ben Hur, El Cid, 55 Days of Peking, The Greatest Story Ever Told, The Agony and the Ecstasy, Khartoun, Will Penny, Planet of the Apes, Julius Caesar, The Hawaiians, The Omega Man, Antony and Cleopatra, Soylent Green, The Three Musketeers, Airport "75, Earthquake, Midway, Two-Minute Warning, The Prince and the Pauper. Trustee Los Angeles Center Theatre Group, Am. Film Inst., 1971—, chmn., 1973; head President's Task Force on Arts and Humanities, 1981—. Served in USAAF, World War II. Recipient Acad. award for best actor in Ben-Hur, 1959; Jean Hersholt award as humanitarian of yr. Am. Acad. Motion Picture Arts and Scis., 1978. Mem. Screen Actors Guild (pres. 1966-71). Office: care George Thomas 25438 W Malibu Rd 1 Malibu CA 90265

HESTON, LILLA ANASTASIA, speech and interpretation educator; b. St. Helen, Mich., Oct. 1, 1927; d. Chester L. and Lilla (Charlton) H. B.S., Northwestern U., 1949, M.A., 1958, Ph.D., 1965. Instr. Vasser Coll., Poughkeepsie, N.Y., 1958-60, Northwestern U., Evanston, Ill., 1961-65, asst. prof., 1965-68, assoc. prof. interpretation, 1968-73, prof. dept. interpretation, 1973—, chmn. dept., 1979—. Editor: Man in the Dramatic Mode, Books 1-6, 1970, Drama Lives!, Books 1-3, 1975; assoc. editor: Quar. Jour. Speech, 1977-80, Lit. in Performance, 1979—. Mem. Speech Communications Assn., AAUP, Ill. Speech and Theatre Assn., Central States Speech Assn. Home: 457 Highcrest Dr Wilmette IL 60091 Office: Dept Interpretation Northwestern U 1979 Sheridan Rd Evanston IL 60201

HESTON, WILLIAM MAY, educational administrator; b. Toledo, Nov. 2, 1922; s. William May and Helen Marie (Lippstreu) H.; m. Marian Cannon Watt, June 17, 1950; children—Mary, Elizabeth, Katherine, Richard. B.Sc. cum laude in Chemistry, Ohio State U., 1943; M.A., Princeton U., 1948, Ph.D. in Chemistry (LeRoy Wiley McKay advanced fellow in phys. chemistry 1949), 1949. With E.I. duPont de Nemours & Co., Inc., 1949-59; dir. office research Western Res. U., 1959-63, asso. chemistry, 1959-67, v.p. research, 1963-64, v.p. student services, 1964-66; vice provost, asso. dean Faculty Arts and Scis., 1966-67; v.p. plans and programs Case Western Res. U., 1967-69; exec. dir. Mental Devel. Center, cons. for spl. programs, 1969; v.p. Hofstra U., 1969-73; exec. dir. Nassau Higher Edn. Consortium, 1973-75, L.I. Regional Adv. Council on Higher Edn., 1975-76, ind. cons., 1976—; assoc. provost N.Y. Inst. Tech., 1977-78; dir. Center for Natural Scis., 1978—, prof. life scis., 1981—; Chmn. Cleve. Regional Com. Comprehensive Mental Health Planning Report, 1964-66; mem. adv. council Ohio Dept. Mental Hygiene and Correction, 1966-69; cons. grad. chemistry research facilities br. NSF, 1965-68, cons. sci. devel. program br., 1968-70; tech. cons. chemistry AID Govt. India, 1965; mem. program project com. Nat. Inst. Dental Research, NIH, 1964-68; spl. cons. Dental Research Inst. program, 1968-70; mem. Dental Research Inst. and spl. program adv. com., 1970-74; cons. to pharmacology-toxicology research program com. Nat. Inst. Gen. Med. Sci., NIH, 1976—; mem. clin. cancer program project rev. subcom. Nat. Cancer Inst., 1981—; cons. Engring. Research Group, Stanford Research Inst. Internat., 1981—. V.p. Cleve. chpt. UNICEF, 1968-69; mem. 12th grade sci. adv. com. Cleve. Bd. Edn., 1967-69; mem. adv. council Natural Sci. Mus., Cleve., 1967-69; mem. health goals com. Cleve. Welfare Fedn., mem. community planning and devel. com., 1965-69, chmn. mental health planning com., 1966-69; mem. sci. adv. com. Nassau County Police Dept., 1969-72; edn. adv. com. Garden City Pub. Sch. System, 1974-75; mem. Garden City Bd. Edn., 1975—, v.p., 1978—; research adv. group Nassau-Suffolk Regional Med. Program, 1974-75; mem. Nassau County Manpower Adv. Council, 1974-75; Sec. bd. trustees N.Y. Ocean Sci. Lab., 1969-72 Sec. bd. trustees N.Y. Ocean Sci. Lab., vice chmn. trustees Sec. bd. trustees N.Y. Ocean Sci. Lab., 1972-74; trustee Cleve. Center Alcoholism, 1961-64, Mental Health Rehab. and Research, 1963-69, Vocat. Guidance and Rehab. Services, 1963-69, Laurel Sch., Cleve., 1967-69;

chmn. bd. dirs. Nassau-Suffolk Community Health Edn. System, 1973-76; bd. dirs. Central Garden City Property Owners Assn., 1973-75; trustee L.I. Library Resources Council, 1975-78, AMD Research Found., 1977-78; v.p. Garden City Hist. Soc., 1976-78, trustee, 1978-79. Served with USNR, 1944-46. Fellow AAAS, Am. Inst. Chemists, Explorers Club; mem. Am. Chem. Soc., N.Y. Acad. Scis., Am. Soc. for Pub. Adminstrn. (mem. chpt. council 1973-75), Soc. for Coll. and Univ. Planning, Hempstead C. of C. (participating dir. 1974-76), Phi Beta Kappa, Sigma Xi, Phi Lambda Upsilon, Phi Eta Sigma. Unitarian (trustee 1963-66). Clubs: Cleveland Skating; Chapoquoit Yacht (West Falmouth, Mass.) (sec. 1969); Rowfant (Cleve.)). Home: 47 Hilton Ave Garden City NY 11530

HETHERINGTON, CHARLES RAY, oil company executive; b. Norman, Okla., Dec. 12, 1919; s. William Leslie and Helen Rowena (Hudgens) H.; m. Rose Cosco Scurlock, June 1967; children: Helen Jane, William Leslie, Childs Pratt, Gail Ann. B.S. in Chem. Engring, U. Okla., 1940, M.S., 1941; Sc.D. in Chem. Engring, M.I.T., 1943. Registered profl. engr., Alta. Research engr. Standard Oil Co. Calif. and Calif. Research Corp., Richmond, 1946-52; cons. engr. Ford, Bacon, Davis, Inc., N.Y.C., after 1946; v.p., mng. dir. Westcoast Transmission Co. Ltd. and Pacific Petroleums Ltd., Vancouver and Calgary, Can., 1959-67; pres., dir. Charles R. Hetherington & Co. Ltd. and Canacrude Oil & Gas Co., Ltd., Calgary, Alta., 1959-67; v.p., dir. West Coast Transmission Co. Ltd., Vancouver, 1967-70, So. and Westcoast Petroleum Co. Ltd.; pres., chief exec. officer Panarctic Oils Ltd., Calgary, 1970—; oil and gas cons. Govt. Queensland, Victoria, Australia; dir. Hetherington Ranches Ltd., Greyhound Lines of Can. Ltd. Contbr. articles to profl. jours. Bd. dirs. Holly Park Condominimum Assn. Mem. Am. Gas Assn., Calgary Petroleum Club. Clubs: Calgary Golf and Country, Calgary Polo, Eldorado Country, Eldorado Polo., Glencoe. Home: 300 Meredith Rd NE Suite 1001 Calgary AB T2E 7A8 Canada Office: 815 8th Ave SW Calgary AB Canada T2P 2H6 *I was raised during the depression by very loving and intelligent parents. They taught me to do my best in each endeavor and the future would look after itself. My first objective was to get an education so I would have a better chance of eating after I left home. From this simple start I have followed this creed of doing my best and it works.*

HETHERINGTON, EILEEN MAVIS, psychologist, educator; b. Nov. 27, 1926. B.A., U. B.C., 1947, M.A., 1948; Ph.D. in Psychology, U. Calif.-Berkeley, 1958. Clin. psychologist B.C. Child Guidance Clinic, 1948-51, sr. psychologist, 1951-52; clin. internship Langley Porter Clinic, 1956-57; instr. psychology San Jose State Coll., 1957-58; asst. prof. Rutgers U., 1958-60; from asst. prof. to prof. U. Wis., 1960-70; prof. psychology U. Va., Charlottesville, 1970—, dept. chmn., 1980—; mem. grant rev. com. Off Child Devel., 1971-77. Mem. editorial bd.: Child Devel., 1966-69, Devel. Psychology, 1968-77, Contemporary and Abnormal Psychology; researcher in personality development, the role of family structure and parent characteristics on normal and deviant behavior in children, the devel. of sex role typing, family therapy. Mem. Am. Psychol. Assn., Soc. Research Child Devel. Office: Dept Phychology U Va Charlottesville VA 22903 *

HETLAND, JAMES LYMAN, JR., banker, lawyer, educator; b. Mpls., June 9, 1925; s. James L. and Evelyn E. (Lundgren) H.; m. Barbara Anne Taylor, Sept. 10, 1949; children: Janice E., James E., Nancy L., Steven T. B.S.L., U. Minn., 1948, J.D., 1950. Bar: Minn. 1950. Law clk. Minn. Supreme Ct., 1949-50; asso. firm Mackall, Crounse, Moore, Helmey & Palmer, Mpls., 1950-56; prof. U. Minn. Coll. Law, 1956-71; v.p. urban devel. First Nat. Bank Mpls., 1971-75, sr. v.p. law and urban devel., 1975—; adj. prof. Hubert Humphrey Inst., U. Minn., 1976—, Bus. Coll. extension, 1975-81, Coll. Law, 1980—; labor arbitrator, 1967—; chmn. Minn. Citizens Council Crime and Delinquency, 1978-83; chmn. adv. coms. Minn. Supreme Ct. Co-author: Minnesota Practice, 3 vols., 1970, Minnesota Jury Instruction Guides, 2d edit., 1974. Chmn. Met. Council Twin Cities, St. Paul, 1967-71, Mpls. Charter Commn., 1963-70; chmn. Mpls. Citizens League, 1963-64, bd. dirs., 1953-67; bd. dirs. Mpls. Downtown Council, 1971—, vice chmn., 1978-82, chmn., 1982-83; chmn. bd. Minn. Zool. Garden, 1978-83; nat. v.p., mem. exec. com. Nat. Mcpl. League, 1979-82, pres., 1982—; vice chmn. Minn. Press Council, 1973-81; vice chmn. bd. Minn. Health Care Cost Coalition, 1980; bd. dirs. Interstudy, 1972-79, chmn., 1974; mem. Bus. Urban Issues Council, Conf. Bd., 1980—; bd. dirs. Freshwater Biol. Research Found., 1971—, Mpls. Community Coll. Found., 1978-83, Minn. Exptl. City, 1972-75, Minn. Campfire Girls, 1974-79, Mpls. YMCA, 1957-76, Health Central, Inc., 1973—; exec. com. Health Central, Inc., 1977—; mem. exec. com. Partnership Dataline U.S.A., 1983. Served with AUS, 1943-46. Mem. ABA, Am. Bankers Assn., Minn. Bar Assn., Hennepin County Bar Assn. Republican. Lutheran. Clubs: Mpls. Rotary, Mpls. Athletic, St. Anthony Athletic, N.W. Tennis Assn. Office: First Bank Pl Minneapolis MN 55480 *Seeking to improve services for urban citizens through new public and private service delivery systems has been a keystone for setting involvement priorities. Effective service delivery systems are essential if an urban society is to preserve a free public-private economic democracy. Involvement and change in the private sector is as important as in the public sector.*

HETLAND, JOHN ROBERT, lawyer, educator; b. Mpls., Mar. 12, 1930; s. James L. and Evelyn (Lundgren) H.; m. Mildred Woodruff, Dec. 1951 (div.); children: Lynda Lee, Robert John, Debra Ann.; m. Anne Kneeland, Dec. 1972; children: Robin T. Kneeland, Elizabeth J. Kneeland. B.S.L., U. Minn., 1952, J.D., 1956. Bar: Minn. bar 1956, Calif. bar 1962. Practice law, Mpls., 1956-59; asso. prof. law U. Calif., Berkeley, 1959-60, prof. law, 1960—; practice law, Berkeley, 1959—; vis. prof. law Stanford U., 1971, 80, U. Singapore, 1972. Author: Hetland, California Real Property Secured Transactions, 1970, Hetland, Commercial Real Estate Transactions, 1972, Hetland, Secured Real Estate Transactions, 1974, Maxwell, Riesenfeld, Hetland and Warren, California Cases on Security Transactions in Land, 2d edit., 1975, 3d edit., 1984, Hetland, Secured Real Estate Transactions, 1977; contbr. articles to legal, real estate and fin. jours. Served to lt. comdr. USNR, 1953-55. Mem. state bars Calif. and Minn., Am. Bar Assn., Order of Coif, Phi Delta Phi. Republican. Home: 20 Redcoach Ln Orinda CA 94563 Office: 2600 Warring St Berkeley CA 94704

HETSKO, CYRIL FRANCIS, ret. lawyer, corp. exec.; b. Scranton, Pa., Oct. 4, 1911; s. John Andrew and Anna (Lesco) H.; m. Josephine G. Stein, Nov. 12, 1932; children—Jacqueline V. (Mrs. Charles F. Kaufer), Cyril M., Cynthia F. (Mrs. William J. Rainey). Jeffery F. A.B., Dickinson Coll., 1933; J.D., U. Mich., 1936. Bar: Pa. bar 1937, N.Y. bar 1938, U.S. Supreme Ct. bar 1965. Asso. firm Chadbourne, Parke, Whiteside & Wolff, 1936-55, partner, 1955-64; gen. counsel Am. Brands, Inc. (formerly Am. Tobacco Co.), 1964-77, v.p., 1965-69, sr. v.p., 1969-77, also former dir.; former dir. Acme Visible Records, Inc., Acushnet Co., Am. Brands Export Corp., Am. Tobacco Internat. Corp., James B. Beam Distilling Co., James B. Beam Distilling Internat. Co., Duffy-Mott Co., Inc., Gallaher Ltd. (Gt. Britain), Master Lock Co., Master Lock Export, Inc., Swingline, Inc., Andrew Jergens Co., Sunshine Biscuits, Inc., Swingline Export Corp., Wilson Jones Co. Mem. Am., Fed., N.Y. State bar assns., Assn. Bar City N.Y., U.S. Trademark Assn. (dir. 1959-67, 68-72, 73-77, pres. 1965-66, hon. bd. chmn. 1966-67, mem. council past presidents 1977—), Order of Coif, Phi Beta Kappa, Phi Delta Theta, Delta Theta Phi. Republican. Presbyn. Clubs: Intrepids, Explorers, Williams (N.Y.C.); Nat. Lawyers (Washington); Ridgewood (N.J.) Country. Home: 714 Waverly Rd Ridgewood NJ 07450

HETTICH, ARTHUR MATTHIAS, editor; b. Bklyn., May 5, 1927; s. Arthur M. and Elsa (Schaeffer) H.; m. Mary Elizabeth Fitz Randolph, Dec. 27, 1942; children: Michael, John, Elizabeth. B.A., Amherst Coll., 1949; M.S. in English, Columbia U., 1950. Editor Thomas Ashwell & Co., N.Y.C., 1950-52; asst. promotion dir. McCall Corp., N.Y.C., 1952-54; v.p. promotion dir. Family Circle, N.Y.C., 1954-66, v.p., editor-in-chief, 1968—; v.p., dir. pub. relations Cowles Communications, N.Y.C., 1966-67. Atuhor: Best of the Best, 1976; editor, pub.: The New York Suburbs, 1960. Served with USNR, 1944-46. Clubs: N.Y. Athletic, Shore Acres Yacht (Mamaroneck). Home: 606 Shore Acres Dr Mamaroneck NY 10543 Office: Family Circle 488 Madison Ave New York NY

HETTLINGER, RICHARD RAYMOND, retail financial executive; b. Chgo., Dec. 11, 1948; s. John Francis and Leona Maryann (Hinch) H.; m. Nancy C. Catalano, Nov. 22, 1969; children: Amy, Matthew. B.S., DePaul U., 1972. C.P.A., Ill. Corp. acct. Marshall Field & Co., Chgo., 1968-72; audit supr. Coopers & Lybrand, Chgo., 1972-76; chief fin. officer Manchester's Dept. Store, Madison, Wis., 1976-77; dir. corp. acctg. Federated Dept. Stores, Inc., Cin., 1977-79; dir. audit Household Merchandising, Chgo., 1979-82; v.p. audit The May Dept. Stores Co., St. Louis, 1982—. Served with USMCR, 1969-75. Mem. Am. Inst. C.P.A.s, Mo. Soc. C.P.A.s. Office: The May Dept Stores Co 611 Olive St Saint Louis MO 63101

HETTRICK, JOHN LORD, banker, manufacturer; b. Lynchburg, Va., Apr. 24, 1934; s. Ames Bartlett and Frances (O'Brian) H.; m. Marica Parkinson Allard, June 22, 1954; children—John Lord, James Parkinson. B.A., Lehigh U., 1956. With Marine Midland Trust Co. Western N.Y. (changed name to Marine Midland Bank-Western 1970), Buffalo, 1957-76; sr. v.p. comml. banking depts., 1968- 69, exec. v.p., 1969-70, pres., 1970-73; vice chmn. bd. Marine Midland Banks, Inc., 1973-75, group exec. v.p., 1976; chmn. bd. WSF Industries, Inc., 1977—; trustee Goldome Bank Savs.; dir. Firstmark Corp. Pres. Jr. Achievement Niagara Frontier, 1967, chmn. bd., 1969-78; active Buffalo United Fund, 1962-65; exec. com. Nat. Jr. Achievement; met. chmn. Nat. Alliance Businessmen.; Bd. dirs. Neighborhood House, Buffalo Fine Arts Acad.; trustee U. Buffalo Found., Buffalo and Erie County Hist. Soc., 1977-78; exec. bd. Nat. Conf. Christians and Jews; co-chmn. Buffalo area Nat. Jewish Hosp. at Denver. Served to capt. AUS. Named Businessman of Year Alumni Sch. Mgmt. State U. N.Y. at Buffalo, 1970. Mem. Greater Buffalo C. of C., Assn. Res. City Bankers. Episcopalian (vestry 1965-68, 69-71, 72-75, warden 1976-78). Clubs: Saturn, Buffalo (Buffalo); Links, Knickerbocker (N.Y.C.). Home: 53 Tudor Pl Buffalo NY 14222 Office: 7 Hackett Dr Tonawanda NY 14150

HETZEL, FREDERICK ARMSTRONG, publisher, editor; b. Pitts., Sept. 6, 1930; s. Louis and Jean Bowman (Armstrong) H.; m. Nancy Miller, Dec. 14, 1957; children: Jean Armstrong, Jennifer Elizabeth, Frederick Armstrong, Emily Miller. B.A., Washington and Jefferson Coll., 1952; M.A., U. Va., 1957. Assoc. editor Inst. Early Am. History and Culture, Williamsburg, Va., 1957-61; asso. editor U. Pitts. Press, 1961-64, dir., 1964—; sec., dir. United Pocahontas Coal Co., 1960-68; dir. Second Nat. Bank, Connellsville, Pa., 1972-75; commentator WQED-FM, 1976-79. Mem. editorial bd.: Western Pa. Hist. Mag., 1981—. Mem. adv. council Internat. Poetry Forum, 1966-74; Bd. dirs., sec. U. Pitts. Book Center, 1969-72, chmn., 1970-72; bd. dirs. Loaves and Fishes Coffee House, 1969-70; trustee Winchester-Thurston Sch., 1969-77, 79-83, mem. exec. com., 1970-77, 79-83, chmn., 1971-74; bd. dirs. Mendelssohn Choir Pitts., 1977-79, Pitts. Dance Council, 1977-83; vice pres. Pitts. Dance Council, 1978-79. Served to 1st lt. AUS, 1952-54; Korea. Decorated Bronze Star. Mem. Assn. Am. Univ. Presses (dir. 1972-74), Am. Hist. Assn., Pitts. History and Landmarks Found., Hist. Soc. Western Pa., Pitts. Bibliophiles (vice chmn. 1970-72, chmn. 1972-73), MLA, Junta, Phi Beta Kappa, Phi Kappa Sigma, Pi Delta Epsilon. Presbyn. Clubs: Pittsburgh Press, University (Pitts.). Home: 1221 Wightman St Pittsburgh PA 15217 Office: 127 N Bellefield Ave Pittsburgh PA 15213

HETZEL, RALPH DORN, JR., economist, artist, educator; b. Corvallis, Oreg., Aug. 18, 1912; s. Ralph Dorn and Estelle (Heineman) H.; m. Marion Dubois, May 1, 1942; children: Otto Joseph, Ralph Dorn III. A.B., Pa. State Coll., 1933; postgrad., U. London, 1935-36. Pvt. sec. to Gov. Pinchot of Pa., 1933-35; engaged in study and spl. research, 1936-37; exec. sec. Nat. Hdqrs. CIO, 1937-40, unemployment dir., 1938-40, econ. dir., 1940-42; assigned cons. on labor Nat. Selective Service Hdqrs., 1942; man power cons. WPB, 1942-43, dep. vice chmn. for manpower requirements, 1943-45, acting vice chmn., 1945; dir. Office of Labor Requirements, Civilian Production Administrn., 1945-46; asst. to sec. commerce U.S. Dept Commerce, 1946-48; asst. to sec. and dir. Office Program Planning, 1948-51; asst. adminstr. for ops. Econ. Stblzn. Agy., 1951; v.p. Motion Picture Assn. Am., Inc., 1951-62, exec. v.p., 1962-63, 66-71, acting pres., 1963-66; exec. v.p. Motion Picture Export Assn., 1954-63, 66-71, acting pres., 1963-66; pres. Am. Motion Picture Export Co. (Africa), Inc., 1963-70, Internat. Fedn. Film Producers Assn., 1963-67; prof. art Kent State U., 1971-76; dean Coll. Fine and Profl. Arts, 1971-76, Blossom Festival Sch., 1973-76; v.p., provost Calif. Inst. Arts, Valencia, 1976-80, mem. faculty, 1976—. One-man exhbn. paintings, Chase Gallery, N.Y.C., 1964, Kent State U., 1972, Pa. State U. Mus. Art, 1973. Mem. adv. council Edward R. Morrow Center Public Diplomacy, 1967—; mem. adv. com. to dept. film Mus. Modern Art, 1966-71; chmn. Internat. Council Fine Arts Deans, 1973, Univ. Arts Commn., 1973-76; trustee Calif. Inst. Arts, 1969-76, Pa. State U., 1956—; bd. govs. Blossom Festival Soc., 1973-76; trustee Akron Art Inst., 1974-76; bd. dirs. Am. Research Inst. Arts, 1976—; trustee Coll. Santa Fe, 1979—. Served from 1st lt. to maj. AUS, 1942-45. Mem. Phi Kappa Phi, Beta Theta Pi. Club: Century Assn. Home: 4411 Gloria Ave Encino CA 91436 Office: Calif Inst Arts 24700 McBean Pkwy Valencia CA 91355

HETZEL, WILLIAM GELAL, management consultant; b. New Rochelle, N.Y., May 19, 1933; s. William Gelal and Nan (Sanes) H.; m. Linda R. Slate, July 23, 1982; children: William Gelal III, Tara L., John F., Janda B. Student, Washington Coll., 1949-51; B.B.A., U. Miami, 1953; postgrad., Xavier U., 1957-58; M.B.A., Northwestern U., 1964. Cons. McKinsey & Co., Inc., Chgo., 1961-64; various sales mgmt. positions Xerox Corp., Chgo., Rochester, N.Y., Louisville, 1964-69; dir. mktg. Maremont Corp., Chgo., 1969-70; pres. Medelco, Inc., Schiller Park, Ill., 1970-72; div. gen. mgr., v.p. ITT Service Industries Corp., Cleve., 1972-74; v.p. Lamalie Assos., Inc., Chgo., 1974-78; sr. v.p. Eastman & Beaudine, Chgo., 1978-81; pres. William Hetzel Assos., Inc., Schaumburg, Ill., 1981—; asso. Cabledata Assos., Menlo Park, Calif., 1975—. Mem. DuPage County (Ill.) Central Rep. Com., 1971-74; pres. pro tem Village of Downers Grove (Ill.), Bd. Local Improvements, 1969-72. Served to lt. (j.g.) USN, 1953-58. Republican. Lutheran. Club: Plaza. Office: 999 Plaza Dr Suite 400 Schaumburg IL 60195

HETZRON, ROBERT, linguist, educator; b. Budapest, Hungary, Dec. 31, 1937; came to U.S., 1966, naturalized, 1973; s. Vilmos Jakab and Olga (Mandel) Herzog; (div); children—Gabriel Fenteany, Rita Ennemore, George Tardenat. Diplome d'hebreu, Ecole Nationale des Langues Orientales, Paris, 1959, diplome d'amharique, 1960; M.A., Hebrew U., Jerusalem, 1964; Ph.D., UCLA, 1966. Asst. prof. Hebrew U. Calif., Santa Barbara, 1966-69, asso. prof., 1969-74, prof., 1974—. Author: Ethiopian Semitic, Studies in Classification, 1972, Surfacing, 1975, the Gunnan-Gurage Languages, 1977; editor: Afroasiatic Linguistics, 1974—; contbr. articles to profl. jours. Humanities Inst. summer fellow, 1970, 74; Guggenheim fellow, 1976-77; NSF grantee, 1980-81. Mem. N.Am. Conf. on Semitic Linguistics (founder), Internat. Linguistic Assn., Linguistic Soc. Am., Societe de Linguistique de Paris. Office: Dept Germanic and Slavic U Calif Santa Barbara CA 93106

HEUBAUM, WILLIAM LINCOLN, lawyer; b. Chgo., Jan., 11, 1938; s. Lincoln William and Hazel Lillian (Kvilvang) H.; m. Mary Lynn Gilbert, June 19, 1965; children: Karl Franz, Joy Ann. B.S. (Forrestel scholar), Northwestern U., 1959, J.D. (Kosmerl scholar), 1965. Bar: Ill. bar 1965, Iowa bar 1973, Nebr. 1982. Atty. Hopkins, Sutter, Mulroy, Davis & Cromartie, Chgo., 1965-72; v.p., sec., gen. counsel Iowa Beef Processors, Inc., Dakota City, Nebr., 1972-82; ptnr. Bikakis, Heubaum, Titus, Vohs & Storm, Sioux City, Iowa, 1983—; Lectr. Chgo. Bar Assn. Continuing Legal Edn. Com. Mem. Local Bd. 12; asso. govt. appeal agt. Local Bd. 30, Ill. Selective Service System, 1967-72. Served to lt. Supply Corps USNR, 1959-62. Mem. Am., Ill., Iowa, Fed. bar assns., Am. Soc. Corporate Secs., Phi Alpha Delta. Republican. Methodist. Clubs: Mason, Moose. Home: 4021 Country Club Blvd Sioux City IA 51104 Office: Suite 340 Ins Exchange Bldg Sioux City IA 51101

HEUBERGER, OSCAR, chemist; b. Bern, Switzerland, May 30, 1924; came to U.S., 1951, naturalized, 1957; s. Oscar and Dora (Stoekli) H.; m. Elizabeth L. Hawkins, Mar. 19, 1955; children: Peter, Mark. M.Chem. Engring., Swiss Fed. Inst. Tech., Zurich, 1947, Ph.D. in Organic Chemistry, 1949; postgrad., Imperial Coll., London, 1950-51. With E.I. duPont de Nemours & Co., Inc., 1951—, research mgr., Wilmington, Del., 1969-74; dir. Benger Lab., Waynesboro, Va., 1974—. Recipient Silver medal Swiss Fed. Inst. Tech., 1949. Mem. Am. Chem. Soc. Address: 830 Fairway Dr Waynesboro VA 22980

HEUER, GERALD ARTHUR, mathematician, educator; b. Bertha, Minn., Aug. 31, 1930; s. William C.F. and Selma C. (Rosenberg) H.; m. Jeanette Mary Knedel, Sept. 5, 1954; children—Paul, Karl, Ruth, Otto. B.A., Concordia Coll., 1951; M.A., U. Nebr., 1953; Ph.D., U. Minn., 1958. Math. instr. Hamline U., 1955-56; math. instr. Concordia Coll., 1956-57, asst. prof., 1957-58, asso. prof., 1958-62, prof., 1962—, chmn. dept., 1963-70, research prof., 1970-71; mathematician Remington Rand Univac, summer 1958; vis. prof. U. Nebr., 1960-61; mathematician Control Data Corp., summers 1960-62, cons., 1960-63; vis. lectr. Math. Assn. Am., 1964-66; cons. NSF-AID, India, 1968-69; guest speaker Minn. sect. Math. Assn. Am., 1956, Neb. sect., 1961, No. Central sect., 1974; vis prof.-scholar Math. Inst., Cologne (Germany) U., 1973-74; vis. prof. dept. pure and applied math. Wash. State U., Pullman, 1980-81. Reviewer: Zentralblatt fur Mathematik, Berlin, 1967—, Math. Revs, Ann Arbor, Mich., 1978—; Contbr. articles profl. jours. NSF faculty fellow, 1966-67; NSF research grantee, 1963, 64, 66; Bush research scholar Concordia Coll., 1983-84. Mem. Math. Assn. Am. (pres. Minn. sect. 1959-60, nat. bd. govs. 1971-73), Am. Math. Soc., Nat. Geog. Soc., Soc. Indsl. and Applied Math., Deutsche Mathematiker-Vereinigung e. U. (Berlin), Österreichische Mathematische Gesellschaft (Vienna), Sigma Xi. Lutheran. Home: 1216 S Elm St Moorhead MN 56560

HEUER, KENNETH JOHN, publishing company executive; b. Yonkers, N.Y., Jan. 30, 1927; s. Lester Frederick and Ida Antoinette (Fechner) H. Student, Amherst Coll., 1945-48; B.A., New Sch. Social Research, 1961. Head sci. dept. Collegiate Sch. for Boys, N.Y.C., 1948; lectr. Am. Museum-Hayden Planetarium, N.Y.C., 1948-53; sci. editor Viking Press, N.Y.C., 1953-60, Thomas Y. Crowell Co., 1960-61; editor-in-chief trade sci. dept. Macmillan Co., N.Y.C., 1961-63; dir. sci. book dept. Charles Scribner's Sons, N.Y.C., 1963-76, v.p., 1974—; N.Y. editor Cornell U. Press, Ithaca, 1980-82. Author: Men of Other Planets, 1951, The End of the World: A Scientific Inquiry, 1953, Wonders of the Heavens, 1954, An Adventure in Astronomy, 1958, City of the Stargazers, 1972, Rainbows, Halos and Other Wonders: Light and Color in the Atmosphere, 1978 (Nat. Sci. Tchrs. Assn. sci. book award), Thunder, Singing Sands, and Other Wonders: Sound in the Atmosphere, 1981 (Nat. Sci. Tchrs. Assn. sci. book award, N.Y. Acad. Scis. sci. book award); Contbr. articles nat. periodicals. Asso. benefactor Am. Mus. Natural History, N.Y.C. Fellow Royal Astron. Soc. (London); mem. Explorers Club. Home: 451 W 21st St New York NY 10011

HEUER, MICHAEL ALEXANDER, dentist, educator; b. Grand Rapids, Mich., Apr. 27, 1932; s. Harold Maynard and Gwendolyn Ruth (Kremer) H.; m. Barbara Margaret Naines, Nov. 23, 1955; children—Kristan M., Karin E., Katrina A. D.D.S., Northwestern U., 1956; M.S., U. Mich., 1959. Practice dentistry specializing in endodontics, Chgo., 1959—; asst. prof. Northwestern U., 1960-66; asso. prof. Loyola U., Chgo., 1968-73; prof., chmn. dept. endodontics Northwestern U., 1974-83, assoc. dean acad affairs, 1983—; dir. Am. Bd. Endodontics, 1971-77, sec.-treas., 1973-76, pres., 1976-77; chmn. subcom. Am. Nat. Standards Inst.; mem. com. on advanced edn. Commn. on Accreditation of Dental Edn., 1974-77. Contbr. articles in field to profl. jours. Served with USNR, 1956-58. Fellow Am. Coll. Dentistry, Internat. Coll. Dentistry, Am. Assn. Endodontists (exec. council 1967-71, sec. 1979—); mem. ADA (mem. council dental materials and devices 1972-78, chmn. 1977-78), AAAS, Internat. Assn. Dental Research, Am. Assn. Dental Schs., Chgo. Odontographic Soc. (pres. 1982-84), Edgar D. Coolidge Endodontic Soc. (trustee), Phi Eta Sigma, Omicron Kappa Upsilon, Chi Psi, Delta Sigma Delta. Home: 156 Timber Ridge Lake Barrington Shores Barrington IL 60010 Office: Dental Sch Northwestern U Chicago IL 60611

HEUER, ROBERT MAYNARD, II, opera company executive; b. Detroit, Nov. 27, 1944; s. Robert Maynard and May Elizabeth (Quinn) H. Student, Capital U., 1963-64; B.A., Wayne State U., 1976. Youth dir. Grace Lutheran Ch., Detroit, 1964-66; costume designer, prodn. mgr. U. Windsor, Ont., Can., 1967-69; program coordinator Detroit Youtheatre, Detroit Inst. Arts, 1970-71; mng. dir. Mich. Opera Theatre, Detroit, 1971-79; prodn. dir. Greater Miami (Fla.) Opera, 1979—; cons. Nat. Endowment Arts; trustee Miami Stage Employees Health and Welfare Pension Funds. Bd. dirs. Morningside Civic Assn.; mem. Com. for Renovation of Miami Beach Theater of Performing Arts. Mem. Opera Am., So. Opera Conf. (bd. dirs.). Home: 5955 N 6th Ave Miami FL 33137 Office: 1200 Coral Way Miami FL 33145

HEUERMAN, RICHARD ARNOLD, rubber company executive; b. Toledo, Ohio, May 17, 1930; s. Clarence John and Lucy Clara (Kinker) H.; m. Lois Anne Mahlerwein, Sept. 1, 1952; children: Paul Kevin, Mark Richard. A.B., Capital U., 1952; J.D., U. Toledo, 1956; A.M.P., Harvard U., 1972. Bar: Ohio 1956, Mich. 1957. Atty. Dow Corning Corp., Midland, Mich., 1956-63, mgr. legal dept., 1963-67, asst. sec., 1963-73, gen. counsel, 1967-73, treas., 1972-73; v.p., treas. B.F. Goodrich Co., Akron, Ohio, 1973, sec., 1974-79, v.p., gen. counsel, 1973—; dir. Huntington Nat. Bank, Akron, 1982—. Exec. com., trustee Akron (Ohio) Gen. Med. Ctr., 1974—; trustee Akron Gen. Devel. Found., 1977—; exec. com., bd. regents Capital U., Columbus, Ohio, 1978—; bd. visitors Capital U. Law Sch., Columbus, 1982—; trustee Akron Bluecoats Inc. Mem. ABA, Ohio State Bar

Assn., State Bar Mich. Clubs: Cascade (Akron, Ohio); Birchwood Country (Harbor Springs, Mich.); Board Room (N.Y.C.). Office: B F Goodrich Co 500 S Main St Akron OH 44318

HEUERMANN, LAURA HALL, lawyer; b. Brookings, S.D., July 19, 1919; d. George Porter and Ethel Myrtle (King) Hall; m. William H. Heuermann, May 13, 1947; children: Marcia Heuermann Hartshorn, Terry Lee, Laurie Li, William Hall. Grad., Mankato Comml. Coll., 1939; student, S.D. State U.; B.B.A., S.D. U., 1943, J.D., 1948. Bar: S.D. 1948. Tchr. Volga (S.D.) High Sch., 1943-46; mem. faculty Law Sch., S.D. U., Vermillion, summer, 1948; practiced in, Kennebec, S.D., 1949-54, Sioux Falls, S.D., 1954—; partner Heuermann & Heuermann, 1954-59, individual practice, 1959—; states atty., Lyman County, S.D., 1951-52. Pres. V.F.W. Aux., Sioux Falls, S.D., 1959-60, chaplain, 1962-70; pres. Emerson Elementary Sch., PTA, 1960-61, PTA, Lincoln High Sch., Sioux Falls, 1971-72; hon. mem. Girl's Club, Sioux Falls, 1972—; mem. bd. Family Service, 1956-63; mem. S.D. Bicentennial Commn., 1974-77; pres. Sioux Falls chpt. AFS Internat./Intercultural Programs, 1974-79; mem. exec. bd. Estate Planning Council, Sioux Falls, 1975-79; ambassador Diplomatic Corps State S.D., 1975—; bd. dirs. Sioux Falls Coll. Found., 1979—. Glory House, 1983—. Named Lady of Year Social Ministry Bd. Sioux Falls, 1975. Mem. S.D. State Bar, Minnehaha County Hist. Soc. (life), Sioux Valley Geneal. Soc., Nat. Trust for Historic Preservation, Sioux Falls Zool. Soc., Nat. Parks and Conservation Assn., P.E.O., LWV (mem. S.D. state bd. 1968-71), Soroptimist Internat. (officer N. Central region 1974-78), Internat. Thespian Soc. (hon. mem.), Sioux Empire Kennel Club, Kappa Beta Pi. Baptist. Address: 1601 E 26th St Sioux Falls SD 57105

HEULE, ROBERT K., oil pipeline company executive. Pres., chief exec. officer Interprovincial Pipe Line Ltd., Toronto, Ont., Can. Office: Interprovincial Pipe Line Ltd 1 First Canadian Pl Toronto ON Canada M5X 1A9§

HEULE, ROBERT KNEELAND, pipeline company executive; b. Duluth, Minn., Aug. 25, 1925; s. Harold H. and Edna L. H.; m. Dorothy Jane Johnson, July 2, 1949; children: Mark K., Michael D., Laurie J. B.S.M.E., U. Minn., 1945. Registered profl. engr. Project engr. Lakehead Pipe Line Co., Superior, Wis., 1950-66, gen. mgr., Superior, 1966-70; v.p. lakehead Pipe Line Co., Superior, 1970-77; pres. Lakehead Pipe Line Co., Superior, 1977—, chmn. bd., 1983—; dir. Interprovincial Pipe Line, Toronto, Lakehead Pipe Line Co., Superior, Chem. Bank of Can., Toronto. Served to lt. USNR, 1943-46, 51-53. Mem. Can. Petroleum Assn. (exec. com. pipeline div.), Am. Petroleum Inst., Assn. Oil Pipe Lines. United Ch. of Can. Club: National (Edmonton, Alta., Can.). Home: 1142 Morrison Heights Dr Oakville ON Canada L6J 4J1 Office: Interprovincial Pipe LineLtd 1 First Canadian Pl Toronto ON Canada

HEUMANN, KARL FREDRICH, chemist, editor; b. Chgo., Mar. 3, 1921; s. Karl George and Anna Elise (Heiler) H.; m. Doris B. Wilkinson, Mar. 24, 1947; children: David Wilkie, Elise Ann, Erika Jean. B.S., Iowa State Coll., 1942, M.S., 1943; Ph.D., U. Ill., 1951. Chemist tech. information sect. Minn. Mining & Mfg., St. Paul, 1950-52; dir. chem.-biol. coordination center NRC, 1952-55; dir. research Chem. Abstracts Service, Ohio State U., Columbus, 1955-59; dir. office documentation Nat. Acad. Scis., 1959-66; asst. exec. editor Fedn. Proc., Fedn. Am. Socs. for Exptl. Biology, 1966-67, exec. editor, 1967—, dir. editorial and info. services, 1969-73, dir. publs., 1973—; pres. Am. Documentation Inst., 1959; v.p. Fedn. Internationale de Documentation, 1961-64; Sec. Council Biology Editors, 1969-73, chmn., 1974-75. Served to lt. (j.g.) USNR, 1944-46. Mem. Am. Chem. Soc. (chmn. div. chem. lit. 1960), AAAS, Spl. Libraries Assn. Home: 6410 Earlham Dr Bethesda MD 20817 Office: 9650 Rockville Pike Bethesda MD 20814

HEUSI, JOE DUANE, insurance company executive; b. Defiance, Ohio, June 12, 1942; s. Oscar Joseph and Ernestine (Penrod) H.; m. Frances Jean Hyland, Aug. 15, 1964; children: Richard Duane, Michael David. B.Music, Baldwin Wallace Coll., 1964, B.Music Edn., 1965; M.S., Columbia U., 1979. Tchr. Bedford (Ohio) Pub. Schs., 1965-66, Berea (Ohio) Pub. Schs., 1966-69; career account rep. Variable Annuity Mktg. Co., Cleve., 1968-71, v.p., regional mgr., Cranford, N.J., 1971-80, v.p. mktg. services, 1980-81, sr. v.p. mktg., Houston, 1981-83, pres., 1983—, dir., 1981—; chmn. Variable Annuity Life Ins. Co.; dir., pres. Tomed Opportunity Fund, Valic Capital Accumulation Fund, Houston, 1983—, Separate Accounts One and Two, 1983—. Chmn., dir. Concert Chorale of Houston, 1983. Mem. Am. Mgmt. Assn., Phi Mu Alpha, Sinfonia, Sigma Phi Epsilon. Home: 650 W Forest Dr Houston TX 77079 Office: Variable Annuity Life Ins Co 2727 Allen Pkwy Houston TX 77019

HEUSON, WILLIAM GEORGES, finance educator; b. St Louis, Sept. 6, 1921; s. Georges H. and Lee (Miesenbach) H.; m. Jane E. Spiegelhalter, June 30, 1954; 1 dau., Andrea. B.A., St. Louis U., 1942, M.S., 1947, Ph.D., 1954. Instr. finance St. Louis U., 1947-48; mem. faculty U. Miami, 1948—, prof. finance, 1954—; mem. faculty Sch. Banking of South, La. State U., 1961—, Mortgage Banking Sch., Northwestern U., 1963—, Sch. Mortgage Banking U. Miami, 1969—, Sch. Mortgage Banking U. Notre Dame, 1973—, Sch. Banking, Fla. Bankers Assn., 1981, edn. dir., 1983; cons. to industry, 1952—. Author: Public Finance, 1962, Investing in Mortgages, 1961. Mem. Local Govt. Study Commn., 1970—, South Miami Capital Improvement Com., 1973—; mem. adv. bd. Zool. Soc. Fla. Faculty; adviser Young Republicans, 1964—; Trustee Mus. of Sci., 1975—, Met. Dade County Water and Sewer Bd., 1975—, Mercy Hosp., Miami, 1976—; mem. exec. com. Jr. Orange Bowl Com., 1976—. Served to lt. USNR, 1941-46. Mem. Am., So. econs. assns., Am., So. finance assns., Am. Acad. Polit. and Social Scis., Econ. Soc. S. Fla., Soc. Financial Analysts Miami, Order Artus, Alpha Kappa Psi, Omicron Delta Gamma, Beta Gamma Sigma, Lambda Chi Alpha (Order of Merit 1962). Home: 5978 Miller Rd South Miami FL 33155 Office: Box 8094 Coral Gables FL 33124 *I regret those days when I have not helped a friend or stranger find a new dimension in understanding his fellow man.*

HEWES, HENRY, drama critic; b. Boston, Apr. 9, 1917; s. Henry Fox and Margaret (Warman) H.; m. Jane Fowle, Aug. 21, 1945; children—Henry Fox, Tucker Fowle, Havelock. B.S., Columbia, 1948. Staff writer N.Y. Times, 1949-51; drama editor Saturday Review, 1952-73, drama critic, 1954-77, critic-at-large, 1977; drama critic Internat. Theatre Yearbook, 1978—; lectr. Sarah Lawrence Coll., 1955-56, Columbia, 1956-57, Salzburg Seminar in Am. Studies, 1970, New Sch. for Social Research, 1972—; exec. sec. Bd. Standards and Planning for Living Theatre, 1956-66, Am. Theatre Planning Bd., 1966—; mem. Pulitzer Prize Jury for Drama, 1968, 81; chmn. Margo Jones Award Com., 1967—, Joseph Maharam Award Com., 1965—; cons. Bicentennial World Theatre Season, 1974; Bd. dirs. Am. Theatre Wing, 1972—; mem. adv. council Theater Hall of Fame, 1972—. Adapter: play La Belle Aventure (produced as Accounting for Love), London, 1954; adaptor, dir.: Tennessee Williams' Three Players of a Summer Game, Westport, Conn., 1955, (with Siobhan McKenna) Exptl. Hamlet, N.Y.C., 1957, Our Very Own Hole in the Ground, N.Y.C., 1972; adapter, dir.: Watergate version Measure for Measure, Gt. Lakes Shakespeare Festival, 1974; moderator: (1976) Am. Theatre Wing TV Seminars; Editor: The Best Plays of 1963-64. Served as tech. sgt. USAAF, 1941-45. Mem. N.Y. Drama Critics Circle (v.p. 1969-71, pres. 1971-73), Drama Desk (pres. 1967-74), Am. Theatre Critics Assn. (exec. sec. 1973—), ANTA (exec. dir. Greater N.Y. chpt. 1953-58), Internat. Assn. Theatre Critics, New Drama Forum, Critics Circle, London. Address: 1326 Madison Ave New York NY 10028

HEWES, LAURENCE ILSLEY, III, lawyer; b. Palo Alto, Cal., Sept. 18, 1933; s. Laurence Ilsley, Jr. and Patricia Esther (Jackson) H.; m. Mary Clarke Darling, Oct. 1, 1960; children: Laurence Ilsley IV, Henry Patrick Darling, Mary Clarke Danforth. A.B., Yale U., 1956, LL.B., 1959. Bar: D.C. 1961. Asso. counsel Subcom. on Migratory Labor, Senate Com. on Labor and Pub. Welfare, Washington, 1961-62; atty. office of chief counsel Area Redevel. Adminstrn., U.S. Dept. Commerce, Washington, 1962; counsel Pres.'s Com. on Equal Opportunity in Armed Forces, Washington, 1962-63; asso. Hydeman & Mason, Washington, 1963-66, partner, 1966-72, Boasberg, Hewes & Klores, Washington, 1972-80, Wald, Harkrader & Ross, 1980—. Contbr. articles to profl. jours., chpts. to books. Trustee Friends of Superior Ct. of D.C., 1973—, Wooster Sch., 1981—. Served with USAF, 1959-66. Mem. ABA, D.C. Bar Assn. Democrat. Clubs: Yale (N.Y.C.); Cosmos, University (Washington); Bronxville Field (N.Y.); Mountainview Country (Greensboro, Vt.). Home: 1821 Randolph St NW Washington DC 20011 Office: 1300 19th St NW Washington DC 20036

HEWES, LAURENCE ILSLEY, JR., natural resources economist; b. Kingston, R.I., Apr. 17, 1902; s. Laurence Ilsley and Agnes Bancroft (Danforth) H.; m. Patricia Esther Jackson, Jan. 29, 1932 (dec. 1976); 1 son, Laurence Ilsley; m. Martha Odle Overholser, Aug. 1, 1979. B.Sc., Dartmouth Coll., 1924; Ph.D., George Washington U., 1946; M.P.A., Harvard U., 1956. Engaged in investment banking, San Francisco, 1925-33, asst. to undersec. agr., 1935; asst. to adminstr. Farm Security Adminstrn., 1935-39, regional dir., San Francisco, 1939-44; West Coast dir. Am. Council Race Relations, San Francisco, 1944-47; land reform adviser Hdqrs. SCAP, Tokyo, Japan, 1947-49; chief land settlement and agrl. economist Bur. Reclamation, Denver, 1950-59; chief forecasts and econs. U.S. Outdoor Recreation Resources Rev. Commn., 1959-62; asst. to adminstr. Office Rural Areas Devel., USDA, 1962-63; rural devel. adviser AID mission to India, New Delhi, 1963-65; chief natural resources conservation Rural Community Devel. Service, USDA, Washington, 1965-68; Sr. cons. UN Devel. Program, World Bank, FAO, with assignment, Ethiopia, Panama, India, Pakistan, Ceylon, South Vietnam, Mexico, Brit. Honduras, Nicaragua, Tanzania, 1968—; vis. fellow Center for Study Democratic Instns., Santa Barbara, Calif., 1972, 73, assoc., 1976-77; Mem. U.S. Inter Agy. Com. Post Def. Planning, 1939-41, Dept. Agr., War Bd. Calif. and Ariz., 1941-43; U.S. rep. Mexican Labor Transp. Negotiations, 1942-43; exec. sec. land and water policy com. Dept. Agr., 1965-68. Author: Japanese Land Reform Program, 1950, Japan-Land and Men, 1955, Boxcar in the Sand, 1957, Rural Development: World Frontiers, 1974. Recipient Disting. Service award Dept. Agr., 1968. Mem. Artus, Sigma Nu. Presbyterian. Club: Cosmos (Washington). Home: 1937 Rosewood Valley Dr Brentwood TN 37027

HEWETT, ARTHUR EDWARD, real estate developer; b. Dallas, Oct. 16, 1935; s. Arthur Elton and Clara Mae (Wagoner) H.; m. Helen Yvonne Barry, May 20, 1959; children: Julie, Matthew, Clara. B.B.A., So. Methodist U., 1957, LL.B., 1965. Bar: Tex. bar 1965. Asst. to exec. v.p. Diversa, Inc., Dallas, 1960-61; asst. to pres. RichPlan Corp., Dallas, 1961-62; mng. ptnr. firm Hewett Johnson Swanson & Barbee, 1970-80; pres. Thompson Realty Corp., Dallas, 1980-84; pres., chief exec. officer Republic Property Group, Inc., 1984—; dir. Inter First Bank Park Cities, Instacom, Inc., Tex. Internat. Co. Trustee Episc. Sch. Dallas. Served with USNR, 1957-60. Mem. Tex. Bar Assn. Presbyn. Club: City. Home: 3705 Euclid Ave Dallas TX 75205 Office: 8235 Douglas Suite 1350 Dallas TX 75225

HEWETT, ED ALBERT, economist; b. Columbia, Mo., Sept. 2, 1942; s. Edward and Esther Virginia (Lawrence) H.; m. Nancy Anna Maisto, Dec. 29, 1963. Student, Hasting Coll., 1960-62; B.S., Colo. State U., 1964, M.S., 1966; Ph.D. and Cert. in Russian, U. Mich., 1971. From asst. prof. to assoc. prof. econs. U. Tex., Austin, 1971-81; vis. scholar Inst. for World Econs., Budapest, 1974; vis. lectr. dept. econs. U. Pa., Phila., 1977-78; vis. scholar Harvard Russian Research Center, Cambridge, Mass., 1979; sr. fellow Brookings Instn., Washington, 1981—; mem. bd. Internat. Research and Exchanges Bd., N.Y.C., 1979—. Author: Foreign Grade prices in CMEA, 1974, Energy, Economics and Foreign Policy in the Soviet Union, 1984; co-editor: Soviet Economy, 1984—. Mem. Am. Econs. Assn., Am. Assn. Advancement Slavic Studies, Assn. for Comparative Econ. Systems (exec. com. 1979-81). Office: 1775 Massachusetts Ave Washington DC 20036

HEWETT, JOHN BRAND, sch. adminstr.; b. Boston, Nov. 27, 1931; s. Merritt Alfred and Gaynor (Br) H.; m. Lisa Landon, Apr. 3, 1954; children—John Brand, Sabrina. Grad., Milton Acad. Boys' Sch., 1949; B.A., Williams Coll., 1953; M.A. L.S., Wesleyan U., 1963. Tchr., adminstr. Gilman Sch., Balt., 1957-66; headmaster Bordentown (N.J.) Mil. Inst., 1966-72, Bordentown/Lenox (Mass.) Sch., 1972-73; asst. headmaster Lawrence Country Day Sch., N.Y., 1973-74; headmaster Perkiomen Sch., Pennsburg, Pa., 1974—. Mem. exec. com. Burlington council Boy Scouts of Am., 1969—; civilian adviser Jr. ROTC Adv. Bd., 1st U.S. Army, 1971—; Chmn. bd. dirs. Greensboro Free Library, 1966—. Served to comdr. USNR, 1953-57. Mem. Boarding Sch. Assn. Middle Atlantic States (exec. bd. 1970-71, v.p. 1971-72, sec.-treas. 1976-77, pres. 1977-78), Assn. Mil. Colls. and Schs. (exec. bd. 1971-72), Pa. Assn. Ind. Schs. (dir. 1981—). Clubs: Williams American Alpine (N.Y.C.); Greensboro (Vt.) Country. Home: 202 Seminary St Pennsburg PA 18073

HEWITT, DON S., TV news producer; b. N.Y.C., Dec. 14, 1922; s. Ely S. and Frieda (Pike) H.; children—Jeffrey, Steven, Jill, Lisa; m. Marilyn Berger, Apr. 14, 1979. Student, N.Y. U., 1941. Corr.-spl. assignment War Shipping Adminstrn., World War II; producer 1st Kennedy-Nixon TV debate, 1960; producer-dir. A Conversation with President Kennedy, 1962, A Conversation with President Johnson, 1964; exec. producer (CBS Evening News with Walter Cronkite), 1961-64; producer-dir. CBS News coverage Eisenhower in Europe and India, 1960-61, President Kennedy in Europe, 1962-63, also polit. convs. and inaugurations; CBS News producer Cape Canaveral, 1960-65; exec. producer CBS News, 60 Minutes (with Mike Wallace, Morley Safer, Dan Rather, Harry Reasoner and Ed Bradley), 1968—. *Never take yourself too seriously.*

HEWITT, EDWIN, mathematician, educator; b. Everett, Wash., Jan. 20, 1920; s. Irenaeus Prime and Margaret (Guthrie) H.; m. Carol Blanchard, Mar. 4, 1944 (div. Apr. 1962); children: Margaret, Elizabeth; m. Pamela Jones Meyer, May 28, 1964 (div. Oct. 1973). A.B., Harvard, 1940, M.A., 1941, Ph.D., 1942. Ops. analyst USAAF, 1943-45; Guggenheim fellow, mem. Inst. Advanced Study, 1945-46, 55-56; asst. prof. math. Bryn Mawr Coll., 1946-47; lectr. U. Chgo., 1947-48; mem. faculty U. Wash., 1948—, prof. math., 1954—; vis. prof. U. Uppsala, Sweden, 1951-52, Australian Nat. U., Canberra, 1963, 70, 76, U. Tex., 1972-73, Math. Inst. of Acad. Scis., USSR, 1969-70, 73, 76, U. New S. Wales, 1976, 78, 82, U. Erlangen-Nürnberg, 1975-76, U. Hokkaido (Japan), 1982; Mem. div. math. NRC, 1957-69, exec. com, 1960-62, 67-69; mem. U.S. Nat. Com. for Math., 1973-77, chmn., 1975-77. Author: Theory of Functions of a Real Variable, 1961, (with Kenneth A. Ross) Abstract Harmonic Analysis I, 1963, Vol. II, 1970, (with Karl R. Stromberg) Real and Abstract Analysis, 1965; also research papers. Recipient Alexander von Humboldt Found. prize, 1975. Mem. Am. Math. Soc. (council 1955-65), Math. Assn. Am., Phi Beta Kappa, Sigma Xi. Christian Scientist. Home: 5624 56th Ave NE Seattle WA 98105

HEWITT, FRANK SEAVER, electronics executive, lawyer; b. Pitts., Mar. 5, 1941; s. Kenneth Chadbourne and Mary (Seaver) H. A.B., Harvard U., 1963, LL.B., 1966; LL.M. in Comparative Law, NYU, 1967; postgrad., U. Munich, W.Ger., 1967-68. Bar: N.Y. 1967. Asso. Shearman & Sterling, N.Y.C., 1968-71; atty. Mobil Oil Corp., N.Y.C., 1972-74; gen. counsel, sec. Siemens Capital Corp., N.Y.C., 1974-78; corp. counsel, sec. Siemens Corp., N.Y.C., 1978-79, asso. gen. counsel, sec., 1979-82, Siemens Capital Corp., 1982—. Mem. N.Y. State Bar Assn., Bar Assn. City N.Y. Club: N.Y. Athletic. Office: 767 Fifth Ave New York NY 10153

HEWITT, JOHN G., banker; b. Phila., Dec. 1, 1918; s. Carroll B. and Helen (Goorley) H.; m. Loretta Giering, Aug. 15, 1948; children: John P., Joanne G., Frank G., Jane L. B.A., Rutgers U., 1946. Exec. v.p. First Nat. Bank, Jersey City, 1949-63; chmn. Midlantic Nat. Bank/Merchants, Neptune, N.J., 1963—, also dir.; dir. Midlantic Bank, Inc. Bd. dirs. Monmouth County United Fund; bd. dirs. Jersey Shore Med. Center. Mem. N.J. Bankers Assn. Home: 19 Auburn Ct Shadow Lake Village Red Bank NJ 07701 Office: 60 Neptune Blvd Neptune NJ 07753

HEWITT, ROBERT LEE, surgeon, educator; b. Paducah, Ky., Nov. 2, 1934; s. Lee A. and Donis (Brown) H.; m. Patricia M. Stewart, May 1, 1965; children—Heather Edgeworth, Robert Stewart, Whit Butler, Brooke Lee. Student, U. Louisville, 1952-55; M.D., Tulane U., 1959. Diplomate: Am. Bd. Surgery, Am. Bd. Thoracic Surgery. Intern Charity Hosp., Tulane U., New Orleans, 1959-60, resident, 1960-65; faculty Sch. Medicine, 1960—, asst. prof. surgery, 1968-70, asso. prof., 1970-75, prof. surgery, 1975-76, clin. prof. surgery, 1976—; mem. staff Charity, So. Bapt., Tulane U. hosps., Touro Infirmary, all New Orleans; cons. several hosps. Contbr. articles to profl. jours. Mem. leadership forum Met. Area Com. New Orleans, 1971. Served with M.C. AUS, 1966-68. Fellow A.C.S.; mem. Soc. Univ. Surgeons, Am. Assn. Thoracic Surgery, So. Surg. Assn., Oscar Creech, Alton Ochaner, New Orleans surg. socs., Southeastern Surg. Congress, Soc. Vascular Surgery, Soc. Thoracic Surgeons, Internat. Cardiovascular Soc., So. Assn. Vascular Surgery, Assn. Acad. Surgeons, AMA, La., Orleans Parish med. socs., Assn. Mil. Surgeons, New Orleans Grad. Med. Assembly, Alpha Omega Alpha, Omicron Delta Kappa, Phi Kappa Tau, Phi Chi. Episcopalian. Home: 1207 Webster St New Orleans LA 70118 Office: 4440 Magnolia St New Orleans LA 79115

HEWITT, THOMAS FRANCIS, hotel executive; b. Marblehead, Mass., Dec. 7, 1943; s. Ralph Augustine and Shirley Elizabeth (Morris) H.; m. Sharyn Ann Holleran, June 11, 1968; 1 son, Sean Thomas. B.B.A., Bryant Coll., 1967. Gen. mgr. Sheraton LaGuardia, N.Y.C., 1973-74; gen. mgr. Sheraton Heights Hotel, Hasbrouck Heights, N.J., 1974-75, Sheraton Plaza Hotel, Chgo., 1975-78; vice-pres., gen. mgr., area mgr. The Sheraton-Boston Hotel (The Sheraton Corp.), Boston, 1978-81; vice pres., gen. mgr. Sheraton New Orleans Hotel, 1981, sr. v.p., gen. mgr., area mgr., 1983—. Exec. com. Greater New Orleans Tourist and Conv. Commn. Served with AUS, 1968-70. Mem. Hotel Sales Mgrs. Assn., Greater New Orleans Hotel-Motel Assn. (dir.), Am. Hotel and Motel Assn. (vice chmn. internat. travel com.), New Orleans C. of C. (aviation com.). Roman Catholic. Office: 500 Canal St New Orleans LA 70130

HEWITT, VIVIAN ANN DAVIDSON (MRS. JOHN HAMILTON HEWITT, JR), librarian; b. New Castle, Pa., Feb. 17; d. Arthur Robert and Lela Luvada (Mauney) Davidson; m. John Hamilton Hewitt, Jr., Dec. 26, 1949; 1 son, John Hamilton III. A.B. with honors, Geneva Coll., 1943, L.H.D., 1978; B.S. in L.S., Carnegie Library Sch., Carnegie Mellon U., 1944; postgrad., U. Pitts., 1947-48. Sr. asst. librarian Carnegie Library, Pitts., 1944-49; instr., librarian Sch. Library Sci., Atlanta U., 1949-52; with Readers Reference Service, Crowell-Collier Pub. Co., N.Y.C., 1953-55; librarian Rockefeller Found., N.Y.C., 1955-63, Carnegie Endowment Internat. Peace, 1963-83; librarian Mexican Agrl. Program, Rockefeller Found., summer 1958; lectr. spl. librarianship at grad. schs. library sci. and info. throughout, U.S. and Can., 1968—; condr. profl. seminars Am. Mgmt. Assn., 1968-69, Spl. Libraries Assn., 1969, UN Inst. Tng. and Research, 1973, 74; Spl. Libraries Assn. rep. Pacem In Terris Convocation, 1965, White House Conf. Internat. Cooperation Year, 1965, Internat. Fedn. Library Assns., 1970-73, 73-75, 75-77; Spl. Libraries Assn. non-govtl. observer UN, 1964-69; mem. nat. adv. com. Ctr. for the Book, Library of Congress, 1979—. Contbr.: chpt. to The Black Librarian in America, 1970, What Black Librarians Are Saying, 1972, New Dimensions for Academic Library Service, 1975, A Century of Service, 1976, Handbook of Black Librarianship, 1977. Bd. dirs. Graham-Windham, METRO (N.Y. Met. Reference and Research Library Assn.). Recipient Outstanding Community Service awards United Fund of N.Y., 1965-77; Disting. Alumna award U. Pitts.-Carnegie Library Schs. Alumni Assn., 1978; merit award Carnegie Mellon U. Alumni Assn., 1979; Disting. Service to Librarianship award ALA Black Caucus, 1978. Mem. Spl. Libraries Assn. (pres. N.Y. chpt. 1970-71, nat. pres. 1978-79), ALA, Jack and Jill of Am., Inc. (Eastern regional dir. 1967-69), Alpha Kappa Alpha. Democrat. Mem. P.E. Ch. Club: Women's City (N.Y.C.). Home: 862 West End Ave New York NY 10025

HEWITT, WILLIAM ALEXANDER, ambassador; b. San Francisco, Aug. 9, 1914; s. Edward Thomas and Jeannette (Brun) H.; m. Patricia Deere Wiman, Jan. 3, 1948; children: Anna, Adrienne, Alexander. A.B., U. Calif., 1937; LL.D., Augustana Coll., 1963, St. Ambrose Coll., 1964, Knox Coll., 1965. With John Deere Plow Co., San Francisco, 1948-54, v.p., 1950-54; dir. Deere & Co., Moline, Ill., 1951-82, exec. v.p., 1954-55, pres., chief exec. officer, 1955-64, chmn., chief exec. officer, 1964-82; U.S. ambassador to Jamaica, 1982—; dir. Continental Ill. Nat. Bank & Trust Co. of Chgo., 1955-82, Continental Ill. Corp., 1968-82, AT&T., 1962-82, Conoco Inc., 1965-82, Baxter-Travenol Labs., Inc., 1978-82; internat. adv. com. Chase Manhattan Bank, 1965-82; Bd. dirs. Internat. Exec. Service Corps; mem. Bus. Council, Bus. Roundtable, Nat. Council for Humanities, 1975-80; founding mem. Bus. Com. for Arts, Emergency Com. for Am. Trade; an incorporator Nat. Corp. for Housing Partnerships, 1968-70; bd. dirs. Nat. Council for U.S.-China Trade, 1973-80, vice chmn., 1973-75, chmn., 1975-78; dir. U.S.-USSR Trade and Econ. Council; mem. Trilateral Commn., 1973-81. Mem. vis. com. Harvard U. Grad. Sch. Bus. Adminstrn., 1962-67, Harvard U. Grad. Sch. Design, 1967-73; mem. council Stanford Research Inst., 1971-79; mem. vis. com. East Asian studies 102345Harvard U.; mem. Wilson council Woodrow Wilson Internat. Center for Scholars; trustee St. Katharine's-St. Mark's Sch., Davenport, Iowa, 1965-76, Calif. Inst. Tech.; bd. govs. Am. Nat. Red Cross, 1967-70; trustee Carnegie Endowment for Internat. Peace, 1971-75, Nat. Safety Council, Council of Americas, Mus. Modern Art, N.Y.C.; bd. dirs. UN Assn., 1970-73; governing mem. Ill. Council on Econ. Edn., 1970-77; hon. mem. Smithsonian Nat. Assos. Bd. Served as lt. comdr. USNR, 1942-46. Laureate Lincoln Acad. Ill. Fellow Am. Soc. Agrl. Engrs.; mem. Soc. Automotive Engrs., Farm and Indsl. Equipment Inst., Conf. Bd., Internat. C. of C. (trustee U.S. council),

Com. for Econ. Devel. (hon. trustee), A.I.A. (hon.), Council on Fgn. Relations, Internat. Council of Asia Soc., Atlantic Inst. for Internat. Affairs, Alpha Delta Phi. Clubs: Pacific-Union, Bohemian (San Francisco); Burlingame (Cal.); Country, Chicago, Pilgrims of U.S. Home: 3800 Blackhawk Rd Rock Island IL 61201

HEWITT, WILLIAM LANE, educator, physician; b. Hebron, Nebr., Nov. 25, 1916; s. William Thomas and Iva Lee (Lane) H. B.A., 1938; M.D., 1942. Intern San Francisco City and County Hosp., 1942-43; resident Evans Meml. Hosp., Mass. Meml. Hosp., 1943-45; mem. staff div. infectious diseases NIH, 1945-48; instr. medicine Boston U. Sch. Medicine, 1948-51; faculty U. Calif. at Los Angeles Med. Sch., 1951—, prof. medicine and infectious diseases, 1958—, chief div., 1953—; acting chief medicine Harbor Hosp., Torrance, Calif., 1965-66. Mem. A.C.P., Western Assn. Physicians, Western Soc. Clin. Investigation, Alpha Omega Alpha. Home: 20109 Big Rock Dr Malibu CA 90265

HEWLETT, C(ECIL) JAMES, interior designer; b. Russell, N.Y., Apr. 24, 1923; s. Orin Stanley and Grace Josephine (Heffernan) H. Student, U. Md., 1949-51, Syracuse U., 1953-60. Mem. design staff Colony Shop, Syracuse, N.Y., 1952-55, Sagenkahn Co., Syracuse, 1955-61; design dir. Halle Bros. Co., Cleve., 1961-72, Nahan Co., New Orleans, 1973-75; pvt. practice interior design New Orleans, 1975-76; partner Hewlett Mack Design Assos., New Orleans, 1977—; design dir. Hemenway Co., Inc., New Orleans, 1976-77; lectr. various profl. groups, nat. convs. Contbr. articles to profl. publs. Trustee, chmn. Found. for Interior Design Edn. Research, 1970-74, chmn. futures conf., coll. curricula planning, trustee emeritus, 1981-85; del. Coalition for Nat. Growth Policy, 1971-74; mem. adv. panel Washington Center for Met. Studies, HUD, 1970-74; founder, mem. Nat. Council for Interior Design Qualification, 1969-73. Served with USAAF, 1942-51. Decorated Air medal with 8 oak leaf clusters. Fellow Am. Soc. Interior Designers (governance eval. com.); mem. Nat. Soc. Interior Designers (pres. 1967-69, chmn. bd. dirs. 1969-71), Interior Design Educators Council (hon.), La. Inst. Bldg. Scis. (founding mem.). Office: 4136 Ulloa St New Orleans LA 70119

HEWLETT, HORACE WILSON, former educational administrator, association executive; b. Derby, Conn., July 27, 1915; s. Horace Barnes and Barbara Atwater (Lewis) H.; m. Mary Estelle Lazear, June 24, 1939; children; William Tuthill, Elisabeth Bane. B.A., Amherst Coll., 1936; M.A., Yale U., 1941. Asst. to producer March of Time (cinema), 1936-37; tchr. Curtis Sch., 1937-39, Hill Sch., 1941-43; asst. dir. pub. relations, univ. editor U. Denver, 1946-47; dir. pub. relations Amherst Coll., 1947-58, sec. coll., 1958-77; dir. Western Mass. Broadcasting Council, Inc., 1952—, pres., 1957-79; dir. Mass. Exec. Com. Edn. TV, 1962-71; Pres. Anchor Realty Co., Inc., 1974-77, also dir. Editor: Amherst Alumni News, 1947-77, New Eng. Assn. Rev, 1963-71, In Other Words, 1964. Chmn. Amherst Bicentennial Com., 1959; trustee Jones Library, Amherst, Mass., 1969-84, chmn., 1970-84; bd. overseers Williston Acad., 1955-59, pres., 1958-59; bd. dirs., sec. Wildwood Assn., 1974—. Served to lt. USNR, 1943-46. Mem. Amherst Community Assn. (pres. 1958), Am. Coll. Pub. Relations Assn. (sec.-treas. 1959-60, pres. 1963-64), Am. Oral History Assn., New Eng. Oral History Assn., Chi Phi. Conglist. Club: Rotary (pres. 1958). Home: Middle St Amherst MA 01002

HEWLETT, RICHARD GREENING, historian; b. Toledo, Feb. 12, 1923; s. Timothy Younglove and Gertrude Josephine (Greening) H.; m. Marilyn Eloise Nesper, Sept. 6, 1946. Student, Dartmouth, 1941-43, Bowdoin Coll., 1943-44; M.A., U. Chgo., 1948, Ph.D., 1952. Intelligence specialist USAF Hdqrs., Washington, 1951-52; reports analyst AEC, Washington, 1952-57, chief historian, 1957-75, ERDA, Washington, 1975-77, U.S. Dept. Energy, 1977-80; sr. asso. History Assos., Inc., Germantown, Md., 1980—; regents' lectr. U. Calif., 1982; historiographer Episcopal Diocese of Washington, also Washington Cathedral; chmn. fed. govt. resource group Nat. Coordinating Com. for Promotion of History., 1977-81; Mem. U.S. del. 2d UN Internat. Conf. Peaceful Uses Atomic Energy, 1958. Author: The New World, 1939-46, 1962, Atomic Shield, 1947-52, 1969, Nuclear Navy, 1946-52, 1974. Served with USAAF, 1943-46. Recipient David D. Lloyd prize, 1970; Distinguished Service award AEC, 1973. Mem. Am. Hist. Assn., Orgn. Am. Historians, Soc. History Tech., Am. Nuclear Soc., Nat. Council for Public History, Soc. for History in Fed. Govt. (v.p. 1983). Episcopalian. Club: Cosmos. Home: 7909 Deepwell Dr Bethesda MD 20817 Office: History Assos Inc PO Drawer 730 Germantown MD 20874

HEWLETT, WILLIAM (REDINGTON), institutional administrator, electrical engineer; b. b. Ann Arbor, Mich., May 20, 1913; s. Albion Walter and Louise (Redington) H.; m. Flora Lamson, Aug. 10, 1939 (dec. 1977); children: Eleanor Hewlett Gimon, Walter B., James S., William A., Mary Hewlett Jaffe; m. Rosemary Bradford, 1978. A.B., Stanford U., 1934, E.E., 1939; M.S., MIT, 1936; LL.D., U. Calif., 1966, Yale U., 1976, Mills Coll., 1983; D.Sc. (hon.), Kenyon Coll., 1978, Poly Inst. N.Y., 1978; other hon. degrees. Electromed. researcher, 1936-39; co-founder Hewlett-Packard Co., Palo Alto, Calif., 1939, ptnr., 1939-46, exec. v.p., dir., 1947-64, pres., 1964-77, chief exec. officer, 1969-78, chmn. exec. com., 1977-83, vice chmn. bd. dirs., 1983—, dir.; trustee Carnegie Inst., Washington, 1971, chmn. bd. trustees, 1980—; dir. Utah Internat. Trustee Standord U., 1963-74; mem. Pres.'s Gen. Adv. Com. on Fgn. Assistance, 1965-68, Pres.'s Sci. Adv. Com., 1966-69, San Francisco panel Commn. on White House Fellows, 1969-70; chmn. San Francisco panel Commn. on White House Fellows, 1970; bd. dirs. San Francisco Bay Area Council. Served to lt. col. AUS, 1942-45. Fellow IEEE (pres. 1954), Franklin Inst. (life), Am. Acad. Arts and Scis.; mem. Nat. Acad. Scis., Nat. Acad. Engring., Instrument Soc. Am. (hon. life), Am. Philos. Soc., Calif. Acad. Sci. (Hon. trustee). 1501 Page Mill Rd Palo Alto CA 94304

HEWSON, EDGAR WENDELL, emeritus meteorology educator; b. Amherst, N.S., Can., July 12, 1910; came to U.S., 1948, naturalized, 1956; s. Edgar Ellis and Helen (Bell) H.; m. Julia Elizabeth O'Brien, Aug. 17, 1935; children: David Garnet, Barbara Elizabeth. B.A. Mt. Allison U, 1932; M.A., Dalhousie U., 1933, U. Toronto, 1935; D.I.C., Imperial Coll. Sci. and Tech., London, 1937; Ph.D., U. London, 1937. With Meteorol. Service of Can., Toronto, 1938-48; dir. diffusion project Mass. Inst. Tech. (Round Hill Field Sta.), South Dartmouth, Mass., 1948-53; prof. meteorology U. Mich., Ann Arbor, 1953-68; prof., chmn. dept. atmospheric scis. Oreg. State U., 1969-76, prof., 1976-81, prof. emeritus, 1981—; cons. to industry, govt. agys. Author: (with R.W. Longley) Meteorology, Theoretical and Applied, 1944; also articles. Recipient Am. Wind Energy Assn. award, 1983. Fellow Royal Meteorol. Soc. (Buchan prize 1939), Am. Meteorol. Soc. (award 1969), Royal Soc. Can.; mem. Am. Geophys. Union, Am. Phys. Soc. Research in application of meteorology to solution of air pollution problems; research on aeroallergens, elec. power generation by wind. Home: 4015 Crown Point Dr #301 San Diego CA 92109

HEXNER, PETER EUGEN, consumer goods executive; b. Vienna, Austria, Nov. 27; s. Ervin Paul and Gertrud (Stem) H.; m. Lila M. Fird, Dec. 28, 1951; children: Michael, Holly, Thomas. B.S., U. N.C.; Ph.D. in Physics, U. Va., 1962. Exec. asst. v.p. research and devel. Gillette Co., Cambridge, Mass., 1970-72, dir. advanced tech., 1973-80; dir. research and devel. Braun A.G., Kronberg, W. Ger., 1981—. Contbr. to profl. jours. Served to lt. col. U.S. Army, 1951-70. Mem. Am. Phys. Soc., Phi Beta Kappa, Sigma Xi. Home: 105-1 Trowbridge St Cambridge MA 02138 Office: Braun AG Am Schantzenfeld Postfach 1120 6242 Kronberg (TS) Federal Republic Germany

HEXTER, JACK H., historian, educator; b. Memphis, May 25, 1910; s. Milton J. and Alma (Marks); m. Ruth Mullin, Mar. 29, 1942; children—Christopher, Eleanor, Anne, Richard. B.A., U. Cin., 1931; M.A., Harvard, 1933, Ph.D., 1937; Litt.D. (hon.), Brown U., 1964, U. East Anglia, U. Cin., 1978; L.H.D., Washington U., 1973; LL.D. (hon.), Portland U., 1974. Tchr. U. Cin., 1936, Harvard, summer 1937, Mass. Inst. Tech., 1938, Queens Coll., 1939-57; mem. faculty Washington U., St. Louis, 1957-64, prof. history, 1957-64, chmn. dept., 1957-60, Disting. historian in residence, 1978—; prof. history Yale, 1964-67, Charles J. Stillé prof., 1967-78; dir. Yale Center for Parliamentary History, 1965—; asso. seminars Columbia U., 1948—. Author: The Reign of King Pym, 1941, More's Utopia: The Biography of an Idea, 1952, Reappraisals in History, 1961, The Judaeo-Christian Tradition, 1966, The History Primer, 1971, Doing History, 1971, The Vision of Politics on the Eve of the Reformation, 1973, On Historians, 1979; also articles; co-author: Western Civilization, 1968; transl.: The Monarchy of France (Claude de Seysel), 1981; Assoc. editor: Jour. Brit. Studies, 1961-74, Jour. History of Ideas, Medievalia et Humanistica; co-editor: Utopia, Complete Works of Thomas More, 1965; gen. editor: The Traditions of the Western World, 1967. Trustee Danforth Found., 1973-78. Served with AUS, 1942-46. Guggenheim fellow, 1942, 47, 79; Social Sci. Research Council grantee, 1947, 71; Yaddo fellow, summer 1949; Fulbright Research fellow, 1950, 59-60; Ford fellow, 1953-54; fellow Center Advanced Study in Behaviorial Scis., 1966-67, Inst. for Advanced Study, 1975-76; Mellon fellow Nat. Humanities Center, 1981-83. Mem. New Eng. Hist. Assn. (pres. 1970-71), Econ. History Assn., Econ. History Soc. (Gt. Britain), Am. Conf. Brit. Studies (pres. 1973-75), Royal Hist. Soc., Am. Acad. Arts and Scis. (council 1979—). Home: 4500 McPherson Saint Louis MO 6310 Office:: Washington U Dept History Saint Louis MO 63150

HEXTER, MAURICE BECK, welfare executive; b. Cin., June 30, 1891; s. Max and Sarah (Beck) H.; m. Marguerite Mock, Aug. 11, 1921; 1 dau., Marjorie M. (Mrs. Howard M. Cohen). B.A., U. Cin., 1912, L.H.D. (hon.), 1980; M.A., Harvard U., 1923, Ph.D. in Social Ethics, 1924, U. Dominican Republic, 1955; L.H.D., Brandeis U., 1961, Yeshiva U., 1961, Mt. Sinai Med. Sch., 1980. With Fedn. Jewish Philanthropies of N.Y., 1938—, exec. v.p., 1941-66, exec. cons., 1966—; mem. adv. bd. to Commr. Welfare, N.Y.C.; mem. N.Y.C. Council Against Poverty, 1965—. Mem. grants com. Lois and Samuel Silberman Found.; v.p., treas. Henry Kaufmann Found., N.Y.C.; chmn. bd. overseers Florence Heller Sch. Advanced Studies in Social Work; trustee emeritus Brandeis U.; Am. mem. Jewish Colonization Assn., 1952; pres. Nat. Conf. Jewish Social Work, 1924, Dominican Republic Settlement Assn., 1941. Mem. Nat. Assn. Social Workers. Jewish. Home: 480 Park Ave New York NY 10022 Office: 130 E 59th St New York NY 10022

HEXTER, ROBERT MAURICE, educator; b. Atlanta, Oct. 15, 1925; s. Leo Solomon and Rachel Belle (Schwartz) H.; m. Norma Goldberg, Aug. 29, 1948; children—Claudia Sue, Nancy Joy, Daniel Jonathan. B.A., U. Minn., 1948; M.S., Columbia U., 1950, Ph.D., 1952. Research asst. U. Minn., 1948; teaching asst. Columbia, 1948-50, DuPont fellow, 1950-51, lectr., 1951-52; instr. Cornell U., 1952-54, asst. prof., 1954-57; lectr. U. Pitts., 1964-65; adj. prof. Carnegie Inst. Tech., 1965-67; prof. Carnegie-Mellon U., 1967-69, U. Minn., Mpls., 1969—, chmn. dept. chemistry, 1969-75; dir. Surface Analysis Center, 1979—, research officer Inst. Tech., 1980—; bd. dirs., acting dir. Microelectronics and Info. Scis. Center, 1981-83; corporate research adv. com. Control Data Corp., 1981—; tech. adv. council First Midwest Capital Corp., 1981—; co-dir. NSF Regional Instrumentation Facility in Surface Analysis, 1979—; Cons. in field. Author: (with J.C. Decius) Molecular Vibrations in Crystals, 1977; Contbr. articles to profl. jours. Bd. dirs. North Star Research Inst., 1973—. Served with AUS, 1944-46; PTO. Sr. fellow Mellon Inst., 1957-69; Guggenheim fellow, 1961-62; Fulbright scholar, 1961-62. Mem. Am. Chem. Soc., Am. Phys. Soc., Sigma Xi, Phi Lambda Upsilon, Phi Epsilon Pi-Home: 5117 James Ave S Minneapolis MN 55419

HEY, DENNIS JOHN, neonatologist; b. St. Louis, Sept. 23, 1940; s. Gustav James and Elsie Anna (Ontl) H.; s. Gustav James and Elsie Anna (Ontl) H.; m. Gloria Lee Hainds, May 29, 1965; children: John, Sonya. Student, N.E. Mo. State U., 1962-65; D.O., Kansas City Coll. Osteo. Medicine, 1969. Diplomate: Am. Coll. Osteo. Pediatricians, Nat. Bd. Osteo. Examiners. Intern Bay View Hosp., Bay Village, Ohio, 1969-70; resident in pediatrics Kansas City Coll. Osteo. Medicine, Mo., 1970-72; asst. prof. pediatrics Kansas City Coll. Osteo., Mo., 1973—; dir. newborn and intensive care nursery unit Kansas City Coll. Osteo. Medicine, Mo., 1973—; head dept. pediatrics U. Health Sci., 1981—; fellow in neonatology Children's Mercy Hosp., Kansas City, Mo., 1972-73. Participant: revision manual Standards and Recommendations for Hospital Care for Your New Baby, 1977. Mem. edn. adv. com. Mo. Div. Health Bill, 1976—, State of Mo. Profession Liability Rev. Bd., 1976—. Served with USAF, 1957-62. Mem. Am. Osteo. Assn. (editorial reviewer Jour. 1974—), Mo. Assn. Osteo. Physicians, Jackson County Osteo. Soc. (rep. to Kansas City Pub. Health for Children's Immunizations Program 1978), Southwest Pediatric Soc., Midwest Neonatology Soc. Republican. Baptist. Home: 3712 Beechwood Dr Lee's Summit MO 64063 Office: Univ Health Sci Univ Hosp 2105 Independence Blvd Kansas City MO 64124

HEY, ROBERT PIERPONT, journalist; b. E. Providence, R.I., Jan. 24, 1935; s. Daniel Chase and Grace (Pierpont) H.; m. Nancy Henson, July 4, 1959; 1 dau., Julie. A.B., Harvard U., 1955. Gen. assignment reporter, local edn. reporter Christian Sci. Monitor, Boston, 1960-64, asst. to Am. news editor, then asst. Am. news editor, 1964-67, S.E. U.S. corr., then Washington corr., 1967-76, asst. mng. editor, 1976-79, mng. editor features, Boston, 1979-83, editorial writer, 1983—; with Arkell Safety Bag Co., N.Y.C., 1956-58; with public relations dept. U. Pitts., 1964. Served with AUS, 1958-60. Office: 1 Norway St Boston MA 02115

HEYBORNE, ROBERT LINFORD, electrical engineering educator; b. McCornick, Utah, Apr. 17, 1923; s. Robert Leigh and Junetta (Nielsen) H.; m. Denese Theobald, Aug. 21, 1942; children: Linford, Brenda. B.S. in Elec. Engring., Utah State U., 1949, M.S., 1950; Ph.D. in Elec. Engring., Stanford U., 1967. Chief engr. So. Utah Broadcasting Co., 1949-51, asst. mgr., dir. news, 1953-57; prof. elec. engring. Utah State U., 1957-69; dean U. Pacific Sch. Engring., Stockton, Calif., 1969—; cons. elec. engring. to industry; lectr. NSF Vis. Scientist Program, 1966-67. Contbr. articles to profl. jours. Mem. San Francisco Bay Area Relations With Industry Com., 1969—; chmn. Calif. Engring. Liaison Com., 1974. Served with USNR, 1942-46, 51-52. Named Prof. of Year, Utah State U., 1962, Outstanding Engring. Prof., Phi Kappa Phi, Sigma Tau Logan, 1967, Engr. of Year, No. Calif. Engrs. Council, 1972; NSF sci. faculty fellow, 1963-65. Mem. IEEE, Am. Soc. Engring. Edn. (chmn. Rocky Mountain sect. 1969, nat. developing colls. com. 1969-73, chmn. Pacific S.W. sect. 1975, nat. chmn. coop. edn. div. 1977-78, nat. dir. relations with industry div. 1974-77, accreditation processes com. 1978-81, chmn. council of sects. Zone IV 1982-84), Am. Geophys. Union, Internat. Sci. Radio Union, Sigma Xi. Club: Kiwanian (lt. gov. Utah-Idaho dist. 1957). Home: 7523 Park Woods Dr Stockton CA 95207

HEYBURN, DONALD ELLIOTT, mfg. co. exec.; b. N.Y.C., Feb. 5, 1924; s. Robert E. and Helen A. (Martinez) H.; m. Elizabeth Kirkwood, Apr. 26, 1952; children—Glenn, Karen, David. B.S. in Mech. Engring, Rensselaer Poly. Inst., 1949. With Babcox & WIlcox Co., 1949—; v.p. Fossil Power Generation div., Barberton, Ohio, 1973-80, sr. v.p., group exec. indsl. products and services, Akron, Ohio, 198-; dir. TLT-Babcock, Inc., Diamond Power Co., Ltd., Bailey Japan Co., Ltd. Served with AUS, 1943-46. Decorated Bronze Star; named Ohio Commoedore. Mem. ASME, Atomic Indsl. Forum, Gideons, Sigma Xi, Tau Beta Pi, Pi Tau Sigma. Office: 3330 W Market St Akron OH 44313 *

HEYDEBRAND, WOLF VON, sociology educator; b. Preussenfeld, Germany, June 15, 1930; came to U.S., 1954; s. Georg Von and Sigrid Von (Waldersee) H.; m. Ruth Keiling, Sept. 1954 (div. 1973); 1 child, Gitry V.; m. Sarah Rosenfield, June 1974 (div. 1979). M.A., U. Chgo., 1961, Ph.D., 1965. Asst. prof. sociology U. Chgo., 1964-67; assoc. prof. Washington U., St. Louis, 1967-71; prof. NYU, N.Y.C., 1973—; vis. assoc. prof. Columbia U., 1972-73; co-dir. Comparative Orgn. Research Program, U. Chgo., 1964-67; research assoc. Med. Care Research Ctr., St. Louis, 1967-71; co-prin. investigator Explorat's Health Service, N.Y.C., 1972-74. Author: Hospital Bureaucracy, 1973; editor: Comparative Organizations, 1973; assoc. editor: Am. Jour. Sociology, 1964-67, Contemporary Sociology, 1972-74, Social Problems, 1981—. Grantee NSF, 1964, USPHS, 1967, Nat. Ctr. Health Service, 1972, Russell Sage Found., 1974-75. Mem. Am. Sociol. Assn., Eastern Sociol. Assn. (exec. council 1979-82), Law and Soc. Assn., Internat. Sociol. Assn. Jewish. Office: Dept Sociology NYU 269 Mercer St Room 409 New York NY 10003

HEYER, PAUL OTTO, architect; b. Brighton, Eng., July 8, 1936; came to U.S., 1960; s. Albert Otto and Ivy Winifred (Winter) H.; m. Juliet Ruth Attree, Dec. 23, 1969. B.Arch., Brighton Coll. Art, 1958; M.Arch., U. Mich., 1961, Harvard U., 1962. Registered architect, N.Y., Pa., U.K. Architect Yorke, Rosenberg & Mardall, London, 1959-60, Edward Durell Stone, N.Y.C., 1961-62, Oskar Stonorov, Phila., 1962-63, Edward Durell Stone, N.Y.C., 1963-64, Paul Heyer Architects, 1965—; prof. architecture Pratt Inst., Bklyn.; 1968—, co-chmn. Grad. Architecture, 1979-82, acting dir., 1981-82, dean, 1982—. Author: Architects on Architecture: New Directions in America, 1966, Architects on Architecture: New Directions in America, rev. edit., 1977, Mexican Architecture: The Work of Abraham Zabludovsky and Teodoro Gonzalez de Leon, 1978. Fulbright Found. scholar, 1960; English Speaking Union fellow, 1960; Albert Kahn Found. fellow, 1960; Graham Found. fellow, 1968-69. Mem. Royal Inst. Brit. Architects, AIA. Home: 317 W 84th St New York NY 10024 Office: Pratt Inst Sch Architecture 200 Willougby Ave Brooklyn NY 11205

HEYERDAHL, THOR, anthropologist, explorer, author; b. Larvik, Norway, Oct. 6, 1914; s. Thor and Alison (Lyng) H.; m. Liv Coucheron Torp, Dec. 24, 1936; children—Thor, Bjorn; m. Yvonne Dedekam-Simonsen, Mar. 7, 1949; children—Anette, Marian, Bettina. Realartium, Larvik Coll., 1933; grad. student, U. Oslo; field study, Polynesia, B.C.; library study, U.S., Can., Germany, Norway; Ph.D. (hon.), Oslo U., 1961. Ethnol. collection and research primitive man, his habits, Polynesia and British Columbia, 1937-40; prod. documentary film Kon-Tiki, 1951; leader, organizer Norwegian archeol. expdn., Galapagos, 1953; research Andes region, 1954; prod. film, Galapagos, 1955; leader, organizer Norwegian archaeol. expdn., Easter Island and the East Pacific, 1955-56, Ra expdns.; Mem., lectr. Internat. Congress Americanists, Cambridge, 1952, São Paulo, 1954, San Jose, 1958, Vienna, 1960, Barcelona, Madrid, Sevilla, 1964, Internat. Congress Anthropology and Ethnology, Paris, 1960, Moscow, 1964, Internat. Pacific Sci. Congress, Honolulu, 1961, Tokyo, 1965, Vancouver, 1976. Author: Paa Jakt Efter Paradiset, Oslo, 1938, Kon-Tiki (Am. edit.), 1950, American Indians in the Pacific: The Theory Behind the Kon-Tiki Expedition, 1952, Archaeological Evidence of pre-Spanish visits to the Galapagos Island, 1956, Aku-Aku, The Secret of Easter Island (Am. edit.), 1958, Reports of the Norwegian Archaeological Expedition to Easter Island and the East Pacific: Vol. 1, Archaeology of Easter Island, 1961, Vol. 2, Miscellaneous Papers, 1965, Sea Routes to Polynesia, 1968, The Ra Expeditions, 1972, Fatu-Hiva, Back to Nature (Am. edit.), 1975, Zwischen den Kontinenten, 1975, The Art of Easter Island, 1975, Early Man and The Ocean (Am. edit.), 1979, Tigris, 1979; Contbr.: chpts. to The Quest for America, 1971; also articles to sci. and popular mags. Founder, bd. mem. Kon-Tiki Mus., Oslo; internat. patron United World Colls.; trustee World Wildlife Fund Internat. Decorated grand officer Order Al Merito della Repubblica Italiana; Order of Merit First Class, Egypt; grand officer Royal Alaouites Order, Morocco; Kirll i Metodi Order of 1st Class, Bulgaria; comdr. Order St. Olav, Norway; Order Golden Ark, Netherlands; recipient Retzius medal Royal Swedish Anthrop. and Geog. Soc., 1950, Vega medal, 1962; Mungo Park medal Royal Scottish Geog. Soc., 1951; Oscar for camera achievement Nat. Acad. Motion Picture Arts and Scis., 1951; Prix Bonaparte-Wyse Société de Geographie Paris, 1951; Elish Kane gold medal, Geog. Soc. Phila, 1952; Lomonosov medal Moscow U., 1962; Patron's Gold medal Royal Geog. Soc., 1964; Internat. Pahlavi environ.; prize UN, 1978; named hon. prof. El Instituto Politécnico Nacional, Mexico, others. Fellow N.Y. Acad. Scis.; mem. Belgian, Brazilian, Peruvian, Russian, Swedish (hon.) anthrop. geog. socs., Norwegian Acad. Sci., Norwegian Geog. Soc. (hon.). Sci. expdns. Pacific Islands to test theory that inhabitants of these islands partly originated in prehistoric S. Am.; to conduct expt., replica of prehistoric Inca balsa-wood raft was fashioned, crew 6 Scandinavian scientists, tech. experts, went on-board off Callao, Peru, drifted westward until safely landed on Polynesian Atoll Raroia, Tuamotu Archipelago (direct oversea drift of 4300 miles); meteorol., hydrographic, zool. research carried out during expdn., also tests for Am., Brit. war depts., 1947; attempted to cross Atlantic in papyrus boat Ra I, sailed from Safi, Morocco, 1969, covering 2,800 miles in 56 days; sailed in Ra II from Safi, May 1970, covering 3,270 miles in 57 days, arrived in Barbados, July 1970; leader, organizer Tigris expdn. testing Sumerian type reed ship on 5 month voyage, 1977-78. Address: Colla Micheri Laigueglia Italy *A united mankind in a healthy biosphere.*

HEYING, THEODORE LOUIS, chemical company executive; b. Balt., Oct. 19, 1927; s. Louis Joseph and Marie Elizabeth (Scherder) H.; m. Patricia E. Worthington, Nov. 22, 1952; children: Theodore Louis, Maria T. B.S., Loyola Coll., Balt., 1948; M.S., Holy Cross Coll., Worcester, Mass., 1949; Ph.D. in Chemistry, U. Md., 1953. With Olin Corp., New Haven, 1953—, bus. mgr., 1970-72, dir. research, 1972-82, dir. internat. tech., 1982—; mng. dir. Olin Chems. Ltd., Ireland, 1971-74. Author. Mem. bd. finance, North Haven, Conn., 1966-71, chmn., 1970-71. Served with AUS, 1954-56. Mem. Am. Chem. Soc., Am. Inst. Chemists, Indsl. Research Inst. Republican. Roman Catholic. Patentee in field. Home: 29 Gail Dr North Haven CT 06473 Office: 120 Long Ridge Rd Stamford CT 06904

HEYLIN, MICHAEL, editor; b. London, Aug. 11, 1930; U.S., 1956, naturalized, 1963; s. Henry Brougham and Irene Beyer (Gauntlett) H. B.Sc., U. London, 1954. Research chemist U.S. Gypsum Co., Chgo., 1957-63; with Chem. & Engring. News publ. Am. Chem. Soc., 1963—, bur. head, Chgo., 1967-71, asst. mng. editor, Washington, 1971-73, mng. editor, 1973-77, editor, 1977—. Office: 1155 16th St NW Washington DC 20036

HEYLMAN, WARREN CUMMINGS, architect; b. Spokane, Wash, Sept. 12, 1923; s. William Harry and Jane (Cummings) H.; m. Kathryn Lois Heylman Zimmerman, Dec. 12, 1945; children: William Warren, Ann Heylman Martin. B.S., U. Kan., 1945. Lic. architect, Wash., Idaho. Staff architect Whitehouse & Price Architects, Spokane, 1947-50; prin. Warren Cummings Heylman & Assocs., Spokane, 1952-82, Warren Cummings Heylman & Ptnrs., 1982—. Contbr. articles to profl. jours. Officer, dir. Greater Spokane Coummunity Found., 1977-82; exec. bd. Boy Scouts Am., Spokane, 1972-83. Served to lt. USN, 1942-46. Recipient awards of merit and honor AIA, 1959-83, 1st Award Honor Wash. Concrete Inst., 1968, award excellence Wash. Precast Concrete Industry, 1975, 1st Honor award, 1978, award excellence, 1979, Spl. recognition award Prestressed Concrete Inst., 1979, Honor award Wash. Roadside Council, 1981; named Disting. Citizen, Rotary, 1975. Fellow AIA; mem. Wash. Council Architects (dir. 1980-83). Episcopalian. Home: 3620 West Dr Spokane WA 99204 Office: Warren Cummings Heylman & Partners 511 Parkade Plaza Spokane WA 99201

HEYMAN, DAVID JOHN, foundation executive; b. N.Y.C., Sept. 4, 1922; s. David Melville and Ruth (Stein) H.; m. Geraldine Lederer, July 4, 1945; children: Stephen, Linda, Janet. B.A., Columbia, 1947. Investment analyst Marine Midland Trust Co., 1947-49; asst. to sales mgr. Miami Copper Co., 1949-52; owner Whistle Stop, Inc., Mt. Kisco, N.Y., 1952-55; asso. dir. Home Adv. Council, Inc., N.Y.C., 1955-57; dir. N.Y.C. chpt. WAIF-ISS, 1957-58; project adminstr. research facility Rockland State Hosp., Orangeburg, N.Y., 1958-60; dir. operations Neighborhood Conservation Program, N.Y.C., 1960-62; exec. officer N.Y.C. Rent and Rehab. Adminstrn., 1962-64; engaged in pvt. investment, 1965—; Sec. N.Y. Found., 1955-67, pres., 1967-76, vice chmn., 1977-81; mem. exec. com. Am. Korean Found., 1960-76; pres. Heyman Family Fund; past pres. Internat. Psychiat. Research Fund; past v.p. Internat. Com. Against Mental Illness, 1962-74; past chmn. bd. Nat. Com. Against Discrimination in Housing; past pres. Career Center for Social Service, N.Y.C.; pres. State Communities Aid Assn.; mem. N.Y.C. Bd. Correction, 1957-69; past vice chmn. Nat. Scholarship Service and Fund for Negro Students. Past pres. Barnard Coll. Parents Assn.; vice chmn. Health Ins. Plan Greater N.Y.; bd. dirs. Coop. Assistance Fund, Community Sex Info. Service; bd. dirs., treas. Tougaloo Coll.; adv. bd. Columbia U. Sch. Social Work.; treas. ACLU. Served with AUS, 1942-45. Decorated comdr. Order Toussaint-Louverture, Haiti; Mil. Order of Santa Maria Gloriosa, Italy). Mem. Zeta Beta Tau. Club: Columbia Univ. Home: Route 3 292 Coker Rd Lake Lorman Jackson MS 39213 Office: 485 Madison Ave New York NY 10022

HEYMAN, GEORGE HARRISON, JR., securities company executive; b. N.Y.C., June 29, 1916; s. George H. and Anne (Luxenberg) H.; m. Edythe Forman, Mar. 17, 1946; children: William H., John A. B.B.A., CCNY, 1936; M.B.A., NYU, 1938. Asso. Abraham & Co., N.Y.C., 1936-49, gen. partner, 1949-72; pres., dir. Abraham & Co. Inc., 1972-75; chmn. investment com., mng. dir. Lehman Bros. Kuhn Loeb Inc., 1975-83, adv. dir., 1983—; dir. Lehman Corp.; FGIC Corp.; dir. One William St. Fund. Pres. Fedn. Jewish Philanthropies of N.Y., 1969-71, chmn. bd. trustees, 1977-80; fellow pres.'s council Tulane U.; trustee N.Y. U. Served to capt. AUS, 1941-46. Recipient Louis Marshall medal Jewish Theol. Sem. Am., 1976; Townsend Harris medal Alumni Assn. Coll. City N.Y., 1976. Mem. Beta Gamma Sigma. Clubs: Harmonie, Sunningdale Country. Home: 888 Park Ave New York NY 10021

HEYMAN, IRA MICHAEL, educator, univ. chancellor; b. N.Y.C., May 30, 1930; s. Harold Albert and Judith (Sobel) H.; m. Therese Helene Thau, Dec. 17, 1950; children—Stephen Thomas, James Nathaniel. A.B., Dartmouth, 1951; J.D., Yale, 1956. Bar: N.Y. bar 1956, Calif. bar 1961. Legislative asst. to U.S. Senator Ives, 1950-51; with firm Carter, Ledyard & Milburn, N.Y.C., 1956-57; law clk. to U.S. Circuit Judge Charles Clark, 1957-58, to Supreme Ct. Justice Earl Warren, 1958-59; prof. law U. Calif. at Berkeley, 1959—, prof. city and regional planning, 1966—, vice chancellor, 1974-80, chancellor, 1980—; Vis. prof. Yale Law Sch., 1963-64, Stanford Law Sch., 1971-72. Contbr. articles to profl. jours. Mem. City of Berkeley Charter Rev. Commn., 1972-74; Calif. adv. com. U.S. Commn. Civil Rights, 1962-67. Served to 1st lt. USMCR, 1951-53. Mem. Am. Law Inst. (asst. reporter). Democrat. Home: Univ House U Calif Berkeley CA 94720

HEYMAN, LAWRENCE MURRAY, painter, printmaker; b. Washington, June 30, 1932; s. Philip I. and Gertrude B. H.; m. D. Tania Berchatsky, Aug. 25, 1971; children—Dain, Adam, Nicholas, Latha. B.F.A., Tyler Sch. Fine Arts, Temple U., 1954; B.S. in Edn, Temple U., 1955; M.F.A., Am. U., 1972. Instr. fine arts in printmaking R.I. Sch. Design, 1967-69, asst. prof. fine arts and printmaking, 1972-79, dir. printmaking program, 1976-79; lectr. Am. U., 1971-72. Exhibited in one-man shows, Mickelson Gallery, Washington, 1966, 77, R.I. Sch. Design, 1969, 79, St. John's U., St. Paul, 1980, group shows, including, Providence Art Club, 1974 (prize), 1976), Bibliotheque Nationale, Paris, 1977 (purchase honor), 79), San Francisco Art Museum; represented in permanent collections, Bibliotheque Nationale, Paris, Bklyn. Mus., Brooks Meml. Mus., Tenn., Portland (Oreg.) Art Mus.; U.S. rep. Art in Embassies program exhbn., Istanbul, Turkey, 1976; Commd.: print edits. for Associated Am. Artists, N.Y.C., 1964, 68, 69, Antares Editions d'Art, Paris, 1970, 71, 72, Judith Selkowitz Fine Arts, N.Y.C., 1978. Served with U.S. Army, 1955-57. Mem. Coll. Art Assn., NEA. Home and Office: 182 Raleigh Ave Pawtucket RI 02860

HEYMAN, RALPH EDMOND, lawyer; b. Cin., Mar. 14, 1931; s. Ralph and Florence (Kahn) H.; m. Sylvia Lee Schottenstein, Jan. 2, 1984; children: Michael Cary, Cynthia Ann, Ginger Florence. A.B. magna cum laude (Rufus Choat scholar), Dartmouth Coll., 1953; LL.B. cum laude, Harvard U., 1956; LL.M., U. Cin., 1957. Bar: Ohio 1956, Ill. 1957. Practice in, Cin., 1956-58, Dayton, 1958—; assoc. Freiden & Wolf, 1956-58, Smith & Schnacke and (predecessor firm), 1958-61, partner, 1961—; Lectr. estate planning U. Cin., 1958-61; lectr., participant Southwestern Ohio Tax Inst., 1957—; lectr., moderator Dayton Bar Assn. Tax Insts., 1975-79; dir. and/or gen. counsel Towne Properties, Ltd., Digital Systems Design Corp., Arbor Internat. Group, Inc., Precision Photo Labs., Inc., Aristocrat Products, Inc., K.K. Motorcycle Supply, Inc., The Jams Co. Commr. Bd. Rural Zoning Commn. Montgomery County, 1969-71; Bd. dirs. Jewish Fedn. Dayton; trustee Miami Valley Sch., St. Elizabeth Med. Center Community Health Found. Mem. ABA, Ohio Bar Assn., Dayton Bar Assn. (chmn. tax com.), Cin. Bar Assn., Phi Beta Kappa., B'nai B'rith. Jewish (past pres. Temple Israel, pres. Temple Israel Found.). Clubs: Meadowbrook, Dayton City, Bankers, Standard, Discussion. Office: 2000 Courthouse Plaza Dayton OH 45402

HEYMANN, C(LEMENS) DAVID, author; b. N.Y.C., Jan. 14, 1945; s. Ernest Frederick and Renee K. (Vago) H.; m. Jeanne Ann Lunin, Nov. 10, 1974; 1 dau., Chloe Colette. B.S., Cornell U., 1966; M.F.A., U. Mass., 1969. Lectr. English lit. SUNY, Stony Brook, 1969-74, Antioch Coll., N.Y.C. campus, 1975; mem. judges panel Am. Book Awards, 1979-80, Nat. Book Critics Circle, 1978-79. Author: poetry The Quiet Hours, 1969; Ezra Pound: The Last Rower, 1976, American Aristocracy: The Lives and Times of James Russell, Amy and Robert Lowell, 1980, Poor Little Rich Girl: The Life and Legend of Betty Hutton, 1983; also book revs. and articles for nat. mags., newspapers. Mem. PEN. *Even the village idiot may have something of interest to tell us. Perhaps I am a village idiot. In any event, I shall have my say.*

HEYMANN, PHILIP B., educator, former govt. ofcl.; b. Pitts., Oct. 30, 1932. B.A., Yale U., 1954; LL.B., Harvard U., 1960. Bar: bar. Trial atty. Office Solicitor Gen., Dept. Justice, Washington, 1961-65, asst. atty. gen., 1978-81; dep. adminstr. Bur. Security and Consular Affairs, Dept. State, Washington, 1965, acting adminstr., to 1967; dep. asst. sec. of state for Bur. Internat. Orgns., 1967, exec. asst. to under sec. of state, 1967-69; with Legal Aid Agy. of D.C., 1969; faculty law Harvard U., 1969-78, 81—; asso. prosecutor and cons. to Watergate Spl. Prosecution Force, summers 1973-75. Served with USAF, 1955-57. Office: Harvard Law Sch Cambridge MA 02138

HEYMANN, STEPHEN TIMOTHY, marketing management consultant; b. N.Y.C., Dec. 7, 1940; s. Harold Joseph and Estelle Olga H.; m. Elaine Puciat, June 24, 1962; children: Elizabeth Jill, Michael Carroll, Andrew Harold. B.S. summa cum laude, Wharton Sch., U. Pa., 1962. Div. mgr., mdse. mgr. Sears, Roebuck & Co., Phila., 1962-65; brand mgr. Household Products div. Procter & Gamble Co., Cin., 1965-69; pres., dir. Glendinning Assos., Westport, Conn., 1969-81; dir. Penniman Chems. Inc., Glenco Enterprises Ltd., Glendinning Cos. Inc. Author: More People on Skis, 1972, Like, series of children's books, 1972-74. Mem. Abington (Pa.) Town Council, 1964-65; bd. dirs. Cin. Art Mus., 1968-69, Cin. United Fund, 1967-68; area dir. Ohio Republican Com., 1968; bd. dirs. Boy Scouts Am., 1962-65. Recipient Lost Dutchman award, 1975-78, Wharton Sch. Alumni award, 1979. Mem. Am. Mgmt. Assn., Am. Mktg. Assn., Young Pres. Orgn., Assn. Nat. Advertisers, Phi Beta Kappa. Clubs: Stratton Mountain Assn., Murray Hill Assn., Wharton Grad. Home: 573 Nod Hill Rd Wilton CT 06897 Office: New Eng Cons Group 191 Post Rd W Westport CT 06880

HEYN, ARNO HARRY ALBERT, chemistry educator; b. Breslau, Germany, Oct. 6, 1918; s. Myron and Margarete M.E.C. (Cierpinski) H.; m. Helen A. Pielemeier, Mar. 14, 1942; children: Evan A., Margaret L., Robert E. B.S., U. Mich., 1940, M.S., 1941, Ph.D., 1944. Exptl. chemist Sun Oil Co., Norwood, Pa., 1944-47; from instr. to prof. chemistry Boston U., 1947—; vis. scientist Brookhaven Nat. Lab., summers 1954-56; acad. guest Eidg. Techn. Hochschule, Zurich, 1965, Gesellschaft F. Kernforschung, Karlsruhe, 1973, 80, 81, 82, Landesanst. F. Wasserbiologie, Vienna, 1973; sci. adviser Boston Dist. U.S. FDA, 1967-72. Contbr. articles profl. jours. Fellow AAAS; mem. Am. Chem. Soc. (councilor 1967—, chmn. council com. on constn. and bylaws 1983, 84, chmn. Northeastern sect. 1968), AAUP (treas. Boston U. chpt. 1979-83), Sigma Xi, Phi Lambda Upsilon. Club: Sub Sig Outing (Boston). Home: 21 Alexander Rd Newton Highlands MA 02161 Office: Boston Univ Boston MA 02215

HEYN, ERNEST V., author, former editor; b. N.Y.C., Oct. 30, 1904; s. Herbert Alexander and Frieda (Senner) H.; m. Ethel Kenyon, May 1, 1942; children: Susan (Mrs. Willard F. Lochridge III), Dalma (Mrs. Jeffrey Owen Jones). Ed., Trinity Sch., Horace Mann Sch.; grad. magna cum laude, Princeton U., 1925; postgrad., U. Berlin, Germany. Founder, editor Modern Screen mag., 1931; editor Radio Mirror, 1935, Photoplay, 1938, Liberty mag., 1942; founder, editor Sport mag.; editor True Story mag.; editor-in-chief True Story mag. all Macfadden publs., 1948-51; editor Am. Weekly, 1951-59, Family Weekly, Suburbia Today, 1959-64; asso. pub., editor Popular Sci. Monthly, 1964-71, ret., 1970; chmn. bd. Nat. Provisioner, Inc., 1971—. Author: A Century of Wonders, 100 Years of Popular Science, Fire of Genius, Inventors of the Past Century; Author: (with Alfred W. Lees) Popular Science Leisure Homes, Do-It-Yourself Projects for your own Back Yard, (with Herbert Shuldiner) Popular Science Book of Gadgets; author: (with Evan Powell) Popular Science Book of Home Heating and Cooling, (with Daniel Ruby) Home Alternate Energy Projects; editor: My Most Inspiring Moment, Twelve Sport Immortals, My Favorite True Mystery. Served with AUS, 1942-45. Mem. Sigma Delta Chi. Presbyterian. Clubs: Dutch Treat, Deadline, Overseas Press, New Eng. of N.Y.; Princeton (N.Y.C.). Home: 240 Hillspoint Rd Westport CT 06880 *The Italians say: Dolce far niente which means: "It is sweet to do nothing." Since I am very busy in retirement, with an office and book projects, I say: It is sweet to do nothing, as long as you have something to do.*

HEYNEMAN, DONALD, educator, parasitologist; b. San Francisco, Feb. 18, 1925; s. Paul and Amy Josephine (Klauber) H.; m. Louise Davidson Ross, June 18, 1971; children: Amy J., Lucy A., Andrew P., Jennifer K., Claudia G. A.B. magna cum laude, Harvard U., 1950; M.A., Rice U., 1952; Ph.D., 1954. Instr. zoology UCLA, 1954-56, asst. prof., 1956-60; head dept. parasitology U.S. Navy Med. Research unit, Cairo, also co-dir., Malakal, Sudan, 1960-62; asso. research parasitologist Hooper Found., U. Calif. at San Francisco, 1962-64, asso. prof., 1966-68, prof. parasitology, 1968—, asst. dir. found., 1970—, acting chmn. dept. internat. health, 1976—; research coordinator U. Calif. Internat. Center Med. Research and Tng., Kuala Lumpur, Malaysia, 1964-66; cons. physiol. processes sect. NSF, 1966—; environ. biology div. NIH, 1968—; mem. tropical medicine and parasitology study sect. NIAID-NIH, 1973-76; mem. adv. sci. bd. Gorgas Meml. Inst., 1967—; cons. WHO, 1967, UNDP/WHO, 1978, UN Devel. Program, 1978—, also AID, others. Author: (with R. Boolootian) An Illustrated Laboratory Text in Zoology; An Illustrated Laboratory Text in Zoology; A Brief Version; editor, 1968—, International Dictionary Medicine and Biology; also papers, chpts., revs.; editorial cons.: Am. Jour. Tropical Medicine and Hygiene, Jour. Parasitology Exptl. Parasitology, Sci, 1968—. Served with AUS, 1943-46. Office Naval Research contractee, 1958-60, 71—; NIH grantee, 1966—. Mem. Am. Soc. Parasitologists (council 1970-74, pres. 1982-83), Am. Micros. Soc. (exec. com. 1971-75), Am. Soc. Tropical Medicine and Hygiene (councilor 1981-84), So. Calif. Parasitol. Soc. (pres. 1957-58), No. Calif. Parasitologists (sec.-treas. 1969-72, pres. 1977-78), Phi Beta Kappa. Specialist in parasitology, tropical medicine, internat. health problems. Home: 1400 Lake St San Francisco CA 94118 *A guideline of my research has been the conviction that all living forms and activities are related, so that the study of any one, like the spoke of a wheel, converges equally with the others onto the central axis of life, which we all are seeking.*

HEYNS, ROGER WILLIAM, foundation executive; b. Grand Rapids, Mich., Jan. 27, 1918; s. Garrett and Rosa (Klooster) H.; m. Esther Gezon, Sept. 20, 1941; children—Michael, John, Daniel. Student Hope Coll., 1936-37; A.B., Calvin Coll., 1940; M. Clin. Psychology, U. Mich., 1942, Ph.D., 1948. Instr. psychology U. Mich., 1947-48, asst. prof., 1948-55, asso. prof., 1955-57, prof., 1957-65; dean Coll. Lit., Sci. and Arts, 1958-62; v.p. acad. affairs, 1962-65, prof. psychology and edn., 1971; chancellor U. Calif. at Berkeley, 1965-71; pres. Am. Council on Edn., Washington, 1972-77, William and Flora Hewlett Found., 1977—; Dir. Norton Simon, Inc., Times Mirror Co., Kaiser Steel, Levi-Strauss & Co.; Mem. Nat. Sci. Bd., 1967-76. Bd. dirs. James Irvine Found.; mem. Council on Fgn. Relations, 1978—; trustee Brookings Instn., Center for Advanced Study in Behavioral Scis., 1975-81. Served from pvt. to capt. USAAF, 1942-46. Recipient outstanding tchr. award U. Mich., 1952, faculty distinguished service award, 1958; Clark Kerr award for outstanding service to edn., 1967; Benjamin Ide Wheeler award as Berkeley's Most Useful Citizen, 1969; Robert C. Kirkwood award for greatest service to N. Calif., 1969. Fellow Am. Psychol. Assn.; mem. Phi Beta Kappa, Sigma Xi, Phi Kappa Phi. Office: 525 Middlefield Rd Suite 200 Menlo Park CA 94025

HEYSE, WARREN JOHN, publishing company executive; b. Milw., Oct. 13, 1923; s. Raymond Henry and Harriet Margaret (Regner) H.; m. Roxybelle Brown, July 9, 1949; children: Roxanne, Jennifer, Nanette. B.S., U. Wis., 1948; postgrad., Marquette U. Law Sch., 1949; M.S., UCLA, 1950, U. Minn., 1952. Classified advt. salesman Milw. Jour., 1952-55, retail advt. supr., 1955-59, classified advt. mgr., 1959-66, asst. advt. dir., 1966-68, v.p., dir. mktg., devel., 1968-73; sr. v.p. The Jour. Co., 1973-77, exec. v.p., 1977-83, pres., 1983—, Newspapers Inc. (pub. Milw. Jour.), 1977—; v.p., dir. Tempo Communications, MJE, Perry Printing, Midwestern Relay (all Jour. Co. subs.), 1973—; vice chmn. WTMJ, Inc.; dir. Million Market Newspapers, 1974—, chmn., 1976-77, 82-83; dir. Metro Sunday Newspapers, 1978—; trustee Jour. Stock Trust, 1976—. Gen. chmn. United Way, 1969, bd. dirs., 1970-76; bd. dirs. Vis. Nurses Assn., 1971-76, ARC, 1972-74, Milwaukee County council Boy Scouts Am., 1975—; pres. Milwaukee County council Boy Scouts Am., 1984; bd. dirs. St. Joseph Hosp., 1970—, Greater Milw. Com., 1977—, U. Wis. Found., 1980—, United Performing Arts Fund, 1978—; co-chmn. United Performing Arts Fund, 1979. Served with inf. U.S. Army, 1943-46; ETO. Recipient McGovern award for classified advt., 1979, Wis. Newspaper Pub. of Yr., 1983. Mem. Sigma Alpha Epsilon, Sigma Delta Chi, Kappa Tau Alpha. Methodist. Clubs: Univ.; Bascom Hill Soc. (U. Wis., Madison); Circumnavigator. Office: Jour Co 333 State St Milwaukee WI 53203

HEYSSEL, ROBERT MORRIS, physician, hospital administrator; b. Jamestown, Mo., June 19, 1928; s. Clarence D. and Meta and (Reusser) H.; m. Maria McDaniel, Aug. 7, 1955; children: James Olin, Maria Lisa, Robert Morris, Kurt Frederick, Helen Perrier. B.S., U. Mo., 1951; M.D., St. Louis U., 1953. Postgrad. tng. St. Louis U. Hosp., 1953-56, Barnes Hosp., St. Louis, 1953-56; hematologist, acting dir. dept. medicine Atomic Bomb Casualty Commn., Nagasaki and Hiroshima, Japan, 1956-58; mem. faculty Sch. Medicine, Vanderbilt U., Nashville, 1959-68, dir. div. nuclear medicine, 1962-68, asso. prof. medicine, 1964-68; asso. dean Sch. Medicine, Johns Hopkins U., Balt., 1968-72, dir. health care programs and outpatient services, 1968-72, prof. medicine, 1971—, prof. health care orgn., 1972—; exec. v.p., dir. Johns Hopkins Hosp., 1972-83, pres., 1983—; dir. Union Trust BanCorp, Union Trust Bank, Balt.; chmn. Commonwealth Fund on Acad. Health Ctrs., 1983. Contbr. articles to profl. jours. Pres. Columbia (Md.) Hosp. and Clinics, 1969-74; chmn. health services com. Assn. Am. Med. Colls., 1971-74, mem. gen. assembly, 1974—, mem. exec. council, chmn. council teaching hosps., 1978, chmn., 1984—; chmn. com. on emergency med. services Nat. Acad. Scis., 1973—; mem. Joint Commn. on Prescription Drugs, 1976, Gov's Commn. on High Technology, 1983—; chmn. council teaching hosps. numerous other local, state and nat. coms. on health, medicine and med. edn.; Bd. dirs. East Balt. Community Corp. Recipient USPHS Career Devel. award, 1962; Distinguished Alumnus award U. Mo., 1972. Fellow ACP, Internat. Soc. Hematology; mem. Inst. Med. Nat. Acad. Scis., Assn. Am. Med. Colls. (chmn. elect 1983), Assn. Am. Physicians, Soc. Med. Adminstrs., numerous other sci. assns. Club: Elk Ridge (Balt.). Home: 200 Ridgewood Rd Baltimore MD 21210 Office: 601 N Broadway Baltimore MD 21205

HEYWOOD, STANLEY JOHN, educator; b. Vancouver, B.C., Can., Mar. 18, 1925; came to U.S., 1950, naturalized, 1959; s. John Albert and Lillian (Burton) H.; m. Joan Olive Murton, Aug. 18, 1950; children: John Spencer, Philip Arthur. B.A., U. B.C., 1949, B.Ed., 1949; A.M., U. Chgo., 1952, Ph.D., 1954. Faculty pub. schs., B.C., 1945-47; lectr. adminstrn. RCAF, Royal Mil. Coll., Kingston, Ont., 1951, 52; instr. adminstrn. U. B.C., 1953; research asso. Midwest Adminstrn. Center, U. Chgo., 1954; registrar, chmn. dept. tchr. edn., dir. summer session Coe Coll., 1954-56, adminstrv. asst. to pres., registrar, dir. summer session, 1957-58; dean Coll. Edn., Idaho State U., 1958-66; pres. Eastern Mont. Coll., Billings, 1966-76, prof. edn., 1976—; acad. specialist USIA, Africa, 1976, 79, Bangladesh, Hong Kong, 1982; mem. Carnegie Commn. on Future of Higher Edn., 1969-73; bd. dirs. Am. Assn. State Colls. and Univs., 1968-72; study/speaking tour, Malta, Egypt, Kenya, 1980, Belize, Costa Rica, 1981. Served to flying officer RCAF, 1943-45, 51, 52. Danforth fellow for coll. adminstrs., 1971; Northwest Regional Ednl. Lab. grantee, 1981. Mem. AAUP, Internat. Assn. Univ. Pres., World Future Soc., Phi Delta Kappa. Episcopalian. Address: Dept Edn Eastern Mont Coll Billings MT 59101

HEYWORTH, JAMES O., communications company executive; b. Chgo., Sept. 22, 1942; s. James O. and Jean (Stevens) H.; m. Christine Griffith, Sept. 15, 1968; children: Samuel, Benton, James. B.A., Yale U., 1964; M.B.A., U. Chgo., 1967. Mktg. mgr. Time mag., N.Y.C., 1967-69; asst. bus. mgr. Tome-Life Broadcasting, 1969-72; bus. mgr. Time-Life Cable TV, 1972-73; v.p., treas. Home Box Office, N.Y.C., 1973-76, sr. v.p. fin. and devel., 1976-78, v.p., ops., 1978-79, pres., chief exec. officer, 980-83, dir.; dep. group v.p. Video Time Inc., N.Y.C., 1983—; dir. Time-Life Books, Alexandria, Va., 1980—, Am. TV & Communications Corp., Denver, Tri-Star Pictures, N.Y.C., U.S.A. Cable Network, C-Span, Washington. Served with U.S. Army, 1968-69. Mem. Nat. Cable TV Assn. (dir. Jerry Greene Meml. award 1983, chmn. assocs. com. 1979-83). Office: Time Inc 1271 Ave of Americas New York NY 10020

HIARING, ROBERT DALE, lawyer, federal judge; b. Lake County, S.D., Dec. 21, 1941; s. Lawrence Carl and Helen Vina (Quam) H.; m. Barbara Lynne Hanson, June 6, 1964; 1 dau., Lisa Lynne. A.B., U. S.D., 1967, J.D., 1970. Bar: S.D. 1970, Mont. 1982. Law clk. U.S. Dist. Ct., Rapid City, S.D., 1970-71; asst. U.S. atty. Dist. of S.D., 1971-77, 1st asst. U.S. atty., 1977-78, U.S. atty., 1978-79; fed. adminstrv. law judge, Billings, Mont., 1979—. Mem. S.D. State Bar., Mont. State Bar. Office: Office of Hearings and Appeals - SSA 17 N 26th St Suite 101 Billings MT 59101

HIATT, ARNOLD, shoe manufacturer, importer, retailer; b. May 26, 1927; s. Alexander and Dorothy H.; m. Anne Wechsler. B.A., Harvard U., 1948. Pres., founder Blue Star Shoe Co., Lawrence, Mass., 1952-69; pres., chief exec. officer Stride Rite Corp., Boston, 1969—, chmn. bd., 1982—; dir. Fiduciary Trust Co., Boston, 1972—, also New Republic mag.; corporator Charlestown Savs. Bank, Boston, 1971-72, trustee, 1972-77; dir. Dreyfus Fund. Bd. dirs. Boston Office Cultural Affairs, Am. Orgn. Rehab. Through Tng., Pvt. Industry Council, Mass Advocacy Center, Summerthing of Boston; trustee Com-Jewish Philanthropies, Northeastern U., 1983—; mem. vis. com. Boston U. Sch. Medicine; mem. overseers' com. on univ. resources Harvard U.; mem. corp. Northeastern U., Boston. Mem. Am. Footwear Industries Assn. (dir., chmn. 1980), Young Pres. Orgn. Office: 5 Cambridge Ctr Cambridge MA 02142

HIATT, HOWARD H., educator, physician; b. Patchogue, N.Y., July 22, 1925; s. Alexander and Dorothy (Askinas) H.; m. Doris Bieringer, Nov. 29, 1947; children—Jonathan, Deborah, Frederick. M.D., Harvard, 1948. Intern, then resident medicine Beth Israel Hosp., Boston, 1948-50; research fellow Cornell Med. Coll., 1950-53; clin. investigator USPHS, 1953-55; mem. faculty Harvard Med. Sch., 1955—, H.L. Blumgart prof. medicine, 1963-72, prof. medicine, 1972—; physician-in-chief Beth Israel Hosp., 1963-72; dean Harvard Sch. Pub. Health, 1972—. Mem. Am. Soc. Clin. Investigation, Assn.

Am. Physicians, Am. Acad. Arts and Scis., Inst. Medicine, Alpha Omega Alpha. Home: 22 Hyslop Rd Brookline MA 02146 Office: 677 Huntington Ave Boston MA 02115

HIATT, PETER, library educator; b. N.Y.C., Oct. 19, 1930; s. Amos and Elizabeth Hope (Derry) H.; m. Linda Rae Smith, Aug. 16, 1968; 1 dau., Holly Virginia. B.A., Colgate U., 1952; M.L.S., Rutgers U., 1957, Ph.D., 1963. Head Elmora Br. Library, Elizabeth, N.J., 1957-59; instr. Grad. Sch. Library Service, Rutgers U., 1960-62; library cons. Ind. State Library, Indpls., 1963-70; asst. prof. Grad. Library Sch., Ind. U., 1963-66, asso. prof., 1966-70; dir. Ind. Library Studies, Bloomington, 1967-70; dir. continuing edn. program for library personnel Western Interstate Commn. for Higher Edn., Boulder, Colo., 1970-74; dir. Sch. Librarianship, U. Wash., Seattle, 1974-81, prof., 1974—; prin. investigator Career Devel. and Assessment Center for Librarians, 1979-83; dir. library insts. at various colls. and univs.; adv. project U.S. Office Edn.-ALA, 1977—. Author: (with Donald Thompson) Monroe County Public Library: Planning for the Future, 1966, The Public Library Needs of Delaware County, 1967, (with Henry Drennan) Public Library Services for the Functionally Illiterate, 1967, (with Robert E. Lee and Lawrence A. Allen) A Plan for Developing a Regional Program of Continuing Education for Library Personnel, 1969, Public Library Branch Services for Adults of Low Education, 1964; dir., gen. editor: The Indiana Library Studies, 1970; mem. editorial bd.: Coll. and Research Libraries, 1969-73; co-editor: Leads: A Continuing Newsletter for Library Trustees, 1973-75, Octavio Noda; author chpts., articles on library continuing edn. and staff devel. Mem. ALA (officer), Pacific N.W. Library Assn., Spl. Libraries Assn., Assn. Am. Library Schs. (officer, Outstanding Service award 1979), Am. Soc. Info. Sci., Adult Edn. Assn., ACLU. Home: 19324 8th Ave NW Seattle WA 98177 Office: Grad Sch Library and Info Sci U Wash Seattle WA 98195

HIATT, ROBERT WORTH, former univ. pres.; b. San Jose, Calif., Dec. 23, 1913; s. Elwood B. and Bernice (Bane) H.; m. Elizabeth A. Matthews, July 18, 1938; children—Judith L., Gerald A., William R. B.A., San Jose State Coll., 1936; Ph.D., U. Calif. at Berkeley, 1941. Instr., asst. prof. zoology Mont. State Coll., 1941-43; asst. prof. zoology U. Hawaii, 1943-45, asso. prof., prof., sr. prof., chmn. dept., 1946-55, dean Grad. Sch., dir. research, 1955-63, v.p. acad. affairs, 1963-68, acting pres., 1968-69; exec. dir. U. Hawaii Research Corp., 1969; sci. counselor U.S. embassy, Tokyo, 1970-73; pres. U. Alaska, 1973-78; sci. liaison officer Am. embassy, London, Eng., 1957-58; dir. Hawaii Marine Lab., 1943-55, Eniwetok Marine Biol. Lab., 1952-69, Standard Oil Co. Ohio.; Chmn. adv. com. hydrobiology Office Naval Research, 1951-65, mem. adv. com. on biology, 1951-56; mem. com. on internat. relations Am. Inst. Biol. Sci., 1959-63; mem. Office Instnl. Programs Council, NSF, 1960-66, FAO panel experts on marine fisheries, 1962-69; cons. div. biology and medicine NSF, 1968-69; chmn., editor Proc. Internat. Conf. on Marine Labs., Rome, 1955. Editor: Directory of Hydrobiological Laboratories and Personnel in North America, 1954, World Directory to Hydrobiologic Institutions, 1963; Contbr. articles to sci. jours. Fellow AAAS; mem. Pacific Sci. Assn., Nat. Acad. Sci. (Pacific sci. bd.), Am. Ornithol. Union, Am. Fisheries Soc., Am. Soc. Zoologists, Am. Soc. Ichthyologists and Herpetologists, Soc. Systematic Zoologists, Ecol. Soc. Am., Am. Soc. Limnology and Oceanography. Address: PO Box 4137 Incline Village NV 89450

HIBBARD, GEORGE A., banker; b. Boston, Oct. 9, 1922; s. Bement and Margaret (McCarthy) H.; m. Ann F. Doherty, June 13, 1953; children: Sarah, George, John, Robert, James. B.A., Harvard U., 1944, M.B.A., 1948. With BayBank Middlesex, 1948-50; with BayBanks, Inc., 1950-77, v.p., 1961-69, treas., 1966-74, sr. v.p., 1969-74, pres., dir., 1974-77; pres., chief exec. officer, dir. BayBank Harvard Trust Co., Cambridge, Mass., 1977-82, chmn. bd., chief exec. officer, dir., 1982—. Served with USNR, 1943-46. Mem. Boston Security Analysts Soc. Clubs: Harvard Varsity (past pres.), Wellesley Country (past pres.), Harvard (Boston)). Home: 19 Colgate St Wellesley MA 02181 Office: 1414 Massachusetts Ave Cambridge MA 02138

HIBBARD, HOWARD, art historian, educator; b. Madison, Wis., May 23, 1928; s. Benjamin Horace and Margaret M. (Baker) H.; m. Shirley Irene Griffith, Sept. 14, 1951; children: Claire Alexandra, Susan Giulia, Carla Costanza. B.A., U. Wis., 1949, M.A., 1952; Ph.D., Harvard U., 1958; M.A., Oxford (Eng.) U., 1977. Research fellow Am. Acad. in, Rome, 1956-58; vis. instr. U. Calif., Berkeley, 1958-59; mem. faculty Columbia U., N.Y.C., 1959—, prof. art history, 1966—, chmn. dept. art history and archaeology, 1978-81; vis. disting. scholar CCNY, 1973-74; vis. prof. Yale U., 1976; Slade prof. fine art Oxford U., 1976-77. Author: The Architecture of the Palazzo Borghese, 1962, Bernini, 1965, Bernini e barocco, 1968, Carlo Maderno and Roman Architecture, 1580-1630, 1972, Poussin: The Holy Family on the Steps, 1974, Michelangelo, 1975, Masterpieces of Western Sculpture, from Medieval to Modern, 1977, The Metropolitan Museum of Art, 1980, Caravaggio, 1983; also exhbn. catalogue; book rev. editor: Art Bull., 1961-65; editor-in-chief, 1974-78. Fulbright fellow, Paris, 1949-50; fellow Am. Council Learned Socs., 1962-63, Guggenheim Found., 1965-66, 72-73, Nat. Endowment Humanities, 1967, 79-80. Fellow Am. Acad. Arts and Scis.; mem. Assn. Art Historians Gt. Britain, Coll. Art Assn. Am., Renaissance Soc. Am., Soc. Archtl. Historians (dir. 1963-65). Office: 815 Schermerhorn Hall Columbia U New York NY 10027

HIBBARD, WALTER ROLLO, JR., engineering educator; b. Bridgeport, Conn., Jan. 20, 1918; s. Walter Rollo and Helen S. (Kenworthy) H.; m. Charlotte Tracy, Mar. 21, 1942 (dec. Sept. 1970); children: Douglas, Lawrence, Diana; m. Louise Brembeck, Jan. 29, 1972. A.B., Wesleyan U., Middletown, Conn., 1939; D.Eng., Yale, 1942; LL.D. (hon.), Mich. Technol. U., D.Eng., Mont. Coll. Mineral Sci. and Tech., 1968. Registered profl. engr., Conn., Va., Ohio. From asst. to asso. prof. metallurgy Yale, 1945-51; with research lab. Gen. Electric Co., 1951-65, mgr. alloy studies, 1953-60, mgr. metallurgy and ceramics research, 1960-65; adj. prof. metall. engring. Rensselaer Poly. Inst., 1952-65; dir. Bur. Mines, Dept. Interior, 1965-68; v.p. tech. services Owens Corning Fiberglas Corp., Toledo, 1968-74; with Energy Research and Devel. Office, Fed. Energy Office, 1974; prof. engring., dir. Va. Center for Coal and Energy Research, Va. Poly. Inst. and State U., Blacksburg, 1974—; Dir. Norton Co., Worcester, Mass.; Chmn. materials adv. bd. Nat. Acad. Scis.-NRC, 1965-66; mem. adv. com., engring. div. NSF, 1965-69; chmn. bldg. research adv. bd. NRC, 1975. Editor: (with F.P. Bundy and H.M. Strong) Progress in Very High Pressure Research, 1961, Jour. Materials and Society; Contbr. articles to profl. jours. Mem. vis. com. Vanderbilt U.; asso. fellow Davenport Coll., Yale. Served to lt. USNR, 1942-45. Recipient Yale Engring. Assn. award advancement basic and applied sci., 1959; Wesleyan Disting. Alumnus award, 1979. Fellow Am. Acad. Arts and Scis., Metall. Soc. of Am. Inst. M.E. (pres. 1958), AAAS (chmn. engring. sect. 1975), Am. Ceramic Soc., Am. Soc. Metals; mem. Va. Acad. Sci., Am. Inst. Mining, Metall. and Petroleum Engrs. (Rossiter W. Raymond award 1950, pres. 1967, recipient James Douglas gold medal), Nat. Acad. Engring., Phi Beta Kappa, Sigma Xi, Tau Beta Pi, Alpha Chi Sigma, Alpha Sigma Mu, Delta Tau Delta, Gamma Alpha. Home: 1403 Highland Circle Blacksburg VA 24060 Office: 301 Holden Hall Blacksburg VA 24061

HIBBERT, DONALD R., corporation executive; b. 1926; married. B.A. in Econs., Mich. State U., 1950. With Touche, Ross & Co., 1950-58; v.p., treas. Wyandotte Chem. Corp., 1958-69; treas. Bendix Corp., 1969-70; v.p. fin. Kimberly-Clark Corp., Neenah, Wis., 1970-72, treas., 1971-72, exec. v.p., then exec. v.p., chief fin. officer, 1972-83; sr. exec. v.p. Consumer and Service Cos., Kimberly-Clark Corp., Neenah, Wis., 1983—, dir. Served with USNR, 1943-46. Office: Kimberly-Clark Corp N Lake St Neenah WI 54956 *

HIBBETT, HOWARD SCOTT, educator; b. Akron, Ohio, July 27, 1920; s. Howard Scott and Florence (Line) H.; m. Tomi Kuwayama, Feb. 16, 1946 (div. 1958); children—Mariko, Reiko; m. Akiko Yamagawa, Jan. 20, 1960; 1 son, David. A.B. summa cum laude, Harvard, 1947; Ph.D., 1950. Jr. fellow Harvard Soc. Fellows, 1949-52; from instr. to asst. prof. Oriental langs. U. Calif. at Los Angeles, 1952-58; mem. faculty Harvard, 1958—, prof. Japanese lit., 1963—, chmn. dept. Far Eastern langs., 1965-70; chmn. council on East Asian studies, 1980—. Author: The Floating World in Japanese Fiction, 1959, (with Gen. Itasaka) Modern Japanese: A Basic Reader, 1965; Translator: (J. Tanizaki) The Key, 1961, Seven Japanese Tales, 1963, Diary of A Mad Old Man, 1965, (Y. Kawabata) Beauty and Sadness, 1974; editor: Contemporary Japanese Literature, 1977. Served to 1st lt. AUS, 1942-46. Fulbright research scholar, Japan, 1956-57, 64-65; Guggenheim fellow, 1964-65. Mem. Assn. Asian Studies, Am. Acad. Arts and Scis., Phi Beta Kappa. Home: 220 Pleasant St Arlington MA 02174 Office: 2 Divinity Ave Cambridge MA 02138

HIBBS, LEON, univ. pres.; b. Balko, Okla., Oct. 15, 1930; s. Paschal Otho and Luella (Smith) H.; m. Maxine Parker, Sept. 6, 1950; children—Max, Gaye, Craig, LeAn. B.S., Northwestern Okla. State U., 1952; Ed.M., U. Okla., 1956; M.S., Okla. State U., 1957, Ed.D., 1959. Successively tchr., prin., supt. Greenough schs., Beaver County, Okla., 1952-56; dir. instructional TV Okla. Dept. Edn., 1957-60; dir. course devel., coordinator spl. projects Purdue Research Found., 1960-62; dean edn. Oklahoma City U., 1962-67; pres. Southeastern Okla. State U., 1967—; cons. infield, 1960—. Author: Using the Stereomicroscope, 1964, A Programmed Textbook in Mathematics for Elementary School Teachers, 1966, Living Science, 1966. Chmn. Goals for Durant, 1969—; Chmn. bd. dirs. Southeastern Found., 1967—. Recipient Favorite Faculty award Oklahoma City U., 1965; Student Edn. Assn. award, 1966; fellow NSF, 1956. Mem. Nat., Okla. edn. assns., Durant C. of C. (dir. 1967—). Clubs: Mason, Rotarian (dir. Durant 1967—). Office: Station A Durant OK 74701 *

HIBBS, LOYAL ROBERT, lawyer; b. Des Moines, Dec. 24, 1925; s. Loyal B. and Catharine (McClymond) H.; children: Timothy, Theodore, Howard, Dean. B.A., U. Iowa, 1950, LL.B., 1952. Bar: Iowa 1952, Nev. 1958, U.S. Supreme Ct. 1971. Partner firm Hibbs, Roberts, Lemons & Grundy, Reno, 1972—. Mem. Am. Bar Assn. (standing com. Lawyer Referral Service 1978-79, sec. 1979—, steering com. state dels. 1979—, consortium on legal services and the public 1979-82, Nev. del. to Ho. of Dels. 1978—, bd. govs. 1982—), Iowa Bar Assn., Nev. Bar Assn. (bd. govs. 1968-78, pres. 1977-78), Washoe County Bar Assn. (pres. 1967-68), Greater Reno C. of C. (dir. 1970-73), Phi Alpha Delta. Home: 1489 Foster Dr Reno NV 89509 Office: 350 S Center St Reno NV 89501

HIBBS, RICHARD GUYTHAL, educator; b. Winner, S.D., Feb. 17, 1922; s. George G. and Verna (Smith) H.; m. Dorothy H. Taggart, Aug. 19, 1946; children—Richard Gene, Linda Marie, Mary Jo. Student, Loyola U., Chgo., 1947-49; B.A., U. S.D., 1950; Ph.D., U. Minn., 1955. Instr. anatomy U. Minn. Med. Sch., 1954-55; mem. faculty Tulane U. Med. Sch., New Orleans, 1955-75, asso. prof. anatomy, 1963-66, prof. anatomy, 1966-75; prof. anatomy, head dept. La. State U. Sch. Medicine, Shreveport, 1975—. Served with USMC, 1940-46. Recipient gold award original research Am. Acad. Dermatology and Syphology, 1958, Career Devel. award USPHS, 1960-65, 65-70. Mem. Am. Assn. Anatomists, Am. Physiol. Soc., La. Soc. Electron Microscopy, So. Soc. Anatomists, Sigma Xi. Spl. research electron microscopy of skin and appendages, electron microscopy and histochemistry cardiovascular system. Home: 2949 Curtis Ln Shreveport LA 71109

HIBDON, JAMES EDWARD, economist, educator; b. McAlester, Okla., Sept. 1, 1924; s. William Wesley and Minnie Irene (McBride) H.; m. Mina Mae Gilreath, Aug. 20, 1944; children—Mary Ann, Jennifer Lee. Student, Okla. Bapt. U., 1942-43, Syracuse U., 1943; B.A., U. Okla., 1948, M.A., 1949; Ph.D., U. N.C., 1957. Asst. prof. econs. Ga. State U., 1954-57, asso. prof., 1957-59, Tex. A&M U., 1959-61, U. Okla., Norman, 1961-67, prof., 1967—, chmn. dept. econs., 1971—; vis. scholar U.S. Dept. Commerce, 1977-78. Author: Price and Welfare Theory, 1969; editor: Rev. of Regional Econs. and Bus, 1975—, Okla. Bus. Bull, 1970-71; contbr. articles to profl. jours. Trustee annuity bd. So. Bapt. Conv. Served with AUS, 1943-46, 50-51. Mem. Am. Econs. Assn., So. Econs. Assn., S.W. Econs. Assn. (pres. 1977-78), Midwest Econs. Assn., Southwestern Social Sci. Assn., Western Social Sci. Assn., Beta Gamma Sigma, Omicron Delta Epsilon.

HIBEL, BERNARD, former apparel company executive, consultant; b. N.Y.C., Dec. 22, 1916; s. Jacob and Leah (Singer) H.; m. Annette; children: Laurel, Karen, Miriam. B.B.A. magna cum laude, St. John's U., 1937. C.P.A. Mng. exec. charge contract termination Cleve. Ordnance Dist., 1945-46; mng. acct. Bernard M. Joffe & Co., N.Y.C., 1946-48, Aronson & Oresman (C.P.A.s.), 1948-55; exec. v.p. Kayser-Roth Corp., N.Y.C., 1975-81, also dir.; cons., 1982—; tchr. acctg. Bklyn. Coll., U.S. Army. Served with AUS, 1943-45. Decorated Bronze Star. Mem. Am. Inst. C.P.A.s, N.Y. State Soc. C.P.A.s, Fin. Execs. Inst., Nat. Assn. Accts. Office: 300 E 56th St New York NY 10022

HIBLER, DOUGLAS HARRY, publishing company executive; b. Albuquerque, Feb. 28, 1935; s. Douglas Feldon and Alice Berhman (Hoyl) H.; children: Sheree Lynn, Raymond Tracy. Student extension classes, UCLA, U. Calif., San Diego. Constrn. foreman, 1952-62; pres. BMH Inc. (gen. contractors), 1962-69; advt. sales Petersen Pub. Co., Los Angeles, 1969-74, nat. advt. mgr., 1975-79; pub. Hot Rod mag., 1979—; v.p. Joelen Gen. Contractors, Los Angeles, 1974-75; owner, builder, driver race cars, 1951-79. Republican. Baptist. *

HICHAR, JOSEPH KENNETH, biologist, educator; b. Allentown, Pa., Aug. 5, 1928; s. Nicholas and Paraska (Fenyo) H.; m. Barbara June Gill, Dec. 25, 1955; children: Joseph K., Mark N.G. B.S., U. Pitts., 1950; M.S., Pa. State U., 1952; postgrad., Mass. Inst. Tech., Marine Biol. Lab., Woods Hole, Mass., 1956; Ph.D., Harvard, 1958. Asst. prof. Moravian Coll., Bethlehem, Pa., 1952-53; asst. prof., then asso. prof. State U. N.Y. at Brockport, 1953-55; teaching and research fellow Harvard, 1955-58; asst. prof. zoology Ohio Wesleyan U., 1958-60; instr. biology Brown U., summers 1959-60; prof. biology Parsons Coll., Fairfield, Ia., 1960-65, dean Grad. Sch., 1960-65, Coll. Arts and Scis., 1962-63, dean faculty scis., 1963-65; prof. biology, dean coll., v.p. acad. affairs Hiram Scott Coll., Scottsbluff, Neb., 1965-70; prof. biology State U. N.Y. at Buffalo, 1970—, dean faculty arts and scis., 1970-72, dean faculty natural scis., 1972-75; Fulbright prof. U. Ceylon, 1963-64; U.S. Ednl. Found. in India Univ. lectr., 1963. Contbr. articles to profl. jours. Mem. planning bd. Neb. Ednl. TV Commn. Higher Edn., 1965-70; v.p. Platte Valley Forum, 1967-69, pres., 1969-70; mem. adv. com. liberal arts Erie Community Coll., 1972—; mem. policy com. Neb. Acad. Scis., 1965-70; exec. com. Wyobraska council Boy Scouts Am., 1968-69; mem. Amherst Conservation Adv. Council, 1974-76; Bd. dirs. Scottsbluff-Gering Community Chest, 1968-70; sec., trustee Hiram Scott Coll., 1966-70 sec., trustee Hiram Scott Coll., trustee; trustee Scottsbluff YMCA, 1966-70. Mem. USAR, 1950—; now col. Harvard summer scholar, 1956; grantee NSF, 1959, 60, 65, NRC-Nat. Acad. Scis., 1961, USPHS, 1957-58, NIH, 1960-65, U.S. Office Edn., 1968-69. Fellow A.A.A.S., Acad. Zoology (Agra, India), N.Y. Acad. Scis., Am. Soc. Zoologists; mem. Am. Inst. Biol. Scis., Biophys. Soc. (charter), Am. Assn. Higher Edn., Internat. Inst. Med. Electronics and Biol. Engring., Internat. Fedn. Med. Electronics, Scabbard and Blade, Sigma Xi, Phi Kappa Phi, Chi Beta Phi, Beta Beta Beta, Sigma Phi Epsilon. Conglist. (trustee). Home: 250 Washington Hwy Snyder NY 14226 Office: 1300 Elmwood Ave Buffalo NY 14222

HICK, JOHN HARWOOD, theology educator; b. Scarborough, Yorkshire, Eng., Jan. 20, 1922; s. Mark D. and Mary Aileen (Hirst) H.; m. Joan Hazel Bowers, Aug. 30, 1953; children: Eleanor, Mark, Peter, Michael. M.A., Edinburgh (Scotland) U., 1948, D.Litt hon., 1974; D.Phil., Oxford (Eng.) U., 1950; postgrad., Westminster Theol. Coll., 1950-53; Ph.D., Cambridge U., 1964; Theol. Dr. hon., Uppsala U., Sweden, 1977. Ordained to ministry Presbyterian Ch., 1953. Minister Belford Presbyn. Ch., Northumberland, Eng., 1953-56; asst. prof. philosophy Cornell U., Ithaca, N.Y., 1956-59; Stuart prof. Christian philosophy Princeton Theol. Sem., 1959-64; lectr. divinity Cambridge U., 1964-67; H.G. Wood prof. theology Birmingham U., Eng., 1967-82; Danforth prof. religion Claremont Grad. Sch., Calif., 1979—; James W. Richard lectr. U. Va., 1969; Arthur Stanley Eddington Meml. lectr. Cambridge U., 1972, Stanton lectr., 1974-77; Ingersoll lectr. Harvard U., 1977; Teape lectr., New Delhi, 1975. Author: Faith and Knowledge, 1957, 66, Philosophy of Religion, 1963, 73, 83, Evil and the God of Love, 1966, 77, The Center of Christianity, 1968, 83, Arguments for the Existence of God, 1971, God and the Universe of Faiths, 1973, Death and Eternal Life, 1976, God Has Many Names, 1980, (with Michael Goulder) Why Believe in God, 1983; editor: The Existence of God, 1963, Faith and the Philosophers, 1963, The Myth of God Incarnate, 1977, Truth and Dialogue, 1974. Chmn., pres. All Faiths for One Race, Birmingham, Eng., 1972-73, 80—. Fellow Guggenheim Found., 1963-64; vis. fellow Brit. Acad. Overseas, 1974; Leverhulme Research fellow, 1974; Select preacher Oxford U., 1970; Hulsean preacher Cambridge U., 1969. Mem. Soc. for Study of Theology (pres. 1975-76), Am. Philos. Assn., Am. Acad. Religion, Soc. for Psychical Research, Am. Soc. for Study of Religion, Pacific Coast Theol. Soc. Office: Claremont Grad Sch Claremont CA 91711

HICKCOX, CURTISS BRONSON, anesthesiologist; b. Watertown, Conn., July 14, 1913; s. Frank Bronson and Elizabeth May (Atwood) H.; m. Helen Theresa Burke, June 7, 1941; children: Maryann Elizabeth, Patricia Katherine, Curtiss Bronson, Edward Frank. S.B., Middlebury (Vt.) Coll., 1934; M.D., Tufts Coll., Boston, 1938. Diplomate: Am. Bd. Anesthesiology (dir.; sec.-treas. 1948-58, pres. 1959). Intern Waterbury (Conn.) Hosp., 1938-39, cons. staff, 1955-80; resident in anesthesiology Hartford (Conn.) Hosp., 1939-41, clin. asst., 1942-43, acting chief, 1942-45, asst., 1943-44, asso., 1944-45, acting dir., 1963-64, dir. dept., 1964-73, sr. anesthesiologist, 1959-79, hon. anesthesiologist, 1979—; prof., head dept. anesthesiology Temple U. Med. Sch. and Hosp., 1946-49; med. dir. Hartford Surg. Center, 1976-83; mem. Adv. Bd. Med. Specialists, 1948-59, exec. com., 1958-59. Mem. Am. Soc. Anesthesiologists (bd. dirs. 1943-49, sec. 1946-49), A.M.A., Conn., Hartford County, Hartford med. socs., New Eng., Conn. socs. anesthesiologists, Kappa Delta Rho. Roman Catholic. Home and. Office: 30 Rosedale Rd West Hartford CT 06107

HICKEL, WALTER JOSEPH, construction executive, former governor Alaska; b. nr. Claflin, Kans., Aug. 18, 1919; s. Robert A. and Emma (Zecha) H.; m. Janice Cannon, Sept. 22, 1941 (dec. Aug. 1943); 1 son, Theodore; m. Ermalee Strutz, Nov. 22, 1945; children: Robert, Walter, Jack, Joseph, Karl. Student pub. schs., Claflin; D.Eng., Stevens Inst. Tech., 1970, Mich. Tech. U., 1973; LL.D., St. Mary of Plains Coll., St. Martin's Coll., U. Md., h4Adelphi U., h4U. San Diego, Rensselaer Poly. Inst., 1973, U. Alaska, 1976; D.Pub. Adminstrn., Willamette U. Builder-owner, Traveler's Inn, Anchorage, 1953—, Fairbanks, Alaska, 1955—, Hickel Constrn. Co., Anchorage, 1947—, Hotel Captain Cook, No. Lights Shopping Center, Univ. Shopping Center, Anchorage; chmn. bd. Hickel Investment Co.; gov., State of Alaska, 1966-69, sec. U.S. Dept. Interior, 1969-70; dir. Western Airlines, Rowan Cos., Inc.; mem. world adv. council Internat. Design Sci. Inst.; mem. com. on sci. freedom and responsibility AAAS. Mem. Republican Nat. Com., 1954-64; bd. regents Gonzaga U.; bd. dirs. Salk Inst. Named Alaskan of Year, 1969; recipient DeSmet medal Gonzaga U., 1969, Horatio Alger award, 1972; named Man of Year, Ripon Soc., 1970. Mem. Pioneers of Alaska, Alaska C. of C. (chmn. econ. devel. com.), Equestrian Order Holy Sepulchre, Knights Malta. Clubs: Elks, KC, Capitol Hill, Washington Athletic (Washington). Home: 1905 Loussac Dr Anchorage AK 99503 Office: Hotel Captain Cook 939 W 5th Ave Anchorage AK 99501 *We shall never understand peace, justice and the living of life until we recognize that all people are human and that humans are the most precious things on earth.*

HICKEN, PHILIP BURNHAM, artist; b. Lynn, Mass., June 27, 1910; s. Willis and Lena (Burnham) H.; m. Evangeline Chase, June 5, 1937; Children—Tana Val, Theo Jo. Student Mass. Sch. Art, 1928-32. Nat., internat exhibits, 1936—; lectr. Sch. of Mus. Fine Arts, Boston, Sch. Practical Arts, and Butera Sch. Fine Arts, 1947; instr. Grad. Sch. Design, Harvard, 1950-54; instr. drawing Boston U. Sch. Fine and Applied Arts, 1955-56; chmn. dept. design Sch. Practical Art, Boston, 1956—; chmn. dept. fine arts Art Inst. Boston, 1969—. Represented in permanent collections, Met. Mus. Art, N.Y.C., Library of Congress, Phila. Mus. Fine Art, Nat. Bezalel Mus., Jerusalem, many others, mural, Boston Five Cents Savs. Bank; combat art assignment Okinawa, U.S. Dept. Mil. History, 1970; Easel and mural painter Fed. Art Project. Served as artist AUS, 1942-45. Recipient prizes Black Mountain (N.C.) Art Club, 1943; Springfield (Mass.) Soldier Art, 1944; New Eng. Soldier Art, 1944; Mint Mus., Charlotte, N.C., 1946; 1st Cambridge (Mass.) Art Assn. Ann., 1953; purchase award Bklyn. Mus. Print Ann., 1958; 1st award Nantucket Art Assn. Annual, 1958, 68; Directors award Nat. Soc. Casein Painters, 1963; 1st award Natick (Mass.) Art Festival, 1971, Copley Soc., Boston. Fellow Royal Soc. Arts, London; mem. Nat. Serigraph Soc., Boston Printmakers, Boston Soc. Water Color Painters, Nantucket Artists Assn. Address: 23 Pine St Nantucket MA 02554 *Art is an all consuming religion, a philosophy, a way of life. The driving motivation to create is inherent in its disciples and the compulsive urge to speak in the language of paint refuses denial.*

HICKEN, VICTOR, historian, educator; b. Witt, Ill., Sept. 28, 1921; s. Thomas and Ann (Atherton) H.; m. Mary Patricia O'Connell, Dec. 28, 1943; children—Jeffrey Price, Brian Thomas, Elizabeth Ann, Daniel Joseph. B.Ed., So. Ill. U., 1943; M.A., 4U. Ill., 1947, Ph.D., 1955. Asst. U. Ill., 1950-51; instr. Western Ill. U., Macomb, 1947-50, prof., 1951—, chmn. dept. history, 1967-69, Distinguished prof. history, 1976—; vis. prof. U. Salzburg, Austria, 1971. Author: Illinois in the Civil War, 1966, The Settlement of Western Illinois, 1966, Western Illinois Factbook, 1968, Illinois at War, 1968, The American Fighting Man, 1969, The Purple and the Gold, 1970, The Urbanization of Illinois; The World Is Coming to An End, 1976, Gallery of American Heroes, 3 vols, 1976, Between the Rivers, Vols. I and II, 1982-83, Illinois: Its History and Legacy, 1983. Mem. faculty com. Higher Edn. Planning Commn. Ill. Served to lt. USNR, 1943-46. Mem. Ill. Hist.

Soc. (pres. 1975-76, dir.), Pi Alpha Theta, Pi Gamma Mu. Episcopalian. Club: Macomb Country. Home: 615 Lincoln Dr Macomb IL 61455 *I have always felt that, in doing the best I can with what I have in the way of talent—honestly, decently, and without the thought of pleasing others in order for my own advancement—that my children, when reaching their majority or at least their maturity, would say of their father: "He was really quite a man! He was everything I would want to be."*

HICKERSON, GLENN LINDSEY, aerospace company executive; b. Burbank, Calif., Aug. 22, 1937; s. Ralph M. and Sarah Lawson (Lindsey) H.; m. Jane Fortune Arthur, Feb. 24, 1973. B.A. in Bus. Adminstrn, Claremont Men's Coll., 1959; M.B.A., N.Y. U., 1960. Exec. asst. Douglas Aircraft Co., Santa Monica, Calif., 1963; sec., treas. Douglas Finance Corp., Long Beach, Calif., 1964-67, regional mgr. customer financing, 1967; exec. asst. to pres. Universal Airlines, Inc., Detroit, 1967-68, v.p., treas., asst. sec., 1968-69, pres., 1969-72; v.p., treas., asst. sec. Universal Aircraft Service, Inc., Detroit, 1968-69, chmn. bd., 1969-72; v.p., treas. Universal Airlines Co., Detroit, 1968-69, pres., 1969-72; group v.p. Marriott Hotels, Inc., Washington, 1972-76; dir. sales Far East and Australia Lockheed Calif. Co., 1976-78, dir. mktg. Americas, 1978-79, dir. mktg. Internat., 1979-81; v.p., internat. sales, 1981-83; v.p. comml. mktg. internat. Douglas Aircraft Co., McDonnell Douglas Corp., 1983—. Served to lt. (j.g.) USCGR, 1960-62. H.B. Earhart Found. fellow, 1962. Mem. Internat. Assn. Charter Airlines (exec. com. 1971). Home: 2332 Mandeville Canyon Rd Los Angeles CA 90049 Office: 3855 Lakewood Blvd Long Beach CA 90846

HICKEY, EDWARD HUTCHINS, lawyer; b. Boston, July 22, 1912; s. James M. and Mary (Simpson) H.; m. Ragnhild Tait, Feb. 25, 1941; children: Shelagh (Mrs. George M. Covington), Karen, John. A.B. cum laude, Harvard U., 1933, LL.B., 1936. Bar: Mass. 1936, D.C. 1946, Ill. 1957. Practice in, Boston, 1936-38, Washington, 1938-57, Chgo., 1957—; with Dept. Justice, 1938-42; spl. asst. to Atty. Gen., chief gen. litigation sect., 1945-57; counsel firm Bell, Boyd, Lloyd, Haddad & Burns, 1957—; dir. First Nat. Bank of Winnetka. Trustee Village of Winnetka, 1971-72, pres. village, 1972-74; Pres. Winnetka Community Chest, 1963-64; chmn. Winnetka Bicentennial Com., 1975-76; bd. dirs. Great Books Found., United Charities of Chgo. Served as lt. USNR, World War II. Decorated Presdl. citation. Fellow Am. Coll. Trial Lawyers; mem. Fed. Bar Assn., ABA, Ill. Bar Assn., Chgo. Bar Assn. (chmn. legal aid 1969, chmn. urban affairs 1970), 7th Fed. Circuit Bar Assn. (pres. 1974-75), Nat. Legal Aid and Defender Assn., Am. Law Inst., Am. Judicature Soc., Jud. Conf. U.S. (com. on rules of practice and procedure), Harvard U. Alumni Assn. (dir. 1981-84), Law Club Chgo. Clubs: Attic, Harvard (pres. 1973-75), University (Chgo.)). Home: 823 Humboldt Ave Winnetka IL 60093 Office: Bell Boyd Lloyd Three First National Plaza 70 W Madison St Chicago IL 60602

HICKEY, EDWARD VINCENT, JR., White House official; b. Dedham, Mass., July 15, 1935; s. Edward Vincent and Marion Rosaire (Caulfield) H.; m. Barbara Ann Burke, June 6, 1959; children: Edward V. III, Michael F., Joseph G., Paul V., John D., David T., Daniel J. B.S. in Bus. Adminstrn., Boston Coll., 1960; grad., Treasury Law Enforcemtn Officers Sch., 1964, U.S. Secret Service Spl. Agt. Sch., 1965. Juvenile officer Mass. Youth Authority, Boston, 1960-64; spl. agt. U.S. Secret Service, Boston, 1964-69; exec. dir. Calif. State Police, Sacramento, 1969-74; asst. dir. Office of Security, Dept. of State, Washington, 1974-78; sr. regional security officer Dept. of State, London, 1978-80; asst. to Pres., dir. spl. support services The White House, Washington, 1981—. Served to cpl. U.S. Army, 1954-56. Recipient Dirs. Honor award U.S. Secret Service, 1974. Mem. Internat. Assn. Chiefs of Police, Boston Coll. Alumni Assn., Friendly Sons of Saint Patrick (Washington chpt.). Republican. Roman Catholic. Office: The White House 1600 Pennsylvania Ave NW Washington DC 20500

HICKEY, FRANK G., electronic components and equipment manufacturing company executive; b. 1927. B.S. in Bus. Adminstrn., U. Dayton, 1950. Vice pres. Tait Mfg. Co., 1953-63; pres. Fairbanks-Morse Pump div. Colt. Industries Inc., 1963-65; with Gen. Instrument Corp., N.Y.C., 1965—, corp. v.p. capacitor group, 1966-70, exec. v.p. components group, 1970-72, pres., chief operating officer, 1972-74, chief exec. officer, pres., 1975—, chmn., 1975—, also dir. Served with USN, 1945-46. Office: Gen Instrument Corp 1775 Broadway St New York NY 10019 *

HICKEY, HOWARD WESLEY, educator; b. Bozeman, Mont., Oct. 20, 1930; s. Wesley Grandon and Frances Mildred (Howard) H.; m. Kay Young, July 1, 1976; children—Darcianne, Benjamin, Morris, Stuart, Bryan; 1 dau. by previous marriage, Brooks. B.A., Western Wash. U., 1953, M.Ed., 1958; M.A., Bowdoin Coll., 1962; Ph.D., Mich. State U., 1968. Dir. fed. programs Puyallup (Wash.) Schs., 1962-66; asst. prof. elem. edn. Mich. State U., East Lansing, 1968-71; asso. prof., dir. Mott Inst. for Community Improvement, Mich. State U., 1971-77, prof. higher edn., 1978—; cons. in field. Author: (with Curt Van Voorhees) Role of the School in Community Education, 1969; asso. editor: Community Edn. Jour, 1971-74; contbr. articles to profl. jours. NSF fellow, 1958, 61-62; Mott fellow, 1966-67. Mem. Nat. Community Edn. Assn., Nat. Soc. Study Edn., Phi Delta Kappa. Episcopalian. Club: Rotary (pres. 1965-66). Home: 3885 Binghamton St Okemos MI 48864 Office: 420 Erickson Hall East Lansing MI 48824

HICKEY, JAMES ALOYSIUS, archbishop; b. Midland, Mich., Oct. 11, 1920; s. James P. and Agnes (Ryan); s. James P. and Agnes (Hickey). J.C.D., Lateran U., Italy, 1950; S.T.D., Angelicum U., Italy, 1951; M.A., Mich. State U., 1962. Ordained priest Roman Catholic Ch., 1946; sec. to, Bishop of Saginaw, 1951-60; rector St. Paul Sem., Saginaw, Mich., 1960-68; aux. bishop, Saginaw, 1967-69; chmn. bishops' com. on Priestly Formation, 1968-69; rector N.Am. Coll., Rome, 1969-74; bishop of Cleve., 1974-80, archbishop of Washington, 1980—; chancellor Cath. U. Am., 1980—; mem. Central Com. for 1975 Holy Year, 1973-75; chmn. Bishop's Com. Pastoral Research and Practices, 1974-77, Bishop's Com. for Doctrine, 1979-82; chmn. bd. trustees Nat. Shrine of Immaculate Conception, 1980—. Address: Archdiocese of Washington Archdiocesan Pastoral Center PO Box 29260 Washington DC 20017

HICKEY, JOHN THOMAS, electronics company executive; b. Chgo., Oct. 28, 1925; s. Matthew J., Jr. and Naomi (Pope) H.; m. Joanne R. Keating, Sept. 17, 1949; children: Kathleen Hickey Coakley, John, Michael, James, Roger. B.S. in Commerce, Loyola U., Chgo., 1948; M.B.A., U. Chgo., 1952. With Motorola Inc. (and subs.), 1948—, gen. mgr. semicondr. div., 1955-58, asst. to pres., 1958-62, dir. long range planning, 1962-65, v.p. planning, 1965-70, v.p. finance, sec., 1970-74, sr. v.p., chief fin. officer, dir., 1974-84, exec. v.p., chief fin. officer, dir., 1984—; dir. Hickey & Co., Chgo., Benefit Trust Life Ins. Co. Mem. adv. com. to sch. bus. U. Ill., Champaign-Urbana. Served with AUS, 1944-46. Club: Skokie Country (Glencoe). Home: 614 South Ave Glencoe IL 60022 Office: 1303 E Algonquin Rd Schaumburg IL 60196

HICKEY, LEO J(OSEPH), museum director, educator; b. Phila., Apr. 26, 1940; s. James J(oseph) and Helen Marie (Schwartz) H.; m. Judity McKendry, June 29, 1968; children: Geoffrey Alan, Damian Michael, Jason Alexander. B.S., Villanova U., 1962; M.A., Princeton U., 1964; postgrad., Rutgers U., 1963-65; Ph.D., Princeton U., 1967; M.A. (privatim), Yale U., 1983. Postdoctoral fellow NRC-Smithsonian Inst., Washington, 1966-69, assoc. curator, 1969-80; chmn. exhibits. com. Natural History Mus., Smithsonian, 1973-75, curator, 1980-82; prof. biology and geology Yale U., New Haven, Conn., 1982—; dir. Peabody Mus., Yale U., 1982—; adj. prof. botany U. Md., College Park, 1981—; adj. prof. geology U. Pa., Phila., 1982—; past pres., pres., v.p. Yellowston-Bighorn Research Assn., Red Lodge, Mich., 1979—; dir. Mus. of Am. Theatre, New Haven, Conn., 1983—. Author: Stratigraphy and Paleobotany of Golden Valley Formation, 1977; co-author: Early Evolution of Flowering Plants, 1976-77 (H.A. Gleason award 1977); author: classification system Leaf Architecture, 1972. Recipient best paper award Geol. Soc. Washington, 1981, Disting. Alumnus award Villanova U., 1982; grantee Smithsonian Research Found., 1972-76, Nat. Geog. Soc., 1979. Mem. Geol. Soc. Am., Bot. Soc. Am., AAAS, Internat. Assn. Plant Taxonomists, Paleontol. Soc. Democrat. Roman Catholic. Club: Moreys (New Haven). Home: 82 Blake Rd Hamden CT 06517 Office: Peabody Mus of Natural History PO Box 6666 New Haven CT 06511

HICKEY, MARGARET A., editor; b. Kansas City, Mar. 14, 1902; d. Charles L. and Elizabeth (Wynne) H.; m. Joseph T. Strubinger, Oct. 20, 1935 (dec. Oct. 1973). J.D., U. Mo., 1928; LL.D., Cedar Crest Coll., 1952, MacMurray Coll., 1957; L.H.D., Wilson Coll., 1962; Litt.D., St. Mary's Coll. Notre Dame, 1964; D.Ed., Culver-Stockton Coll., 1966; LL.D., U. Mo. at St. Louis, 1975. Bar: bar 1928. Pvt. practice of law, 1928-33; founder, dir. Miss Hickey's Sch. for Secretaries, St. Louis, 1933-69; editor Ladies Home Jour., N.Y.C.; Apptd. chmn. nat. women's adv. com. and observer Labor-Mgmt. Com., War Manpower Commn., 1942-45; sec. nat. citizens com. U.S. Office Edn.; mem. exec. com. Nat. Social Welfare Assembly; v.p.; mem. adv. bd. Point Four Program, 1950-52; mem. President's adv. com. Vol. Fgn. Aid, AID, 1952—, vice-chmn., 1962-73, chmn., 1973-76; com. White House Conf. Edn.; bd. govs. A.R.C., 1947-53, 55-60, vice chmn. bd., 1947-53, 59-61, dep. to chmn., 1960-73; vice chmn. med. and social adv. com. League Red Cross Socs.; mem. Nat. Manpower Council; mem. bd. Nat. Health Council, 1948-56; mem. President's Nat. Com. White House Conf. Children and Youth, 1960; pres. Nat. Conf. Social Work, 1956-57; chmn. organizing com. Internat. Conf. Social Work, 1966; chmn. Nat. Citizens Council Status Women, 1964-66; mem. commn. social scis. NSF, 1968-69. Pub. affairs editor: Ladies Home Jour. Mem. bd. overseers Brandeis U.; mem. vis. com. Grad. Sch. Edn., Harvard; trustee Tuskegee Inst. Am. Youth Found.; bd. dirs. Nat. Assn. for Mental Health, 1970-76. Recipient Benjamin Franklin award for distinguished pub. service journalism, 1953; St. Louis Woman of Achievement award, 1957; Distinguished Alumni award U. Mo. Kansas City, 1972. Mem. Internat. Fedn. Bus. and Profl. Women (chmn. UN com., v.p.), Nat. Fedn. Bus. and Profl. Women (hon. pres.), Am. Newspaper Women's Club, Nat. Fedn. Press Women, Mo. Bar, Women's Bar Assn., Kappa Beta Pi. Home: 3940 E Timrod Apt 207 Tucson AZ 85711 Office: 3 Park Ave New York NY 10022

HICKEY, MATTHEW JOSEPH, III, investment banker; b. Chgo., Oct. 26, 1929; s. Matthew Joseph and Naomi (Pope) H. Student, Holy Cross Coll., 1947-48; B.Sc., Loyola U., Chgo., 1950. With Hickey & Co., Chgo., 1950—, v.p., 1954-69, pres., dir., 1969—; mem. Midwest Stock Exchange, 1950—; chmn. Matickey Corp., Chgo.; pres. MJH Corp.; dir. Uptown Fed. Savs. & Loan Assn., Chgo., Greif Bros. Corp., Delaware, Ohio, River Woods Inc., Spring Green, Wis., Soterra Inc., Delaware, Ohio.; Mem. bd. govs. Chgo. Assn. Stock Exchange Firms, 1955-61, treas., 1958-59, vice chmn., 1960-61. Mem. citizens bd. Loyola U., 1959—, Mundelein Coll., 1959—, De Paul U., 1960—; fin. chmn. Chgo. Red Cross, 1955-57; bd. dirs., asst. sec. Hundred Club Cook County, Chgo.; trustee St. Joseph's Coll., Rensselear, Ind., Sch. St. Maur, Atchinson, Kans. Served with AUS, 1951-54. Mem. AIM, Presidents Assn. (dir. Chgo.), U.S. Naval Inst. (dir.), Chgo. Athletic Assn. (dir., v.p.), Bond Club Chgo., Municipal Bond Club, Chgo. Security Traders Assn., SAR, Wedgwood Soc. (dir. Chgo.), President's Assn. (Chgo.), Sovereign Mil. Order Knights of Malta. Roman Catholic. Clubs: Chgo. Athletic, Chgo. Yacht (Chgo.); Palm Bay, Racquet (Miami, Fla.); Jockey (Acapulco, Mex.); Oyster Pond Yacht (Sint Maarten, Dutch West Indies); Le Mirador Country (Lake Geneva, Switzerland). Home: 1340 N Astor St Chicago IL 60610 Office: 135 S LaSalle St Chicago IL 60603 *With all the give and take in life, I aspire to think of everyday as Christmas.*

HICKEY, ROBERT CORNELIUS, surgeon, educator; b. Hallstead, Pa., Dec. 9, 1917; s. Cornelius E. and Jennie (Murphy) H.; m. Rose Van Vranken, June 11, 1942; children: Kathryn Ann (Mrs. Geoffrey White), Robert C., Stephen P., Dennis V., Sarah E. B.S., Cornell U., 1938, M.D., 1942; postgrad., State U. Iowa, U.S. Naval Hosp., San Diego, Meml. Hosp. Cancer and Allied Diseases, N.Y.C. Diplomate: Am. Bd. Surgery. Staff U. Hosp. and State U. Iowa, 1951-62, successively asso. surgery, clin. asst. prof., asso. prof., 1951-57, prof. surgery, 1957-62, asso. dean research in medicine, 1955-62; asso. dir. research U. Tex. M.D. Anderson Hosp. and Tumor Inst., 1962-63, dir., 1969—, exec. v.p., 1976—; prof. surgery U. Tex., 1962-63, 68—; prof., chmn. dept. surgery U. Wis. Med. Sch., Madison, 1963-68; cons. surgeon gen. USPHS, 1959-68. Dir. Iowa div. Am. Cancer Soc., 1954-62; pres. Iowa div., 1959-60; dir.-at-large Tex. div., 1968—; mem. U.S. nat. com. Internat., Union Against Cancer, 1977—; mem. nat. cancer adv. com. USPHS, 1980—. Served to lt. M.C. USNR, 1943-46. Fellow A.C.S. (gov. 1968-71, vice chmn. bd. govs. 1971-73, chmn. bd. 1973-74, pres. So. Tex. chpt.); mem. Houston Surg. Soc., Am. Soc. Clin. Oncology, AAAS, AAUP, Am. Radium Soc. (v.p. 1964-65), Central Surg. Assn., AMA, N.Y. Acad. Scis., James Ewing Soc. (v.p. 1964-65), Western Surg. Assn. (v.p. 1973-74), Iowa Acad. Surgery (pres. 1962), Am. Surg. Assn., Soc. Surgery Alimentary Tract (v.p. 1977—), Tex. Surg. Soc., Sigma Xi. Home: 435 Tallowood Dr Houston TX 77024

HICKEY, SISTER RUTH CECELIA, religious administrator; b. Erie, Pa., July 28, 1914; d. Sherman Sylvester and Nell (McKinney) H. Grad., St. Vincent's Sch. Nursing, Toledo, 1936; B.S., d'Youville Coll., U. Montreal, 1949; postgrad., Cath. U., 1950, U. B.C.; M.A., Columbia U., 1954. Head nurse medicine-surgery St. Vincent Hosp. and Med. Center, Toledo, 1936-38, nursing service and asst. adminstr., 1956-62, adminstr., 1962-69; nursing cons., 1969—; asso. exec. dir. St. Boniface Gen. Hosp., Winnipeg, Man., Can., 1973-79, v.p., 1974-79, Taché Nursing Center, Winnipeg, 1974-79; regional sec. Can. Religious Conf., Winnipeg, 1979—; nursing instr. St. Mary's Hosp., Montreal, 1940-42; supr. obstetrics, surgery St. Peter's Gen. Hosp., New Brunswick, 1942-47; dir. sch. nursing and nursing service Regina Grey Nuns Hosp., Regina, Sask., Can., 1955-56. Bd. dirs., v.p. Bd. Catholic Hosps. Can., 1974—; bd. dirs. Canadian Council Hosp. Accreditation; bd. govs. U. Man., 1976—; bd. dirs. Sara Riel Corp., 1983—. Named Toledo Woman of Year, 1969. Fellow Am. Coll. Hosp. Adminstrs.; mem. Am. Acad. Med. Adminstrs., Canadian Hsop. Assn. (dir.), Am.), Ohio hosp. nurses assns., Am., Ohio nurses assns., Nat. Assembly Women Religious Edn., Cath. Health Assn. Man. (pres. 1974—). Address: #2 366 Enfield Crescent Winnipeg MB R2H 1C7 Canada

HICKLER, ROGER BALDWIN, physician, educator; b. Medford, Mass., Oct. 26, 1925; s. Walter Rol and Rosalie Baldwin (Dunlap) H.; m. Dorothy Masterton, July 27, 1974; children—Luisa, Mathew, Sarah, Samuel. Student, M.I.T., 1943-45; M.D., Harvard U., 1949. Diplomate: Am. Bd. Internal Medicine. Intern Peter Bent Brigham Hosp., Boston, 1949-50, resident, 1952-54; practice medicine, specializing in internal medicine, Worcester, Mass., 1971—; dir. hypertension unit Peter Bent Brigham Hosp., 1961-69; chief of medicine Framingham Union Hosp., 1969-71; prof., chmn. dept. medicine U. Mass. Med. Sch., 1971-77; Lamar Soutter Disting. prof. medicine, dir. unit for study of aging Med. Center, 1977—. Contbr. articles to med. jours. Served with USNR, 1950-52. Recipient Research Career award NIH, 1961-66; investigator Howard Hughes Med. Inst., 1966-69. Fellow A.C.P., Am. Coll. Cardiology; mem. Am. Soc. Clin. Investigation, Am. Heart Assn. (adv. bd. Council for High Blood Pressure Research), Nat. Hypertension Council (adv. council). Unitarian. Home: 339 Boston Rd Sutton MA 01527 Office: 55 Lake Ave N Worcester MA 01605

HICKLIN, ROBERT MCLEAN, textile co. exec.; b. Richburg, S.C., May 10, 1925; s. Ira Kell and Helen (McRae) H.; m. Jean Ellen Horton, Oct. 2, 1948; children—Robert, David Mark, Ann Ivy, Ira Kell. B.S. in Textile Engring, Clemson U., 1948. Trainee, Springs Mills, Lancaster, S.C., 1948-49; various mgmt. positions Reeves Bros. Inc., Spartanburg, S.C., 1949—, exec. v.p., dir., 1968—. Served with USNR, 1943-46. Presbyn. Office: PO Box 892 Spartanburg SC 29304

HICKLING, M. ANTHONY, legal educator; b. Scunthorpe, Lincolnshire, Eng., June 3, 1934; s. Bertram and Clara (Dixon) H.; m. Margaret Burtch, May 18, 1963; children: Robert Ann, Robert Anthony, James Stephen Burtch. LL.B., King's Coll., London U., 1955, Ph.D., 1958, LL.D., 1976. Asst. lectr., then lectr. King's Coll. Faculty Law, 1960-66; assoc. prof. U. B.C. Faculty Law, Vancouver, 1966-69, prof. law, 1974—; prof. U. Western Ont. Faculty Law, 1969-74; labour arbitrator. Author: Labour Disputes and Unemployment Insurance in England and Canada, 1975; Editor: Western Labour Arbitration Cases; editor: Citrine's Trade Union Law, 1967. Served with Brit. Army, 1958-60. Mem. Can. Assn. Law Tchrs., Can. Bar Assn., Soc. Public Tchrs. Law, Brit. Inst. Internat. and Comparative Law. Mem. United Ch. Can. Office: 1822 East Mall Vancouver BC V6T 1Y1 Canada *

HICKMAN, BERT GEORGE, JR., economist, educator; b. Los Angeles, Oct. 6, 1924; s. Bert George and Caroline E. (Douglass) H.; m. Edythe Anne Warshauer, Feb. 9, 1947; children: Wendy Elizabeth, Paul Lawrence, Alison Diane. B.S., U. Calif.-Berkeley, 1947, Ph.D., 1951. Instr. Stanford U., 1949-51; research asso. Nat. Bur. Econ. Research, 1951-52; asst. prof. Northwestern, 1952-54; mem. sr. staff Council Econ. Advisers, 1954-56; research asso. Brookings Instn., 1956-58, mem. sr. staff, 1958-66; prof. Stanford U., 1966—; vis. prof. U. Calif. at Berkeley, 1960, London Grad. Sch. Bus Studies, 1972-73, Kyoto U., 1977; NSF fellow Netherlands Econometric Inst., Rotterdam, 1964-65; Ford Found. Faculty research fellow, 1968-69; mem. com. econ. stability Social Sci. Research Council, 1959-61, chmn., 1962—. Author: Growth and Stability of the Postwar Economy, 1960, Investment Demand and U.S. Economic Growth, 1965, (with Robert M. Coen) An Annual Growth Model of the U.S. Economy, 1976; Editor: Quantitative Planning of Economic Policy, 1965, Econometric Models of Cyclical Behavior, 1972; co-editor: Global International Economic Models, 1983; editor: Global Econometrics, 1983; Contbr. articles to profl. jours. Served with USNR, 1943-46. Fellow Econometric Soc.; mem. Am. Econ. Assn. (chmn. census adv. com. 1968-71, tech. subcom. to rev. bus. cycle devels. 1962-68), Phi Beta Kappa, Phi Eta Sigma. Home: 904 Lathrop Dr Stanford CA 94305

HICKMAN, CLEVELAND PENDLETON, JR., educator; b. Greencastle, Ind., Oct. 29, 1928; m. Ethel Rae Rickenbacher, Aug. 19, 1950; children: Andrew Richard, Diane Elaine. A.B., DePauw U., 1950; M.S., U. N.H., 1953; Ph.D. in Zoology (B.C. Elec. scholar), U. B.C., 1958. Demonstrator zoology DePauw U., Greencastle, 1948-50; asst. in biology U. N.H., 1950-52; fishery researcher U. Wash., Seattle, 1954-55; asst. in zoology U. B.C., 1955-58; asst. prof. U. Alta., 1958-63, asso. prof., 1963-67; asso. prof. biology Washington and Lee U., Lexington, Va., 1967-70, prof., 1970—. Author: (with F.M. Hickman and L.S. Roberts) Biology of Animals, 3d edit, 1982, Integrated Principles of Zoology, 6th edit, 1979, (with William S. Hoar) A Laboratory Companion for General and Comparative Physiology, 3d edit, 1983; contbr. numerous articles to profl. jours. Nat. Research Council Can. grantee, 1959-67; sr. research fellow, 1965-66; NIH grantee, 1962-65; NSF grantee, 1970-74. Office: Dept Biology Washington and Lee U Lexington VA 24450

HICKMAN, DARRELL DAVID, state justice; b. Searcy, Ark., Feb. 6, 1935; s. James Paul and Mildred Margaret (Jackson) H.; m. Kerry Lee Hardcastle, Oct. 16, 1971; children: Dana, David, Torrie. Student, Harding Coll., Searcy, 1952-55; LL.B., U. Ark., 1958. Bar: Ark. 1958. Pvt. practice, Searcy, 1964-70, dep. pros. atty., White and Woodruff counties, 1965; chancery judge 1st Chancery Circuit, 1972-76; asso. justice Ark. Supreme Ct., 1977—. Served with USN, 1958-64. Judge Freedoms Found. awards, 1977. Mem. Ark. Bar Assn. Mem. Ch. of Christ. Office: Justice Bldg Little AR 72201 *

HICKMAN, FREDERIC W., lawyer; b. Sioux City, Iowa, June 30, 1927; s. Simeon M. and Esther (Nixon) H.; m. Katherine Heald, July 15, 1964; children: Mary, Sara. A.B., Harvard U., 1948; LL.B. magna cum laude, 1951. Bar: Ill. 1951. Asso. firm Sidley & Austin, Chgo., 1951-55; partner firm Hopkins & Sutter, Chgo., 1956-71, 75—; asst. sec. for tax policy Dept. Treasury, Washington, 1972-75; tech. adv. on taxation Am. Enterprise Inst.; draftsman Ill. Income Tax, 1969; lectr. on taxation. Mem. Ill. Humanities Council, 1977-82; mem. Citizens Commn. on Public Sch. Fin., 1977-78; trustee Am. Conservatory Music, 1980—; bd. dirs. Winnetka Community House, 1980—. Served with USN, 1945-46. Mem. ABA (chmn. com. on depreciation 1966-68, com. on capital formation 1976-78, council 1980-83), Internat. Fiscal Assn. (dir. 1973-77). Republican. Methodist. Clubs: Comml., Union League, Mid-Day, Cliff Dwellers, Law, Legal (Chgo.) (pres. 1980-81); Chikaming Country (Lakeside, Mich.); Capitol Hill [(Washington). Home: 888 Tower Rd Winnetka IL 60093 Office: 3 First Nat Plaza Chicago IL 60602

HICKMAN, J. KENNETH, accounting company executive; b. Bklyn., July 8, 1928; s. Walter E. and Mildred C. (Ehrhardt) H.; m. Irene A. Davis, May 12, 1956; children: Patricia, Carolyn, Beth. B.S. cum laude, Fordham U., 1951. Salesman Charles W. Sommer & Bro., Inc., N.Y.C., 1946-51; with Arthur Andersen & Co. (C.P.A.s), 1953—; mng. partner Newark office, 1963-72, N.Y. office, 1972—. Trustee Regis High Sch., N.Y.C., chmn. bd. trustees, N.Y.C., 1982—; trustee, mem. council Fordham U.; advisory council Fordham U. Coll. Bus. Adminstrn.; mem. advisory council Grad. Sch., Rutgers U. Served as 1st lt. AUS, 1951-53. Mem. Nat. Fgn. Trade Council (dir. 1980—, chmn. European Communities com. 1981—), Bus. Council Internat. Understanding (dir. 1981—), Fordham U. Alumni Fedn. (nat. chmn. 1973-75), Am. Inst. C.P.A.s, N.J. Soc. C.P.A.s (trustee 1971-73), N.Y. State Soc. C.P.A.s, Nat. Assn. Accts., Am. Accounting Assn., Ireland-U.S. Council for Commerce and Industry (trustee 1978—, v.p. 1979—), Alpha Kappa Psi, Beta Gamma Sigma. Clubs: Economic (N.Y.); Board Room (N.Y.C.); Beacon Hill (Summit). Home: 45 Templar Way Summit NJ 07901 Office: 1345 Ave of Americas New York NY 10105

HICKMAN, JAMES BLAKE, chemistry educator; b. Charleston, W.Va., Nov. 29, 1921; s. James Howard and Bessie (Barnsgrove) H.;

m. Martha Louise Hornor, June 25, 1948. B.S. in Chemistry, W.Va. U., 1942, M.S., 1943; Ph.D., Pa. State U., 1950. Chemist Carbide and Carbon Chem. div. (Union Carbide and Carbon), South Charleston, W.Va., 1943-45; instr. chemistry W.Va. U., 1946-49, 50-51; asst. prof. chemistry, 1951-56, asso. prof., 1956-62, prof. chemistry, 1962-83, prof. emeritus, 1983—; dir. NSF Summer insts., 1959—; cons. chem. info. retrieval, 1983—; dir. NSF Acad. Year Insts., 1961-65. Author Physical Science, 1966, The Nature of Science, 1970. Fellow AAAS, Am. Inst. Chemists; mem. Am. Chem. Soc., Royal Soc. Chemistry, W.Va. Acad. Sci. (pres. 1968-69), Phi Beta Kappa, Sigma Xi, Phi Lambda Upsilon. Republican. Baptist. Research on behavior of mixtures of non-electrolytes and sci. info. retrieval. Home: 145 Waitman St Morgantown WV 26505 *I thank God that learning and mental growth, which must go on as long as one lives, have served in my mind to make everything more beautiful and fascinating—seeing a scientific law illustrated in some commonplace event delights me now more than the first time I saw it so illustrated. A teacher must teach—35 years of formal teaching may be enough, but leaving the classroom can be an opportunity to address a wider audience of colleagues and of any who wish to learn.*

HICKMAN, JAMES CHARLES, educator; b. Indianola, Iowa, Aug. 27, 1927; s. James C. and Mabel L. (Fisher) H.; m. Margaret W. McKee, June 12, 1950; children—Charles Wallace, Donald Robert, Barbara Jean. B.A., Simpson Coll., 1950; M.S., U. Iowa, 1952, Ph.D., 1961. Actuarial asst. Bankers Life Co., Des Moines, 1952-57; asst. prof. dept. statistics U. Iowa, 1961-64, asso. prof., 1964-67, prof., 1967-72; prof. bus. and statistics U. Wis., Madison, 1972—; mem. panel of cons. on social security fin. Senate Fin. and House Ways and Mean Com., 1975-76; mem. adv. com. to Joint Bd. for Enrollment of Actuaries, 1976-78. Served with USAAF, 1945-47. Recipient Alumni Achievement award Simpson Coll., 1979; David Halmstad award for actuarial research Actuarial Ednl. Research Fund, 1979. Fellow Soc. Actuaries (v.p. 1975-77); mem. Casualty Actuarial Soc., Am. Acad. Actuaries, Am. Statis. Assn. Presbyterian. Home: 4917 Woodburn Dr Madison WI 53711 Office: 1155 Observatory Dr Madison WI 53706

HICKMAN, JOHN HAMPTON, III, entrepreneurial industrialist, investment banker, educator; b. Wilmington, Del., May 19, 1937; s. John Hampton Jr. and Martha (Barnett) H.; m. Barbara Spurlin; children: Erica Delius Hickman-Downs, Gretchen Leigh, Rochanya Charlotte Hickman-Generous, John Hampton IV. Student, Randolph-Macon Coll., 1954-56; A.B., Brown U., 1959; certificate in Chinese, Yale U., 1960, J.D., 1962. Investment banker McDonnell & Co., N.Y.C., 1964-68; partner investment banking firm J.H. Hickman & Co., 1969—; chmn. bd., chief exec. officer Seilon, Inc., 1968-69; chmn., chief exec. officer Nev. Nat. Bank, Reno, 1968—; chmn. Thomson Internat. Co., Thibodaux, La., 1968-69; chmn. bd., chief exec. officer Lockwood Corp., Gering, Nebr., 1968-69; chmn. bd. C.R. Burr & Co. (name now United Nurseries Corp.), Middlefield, Conn., 1972-75, Buffalo Capital Corp. (mcht. banking firm), N.Y., 1984—; founder chmn. bd. Peninsula Corp., Melfa, Va.; chmn. bd., pres. Nev. Nat. Bancorp, Las Vegas, 1968-69; pres. Delanair, Inc. (name now Nexus Industries), N.Y.C., 1969-70; dir., chmn. fin. com. Aberdeen Petroleum (name now Adobe Oil & Gas Co.), Tulsa, 1970-73; dir. Dissen & Juhn Corp., Webster, Nat. Health Care Affiliates, Inc., Buffalo; chmn. The Rochester Fund, 1978-81; mem. faculty M.B.A. program U. Conn.; vis. exec. U. N.C., Boone; prof. bus., chmn. dept. mgmt. Tenn. Wesleyan Coll.; prof., chmn. dept. mgmt. studies Rochester Inst. Tech., 1977-83; vis. prof. La. State U., Barry U., Miami, Fla. Author: Financing in the Entrepot Capital Market, 1968, East-West Investments, 1969, Spin-Offs As A Management Tool, Corporate Reorganization, 1972; Contbr.: Business Handbook for Photographers, 1980; articles to profl. jours. Trustee, chmn. finance com. Oceanic Soc., Stamford, Conn., 1973—; trustee N.Y. State Assn. for Human Services, 1977-80; bd. dirs. Genessee Valley Arts Found., Rochester, 1978-84; mem. Yale U. Alumni Assembly, 1976-79. Mem. Am. Mgmt. Assn. (world council pres.'s assn., lectr., editor publs.), Internat. Law Assn. (Am. br.), Fin. Execs. Inst. Clubs: Rochester Yacht, Univ., Yale of Eastern Conn. (pres.); Mid-day (Buffalo)). Office: Mount Morris Rd Geneseo NY 14454 *Fortitude is the most important virtue. Without it, life is an intolerable and disappointing series of surrenders—fortitude is what gives life dignity, even nobility. That so few dare to be eccentric is a central danger of the times.*

HICKMAN, LEON EDWARD, lawyer, business executive; b. Sioux City, Iowa, July 27, 1900; s. Charles Addison and Edith (Fogg) H.; m. Mayme Hoyt, Aug. 12, 1926; children: Hoyt Leon, Herbert Wilbur. A.B., Morningside Coll., 1922, LL.D., 1944; J.D., Harvard U., 1925; LL.D., Western Md. Coll., 1958, W.Va. Wesleyan Coll., 1960; L.H.D., S.D. Sch. Mines and Tech., 1956; D.B.A., Tenn. Wesleyan Coll., 1965. Bar: Pa. 1926. Partner Smith, Buchanan & Ingersoll and predecessor firms, Pitts., 1930-51; counsel firm Eckert, Seamans, Cherin & Mellott, Pitts., 1976—; v.p., gen. counsel Aluminum Co. Am., 1951-60, exec. v.p., 1959-67, exec. com., 1951-67, chmn. finance com., 1963-67, dir., 1951-71, Payless Cashways, Inc. Chmn. Action Housing, Inc., 1969-75, Pa. Housing Commn., 1970-71, Southwestern Pa. Regional Planning Commn., 1963-77; chmn. Gov's Commn. to Revise Pub. Employee Laws Pa., 1968; coordinating council United Meth. Ch., 1952-64, vice chmn. coordinating council, 1968-72, vice chmn. jud. council, 1964-72; trustee Morningside Coll., 1938-71, pres. bd. trustees, 1962-71. Mem. Am., Pa., Allegheny County bar assns., Assn. Bar City N.Y., Am. Law Inst. Republican. Clubs: Mason., Duquesne (Pitts.); Harvard-Yale-Princeton Western Pa., St. Clair Country. Home: 829 Osage Rd Pittsburgh PA 15243 Office: 600 Grant St Pittsburgh PA 15219

HICKOK, RICHARD SANFORD, accountant; b. Elizabeth, N.J., Nov. 3, 1925; s. Ernest Sherlock and Amy (McFadden) H.; m. Janet E. Allsopp, Sept. 24, 1948; children: Sanford, Steven, Jonathan, Wendy. B.S. in Econs, U. Pa., 1948. C.P.A., N.Y., N.J., Ohio, Tex., La. With firm Main Hurdman, N.Y.C., 1948—, partner, 1958—, mem. policy bd., 1971—, mng. partner, 1975—, chmn., 1980—; pres. Klynveld Main Goerdeler (internat. firm), 1981—; dir. Gen. Refactories, Dollar Dry Savs. Bank. Contbr. articles to profl. jours. Trustee Fin. Accounting Found., 1978-80. Served to lt. (j.g.) USNR, 1943-47. Mem. Am. Inst. C.P.A.'s (mem. council), N.Y., N.J., Ohio, Tex. State socs. C.P.A.'s. Clubs: Univ., Pilgrims (N.Y.C.); Econ., Baltusrol Golf, Eastward Ho. Home: Tempe Wick Rd Morristown NJ 07960 Office: Park Ave Plaza 55 E 52d St New York NY 10055

HICKS, ALLEN MORLEY, hosp. adminstr.; b. Toronto, Iowa, May 11, 1928; s. Perle and Grace (Mowry) H.; m. Sue Hicks; children by previous marriage—David, Dennis, Wendy, Patricia. Student, Long Beach City Coll., 1949-50; B.S., U. Iowa, 1952, M.S., 1954. Adminstrv. resident St. Lukes Hosp., Davenport, Ia., 1953-54; adminstr. Schmitt Meml. Hosp., Beardstown, Ill., 1954-57, Pekin (Ill.) Meml. Hosp., 1957-63, Ill. Masonic Hosp. and Med. Center, Chgo., 1963-72; pres. Community Hosp., Indpls., 1972—; Preceptor masters degree program in health and hosp. adminstrn. Adminstrn. U. Iowa; chmn. com. extended care Council on Assn. Service, 1963; pres. Chgo. Hosp. Council, 1970-71. Campaign chmn., bd. dirs., chmn. indsl. div. United Fund, Pekin, Ill., 1959-64; pres. Tazwell County United Cerebral Palsy, 1960-61; chmn. Cancer Crusade, Pekin, 1960-61; service chmn. Tazewell County, 1958-60; chmn. bd. Tomahawk dist. Creve Coeur council Boy Scouts Am., 1963-64; Bd. dirs. Cancer Soc., Hosp. Research and Devel. Inst., Inc. Served with USNR, 1945- 49, 51-52. Recipient Outstanding Young Man of Year award State Ill., 1960; Distinguished Service award Pekin Jr. C. of C., 1960; Boss of Year award Marquette chpt. Nat. Secs. Assn., 1962. Mem. Am. Hosp. Assn. (del. 1971—, chmn. com. community relations), Ill. Hosp.Assn. (trustee, chmn. com. personnel relations), Am. Coll. Hosp. Adminstrs., Am. Assn. Maternal and Infant Health, Ill. Welfare Assn., Ill. C. of C., Am. Legion, Am. Vets., Beta Gamma Sigma. Presbyn. (elder, trustee). Clubs: Mason, Elk, Kiwanian. Home: 5305 Hawthorne Dr Indianapolis IN 46226 Office: 1500 N Ritter Ave Indianapolis IN 46219

HICKS, BYRON ADNA, banker; b. Moneta, Va., Aug. 30, 1916; s. Wesley Peters and Sally Walthal (Holl) H.; m. Agnes Rose Cunningham, Apr. 20, 1940; children: Martha Holland, Celia Parry. Student, Roanoke Coll., 1934-35; B.S. in Econs, U. Va., 1938; postgrad., Stonier Grad. Sch. Banking, Rutgers U., 1950-52. With Univ. Credit Co., Raleigh, N.C., 1939-42, Hercules Powder Co., Radford, Va., 1942-43; with First Nat. Exchange Bank of Va., Roanoke, 1946—, chmn. bd., chief exec. officer, 1977—; also dir., mem. exec. com., mem. trust com.; with Dominion Bankshares Corp., Roanoke, 1967—, pres., chief adminstrv. officer, 1973-77, pres., chief exec. officer, 1977-81, chmn., chief exec. officer, 1981—, also dir., mem. exec. com. Bd. dirs., chmn. finance com. Community Hosp. of Roanoke Valley; trustee, mem. exec. com. Roanoke Coll.; trustee Va. Bapt. Children's Home, Va. Found. Ind. Colls. Served to lt. USNR, 1943-46. Baptist. Home: 2726 Cornwallis Ave SE Roanoke VA 24014 Office: PO Box 13327 Roanoke VA 24040

HICKS, CHARLES ROBERT, educator; b. Syracuse, N.Y., Apr. 7, 1920; s. Seward Bliss and Abbie (Teeple) H.; m. Ruth Frances Muller, June 13, 1942; children—William Seward, Robert Peter, John Charles. A.B., Syracuse U., 1942; M.A., 1944, Ph.D., 1953. Grad. instr. Syracuse U., 1942-44, instr. math. and edn., 1946-53; quality control engr. Eastman Kodak Co., 1944-46; mem. faculty Purdue U., Lafayette, Ind., 1953—, prof. edn., head dept., 1964-74, prof. edn. and statistics, 1974—, dir. tchr. edn., 1970-74; cons. in field, 1946—. Mem. Lafayette Bd. Edn., 1973-79; Trustee Judson Coll., Elgin, Ill., 1970—. Fellow Am. Soc. Quality Control (Brumbaugh award 1957, nat. v.p. 1969-71); mem. Am. Statis. Assn., Comparative and Internat. Edn. Soc., Biometric Soc., Phi Beta Kappa, Phi Delta Kappa. Baptist. Club: Kiwanian (past pres. Harrison club Lafayette, lt. gov. Sagamore div. 1975-76). Home: 1016 S 22d St Lafayette IN 47905

HICKS, CLIFFORD BYRON, mag. editor; b. Marshalltown, Iowa, Aug. 10, 1920; s. Nathan LeRoy and Kathryn Marie (Carson) H.; m. Rachel G. Reimer, May 12, 1945; children—David P., Douglas L., Gary R. B.S. cum laude, Northwestern U., 1942. With Popular Mechanics mag., Chgo., 1945—, editor, 1960-63, spl. publs. editor, 1963—. Author: Do-It-Yourself Materials Guide, 1955, First Boy on the Moon, 1958, The Marvelous Inventions of Alvin Fernald, 1960, Alvin's Secret Code, 1963, The World Above, 1965, Alvin Fernald, Foreign Trader, 1966, Alvin Fernald, Mayor for a Day, 1969, Peter Potts, 1972, Alvin Fernald, Superweasel, 1974, Alvin's Swap Shop, 1976, Alvin Fernald, TV Anchorman, 1980, The Wacky World of Alvin Fernald, (1981); also author fiction and non-fiction in mags.; Editor: Popular Mechanics Do-It-Yourself Ency. Served to maj. USMCR, 1942-45. Decorated Silver Star. Mem. Soc. Midland Authors, Sigma Delta Chi. Home: Rte 1 Box 171 Brevard NC 28712 Office: 10 Times Arcade Brevard NC 28712

HICKS, DAVID, opera producer, director; b. Phila., June 3, 1937; s. Paul W. and Mary (Ploucher) H. B.S. in Music, Temple U., 1959. Acting faculty Am. Opera Center, Juilliard Sch. Music, 1978—. Appeared as singer with various opera cos., including N.Y.C. Opera and cos. in Phila., Cin., Balt., Hartford, Conn., until 1970; concert artist Community Concerts, throughout U.S., 1962-70; asst. dir., N.Y.C. Opera, 1967-73; free-lance dir., 1973—; artistic dir., Florentine Opera, Milw., 1980—; dir. opera prodns., Acad. Vocal Arts, Phila., 1973-77. Mem. Am. Guild Musical Artists (bd. govs. 1965-75). Office: care Robert Lombardo Assocs 61 W 62d St New York NY 10023

HICKS, DONALD ALDEN, aerospace company executive; b. Ely, Nev., Feb. 20, 1925; s. William John and Mary Josephine (Williams) H.; m. Mary Lou Hansen, Aug. 26, 1972; children: Pamela Leigh, Janine Elizabeth. A.B., U. Calif. at Berkeley, 1950, M.A., 1954, Ph.D., 1956. Physicist Lawrence Radiation Lab., 1954-56; chief sect. applied physics aerospace group Boeing Co., Seattle, 1956-61; v.p.-tech. Ventura div. Northrop Corp., Los Angeles, 1961-65; v.p., mgr. dept. applied research Nortronics div., 1965-67; v.p. corp. research, mgr. Northrop Corp. Labs., 1967-70; corp. v.p., mgr. Northrop Research & Tech. Center, 1970-74; sr. v.p. mktg. and tech. Northrop Corp., 1974—; mem. Def. Sci. Bd. councilors Sch. Engring. U. So. Calif.; bd. dirs. John Tracy Clinic.; mem. adv. bd. U. Calif.-Berkeley Coll. Engring. Served with inf. AUS, 1943-46. Office: 1800 Century Park E Los Angeles CA 90067

HICKS, DONOVAN BLAKE, container, industrial and technical products manufacturing company executive; b. Laramie, Wyo., Nov. 19, 1937; s. Elzy Marvin and Vivian Vera (Blakeman) H.; m. Sally Sue Warren, Aug. 30, 1958; children: Warren Earl, Whitney Anne. B.S. in Physics, Colo. State U., 1960. With Ball Corp., Boulder, Colo., 1961-80, Broomfield, Colo., 1980—, dir. sci. and application aerospace div., 1972-77, pres. aerospace div., 1977-80, group v.p. tech. products group, 1980—; dir. Radio Physics Inc., Boulder. Served to 2d lt. U.S. Army, 1960-61. Recipient Skylab Achievement award NASA, 1974, Disting. Engring. Achievement award Soc. Mfg. Engrs., Denver, 1980. Mem. AAAS, Am. Def. Preparedness Assn. (pres. Colo.-Wyo. chpt. 1982—), Am. Electronics Assn. (chmn. Colo. council 1980-81, 83-84), Nat. Space Club (gov. 1977-80). Democrat. Episcopalian. Lodge: Kiwanis. Office: Ball Corp PO Box 589 Broomfield CO 80020

HICKS, EDWARD JAMES, communications executive; b. Halifax, N.S., Can., Nov. 3, 1939; s. Charles Edward and Mary Helen (Burke) H.; m. Dorothy Isner, July 23, 1962; children: Colin, Jacqueline, Catherine. Grad. high sch. Gen. acct. Maritime Tel.&Tel. Co., Ltd., Halifax, 1964-69, treas., 1969-73, sec.-treas., 1973-75; v.p. fin. Maritime Tel. & Tel. Co., Ltd., 1975-82; v.p. fin. and adminstrn. Maritime Tel.&Tel. Co., Ltd., 1982—; v.p. fin. The Island Telephone Co., Ltd., Charlottetown, P.E.I., 1975-82, dir., 1975—; pres., dir. Maritime Computers, Ltd. Provincial treas. Boy Scouts, 1979-82; bd. dirs. Halifax YMCA, 1975-80. Fellow Soc. Mgmt. Accts. (registered); mem. Fin. Execs. Inst. (pres. Maritime chpt. 1979-80). Home: 3143 Mayfield Ave Halifax NS B3L 4B3 Canada Office: 1505 Barrington St Halifax NS B3J 2W3 Canada

HICKS, EDWIN HUGH, accountant; b. Detroit, Jan. 15, 1932; s. Willis and Anna (Dunlop) H.; m. Joan Marie Mayer, July 26, 1958; children—Scott Mayer, Sharon Anne, Douglas Edwin. B.B.A., U. Mich., 1953; M.B.A., 1956. C.P.A., Mich., Ohio. Supr. Touche, Ross, Bailey & Smart, Detroit, 1956-63; mgr. tax dept. Am. Motors Corp., Detroit, 1963-67; gen. tax mgr. Massey Ferguson, Inc., Des Moines, 1967-69, treas., 1969-70; mgr. Touche Ross & Co., Cleve., 1970, partner, 1971—, partner-in-charge Cleve., 1972-76, dir. tax ops., 1979—. Served with U.S. Army, 1953-55. Mem. Am. Inst. C.P.A.'s, Mich. Assn. C.P.A.'s, Ohio Soc. C.P.A.'s, Fin. Execs. Inst., Nat. Assn. Accountants, Delta Sigma Pi, Phi Kappa Phi, Beta Alpha Psi. Lutheran. Home: 20950 Fairmount Blvd Shaker Heights OH 44118 Office: Ohio Savs Plaza Cleveland OH 44114

HICKS, ELE WYATTE, management consultant; b. El Dorado, Ark., May 7, 1926; s. John Wesley and Sara Martha (Wilson) H.; m. Shirley Jean Merrill, July 3, 1947; children: Constance Anne, Victoria Kathleen, Mark Wyatte, David Owen. B.A., U. Mo., 1944; M.A., U. Mich., 1949. Sales promotion exec. McCannErickson, Inc., N.Y.C., 1947-48; advt. sales promotion mgr. Libbey-Owens-Ford Glass Co., Toledo, 1948-53; v.p., acct. supr. Benton & Bowles, Inc., N.Y.C., 1953-61; exec. v.p., mng. dir. J. Walter Thompson Co., N.Y.C., 1961-76, also dir.; chmn., dir. Barickman Advt. Inc. (now Doyle Dane Bernbach Inc.), 1976-78; mng. dir., dir. Compton Communications Inc., N.Y.C., 1978-80; corp. exec. v.p., dir. Creamer Inc., N.Y.C., 1980-82; pres. Wyatte Hicks Ptnrs. Inc., Mgmt. Cons.; dir. Ross Roy N.Y./Compton, Klemtner Advt., Rumrill-Hoyt Inc.; mem. N.Y. Advt. Rev. Bd.; lectr., panelist seminars Am. Mgmt. Assn.; leader seminars on high tech. mktg. Served with U.S. Army, 1944-47. Decorated Army Commendation medal, Bronze Star, Silver Star. Mem. Am. Assn. Advt. Agys. (bd. govs. 1972-76), Econ. Club N.Y. Republican. Presbyterian. Clubs: New Canaan (Conn.); Field; Genessee Valley (Rochester, N.Y.); Sky (N.Y.C.). Home: Sleepy Hollow Rd New Canaan CT 06840 Office: 575 Madison Ave New York NY 10022

HICKS, HENRY DAVIES, university president, Canadian legislator; b. Bridgetown, N.S., Can., Mar. 5, 1915; s. Henry Brandon and Annie May (Kinney) H.; m. Paulene Banks, Dec. 28, 1945 (dec. Feb. 1964); m. Margaret Gene Morison, Apr. 15, 1965; children: Catherine Kinney, Henry Randolph Harlow, John George Herbert, Paulene Jane Francess. B.A. With honours in Chemistry, Mt. Allison U., 1936; B.Sc., Dalhousie U., 1937, LL.D.; B.C.L., Oxford U., 1940, M.A. (Rhodes scholar), 1944; D.Ed., St. Anne's; LL.D., Mt. Allison U.; D.C.L., King's Coll., U. N.B.; D.Lit., Acadia U.; D.H.L., Mt. St. Vincent U. Bar: bar 1941, Apptd. Queen's counsel 1957. With Orlando & Hicks, Bridgetown, N.S., Can., 1946-50; dean arts and sci. Dalhousie U., Halifax, N.S., 1960-61, v.p., 1961-63, pres., vice chancellor, 1963-80. Mem. Canada Council, 1963-69; bd. dirs. Assn. Univs. and Colls. Can., 1966-69, 70-72, 74-75; rep. on bd. govs. U. Guyana, 1970-75; pres. Assn. Atlantic Univs., 1968-72; Canadian del. 28th gen. assembly UN, 1973; Mem. N.S. Legislature, 1945-60, minister edn., 1949-54, provincial sec., 1954, premier, 1954-56; leader Liberal Party in N.S., 1954; leader Her Majesty's loyal opposition, 1956-60; mem. Senate of Can., 1972—. Served as capt. Royal Canadian Arty., 1941-45. Invested companion Order Can., 1970. Fellow Royal Philatelic Soc. London, Royal Philatelic Soc. Can.; mem. Aesculapius Fishing Assn. Clubs: Saraguay, Halifax. Home: 6446 Coburg Rd Halifax NS B3H 2A7 Canada

HICKS, IRLE RAYMOND, retail food chain exec.; b. Welch, W.Va., Dec. 21, 1928; s. Irle Raymond and Mary Louise (Day) H. B.A., U. Va., 1950. Bus. mgr. Hicks Ford, Covington, Ky., 1952-58; acct. Firestone Plantations Co., Harbel, Liberia, 1958-60; auditor Kroger Co., Cin., 1960-66, gen. auditor, 1966-68, asst. treas., 1968-72, treas., 1972—. Bd. dirs. Old Masons' Home Ky. Served with AUS, 1950-52. Mem. Fin. Execs. Inst., Bankers Club, Alpha Kappa Psi, Phi Kappa Psi. Episcopalian. Clubs: Mason., Cincinnati. Home: 454 Oliver Rd Cincinnati OH 45215 Office: 1014 Vine St Cincinnati OH 45202

HICKS, JOSEPH ROBERT, former rubber company executive; b. Bloomsburg, Pa., Aug. 27, 1922; s. Joseph Arch and A and da (Correll) H.; m. Mary Rita Schlitzer, Dec. 12, 1946; children: Robert William, Nancy Jane (Mrs. Roger Freed), Jeffrey Alan, Thomas Joseph, Joanne Elizabeth. B.A. in Commerce and Finance, Pa. State U., 1943. With Gen. Electric Co., 1946-62, dist. mgr. finance and service operation, Cleve., 1957-62; asst. comptroller Goodyear Tire & Rubber Co., Akron, Ohio, 1962-64, comptroller, 1964-68, v.p., comptroller, 1968-76; pres., chief exec. officer Goodyear Can. Inc., Toronto, Ont., 1976-78, now dir., corp. exec. v.p. fin., 1978-80, group exec. v.p., 1981-82; dir. The Stanley Works, 1983—. Trustee Children's Med. Center of Akron, 1980—. Served with AUS, 1943-46. Mem. Financial Execs. Inst. (bd. dirs. Cleve. 1967-76, 79-82), Pa. State U. Alumni Council (exec. com. 1967-72, 76-77), NAM (dir. 1980-82), Delta Chi. Clubs: Portage Country (Akron); Toftrees (University Park, Pa.); Wyndemere Country (Naples, Fla.). Home: 2375 Covington Rd Akron OH 44313

HICKS, KENNETH WILLIAM, bishop; b. LaHarpe, Kans., June 18, 1923; s. Earl Franklin and Ertie Leona (Williams) H.; m. Lila Elaine Goodwin, Aug. 11, 1946; children—Linda Diane, Debra Dawn. B.A., York (Nebr.) Coll., 1947; M.Th., Iliff Sch. Theology, Denver, 1953; D.D. (hon.), Nebr. Wesleyan U., 1970, Westmar Coll., LeMars, Iowa, 1977, LL.D., Philander Smith Coll., 1978. Ordained to ministry United Methodist Ch., 1952; pastor chs. in, Nebr. and Colo., 1945-68; dist. supt. Central dist. United Meth. Ch., Kearney, Nebr., 1968-73; sr. pastor Trinity United Meth. Ch., Grand Island, Nebr., 1973-76; bishop Ark. area United Meth. Ch., Little Rock, 1976—. Trustee So. Meth. U., St. Paul Sch. Theology, Kansas City, Mo., Hendrix Coll., Conway, Ark., Meth. Hosp., Memphis, Philander Smith Coll., Little Rock, Lydia Patterson Inst., El Paso, Lydia Patterson Inst., Tex., Meth. Children's Home, Little Rock; chmn. United, Negro Coll. Fund Ark., 1977. Named Alumns of Year Iliff Sch. Theology, 1977. Democrat. Clubs: Lions, Rotary, Shriners. Office: 723 Center St Little Rock AR 72201 *To love others, we must first have a sense of what it is to love one's self; otherwise, a fragmented self will generate a fragmented, untrusting response. The world will be helped through selfless giving of persons who know inner security.* *

HICKS, LESLIE HUBERT, educator; b. Washington, Aug. 26, 1927; s. Leslie Hubert and Ruth Thornton (Daves) H.; m. Margaret B. Smith, Dec. 8, 1956; 1 son, Stephen Leslie. B.S., Howard U., 1949; M.A., U. Wis., 1952, Ph.D., 1954. Instr. to prof. psychology Howard U., Washington, 1954-68, prof., chmn. dept. psychology, 1970—; adminstrv. officer sci. affairs Am. Psychol. Assn., 1968-70; fellow Center Advanced Study in Behavioral Scis., Stanford, Calif., 1978-79; spl. fellow dept. anatomy UCLA, 1959-62; exchange scientist to Soviet Union, 1963, 65, 76; cons. NIMH, Ednl. Testing Service, Social Rehab. Service, HEW. Served with AUS, 1946-47. Fellow AAAS, Am. Psychol. Assn.; mem. Soc. for Neuroscis., Phi Beta Kappa, Sigma Xi. Home: 9344 Harvey Rd Silver Spring MD 20910 Office: Psychology Dept Howard U Washington DC 20059

HICKS, ORTON HAVERGAL, coll. adminstr.; b. Mpls., Nov. 6, 1900; s. Eliphalet G. and Mabel (Pease) H.; m. Lois Paddock, Jan. 19, 1924; children—Orton H., Caryl Ann (Mrs. William G. Clark), Wendy Joan (Mrs. Milo G. Coerper). Grad., Shattuck Sch., 1917; A.B., Dartmouth, 1921; M.B.A., Tuck Sch., 1922. Salesman Eastman Kodak Co., 1922-26; pres. Films, Inc., 1927-38, Seven Seas Film Corp., 1938-45; dir. Loew's Internat. Corp., 1945-58, Barnett Internat. Corp., Ency. Brit. Films, Inc.; v.p. Dartmouth, 1958—; Cons. WPB, 1941-42. Trustee Shattuck Sch. Served to lt. col. Signal Corps AUS, 1942-45. Clubs: University, Military Naval, Dartmouth (N.Y.C.); Creek (Locust Valley, N.Y.); Hanover Country. Home: 6 Rope Ferry Rd Hanover NH 03755

HICKS, PAUL B., JR., petroleum company executive; b. Norfolk, Va., Oct. 3, 1925; s. Paul B. and Maerose (Rausch) H.; m. Lucile Green, Nov. 28, 1953; children: Paul Burton III, Peter David, Thomas Patrick. B.A., U. Va., 1950. Sales rep. Texaco Inc., 1953-57, dist. supr. merchandising, 1957-60, dist. sales mgr., Chgo., 1960-62, asst. div. sales mgr., 1962, mgr. merchandising, N.Y.C., 1962, div. sales mgr., Columbus, Ohio, 1963-65, asst. to pres., N.Y.C., 1965-66, gen. mgr.

sales dept. U.S., 1966-69, v.p. sales dept., U.S., 1969-72, v.p. worldwide sales, 1972-75, v.p. pub. relations and personnel, 1975-77, v.p. pub. relations and advt., 1977-83; pres. Texaco Europe, 1983—; pres., dir. Texaco Services (Europe) Ltd.; dir. Texaco Ltd., Texaco A.G. Mem. Zeta Psi. Clubs: Winged Foot Golf, Milbrook Country, Farmington (Va.) Country. Home: 100 Woodside Dr Greenwich CT 06830 Office: Texaco Inc 2000 Westchester Ave White Plains NY 10650

HICKS, R. V., lawyer; b. Windsor, Ont., Can., Jan. 16, 1917; s. Robert and Iva (Haight) H.; m. Mary C. Reginald, June 24, 1944; children: Peter Robert, Douglas Reginald, Nancy Kathryn. B.A. Gov. Gen.'s medal, U. Western Ont., 1939; postgrad. in law, Osgoode Hall. Bar: Ont. bar 1942, Queen's counsel 1953. Sr. ptnr. Hicks, Morley, Hamilton, Stewart, Storie.; Dir. CKR Ltd., Wabasso Inc., St. Lawrence Cement Ltd., Gray Coach Lines Ltd.; part-time mem. Fed. Pub. Service Arbitration Tribunal, 1968-72; dir. project on communications and info. Com. on Govt. Productivity in Ont., 1972. Bd. dirs., past pres. Stratford Festival Theatre Found.; past pres. Bd. of Trade of Met. Toronto.; past bd. dirs. Toronto Symphony Orch., Ont. Chamber Commn. Mem. Canadian Bar Assn. United Ch. Can. Home: 2 Hunthill Ct Islington ON Canada M9A 4A2 Office: PO Box 371 1201 Toronto Dominion Centre Toronto ON Canada M5K 1KS

HICKS, TYLER GREGORY, publishing company executive; b. N.Y.C., June 21, 1921; s. Ernest Tyler and Mary B. (O'Brien) H.; m. Saretta M. Gratke, Feb. 23, 1946 (dec. Mar. 1974); children: Gregory T., Barbara L., Steven D.; m. Mary T. Shanley, Aug. 29, 1975. Engr. Merport Realty Co., 1942-46; design engr. Lockwood-Greene Engrs. Inc., 1946-49; editor-in-chief Profl. and Reference Books div. McGraw-Hill Co., N.Y.C., 1962—; instr. Cooper Union, N.Y.C.; owner Internat. Engring. Assocs.; pres. Internat. Wealth Success Inc., Rockville Centre, N.Y.; lectr. in field. Author: How To Borrow Your Way to a Great Fortune, 1970, Magic Mind Secrets for Building Riches Fast, 1971, Standard Handbook of Engineering Calculations, 1972, How to Make One Million Dollars in Real Estate in Three Years Starting with No Cash, 1976, Tyler Hicks' Encyclopedia of Wealth-Building Secrets, 1980, How to Borrow Your Way to Real Estate Riches, 1981, Business Capital Sources, 1984, Financial Broker, Finder, Business Broker Complete Success Kit, 1984, Real Estate Riches Success Kit, 1984, Complete Business Borrowers Success Kit, 1984, 101 Ways to 100% Financing of Business and Real Estate, 1984; co-author: Handbook of Electric Power Calculations, 1984, Handbook of Chemical Engineering Calculations, 1984; co-editor: Standard Handbook of Consulting Engineering, 1984. Mem. IEEE, ASME, U.S. Naval Inst., Internat. Oceanographic Found. Clubs: Rockville Links Golf, Huntington Yacht. Home: 24 Canterbury Rd Rockville Ctr NY 11570 Office: McGraw-Hill 1221 Ave of Americans New York NY 10020 *Z The clearest and strongest thought permeating my life is based on my own experience and observation of lives of thousands of people throughout the world. This thought is: Men and women can achieve in life whatever goals they set for themselves if a person combines careful planning and analysis of each objective with mental images of successful achievement. This approach seems to work everywhere—for everyone. Choosing to do what one enjoys also contributes to success because better performance occurs when people like what they're doing. Helping others achieve their goals in life brings great rewards to both the helper and the person assisted.*

HIDALGO, EDWARD, lawyer, former secretary U.S. Navy Dept.; b. Mexico City, Oct. 12, 1912; U.S., 1918, naturalized, 1936; s. Egon and Domitila (Hidalgo) Kunhardt; m. Karen Dane Jernstedt, Jan. 22, 1961; children: Joanne, Edward, Richard, Tila. B.A. magna cum laude, Holy Cross Coll., 1933; J.D., Columbia U., 1936; civil law degree, U. Mexico Law Sch., 1959. Bar: N.Y. 1936, Mexico 1959, D.C. 1976. Law clk. 2d Circuit Ct. Appeals, N.Y., 1936-37; assoc. Wright, Gordon Zachry & Parlin, N.Y.C., 1937-42; mem. Eberstadt Com. on Unification of Mil. Services, Washington, 1945; spl. asst. to Sec. of Navy James Forrestal, Washington, 1945-46; partner Curtis, Mallet-Provost, Colt & Mosle, 1946-48; founder, sr. partner Barrera, Siqueiros & Torres Landa, Mexico City, 1948-65; spl. asst. to Sec. of Navy Paul H. Nitze, Washington, 1965-66; partner Cahill, Gordon & Reindel, Paris, 1966-72; spl. asst. econ. affairs to dir. USIA, Washington, 1972; gen. counsel Congl. liaison USIA, 1973-76; asst. sec. for manpower, res. affairs and logistics U.S. Navy Dept., Washington, 1977-79, sec., 1979-81. Served with USNR, 1942-46. Decorated Bronze Star Royal Order of Vasa (Sweden); Order of Aztec Eagle (Mex.). Roman Catholic. Clubs: Chevy Chase, Met. Office: 1828 L St NW Suite 1111 Washington DC 20036

HIDORE, JOHN JUNIOR, geographer, educator; b. Cedar Falls, Iowa, July 6, 1932; s. John Henry and Vearle Lluela (Thomas) H.; m. Ruth Olive Norton, June 6, 1954; children—Jill Helen, John Warren. B.A. in Math. and Earth Sci, State Coll. Iowa, Cedar Falls, 1954; M.A. in Phys. Geography, U. Iowa, 1958, Ph.D., 1960. Instr. geography U. Wis., Madison, 1960-62; asst. prof. Okla. State U., Stillwater, 1962-64, asso. prof., 1964-66; dir. NDEA Inst. Geography, 1966; asso. prof. U. Ind., Bloomington, 1966-68, acting chmn., 1968-71, prof., 1972-80; prof. and head dept. geography U. N.C., Greensboro, 1980—; vis. prof. U. Ife, Nigeria, 1971-72, U. Khartoum, Sudan, 1974-75, Ben Gurion U. of Negev, Beer Sheva, Israel, 1978. Author: Introduction to Physical Geography, 1967, A Geography of the Atmosphere, 1972, Physical Geography: Earth Systems, 1974, A Workbook of Weather Maps, 1976, Physical Geography: A Laboratory Manual, 1978; contbr. articles, abstracts and book revs. to profl. jours. Home: 6 W Oak Ct Greensboro NC 27407 Office: Dept Geography U NC Greensboro NC 27412

HIEATT, ALLEN KENT, educator; b. Indpls., Jan. 21, 1921; emigrated to Can., 1968; s. Allen Andrew and Violet Rose (Kent) H.; m. Constance Bartlett, Oct. 25, 1958; children by previous marriage: Alice Allen, Katherine Marsh. A.B., U. Louisville, 1943; Ph.D., Columbia U., 1954. Lectr. Columbia U., N.Y.C., 1944-45, instr., 1945-55, asst. prof., 1956-59, assoc. prof., 1960-69; prof. English U. Western Ont., London, 1969—; sr. founding editor Spenser Newsletter, London, Ont., 1970-75. Editorial bd.: Duquesne Studies, Pitts., 1976—, Renaissance and Reformation, 1977—, Spenser Studies, 1979—; sr. co-editor: Spenser Ency., 1981—; author: Short Time's Endless Monumet, 1960, Chaucer, Spenser, Milton, 1975; translator: (with M. Lorch) Lorenzo Valla, On Pleasure, 1977. Cutting fellow, 1946-47; leave grantee Can. Council, Oxford, Eng., 1977-78; research fellow Social Sci. and Humanities Research Council of Can., 1981—. Mem. MLA (chmn. div. English lit. Renaissance 1978-79), Spenser Soc. (pres.), Renaissance Soc. Am. (chmn. north central div. 1973-79). Home: 2 Grosvenor St London ON Canada N6A 1Y4 Office: Dept English Univ Western Ont London ON Canada N6A 3K7

HIEATT, CONSTANCE BARTLETT, English language educator; b. Boston, Feb. 11, 1928; d. Arthur Charles and Eleonora (Very) Bartlett; m. Allen Kent Hieatt, Oct. 25, 1958. Student, Smith Coll., 1945-47; A.B., Hunter Coll., 1953, A.M., 1957; Ph.D., Yale U., 1959. Lectr. City Coll., CUNY, 1959-60; from asst. prof. to asso. prof. English Queensborough Community Coll., CUNY, 1960-65; asso. prof. St. John's U., Jamaica, N.Y., 1965-69; prof. English U. Western Ont. (Can.) London, 1969—. Author: The Canterbury Tales of Geoffrey Chaucer, 1964, The Realism of Dream Visions, 1967, Beowulf and Other Old English Poems, 1967, Essentials of Old English, 1968, (with Sharon Butler) Pleyn Delit: Medieval Cookery for Modern Cooks, 1976, rev. edit., 1979, Karlamagnus Saga, Vols. I and II, 1975, 1975, Vol. III, 1980, Sir Gawain and the Green Knight, 1967, The Knight of the Lion, 1968, The Knight of the Cart, 1969, The Joy of the Court, 1971, The Sword and the Grail, 1972, The Castle of Ladies, 1973, The Minstrel Knight, 1974; Contbr. articles to scholastic jours. Yale U. fellow, and Lewis-Farmington fellow, 1957-59; Can. Council and Social Sci. and Humanities Research Council grantee. Fellow Royal Soc. Can.; mem. MLA, Medieval Acad. Am., Internat. Arthurian Assn., Societe Rencesvals, Internat. Saga Assn., Children's Lit. Assn., Soc. Advancement of Scandinavian Studies, Assn. Canadian Univ. Tchrs. English, New Chaucer Soc., Anglo-Norman Text Soc. Anglican. Home: 2 Grosvenor St London ON N6A 1Y4 Canada Office: Dept English Univ Western Ont London ON N6A 3K7 Canada

HIEBERT, ERWIN NICHOLAS, historian, educator; b. Waldheim, Sask., Can., May 27, 1919; s. Cornelius Nicholas and Tina (Harms) H.; m. Elfrieda Franz, June 3, 1943; children: Catherine, Margaret, Thomas. B.A., Bethel Coll., 1941; M.A., U. Kans., 1943; M.S., U. Chgo., 1949; Ph.D. in Phys. Chemistry and History Sci, U. Wis., 1954. Research chemist Standard Oil Co., Ind., also Manhattan Project, 1943-46, Inst. Study Metals, U. Chgo., 1947-50; mem. faculty U. Wis., 1957-70, prof. history of sci., 1963-70, Harvard U., 1970—; Fulbright lectr. Max Planck Inst. Physics, Göttingen, Germany, 1954-55; Am. specialist U. Kabul, Afghanistan, summer 1961; vis. prof. Inst. Advanced Studies, Princeton, 1961-62, 68-69, U. Tübingen, Germany, 1964-65, Harvard U., 1965-66. Author: The Impact of Atomic Energy, 1961, Historical Roots of the Principle of Conservation of Energy, 1962; also numerous articles. Fellow AAAS; mem. Am. Chem. Soc., Am. Phys. Soc., History Sci. Soc., Am. Acad. Arts and Scis., Sigma Xi. Mennonite. Home: 40 Payson Rd Belmont MA 02178 Office: Dept History of Sci Sci Center 235 Harvard Univ Cambridge MA 02138

HIEBERT, RAY ELDON, journalism educator, author, consultant; b. Freeman, S.D., May 21, 1932; s. Peter Nicholas and Helen (Kunkel) H.; m. Roselyn Lucille Peyser, Jan. 30, 1955; children: David, Steven, Emily, Douglas. B.A., Stanford U., 1954; M.S., Columbia U., 1957; M.A., U. Md., 1961, Ph.D., 1962. Editorial work Los Angeles Examiner, Washington Times-Herald, L.I. Press, Am. Banker, 1950-57; instr. U. Minn., Duluth, 1957-58; faculty Am. U., 1958- 67, prof. journalism, chmn. dept. journalism, pub. relations and broadcasting, 1962-67; dir. Washington Journalism Center, 1965-68; head dept. journalism U. Md., College Park, 1968-72; dean Coll. Journalism, 1973-79, prof., 1980—; pres. Communication Research Assocs., 1979—; Editorial cons., speech writer Dept. Commerce, 1961-63; cons. Labor Dept., 1969, HUD, 1970-71, U.S. CSC, 1973-75, Liberian Broadcasting System, 1982, Nat. Orgn. on Disability, 1982—, U.S. Voice of Am., 1983—. Author: Books in Human Development, 1965, The Press in Washington, 1966, Courtier to the Crowd, 1966, Journalism Handbook, The Boy Scouts of America, 1976; co-author: Franklin Delano Roosevelt, 1968, The Voice of Government, 1968, Thomas Edison, 1969, The Stock Market Crash, 1970, Atomic Pioneers, 1970, The Political Image Merchants, 1971, Mass Media, 1974, A Grateful Remembrance: The Story of Montgomery County, Maryland, 1976, Mass Media II, 1979, Informing the People, 1981; Editor: John Wiley Series on Government and Communication, 1966-76, Radio TV News Dirs. Assn. Communicator, 1971-78, Public Relations Rev, 1975—, Social Sci. Monitor, 1979—, Longman Series on Public Communication, 1979—. Vice chmn. Montgomery County Citizens Cable-TV Commn.; mem. nat. communications com. Boy Scouts Am., 1974—; Trustee Found. for Public Relations Edn. and Research, 1969-79; bd. dirs. Center Policy Process, Washington, 1978-80; mem. nat. public affairs com. ARC, 1981—. Served with AUS, 1954-56. Recipient Tchr. of Year award Public Relations Soc. Am., 1978; Fulbright fellow to Africa, 1982. Mem. Am. Studies Assn., Am. Soc. Journalism Sch. Adminstrs., Assn. Edn. in Journalism, Am. Assn. Schs. and Depts. Journalism (exec. com. 1974-75), Nat. Conf. Social Welfare (audio-visual bd. 1974-75), AAUP, Pub. Relations Soc. Am., Authors Guild, Nat. Press Club, Overseas Press Club, Sigma Delta Chi (pres. Md. chpt. 1977-78), Kappa Tau Alpha, Phi Kappa Phi. Club: Cosmos (Washington). Home: 10615 Harper Ave Silver Spring MD 20901 Office: U Md College Park MD 20742 *I believe peace can only come from understanding, and understanding requires communication. As life grows more complex, communication is becoming more difficult. Our survival may depend on improving our dialogue, not only with parents, children, friends and colleagues, but with strangers and enemies as well. Our technologies are making the world into one neighborhood. We are all one family. More than ever we need to listen carefully and speak clearly if we are to understand each other.*

HIEGEL, JERRY M., food company executive; b. Davenport, Iowa, 1927; married. B.S., St. Ambrose Coll., 1949; M.B.A., U. Wis., 1950. With Des Moines Register, 1946; with Oscar Mayer & Co. Inc., Madison, Wis., 1946—, asst. sales mgr. and gen sales mgr. Western div., 1962-66, v.p. sales, 1966-70, v.p. mktg., 1970-71, group v.p., 1971-73, exec. v.p., 1973-77, pres., 1977—, chief exec. officer, 1980—, also dir.; group v.p. parent co. Gen. Foods Corp., 1981-82, exec. v.p., 1982—; dir. First Wis. Corp., Wis. Telephone Co. Wis. vol. state chmn. U.S. Savs. Bonds, 1980-84; mem. AID-President's Task Force on Internat. Pvt. Enterprise, 1983; bd. dirs. Wis. Taxpayers Alliance, 1984. Served with USN, 1945-46. Mem. Am. Meat Inst. (exec. com., dir., vice chmn.). Office: 910 Mayer Ave PO Box 7188 Madison WI 53707

HIEMSTRA, ROGER, adult educator, writer; b. Plainwell, Mich., Sept. 15, 1938; s. Calude and Frances (Anson) H.; m. Janet Louise Wemer, June 23, 1963; children: Nancy, David. A.A., Pasadena City Coll., Calif., 1958; B.S., Mich. State U., 1964; M.S., Iowa State U., 1967; Ph.D., U. Mich., 1970. Mott Intern Flint (Mich.) Community Schs., 1968-69; program coordinator Wayne State U., Detroit, 1969-70; dept. asst. U. Mich., Ann Arbor, 1969-70; prof. adult edn. U. Nebr., Lincoln, 1970-76; prof., chmn. adult edn. Iowa State U., Ames, 1976-80; prof. adult edn. Syracuse (N.Y.) U., 1980—, chmn. dept. adult edn., 1980—; chmn. Commn. Profl. Adult Edn., Washington, 1981-83. Co-author, editor: Changing Approaches to Studying Adult Education, 1980; author: The Educative Community, 1972, Lifelong Learning, 1976; sr. editor: Lifelong Learning: The Adult Years, Washington, 1980-83. Served with USNR, 1960-62. Mem/ Adult Edn. Assn. USA (exec. bd. 19678-82, service award 1981, mem., leadership award 1980, membership award 1979), Am. Assn. Adult and Continuing Edn. (editor 1980-83). Democrat. Unitarian. Office: Syracuse U 356 Huntington Hall NY Syracuse 13210

HIERONYMUS, CLARA BOOTH WIGGINS, journalist; b. Drew, Miss., July 25, 1913; d. Bruce Charles and Maude (Watson) Wiggins; m. Senator Cleo Hieronymus, Apr. 24, 1937; children—Bruce Lee, Jane (Mrs. David Piller). B.A. cum laude, U. Tulsa, 1932; M.S.W., U. Okla., 1936. Employment sec. and counselor YWCA, Tulsa, 1936-38; labor market analyst Okla. Employment Service, also instr. sociology U. Tulsa, 1938-50; free-lance writer, Nashville, Tennessean, 1951-56, art and drama critic, home furnishings editor, 1956—; mem. rotating faculty Nat. Critics Inst., 1975-77; book review radio sta. KFMJ, Tulsa, 1938-45; speaker before groups, 1950—. Author: (with Barbara Izard) On Stage and Off. Mem. panel jurors for selection Am. children's theaters to perform at Internat. Conf. U.S.A., 1972; Bd. dirs. Samaritans, Inc., 1967-76, pres., 1967-69; bd. dirs. Middle Tenn. chpt. Nat. Arthritis Found., 1967-70; charter mem. bd. Middle Tenn. Historic Sites Fedn., 1968-70; mem. Tenn. Fine Arts Center and Bot. Gardens, 1959—; mem. adv. bd. O'More Coll. Design, 1970—, Nashville Ballet Soc., 1977-79; founder, life mem. O'More Design Guild, 1970—. Recipient Dorothy Dawe award Am. Furniture Mart, 1960, 63, 66, 69; Dallas Market Center award, 1965; named Woman of Year in Communications Bus. and Profl. Women's Club, Nashville, 1966; named to Mayor's Com. Community Excellence, 1982; Gov.'s award in arts, 1980; honored by Links, Inc., 1982; named Pride of Tenn., 1982. Mem. Am. Soc. Interior Designers (press asso.), Nashville Children's Theatre, Assn. Internationale du Theatre pour L'Enfance et Jeunesse, Am. Theater Critics Assn. (founding mem., governing bd. 1974—, nat. chmn. 1980—). Democrat. Methodist. Clubs: Centennial, Le Petit Salon (Nashville). Named among 10 best and most rep. women in critical profession today in Women in American Theater (Helen Krich Chinoy and Linda Walsh Jenkins), 1981. Home: 2200 Hemingway Dr Nashville TN 37215 Office: 1100 Broad St Nashville TN 37202

HIERONYMUS, EDWARD WHITTLESEY, lawyer; b. Davenport, Iowa, June 13, 1943. B.A. cum laude, Knox Coll., 1965; J.D. with distinction, Duke U., 1968. Bar: Calif. 1969, Iowa 1968. Ptnr. O'Melveny & Myers, Los Angeles, 1974—. Contbr. articles on law to profl. jours. Exec. sec. Los Angeles Com. Fgn. Relations, 1975—. Served with Judge Adv. Gen. U.S. Army, 1965-74. Mem. ABA (award for profl. merit 1968), Calif. Bar Assn., Los Angeles County Bar Assn., Iowa Bar Assn. Office: 400 S Hope St Los Angeles CA

HIESINGER, KATHRYN BLOOM, museum curator; b. Houston, Mar. 7, 1943; d. Benjamin and Adele Ray (Freundlich) Bloom; m. Ulrich W. Hiesinger, Sept. 14, 1968; children—Margaret A., William M.B. A.B., Wellesley Coll., 1965; A.M. (tuition fellow 1966-68, teaching fellow 1966-68, Sachs research fellow 1968-69, Whitney Cromwell scholar 1969-71), Harvard U., 1966, Ph.D., 1971. Mem. staff Phila. Mus. Art, 1971—, asst. curator Mediaeval and Renaissance decorative arts and painting before 1900, 1971-73, asso. curator European decorative arts after 1700, 1973, curator European decorative arts after 1700, 1974—; lectr. Inst. Fine Arts at N.Y. U., U. Pa., Moore Coll. Art. Contbr. exhbn. catalogues, profl. jours. Harry D.M. Grier Meml. fellow, 1973; travel grantee Nat. Mus. Act, 1979-80. Office: Phila Mus Art Box 7646 Philadelphia PA 19101

HIETT, EDWARD EMERSON, glass co. exec.; b. Toledo, Nov. 24, 1922; s. Stanley J. and Clara I. (Jones) H.; m. Margaret J. Winter, July 1, 1944; 1 dau., Katherine L. B.B.A., U. Mich., 1946, M.B.A., LL.B., 1949. Bar: Ohio bar 1949. Practice in, Toledo, 1949-52; mem. legal dept. Libbey-Owens-Ford Co., Toledo, 1952—, sec., 1963-78, asst. gen. counsel, 1963-73, v.p. gen. counsel, 1973-78; sr. counsel Owens-Corning Fiberglas, 1978—; lectr. econs., bus. law U. Toledo, 1949-69. Served as officer USNR, 1942-46. Mem. Am., Ohio, Toledo bar assns. Clubs: Tennis, Racquet, Toledo (Toledo). Home: 3723 Brookside Rd Toledo OH 43606 Office: 26 Fiberglas Tower Toledo OH 43659

HIGDON, ERNEST D., labor union official. Pres., sec.-treas. Coopers' Internat. Union N.Am. Office: 224 Executive Park Louisville KY 40207§

HIGGINBOTHAM, A. LEON, JR., judge; b. Trenton, N.J., Feb. 25, 1928; s. Aloyisus Leon and Emma Lee (Douglass) H.; m. Jeanne Louise Foster, Aug. 21, 1948; children: Stephen Lee, Karen Lee, Kenneth Lee. Student, Purdue U., 1944-45; B.A., Antioch Coll., 1949; LL.B., Yale U., 1952, M.A. (hon.); 35 hon. degrees. Bar: Pa. 1953. Asst. dist. atty., Philadelphia County, 1953-54; partner firm Norris, Green, Harris & Higginbotham, Phila., 1954-62; spl. dep. atty. gen. Commonwealth of Pa., 1956-62; spl. hearing officer for conscientious objectors U.S. Dept. Justice, 1960-62; commr. Pa. Human Relations Commn., 1961-62, FTC, 1962-64; U.S. dist. judge Eastern Dist. Pa., Phila., 1964-77; judge U.S. Ct. Appeals 3d Circuit, 1977—; adj. prof. Wharton Grad. Sch., U. Pa., 1970—; lectr.-in-law Law Sch., 1971—; lectr. Yale U., 1975; vis. lectr. Law Sch., U. Mich., 1976; lectr.-in-law Harvard Law Sch., 1983—. Author: In the Matter of Color: Race and the American Legal Process; The Colonial Period, 1978; contbr. numerous articles to profl. jours. Vice chmn. Nat. Commn. on Causes and Prevention of Violence; trustee U. Pa.; bd. dirs. Christian St.; br. YMCA, Robin Hood Dell Concerts, Inc.; citizen regent Smithsonian Instn. Recipient Nat. Human Relations award Nat. Conf. Christians and Jews, 1968, William C. Menninger Meml. medallion, 1969, Samuel S. Fels award Sch. Dist. Phila., 1969, Russwurm award Nat. Newspaper Pubs. Assn., 1969, Citation of Merit award Law Sch., Yale, 1975, Martin Luther King award, 1976; named One of Ten Most Outstanding Young Men in Am., 1964, Most Outstanding Young Man in Govt., 1964, Most Outstanding Young Man Phila., 1964, Outstanding Layman of Year YMCA, 1970. Office: US Court House 6th and Market Sts Philadelphia PA 19106

HIGGINBOTHAM, PATRICK ERROL, judge; b. Ala. Student, Arlington State Coll., 1956-57, North Tex. State U., 1958, U. Tex., 1958; B.A., U. Ala., 1960, LL.B., 1961. Bar: Ala. 1961, Tex. 1962, U.S. Supreme Ct. 1962. Partner firm Coke & Coke, Dallas, 1964-75; judge U.S. Dist. Ct. for No. Dist. Tex., Dallas, 1976-82, U.S. Ct. Appeals for 5th circuit, 1982—; lectr. on Constl. law, fed. complex litigation So. Meth. U. Law Sch., 1971—, lectr. constl. law, 1981—; mem. faculty Am. Inst. Banking, Fed. Jud. Center, Washington, Columbia U. Trial Seminar, Nat. Inst. Trial Advocacy; lectr. in field; conferee Am. Assembly, 1975, Pound Conf., 1976. Contbr. articles, revs. to profl. publs.; note editor: Ala. Law Rev, 1960-61; adv.: Human Rights Jour; narrator: one-hour video tape Law in Changing Soc, 1977. Chmn. bd. First United Methodist Ch., Richardson, Tex. Named Outstanding Alumnus U. Tex., Arlington, 1978, One of Nation's 100 Most Powerful Persons for the 80's Next Mag. Fellow Am. Bar Found.; mem. Am. Bar Assn. (chmn. com. to compile fed. jury charges antitrust sect., mem. council antitrust sect.), Dallas Bar Assn. (dir., chmn. coms. legal aid, civic affairs), Dallas Bar Found. (dir.), Continuing Legal Edn. (chmn. subcom. civil litigation), Am. Law Inst., S.W. Legal Found., Am. Judicature Soc. (dir.), Farrah Law Soc., Bench and Bar, Omicron Delta Kappa. Office: 1100 Commerce St Room 13E23 Dallas TX 75242 *

HIGGINBOTHAM, ROBERT DON, history educator; b. Fresno, Calif., May 22, 1931; s. E.B. and Maude (Myers) H.; m. Mary Stone, Dec. 22, 1957 (dec.); children: Robert, Lawrence, David; m. 2d Katherine Jenner, July 21, 1980. A.B., Washington U., St. Louis, 1953, A.M., 1954; Ph.D., Duke U., 1958. Mem. faculty Duke U., Durham, N.C., 1957-58, Coll. William and Mary, Williamsburg, Va., 1958-59, Longwood Coll., Farmville, Va., 1959-60, La. State U., Baton Rouge, 1960-67; prof. U. N.C., Chapel Hill, 1967—. Author: Daniel Morgan, 1961, War of American Independence, 1971, Atlas of the American Revolution, 1974; editor: Papers of James Iradell, 1976, Reconsiderations on the Revolutionary War, 1978. Recipient Civilian Disting. Service medal U.S. Army, 1976, award for outstanding book on Am. Revolution Am. Revolution Round Table; Nat. Hist. Pub. Commn. grantee, 1967, 68. Mem. Am. Hist. Assn. (bd. editors 1979-80), So. Hist. Assn., Orgn. Am. Historians, Phi Beta Kappa. Democrat. Episcopalian. Home: 706 Churchill St Chapel Hill NC 27514 Office: Dept History U NC Chapel Hill NC 27514

HIGGINBOTHAM, WILLIAM HENRY, mgmt. cons.; b. Jefferson City, Mo., Apr. 19, 1909; s. William Barber and May (Pritchard) H.; m. Mildred Catherine Winsby, Mar. 4, 1944 (dec. Dec. 1959);

children—Cynthia, Pamela (dec. Dec. 1974), Ronald; m. Suzanne Guge, Oct. 4, 1970. B.S., Washington U., St. Louis, 1953. Personnel dir. Rice-Stix Dry Goods Co., St. Louis, 1945-50; personnel mgr. White Rodgers Co., St. Louis, 1950-58; v.p. indsl. relations, dir. Century Electric Co., St. Louis, 1958-63; mgmt. cons. in pvt. practice, St. Louis, 1963—; mem. faculty St. Louis U., 1945-50, So. Ill. U., 1963-67; speaker; mem. faculty Creative Edn. Found., Buffalo, 1963—; Bd. dirs. Jr. Achievement of Miss. Valley, Inc. Mem. Am. Soc. Tng. and Devel. (past officer St. Louis chpt.), Am. Soc. Personnel Adminstrn., Assn. Mgmt. Cons. (bd. trustees, nat. pres.), Creative Leadership Council of Creative Edn. Found., Indsl. Relations Assn. Greater St. Louis, Exec. Assn. Grad. Sch. Bus. Columbia U., Inst. Mgmt. Cons. (certified), Mgmt. Devel. Study Group. Republican. Christian Scientist. Club: Rotary (Clayton, Mo.). Home: 890 Judson Manor Dr Saint Louis MO 63141 Office: 7701 Forsyth Blvd Saint Louis MO 63105 *Competition should be only with oneself. In this way one grows from within, strengthens his natural powers, makes fuller use of his talents and therefore improves his performance in the service of others.*

HIGGINBOTTOM, SAMUEL LOGAN, manufacturing company executive; b. North Lawrence, Ohio, Oct. 5, 1921; s. Samuel Bradlaugh and Vera Abbie (Gutchess) H.; m. Fair Steinschneider, Aug. 30, 1947; children: Samuel Logan, Marie Fair, Michele Rowan Maclaren. B.S. in Civil Engring, Columbia, 1943; grad. Advanced Mgmt. Program, Harvard U. Design engr. Parsons, Brinckerhoff, Hogan & McDonald, N.Y.C., 1945-46; v.p. engring., flight, test and inspection Trans World Airlines, Inc., 1946-64; v.p. engring. and maintenance Eastern Air Lines, Inc., 1964-67, v.p. operations group, 1967-69, sr. v.p., 1969, exec. v.p., 1969-70, pres., chief operating officer, 1970-73; chmn., pres., chief exec. officer Rolls-Royce Inc., N.Y.C., 1974—; dir. Rolls-Royce Ltd., also dir. various subs.; Lifetime Communities, Inc. Chmn. bd. trustees Columbia U.; mem. council Internat. Exec. Service Corps. Served to capt. USAAF, World War II; ETO. Decorated hon. comdr. Order Brit. Empire; recipient Egleston medal Columbia U. Engring. Sch., 1977. Fellow Am. Inst. Aeros. and Astronautics; mem. Soc. Automotive Engrs., Newcomen Soc. N.Am., Conquistadores del Cielo, Theta Tau, Tau Beta Pi, Psi Upsilon. Roman Catholic. Clubs: Wings (pres. 1980-81), River, Sky (N.Y.C.); Riverside Yacht, Stanwich. Home: 5 Conant Pl Darien CT 06820 Office: 375 Park Ave New York NY 10152

HIGGINS, ANDREW JACKSON, state supreme ct. justice; b. Platte City, Mo., June 21, 1921; s. Andrew Jervy and Frances Beverly H.; m. Laura Jo-an Brown, Oct. 30, 1948; children—Susan Louise, Laura Frances. A.B., Central Coll., 1943; LL.B., Washington U., St. Louis, 1948. Bar: Mo. bar 1948. Practice law Platte City, 1948-60; former pros. atty., 2Platte County, former mayor, Platte City; judge Jud. Circuit 6, 1960-64; commr. Mo. Supreme Ct., 1964-81, Jefferson City, asso. justice, 1981—. Past chmn. Platte County Democratic Central Com. Served with USN, 1943-46. Mem. Sigma Alpha Epsilon, Delta Theta Phi. Office: Supreme Ct Bldg Jefferson City MO 65101 *

HIGGINS, ANNE VOLZ, presidential assistant; b. N.Y.C., Oct. 7, 1939; m. George B. Higgins, 1968. B.A., George Washington U., 1974. Exec. sec. Office of Richard Nixon, N.Y.C., 1965-69; staff asst. to Pres. Nixon and Ford; dep. dir. corr., dir. Office of Presdl. Corr., Washington, 1969-77; mem. ad hoc Com. in Def. of Life, Washington, 1977-78, 79-80; exec. dir. Ams. for Constl. Conv., Washington, 1978-79; spl. asst. to pres. for correspondence The White House, Washington, 1981—. Office: Office of Asst to Pres and Dep Chief of Staff 1600 Pennsylvania Ave NW Washington DC 20500

HIGGINS, COLIN, writer, theater director; b. Noumea, New Caledonia, July 28, 1941; s. John Edward and Joy (Kelly) H. Student, St. Anthony's Coll., Robertson, N.S.W., Australia, 1958; B.A., Stanford U., 1967; M.F.A., UCLA, 1970. Writer: screenplay Harold and Maude, Paramount Pictures Corp., 1971; writer: stage play Harold et Maude, Jean-Louis Barrault's Co., Paris, 1973, (with Dennis Cannan) The IK, Peter Brook's Theater, Paris, 1974; screenplay Silver Streak, 20th Century-Fox, 1976; writer, dir.: Foul Play, Paramount Pictures Corp., 1978; writer (with Patricia Resnick) screenplay; dir.: Nine to Five, 20th Century-Fox, 1980; writer, dir. The Best Little Whorehouse in Texas, Universal Pictures-RKO, 1982; Author: Harold and Maude, 1971, Avon, 1972. Served with U.S. Army, 1962-65. Mem. Writers Guild Am. West, Inc., Dirs. Guild Am., Acad. Motion Picture Arts and Scis. Democrat. Roman Catholic. Office: Michael Ovitz Creative Artists Agy 1888 Century Park E Los Angeles CA 90067

HIGGINS, DICK, author, publisher; b. Cambridge, Eng., Mar. 15, 1938; s. Carter Chapin and Katharine (Bigelow) H.; m. Alison Knowles, May 31, 1960 (div. 1970); children: Hannah and Jessica (twins). Student, Yale, 1957; B.S., Columbia, 1960; postgrad., Manhattan Sch. Printing, 1960-61; A.M. in English, N.Y. U., 1977. Active in Happenings (Theater) movement, 1958-60; co-founder Fluxus movement, 1961—; U.S. editor De-Collage Mag., Germany, 1962—; founder Something Else Press, N.Y.C., 1964, pub., 1964-74; prof. publishing Calif. Inst. Arts, 1970-71; founder Unpub. Edits. (name now Printed Edits.), West Glover, Vt., 1973—; fellow Center for 20th Century Studies, U. Wis., Milw., 1977. Author (with Richard Maxfield); first electronic opera Stacked Deck, 1958-59; What Are Legends, 1960, Jefferson's Birthday/Postface, 1964, FOEW & OMBWHNW, 1968, Die Fabelhafte Geträume von Taifun-Willi, 1969, Computers for the Arts, 1970, Amigo, 1972, A Book about Love & War & Death, 1972, The Ladder to the Moon, 1973, For Eugene in Germany, 1973, Modular Poems, 1975, Classic Plays, 1976, Legends and Fishnets, 1976, George Herbert's Pattern Poems: In Their Tradition, 1977, Everyone Has Sher Favorite (His or Hers), 1977, A Dialectic of Centuries: Notes Towards a Theory of The New Arts, 1978, The Epickall Quest of the Brothers Dichtung, 1978, Hymns to the Night, 1978, some recent snowflakes (and other things), 1979, A Dialectic of Centuries, 1979, Piano Album, 1980, Of Celebration of Morning, 1980, Ten Ways of Looking at a Bird, 1981, 26 Mountains for Viewing the Sunset From, 1981, Sonata for Prepared Piano, 1982, Variations on a Natural Theme, 1982, Selected Early Works, 1982; also numerous plays, movies; transl.: Novalisi Hymns to the Night, 1978; Editor: (with Wolf Vostell) Pop Architektur, 1969, Fantastic Architecture, 1971. Mem. N.Y. Audiovisual Soc. (v.p.), N.Y. Mycol. Soc., Am. Mongolian Soc. Home: PO Box 27 Barrytown NY 12507 *My life is my work; my work is my life. Everything I do is intermedia—media between two or more other media.*

HIGGINS, EDWARD ALOYSIUS, journalist; b. St. Louis, Aug. 22, 1931; s. Edward Aloysius and Elsie (Gummersbach) H.; m. Mary Suzanne Vallar, May 15, 1954; children—Nancy Elizabeth, David Francis, Carol Marie. A.B., St. Louis U., 1953; Stanford Journalism fellow, Stanford, 1968-69. Gen. assignment reporter St. Louis Post-Dispatch, 1953-62, 63-67, asst. city editor, 1962-63, editorial writer, 1967—. Home: 1318 Christine Ave Des Peres MO 63131 Office: 900 N Tucker Blvd Saint Louis MO 63101

HIGGINS, GEOFFREY TREVOR, metall. engr., ednl. adminstr.; b. Wigan, Eng., Dec. 15, 1932; came to U.S., 1969; s. William and Muriel Harriet (Yarwood) H.; m. Heather Ann Lumsden, May, 1957; children—Andrew, Jacqueline, Mark, Jill, Peter. B.Sc., Manchester (Eng.) U., 1954, M.Sc., 1955, Ph.D., 1957. Asst. lectr. U. Manchester, 1957-59; sr. sci. officer U.K. Atomic Energy Authority, Culcheth, Eng., 1959-61; sr. lectr. U. Liverpool, Eng., 1961-69; dean Sch. Advanced Studies, profl. metall engring. Ill. Inst. Tech., Chgo., 1969—; cons. to industry. Rep. Lymm (Eng.) Urban Dist. Council, 1963-66. Brit. Steel Corp. grantee, 1965-70; Sci. Research Council grantee, 1966; U.K. Atomic Energy Authority grantee, 1963-70; NSF grantee, 1974-78; U.S. Army Research Office grantee, 1969-72; NASA grantee, 1971-75; Am. Iron and Steel Inst. and Industry grantee, 1973-76. Mem. Metals Soc. (London), Am. Soc. Metals, AIME. Home: 329 Woodland Ave Winnetka IL 60093 Office: 3300 S Federal St Chicago IL 60616

HIGGINS, GEORGE EDWARD, sculptor; b. Gaffney, S.C., Nov. 13, 1930. B.A., U. N.C. Instr. sculpture Parsons Sch. Design, N.Y.C., 1961-62. Vis. prof. Cornell U., 1968, U. Wis., 1968-69, U. Ky., 1969-70, Sch. Visual Arts, N.Y.C., 1964-72. One man shows, Leo Castelli Gallery, N.Y.C., 1960, 63, 66, Richard Feigen Gallery, Chgo., 1964, Mpls. Inst. Art, exhibited group shows Art, USA, 1959, Detroit Inst. Art, 1959-60, Carnegie Inst., 1961, Mus. Modern Art, N.Y.C., 1961, 63, Martha Jackson Gallery, N.Y.C., 1960, Andrew Dickson White Gallery, Bernard Gallery, Paris, France, Whitney Mus., N.Y.C., 1964, 66, Documenta, Kassel, Germany, 1968, Art Inst. Chgo., Brandeis U., Tate Gallery, London, Phila. Mus. Arts, New Sch. Art Center, N.Y.C., Smithsonian Instn., numerous others; represented in permanent collections, Whitney Mus., N.Y.C., Guggenheim Mus., N.Y.C., Albright-Knox Gallery, Buffalo, Houston Mus. Fine Arts, Mus. Modern Art, N.Y.C., Albright Art Gallery, Chase Manhattan Bank, N.Y.C., others. Address: RFD 4 Easton PA 18042

HIGGINS, GEORGE VINCENT, journalist, lawyer, author; b. Brockton, Mass., Nov. 13, 1939; s. John Thompson and Doris (Montgomery) H.; m. Elizabeth Mulkerin, Sept. 4, 1965 (div. Jan. 1979); children:Susan, John; m. Loretta Lucas Cubberley, Aug. 23, 1979. A.B., Boston Coll., 1961, J.D., 1967; M.A., Stanford U., 1965. Bar: Mass. 1967. Reporter Providence Jour., 1962-63; corr. A.P., Springfield, Mass., 1963-64, Boston, 1964-66; asst. atty. gen. Mass., Boston, 1967-70; cons. Nat. Inst. Law Enforcement, Washington, 1970-71; asst. U.S. atty. Mass., Boston, 1970-73, practiced in Boston, 1973—. Author: The Friends of Eddie Coyle, 1972, The Digger's Game, 1973, Cogan's Trade, 1974, A City on a Hill, 1975, The Friends of Richard Nixon, 1975, The Judgment of Deke Hunter, 1976, Dreamland, 1977, A Year or So With Edgar, 1979, Kennedy for the Defense, 1980, The Rat On Fire, 1981, The Patriot Game, 1982, Choice of Enemies, 1983; columnist: Boston Herald Am, 1977-79, Boston Globe, 1979—. Mem. Mass. Bar Assn., Am. Newspaper Guild, Writers Guild Am., mem. exec. com.). Home: 15 Brush Hill Ln Milton MA 02186

HIGGINS, JACK (HARRY PATTERSON), author; b. Newcastle, Eng., July 27, 1929; s. Harry and Henrietta Higgins (Bell) Patterson; m. Amy Margaret Hewitt, Dec. 28, 1958; children: Sarah, Ruth, Sean, Hannah. B.Sc. in Sociology and Social Psychology, London Sch. Econs., 1962. Factory worker, clerical worker, truck driver, 1945-58; lectr. liberal studies Leeds (Eng.) Poly. Inst.; sr. lectr. edn. James Graham Coll.; tutor in edn. Leeds U., 1958-70. Author: The Eagle Has Landed, 1975, Day of Judgement, 1978, Solo, 1980, Luciano's Lake, 1981, Touch of Devil, 1982. Served with Royal Horse Guards, 1947-50. Fellow Royal Soc. Arts. Presbyterian. Office: care David Higham Assos 5-8 Lower John St Golden Sq London W1R 4HA England *

HIGGINS, JAMES GEORGE, business executive; b. Reno, Oct. 25, 1928; s. George N. and Gertrude (Knaster) H.; m. Marilyn Massengale, June 28, 1975; children by previous marriage: Michael, Robert, Jay. B.S., U. Calif.-Berkeley, 1949. Mgmt. trainee Burroughs Adding Machine Co., San Francisco, 1949-51; agt., instr., chief conf. staff IRS, 1951-68; tax mgr. C. Brewer & Co., Ltd., Honolulu, 1968-70, asst. treas., 1970-71, treas., sec., 1971-72, v.p. taxes and ins., sec., 1972-77, v.p. adminstrn., sec., 1977, exec. asst. to pres., 1980-82, exec. asst. to chmn., 1982—. Bd. dirs. Goodwill Industries of Honolulu. Mem. Tax Execs. Inst. (past pres.). Home: 927 Prospect St Apt 1103 Honolulu HI 96822 Office: PO Box 1826 Honolulu HI 96805

HIGGINS, JAMES VICTOR, human geneticist; b. Sandusky, Ohio, Jan. 24, 1933; s. Charles Eugene and Marie Katherine (Olcott) H.; m. Patricia Margaret Braidwood, Sept. 5, 1953; children: Maureen, Kathleen, Michael; m. Kathleen Jane Delp, Aug. 20, 1983. B.S., Mich. State U., 1954; M.S., U. Minn., 1958, Ph.D., 1961. Asst. prof. zoology Mich. State U., 1961-66, asso. prof., 1966-70, prof. pediatrics/human devel. and zoology, 1970—, dir. Genetics Counseling Clinic, 1969—, dir. Cytogenetics Lab., 1969—; vis. asso. prof. med. genetics U. Oreg. Med. Sch., 1968-69. Mem. Am. Soc. Human Genetics, AAAS, Sigma Xi. Research on human cytogenetics and linkage. Home: 4257 Manitou Okemos MI 48864 Office: B240 Life Scis Bldg Mich State U East Lansing MI 48824

HIGGINS, JOHN JOSEPH, banker; b. Everett, Mass., Sept. 9, 1943; s. Doris (Gibbens) H.; m. Justine Mary Stankus, Sept. 18, 1965; children: Jeffrey, Donna, Jennifer. B.A., Northeastern U., 1966. C.P.A., N.Y. State. Mgr. Deloitte, Haskins & Sells, N.Y.C., 1966-75; audit mgr., v.p. Chem. Bank, N.Y.C., 1975-79, v.p., asst. controller, 1979-81, sr. v.p., controller, 1981—. Mem. Am. Inst. C.P.A.s, Bank Adminstrn. Inst. Club: Board Room (N.Y.C.). Office: Chemical Bank 55 Water St New York NY 10041

HIGGINS, PAUL VINCENT, consultant, freelance writer; b. N.Y.C., Oct. 30, 1919; s. Patrick J. and Rose (Degnan) H. B.S., Fordham U., 1941; M.A., NYU, 1948. Mem. faculty dept. English N.Y.U., 1949-51; pub. relations Kollsman Instrument Corp., N.Y.C., 1951-53, Greer Hydraulic Inc., 1953-55; account exec. Gaynor & Ducas Advt. Co., N.Y.C., 1955-57; v.p. O.S. Tyson Advt. Co., N.Y.C., 1957-65, E. H. Weiss Advt. Co., 1965-69; pres. Harrison, Higgins Inc., N.Y.C., 1969-82; cons., N.Y.C., 1982—; lectr. Marymount Coll., N.Y.C., 1982—. Served with U.S. Army, 1942-45. Home: 530 E 72d St New York NY 10021 *I was born a hyphenated American. Like so many sons of immigrants, I aspired to fulfill the dream of my parents and become truly a part of their adopted country. Some partial success has been achieved. But I lost one hyphen to acquire another: Pax-American.*

HIGGINS, PETER THOMAS, foreign service officer; b. Hollywood, Calif., Sept. 19, 1936; s. Thomas Elkin and Frances Lenore (Kanary) H.; m. Betty Louise Hughart, Jan. 16, 1960; children: Carolyn Elizabeth, Mark Thomas, Sean Patrick. B.S. in Fgn. Service, Georgetown U., 1958; postgrad, Nat. War Coll., Washington, 1980. Consular officer Am. Consulate Gen., Guadalajara, Mexico, 1959-61; econ. officer Am. Embassy, Madrid, 1962-64, Lome, Togo, 1967-69; comml. officer Am. Consulate Gen., Barcelona, Spain, 1969-71; econ. officer Am. Embassy, Ottawa, Ont., Can., 1971-74, dep. chief mission, Kigali, Rwanda, 1974-77; consul gen. Am. Consulate Gen., Auckland, N.Z., 1980—. 2d lt. USAR, 1958-59. Club: Rotary (Auckland). Home: 44 Paritai Dr Auckland New Zealand 5 Office: Am Consulate General Private Bag Auckland New Zeland 1

HIGGINS, ROBERT LOUIS, trade assn. exec.; b. Youngstown, Ohio, Apr. 30, 1919; s. John F. and Rosella (Johnson) H.; m. Carol Geary, Jan. 18, 1946; children—Robert Louis, Melinda Jane, Geary Michael, Mark Stuart. B.S. in Elec. Engring, Ohio U., 1949. With Nat. Elec. Contractors Assn., 1949—, exec. v.p., 1960—; Mem. Pres. Nixon's Commn. on Constrn. Industry Collective Bargaining; also for Pres. Ford; mem. Constrn. Industry Collective Bargaining Com., Nat. Constrn. Industry Council, Asso. Splty. Contractors, Inc., Council Indsl. Relations Elec. Contracting Industry, Fed. Com. on Apprenticeship. Co-trustee Nat. Elec. Benefit Fund; mem. bd. Acad. Elec. Contracting. Home: 7713 Glennon Dr Bethesda MD 20817 Office: 7315 Wisconsin Ave Bethesda MD 20814

HIGGINS, STEPHEN E., government official; b. McCracken, Kans., Oct. 19, 1938; s. Samuel L. H. and Maurine (Settles) Walker; m. Cheryl Buckley, Oct. 2, 1971; children: Angela, Tamela, 1 stepson, Warren Callis. B.S. in Bus. Adminstrn., Coll. Emporia, 1961; postgrad., U. Wash., 1968-69. From insp. to dir. Bur. Alcohol, Tobacco & Firearms, U.S. Treasury Dept., Omaha and Washington, 1961—. Recipient Nat. Inst. Pub. Affairs Career Edn, 1968, Meritorious Exec. U.S. Dept. Treasury, 1980. Mem. Internat. Assn. Chiefs of Police (exec. com. 1983). Office: Bur Alcohol Tobacco and Firearms 1200 Pennsylvania Ave NW Washington DC 20226 *

HIGGINS, THERESE, college president; b. Winthrop, Mass., Sept. 29, 1925; d. James C. and Margaret M. (Lennon) H. A.B. cum laude, Regis Coll., 1947; M.A., Boston Coll.; Ph.D., U. Wis.; D.H.L., Emmanuel Coll.; postgrad. in lit. and theology, Harvard U.; LL.D. (hon.), Northeastern U. Joined Congregation of Sisters of St. Joseph, Roman Cath. Ch., 1947; instr. Regis Coll., Weston, Mass., 1963-65, asst. prof., 1965-67, asso. prof., 1968—, pres., 1974—, also trustee. Book reviewer: Boston Globe, 1965—. Trustee Waltham (Mass.) Hosp., 1978—, Cardinal Spellman Philatelic Mus., 1976—; mem. Mass. Gov.'s Commn. on Status Women, 1977-79, Nat. Com. Ecclesial Role Women. U. Wis. research grantee, Eng. Mem. Nat. Cath. Ednl. Assn., AAUW, MLA, AAUP, Assn. Ind. Colls. and Univs. Mass. (exec. com.), New Eng. Colls. Fund, Women's Coll. Coalition (exec. com.), Council Ind. Colls. (dir.). Office: 235 Wellesley St Weston MA 02193

HIGGINS, WILLIAM HENRY CLAY, telecommunications cons.; b. Montclair, N.J., Apr. 26, 1908; s. William H.C. and Grace Eliza (Brown) H.; m. Ruth Henrietta Matz, Aug. 14, 1930; dec. June 1979; m. LaDonna M. Erickson, Oct. 26, 1980. B.S. with distinction in Elec. Engring, Purdue U., 1929, E.E., 1934, D.Engring. (hon.), 1978. Engr. AT&T, N.Y.C., 1929-34; with Bell Telephone Lab., Inc., N.Y.C., 1934-40, Whipanny, N.J., 1940-62, Holmdel, N.J., 1962-73, exec. dir. mil. electronics, 1953-60, exec. dir. electronic switching, 1960-66, v.p. switching systems, 1966-73; cons. North Electric Co., Galion, Ohio, 1973-74, group v.p. research and devel., 1974-77; Del., Ohio, cons. United Telecommunications, Inc., Kansas City, Mo., 1977-78. Contbr.: articles to Bell Lab Record, German Bundespost Yearbook, 1964, History of Engineering and Science in the Bell System, 1973. Fellow IEEE; mem. Sigma Xi (asso.), Tau Beta Pi, Eta Kappa Nu. Republican. Methodist. Home and Office: 20214 126th Ave Sun City West AZ 85375 *Promotion should never be a goal. Promotions come-if deserved. One gets there by earning it-not by wanting it. Some say "being at the right place at the right time" brings success. Those who say so are largely among the unsuccessful.*

HIGGINSON, JAMES JACKSON, lawyer; b. N.Y.C., Dec. 10, 1921; s. James J. and Virginia (Mitchell) H. Grad., Groton (Mass.) Sch., 1940; B.A., Harvard U., 1943, LL.B., 1949. Bar: N.Y. bar 1949, U.S. Supreme Ct. bar 1957. Practiced in, N.Y.C., 1949—; partner firm Appleton, Rice & Perrin, 1969—; Dir. F.H. Prince & Co., Inc. Served to capt. AUS, 1943-46, 50-52. Mem. Am., N.Y. State bar assns., Assn. Bar City N.Y. Home: 800 Fifth Ave New York NY 10021 Office: 444 Madison Ave New York NY 10022

HIGGINSON, THOMAS LEE, lawyer; b. N.Y.C., Jan. 2, 1920; s. James Jackson and Lucy Virginia (Mitchell) H.; m. Theodora Winthrop, Sept. 11, 1948; children: Thomas Lee Jr., Elizabeth, Robert Winthrop. Student, Groton Sch.; A.B., Harvard U., 1942, LL.B., 1949. Bar: N.Y. 1950. Since practiced in N.Y.C.; mem. firm Shearman & Sterling, 1957—; v.p., dir. Hamiltonian Corp.; exec. com., dir. Fiduciary Trust Co. of N.Y. Bd. dirs., sec. Nassau Hosp. Assn.; trustee, sec. The Frick Collection. Served from 2d lt. to maj. AUS, 1942-46. Decorated Bronze Star. Mem. Am., N.Y. State bar assns., Assn. Bar City N.Y. Republican. Episcopalian. Clubs: Brook, Links, Downtown Assn. (N.Y.C.); Piping Rock (L.I.). Office: 53 Wall St New York NY 10005

HIGGS, DEWITT A., lawyer; b. Soldier, Idaho, Dec. 13, 1907; s. DeWitt P. and Vina (Reedy) H.; m. Florence J. Fuller, Dec. 25, 1929; children: Barbara Lee, Craig DeWitt. LL.B., Calif. Western U., 1934. Bar: Calif. 1934, U.S. Supreme Ct 1939. Practice law, specializing trial work, municipal and water law, San Diego; now sr. partner Higgs, Fletcher & Mack; city atty., Chula Vista, 1940-42, 46-47; mem. Jud. Council Calif., 1961-64; Mem. bd. regents U. Calif., 1966-82, chmn., 1968-70, vice chmn., 1970-71. Served lt. comdr. USNR, 1942-45. Fellow Am. Coll. Trial Lawyers, Am. Bar Found.; mem. ABA, San Diego County Bar Assn. (dir. 1938-40, pres. 1940), State Bar of Calif. (bd. govs. 1952-55, pres. 1955), Am. Legion (post comdr. 1947). Club: San Diego Country (Chula Vista). Home: 12 Toyon Ln Chula Vista CA 92010 Office: 2000 Columbia Centre 401 W A St San Diego CA 92101

HIGGS, LLOYD ALBERT, astronomer, observatory adminstrator; b. Moncton, N.B., Can., June 21, 1937; s. Maxwell Lemert and Reta Mae (Jollimore) H.; m. Kathleen Mary Fletcher, Jan. 15, 1966; children: Kevin, Scott, Michelle. B.Sc., U. N.B., Fredericton, 1958; D.Phil., Oxford (Eng.) U., 1961. Research officer NRC Can., Ottawa, Ont., 1961-81; dir. Dominion radio Astrophys. Obs., Penticton, B.C., 1981—; research officer Leiden (Holland) U., 1964-65. Researcher numerous publs. in astronomy. Leader Boy Scouts Can., 1977—. Beaverbrook scholar, 1954-58; Rhodes scholar, 1958-61. Fellow Royal Astron. Soc.; mem. Am. Astron. Soc., Can. Astron. Soc., Royal Astron. Soc. Can. (life mem., editor jour. 1976-80, Service award 1983), Internat. Astron. Union. Office: Dominion Radio Astrophys Obs PO Box 248 Penticton BC Canada V2A 6K3

HIGH, GEORGE BORMAN, foreign service officer; b. Chgo., July 25, 1931; s. Oscar and Harriet (Borman) H.; m. Elizabeth Codman, Jan. 28, 1956; children: Mark Randall, Susan Jane. A.B., Dartmouth Coll., 1953; J.D., Columbia U., 1956. Bar: D.C. 1958. Intern UN, 1955; commd. fgn. ser. officer Dept. State, 1956, intelligence research specialist, Washington, 1956-59; econ. officer, Luanda, Angola, 1959-61; detailed Arabic lang. and area tng. Fgn. Service Inst. Field Sch., Beirut, 1961-62; acting officer-in-charge South Africa, Washington, 1962-63, officer-in-charge Angola-Mozambique affairs, 1962-65, officer-in-charge Madagascar affairs, 1964-65, dep. prin. officer, Guayaquil, Ecuador, 1965-68, polit. officer, Buenos Aires, 1968-72; assigned to U.S. Army War Coll., Carlisle Barracks, Pa., 1972-73; asst. dir. for polit. affairs Office Caribbean Affairs, Washington, 1973-75; fgn. service insp., Washington, 1975-78; dep. chief of mission U.S. Embassy, Brasilia, Brazil, 1978-82, Mexico City, 1982-83; dir. Office of Mex. Affairs, Washington, 1983—. Recipient Meritorious Service award Dept. State, 1972, Superior Honor award Dept. State, 1983. Home: 426 Blair Rd NW Vienna VA 22180

HIGHAM, JOHN, educator; b. N.Y.C., Oct. 26, 1920; s. LLoyd Stuart and Margaret (Windred) H.; m. Eileen Moss, Aug. 26, 1948; children—Margaret, Constance, Jay, Daniel. B.A., Johns Hopkins, 1941; Ph.D., U. Wis., 1949. Instr. history U. Cal. at Los Angeles, 1948-50, asst. prof., 1950-54; asso. prof. Rutgers U., 1954-58, prof., 1958-60;

prof. history U. Mich., Ann Arbor, 1961-67, Moses Coit Tyler Univ. prof., 1968-71, 72-73; vis. asso. prof. Columbia, 1958-59; John Martin Vincent prof. Johns Hopkins, 1971-72, 73—; directeur d'études associé Ecole des Hautes Etudes en Sciences Sociales, Paris, 1981-82. Author: Strangers in the Land, 1955, History: Humanistic Scholarship in America, 1965, Writing American History, 1970, Send These to Me, 1975; Editor: The Reconstruction of American History, 1962, Ethnic Leadership in America, 1978, New Directions in American Intellectual History, 1979. Served with USAAF, 1943-45. Princeton U. Council Humanities fellow, 1960-61; Commonwealth Fund lectr. Univ. Coll., London, 1968; Center Advanced Study Behavioral Scis. fellow, 1965-66; Phi Beta Kappa vis. scholar, 1972-73; mem. Inst. Advanced Study, 1973-74; Fullbright-Hays lectr. Kyoto Am. Studies Seminar, 1974; fellow Woodrow Wilson Internat. Center for Scholars, 1976-77. Mem. Am. Acad. Arts and Scis., Am. Hist. Assn. (council and exec. com. 1971-74, rep. to Am. Council Learned Socs. 1977-80), Orgn. Am. Historians (pres. 1973-74), Mich. Soc. Fellows (sr. fellow 1971-73), New Soc. Letters Lund (Sweden), Am. Antiquarian Soc., Am. Studies Assn., Soc. Am. Historians, Immigration History Soc. (pres. 1979-82). Office: Dept History Johns Hopkins Univ Baltimore MD 21218

HIGHAM, ROBIN, history educator, editor; b. London, June 20, 1925; U.S., 1940, naturalized, 1954; s. Frank) David and Margaret) Anne (Stewart) H.; m. Barbara Davies, Aug. 5, 1950; children: Susan Elizabeth, Martha Anne, Carol Lee. A.B. cum laude, Harvard U., 1950, Ph.D., 1957; M.A., Claremont Grad. Sch., 1953. Instr. Webb Sch. Calif., 1950-52; grad. asst. in oceanic history Harvard U., 1952-54; instr. U. Mass., 1954-57; asst. prof. U. N.C., Chapel Hill, 1957-63; asso. prof. Kans. State U., 1963-66, prof., 1966—; historian Brit. Overseas Airways Corp., 1960-66, 76-78; editor Mil. Affairs, 1968—, Aerospace Historian, 1970—; editor, co-pub. Jour. of West, 1977—; adv. editor Tech. and Culture, 1967—; founder, pres. Sunflower Univ. Press, 1978—; mil. adv. editor Univ. Press Ky., 1970-75; archivist Am. Com. for History Second World War, 1979—, trustee, 1981—; cons. Epic of Flight, Time/Life Books, 1980-82; lectr. in field; mem. publs. com. Conf. Brit. Studies, 1965—, chmn. travel com., 1965-66; sec. Tri-Univ. com. to convert U. Kans. Press to Univ. Press Kans., Lawrence, Manhattan and Wichita, 1966-67, search com., 1970-71; adviser Core Collection for Coll. Libraries, 1971-72; pres. cons. com. Revue Internat. d'Histoire Militaire, 1982—. Author: Britain's Imperial Air Routes, 1918-39, 1960, The British Rigid Airship, 1908-31, 1961, Armed Forces in Peacetime: Britain 1918-39, 1963, The Military Intellectuals in Britain: 1918-1939, 1966, (with David H. Zook) A Short History of Warfare, 1966, The Compleat Academic (Macmillan Book Club choice), 1975, Air Power: A Concise History (selection Mil. Book Soc., History Book Club, Flying Book Club), 1973, (with Mary Cisper & Guy Dresser) A Brief Guide to Scholarly Editing, 1982; editor: Bayonets in the Street, 1969, Civil Wars in the Twentieth Century, 1972, A Guide to the Sources of British Military History, 1971, A Guide to the Sources of U.S. Military History, 1975, supplement, 1981, The U.S. Army in Peacetime: Essays in Honor of the Bicentennial, 1975, Intervention or Abstention, 1975, (with Jacob W. Kipp) Soviet Aviation and Air Power, 1977, Flying Combat Aircraft, vol. 1, 1975, vol. 2, 1978, vol. 3, 1981; cons.: Dictionary of Business Biography, 1980—; contbr. articles to profl. jours. Organizer Gov.'s Conf. on Future of Rural Kans., 1975; chmn., presdl. rep. Pres.'s Com. on Freedom Park and Kans. State U., 1973—. Served with RAF, 1943-46. Named hon. col. Tar Heel Air Force, 1962, Disting. Personality Kans. State U., 1967; Social Sci. Research Council nat. security policy research fellow, 1960-61. Mem. Am. Hist. Assn. (permanent liaison officer with Soc. History Tech.), Am. Aviation Hist. Soc., Aviation and Space Writers Assn., Soc. History Tech. (liaison officer with Am. Hist. Assn.), Friends of RAF Mus. (life mem.), Air Force Hist. Found., U.S. Naval Inst., Soc. Army Hist. Research (corr. mem. council 1980—), Am. Mil. Inst., Orgn. Am. Historians, AIAA (standing com. history 1973—), Am. Com. History Second World War (dir. 1973-75, 79-82, archivist 1977—), U.S. Commn. on Mil. History (chmn. pubs. com.), Internat. Commn. on Mil. History (editorial bd.), Soc. Scholarly Pub. (nat. publs. com. 1980—). Home: 2961 Nevada St Manhattan KS 66502

HIGHBLOOM, LLOYD HENRY, advt. agy. exec.; b. N.Y.C., Aug. 2, 1939; s. Joseph and Rose (Steinberg) H.; m. Maxine Miller, Dec. 22, 1962; children—Marc, David. B.S. in Advt. and Mktg, Fairleigh Dickinsom U., Teaneck, N.J., 1961. With Doyle Dane Bernbach, N.Y.C., 1962—, v.p., then sr. v.p., 1972-80, group sr. v.p., 1980—, also dir. Home: Millwood Rd Mt Kisco NY 10549 Office: 437 Madison Ave New York NY 10022

HIGHET, GILBERT KEITH MACINNES, lawyer; b. Oxford, Eng., May 20, 1933; came to U.S., 1938, naturalized, 1951; s. Gilbert and Helen (MacInnes) H.; m. Nancy Bryan Blair (Trask), Oct. 11, 1976; 1 dau., Mary Marshall MacInnes; children by previous marriage: Ian Douglas, Eliot Chace; stepsons: Nicholas Randolph Trask (dec. 1980), Ethan Barber Trask. B.A. magna cum laude in English, Harvard U., 1954, LL.B., 1960; postgrad, Balliol Coll., Oxford, Eng., 1956-57. Bar: N.Y. 1962, D.C. 1973. Lectr. law Ghana Sch. Law, Accra, 1961; asso. firm Sullivan & Cromwell, N.Y.C., 1961-63; counsel Internat. Ct. of Justice, The Hague, 1963-66, 80—; assoc. firm Curtis, Mallet-Prevost, Colt & Mosle, N.Y.C., 1966-68; partner Curtis, Mallet-Prevost, Colt & Mosle, 1968—. Dir., v.p. The Am. Ditchley Found., N.Y.C. Served to 1st lt. USMCR, 1954-56. Mem. ABA; Mem. Assn. Bar City N.Y., Am. Soc. Internat. Law (exec. council, v.p. 1983—), Am. Law Inst., Internat. Law Assn., Council on Fgn. Relations, Am. Fgn. Law Assn. (dir. 1978), Fed. Bar Council (trustee 1976). Presbyterian. Clubs: Century, Edgartown Yacht, Englewood Field, India House. Home: 280 N Woodland St Englewood NJ 07631 also River Rd Deep River CT 06417 Office: 101 Park Ave New York NY 10178

HIGHFILL, WILLIAM CARL, librarian; b. Hontubby, Okla., Aug. 12, 1935; s. William Herman and Rosemary (Kemmerer) H.; m. Claudia Thompson, Oct. 5, 1957; children—Sarah Elizabeth, William Clinton, James Kemmerer. A.B. in English, Okla. Baptist U., 1957; M.S. in L.S, Kans. State Tchrs. Coll., 1961, Ph.D., U. Ill., 1969. Tchr., librarian Isabel (Kans.) High Sch., 1957-59, Chase County Community High Sch., Cottonwood Falls, Kans., 1959-62; asst. librarian Kans. State Tchrs. Coll., Emporia, 1962-65, vis. instr. dept. librarianship, 1966, 68; dir. library East Tex. State U., 1969-73; univ. librarian Auburn (Ala.) U., 1973—; del. White House Conf. on Libraries, 1980. Trustee Auburn Public Library, 1974-77. HEA fellow, 1966, 68. Mem. ALA, Ala. Library Assn. (pres. 1979-80), Southeastern Library Assn., Phi Beta Mu, Phi Kappa Phi. Democrat. Office: Ralph Brown Draughon Library Auburn University Auburn AL 36849

HIGHLAND, CECIL BLAINE, JR., newspaper pub., lawyer, banker; b. New Martinsville, W.Va., Nov. 23, 1918; s. Cecil Blaine and Ella C. (Clark) H.; m. Barbara Brennan, June 4, 1955; 1 dau., Ellen Brennan. A.B., W.Va. U., 1939; J.D., Harvard, 1949. Bar: W.Va. bar 1949. Practiced in, Clarksburg, 1949—; now partner firm McNeer, Highland and McMunn.; Pres. Empire Nat. Bank, Clarksburg, 1957—, also dir.; dir. Clarksburg Pub. Co., 1949—, pres., gen. mgr., treas., 1957—; pub. Clarksburg Exponent, Clarksburg Telegram & Sunday Exponent-Telegram, 1957—. Served with AUS, 1940-46; lt. col. Res. ret. Mem. Am., W.Va., Harrison County bar assns., Am. Legion, Harvard, W.Va. law sch. assns., Phi Beta Kappa, Phi Kappa Psi. Republican. Episcopalian. Clubs: Mason (32 deg., Shriner), Elk.). Office: Empire Nat Bank Clarksburg WV 26301

HIGHLEYMAN, SAMUEL LOCKE, III, lawyer; b. Kansas City, Mo., June 1, 1928; s. Samuel Locke and Kate (Reynolds) H. B.B.A., U. Miami, Fla., 1951, M.A. in Econs., 1954; J.D., Yale U., 1957; diploma, Columbia U., 1962. Bar: Calif. 1957, N.Y. 1972, U.S. Supreme Ct. 1965. Assoc. firm Craveth, Swaine & Moore, N.Y.C., 1956, firm O'Melveny & Myers, Los Angeles, 1957-64; ptnr. firm Coudert Bros., N.Y.C., 1964—; cons., dir. various firms. Vestryman All Saints Episcopal Ch., Pasadena, Calif., 1959-63; vestryman, chancellor St. Bartholemew's Ch., N.Y.C., 1980—. Capt. USAF, 1951-53. Clubs: Union League, Racquet and Tennis, Sky, Le Club (N.Y.C.); California (Los Angeles); Annabel's (London). Office: Coudert Bros 200 Park Ave New York NY 10166

HIGHSAW, JAMES LEONARD, JR., lawyer; b. Memphis, Jan. 6, 1914; s. James Leonard and May (Baker) H.; m. Jane Fillmore Dunlap, June 20, 1945; children: Rhoda Jane (Mrs. Alan P. Agle), James Leonard III, Carol Anne. A.B., Princeton, 1935; J.D., Harvard U., 1941. Bar: Tenn. 1940, D.C. 1954. Staff atty. Nat. Home Loan Bd., 1941-44, CAB, 1944-48, chief intercarrier relationship, 1948-51, chief litigation, 1951-55; partner firm Mulholland, Hickey & Lyman, Washington, 1955-69; sr. partner Highsaw & Mahoney, Washington, 1970-76, Highsaw & Mahoney, P.C., 1976—; lectr. aviation law Am. U. Law Sch. Chmn. Drummond (Md.) Citizens Com., 1966-76. Author articles in field. Mem. ABA (co-chmn. equal employment opportunity com. 1977-79), Fed. Bar Assn., D.C. Bar Assn., Phi Beta Kappa. Democrat. Presbyterian. Home: 4601 Drummond Ave Chevy Chase MD 20815 Office: 1050 17th St NW Washington DC 20036

HIGHSMITH, SHELBY, lawyer; b. Jacksonville, Fla., Jan. 31, 1929; s. Isaac Shelby and Edna Mae (Phillips) H.; m. Mary Jane Zimmerman, Nov. 25, 1972; children—Holly Law, Shelby. A.A., Ga. Mil. Coll., 1948; B.A., J.D., U. Kansas City, 1958. Bar: Fla. bar 1958. Trial atty., Kansas City, Mo., 1958-59, Miami, Fla., 1959-70, circuit judge, Dade County, Fla., 1970-75; sr. ptnr. firm Highsmith, Strauss, & Glatzer (P.A.), Miami, 1975—. Chief legal adviser Gov.'s War on Crime Program, 1967-68; spl. counsel Fla. Racing Commn., 1969-70; mem. Inter-Agy. Law Enforcement Planning Counsel of Fla., 1969-70. Served to capt. AUS, 1949-55. Decorated Bronze Star. Fellow Internat. Soc. Barristers; mem. Am., Dade County bar assns., Fla. Acad. Trial Lawyers, Omicron Delta, Bench and Robe, Torch and Scroll, Phi Alpha Delta. Republican. Methodist. Home: 8540 SW 120th St Miami FL 33156 Office: 3370 Mary St Coconut Grove Miami FL 33133

HIGHSMITH, WILLIAM EDWARD, univ. chancellor; b. Eastland, Tex., Mar. 21, 1920; s. Robert A. and Dollie (Marshall) H.; m. Allene Sugg, Aug. 15, 1953; children—William Edward, John Marshall. A.B., Southeastern Coll., 1942; M.A., La. State U., 1947, Ph.D., 1953. Julius Rosenwald research fellow, 1948-49; instr. history U. Ark., 1949-50, La. State U., 1950-51; dir. Caribbean program La. State U., 1951-54, Gadsden Center U. Ala., 1954-57; prof. Jacksonville U., 1957, dean, 1957-62; pres. Asheville-Biltmore Coll., 1962-69; chancellor U. N.C., Asheville, 1969—; Dir. Duval Safety Council, Jacksonville; chmn. Opportunity Corp. Asheville-Buncombe County. Author articles, reviews. Mem. bd. advisers St. Luke's Hosp. Sch. Nursing; bd. dirs. Greater Asheville Council, United Fund, Asheville Symphony Soc., Asheville Community Concert Assn.; chmn. Mountain Area Health Edn. Center; trustee St. Mary's Coll., Asheville Country Day Sch.; bd. dirs. Art Mus.; bd. dirs., pres. Meml. Mission Hosp.; gen. chmn. Venture in Mission, Diocese of Western N.C.; mem. governing body Western N.C. Health Systems Agy. Served to cpl. USAAF, 1942-46. Mem. So., Miss. Valley hist. assns., Asheville C. of C. (dir.), N.C. Assn. Colls. and Univs. (pres.), Conf. Acad. Deans So. States (sec.-treas. 1961-62), Blue Key, Phi Kappa Phi, Theta Xi (nat. pub. relations com.). Democrat. Episcopalian (vestryman). Clubs: Pen and Plate (pres.), Rotary (pres., dir.). Home: 62 Macon Ave Asheville NC 28801

HIGHTOWER, JACK ENGLISH, Congressman; b. Memphis, Tex., Sept. 6, 1926; s. Walter Thomas and Floy Edna (English) H.; m. Colleen Ward, Aug. 26, 1950; children—Ann, Amy, Alison. B.A., Baylor U., 1949; LL.B., 1951. Bar: Tex. bar 1951. Since practiced in, Vernon; mem. Tex. Ho. of Reps., 1953-54; dist. atty. 46th Jud. Dist. Tex., 1955-61; mem. Tex. Senate, 1965-74, pro tempore, 1972; mem. 94th-97th Congresses from 13th Tex. Dist. Mem. Tex. Law Enforcement Study Commn., 1957; del. White House Conf. Children and Youth, 1970; alt. del. Democratic Nat. Conv., 1968; bd. regents Midwestern U., Wichita Falls, Tex., 1962-64; trustee Baylor U., 1971—. Served with USNR, 1944-46. Named Outstanding Dist. Atty. Tex. Tex. Law Enforcement Found., 1957. Clubs: Masons (grand master Tex. 1972), Lions (pres. Vernon 1961). Home: 2719 Mansard St Vernon TX 76384 Office: 2348 Rayburn House Office Bldg Washington DC 20515

HIGHTOWER, JOE WALTER, chemical engineering educator, consultant; b. Morrilton, Ark., Sept. 14, 1936; s. Walter Eugene and Verda Mae (Poindexter) H.; m. Sallie Turner, Sept. 14, 1936; m. Ann Grekel, May 11, 1980. B.S., Harding Coll., Searcy, Ark., 1959; M.S., Johns Hopkins U., 1961, Ph.D., 1963. Postdoctoral fellow Queens U., Belfast, No. Ireland, 1963-64; research assoc. Mellon Inst., Pitts., 1964-67; assoc. prof. chem. engring. Rice U., Houston, 1967-70, prof., 1970—; cons. Exxon Research & Devel. Co., Linden, N.J., 1970—; sci. adv. bd. Haldor Topsoe A-S, Copenhagan, 1976—; adv. bd. Catalytica Assocs., Stanford, Calif., 1975—; chmn. bd. trustees Gordon Research Conf., 1980-81; chmn. 5 coms. NRC, 1972-78. Editor: Proceedings 4th Internat. Congress on Catalysis, 1972, Procs. 5th Internat. Congress on Catalysis, 1976; editorial bd.: Energy Courses, 1978—, Indsl. and Engring. Chemistry, 1981—; editorial bd: Profl. Design and Devel., 1981—; editorial bd.: Jour. Catalysis, 1984—; contbr. articles to sci. jours. Co-founder, pres. Human Resources Devel. Found., Houston, 1967—. Recipient Jefferson award for pub. service, Houston, 1982. Mem. Am. Chem. Soc. (chmn. petroleum chemistry div. 1974-75, Nat. award in petroleum chemistry 1973, award Southeastern Tex. sect. 1976), Am. Inst. Chem. Engring. Republican. Mem. Ch. of Christ. Home: 2346 Quenby St Houston TX 77005 Office: Rice University PO Box 1892 Houston TX 77251

HIGHTOWER, JOHN BRANTLEY, arts administrator; b. Atlanta, May 23, 1933; s. Edward A. and Margaret (Kimzey) H.; children—Amanda, Matthew. B.A. in English, Yale, 1955; D.F.A., Calif. Coll. Arts and Crafts. Asst. to pub. Am. Heritage Pub. Co., Inc., N.Y.C., 1961-63; exec. asst. N.Y. State Council Arts, N.Y.C., 1963-64, exec. dir., 1964-70; dir. Mus. Modern Art, N.Y.C., 1970-72; pres. Asso. Councils Arts, N.Y.C., 1972-74, South St. Seaport, 1977-83, bd. dirs., 1983—; exec. dir. Richard Tucker Music Found., 1977—; founder, chmn. Advocates for Arts, 1974-77; instr. arts mgmt. Wharton Sch., 1976-77, New Sch., 1976-77; Cultural adviser Rockefeller Mission to Latin Am., 1969; Fulbright fellow, rep. UNESCO Conf. on Performing Arts, Canberra, Australia, 1969; vis. critic in arts adminstrn. Yale Grad. Sch. Drama, 1972-77; chmn. Planning Corp. for Arts, Urban Arts Corps. Bd. dirs. N.Y. State Council on Arts, Poets and Writers, Inst. Art and Urban Resources. Served with USMCR, 1955-57. Recipient N.Y. State award, 1970. Club: Century Assn. (N.Y.C.). Home: 304 W 88th St New York NY 10024

HIGHTOWER, JOHN MURMANN, journalist, educator, writer; b. Coal Creek, Tenn., Sept. 17, 1909; s. James Edward and Mary Elizabeth (Murmann) H.; m. Martha Nadine Joiner, Nov. 19, 1938; children—John Murmann, Leslie, James Edward. Student, U. Tenn., 1927-28. Asso. editor Drug Topics mag., 1929-30; reporter Knoxville (Tenn.) News-Sentinel, 1931-33; reporter, editor Asso. Press, Nashville, 1933-36, assigned, 1936-71, gen. reporting, news editing, 1936-40, Navy Dept. coverage, 1940-42, Dept. State and internat. affairs coverage, 1943-71, spl. corr., 1964-71; covered UN orgn., San Francisco, 1945; opening session UN, London, Eng., 1946, N.Y.C., 1946; European peace treaty sessions Council Fgn. Ministers, London, Moscow, USSR, N.Y.C., 1946-48; orgn. Marshall Plan, North Atlantic Treaty, Japanese Peace Conf., San Francisco, 1951, Bermuda Conf., 1953, Berlin Fgn. Ministers Conf., 1954, Big-Four Summit Conf., Four Power Fgn. Ministers Conf., Geneva, 1955, 2d Bermuda Conf., 1957, NATO Summit Conf., 1957, Berlin, Disarmament Negotiations, Paris Summit, 1960, Kennedy-Khrushchev Meeting, 1961, Manila Summit Conf. on Vietnam, 1966, Paris Peace Talks, 1968; asso. prof. journalism U. N.Mex., Albuquerque, 1971-74. Recipient Pulitzer prize internat. reporting, 1951; Raymond Clapper Meml. award, 1951; Sigma Delta Chi award for nat. reporting, 1951; citation Overseas Press Club, 1955; Am. Acad. Achievement award for Washington corr., 1970; decorated Comdr.'s Cross Order Merit, Fed. Republic Germany; chevalier Légion d'Honneur, France). Club: Gridiron (Washington). Address: 916 Old Santa Fe Trail Santa Fe NM 87501

HIGHTOWER, NEIL HAMILTON, textile manufacturing company executive; b. Atlanta, Dec. 31, 1940; s. William H. and Elinor (Hamilton) H.; m. Kay Trogdon, Aug. 2, 1980; children by previous marriage—Neil Hamilton, John, Heidi. B.S., Ga. Inst. Tech., 1963; Program for Mgmt. Devel., Harvard U. Bus. Sch., 1974. Cost acct. Thomaston (Ga.) Mills, Inc., 1965-66, asst. treas., 1966-73, sr. v.p. indsl. sales, 1973-77, exec. v.p., 1977—, dir., 1980—; dir. C&S Bank of Thomaston. Mem. Thomaston Bd. Edn., 1972-79, chmn., 1978-79; Bd. dirs., treas Textile Edn. Found., 1981, v.p., 1982, pres., 1983. Served to 1st lt. AUS, 1963-65. Mem. Textile Traffic Assn. (pres. 1980-81), Ga. Textile Mfrs. Assn. (dir.), Am. Yarn Spinners Assn. (dir.), Textile Edn. Found. (dir.), So. Indsl. Relations Conf. (dir. 1981—). Methodist. Club: Kiwanis. Home: 304 Cherokee Rd Thomaston GA 30286 Office: Thomaston Mills Inc PO Box 311 Thomaston GA 30286

HIGHWATER, JAMAKE, author, lecturer; b. Mont., Feb. 14, 1942; s. Jamie and Amana (Bonneville) H. Lectr. primal culture various univs. in, U.S. and Can., 1970—; grad. lectr. N.Y. U. Continuing Edn., 1979—; asst. prof. Grad. Sch. Architecture, Columbia U., 1983; cons. N.Y. State Council on the Arts, 1975—; founding mem. Indian Art Found., Santa Fe, 1980—, Cultural Council, Am. Indian Community House, N.Y.C., 1976, pres., 1976-78; mem. task force on individual artist N.Y. State Council on Arts, 1981, mem. lit. panel, 1982-83. Host, narrator and writer of: TV series Native Land, Public Broadcasting Service Network, 1983; Author: Indian America: A Cultural and Travel Guide, 1975, Song From the Earth: American Indian Painting, 1976 (Anisfield-Wolf award in race relations 1980), Ritual of the Wind: No. American Indian Ceremonies, Music and Dances, 1977, Many Smokes, Many Moons, 1978 (Jane Addams Peace Book award), Dance: Rituals of Experience, 1978; novel Journey to the Sky: Stephens and Catherwood's Rediscovery of the Maya World, 1978; The Sweet Grass Lives On: 50 Contemporary North American Indian Artists, 1980, Masterpieces of American Indian Painting, 8 vols, 1978-80, The Primal Mind: Vision and Reality in Indian America, 1981 (Virginia McCormick Scully Lit. award 1982); novels Anpao: An American Indian Odyssey (Newbery Honor award 1978), 1977 (Named Best Book for Young Adults, ALA 1978), The Sun, He Dies: The End of the Aztec World, 1980 (named Best Book for Young Adults, Sch. Library Jour. 1980); On popular music Rock and Other Four Letter Words, 1968, Mick Jagger: The Singer Not the Song, 1973; contbr. critiques to various lit. jours.; classical music editor: Soho Weekly News, 1975-79; sr. editor: Fodor Travel Guides, 1970-75; contbg. editor: N.Y. Arts Jours, 1978—, Indian Trader, 1977-80, Stereo Rev, 1972-79, Native Arts/West, 1980-81. Mem. art task panel President's Commn. on Mental Health, 1977-78. Named Hon. Citizen of Okla., 1977. Mem. AFTRA, Authors Guild, Dramatists Guild, Authors League, PEN. (exec. bd. Am. Ctr. 1983-84). Office: care Alfred Hart 419 E 57th St New York NY 10022 *I attempt in my writing and lecturing to use American Indians as a metaphor for a separate, primal reality which is alternative to Western mentality and possesses significance and vitality in its own distinctive values and traditions.*

HIGINBOTHAM, WILLIAM ALFRED, physicist; b. Bridgeport, Conn., Oct. 25, 1910; m. Julie Ann Burritt, July 9, 1949 (dec. June 1971); children: Julie Eileen (Mrs. Schletter), Robin Ann Higinbotham Clark, William Burritt; m. Margaret A. Miller, Dec. 29, 1976 (dec. 1982). A.B., Williams Coll., 1932, D.Sc., 1963; postgrad., Cornell U., 1932-40. Radar research Radiation Lab., Mass. Inst. Tech., 1941-43; with Manhattan Project, Los Alamos, 1943-45, head electronics group, 1944-45; chmn. Fedn. Am. Scientists, Washington, 1946, 59, 63, exec. sec., 1947, vice-chmn., 1948, 51; asso. head electronics div. Brookhaven Nat. Lab., 1947-51, head instrumentation div., 1951-68; sr. physicist Tech. Support Group, 1968—. Fellow Am. Phys. Soc., IEEE, Am. Nuclear Soc., AAAS; mem. Inst. Nuclear Materials Mgmt. Invented Higinbotham scaler circuit. Home: 11 N Howell's Pt Road Bellport NY 11713 Office: Brookhaven Nat Lab Upton NY 11973

HIGLEY, BRUCE WADSWORTH, orthodontist; b. Iowa City, Dec. 1, 1928; s. Lester Bodine and Harriet (Wadsworth) H.; m. Marta Beatriz Velasco, Sept. 23, 1966. D.D.S., State U. Iowa, 1952, M.S., 1953; student, Grinnell Coll., 1946-48, orthodontic certificate, 1953. Research, instr. Iowa Dental U., 1952-53; practice dentistry, specializing in orthodontics, South Miami, Fla., 1955—; Owner, chmn. bd. M.B.H. Enterprises, Inc., Miami, Fla., 1960—. Vice chmn. dist. council Boy Scouts Am., 1959-62; Mem. Personnel Bd., South Miami, 1959. Served as 1st lt. Dental Corps AUS, 1953-55. Mem. Am. Assn. Orthodontics, Fla. Orthodontic Soc., So., Miami socs. orthodontists, Fla., Am. socs. dentistry for children, Fla., Fla. East Coast, Miami dental socs., Am., S. Dade dental assns., Fedn. Dentaire Internat., English Royal Acad., C. of C. (past dir., sec., treas.), Psi Omega, Omicron Kappa Upsilon. Presbyn. (deacon). Clubs: Rotarian (pres. 1961-62), Elk., Coral Reef Yacht, Coral Gables Country, Royal Palm Tennis; Bankers, Executive (Miami); Army-Navy. Home: 2000 Brickell Ave Miami FL 33129 Office: 7210 Red Rd South Miami FL 33143

HIGUCHI, TAKERU, chemistry educator; b. Los Altos, Calif., Jan. 1, 1918; s. Iekichi and Chiye (Shiki) H.; m. Aya Toki, Jan. 1, 1944; children: Kenji W., Junji H., Chie S., Peter T. A.B., U. Calif. at Berkeley, 1939; Ph.D., U. Wis., 1943; D.Sc. (hon.), U. Mich., 1967, Eidgenössische Technische Hochschule, Zurich, 1978, U. Ill., 1980, Phila. Coll. Pharmacy and Sci., 1982. Research asso. U. Wis., 1943-44; research chemist Office Rubber Research, U. Akron, 1944-47; mem. faculty U. Wis., 1947-67, prof. pharm. chemistry, 1954-64, Edward Kremers prof., 1964-67; Regents distinguished prof. chemistry and pharmacy U. Kans., Lawrence, 1967—; Pres. INTERx Research Corp., 1972—; v.p. Merck Sharp & Dohme Research Labs.; revision com. U.S. Pharmacopoeia, 1960-70; David E. Guttman Meml. lectr. U. Ky., 1978; Rachelle lectr. Calif. State U., Long Beach, 1979; Allen I. White lectr. Wash. State U., 1982. Author numerous papers in field. Co-recipient Ebert prize Am. Pharm. Assn., 1951, 52, winner, 1954; recipient Sturmer Lectr. award PCPS chpt. Rho Chi, 1956; Research Achievement award phys. pharmacy Am. Pharm. Assn. Found., 1962; Justin Power award pharm. analysis, 1964; research achievement award in stimulation of research, 1967; hon. citation U. Wis., 1969;

award for advancement indsl. pharmacy, 1974; Internat. Surfactant Chemistry prize Italian Oil Chemists' Soc., 1974; Scheele lectr. award Pharm. Soc. Sweden, 1970; Rho Chi lectr., 1971; Recipient Kolthoff Gold medal award Am. Pharm. Assn. Acad. Pharm. Scis., 1977; Volwiler award Am. Assn. Colls. Pharmacy, 1978; Citation for Disting. Service U. Kans., 1982, Roland T. Lakey award Wayne State U., 1982. Fellow Acad. Pharm. Scis.; mem. Am. Chem. Soc. (Midwest award 1975), Am. Pharm. Assn. (life mem.; past chmn. sci. sect., Remington Honor medal 1983), Am. Oil Chemists Soc., Internat. Assn. Dental Research, Chem. Soc. (London, Eng.), Acad. Pharm. Scis. (pres. 1965-67), Japanese Pharm. Soc. (hon.), Victorian Pharm. Soc. Australia (hon.), Mexican Assn. Students Pharmacy (hon.), Phi Beta Kappa (hon.), Sigma Xi, Rho Chi. Home: 2811 Schwarz Rd Lawrence KS 66044

HIGUCHI, WILLIAM IYEO, pharmaceutics educator; b. San Jose, Calif., Mar. 16, 1931; s. Iyekichi H. and Chiye (Higuchi); m. Setsuko Saito; children: Kenneth, Shirley Ann, Robert I., John. B.A. in Chemistry, San Jose State Coll., 1952, Ph.D., U. Calif.-Berkeley, 1956. Assoc. prof. pharm. chemistry U. Mich., 1962-65, prof. pharm. chemistry, 1965-82, prof. pharm. chemistry and dentisty, 1966-82, Albert B. Prescott Disting. prof. pharmacy, 1976-82, Disting. prof. harmaceutics, chmn. dept. pharmaceutics, 1982. Contbr. numerous articles, chpts. to profl. publs.; mem. editorial bd.: Pharmacy Internat., Cambridge, Eng., 1982. Recipient Phi Lambda Upsilon Teaching award U. Mich., 1968; sr. fellow U. Mich. Soc. Fellows, 1979-83. Fellow Acad. Pharm. Scis. (vice chmn. 1971, chmn. 1972); mem. Am. Pharm. Assn. (Ebert prize 1968, 70, Research Achievement award in Phys. Pharmacy 1970, co-recipient Ebert prize 1980, 83), Am. Chem. Soc., AAAS, Internat. Assn. Dental Research, Sigma Xi, Rho Chi, Phi Upsilon Pi, Phi Kappa Phi. Office: Dept Pharmaceutics Coll Pharmacy U Utah Salt Lake City UT 814112

HILBERG, RAUL, political scientist; b. Vienna, Austria, June 2, 1926; came to U.S., 1939, naturalized, 1944; s. Michael and Gisela H.; m. Christine Hemenway, 1964 (div. 1973); children—David, Deborah; m. Gwendolyn Montgomery, 1980. B.A., Bklyn. Coll., 1948; Ph.D., Columbia U., 1955. Research specialist War Documentation Project, Washington, 1951-52; lectr. Hunter Coll., 1954, U. P.R., 1954-55; John G. McCullough prof. polit. sci. U. Vt., Burlington, 1956—. Author: The Destruction of the European Jews, 1961, Special Trains to Auschwitz, 1981; editor: Documents of Destruction, 1971, (with Stanislaw Staron and Joseph Kermisz) The Warsaw Diary of Adam Czerniakow, 1979. Mem. Pres.'s Commn. on the Holocaust, 1978-79; mem. U.S. Holocaust Meml. Council, 1980—. Served with U.S. Army, 1944-46. Recipient Anisfield-Wolfe award Saturday Rev., 1967. Mem. Am. Soc. Internat. Law. Home: 236 Prospect Pkwy Burlington VT 05401 Office: Dept Polit Sci U Vt Burlington VT 05405

HILBERRY, NORMAN, nuclear engineering educator, consultant; b. Cleve., Mar. 11, 1899; s. Howard King and Bertha (Sabin) H.; m. Ann Hepburn, May 21, 1927; 1 dau., Joan Pryde Hilberry. A.B. in Physics, Oberlin Coll., 1921, Ph.D., U. Chgo., 1941; LL.D., Elmhurst Coll., 1961, Marquette U., 1962; D.Sc., Monmouth Coll., Ill., 1962. Asst. physics U. Chgo., 1922-25; instr. Physics Washington Sq. Coll., N.Y.U., 1925-28; asst. prof. Coll. Arts and Scis., 1928-42; asst. project dir. Metall. Project, U. Chgo., 1942-46; assoc. dir. Argonne Nat. Lab, Argonne, Ill., 1946-49, dep. dir., 1949-57, dir. lab., 1957-61, sr. scientist, 1961-64; dir. Sch. Nuclear Sci. and Engring., 1955-56; prof. dept. nuclear and energy engring. U. Ariz., 1964—; commr. Ariz. AEC, 1969-80; participated in U. Chgo.-Dept. of State cosmic ray expdn. to, S.A., 1941, in constrn. and operation first chain reacting pile, 1942; head IAEA Mission to Latin Am., 1958; mem. Nat. Acad. Scis.-NRC advisory panel to U.S. Office Emergency Preparedness, 1968-73; mem. pub. understanding sci. subcom. com. sci. and soc. NSF, 1977-80; mem. State Dept. ad hoc adv. com. on U.S. policy toward IAEA, 1962. Recipient Arthur Holly Compton award Am. Nuclear Sci., 1967; citation for meritorious service U.S. AEC, 1969. Fellow Am. Phys. Soc., AAAS, Am. Nuclear Soc. (pres. 1965-66, dir. 1958-61, 65-68); mem. Nuclear Medicine Soc. (hon. life), Western Soc. Engrs. (hon. life), Am. Soc. Engring. Edn. (dir. atomic indsl. forum 1961-68), Research Soc. Am. (gov. 1956-59), Sigma Xi, Tau Beta Pi. Home: 6434 E Santa Aurelia Tucson AZ 85715

HILBERT, BERNARD CHARLES, ret. union ofcl.; b. Galion, Ohio, Jan. 7, 1921; s. Charles Edward and Helena Ann (Requet) H.; m. Elizabeth Sykes, Sept. 14, 1962; four children by previous marriage. Student, Woodbury Coll. of Bus., Los Angeles, 1939-40. Telegrapher, train dispatcher, asst. chief train dispatcher Spokane, Portland & Seattle Ry. (now Burlington No.), Portland, Oreg., 1946-63; local chmn. Am.Train Dispatchers Assn., Berwyn, Ill., 1952-59, gen. chmn., 1959-63, internat. v.p., 1963-76, internat. pres., 1976-81, now ret. Pres. local unit PTA, Portland, 1956-57; active Portland Area council Boy Scouts Am.; mem. City Council, Troutdale, Oreg., 1968-72. Served with Signal Corps AUS, 1943-46. Mem. Ry. Labor Execs. Assn., Am. Radio Relay League. Democrat. Clubs: Masons, Order Eastern Star, Elks. Amateur radio operator. Home: 16830 NE Flanders St Portland OR 97230

HILBERT, ROBERT BACKUS, county water utility adminstr.; b. Pleasant Grove, Utah, Jan. 4, 1929; s. Rudy and Sarah M. (Whitecar) H.; m. Dora Jean Davis, Aug. 26, 1949; children—Susan Jean (Mrs. Barry Bernards), Robert Jeffrey, Richard Wayne, Robert Layne. Student, U. Utah at Salt Lake City, 1946-47. Engring. aide U.S. Bur. Reclamation, Salt Lake City, 1947-52; field engr. Templeton, Linke & Alsup (cons. engrs.), Salt Lake City, 1952-54; gen. mgr., sec.-treas. Salt Lake County Water Conservancy Dist., Salt Lake City, 1954—; Pres., chmn. bd. dirs. Central Utah Water Conservancy Dist., Orem, 1964—; chmn. State of Utah Safe Drinking Water Commn., 1979—. Mem. water policy task force of nat. resource com. Utah State Legislature, 1974—. Served with AUS, 1950-52. Named Water Utility Man of the Year Intermountain sect. Am. Water Works Assn., 1969; named Am. Water Works Assn. leader to Goodwill People to People Tour of Iron Curtain Countries, 1972. Mem. Am. Water Works Assn. (dir. 1969-72, pres. 1974-75), Utah Water Users Assn. (pres. 1970-73), Salt Lake County Water Users Assn. (dir. 1968-77), Salt Lake County Water and Wastewater Assn. (pres. 1971-72). Democrat. Mem. Ch. of Jesus Christ of Latter-day Saints. Home: 4888 Andlor St Salt Lake City UT 84117 Office: 3495 S 300 West St Salt Lake City UT 84115

HILBORN, MICHAEL G., real estate development executive, lawyer; b. Chgo., May 10, 1943; s. Harold and Isabelle H.; m. Helene Wiczer, June 26, 1966; children: Harold, Jamie, Jeremy. B.S. in Accountancy, U. Ill., 1965; J.D., DePaul U., 1968. Bar: Ill. 1968. Atty. firm Tenney & Bentley, Chgo., 1968-72; atty. Urban Investment & Devel. Co., Chgo., 1972-76, asst. gen. counsel, 1976-79, v.p., gen. counsel, sec., 1979-82, sr. v.p., gen. counsel, sec., 1983—. Mem. Ill. Soc. C.P.A.s, Ill. Bar Assn., Chgo. Bar Assn., Am. Bar Assn., Decalogue Soc. Lawyers. Office: 333 W Wacker Dr Chicago IL 60606

HILBRECHT, NORMAN TY, lawyer, state legislator; b. San Diego, Feb. 11, 1933; s. Norman Titus and Elizabeth (Lair) H.; m. Mercedes L. Sharratt, Oct. 24, 1980. B.A., Northwestern U., 1956; J.D., Yale U., 1959. Bar: Nev. 1959, U.S. Supreme Ct. 1963. Atty., asso. firm Jones, Wiener & Jones, Las Vegas, 1959-62; asso. counsel Union Pacific R.R., Las Vegas, 1962; partner firm Hilbrecht & Jones, Las Vegas, 1962-69; pres. Hilbrecht, Jones, Schreck & Bernhard, 1969-83, Norman Ty Hilbrecht & Assocs, 1983—; assemblyman Nev. Legislature, 1966-72, minority leader, 1971-72; mem. Nev. Senate, 1974-78; asst. lectr. bus. law U. Nev., Las Vegas. Mem. labor mgmt. com. NCCJ, 1963; mem. Clark County (Nev.) Democratic Central Com., 1959—, 1st vice chmn.; del. Western Regional Assembly on Ombudsman; chmn. Clark County Dem. Conv., 1966, Nev. Dem. Conv., 1966; pres. Clark County Legal Aid Soc., 1964, Nev. Legal Aid and Defender Assn., 1965—. Served to capt. AUS, 1952—. Named Outstanding State Legislator Eagleton Inst. Politics, Rutgers U., 1969. Mem. Am. Judicature Soc., Am. Bar Assn., Clark County Bar Assn., Am. Assn. Rev. Appraisers, Am. Acad. Polit. and Social Sci., Am. Trial Lawyers Assn., State Bar Nev., Nev. Trial Lawyers (pres. So. chpt., state v.p.), Fraternal Order Police Assos. (v.p.), Phi Beta Kappa, Delta Phi Epsilon, Theta Chi, Phi Delta Phi. Lutheran. Office: 723 S Casino Center Blvd Las Vegas NV 89101

HILBURN, (CHARLES) ROBERT, music critic; b. Natchitoches, La., Sept. 25, 1939; s. Charles M. and Alice Marie (Taylor) Nelms; m. Ruthann Marie Schlegel, Nov. 19, 1958 (div. Oct. 1983); children: Kathleen Marie, Charles Robert, II. B.A. in Journalism, Calif. State U., Northridge, 1961. Reporter Valley Times Today, North Hollywood, Calif., 1961-64; public info. officer Los Angeles Bd. Edn., 1964-70; pop music critic Los Angeles Times, 1970—; music critic Playboy's TV Mag., 1982—; mem. adv. panel jazz, folk, popular and rock music U.S. Internat. Communication Agy., Dept. State, 1976-79. Author: Rolling Stone Anthology; Contbr. articles to mags., newspapers. Recipient award Los Angeles Press Club, 1972. Address: Los Angeles Times Times-Mirror Sq Los Angeles CA 90053

HILBURN, EARL DRAYTON, communications executive, consultant; b. Mpls., Apr. 16, 1920; s. Earl D. and Jess U. (Neutson) H.; m. Charlotte B. Johnson, Sept. 16, 1940; children: Scott L., Bruce J. Student, U. Wis., 1938-40; Indpls. extension br., Purdue U., 1943-44. Communications dept. United Air Lines, 1940-42; sr. engr. test equipment dept. RCA, Indpls., 1942- 44, field engr., Camden, N.J., 1944-46; project engr. Melpar, Inc., Alexandria, Va., 1946-47, cons., 1947-50, asst. to exec. v.p., 1950-53; (became subsidiary Westinghouse Air Brake Co. 1953); v.p. govt. contracts Westinghouse Air Brake Co., 1953-56; v.p. Link Aviation Inc., Binghamton, N.Y., 1956-60; pres., dir. Burtek, Inc., Tulsa, 1960-62; v.p., gen. mgr. electronics div. Curtiss-Wright Corp., 1962-63; dep. to asso. adminstr. and gen. mgr. NASA, 1963-66; v.p., asst. to pres. Western Union Telegraph Co., N.Y.C., 1966-69, exec. v.p., 1969-70, pres., 1970-77, Western Union Corp., 1977-81, cons., 1981—; cons. NASA, 1981—, SIAC, 1981—; dir. Hudson City Savs. Bank; Bd. dirs. Nat. Space Inst.; chmn. adv. com. Internat. Assn. Satellite Users. Mem. Armed Forces Communications and Electronics Assn., U.S. C. of C. (chmn. communications com., dir. 1970-76), U.S. Power Squadron. Clubs: Internat., Nat. Aviation (Washington); Skytop (Pa.); Apple Ridge Country (Mahwah, N.J.); Ocean Reef (Key Largo, Fla.). Address: F-305 1550 NE Ocean Blvd Stuart FL 33494

HILDEBRAND, RICHARD ALLEN, bishop; b. Winnsboro, S.C., Feb. 1, 1916; s. Benjamin Franklin and Agnes Luvenia (Brogdon) H.; m. Anna Beatrix Lewis, Dec. 3, 1942; 1 dau., Camille Ylonne. A.B., Allen U., 1938; B.D., Payne Theol. Sch., 1941; S.T.M., Boston U., 1948; D.D., Wilberforce U., 1953; LL.D. (hon.), Morris Brown Coll., 1975. Ordained to ministry African Meth. Episcopal Ch., 1936, elected bishop, 1972; pastor chs., Columbia and Sumter, S.C., 1936-38, Jamestown and Akron, Ohio, 1938-45, Providence, 1945-48, Bayshore, N.Y., 1948-49, Wilmington, Del., 1949-50; pastor Bethel A.M.E. Ch., N.Y.C., 1950-65, Bridge St. A.M.E. Ch., Bklyn., 1965-72; presiding bishop 6th Dist. A.M.E. Ch., Ga., 1972-76, 1st Dist., Phila., 1976—; pres. Atlanta N. Ga. Conf. A.M.E. Fed. Credit Union, 1972-76, Council of Bishops A.M.E. Ch., 1977—. Chmn. Chs. for New Harlem Hosp., N.Y.C., 1957-65; pres. Manhattan Dirs. Protestant Council, N.Y.C., 1956-60; chmn. bd. dirs. Morris Brown Coll., Turner Sem. Interdenominational Theol. Center, 1972-76, Payne Theol. Sem., 1976—. Mem. NAACP (pres. N.Y.C. br. 1962-64), Alpha Phi Alpha. Club: Masons. Home: 5921 Overbrook Ave Philadelphia PA 19131 Office: 1 Bala Ave Suite 3C Bala Cynwyd PA 19004 *I believe that if a person always does what he truly believes to be right, ultimately he will be victorious.*

HILDEBRAND, ROGER HENRY, physicist, astrophysicist; b. Berkeley, Calif., May 1, 1922; s. Joel Henry and Emily (Alexander) H.; m. Jane Roby Beedle, May 28, 1944; children: Peter Henry, Alice Louise, Kathryn Jane, Daniel Milton. A.B. in Chemistry, U. Calif.-Berkeley, 1947, Ph.D. in Physics, 1951. Physicist, Radiation Lab., U. Calif.-Berkeley, 1942-51; Physicist Tenn. Eastman Corp., Oak Ridge Nat. Lab., 1945; asst. prof. physics Enrico Fermi Inst., U. Chgo., 1952-55, asso. prof., 1955-60, prof., 1960—, prof. dept. astronomy and astrophysics, 1978—; dir. Enrico Fermi Inst., 1965-68, dean coll., 1969-73; asso. lab. dir. for high energy physics Argonne (Ill.) Nat. Lab., 1958-64; chmn. sci. policy com. Stanford Linear Accelerator Center, Calif., 1962-66; mem. physics adv. com. Nat. Accelerator Lab., 1967-69; mem. sci. and ednl. adv. com. Lawrence Berkeley Lab., 1972-80; chmn. com. to rev. U.S. medium energy sci. AEC and NSF, 1974; chmn. airborne obs. users group NASA, 1983—. Guggenheim fellow, 1968-69. Fellow Am. Phys. Soc.; mem. Midwestern Univs. Research Assn. (dir. 1956-58, 62-68), Sierra Club, Phi Beta Kappa, Sigma Xi. Office: Enrico Fermi Inst U Chgo 5630 S Ellis Ave Chicago IL 60637

HILDERBRANDT, DONALD FRANKLIN, II, landscape architect, artist; b. Bloomsburg, Pa., Aug. 30, 1939; s. Donald Franklin and Beatrice May (Kirchman) H.; m. M. Coroline Housenick, Aug. 27, 1960; children: Mark Berwind, John Thomas, Johanna Lynn. B.S. in Landscape Architecture, Pa. State U., 1961; M., in Landscape Architecture, U. Mich., 1963. Rigistered landscape architect, Md. Sr. designer, assoc. Johnson, Johnson & Roy, Inc., Ann Arbor, Mich., 1963-68; chief landscape architect The Rouse co., Columbia, Md., 1968-71; founder, prin. Land Design-Research, Inc., Columbia, 1971—; vis. lectr. Pa. State U., University Park, 1968—; mem. design arts program panel, cons. NEA, Washington, 1983—. Author: Cost Effective Site Planning, 1976 (award 1978), New Life for Maryland's Old Towns, 1979 (award 1980), Cuyahoga Valley, 1975 (award 1976). Pa. State U. Alumni Assn. fellow, 1983; recipient Design award, spl. mention HUD, 1974, Grand award Associated Landscape Contractors Am., 1978. Fellow Am. Soc. Landscape Architects (nat. awards jury mem. 1975, 81). Democrat. Episcopalian. Home: 11101 Youngtree Ct Columbia MD 21044

HILDRETH, CLIFFORD, educator; b. McPherson, Kans., Dec. 8, 1917; s. George W. and Lillian Belle (Huenergardt) H.; m. Mary Louise McGee, Jan. 1, 1942; children: Richard, Robert, Susan, Mary. A.B., U. Kans., 1939; M.S., Iowa State U., 1941, Ph.D., 1947. Asst. prof., then asso. prof. econs. Iowa State U., 1946-48; asst. prof., then asso. prof. econs. and mem. Cowles Commn., U. Chgo., 1949-52; prof. agrl. econs. N.C. State U., 1953-55, Mich. State U., 1955-58, prof. econs., head dept., 1958-60, prof. econs. and agrl. econs., 1960-64; prof. econs., statistics and agrl. econs. U. Minn., 1964—; Fulbright lectr. U. Tokyo, Hitotsubashi U., Keio U., Tokyo, Japan, 1970; mem. com. nat. stats. Nat. Acad. Sci., 1975-81; Fellow Center Advanced Study Behavioral Scis. Stanford, Calif., 1961-62. Author: (with Frank Jarrett) A Statistical Study of Livestock Production and Marketing, 1955. Served to lt. USNR, 1943-46. Fellow Econometrics Soc., Am. Statis. Assn. (editor jour. 1960-65, v.p. 1968-69, pres. 1973), Inst. Math. Statistics; mem. Am. Econ. Assn., Am. Agrl. Econ. Assn. Home: 2163 Berkeley Ave Saint Paul MN 55105

HILDRETH, EUGENE A., physician, educator; b. St. Paul, Mar. 11, 1924; s. Eugene A. IV and Lila K. (Clator) H.; m. Dorothy Anne Myers, Mar. 23, 1946; children: Jeffrey Reed, William Myers, Anne Sarver, Katherine Clator. B.S., Washington Jefferson Coll., 1943; M.D., U. Va., 1947. Diplomate: Am. Bd. Internal Medicine (mem. 1969-72, 75—, cons., com. mem. 1972-75), Am Bd. Allergy and Immunology (founding com. 1970, mem. 1970-72, 1st co-chmn.). internal medicine 1970-71, cons. 1972—). Intern Johns Hopkins, 1947-48; resident in medicine Hosp. U. Pa., 1948-49, USPHS Postdoctoral Research fellow in cardio-vascular disease, 1949-51, chief resident in medicine, 1953-54, fellow in allergy and immunology, 1954-58, faculty, 1954-69, 71—; instr. medicine U. Pa., Phila., 1953-54, asso. medicine, 1954-55, asst. prof. medicine, 1955-60, asso. prof., 1960-69, asso. dean, 1964-69, prof. clin. medicine, 1971—, acting chmn. dept. research medicine, 1960-64; chmn. dept. medicine Reading (Pa.) Hosp. and Med. Center.; Cons. project site visits USPHS, 1965-70, rev. devel. new methods research in chronic pulmonary disease, 1967-69; cons. VA Hosp. Phila., 1955—; nat. adv. com. Medic Alert Found. Internat., 1964-83; cons. Citizens' Com. to Study Grad. Med. Edn., 1966; Am. Bd. Med. Spltys. rep. of subsplty. Bd. Allergy and Immunology of Am. Bd. Internal Medicine, 1969-72; chmn. certifying exam. com. Am. Bd. Internal Medicine, 1978-81, mem. exec. com., 1978-82; chmn., 1981-82; mem. rep. Am. Bd. Med. Spltys., 1976—, chmn. nominating com., 1979-80, mem. evaluation procedures study com., 1979—; mem. med. adv. bd. Lupus Found. Del. Valley, 1979—; chmn. Federated Council Internal Medicine; appeals bd. liaison Council of Grad. Med. Edn., 1980—. Co-author: Low Fat Diet, 1953, also research articles, chpts. in textbooks.; Editorial bd.: Annals Internal Medicine, 1960-68, Postgrad. Medicine, 1969-75, Jour. Berks County Med. Soc, 1969-73, Internal Medicine Digest, 1971-75. Served with USNR, 1943-45, 51-53. John and Mary R. Markle scholar in acad. medicine, 1958-63; USPHS Research grantee. Fellow Am. Clin and Climatologic Assn., A.C.P.; mem. Peripatetic Soc., AAAS, Fedn. Am. Socs. for Exptl. Biology, N.Y. Acad. Scis., Am. Heart Assn., Inst. Medicine of Nat. Acad. Scis. (nominating com. 1982—), Pa. Thoracic Soc., Phila. Art Mus., AMA, Am. Acad. Allergy, Nat. Kidney Found. Home: RD 3785 Mohnton PA 19540 Office: Reading Hosp and Medical Center Reading PA 19603

HILDRETH, JAMES ROBERT, air force officer; b. Pine Bluff, Ark., May 4, 1927; s. William Wilson and Martha Leah (Chidester) H.; m. Beth Dixon Baker, July 12, 1955; children: John Baker, William Reid, Margaret Leah, Mark Dixon, Amy Beth. B.A. cum laude, La. Poly. Inst., 1952. Commd. 2d lt. USAF, 1952, advanced through grades to maj. gen., 1976; comdr. 4th Tactical Fighter Wing, 1970-72, dep. comdr. 13th Air Force, 1973-75, sr. Air Force rep. Weapons Systems Evaluation Group, Office of Sec. Def., 1975-76, comdr. Tactical Fighter Weapons Center, 1976-79, comdr. 13th Air Force, 1979—. Pres. So. Nev. Fed. Exec. Agy., 1975-76; mem. adv. bd. United Way, Las Vegas, Nev., 1975-79; bd. dirs. Las Vegas C. of C., 1976-79; dist. chmn. Boy Scouts Am., 1979—. Decorated D.S.M., Silver Star, Legion of Merit, D.F.C., Bronze Star, Air medal, Air Force Commendation medal, Purple Heart, others. Methodist. Clubs: Masons, Rotary. Home: 315 Branch St Spring Hope NC 27882 Office: 103 Pine St Spring Hope NC

HILDRETH, R(OLAND) JAMES, foundation executive, economist; b. Des Moines, Nov. 26, 1926; s. Roland James and Emma (Lehman) H.; m. May Helen Carlson, June 8, 1947; children: Christine, Jeffrey, Paul. B.S., Iowa State U., 1949; M.S. in Indsl. Econs., 1950; Ph.D. in Econs., 1954; postgrad. in econs., U. Minn., 1950-52. Instr. Augsburg Coll., Mpls., 1950-52; asst. prof. agrl. econs. and sociology Tex. A&M U., 1954-58; with Tex. Agr. Experiment Sta., 1954-62, research coordinator W. Tex., 1958-59, asst. dir., 1959-62; asso. mgr., dir. Farm Found., Chgo., 1962-70, mgr., dir., 1970—; dir. Gifford-Hill & Co., Inc., Dallas; joint council Food and Agrl. Scis., USDA, 1978—; cons. council edn. Am. Veterinary Med. Assn., 1977—. Contbg. author: Changing Patterns in Fertilizer Use, 1968; Editor: Readings in Agricultural Policy, 1967; Co-editor, contbg. author: Methods for Land Economics Research, 1966. Mem. nat. council Boy Scouts Am., 1973-75; mem. advisory com. Council on Rural Health, AMA, 1970-77; mem. advisory council on consumer affairs Am. Bankers Assn., 1971-73; mem. citizens advisory com. Coll. Phys. Edn., U. Ill., 1966-69; bd. dirs. Lutheran Gen. Hosp., Park Ridge, Ill., 1970-82, Nat. Center for Vol. Action, 1970-72. Served with U.S. Army, 1945-47. Recipient Henry A. Wallace award Iowa State U., 1981. Fellow Am. Agrl. Econs. Assn. (pres. 1977-78); Mem. Internat. Assn. Agrl. Economists (sec.-treas. 1973—), Am. Country Life Assn. (past pres.). Home: 381 Poplar Ave Elmhurst IL 60126 Office: 1211 W 22d St Oak Brook IL 60521

HILEMAN, CHARLES CLEMENS, III, lawyer; b. Greensburg, Pa., Sept. 3, 1924; s. Charles Clemens H. and Louise D. Landis; m. Margaret McKay, 1947; children: Jane, Susan Hileman Malone, Peter M. B.A., Allegheny Coll., 1947; J.D., U. Pa., 1950. Bar: Pa. 1951, U.S. Supreme Ct. 1976, U.S. Ct. Appeals (3d cir.) 1951, U.S. Dist. Ct. (ea. and mid. dists.)Pa. 1951. Law clk. to judge U.S. Ct. Appeals (3d cir.), 1950-51; law clk. to justice Harold H. Burton U.S. Supreme Ct., 1951-52; assoc., then ptnr. Schnader, Harrison, Segal & Lewis, Phila., 1952—. Trustee Allegheny Coll. Served with inf. U.S. Army, 1943-46. Decorated Bronze Star medal. Fellow Am. Bar Found.; mem. ABA, Pa. Bar Assn., Phila. Bar Assn. Democrat. Presbyterian. Club: Racquet. Office: 1600 Market St Philadelphia PA 19102

HILEMAN, DONALD GOODMAN, college dean; b. Anna, Ill., Sept. 8, 1925; s. Turner Clifford and Mary (Goodman) H.; m. Shirley Ann Rau, Aug. 28, 1948; children: David, Mark, Mike, Kathryn. Student, Carthage Coll., 196-48; B.S. in Journalism, U. Ill., 1949, M.S., 1951, Ph.D. in Mass Communications, 1955. Instr. U. Ill., 1949-52; asst. prof. bus. adminstrn. Wash. State U., Pullman, 1952-55; asso prof. journalism So. Ill. U., 1955-69; chmn. dept. advt. U. Tenn., 1969-70, dean Coll. communications, 1970—; vis. prof. U. S.C., fall 1980. Author: (with Billy I. Ross) Towards Professional in Advertising, 1969; Editor: Linage, 1963-70; Contbr. articles profl. jours. Mem. synod ethics com. Presbyn Ch. Ill., 1960-62; mem. Council pub. relations Boy Scouts Am., 1958-68; Bd. dirs., asso. Danforth Found.; pres. Helen Ross McNabb Mental Health Ctr., 1982-83. Served with USNR, 1943-46. Recipient spl. awards U. Ill., 1967, Tex. A. and M. Coll., 1969; Distinguished Service award Am. Motel Assn. Ill.; Phi Eta Sigma Outstanding Tchr. award U. Tenn., 1980. Fellow Am. Assn. Advt. Agys., Direct Mail Advt. Assn., Splty. Advt. Assn., Advt. Age Creative Workshop; mem. Am. Advt. Fedn. (silver medal), Assn. Schs. Journalism and Mass Communication (nat. pres. 1983-84), Assn. Edn. in Journalism, Am. Marketing Assn., AAUP, Am. Acad. Advt., Alpha Delta Sigma (exec. dir. 1961-70, recipient 6th Key, spl. awards). Home: 5109 Angeles Dr Knoxville TN 37918 *People are the most important element of our existence. All that we do should be done to help individuals achieve greater meaning and personal satisfaction in living.*

HILER, EDWARD ALLAN, agrl. engr.; b. Hamilton, Ohio, May 14, 1939; s. Earl and Thelma H.; m. Patricia Ann Burke, Jan. 30, 1960; children—Karen, Richard, Scott. B.S., Ohio State U., 1963, M.S., 1966, Ph.D. (USPHS fellow 1964-65), 1966. Registered profl. engr., Tex. Instr. Ohio State U., 1962-64, Ohio Agrl. Research and Devel.

Center, 1965-66; Mem. faculty Tex. A. and M. U., 1966—, prof. agrl. engring., 1973—, chmn. dept., 1974—. Contbr. articles profl. jours. Recipient Disting. Service award Tex. A&M U., 1974, Faculty Disting. Achievement award, 1973; named Disting. Alumnus Ohio State U. Coll. Engring., 1978. Fellow AAAS; mem. Am. Soc. Agrl. Engrs. (Paper award 1972, 74, Young Researcher award 1977, Disting. Young Agrl. Engr. award 1975), Am. Soc. Engring. Edn., Am. Geophys. Union, Council Sgrl. Sci. and Tech., Tex. Soc. Profl. Engrs., Sigma Xi (chpt. Disting. Mem. award 1975). Presbyterian. Office: Dept Agrl Engring Tex A&M U College Station TX 77843

HILER, JOHN PATRICK, congressman, former foundry executive; b. Chgo., Apr. 24, 1953; s. Robert J. and Margaret F. H. B.A., Williams Coll., 1975; M.B.A., U. Chgo., 1977. Mktg. dir. Charles O. Hiler and Son, Inc., Walkerton, Ind., 1977-80, Accurate Castings Co., La Porte, 1977-80; Mem. 97th-98th congresses from 3d Ind. Dist. Chmn. LaPorte City Republican Com., 1979; del. Ind. Rep. Conv., 1978, 80; trustee LaLumiere Sch., LaPorte; del. White House Conf. Small Bus., 1980. Mem. LaPorte C. of C. Roman Catholic. Club: LaPorte County Rep. Men's. Office: River Glen Office Plaza 501 E Monroe Room 120 South Bend IN 46601 also 316 Cannon House Office Bldg Washington DC 20515

HILF, RUSSELL, biochemist; b. Bklyn., Aug. 13, 1931; s. Jerome Joseph and Sydel Ruth (Kaufman) H.; m. Beverly Sydelle Polak, May 29, 1955; children: Elise Rachel, Merrill Jean, Lawrence Michael. B.S., CCNY, 1952; M.S., Rutgers U., 1953, Ph.D., 1955. Head biochemistry sect., nutrition div. QM Food and Container Inst., Chgo., 1958-59; head, cancer endocrinology sect. Squibb Inst. for Med. Research, New Brunswick, N.J., 1959-69; prof. biochemistry dept. U. Rochester Sch. Medicine and Dentistry, N.Y., 1969—; chmn. diagnosis working group Breast Cancer Task Force, Nat. Cancer Inst., NIH, 1978-80; mem. merit rev. bd. in oncology VA, 1979—. Editor: (with J.A. Kellen) Influences of Hormones in Tumor Development, 1979; asso. editor: Cancer Research, 1967-78, 83—; mem. editorial adv. bd.: Biochemical Pharmacology, 1973—; internat. adv. bd.: Cancer Biochemistry BioPhysics, 1974—; Contbr. articles to profl. jours. Served with Med. Service Corps U.S. Army, 1955-58. Nat. Cancer Inst. grantee, 1969—; Am. Cancer Soc. grantee, 1970-75. Fellow N.Y. Acad. Sci.; mem. Am. Soc. Biol. Chemists, Am. Assn. for Cancer Research, Endocrine Soc., Am. Physiol. Soc., Soc. Exptl. Biology and Medicine, AAAS. Home: 85 Willowcrest Dr Rochester NY 14618 Office: 601 Elmwood Ave Rochester NY 14642

HILFORD, LAWRENCE B., video company executive; b. N.Y.C., June 17, 1934; s. Norman and Diana (Barlis) H.; m. Lynn Sherr, Jan. 11, 1980; children: Jeffrey, Andrew, James. B.A., Yale U., 1955; M.B.A., Harvard U., 1959. Pres. Cartridge Rental Network, N.Y.C., 1972-73, Hilford Bus. Services, 1981-82; exec. v.p., dir. Viacom Internat. Inc., N.Y.C., 1973-77; sr. v.p. Columbia Pictures Industries, N.Y.C., 1979-81; pres., chief exec. officer CBS-Fox Video, N.Y.C., 1983—; adj. prof. NYU, N.Y.C., 1981-83. Office: CBS-Fox Video 1211 Ave of the Americas New York NY 10036

HILGARD, ERNEST ROPIEQUET, psychologist; b. Belleville, Ill., July 25, 1904; s. George Engelmann and Laura (Ropiequet) H.; m. Josephine Rohrs, Sept. 19, 1931; children—Henry Rohrs, Elizabeth Ann. B.S., U. Ill., 1924; Ph.D., Yale, 1930; D.Sc., Kenyon Coll., 1964; LL.D., Centre Coll., 1974. Asst. instr. in psychology Yale U., 1928-29, instr., 1929-33; successively asst. prof., asso. prof., prof. psychology Stanford, 1933-69, emeritus prof., 1969—, exec. head dept., 1942-50, dean grad. div., 1951-55; Bd. dirs., pres. Ann. Reviews, Inc., 1948-73; With USDA, Washington, 1942, OWI, 1942-43, Office Civilian Requirements, WPB, 1943-44; Collaborator, div. child devel. and tchr. personnel Am. Council Edn., 1940-41; nat. adv. mental health council USPHS, 1952-56; fellow (Center Advanced Study Behavioral Scis.), 1956-57; Mem. U.S. Edn. Mission to Japan, 1946. Author: several books, latest Theories of Learning, 1948, rev. edit., 1981, Introduction to Psychology, 1953, revised edit., 1983, Hypnotic Susceptibility, 1965, Hypnosis in the Relief of Pain, 1975, Divided Consciousness, 1977, American Psychology in Historical Perspective, 1978. Bd. curators Stephens Coll., Mo., 1953-68. Recipient Warren medal in exptl. psychology, 1940; Wilbur Cross medal Yale U., 1971; Gold medal Am. Psychol. Found., 1978. Hon. fellow Brit. Psychol. Assn.; mem. Am. Psychol. Assn. (pres. 1948-49), Am. Acad. Arts and Scis., Nat. Acad. Edn., Soc. Psychol. Study Social Issues (chmn. 1944-45), AAAS, Nat. Acad. Scis., Am. Philos. Soc., Internat. Soc. Hypnosis (pres. 1973-76, Benjamin Franklin gold medal 1979), Sigma Xi. Home: 850 Webster Palo Alto CA 94301

HILINSKI, CHESTER C., lawyer; b. Bethlehem, Pa., Mar. 26, 1917; s. Andrew and Mary (Dziki) H.; m. Bernice F. Slabinski, June 29, 1944; children: John, Susan, Andrew, Mark. B.S. in Econs., U. Pa., 1938, J.D., 1941. Bar: Pa. 1941. Law clk. to presiding justice Pa. Supreme Ct., Phila., 1941-42; assoc. Dechert Price & Rhoads, Phila., 1943-50, ptnr., 1951—, sr. ptnr., 1967—; pres. Internat. Fiscal Assn., U.S. br., N.Y.C., 1982-83; lectr. Villanova U. Law Sch., Pa., 1983-84. Contbr. articles to profl. jours. Bd. dirs., v.p. Connelly Found., Phila., 1978—; commr. Abington Twp., Pa., 1954-56. Mem. Pa. State (chmn. tax sect. adminstrv. practice com 1971-72), Pa. State Bar Assn., Phila. Bar Assn. Republican. Roman Catholic. Clubs: Union League (Phila.); Commonwealth (Gwynedd,Pa.). Home: 789 Arden Rd Jenkintown PA 19046 Office: Dechert Price & Rhoads 3400 Centre Sq SW 1500 Market St Phila PA 19102

HILKER, ROBERT RICHARD, broadcasting executive; b. Winston-Salem, N.C., Apr. 25, 1927; s. Arthur Henry and Katie Shuttie (Leigh) H.; m. Janie Juanita Christy, Nov. 15, 1974; children: Carolyn, Janet, Robert Richard. Organizer, chmn., chief exec. officer Suburban Radio Group, 1954—; operators Sta. WEGO, WPEG, Concord, N.C., WSVM, Valdese, N.C., WCGC, Belmont, N.C., WJJJ, Christiansburg, Va., WVVV, Blacksburg, Va., WYNR, WPIQ, Brunswick, Ga.; part-owner C.A.T.V. Systems, North Mecklenburg, Corneilus, Davidson, Mooresville, Huntersville, N.C. Pres. Belmont United Fund, 1979-80. Served with USNR, 1944-46. Mem. N.C. Assn. Broadcasters (pres. 1960), Belmont C. of C. (past pres.), Belmont Mchts. Assn. (past pres.), Nat. Assn. Broadcasters (dir. 1971-76, 80-84). Democrat. Presbyterian. Clubs: Gaston Country, Cowans Ford Country, Belmont Kiwanis. Office: Box 888 Belmont NC 28012

HILKER, WALTER ROBERT, JR., lawyer; b. Los Angeles, Apr. 18, 1921; s. Walter Robert and Alice (Cox) H.; m. Ruth Margaret Hibbard, Sept. 7, 1943; children: Anne Katherine, Walter Robert III. B.S., U. So. Calif., 1942, LL.B., 1948. Bar: Calif. 1949. Since practiced in Los Angeles; partner Parker, Milliken, Kohlmeier, Clark & O'Hara, 1955-75; now of counsel Pacht, Ross, Warne, Bernhard & Sears, Newport Beach, Calif. Trustee Bella Mabury Trust; bd. dirs. Houchin Found., Virginia Steele Scott Found. Served to lt. USNR, 1942-45. Decorated Bronze Star. Mem. Am., Calif., Los Angeles, Orange County bar assns. Republican. Clubs: Spring Valley Lake Country (Apple Valley, Calif.); Balboa Bay (Newport Beach, Calif.). Home: 21 Rustling Wind Irvine CA 92715 Office: 500 Newport Center Dr Newport Beach CA 92660

HILL, ALBERT ALAN, government official; b. Palo Alto, Calif., Feb. 1, 1938; s. Albert Andrew and Margaret (Larsen) H.; m. Mary Jeanette Smith, June 17, 1961; children: Andrew Alan, Timothy Brewster, Michael Ralph. A.B., Coll. Pacific, 1960. Asst. to minority leader Calif. Senate, 1962-65; state info. officer Republican State Central Com., 1965-69; asst. to sec. resources, then dep. sec. agr. and services Calif. State Govt., 1969-74; mgr. Purves Supply Co., 1974-76; chief exec. officer Hill Bldg. Spltys., Inc., 1976-81; chmn. Council Environ. Quality, 1981—. Pres. Marin Rep. Council, 1975. Recipient Disting. Alumnus award U. Pacific, 1981. Episcopalian. Club: Commonwealth of Calif. Lodge: Elks. Office: 722 Jackson Pl NW Washington DC 20006

HILL, ALBERT GORDON, physicist, educator; b. St. Louis, Jan. 11, 1910; s. Glenn C. and Alberta (Boogher) H.; m. Ruth Harriet Parker. B.S., Washington U., St. Louis, 1930, M.S., 1934; Ph.D., U. Rochester, 1937. Mem. tech. staff Bell Telephone Labs., 1930-32; fellow in physics U. Rochester, 1934-37; instr. physics M.I.T., 1937-41, staff mem., 1942-46, asso. prof. physics, 1946-47, prof. physics, 1947-75, lectr. in polit. sci., 1965-75, dir., 1949-52, 1952-55, chmn. physics council, 1967-70, v.p. for research, 1970-75, cons. to pres., 1975—, dir., 1975-78; chmn. bd. dirs. C. Stark Draper Lab., Inc., 1970—; physicist Research Corp., 1941; adviser SHAPE Air Def. Center, 1955-63; dir. research (Weapons Systems Evaluations Group), 1955-58; v.p. Inst. Def. Analyses, Washington, 1956-59, trustee, 1956-61. Author: (with L. N. Ridenour and Ralph Shaw) Bibliography in an Age of Science, 1951. Trustee Asso. Univs., Inc., 1970-74, Detroit Inst. Tech., 1974-78. Recipient Presdl. Certificate of Honor, 1948; Distinguished Civilian Service award USAF, 1955, Am. Ordnance Assn., 1956; Meritorious Civilian Service award Office of Sec. of Def. Fellow Am. Phys. Soc., IEEE, Am. Acad. Arts and Sci., Benjamin Franklin fellow Royal Soc. Arts. Inventor, systems engr. communication system Norway to Turkey, also ballistic missile detection radar in Eastern Turkey. Home: 11171 Oakdale Rd Boynton Beach FL 33437 Office: 555 Technology Sq Cambridge MA 02139 also 77 Massachusetts Ave Cambridge MA 02139 *I firmly believe in the eternal verity of Mother Nature and in the inherent dignity of all mankind.*

HILL, ALFRED, lawyer, educator; b. N.Y.C., Nov. 7, 1917; m. Dorothy Turck, Aug. 10, 1960; 1 dau., Amelia. B.S., Coll. City N.Y., 1937; LL.B., Bklyn. Law Sch., 1941; S.J. D., Harvard U., 1957. Bar: N.Y. State bar 1943, Ill 1958. With SEC, 1943-52; prof. law So. Meth. U., 1953-56, Northwestern U., 1956-62, Columbia U., 1962-75, Simon H. Rifkind prof. law, 1975—. Contbr. articles on torts, conflict of laws, fed. cts. to legal jours. Mem. Am. Law Inst. Home: 152 Highwood Ave Tenafly NJ 07670 Office: Columbia Law Sch New York NY 10027

HILL, ALTON DAVID, JR., geography educator; b. Biwabik, Minn., Jan. 22, 1933; s. Alton David and Fern Elizabeth (Swanson) H.; m. Myhra Carleen Diedrick, Dec. 27, 1957; children: Kelly, Graham, Tiffany. B.A., U. Colo., 1954, M.A., 1959; Ph.D., U. Chgo., 1964. Instr. San Francisco State Coll., 1962-63; asst. prof. Antioch Coll., Yellow Springs, Ohio, 1963-68; assoc. prof. geograph U. Colo., Boulder, 1968-71; acting dir. Ctr. for Edn. in Social Scis., U. Colo., Boulder, 1969-70; prof. Ctr. For Edn. in Social Scis., U. Colo., Boulder, 1971—; prof., chmn. dept. geography Ctr. for Edn. in Social Scis., U. Colo., Boulder, 1982—; mem. sci. edn. policy research group Colo. State Dept. Edn., 1983-84; vis. geog. scientist Assn. Am. Georgraphers, 1983-84; mem. assessment com. Council on Learning, New Rochelle, N.Y., 1978-80; geography cons. Houghton-Mifflin Co., Boston, 1972-76. Author: The Changing Landscape, 1964; editor: Latin American Development, 1973, The Quality of Life, 1973. Chmn. City of Boulder Human Relations Commn., 1978. Served to lt. USAF, 1955-57. Danforth assoc., 1978-84; Ford Found. fellow, 1964, 67; NSF grantee, 1970-75. Mem. Am. Assn. Geographers (councillor 1980-83), Nat. Council for Geog. Edn. (exec. bd. dirs. 1972-75, Jour. Geography 1980), Conf. Latin Am. Geographers (chmn. 1973), Social Sci. Edn. Consortium, Internat. Assn. Univ. Presidents (assoc.). Home: 3695 Longwood Ave Boulder CO 80303 Office: Dept Geography U Colo Campus PO Box 260 Boulder CO 80309

HILL, ALWYN SPENCER, educator; b. Logan, Utah, June 4, 1925; s. Reuben Lorenzo and Theresa (Snow) H.; m. Beth Elaine Powell, July 17, 1946; children—Gregory Spencer, Michael Bleak, Theresa Jeanine, Marybeth, Rebecca Ann, Donald Reuben. B.S., Utah State U., 1949; postgrad., U. Utah, 1951-52, 55; M.S., U. Wis., 1951, Ph.D., 1960. Tchr. Latter-day Saints Sem., Malad, Ida., Salt Lake City, 1951-56; teaching asst. U. Utah, U. Wis., 1956-59; asst. prof. polit. sci. Drury Coll., Springfield, Mo., 1959-61; chmn. dept. social sci. Eastern N.Mex. U., 1961-65, chmn. dept. social scis., 1967-69; asso. prof. polit. sci. U. Nev., 1965-67, prof. polit. sci., 1978—, Mich. Technol. U., Houghton, 1969-78, head dept. social scis., 1969-78; Govt. intern dir. N.Mex., 1962; mem. staff Commn. for Study Statewide Problems Higher Edn., N.Mex., 1963-64; project dir. State-wide Survey Libraries, Nev., 1966-67. Contbr. articles to profl. jours. Served with AUS, 1944-46. Named Tchr. of Year Eastern N.Mex. U., 1964. Mem. Am. Polit. Sci. Assn. Home: 304 Agate Houghton MI 49931

HILL, ANDREW E., petroleum company executive; b. 1935; married. B.A., U. St. Thomas, 1957. With Signal Oil & Gas Co., 1957-70, The Oil Shale Co., 1970-71, Charter Internat. Oil Co., 1971-73, Goldking Refining Co., 1973—; chmn. bd., chief exec. officer Hill Petroleum Co., 1975—, also dir. Office: Hill Petroleum Co Inc 921 Main St Suite 1900 Houston TX 77002 *

HILL, ARTHUR, actor; b. Can.; m. Peggy Hassard; children—Douglas, Jennifer. Studied law, U. B.C. Performed in plays including Matchmaker, Home of the Brave, The Male Animal, Look Homeward Angel, Man and Superman, The Country Girl, All the Way Home; performed in plays including The Gang's All Here, Who's Afraid of Virginia Woolf?, 1962-63; numerous TV appearances; appeared: motion pictures A Little Romance, Ugly American, Moment to Moment, Harper, The Chairman, Andromeda Strain, Killer Elite, A Bridge Too Far, The Champ. Served with RCAF, 1942-45. Recipient Tony award as best actor, 1962-63. Address: Creative Artists Agy 1888 Century Park E Suite 1400 Los Angeles CA 90067 *

HILL, BENJAMIN HARVEY, JR., lawyer; b. Atlanta, Apr. 10, 1939; s. Benjamin Harvey and Emily S. H.; m. Sarah H. Hill, Aug. 31, 1963; children: Benjamin Harvey, Robert Marcus. B.A., Yale U., 1961; LL.B., U. Va., 1964. Bar: Ga. 1964. Asso. Alston & Bird, Atlanta, 1964-69; partner Alston, Miller & Gaines, 1969—. Mem. Am., Ga., Atlanta bar assns. Home: 3210 W Andrews Dr NW Atlanta GA 30305 Office: 12th Floor C & S Nat Bank Bldg Atlanta GA 30335

HILL, BENNETT DAVID, educator, Benedictine monk; b. Balt., Sept. 27, 1934; s. David Bennett and Muriel Vincent (Clarke) H. A.B., Princeton U., 1956, Ph.D., 1963; A.M., Harvard U., 1958. Instr. history Princeton U., 1960-62; asst. prof. U. Western Ont., 1962-64, U. Ill., Urbana, 1964-67, assoc. prof., 1967-75, prof., 1975-81, chmn. dept. history, 1978-81; joined Order of St. Benedict, 1981. Author: English Cisterican Monasteries and Their Patrons in the Twelfth Century, 1968; co-author: A History of Western Society, 1979, 2d edit., 1982; editor: A History of World Societies, 1983, Church and State in the Middle Ages, 1970; contbr. in field. Am. Council Learned Socs. fellow, 1970-71. Mem. Mediaeval Acad. Am., Am. Cath. Hist. Assn. Roman Catholic. Office: St Anselm's Abbey 4501 South Dakota Ave NE Washington DC 20017

HILL, BOBBY LEE, lawyer, state legislator; b. Wilkes County, Ga., July 24, 1941; s. Birl D. and Fannie M. (Hubbard) H.; 1 son, Ashley Conrad. B.S. cum laude, Savannah State Coll., 1963; J.D., Howard U., 1966. Bar: Ga. 1967. Youth field dir. Region V, NAACP, Ga., 1963-66; mem. Legal Def. and Edn. Fund, Inc., Lawyers Inst., Airlie, Va., 1966, cooperating counsel, N.Y.C., 1966—; asst. in law firm Van Arkle & Kaiser, Washington, 1966; sr. partner firm Hill, Jones & Farrington, Atlanta and Savannah, Ga., 1971—; pres., partner Hill, Jones & Assos.; mem. Ga. Gen. Assembly, 1968—; mem. edn., judiciary and welfare coms., chmn. Black Caucus.; Chmn. bd. IDEA, Inc.; mem. advisory bd. Exec. Inns of Am.; lectr. Race Relations Inst., London, Eng. Del., U.S. Youth Council, 1966; mem. World Law Funds Forum on War Prevention and World Order at Sarah Lawrence Coll., Bronxville, N.Y., 1966; freelance writer, photographer So. News Syndicate, Columbus, Ga.; mem. Dublin Conf. for Enforceable World Law to Prevent War, N.Y.C., 1966; del. World Assembly Youth, Tokyo, Japan, 1966. Bd. dirs. Nat. Assembly for Social Policy and Devel., UN Assn. U.S.A.; mem. citizens adv. com. on community improvement and urban renewal, Chatham County; mem. state advisory bd. ACLU; mem. advisory bd. Ga. Service Center for Elected Ofcls. div. Clark Coll. Pub. Center; del. Dem. Nat. Conv., 1976. Recipient award for outstanding achievement in politics Savannah State Coll. Nat. Alumni Assn., 1969, Distinguished Alumnus award Student Bar Assn., Howard U., 1969, Maj. Richard Wright award, 1972. Mem. Am., Ga., Savannah bar assns., Ga. Assn. Black Elected Ofcls. (pres. 1978-80), Savannah Area C. of C., Beta Phi Lambda (Man of Year 1969-70), Alpha Phi Alpha. Appeared before U.S. and Ga. Supreme Cts. in cases which overturned death penalty in U.S. and Ga. Address: 208 E 34th St Savannah GA 31401 *I believe.*

HILL, BOYD H., JR., medieval history educator; b. Dunedin Isles, Fla., Feb. 21, 1931; s. Boyd Howard and Minnie Cauthen (Buchanan) H.; m. Alette Louise Olin, Jan. 26, 1956; children: Boyd Buchanan, Michael Howard. A.B., Duke U., 1953; M.A., U. N.C., 1957, Ph.D., 1963; postgrad., UCLA, 1957-58. Instr. La. State U., Baton Rouge, 1962-64; asst. prof. medieval history U. Colo., Boulder, 1964-66, assoc. prof., 1967-71, prof., 1971—; vis. asst. prof. UCLA, 1966-67. Author: Medieval Monarchy in Action, 1972; editor: The Rise of the First Reich, 1969, The Western World, 1974; contbr. articles to profl. jours. Served with U.S. Army, 1953-55. Wellcome Hist. Med. Library fellow, 1962; Am. Philos. Soc. grantee, 1968; Council Research and Creative Work U. Colo. grantee, 1980. Mem. Am. Hist. Assn. (councillor Pacific Coast br. 1971-74), Medieval Acad. Am. (councillor 1973-76), Rocky Mountain Medieval and Renaissance Assn. (pres. 1983), Phi Kappa Psi. Democrat. Presbyterian. Home: 275 29th St Boulder CO 80303 Office: Dept History U Colo Campus Box 234 Boulder CO 80309

HILL, BRUCE MARVIN, scientist, educator; b. Chgo., Mar. 13, 1935; s. Samuel and Leah (Berman) H.; m. Linda Ladd, June 18, 1958; children—Alec Michael, Russell Andrew, Gregory Bruce; m. Anne Edith Gardiner Bruce, Aug. 5, 1972. B.S., U. Chgo., 1956; M.S., Stanford U., 1958, Ph.D., 1961. Mem. faculty U. Mich., Ann Arbor, 1960—, assoc. prof. stats. and probability theory, 1964-70, prof., 1970—; vis. prof. bus. Harvard U., 1964-65; vis. prof. systems engring. U. Lancaster, U.K., 1968-69; vis. prof. stats. U. London, 1976; vis. prof. econs. U. Utah, 1979; cons. IBM. Editor Jour. Am. Statis. Assn., 1977-83, Jour. Bus. and Econ. Stats, 1982—; Contbr. articles to profl. jours., chpts. to books on stats. Ford Corp. NSF grantee, 1962-69, 81-83; USAF grantee, 1971-73. Fellow Am. Statis. Assn., Inst. Math. Stats.; mem. AAUP, Research Club U. Mich., Psi Upsilon, Sigma Chi. Home: 1657 Glenwood Ann Arbor MI 48104 Office: Dept Statistics U Mich Ann Arbor MI 48104

HILL, CARL MCCLELLAN, university president; b. Norfolk, Va., July 27, 1907; s. William F. and Sarah A. (Rowe) H.; m. Mary E. Elliott, Sept. 21, 1927 (dec.); 1 dau., Doris E. McGhee; m. Helen C. Rose, Aug. 2, 1970; son, Ernest Rose. B.S., Hampton Inst., 1931; M.S., Cornell U., 1935, Ph.D., 1941; postgrad., U. Pa., summers 1938-40; LL.D., U. Ky., 1966; D.Sc., U. Louisville, 1975, Eastern Ky. U., 1975. Asst. prof. chemistry Hampton Inst., 1931-41; asso. prof. chemistry Greensboro (N.C.) Agr. and Tech. U., 1941-44; prof. chemistry Tenn. State U., 1944-62, head dept. chemistry, 1944-51; chmn. Sch. Arts and Scis., 1951-58, dean sch., dean faculty, 1958-62; pres. Ky. State U., Frankfort, 1962-75, Hampton (Va.) Inst., 1976-78; Dir. United Va. Bank. Supt.; chem. research projects TVA, Research Coop., USAF Research and Devel. Command, NSF. Author: General College Chemistry, Laboratory Experiments in Organic Chemistry; Contbr. articles to profl. jours. Bd. commrs. Nat. Commn. Accrediting; mem. Ky. Med. Scholarship Bd., Ky. Authority Ednl. TV, Ky. Council on Pub. Higher Edn.; mem. gen. exec. bd. Presbyn. Ch. U.S.; Bd. dirs. Ky. Heart Assn., Am. Heart Assn., Blue Cross Hosp. Plan, Salvation Army; trustee Stillman Coll., Centre Coll.; mem. bd., exec. com. So. Regional Edn. Bd., 1972-75; sec.-treas. Council on Coop. Coll. Projects, 1964-75; chmn. adv. com. Hampton (Va.) City Coliseum; mem., chmn. Norfolk (Va.) Presbytery Higher Edn. Ministries Com.; mem. nominations com. Synod of Virginias; mem. religion and medicine com. Eastern Va. Med. Sch. Recipient Mfg. Chemists Assn. coll. chem. tchrs. award, 1962. Fellow AAAS, Am. Inst. Chemists, Tenn. Acad. Sci.; mem. Am. Chem. Soc., NEA, N.Y., Ky. acads. sci., Ky. C. of C. (dir.), Sigma Xi, Omega Psi Phi. Lodge: Masons. Home: 431 Elizabeth Lake Dr Hampton VA 23669

HILL, CARL PAUL, food company executive; b. Bay City, Mich., Apr. 25, 1942; s. Monica Cecelia and O'Neal (Hill); (div); children: Heather, Alison, Gretchen, Mitchell. B.S. in Bus. Adminstrn., Central Mich. U., 1967. Regional sales mgr. Dow Chem. Co., Mpls., 1967-68; v.p. sales Totino Foods, Mpls., 1968-69; regional v.p. Perk Foods, Mpls., 1969-70; sr. v.p. mktg. and sales Jeno's, Inc., Casselberry, Fla., 1970-72, pres., 1972-78, vice chmn. bd., 1978—, also dir.; pres. Poulucci Enterprises, 1978—; dir. Aerodrome, Inc., Miller Hill State Bank; cons. food industry Bus. Cons. Inc. Indsl. devel. dir., Austin, Minn., 1973-78. Office: Jenos Inc 100 Live Oak Gardens PO Box 200 Casselberry FL 32707

HILL, CLINTON, artist; b. Payette, Idaho, Mar. 8, 1922; s. Samuel Edgar and Iva Marie (Horn) H. B.S. U. Oreg., 1947; postgrad., Bklyn. Mus. Sch., 1949-51, Academie de la Grande Chaumiere, Paris, France, 1951, Instituto d'Arte Statale, Florence, Italy, 1951-52. Prof. Queens Coll., N.Y.C., 1968—. Artist: one-man show Marilyn Pearl Gallery, N.Y.C., 1979, 80, 83, Montclair Mus., N.J., 1981, Galleria Blu, Milan, Italy, 1984; represented in permanent collection, Mus. Modern Art, N.Y.C., Met. Mus., N.Y.C., Phila. Mus., Albright Knox Gallery, Buffalo, Nat. Gallery of Australia, Canberra, Bklyn. Mus., Phoenix Art Mus., others. Served to lt. (j.g.) USN, 1943-47. Fulbright grantee, India, 1956; Creative Artists Pub. Service grantee, 1975; Nat. Endowment for Arts grantee, 1976, 80. Home: 178 Prince St New York NY 10012

HILL, CLYDE CECIL, JR., retired manufacturer; b. Ashtabula, Ohio, Nov. 25, 1914; s. Clyde Cecil and Nancy Elizabeth (Humphrey) H.; m. Ruth Helen Westfall, May 10, 1941; children: Nancy (Mrs. Jay MacDonald Davis), Thomas, Susan (Mrs. Emilio Cabrera), Barbara (Mrs. Lee Behrman). A.B., Ohio Wesleyan U., 1937. C.P.A., Pa. With Ernst & Ernst, Cleve. and Pitts., 1937-42; controller Clark div. Dresser Industries, Inc., Olean, N.Y., 1942-53, treas., 1953-57, asst. treas. parent co., Dallas, 1957-70, treas., 1970-79, ret., 1979; former officer affiliated cos. Pres., dir. YMCA, Olean, 1950-53, Community Chest,

1948-51; mem. adv. bd. Salvation Army, 1950-53; officer dir. council Boy Scouts Am., 1948-51; adv. council Dallas Community Chest Trust Fund, Inc., 1973; mem. Dallas Crime Commn., Cotton Bowl Council; bd. dirs. Tex. Soc. Prevention Blindness, 1979-81; also officer Dallas chpt.; bd. dirs. Dallas Council World Affairs, 1978-80, Dallas Summer Musicals, 1977-79; trustee Amyotrophic Lateral Sclerosis Soc. Am., 1980—. Mem. Financial Execs. Inst. (v.p. Dallas chpt. 1971, pres. 1972-73), Dallas Central Bus. Dist. Assn. (dir. 1977-79), Dallas C. of C. (dir. 1975-79), Olean C. of C. (past officer, dir.), Phi Gamma Delta, Omicron Delta Kappa. Republican. Methodist. Clubs: Olean (pres., dir. 1945-48), Rotary (dir. 1981-83), Dallas, Brookhaven Country (Dallas). Home: 4431 Alta Vista Ln Dallas TX 75229

HILL, DELMAS CARL, sr. judge; b. Wamego, Kans., Oct. 9, 1906; s. Ray G. and Elfie E. (Smith) H.; m. Katherine V. Hooven, July 29, 1933 (dec. Jan. 1978); m. Wilma B. Jennings, Mar. 4, 1981. LL.B., Washburn Coll., 1929; LL.D., 1958. Bar: Kan. bar 1929. Practiced in, Wamego, 1929-43, 46-49, county atty., Pottawatomie County, Kans., 1931-34; asst. U.S. atty., Dist. Kans., 1934-36; gen. counsel Kans. State Tax Commn., 1937-39; chmn. Democratic State Com., 1946-48; U.S. dist. judge, 1949-61, U.S. circuit judge, 10th circuit, 1961-77, sr. judge, 1977—. Served with AUS, 1943-46; prosecution staff in trial of Gen. Yamashita, 1945; Manila, P.I. Episcopalian. Home: 5051 E Lincoln Wichita KS 67218

HILL, DEREK LEONARD, chemistry educator; b. Croydon, Eng., Dec. 6, 1930; came to U.S., 1957; s. Leonard David and Jessie (Hoare) H.; m. Sandra Hale Cloke, Aug. 23, 1958; children: Lauren, Brenda, Amanda, Sharon. B.Sc., U. London, 1953, Ph.D., 1957; D.I.C., Imperial Coll., 1957. Asst. exptl. officer AEC U.K., 1956-57; research asso. Rensselaer Poly. Inst., 1957-59, asst. prof. chemistry, 1959-61; sr. lectr. phys. chemistry U. Hong Kong, 1961-68; asso. prof. chemistry SUNY-Brockport, 1968-71, prof. chemistry, 1971, chmn. dept., 1970-79, dean faculty nat. math. sci., 1979-82. Mem. Am. Chem. Soc., Chem. Soc. (London), Electrochem. Soc., Sigma Xi. Home: 123 Sherwood Dr Brockport NY 14420

HILL, DONALD WALTER, educator; b. Hazleton, Pa., Jan. 13, 1922; s. Richard Joseph and Anna Martha (Lohrke) H.; m. Elsa Louise Schiel, May 14, 1949; children—Douglas Warren, Randall Richard, Jane Louise, Christine Lois. Student, Wilkes Coll., 1947-48, 49-50; B.S., Bucknell U., 1953; M.S., Cornell U., 1955; Ph.D., Am. U., 1964. Lab. analyst Pa. Power and Light Co., 1940-42; flight radio engr. TWA, 1944; transmission engr. Am. Tel. & Tel., 1944-50; comml. engineer, marketing research, 1954-58; instr. Bucknell U., 1952-53; grad. asst. Cornell U., 1953-54; asst. prof. Rollins Coll., Winter Park, Fla., 1958-59; vis. lectr. Am. U., 1959-61; asst. prof. Lehigh U., 1961-62; mem. faculty Rollins Coll., 1962—, dean adminstrv. affairs, 1965-66, dean of coll., 1966-71, prof. econs., 1966—; coordinator M.B.A. program, 1977-80; acting dean Crummer Sch. Fin. and Bus. Adminstrn., 1978-79; Pres. Internat. Group Travel Orgn., 1972—; Chmn. planning council Assn. Mid Fla. Coll., 1966-71; rep. to Am. Council Edn., Am. Assn. Coll., 1966-71; rep. So. Assn. Colls. and Sch., 1966-71. Served with USCGR, 1942-44. Gen. Electric fellow U. Chgo., 1963; Republic Steel fellow Case Inst. Tech., 1965; Ford fellow Duke, 1964. Mem. Am., So. econs. assns., Tau Kappa Epsilon, Omicron Delta Kappa, Psi Chi, Delta Mu Delta. Republican. Methodist. Home: 1085 Park Ave N Winter Park FL 32789

HILL, DOUGLAS FRANKLIN, rubber company executive; b. Aurora, Ill., Jan. 20, 1933; s. Wayne W. and Edna C. (Browning) H.; m. Shirley M. Ellis, Aug. 3, 1956; children: Geoffry, Mark, Monique. B.S., Am. Grad. Sch. Internat. Mgmt., Glendale, Ariz., 1958, Ariz. State U., 1957; postgrad., Stanford U., 1975. Pres. Goodyear Mexico, Mexico City, 1971-74; regional dir. Goodyear Internat. Corp., Akron, Ohio, 1974-79, v.p., 1979-80, exec. v.p., 1980—; v.p. Goodyear Tire & Rubber, Akron, 1980—. Served to cpl. U.S. Army, 1953-54; ETO. Republican. Methodist. Club: Fairlawn Country (Akron). Home: 4240 Derrwood Dr Akron OH 44313 Office: Goodyear Internat Corp 1144 E Market St Akron OH 44316

HILL, DOUGLAS GREEN, musician; b. Tulsa, Oct. 7, 1930; s. Israel Phillip and Mabel (Turner) H.; m. Kathryn Thomas, Oct. 21, 1951 (dec.); children—Cynthia Ann, Barbara Diane, Lawrence Thomas. B.Music Edn., U. Tulsa, 1951, M.M., 1957; postgrad., U. N.M. Mem. string bass and tuba. sect. Tulsa Symphony Orch., 1945-52, 54-57, New Orleans Symphony, 1949-50, El Paso Symphony, 1950, N.Mex. Symphony, 1961-78; string bassist Fred Waring Orch., 1950-51; tuba player N.Mex. Brass Ensemble, 1961-68, N.Mex. Symphony Brass Ensemble, 1968-78, Santa Fe Opera, 1962-72, Albuquerque Opera Theater, 1974-80; condr. Albuquerque Civic Light Opera, 1973-74; Elementary band specialist Albuquerque Pub. Schs., 1960—; instr. low brass and strings U. Albuquerque, 1967-70; Del. conf. on art in Ams. UNESCO, 1959. Served with AUS, 1952-54. Mem. Am. Fedn. Musicians, Music Educators Nat. Conf., N.Mex. Music Educators Assn., Phi Mu Alpha, Kappa Kappa Psi. Home: 9024 Aspen NE Albuquerque NM 87112 Office: PO Box 25704 Music Dept Albuquerque Public Schs Albuquerque NM 87125

HILL, DRAPER, editorial cartoonist; b. Boston, July 1, 1935; s. L. Draper and Jean Hutchins (Thompson) H.; m. Sarah Randolph Adams, Apr. 22, 1967; children: Jennifer Randolph, Jonathan Draper. B.A. magna cum laude, Harvard, 1957; postgrad, Slade Sch. Fine Arts, Univ. Coll., London, Eng., 1960-63. Reporter and cartoonist Quincy (Mass.) Patriot Ledger, 1957-60; editorial cartoonist Worcester (Mass.) Telegram, 1964-71, Comml. Appeal, Memphis, 1971-76, The Detroit News, 1976—; dir. Play of Month Guild, N.Y.C., 1958-82; instr. drawing Worcester Art Sch., 1967-71. Author: Mr. Gillray, The Caricaturist, 1965, Fashionable Contrasts, 1966, (with James Roper) The Decline and Fall of the Gibbon, 1974, The Satirical Etchings of James Gillray, 1976; also catalogues. Mem. adv. bd. Swann Found. for Caricature and Cartoon, N.Y.C., 1980—. Mem. Assn. Am. Editorial Cartoonists (2d v.p. 1972-74, 1st v.p. 1974-75, pres. 1975-76), Club of Odd Vols. Home: 368 Washington Rd Grosse Pointe MI 48230 Office: 615 W Lafayette Blvd Detroit MI 48231

HILL, EDWIN HOLLIS, JR., retail liquor company executive; b. Miami, Fla., Nov. 21, 1932; s. Edwin Hollis and Lillian Dorothy (Hampton) H.; children: Edwin Hollis III, John Hampton, Wendy Pace. Student, Rollins Coll., 1950-51; B.A., U. Miami, Coral Gables, 1954. With Hill Bros., Inc., Miami, 1957—, pres., 1965-69, 72—, chmn. bd., 1965—. Active Orange Bowl Com., 1965—, United Fund Dade County, 1969—; adv. bd. Salvation Army, 1965-71; Bd. dirs. Miami Heart Inst., ARC, 1969-71, Big Bros., Jr. Achievement, Nat. Conf. Christians and Jews, Miami Crime Commn. Served to capt. USAF, 1954-57. Mem. Miami C. of C., Young Pres.' Orgn., Econ. Soc. Methodist. Clubs: Coral Reef Yacht, University (Miami); Biscayne Bay Yacht, Rod and Reel, Riviera Country. Office: 3575 NW 60th St Miami FL 33142

HILL, FRANCIS FREDERICK, gas co. exec.; b. Portland, Oreg., Dec. 13, 1908; s. James F. and Bertha M. (McIntire) H.; m. Barbara Jean Campbell, Dec. 25, 1941; children—Cinda, Jeffrey. J.D., U. Oreg., 1933. Bar: Oreg. bar 1933. With firm Laing, Gray & Smith (and predecessors), Portland, 1936-55, partner, 1941-55; partner firm Smith, Gray, Hill & Rodgers, 1955-61; v.p., gen. counsel Northwest Natural Gas Co., Portland, 1961, pres., dir., 1962—, chmn., 1975-77; dir. First Nat. Bank of Oreg. Mem. emergency adv. com. for natural gas Dept. Interior.; Mem. econ. stblzn. group Oreg. Office Emergency Planning.; Bd. dirs. Portland Rose Festival Assn., 1950-56, N.W. Hosp. Service-Blue Cross, 1965-77; bd. dirs. Good Samaritan Found.; mem. adv. bd. St. Vincent Hosp. and Med. Center. Served to lt. comdr. USNR, 1942-46. Mem. Am., Oreg., Multnomah bar assns., Am. Gas Assn. (dir. 1966-70), Pacific Coast Gas Assn. (pres. 1969, dir. 1965-71). Presbyn. Clubs: Internat., Arlington, Waverley (Portland). Home: 127 SW Kingston Ave Portland OR 97201 Office: 200 SW Market St Suite 1900 Portland OR 97201

HILL, FRANK WHITNEY, JR., ins. co. exec; b. Topeka, Aug. 4, 1914; s. Frank Whitney and Blanche (Scott) H.; m. Mary Louise Booth, May 18, 1940; children—Frank Whitney III, Marilyn Louise, Barbara Jane. Student, U. Kans., Kansas City Sch. Law. With Equitable Life Assurance Soc. U.S., 1946—, field asst., Peoria, Ill., asst. agy. mgr., dist. mgr., Bloomington, Ill., agy. mgr., Albany, N.Y., 1946-58, field v.p., N.Y.C., 1958-61, v.p. agy. affairs, 1961-61, agy. mgr., Pitts., 1962—; Former mem. nat. bd. Gen. Agts. and Mgrs. Conf. Chmn. life div. Greater Alegehny United Fund; gen. chmn. Greater Albany Community Chest Fund, 1957-8. Mem. Albany Gen. Agts. and Mgrs. Assn. (past pres.), Pitts. Gen. Agts. and Mgrs. Assn. (pres.), Pitts. Life Underwriters Assn. Club: Duquesne. Home: 17326 Tam O'Shanter Dr Poway CA 92064 Office: 1333 Camino Del Rio S Suite 200 San Diego CA 92108

HILL, FREDRIC WILLIAM, poultry scientist, nutrition educator; b. Erie, Pa., Sept. 2, 1918; s. Vaino Alexander and Mary Elvira (Holmstrom) H.; m. Charlotte Henrietta Gummoe, Apr. 1, 1944; children: Linda Charlotte, James Fredric, Dana Edwin. B.S., Pa. State U., 1939, M.S., 1940; Ph.D., Cornell U., 1944. Research asst. Pa. State U., 1939-40, Cornell U., 1940-44; head nutrition div. research labs. Western Condensing Co., Appleton, Wis., 1944-48; assoc. prof., then prof. animal nutrition and poultry husbandry Cornell U., 1948-59; prof. poultry husbandry, chmn. dept. U. Calif. at Davis, 1959-65, prof. nutrition, 1965—, chmn. dept. nutrition, 1965-73, assoc. dean Coll. Agr., 1965-66, assoc. dean research Coll. Agr., 1976-80, coordinator internat. programs Coll. Agr., 1976-80; Mem. subcom. hormonal relationships and applications com. on Animal Nutrition, NRC, 1953, subcom. poultry nutrition, 1953-74; mem. Food and Nutrition Bd., 1975-78; commr. Calif. Poultry Improvement Commn., 1959-65; participant 8th Easter Sch. Agrl. Scis., U. Nottingham, Eng., 1961, World Conf. Animal Prodn., Rome, Italy, 1963, U.S. AID-Nat. Acad. Sci. Seminar on Protein Foods, Bangkok, 1970, USIA Asia Seminars on Food, Population and Energy, 1974-75; Japan Soc. Promotion Sci. vis. prof. Nagoya U., 1974-75; vis. scientist FDA, 1975, Nutrition Inst., USDA, 1975; cons. Institut National de Recherche Agronomique, France, 1982. Contbr. articles profl. jours.; Editorial bd.: Poultry Sci. Jour, 1960-64; editorial bd.: Jour. of Nutrition, 1964-68; editor, 1969-79. Fellow Danforth Found., 1938; recipient Nutrition Research award Am. Feed Mfrs. Assn., 1958, Newman Internat. Research award British Poultry Assn., 1959; Guggenheim Found. fellow, 1966-67; Alumni fellow Pa. State U., 1983. Fellow AAAS, Poultry Sci. Assn. (Research prize 1957, Borden award 1961); mem. Soc. Exptl. Biology and Medicine, Nutrition Soc. (Gt. Britain), Council Biology Editors, World's Poultry Sci. Assn., Am. Inst. Nutrition (councillor 1982-85), Am. Inst. Biol. Scis., Am. Soc. Animal Sci., Am. Chem. Soc., Sigma Xi, Phi Eta Sigma, Gamma Sigma Delta, Phi Kappa Phi, Delta Theta Sigma, Gamma Alpha. Clubs: Cosmos (Washington); El Macero (Calif.). Home: 643 Miller Dr Davis CA 95616

HILL, GEORGE JACKSON, III, advertising agency executive; b. Cambridge, Mass., Nov. 21, 1932; s. George Jackson Hill Jr. and Elizabeth Cary (Heath) H.; m. Virginia Graham Drew, Dec. 10, 1960; children: David Winslow, John Drew, Peter Bigelow Heath. A.B., Harvard U., 1954. Copywriter Dickie-Raymond, Boston, 1960-62, Bresnick Co., 1962-64; copy supr. Kenyon & Eckhardt, Boston, 1964-66; copy group head BBDO, Boston, 1966-68; chmn., creative dir. Hill, Holliday, Connors, Cosmopulos, Inc., Boston, 1968—; mem. corp. Children's Mus., Boston, 1975—. Served with AUS, 1950-53. Clubs: Fox, Bedham Country and Polo. Home: 188 Village Ave Dedham MA 02026 Office: Hill Holliday Connors Cosmopulos Inc 200 Clarendon St Boston MA 02116

HILL, GEORGE JAMES, surgeon, educator; b. Cedar Rapids, Iowa, Oct. 7, 1932; s. Gerald Leslie and Essie Mae (Thompson) H.; m. Helene Zimmermann, July 16, 1960; children: James Warren, David Hedgcock, Sarah, Helena Rundall. A.B., Yale U., 1953; M.D., Harvard U., 1957. Intern N.Y. Hosp., 1957-58; fellow and resident in surgery Peter Bent Brigham hosp. and Harvard Med. Sch., 1958-61, 63-66; instr. surgery U. Colo., 1966-67, asst. prof., 1967-72, asso. prof., 1972-73; prof. Washington U., 1973-76; prof., chmn. Marshall U., 1976-81; prof., dir. surg. oncology U. of Medicine & Dentistry of N.J.-N.J. Med. Sch., Newark, 1981—. Author: Leprosy in Five Young Men, 1970, Outpatient Surgery, 1973, 2d edition, 1980, Clinical Oncology, 1977; contbr. articles in field to profl. jours. Pres. Tri-State Area council Boy Scouts Am., Huntington, W.Va., 1980-81; pres. W.Va. div. Am. Cancer Soc., 1980-81. Served with USPHSR, 1961-63; Served with USNR, 1976—. Damon Runyon fellow, 1958. Mem. A.C.S., Soc. Univ. Surgeons, Soc. Surg. Oncology, Central Surg. Assn., Am. Assn. Cancer Research. Republican. Episcopalian. Clubs: Harvard (Boston); Univ. (Denver); Army and Navy (Washington); Explorers, Harvard (N.Y.C.). Lodge: Rotary. Office: 100 Bergen St Newark NJ 07103

HILL, GEORGE RICHARD, educator; b. Ogden, Utah, Nov. 24, 1921; s. George Richard and Elizabeth (McKay) H.; m. Melba Parker, Aug. 25, 1941; children: George Richard IV, Margaret Hill Nielson, Robert Parker, Carolyn Hill Allen, Susan Hill Mann, Nancy Hill Bauman, David Parker. A.B. in Chemistry, Brigham Young U., 1942, D.Sc. (hon.), 1980; Ph.D. in Phys. and Inorganic Chemistry, Cornell U., 1946. Chemist Am. Smelting & Refining Co., 1937-42; asst., part-time instr. Cornell U., 1942-46; project dir. Air Force Combustion Research, 1952-57; dir. Office Coal Research, Dept. Interior, Washington, 1972-73; mem. faculty U. Utah, 1946-72, prof. chemistry, 1950-72, chmn. fuels engring., 1951-65; dean Coll. Mines and Mineral Industries, U. Utah, 1966-72; Envirotech. endowed prof. U. Utah, 1977-82, Eimco endowed prof., 1982—; dept. dir. fossil fuels Electric Power Research Inst., Palo Alto, Calif., 1973-77, dir. fossil fuel power plants dept., 1976-77; project dir. Air Force Office Sci. Research, 1956-61, Equity Oil Shale Research, 1961; mem. NRC com. Mineral and Energy Resources, 1976-81; mem. fossil energy adv. com. Dept. Energy, 1977—; vice chmn. Utah Council Energy Conservation and Devel., 1978-83; chmn. Utah Task Force on Power Plant Siting, 1978; chmn. editorial com. NRC, 1977-81; com. chmn. Chemistry of Coal Utilization, 1981. Contbr. papers on kinetics of coal conversion, oil shale, corrosion, catalysis. Mem. exec. bd. region XII Boy Scouts Am., 1961; chmn. Explorer activities sect. 6, 1959-61; mem. Explorer com., nat. exec. bd., 1965-72; Bd. dirs. Deseret Gymnasium, 1967. Recipient Silver Beaver, Silver Antelope awards Boy Scouts Am.; Distinguished Service award Utah Petroleum Council, 1968; Outstanding Profl. Engr. award Utah Engring. Council, 1970. Fellow Am. Inst. Chemists; mem. AAAS, AIME, Am. Chem. Soc. (Utah award Salt Lake sect. 1969, Henry H. Storch award 1971), Am. Inst. Chem. Engrs., Sigma Xi, Phi Kappa Phi, Sigma Pi Sigma, Alpha Phi Omega. Home: 1430 Yale Ave Salt Lake City UT 84105 *There's no limit to the amount of good you can do if you don't care who gets the credit.*

HILL, GEORGE ROY, film dir.; b. Mpls., Dec. 20, 1922; s. George Roy and Helen Frances (Owens) H.; m. Louise Horton, Apr. 7, 1951. B.A., Yale U.; B.Litt., Trinity Coll., Dublin, Ireland. (Winner 2 Emmy nominations for A Night to Remember, also nominated for The Helen Morgan Story, Child of Our Time, nominated Acad. award Best Dir. for Butch Cassidy and the Sundance Kid 1969, winner Acad. award for Best Dir. of The Sting 1973); Stage Acting deput in The Devil's Disciple, Dublin, 1948; other stage appearances include The Creditors, 1950; tour with, Margaret Webster's Shakespeare Repertory Co.; writer: actor teleplay My Brother's Keeper, 1953; writer, producer, dir.: teleplays Judgment at Nuremberg, 1957; dir.: Broadway play Look Homeward, Angel, 1957, The Gang's All Here, Period of Adjustment, Greenwillow, 1960, Henry, Sweet Henry, 1967; off-Broadway show Moon on a Rainbow Shawl, 1962; films Period of Adjustment, 1962, Toys in the Attic, 1963, The World of Henry Orient, 1964, Hawaii, 1966, Thoroughly Modern Millie, 1967, Butch Cassidy and the Sundance Kid, 1969, Slaughterhouse-Five, 1972, The Sting, 1973, The Great Waldo Pepper, 1975, Slap Shot, 1977, A Little Romance, 1979, The World According to Garp, 1981. Served as pilot USMC, World War II and Korean War. Office: Pan Arts Prodns Corp 4000 Warner Blvd Burbank CA 91522

HILL, GEORGE WATTS, banker; b. N.Y.C., Oct. 27, 1901; s. John Sprunt and Annie Louise (Watts) H.; m. Ann McCulloch, Sept. 30, 1924 (dec.); children: George Watts, Ann Dudley, John Sprunt; m. Anne Gibson, June 14, 1975. B.S. in commerce, U. of N.C., 1922; student, U. of N.C. Law Sch., 1922-24. Bar: N.C. bar 1924. Pres. Central Carolina Bank & Trust Co., 1932-49, chmn. bd., 1949—; pres. Home Security Life Ins. Co., 1934-39, chmn. bd. dirs., 1939-76. Pres. Watts Hosp., 1937-62; Mem. City Council, Durham, 1928-36; Mem. exec. com. American Guernsey Cattle Club, 1934-56; Trustee and mem. exec. com. U. N.C., 1956-72, bd. govs., 1972-81; sec. Research Triangle Found. N.C., 1958-82; chmn. bd. govs. Research Triangle Inst., 1959—; co-founder N.C. Blue Cross-Blue Shield, 1933, trustee, 1933-74; Leader orgn. coop. mktg. and farm orgns. Served as major AUS, 1943-45. Home: Raleigh Rd Chapel Hill NC 27514 Office: Central Carolina Bank Bldg Durham NC 27702

HILL, GRAHAM RODERICK, librarian; b. Richmond, Surrey, Eng., Apr. 4, 1946; s. Herbert Edgar and Elsie (Davies) H.; m. Penelope Mary Potts, Aug. 31, 1968; 1 dau., Lindsay. B.A., U. Newcastle-on-Tyne, 1968; M.A., U. Lancaster, 1969; M.L.S., U. Western Ont., 1970. With Univ. Libraries, McMaster U., Hamilton, Ont., Can., 1971—, assoc. univ. librarian, 1977-79, univ. librarian, 1979—; mng. editor, treas. Cromlech Press Inc., 1975—. Recipient various grants. Mem. Can. Assn. Research Libraries (sec.-treas. 1981—), Ont. Council Univ. Libraries (vice chmn. 1982-84). Home: 15 Forestview Dr Dundas ON L9H 6M9 Canada Office: McMaster U 1280 Main St W Hamilton ON L8S 4L6 Canada

HILL, HAMLIN LEWIS, JR., English educator; b. Houston, Nov. 7, 1931; s. Hamlin Lewis and Marguerite (Courtin) H.; m. Arlette Crawford, Dec. 27, 1952; children: Cynthia, Joe Scott, Sondra June, William Christian. Student, U. Tex., 1949-51, 1953-54, M.A., 1954; B.A., U. Houston, 1953; Ph.D., U. Chgo., 1959. Instr. English U. N.Mex., 1959-61, asst. prof., 1963-65, asso. prof., 1965-68; asst. prof. English, U. Wyo., 1961-63; prof. English U. Chgo., 1968-75, U. N.Mex., Albuquerque, 1975—, chmn. dept., 1979—; vis. prof. U. Nebr., 1960, U. Calif. at Berkeley, 1965, Stanford, 1972-73; dir. Summer Seminar for Coll. Tchrs., Nat. Endowment for Humanities, 1977, 81, Seminar in Residence for Coll. Tchrs., 1978-79; mem. Am. lit. selection com. Council Internat. Exchange of Scholars, 1981—; Fulbright fellow U. Copenhagen, 1966-67; Fulbright prof. U. Würzburg, 1980; acad. specialist, India, 1983. Author: Mark Twain and Elisha Bliss, 1964, Mark Twain: God's Fool, 1973, (with Walter Blair) America's Humor, 1978; Editor: The Art of Huckleberry Finn, 1962, A Connecticut Yankee in King Arthur's Court, 1963, Mark Twain's Letters to His Publishers, 1967, Roughing It, 1981, Wapping Alice by Mark Twain, 1981; mem. editorial bd.: The Lovingood Papers, 1965-67, Am. Lit. Realism, 1972—, Studies in Am. Humor, 1974—, The Old Northwest, 1974—, Am. Lit., 1982—; Contbr. articles, revs. to scholastic jours. Am. Council Learned Socs. grantee-in-aid, 1963, 65, 67; Guggenheim fellow, 1971-72. Mem. MLA, Am. Humor Studies Assn., Theta Xi. Democrat. Episcopalian. Home: 10506 San Marino Pl NE Albuquerque NM 87111

HILL, HAROLD EUGENE, retired educator; b. Keokuk, Iowa, Sept. 7, 1918; s. Grover Clevel and Letha Agnes (McKinney) H.; m. Dorothy May Crays, July 4, 1941; children: Sandra Lu, Wade Crays, Kathy Lynn. B.S., U. Ill., Urbana, 1940, M.S., 1954. Writer, announcer, dir., producer, program dir. Sta.-WILL-AM-FM-TV, Urbana, 1946-54; mem. faculty U. Ill., Urbana, 1946-56; sportscaster Sta. WDWS, Champaign, Ill., 1950-55; exec. v.p., treas. Nat. Assn. Ednl. Broadcasters, Washington, 1954-66; asso. dir. Edn. Media Center, U. Colo., Boulder, 1967-72, asso. prof. speech and drama, 1967-72, prof. communication, 1972-80, chmn. dept. communication, 1976-80, prof. broadcast journalism, 1980-84, prof. emeritus, 1984—; bd. dirs. Nat. Center Communication Arts and Scis., Sta. KRMA-TV (public TV), 1967-84, Sta. KGNU (public radio), 1977-79; subchmn. new tech. Colo. Commn. on Higher Edn., 1979-82; trustee Ednl. Communication Found. TV editor: AV Guide, 1968-74; editorial bd.: Audiovisual Communications Rev, 1974, Audiovisual Instrn, 1975. Chmn. ednl. adv. com. Champaign Schs., 1950-52. Served to maj. U.S. Army, 1940-46. Named Hon. Citizen, Tex., Louisville, New Orleans, hon. Ky. Col., La. Col. Mem. Assn. Ednl. Communication and Tech. (Disting. Service award 1978, dir., pres., book rev. editor, editorial bd. assn. jour. 1977—), Ednl. Media Council (exec. dir.), Western Ednl. Soc. Telecommunications (dir.), Speech Communication Assn., Nat. Assn. Ednl. Broadcasters (dir.), Colo. Ednl. Media Assn. (dir., pres.), Broadcast Edn. Assn., Colo. Broadcasters Assn., Colo. Drama and Speech Assn. (dir.), Colo. Media Dirs., Sigma Delta Chi, Alpha Kappa Psi, Kappa Tau Alpha. Democrat. Episcopalian. Club: Exchange (pres. Ill. State Exchange Clubs 1956). Office: Sch Journalism Box 287 U Colo Boulder CO 80309 *I have always lived by the tenet that the most satisfying "Road to Achievement" is through helpfulness & loyalty to others. Service is much more fulfilling to me than material rewards. Belief in the honesty & goodness of my fellows has caused me to have a lasting faith in friends, family, and perhaps most importantly, myself—A belief that they, and I, can accomplish any worthwhile task we set for our selves, and we can be anything we want to be.*

HILL, HAROLD NELSON, JR., state justice; b. Houston, Apr. 26, 1930; s. Harold Nelson and Emolyn Eloise (Geeslin) H.; m. Betty Jane Fell, Aug. 16, 1952; children—Ward, Douglas, Nancy. B.S. in Commerce, Washington and Lee U., Lexington, Va., 1952; LL.B., Emory U., 1957. Bar: Ga. 1957. Assoc., then partner firm Gambrell, Harlan, Russel, Moye & Richardson, 1957-66; asst. atty. gen., Ga., 1966-68, exec. asst. atty. gen., 1968-72; partner firm Jones, Bird & Howell, 1972-74; assoc. justice Supreme Ct. Ga., 1975—, now chief justice. Served with AUS, 1952-54. Fellow Am. Bar Found.; Mem. Am. Law Inst., State Bar Ga., Lawyers Club Atlanta, Old War Horse Lawyers Club. Methodist. Office: 533 State Judicial Bldg Atlanta GA 30334

HILL, HENRY ALLEN, educator, physicist; b. Port Arthur, Tex., Nov. 25, 1933; s. Douglas and Florence (Kilgore) H.; m. Ethel Louise Eplin, Aug. 23, 1954; children—Henry Allen, Pamela Lynne,

Kimberly Renee. B.S., U. Houston, 1953; M.S., U. Minn., 1956, Ph.D., 1957; M.A. (hon.), Wesleyan U., 1966. Research asst. U. Houston, 1952-53; teaching asst. U. Minn., 1953-54, research asst., 1954-57; research asso. Princeton, 1957-58, instr., then asst. prof., 1958-64; asso. prof. Wesleyan U., Middletown, Conn., 1964-66, prof. physics, 1966-74, chmn. dept., 1969-71; prof. physics U. Ariz., 1966—. Contbr. articles to profl. jours. Sloan fellow, 1966-68. Mem. Am. Phys. Soc., Am. Astron. Soc., Royal Astron. Soc., Optical Soc. Am. Research on nuclear physics, relativity and astrophysics. Home: 340 S Avenida de las Palmas Tucson AZ 85716

HILL, HENRY PARKER, accountant; b. N.Y.C., Jan. 20, 1918; s. Henry Parker and Hermione (Graf) H.; m. Patricia Andersen, Oct. 3, 1943; children: Henry Parker, Robert Scott. B.S., U. Pa., 1940. C.P.A., N.Y. With Price Waterhouse & Co. (C.P.A.s), 1940-76, partner, 1956-76; adj. prof. acctg. N.Y. U. Grad. Sch. Bus. Adminstrn.; vis. prof. acctg. Amos Tuck Sch. Bus. Adminstrn., Dartmouth, 1977-79. Author: (with others) Sampling in Auditing, 1962; also articles.; Editor-in-chief: Jour. Acctg. Auditing and Fin, 1977—. Served to lt. USNR, 1943-45. Mem. Am. Inst. C.P.A.s (chmn. com. banking 1962-64), N.Y. State Soc. C.P.A.s, Delta Phi, St. Elmo. Clubs: New York Yacht, Nassau Country; Shelter Island Yacht, Gardiner's Bay Country (Shelter Island, N.Y.). Home: 66 Cobbetts Ln Shelter Island NY 11964 also 14A Washington Mews New York NY Office: 40 W 4th St New York NY 10003

HILL, HEYWARD GIBBES, diplomat, retired foreign service officer; b. Hammond, La., Jan. 16, 1900; s. Samuel Lindsay and Kate Turpin (McKnight) H. Ed., La. State U., 1916-20; also private tutors in, France and Switzerland. Apptd. fgn. service officer, vice consul and sec. in the diplomatic service, 1930; fgn. service Sch. Dept. State, 1930; vice consul, Kobe, Japan, 1930, temporary vice consul, Taihoku, 1931, vice consul, Kobe, 1931, vice consul, Yokahama, 1931, vice consul, Buenos Aires, 1933; asst. sec. Am. del. 7th Internat. Conf. of Am. States, Montevideo, 1933; sec. Am. del. Pan Am. Comml. Conf., Buenos Aires, 1935, Chaco Peace Conf., 1935-36; vice consul, Geneva, Switzerland, 1936, consul, 1937; sec. Am. del. Intergovernmental Com. on Polit. Refugees meeting, Evian, France and London, 1938, Eighth Internat. Conf. Am. States, Lima, Peru, 1938; consul, Basel, Switzerland, 1939, second sec. embassy, Panama, 1939; 2d sec. embassy for duty with U.S. rep. to Politico-Mil. Commn., Algiers, 1943; temporarily detailed European div. Dept. of State, 5 mos. in 1944; 1st sec. embassy, Ankara, Turkey, June, 1945, counselor of embassy, charge d' affaires, Jidda, Saudi Arabia, 1949-50, consul gen., Marseilles, France, 1951-54, counselor of embassy, consul gen., Manila, P.I., 1954-56, consul gen., Alexandria, Egypt, U.A.R., 1957-61. Decorated comdr. Order St. Mark, 1961. Clubs: University (Washington); Athens Lawn Tennis. Address: Hilton Hotel Athens Greece *Have good health. Early in life, find out what is bad for the health, and avoid it. Find out what is good for the health, and emphasize it. Without the basis of good health, nothing is worth very much. Also, be kind and helpful to others. It will always pay off in the end.*

HILL, IRA D., biochemist; b. Knox City, Tex., Aug. 16, 1934; s. Wilburn C. and Susie Avanell (Ruckman) H.; m. W. June Brown, Oct. 14, 1955; children: Haley, Holly. B.S., Abilene Christian U., 1956; M.S., Purdue U., 1958; Ph.D., U. Tex., 1962. Research biochemist Sun Oil Co., Marcus Hook, Pa., 1961-66; mgr. corp. research Tenneco Chems. Co., Piscataway, N.J., 1966-70; mgr. research and devel., environ. planning Monsanto Indsl. Chem. Co., St. Louis, 1970-74; v.p., dir. research and devel. Internat. Flavors & Fragrances, Inc., Union Beach, N.J., 1974—, v.p. tech., 1979—. Contbr. tech. articles to profl. jours. Mem. Am. Chem. Soc., Soap and Detergent Assn., Indsl. Research Inst., Dirs. Indsl. Research. Mem. Ch. of Christ. Home: Clay Ct Locust NJ 07760 Office: 1515 Hwy 36 Union Beach NJ 07735

HILL, IRVING, judge; b. Lincoln, Nebr., Feb. 6, 1915; s. Nathan and Ida (Ferder) H.; m. Maydee Taylor, June 23, 1939; children: Lawrence N., Steven C., Richard F. A.B., U. Nebr., 1936; J.D., Harvard U., 1939; L.H.D., Hebrew Union Coll., 1976. Bar: Nebr. 1939, D.C. 1942, Calif. 1946. Spl. asst. to U.S. atty. gens. Biddle and Clark, Dept. Justice, Washington, 1942-46; legal adviser U.S. del. UN Social and Econ. Council, 1946; individual practice law, Beverly Hills, Calif., 1946-61; judge Calif. Superior Ct., 1961-65; U.S. dist. judge, Los Angeles, 1965—, chief judge, 1979-81. Pres. Jewish Fedn.-Council Greater Los Angeles, 1960-63; v.p. Council Jewish Fedns. and Welfare Funds, 1962-65; dir. gen. bd. United Way, Los Angeles County, 1963-74. Served to lt. (j.g.) USNR, 1944-46. Mem. Phi Beta Kappa. Office: US Court House 312 N Spring St Los Angeles CA 90012

HILL, ISAAC WILLIAM, writer, retired newspaper editor; b. Opelika, Ala., Aug. 8, 1908; s. Isaac W. and Laura (Jones) H.; m. Catherine H. Dawson, June 25, 1932 (dec. Sept. 1974); children: Catherine R., Joyce E.; m. Louise B. Andrews, June 22, 1979. A.B., Washington and Lee U., 1929. Reporter-editor Mobile Press, 1929-30; deskman Washington Evening Star, 1930-37, city editor, 1937-49, news editor, 1949-54, asst. mng. editor, 1954-62, mng. editor, 1962-68, asso. editor, 1968-73; Washington corr. Editor and Pub. mag., 1974-81; book editor Island Packet newspaper, Hilton Head Island, S.C., 1983—; lectr. newspaper personnel Am. Press Inst., Columbia, 1955-73. Co-author: Mirror of War, 1961; also short stories and articles in popular mags. Mem. Am. Soc. Newspaper Editors (dir. 1972-73), AP Mng. Editors Assn. (pres. 1967, chmn. new tech. com. 1969-72), Newspaper Comics Council, Lambda Chi Alpha, Pi Delta Epsilon, Sigma Delta Chi. Presbyterian. Clubs: Circus Saints and Sinners (v.p. P.T. Barnum tent); Nat. Press, Chevy Chase (Washington). Home: 30 Gloucester Rd Hilton Head Island SC 29928 *The key to living life as it should be lived is to learn to work up steam without generating any fog.*

HILL, JAMES CLINKSCALES, judge; b. Darlington, S.C., Jan. 8, 1924; s. Albert Michael and Alberta (Clinkscales) H.; m. Mary Cornelia Black, June 7, 1946; children: James Clinkscales, Albert Michael. B.S. in Commerce, U. S.C., 1948; J.D., Emory U., 1948. Bar: Ga. 1948, U.S. Supreme Ct. 1969. Assoc. Gambrell, Russell, Killorin & Forbes, Atlanta, 1948-55, partner, 1955-63, Hurt, Hill & Richardson, Atlanta, 1963-74; U.S. dist. judge No. Dist. Ga., 1974-76; U.S. circuit judge 5th Circuit, Atlanta, 1976-81, 11th Circuit, 1981—. Served with USAAF, 1943-45. Fellow Am. Coll. Trial Lawyers, Am. Bar Found.; mem. ABA, Am. Law Inst., World Assn. Judges, State Bar Ga., Atlanta Bar Assn., Am. Judicature Soc. Republican. Baptist. Clubs: Lawyers of Atlanta, Old War Horse Lawyers. Office: US Courthouse Room 240 56 Forsyth St NW Atlanta GA 30303

HILL, JAMES NEWLIN, anthropological archaeologist, educator; b. Pomona, Calif., Nov. 30, 1934; s. Mason Lowell and Katharine Norris (Maple) H.; (div.)children: Kraig Mason, Laura Katharine, Karlyn McLeod. B.A., Pomona Coll., 1957; M.A., U. Chgo., 1963, Ph.D., 1965. Asst. prof. anthropology UCLA, 1965-71, asso. prof., 1971-76, prof., 1976—; cons. in contract archaeology. Editor: Explanation of Prehistoric Change, 1977, (with Joel Gunn) The Individual in Prehistory, 1977; author articles in field. Served with USN, 1957-60. NSF grantee, 1962-64, 78-80. Mem. Am. Anthrop. Assn., AAAS, Soc. Am. Archaeology. Democrat. Home: 20540 Stagg St Canoga Park CA 91306 Office: 405 Hilgard Ave Los Angeles CA 90024

HILL, JAMES SCOTT, lawyer; b. Boston, Mar. 21, 1924; s. Benjamin B. and Dorothy (Scott) H.; m. Sally C. Foss, June 28, 1945; children: Richard B., Chessye F., Cynthia C., Michael O. B.A., Williams Coll., 1947; LL.B., Columbia U., 1949. Bar: N.Y. 1949, N.J. 1958. Asso. firm Baldwin, Todd & Lefferts, N.Y.C., 1949-50; sec., atty. Johnson & Johnson, N.J., 1950-66; v.p., sec., gen. counsel Celanese Corp., N.Y.C., 1966-74; v.p., gen. counsel, dir. Liggett & Myers, Durham, N.C., 1974-76; v.p. law and govt. affairs CBS Inc., N.Y.C., 1976-78; v.p. law and regulatory affairs Am. Hosp. Supply Corp., Evanston, Ill., 1978-81; of counsel Shanley & Fisher, Attys., 1981—; Judge, Princeton (N.J.) Twp., 1959-65. Treas. N.J. Republican Finance Com., 1965-70; Trustee, v.p. Princeton Hosp., 1962-68. Served to 1st lt. USAAF, 1943-46. Mem. Chi Psi. Republican. Episcopalian (warden). Clubs: Met. (Washington); Princeton (N.Y.C.); Mid-Ocean (Bermuda). Home: 155 Lambert Dr Princeton NJ 08540 Office: 22 Chambers St Princeton NJ 08540

HILL, JAMES STANLEY, computer cons.; b. Merrickville, Ont., Can., July 24, 1914; m. Doris C. Huelster, 1938; children—George, Janice, Mary, Beverly, Richard. With Minn. Mut. Life Ins. Co., 1930-69, sr. v.p., 1966-69; pres. Digiplan, Inc., Mahtomedi, Minn., 1969—. Treas. Minn. High Sch. Math. Contest Com.; chmn. bd. United Hosp. Mem. Soc. Actuaries (bd. govs., v.p.), Internat. Congress Actuaries. Home: 70 Spruce St Mahtomedi MN 55115 Office: Digiplan Inc 70 Spruce St Mahtomedi MN 55115 *To live each day free from guilt, worry and fear, with opportunities to serve and love others and to exercise both mind and body vigorously—with these goals (and it's taken me over 60 years to come even close), the other things (money, recognition, love from others, and appreciation) come automatically. Christ and others have said it better, but the important thing is: It Works.*

HILL, JIMMIE DALE, government official; b. Fort Worth, Tex., Dec. 28, 1933; s. William Haden and Myrtle Maude H.; m. Martha Lea Hoad, May 26, 1956; children: William, Loretta, Carol, Patricia. Student, DelMar Coll., 1955-57, U. Okla., 1957-58, U. Wichita, 1963-64. Enlisted in U.S. Air Force, 1951, advanced through grades to maj., 1974; comptroller for space systems acquisition, Los Angeles, 1963-70; adv. CIA, 1970-73; ret., 1974; spl. asst. to undersec. Air Force, Washington, 1974-78; dir. Office of Space Systems, Dept. Air Force, 1978-82; dep. undersec. Air Force Space Systems, 1982—. Scoutmaster Boy Scouts Am., 1971-76. Decorated Legion of Merit.; Recipient Disting. Civilian Service medal Dept. Def., 1974, 76; recipient Presdl. Rank award of Meritorious Exec., 1980, Presdl. Rank of Disting. Exec., 1981, Air Force sr. exec. award, 1982. Mem. Air Force Assn., Fed. Exec. Inst. Alumni Assn. Methodist. Home: 7920 Lewinsville Rd McLean VA 22102 Office: OSAF SAF/USS Pentagon Washington DC 20330 *Choose an occupation or profession because you like it, not for recognition and reward. For if you're happy in your work, with loyalty, dedication and hard work, ample recognition and reward will follow.*

HILL, JOHN (ELISHA HILL), utility exec.; b. Marshall County, Ala., Jan. 28, 1926; s. William Homer and Bernice Izella (Dendy) H.; m. Mary Inez Wright, Feb. 16, 1950; children—Joan Frances Hill Mitchell, Jane Denise. B.S., U. Ala., 1949. News editor The Monroe Jour., Monroeville, Ala., 1949-51; comml. mgr. Ala. Electric Coop., Inc., Andalusia, 1951-66, pres., 1979—; gen. mgr. Covington Electric Coop., Andalusia, 1966—; dir. Ala. Rural Electric Assn. of Coops. Chmn. Andalusia City Bd. Edn., 1977-81; mem. Andalusia Indsl. Devel. Bd., 1973—. Mem. Andalusia Area C. of C. (dir.), Phi Beta Kappa. Baptist. Club: Kiwanis (past pres., lt. gov.). Office: PO Box 1357 Andalusia AL 36420

HILL, JOHN ALEXANDER, hospital corporation executive; b. Shawnee, Okla., Feb. 24, 1907; s. John E. and Mary B. (Cheek) H.; m. Margaret M. Mikesell, June 14, 1929; children: Mary (Mrs. Lowell R. King), John, Jane. A.B., U. Denver, 1928, LL. D., 1965. With Aetna Life Ins. Co. as group rep., Denver, 1928-30, mgr. group and pension depts., Detroit, 1930-33, dist. supr., 1933-36; gen. agt. John A. Hill & Assos., Toledo, 1936-58, sr. v.p., Hartford, Conn., 1958-62; pres. Aetna Life & Casualty, 1962-70; pres., dir. Hosp. Corp. Am., Nashville, 1970-72, vice chmn., 1973-74, chmn., 1974—; chmn. Parthenon Ins. Co., Nashville; chmn., dir. Am. Life Ins. Co. N.Y.; dir. Am. Integrity Corp., Phila., Wells Fargo Mortgage Investors, Los Angeles, 3d Nat. Corp., Nashville, Advest, Inc., Hartford, Conn.; vice chmn. Southlife Holding Co., Nashville. Pres. Toledo Community Chest, 1952; chmn. Toledo chpt. ARC, 1946-49; Bd. dirs. Greater Hartford Community Chest; chmn. bd. govs. Inst. for Living, Hartford; trustee Cheekwood Mus., Nashville. Mem. Million Dollar Round Table, Toledo C. of C. (pres. 1953), Beta Theta Pi. Republican. Episcopalian. Clubs: Links, University (N.Y.C.); University, Belle Meade Country (Nashville). Home: Belle Meade Towers Nashville TN 37203 Office: One Park Plaza Nashville TN 32703

HILL, JOHN DEKOVEN, architect; b. Cleve., May 19, 1920; s. John deKoven and Helen Elizabeth (Muckley) H.; m. Heloise Fichter, 1957; 1 son, Christopher deKoven. Taliesin fellow, Frank Lloyd Wright Sch. Architecture, 1938-42. Asso. of Frank Lloyd Wright, 1942-59; editorial dir. House Beautiful mag., 1953-63; dir. Joel Design Projects, N.Y.C., 1956-63; mem. Taliesin Asso. Architects, 1959—. Designer domestic and comml. bldgs. and interiors; writer; critic architecture and, aesthetics, recent designs include restoration of bldgs. by, Frank Lloyd Wright. Sec., dir. Frank Lloyd Wright Found., 1963—. Address: Taliesin West Scottsdale AZ 85261 Taliesin Spring Green WI 53588

HILL, JOHN HOWARD, lawyer; b. Pitts., Aug. 12, 1940; s. David Garrett and Eleanor Campbell (Musser) H. B.A., Yale U., 1962, J.D., 1965. Bar: Pa. 1965, U.S. Dist. Ct. (we dist.) Pa. 1965, U.S. Ct. Appeals (3d cir.) 1965, U.S. Supreme Ct. 1982. Assoc. Reed, Smith, Shaw & McClay, Pitts., 1965-75, ptnr., 1975—. Mem. Travelers Aid Soc. Pitts., 1973—, treas., 1982—. Mem. ABA, Pa. Bar Assn., Allegheny County Bar Assn., Hosp. Assn. Pa., Pa. Soc., World Affairs Council, Pitts. Symphony Soc., Pitts Opera Assn., Phi Gamma Delta. Clubs: Duquesne, Fox Chapel Golf (Pitts.); Rolling Rock (Ligonier, Pa.). Home: 1200 Resaca Pl Pittsburgh PA 15212 Office: 747 Union Trust Bldg Pittsburgh PA 15230

HILL, JOHN HUB, industrialist; b. Paris, Tex., Nov. 8, 1905; s. Joe Wilson and Tommie (Roberts) H.; m. Alstacheia Walker, June 6, 1953. Student, Paris Bus. Coll., 1923-25. Classer-buyer McFadden Cotton Co., Paris, 1925-26; salesman House Jewelry Co., Paris, 1926-27, Dallas Paper and Box Co., 1927-28, Acme Brick Co., Dallas, 1928-32, div. mgr. sales, 1932- 51; propr. Hub Transp. Co., Dallas, 1933-40; pres. Houston-Harris Co., 1944-48, Hub Devel. Corp., 1944-48, Hub Improvement Corp., 1944-48, Denton Housing Corp., 1944-48, Sherman Housing Corp., 1944-48, Clearview Bldg. Corp., 1947-55, Clearview Park, Inc., 1948-55, Dodd Corp., 1950-60, Hill-Elliott, Inc., Dallas, 1950—, Lakewood Terrace, Inc., 1950-70, Bergstrom Corp., 1951-58, Sill Corp., 1951-60, Hub Hill, Inc., Dallas, 1960—, Hill-Elliott Investment Co., 1960—, Tex-Ariz. Motor Freight, Inc., 1964-65; partner Sherman Bldg. and Supply Co., 1945-58, Jenkins Wholesale Lumber Co., 1946-50, Cavalier Lodge Motor Hotel, 1947-61, Hub Investment Co., 1948-65, Goodhue Bldg. Co., 1950-52, Lufkin Pine Lumber Co., 1950-54, Don Elliott Gen. Contractor, Dallas and Sherman, Tex., 1955—, Rio Grande Valley farming interests, McAllen and Edinburg, Tex., 1961—; pres., dir. Builders Loan Co., 1955-71; chmn. exec. com. Strickland Transp. Co., Inc., Dallas, 1967-78; pres., chmn. Tex. Bankers Investment Co., Dallas, 1968—; dir. Dallas Title and Guaranty Co., 1955-71, Mercantile Security Life Ins. Co., Dallas, 1956-69, Mercantile Nat. Bank, 1962—; pres. Wherry Mil. Housing Assn., 1958-61; chmn. bd., chmn. exec. com. Acme Brick Co., 1959-68; an organizer, mem. exec. com., dir. Park Cities Bank & Trust Co., 1959-62; developer, chmn. bd. Penn Towers, Inc., 1960-61; v.p., dir. L.M.S. Corp., 1961-65; dir. Transport Ins. Co., 1969—, exec. com., investment com., 1971—; dir. Transport Mgmt. Co., 1969—; exec. com., investment com., 1971—; dir. Transport Life Ins. Co., 1969—, Am. Commonwealth Devel. Co., 1969—; Mem. nat. adv. council Small Bus. Adminstrn., 1966—, chmn. Tex. adv. council, 1962-67. Bd. dirs. Dallas Civic Opera, 1961-69, Children's Med. Center, Dallas, 1961-73, Tex. Council for Wildlife Protection, 1968—, Dallas County Community Coll. Dist. Found., 1974—; mem. adv. bd. Salvation Army, 1977—; bd. visitors Tex. U.-M.D. Anderson Hosp. and Tumor Inst., Houston, 1968—; mem. citizens council Scott and White Hosp., Temple, Tex., 1962-65; bd. dirs., mem. exec. com. Western Hwy. Inst., 1971-78; mem. chancellor's council U. Tex. System, 1973—; mem. devel. council Baylor Coll. Dentistry, 1973—; bd. devel. Dallas Bapt. Coll., 1970—; mem. exec. com. S.W. Center for Advanced Studies Devel., 1968—; mem. adv. council Bishop Coll., Dallas, 1967—, others. Mem. Dallas Council World Affairs, Tex. Bur. Econ. Understanding, Dallas C. of C., North Dallas C. of C., Dallas East C. of C., Oak Cliff C. of C., East Tex. C. of C., Lamar County C. of C. (hon. life mem.), U.S. C. of C., Tex. Research League, Newcomen Soc. N.Am., Internat. Platform Assn., Trinity Improvement Assn., Navy League U.S., Am. Trucking Assn. (bd. govs. common carrier conf. 1964-65, mem. Com. 100 1968—), Ind. Producers Assn., Am., Nat. Structural Clay Products Assn., Mid-Continent Oil and Gas Assn., Tex. Ind. Producers and Royalty Owners Assn., Southwest Clay Products Assn., Dallas Real Estate Bd., Tex. Real Estate Assn., Nat. Assn. Real Estate Bds., Dallas Execs. Club, Dallas Petroleum Club, Ins. Club Dallas, Transp. Assn. Am., Admirals Club Am. Airlines. Methodist (past steward). Clubs: National Capital Democratic (Washington); Dallas Country, Dallas Athletic, Dallas Athletic Country, Imperial, Lancers (Dallas); St. Anthony (San Antonio). Home: 4209 Bordeaux St Dallas TX 75205 Office: Mercantile Bank Bldg Dallas TX 75201

HILL, JOHN LUKE, lawyer; b. Breckenridge, Tex., Oct. 9, 1923; s. John L. and Jessie H.; m. Elizabeth Ann Graham, 1947; children: Melinda (Mrs. Mike Perrin), Graham, Martha (Mrs. Bill Clark). Student, Kilgore Jr. Coll.; LL.B., U. Tex.-Austin, 1947. Individual practice law; sec. state, Tex., 1966-68, atty. gen., Austin, 1973-80. Bd. dirs. Girlstown U.S.A., Young Life. Served to lt. USNR, 1943-45. Recipient Gold medal as U.S. lawyer contbg. most to law sci. movement Law Sci. Acad., 1960; named Most Outstanding Atty. Gen. in U.S. Washington Monthly, 1975. Fellow Am. Coll. Trial Lawyers, Internat. Acad. Trial Lawyers, Tex. Bar Found.; mem. Nat. Coll. Dist. Attys. (bd. regents). Methodist. Office: 1500 United Bank Tower Austin TX 78701 *

HILL, JOHN PAUL, psychologist, educator; b. Michigamme, Mich., July 20, 1936; s. William A. and Vieno M. (Kulju) H. A.B., Stanford U., 1958; Ph.D., Harvard U., 1964. From asst. prof. to assoc. prof. child psychology and psychology Inst. Child Devel., U. Minn., Mpls., 1963-70; prof. human devel. and family studies, assoc. dean research and grad. edn. Coll. Human Ecology, Cornell U., 1971-73, prof., chmn. dept. human devel. and family studies, 1973-77; sr. research scientist, dir. Project on Social Relations in Early Adolescence, Boys Town Center for Study of Youth Devel., Omaha, 1977-81; prof. psychology Va. Commonwealth U., Richmond, 1981, chmn. dept., 1981-84; cons. in field. Author: Understanding Early Adolescence: A Framework, 1980; Co-editor: Adolescence and Youth in Prospect, 1977; Editor: Minnesota Symposia on Child Psychology, 1966-71; assoc. editor: Developmental Psychology, 1969-73. Chmn. adv. com. Children's Theatre Co., Mpls. Inst. Arts, 1967-70. Woodrow Wilson fellow, 1958. Fellow Am. Psychol. Assn.; mem. Soc. Research Child Devel., Internat. Soc. Study Behavioral Devel., Soc. for Research on Adolescence (pres.-elect 1984-86), Phi Beta Kappa, Delta Sigma Rho. Home: 2103 Park Ave Richmond VA 23220 Office: Dept Psychology Va Commonwealth U 810 W Franklin St Richmond VA 23284

HILL, JOHN RUTLEDGE, JR., construction materials company executive; b. Dallas, Oct. 13, 1922; s. John Rutledge and Catharine (Scarborough) H.; m. Peggy Sloan, May 5, 1962; children: John Rutledge III, Nancy, Cynthia, Sara. B.S. in Civil Enging, Tex. A. and M. U., 1947. With Gifford-Hill & Co., Inc., Dallas, 1946—, chief engr., 1952-58, 1st v.p., 1958-68, exec. v.p., 1968-69, chmn. bd., chief exec. officer, 1969—; dir. InterFirst Bank-Dallas, Dorchester Gas Corp. Pres. Timberlawn Found., 1968-70, now bd. dirs. Served with 13th and 82d Airborne divs. AUS, 1943-46. Mem. Tex. Soc. Profl. Engrs., Chi Epsilon. Presbyterian. Clubs: Dallas Country, City (pres. 1966-73). Home: 3653 Maplewood St Dallas TX 75205 Office: 300 E Carpenter Freeway PO Box 47127 Dallas TX 75247

HILL, JOHN WILLIAM, architect, educator; b. Ft. Leavenworth, Kans., Feb. 4, 1930; s. Ira Benjamin and Anna (Storck) H.; m. Carol Wheeler, June 10, 1952; children: Lucy, Robin, Orissa, Eriksson; m. Catherine Mahan, June 17, 1978; 1 son, Wilson John Mahan. B.A., Rice U., 1951, B.Arch., 1952; M.Arch., U. Pa., 1959. Asst. prof. La. State U., 1959-61; asso. prof. U. Ky., 1961-67; prof. Sch. Architecture, U. Md., College Park, 1967—, dean, 1967-82; partner Graves-Hill & Assocs., Lexington, Ky., 1962-67, Hill, Lewis & Assos. (Architects), Chevy Chase and Balt., Md., 1969-78, Chesapeake Design Group (architects), Washington, Balt., 1978—; mem. Gov.'s Cons. Com. on Historic Preservation, 1968—, Environ. Research Guidance Com., State of Md., 1975-78. Important works include Crossen House, Lexington (1st Honor award Ky. Soc. Architects 1967), Calvert Heights Housing, Chestertown, Md. (Design award Washington Met. chpt. AIA 1980), housing for elderly, Sudlersville, Eastern Shore of Md. (Design award Balt. chpt. AIA 1980). Mem. design adv. panel, City of Balt., 1968—; bd. dirs. CADRE Corp., pres., 1980—. Served from ensign to lt. (j.g.) USN, 1952-55. Research grantee Dept. Def., 1964-65, AIA, 1965, Higher Edn. Act of 1965, 1977. Fellow AIA. Club: 14 W. Hamilton St. Office: Sch Architecture U Md College Park MD 20742 *My interests center around the problems of maintaining existing environmental values in the development of new projects, especially in the central areas of small and large towns. These interests find expression in architectural design projects, town revitalization studies, consulting on architectural preservation and in my teaching and writing.*

HILL, JOSEPH MCCRIGHT, manufacturing executive; b. Snyder, Tex., Nov. 10, 1930; s. Leslie Augustus and Bessie Lou (McCright) H.; m. Ruth Ann Benton, Sept. 27, 1958; children: Lena Elizabeth, Joseph McCright. B.B.A., Tex. Tech U., 1953, M.B.A., 1958. C.P.A., Tex. Staff acct. Peat Marwick Mitchell & Co., 1958-62; controller Rangaire Corp., Cleburne, Tex., 1962-66, v.p., 1966-73, treas., 1966-73, pres., 1973—, also dir.; Mem. adv. council Coll. Bus., U. Tex., Arlington, 1978—; mem. acctg. adv. council Tex. Tech U., 1978-81. Served with USN, 1953-57. Mem. Tex. Soc. C.P.A.s, Am. Inst. C.P.A.s, Nat. Assn. Security Dealers (gov. 1981-84). Methodist. Home: 2313 Lakeshore Dr Cleburne TX 76031 Office: 500 S Wilhite St Cleburne TX 76031

HILL, KATHLEEN LOUISE (KAY HILL), author; b. Halifax, N.S., Can., Apr. 7, 1917; d. Henry and Margaret Elizabeth (Ross) H. Grad. high sch. Steno-sec. various comml. firms, 1935-57. Free lance writer for radio, TV, juvenile books and stage, 1957—; Author: Glooscap and His Magic, 1963, Badger The Mischief Maker, 1965, And

Tomorrow the Stars, 1968, More Glooscap Stories, 1970, Joe Howe, The Man Who Was Nova Scotia, 1980 (Evelyn Richardson lit. award 1981). Recipient Vickey Metcalf award; Can. Council grantee for research on biography of Cabot, 1965, also biography Joseph Howe, 1973. Address: 1137 Ketch Harbor Rd Ketch Harbour NS B0J 1X0 Canada

HILL, KENNETH DOUGLAS, restaurant executive; b. Owesse, Mich., Feb. 8, 1934; s. Douglas and Margaret H.; m. Elizabeth Jane Kundere, Nov. 26, 1960; 1 son, Michael Scott. B.A., Mich. State U., 1952-56. Asst. mgr. Golden Ox Restaurant, Kansas City, Mo., 1956-58; mgmt. trainee John R. Thompson Co., Skokie, Ill., 1958-59; asst. mgr. Holiday Inn Chain, Wichita Falls, Tex., 1959-60; gen. mgr. Cheshire Inn & Lodge, St. Louis, 1960-66; pres. Gilbert-Robinson Inc., Kansas City, Mo., 1967—. Mem. Mayor's Corps of Progress, Kansas City, Mo. Recipient Nat. Spirit of Life award City of Hope, 1982. Mem. Nat. Restaurant Assn. (bd. dirs.), Am. Hotel and Motel Assn. (bd. dirs.), Nat. Inst. Food Service Industry (bd. dirs.), Mo. Restaurant Assn. (bd. dirs., past pres. Kansas City chpt.), Young Pres. Orgn., Mo-Kan. Fleet Res. Assn. (hon.), Kansas City C. of C., Kansas City Conv. and Visitors Bur. (hon.). Republican. Congregationalist. Club: Winnebago Yacht (Lake Winnebago, Mo.). Home: 272 N Winnebago Dr Lake Winnebago MO 64034 Office: Gilbert-Robinson Inc PO Box 16000 Kansas City MO 64112

HILL, KENNETH MARTIN, advertising agency executive; b. Lebanon, Tenn., Jan. 29, 1913; s. Homer Allen and Lois (Ayers) H.; m. Josephine Lucas, Apr. 4, 1938; 1 dau., Margaret Diane. Ed., Huron (S.D.) Coll. With Internat. Harvester, 1935-42, Montgomery Ward, 1942-49, Aubrey, Finlay, Marley & Hodgson, Inc., Chgo., 1950-63; exec. v.p., dir., mem. mgmt. com. The Griswold-Eshleman Co., 1963-69; cons. corp. communications J. Walter Thompson Co., Chgo., 1970-71; pres., dir. Spare Room Corp., Clearwater, Fla., 1973—; mng. dir. Internat. Fedn. Advt. Agys., Sarasota, 1973—. Episcopalian. Clubs: Univ., Field (Sarasota); Longboat Key Golf and Tennis (Longboat Key, Fla.). Home: 374 Bobwhite Dr Sarasota FL 33577 Office: Ellis Bank Bldg Suite 1115 Sarasota FL 33577

HILL, KNOX CALVIN, philosophy educator; b. Oak Park, Ill., Dec. 15, 1910; s. Howard Copeland and Hermione (Irel) H.; m. Pauline Willis, June 19, 1939; children: Virginia, Joan, Thomas, Susan. B.S., U. Chgo., 1930, M.A., 1936, Ph.D., 1954. Mem. faculty U. Chgo., 1939—, prof. philosophy, 1962—, chmn. coll. staff, 1961-71, also dir. undergrad. programs in philosophy, sec. faculties, 1969-80; vis. prof. U. P.R., 1957. Author: Interpreting Literature, 1966; Mng. editor: Jour. Gen. Edn, 1956-60; Contbr. profl. jours. Served to lt. col. AUS, 1942-46; col. Res. Decorated Bronze Star; recipient Quantrell Teaching prize U. Chgo., 1952; Ford Found. fellow, 1952-53. Mem. Am. Philos. Assn., Sigma Alpha Epsilon. Clubs: Quadrangle (U. Chgo.); Cliff Dwellers (Chgo.). Home: 5834 S Stony Island Ave Chicago IL 60637

HILL, LOUIS ALLEN, JR., university dean; b. Okemah, Okla., May 18, 1927; s. Louis Allen and Gladys Adelia (Dietrich) Hill W.; m. Jeanne Rose Murray, June 14, 1951; children: Dawn, David, Dixon. B.A., Okla. State U., 1949, B.S.C.E., 1954, M.S.C.E., 1955; Ph.D., Case Inst. Tech., 1965. Registered profl. engr., Okla., Ohio, Ariz. Engr. Lee Hendricks Engring., Tulsa, 1955-57; engr. in charge Hudgins, Thompson, Ball & Assocs., Oklahoma City, 1957-58; asst. prof. civil engring. Ariz. State U., 1958-66, assoc. prof., 1966-70, prof., 1970-74, chmn. dept. civil engring., 1974-81; dean Coll. Engring. U. Akron, 1981—; chmn. Ohio Engring. Dean's Council; staff engr. Salt River Project, Ariz., 1962; cons. in field. Author: Fundamentals of Structures, 1975, Compendium of Structural Aids, 1975, Structured Programming in Fortran, 1981; contbr. numerous articles to profl. jours.; designer numerous bridges, hwys. Ch. leader-tchr. 1st Baptist Ch., 1981—; pres. Global Energy Soc. for Eradication of Poverty and Hunger. Served to capt. C.E. U.S. Army, 1945-47, 51-54; Philippines, Japan. Fellow Continental Oil Co., 1955; faculty fellow NSF, 1963. Fellow ASCE; mem. Nat. Soc. Profl. Engrs., Am. Soc. Engring. Edn. (Western Electric Fund award 1967), Assn. Computing Machinery, AAAS, Sigma Xi, Tau Beta Pi, Omicron Delta Kappa. Republican. Office: Coll Engring U Akron Akron OH 44325

HILL, LUTHER LYONS, JR., ins. co. exec.; b. Des Moines, Aug. 21, 1922; s. Luther Lyons and Mary (Hippee) H.; m. Sara S. Carpenter, Aug. 12, 1950; children—Luther Lyons III, Mark L. B.A., Williams Coll., 1947; LL.B., Harvard, 1950. Bar: Ia. bar 1951. Since practiced in, Des Moines; law clk. Justice Hugo L. Black, 1950-51; asso., partner Henry & Henry, 1951-69; mem. legal staff Equitable Life Ins. Co. of Iowa, 1952—, exec. v.p., 1969—, gen. counsel, 1970—; dir. Des Moines Register & Tribune Co., Mpls. Star & Tribune Co. Past pres. United Community Services Greater Des Moines; trustee, past chmn. Simpson Coll., Indianola, Ia. Served with AUS, World War II. Home: 2801 Park Ave Des Moines IA 50321 Office: 604 Locust St Des Moines IA 50306

HILL, MELVIN JAMES, oil company executive; b. Santa Ana, Cal., May 19, 1919; s. Albert Frederick and Alice Lucile (Moody) H.; m. Daphne G. Langston, Mar. 1, 1947; children: Patricia (Mrs. Frederick G. Fidura), Candace A. A.B., U. Cal. at Berkeley, 1941. With Western Gulf Oil Co., Cal., 1941-56, Gulf Research & Devel. Co., Harmarville, Pa., 1956-63; with Gulf Oil Corp., Pitts., 1963-75, v.p., 1971-74, sr. v.p., 1974-75, exec. v.p., 1981—; pres. Gulf Energy and Minerals Co.-Internat., Houston, 1975-78, Gulf Exploration & Prodn. Co., 1978-81. Mem. Am. Petroleum Inst., Am. Assn. Petroleum Geologists, Am. Inst. Profl. Geologists, Geol. Soc. Am., Soc. Exploration Geophysicists, Am. Geophys. Union. Home: 507 Fall River St Houston TX 77024 Office: 4 Gulf Tower Houston TX 77002

HILL, NORMAN JULIUS, publisher, author, editor; b. Bklyn., July 21, 1925; s. Jacob and Rose (Fogel) H.; m. Lili Fenyves, 1950 (div. 1976); children: Emily, Andrew David.; m. Mary Guest, 1982. B.S.S. cum laude, CCNY, 1947; grad., Am. Acad. Dramatic Arts, 1967. Copy chief, account exec. S. Gross & Assocs., Norfolk, Va., 1947-48; disc jockey Sta. WLOW, Norfolk, 1947; promotion mgr. Sport Mag., N.Y.C., 1949-51; promotion dir. Popular Library, Inc., 1951-55, v.p., asst. to pub., 1955-60; founder, pres. Webster's Red Seal Publs., Inc., N.Y.C., 1960—, Webster's Crosswords mag., 1960; v.p. Barkas & Shalit, Inc., N.Y.C., 1962-65; circulation promotion dir. McCall's and Redbook mags., N.Y.C., 1965-68; pub. relations dir. McCall Pub. Co., N.Y.C., 1968-70; editor Crossword Mags., Popular Library, 1963-75, Crossword Mags., CBS Publs., Inc., N.Y.C., 1975—; exec. pub. Genesis Publs., Inc., N.Y.C., 1975-78; cons. McCall's, 1977; editor TV Guide Crosswords Mag., 1979—, Woman's Day Crosswords Mag., 1981—. Author: Webster's Crossword Book, 1961, Israel Will Win, 1970, Marijuana: Teenage Killer, 1970, 165 Temples Desecrated, 1970, The Lonely Beauties, 1971, Free Sex: a Delusion, 1971, The Violent Women, 1971, Modern Dictionary of Synonyms and Antonyms, 1971, Webster's Red Seal Crossword Dictionary, 1972, The Black Panthers, 1972, How to Solve Crossword Puzzles, 1974, TV Guide Book of Crossword Puzzles, 6 through 10, 1979; contbr.: articles to N.Y. Times, Saturday Rev., Variety, Athletic Jour. Served with inf. U.S. Army, 1943-46. Recipient cert. of commendation UNICEF, 1961, award for outstanding book advertisement Pubs. Weekly, 1955, 56, award for service Boys Clubs Am., 1956, citations Fed. CD Adminstrn., 1954, Theodore Roosevelt Centennial Commn., 1958. Mem. Authors Guild, Am. Soc. Journalists and Authors (past dep. treas.), Authors League, Sigma Alpha Mu. Home and Office: 210 E 68th St New York NY 10021

HILL, ORION ALVAH, JR., banker; b. Sweetwater, Tex., May 6, 1920; s. Orion Alvah and Lillian (Reynolds) H.; m. Portia Joy Myhre, June 14, 1941; children: Gretchen Annette (Mrs. Phillip John Peterson), Orion Ellsworth, John Adrian, Brian Adair. A.B. in Econs, U. Calif. at Berkeley, 1943; grad., U. Wis. Bank Adminstrn. Inst. Sch., 1961. Chartered bank auditor, 1969; certified internal auditor, 1973. With Wells Fargo Bank (N.A. and predecessor), 1941—, gen. auditor, 1968—, Wells Fargo & Co., 1970-82, sr. v.p., 1982—; on leave with Bank Am. Samoa, mgr., cashier, 1954-56; dir. budget and finance, treas. Govt. Am. Samoa and; dir. Bank Am. Samoa, 1956-58; Speaker in field, 1947—. Contbr. articles in profl. jours. Served with USNR, 1944-46. Mem. Inst. Internal Auditors (pres. San Francisco chpt. 1968-69, regional v.p. 1972-73, internat. dir. 1972-77, 79-80), Bank Adminstrn. Inst. (pres. San Francisco chpt. 1969-70, chmn. nat. audit com., nat. dir. 1972-74), U. Calif. Alumni Assn. Republican. Methodist. Clubs: Commonwealth Cal., San Francisco Commercial. Home: 1040 Bella Dr Napa CA 94558 Office: 425 Market St San Francisco CA 94144

HILL, PAMELA, television exec.; b. Winchester, Ind., Aug. 18, 1938; d. Paul and Mary Frances (Hollis) Abel; m. Tom Wicker, Mar. 9, 1974; 1 son, Christopher; stepchildren—Cameron Wicker, Grey Wicker, Lisa Freed, Kayce Freed. B.A., Bennington Coll., 1960; postgrad., Universidad Autonoma de Mexico, 1961, U. Glasgow, 1958-59. Fgn. affairs analyst Nelson A. Rockefeller Presdl. Campaign, 1961-64; researcher, asso. producer, dir., producer NBC News, 1965-73, dir., 1969-72, producer, 1972, Closeup Documentary series ABC News, N.Y.C., 1973-78, exec. producer Closeup, 1978—; v.p. ABC News, 1979—. (Recipient Emmy award for best documentary 1974, Emmy award for best direction of a documentary 1974, 4 News Emmys 1981); Author: American Foreign Policy, 1945-65, 1968; Contbr.: photographs to Catching Up With America, 1969. Trustee Bennington Coll. George Foster Peabody award, 1974; DuPont Columbia award to Closeup, 1981; Clarion award, 1981; Nat. Press Club award for best consumer reporting, 1975; Christopher award, 1979, 80; Gabriel award, 1980; Headliners award, 1980; N.Y. State Broadcasting award, 1979; Matrix award, 1980; others. Mem. Dirs. Guild, Writers Guild, Nat. Acad. Television Arts and Scis. Office: ABC News 7 W 66th St New York NY 10023

HILL, PAUL DRENNAN, banker; b. Bklyn., Jan. 8, 1941; s. John Drennan and Margaret Henrietta (Gens) H.; m. Ann Kilbourne Patch, June 6, 1964; children: Hal Chase, John Andrew. B.A., Williams Coll., 1962; J.D., Columbia U., 1966. Bar: Ga. 1966. Mgmt. asso. Time Inc., 1962-63; partner firm Gambrell, Russell & Forbes, Atlanta, 1970-75; sr. v.p., gen. counsel First Atlanta Corp., 1975-78, exec. v.p., chief fin. officer, 1978—, also dir.; dir. 1st Nat. Bank Atlanta; adj. prof. Emory U. Law Sch. Trustee Met. Atlanta Crime Commn., 1980-82; v.p., trustee Atlanta Bot. Garden, 1979—; mem. Downtown Task Force for Met. Atlanta, Ga. Commn. on Continuing Lawyer Competency. Served with USAR, 1963. Mem. ABA, Am. Inst. Banking, Conf. Board (exec. conf.), Ga. Bar Assn. (chmn. corp. and banking law sect. 1974, mem. corp. counsel sect.), Atlanta Bar Assn. (chmn. continuing legal edn. com. 1981-82). Congregationalist. Club: Brookwood Hills Community. Office: 2 Peachtree St PO Box 4148 Atlanta GA 30302

HILL, PHILIP GRAHAM, mechanical engineering educator; b. Vancouver, C., Can., July 18, 1932; s. Thomas and Elizabeth Helen (Taylor) H.; m. Marguerite Anne Goff, June 27, 1959; children: Lorilee, Patricia, Graham. B.Sc. with honors, Queen's U., 1953; M.S., U. Birmingham, 1955; Sc.D., Mass. Inst. Tech., 1958. Asst. prof. Mass. Inst. Tech., 1958-65, asso. prof., 1965-67; prof. mech. engring. Queen's U., Kingston, Ont., Can., 1968-75, head dept., 1968-73; prof. mech. engring. U. B.C., Vancouver, 1976—, head dept., 1978-83; Commonwealth vis. prof. U. Sheffield and Cambridge, Eng., 1973-74. Author: (with C.R. Peterson) Mechanics and Thermodynamics of Propulsion, 1965, (with J.H. Keenan, F.G. Keyes, J.G. Moore) Steam Tables, 1969, Power Generation: Resources Hazards, Technology and Costs, 1977; Contbr. articles to profl. jours. Guggenheim fellow, 1962-63. Fellow Royal Soc. Can.; mem. ASME, Assn. Profl. Engrs. Province Ont. and B.C., Can. Soc. Mech. Engrs. Home: 2037 Allison Rd Vancouver BC Canada

HILL, RALPH HAROLD, wholesale grocery company executive; b. Miller, Mo., Dec. 22, 1914; s. Richard Henry and Geneva Gertrude (Woodard) H.; m. Velma Lee Friar, Sept. 20, 1937; children: James Ralph, Richard Lee, Janice Louise. Student. With San Diego div. Alfred M. Lewis, Inc., Riverside, Calif., 1935—, mgr. dept. frozen food, 1953-56, mgr. Ariz. div., Phoenix, 1956-63, pres., chief exec. officer, Riverside, 1963-82, chmn. bd., 1982—; dir. M&M, Los Angeles. Served with USNR, 1943-45. Mem. So. Calif. Grocers Assn., Pres. Assn., Am. Mgmt. Assn., Riverside C. of C. (bd. dirs. 1970-76, pres. 1974-75). Lodge: Rotary (pres. 1972-73). Office: Alfred M Lewis Inc 3021 Franklin Ave Riverside CA 92520

HILL, REUBEN LORENZO, JR., sociologist, educator; b. Logan, Utah, July 4, 1912; s. Reuben Lorenzo and Mary Theresa (Snow) H.; m. Marion Ensign, Sept. 9, 1935; children: Judith Ann Hill Wright, David Reuben, Susan Hill Oppegaard, Gladys Paulena Hill McBeth, George Richard. B.S., Utah State U., 1935, H.H.D., 1977; Ph.M., U. Wis., 1936, Ph.D., 1938; postgrad., U. Chgo., 1941; Dr. honoris causa, U. Louvain, Belgium, 1970. From instr. to asst. prof. social edn. U. Wis., 1938-42; prof. sociology, head dept. U. S.D., 1942-44; asso. prof. sociology Iowa State U., 1944-49; research prof. sociology U. N.C., 1949-53, 54-57; dir. Minn. Family Study Center; prof. sociology and child devel. U. Minn., 1957-61, 62-64, 66-68; research program dir., prof. sociology Minn. Family Study Center, 1968-70, 71-73, Regents' prof. family sociology, 1973-83, Regent's prof. emeritus, 1983—; fellow Center for Advanced Study in Behavioral Scis., 1970-71; vis. prof. sociology Fla. State U., 1984; program cons. population Ford Found., 1964, 65-66; Fulbright sr. lectr. in family sociology Cath. U. Louvain, 1961-62; dir. family research, vis. prof. sociology U. P.R., 1953-54; dir. Groves' Conf. Marriage, 1950-57; cons. nat. orgns. Author: (with H. Becker) Marriage and Family, 1942, (with E.M. Duvall) When You Marry, 1945, rev. edit., 1967, Families Under Stress, 1949, (with W. Waller) The Family: A Dynamic Interpretation, 1951, (with J. Moss, C. Wirths) Eddyville's Families, 1953, (with Howard Becker) Family, Marriage and Parenthood, rev. edit., 1955, (with J.M. Stycos, K. Back) The Family and Population Control: A Puerto Rican Experiment in Social Change, 1959, (with E.M. Duvall) Being Married, 1960, (with E. Driver and M. Nag) Needed Research in Population and Family Planning in India, 1968, (with Rene Konig) Families in East and West: Socialization Process and Kinship Ties, 1970, Family Development in Three Generations, 1970, (with others) Family Problem Solving, 1971, Family Economic Behavior: Problems and Prospects, 1973, (with W. Burr, Ivan Nye, I. Reiss) Contemporary Theories About the Family, 1979, (with T. Caplow and others) Middletown Families: Half a Century of Change and Continuity, 1981. Recipient Helen DeRoy award, 1956; Ernest Burgess award, 1963. Fellow Am. Sociol. Assn. (chmn. com. on internat. cooperation 1966-70); mem. Nat. Council Family Relations (dir.), Sociol. Research Assn., Internat. Sociol. Assn. (chmn. family research 1959-70, pres. 1970-74). Mem. Ch. Jesus Christ of Latter-day Saints. Home: 3906 Xerxes Ave S Minneapolis MN 55410

HILL, REY MARSHALL, former government official; b. Beaver, Utah, Mar. 3, 1912; s. Charles Washington and Esther (Burgess) H.; m. Mary Howell, Aug. 9, 1935; 1 dau., Lorna Rey (Mrs. Michael R. Anderberg). B.S., U. Utah, 1935. Staff statistician Utah Planning Bd., Salt Lake City, 1934-39; asst. economist U.S. Soil Conservation Service, Albuquerque, 1939-42; program officer Inst. Interam. Affairs, San Jose, Costa Rica, 1942-44, Washington, 1944-48, asst. dir. food supply div., 1948-50, dir. div. agr. and natural resources, 1950-52; asso. dir. for Latin Am. Fgn. Operations Adminstrn., Washington, 1952-54; asst. regional dir. for Near East of Ford Found., Beirut, Lebanon, 1954-58; dir. U.S. operations mission to Bolivia ICA, LaPaz, Bolivia, 1958-61, regional dir. for Latin Am., Washington, 1961; rep. for Iran of Ford Found., Tehran, 1961-64, dep. rep., New Delhi, India, 1964-68; dep. dir. U.S. AID mission to Thailand, Bangkok, 1968-69, dir., 1969-73; vis. lectr. AID, Calif. Poly. State U., 1973-75; internat. devel. cons. AID, 1975—; minister-counselor Am. embassy, Bangkok.; Chmn. bd. dirs. Calabrian Corp. Thailand, Ltd., Bangkok. Columnist, Valley Ctr. Roadrunner. Mem. advisory com. Musa Alami Found. of Jericho; bd. dirs. San Diego County Planning Group for Valley Center, Calif., 1980-83, Valley Center Community Recreation, Inc. Mem. Soc. Internat. Devel. (v.p. Thailand chpt. 1970-71). Home: 1250 Portola Ave Escondido CA 92026 *A small group of U.S. Government employees, living in the vicinity of Albuquerque in 1942, pioneered the humanitarian aspects of U.S. foreign assistance. Hugh Calkins, a government official there, was called by Nelson Rockefeller, coordinator of Interamerican affairs, to become the regional director for Central America of a development program ostensibly to offset the German influence. He assembled a group of his former associates, me among them, to work in the area. That group discovered for America that poor people in those countries needed help, and they guided the program toward that end. When the War ended, this group's efforts were extended to Asia and Africa by President Truman. It was called Point Four. A thread of that effort remains. My working life has been devoted to making sure that the thread does not break.*

HILL, RICHARD ALLEN, pharm. co. exec.; b. Springfield, Ohio, Aug. 14, 1932; s. Kenneth C. and Isabel (Sweeney) H.; m. Vivian J. King, Jan. 28, 1956; children—Kenneth Charles, Cynthia Marie, David Gordon. B.S. in Pharmacy, U. Fla., 1956, M.S., 1958, Ph.D., 1960, B.S. in Chem. Engring, 1960. With E.R. Squibb & Sons, 1964-76, dir. engring. and tech. services, Princeton, N.J., 1971-75, dir. tech. adminstrn., 1975-76; dir. devel. Norwich-Eaton Pharms., Norwich, N.Y., 1976-78, v.p. devel., 1978-80, v.p. research and devel., 1980—. Contbr. chpt. to book, articles to profl. publs. Vice pres. George Washington council Boy Scouts Am., 1974-76; mem. Drug Abuse Council, Norwich, 1977-81, chmn., 1979-81. Served with U.S. Army, 1952-54; Korea. Am. Found. Pharm. Edn. fellow, 1956-58; NSF fellow, 1958-60. Mem. Am. Pharm. Assn., Acad. Pharm. Scis., Pharm. Mfrs. Assn., Blue Key, Sigma Xi, Sigma Tau, Phi Kappa Phi, Gamma Sigma Epsilon, Rho Chi, Kappa Psi. Home: 31 Newton Ave Norwich NY 13815 Office: PO Box 191 Norwich NY 13815

HILL, RICHARD DEVEREUX, banker; b. Salem, Mass., Nov. 6, 1919; s. Robert W. and Grace (Dennis) H.; m. Polly Bergstedt, Sept. 13, 1947; children: Steven D., Johanna Hill Simpson, Richard Devereux. A.B., Dartmouth Coll., 1941; M.C.S., Amos Tuck Sch. Adminstrn. and Finance, 1942; postgrad., Rutgers U. Stonier Grad. Sch. Banking, 1951; LL.D., Babson Coll., Northeastern U., Salem State Coll. With Bank of Boston, 1946—, loan officer, 1948-51, asst. v.p., 1951-55, v.p., 1955-65, exec. v.p., 1965-66, pres., 1966-71, chmn. bd., chief exec., 1971-83, chmn. exec. com., 1983—; also dir.; pres., dir. Bank of Boston Corp., 1970-71, chmn. bd., chief exec. officer, 1971-83, chmn. exec. com., 1983—; dir. Polaroid Corp., John Hancock Mut. Life Ins. Co., Raytheon Co., NYNEX, Boston Edison Co., Fed. Res. Bank, Boston, 1978-80; pres. fed. adv. council Fed. Res. System, 1977; chmn. Inst. Internat. Fin. Inc. Former chmn. transp. com. New Eng. Council; mem. vis. com. Sloan Sch. Mgmt., Mass. Inst. Tech., 1967-70; mem. Greater Boston adv. bd. Salvation Army; chmn. investment com. Dartmouth Coll.; trustee Boston Urban Found., U.S.S. Constitution Mus. Found.; overseer Crotched Mountain Found.; former chmn. Bus. Council for Internat. Understanding; vice-chmn. adv. council Japan-U.S. Econ. Relations; mem. corp. Northeastern U.; pres. Mus. Fine Arts, Boston. Served to lt. comdr. USNR, 1942-46; PTO. Mem. Internat. Monetary Conf. (dir.), Transp. Assn. Am. (dir., past chmn. investor panel), Assn. Res. City Bankers (past pres.), Am. Inst. Banking (adv. com. Boston chpt.), Dartmouth Alumni Assn. Boston (past v.p.), New Eng. Exeter Alumni Assn. (past pres.), Sigma Nu. Republican. Congregationalist. Clubs: Algonquin, Commercial, Somerset (Boston); Eastern Yacht (Marblehead); Federal; Economic (N.Y.C.); Royal Bermuda Yacht., Coral Beach and Tennis. Lodge: Masons. Home: Sargent Rd Marblehead MA 01945 Office: 100 Federal St Boston MA 02110

HILL, RICHARD EARL, college president; b. Clintonville, Wis., Mar. 30, 1929; s. Lyle Earl and Gladness Josephine (Love) H.; m. Marilyn Jean Thompson, June 5, 1951; children: Mark R., Kenneth L., Richard Earl, Joy A., Sarah J. B.A., Carroll Coll., Waukesha, Wis., 1951, L.H.D., 1974; M.Div., McCormick Theol. Sem., 1956. Ordained to ministry Presbyterian Ch., 1956; pastor chs. in, Wis., 1955-62; pastor Frame Meml. Presbyn. Ch., Stevens Point, Wis.; also univ. pastor U. Wis., Stevens Point, 1962-69; asst. to pres. Carroll Coll., 1969-74; pres. Huron (S.D.) Coll., 1974-77, Lakeland Coll., Sheboygan, Wis., 1977—; pres. S.D. Fedn. Pvt. Colls., 1977; exec. com. Colls. Mid-Am., 1975-77; mem. 6th Congl. Dist. Acad. Selection Com., 1978—; v.p. Wis. Found. Ind. Colls., 1983—. Mem. Am. Assn. Colls., Council Advancement and Support Small Colls., Council Advancement and Support Edn., Wis. Assn. Ind. Colls. and Univs. (pres. 1980-83), Am. Mgmt. Assn., Pi Kappa Delta, Pi Gamma Mu. Club: Rotary. Address: Lakeland Coll Sheboygan WI 53081

HILL, RICHARD JOHNSON, sociologist, university administrator; b. N.Y.C., Sept. 9, 1925; s. Archie S. and Esther (Johnson) H.; m. Barbara Joyce Beall, June 21, 1947; children: Suzan Elizabeth, Laura Kathryn. Student, Rutgers U., 1946-48; A.B., Stanford U., 1950, M.A., 1951; Ph.D., U. Wash., 1955. Mem. labs. staff Bell Telephone Labs., N.Y.C., 1955-56; asst. prof. sociology UCLA, 1956-60; assoc. prof. sociology U. Tex., Austin, 1960-62, prof., 1962-65; prof. sociology Purdue U., Lafayette, Ind., 1965-71, U. Oreg., 1971—, head dept. sociology, 1972-75, dean, 1978-80, acting v.p. for acad. affairs, provost Sch. of Community Service and Public Affairs, 1980-81, v.p. acad. affairs, provost, 1981—; cons. NSF, NIMH. Author: Public Leadership, 1961, Sociological Measurement, 1967; Asso. editor: Sociological Methodology, 1968-71; Editor: Sociometry, 1966-70; Contbr. articles to profl. jours. Bd. dirs. Purdue-Calument (Ind.) Devel. Found.; bd. dirs. Inst. for Policy Analysis, Eugene, Oreg. Served with USMC, 1942-46. Mem. Am. Sociol. Assn. (council 1977-79), Pacific Sociol. Assn. (pres. 1974-75), Am. Statis. Assn., Psychometric Soc., Sociol. Research Assn., Phi Beta Kappa. Home: 30729 Fox Hollow Rd Eugene OR 97405 Office: Office of the Provost U Oregon Eugene OR 97403 *A principle that has guided many of my decisions was stated first by a rural American whose name is unknown to me. That fundamental, pragmatic statement was "Son, if it works don't mess with it".*

HILL, RICHARD KEITH, chemistry educator; b. Erie, Pa., June 1, 1928; s. Ranald Keith and Lois Rebecca (Bingham) H.; m. Joan Ethel Caine, Aug. 7, 1954; children: Julie Bingham, Sybil Anne, Holly Caine, Ellen McBride. B.S. in Chemistry, Pa. State U., 1949; M.A., Harvard, 1950, Ph.D., 1954. Instr. chemistry Princeton, 1953-56, asst. prof., 1956-62, asso. prof., 1962-68; prof. chemistry U. Ga. at Athens, 1968—, Gen. Beaver teaching prof., 1978-82, acting chmn. dept., 1969-71, 77-78; NATO Sr. fellow in sci., Cambridge, Eng., 1976; Mem. Medicinal Chemistry Study Sect. A, NIH, 1968-72, Fulbright fellowship chemistry panel, 1970-73. Mem. Bd. Edn., Rocky Hill, N.J., 1968. Alfred P. Sloan Found. research fellow, 1961-65; NSF sr. postdoctoral fellow, 1965-66. Fellow AAAS; Mem. Am. Chem. Soc., Chem. Soc. London. Home: 115 Broomsedge Trail Athens GA 30605

HILL, ROBERT HUNTER, pediatrician; b. Lausanne, Switzerland, Aug. 13, 1926; s. Thomas William and Rosalind (Liddell) H.; m. Helen Allen, Feb. 10, 1957; children—Louise Anne, Robert, Diana. B.M., B.Ch., Winchester Coll. Oxford (Eng.) U., 1950, M.A., 1952. Prof., head dept. pediatrics B.C. Children's Hosp. and U. B.C.; med. dir. Sunny Hill Hosp. for Children, 1964-81. Fellow Royal Can. Physicians; mem. Am. Acad. Pediatrics, Can. Med. Assn., Can. Pediatric Assn., North Pacific Pediatric Soc. (pres.). Club: Royal Vancouver Yacht. Address: 4911 Connaught Dr Vancouver BC V6M 3E8 Canada

HILL, ROBERT LELAND, economics educator; b. Coffeyville, Kans., July 12, 1922; s. Earl Winfred and Mary Greenshields (Latta) H.; m. Ann Elizabeth Rowe, 1977. B.A. in Econs., U. Mo. at Kansas City, 1949, M.A., 1951; Ph.D., Georgetown U., 1958. Economist Fed. Res. Bd., 1955-59; sr. asso. Cresap, McCormick & Paget, N.Y.C., 1959-61; economist deptl. planning staff Dept. Commerce, 1961; dir. Office Emergency Readiness, 1962-65; prof. econs., chmn. econs. dept. Lynchburg (Va.) Coll., 1965—, dir. program plans and research, 1965-68, William R. Perkins Jr. prof. econs., 1969—, dir. Ctr. Econ. Edn., 1981—; Dir. Greater Lynchburg Transit Co., 1974-79, pres., 1976-79, Va. Assn. Pub. Transit Ofcls., 1977; Mem. adv. bd. Va. Erosion and Sedimentation Control, 1974-76; Bd. dirs. Robert E. Lee Water and Soil Conservation Dist., 1972—. Contbr. articles, reports to profl. lit. Served with AUS, 1942-45. Mem. Am. Econ. Assn., Va. Assn. Economists (pres. 1975-76), Order DeMolay, Gold Key Soc., Delta Xi. Lodge: Masons. Home: 1830 Rivermont Ave Lynchburg VA 24503

HILL, ROBERT MASON, banking consultant; b. Elizabeth, N.J., Aug. 18, 1922; s. Roger W. and Margaret (Himmelberger) H.; m. Evelyn Cronn, May 13, 1949; 1 son, Robert Mason. A.B., Princeton U., 1947. With Guaranty Trust Co., N.Y.C., 1947-58, 2d. v.p., 1958; asst. v.p. Morgan Guaranty Trust Co. (merger Guaranty Trust Co. and J.P. Morgan & Co.), N.Y.C., 1959-61, v.p., 1961-70, sr. v.p., 1970-82; pres. RMH Group, Inc., internat. banking cons.; dir. Binney & Smith, Inc., Saudi Internat. Bank (Nassau) Ltd. Trustee Morristown (N.J.) Meml. Hosp. Served with U.S. Army, 1943-46. Mem. Internat. C. of C. (U.S. council). Clubs: Campus (Princeton, N.J.); Morris County Golf (Convent Station, N.J.); Mid-Ocean (Bermuda). Home: Village Rd New Vernon NJ 07976 Office: Box 134 New Vernon NJ 07976

HILL, ROBERT WAYNE, utility executive; b. Richmond, Ind., July 10, 1927; s. H. Wayne and Kathryn G. (Weimer) H.; m. Bonnie J. Dishman, June 22, 1948; children: Robert W., Susan Jane Hill deArmendi. B.S.E.E., Purdue U., 1951. Registered profl. engr., Ind. Engr. in charge elec. distn. Indpls. Power & Light Co., 1970-73, asst. v.p. engring. and constrn., 1973-77, v.p. transp. and distbn., 1977-79, sr. v.p. ops., 1979-80, exec. v.p., 1980-81, pres., chief operating officer dir., 1981—. Mem. exec. bd. East Central Area Reliability Agreement, Canton, Ohio; dir. Ind. Electric Assn., Ind. Repertory Theatre; bd. dirs. Greater Indpls. Progress Com., Indpls. Growth Project. Served with USN, 1945-46. Mem. Indpls. C. of C., Am. Mgmt. Assn. (pres.'s assn.), Eta Kappa Nu. Clubs: Crooked Stick Golf, Columbia, Indpls. Athletic, Skyline, Greenfield Elks. Office: Indianapolis Power & Light Co 25 Monument Circle Indianapolis IN 46206

HILL, RODNEY FLEMING, bank holding company executive; b. Willard, Ohio, Sept. 29, 1927; s. Fleming T. and Dora M. (Crites) H.; m. Margaret Virginia Burns, May 26, 1982. B.A., Ohio Wesleyan U., 1951; postgrad., U. Pitts, 1954-56; student, U. Wis. Grad. Sch. Banking, 1974-76. Asst. v.p. St. Louis County Bank, Clayton, Mo., 1966-68, v.p., 1969-74, sr. v.p., 1975-79, County Nat. Bancorp., Clayton, 1972-82; exec. v.p. County Tower Corp., Clayton, 1982—; chief exec. officer County Realty Corp.; dir. County Bank of House Springs, Mo., County Bank of Louisiana, County Bank of Richmond Heights, County Bank of Manchester. Trustee Leukemia Soc. Am., 1983; bd. mgrs. Brentwood (Mo.) YMCA, 1981. Served to 1st lt. USAF, 1951-53. Mem. Robert Morris and Assocs., Am. Inst. Banking, Res. Officers Assn. (chpt. pres. 1968-69), Ret. Officers Assn. Republican. Presbyterian. Clubs: Clayton (dir.); Glen Echo Country (St. Louis)). Office: County Tower Corp 8000 Forsyth St Clayton MO 63105

HILL, ROLLA B., pathologist; b. Balt., June 11, 1929; s. Rolla B. and Claire (McDowell) H.; children—Claire, Paul, Helen. B.A., U. Rochester, 1950, M.D., 1955. Mem. pathology faculty Yale U., New Haven, 1959-61, U. Colo., Denver, 1961-69, U. Calif., Davis, 1968-69; chmn. dept. pathology Upstate Med. Center SUNY, Syracuse, 1969—. Co-author: The Gastrointestinal Tract, 1977, Principles of Pathobiology, 3rd edit, 1980, Environmental Pathology, 1981. Served with M.C. U.S. Army, 1956-58. Mem. Am. Assn. Pathologists (pres.), Council Acad. Socs. (chmn.), Assn. Pathology Chmn. (pres.), Internat. Acad. Pathologists, Am. Soc. Clin. Pathology, Coll. Am. Pathologists, AAAS, Assn. Am. Med. Colls., Am. Gastroent. Assn. Home: 302 Brookford Rd Syracuse NY 13224 Office: 766 Irving Ave Syracuse NY 13210

HILL, SAMUEL RICHARDSON, JR., university president, medical educator; b. Greensboro, N.C., May 19, 1923; s. Samuel Richardson and Nona (Sink) H.; m. Janet Redman, Oct. 28, 1950; children: Susan Dustin, Samuel Richardson III, Elizabeth, Margaret Hanes. B.A., Duke U., 1943; M.D., Bowman Gray Sch. Medicine, 1946; D.Sc. (hon.), U. Ala., 1975, Wake Forest U., 1979. Intern medicine Peter Bent Brigham Hosp., Boston, 1947-48, asst. resident medicine, 1948-49, asst. medicine, 1949-50; teaching fellow medicine Harvard Med. Sch., 1948-49, research fellow medicine, also Dazian Med. Found. research fellow, 1949-50; chief resident medicine N.C. Bapt. Hosp., also instr. medicine Bowman Gray Sch. Medicine, 1950-51; asst. medicine Harvard Med. Sch., also Peter Bent Brigham Hosp., 1953-54; asst. prof. medicine, dir. metabolic and endocrine div. Med. Coll. Ala., also chief metabolic div. VA Hosp., Birmingham, 1954-57; assoc. prof. medicine, dir. metabolic and endocrine div. U. Ala. Med. Center and VA Hosp., Birmingham, 1957-62; prof. medicine, dean U. Ala. Med. Coll., 1962-68, prof. medicine, 1968—; v.p. for health affairs, dir. Med. Center, 1968-77; pres. U. Ala., Birmingham, 1977—; dir. med. edn. program U. Ala. System, 1972-79; dir. Birmingham br. Fed. Res. Bank of Atlanta, 1981-83, chmn. Birmingham br., 1983; dir. Vulcan Materials Co., 1981—. Contbr. articles to med. jours. Bd. regents Nat. Library Medicine, 1978-80, chmn. bd. regents, 1979-80. Served to maj. M.C. USAF, 1951-53. Fellow A.C.P. (Willard O. Thompson Meml. traveling scholar 1960), AAAS, Royal Soc. Medicine; mem. Soc. Exptl. Biology and Medicine, Am. Fedn. Clin. Research (pres. 1961-62), Endocrine Soc., Am., Ala. diabetes socs., N.Y. Acad. Scis., Mass., Jefferson County med. socs., Am. Thyroid Soc., AMA, Inst. Medicine of Nat. Acad. Scis., So. Soc. Clin. Investigation, Med. Assn. State Ala. (councillor), Assn. Am. Med. Colls., Assn. for Acad. Health Centers (pres. 1972), Sigma Xi, Alpha Omega Alpha. Episcopalian. Home: 4101 Altamont Rd Birmingham AL 35213 Office: Office of Pres U Ala in Birmingham Univ Sta Birmingham AL 35294

HILL, STEPHEN M., paper company executive; b. Wisconsin Rapids, Wis., Mar. 9, 1930; s. Earl M. and Martha E. (Piske) H.; m. Joyce D. Brown, Nov. 28, 1953; children: Barbara L., Sarah L. B.B.A., U. Wis.-Madison, 1951; M.B.A., U. Pa., 1954. Chartered fin. analyst. Econ. analyst Allis-Chalmers Corp., Milw., 1954-58; instr. U. Wis.-Milw., 1958-59; investment analyst Newton & Co., Milw., 1959-64; treas. Securities Counsel, Inc., Jackson, Mich., 1964-75; sr. v.p., treas. NAC, Atlanta, 1975-76; treas. Great No. Nekoosa Corp., Stamford, Conn., 1977—; trustee Equitable Research Assn., Neenah, Wis., 1974. Vice-pres., treas. Jr. Achievement Stamford, 1982-83. Served with U.S. Army, 1951-53; France. Republican. Office: 75 Prospect St Stamford CT 06904

HILL, TERRELL LESLIE, chemist, biophysicist; b. Oakland, Calif., Dec. 19, 1917; s. George Leslie and Ollie (Moreland) H.; m. Laura Etta Gano, Sept. 23, 1942; children: Julie Lisbeth Eden, Carolyn Jo (Mrs. Gary Lineburg), Ernest Evan. A.B., U. Calif. at Berkeley, 1939, Ph.D., 1942; postgrad., Harvard U., 1940. Instr. chemistry Western Res. U., 1942-44; research asso. radiation lab. U. Calif. at Berkeley, 1944-45; research asso. chemistry, then asst. prof. chemistry U. Rochester, 1945-49; chemist U.S. Naval Med. Research Inst., 1949-57; prof. chemistry U. Oreg., 1957-67, U. Calif. at Santa Cruz, 1967-71, adj. prof., 1977—, vice chancellor for scis., div. natural scis., 1968-69; research chemist NIH, Bethesda, Md., 1971—; Mem. biophysics study sect. USPHS, 1954-57; chemistry panel NSF, 1961-64. Author: Statistical Mechanics, 1956, Statistical Thermodynamics, 1960, Thermodynamics of Small Systems, Vol. I, 1963, Vol. II, 1964, Matter and Equilibrium, 1965, Thermodynamics for Chemists and Biologists, 1968, Free Energy Transduction in Biology, 1977, also research papers. Guggenheim fellow Yale, 1952-53; recipient Arthur S. Flemming award U.S. Govt., 1954; Distinguished Civilian Service award U.S. Navy, 1955; award Washington Acad. Scis., 1956; Disting. Service award USPHS, 1981, U. Oreg., 1983; Sloan Found. fellow, 1958-62. Mem Nat. Acad. Scis., Am. Chem. Soc. (Kendall award 1969), Biophys. Soc., NAACP, ACLU, Phi Beta Kappa. Home: 9626 Kensington Pkwy Kensington MD 20895

HILL, THOMAS BOWEN, JR., lawyer; b. Montgomery, Ala., Nov. 11, 1903; s. Thomas Bowen and Lida Tunstall (Inge) H.; m. Mildred Ellen Abrams, Sept. 22, 1925; children: Thomas Bowen, III, Mildred Inge, Luther Abrams, William Inge, II. A.B., U. Ala., 1922, LL.B., 1924, LL.D. (hon.), 1978. Bar: Ala. 1924. Asso. prof. German U. Ala., 1923-24; since practiced in, Montgomery; sr. mem. firm Hill, Hill, Carter, Franco, Cole & Black (and predecessor firm), 1947—; spl. chief justice Supreme Ct. Ala., 1966, 67, 68; Chmn. bd. Union Bank & Trust Co., Montgomery., 1954-76, chmn. emeritus for life, 1976—, also dir. Former mem. bd. dirs. Montgomery YMCA, Children's Protective Home; vice chmn. U. Ala. Found.; bd. dirs. U. Ala. Law Sch. Found. Recipient George Washington Honor medal Freedoms Found., 1970, Daniel J. Meador Outstanding Alumnus award U. Ala. Sch. Law, 1975; named to Ala. Acad. of Honor, 1977. Fellow Am. Coll. Trial Lawyers, Internat. Acad. Trial Lawyers, Am. Bar Found.; mem. ABA (ho. of dels.), Ala. Bar Assn. (v.p. 1951-52, pres. 1952-53, mem. bd. commrs. 1953-80), Montgomery County Bar Assn. (past pres.), Farrah Law Soc. (charter), Ala. Bible Soc. (dir.), Ala. C. of C. (dir.), Am. Judicature Soc., Ala. Motorists Assn. (dir.), Phi Beta Kappa, Phi Alpha Delta. Episcopalian (vestryman, sr. warden). Clubs: Mason (Shriner), Kiwanian (past pres. Montgomery). Home: 1831 Hillwood Dr Montgomery AL 36106 Office: PO Box 116 Montgomery AL 36101

HILL, THOMAS BOWEN, III, lawyer; b. Montgomery, Ala., Oct. 21, 1929; s. Thomas Bowen, Jr. and Mildred (Abrams) H.; m. Maria Paschall, Dec. 29, 1955; children: Thomas Bowen IV, Mason P., William III, Chappell H. B.S., U. Ala., 1951, LL.B., 1953. Bar: Ala. 1953. Since practiced in, Montgomery; mem. firm Hill, Hill, Carter, Franco, Cole & Black, 1953—, partner, 1957—; dir., gen. counsel So. United Life Ins. Co.; dir. Union Bank & Trust Co.; Mem. Gov.'s staff, 1963—. Trustee YWCO. Recipient Algernon Sydney Sullivan medallion as outstanding male grad. U. Ala., 1953. Mem. ABA, Ala. Bar Assn. (com. chmn.), Montgomery County Bar Assn. (past pres.), Am. Coll. Mortgage Attys., U. Ala. Nat. Alumni Assn. (past v.p.), Montgomery C. of C. (dir.), Men of Montgomery, Ala. Assn. Canterbury Clubs, Druids, Jasons, Quadrangle, Tau Kappa Alpha, Phi Delta Phi, Alpha Tau Omega, Omicron Delta Kappa. Presbyn. (deacon). Club: Kiwanian. (past pres.). Home: 3721 Vaughn Rd Montgomery AL 36106 Office: PO Box 116 Montgomery AL 36101

HILL, TOM, artist; b. Terrell, Tex., July 21, 1922; s. Thomas T. and Lucy Winston (Paine) H.; m. Barbara Smerchek; 3 children. Student, Art Ctr. Coll. Design, Loa Angeles, 1941-43. One Man Shows, Honolulu Acad. Arts, 1945, U. Okla., Tribune Tower, Chgo., 1953, Settlers West Galleries, 1976-84, group shows, Los Angeles Artists Assn., 1946, Am. Watercolor Soc., 1954—, NAD, 1974—, Nat. Acad. Western Art, 1978—; represented: permanent collections NAD, N.Y.C., Copley Collection, San Diego, W. Tex. U.lection, Lubbock; authorented: Color for the Water Color Painter, 1975, 82, The Watercolor Painters Problem Book, 1979. Recipient numerous awards for painting. Mem. Am. Watercolor Soc., Nat. Acad. Design, Nat. Acad. Western Art.

HILL, WALTER, film director, writer; b. Long Beach, Calif., Jan. 10, 1942. Student, Mich. State U. Screenplays include Hickey and Boggs, 1972, The Getaway, 1972, The Thief Who Came to Dinner, 1973, The Mackintosh Man, 1973, The Drowning Pool, 1975, The Warriors, 1979; writer, dir.: Hard Times, 1975, The Driver, 1978, Southern Comfort, 1981; producer: Alien, 1979; dir.: The Long Riders, 1980, 48 Hours, 1982. Office: care Internat Creative Mgmt 8899 Beverly Blvd Los Angeles CA 90048 *

HILL, WARREN GARDINER, former educator; b. Brooklyn, N.S., Can., Oct. 19, 1918; came to U.S., 1922, naturalized, 1942; s. Andrew William and Hannah (Walker) H.; m. Catherine Lewis, Aug. 26, 1942; children—Senetta Louise, Charles Douglas. B.S., Gorham State Tchrs. Coll., 1939; Ed.M., Boston U., 1941; Ed.D., Columbia, 1947; L.H.D., Bowdoin Coll., 1961; D.Sc., U. Me., 1964; H.H.D., Franklin Pierce Coll., 1973; LL.D., U. Maine, Portland/Gorham, 1977. Prin. Islesford (Me.) Elementary Sch., 1939-40; instr. math., sci. Gorham State Tchrs. Coll., 1941-42; asst. to pres., acting pres. New Haven State Tchrs. Coll., 1947-55; chief bur. fed.- state-local relations Conn. Dept. Edn., 1955-56; commr. edn., Me., 1956- 63; pres. Trenton (N.J.) State Coll., 1963-66; chancellor Higher Edn., State Conn., 1966-74; dir. In-Service Edn. Program, Edn. Commn. of States, Denver, 1974-76, exec. dir., 1976-80; mem. Sec. of Navy's Adv. Bd. on Edn. and Tng.; mem. adv. bd. U. Mid-Am.; trustee BACCHUS; mem. bd. advisers Inst. for Lifelong Learning, Harvard U.; Past chmn. Nat. Commn. Tchr. Edn. and Profl. Standards; past chmn. Catalyst in Edn., Armed Forces Adv. Com.; past vice chmn. Edn. Commn. States. Served as lt. USCGR, 1942-46; as lt. comdr. USNR, 1952-56. Mem. Am. Assn. Sch. Adminstrs. Conglist. Club: Mason. Home: 62 Old Salt Works Rd Westbrook CT 06498

HILL, WILLIAM CHARLES, state justice; b. Newark, May 10, 1917; s. William Herbert and Alice Anna (de Groote) H.; m. Grace Giarratano, May 2, 1942; children: Carol, Pamela, Elizabeth. B.A., N.Y. U., 1939, J.D., 1941; M.A., U. Vt., 1967. Bar: N.Y. bar 1942, Vt. bar 1947. Practiced in, N.Y., Vt., 1942-59; judge Vt. Superior Ct., 1959-76, chief judge, 1972-76; justice Vt. Supreme Ct., 1976—; vis. lectr. polit. sci. Trinity Coll., Burlington, Vt., 1973—; mem. Vt. Ho. of Reps., 1953-57. Contbg. author: New Eng. Politics. Served with U.S. Army, 1942-46; lt. col. JAGC U.S. Army Res., 1946-72. Mem. Vt. Bar Assn. Republican. Club: Masons. Address: PO Box 680 RD 1 Hinesburg VT 05461

HILL, WILLIAM EDWIN, business executive; b. N.Y.C., Nov. 5, 1910; s. William Edwin and Alice I. (Haggerty) H.; m. Jane E. Herrmann, June 4, 1938; children: Alice Susan (Mrs. John S. McLaughlin), Sarah Knipe. B.S., Sheffield Sci. Sch., Yale U., 1932. Indsl. cons. engr., instr. Ruston Acad., Havana, Cuba, 1932-36; mgr. comml. dept. Am. Standard Corp., N.Y.C., 1936-38; founder Turck, Hill & Co., Inc. (indsl. engrs.), N.Y.C., 1938; founder, pres. William E. Hill & Co., Inc., N.Y.C., 1953-70; also dir.; chmn. Hill-Fantus (S.A.), Paris, France, 1972-75; chmn. mgmt. cons. div. Dun & Bradstreet Corp., 1970-75; counsel to William E. Hill & Co., Inc., 1976-79; chmn. Hayes/Hill Inc., 1979—; dir. 123 E. 74th St. Corp.; past dir. N.Am. Reins. Co., N.Am. Reassurance Co., Dead River Co., Iroquois Brands Ltd., Eltra Corp., Swiss Re Holding (N.A.) Inc., Bangor Punta Corp.; past trustee Emigrant Savs. Bank; mem. exec. com. Mktg. Sci. Inst., 1971-76. Contbr. articles to mgmt. publs. Pres. Catholic Youth Orgn., 1946-49; exec. com., dir. Boys Clubs Am.; trustee Wells Coll., 1964-73; mem. exec. com., trustee Children's Aid Soc.; founder Yale Sch. Orgn. and Mgmt.; overseer Thayer Sch. of Dartmouth Coll., 1973-75; mem. Yale Alumni Fund. Recipient Silver Keystone award Boys Clubs Am.; award Colony Found.; joint award Boys' Clubs Am. and Children's Aid Soc. Mem. Nat. Inst. Social Scis. (v.p. 1960-75), Pilgrim Soc. Clubs: Links, Anglers; Univ., Sky (N.Y.C.); Chgo. Home: 125 E 74th St New York NY 10021 also Old Black Point Niantic CT 06357 Office: 220 E 42d St New York NY 10017

HILL, WILLIAM LEON, advertising executive; b. Greensburg, Pa., Sept. 4, 1932; s. Leon McDonald and Hanna Clara (Schaffer) H.; m. Rae Ellen Warren, Mar. 3, 1956; children: Shaun, Tamara, Schaffer, Christian. Asso. Fine Arts, Amarillo (Tex.) Jr. Coll., 1952; B.F.A., Kansas City (Mo.) Inst. Art, 1956. Graphic designer Mel Richmon Assos., Phila., 1957; art dir. Degarmo Advt., N.Y.C., 1958-59, Bloom Advt. Agy., Dallas, 1959-64, creative dir., 1965—, exec. v.p., 1973-80, pres., 1980—, Hill Communications, 1981—; cons. in field. Bd. dirs. Evangelical Communications Research Found., Suicide Prevention Dallas. Served with USNR, 1950-58. Recipient numerous awards, including Golden Egg award; named one of top 100 creative people in advt., 1972, 75, 81. Mem. Assn. Visual Communication (dir. 1966-68, named Dir. of Year 1968), Dallas C. of C. Episcopalian. Club: Dallas Athletic. Home: 300 Sutton Pl Richardson TX 75080

HILL, WILLIAM THOMAS, natural resources company executive; b. Covington, Ky., Apr. 8, 1925; s. William Thomas and Bertha katherine (Paine) H.; m. Jo Law, Sept. 16, 1950; children: Pamela Kay, Leigh Anne, Lisa Karen. B.A., U. Tenn., 1950, M.S., 1951, Ph.D., 1971. Geologist Tenn. Geol. Survey, Knoxville, 1951-52; prof. geology U. Tenn., Knoxville, 1952-54; exploration mgr. Putman & Assocs., Maryville, Tenn., 1954-59; geologist, mgr. N.J. Zinc Co., Morristown, Tenn., 1959-69; project mgr. NJ-Elmwood Mine, Carthage, Tenn., 1969-74; mgr., dir. Enjex Mineracao, Rio de Janerio, Brazil, 1974-76; v.p. N.J. Zinc Exploration Co., Bethlehem, Pa., 1976-79, pres., Nashville, 1979—; v.p. exploration G & W Natural Resources Co., Nashville, 1981—. Served with USN, 1943-46; PTO. Mem. Soc. Econ. Geologists, Am. Inst. Mining, Prospectors and Developers Assn., Sociedada Brasileira de Geologia. Presbyterian. Lodge: Lions. Home: 100 Jackson Ln Hendersonville TN 37075 Office: G & W Natural Resources Co 1 Commerce Pl Nashville TN 37239

HILL, WILMER BAILEY, lawyer; b. Washington, May 18, 1928; s. Wilmer A. and Matilda F. (Nabor) H.; m. Joan C. Brunelle, June 24, 1967; children: Stuart Michael, Stephen Mark. A.B., Dartmouth Coll., 1950; LL.B., J.D., Georgetown U., 1953. Bar: D.C. 1956. Sec.-treas., dir. Ames, Hill & Ames, Washington, 1955-81. Vice-pres. Brookdale Citizens Assn., 1975-76. Served with AUS, 1953-55. Mem. Am., Fed. bar assns., Bar Assn. D.C., Motor Carrier Lawyers Assn. (treas. 1978-80, v.p. 1980-83, pres.-elect 1983-84), Assn. ICC Practitioners, Am. Conservative Union, Sigma Phi Epsilon, Delta Theta Phi. Republican. Methodist. Clubs: University, Kenwood Golf and Country, Bryce Mountain Ski and Country. Home: 5016 Westport Rd Chevy Chase MD 20815 Office: 1030 15th St NW Washington DC 20005

HILL, WINFRED FARRINGTON, educator; b. Chelsea, Mass., May 23, 1929; s. Roy Wesley and Lura Lois (Cole) H.; m. Libby May Kaplan, June 14, 1957; children—Alison Renee, Linda Suzanne. A.B., Yale, 1950; M.A., Northwestern U., 1951; Ph.D., Stanford, 1954. Instr. psychology Harvard, 1956-57; faculty Northwestern U., 1957—, Evanston, Ill., prof. psychology, 1968—. Author: Learning: A Survey of Psychological Interpretations, 1963, 3d edit., 1977, Psychology, Principles and Problems, 1970, Principles of Learning: A Handbook of Applications, 1981. Served with AUS, 1954-56. Research grantee NSF, 1958-64, Nat. Inst. Mental Health, 1965-68; Center Advanced Studies Behavioral Scis. fellow, 1966-67. Fellow Am. Psychol. Assn., A.A.A.S.; mem. Midwestern Psychol. Assn. (sec.-treas. 1970-73, pres. 1974-75), Am. Assn. U. Profs., Psychonomic Soc., Sigma Xi. Home: 2715 Woodland Rd Evanston IL 60201

HILLAIRE, MARCEL, actor; b. Cologne, Germany, Apr. 23, 1908; came to U.S., 1948, naturalized, 1954; s. Paul and Sofie (Lion) von Hiller. Grad. pub. schs., Cologne, Germany. Appeared numerous movies, TV, 1948—; appeared as Cooking Prof. in: Sabrina, 1953; appeared as: TV series Adventures in Paradise, 1959-61. Mem. Screen Actors Guild. Address: 637 1/2 Burnside Ave Los Angeles CA 90036 *Success or no success: I always tried to see both as possibilities of a destiny and therefore gave them both a kind of an inward smile. That smile has seldom faded and I'll see to it that it won't.*

HILLARD, JAMES MILTON, librarian; b. Nortonville, Ky., Sept. 27, 1920; s. Cornelius and Leona L. (Hicks) H.; m. Ella Louise Winzenried, Dec. 23, 1944; children: James Randolph, Jerrold Manley. B.A. with high honors, Ohio U., 1947; M.S. in L.S. with honors, U. Ill., 1948. Asst. librarian Free Pub. Library, Summit, N.J., 1948-50; city librarian Carnegie City Library, Ft. Smith, Ark., 1950-52; dir. Curtis Meml. Library, Meriden, Conn., 1952-55; asso. librarian U.S. Mil. Acad., West Point, N.Y., 1955-57; dir. Daniel Library, The Citadel, Charleston, S.C., 1957—. Author: Where to Find What, 1975, 2d edit., 1984, Where to Find More, 1977; Contbr. articles to profl. jours. Served with AUS, 1942-46. Mem. ALA, Southeastern Library Assn., S.C. Library Assn. (sec. 1960, treas. 1965-78), AAUP. Club: Exchange. Address: 203 Carolina Blvd Isle of Palms SC 29451

HILLARD, ROBERT ELLSWORTH, public relations cons.; b. St. Paul, Nov. 17, 1917; s. Homer Ellsworth and Barbara Mary (Smith) H.; m. Nancy Jane Oxenhandler, Dec. 30, 1973. B.A. summa cum laude, U. Minn., 1940. Reporter Des Moines Tribune, 1939-40; rotogravure editor Des Moines Register, 1940-41; feature editor St. Louis Star-Times, 1941, 45-46; partner Fleishman-Hillard, Inc., St.

Louis, 1946-74, sr. partner, 1974—. Pres. Urban League St. Louis, 1950-52, Health and Welfare Council Met. St. Louis, 1957-59, Family and Children's Service Greater St. Louis, 1960-62. Served as lt. USNR, 1942-45; PTO. Mem. Public Relations Soc. Am. (accredited), St. Louis Public Relations Soc. (pres. 1953-56), Phi Beta Kappa, Sigma Delta Chi, Beta Theta Pi. Clubs: St. Louis, Stadium (St. Louis). Home: Box 104 Caledonia MO 63631 Office: One Memorial Dr Saint Louis MO 63102

HILLAS, ROGER S., banker; b. 1927; married. A.B., Dartmouth Coll.; postgrad., Wharton Sch. Fin., U. Pa. With Provident Nat. Bank, Phila., 1951—, v.p., 1960-64, exec. v.p. coml. div., 1964-69, pres., chief adminstrv. officer, 1969-75, chmn. bd., chief exec. officer, 1975—, pres., 1980—, dir.; pres. parent co. Provident Nat. Corp., 1969-75, chief exec. officer, 1973—, chmn. bd., 1975—, dir.; dir. Fed. Res. Bank Phila., Lease Financing Corp., P.H. Glatfelter Co., Goodall Co., Phila. Facilities Mgmt. Corp., Consol. Rail Corp., Provident Mut. Life Ins. Co. Treas., bd. overseers William Penn Charter Sch.; trustee Temple U. Office: Provident Nat Bank Broad and Chestnut Sts Philadelphia PA 19101 *

HILLBERRY, BEN(NY) M(AX), mechanical engineering educator; b. Riverton, Wyo., Dec. 17, 1937; s. Phil J. and Georgie K. (Renner) H.; m. Carol Ann Kohn, June 4, 1960; children: Julie Ann, Jeanne Marie, Jennifer Lynn, Joellen Elizabeth. B.S. in Mech. Engring, Iowa State U., 1961, M.S., 1964, Ph.D., 1967. Registered profl. engr., Ind., Ohio. Product engr. Gen. Motors Corp., Dayton, Ohio, 1961-62; instr. Iowa State U., 1962-66, asst. prof., 1967; research engr. Gen. Electric Co., Schenectady, 1966; asst. prof. Purdue U., West Lafayette, Ind., 1967-70, asso. prof., 1970-75, Alcoa prof. engring., 1973-75, prof., 1975—, chmn. design, 1977; Prince scholar Ariz. State U.; v.p. GLN Co.; dir. Hillberry Cattle Co., Linsley Enterprises; cons. numerous indsl. firms. Editor: Measurement of Dynamic Properties of Elastomers, 1973; Contbr. tech. articles to profl. jours. Gen. Motors Corp. fellow, 1962. Mem. ASTM (exec. com. for fatigue 1974-81), ASME, Soc. Automotive Engrs. (Gen. Materials Council, Arch T. Cowell award of merit 1972). Roman Catholic. Patentee in field. Home: 246 Lincoln St West Lafayette IN 47906 Office: Sch Mech Engring Purdue U West Lafayette IN 47907

HILLBRUNER, ANTHONY, educator, scholar, critic; b. Chgo., Feb. 10, 1914; s. Walter and Hedwig (Senk) H.; m. Laura Zino, Nov. 26, 1942; children—Anthony James, Tina Laurie. B.S., Northwestern U., 1949, M.A., 1950, Ph.D., 1953. Inst. U. Denver, 1950-51, U. Oreg., 1951-52, Stanford U., 1952-54; mem. faculty Calif. State U., Los Angeles, 1954—, now prof. rhetoric emeritus and Am. studies, dir. Am. studies program, 1954-69; vis. prof. Whittier Coll., 1962, Pa. State U., 1963; cons. Los Angeles County Execs., 1965-70, univ. presses, 1979—; vis. scholar U. Cambridge, Eng., 1972, U. Oxford, 1979. Author: Critical Dimensions, 1966; Contbr. articles to profl. jours., chpts. to books. Grantee Calif. State U. Found., 1965. Mem. Am. Studies Assn., Speech Communication Assn., Western Speech Communication Assn. (Disting. Service award 1981), Center Study Democratic Instns. Home: 407 N Mission Dr San Gabriel CA 91775 Office: 5151 State College Dr Calif State U Los Angeles CA 90032 *The concept of equality, as an integral part of American society, has been influential in my life and work. It suggests no preferential treatment for anyone. I have utilized egalitarianism from my earliest writings on its rhetorical influence, to today, when I use it as a touchstone in analyzing the rhetoric of politics, religion, the law, and society in general. This archetypal theme is most significant as one of the foundations of our Republic. It needs, however, to be coupled to two other seminal concepts: liberty and brotherhood. Without them, America would not be the blessed land that it is.*

HILLCOURT, WILLIAM (VILHELM HANS BJERREGAARD-JENSEN), author, editor; b. Aarhus, Denmark, Aug. 6, 1900; came to U.S., 1926, naturalized, 1939; s. Johannes Hans and Andrea Kristina (Pedersen) Bjerregaard-Jensen; m. Grace Constance Brown, June 3, 1933. Prep. edn., Aarhus Latinskole; M.Sc., Pharm. Coll., Copenhagen, 1924. While studying pharmacy became editor ofcl. Danish Scout mag. (and started to write boy's fiction); journalist, asst. editor Ferslew Newspapers, Copenhagen, 1924, corr. on tour of Europe and Am., arriving in U.S., 1926; mem. nat. staff Boy Scouts Am., 1926-65, asst. to dir. publs., 1927-44; mng. editor Scouting mag., 1927-31; feature writer, asst. editor, contbg. editor Boys' Life mag., 1932—; nat. dir. Scoutcraft, 1944-54, asst. to dir. program, 1954-56, nat. dir. program resources, 1956-65; Attended World Scout Jamborees, 1920, 24, 29, 33, 37, 47, 51, 55, 63, 67, 71, 75, 79, 83, Nat. Jamborees, 1937, 50, 53, 57, 60, 64, 69, 73, 77, 81. Author: Handbook for Patrol Leaders, 1929, (with James E. West) The Scout Jamboree, 1933, Handbook for Scoutmasters, 1936, Scout Field Book, 1944, Field Book of Nature Activities, 1950, Boy Scout Handbook, 1959, 65, Field Book of Nature Activities and Conservation, 1961, (with Olave, Lady Baden-Powell) Baden-Powell—The Two Lives of a Hero, 1964, Physical Fitness for Boys, Physical Fitness for Girls, 1967, Fun with Nature Hobbies, 1970, Field Book of Nature Activities and Hobbies, 1970, Golden Book of Camping, 1971, Outdoor Things to Do, 1975, Norman Rockwell's World of Scouting, 1977, Official Boy Scout Handbook, 1979, Handbook for Patrol Leaders, Silver Jubilee edit, 1979; pamphlets, mag. articles; editor: The 1929 World Jamboree Book, 1929, World Brotherhood Editions of Baden-Powell's Aids to Scoutmastership, 1944, Scouting for Boys, 1946. Spl. instr. U.S. Army 2d Service Command Tactical Sch., 1941-45. Recipient Medal of Merit, Danish Boy Scout Assn.; Cert. of Merit award Freedoms Found., 1951; Honor Medal awards, 1953-57; Badge of Honor, Norwegian Boy Scout Assn.; medal of Honor, Danish Boy Scout Assn.; Silver Horse, Venezuelan Boy Scout Assn.; Silver Wolf, Brit. Boy Scouts Assn.; Silver Hawk, Boy Scouts of Japan; Silver Beaver, Silver Buffalo Disting. Eagle award Boy Scouts Am.; other Scout decorations. Mem. Authors League Am. Home: 8104 E Seneca Turnpike Manlius NY 13104

HILLE, STANLEY JAMES, university dean; b. New London, Minn., Mar. 19, 1937; s. Sigurd Munson and Jennie (Stromme) H.; m. Gail Anne Bekowies, Sept. 12, 1964; children: Erik, Peter, Kirsten, Julia, Jennifer. B.B.A. with distinction, U. Minn., 1959, M.B.A., 1962, Ph.D., 1966. Instr. U. Minn., 1962-65; asst. prof. Coll. Bus. and Mgmt. U. Md., 1965-71, prof., chmn. dept. transp., bus. and public policy, 1971-74; prof. transp. U. Ala., 1974-78; dean Coll. Bus. Adminstrn., Kent State U., 1978-81, Coll. Bus. and Public Adminstrn., U. Mo., Columbia, 1981—; cons. to fed. and state gys., pvt. firms. Contbr. numerous articles to profl. publs. Recipient Teaching award U. Md., 1967; Norfolk and Western fellow, 1967; Gt. No. Ry. Found. fellow, 1974. Mem. Am. Soc. Traffic and Transp., Kent C. of C. (dir.), Delta Nu Alpha (Nat. Man of Yr. 1978). Lodges: Masons.; Rotary. Office: Coll Bus and Public Adminstrn U Mo Columbia MO 65211

HILLEGASS, CLIFTON KEITH, publisher; b. Rising City, Nebr., Apr. 18, 1918; s. Pearl Clinton and Rosena Christina (Dechert) H.; m. Mary D. Patterson, Apr. 17, 1968; children: James C., Linda L., Diane (Mrs. Michael Nolan). B.S., Midland Coll., Fremont, Nebr., 1937; grad. student, U. Nebr., 1937-39. With Nebr. Book Co., Lincoln, 1939—, mgr. wholesale div., 1946-64, cons., 1964—; founder, pres. Cliff's Notes, Inc. (study aids), Lincoln, 1958-83, chmn., 1983—. Mem. Nebr. Centennial Commn., 1967; Bd. dirs. Bryan Meml. Hosp., 1967-71; sec. bd. govs. Nebr. Wesleyan U. Served with USAAF, 1942-45. Presbyterian. Office: care Cliff's Notes Inc 1701 P St Lincoln NE 68508 *

HILLEMAN, MAURICE RALPH, virus research scientist; b. Miles City, Mont., Aug. 30, 1919; s. Robert A. and Edith (Matson) H.; m. Lorraine Witmer, Aug. 3, 1963; children—Jeryl Lynn, Kirsten Jeanne. B.S., Mont. State U., 1941, D.Sc., 1966; Ph.D., U. Chgo., 1944; D.Sc., U. Md., 1968. Asst. bacteriologist U. Chgo., 1942-44; research asso. virus labs. E.R. Squibb & Sons, 1944-47, chief virus dept., 1947-48; chief research and diagnostic sects. virus and rickettsial diseases Army Med. Service Grad. Sch., Walter Reed Army Med. Center, 1948-56, asst. chief lab. affairs, 1953-56; chief respiratory diseases Walter Reed Army Inst. Research, Washington, 1956-57; dir. virus and cell biol. research Merck Inst. Therapeutic Research, Merck & Co. Inc., 1957-66, exec. dir., 1966-71, v.p., 1971-78, sr. v.p., 1978—; dir. virus and cell biology research, v.p. Merck, Sharp & Dohme Research Labs., 1970-78, sr. v.p., 1978—; vis. investigator Hosp. of Rockefeller Inst. for Med. Research, 1951; vis. prof. bacteriology U. Md., 1953-57; adj. prof. virology pediatrics Sch. Medicine U. Pa., 1968—; cons. Children's Hosp. of Phila., 1968—; mem. council div. biol. scis. Pritzker Sch. Medicine, 1977—; John Herr Musser lectr. Musser-Burch Soc., Tulane U. Sch. Medicine, 1969, 19th Graugnard lectr., 1978; Mem., spl. cons. panel respiratory and related viruses USPHS, 1960-64; mem. Nat. Cancer Inst. primate study group, 1964-70; mem. council analysis and projection Am. Cancer Soc., 1971-76; mem. expert adv. panel on virus diseases WHO, 1952—; bd. dirs. W. Alton Jones Cell Sci. Center, Lake Placid, N.Y., 1980-82; mem. overseas med. research labs. com. Dept. Def., 1980; mem. virology dept. rev. com. Am. Type Culture Collection, 1980. Editorial bd.: Internat. Jour. Cancer, 1964-71, Inst. Sci. Information, 1968-70, Am. Jour. Epidemiology, 1969-75, Infection and Immunity, 1970-76, Excerpta Medica, 1971—, Proc. Soc. Exptl. Biology and Medicine, 1976—, Jour. Antiviral Research, 1980—; Contbr. 400 articles to sci., profl., med. jours. Phi Kappa Phi fellow, 1941-42; Koessler fellow, 1943-44; Recipient Howard Taylor Ricketts prize, 1945; Distinguished Civilian Service award sec. def., 1957; Walter Reed Army Med. Incentive award, 1960; Dean M. McCann award, 1970; Procter award, 1971; Achievement award Indsl. Research Inst., 1975. Fellow Am. Acad. Microbiology, Am. Acad. Arts and Scis.; mem. Am. Soc. Microbiology, Soc. Exptl. Biology and Medicine (mem. editorial and publs. com. 1977—), Tissue Culture Assn. (mem. council 1977—), Am. Assn. Immunologists, Am. Assn. Cancer Research, Infectious Diseases Soc., Permanent sect. Microbiol. Standardization Internat. Assn. Microbiol. Socs. Office: Merck Sharp & Dohme Research Labs West Point PA 19486 *Once the problem is defined and the facts are known, decision and action are little more than the implementation of the obvious.*

HILLENBRAND, DANIEL A., manufacturing company executive; b. 1923; married. Student, Purdue U. With Hillenbrand Industries, Inc., Batesville, Ind., 1946—, dir. purchasing, 1946-64, v.p., dir. mktg., 1964-69, pres. subs. Batesville Casket Co., 1969-72, chmn. bd., pres., chief exec. officer parent co., 1972-81, chmn. bd., chief exec. officer, 1981—, also dir. Office: Hillenbrand Industries Inc Hwy 46 East Batesville IN 47006 *

HILLENBRAND, MARTIN JOSEPH, diplomat, educator; b. Youngstown, Ohio, Aug. 1, 1915; s. Joseph John and Mary Magdalene (Walter) H.; m. Faith Stewart, June 27, 1941; children: Ruth Marie, David Martin, John Steven. A.B., U. Dayton, 1937, Litt.D. (honoris causa), 1963; M.A., Columbia U., 1938, Ph.D., 1948; postgrad., Harvard U., 1949-50; LL.D. (hon.), U. Md., 1973. Joined fgn. service, 1939, vice consul, Zurich, Switzerland, 1939, Rangoon, Burma, 1940, Calcutta, India, 1942, Lourenco Marques, S.E. Africa, 1944, fgn. service officer, Bremen, Ger., 1945, consul, 1946; officer in charge div. govt. and adminstrn. Bur. German Affairs, Dept. State, 1950-52, 1st sec., Paris, 1952-56, U.S. polit. adviser, Berlin, 1956-58; dir. Office of German Affairs Dept. State, 1958-62, dir. Berlin Task Force, 1962-63; minister, dep. chief of mission, Bonn, Ger., 1963-67, ambassador to Hungary, 1967-69; asst. sec. for European affairs Dept. State, 1969-72; ambassador to Fed. Republic Germany, 1972-76; dir. gen. Atlantic Inst. Internat. Affairs, Paris, 1977-82; Dean Rusk prof. internat. relations U. Ga., Athens, 1982—, dir. Global Policy Studies, 1983—; chmn. Fulbright Commn. for Ger., 1963-67; chmn. U.S. del. Four Power Working Group on Ger. and Berlin, 1959; mem. del. Fgn. Ministers Conf., Geneva, 1959; head or mem. U.S. del. numerous internat. meetings and confs. Author: Power and Morals, 1949; co-author: Zwischen Politik und Ethik, 1968; co-author, editor: The Future of Berlin, 1980. Decorated Grand Cross of Merit, W.Ger., others. Mem. Internat. Studies Assn., Council Fgn. Relations, Atlantic Council (dir.), Am. Fgn. Service Assn. Roman Catholic. Office: Ctr Global Policy U Ga Athens GA 30602

HILLENBRAND, W. AUGUST, manufacturing company executive; b. 1940; married. B.S. in Mgmt., St. Joseph's Coll., 1965. With Hillenbrand Industries, Batesville, Ind., 1958—, asst. to pres., 1965-70, v.p. ops., 1970-79, exec. v.p., 1979-81, pres., chief operating officer, 1981—, also dir. Office: Hillenbrand Industries Inc Hwy 46 East Batesville IN 47006 *

HILLER, ARTHUR, motion picture director; b. Edmonton, Alta., Can., Nov. 22, 1923. Ed. univs., Alta., Toronto and B.C.; F.V.Ch.C., Victoria Coll., Glasgow, 1967; M.A. in Psychology; L.H.D., London Inst. Applied Research, 1973. TV prodns. include Naked City; films include Americanization of Emily, 1965, Popi, 1968, Out of Towners, 1969, Love Story, 1970, Plaza Suite, 1970, The Hospital, 1971, Man of La Mancha, 1972, The Man in the Glass Booth, 1974, W.C. Fields and Me, 1975, Silver Streak, 1976, The In-Laws, 1979, Author! Author!, 1982. Decorated comdr. Internat. Order Sursam Corda; doctor laureate Imperial Order Constantine, Brussels, 1972; recipient Can. radio awards, 1951, 52; awards for edn. by radio Ohio U., 1952, 53; best dir. nomination Nat. Acad. TV Arts and Scis., 1962, Acad. Motion Picture Arts and Scis., 1970; Golden Globe award for best dir., 1970; Dir.'s award Dirs. Guild Am., 1970; Best Dir. award N.Y. Fgn. Press, 1970. Address: care The Gersh Agy 222 N Canon Dr Beverly Hills CA 90210

HILLER, LEJAREN ARTHUR, JR., composer, educator; b. N.Y.C., Feb. 23, 1924; s. Lejaren and Sara Anita (Plummer) H.; m. Elizabeth Halsey, Apr. 18, 1945; children—Amanda, David. B.A., Princeton U., 1944, M.A., 1946, Ph.D., 1947; M.Mus., U. Ill., 1958. Research chemist E.I. duPont de Nemours & Co., Inc., Waynesboro, Va., 1947-52; research assoc., asst. prof. dept. chemistry U. Ill., Urbana, 1953-58, asst. prof., 1958-61, assoc. prof. music, 1961-65, prof. music, 1965-68; also dir. exptl. music studio; Slee prof. music SUNY-, Buffalo, 1968-81, Birge-Cary prof. music, 1981—; co-dir. Center for Creative and Performing Arts, 1968-74; lectr. Darmstadt Ferienkurse für Neue Musik, 1963, 65, 69; sr. Fulbright lectr. music, Poland, 1973-74, Brazil, 1980. Author: (with L.M. Isaacson) Experimental Music, 1959, (with R.H. Herber) Principles of Chemistry, 1960, Informationstheorie und Computermusik, 1964; Composer 45 scores written, prior to 1964; Third Violin Sonata, 1970, A Cenotaph for 2 Pianos, 1971, Piano Sonata 6, Rage Over the Lost Beethoven, 1972, (with Ravi Kumra) Algorithms II for 9 Instruments and Tape, 1972, Sixth String Quartet, 1972, 6 Easy Pieces for Violin and Piano, 1974, A Portfolio for Diverse Performers and Tape, 1974, Malta for Tuba and Tape, 1975, Electronic Sonata, 1976, Midnight Carnival, 1976, Persiflage for Flute, Oboe and Percussion, 1977, Ponteach for Narrator and Piano, 1977, Diabelskie Skrzypce for Stringed Instrument and Harpsichord, 1978, An Apotheosis of Archaeopterix for Piccolo and Berimbau, 1979, Seventh String Quartet, 1979, Minuet and Trio for 6 performers, 1980, Lembrança da Bahia for Tape, 1981; Contbr. articles to profl. jours. Mem. Am. Soc. U. Composers, ASCAP., Am. Music Center. Home: 359 Berryman Dr Snyder NY 14226 Office: Dept Music SUNY Buffalo NY 14260

HILLER, WENDY, actress; b. Stockport, Eng.; d. Frank and Marie (Stone) H.; m. Ronald Gow, Feb. 25, 1937; children: Ann, Anthony. Ed., Winceby Sch. Broadway debut in Love on the Dole, 1935; stage appearances in N.Y. include The Heiress, 1947, Moon for the Misbegotten, 1957, Flowering Cherry, 1959, Aspern Papers, 1961-62; London appearances include: Tess of the d'Urbervilles, 1947, Ann Veronica, 1949, The Heiress, 1950, Shakespeare at the Old Vic, 1955-56, John Gabriel Borkman at the National, 1975; appeared in: play Waters of the Moon, Haymarket Theatre, London, 1951, revival 1979, Wings of the Dove, Haymarket Theatre, London, 1963, Crown Matrimonial, Haymarket Theatre, London, 1973, Aspern Papers, Haymarket Theatre, London, 1984; motion pictures include Pygmalion, 1939, Major Barbara, 1941, I Know Where I'm Going, 1945, Separate Tables, 1958 (Acad. award for Best Supporting Actress 1958), Sons and Lovers, 1960, Toys in the Attic, 1963, A Man for All Seasons, 1966, David Copperfield, 1969; appeared in: Murder on the Orient Express, 1973; motion pictures include Voyage of the Damned, 1976, Elephant Man, 1980. Decorated Order Brit. Empire, 71, dame Brit. Empire, 1975. Office: care ICM 388/396 Oxford St London WI England

HILLER, WILLIAM ARLINGTON, agricultural executive; b. East Stroudsburg, Pa., Jan. 15, 1928; s. John Jacob and Marguetite Laura H.; m. Joan Drake, June 2, 1947; children: William A., Joel, Jay S. B.S. cum laude, Upper Iowa U., 1950; M.S., Pa. State U., 1952. Mgmt. trainee Agway Inc., Lakewood, N.J., 1951-53, retail store mgr., 1953-71, v.p. corp. mktg., Syracuse, N.Y., 1971-73, group v.p., 1973-79, asst. gen. mgr., 1979-81, pres., chief exec. officer, 1981—; chmn. bd. Texas City Refinery, Agway Ins. Co.; trustee Syracuse Savs. Bank; dir. Pass & Seymour, Syracuse, Nat. Council Farmer Coops. Trustee Crouse-Irving Meml. Hosp., Syracuse, Upper Iowa U., Fayette; pres. Hiawatha Council Boy Scouts Am., Syracuse; mem. adv. council Cornell Coll. Agrl. and Life Scis. Recipient Silver Beaver award Boy Scouts Am., 1981. Mem. Alpha Zeta. Office: Agway Inc 333 Butternut Dr De Witt NY 13214

HILLERBRAND, HANS JOACHIM, historian, univ. adminstr.; b. Gersheim, Germany, Sept. 13, 1931; s. Johann and Louise (Feiler) H.; m. Bonnie Brunk, Nov. 13, 1954; children—Eric, Michael, Stephan. Student, Goshen (Ind.) Coll., 1951-53; Ph.D., U. Erlangen, Germany, 1957; LL.D., Montclair State Coll., 1978. Prof. Goshen Coll., 1957-59, Duke, 1959-70; prof. City U. N.Y., 1970—, dean Grad. Sch., 1972-77, v.p., provost, 1977-81, So. Meth. U., Dallas, 1981—. Author: Bibliography of Anabaptism, 1962, The Reformation, 1965, Fellowship of Discontent, 1967, Men and Ideas in the 16th Century, 1968, The World of the Reformation, 1974; Editor: Archive for Reformation History; mem. editorial bd. various profl. jours. Trustee Montclair State Coll., 1980-81, Scarritt Coll., 1979—. Mem. various profl. socs. Home: 9605 Robin Meadow Dallas TX 75243 Office: Office of Provost So Meth U Dallas TX 75275

HILLERICH, JOHN ANDREW, III, corp. exec.; b. Louisville, Oct. 27, 1940; s. John Andrew, Jr. and Gertrude (Hart) H.; children—John Andrew, IV, Holly Ann. B.A., Vanderbilt U., 1961. With Hillerich & Bradsby Co. (mfrs. baseball bats and golf clubs), Louisville, 1961—, asst. to mgr. timber div., then v.p. corp. affairs, 1965-70, chmn. bd., 1970, now pres., dir. Bd. dirs. Goodwill Industries Ky. Office: Hillerich & Bradsby Co PO Box 35700 Louisville KY 40232 *

HILLERMAN, JOHN BENEDICT, actor; b. Denison, Tex.; s. Christopher Benedict and Lenora JoAnn (Medlinger) H. Student, U. Tex., 1949-52. Stage actor: including Broadway shows such as Lady of the Camellias, The Great God Brown; summerstock; off-Broadway shows including Death of a Salesman, The Lion in Winter, The Little Foxes, Come Blow Your Horn, Caligula, Rhinoceros, The Fourposter, The Lark, The Devil's Disciple; with, Am. Theatre Wing, N.Y.C., 1958-59, Theatre Club, Washington, 1965-69; actor in: films including Chinatown, The Last Picture Show, Whats Up, Doc?, Paper Moon, At Long Last Love, Lawman, Blazing Saddles; actor: TV series including Magnum, P.I, Ellery Queen, Betty White Show, One Day at a Time; frequent guest roles: TV series and movies including Battles, The FBI, Mannix, Maude, Kojak, Serpico, Little House on the Prairie, Love Boat, Soap, Lou Grant, The Law, Relentless, Betrayal, Marathon. Served with USAF, 1953-57. Mem. Acad. Motion Picture Arts and Scis., Acad. TV Arts and Scis., Screen Actors Guild, AFTRA, Actors Equity Assn. Office: 10350 Santa Monica Blvd Suite 350 Los Angeles CA 90025 *As one who has always suffered from a low threshold of boredom, I have discovered over the years that the best antidote to that unhappy conditon is work. I am fortunate that acting, for me, is work of the most pleasurable kind. But work, whatever it may be, is the last refuge from boredom.*

HILLERS, DELBERT ROY, Near East language educator; b. Chester, S.D., Nov. 7, 1932; s. William Albert and Emma Rose (Gienapp) H.; m. Patricia Mays Turnbaugh, June 29, 1958; children: Eve Elizabeth, Samuel Thomas. Diploma, Concordia Coll., Milw., 1952; B.A., Concordia Sem., St. Louis, 1954, B.D., 1957; M.A., Johns Hopkins U., 1958, Ph.D., 1963. Instr. Hebrew and ancient Near East studies Concordia Sr. Coll., Fort Wayne, Ind., 1958-60; asst. prof. Johns Hopkins U., Balt., 1963-66, assoc. prof., 1966-70, prof., 1970—; W.W. Spence prof. Semitic Langs. John Hopkins U., Balt., 1971—; acting chmn. dept. Near Eastern Studies Johns Hopkins U., Balt., 1964-70, chmn. dept. Near Eastern Studies, 1976-79; ann. prof. Am. Sch. Oriental Research, Jerusalem, 1968-69. Author: Treaty Curses and the Old Testament Prophets, 1964, Covenant: The History of a Biblical Idea, 1969, Lamentations, The Anchor Bible, 1972, Micah, Hermeneia Series, 1983; mem.: Revised Standard Version Old Testament Com., 1983—. Fellow Johns Hopkins U., 1961-63, 1957-58; Schaff lectr. Pitts. Theol. Sem., 1970. Mem. Soc. Bibl. Lit., Am. Schs. Oriental Research (trustee Amman Ctr.), Am. Oriental Soc. Home: 604 Hollen Rd Baltimore MD 21212 Office: Dept Near Eastern Studies Johns Hopkins U. 34th and Charles Sts Baltimore MD 21218

HILLESTAD, ALBERT WILLIAM, bishop Episcopal Ch.; b. New Richmond, Wis., July 11, 1924; s. Evar and Elenora H.; m. Carol Joyce Hutchens, June 19, 1954; children—Mary Harriet, Michael Evar, Elizabeth Ann, William Joseph, James Frederick, Christina Louise, Paul Eric. B.A., U. Wis., Madison, 1947; M.Div., Seabury Western Theol. Sem., 1950; D.D., Nashotah House Sem., 1972. Ordained priest Episcopal Ch., 1950, consecrated bishop, 1972; curate ch., La Crosse, Wis., 1950-51, rector ch., Chgo., 1951-57, Carbondale, Ill., 1964-72, vicar ch., Oconoto, Wis., 1957-64; Episcopal chaplain Menard and Vienna (Ill.) State Penitentiaries, 1965-72; archdeacon, Cairo, Ill., 1967-72; bishop, coadjutor Diocese of Springfield, Ill., 1972, bishop, 1972—. Office: 821 S 2d St Springfield IL 62704 *

HILLHOUSE, GORDON EMERSON, oil company executive; b. Barnsdall, Okla., Feb. 27, 1925; s. Noval C. and Gladys (Dodd) H.; m. Bobbie Watts, Oct. 7, 1950; children: David, Brent. Student, Purdue

U., 1943; B.S. in Mech. Engring, U. Okla., 1949; grad., Advanced Mgmt. Program, Harvard, 1971. With Sunray D-X Oil Co. (name now Sun Co., Inc.), Tulsa, 1949—, mgr. engring., 1961-64, dir. systems and ops. research, 1964-66, v.p. prodn., 1966-68, asst. merger mgr., 1968-69, dir. corp. materials mgmt., 1969-71, project leader, 1971-72; pres., dir. Sun Oil Internat., Inc., 1972-74, corp. v.p., 1974, now exec. v.p., dir.; dir. Suncor Inc., Can., Sun Oil Co. Del., Sun Oil Co. Canada, Ltd., Sun Exploration and Prodn. Co., Sun Oil Co. Pa. Trustee U. Okla. Found.; bd. dirs. Phila. Urban Coalition, Franklin Research Ctr.; bd. mgrs. Franklin Inst. Served with AUS, 1943-46. Mem. Am. Petroleum Inst. (bd. dirs.), Soc. Petroleum Engrs., AIME, Inst. Mining, Metall. and Petroleum Engrs. Club: Aronimink Golf. Office: 100 Matsonford Rd Radnor PA 19087

HILLIARD, JAMES HENNING, investment company executive; b. Louisville, May 25, 1916; s. Isaac and Helen Cochran (Donigan) H.; m. Mary Wheeler, Apr. 7, 1947; children—Helen D., Margaret W., Mary G. Grad., Woodberry Forest Sch., 1934; B.S., U. Va., 1938, LL.B., 1940. Bar: Va. bar 1939, Ky. bar 1939. Practiced in Louisville, 1940-42, 45-48; partner J.J.B. Hilliard & Son, Louisville, 1948-65; chmn. J.J. B. Hilliard & W.L. Lyons, Inc., Louisville, 1965—; dir. Belknap Inc., Spalding Services, Inc., Brown Forman Distillers Corp., Louisville Cement Co., Vt. Am. Corp., Roll Forming Corp., Shelbyville, Ky.; Gov. N.Y. Stock Exchange, 1968-71. Chmn. bd. dirs. Norton Children's Hosps., Inc.; regent Ky. State U.; bd. overseers U. Louisville; trustee Bernheim Found., Shakertown at Pleasant Hill. Served with USAAF, 1942-45. Mem. Better Bus. Bur. (pres. 1956-58), Louisville C. of C. (pres. 1962), Securities Industry Assn. (dir. 1971-74, chmn. 1974), Assn. Stock Exchange Firms (bd. govs. 1962-66), Beta Theta Pi, Omicron Delta Kappa, Phi Alpha Delta. Republican. Episcopalian (trustee Ky. diocese). Clubs: Pendennis, Louisville Country, River Valley, Jefferson; River (N.Y.C.); Mill Reef (Antigua). Home: 4506 Upper River Rd Louisville KY 40222 Office: 545 S 3d St Louisville KY 40202

HILLIARD, JOHN EVELYN, educator; b. London, Eng., May 14, 1926; s. John Perry and Dorothy (Eyre) H. B.Eng., Liverpool U., Eng., 1947, Ph.D., 1950. Research asso. Mass. Inst. Tech., 1950-56; metallurgist Gen. Elec. Research Lab., Schenectady, 1956-62; prof. materials sci. Northwestern U., 1962—, Walter P. Murphy prof., 1971—. Office: Dept Materials Sci and Engring Technol Inst Northwestern U Evanston IL 60201

HILLIARD, ROBERT GLENN, lawyer, insurance company executive; b. Anderson, S.C., Jan. 18, 1943; s. Baz Robert and Louise (Holcombe) H.; m. Heather Ann Prevost, Apr. 1, 1966; children: Kathryn Louise, Nancy Ann. B.A., Clemson U., 1965; J.D., George Washington U., 1968. Bar: S.C. 1969. Atty., asst. sec. Liberty Corp., Greenville, 1970-75, v.p., gen. counsel, sec., 1975—; atty., legal dept. Liberty Life Ins. Co., Greenville, S.C., 1968-75, sec., 1975-78, v.p., gen. counsel, sec., 1978-82, pres., 1982—, also dir.; atty. Cosmos Broadcasting Corp., Greenville, 1970-75, v.p., gen. counsel, sec., 1975-82, now dir., Liberty Corp.; dir. S.C. Life & Health Ins. Guaranty Assn., N.C. Life & Health Ins. Guaranty Assn.; state v.p. Am. Council Life Ins.; former pres., dir. Assn. S.C. Life Ins. Cos. Bd. dirs. Greenville Assn. for Retarded Children; bd. dirs., vice chmn. YMCA Camp Greenville Mgmt. Bd.; project chmn. Foothills Trail project Sierra Club. Mem. Am., S.C., Greenville County bar assns., Am. Soc. Corporate Secs., Fedn. Ins. Counsel, Assn. Life Ins. Counsel, Internat. Assn. Ins. Counsel, Life Insurers Conf., Sierra Club. Presbyterian. Clubs: Summit (Columbia, S.C.); Greenville Country, Poinsett. Home: 124 E Tallulah Dr Greenville SC 29605 Office: PO Box 789 Greenville SC 29605

HILLIARD, SAM BOWERS, geography educator; b. Hart County, Ga., Dec. 21, 1930; s. Asa Farris and Flora Elizabeth (Bowers) H.; m. Joyce Collier, June 4, 1955; children—Steven Glen, Anita Joy. A.B., U. Ga., 1960, M.A., 1962; M.S., U. Wis., 1963, Ph.D., 1966. Electrician Savannal River Valley plant Dupont Co., Aiken, S.C., 1954-59; teaching asst. U. Wis., 1961-65, instr., Milw., 1965-67; asst. prof. geography So. Ill. U., 1967-71; prof. La. State U., Baton Rouge, 1971—, Alumni prof., 1983—, chmn. dept. geography, 1976-79, dir. Sch. Geosci., 1977-79. Author: Hog Meat and Hoecake: Food Supply in the Old South, 1972, also articles in profl. jours. Served with U.S. Navy, 1950-54. Mem. Assn. Am. Geographers, Agrl. History Assn., Am. Geog. Soc., So. History Assn. Office: Geology 255 Louisiana State U Baton Rouge LA 70803

HILLIER, J(AMES) ROBERT, architect; b. Toronto, Ont., Can., July 24, 1937; came to U.S., 1941, naturalized, 1961; s. James and Florence (Bell) H.; m. Susan Baldwin Smith, June 17, 1961; children—Kimberly, James Baldwin. B.A., Princeton U., 1959, M.F.A., 1961. Project designer J. Labatut (Architect), Princeton, N.J., 1961-62; project mgr. Fulmer & Bowers, Princeton, 1966-72; prin. J. Robert Hillier (Architects/Planners), Princeton, 1966-72; pres. The Hillier Group (Architects), Princeton, 1972—; dir. First Nat. Bank Princeton, Sedden Island Devel. Corp. Prin. works include Bryant Coll. campus, Smithfield, R.I., 1969, Rutgers U. Athletic Center, Piscataway, N.J., 1977, Butler Hosp, Providence, 1978, N.J. State Justice Complex, Trenton, 1981, Harbor Island Design, Tampa, Fla., 1981, Beneficial Corp. Complex, 1982. Recipient various design awards. Fellow AIA (v.p. N.J. chpt. 1974); mem. Nat. Council Archtl. Registration Bds. Clubs: Princeton Quadrangle, Nassau, Princeton of N.Y. Home: 87 Ridgeview Circle Princeton NJ 08540 Office: 777 Alexander Rd Princeton NJ 08540

HILLIKER, JOHN ARTHUR CHARLES, trust company executive; b. Toronto, Ont., Can., Feb. 17, 1928; s. Arthur Ellwood and Kathleen (Keyes) H.; m. Barbara Doreen Kenny, Feb. 20, 1954; children: Nancy Lynne Hilliker Luks, David John. B.A., U. Toronto, 1951; postgrad., U. Alta., Calgary, Harvard U. Mgr. Canadian Imperial, Montego Bay, Jamaica, 1960-61; sr. asst. mgr. Bank of Commerce, Vancouver, B.C., Can., 1961-64, mgr., Ottawa, Ont., 1954-65, asst. gen. mgr., Toronto, 1965-70, from sr. v.p. to vice chmn. head office, 1971-82; chmn., pres., chief exec. officer Can. Permanent Trust Co., Toronto, 1982—; dir. Leitch Transport Co., Toronto, St. Lawrence Starch Co.; pres., trustee Can. Permanent Income Investments. Bd. dirs. St. George's Coll., Toronto. Clubs: Granite; Rosedale (Calif.); Toronto (Toronto); Vancouver; Rideau (Ottawa). Home: 22 McGlashan Ct Toronto ON Canada M5M 4M6 Office: Canada Permanent Trust Co 320 Bay St Toronto ON Canada M5H 2P6

HILLILA, BERNHARD HUGO PAUL, educator; b. Gwinn, Mich., May 21, 1919; s. Hugo Mathias and Hannah Maria (Mattonen) H.; m. Esther Pauline Halttunen, June 28, 1944; children—Esther Pauline Nelson, Sarah Christine, Martin Bernhard. Grad., Suomi Coll., Hancock, Mich., 1938, Suomi Theol. Sem., 1941; B.A., Boston U., 1943; M.A., Western Res. U., 1945, postgrad., 1945-46; Ed.D., Columbia, 1955. Ordained to ministry Luth. Ch., 1941; pastor, Maynard, Mass., 1941-43, Fairport Harbor, Ohio, 1943-46, Bklyn., 1946-49, 52-57; instr. Wagner Coll., S.I., 1948-49; pres. Suomi Coll. and Theol. Sem., 1949-52; pastor, Warren, Ohio, 1957-60; dean, prof. practical theology Hamma Div. Sch., Wittenberg U., 1960-64, dir. grad. div., 1961-63; dean Calif. Luth. Coll., Thousand Oaks, Calif., 1964-68; prof. edn. Valparaiso (Ind). U., 1968—; lectr. Purdue U., 1969-73; Vice pres. Finnish Evang. Luth. Ch., 1955-60; mem. Joint Commn. Luth. Unity, 1956-62, Inter-Luth. Consultation Commn., 1962-66; councillor Nat. Luth. Council, 1962-66; del. Luth. World Fedn. Assembly, 1957; Mem. Mich. Tb Sanatorium Commn., 1950-52. Editor: The Luth. Counselor, 1942-44; author: The Sauna Is, 1979; project dir.: Public Art and Porter County, 1977-78. Mem. NEA, Am. Psychol. Assn., Phi Delta Kappa. Home: 703 Hastings Terr Valparaiso IN 46383

HILLIS, MARGARET, musician; b. Kokomo, Ind., Oct. 1, 1921; d. Glen R. and Bernice (Haynes) H. B.A., Ind. U., 1947; grad. student choral conducting, Juilliard Sch. Music, 1947-49; D.Mus. (hon.), Temple U., 1967, Ind. U., 1972, Carthage Coll., 1979, Wartburg Coll., 1981, D.F.A., St. Mary's Coll., 1977, Lake Forest Coll., 1980. Dir., Met. Youth Chorale, Bklyn., 1948-51; asst. condr., Collegiate Choral, N.Y.C., 1952-53; mus. dir., condr., Am. Concert Choir, N.Y.C., 1950—, Am. Concert Orch.; condr., instr., Union Theol. Sem., 1950-60, Juilliard Sch. Music, 1951-53; dir. choral dept., Third St. Music Sch. Settlement, 1953-54; founder, music dir., Am. Choral Found., Inc., 1954—; choral dir., N.Y.C. Opera Co., 1955-56, Chgo. Mus. Coll. of Roosevelt U., 1961-62; condr., choral dir., Santa Fe Opera Co., 1958-59, Chgo. Symphony Chorus, 1957—; music dir., N.Y. Chamber Soloists, 1956-60; choral condr., Am. Opera Soc., N.Y.C., 1952-68; mus. asst. to music dir., Chgo. Symphony Orch., 1966-68; music dir., condr., Kenosha Symphony Orch., 1961-68; condr., choral dir., Cleve. Orch. Chorus, 1969-71; prof. conducting, dir. choral orgns., Northwestern U. Sch. Music, 1970-77; vis. prof. conducting, Ind. U., 1978—; resident condr., Chgo. Civic Orch., 1967—; music dir., Choral Inst., 1968-70, 75; mus. dir., condr., Elgin (Ill.) Symphony Orch., 1971—; condr., Chgo.'s Do-It-Yourself Messiah, 1976—; dir. choral activities, San Francisco Symphony Orch., 1982-83; guest condr., Chgo. Symphony, Cleve. Orch., Minn. Orch., Nat. Symphony Orch., others.; (Grammy award for best choral performance of 1977 (Verdis' Requiem) 1978, for best choral performance of 1978 (Beethoven's Missa Solemnis) 1979, for best choral performance of 1979 (Brahms' Ein Deutsches Requiem) 1980, for best choral performance of 1982 (Berlioz' La Damnationde Faust) 1983). Artists' adviser Nat. Fedn. Music Clubs Youth Auditions, 1966-70; mem. vis. com. dept. music U. Chgo., 1971—; chmn. choral panel Nat. Endowment for Arts, 1974—; hon. mem. Roosevelt U. Council of 100, 1976—; adv. bd. Cathedral Choral Soc. Washington Cathedral, 1976—. Civilian flight instr. USN CAA, WTS, World War II. Recipient Golden Plate award Am. Acad. Achievement, 1967; Alumnus of Year award Ind. U. Sch. Music Alumni, 1969; Steinway award, 1969; Chgo. YWCA Leader Luncheon I award, 1972; Friends of Lit. award, 1973; SAI Found. Circle of 15 award, 1974; Woman of Yr. in Classical Music award Ladies Home Jour., 1978; Leadership for Freedom award; Women's Scholarship Assn. Roosevelt U., 1978. Mem. Nat. Fedn. Music Clubs (hon., citation for contbns. to musical life of nation 1981), Am. Choral Dirs. Assn., Assn. Choral Condrs., Am. Music Center, P.E.O., Sigma Alpha Iota (hon.), Pi Kappa Lambda (hon.), Kappa Kappa Gamma (Alumni Achievement award 1978), Assn. Profl. Vocal Ensembles, Am. Symphony Orch. League, Nat. Soc. Lit. and Arts. Club: Musicians of Women (hon.). Office: Am Choral Found Inc: 130 W 56th St New York NY 10019 also 220 S Michigan Ave Chicago IL 60604

HILLMAN, BILL (CLARENCE WILLIAM), labor union executive; b. Rexburg, Idaho, Dec. 10, 1922; s. Clarence Lynn and Reva (Baird) H.; m. Virginia Carney, June 1948 (div. 1950); 1 son, Robert W.; m. Martha Ruth Apollonio, Dec. 31, 1959; children: Kenneth W., Nancy A. A.A., Boise Jr. Coll., 1942; B.A., U. Calif., 1949. Reporter Sta. KPIX, San Francisco, 1949—; corr. Voice of Am., San Francisco, 1956-72; lst v.p. AFTRA, N.Y.C., 1976-79, pres., 1979—. Office: AFTRA 1350 Avenue of the Americas New York NY 10019 *In my union, AFTRA, member participation and democracy are prized. That has made it possible for outstanding performances such as Eddie Cantor and Lawrence Tibbett to become presidents of AFTRA and to emerge as union leaders. As their successor, my success is due to the system they helped create.*

HILLMAN, DONALD ARTHUR, pediatrician, educator; b. Montreal, Que., Canada, June 25, 1925; s. Daniel and BerthaJean (Smith) H.; m. Elizabeth Sloman, Dec. 29, 1956; children: Alison, Jamie, Donald, Alan, Elizabeth. B.S., McGill U., Montreal, 1949, M.D., 1951, Ph.D. in Endocrinology, 1961. Assoc. prof. McGill U., 1958-76, assoc. dean, 1971-74; prof. discipline pediatrics, chmn. discipline pediatrics Meml. U. Nfld., St. John's, Nfld., Canada, 1976—; physician in chief Janeway Child Health Centre, St. John's, Nfld., Canada, 1976—. Served with Can. Army, 1943-46. Home: 102 New Cove Rd Saint Johns NF Canada A1A 2C4 Office: Discipline of Pediatrics Medicine Meml U of Nfld Saint Johns NF Canada A1B 3V6

HILLMAN, DOUGLAS WOODRUFF, federal judge; b. Grand Rapids, Mich., Feb. 15, 1922; s. Lemuel Serrell and Dorothy (Woodruff) H.; m. Sally Jones, Sept. 13, 1944; children: Drusilla W., Clayton D. Grad., Phillips Exeter Acad., 1941; A.B., U. Mich., 1946, LL.B., 1948. Bar: Mich. 1948, U.S. Supreme Ct. 1967. Asso. firm Lilly, Luyendyk & Snyder, Grand Rapids, 1948-53; partner firm Luyendyk, Hainer, Hillman, Karr & Dutcher, Grand Rapids, 1953-65, Hillman, Baxter & Hammond, 1965-79; U.S. dist. judge Western Dist. Mich., Grand Rapids, 1979—; instr. Nat. Inst. Trial Advocacy, Boulder, Colo. Chmn. Grand Rapids Human Relations Commn., 1963-66; chmn. bd. trustees Fountain St. Ch., 1970-72; pres. Family Service Assn., 1967. Served as pilot USAAF, 1943-45. Decorated D.F.C., Air medal.; Recipient Annual Civil Liberties award ACLU, 1970. Fellow Am. Bar Found.; Mem. Am. Bar Assn., Mich. Bar Assn. (chmn. client security fund), Grand Rapids Bar Assn. (pres. 1963), Am. Coll. Trial Lawyers (Mich. chmn. 1979), 6th Circuit Jud. Conf. (life), Internat. Acad. Trial Lawyers, Fedn. Ins. Counsel, Internat. Assn. Ins. Counsel, Internat. Soc. Barristers (pres. 1977-78), Nat. Bd. Trial Advocacy. Clubs: M (U. Mich.); University (Grand Rapids); Rotary, Torch. Office: 110 Michigan St NW 682 Grand Rapids MI 49503

HILLMAN, G. ROBERT, journalist; b. Peoria, Ill., Jan. 30, 1951; s. Glenn Robert and Marjorie Irene (Mooberry) H. B.S., U. Ill., 1972. Investigative reporter Chgo. Today, 1972, Chgo. Sun-Times, 1972-75, Springfield bur. chief, 1975-83, nat. corr., 1983—. Contbr.: articles to N.Y. Times, Newsweek, World Book Ency. Recipient Med. Journalism award Ill. State Med. Soc., Chgo., 1973, Stick-O-Type award Chgo. Newspaper Guild, 1982, awards AP, UPI, Lincoln U., Jefferson City, Mo. Mem. U. Ill. Alumni Assn. (life). Mem. United Ch. of Christ. Club: Chgo. Press. Home: 2250 N Wayne Ave Chicago IL 60614 Office: Chgo Sun-Times 401 N Wabash Ave Chicago IL 60611

HILLMAN, HENRY L., business executive; b. Pitts., Dec. 25, 1918; s. J.H. (Jr.) and Juliet Cummins (Lea) H.; m. Elsie Mead Hilliard, May 12, 1945; children: Lea, Audrey, Henry, William. A.B., Princeton U., 1941. Chmn. bd. Hillman Co., Copeland Corp.; dir. Chem. N.Y. Corp., Nat. Steel Corp., Pitts. Nat. Corp., Cummins Engine Co., Inc., Nat. Steel Corp., Gen. Electric Co. Mem. exec. com. Allegheny Conf. on Community Devel., Pitts. Regional Planning Assn.; pres. Hillman Found.; trustee U. Pitts., Children's Hosp. of Pitts., Carnegie Inst.; mem. Bus. Council. Served from ensign to lt., naval aviator USNR, 1942-45. Clubs: Duquesne, Pitts. Golf (Pitts.); Fox Chapel Golf; Rolling Rock (gov.), Laurel Valley Golf (Ligionier, Pa.); Links, Princeton (N.Y.C.); Augusta Nat. Golf (Ga.). Home: Morewood Heights Pittsburgh PA 15213 Office: Grant Bldg Pittsburgh PA 15219

HILLMAN, HOWARD BUDROW, author, consultant; b. Hollywood, Calif, Dec. 8, 1934; s. Donald Edward and Rebecca (Budrow) H. B.A., Calif. State U.-Long Beach, 1959; M.B.A., Harvard U., 1961. Pres. Nat. Acad. Sports, N.Y.C., 1961-66, Howard Hillman Co., 1966—; v.p. Am. Film Theatre, N.Y.C., 1972-74; lectr. and cons. in field. Author: The Complete New Yorker, 1972, The Art of Winning Foundation Grants, 1975, The Art of Winning Government Grants, 1977, The Diner's Guide to Wine, 1978, The Book of World Cuisines, 1979, The Art of Winning Corporate Grants, 1980; AUTHOR: The Art of Writing Business Reports and Proposals, 1980; author: The Cook's Book, 1981, Kitchen Science, 1981; Great Peasant Dishes of the World, 1983; author: The Gourmet Guide to Beer, 1983, The Art of Dining Out, 1984, The Macmillan Complete Computer Buyer's Checklist, 1984; contbr. articles to various mags., newspapers and jours.; guest radio, TV talk shows. Served with U.S. Army, 1954-56. Episcopalian. Club: Harvard (N.Y.). Home and Office: 220 E 63d St New York NY 10021

HILLMAN, MELVILLE ERNEST DOUGLAS, chemist; b. Winnipeg, Man., Can., Aug. 3, 1926; came to U.S., 1954, naturalized, 1976; s. Frank Ernest and Elizabeth (Grindlay) H.; m. Marion Louise Pettingill, Nov. 22, 1974; stepchildren: Robert F. James, Deborah L. Wasylak, Lorraine Maillot. B.A. with honors, U. B.C., 1952, M.Sc., 1954; Ph.D., Ohio State U., 1958. Research chemist E.I. DuPont de Nemours & Co., Wilmington, Del., 1958-61, Chevron Research, Richmond, Calif., 1961-64; research supr. W.R. Grace Co., Columbia, Md., 1964-68; group leader Celanese Research Co., Summit, N.J., 1968-71; program leader Ethicon, Inc., Somerville, N.J., 1971-73; prin. research scientist Battelle Columbus Labs., Ohio, 1973-75, sr. research scientist, 1975-79, research leader, 1979—; cons. in field. Contbr. articles to profl. jours.; patentee in field. Fellow Socony-Mobil, 1955-56, Lubrizol, 1956-57, DuPont, 1957-58. Mem. Am. Chem. Soc., N.Y. Acad. Scis., N.Y. Catalyst Soc., Sigma Xi, Phi Lambda Upsilon. Baptist. Home: 3317 Darbyshire Dr Columbus OH 43220 Office: Battelle Columbus Labs 505 King Ave Columbus OH 43201

HILLMAN, RICHARD EPHRAIM, educator, pediatrician; b. Pawtucket, R.I., Oct. 6, 1940; s. Harold S. and Anne (Chernick) H.; m. Laura S. Smith, June 14, 1970; children: Helena, Stuart, Noah, Paul, Andrew, Anne. A.B., Brown U., 1962; M.D., Yale U., 1965. Diplomate: Am. Bd. Med. Examiners, Am. Bd. Pediatrics, Am. Bd. Human Genetics. Intern Grace-New Haen Hosp., 1965-66; resident Grace-New Haven Hosp., 1966-67; asst. prof. pediatrics Washington U., St. Louis, 1971-75, assoc. prof., 1975-78, prof. pediatrics, 1981—, assoc. prof. genetics, 1977-81, prof. genetics, 1981—; chmn. Mental Retardation Research Com. NICHHD, Bethesda, Md., 1983—. Lt. comdr. USN, 1969-71. Fellow Am. Acad. Pediatrics; mem. Soc. Pediatric Research (council), Am. Pediatric Soc., Am. Soc. Clin. Investigation, Soc. for Inherited Metabolic Disorders (pres.). Office: Div Med Genetics Washington Univ Sch Medicine 660 S Euclid Ave Saint Louis MO 63110

HILLMAN, STANLEY ERIC GORDON, former corporate executive; b. London, Eng., Oct. 13, 1911; came to U.S., 1951, naturalized, 1957; s. Percy Thomas and Margaret Eleanor Fanny (Lee) H.; m. May Irene Noon, May 2, 1947; children: Susan, Deborah, Katherine. Ed., Holyrood, Tonbridge schs., Eng. With Brit.-Am. Tobacco Co., Ltd., London, Shanghai, 1933-47; dir. Hillman & Co., Ltd., Cosmos Trading Co., FED Inc., U.S.A., Airmotive Supplies Co. Ltd., Hong Kong, 1947-52; v.p. Gen. Dynamics Corp., 1953-61; v.p., group exec. Am. Machine & Foundry Co., N.Y.C., 1962-65; v.p., dir. Gen. Am. Transp. Corp., 1965-67; pres., vice chmn., dir. IC Industries, 1968-78; bankruptcy trustee Chgo., Milw., St. Paul & Pacific R.R., 1978-79; dir. Bell & Howell, Avco Corp., SFN Cos., Bandag Corp., Conrail Corp. Trustee Gen. Growth Properties. Clubs: Chgo., Mid Am. (Chgo.); Onwentsia, Royal Poinciana. Home: 533 N Mayflower Rd. Lake Forest IL 60045

HILLS, CARLA ANDERSON, lawyer, former secretary housing and urban development; b. Los Angeles, Jan. 3, 1934; d. Carl H. and Edith (Hume) Anderson; m. Roderick Maltman Hills, Sept. 27, 1958; children: Laura Hume, Roderick Maltman, Megan Elizabeth, Alison Macbeth. A.B. cum laude, Stanford U., 1955; student, St. Hilda's Coll., Oxford (Eng.) U., 1954; LL.B., Yale U., 1958; hon. degrees, Pepperdine U., 1975, Washington U., 1977, Mills Coll., 1977, Lake Forest Coll., 1978, Williams Coll., 1981. Bar: Calif. 1959, U.S. Supreme Ct. 1965. Asst. U.S. atty. civil div., Los Angeles, 1958-61; partner firm Munger, Tolles, Hills & Rickershauser, Los Angeles, 1962-74, Latham, Watkins & Hills, Washington, 1978—; asst. atty. gen. civil div. Justice Dept., Washington, 1974-75; sec. HUD, 1975-77; dir. IBM Corp., Corning Glass Works, Am. Airlines, Fed. Nat. Mortgage Assn., Signal Cos., Inc., Rand Corp., Standard Oil Co. Calif.; adj. prof. Sch. Law, UCLA, 1972; mem. Trilateral Commn., 1977—, Am. Com. on East-West Accord, 1977-79, Internat. Found. for Cultural Cooperation and Devel., 1977—, Fed. Acctg. Standards Adv. Council, 1978-80; bd. dirs. Internat. Exec. Service Corps.; mem. corrections task force Los Angeles County Sub-Regional; adv. bd. Calif. Council on Criminal Justice, 1969-71; mem. standing com. discipline U.S. Dist. Ct. for Central Calif., 1970-73; mem. Adminstrv. Conf. U.S., 1972-74; mem. exec. com. law and free soc. State Bar Calif., 1973; bd. councillors U. So. Calif. Law Center, 1972-74; trustee Pomona Coll., 1974-79, U. So. Calif., Brookings Instn.; mem. at large exec. com. Yale Law Sch., 1973—; mem. com. on Law Sch. Yale Univ. Council; Gordon Grand fellow Yale U., 1978; mem. Sloan Commn. on Govt. and Higher Edn., 1977-79; mem. advisory com. Princeton U., Woodrow Wilson Sch. of Pub. and Internat. Affairs, 1977—. Co-author: Federal Civil Practice, 1961; co-author, editor: Antitrust Adviser, 1971; contbg. editor: Legal Times, 1978—; mem. editorial bd.: Nat. Law Jour, 1978—. Trustee U. So. Calif., 1977-79, Norton Simon Mus. Art, Pasadena, Calif., 1976—, Lawyers Com. for Civil Rights under Law, 1978—, Urban Inst., 1978-80; chmn. Urban Inst., 1983—; co-chmn. Alliance To Save Energy, 1977—; vice chmn. adv. council on legal policy Am. Enterprise Inst., 1977—; bd. visitors, exec. com. Stanford U. Law Sch., 1978—; bd. dirs. Am. Council for Capital Formation, 1978—; mem. adv. com. M.I.T.-Harvard U. Joint Center for Urban Studies, 1978—; bd. govs. Nat. ARC, 1975—. Fellow Am. Bar Found.; mem. Los Angeles Women Lawyers Assn. (pres. 1964), ABA (chmn. publs. com. antitrust sect. 1972-74, council 1974, 77—, chmn. 1982-83), Fed. Bar Assn. (pres. Los Angeles chpt. 1963), Los Angeles County Bar Assn. (mem. fed. rules and practice com. 1963-72, chmn. issues and survey 1963-72, chmn. sub-com. revision local rules for fed. cts. 1966-72, mem. jud. qualifications com. 1971-72), Am. Bar Inst. Clubs: Yale of So. Calif. (dir. 1972-74); Yale (Washington)). Office: 1333 New Hampshire Ave NW Suite 1200 Washington DC 20036

HILLS, FREDERIC WHEELER, editor, publishing company executive; b. East Orange, N.J., Nov. 26, 1934; s. Frederic Wheeler and Mildred Chambers (Hood) H.; m. Patricia Schulze, Jan. 17, 1958 (div. Dec. 1973); children: Christina, Bradford; m. Kathleen Matthews, Apr. 21, 1980. B.A., Columbia U., 1956; M.A., Stanford U., 1959. Editor F.W. Dodge Corp., San Francisco, 1959-60, N.Y.C., 1960-61; editor McGraw-Hill Book Co., N.Y.C., 1961-68, editor-in-chief, 1968-72, 1972-78; mem. editorial bd. Simon & Schuster Book Co., N.Y.C., 1979—, v.p., 1981—. Served with AUS, 1958. Mem. A.C.L.U., Assn. Am. Publishers. Home: 380 Clinton St Brooklyn NY 11231 Office: 1221 Ave of the Americas New York NY 10020

HILLS, GEORGE BURKHART, JR., business executive; b. Jacksonville, Fla., July 17, 1925; s. George Burkhart and Anna Donna (McEnerny) H.; m. Sarah Anne Davis, Sept. 6, 1947; children: George Burkhart III, Barrett Davis, Sarah Kathryn, Margaret Anne, Harland Andrew. B.Mech. Engring., Ga. Inst. Tech., 1946; B.Indsl. Engring., U. Fla., 1947, M.S. in Engring., 1949; postgrad., Advanced Mgmt. Program, Harvard Bus. Sch., 1972. With St. Joe Paper Co., Port St. Joe, Fla., 1949-50; with MacMillan Bloedel Ltd., Vancouver, B.C., Can., 1950-61; pres., chief exec. officer MacMillan Bloedel (USA) Inc., Stamford, Conn., 1974-77; with Stone Container Corp., Chgo., 1961-64, sr. v.p., 1977—; with The Continental Group, Inc., N.Y.C., 1964-73; Mem. nat. adv. bd. Ga. Inst. Tech.; mem. bus. adv. council Roosevelt U. Served to lt. (j.g.) USNR, 1943-46. Mem. TAPPI, Am. Paper Inst., Newcomen Soc. N.Am., Phi Delta Theta, Tau Beta Pi, Phi Kappa Phi. Republican. Episcopalian. Club: Exmoor Country (Highland Park, Ill.). Home: 289 E Foster Pl Lake Forest IL 60045 Office: 360 N Michigan Ave Chicago IL 60601

HILLS, LEE, newspaperman; b. Granville, N.D., May 28, 1906; s. Lewis Amos and Lulu Mae (Loomis) H.; m. Leona Haas, Dec. 25, 1933 (dec.); 1 son, Ronald Lee; m. Eileen Whitman, June 4, 1948 (dec. 1961); m. Tina S. Ramos, Oct. 31, 1963. Student, Brigham Young U., 1924-25, U. Mo., 1927-29; LL.B., Oklahoma City U., 1934; Sc.D. in Bus. Adminstrn, Cleary Coll., 1958; L.H.D. (hon.), U. Utah, 1969; LL.D., Eastern Mich. U., 1969. Bar: Okla. bar 1935. News reporter News-Adv., Price, Utah, 1924-25, editor, 1926; reporter Oklahoma City Times, 1929-32; polit. writer Okla. News, 1932-35, editor, 1938-39; reporter, copyreader Cleve. Press, 1935-36, news editor, 1940-42; chief editorial writer, asso. editor Indpls. Times, 1936-37; asso. editor Memphis Press-Scimitar, 1939-40; mng. editor Miami (Fla.) Herald, 1942-51, exec. editor, 1951-66, asso. pub., 1966-69, pub., 1970-79, editorial chmn., 1979-81, editorial chmn. emeritus, 1981; exec. editor Detroit Free Press, 1951-69; leave as war corr., Europe, 1945; pub. Detroit Free Press, 1963-79, pres., 1967-73, editorial chmn., 1979-81, editorial chmn. emeritus, 1981; exec. editor Knight Newspapers, Inc., 1959-66, exec. v.p., 1966-67, pres., 1967-73, chmn. exec. com., 1969-73, chmn. operation com., 1973-74; chmn. bd., chief exec. officer Knight-Ridder Newspapers, Inc., 1973-76, chmn. bd., editorial chmn., 1976-79, editorial chmn., 1979-81, editorial chmn. emeritus, 1981. Pres. Detroit Arts Commn., 1966-79; trustee Founders Soc., Detroit Inst. Arts., Knight Found., Akron, Ohio, Ctr. for Fine Arts, Miami. Recipient Maria Moors Cabot Gold medal for distinguished contbn. inter-Am. relations Columbia, 1946; Pulitzer prize in journalism, 1956. Mem. Internat. Press Inst., Inter-Am. Press Assn. (dir., pres. 1967-68), Mich. Press Assn., Am. Soc. Newspaper Editors (pres. 1962-63), Am. Newspaper Pubs. Assn., AP Mng. Editors Assn. (past pres.), Fla. AP Assn. (past pres.), Sigma Delta Chi (past pres.). Clubs: Nat. Press, Washington Press; Renaissance, Grosse Pointe (Detroit); Miami, Bath (Miami, Fla.); Bankers. Home: 4450 Banyan Lane Miami FL 33137 Office: 1 Herald Plaza Miami Herald Miami FL 33101

HILLS, PATRICIA GORTON SCHULZE, curator; b. Baraboo, Wis., Jan. 31, 1936; d. Hartwin A. Schulze and Glennie Gorton Baker; m. Frederic W. Hills, Jan. 17, 1958 (div. Feb. 1974); children: Christina, Bradford; m. Guy Kevin Whitfield, Jan. 3, 1976; 1 son, Andrew. B.A., Stanford U., 1957; M.A., Hunter Coll., 1968; Ph.D., N.Y. U., 1973. Curatorial asst. Mus. Modern Art, N.Y.C., 1960-62; guest curator Whitney Mus. Am. Art, 1971-72, asso. curator 18th and 19th Century art, 1972-74; vis. asst. prof. art dept. Hunter Coll., 1973; adj. asso. prof. fine arts Inst. Fine Arts NYU, 1973-74; asso. prof. fine arts and performing arts York Coll., CUNY, 1974-78; asso. prof. dept. art history Boston U., 1978—; adj. asso. prof. Grad. Sch. Arts and Scis., Columbia U., 1974-75; adj. curator Whitney Mus. Am. Art, 1974—. Author: Eastman Johnson, 1972, The American Frontier: Images and Myths, 1973, The Painters' America: Rural and Urban Life, 1810-1910, 1974, Turn-of-Century America: Paintings, Graphics, Photographs, 1890-1910, 1977, Social Concern and Urban Realism: American Painting of the 1930s 1983; co-author: The Figurative Tradition and the Whitney Mus. Am. Art, 1980. Danforth Found. grad. fellow for women, 1968-72; John Simon Guggenheim Meml. Found. fellow, 1982-83; Charles Warren Ctr. for Studies in Am. History fellow, 1982-83. Mem. Coll. Art Assn., Inst. Research in History, Women's Caucus for Arts (co-chairperson Boston chpt.), Dunlap Soc. Home: 36 Harrison St Brookline MA 02146 Office: 945 Madison Ave New York NY 10021

HILLS, RODERICK M., lawyer, business executive, former government official; b. Seattle, Mar. 9, 1931; s. Kenneth Maltman and Sarah (Love) H.; m. Carla Anderson, Sept. 27, 1958; children: Laura, Roderick, Megan, Allison. A.B., Stanford U., 1952, LL.B., 1955. Bar: Calif. 1957, U.S. Supreme Ct. 1960. Law clk. to Justice Stanley F. Reed U.S. Supreme Ct., 1955-57; ptnr. Munger, Tolles, Hills & Rickershauser, Los Angeles, 1962-75; chmn. Republic Corp., Los Angeles, 1971-75; counsel to Pres. U.S., 1975; chmn. SEC, 1975-77; chmn., chief exec. officer Peabody Coal Co., St. Louis and Washington, 1977-78; ptnr. Latham, Watkins & Hills, Washington, 1978-82; chmn. Sears World Trade, Inc., Washington, 1982—; vis. prof. law Harvard U., 1969-70; lectr. law Stanford U., 1960-69; chmn. bd. Republic Corp., Century City, 1971-75; dir. Anheuser-Busch, Inc. Fed. Mogul Corp., Santa Fe Internat., Alexander & Alexander. Bd. editors, comment editor: Stanford Law Rev, 1953-55. Trustee Claremont U. Center, Com. Econ. Devel. Mem. ABA, Los Angeles County Bar Assn., State Bar Calif., Order of Coif, Phi Delta Phi. Club: Chancery (Los Angeles). Home: 3125 Chain Bridge Rd Washington DC 20016 Office: 1211 Connecticut Ave NW Suite 810 Washington DC 20036

HILLWAY, TYRUS, English educator, author; b. Mpls., Jan. 5, 1912; s. William H. and Martha (Milbrett) H.; m. Hazel Andrews, Aug. 28, 1937; children: Holly Ann, Richard Andrews. A.B., Willamette U., 1934; M.A., U. Calif., 1939; Ph.D., Yale, 1944; postgrad., U. Oreg., 1934, Harvard, 1942. Tchr. Oreg. State Sch. for Blind, Salem, 1934-38; bus. experience, Berkeley, Calif., 1938-40; dean evening div. Hillyer Coll., Hartford, Conn., 1940-44; dir. ednl. counseling and planning Bridgeport (Conn.) Program Postwar Readjustment, 1944-46; pres. Mitchell Coll., New London, Conn., 1946-51; asso. prof. edn. U. No. Colo., Greeley, 1951-54, prof. edn., 1954-66, asst. to pres., 1966-69, prof. higher edn., 1966-73, dir. acad. devel., 1969-71; Fulbright guest prof. U. Vienna, Austria, 1964-65; guest prof. U. Salzburg, Austria, 1970-71, prof. English, chair Am. studies, 1973-77; vis. prof. English U. Denver, 1977-78; co-dir. Nat. Project Improving Academic Adminstrn., 1977—; Mem. U.S. Mil. Manpower Com.; Former pres. Conn. Conf. Jr. Colls.; mem. com. standards Conn. Council Higher Edn., 1946-51; mem. com. accreditation New Eng. Jr. Coll. Council, 1948-51; mem. adv. com. Conn. Gov's. Commn. Edn., 1949-50. Author: Melville and the Whale, 1950; play Captain Ahab, 1951; Introduction to Research, 1956, rev., 1964, American Two-Year College, 1958, Education in American Society, 1961, Herman Melville, 1963, rev., 1979, Handbook of Educational Research, 1969, Evidences of Neo-Romanticism in Contemporary Western Culture, 1976; Editor: (with Luther S. Manfield) Moby Dick Centennial Essays, 1953, American Education, 1964; Contbr. to lit. anthologies, periodicals, Ency. Americana, Collier's Ency.; Authority on life and work of Herman Melville; contbg. author: A Century of Higher Education, 1962, American Studies Abroad, 1975, The Endless, Winding Way in Melville, 1981 (honored by Essays in Honour of Professor Tyrus Hillway (edited by Erwin A. Stürzl) 1977). Conn. state chmn. Am. Youth Hostels, 1947; Trustee Estes Park Center for Edn. and Research, Austro-America Inst. of Edn. Am. Philos. Soc. research grantee, 1959, 61, 64; Recipient 1st Distinguished Scholar award U. No. Colo., 1972. Mem. Soc. Advancement Edn., Modern Lang. Assn. Am., Melville Soc. (co-founder, sec. 1945-59, pres. 1960), Citizens Com. Hoover Report, Yale Library Assos., Austrian Assn. Am. Studies (chmn. 1974-75), Sigma Chi. Address: 1221 Prospect Mountain Rd Moraine Route Estes Park CO 80517

HILLYARD, IRA WILLIAM, university administrator, pharmacologist; b. Richmond, Utah, Mar. 23, 1924; s. Neal Jacobsen and Lucille (Duce) H.; m. Venice Lenore Williams, July 10, 1945 (dec.); children: Christine, Kevin, Eric; m. Norma Larsen, May 1, 1970. B.S., Idaho State U., 1949; M.S., U. Nebr., 1951; Ph.D., St. Louis U., 1957. Pharmacologist Mead Johnson Co., Evansville, Ind., 1957-59; sr. pharmacologist, sect. leader Warner-Lambert Research Inst., Morris Plains, N.J., 1959-69; asso. prof. pharmacology Idaho State U. Coll. Pharmacy, Pocatello, 1969-73, 77-79, dean, 1979—; dir. pharmacology and toxicology ICN Pharms., Irvine, Calif., 1973-77, cons., 1977-80, Pennwalt Pharm. Co., Rochester, N.Y., 1978-83. Contbr. articles to profl. jours. Served with USN, 1945, 51-53. Decorated Purple Heart. Fellow Am. Found. Pharm. Edn.; mem. Western Pharmacology Soc., Am. Assn. Colls. Pharmacy, Am. Soc. Pharmacology and Exptl. Therapeutics, N.Y. Acad. Scis., Sigma Xi, Rho Chi, Phi Delta Chi. Mormon. Club: Rotary. Home: 2750 Mt Borah Pl Pocatello ID 83201 Office: Idaho State U Box 8288 Pocatello ID 83209 *I firmly believe that we make individual contributions to the welfare and progress of mankind only if every action is based on truth. If we remain honest and open-minded in our approach, truth will always be recognized and those challenging decisions which must precede every action, will be correctly made even though each decision may not always be agreeable to us or to others. In the end, however, if truth prevails, progress will be made because we will all recognize the correctness of what is said or done.*

HILLYER, EDWARD JAMES, dancer; b. Oakland, Calif., Sept. 3, 1958; s. Floyd Donald and Mary Carina (Best) H. Student, Nat. Acad. Arts High Sch. Apprentice Les Grand Ballets Canadiens, Montreal, 1976, mem. corps de ballet, 1977, demi-soloist, 1978, soloist, 1980, prin. dancer, 1982—. Prin. lead: film Miraculous Mandarin, 1981. Scholar Ford Found., Oakland, Calif., 1970. Home: 181 Quebes Outremont PQ Canada H2V 3V8 Office: Les Grands Ballets Canadiens 4816 rue Rivard Montreal PQ Canada H2J 2N6

HILLYER, KAZUKO TATSUMURA, impressario; b. Osaka, Japan; m. Raphael Hillyer; 1 dau., Reiko. Student, Toho Acad. Music; B.A., Boston U.; M.A. in Musicology, N.Y. U. Founder, mgr. Pacific World Artists Inc., 1968—; arranged tours Los Angeles Philharmonic, Cleve. Orch., Noh Nat. Theater, Black Theatre Prague, Budapest Philharmonic; founder, mgr. Kazuko Hillyer Internat., N.Y.C., 1972—; presented 1st Internat. Festival Chamber Music, 1973; took Met. Opera on 1st tour, Asia, 1975; founder, mgr. Concert Arts Soc., 1976; initiator Beacon Theater Project, 1977; lectr. arts mgmt. Office: 250 W 57th St New York NY 10107

HILSMAN, ROGER, educator; b. Waco, Tex., Nov. 23, 1919; s. Roger and Emma (Prendergast) H.; m. Eleanor Willis Hoyt, June 22, 1946; children—Hoyt R., Amy, Ashby, Sarah. B.S., U.S. Mil. Acad., 1943; M.A., Yale, 1950, Ph.D., 1951. Commd. 2d lt. U.S. Army, 1943, advanced through grades to maj., 1951; with (Merrill's Marauders), Burma, 1944, comdg. officer, 1944-45; asst. chief Far East intelligence operations, Hdqrs. OSS, Washington, 1945-46; spl. asst. to exec. officer CIA, 1946-47; planning officer NATO affairs, Joint Am. Mil. Adv. Group, London, Eng., 1950-52; internat. politics br. Hdqrs. U.S. European Command, 1952-53; resigned, 1953; research fellow Center Internat. Studies, Princeton, 1953-54, research asst., 1954-55; research asso., lectr. Woodrow Wilson Sch.; lectr. internat. relations Columbia, 1958; research asso. Washington Center Fgn. Policy Research, lectr. internat. affairs Sch. Advanced Internat. Studies, Johns Hopkins, 1957-61; prof. govt. Columbia, 1964—; chief fgn. affairs div., legislative reference service Library Congress, 1956-58, dep. dir. for research, 1958-61; dir. bur. intelligence and research State Dept., 1961-63; asst. sec. state Far Eastern affairs, 1963-64; Lectr. Nat. War Coll., Army War Coll., Indsl. Coll. Armed Forces. Author: Strategic Intelligence and National Decisions, 1956, To Move a Nation, 1967, The Politics of Policy Making in Defense and Foreign Affairs, 1971, The Crouching Future: International Politics and U.S. Foreign Policy—A Forecast, 1975, To Govern America, 1979; Co-author: Military Policy and National Security, 1956, Alliance Policy in the Cold War, 1959, NATO and American Security, 1959, Foreign Policy in the Sixties, 1965. Rockefeller fellow, 1958. Mem. Am. Polit. Sci. Assn. (pres. D.C.). Home: Hamburg Cove Lyme CT 06371

HILSMAN, WILLIAM JOSEPH, army officer; b. St. Louis, Mar. 13, 1932; s. William E. and Mary L. (Hayes) H.; m. Emily Jean Butler, Feb. 11, 1956; children: Karen Marie, Allison Ann, Donna Jeanne, William Mark. B.S., U.S. Mil. Acad., 1954; M.S. in Elec. Engring., Northeastern U., 1962; grad., U.S. Army Command and Gen. Staff Coll., 1966, Indsl. Coll. of Armed Forces, 1972. Commd. 2d lt. U.S. Army, advanced through grades to lt. gen.; exec. officer 121st Signal Bn., 1st Inf. Div., Pacific-Vietnam, 1966-67; signal systems plans officer mgmt. info. systems officer Office of asst. Vice Chief of Staff, Washington, 1967-68; chief research team of info. systems group Mgmt. Info. Systems Directorate, Office of Asst. Vice Chief of Staff, Washington, 1968-69; comdr. 144th Signal Bn., 4th Armored Div., Europe, 1969-71; chief Tng. Support Div., U.S. Army Combat Arms Tng. Bd., U.S. Army Inf. Center, Ft. Benning, Ga.; also spl. asst. to dep. chief of staff for tng. and schs., comdr. 1st Signal Group, Fort Lewis, Wash., 1973-75; project mgr. Army Tactical Data Systems, provisional comdr., Army Communications Research and Devel. Command, Ft. Monmouth, N.J., 1975 1977; comdg. gen. U.S. Army Signal Center and Ft. Gordon, Ga., from 1977; now dir. Def. Communications Agy., Washington. Decorated Legion of Merit with two oak leaf clusters, Bronze Star with two oak leaf clusters. Mem. Assn. U.S. Army, Armed Forces Communications and Electronics Assn. Roman Catholic. Lodge: Kiwanis. Office: Def Communications Agy Dept Army Washington DC 20305

HILTNER, WILLIAM ALBERT, astronomy educator; b. Continental, Ohio, Aug. 27, 1914; s. John Nicholas and Ida Lavina (Schafer) H.; m. Ruth Moyer Kreider, Aug. 12, 1939; children—Phyllis Anne, Kathryn Jo, William Albert, Stephen Kreider. B.S., U. Toledo, 1937; M.S., U. Mich., 1938, Ph.D., 1942. Mem. faculty U. Chgo., 1943-70, prof. astronomy, 1955-70; dir. Yerkes Obs., 1963-66; acting dir. Cerro Tololo Inter-Am. Obs., 1966-67; prof. U. Mich. at Ann Arbor, 1970—, chmn. dept. astronomy, 1970-82; Bd. dirs. Assn. Univs. for Research Astronomy, 1959-71, 74—, pres. bd., 1968-71. Co-author: Photometric Atlas of Stellar Spectra, 1946; Editor: Astronomical Techniques, 1962. NRC fellow, 1942-43. Mem. Astron. Soc. Pacific, Am. Astron. Soc. (councilor 1962-65), A.A.A.S. Home: 801 Berkshire Ann Arbor MI 48104

HILTON, ALICE MARY, cons. in cybernetics and computing systems, author; b. N.Y.C., June 18, 1927; d. Frederick O. and Thea (von Weber) H.; m. Herbert Layton Hayward, Sept. 7, 1947; children—Barbara Mary Hilton-Hayward, Kathryn Anne Hilton-Hayward. B.A. with honors; M.A., D.Phil., U. Oxford, Eng.; Ph.D. in Math. and Elec. Engring, U. Calif.; postgrad., Sorbonne, Columbia. Computing systems analyst Electrodata Corp. (name now Burroughs Corp.), Pasadena, Cal., 1951-55; dir. publs. and pub. relations Underwood Corp., N.Y.C., 1955-57; cons. computing-machine applications in industry, sci. research, govt., medicine, art history A.M. Hilton & Assos., N.Y.C., 1958—; pres. Inst. Cybercultural Research, N.Y.C., 1964—; Asso. prof. dept. philosophy Queens Coll., City U. N.Y., N.Y.C., 1970—; computing systems cons., N.Y.C., 1956—; prof. Mary Mt. Manhattan Coll.; vis. scholar U. Oxford; vis. prof. U. N.C.; Pres. A.R.T.S. (Art Registration Terminals System), UNESCO; lectr. Met. Mus. Art, N.Y.C. Author: Computing Machines in Control Systems, 1961, Logic, Computing Machines and Automation, 1963, Human Beings and Their Machines, 1965, The Evolving Society, 1966, Against Pollution and Hunger, 1974, Art-in-Context: The Logic of Gothic Art, 1979; Editor: The Cybercultural Review, 1968—, The Feedback Newsletter, 1964—, The Age of Cyberculture: The Challenge of Leisure and Abundance; Contbr. numerous essays on cybernetics and social change to profl. jours. Recipient A.N. Ribero Sanches award Govt. of Portugal, 1968; Distinguished Achievement award Inst. Cybercultural Research, 1964; Guggenheim fellow. Mem. Am. Math. Soc., Assn. for Computing Machinery, IEEE, Authors League, Fedn. Am. Scientists, Am. Soc. for Cybernetics, Cybernetica, British Computer Soc., Soc. for Social Responsibility in Sci. (past pres.), Internat. Com. on Museums, Mind Assn. Office: 420 E 72d St New York NY 10021

HILTON, ANDREW CARSON, mfg. co. exec.; b. D'Lo, Miss., Nov. 20, 1928; s. A.C. and Pearl (Walters) H. B.A., U. Md., 1952; M.A., George Washington U., 1953; Ph.D., Western Res. U., 1956. Former research asso. Personnel Research Inst., Western Res. U.; cons. Psychol. Corp., N.Y.C.; dir. personnel relations Raytheon Co.; then dir. personnel Internat. Tel.& Tel. Corp.; sr. v.p. adminstrn. Colt Industries Inc, N.Y.C., 1963—. Contbr. articles to profl. jours. Corporate trustee Colt Industries Found. Served with USAF, 1946-49. Mem. Am. Psychol. Assn., N.Y. Acad. Scis. Club: University (N.Y.C.). Office: 430 Park Ave New York City NY 10022

HILTON, BARRON, hotel exec.; b. 1927; s. Conrad Hilton. Founder, pres. San Diego Chargers (Am. Football League), until 1966; v.p. Hilton Hotels Corp., 1954, pres., chief exec. officer, 1966—, chmn., 1979—, also dir.; mem. gen. adminstrv. bd. Mfrs. Hanover Trust Co., N.Y.C. Address: care Hilton Hotels Corp 9880 Wilshire Blvd Beverly Hills CA 90210 *

HILTON, ERIC MICHAEL, hotel industry executive; b. Dallas, July 1, 1933; s. Conrad N. and Mary (Barron) H.; m. Patricia Skipworth, Aug. 14, 1954; children: Eric Michael, Beverly, Linda, Joseph B. Student, U. Tex., 1950-51, Cornell Hotel Sch., 1953-54. Various exec. position Dallas Statler Hilton, 1955-59; resident mgr. Dreshler Hilton, Columbus, Ohio, 1959-60; gen. mgr. Aurora Hilton, Ill., 1960-61; resident mgr. Shamrock Hilton, Houston, 1961-66; SW sales mgr. Hilton Hotels Corp., Houston, 1966-69; SW regional mgr. Hilton Inns, Inc., Houston, 1969-72, divisional v.p., 1972; sr. v.p. internat. real estate devel. Hilton Hotels Corp., Beverly Hills, Calif.; dir. Greenspoint Bank, Houston. Pres. N. Braes Bayou Little League, 1963; exec. v.p. Houston Trade and Travel Fair, 1963; chmn. Sponsors Club, PineOak Horse Show, 1964; bd. dirs. Harris County Cancer Soc., Tex., 1964, Houston Livestock Show and Rodeo, 1964, Conrad N. Hilton Found., Beverly Hills, Calif., 1968—, Fun Football, 1963, Lifemark Corp., 1978—, Am. Contract Bridge League, 1973; pres. dist. 16 Am. Contract Bridge League, 1974; trustee Allen Acad., Bryan, Tex., 1970—, Little League Found., 1977—. Served with U.S. Army, 1953-55. Mem. Airline Passengers Assn. (nat. adv. bd. 1970—), Future Bus. Leaders Assn., Phi Beta Lambda. Office: Hilton Hotels Corp 9880 Wilshire Blvd Beverly Hills CA 90210

HILTON, GRAEMER KEENHOLTS, manufacturing company financial executive; b. Altamont, N.Y., Oct. 26, 1921; s. Stanley G. and Anita K. (Keenholts) H.; m. Joan Mather, July 3, 1948; children: Thomas J., John M., Peter M., Kathleen A. B.S. in Bus. Adminstrn, Albany Coll., 1943. Acctg./audit staff Gen. Electric, Schenectady, 1946-61, mgr. cost acctg., 1961-63; mgr. fin. and adminstrn. Standard Steel div. TMCA, Burnham, Pa., 1963-69, v.p., gen. mgr., 1969-72, pres., 1972-75; v.p., controller Allegheny Internat., Inc., Pitts., 1975-79, sr. v.p., controller, 1979-81, exec. v.p., chief fin. officer, 1981—, dir., 1981—; dir. Wilkinson Sword Group, Ltd., U.K. Titanium Metals Corp., Liquid Air Corp. Treas., v.p. Lewistown (Pa.) Hosp., 1964-74. Served with U.S. Army, 1943-46. Mem. Fin. Execs. Inst., Machinery and Allied Products Inst. Clubs: Duquesne, Pittsburgh Field, Pittsburgh Athletic Assn., The Plaza, Les Ambassadeurs. Office: Two Oliver Plaza PO Box 456 Pittsburgh PA 15230

HILTON, JAMES GORTON, pharmacologist; b. Balt., Sept. 21, 1923; s. George Edward and Ethel Alberta (Schaeffer) H.; m. Elizabeth Earline Lindsay, Sept. 21, 1946; children: James Lindsay, William Edward. B.S. in Chemistry, Va. Poly. Inst., Blacksburg, 1947; M.S. in Pharmacology, U. Tenn., 1952, Ph.D., 1954. Teaching fellow dept. pharmacology U. Tenn., Memphis, 1950-53; asst. prof. to asso. prof. pharmacology U. Miss., Oxford and Jackson, 1953-58; asso. prof. pharmacology Marquette U., Milw., 1959-61; with U. Tex., Galveston, 1961—, prof., 1963—, acting chmn. dept. pharmacology and toxicology, 1979-82; chief div. pharmacology Shriners Burn Inst., Galveston, 1976—. Contbr. in field. Served with USNR, 1941-46. Fellow Am. Heart Assn.; mem. Am. Physiol. Soc., Am. Soc. Pharmacology and Exptl. Therapeutics, Internat. Soc. Burn Injuries, Peruvian Pharmacology Soc., Am. Burn Assn. Episcopalian. Club: Masons. Home: 2626 Gerol Ct Galveston TX 77551 Office: 610 Texas Ave Galveston TX 77550

HILTON, ORDWAY, document examiner; b. Chgo., July 14, 1913; s. Charles Ordway and Hazel Beatrice (Horner) H.; m. Lillie Lee Atkinson, Mar. 27, 1939. B.S. with honors, Northwestern U., 1935, M.A., 1937. Diplomate: Am. Bd. Forensic Document Examiners. Research statistician Armour & Co., Chgo., 1937-38; statis. analyst A.C. Neilsen, Chgo., 1938; document examiner Chgo. Police Crime Lab., Chgo., 1938-41; asso. Elbridge W. Stein (examiner questioned documents), N.Y.C., 1946-50; pvt. practice as questioned document examiner, N.Y.C., 1951-79, Landrum, S.C., 1979—; lectr. short course for pros. attys. Northwestern U. Sch. Law, 1949-79; lectr. questioned documents Georgetown U., Washington, summers 1973, 74; convenor, v.p. Internat. Meeting in Questioned Documents, London, 1963, convenor, presiding officer, Copenhagen, Denmark, 1966; chmn. questioned document sect. 8th Internat. Meeting in Forensic Scis., 1978. Author: Scientific Examination of Questioned Documents, 1956, rev. edit., 1982; police sci. editor: Jour. Criminal Law and Criminology, 1941-44, Jour. Criminal Law, Criminology and Police Sci, 1947-72; asso. editor for police sci.: Jour. Police Sci. and Adminstrn, 1973-78; questioned document editor: Forensic Sci. Internat, 1978—; contbr. articles to profl. publs. Vestryman Ch. of Holy Cross, Tryon, N.C., 1981-83. Served with USNR, 1935-36, 41-46. Recipient award of merit Am. Acad. Forensic Scis., 1973; H. Ward Smith Meml. award, 1978. Fellow Am. Acad. Forensic Scis. (pres. 1959, Questioned Document Sect. award 1979); mem. Am. Soc. Questioned Document Examiners (pres. 1960-62). Episcopalian (trustee Trinity Ch. Assn. N.Y.C. 1956-73). Home and Office: PO Box 592 Landrum SC 29356

HILTON, PETER JOHN, mathematician, educator; b. London, Eng., Apr. 7, 1923; s. Mortimer and Elizabeth (Freedman) H.; m. Margaret Mostyn, Sept. 14, 1949; children—Nicholas, Timothy. M.A., Oxford (Eng.) U., 1948; D.Phil., 1950; Ph.D., Cambridge (Eng.) U., 1952; D.Hum. (hon.), No. Mich. U., 1977, D.Sci., Meml. U. Nfld., 1983. Lectr. Manchester (Eng.) U., 1948-52, sr. lectr., 1956-58; lectr. Cambridge U., 1952-55; Mason prof. pure math. Birmingham (Eng.) U., 1958-62; prof. math. Cornell U., 1962-71, U. Wash., 1971-73; Beaumont prof. Case Western Res. U., 1972-82; Disting. prof. SUNY, 1983—; guest prof. Eidgenössische Technische Hochschule, Zurich, Switzerland, 1966-67, 81-82, Courant Inst. Math. Scis., N.Y. U., 1967-68, Ohio State U., 1977; vis. fellow Battelle Seattle Research Center, 1970-71, fellow, 1971—; co-chmn. Cambridge Conf. on Sch. Math., 1965; chmn. com. applied math. tng. NRC, 1977—; sec. Internat. Commn. Math. Instruction, 1979-82. Author: Homotopy Theory, 1953, (with S. Wylie) Homology Theory, 1960, Homotopy Theory and Duality, 1966, (with H.B. Griffiths) Classical Mathematics, 1970, General Cohomology Theory and K. Theory, 1971, (with U. Stammbach) Course in Homological Algebra, 1971, Le Langage des Categories, 1973, (with Y.C. Wu) Course in Modern Algebra, 1974, (with G. Mislin and J. Roitberg) Localization of Nilpotent Groups and Spaces, 1975, (with J. Pedersen) Fear No More, 1982; Editor: Ergebnisse der Mathematik, 1964—, Ill. Jour. Math, 1962-68, Jour. Pure and Applied Algebra, 1970-75, Topics in Modern Topology, 1968; Contbr. articles to profl. jours. Recipient Silver medal U. Helsinki, Finland, 1975. Mem. Am. Math. Soc., Math. Assn. Am. (1st v.p. 1978—), Math Soc. Belgium (hon.), Am., London Math. Soc., Cambridge Philos. Soc., Brazilian Acad. Scis. (hon.). Home: 4172 42d Ave NE Seattle WA 98105 Office: Battelle Seattle Research Center 4000 NE 41st St Seattle WA 98105

HILTON, ROBERT PARKER, naval officer; b. Atlanta, Mar. 17, 1927; s. William Linwood and Elizabeth Shumate (Parker) H.; m. Joan Maxine Mader, Sept. 3, 1955; children: Robert Parker, Wendy Muriel. B.A., U. Miss., 1948; M.A. in Russian Affairs, Georgetown U., 1964; postgrad., Sino-Soviet Inst. George Washington U., 1964-68. Commd. ensign U.S. Navy, 1948, advanced through grades to rear adm., 1972; service in, Korea, Japan, Vietnam, Italy, Belgium; asst. chief staff logistics CINCSOUTH, Naples, Italy, 1972-74; dep. dir. force devel. and strategic plans Office Joint Chiefs Staff, 1974-76; dir. East Asia and Pacific region Office Sec. Def., Washington, 1976-77; dir. Strategy plans and policy div. OPNAV (OP60), 1977-78; asst. dep. CNO, Plans and Policy, 1979; dep. asst. chief staff Plans and Policy SHAPE, 1979—. Decorated D.S.M., D.D.S.M., Legion of Merit, Bronze Star, Joint Service Commendation medal. Mem. U.S. Naval Inst., Nat. Trust Historic Preservation, Pi Sigma Alpha, Pi Kappa Phi, Phi Delta Theta. Episcopalian. Clubs: Masons, Army Navy Country. Home: 3628 Orlando Pl Alexandria VA 22305 Office: Vice Director for Operations (J-3) OJCS Pentagon Washington DC 20301 *Many times as a commanding officer and later as a flag officer, I have had the opportunity, and even been encouraged, to violate a rule or regulation to my own advantage. My answer, and my advice to a junior officer, has always been to enforce the law, not break it.*

HILTON, RONALD, educator; b. Torquay, Eng., July 31, 1911; came to U.S., 1937, naturalized, 1946; s. Robert and Elizabeth Alice (Taylor) H.; m. Mary Bowie, May 1, 1939; 1 dau., Mary Alice Taylor. B.A., Oxford U., Eng., 1933, M.A., 1936; student, Sorbonne, Paris, 1933-34, U. Madrid, 1934-35, U. of Perugia, Italy, 1935-36, U. Calif., 1937-39. Dir. Comité Hispano Ingles Library, Madrid, 1936; asst. prof. modern langs. U. of B.C., 1939-41; asso. prof. Romanic langs. Stanford, 1942-49, prof., 1949—; dir. Inst. Hispanic Am. and Luso-Brazilian studies; hon. prof. U. de San Marcos, Lima, Peru; vis. prof. U. Brazil, 1949; cultural dir. U. of Air, KGEI, San Francisco.; Founder exec. dir. Calif. Inst. Internat. Studies. Author: Campoamor, Spain and the World, 1940, Handbook of Hispanic Source Materials in the U.S, 1942, 2d edit., 1956, Four Studies in Franco-Spanish Relations, 1943, La América Latina de Ayer y de Hoy, 1970, The Scientific Institutions of Latin America, 1970, The Latin Americans, Their Heritage and Their Destiny, 1973; Asso. editor for: Who's Who America; editor: The Life of Joaquim Nabuco, 1950, The Movement Toward Latin American Unity, 1969, World Affairs Report, 1970—. Decorated officer Cruzeiro do Sul, Brazil). Mem. Am. Assn. Tchrs. Spanish, Hispanic Soc. of Am., Am. Acad. Franciscan History. Home: 766 Santa Ynez St Stanford CA 94305

HILTS, JOHN WARREN, industrial relations executive; b. Los Angeles, May 14, 1923; s. Joseph Earle and Lillian Mary (Gibson) H.; m. Phyllis Ruth Overton, June 27, 1945; children: Jill Robyn, Judith, Nancy Suzanne Sunsire. B.S., U. So. Calif., 1949; M.S., Calif. State U.-Los Angeles, 1972. Single and multi-engine comml. pilot. Dist. mgr. Pacific Fin. Corp., Los Angeles, 1949-60; ptnr. Overton Labs., Hollywood, Calif., 1960-62; dist. mgr. Pacific Fin. Loans, Los Angeles, 1962-70; v.p. Transam Fin. Corp., Los Angeles, 1970—. Contbr. articles to profl. jours. Active Jr. Achievement Program, United Fund; bd. dirs. Glendale chpt. Am. Field Service. Served with USNR, 1943-47. Mem. Calif. Loan and Fin. Assn. (dir., chmn. pub. affairs), Wash. Conusmer Fin. Assn. (dir.). Clubs: Am. Legion, Oakmont Country (Glendale, Calif.). Home: 2981 Country Club Dr Glendale CA 91208 Office: 1150 Olive St Los Angeles CA 90015

HILTS, MARGARETE LOUISE, modern language educator; b. Otsego, Mich., Dec. 4, 1912; d. Karl Frederick and Emma (Stiefel) Ambs; m. David Glenn Hilts, Nov. 22, 1956. B.A., Andrews U., 1935; postgrad., U. Mexico, 1940, 45, Sorbonne, Paris, France, 1950; M.A., U. So. Calif., 1941; Ph.D., Western Res. U., 1956. Tchr. English and French Fletcher (N.C.) Acad., 1935-38; tchr. German and Spanish So. Calif. Jr. Coll., Arlington, 1938-44; chmn. modern lang. dept. La Sierra Coll., Riverside, Calif., 1944-67; prof. modern langs. Loma Linda U., Riverside, Calif., 1967—, chmn. dept., 1967-78; Mem. liaison com. for modern langs., Calif., 1969-70. Editor: (jour. Adventist lang. tchrs.) Alta Vox, 1971-75. Fulbright-Hayes grantee study in France, 1964. Mem. Modern Lang. Assn., Am. Assn. Tchrs. French, Am. Council Teaching Fgn. Langs. Seventh-Day Adventist (mem. bd. higher edn. 1970-76). Home: 11636 Richmond St Riverside CA 92505

HILTY, WILLIAM JACOB, association executive; b. Bucyrus, Ohio, Dec. 1, 1921; s. Harold Eugene and Gladys Marie (Heinien) H.; m. Davelyn Lawrence, July 15, 1942; children: Harold Lawrence, Amanda Sue, Melissa Kay, Laura Ann. B.B.A., Fenn. Coll., 1948. Advt. mgr. Flexible Bus. Co., Loudonville, Ohio, 1948-51; account exec. Fuller & Smith & Ross, Cleve., 1951-55; dir. communications Am. Soc. Metals, Metals Park, Ohio, 1955-59, IEEE, N.Y.C., 1969-71; mng. dir. expositions and publs. Soc. Mfg. Engrs., Dearborn, Mich., 1971-81, exec. v.p., gen. mgr., 1981—; dir. Mfg. Engring. Edn. Found. Served to maj. USAF, 1941-45; ETO. Mem. Nat. Assn. Exposition Mgrs. (pres. 1970). Home: 2228 W Settlers Way The Woodlands Houston TX 77380 Office: Society of Manufacturing Engineers PO Box 930 Dearborn MI 48121

HILTZ, LEROY COLSON, union official; b. Halifax, N.S., Can., Mar. 31, 1943; s. Colson Norman and Ruby Irene (Evans) H.; m. Edna Irene Getson, Aug. 17, 1962; children: Sharon Irene, Barbara Anne, Ramona Lynn. Clk. Dept. Fisheries, Halifax, 1959-61, Dept. Vets. Affairs, 1961-64; letter carrier Post Office Dept., Halifax, 1964-70, postal clk., Charlottestown, P.E.I., 1970-76; nat. sec., treas. Can. Union Postal Workers, Ottawa, Ont., 1976—; sec., treas. P.E.I. Fedn. of Labour, Charlottestown, 1974. Scholar Dept. Labour Can., 1973. Democrat. Home: 2152 Beaconwood Dr Gloucester ON Canada K1J 8M4 Office: Can Union Postal Workers 280 Metcalfe St Ottawa ON Canada K2P 1R7

HIMEL, CHESTER MORA, entomologist, educator; b. Des Plaines, Ill., Mar. 10, 1916; s. Charles Maurice and Mary Eleanor (Mora) H.; m. Ann Walter, June 21, 1943; children: Barbara Holly Himel Pietrowski, Shelley Jeanne Himel Scharnberg. B.S. in Chemistry, U. Chgo., 1938; Ph.D. in Organic Chemistry, U. Ill., 1942. Research chemist E.I. duPont de Nemours & Co., Wilmington, Del., 1942-43, Allied Chem. Co., N.Y.C., 1943-44; research group leader Phillips Petroleum Co., Bartlesville, Okla., 1944-49; sr. organic chemist, dir. organic research div. Stanford Research Inst., 1949-65; research prof. entomology U. Ga., Athens, 1965—; chmn. bd. Environ. Chem. Co., 1979—; indsl. cons. Intra-Sci. Contbr. articles to sci. jours., chpt. in book. Research Found. fellow, 1968—; grantee NIH, Office Naval Research, Dept. Agr., EPA, Army Med. Research and Devel. Command. Mem. Entomol. Soc. Am., Am. Chem. Soc., AAAS, Ga. Entomol. Soc., Sigma Xi, Gamma Sigma Delta. Episcopalian. Holder 43 U.S. patents. Home: 165 Xavier Dr Athens GA 30606 Office: Dept of Entomology University of Georgia Athens GA 30602

HIMELICK, ALAN EDWARD, advertising agency executive; b. Lakewood, Ohio, May 27, 1929; s. Francis Herbert and Harriet Grace (Woodward) H. B.S. in Journalism, Ohio U., 1951, M.A., 1951. Advt. mgr. Tectum Corp:, Newark, Ohio, 1954-56; account exec. Griswold-Eshelman Co., Cleve., 1956-57; copywriter J.M. Mathes Inc., N.Y.C., 1957-63; copywriter-creative supr. Young & Rubicam, Inc., N.Y.C., 1963-70, sr. v.p., creative dir., 1970—. Trustee, bd. mgrs. New Milford Hosp., 1982—; vice chmn. Children's Ctr., New Milford, Conn., 1982—; v.p. Merryall Community Ctr., New Milford, 1983—. Served with USN, 1951-53. Mem. Sigma Delta Chi, Delta Tau Delta. Republican. Espicopalian. Office: Young & Rubicam 285 Madison Ave New York NY 10017

HIMELSTEIN, PHILIP NATHAN, psychology educator; b. N.Y.C., Sept. 25, 1923; s. Isidore and Martha (Feinberg) H.; m. Peggy Donn, June 1, 1952; children: Steven Mark, Carol Sue, Roger Alan. A.B., N.Y. U., 1949, A.M., 1950; Ph.D., U. Tex., 1955. Diplomate: Am. Bd. Profl. Psychology. Clin. psychologist Salem (Va.) VA Hosp., 1955-56; research psychologist USAF, 1956-58; faculty U. Ark., Fayetteville, 1958-63; asso. prof. N.Mex. State U., Las Cruces, 1963-65; prof. psychology U. Tex., El Paso, 1965—, chmn. dept., 1966-71; clin. psychologist El Paso Psychiat. Clinic, 1971-78; clin. asso. prof. psychiatry Tex. Tech. U. Sch. Medicine, 1978-80; adj. prof. Sch. Psychology, Fla. Inst. Tech., Melbourne, 1977—. Co-editor: Readings on the Exceptional Child, 1962, 2d edit., 1972, Handbook of Gestalt Therapy, 1976. Served with USAAF, World War II. Fellow Am. Psychol. Assn., Soc. Personality Assessment; mem. El Paso Psychol. Assn. (pres. 1971-72), Am. Soc. Clin. Hypnosis, Soc. Exptl. and Clin. Hypnosis, Sigma Xi, Phi Kappa Phi. Home: 331 Rainbow Circle El Paso TX 79912

HIMES, CHESTER BOMAR, author; b. Jefferson City, Mo., July 29, 1909; s. Joseph Sandy and Estelle (Bomar) H.; m. Lesley Packard. Student, Ohio State U., 1926-27. (Rosenwald fellow creative writing 1944-45); Author: If He Hollers Let Him Go, 1945, Lonely Crusade, 1947, Cast The First Stone, 1952, The Third Generation,, The Primitive, 1956, Pinktoes, 1965, Cotton Comes to Harlem, 1968, The Heat's On, 1968, Run Man Run, 1968, Blind Man With a Pistol, 1969, French edit., 1982, Hot Day, Hot Night, Pinktoes, 1961, A Rage in Harlem, All Shot Up, 1960, The Real Cool Killers, 1969, The Crazy Kill, Quality of Hurt: The Autobiography of Chester Himes (1st vol.), 1972, 2d vol, My Life of Absurdity, U.S.A, 1976, Black on Black-Baby Sister: A Black Greek Tragedy and Selected Writings, 1973, A Case of Rape, U.S.A, 1980, also numerous articles. Address: care Roslyn Targ 250 W 57th St New York NY 10019

HIMES, NORMAN STEPHEN, banker, data processing executive; b. Pitts., June 5, 1943; s. Norman and Terry Griffith (Powell) H.; m. Patti M. Miller, Aug. 27, 1966; children: N. Stephen, Pamela J. B.A., U. Pitts., 1965, M.B.A., 1971; postgrad. Stonier Grad. Sch. Banking, Rutgers U., 1978. Mktg. rep. IBM Corp., Pitts., 1965-69; regional mgr. University Computing Co., Pitts., 1969-71; various positions, v.p. Equibank N.A., Pitts., 1971-79; sr. v.p. ACS Inc. (Mercantile Tex. Corp.), Dallas, 1979-80; exec. v.p. Flagship Banks Inc., Tampa, Fla., 1980—; dir. Flagship Central Acctg. Inc., Haines City, Fla., Flagship Central Bookeeping Inc., Stanford, Fla.; pres., dir. Flagship Data Systems Corp., Tampa, 1982—. Bd. dirs. CVST Swim Team, Tampa; mem. Cable TV Commn., Upper St. Clair, Pa., 1978. Mem. Tampa Bay Area Tech. Research and Devel. Exchange, Tampa C. of C. (com. of 100). Republican. Presbyterian. Clubs: Avila Golf and Country, Carrollwood Golf and Tennis. Home: 16403 Brieva Ct Tampa FL 33612 Office: Flagship Banks Inc 5404 Hoover Blvd Tampa FL 33614

HIMMELBERG, CHARLES JOHN, III, mathematics educator, researcher; b. North Kansas City, Mo., Nov. 12, 1931; s. Charles John and Magdalene Caroline (Batliner) H.; m. Mary Patricia Hennessy, Jan. 27, 1962; children: Charles, Ann, Mary, Joseph, Patrick. B.S., Rockhurst Coll., 1952; M.S., U. Notre Dame, 1955, Ph.D., 1957. Assoc. analyst Midwest Research Inst., Kansas City, Mo., 1957-59; asst. prof. math. U. Kans.-Lawrence, 1959-65, assoc. prof., 1965-68, prof., 1968—, chmn. dept. math., 1978—. Mem. editorial bd.: Rocky Mountain Jour. Math; contbr. articles to profl. jours. Mem. Am. Math. Soc., Math. Assn. Am. Roman Catholic. Office: Dept Math U Kans Lawrence KS 66045

HIMMELBLAU, DAVID MAUTNER, chemical engineer; b. Chgo., Aug. 29, 1923; s. David and Roda (Mautner) H.; m. Betty H. Hartman, Sept. 1, 1948; children—Andrew, Margaret Ann. B.S., MIT, 1947; M.B.A., Northwestern U., 1950; Ph.D., U. Wash., 1957. Cost engr. Internat. Harvester Co., Chgo., 1946-47; cost analyst Simpson Logging Co., Seattle, 1952-53; mgr. Excel Battery Co., Seattle, 1953-54; teaching asst., instr. U. Wash., Seattle, 1955-57; successively asst. prof., asso. prof., prof. chem. engring. U. Tex., Austin, 1957—, chmn. dept., 1973-77; pres. RAMAD Corp., CACHE Corp. of Mass., Univ. Fed. Credit Union, 1964-68. Author: Basic Principles and Calculations in Chemical Engineering, 1962, 67, 74, 82, Process Analysis and Simulation, 1968, Process Analysis by Statistical Methods, 1970, Applied Nonlinear Programming, 1974; contbr. numerous articles in field to profl. jours. Served with U.S. Army, 1943-46, 51-52. NSF grantee, 1957-81; NATO Sci. Com. grantee, 1969. Mem. Am. Inst. Chem. Engrs. (dir. 1973-76), Am. Chem. Soc., Am. Math. Soc., Ops. Research Soc. Am., Soc. Indsl. and Applied Mathematics, Sigma Xi, Delta Mu Delta. Club: Headliners (Austin). Home: 4609 Ridge Oak Dr Austin TX 78731 Office: Univ Texas Coll Engring Austin TX 78712

HIMMELFARB, GERTRUDE (MRS. IRVING KRISTOL), author, educator; b. N.Y.C., Aug. 8, 1922; d. Max and Bertha (Lerner) H.; m. Irving Kristol, Jan. 18, 1942; children—William, Elizabeth. B.A., Bklyn. Coll., 1942; M.A., U. Chgo., 1944, Ph.D., 1950; L.H.D., R.I. Coll., 1976; Litt. D., Smith Coll., 1977, Lafayette Coll., 1978, Jewish Theol. Sem., 1978. Distinguished prof. history Grad. Sch., City U. N.Y., 1965—. Author: Lord Acton: A Study in Conscience and Politics, 1952, Darwin and the Darwinian Revolution, 1959, Victorian Minds, 1968, On Liberty and Liberalism—The Case of John Stuart Mill, 1975; editorial bd.: Am. Scholar, This World,, Albion. Trustee Nat. Humanities Center; bd. Internat. Council Future of Univ.; mem. council Nat. Endowment Humanities. Recipient Rockefeller Found. award, 1962-63, 63-64, 80-81; Guggenheim fellow, 1955-56, 57-58; sr. fellow Nat. Endowment for Humanities, 1968-69; Am. Council Learned Socs. fellow, 1972-73; Phi Beta Kappa vis. scholar, 1972-73; Woodrow Wilson Center fellow, 1976-77. Fellow Royal Hist. Soc., Am. Acad. Arts and Scis., Soc. Am. Historians (dir.); mem. Am. Hist. Assn., Conf. on Brit. Studies. Office: City U NY 33 W 42d St New York NY 10036

HIMMELFARB, JOHN DAVID, artist; b. Chgo., June 3, 1946; s. Samuel and Eleanor (Gorecki) H.; m. Mary Louise Day. A.B., Harvard U., 1964; M.A., Grad. Sch. Edn., 1970. One-man shows, Ill. Arts Council, Chgo., 1974, Graphics I&II, Boston, Ill. Center, Chgo., 1975, U. Nebr., Omaha, 1976, Dorothy Rosenthal Gallery, Chgo., Ill. State Mus., Springfield, 1978, Albrecht Mus. Art, St. Joseph, Mo., Ball State U., Sheldon Meml. Art Gallery, Ill. Wesleyan U., 1979, Terry Dintenfass Inc., N.Y.C., 1979, 83, Gallery 72, Omaha, 1979, Fountain Gallery, Portland, Oreg., 1980, Hull Gallery, Washington, Barbara Ballein Gallery, Chgo., 1982, group shows include, Minn. Mus. Art, Ill. State Mus., Bklyn. Mus., Okla. Art Center, Art Inst. Chgo., El Paso Art Mus., Nat. Mus. Am. Art; represented in permanent collections, Art Inst. Chgo., Nat. Collection Fine Art, Fogg Mus. Art, Cleve. Mus. Art, Mpls. Inst. Art, Portland Mus. Art, Ill. State Mus., Bklyn. Mus., Balt. Mus. Art, Des Moines Art Center, univs. Wis., Minn., Oreg., Western Ill., Iowa, others. Home: 908 W 19th St Chicago IL 60608

HIMMELFARB, MILTON, editor, educator; b. Bklyn., Oct. 21, 1918; s. Max and Bertha (Lerner) H.; m. Judith Siskind, Nov. 26, 1950; children: Martha, Edward, Miriam, Anne, Sarah, Naomi, Dan. B.A., CCNY, 1938, M.S., 1939; B.Hebrew Lit., Jewish Theol. Sem. Coll., 1939; diplôme, U. Paris, 1939; postgrad., Columbia U., 1942-47. Dir. information and research Am. Jewish Com., N.Y.C., 1955—; editor Am. Jewish Year Book, N.Y.C., 1959—; contbg. editor Commentary mag., N.Y.C., 1960—; Vis. prof. Jewish Theol. Sem., N.Y.C., 1967-68, 71-72; vis. lectr. Yale, 1971; vis. prof. Reconstructionist Rabbinical Coll., Phila., 1972-73. Author: The Jews of Modernity, 1973. Office: 165 E 56th St New York City NY 10022

HIMMS-HAGEN, JEAN MARGARET, biochemist; b. Oxford, Eng., Dec. 18, 1933; d. Frederick Hubert and Margaret Mary (Deadman) Himms; m. Paul Hagen, Sept. 29, 1956; children: Anna, Nina. B.Sc., U. London, 1955; Ph.D., Oxford U., 1958. Postdoctoral fellow Harvard U., 1958-59; asst. prof. biochemistry U. Man., 1959-64; asso. prof. biochemistry Queen's U., 1964-67, U. Ottawa, 1967-71, prof., 1971—, acting chmn. dept., 1975-77, chmn. dept., 1977-82. Contbr. articles to sci. jours.; reviews to Annual Reviews Physiology. Recipient research grants Med. Research Council, 1960—, career award, 1968-77, Bond award Am. Oil Chemists Soc., 1972. Fellow Royal Soc. Can.; mem. Canadian Biochem. Soc. (Ayerst award 1973), Am. Soc. Pharmacology and Exptl. Therapeutics, Am. Inst. Nutrition, Endocrine Soc., Biochem. Soc. U.K., Canadian Physiol. Soc. Home: 233 Tudor Pl Ottawa ON Canada K1L 7Y1 Office: Dept Biochemistry University Ottawa 451 Smyth Rd Ottawa ON Canada K1H 8M5

HINCHLIFFE, STEPHEN FREEMAN, JR., mfg. co. exec.; b. Los Angeles, July 18, 1933; s. Stephen Freeman and Katherine Morris (Gruettner) H.; m. Ann Louise Hoffmann, June 7, 1956; children—Lisa, Stephen, John. B.A., Occidental Coll., 1955; M.B.A. with distinction, Harvard, 1957. Asso. McKinsey & Co., Inc, Los Angeles, 1960-64; chief exec. officer The Leisure Group, Inc, Los Angeles, 1964—. Bd. dirs. Met. YMCA, Los Angeles, Ind. Colls. So. Calif.; trustee Occidental Coll. Served to lt. AUS, 1957-60. Mem. Mchts. and Mfrs. Assn. Los Angeles (dir.). Home: 3825 Paseo Del Campo Palos Verdes Estates CA 90274 Office: 445 S Figueroa St Los Angeles CA 90017

HINCHMAN, ROGER WALWORTH, minerals and chemical company executive; b. San Francisco, Mar. 10, 1911; s. William Brown and Metha Matilda (Peterson) H.; m. Jean Markham, Aug. 13, 1956; children: David, Marina, Barbara Joan, Jennifer. B.S. in Mech. Engring, U. Calif.-Berkeley, 1935. With sales dept. E.I. DuPont de Nemours & Co., Inc., San Francisco, 1935-45; with U.S. Borax & Chem. Corp., N.Y.C., 1945—, gen. sales mgr., 1960-75, asst. to exec. v.p., 1975—. Bd. dirs., chmn. bd. Porcelain Enamel Inst., 1970—, pres., 1968-69. Home: 5805 Berkeley Rd Goleta CA 93117 Office: 3075 Wilshire Blvd Los Angeles CA 90010

HINCKLEY, CHARLES CLARENCE, insurance company executive; b. Wausau, Wis., Feb. 11, 1933; s. Clarence Charles and Ada Marie (Kronenwetter) H.; m. Ellen Ann Conaghan, July 29, 1961; children: Charles III, Molly, Andrew, Alison. B.S., Marquette U., 1955, J.D., 1958; LL.M., Wayne State U., 1973. Bar: Wis. 1958, Ohio 1974. With Northwestern Mut. Life Ins. Co., Milw., 1958-61, Home Life Ins. Co., N.Y., 1964-73, Union Central Life Ins. Co., Cin., 1961-64, 73—, assoc. gen. counsel, v.p., gen. counsel, sr. v.p., exec. v.p., 1973-83, pres., 1983—. Contbr. articles to profl. jours. Div. chmn. YMCA Capital Campaign, Cin., 1981; pres. bd. Cath. Social Services, S.W. Ohio; trustee Summit Country Day Sch., 1981—, Community Chest and Council, Cin., 1983—. Mem. Assn. Life Ins. Counsel, ABA, Assn. Life Underwriters, Nat. Assn. Life Underwriters, Ohio Assn. Life Underwriters., Million Dollar Round Table (life). Clubs: Cin. Country; Queen City Commonwealth (Cin.). Home: 3160 Victoria Ave Cincinnati OH 45208 Office: Union Central Life Insurance Co PO Box 179 Cincinnati OH 45201

HINCKLEY, G(EORGE) F(OX) STEEDMAN, airline exec.; b. Mt. Kisco, N.Y., Nov. 3, 1931; s. Albert Pope and Katherine (Steedman) H.; m. Ingrid Annette Mjornell, Aug. 12, 1967; children—G. F. Steedman, Annalisa M., Katherine S. P. B.A., Princeton U., 1953; postgrad., Program for Mgmt. Devel., Harvard U. Bus. Sch., 1960. Project coordinator missile div. Chrysler Corp., Detroit, 1957-58; with Overseas Nat. Airways, 1958-63, 65—, exec. v.p., N.Y.C., 1965-66, pres., chmn. bd., 1966-77, hon. chmn., 1977—; v.p. Saturn Airways, San Antonio, 1964; pres. Delta Queen Steamboat Co. subs. Overseas Nat. Airways, 1973-76, chmn., 1969-76; pres., chmn. United Air Carriers, Inc., 1978—; chmn. Overseas Nat. Airways, Inc., 1979—; dir. Cannon Shoe Corp.; chmn. 1Flight Safety Found., 1976-77; farmer Va. Served with USAF, 1953-57. Episcopalian. Home: 105 Barrett Rd Lawrence NY 11559 Office: Overseas Nat Airways Inc Kennedy Internat Airport Jamaica NY 11430

HIND, HARRY WILLIAM, pharmaceutical company executive; b. Berkeley, Calif., June 2, 1915; s. Harry Winnam and B.J. (O'Connor) H.; m. Diana Vernon Miesse, Dec. 12, 1940; children—Leslie Vernon Hind Daniels, Gregory William. B.S., U. Calif., Berkeley, 1939; LL.D., U. Calif.-Berkeley, Berkeley, 1968; D.Sc., Phila. Coll. Pharmacy, 1982. Founder Barnes-Hind Pharms., Inc., Sunnyvale, Calif., 1939—, now chmn. bd. dirs. Contbr. articles to profl. jours. Mem. chancellor's assocs. U. Calif. Recipient Ebert award for pharm. research, 1948; Eye Research Found. award, 1958; Helmholtz Ophthalmology award for research, 1968; Carbert award for sight conservation, 1973; Alumnus of Yr. award U. Calif., 1965. Fellow AAAS; Mem. Am. Pharm. Assn. (past pres. No. Calif. br.), Am. Chem. Soc., Calif. Pharm. Assn., N.Y. Acad. Scis., Sigma Xi, Rho Chi, Phi Delta Chi. Club: Los Altos

Country. Designer ph meter. Home: 1448 Club View Ter Los Altos CA 94022 Office: 895 Kifer Rd Sunnyvale CA 94086

HIND, JOSEPH EDWARD, JR., educator; b. Chgo., Apr. 2, 1923; s. Joseph Edward and Dorothy Elsie (Burmester) H.; m. Ruth Anita Lueders, Sept. 12, 1947; children—David, Thomas, Susan. B.S. in Elec. Engring, Ill. Inst. Tech., 1944; Ph.D. in Psychology, U. Chgo., 1952. Asst. mfg. engr. Western Electric Co., Chgo., 1944-45; radar engr. Naval Research Lab., Washington, 1945; research asst. in otolaryngology U. Chgo., 1947-53; research asso. Central Inst. for Deaf, St. Louis, 1953-54; mem. faculty U. Wis. Med. Sch., Madison, 1954—, prof. neurophysiology, 1964—, chmn. dept. neurophysiology, 1973—; Cons., communicative scis. study sect. NIH, 1962-66, 1969-73. Contbr. articles to profl. jours. Served with USNR, 1945. Fellow Acoustical Soc. Am.; mem. Am. Physiol. Soc., A.A.A.S., Soc. for Neuroscience, Internat. Brain Research Orgn., Sigma Xi, Tau Beta Pi, Eta Kappa Nu. Lutheran. Research in auditory neurophysiology, emphasizing electrophysiol. studies; application of digital computers to biomed. research. Home: 5410 S Hill Dr Madison WI 53705

HINDEN, STANLEY JAY, newspaper editor; b. N.Y.C., Jan. 27, 1927; s. Edward I. and Rose (Kroshinsky) H.; m. Sara Leopold, May 24, 1953; children: Alan, Lawrence, Pamela. B.A., Syracuse U., 1950. Successively reporter, polit. editor, editor editorial pages, nat. corr. Washington Newsday, Garden City, N.Y., 1952-71; successively exec. editor, editor Nat. Jour., Washington, 1971-73; editorial page features editor, editor Dist., Md. and Va. weekly sects. Washington Post, 1973—, also dep. Met. editor. Contbr.: polit. column. Inside Politics, Newsday, 1955-65. Served with AUS, 1945-46. Home: 10 Kirkwall Ct Potomac MD 20854 Office: 1150 15th St NW Washington DC 20005

HINDERAKER, IVAN, political science educator; b. Hendricks, Minn., Apr. 29, 1916; s. Theodore and Clara (Hanson) H.; m. Evelyn Birkholz, June 7, 1941; 1 son, Mark. B.A., St. Olaf Coll., 1938; M.A., U. Minn., 1942, Ph.D., 1949. Research asst. Minn. League Municipalities, 1939-40; asso. budget examiner U.S. Bur. Budget, 1942-43; mem. faculty U. Calif. at Los Angeles, 1948—, prof. polit. sci., 1956—, chmn. dept., 1960-62; vice chancellor acad. affairs U. Calif. at Irvine, 1962-64; chancellor U. Calif. at Riverside, 1964-79, chancellor emeritus, 1979—; asso. dir. Citizenship Clearing House, Law Center, N.Y. U., 1956-57; asst. to sec. Dept. Interior, 1959-60. Author: Party Politics, 1956. Mem. Minn. Ho. of Reps. from Lincoln County, 1941-43, Calif. Transp. Commn., 1978—; chmn. Calif. Transp. Commn., 1982—. Served to 1st lt., pilot USAAF, 1943-46. Mem. Am. Polit. Sci. Assn., Western Polit. Sci. Assn. (pres. 1962-63). Home: 943 Goldenrod Ave Corona Del Mar CA 92625 Office: U Calif: Riverside CA 92502

HINDERER, WALTER HERMANN, German language educator; b. Ulm, Swabia, Germany, Sept. 3, 1934; came to U.S., 1966; s. Ludwig H. and Anna K. (Dangel) H.; m. Dietlinde M. Reim, Sept. 25, 1966. Abitur, Kepler Gymnasium, Ulm, 1954; Ph.D., U. Munich, 1960. Dir. acad. div. R. Piper & Co., Munich, 1961-66; asst. prof. German Pa. State U., 1966-69; assoc. prof. German. U. Colo., 1969-71; prof. German U. Md., 1971-78; prof. Princeton U., 1978—; vis. prof. Stanford U., 1970-71. Author: Elemente der Literaturkritik, 1976, Buchner-Kommentar zum dichterischen Werk, 1977, Uber deutsche Literatur und Rede: Historische Interpretationen, 1981, Der Mensch in der Geschichte: Eine Interpretation von Scillers Wallenstein, 1980; editor: numerous books including Goethe's Dramen: Neue Interpretationen, 1980, Kleists dramen: Neue Interpretationen, 1981, Hineich von Kleist: Plays, 1982, Literarische Profile: Deutsche Dichter von Grimmelshausen bis Brect, 1982, Friedrich Schiller: Plays, 1983; mem. editorial bd.: Ottendorfer Series, 1975—, German Library, 1978—. Recipient faculty award for research U. Md., 1971; fellow Inst. Research in Humanities, U. Wis.-Madison, 1976-77. Mem. Am. Assn. Tchrs. of German, MLA (chmn., sec. 19th century German lit. 1976, 78, 83), Internationale Vereinigung fur Germanische Sprach und Literaturwissenschaft, Am. Soc. for 18th Century Studies, Schiller-Gesellschaft, Buchner Soc., Goethe Soc. (pres. 1977-78), Brecht Soc. Home: 17 Batberry Rd Princeton NJ 08540 Office: Princeton U 230 E Pyne St Princeton NJ 08544

HINDLE, BROOKE, history educator; b. Drexel Hill, Pa., Sept. 28, 1918; s. Howard Brooke and Marion (Manchester) H.; m. Helen Elizabeth Morris, Aug. 21, 1943; children: Margaret Joan (Mrs. Robert M. Hazen), Donald Morris. Student, Mass. Inst. Tech., 1936-38; A.B. magna cum laude, Brown U., 1940; A.M., U. Pa., 1942, Ph.D., 1949. Asst. in history U. Pa., 1941-42, 45-48; research asso. Inst. Early Am. History and Culture, 1948-50; asso. prof. history N.Y. U., 1950-61, prof., 1961-74, chmn. dept. history, 1965-67, dean, 1967-69, head univ. dept. history, 1970-74; dir. Nat. Mus. Am. History, Smithsonian Instn., Washington, 1974-78, sr. historian, 1978—; vis. prof. M.I.T., 1971-72, U. Central Fla., 1981, U. Del., 1982; sr. resident scholar Eleutherian Mills-Hagley Found., 1969-70, mem. adv. com., 1971-74, trustee, 1974—. Author: The Pursuit of Science in Revolutionary America, 1956, David Rittenhouse, 1964, Technology in Early America, 1966, Emulation and Invention, 1981; co-author: Charles Willson Peale and His World, 1982; editor: America's Wooden Age, 1975, Early American Science, 1976, The Scientific Writings of David Rittenhouse, 1980, Material Culture of the Wooden Age, 1981. Served to lt. USNR, 1942-45; PTO. Guggenheim fellow, 1964-65. Fellow AAAS (past mem. council, past chmn. sect. L), Early Am. Industries Soc., Inst. Early Am. History and Culture (past mem. council); mem. Am. Antiquarian Soc., Am. Philos. Soc., Internat. Acad. History of Sci. (corr.), Mass. Hist. Soc. (corr.), History of Sci. Soc. (past sec., council mem.), Orgn. Am. Historians, Am. Hist. Assn., Soc. for History Tech. (past pres., mem. exec. council), Phi Beta Kappa. Club: Cosmos (Washington). Home: 5114 Dalecarlia Dr Bethesda MD 20816 Office: Nat Mus Am History Smithsonian Instn Washington DC 20560

HINDMAN, HUGH DAVID, JR., educator; b. Toledo, Apr. 18, 1927; s. Hugh David and Alpha (Westphal) H.; m. Nancy Nafzger, June 12, 1953; children: Karen, Melanie, Melissa. B.S. in Edn, Miami U., Oxford, Ohio, 1950; M.A. in Athletic Adminstrn, Ohio U., 1960. Coach Grandview High Sch., Columbus, Ohio, 1950-53, North High Sch., Columbus, 1953-58; offensive line coach Ohio U., Athens, 1958-63, Ohio State U., Columbus, 1963-70; asso. dir. athletics, 1970-77, dir. athletics, 1977—; dir. Scioto Savs. and Loan, Ohio State Life Ins. Co.; mem. football rules com. nat. Collegiate Athletic Assn.; dir. (Big Ten Conf.), 1977—. Chmn. exec. com. Central Ohio Heart Assn. Served with USNR, 1945-46. Republican. Presbyterian. Clubs: Touchdown (Washington); Columbus Maennerchor, Columbus Athletic, Gyro, Muirfield Village Golf, Masons, Shriners. Office: Ohio State U 410 W Woodruff St Columbus OH 43210

HINDS, CHARLES FRANKLIN, librarian; b. Henderson, Ky., Oct. 31, 1923; s. Charles Fretwell and Ruth Alice (Carson) H.; m. Doris May Rooney, June 8, 1946; 1 son, Joseph James. A.B., U. Ky., 1950, M.A., 1958, M.S. in L.S, 1968, postgrad., 1968; postgrad., U. Louisville, 1950-52, 53-56; certificate in archival adminstrn., Am. U., 1961. Auditor freight accounts Louisville & Nashville R.R., 1941-53; instr. Male High Sch., Louisville, 1953-56; dir. Ky. Hist. Soc., Frankfort, 1956-59; field rep. U. Ky. Libraries, Lexington, 1959-60; dir. Ky. Archives and Records Service, Frankfort, 1960-67; instr. Ky. State U., Frankfort, 1966-67, 73—; asso. prof., dir. libraries Murray (Ky.) State U., 1967-73; state librarian, dir. Ky. Dept. Libraries and Archives, Frankfort, 1973-77; prin. asst. Ky. Edn. and Arts Cabinet, 1977—; chmn. Ky. Library and Archives Commn., 1973-77; pres. Hinds Archives Enterprises, Frankfort, 1978—; cons. in field. Editor: Catalog of Federal Programs, Education and Arts, 1978. Pres.-elect Frankfort Arts Found., 1983-84. Served with AUS, 1941-45. Decorated Bronze Star. Mem. Ky. Microfilm Assn. (pres. 1974-75), Ky. Geneal. Soc. (pres. 1978-79), Ky. Assn. Pub. Annuitants (pres. 1983-84). Democrat. Episcopalian. Clubs: Rotary. (pres. 1982-83), Rotary (history and archives com. 1983-84). Home: 320 Meadow Ln Frankfort KY 40601 Office: State Office Bldg Frankfort KY 40601

HINDS, JACKSON CEIVERS, utility company executive; b. Brownsville, Tex., Aug. 28, 1921; s. Jackson Ceivers and Tallulah G. (Raffo) H.; m. Artie Lee Page, June 18, 1946; children: Stephen Randolph, Page Aline, Denise Jacqueline. B.B.A., U. Tex., 1942, LL.B., 1948; postgrad. indsl. adminstrn., Harvard U., 1943, M.B.A., 1947. Bar: Tex. bar 1948. Since practiced in, Houston; with firm Fulbright, Crooker, Freeman, Bates & Jaworski, 1948-56; gen. counsel Houston Natural Gas Corp. (and subs.), 1956-69, sr. v.p., dir., 1962-67, exec. v.p., dir., 1967-69; pres. United Gas Distbn. Co., Houston, 1969—; now chmn. bd., chief exec. officer Entex Co., Houston; dir. Univ. Savs. & Loan Assn, Houston, Bank of Southwest, Kroger Stores, Inc., Cin. Pres. Houston Housing Devel. Corp., 1968—; chmn. Mayor Houston Adv. Com. on Housing, 1967—; bd. dirs. meml. Hosp., Houston. Served to lt. USNR, 1942-46. Decorated Bronze Star. Mem. Am., Tex., Houston, Fed. Power Communications bar assns., Am., So. gas assns. Office: Entex Co 1200 Milam Houston TX 77002

HINDS, WILLIAM EDWARD, comic strip artist; b. Houston, Apr. 21, 1950; s. Edward and Dorothy (McGuire) H. B.F.A., Stephen F. Austin U., 1972. Free-lance artist, Houston, 1970-73; staff artist, Houston Chronicle, 1973-76; co-creator: books include Tank McNamara Chronicles, And I Am Tank McNamara With Sports News, If I Quit Baseball Will You Still Love Me, Shout Tank Shout, Tank McNamara, God Intended Blond Boys to be Quarterbacks. Mem. Nat. Cartoonist Soc., Tau Kappa Epsilon. Address: care Universal Press Syndicate 4400 Johnson Dr Fairway KS 66205 *

HINDUS, MILTON, writer, educator; b. N.Y.C., Aug. 26, 1916; s. Meyer and Minnie (Slutsky) H.; m. Eva Tenenbaum, Aug. 30, 1942; 1 dau., Myra Gladys. B.A., Coll. City N.Y., 1936, M.S., 1938; postgrad., Columbia, 1938-39, U. Chgo., 1947-48. Lectr. lit. Hunter Coll. and New Sch., 1943-46; asst. prof. humanities Coll. U. Chgo., 1946-48; asst. prof. English Brandeis U., Waltham, Mass., 1948-54, asso. prof., 1954-62, prof., 1962—; summer faculty N.Y. U., U. Calif. at Los Angeles, City U. N.Y. Author: The Crippled Giant, 1950, The Proustian Vision, 1954, Leaves of Grass: One Hundred Years After, 1955, A Reader's Guide to Marcel Proust, 1962, F. Scott Fitzgerald: An Introduction and Interpretation, 1968, The Old East Side, 1969, Walt Whitman: The Critical Heritage, 1971, A World at Twilight, 1971, Charles Roznikoff: A Critical Essay, 1977, The Worlds of Maurice Samuel: Selected Writings, 1977, The Broken Music Box, 1980; Contbr. book reviews to newspapers and mags.; Editor: sect. Am. lit. Ency. Judaica, 1968—. Recipient Walt Whitman prize Poetry Soc. Am., 1959. Mem. Am. Assn. U. Profs. (chpt. pres.), Modern Lang. Assn., Jewish Publns. Soc. Am., Jewish Faculty Group Greater Boston (chmn.). Home: 24 Stiles Terr Newton Centre MA 02159 Office: Dept English Brandeis U Waltham MA 02154

HINE, CHARLES HENRI, II, physician, educator; b. Toledo, Mar. 31, 1916; s. Charles Henry and Grace (Gibson) H.; m. Betty Dixon, Aug. 11, 1945; children—Holly Elizabeth, Charles Henri III. B.A., St. Norbert Coll., 1937; M.A., U. Wis., 1938, Ph.D. (Alumni Research fellow), 1942, M.D., 1943. Chief toxicology sect. U.S. Naval Med. Research Inst., 1946-47; acting chief, head toxicologists U.S. Naval Def. Lab., San Francisco Naval Shipyards, 1947; practice medicine specializing in occupational medicine and toxicology, San Francisco, 1947—; faculty U. Calif. Sch. Medicine, San Francisco, 1947—, clin. prof. toxicology and occupational medicine, 1964—; dir. occupational med. service, chief div. occupational medicine; toxicologist, coroner, City and County of San Francisco, 1950—; pres., dir. Hine Inc., San Francisco, 1961—; cons. toxicologist Calif. Dept. Pub. Health, 1955-75. Contbg. author: Industrial Hygiene and Toxicology, 1962; Contbr. articles to profl. jours. Fellow Am. Acad. Forensic Scis., Am. Acad. Occupational Medicine; mem. Calif. Acad. Preventive Medicine, Am. Indsl. Hygiene Assn., AMA, Am. Occupational Med. Soc., Am. Soc. for Pharmacology and Exptl. Therapeutics, Soc. Toxicology. Home: 60 King Ave Piedmont CA 94611 Office: Sch Medicine U Calif 3d and Parnassus Sts San Francisco CA 94122

HINE, DARYL, poet; b. Burnaby, B.C., Can., 1936; came to U.S., 1965; s. Robert Fraser and Elsie (James) H. Student, McGill U., 1954-57; M.A., U. Chgo., 1965, Ph.D., 1967. Asst. prof. U. Chgo., 1967-69, vis. prof., 1978. Editor: Poetry Mag, 1968-77; Author: poems Five Poems, 1954, The Carnal and the Crane, 1957, The Devil's Picture Book, 1960, The Wooden Horse, 1965, Minutes, 1968, Resident Alien, 1975, In & Out, 1975, Daylight Saving, 1978, Selected Poems, 1981; novel The Prince of Darkness and Company, 1961; travel book Polish Subtitles, 1962; play The Death of Seneca, 1970; translator: The Homeric Hymns and The Battle of the Frogs and the Mice, 1972, Theocritus: Idylls and Epigrams, 1982; editor: Lockhart Library of Translation, Princeton U. Press, 1983—. Recipient award Am. Acad. Arts and Letters, 1982; Guggenheim fellow, 1980.

HINE, GILBERT CLARENDON, lawyer, consultant; b. Lancaster, Pa., July 27, 1917; s. Cecil C. and Frances (Julian) H.; m. Evelyn Messenger, June 16, 1945; children: Gilbert Clarendon, Sarah, Cecily, Isabel, Julian. A.B., Gettysburg Coll., 1939; J.D. with honors, U. N.C., 1941. Bar: N.C. 1941, Tex. 1980. Practice in Charlotte, 1941-42, San Antonio, 1980—; asso. Tillett & Campbell, 1941; editor Prentice Hall, Inc., N.Y.C., 1946; mgr. tax dept. H.J. Heinz Co., Pitts., 1947-50; asst. trust officer Security Trust Co., Miami, Fla., 1951; trust officer Wachovia Bank & Trust Co., Winston-Salem, N.C., 1951-60; v.p., sr. trust officer Nat. Bank Westchester, 1960-61; sr. v.p., exec. trust officer Nat. Bank of Commerce, San Antonio, 1961-80; dir., mem. audit com. Weatherford Internat., Inc., 1971-83; lectr. in field. Contbr. articles to trade publs. Chmn. bd. dirs. Winston-Salem chpt. ARC, 1951-56; exec. sec. Winston-Salem Found.; pres. Town North YMCA, San Antonia; sec. bd. dirs. Boysville, Inc.; mem. trustees com. San Antonio Area Found., 1964-79, chmn., 1975-79; treas. bd. dirs., exec. com. South Tex. Health Info. Center, 1970-77. Served to capt. USAAF, 1941-46; ETO. Decorated Air medal, Bronze Star. Mem. Am. Bankers Assn. (exec. com. trust div. 1973-76), Tex. Bankers Assn. (sec.-treas. 1969-71). Episcopalian. Club: Kiwanis. Home and office: 3215 Northridge St San Antonio TX 78209 *How well you listen determines how well you communicate with others. Excellence in this is no accident. It takes conscious effort, thoughtful care and constant practice. It is the foundation for successful service to others. An orderly life stems from an orderly mind.*

HINE, JACK, educator, chemist; b. Coronado, Calif., July 2, 1923; s. Virgil Sylvester and Mildred Virginia (Wing) H.; m. Mildred Halacek, May 24, 1946; 1 dau, Katherine; m. Myra Safley Baker, June 24, 1978. B.S., U. Ark., 1944; Ph.D., U. Ill., 1948; LL.D., Lewis Coll., 1965. Asst. research chemist Cities Service Oil Co., Okmulgee, Okla., 1943-45; research asso. Mass. Inst. Tech., 1947-48; postdoctoral fellow Harvard, 1948-49; asst. prof. chemistry Ga. Inst. Tech., 1949-51, asso. prof., 1951-54, prof., 1954-58, Regents prof., 1958-65; prof. chemistry Ohio State U., 1965—; Cons. NIH Medicinal and Organic Chemistry Fellowship Rev. Com., 1964-68. Author: Physical Organic Chemistry, 1956, 62, Divalent Carbon, 1964, Structural Effects on Equilibria in Organic Chemistry, 1975; Editorial adv. bd.: Jour. Organic Chemistry, 1965-70. Alfred P. Sloan Research fellow, 1956-60. Mem. Am. Chem. Soc. (Fla. award 1962, Herty medal 1963, exec. com. div. organic chemistry 1963-65), Chem. Soc. London., Am. Phys. Soc., Société Chemique de France, AAAS, Faraday Soc., Phi Beta Kappa, Sigma Xi, Phi Kappa Phi, Alpha Chi Sigma, Phi Lambda Upsilon, Omicron Delta Kappa, Pi Mu Epsilon. Unitarian. Home: 2930 North Star Rd Upper Arlington OH 43221 Office: 140 W 18th Ave Columbus OH 43210

HINE, JAMES SPENCER, advertising agency executive; b. Millburn, N.J., Feb. 13, 1939; s. Louis Phillips and Ethel May (Spencer) H.; m. Beverly Ann, May 26, 1962 (div.); children: Susan, James D.; m. Linda Murphy, June 21, 1975; 1 son, James C. B.A., Colgate U., 1961; M.B.A., Upsala U., 1965. Account exec. Benton & Bowles, N.Y.C., 1964-67; account supt. Ted Bate, N.Y.C., 1967-69; account group supr. Doyle Dane Bernbach, N.Y.C., 1969-71; v.p., account group supr. Bloom Advt., Dallas, 1975-76; account group supr. Glenn, Bozell & Jacobs, Dallas, 1975-76; v.p., gen. mgr. Ogilvy and Mather, Houston, 1976—. Bd. dirs. Houston Better Bus. Bur., 1982—. Served to 1st lt. U.S. Army, 1961-69. Club: Forum (Houston). Home: 611 Marshall St Houston TX 77006 Office: Ogilvy and Mather 1 Allen Ctr Houston TX 77002

HINE, ROBERT VAN NORDEN, JR., historian, educator; b. Los Angeles, Apr. 26, 1921; s. Robert Van Norden and Elizabeth (Bates) H.; m. Shirley M. McChord, June 24, 1949; 1 dau., Allison. B.A., Pomona Coll., 1948; M.A., Yale U., 1949, Ph.D., 1952. Instr. history U. Calif., Riverside, 1954-55, asst. prof., 1955-61, asso. prof., 1961-66, prof., 1966—. Author: California's Utopian Colonies, 1953, Edward Kern and American Expansion, 1962, Bartlett's West: Drawing the Mexican Boundary, 1968, The American Frontier: Readings and Documents, 1972, The American West: An Interpretive History, 1973, Community on the American Frontier: Separate But Not Alone, 1980, California Utopianism: Contemplations of Eden, 1981; Editor: William Andrew Spalding, Los Angeles, Newspaperman: An Autobiographical Account, 1961, Soldier in the West: Letters of Theodore Talbot during his Services in California, Mexico and Oregon, 1845-53, 1972; Contbr. articles to profl. jours. Recipient Harbison award for disting. teaching Danforth Found., 1968; Huntington Library fellow, 1953, 60; Guggenheim fellow, 1958, 68; Nat. Endowment for Humanities sr. fellow, 1977. Mem. Am. Hist. Assn. (mem. council Pacific Coast br.), Western History Assn., Orgn. Am. Historians, Phi Beta Kappa. Office: Dept History Univ Calif Riverside CA 92521

HINER, LOUIS CHASE, newspaperman; b. Astoria, Oreg., Apr. 19, 1919; s. Louis Chase and Rubye Marie (Isaac) H.; m. Phyllis Clark, Mar. 24, 1950; children: Gregory C., Bradley C.; 1 dau. by previous marriage, Mary Carolyn Hiner Koon. Student, Ind. U., 1937-39, 41-42. City editor Rushville (Ind.) Republican, 1942; editor Martinsville (Ind.) Reporter, 1946-47; with Indpls. News, 1947—, statehouse reporter, polit. and feature writer, 1947-52, aviation editor, 1949-52, Washington corr., columnist, 1953—, reporter presdl. campaigns, 1948—, reporter nat. polit. convs., 1952—; Washington corr. Gary (Ind.) Post-Tribune, 1956-67; Washington corr., columnist Phoenix Gazette, 1955—, Muncie (Ind.) Eve. Press, 1953—. Served as pilot USAAF, 1943-46. Mem. White House Corrs. Assn., Ind. Hist. Soc., Ariz. Soc. of Washington, Am. Legion, Ind. Soc. of Washington, Sigma Delta Chi, Kappa Kappa Psi. Clubs: Nat. Press (Washington); Elks. Home: 3426 Farm Hill Dr Falls Church VA 22044 Office: 1000 Nat Press Bldg Washington DC 20045

HINER, ROBERT L., transportation executive; b. Clinton County, Ind., Nov. 7, 1902; s. Ward Beecher and Vienna Susan (Fleming) H.; m. Margaret Stowers, Oct. 24, 1927; 1 son, Dan Stowers (dec. 1979). Student, Ind. U., 1923. With Am. Red Ball Transit Co., Inc., Indpls., 1925—, now chmn. bd.; lectr. traffic orgns. and lit. groups; bd. dirs. Household Goods Carriers Bur., Am. Movers Conf. of Washington. Author: Songs of Life, 1971, On Wings of Words, 1976; Contbr. articles to profl. jours. Ky. Col.; Recipient Hanson H. Anderson award. Mem. Nat. Def. Transp. Assn. (life), Am. Truck Hist. Soc. (bd. govs., Spl. Citation 1980), Ind. Hist. Soc., Traffic Club N.Y.C., Ind. State, Indpls. chambers commerce, Indpls. Museum Art. Clubs: Masons, Highland Golf and Country, Indpls. Athletic. Home: 6430 Central Ave Indianapolis IN 46220 Office: PO Box 1127 Indianapolis IN 46206

HINERFELD, NORMAN MARTIN, manufacturing company executive; b. N.Y.C., May 17, 1929; s. Benjamin B. and Anne (Blitz) H.; m. Ruth Jean Gordon, Dec. 25, 1952; children—Lee Ann, Thomas Benjamin, Joshua Gordon. A.B., Harvard, 1951, M.B.A., 1953. Security underwriter, underwriting dept. Goldman Sachs & Co., 1953; asst. to pres. Julius Kayser & Co., 1955-56, Catalina, Inc., 1956-57, v.p. mfg., 1957-64, sr. v.p., 1964-67; v.p. Kayser-Roth Corp., 1964-67, exec. v.p., 1967-74, mem. exec. com., 1972—, pres., chief operating officer, 1974-76, dir., 1958—, chmn. exec. com., 1976—; dir. Supermarkets Gen. Corp.; Chmn. Center Council Center for Study Democratic Instns.; mem. U.S.A.-BIAC to OECD, 1978—; mem. exec. com. Dist. Export-Council U.S. Dept. Commerce, 1978—; Mem. Adv. Council on Japan-U.S. Econ. Relations, 1980—. Author: (with D. Moross) Automation-Challange to Management, 1953. Served from 2d lt. to 1st lt. AUS, 1953-55. Mem. Am. Arbitration Assn. (chmn. exec. com. 1983—), Am. Apparel Mfrs. Assn. (dir., past pres., mem. exec. com.), Nat. Knitted Sportswear Assn. (exec. com., dir.), U.S. C. of C. (chmn. task force on tech. transfer 1975-79, chmn. export policy task force 1979—). Patentee self-programmed automatic machinery. Home: 11 Oak Ln Larchmont NY 10538 Office: 640 Fifth Ave New York NY 10019

HINERFELD, ROBERT ELLIOT, lawyer; b. N.Y.C., May 29, 1934; s. Benjamin B. and Anne (Blitz) H.; m. Susan Hope Slocum, June 27, 1957; children: Daniel Slocum, Matthew Ben. A.B., Harvard U., 1956, J.D., 1959. Bar: Calif. 1960. Asst. U.S. atty So. Dist. Calif., 1960-62; assoc. lawyer Leonard Horwin, Beverly Hills, Calif., 1962-66; mem. Simon, Sheridan, Murphy, Thornton & Hinerfeld, Los Angeles, 1967-74, Murphy, Thornton, Hinerfeld & Cahill, 1975—; referee State Bar Ct., 1979—; arbitrator bus. panel Los Angeles Superior Ct., 1979—; judge pro tempore Beverly Hills Municipal Court, 1967-74; clin. lectr. U. So. Calif. Law Center, 1980—. Contbr. articles to profl. jours. Trustee Westland Sch., Los Angeles, 1970-75, Pacific Hills Sch., Los Angeles, 1971-72. Mem. ABA, Fed. Bar Assn., Los Angeles County Bar Assn. (spl. com. judicial evaluation 1978—, arbitration com. 1981—), Beverly Hills Bar Assn., State Bar Calif. (mem. com. on criminal law and procedure, chmn. spl. com. revision fed. criminal code, mem. disciplinary investigation panel dist. 7 1977-80, hearing referee State Bar Ct. 1981—, exec. com. litigation sect. 1983—), Am. Arbitration Assn. (arbitrator comml. panel 1966—), Calif. Acad. Appellate Lawyers. (membership com. 1983—). Clubs: Harvard Club So. Calif. (N.Y.C.) (dir. 1974-83, sec. 1978-80); Harvard (N.Y.C.)). Home: 131 S Cliffwood Ave Los Angeles CA 90049 Office: 7447 N Figueroa St Los Angeles CA 90041

HINERFELD, RUTH J., civic organization executive; b. Boston, Sept. 18, 1930; m. Norman Hinerfeld, children: Lee, Tom, Josh. A.B., Vassar Coll., 1951; grad., Program in Bus. Adminstrn., Harvard-Radcliffe Coll., 1952. With LWV, 1954—, UN observer, 1969-72, chairperson internat. relations com., 1972-76, 1st v.p. in charge legis. activities, 1976-78, pres., 1978-82; dir. LWV Overseas Edn. Fund., 1975-76, trustee, 1975—; chairperson LWV Edn. Fund, 1978-82; mem. White House Adv. Com. for Trade Negotiations, 1975-82; sec. UN Assn. of U.S., 1975-78, vice chmn., 1983—, bd. govs., bd. dirs., 1975—; mem. econ. policy council; mem. exec. com., dir. Overseas Devel. Council; mem. U.S. del. auspices of Nat. Com. on U.S.-China Relations and Chinese People's Inst. Fgn. Affairs, 1978. Mem. council Nat. Mcpl. League, 1977-80; del.-at-large Internat. Women's Year Conf., Houston, 1977; mem. exec. com. Leadership Conf. on Civil Rights, 1978-82; trustee Citizens Research Found., 1978—; mem. Nat. Petroleum Council, 1979-82; mem. U.S. del. to World Conf. on UN Decade for Women, 1980; mem. adv. com. Nat. Inst. for Citizen Edn. in the Law, 1981—; mem. North South Roundtable, 1978—. Recipient Disting. Citizen award Nat. Mcpl. League, 1978; Outstanding Mother award Nat. Mother's Day Com., 1981; Aspen Inst. Presdl. fellow, 1981. Mem. Council on Fgn. Relations, Phi Beta Kappa. Office: 11 Oak Ln Larchmont NY 10538

HINES, ANDREW HAMPTON, JR., industry executive; b. Lake City, Fla., Jan. 28, 1923; s. Andrew Hampton and Louise (Howl) H.; m. Ann Groover, June 28, 1947; children: Hampton, Elizabeth, Brad, Daniel. B.M.E. with high honors, U. Fla., 1947. Registered profl. engr., Fla. Research and devel. Gen. Electric Corp., 1947-51; Chmn. bd., pres. Fla. Progress Corp., St. Petersburg, 1982—; also chmn. bd., chief exec. officer subs. Fla. Power Corp., 1951—; chmn. bd. Landmark Union Trust Bank; dir. Landmark Banking Corp. of Fla., Breeder Reactor Corp.; former chmn. Nat. Electric Reliability Council; bd. dirs., past pres. Southeastern Electric Exchange.; mem. com. on utilities U.S. Nat. Com., World Energy Conf. Bd. overseers Stetson U. Coll. Law; trustee, mem. exec. com. Rollins Coll.; trustee Eckerd Coll.; co-chmn. industry cluster Fla. A&M U.; bd. dirs. U. Fla. Found. Served as 2d lt. USAAF, 1944-45; maj. Res. (ret.). Decorated Air medal. Fellow ASME; mem. Fla. Blue Key, Sigma Tau, Phi Kappa Phi, Tau Beta Pi, Beta Gamma Sigma. Methodist (Sunday sch. tchr.). Clubs: St. Petersburg Yacht, Lakewood Country (St. Petersburg); Citrus (Orlando, Fla.). Office: PO Box 33042 Saint Petersburg FL 33733

HINES, EDWARD, lumber company executive; b. Evanston, Ill., May 21, 1935; s. Charles M. and Florence (Notz) H.; m. Marcia McMillan, Dec. 28, 1963; children: Edward, Elizabeth, Heather. B.A., Williams Coll., 1957. With Edward Hines Lumber Co., Chgo., v.p., 1969-73, sr. v.p., 1973-78, exec. v.p., 1978-81, pres., chief exec. officer, 1981—; v.p., dir. So. Mineral Corp., Oreg. and Northwestern R.R., No. Mineral Corp. Pres. Northfield Schs. and Park Bd. Caucus; bd. dirs. Chgo. Boys' Club; mem. Northfield Sch. Bd. Mem. Pres.'s Assn. Republican. Roman Catholic. Clubs: Irish Fellowship, Univ., Glen View, Econ., Indian Hill. Office: Edward Hines Lumber Co 200 S Michigan Ave Chicago IL 60604 *

HINES, GERALD D., bank executive. Chmn. Fed. Res. Bank Dallas. Office: Fed Res Bank Dallas 400 S Akard St Dallas TX 75222§

HINES, GREGORY OLIVER, actor; b. N.Y.C., Feb. 14, 1946; s. Maurice Robert and Alma Iola (Lawless) H.; m. Pamela Koslow, Apr. 12, 1981; children: Daria Hines, Jessica Koslow, Zachary Evan. Appeared with, Hines Kids, 1949-55, Hines Bros., 1955-63, Hines, Hines and Dad, 1963-73; appeared in: Severance, 1974-77, Eubie!, 1978, Comin' Uptown, 1980, Sophisticated Ladies, 1981—; appeared in films: Wolfen, 1981, History of the World Part I, 1981, The Deal of the Century, 1983. 3 Tony nominations, 1979, 80, 81; Recipient Theater World award, Tor award, Dance Educators Am. award. Mem. Actors Equity, Screen Actors Guild, AFTRA.

HINES, HOWARD HARRY, social scientist; b. Iowa City, June 30, 1922; s. Harry Matlock and Leona (Fisher) H. B.A., U. Iowa, 1942; A.M., Harvard U., 1948, Ph.D., 1950. Tchr. econs. U. Iowa, 1947, Bowdoin Coll., 1948, Harvard U., 1948-50, U. Minn., 1957; from asst. prof. to prof. econs. Iowa State U., 1950-62; program dir. for econs. NSF, 1962-64, div. dir. for social scis., 1964-76, spl. asst. to dir., 1977-79, dir. Coll. Research Instrumentation Program, 1979—; acting asst. prof. bus. adminstrn. U. Calif. at Berkeley, 1955-56; vis. prof. econs. Cornell U., 1976-77. Served with AUS, 1943-46. Mem. Am., Midwest econ. assns., Royal Econ. Soc., Phi Beta Kappa, Delta Sigma Rho. Home: 2020 F St NW Washington DC 20006 Office: Nat Science Found Washington DC 20550

HINES, JAMES HERMAN, banker; b. Jackson, Miss., Sept. 8, 1914; s. Hulon H. and Ava O. H.; m. Martha Hamilton, Dec. 25, 1942; children: Martha H. Botts, Linda Hines White, Julia G. Hines Ditmore. Student, Jackson Sch. Law, 1935-36, Sch. Banking of South, La. State U., 1950-53; grad., Advanced Mgmt. Program, Harvard U. Sch. Bus., 1966. With Deposit Guaranty Nat. Bank, Jackson, 1936—, pres., 1973-75, chmn., chief exec. officer, 1975-79. Mem. governing and adv. bd. St. Dominic-Jackson Hosp.; co-chmn. 5 Million Capital Funds Campaign for Miss. Coll., 1976-78; treas., trustee Millsaps Coll.; also state chmn. 1982 7 million capital fund campaign; bd. dirs. Jackson State U. Found., YMCA of Jackson; chmn. bd., trustee Piney Woods Country Life Sch.; pres. Miss. Higher Edn. Assistance Corp.; mem. Mayor's Task Force Job Opportunities for Youth; chmn. Miss. affiliate Am. Heart Assn. Fund campaign, 1980-82; chmn. bd. Miss. affiliate Am. Heart Assn., 1983-84. Served to maj. AUS, 1941-46. Mem. Mid Continent Oil and Gas Assn. (dir.). Episcopalian. Club: North Jackson Kiwanis (past lt. gov.). Office: 1547 Deposit Guaranty Bldg Jackson MS 39205

HINES, JAMES RODGER, surgeon; b. Kewanna, Ind., Sept. 16, 1923; s. Michael and Ella (Costello) H.; m. Hollis Burke, July 6, 1957; children: James, Rachel, John, Matthew, Eliza. Student, U. Notre Dame, 1941-43; B.S., U. Ill., 1944, M.D., 1946; M.S. in Surgery, Northwestern U., 1951. Intern Northwestern Univ. Hosp., 1946-47, resident in surgery, 1947-51, staff surgeon, 1954—, chief gen. surgery, 1969—; vice chief of staff Northwestern Meml. Hosp., chief of staff, 1984-86; prof. surgery Northwestern U. Med. Sch., 1969—, now vice-chmn. dept. surgery, dir. grad. tng. surgery. Served with AUS, 1943-46, 52-54. Decorated Bronze Star; named Northwestern U. Med. Sch. Tchr. of Year, 1971; Abbott fellow, 1948-51. Mem. Ill. Surg. Soc. (pres. 1977), Chgo. Surg. Soc. (pres. 1982), Western Surg. Soc., Am. Surg. Assn., Central Surg. Assn., Internat. Surg. Soc., Soc. Surgery Alimentary Tract, ACS, Alpha Omega Alpha. Research peptic ulcer disease, breast cancer, parathyroid disease, calcium metabolism; developed gastric outlet operation. Home: 715 Sheridan Rd Winnetka IL 60093 Office: 251 E Chicago Ave Chicago IL 60611

HINES, JEROME, opera singer; b. Hollywood, Calif., Nov. 8, 1921; s. Russell Ray and Florence Mildred (Link) Heinz; m. Lucia Evangelista, July 23, 1952; children: David Jerome, Andrew, John, Russell. B.A. in Chemistry and Math, UCLA; Ph.D. (hon.), Whitworth Coll., Bloomfield Coll., Taylor U., Stevens Inst. Tech. Chemist Union Oil Co. of Los Angeles, 1944-45. Began as singer with the, Civic Light Opera Co. of Los Angeles, 1940, San Francisco Opera Co., 1941; Hollywood Bowl soloist, 1942, 47, Opera Assn. of Golden West, 1943; with, New Orleans Opera Co., 1942, 46, 67, 83; leading basso, Met. Opera Co., 1946—, La Scala, Milan, Bolshoi, Moscow, Teatro Colón, Buenos Aires; performed in, Glyndebourne, Edinburgh festivals, 1953, Munich Opera Festival, 1953, 54, Wagner Opera Festival, Bayreuth, Germany, 1958, 59, 60, 61, 63; toured, Soviet Union 4 times.; Recording artist, London, EMI, Columbia, Victor, Word recording cos.; Author: This is My Story, This is My Song, 1968, Tim Whosoever, 1970, Great Singers on Great Singing; also articles on math. research; composer: opera I Am the Way; 30 songs. Recipient Caruso Scholarship, Cornelia Bliss Scholarhip. Address: care Shaw Concerts Inc 1995 Broadway New York NY 10023

HINES, LAWRENCE GREGORY, educator; b. Leavenworth, Kans., Oct. 31, 1915; s. Michael Joseph and Louise Ann (Rokoski) H.; m. Ann Williston Philips, Nov. 27, 1937; 1 son, Terence Michael. A.B., U. Kans., 1938; A.M., U. Minn., 1942, Ph.D., 1947; A.M., Dartmouth, 1953. Teaching asst. U. Minn., 1940-41; research asst. Employment Stblzn. Research Inst., 1941-42, instr. econs., 1942-46, asst. prof. econs., summer 1947, Dartmouth, 1947-53, prof., 1953—, chmn. div. social scis., 1959-62, chmn. dept. econs., 1963-65, asso. chmn., 1974—; Cons. Fed. Res. Bank of Boston; also econ. cons., water control div. USPHS; vis. prof. econs. U. Mich., summer 1948; lectr. econs. George Washington U., summer 1949; Mem. Fed. Interagy. Com. Evaluation Standards; vice-chmn. subcom. evaluation standards Northeastern Resources Com. Author: The Size, Shape and Distribution of Economic Income, 1952, Environmental Issues, 1973, The Persuasion of Price, 1976; Contbr. articles to profl. publs. Served as air intelligence specialist Office Naval Intelligence, 1946-47; Washington. Recipient Ford Found. essay prize award, 1958; NSF grantee, 1965-66. Fellow Royal Econ. Soc.; mem. Regional Sci. Assn., Am. Econ. Assn., Am. Assn. U. Profs. (nat. council mem.), Soil Conservation Soc. Am., Quetico-Superior Found. Home: 5 Kingsford Rd Hanover NH 03755

HINES, MARION ERNEST, electronic engineer; b. Bellingham, Wash., Nov. 30, 1918; s. William Robert and Zella (Mudge) H.; m. Julie Warren Viele, May 3, 1947; children: Sheldon, Julian, Hadley. B.S. in Applied Physics, Calif. Inst. Tech., 1940, 1941, M.S. in E.E., 1946. Mem. tech. staff Bell Telphone Labs., Inc., Murray Hill, N.J., 1946-60; v.p. M-A-Com Inc., Burlington, Mass., 1960—. Contbr. articles in field to profl. jours.; patentee in field. Maj. AC U.S. Army, 1940-45. Life fellow IEEE (Microwave prize 1971, 78, J.J. Ebers award Electron Devices Soc. 1976, Lamme medal 1983, Microwave Career award 1983). Home: 752 Wellesley St Weston MA 02193 Office: MA-Com Inc South Ave Burlington MA 01803

HINES, MERRILL ODOM, surgeon; b. Jackson, Miss., Nov. 17, 1909; s. Hulon Hunter and Ava Ione (Odom) H.; m. Margaret McLaurin Davis, Aug. 24, 1937; children: Margaret Anne, Merrill Odom. B.S., Millsaps Coll., 1931; M.D. (Commonwealth fellow from Miss.), Tulane U., 1936. Diplomate: Am. Bd. Proctology (mem. bd. 1956—), Am. Bd. Colon and Rectal Surgery (v.p. 1960-61, pres. 1961-63). Intern Baroness Erlanger Hosp., Chattanooga, 1936-37, resident, 1937-38, chief resident surgery, 1938-39; staff surgeon Tylertown (Miss.) Hosp., 1939-42; mem. staff Alton Ochsner Clinic and Ochsner Found. Hosp., New Orleans, 1945—, head dept. proctology, 1945-62, Ochsner Found. Hosp., 1947-62, pres. staff, 1951-52; asst. med. dir. Ochsner Clinic, 1954-60, mem. bd. mgmt., med. dir., 1960-75; sr. vis. surgeon Charity Hosp., New Orleans, 1956—; courtesy staff Sara Mayo Hosp., New Orleans, 1954-70; sr. asso. surgery Touro Infirmary, New Orleans, 1953-64; courtesy staff Flint-Goodrige Hosp., New Orleans, 1949-74; faculty clin. surgery Tulane u. Med. Sch., 1949—; prof. Tulane U. Med. Sch., 1964—; cons. Ill. Central Hosp., New Orleans, 1960-70, Ill. Central R.R., 1958—; cons. group practice of medicine Dept. Health, Edn. and Welfare, 1966-70; mem. Govt. Health Ins. Benefits Adv. Council, 1968-71; mem. nat. drug adv. com. FDA, 1972-74; cons. subcom. on physicians' reimbursement HIBAC, 1971-74; mem. Coordinating Council on Med. Edn., 1972-76. Mem. editorial bd.: Jour. Diseases Colon and Rectum, 1957-77. Bd. dirs. Am. Cancer Soc. Greater New Orleans, 1957—, sec., 1957-58, v.p., 1959-60, pres., 1961-62, mem. exec. com., 1962—; mem. La. State Bd. Nurse Examiners, 1962-66; co-chmn. health com. New Orleans C. of C., 1962-68; mem. Adv. Bd. Med. Spltys., 1962-72, mem. exec. com., 1968-70; regent Inst. for Profl. Standards, 1974-76; Trustee Alton Ochsner Med. Found., sec.-treas., 1963-70, pres., 1970-74, chmn. bd. trustees, chmn. exec. com. trustees, 1974-80; mem. La. State Manpower Council, chmn., 1976—; mem. La. State Coordinating Council, 1976—. Served to capt. M.C. AUS, 1942-44. Recipient One of 10 Outstanding Persons award Greater New Orleans area Inst. for Human Understanding, 1983. Fellow A.C.S. (bd. govs. 1966-75, pres. La. chpt. 1972-73); mem. AMA (chmn. sec. proctology 1963, alt. del. and del. 1963-80, Disting. Service award 1983), So. Med. Assn. (treas. 1954—), Orleans Parish Med. Soc., La. Med. Soc., Am. Proctologic Soc. (pres. 1961-62), Mid West Proctologic Soc., Southeastern Proctologic Soc. (pres. 1954), New Orleans Surg. Soc. (treas. 1945, dir. 1977-78), Southeastern Surg. Soc., La. Surg. Soc., Alton Ochsner Surg. Soc., Alumni Alton Ochsner Med. Found. Fellows Assn. (1st pres. 1954-56), New Orleans Grad. Med. Assembly, Alpha Omega Alpha. Democrat. Methodist (chmn. ofcl. bd. 1957-59). Clubs: Louisiana, Round Table, International House (New Orleans). Home: 1634 Robert St New Orleans LA 70115 Office: 1514 Jefferson St New Orleans LA 70121

HINES, PATRICK, actor, stage director; b. Burkeville, Tex., Mar. 17, 1930; s. Ruben Mainer and Edice (Miller) H. A.A., Del Mar Coll., 1949; B.F.A., U. Tex., 1952. Actor in 40 Shakespearean prodns., Stratford, Conn., 1956-66; actor: Broadway prodns. including Great God Brown, 1959, A Passage to India, 1962, The Devils, 1965, Cyrano, 1973, Tex. Trilogy, 1976, Caesar and Cleopatra, 1979, Amadeus, 1980-83 (Dramalogue award for disting. performance 1981); actor in films: 1776, 1972, W.W. and the Dixie Dance Kings, 1977, Brinks Job, 1978, King, 1978, Amadeus, Prague, Czechoslovakia, 1983; assoc. dir., Am. Shakespeare Festival, Stratford, Conn., 1960-61; dir., Oreg. Shakespeare Festival, 1968-69; guest artist, So. Meth. U., 1978, U. Tex., 1979. Served with U.S. Army, 1954-56. Nominee Jefferson award, Chgo., 1978. Mem. Actors Equity, Screen Actors Guild, AFTRA. Democrat. Methodist. Address: 46 W 95th St New York NY 10025
Mine is a profession in which many people of many talents work closely together to create a production which comes from the author's words. Before accepting an engagement some questions come to mind: does the play reflect human nature and the human condition; does the play contain graceful, speakable language; does it challenge and excite; do others involved in various aspects of the production have talent, integrity and wit? Perhaps then the project is worthwhile.

HINES, PAUL GARRY, investment company executive; b. Schenectady, July 30, 1937; s. John F. and Helen (McGarry) H.; m. Judith Ann Albergotti, June 2, 1979; children: Erin, Lucas, Tara, Nina, Gael. B.A. in Econs, Harvard U., 1959, M.B.A. in Fin. and Mgmt, 1963. C.P.A., N.Y. State. Assoc. Arthur Young & Co. C.P.A.s, N.Y.C., 1963-66; v.p. Mgmt. Analysis Center, N.Y.C., 1966-70, E.F. Hutton & Co. Inc., 1970-74, sr. v.p., dir., 1974-83, exec. v.p., dir., mem. exec. com., 1983—; chmn. Hutton Ins. Group; pres. Hutton Venture Ptnrs., Inc.; pres. Wall St. Planning Group, 1975. Treas. Found. Religion and Mental Health, 1979—. Served to lt. (j.g.) USNR, 1959-61. Mem. Am. Inst. C.P.A.s, N.Y. State Soc. C.P.A.s. Clubs: India House, N.Y. Athletic, Harvard, N.Y. Yacht (N.Y.C.). Home: 12 Flying Cloud Rd Stamford CT 06902 Office: 1 Battery Park Plaza New York NY 10004

HINES, WILLIAM EUGENE, banker, orgn. ofcl.; b. N.Y.C., July 5, 1914; s. William J. and Alice M. (Callahan) H.; m. Dorothy H. Moore, June 4, 1949; children—Alice M., Dorothy H., Margaret M., William J., Elizabeth A., Robert J. Student, Columbia; grad., Rutgers U. Grad. Sch. Banking, 1948. With Bankers Trust Co., N.Y.C., 1950—, asst. v.p., 1958-63, v.p., 1963—; instr. Am. Inst. Banking, 1948-64, Am. Youth Hostels, 1954-65, former chmn., now dir. Mem. N.Y. Soc. Security Analysts, Accountants Club N.Y.C., Nat. Assn. Mental Health (nat. treas., dir. 1966, nat. trustee). Clubs: Shinnecock Yacht (commodore 1974-76, treas. 1980—. Home: 6 Edgewood Rd Scarsdale NY 10583 Office: 280 Park Ave New York NY 10022

HINES, WILLIAM MEREDITH, JR., journalist, science writer; b. San Jose, Calif., Sept. 11, 1916; s. William Meredith and Ethel (Sain) H.; m. Judith E. Randal, 1983. Student, Guilford (N.C.) Coll., 1936-37. Editorial positions with Boston Transcript, 1936-37, U.P.A., 1937-40, Chattanooga Times, 1940-41; mem. staff Washington Evening Star, 1950-68, sci. editor, 1957-68; with Field Enterprises, Inc., 1968—; sci. editor Chgo. Sun-Times, 1969—; sci. corr. Westinghouse Broadcasting Co., 1968—, Die Welt, Hamburg, West Germany, 1969-73; fellow Harvard Sch. Pub. Health, 1983. Author: Conquest of the Moon, 1964. Served to 1st lt. AUS, 1941-46. Recipient Sci. Writing award AAAS-Westinghouse Found., 1959, 60, 61, 65; Atomic Indsl. Forum award, 1965; Robert S. Ball award Aviation-Space Writers Assn., 1966. Club: Washington Press. Home: Mouse Trap Farm Route 1 Lovettsville VA 22080 Office: Nat Press Bldg Washington DC 20045

HINGLE, PAT, actor; b. Miami, Fla., July 19, 1924; s. Clarence M. and Marvin (Patterson) H.; m. Julia Wright, Oct. 25, 1979; children—Jody, Billy, Molly. B.F.A., U. Tex., 1949; PH.D. (hon.), Otterbein Coll., 1974. Numerous acting roles, among latest being End as a Man, 1953, Festival, 1954, Cat on a Hot Tin Roof, 1955, Girls of Summer, 1956, Dark at the Top of the Stairs, 1957, J.B, 1958, The Deadly Game, 1960, Macbeth, 1961, Troilus and Cressida, 1961, Strange Interlude, 1963, Blues for Mr. Charlie, 1964, A Girl Could Get Lucky, 1964, The Glass Menagerie, 1965, The Odd Couple, 1966, Johnny No-Trump, 1967, The Price, 1968, Childs Play, 1970, The Selling of the President, 1972, That Championship Season, 1973, The Lady from the Sea, 1976, Norma Rae, 1979, When You Comin' Back, Red Ryder, 1979, Thomas A. Edison, Reflections of a Genius, 1978, A Life, 1980. Served with USNR, 1942-46, 51-52.

HINICH, MELVIN JAY, government and economics educator; b. Pitts., Apr. 29, 1939; s. Joseph and Sara (Rubinstein) H.; m. Sonje Gregg, Sept. 14, 1966; 1 dau., Amy Sara. B.S., Carnegie Inst. Tech., 1959, M.S. in Math, 1960; Ph.D. in Statistics, Stanford, 1964. Asst. prof. indsl. adminstrn. Carnegie Inst. Tech., 1963-68; asso. prof. indsl. adminstrn., statistics, 1968-70; prof. statistics, polit. economy Carnegie Mellon U., 1970-74; prof. econs. dept. Va. Poly. Inst. and State U., Blacksburg, 1974-83; prof. govt. and econs. U. Tex., Austin, 1982—; Fairchild disting. scholar Calif. Inst. Tech. Inc., Pasadena, 1975-76; cons. Teledyne-Isotopes, Inc., Internat. Research & Tech., Inc., FDA, Air Pollution Control-Allegheny County Health Dept., U.S. Naval Coastal Systems Center, Tracor Applied Scis.; cons. task force on regulatory reform U.S. Senate Govt. Ops. Com. Author: Introduction to Continuous Probability, 1969, Consumer Protection Legislation and the U.S. Food Industry, 1980, The Spatial Theory of Voting: An Introduction, 1983; mem. editorial bd.: Jour. Math. Soc; assoc. editor: Jour. Am. Statis. Assn.; Contbr. articles to profl. jours. Fellow Inst. Math. Statistics; mem. Am. Statis. Assn., Am. Polit. Sci. Assn., Pub. Choice Soc., Am. Econ. Assn., Econometric Soc., Sigma Xi. Home: 3902 Cresthill Dr Austin TX 78731

HINKLE, B. J., food company executive; b. Springfield, Mo., July 21, 1922; s. Sam J. and Sallie J. (Best) H.; m. Margaret Ann Herschberger, Mar. 19, 1955; children—Susan, David, James. B.S. in Bus. Adminstrn, U. Kans., 1949. Mgr. systems and procedures Interstate Brands Corp., Kansas City, Mo., 1955-63, asst. treas., 1963-68, controller, 1968-70, treas., 1970-71, v.p. fin., 1971-72, dir., 1971—, exec. v.p., chief operating officer, 1972-73, pres., chief exec. officer, 1973-77, chmn. bd., chief exec. officer, 1977-80, chmn. bd., chief adminstrv. officer, 1980—; dir. Interstate Bakeries Corp., Kansas City, Mo. Served with M.C. U.S. Army, 1942-45. Mem. Am. Bakers Assn. (br. gov. 1973—, chmn. 1981-82), Wheat Industry Council, Alpha Kappa Psi, Sigma Nu. Clubs: Kansas City, Perry Yacht, Woodside Racquet, Wolf Creek Golf. Home: 8108 Dearborn St Prairie Village KS 66208 Office: PO Box 1627 Kansas City MO 64141

HINKLE, BARTON LESLIE, chem. co. exec.; b. Miami Beach, Fla., Nov. 2, 1925; s. Frank Leslie and Kathryn Barton (Paddock) H.; m. Christine Smith, Aug. 22, 1949 (dec. Aug. 1955); m. Sabrena Sanford, Apr. 4, 1959; children—Karen, Douglas, Jean, Maria, Elizabeth. B.S. in Chem. Engring, Purdue U., 1949; M.S., Inst. Textile Tech., 1951; Ph.D., Ga. Inst. Tech., 1953. Research asst. Ga. Inst. Tech. Exptl. Sta., Atlanta, 1951-53; research engr. E.I. duPont de Nemours & Co., Inc., Richmond, Va., 1953-55, research supr., 1955-57, tech. supt., 1957-61, mfg. supt., 1961-62, asst. plant mgr., 1962-64, plant supt., Clinton, Iowa, 1964-69, product mgr., Wilmington, Del., 1969-71, lab. mgr., 1971-75, adminstrv. and planning asst., 1976-77, personnel mgr., 1977—. Sr. warden, vestryman St. Davids Episcopal Ch., 1975-78. Served with AUS, 1944-46; ETO. Republican. Patentee in field aerosol electrification, viscous polymers, cellophane. Home: 3330 Coachman Rd Wilmington DE 19803 Office: E I duPont de Nemours & Co Inc Wilmington DE 19898

HINKLEY, LEO THOMAS, JR., manufacturing company executive; b. Springfield, Mass., Mar. 23, 1926; s. Leo Thomas and Alice (McMahon) H.; m. Anna Marie Cantalini, June 30, 1951; children—Maureen, Leo, Margaret, Mary, Michael, James, Martha Ann. B.S., Holy Cross Coll., 1950; postgrad., Stanford Bus. Sch., 1969. C.P.A., Mass. Acct. Scovell, Wellington & Co. (C.P.A.'s), Springfield, 1950-60; treas. Savage Arms Co., Westfield, Mass., 1960-63; asst. treas. Am. Hardware Corp., New Britain, Conn., 1963-64; asst. controller Emhart Corp., Bloomfield, Conn., 1964-67, controller, 1967-69, v.p., controller, 1969-76; v.p. finance Emhart Industries, Inc., 1976, v.p. adminstrn., 1976-79; v.p. Emhart Corp., 1979—. Served with AUS, 1944-45. Decorated Purple Heart. Mem. Am. Inst. C.P.A.s, Fin. Execs. Inst. Clubs: Quechee, Quechee Lakes (Vt.) Country, Farmington (Conn.) Country. Home: 179 Wood Pond Rd West Hartford CT 06107 Office: 426 Colt Hwy Farmington CT 06032

HINMAN, CHARLES B., artist; b. Dec. 29, 1932. B.F.A., Syracuse U., 1955; student, Art Students League, N.Y.C., 1955-56. Exhibited one man shows, Richard Feigen Galleries, N.Y.C., Chgo., Los Angeles, 1964—, Tokyo (Japan) Gallery, Denise Rene Gallery, N.Y.C., Denise Rene Gallery, Paris, Denise Rene Gallery, Dusseldorf, Irving Galleries, Palm Beach, Bellman Gallery, N.Y.C.; exhibited group shows, Am. Fedn. Arts, Nat. Collection Fine Arts, N.Y. State Council Arts, Whitney Mus.; represented in permanent collections, Mus. Modern Art, N.Y.C., Weatherspoon Gallery Assn., Larry Aldrich Mus. Contemporary Art, Los Angeles County Mus., Detroit Inst. Art, Mus. Modern Art, Nagaoka, Japan, Whitney Mus., Albright Knox Gallery. Address: 231 Bowery New York NY 10002

HINMAN, FRANK, JR., urologist, educator; b. San Francisco, Oct. 2, 1915; s. Frank and Mittie (Fitzpatrick) H.; m. Marion Modesta Eaves, Dec. 3, 1948. A.B. with great distinction, Stanford U., 1937; M.D., Johns Hopkins U., 1941. Diplomate Am. Bd. Urology (trustee 1979—). Intern Johns Hopkins Hosp., 1941-42; resident Cin. Gen. Hosp., 1942-44, U. Calif. Hosp., 1945-47; practice medicine specializing in urology, San Francisco, 1947—; asso. clin. prof. urology U. Calif. - San Francisco, 1954-62; clin. prof. U. Calif.- San Francisco, 1962—; urologist-in-chief Children's Hosp., 1957—; mem. adv. council Nat. Inst. Arthritis, Diabetes, Digestive and Kidney Diseases, 1983—. Served to lt. USNR, 1944-46. Fellow A.C.S. (regent 1972-80, vice-chmn. 1978-79, v.p. 1982-83), Am. Acad. Pediatrics; mem. Am. Urol. Assn., Am. Assn. Genito-Urinary Surgeons (pres. 1981), Clin. Soc. Genito-Urinary Surgeons (pres. 1979), Internat. Urol. Soc. (pres. Am. sect. 1980—), Internat. Nephrological Soc., Am. Assn. Clin. Urologists, Am. Fedn. Clin. Research, Soc. Pediatric Urology (founder, pres. 1971), Soc. Univ. Urologists (founding mem., pres. 1973), Urodynamics Soc. (founding mem., pres. 1980—), Pan Pacific Surg. Assn. (v.p. 1980—), Internat. Continence Soc.; corr. mem. Brit. Assn. Urologic Surgeons, Société Française d'Urologie, Australasian Soc. Urologic Surgeons, Phi Beta Kappa, Alpha Omega Alpha. Clubs: Bohemian, St. Francis Yacht, San Francisco Yacht. Home: 1000 Francisco St San Francisco CA 94109 Office: U of Calif Med Center San Francisco CA 94143 *Devoting two afternooons each week to research, teaching and other academic pursuits, uninterrupted by surgery and clinical practice, can result in satisfying advances.*

HINMAN, GEORGE LYON, lawyer; b. Binghamton, N.Y., Sept. 25, 1905; s. Harvey D. and Phebe (Brown) H.; m. Barbara Davidge, Sept. 12, 1929; children: Constance, Martha, Virginia, Harvey II. A.B., Princeton U., 1927; LL.B., Harvard U., 1930; LL.D., Union Coll., 1962; L.H.D., Elmira Coll., 1950; D.C.L., Colgate U., 1967. Bar: N.Y. 1930. Practice law, Binghamton; assoc. Hinman, Howard & Kattell, 1930-37, partner, 1937—; mem. adv. bd. IBM, dir., 1949-76; adv. dir. Russell Reynolds Assocs., Inc.; former dir. various cos. including IBM World Trade Corp., N.Y. Telephone Corp.; counsel N.Y. State Temp. Commn. on Constl. Conv. and Spl. Legis. Com. on Constl. Revision and Simplification, 1956-58; exec. asst. to gov. N.Y., 1958-59. Mem. Lt. Gov.'s Com. on Tchrs. Salaries, 1951; mem. N.Y. Atty.-Gen.'s Com. on Ethical Standards in Govt.; Republican nat. committeeman for N.Y., 1959-77; del.-at-large Rep. Nat. Conv., 1960, 64, 76; trustee Elmira Coll., 1950-63, SUNY, 1965-70, Colgate U., 1960-70, Harriet Ford Dickenson Found., A. Lindsay and Olive B. O'Connor Found.; former trustee Edward John Noble Found.; chmn. nat. com. Nelson A. Rockefeller Center for Social Scis., Dartmouth Coll.; bd. regents SUNY, 1948-50. Mem. ABA, N.Y. State Bar Assn. (chmn. banking law sect. 1954). Clubs: Harvard, Century Assn., Links, Pilgrims (N.Y.C.); Binghamton City, Edgartown Yacht, Edgartown Golf; Links Golf (L.I.). Home: Hawleyton Rd Binghamton NY 13903 also 201 E 62d St New York NY 10021 Office: Security Mut Bldg Binghamton NY 13901

HINNANT, A(UGUSTUS) RAY(MOND), judge; b. nr. Columbia, S.C., Mar. 2, 1919; s. Julius Josiah and Harriet Rebecca (Douglass) H.; m. June Elizabeth Bellinger, Dec. 26, 1939; children—Carol (Mrs. Gary Michael Davis), Kathryn. LL.B., U. S.C., 1956. Bar: S.C. bar 1955. J.D., 1970; sales rep. Meinecke & Co., N.Y.C., 1938-41, 46-51; judge probate ct., Richland County, S.C., 1955—. Pres. Richland County Mental Health Assn., 1962-63; Mem. S.C. Ho. of Reps., 1948-50. Served with AUS, 1941-46, 51-53. Mem. Am., S.C., Richland County bar assns., S.C. Probate Judges Assn. (pres. 1967-68), Am. Judicature Soc., Nat. Coll. Probate Judges, Assn. U.S. Army (pres. Columbia 1963-64), Phi Delta Phi. Democrat. Methodist. Clubs: Lion., Columbia Exchange (v.p. 1960-61). Home: 6215 Gill Creek Rd Columbia SC 29206 Office: Courthouse Columbia SC 29201

HINOJOSA, BERRONES ALFONSO, bishop; b. Monterrey, Mex., Oct. 7, 1924; s. Emilio H. and Guadalupe (Berrones). Th.D., Gregorian U., Rome, 1951. Ordained priest, Roman Catholic Ch., 1949. Prof. theology Seminario de monterrey; bishop Cludad Victoria (Mex.). Home: Caretera Nacional KM 701 Cludad Victoria Mexico 87000 Office: 15 Hidalgo y Juarez Ciudad Victoria Mexico 87000

HINOJOSA, RICARDO H., federal judge. Judge U.S. Dist. Ct. (so. dist.) Tex. Office: US Dist Ct PO Box 1072 Brownsville TX 78520§

HINOJOSA BERRONES, ALFONSO, bishop; b. Monterrey, Mex., Oct. 7, 1924; s. Emilio Hinojosa and Guadalupe Berrones. Th.D., Gregorian U., Rome. Prof. theology Seminario de Monterrey; ordained priest Roman Catholic Ch.; now bishop of Ciudad Victoria, Mex. Home: Carretera Nacional KM 701 Ciudad Victoria Tamps87000 Mexico Office: 15 Hidalgo y Juárez Ciudad Victoria 87000 Mexico

HINOJOSA-SMITH, ROLAND, English educator, writer; b. Mercedes, Tex., Jan. 21, 1929; s. Manuel Guzman and Carrie Effie (Smith) Hinojosa; m. Patricia Louise Mandley, Sept. 1, 1963; children: Clarissa Elizabeth, Karen Louise. B.S., U. Tex., 1953; A.M., N.Mex. Highlands U., 1963; Ph.D., U. Ill., 1969. Chmn. dept. modern langs. Tex A&I U., Kingsville, 1970-74, dean Coll. Arts and Scis., 1974-76; v.p. acad. affairs Tex. A&I U., Kingsville, 1976-77; prof. English U. Minn., Mpls., 1977-81, U. Tex., Austin, 1981—. Author: Estampas del Valle, 1973 (Quinto Sol 1973), Klail City, 1976 (Casa de los Americas 1976), Korean Love Songs, 1978, The Valley, 1983. Served to 2d lt. U.S. Army, 1951-53. Ford fellow, 1979. Fellow Soc. Spanish and Spanish Am. Studies; mem. MLA, Am. PEN, Academia Real de al Lengua, Hispanic Soc. Democrat. Roman Catholic. Home: 7502 Daugherty St Austin TX 78758 Office: Dept English U Tex Austin TX 78712

HINRICHS, JERALD RAY, insurance company executive; b. Fairmont, Minn., June 2, 1933; s. Harry Edward and Evelyn L. (Jaqua) H.; m. Betty JoAnn Harris, Sept. 5, 1953; children: Jay Scott, Jill Annette, Jana Lynn. B.S., Mankato (Minn.) State U., 1955; C.L.U., Am. Coll. Life Underwriters, 1970. Agt. to gen. mgr. N.Y. Life Ins. Co., Mpls. and Kansas City, 1959-70, gen. mgr., Wichita, Kans., 1970-78, regional v.p., Kansas City, 1979-80, v.p., N.Y.C., 1980-82, sr. v.p., 1982—. Served with U.S. Army, 1956-58. Mem. Am. Coll. Life Underwriters, Life Underwriters Assn., Gen. Arts and Mgrs. Assn. (pres. Wichita 1970-83, Nat. Mgmt. award 1975-80), Sales and Mktg. Execs. Assn. (local pres. 1975). Republican. Roman Catholic. Club: K.C. (local pres. 1958-59). Home: 148 Weeburn Dr New Canaan CT 06840 Office: New York Life InsuranceCo 51 Madison Ave New York NY 10010

HINSEY, JOSEPH, IV, lawyer; b. Palo Alto, Calif., Oct. 17, 1931; s. Joseph Clarence and Sarah (Callen) H.; m. Phyllis Heartt LaRue, June 23, 1956; children—Carolyn Jeanne, Nancy Alison, Sara Ruth. A.B., Cornell U., 1953, LL.B., 1955; M.B.A., Harvard U., 1957. Bar: N.Y. bar 1956. Assoc. firm White & Case, N.Y.C., 1957-65, ptnr., 1965—; mem. legal adv. com. N.Y. Stock Exchange., 1978-83. Editor: The Business Lawyer, 1981-82. Mem. Am. Bar Assn. (chmn. bus. mgmt. liability ins. com. 1972-80, corp. banking and bus. law sect. 1983—1972-80, chmn. audit com. 1973-80), N.Y. State Bar Assn. (exec. com. corp. banking and bus. law sect. 1977—, com. corp. law 1970—), Assn. Bar City N.Y., Am. Law Inst. (cons. corp. govt. project), Am. Inst. C.P.A.s (auditing standards adv. council 1980-83). Home: 130 Old Army Rd Scarsdale NY 10583 Office: 14 Wall St New York NY 10005

HINSHAW, CARROLL ELTON, economist; b. Texarkana, Aug. 2, 1936; s. Curtis Tillman and Loma Dean (Roberts) H.; m. Jane A. Simpson, Aug. 11, 1958; children—Stephen, Rebecca, Carroll. B.B.A., Baylor U., 1958; Ph.D., Vanderbilt U., 1966. Asso. prof. La. Coll., 1962-64; asst. prof. Vanderbilt U., 1966-72; asso. prof. econs., 1972—, asst. dean, 1970-72, asso. dean, 1972-74; vis. asst. prof. Getulio Vargas Found., Rio de Janeiro, Brazil, 1967-69; cons. in field. Author: Forecasting and Recognizing Business Cycle Turning Points, 1968; Contbr. articles to profl. jours. H.B. Earhart fellow, 1965-66. Mem. Am. Econ. Assn. (sec. 1976—), Am. Council Learned Socs., So. Econ. Assn., AAUP, Am. Soc. Assn. Execs., Beta Alpha Psi, Omicron Delta Epsilon. Baptist. Home: 151 Windsor Dr Nashville TN 37205 Office: 1313 21st Ave S Nashville TN 37212

HINSHAW, DAVID BURDG, physician, educator; b. Whittier, Calif., Nov. 24, 1923; s. Lindsey and Hazel Grace (Burdg) H.; m. Mildred Helen Benjamin, Dec. 23, 1943; children: David Burdg, Kathleen Marie, Daniel Benjamin. Student, La S'erra Coll., Riverside, Cal., 1940-43; M.D., Loma Linda U., 1946. Intern White Meml. Hosp., Los Angeles, 1946-47; fellow Loma Linda U., 1947-48; resident surgery VA Hosp., Portland, Oreg., 1950-54; mem. faculty Loma Linda U. Sch. Medicine, 1954—, prof. surgery, chmn. dept., 1961-78, dean, 1962-75; chief surgery service Jerry L. Pettis Meml. VA Hosp.; dean Oral Roberts U. Sch. Medicine, Tulsa, 1982—. Contbr. articles to med. jours. Served with M.C. AUS, 1948-50. Mem. A.C.S. (gov.), Soc. Univ. Surgeons, Am., Western, Pacific Coast surg. assns., Soc. Internat. Surgery, Internat. Cardiovascular Soc., Soc. Surgery Alimentary Tract, AMA, Okla. Med. Soc., San Bernardino County Med. Soc. Home: 8779 S Richmond Ave Tulsa OK 74137

HINSHAW, EDWARD BANKS, broadcasting company executive; b. Aurora, Ill., Feb. 27, 1940; s. Lorenzo M. and Emily (Roach) H.; m. Victoria Leone Biggers, Jan. 16, 1965; children: Eric, Brian. Student, Harvard Coll., 1958-59, U. Minn., 1959-62. Announcer Sta. KSTP-Radio-TV, Mpls., 1959-64; announcer Voice of America, Washington, 1964-65; reporter, anchorman Sta. WTMJ, Inc., Milw., 1965-70, editorialist, 1970-74, editorial dir., 1974—, mgr. public affairs, 1979—; instr. broadcast journalism U. Wis., Whitewater, 1976, 79. Trustee 1st Amendment Congress, 1980-83. Recipient DuPont-Columbia Citation in Broadcast Journalism, 1978; Abe Lincoln Merit award So. Baptist Radio-TV Commn., 1978; NCCJ Gold Media Medallion, 1977. Mem. Nat. Broadcast Editorial Assn. (pres. 1980-81), Sigma Delta Chi (Disting. Service award 1977). Office: 720 E Capitol Dr Milwaukee WI 53201

HINSHAW, ERNEST THEODORE, JR., Olympics executive, former financial executive; b. San Rafael, Calif., Aug. 26, 1928; s. Ernest Theodore and Ina (Johnson) H.; m. Nell Marie Schildmeyer, June 24, 1952; children: Marc Christopher, Lisa Anne, Jennifer, Amy Lynn. A.B., Stanford U., 1951, M.B.A., 1957. Staff asst. to pres. Capital Research and Mgmt. Co., Los Angeles, 1957-58, dir. planning, 1967-68; fin. analyst Capital Research Co., Los Angeles, N.Y.C., 1958-68, v.p., 1962-71, mgr. N.Y.C. office, 1962-66; dir., exec. v.p. Am. Funds Service Co., Los Angeles, 1968-69, pres., 1969-72, chmn. bd., 1972-82; dir. pres. Capital Data Systems, Inc., Los Angeles, 1971-73, chmn., 1973-79; v.p. Capital Group, Inc., Los Angeles, 1973-83; sr. v.p. Growth Fund Am., 1973-74, pres., 1974-76, chmn. bd., 1976-82, now dir.; sr. v.p. Income Fund Am., 1973-74, pres., dir., 1974-76, chmn. bd., 1976-82, now dir.; commr. yachting 1984 Olympic games Los Angeles Olympic Organizing Com., 1980—; dir. Capital Research & Mgmt. Co., 1972-83; mem. guest faculty Northwestern U. Transp. Center, 1965-66; mem. ops. com. Investment Co. Inst., 1970-74. Served to 1st lt. USMC, 1951-53. Mem. Soc. Airline Analysts (sec. 1965-66), Los Angeles Soc. Fin. Analysts, N.Y. Soc. Security Analysts, Am. Statis. Assn., Town Hall Calif., Nat. Kite Class (pres. 1968-69), Lido 14 Internat. Class Assn. (pres. 1978-79), Assn. Orange Coast Yacht Clubs (commodore 1976), So. Calif. Yachting Assn. (commodore 1979), B.O.A.T., Inc. (dir. 1977-81), Pacific Coast Yachting Assn. (dir. 1979-80), U.S. Yacht Racing Union (dir. 1980-81). Democrat. Clubs: Wall Street (N.Y.C.); University (Los Angeles); Lido Isle Yacht (Newport Beach, Calif.) (commodore 1973); St. Francis Yacht (San Francisco); Ft. Worth Boat. Home: 729 Via Lido Soud Newport Beach CA 92663

HINSHAW, HORTON CORWIN, physician; b. Iowa Falls, Iowa, 1902; s. Milas Clark and Ida (Bushong) H.; m. Dorothy Youmans, Aug. 6, 1924; children—Horton Corwin, Barbara (Mrs. Barbara Baird), William, Dorothy (Mrs. Gregory Patent). A.B., Coll. Idaho, 1923, D.Sc., 1947; A.M., U. Calif., 1926, Ph.D., 1927; M.D., U. Pa., 1933. Diplomate: Am. Bd. Internal Medicine, Nat. Bd. Med. Examiners. Asst. prof. zoology U. Calif., 1927-28; adj. prof. parasitology and bacteriology Am. U., Beirut, Lebanon, 1928-31; instr. bacteriology U. Pa. Sch. Medicine, 1931-33; fellow, 1st asst. medicine. Mayo Found., U. Minn., 1933-35, asst. prof., 1937-46, asso. prof., 1946-49; cons. medicine Mayo clinic, 1935- 49, head sec. medicine, 1947-49; clin. prof. medicine, head div. chest diseases Stanford Med. Sch., 1949-59; clin. prof. medicine U. Calif. Med. Sch., 1959-79, emeritus prof., 1979—; chief thoracic disease service So. Pacific Meml. Hosp., 1958-69; dir. med. services and chief staff Harkness Community Hosp. and Med. Center, San Francisco, 1968-75; Dir. med. operations Health Maintenance No. Calif., Inc.; Mem. Calif. Com. Regional Med. Programs, 1969-75. Author: Diseases of the Chest, rev. edit., 1980; co-author: Streptomycin in Tuberculosis, 1949; Contbr. over 215 articles to med. publs. Del. various internat. confs., 1928-59. Fellow A.C.P., Am. Coll. Chest Physicians; hon. mem. Miss. Valley Med. Assn.; mem. Nat. Tb Assn. (bd. dirs., chmn. com. therapy, v.p. 1946- 47, 67-68, research com.), Am. Thoracic Soc. (pres. 1948-49, hon. life 1979), Am. Clin. and Climatol. Soc., Minn. Med. Assn., Am. Bronchoesophalogical Assn., A.M.A., Am. Soc. Clin. Investigation, Central Soc. Clin. Research, Soc. Exptl. Biology and Medicine, Aero-Med. Assn., Am. Lung Assn. (hon., Hall of Fame 1980), Minn. Soc. Internal Medicine, Sigma Xi, Phi Sigma, Gamma Alpha.; Mem. Soc. of Friends. Co-discoverer anti-Tb chemotherapy, exptl. and clin., with several drugs. Home: Box 546 512 San Rafael Ave Belvedere CA 94920 Office: 450 Sutter St San Francisco CA 94108 *Scientific research is a game, played like many others. Whether dealing with atoms, guinea pigs or humans the contest is to penetrate the secrets of nature by arranging facts in a logical sequence. Many attempts fail, but well documented failures help scientists who follow. Satisfaction is supreme in scientific medical research when victory is shared by countless potential victims of such diseases as tuberculosis and leprosy.*

HINSHAW, LERNER BRADY, physiology educator; b. San Diego, June 9, 1921; s. Lerner Andrew and Ruth Anna (Brady) H.; m. Alice E. Larson, June 28, 1946; children: Mark L., Carol J., Roger W., Paul B. B.A., U. So. Calif., 1949, M.S., 1952, M.A., 1953, Ph.D., 1955. Instr. U. Minn. Med. Sch., Mpls., 1955-59, asst. prof., 1959-61; research physiologist Civil Aeromed. Research Inst., Oklahoma City, 1961-65; prof. physiology and biophysics, research prof. surgery Med. Center U. Okla., Oklahoma City, 1965—; med. investigator VA Hosp., Oklahoma City, 1965—; prof. biology Oklahoma City U., 1965-71; chmn. research adv. group VA, Washington, 1974-75, mem. research adv. com., 1975-76. Editorial bd.: Circulatory Shock, 1974—; Contbr. articles to profl. jours. Pres. PTA Council, Norman, 1969-71; mem. Norman Civic Improvement Council, 1969-71; bd. dirs. Okla. Heart Assn., 1971, 78. Served to capt. C.E. AUS, 1942-46; ETO. Life Ins. Med. Research fellow, 1955-57; Recipient Lederle Med. Faculty award, 1959-62; apptd. VA research career scientist. Mem. Am. Physiol. Soc. (circulation group), Soc. Exptl. Biol. Medicine, Western Soc. Clin. Research, Central Clin. Soc., Am. Soc. Pharm. and Exptl. Therapeutics, Am. Heart Assn. (med. adv. bd. council circulation), Soc. Clin. Care Medicine, Internat. Inflammation Club. Presbyn. Home: 401 Merkle Dr Norman OK 73069 *My view as a medical investigator (researcher): I see myself as standing on the periphery of a fantastically exciting universe. What is behind me is known; what is beyond me is the unknown. What I clearly perceive is that the unknown is infinitely greater than all that I now know. As I zero in on a fragment of the truth ahead of me, I know I must keep a proper perspective of what I think the entire truth must be. At this point, my faith to comes into harmony with my scientific endeavors. I believe that a divine thread runs through all of reality, not only in theology, but in science also.*

HINSHAW, RANDALL (WESTON), economist, educator; b. La Grange, Ill., May 9, 1915; s. Virgil Goodman and Evelyn (Piltz) H.; m. Pearl Electa Stevens, June 19, 1949; children: Frederic Randall, Robert Louis, Elisabeth Mary. A.B., Occidental Coll., 1937, M.A., 1939; Ph.D., Princeton U., 1944. Teaching fellow Harvard, 1942-43; asst. prof. Amherst Coll., 1946-47; vis. prof. Yale, 1957-58, Oberlin Coll., 1958-59, U. So. Calif., 1963-64, Bologna Center, Johns Hopkins, 1965-67, 71, Disting. vis. prof. econs., 1983; prof. econs. Claremont Grad. Sch., 1960-82, prof. econs. emeritus, 1982—, chmn. dept., 1967-69, 77-79; dir., chmn. planning com. Bologna-Claremont biennial internat. monetary conf. series, 1967—; economist div. internat. finance Fed. Res. Bd., 1943-46, 47-52; Spl. adviser, U.S. rep. various internat. confs. and coms. U.S. Mission to NATO (USRO), Paris, 1952-57. Author: The European Community and American Trade, 1964, Monetary Reform and the Price of Gold, 1967, The Economics of International Adjustment, 1970, Inflation as a Global Problem, 1972, Key Issues in International Monetary Reform, 1975, Stagflation—An International Problem, 1977, Domestic Goals and Financial Interdependence, 1980, Global Monetary Anarchy, 1981, Global Economic Priorities, 1983; contbr. articles to various jours. South East Club fellow Princeton, 1940-41. Mem. Am. Econ. Assn., Western Econ. Assn., Council Fgn. Relations, Phi Beta Kappa. Home: 755 W 8th St Claremont CA 91711

HINSHAW, VIRGIL GOODMAN, JR., philosopher, educator; b. LaGrange, Ill., Nov. 3, 1919; s. Virgil Goodman and Evelyn (Piltz) H.; m. Alene Kinsey Pryor, June 12, 1950; children: Stephen, Sally. B.A., Stanford U., 1941; M.A., State U. Iowa, 1942, Princeton U., 1943, Ph.D., 1945. Asst. State U. Iowa, Iowa City, 1941-42; instr. philosophy Ohio State U., Columbus, 1946-47, asst. prof., 1947-53, asso. prof., 1953-60, prof., 1960-81, prof. emeritus, 1981—, dir. grad. studies, 1968-71, vice chmn., 1971-80; cons. Office Naval Research, 1958-59, 62, Congress Neurol. Surgeons, 1964, Wright Patterson AFB, 1983. Contbr. articles to profl. jours. Bd. govs. Arthritis Found. Central Ohio. Mem. Am. Philos. Assn., Assn. Symbolic Logic, AAAS, AAUP, Philosophy of Sci. Assn., Ohio Coll. Assn. (sect. pres. 1955-58), N.Y. Acad. Scis., Assn. Princeton U. Grad. Alumni. (governing bd. 1975—), Phi Beta Kappa. Democrat. Methodist. Home: 1573 Kirkley Rd Columbus OH 43221 *At the moment I can only repeat what, nearing eighty years of age, one of my many gifted teachers said about ". . . love, Christian love or compassion. If you feel this, you have a motive for existence, a guide in action, a reason for courage, an imperative necessity for intellectual honesty." (Bertrand Russell, The Impact of Science on Society, 1959)*

HINSON, HOWARD HOUSTON, petroleum company executive; b. Fletcher, Okla., Mar. 3, 1913; s. Jasper Lafayette and Dana (Wunsch) H.; m. Louise Lawson, May 31, 1934 (dec.); children: Barbara Ann Hinson Brightwell, Larry Howard; m. Doris Lloyd Findley, 1976. B.S., Tex. Tech Coll., Lubbock, 1934, M.S., 1945; postgrad., Advanced Mgmt. Program, Harvard U. Registered profl. engr., Tex. Jr. petroleum engr. helium plants U.S. Bur. Mines, Tex., 1936-40, asst. petroleum engr., 1940-42, asso. petroleum engr., 1942-43, petroleum engr., 1943-44, sr. petroleum engr., 1944-47, asst. supervising engr., 1947-48; chief prodn. research engr. Continental Oil Co., 1948-50, asst. mgr. prodn., 1950-52, southwestern regional gen. mgr., 1952, v.p. fgn. dept., 1953-57, dir., 1958-66, v.p. fgn. exploration and prodn., 1957-61, v.p., gen. mgr. internat. exploration, prodn., 1961-66, cons., 1966-68; pres., dir. Imperial-Am. Mgmt. Co., Houston, 1968-69; partner Hinson & Hall, 1969-72, Hinson, Hall & Smith, 1971-72; pres. Tex. Pacific Oil Co., Inc., Dallas, 1972-82. Contbr. articles to profl. jours. Bd. dirs. Dallas Council World Affairs. Recipient Distinguished Engr. award Tex. Tech U., 1975, Distinguished Alumnus award, 1976. Mem. Am. Petroleum Inst., Soc. Petroleum Engrs., Ind. Petroleum Assn., Inst. Mining and Metall. Engrs., Am. Assn. Petroleum Geologists, Pres.'s Assn. N.Y., Mid-Continent Oil and Gas Assn. (dir. 1976), Tau Beta Pi. Clubs: Petroleum, Plaza (Dallas); Willowbrook Holytree (Tyler, Tex.); Ramada (Houston); Fort Worth. Office: 9400 N Central Expressway Dallas TX 75231

HINTIKKA, KAARLO JAAKKO, philosopher; b. Helsingin pitäjä, Finland, Jan. 12, 1929; s. Toivo Juho and Lempi J. (Salmi) H.; m. Merrill Bristow Provence, Feb. 11, 1978. Cand. Phil. Lic. Phil., U. Helsinki, Finland, 1952, Dr.Phil., 1956; exchange student, Williams Coll., 1948-49; post-doctoral scholar, Harvard U., 1954. Jr. fellow Soc. Fellows, Harvard U., 1956-59; prof. philosophy U. Helsinki, 1959-70; research prof. Acad. Finland, 1970-81; vis. prof. Brown U., 1962, U. Calif., Berkeley, 1963, Hebrew U. Jerusalem, 1974; prof. philosophy Stanford U., part-time 1964-82, Fla. State U., 1978—; John Locke lectr. Oxford (Eng.) U., 1964; fellow Center for Advanced Study in Behavioral Scis., 1970-71; fgn. mem., mem. Forschungsrat of Internationales Forschungszentrum, Salzburg, Austria, 1966—. Author: Knowledge and Belief, 1962, Models for Modalities, 1969, Tieto on Valtaa, 1969, Logic, Language-Games and Information, 1973, Time and Necessity, 1973, Knowledge and the Known, 1974, (with U. Remes) The Method of Analysis, 1974, The Intentions of Intentionality, 1975, The Semantics of Questions and the Questions of Semantics, 1976, Aristotle on Modality and Determinism, 1977; contbr. over 200 articles to profl. jours.; Editor-in-chief: Internat. Jour. Synthese, 1965-76, 82—; editor: Synthese Library, 1965—, Acta Philosophica Fennica, 1973-79, Synthese Language Library, 1976—, (with Patrick Suppes) Aspects of Inductive Logic, 1966, Philosophy of Mathematics, 1969, (with Donald Davidson) Words and Objections, 1969, (with Patrick Suppes) Information and Inference, 1970, (with others) Approaches to Natural Language, 1973, Rudolf Carnap, Logical Empiricist, 1976, (with others) Essays on Wittgenstein in Honor of G.H. von Wright, 1976, (with Robert Butts) Procs. Fifth Internat. Congress Logic, Methodology and Philosophy of Science (4 vols.), 1977. Decorated comdr. Order of the Lion, Finland; recipient Wihuri Internat. prize, 1976; Guggenheim fellow, 1979-80. Mem. Assn. Symbolic Logic (v.p. 1968-70), Internat. Inst. Philosophy, Internat. Union History and Philosophy Sci. (v.p. 1971-75, pres. 1975), Finnish Acad. Sci. and Letters (council 1972-79), Philosophy of Sci. Assn. (governing bd. 1970-72), Societas Scientiarum Fennica, Internat. Fedn. Philos. Socs. (governing bd. 1978—), Am. Philos. Assn. (v.p. Pacific div. 1974-75, pres. 1975-76), Am. Acad. Arts and Scis. (council for philos. studies 1982—). Home: 3086 Waterford Dr Tallahassee FL 32308 Office: Dept Philosophy Florida State U Tallahassee FL 32306 also Inst Philosophy Unioninkatu 40 B 00170 Helsinki 17 Finland

HINTON, CLAUDE WILLEY, genetics educator; b. Gatesville, N.C., Aug. 1, 1928; s. Claude W. and Addie (Hudgins) H.; m. Jean Marie Belmont, Dec. 26, 1952; children: Rebecca, Claire. A.B., U. N.C., 1948, M.A., 1950; Ph.D., Calif. Inst. Tech., 1954. Research assoc. in biology Oak Ridge Nat. Lab., 1954-55; asst. prof. to prof. zoology U. Ga., 1955-68; Mateer prof. biology Coll. of Wooster, Ohio, 1968—; summer vis. prof. U. Wash., 1962, U. Oreg., 1965; vis. investigator genetics sect. div. plant industry Commonwealth Sci. and Indsl. Orgn., Canberra, Australia, 1972-73; vis. investigator biology U. Calif. at San Diego, 1977-78; vis. scientists U. N.C., Chapel Hill, 1982-83; cons. in field, 1949—. Predoctoral fellow AEC, 1950-52, USPHS, 1952-54. Fellow AAAS; mem. Genetics Soc. Am., Soc. Am. Naturalists, Am. Genetic Assn. Research on chromosome behavior and its genetic control in Drosophila. Home: 510 Beechwood Ave Wooster OH 44691

HINTON, DEANE ROESCH, ambassador; b. Fort Missoula, Mont., Mar. 12, 1923; s. Joe A. and Doris (Roesch) H.; m. Angela E. Peyraud, May 10, 1946 (div. 1971); children: Deborah, Christopher, Jeffrey, Joanna, Veronica; m. Miren de Aretxabala, Dec. 6, 1971 (dec. Nov. 1979); stepchildren: Pedro, Guillermo, Miren, Maria, Juan, Sebastian; m. Patricia Lopez, Feb. 14, 1983. Grad., Elgin (Ill.) Acad., 1940; B.A., U. Chgo., 1943, postgrad., 1946; postgrad., Fletcher Sch. Law and Diplomacy also Harvard U., 1951-52. Apptd. fgn. service officer, 1946; with Dept. State, Washington, 1946, 51-52, 55-58; 3d sec., vice consul, Damascus, 1947-48, 2d sec., vice consul, 1948-49, vice consul, Mombasa, Kenya, 1949, consul, 1949-51, 2d sec., consul, Paris, France, 1952-55; attache U.S. Mission to European Communities, Brussels, Belgium, 1958-59, 1st sec., 1959-61; grad. Nat. War Coll., 1962; chief commodity programming div. Dept. State, 1962-63; dir. Office Atlantic Polit. Econ. Affairs, 1963-67, AID mission to, Guatemala, 1967-69, Chile, econ. counselor, Santiago, 1969-71; asst. dir. Council Internat. Econ. Policy, Washington, 1971-73, dep. dir., 1973-74; ambassador to Zaire, Kinshasa, 1974-75; U.S. rep. U.S. mission to European Communities, Brussels, 1976-79; asst. sec. state for econs. and bus., 1980-81, ambassador to El Salvador, San Salvador, 1981-83, ambassador to Pakistan, Islamabad, 1983—; professorial lectr. Am. U., Washington. Served to 2d lt. AUS, 1943-45. Recipient Dept. State Superior Service award, 1967, Presdl. award for disting. diplomatic service, 1983. Mem. Council Fgn. Relations, Fgn. Service Assn., Royal Central Asian Soc., Soc. Internat. Devel. Office: Am Embassy-Islamabad Dept State Washington DC 20520

HINTON, S(USAN) E(LOISE), author; b. Tulsa, 1948; m. David Inhofe, 1970. Grad., U. Tulsa, 1970. Author teen-age fiction; books include The Outsiders, 1967, That Was Then, This Is Now, 1971, Rumble Fish, 1975, Tex, 1979; screen play Rumble Fish. Recipient Media and Methods Maxi award, 1975; Nat. Book award nominee, 1981. Office: care Press Relations Delacorte Press 1 Dag Hammarskjold Plaza New York NY 10017

HINTON, WARREN S., hospital consultant; b. Wichita, Kans., Nov. 19, 1921; s. Joseph Robert and Callie (Stickley) H.; m. Patricia Head, Sept. 25, 1954; children: Heidi, Walter. Student, Friends U., Wichita, 1945-46, 47-48; A.B., Kans. U., 1949; M.H.A., St. Louis U., 1952. Adminstrv. resident Menorah Hosp., Kansas City, Mo., 1951-52; asst. adminstr. Meth. Hosp. and Med. Center, St. Joseph, Mo., 1952-61, adminstr., 1961-70; exec. dir. Meth. Med. Center, 1970-80, pres., 1980-81; mem. faculty U. Mo., Columbia.; Mem. Area II Health Systems Agy., 1975-81, pres., 1976-78; mem. Mo. Bd. Health, 1975—, pres., 1978—. V.p. bd. hosps. and homes Mo.-West Conf. United Meth. Ch., 1963-70. Served with AUS, 1942-45. Fellow Am. Coll. Hosp. Adminstrs.; mem. Mid-West Hosp. Assn. (treas. 1971-72, pres. 1973-74), Am. Hosp. Assn. (life mem.; ho. of dels. 1970-73), Mo. Hosp. Assn. (pres. 1970-71), Am. Protestant Hosp. Assn. (trustee 1975-81). Methodist. Club: Mason (Shriner). Home and Office: Box 236 Amity MO 64422

HINTZ, ROBERT LOUIS, railroad executive; b. Chgo., May 25, 1930; s. Louis A. and Gertrude V. (Herman) H.; m. Gloria Mae Safbom, Nov. 12, 1955; children—Cary, Leslie, David, Erin. B.S. in Bus. Adminstrn. magna cum laude, Northwestern U., 1960, M.B.A., 1965. With Chessie System Inc., 1963—; internal audit officer C. & O. Ry., Cleve., 1963-65; staff asst. to v.p. C. & O. Ry.-B. & O. R.R., Cleve., 1965-68, asst. to v.p., 1968-70, comptroller, Balt., 1970-72, asst. to pres. parent co., Cleve., 1972-74, v.p. corporate services, 1974-76, v.p. fin., 1976-78, sr. v.p. fin., 1978-80, CSX Corp., Richmond, Va., 1980—; dir. Aviation Enterprises, Chesapeake and Ohio R.R., Robertshaw Control Co., Balt. and Ohio R.R., Third Nat. Bank Corp., Western Md. R.R., Nat. Mine Services, Seaboard Coast Line R.R., Louisville and Nashville R.R. Co. Trustee St. Joseph's Villa; bus. adv. council Va. Poly. Inst., Va. Commonwealth U., U. Richmond. Served with USAF, 1950-54. Mem. Am. Mgmt. Assn. (fin. council), Fin. Execs. Inst. Roman Catholic. Clubs: Lakewood Country, Hermitage Country, Commonwealth., Country of Va. Home: 10002 Walsham Ct Richmond VA 23233 Office: Fed Reserve Bldg Richmond VA 23261

HINZ, CARL FREDERICK, JR., physician, educator; b. Cleve., Apr. 9, 1927; s. Carl Frederick and Marie (Jones) H.; m. Joan Herndon, June 5, 1953; children—Elizabeth, Richard, Catherine, Gretchen. B.S., Western Res. U., 1948, M.D., 1951. Faculty dept. medicine Western Res. U. Sch. Medicine, Cleve., 1953-67, asst. prof., 1961-67, research asso. dir. research in med. edn., 1964-67; prof., asso. dean U. Conn. Sch. Medicine, 1967—, acting head dept. medicine, 1979-80; mem. Conn. Med. Exam. Bd., 1976-80. Markle scholar, 1959-64. Mem. Am. Soc. Clin. Investigation, Am. Assn. Immunologists, Am. Soc. Hematology, Central Soc. Clin. Research, Am. Fedn. Clin. Research, Conn. Med. Soc., Hartford County Med. Assn. (dir. 1976—), Conn. Lung Assn. (pres. 1979-81). Home: 11 Highwood Dr Avon CT 06001 Office: U Conn Sch Medicine Farmington CT 06032

HINZE, WILLIAM JAMES, geophysics educator; b. Milw., July 26, 1930; s. Walter G. and Loraine K. (Rasmussen) H.; m. Marilyn A. Thornburg, June 21, 1956; children: Laura Lynn, Linda Maria. B.S., U. Wis., 1951, Ph.D., 1957. Staff geophysicist Jones & Laughlin Steel Co., Negaunee, Mich., 1953-58; prof. geophysics Mich. State U., East Lansing, 1958-71, Purdue U., West Lafayette, Ind., 1971—. Mem. Soc. Exploration Geophysicists, Am. Geophys. Union, Sigma Xi, Geol. Soc. Am. (chmn. geophysics div. 1983). Research interests: potential-field exploration geophysics and intra-plate tectonics. Home: 30 Brook Hollow West Lafayette IN 47906 Office: Purdue Univ Dept Geoscis West Lafayette IN 47907

HIPP, FRANCIS MOFFETT, insurance executive; b. Newberry, S.C., Mar. 3, 1911; s. William Frank and Eunice Jane (Halfacre) H.; m. Mary M. Looper, Nov. 10, 1935 (dec. 1962); children: Mary Elizabeth (dec.), William, John, Mary Jane; m. Shirley A. Mattoon, May 11, 1964. Student, The Citadel, 1929-31; A.B., Furman U., 1933, LL.D., 1968; LL.D., U. S.C., 1964, The Citadel, 1968, Clemson U., 1980, Benedict Coll., 1983. With Liberty Life Ins. Co., 1933—, asst. treas., 1936-41, v.p., 1942, pres., chmn. bd., 1943—; chmn. bd. Liberty Corp., 1977—, pres., chmn. bd., Greenville, S.C., 1976-77; dir. United Fidelity Life Ins. Co.; chmn. exec. com., dir. Cosmos Broadcasting Corp., Greenville; dir. S.C. Nat. Corp., Columbia; dir. emeritus S.C. Electric & Gas Co., Columbia.; Mem. S.C. Devel. Bd., 1955—, chmn., 1959-63; state v.p. Am. Life Conv., 1947-57, mem. exec. com., 1957-63, Life Insurors Conf., 1961-64. Trustee S.C. Found. Ind. Colls., Queens Coll., N.C., The Citadel Devel. Found.; nat. adv. council Bus. Partnership Found. of U. S.C.; nat. bd. govs. Inst. Living, Hartford; chmn. Palmetto Found., Columbia, Palmetto Bus. Forum. Recipient Businessman of Yr. award S.C. C. of C., 1980. Mem. Newcomen Soc., Kappa Alpha, Beta Gamma Sigma. Presbyn. Clubs: Greenville Country, Poinsett, Green Valley Country (Greenville, S.C.); Augusta (Ga.); Nat. Golf; Summit (Columbia). Home: 33 W Avondale Dr Greenville SC 29609 Office: Wade Hampton Blvd Greenville SC 29602

HIPP, FREDERICK RICHARD, restaurant company executive; b. Buffalo, Apr. 5, 1950; s. Frederick Adam and Kathleen (Dunning) H.; 1 son, Adam. B.B.A., Ohio U.-Athens, 1972. Dir. restaurant systems S & A Restaurants, Inc., Dallas, 1971-78; pres. RDS Inc., Dallas, 1978-80; exec. v.p. Gilbert/Robinson, Inc., Kansas City, Mo., 1980—. Mem. Nat. Restaurant Assn. (mem. steering com. 1978), Mo. Restaurant Assn. Republican. Episcopalian. Home: 721 W 49th Terr Kansas City MO 64112 Office: Gilbert/Robinson Inc 47th St and Main St Kansas City MO 64112

HIPP, WILLIAM HAYNE, insurance and broadcasting executive; b. Greenville, S.C., Mar. 11, 1940; s. Francis Moffett and Mary Matilda (Looper) H.; m. Anna Kate Reid, June 14, 1963; children: Mary Henigan, Francis Reid, Anna Hayne. B.A., Washington and Lee U., 1962; M.B.A., U. Pa., 1965; grad., Harvard U. Program Mgmt. Devel., 1971. With Met. Life Ins. Co., 1965-69; v.p. Liberty Life Ins. Co., Greenville, S.C., 1969-74, sr. v.p. investments, 1975-77, exec. v.p., 1977-79, chmn. bd., 1979—; vice chmn., chief exec. officer Liberty Corp., 1979—, pres., 1981—; dir. Textile Hall Corp., Cosmos Broadcasting Co., Columbia, S.C., S.C. Electric & Gas Co., Dan River, Inc., S.C. Nat. Bank. Trustee, vice chmn. Nat. Urban League, 1979—; trustee Greenville County Found., 1978-83, Episcopal High Sch., Alexandria, Va., 1982—; pres. Met. YMCA, 1979; trustee Greenville County Sch. System, 1975; bd. dirs. Am. Council Life Ins., 1979-83, S.C. State Devel. Bd., 1980—, S.C. C. of C., 1983. Office: PO Box 789 Greenville SC 29602

HIPPLE, JAMES BLACKMAN, diversified energy company executive; b. Pierre, S.D., Oct. 14, 1934; s. James Bowman and Leola (Blackman) H.; m. Jeanette Pellerin, May 10, 1958; children—Carolyn Jean, Leah Margaret. B.S., La. State U., 1957. C.P.A., La., Tex.; cert. data processor; cert. internal auditor. With Tex. Eastern Corp., Houston, 1957—, asst. sec.-asst. treas., 1969-76, treas., 1976-81, comptroller, 1981—. Served to 1st lt. AUS, 1958-60. Mem. Inst. Internal Auditors (pres. Ark.-La.-Tex. chpt. 1967), La. Soc. C.P.A.'s (dir. Shreveport chpt. 1967), Fin. Execs. Inst., Tex. Soc. C.P.A.'s. Address: PO Box 2521 Houston TX 77252

HIPPLE, WALTER JOHN, educator, coll. ofcl.; b. Chgo., Mar. 14, 1921; s. Walter John and Emilie (Scheu) H.; m. Anne Ruth Poier, Nov. 27, 1962; children—Heidi Kristina, Ethan John. B.A., U. Chgo., 1947, M.A., 1948, Ph.D., 1954; postdoctoral, Courtauld Inst., U. London, 1957, Cambridge (Eng.) U., 1961-62. Lectr. Roosevelt U., 1948; instr. U. Chgo., 1948-50, U. Ark., 1951-52; asst. prof. U. Fla., 1952-56; asso. prof. Cornell Coll., 1957-61; prof. U. Pacific, 1962, Idaho State U., 1963, U. So. Calif., summer 1963; chmn. dept. humanities, prof. Ind. State U., Terre Haute, 1963-72; dean coll. Shimer Coll., Mt. Carroll, Ill., 1972-76; acad. v.p. West Chester (Pa.) State Coll., 1976-77, prof. philosophy, 1977—, asso. to pres., 1977-79, dir. of honors, 1979—; Chmn. Com. on Humanities in Secondary Schs. Ind., 1965-69. Author: The Beautiful, The Sublime, and the Picturesque in Eighteenth-Century British Aesthetic Theory, 1957; Editor: An Essay on Taste (1759) by Alexander Gerard with an Introduction by Walter J. Hipple, Jr, 1963; Contbr. articles to profl. jours. Served with Signal Corps attached to Air Corps AUS, 1943-45. Guggenheim fellow, 1961-62. Mem. Modern Lang. Assn., Am. Philos. Assn., Am. Soc. Aesthetics. Home: RD 1 Box 380 Fairville Rd Chadd's Ford PA 19317

HIPPS, JOHN ROBERT, manufacturing company executive; b. Kansas City, Mo., Oct. 21, 1939; s. Robert Lawrence and Mary Thelma (Jackson) H.; m. Geraldine McGraw Wack, Dec. 21, 1962; children: Robert Otis, Matthew McGraw. A.B., Yale U., 1961; M.B.A., Stanford U., 1963. Accountant Price Waterhouse & Co. (C.P.A.'s), N.Y.C., 1963-68; exec. v.p. Livingston Audio Products Corp., Fairfield, N.J., 1968-69; v.p. finance Burton, Dana, Westerlund, Inc., N.Y.C., 1970-71; v.p. co. devel. U.S. Industries, Inc., N.Y.C., 1972-73; v.p., treas. Neptune Internat. Corp., Atlanta, 1973-78, Gen. Signal Corp., 1978—. Clubs: Capital City (Atlanta); Field (New Canaan, Conn.). Home: 57 Ramhorne Rd New Canaan CT 06840 Office: Two High Ridge Park Stamford CT 06904

HIRES, THOMAS LOUIS, SR., home mfr.; b. Tampa, Fla., Apr. 22, 1930; s. David Louis and Wilda Ann (Griffin) H.; m. Ruby Lee Mills, Dec. 10, 1974; children—Thomas Louis, Kimberly Ann. Student, Tampa public schs. Clk. Am. Can Co., Tampa, 1947-50; sales rep. Gerber Products Co., Daytona Beach, Fla., 1955, Jim Walter Homes, Tampa, 1955—; now pres.: sr. v.p., dir. Jim Walter Corp. Mem. Fla. Game and Fresh Water Fish Commn., 1979-83. Served with USNR, 1950-54. Democrat. Baptist. Home: 4201 Fairway Circle Tampa FL 33624 Office: 1500 N Dale Mabry Hwy Tampa FL 33614

HIRO, YASUHIRO WAKABAYASHI, photographer; b. Shanghai, China, Nov. 3, 1930; came to U.S., 1954; s. Takeo H. and Fuji (Wakabayashi); m. Elizabeth K. Clark, May 9, 1959; children: Gregory Thomas, Hiro Clark. Student, New Sch. Social research, N.Y.C., 1956, Alexy Brodovitch's Design Lab., 1956-64. Freelance photographer, N.Y.C., 1957—; mem. photography staff Harpers Bazaar, N.Y.C., 1958-74; under contract Conde Nast Publs., 1981—; lectr. in field. Photographer: spl. mag. issues Camera, 1965, Zoom, 1972, Am. Photographer, 1982. Recipient Newhouse citation Syracuse U., N.Y., 1972. Mem. N.Y. Art Dirs. Club (Gold medal 1968, Gold medal 1969), Am. Soc. Mag. Photographers (Photographer fo Yr. 1969), soc. Photographers in Communications. Office: 50 Central Park West New York NY 10023

HIRONAKA, HEISUKE, educator; b. Yamaguchi-Ken, Japan, Apr. 9, 1931; came to U.S., 1957; s. Taisuke and Matsue (Minamimoto) H.; m. Wakako Kimoto, Aug. 1, 1960; children—Eriko, Jo. M.S., Kyoto U., 1957, D.Phil., 1963; Ph.D., Harvard, 1960. Lectr. math. Brandeis U., Waltham, Mass., 1960-61, asst. prof., 1961-63, asso. prof., 1963-64; prof. Columbia, 1964-68, Harvard, 1968—. Fulbright scholar, 1957; A.P. Sloan fellow, 1963; Research Corp. fellow, 1963; Guggenheim fellow, 1971; recipient Fields prize, 1970; Japan Acad. award, 1970; Order of Culture, Japan, 1975. Mem. Am. Acad. Arts and Scis., Japan Acad., Japan Math. Soc., Am. Math. Soc., French Acad. Scis. Home: 7 Chauncy St Cambridge MA 02138 Office: Dept Math Harvard U Cambridge MA 02138

HIROSE, TERUO TERRY, surgeon; b. Tokyo, Jan. 20, 1926; s. Yohei and Seiko (Ogushi) H.; m. Tomiko Kodama, June 1, 1976; 1 son, George Philamore. B.S., Tokyo Coll., 1944; M.D., Chiba U., Japan, 1948, Ph.D., 1958. Diplomate: Am. Bd. Surgery, Am. Bd. Thoracic Surgery. Intern Chiba U. Hosp., 1948-49, resident in surgery, 1949-52, Am. Hosp., Chgo., 1954; resident in thoracic surgery Hahnemann Med. Coll., Phila., 1955-56, N.Y. Med. Coll., N.Y.C., 1961-62; practice medicine specializing in surgery, Chiba, Japan, 1952-53; chief of surgery Tsushimi Hosp., Hagi, Japan, 1958-59; asst. prof. surgery Chiba U., 1959; research fellow advanced cardiovascular surgery Hahnemann Hosp., Phila., 1959; teaching fellow surgery N.Y. Med. Coll., 1959-60, instr., 1961-62; practice medicine specializing in surgery, N.Y.C., 1965—, N.J., 1975—; dir. cardiovascular lab. St. Barnabas Hosp., N.Y.C., 1965—, sr. attending surgeon, 1965—; chief vascular surgery Union Hosp., Bronx, N.Y., 1966-67; attending surgeon Flower and Fifth Ave Hosp., N.Y.C., 1973—, Jewish Hosp. Med. Center, Bklyn., 1976—, St. Vincent Hosp., N.Y.C., 1976—, Mamonides Hosp., Bklyn., 1976-78, Passaic Gen. Hosp., 1977—, Westchester (N.Y.) County Hosp., 1977-78, Yonkers (N.Y.) Profl. Hosp., 1978-79, Westchester Sq. Hosp., 1978—, Yonkers Gen. Hosp., 1980—, St. Joseph Hosp., Yonkers, 1980—; clin. prof. surgery N.Y. Med. Coll., 1974—. Contbr. articles in field of cardiovascular surgery to Am. and Japanese med. jours. Recipient Hektoen Bronze medal AMA, 1965, Gold medal, 1971. Fellow Am. Coll. Angiology, Am. Coll. Chest Physicians, A.C.S., Am. Coll. Cardiology, Internat. Coll. Surgeons, N.Y. Acad. Medicine; mem. Am. Assn. Thoracic Surgery, N.Y. Soc. Thoracic Surgery, Pan-Pacific Surg. Assn., Internat. Cardiovascular Soc., Am. Geriatric Soc., Am. Fedn. Clin. Research. Inventor single pass low prime oxygenator; pioneer aortocoronary direct bypass surgery, open heart surgery without blood transfusion. Office: 1625 St Peters Ave Bronx NY 10461 *One should respect another's religion or creed and offer assistance regardless of whether or not one is in agreement with the other's belief, provided that belief harms no other.*

HIROSHIMA, KOJI EDMUND, trading company executive; b. N.Y.C., Oct. 10, 1924; s. Takashi and Sakura (Yamamoto) H.; m. Shigeko Ogata, Oct. 17, 1948; children: Junko Clara, Yuji Edward. B.A., Waseda U., Tokyo, 1948; postgrad., U. Tex., 1950. Office mgr. A. Campdera Inc., Osaka, Japan, 1952-54; mgr. Marubani Mex. S.A. DE C.V., Mexico City, 1955-63; pres. Marubeni Cotton Corp., Dallas, 1963-66; asst. gen. mgr. internat. div. Marubeni Corp., Toyko, 1966-71; v.p. Marubeni Am. Corp., N.Y.C., 1971-76, sr v.p., sec., 1976—; pres., dir. Macklen Enterprises Inc., Lake Park, Fla., 1978—; sec. Wateree Textile Corp., Lugoff, S.C., 1976—; dir. Martec Internat. Elec. Corp., Wellesley, Mass. Served with Japanese Navy, 1944-45. Recipient hon. citizenship New Orleans, 1971, State of Tex., 1951, State of W.Va., 1975. Clubs: Scarsdale Golf (Hartsdale, N.Y.); Squadron A, Sky (N.Y.C.). Home: 200-B High Point Dr Hartsdale NY 10530 Office: Marubeni Am Corp 200 Park Ave New York NY 10166

HIRS, JAMES MCDAVID, banker; b. Mobile, Oct. 12, 1934; s. Edward Adolph and Jamie (McDavid) H.; m. Mary Lucy McKnight, Apr. 23, 1960; children—Jamie H., Louise N., Leigh M. B.S., U. Ala., 1956. With Am. Nat. Bank & Trust Co., Mobile, since 1967, pres., 1978—; dir. Gulf Coast Public Broadcasting, Inc. Bd. dirs. America's Jr. Miss Pageant, Mobile Carnival Assn., St. Paul's Episcopal Sch., Mobile, Mobile Community Chest. Office: PO Box 1628 Mobile AL 36629

HIRSCH, BARRY, corp. exec., lawyer; b. N.Y.C., Mar. 19, 1933; s. Emanuel M. and Minnie (Levenson) H.; m. Myra Seiden, June 13, 1963; children—Victor Terry II, Neil Charles Seiden, Nancy Elizabeth. B.S., U. Mo., 1954, B.A., 1954; J.D., U. Mich., 1959; LL.M., N.Y. U., 1964. Bar: N.Y. bar 1960. Asso., then partner firm Seligson & Morris, N.Y.C., 1960-69; v.p., sec., gen. counsel dir. B.T.B. Corp., 1969-71; v.p., sec., gen. counsel Loews Corp. (and subsidiaries), 1971—; pres., dir. 1036 Park Corp., 1969-71. Dir. Manhattan Fund, Liberty Fund, Hemisphere Fund, CL Assets, Inc. Served to 1st lt. AUS, 1954-56. Mem. Am. Bar Assn., Assn. Bar City N.Y., N.Y. State Bar Assn., Zeta Beta Tau, Phi Delta Phi. Home: 1010 Fifth Ave New York NY 10028 Office: 666 Fifth Ave New York NY 10103

HIRSCH, CHARLES BRONISLAW, educator; b. Bklyn., Jan. 23, 1919; s. Hugo G. and Mary (Romanitch) H.; m. Patricia Parsons, June 1, 1941; children: Judith Rae, Susan Kathryn, Cynthia Jean. B.A. in History, Atlantic Union Coll., Mass., 1948; M.A. in History and Polit. Sci, Ind. U., 1949, Ph.D., 1954. Instr. State Tchrs. Coll., New Britain, Conn., 1950-51; asso. prof., chmn. dept. social scis., dir. pub. relations La Sierra Coll., Arlington, Calif., 1951-57; prof. history, chmn. dept. Columbia Union Coll., Washington, 1957-59, pres., 1959-65; v.p. acad. adminstrn. Andrews U., Berrien Springs, Mich., 1965-66; sec. dept. edn. Gen. Conf. Seventh-day Adventists, Washington, 1966-74; dir. office edn. Columbia Union Conf., Takoma Park, Md., 1974-75, N.Am., 1975—; dir. Office Edn., World Hdqrs. Seventh-day Adventists Ch., 1980; dir. Internat. Ins. Co., Takoma Park, Md., Gen. Conf. Risk Mgmt. Services. Chmn. bd. trustees Andrews U.; exec. sec. N.Am. Bd. Edn. K-12, 1975-80; chmn. Home Study Internat., Washington, Seventh-Day Adventists Internat. Bd. Edn. Served with AUS, 1941-45; ETO. Decorated Bronze Star. Mem. Am. Hist. Assn., Orgn. Am. Historians, Am. Assn. Sch. Adminstrs., Am. Polit. Sci. Assn., Phi Alpha Theta. Club: Rotary. Home: Route 1 Box 358 Warsaw VA 22572

HIRSCH, ELROY LEON, university administrator; b. Wausau, Wis., June 17, 1923; s. Otto Peter and Mayme Sabena (Magnuson) H.; m. Ruth Katherine Stahmer, June 27, 1946; children—Win Stephen, Patricia Caroline. Student, U. Wis., 1941-42, 47, U. Mich., 1943-44; B.A., Baldwin Wallace U., 1951. Profl. football player Chgo. Rockets, 1946-48, Los Angeles Rams, 1949-57; with Union Oil Co. of Cal., 1958-60; gen. mgr. and asst. to pres. Los Angeles Rams, 1960-69; dir. athletics U. Wis., Madison, 1969—. Hon. chmn. Cancer Crusade, Multiple Sclerosis, Muscular Dystrophy, Big Bros. Served with USMCR, 1943-46. Selected to All Profl. Football Team of Last Fifty Years; enshrined in Collegiate Football Hall of Fame, Profl. Football Hall of Fame. Mem. Nat. Assn. Collegiate Dirs. of Athletics. Home: 50 Oak Creek Trail Madison WI 53717 Office: 1440 Monroe St Madison WI 53706

HIRSCH, ERIC DONALD, JR., English educator; b. Memphis, Mar. 22, 1928; s. Eric Donald and Leah (Aschaffenburg) H.; m. Mary Monteith Pope, June 15, 1958; children: John, Frederick, Elizabeth. B.A., Cornell U., 1950; M.A., Yale U., 1955, Ph.D. (Fulbright fellow), 1957. Instr. Yale, 1956-61, asst. prof. English, 1961-64, asso. prof., 1964-66; prof. U. Va., Charlottesville, 1966—, chmn. dept. English, 1968-71, 81-83, dir. composition, 1971—, Kenan prof. English, 1973—; bd. dirs. U. Press.; Lectr. in field; supervising com. English Inst., 1972-74; mem. nat. adv. council N.Y. Regent's Competency Tests in Writing, 1979; advisor Nat. Council Ednl. Research, 1983. Author: Wordsworth and Schelling, A Typological Study of Romanticism, 1960, Innocence and Experience, an Introduction to Blake, 1964 (Explicator award), Validity in Interpretation, 1967, The Aims of Interpretation, 1976, The Philosophy of Composition, 1977; Adv. bd.: Jour. Basic Writing, Blake Studies, Critical Inquiry, New Lit. History; adv. bd.: Lit. in Performance; contbr. articles to profl. jours. Served with USNR, 1950-52. Morse fellow, 1961-62; Guggenheim fellow, 1964-65; sr. fellow NEH, 1971, 80-81; fellow Center for Humanities Wesleyan U., 1973, Council Humanities Princeton U., 1976, Center for Advanced Study in Behavioral Scis., 1980-81, Humanities Research Ctr., Australian Nat. U., 1982; Bateson lectr. Oxford U., 1983. Mem. Am. Acad. Arts and Scis. (supervisory com. 1981—); mem. MLA, Byron Soc. Home: 2006 Pine Top Rd Charlottesville VA 22903

HIRSCH, GEORGE AARON, publisher; b. N.Y.C., June 21, 1934; s. George J. and Sylvia (Epstein) H.; m. Brenda Baldwin Walker (div.); children: David Aaron, William George. A.B. magna cum laude,

Princeton U., 1956; M.B.A., Harvard U., 1962. With Time-Life Internat., 1962-67; founder, pres., treas., dir. New York Mag. Co., 1967-71, pub. New York mag.; chmn., pres., chief exec. officer New Times Communications Corp. (founder, pub. New Times Mag.), 1973-79, founder, pub. New Times Mag.; founder, pub. The Runner mag., 1978—; TV sports commentator, 1979—. Mem. Publ. bd.: Princeton Alumni Weekly, 1979—. Hon. mem. exec. com. Princeton Alumni Council. Served as officer USNR, 1957-60. Club: Century Assn. Home: 246 E 32d St New York NY 10016

HIRSCH, HAROLD SELLER, manufacturing executive; b. Portland, Oreg., Sept. 3, 1907; s. Max S. and Clementine (Seller) H.; m. Barbara Honeyman, May 25, 1934 (div.); children—Frederic S., Janet H.; m. Elizabeth Blair, Nov. 5, 1949. A.B., Dartmouth Coll., 1929. With White Stag Mfg. Co., Portland, Oreg., 1929—, pres., 1954-64, chmn. bd., 1964-70, chmn. exec. com., 1970—; dir. Liberty Communications Inc., to 1975, Warnaco, Inc., 1966-78, hon. dir., 1978-80; dir. Warnaco Fund, Inc., 1974-80. Commr. Port of Portland, 1961-69, treas., 1962, sec., 1963, v.p., 1966, pres., 1967; mem. nat. adv. council Nature Conservancy; Portland met. chmn. Nat. Alliance Businessman, 1970-71; pres. Oreg. Mental Health Assn.; treas. Boys and Girls Aid Soc. Oreg.; mem. Dartmouth Coll. Alumni Council, 1960-61; v.p. Dartmouth Alumni Assn., 1969—; bd. dirs. Oreg. Ceramic Studio, Portland Art Mus. Sch., Portland Civic Theatre, Council Social Agys.; bd dirs. Portland Youth Symphony Orch., 1973-79, v.p., 1978-79, 80—; bd. dirs. Oreg. chpt. Nature Conservancy Found., 1972-79, v.p., 1977-79; trustee Pacific Internat. Livestock Expn., 1974—; mem. SSS Bd., Portland, 1942-43; spl. cons. O.Q.M.G., Research and Devel. Div., Washington, 1943-44; Pres., trustee Gabel Country Day Sch., Portland; trustee Reed Coll., sec., 1972-77; pres. Hirsch Found., 1966-77; bd. dirs. Isam and Rose White Found., 1966-78, pres., 1971-77; bd. dirs., treas. Neskowin Coast Found., 1970-77; bd. dirs. Parry Center, 1970-76, World Affairs Council, 1975-79; bd. dirs., treas. Neskowin Community Assn., 1970—; dir. Oreg. chpt. NCCJ, 1977—, sec., 1980—; bd. dirs. Contemporary Crafts, 1979—; mem. St. Vincent Med. Found.; bd. overseers Oreg. Health Scis. U., 1981—. Mem. Oreg. Men's Apparel Assn. (pres.), Pacific N.W. Apparel Mfrs. Assn. (pres.), United World Federalists (nat. adv. bd.), Jewish Hist. Soc. Oreg. (dir. 1975—, treas. 1975-79, 81—), Ski Industries Am. (pres. 1963-65, hon. chmn. 1965-69, hon. dir.), Nat. Ski Patrol (hon.), U.S. Ski Writers Assn. (hon.), Japanese Garden Soc. Oreg. (dir., fin. v.p. 1974—), Beta Gamma Sigma, Alpha Kappa Psi. Clubs: Multnomah Athletic, Univ., Lang Syne Soc. Office: care Hirsch Interests Morgan Bldg Portland OR 97205

HIRSCH, JAMES GERALD, physician, scientist, foundation executive; b. St. Louis, Oct. 31, 1922; s. Mack J. and Henrietta B. (Schiffman) H.; m. Marjorie Manne, June 6, 1943 (div. 1974); children: Ann I., Henry J.; m. Beate I. Fried, 1974; 1 dau., Rebecca A. B.S., Yale U., 1942; M.D., Columbia U., 1946. Intern, then asst. resident physician Barnes Hosp., St. Louis, 1946-48; NRC fellow Rockefeller U., N.Y.C., 1950-52, asst. prof. medicine and microbiology, 1952-56, assoc. prof., 1956-60, prof., mem. inst., 1960-81, dean grad. studies, 1972-80; pres. Josiah Macy, Jr. Found., N.Y.C., 1981—. Chmn. div. med. scis. Assembly Life Scis., NRC.; Mem. bd. Macy Found.; chmn. bd. Trudeau Inst. Served to capt. USAF, 1948-50. Mem. Harvey Soc., Am. Assn. Immunologists, Soc. Am. Bacteriologists, Am. Acad. Microbiology, Soc. Exptl. Biology and Medicine, AAAS, Inst. Medicine, Am. Soc. Clin. Investigation, Assn. Am. Physicians, Nat. Acad. Sci., Alpha Omega Alpha. Office: 44 E 64th St New York NY 10021

HIRSCH, JAY G., psychiatrist; b. Cleve., Aug. 6, 1930; s. Abe and Bertha (Gusman) H.; m. Renee B. Schwartz, Oct. 10, 1962; children—Deborah, David, Lauren, Susan. B.S., U. Cin., 1950, M.D., 1954. Intern Phila. Gen. Hosp., 1954-55; resident U. Ill. Hosps., 1957-60; practice medicine specializing in psychiatry and child psychiatry, Chgo., 1960-70, Highland Park, Ill., 1970—; resident Inst. Juvenile Research, Chgo., 1960-62, research child psychiatrist, 1962-66, chief div. preventive psychiatry, 1966-70; dir. Melampus Ltd.; mem. faculty U. Ill. Coll. Medicine, Chgo., 1959—, asso. prof. psychiatry, 1970-74, prof., 1974—, dir. edn. in child psychiatry and related disciplines, 1973-77; cons. to agys., schs.; mem. Ill. Mental Health Planning Bd., 1967-69, Ill. Comprehensive Health Planning Agy. Bd., 1971-74. Bd. editors: Jour. Child Psychiatry, 1972-77; contbr. articles to profl. jours., chpts. to books. Vice pres. Kenneth P. Montgomery Found., Chgo., 1965-71; bd. dirs. Dr. Martin L. King Family Center, Chgo., 1969-74, Urban Dynamics/Inner City Fund, Chgo., 1970-75. Served to capt. USAF, 1955-57. Fellow Am. Psychiat. Assn., Am. Acad. Child Psychiatry, Am. Orthopsychiat. Assn.; mem. AMA, Soc. Research in Child Devel., AAAS, Phi Beta Kappa, Alpha Omega Alpha. Home: 591 Stonegate Terr Glencoe IL 60022 Office: 1971 2d St Highland Park IL 60035 also U Ill Dept Psychiatry 912 S Wood St Chicago IL 60612

HIRSCH, JOHN ARTHUR, stockbroker; b. West Long Brach, N.J., Apr. 3, 1939; s. Chester A. and Edith (Brukenfeld) H.; m. Mariellen Mercke, July 7, 1963 (div. 1981); children: Elisabeth Stewart, Nancy Evans; m. Elizabeth Galt, Nov. 2, 1982. B.A., Rollins Coll., 1961. Ptnr. Bear Stearns & Co., N.Y.C., 1975—. Office: Bear Stearns & Co 55 Water St New York NY 10041

HIRSCH, JOHN STEPHEN, artistic director; b. Siofok, Hungary, May 1, 1930; emigrated to Can., 1947; s. Joseph and Ilona (Horvath) H. Student, Israel Gymnasium in, Budapest; D.Litt. (hon.), U. Man., 1966; also hon. fellow, Univ. Coll.; LL.D. (hon.), U. Toronto, 1967. Cons. Nat. Endowment for Arts, Visions-New Am. Theatre Project; cons. bldg. com. Nat. Arts Centre; mem. corp. Nat. Theatre Sch.; also gov.; lectr. Columbia, N.Y. U.; Plaunt lectr. Carleton U.; design cons. Nat. Museums Can. Discovery Train, 1978; theatre cons. Can. Council, Ont. Arts Council, 1978; cons. BBC/PBS Shakespeare Project for Children's TV, 1978; cons. artistic dir. Seattle Repertory Theatre, 1979—. Dir. first play: The Time of Your Life at Little Theatre, Winnipeg, Man., Can., 1951; dir., Stratford Shakespearean Festival, Ont., 1965, The Cherry Orchard, Henry VI, 1966, Richard III, The Tempest, 1982, A Midsummer Night's Dream, The Three Musketeers, 1968, Satyricon, 1969; dir. first play in New York: Federico Garcia Lorca's Yerma, Vivian Beaumont, for Repertory Theater of Lincoln Center, 1966; and since directed for this company: Galileo, 1967, St. Joan, 1968, The Time of Your Life, 1969, Beggar on Horseback, 1970, Playboy of the Western World, Antigone, 1971; dir.: Broadway prodn. of We Bombed in New Haven, 1968, AC/DC, for Chelsea Theater Center of Bklyn., 1970; for Theatre du Nouveau Monde, Mere Courage, 1964, for the Habimah, Tel Aviv, Israel, The Seagull, 1970; asso. artistic dir., Stratford (Ont.) Shakespearean Festival, 1967-69; artistic dir., Stratford (Ont.) Shakespearean Festival, 1981—; founder, Rainbow Stage, Theatre 77, Man. Theatre Centre; entered film prodn. in Can. with: In The Shadow of the City, 1955; first directed on TV, in 1954; and has since directed: The Three Musketeers; co-artistic dir., Stratford Festival Theatre, 1968-69; dir.: Midsummer Nights Dream, Mpls. Theatre, 1972, The Dybbuk, Los Angeles prodn. Mark Taper Forum, 1975, Maggie Smith in The Three Sisters, Stratford Festival, 1976, The Tempest, Mark Taper Forum, 1979, Number Our Days, Mark Taper Forum, 1979; exec. producer: Sarah, 1976; head TV drama, English service div. CBC, 1976-78; cons., 1978; producer, CBC, Toronto and Winnipeg; dir.: Saint Joan, 1979, History of the American Film, Nat. Arts Centre, Ottawa, 1979; Author: children's plays Rupert the Great; puppet plays Peter the Snowman, 1952, The Dog Who Never Learned; New Translation and Adaptation of Ansky's The Dybbuk.; Contbr. articles to profl. jours. Bd. dirs. Theatre Communications Group, Royal Winnipeg Ballet, Nat. Ballet Can. Recipient Order of Can. medal, Outer Circle Critics award for St. Joan, Obie award for AC/DC, Canadian Authors Assn. award for transl. and adaptation The Dybbuk. Office: Stratford Festival Can Stratford ON Canada

HIRSCH, JOSEPH, artist; b. Phila., Apr. 25, 1910; s. Charles S. and Fannie (Wittenberg) H.; m. Ruth L. Schindler, Oct. 30, 1938; children: Charles, Paul; m. 2d Genevieve Baucheron, July 19, 1955; 1 son, Frederic Henri-Joseph. Student, Phila. Coll. Art, 1927-31. Instr. painting Art Students League, 1959-67, 76—, NAD, 1974—; vis. artist U. Utah, 1959, Dartmouth Coll., 1966, Brigham Young U., 1971. Exhibited paintings, prin. museums, galleries, U.S., 1934—, one-man shows, N.Y.C., Paris, Phila., Chgo., Beverly Hills, 1934—; represented permanent collections; war artist corr., AUS, USNR, 1943-44. Woolley fellow Inst. Internat. Edn., Paris, 1935; Guggenheim fellow, 1942, 43; Nat. Inst. Arts and Letters grantee, 1947; Fulbright research fellow, France, 1949; Disting. Bicentennial prof. as artist-in-residence U. Utah, 1975—; recipient 4th prize Met. Mus. Art, 1951, Altman prizes figure painting NAD, 1959, 66, 78, Purchase prize Butler Inst., 1965, Carnegie prize NAD, 1968, Purchase awards Davidson Coll., Nat. Print Competition, 1972, 73, Print Purchase award Okla. Art Ctr., Oklahoma City, 1974. Mem. Artists Equity Assn. (founder, 1st treas.), NAD, Century Assn., Nat. Inst. Arts and Letters (life). Home: 90 Riverside Dr New York NY 10024 Office: care Kennedy Galleries 40 W 57th St New York NY 10019

HIRSCH, JUDD, actor; b. N.Y.C., Mar. 15, 1935; s. Joseph Sidney and Sally (Kitzis) H. B.S. in Physics, Coll. City N.Y., 1960. Broadway appearance in Barefoot in the Park, 1966, Knock Knock, 1975-76 (Drama Desk award for best featured actor); off-Broadway appearances in Scuba Duba, 1967, 69, Mystery Play, 1972, Hot L Baltimore, 1973, King of the United States, 1972, Chapter Two, 1977-78, Talley's Folly, 1979-80 (Obie award); mem., Theatre of Living Arts, Phila., 1969-70; appearance in Peterpat, Houston and Ft. Worth, 1970; TV appearances include The Law, 1974, The Keegans, 1975, Fear on Trial, 1975, Two Brothers, 1975, Valentino, 1975, Medical Story, 1975, Delvecchio series, 1976-77, Rhoda, 1977, The Last Resort, 1979, The Halloween That Almost Wasn't, 1979; star: TV series Taxi, 1978—; films include King of the Gypsies, 1978, Ordinary People, 1980. Mem. Screen Actors Guild, Actors Equity Assn., AFTRA. Home: New York NY also Los Angeles CA Office: care Artists Agy 190 N Canyon Dr Beverly Hills CA 90210

HIRSCH, LAWRENCE LEONARD, physician, educator; b. Chgo., Aug. 20, 1922; m. Donna Lee Sturm; children: Edward, Sharon. B.S., U. Ill.-Urbana, 1943; M.D., U. Ill.-Chgo., 1950. Diplomate: Am. Bd. Family Practice. Intern. Ill. Masonic Med. Ctr., Chgo., 1950-51; practice medicine specializing in family medicine, Chgo., 1951-70; dir. ambulatory care Ill. Masonic Med. Ctr., Chgo., 1970-71, dir. family practice residency program, 1971-75; prof., chmn. dept. family medicine Chgo. Med. Sch., 1975—; mem. med. examining com. State of Ill., 1982—; bd. dirs. Ill. Council for Continuing Med. Edn., 1981—; cons. recombinant DNA Abbott Labs., 1980—; lectr. in field; staff pres. Ill. Masonic Med. Ctr., 1969. Book rev. editor: Soc. of Tchrs. Family Medicine, 1979—; book reviewer: Jour. AMA, 1969—; contbr. articles to profl. jours. Bd. dirs. Mid-Am. chpt. ARC, Chgo., 1978—; nat. pres. Alpha Phi Omega, Kansas City, Mo., 1974-78; exec. com. Chgo. Found. Med. Care, 1977—, Ill. State Inter-Ins. Exchange, 1975—. Served with U.S. Army, 1943-46. Recipient Silver Beaver award Boy Scouts Am., 1963, Silver Antelope award Boy Scouts Am., 1967, Disting. Eagle award, 1969, Brotherhood award Lakeview Interfaith Council, 1968, Physician Speaker award AMA, 1981. Fellow AAAS, Am. Acad. Family Physicians (mem. congress of dels.); mem. Chgo. Med. Soc. (pres. 1979), Ill. Acad. Family Physicians (pres. 1977), Assn. Depts. Family Medicine (exec. com.). Democrat. Unitarian. Club: Kiwanis (dir.). Lodges: Masons; Shriners. Office: Chicago Med Sch 3333 Green Bay Rd North Chicago IL 60064

HIRSCH, PHILIP FRANCIS, pharmacologist; b. Stockton, Calif., June 24, 1925; s. Harold and Elsa (Frohman) H.; m. Eugenia Isaeff, Sept. 21, 1956; children—Steven, Lisa, Kenny, Nancy. B.S. in Chemistry, U. Calif., Berkeley, 1950, Ph.D. in Physiology, 1954. Lectr. physiology U. Calif., Berkeley, 1954-55; instr. pharmacology Sch. Dental Medicine, Harvard U., Cambridge, Mass., 1955-57, asso. in pharmacology, 1957-63, asst. prof. pharmacology, 1964; physiologist Lawrence Livermore Lab., 1964-66; asso. prof. pharmacology Sch. Medicine, U. N.C., Chapel Hill, 1966-70, prof., 1970—, dir., 1975—; mem. gen. medicine B study sect. NIH, 1974-78. Contbr. articles to profl. jours. Bd. dirs. YMCA, Chapel Hill, 1981—. Served with AUS, 1943-46. Mem. AAAS, Endocrine Soc., Am. Soc. Pharmacology and Exptl. Therapeutics, Internat. Assn. Dental Research, Sigma Xi. Home: 2008 S Lake Shore Dr Chapel Hill NC 27514 Office: Dental Research Center 210-H U of NC Chapel Hill NC 27514

HIRSCH, RAYMOND ROBERT, chemical executive, lawyer; b. St. Louis, Mar. 20, 1936; s. Raymond Winton and Olive Frances (Gordon) H.; m. Joanne Therese Dennis, Jan. 30, 1960; children: Amy Elizabeth, Thomas Christopher, Timothy Joseph, Mary Patricia. LL.B., St. Louis U., 1959. Bar: Mo. 1959. With Treasury Dept., 1960-62, Petrolite Corp., St. Louis, 1962—, sec., 1971—, v.p., gen. counsel, 1973-82, sr. v.p., gen. counsel, 1982—. Mcpl. judge City of Bridgeton, Mo., 1970-73; mem. City of Des Peres Planning and Zoning Commn., 1974-78; mem. bd. edn. Spl. Sch. Dist. St. Louis County, 1981—. Mem. Mo. Air N.G., 1959-60. Mem. ABA, Am. Soc. Corp. Secs., Mo. Bar Assn., Bar Assn. St. Louis. Roman Catholic. Clubs: Algonquin Golf, Missouri Athletic. Home: 1623 Wendover Ln Saint Louis MO 63131 Office: 100 N Broadway Saint Louis MO 63102

HIRSCH, RICHARD GEORGE, rabbi; b. Cleve., Sept. 13, 1926; s. Abe and Bertha (Gusman) H.; m. Bella Rosencweig, Sept. 5, 1954; children—Ora Hirsch Pescovitz, Raphael, Ammiel, Emmet. B.A., U. Cin., 1947; B.H.L., Hebrew Union Coll.-Jewish Inst. Religion, Cin., 1948, M.H.L., 1951, D.D., 1976. Rabbi Temple Emanuel, Chgo., 1951-53, Denver, 1953-56; regional dir. Union Am. Hebrew Congregations, Chgo., 1956-61; dir. Union Am. Hebrew Congregations Religious Action Center, Washington, 1962-73; exec. dir. World Union Progressive Judaism, Jerusalem, 1973—; vis. lectr. Hebrew Union Coll. Jewish Inst. Religion; mem. exec. com. World Zionist Orgn., Central Conf. Am. Rabbis. Author: Judaism and Cities in Crisis, 1961, There Shall Be No Poor, 1964, The Way of the Upright, 1967, Thy Most Precious Gift, 1969. Sec. Citizens Crusade Against Proverty, 1964-68. Office: 13 King David St Jerusalem Israel

HIRSCH, ROBERT LOUIS, oil company executive; b. Evanston, Ill., Mar. 6, 1935; s. Louis Aaron and Dorothy Jean (Block) H.; m. Evelyn Podhouser, Feb. 1, 1959; children—Allen, Lauri, Scott. B.S., U. Ill., 1958, Ph.D., 1964; M.S., U. Mich., 1959. Research engr. Atomics Internat., 1959-60; physicist, later dir. ITT Indsl. Labs., Ft. Wayne, Ind., 1964-68; sr. physicist controlled thermonuclear research AEC (now Dept. Energy), Washington, 1968-72; div. dir. 1972-76; asst. adminstr. solar, geothermal and advanced energy systems ERDA, 1976-77; dep. mgr. sci. and tech. dept. Exxon Corp., 1977; gen. mgr. exploratory petroleum research Exxon Research and Engrng. Co., 1977-80, mgr. Synthetic Fuels Research Lab., Baytown, Tex., 1980-83; v.p., mgr. exploration and prodn. research Arco Oil and Gas Co., Dallas, 1983—; mem. U.S.-USSR Joint Commn. on Peaceful Uses of Atomic Energy; chmn. U.S. del. U.S.-USSR Joint Fusion Power Coordinating Com.; mem. Internat. Fusion Research Council; vice chmn. com. on sci., engring. and tech. Fed. Coordinating Council for Sci., Engrng. and Tech.; cons. in field. Contbr. articles to profl. jours. Recipient Meritorious award William Jump Found., 1971, Distinguished Service award AEC, 1974, spl. achievement award Fusion Power Assocs., 1982; Spl. Achievement award ERDA, 1976, 77; commendation NASA, 1982; AEC Spl. fellow, 1960-63. Fellow AAAS; mem. Am. Nuclear Soc. (chmn. fusion tech. group, dir. 1975-76, 78-79, outstanding tech. achievement award 1983), Am. Petroleum Inst., Am. Phys. Soc., Soc. Petroleum Engrs. of AIME, N.Y. Acad. Scis., Phi Epsilon Pi. Patentee in field. Home: 6309 Misty Trail Dallas TX 75248 Office: Arco Oil and Gas Co PO Box 2819 Dallas TX 75221

HIRSCH, ROBERT W., apparel manufacturer; b. N.Y.C., Nov. 23, 1934; s. Lawrence W. and Ruth (Halper) H.; m. Shauna Weston, Jan. 26, 1980; children by previous marriage: Betsy, Margo, Stephen. B.S., Yale U., 1956. Buyer Bloomingdale's, N.Y.C., 1956-61; asst. sales mgr. Donmoore, Inc., N.Y.C., 1961-65; various positions to pres. BTK Industries, Inc., El Paso, Tex., 1965—. Mem. Am. Apparel Mfrs. Assn. (dir.), Boys. Apparel Mfrs. Assn. (dir.), Southwestern Apparel Mfrs. (dir.). Home: 916 Thunderbird St El Paso TX 79912 Office: BTK Industries Inc 4171 N Mesa St Bldg D El Paso TX 79902

HIRSCH, ROBERT WILLIAM, lawyer; b. Tripp, S.D., Oct. 12, 1925; s. Raymond and Linda (Schmiedt) H.; m. Doris J. Brosz, Aug. 10, 1947 (dec. Dec. 1963); children: John, James, Jayne, Sarah; m. Lyla Voorhees, Feb. 19, 1968. B.A. in Math, U. S.C., 1946; J.D., U. S.D., 1949; LL.D., Concordia Theol. Sem., Springfield, Ill. Bar: S.D. 1949. Atty., Tripp, 1950-68; state's atty. Hutchinson County, 1953-57. Scoutmaster Sioux council Boy Scouts Am., 1949-65; past chmn., former mem. exec. bd. Legislative Research Council; mem. Constl. Revision Commn.; Chmn. Young Republicans, Hutchinson County (S.D.), 1949-52; mem. S.D. Senate, 1956-69; majority leader, 1968-69; Mem. nat. bd. dirs. Lutheran Ch.-Mo. Synod, 1969-81. Served with USNR, 1943-47; mem. S.D. N.G. Mem. Luth. Laymen's League (internat. pres. 1964-68, award of merit 1975), S.D., Am. bar assns., Am. Trial Lawyers Assn., Jud. Council S.D., Phi Kappa Delta, Phi Delta Phi, Phi Mu. Home: Route 1 Box 520 Yankton SD 57078 Office: 311 W 3d St Yankton SD 57078

HIRSCH, ROSEANN CONTE, editor; b. N.Y.C., Feb. 5, 1941; d. Frank and Anna (Burzycki) Conte; m. Barry J. Hirsch, Oct. 1, 1967; children: Brian Christopher, Nicholas Benjamin, Jonathan Alexander. Student, Boston U., 1958-61. Editorial asst. Grolier, Inc., 1962-64; asso. editor Ideal Pub. Corp., N.Y.C., 1968, editor, 1968-74, Sterling's Mags., Inc., N.Y.C., 1975-76, editorial dir., 1976-78, Hearst Spl. Pubns., Hearst Corp., N.Y.C., 1978-84; v.p. Ultra Communications, Inc., N.Y.C., 1984—. Editor: Young & Married Mag, 1976-77, 100 Greatest American Women, Good Housekeeping's Moms Who Work; contbr. articles to various mags. Mem. Nat. Acad. TV Arts and Scis. Home: 1172 Park Ave New York NY 10028 Office: Hearst Spl Publs 959 8th Ave New York NY 10019

HIRSCH, WERNER ZVI, educator; b. Linz, Germany, June 10, 1920; came to U.S., 1946, naturalized, 1955; s. Waldemar and Toni (Morgenstern) H.; m. Hilde E. Zwirn, Oct. 30, 1945; children—Daniel, Joel, Ilona. B.S. with highest honors, U. Calif., 1947, Ph.D., 1949. Instr. econs. U. Calif., 1949-51; econ. affairs officer UN, 1951-52; economist Brookings Instn., Washington, 1952-53; asst. research dir. St. Louis Met. Survey, 1956-57; prof. econs. Washington U., St. Louis, 1953-63; economist Resources for Future, Inc., Washington, 1958-59; dir. Inst. Govt. and Pub. Affairs, U. Calif. at Los Angeles, also prof. econs., 1963—; scholar in residence Rockefeller Study Center, 1978; cons. Rand Corp., 1958—, U.S. Senate Com. on Pub. Works, 1972, Calif. Senate Select Com. on Structure and Adminstrn. Pub. Edn., 1973, Joint Econ. Com. of Congress, 1975-76, OECD, 1977-80, Edmund G. Brown Inst. Govt., 1981—; mem. com. to improve productivity of govt. Com. Econ. Devel., 1975-76; chmn. Los Angeles City Productivity Adv. Com., 1982—. Author: Introduction to Modern Statistics, 1957, Analysis of the Rising Costs of Education, 1959, Urban Life and Form, 1963, Elements of Regional Accounts, 1964, Regional Accounts for Public Decisions, 1966, Inventing Education for the Future, 1967, The Economics of State and Local Government, 1970, Regional Information for Government Planning, 1971, Fiscal Crisis of America's Central Cities, 1971, Program Budgeting for Primary and Secondary Public Education, 1972, Governing Urban America in the 1970s, 1973, Urban Economic Analysis, 1973, Local Government Program Budgeting: Theory and Practice, 1974, Recent Experiences with National Planning in the United Kingdom, 1977, Law and Economics: An Introductory Analysis, 1979, Higher Education of Women: Essays in Honor of Rosemary Park, 1978, Social Experimentation and Economic Policy, 1981, The Economics of Municipal Labor Markets, 1983; assoc. editor: Jour. Am. Statis. Assn, 1980—. Bd. dirs. Calif. Council Environ. and Econ. Balance, 1973—; pres. Town Hall West of Calif., 1974-79, Friends of Graphic Arts. Mem. Am., Western econ. assns., Am. Farm Econ. Assn., Western Region Sci. Assn. (dir., pres. 1978-80), Town Hall (chmn. econ. sect.), Los Angeles World Affairs Council, Phi Beta Kappa, Sigma Xi. Home: 11601 Bellagio Rd Los Angeles CA 90049

HIRSCHBERG, GERT K., lawyer, educator; b. Berlin, Germany, Aug. 21, 1926; came to U.S., 1939, naturalized, 1945; s. Rudolph S. and Elsie (Cohn) H.; m. Eleanor Zoltan, Sept. 2, 1951; children: Janis, Vicki, Leslie. B.A., U. So. Calif., 1948; J.D. cum laude, Southwestern U., 1950. Bar: Calif. bar 1951. Practice law, Los Angeles, 1951—; mem. firm Goodman, Hirschberg & King, Los Angeles, 1952-78; faculty Southwestern U. Sch. Law, 1965-80, prof. law, 1967-80; mem. faculty U. West Los Angeles Sch. of Law, 1980—; Referee Juvenile Ct., Los Angeles Superior Ct., 1972-75. Served with AUS, 1944-46. Mem. State Bar Calif. (mem. disciplinary bd. 1976—, presiding referee disciplinary bd. 1978-79, presiding referee State Bar Ct. 1979, bd. govs. 1980—, v.p. 1982-83). Home: 3329 Club Dr Los Angeles CA 90064 Office: Law Offices Gert K Hirschberg 3550 Wilshire Blvd Los Angeles CA 90010

HIRSCHBERG, JOSEPH GUSTAV, educator, physicist; b. Chgo., Apr. 13, 1921; s. Joseph Gustav and Lillian (Kahn) H.; m. Ginette Henriette Tetard, Apr. 26, 1947; children—Dorothy Jean, Joseph Gerald, Anne Marie, Lynn Susan. A.B., Dartmouth, 1943; M.S., U. Wis., 1951, Ph.D., 1952. Research asso. U. Wis., 1953-57; head optical group, also research physicist Plasma Physics Lab., Princeton, 1958-65; professeur d'Echange U. Paris, France, 1963; prof. physics U. Miami, Fla., 1965—, chmn. dept., 1965-72, dir. optical physics lab., 1968—; contractor Langley Research Center, NASA, 1966-69. Served to capt. USAAF, 1943-47. Fellow Am. Phys. Soc., Optical Soc. Am.; mem. A.A.A.S., Fla. Acad. Scis., Phi Beta Kappa, Sigma Xi, Sigma Pi Sigma. Co-discoverer telluric sodium absorption in solar radiation; inventor optical spectroscopic devices. Home: 1046 Alfonso Ave Coral Gables FL 33146

HIRSCHFELD, ALBERT, artist; b. St. Louis, June 21, 1903; s. Isaac and Rebecca (Rothberg) H.; m. Florence Ruth Hobby, July 13, 1927;

m. Dorothy Dolly Haas, May 8, 1943; 1 dau., Nina. Student, Nat. Acad., Art Students Leaque, County Council, London, Julienne's, Paris. Theatre corr. in Moscow for N.Y. Herald Tribune, 1927. Sculptor one-man exhbns. include, Newhouse Gallery, 1928, Waldorf Astoria, 1932, Morgan Gallery, 1936, Guy Mayer Gallery, 1942, John Heller Gallery, 1959, Hammer Gallery, 1967, Mus. City N.Y., 1973, Margo Feiden Gallery, Wako Galleries, Tokyo, 1975; theater caricaturist, N.Y. Times, 1925—; represented in permanent collections, St. Louis Art Mus., Butler Inst. Am. Art, Whitney Mus. Am. Art, N.Y.C., Cleve. Art Mus., N.Y.C. Mus., N.Y. Pub. Library, Fogg Mus., Bklyn. Mus., Met. Mus. Art, Mus. Modern Art, Davenport Municipal Art Gallery, Mus. U. Wis., Lincoln Center Mus. Performing Arts, N.Y.C., murals in, Fifth Ave. Playhouse, Manhattan Playbill Room, N.Y.C., Am. Pavilion, World's Fair, Brussels, 1958; (Spl. Tony award for theatre caricature 1974); Author: Manhattan Oases, 1932, Harlem, 1942; musical comedy Sweet Bye and Bye, 1946; The American Theatre, 1961, (with S.J. Perelman) Westward Ha, 1949, Show Business is No Business, 1951, Hirschfeld Folio, 1964, The World of Hirschfeld, 1970, (with Brooks Atkinson) The Lively Years, 1973, Rhythm; folio 10 lithographs Hirschfeld by Hirschfeld, 1979; The Entertainers, 1977. Recipient Am. Specialist grant U.S. State Dept., 1960; Creative award Art Inst. Boston, 1976. Home: 122 E 95th St New York NY 10028

HIRSCHFELD, GERALD J., cinematographer; b. N.Y.C., Apr. 25, 1921; s. Ralph and Kate (Zirker) H.; m. Sarnell Ogus, June 5, 1945 (div. June 1972); children—Alec, Marc, Eric, Burt; m. Julia Warren Tucker, July 28, 1981. Student, Columbia U., 1938-40. Pres. GJH Productions Calif., Inc.; v.p., dir. MPO Videotronics, Inc.; instr. New Inst. Film; Free-lance dir., cameraman, cinematographer. Cinematographer for films including: Neighbors, My Favorite Year, To Be or Not To Be. Served with Signal Corps U.S. Army, 1941-45. Mem. Dirs'. Guild Am., Am. Soc. Cinematographers, Acad. Motion Picture Arts and Scis., Internat. Photographers' Union. Address: 904 High View Dr Arroyo Grande CA 93420

HIRSCHFELD, RONALD COLMAN, consulting engineer; b. Amsterdam, N.Y., Nov. 23, 1930; s. John Anton and Catherine (Schuyler) H.; m. Erma Lou Jones, Aug. 8, 1964; children: Amy Karen, Carl Schuyler. B.S. in Civil Engring, Union Coll., 1950; S.M., Harvard U., 1951, Ph.D., 1958. Teaching fellow Harvard U., 1951-54, instr. soil mechanics, 1958-60, asst. prof., 1960-64; assoc. prof. civil engring. M.I.T., 1964-72; prin. Geotech. Engrs. Inc., Winchester, Mass., 1970—, pres., 1974-78, 82—; Mem. dean's adv. council Sch. Engring., U. Mass., 1978—. Co-editor: Embankment-Dam Engineering, 1963. Bd. dirs. Winchester A Better Chance Inc., 1979—; chmn. governing bd. Winchester Unitarian Soc., 1981-82. Served with USN, 1954-57. Mem. ASCE (pres. Mass. sect. 1973-74, nat. dir. 1981—), Am. Cons. Engrs. Council (pres. New Eng. 1982-83, nat. dir. 1983—), Assn. Engring. Geologists (chmn. New Eng. sect. 1971-73, nat. dir. 1972-73), Geol. Soc. Am., U.S. Com. on Large Dams, Internat. Soc. Soil Mechanics and Found. Engring. (sec. U.S. Nat. Com. 1961-69), Internat. Soc. for Rock Mechanics. Unitarian. Home: 47 Emerson Rd Winchester MA 01890 Office: 1017 Main St Winchester MA 01890

HIRSCHFELD, TOMAS BENO, chemical engineer; b. Montevideo, Uruguay, Dec. 20, 1939; came to U.S., 1966, naturalized, 1974; s. Rudolf Georg Herman and Ruth (Nordon) H.; m. Judith Berggrun, Nov. 3, 1963; children: Noemi Brenda, Dinorah Jael, Susan Deborah. B.Sc., Vasquez Acevedo Coll., 1956; Ph.D., Nat. U. Uruguay, 1965. Asst. prof. spectrochemistry Nat. U. Uruguay, 1965-68; vis. scientist N.Am. Aviation Co., Thousand Oaks., Calif., 1966-67; staff scientist Block Engring. Co., Cambridge, Mass., 1969-71, chief scientist, 1971-79; scientist Lawrence Livermore (Calif.) Lab., 1979—; prof. Ind. U., Bloomington, 1977—. Author; Asso. editor: Jour. Applied Spectroscopy. Trustee Temple Beth Sholom, Framingham, Mass., 1974-79, chmn. sch. com., 1975-76. Recipient IR-100 award Indsl. Research mag., 1975, 77, 81, 83. Fellow Optical Soc. Am. (editorial adv. bd. of jour.); sr. mem. IEEE; mem. Am. Chem. Soc., Coblentz Soc. (governing bd.), Soc. Applied Spectroscopy (Meggers award 1978), Canadian Spectroscopic Assn., Soc. Photo-Instrumentations Engrs., Soc. Automated Cytology. Jewish. Club: B'nai B'rith. Patentee in field. Home: 1262 Vancouver Way Livermore CA 94550 Office: PO Box 808 Mail Stop L-322 Livermore CA 94550 *Inspiration must precede perspiration.*

HIRSCHFIELD, ALAN J., motion picture company executive. B.S., U. Okla.; M.B.A., Harvard U. Vice-pres. Allen & Co., Inc., 1959-67; v.p.-fin., dir. Warner Bros. Seven Arts, Inc., 1967-68; with Am. Diversified Enterprises, Inc., 1968-73; pres., chief exec. officer Columbia Pictures Industries, N.Y.C., 1973-78; vice chmn., chief operating officer 20th Century-Fox Film Corp., Los Angeles, 1979-81, chmn. bd., chief exec. officer, 1981—, also dir.; cons. Warner Communications Inc., N.Y.C., 1979—; mem. N.Y. State TV and Adv. Bd.; dir. Straight Arrow Publs. Inc., John B. Coleman Co. Bd. dirs. Film Soc. of Lincoln Center, Cancer Research Inst., Will Rogers Meml. Fund. Office: 20th Century-Fox Film Corp Box 900 Beverly Hills CA 90213 *

HIRSCHFIELD, ROBERT SIDNEY, political science educator; b. St. Louis, Sept. 1, 1928; s. Charles and Rose (Susman) H. A.B., Harvard U., 1950, LL.B., 1953, M.A., 1954; Ph.D., NYU, 1958. Teaching asst. Harvard U., 1953-54; instr. NYU, 1955-57, Hunter Coll., CUNY, 1958-60, asst. prof., 1961-63, asso. prof., 1964-66, prof., 1967—, chmn. polit. sci. dept., 1968—, dir. CUNY internship program, 1968—; dir. Center for Edn. in Politics Hunter Coll., City U. N.Y., chmn. univ. senate, 1968-71; Staff dir. N.Y. State Joint Legisl. Com. on Higher Edn., 1965-66. Author: The Constitution and the Court, 1962, The Power of the Presidency, 1968, rev. edit., 1973, 82, Selection/Election: A Forum on the American Presidency, 1982. Chmn. bd. N.Y. State Facilities Devel. Corp., 1979—; host, producer Cityscope; mem. N.Y.C. Commn. on Status of Women, 1975-81. Mem. Am. Polit. Sci. Assn., AAUP, Pi Sigma Alpha. Home: 67 Riverside Dr New York NY 10024 Office: Polit Sci Dept Hunter College 695 Park Ave New York NY 10021

HIRSCHHORN, AUSTIN, lawyer; b. Detroit, Feb. 20, 1936; s. Herman and Dena Grace (Ufberg) H.; m. Susan Carol Goldstein, June 30, 1963; children—Laura Elsie, Carol Helen, Paula Gail. B.A. with honors, Mich. State U., 1957; LL.B., Wayne State U., 1960. Bar: Mich. bar 1960. Since practiced in, Detroit; atty. Arnold M. Gold Law Offices, 1960-63; partner Gold & Hirschhorn, 1963-65; individual practice, 1965-68, 79-80; partner firm Boigon, Hirschhorn & Winston, 1968-69, Boigon & Hirschhorn, 1969-78, Zemke & Hirschhorn (P.C.), 1980—; lectr. Inst. Continuing Legal Edn., Mich. Trustee City Sch. Detroit. Served with AUS, 1960-62. Mem. Am., Detroit, Oakland County bar assns., State Bar Mich., Comml. Law League Am., Am. Judicature Soc. Jewish. Home: 26903 York Huntington Woods MI 48070 Office: 3000 Town Center Suite 2301 Southfield MI 48075

HIRSCHHORN, KURT, pediatrics educator; b. Vienna, Austria, May 18, 1926; came to U.S., 1940, naturalized, 1945; s. Emanuel and Helen (Mayberger) H.; m. Rochelle Reibman, Dec. 20, 1952; children—Melanie D., Lisa R., Joel N. Student, U. Pitts., 1944; B.A., N.Y. U., 1950, M.D., 1954, M.S. (Bergquist fellow), 1958. Intern Bellevue Hosp., N.Y.C., 1954-55, resident, 1955-56; fellow N.Y. U., 1956-57, U. Upsala, Sweden, 1957-58; instr. N.Y. U. Sch. Medicine, 1956-58, asst. prof., 1958-63, asso. prof., 1963-66; Arthur J. and Nellie Z. Cohen prof. genetics and pediatrics Mt. Sinai Sch. Medicine, City U. N.Y., 1966-76, Herbert H. Lehman prof., chmn. pediatrics, 1977—; adj. prof. biology N.Y. U., 1966-74; Established investigator Am. Heart Assn., 1960-65; career scientist N.Y.C. Health Research Council, 1965-75. Author numerous sci. publs.; Editor: (with Harry Harris) Advances in Human Genetics, 1969—; editorial bd. 16 sci. jours. Mem. council Village Community Sch., 1968-73, chmn., 1972-73. Served with AUS, 1944-47. Recipient Rudolph Virchow medal, 1974, Alumni Achievement award NYU Sch. Medicine, 1982. Fellow A.A.A.S.; mem. Am. Soc. Clin. Investigation, Am. Assn. Physicians, Am. Pediatric Soc., Am. Soc. Human Genetics (pres. 1969, dir.), Am. Assn. Immunologists, Harvey Soc. (v.p. 1979-80, pres. 1980-81, council 1981-84), Genetics Soc. Am., Environmental Mutagen Soc. (council), Inst. for Soc. Ethics and Life Scis. (dir.), Am. Soc. Pediatric Chmn. (council 1983—). Home: 29 Washington Sq New York City NY 10011 Office: Mt Sinai Sch Medicine 100th St and Fifth Ave New York City NY 10029

HIRSCHMAN, ALBERT OTTO, educator, political economist; b. Berlin, Apr. 7, 1915; s. Carl and Hedwig (Marcuse) H.; m. Sarah Chapiro, June 22, 1941; children: Catherine Jane, Elisabeth Nicole. Student, Sorbonne, H.E.C., London Sch. Econs., 1933-36; Dr. Econ. Sc., U. Trieste, 1938; LL.D. (hon.), Rutgers U., 1978; Rockefeller fellow, U. Calif.-, Berkeley, 1941-43. Economist Fed. Res. Bd., Washington, 1946-52; fin. adviser Nat. Planning Bd., Bogotá, Colombia, 1952-54; pvt. econ. cons., Bogotá, 1954-56; research prof. econs. Yale U., 1956-58; prof. internat. econ. relations Columbia U., 1958-64; prof. polit. economy Harvard U., 1964-74, Littauer prof. polit. economy, 1967-74; prof. Inst. for Advanced Study, Princeton U., 1974—; fellow Center Advanced Study Behavorial Scis., 1968-69; mem. Inst. for Advanced Study, 1972-73. Author: National Power and the Structure of Foreign Trade, 1945, The Strategy of Economic Development, 1958, Journeys Toward Progress: Studies of Economic Policy-Making in Latin America, 1963, Development Projects Observed, 1967, Exit, Voice, and Loyalty: Responses to Decline in Firms, Organizations and States, 1970, A Bias for Hope: Essays on Development and Latin America, 1971, The Passions and the Interests: Political Arguments for Capitalism before Its Triumph, 1977, Essays in Trespassing: Economics to Politics and Beyond, 1981, Shifting Involvements: Private Interest and Public Action, 1982; editor: Latin American Issues-Essays and Comments, 1961; contbr. articles to profl. jours. Served with AUS, 1943-45. Recipient Frank E. Seidman Disting. award in polit. economy, 1980, Talcott Parsons prize for social sci., 1983. Mem. Am. Econ. Assn., Council Fgn. Relations, Am. Acad. Arts and Scis., Am. Philos. Soc. Address: Inst For Advanced Study Princeton NJ 08540

HIRSCHMAN, SHALOM ZARACH, physician; b. Troy, N.Y., Aug. 5, 1936; s. Meyer and Anne H.; m. Donna Tobi Adelman, July 11, 1965; children: Orin, Raquel. B.A., Yeshiva U., 1957; M.D., Albert Einstein Coll. Medicine, 1961; Ph.D. equivalent, NIH Grad. Sch., 1966. Intern medicine Mass. Gen. Hosp., Harvard Med. Sch., 1961-62, resident, 1962-63; research assoc. NIH, Nat. Insts. Arthritis, Metabolic and Digestive Diseases, 1963-65, sr. investigator, 1965-66; NIH fellow in medicine Columbia-Presbyn. Med. Center, N.Y.C., 1966-67; sr. investigator Nat. Cancer Inst., NIH, 1967-69; instr. medicine George Washington U. Sch. Medicine, 1963-65; assoc. prof. medicine, dir. div. infectious diseases Mt. Sinai Sch. Medicine, CUNY, N.Y.C., 1969-71, prof. medicine, dir. div. infectious diseases, 1971—; attending physician Mt. Sinai Hosp., N.Y.C., 1971—; mem. merit rev. bd. VA, 1976-79; mem. virology and microbiology exec. bd. Am. Cancer Soc. Founder, trustee Touro Coll., Touro Law Sch., N.Y.C., 1970. Served with USPHS, 1963-69. NIH fellow, 1964; research grantee, 1970. Fellow A.C.P., Am. Soc. Infectious Diseases, Am. Coll. Clin. Pharmacology, Royal Coll. Hygiene and Tropical Medicine; mem. Am. Biophys. Soc., Am. Soc. Microbiology, Am. Soc. Liver Diseases, Soc. Exptl. Biology and Medicine, Am. Soc. Clin. Investigation, Assn. Am. Physicians, Am. Fedn. Clin. Research, AAAS, N.Y. Acad. Scis. (chmn. microbiology sect. 1975). Office: 1 Gustave Levy Pl New York NY 10029

HIRSCHOWITZ, BASIL ISAAC, physician; b. Bethal, S. Africa, May 29, 1925; came to U.S., 1953, naturalized, 1961; s. Morris and Dorothy (Drieb) H.; m. Barbara L. Burns, July 6, 1958; children: David E., Karen, Edward A., Vanessa. B.Sc., Witwatersrand U., Johannesburg, 1943, M.B., B.Ch., 1947, M.D., 1954. Intern, resident Johannesburg Gen. Hosp., 1948-50; house physician Postgrad. Med. Sch., London, Eng., 1950; registrar Central Middlesex Hosp., London, 1951-53; instr., asst. prof. U. Mich., 1953-56; asst. prof. Temple U., 1957-59; asso. prof. medicine, dir. div. gastroenterology U. Ala. Med. Center, Birmingham, 1959-64, prof. medicine, asso. prof. physiology, 1964-70, prof. physiology, 1970—; dir. gastroenterology dept. medicine U. Ala. Hosp. and Clinics, 1959—. Fellow AAAS, A.C.P., Royal Coll. Physicians (Edinburgh), Royal Coll. Physicians (London); mem. South African, Brit., Ala. med. assns., Med. Research Soc. Gt. Britain, Am. Fedn. Clin. Research, So. Soc. Clin. Investigation, Am. Physiol. Soc., Biophys. Soc., Am. Gastroent. Assn., Ala. Acad. Sci., Am. Soc. Gastro-Intestinal Endoscopy (Schindler medal 1974), Brit. Soc. Gastro-Intestinal Endoscopy (hon.), William Beaumont Soc. (Eddy Palmer award for contbns. to endoscopy 1976), Soc. Exptl. Biology and Medicine, Sigma Xi, Alpha Omega Alpha. Office: U Ala Med Center Birmingham AL 35294

HIRSH, ALBERT, concert pianist, educator; b. Chgo., July 1, 1915; s. Louis and Sonia (Weinberg) H.; m. Mildred Rigby Wile, May 18, 1937; children: Oliver, Conrad, Ethan. Studied under, Djane Lavoie-Herz. Concert pianist, 1933—, performer throughout, U.S., Can., Mexico, West Indies and Europe; prof. music, artist-in-residence U. Houston, 1950—; mem. faculty Am. Inst. Mus. Studies, Graz, Austria, 1974-81. Mem. Mcpl. Art Commn., Houston, 1966-71; mem. adv. council Miller Theatre, Houston, 1972—. Served with U.S. Army, 1944-46. Mem. AAUP, AFL-CIO, Phi Mu Alpha, Phi Kappa Phi. Jewish. Office: Sch Music U Houston Houston TX 77004

HIRSH, ALLAN THURMAN, JR., publishing executive; b. Cumberland, Md., Aug. 19, 1920; s. Allan Thurman and Ellinor Goldsmith (Ottenheimer) H.; m. Eleanor B. Rosenthal, June 17, 1944; children: Helene, Allan III, Eleanor. B.S. in Econs., Johns Hopkins U., 1941. C.P.A., Md. Acct., Burke Landsberg Gerber, Balt., 1941-42; with Ottenheimer Pubs., Inc., Balt., 1946—, pres., 1960—; v.p. Allan Pubs., Inc., Balt., 1980—. Bd. dirs. Balt. Hebrew Congregation, 1960-63, 83—; asso. Jewish Charities, Balt., 1972-79; pres. Forest Park High Sch. PTA, 1968, Balt. City Coll. PTA, 1971, Hebrew Burial and Social Service Soc., 1972-79. Served with USN, 1942-46. Mem. Assn. Am. Pubs. Democrat. Jewish. Clubs: Suburban (Balt.) (dir. 1974-76, v.p. 1976-79. Home: 11 Slade Ave Baltimore MD 21208 Office: 300 Reisterstown Rd Pikesville MD 21208

HIRSH, IRA JEAN, scientist, educator; b. N.Y.C., Feb. 22, 1922; s. Ellis Victor and Ida (Bernstein) H.; m. Shirley Helene Kyle, Mar. 21, 1943; children—Eloise, Richard, Elizabeth, Donald. A.B., N.Y. Coll. for Tchrs., 1942; A.M., Northwestern U., 1943; M.A., Harvard, 1947, Ph.D., 1948. Research asst. psycho-acoustic lab. Harvard, Cambridge, Mass., 1946-47, research fellow, 1947-51; with Central Inst. for Deaf, St. Louis, 1951—, asst dir. research, 1958-65, dir., 1965-83; dir. emeritus Central Inst. Deaf, 1983—; mem. faculty or adminstrn. Washington U., St. Louis, 1951—, prof. psychology, 1961—, dean faculty arts and scis., 1969-73; vis. prof. U. Paris, France, 1962-63; U.S. del Internat. Standards Orgn., 1962-76; mem. Internat. Acoustics Commn., 1969-75; chmn. behavioral scis. and edn. NRC, 1982—. Author: The Measurement of Hearing, 1952; Contbr. articles to profl. jours. Served with USAAF, 1943-45; Served with AUS, 1945-46. Recipient Biennial award Acoustical Soc. Am., 1956, Assn. Honors Am. Speech and Hearing Assn., 1968. Fellow Acoustical Soc. Am. (pres. 1967-68), Am. Psychol. Assn., Am. Speech and Hearing Assn. (exec. council 1958-61, 65-68); mem. Nat. Acad. Sci. Home: 6629 Waterman Ave Saint Louis MO 63130

HIRSHEN, SANFORD, architect, educator; b. N.Y.C., Feb. 6, 1935; s. Harry and Mildred (Zaidman) H.; m. Vivian Ann Greenberg, June 2, 1957; children: Richard K., Julie M. A.B., Columbia Coll., 1957; B.Arch., Columbia U., 1959. Lic. architect. With various archtl. firms, 1960-65; ptnr. Hirshen Gammill Trumbo, Architects, Berkeley, 1967—. Served with U.S. Army, 1959-60. Fellow AIA. Democrat. Jewish. Home: 2832 Benvenue St Berkeley CA 94705 Office: Hirshen Gammill Trumbo 2927 Newbury St Berkeley CA 94703

HIRSHFIELD, JAY LEONARD, physicist; b. Washington, Oct. 24, 1931; s. Milton Oliver and Tema (Marmelstein) H.; m. Marjorie Sandra Melnick, Aug. 19, 1957; children—David Eric, Andrew Marc, James Rodney, Louis Russell. B.S., U. Md., 1952; M.S., U.S. Air Force Inst. Tech., 1954, Ohio State U., 1956; Ph.D., MIT, 1960; M.A. (hon.), Yale U., 1968. Research asso. physics M.I.T., 1960-61; NATO postdoctoral fellow FOM Inst., Jutphaas, Netherlands, 1961-62; mem. faculty dept. physics Yale U., 1961—, prof. applied physics, 1968—; pres. Omega-P. Inc.; cons. Raytheon, United Technologies, Naval Research Lab.; vis. prof. physics Hebrew U. Jerusalem, 1972-73, 78-79; hon. prof. physics Chengdu Inst. Radio Engrs. (People's Republic of China), 1983. Served to lt. USAF, 1952-57. Guggenheim fellow, 1968. Mem. Am. Phys. Soc. Home: 55 Killdeer Rd Hamden CT 06517 Office: PO Box 2159 Yale Station New Haven CT 06520

HIRSHSON, STANLEY PHILIP, history educator; b. Bklyn., June 8, 1928; s. Morris M. and Rose (Gallant) H.; m. Claire Shibin, Nov. 21, 1965; 1 son, Mark Robert; m. Janet N. Feldman, Mar. 4, 1974; 1 son, Scott Garad. A.B., Rutgers U., 1950; M.A., Columbia U., 1951, Ph.D., 1959. Lectr. history Seton Hall U., South Orange, N.J., 1957-59; asst. prof. Paterson (N.J.) State Coll. (now William Paterson Coll.), 1959-62; asso. prof. Queens Coll., City U. N.Y., Flushing, 1963-66, prof., 1966—. Author: The Lion of the Lord, A Biography of Brigham Young, 1969, Grenville M. Dodge, Soldier, Politician, Railroad Pioneer, 1967, Farewell to the Bloody Shirt, Northern Republicans and the Southern Negro, 1962, My History Is Holy, A Biography of Mary Baker Eddy. Served with AUS, 1946-47, 53-55. Am. Council Learned Socs. fellow, 1962-63; Guggenheim fellow, 1966-67; Rockefeller Found. fellow, 1981-82. Home: 59 Wilson Pl Closter NJ 07624 Office: Dept History Queens Coll Flushing NY 11367

HIRST, HESTON STILLINGS, former ins. co. exec.; b. Concord, N.H., Nov. 8, 1915; s. Edgar Clarkson and Mary Walker (Stillings) H.; m. Ruth Elizabeth Galway, Sept. 9, 1939; children—Ann, Edgar, George. A.B., Dartmouth Coll., 1936, postgrad., 1937. Chem. engr. Factory Mut. Engring. Corp., 1937-44; chief engr. Blackstone Mut. Ins. Co., 1945-49, sec., asst. treas., 1949-52, v.p., sec., 1952-65, exec. v.p., 1965-68; sr. v.p. engring.-underwriting MFB Mut. Ins. Co., Providence, 1968-72; sr. v.p., sec. corp. affairs Allendale Mut. Ins. Co., Johnston, R.I., 1972-81; ret., 1981; sr. v.p., sec. corp. affairs Affiliated FM Ins. Co., Appalachian Ins. Co., New Providence Corp. Mem. Republican Town Com., Barrington, R.I., 1952-76, Com. on Appropriations, Barrington, 1961-70; town moderator, Barrington, 1970-76. Mem. Am. Chem. Soc., Soc. Fire Protection Engrs., Providence Engring. Soc., Dartmouth Soc. Engrs. Republican. Unitarian. Clubs: Turks Head, Univ. (Providence).

HIRST, JULIAN FRAVEL, city ofcl.; b. Purcellville, Va., Mar. 3, 1921; s. Julian Terry and Katherine Ethel (Fox) H.; m. Margaret Jane Fagan, May 11, 1946; children—Julian Terry, David Townshend, Jane Elizabeth. B.S., Va. Mil. Inst., 1941. San. engr. Va. Dept. Health, 1941-42; engr. So. Ry. Co., Washington, 1946-49; town mgr., Town of Pearisburg, Va., 1949-52, Town of Pulaski, Va., 1952-56, city mgr., City of Martinsville, Va., 1956-65, City of Roanoke, Va., 1965-72, City of Norfolk, Va., 1975—. Exec. dir. Va. Municipal League, 1973-75, also pres.; vice chmn. Va. Council on Criminal Justice, 1967-78. Served to lt. col. USAAF, 1942-46; ETO.; Recipient. State Meritorious Service citation Va. N.G., 1967. Mem. Internat. City Mgmt. Assn. (pres. Va. sect., 30-Yr. Service citation). Episcopalian. Clubs: Lions (former dep. dist. gov.), Kiwanis.). Home: 500 Colonial Ave Norfolk VA 23507 Office: 1101 City Hall Bldg Norfolk VA 23501

HIRST, WILLIAM, JR., financial executive; b. Phila, Sept 5, 1920; s. William and Mary (Davie) H.; m. Mary E. Bortz, Apr. 12, 1952; children: Leslie, W. Bradley, Donald L., James C. Jonathan D. B.S., U. Pa., 1947. With Chase Bag Co., Greenwich, Conn., 1947-74, v.p., 1968-71, dir., 1967-74, sr. v.p., treas., 1971-74; treas., chief financial officer ATI, Inc., 1974-82; v.p. fin. Light Communications Corp., 1983—; sec.-treas., dir. Arkell Safety Bag Co., 1963-74, Strawberry Hill Press, 1970-74; both Greenwich. Served with USNR, 1942-46. Mem. Nat. Assn. Accountants, Financial Exec. Inst., Sigma Alpha Epsilon. Home: 58 Fallow Field Ln Fairfield CT 06430 Office: 25 Van Zant St Norwalk CT 06855

HIRTH, JOHN PRICE, metallurgical engineering educator; b. Cin., Dec. 16, 1930; s. John Willard and Betty Ann (Price) H.; m. Martha Joan Davis, Nov. 28, 1953; children: John Marcus, Laura Ellen, James Gregory, Christina Louise. B. Metall. Engring., Ohio State U., 1953; M.S., Carnegie-Mellon U., 1953, Ph.D., 1957. Asst. prof. metall. engring. Carnegie-Mellon U., Pitts., 1958-61; Mershon prof. Ohio State U., 1961-67; vis. prof. Stanford, 1967-68; prof. Ohio State U., Columbus, 1967—; Aizen vis. prof. Nat. U. Mex., Mexico City, 1976; cons. in field; vis. adv. com. Nat. Bur. Standards, 1969-72, Argonne Nat. Lab., 1970-73, Cornell U., 1971-74, Carnegie-Mellon U., 1967-76; bd. overseers Acad. for Contemporary Problems, 1971-76. Author: Condensation and Evaporation, 1964, Theory of Dislocations, 1968, 82; editor: Scripta Metallurgica, 1974—. Served with USAF, 1953-55. Fulbright fellow Bristol U., Eng., 1957-58. Fellow Am. Soc. Metals (Stoughton award 1964, Campbell lectr. 1972), AIME (Hardy medal 1960, Mehl medal 1980, Mathewson medal 1982), Am. Soc. Engring. Edn. (McGraw award 1967); mem. Nat. Acad. Engring., Sigma Xi. Club: Ohio State Rugby Football. Home: 4062 Fairfax Dr Columbus OH 43220 Office: Dept Metall Engring Ohio State U Columbus OH 43210

HISER, HAROLD RUSSELL, JR., pharmaceutical company executive; b. Decatur, Ill., Oct. 21, 1931; s. Harold Russell and Dorothy Marie (Anderson) H.; m. Marguerite Lawrence West, June 20, 1961; children: Elizabeth Lawrence, Samuel West, John Anderson. B.S.E., Princeton U., 1953. Treas. Inco Ltd., N.Y.C., 1972-77; controller, 1977-79; v.p., treas. F.W. Woolworth Co., N.Y.C., 1979-81; sr. v.p. fin. Schering Plough Corp., Madison, N.J., 1981—. Office: One Giralda Farms Madison NJ 07940

HISEY, R. WARREN, paper manufacturing company executive; b. Chgo., 1931; married. B.A., Middlebury Coll., 1952; M.S., Ph.D., Inst. Paper Chemistry, 1955. Chief engr. S.D. Warren, 1955-65; v.p. mfg. Brown Co., 1965-69; gen. mgr. staff ops. paper group The Continental Group, Inc., Stamford, Conn., 1969-71, gen. mgr. consumer products, 1971-73, v.p., gen. mgr. bleached products div., 1973-75, pres. Continental Forest Industries div., 1975—, corp. exec. v.p. bleached systems div., 1976—; dir. Hospitality, Inc. Bd. dirs. Pulp and Paper Found. U. Maine. Mem. TAPPI (dir.). Office: Continental Forest Industries 21 Harbor Plaza Stamford CT 06904 *

HISLOP, MERVYN WARREN, health administrator, psychologist; b. Vancouver, B.C., Apr. 26, 1937; s. George and Freda (Wickenden) H.; m. Marilyn Gail Johnson, July 28, 1965; children: Lawren Nyall, Mylene Lorelle. B.A. with honors, U. B.S., 1965; M.A., McMaster U., 1967, Ph.D., 1970. Registered cert. psychologist, Ont., B.C.; cert. health adminstr. Dir. behaviour mgmt. services Surrey Place Centre, Ministry of Health, Toronot, Ont., 1970-73; dir. psychol. services Woodlands Ministry of Human Resources, New Westminster, B.C., 1973-78; coordinator life edn. program New Westminster, 1975-77; exec. dir. Riverview Hosp. Ministry of Health, Port Coquitlam, B.C., 1978—; research proposal submission cons. Can. Council, 1973; mem. edn. adv. com. Douglas Coll., 1983—. Demonstration model grantee Province Ont., 1971; province Ont. grad. fellow McMaster U., 1969; recipient David and Jean Bolocan Meml. prize U. B.C., 1965. Mem. Can. Coll. Health Service Execs., Can. Inst. Law and Medicine, Health Adminstrs. Assn. B.C., B.C. Health Assn., Hosp. Adminstrs. Councils Greater Vancouver and Fraser Valley, Can. Psychol. Assn., B.C. Psychol. Assn. (mem. com. 1974-76). Home: 3009 Fleet St Coquitlam BC Canada V3C 3S1 Office: Riverview Hosp British Columbia Ministry of Health 500 Lougheed Hwy Port Conquitlam BC Canada V3C 1J0

HITCH, CHARLES JOHNSTON, economist, institution executive; b. Boonville, Mo., Jan. 9, 1910; s. Arthur Martin and Bertha (Johnston) H.; m. Nancy Winslow Squire, Mar. 20, 1942; 1 dau., Caroline Winslow. A.A., Kemper Mil. Sch., 1929; B.A. with highest distinction, U. Ariz., 1931, LL.D., 1962; postgrad., Harvard, 1931-32; B.A. with first class honors (Rhodes scholar), Oxford U., 1934, M.A., 1938; D.Sc. in Commerce, Drexel U., 1963; LL.D., U. Pitts., 1968, U. Mo., 1968, George Washington U., 1976; D.Engring., Colo. Sch. Mines, 1979; L.H.D. honoris causa, U. Judaism, 1973. Began as fellow, praelector, tutor Queen's Coll., Oxford U., 1935-48; gen. editor Oxford Econ. Papers, 1941-48; vis. prof. U. São Paolo, Brazil, 1947; chief econs. div. Rand Corp., 1948-61, dir. research program; asst. sec. def. (comptroller), Washington, 1961-65; v.p. bus. and finance U. Calif., 1965-66, v.p. of adminstrn., 1966-67, pres. univ., 1968-75; prof. econs. U. Calif. at Berkeley, 1965-75; now emeritus; pres. Resources for the Future, 1975-79, also dir.; vis. prof. U. Calif. at Los Angeles, 1949-50; Irving Fisher research prof. Yale, 1957; Staff economist Mission for Econ. Affairs, U.S. Embassy, London, 1941-42; staff economist planning com. WPB, 1942-43; chief stblzn. controls div. Office War Moblzn. and Reconversion, 1945-46; chmn. gen. adv. com. ERDA, 1975-77; mem. Energy Research Advisory Bd. Dept. Energy, 1978—, Assembly Engring., NRC, 1975-78, Nat. Petroleum Council, 1975-78; mem. advisory council Gas Research Inst., 1976—, Electric Power Research Inst., 1978—; dir. Aerospace Corp., 1975-82. Author: The Economics of Defense in the Nuclear Age, 1960, Decision Making for Defense, 1965; Editor: Introduction to Economic Analysis and Policy, 1938, Energy Conservation and Economic Growth, 1978. Trustee Asia Found., Center Biotech. Research; bd. dirs. Am. Council on Edn., 1971-74. Served as 1st lt., OSS U.S. Army, 1943-45. Recipient Pub. Service award U.S. Navy, 1965; Phi Beta Kappa vis. scholar, 1977-78; Hon. fellow Queen's Coll., Oxford, Worcester Coll., Oxford. Fellow AAAS, Am. Acad. Arts and Scis., Econometric Soc.; mem. Am. Econ. Assn. (v.p. 1965), Royal Econ. Soc., Ops. Research Soc. Am. (council 1955-58, pres. 1959-60), Council Fgn. Relations, Nat. Acad. Pub. Adminstrn., Phi Beta Kappa. Democrat. Presbyn. Clubs: Bohemian (San Francisco); Cosmos (Washington). Home: 1515 Oxford St Berkeley CA 94709 Office: Lawrence Berkeley Lab U Calif Berkeley CA 94720

HITCH, HENRY ATWOOD, JR., banker; b. Salisbury, Md., Feb. 10, 1923; s. Henry Atwood and Rosalee (Harrell) H.; m. Rosalie Lowe, Aug. 16, 1947; children: Henry Atwood, III, James M., R. Todd. Student, Cornell U., 1943; B.S. in Commerce, U. Va., 1947; grad. with honors, Pacific Coast Banking Sch., U. Wash., 1970. With First Interstate Bank of Casper, Wyo., 1958-74, pres., chief exec. officer, 1974—; dir. Western Bancorp Mortgate Co., Denver; Bd. dirs. Pacific Coast Banking Sch., 1974—, First Interstate Investment Services, Inc., Los Angeles. Bd. dirs. Casper Coll. Found., Inc., 1975—, pres., 1979—; mem. Downtown Improvement Com., 1972-73; state fin. chmn. John Wold's U.S. congressional and senatorial campaigns, 1968, 70; bd. dirs. Casper Petroleum Club, 1968-69, 1978—, sec.-treas., 1968, 1st v.p., 1979, treas., 1980; dr. chmn. United Fund, 1959, pres., 1960, mem. bd., exec. com., 1960-63; bd. dirs. Casper Family YMCA, 1965-68, Community Recreation, Inc., 1957-68; pres. Community Recreation, Inc., 1968-70, sec., treas., 1970-78; mem. Casper Bd. Public Utilities, 1976-79; trustee Iliff Sch. Theology, Denver, 1979-80. Served as 2d lt. USAF, 1943-45. Mem. Wyo. Bankers Assn. (pres. 1982-83), C. of C. (dir. 1962-65). Clubs: Casper Country (dir. 1960-63, pres. 1963), Kiwanis (pres. 1964). Home: 1800 Brookview Dr Casper WY 82604 Office: PO Box 40 Casper WY 82602

HITCH, HORACE, lawyer; b. Princeton, Ind., July 3, 1921; s. Horace and Edith Mae (Ervin) H.; m. Helen Tuttle, Oct. 7, 1943; children: Peter H., Thomas E. B.Sc., U. Minn., 1942, LL.B., 1947. Bar: Minn. 1947. Ptnr. Dorsey & Whitney, Mpls., 1947—. Chancellor Episcopal Diocese Minn., 1974—. Served with USNR, 1942-46, 51-52. Mem. Minn. Bar Assn., Am. Judicature Soc., ABA. Clubs: Minikada, Mpls. Office: 2200 1st Bank Pl E Minneapolis MN 55402

HITCH, THOMAS KEMPER, economist; b. Boonville, Mo., Sept. 16, 1912; s. Arthur Martin and Bertha (Johnston) H.; m. Margaret Barnhart, June 27, 1940 (dec. Nov. 1974); children: Hilary, Leslie, Caroline, Thomas; m. Mae Okudaira. Student, Nat. U. Mexico, 1932; A.B., Stanford U., 1934; M.A., Columbia U., 1946; Ph.D., U. London, 1937. Mem. faculty Stephens Coll., Columbia, Mo., 1937-42; spl. study commodity markets Commodity Exchange Adminstrn., Dept. Agr., 1940; acting head current bus. research sect. Dept. Commerce, 1942-43; labor adviser Vets. Emergency Housing Program, 1946-47; economist labor econs. Pres.'s Council Econ. Advisers, 1947-50; dir. research Hawaii Employers Council, Honolulu, 1950-59; sr. v.p., mgr. research div. First Hawaiian Bank, 1959-82; chmn. Hawaii Gov.'s Adv. Com. on Financing, 1959-62; chmn. research com. Hawaii Vistors Bur., 1962-69; chmn. Mayor's Fin. Adv. Com., 1960-68; chmn. taxation and fin. com. Constl. Conv. Hawaii, 1968. Contbr. articles to profl. jours. Trustee Tax Found. of Hawaii, 1955-80, pres., 1968; trustee McInerny Found.; chmn. Hawaii Joint Council Econ. Edn., 1964-68. Served as lt. O.R.C., 1933-38; as lt. USNR, 1943-46. Mem. C. of C. Hawaii (chmn. bd. 1971), Nat. Assn. Bus. Economists, Am., Hawaii econs. assns., Indsl. Relations Research Assn., Am. Statis. Assn., Phi Beta Kappa, Pi Sigma Alpha, Alpha Sigma Phi. Clubs: Waialae Country (pres. 1979), Pacific.). Home: 5329 Olapa St Honolulu HI 96821 Office: First Hawaiian Bank Honolulu HI 96847

HITCHCOCK, DONALD SIMON, architectural engineering company executive; b. Putnam County, Ohio, May 12, 1929; s. George Clinton and Teresa Fern (Ridenour) H.; m. Gwenna F. Hicks, July 4, 1955; children: Thomas, Michael, James. B.S. in Engring, U.S. Mcht. Marine Acad., 1951; M.M. in Fin., Northwestern U., 1980. Registered profl. engr., Ill., Ohio, Ind., W.Va. Sr. engr. Central Foundry div. Gen. Motors Corp., Defiance, Ohio, 1955-69; exec. v.p. Lester B. Knight & Assos., Inc. (architects/engrs.), Chgo., 1970—. Past pres. Anthony Wayne Sch. PTA, Defiance; past mem. Traffic Safety Commn., Western Springs, Ill.; trustee Foundry Edn. Found. Served to lt. (j.g.) USNR, 1951-54. Mem. Foundry Equipment Mfrs. Assn. (pres.), Nat. Soc. Profl. Engrs., Am. Foundrymen's Soc., Western Soc. Engrs., Ill. Soc. Profl. Engrs., Lake County Contractors Assn., Chgo. Bldg. Congress (dir.). Presbyterian. Clubs: Chgo. Athletic Assn., Tower, Economic (Chgo.); La Grange Country. Home: 3801 Central Ave Western Springs IL 60558 Office: 549 W Randolph St Chicago IL 60606

HITCHCOCK, EDWARD KEITH, insurance company executive; b. Lima, Peru, Mar. 6, 1941; came to U.S., 1943; s. Alonzo David and Bessie (Light) H.; m. Jean Grace Miller, June 30, 1963; children: Keith David, Stephen Jon. B.A., in Econs. and Psychology, Stanford U., 1963; M.B.A. in Fin., Stanford U., 1965. Mgr. long range planning Allstate Ins., Northbrook, Ill., 1965-71; v.p. fin. Calif. Life Ins. Co., Oakland, 1971-72; v.p. fin. services and planning Indsl. Indemnity Co., San Francisco, 1972—; dir. Realty Counsel, Walnut Creek, 1981-83. Treas. Evang. Free Ch., Walnut Creek, 1982-83, bd. dirs., Walnut Creek, 1980-83. Mem. Planning Execs. Inst., Ins. Acctg. and Statis. Assn. Club: Bankers (San Francisco). Home: 324 Lowell Ln Lafayette CA 94549 Office: Industrial Indemnity Co 255 California St San Francisco CA 94119

HITCHCOCK, ETHAN ALLEN, lawyer; b. Milton, Mass., July 12, 1909; s. George Collier and Elizabeth (Fiske) H.; m. Elizabeth French, 1937 (dec.); children: Constance, Mary Elizabeth Bigham; m. Jane Chace Nicholas, 1976. Grad., St. Louis Country Day Sch., 1927; A.B., Yale U., 1931; LL.B., Harvard U., 1934. Bar: N.Y. 1935. Practiced in, N.Y.C., 1934-41, 46—; partner firm Webster & Sheffield, 1961—; chmn. bd. dirs. Olivetti Corp. Am., 1959-78. Pres. bd. Lenox Hill Neighborhood Assn., 1938-40, Brearley Sch., 1954-60; mem. Yale U. Council; chmn. Com. on Med. Affairs, 1970-75; trustee Lenox Hill Hosp., 1950-70, WNET/Thirteen Ednl. Broadcasting Corp., 1967-82; chmn. WNET/Thirteen Ednl. Broadcasting Corp., 1968-81; vice chmn. bd. dirs. N.Y. Philharm., 1965-74; bd. govs. Pub. Broadcasting Service, 1973-75; bd. dirs. Moblzn. for Youth, 1965-68; chmn. bd. dirs. MFY Legal Services, 1968-70; v.p., bd. dirs. Alzheimer's Disease and Related Disorders Assn. Inc., 1982—. Served from lt. to lt. comdr. USNR, 1941-46. Mem. Chi Psi. Home: Vliettown Rd Box 147 Oldwick NJ 08858 Office: One Rockefeller Plaza New York NY 10020

HITCHCOCK, GEORGE PARKS, editor; b. Hood River, Oreg., June 2, 1914; s. George Parks and Constance Leland (Henderson) H. B.A. cum laude, U. Oreg., 1935. Editor San Francisco Rev., 1958-63, Kayak mag., Santa Cruz, Calif., 1964—; lectr. lit. U. Calif. at Santa Cruz, 1969—; Bd. dirs. Coordinating Council Lit. Mags., 1968-74. Author: Another Shore, 1972, Tactics of Survival, 1962, Notes of the Siege Year, 1974, The Rococo Eye, 1968, The Dolphin With a Revolver in Its Teeth, 1968, Lessons in Alchemy, 1975, Mirror on Horseback, 1979, The Piano Beneath the Skin, 1980, Five Plays, 1981. Recipient Nat. Endowment Arts award. Home: 325 Ocean View Santa Cruz CA 95062

HITCHCOCK, HENRY PERRY, dentist, educator; b. Sanford, Maine, Apr. 8, 1921; s. Henry Sylvester and Cassilena (Perry) H.; m. Anna Ruth Gant, Dec. 19, 1948; children—Henry Malcolm (dec.), Edgar Perry, George Samuel, Amy Ruth. Student, Am. Internat. Coll., 1940-42; D.M.D., Tufts Coll., 1946; M.S.D., U. Ala., 1958. Diplomate: Am. Bd. Orthodontics. Pvt. dental practice, Belchertown, Mass., 1946; instr., asst. prof., asso. prof., prof. dentistry U. Ala. Sch. Dentistry, Birmingham, 1948-75, chmn. dept. orthodontics, 1964-75; prof. orthodontics U. Tex. Dental Sch., San Antonio, 1975—, chmn. dept., 1975—; pvt. practice orthodontics, Birmingham, 1951-58; vis. prof. Zahnarztliches Institut, U. Zurich, Switzerland, 1969-70; cons. cleft palate team State of Ala., VA Hosp., Birmingham. Author: Orthodontics for Undergraduates, 1974; Contbr.: chpt. to Clinical Pedodontics, 1967, 73. Served to capt. AUS, 1946-48. Mem. Am. Dental Assn., Am. Assn. Orthodontists, Sociedad Colombiana de Ortodontia (hon.), Omicron Kappa Upsilon. Office: Dental Sch Health Sci Center Floyd Curl Dr San Antonio TX 78284

HITCHCOCK, HENRY RUSSELL, educator, architectural historian; b. Boston, June 3, 1903; s. Henry Russell and Alice Whitworth (Davis) H. Student, Middlesex Sch., 1917-20; A.B., Harvard U., 1924, M.A., 1927, Harvard Sch. of Architecture, 1923-24; D.F.A., N.Y. U., 1969; Litt.D., U. Glasgow, 1973; L.H.D., U. Pa., 1976; D.H.L., Wesleyan U., 1979. Asst. prof. art Vassar Coll., 1927-28; asst. prof. art Wesleyan U., Middletown, Conn., 1929-41, asso. prof., 1941-47, prof., 1947-48; prof. art Smith Coll., 1948-61, Sophia Smith prof. art, 1961-68; prof. art U. Mass., Amherst, 1968; adj. prof. Inst. Fine Arts, N.Y.U., 1969—; dir. Smith Coll. Museum Art, 1949-55; lectr. architecture MIT, 1946-48; vis. lectr. architecture Yale U., 1952-53, 59-60, 69, Cambridge (Eng.) U., 1962, Harvard, 1965; tchr. Conn. Coll., 1934-42; lectr. Inst. Fine Arts, N.Y.U., 1940, vis. lectr., 1951, 57; Mathews lectr. Columbia U., 1971; prin. investigator Am. Capitols Research Project, 1971; Civilian employee Navy Dept., 1942; tech. author Pratt & Whitney Aircraft, 1943-45. Prepared archtl. exhbns., Mus. Modern Art, N.Y.C., Mus. Modern Art, Springfield, Mass., Mus. Modern Art, Hartford, Conn., Worcester, Buffalo and Providence Mus.; circulated archtl. exhbns. from, Wesleyan; Author: Frank Lloyd Wright, 1928, Modern Architecture, 1929, J.J.P. Oud, 1931, Modern Architects, (with others), 1932, The International Style, (with Philip Johnson), 1932, The Architecture of H.H. Richardson, 1936, Modern Architecture in England, (with others), 1937, Rhode Island Architecture, 1939, In the Nature of Materials, the Buildings of Frank Lloyd Wright, 1942, American Architectural Books, 1946, Painting Toward Architecture, 1948, Early Victorian Architecture in Britain, 1954, Latin-American Architecture since 1945, 1955, Architecture: 19th and 20th Centuries, 1958, paperback edit., 1971, rev. edit., 1977, German Rococo: The Zimmermann Brothers, 1968, Rococo Architecture in Southern Germany, 1968, (with William Seale) Temples of Democracy, 1976, Netherlandish Scrolled Gables of the 16th and Early 17th Centuries, New York, 1978, German Renaissance Architecture, 1981, also articles U.S., foreign mags. Guggenheim fellow, 1945-46; recipient Am. Council Learned Socs. award, 1961, AIA award merit, 1978; Benjamin Franklin award Royal Soc. Arts, London, 1979. Fellow Pilgrim Soc.; hon. corr. mem. Royal Inst. Brit. Architects, London; mem. Coll. Art Assn., Soc. Archtl. Historians (dir., nat. pres., pres. N.Y. chpt. 1970-73), Royal Soc. Arts (London) (Franklin fellow), Victorian Soc. (London), Victorian Soc. Am. (pres. 1970-74), AAUP, Soc. Preservation N.E. Antiquities. Democrat. Unitarian. Club: Century (N.Y.C.). Home: 152 E 62d St New York NY 10021

HITCHCOCK, JOHN THAYER, educator, anthropologist; b. Springfield, Mass., June 29, 1917; s. Arthur Cornwall and Ruth Harriet (Thayer) H.; m. Patricia Jennings, Nov. 27, 1947; children—Emily Robertson, Marion Thayer, Benjamin Jennings; m. Catharine McClellan, June 6, 1974. B.A., Amherst Coll., 1939; M.A., U. Chgo., 1941; Ph.D., Cornell U., 1956. Instr. Amherst Coll., 1946-48; acting asst. prof. anthropology U. Calif. at Berkeley, 1957-58; asst. prof. anthropology U. Calif. at Los Angeles, 1958-63, asso. prof., 1963-66; prof. anthropology and South Asian studies U. Wis., Madison, 1966—, chmn. Nepal studies program.; Bd. dirs. Anthrop. Film Research Inst. Author: The Rajputs of Khalapur, 1966, The Magars of Banyan Hill, 1966; Editor: Spirit Possession in the Nepal Himalaya, 1976; Producer: ethnographic films North Indian Village, 1956, Gurkha Country, 1966, Himalayan Farmer, 1966, Himalayan Shaman, 1966. Mem. nat. adv. com. Amnesty Internat. Served to lt. USNR, 1941-45. Decorated D.F.C.; Henry P. Field fellow, 1940-41; Ford Found. fellow, 1953-55; NSF grantee, 1960-62; Nat. Inst. Mental Health grantee, 1966-68; Wenner-Gren Found. grantee, 1965. Mem. Nepal Studies Assn. (pres.), Royal Anthropol. Inst., Am. Anthrop. Assn., Himalayan Club, A.A.A.S., Assn. for Asian Studies, Alpha Delta Phi, Phi Beta Kappa. Research Ute Indians, 1952, India, 1953-55, Nepal, 1960-62, 66-68. Address: Dept Anthropology U Wis Madison WI 53706

HITCHCOCK, RICHARD ELONZO, lawyer; b. Bakersfield, Calif., Apr. 16, 1925; s. Arthur Ralph and Erma (Davis) H.; m. Wilma Ann Tieck, Feb. 24, 1945; children: Richard Scott, Carol Ann (Mrs. Brian W. Aherne), Sara Tieck (Mrs. James Watson). Student, Bakersfield Coll., 1946; B.A., U. Calif.-Berkeley, 1948; J.D., Hastings Coll. Law, 1951. Bar: Calif. bar 1952. Claims rep. Cal-Farm Ins. Co., 1951-53; practiced in, Bakersfield, 1953—, pvt. practice, 1953-58, dep. dist. atty., 1958-65; asso. Borton, Petrini, Conron & Brown, 1965-69; partner Borton, Petrini & Conron, 1969—. Trustee Kern County Law Library, 1978—. Served to 2d lt. USAAF, 1943-45. Mem. Def. Research Inst., ABA, Kern County Bar Assn. (past pres.), Calif. State Bar, Kern County Peace Officers Assn. (past pres.), Assn. Def. Counsel (2d v.p., dir.). Presbyn. (elder, trustee). Home: 4305 Park Circle Dr Bakersfield CA 93309 Office: 1800 30th St Bakersfield CA 93301

HITCHCOCK, WALTER ANSON, cons., retired educational administrator; b. Shelton, Wash., Dec. 9, 1918; s. Paul H. and Hazel (Boyington) H.; m. Helen Nadine Rainbolt, Mar. 13, 1944; children: Paul H., Walter Anson, Larry W. B.A. in Bus. Adminstrn, Wash. State U., 1940, B.Ed., 1941, M.A. in Edn, 1948; postgrad., U. Okla., 1943-44, summer 1946; Ed.D., Wash. State U., 1966. Tchr. bus. subjects Omak (Wash.) Sr. High Sch., 1941-42; counselor Weatherwax Sr. High Sch., Aberdeen, Wash., 1946-47; prin. Wilbur (Wash.) High Sch., 1947-49; supt. schs., Nespelem, Wash., 1949-50, Wilbur, 1950-55, Moxee, Wash., 1955-59, West Valley schs., Spokane, 1959-66, Kennewick schs., 1966-69; dep. supt. Spokane city schs., 1969-72, supt., 1972-80, ret., 1980; assoc. Interpacific Investors Services (fin. planners), 1980—; Mem. advisory com. on tchr. edn. Eastern Wash. State U., 1959-63, chmn. ednl. imperatives, 1984—; adminstrv. advisory com. State Sch. Supt., mem. spl. edn. com., 1976-79; mem. Wash. State Ednl. TV Adv. Com., 1972-74; mem. spl. edn. adv. com. Central Wash. State U., 1975-79. Mem. Tri-Cities United Community Services, 1967-69, v.p., 1968; mem. Benton-Franklin Govtl. Conf., 1968-69; Bd. dirs. Expo 74, 1972-75, United Way of Spokane County, 1972-79, Inland Empire Red Cross, Inland Empire council Boy Scouts Am., Spokane Area Youth Com.; mem. panel on aging Eastern Wash. Area Agy. on Aging, 1984—. Served with AUS, 1942-45. Mem. Am. Assn. Sch. Adminstrs. (mem. SASA-AASA relations com. 1971-74), NEA, Wash. Edn. Assn. (bd. dirs. dept. adminstrn. and supervision 1968-69), Inland Empire Edn. Assn. (pres. 1972-73), Kennewick Edn. Assn., Northwest Regional Sch. Adminstrs. (chmn.), Yakima Valley Sch. Adminstrs. (chmn.), Spokane Area Supts. Assn. (pres.), Lincoln-Adams Bi-County Activities Assn. (pres.), Wash. Assn. Sch. Adminstrs. (pres. 1969-70, mem. exec. com.), Phi Kappa Phi, Alpha Kappa Psi, Phi Delta Kappa, Sigma Phi Epsilon. Presbyterian. (trustee 1957-59, ruling elder). Clubs: Lion., Wilbur Commercial (pres. 1952-54), Kiwanis (trustee 1961-63, 67-69, 72-76). Office: Northtown Office Bldg Spokane WA 99205

HITCHING, HARRY JAMES, lawyer; b. N.Y.C., Nov. 20, 1909; s. Harry and Sara (James) H.; m. Virginia Wyber, June 1933 (dec. Feb. 12, 1972); children: Virginia B. (Mrs. Daniel Andrews), James F.; m. Jeanne Austin Buckner, Aug. 25, 1972. A.B., Columbia, 1929, LL.B. (Kent scholar), 1931, J.D., 1969. Bar: N.Y. 1932, Tenn. 1938, Ga. 1969. Pvt. practice, N.Y.C., 1931-37; prin. atty. TVA, 1937-40, asst., gen. counsel, 1940-44; mem. firm Miller and Martin, Chattanooga, 1944-46; partner Miller, Martin and Hitching, 1946—; Gen. counsel Skyland Internat. Corp., Benwood Found., Chattanooga Area Regional Transp. Authority; div. counsel Vulcan Materials Co.; dir. Krystal Co. Mem. Miller Park Bd.; Chmn. bd. Tonya Meml. Found., Estate Planning Council Chattanooga; chmn. advisory bd. Chattanooga Salvation Army; bd. dirs. Chattanooga Opthalmol. Found., Community Found. Greater Chattanooga. Served to ensign USCGR, 1943-45. Mem. ABA, Tenn. Bar Assn., Ga. Bar Assn., Chattanooga Bar Assn. (v.p.), Chattanooga C. of C. (treas., dir.), Newcomen Soc. N.Am. Episcopalian. Clubs: Lookout Mountain Fairyland; Mountain City, Lookout Mountain Golf, Geology, Torch (Chattanooga) (pres.). Home: 1701 Wood Nymph Trial Lookout Mountain GA 37350 Office: Volunteer State Life Bldg Chattanooga TN 37402

HITCHINGS, WILLARD GRANT, hospital administrator; b. Syracuse, N.Y., Apr. 28, 1917; s. Raymond Clark and lina (King) H.; m. Gladys Alice Radney, May 22, 1943; children: Andrea, Scott. B.S., U. Iowa Bus. Adminstrn., 1940. Chief hosp. ops div. VA, Columbus, Ohio, 1948-49, field supt., Washington, 1949-50, asst. dir. hosps., Bronx, N.Y., Fayetteville, Ark., Providence, Tupper Lake, N.Y., Richmond, Va., 1951-70, hosp. dir., Miles City, Mont., 1970-71; dir. VA Med. Ctr., Dayton, Ohio, 1971—; assoc. clin. prof. community medicine Wright State U. Sch. Medicine, Dayton; mem. Statewide Health Coordinating Council, Columbus, 1978—. Mem. Dayton Mil. Affairs Com., 1980—. Served to capt. USAAF, 1942-45. Fellow Am. Coll. Hosp. Adminstrs.; mem. Fed. Exec. Assn. (chmn. Dayton chpt. 1977, 79, 81, 83), Greater Dayton Area Hosp. Assn., Dayton C. of C. Lodge: Rotary. Home: 4230 Lotz Rd Kettering OH 45429 Office: VA Med Ctr 4100 W Third St Dayton OH 45428

HITCHNER, DELL GILLETTE, political scientist, educator; b. Kansas City, Mo., Aug. 31, 1914; s. F.G. and Ouida M. (Kelley) H.; m. Kathleen D. Enlow, Sept. 3, 1938; children—Camilla (Mrs. C.H. Fulton), Nancy (Mrs. Gary A. Uderitz), Stuart. A.B., U. Wichita, 1936, A.M., U. Mo., 1937; Ph.D., U. Wis., 1940. Mem. faculty Coe Coll., 1940-44, asst. prof., 1943-44; asso. prof. U. Wichita, 1946; asst. prof. U. Wash., Seattle, 1947-51, asso. prof. polit. sci., 1951-63, prof. polit. sci., 1963-80, prof. emeritus, 1980—, acting exec. officer, 1957-59; vis. prof. U. Nebr., 1946, U. Utah, 1952; U.S. specialist Am. Embassy, London, 1956-57; vis. mem. London Sch. Econs. and Polit. Sci., 1957. Author: (with W.H. Harbold) Modern Government, 1962, 3d edit., 1972, (with C. Levine) Comparative Government and Politics, 1967, 2d edit., 1981; contbr. articles to profl. jours. Sec. Seattle Com. on Fgn. Relations, 1948-64. Served as sgt. inf. AUS, 1944-46; PTO. Mem. Am. Polit. Sci. Assn., Pacific N.W. Polit. Sci. Assn. (pres. 1967-68), AAUP. Republican. Home: 3844 NE 98th St Seattle WA 98115

HITE, JAMES TILLMAN, III, transportation company executive; b. Leesville, S.C., July 1, 1938; s. James Tillman, Jr. and Sarah Annette (Rikard) H.; m. Mary Ann Fulmer, June 27, 1961; children: James Tillman IV, John Lawrence. B.A., U. S.C., 1960. Salesman DuPont Co., 1961-64; exec. v.p., chief operating officer KTVE-TV, 1964-68;

with Fuqua Industries, Inc., 1964—, dir. market devel., 1968-69; pres. subs. Yarbrough Mfg. Co., Arlington, Tex., 1969-72, Arlington, 1972-75, Grand Rapids, Mich., 1975-78, exec. v.p. parent co., 1978-80, chmn. bd., 1980—, also dir.; dir. Fuqua Industries, Inc., Old Kent Bank & Trust Co., Trucking Mgmt., Inc., Arlington Bank Commerce, Yarbrough Mfg. Co., Fuqua Homes Inc., Nat. Prepaid Legal Services, Inc. Bd. dirs. Ark. Edn. Bd., 1966-68, Sentry Indsl. Dist., 1972, Ark. Ednl. TV, 1966-68; chmn. Ark. C. of C. City Expansion, 1967, Gov.'s Bus. Adv. Council; trustee ATA Found. Served as officer USMCR, 1959-61. Mem. Am. Soc. Packaging Engrs., Am. Soc. Bankers, Regular Common Carrier Conf. (dir.), Am. Trucking Assns. (exec. com., v.p.-at-large, vice-chmn.), Mich. Trucking Assn. (dir.), Eastern Central Bur. (dir.), Young Pres.'s Orgn. Home: 1401 Mt Paran Rd NW Atlanta GA 30327 Office: 110 Ionia Ave SE Grand Rapids MI 49503

HITE, SHERE D., author, cultural historian; b. St. Joseph, Mo. B.A. cum laude, U. Fla., 1964; M.A., 1968; postgrad., Columbia U., 1968-69. Dir. feminist sexuality project NOW, N.Y.C., 1972-78; dir. Hite Research Internat., N.Y.C., 1978—; instr. female sexuality N.Y. U., 1977—; lectr. Harvard U., McGill U., Columbia U., also numerous women's groups, internat. lectr., 1977-83; mem. adv. bd. Am. Found. Gender and Genital Medicine, Johns Hopkins U. Author: Sexual Honesty: By Women For Women, 1974, The Hite Report: A Nationwide Study of Female Sexuality, 1976, The Hite Report on Male Sexuality, 1981; cons. editor: Jour. Sex Edn. and Therapy, Jour. Sexuality and Disability. Mem. NOW, Am. Hist. Assn., Am. Sociol. Assn., AAAS, Acad. Polit. Sci., Women's History Assn., Soc. for Sci. Study Sex, Womens Health Network. Office: PO Box 5282 FDR Sta New York NY 10022 *I am dedicated to improving women's situation, here and around the world. I am also trying to express an esthetic ideal through my work and how I live my life. I feel I have only begun to do all the things I want to do. What makes life exciting? Wit, beauty and purpose.*

HITESMAN, WALTER WOOD, JR., publishing consultant; b. Baton Rouge, Aug. 9, 1918; s. Walter Wood and Anna (Allen) H.; m. Betty Parker, Oct. 8, 1948; 1 son, Jonathon. B.A., La. State U., 1939, postgrad., 1939-40. News editor Baton Rouge Advocate, 1939-40; bus. mgr. comml. printing div. McCall Corp., 1946-48; mng. dir. Reader's Digest, Can., 1948-60; v.p. Reader's Digest Assn., Inc., Pleasantville, N.Y., 1960-69, sr. v.p., 1969-70, exec. v.p., 1970-71, 1st v.p., 1971-73, pres., 1973-74, dir., 1965-74; sr. v.p. Eastern Air Lines, N.Y.C., 1974-75; chmn. Am. Econ. Found., N.Y.C., 1976-77; publishing cons., 1977—; Treas. Acad. Am. Poets. Bd. dirs. Marine Mil. Acad., Boscobel Restoration, Inc., Boys Clubs Am., Environ. Law Inst. Served to lt. col. USMCR, 1940-46. Named Direct Mail Mktg. Man of Year, 1969; Alumnus of Year, La. State U., 1974. Mem. Pilgrims of U.S., Sigma Pi, Sigma Delta Chi. Republican. Episcopalian. Clubs: Chappaquiddick Beach, Edgartown (Mass.) Yacht, Edgartown Golf (pres.). Home: PO Box 178 Edgartown MA 02539

HITSCHFELD, WALTER FRANCIS, educator; b. Vienna, Austria, Apr. 25, 1922; s. Alois and Amelie (Brahms) H.; m. Irma Morissette, Sept. 6, 1947; children: Paul Alois, Charles Philip. Student, St. Francis Xavier U., Antigonish, N.S., 1939-43; B.A.Sc., U. Toronto, 1946; Ph.D., McGill U., 1950. Faculty Loyola Coll., Montreal, Que., Can., 1946-51; faculty McGill U., Montreal, 1950—, vice prin. research, 1974-80, dean grad. studies, 1971-80. Contbr. articles to profl. jours. Recipient Patterson medal Atmospheric Environment Service. Fellow Am., Royal, Canadian meteorol. socs., Canadian Assn. Physicists, Royal Soc. Can. Home: 4021 Grand Blvd Montreal PQ Canada H4B 2X4

HITT, DAVID H., hospital executive; b. Tuscaloosa, Ala., May 14, 1925; m. Frances Ford, Aug. 12, 1949; children: David Hamilton, Kathryn Ann. M.S. in Commerce and Bus. Adminstrn, U. Ala.; M.H.A., U. Minn. Hosp. adminstr., 1947—; with Baylor U. Med. Center, 1952-79; various mgmt. positions, including chief exec. officer James A. Hamilton Assocs. (hosp. consultants), Dallas, 1979-84; pres. Meth. Hosps. of Dallas, 1984—; dir. Swiss Ave. Bank; pres. Dallas Hosp. Council, 1959; mem. adminstrv. bd. Council Teaching Hosps. of Assn. Am. Med. Colls., 1972-79; v.p. Community Council Greater Dallas; assoc. clin. prof. Washington U., St. Louis.; adj. assoc. prof. Trinity U., San Antonio. Contbr. numerous articles to profl. jours. Mem. exec. bd. council Boy Scouts Am. Recipient Earl M. Collier award Distinguished Hosp. Adminstrn. Tex., 1973; Dean Conley award.; Silver Beaver award Boy Scouts Am. Fellow Am. Coll. Hosp. Adminstrn. (past regent); mem. Am. Hosp. Assn. (trustee, past chmn. council financing), Tex. Hosp. Assn. (trustee, treas., v.p., pres., chmn. ho. of dels. 1967), Am. Protestant Hosp. Assn. (past trustee), Alumni Assn. U. Minn. Program Hosp. Adminstrn. (past pres.). Clubs: Exchange (East Dallas) (pres. 1957); Masons (32°, KT), Shriners, K.T., Dallas Wood and Waters. Home: 7231 Twin Tree Ln Dallas TX 75214

HITT, JOHN CHARLES, JR., university provost; b. Houston, Dec. 7, 1940; s. John Charles and Mary W. (Green) H.; m. Martha Ann Halsted, Dec. 23, 1961; children: John Charles, Sharon Aileen. A.B. cum laude, Austin Coll., 1962; M.S. (Danforth fellow, NSF fellow), Tulane U., 1964, Ph.D., 1966. Cert. psychologist, Tex. Asst. prof. psychology Tulane U., 1966-69; assoc. prof. psychology Tex. Christian U., Ft. Worth, 1969-77, assoc. dean of univ., 1972-77; v.p. Tex. Christian U. Research Found., 1974-77; dean Grad Sch. Tex. Christian U., 1975-77; v.p. acad. affairs Bradley U., Peoria, Ill., 1977—, provost, 1981—. Mem. bd. co-editors: Psychological Research, 1973-76; contbr. articles in psychology and neuroscience to scholarly jours. Chmn. com. on social scis. Austin Coll. 125th Anniversary Commn., 1973-74; charter mem. Austin Coll. Bd. Edn. Visitors, 1976; Tex. Christian U. rep. Leadership Ft. Worth, 1973-74; program chmn. Forum Ft. Worth, 1976-77; mem. Tarrant County United Way Budget Com., 1975-77, Forward Ft. Worth, 1976-77; chmn. loaned exec. program Heart of Ill. United Way, 1979, chmn. edn. unit, 1980; bd. dirs. Greater Peoria YMCA, 1980—, Inst. Phys. Medicine and Rehab., Peoria, 1981—, Heart of Ill. United Way, 1983—. Mem. Am., Midwestern psychol. assns., Psychonomic Soc., Soc. Neuroscience, AAAS, Am. Assn. Higher Edn., Sigma Xi, Alpha Chi, Psi Chi, Phi Kappa Phi. Democrat. Episcopalian. Home: 1508 W Thames Ave Peoria IL 61614 Office: Bradley U Peoria IL 61625

HITT, PETER, architect; b. Detroit, Apr. 16, 1932; s. Eldridge and Christine (Noeker) H.; m. Betsy Buell, Dec. 29, 1959; children—Peter David, Jeffrey Buell. B.A. in Econs, Colgate U., 1954; B.Arch. cum laude, Syracuse (N.Y.) U., 1962. Designer C.F. Murphy Assos., Chgo., 1962-63; draftsman Suter & Johnson, Evanston, Ill., 1963-64; sr. v.p., gen. mgr. Perkins & Will, Chgo., 1964—. Prin. works include U. S. Army Hosp, Ft. Campbell, Ky., Heritage Hosp, Taylor, Mich., Tucson Med. Center, Fed. Plaza, Milw., First Fed. Savs. & Loan Assn. of Chgo, South Central Bell Telephone Hdqrs, Nashville, Tenn. Past mem. Village of Wilmette (Ill.) Planning Commn.; Active fund raising for Colgate U., United Fund Chgo. Served with capt. USAF, 1954-57. Mem. AIA, Colgate U. Alumni Assn. (past pres. Chgo. chpt.). Club: Union League (Chgo.). Home: 1202 Lake Ave Wilmette IL 60091 Office: Perkins and Will 2 N LaSalle St Chicago IL 60602

HITTINGER, WILLIAM CHARLES, electronics co. exec.; b. Bethlehem, Pa., Nov. 10, 1922; s. John Tilghman and Pearl (Heimbach) H.; m. Elizabeth Herman, July 9, 1944; children—Patricia, William, David, Nancy. B.S. with honors in Metall. Engring, Lehigh U., 1944, D.Engring. (hon.), 1973. Engr. Western Electric Co., 1946-52; prodn. mgr. Semiconductor div. Nat. Union Radio Corp., 1952-54; exec. dir. Bell Telephone Labs., 1954-66; pres. Bellcomm Inc., Washington, 1966-68, Gen. Instrument Corp., N.Y.C., 1968-70; v.p., gen. mgr. RCA Corp., Somerville, NJ., 1970-72, exec. v.p., N.Y.C., 1972—, also dir.; dir. Am. Fletcher Nat. Bank, Am. Fletcher Corp., Indpls. Bd. dirs. Bethlehem (Pa.) Fgn. Policy Assn., 1960-62, Nat. Action Council for Minorities in Engring., Inc.; trustee Lehigh U. Served to capt. AUS, 1943-46. Named hon. citizen, Bethlehem, 1966. Fellow I.E.E.E.; mem. Nat. Acad. Engring., Omicron Delta Kappa, Phi Gamma Delta. Home: 149 Bellevue Ave Summit NJ 07901 Office: David Sarnoff Research Center Princeton NJ 08540

HITTLE, JAMES D., government and business consultant; b. Bear Lake, Mich., June 10, 1915; s. Harry F. and Margaret Jane (McArthur) H.; m. Edna Jane Smith, Dec. 9, 1939 (dec. 1969); children: Harry McArthur, James Richard; m. Patricia Ann Herring, Sept. 5, 1970. B.A., Mich. State U., 1937; M.S. in Oriental History and Geography, U. Utah, 1952. Commd. 2d lt. USMC, 1937, advanced through grades to brig. gen., 1958, legis. asst. to comdt., 1952-58; asst. to sec. def. legis. affairs, 1958-60, retired, 1960; dir. nat. security and fgn. affairs VFW, 1960-67; syndicated columnist Copley News Service, 1964-69; mil. commentator MBS, 1964-69; dir. DISC, Inc., 1960-67; spl. counsel Senate Armed Services Com., 1968-69; cons. House Armed Services Com., 1968-69; founder, dir. D.C. Nat. Bank, 1965-69; asst. sec. navy for manpower and res. affairs, 1969-71; sr. v.p. govt. affairs Pan Am. World Airways, Washington, 1971-73; cons. to adminstr. VA, 1973-77; cons. to pres. Overseas Pvt. Investment Corp., 1974-75; participant comml. air mgmt. survey S.E. Asian Transp. and Communications Commn., 1975; cons. Gleason Assos. Inc., 1974—, Vought Corp., 1975—, Marriott Corp., 1978—; comdt. U.S. Marine Corps, 1979-81; sec. U.S. Navy, 1981-82; counselor to Sec. of Navy, 1982. Author: History of the Military Staff, 1949; also articles.; Editor: Jomini's Art of War, 1945; columnist: Navy Times, 1974—. Bd. dirs. Stafford County (Va.) Indsl. Devel. Authority, 1974—; vice chmn. Belleau Woods U.S. Mil. Cemetary Meml. Day Services, 1978—. Decorated Legion of Merit, Purple Heart; Medal of Combat Merit, France; Cross of Chevalier; Mil. Order European Vets.; recipient Alfred Thayer Mahan award Navy League U.S., 1960, Scroll of Honor, 1967; silver medal City of Paris, 1961; gold medal, 1972; George Washington award Freedom Found., 1967, 69; Selective Service System Distinguished Service award, 1971; U.S. Navy Distinguished Service award, 1971; Meritorious Pub. Service citation U.S. Marine Corps, 1981. Mem. VFW, Am. Legion, Brit. Legion (hon.), La. State Hist. Soc. (hon. life), Mil. Order World Wars, Clan MacArthur Soc. Am., Navy League, U.S. Marine Corps League (legis. com. 1980—), Battleship Assn. U.S., Phi Kappa Phi, Phi Kappa Delta. Club: Army-Navy (pres. Washington 1983—). Mailing Address: 3137 S 14th St Arlington VA 22204

HITTLE, RICHARD HOWARD, energy company executive; b. Columbus, Nebr., Apr. 30, 1923; s. Arthur Howard and Frieda Margaret (Poppe) H.; m. Catherine Louise Dethlefsen, May 11, 1951; children: Ann-Louise, Thomas Woodford, Bradley Arthur. Student, Cambridge (Eng.) U., 1945; B.S., U. Denver, 1950, LL.B., 1951; M.B.A., Harvard U., 1955. With Conoco Inc., 1955—, mgr. internat. acquisitions, 1964-75; pres. Continental Overseas Oil Co., N.Y.C. also Stamford, Conn., 1969-75; gen. mgr., v.p. internat. govt. affairs Conoco, Inc., Stamford, 1975-83, Wilmington, Del., 1983—; Bd. govs. Middle East Inst., Washington; mem. industry sector adv. com. on energy U.S. Govt.; rep. to Council on Fgn. Relations. Mem. president's council on Near East studies NYU; trustee Beirut U. Coll. Served with AUS, 1943-46; Served with USAF, 1951-53. Mem. Asia Soc., Japan Soc., U.S.-Arab C. of C. (dir., pres.), Egyptian Am. C. of C. (dir.), Norwegian Am. C. of C. (dir.). Republican. Lutheran. Clubs: Harvard (N.Y.C.); Stanwich, Rocky Point (Greenwich, Conn.); Dorset Field. (Vt.); Metropolitan (Washington). Home: 3 Hendrie Dr Old Greenwich CT 06870 Office: 1007 Market St Wilmington DE 19898

HIXON, PHILIP EDWARD, publishing company executive; b. N.Y.C., Jan. 6, 1932; s. Harry and Augusta (Talianoff) H.; m. Helene Adele Liff, Oct. 3, 1953; children: Dawn Jeri, Neil Mark, Jonathan David. B.Chem. Engring., NYU, 1953; M.B.A., L.I.U., 1974; postgrad., Cornell U., 1954. Founder, pres. Rolor Corp., Syosset, N.Y., 1956-67; gen. mgr. Rolor div. Itek Corp., Syosset, 1967-69; ptnr. Snyder-Hixon Assocs., N.Y.C., 1970—; publ. Cambridge Sci. Abstract, Washington, 1973—; pres. Disclosure Inc., Washington, 1977—; pres., dir. Nat. Standards Assn., Washington, 1976—. Served to 1st lt. USAF, 1953-56. Recipient Student Medal Am. Inst. Chemists, 1953. Fellow Am. Inst. Chemists; mem. Am. Inst. Chem. Engrs. (chpt. pres. 1952-53), Am. Inst. Photog. Scientists. Jewish. Clubs: Georgetown, University. Office: Disclosure Inc 5161 River Rd Bethesda MD 20816

HIXON, ROBERT CHARLES, retired army officer; b. Camp Bragg, N.C., Feb. 12, 1922; s. Charles Edward and Edna Grace (Wickham) H.; m. Patricia Jean Laske, Aug. 15, 1981; children: Robert Charles, Thomas Edward, James Andrew, William Oliver. Student, Mich. State Coll., 1940-42; B.S., U. Md., 1958; M.A., George Washington U., 1960. Commd. 2d lt. U.S. Army, 1943, advanced through grades to maj. gen., 1972; staff officer, exec. officer 555 F.A. Bn., 5th Regt. Combat Team, Korea, 1953-54; spl. asst. to dep. chief of staff for personnel Dept. Army, 1958-60; comdr. 2d Bn., 16th Arty., 4th Armored Div., Germany, 1961-63; liaison officer, legis. asst. Office Asst. Sec. Def. for mil. assistance, 1964-65; exec. officer Office Asst. Sec. Def. for Internat. Security Affairs, 1966-67; comdr. 46th F.A. Group, Ft. Carson, Colo., 1967-68; mil. asst. to Sec. Def., 1968-69; comdr. IV Corps Arty., Vietnam, 1969-70; chief of staff XXIV Corps, 1970-71; comdg. gen., Ft. Jackson, S.C., 1972-74; comdr. U.S. Mil. Assistance Command, Thailand, 1974-75; chief of staff Hdqrs. U.S. Army Tng. and Doctrine Command, Ft. Monroe, Va., 1975-79. Bd. dirs. Assembly Against Hunger and Malnutrition, Army Emergency Relief Soc.; mem. Va. Gov.'s Task Force Food and Nutrition Policy; dir. personnel Christopher Newport Coll. Decorated D.S.M. with one oak leaf cluster, Silver Star medal, Legion of Merit with 2 oak leaf clusters, D.F.C., Bronze Star medal with oak leaf cluster, Air medal with V device and 17 oak leaf clusters, Joint Services Commendation medal, Army Commendation medal; Nat. Order Vietnam (5th class); Order Mil. Merit, Korea. Mem. U.S. Parachutist Assn., Assn. U.S. Army, Nat. Rifle Assn., Sigma Alpha Epsilon. Episcopalian. Home: 30 Rivergate Dr Poquoson VA 23662

HJALMARSON, GORDON ROSS, publishing company executive; b. Dauphin, Man., Can., Apr. 9, 1926; came to U.S., 1942, naturalized, 1950; s. John I. and Holmfridur J. (Johnson) H.; m. Carroll L. Clark, Aug. 9, 1952; children: Gordon Ross II, Melissa Anne, John Clark, Eric Alexander. B.A., Pomona Coll., 1949; M.A., San Francisco State U., 1951; postgrad., U. So. Calif., 1953-54. Sch., univ. tchr., 1951-58; with Houghton Mifflin, Boston, 1958-73, asso. dir. sch. depts., 1968-69, dir. dept., 1969-73, v.p., mem. exec. com., 1973, also dir., 1970-73; pres., dir. Scott, Foresman & Co., Glenview, Ill., 1973-76, chmn. bd., chief exec. officer, 1976—; chmn. bd., chief exec. officer, pres. SFN Cos., Inc., 1980-83; holding co. for William Morrow Co., N.Y.C., Silver Burdett Co., Morristown, N.J., Southwestern Pub. Co., Cin., Fleming H. Revell Co., Old Tappan, N.J., Scott, Foresman & Co., Glenview, Ill., Univ. Park Press, Balt.; chmn., dir. GLC Ltd., Toronto, Gage Pubs. Toronto; Asso. pres.'s com. Northwestern U., Nat. Coll. Edn., Evanston, Ill., U. Chgo., U. Ill. Trustee, mem. pres.'s com. Pomona (Calif.) Coll. Named First Disting. Alumnus of Yr. San Francisco State U., 1979, Top Chief Exec. Officer in Pub. Industry Wall St. Transcript, 1980. Mem. Chgo. Council Fgn. Relations, Chgo. Assn. Commerce and Industry, Pres.'s Assn., Assn. Am. Pubs. (dir., sec. exec. council), C. of C. of U.S. Clubs: Masons, Wellesley Country; Union (Boston); Econ., Chicago, Executive (Chgo.); President's (N.Y.C.); Sunset Ridge Country. Home: 119 Abingdon Ave Kenilworth IL 60043 Office: 4710 Valdina Way San Diego CA 62124

HJELLUM, JOHN, lawyer; b. Aurland, Sogn, Norway, Mar. 29, 1910; s. Olav Iversen and Belle (Ohnstad) H.; m. Helen Jeanette Fodness, May 12, 1935; children: Janice Ann, Joan Mae, John II. LL.B., J.D., U. N.D., 1934. Bar: N.D. 1934. Since practiced in Jamestown; mem. firm Hjellum, Weiss, Nerison, Jukkala, Wright & Paulson; investigator fed. violations Dept. Justice, 1934; asst. states atty., Stutsman County, N.D., 1943-45, states atty., 1948-50; sec. N.D. Broadcasting Co., 1950-62; sec., dir. N.Am. Uranium Inc., Jamestown, N.D., 1954-69. Active community drives.; chmn. N.D. Eisenhower for Pres. group, also N.D. Citizens for Eisenhower-Nixon; vice chmn. Stutsman County Republican Orgn., 1955-58; mem. Stutsman County Central Com., 1958-62; del. Rep. Nat. Conv., 1952; trustee Jamestown Coll., 1967-75; chmn., trustee N.D. Ind. Coll. Fund, 1957-68. Served with CIC, AUS, 1944-45. Fellow Internat. Acad. Trial Lawyers (dir. 1969-75, 78—); mem. ABA, Internat. Bar Assn., N.D. Bar Assn. (pres. 1957-58), 4th Jud. Dist. Bar Assn. (pres. 1949-50), Stutsman County Bar Assn. (pres. 1940-41, 49-50), Am. Legion, VFW, Order of Coif (hon.), Lambda Chi Alpha, Phi Delta Phi, Kappa Kappa Psi. Methodist (chmn. bd. 1946-76). Club: Masons. Home: 916 2d Ave NW Jamestown ND 58401 Office: PO Box 1132 Jamestown ND 58401

HJORT, HOWARD WARREN, consultant; b. Plentywood, Mont., Dec. 20, 1931. B.S., Mont. State U., 1958, M.S., 1959; postgrad., N.C. State U. Staff economist Office of Sec. Agr., Washington, 1963-65, spl. asst. to under sec., 1965; dir. staff for program planning and analysis Office of Sec., 1965-69; planning and mgmt. adviser with Ford Found., India, 1969-72; dir. Office of Econs., Policy Analysis and Budget, 1977-81; co-founder Schnittker Assos. (agrl. cons.), Washington, 1972-77; ptnr. EPI (McLean), Va. Home: 1817 Briar Ridge Ct McLean VA 22101 Office: 6723 Whittier Ave Suite 101 McLean VA 22101

HJORTSBERG, WILLIAM REINHOLD, author; b. N.Y.C., Feb. 23, 1941; s. Helge Reinhold and Ida Anna (Welti) H.; m. Marian Souidee Renken, June 2, 1962 (div. 1982); children—Lorca Isabel, Max William.; m. Sharon Leroy, July 21, 1982. B.A., Dartmouth Coll., 1962; postgrad., Yale Drama Sch., 1962-63, Stanford U., 1967-68. Author: Alp, 1969, Gray Matters, 1971, Symbiography, 1973, Toro! Toro! Toro!, 1974, Falling Angel, 1978; author: film Thunder and Lightning, 1977; co-author: TV film Georgia Peaches, 1980; Contbg. editor: Rocky Mountain mag, 1979; contbr.: fiction to Realist, Playboy, Cornell Rev., Penthouse, Oui, Sports Illustrated; also articles.; criticism to N.Y. Times Book Rev. Wallace Stegner fellow, 1967-68; Nat. Endowment Arts grantee, 1976. Mem. Authors Guild, Writers Guild Am. Office: care Robert Dattila Phoenix Literary Agy Inc 150 E 74th St New York NY 10021

HLADKY, JOSEPH FRANK, JR., newspaper publisher, broadcasting executive; b. Cedar Rapids, Iowa, Aug. 25, 1910; s. Joseph Frank and Laura (Krchmar) H.; m. Jane Miller, Sept. 15, 1935; children: John Miller, Joseph Frank. Student, Coe Coll., Cedar Rapids, 1928-29, U. Iowa, 1930-31. Engaged in vending machine bus., 1931-35, newspaper publ., 1935—, broadcasting, 1947—; chmn. bd. Gazette Co. (pubs. Cedars Rapids Gazette), Cedar Rapids TV Co.; past chmn. bd. govs. ABC-TV Affiliates; dir. Mchts. Nat. Bank, Cedar Rapids, Iowa Nat. Mut. Ins. Co. Chmn. Cedar Rapids Airport Commn., 1973—, Cedar Rapids Hwy. Com., 1960—; mem. Iowa Devel. Commn., 1964—, Cedar Rapids Civic Planning Com., 1962—; bd. dirs. St. Luke's Methodist Hosp., Cedar Rapids, 1961—, Cedar Rapids Met. YMCA, 1969—; trustee Coe Coll., 1968—. Recipient Master Editor and Pub. award, 1970; Community Recognition award, 1981; named Boss of Year, 1964. Mem. Am. Soc. Newspaper Editors, Am. Newspaper Pubs. Assn., Inland Daily Press Assn., AP, Nat. Assn. Broadcasters, Iowa Daily Press Assn. (past pres.), Cedar Rapids C. of C. (past pres.), Sigma Delta Chi. Clubs: Nat. Press (Washington); Cedar Rapids Country, Elmcrest Country, Sombrero Golf and Country, Marathon Yacht, Marathon. Lodges: Shriners; Elks; Royal Order Jesters. Office: 500 3d Ave SE Cedar Rapids IA 52401 *

HLASS, I. JERRY, government official; m. Helen Mae Diller, Dec. 21, 1963; 1 son, George O. B. Mech. Engring., N.C. State U., 1949; M. Engring. Adminstrn., George Washington U., 1971. Dir. space shuttle facilities NASA, Washington, 1971-76, mgr. nat. space tech. labs., Bay St. Louis, Miss., 1976—. Mem. Nat., Miss. socs. profl. engrs. Methodist. Office: Nat Space Tech Labs NSTL Station MS 39529 *

HLAVACEK, ROY GEORGE, editor; b. Chgo., Sept. 17, 1937; s. George Louis and Lillian Barbara (Vasovic) H.; m. Nancy Elaine Wroblaski, Aug. 3, 1963; children: Carrie Lee, Alexander Michael. B.S., U. Ill., 1960; M.B.A., U. Chgo., 1969. Project engr. Research and Devel. Center, Swift & Co., Chgo., 1960-65; v.p., editor/pub. Food Processing mag., Foods of Tomorrow mag. Food Publs. div. Putman Pub. Co., Chgo., 1965—. Commr. Oak Park (Ill.) Landmarks Commn., 1972-79, chmn., 1976-79; treas. Oak Park Bicentennial Commn., 1973-76, Ernest Hemingway Found. of Oak Park, 1983—. Mem. Inst. Food Technologists (councilor 1975-81, chmn. Chgo. sect.), ASME, Pi Tau Sigma, Sigma Tau. Patentee in field. Home: 904 Forest Ave Oak Park IL 60302 Office: 301 E Erie St Chicago IL 60611

HLAVKA, EDWIN JOHN, financial company executive; b. Chgo., Aug. 21, 1937; s. Edwin Frank and Frances Marian (Forker) H.; m. Catherine Beverly McGunn, Aug. 25, 1962; children: Susan Claire, Edwin John. B.S. in Fin., Northwestern U., 1959, M.B.A., U. Chgo., 1961. Budget dir. Am. Photocopy Equipment Co., Chgo., 1961-64; acctg. officer, 2d v.p. Continental Ill. Corp., Chgo., 1965-71, v.p., internat. audit mgr., 1972-73, v.p., 1974-82, sr. v.p., auditor, 1983—. Treas., bd. dirs. MacNeal Meml. Hosp., Berwyn, Ill., 1978—. Mem. Bank Adminstrn. Inst. (chmn. audit com. 1980-81), Inst. Internal Auditors. Roman Catholic. Home: 4825 Fair Elms Ave Western Springs IL 60558 Office: Continental Ill Corp 231 S LaSalle St Chicago IL 60693

HNILICA, LUBOMIR SIDONIUS, biochemist, pathologist, educator; b. Hodonin, Czechoslovakia, Jan. 26, 1929; came to U.S., 1961, naturalized, 1968; s. Andrew and Vlasta (Hajkova) H.; m. Violette E. Schlatter, Aug. 2, 1963; children—Mark Andrew, Keith Allen, Rebecca Jean. B.A., State Gymnasium, Hodonin, 1948; Ph.D., Masaryk U., Czechoslovakia, 1952; D.Sc., Czechoslovak Acad. Scis., Prague, 1969. Asst. prof. biochemistry U. Tex. System Cancer Center, Houston, 1963-65, asso. prof., 1965-70, prof., chief sect. biochem. control mechanisms, 1970-75; asso. dir. research Vanderbilt U. Cancer Research and Treatment Center, Nashville, 1977—, prof. biochemistry and pathology, Mary Geddes Stahlman prof. cancer research, 1975—. Contbr. chpts. to books, articles to profl. jours. WHO fellow, 1960-61; recipient various grants. Mem. Am. Soc. Biol. Chemists, Am. Soc. for Cell Biology, Am. Assn. for Cancer Research. Methodist. Home: 1713

Warfield Dr Nashville TN 37215 Office: Dept Biochemistry Vanderbilt U Sch Medicine Nashville TN 37232

HO, CHIEN, biological sciences educator; b. Shanghai, China, Oct. 23, 1934; came to U.S., 1953; s. Ping Yin and Chin Hwa (Chiu) H.; m. Nancy Tseng, Dec. 21, 1963; children: Jeanette, Carolyn. B.A., Williasm Coll., 1957; Ph.D., Yale U., 1961. Research chemist Linde Co., Union Carbide, Tonawanda, N.Y., 1960-61; research assoc. depts. chemistry and biology MIT, Cambridge, 1961-64; asst. prof. U. Pitts., 1964-67, assoc. prof., 1967-70, prof. biol. scis., 1971-79; prof. and head dept. biol. scis. Carnegie-Mellon U., Pitts., 1979—; mem. adv. com. NSF, Washington, 1980-83; chmn. NMR adv. com. Stanford (Calif.) U., 1975-82; mem. biophys. study sect. NIH, Bethesda, Md., 1974-78, chmn. biotech. research rev. com., 1979-82. Contbr. articles to profl. jours. Guggenheim fellow, 1970-71. Mem. Am. Chem. Soc., Am. Soc. Biol. Chemists, AAAS, Academia Sinica, Sigma Xi. Home: 2034 Garrick Dr Pittsburgh PA 15235 Office: Dept Biol Scis Carnegie-Mellon U 4400 Fifth Ave Pittsburgh PA 15213

HO, CHINN, investment banker; b. Waikiki, Honolulu, Feb. 26, 1904; s. Ti Yuen and Lan (Kam) H.; m. Betty Ching, Oct. 13, 1934; children—Stuart, Dean, Karen, John, Robin, Heather. Student, U. Hawaii Extension, 1925-26; LL.D. (hon.), U. Guam, 1980, H.H.D., U. Hawaii, 1983. Various positions Bishop Bank, Duisenberg Wichman & Co., Swan Culbertson & Fitz, Philippines) and; Dean Witter & Co., Honolulu, 1924-43; chmn. bd., dir. Capital Investment of Hawaii, Inc., 1944—; chmn. bd. Gannett Pacific Corp. (Honolulu Star-Bull., Inc., Guam Publs., Inc.); pres., dir. Makaha Valley, Inc.; internat. adv. bd. Sing Tao Newspapers, Hong Kong; dir. Host Internat., Inc., Victoria Ward, Ltd., Pacific Ins. Co.; mng. trustee Mark A. Robinson Trust, Mark A. Robinson Estate. Civilian aide to sec. of army, Hawaii, 1965-71. Named Optimist of Year, Hawaii, 1956, Father of Year, 1961, Sportsman of Year, 1964, Salesman of Year, Hawaii, 1966; recipient Golden Plate award Am. Acad. Achievement, 1968; Golden Eagle award, 1971; Nat. Jewish Hosp. honor award, 1972; Citizen of Year in Hawaii award, 1974; Golden Bear award Calif. Parks and Recreation Commn., 1981. Mem. Bishop Mus. Assn. (past pres.), Honolulu Stock Exchange (past pres.), Hawaii Visitors Bur. (past pres.), Honolulu Realty Bd. Club: Waialae Country. Office: 239 Merchant St Honolulu HI 96813

HO, PING-TI, educator, historian; b. Tientsin, Hopei, China, Sept. 1, 1917; naturalized, 1982; s. Shou- ch'ûan and Yung-Lan (Chang) H.; m. Ching-lo Shao, July 3, 1940; children—Sidney K'o-yûeh, Bartlet K'o-chûn. B.A., Nat. Tsing-Hua U., Peiping, China, 1938; Ph.D., Columbia, 1952; LL.D. (hon.), Chinese U., Hong Kong, 1975, L.H.D., Lawrence U., 1978. Instr. history Tsing-hua U., 1939-45; from instr. to prof. history and Asian studies U. B.C., 1948-63; prof. Chinese history and instns. U. Chgo., 1963-65, James Westfall Thompson prof. history, 1965—; Mem. Council of Sino-Am. Coop. in Humanities and Social Studies, 1966-69; Sino-Am. Boxer Fund Scholar, 1945-48. Author: Studies on the Population of China, 1368-1953, 1959, The Ladder of Success in Imperial China, 1368-1911, 1962, (in Chinese) Landsmannschaften in China, 1966, The Loess and the Origin of Chinese Agriculture, 1969, The Cradle of the East: An Inquiry into the Indigenous Origins of Techniques and Ideas of Neolithic and Early Historic China, 5000-1000 B.C, 1975, also numerous articles.; Mem. editorial: Tsing-Hua Jour. Chinese Studies, 1964—. Fellow AAAS, Am. Acad. Arts and Scis.; mem. Assn. Asian Studies (pres. 1975-76). Home: 4741 S Woodlawn Av Chicago IL 60615

HO, THOMAS INN MIN, computer scientist, educator; b. Honolulu, Oct. 17, 1948; s. Herbert Low Seu and Rose (Lee) H.; m. Jean Joan Kwan, Aug. 26, 1971; 1 son, Brian Koon Leong. B.S., Purdue U., 1970, M.S., 1971, Ph.D., 1974. Asst. prof. computer sci. and mgmt. Purdue U., West Lafayette, Ind., 1975-78, asso. prof., 1978—, head computer tech., 1978—; cons. in field. Contbr. articles to profl. jours. NSF fellow, 1970-72. Mem. Assn. Computing Machinery, Data Processing Mgmt. Assn., Soc. for Info. Mgmt., Phi Kappa Phi. Office: Computer Tech Dept Purdue U West Lafayette IN 47907

HO, YHI-MIN, university administrator, educator; b. Nanking, China, Nov. 18, 1934; came to U.S., 1958, naturalized, 1972; s. Yung-Tung and Hsing-In H.; m. Shu-Fen Ma, Nov. 23, 1962; Andrew M., Katherine. B.A. in Econs., Nat. Taiwan U., 1955, M.S., Utah State U., 1961, Ph.D., Vanderbilt U., 1965. Mem. managerial staff mktg. div. Chinese Petroleum Corp., 1955-58; asst. prof. U. So. Miss., 1963-65, U. Houston, 1965-66, Tulane U., New Orleans, 1966-70; chmn.dept. econs. and bus. adminstrn. U. St. Thomas, Houston, 1970—, acting dean Cameron Sch. Bus., 1978-80, dean, 1980—; dir. Asian Am. Nat. Bank, 1982—. Author: Agricultural Development of Taiwam, 1903-1960, 1966; contbr. articles to profl. jours. Mem. Council Chinese Orgns., Houston, 1977—; adminstrv. bd. Houston-Taipei Soc., Inc., 1978—; bd. dirs. Chinese Community Ctr., Inc., Houston, 1979—; bd. dirs Chinese Community Culture Center, Houston, 1982—. Ford scholar, 1960-61; Rockefellow fellow, 1961-63; NSF grantee, 1973-75. Mem. Am. Econ. Assn., So. Econ. Assn., Western Econ. Assn. Office: Univ of St Thomas 3812 Montrose Blvd Houston TX 77006

HO, YU-CHI, educator; b. China, Mar. 1, 1934; s. Chin-Woo and Ching-Yi (Pan) H.; m. Sophia Hu, Oct. 10, 1959; children—Adrian, Christine, Lara. S.B., Mass. Inst. Tech., 1953, S.M., 1955; Ph.D., Harvard, 1961. Sr. engr. Bendix Corp., 1955-58; asst. prof. elec. engring. Harvard, 1961-65, asso. prof., 1965-69, Gordon McKay prof., 1969—; Mem. Army Sci. Adv. Panel, 1968-74. Guggenheim fellow, 1970; USA-USSR Sr. Exchange fellow, 1973. Fellow I.E.E.E. Office: Pierce Hall Harvard Univ Cambridge MA 02138

HOADLEY, IRENE BRADEN (MRS. EDWARD HOADLEY), librarian; b. Hondo, Tex., Sept. 26, 1938; d. Andrew Henry and Theresa Lillian (Lebold) Braden; m. Edward Hoadley, Feb. 21, 1970. B.A., U. Tex., 1960; A.M.L.S., U. Mich., 1961, Ph.D., 1967; M.A., Kans. State U., 1965. Cataloger Sam Houston State Tchrs. Coll. Library, Huntsville, Tex., 1961-62; head circulation dept. Kans. State U. Library, Manhattan, 1962-64; grad. asst. U. Mich. Dept. of Library Sci., 1964-66; librarian gen. adminstrn. and research Ohio State U. Libraries, Columbus, 1966-73, asst. dir. libraries adminstrv. services, 1973-74; dir. of libraries Tex. A. and M. U. Library, College Station, Tex., 1974—; dir. Higher Edn. Act Inst. Quantitative Methods in Librarianship, Ohio State U., summer 1969; instr. inst. U. Calif. at San Diego, 1970, summer; Mem. steering com. Gov's. Conf. on Library and Info. Services, Ohio, 1973-74, joint chairperson, 1974; mem. adv. com. Library Services and Constrn. Act Cuyahoga County Pub. Library, Cleve., 1973. Author: (with others) Physiological Factors Relating to Terrestrial Altitutes: A Bibliography, 1968; Editor: (with Alice S. Clark) Quantitative Methods in Librarianship: Standards, Research, Management, 1972; Contbr. articles to profl. jours. Recipient Scarecrow Press award for library lit., 1971; Distinguished Alumnus award Sch. Library Sci., U. Mich., 1976. Mem. ALA, Ohio Library Assn. (chmn. constn. com. 1967-68, chmn. election tellers com. 1969, asst. gen. chmn. local conf. com. 1969-70, sec. 1970-71, v.p., pres.-elect 1971-72, chmn. budget advisory com. 1971-72, pres. 1972-73, bd. dirs. 1970-75), Tex. Library Assn. (com. on White House conf. 1975-77, vice chmn., chmn. coll. and univ. div. 1977-78, exec. bd. 1978-81), Assn. Research Libraries (bd. dirs. 1978-81, search com. for exec. dir. 1980), Midwest Fedn. Library Assns. (exec. bd. 1973-74, chairperson program com. 1974), Phi Kappa Phi, Phi Alpha Theta, Pi Lambda Theta, Beta Phi Mu, Phi Delta Gamma. Home: Route 5 Box 1048 College Station TX 77840

HOADLEY, PETER GEORGE, civil engineering educator; b. Media, Pa., Dec. 30, 1934; s. George B. and Mary B. (Betts) H.; m. Susan Elise Redmile, Mar. 25, 1972. B.S. in Civil Engring., Duke U., 1957; M.S., U. Ill., 1960, Ph.D., 1961. Registered profl. engr., Tenn. Asst. prof. Vanderbilt U., Nashville, 1961-64, assoc. prof., 1964-68, prof. civil engring., 1968—, chmn. dept., 1968-72, 75-80—; project engr. D'appolonia Inc., Pitts., 1973-74. Co-author: Computer Methods of Structural Analysis, 1969. Mem. Bldg. Codes Appeals Bd., Nashville, 1976-80; pres. Council of Hearing Impaired, Nashville, 1964. White House fellow (nat. finalist), 1971. Mem. ASCE (pres. Nashville sect. 1971), Am. Soc. Engring. Edn. (pres. civil engring. div. 1976). Quaker. Office: Vanderbilt U Dept Civil Engring Nashville TN 37235

HOADLEY, WALTER EVANS, economist, financial executive; b. San Francisco, Aug. 16, 1916; s. Walter Evans and Marie Howland (Preece) H.; m. Virginia Alm, May 20, 1939; children: Richard Alm, Jean Elizabeth (Mrs. Richard A. Price, Jr.). A.B., U. Calif., 1938, M.A., 1940, Ph.D., 1946; Dr.C.S., Franklin and Marshall Coll., 1963; LL.D. (hon.), Golden Gate U., 1968, U. Pacific, 1979; hon. degree, El Instituto Tecnologico Autonomo de Mexico, 1974. Collaborator U.S. Bur. Agrl. Econs., 1938-39; research economist Calif. Gov.'s Reemployment Commn., 1939, 1941; research economist, teaching fellow U. Calif., 1938-41, supr. indsl. mgmt. war tng. office, 1941-42; econ. adviser U. Chgo. Civil Affairs Tng. Sch., 1945; sr. economist Fed. Res. Bank Chgo., 1942-49; economist Armstrong Cork Co., Lancaster, Pa., 1949-54, treas., 1954-60, v.p., treas., 1960-66, dir., 1962—; sr. v.p., chief economist, mem. mng. com. Bank of Am. NT & SA, San Francisco, 1966-68, exec. v.p., chief economist, mem. mng. com., mem. mgmt. adv. council, chmn. subs., 1968-81; ret., 1981; sr. research fellow Hoover Inst., Stanford U., 1981—; econ. commentator Sta. KRON-TV, San Francisco, 1981—; dir. Lucky Stores, Pacific Gas Transmission, Robert A. McNeil Corp., Soule Steel, Selected Funds, PLM Inc.; dep. chmn. Fed. Res. Bank, Phila., 1960-61, chmn., 1962-66, Conf. Fed. Res. Chairmen, 1966; faculty Sch. Banking U. Wis., 1945-49, 55, 58-66; adviser various U.S. Govt. agys.; spl. adviser U.S. Congl. Budget Office, 1975—; mem. pub. adv. bd. U.S. Dept. Commerce, 1970-74; mem. White House Rev. Com. for Balance Payments Statistics, 1963-65, Presdl. Task Force on Growth, 1969-70, Presdl. Task Force on Land Utilization, Presdl. Conf. on Inflation, 1974. Columnist: Dun's Bus. Month. Mem. Meth. Ch. Commn. on World Service and Fin. Phila. Conf., 1957-64, chmn. investment com., 1964-66; bd. dirs., exec. com. Internat. Mgmt. and Devel. Inst., 1976—; trustee Pacific Sch. Religion, 1968—; adviser Nat. Commn. to Study Nursing and Nursing Edn., 1968-73; trustee Duke U., 1968-73, pres.'s assoc., 1973-80; trustee Golden Gate U., 1974—, chmn. investment com., 1977—; trustee Conservation Found., 1974—; mem. periodic chmn. adminstrv. bd. Trinity United Meth. Ch., Berkeley, Calif., 1966—; mem. bd. overseers vis. com. Harvard Coll. Econs., 1969-74; chmn. investment com. Calif.-Nev. Meth. Found., 1968-75, mem., 1976—; mem. Calif. Gov.'s Council Econ. and Bus. Devel., 1978—, chmn., 1980—; trustee Hudson Inst., 1979—; co-chmn. San Francisco Mayor's Fiscal Adv. Com., 1978-81; spl. adviser Presdl. Cabinet Com. Innovation, 1978-79. Fellow Am. Statis. Assn. (v.p. dir. 1952-54, pres. 1958), Nat. Assn. of Bus. Economists, Internat. Acad. Mgmt.; mem. Am. Fin. Assn. (dir. 1955-56, pres. 1969), Conf. Bus. Economists (chmn. 1962), C. of C. of U.S., Internat. C. of C. (vice chmn. commn. on internat. monetary relations, trustee, chmn. com. on internat. monetary affairs U.S. council), Internat. Conf. Comml. Bank Economists (chmn. 1978-81), Am., Western Econ. Assns., Am. Marketing Assn., Fin. Analysts San Francisco, Conf. Bd. (econ. forum), Am. Bankers Assn. (chmn. urban and community affairs com. 1972-73, mem. econ. adv. council 1976-78), Nat. Bur. Econ. Research (dir.), Western Fin. Assn., dir., mem. steering com., U. Calif. Alumni Council (chmn. investment com. 1983—), Phi Beta Kappa (v.p. Western region), Kappa Alpha. Clubs: St. Francis Yacht, Commonwealth, Pacific Union, Bankers (San Francisco); Silverado Country. Office: Bank of America Center San Francisco CA 94104 *I've learned that most professional thinking is dominated by problems and potential crises, ignoring that often things can and do go unexpectedly right as well as wrong—and that few really important decisions are ever made except in or near crisis.*

HOAG, ARTHUR HOWARD, JR., architect; b. Lakewood, Ohio, May 19, 1923; s. Arthur Howard and Ada Rose (Keyse) H.; m. Nancy Louise Elliott, May 26, 1949; children—Patricia, Victoria, Lawrence, Daniel, Leslie, Jeffery. Student, U. Tex., 1942-43, 47-48, Wooster Coll., 1943, Fenn Coll., 1949, Whitman Coll., 1944, St. Mary's Coll., 1944, U.S. Mcht. Marine Acad., 1945, Western Res. U., 1948-49. Field engr., asso. architect McGeorge-Hargett & Assos., 1949-59; architect, partner McGeorge-Hargett & Hoag, 1959-62, Hargett-Hoag Assos., 1962-64; sr. partner Hoag-Wismar Partnership, Cleve., 1965—; chmn. exec. com. treas. HWH Affiliates Inc.; dir. Citizens Fed. Savs. & Loan of Cleve.; Pres. Architects Soc. of Ohio Found., Inc., 1972-77. Served with USNR, 1942-45. Recipient award of merit Architects Soc. Ohio, 1965, Top Ten Plant award, 1963, 68; elected to Constrn. Hall of Fame Cleve. Engring. Soc., 1977. Fellow AIA; mem. Architects Soc. Ohio (pres. 1970, chmn. com. on architecture commerce and industry 1974), Ohio Motorists Assn. (dir.). Clubs: Cleveland Athletic, Cleve. Yachting; South Orlando Rotary, Sweetwater Country, Citrus (Orlando, Fla.). Home: Route 1 Box 95 Mount Dora FL 32757 Office: 1150 W 3d St Cleveland OH 44113 also 1200 Edgewater Dr Orlando FL 32804

HOAG, DAVID GARRATT, elec. engr.; b. Boston, Oct. 11, 1925; s. Alden Bomer and Helen Lucy (Garratt) H.; m. Grace Edward Griffith, May 10, 1952; children—Rebecca Wilder, Peter Griffith, Jeffrey Taber, Nicholas Alden, Lucy Seymour. B.S., MIT, 1946, M.S., 1950. Staff engr. Mass. Inst. Tech. Instrumentation Lab., Cambridge, 1946-57; tech. dir. Polaris Missile Guidance, 1957-61; tech. dir., program mgr. Apollo Spacecraft Guidance, 1961-74; advanced system dept. head C.S. Draper Lab., Inc., 1974—; Reviewer children's sci. book com. Harvard U., 1965—. Incorporator, bd. dirs. Medway Community Nursery Sch. Served with USN, 1943-46. Recipient Pub. Service award NASA, 1969, Spl. award Royal Inst. Navigation, Britain, 1970. Fellow Am. Inst. Aeros. and Astronautics (Louis W. Hill Space Transp. award 1972, chmn. New Eng. sect. 1979-80); mem. Nat. Acad. Engring., Inst. Navigation (Thurlow award 1969, pres. 1978-79), Internat. Acad. Astronautics (asso. editor ACTA Astronautica 1973—). Home: 116 Winthrop St Medway MA 02053 Office: CS Draper Lab Inc 555 Technology Sq Cambridge MA 02139

HOAG, FRANK STEPHEN, JR., publisher; b. Pueblo, Colo., June 11, 1908; s. Frank S. and Louise (Allebr) H.; m. LeVert Wiess, June 15, 1935. B.A., Princeton, 1931; Litt.D (hon.), So. Colo. State Coll., 1965. Pres. Pueblo Star-Jour. and Chieftain, 1943—; Formerly mem. audit com. Asso. Press.; Dir. Minnequa Bank, Pub. Service Co. Colo.; Dir., v.p. Colo. Public Expenditures Council; formerly mem. Colo. Commn. Higher Edn. Trustee Colo. Coll., Colorado Springs; bd. dirs. USAF Acad. Found., Colorado Springs; trustee Parkview Episcopal Hosp., Pueblo Devel. Found.; trustee, past pres. U. So. Colo. Found. DeMolay Legion of Honor.; Named Citizen of Year Colo. Assn. Real Estate Bds., 1971. Mem. Pueblo C. of C. (past pres.), Am. Soc. Newspaper Editors, Colo. Press Assn. (past pres.), Am. Newspaper Pubs. Assn., Sigma Delta Chi. Presbyn. Clubs: Mason (32 deg.), Rotarian (past pres.), Elk.). Home: 305 Argyle St Pueblo CO 81004 Office: 825 W 6th St Pueblo CO 81002

HOAG, PAUL STERLING, architect; b. Spokane, Aug. 7, 1913; s. Percival Doane and Emma Imogen (Rusk) H.; m. Mary Jane Ackley, 1934 (div. 1935); m. 2d Betty Jane Lochrie, Dec. 28, 1937 (div. Nov. 1965); children: Suzanne Hoag Lacabe, Peter L., Jane Elizabeth Hoag Brown, Robert Doane; m. 3d Nancy Jean Lawrence, Oct. 21, 1967. Student, Washington State Coll., Pullman, 1930-31, Stanford U., 1931-32. Lic. architect, Calif., Colo., Tex. Gen. mgr. Hoag X-Ray Co., Spokane, 1933-42; tooling designer Boeing Aircraft Co., Renton, Wash., 1942; prodn. mgr. Brown Industries, Spokane, 1943-44; asst. plant engr. Weyerhaeuser Timber Co., Longview, Wash., 1944-45; draftsman apprentice Richard Neutra, Los Angeles, 1945-46, Paul Hunter, 1946-48; prin. Paul Sterling Hoag, Los Angeles, 1948—; instr. advanced design studio So. Calif. Inst. Architecture, Santa Monica, Calif., 1975. Architect works, Palcon Plastics plant div. Becton-Dickenson & Co. Architect mem. Bel-Air Archtl. Com., Los Angeles, 1979—, San Vicente Design Rev. Bd., Los Angeles, 1980—. Fellow AIA. Episcopalian. Home: 1541 Casale Rd Pacific Palisades CA 90272 Office: Paul Sterling Hoag 11973 San Vicente Blvd Los Angeles CA 90049 *The most exciting discovery of my professional life was Carl Jung's revelatory concept of "archaic memories" because it enabled me to understand how intuitive disign makes it possible to create building forms and interior spaces which are free of fashion and therefore timelessly meaningful, my constant goal.*

HOAGLAND, ALBERT SMILEY, electrical engineer; b. Berkeley, Calif., Sept. 13, 1926; s. Dennis Robert and Jessie Agnes (Smiley) H.; m. Janine Maryse Simart, May 23, 1950; children: Catherine, Nicole, Richard. B.S., U. Calif.-Berkeley, 1947, M.S., 1948, Ph.D., 1954. Registered profl. engr., Calif. Asst. prof. elec. engring. U. Calif.-Berkeley, 1954-56; sr. engr. IBM, San Jose, Calif., 1956-59; mgr. engring sci. San Jose Research Lab., 1959-62; sr. tech. cons. IBM World Trade, The Hague, Holland, 1962-64; mgr. engring. sci. IBM Research Center, N.Y.C., 1964-68, dir. tech. planning research div., 1968-71, corporate program coordinator, Boulder, Colo., 1971-76; mgr. exploratory magnetic rec. San Jose Research Lab., 1976-82; tech. adv. gen. products div., 1982—; lectr. computer design U. Calif.-Berkeley, 1948-54, 56-62; adj. prof. U. Calif.-San Diego, 1983—; cons. State Calif., 1955-56, IBM, 1954-56; chmn. Nat. Computer Conf. Bd., 1976-78; adj. prof. Harvey Mudd Coll. Author: Digital Magnetic Recording, 1963; Contbr. articles on computer sci. to profl. publs. Trustee Charles Babbage Inst. Served with USNR, 1943-46. Recipient best paper award IEEE, 1957. Fellow IEEE (dir. 1974-77); mem. Am. Fedn. Info. Processing Socs. (dir. 1969-75, pres. 1978—), IEEE Computer Soc. (pres. 1971-73), Research Soc. Am. (pres. Sequoia chpt. 1962-63), Sigma Xi, Phi Beta Kappa, Eta Kappa Nu, Tau Beta Pi. Club: Golden Bear. Patentee in field. Home: 13834 Upper Hill Dr Saratoga CA 95070 Office: IBM 5600 Cottle Rd San Jose CA 95193

HOAGLAND, DONALD WRIGHT, lawyer; b. N.Y.C., Aug. 16, 1921; s. Webster Comley and Irene (Wright) H.; m. Mary Tiedeman, May 14, 1949; children—Peter M., Mary C., Sara H., Ann W. B.A., Yale, 1942; LL.B., Columbia, 1948. Bar: N.Y. 1948, Colo. 1951. Asso. firm Winthrop, Stimson, Putnam & Roberts, N.Y.C., 1948-51; ptnr. Davis, Graham & Stubbs, Denver, 1951-63, 66—; with AID, 1964-66, asst. adminstr. devel. finance and pvt. enterprise, 1965-66, cons., 1967—; Lectr. U. Denver Sch. Law, 1971—; Chmn. bd. Bi-Nat. Devel. Corp., 1968-70; dir. Centennial Fund, Inc., 1959-63, 2d Centennial Fund, Inc., 1959-63, Gryphon Fund, Inc., 1959-63. Mem. Denver Planning Bd., 1955-61, 67-70; chmn., 1959-61; Bd. dirs., vice chmn. Denver Art Mus., 1959-63, 72-76, 79-82; bd. dirs. Colo. Urban League, 1960-63, 66-72, chmn. bd., 1968-72; bd. dirs. Vols. Tech. Assistance, 1970—, Legal Aid Soc. Colo., 1972—; pres. Legal Aid Soc. Colo., 1975-79; trustee Phillips Exeter Acad., 1960-67, Am. U., Washington, 1982—; chmn. bd. dirs. Legal Aid Found. Colo., 1983—; bd. dirs., vice chmn. bd. Denver chpt. A R C, 1959-61; chmn. bd. trustees Social Sci. Found. Denver U. Served as dive bomber pilot USNR, 1943-45. Decorated Air medal with oak leaf cluster. Mem. Am., Colo., Denver bar assns., Am. Soc. Internat. Law, Soc. Internat. Devel. Home: 2250 S Columbine St Denver CO 80210 Office: Colo Nat Bldg Denver CO 80202

HOAGLAND, EDWARD MORLEY, author; b. N.Y.C., Dec. 21, 1932; s. Warren Eugene and Helen Kelley (Morley) H.; m. Amy J. Ferrara, 1960 (div. 1964); m. Marion Magid, Mar. 28, 1968; 1 dau., Molly. A.B. cum laude, Harvard U., 1954. Mem. faculty New Sch. for Social Research, N.Y.C., 1963-64, Rutgers (N.J.) U., 1966, Sarah Lawrence Coll., Bronxville, N.Y., 1967, 71, CUNY, 1967, 68, U. Iowa, 1978, 82, Columbia U., 1980, 81. Author: Cat Man, 1956, The Circle home, 1960; auhtor: The Peacock's Tail, 1965; author: Notes from the Century Before: A Journal from British Columbia, 1969, The Courage of Turtles, 1971, Walking the Dead Diamond River, 1973 (Nat. Book award nominee), The Moose on the Wall: Field Notes from the Vermont Wilderness, 1974, Red Wolves and Black Bears, 1976, African Calliope: A Journey to the Sudan, 1979 (Am. Book award and nominee, Nat. Book Critics Circle award), The Edward Hoagland Reader, 1979, The Tugman's Passage, 1982; essays and stories for publs. including, New York Times, Village Voice, New Yorker, Atlantic, Nation, Vanity Fair, Am. Heritage, and Sat. Rev., commentary, Harper's; contbr. nature editorials, N.Y. Times, editorial page, N.Y. Times, 1979—. Served with U.S. Army, 1955-57. Houghton Mifflin Lit. fellow, 1954; AAAL traveling fellow, 1964; Guggenheim fellow, 1964, 75; recipient Longview Found. award, 1961, O. Henry award, 1971, lit. citation Brandeis U. Creative Arts Awards Commn., 1972, N.Y. State Council on Arts award, 1972, Harold D. Vursell award AAAL, 1981, Nat. Endowment Arts award, 1982. Mem. AAAL. Office: care Random House 201 E 50th St New York NY 10022

HOAGLAND, JAMES LEE, electrical distribution executive; b. Oak Park, Ill., Nov. 2, 1922; s. Walter P. and Lola L. (Lee) H.; m. Florence E., Jan. 15, 1947; children: James, Edward, John, Peter. B.A., Colgate U., 1944. With Graybar Electric Co., 1946—, regional mgr., Chgo., 1972-75, v.p., 1975-78, exec. v.p., N.Y.C., 1979-80, pres., chief exec. officer, 1980—, also dir.; dir. Centerre Bank N.A. Bd. dirs. St. Louis Symphony, Met. St. Louis YMCA, Arts and Edn. Council. Served with USNR, 1942-46. Clubs: St. Louis, Log Cabin, Old Warson Country; Union League (N.Y.C.).

HOAGLAND, JIMMIE LEE, newspaper editor; b. Rock Hill, S.C., Jan. 22, 1940; s. Lee Roy and Edith Irene (Sullivan) H.; m. Elizabeth Becker, 1979; children—Laura Lee, Lily Hue. A.B. in Journalism, U. S.C., 1961; student, U. Aix-en-Provence, France, 1961-62. Reporter Evening Herald, Rock Hill, 1960; copy editor N.Y. Times Internat. Edit., Paris, France, 1964-66; reporter Washington Post, 1966-69, Africa corr., 1969-72, Middle East corr., 1972-75, Paris corr., 1975-77, fgn. editor, 1979-81, asst. mng. editor, 1981—. Author: South Africa: Civilizations in Conflict, 1972. Mem. pres. adv. council U. S.C. Served with USAF, 1962-64. Recipient Pulitzer prize internat. reporting, 1970; Overseas Press Club award internat. reporting, 1977; Ford Found. fellow Columbia U., 1968-69. Mem. Council on Fgn. Relations, Phi Beta Kappa, Pi Kappa Alpha. Office: 1150 15th St NW Washington DC 20005

HOAGLAND, KARL KING, JR., lawyer; b. St. Louis, Aug. 21, 1933; s. Karl King and Mary Edna (Parsons) H.; m. Sylvia Anne Naranick, July 13, 1957; children: Elizabeth Parsons, Sarah Stewart, Karl King, III, Alison Thomson. B.S. in Econs, Wharton Sch., U. Pa., 1955; LL.B., U. Ill., 1958. Bar: Ill. 1958. Partner firm Hoagland, Maucker, Bernard & Almeter, Alton, 1960—; gen. counsel, asst. sec., dir. Jefferson Smurfit Corp.; dir., Millers' Mut. Ins. Assn. Ill. Asst. editor: U. Ill. Law Forum, 1957-58. Trustee, treas. Monticello Coll. Found., 1965—. Served with USAF, 1958-60. Mem. Am., Ill., Madison County, Alton-Wood River bar assns., Order of Coif, Beta Gamma Sigma. Episcopalian. Clubs: Lockhaven Country (Alton); Mo. Athletic (St. Louis). Home: PO Box 130 Alton IL 62002 Office: 401 Alton St Alton IL 62002

HOAGLAND, LAURANCE REDINGTON, JR., investment counselor; b. Palo Alto, Calif., Dec. 18, 1936; s. Laurance Redington and Naomi Ann (Carpenter) H.; m. Grace Updegraff Mohns, Sept. 5, 1959; children: Laurance Redington, III, Craig C., David B., Edward L. A.B., Stanford U., 1958; B.A., Oxford (Eng.) U., 1960, M.A., 1963; M.B.A., Harvard U., 1962. Chartered financial analyst. With Irwin Mgmt. Co., Columbus, Ind., 1962-74, v.p., portfolio mgr., 1965-74; exec. dir. fin. services Cummins Engine Co., Columbus, 1975, v.p., treas., 1975-80; founder, prin. Anderson, Hoagland and Co., investment mgmt. co., St. Louis, 1980—. Bd. dirs. Driftwood Valley Arts Council, 1975-78, treas., 1975-76; bd. dirs. Columbus Dance Workshop, 1978-80; pres. Columbus Tennis Assn., 1972-73; dir. bd. pensions Presbyn. Ch. U.S., 1981—. Mem. Soc. Chartered Financial Analysts. Home: 28 Twin Springs Ln Saint Louis MO 63124 Office: 8850 Ladue Rd Saint Louis MO 63124

HOAGLAND, MAHLON BUSH, educator, biochemist; b. Boston, Oct. 5, 1921; s. Hudson and Anna (Plummer) H.; m. Olley Virginia Jones, Jan. 10, 1961; children by previous marriage—Judith, Mahlon Bush, Robin. Student, Williams Coll., 1940-41, Harvard U., 1941-43, M.D., 1948; Sc.D. (hon.), Worcester Poly. Inst., 1973. From research fellow to asst. prof. medicine Harvard Med. Sch. at Mass. Gen. Hosp., 1948-60; asso. prof. bacteriology and immunology (Med. Sch.), 1960-67; prof. biochemistry, chmn. dept. Dartmouth Med. Sch., 1967-70; research prof. U. Mass. Med. Sch., 1970—; dir. Worcester Found. for Exptl. Biology, Shrewsbury, Mass., 1970—; research asso. Carlsberg Labs., Copenhagen, Denmark, 1951-52, Cavendish Labs., Cambridge, Eng., 1957-58; Exec. sec. com. research Mass. Gen. Hosp., 1954-57; cons. NIH, 1961-64, Am. Cancer Soc., 1965-68; bd. sci. counsellors Nat. Heart and Lung Inst., 1972-74; Bd. dirs. Mass. div. Am. Cancer Soc.; Scholar cancer research Am. Cancer Soc., 1953-58. Contbr. articles to profl. jours. Fellow Am. Acad. Arts and Scis.; mem. Am. Soc. Biol. Chemists (Franklin medal 1976). Research on mechanism of carcinogenic action of beryllium, mechanism of synthesis of coenzyme A; discovery mechanism of amino acid activation and role of transfer ribonucleic acid in protein synthesis. Home: 234 Gulf St Shrewsbury MA 01545 Office: Worcester Found Shrewsbury MA 01545

HOAGLUND, GLENN CARL, beef company executive, engineer; b. Chgo., May 16, 1937; s. Reuben Athur H. and Margaret Ann (Hoaglund); m. Cherie Ann Morice, Aug. 25, 1960; children: Pamela May, Richy Allen, Dennis Dean. A.A., Belleville Jr. Coll., 1957; ASME, Mo. Sch. Mines, 1960. Plant engr. Pet Foods, Greenville, Ill., 1960-64; plant constrn. engr. Falstaff Brewing, Galveston, Tex., 1964-68; dir. engring. Iowa Beef Processing, Dakota City, Nebr., 1968-78; pres. TASCO, Amarillo, Tex., 1974-78; group v.p. IBP Inc., Dakota City, 1978—; chmn. bd. TASCO, Amarillo, 1974. Office: IBP Inc PO Box 511 Dakota City NE 68731

HOAGLUND, JAMES BARRON, manufacturing company executive; b. Mpls., Sept. 15, 1924; s. Arthur William and Mary McCullough (Barron) H.; m. Mary Evans Lamb, Sept. 10, 1946; children: John Bjorn, Judith Ann, Nora Ellen. B.S. in Elec. Engring., MIT, 1945, 1947. Tech. dir. ITT, N.Y.C., 1969-72; v.p. corp. planning McQuay-Perfex Inc., Mpls., 1972-74, exec. v.p., 1979-82, pres., 1982, McQuay Group, 1974-79; chmn., chief exec. officer McQuay Inc., Mpls., 1983; dir. Pentair, Inc., 1984. Patentee (rooftop multizine air conditioning units). Bd. dirs. North Star found., Mpls., 1983. Served to ensign USNR, 1943-46. Mem. ASHRAE, Air Conditioning and Refrigeration Inst. (bd. dirs 1979—). Republican. Clubs: Mpls.; Interlachen Country (Edina). Home: 5133 Wooddale Ave S Edina MN 55424 Office: McQuay Inc 13600 Industrial Park Blvd Minneapolis MN 55441

HOAK, JOHN CHARLES, physician, educator; b. Harrisburg, Pa., Dec. 12, 1928; s. John Andrew and Anna Bell (Holley) H.; m. Dorothy Elizabeth Witmer, Dec. 21, 1952; children: Greta Elizabeth, Laurinda Elaine, Thomas Emory. B.S., Lebanon Valley Coll., 1951; M.D., Hahnemann Med. Coll., 1955. Diplomate: Am. Bd. Internal Medicine. Intern Harrisburg Polyclinic Hosp., 1955-56; resident internal medicine VA Hosp., Iowa City, 1958, U. Iowa Hosps., 1958-61, research fellow blood coagulation, 1958-59; mem. faculty U. Iowa Med. Sch., 1961-62, 63—, asso. prof. internal medicine, 1967-70, prof., 1970—, dir. div. hematology, 1970-72, dir. div. hematology-oncology, 1973—; vis. research staff Sir William Dunn Sch. Pathology, Oxford (Eng.) U., 1962-63; prin. research and tng. grants Nat. Heart and Lung Inst., assoc. dir. Specialized Center for Research in Atherosclerosis U. Iowa, 1970—; Research fellow, then advanced research fellow Am. Heart Assn., 1961-63. Editorial bd.: Jour. Lab. and Clin. Medicine, 1972-78; Contbr. articles to profl. jours. Fellow ACP; mem. Am. Soc. Hematology, Internat. Soc. Thrombosis and Haemostasis, Am. Heart Assn., Am. Fedn. Clin. Research, Central Soc. Clin. Research, Phi Alpha Epsilon, Alpha Omega Alpha., Assn. Am. Physicians. Office: Dept Medicine U Iowa Hosps and Clinics Iowa City IA 52242

HOAR, SAMUEL, lawyer; b. Boston, Oct. 14, 1927; s. Samuel and Helen (Warren) H.; m. Martha Ford, June 30, 1951; children: Samuel, Rebecca Phelps Hoar Meissner, Andrew Willard. A.B., Harvard U., 1951, LL.B., 1954. Bar: Mass. 1954. Assoc. firm Goodwin, Procter & Hoard, Boston, 1954-58, 60-62, partner, 1963—; asst. U.S. atty. U.S. Atty.'s Office, Mass., 1958-60; spl. asst. atty. gen. Criminal div. Atty. Gen.'s Office for Commonwealth of Mass., Boston, 1963-67. Mem. exec. com., sec., bd. dirs. U.S. Equestrian Team; chmn. Bldg. Code Com., Wenham, Mass., 1954; mem. Planning Bd., Town of Wenham, 1954-63, Essex (Mass.) Conservation Commn.; mem., chmn. Essex Fin. Com., 1966-69; mem. Essex Bd. Selectmen, 1969-76; town moderator Essex, 1976-82. Served with AUS, 1946-47. Mem. Am. Bar Assn., Mass. Bar Assn., Boston Bar Assn., Essex County Bar Assn., Am. Coll. Trial Laws (past chmn. Mass. state com.), Am. Bar Found. Republican. Episcopalian. Clubs: Mason., Somerset, Boston Racquet. Home: Apple St Essex MA 01929 Office: Goodwin Procter & Hoar 28 State St Boston MA 02109

HOAR, TIMOTHY STURDEE, oil company executive; b. Moncton, N.B., Can., May 31, 1947; s. Harry Earl and Norah Beverly (Macquarie) H.; m. Rosella LeBlanc; children: Stacey Anne, Shanda Lynn. B.A., U. N.B., 1970, LL.B., 1972. Bar: Called to N.B. bar 1972, Alta. bar 1975. Atty. Chevron Standard Ltd., Calgary, 1972-75; solicitor Home Oil Co. Ltd., Calgary, 1975-79, corp. sec., 1979-82; also corp. sec. subs. Scurry-Rainbow Oil Ltd., Plains Petroleums Ltd., (both Calgary); v.p., gen. consul, corp. sec. Geocrude Energy Inc., Calgary, 1982—; also v.p., gen. consul, corp. sec. subs. Pan Cava Resources Ltd., Pan Cava Minerals, Inc. Asso. dir. Stampeder Football Club Ltd. Mem. Can. Bar Assn., Law Soc. Alta., Barristers Soc. N.B., Calgary Bar Assn. Club: Calgary Petroleum. Office: 3300 Bow Valley Square Two 205 5th Ave SW Calgary AB Canada T2P 2V7

HOAR, WILLIAM STEWART, zoologist, educator; b. Moncton, N.B., Can., Aug. 31, 1913; s. George W. and Nina (Steeves) H.; m. Margaret MacKenzie, Aug. 13, 1941; children: Stewart George, David Innes, Kenzie Margaret, Melanie Frances. B.A. hon., U. N.B., 1934, D.Sc., 1965; M.A., U. Western Ont., 1936, D.Sc. (hon.), 1978; Ph.D., Boston U., 1939; D.Sc. (hon.), Meml. U. Nfld., 1967, St. Francis Xavier U., 1976, LL.D., Simon Fraser U., 1980, Toronto U., 1981. Asst. prof. biology U. N.B., 1939-42, prof. zoology, 1943-45; research assoc. U. Toronto, 1942-43; prof. zoology and fisheries U. B.C., Vancouver, 1945-64, head dept. zoology, 1964-71, prof., 1971—; research scientist Fisheries Research Bd. Can., 1935-57. Author: General and Comparative Physiology, 3d edit, 1983; Sr. editor 9-vol. treatise on fish physiology.; Contbr. articles to profl. jours. Decorated Order of Can.; recipient Flavelle medal, 1965, Fry medal, 1974. Fellow Royal Soc. Can., Canadian, U.S. socs. zoology and physiology. Home: 3561 W 27th Ave Vancouver BC V6S 1P9 Canada

HOARE, RICHARD DAVID, educator; b. Rosiclare, Ill., May 14, 1927; s. Bert J. and Bess (Wright) H.; m. Roselea Lillian Tate, Nov. 14, 1947 (div. 1971); children—Thomas, Stephen, Michael; m. Mary Ann Goodman, Dec. 19, 1971; 1 son, Bradley. A.B., Augustana Coll., 1951; M.A., U. Mo., 1953, Ph.D., 1957. With U.S. Geol. Survey, Alaska, 1949, 50, 51, 52; geologist Cartier Mining Co., Que., Can., 1956; asst. prof. U. Mo., summers 1957, 58; mem. faculty Bowling Green (Ohio) State U., 1957—, now prof. geology. Contbr. articles to profl. jours. Served with AUS, 1945-47. Mem. Ohio Acad. Sci., Palaeontol. Assn., Paleontol. Soc., Soc. Econ. Mineralogists and Paleontologists, Sigma Xi. Home: 1337 Clark St Bowling Green OH 43402

HOARE, TYLER JAMES, sculptor; b. Joplin, Mo., June 5, 1940; s. Melvin James and Dorotha Maude (Beadle) H.; m. Kathy Joyce Quinn, Mar. 9, 1963; 1 dau., Janet Elaine. Student, U. Colo., 1959-60, Sculpture Center, N.Y.C., 1960-61, Calif. Coll. Arts and Crafts, 1965-67; B.F.A., U. Kan., 1963. Instr. extension U. Calif. at Berkeley, 1973—; guest lectr. San Francisco Art Inst., San Francisco State Coll. Exhibited one man shows, New Center U.S. Art Gallery, Kansas City, Mo., 1964, Jewish Community Center Gallery, Kansas City, Studio C, Berkeley, Calif., 1965, Derby Gallery, Berkeley, Lucien Labaudt Gallery, San Francisco, 1966, U. Calif. at Berkeley, 1966, 67, Free U. Berkeley Gallery, Fredric Hobb's San Francisco Art Center, 1967, Green Gallery, San Francisco, 1968, St. Mary's Coll., 1969, John Bolles Gallery, San Francisco, 1969, 71, San Francisco State Coll., 1970, Camberwell Sch. Art, London, Eng., 1971, State U. N.Y. at Albany, Atherton Gallery, Menlo Park, Calif., 1972, Stanford, 1973, Studio Nine, Benicia, Calif., 1982, Solano Community Coll., Suison City, Calif., 1983; exhibited numerous group shows, 1963—, including, Oakland (Calif.) Mus., Pasadena (Calif.) Mus., Calif. Palace of Legion of Honor, San Francisco, San Francisco Mus., Library of Congress, Pratt Graphics Center, Los Angeles County Mus., Cin. Mus.; represented permanent collections, USIA, Washington, State U. N.Y. at Albany, Oakland Mus., Calif. Coll. Arts and Crafts, others. Mem. San Francisco Arts Guild, Richmond (Calif.) Art Center. Address: 30 Menlo Pl Berkeley CA 94707

HOATH, JAMES ROBERT, economist; b. Anthony, Kans., Sept. 3, 1919; s. James Clinton and Mabel Verene (Sluss) H.; m. Marjorie Bernice Kincaide, Feb. 27, 1948; children: James Irven, Gregory Leon, Bryan Douglas. B.S., Kans. State U., 1941, M.A., 1949; postgrad., U. Chgo., 1951; Ph.D., U. Nebr., 1959. Asst. prof. econs. Kans. State U., Manhattan, 1952-60; lectr. econs. U. Wis. project at Gadjah Madah U., Jogjakarta, Indonesia, 1960-63; chief of party Nat. Lutheran Council-Ford Found. Project Nommensen U., Medan, North Sumatra, 1963-64; lectr. econs. U. Nebr. at Lincoln, 1964-65; chief research div. Office of Programs, U.S. AID, Bangkok, Thailand, 1965-71; program analyst Office of Research and U. Relations, Tech. Assistance Bur., AID, Washington, 1971-73, econ. research adviser, 1973-77; area coordinator AID, Surabaya, Indonesia, 1977-80; ret., 1980; team leader consultants to East Java Gov.'s Office, Resources Mgmt. Internat., Surabaya, 1981-82; project mgmt. cons. Project Citanduy, West Java, Indonesia. Author studies on banking in Indonesia, rural devel. in Thailand. Served to maj. AUS, 1942-46; PTO. Decorated Bronze Star. Mem. Am. Econ. Assn., Assn. Asian Studies, Delta Sigma Phi. Democrat. Methodist. Address: 3106 Cunningham Dr Alexandria VA 22309

HOBAN, GEORGE SAVRE, lawyer; b. Faribault, Minn., Nov. 20, 1914; s. George W. and Margaret (Savre) H.; m. June Tullar, Feb. 4, 1939; children: William J., Robert G. B.A., Ripon Coll., 1936; J.D., Northwestern U., 1938. Bar: Ill. 1938. Practiced in, Chgo., 1938-80; partner firm Hinshaw, Culbertson, Moelmann, Hoban & Fuller, 1949-80; ret., 1980. Trustee Ripon Coll., 1965-80, hon. trustee, 1981—; trustee N.W. Community Hosp., Arlington Heights, Ill., 1963-70, Ravenswood Hosp. Med. Center, 1970-80; hon. trustee Ravenswood Hosp. Med. Center, 1981—. Served to capt. AUS, 1942-46. Mem. Am., Ill., Chgo. bar assns., Am. Acad. Orthopaedic Surgeons (hon.), Ill. C. of C. (chmn. legis. com. 1963-64), Phi Delta Phi. Club: Kingsway Country. Home: 3025 Guadalupe Dr Punta Gorda FL 33950 Office: 69 W Washington St Chicago IL 60602

HOBAN, RUSSELL CONWELL, author; b. Lansdale, Pa., Feb. 4, 1925; s. Abram and Jennie (Dimmerman) H.; m. Lillian Aberman, Jan. 31, 1944; children: Phoebe, Brom, Esmé, Julia; m. Gundula Ahl, Aug. 14, 1975; children—Jachin, Benjamin, Wieland. Student, Phila. Mus. Sch. Indsl. Art, 1941-43. Gen. illustrator, Wexton Co., N.Y.C., 1950-52; TV art dir., Batten, Barton, Durstine & Osborne, N.Y.C., 1952-57; free-lance illustrator and author children's books, 1957-65; copywriter, Doyle Dane Bernbach, N.Y.C., 1965-67; author: children's books What Does it Do and How Does it Work?, 1959, The Atomic Submarine, 1960, Bedtime for Frances, 1960, Herman the Loser, 1961, The Song in My Drum, 1962, London Men and English Men, 1963, Some Snow Said Hello, 1963, A Baby Sister for Frances, 1964, Nothing to Do, 1964, Bread and Jam for Frances, 1964, The Sorely Trying Day, 1964, Tom and the Two Handles, 1965, The Story of Hester Mouse, 1965, What Happened When Jack and Daisy Tried to Fool the Tooth Fairies, 1965, Goodnight, 1966, Henry and the Monstrous Din, 1966, Charlie the Tramp, 1966, The Little Brute Family, 1966, Save My Place, 1967, The Mouse and His Child, 1967, The Pedalling Man and Other Poems, 1968, The Stone Doll of Sister Brute, 1968, A Birthday for Frances, 1968, Ugly Bird, 1969, Best Friends of Frances, 1969, Harvey's Hideout, 1969, The Mole Family's Christmas, 1969, A Bargain for Frances, 1970, Emmet Otter's Jug-Band Christmas, 1971, Egg Thoughts and Other Frances Songs, 1972, The Sea-Thing Child, 1972, Letitia Rabbit's String Song, 1973, How Tom Beat Captain Najork and his Hired Sportsmen, 1974, Ten What?, 1974, Dinner at Alberta's, 1975, Crocodile and Pierrot, 1975, A Near Thing for Captain Najork, 1975, The Twenty Elephant Restaurant, 1977, Arthur's New Power, 1978, The Dancing Tigers, 1979, La Corona and Other Tin Tales, 1979, Ace Dragon Ltd, 1980, Flat Cat, 1980, The Serpent Tower, 1981, The Great Fruit Gum Robbery, 1981, They Came from Aargh!, 1981, The Flight of Bembel Rudzuk, 1982, The Battle of Zormla, 1982, Jim Frog, 1983, Big John Turkle, 1983; adult fiction The Lion of Boaz-Jachin and Jachin-Boaz, 1973, Kleinzeit, 1974, Turtle Diary, 1975, Riddley Walker, 1980, Pilgermann, 1983 (John W. Campbell Meml. award for best sci. fiction novel 1981). Served with U.S. Army, 1943-45. Decorated Bronze Star.; Recipient Whitbread Children's book award for How Tom Beat Captain Najork and his Hired Sportsmen, 1974. Mem. Soc. Authors, P.E.N. Office: c/o David Higham Assos Ltd 5-8 Lower John St Golden Sq London W1R 4HA England

HOBBIE, RUSSELL KLYVER, physicist; b. Albany, N.Y., Nov. 3, 1934; s. John Remington and Eulin Pomeroy (Klyver) H.; m. Cynthia Ann Borcherding, Dec. 28, 1957; children: Lynn Katherine, Erik Klyver, Sarah Elizabeth, Ann Stacey. B.S. in Physics, Mass. Inst. Tech., 1956; A.M., Harvard U., Ph.D., 1960. Research asso. U. Minn., 1960-62, mem. faculty, 1962—, prof. physics, 1972—, assoc. dean, 1983—, dir. Space Sci. Center, 1979—84. Author: Intermediate Physics for Medicine and Biology, 1978. Mem. Am. Assn. Physics Tchrs. (exec. bd. 1980-83), Am. Phys. Soc., Am. Assn. Physicists in Medicine, AAAS., Biophys. Soc. Home: 2151 Folwell St St Paul MN 55108 Office: 106 Lind Hall 207 Church St SE Minneapolis MN 55455

HOBBING, JEFFREY W., petroleum company executive. Exec. v.p. Charter Oil Co. Office: Charter Oil Co 21 W Church St Jacksonville FL 32202§

HOBBS, CARL FREDRIC, artist, filmmaker, author; b. Phila., Dec. 30, 1931; s. Robert Frederic and Gertrude (Madison) H.; children: Leslie Newbold, Mary Alison. Student, Cornell U., 1949-53, Academia de San Fernando de Belles Artes, Madrid, 1955-56. Pres. Fredric Hobbs Films, Inc., 1975—; chmn., chief exec. officer Virginia City (Nev.) Restoration Corp., 1974—. Writer, dir., producer 6 feature films; author: Richest Place on Earth, 1978, Eat Your House: Art Eco Guide to Self Sufficiency, 1980, American Paradise, 1982, also articles.; one-man shows include, Calif. Palace Legion of Honor, San Francisco, 1958, Mus. Sci. and Industry, Los Angeles, 1976, San Francisco Mus. Modern Art, 1980-81, group shows include, Nat. Fine Arts Collection Smithsonian Inst., Washington, 1964, The Hwy. Traveling Exhbns. Inst. Contemporary Art, Phila., 1970; group shows include travelling multi-media exhbn. Future Now, 1981-85; represented in permanent collections, Mus. Modern Art, Met. Mus. Art, Finch Collections Mus., N.Y.C., Oakland Mus. Art, Calif., San Francisco Mus. Modern Art, Spencer Meml. Ch., Bklyn. Served to 1st lt. USAF, 1953-55. Democrat. Episcopalian. Clubs: Commodore, Virginia City Yacht (commodore). *To create a work of art is an act of faith in the human spirit and in God. Art must always transcend materialist values and monuments to success. It is often the work of fools and children yet it is the ultimate reality.*

HOBBS, EDWARD HENRY, political science educator; b. Selma, Ala., Jan. 14, 1921; s. Edward Henry and Mary Olivia (Dannelly) H.; m. Marleah Marguerite Kaufman, Dec. 23, 1943; children: Milton Dannelly, Miriam Kaufman, Edward Henry, Vivian Blair. A.B. in Am. History, U. N.C., 1943; M.A. in Polit. Sci, U. Ala., 1947; So. Regional Tng. Program in Pub. Adminstrn. advanced scholar, 1947-48; M.A., Harvard, 1949, Ph.D., 1951. Instr. U. Ala., 1946-47; faculty U. Miss., 1949-67, acting chmn. dept. research in bus. and pub. adminstrn., prof. polit. sci., 1957-59, chmn. dept., prof., 1959-61, chmn. dept. research in bus. and govt., prof. polit. sci., 1961-67; dean Sch. Arts and Scis., Auburn U., 1967—; Corr. So. Regional Tng. Program in Pub. Adminstrn., 1955—. Author: Behind the President: A Study of Executive Office Agencies, 1954, Yesterday's Constitution Today: An Analysis of the Mississippi Constitution of 1890, 1960, Legislative Apportionment in Mississippi, 1956, Executive Reorganization in the National Government, 1953, A Manual of Mississippi Municipal Government, 1962, (with others) Mississippi in Maps-Industry, Resources and Agriculture, 1959, A Directory of Mississippi Municipalities, 3d edit, 1962, Money for Miles in Mississippi: A Highway Finance Report, 1962, also articles.; Co-author: A Compendium of Selected Information on Mississippi Municipalities, 1966, Power in American State Legislatures, 1967; Co-compiler: Annotated Bibliography on Mississippi Economy, Business, Industry and Government, 1950-1963, 1964; project dir., co-author: Arts and Sciences Council Report to Alabama Commn. on Higher Edn, 1972; Editor: Mississippi's Workmen's Compensation: Selected Cases, 1964, U.S.A. and the World's Three Biggest Economic Myths, 1965; Contbr. numerous articles in acad. and profl. jours. Chmn. Oxford (Miss.) Planning Commn., 1959-67; chmn. Oxford Council Aging, 1959; cons. Miss. Council Aging, 1957; pres. Miss. Research Clearing House, 1957-58; bd. dirs. Miss. Planning Conf., 1959-64; chmn. campaign dist. II Miss. Mental Health Assn., 1960; corr. Nat. Municipal League, 1955-67, Conf. Met. Area Problems, 1958—; bd. dirs. Miss. Heart Assn.; co-chmn. univ. relations com. Citizens' Conf. on Ala. State Govts., 1973; bd. dirs. Citizens' Com. for Constl. Conv., 1977; moderator Conf. on Pres. Truman's Orgn. and Adminstrn. of Presidency, Kansas City, Mo., 1977; chmn. Council of Deans of Arts and Scis. Ala. Commn. on Higher Edn., 1983—. Served to lt. USNR, World War II; capt. in Res. Nat. fellow to 2d Summer Inst. in Social Gerontology U. Calif. at Berkeley, 1959. Mem. So. Polit. Sci. Assn., So. Pub. Adminstrn. Research Council, Am. Soc. Pub. Adminstrn. (nat. adv. com. 1957—), Am. Polit. Sci. Assn., Oxford-Lafayette County C. of C., Pi Sigma Alpha (nat. exec. com. 1958—), Delta Kappa Epsilon, Omicron Delta Kappa (honoris causa 1955), Phi Kappa Phi (chpt. pres.). Presbyn. (elder). Club: Rotarian. Home: 926 Terrace Acres Auburn AL 36830

HOBBS, ESTEL MILTON, petroleum co. exec.; b. Louisville, May 21, 1937; s. Estel G. and Lillian M. (Brutscher) H.; m. Norma Lee Smith, Aug. 29, 1959; children: Tracy Leigh, Todd Milton. B.S., Eastern Ky. U., 1959; M.S., Purdue U., 1963; postgrad., Marshall U., 1973-74. Sr. research chemist Texaco Inc., Port Arthur, Tex., 1965-68; research chemist Ashland Petroleum Co. div. of Ashland Oil Inc., Ky., 1968-70, research group leader, 1970-73, mgr. dept. research and devel., 1973—; dir. Automotive and Product Applications Labs., 1981; mem. chemistry adv. com. Marshall U. Vice pres. Belhaven Civic League, Russell, Ky., 1973; elder, dir., chmn. 1st Christian Ch., Ashland. Served to capt. Ordnance Corps U.S. Army, 1962-65. Mem. Nat. Mgmt. Assn., Am. Chem. Soc., Am. Petroleum Inst., Indsl. Research Inst., Assn. Research Dirs., Soc. Automotive Engrs., Tri-State Catalyst Club. Republican. Clubs: Ashland Oil Forum, Tranquilan Swim. Home: 211 Erwin Rd Ashland KY 41101 Office: Ashland Oil Inc PO Box 391 Ashland KY 41101 *The miracle of the universe is man's mind. To waste intellect is a tragedy. Everyday should be a creative and learning experience which is fun rather than a dreaded task. I cannot imagine living without an ever present curiosity about why and how things happen.*

HOBBS, FRANKLIN WARREN, IV, investment banker; b. Manchester, N.H., July 30, 1947; s. Franklin W. and Margery (Baird) H.; m. Linda Barton Read, Nov. 26, 1973; children: Nicholas Baird, Ashley Read. A.B. magna cum laude in Am. History, Harvard U., 1969, M.B.A., 1972. Mng. dir. mergers and acquisitions Dillon, Read & Co. Inc., N.Y.C., 1972—. Mem. U.S. Olympic Team, 1968, 72. Episcopalian. Club: Harvard of N.Y.C. (bd. mgrs.). Office: Dillon Read & Co Inc 535 Madison Ave New York 10022

HOBBS, GERALD STEPHEN, publisher; b. N.Y.C., Nov. 5, 1941; s. Martin Joseph and Mary Theresa (Keane) H.; m. Susan E. Haunfelder, Apr. 4, 1970; children: Peter Laurence, Meredith Anne. Student, Am. Inst. Banking, 1962-64, N.Y. U., 1971. With Procter & Gamble, Inc., 1967-70; with Billboard Publs., Inc., N.Y.C., 1970—;

pub. Am. Artist, 1974—, Am. Artist Bus. Letter, 1974—, Indsl. Design, 1975—, Am. Artist Diary, 1975—, The Artist (English mag.), 1975—, The Am. Artist Collection, 1976—, Interiors, Residential Interiors, 1978—; v.p. Billboard Publs., Inc., 1978-81, exec. v.p., 1981—, also dir.; group pub. Billboard mag., 1980—, Musician mag., 1980—. Served with N.Y. N.G., 1966-72. Mem. Nat. Art Materials Trade Assn., Art Materials Mfrs. Assn. (dir.), Nat. Arts Club, Mag. Pubs. Assn., Am. Bus. Press (chmn. merchandising com.), Scarsdale Art Assn., Artist Fellowship, Internat. Soc. Artists (dir. 1977). Club: Sky. Home: 33 Thornbury Rd Scarsdale NY 10583 also Southampton NY 11968 Office: 1 Astor Plaza New York NY 10036

HOBBS, GRIMSLEY TAYLOR, coll. pres.; b. Greensboro, N.C., June 14, 1923; s. Richard J. M. and Gretchen (Taylor) H.; m. Lois Ann Hunkele, Nov. 1, 1943; children—Grimsley Taylor, Louise B. Ruffin M., Herbert J., Richard M., Elise M. B.A., Guilford (N.C.) Coll., 1947; M.A., Haverford Coll., 1948; Ph.D. in Philosophy, Duke, 1955. Mem. faculty Earlham (Ind.) Coll., 1951-65, prof., chmn. philosophy, 1958-65; pres. Guilford Coll., 1965—; Exec. com. Piedmont Univ. Center; mem. exec. com., vice chmn. Ind. Coll. Funds of N.C.; past chmn. Assn. Friends Colls. Contbr. to profl. jours. Bd. dirs. YMCA. Served USAAF, 1943-46. Ford Found. Postdoctoral fellow, 1955; recipient Doan Distinguished Prof. award Earlham Coll., 1960. Mem. Am. Philos. Assn., Ind. Philos. Assn. (past pres.), Am. Assn. Higher Edn., N.C. Assn. Ind. Colls. and Univs., Am. Council on Edn., C. of C. (dir.). Democrat. Mem. Soc. of Friends. Clubs: Rotarian (pres. 1973-74, dir. Office: 5800 W Friendly Ave Greensboro NC 27410 *

HOBBS, J. EDWIN, utility executive; b. Salisbury, Md., Dec. 9, 1916; s. Woodland Page and Annie Brown (Leigh) H.; m. Afton Hepworth, Sept. 10, 1946; children: Steven Edwin, Alan Robert, Walter James, Ann, Ellen. Student public schs. With Delmarva Power & Light Co. (and predecessors), Salisbury, 1933-81, mgr. ops., then v.p., pres. subs. cos., 1966-79, asst. to chmn. bd., 1980-81, ret., 1981. Served to capt. AUS, 1943-46, 51-52. Decorated Bronze Star. Sr. mem. IEEE (past chmn. Eastern Shore sect.); mem. Md. C. of C. (dist. v.p. 1978-81), Salisbury Area C. of C. (pres. 1971). Republican. Club: Salisbury Kiwanis (pres. 1961). Office: PO Box 1739 Salisbury MD 21801 *

HOBBS, JAMES ALLEN, insurance executive; b. Richmond, Ind., July 28, 1930; s. Vernon D. and Benona H. (Heath) H.; m. Ann House, Dec. 27, 1952; children: Alan, Larry. B.S. in Bus, Ind. U., Bloomington, 1952. With Lafayette Life Ins. Co., Ind., 1954—, sr. v.p., sec., dir., 1968—. Bd. dirs. Lafayette Parks and Recreation Dept. Served with USAF, 1952-54. Fellow Life Mgmt. Inst.; mem. Lafayette C. of C. (dir.), Life Office Mgmt. Assn. Republican. Methodist. Office: 2203 S 18th St Box 7007 Lafayette IN 47903

HOBBS, JAMES BEVERLY, business administration educator, writer; b. Topeka, Kans., Sept. 9, 1930; s. Kenneth Beverly and Ida (Burkholder) H.; m. Peggy Genevieve Whitney, Nov. 2, 1957; children: David Beverly, Nancy Ruth. A.B., Harvard U., 1952; M.B.A., U. Kans., 1957; D.B.A., Ind. U., 1962. Fin. analyst Hotpoint div. Gen. Electric Co., Chgo., 1957-60; asst. prof. mgmt. and acctg. Kans. State U., 1962-66; assoc. prof. mgmt. and acctg. Lehigh U., 1966-70, prof., 1970-79, Frank L. Magee disting. prof. bus. adminstrn., 1979—, chmn. dept. mgmt., fin., mktg. and law, 1970-75, chmn. dept. mgmt., fin. and mktg., 1982—; assoc. dean Kans. State U., 1964-66. Author (with others) Financial Accounting, 1984. Served to sgt. U.S. Army, 1952-54; Korea. Mem. Am. Acctg. Assn., Acad. Mgmt., Phi Kappa Phi, Beta Gamma Sigma, Beta Alpha Psi. Unitarian. Home: RD 3 Box 187 Black River Rd Bethlehem PA 18015 Office: Lehigh U Drown Hall 35 Bethlehem PA 18015

HOBBS, LEWIS MANKIN, astronomer; b. Upper Darby, Pa., May 16, 1937; s. Lewis Samuel and Evangeline Elizabeth (Goss) H.; m. Jo Ann Faith Hagele, June 16, 1962; children: John, Michael, Dara. B.Engring. Physics, Cornell U., 1960; M.S., U. Wis., 1962, Ph.D. in Physics, 1966. Jr. astronomer Lick Obs., U. Calif., Santa Cruz, 1965-66; mem. faculty U. Chgo., 1966—, prof. astronomy and astrophysics, 1976—; also dir. Yerkes Obs., Williams Bay, Wis., 1974-82; bd. dirs. Assn. Univs. Research in Astronomy, Tucson, 1974—; mem. astronomy com. of bd. trustees Univs. Research Assn., Inc., Washington, 1979—, chmn., 1979-81. Contbr. to profl. jours. Bd. dirs. Mil. Symphony Assn. of Walworth County, 1972—. Alfred P. Sloan scholar, 1955-60. Mem. Am. Astron. Soc., Am. Phys. Soc., Internat. Astron. Union, Wis. Acad. Scis. Arts and Letters. Home: 18 Highland St Williams Bay WI 53191 Office: Yerkes Obs U ChgoBox 258 Williams Bay WI 53191

HOBBS, MARCUS EDWIN, educator; b. Chadbourn, N.C., Aug. 11, 1909; s. Julius Charles and Maude Elizabeth (Player) H.; m. Sarah Ferguson Blanchard, July 3, 1937; children—Sarah Lillian, Joan Elizabeth. A.B., Duke U., 1932, M.A., 1934, Ph.D., 1936. Indsl. research fellow tobacco Duke, 1931-33, instr. chemistry, 1936, asst. prof., 1942, asso. prof., 1945, prof., 1950—, univ. disting. service prof. emeritus, 1978—, chmn. dept. chemistry, 1951-54, dean, 1954-58, dean of univ., 1958-64, vice provost, 1960-64, provost, 1969-71, charge spl. sources of chemistry of explosives, 1941-42; research asso. Nat. Def. Research Com., George Washington U., 1942-45, civilian cons., 1942-44, 1943-45; adviser Office Ordnance Research, 1951-61, chief scientist, acting, 1951-52; Dir. N.C. Blue Cross and Blue Shield, Inc., 1967-81, chmn. exec. com., 1978-81; Mem. advisory council Army Research Office, 1970-76; mem. adv. com. jr. sci. and humanities symposia Dept. Army, 1974-77, adviser, 1980—; mem. NSF adv. panel U.S.-Japan Coop. Service Program, 1963-65; adv. com. utility research and devel. U.S. Dept. Agr., 1964-70; mem. N.C. Bd. Sci. and Tech., 1963—; Chmn. exec. com. Research Triangle Inst., 1965-70, 77—, mem. exec. com., 1965—. Contbr. articles to profl. jours. Recipient Army-Navy Certificate of Merit for sci. work with OSRD during World War II, 1957; Outstanding Civilian Service medal Dept. Army, 1959; Cigar Industry Research award, 1959. Fellow AAAS; mem. Am. Chem. Soc. (chmn. N.C. sect. 1946), AAUP, Phi Beta Kappa, Sigma Xi, Phi Lambda Upsilon, Sigma Pi Sigma, Sigma Chi. Club: Rotary (Durham) (pres. 1978-79). Home: 115 Pinecrest Rd Durham NC 27705

HOBBS, MICHAEL EDWIN, broadcasting company executive; b. Washington, Nov. 26, 1940; s. Robert Boyd and Barbara Alberta (Davis) H. A.B. cum laude, Dartmouth Coll., 1962; J.D., Harvard U., 1965. Bar: Mass. bar 1966. Staff counsel, asst. to gen. mgr. WGBH Ednl. Found., Boston, 1966-67; exec. asst. ednl. TV stas. Nat. Assn. Ednl. Broadcasters, Washington, 1967-70; sec. Public Broadcasting Service, Washington, 1970—, gen. counsel, 1970-71, dir. adminstrn., 1970-73, v.p., 1973, sr. v.p., 1976—. Mem. Am. Bar Assn. (com. on patent trademark and copyright law), Mass. Bar Assn., Am. Judicature Soc., Nat. Assn. Ednl. Broadcasters, Phi Beta Kappa. Clubs: George Town., Seven River Yacht. Home: 419 Cameron St Alexandria VA 22314 Office: 475 L'Enfant Plaza SW Washington DC 20024

HOBBS, RANALD PURCELL, publisher; b. Bartlett, N.H., Sept. 14, 1907; s. Don P. and Blanche (Stevens) H.; m. Vera Ingeborg Andren, June 27, 1936; children: Ranald D., Linda A. A.B., Dartmouth Coll., 1930. With The Macmillan Co., 1935-43; with Rinehart & Co., Inc., 1943-60, exec. v.p., 1955-60, Bobbs-Merrill Co., Inc., 1960-61; pres. Hobbs Internat., Inc., 1962-63, Hobbs, Dorman & Co., Inc., 1964-73, Hobbs/Context Corp., 1973-77, Cowles Book Co., Inc., 1968-69; v.p., treas. BCMA Assos. Inc., 1971—; Mem. Darien (Conn.) Bd. Edn., 1948-55, chmn., 1950-52; chmn. coll. sect. Am. Textbook Pubs. Inst., 1954-55, bd. dirs., 1956-59, sec., 1957, treas., 1958; regional v.p. United Student Aid Funds, Inc., 1973-77. Clubs: Union League, Dartmouth of S.W. Florida, Dutch Treat. Home: 1930 Gulf Shore Blvd N Apt D-301 Naples FL 33940 Office: 485 Fifth Ave New York NY 10017

HOBBS, ROBERT WESLEY, astronomer; b. Chester, W.Va., Jan. 28, 1938; s. Harry S. and Sarah Caughey H.; children: David, Anne Marie. B.S., Case Inst. Tech., 1960; M.S., U. Mich., 1962, Ph.D. in Astronomy, 1964. With Naval Research Lab., Washington, 1964-69, head millimeter wave radio astronomy sect., 1966-69; with Goddard Space Flight Center, NASA, Greenbelt, Md., 1969-82, head obs. and data analysis br., 1977-82; chief scientist Eastern region Computer Tech. Assocs., Landover, Md., 1982—. Contbr. articles on systems engring. to profl. jours. Mem. Am. Astron. Soc., Internat. Sci. Radio Union, Internat. Astron. Union.

HOBBS, TRUMAN MCGILL, lawyer, judge.; b. Selma, Ala., Feb. 8, 1921; s. Sam F. and Sarah Ellen (Greene) H.; m. Joyce Cummings, July 9, 1949; children—Emilie C., Frances John, Dexter Cummings, Truman McGill. A.B., U. N.C., 1942; LL.B., Yale, 1948. Bar: Ala. bar 1948. Practiced in, Montgomery, 1951—; law clk. U.S. Supreme Ct., 1948-49; partner Hobbs, Copeland, Franco & Screws, from 1951; now U.S. dist. judge, Montgomery.; Chmn. Ala. Unemployment Appeal Bd., 1952-58. Pres. United Appeal Montgomery, Montgomery County Tb Assn.; v.p. Ala. Com. for Better Schs.; Chmn. Montgomery County Exec. Democratic Com., 1970. Served to lt. USNR, 1942-46; ETO, PTO. Decorated Bronze Star medal. Fellow Am. Coll. Trial Lawyers; mem. Internat. Acad. Trial Lawyers, Ala. Plaintiffs Lawyers Assn. (past pres.), Ala. Bar Assn. (pres. 1970-71), Montgomery County Bar Assn. (past pres.). Home: 2301 Fernway Dr Montgomery AL 36111 Office: PO Box 4954 Montgomery AL 36101

HOBBS, WILLIAM DAVID, ret. tobacco co. exec.; b. Eden, N.C., Dec. 22, 1915; s. Edward Victor and Grace B. (Stocks) H.; m. Jane Farr, Mar. 1, 1943; children—William David, Jane (Mrs. Gary S. Dean). Student, Davidson (N.C.) Coll., 1934-36. With R.J. Reynolds Tobacco Co., Winston-Salem, N.C., 1936-80, pres., 1972-75, 79-80, chmn. exec. com., dir., 1975-80; now ret. exec. v.p.; dir. R.J. Reynolds Industries; chmn. Winston-Salem city bd. N.C. Nat. Bank; dir. 1st Fed. Savs. and Loan Assn. Officer Winston-Salem Citizens Coalition, 1971, 73—; chmn. United Fund campaign Forsyth County, 1956; Mem. gdv. bd. Winston-Salem Salvation Army, 1968-72; bd. visitors Davidson (N.C.) Coll., 1980—, Babcock Grad. Sch. Mgmt., Wake Forest U., Winston-Salem, N.C. Served to capt. AUS, 1941-46. Episcopalian. Clubs: Forsyth Country (Winston-Salem); Bermuda Run Country (Clemmons, N.C.) *

HOBBY, OVETA CULP, newspaper publisher; b. Killeen, Tex., Jan. 19, 1905; d. I.W. and Emma (Hoover) Culp; m. William P. Hobby, Feb. 23, 1931 (dec. 1964); children: William, Jessica (Mrs. Henry Gatto Jr.). Student, Baylor Coll., L.H.D., 1956; L.H.D., Bard Coll., 1950, Lafayette Coll., 1954; LL.D., Baylor U., 1943, Sam Houston State Tchrs. Coll., 1943, U. Chattanooga, 1943, Bryant Coll., 1953, Ohio Wesleyan U., 1953, Columbia U., 1954, Smith Coll., 1954, Middlebury Coll., 1954, U. Pa., 1955, Colby Coll., 1955, Farleigh Dickinson U., Western Coll.; D.Litt., Colo. Women's Coll., 1947, C.W. Post Coll., 1962. Parliamentarian Tex. Ho. of Reps., 1926-31, 39, 41; research editor Houston Post, from 1931, successively lit. editor, asst. editor,v.p., exec. v.p.,editor, 1931-53, editor, pub., 1952-53, pres., editor, 1955-65, chmn. bd., editor, 1965—; dir. Sta. KPRC AM-TV, 1945-53, 55-69, chmn. bd., 1970—; chmn. bd., dir. Channel Two TV Co., 1970—; vice chmn. Channel 5-TV, Nashville; chief women's interest sect. War Dept. Bur. Pub. Relations, 1941-42; apptd. dir. WAAC, 1942; commd. col. AUS, 1943-45; dir. WAC, 1943-45; fed. security adminstr., 1953; sec. HEW, 1953-55. Author: textbook Mr. Chairman; synicated columnist: Mr. Chairman. Sponsor Clark Sch. for Deaf; trustee Eisenhower Birthplace Meml. Park; mem. Pres.'s Com. on Employment for Physically Handicapped, Com. on Civilian Nat. Honors; trustee Eisenhower Exchange Fellowship; bd. dirs. Houston Symphony Soc.; mem. S.W. adv. bd. Inst. Internat. Edn.; mem. Com. of 75, U. Tex., 1958—; mem. So. regional com. Marshall Scholarship, 1957—; mem. Rockefeller Bros. Fund Spl. Studies project; bd. dirs. Com. Econ. Devel.; mem. nat. bd. devel. Sam Rayburn Found.; mem. Crusade for Freedom, Inc.; nat. bd. Eleanor Roosevelt Meml. Found.; trustee Rice U. Decorated Phillippine Mil. Merit medal, 1947; recipient Disting. Service medal, 1944, Pub. of Yr., 1960, Honor Nat. Jewish Hosp., 1962, Living History Research Inst. Am., 1960. Mem. Soc. Rehab. Facially Disfigured, So. Newspaper Pubs. Assn. (pres. 1949), Acad. Tex. (charter), Gamma Alpha Chi (hon. vice chmn.). Episcopalian. Clubs: Houston Country, Bayou, Ramada, Jr. League (Houston). Office: Houston Post 4747 Southwest Freeway Houston TX 77001

HOBBY, WILLIAM PETTUS, state official, newspaper and broadcast executive; b. Houston, Jan. 19, 1932; s. William Pettus and Oveta (Culp) H.; m. Diana Poteat Stallings, Sept. 11, 1954; children: Laura Poteat, Paul William, Andrew Purefoy, Katherine Pettus. B.A., Rice U., 1953. Asst. sec.-treas. Houston Post, 1957-59, assoc. editor, 1959-60, mng. editor, 1960-63, exec. editor, 1963-73; exec. v.p. Houston Post Co., 1963-65, pres., 1965-83; vice chmn. Channel Two TV Co., KPRC Radio Co., Houston, 1970-83, chmn., chief exec. officer, 1983—; chmn. bd., chief exec. officer Channel Five TV, Nashville, 1975—, Channel Eleven TV, Meridian, Miss., Channel Four TV, Tucson; pres. H & C Communications, Inc., 1979-83, chmn. bd., chief exec. officer, 1983—; lt. gov., Tex., 1973—; Chmn. Nat. Conf. Lt. Govs., 1976-77; Parliamentarian Tex. Senate, 1959. Served to lt. (j.g.) USNR, 1953-57. Mem. Am. Soc. Newspaper Editors, Tex. Hunter and Jumper Assn. (dir. 1953—, pres. 1959-60), Houston Symphony Soc., Jefferson Davis Assn., Hobby Found., Catto Found., Houston C. of C. Office: State Capitol Austin TX 78711 Office: H & C Communications Houston TX 77056

HOBDAY, JOHN CHARLES, foundation administrator; b. Richmond, Surrey, Eng., July 7, 1935; emigrated to Can., 1952, naturalized, 1967; s. Stephen Henry and Kathleen Hawtrey (White) H.; m. Helga Stock, June 21, 1961; children: Heidi Andrea, Oliver John, Tina Karina. Ed., Rugby Sch., Eng. Producer, dir. radio drama and features CBC, 1957-64; theatre dir. Confedn. Centre for Arts, Charlottetown, P.E.I., Can., 1966-68; adminstrv. dir. Neptune Theatre, Halifax, N.S., Can., 1968-71; nat. dir. Can. Conf. Arts, Toronto and Ottawa, Ont., 1971-82; exec. dir. corp. donations Joseph E. Seagram and Sons, Ltd., Montreal, Que., Can., 1982—; exec. dir. Samuel and Saidye Bronfman Family Found., Montreal, 1983—; mem. adv. com. on culture and communications UNESCO. Freelance writer, actor, dir., lectr. Mem. Assn. Cultural Execs., Assn. Can. Radio and TV Artists, Inst. Assn. Execs., Royal Soc. Arts. Office: 1430 Peel St Montreal PQ H3A 1S9 Canada

HOBERECHT, EARNEST, abstract company executive, former newspaper executive; b. Watonga, Okla., Jan. 1, 1918; s. Earnest Trevar, Sr. and Grace (Woolman) H.; m. Katherine Row, Aug. 1939 (div. 1940); m. Mary Jane Royal, Nov. 16, 1940 (div. 1945); m. Laurette Heger, May 6, 1959 (div. June 1969); children: Antonia, Earnest Trevar III, Nathalie, Shelley; m. Mary Ann Shaklee Karns, Apr. 26, 1970. B.A., U. Okla., 1941. Reporter, Watonga Republican, 1935; pub. Reflector mag. Watonga, 1936; also part-time staff Oklahoma City News, Daily Oklahoman, Oklahoma City, 1937-41; reporter Memphis Press-Scimitar, 1941-42; laborer Navy Yard, Pearl Harbor, Hawaii, 1942-43; editor Pearl Harbor Bull., 1944-45; war corr. Pacific, UP, 1945, staff Tokyo bur., 1945-48, chief corr., mgr. Tokyo bur., 1948-51, gen. mgr. Asia, 1951-66; v.p. UPI, 1953-66; chief UP War Corrs. in Korea, 1950-53; pres. Okla. Land Trust, Blaine County Abstract Co.; chmn. Watonga Abstract Co., Inc., 1972—; owner Earnest Hoberecht Ins. Free-lance writer; Author: Tokyo Romance English and Japanese, 1947; (pub. in Japanese) Tokyo Diary, 1947, Democratic Etiquette, 1948; Fifty Famous Americans, 1949, Shears of Destiny, 1949, Asia In My Beat, 1961; pres., editor-in-chief: Gt. American News, 1979. Named to Okla. Jour. Hall of Fame, 1972, Okla. Hall of Fame, 1977. Mem. Fgn. Corrs. Club, Sigma Delta Chi. Presbyterian. Clubs: Koganei Country (Tokyo); Karuizawa (Japan) Country. Home: 1317 N Noble Ave Watonga OK 73772 Office: Okla Land Trust 100 W Main St Watonga OK 73772

HOBERMAN, BERNARD GILBERT (BEN HOBERMAN), radio sta. exec.; b. Chisholm, Minn., July 21, 1922; s. Max and Faye (Bernstein) H.; m. Jacklyn Kanter, Aug. 22, 1948; children—Thomas, David, Joan. Announcer-salesman radio sta. WMFG, Hibbing, Minn., 1940-42; asst. gen. mgr. radio sta. WELI, New Haven, Conn., 1946-48; gen. mgr. radio sta. WDET-FM, Detroit, 1948-50; account exec. WXYZ-TV, Detroit, 1950-58; gen. mgr. radio sta. WABC, N.Y.C., 1958-60; v.p., gen. mgr. radio sta. KABC, Los Angeles, from 1960; pres. ABC Radio, N.Y.C., 1979—; dir. Mfrs. Bank Los Angeles.; Vice pres. Braille Inst. Am., 1968-75; mem. community relations com. Jewish Fedn.-Council Greater Los Angeles, 1965—; mem. Los Angeles County Commn. on Jud. Procedures, 1967-68. Adv. bd. Big Bros. Greater Los Angeles, 1965—; bd. dirs. Inst. Cancer and Blood Research, 1970-74, Los Angeles Better Bus. Bur., 1970-72; trustee City of Mope, Los Angeles. Served with AUS, 1943-46; ETO. Decorated Bronze Star; named Innovator of Year U. San Francisco, 1972, Citizen of Year Guardians of Jewish Home for Aged, 1974. Mem. Cal. Broadcasters Assn. (dir. 1973-75), So. Cal. Broadcasters Assn. (chmn. 1971-74), Hollywood Radio and TV Soc. (pres. 1968-69), Pacific Radio Pioneers, Los Angeles C. of C. (mem. communications com. 1974-75). Jewish religion (past dir. synagogue). Club: Brentwood Country (pres. 1971-73). Office: care ABC Radio 1330 Ave of Americas New York NY 10019 *

HOBERMAN, HENRY DON, biochemist, physician, educator; b. Bridgeport, Conn., Apr. 23, 1914; s. Samuel William and Olga Ruth (Paley) H.; m. Hilda Hortensia Carnicero, Oct. 18, 1974; children by previous marriage—John, David, Ruth, Michael. A.B., Columbia U., 1936, Ph.D., 1942; M.D., Harvard, 1946. Research asso. Harvard U. Med. Sch.; tutor in biochem. scis. Harvard U., 1942-44; research asso. Yale U. Sch. Medicine, 1946-48, asst. prof. biol. chemistry, 1948-53; asso. prof. biochemistry Albert Einstein Coll. Medicine, Bronx, N.Y., 1953-58, prof., 1958—; Vis. prof. Wenner-Gren Inst., Stockholm, Sweden, 1964, 65, Biochem. Inst., Royal U. Stockholm, 1967, 70, Inst. Phys. Biochemistry, U. Munich, Germany, 1967; vis. scientist Weizmann Inst. Sch., 1961, 67; Cons., research com. Nat. Inst. Alcohol Abuse and Alcoholism, 1974-75; mem. sect. of fellowships, com. on growth NRC, 1948-53. Contbr. articles to profl. jours. Alexander Browne Coxe fellow, 1946-47; Markle scholar, 1948-53; Commonwealth fellow, 1967-68; Am. Scandinavian Soc. fellow, 1970; NSF grantee, 1955-74; NIH grantee, 1948-75; Am. Cancer Soc. grantee, 1948-53; Jane Coffin Childs Meml. Fund grantee, 1952-53. Mem. Am. Soc. Biol. Chemists, Am. Chem. Soc., Harvey Soc., Am. Scandinavian Soc., Sigma Xi. Home: 3 Winchester Oval New Rochelle NY 10805 Office: 1300 Morris Park Ave Bronx NY 10461

HOBLER, HERBERT WINDSOR, broadcasting executive; b. St. Louis, Sept. 25, 1922; s. Atherton Wells and Ruth Charles (Windsor) H.; m. Mary Fitz Randolph, Mar. 25, 1944; children: Randolph W., Deborah H. Kahane, Mary H. Hyson, Nancy Trani. B.A., Princeton U., 1944. Salesman, Mut. Broadcasting System, 1946-49; sales exec. NBC-TV, 1952-54, CBS-TV, 1954-59; v.p. TelePrompter Corp., N.Y.C., 1954-59, Videotape Prodns., 1959-65; founder, chmn. Nassau Broadcasting Co., Princeton, N.J., 1963—; chmn. Dow Jones Radio 2, Inc., Princeton, 1981—, Cable One, Trenton, N.J., 1981—. Chmn., Am. Boychoir Sch.; v.p. Tiger Inn. Served with USAAF, 1943-45. Named Broadcaster of Yr., So. Bapt. Radio-TV Commn., 1975; Man of Yr., Princeton United Fund, 1976; Citizen of Yr., Princeton C. of C., 1980. Mem. Nat. Assn. Broadcasters (past dir.), N.J. Broadcasters Assn. (past dir.), N.J. Cable TV Assn. (past dir.). Republican. Presbyterian. Club: Nassau. Office: Box 1350 Princeton NJ 08540
Through a broadcast frequency I saw a way to serve the public at large. The company was founded, its directors and private stockholders selected first to serve the community and second to make a profitable business.

HOBLIN, PHILIP J., JR., securities company executive; b. S.I., N.Y., July 31, 1929; s. Philip J. and Mary A. (Brown) H.; m. Eileen P. Killilea, Jan. 10, 1959; children: Philip, Monica, Michael. B.S., Fordham U., 1951, LL.D., 1957. Bar: N.Y. 1957. Regional atty. Bache & Co., N.Y.C., 1958-63; exec. v.p., gen. counsel Shearson/Am. Express (and predessor), 1963—; Co-chmn. Law Center, Inst. Finance, N.Y.C., 1972—; mem. Joint Industry Com. Securities Protection, 1969; mem. bd. arbitration N.Y. Stock Exchange; chmn. arbitration com. Chgo. Bd. Options Exchange, 1977-78, mem. conduct com., 1979-80; arbitrator Nat. Assn. Securities Dealers, also; mem. bus. conduct com. dist. 12, 1974-77; mem. Securities Industry Com. on Arbitration, 1977-81. Author: Arbitration Can Be Broker's Solution to Disputes, 1972, also law rev. articles. Bd. advisers Xavier High Sch., N.Y.C., 1969; pres. Sons of Xavier, 1977-79. Served as spl. agt. USAF, 1951-53; col. Res. (ret.). Mem. Security Industry Assn. (pres. compliance div. 1970-72), Am. Bar Assn., N.Y. County Lawyers Assn., Am. Legion, Res. Officers Assn. (v.p. air N.Y. State chpt. 1973-74, sec. judge adv. gen. N.Y.C. chpt.). Clubs: K.C., Elks. Home: 15 Lancaster Dr Suffern NY 10901 Office: 14 Wall St New York NY 10005

HOBLITZELL, ALAN PENNIMAN, JR., banker; b. St. Louis, June 13, 1931; s. Alan Penniman and Dorothy (May) H.; m. Louise Perkins; children: Jean, Priscilla S., Marjorie. B.S., Princeton U., 1953; postgrad., Rutgers U. Grad. Sch. Banking, 1956, Harvard U. Bus. Sch., 1966. With Md. Nat. Bank, Balt., 1956—, sr. v.p., 1969-72, exec. v.p., 1972-76, pres., 1976—, chief exec. officer, 1979—; dir. Ryland Group, Fidelity & Deposit Co. of Md., PHH Group, Inc., London Interstate Bank. Treas. Mcpl. Arts Soc.; trustee Md. Inst. Served with U.S. Army, 1953-56. Mem. Res. City Bankers, Robert Morris Assn. Clubs: Green Spring Valley Hunt, Center, Merchants. Office: Md Nat Bank 10 Light St Baltimore MD 21203

HOBLITZELLE, GEORGE KNAPP, state legislator; b. St. Louis, Sept. 28, 1921; s. Harrison and Mary D. (Jones) H.; m. Katharine L. Wells, Nov. 18, 1950; children—Katharine, Laura Trimble, Lucy. A.B., Princeton, 1943. With Gen. Steel Industries, Inc., 1946-73, successively spl. apprentice, asst. to v.p., treas., 1946-53, sec., asst. to pres., 1953-60, v.p., 1960-65, v.p., sec., 1965-73; mem. Mo. Ho. of Reps., 1973—. Bd. dirs. Arts and Edn. Council Greater St. Louis; trustee St. Louis Art Mus. Served to capt. F.A. AUS, 1943-46, 51-53; ETO. Decorated Bronze Star. Mem. Nat. Def. Transp. Assn. Episcopalian. Home: 35 Glen Eagles Dr Saint Louis MO 63124 Office: State Capitol Jefferson City MO 65101

HOBSON, BURTON HAROLD, publishing company executive; b. Galesburg, Ill., Apr. 16, 1933; s. Burt and Geneva (Sornberger) H.; m. Maxine C. Meyer, Aug. 9, 1953; children: Alice L., Andrew J., Mark R. B.A., U. Chgo., 1953. Mgr. collector's coin dept. Marshall Field & Co., Chgo., 1953-61; sales mgr. Sterling Pub. Co., Inc., N.Y.C., 1961-66, v.p. sales, 1966-72, exec. v.p., 1972-79, pres., 1979—, dir., 1966—; dir. Printed Arts Corp., Port Washington, N.Y., Oak Tree Press Co., Ltd., Sydney, Australia. Author: (with Fred Reinfeld) Manual for Coin Collectors and Investors, 1963, Picture Book of Ancient Coins, 1963, U.S. Commemorative Coins and Stamps, 1964, Catalogue of the World's Most Popular Coins, 1965, What You Should Know about Coins and Coin Collecting, 1965, Hidden Values in Coins, 1965, International Guide to Coin Collecting, 1966, Coins You Can Collect, 1966, Coin Identifier, 1966, Coin Collecting As a Hobby, 1967, (with Robert Obojski) Illustrated Encyclopedia of World Coins, 1970, Catalogue of Scandinavian Coins, 1970, Historic Gold Coins of the World, 1971, Coin Collecting for Beginners, 1970, Stamp Collecting for Beginners, 1970, Coins and Coin Collecting, 1971. Recipient Robert Friedberg award for Numismatic Lit., 1972. Mem. Am. Numismatic Soc., Delta Upsilon. Club: Nat. Arts (N.Y.C.). Home: 4 Warwick Pl Port Washington NY 11050 Office: Sterling Pub Co 2 Park Ave New York NY 10016

HOBSTETTER, JOHN NORMAN, educator, scientist; b. Dayton, Ohio, Feb. 19, 1917; s. John Herman and Mary (Young) H. B.S., MIT, 1939; D.Sc., Harvard U., 1945. Asst. prof. Harvard U., 1947-52; mem. tech. staff Bell Telephone Labs., Murray Hill, N.J., 1952-58; asso. prof. U. Pa., Phila., 1958-59, prof., 1960-82, prof. emeritus, 1982—, dir. lab. for research on structure of matter, 1960-67, vice provost for research, 1967—, dean Grad. Sch., 1968-70, asso. provost, 1970-78. Author: Effect of Imperfections on Geranium and Silicon, 1959, Mechanical Properties of Semiconductors, 1960, Theory of Nucleation in Solid-Solid Transformations-Decomposition of Austenite by Diffusional Processes, 1962; also articles. Recipient Army-Navy cert. of appreciation, 1946. Mem. AIME, Am. Phys. Soc., AAAS, Sigma Xi, Alpha Chi Sigma, Omicron Kappa Upsilon. Home: Cape May Ave Sewell NJ 08080

HOCH, EDWARD DENTINGER, author; b. Rochester, N.Y., Feb. 22, 1930; s. Earl George and Alice Mary (Dentinger) H.; m. Patricia Ann McMahon, June 5, 1957. Student, U. Rochester, 1947-49. Research asst. Rochester (N.Y.) Public Library, 1949-50; circulation asst. Pocket Books, N.Y.C., 1952-54; public relations writer Hutchins Advt. Co., Rochester, N.Y., 1954-68. Author: The Shattered Raven, 1969, The Judges of Hades, 1971, The Transvection Machine, 1971, The Spy and the Thief, 1972, City of Brass, 1972, The Fellowship of the Hand, 1973, The Frankenstein Factory, 1975, The Thefts of Nick Velvet, 1978, The Monkey's Clue and the Stolen Sapphire, 1978, All But Impossible, 1981; Editor: Dear Dead Days, 1972; editor: Best Detective Stories of the Year, 1976-81, All But Impossible, 1981, Year's Best Mystery and Suspense Stories, 1982-84. Served with U.S. Army, 1950-52. Mem. Mystery Writers Am., Inc. (dir., Edgar award 1967, Edgar scroll 1980, pres. 1982), Sci. Fiction Writers Am., Authors Guild, Crime Writers Assn. (Gt. Brit.). Roman Catholic. Home and Office: 2941 Lake Ave Rochester NY 14612 *After publishing over 600 short stories and 20 books, I have to admit that I write primarily to entertain. But I've yet to decide whether it's more to entertain the reader or myself.*

HOCH, FRANK WILLIAM, banker; b. White Plains, N.Y., May 14, 1921; s. Herman and Hanny (von Salis) H.; m. Lisina de Schulthess, Aug. 14, 1951; children: Steven George, Alix Monica, Daphne Lisina, Roland Eric. Student, Kantonales Gymnasium, Zurich, Switzerland; LL.D., U. Geneva, Zurich U., Switzerland Law Sch., 1947. With Brown Bros. Harriman & Co., N.Y.C., 1947—, partner, 1960—; vice chmn., dir. Immobilien gesellschaft Lehndorff GmbH & Cie., Hamburg; dir. Christiana Gen. Ins. Corp., Société d'Investissement et de Gestion, Paris, Sandoz Inc., Sandoz U.S., Inc., DESCO Holding AG, Zurich, Girard Perregaux Corp., N.Y., Kleinwort Benson Internat. Fund, Volkart Bros. Holding AG, Winterthur; mem. adv. bd. Lehndorff Properties (USA) Ltd. Mem. Am.-Swiss Assn., Am. Council on Germany (dir.), Internat. C. of C. (trustee U.S. council), Council on Fgn. Relations. Home: Matthiessen Park Irvington-on-Hudson NY 10533 Office: 59 Wall St New York NY 10005

HOCH, FREDERIC LOUIS, med. educator; b. Vienna, Austria, Apr. 14, 1920; came to U.S., 1922, naturalized, 1928; s. Samuel and Dore (Glinert) H.; m. Martha Louise Ludwig, Apr. 8, 1961. B.S., CCNY, 1939; M.D., N.Y. U., 1943; M.S., M.I.T., 1951. Intern Michael Reese Hosp., Chgo., 1943; resident in pathology Tufts Med. Sch., Boston, 1947; research asso. in biology M.I.T., 1948-51; research fellow in biochemistry Mass. Gen. Hosp., Boston, 1951-53; research asso., asst. prof. medicine Harvard Med. Sch., Boston, 1953-66; jr. asso., sr. asso. medicine Peter Brent Brigham Hosp., Boston, 1953-66; asso. prof. internal medicine and biol. chemistry U. Mich. Med. Sch., Ann Arbor, 1967-77, prof. internal medicine and biol. chemistry, 1977—. Author: Energy Transformations in Mammals: Regulatory Mechanisms, 1971. Served to capt. M.C. U.S. Army, 1944-46. Fellow Baruch Found., 1948, NIH, 1949-51, Jane Coffin Childs Found., 1951-53, Howard Hughes Med. Inst., 1954. Mem. AAAS, Am. Chem. Soc., Biochem. Soc. (London), Am. Soc. Biol. Chemistry, Am. Thyroid Assn., Endocrine Soc., Central Soc. Clin. Research, Mich. State Med. Soc., Phi Beta Kappa, Sigma Xi. Office: 7696 Kresge Med Bldg U Mich Med Sch Ann Arbor MI 48109

HOCH, GEORGE EDWARD, biologist, educator; b. Brookings, S.D., Mar. 11, 1931; s. Alfred A. and Rose Mary (Sullivan) H.; m. Kathleen Ann McCullough, Apr. 9, 1953; children—Gregory, Marie, Lambert, Ellen, James, Ann, Kathryn, George. B.S. in Chemistry, S.D. State U., 1952; Ph.D. in Biochemistry, U. Wis., 1958. Scientist Research Inst. for Advanced Studies, Balt., 1958-64; vis. asso. prof. biophysics Johnson Research Found., U. Pa., 1964-65; asso. prof. biology U. Rochester, N.Y., 1965-70, prof., 1970—, chmn. dept., 1978—; vis. research biologist U. Calif., San Diego, 1979; sr. fellow Carnegie Inst., Washington, 1980. Served with U.S. Army, 1954-55. Office: Dept Biology U Rochester Rochester NY 14627

HOCH, ORION LINDEL, corporate executive; b. Canonsburg, Pa., Dec. 21, 1928; s. Orion L.F. and Ann Marie (McNulty) H.; m. Jane Lee Ogan, June 12, 1952 (dec. 1978); children: Andrea, Brenda, John; m. Catherine Nan Richardson, Sept. 12, 1980; 1 son, Joe. B.S., Carnegie Mellon U., 1952; M.S., UCLA, 1954; Ph.D., Stanford U., 1957. With Hughes Aircraft Co., Culver City, Calif., 1952-54, Stanford Electronics Labs., 1954-57; sr. engr., dept. mgr., div. v.p., div. pres. (Litton Electron Tube div.), San Carlos, Calif., 1957-68, group exec., 1968-70; v.p. Litton Industries, Inc., Beverly Hills, Calif., 1970, sr. v.p., 1971-74; pres. Intersil, Inc., Cupertino, Calif., 1974-82, Litton Industries, Inc., Beverly Hills, 1982—; dir. Priam Corp., Mesurex Corp., Maxim Integrated Products. Served with AUS, 1946-48. Mem. IEEE, Am. Electronics Assn. (bd. dirs.), Sigma Xi, Tau Beta Pi, Phi Kappa Phi. Home: 707 N Palm Dr Beverly Hills CA 90210 Office: 360 N Crescent Dr Beverly Hills CA 90210

HOCHBAUM, GODFREY MARTIN, behavioral scientist, educator; b. Vienna, Austria, Nov. 19, 1916; came to U.S., 1938, naturalized, 1942; m. Jean Fent, Nov. 14, 1942. B.A. in Psychology, Am. U., 1947, M.A., George Washington U., 1949; Ph.D. in Psychology and Sociology, U. Minn., 1953. Research psychologist, asst. chief behavioral sci. sect., chief sect. USPHS, 1952-67, dep. dir. social and econ. analysis div., 1967-68; dir. Office Internat. Health Research, Nat. Center Health Services Research and Devel., 1968-72; prof. dept. health edn. Sch. Public Health, U. N.C., Chapel Hill, 1972—; cons. WHO, Pan Am. Health Orgn., Am. Lung Assn., Nat. Cancer Inst., Nat. Heart and Lung Inst.; Bur. Health (Center for Disease Control, USPHS), Nat. Center for Health Services Research (USPHS), Nat. Center Health Edn., VA. Editorial reviewer: Public Health Reports, Chronic Diseases; editorial bd.: Brit. Jour. Health Edn, Health Edn. Quar.; author: Health Behavior, 1970; contbr. chpts. to books, articles to profl. jours. Served with Armed Forces, 1941-45. Recipient Nat. Honor award Eta Sigma Gamma., Mayhew Derryberry award Delta Omega Soc. Fellow Am. Public Health Assn.; mem. Am. Psychol. Assn., Soc. Public Health Educators, AAAS, Internat. Union Health Edn., Am. Sch. Health Assn., Assn. for Advancement Health Edn. Home: 306 Azalea Dr Chapel Hill NC 27514

HOCHBERG, BAYARD ZABDIAL, lawyer; b. N.Y.C., May 16, 1932; s. Abraham and Sonia (Pincus) H.; m. Arlene Beethoven, Feb. 15, 1953; children: Ronny Mark, Randy Jean, Elizabeth Joyce. B.A., City Coll. N.Y., 1953; LL.B., J.D., U. Va., 1958. Bar: Md. 1958, Va. 1958. Law bailiff to Hon. Joseph Allen, Supreme Bench of Balt., 1958-59; asso. law office Paul Berman, Esq., Balt., 1959-68; ptnr. Levin, Hochberg & Chiarello, Balt., 1968-82; sr. ptnr. Hochberg, Chiarello, Costello & Dowell, Balt., 1983—. Mem. editorial bd.: Va. Law Rev, 1956-58. Served to maj. U.S. Army Res., 1953-75. Fellow Am. Coll. Trial Lawyers; mem. ABA (Md. del. standing com. on state legis. 1970-73, tort and ins. practice sect. 1979—), Md. Bar Assn. (chmn. ins., negligence and workmens compensation sect. 1973, exec. bd., state-city medicolegal com. 1979—, chmn. 1983—), Balt. Bar Assn. (chmn. legis. com. 1968-69, bd. govs. 1969-70, mem. jud. adminstrn. com. 1980—), Md. Trial Lawyers Assn. (bd. govs. 1970-76, co-chmn. com. on legis. 1970-72, v.p. Balt. 1975, Amicus brief com. 1979—), Order of Coif. Home: 710 Cliveden Rd Baltimore MD 21208 Office: 330 N Charles St Suite 204 Baltimore MD 21201

HOCHBERG, JOEL MORTON, advertising agency executive; b. N.Y.C., Feb. 20, 1939; s. Aaron and Laura (Cohen) H.; m. Barbara Jaslow, Dec. 25, 1966; 1 dau., Lauren Shelby. B.S., N.Y. U., 1960, M.A., 1962. Copywriter Leo Burnett Co., Chgo., 1964-65, creative dir., v.p., 1967-76; copy supr. Grey Advt., N.Y.C., 1965-67; exec. v.p., dir. creative services Needham, Harper & Steers, Inc., Chgo., 1976—; mem. bd. Film Center of Art Inst. Chgo.; sustaining fellow Art Inst. Chgo. Pres. Chgo. Sinfonietta, 1980—; bd. dirs. Orch. of Ill.; governing bd. Cinema Chgo. Recipient 1st prize N.Y.C. Cancer Com. Script Writing Contest, 1956, Clio award Am. Commls. Festival, 1970, 76, 78, 79, Gold Lion award Internat. TV Festival, 1970; named to Advt. Hall of Fame. Mem. Chgo. Art Inst., Chgo. Symphony Soc., Shedd Aquarium. Home: 20 E Cedar St Chicago IL 60611 Office: 303 E Wacker Dr Chicago IL 60601 *Two essential qualities for success in life: Be yourself and don't lose your sense of humor.*

HOCHBERG, JULIAN, psychologist; b. July 10, 1923; s. Edward and Dora (Weiner) H.; m. Virginia Loring Brooks, July 1, 1955; children—Joanne Deborah Susan, Jonathan Andrew, Jennifer Ellen. B.S. in Physics, CCNY, 1945; M.A., U. Calif., Berkeley, 1947, Ph.D. in Psychology, 1949. Mem. faculty Cornell U., Ithaca, N.Y., 1949-65, N.Y. U., N.Y.C., 1965-69; prof. psychology Columbia U., N.Y.C., 1969—. Guggenheim fellow, 1967-68. Fellow Am. Psychol. Assn. (Disting. Sci. Contbn. award 1978), Nat. Acad. Sci. Home: 460 Riverside Dr New York NY 10027 Office: 406 Schermerhorn Columbia U New York NY 10027

HOCHBERG, MELVIN, pharmaceutical company executive; b. N.Y.C., Feb. 12, 1920; s. Max and Sarah (Deutsch) H.; m. Ruth Kahn, June 14, 1945; children: Phyllis Ann, Mitchell Alan. B.S., CCNY, 1940; M.A., Columbia U., 1943; Ph.D., NYU, 1949. Prin. research chemist Food & Drug Research Lab., Long Island City, N.Y., 1940-46; v.p., dir. Nopco Chem. Co., Harrison, N.J., 1947-67; v.p. Diamond Shamrock, Cleve., 1967-70; pres. Rachelle Labs., Long Beach, Calif., 1970—. Contbr. numerous articles to profl. jours. Fellow Am. Inst. Chemists; mem. AAAS, N.Y. Acad. Sci., Am. Chem. Soc., Sigma Xi, Phi Beta Kappa, Phi Lambda Epsilon. Home: 30035 Avenida Elegante Rancho Palos Verdes CA 90274 Office: Rachelle Labs Inc 700 Henry Ford Ave Long Beach CA 90801

HOCHBERGER, SIMON, educator; b. York, Pa., Aug. 29, 1912; s. Charles Michael and Lena (Freireich) H.; m. Bella Hirschfield, Dec. 26, 1937; 1 son, Charles Michael. B.Jour. (Eugene Field scholar), U. Mo., 1933, M.A., 1935. Engaged in publicity and pub. relations, 1933-34, 35-37; mem. faculty U. Miami, Fla., 1937—, prof. journalism, chmn. dept., 1947-66, prof. mass communications, chmn. dept., 1966-72, prof. communications, 1972-78, emeritus, 1978—; vis. prof. U. Nev., Reno, 1962, 69, 71-72, 73, 74; asso. editor Fla. Tchr. mag., 1937-42; book reviewer Miami News, 1939-40, 48-51; editorial adviser, manuscript editor Glade House Book Pubs., Miami, 1942-45; copy editor, Sunday mag. writer, editorial writer Nashville Tennessean, 1946-47, 53; asso. editor, drama reviewer Playtime mag., Miami, 1957, Beachcomber mag., 1957-59; v.p. Beachcomber Pub. Co., Inc., Miami, 1957- 59; mem. editorial bd. Journalism Educator, 1958-65; editorial cons., 1940—. Editor: (with Lambert Greenawalt) The Student's Macbeth, 1954, 2d edit., 1959; Author articles and revs.; editor and or editorial cons. Mem. pub. information com. Heart Assn. Greater Miami, 1967-71; editorial cons. Dade County (Fla.) Bd. Pub. Instrn., 1970-71. Recipient Gold Key award Columbia Scholastic Press Assn., 1949. Mem. Am. Soc. Journalism Sch. Adminstrs. (sec.-treas. 1962-65, chmn. internat. relations com.), Assn. Edn. Journalism (nat. dep. sec.-treas. 1962-65), Mo. Hist. Soc. (life), AAUP, Inter-Am. Press Assn. (asso.), Am. Acad. Polit. and Social Sci., Phi Kappa Phi (pres. U. Miami chpt. 1961-62), Iron Arrow, Omicron Delta Kappa, Kappa Tau Alpha (mem. nat. council 1958-78, nat. sec. 1968-70), Soc. Profl. Journalists, Sigma Delta Chi (life). Clubs: Univ. Miami Faculty (v.p. 1959-61, bd. dirs. 1959-63. Home: 5329 Granada Blvd Coral Gables FL 33146

HOCHE, PHILIP ANTHONY, life insurance company executive; b. Cape Girardeau, Mo., Jan. 29, 1906; s. Philip Aloysius and Mary Edith (Meyers) H.; m. Angela Genevieve Hayes, Jan. 2, 1941; children—A. Henry, John Philip. B.A., Southeast Mo. State U., 1926. Sales rep. Sherwin-Williams Co., Chgo., 1926-31; asst. ednl. dir. New Eng. Mut. Life Ins. Co., Chgo., 1932-39; gen. agt. Kansas City Life Ins. Co., Bloomington, Ill., 1940-43, Orlando, Fla., 1946—; Mem. ins. bd., Winter Park, Fla., 1965-76, chmn., 1973-76, mem. ins. bd., Orlando, Fla., 1976-81; trustee Life Underwriters Tng. Council, 1956-59, Nat. Assn. Life Underwriters, 1961-63, sec., 1964, v.p., 1965, pres., 1966; also life mem. nat. council; chmn. Fla. Life Underwriters Polit. Action Com., 1970-81. Pres. Orange County (Fla.) Heart Assn., 1963-64; chmn. fund raising adv. com. So. region Am. Heart Assn., 1969, 71; gov.'s ambassador good will for Fla., 1965-66; pres. Central Fla. Estate Planning Council, 1957-58, 68-69; Life mem. bd. dirs. Fla. affiliate Am. Heart Assn., chmn., 1976-77. Served to lt. comdr. USNR, 1943-45. Recipient C.G. Snead Meml. award Fla. Assn. Life Underwriters, 1961. Mem. Am. Soc. C.L.U., Guild Former Pipe Organ Pumpers, Navy League, Am. Mensa Ltd. Clubs: University, Rotary (pres. 1958-59), Rotary (Man of Yr. award 1959), Rotary (sec. 1972-83); Rotary (Winter Park) (Paul Harris fellow). Home: 1431 Temple Dr Winter Park FL 32789 Office: 1320 Lang St PO Box 6606 Orlando FL 32853

HOCHGURTEL, JEROME LEO, banker; b. Racine, Wis., May 3, 1932; s. Leo Sylvester and Helen (Navitzky) H.; m. Peggy Albright, Aug. 24, 1957; children: Julie, Jeanne, Sue Ellen. B.S., Marquette U., 1958. C.P.A., Wis. Sr. accountant Arthur Andersen & Co., Milw., 1958-62; v.p., controller Wauwatosa State Bank, Wis., 1962-70; sr. v.p., controller Marine Nat. Exchange Bank, Milw., 1970-77, sr. v.p. personal banking, 1977-80, sr. v.p. planning, 1980—; v.p. planning Marine Corp., Milw., 1975-77, 80—. Served with AUS, 1951-54. Mem. Am. Inst. C.P.A.s, Wis. Inst. C.P.A.s, Fin. Execs. Inst. (pres. Milw. chpt. 1983-84), Bank Adminstrn. Inst. (pres. Milw. chpt. 1970-71), Beta Gamma Sigma, Beta Alpha Psi.

HOCHMAN, RICHARD HAROLD, investment banking firm executive; b. Bklyn., Oct. 15, 1945; s. Albert A. and Frances G. (Roth) H.; m. Carol J. Schwartz, June 15, 1980. B.A., Johns Hopkins U., 1967; M.B.A., Harvard U., 1969. E. F. Hutton & Co., N.Y.C., 1969—, 1st v.p., 1974-79—; sr. v.p. E. F. Hutton, N.Y.C., 1980—; dir. West Chem. Products, Princeton, N.J., Zebec, Sunnyvale, Calif. Mem. Investment Assn. N.Y., N.Y. Soc. Security Analysts, Fin. Analysts Assn., Phi Beta Kappa. Clubs: Harmonie, India (N.Y.C.). Office: E F Hutton & Co One Battery Park Plaza New York NY 10004

HOCHMANN, JOHN LEONARD, publisher; b. N.Y.C., July 26; s. Benjamin and Ann C. (Beer) H. B.A., Cornell U. Editor Time-Life Books, Time, Inc., N.Y.C., 1962-66; sr. editor Praeger Pubs., N.Y.C., 1966-74; exec. editor Harry N. Abrams, Inc., N.Y.C., 1974-76; pres. John L. Hochmann Books, N.Y.C., 1976—, Artnews Books, 1980—. Trustee Goodspeed Opera House, East Haddam. Conn. Salzburg Seminar fellow, 1958. Mem. Am. P.E.N. Club: Univ. (N.Y.C.). Office: 15 W 37th St New York NY 10018 Office: 122 E 42d St New York NY 10022 *Publishing is a business; literature a happy accident.*

HOCHMUTH, ROBERT MILO, biomed. engr., educator; b. Berkeley, Calif., May 29, 1939; s. Harold Robert and Marjorie Evelyn (Strawn) H.; m. Doris Ann Schwartz, June 5, 1964; 1 dau., Carolyn Ann. B.S., U. Colo., 1961; M.S., Ohio State U., 1962; Ph.D., Brown U., 1967. Mem. faculty dept. chem. engring. Washington U., St. Louis, 1967-78, prof., 1975-78; prof. dept. biomed. engring. Duke U., Durham, N.C., 1978—; cons. Nat. Heart, Lung and Blood Inst. Mem. editorial bd.: Biophysical Jour, 1980—, Critical Revs. in Bioengring, 1977—; contbr. articles to profl. jours. NSF fellow, 1961-62; Brown U. fellow, 1962-63; NIH research career devel. grantee, 1973-78. Mem. Biophys. Soc., Soc. Rheology, Biomed. Engring. Soc., AAAS, Red Cell Club. Research on elastic and viscous properties of red cell membranes, cellular biomechanics. Office: Duke Univ Durham NC 27706

HOCHSCHILD, ADAM MARQUAND, writer, commentator; b. N.Y.C., Oct. 5, 1942; s. Harold K. and Mary (Marqu) H.; m. Arlie Russell, June 26, 1965; children: David, Gabriel. A.B. cum laude, Harvard U., 1963; postgrad., U. Geneva. Reporter San Francisco Chronicle, 1965-66; writer, editor Ramparts mag., 1967-68, 73-74; commentator Nat. Pub. Radio, 1982—; bd. dirs. Nuclear Times mag., 1982—; mem. McGovern Presdl. Nat. Campaign staff, Washington, 1972. Freelance writer nat. mags., 1966—; co-founder, since editor, writer: Mother Jones mag, San Francisco, 1974—; lectr. in field. Bd. dirs. Found. Nat. Progress, 1976—, Campaign for Peace and Democracy East and West; mem. interim nat. com. Citizens Party, 1979-80; mem. Commn. on U.S.-Central Am. Relations. Served with U.S. Army, 1964. Recipient cert. of excellence Overseas Press Club, N.Y.C., 1981. Office: Mother Jones 1663 Mission San Francisco CA 94103

HOCHSTADT, HARRY, mathematician, educator; b. Vienna, Austria, Sept. 7, 1925; s. Samuel and Amalie (Dorn) H.; m. Pearl Schwartzberg, Mar. 29, 1953; children—Julia Phyllis, Jesse Frederick. B.Chem. Engring., Cooper Union, 1949; M.S., N.Y. U., 1950, Ph.D., 1956. Research engr. W. L. Maxson Corp., N.Y.C., 1951-57; mem. faculty Poly. Inst. Bklyn., 1957—, prof. math., 1961—, head dept., 1963—, dean arts and scis., 1974-76, dir. inst. relations, 1976—. Author: Special Functions of Mathematical Physics, 1961, Differential Equations, A Modern Approach, 1964, The Functions of Mathematical Physics, 1971, Integral Equations, 1973; Translation editor: Linear Equations of Mathematical Physics (Mikhlin), 1967; adv. editor: Wiley-Intersci. Series on Pure and Applied Mathematics. Served with inf. AUS, 1943-45. Decorated Bronze Star, Combat Inf. badge. Mem. Am., London math. socs., Math. Assn. Am., Soc. Indsl. and Applied Math. (editor Jour. Applied Math.), Sigma Xi, Tau Beta Pi. Home: 126 Joralemon St Brooklyn NY 11201

HOCHSTADT, JOY, biomedical research scientist, hospital administrator; b. N.Y.C., May 6, 1939; d. Julius Louis and Edith (Tabatchnick) H.; m. Harvey Leon Ozer, Feb. 3, 1960; 1 dau., Juliane Natasha Hochstadt-Ozer. A.B. in Zoology, Barnard Coll., 1960; A.M. in Biologic Scis. (grad. fellow 1961-62), Stanford U., 1963; vis. fellow in tumor biology, Karolinska Inst., Stockholm, 1964-65; research fellow in biol. chemistry, Harvard U., 1965-66; Ph.D. in Microbiology, Georgetown U., 1968; postdoctoral fellow NIH, 1968-70. Instr. biology Coll. San Mateo, Calif., 1962-63; teaching asst. microbiology Georgetown Med. Sch., 1967-68; established investigator Am. Heart Assn.; lab. biochemistry Nat. Heart and Lung Inst., Bethesda, Md., 1970-72; sr. scientist Worcester Found. Exptl. Biology, Shrewsbury, Mass., 1972-76; adj. prof. biochemistry Central New Eng. Coll., Worcester, Mass., 1974-75; vis. prof. membrane research Weizmann Inst. Sci., Rehovot, Israel, 1976; vis. prof. biochemistry and biophysics U. R.I., Kingston, 1976-77; research prof. microbiology N.Y. Med. Coll., Valhalla, 1977-81; dir. Div. Clin. Biochemistry, Cath. Med. Center, Queens, 1981—; chmn. com. to distribute and administer instl. award Am. Cancer Soc., 1973-74; mem. NSF postdoctoral fellowship evaluation panel in biology NRC, 1975—, NATO postdoctoral fellowship evaluation panel, 1978—; mem. cell biology study sect. NIH, 1979—, BIA fellowship com., 1979—. Editorial bd.: Jour. Bacteriology, 1975-80; contbr. research papers, methods articles and monographs to profl. lit. Co-dir. women's project Worcester chpt. Civil Liberties Union Mass., 1974-75; mem. nat. policy com. Profl. Women's Caucus, 1970-73; mem. alumnae council Barnard Coll., 1975—. Recipient Stanford Grad. award, 1963; Cancer Internat. Research Coop. Snell scholar, 1965; predoctoral trainee USPHS, 1966-67; predoctoral fellow USPHS, 1967-68; postdoctoral fellow USPHS, 1968-70; spl. trainee USPHS, 1973; Am. Heart Assn. investigatorship, 1970-75; NIH grantee, 1973—; NSF grantee, 1978—; Travel award to Stockholm, Am. Soc. Biol. Chemists, 1973, to Hamburg, 1976; Travel award to Jerusalem, Am. Soc. Microbiology, 1973. Fellow Am. Acad. Microbiology, Am. Inst. Chemists (profl. opportunities com., legis. com.); mem. Am. Heart Assn. (basic sci. council), Am. Soc. Microbiology (status of women com. 1970-73, sec. physiology div. 1972-74, mem. divisional nominating com. 1973), Am. Soc. Biol. Chemists, Am. Assn. Clin. Chemists, AAAS, Am. Soc. Clin. Research, Am. Chem. Soc., Genetics Soc. Am., Harvey Soc., Am. Assn. Cancer Research, N.Y. Acad. Scis., Fedn. Am. Scientists, Assn. Women in Sci. (affirmative goals and actions com. 1973-75). Discoverer that penicillinase is involved in bacterial cell wall metabolism (differentiation to spore wall in bacillus); elucidator of mechanisms of utilization of several purines and pyrimidines in bacterial and animal cells; developer of first cell-free vesicle system permitting study of nutrient transport across membranes isolated from mammalian cells in culture; identifier transport changes with growth, quiescence and reactivation involve membrane alterations; viral transformation, differentiation, recombinant DNA gene cloning. Home: 300 Central Park W New York NY 10024 also Spur Rd Roaring Brook Lake Putnam Valley NY 10579 Office: Dept Pathology Cath Med Center of Bklyn and Queens Inc 88-25 153d St Queens NY 11432 Office: Cell Genetics Research Lab St Anthony's Hosp 89-15 Woodhaven Blvd Woodhaven NY 11421

HOCHULI, PAUL RICHARD, banker; b. Newark, July 3, 1928; s. Henry W. and Elsie (Kreisel) H.; m. Audrey K. Walker, Aug. 26, 1950; children: Joan Carol, Carolyn Ann, Richard Paul. A.B. in Econs, Union Coll., Schenectady, 1949. With Gen. Electric Co., 1949-67; treas. Popular Mdse. Co., Inc., Passaic, N.J., 1967-69; auditor Seamen's Bank for Savs., N.Y.C., 1969-71, v.p., 1971-75, sr. v.p., 1975—, treas., 1972-81. Presbyterian (trustee 1967-69, elder 1970—). Home: 230 Mulberry Pl Ridgewood NJ 07450 Office: 30 Wall St New York City NY 10005

HOCHWALD, WERNER, educator, economist; b. Berlin, Germany, Jan. 21, 1910; s. Moritz and Elsa (Stahl) H.; m. Hilde Landenberger, Jan. 28, 1938 (dec. June 1958); children: Miriam Ruth, Eve Fay. Student, U. Freiburg, 1928-29; LL.B., U. Berlin, 1933; B.S., Washington U., St. Louis, 1940, A.M., 1942, Ph.D., 1944. Counsel Com. on Aid and Reconstrn., 1933-38; instr. ASTP, 1942-44; instr. to asso. prof. Washington U., St. Louis, 1944-49, prof., 1950—, chmn. dept. econs., 1955-63, Tileston prof. polit. economy, 1958—; Kennedy Disting. prof. econs. U. of the South, 1981; cons. Fed. Res Bank of St. Louis, 1947-58; mem. citizens budget com., St. Louis. Author: Local Impact of Foreign Trade, 1960, An Economist's Image of History, 1968, The Rationality Concept in Economic Analysis, 1971; Contbg. author: Twentieth Century Economic Thought, 1950, Studies in Income and Wealth, 1957, Local Economic Activity and Foreign Trade, 1958, Design of Regional Accounts, 1962, Southern Economic Development, 1964, The Idea of Progress, 1973, Encyclopedia of Economics, 1981. Mem. Am. Econ. Assn., So. Econ. Assn. (pres. 1966-67), Midwest Econ. Assn., Nat. Bur. Econ. Research, Am. Statis. Assn. (nat. council 1950-52), Econometric Soc., Econ. History Assn., Internat. Assn. for Research in Income and Wealth, Phi Beta Kappa (chpt. pres.). Home: 6910 Cornell Ave University City MO 63130 Office: Dept Econs Washington U Saint Louis MO 63130

HOCHWALT, CARROLL ALONZO, research chemist; b. Dayton, Ohio, Apr. 29, 1899; s. Albert Frederick and Adele (Butz) H.; m. Pauline Burkhardt, Sept. 27, 1922; children—Carroll A., Richard, Paula (Mrs. Robert E. Morie). B.Ch.E., U. Dayton, 1920, D.Sc., 1935; D.Sc., Washington U., St. Louis, 1962, St. Louis U., 1964; LL.D. (hon.), Cath. U. Am., 1981. Research chemist Gen. Motors Corp., Dayton, 1920-24; prodn. mgr. Ethyl Gasoline Corp., Dayton, 1924-25; v.p. Thomas & Hochwalt Labs., Dayton, 1926-36; asso. dir. central research dept. Monsanto Chem. Co., St. Louis, 1936-45, dir., 1945-48, coordinator research, devel. and engring., v.p., 1947-64, dir., 1949-64; pres. Chemstrand Corp., 1949-50, dir., 1949-64, St. Louis Regional Commerce and Growth Assn., 1964-74; chmn. mgmt. com. Argus Chem. Corp. subs. Witco Chem. Co., Inc., N.Y.C., 1964-74; dir. Nat. Computer Service, Inc., Petrolite Corp., both St. Louis; cons. to policy com. Mallinckrodt Chem. Works, St. Louis, 1969-77; mem. tech. adv. com. Mallinckrodt Inc., St. Louis, 1981—; mem. Manhattan Project on atomic bomb research; also mem. Div. 8., NDRC, World War II; mem. ordnance adv. com. research and devel. div. Dept. Army; ofcl. witness Operation Crossroads, Bikini Atoll, 1946; mem. Gov.'s adv. com. Mo. State Tech. Services Program, 1966-70, Greater St. Louis Arts and Edn. Council, 1963-69. Mem. lay bd. trustees St. Louis U., chmn., 1963-66, mem. pres.'s council, 1957—; trustee Cath. U. Am., chmn. bd. trustees, 1968-70, U. Dayton, 1955-73, Charles F. Kettering Found., 1948-73; mem. Am. sponsors com. Am. Coll. in Paris, France, Cath. Commn. Intellectual and Cultural Affairs, 1952—; adv. bd. Internat. Inst., 1964—. Recipient Midwest award Am. Chem. Soc., 1956; Brotherhood citation NCCJ, 1969; Cardinal Gibbons award Cath. U. Am., 1970; Am. Sect. medal Soc. Chem. Industry, 1971. Mem. Am. Chem. Soc., Soc. Chem. Industry, Electrochem. Soc., Am. Inst. Chem. Engrs., AAAS, Am. Phys. Soc., Am. Ordnance Assn., Sigma Xi, Tau Beta Pi. Clubs: St. Louis, Bogey. Home: 7 Upper Ladue Rd Saint Louis MO 63124

HOCK, DEE WARD, credit card company executive; b. Utah. Hod carrier, 1949-51, various jobs, 1951-65; mgr. bank card program, com. chmn. bank card program Rainier Bank, Seattle, from 1965; now pres., chief exec. officer Visa Internat., Visa U.S.A., San Francisco. Office: Visa Internat 101 California St San Francisco CA 94111 *

HOCK, NICHOLAS GEORGE, magazine publisher; b. Vienna, Austria, June 8, 1917; came to U.S., 1939, naturalized, 1943; s. Oskar and Katherina (Popovic) H.; m. Doris Moore, Oct. 31, 1945; children—Elizabeth R., Karin M., Meredith P., George A., Christopher C., James R. Student, Alliance Francaise, Paris, 1937. With Saks Fifth Ave., N.Y.C., 1940-41, 46-47, A. de Pinna Co., 1947-48; pubs. rep. A.M. Willcox & Assos., N.Y.C., 1948-50; advt. mgr. Sports Age mag., 1950-57; dist. mgr. Rock Products mag., N.Y.C., 1957-60; advt. dir. Ski mag., asso. pub. Ski Business mag., N.Y.C., 1960-64; asso. pub., advt. dir. Skiing mag., 1964-69; dir. advt. and sales promotion Lange Co., Broomfield, Colo., 1969-72; v.p. new bus. Henderson-Bucknum Advt., Denver, 1972-73; pub. Guide to Cross Country Skiing, Ski Bus. mag., Times-Mirror Mags., Inc., N.Y.C., 1973-82, Ski mag., 1973-77; also v.p. Cross Country Ski mag., Ski Bus. mag., 1977-82; pres., pub. Ski Bus., Darien, Conn., 1982—. Served to 2d lt. AUS, 1941-45. Republican. Lutheran.

HOCKADAY, IRVINE O., JR., greeting card company executive; b. Ludington, Mich., Aug. 12, 1936; s. Irvine Oty and Helen (McCune) H.; m. Mary Ellen Jurden, July 8, 1961; children: Wendy Helen, Laura DuVal. A.B., Princeton U., 1958; LL.B., U. Mich., 1961, J.D., 1961. Bar: Mo. bar 1961. Atty. firm Lathrop, Righter, Gordon & Parker, Kansas City, 1961-67; atty., asst. gen. counsel, asst. to pres., v.p. Kansas City So. Industries, Inc., 1968-72, pres., chief ops. officer, 1972-81, pres., chief exec. officer, 1981-83; also dir., mem. exec. com.; chmn. exec. com., dir. Kansas City So. Ry. Co., chmn. bd., 1981-83; mem. exec. com., dir. Hallmark Cards, Inc., exec. v.p., mem. Office of Chmn., 1983—; dir. Lincoln Nat. Corp., Lincoln Nat. Life Ins. Co., United Mo. Bancshares, McNally Pitts. Co. Mem. exec. com. Midwest Research Inst.; trustee Menninger Found., Topeka. Clubs: Kansas City, Kansas City Country. Office: Hallmark Cards Inc 2501 MCGEE TRAFFICWAY Kansas City MO 64141

HOCKEIMER, HENRY ERIC, aerospace company executive; b. Winzig, Germany, Apr. 3, 1920; came to U.S., 1946, naturalized, 1951; s. Erich and Gertrude (Masur) H.; m. Margaret Feeny, May 26, 1956; children: Ellen Patricia, Henry Eric. Student, RCA Insts., 1946-47; electronics and bus. mgmt., N.Y.U., 1948-51. With Philco-Ford Corp., Phila., 1947—, gen. mgr. communications and tech. services div., 1962-63, corp. v.p., 1963-72, v.p., gen. mgr. refrigeration products div., Connorsville, Ind., 1972-75; pres. Ford Aerospace & Communications Corp., Dearborn, Mich., 1975—; v.p. Ford Motor Co., 1981—. Mem. Pres.'s Nat. Security Telecommunications Adv. Com.; Bd. dirs. Nat. Sci. Ctr. for Communications and Electronics Found., Inc., Detroit Symphony, Hampton Inst.; mem. adv. council Miami of Ohio U. Mem. Franklin Inst., Nat. Security Indsl. Assn., Am. Def. Preparedness Assn., Assn. U.S. Army, Air Force Assn., Navy League U.S., Am. Mgmt. Assn., Engring. Soc. Detroit, Armed Forces Communications and Electronics Assn., Electronic Industries Assn. Clubs: Renaissance, Fairlane, Detroit Econ., Nat. Space. Home: 50 Harlan Dr Bloomfield Hills MI 48013 Office: 300 Renaissance Center PO Box 43342 Detroit MI 48243

HOCKENBROCHT, DAVID WILLIAM, mfg. and oil co. exec.; b. Williamsport, Pa., Mar. 17, 1935; s. William Robert and May Elizabeth (Dietrick) H.; m. Joan Carol Ferguson, Aug. 4, 1956; children—Robin Gaye, Douglas David. B.S., Allegheny Coll., 1957; M.B.A., Western Res. U., 1965. Gen. mgr. subs. Standard Oil Co. of Ohio, Cleve., 1957-68; v.p. mktg. Curtis-Noll Corp., Cleve., 1968-71; pres. Auto & Acro Inc., Cin., 1971-73; dir. corp. acquisitions Firestone Tire & Rubber Co., Akron, Ohio, 1973-78; pres., chief operating officer, dir. Sparton Corp., Jackson, Mich., 1978—, also dir. Served to capt. USAF, 1958-60. Republican. Mem. Free Methodist Ch. Office: 2400 E Ganson St Jackson MI 49202

HOCKIN, ALAN B., bank executive. Exec. v.p. investments Toronto Dominion Bank, Ont., Can. Office: Toronto-Dominion Centre Toronto ON Canada M5K 1A2§

HOCKING, JAMES ROBERT, investment company executive; b. Chgo., Oct. 20, 1929; s. Frank and Zada (Bone) H.; m. Jane Hasselman, Dec. 19, 1954; children: Scott Pearce, Leslie Beth, Jennifer Ann, Rachel Elizabeth, Douglas Wyatt. B.S., U.S. Naval Acad., 1953; M.B.A., U. Chgo., 1964. Chartered fin. analyst. Mem. trust adminstrn. and ops. dept. Continental Ill. Nat. Bank, Chgo., 1960-70, v.p., dir. investment research, 1970-72; v.p. John Hancock Mut. Life Ins. Co., Boston, 1972-76, sr. v.p., 1976-80; chmn. Schroder Capital Mgmt. Inc., N.Y.C., 1980—; exec. v.p. J. Henry Schroder Bank & Trust Co.; chmn., dir. Cheapside Dollar Fund; pres., dir. Naess & Thomas Spl. Fund; dir. London Am. Energy Investments Ltd. Vestryman Parish of Trinity Ch. in City of N.Y. Served with USN, 1953-59. Mem. Fin. Analysts Fedn., N.Y. Soc. Analysts. Clubs: University (Boston); Weston Golf, Racquet and Tennis. Home: 430 E 84th St New York NY 10028 Office: One State St New York NY 10004

HOCKING, JOHN GILBERT, mathematics educator; b. Caspian, Mich., Sept. 26, 1920; s. John Pearce and Ethel (Faragher) H.; m. Virginia Marilynn Yinger, Mar. 6, 1944; children: Claudia Megan, John Chadwick, Judith Wendell, Nancy Reid (Mrs. Ara Y. Nigogossian). B.S. with distinction, U. Mich., 1946, M.S., 1948, Ph.D., 1953. Mem. faculty dept. math. Mich. State U., East Lansing, 1951—, prof., 1964—; vis. lectr. U. B.C., Vancouver, Can., 1956; Fulbright guest lectr. U. Tubingen, Germany, 1962-63; vis. prof. Westfield Coll., U. London, Eng., 1970-71, Univ. Coll., Dublin, Ireland, 1977-78, East China Normal U., Shanghai, 1981. Author: (with G.S. Young) Topology, 1961, Calculus, 1970; Editor conf. proc.: Topology of Manifolds, 1969. Served with USAAF, World War II; CBI. Mem. Am. Math. Soc., Math. Assn. Am., Phi Beta Kappa, Sigma Xi. Home: 4205 Meridian Rd Okemos MI 48864 Office: Math Dept Mich State U East Lansing MI 48824

HOCKNEY, DAVID, artist; b. Bradford, Yorkshire, Eng., July 9, 1937; s. Kenneth and Laura H. Attended, Bradford Coll. Art, 1953-57, Royal Coll. Art, 1959-62. Lectr. U. Iowa, 1964, U. Colo., 1965, U. Calif. Berkeley, 1967, UCLA, 1966, hon. chair of drawing, 1980. Exhibited in one-man shows, Kasmin Gallery, 1963, Mus. Modern Art, N.Y.C., 1964, 68, Stedelijk Mus., Amsterdam, Netherlands, 1966, Andre Emmerich Gallery, N.Y.C., 1972, Musee des Arts Decoratifs, Paris, 1974, Mus. Gerona, Spain, 1976, Goteborg (Sweden) Mus., Gulbenkian Found., Lisbon, Spain, 1977; designer: Rake's Progress, Glyndebourne, Eng., 1975; sets for Magic Flute, Glyndebourne, 1978, Met. Opera House, 1979; Author: David Hockney by David Hockney, 1976, David Hockney: Travels with Pen, Pencil and Ink, 1978, Paper Pools, 1980, David Hockney Photographs, 1982; illustrator: Six Fairy Tales of the Brothers Grimm, 1969. Recipient Guinness award and 1st prize for etching, 1961, Gold medal Royal Coll. Art, 1962, Graphic prize Paris Biennale, 1963, 1st prize 8th Internat. Exhbn. Drawings, Lugano, Italy, 1964, 1st prize John Moores Exhbn., Liverpool, Eng., 1967. Office: Knoedler Gallery 143 New Bond St London W 1 England *

HOCOTT, CLAUDE RICHARD, petroleum engineer, educator; b. Excelsior, Ark., Nov. 16, 1909; s. James Richard and Leona (Griffin) H.; m. Edna Rae Gunn, June 7, 1937; children: Elaine, Gail. A.A., Pan Am. U.; B.S., U. Tex., 1933, M.S., 1934, Ph.D., 1937. Instr. U. Tex., Austin, 1934-37, prof. engring., 1974-79, prof. emeritus, 1979—; research engr. Humble Oil & Refining Co., 1937-64; v.p. Esso Prodn. Research Co., 1964-70; exec. v.p. Exxon Prodn. Research Co., 1970-74. Mem. Soc. Petroleum Engrs., Am. Inst. Chem. Engrs., Am. Assn. Petroleum Geologists. Home: 4538 Ivanhoe St Houston TX 77027 Office: Dept Petroleum Engring U Tex Austin TX 78712

HOCUTT, MAX OLIVER, educator; b. Berry, Ala., July 3, 1936; s. Harry Juell and Edith Pauline (Skelton) H.; m. Dorothy Lois Etheredge, Nov. 22, 1957; children—James Max, Cassandra Diane. B.A. with honors in philosophy (honors scholar), Tulane U., 1957, M.A., 1958; Ph.D. (So. Fellowships Career Teaching fellow), Yale, 1960. Instr. U. South Fla., Tampa, 1960-62, asst. prof., chmn. dept. philosophy, 1962-65; asso. prof. U. Ala., 1965-70, prof., 1970—, chmn. dept., 1978—; vis. fellow Princeton U., 1979; Bd. dirs. ACLU, University, 1969. Author: The Elements of Logical Analysis and Inference, 1979, First Philosophy, 1980; contbr. articles to profl. jours. Mem. Ala. Philos. Soc. (pres. 1967), So. Soc. Philosophy and Psychology, Am. Philos. Assn., Phi Beta Kappa. Home: 1231 Northwood Lake Northport AL 35476 Office: Dept Philosophy University AL 35486

HODAPP, LEROY CHARLES, bishop; b. Seymour, Ind., Nov. 11, 1923; s. Linden Charles and Mary Marguerite (Miller) H.; m. Polly Anne Martin, June 12, 1947; children: Anne Lynn Hodapp Gates, Nancy Ellen Hodapp Wichman. A.B., U. Evansville, Ind., 1944, D.D., 1961; B.D., Drew Theol. Sem., Madison, N.J., 1947; L.H.D., Ill. Wesleyan U., 1977; D.D., McKendree Coll., 1978, Wiley Coll., 1980. Ordained to ministry Methodist Ch., 1947; pastor chs. in Ind., 1947-65; supt. Bloomington (Ind.) Dist. Meth. Ch., 1965-67, supt. Indpls. West Dist., 1967-68, supt. Indpls. N.E. Dist., 1968-70; dir. S. Ind. Conf. Council, 1970-76; bishop Ill. area United Meth. Ch., Springfield, 1976—; pres. United Meth. Gen. Bd. Ch. and Soc., 1980—. Co-editor: Change in the Small Community, 1967. Democrat. Home: 90 Pebble Beach Dr Springfield IL 62704 Office: 501 E Capitol Ave Springfield IL 62701

HODDER, WILLIAM ALAN, fabricated metal products co. exec.; b. Lincoln, Nebr., May 6, 1931; s. Ernest Chesley and Velma Catherine (Warren) H.; m. Suzanne Holmes, Apr. 3, 1954; children: Kent, Laurie, Susan, Mark, Beth. B.A., U. Nebr., 1954; grad., Programs and Mgmt. Devel. Program, Harvard, 1961. Mktg. positions IBM Corp., 1954-66; v.p. orgn. planning and devel. Dayton Co., Mpls., 1966-68; sr. v.p. Dayton Hudson Corp., 1970-73, dir., 1971-73; pres. Target Stores, 1968-73; pres., dir. Donaldson Co., Inc., Mpls., 1973—, chief exec. officer, 1982—; dir. Norwest Corp., Sci. Computers, Inc., Tennant Co., Northwestern Nat. Life Ins. Co.; mem. Minn. Project on Corp. Responsibility. Trustee Mpls. Soc. Fine Arts, Macalester Coll.; bd. overseers Coll. Bus. Adminstrn., U. Minn. Served with AUS, 1954-56. Mem. Young Pres. Orgn., Chief Execs. Orgn., Inc., Soc. Automotive Engrs., Harvard Bus. Sch., Club Minn. (dir., past pres.). Clubs: Minneapolis, Minikahda. Home: 11 Circle West Edina MN 55436 Office: 1400 W 94th St PO Box 1299 Minneapolis MN 55440

HODDY, GEORGE WARREN, industrialist; b. Columbus, Ohio, Mar. 7, 1905; s. Arthur H. and Mary E. (Lutz) H.; m. Lois L. Mitchell, May 30, 1947; children: John, Peter, Matthew, Elizabeth Hoddy Howe, Rebekah Hoddy Patton, Melissa, Hoddy Teachworth. B.E.E., Ohio State U., 1926, E.E., 1932; Ph.D. in Modern Industry (hon.), Sunshine U., Pinellas County, Fla., 1968. Elec. engr. Day-Fan Electric Co., Dayton, Ohio, 1926-29, Robbins & Myers, Inc., Springfield, Ohio, 1929-31; chief engr. Pioneer div. Master Electric Co., Dayton, 1932-34; v.p., gen. mgr. Redmond Co., Inc., Owosso, Mich., 1934-43; pres., gen. mgr., chief exec. officer Universal Electric Co., Owosso, 1942-71, chmn. bd., dir. internat. relations, 1971-79, vice chmn., 1979—; chmn., dir. Am. Universal Electric (India), Ltd., New Delhi, 1962—; vice chmn., dir. Intertherm, Inc., 1972-80, chmn., 1980—, Universal Electric Ltd., Gainsborough, Eng., 1974—, Universal Electric Export, 1973—; pres. Fiji Marina, Los Angeles, 1968-76; pres., dir. Ventrola Mfg. Co., Owosso, 1968-76. Mem. Owosso Public Sch. Bd., 1957-76, pres., 1975-76; bd. dirs. Shiawassee United Way, 1956-59; bd. dirs., pres. Shiwassee Found., 1973-77; bd. dirs. Shiawassee County Mental Health Bd., 1963-67, Owosso Community Concert Assn., 1946-53, United Cerebral Palsy Assn., 1963-65, Mich. Accident Fund, 1945-61; mem. Owosso Charter Revision Commn., 1956-57, Owosso Citizens Com. Juvenile Delinquency, 1967; chmn. Shiwassee County chpt. U.S. Savs. Bonds, 1971-80; trustee Meml. Hosp., Owosso, 1948—, pres., 1954-58; trustee Flint Osteo. Hosp., 1958—; trustee, chmn. exec. com. John Wesley Coll., Owosso, 1980-81. Recipient Silver Beaver award Tall Pine council Boy Scouts Am., 1958, Disting. Alumnus award Ohio State U. Coll. Engring., 1970, Alumni Citizenship award Ohio State U., 1975, also other awards. Mem. NAM, U.S. C. of C., Mich. Mfrs. Assn., Owosso Corunna Area C. of C. (dir. 1948-61, adv. bd. 1961-78), Ohio State U. Alumni Assn., Newcomen Soc., Sigma Xi, Tau Beta Pi, Pi Mu Epsilon, Eta Kappa Nu, Lambda Chi Alpha. Republican. Congregationalist. Clubs: Owosso City, Shriners, Masons. Patentee in field. Home: 508 W Williams St Owosso MI 48867 also Lakeside Rd Cedarville MI 49719 Office: 300 E Main St Owosso MI 48867

HODDY, RAYMOND ARTHUR, industrial consultant; b. Corning, Ohio, Aug. 31, 1921; s. Arthur H. and Mary Elizabeth (Lutz) H.; m. Audrey Mae Wing, June 23, 1944; children: George Raymond, Jerry Robert, Mary Elizabeth, Martha Ann. Student in elec. engring., Ohio State U., 1938-41. Design engr. A.G. Redmond Co., Owosso, Mich., 1941-42; mfg. engr. Universal Electric Co., Owosso, 1942-71, pres., 1971-77, also dir.; gen. mgr. Ray-O-Vac. div. ESB Inc., 1974-77; exec. v.p. ESB Inc., Phila., 1977-79, also dir.; indsl. cons., 1979—. Vice chmn. Tall Pine council Boy Scouts Am., 1950-70; chmn. adv. bd. Salvation Army, 1955-70. Recipient Silver Beaver award Boy Scouts Am., 1964, Meritorious citation Salvation Army, 1965. Mem. Tau Beta Pi. Republican. Methodist. Club: Hiawatha Sportsman's. Patentee electric motors. Home and office: PO Box 154 Millecoquins Lake Rd Engadine MI 49827

HODEL, DONALD PAUL, govt. ofcl.; b. Portland, Oreg., May 23, 1935; s. Philip E. and Theresia Rose (Brodt) H.; m. Barbara Beecher Stockman, Dec. 10, 1956; children: Philip Stockman (dec.), David Beecher. B.A., Harvard Coll., 1957; J.D., U. Oreg., 1960. Bar: Oreg. 1960. Treas., Harvard Young Republican Club, 1955-56, pres., 1956-57; precinct organizer Clackamas County Rep. Central Com., Oreg., 1964, sec., 1964-65, chmn., 1965-66, Oreg. Rep. State Central Com., 1966-67; alt. del. Rep. Nat. Conv., 1968; dep. adminstr. Bonneville Power Adminstrn., 1969-72, adminstr., 1972-77; pres. Nat. Elec. Reliability Council, Princeton, N.J., 1978-80, Hodel Assos. Inc., 1978-81; undersec. Dept. Interior, Washington, 1981-82; sec. Dept. Energy, 1982—; atty. Daview, Biggs, Strayer, Stoel & Boley, 1960-63, Ga. Pacific Corp., 1963-69. Mem. Oreg. Bar Assn., Multnomah Bar Assn. Lutheran. Office: Dept of Energy Office of the Sec 1000 Independence Ave SW Washington DC 20585 *

HODES, BERNARD S., advertising agency executive; b. Newark, Dec. 27, 1931; s. Irving H. and Shirley (Baron) Ettenberg; 1 son, Jeffrey; m. Bonnie; stepchildren: Viki, Wendy. Student, NYU, 1954-58. Advt. exec. various agys., N.Y.C., 1954-70; pres. Bernard Hodes Advt., N.Y.C., 1970—; chmn., prin. Galleri Bellman, N.Y.C.; pres. The Maestro restaurant, N.Y.C.; dir. Community Guidance Service, N.Y.C., 1979—. Author: Principles and Practice of Recruitment Advertising: A Guide for Personnel Professionals, 1982. Club: Friars. Office: Bernard Hodes Advt 555 Madison Ave New York NY 10022

HODES, HORACE LOUIS, pediatrician, educator; b. Phila., Dec. 21, 1907; s. Morris and Anna (Jacobson) H.; m. Anne E. Reber, June 10, 1931; children—Ruth Anne, David Samuel. A.B., U. Pa., 1927, M.D., 1931. Intern, asst. resident Children's Hosp., Phila., 1931-33, chief resident, 1934-35; asst. resident pediatrics Johns Hopkins Hosp., 1933-34, dir. pediatric dispensary, 1935-36; asst. pathology and bacteriology Rockefeller Inst. Med. Research, 1936-38; lectr. epidemiology, sch. hygiene Johns Hopkins, 1938-49, asst. prof. pediatrics, 1938-45, asso. prof., 1945-49; dir. Sydenham Hosp., Balt., 1938-49; dir. med. research Balt. Health Dept., 1938-49; dir. pediatrics dept. Mt. Sinai Hosp., N.Y.C., 1949-76; clin. prof. pediatrics Columbia U., 1949-70; prof., chmn. dept. pediatrics Mt. Sinai Med. Sch., 1964-76, Distinguished Service prof., 1976—; Advisory council N.Y. Pub. Health Research Inst.; med. adv. bd. Hebrew U.; Mem. commn. control measles and mumps U.S. Army, 1940-42; cons. sec. of war. Co-author: Common Contagious Diseases, 1956; Editorial bd.: Pediatrics; Contbr. to profl. jours. Served as lt. comdr. USNR, 1942-46; officer charge virus lab.; Guam. Mem. Am. Pediatric Soc. (pres. 1974-75, Howland medal and award 1982), Soc. Pediatric Research (pres. 1951-52), Am. Acad. Pediatrics (Mead-Johnson award 1946), Soc. Explt. Biology and Medicine, N.Y. Acad. Scis., N.Y. Acad. Medicine, Pediatric Travel Club. Home: 41 Sutton Crest Manhasset NY 11030 Office: Mount Sinai Hosp 11 E 100th St New York NY 10029

HODES, LINDA, dance company director; b. N.Y.C.; d. Albert and Lily Margolies; children: Catherine, Martha, Tal. Tchr. Martha Graham Studio, Neighborhood Playhouse, Juilliard Sch., Batsheva Dance Sch., Israel, Rubin Acad. Prin. dancer, Martha Graham Dance Co., N.Y.C., Glen Tetley Dance Co., Paul Taylor Dance Co., Batsheva Dance Co., Israel; now asso. artistic dir., Martha Graham Dance Co., N.Y.C., Martha Graham Sch.; asst. dir.: Dance in Am, Martha Graham Dance Center Prodns. Jewish. Office: 316 E 63d St New York NY 10021

HODES, MARION EDWARD, physician, educator; b. N.Y.C., Aug. 6, 1925; s. Louis and Esterre (Berman) H.; m. Halina Zora Markowicz, Nov. 23, 1949; children: Marquis Z., Zachary I., Jonathan E., Abigail J. Student, Cornell U., 1941-43, U. Rochester, 1943-44; M.D., U. Buffalo, 1947; Ph.D., Columbia, 1955. Intern Jewish Hosp., Bklyn., 1947-48; officer-in-charge dept. physiol. chemistry U.S. Naval Med. Sch., 1951-52; resident Goldwater Meml. Hosp., N.Y.C., 1955-56; faculty Ind. U. Sch. Medicine, Indpls., 1956—, prof. medicine and biochemistry, 1966-72, prof. med. genetics and medicine, 1972—; sr.

Fogarty Internat fellow, Lady Davis vis. prof. Hebrew U., 1977-78; cons. Eli Lily & Co., 1958-62; med. cons. City of Hope Med. Center.; mem. adv. screening com. for sr. Fulbright awards in life scis. Council Internat. Exchange of Scholars, 1981-84. Trustee, mem. exec. counsel of sci. adv. bd. Israel Cancer Research Fund. Served with USNR, 1943-45, 50-52. Eleanor Roosevelt fellow, 1962-63; Guggenheim fellow, 1969-70; Leukemia Soc. scholar, 1961-66. Fellow Ind. Acad. Sci.; mem. AAAS, Am. Assn. Cancer Research, Am. Soc. Biol. Chemists, Am. Assn. Clin. Chemists, Am. Chem. Soc., Am. Soc. Microbiology, Central Soc. for Clin. Research, Am. Soc. Human Genetics, Am. Fedn. Clin. Research, N.Y. Acad. Sci., Sigma Xi. Home: 648 Edgemere Dr Indianapolis IN 46260 Office: 702 Barnhill Dr Indianapolis IN 46223

HODES, SCOTT, lawyer; b. Chgo., Aug. 14, 1937; s. Barnet and Eleanor (Cramer) H.; children—Brian Kenneth, Valery Jane. A.B., U. Chgo., 1956; J.D., U. Mich., 1959; LL.M., Northwestern U., 1962. Bar: Ill. bar 1959, D.C. bar 1962, N.Y. bar 1981. Partner firm Arvey, Hodes, Costello & Burman, Chgo., 1961—; dir. First Investors Life Ins. Co. N.Y., Richardson Electronics, Ltd. Author: The Law of Art and Antiques, 1966, What Every Artist and Collector Should Know About the Law, 1974; Assoc. news editor: Fed. Bar News, 1963-70; co-editor: Conf. Mut. Funds, 1966; Contbr. articles to profl. jours. Chmn. Philippine Exchange Nurses award com., 1966; nat. chmn. Lawbooks U.S.A., 1962-73; co-chmn. Chgo. World Friendship Day, 1967; mem. Ill. Arts Council, 1973-75; Committeeman Ill. 9th Dist. Democratic Com., 1970-82; Bd. dirs. United Cerebral Palsy of Chgo., Michael Reese Hosp. Research Inst., 1965-73, Found. of Fed. Bar Assn., 1970—; governing bd. Chgo. Symphony Soc., 1978—; governing mem. Art Inst. Chgo., 1980—; mem. com. on internat. investment and tech. Dept. State, 1980-83. Served to capt. AUS, 1962-64. Decorated Army Commendation medal; named one of Chicago's ten outstanding young men Jr. Assn. Commerce and Industry, 1968. Mem. ABA, Fed. Bar Assn. (chmn. council financing 1966-71, chmn. younger lawyers div. 1963-64, nat. council 1965—, Distinguished Service award 1971, 75), Ill. Bar Assn., Chgo. Bar Assn., Chgo. Art Inst. (life), Chgo. Hist. Soc. (life), Judge Adv. Gens. Assn. (life), Zeta Beta Tau, Tau Epsilon Rho. Jewish. Clubs: Masons (32 deg.), Standard, Econ. (Chgo.). Home: 1540 Lake Shore Dr Chicago IL 60610 Office: 180 N LaSalle St Chicago IL 60601

HODGDON, HERBERT JAMES, savings and loan executive; b. New Bedford, Mass., Mar. 6, 1924; s. Herbert James and Edna M. (Niles) H.; m. Carol Jane Murphy, Feb. 12, 1944; 1 dau., Janis Elizabeth. Student, Occidental Coll., 1946, U. Cin., 1943-44, Ind. U., 1943. With Security First Nat. Bank Los Angeles, 1946, Bank of Ceres, Calif., 1946-51; with Stanislaus-Merced (Calif.) Savs. and Loan Assn., 1951-63, exec. v.p., 1962-63, Stanislaus-Merced (Calif.) Savs. and Loan Assn. (merged with State Savs. & Loan Assn.), Stockton, Calif., 1963, pres., 1964-70, vice chmn., 1970-72; pres. First Channel Corp., Stockton, 1962-72, Norco Service Co., Los Angeles, 1966-72, Budget Industries, Inc., 1970-72, Budget Finance Plan, 1970-72; pres., dir. Homestead Savs & Loan Assn., San Francisco, 1973-75; exec. v.p., dir. Homestead Financial Corp., San Francisco, 1973-75; sr. v.p. real estate devel. USLIFE Savs. and Loan Assn., Los Angeles, 1975-80; exec. v.p. USLIFE Devel. Corp. of Calif., Los Angeles, 1977-80; v.p., dir. S.H. Bulmer & Assocs., Inc., Sherman Oaks, Calif., 1980-83; pres., chief exec. officer Woodland Savs. Bank, Woodland Hills, Calif., 1983—. Past mem. citizens adv. com. city, Merced; past chmn. Merced County March of Dimes; active local chpts. Am. Cancer Soc., United Givers; charter pres. Stockton Jr. Achievement, 1966, bd. dirs. Western region, 1966-70, also nat. bd. dirs.; Past chmn. Merced County Republican Central Com. Served with inf. AUS, 1942- 45; ETO. Mem. U.S. Savs. and Loan League, Calif. Savs. and Loan League (past dir., vice chmn. govtl. relations com.), Calif. C. of C. (past exec. com. San Joaquin Valley council), Merced C. of C. (past pres.), Stockton C. of C. (past v.p.), Am. Mgmt. Assn., President's Assn., Merced Pilots Assn. (past pres.), Am. Legion. Clubs: Commonwealth (San Francisco); University (Los Angeles); Friars (Beverly Hills). Home: 5501 Round Meadow Rd Hidden Hills CA 91302 Office: 4558 Sherman Oaks Ave Sherman Oaks CA 91403

HODGE, CARLETON TAYLOR, linguist, educator; b. Springfield, Ill., Nov. 27, 1917; s. Clarence Sim and Nina Maude (Eaton) H.; m. Patricia Eileen Sutcliffe, June 2, 1943; children: Philip, Nina, Nicholas, Charles. A.B. (Rector scholar), DePauw U., 1939; postgrad., U. Mich., summers 1939-40; Ph.D. (Harrison fellow), U. Pa., 1943. Instr. Ind. U., 1943-44, prof. linguistics, dir. intensive lang. tng. center, 1964-68, prof. linguistics and anthropology, 1968-83, prof. emeritus, 1983—, acting chmn. dept. linguistics, 1965-66; asso. chmn. Research Center for Lang. Scis. (Ind. U.), 1969-73; instr. U. Pa., 1945-46, Fgn. Service Inst., Washington, 1946-47, asst. prof. linguistics, 1947-49, sci. linguist, 1949-64, asso. prof., 1949-62, head dept. Nr. Eastern and African langs., 1955-62, prof., 1962-64; vis. lectr. Johns Hopkins U., 1950, Am. U., 1962; vis. prof. Brandeis U., 1963-64, U. Mich., 1965, No. Ariz. U., 1968, 69; cons. in field. Author: Outline of Hausa Grammar, 1947, (with Umaru) Hausa Basic Course, 1963, (with Jankovic) Serbocroatian Basic Course, Vol. I, 1965, Vol. II, 1969; editor: Afroasiatic: A Survey, 1971, Papers on the Manding, 1971. Local preacher Methodist Ch., 1938—; pastor Providence charge Alexandria (Va.) Dist., 1947-48. Am. Council Learned Socs. fellow, 1944-46. Mem. Linguistic Soc. Am., Am. Oriental Soc., Soc. Bibl. Lit., Am. Schs. Oriental Research, Egypt Exploration Soc., Am. Research Center in Cairo, Linguistic Soc. India, West African Linguistic Soc., Linguistic Assn. Can. and U.S., Phi Beta Kappa. Home: 3291 S Spring Branch Rd Bloomington IN 47401 Office: Lindley 401 Ind U Bloomington IN 47405

HODGE, EDWIN, JR., manufacturing company executive; b. Henderson, Ky., Aug. 26, 1890; s. Edwin and Frances A. (Ditto) H.; m. Emma L. Clyde, June 10, 1915; children—Mrs. Margaret Dauler, Mrs. Frances Gordon, Mrs. Emma Sarosdy. B.S., Va. Mil. Inst., Lexington, 1910; LL.D., Thiel Coll., 1951, Washington and Jefferson Coll., 1962. Chmn., dir. Neville Chem. Co.; dir. Neville Cindu Chemie N.V., Uithoorn, Holland.; Mem. Greater Pitts. Airport Adv. Com.; Bd. dirs. emeritus Children's Hosp., Pitts.; emeritus mem. exec. com. Thiel Coll.; pres. Am. Ry. Car Inst., 1943-45, Drop Forging Assn., 1942-44. Episcopalian. Clubs: Mason. Clubs: Pitts. Athletic Assn., Duquesne Fox Chapel Golf (Pitts.); Laurel Valley Golf Rolling Rock (Ligonier, Pa.); Port Royal Beach, Hole-in-the-Wall Golf (Naples, Fla.). Home: RD 2 Ligonier PA 15658 Office: 3 Gateway Center 401 Liberty Ave Pittsburgh PA 15222

HODGE, JAMES LEE, educator; b. Harrisburg, Pa., Sept. 18, 1935; s. Earl Henry and Catherine Margaret (Ferber) M.; m. Janice Ellen Dunn, June 21, 1958; children: Geoffrey Lee, Stephen Charles. A.B., Tufts U., 1957; A.M., Pa. State U., 1960, Ph.D., 1961. Grad. asst. Pa. State U., 1957-60; instr. German Bowdoin Coll., Brunswick, Maine, 1961-63, asst. prof., 1963-68, asso. prof., 1968-74, prof., 1974—, George Taylor Files prof. modern langs., 1977, chmn. dept. German, 1974—. Author: Portable German Tutor, 1970; editor: (with Buehue and Pinto) Helen Adolf Festschrift, 1968; mem. editorial staff: German Quar, 1976—; contbr. articles in field to profl. jours. Cubmaster Pine Tree council Boy Scouts Am., Brunswick, 1974. NDEA grantee, 1966-67; Bowdoin Mellon grantee, 1977. Mem. Am. Assn. Tchrs. German, MLA. Republican. Home: 37 Meadowbrook Rd Brunswick ME 04011 Office: Bowdoin Coll Brunswick ME 04011

HODGE, JAMES ROBERT, psychiatrist; b. Martins Ferry, Ohio, Jan. 28, 1927; s. Robert Gabriel and Ethel Melissa (Ashton) H.; m. Marilyn Jane Dinklocker, June 10, 1950; children: Sharon, Scott. B.S., Franklin and Marshall Coll., 1946; M.D., Jefferson Med. Coll., 1950; M.A., U. Akron, 1981. Intern U.S. Naval Hosp., St. Albans, N.Y., 1950-51; resident Menninger Sch. Psychiatry, Topeka, 1951-52, U.S. Naval Hosp., Oceanside, Calif., 1952-53, Univ. Hosps., Cleve., 1954-55; USPHS fellow in adult psychiatry Sch. Medicine Case-Western Res. U., 1955-56; practice medicine specializing in psychiatry, Akron, Ohio, 1956—; head psychiatry Akron City Hosp., 1962-75, cons. staff, 1975-79, chmn. dept. psychiatry, 1979—; adj. prof. psychology U. Akron, 1963—; prof. psychiatry Northeastern Ohio Univs. Coll. Medicine, 1980—; mem. council chiefs psychiatry Northeastern Ohio U. Coll. Medicine, Akron, 1974-76, 79—, dir. psychiat. residency tng. program, 1981-83, chmn. council of psychiatry, 1982—; grad. faculty in psychology Fla. Inst. Tech., 1976-83. Author: Practical Psychiatry for the Primary Physician, 1975, also articles in med. and psychiat. jours.; feature writer: Med. Times mag; producer: movie The Use of Hypnosis in Psychotherapy, 1975. Served to lt. USNR, 1944-45, 50-51, 52-54. Recipient spl. recognition award Ohio Psychiat. Assn., 1976, Meritorious Service award Ohio Psychiat. Assn., 1981. Fellow Am. Psychiat. Assn., Am. Soc. Clin. Hypnosis, Internat. Soc. Clin. and Exptl. Hypnosis, Acad. Psychosomatic Medicine, Am. Coll. Psychiatrists; mem. Am. Psychol. Assn., Ohio Psychiat. Assn. (pres. 1980-81), Central Neuropsychiat. Assn. Home: 295 Pembroke Rd Akron OH 44313 Office: Dept Psychiatry Akron City Hosp 525 E Market St Akron OH 44309 *I try to lead a balanced life of work, play, love and worship. I try to do well and do good, keeping an open mind for new ideas and new experiences which allow me to be both traditional and innovative. When I do that, opportunities arise.*

HODGE, JERRY H., pharmacist, mayor; b. Carnegie, Okla., Sept. 7, 1942; s. Robert H. and Creda Arvona (Ainsworth) H.; m. Ellen Hope Williams, Nov. 16, 1975; 1 dau., Sunny Hope; children by previous marriage—Jerry Heath, Ryan Craig. B.S. in Pharmacy, Southwestern State U., 1965. Owner Maxor Drugs, Amarillo, Tex., 1966—, pres., 1969—, Devil Oil, Inc., 1977—; pres., chief exec. officer Sunn Miss Corp.; dir. Palo Duro Savs. & Loan.; mem. Tex. Bd. Pharmacy; mayor City of Amarillo. Bd. dirs. Amarillo Sr. Citizens Assn., 1975-77, Am. Cancer Soc., 1970-71, Tex. Municipal Retirement System. Recipient Disting. Alumni award S.W. State U., 1979. Mem. Tex. Panhandle Pharm. Assn. (pres. 1973-74), Am. Soc. Cons. Pharmacists, Am. Pharm. Assn., Amarillo Exec. Assn., Amarillo Flag Football Assn. (founder), Golden Spread Tex. Longhorn Breeders Assn. (pres.). Home: 32 Oldham Circle Amarillo TX 79109 Office: 25 Medical Dr Amarillo TX 79106

HODGE, PAUL WILLIAM, astronomer, educator; b. Seattle, Nov. 8, 1934; s. Paul Hartman and Frances (Bakeman) H.; m. Ann Uran, June 14, 1962; children—Gordon, Erik, Sandra. B.S., Yale, 1956; Ph.D., Harvard, 1960. Lectr. Harvard, 1960-61; asst. prof. astronomy U. Calif. at Berkeley, 1961-65; asso. prof. U. Wash., Seattle, 1965-69, prof. astronomy, 1969—; fellow Mt. Wilson, Palomar Obs., Calif. Inst. Tech., Pasadena, 1960-61; physicist Smithsonian Astrophys. Obs., Cambridge, Mass., 1956-74. Author: Solar System Astrophysics, 1964, Galaxies and Cosmology, 1966, The Large Magellanic Cloud, 1967, Concepts of the Universe, 1969, The Revolution in Astronomy, 1970, Galaxies, 1972, Concepts of Contemporary Astronomy, 1974, The Small Magellanic Cloud, 1977, An Atlas of the Andromeda Galaxy, 1981, Interplanetary Dust, 1982. Mem. Am. Astron. Soc., Internat. Astron. Union, Meteoritical Soc., AAAS (pres. sect. D 1978-79, 83-84), Astron. Soc. Pacific (v.p. 1974-75). Office: Dept Astronomy FM-20 U Wash Seattle WA 98195

HODGE, PHILIP GIBSON, JR., mechanical engineering educator; b. New Haven, Nov. 9, 1920; s. Philip Gibson and Muriel (Miller) H.; m. Thea Drell, Jan. 3, 1943; children: Susan E., Philip T., Elizabeth M. A.B., Antioch Coll., 1943; Ph.D., Brown U., 1949. Research asst. Brown U., 1947-49, asso., 1949; asst. prof. math. UCLA, 1949-53; asso. prof. applied mechs. Poly. Inst. Bkly., 1953-56, prof., 1956-57; prof. mechanics Ill. Inst. Tech., 1953-71, U. Minn., Mpls., 1971—; Russell Severance Springer vis. prof. U. Calif., 1976; sec. U.S. Nat. Com./Theoretical and Applied Mechanics, 1982—. Author: 5 books, the most recent being Limit Analysis of Rotationally Symmetric Plates and Shells, 1963, Continuum Mechanics, 1971; research numerous publs. in field, 1949—; tech. editor: Jour. Applied Mechanics, 1971-76. NSF sr. postdoctoral fellow, 1963. Mem. ASME (hon.), Nat. Soc. Profl. Engrs., Nat. Acad. Engring. Mem. Democratic Farm Labor Party. Home: 2962 W River Pkwy Minneapolis MN 55406 Office: 107 Akerman Hall U Minn Minneapolis MN 55455

HODGE, RAYMOND JOSEPH, engring. and archtl. co. exec.; b. N.Y.C., May 15, 1922; s. Christopher George and Lucy Agnes (Madden) H.; m. Lorraine Cecelia Remmert, Aug. 5, 1950; children—Christopher, Susan, Raymond, Patricia. B.C.E., Manhattan Coll., 1944; M.C.E., Cornell U., 1948. With Tippetts-Abbett-McCarthy-Stratton (Cons. Engrs., Architects and Planners), 1953—, partner, Washington, 1968—; asst. prof. Cornell U., 1948-51; pres. Am. Chamber El Salvador, 1963-65. Served to lt. comdr. USNR, 1943-46, 51-53. Recipient Engring. News-Record award for Dallas/Ft. Worth Airport, 1974, Civil Engring. award, 1974. Fellow ASCE, Australian Instn. Engrs., Am. Cons. Engrs. Council; mem. Am. Rd. and Transp. Builders Assn. (pres. planning and design div. 1974), Am. Ins. Mining Engrs., Soc. Am. Mil. Engrs. Roman Catholic. Club: Congressional Country. Home: 10108 Garden Way Potomac MD 20854 Office: 1101 15th St NW Washington DC 20005

HODGE, VERNE ANTONIO, judge; b. St. Thomas, V.I., Nov. 16, 1933; s. John Wesley and Idalia Victoria Stout; m. Maude Almida Hoheb, July 7, 1956; children: Verne Jr., Bridget, Teresa. B.S. magna cum laude, Hampton Inst., 1956; J.D. cum laude, Howard U., 1969. Bar: V.I. 1969, D.C. 1969, U.S. Dist. Ct. (3d cir.) 1970, U.S. Supreme Ct. 1973. Internal auditor, internal revenue agt. V.I. Govt., 1958-61; pub. accountant, comptroller Mannassah Busline, Inc., St. Thomas, 1961-65; bus. mgr., personnel dir. V.I. Dept. Pub. Works, 1965-66; private practice law, V.I., 1969-73, atty. gen., 1973-76; presiding judge Territorial Ct. of V.I., St. Thomas, 1976—; past chmn. Eastern region Nat. Assn. Attys. Gen.; Mem. V.I. Indsl. Incentive Bd., 1963-64, V.I. Bd. Elections, 1964-66. Author: The Need for Constitutional Courts in U.S. Territories, 1968, The Mirror Theory and Its Effects, 1969. Served to 1st lt., inf. U.S. Army, 1956-58. Recipient Am. Jurisprudence awards in state, local and fed. taxation, 1968-69, certificate in advanced income tax law Internal Revenue Service, 1960, award of merit 9th Inf. Div. U.S. Army, 1958. Mem. Am. Judges Assn., Am., Nat., V.I. bar assns. Democrat. Lutheran. Club: Dukes Civic and Social (treas. 1961). Office: Territorial Ct PO Box 70 Saint Thomas VI 00801 *Nothing is so complicated that it cannot be simplified by hard work.* *

HODGELL, MURLIN RAY, univ. dean; b. Mankato, Kans., Jan. 6, 1924; s. Ray Darius and Lora Henrietta (Overman) H.; m. Billie RoJean Seward, July 20, 1947; children—Janet, Kristen, Kevin. B.S., Kans. State U., 1949; M.S., U. Ill., 1952; M.R.P., Cornell U., 1956, Ph.D., 1959. Licensed architect, engr. and planner. Prof. U. Ill., 1950-54, Kans. State U., 1957-63; chmn. dept. city and regional planning Rutgers U., 1963-64; dir. Sch. Architecture, U. Nebr., 1964-69; dean Coll. Environ. Design, U. Okla., 1969—; prin. Hodgell Assos. in Architecture, Engring. and Planning.; City planning dir., Manhattan, Kans., 1957-58, planning commr., 1959-63; dir. Kans. State U. Center Community Devel., 1959-63. Author: Contemporary Farmhouses, 1956, Forgotten Millions, 1959, Zoning, 1957. Trustee Weigal Found., Leonard Bailey Found. Served to lt. (j.g.) USNR, 1943-45. Named Kan. Outstanding Young Man of Yr. Kans. Jr. C. of C., 1959, Man of Yr., Manhattan, Kans., 1960; recipient citation distinguished community service Lane-Bryant Found., 1960. Fellow ASCE; mem. Am. Inst. Planners, AIA, Am. Soc. Planning Ofcls., Assn. Collegiate Schs. Architecture, Asso. Schs. Constrn. Home: 1301 Avondale St Norman OK 73069

HODGELL, ROBERT OVERMAN, artist, art educator; b. Mankato, Kans., July 14, 1922; s. Ray Darius and Lora Henrietta (Overman) H.; m. Lois Adele Partridge, 1946 (div. 1953); 1 dau., Patricia Christine; m. 2d Joan Van Tassel, May 13, 1968. B.S., U. Wis., 1948, M.S. in Applied Art, 1948; postgrad., Dartmouth Coll., State U. Iowa, 1952-53, U. Ill., 1954. Artist-in-residence, instr. Des Moines Art Center, 1949-53; illustrator Our Wonderful World Ency., Urbana, Ill., 1953-56; art dir. Editorial and Communication Services, U. Wis., Madison, 1957-59; artist-in-residence, assoc. prof. art Eckerd Coll., St. Petersburg, Fla., 1961-77; co-owner Joan Hodgell Gallery, Sarasota, Fla., 1977—. Served to lt. (j.g.) USNR, 1943-46; PTO. Mem. NAD. Methodist. Home: 4809 Featherbed Ln Sarasota FL 33581

HODGEN, MAURICE DENZIL, university administrator; b. Timaru, New Zealand, Aug. 7, 1929; s. William Arnold and Lindsey Frances (Neill) H.; m. Rhona Brandstater, June 20, 1951; children: Philip Denzil, Victoria Anne. Student, Avondale Coll., Cooranbong, Australia, 1948-50; B.S., Pacific Union Coll., 1953; M.A., Columbia U., 1956, Ed.D., 1958. Asst. prof. La Sierra Coll., Riverside, Calif., 1958-64; lectr. Solusi Coll., Bulawayo, Zimbabwe, 1964-66; dir. tchr. edn. Helderberg Coll., Somerset W., S. Africa, 1966-68; asso. prof. Sch. Edn., Loma Linda (Calif.) U., 1968-72, prof., 1972—, dean, 1978—. Served with U.S. Army, 1953-55. Mem. History of Edn. Soc., John Dewey Soc., Religious Edn. Assn., Am. Acad. Polit. and Social Sci. Seventh-day Adventist. Office: Grad Sch Loma Linda U Loma Linda CA 92350

HODGES, CLARENCE EUGENE, government official; b. Goldsboro, N.C., Oct. 1, 1939; s. Alphine (Lewis); m. Yvonne Ethyl Mitchell, July 3, 1958; children: Clarence Eugene Jr., Cortney Elliott, Cassandra Eileen, Cathleen Evon. B.A., U. Iowa-Fayette; M.A., Occidental Coll., Los Angeles, 1974; cert. in advanced bus., Hamilton Inst., N.Y.C., 1966. Social worker Mo. Dept. Welfare, St. Louis, 1962-64, caseworker supr., 1964-66; dir. social services Kinloch Sch. Dist., Mo., 1966-67; exec. dir. St. Louis Employment, 1967-73; dir. Ind. Dept. Human Resources, Indpls., 1974-76; asst. to U.S. Senator Richard Lugar of Ind., Washington, 1977-81; commr. for children and families HHS, Washington, 1981—; pres. Profls. Diversified Indpls., 1980-81; vis. prof. Washington U., St. Louis; mem. Presdl. Personnel Task Force, 1982-83. Columnist, St. Louis Argus, 1968-73. Trustee Oakwood Coll., Ala., 1982-83. Served with USAF, 1956-60. Named Man of Yr. Nat. Profl. Negro Women, 1976, Ind. Disting. Citizen Ind. Bicentennial Com., 1976; recipient Leadership award, 1981. Mem. NAACP (v.p. 1966-67), CORE (pres., chmn. 1967-68). Republican. Adventist. Home: 14212 Burning Bush Ln Silver Spring MD 20906 Office: US Department of Health and Human Serv ices 200 Independence Ave SW Washington DC 20201

HODGES, DAVID ALBERT, electrical engineering educator; b. Hackensack, N.J., Aug. 25, 1937; s. Albert R. and Katherine (Rogers) H.; m. Susan Spongberg, June 5, 1965; children: Jennifer, Alan. B.E.E., Cornell U., 1960; M.S., U. Calif., Berkeley, 1961, Ph.D. in Elec. Engring, 1966. Mem. tech. staff Bell Telephone Labs., Murray Hill, N.J., 1966-69, head system elements research dept., Holmdel, N.J., 1969-70; asso. prof. dept. elec. engring. and computer scis U. Calif., Berkeley, 1970-74, prof., 1974—. Contbr. articles to profl. jours. Trustee Deep Springs (Calif.) Coll., 1973-76; trustee Telluride Assn., Ithaca, N.Y., 1957-74, pres., 1967-69. Fellow IEEE.; mem. Nat. Acad. Engring. Patentee in field. Office: Dept Elec Engring and Computer Scis Univ of Calif Berkeley CA 94720

HODGES, ELMER BURKETT, lawyer; b. College View, Nebr., July 11, 1903; s. Charles Huntley and Mabel Gertrude (Blocher) H.; m. Maebelle Parsons, May 28, 1948; children: Deborah, Richard. Student, Jr. Coll. of Kansas City, Mo., 1921-23; LL.B., Kansas City Sch. Law, 1927. Bar: Mo. 1927, U.S. Supreme Ct 1940. Asst. county counselor, Jackson County, Mo., 1929-35; mem. firm Gage, Hodges, Park & Kreamer, 1960-69; partner Gage and Tucker, Kansas City, 1970-79, of counsel, 1980—; sec. Parmelee Industries, Inc., U.S. Safety Service Co., Countryside Fund, Inc. Mem. Am., Mo. bar assns., Lawyer's Assn. Kansas City, SAR. Republican. Mem. Christian Ch. Clubs: Kansas City, Mission Hills Country, Owl, Creek (Kansas City, Mo.); Westport Investors. Home: 5512 Central St Kansas City MO 64113 Office: Mutual Benefit Life Bldg Kansas City MO 64108

HODGES, JOHN HENDRICKS, physician, educator; b. Harpers Ferry, W.Va., Aug. 1, 1914; s. Joseph Howard and Edna (Hendricks) H.; m. Elizabeth May Wallace, Jan. 27, 1940; 1 son, John Hendricks. B.S., Cath. U. Am., 1935; M.D., Jefferson Med. Coll., Phila., 1939. Diplomate: Am. Bd. Internal Medicine. Intern Phila. Gen. Hosp., 1939-41; gen. practice, Martinsburg, W.Va., 1941-42; resident medicine Jefferson Med. Coll. Hosp., 1942-46; mem. faculty Jefferson Med Coll., 1944—, Ludwig A. Kind prof. medicine, 1964-79, emeritus, 1979—, dir. div. gen. medicine, 1944-77; cons. hematology Lankenau Hosp., Phila., 1963—; pres. Henry K. Mohler Physicians Office, Phila., 1955-75; S. Weir Mitchell assoc., treas. Coll. Physicians of Phila.; assoc. Cardeza Found. Editor: Manual for Laboratory Medicine, 11th edit, 1966; Contbr. articles to med. jours. Bd. dirs. Mercy Catholic Med. Center, 1972-82; trustee Thomas Jefferson U., 1978—, Physicians Rev. Bd. of United Fund. Mary Markle Found. fellow tropical medicine, 1944; recipient Christian R. and Mary F. Lindback Found. award excellence teaching, 1966; Ann. award in medicine Catholic U. Am., 1969; portrait presented to Thomas Jefferson U., 1981. Fellow A.C.P.; mem. AMA, Am. Heart Assn., Am. Thoracic Soc., Pa., Phila., Montgomery County med. socs., Am. Soc. Tropical Medicine and Hygiene, Internat., Am., Phila. socs. hematology, Internat. Soc. Internal Medicine, Alumni Assn. Jefferson Med. Coll. (past pres.), Meigs Med. Assn. (past pres.), Sigma Xi, Alpha Omega Alpha, Phi Eta Sigma, Nu Sigma Nu. Home: 436 Sabine Ave Wynnewood PA 19096

HODGES, JOHN RAYMOND, educator; b. Little Rock, Aug. 30, 1925; s. James Clevel and Ruby Mae (Magda) H.; m. Mary Lucia DiMeglio, Nov. 29, 1952 (dec. Mar. 1976); children—Lucia Lena, Raymond Francis, Carol Jean; m. Blanche P. Meriwether, May 10, 1979. Student, Little Rock Jr. Coll., 1942-43, Ark. A. and M. Coll., 1943-44; B.S., Tulane, 1947, M.S., 1950; Ph.D., George Peabody Coll., 1963. Tchr. Little Rock Jr. Coll., 1950-57; asst. prof. math. Little Rock U., 1957-63, asso. prof., 1963-66, prof., 1966—; head dept. math. and computer sci. U. Ark. at Little Rock, 1968-77, cons. drug systems research, 1964-65. Served with USNR, World War II, Korean War. Mem. Math. Assn. Am., Ark. Acad. Sci., AAAS, Naval Res. Assn., Sigma Xi. Roman Catholic. Home: 2603 Arkansas Valley Dr Little Rock AR 72212

HODGES, JOSEPH HOWARD, bishop; b. Harpers Ferry, W.Va., Oct. 8, 1911; s. Joseph Howard and Edna Belle (Hendricks) H. Student, St. Charles Coll., Catonsville, Md., 1928-30, North Am. Coll., Rome, Italy, 1930-36; D.D. (hon.), North Am. Coll., Rome, Italy, 1952. Ordained priest Roman Cath. Ch., Rome, 1935; asst. Sacred Heart Ch., Danville, Va., 1936-39, St. Andrew's Ch., Roanoke, Va., 1939-45; adminstr. St. Mary's Ch., Richmond, Va.; also dir. Diocesan Missionary Fathers, 1945-55; pastor St. Peter's Ch., Richmond, 1955-61; consecrated Titular Bishop of Rusadus, and Aux. Bishop of the Cath. Diocese of Richmond, 1952; vicar gen. Diocese of Richmond, 1958-61; coadjutor bishop and vicar gen. Diocese of Wheeling-Charleston, W.Va., 1961, bishop, 1962—. Office: 1300 Byron St PO Box 230 Wheeling WV 26003

HODGES, LUTHER HARTWELL, JR., banker, former govt. ofcl.; b. Leaksville, N.C., Nov. 19, 1936; s. Luther Hartwell and Martha Elizabeth (Blakeney) H.; m. Dorothy Emile Duncan, Feb. 15, 1958; children—Anne Houston, Luther Hartwell III. A.B. in Econs, U. N.C., 1957; M.B.A., Harvard, 1961. Mem. faculty U. N.C., Chapel Hill, 1961-62; with N.C. Nat. Bank, 1962-77, exec. v.p., 1970-72, vice-chmn., 1973-74, chmn. bd., 1974-77; prof. Grad. Sch. Bus. Adminstrn., Duke U., 1978-79; dep. sec. commerce Dept. Commerce, Washington, 1979-80; chmn. bd. Nat. Bank of Washington, 1980—; dir. Burris Industries, Lincolnton, N.C., J.B. Ivey & Co., Charlotte, Pic 'n Pay Corp., Charlotte.; Chmn. Mecklenburg County (N.C.) Democratic Com., 1969; candidate U.S. Senate, 1978; bd. govs. U. N.C.; bd. dirs. Friends of Library U. N.C., N.C. Citizens Assn., Bus. Found. N.C., Research Triangle Found. N.C. Author: (with Joe S. Floyd) Financing Industrial Growth, 1962, (with Rollie Tillman, Jr.) Bank Marketing-Text and Cases, 1968; zk3Managing Corporate Social Performance, 1980. Served with USNR, 1957-59. Mem. Charlotte C. of C. Clubs: Charlotte Country; Linville (N.C.) Golf, Grandfather Golf and Country (Linville).

HODGES, MARGARET MOORE, author, educator; b. Indpls., July 26, 1911; d. Arthur Carlisle and Anna Marie (Mason) Moore; m. Fletcher Hodges, Jr., Sept. 10, 1932; children: Fletcher III, Arthur Carlisle, John Andrews. A.B. with honors, Vassar Coll., 1932; M.L.S.; Carnegie Library Staff scholar, Carnegie Inst. Tech., 1958. Lectr. U. Pitts. Grad. Sch. Library and Info. Services, 1964-68, asst. prof., 1968-72, assoc. prof., 1972-75, prof., 1975-77, emeritus, 1977—. Children's librarian, radio and TV storyteller, Carnegie Library Pitts., 1953-64; story specialist, Pitts. Pub. Schs., 1964-68; also storyteller, WQED Schs. Services Dept. NIT network, 1965—; Author: juvenile One Little Drum, 1958, What's for Lunch, Charley?, 1961, Club Against Keats, 1962, Tell It Again, 1963, Secret in the Woods, 1963, Wave, 1964 (runner-up Caldecott award), Hatching of Joshua Cobb, 1967, Constellation, a Shakespeare Anthology, 1968, Sing Out, Charley!, 1968, Lady Queen Anne, 1969 (named Best Book for Young Adults by Ind. Author, Ind. U. Writers Conf.), Making of Joshua Cobb, 1971, Gorgon's Head, 1972, Hopkins of the Mayflower, 1972, Fire Bringer, 1972, Persephone and the Springtime, 1973, Baldur and the Mistletoe, 1974, Freewheeling of Joshua Cobb, 1974, Knight Prisoner, The Tale of Sir Thomas Malory and His King Arthur, 1976, The High Riders, 1980, The Little Humpbacked Horse, 1980, The Avenger, 1982; co-editor: adult Elva S. Smith's The History of Children's Literature, 1980. Mem. ALA (Newbery-Caldecott com. 1960), Pa. Library Assn., Am. Assn. Library Schs., Pitts. Bibliophiles, Zonta Internat., Distinguished Daus. Pa. Republican. Episcopalian. Home: 5812 Kentucky Ave Pittsburgh PA 15232 Office: Library and Information Scis. Bldg U Pitts Bellefield Ave Pittsburgh PA 15260

HODGES, MARY DORIS, hosp. adminstr.; b. Peoria, Ill, Sept. 30, 1912; d. Samuel G. and Edna G. (Wright) H. B.S., Ind. U., 1968. Registered record librarian. Med. record librarian trainee St. Elizabeth Hosp., Lafayette, Ind., 1930-33; chief med. record librarian St. Alexis Hosp., Cleve., 1933-38, St. Joseph Hosp., Memphis, 1938-43, St. Margaret Hosp., Hammond, Ind., 1943-68, hosp. adminstr., 1968—; dir. Sch. Med. Record Technicians, 1962-67; Pres. N.W. Ind. Hosp. Council, 1970-71. Fellow Am. Acad. Med. Adminstrs.; mem. Am. Med. Record Assn., Am. Mgmt. Assn. Address: 5454 Hohman Ave Hammond IN 46320

HODGES, RALPH DORE, JR., assn. exec.; b. Fresno, Calif., Oct. 5, 1920; s. Ralph Dore and Viola Agnes (MacDonald) H.; m. Dorothy Ellen Chamberlain, Dec. 6, 1942; children—Don, Tom, Karen. Student, Pasadena Jr. Coll., 1938-40; B.S., U. Calif., 1946; LL.B., Cath. U. Am., 1965; grad., Advanced Mgmt. Program, Harvard U., 1971. Forest engr. Harbor Plywood Corp., 1947-49, Western Pine Assn., 1950-55, Wetsel-Oviatt Lumber Co., 1955-59; with Nat. Forest Products Assn., Washington, 1959—, v.p. forestry and govt. affairs, 1966-69, v.p., gen. mgr., 1969-72, exec. v.p., 1972—; mem. U.S. Pres.'s Adv. Panel on Timber and Environ. Served with USNR, 1942-46. Mem. Am. Bar Assn., Soc. Am. Foresters, Forest History Soc., Am. Forestry Assn., Am. Soc. Assn. Execs. Clubs: University, Capitol Hill, Harvard Bus. Sch., Harvard. Home: 4516 30th St NW Washington DC 20008 Office: 1619 Massachusetts Ave NW Washington DC 20036

HODGES, RAYMOND DALE, cons. engr.; b. Eupora, Miss., Feb. 12, 1928; s. Russell Ruben and Grace Mae (Collum) H.; m. Violet D. Bates, Aug. 2, 1947; children—Dale, Kathy, Patty, Carol, Alan. B.S. in Civil Engring, Miss. State U., 1949. Engr. U.S.C.E., New Orleans, 1949-51, chief civil engr. sect. airbase design, French Morocco, 1951-55; with Pan Am. Engrs., Inc., 1955—, pres., Baton Rouge, 1976—, Miss. Gas Corp.; partner System Operators. Mem. La. Engrs. Soc., ASCE, Am. Council Engring. Cons. (pres. La. 1974, nat. dir. 1976), Nat. Soc. Profl. Engrs., Miss. Engrs. Soc., Am. Arbitration Assn., Profl. Engrs. in Pvt. Practice. Democrat. Baptist. Club: Kiwanis (dir.). Home: Rt 2 Box 4 Zachary LA 70791 Office: 2708 N Acadian Thruway W Baton Rouge LA 70805 *Happiness and success have been mine because of my life commitment to Christ. I believe an employer or client is entitled to my best effort on his behalf. Every person is entitled to dignity, respect, and fair treatment. My goal is to continue to serve mankind through the engineering profession and as an individual.*

HODGES, ROBERT EDGAR, physician, educator; b. Marshalltown, Iowa, July 30, 1922; s. Wayne Harold and Blanche Emma (McDowell) H.; m. Norma Lee Stempel, June 8, 1946; children: Jeannette Louise, Robert William, Karl Wayne, James Wolter. B.A., State U. Iowa, 1944, M.D., 1947, M.S. in Physiology, 1949. Diplomate: Nat. Bd. Med. Examiners, Am. Bd. Internal Medicine. Intern Meml. Hosp., Johnstown, Pa., 1947-48; fellow physiology, also obstetrics and gynecology, then resident in internal medicine State U. Iowa Hosp., 1948-52, dir. metabolic ward, 1952-71; mem. faculty State U. Iowa Med. Sch., 1952-71, prof. internal medicine, 1964-71, chmn. com. nutritional edn., adminstrn. grad. ednl. program nutrition, 1968-71; mem. liaison com. Maximum Security Hosp., Iowa City, 1966-71; prof. internal medicine, chief sect. nutrition U. Calif. Med. Sch., Davis, 1971-80, U. Nebr. Coll. Medicine, Omaha, 1980-82; prof. and dir. nutrition program, dept. family medicine, prof. dept. internal medicine U. Calif. Irvine Sch. Medicine, 1982—; mem. nutrition study sect. NIH, 1964-68; chmn. subcom. ascorbic acid and pantothenic acid ARC, 1966-68; mem. com. nutrition overview and adjustment of food on demand Nat. Acad. Scis.-NRC, 1976; cons. to hosps., other govt. agencies. Author: Nutrition in Medical Practice, 1980, also articles.; Editor: Human Nutrition, A Comprehensive Treatise, 1980; Mem. editorial bds. med. jours. Served to capt. M.C. AUS, 1943-46, 54-56. Fellow ACP; mem. AMA, Am. Heart Assn. (fellow councils atherosclerosis, epidemiology; chmn. com. nutrition 1966-68), Am. Bd. Nutrition (pres. 1973-74), Internat. Soc. Parenteral Nutrition, Am. Soc. Parenteral and Enteral Nutrition, Soc. Exptl. Biology and Medicine, Am. Fedn. Clin. Research, Am. Inst. Nutrition, Am. Soc. Clin. Nutrition (pres. 1966-67), Nutrition Soc. (London). Home: 1323 Fairway Orange CA 92666 Office: Dept Internal Medicine U Calif Irvine Sch Medicine 101 City Dr South Orange CA 92668

HODGES, ROBERT MANLEY, pharm. co. exec.; b. Llandrindod, Wales, July 13, 1924; came to U.S., 1955, naturalized, 1964; s. Joseph Henry and Lalla Jane (Mostyn) H.; m. Nan Powell Jones, Dec. 21, 1957; children—Robert, Jonathan, Daniel, Edward. B.Sc., U. Wales, 1950, M.B., B.Chir., 1953. Diplomate: Royal Coll. Obstetrics and Gynecology. Instr. U. Wash. Med. Sch., 1958-63; dir. Office New Drugs, med. officer U.S. FDA, Washington, 1963-68; dir. clin. research Parke, Davis & Co., Detroit, 1968-70, v.p. research and devel., 1970—, also dir.; Mem. Drug Rev. Bd. Nat. Acad. Scis., 1972-76. Author numerous sci. publs. Served with Brit. Army, 1942-47. Fellow Am. Coll. Obstetrics and Gynecology. Office: 2800 Plymouth Rd Ann Arbor MI 48106

HODGES, THOMAS KENT, plant physiologist; b. Bedford, Ind., Oct. 18, 1936; s. Ollie Russell and Frances M. (Foster) H.; m. Sharon Ann Fultz, June 9, 1957; children: Christine Ann, Cynthia Lynne, Scott Russell. B.S., Purdue U., 1958; M.S., U. Calif., Davis, 1960, Ph.D., 1962. Postdoctoral fellow U. Ill., Urbana, 1962-63, asst. prof., then asso. prof. plant physiology, 1963-71; vis. prof. botany U. Calif., Davis, 1968-69; mem. faculty Purdue U., 1971—, prof. plant physiology, 1973—, head dept. botany and plant pathology, 1977-82; program mgr. plant biology grants Dept. Agr., 1981. Author papers in field. Recipient Daryl Snyder award Farm House Frat., 1976. Mem. Am. Soc. Plant Physiologists (Charles Albert Shull award 1975), Sigma Xi, Pi Alpha Xi, Phi Sigma, Alpha Zeta. Office: Lilly Hall Purdue U West Lafayette IN 47907

HODGES, THOMPSON GENE, librarian; b. Clinton, Okla., Jan. 30, 1913; s. Kiah and Allie Lee (Thompson) H.; m. Claire Surbeck, June 19, 1935 (dec. 1979); 1 son, Thompson Gene; m. Dorothea Arnold Ray, 1980. B.S., U. Okla., 1934, M.L.S., 1955; B.D., McCormick Theol. Sem., Chgo., 1939. Ordained to ministry Presbyn. Ch., 1939; minister supply Ch. of Scotland, 1939; pastor, Pawhuska and Lawton, Okla., 1939-47; aquisitions librarian U. Okla., 1955-58; dean library services Central State U., Edmond, Okla., 1958-76, dean emeritus, 1976—; library cons. Univ. Microfilms, 1977; vis. prof. bibliography U. Okla., 1980-81; library cons. Mem. ALA, Southwestern Library Assn., Okla. Library Assn. (pres. 1965-66), Okla. Ednl. Assn., Kappa Sigma, Beta Phi Mu, Kappa Kappa Psi. Home and Office: 415 Macy St Norman OK 73071

HODGES, WALTER PAUL, oil co. exec.; b. Ft. Smith, Ark., Feb. 24, 1921; s. Walter H. and Mae (Williams) H.; children—Jeffery Paul, David Steven. B.S., U. Ark., 1942. C.P.A., Okla. With Haskins & Sells (C.P.A.s), Tulsa, 1945-49; with Deep Rock Oil Corp., Tulsa, 1949-54; asst. controller Forest Oil Corp., Bradford, Pa., 1954-58; sr. v.p. finance, dir. Quaker State Oil Refining Corp., Oil City, Pa., 1958-75, exec. v.p., 1975—. Served as 1st lt. USAAF, 1942-45. Mem. Am. Inst. C.P.A.s, Okla. Soc. C.P.A.s, Pa. Inst. C.P.A.s, Am. Petroleum Inst., Pa. Grade Crude Oil Assn., Inst. Internal Auditors, Fin. Execs. Inst. Home: 4 Chautauqua Ct Oil City PA 16301 Office: PO Box 989 Oil City PA 16301

HODGES, WILLIAM TERRELL, judge; b. Lake Wales, Fla., Apr. 28, 1934; s. Haywood and Clara Lucy (Murphy) H.; m. Peggy Jean Woods, June 8, 1958; children: Judson, Daniel, Clay. B.S.B.A., U. Fla., 1956, LL.B., 1958, J.D., 1967. Bar: Fla. 1959. Mem. firm Macfarlane, Ferguson, Allison & Kelly, Tampa, 1958-71; instr. bus. law U. South Fla., Tampa, 1961-66; judge U.S. Middle Dist. of Fla., Tampa, 1971—, now chief judge, 1971—. Exec. editor, U. Fla. Law Rev., 1957-58. Mem. Am., Tampa-Hillsborough County bar assns., Fla. Bar (chmn. grievance com. 1967-70, chmn. uniform comml. code com. 1970-71), Am. Judicature Soc. Office: PO Box 2908 Tampa FL 33601 *

HODGETTS, JOHN EDWIN, educator; b. Omemee, Ont., Can., May 28, 1917; s. Alfred Clark and Mary Elsie (Birnie) H.; m. Ella Ruth Woodger, June 26, 1943; children: Edwin C., P. Geoffrey, E. Anne. B.A., U. Toronto, Ont., 1939, M.A. (Rhodes scholar), 1940; Ph.D., U. Chgo., 1946; LL.D., Mt. Allison U., N.B., 1970, Queens U., Ont., 1973, Carleton U., Ont., 1982; D.Litt., Meml. U., Nfld., 1971. Lectr. polit. sci. U. Toronto, 1943-45, prof., 1965-82, prof. emeritus, 1982—; prin. Victoria Coll., 1967-70; pres. Victoria U., 1970-72; lectr. to prof., Hardy prof., chmn. dept. polit. studies Queens U., 1945-65; editor Queens Quar., 56-58; editorial dir. Royal Commn. on Govt. Orgn., 1960-62; vis. prof. Can. studies Northwestern U., 1975; vis. Killam prof. Dalhousie U., N.S., 1975-76; vis. Henrietta Harvey prof. Meml. U. Nfld., 1976-77; Chmn. acad. adv. panel Can. Council, 1966-69; vice chmn. Toronto Sch. Theology, 1973—; mem. Royal Commn. Fin. Mgmt. and Accountability Com., 1976. Author: The Canadian Public Service: A Physiology of Government, 1973, (with others) The Biography of an Institution, 1972. Nuffield Traveling fellow, 1949; Skelton-Clark fellow Queens U., 1954-55; Sr. Can. Council fellow, 1962-63; recipient Vanier Gold medal Inst. Pub. Adminstrn. Can., 1981. Fellow Royal Soc. Can.; mem. Can. Polit. Sci. Assn. (pres. 1970-71), Internat. Polit. Sci. Assn. (exec. council 1958-64), Inst. Pub. Adminstrn. Can., Phi Delta Theta. Home: Rural Rt 1 Mahone Bay NS Canada

HODGINS, JACK STANLEY, author; b. Comox Valley, Vancouver Island, B.C., Can., Oct. 3, 1938; s. Stanley H. and Reta A. (Blakely) H.; m. Dianne Child, Dec. 17, 1960; children: Shannon, Gavin, Tyler. B.Ed., U. B.C., 1961. Tchr. high sch. English and creative writing, Nanaimo, B.C., 1961-79; tchr. workshops, cons. and speaker in field, 1976—; writer-in-residence Simon Fraser U., Vancouver, 1977, U. Ottawa (Ont.), 1979; vis. prof. U. Victoria. Author: fiction Spit Delaney's Island, 1976 (B.C. Eaton's Book award 1977), The Invention of the World, 1977 (Gibson's First Novel award 1978), The Resurrection of Joseph Bourne, 1979 (Gov. Gen. Can. award fiction 1980); The Barclay Family Theatre, 1981; textbook Teaching Short Fiction, 1978; editor: The Frontier Experience, 1976, The West Coast Experience, 1976; co-editor: Voice and Vision, 1971; contbr. articles mags., newspapers. Recipient President's medal U. Western Ont., 1973, Periodical Distbrs. award, 1979; grantee Can. Council, 1973, 80. Mem. Writers Union Can. Address: 5534 Rutherford Rd Nanaimo BC V9S 5N7 Canada

HODGKIN, JOHN PEASE, finance company executive; b. Chentu, Szechuan, China, Jan. 12, 1909; came to U.S., 1931, naturalized, 1946; s. Henry Theodore and Elizabeth Joy (Montgomery) H.; m. Ruth Sherlock Walenta, July 2, 1934 (dec. Dec. 1961); children: Margaret, Christopher; m. Elizabeth Davis, Jan. 12, 1963 (dec. Dec. 1974). B.A. in Econs. with honors, Kings Coll., Cambridge (Eng.) U., 1931. C.P.A., Pa., 1947. Tchr. math., Hudson, Ohio, 1931-32, tchr. math. and French, Newtown Square, Pa., 1932-34; activities sec. Internat. House, N.Y.C., 1935; accountant Price Waterhouse & Co. (C.P.A.'s), Phila., 1936-60; with Office Messrs. Rockefeller, N.Y.C., 1960-67; treas. Rockefeller Brothers Fund, Inc., 1961-67, Rockefeller Brothers Inc., 1961-67, Martha Baird Rockefeller Fund Music, Inc., 1962-67; fin. asst. office of Stewart R. Mott, 1967—; v.p. Spectemur Agendo, Inc., 1967—; dir. Revels, Inc., Oram Group, Inc.; author, lectr. on taxes. Founding mem., past pres. Bryn Gweled Homesteads, Southampton; treas. Country Dance Soc., N.Y.C., 1963-83; dir., treas. N.Y. Pro Musica Antiqua, 1970—, Pinewoods Camp, Inc., Plymouth, Mass., 1975-76. Mem. Fin. Execs. Inst., Am., Pa. insts. C.P.A.'s., Soc. Friends (elder). Home: 124 E 24th St New York NY 10010 Office: 515 Madison Ave New York NY 10022 *I try to be considerate of others at all times. I dislike violence and try to avoid confrontations. I think I have a logical mind and I seek always to find a rational and reasonable solution to any problem. I feel that I have been particularly fortunate in my family, friends, and business associates. I have been the recipient of many kindnesses which I could not repay directly. I have tried to pass these on without direct recompense to others who may, in some future time, again help others. I aim to moderation in all things and concerned co-operation with others.*

HODGKINSON, CHARLES PAUL, physician; b. New Castle, Pa., Apr. 13, 1907; s. William Henry and O'Rilla Laura (Lambert) H.; m. Amy Virginia Walker, Jan. 22, 1929; children—Charles Paul II, Grace Ann; m. Mary McClure Stearns, Apr. 1972. Student, U. Pitts. Sch. Pharmacy, 1925-28, U. Pitts. Pre-Med. Sch., 1929-32, U. Buffalo Med. Sch., 1932-33; M.D. (W. Wayne Babcock Gold medal, Temple U. Faculty prize 1936), Temple U., 1936; M.S. in Obstetrics and Gynecology, U. Mich., 1940. Diplomate: Am. Bd. Obstetrics and Gynecology. Intern Henry Ford Hosp., Detroit, 1936-37, resident gen. surgery, 1937-39, resident gynecology and obstetrics, 1939-42, chmn. dept. gynecology and obstetrics, 1952-73, staff, 1973-75, cons. dept. gynecology-obstetrics, 1975—, sec. adv. bd., 1952-68, hon. emeritus asso. dept., 1979—; clin. prof. dept. obstetrics and gynecology Wayne State U. Sch. Medicine, Detroit, U. Mich., 1973—; Sec.-treas. Am. Assn. Obstetricians and Gynecologists Found., Inc., 1965-75. Contbr. numerous articles to tech. jours. Served to capt. M.C. AUS, 1942-46. Recipient Cum Laude award Radiol. Soc. N.Am., 1952; Hektoen medal AMA, 1967. Fellow Am. Gynecol. Soc., Am. Assn. Obstetricians and Gynecologists; mem. Am. Acad. Obstetricians and Gynecologists (sec. 1953-55, 1st award for sci. display 1953), Am. Coll. Obstetricians and Gynecologists (sec. 1955-57, pres. 1960-61, Distinguished Service award 1978), Mich. Soc. Obstetricians and Gynecologists (pres. 1959-60), Central Assn. Obstetricians and Gynecologists (Ann. Prize award 1952, pres. 1966-67), A.C.S. (gov. 1958-61, 63-66, certificate of merit 1957), AMA (certificate of merit 1953, 73), Central Travel Club Obstetricians and Gynecologists (council 1959-62), Gynecologic Urology Soc. (pres. 1980-81), AAAS; hon. mem. S.W. Obstet. and Gynecol. Soc., Kansas City Gynecol. Soc., Ky. Obstet. and Gynecol. Soc., Pitts. Soc. Obstetricians and Gynecologists. Home: 249 Kenwood Ct Grosse Pointe Farms MI 48236 Office: 2799 W Grand Blvd Detroit MI 48202

HODGKINSON, ROBERT, anesthesiologist; b. Bolton, Eng., Feb. 2, 1922; came to U.S., 1952, naturalized, 1957; s. Robert and Mary (Shephard) H.; m. Ottillia Mathias, Aug. 7, 1974; children: Rima Stella, Sylvia Roxana. M.A., Cambridge U., 1944; M.D., 1946. Intern, Plymouth, Eng., 1946-47; resident Townley Hosp., Eng., 1947-50; practice medicine specializing in anesthesiology; mem. staff Med. Center Hosp; faculty U. Tex., San Antonio, 1975—, prof. anesthesiology, 1981—. Editor: Obstetric Anesthesia Digest. Served to capt. Brit. Army, 1950-52. Mem. AMA, Am. Soc. Anesthesiologists, Soc. Obstetric Anesthesia and Perinatology. (pres.). Home: 7527 Wild Eagle St San Antonio TX 78255 Office: Univ Tex Health Science Center San Antonio TX 78284

HODGMAN, JOAN ELIZABETH, neonatologist; b. Portland, Oreg., Sept. 7, 1923; d. Kenneth E. and Ann (Vannet) H.; m. Amos N. Schwartz, Jan. 30, 1949; children—Ann Vannet, Susan Lynn. B.A., Stanford U., 1943; M.D., U. Calif., San Francisco, 1946. Intern in pediatrics U. Calif. Hosp., San Francisco, 1946-47; resident in pediatrics Harbor Gen. Hosp., Torrance, Calif., 1947-48, Los Angeles County-U. So. Calif. Med. Center, 1948-50; practice medicine specializing in pediatrics, S. Pasadena, Calif., 1950-52; mem. faculty U. So. Calif. Med. Sch., 1952—, prof. pediatrics, 1969—; dir. newborn div. Los Angeles County-U. So. Calif. Med. Center, 1955—; chmn. med. adv. com. Nat. Found.-March of Dimes, 1972-75; adv. com. Western sect. UNICEF, 1975; med. adv. com. Calif. Legislature, 1970; cons. Calif. Health Dept. Author articles in field, chpts. in books. Recipient cert. appreciation Am. Cancer Soc., 1964, Cameo of Committent award B'nai B'rith, 1969, Meritorious award Nat. Found.-March of Dimes, 1969; named Woman of Year Calif. Museum Sci. and Industry, 1974, Los Angeles Times, 1976. Mem. Am. Pediatric Soc., Am. Acad. Pediatrics, Am. Thoracic Soc., Western Soc. Pediatric Research, Southwestern Pediatric Soc., Calif. Perinatal Assn., Calif. Med. Assn., Los Angeles County Med. Assn., Los Angeles Pediatric Soc. Home: 494 Stanford Dr Arcadia CA 91006 Office: 1240 Mission Rd Los Angeles CA 90033

HODGSON, ALLAN ARCHIBALD, aluminum company executive; b. Montreal, Que., Can., Oct. 13, 1937; s. Jonathan Archibald and Anne Churchill (Hyde) H.; m. Victoria Webster; children: Lucinda Nora, Jonathan Welbourn, Anne Gregory. B.A. with Honors, McGill U., 1958; grad. advanced mgmt. program, Harvard U., 1976. Dir. investment research C.J. Hodgson & Co., Inc., Montreal, 1964-67; asst. treas. Alcan Aluminium Ltd., Montreal, 1969-72; fin. dir. Indian Aluminium Co. Ltd., Calcutta, India, 1972-76; treas. Aluminum Co. Can. Ltd., Montreal, 1976-80, Alcan Aluminium Ltd., 1980-82, v.p., chief fin. officer, 1982—. Clubs: Bengal, Univ. (Montreal). Home: 523 Argyle Ave Westmount PQ H3Y 3B8 Canada Office: Alcan Aluminium Ltd 1188 Sherbrooke St W Montreal PQ H3A 3G2 Canada

HODGSON, CHARLES ARTHUR, advt. exec.; b. East St. Louis, Ill., Jan. 7, 1920; s. Edward Stith and Gertrude (Niebling) H.; m. Mary E. Greene, Apr. 22, 1944 (dec. 1958); children—Cynthia Ann, Marilyn Elizabeth, Kathryn Ellen; m. Jean E. Buettner, Sept. 17, 1960; 1 son, Jeffrey Charles. B.S., Washington U., St. Louis, 1941. Partner Eggers-Ranking Advt., St. Louis, 1947-49; chmn. bd. Batz-Hodgson-Neuwoehner Advt., St. Louis, 1950—; v.p. Dooley's Ltd. Served with USNR, 1943-46. Mem. Advt. Club St. Louis, Media Club. Presbyn. (elder). Club: Algonquin Golf (St. Louis). Home: 332 McDonald Pl Webster Groves MO 63119 Office: 910 N 11th St Saint Louis MO 63101

HODGSON, CHARLES CLARK, lawyer; b. Kane, Pa., Oct. 24, 1906; s. J. Keene and Honora (Clark) H.; m. Helen G. Day, Jan. 6, 1937; children—Charles Clark, Helen (Mrs. Kerry L. Overlan), Stephen J., Richard J. A.B., Holy Cross Coll., 1927; LL.B., Temple U., 1939. Bar: Pa. bar 1931. Since practiced in, Phila.; partner firm Stradley, Ronon, Stevens & Young, 1945—; instr. bus. law U. Pa., 1940-52; Chmn. Phila. Parking Authority, 1953-55. Bd. dirs. Big Brother Assn., 1955—. Mem. ABA, Pa. Bar Assn., Phila. Bar Assn. (bd. govs. 1954-55, com. censors 1960-62, chmn. com. specialization 1968-69). Democrat. Roman Catholic. Club: Phila. Cricket. Home: 107 W Willow Grove Ave Philadelphia PA 19118 Office: 1100 One Franklin Plaza Philadelphia PA 19102

HODGSON, MATTHEW MARSHALL NEIL, publishing company executive; b. Washington, June 28, 1926; s. Hal King and Georgia

Frances (Gregory) H.; m. Patricia Kindelan, Jan. 8, 1967; children: Laura Ann, Edward Telfair. A.B., U. N.C., 1949. With Appleton-Century-Crofts, Inc., 1949-55; sr. editor Houghton Mifflin Co., Boston, 1955-68; developmental editor U. Press of Ky., Lexington, 1968-70; dir. U. N.C. Press, Chapel Hill, 1971—; Bd. dirs. Assn. Am. U. Presses, 1973-74, pres., 1978-79; bd. dirs. N.C. Art Soc. Served with USNR, 1944-45. Mem. Phi Gamma Delta. Clubs: Century Assn. (N.Y.C.); Long Hope Trout (N.C.). Home: 2474 Foxwood Dr Chapel Hill NC Office: U NC Press Chapel Hill NC 27514

HODGSON, PAUL EDMUND, surgeon; b. Milw., Dec. 14, 1921; s. Howard Edmund and Ethel Marie (Niemi) H.; m. Barbara Jean Osborne, Apr. 22, 1945; children: Ann, Paul. Student, Beloit Coll., 1939-42; M.D. cum laude, U. Mich., 1945. Diplomate: Am. Bd. Surgery. Intern U. Mich. Hosp., 1945-46, resident in surgery, 1948-52; mem. faculty dept. surgery U. Mich., 1952-62, assoc. prof., 1956-62; prof. surgery U. Nebr. Coll. Medicine, Omaha, 1962—, asst. dean for curriculum, 1966-72, chmn. dept. surgery, 1972-84; Trustee Beloit Coll., 1977-80. Served to capt. M.C. U.S. Army, 1946-48. Mem. A.C.S., Frederick A. Coller Surg. Soc., Soc. Univ. Surgeons, Central Surg. Assn., Soc. Surgery Alimentary Tract, Am. Assn. Surgery Trauma, Western Surg. Assn., Am. Surg. Assn. Presbyterian. Office: Univ of Nebr Med Center 42d and Dewey Ave Omaha NE 68105

HODGSON, PETER JOHN, music educator; b. Birmingham, Eng., Apr. 6, 1929; came to U.S., 1965, naturalized, 1974; s. Eric Christopher and Dorothy (Price) H.; m. Mary Thatcher, 1958; 1 son, Michael. Mus.B., U. London, 1964; Mus.M., Royal Coll. Music, 1965; Ph.D. in Music (Univ. fellow), U. Colo., 1970. Resident music master Univ. Sch., Victoria, B.C., Can., 1952-55; mem. faculty, adminstr. Mt. Royal Coll., Calgary, Alta., Can., 1955-65; mem. faculty Banff (Alta.) Sch. Fine Arts, 1960-66; mem. faculty, adminstr. Sch. of Music, Ball State U., Muncie, Ind., 1968-78; dean New Eng. Conservatory of Music, 1978-83; prof. music, chmn. dept. music Tex. Christian U., Ft. Worth, 1983—. Author: Music of Herbert Howells, 1971, Toward an Understanding of Renaissance Musical Structure, 1972. Served with Brit. Army, 1947-49. Recipient award Brit. Council, 1964. Home: 4017 Toledo Ave Fort Worth TX 76133 Office: Dept Music Tex Christian U Fort Worth TX 76133

HODGSON, RICHARD, communications company executive; b. Anyox, C., Can., Jan. 7, 1917; s. Arthur R. and Mabel (Malmstrom) H.; m. Geraldine Reed, Nov. 26, 1945; children: Philip, Morgan, Brooke, Peter. A.B. in Engring, Stanford U., 1937; M.B.A., Harvard U., 1939. With Radiation Lab., Mass. Inst. Tech., 1942-45; head engr. mgmt. div. Brookhaven Nat. Lab., AEC, 1946; dir. TV Paramount Pictures, 1947-50; pres., dir. Chromatic TV Labs., 1950-56; exec. v.p. Fairchild Camera & Instrument Corp., Syosset, L.I., 1955-62, pres., dir., 1962-68; corp. sr. v.p., group mgr. ITT Corp., 1968-80; dir. Research-Cottrell Inc., Intel Corp., NBI Inc., Applicon Inc., Mech-El Inc., McCowan Assos. Inc.; Expert cons. U.S. sec. war, 1943-45. Mem. IEEE (sr.), Tau Beta Pi. Home: Ponus Ridge Rd New Canaan CT 06840

HODGSON, THOMAS RICHARD, health care executive; b. Lakewood, Ohio, Dec. 17, 1941; s. Thomas Julian and Dallas Louise (Livesay) H.; m. Susan Jane Cawrse, Aug. 10, 1963; children—Michael, Laura, Anne. B.S. in Chem. Engring, Purdue U., 1963; M.S.E., U. Mich., 1964; M.B.A., Harvard U., 1969. Devel. engr. E.I. Dupont, 1964; asso. Booz-Allen & Hamilton, 1969-72; with Abbott Labs., North Chicago, Ill., 1972—, gen. mgr. Faultless div., 1976-78, v.p. gen. mgr. Hosp. div., 1978-80, pres. Hosp. div., 1980—. Mem. bus. adv. council U. Ill.-Chgo. Served with Chem. Corps U.S. Army, 1965-67. Baker scholar; NSF fellow. Mem. Phi Eta Sigma, Tau Beta Pi. Club: Economic of Chgo. Home: 715 Forest Hill Rd Lake Forest IL 60045 Office: Abbott Labs Abbott Park North Chicago IL 60064

HODKINSON, SYDNEY PHILLIP, clarinetist, composer, conductor; b. Winnipeg, Man., Can., Jan. 17, 1934; s. Ernest and Irene (Pilgrim) H.; m. Elizabeth Jane Deischer, July 22, 1955; children—Mark, Scott, Grant. B.Mus., U. Rochester, N.Y., 1957, M.Mus., 1958; D.Mus.Arts, U. Mich., 1968. Mem. faculty U. Va., 1958-63, Ohio U., Athens, 1963-66, U. Mich., Ann Arbor, 1968-73; currently prof. conducting and ensembles Eastman Sch. Music, Rochester, N.Y., and; U. Rochester. Artist-in-residence, Mpls.-St. Paul, 1970-72; composer numerous works for brass, woodwinds, strings and percussion, 1964—; artist various recs. Guggenheim fellow, 1978-79; grantee U. Va., 1961, Ohio U., 1964, Can. Council, 1966, 69, 77-78, Danforth Found., 1966-68, U. Mich., 1969, 70-73, Ford Found., 1970-72, Nat. Endowment Arts, 1975-78, Martha Baird Rockefeller Found., 1976. Mem. Broadcast Music Inc., Nat. Assn. Am. Composers and Conductors, Am. Music Center, Music Educators' Nat. Conf., Am. Soc. Univ. Composers, Am. Fedn. Musicians, Coll. Music Soc., Phi Mu Alpha Sinfonia. Home: 18 Timber Ln Fairport NY 14450 Office: 26 Gibbs St Rochester NY 14604

HODNE, THOMAS HAROLD, JR., architect, educator; b. Mpls., May 14, 1927; s. Thomas Harold and Martha (Loff) H.; m. Patricia Doyle, Sept. 10, 1948 (div. Apr. 1979); children: Thomas III, Kevin, Mark, Joanne, Christina, Hans, Katrina; m. 2d Joy Murphy, Oct. 1, 1981; children: Eva, Soren. B.A., U. Minn., 1955, B.Arch., 1955; M.Arch., MIT, 1956. Registered architect, Alaska, Iowa, Mich., Minn., Nebr., N.Y., N.D., S.D., Man., Nat. Council Architecture Registration Bds. Architect, owner Hodne Assocs., Inc., Mpls., 1960-68; prof. dept. architecture U. Minn., Mpls., 1965-83; architect, owner Hodne-Stageberg Ptnrs., Mpls., 1968-82, Thomas Hodne Architects, 1982—; prof., head dept. architecture U. Man., Winnipeg, 1983—; urban design, planning cons. U. Iowa, Iowa City, 1973—. Mem. Com. Urban Environment, Mpls., 1978-83. Served with U.S. Navy, 1945-46. Fellow AIA; mem. Minn. Soc. Am. Inst. Architects, Am. Inst. Cert Planners, Man. Architect Assn., Royal Archtl. Inst. Can. Roman Catholic. Home: 2520 Stevens Ave S Minneapolis MN 55404 Office: Thomas Hodne Architects Inc 2404 Stevens Ave Minneapolis MN 55404 Office: 30 West Gate Winnipeg MB Canada R3C 2E1

HODNETT, EDWARD, writer; b. Sag Harbor, L.I., N.Y., Oct. 15, 1901; s. John and Mary (Radigan) H.; m. Jessie Patrick, 1923; 1 child, Grey. A.B., Columbia U., 1922, Ph.D., 1935. Tchr. English Columbia U., 1922-40; editor Columbia U. Press, 1936-42, Columbia U. Quar., 1940-41; prof. English, dean (Coll. Arts and Scis.), U. Newark, 1940-42; editor Houghton Mifflin Co., 1945-46; v.p. U. Mass., 1946-48; pres. Fenn Coll., 1948-51; prof. English Ohio U., 1951-57; head pub. relations Dow Corning Corp., 1957-66. Author: Plain English, 1931, English Woodcuts: 1480-1535, 1935, Problem Solving, 1955, Industry-College Relations, 1955, Poems to Read Aloud, 1957, Working with People, 1959, Which College for You?, 1960, So You Want to Go into Industry, 1960, The Cultivated Mind, 1963, Effective Presentations, 1967, Marcus Gheeraerts the Elder, 1971, Addenda et Corrigenda, English Woodcuts, 1480-1535, 1973, Francis Barlow, 1978, Aesop in England, 1979, Image & Text, 1982; Editor: A Tale of a Tub (Swift), 1930, Introduction to Caxton's Fables of Aesop 1484, 1976. Served to lt. comdr. USNR, World War II. Address: 910 S The Willoughby 4515 Willard Ave Chevy Chase MD 20815

HODNETTE, ROBERT EDWARD, JR., judge; b. Ft. Deposit, Ala., May 17, 1913; s. Robert Edward and Clara Martha (Brooks) H.; m. Agnes Nowling, Apr. 29, 1955; 1 dau., Martha Sue. Student, Auburn U., 1930-32; J.D., U. Ala., 1935; LL.M., U. Chgo., 1946; grad., Nat. Coll. State Judiciary, 1971. Bar: Ala. 1935. Practiced in, Atmore, 1935-38, Mobile, 1947-50, 59-70; atty. claim dept. Aetna Ins. Cos., Louisville, 1939-40; asst. U.S. atty. So. Dist. Ala., Mobile, 1950-52; mem. firm Holberg, Tulley and Hodnette, 1959-70; circuit judge, Mobile, 1970—, presiding judge, 1982—; Dir. Jefferson Fed. Savs. & Loan Assn.; chmn. Mobile Fed. Savs. & Loan Assn., 1956—; chmn. adv. com. on criminal procedure Ala. Supreme Ct., 1974—. Served with AUS, 1940-46; ETO. Decorated Bronze Star, Purple Heart; Croix de Guerre, Belgium). Mem. Ala. Circuit Judges Assn. (pres. 1982-83), Mobile, Ala., Am. bar assns., Internat. Acad. Trial Judges, VFW, Pi Kappa Alpha, Phi Alpha Delta. Methodist. Home: 2456 Venetia Rd Mobile AL 36605 Office: County Court House Mobile AL 36602 *My main interests are directed towards improving judicial standards and procedures so that courts will function more simply, speedily and impartially.*

HODOUS, ROBERT POWER, bank holding company executive; b. Zanesville, Ohio, July 29, 1945; s. Robert Frank and Nancy Aurelia (Power) H.; m. Susan Cottrell Birkhead, Feb. 1, 1969; children: Robert Everett, Shannon Alycia. B.A., Miami U., Oxford, Ohio, 1967; J.D., U. Va., Charlottesville, 1970. Bar: Va. 1970. Asso. firm McGuire, Woods & Battle, Charlottesville, 1970-71; trust officer Nat. Bank & Trust Co., 1971-75; sec. Jefferson Bankshares, Inc. (formerly NB Corp.), Charlottesville, 1975—. Chmn. profl. div. Thomas Jefferson Area United Way, 1973, vice-chmn., 1978-79, campaign chmn., 1979-80, v.p. planning, 1981, pres., 1983; bd. dirs. Central Va. chpt. ARC, 1972-78, treas., 1972-75, chmn., 1975-77; commr. Charlottesville Redevel. and Housing Authority, 1974-78; mem. Region X Community Mental Health and Retardation Services Bd., 1973-79, chmn., 1974-76, mem. exec. com., 1976-78; chmn. recreation precinct Charlottesville City Democratic Com., 1971. Mem. Am., Charlottesville-Albemarle bar assns., Va. State Bar. Roman Catholic. Club: Fairview Swim. Home: 1309 Lester Dr Charlottesville VA 22901 Office: 123 E Main St Charlottesville VA 22901 *To me success is indicated by feelings of personal peace and satisfaction, not by external possessions. My goals are to do my best in contributing to the success of endeavors in which I become involved and to remember that the people involved in activities are the most important part of the activities. I feel my family is my most important endeavor. I hope never to become so involved in activities that I cannot enjoy my family, my surroundings and people I meet, or that I cannot spend the time necessary to do well those activities in which I am involved.*

HODSOLL, FRANCIS S.M., government official; b. May 1, 1938; m. Margaret McEwen. B.A., Yale U.; M.A., Cambridge U.; J.D., Stanford U. Bar: D.C. Assoc. Sullivan and Cromwell, N.Y.C.; spl. asst. to adminstr. EPA, Washington, asst. sec. for energy and strategic resource policy; asst. to undersec. commerce Dept. Commerce, Washington; fgn. service officer; dep. U.S. spl. rep. for nonproliferation Dept. State; coordinator debate preparation Reagan-Bush campaign, 1980; dep. asst. to pres. The White House, 1981; chmn. Nat. Endowment Arts, Washington, 1981—. Office: Nat Endowment for Arts 1100 Pennsylvania Ave NW Washington DC 20506 *

HODSON, KENNETH JOE, criminal justice consultant, lawyer, retired army officer; b. Crestline, Kans., Apr. 27, 1913; s. Charles Asa and Lillian (Raymer) H.; m. Helen J. Butterfield, Nov. 29, 1935 (dec. 1965); children: Terrie Loua, Kenneth Joe, Kay Altie, David Michael; m. Marjorie Bell, Sept. 8, 1968. A.B., U. Kans., 1935, LL.B., 1937; grad., Judge Adv. Gen. Sch., 1944, Army Command and Gen. Staff Coll., 1954, Army War Coll., 1958. Bar: Wyo. 1938. Practiced in, Jackson, 1938-41; commd. 2d lt. arty. U.S. Army, 1934, advanced through grades to maj. gen., 1967; arty. officer, 1941-42; judge adv. Dept. Army, Trinidad, Europe and Japan, 1942-62; faculty Judge Adv. Gen. Sch., 1951-53; U.S. chmn. U.S.-Japan Criminal Juris Com., 1955-57; asst. judge adv. gen. for mil. justice U.S. Army, 1962-67, judge adv. gen., 1967-71; chief judge U.S. Army Ct. Mil. Rev., 1971-74; ret., 1974; exec. dir. Nat. Commn. for Rev. of Fed. and State Laws on Wiretapping and Electronic Surveillance, 1974-76; criminal justice cons., 1976—. Co-editor: Am. Criminal Law Quar, 1963-67; Contbr. mil. legal articles to profl. publs. Decorated Legion of Merit; D.S.M. Mem. ABA (spl. com. standards for adminstrn. criminal justice 1964-73, spl. com. on youth edn. for citizenship 1971-74, mem. spl. com. adminstrn. criminal justice 1974-75, chmn. standing com. on assn. standards for criminal justice 1975-80, vice chmn. 1980—, chmn. criminal justice sect. 1964-65, sec. 1965-80, mem. ho. of dels. 1971-79), Fed. Bar Assn. (past pres. Pentagon chpt.; nat. council), Am. Judicature Soc., Internat. Acad. Trial Lawyers, Inst. Jud. Adminstrn., Judge Advs. Assn. (dir. 1960—). Home: 2931 Garfield St NW Washington DC 20008

HODSON, THOMAS WILLIAM, health care company executive; b. Phila., Nov. 25, 1946; s. William K. and Marguerite M. (Hendrick) H.; m. Constance Stirling, July 5, 1969; children: Hollistir S., Andrew S. B.S. in Bus. Adminstrn. and Econs, Lehigh U., Bethlehem, Pa., 1968; M.B.A., Harvard U., 1974. With Baxter Travenol Labs., Inc., 1974—, treas., Deerfield, Ill., 1980-84, v.p., 1984—. Served to lt. USNR, 1969-72. Roman Catholic. Home: 911 Forest Glen W Winnetka IL 60093 Office: 1 Baxter Pkwy Deerfield IL 60015

HODSON, WILLIAM ALAN, pediatrician; b. Winnipeg, Man., Can., June 27, 1935; came to U.S., 1961; s. Douglas Cecil and Grace Evelyn (Stewart) H.; m. Judith Ann Welsh, Oct. 29, 1960; children: Jeffrey Alan, Elizabeth Andrea, Douglas Alexander. M.D., U. Man., 1959; M.M.Sc., Ohio State U., 1964; postgrad., Johns Hopkins U., 1964-66. Intern Winnipeg Gen. Hosp., U. Man., 1959-60; fellow in respiratory disease U. Man., 1960-61; resident in pediatrics Ohio State U., 1961-64; postdoctoral fellow in neonatal and respiratory disease Johns Hopkins U., 1964-66; mem. faculty U. Wash. Med. Sch., Seattle, 1966—, prof. pediatrics, 1975—, dir. neonatal clin. research center, 1967-69, head div. neonatal biology, 1970—; chief newborn service Children's Orthopedic Hosp. and Med. Center, 1975—; dir. Wash. Regional Perinatal Care Program, 1975—; cons. in field. Author Intensive Care of The Newborn, numerous papers in field.; Editor: Development of the Lung, 1977; co-editor sects. med. books. Fellow Fogarty Coll. Med. Sch., London, 1982-83. Mem. Am. Thoracic Soc. (chmn. sci. assembly pediatrics 1973-74), Soc. Pediatric Research, Am. Pediatric Soc., Perinatal Research Soc., Am. Fedn. Clin. Research, AAAS, Internat. Primatological Soc., Am. Acad. Pediatrics, Am. Heart Assn. (cardiopulmonary council), Am. Soc. Primatologists, Am. Physiol. Soc., N. Pacific Pediatric Soc., Wash. Thoracic Soc., Wash. Soc. Pediatrics, King County Med. Soc. Office: Dept Pediatrics RD-20 U Wash Med Sch Seattle WA 98195

HOEBEL, BARTLEY GORE, educator; b. N.Y.C., May 29, 1935; s. Edward Adamson and Frances (Gore) H.; m. Cynthia A. Eney, June 22, 1962; children—Valerie, Carolyn, Brett. A.B., Harvard, 1957; postgrad., Rockefeller Inst., 1957-60; Ph.D., U. Pa., 1962. Mem. faculty psychology dept. Princeton, 1962—, prof, 1970—. Contbr. articles to tech. jours. and books. Fellow AAAS, Am. Psychol. Assn.; mem. Neurosci. Soc. Unitarian. Home: 207 Hartley Ave Princeton NJ 08540

HOEBEL, EDWARD ADAMSON, anthropologist, educator; b. Madison, Wis., Nov. 16, 1906; s. Edward Charles and Kathryn (Arnold) H.; m. Frances Elizabeth Gore, June 20, 1930 (dec. July 1962); 1 son, Bartley Gore; m. Irene Holth, Aug. 26, 1963; 1 dau., Sue Dunbar (dec.). A.B., U. Wis., 1928; student, Cologne, Germany, 1928-29; A.M., NYU, 1931; Ph.D., Columbia, 1934. Instr. sociology NYU, 1929-35, asst. prof. sociology and anthropology, 1935-41, assoc. prof., 1941-48; lectr. anthropology, dept. psychiatry Sch. Medicine, NYU, 1946-48; vis. prof. various schs.; prof., head dept. anthropology U. Utah, 1948-54, dean Univ. Coll., 1953-54; prof. anthropology, chmn. dept. U. Minn., 1954-68, Regent's prof., 1966-72, emeritus, 1972—, adj. prof. law, 1972-81; Fulbright prof. Oxford (Eng.) U., 1956-57, Cath. U., The Netherlands, 1970; Research fellow Lab. Anthropology, Santa Fe; dir. Social Sci. Research Council; adv. panel social sci. research NSF, 1958-60; sr. specialist Inst. Advanced Study, East-West Center Cultural and Tech. Interchange, Honolulu, 1964-65; mem. Gov.'s Commn. Human Relations, 1955-64; behavioral scis. panel Nat. Inst. Gen. Med. Sci., 1962-66; spl. officer Dept. State, ACDA, 1969-73; Conf. Bd. for Internat. Exchange Persons NRC, 1966-70; Research fellow Columbia U. Council Research in Social Scis., Am. Council Learned Socs.; fellow Center Advanced Studies Behavioral Scis., 1960-61. Author: several books, including (with K.N. Llewellyn) The Cheyenne Way: Conflict and Case Law in Primitive Jurisprudence, 1941; (with others) Social Meaning of Legal Concepts: Inheritance, 1948, Man in the Primitive World: An Introduction to Anthropology, 1949, (with E. Wallace) The Comanches, 1952, The Law of Primitve Man: A Study in Comparative Legal Dynamics, 1954, The Cheyennes: Indians of the Great Plains, 1961, rev. edit., 1978, Anthropology: The Study of Man, 1966, rev., 1972, (with E.L. Frost) Social and Cultural Anthropology, 1975, The Plains Indians: A Critical Bibliography, 1978, (with Thomas Weaver) Anthropology and the Human Experience, 1979; also articles, revs. in legal, hist. and anthrop. jours.; Assoc. editor: Law and Soc. Rev, 1969-73, Jour. Natural Law, 1960-65, Am. Indian Quar, 1972—. Trustee Sci. Mus. Minn. Fellow AAAS; mem. Am. Philos. Soc., Am. Ethnol. Soc. (pres. 1947), Am. Anthrop. Assn. (pres. 1956-57), Assn. Am. Indian Affairs (dir. 1945-56), Explorers Club, Alpha Kappa Lambda, Alpha Kappa Delta, Phi Kappa Phi. Club: Skylight. Home: 2273 Folwell Saint Paul MN 55108

HOEBER, PAUL B., publisher; b. N.Y.C., Oct. 11, 1914; s. Paul B. and Catherine (Putzel) H.; m. Elizabeth Price, June 20, 1940; children—Paul Richard, Thomas Edward. Student, Antioch Coll., 1931-34, Am. U. Sch. Pub. Affairs, 1934-37. With Paul B. Hoeber, Inc. (med. book dept. Harper & Bros.), 1937-69, pres., 1945-69; exec. v.p. Am. Elsevier Pub. Co., 1970-72, pres., 1972-75; chmn. bd. Agathon Press, Inc., 1975—; pres. APS Publs., Inc., 1975—. Served with USNR, 1942-45; South Atlantic Fleet; Served with USNR, 1942-43; South Atlantic Fleet; inactive Res. Democrat. Clubs: Players, Overseas Press (N.Y.C). Home: 350 Central Park W New York NY 10025 Office: 15 E 26th St New York NY 10010

HOECKER, DAVID, engineering executive; b. Cin., July 7, 1948; s. Vernon and Ruth (Schnake) H.; m. Susan Ameling, Aug. 15, 1970; children: Sarah, Paul. B.S., Rose Poly. Inst., Terre Haute, Inc., 1969; M.S.I.A., Purdue U., 1970. Cert. quality mengr. Project mgr. Timken Co., Canton, Ohio, 1970-73, gen. supr., 1973-78, chief quality control engring., Lincolnton, N.C., 1978-82, chief engr. engring. services., Canton, Ohio, 1982—. Vice pres. Canton Jaycees, 1973-74, Trinity United Ch. of Christ, 1983-84; dir. Young Life, Canton, 1975-78. Named Spoke of Yr. Canton Jaycees, 1972, Key Man Canton Jaycees, 1974. Sr. mem. Am. Soc. Quality Control (sec. Charlotte sect. 1980-81, treas. 1981), Soc. Mfg. Engrs. Republican. Club: Carriage Hill (Canton). Office: Timken Co 1835 Dueber Ave SW Canton OH 44706

HOEFER, JOHN HENRY, advertising agency executive; b. St. Cloud, Minn., Nov. 12, 1915; s. John James and Marie E. (De Longchamps) H.; m. Katherine Adele Foster, Sept. 9, 1939; children: Carolyn (Mrs. John Pelkan), Susan (Mrs. Peter Witter), John Foster, William Edward. A.B., U. Calif. at Berkeley, 1938; M.B.A., Stanford U., 1940. Pres. Hoefer, Dieterich & Brown, Inc. (merged with Chiat/Day Inc. 1980), San Francisco, 1967-80, chmn. bd., 1967-80; chmn. Chiat/Day/Hoefer, Inc., advt., San Francisco, 1980—; chmn. bd. John H. Hoefer Co., 1965—, Advt. Prodns., Inc., 1965—; gen. partner John H. Hoefer & Assos. (real estate holding co.); trustee Pacific Real Estate Investment Trust, Menlo Park, Calif.; dir. Lucky Stores, Inc. Served to rear adm. USNR, 1940. Mem. Advt. Assn. of West (past pres.), San Francisco Advt. Club (past pres.), Am. Assn. Advt. Agys. (past sec.-treas., dir.), Advt. Council (dir.), San Francisco C. of C. (v.p. 1968—), San Francisco Better Bus. Bur. (past pres.), U. Calif.-Berkeley Alumni Assn. (councillor). Episcopalian. Home: 32 Peninsula Rd Belvedere CA 94920 Office: 414 Jackson Sq San Francisco CA 94111

HOEFLIN, RUTH MERLE, univ. dean; b. Ft. Dodge, Iowa, Jan. 4, 1918; d. Herbert and Edna (Mathias) H. B.S., Iowa State U., 1940; M.A., U. Mich., 1945; Ph.D., Ohio State U., 1950. Nursery sch. tchr., Detroit, 1940-42, 43-44; recreation dir. Home for Delinquents, Detroit, 1942-43; instr. Merrill-Palmer Sch., Detroit, 1944-46; asst. prof. home life dept. Okla. State U., 1946-47; asso. prof. child devel. Ohio State U., 1947-57; prof. family and child devel., head dept. Kans. State U., 1957-60, asso. dean, 1960-74, acting dean, 1974-75, dean, 1975—; speaker, condr. family life insts. Sec. Nat. Council Family Relations, 1962-63; Kans. chmn. middle state project for family life edn. Am. Social Health Assn. Author: Essentials of Family Living, 1960, Careers in Home Economics, 1970, also research bulletins, articles; co-author: monograph Society for Research in Child Development, 1959, Careers for Professionals: New Perspectives in Home Economics, 1981. Recipient Diamond Anniversary award for distinguished service in home econs. Ohio State U.; Alumni award in home econs. Iowa State U. Mem. AAUP, Soc. Research Child Devel., Am. Home Econs. Assn. (pres. 1981-82), North Central Home Econs. Assn. (chmn.), Kans. Home Econs. Assn. (pres.), Assn. Adminstrs. Home Econs. (chmn.), Mortar Bd., Phi Upsilon Omicron, Omicron Nu, Phi Kappa Phi, Pi Lambda Theta. Home: 3100 Arbor Dr Manhattan KS 66502

HOEFLING, JOHN ALAN, former army officer, corporation executive; b. Milw., Sept. 3, 1925; s. Frederick Adolph and Lorraine (Braun) H.; m. Patricia Eileen Flynn, Apr. 12, 1947; children: Peggy Ann, Mary Kathleen, John Patrick. B.S., U.S. Mil. Acad., 1946; M.B.A., U. Ala., 1957; M.S. in Indsl. Relations, George Washington U., 1965; grad., Advanced Mgmt. Program, Harvard U., 1970. Commd. 2d lt. U.S. Army, 1946, advanced through grades to maj. gen., 1974; service in, Japan, Korea, Germany, Vietnam, India, U.S. def. rep. to India, New Delhi, 1970-72, asst. div. comdr., 1972-74, coordinator Army Security Assistance, Washington, 1974-76; program gen. mgr. Vinnell Corp., 1976-79; v.p. Litton Data Command Systems and v.p., gen. mgr. Litton Saudi Arabia Ltd., 1979-84; v.p. Litton Data Command, Washington, 1980—. Pres. Republicans Abroad, 1980-82. Decorated D.S.M., Silver Star, Legion of Merit, D.F.C., Soldier's medal, Bronze Star. Mem. Assn. U.S. Army 3d Armored Div. (pres. 1972-74), Army Athletic Assn., Harvard Bus. Sch. Assn. Roman Catholic. Address: Litton Data Command Systems 1755 Jefferson Davis Hwy Suite 902 Arlington VA 22202

HOEFLINGER, NORMAN CHARLES, clergyman; b. Hawthorne, N.Y., Dec. 19, 1925; s. Herman George and Mabel Magdalena (Stenstrom) H.; m. Virginia Louise Murphrey, June 12, 1950; children—Laurel (Mrs. Robert Clausing), Fern (Mrs. Gary Vander Hart), Sara, Heidi. Student, U. Colo., 1948-50; B.A., U. Denver, 1951;

B.D., Westminster Theol. Sem., Phila., 1955. Ordained to ministry Ref. Ch. in U.S., 1955; pastor Odessa Ref. Ch., Artas, S.D., 1955-61, Salem-Ebenezer Ref. Ch., Manitowoc, Wis., 1961-73, Minot (N.D.) Ref. Ch., 1973-76, Menno, S.D., 1976-82, Hope Ref. Ch., Kansas City, Mo., 1982—; stated clerk Ref. Ch. in U.S., 1957-61, pres., 1966-78; Trustee Westminster Theol. Sem., 1964—, Hope Haven, Rock Valley, Iowa. Editor: Ref. Herald, 1956-59, 61-74. Served with USNR, 1944-46. Address: 4206 N Colorado Kansas City MO 64117

HOEFT, JULIUS ALBERT, JR., publishing company executive; b. Buffalo, Aug. 5, 1946; s. Julius Albert and Imogene (Belton) H.; m. Margaret Hill, Aug. 24, 1968; children: Kelly, Kathleen. B.S., U. Dayton, 1968. Vice pres. sales Eastern div. Pepsi-Cola Co., Purchase, N.Y., 1977-79; v.p. sales Harlequin Enterprises, Toronto, Ont., Can., 1979-81; pres. Harlequin Sales Corp., White Plains, N.Y.; v.p., dir. sales and mktg. Bantam Books, N.Y.C., 1981—. Commr. Ridgefield Youth Com., Conn., 1983-84. Served to capt. U.S. Army, 1969-72. Mem. Periodicals Inst. (sec. 1982-84). Republican. Roman Catholic. Home: 21 Red Oak Ln Ridgefield CT 06877 Office: Bantam Books 666 Fifth Ave New York NY 10103

HOEG, DONALD FRANCIS, chemist; b. Bklyn., Aug. 2, 1931; s. Harry Herman and Charlotte (Bourke) H.; m. Patricia Catherine Fogarty, Aug. 30, 1952; children—Thomas Edward, Robert Francis, Donald John, Marybeth, Susan Catherine. B.S. in Chemistry summa cum laude, St. John's U., N.Y., 1953, Ph.D., Ill. Inst. Tech., 1957. Fellow in chemistry and chem. engring. Armour Research Found., 1953-54; grad. research asst. Ill. Inst. Tech., 1954-56; research chemist W.R. Grace & Co., 1956-58, sr. research chemist, 1958-61; group leader addition polymer chemistry Roy C. Ingersoll Research Center, Borg-Warner Corp., Des Plaines, Ill., 1961-64, mgr. polymer chemistry, 1964-66, asso. dir., head chem. research dept., 1966-75, dir., 1975—; mem. solid state scis. adv. bd. Nat. Acad. Scis.; Bd. overseers Lewis Coll. Scis. and Letters of Ill. Inst. Tech., 1980—; bd. dirs. Ill. Inst. Tech. Alumni, 1979-82, Mt. Prospect Combined Appeal, 1963-65. Bd. editors: Research Mgmt. Mag, 1979—; contbr. numerous articles tech. publs., chpts. in books. TaPing Lin scholar, 1955-56; AEC asst., 1954; Armour Research Found. fellow, 1953-54; Ill. Inst. Tech. Achievement award, 1983. Mem. Am. Chem. Soc., AAAS, N.Y. Acad. Scis., Dirs. Indsl. Research, Am. Mgmt. Assn., Research Dirs. Assn. Chgo. (pres. 1977-78), Sigma Xi. Patentee in field. Office: Roy C Ingersoll Research Center Wolf and Algonquin Rds Des Plaines IL 60018 *I've counseled myself that all ideas and concepts, no matter how seemingly difficult, are products of man's mind, and, therefore fundamentally understandable.*

HOEHLER, FRED KENNETH, JR., labor studies institute administrator; b. Cin., Nov. 18, 1918; s. Fred Kenneth and Dorothy Scovil (Stevens) H.; m. Lisa G. Portman, Apr. 27, 1979; children: Fred Kenneth III, Daniel Price. B.S., U. Ariz., 1942; M.A., U. Chgo., 1947. Asst. prof. pub. adminstrn. U. P.R., 1947-49; asst. prof. polit. sci. Pa. State U., 1949-54; asst. dir. social security dept. AFL-CIO, Washington, 1954-56; prof., assoc. dir. Sch. Labor and Indsl. Relations, Mich. State U., East Lansing, 1956-70; dir. George Meany Ctr. for Labor Studies, Washington, 1969—; edn. dir. United Steelworkers Am., Pitts., 1965-67; faculty mem. Salzburg Seminar in Am. Studies, 1978; Mem. Gov.'s Study Commn. on Workmen's Compensation, Lansing, 1960-62; mem. Nat. Commn. on Higher Edn. Issues, 1981-82; cons. community action orgn. OEO, 1964-65; advance study program Brookings Instn., 1962-71. Trustee U.Mid-Am., 1976-82; chmn. bd. dirs. Am. Open U., 1982—. Served with USAAF, 1943-46. Received citation pub. service U. Chgo., 1971. Mem. Univ. Labor Edn. Assn. (chmn. 1961), Nat. Inst. Labor Edn. (bd. dirs. 1961-65). Office: 10000 New Hampshire Ave Silver Spring MD 20903

HOEHN, ELMER L., lawyer; b. Memphis, Ind., Dec. 19, 1915; s. Louis and Agnes (Goss) H.; m. Frances Cory, June 10, 1943; children: Kathleen Cory, G. Patrick. B.S., Canterbury Coll., 1936, Northwestern U., 1937; J.D., U. Louisville, 1940. Bar: Ky. 1940, D.C. 1969, U.S. Supreme Ct. 1969, U.S. Ct. Appeals 1970, Ind. bar 1981. Prof. bus. and law Jeffersonville (Ind.) High Sch., 1937-41, Ind. U., 1940-41; with legal and personnel div. Am. Barge Lines, 1942-44; realtor, Ind., 1949—; apptd. dir. by Gov. Ind. Oil and Gas, 1949-53; apptd. adminstr. by Pres. U.S. Oil Import Adminstrn., 1965-69; sec.-treas. Am. Assn. Oil Well Drilling Contractors, 1956-60; exec. sec. Ind. Oil Producers and Land Owners Assn., 1953-64; pvt. practice law, Washington, 1969—; cons. petroleum, natural resources, energy and environment. Mem. Ind. Gen. Assembly, 1945- 49, minority floor leader, 1947, chief clk., 1949; Democratic chmn., Clark County, Ind., 1945-52; Ind. del. Dem. Nat. Conv., 1964, 8th Congl. Dist., 1952-58; mem. Ind. Dem. Exec. Com., 1952-58, Ind. and Mid-west campaign mgr., LBJ campaign for president, 1960. Named hon. citizen, Ind., Tex., Ky., Nebr., S.D., La., Okla. Mem. Am., Fed., Ky., D.C., Ind. bar assns., Am. Petroleum Inst., Sigma Delta Kappa. Roman Catholic. Clubs: Nat. Lawyers, Nat. Press (Washington); Ind. Legislators (Indpls.); Elks Country (Jeffersonville). Home: 5914 Woodley Rd McLean VA 22101 also 19 Blanchel Terr Jeffersonville IN 47130 Office: 1523 L St NW Washington DC 20005 also 1415 S Clark Blvd Jeffersonville IN 47130

HOEKENGA, EARL NELSON, trucking company executive; b. Muskegon, Mich., Feb. 15, 1916; s. Gerrit and Esther A. (Bergren) H.; m. Helen Mary Beattie, June 14, 1941; children: David E., Ann H., Linda E., Gretchen B., Christian M., Trena M. A.B. in Econs., Mich. State U., 1939. With Ernst & Ernst (C.P.A.s), Grand Rapids, Mich., 1941-43, George F. Alger Co., Detroit, 1946-55; prin. A.T. Kearney & Co., Chgo., 1956-64; with Ryder Truck Lines, Inc., Jacksonville, Fla., 1964—, pres., chmn. bd., 1970—, also dir.; pres. PIE, 1971-73; pres., treas. Bridgestone, Inc., 1981—; chmn., chief exec. officer Universal Select, Inc., 1983—; dir. Pacific Intermountain Express, Inc., Byrns Motor Express, Ltd., Transp. Teleprocessing Systems, Inc., RTL Holdings, Inc., Helms Salvage, Inc., Atlantic Nat. Bank. Bd. dirs. United Way Jacksonville, Jr. Achievement Jacksonville, YMCA; trustee Edward Waters Coll., Jacksonville, Jacksonville U.; bd. govs. Jacksonville Area C. of C.; mem. ofcl. bd. Lakewood Meth. Ch., Jacksonville. Served to capt. USAAF, 1943-46. Decorated cert. meritorious service; recipient Disting. Alumni award Mich. State U., 1977; also named Outstanding Bus. Alumnus, 1979; Top Mgmt. award Jacksonville Sales Execs., 1978. Mem. Central and So. Motor Freight Assn. (dir., pres.), Acctg. and Statis. Soc. (hon. life), Mich. Truck Assn. (v.p.-at-large, exec. com.; trustee found., vice chmn. 1977—), Am. Trucking Assn., Regular Common Carrier Conf. (chmn. 1976-77), Trucking Mgmt. Inc. (exec. com., dir.). Republican. Clubs: River, San Jose Country. Home: 2317 Miller Oaks Dr S Jacksonville FL 32217 Office: 812 Barnett Bank Bldg Jacksonville FL 32209 *The late Vince Lombardi, former coach of Green Bay, had a simple but effective plan for winning football games—do the basics of blocking and tackling and keep doing it 60 minutes every hour. Running a business is comparable. There are no fancy plays that will make you win—it's doing the basics and doing them every day; it's quality products, fair pricing, good employee relations and public concern—it's just that simple.*

HOEL, LESTER A., civil engineering educator; b. Bklyn., Feb. 26, 1935; s. Johannes and Julia (Michelsen) H.; m. Unni Sonja Blegen, Jan. 24, 1959; children: Julie Britt, Sonja Leslie, Lisa Maureen. B.C.E., City Coll., N.Y., 1957; M.S. in Civil Engring, Bklyn. Poly. Inst., 1960; D.Eng., U. Calif. at Berkeley, 1963. Registered profl. engrs. Calif., Pa., Va. Asst. prof. engring. San Diego State Coll., 1962-64; Fulbright research scholar Inst. Transport Economy, Oslo, Norway, 1964-65; prin. engr. Wilbur Smith & Assos., San Francisco, 1965-66; faculty Carnegie-Mellon U., Pitts., 1966-74, prof. civil engring., 1970-74; asso. dir. Transp. Research Inst., 1966-74; Hamilton prof., chmn. dept. civil engring. U. Va., 1974—; staff cons. Gen. Analytics, Inc., 1971-78; Cons. P.R. Planning Bd., 1969-70. Editor: Public Transportation: Planning, Operations and Management, 1979; Mem. editorial bd.: Transp. Research; Author tech. papers, books and articles. Chmn. bd. mgmt. YMCA, 1968-69; mem. Churchill Boro Planning Commn., 1972-74. Recipient Alumni award in Civil Engring. Coll. City N.Y., 1957; Pyke Johnson award Transp. Research Bd., 1977; Fulbright travel grantee, 1964-65. Mem. ASCE (Huber research prize 1976), Am. Scandinavian Found., Inst. Transp. Engrs., Transp. Research Bd. (exec. com.), Am. Soc. Engring. Edn., Sigma Xi, Chi Epsilon, Tau Beta Pi. Home: 1703 Old Forge Rd Charlottesville VA 22901

HOEL, PAUL (GERHARD HOEL), statistician, educator; b. Iola, Wis., Mar. 23, 1905; s. Carl S. and Inga (Loken) H.; m. Hazel Bessie Helvig, Sept. 7, 1932; children—David, Carlton, Marie. A.B., Luther Coll., 1926; postgrad., U. Pitts., 1926-27; M.A., U. Minn., 1929, Ph.D., 1933. Instr. Rose Poly. Inst., 1933-36; instr. Oreg. State U., 1936-39; from instr. to prof. U. Cal. at Los Angeles, 1939—. Author: Introduction to Mathematical Statistics, 4 edits, 1947-71, Elementary Statistics, 4 edits, 1960-76, (with R. Jessen) Basic Statistics for Business and Economics, 2d edit, 1977, (with C. Stone and S. Port) Probability, Statistics, Stochastic Processes, 3 vols, 1970. Am.-Scandinavian Found. fellow, Norway, 1936-37; Fulbright research fellow, Norway, 1953-54. Home: 1726 Westridge Rd Los Angeles CA 90049

HOELTERHOFF, MANUELA VALI, editor, critic; b. Hamburg, W.Ger., Apr. 6, 1949; came to U.S., 1957; d. Heinz Alfons and Olga Christine (Goertz) H. B.A., Hofstra U., 1971; M.A., NYU, 1973. Assoc. editor Arete Pub. Co., Princeton, N.J., 1977-80; editor-in-chief Art and Auction Mag., N.Y.C., 1979-81; arts editor Wall Street Jour., N.Y.C., 1981—. Recipient Pulitzer prize Columbia U., 1983, citation for disting. commentary Am. Soc. Newspaper Editors, 1982, 83. Office: Wall Street Jour 22 Cortlandt St New York NY 10007

HOENACK, AUGUST FREDERICK, architect; b. N.Y.C., Apr. 1, 1908; s. Hugo H. and Hulda (Kilian) H.; m. Mary Margery Course, June 14, 1939; children—Stephen A., Judith (Mrs. Paul Schultz), Francis A., August Jeremy. B.Arch., Pratt Inst., 1938; student, Columbia, 1930-31; postgrad., George Washington U., 1940-41. Architect PBA, Washington, 1938-41; asso. architect hospital facilities USPHS, Washington, 1942-46, asst. chief, 1946-55, chief architecture, engring. equipment br., 1955-68; v.p. firm Jensen & Halstead (Architects, Engrs. & Consultants), Chgo., 1968-73; asso. Dalton, Dalton, Litte, Newport, Bethesda, Md., 1973—. Contbr. profl. jours. Recipient Superior Service award HEW, 1967, Outstanding Alumnus award Pratt Inst., 1968. Fellow AIA (mem. health environment com. 1960-67), Am. Assn. Hosp. Planning (Distinguished Service to Hosp. Design award 1967), Am. Hosp. Assn., Internat. Hosp. Fedn. Home: 8409 Seven Locks Rd Bethesda MD 20817

HOENEMEYER, FRANK JOSEPH, insurance company executive; b. Cin., Nov. 1, 1919; s. Frank Joseph and Irene (Perry) H.; m. Lucille F. De Jaco, Nov. 14, 1942; children: Frank, Cheryl, Marylyn, David. B.S., Xavier U., Cin., 1941, LL.D., 1974; M.B.A., Wharton Sch. of U. Pa., 1947, Rider Coll., 1982. With Prudential Ins. Co., Newark, 1947—, v.p., 1958-64, 64, sr. v.p., 1964-65, exec. v.p. investments, 1965-81, vice chmn., 1981—, also dir.; dir. Cin. Inc., Hambros Ltd. Trustee Xavier U. Served to lt. col. USAAF, 1941-46. Club: Essex. Home: 7 Harwood Dr Madison NJ 07940 Office: Prudential Plaza Newark NJ 07101

HOENER, ARTHUR, artist, educator; b. Bklyn., June 4, 1929; s. Clarence Morton and Ella (Long) H.; m. Margaret Franklin, Nov. 19, 1951; children: Arthur, Carolyn, Irene, Donna, Ginny. Student, Cooper Union, 1949-52; B.F.A., Yale U., 1956, M.F.A., 1958. Asst. prof. art Boston U., 1957-60; pres., creative dir. Sage Advt., Inc., Brookline, Mass., 1960-65; freelance designer, design cons., 1965—; prof. design, chmn. design dept. Mass. Coll. Art, Boston, 1960-70; prof. art, design Hampshire Coll., Amherst, Mass., 1970—. Moderator, producer: program Studio Talk, Eastern Ednl. Network, WGBH-FM, Boston, 1963-67; one-man shows include, Peter Cooper Gallery, N.Y.C., 1957, Nexus Gallery, Boston, 1958, 59, 60, Obelisk Gallery, Boston, 1966, San Diego U., 1977, Art Inst., Boston, 1979, Hampshire Coll., 1981; exhibited group shows, Phila. Coll. Art, 1950, Corcoran Gallery, 1959, Worcester (Mass.) Art Mus., 1981. Trustee Unitarian Soc., Northampton, 1974-76. YADDO fellow, 1968; recipient Boston Art Dirs. Club award distinctive merit, 1964, 67, 68. Mem. New Eng. Contemporary Artists (chmn. 1963-67). Home: 289 Elm St Northampton MA 01060 Office: Dept Art Hampshire Coll Amherst MA 01002

HOENIGER, FREDERICK JULIUS DAVID, educator; b. Goerlitz, Germany, Apr. 25, 1921; naturalized, 1946; s. George and Elli (Dohne) H.; m. Judith Whitaker, Sept. 13, 1954; children—Brian, Cathleen. B.A., U. Toronto, Can., 1946, M.A., 1948; Ph.D., U. London, Eng., 1954. Lectr. U. Sask. (Can.), Saskatoon, 1946-47; lectr. English dept. Victoria Coll., U. Toronto, 1948-51, 53-55, asst. prof., 1955-61, asso. prof., 1961-63, prof., 1963—, chmn. dept., 1969-72; Dir. Centre for Reformation and Renaissance Studies, Toronto, 1964-69, 75-79. Gen. editor: Revels Plays, 1971—; Editor: (with Thomas P. Harrison) The Fowles of Heaven, 1972. Brit. Council scholar, 1951-53; Guggenheim fellow, 1964-65. Mem. Renaissance Soc. Am. (coordinating sec. No. Central br. 1965-73), Canadian Soc. Renaissance Studies (pres. 1976-78), World Centre for Shakespeare Studies. Club: Toronto Field Naturalist (pres. 1960-62). Home: 133 Roxborough Dr Toronto ON M4W 1X5 Canada

HOENIGSWALD, HENRY MAX, educator; b. Breslau, Germany, Apr. 17, 1915; s. Richard and Gertrud (Grunwald) H.; m. Gabriele Schoepflich, Dec. 26, 1944; children: Frances Gertrude, Susan Ann. Student, U. Munich, 1932-33, U. Zurich, 1933-34, U. Padua, 1934-36; D.Litt., U. Florence, 1936, Perfezionamento, 1937; L.H.D. (hon.), Swarthmore Coll., 1981, M.A., U. Pa., 1971. Staff mem. Istituto Studi Etruschi, Florence, 1936-38; lectr., research asst., instr. Yale U., 1939-42, 44-45; lectr., instr. Hartford Sem. Found., 1942-43, 45-46; lectr. Hunter Coll., 1942-43, 46; lectr. charge Army specialized tng. U. Pa., Phila., 1943-44, asso. prof., 1948-59, prof. linguistics, 1959—, chmn. dept. linguistics, 1963-70, co-chmn., 1978-79; P-4 Fgn. Service Inst., Dept. State, 1946-47; asso. prof. U. Tex., 1947-48; Collitz prof., 1955; sr. linguist Deccan Coll., India, 1955; Fulbright lectr., Kiel, summer 1968, Oxford U., 1976-77; corp. vis. com. fgn. lits. and linguistics MIT, 1968-74; chmn. overseers com. to visit dept. linguistics Harvard U., 1978—; vis. assoc. prof. Georgetown U., 1952-53, 54, Princeton U., 1959-60; vis. prof. Yale U., 1961-62; mem. Seminar, Columbia U., 1965—; fellow St. John's Coll., Oxford U., 1976-77; cons. Etymological Dictionary of Old High German, 1980—. Author: Spoken Hindustani, 1946-47, Language Change and Linguistic Reconstruction, 1960, Studies in Formal Historical Linguistics, 1973; Editor: Am. Oriental Series, 1954-58, The European Background of American Linguistics, 1977; assoc. editor: Folia Linguistica Historica, 1979—, Indian Jour. Linguistics, 1977—; cons. editor: Jour. History of Ideas, 1978—; adv. bd.: Jour. Indo-European Studies, 1973—, Lang. and Style, 1968—. Am. Council Learned Socs. fellow, 1942-43, 44; Guggenheim fellow, 1950-51; Newberry Library fellow, 1956; NSF and Center Advanced Study Behavioral Scis. fellow, 1962-63. Mem. Am. Philos. Soc., Am. Acad. Arts and Sci., Linguistic Soc. Am. (pres. 1958, com. research 1972-84, com. library 1984—, com. archives 1983—), Am. Oriental Soc. (editor 1954-58, pres. 1966-67), Philol. Soc. (London), Linguistic Soc. India, Societas Linguistica Europaea, Linguistics Assn. Gt. Britain, Indogermanische Gesellschaft, Am. Philol. Assn., Archaeol. Inst. Am., Società di linguistica Italiana, Internat. Linguistic Assn.; mem. MLA. Home: 908 Westdale Ave Swarthmore PA 19081 Office: 618 Williams Hall U Pa Philadelphia PA 19104

HOENMANS, PAUL JOHN, oil company executive; b. Humboldt, Sask., Can., Aug. 22, 1932; came to U.S., 1965; s. Paul Ferdinand and Barnadine (Gentges) H.; m. Rhoda J. Main, June 29, 1957; children: John Paul, Jill Kendal, Dina Eugenie. B.S. in Civil Engring., U. B.C., Vancouver, 1954. Gen mgr. Mobil Oil A.G., Hamburg, West Germany, 1975-78; pres. Mobil Europe Inc., London, 1978-79; exec. v.p. exploration and producing Mobil Oil Corp., N.Y.C., 1979-82, exec. v.p. mktg.and refining, 1983, pres. mktg. and refining, 1983—, dir. Chmn. for Mobil Corp. United Way, N.Y.C., 1981. Mem. AIME, Assn. Profl. Engrs. Alta. (Can.). Roman Catholic. Office: Mobil Oil Corp 150 E 42d St New York NY 10017

HOERNER, ROBERT JACK, lawyer; b. Fairfield, Iowa, Oct. 12, 1931; s. John A. and Margaret (Simmons) H.; m. Susan Patricia Warren, Aug. 27, 1980; children: John Andrew, Timothy Chandler, Blayne Marie, Michelle Margaret. B.A., Cornell Coll., 1953; J.D., U. Mich., 1958. Bar: Ohio 1960, U.S. Supreme Ct. 1964. Law clk. to Chief Justice Earl Warren, U.S. Supreme Ct., Washington, 1958-59; chief evaluation sect. antitrust div. Dept. Justice, Washington, 1963-65; ptnr. Jones, Day, Reavis & Pogue, Cleve., 1967—. Contbr. articles to legal jours. Mem. ABA, Ohio Bar Assn., Cleve. Bar Assn. Home: 8 Oakshore Dr Bratenahl OH 44108 Office: Jones Day Reavis & Pogue 1700 Huntington Bldg Cleveland OH 44115

HOERNI, JEAN AMÉDÉE, electronics cons.; b. Geneva, Sept. 26, 1924; U.S., 1953, naturalized, 1959; s. Robert and Jeanne (Berthoud) H.; m. Ruth Carmona, May 18, 1976; children—Michael, Anne, Susan. B.S., U. Geneva, 1947, Ph.D., 1950; Ph.D., Cambridge U., 1952. Founder, research physicist Fairchild Semiconductor Corp., 1957-61; v.p. Teledyne, Inc., Mountain View, Calif., 1961-63; cons., Los Altos, Calif., 1963-67; founder, pres. Intersil, Inc., Cupertino, Calif., 1967-75; electronics cons., Hailey, Idaho, 1975—; founder, dir. Telmos, Inc., Santa Clara, Calif., 1981—. Recipient John Scott medal City of Phila., 1966; Longstreth medal Franklin Inst., 1969. Fellow IEEE. Patentee in field. Home and office: East Fork Rd Hailey ID 83333 PO Box 1349 Hailey ID 83333

HOERR, STANLEY OBERMANN, surgeon; b. Chgo., Sept. 29, 1909; s. Charles Ferdinand and Lillie Sophia (Obermann) H.; m. Janet Urie, July 9, 1932; children: Mary Hoerr Meyer, Joan Hoerr Schilling, Stanley O., Charls M., Mark R. A.B., Antioch Coll., 1932; M.D., Harvard U., 1936. Diplomate: Am. Bd. Surgery. Intern, resident Peter Bent Brigham Hosp., Boston, 1936-42; pathology resident Huntington Meml. Hosp., Boston, 1938-39; asso. in surgery Peter Bent Brigham Hosp., 1945-47; asso. prof. surgery Ohio State U. Sch. Medicine, 1947-50; surg. staff Cleve. Clinic Found., 1950-74, chmn. div. surgery, 1956-71, resident emeritus staff, 1979—; chmn. dept. surgery Fairview Gen. Hosp., Cleve., 1974-79. Contbr. articles to profl. jours., textbooks. Served from capt. to maj. AUS, 1942-45; ETO. Fellow ACS (gov. 1963-72, 2d v.p. 1970-71, pres. Ohio chpt. 1963, Disting. Service award 1979); mem. AMA (sec. sect. gen. surgery 1965-68, chmn. sect. 1973-75), Am. Surg. Assn., Central Surg. Assn. (pres. 1970-71), Internat. Surg. Soc., Eastern Surg. Soc. (pres. 1975-76), Soc. Surgery Alimentary Tract (pres. 1971-72), Soc. Univ. Surgeons, Whipple Surg. Soc., Am. Gastroent. Assn., Cleve. Surg. Soc. (pres. 1958), Cleve. Med. Library Assn. (trustee 1973-83, pres. 1977-78, 80-81), Cleve. Acad. Med. (Disting. Service award 1974). Clubs: Pasteur, Rowfant, Harvard (Cleve.). Home: 997 Richmond Rd Lyndhurst OH 44124 Office: 9500 Euclid Ave Cleveland OH 44106

HOESCHLER, LINDA LOVAS, computer systems company executive; b. Joplin, Mo., July 19, 1944; d. Stephen Edward and Hildur (Wederquist) Lovas; m. John Gregory Hoeschler, Aug. 27, 1966; children: Kristen Bowe, Frederick Reeves. B.A., Barnard Coll., 1966; M.A., New Sch. for Social Research, 1968. Editorial asst. Macy Westchester Newspapers, Inc., summers 1964-66; research asst. Columbia U., N.Y.C., 1966-67; editor New Sch. for Social Research, N.Y.C., 1966-68; dir. Hull House Ctr., Chgo., 1967-68; free-lance writer, editor, lectr., 1969-76; mng. editor Minn. Gov's Commn. on Arts, St. Paul, 1976-77; arts grants coordinator Dayton-Hudson Found., Mpls., 1977-78; dir. communications Dayton-Hudson Corp., Mpls., 1978-80, v.p. communications, 1980-82; regional mgr. B. Dalton Bookseller subs. (Dayton-Hudson Corp.), Mpls., 1982-83; mem. adv. bd. Nat. Computer Systems, Mpls., 1981-83, group v.p., 1983—. Author music, dance and book criticism, Mpls. star and St. Paul Pioneer Press; producer concerts, Bach Soc., 1970-74; author (with Jimmie Powell), Minnesota: State of the Arts, 1977; author, editor ann. reports, St. Paul Arts-Sci. Council, 1971-72, 73-74 (Printing Industries Am. Graphics 1973). Bd. dirs., chmn. long-range planning Minn. Dance Theatre, Mpls., 1979-81; bd. dirs. Milkweed Chronicale, Mpls., 1979—, Plymouth Music Series, Mpls., 1979—; bd. dirs., mem. exec. com., fin. com. and books com. Am. Council for Arts, N.Y.C., 1981—; mem. Minn. Gov's Commn. on Edn. for Econ. Growth. Herbert Lehman fellow, 1966-68. Mem. Women's Econ. Roundtable. Mem. Democratic Farm Labor Party. Congregationalist. Club: Mpls. Home: 1630 Edgcumbe Rd St. Paul MN 55116 Office: Nat. Computer Systems 4401 W 76th St Minneapolis MN 55435

HOESSLE, CHARLES HERMAN, zoo director; b. St. Louis, Mar. 20, 1931; m. Marilyn Mueller, Jan. 5, 1952; children: Maureen, Kirk, Tracy, Bradley. A.A., Harris Tchrs. Coll., 1951; student, Am. Assn. Zool. Parks and Aquariums Zoo Mgmt. Sch., 1976-77. Reptile keeper St. Louis Zoo, 1963, asst. curator, 1964; curator reptiles and curator edn. St. LouisZoo, 1968-69; gen, curator and dep. dir. St. Louis Zoo, 1969-82, dir., 1982—; adj. prof. dept. biology St. Louis U., 1973-74, 81-82, 83; owner, operator Exotic Pet Shop, St. Louis; host St. Louis Zoo Show, 1968-78. Chmn. Reptile Study Merit Badge Counselors, St. Louis; state chmn. UN Day, 1982. Served with U.S. Army, 1952-54. Mem. Am. Assn. Zool. Parks and Aquariums (bd. dirs. 1977-79), St. Louis Naturalists Club, Internat. Union Dirs. Zool. Gardens. Club: Rotary. Home: 7934 Croydon St. Louis MO 63123 Office: St Louis Zool Park Forest Park St. Louis MO 63110

HOETKER, WILLIAM JAMES, English education educator; b. St. Louis, July 23, 1932; s. Carl Henry and Mary O'Neill H.; children: William, Glenn, Morna. B.S., S.E., Mo. State U., 1953; M.A., Washington U., St. Louis, 1960, Edn.D., 1967. Tchr. English Clayton High Sch., Mo., 1960-65; dir. theater research Cemrel, Inc., St. Louis, 1967-70; assoc. prof. English U. Ill., 1970-73; prof. English edn. Fla. State U., Tallahassee, 1973—, prof. curriculum and instrn. Coll. Edn., 1978—; vis. prof. U. B.C., 1975. Assoc. editor: Research in Teaching of English, 1973-77; contbr. articles to profl. jours. Mem. Nat. Council Tchrs. English, Assn. Supervision and Curriculum Devel. Democrat.

Home: 1226 Pepper Dr Tallahassee FL 32304 Office: Fla State U 209 Edn Tallahassee FL 32306

HOEVELER, WILLIAM M., judge; b. Aug. 23, 1922; m. Mary Griffin Smith, 1950; 4 children. Student, Temple U., 1941-42; B.A., Bucknell U., 1947; LL.B., Harvard U., 1950. Bar: Fla. bar 1951. Practice law, Miami, Fla., 1951—; firm individual practice law; judge U.S. Dist. Ct. for Fla. So. Dist., 1977—; mem. U.S. Dist. Ct. Com. for Rev. Local Rules; lectr. in field. Incorporator, bd. dirs. Youth Industries, Inc.; mem. vestry St. Stephens Episcopal Ch., 1973-75, chancellor, 1973—. Served to lt. USMC, 1942-46. Mem. Am. Judicature Soc., Fla. Bar (personal injury and wrongful death adv. com. 1976), Phila. Bar Assn., Dade County (Fla.) Bar Assn. (chmn. charity drives com. 1966), Am. Bar Assn. (chmn. com. on products, profl. and gen. liability law 1972-73, program chmn. sec. ins., negligence and compensation law 1975, mem. sect. governing council 1975-78, mem. governing com. of forum com. on constrn. industry), Omicron Delta Kappa. Office: PO Box 013660 Flagler Sta Miami FL 33101 *

HOFACRE, WILLIAM MARION, food co. exec.; b. Axtell, Kans., July 29, 1933; s. Michael Howard and Nellie Marie (Wilson) H.; m. Janet Elizabeth Hemmer, June 12, 1959; children—Michael Lane, Tracey Elizabeth. B.S. in Bus. Adminstrn, U. Nebr., 1957; M.B.A., Mich. State U., 1967. Internal auditor Bendix Corp., South Bend, Ind., 1957-63, controller, Detroit, 1963-67, Itek Corp. bus. products div., Rochester, N.Y., 1967-69; corporate controller Am. Air Filter, Louisville, 1969-70; v.p., controller Daniel Internat. Corp., Greenville, S.C., 1970-74, v.p. fin., 1974-78, Oscar Mayer & Co., 1978—, also dir. Served with AUS, 1953-55. Mem. Financial Execs. Inst., Delta Sigma Pi. Mem. Ch. of Christ. Clubs: Maple Bluff Country, Cherokee Park Country, Madison; Met. (Chgo.). Home: 1545 Comanche Glen Madison WI 53704 Office: 910 Mayer Ave Madison WI 53707

HOFELDT, JOHN W., lawyer; b. Elkhart Lake, Wis., Sept. 6, 1920; s. Johann Heinrich and Matilda A. (Kuester) H.; m. Marion Ruth Meyer, Nov. 27, 1943; children: Nancy R. Hofeldt Werley, William A., Mark R. Ph.B., U. Wis.-Madison, 1943, LL.B. (editor Law Rev. 1946-47), 1947. Bar: Ill. 1948. Since practiced in, Chgo.; partner firm Haight, Hofeldt, Davis & Jambor (and predecessors), 1955—; lectr. John Marshall Grad. Sch., Chgo., 1974-82. Mem. Ill. Sch. Dist. 194 Bd. Edn., 1964-72. Served with USN, 1943-46. Mem. Am., Wis., Ill. bar assns., Bar Assn. 7th Fed. Circuit, Patent Law Assn. Chgo. Republican. Clubs: Masons, Shriners, Union League (Chgo.). Home: 900 Sunset Dr Glenwood IL 60425 Office: 55 E Monroe St Chicago IL 60603

HOFF, DAVID DANIEL, lawyer; b. Seattle, Feb. 22, 1938; s. Edward Morton and Rose Frances (Rubin) H.; m. Valerie Margaret Knecht, Nov. 25, 1978; children—James B., Paula J., Deana L., Mack H. B.A. in Polit. Sci, U. Wash., Seattle, 1959, J.D., 1962. Bar: Wash. bar 1962. Law clk. to justice Wash. Supreme Ct., 1962-63; practice in, Seattle, 1963—; partner firm Ridell, Williams, Ivie, Bullitt & Walkinshaw, 1981—; instr. real estate securities Wash. Real Estate Ednl. Found., 1973—; pres. Western States Bar Conf., 1981-82; chmn. Fed. Jud. Nominating Com. Western Wash., 1980; police intelligence auditor City of Seattle, 1980—; mem. Wash. Securities Adv. Com., 1974-79. Mem. Am. Bar Assn., Am. Arbitration Assn., Wash. Bar Assn. (pres. 1978-79), Seattle-King County Bar Assn. Clubs: Rainier, College. Home: 265 SW 192d St Seattle WA 98166 Office: 4400 Seattle First Nat Bank Bldg Seattle WA 98154

HOFF, GERHARDT MICHAEL, lawyer, insurance company executive; b. Vienna, Austria, June 12, 1930; came to U.S., 1951, naturalized, 1955; s. Erich Theodor and Vilma (Frank) Klockenhoff; m. Lisa Decristoforo, June 1, 1970; children: Michael, Elizabeth, Anne Christine. Student, U. Munich (Ger.) Law Sch., 1948-51, Columbia U., 1951-52; LL.B., N.Y. U., 1958; LL.M., Emory U., 1982; C.L.U., 1961. Bar: Mass. 1959, D.C. 1968, Ga. 1984. With Mass. Mut. Life Ins. Co. and Variable Annuity Life Ins. Co., 1958-67; v.p. Variable Annuity Life Ins. Co. Am., Washington, 1967-70; mem. staff financial services group ITT Corp., 1968-69; pres. ITT Hamilton Life Ins. Co., also Variable Annuity Ins. Co., St. Louis, 1970-72, Sun Life Ins. Co. Am., Balt., 1972-78, 81-83, chief exec. officer, 1978-83; pres. Sun Life Group Am., Inc., Atlanta, 1978-83; dir. Kaufman & Broad, Inc., Los Angeles, 1976-83; Chmn. Balt. Urban Coalition, 1976-77. Served with AUS, 1955-57. Decorated Commendation ribbon with pendant. Mem. Am. Soc. C.L.U.'s, Am. Bar Assn. Presbyterian. Clubs: Cherokee Country, Capital City (Atlanta). Office: 27 W Wesley Ridge Atlanta GA 30327 *We'll get along better with others if we recognize their right to be hard or easy on themselves, depending on their own choice of priorities.*

HOFF, MARCIAN EDWARD, JR., electronics engineer; b. Rochester, N.Y., Oct. 28, 1937; s. Marcian Edward and Mary Elizabeth (Fitzpatrick) H.; m. Judith Schless Rytand, May 19, 1977; children: Carolyn, Lisa, Jill. B.E.E., Rensselaer Poly. Inst., Troy, N.Y., 1958; M.S., Stanford U., 1959, Ph.D., 1962. Research asso. Stanford U., 1962-68; mgr. applications research Intel Corp., Santa Clara, Calif., 1968-83; v.p. research and devel. Atari Inc., Sunnyvale, Calif., 1983—. Author articles on adaptive systems, microcomputers. NSF fellow, 1958—; recipient Stuart Ballantine medal Franklin Inst., 1979. Mem. IEEE (Clido Brunetti award 1980), Sigma Xi, Eta Kappa Nu, Tau Beta Pi. Patentee track circuits, electrochem. memory, digital filters, integrated circuits. Home: 1075 Astoria Dr Sunnyvale CA 94087 Office: Atari Inc 1196 Borregas Ave Sunnyvale CA 94086

HOFF, MARGO, painter, printmaker, muralist; b. Tulsa, June 14, 1912; d. C.W. and Ada Almeda (Hayes) H.; m. George Buehr, 1940 (dec.); 1 dau., Mia. Student, U. Tulsa, Art Inst. Chgo., Pratt Graphics; hon. D.F.A., St. Mary's Coll., 1969. Pub. collections, Met. Mus. Art, Whitney Mus. Am. Art, Nat. Gallery Art, Washington, Victoria and Albert Mus., London, Smithsonian Instn., Washington, gallery exhbns. and one-man shows, Wildenstein Gallery, Paris, Betty Parson Gallery, N.Y.C., Fairweather Hardin Gallery, Chgo., Itau Gallery, San Paolo, Brazil, Art Inst., Chgo.; commd. work Mural, Mayo Clinic, Rochester, Minn., Murals, Govt. Bldg., Plattsburgh, N.Y., Wall constrn., Home Fed. Bank, Chgo., Canvas collage, Peat-Marwick-Mitchell, Washington, Ben Franklin Bank, Houston; artist-in-residence or vis. artist assignments, Am. U. Beirut, R.I. Sch. Design, Art Sch. U. Denver, Goretti Sch., Ft. Portal, Uganda; (work in other fields) mosaic pool, Del E. Bldg., Chgo., Stage curtain and costumes, Murray Louis Dancer, illustrations 3 books, tapestry designs woven by Addis Ababa Workshop; slide projections Carmina Burana Ethiopa, Notre Dame Theatre. Home: 218 E 12th St New York NY 10003 Office: 114 W 14th St New York NY10011

HOFF, NICHOLAS JOHN, mechanical and aerospace engineer; b. Magyarovar, Hungary, Jan. 3, 1906; came to U.S., 1939, naturalized, 1944; s. Miklos and Lenke H.; m. Vivian Church, July 20, 1940 (dec. Apr. 1969); m. Ruth Kleczewski, Nov. 17, 1972; 1 dau., Karen Brandt. M.E., Fed. Poly. Inst. Zurich, Switzerland, 1928, Dipl.-Ing., 1928; Ph.D. in Engring. Mechs, Stanford U., 1942. Airplane designer, Hungary, 1928-38; research asst. Stanford U., 1939-40, head dept. aeros., 1957-71, prof. aeros., 1957-71, prof. emeritus, 1971—; instr. aeros. Poly. Inst. Bklyn., 1940-41, asst. prof., 1941-43, asso. prof., 1943-46, prof., 1946-57, head dept. aeros., 1950-57; vis. prof. Monash (Australia) U., 1971, Ga. Inst. Tech., 1973, Cranfield (Eng.) Inst. Tech., 1974-75, Poly. Inst. Zurich, 1975; Clark/Crossan prof. engring. Rensselaer Poly. Inst., 1976-79, vis. Disting. prof., 1979-81; cons. to govt. and industry. Author: The Analysis of Structures, 1956; editor: books, including High Temperature Effects in Aircraft Structures, 1958, Creep in Structures, 1962; contbr. numerous articles on structural and stress analysis, aeros. to profl. jours. Fellow AIAA (hon., Pendray award 1971, Structures, Structural Dynamics, and Materials award 1971), ASME (hon., Worcester Reed Warner medal 1967, ASME medal 1974), Royal Aero. Soc. (Gt. Britain); mem. ASCE (life, von Karman medal 1972), Aero. Soc. India (hon.), U.S. Nat. Acad. Engring., Internat. Acad. Astronautics (corr.). Office: Dept Aeros and Astronautics Stanford U Stanford CA 94305

HOFF, SYD(NEY), cartoonist, author; b. N.Y.C., Sept. 4, 1912; s. Ben and Mary H.; m. Dora Berman, May 31, 1937; children: Susan Gross, Bonnie Stillman. Student, Nat. Acad. Design. Cartoonist: Laugh It Off Comic Strip, King Features Syndicate, 1957-71; Cartoonist appearing in: Playboy Mag.; author: The Man Who Loved Animals, 1982, The Young Cartoonist, 1983, Happy Birthday, Henrietta!, 1983; illustrator: children's books including Oliver; author: juvenile fiction Irving and Me; short stories. Mem. Authors Guild. Address: Box 2463 Miami Beach FL 33140 *

HOFF, WILLIAM BRUCE, JR., lawyer; b. Parkersburg, W.Va., Sept. 13, 1932; s. William Bruce and Edith Virginia (Stalnaker) H.; m. Catherine Louise McCue, Feb. 20, 1954; children: William Bruce, David Franklin, Jennifer, Catherine. A.B. with honors, W.Va. U., 1954; L.L.B., Harvard U., 1957. Bar: Ill. 1958, U.S. Supreme Ct. 1972. Assoc. Mayer, Brown & Platt, Chgo., 1957-66, ptnr., 1967—. Chmn. Winnetka (Ill.) Caucus Com., 1969-70. Mem. Am. Coll. Trial Lawyers, ABA, Chgo. Bar Assn., 7th Circuit Bar Assn., Phi Beta Kappa. Home: 1340 Scott Ave Winnetka IL 60093 Office: Mayer Brown & Platt 231 S LaSalle St Chicago IL 60604

HOFFA, HARLAN EDWARD, art education educator; b. Kalamazoo, June 23, 1925; s. Leolan William and Pearl (Foster) H.; m. Marian Perko, Aug. 10, 1946 (div. 1971); children: Kathryn Jane, Thomas Scott; m. Suzanne Aldridge Dudley, Sept. 11, 1971. B.S., Wayne U., 1948; M.Ed., 1949; Ed.D., Pa. State U., 1959. Tchr. Evanston (Ill.) pub. schs., 1949-51; instr. art edn. Ohio State U., 1951-53; asst. prof. art State U. Coll. at Buffalo, 1953-59; asso. prof. fine arts and edn. head dept. Boston U., 1959-65; art edn. specialist U.S. Office Edn., 1964-67; prof. edn. and fine arts, chmn. art edn. program Ind. U., 1967-70; prof., head dept. art edn. Pa. State U., 1970-76, head div. art and music edn., 1976-79, acting dir. Sch. Visual Arts, 1979-80. Served with AUS, 1943-45. Mem. Nat. Art Edn. Assn. (pres. 1971-73). Home: 519 Cricklewood Dr Toftrees State College PA 16801 Office: Chambers Bldg Pa State U University Park PA 16802

HOFFBERGER, JEROLD CHARLES, corporation executive; b. Balt., Apr. 7, 1919; s. Samuel H. and Gertrude (Miller) H.; m. Alice Berney, June 10, 1946; children: David B., Richard J., Carol S., Charles P. Grad., Tome Sch., 1937, U. Va., 1940. Pres., dir. Nat. Brewing Co., Balt., 1947-75; pres., chmn. bd., chief exec. officer Carling Nat. Breweries, Inc., Balt., 1975-78; dir., chmn. exec. com. Fairchild Industries; dir. BTR Realty, Inc., Dayco, Inc., Real Estate Holding Co., Md. Nat. Bank; chmn., pres. Balt. Orioles, 1965-79, pres., 1979-83; chmn. bd. Diversified Resource Mgmt. Ltd., 1978—. Trustee United Jewish Appeal; bd. dirs. Hoffberger Found.; pres. Council Jewish Fedns. and Welfare Funds, 1975-78; chmn. United Israel Appeal, 1978-83; chmn. bd. Jewish Agy.; trustee Johns Hopkins Hosp., Balt. Served to capt. AUS, World War II. Mem. U. Va. Alumni Assn., Nat. Steeplechase and Hunt Assn. (past steward), Phi Epsilon Pi. Jewish. Clubs: Suburban Country, Mchts. Office: 25 S Calvert St Baltimore MD 21201

HOFFBERGER, LEROY EDWARD, lawyer; b. Balt., June 8, 1925; s. Jack H. and Mildred G. (Rosenstein) H.; m. Hildegard Voss, Aug. 9, 1967; children: Jack W., Douglas M. A.B., Princeton U., 1947; LL.B., U. Md., 1950. Bar: Md. 1950. Since practiced in, Balt.; of counsel firm Gordon, Feinblatt, Rothman, Hoffberger & Hollander, 1972—; pres., dir. CPC, Inc., Keystone Realty Co., Inc., O-W Fund, Inc., Real Estate Holding Co.; treas., dir. Blum's Inc.; gen. partner Churchill Investments, First Assos. Limited Partnership, World-Wide Rights Co.; dir. Motor Freight Express, Mchts. Mortgage Co., BTR Realty, Inc., Equitable Bancorp., Equitable Bank N.A., Formula 16 Limited. Pres., bd. dirs. Hoffberger Found.; bd. dirs. Asso. Jewish Charities Balt. Served to lt. (j.g.) USNR, World War II. Recipient award of merit, City of Balt., 1966. Mem. Am., Md., Balt. bar assns. Jewish. Clubs: Suburban; Tower (Princeton); Bucks (London). Home: 16 E Mt Vernon Pl Baltimore MD 21202 Office: 900 Garrett Bldg Baltimore MD 21202

HOFFBERGER, STANLEY ALAN, developer; b. Balt., Aug. 7, 1929; s. Jack H. and Mildred (Rosenstein) H.; m. Judith Rosenberg, Feb. 12, 1955; children: Jeffrey Alan, Russell Jay. A.B. cum laude, Princeton U., 1951. Vice pres. Merchants Terminal Corp., Balt., 1954-58, dir., 1962—; pres. Pompeian, Inc., Balt., 1964-68, chmn. bd., 1968-69; also dir.; pres. The Solarine Co., Laco Corp., Laco Products, Inc., C.W. Abbott, Inc., 1969-71; v.p. comml. div. Ervin Atlantic Co., Bethesda, Md., 1972-75; v.p., dir. R.B.H., Inc., 1970—; pres. Aspen Hill Tennis, Inc., 1978—. Dir. O.W. Fund.; Bd. dirs. Community Psychiatric Clinic, 1978—. Served with AUS, 1951-54. Jewish. Home: 4201 Cathedral Ave NW Apt 704-W Washington DC 20016

HOFFENBERG, MARTIN, air freight transportation company executive; b. Bklyn., Jan. 12, 1945; s. Harry and Bernice H. B.A., Bklyn. Coll., 1965; J.D., St. John's U., 1968. Bar: N.Y. bar 1969. Atty. Nat. Assn. Securities Dealers, Inc., N.Y.C., 1969; mem. firm Germaise and Quinn, N.Y.C., 1968-70; v.p. adminstrn., sec., gen. counsel Air Express Internat. Corp., Stamford, Conn., 1970-83, also dir.; pres. Transept Systems, Inc. Mem. Am. Bar Assn., N.Y. State Bar Assn. Home: 415 E 52d St Apt 26 New York NY 10022 Office: Suite 1100 225 W 34th St New York NY 10001

HOFFER, PAUL B., nuclear medicine physician, educator; b. N.Y.C., Apr. 9, 1939; m. Vicki Kornbluth; children: Marjorie, Joanne, Ilene, Suzanne. Student, Union Coll., 1956-59; M.D., U. Chgo., 1963; M.S., Yale U., 1977. Diplomate: Am. Bd. Radiology, Am. Bd. Nuclear Medicine. Resident in radiology U. Chgo., 1966-69, radiologist, 1969-70, dir. nuclear medicine, 1970-74; prof., dir. nuclear medicine U. Calif.-San Francisco, 1974-77, Yale U., New Haven, 1977—. Editor: Gallium 67 Imaging, 1978, Yearbook of Nuclear Medicine, 1981—; inventor radiation camera system, 1973. Served to lt. comdr. USN, 1964-66. Recipient Meml. medal Assn. Univ. Radiologists, 1968; James Picker Found. scholar, 1969-72. Mem. Soc. Nuclear Medicine (v.p. 1980-81), Commn. on Nuclear Medicine, Am. Coll. Radiology, Am. Coll. Physicians, Radiol. Soc. N.Am., AAAS. Jewish. Home: 10Briar Ln Hamden CT 06511 Office: Yale U Sch Medicine 333 Cedar St New Haven CT 06510 *The more I've done, the more I've been asked to do and the less time I've had available to do it. Sooner or later everyone must set priorities as well as goals. We must not only know what we want but also what we are willing to sacrifice for it.*

HOFFLEIT, ELLEN DORRIT, astronomer; b. Florence, Ala., Mar. 12, 1907; d. Fred and Kate (Sanio) H. A.B., Radcliffe Coll., 1928, M.A., 1932, Ph.D., 1938. From research asst. to astronomer Harvard Coll. Obs., 1929-56; mathematician Ballistic Research Labs., Aberdeen Proving Ground, Md., 1943-48; tech. expert, 1948-62; lectr. Wellesley Coll., 1955-56; mem. faculty Yale U., 1956—, sr. research astronomer, 1974—; dir. Maria Mitchell Obs., Nantucket, Mass., 1957-78; mem. Hayden Planetarium Com., N.Y.C., 1975—; editor Meteoritical Soc., 1958-68. Author: Some Firsts in Astronomical Photography, 1950, Yale Bright Star Catalogue, 4th edit, 1982; also research papers. Recipient Caroline Wilby prize Radcliffe Coll., 1938, Grad. Soc. medal, 1964; certificate appreciation War Dept., 1946; alumnae recognition award Radcliffe Coll., 1983. Mem. Internat. Astron. Union, Am. Astron. Soc., AAAS, Am. Geophys. Union, Meteoritical Soc., Am. Assn. Variable Stars Observers, Am. Def. Preparedness Assn., Nantucket Maria Mitchell Assn., Nantucket Hist. Soc. (hon.), Phi Beta Kappa, Sigma Xi. Home: 255 Whitney Ave New Haven CT 06511 Office: Yale U Obs Box 6666 New Haven CT 06511 *The guiding motto of my life has been, "Work for the work's sake and it will become a part of you./Work for the sake of worldly gain and you sell your soul to the Devil." Love for research and boundless perseverance have enabled me to achieve, not all that I might have wished, but far more than I would ever have dared to expect on the basis of mediocre high school grades.*

HOFFMAN, ALFRED JOHN, mutual fund executive; b. Amarillo, Tex., Apr. 16, 1917; s. Kurt John and Mabel (Beven) H.; m. Falice Mae Pittinger, Jan. 5, 1946; children: Susan Terry, Joh. J.D., U. Mo., 1942. Atty., Prudential Ins. Co. Am., 1946-50, Kansas City Fire & Marine Ins. Co., 1950-59; pres., dir. Jones & Babson, Inc., Kansas City; David L. Babson Growth Fund, Inc., Kansas City, Babson Tax Free Income Fund, Babson Money Market Fund; trustee Babson (D.L.) Bond Trust; vice chmn., dir. Am. Cablevision of Kansas City; pres. dir. UMB Bond Fund, UMB Stock Fund, others; dir. Frankona Am. Life Reins. Co. Served with USN, 1942-46. Mem. Am., Mo. bar assns. Home: 6701 High Dr Hills Mission KS 66208 Office: 2440 Pershing Rd Kansas City MO 64108

HOFFMAN, ALLAN SACHS, chemical engineer, educator; b. Chgo., Oct. 27, 1932; s. Saul A. and Frances E. (Sachs) H.; m. Susan Carol Freeman, July 29, 1962; children: David, Lisa. B.S. in Chem. Engring, Mass. Inst. Tech., 1953, M.S., 1955, Sc.D., 1957. Instr. chem. engring. Mass. Inst. Tech., Cambridge, 1954-56, asst. prof., 1958-60, asso. prof., 1965-70; research engr. Calif. Research Corp., Richmond, 1960-63; asso. dir. research Amicon Corp., Cambridge, 1963-65; prof. chem. engring. U. Wash., Seattle, 1970—; asst. dir. Center for Bioengring., 1973—; Cons. to various govtl., indsl. and acad. orgns., 1958—. Author: (with W. Burlant) Block and Graft Copolymers, 1960; Contbr. numerous articles on chem. engring. to profl. jours.; Patentee in field. Kimberly Clark fellow, 1954-55; Visking fellow, 1955-56; Fulbright fellow, 1957-58; Battelle fellow, 1970-72; UN adviser to Mexican govt., 1973-74. Mem. Am. Chem. Soc., Am. Inst. Chem. Engrs., Am. Soc. for Artificial Internal Organs, Internat. Soc. Artificial Internal Organs, Soc. for Biomaterials (pres. 1983-84), Biomed. Engring. Soc. Home: 4528 W Laurel Dr NE Seattle WA 98105 Office: Bioengineering Center FL 20 Univ Wash Seattle WA 98195

HOFFMAN, ARTHUR SAMUEL, govt. ofcl.; b. Camden, N.J., June 22, 1926; s. Louis and Rose (Wessel) H.; m. Roberte Anne Piot de Cesse, Nov. 13, 1950; children—Richard, Alan, Sidney, Elisabeth. A.B., Oberlin Coll., 1947; student, U. Minn., 1945; M.A., Johns Hopkins, 1948; Docteur es scis. politiques, U. Geneva, Switzerland, 1951. Corr. Camden-Phila. newspapers, Western Europe, 1949; econ. and polit. officer Dept. State, Germany, 1950-51, Czechoslovakia, 1957-59; information and cultural officer Dept. State and USIA, Germany, 1951-54, Japan, 1954-56, Washington, 1956, 62-65, 70-73, France, 1959-62, Turkey, 1966-68, Vietnam, 1969-70; acting dir. Edward R. Murrow Center Pub. Diplomacy, Fletcher Sch., Tufts U., 1965-66; chief planning and operational policy USIA, Washington, 1970, asso. dir. policy and plans, 1970-73; public affairs counselor US Mission to European Communities, Brussels, 1973-77; regional econ. info. adv. U.S. Mission to OECD, Paris, 1979-81; asst. dir. NATO Info. Service, Brussels, 1981—; mem. NATO Fellowship Awards Com., 1979—; lectr. univs., 1965-66; lectr. European, Australian and African univs., 1974-81. Producer television program on communications satellites, WGBH, Boston, 1966; Author: Speech, American Legion Oratory Anthology, 1944; Co-editor: Communications Satellites Seminar papers, 1967; editor: International Communication and the New Diplomacy, 1968; editor, contbr.: Japan and the Pacific Basin, 1980; Contbr.: articles U.S. newspapers and KYKLOS Mag, Zurich, 1949, Tunisie Economique, Tunis, 1979, Cronache Economiche, Turin, 1980. Served with AUS, 1944-46. Fellow Battelle Seattle Research Center, 1975. Address: NATO 1110 Brussels Belgium

HOFFMAN, ARTHUR WOLF, educator; b. S.I., N.Y., Mar. 13, 1921; s. William Herny and Esther Matilda (Wofl) H.; m. Joyce Faythe Lake, Aug. 13, 1949; children: Ruth, Gail, Susan. B.A., Wesley U., 1942; M.A. in English, Yale U., 1949, Ph.D., 1951. Instr. English Yale U., New Haven, 1949-53; asst. prof. English Syracuse U., N.Y., 1953-57, assoc. prof., 1957-62, prof., 1962—, chmn. dept. English, 1974-79. Author: John Dryden's Imagery, 1962; co-editor: Reading Poetry, 1968. Fellow Am. Council Learned Socs., 1961-62; Syracuse U. Humanities Research grantee, summer 1980. Lutheran. Office: Dept English Syracuse U 401 Hall of Langs Syracuse NY 13210

HOFFMAN, CALVIN, poet; b. Phila., Nov. 1, 1916; s. Henry Michael and Rachel Elizabeth (Greentrees) H.; m. Rosemary Galowin, Nov. 15, 1941 (dec. Sept. 29, 1979). B.A., Columbia, 1937. Reporter UPI, N.Y.C., 1937-40; free lance book reviewer, 1940-43; Spl. lectr. Cambridge (Eng.) U., 1956-75, U. Birmingham, Eng., 1955-75, U. Calif. at Los Angeles, 1960-65. Scenarist, Metro Goldwyn Mayer, Hollywood, Calif., 1943-46; drama critic Broadway (N.Y.) plays, 1946-60; poet, author, 1960—; Author: Stigma, 1939, Science Isn't God, 1941, This Mad Peace, 1945, The Engulfing Tide, 1948, Condemned to Live, 1951, Of Love Enriched, 1954, The Murder of the Man Who Was Shakespeare, 1955, Maude Morgan, 1956, Sunset, 1958, Bondage, 1961, Expense of Spirit, 1965, Paid in Blood, 1968, Beaded With Roses, 1970, Time Must End, 1972, Of Pleasures Unknown, 1974, The Undying Quest: Was It Shakespeare or Marlowe?, 1975, The Warring Winds, 1976, Amber Waves, 1977, Man Hates Man, 1978, Wave of Doom, 1980. Mem. Marlowe Soc. Gt. Britain (named hon. chmn. 1958), Marlowe Clubs Am. (named hon. pres. 1959), Shakespeare Action Com. (dir. London 1958-66), Poetry Soc. Am., Elizabethan Soc., Dante Alighieri Soc., English Speaking Union, Renaissance Soc. Am. Home: 1433 Flower Dr Sarasota FL 33579

HOFFMAN, CARTER OSBURN, investment banker; b. Balt., Sept. 3, 1927; s. Johns Janney and Margaret (Osburn) H.; m. Ann Cameron Marburg, June 24, 1950; children—Carter Osburn, Mary M., Carolyn Janney. Student, Johns Hopkins U., Wharton Sch. Fin., U. Pa.; certificate advanced investment studies, Internat. Banking Assn. Rep. Mead, Miller & Co. (Stockbrokers), Balt., 1948-57; asst. investment trust officer Equitable Trust Co., Balt., 1957-61; with T. Rowe Price Assos., Inc., Balt., 1961—; v.p., also dir.; Rowe chmn. Rowe Price New Income Fund, Inc.; also Rowe Price Prime Res. Fund, 1981—. Served with U.S. Army, 1946-48. Republican. Episcopalian. Clubs: Elkridge, Bachelors Cotillion, Center (Balt.). Office: T Rowe Price Assos 100 E Pratt St Baltimore MD 21202 *

HOFFMAN, DANIEL, literature educator, poet; b. N.Y.C., Apr. 3, 1923; s. Daniel and Frances (Beck) H.; m. Elizabeth McFarland, May

22, 1948; children: Kate, Macfarlane. B.A., Columbia, 1947; M.A., Columbia U., 1949, Ph.D., 1956. Instr. English Columbia U., 1952-56; vis. prof. Am. lit. Faculté des Lettres, Dijon, France, 1956-57; asst. prof. to prof. English Swarthmore Coll., 1957-66; prof. English U. Pa., 1966—, poet-in-residence, 1978—, Felix E. Schelling prof. English lit., 1983—; fellow Ind. U. Sch. Letters, 1959; George Elliston lectr. poetry U. Cin., 1964; lectr. 6th Internat. Sch. Yeats Studies, Sligo, Ireland, 1965; cons. poetry Library of Congress, 1973-74, hon. cons. in Am. letters, 1974-77. Author: poetry An Armada of Thirty Whales, 1954, A Little Geste and Other Poems, 1960, The City of Satisfactions, 1963, Striking the Stones, 1968, Broken Laws, 1970, The Center of Attention, 1974, Able Was I Ere I Saw Elba, 1977, Brotherly Love, 1981; criticism Paul Bunyan: Last of the Frontier Demigods, 1952, The Poetry of Stephen Crane, 1957, Form and Fable in American Fiction, 1961, Barbarous Knowledge, 1967, Poe Poe Poe Poe Poe Poe Poe, 1972; Editor: The Red Badge of Courage, 1957, American Poetry and Poetics, 1962, Ezra Pound and William Carlos Williams, 1983; editor, contbr.: The Harvard Guide to Contemporary American Writing, 1979. Served to 1st lt. USAAF, 1943-46. Decorated Legion of Merit; recipient Poetry Center Introductions prize, 1951; Yale Series of Younger Poets award, 1954; Ansley prize, 1957; Lit. award Athenaeum of Phila., 1963, 83; medal for excellence Columbia U., 1964; Nat. Inst. Arts and Letters award in poetry, 1967; meml. medal Hungarian PEN, 1980; poetry grantee Ingram Merrill Found., 1971-72; fellow Am. Council Learned Socs., 1961-62, 66-67; Nat. Endowment for Humanities, 1975-76; Guggenheim Meml. Found., 1983-84. Mem. Modern Lang. Assn., Acad. Am. Poets (chancellor 1972—), English Inst. Clubs: Century (N.Y.C.); Franklin Inn (Phila.). Office: Dept English U Pa Philadelphia PA 19104

HOFFMAN, DARLEANE CHRISTIAN, national laboratroy administrator, researcher; b. Terril, Iowa, Nov. 8, 1926; d. Carl Benjamin and Elverna (Kuhlman) Christian; m. Marvin Morrison Hoffman, Dec. 26, 1951; children: Maureane R., Daryl K. B.S., Iowa State U.-Ames, 1948, Ph.D., 1951. Chemist Oak Ridge Nat. Lab., 1952-53; staff mem. Los Alamos Sci. Lab., 1953-71, assoc. leader radiochemistry group, 1971-79, div. leader Chem.-Nuclear Chem. div., 1979-82, div. leader Isotope & Nuclear Chem. Div., 1982—; panel leader, speaker Los Alamos Women in Sci., 1975, 79, 82; mem. subcom. on nuclear and radiochemistry NRC, 1978-81, chmn. subcom. on nuclear and radiochemistry, 1982-84. Contbr. numerous articles in field to profl. jours. Recipient Alumni Citation of Merit Coll. Scis. and Humanities, Iowa State U., 1978; fellow NSF, 1964-65, Guggenheim Found., 1978-79. Fellow Am. Inst. Chemists; mem. Am. Chem. Soc. (chmn. nuclear chemistry and technology div. 1978-79, John Dustin Clark award Central N.Mex. sect. 1976, award for Nuclear Chemistry 1983), N.Mex. Inst. Chemists (pres. 1976-78), Am. Phys. Soc., AAAS. Methodist. Home: 3 Acoma Ln Los Alamos NM 87544 Office: Isotope & Nuclear Chemistry Div Los Alamos Nat Lab Los Alamos NM 87454

HOFFMAN, DONALD HOWARD, railroad executive; b. Pitts., Apr. 6, 1933; s. Howard Alfred and Helen Aline (Dickson) H.; m. Mary Lovina Lamb, Sept. 17, 1955; children: Thomas, James, Timothy, Michael. B.S., W. Va. U., 1954; postgrad., Grad. Sch. Bus. U. Pitts., 1957, Grad. Sch. Bus. Adminstrn. Harvard U., 1977. With U.S. Steel Corp., 1957-83, gen. mgr. labor relations, 1973-78, v.p. personnel, 1978-83, pres., 1983—, Bessemer and Lake Erie R.R. Co. and affiliated cos., Monroeville, Pa., 1983—, Missabe and Iron Range Ry. Co., Duluth, Minn., 1983—, Elgin, Joliet and Eastern Ry. Co., Joliet, Ill., 1983—, Pitts. & Conneaut Dock Co., Conneaut, Ohio, 1983—. Chmn. bd. Port Authority of Allegheny County, 1977-81; bd. dirs. S.W. Pa. Regional Planning Commn., 1979—, Indsl. Relations Assn., 1979—, State Transp. Adv. Com., 1980-82, St. Clair Meml. Hosp., Pitts., 1980—, Greater Pitts. Bus. Devel. Corp., 1981—. Served to capt. USAF, 1954-57. Mem. Assn. Am. R.R.s (dir. 1983—), Western R.R. Assn. (dir. 1983), Traffic Club Pitts. Republican. Roman Catholic. Clubs: Duquesne, Chartiers Country (Pitts.); Kitchi Gammi (Duluth); Rolling Rock, Laurel Valley Golf (Ligonier, Pa.). Home: 519 N Meadowcroft Ave Pittsburgh PA 15216 Office: 135 Jamison Ln PO Box 68 Monroeville PA 15146

HOFFMAN, DONALD M., lawyer; b. Los Angeles, Aug. 27, 1935; s. Henry Maurice and Viola Gertrude (Rothe) H. B.S., UCLA, 1957, LL.B., 1960. Bar: Calif. 1961. Practiced in, Los Angeles, 1961—; partner firm Greenwald, Hoffman & Meyer, 1964—. Charter mem., pres. Wilshire Estate Planning Council. Served to 2d lt. U.S. Army. Mem. Am., Los Angeles County bar assns., Phi Alpha Delta, Beta Gamma Sigma. Club: Jonathan. Home: 3520 St Elizabeth Rd Glendale CA 91206 Office: 3345 Wilshire Blvd Suite 1106 Los Angeles CA 90010

HOFFMAN, DUSTIN, actor; b. Los Angeles, Aug. 8, 1937; s. Harry Hoffman; m. Anne Byrne, May 4, 1969 (div.); children: Karina, Jenna; m. Lisa Gottsegen, Oct. 21, 1980; children: Jacob, Rebecca. Ed., Santa Monica City Coll., Pasadena Playhouse. Stage debut: Sarah Lawrence Coll. prodn. of Yes Is For a Very Young Man; Broadway debut: A Cook for Mr. General, 1961; appeared in: Noon and Night, Am. Place Theatre, N.Y.C., 1964-65; also: Journey of the Fifth Horse, 1966 (Obie award); Star Wagon, 1966, Fragments at, Berkshire Theatre Festival, Stockbridge, Mass., 1966, Eh?, 1966-67 (Drama Desk, Theatre World, Vernon Rice awards); (Broadway) Jimmy Shine, 1968-69; dir.: All Over Town, 1974; recorded: Death of a Salesman, Caedmon Records (Drama Desk award 1984); appeared in films: (motion pictures) The Graduate (Oscar nominee); Midnight Cowboy, John and Mary, 1969, Little Big Man, 1971, Who Is Harry Kellerman and Why Is He Saying Those Terrible Things About Me?, 1971, Straw Dogs, 1972, Alfredo, Alfedo, Papillion, 1973, Lenny, 1974 (Oscar nominee), All the President's Men, 1975, Marathon Man, 1976, Straight Time, 1978, Agatha, 1979, Kramer vs. Kramer, 1979 (N.Y. Film Critics award as best actor), Tootsie, 1982 (Golden Globe award as best actor). Address: care Punch Prodns 711 Fifth Ave New York NY 10022

HOFFMAN, EDWARD FENNO, III, sculptor; b. Phila., Oct. 20, 1916; s. Edward Fenno and Elizabeth Rodman (Wright) H.; m. Nadine Kalpaschnikoff, June 8, 1946; children—Susan Rush Johns, David Fenno, Cynthia Logan Carosso. Student, Pa. Acad. Fine Arts, 1946-50. One-man shows, Grand Central Galleries, N.Y.C., 1956, 70, Galerie Internationale, N.Y.C., 1977, group shows include, Nat. Sculpture Soc., N.Y.C., 1956—, NAD, N.Y.C., 1957—; represented in permanent collections, Am. Cathedral, Rome, Italy, Weightlifters Hall of Fame, York, Pa., Phila. Mus. Art, Pa. Acad. Fine Arts, Garden of Coll. Physicians, Phila., Our Lady of Grace Ch., Greensboro, N.C., others; sculptor in residence, Henry Clews Meml. Art Found., France, 1952-55. Served with U.S. Army, 1940-45. Tiffany Found. grantee, 1951; Recipient Barnet prize NAD, 1951, Speyer prize NAD, 1973, Thomas R. Proctor prize, 1982, Watrous gold medal, 1972; Mrs. Newington award Hudson Valley Art Assn., 1983. Fellow Nat. Sculpture Soc. (1st v.p. 1973-76, Silver medal 1973, Hexter prize 1979); mem. NAD, Allied Artists Am., Am. Artists Profl. League (prize 1981), Artists Equity. Republican. Episcopalian. Home: 353 Oak Terr Wayne PA 19087 Office: 501 Conestoga Rd Wayne PA 19087 *To be aware of and act on intuitive impressions; to recognize opportunities; to be able to concentrate one's whole mind on the problem; to look for and find the best in those one comes in contact with; and above all, to work diligently and with sustained effort. These are qualities I feel have achieved what success I have.*

HOFFMAN, EDWIN KARL, retail co. exec.; b. Chgo., June 29, 1922; s. Joseph M. amd and Mildred (Page) H.; m. Gladys Steigerwaldt, Nov. 6, 1943; children—Mark Joseph, Kimberly Anne. B.S., Northwestern U., 1947. Trainee Carson Pirie Scott & Co., Chgo., 1948-52, div. mdse. mgr. ready-to-wear, 1951-52; gen. mdse. mgr. De Pinna, N.Y.C., 1952-55; div. mdse. mgr. women's ready-to-wear The Higbee Co., Cleve., 1955-58, gen. mdse. mgr., 1958, v.p., 1958-62, pres., 1962-67, John Wanamaker, Phila., 1967-68; exec. v.p., gen. mgr. Woodward & Lothrop, Washington, 1968, pres., 1969-78, chmn., chief exec. officer, 1978—, also dir.; dir., mem. exec. com. Asso. Merchandising Corp.; dir. Am. Security & Trust Co., Chesapeake & Potomac Telephone Co., Potomac Electric Power Co.; mem. Met. Washington Bd. Trade. Bd. dirs. Nat. Symphony Orch. Assn.; trustee Meridian House Found., Fed. City Council. Served with AUS, 1942-45. Clubs: Union League (N.Y.C.); Columbia Country, University, Burning Tree, Pine Valley, Georgetown, 1925 F Street (Washington). Office: Woodward & Lothrop 11th and F Sts NW Washington DC 20013

HOFFMAN, ELLIOT LEE, lawyer; b. Bklyn., June 29, 1930; s. Harry Edward and Kate (Hackmyer) H.; m. Nancy Bookman, Apr. 19, 1962; children: Robert Harris, Alexandra deF. Hendricks. A.B. magna cum laude, Harvard U., 1951; LL.B. with honors, Yale U., 1954. Bar: N.Y. 1955, U.S. Dist. Ct. 1956, U.S. Ct. Appeals 1956, U.S. Supreme Ct. 1973. Law asst., asso. judge Charles W. Froessel, N.Y. Ct. Appeals, Albany and N.Y.C., 1954-56; asst. U.S. atty. So. Dist. N.Y., N.Y.C., 1956-58; practiced law, N.Y.C., 1958-60, 65—; counsel N.Y. State Com. of Investigation, 1960-61; partner Beldock, Levine & Hoffman, 1965—; copyright lectr. Temple U., 1976, New Sch. Social Research, 1977, New Eng. Sch. Law, 1983; dir. Entertainment Corp. Am., Premier Talent Agy., Above Average Prodns. Inc., Broadway Video Corp., N.Am. Soccer League; mem. exec. com., v.p. Phila. Fury Soccer Team, 1977-81. Editor: Yale Law Jour, 1954. Mem. community council Town of Kent, Carmel, N.Y., 1974—; counsel, advisor Newport Jazz Festival, 1960—; Trustee Newport Folk Found., N.Y. Studio Sch.; bd. dirs. N.Y. Jazz Repertory Co.; mem. Olympia Brass Band of New Orleans, 1980—. Mem. N.Y. State Bar Assn., N.Y. State Dist. Attys. Assn., Harvard Alumni Assn., Am. Arbitration Assn., Mid-Hudson R/C Soc., Phi Beta Kappa. Democrat. Jewish. Club: Harvard (N.Y.C.). Home: 72 Bank St New York City NY 10014 Office: 565 Fifth Ave New York City NY 10017

HOFFMAN, GENE, food company executive; b. East St. Louis, Ill., July 29, 1927; s. Edmund H. and Bee (Hood) H.; m. Nancy P. Claney, Oct. 27, 1951; children: Kim Elizabeth, Keith Murdock. B.J. in Advt, U. Mo., 1948. Asst. advt. mgr. Montgomery Ward Co., 1948; copywriter, asst. advt. promotion mgr. Chgo. Tribune, 1949-50; promotion mgr. Phila. Bull., 1951-56; with The Kroger Co., 1956-77, gen. mgr., 1956-61, dir. mktg. processed foods div., Cin., 1961-63, v.p., gen. mgr., 1964-66, corporate v.p., 1966, v.p. food mfg. divs., 1966-69; pres. Kroger Food Processing, 1969-72, Kroger Brands Co., 1972-74; sr. corp. v.p. parent company, 1974-75, corp. pres., 1975-77; also dir.; with Super Valu Stores, Inc., 1977—; pres. Super Valu Wholesale Food Cos., 1977—; sr. corp. v.p. Super Valu Stores Inc.; dir. Americana Mag., Hybridoma Scis., Inc., Rural Ventures, Inc., 1st Nat. Bank of Anniston, Lewis Grocer Co., Vital Resources, Inc., Warner Nat. Corp., Home State Savs. Assn.; Bd. govs. ATO Found. Served with AC USNR, 1945-46. Mem. Am. Mgmt. Assn., Food Mktg. Inst., Greater Cin. C. of C. (v.p., dir.), AIM, Alpha Delta Sigma, Alpha Tau Omega. Episcopalian. Clubs: Interlachen Country, Comml., Cin., Hyde Park Golf and Country, Queen City, Bankers (Cin.); Tonka Racquets, Camargo Racquet. Office: Bryant Lake Valley View Rd PO Box 990 Minneapolis MN 55440

HOFFMAN, GEORGE W(ALTER), educator; b. Vienna, Austria, June 19, 1914; came to U.S., 1939, naturalized, 1943; s. Albert W(ilhelm) and Hedwig (Weihs) H.; m. Viola Smith, Sept. 30, 1944; children: Jeane (Mrs. Hugh Pendery), A. Michael. Student, U. Vienna, 1934-36; Ph.D., U. Mich., 1950, Harvard U., 1946-47. Asst. editor Wirtschaftlicher Beobachter, Vienna, 1935-38; instr. Ind. U., 1946-47; grad. asst. U. Mich., 1948-49; asst. prof. U. Tex., Austin, 1949-53, asso. prof., 1953-60, prof., 1961—, chmn. dept., 1978-82; vis. prof. U. Vt., summer 1948, U. Mich., also Pa. State Coll., 1952, U. R.I., 1959, Ind. U., 1967, Kent State U., 1968, U. Munich, 1962, U. Heidelberg, 1972; vis. lectr. numerous European countries, also U. Wash., Portland State U., Ind. U., U. Nebr., Kent State U.; dir. Am. Assn. Geographers program, Yugoslavia, 1971; Exec. sec. Austin Com. Fgn. Relations, 1954-75, chmn. bd. dirs., 1975-81; mem. Nat. Citizens Commn. Internat. Cooperation, Commn. Research Devel. Internat. Instns.; mem. acad. adv. bd. Kennan Inst. for Advanced Russian Studies, Woodrow Wilson Center for Scholars, 1974-77; bd. dirs., mem. exec. com. RFE-RL, Inc., 1977-81. Author books, articles in field.; Mem. bd. editors: The East European Quarterly, 1967—; editorial advisor: F.A. Praeger, 1968-72, Standard Ednl. Corp, Chgo., 1966-80; co-editor: Searchlight Books, 1961—; editorial bd.: Comparative Communism, 1974-81, East European/Soviet Series; mem. adv. com.: Polit. Geography quar. Served with AUS, 1943-45. Recipient Polit. Geography Contbn. award Nat. Council Geographic Edn., 1953, 58; Internat. Relations award St. Mary's U., 1962; Thomas Jefferson award, 1978; NSF-IREX Travel grants, 1973; Am. Council Learned Socs. Travel award, 1970; Research award, 1972; Fulbright award, 1962, 72; Am. Philos. Soc. Research awards, 1957, 62, 69; NSF Research award, 1964-67, 67-69; Nat. Acad. Scis. Travel award, 1964, 76. Fellow Royal Geog. Soc. (London); mem. Assn. Am. Geographers (chmn. com. Eastern Europe, chmn. com. internat. cooperation, chmn. Am.-German Project), Am. Geog. Soc., AAAS, Am. Assn. Advancement Slavic Studies (dir., chmn. research and devel. com. 1972-76, council 1972-76, 80), Nat. Council Geog. Edn., Osterreichische Geographische Gesellschaft, Südost Europa Gesellschaft (Munich), Tex. Assn. Coll. Teachers (pres. Austin chpt. 1969-70), AAUP (sec.-treas. U. Tex. chpt. 1969-70), Phi Kappa Phi, Tex. Council Geography Tchrs. (pres. 1954-55, dir. 1955-58), Pi Kappa Alpha. Mem. Christian Ch. (deacon 1958-60). Home: 1801 Lavaca Austin TX 78701

HOFFMAN, GRACE, dramatic mezzo-soprano; b. Cleve., Jan. 14, 1925. Studied with, Friedrich Schorr, Manhattan Sch. Music, Giuseppe Gentile (Grant Garnell), Mario Basiola, Milan, Lila Robeson, Western Res. U., Maria Wetzelsberger, Stuttgart. Prof. voice Hochschule für Musik, Stuttgart, from 1978. Stage debut in: Cavalleria Rusticana, N.Y.C., 1951; with, Zurich Mcpl. Opera, 1953-55, Stuttgart (Germany) State Opera, 1955—; guest appearances include, La Scala, Covent Garden, Vienna, Covent Garden, Munich, Covent Garden, San Francisco, Met. Opera, Beyreuth Festivals, 13 yrs, numerous others, numerous recordings including, London Records in, Strauss' Salome, by Vox in Mahler's Das Lied von der Erde. Recipient Blanche Thebom scholarship; Vercelli prize; Outstanding Service medal State of Baden-Württemberg, 1978; given title Württembergische Kammersängerin, 1960, title of Austrian Kammersängerin, 1980; Fulbright scholar. Office: care Staatsoper Postfach 982 7 Stuttgart Federal Republic Germany *

HOFFMAN, HAROLD WAYNE, advertising agency executive; b. Brinkman, Okla., Feb. 9, 1930; s. Alva Webster and Willie Anna (Cochran) H.; m. Helen Louise Fleming, Dec. 30, 1974; children: Kimberly Jean, Harold. A.A., Compton Jr. Coll., 1950; B.J., U. Okla., 1955. Pub. relations supr. Magnolia Petroleum Co., Dallas, 1955-60; advt. mgr. Collins Radio Co., Dallas, 1960-62; pres. Falcon Internat. Corp., Dallas, 1962—; account exec. Bloom Agy., Dallas, 1966-68; v.p. Albert Frank-Guenther Law (advt. agy.), Dallas, 1968-72; owner, operator Hoffman Agy., Dallas, 1972—. Theatrical film producer, writer, dir. as pres., treas., Falcon Internat. Corp.; Free, White & 21, Under Age, Trial of Oswald, The Black Cat, Story of Life; Author: Profession Portrait Tips; Writer: motion picture script 2880 for TV; others.; Composer: title song for movies The Other Side of Bonnie & Clyde; Nature photographer. Pres. Dallas Dance Council, 1974-75; pres. Tex. Civic Ballet Co., 1972-74; dir. Beautify Greater Dallas Assn., 1959. Served with AUS, 1951-53. Recipient Nat. 1st award, Civic Portfolio Jaycees, 1958; Producer's award Box Office mag., 1963. Mem. Am. Soc. Mag. Photographers. Democrat. Methodist. Home and Office: 17347 Stedman Dr Dallas TX 75252

HOFFMAN, HARRY THEODORE, retail executive; b. Bklyn., Oct. 28, 1927; s. Harry Theodore and Alice Audley (White) H.; m. Norma Olson, Oct. 20, 1951; children: Jan, Harry, Loren. B.A., Colgate U., 1950. Agt. FBI, Atlanta and Washington, 1951-54; sales mgr. Procter & Gamble, N.Y.C., 1954-59; mktg. mgr. Bell & Howell, N.C., N.Y., Ohio and; Chgo., 1959-66; dir. mktg. Demco, Madison, Wis., 1966-68; pres., chief exec. officer Ingram Book Co., 1968-79, Waldenbooks, Stamford, Conn., 1979—. Served with airborne inf. U.S. Army, 1946-47. Office: Waldenbooks 201 High Ridge Rd Stamford CT 06904

HOFFMAN, HOWARD STANLEY, experimental psychologist, educator; b. N.Y.C., May 23, 1925; s. Melvin Leo and Henrietta (Rosenthal) H.; m. Alice Marie Cruikshank, June 7, 1961; children: Randall, Gwendolyn, Russell, Franklin, Daniel, Martha. B.A., New Sch. for Social Research, N.Y.C., 1952; M.A., Bklyn. Coll., 1953; Ph.D., U. Conn., 1957. Research fellow in auditory perception U. Conn., 1953-56, instr. dept. statistics, 1956-57; asst. to prof. psychology Pa. State U., 1957-70; prof. psychology Bryn Mawr Coll., 1970—; mem. exptl. psychology research rev. com. NIMH, 1968-72, chmn. basic behavioral processes research rev. com., 1979-83. Bd. editors: Jour. Exptl. Analysis Behavior, 1966-69, Jour. Exptl. Psychology, Animal Behavior Processes; reviewer: Jour Comparative and Physiol. Psychology. Served with AUS, 1943-45. Fellow Am. Psychol. Assn., AAAS; mem. Eastern Psychol. Assn., AAUP, Sigma Xi, Phi Kappa Phi, Psi Chi. Home: 265 Hathaway Ln Wynnewood PA 19096 Office: Dept Psychology Bryn Mawr Coll Bryn Mawr PA 19010

HOFFMAN, IRWIN, orchestra conductor; b. N.Y.C., Nov. 26, 1924; s. Harry and Augusta (Cohen) H.; m. Esther Glazer, Feb. 21, 1946; children: Joel H., Gary, Toby, Deborah. Student, Juilliard Sch. Music, 1942-43, 45-48; Mus. D. (hon.), U. Tampa, 1984. Teaching fellow Juilliard Sch. Music, 1948. Condr., Phila. Orch. at Robin Hood Dell, summer 1942; condr., Bronx (N.Y.) Symphony, 1948-52, Yonkers (N.Y.) Philharmonic, 1950-52, Westchester (N.Y.) Chamber Orch., for Martha Graham Dance Co., 1949-50; condr., mus. dir., Vancouver (B.C., Can.) Symphony Orch., 1952-64; asso. condr., Chgo. Symphony Orch., 1964-68; acting music dir., 1968-69; condr., 1969-70; prin. condr., Grant Park, Chgo., 1965-73; permanent condr., Belgian Radio and TV Symphony Orch., 1973-76; music dir., Fla. Orch., 1968—, Flagstaff (Ariz.) Festival of Arts, 1983; condr., St. Louis Little Symphony, summers 1959-64; lectr., condr., U. B.C., State Coll. Wash., 1958; guest condr., Toronto, Vancouver, Chgo., Israel Philharmonic, 1960, Dallas Symphony, 1962, Dallas Symphony, Brazil, 1962, 78, St. Louis Symphony Orch., 1963, Miami and Tampa symphonies, 1967; protege, Serge Koussevitzky, Tanglewood, 1948-50; guest condr., BBC Symphony, Manchester, Eng., 1968, Brussels (Belgium), Radio Orch., 1968, Strasbourg (France) Radio Orch., BBC Welsh, 1969-82, BBC Scottish, 1971-82, BBC No. Orch., Orch. Nat., France, 1970, Orch. Philharmonique, France, Orch. Nat., Peru, Philharmonia Orch., Eng., 1971, Chgo., Vancouver symphonies, N.J., Denver, Costa Rica, 1977-78, N.J., Denver, Costa Rica, Chgo., 1977, Montevideo (Uruguay) Nat., 1979, Buffalo symphonies, 1980-81, New Orleans Philharm., 1981; Composer two string quartets, violin sonata, others.; Collector autography music manuscripts, mus. memorablia. Served with AUS, 1943-45. Office: 26 2d St N Saint Petersburg FL 33701

HOFFMAN, IRWIN D., artist; b. Boston, Mar. 8, 1901; s. Jacob Hillel and Minna (Aronson) H.; m. Dorothea Gabriel Geyer, 1930. Ed., Boston pub. schs.; student, Boston Mus. Fine Arts Sch., 1917-24; Page Travelling fellow, Amsterdam, 1924-26. Painter and etcher, N.Y.C., 1927—, best known for paintings and etchings of mining scenes; executed murals for, Mining Exhibit, Golden Gate Internat. Expn., San Francisco, History of Medicine mural for Mary Hitchcock Meml Hosp., Hanover, N.H., Colo. Sch. Mines, Golden.; five one-man shows, N.Y.C.; executed retrospective, Boston Public Library, 1981; painted portraits:: Pres. Hector Trujillo of Dominican Republic, 1956; painted: portrait Cardinal Spellman, Justice Frankfurter, Dr. Samuel Belkin, Mischa Elman, Dr. Bela Schick, David Ben Gurion, 1964, former gov. Vt. Ray Keezer, Jr., 1972, Dr. Abraham Heschel, Victor Hammer, 1980; numerous others. Recipient Henry F. Noyes prize for etching, ann. exhibit Soc. Am. Etchers, 1937. Mem. Soc. Am. Etchers. Hoffman Auditorium dedicated in his honor Central Israel Orphan Home for Girls, Jerusalem, 1981. Studio: 54 W 74th St New York NY 10023

HOFFMAN, JACK LEROY, lawyer; b. Portland, Oreg., Aug. 30, 1922; s. Daniel William and Lillian (Huget) H.; m. Lynne M. Parks; children—Kenneth J., William S. A.B., Linfield Coll., 1946; J.D., U. Oreg., 1949. Bar: Oreg. bar 1949. Asst. statute reviser, Oreg., 1949-50, practice in, Portland, 1950—; mem. firm Bullivant, Wright, Leedy, Johnson, Pendergrass & Hoffman, 1950—. Mem. dist. com. local Boy Scouts Am., 1965-67; Bd. dirs. Oreg. Lung Assn., 1957—, mem. exec. com., 1961—, pres., 1969-71; bd. dirs. Am. Lung Assn., 1963-77, 79—, exec. com., 1971-77, sec., 1971-74, pres.-elect, 1974-75, pres., 1975-76. Served to 1st lt. USAAF, World War II; to capt. USAF; Korea. Mem. ABA, Oreg. Bar Assn. (chmn. legal ethics com. 1968-69), Multnomah County Bar Assn. (chmn. jud. selection com. 1970-71, v.p. 1971-72), Am. Judicature Soc., Phi Alpha Delta. Clubs: Rotary, City, Multnomah Athletic (Portland). Home: 1335 SW Upland Dr Portland OR 97221 Office: 1000 Willamette Center 121 SW Salmon St Portland OR 97204

HOFFMAN, JAMES R., bishop; b. Fremont, Ohio, June 12, 1932. Ed., Our Lady of Lake Minor Sem., Wawasee, Ind., St. Meinrad Coll., Mt. St. Mary Sem., Norwood, Ohio, Cath. U. Am. Ordained priest Roman Cath. Ch., 1957; ordained titular bishop of Italica and aux. bishop of Toledo, 1978, apptd. bishop of Toledo, 1980. Office: Bishop's Residence 2544 Parkwood Ave Toledo OH 43610 *

HOFFMAN, JANE, actress theatrical director; b. Seattle, July 24, 1911; d. Samuel Lewis and Marguerite (Kirschbaum) H.; m. James W. McGlone (dec.); m. William Friedberg, 1945 (div. 1949); m. Richard McMurray, 1950 (div. 1969); 1 son, Samuel H. B.A., U. Calif.-Berkeley, 1931. Charter mem., mem. bd. Ensemble Studio Theatre, 1972, dir., 1983. Debut Tis of Thee, N.Y.C., 1940; appeared Crazy with the Heat, 1941, A Temporary Island, N.Y.C., 1948, A Story for Two Strangers, 1948, Two Blind Mice, 1949, The Rose Tatto, Westport, Conn., 1951, The Crucible, 1953, Good Woman and Setzuan, Phoenix, 1956, The Third Best Sport, 1958, The Sandbox, 1960, Rhinoceros, 1961, Mommy (American Dream 1961), Mother Courage and Her Children, 1963, Fair Game for Lovers, 1964, A Murderer Among Us, 1964, The Child Buyer, 1964; (appeared) repertory groups, 1965-67, toured, Stanford Reperitory Theatre, 1965-67; appeared Richard III, Lincoln Ctr, N.Y.C., 1969, The Increased Difficulty of Concentration, 1969, Murder Among Friends, 1975; (appeared) movies A Hatful of Rain, 1957, Ladybug, Ladybug, Up the Sandbox, Black Harvest, Day of the Locust; TV Alcoa Hour, Love of Life, 1971-75, Phyllis. Mem. Actors Studio (founding mem.). Home: 16 St Lukes Pl New York NY 10014

HOFFMAN, JEROME A., lawyer; b. Phila., Apr. 10, 1938; s. Leon and Katherine H.; m. Sandra J. Hoffman, Oct. 11, 1946; children: Alisa, Sharon, David. B.S. in Econs., U. Pa., 1959, J.D., 1962. Bar: Pa. 1963. Assoc. Becker & Becker, 1963-64; with Smith Kline Corp., 1965-72; ptnr. Dechert Price & Rhoads, Phila., 1972—. Mem. ABA, Phila. Bar Assn. Office: Centre Square W Suite 3400 Philadelphia PA 19102

HOFFMAN, JOHN ERNEST, JR., lawyer; b. N.Y.C., May 1, 1934; s. John E. and Effe K. (Dooling) H.; m. Jean Wheeler, Aug. 13, 1955; children: Jean E., John E., Katherine, Carolyn W., Christine D. A.B. cum laude, Princeton U., 1955; J.D., Harvard U., 1960. Bar: N.Y. 1961, U.S. Dist. Ct. (so. and ea. dists.) N.Y. 1962, U.S. Dist. Ct. (we. dist.) N.Y. 1963, U.S. Ct. Appeals (2d cir.) 1963, U.S. Supreme Ct. 1963, U.S. Ct. Appeals (3d cir.) 1974. Assoc. Shearman & Sterling, 1968, ptnr., 1968—. Contbr.: chpt. to Private Investors Abroad, 1980. Served to 1st lt. U.S. Army, 1955-57. Mem. ABA, N.Y. Bar Assn., N.Y.C. Bar Assn., Am. Soc. Internat. Law. Congregationalist. Club: University (N.Y.C.). Home: 300 Millwood Rd Chappaqua NY 10514 Office: Shearman & Sterling 153 E 53d St New York NY 10022

HOFFMAN, JOHN RALEIGH, physicist; b. Evansville, Ind., July 7, 1926; s. John Henry and Ruth Margaret (Bryant) H.; m. Phyllis Christine Reindel, July 5, 1950; children: John Russell, Gary Paul. B.S., U. Richmond (Va.), 1949; M.S., U. Fla., 1951, Ph.D., 1954. Research asst. U. Fla., 1950-54; research scientist Sandia Corp., Albuquerque, 1954-57; project supr. Kaman Nuclear Co., Colorado Springs, 1957-68; v.p. Kaman Scis. Corp., Colorado Springs, 1968—. Served with USNR, 1944-46. Mem. Am. Phys. Soc., IEEE. Republican. Presbyterian. Home: 5020 Lyda Ln Colorado Springs CO 80904 Office: 1500 Garden of Gods Rd Colorado Springs CO 80907

HOFFMAN, JOSEPH FREDERICK, educator; b. Oklahoma City, Mar. 7, 1925; s. Henry Raymond and Rena Virginia (Crossman) H.; m. Elena Citkowitz, Mar. 30, 1974. B.S., U. Okla., 1947, M.S., 1948; M.A., Princeton, 1951, Ph.D., 1952; M.A. (hon.), Yale, 1965. Lectr., research asso. Princeton, 1953-56; head sect. membrane physiology, lab. kidney and electrolyte metabolism Nat. Heart Inst., NIH, 1957-65; prof. physiology Yale, 1965—, chmn. dept. physiology, 1973-79, Eugene Higgins prof. physiology, 1974—. Mem. Nat. Acad. Scis. Home: 410 Livingston St New Haven CT 06511

HOFFMAN, JULIEN IVOR ELLIS, pediatric cardiologist, educator; b. Salisbury, South Rhodesia, July 26, 1925; came to U.S., 1957, naturalized, 1967; s. Bernard Isaac and Minrose (Bermant) H. B.Sc., U. Witwatersrand, Johannesburg, South Africa, 1944; B.Sc. Hons., 1945; M.B., B.Ch., 1949; M.D., 1970. Intern, resident internal medicine, South Africa and Eng., 1950-56; research asst., postgrad. Med. Sch., London, 1956-57; fellow pediatric cardiology Boston Children's Hosp., 1957-59; fellow Cardiovascular Research Inst., San Francisco, 1959-60; asst. prof. pediatrics, internal medicine Albert Einstein Coll., N.Y., 1962-66; assoc. prof. pediatrics U. Calif. at San Francisco, 1966-70, prof., 1970—; sr. mem. Cardiovascular Research Inst., U. Calif. at San Francisco, 1966—; mem. bd. examiners, sub-bd. pediatric cardiology Am. Bd. Pediatrics, 1973-78; chmn. Louis Katz Award Com., Basic Sci. Council, Am. Heart Assn., 1973-74; George Brown Meml. lectr. Am. Heart Assn., 1977; George Alexander Meml. lectr. Royal Coll. Physicians (Edinburgh), 1978; Lilly lectr. Royal Coll. Physicians (London), 1981; Isaac Starr lectr. Cardiac Systems Dynamics Soc., Eng., 1982. Fellow Royal Coll. Physicians; mem. Am. Physiol. Soc., Am. Pediatric Soc., Soc. Pediatric Research. Extensive research into congenital heart disease and coronary blood flow. Home: 438 Boynton Ave Berkeley CA 94707 Office: 1403 HSE U Calif Med Center San Francisco CA 94143

HOFFMAN, KENNETH MYRON, mathematician, educator; b. Long Beach, Calif., Nov. 30, 1930; s. Myron Grant and Madge (Harrison) H.; children: Donna, Laura, Robert. A.A., John Muir Coll., 1950; A.B., Occidental Coll., 1952; M.A., UCLA, 1954, Ph.D., 1956. Instr. math. Mass. Inst. Tech., Cambridge, 1956-59, asst. prof., 1959-61, asso. prof., 1961-63, prof., 1963—, chmn. pure math., 1968-69; chmn. Commn. on Edn., 1969-71, head dept. math., 1971-79; exec. dir. Commn. on Resources for Math. Sci., NRC, 1981—. Author: (with Ray Kunze) Linear Algebra, 1961, Fundamentals of Banach Algebras, 1962, Banach Spaces of Analytic Functions, 1962, Analysis in Euclidean Space, 1975; Contbr.: articles to profl. jours. Mailing Analysis in Euclidean Space. Fellow Alfred P. Sloan Found., 1964-66. Mem. AAAS (council), Am. Math. Soc. (past mem. council), Phi Beta Kappa. Office: Mass Inst Tech Cambridge MA 02139

HOFFMAN, LARRY RONALD, botanist, educator; b. Sigourney, Iowa, May 12, 1936; s. Rufus Harold and Edna Lou (Kuhn) H.; m. Margaret Ann Sankey, Aug. 2, 1959; children: Jennifer, Michael, Christopher. B.S., Iowa State U., 1958; Ph.D., U. Tex., 1961; NSF postdoctoral fellow, U. Leeds, Eng., 1961-62. Asst. prof. botany U. Ill., Urbana, 1962-68, asso. prof., 1968-75, prof., 1975—. Mem. bd. reviewers, Transactions Am. Micros. Soc., 1966—; mem. editorial bd.: Jour. Phycology, 1979-81; editorial bd. rep.: Am. Jour. Botany, 1977-79; contbr. articles to profl. jours. Recipient Darbaker prize Bot. Soc. Am., 1975. Mem. Phycological Soc. Am. (v.p. 1975, 80, pres. 1981, trustee 1983—), Am. Inst. Biol. Scis. (bd. govs. 1980-82), Am. Microscopical Soc., Botanical Soc. Am., Brit. Phycological Soc., Internat. Phycological Soc. Home: 1509 Rutledge St Urbana IL 61801 Office: Dept Botany Morrill Hall U Ill 505 S Goodwin Ave Urbana IL 61801

HOFFMAN, LOIS WLADIS, psychologist, educator; b. Elmira, N.Y., Mar. 25, 1929; d. Gustave and Etta (Wladis) Wladis; m. Martin Leon Hoffman, June 24, 1951 (div.); children—Amy Gabrielle, Jill Adrienne.; m. Herbert Zimiles, Oct. 25, 1981. B.A. cum laude, U. Buffalo, 1951; M.S., Purdue U., 1953; Ph.D., U. Mich., 1958. Research fellow sociology Purdue U., 1951-53; Flint Met. research fellow sociology U. Mich., Ann Arbor, 1953-54; asst. study dir. Survey Research Center, 1954-55; research asst. Research Center for Group Dynamics, 1955-56, research asso., 1956-60, cons. psychol. clinic, 1959-60; lectr. psychology, 1967-72, asso. prof., 1972-75, prof., 1975—; co-editor Rev. Child Devel. Research, Soc. Research in Child Devel., Ann Arbor, 1962-66; cons. OEO, 1968-70. Author: (with F. Ivan Nye) The Employed Mother in America, 1963, Working Mothers, 1974; editor: (with Martin L. Hoffman) Review of Child Development Research, Vol. 1, 1964, Vol. 2, 1966 (Family Life Book award Child Study Assn. Am. 1965), (with Mednick and Tangri) Women and Achievement; contbr. articles to profl. jours. Mem. Am. Psychol. Assn., Am. Sociol. Assn., Soc. Research in Child Devel., Soc. Psychol. Study of Social Issues (pres. 1983-84), Population Assn. Am., Phi Beta Kappa, Phi Kappa Phi. Address: 1307 Baldwin Ave Ann Arbor MI 48104

HOFFMAN, MICHAEL EUGENE, editor, publisher, museum curator; b. N.Y.C., July 5, 1942; s. Myron Block and Dorothy (Steinfeld) H.; m. Katharine Perkins Carter, Dec. 23, 1967 (dec.); children: Matthew, Sarah. B.A., St. Lawrence U., 1964. Editor, pub. Aperture, Inc., Millerton, N.Y., 1965—; in charge Alfred Stieglitz Center, Phila. Museum Art, 1968—; exec. dir. Paul Strand Found., 1980—. Editor, dir. pub. numerous books and periodicals of photography; dir. photog. exhbns., U.S. and abroad. Served to 1st lt. U.S. Army, 1964-65. Mem. Soc. Photog. Edn. Office: Aperture Inc Elm St Millerton NY 12546 also 20 E 23d St New York NY 10010

HOFFMAN, NEIL JAMES, art school president; b. Buffalo, Sept. 2, 1938; s. Frederick Charles and Isabella Dias (Murchie) H.; m. Sue Ellen Jeffery, Dec. 30, 1960; children: Kim, Amy, Lisa. B.S., SUNY-Buffalo, 1960, M.S., 1967. Chmn. unified arts dept. Grand Island Pub. Schs. (N.Y.), 1968-69; assoc. dean, asst. prof. Coll. Fine and Applied Art Rochester Inst. Tech. (N.Y.), 1969-74; dir. program in artisanry Boston U., 1974-79; dean, chief adminstrv. officer Otis Art Inst., Parsons Sch. Design, Los Angeles, 1979-83; pres. Sch. Art Inst. Chgo., 1983—; cons. arts, prof. photographer; mem. local arts councils, local arts orgns., state arts orgns., nat. arts orgns. Bd. dirs., v.p. Pasadena Children's Mus. Kidspace, 1980-82; bd. dirs. Geisen Trust, 1980—; mem. evaluation team Western Assn. Schs. and Colls., 1982—; bd. dirs. Idyllwild Sch. Music and Arts, 1983. Mem. Phi Delta Kappa. Office: Sch Art Inst Chgo Columbus and Jackson Chicago IL 60603

HOFFMAN, OSCAR ALLEN, forest products company executive; b. Newark, Feb. 4, 1920; s. Ernest Benjamin and Edith Marie (Meyers) H.; m. Carolyn Ruth Layman, May 10, 1947 (div.); children: Peter Miles, Jared Mark; m. Geri McReynolds, Aug. 21, 1956. A.B., Drew U., 1943; M.S., Syracuse U., 1945; Ph.D., Stanford U., 1948. Sect. leader MIT-Naval Ops. research group, Washington, 1948-54; mgr. ops. AMF, Greenwich, Conn., 1954-58; v.p., spl. asst. to pres. Champion Internat. Corp., Stanford, Conn., 1958—; chief ops. research Turkish Gen. Staff, Ankara, summer 1956. Commr. fin. City of Stamford, 1978-82. Mem. Ops. Research Soc. Am. (founding mem.), Inst. Mgmt. Sci. Republican. Episcopalian. Home: 54 Shelter Rock Rd Stamford CT 06903 Office: Champion Internat Corp 1 Champion Plaza Stamford CT 06921

HOFFMAN, PAUL FELIX, field geologist; b. Toronto, Ont., Canada, Mar. 21, 1941; s. Samuel and Dorothy Grace (Medhurst) H.; m. Erica Jean Westbrook, Dec. 4, 1976; 1 son, Guy Samson. B.S., McMaster U., 1964; M.A., Johns Hopkins U., 1965, Ph.D., 1970. Lectr. Franklin & Marshall Coll., Lancaster, Pa., 1968-69, U. Calif., Santa Barbara, 1971-72; vis. prof. U. Tex., Dallas, 1978; research scientist Geol. Survey Can., Ottawa, Ont., 1969—; dist. lectr. Am. Assn. Petroleum Geologists, 1979-80; mem. Internat. Union Geol. Scis. Commn. on Precambrian Stratigraphy, 1976, Internat. Commn. Lithosphere Working Group on Proterozoic Lithopheric Evolution, 1980. Fairchild Found. vis. scholar Calif. Inst. Tech., 1974-75. Fellow Royal Soc. Can.; mem. Geol. Assn. Can., Am. Geophys. Union, Geol. Soc. Am., Soc. Econ. Paleontologists and Mineralogists. Home: 153 Beech St Ottawa ON Canada K1Y 3S9 Office: Geol Survey of Can 588 Booth St Ottawa ON Canada K1A 0E4

HOFFMAN, PHILIP EISINGER, lawyer, real estate company executive; b. N.Y.C., Oct. 2, 1908; s. David S. and Hildegarde (Eisinger) H.; m. Florence L. Lehman, Sept. 9, 1933 (dec.); children: David L., Lynn B. (Mrs. Roger L. Manshel); m. Bee Beham, June 18, 1972. A.B. cum laude, Dartmouth Coll., 1929; LL.B., Yale U., 1932. Bar: N.Y. 1933. Since practiced in, N.Y.C., corp. law practice, 1933-42, 45—; partner Goodell, Hoffman & Spark, 1937-42, Hoffman & Tuck, 1962—; chmn. exec. com. U.S. Realty & Investment Co., Newark, 1962—; also dir.; dir. Comml. Mortgage Co., Ray Miller, Inc., Realty Capital Corp., Ltd., Toronto, Ont., Can.; Mem. N.J. Commn. on Civil Rights, 1969-75, Bipartisan Conf. on Civil Rights, 1960—, mem. N.J. adv. com., 1964-69; N.J. adv. com. U.S. Commn. on Civil Rights, 1969-75; U.S. rep. Human Rights Commn. UN, 1972-75; chmn. Community Relations Council Essex County, N.J., 1960-63; co-chmn. housing com. Com. of Concern Newark, 1967-69; asst. gen. counsel WPB, Washington, 1942-45; hearing commr. Nat. Prodn. Authority, 1950-53; chmn. coodinating com. Retail Jewelry Industry, 1954-60; Chmn. bd. govs. Am. Jewish Com., 1963-67, pres., 1969-73, hon. pres., 1973—, chmn. nat. exec. bd., 1967-68; hon. chmn. Appeal for Human Relations, 1962—; mem. exec. com. Nat. Community Relations Adv. Council, 1966-73, Am. Israel Pub. Affairs Com., 1969-73; chmn. adminstrv. council Jacob Blaustein Inst. for Advancement Human Rights, 1975—; trustee Leonard M. Sperry Research Center, East Orange Gen. Hosp., Jewish Community Council Essex County; chmn. bd. dirs. Nat. Assn. for Visually Handicapped, 1978-79; bd. dirs. Am. Friends of Jerusalem Mental Health Center, 1973-76; bd. govs. Hebrew U. Jerusalem, 1973—, Internat. League for Human Rights, 1975—, Com. for Econ. Growth in Israel, 1975; v.p. acad. affairs Am. Friends of Hebrew U., 1978—. Recipient numerous awards in human relations field. Mem. Am. Bar Assn., Assn. Bar City N.Y., N.Y. County Lawyers Assn., Phi Beta Kappa. Jewish. Clubs: 744 (Newark); Mountain Ridge Country (Caldwell, N.J.). Home: Claridge 1 Verona NJ 07044 Office: 909 Broad St 5th Floor Newark NJ 07102

HOFFMAN, PHILIP GUTHRIE, medical center administrator, former university president; b. Kobe, Japan, Aug. 6, 1915; s. Benjamin Philip and Florence (Guthrie) H. (parents Am. citizens); m. Mary Elizabeth Harding, Aug. 31, 1939; children: Philip Guthrie, Mary Victoria Hoffman Forsyth, Ruth Ann Hoffman Gabler, Jeanne Hoffman Camp. Student, George Washington U., 1936-37; A.B., Pacific Union Coll., 1938; M.A., U. So. Calif., 1942; Ph.D., Ohio State U., 1948; H.H.D. (hon.), Jacksonville U., LL.D., U. Americas, U. Akron, L.H.D., Pikeville Coll., Marshall U., D.L., Kyung Hee U., Korea, D.H.C., Autonomous U., Guadalajara (Mex.), Litt.D., U. St. Thomas, 1979. Credit mgr. Harding Sanitarium, Worthington, Ohio, 1938-40; instr. history Ohio State U. Columbus, 1946-49; asst. prof. history U. Ala., Tuscaloosa, 1949-51, assoc. prof., 1951-53, dir. arts and scis. extension services, 1949-53; dean, assoc. prof. history gen. extension div. Oreg. System Higher Edn., Portland, 1953-55; prof. history Portland State Coll., Oreg., 1955-57, dean faculty, 1955-57; v.p., dean faculties, prof. history U. Houston, 1957-61, pres., 1961-79, pres. emeritus, 1979—; cons. Mitchell Energy and Devel. Corp., Houston, 1980-81; pres. Tex. Med. Ctr. Inc., Houston, 1981—; dir. Fed. Res. Bank Dallas. Mem. Nat. Commn. on Accrediting, Am. Council on Edn., 1970—, Coll. Entrance Exam. Bd. Served to lt. USNR, 1943-45. Recipient Centennial Achievement award Ohio State U., Merit award U. So. Calif., 1975. Mem. Tex. Hist. Assn., Gulf Hist. Assn., Am. Hist. Assn., Assn. Tex. Coll. and Univs. (pres.), Assn. Urban Univs. (pres. 1965-66), Nat. Assn. State Univs. and Land-Grant Colls. (dir. 1971—), So. Univ. Conf. (pres. 1976-77), Phi Kappa Phi, Phi Alpha Theta (nat. pres. 1952-54), Omicorn Delta Kappa. Clubs: Petroleum, Torch (Houston); Houston; River Oaks (Houston). Lodge: Rotary. Home: 2929 Buffalo Speedway #608 Houston TX 77098

HOFFMAN, RICHARD JOEL, investment banker; b. Boston, Nov. 17, 1940; s. Sidney William and Mary C. H.; m. Sheila Ethel Beda, Nov. 3, 1962; children: Lisa Ann, Robert Spencer. B.S. in Bus. Adminstrn. cum laude, Suffolk U., Boston, 1968; M.B.A., Harvard U., 1970. Analyst Mitchell Hutchins Co., N.Y.C., 1970-72; internat. portfolio mgr. Oppenheimer Mgmt. Co., N.Y.C., 1972-76; chief investment strategist, mng. dir. Merrill Lynch White Weld Capital (div. Merrill Lynch, Pierce, Fenner & Smith), N.Y.C., 1976-83; pres. R.J. Hoffman & Co., Inc., West Orange, N.J., 1983—. Author articles in field. Mem. N.Y. Soc. Security Analysts. Republican. Jewish. Office: 101 Old Short Hills Rd West Orange NJ 07052

HOFFMAN, RICHARD WILLIAM, banker; b. Rice Lake, Wis., Feb. 8, 1918; s. William A. and Anna (Amundson) H.; m. June M. Weink, June 27, 1948; children: William H., Stephen C. B.A., U. Wis., 1939; M.B.A., 1954; postgrad., Grad. Sch. Banking, U. Wis., 1952, BAI Sch. for Bank Auditors and Comptrollers, 1957; grad. certificate, Am. Inst. Banking, 1960. With First Wis. Nat. Bank Milw., 1939-83, asst. v.p., asst. comptroller, 1959-63, v.p., comptroller, 1963-70, 1st v.p., 1970-83; v.p. First Wis. Corp., 1965-83; instr. Duke U., 1943-45, Army Finance Sch., Ft. Benjamin Harrison, 1945, Am. Inst. Banking, 1946-62, U. Wis., 1946-62, BAI Sch. Bank Adminstrn., 1956-77. Mem. Polit. Edn. and Action League, 1962-68; adv. com. Pub. Expenditure Survey Wis., 1963—; asso. div. chmn. Milw. County United Fund, 1960-63; mem. Milw. Am. Revolution Bicentennial Commn., 1975-76. Served to maj., Finance Corps AUS, 1941-46. Mem. Am. Inst. Banking, Am. Inst. C.P.A.'s, Assn. Bank Holding Cos., Army Finance Assn., Am. Econ. Devel. Council, Pub. Affairs Council, Am. Legion, Fin. Execs. Inst. (nat. adv. council), Bank Adminstrn. Inst., Nat. Alumni Assn. BAI Sch., Nat. Assn. Bus. Economists, Wis. Bus. Econs. Assn., Gt. Lakes Area Devel. Council, Res. Officers Assn., Wis. Bankers Assn., Wis. Econ. Devel. Assn. (dir.), Wis. Inst. C.P.A.'s, Wis. Mfrs. and Commerce (mining com.), Met. Milw. Assn. Commerce (area devel. com.), Beta Alpha Psi, Beta Gamma Sigma. Clubs: Badger Bankers, Milwaukee Athletic, Milwaukee Press, University, Wisconsin Alumni. Home: 7103 N Crossway Rd Fox Point WI 53217

HOFFMAN, RONALD, medical educator, physician; b. Passaic, N.J., June 17, 1945; s. Moris and Sarah (Wishna) H.; m. Laura Provisor, July 7, 1968; children: Judith Helaine, Michael Nathaniel. B.A., NYU, 1967, M.D., 1971. Diplomate: Nat. Bd. Med. Examiners, Am. Bd. Internal Medicine, Am. Bd. Hematology. Intern Montreal Gen. Hosp., 1971-73; resident in medicine Stanford U. Hosp., Palo Alto, Calif., 1973-74; fellow in hematology Mt. Sinai Hosp., N.Y.C., 1974-76; spl. hematology research fellow Mt. Sinai Hosp, N.Y.C., 1976-77; assoc. prof. Yale U. Sch. Medicine, New Haven, 1977-80, assoc. prof. medicine, 1980-82; prof. medicine, chief hematology, oncology Ind. U. Sch. Medicine, Indpla., 1982—. Contbr. numerous articles to profl. jours. Recipient Daniel P. Statz Mt. Sinai Hosp, 1976, Outstanding paper presentation N.Y. Blood Club, 1977, research career devel. NIH, 1980-85. Mem. Am. Fedn. Clin. Research, Am. Soc. Hematology (chmn. erythropoietin and cell proliferation subcom 1982), Internat. Soc. Exptl. Hematology, AAAS, Am. Soc. Clin. Investigation, Phi Beta Kappa, Sigma Xi. Democrat. Jewish. Office: Clin Cancer Research Ctr Ind U Sch Medicine 379 - 541 Clinical Dr Indianapolis IN 46223

HOFFMAN, RONALD ROBERT, aluminum company executive; b. Allentown, Pa., Mar. 20, 1934; s. Josiah Stephen and Gladys Elizabeth (McNabb) Hoffman D.; m. Shirley A. Carlson, June 25, 1955; children: Kerry Carlson Hoffman Phillips, Craig Martin. B.S., Lehigh U., 1954. Sales engr. Aluminum Co. Am., Cleve., 1954-65, br. sales mgr., South Bend, Ind., 1965-66, div. mgr. transp. industry sales, Pitts., 1966-68, asst. dist. sales mgr., Los Angeles, 1968-69, industry mgr. transp., Pitts, 1969-72, gen. mgr. industry sales, Pitts., 1972-75, v.p., 1975—; dir. Taylor Chair Co., Bedford, Ohio, 1979—. Bd. dirs. Wesley Inst., Bethel Park, Pa., Lehigh U., Bethlehem, Pa. Office: Aluminum Co Am 1501 Alcoa Bldg Pittsburgh PA 15219

HOFFMAN, S. JOSEPH, advt. agy. exec.; b. Haverhill, Mass., Feb. 19, 1920; s. Joseph H. and Bessie (Milhendler) H.; m. Ruth V. Wicks, Nov. 17, 1951; children—Jane, David, Drew. Student, Boston U., 1940; B.S., Ind. U., 1943. Pres. Duro Specialty Co., Lynn, Mass., 1945-50; with Ingalls Assos., Inc., Boston, 1950—, copywriter, 1950-56, copy chief, 1956-59, partner, 1959-64, prin., exec. v.p., 1964-78, pres., 1978—, Adgroup Internat. Inc., Montreal, Que., Can., 1972-74. Mem. Andover Indsl. Commn., 1966—. Served with AUS, 1942-44. Mem. New Eng. Broadcasting Assn., Boston/New Eng. Acad. TV Arts and Scis. (bd. govs.), Boston Advt. Club. Club: Tennis and Racquet (Boston). Home: 28 Hidden Way Andover MA 01810 Office: 857 Boylston St Boston MA 02116

HOFFMAN, TERRENCE WILLIAM, chemical engineer, educator; b. Kitchener, Ont., Can., Jan. 3, 1931; s. Otto William and Dorothy Violet (Rutty) H.; m. Mary Winnifrid Joyce Woodside, Jan. 29, 1954; children: David, Eric, Jane, Thomas. Student, Royal Mil. Coll., Kingston, Ont., 1948-52; B.Sc. in Chem. Engring, Queen's U., Kingston, 1953, M.Sc., 1955, Ph.D., McGill U., 1959. Lectr. Royal Mil. Coll., 1953-55, McGill U., 1955-58; asst. prof. McMaster U., Hamilton, Ont., 1958-64, assoc. prof., 1964-68, prof. chem. engring., 1968-82, chmn. dept., 1965-71, part-time prof., 1982—; sr. indsl. fellow Polysar, Ltd., Sarnia, Ont., 1979-80, prin. chem. engr., 1982—. Author: (with others) Chemical Plant Simulation, 1971. Served with Royal Canadian Navy, 1948-52. Recipient Erco award Canadian Soc. Chem. Engring., 1970; Ford Found. fellow engring. practice Hercules, Inc., Wilmington, Del., 1966-67. Fellow Chem. Inst. Can. Home: 2555 Lakeshore Rd Bright's Grove ON Canada N0N 1C0

HOFFMAN, THOMAS HENRY, foodservice distribution company executive; b. Cleve., Sept. 21, 1939; s. Henry Herman and Irene (Kiss) H.; m. Nancy Elizabeth Thomas, Dec. 30, 1960; children: Pamela, Matthew, Danielle. B.E.E., Ohio State U., 1962; M.B.A., Harvard U., 1964. Asst. to pres. H.A. Johnson Co., Boston, 1964-67, v.p., gen. mgr., 1967-70; gen. mgr. Shintron Co. Inc., Cambridge, Mass., 1971-72; pres. Internat. Foodservice, Miami Inc. (Fla.), 1973-81; gen. mgr. CFS Continental, Miami, 1981—. Home: 349 South Dr Miami Springs FL 33166 Office: PO Box 1600 Hialeah FL 33011

HOFFMAN, WAYNE MELVIN, airline official; b. Chgo., Mar. 9, 1923; s. Carl A. and Martha (Tamillo) H.; m. Laura Majewski, Jan. 26, 1946; children—Philip, Karen, Kristin. B.A. summa cum laude, U. Ill., 1943, J.D. with high honors, 1947. Bar: Ill. bar 1947, N.Y. bar 1958. Atty. I.C. R.R., 1948-52; with N.Y.C. R.R. Co., 1952-67, exec. asst. to pres., 1958-60, v.p. freight sales, 1960-61, v.p. sales, 1961-62, exec. v.p., 1962-67; chmn. N.Y. Central Trans. Co., 1960-67, Flying Tiger Line, Inc., 1967—, N.Am. Car Corp., 1971—; chmn., chief exec. officer Tiger Internat., Inc.; trustee Aerospace Corp., 1975—; chmn. Hungry Tiger Inc.; dir. Rohr Industries; dir. Kaufman & Broad, Inc.; mem. vis. com. Grad. Sch. Mgmt., U. Calif. at Los Angeles, 1972—; mem. bus. adv. com. Northwestern U. Transp. Center, 1972—. Served to capt. inf. AUS, World War II. Decorated Silver Star, Purple Heart with oak leaf cluster. Mem. Am. Bar Assn., Internat. Air Transport Assn. (exec. com.), Phi Beta Kappa. Clubs: Calif.; Regency, Bel Air Country (Los Angeles); Eldorado Country (Indian Wells, Calif.); Bohemian (San Francisco). Home: 425 N Barrington Ave Los Angeles CA 90049 Office: 1888 Century Park East Los Angeles CA 90067

HOFFMAN, WILLIAM BERTRAND, glass company executive; b. Richmond Hill, N.Y., Dec. 29, 1919; s. William Albert and Hermine Catherine H.; m. Ann Marie Gutekunst, Aug. 31, 1941; children: Susan Anne, William Craig, Linda Marie. Cert. bus. adminstrn., Rutgers U., 1942. Acct., Fidelity Union Trust Co., Newark, 1941-42, Bendix Aviation Corp., Teterboro, N.J., 1942-47; controller Acme Pattern & Machine Co., Buffalo, 1947-50; pres., chief exec. officer Binswanger Glass Co. (div. Nat. Gypsum Co.), Memphis, 1950—. Served with AUS, 1943-46. Republican. Presbyterian. Clubs: Colonial

Country (Memphis); Shriners. Office: Binswanger Glass Co 5885 Ridgeway Pkwy Memphis TN 38117 *

HOFFMAN, WILLIAM HOWARD, construction executive; b. Phillipsburg, N.J., Sept. 17, 1930; s. Howard Ambrose and Lilian (Ackroyd) H.; divorced; children: Deborah, William, Robert, John, Nancy Ann. B.S. in Elec. Engring., Lafayette Coll., 1952. Prodn. foreman E.I. du Pont de Nemours & Co., Inc., Kinston, N.C., 1952-56; dir. mktg. Am. Machine & Foundry Co., York, Pa., 1956-70; sr. v.p. constrn. Nat. Corp. for Housing Partnerships, Washington, 1970—; mem. Nat. Inst. Bldg. Scis., Washington, 1980—, nat. exec. com., 1982—. Republican. Clubs: Washington Country (Gaithersburg, Md.); Nautilus Boating (Galesville, Md.); Chevy Chase Athletic (Md.). Home: 6113 Walhonding Rd Bethesda MD 20816 Office: Nat Corp for Housing Partnerships 1133 15th St NW Washington DC 20005

HOFFMAN, WILLIAM M., playwright, editor; b. N.Y.C., Apr. 12, 1939; s. Morton and Johanna (Papiermeister) H. B.A. cum laude, CCNY, 1960. Drama editor Hill & Wang Corp., N.Y.C., 1961-68; lectr. Eugene O'Neill Found., 1971; lit. adviser Scripts mag., N.Y.C., 1971-75; vis. lectr. U. Mass. at Boston, 1973; playwriting cons. Creative Artists Pub. Service, 1975-76; vis. lectr. Hofstra U., 1980, 82, 83. Editor: N.Am. Plays series, 3 vols., 1968—, Gay Plays, 1978; author: (plays) Thank You, Miss Victoria, 1970; plays From Fool to Hanged Man, 1981, Luna, 1971, Saturday Night at the Movies, 1973, A Quick Nut Bread to Make Your Mouth Water, 1973, XXXXX, 1973, The Last Days of Stephen Foster, 1978, Whistler: 5 Portraits, 1979, Cornbury, 1978; (poetry) The Cloisters (song cycle), 1968; 31 New American Poets, 1970, Fine Frenzy, 1972; artist-in-residence, Lincoln Center Student Program, 1971-72; playwright in residence, La Mama, N.Y., 1978, ACT, San Francisco; Contbr. to profl. jours. MacDowell Colony fellow, 1971; PEN grantee, 1973; Guggenheim fellow, 1974; Nat. Endowment for Arts librettist grantee, 1975; Nat. Endowment for Arts creative writing fellow, 1976. Mem. ASCAP, N.Y. Theatre Strategy, Circle Repertory Co. Playwrights Workshop, P.E.N., Phi Beta Kappa. Commd. by Met. Opera to write libretto for centennial season, 1983-84. Home: 199 Prince St New York NY 10012 Office: care Luis San Jurjo Internat Creative Mgmt 40 W 57th St New York NY 10019

HOFFMANN, CHARLES, economist, educator; b. N.Y.C., Jan. 10, 1921; s. William and Regine (Jonkler) H.; m. Shireley Meretsky, July 26, 1953; children: Richard, Brian. B.A. magna cum laude in Econs. and History, Queens Coll., 1942; M.A. in Econs., Columbia U., 1947, Ph.D., 1954. Economist OPA, Washington and N.Y.C., 1942, 46; mem. faculty dept. econs. Queens Coll. CUNY, 1947-63; prof. econs., asst. to v.p., provost social behavioral scis. SUNY-Stony Brook, 1963-70, asst. acad. v.p., 1970-74; dean social scis. div., prof. econs. Queens Coll. CUNY, 1979—. Author: Economic Principles and Public Issues, 1958, Work Incentive Practices and Polities in the People's Republic China, 1953-65, The Depression of the Nineties, 1970, The Chinese Worker, 1974; contbr. articles to profl. jours. Served with USNR, 1942-46. Mem. AAAS, Columbia U. Seminar on Modern China, Phi Beta Kappa, Omicron Delta Epsilon, Kappa Delta Pi. Office: Social Scis Div Queens Coll Kissena Blvd Flushing NY 11367

HOFFMANN, CHARLES WESLEY, educator; b. Sioux City, Iowa, Nov. 25, 1929; s. John Wesley and Gertrude J. (Giessen) H.; m. Barbara Brandel Frank, Aug. 11, 1954; children: Eric Gregory, Karla Jennifer. B.A., Oberlin Coll., 1951; M.A., U. Ill., 1952, Ph.D., 1956. Fulbright fellow U. Munich, Germany, 1953-55; Instr. German UCLA, 1956-58, asst. prof., 1958-64; asso. prof. Ohio State U., 1964-66, prof., 1966—, chmn. dept. German, 1969-77. Author: Opposition Poetry in Nazi Germany, 1962, Survey of Research Tool Needs in German Language and Literature, 1978; also: articles on 20th Century German lit; Adv. editor: Dimension, 1968-74. Recipient Distinguished Teaching award UCLA, 1962; Fulbright grantee, Germany, 1981. Mem. MLA, Am. Assn. Tchrs. German, ACLU, AAUP. Home: 291 McCoy Ave Worthington OH 43085 Office: Dieter Cunz Hall Columbus OH 43210

HOFFMANN, DONALD, art critic; b. Springfield, Ill., June 24, 1933; s. George C. and Ines (Catron) H.; m. Theresa Cecelia McGrath, Apr. 12, 1958; children—George, Alan, Eric, Michael, Valerie. Student, U. Chgo., 1949-53, U. Kansas City, Mo., 1958. Mem. staff Kansas City (Mo.) Star, 1956—, art critic, 1965—; Mem. journalism adv. com. Fulbright Scholarship Program, 1968-70; Younger Humanist fellow Nat. Endowment Humanities, 1970-71. Editor: The Meanings of Architecture-Buildings and Writings by John Wellborn Root, 1967; Author: The Architecture of John Wellborn Root, 1973, Frank Lloyd Wright's Fallingwater, 1978; Asst. editor: Jour. Soc. Archtl. Historians, 1970-72; Contbr. jours. in field. Art Critic's fellow-grantee Nat. Endowment for Arts, 1974. Mem. Soc. Archtl. Historians (bd. dirs. 1968-70), Coll. Art Assn. Am., Art Inst. Chgo. (life). Home: 6441 Holmes St Kansas City MO 64131 Office: 1729 Grand Ave Kansas City MO 64108

HOFFMANN, LUDWIG CARL, maritime cons.; b. N.Y.C., Sept. 8, 1906; s. Theodore Henry and Mathilde Millosine (Ebbighausen) H.; m. Helen M. Boudrot, Apr. 18, 1931; children—Theodore Henry, Ludwig Carl. Student, N.Y. State Maritime Coll., 1924-25, U.S. Naval Acad., 1926-27; B.S., Mass. Inst. Tech., 1929; postgrad., U. Md., 1960. Marine engr. shipbldg. div. Bethlehem Steel Co., Quincy, Mass., 1930-33, Navy Dept., Washington, 1933-38; marine engr. Maritime Adminstrn., Dept. Commerce, Washington, 1938-56, chief Office, 1957-68, asst. adminstr. operations, 1969-73; asst. instr. Mass. Inst. Tech., Cambridge, 1929-30; cons. Presdl. Commn. Am. Shipbldg., 1973; maritime cons., 1973-77; v.p. Lowry & Hoffmann Assos., Inc., 1977—; adviser, maritime safety com. Intergovtl. Maritime Consultative Orgn.; mem. tech. com. Am. Bur. Shipping. Recipient Gold medal Dept. Commerce, Silver medal. Life fellow Soc. Naval Architects and Marine Engrs. (David Taylor Gold medal for naval architecture); mem. Am. Soc. Naval Engrs., Propeller Club U.S. Home and Office: 6618 Malta Ln McLean VA 22101

HOFFMANN, OSWALD CARL JULIUS, clergyman; b. Snyder, Nebr., Dec. 6, 1913; s. Carl John and Bertha (Seidel) H.; m. Marcia Rosalind Linnell, June 23, 1940; children: Peter, Paul, John, Katharine Ann. Student, Luther Inst., Chgo., Concordia Coll., Milw. and St. Paul; M.A., U. Minn., 1935; B.D., Concordia Sem., St. Louis, 1936, D.D., 1952; LL.D., Valparaiso U., 1952; L.H.D. Philippine Christian U., 1982. Instr. Bethany Luth. Coll., Mankato, Minn., 1936-40; also dean of men, dir. music, head English dept.; chmn. Minn. Jr. Coll. Conf. Forensic Festival; ordained to ministry Luth. Ch., 1939; pastor English Luth. Ch., Cottonwood, Minn., 1939-40; instr. U. Minn., 1940-41; prof. Concordia Collegiate Inst., Bronxville, N.Y., 1941-48; dir. pub. relations dept. Luth. Ch., Mo. Synod, 1948-63; asst. pastor St. Matthew Luth. Ch., Manhattan, 1948-63; bd. dirs. Aid Assn. for Luths.; pres. Luth. Council in U.S.A., 1970-73; speaker Internat. Luth. Hour, 1955—; sec. Luth. Church Prodns.; Mem. nat. religious adv. com. Fed. Civil Def. Adminstrn.; pres. Nat. Religious Publicity Council, 1953-55, United Bible Socs., 1977—; Bd. dirs. Wheat Ridge Found., Found. Reformation Research. Supervised: prodn. of films Question Seven and Martin Luther; editorial asso.: Am. Lutheran mag; mem. bd.: nat. TV program. This is the Life; Author: The Passion Journey, 1956, The Joyful Way, 1958, Life Crucified, 1959, God Is No Island, 1969, Hurry Home Where You Belong, 1970, God's Joyful People—One in the Spirit, 1973, The Lord's Prayer, 1982. Named Clergyman of Yr. Religious Heritage Am., 1973; recipient Sec. Def. award, 1980, Gold Angel award as Internat. Clergyman of Yr. Religion in Media, 1982. Mem. Am. Philol. Assn., Am. Bible Soc. (life, bd. mgrs.). Home: 586 Oak Valley Dr Saint Louis MO 63131 Office: 2185 Hampton Ave Saint Louis MO 63139

HOFFMANN, PETER CONRAD WERNER, educator; b. Dresden, Germany, Aug. 13, 1930; emigrated to came to Can., 1970; s. Wilhelm and Elfriede Frances (Müller) H.; m. Helga Luise Hobelsberger, July 22, 1959; children: Peter Friedrich Georg Wilhelm, Susan Judith Gudula. Student, U. Stuttgart, 1953-54, U. Tübingen, 1954-55, U. Zurich, 1955, Northwestern U., 1955-56; Ph.D., U. Munich, 1961. Prof. McGill U., Montreal, Que., Can. Author: Widerstand, Staatsstreich, Attentat: Der Kampf der Opposition gegen Hitler, 1969, Die Sicherheit des Diktators: Hitlers Leibwachen, Schutzmassnahmen, Residenzen, Hauptquartiere, 1975, The History of the German Resistance 1933-45, 1977, Hitler's Personal Security, 1979, Widerstand gegen Hitler, 1979. Mem. Deutsche Schillergesellschaft, Canadian Com. History Second World War, Württembergischer Geschichts- und Altertumsverein, Sigma Alpha Epsilon. Home: 4332 Montrose Ave Montreal PQ Canada H3Y 2A9

HOFFMANN, ROALD, chemist, educator; b. Zloczow, Poland, July 18, 1937; came to U.S., 1949, naturalized, 1955; s. Hillel and Clara (Rosen) Safron (stepson Paul Hoffmann); m. Eva Börjesson, Apr. 30, 1960; children: Hillel Jan, Ingrid Helena. B.A., Columbia U., 1958; M.A., Harvard U., 1960, Ph.D., 1962; D.Tech. (hon.), Royal Inst. Tech., Stockholm, 1977, D.Sc., Yale U., 1980, Columbia U., 1982, Hartford U., 1982, CUNY, 1983, U. P.R., 1983. Jr. fellow Soc. Fellows Harvard, 1962-65; asso. prof. Cornell U., Ithaca, N.Y., 1965-68, prof., 1968-74, John A. Newman prof. phys. sci., 1974—. Author: (with R.B. Woodward) Conservation of Orbital Symmetry, 1970. Recipient award in pure chemistry Am. Chem. Soc., 1969, Arthur C. Cope award, 1973; Fresenius award Phi Lambda Upsilon, 1969; Harrison Howe award Rochester sect. Am. Chem. Soc., 1970; ann. award Internat. Acad. Quantum Molecular Scis., 1970; Pauling award, 1974; Nobel prize in chemistry, 1981; inorganic chemistry award; Am. Chem. Soc., 1982. Mem. Nat. Acad. Scis., Am. Acad. Arts and Scis., Internat. Acad. Quantum Molecular Scis. Home: 4 Sugarbush Ln Ithaca NY 14850

HOFFMANN, STANLEY, educator, political scientist; b. Vienna, Austria, Nov. 27, 1928; came to U.S., 1955, naturalized, 1960; m. Inge Schneier. Grad., Inst. d'Etudes Politiques, Paris, 1948; doctorate, Paris Law Sch., 1953; M.A. in Govt, Harvard, 1952. Research Fond. Nationale des Sciences Politiques, Paris, 1952-53, 55; mem. faculty Harvard, 1955—, prof. govt., 1963—, Douglas Dillon prof. civilization of France, 1980—; chmn. Center for European Studies, 1969—; mem. faculty Center Internat. Affairs, 1971—; prof. associé Inst. d'etudes Politiques, Paris, 1975-76. Author: Organisations Internationales et Pouvoirs Politiques des Etats, 1954, Le Mouvement Poujade, 1956, The State of War, 1965, Gulliver's Troubles, 1968, Decline or Renewal?, 1974, Primacy or World Order, 1978, Duties Beyond Borders, 1981, Dead Ends, 1983; co-author: In Search of France, 1963, The Relevance of International Law, 1968, La Politique des Sciences Sociales en France, 1975, The Fifth Republic at Twenty, 1981, Living with Nuclear Weapons, 1983; Editor: Contemporary Theory in International Relations, 1960, Conditions of World Order, 1968. Fellow Center Advanced Study Behavioral Scis., Stanford, Calif., 1965-66. Mem. Council Fgn. Relations, Am. Acad. Arts and Scis., Am. Polit. Sci. Assn., Am. Philos. Soc., Am. Soc. Internat. Law, Assn. Française de Science Politique. Home: 91 Washington Ave Cambridge MA 02140

HOFFMANN, THOMAS RUSSELL, educator; b. Milw., Sept. 10, 1933; s. Alfred C. and Florence M. (Morlock) H.; m. Lorna G. Gruenzel, Aug. 31, 1957; 1 son, Timothy Jay. B.S., U. Wis., 1955; M.S., 1956, Ph.D., 1959. Engring. trainee Allis-Chalmers Mfg. Co., 1956-59; asst. prof. U. Wis. Sch. Commerce, 1959-63; mem. faculty U. Minn. Sch. Mgmt., Mpls., 1963—, prof., 1965—, chmn. dept. mgmt. scis., 1969-78; dir. West Bank Computer Center, 1971—; cons. to industry. Fellow Am. Prodn. and Inventory Control Soc. (pres. Twin Cities chpt.), 1970-71. Author: Production Management and Manufacturing Systems, 2 edits, 1967-71, (with others) Fortran 77: A Structured, Disciplined Style, 1978, 83, Production and Inventory Management, 1983; Contbr. papers to profl. lit. Mem. Assn. Computing Machinery, Ops. Research Soc. Am., Inst. Mgmt. Scis. Lutheran (chmn. long range planning com. 1971, pres. 1974, treas. 1977-82). Home: 4501 Sedum Ln Edina MN 55435 Office: Mgmt and Econs Bldg U Minn Minneapolis MN 55455

HOFFMANN, WILLIAM FREDERICK, astronomer, educator; b. Manchester, N.H., Feb. 26, 1933; s. Maurice and Charlotte (Hibbs) H.; m. Silke Elisabeth Margaretha Schneider, June 5, 1965; children: Andrea Charlotte, Christopher James. A.B. in Physics, Bowdoin Coll., 1954; Ph.D., Princeton U., 1962. Instr. physics Princeton U., 1958-61; research asso. NASA Goddard Inst. Space Studies, N.Y.C., 1962, staff astronomer, 1965-73; instr. physics Yale U., 1963-65; adj. asso. prof. astronomy Columbia U., 1970-73; prof. astronomy U. Ariz., 1973—, astronomer Stewart Obs., 1973—, project scientist multiple mirror telescope, 1973-79, project scientist sub-millimeter telescope, 1983—; Pres. Spuyten Duyvil Assn., N.Y.C., 1971. Editor: (with H.Y. Chiu) Gravitation and Relativity, 1964. NSF fellow, 1954; Danforth fellow, 1954-58; recipient NASA Exceptional Sci. Achievement medal, 1972. Mem. Am. Phys. Soc., Am. Astron. Soc., AAAS, Phi Beta Kappa, Sigma Xi. Club: Sierra. Home: 4225 E Kilmer St Tucson AZ 85711 Office: Steward Observatory University of Arizona Tucson AZ 85721

HOFFMEISTER, DONALD FREDERICK, zoology educator; b. San Bernardino, Calif., Mar. 21, 1916; s. Percival George and Julia Bell (Hillgartner) H.; m. Helen E. Kaatz, Aug. 11, 1938; children: James Ronald, Robert George. A.B., U. Calif.-Berkeley, 1938, M.A., 1940, Ph.D., 1944. Research, curatorial asst. Museum Vertebrate Zoology, U. Calif. at Berkeley, 1941-44, teaching asst. zoology at univ., 1943-44; asso. curator modern vertebrates Mus. Natural History, U. Kans., 1944-46, asst. prof. zoology at univ., 1944-46; dir. Mus. Natural History, U. Ill., 1946—, mem. faculty univ., 1946—, prof. zoology, 1959—; research asso. Mus. No. Ariz., 1969—. Author: Mammals, 1955, 1963, Fieldbook of Illinois Mammals, 1957, Zoo Animals, 1967, Mammals of Grand Canyon, 1971; also articles, reports. Mem. Am. Soc. Mammalogists (sec. 1946-52, v.p. 1961-64, pres. 1964-66), Midwest Museum's Conf. (exec. v.p. 1962-63, pres. 1963-64), Am. Assn. Museums (council 1973-76), Assn. Sci. Mus. Dirs. Home: 1505 W Charles St Champaign IL 61821 Office: Museum Natural History Univ Illinois Urbana IL 61801

HOFFSTOT, HENRY PHIPPS, JR., lawyer; b. Pitts., Nov. 13, 1917; s. Henry Phipps and Marguerite (Martin) H.; m. Barbara Drew, Apr. 17, 1948; children: Thayer Drew Hoffstot Unterman, Henry Phipps, III. A.B., Harvard U., 1939, LL.B., 1942. Bar: Pa. bar 1942. Asso. firm Reed Smith Shaw & McClay, Pitts., 1946-55, partner, 1956—; pres., dir. Pennsgrove Water Supply Co., 1967—; Active Commn. for Study of Common Body of Knowledge for C.P.A.'s, N.Y., 1965-67, Nat. Parks Centennial Commn., 1971-73; trustee Carnegie Library, Pitts., 1966—, v.p., 1970—; trustee Carnegie Inst., 1966—, sec., 1968—; supervising com. Bellefield Boiler Plant, 1967—, chmn., 1978—. Trustee Family and Children's Service, 1962-68, 69-75, 77-83, pres., 1964-66; trustee Pitts. Regional Library Center, 1967—, St. Edmunds Acad., 1964-72; pres. St. Edmunds Acad., 1968-70; bd. dirs. Community Chest of Allegheny County, 1962-68, exec. com., 1968-69; bd. dirs. Mendelssohn Choir, Pitts., 1958—, treas., 1959-61; bd. dirs. Pitts. Chamber Music Soc., 1968—, Vis. Nurse Assn. of Allegheny County, 1948—; pres. Vis. Nurse Assn. of Allegheny County, 1957-60, 66-67, 79-83; mem. council Am. Mus. in Britain, 1979—. Served with inf. AUS, 1942-46. Fellow Am. Bar Found.; mem. ABA, Pa. Bar Assn., Allegheny County Bar Assn., Am. Coll. Probate Counsel, Am. Law Inst., SAR (pres. Pitts. chpt. 1978-79). Presbyterian. Clubs: Economic (dir. 1978-79), Duquesne, Harvard-Yale-Princeton, Pitts. Golf (Pitts.); Rolling Rock, Harvard (N.Y.C.); Everglades (Palm Beach)). Home: 5057 5th Ave Pittsburgh PA 15232 Office: Reed Smith Shaw & McClay PO Box 2009 Pittsburgh PA 15230

HOFHEINZ, ROY MARK, JR., political science educator; b. Houston, Dec. 18, 1935; s. Roy Mark and Irene (Cafcalas) H.; m. Harriet Parker, June 15, 1963 (div. Dec. 1980); m. Susan Hart Nicholson, May 2, 1981; children: Frederick, Irene. B.A., Rice U., 1957; M.A. (Rhodes scholar), Exeter Coll., Oxford U., 1959; Ph.D. (Nat. Def. Fgn. Lang. fellow), Harvard, 1966. Prof. govt. Harvard, Cambridge, Mass., 1966-81; dir. Fairbank Center for East Asian Research, 1977-80; mem. Centre on Scholarly Communication with People's Republic of China, 1976—. Author: Broken Wave: The Chinese Communist Peasant Movement, 1977, (with Kent E. Calder) The Eastasia Edge, 1982; Contbr. articles to profl. jours. Ford Fgn. Area Tng. fellow, 1959-61; Ford faculty fellow in polit. sci., 1970. Mem. Assn. Asian Studies, Am. Polit. Sci. Assn.

HOFLEY, BERNARD C., lawyer; b. Winnipeg, Man., Can., Dec. 16, 1928; s. Roy and Leocadie (Viller) H.; m. Micheline Fournier, Feb. 18, 1958; children—Bernard Charles, Charles Viller, Marc Arthur. B.A., St. Paul's Coll., Winnipeg, 1951; LL.B., Man. Law Sch., 1955. Bar: Called to Man. bar 1955, created Queen's counsel 1980. Legal officer Dept. Justice, Ottawa, Ont., Can., 1955-58; pvt. Sec. to minister of nat. def., 1958-60; with Fournier, Papillon Ltee, Quebec, 1960-64; exec. asst. to gen. mgr. Can. Corp. for World Exhbn. (Expo '67), 1964-67; gen. mgr. Schweppes-Powell Ltd., 1967-69; asst. dep. solicitor gen. for research and systems devel. Govt. of Can., Ottawa, 1969-78; registrar Supreme Ct. of Can., Ottawa, 1978—. Bd. dirs. Ottawa Boys and Girls Club; founding mem. Le Cercle Universitaire, Ottawa. Recipient Centennial medal. Office: Supreme Ct of Can Wellington St Ottawa ON K1A 0J1 Canada

HOFMANN, HANS, educator, author; b. Basel, Switzerland, Aug. 12, 1923; came to U.S., 1951, naturalized, 1956; s. Oscar and Henriette (Burbiel) H.; m. Emilie Scott Welles, Oct. 15, 1955; children—Elizabeth Scott, Mark Lawrence, David Hans, Scott Cluett. A.B., Thurg. Kantonsschule, 1943; B.D., U. Basel, 1948; Th.D., U. Zurich, 1953. Mem. faculty Princeton Theol. Sem., 1953-57, asso. prof., 1956-57; mem. faculty Harvard Div. Sch., 1957-62, prof. theology, 1961-62, Ingersoll lectr. at univ., 1956-57; leader Danforth seminar religion and bus. ethics Grad. Sch. Bus. Adminstrn., 1958, dir. project religion and mental health at univ., 1957-61; inaugural Thorp lectr. Cornell U., 1955-56; exec. dir. Center Study Personality and Culture, Inc., Cambridge, Mass., 1964-66; pres. Inst. for Human Devel., Cambridge, 1966—; ordained to ministry United Ch. Christ, 1957; cons. dept. internat. affairs Nat. Council Chs. Author: The Theology of Reinhold Niebuhr, 1955, Religion and Mental Health, 1961, Incorporating Sex, 1967, Breakthrough to Life, 1969, Discovering Freedom, 1969; Editor: Making the Ministry Relevant, 1960, The Ministry and Mental Health, 1960, Sex Incorporated, 1967. Mem. bd. overseers Shady Hill Sch., Cambridge. Mem. Internat. Platform Assn., Nat. Cum Laude Soc. (hon. mem.), Nat. Inst. Arts and Letters, English-Speaking Union, Soc. Sci. Study Religion, Am. Soc. Christian Social Ethics, Fedn. Am. Scientists, AAUP, Signet Soc. Home: 110 Evening Glow Pl Sedona AZ 86336 *It is simply amazing how much more can be achieved when one learns to flow with the life forces, participate rather than obstruct the inevitable life development, and to infuse with understanding enlightenment all that cannot be dealt with constructively through confrontation and mere power play. Human development through growth in awareness, understanding, and creative self-expression in union with natural development represents therefore the most needed and promising breakthrough for all of us in our immediate future and the very goal to which I have dedicated myself fully and with great joy.*

HOFMANN, JOHN RICHARD, JR., lawyer; b. Oakland, Calif., June 24, 1922; s. John Richard and Esther (Starkweather) H.; m. Mary Macdonough, Feb. 6, 1954; children: John Richard, Gretchen, Sarah W., Joan Macdonough. A.B., U. Calif.-Berkeley, 1943; J.D., Harvard U., 1949. Bar: Calif. 1950. Assoc. Pillsbury, Madison & Sutro, San Francisco, 1949-58, ptnr., 1959—; city atty. City of Belvedere (Calif.), 1957-58. Mem. ABA, Calif. Bar Assn., San Francisco Bar Assn. Office: Pillsbury Madison & Sutro PO Box 7880 225 Bush St San Francisco CA 94120

HOFMANN, KLAUS, biochemistry educator, researcher; b. Karlsruhe, Germany, Feb. 21, 1911; came to U.S., 1938; s. Fritz and Marianne (Bally) H.; m. Paula Blum, 1936 (div.); 1 dau., Suzanne Elisabeth; m. Frances Mary Finn, Feb. 26, 1965. Ph.D., Fed. Inst. Tech., Zurich, Switzerland, 1936. Postdoctoral fellow Rockefeller Inst. Med. Research, N.Y.C., 1938-40, Cornell Med. Coll., 1940-42; guest worker Ciba Pharm. Co., Summit, N.J., 1942-44; asst. research prof. U. Pitts., 1944-45, assoc. prof., 1945-47, research prof., 1947-52, chmn. biochemistry dept. Med. Sch., 1952-64, prof. exptl. medicine and biochemistrry, dir. Protein Research Lab., 1964—. Author: Chemistry of Imidazole, 1953, Fatty Acid Metabolism in Microorganisms, 1963; contbr. numerous articles to profl. jours. Recipient Chancellor's medal U. Pitts., 1963, Borden award, 1963, Sr. U.S. Scientist award Alexander von Humboldt-Stiftung, Germany, 1976-77, Alan E. Pierce award Pierce Chem. Co., 1981. Fellow Japan Soc. Promotion of Sci.; mem. Nat. Acad. Scis., Am. Chem. Soc. (Pitts. award Pitts. sect. 1962), Am. Soc. Biol. Chemists, AAAS, Endocrine Soc., Swiss Chem. Soc. Home: 1467 Mohican Dr Pittsburgh PA 15228 Office: Univ Pittsburgh 3550 Terrace St Pittsburgh PA 15261

HOFMANN, PAUL BERNARD, hosp. adminstr.; b. Portland, Oreg., July 6, 1941; s. Max and Consuelo Theresa (Bley) H.; m. Lois Bernstein, June 28, 1969; children—Julie, Jason. B.S., U. Calif., Berkeley, 1963, M.P.H., 1965. Research asso. in hosp. adminstrn. Lab. of Computer Sci., Mass. Gen. Hosp., Boston, 1966-68, asst. dir., 1968-69; asst. adminstr. San Antonio Community Hosp., Upland, Calif., 1969-70, asso. adminstr., 1970-72; dep. dir. Stanford (Calif.) U. Hosp., 1972-74, dir., 1974-77; exec. dir. Emory U. Hosp., Atlanta, 1978—; instr. computer applications Harvard U., 1968-69; lectr. hosp. adminstrn. UCLA, 1970-72, Stanford U. Med. Sch., 1972-77; asso. prof. Emory U. Sch. Medicine, Atlanta, 1978—. Contbr. articles to profl. jours. Served with U.S. Army, 1959. Fellow Am. Coll. Hosp. Adminstrs. (recipient Robert S. Hudgens meml. award 1976); mem. Am. Hosp. Assn., Assn. Univ. Programs in Health Adminstrn., U. Calif. Alumni Assn. Home: 2767 Briarlake Woods Way Atlanta GA 30345 Office: Emory U Hosp 1364 Clifton Rd NE Atlanta GA 30322

HOFMANN, PAUL LEOPOLD, foreign correspondent; b. Vienna, Austria, Nov. 20, 1912; emigrated to U.S., 1959, naturalized, 1968; s. Joseph Martin and Ida Anna (Pirkmayr) H. Dr. Jur., Vienna U., 1936. With N.Y. Times, N.Y.C., 1945—, fgn. corr., Italy, France, Nigeria,

Zaire, other countries, 1956-74; chief UN Bur., 1974-76, Vienna corr., 1976-78, roving corr., Rome, 1978—. Author: Rome: The Sweet, Tempestuous Life, 1982, Oh Vatican!, 1984. Roman Catholic. Home: 25 Viale Platone 00136 Rome Italy

HOFMANN, RICHARD DEACON, packaging company executive; b. Phila., Aug. 31. 1940; s. Charles E. and Lois (Deacon) H.; m. Mary Joan McGonigal, Aug. 10, 1963; children Richard Deacon, Elizabeth Anne, Patricia Anne, John C. B.A., Dartmouth Coll., 1962; M.B.A., U. Pa., 1964. With Continental Group, Inc., 1963—, corp. v.p., 1979—; pres. Continental Can Co., 1981-82; chief operating officer Continental Packaging Co., 1982-83; exec. v.p. chief planning officer The Continental Group, Inc., 1983—. Bd. dirs., exec. officer Keep Am. Beautiful; mem. Wharton grad. exec. bd. U. Pa. Mem. U.S. Brewers Assn. (assoc. dir.), Can Mfrs. Inst. (dir.). Clubs: Stamford Yacht (Conn.); Wee Burn Country (Darien, Conn.). Office: Continental Group Inc 1 Harbor Plaza Stamford CT 06904

HOFMANN, THEO, biochemist, educator; b. Zurich, Switzerland, Feb. 20, 1924; emigrated to Can., 1964, naturalized, 1969; s. Edwin and Hedwig (Moos) H.; m. Doris Topham Forbes, July 15, 1953; children: Martin Ian, Tony David, Peter Adrian. Diploma chem. engring., Swiss Fed. Inst. Tech., Zurich, 1947, Dr. Sc. Tech., 1950. Research asst. U. Aberdeen, Scotland, 1950-52; sci. officer Hannah Dairy Research Inst., Ayr, Scotland, 1952-56; lectr. Sheffield (Eng.) U., 1956-64; prof. biochemistry U. Toronto, Ont., Can., 1964—; vis. asso. prof. U. Wash., 1962-63; vis. scientist Commonwealth Sci. and Indsl. Research Orgn., Sydney, Australia, 1971-72; vis. prof. div. natural scis. U. Calif.-Santa Cruz, 1981. Asso. editor: Can. Jour. Biochemistry, 1968-71; Contbr. numerous articles to profl. jours. Med. Research Council (Can.) grantee, 1964—. Mem. Can. Biochem. Soc., Am. Soc. Biol. Chemists, Biochem. Soc. Research in function and evolution of enzymes. Home: 199 Arnold Ave Thornhill ON L4J 1C1 Canada Office: Dept of Biochemistry U of Toronto Toronto ON M5S 1A8 Canada

HOFMEYER, GEORGE AUGUST, paper co. exec.; b. New Milford, N.J., Nov. 1, 1921; s. George August and Anna (Schwern) H.; m. Adele Helen Mulch, Mar. 9, 1947; children—Ridge, Holly. B.S., N.Y. U., 1955. C.P.A., N.J. Staff accountant S.D. Leidesdorf & Co. (C.P.A.'s), N.Y.C., 1955-62; staff accountant Fed. Paper Bd. Co., Montvale, N.J., 1962-65, asst. to controller, 1965-68, controller, 1968-77, dir. internal auditing, 1977—. Mem. Am. Inst. C.P.A.'s, Inst. Internal Auditors. Home: 77 Venus Dr Closter NJ 07624 Office: 75 Chestnut Ridge Rd Montvale NJ 07645

HOFSISS, JACK BERNARD, stage, film and television director; b. Bklyn., Sept. 28, 1950; s. Christian Leo and Cecilia Kathleen (Loughlin) H. A.B., Georgetown U., 1971. Dir. Washington Theatre Club, 1972-73, Folger Theatre Group, Washington, 1971, N.Y. Shakespeare Festival, N.Y.C., 1976, Am. Nat. Theatre Acad., 1977-79; ANTA; lectr. Columbia U. Dir.: play The Elephant Man, N.Y.C. (Tony award 1979); (Obie award 1979, Outer Critics Circle award 1979, New Drama Forum award 1979, Broadway Drama Guild award 1979); dir.: play Poor Little Lambs, 1982, Total Abandon, 1983; film I'm Dancing As Fast As I Can, 1982, Family Secrets, 1983; also dir. TV shows. Mem. Dirs. Guild Am., Soc. Stage Dirs. and Choreographers (exec. bd.). Office: care of Joan Hyler William Morris Agency 1300 Ave Americas New York NY

HOFSTAD, RALPH PARKER, dairy company executive; b. Phila., Nov. 14, 1923; s. Ottar and Amelia (Davis) H.; m. Adeline Smedstad, June 14, 1947; children: Diane (Mrs. Roger Dunker), Barbara (Mrs. Dan McClanahan), James, Ron, Tom, Susan. Student, Hamline U., 1942-43, Gustavus Adolphus Coll., 1943-44, Northwestern U., 1944, U. Minn., 1946-47; B.B.A., Northwestern U., 1948. Accountant F S Services, Bloomington, Ill., 1948-51, mgmt. ops., 1953-65; pres. Farmers Regional Coop (Felco), Ft. Dodge, Iowa, 1965-70; sr. v.p. agrl. services Land O' Lakes Inc., Ft. Dodge, 1970—, pres., Mpls., 1974—; dir. Mut. Service Ins. Cos., St. Paul, Hon Industries, Muscatine, Iowa, Control Data Corp., Mpls., Nat. Milk Producers Fedn., Washington, 1977—; Bd. dirs. Nat. Council Farmer Coops., Washington, 1973—, Goodwill Industries Am., 1977—; chmn. Internat. Energy Coop., Inc., 1979-80, bd. dirs., 1974—. Served with USNR, 1943-46. Methodist. Home: 6608 Field Way Edina MN 55436 Office: Land O'Lakes Inc PO Box 116 Minneapolis MN 55440

HOFSTADTER, DOUGLAS RICHARD, computer scientist, educator; b. N.Y.C., Feb. 15, 1945; s. Robert and Nancy (Givan) H. B.S. in Math. with distinction, Stanford U., 1965; M.S., U. Oreg., 1972, Ph.D. in Physics, 1975. Asst. prof. computer sci. Ind. U., Bloomington, 1977-80, assoc. prof., 1980-84; Walgreen prof. Cognitive Sci. U. Mich., Ann Arbor, 1984—. Author: Gödel, Escher, Bach: an Eternal Golden Braid, 1979; editor: (with Daniel C. Dennett) The Mind's I, 1981; columnist: Metamagical Themas in Sci. Am., 1981-83. Recipient Pultizer prize for gen. nonfiction, 1980; Am. Book award, 1980; Guggenheim fellow, 1980-81. Mem. Assn. for Computing Machinery, Cognitive Sci. Soc., Am. Assn. Artificial Intelligence. Office: Dept Psychology U Mich Ann Arbor MI

HOFSTADTER, ROBERT, physicist, educator; b. N.Y.C., Feb. 5, 1915; s. Louis and Henrietta (Koenigsberg) H.; m. Nancy Givan, May 9, 1942; children: Douglas Richard, Laura James, Mary Hinda. B.S. magna cum laude (Kenyon prize), Coll. City N.Y., 1935; M.A. (Procter fellow), Princeton U., 1938; Ph.D., Princeton U., 1938; LL.D., City U. N.Y., 1961; D.Sc., Gustavus Adolphus Coll., 1963; Laureate Honoris Causa, U. Padua, 1965; D.Sc., Carleton U., Ottawa, Can., 1967, Seoul Nat. U., 1967; Honoris Causa, U. Clermont-Ferrnad, 1967; D. Rerum Naturalium honoris causa, Julius Maximilians U., Würzburg, W. Ger., 1982, Johannes Gutenberg U. Mainz (W. Ger.), 1983. Coffin fellow Gen. Electric Co., 1935-36; Harrison fellow U. Pa., 1939; instr. physics Princeton U., 1940-41, CCNY, 1941-42; physicist Norden Lab. Corp., 1943-46; asst. prof. physics Princeton U., 1946-50; assoc. prof. physics Stanford U., 1950-54, prof., 1954—, Max H. Stein prof. physics, 1971—, dir. high energy physics lab., 1967-74; dir. John Fluke Mfg. Co. Author: (with Robert Herman) High-Energy Electron Scattering Tables, 1960; Editor: Investigations in Physics, 1958-65, Electron Scattering and Nucleon Structure, 1963; Co-editor: Nucleon Structure, 1964; Asso. editor: Phys. Review, 1951-53; mem. editorial bd.: Review Sci. Instruments, 1953-55, Reviews of Modern Physics, 1958-61. Calif. Scientist of Year, 1959; co-recipient of Nobel prize in physics, 1961; Townsend Harris medal Coll. City N.Y., 1961; Guggenheim fellow, Geneva, Switzerland, 1958-59; Ford Found. fellow. Fellow Am. Phys. Soc., Phys. Soc. London; mem. Nat. Acad. Scis., Am. Acad. Arts and Scis., AAUP, Phi Beta Kappa, Sigma Xi. Home: 639 Mirada Ave Stanford CA 94305

HOFSTATTER, LEOPOLD, physician, researcher; b. Vienna, Austria, Mar. 11, 1902; came to U.S., 1938, naturalized, 1944; s. Leopold H. and Josefine (Eibuschuetz) H.; m. Lilli Schwarz, Apr. 16, 1930; m. Theresa Adams Mayer, Sept. 4, 1971. M.D., U. Vienna, 1926. Intern Allgemeines Krankenhaus Wien, Vienna, 1927-28; resident Maria Theresian Schloessel, 1930-33, St. Louis State Hosp., 1941-42; mem. staff St. Vincent's Hosp., 1948—; asst. supt. St. Louis State Hosp., 1942-62, chief gen. med., surg. div., 1960-62; supt. St. Louis State Sch. and Hosp., 1962-67; sr. cons. resident tng. program Mo. Inst. Psychiatry, 1967-69, med. dir., 1972-74; supt. St. Louis State Hosp. Complex, 1970-72; clin. prof. psychiatry U. Mo. Fellow Am. Psychiat. Assn. (life); mem. Mo. Hosp. Physicians Assn. (past pres.), Sci. Research Assn. Am., Eastern Mo. Psychiat. Soc., Sigma Xi. Home: 768 Glenvista Glendale MO 63122 Office: 5400 Arsenal St Saint Louis MO 63139

HOFSTETTER, HENRY W, optometrist, educator; b. Windsor, Ohio, Sept. 10, 1914; s. Kaspar and Augusta (Kresin) H.; m. Frances Jane Elder, July 5, 1941; children—Ann Kresin, Susan Claire. Student, Western Res. U., 1931-33, Kent State U., 1933; B.S., Ohio State U., 1939, M.S., 1940, Ph.D., 1942; D.Optometric Sci., Los Angeles Coll. Optometry, 1954, Mass. Coll. Optometry, 1968; Sc.D., Pa. Coll. Optometry, 1969; D.Sci., U. Waterloo, Can., 1977. Elementary sch. tchr. Middlefield (Ohio) Pub. Sch., 1933-36; faculty Ohio State U., 1942-48, asso. prof., 1947-48; dean Los Angeles Coll. Optometry, 1948-52; prof. optometry Ind. U., Bloomington, 1952-75, Rudy prof. optometry, 1975-80, emeritus, 1980—, dir. div. optometry, 1952-70; nat. cons. in optometry surgeon gen. of USAF, 1972-77; chmn. tech. adv. com. Illuminating Engring. Research Inst.; mem. U.S. nat. com. Commn. Internationale d L'Eclairage; vis. prof. optometry U. Waterloo (Can.), fall 1980; acting dean Sch. Optometry, Inter-Am. U. P.R., 1981; Mem. Nat. Adv. Council on Edn. for Health Professions, 1964-67; mem. Ind. Commn. for Handicapped; mem. com. on vision Armed Forces NRC, 1961—; dir. Contact Lens Testing Bur. Contact Lens Mfrs. Assn., 1983—. Author: Optometry, 1948, Industrial Vision, 1956, (with M. Schapero, David Cline) Dictionary of Visual Science, 1960, 2d edit., 1968, (with Cline and John Griffin), 3d edit., 1980, also over 360 articles.; Editor newsletter: Optometric Hist. Soc., 1970—. Recipient medal Internat. Optical League, 1968, Centennial Achievement award Ohio State U., 1970, Der Deutscher Preis für Optometrie, 1973, Orion award Armed Forces Optometric Soc., 1974. Fellow Am. Public Health Assn., AAAS, Sociedad Americana de Oftalmologia y Optometria, Optometric Hist. Soc. (pres. 1970-74), Optical Soc. Am.; mem. Illuminating Engring. Soc., Am. Optometric Assn. (disting. mem., past pres., Apollo award 1973), South African Optometric Assn. (chmn. commn. on edn. 1980), Am. Acad. Optometry (Charles F. Prentice medal 1976), Soc. for Internat. Devel., Assn. Schs. and Colls. Optometry (past pres.). Research on graphical analysis of relationship between accommodation and convergence of eyes and application to clin. techniques, accommodation fatigue and age-amplitude relationships, heredity in astigmatism, stereopsis, internat. optometric edn. Home: 2615 Windermere Woods Dr Bloomington IN 47401

HOGAN, BEN, golfer, business executive; b. Dublin, Tex., Aug. 13, 1912; m. Valerie Fox, Apr. 14, 1935. Attended Ft. Worth pub. schs. Profl. golfer, 1931-70; former chmn. Ben Hogan div. AMF, Inc., White Plains, N.Y., now chief exec. officer, Ft. Worth. Author: Power Golf, 1948. Served to lt. USAAF, 1943-45. Recipient Ryder Cup, 1947, 49; named Golfer of Year, 1948, 50, 51, 53; named to PGA Hall of Fame, 1953. Winner 4 U.S. Open Championships, 2 Masters, 1 Brit. Open, and Profl. Golfers' Assn. Championship, 1946, 48. Address: Ben Hogan Co 2912 W Pafford St Fort Worth TX 76110 *

HOGAN, CLARENCE LESTER, electrical engineer; b. Great Falls, Mont., Feb. 8, 1920; s. Clarence Lester and Bessie (Young) H.; m. Audrey Biery Peters, Oct. 13, 1946; 1 dau., Cheryl Lea. B.S. in Chem. Engring., Mont. State Coll., 1942; M.S. in Physics, Lehigh U., 1947, Ph.D., 1950; A.M. (hon), Harvard U., 1954; D.Eng. (hon.), Mont. State U., 1967, Lehigh U., 1971, D.Sc., Worcester Poly. Inst., 1969. Research chem. engr. Anaconda Copper Mining Co., 1942-43; instr. physics Lehigh U., 1946-50; tech. staff Bell Telephone Labs., 1950-52, sub. dept. head, 1952-53; asso. prof. Harvard U., 1953-57, Gordon McKay prof. applied physics, 1957-58; gen. mgr. semi-conductor products div. Motorola, Inc., Phoenix, 1958-60, v.p., 1960-66, exec. v.p., 1966-68; pres., chief exec. officer Fairchild Camera & Instrument Corp., Mountain View, Calif., 1968-74, vice chmn. bd., 1974-79, tech. adviser to pres., 1979—; dir. First Interstate Bank, Rolm Corp., Tab Products Co., Timeplex, Inc., Varian Assocs., Osborne Computer Corp., Semicondr. Specialists.; Gen. chmn. Internat. Conf. on Magnetism and Magnetic Materials, 1959, 60; materials adv. bd. Dept. Def., 1955-57; adv. council dept. elec. engring. Princeton U., 1962-68; adv. council NASA-Electronic Research Council, 1967-70; adv. bd. Coll. Engring., U. Calif.-Berkeley, 1974—; mem. nat. adv. bd. Desert Research Inst., 1976-80; vis. com. Lehigh U., 1966, trustee, 1971-80; vis. com. dept. elec. engring. and computer sci. MIT, 1975—; adv. council div. engring. Stanford U., 1976—; mem. sci. and edn. adv. com. Lawrence Berkeley Lab., 1978-82; mem. Pres.'s Export Council, 1976-80; mem. adv. panel to tech. adv. bd. U.S. Congress, 1976-80; Trustee Western Electronic Edn. Fund; governing bd. Maricopa County Jr. Coll., 1966-68; bd. regents U. Santa Clara. Served from ensign to lt. (j.g.) USNR, 1943-46. Recipient Community Service award NCCJ, 1978, medal of achievement Am. Electronics Assn., 1978; named Bay Area Outstanding Businessman of Year San Jose State Coll., 1977, One of 10 Greatest Innovators in Past 50 Yrs. Electronics Mag., 1980; Berkeley citation U. Calif., Berkeley, 1981. Fellow IEEE (exec. v.p. 1978, Frederik Philips medal 1976), AAAS, Instn. Elec. Engrs. (London, hon.); mem. Am. Phys. Soc., Nat. Acad. Engring., Sigma Xi, Tau Beta Pi, Phi Kappa Phi, Kappa Sigma. Home: 36 Barry Ln Atherton CA 94025 Office: 464 Ellis St Mountain View CA 94042

HOGAN, CLAUDE HOLLIS, lawyer; b. Bishop, Calif., Mar. 2, 1920; s. Claude Hollis and Emma Janet (Slade) H.; m. June Cunningham, June 12, 1946; children: David, Patricia. A.B., Coll. of Pacific, 1942; LLB., Yale U., 1948. Bar: Calif. 1949. Assoc. Pillsbury, Madison & Sutro, San Francisco, 1948-58, ptnr., 1959—. Contbr. articles to profl. jours. D. dirs. Ernest D. van Loben Sels--Eleanor Slate vol Loben Sels Charitable Found., San Francisco, 1964—; pres. Ernest D. van Loben Sels-Eleanor Slate vol Loben Sels Charitable Found., San Francisco, 1971—; mem. San Francisco Lawyers Com. on Urban Affairs, 1973—, com-chmn., 1978; bd. dirs. Legal Aid Soc. San Francisco, 1974—; trustee Lawyers Com. for Civil Rights under Law, 1980—. Mem. State Bar Calif. (exec. com. taxation sect. 1975-76, bd. legal specialization 1981—), ABA, Bar Assn. San Francisco (chmn. taxation sect. 1970, dir. 1978, pres. found. 1983—), Internat. Fiscal Assn., Am. Judicature Soc., Calif. C. of C. (tax com. 1973—). Office: Pillsbury Madison & Sutro Standard Oil Bldg 225 Bust St San Francisco CA 94104

HOGAN, COLEMAN FRANCIS, manufacturing company executive; b. Boston, Apr. 1, 1917; s. Patrick J. and Annie M. (McKeone) H.; m. Margaret M. Lawrence, Feb. 27, 1943. B.B.A., Northeastern U., 1952. Works accountant, comptroller Walworth Co., N.Y.C., 1946-59; treas. Sucrest Co., N.Y.C., 1960-61; pres. Davidson Rubber Co., Dover, N.H., 1961-65; chmn. bd. McCord Corp., Detroit, 1965—; pres. Hogan Assocs.; asso. trustee Coll. of Holy Cross; mem. corp., trustee Bentley Coll.; mem. nat. council Northeastern U. Served to capt. USAAF, 1942-46. Mem. Financial Execs. Inst., Nat. Assn. Accountants. Club: Algonquin. Home: 72 High St Exeter NH 03833 Office: 72 High St Exeter NH 03833

HOGAN, CURTIS JULE, union exec.; b. Greeley, Kans., July 25, 1926; s. Charles Leo and Anna Malene (Roussello) H.; m. Lois Jean Ecord, Apr. 23, 1955; children—Christopher James, Michael Sean, Patrick Marshall, Kathleen Marie, Kerry Joseph. B.S. in Indsl. Relations, Rockhurst Coll., 1950; postgrad., Georgetown U., 1955, U. Tehran, 1955-57. With Gt. Lakes Pipeline Co., Kansas City, 1950-55; with Internat. Fedn. Petroleum and Chem. Workers, Denver, 1955—, gen. sec., 1973—; cons. in field; lectr. Rockhurst Coll., 1951-52. Contbr. in field. Served with U.S. Army, 1945-46. Mem. Internat. Indsl. Relations Assn., Indsl. Relations Research Assn., Oil Chem. and Atomic Workers Internat. Union. Office: PO Box 6565 Denver CO 80206

HOGAN, EDWARD LEO, neurologist; b. Arlington, Mass., July 26, 1932; s. Patrick Francis and Margaret Mary (McSweeney) H.; m. Gail Manning, July 1, 1961; children—Patrick, Mary Ellen, Timothy, Maura, Michael. B.S. in Biochemistry, Tufts U., 1953, M.D., 1957. Diplomate: Am. Bd. Psychiatry and Neurology. Intern Barnes Hosp., St. Louis, 1957-58; resident in neurology Boston City Hosp., 1959-64; instr. Washington U. Med. Sch., St. Louis, 1957-58; asst. in neurology Harvard U. Med. Sch., 1965-66; mem. faculty U. N.C. Med. Sch., 1966-73, asso. prof. neurology, 1969-73, asso. prof. biochemistry, 1972-73, asso. dir. neurobiology program faculty, 1971-73; prof. neurology, chmn. dept., prof. biochemistry Med. U. S.C., Charleston, 1973—; dir. Muscular Dystrophy Assn. clinic, 1978—; mem. merit rev. bd. neurobiology VA, 1976-79; mem. neurology study sect. NIH, 1981—. Author papers in field, chpts. in books. Chmn. med. fund Tufts U., 1973-79; exec. com. Low Country chpt. Muscular Dystrophy Assn., 1978—. Served as officer M.C. U.S. Army, 1961-63. Fellow Am. Acad. Neurology; mem. Am. Neurol. Assn., Assn. Univ. Profs. Neurology., Am. Soc. Biol. Chemists, Am. Soc. Neurochemistry, Internat. Soc. Neurochemistry, Soc. Neurosci., Assn. Research Nervous and Mental Disease, So. Clin. Neurol. Soc., N.Y. Acad. Scis., S.C. Neurol. Soc. (pres. 1978-79), Phi Beta Kappa, Sigma Xi, Alpha Omega Alpha. Roman Catholic. Home: 10 Legare St Charleston SC 29401 Office: Dept Neurology Med Univ SC 171 Ashley Ave Charleston SC 29425

HOGAN, ERNEST LYNN, JR., ins. co. exec.; b. Davy, W.Va., Apr. 10, 1913; s. Ernest Lynn and Edna (Harris) H.; m. Mildred Shepard, Jan. 18, 1936; 1 dau., Dorothy S. Nazzaro. Student, W.Va., Bus Sch., 1932-33, Oxford Bus. Sch., 1933-34. With Peoples Life Ins. Co., Washington, 1935—, agt., 1935-37, asst. mgr., 1937-41, dist. mgr., 1941-47, div. supt. agts., 1947-54, supt. agts., 1954-57, asst. v.p., 1957-59, 2nd v.p., 1959-63, v.p. agy., 1963-68, exec. v.p., 1968-70, pres., 1970—, chief exec. officer, 1973—, chmn. bd., 1974—; also dir., mem. exec., fin. coms.; chmn. bd., mem. exec. and fin. coms. Home Life Ins. Co. Am., Washington.; Treas. Life Underwriter Tng. Council, 1971-79. Mem. Life Ins. Agy. Mgmt. Assn. (bd. dirs. 1969-72), Nat. Assn. Life Underwriters, Gideons. Baptist. Clubs: Elk, Kiwanian., University (Washington); Loudoun Golf and, Country (Purcellville). Office: 601 New Hampshire Ave NW Washington DC 20048

HOGAN, HENRY LEON, III, business executive, retired air force officer; b. Cin., Feb. 7, 1920; s. H. Leon and Helen (Bolan) H.; m. Anne Surkamp, June 1, 1943; children: Robin (Mrs. Jon H. Brosseau), Christine, James A., Patricia, Elizabeth (Mrs. Barry W. Barksdale). B.S., U.S. Mil. Acad., 1943; grad., Nat. War Coll., 1960. Commd. 2d lt. USAAF, 1943; advanced through grades to maj. gen. USAF, 1970; pilot 483d Bombardment Group, Italy, World War II; mil. aide to secs. of USAF, 1953-55; dep. comdt. cadets U.S. Air Force Acad., Colo., 1955-59; dep. comdr. maintenance, vice comdr. 68th Bombardment Wing, Lake Charles, La., 1960-62; wing comdr. 84th Bombardment Wing, Little Rock, 1962-63; asst. to chmn. Joint Chiefs of Staff, Washington, 1963-65; comdr. 810th Air div. SAC, Minot, N.D., 1965-68; dep. dir., then dir. info. Office Sec. USAF, Washington, 1968-72; exec. v.p. Circulation, Inc., Melbourne, Fla., 1973—; dir. Cert. Audit of Circulations, Inc. Decorated D.S.M., Legion Merit with oak leaf cluster, D.F.C., Air medal with four oak leaf clusters. Home: 670 Grant Ct Satellite Beach FL 32937

HOGAN, ILONA MODLY, lawyer; b. Erlangen, W. Ger., Nov. 23, 1947; came to U.S., 1951, naturalized, 1960; d. Stephen Bela and Gunda Pauline (Gastiger) Modly; m. Lawrence J. Hogan, Mar. 16, 1974; children: Matthew Lawrence, Michael Alexander, Patrick Nicholas, Timothy Stefan. Student, Marymount Coll., 1965-67; A.B. in Internat. Affairs, George Washington U., 1969; J.D., Georgetown U., 1974. Bar: D.C. 1975, Md. 1975. Intern and clk. AID, 1965-69; adminstrv. and legis. asst. to mem. Ho. of Reps. from Md., 1969-72; editor Legis. Digest, Ho. of Reps., Washington, 1972-73; asso. and law clk. firm Trammell, Rand, Nathan and Lincoln, Washington, 1972-74; Washington counsel Alliance of Metalworking Industries, 1975—, exec. dir., 1980—; mng. partner firm Hogan and Hogan, Washington, 1974—; pres. AMCOM Media, Inc., Landover, Md., 1977—; internat. bd. advs. Nat. Bank Washington, 1981—. Contbr. articles to legal jours. Mem. Prince George's County (Md.) Econ. Devel. Adv. Com., 1979—; co-chmn. Greater SE Community Hosp. Center for Aging, 1979—; mem. Lawyers Steering Com. for Reagan-Bush, 1980. Mem. ABA, Md. Bar Assn., Prince George's County Bar Assn. (mem. exec com. 1977—), Bar Assn. D.C., Am. Soc. Assn. Execs., NAM, U.S. C. of C. Republican. Roman Catholic. Home: 8400 Hillview Rd Landover MD 20786 Office: 1100 17th St NW Washington DC 20036

HOGAN, JAMES CHARLES, Classicist, educator; b. Hydro, Okla., Jan. 10, 1936; s. Charles Henry and Ruby (Crandall) H.; m. Aurelia McBee, Oct. 1, 1970; children—Ashley, Kathleen, Maxwell, Ada. B.A., U. Okla., 1958; M.A., Cornell U., 1961, Ph.D., 1966. Asst. prof. Classics, acting chmn. dept. Converse Coll., Spartanburg, S.C., 1961-63; asst. prof. Washington U., St. Louis, 1965-66; asso. prof. U. Okla., 1966-69; Frank T. McClure prof. Classics Allegheny Coll., Meadville, Pa., 1969—. Author: A Guide to the Iliad, 1979; Contbr. articles profl. publs. Fellow Nat. Endowment for Humanities, 1975-76. Mem. Am. Philol. Assn., Phi Beta Kappa. Democrat. Home: 292 Church St Meadville PA 16335 Office: Box 102 Allegheny Coll Meadville PA 16335

HOGAN, JAMES JOHN, bishop; b. Phila., Oct. 17, 1911; s. James F. and Mary E. (Molloy) H. B.A., St. Mary's Sem., Balt., 1934; S.T.L., Gregorian U., Rome, Italy, 1938; J.C.D., Cath. U. Am., 1941. Ordained priest Roman Cath. Ch., 1937; diocesan ofcl. and consultor Diocese of Trenton, N.J.; chancellor of diocese, auxiliary bishop of Trenton; pastor St. Catharine's Ch., Spring Lake, N.J.; now bishop Diocese of Altoona, Johnston, Pa. Office: Box 126 Hollidaysburg PA 16648 *

HOGAN, JOHN DONALD, insurance company executive; b. Binghamton, N.Y., July 16, 1927; s. John D. and Edith J. (Hennessy) H.; m. Beatrice Hinman, June 5, 1950 (div. 1950); children: Thomas P., James E.; m. 2d Anna Craig, Nov. 26, 1976. A.B., Syracuse U., 1949, M.A., 1950, Ph.D., 1952. Registered prin. Nat. Assn. Securities Dealers. Prof. econs., chmn. dept. Bates Coll., Lewiston, Maine, 1953-60; dir. edn. fin. research State of N.Y., 1959, chief mcpl. fin., 1960; staff economist, dir. research Northwestern Mut. Life Ins. Co., Milw., 1960-68; v.p. Nationwide Ins. Cos., Columbus, Ohio, 1968-76; dean Sch. Bus. Asminstrn. Central Mich. U., Mt. Pleasant, 1976-79; v.p. Am. Productivity Center, Houston, 1979-80; pres., chmn., chief exec. officer Variable Annuity Life Inst. Co., Houston, 1980-83, dir.; sr. v.p. investment Am. Gen. Corp., Houston, 1983—; dir. Am. Gen. Life Ins. Co. Tex., Houston, 1980—, Am. Gen. Life Ins. Co. Del., 1980—, Pioneer Security Life Ins. Co., 1980—. Author: American Social Legislation, 1965, U.S. Balance of Payments and Capital Flows, 1967, School Revenue Studies, 1959, Fiscal Capacity of the State of Maine, 1958, American Social Legislation, 1973; editor: Dimensions of Productivity Research (2 vols.), 1981; contbr. articles to jours., abstracts to profl. meetings. Bd. dirs. Goodwill Industries, Columbus, 1972-76, chmn. capital fund drive, Columbus, 1974-75; mem. Houston Com. on Fgn. Relations, 1980—. Served with U.S. Army, 1944-46; ETO; served to capt. (ret.) USAR. Fellow Syracuse U., 1950-52; recipient Best Article award Jur. Risk and Ins., 1964; Maxwell Centennial lectr. Maxwell Grad. Sch., Syracuse U., 1970. Mem. Acad. Mgmt., Am. Econ. Assn., Inst. Mgmt. Scis., Nat. Assn. Bus. Economists, Nat. Tax Assn. (dir. 1981—), Inst. Research in Econs. of Taxation, Columbus C. of C. (chmn. econ. policy com. 1972-76). Clubs: Columbus Athletic; Heritage, Texas (Houston). Home: 701 Magdalene Houston TX 77024 Office: Am Gen Corp 2727 Allen Pkwy Houston TX 77019

HOGAN, JOSEPH CHARLES, university dean; b. St. Louis, May 26, 1922; s. Joseph D. and Anna (Lange) H.; m. Mary Elizabeth Carrere, June 21, 1944; children: Joseph Charles (dec.), Mary E., Susan L., Thomas C., Stephen J., Michael C., Martha A., William G., Daniel C. B.S. in Elec. Engring, Washington U., 1943; M.S., U. Mo., 1949; Ph.D.; univ. fellow 1951-53, U. Wis., 1953. Registered profl. engr., Mo., Ind. Instr. U. N.D., 1947; mem. faculty U. Mo., Columbia, 1947-67, prof., 1958-67, dean engring., 1961-67; prof., dean engring. U. Notre Dame, 1967-83; engr. Commonwealth Assos., Inc., summers 1953-54; dean emeritus U. Notre Dame, 1983—; cons. Columbia Water & Light Dept., 1954-56, North Central Assn., 1967—, Whirlpool Corp., 1971—; dir. Weldun Tool & Engring. Co., Bridgeman, Mich., TII, Inc., Copiaque, N.Y., Mac Engring. & Equipment, Inc., Benton Harbor, Mich.; Chmn. water and light adv. bd., City of Columbia, 1957-61. Contbr. research articles profl. jours. Served as ensign USNR, 1943-45. Mem. IEEE (sr. mem.), Nat., Mo., Ind. socs. profl. engrs., Am. Soc. Engring. Edn. (v.p. 1974-75, dir. 1973-75, pres. elect 1981-82, pres. 1982-83), Engrs. Council for Profl. Devel. (dir. 1974-79), Sigma Xi, Tau Beta Pi, Eta Kappa Nu., Theta Xi. Home: 2516 S Twyckenham Dr South Bend IN 46614 Office: Coll Engring U Notre Dame Notre Dame IN 46556

HOGAN, MARK, investment company executive; b. Chgo., Jan. 27, 1931; s. Mark Anthony and Alice (Glavin) H.; children—Cary Lucile, Mark, Lisa, Matthew, Michael. A.B., Georgetown U., 1952. Vice pres. Koelbel & Co., Denver, 1954-64; pres. Hogan/Stevenson Realtors, 1964-74, Mark Hogan Investment Co., 1974—; Mem. Colo. Ho. of Reps., 1962-66, majority whip, 1964-66; lt. gov. of Colo., 1966-70; chmn. bd. Colo. Rockies Hockey Team.; Democratic candidate for gov., 1970; mem. Nat. Dem. Policy Council, state chmn., 1979-81; bd. dirs. Cath. Charities, Met. Denver YMCA; trustee Loretto Heights Coll., 1964-68; bd. govs. Georgetown U., 1981—. Served to lt. (j.g.) USNR, 1952-54. Named Colo. Young Man of Year, 1957-58. Clubs: Denver, Univ., Hiwan Country, Cherry Hills Country (Denver). Home: 672 Clarkson Denver CO 80218 Office: 555 E 8th Ave Denver CO 80203

HOGAN, MERVIN BOOTH, mechanical engineer, educator; b. Bountiful, Utah, July 21, 1906; s. Charles Ira and Sarah Ann (Booth) H.; m. Helen Emily Reese, Dec. 27, 1928; 1 son, Edward Reese. B.S., U. Utah, 1927, M.E., 1930; M.S., U. Pitts., 1929; Ph.D., U. Mich., 1936, postgrad.; Sterling fellow, Yale U., 1937-38. Registered profl. engr., Conn., Mich., N.Y., Utah, Va.; chartered engr., U.K. Design engr. Westinghouse Electric Corp., East Pittsburgh, Pa., 1927-31; asst. prof. mech. engring. U. Utah, 1931-36, asso. prof., 1936-39, prof., 1939-56, chmn. dept. mech. engring., 1951-56, prof., 1971-76, prof. emeritus, 1976—; mgr. product design engring. Gen. Electric Co., Syracuse, N.Y., 1956-65, mgr. design assurance engring., Phoenix, 1965-70, cons. engr., Waynesboro, Va., 1970-71. Author: Mormonism and Freemasonry: The Illinois Episode, 1977, The Origin and Growth of Utah Masonry and Its Conflict with Mormonism, 1978, Mormonism and Freemasonry under Covert Masonic Influences, 1979, Freemasonry and the Lynching at Carthage Jail, 1981, Freemasonry and Civil Confrontation on the Illinois Frontier, 1981, The Involvement of Freemasonry with Mormonism on the American Midwestern Frontier, 1982; contbr. articles to engr. jours., numerous articles to Masonic publs. Fellow ASME, Inst. Mech. Engrs. (London), Yale Sci., Engring. Assn.; mem. IEEE (sr.), Nat. Eagle Scout Assn., DeMolay Legion of Honor, S.R. in State N.Y., Utah Soc. SAR (pres. 1983-84), Sigma Xi, Phi Kappa Phi, Tau Beta Pi, Pi Tau Sigma, Sigma Nu, Theta Tau, Alpha Phi Omega, Phi Lambda Epsilon. Clubs: Aztec, Timpanogos, Rotary, Masons (33 deg.), Shriners, Prophets, KT, DeMolay. Home: 921 Greenwood Terr Salt Lake City UT 84105 Office: 3008 Merrill Engring Bldg U Utah Salt Lake City UT 84112

HOGAN, TERRENCE PATRICK, psychologist, university administrator; b. Dubuque, Iowa, May 10, 1937; s. Clement Joseph and Clarissa Elizabeth (Theis) H.; m. Elizabeth Anne Gonner, May 15, 1963; children: Maureen Anne, Timothy Patrick, Sean Michael. B.A., Loras Coll., 1959; M.A., Cath. U. Am., 1961, Ph.D., 1963. Chief clin. psychologist VA Hosp., Clinton, Iowa, 1963-65; asst. prof. Bradley U., Peoria, Ill., 1965-67; pvt. practice psychology, Marshfield, Wis., 1967-69; from asst. prof. to prof. psychology, dir. clin. tng. U. Man. (Can.), Winnipeg, 1969-77, asso. dean arts, prof. psychology, 1977-80, dean Faculty Grad. Studies, prof. psychology, 1980-82, assoc. acad. v.p., 1982—; cons. Health Scis. Centre, Winnipeg, Man. Telephone Service, Winnipeg. Author: (with Richard I. Hartman and John T. Wholihan) Modern Business Administration: An Introduction, 1969, (with Gerald Erickson) Family Therapy: An Introduction to Theory and Techniques, 2d edit., 1981. Recipient several grants. Fellow Can. Psychol. Assn. (pres. 1982-83); mem. Am. Psychol. Assn., Social Sci. Fedn. Can. (dir.), Psychol. Assn. Man., Man. Psychol. Soc., Soc. Personality Assessment, Delta Epsilon Sigma, Sigma Xi, Psi Chi. Roman Catholic. Home: 118 King's Dr Winnipeg MB R3T 3E5 Canada Office: 202 Adminstrn Bldg U Man Winnipeg MB R3T 2N2 Canada

HOGAN, THOMAS FRANCIS, district judge; b. Washington, May 31, 1938; s. Bartholomew W. and Grace (Gloninger) H.; m. Martha Lou Wyrick, July 16, 1966; 1 son, Thomas Garth. A.B., Georgetown U., 1960, J.D., 1966; postgrad., George Washington U., 1960-62. Bar: Md. 1966, U.S. Dist. Ct. D.C. 1967, D.C. 1967, U.S. Ct. Appeals (D.C. cir.) 1972, U.S. Dist. Ct. Md. 1973, U.S. Supreme Ct. 1973. Law clk. to presiding judge U.S. Dist. Ct. D.C., 1966-67; counsel Nat. Commn. on Reform of Fed. Criminal Laws, Washington, 1967-68; ptnr. McCarthy & Wharton, Rockville, Md., 1968-75, Kenary, Tietz & Hogan, Rockville, 1975-81, Furey, Doolan, Abell & Hogan, Chevy Chase, Md., 1981-82; U.S. dist. judge U.S. Dist. Ct. D.C., Washington, 1982—; asst. prof. Potomac Sch. Law, Washington, 1977-79. Pub. mem. Officer Evaluation Bd. U.S. Fgn. Service, 1973; chmn. Christ Child Inst. for Disturbed Children, 1975; bd. dirs. Providence Hosp., Washington. Recipient cert. recognition and appreciation for vol. services Montgomery County Govt., 1976, cert. appreciation Christ Child Soc., 1976; St. Thomas More fellow Georgetown U. Law Ctr., 1965-66. Mem. ABA (Md. chmn. Drug Abuse Edn. Program, Young Lawyers sect. 1970-73, mem. Litigation sect.), Bar Assn. D.C. (mem. com. on D.C. cts.), Md. State Bar Assn. (Litigatin sect.), Montgomery County Bar Assn. (chmn. legal ethics com. 1973-74, lawyer referral service com. 1974-75, adminstrn. justice com. 1979-82, bd. govs. 1977-78), Nat. Inst. for Trial Advocacy Assocs., Def. Research Inst., Md. Assn. Def. Trial Counsel, Md. Trial Lawyers Assn., Georgetown U. Alumni Assn., Smithsonian Assocs., John Carroll Soc. Clubs: Barristers, Chevy Chase. Home: 5512 Grove St Chevy Chase MD 20815 Office: US Dist Ct US Courthouse 3d and Constitution Ave NW Washington DC 20001

HOGAN, TIMOTHY S., judge; b. Wellston, Ohio, Sept. 23, 1909; s. Timothy S. and Mary Adele (Deasey) H.; m. Evalon Roberts, Dec. 27, 1934; children—Nancy Ann (Mrs. Fred Dutton), Margaret M. (Mrs. John H. Wyant), Timothy S. III. A.B., Xavier U., 1930, LL.D., 1976; J.D., U. Cin., 1931. Bar: Ohio bar 1931. Pvt. practice with firm Cohen, Baron, Todd & Hogan, Cin., 1931-66; spl. counsel, atty. gen., Ohio, 1937-41, 48-50, U.S. dist. judge So. Dist. Ohio, Cin., 1966—, chief judge, 1976-78; lectr. trial practice U. Cin. Law Sch., 1950-62. Mem. Clermont (Ohio) County Planning Commn., 1958-62; Del.-at-large Ohio Democratic Nat. Conv., 1952. Served to lt. col. USAAF, 1942-46. Mem. Fed., Ohio, Cin., Clermont County bar assns., Order of Coif. Roman Catholic. Home: 3810 Eileen Dr Cincinnati OH 45209 Office: US Post Office and Court House Cincinnati OH 45202

HOGAN, WILLIAM JOSEPH, financial executive; b. St. Louis, Aug. 1902; s. Joseph and Johanna (Grainey) H.; m. Verna L. Coultas, July 12, 1925 (dec.); 1 son, William J.; m. Jean Miller, Aug. 27, 1955; 1 dau., Mary Elizabeth. Student, St. Louis U., 1920-26, LL.D. (hon.), 1980. Mem. controller's staff Firestone Tire & Rubber Co., Akron, Ohio, 1929-43; treas., controller, dir. H.J. Heinz Co., Pitts., 1943-47; v.p., treas. AM. Airlines, Inc., N.Y.C., 1947-54, sr. v.p. fin., 1954-58, exec. v.p., chmn. fin. com., dir., 1958-67; chmn. fin. com., exec. v.p., dir. Interpublic Group Cos., 1968-74, chmn. audit and compensation coms., dir., 1974—; pres., dir. Victory Carriers, Inc., 1968-78; chmn. audit and compensation coms., dir. Raytheon Co.; dir., chmn. audit coms. Intercontinental Hotels Corp. Knight of Malta; recipient Alumni Achievement award St. Louis U., 1963. Clubs: Union League, Links (N.Y.C.); Clove Valley Rod and Gun, Winged Foot Golf; Ekwanak Golf (Manchester, Vt.). Home and Office: 34 Greenfield Ave Bronxville NY 10708

HOGAN, WILLIAM T., university president; b. Lowell, Mass., Feb. 4, 1933; m., 1959; 3 children. B.S., Northeastern U., 1955; M.S., MIT, 1959; Ph.D. in M.E., Northeastern U., 1965. Mech. engr. Gen. Electric, 1955-56; mech. design engr. Redstone Arsenal, Ala., 1956-58; sr. scientist Avco Corp., 1961-63, Lowell Technol. Inst. (now U. Lowell (Mass.), 1963—, assoc. prof. mech. engring. to prof. and head dept. to dean engring., pres., 1981—. Office: Office of the Pres U Lowell Lowell MA 01853 *

HOGAN, WILLIAM WALTER, public policy educator, administrator, consultant; b. Holyoke, Mass., Mar. 3, 1944; s. William Walter and Betty Ethel (Roebaugh) H.; m. Mari-Ann Gertrude Martenson, Mar. 4, 1967; children: Christine, Kevin. B.S., U.S. Air Force Acad., 1966; M.B.A., UCLA, 1967, Ph.D., 1971; A.M. hon., Harvard U., 1978. Dep. asst. adminstr. Fed. Energy Adminstrn., Washington, 1975-76; adj. prof. Stanford U., 1976-78; prof. polit. economy Harvard U., 1978—, dir. Energy and Environ. Policy Ctr., 1978—, chmn. pub. policy program, 1982—; dir. Putnam, Hayes and Bartlett, Cambridge, Mass., 1980—; mem. adv. council Gas Research Inst., 1983—. Served to capt. USAF, 1962-74. Mem. Ops. Research Soc. (dept. editor 1978-82), Inst. Mgmt. Scis., Internat. Assn. Energy Economists (mem. editorial bd. 1978—), Math. Programming Soc. Club: Cosmos. Home: 345 Marsh St Belmont MA 02178 Office: John F Kennedy Sch Government Harvard Univ 79 John F Kennedy St Cambridge MA 02138

HOGARTH, GRACE WESTON ALLEN, publisher, author; b. Newton, Mass., Nov. 5, 1905; d. John Weston and Caroline (Hills) Allen; m. William David Hogarth, Aug. 22, 1936 (dec. Sept. 1965); children: David Allen, Caroline Mary Hogarth Barron; m. Philip Livermore Sayles, May 22, 1971 (div. Sept. 1977). Student, U. Calif.-Berkeley, 1924-25; A.B., Vassar Coll., 1927; postgrad., Mass. Sch. Art, 1927-28, Yale U., 1928-29. With Oxford U. Press, N.Y.C. and London, 1929-38; dir. Longman Young Books, 1968-73. Editor: children's books Chatto and Windus, London, 1938-39, Houghton Mifflin, Boston, 1940-43; scout, London, 1943-47, various pubs., London, 1947-56; editor children's books, Constable & Co., Ltd., London, 1956-63; mng. dir., Constable Young Books, London, 1963-68, Longman Young Books, London, 1968; dir., Longman Young Books, London, 1968-73; editor-in-chief: Am. Edn. Pubs, Middletown, Conn., 1968-71; gen. editor: Classics for Today, William Collins Pubs., London, 1971—; Author: A Bible ABC, 1940, Lucy's League, 1950, John's Journey, 1952, The Funny Guy, 1955, As a May Morning, 1958, A Sister for Helen, 1976, This to be Love, 1949, The End of Summer, 1951, Children of This World, 1953; Editor: Illustrators of Children's Books, vol. IV, 1978. Bd. govs. N. London Collegiate Sch., 1965-71, Camden Sch. for Girls, 1965-71. Mem. English Speaking Union. Clubs: Vassar Coll., Boston, London. Home: 53 Ainger Rd London NW3 England

HOGE, JAMES FULTON, JR., newspaper editor; b. N.Y.C., Dec. 25, 1935; s. James Fulton and Virginia (McClamroch) H.; m. Alice Patterson Albright, June 2, 1962 (div. 1971); children: Alicia McClamroch, James Patrick, Robert Warren; m. Sharon Leigh King, Jan. 4, 1981. B.A. in Polit. Sci, Yale U., 1958; M.A. in Modern Am. and European History, U. Chgo., 1961, Harvard U. Advanced Mgmt. Program, 1980. Fin. writer Chgo. Sun Times, 1958-62; writer Am. Polit. Sci. Assn. Congl. fellow, 1962-63; Washington corr. Chgo. Sun Times, 1963-65, city editor, 1965-67, mng. editor, 1967-68, exec. editor, 1968, editor, 1968-76; editor in chief Chgo. Sun Times and Chgo. Daily News, 1976-78; exec. v.p., editor in chief Chgo. Sun-Times, 1978, pub., 1978-84; chmn., chief exec. officer N.Y. News, Inc., 1984—; pub. N.Y. Daily News, 1984—; chmn. exec. council Adlai Stevenson Center; adv. council Aspen Program Communications and Soc., Am. Council on Germany; mng. com. U.S.-South Africa Leader Exchange Program; mem. German Marshall Fund, Trilateral Commn.; bd. dirs. Eisenhower Exchange Fellowships, Children's Meml. Hosp., Chgo. Theatre Group (Goodman Theatre), Landmarks Preservation Council; mem. Japan-U.S. Friendship Commn. Bd. dirs. Mus. Contemporary Art. Mem. Chgo. Council Fgn. Relations (vice-chmn., chmn. exec. com. of com. on fgn. affairs), Council Fgn. Relations (N.Y.C.) (dir.), Sigma Delta Chi. Clubs: Tavern, Econ., Execs., Arts, Comml., Headline (Chgo.). Office: New York Daily News New York New Inc 220 E 42d St New York NY 10017

HOGENDORN, JAN STAFFORD, economist, educator; b. Lahaina, Hawaii, Oct. 27, 1937; s. Paul Earl and Helen (Stafford) H.; m. Dianne Hodet, Sept. 6, 1960; 1 son, Christiaan Paul. B.A., Wesleyan U., 1960; M.Sc., London Sch. Econs., 1962, Ph.D., 1966; postgrad., Harvard U., 1963. Instr. Boston U., 1963-64; asst. prof. Colby Coll., Waterville, Maine, 1966-69, assoc. prof., 1970-76, prof., 1976—, Grossman prof. econs., 1977—; vis. assoc. prof. Robert Coll., Istanbul, Turkey, 1971-72; Ford Found. lectr., 1971-72; vis. prof. Ahmadu Bello U., Nigeria, 1975; research assoc. U. Birmingham, Eng., 1980. Author: Managing the Modern Economy, 1972, Managing the Modern Economy, 2d edit., 1975, Markets in the Modern Economy, 1975, Modern Economics, 1976, Nigerian Groundnut Exports, 1978, The New International Economcis, 1979, The Uncommon Market, 1979, The Grossman Lectures at Colby College, 1984, (editorial bd.) Slavery and Abolition, 1981—. Fellow Fulbright Found., 1960-61, Danforth Found., 1965-66, Inst. Internat. Edn., 1983; grantee Mellon Found., Am. Council Learned Socs., Social Sci. Research Council. Mem. Am. Econ. Assn., Royal Econ. Soc., African Studies Assn. Unitarian. Home: RFD 1 North Vassalboro ME 04962 Office: Colby Coll Mayflower Hill Waterville ME 04901

HOGG, BENJAMIN GREGORY, educator; b. Winnipeg, Man., Can., July 26, 1924; s. David Cochran and Harriet Olwen (Gregory) H.; m. Emile Shipel, June 1, 1949; chidlren—Kristine, David. B.Sc. with honors, U. Man., 1946; M.A., Weslayan U., 1947, Ph.D., McMaster U., 1953. Def. research scientist, 1949-51; asst., then asso. prof. Royal Mil. Coll., 1954-57; asso. prof. U. Man., 1957-64, prof., 1964-72, dean grad. studies, 1969-72, prof., acad. v.p., 1972-78, prof., 1978—; exchange prof. Max Planck Inst., Mainz, W. Ger., 1965, Inst. Chem. Physics, Moscow, 1970, Centre d'Etude Nucleaire, France, 1979. Contbr. articles to profl. jours. Fellow Royal Soc. Can.; mem. Can. Assn. Physicists, Can. Assn. Univ. Tchrs., Sigma Xi. Home: 1587 Wolseley Ave Winnipeg MB R3G 1J2 Canada Office: 515 Portage Ave Winnipeg MB R3B 2E9 Canada

HOGG, DAVID CLARENCE, physicist; b. Vanguard, Sask., Can., Sept. 5, 1921; came to U.S., 1953, naturalized, 1964; s. Francis Sandison and Frances Katherine (Gadsby) H.; m. Jean E. MacMillan, Feb. 15, 1947; children—David Randal, Rebecca Jean. B.Sc., U. Western Ont. (Can.), London, 1949; M.Sc., McGill U., Montreal, Que., Can., 1951, Ph.D., 1953. With Bell Telephone Labs., 1953-77, head atmospheric physics research, 1966-72, head antenna and propagation research, Holmdel, N.J., 1972-77; chief environ. radiometry wave propagation lab. Environ. Research Lab., NOAA, Boulder, Colo., 1977-83, chief radio metrology, 1983—. Research, numerous publs. on microwaves, optics, satellite communications and remote sensing; patentee microwave antennas. Served with Can. Army, 1940-45. Fellow IEEE; mem. AAAS, Nat. Acad. Engring., Union Radio Scientifique Internationale. Episcopalian. Office: NOAA WAve Propagation Lab Environ Research Lab Boulder CO 80302

HOGG, EUGENE RAY, manufacturing executive; b. Middletown, Ohio, May 29, 1934; s. Clarence O. and Ollie M. H.; m. Marion Lee Bommershine, Nov. 21, 1953; children: Belinda L., Bonita J., Bettina E., Brent C. B.S. in Math., Miami U., Oxford, Ohio, 1956. Engring. group leader Gen. Electric Co., Evendale, Ohio, 1956-61; chief engr., gen. mgr. Parker Hannifin Corp., Cleve., 1961-76; group v.p., corp. officer A-T-O Inc., Willoughby, Ohio, 1976-81; pres., chief exec. officer LaBonte Precision, Inc., Ft. Lauderdale, Fla., 1981—. Mem. Am. Mgmt. Assn., Nat. Fluid Power Assn. Republican. Presbyterian.

HOGG, ROBERT VINCENT, JR., educator, mathematical statistician; b. Hannibal, Mo., Nov. 8, 1924; s. Robert Vincent and Isabelle Frances (Storrs) H.; m. Carolyn Joan Ladd, June 23, 1956; children—Mary Carolyn, Barbara Jean, Allen Ladd, Robert Mason. B.A., U. Ill., 1947; M.S., U. Iowa, 1948, Ph.D., 1950. Asst. prof. math. U. Iowa, Iowa City, 1950-56, asso. prof., 1956-62, prof. math., 1962-65, chmn. dept. statistics, prof. statistics, 1965—. Co-author: Introduction to Mathematical Statistics, 1959, 4th edit., 1978, Finite Mathematics and Calculus, 1974, Probability and Statistical Inference, 1977; Asso. editor: Am. Statistics, 1971-74, Jour. Am. Statis. Assn, 1978-80; Contbr. articles to profl. jours. Served with USNR, 1943-46. NIH research grantee, 1966-68, 75-78; NSF research grantee, 1969-74. Fellow Inst. Math. Statistics (program sec., exec. bd. 1968-74), Am. Statis. Assn. (pres. Iowa sect. 1962-63, council 1965-66, 73-74, vis. lectr. 1965-68, 77—, chmn. tng. sect. 1973); mem. Math. Assn. Am. (pres. Iowa sect. 1964-65, gov. Iowa dist. 1971-74, vis. lectr. 1976-81), Internat. Statis. Inst., Sigma Xi (pres. Iowa chpt. 1970-71), Pi Kappa Alpha. Episcopalian (vestryman 1958-60, 66-68). Club: Rotarian. Home: Rural Route 6 Box 219A Iowa City IA 52240

HOGG, RUSSELL E., corporation executive; b. Providence, R.I., Apr. 28, 1928; s. Walter and Julie H.; m. Dorothy Hogg; 1 son, Jason. B.S., U. R.I., 1951; postgrad., Harvard U. Grad. Sch. Bus. Adminstrn., 1965. With Joseph E. Seagram's & Sons, 1951-54; agt. FBI, 1954-61; sr. fin. officer Am. Airlines, 1961-70; with Am. Express Co., 1970-78, sr. v.p., internat. gen. mgr. card div., London; sr. v.p., operating group exec. MacMillan, Inc., N.Y.C., 1978-80; pres., chief exec. officer MasterCard Internat., Inc., N.Y.C., 1980—; dir. Reichold Chems., Inc., Fincorp Ltd.; trustee Am. Health Found. Clubs: Union League (N.Y.C.); Sleepy Hollow Country (Scarborough, N.Y.). Office: MasterCard Internat Inc 888 7th Ave New York NY 10106

HOGG, THOMAS CLARK, anthropologist; b. Bozeman, Mont., Nov. 29, 1935; s. William Vernon and Florence (Magby) H.; m. Barbara Barker, Mar. 23, 1958; children: Kathleen Marie, Amy Elizabeth. B.S., U. Oreg., 1958, M.A., 1963, Ph.D., 1965. Mem. faculty Oreg. State U., Corvallis, 1965—, prof. anthropology, 1975—, chmn. dept., 1972-81, coordinator contract research program, 1976—, asst. to v.p. for research, 1981-83, E.P. Ritchie Disting. prof., 1971. Author papers in field. Bd. dirs. Pacific Crest Research and Services Corp. Fellow Am. Anthrop. Assn.; asso. Current Anthropology. Democrat. Unitarian. Home: 3210 NW Fillmore St Corvallis OR 97330 Office: Dept Anthropology Oreg State Univ Corvallis OR 97331 *Perhaps the greatest struggles for educators are to become able to honestly listen and respond to the concerns and needs of students and the public we serve. We must also learn to publicly laugh at ourselves. My own goals in research and teaching are to develop and foster a sense of the genius of other people and to make the inquiry to discover its character.*

HOGG, TONY JEFFERSON, editor; b. London, Eng., Jan. 27, 1925; came to U.S., 1953; s. Richard Jefferson and Lilian (Currie) H.; m. Elizabeth Moroney Maxon, Aug. 25, 1957; 1 son, John Jefferson. Ed. Brit. pvt. schs. Contbg. editor Road and Track, 1961—, editor, 1975-79, editor-in-chief, 1979—; tech. editor, 1963-65; automotive editor Esquire mag., from 1970; editor, pub. Sci. and Mechs., N.Y.C., 1969-74. Writer and; photographer; contbr. articles to numerous mags. Mem. Am. Soc. Mag. Editors, Soc. Automotive Engrs. Home: 231 Kings Pl Newport Beach CA 92663 Office: 1499 Monrovia Newport Beach CA 92663

HOGG, WILBUR EMORY, bishop; b. Balt., Aug. 28, 1916; s. Wilbur Emory and Ida May (Spath) H.; m. Lota Winchell Curtiss, Sept. 6, 1947. A.B., Brown U., 1938; Th.M., Phila. Div. Sch., 1941; D.D., Gen. Theol. Sem., 1977. Ordained priest Episcopal Ch.; curate St. Mary's Ch., Burlington, N.J., 1941-43, rector, 1943-51; fellow, tutor Gen. Theol. Sem., N.Y.C., 1953-54; rector Ch. St. Mary the Virgin, Falmouth Foreside, Maine, 1954-68; dean St. Luke's Cathedral, Portland, Maine, 1968-73; bishop Diocese of Albany, N.Y., 1974—; chaplain, tchr. St. Mary's Hall, Burlington, N.J., 1943-51. Served with U.S. Army, 1945-46, 51-53. Fellow Coll. Preachers Washington; mem. Order Holy Cross (asso.). Episcopalian. Club: Fort Orange (Albany). Office: 662 S Swan St Albany NY 12210 *

HOGGARD, JAMES CLINTON, clergyman; b. Jersey City, Aug. 9, 1916; s. Jeremiah Matthew and Symera (Cherry) H.; m. Eva Stanton, Dec. 10, 1949; children: James Clinton, Paul Stanton. B.A., Rutgers U., 1939; M.Div., Union Theol. Sem., 1942; D.D., Livingstone Coll., 1956. Ordained to ministry African Meth. Episcopal Zion Ch., 1939; pastor St. Francis A.M.E. Zion Ch., Mt. Kisco, N.Y., 1940-42, Instnl. A.M.E. Zion Ch., Yonkers, N.Y., 1942-51, Little Rock A.M.E. Zion Ch., Charlotte, N.C., 1951-52; sec., treas., bd. fgn. missions, editor The Missionary Seer (A.M.E. Zion Ch., Washington), 1952-60, N.Y.C., 1960-72; bishop A.M.E. Zion Ch., Indpls., 1972—. Contbr. articles to ch. publs. Vice chmn. Mcpl. Housing Authority, Yonkers, 1945-51;

mem. governing bd. Nat. Council Chs. U.S.A., 1950-72; mem. exec. com. World Meth. Council, 1948—; pres. Ind. Interreligious Commn. Human Equality, 1975-76. Mem. Commn. Ecumenical Studies, ACLU, Alpha Phi Alpha, Sigma Pi Phi. Clubs: Kiwanis, Elks, Masons. Office: 1100 W 42nd St Indianapolis IN 46208 *From childhood, with Christian parents motivating me, I have tried to live and let live; to love God and serve Him and to love my neighbor as I would love myself.* *

HOGGARD, LARA GULDMAR, condr., educator; b. Kingston, Okla., Feb. 9, 1915; s. Calvin Peter and Eva Lillian (Smith) H.; m. Mildred Mae Teeter, Sept. 11, 1943; 1 dau., Susan. B.A., Southeastern Tchrs. Coll., 1934; M.A., Columbia U., 1940, Ed.D., 1947. Supr. music Durant (Okla.) Public Schs., 1934-39; dir. choral activities, opera and oratorio U. Okla., 1940-43; asso. founder, prin. instr. Waring Summer Choral Workshops, 1948-52; co-editor Shawnee Press, Del. Water Gap, Pa., 1946-52; dir. music and music edn. research Ala. Edn. Found., Birmingham, 1955-60; founder Nat. Young Artist Competition, Midland-Odessa, 1962—; William Rand Kenan prof. music U. N.C., Chapel Hill, 1967-80; Fuller E. Callaway prof. music Columbus Coll., U. Ga., 1981—. Condr.: NBC-USN Navy Hour, 1945; asso. condr., Waring's Pennsylvanians, 1946-52; condr., dir.: Festival of Song, Civic Music and Nat. Concert Artists Corp., nat. touring concert group, 1952-53; condr., musical dir., Midland-Odessa (Tex.) Symphony Orch. and Chorale, 1962-67; condr. numerous music festivals in, Am., Europe; artistic dir., Youth and Music in Vienna (Austria) Festival, 1953, Festival of Three Cities, Vienna-Budapest-Prague, Youth and Music in Vienna Festival, 1954; guest lectr. and condr at univs. and conservatories in, Am. and Europe; dir., N.C. Summer Insts. In Choral Art, 1953—; condr.: several mus. premieres, including Behold the Glory (Talmadge Dean), With Louisville Orch., 1964, Light in the Wilderness (Dave Brubeck), Chapel Hill, 1968, numerous others.; Author: Improving Music Reading, 1947, Exploring Music, 1967; editor: an oratorio Light in the Wilderness (Davd Brubeck), 1964; composer-arranger-editor 37 choral publs.; composer: Le Jongleur, CBS-TV, 1951. Served to lt. (j.g.) USN, 1943-45; PTO. Recipient award for outstanding service to music in Ala. Ala. Fine Arts Festival, 1958, citation for outstanding service to fine arts in Tex. Tex. Senate and Gov.; Tanner award U. N.C., 1972; Ten Best Profs. award, 1978; Order Long Leaf Pine Gov. N.C., 1980. Mem. Music Educators Nat. Conf. (life; Master Builder), Am. Choral Dirs. Assn. (life, award for contbn. to music in N.C. 1976), AAUP, N.C. Music Educators Assn. (hon. life), N.C. Lit. Soc. (life), Phi Mu Alpha Sinfonia (nat. hon. life), W.Tex. C. of C. Democrat. Presbyterian. Club: Rotary. Home: 802 Cedar Falls Ln Chapel Hill NC 27514 *Creativity within the individual is our best weapon against conformity and robotism. The arts challenge and elevate both the intellect and the spirit. Sensitivity and respect for the true, the good and the beautiful, stand in defiance of three attitudes which must not prevail, if civilization is to survive: bigotry, arrogant ignorance, and acceptance or approval of mediocrity.*

HOGIN, PHILIP EDWARD, manufacturing company executive; b. Oak Park, Ill., May 4, 1920; s. Ralph M. and Loretta (Murphy) H.; m. Betty Jane Harrison, Nov. 5, 1949; children: Harrison David, Christen Evangeline, Lauretta Joann, Sarah Elizabeth. B.S. in Engring, Cornell U., 1942; M.S. in Indsl. Mgmt. (Alfred P. Sloan fellow), Mass. Inst. Tech., 1954. Registered profl. engr., N.Y., N.J., Ill., Conn. With Western Electric Co., 1942-48, 50—, gen. mgr. service div., central region, 1963-64, v.p. staff, mfg. div., 1964-65, v.p. pub. relations, 1965-66, v.p. mfg., 1966-67, exec. v.p., dir., 1967—; mem. tech. staff Bell Telephone Labs., 1948-50; dir. Teletype Corp., Phoenix Mut. Life Ins. Co., Sandia Nat. Labs. Served to lt. (j.g.) USNR, 1944-46. Mem. Soc. Sloan Fellows, Phi Kappa Sigma, Kappa Tau Chi. Club: Field of Greenwich (Conn.). Office: Western Electric Co 222 Broadway New York NY 10038

HOGLUND, FORREST EUGENE, petroleum co. exec.; b. Lawrence, Kans., July 1, 1933; s. Roy A. and Edna M. (McMichael) H.; m. Sally Sue Roney, June 19, 1956; children—Kelly M., Shelly L., Kristan K. B.S. in Mech. Engring, U. Kans., 1956. With Exxon Corp., 1957—, mgr., 1970-73, v.p. ops., 1973-76, v.p. gas, 1976-77; pres. Tex. Oil and Gas, 1977—. Served with C.E. U.S. Army, 1957-58. Mem. Am. Petroleum Inst., AIME, Tau Beta Pi, Pi Tau Sigma, Sigma Tau, Omicron Delta Kappa. Presbyterian. Clubs: Darien Country (bd. govs. 1977—); Petroleum (Dallas)). Home: 4330 Armstrong Pkwy Dallas TX 75205 Office: 3100 Fidelity Union Tower Dallas TX 75201

HOGLUND, PETER KLINGER, locomotive manufacturing executive; b. Detroit, Jan. 13, 1927; s. Elis Sterner and Helen (Klinger) H.; m. Janet Ann Allen, Apr. 26, 1952; children: William A., Thomas K. B.S. in Mech. Engring., Princeton U., 1949. Various positions Electro-Motive and Euclid divs. Gen. Motors Corp., 1949-58; mng. dir. Euclid (Gt. Britain) Ltd., 1958-64; mgr. forward planning overseas ops. div. Gen. Motors, 1964-68; asst. to mng. dir. Adam Opel GMC, Germany, 1968; gen. mgr. TEREX (formerly Euclid), Hudson, Ohio, 1968-74, corp. v.p., gen. mgr., 1974—. Served with USN, 1945-46. Republican. Clubs: Sea Pines (Hilton Head, S.C.); Larchmont N.Y.) Yacht, Hinsdale (Ill.) Golf. Office: Electro-Motive Div Gen Motors Corp LaGrange IL 60525

HOGLUND, RICHARD FRANK, research and technical executive; b. Chgo., Mar. 22, 1933; s. Reuben Ture and Margaret Mabel (Thayer) H.; m. Arlene Diana Bieniasz, Jan. 7, 1956; children—Terrence, David, Mark. Student, Valparaiso U., 1949-51; B.S. in Mech. Engring, Northwestern U., 1954; M.S. in Mech. Engring. (Gen. Electric fellow), Northwestern U., 1955; Ph.D. (Royal Cabell fellow), Northwestern U., 1960. Dept. head Ford Aeronutronic, 1960-63; asso. prof. aerospace engring., lab. dir. Purdue U., 1963-69; prof. aerospace engring. Ga. Inst. Tech., 1969; chief scientist Atlantic Research Corp., 1969-72; head ocean monitoring and control, chief advanced concepts tech. Def. Advanced Research Research Projects Agy., 1972-75; staff scientist Phys. Dynamics, Inc., Arlington, Va., 1975-77; v.p. Ops. Research, Inc., Silver Spring, Md., 1977; dep. asst. sec. of navy for research and advanced tech. and concepts Dept. Navy, Washington, 1977-80; sr. v.p. ORI, Inc., Silver Spring, Md., 1980—. Contbr. articles to profl. jours.; editor: Energy Sources and Energy Conversion, 1967. Recipient Def. Meritorious Civilian Service medal Dept. Def., 1975. Home: 2353 Nashua Ct Reston VA 22091 Office: 1400 Spring St Silver Spring MD 20910

HOGNESS, JOHN RUSTEN, physician, association executive; b. Oakland, Calif., June 27, 1922; s. Thorfin R. and Phoebe (Swenson) H. Student, Haverford Coll., 1939-42, D.Sc. (hon.), 1973; B.S., U. Chgo., 1943, M.D., 1946; D.Sc. (hon.), Med. Coll. Ohio at Toledo, 1972; LL.D., George Washington U., 1973; D.Litt., Thomas Jefferson U., 1980. Diplomate: Am. Bd. Internal Medicine. Intern medicine Presbyn. Hosp., N.Y.C., 1946-47, asst. resident, 1949-50; chief resident King County Hosp., Seattle, 1950-51; asst. U. Wash. Sch. Medicine, 1950-52, Am. Heart Assn. research fellow, 1951-52, mem. faculty, 1954-71, prof. medicine, 1964-71, med. dir. univ. hosp., 1958-63, dean, chmn. bd. health scis., 1964-69, exec. v.p. univ., 1969-70; dir. Health Scis. Center, 1970-71; pres. Inst. Medicine, Nat. Acad. Scis., 1971-74, mem., 1971—; prof. medicine George Washington U., 1972-74, disting. professional lectr. dept. medicine; pres. U. Wash., Seattle, 1974-79, prof. medicine, 1974-79; pres. Assn. Acad. Health Centers, 1979—; mem. commr.'s adv. com. on exempt orgns. IRS, 1969-71; mem. adv. com. for environ. scis. NSF, 1970-71; adv. com. to dir. NIH, 1970-71; mem. Nat. Cancer Adv. Bd., 1972-76, Nat. Sci. Bd., 1976-82; trustee China Med. Bd.; mem. selection com. for Rockefeller pub. service awards Princeton U., 1976-82; chmn. med. injury compensation study steering com. Inst. Medicine, Nat. Acad. Scis.; mem. council for biol. scis. Pritzker Sch. Medicine, U. Chgo., 1977—; chmn. adv. panel on cost-effectiveness of med. techs. Office Tech. Assessment, U.S. Congress, 1978-80; mem. Council Health Care Tech., HEW; adv. panel for study fin. grad. med. edn. Dept. Health and Human Services, 1980—. Contbr. articles to profl. jours. Served with AUS, 1947-49. Recipient Disting. Service award Med. Alumni Assn. U. Chgo., 1966, Profl. Achievement award Alumni Assn. U. Chgo., 1973; Convocation medal Am. Coll. Cardiology, 1973; Cartwright medal Columbia U. Coll. Physicians and Surgeons, 1978. Fellow ACP, Am. Acad. Arts and Scis.; mem. Assn. Am. Physicians, Assn. Am. Med. Colls. (exec. council, chmn.-elect council of deans 1968-69), Inst. of Medicine, Nat. Acad. Scis., Alpha Omega Alpha. Office: 11 DuPont Circle Washington DC 20036

HOGNESTAD, EIVIND, civil engineer; b. Time, Norway, July 17, 1921; came to U.S., 1947, naturalized, 1954; s. Hans E. and Dorthea (Norheim) H.; m. Andree S. Hognestad, Apr. 4, 1964; children: Hans E., Marta Marie, Kirsten Andree. M.Sc., Norwegian Tech. U., 1947, D.Sc., 1952; M.Sc., U. Ill., 1949. Research asst. to asso. prof. U. Ill., 1947-53; mgr. structural devel. sect. Portland Cement Assn., Skokie, Ill., 1953-66, dir. engring. devel. dept., 1966-74, dir. tech. and sci. devel., 1974—; cons. offshore devel. petroleum fields various oil cos. and contractors., condr. field and lab. investigations of concrete structures. Contbr. to: Ency. Brit, 1966, also over 100 articles on structural engring. and concrete tech. to tech. jours. Served with Royal Norwegian Navy, 1944-46. Fellow Am. Concrete Inst. (chmn. com. 357 offshore concrete structures, Wason medal 1956, Henry L. Kennedy award 1971, hon. mem. 1976, Alfred E. Lindau award 1977, Delmar L. Bloem award 1980), ASCE (past chmn. adminstrv. com. on masonry and reinforced concrete, Research prize 1956, Chgo. Civil Engr. of Yr. award 1977, Arthur J. Boase award 1981); mem. Nat. Acad. Engring., Prestressed Concrete Inst. o3(past chmn. tech. activities com.), European Concrete Com., Internat. Prestressing Fedn., Structural Engring. Soc. P.R. (hon.), Norwegian Acad. Engring., Royal Norwegian Acad. Sci. Home: 2222 Prairie St Glenview IL 60025 Office: 5420 Old Orchard Rd Skokie IL 60077

HOGUE, ALEXANDRE, artist; b. Memphis, Mo., Feb. 22, 1898; s. Charles Lehman and Mattie (Hoover) H.; m. Maggie Joe Watson, July 16, 1938; 1 dau., Olivia. Mem. summer faculty Tex. State Coll. for Women, 1931-42; head art dept. Hockaday Jr. Coll., 1936-42; tech. illustrator N.Am. Aviation, 1942-45; head dept. art U. Tulsa, 1945-63, prof. art, 1963-68, emeritus prof. art, 1969—. Has exhibited art works both, internationally and U.S. including, Mus. of Modern Art, Art Inst., Chgo., Whitney Mus. Am. Art, Corcoran Gallery Art, Met. Mus. Art, Carnegie Internats., Pitts., Internat. at Jeu de Paume, Venetian Biennial, Hayward Gallery Art, London, Tate Gallery, London, Berlin Acad. Arts, 1980, Kunstverein, Hamburg, 1981, Haus der Kunst, Munich, W. Ger., 1983, Kunstverein, also in all Latin Am. capitals, Can., Eng., France, Portugal, Italy and Scotland.; Works reproduced in various art jours. and books.; Represented in collections, U. Ariz. Mus. Art, Tucson, Musee National d'Art Moderne, Paris, Library of Congress, Dallas Mus. Art, Philbrook Art Center, Tulsa, Gilcrease Mus. History and Art, Tulsa, Okla. State Coll. Art, Springfield (Mo.) Art Mus., Sheldon Meml. Gallery Art, Lincoln, Nebr., Weatherspoon Gallery of Art at U. N.C., Greensboro, Okla. Art Center, Oklahoma City, Phoenix Mus. Art, Carl Millesvag, Lidingo, Sweden, Nat. Mus. Am. Art; papers in Archives Am. Art, Washington and Hogue Collection, U. Tulsa Library. Home: 4052 E 23d St Tulsa OK 74114 *Art is ever-changing, and those who resist change are doomed to oblivion and painful unhappiness.*

HOGUE, JAMES LAWRENCE, clergyman; b. Wellsburgh, W.Va., June 9, 1923; s. Dewey Talmadge and Mary Inez (Lawrence) H.; m. Ethel Florence Park, Sept. 15, 1945; children: James Lawrence, Kelsey Graham, Kerrilee, Janiel Louise. B.D., Louisville Presbyn. Sem., 1951; B.S. in Bus. Adminstrn. (Bank of Maryville Econ. award 1948), Maryville (Tenn.) Coll., 1948. Ordained to ministry United Presbyn. Ch., 1951; pastor chs. in, Ind., 1951-52, 60-64; dir. Washington County Student Tng. Parish, Salem, Ind., 1953-59; field adminstr. Synod Colo.; Bd. Nat. Missions United Presbyn. Ch., 1964-68; exec. dir. Synod of Sierra, Sacramento, 1968-72; dir. Council Adminstrv. Services, N.Y.C., 1972-80; v.p. Hogue and Assos. (accountants), Steamboat Springs, Colo., 1980—. Served as aviator USNR, 1942-46. Mem. Am. Mgmt. Assn., Am. Philatelic Soc., Aircraft Owners and Pilots Assn. Republican. Clubs: Rotary (charter dir. Salem), Masons, Odd Fellows. Home: PO Box 880220 Steamboat Plaza CO 80488 Office: 10 Sundance Plaza PO Box 771182 Steamboat Springs CO 80477

HOGUET, ROBERT LOUIS, investment banker, broker; b. N.Y.C., Dec. 23, 1908; s. Robert Louis and Louise Robbins (Lynch) H.; m. Constance M. Roberts, Aug. 3, 1940; children—Robert Louis III, Constance Middleton, George Roberts. A.B., Harvard U., 1931, M.B.A., 1933. With office of sec. U.S. Treasury Dept., Washington, 1933-35; with First Nat. City Bank, 1935-69, v.p., 1947-58, sr. v.p., 1958-62, exec. v.p., vice chmn. trust bd., 1962-69; dir. Internat. Banking Corp., N.Y.C., 1964-70, 1st Nat. City Trust Co., Can., 1964-70, N.Y. London Trustee Co., Ltd., 1964-70, Anaconda Co., 1964-67, Consumers Power Co., 1950-55, 60-65; chmn. Tucker, Anthony & R.L. Day, Inc., 1970—; past dir. London Guarantee and Accident Co., N.Y.C., Phoenix Assurance Co. Mem. bd. mgrs. Hosp. Spl. Surgery, N.Y.C.; bd. dirs. Lincoln Center Performing Arts, 1963-72; chmn., bd. dirs. Repertory Theatre, 1963-72; bd. dirs. French Inst., Fedn. French Alliances; trustee Barnard Coll., N.Y.C., 1955-80, Aspen Inst. Humanistic Studies; bd. overseers Harvard Coll., 1965-71. Served from lt. to comdr. USNR, 1942-45. Mem. Council Fgn. Relations. Clubs: Links, Century, Downtown Assn., River (N.Y.C.); Piping Rock, Maidstone. Home: 1 E 66th St New York NY 10021 Office: 120 Broadway New York NY 10005

HOHAGE, FREDERICK WILLIAM, automobile parts company executive; b. Wuppertal-Barmen, W. Ger., Apr. 16, 1938; came to U.S., 1975; s. Hugo and Emmy (Englemann) H.; m. Christa M. Muller, Dec. 4, 1970. B.A., U. Nottingham, Eng., 1960; A.M.P., Harvard Bus. Sch., 1970. With Hoover Europe, London, Dusseldorf, 1961-63, Robert Bosch GmbH, Stuttgart, Germany, 1964-69, dir., Hamburg, 1970-71, Robert Bosch S.P.A., Milan, Italy, 1972-75; exec. v.p. Robert Bosch Corp., Broadway, Ill., 1976-78; chmn. bd., pres., chief exec. officer Robert Bosch (Can.) Ltd., Mississauga, Ont., Can., 1979—; pres., chief exec. officer Robert Bosch Sales Corp., Broadview, 1979-83; pres. sales group, corp. exec. v.p. Robert Bosch Corp., 1984—; dir. Boge of Am., Inc., Irvine, Calif., 1980—, Keiper Recaro Inc., Battle Creek, Mich., 1982—. Served to lt. German Air Force, 1960-61. Mem. Automobile Sales Council, Motor and Equipment Mfrs. Assn., Assn. Diesel Specialists, Automobile Service Industry Assn. Clubs: Sea Pines (Hilton Head, S.C.); Oak Brook Bath & Tennis (Ill.). Home: 14 Concord Dr Oak Brook IL 60521 Office: Robert Bosch Corp 2800 S 25th Ave Broadview IL 60153

HOHENBERG, JOHN, journalist, educator; b. N.Y.C., Feb. 17, 1906; s. Louis and Jettchen (Scheuermann) H.; m. Dorothy Lannuier, Oct. 16, 1928 (dec. Sept. 2, 1977); m. JoAnn Fogarty, Mar. 9, 1979; children: Pamela Jo, Eric. Student, U. Wash., 1922-24; Litt.B., Columbia U., 1927; postgrad., U. Vienna, 1928; L.H.D., Wilkes Coll., 1971. Reporter Seattle Star, 1923-24; writer N.Y. World, 1925; fgn. corr. N.Y. Evening Post, Vienna, Paris, asst. city editor, 1928-33; fgn. corr. U.P., Vienna, 1927-28; writer nat. politics N.Y. Jour.-Am., 1933-42; UN, Washington and fgn. corr. N.Y. Post, 1946-50; lectr. English Columbia, 1948, asso. in journalism, 1949-50, prof. journalism, 1950-74, prof. emeritus, 1974—; Meeman lectr. U. Tenn., 1975, Meeman Disting. prof. journalism, 1976-77, 78-81; Gannett profl. in residence U. Kans., 1977-78; Gannett disting. prof. journalism U. Fla., 1981-82; Nieman Found. lectr. Harvard U., 1981; vis. prof. U. Miami, 1982-83; Newhouse disting. prof. Newhouse Sch. Pub. Communications, Syracuse U., 1983-84; adminstr. Pulitzer Prizes and sec. Pulitzer Prize Bd., 1954-76, journalism juror, 1982; spl. cons. to Sec. USAF, 1953-63, to German Marshall Fund, 1980; Am. specialist lectr. State Dept. in 10 Asian countries, 1963-64; discussion leader Internat. Press Inst., New Delhi, 1966; sr. specialist East-West Center, Honolulu, 1967; mem. Japanese-Am. Assembly, Shimoda, Japan, 1967; vis. prof. Chinese U. of Hong Kong, 1970-71; lectr. 10 Asian countries for USIA, 1982. Author: The Pulitzer Prize Story, 1959, The Professional Journalist, 1960, rev. edit., 1968, 73, 78, 82, Foreign Correspondence—The Great Reporters and Their Times, 1964, The New Front Page, 1965, Between Two Worlds: Policy, Press and Public Opinion in Asian-American Relations, 1967, The News Media: A Journalist Looks at His Profession, 1968, Free Press/Free People: The Best Cause, 1971, New Era in the Pacific: An Adventure in Public Diplomacy, 1972, The Pulitzer Prizes: A History of the Awards in Books, Drama, Music and Journalism Based on Private Records over Six Decades, 1974, A Crisis For the American Press, 1978, The Pulitzer Prize Story II, 1980. Served with AUS, 1943-45. Recipient Pulitzer Prize Spl. award for services to Am. journalism, 1976; Disting. Service prizes for books: Foreign Correspondence, Between Two Worlds and A Crisis for the American Press Sigma Delta Chi/Soc. Profl. Journalists, 1965, 68, 79; Sigma Delta Chi award for Most Disting. Teaching of Journalism, 1974; Gold Key award Columbia Scholastic Press Assn., 1974; inducted into Journalism Hall of Fame Deadline Club of New York, 1981; Pulitzer traveling scholar Europe, 1927-28; research fellow Council Fgn. Relations in, 10 Asian countries, 1964; Knight Found. grantee for free press study, 1969-70; Ford Found. travel study grantee, Asia, 1971; Gannett Found. grantee for 1st amendment study, 1976-77. Mem. Council Fgn. Relations, Am. Assn. Edn. Journalism, Internat. Press Inst., Columbia Journalism Alumni Assn. (pres. 1954), Authors League Am. Home: 7700 Gleason Rd Apt 31C Knoxville TN 37919 Home: Box 134 Aquebogue NY 11931

HOHENBERGER, FRED L., food wholesale distribution company executive. Pres., treas. Associated Grocers Co. St. Louis, Mo. Office: Associated Grocers Co St Louis Mo 5030 Berthold Ave St Louis MO 63110§

HOHENDAHL, PETER UWE, comparative literature and German language and literature educator; b. Hamburg, Germany, Mar. 17, 1936; came to U.S., 1964; s. Wilhelm and Emilie (Uelschen) H.; m. Iky Maria Zoetelief, July 2, 1965; children: Deborah, Gwendolyn. Student, U. Bern, Switzerland, 1955, U. Hamburg, 1955-57, 59-63, Ph.D., 1964; student, U. Goettingen, Germany, 1958. Asst. prof. Pa. State U., 1965-68; assoc. prof. Washington U., St. Louis, 1968-69, prof., 1970-77, head dept., 1972-77; prof. comparative lit. and German Cornell U., Ithaca, N.Y., 1977—; Merton vis. prof. Berlin U., 1976. Author: Literaturkritik and Oeffentlichkeit, 1974, Der europaische Roman der Empfindsamkeit, 1977, The Institution of Criticism, 1982; mem. editorial bd.: Studies in 20th Century Lit., 1979—, German Quar., 1983—. Fellow Harvard U., 1964-65, Ctr. for Interdisciplinary Research, Bielefeld, 1981, Guggenheim Found., 1983—. Mem. MLA, Am. Assn. Tchrs. German, Internat. Heine Soc. (exec. council 1982—). Home: 81 Genung Rd Ithaca NY 14850 Office: Cornell Univ Ithaca NY 14853

HOHENEMSER, CHRISTOPH, physics educator, researcher; b. Berlin, May 29, 1937; U.S., 1947; s. Kurt H. and Katherine (Dietrich) H.; m. Anne S. Holland, June 20, 1960; children: Lisa, Julia. B.S. with honors, Swarthmore Coll., 1958; PH.D., Washington U., St. Louis, 1963. Research assoc. Washington U., St. Louis, 1963-64; instr., asst. prof. Brandeis U., Waltham, Mass., 1964-71; assoc. prof. physics Clark U., Worcester, Mass., 1971-76, prof., 1976—, chmn. dept. physics, Worcester, 1979-83, chmn. sci., tech. and soc. program, Worcester, Mass., 1971—, dir. Ctr. for Tech., Environ. and Devel, 1983—; vis. sci. U. Groningen, Netherlands, 1973-74, 78-79. Co-editor: Risk in Technological Society, 1982; contbr. 90 articles on physics and tech. assessment to jours. Recipient Bronze medal UN Environ. Programme, 1982; NSF research grantee, 1971—. Mem. Am. Phys. Soc., AAAS, Soc. Risk Analysis, Sigma Xi. Home: 146 Mill Rd Littleton MA 01460 Office: Dept Physics Clark U 950 Main St Worcester MA 01610

HOHENRATH, WILLIAM EDWARD, banker; b. Sea Cliff, N.Y., Mar. 9, 1922; s. Daniel and Ethyle Josephine (Ziegler) H.; m. Vivian Haynes, Sept. 15, 1945 (div. Sept. 1967); 1 dau., Donna; m. Lois Pelletier, Mar. 8, 1969; stepchildren—Jeanne M., Renee T., Michelle A., Anthony J. Grad., Am. Inst. Banking, 1948; B.S. magna cum laude, N.Y. U., 1958, M.B.A., 1968. With Williamsburgh Savs. Bank, Bklyn., 1941—, v.p., 1969-71, sr. v.p., 1971—. Mem. exec. com. Downtown Bklyn. Devel. Assn.; mem. Govt./Bus. Joint Econ. Devel. Com. of L.I., Nassau County Republican Com., 1965-69; Bd. dirs. Bklyn. Tb and Respiratory Disease Assn., 1970—. Mem. Bklyn. Savs. Banks (chmn. marketing com. 1972—), Savs. Banks Assn. N.Y. State (exec. com. 1972—), Am. Inst. Banking (pres. N.Y.C. chpt. 1966, chmn. trustees 1971-73, asso. councilman 1969—), Levittown C. of C. (pres. 1964-65), Bklyn. C. of C. (dir.). Home: 5 Straight Ln Levittown NY 11756 Office: 1 Hanson Pl Brooklyn NY 11243 *There are two things I try never to forget. 1. That all people do all things for some kind of self serving reason. This thought not only deflates ones own ego but helps one to understand another. 2. Failure to appreciate and put into perspective each of life's experiences, bitter or sweet, is only to cheat yourself.*

HOHLER, G. ROBERT, fund raising consultant; b. Boston, Sept. 24, 1932; s. Robert Anthony and Eileen (Dutcher) H.; children: Robert Tillman, Cynthia Ann, Julie Barbara. B.A. magna cum laude, Northeastern U., 1960. Asst. to dep. comptroller Harvard, 1956-60; dir. office information Unitarian Universalist Assn., Boston, 1960-63; exec. dir. Laymen's League, 1963-69; community relations staff Polaroid Corp., 1967-70; dir. devel. Putney (Vt.) Sch., 1970-76; dir., partner Resource Devel. Assos., Brattleboro, Vt., 1976-77; dir. devel. and communication Oxfam-Am., 1978-82; Pres. Liberty Tree Assoc., cons. vol. orgns., 1966—; pres. Robert Hohler Assocs., Orgn. Devel., Communications and Fund Raising, 1971; editor Respond mag., 1966-70, Challenge mag., 1964-65, Putney Post, 1970-76. Author: You Can't Jail Us All, 1964, My Father Played for Me, 1977, Cambodia: Does It Have a Future, 1980. Founding mem. Citizens Boston Schs., 1961; founder Bostonian of Year award, 1960; founder, mem. bd. Boston Center for Arts, 1970—; del., vice-chmn. Vt. del. Nat. Democratic Conv., 1976. Hon. distinguished minister congregation Arlington St. Ch., 1967. Mem. Nat. Soc. Fund Raising Execs., N.E. Direct Mktg. Assn. Home: PO Box 381 Brattleboro VT 05301 Office: Robert Hohler Assocs 121 Mount Vernon St Boston MA 02108

HOHN, HARRY GEORGE, lawyer, insurance company executive; b. N.Y.C., Mar. 1, 1932; s. Harry George and Violia (Meehan) H.; m. Janet Jean LaRosa, June 19, 1954; children: Cynthia, Jennifer, Nancy, Patricia. B.S., NYU, 1953, LL.M., 1959; J.D., Fordham U., 1956. Bar: N.Y. 1956, U.S. Supreme Ct. 1976. Asst. gen. counsel N.Y. Life Ins. Co., N.Y.C., 1968, 2d v.p. corporate planning, 1968-72, assoc. gen. counsel, 1972-74, v.p., assoc. gen. counsel, 1974-77, sr. v.p., gen. counsel, 1977-82, exec. v.p., gen. counsel, 1982-83, exec. v.p., 1983—. Editor: Fordham Law Rev, 1955-56; contbr. articles to, Practising Law Inst. Mem. Am., N.Y. State bar assns., Assn. Bar City N.Y., Assn. Life Ins. Counsel (bd. govs.). Republican. Roman Catholic. Home: 9 Walworth Ave Scarsdale NY 10583 Office: 51 Madison Ave New York NY 10010

HOHN, RICHARD GREGORY, ins. co. exec.; b. N.Y.C., June 12, 1936; s. Harry George and Viola Mary (Meehan) H.; m. Jane Margaret Rushford, July 4, 1964; children—Richard Gregory, Christina Marie. B.B.A., Iona Coll., 1962; J.D., Fordham U., 1966. Bar: Ind. bar 1967, N.Y. State bar 1970. Staff atty. Assos. Investment Co., South Bend, Ind., 1966-68; asst. gen. counsel U.S. Life Ins. Co., N.Y.C., 1969-71; v.p., sec. USLIFE Corp., N.Y.C., 1971-76, v.p.-counsel, sec., 1977-79; pvt. practice, N.Y.C., 1979—. Served with AUS, 1955-58. Mem. Am., N.Y. State bar assns., New York County Lawyers Assn. Home: 6 Oakwood Dr Allendale NJ 07401 Office: 111 W 57 St New York NY 10019

HOHNSTEDT, LEO FRANK, chemist, educator; b. Alton, Ill., June 12, 1924; s. Leo Thomas and Esther (Paris) H.; m. Margaret Mary Gorman, Aug. 13, 1960. B.S. in Chemistry, St. Louis U., 1949; Ph.D., U. Chgo., 1955. Instr. chemistry St. Louis U., 1954-55, asst. prof., 1955-60, asso prof., 1963-69, prof., 1969—, chmn. chemistry dept., 1966-77; asso. prof. Poly. Inst. Bklyn., 1960-61; weapon systems analyst Weapon Systems Evaluation Div., Inst. for Def. Analysis, Washington, 1961-63. Served with AUS, 1943-46. Named Alumni Chemist of Yr. St. Louis U. Alumni Chemists, 1970. Fellow AAAS, Am. Inst. Chemists; mem. Am. Chem. Soc., Inst. for Theol. Encounter with Sci. and Tech., St. Louis Soc. Analysts, VFW, Sigma Xi, Phi Lambda Upsilon, Pi Mu Epsilon, Alpha Chi Sigma. Roman Catholic. Club: K.C. (4th deg.). Home: 1114 Danforth St Alton IL 62002 Office: 221 N Grand St Saint Louis MO 63103

HOIBY, LEE, composer, concert pianist; b. Madison, Wis., Feb. 17, 1926; s. Henry and Violet (Smith) H. B.Mus., U. Wis., 1947; M.A., Mills Coll., Oakland, Calif., 1952; diploma, Curtis Inst., Phila., 1952; D.F.A. (hon.), Simpson Coll., Indianola, Iowa, 1983. Composer: operas The Scarf, 1955, A Month in the Country, 1964, Summer and Smoke, 1970, Something New For the Zoo, 1979, The Italian Lesson, 1980; ballet After Eden, 1967; oratorio Galileo Galilei, 1975, Piano Concerto 2, 1979; also chamber, choral and theatre music, songs. Recipient Am. Acad. Arts and Letters award, 1957; Fulbright fellow, 1952; Guggenheim fellow, 1958; Rockefeller Found. grantee, 1979; NEA fellow, 1980. Mem. ASCAP, Musicians Union, Am. Guild Organists (hon.).

HOIE, CLAUS, artist; b. Stavanger, Norway, Nov. 3, 1911; came to U.S., 1924, naturalized, 1942; s. Claus and Marie (Foss) H.; m. Helen Hunt Bencker, Nov. 17, 1956. Student, Pratt Inst., 1930-33, Ecole des Beaux Arts, Paris, 1945. Art dir., designer, illustrator various advt. and pub. firms in, N.Y.C., 1933-41, 46-62; painter, graphic artist, 1962—; exhibited in one man shows at, Denver Art Mus., 1943, Saltpeter Gallery, N.Y.C., 1962, 63, Monmouth (N.J.) Art Center, 1970, Benson Gallery, Bridgehampton, N.Y., 1972, 77, 80, Southampton Coll., 1972, Guild Hall Mus., East Hampton, N.Y., 1973, Upstairs Gallery, East Hampton, 1973, 74, Norwegian-Am. Mus., 1975, U. Minn. Galleries, Mpls., 1976, Akershus Mus., Oslo, 1982, group shows at, Chgo. Art Inst., 1946, Nat. Acad., 1956, 68, 70, 80, 81, 83, Am. Water Color Soc., 1960-80, 82, L.I. Painters, 1972, 75, Nat. Inst. Arts and Letters, 1975, numerous others; represented in permanent collections, Bklyn. Mus., Norfolk Mus., Okla. Mus. Art, Butler Inst., East Hampton Guild Hall Mus., U. Minn., Centre Coll. Ky., Norwegian-Am. Mus., Brigham Young U.; Contbr. articles to profl. jours. Served with AUS, 1942-45; ETO. Decorated Bronze Star medal; recipient Nat. Inst. Arts and Letters award for painting, 1975. Mem. N.A.D., Soc. Illustrators, Am. Watercolor Soc. (v.p. 1960-62, Gold medal of honor 1962). Episcopalian. Club: Devon Yacht (East Hampton). Home: 20 W 12th St New York NY 10011

HOILAND, ANDREW CALVIN, architect; b. Great Falls, Mont., Aug. 3, 1926; s. Andrew C. and Ida (Mohundro) H.; m. Patricia Ruth Willits, Aug. 13, 1950; children: William H., Richard C., Diana Ruth. B.S. in Architecture, Mont. State Coll., 1949. Draftsman A.V. McIver (architect), Great Falls, 1949-52; prin. A. Calvin Hoiland (architect), Great Falls, 1952-54; partner Hoiland & Lund (architects), Great Falls, 1953-63, Hoiland-Zucconi (architects), 1964-74, A. Calvin Hoiland (Architect), 1974—; Pres. Mont. Bd. Archtl. Examiners, 1968. Asso. editor: Am. Architects Directory, 1969-70; editorial adv. bd. Symposia mag., 1968-78; Important works include: master plan for Great Falls swimming pools, 1963, 1967; master plan for prison facilities Mont. State Prison, 1968; Mountain View Sch., Great Falls, 1968-69, Great Falls fire stas., 1969-71, Gregson Hot Springs swimming pools, 1972, Great Falls PCA-FLBA Office, 1978, I.F.G. Leasing Bldg, Great Falls, 1980; master plan for prison facilities, Great Falls, 1980. Chmn. charity ball for Great Falls Rehab. Center, 1961-62; chmn. master plan com. Great Falls Swimming Pool, 1962-65; chmn. adv. council Great Falls chpt. DeMolay.; Bd. dirs. Great Falls Camp Fire Girls. Served with USAAC, World War II. Named to Legion of Honor Order DeMolay, 1956, Cross of Honor, 1976. Mem. AIA (pres. Mont. 1961-62, editor Mont. publ. 1965-71), Great Falls Soc. Architects (charter pres. 1953), Mont. Tech. Council (charter pres. 1960-61), Sigma Chi. Methodist (chmn. bd. trustees, mem. bldg. com. Wesley Center, mem. Mont. bd. missions). Clubs: Masons (master 1979), Shriners, Kiwanis (pres. Great Falls 1964). Home and Office: 2826 3d Ave S Great Falls MT 59405 *I believe we should learn from the past, enjoy the present, and prepare for the future.*

HOKENSTAD, MERL CLIFFORD, JR., social work educator; b. Norfolk, Nebr., July 21, 1936; s. Merl Clifford and Flora Diane (Christian) H.; m. Dorothy Jean Tarrell, June 24, 1962; children: Alene Ann, Laura Rae, Marta Lynn. B.A. summa cum laude, Augustana Coll., 1958; Rotary Found. fellow, Durham (Eng.) U., 1958-59; M.S.W., Columbia U., 1962; Ph.D., Brandeis U., 1969, Inst. Ednl. Mgmt., Harvard U., 1977. With Lower East Side Neighborhood Assn., N.Y.C., 1962-64; community planning asso. United Community Services, Sioux Falls, S.D., 1964-66; instr. Augustana Coll., Sioux Falls, 1964-66; research asso. Ford Found. Project on Community Planning for Elderly, Brandeis U., Waltham, Mass., 1966-67; prof., dir. Sch. Social Work, Western Mich. U., Kalamazoo, 1968-74; prof., dean Sch. Applied Social Scis., Case Western Res. U., Cleve., 1974-83, Ralph and Dorothy Schmitt prof., 1983—; vis. prof. Inst. Sociology, Stockholm U., 1978, Fulbright lectr., 1980; vis. prof. Nat. Inst. Social Work, London, 1981. Author: Participation in Teaching and Learning: An Idea Book for Social Work Educators; editor: Meeting Human Needs: An International Annual, Vol. V; contbr. articles to profl. jours. Mem. alcohol tng. rev. com. Nat. Inst. Alcoholism and Alcohol Abuse, 1974-78; workshop leader Am. Assn. State Colls. and Univs., 1974; chmn. U.S. com. XVIII Internat. Congress Schs. Social Work, 1976; Chmn. Kalamazoo County Community Mental Health Services Bd., 1971, vice chmn., 1972; mem. edn. and tng. task force Mich. Office Drug Abuse and Alcoholism, 1972-73; mem. Mich. Assn. Mental Health Bds., 1972; bd. dirs. Cleve. United Way Services, 1982—, del. assembly, 1974-82, mem. periodic rev. oversight com., 1982—, mem. leadership devel. com., 1978—; bd. dirs. Kalamazoo United Way, 1968-72; trustee Cleve. Internat. Program for Youth Workers and Social Workers; mem. program devel. com. Cleve. Center on Alcoholism, 1976; trustee Alcoholism Services Cleve., Inc., 1977—, v.p., 1982—; trustee Citizens League Greater Cleve., 1978—, Community Info./Vol. Action Ctr., 1982—; chmn. leadership devel. com. Community Info./Vol. Action Ctr., 1984—. Named Outstanding Alumnus, Augustana Coll., 1980; NIMH trainee, 1960-62; Vocat. Rehab. trainee, 1966; Gerontology trainee, 1967; Rotary Found. fellow, 1958-59. Mem. Acad. Cert. Social Workers, Am. Assn. Higher Edn., Am. Pub. Welfare Assn., Internat. Assn. Schs. Social Work (exec. bd., treas. 1978—), Internat. Council on Social Welfare (dir. U.S. com. 1982—), Council on Social Work Edn. (del. 1972-75, 77-83, chmn. ann. program meeting 1973, chmn. com. on nat. legis. and adminstrv. policy 1975-79, mem. nominating com. 1978-81, internat. com. 1980—, chmn. com. 1982-84, dir. 1979-82, exec. com. 1980-81), Nat. Assn. Social Workers, Nat. Conf. on Social Welfare (dir. 1978-80, chmn. Sect. V program com. 1977-78), World Future Soc. (area coordinator 1972-74). Democrat. Episcopalian. Home: 2917 Weymouth Rd Shaker Heights OH 44120 Office: 2035 Abington Rd Cleveland OH 44106

HOKIN, LOWELL EDWARD, biochemist, educator; b. Chgo., Sept. 20, 1924; s. Oscar E. and Helen (Manfield) H.; m. Mabel Neaverson, Dec. 1, 1952 (div. Dec. 1973); children—Linda Ann, Catherine Esther, Samuel Arthur; m. Barbara M. Gallagher, Mar. 23, 1978. Student, U. Chgo., 1942-43, Dartmouth, 1943-44, U. Ill. Sch. Medicine, 1946-47; M.D., U. Louisville, 1948; Ph.D., U. Sheffield, Eng., 1952. Postdoctoral fellow dept. biochemistry McGill U., 1952-54, faculty, 1954-57, asst. prof., 1955-57; mem. faculty U. Wis.-Madison, 1957—, prof. physiol. chemistry, 1961-68, prof., chmn. dept. pharmacology, 1968—. Editor: Metabolic Transport, Metabolic Pathways, Vol. VI, 1972; Contbr. numerous articles to tech. jours., chpts. to numerous books on phospholipids, biol. transport, pancreas. Mem. Am. Soc. Biol. Chemists, Biochem. Soc. (U.K.), A.A.A.S., Am. Chem. Soc., Am. Soc. Pharmacology and Exptl. Therapeutics. Home: 5 Nokomis Ct Madison WI 53705

HOLABIRD, JOHN AUGUR, JR., architect; b. Chgo., May 9, 1920; s. John Augur and Dorothy (Hackett) H.; m. Donna Katharine Smith, Nov. 25, 1942 (div. 1969); children—Jean, Katharine, Polly, Lisa (dec.); m. Marcia Stefanie Fergestad, June 28, 1969; children—Ann, Lynn. B.A., Harvard, 1942, M.Arch., 1948. Archtl. designer Holabird & Root, Chgo., 1948-49, 55-64, asso. firm, 1964-70, partner, 1970—; tchr. drama Francis Parker Sch., Chgo., 1949-55; stage designer NBC-TV, 1955. Major: archtl. works include Francis Parker Sch, Chgo., Ravinia Stage and Restaurant, Highland Park, Ill., 1970, Bell Telephone Labs, Naperville, Ill., 1975, Canal Bldg, Chgo., 1974. Pres. Park W. Community Assn., 1962; dir. Lincoln Park Conservation Assn., 1960-64, Corlands, 1979—; commr. Chgo. Commn. on Historic and Archtl. Landmarks, 1981—; bd. dirs. Lincoln Park Community Conservation, 1964; trustee Francis Parker Sch., Ravinia Festival Assn., Ill. Inst. Tech., 1980—. Served with U.S. Army, 1942-45. Decorated Silver Star, Bronze Star; Fourragère, Belgium; Order of William, Netherlands). Fellow AIA (pres. Chgo. chpt. 1977—). Ind. Democrat. Clubs: Tavern, Arts, Met., Harvard (dir. 1974—). Home: 2715 Pine Grove Ave Chicago IL 60614 Office: 300 W Adams St Chicago IL 60606

HOLADAY, ALLAN GIBSON, educator; b. Grand Ledge, Mich., Jan. 16, 1916; s. Robert Clayton and Effie (Hooks) H.; m. Ruby Roxane Lees, Sept. 30, 1945; children—Allan Scott, Bruce Lees. B.A., Miami U., Oxford, Ohio, 1938; M.A. (Grad. fellow), Cornell U., 1939; Ph.D. (Grad. Council fellow), George Washington U., 1943. Instr. English U. Ill. at Urbana, 1942-47, asst. prof., 1947-53, asso. prof., 1953-57, prof., 1957-80, emeritus, 1980—. Author, editor: Thomas Heywood's The Rape of Lucrece, 1950, The Plays of George Chapman, 1970; Co-editor: The Life of Lazarillo de Tormes, 1955; editor: Illinois Studies in Language and Literature; Contbr. articles profl. jours. Mem. Modern Lang. Assn., Modern Humanities Research Assn., Cambridge Bibliog. Soc., Am. Assn. U. Profs., Phi Beta Kappa, Phi Eta Sigma, Delta Phi Alpha. Home: 1132 South St Culver IN 46511

HOLAHAN, RICHARD VINCENT, former mag. and book publisher; b. Darien, Conn., Dec. 4, 1909; s. Michael Joseph and Margaret (Callery) H.; m. Pamela Crawford, Mar. 4, 1938; children—Michael N., Thomas R., Richard J., Stephen C., David W. B.S., Yale U., 1933. With Time, Inc., 1936-50; bus. mgr. Fortune mag., 1943-50; prodn. dir. Street & Smith Publs., 1950-53; plant mgr. O.E. McIntyre, Inc., Westbury, N.Y., 1953-56; with Scholastic Mags., Inc., N.Y.C., 1956-74, v.p., 1960-74; pres. Advanced Typographic Systems, Inc., N.Y.C., 1975—. Sec. Stamford Planning Bd., 1949-51; chmn. Stamford Bd. Finance, 1951-54, Huntington Planning Bd., 1960-67; town councilman, Huntington, 1970-77; mem. bd. Met. Transp. Authority, N.Y.C., 1978—; Trustee Performing Arts Found., Huntington; chmn. Yale Alumni Bd., 1952-54. Mem. Vernon Hall, Phi Gamma Delta. Clubs: Yale (N.Y.C.); Huntington Country. Home: 162 Bay Ave Huntington NY 11743

HOLBEIN, BRUCE EDWARD, microbiologist, company executive; b. Arnprior, Ont, Can., May 12, 1950; s. Edward Rutley and Marion (Heins) H.; m. Sharon Marie Griffin, Aug. 14, 1971; children: Marc, Paul. B.S. in Agr., U. Guelph, (Ont.), 1973, Ph.D., U. Grelph, 1977. Scientist Fed. Govt. Can., Medicine Hat, Alta., 1976-79; asst. prof. McGill U., Montreal, Que., 1979-83, assoc. prof., 1983—; pres. DeVoe-Holbein Can. Inc., Montreal, 1982—; supervisory dir. DeVoe-Holbein Internat. N.V., Curacao, 1983—. Contbr. articles on iron and bacterial infection to profl. jours. Grantee Nat. Cancer Inst., 1982—, Med. Research Council Can., 1981, Natural Sci. Engring. Research Council Can., 1974-76, 81—. Mem. Can. Soc. Microbiology, Am. Soc. Microbiology. Office: McGill U Dept Microbiology-Immunology 3773 University St Montreal PQ Canada H3A 2B4

HOLBERG, RALPH GANS, JR., lawyer; b. Mobile, Nov. 5, 1908; s. Ralph G. and Lillian (Frohlichstein) H.; m. Amelia Schwarz, Feb. 16, 1938; children: Ralph G. III, Robert S. J.D., U. Ala., 1932. Bar: Ala. 1932. Since practiced in, Mobile; partner firm Holberg, Tully, Holberg & Danley. Pres. Mobile County chpt. ARC, 1954-55; chmn. Southeastern area council, 1957-58; bd. mem. emeritus Mobile County chpt., Ala. nat. v.p., 1960-61, mem. nat. bd. govs., 1965-68, 68-71; chmn. bd. Mobile County Bd. Pensions and Security, 1947-77, Mobile Gen. Hosp., 1963-67; chmn. Mobile Gen. Hosp., 1965-67; mem. Ala. Docks Adv. Bd., 1962-69, 3d Army Area Adv. Com., Gov. Ala. Com. Adult Edn. Negroes, 1949; chmn. Mobile Pub. Library Bd., 1954-55; past appeal agt. local selective service bd.; past pres. Estate Planning Council Mobile, 1971-72, Hon. Fellows Mobile Coll., 1972-73; mem. nat. adv. council Nat. Multiple Sclerosis Soc., 1973—; alt. Mobile Hist. Devel. Commn., 1973-76; pres. Old Shell Rd. PTA, 1954-55, Ala. Jr. C. of C., 1935; mem. bd. Mobile Community Chest and Council, 1965-71; trustee Mobile YWCA, 1978—; bd. dirs. Gordon Smith Ctr., 1973—. Served to lt. USNR, 1944-46. Recipient Disting. Service Key Mobile Jr. C. of C., 1938; named Mobilian of Year, 1963. Fellow Am. Coll. Probate Counsel; mem. ABA, Ala. Bar Assn., Mobile Bar Assn. (pres. 1942), VFW, Ala. Hist. Assn. (exec. com. 1981—), SCV, Am. Legion (post comdr. 1947-48), Mobile Jaycees (pres. 1934), Mobile Area C. of C. (dir. 1962-65, 71-74, 81), Mobile Hist. Preservation Soc. (dir. 1974-77), Mobile's Azalea Trail (pres. 1934-35), Navy League, Am. Council Judaism (nat. adv. bd. 1955—), Spring Hill Ave. Temple (past pres., mem. bd.), Zeta Beta Tau. Clubs: Exchange (charter, past pres.), Internat. Trade, Touchdown (past mem. bd.), Mobile Country.). Home: Apt 216 217 Berwyn Dr W Mobile AL 36608 Office: Suite 701 Commerce Bldg Mobile AL 36602

HOLBERT, THEODORE FRANK, banker; b. Sussex, N.J., July 15, 1921; s. Theodore M. and Charlotte (Lawrence) H.; m. Florence M. Conrad, June 8, 1948 (dec. Feb. 1970); children: Amy, Amanda, Philip; m. Jacqueline M. Roy, Feb. 2, 1974. B.A., Denison U., 1947; postgrad., Rutgers U., 1954. Vice pres., dir. Farmers Nat. Bank, Sussex, 1947-63; exec. v.p., dir. Bank of Sussex County, Franklin, N.J., 1963- 69; sr. v.p., dir., mem. exec. com. Nat. Community Bank, Rutherford, N.J., 1970—; dir. Arcadia Nat. Bank, Secaucus, N.J. Pres. Sussex County Bd. Realtors, 1958; Councilman, Boro of Sussex, 1949-59; Pres. High Point Regional Bd. Edn.; trustee, treas. Alexander Linn Hosp., Sussex. Served with USAAF, 1943-46; ETO. Mem. Am., N.J. bankers assns., N.J. Agr. Soc., Kappa Sigma. Republican. Episcopalian. Lodges: Masons; Rotary. Office: 59 Main St Sussex NJ 07461

HOLBIK, KAREL, economics educator; b. Czechoslovakia, Sept. 9, 1920; came to U.S., 1948, naturalized, 1952; s. Karel and Catherine (Krouzel) H.; m. Olga Rehackova, Sept. 10, 1956; 1 son, Thomas. J.D., Charles U., Prague, 1947; M.B.A., U. Detroit, 1949; Ph.D., U. Wis., 1956. Researcher Bank of Am., San Francisco, 1951-53; teaching asst. in banking U. Wis., 1953-55; asst. prof. econs. Lafayette Coll., Easton, Pa., 1955-58; prof. econs. Boston U., 1958—; cons. U.S. Naval War Coll., Newport, R.I., 1963-64; vis. prof. U. Brussels, 1969-70; chief sect. for devel. fin. instns. UN, 1976-80; Fulbright sr. scholar U. Tunis, 1983-84. Author: Italy in International Cooperation, 1959, Postwar Trade in Divided Germany, 1964, The United States, The Soviet Union and the Third World, 1968, Monetary Policy in Twelve Industrial Countries, 1973, Industrialization and Employment in Puerto Rico, 1975; others. Mem. Am. Econ. Assn., Am. Fin. Assn. Home: 313 Country Club Rd Newton MA 02159 Office: Econs Dept Boston U Boston MA 02215 *It appears that America, more than any other country, challenges human capabilities and permits individual dreams to come true.*

HOLBROOK, ANTHONY, manufacturing company executive; b. 1940; married. With Advanced Micro Devices Inc., Sunnyvale, Calif., 1973—, exec. v.p., chief operating officer. Office: Advanced Micro Devices Inc 901 Thompson Pl Sunnyvale CA 94086 *

HOLBROOK, CLYDE AMOS, theologian; b. Greenfield, Mass., Mar. 20, 1911; s. Fred Earl and Adella (Caswell) H.; m. Dorothy Bush Wheeler, Dec. 27, 1937; children—Richard Clyde, Arthur Wheeler, Deborah. A.B., Bates Coll., 1934; B.D., Colgate-Rochester Div. Sch., 1937; Ph.D., Yale U., 1945; postgrad. univs., St. Andrews and Basel, 1956; S.T.D., Denison U., 1969; H.H.D., Oberlin Coll, 1982. Ordained to ministry Baptist Ch., 1937; pastor, Weston, Conn., 1937-42, New Haven, 1942-45; dean of chapel, asso. prof. religion Colo. Coll., 1945-49; asso. prof. religion Denison U., 1949-51; prof. religion Oberlin Coll., 1951—, chmn. dept., 1951-75, prof. Christian ethics, 1951-56; Danforth chair of religion, 1957, ret., 1977; prof. Union Theol. Sem., summer 1961; vis. prof. religion U. Va., spring 1980; disting. vis. prof. religion Oberlin Coll., 1980-81; Colgate-Rochester fellow Yale U., 1937-40; sr. fellow Council of Humanities, Princeton U., 1961-62; Past mem. commn. on higher edn. Nat. Council of Chs. of Christ. Author: Faith and Community, 1959, Religion a Humanistic Field, 1963, Jonathan Edwards: Original Sin, 1970, The Ethics of Jonathan Edwards, 1973, The Iconoclastic Deity, 1984; Co-author: The Humanities at Oberlin, 1958, A Handbook of Christian Theologians, 1965, A Heritage of Christian Thought, 1965, Black Theology II, 1978, Encyclopedic Dictionary of Religion, 1979; editorial bd.: Jour. Bible and Religion, 1969. Trustee Oberlin Shansi Meml. Assn., 1956—, v.p., 1960-68, pres., 1968-72. Recipient E. Harris Harbison award, 1966-67; fellow Acad. Sr. Profls., 1982. Mem. Soc. Christian Ethics, Am. Acad. Religion (pres. 1963), Soc. Values in Higher Edn., Am. Theol. Soc., Phi Beta Kappa. Mem. United Ch. of Christ. Home: 21 Hawthorne Dr Oberlin OH 44074

HOLBROOK, DONALD BENSON, lawyer; b. Salt Lake City, Jan. 5, 1925; s. Robert Sweeten and Kinnie (Benson) H.; m. Betty J. Gilchrist, Apr. 23, 1949; children: Mark, Thomas, Gregory, Mary. Student, Colo. Coll., 1943; LL.B., U. Utah, 1952, J.D., 1965. Bar: Utah 1953. Clk. Chief Justice James A. Wolfe, Utah Supreme Ct., 1953-55; asst. city atty. Salt Lake City, 1955-57; pres. firm Jones, Waldo, Holbrook and McDonough, Salt Lake City, 1958—; dir. Kearns-Tribune Corp.; commr. Utah bar, 1983; adviser Mountain Bell. Mem. exec. com. Democratic Party, Utah, 1955-65; chmn. antitrust and monopoly sub-com. Western States Dem. Conf., 1962-66; campaign mgr. Gov. Calvin L. Rampton, 1964-68; chmn. resolutions com. Utah Dem. Conv., 1968; Dem. candidate U.S. Senate, 1974; Vice chmn., then chmn. finance com. bd. regents U. Utah, 1965-67, chmn. bd. regents, 1967-68; mem. Utah Bd. Regents, chmn., 1974—; chmn. Western Interstate Commn. Higher Edn., 1979. Served to 1st lt. USMCR, 1943-45. Fellow Internat. Acad. Trial Lawyers, Am. Bar Found.; mem. Utah Bar Assn. (chmn. com. World Peace through Law 1964, mem. com. jud. retirement 1968), ABA (gen. chmn. Rocky Mountain meeting 1962, mem. com. banking and bus. law 1962—), Salt Lake County Bar Assn. (pres. 1964-65), Order of Coif, Beta Theta Phi, Phi Kappa Phi. Clubs: Alta, Univ. (Salt Lake City). Home: 1752 Laurelhurst Dr Salt Lake City UT 84108 Office: 800 Walker Bank Bldg Salt Lake City UT 84111

HOLBROOK, DOUGLAS C., union official; b. Coeburn, Va., Mar. 31, 1934; m. Jackie Holbrook; children: Douglas, Kevin. Student, Wayne State U. With Chrysler Corp., Detroit, U.S. Postal Service, 1956—; pres. Detroit local Am. Postal Workers Union, 1966-81; sec.-treas. Am. Postal Workers Union, Washington, 1981—; trustee, editor Detroit Postal Worker; chmn. Pres.'s Conf.; founder Save Our Annuity Retirement Coalition of Mich. Office: Am Postal Workers Union-AFL-CIO 817 14th St NW Washington DC 20005

HOLBROOK, ELIZABETH BRADFORD, artist, educator; b. Hamilton, Ont., Can., Nov. 7, 1913; d. William Ashford and Alma Victoria (Carpenter) Bradford; m. Joan Grant Holbrook, Aug. 3, 1936; children: John David, Elizabeth Jane, William Howard (dec.). Student, Hamilton Tech. Inst. Fine Arts, 1929-32; grad., Ont. Coll. Art, Toronto, 1935; postgrad., Royal Coll. Art, London, 1935-36. Asst. in studio Emanuel Hahn, Toronto, 1935-40, Carl Milles (Cranbrook Sch Art), Bloomfield Hills, Mich., 1947-48; instr. sculpture Dundas Valley Sch. Art, 1965-70. One-woman shows, Art Gallery, Hamilton, 1974, Sisler Gallery, Toronto, 1976, McMaster U. Art Gallery, Hamilton, 1979, group shows, Royal Can. Acad., M, Montreal Mus. Fine Arts, Ont. Soc. Artists, London Art Gallery and Mus., others; represented permanent collections, Nat. Portrait Gallery, Washington, Nat. Gallery of Can., Ottawa, Gallery of Parliament Bldgs., Ottawa, Art Gallery, Hamilton, McMasters U., Chedokee Gen. Hosp., Hamilton, U. Syracuse Library, N.Y., pvt. collections. Bd. dirs. Can. Hunter Improvements Soc., Toronto, 1960-80; sr. judge Can. Horse Show

Assn., 1965-75. Recipient Lt. Gov.'s medal Ont. Coll. Art, 1935, Gold medal for portrait sculpture Nat. Sculpture, 1969. Mem. Royal Can. Acad. Art (mem. council 1983—), Ont. Soc. Artists, Sculptors Soc. Can. Home: 1177 Mineral Springs Rd Rural Route 3 Dundas ON Canada L9H 5E3

HOLBROOK, GEORGE EDWARD, chemical engineer; b. St. Louis, Mar. 4, 1909; s. Edward M. and Doretta C. (Krentler) H.; m. Dorothy H. Williams, June 12, 1933; children: James E., Thomas E. B.S., U. Mich., 1931, M.S., 1932, Ph.D., 1933, D.Sc., 1967. With E.I. duPont de Nemours & Co., Inc., Wilmington, Del., 1933-76, asst. gen. mgr. organic chems. dept., 1955-56, gen. mgr. elastomer chems. dept., 1957-58, v.p., dir., mem. exec. com., 1958-69, dir., mem. finance, bonus and salary coms., 1970-76; Bd. dirs. Del. Research Found., Devel. Council U. Mich.; mem. adv. bd. residencies in engring. Ford Found.; mem. chem. engring. adv. bd. U. Rochester, U. Del.; adv. bd. Ford Found.; bd. overseers Newark Coll. Engring.; bd. engring. edn. U. Pa.; exec. com. Office Critical Tables, Nat. Acad. Scis.; governing bd. NRC, also exec. com. engring. div.; exec. com. engring. div.; exec. com. Hwy. Research Bd.; dir. Chem. Bur. Nat. Prodn. Authority, 1952. Contbr. articles to profl. jours. Vice-chmn. bd. trustees St. Francis Hosp. Fellow Am. Inst. Chem. Engrs. (pres. 1958, treas. 1963-69, Profl. Progress award 1953, Founders' award 1961, Van Antwerpen award 1980, Eminent Engr. 1983); mem. Engrs. Joint Council (v.p., dir., mem. exec. com. 1960-61), Mfg. Chemists Assn. (dir., mem. exec. com. 1960-61), Am. Chem. Soc. (com. on corp. assn. 1967-70), Soc. Chem. Industries, Am. Phys. Soc., AAAS, N.Y. Acad. Sci., Franklin Inst., Instn. Chem. Engrs. London (hon.), Nat. Acad. Engring. (charter; mem. exec. com. 1964), U.S. Power Squadron, Sigma Xi, Tau Beta Pi, Phi Lambda Upsilon, Phi Kappa Phi, Phi Eta Sigma, Iota Alpha. Clubs: Chemists; Univ. (Ann Arbor); Miles River Yacht, DuPont Country, Wilmington Country. Home: Box 606 Cokesbury Village Hockessin DE 19707

HOLBROOK, HAL, actor; b. Cleve., Feb. 17, 1925; s. Harold Rowe and Aileen (Davenport) H.; m. Ruby Elaine Johnston, Sept. 22, 1945 (div.); children—Victoria, David; m. Carol Rossen; 1 dau., Eve. Student, Suffield Acad., 1933-37, Culver Mil. Acad., 1938-42; B.A. with honors, Denison U., 1948. Played summer stock cos., 1947-53; organized (with wife) two-person stage prodn., touring high schs., clubs, univs., 1948-53, repertoire included scenes from, Shakespeare, Mollere, Victoria Regina, Elizabeth the Queen; and a sketch based on Mark Twain's short story An Encounter with an Interviewer; appeared TV as Abraham Lincoln, 1953; assembled: solo show Mark Twain Tonight, 1953; night club performances, 1955-56; on tour U.S. TV appearances, 1954-59, in N.Y.C., 1959, 66; on tour, 1960-63, TV spl., CBS, 1967; recording: theatre presentation Mark Twain Tonight, 1959, 61, 67; concert engagements, U.S., Can., Vancouver Festival, Edinburgh Festival, Saudi Arabia, European tour auspices, Dept. State with ANTA, 1959-60; performed: two-character play Do You Know the Milky Way, Vancouver, also N.Y.C., 1961, Am. Shakespeare Festival, Stratford, Conn., 1962; toured: Mark Twain Tonight, 1964—; appeared in: play The Glass Menagerie, N.Y.C., 1965; also TV, (movies) The Whole World is Watching, 1969, A Clear and Present Danger, 1970, Travis Logan, Suddenly Single, Goodbye Raggedy Ann, That Certain Summer, 1971-72 (Emmy nomination best actor in a drama), The Pueblo, 1973 (Emmy awards for best actor in a drama, actor of year in a spl.), Sandburg's Lincoln, 1974-75 (Emmy award outstanding lead actor in a ltd. series), Our Town, 1977 (Emmy nomination outstanding lead actor in a drama or comedy spl.), The Awakening Land, 1978 (Emmy nomination outstanding lead actor in ltd. series), When Hell Was In Session, 1979, The Senator, NBC, 1970-71 (Emmy award, Best actor in dramatic series); plays Abe Lincoln in Illinois, N.Y.C., 1963; appeared: Tartuffe, Lincoln Center Repertory Co., 1963-65; appeared in play: the Apple Tree, N.Y.C., 1967, I Never Sang for My Father, 1968, Man of La Mancha, 1968, Does a Tiger Wear a Necktie, 1969, Lake of the Woods, 1972; appeared in: motion picture The Group, 1965, Wild in the Streets, 1968, The People Next Door, 1970, The Great White Hope, 1970, They Only Kill Their Masters, 1972, Magnum Force, 1973, The Girl from Petrovka, 1974, Midway, 1976, All the President's Men, 1976, Rituals, 1977, Julia, 1978, Capricorn I, 1978, Natural Enemies, 1979; (Tony award 1966); Author: Mark Twain Tonight, 1959. Mem. com. on internat. cultural exchange Nat. Council on Arts and Govt. Served with C.E. AUS, 1943-46. Recipient Vernon Rice Meml. award, 1959, Outer Circle award, 1959; spl. citation for Mark Twain Tonight N.Y. Drama Critics Circle, 1966; Torch of Liberty award Anti-Defamation League B'nai B'rith, 1972. Mem. Mark Twain Meml. Assn. Club: Players (N.Y.C.). Address: Bresler Wolff Cota Livingston 10000 Santa Monica Blvd Suite 305 Los Angeles CA 90067

HOLBROOK, HOLLIS HOWARD, educator, painter, sculptor; b. Natick, Mass., Feb. 7, 1909; s. Goldwin P. and Jessie (Underwood) H.; m. Vivian Alma Nicholas, June 26, 1937; children: Ferris, Nicholas (dec.), Peter W. Student, Boston U. Evening Sch., 1928-30, Mass. Sch. Art, 1930-34; B.F.A., Yale U., 1936. Designer, Dennison Mfg. Co., Framingham, Mass., 1929-30; illustrator AP, N.Y.C., 1943; designer Warren Telechron Co., 1943; tchr. art U. Fla., 1938, successively instr., asst. and asso. prof., prof., 1947-48, 51-79, head prof., 1948-51; instr. Penland (N.C.) Sch. Art, summer 1971-78, artist-scholar, 1975. One-man show, Shillard Smith Art Center, Clearwater, Fla., 1975, Daytona (Fla.) Mus. Arts and Scis., 1980; exhibited in group shows, Pa. Acad. Ann., 1961, Ill. Biennial, Delgado Mus., 1963, Corcoran Bienniel, 1965, Norton Gallery, Palm Beach, Fla., 1971, Bklyn. Mus. Art, 1980; represented in collections including, Canton (Ohio) Art Inst., Sheldon Swope Art Gallery, U. Ga. Mus., Richmond (Va.) Library, Norfolk (Va.) Mus. Arts and Scis., U. Fla., Coll. William and Mary, Walter Chrysler Jr., So. Coll., Lakeland, Fla., Clemson U., Daytona Mus. Arts and Scis., frescoes in, Biblioteca Michoacan, Mexico, murals, Fountain of Youth Mus., St. Augustine, Fla., Library of U. Fla., murals (awarded by govt. in competitions) in post offices, Natick, Mass., Haleyville, Ala., Jeanerette, La., mural series, adminstrn. bldg., R.I. Coll. Edn., Providence, 18 panels in Post Office, Ocala, Fla., 1963; John Eliot mural in pub. library, Natick. Mem. Gainesville Cultural Commn., 1973-76. Served USN, 1944-45. Recipient Honor award Columbia Mus. Art, 1960, Atwater Kent award Soc. Four Arts, 1964, 1st award for painting Southeastern Ann., 1967; U. Fla. Grad. Sch. grantee for creative work, 1965. Fellow Royal Soc. Arts; mem. Fla. Edn. Assn. (art sect. sec. 1943), So. States Art League (dir. 1946-48), Fla. Fedn. Art (pres. 1947), Fla. Artists Group (pres. 1948-51), Nat. Soc. Mural Painters. Home: 1710 SW 35th Pl Gainesville FL 32608

HOLBROOK, RICHARD DRAPER, high technology company executive; b. Attleboro, Mass., June 28, 1920; s. Winford Franklin and Bessie Emeline (Lancaster) H.; m. Georgia Lois Wallace, Feb. 16, 1946; children: Troy, Lisa Holbrook Kaye, Mark Richard. B.SC. In Chemistry, Brown U., 1942, Ph.D. in Physics, 1950. Assoc. group head GMX div. Los Alamos Sci. Lab., 1949-53; assoc. dept. head Rand Corp., Santa Monica, Calif., 1953-61; dep. chif ballistic missle div. Advanced Research Project Agy. U.S Dept. Def., Washington, 1958-59; cons. Advanced Research Projects Agy. U.S Dept., Washington, 1959-64; dir. Mil. Research and Devel. Ctr., Bangkok, Thailand, 1965-68; exec. v.p. Flow Gen. Inc., McLean, Va., 1978—; pres. Gen. Research Corp., McLean, Va., 1981-82. Served to capt. AUS, 1943-46. Decorated Knight Comdr. Crown of Thailand, 1968; recipient Civilian Meritorious Service medal U.S. Dept. of Def., 1968. Mem. Sigma Xi. Republican. Episcopalian. Club: Royal Bangkok Sports. Home: 6532 79th St Cabin John MD 20818 2d Home: 636 Ricardo Ave Santa Barbara CA 93109 Office: Flow General Inc 7655 Old Spring House Rd McLean VA 22102

HOLBROOK, ROBERT SUMNER, economist, educator; b. Los Angeles, June 30, 1932; s. Harry Irving and Margaret (Avery) H.; m. Carol Ann Riggs, Oct. 24, 1954 (div. Apr. 1984); children: David, Kirsten. Student, Calif. Inst. Tech., 1950-52; A.B., U. San Francisco, 1961; M.A. in Stats., U. Calif., Berkeley, 1964; Ph.D. in Econs., 1965. Mechanic, IBM, San Francisco, 1956-61; asst. prof. econs. U. Mich., Ann Arbor, 1965-70, asso. prof., 1970-75, prof., 1975—, asso. dean, 1978-81, asso. v.p. acad. affairs, 1981—; cons. Govt. of P.R., 1975, 78, U.S. Dept. Treasury, 1977; vis. economist Bank of Can., 1971-72. Contbr. articles to profl. jours. Served with USAF, 1952-56. NDEA fellow, 1961-64; Ford Found. dissertation fellow, 1964-65. Mem. Am. Econ. Assn., Royal Econ. Soc., Am. Fin. Assn. Home: 520 Oswego St Ann Arbor MI 48104 Office: Dept Econs U Mich Ann Arbor MI 48109

HOLBROOKE, RICHARD CHARLES ALBERT, executive; b. N.Y.C., Apr. 24, 1941; s. Dan and Trudi (Moos) H.; children: David Dan, Anthony Andrew. B.A., Brown U., 1962; postgrad., Princeton, 1969-70. Joined Fgn. Service, 1962; served in, Vietnam, 1963-66; mem. White House staff, 1966-67; assigned State Dept. and; staff Paris (France) peace talks, 1968-69; dir. Peace Corps, Morocco, 1970-72; mng. editor Fgn. Policy mag., 1972-77; dir. publs. Carnegie Endowment for Internat. Peace, 1973-76; cons. Commn. Orgn. Govt. for Conduct of Fgn., 1974-75; coordinator fgn. policy and def. issues Carter-Mondale Presdl. Campaign, 1976; contbg. editor Newsweek Internat., 1976; asst. sec. for East Asian and Pacific affairs Dept. State, Washington, 1977-81; v.p. Public Strategies, Washington, 1981—; sr. advisor Lehman Bros., 1981—; columnist Asian Wall St. Jour., 1981—; Trustee Internat. Voluntary Services; mem. Trilateral Commn. Author: vol. The Pentagon Papers, 1967; Contbr. numerous articles to, N.Y. Times, Washington Post, Wall St. Jour., Atlantic, numerous other mags. and jours. Mem. Council Fgn. Relations, Inst. Strategic Studies. Home: 1215 29 St NW Washington DC 20007 Office: 2550 M St NW Washington DC 20037

HOLCK, FREDERICK H. GEORGE, clergyman, educator; b. Neuenburg, Germany, June 6, 1927; came to U.S., 1963, naturalized, 1968; s. Edward W. and Elizabeth L. (Luger) H.; m. Miriam I. Ahlgren, Jan. 23, 1954; children: Mark, Christopher, Thomas, David, Timothy. Student, U. Heidelberg, 1947-49, U. Tuebingen, 1949-52; Lic. Phil. in Philosophy summa cum laude, U. Salzburg, 1953; Ph.D. in Comparative Religion summa cum laude, U. Salzburg, 1954. Tutor, Helsinki, 1954-56; parish minister Lutheran State Ch., Germany, 1956-57; sr. lectr. Peshawar U., Pakistan, 1957-59; parish minister in, Can., 1960-62; prof. theology and history of religions Luth. Theol. Sem., Saskatoon, Sask., Can., 1962-63; asst. prof. religion and human devel. Lake Erie Coll., Painesville, Ohio, 1963-66; asst. prof. religion and Oriental philosophy Cleve. State U., 1966-68, assoc. prof., acting chmn. dept. philosophy and religion, 1968-70, prof., chmn. dept. religion, 1970-80, dir. Asian Studies Program, 1969-80, dir. Extended Campus Coll., 1982—; acad. v.p., dean coll. N.C. Wesleyan Coll., Rocky Mount, N.C., 1980-82. Editor: Ohio Jour. Religious Studies, 1972-80; Co-author, editor: Death and Eastern Thought, 1974; co-editor internat. editorial bd.: Ency. Hinduism, 1979-82; contbr. articles to profl. jours. and encys. Mem. Archtl. and Zoning Bds., Kirtland Hills, Ohio, 1970-72; bd. dirs. Greater Cleve. Counseling Service-Interch. Council, 1978-80, v.p., 1982—; mem. adv. bd. World Fellowship Religions, 1978-82. Mem. Am. Acad. Religion, Ohio Acad. Religion (pres. 1974-75), Am. Philos. Assn., Nat. Alliance for Family Life (clin. mem., pres. S.E. region 1981-82). Club: Rotary. Home: 7031 Waite Hill Rd Waite Hill OH 44094 Office: Cleve State U Cleveland OH 44115

HOLCOMB, DONALD FRANK, physicist; b. Chesterton, Ind., Nov. 8, 1925; s. Roger L. and Ethel (Frank) H.; m. Barbara Page, Aug. 26, 1950; children: Douglas Page, Jane D., Nancy M. A.B., DePauw U., 1949; M.S., U. Ill., 1950, Ph.D., 1954. Instr. U. Ill., 1954; mem. faculty Cornell U., 1954—, prof. physics, 1962—, dir. lab. atomic and solid state physics, 1964-68, chmn. dept. physics, 1969-74, 82, trustee, 1976-81; cons. Corning Glass Research Lab., 1959-64, Central Inst. Indsl. Research, Oslo, Norway, 1962. Contbr. profl. jours. Served with USNR, 1944-46. Sr. vis. fellow NATO, 1962; Guggenheim fellow, 1968-69; Sci. Research Council sr. fellow, 1978. Fellow Am. Phys. Soc.; mem. Am. Assn. Physics Tchrs., Sigma Xi. Presbyterian. Spl. research solid state physics, chem. physics. Home: 141 Northview Rd Ithaca NY 14850

HOLCOMB, GEORGE RUHLE, anthropology educator; b. Kankakee, Ill., Oct. 25, 1927; s. William Irving and Rosa (Ruhle) H.; m. Ellen Jean Kaia Jacobsen, Aug. 3, 1952; children: Kaia Christine, Ellen Elizabeth, Carolyn Jean. B.A., U. Wis., 1950, M.A., 1952, Ph.D., 1956. Teaching asst. U. Wis., 1951-53, research asst., 1953-54; instr. anatomy Sch. Medicine Creighton U., 1954-57; asst. prof. anatomy Sch. Medicine, U. N.C., Chapel Hill, 1957-68, prof. anthropology, 1968—, asso. dean, 1962-65, dean research adminstrn., 1965-82; bd. dirs. Oak Ridge Asso. Univs.; mem., chmn. conf. com. Nat. Conf. on Advancement of Research; trustee South-East Consortium for Internat. Devel. Contbr. articles to sci. jours. Served with AUS, 1946-47. Fellow A.A.A.S., Am. Anthrop. Assn.; mem. Nat. Council U. Research Adminstrs. (past pres.), Am. Assn. Phys. Anthropologists, Am. Assn. Anatomists, Sigma Xi. Club: Cosmos. Home: 302 Burlage Circle Chapel Hill NC 27514

HOLCOMB, HENRY JARMAN, journalist; b. Dallas, May 23, 1942; s. Luther Jenkins and Elaine (Parks) H.; m. Pamela Darnell, June 22, 1963 (div. 1969); m. Christine E. Malarin, Oct. 2, 1971; 1 dau., Jennifer. Student, Baylor U., Waco, Tex., 1963. Reporter, columnist Orange Leader, Tex., 1964-67; asst. mng. editor The Baytown Sun, Tex., 1967-68; reporter Houston Post, 1968-72; city editor Cin. Post, 1972-77; chief asst. news editor Detroit News, 1977-79; mng. editor Fort Worth Star-Telegram, 1979—; fgn. editor Phila. Inquirer, 1977-78. Pres. Parenting Guidance Ctr., Fort Worth, 1983. Recipient Investigative Reporting award UPI Editors Assn., 1972, Continuing Excellence award Headliner Club, Fort Worth, 1969. Mem. Soc. Profl. Journalists. Clubs: Headliners (dir.), Century II (Fort Worth)). Home: 4279 Balboa Fort Worth TX 76133 Office: Fort Worth Star-Telegram 400 W 7th St Fort Worth TX 76102

HOLCOMB, M. STASER, naval officer; b. Detroit, Jan. 18, 1932; s. Maurice Staser and Uva Virginia (Spratt) H.; m. Joanne Partridge Williams, June 20, 1955; children: Richard Staser, Helen Rae, Donald Alan, Ross Douglas, Sally Elizabeth. B.S., U.S. Naval Acad., 1953; M.S. in Physics, U.S. Naval Postgrad. Sch., 1960. Commd. ensign U.S. Navy, 1953, designated naval aviator, 1954, advanced through grades to vice adm., 1979; anti-submarine warfare specialist; assigned Office Sec. Def. for systems analysis, 1964-67; comdr. carrier ASW squadron, 1970; comdr. USS Guam, 1973-74; dir. Navy systems analysis, 1974-75; mil. asst. to sec. def., 1976-77; comdr. Carrier Group One, 1978-79; dir. Navy program planning, 1979-81; comdr. U.S. 7th Fleet, 1981-83. Active local Boy Scouts Am. Decorated D.S.M., Legion of Merit, Joint Service commendation medal, Navy Commendation medal., Order Nat. Security (Korea), Order Rising Sun (Japan). Mem. U.S. Naval Inst., Council Fgn. Relations, Sigma Xi. Club: Seattle Tennis. Home: 7 N Audley St London England Office: Dep CdNC US Naval Forces Europe London W1

HOLCOMB, RICHARD YOUNG, lawyer; b. Fayetteville, Ark., Jan. 28, 1915; s. Bruce and Daisy (Young) H.; m. Sylvia Wooster, Aug. 24, 1946; children: Bruce, Martha. A.B., U. Ark., 1935; LL.B., Columbia U., 1938. Bar: N.Y. 1938. Ptnr. Donovan Leisure Newton & Irvine, N.Y.C., 1938—; village atty. Village of Ardsley, N.Y., 1957. Served to capt. U.S. Army, 1941-46; ETO. Mem. ABA, Assn. Bar City N.Y., N.Y. State Bar Assn. Democrat. Presbyterian. Club: Hemisphere. Home: Roland Rd Irvington NY 10533 Office: 30 Rockefeller Plaza New York NY 10112

HOLCOMB, WILLIAM A., oil and gas exploration, pipeline executive; b. Lockhart, Tex., Oct. 31, 1926; s. William A. and Annie O. (Pyl) H. B.B.A., U. Tex., 1949; J.D., U. Houston, 1963. Bar: Tex. bar 1963. Acctg. supr. Fireman's Fund-Am. Ins. Companies, 1950-51; mgr. ins. dept. Transcontinental Gas Pipe Line Corp., 1959-72; asst. treas.-asst. sec. Transco Companies, Inc., Houston, 1972-74, corp. sec. and/ or asst. corp. sec. co. and various subsidiaries, 1977-82; cons., real estate broker, 1983—. Served with AUS, 1944-46. Life mem. Tex. Assn. Bus.; mem. State Bar Tex., Am. Bar Assn., Am. Mgmt. Assn., Am. Gas Assn., Interstate Natural Gas Assn. Am., Am. Soc. Corp. Secs., Mus. Natural Sci., Houston Bd. Realtors, Houston C. of C. (past chmn. ins. com.), Afton Oaks Civic Club, U. Tex. Ex-Students Assn. Club: University (Houston). Home: 3134 Newcastle St Houston TX 77027 Office: 602 Harold Houston TX 77006

HOLCOMBE, ROBERT SWAINE, lawyer, cons. co. exec.; b. Bronxville, N.Y., July 9, 1942; s. Marshall Maynard and Vivian (Swaine) H.; m. Martha Jane Downes, June 4, 1966; children—Robert Swaine, Kathryn E., Samuel D. A.B., Princeton U., 1964; J.D., Columbia U., 1968, M.B.A., 1968. Bar: N.Y. State bar 1969. Asso. firm Dewey, Ballantine, Bushby, Palmer & Wood, N.Y.C., 1968-77; asst. gen. counsel, corporate sec. Indian Head Inc., N.Y.C., 1977-79; v.p., gen. counsel Planning Research Corp., Washington, 1979—. Mem. Am. Bar Assn., N.Y. State Bar Assn. Republican. Clubs: Westwood Country, Regency Racquet. Home: 1029 Union Church Rd McLean VA 22102 Office: 1500 Planning Research Dr McLean VA 22102

HOLCOMBE, WILLIAM ALLEN, newspaper executive; b. Phila., July 8, 1924; s. Albert Thomas and Alice Collet (Cunningham) H.; m. Jane Ellen Rauch, Jan. 10, 1959; children: Polly Ellen and Susan Jane (twins). B.A., U. Mo., 1948. Mem. mgmt. Course staff Am. Mgmt. Assn., N.Y.C., 1952-57; mgr. labor relations Cin. Enquirer, 1957-60; asst. to mng. editor N.Y. Times, 1960-68; asst. bus. mgr. Cleve. Press, 1968-76, bus. mgr., 1976-81; v.p., gen. mgr. Pitts. Press Co., 1981—; dir. Sunday Metro Inc., N.Y.C. Bd. dirs. Pitts Symphony Assn., Better Bus. Pitts.; v.p. Golden Triangle Assn. Served with AUS, 1943-45; PTO. Decorated Purple Heart, Combat Inf. Badge. Mem. Am. Newspaper Pubs. Assn., Pa. Newspaper Pubs. Assn., Pitts. C. of C. (dir. 1981—). Republican. Clubs: Duquesne, Chartiers Country, Pitts. Press; Allegheney (Pitts.). Office: Pitts Press Co 34 Blvd of Allies Pittsburgh PA 15230

HOLDEN, DAN A., manufacturing company human resources executive; b. Sheboygan, Wis., Nov. 7, 1937; s. Frank Pierce and Dorothy (Kubel) H.; m. Delores Donna Gray, June 30, 1964; children: Scott D., Kevin A. B.A., Ripon Coll., 1960; M.A., Ind. U., 1964. Dir. compensation Internat. Harvester, Chgo., 1978-80, 81—, v.p. human resources agrl. equipment group, 1980-82. Served to 1st lt. U.S. Army, 1961-63. Mem. Am. Compensation Assn., Conf. Bd. Council on Compensation. Republican. Lutheran. Home: 45 Kathleen Dr Des Plaines IL 60016 Office: Internat Harvester 401 N Michigan Ave Chicago IL 60611

HOLDEN, DONALD, publishing company executive; b. Los Angeles, Apr. 22, 1931; s. Mack and Miriam (Epstein) H.; m. Wilma Shaffer, Jan. 10, 1954; children: Wendy, Blake. B.A., Columbia U., 1951; M.A., Ohio State U., 1952. Teaching asst. English Ohio State U., Columbus, 1951-52; dir. pub. relations Phila. Coll. Art, 1953-55; dir. pub. relations and personnel Henry Dreyfuss (indsl. designer), N.Y.C., 1956-60; assoc. mgr. pub. relations Met. Mus. Art, N.Y.C., 1960-61; art cons. Fortune mag., N.Y.C., 1962; editorial dir. Watson-Guptill Publs. (art books), 1963-79, Am. Artist mag., N.Y.C., 1971-75; lectr. in field. Author: Art Career Guide, 1961, rev. edits., 1967, 73, 83, Whistler Landscapes and Seascapes, 1969; under pseudonym Wendon Blake: Acrylic Watercolor Painting, 1970, Complete Guide to Acrylic Painting, 1971, Creative Color: A Practical Guide for Oil Painters, 1972, rev. edit, 1983, Landscape Painting in Oil, 1976, The Watercolor Painting Book, 1978, The Acrylic Painting Book, 1978, The Oil Painting Book, 1979, The Portrait and Figure Painting Book, 1979, The Drawing Book, 1980, The Color Book, 1981, Complete Guide to Landscape Painting in Oil, 1981, Painting in Alkyd, 1982; Contbr. articles to profl. publs.; editorial cons., Watson-Guptill Publs., 1979—; drawings exhibited in one-man exhbns., sculpture and drawings in numerous group shows. Mem. Authors Guild, N.Y. Artists Equity Assn., Am. Inst. Graphic Arts, Nat. Art Edn. Assn., Phi Beta Kappa. Club: Century Assn. Whistler book selected for White House Library by Assn. Am. Pubs., 1975. Home: 128 Deertrack Ln Irvington-on-Hudson NY 10533 Office: Watson-Guptill Publs 1515 Broadway New York NY 10036

HOLDEN, JAMES PHILLIP, lawyer; b. Pueblo, Colo., June 10, 1932; s. John Otis and Irene Agnes (Cronan) H.; m. Mary O'Toole, Sept. 20, 1958; children: James P., Edward J., Richard T. B.S., U. Colo., 1953; J.D., Georgetown U., 1960. Bar: D.C., U.S. Ct. Appeals (D.C. cir.), U.S. Ct. Appeals (4th cir.), U.S. Supreme Ct., U.S. Tax Ct. Assoc. Steptoe & Johnson, Chartered, Washington, 1960-64, ptnr., 1965—; adj. prof. Georgetown U. Law Ctr.; mem. adv. group to commr. IRS, 1979-80. Author: (with Bernard Wolfman) Ethical Problems in Federal Tax Practice, 1981. Served to lt. USN, 1954-60. Mem. ABA. Clubs: Metropolitan (Washington); Chevy Chase (Md.). Office: 1250 Connecticut Ave NW Washington DC 20036

HOLDEN, JAMES STUART, judge; b. Bennington, Vt., Jan. 29, 1914; s. Edward Henry and Mary Anstiss (Thayer) H.; m. Helen Elizabeth Vetal, Mar. 3, 1941; children: Susan (Mrs. Spaeth), Peter Vetal, James Stuart. A.B., Dartmouth, 1935; LL.B., Union U., 1938. Bar: Vt. bar 1938. Practice in, Bennington, 1938-41, 46-48, state's atty., Bennington County, 1946-48; chmn. Vt. Pub. Service Commn., 1948-49; superior judge State, 1949-56; assoc. justice Supreme Ct. Vt., 1956-63, chief justice, 1963-72; U.S. dist. judge for Dist. of Vt., 1972-84, sr. U.S. dist. judge for, 1984—; Chmn. Vt. Statutory Revision Commn., 1957-62; chmn. provisional com. to establish Nat. Center for State Cts., 1971. Trustee Vt. State Library, 1959—. Served to maj. 43d Inf. Div. AUS, 1941-46. Mem. 43d Inf. Div. Vets. Assn. (past comdr.), Am., Vt. bar assns., Conf. Chief Justices (vice chmn. 1969-70, chmn. 1971—), Am. Judicature Soc., Inst. Jud. Adminstrn., Am. Law Inst. Protestant Episcopalian. Home: North Bennington VT 05257

HOLDEN, JOHN BERNARD, educator; b. DeCliff, Ohio, Sept. 18, 1910; s. William Edward and Elsie Mae (Kohn) H.; m. A. Alberta Stegemiller, Feb. 2, 1941; children: John Bernard, Peggy Ann, Charles Eugene. B.S., Ohio U., 1932; M.A., Ohio State U., 1936, Ph.D., 1955. Prin., tchr. Ohio schs., 1932-37; head history and speech dept. Wyoming (Ohio) Schs., j71937-41; dir. adult edn., tchr. speech and history, Hamilton, Ohio, 1941-50; cons. continuing edn. Mich. State U., 1950-56; specialist gen. adult edn. U.S. Office Edn., 1956-58; dir. Grad. Sch., U.S. Dept. Agr., 1958-81; pres. Beacon Coll., Washington, 1982—; Pres. World Federalist Ednl. Fund, 1968-72. Author: Score Card for Community Adult Education Program, 1951; Contbr.: chpt. to Materials and Methods in Adult Education; articles to edn. publs. Served with AUS, 1944-46. Recipient Spl. Merit award Nat. Assn. Pub. Sch. Adult educators, 1955; Meritorious award Adult Edn. Assn. Mich., 1956; Distinguished Alumni award Ohio U., 1964; Delbert Clark adult edn. award, 1966; Distinguished Adult Educator award Adult Edn. Assn. Greater Washington, 1975. Mem. Ohio Tchrs. Speech Assn. (past pres.), Ohio Adult Edn. Assn. (past pres.), Adult Edn. Assn. Mich. (past pres.), Adult Edn. Assn. U.S. (exec. bd., past chmn. nat. pub. relations and membership, pres. 1964-65), United World Federalists (chmn. Washington chpt. 1958-60), Phi Delta Kappa, Kappa Kappa Tau, Tau Kappa Alpha. Clubs: Cosmos, Internat. (Washington). Home: 510 N St SW Washington DC 20024

HOLDEN, MATTHEW, JR., political scientist, educator, economic and political consultant; b. Mound Bayou, Miss., Sept. 12, 1931; s. Matthew and Estelle (Welch) H.; m. Dorothy Amanda Howard, June 29, 1963; 1 son, John Matthew Alexander; 1 stepson, Paul C. Hendricks. Student, U. Chgo., 1946-50; B.A., Roosevelt U., 1952; M.A., Northwestern U., 1956, Ph.D., 1961. Mem. faculty Wayne State U., Detroit, 1961-69, assoc. prof., 1966-67, prof., 1967-69; asst. prof. U. Pitts., 1963-66; prof. polit. sci. U. Wis.-Madison, 1969-81; commr. Pub. Service Commn. Wis., Madison, 1974-77; mem. U.S. Air Quality Adv. Bd., 1971-74; commr. Fed. Energy Regulatory Commn., Washington, 1977-81; Henry L. and Grace M. Doherty prof. govt. and fgn. affairs U. Va., Charlottesville, Va., 1981—; dir Atlantic City Electric Co, N.J.; mem. panel on comml. arbitration Am. Arbitration Assn., N.Y.C., 1982. Author: The Divisible Republic, 1973; editor: Varieties of Political Conservatism, 1974; contbr.: numerous articles to profl. jours. Served with U.S. Army, 1955-57; Korea. Mem. Nat. Acad. Pub. Adminstrn., Am. Polit. Sci. Assn. (v.p. 1977, award for scholarship, teaching and service to the profession 1982), Nat. Acad. Scis., Assembly of Behavior and Social Scis., Mid.-Am. Regulatory Commrs. (v.p. 1977), Nat. Assn. Regulatory Commrs. (exec. com. 1979-81). Democrat. Episcopalian. Home: 1934 Lewis Mountain Rd Charlottesville VA 22903 Office: Dept of Govt and Fgn Affairs Charlottesville VA 22903

HOLDEN, PATRICK CORNISH, aluminum company executive; b. Chepstow, Eng., Feb. 4, 1924; came to U.S., 1963, naturalized, 1968; s. Hugh Capel and Margaret Knight Bruce H.; m. Jean Margaret Fisher, July 1, 1950; children: Richard, Mark, David, Jennifer. M.A. in Mech. Scis., Trinity Coll., Cambridge U., 1944; diploma, Centre d'Etudes Industrielles, Geneva, 1949. Mktg. and sales positions Alcan Aluminum Ltd., London, Toronto, Ont., Can.; and Montreal, Que., Can., N.Y. and Cleve., 1948-71; pres. Alcan Services div. Alcan Aluminum Corp., Cleve., 1971-78, 1978—. Served to maj. Brit. Airborne Forces, 1944-47. Episcopalian. Clubs: Hudson Country, Western Res., Racquet. Home: 40 N Hayden Pkwy Hudson OH 44236 Office: 100 Erieview Plaza Cleveland OH 44114

HOLDEN, RAYMOND THOMAS, physician; b. Washington, Apr. 11, 1904; s. Raymond Thomas and Celeste Selma (Moritz) H.; m. Mary Lightle, Oct. 9, 1958; 1 dau., Mary Elliott. Student, U. Notre Dame, 1922-24; M.D., Georgetown U., 1928, D.Sc. (hon.), 1980. Diplomate: Am. Bd. Obstetrics and Gynecology. Intern Providence Hosp., Washington, 1928-29, asso., then attending obstetrician and gynecologist, 1932-56, cons., 1956—; resident Columbia Hosp. for Women, Washington, 1929-30, asst., asso., attending staff, 1933, chief med. staff, 1952-54, 62-64, acting adminstr., 1958-59; preceptorship Dr. R.Y. Sullivan Georgetown U. Sch. Medicine, 1930-32; asso., attending obstetrics and gynecology D.C. Gen Hosp., 1932-47; asst., asso., also attending obstetrics and gynecology Georgetown U. Hosp., 1933—; from clin. instr. to clin. prof. obstetrics and gynecology Georgetown U. Sch. Medicine, 1933—; cons. obstetrics and gynecology U.S. Naval Hosp., Bethesda, Md., 1948-68. Bd. dirs., exec. com. Tb Assn. D.C., 1947-49; bd. dirs., exec. com. D.C. div. Am. Cancer Soc., 1950-56; mem. Health Facilities Planning Council, Washington, 1964—; bd. dirs. D.C. chpt. ARC, mem. exec. com., 1975—; Trustee Columbia Hosp. for Women. Served to capt., M.C. USNR, 1942-46; rear adm. Res. Fellow A.C.S., Am. Coll. Obstetrics and Gynecologists; mem. AMA (D.C. mem. Ho. Dels. 1952-68, chmn. com. on human reproduction 1964-68, trustee 1968-77, vice chmn. 1974-75, chmn. 1975-77), D.C. Med. Soc. (chmn. exec. bd. 1951-52, pres. 1946-47), Washington Gynecology Soc. (sec. 1950-54, pres. 1956), So. Med. Assn., Assn. Profs. Gynecology and Obstetrics, Am. Legion, Alpha Omega Alpha. Clubs: Fifty Year of Am. Medicine (pres. 1979-80), Chevy Chase, Metropolitan. Home: 5120 Watson St NW Washington DC 20016 Office: 3800 Reservoir Rd N W Washington DC 20007

HOLDEN, REUBEN ANDRUS, coll. pres.; b. Louisville, Sept. 2, 1918; s. Reuben Andrus and Grace (Morgan) H.; m. Elizabeth C. Walker, June 23, 1951; children—Grace Morgan, Reuben Andrus 5th, George H. Walker, Mary Carter. B.A., Yale U., 1940, M.A., 1948, Ph.D., 1951, L.H.D., 1971. Asst. to dean of coll. Yale U., 1946-47, asst. to pres., 1947-52, sec. of univ., 1953-71; pres. Warren Wilson Coll., Swannanoa, N.C., 1971—; dir. Asheville bd. N.C. Nat. Bank; trustee Conn. Savs. Bank, 1955-71; Mem. adv. council fin. aid HEW.; Civilian aide to sec. army, 1962-68. Bd. dirs. New Haven YMCA, 1960-71; bd. dirs. Community Progress, Inc., 1962-65, pres., 1965-68; bd. dirs. Blue Ridge Assembly, 1972—, Swannanoa Med. Center, 1973-81, Asheville Area Red Cross, 1974-79, Asheville United Way, 1977-80; Trustee Asheville Sch., 1948-74, Hopkins Grammar Sch., 1952-71, Edward W. Hazen Found., 1966-74; chmn. Edward W. Hazen Found., 1970-73; trustee Jane Coffin Childs Fund Med. Research, Charles A. Coffin Fund, Foote Sch., 1964-71; pres. Foote Sch., 1968-71; trustee Ind. Coll. Funds Am., 1976-79; v.p. Ind. Coll. Fund of N.C., 1980—; chmn. Swannanoa Council, 1981—. Served with AUS, 1941-46; CBI. Decorated Bronze Star, U.S.; Spl. Breast of Yun Hwei, China; Distinguished Civilian award. Mem. Culinary Inst. Am. (gov. 1948-73, chmn. 1968-70), Yale-in-China Assn. (trustee 1947—, pres. 1966-72), Phi Beta Kappa. Presbyterian. Clubs: Rotarian., Yale r2(N.Y.C.); Graduates (New Haven); Pen and Plate (Asheville). Home: Warren Wilson Coll Swannanoa NC 28778

HOLDEN, WILLIAM DOUGLAS, surgeon; b. Pittsfield, Mass., Aug. 25, 1912; s. Harry and Katherine C. (MacInnis) H.; m. Janet Cobb, Dec. 28, 1936; children—John, Frank, Katherine. A.B., Cornell U., 1934, M.D., 1937. Instr. surgery Case-Western Res. U. Med. Sch., 1946-47, sr. instr. surgery, 1947-48, asst. prof., 1948-49, asso. prof., 1948-49, Oliver H. Payne prof. surgery, 1950-77, prof. surgery, 1977—; dir. surgery Univ. Hosps., Cleve., 1950-77, mem. staff, 1977—. Contbr. profl. jours. Mem. Am., Central surg. assns., Soc. U. Surgeons, Soc. Vascular Surgery. Home: 2195 Demington Dr Cleveland Heights OH 44106 Office: Lakeside Hospital Cleveland OH 44106

HOLDEN, WILLIAM P., manufacturing company executive; b. N.Y.C., Sept. 5, 1933; s. Nicholas and Agnes (McNamara) H.; m. Jean Anne Peter, Sept. 3, 1960; 1 son, Gregory. B.B.A., Pace U., 1962. Budget dir. Reeves Bros., Inc., N.Y.C., 1956-63; asst. to pres. Comfy, Inc. (subs. Reeves Bros. Inc.), N.Y.C., 1963-67; group controller Dorr-Oliver Inc., Stamford, Conn., 1967-69, corporate controller, 1969-73, treas., corporate controller, chief financial officer, 1973-76, v.p. finance, 1976-81, v.p. internat., 1981-82; v.p. chief fin. officer, sec. Moore Spl. Tool Co.,-Inc., 1982—; dir. Nat. Filter Media Corp., Moore AG. Served with USAF, 1952-56. Mem. Financial Execs. Inst. (dir. So. Conn. chpt. 1976, 81, pres. So. Conn. chpt. 1979), MAPI Fin. Council III. Home: 2755 Congress St Fairfield CT 06430 Office: 77 Havemeyer Ln Stamford CT 06904 *The greatest success a person can achieve is to know that the level of achievement realized was attained after exerting one's best efforts without sacrificing honesty, integrity, character, or individuality.*

HOLDER, ANGELA RODDEY, lawyer, educator; b. Rock Hill, S.C., Mar. 13, 1938; d. John T. and Angela M. (Fisher) Roddey; 1 son, John Thomas Roddey Holder. Student, Radcliffe Coll., 1955-56; B.A., Newcomb Coll., 1958; postgrad., Faculty of Law-King's Coll., London, 1957-59; J.D., Tulane U., 1960; LL.M., Yale U., 1975. Bar: La. 1960, S.C. 1960, Conn. 1981. Counsel Roddey, Sumwalt & Carpenter, Rock Hill, S.C., 1960—; atty. criminal div. New Orleans Legal Aid Bur., 1961-62; counsel York County (S.C.) Family Ct., 1962-64; asst. prof. polit. sci. Winthrop Coll., Rock Hill, 1964-74; research assoc. Yale Law Sch., 1975-77, exec. dir. program in law, sci. and medicine, 1976-77; lectr. dept. pediatrics Yale Med. Sch., 1975-77, asst. clin. prof. pediatrics and law, 1977-79, assoc. clin. prof., 1979-83, clin. prof., 1983—; counsel for medicolegal affairs Yale-New Haven Hosp. and Yale Med. Sch., 1977—. Author: The Meaning of the Constitution, 1968, Medical Malpractice Law, 1975, 2d edit. 1978, Legal Issues in Pediatrics and Adolescent Medicine, 1977; contbg. editor: Prism mag.; contbg. editor., AMA; mem. editorial bd.: IRB; Law, Medicine and Health Care; contbr. articles to profl. jours. Mem. Rock Hill Sch. Bd., 1967-68; bd. dirs. Family Planning Clinic, chmn., 1970-73. Mem. ABA, S.C. Bar Assn. (medico-legal com. 1973—), La. Bar Assn., Soc. Med. Jurisprudence, Am. Soc. Hosp. Attys., Am. Soc. Law and Medicine (treas. 1981-83, sec. 1983—). Democrat. Episcopalian. Home: 23 Eld St Apt B New Haven CT 06511 Office: Yale-New Haven Hosp 789 Howard Ave New Haven CT 06504

HOLDER, GEOFFREY, dancer, actor, choreographer, director; b. Port-of-Spain, Trinidad, Aug. 1, 1930; s. Arthur and Louise (De Frense) H.; m. Carmen de Lavallade, June 26, 1955; 1 son. Ed., Queens Royal Coll., Port-of-Spain; student native dances in, W.Indies. Stage debut as mem., Roscoe Holder's Dance Co., Trinidad, 1942; formed own dance co., 1950; toured, P.R. and the Caribbean, 1953; U.S. debut; Broadway debut: House of Flowers, 1954; solo dancer with, Met. Opera, N.Y.C., 19S6-57; dramatic debut: Waiting for Godot, 1957; solo dancer: Show Boat, 1957, concerts with, Geoffrey Holder Dance Co., N.Y.C., 1956-60; appeared at, Festival of Two Worlds, Spoleto, Italy, 1958, Festividadi Ballet Hispanico, N.Y., 1979; choreographer: Brouhaha, 1960; Actors Studio prodn. Mhil Daiim, 1964, I Got a Song, 1974; dancer with, Josephine Baker's Revue, 1964; choreographer; costume designer: Three Songs for One; and costume designer: The Twelve Gates, 1964; dir., costume designer: The Wiz, Broadway, 1975; dir., costume designer, choreographer: Timbuktu, 1978; movie appearances include: All Night Long, 1961, Everything You've Always Wanted to Know About Sex, 1972, Live and Let Die, 1973, Swashbuckler, 1976, Annie, 1982; appeared in night clubs; TV appearances include: The Man Without a Country; paintings exhibited, Barbados Mus., San Juan, P.R., Barone Gallery, N.Y.C., Gallery of Brooks Atkinson Theatre, N.Y.C., Gropper Gallery, Cambridge, Mass., Griffin Gallery, N.Y.C., Grinnel Galleries, Detroit; recorded albums of W. Indian songs and album of Song Stories; author: Black Gods, Green Islands, 1957, Geoffrey Holder's Caribbean Cookbook, 1974; contbr.: articles to Playbill; others. (Guggenheim fellow in painting 1957); (Drama Desk award for The Wiz 1975, Tony award for best dir. of a musical, The Wiz 1975, also for costume design.). Recipient United Caribbean Youth award, 1962, Monarch award Nat. Council Culture and Art, 1982. Mem. AFTRA, Screen Actors Guild, Actors Equity Assn., AGVA. Address: care Donald Buchwald Assos 10 E 44th St New York NY 10017 *

HOLDER, HAROLD DOUGLAS, citrus and land company executive; b. Anniston, Ala., June 25, 1931; s. William Chester and Lucile (Kadle) H.; m. Shirlee Heiden, Apr. 5, 1971; children: Debra Holder Greene, Harold Douglas, Robert Douglas. Student, Anniston Bus. Coll., 1949, Jacksonville State U., 1954-57, Druitt Sch. Speech, 1962. Dept. mgr. Sears, Roebuck & Co., Anniston, 1954-57, merchandising mgr., Atlanta, 1957-59, dir. coll. recruiting, 1959-61, dir. exec. devel. program, 1961, asst. personnel dir., 1962-63, store mgr., Cocoa, Fla., 1965-67, Ocala, Fla., 1963-65, asst. zone mgr., Atlanta, 1967-68, asst. gen. mgr. mdse., 1968-69; sales promotion mgr. Sears in South, 1968; pres. Cunningham Drug Stores, Inc., Detroit, 1969-70, also dir.; v.p. Interstate Stores, 1971; pres. Rahall Communications Corp., 1971-73, also dir.; chmn. bd., chief exec. officer, dir. Am. Agronomics Corp., 1973—; chmn. exec. com., dir. Coastland Corp., Fla.; pres., dir. Golden Harvest, Inc.; dir. Kaplan Industries, Inc., Miracle Inc. of Bevard Co., CSI Electronics, Inc., Sun City Industries, Inc., Mega Com, Inc., Key West Harbour Devel. Corp., Westbank Enterprises Inc.; dir., treas. Bay Capital Corp. of Tampa; chmn. exec. com. Cutler-Fed., Inc.; pres. Harold Holder Leasing. Author: Don't Shoot, I'm Only a Trainee, 1975. Chmn. United Appeal, Ocala, Fla., 1964 Chmn. United Appeal, Cocoa, Fla., 1966; bd. dirs. United Way Hillsborough County (Fla.); Chmn. Heart Fund Drive, Ocala, 1964, Marion (Fla.) Com. of 100.; bd. dirs. So. Coll. Placement Assn., Am. Acad. Achievement; Bd. dirs. Marion chpt. ARC, Opera Arts Assn.; exec. com. SHARE, U. Fla.; chmn. bd. trustees Eckerd Coll.; trustee U. Tampa. Served with USMC, 1950- 53. Endowed Harold D. Holder chair of mgmt. Eckerd Coll.; Recipient Disting. Service award Marion County 4-H Club, 1965. Mem. Newcomen Soc., Chief Execs. Forum, C. of C. (chmn. beautification com., retail bus. com.), Young Pres. Orgn. (past chmn. Fla. chpt.). Episcopalian. Clubs: University, Palma Ceia Golf and Country, Tampa (Tampa, Fla.); St. Petersburg Yacht. Home: 5002 Shore Crest Circle Tampa FL 33609 Office: 4600 W Cypress St Suite 300 Tampa FL 33607

HOLDER, LEE, college dean; b. Upland, Calif., Jan. 19, 1932; s. Lee Newcomer and Mattie Beatrice (Richards) H.; m. Charlotte Rosa LaVars, Feb. 15, 1954; children: Lee Kurt, Liese Anne, Lawrence Keith, Lon Karl, Laurie Kristin. B.S., U. Calif.-Berkeley, 1953, M.P.H., 1958; postgrad., U. Wyo., 1961-63; Ph.D., U. Mich., 1968. With Oakland (Calif.) City Health Dept., 1956-57; dir. health edn. Monterey County (Calif.) Health Dept., 1958-59; asst. dir. health edn. Wyo. Health Dept., 1959-63; dir. community action studies project Nat. Commn. on Community Health Services; asso. pub. health adminstrn. Johns Hopkins, 1963-66; asso. prof. U. N.C., Sch. Pub. Health; dir. Planning and Evaluation Regional Med. Program N.C., 1968-71; dean Coll. Allied Health Professions; prof. community medicine U. Tenn., Memphis, 1972-82; dean Coll. Allied Health, prof. health edn. U. Okla., Oklahoma City, 1982—; adj. prof. polit. sci. Memphis State U., 1972-82; Cons. in health planning, Toledo, Idaho Falls, Idaho, Franklin, N.C.; cons. Gov.'s Task Force on Health, W.Va.; Chmn. Area-wide Council on Aging, 1974-76, Memphis Area Vocat. Tech. Edn. Coordinating Com., 1973-74; manpower cons. Nat. Assn. Partners of Ams., Caracas, Venezuela, 1976—, Jordanian Royal Med. Services, Amman, 1977, U. Riyadh, Saudi Arabia, 1980—; mem. Health Systems Agy. Contbr. articles to profl. jours. Chmn. Community Planning Council; bd. dirs. Memphis United Way, United Health Services N.C., Vis. Nurses Assn. Memphis; past pres. Vol. Center Memphis. Served with AUS, 1953-55; col. Res. ret.; USPHS trainee, 1957, 66-68. Fellow Am. Pub. Health Assn., Soc. Pub. Health Educators, Royal Soc. Health, Am. Soc. Allied Health Professions (pres. 1979-80, dir., editorial bd. Jour. Allied Health 1973-80); mem. Council Ednl. Instns. (chmn. 1976), Res. Officers Assn., Am. Legion, Mil. Order World Wars, Phi Kappa Phi, Delta Omega, Alpha Eta (pres. 1978). Clubs: Odd Fellow, Kiwanis. Home: 3008 Charing Cross Rd Oklahoma City OK 73120 Office: 801 NE 13th St Oklahoma City OK 73190

HOLDER, THOMAS MARTIN, physician; b. Corinth, Miss., Sept. 1, 1926; s. Solomon Smith and Ethel Edna (Martin) H.; m. Kathryn Anderson Robinson, June 6, 1953; children: Jean Celeste, Thomas Martin Jr., Kathryn Hendry. Student, U. Miss., 1944, 46-48; M.D., Bowman Gray Sch. Medicine, Wake Forest U., 1952. Diplomate: Am. Bd. Surgery, Am. Bd. Thoracic Surgery. Intern Jefferson Med. Coll. Hosp., Phila., 1952-53, resident surgery, 1953-54, 58-59; resident pediatric surgery Childrens Hosp. Med. Center, Boston., 1954-57, 58-59; practice medicine specializing in pediatric surgery, Kansas City, Mo., 1960—; surgeon-in-chief Childrens Mercy Hosp., 1960-63, chief thoracic and cardiovascular surgery, 1972—; head sect. pediatric surgery U. Kan. Med. Center, 1963-72, prof. surgery, 1960-72; clin. prof. surgery U. Mo., Kansas City, 1972—; vis. scientist McIndoe Labs., Queen Victoria Hosp., East Grinstead, Sussex, Eng., 1969-70. Author, editor textbooks; contbr. articles to profl. jours. Served with USNR, 1944-46. Mem. Am. Acad. Pediatrics (chmn. surg. sect.), Am. Pediatric Surg. Assn. (pres.), Am., Central surg. assns., Brit. Assn. Pediatric Surgeons, Am. Assn. Thoracic Surgery, Soc. U. Surgeons, A.C.S. Home: 6125 Mission Dr Shawnee Mission KS 66208 Office: 4400 Broadway Kansas City MO 64111

HOLDERMAN, JAMES BOWKER, university president; b. Morris, Ill., Jan. 29, 1936; s. Samuel James and Helen Boynton (Bowker) H.; m. Carolyn Meadors, Aug. 16, 1959; children: Elizabeth, Nancy, Jamie. B.A. with Honors, Denison U., 1958; Ph.D., Northwestern U., 1961. Asst. prof. govt. U. Ill., Urbana, 1961-63, asst. prof. polit. sci., 1965-67, asso. prof., 1967-69; asst. supt. pub. instrn., State of Ill., 1963-65; vice-chancellor U. Ill., Chgo., 1968-69; exec. dir. Bd. of Higher Edn. State of Ill., Chgo., 1969-73; v.p. for edn. Lilly Endowment, Inc., Indpls., 1973-76; sr. v.p., dir. pub. policy div. Acad. for Ednl. Devel., 1976-77; pres. Inst. for Pub. Policy Devel., Indpls., 1977, U. S.C., 1977—; Mem. task force on Financing of Higher Edn. Nat. Council of Ind. Colls., 1972—; mem. task force on statewide planning Edn. Commn. of the States, 1969-70; mem. task force on coordinating governance and structure of postsecondary edn., 1972—; gov. mem. Ill. Council on Econ. Edn., 1969-73; mem. Elmhurst (Ill.) Bd. Edn., 1968-73, pres., 1971-73; chmn. ednl. adv. com. Inst. Internat. Edn.; mem. panel on women Am. Council on Edn., 1978—. Contbr. articles to profl. jours. Trustee North Central Coll., Naperville, Ill., 1974, Denison U., Granville, Ohio, 1973-74; bd. dirs. Friends of Our Little Bros., Cuernavaca, Mex., 1976—, United Way of Midlands, Columbia, S.C., 1978—, Citizenship Clearing House fellow in state govt., 1960; chmn. UNESCO, 1981; ambassador to U.S.A. Internat. Conf. for ARC, 1981; mem. President's Council for Internat. Youth Exchange, 1982, World Communications Yr., 1983, Investment Policy Adv. Com., 1983. Decorated comdr.'s cross Order of Merit (W.Ger.), 1983; Ford Found. fellow, 1973; named Chicagoan of the Year in Govt. and Polit. Sci. Chgo. Jr. Assn. Commerce and Industry, 1967. Mem. Am., Midwest Polit. Sci. Assns., Ill. Agrl. Assn., Assn. of State Higher Edn. Exec. Officers, AAAS, Delta Upsilon, Omicron Delta Kappa, Blue Key, Mortar Board, Phi Beta Kappa, Phi Sigma Alpha, Phi Alpha Theta. Clubs: Tavern (Chgo.); Univ. (Chgo., N.Y.); Summit. Home: Pres's House Univ SC Columbia SC 29208 Office: Office of Pres Univ SC Columbia SC 29208

HOLDERNESS, ALGERNON SIDNEY, JR., lawyer; b. Wilmington, Del., Mar. 31, 1938; s. Algernon Sidney and Mary Elizabeth (Crockett) H.; m. Sheila Ann Garvan, June 1, 1963; children: Claire Crockett, Julia Simms. B.A. magna cum laude, Yale U., 1959, LL.B., 1962. Bar: N.Y. Bar 1964. Asso. firm Milbank, Tweed, Hadley & McCloy, N.Y.C., 1964-72, partner, 1973—. Bd. editors: Yale Law Jour, 1960-62. Pres. bd. mgrs. Bklyn. Central br. YMCA Greater N.Y., 1980—, mem. exec. com. bd. dirs., 1982—; bd. govs. Bklyn. Heights Assn., 1979, exec. com., 1981; mem. N.E. regional bd. YMCA of U.S.A., 1982-83, mem. east field com., 1983—, mem. nat. bd., 1984—. Mem. Am. Law Inst., N.Y. State Bar Assn., Assn. Bar City of N.Y., Order of Coif, Phi Beta Kappa. Clubs: Yale, Wall St. (N.Y.C.); Grads. (New Haven); Heights Casino (Bklyn.). Office: 1 Chase Manhattan Plaza New York NY 10005

HOLDGRAF, EARL WESLEY, engineering company executive; b. Aurora, Nebr., Aug. 8, 1924; s. Paul George and Ida Elizabeth (Peterson) H.; m. Dorothy Nieman, Oct. 26, 1946; 1 son, Richard Paul. B.S. in Chem. Engring., Northwestern U., 1945. Registered profl. engr., Mass., Ky. Lectr. CCNY, N.Y.C., 1947-51; asst. mgr. process engring. Lummus Co., Bloomfield, N.J., 1951-63; v.p., mgr. engring. Stone & Webster Engring. Co., Boston, 1963-72; sr. v.p. hydrocarbon group Dynalectron Corp., McLean, Va., 1972—; chmn. bd. dirs. HRI Inc., McLean, Va., 1982—, Hydrocarbon Research Inc., 1980—. Bd. dirs. Fairfax Opportunities Unltd., Springfield, Va. Served with USNR, 1943-46. Mem. Am. Inst. Chem. Engrs., Sigma Xi, Phi Lambda Upsilon, Sigma Phi Epsilon. Home: 8451 Sparger St McLean VA 22102 Office: Dynalectron Corp 1313 Dolly Madison Blvd McLean VA 22101

HOLDHEIM, WILLIAM WOLFGANG, comparative literature educator; b. Berlin, Germany, Aug. 4, 1926; came to U.S., 1947, naturalized, 1953; s. Hugo and Margarete (Lehmann) H.; m. Evelyn M. Stanislawski, Sept. 6, 1954; children: Sylvia, Robert. B.A. summa cum laude, UCLA, 1949, M.A., 1951; Ph.D., Yale U., 1956. Instr. Ohio State U., 1955-57; instr. Brandeis U., 1957-58, asst. prof., 1958-61, assoc. prof., 1961-64; prof. Washington U., 1964-69; prof., chmn. comparative lit. Cornell U., Ithaca, N.Y., 1969—, Frederic J. Whiton prof. liberal studies, 1974—. Author: Benjamin Constant, 1961, Theory and Practice of the Novel, 1968, Der Justizirrtum als literarische Problematik, 1969, Die Suche nach dem Epos, 1978. Mem. Phi Beta Kappa, Pi Delta Phi. Home: 706 Cayuga Hts Rd Ithaca NY 14850

HOLDREN, JOHN RICHARD, supermarket executive; b. Anderson, Ind., Feb. 17, 1925; s. Henry R. and Della Jane (Reynolds) H.; m. Dorothy Jane Chitwood, Oct. 24, 1948 (dec. 1976); children: Teresa Jane, Jerri Lynn; m. Carol Ann Blitz, July 12, 1978. Student, Ind. U. V.p. Hanks Supermarkets Inc., Anderson, Ind., 1948-59, Garden City Foods Inc., Logansport, Ind., 1958-61; pres. Conren Inc., Terre Haute, Ind., 1961—; dir. Payless Supermarkets Inc., Anderson; dir. Terra State Realty Inc., Ultra Steak Inc. Bd. dirs. Ind. State U.Found., Terre Haute, 1980—. Served with U.S. Army, 1943-46. Mem. Food Mktg. Inst. (operating execs. council). Republican. Clubs: Evansville Country, Terre Haute Country. Lodges: Masons; Shriners. Home: 1155 Garden Dr W Terre Haute IN 47802 Office: PO Box 125 Terre Haute IN 47802

HOLDRIDGE, BARBARA, book publisher; b. N.Y.C., July 26, 1929; d. Herbert L. and Bertha (Gold) Cohen; m. Lawrence B. Holdridge, Oct. 9, 1959; 2 children. A.B., Hunter Coll., 1950. Asst. editor Liveright Pub. Corp., N.Y.C., 1950-52; co-founder Caedmon Records,

Inc., N.Y.C., 1952, partner, 1952-60, pres., 1960-62, treas., 1962-70, pres., 1970-75; founder Stemmer House Pubs. Inc., Owings Mills, Md., 1975, pres., 1975—; co-founder, v.p. Shakespeare Rec. Soc., Inc., N.Y.C., 1960—, Theatre Rec. Soc., Inc., 1964—; co-founder History Rec. Soc., Inc., N.Y.C., 1964, pres., 1964-70; lectr. on Ammi Phillips, 1959—. Author: Ammi Phillips, Aubrey Beardsley Designs from the Age of Chivalry; articles on Am. paintings. Recipient Am. Shakespeare Festival award, 1962, N.Y.C. certificate appreciation, 1972; named to Hunter Coll. Hall of Fame, 1972. Mem. Phi Beta Kappa Assocs. Home: Stemmer House Caves Rd Owings Mill MD 21117 Office: 2627 Caves Rd Owings Mills MD 21117

HOLDRIDGE, JOHN HERBERT, diplomat; b. N.Y.C., Aug. 21, 1924; s. Herbert Charles and Marie (Gunther) H.; m. Martha Jane McKelvey, 1949; children: Patricia Holdridge Johnson, David V., Geoffrey M. B.S., U.S. Mil. Acad., 1945; postgrad., Cornell U., Harvard U.; LL.D. (hon.), Elmira (N.Y.) Coll., 1980. Joined U.S. Fgn. Service, 1948; service in Bangkok, Thailand, Hong Kong, Singapore, Beijing, China, A.E. and P. to Singapore, 1975-78; nat. intelligence officer for East Asia CIA, 1979-80; asst. sec. East Asian and Pacific affairs Dept. State, 1981-83; ambassador to Indonesia, 1983—. Served to 1st lt. U.S. Army, 1945-47. Recipient Superior Honor award Dept. State, 1967, Christian Herter award, 1975. Address: Am Embassy Jakarta Indonesia APO San Francisco CA 96356 *

HOLDT, LELAND LAMAR STARK, insurance company executive; b. Sweetwater, Nebr., Apr. 12, 1930; s. Arthur Larsen and Anna Henrietta (Stark) H.; m. Mary Ellen Oelschlager, July 13, 1952; children: Mary Lee, Candace Sue, Mark Leland. B.S. in Bus. Adminstrn., Kearney State Coll., 1971. C.L.U., Pa. With Security Mut. Life Ins. Co., Kearney, Nebr., 1953-66, v.p., agy. dir., Lincoln, Nebr., 1966-71, exec. v.p., 1971-72, pres., 1972-80, chmn. bd., pres., 1980—; dir. Nat. Bank Commerce. Bd. dirs. Nat. Health Inst., Washington, 1975, Nebr. Safety Council, 1959-63, Lancaster County Crusade, 1978—; chmn. Lancaster County Crusade, 1954-57; bd. dirs. Nebr. Wesleyan U., Lincoln, 1980—; gen. chmn. United Way campaign, 1978; bd. dirs. Lincoln Goodwill Industries, pres. bd., 1969. Served with USAF, 1951-53. Recipient Best All-Around Agy. award Security Mut. Life Ins. Co., 1958; named Nebraskan of Month Bus. & Industry mag., 1977, Boss of Year Lincoln Life Ins. Women, 1978, Chief Exec. Officer Lincoln Jr. C. of C., 1980. Mem. Am. Council Life Ins. (Nebr. v.p. 1976-77, bd. dirs. 1977-80), Nat. Assn. Life Underwriters, Am. Soc. C.L.U.s, Ins. Fedn. Nebr. (exec. council 1972—), Lincoln C. of C. (bd. dirs. 1974-78). Republican. Lutheran. Club: Lincoln Country. Lodge: Rotary. Home: 245 N 162d St Lincoln NE 68527 Office: Security Mut Life Ins Co 200 Centennial Mall North Lincoln NE 68501

HOLDT, ROY HOWARD, manufacturing company executive; b. Edgewood, Md., Nov. 19, 1920; s. Jacob S. and Francis (Hansen) H.; m. Shirley Boatwright, Feb. 4, 1984; children by previous marriage: Linda Holdt Greene, Douglas M. Student, Dyke Bus. Coll., 1941, Cleve. State U., 1947. With Lake Erie Chem. Co., Cleve., 1938-40, Apex Elec. Mfg. Co., 1941-56; div. controller White Consol. Industries, Inc., Cleve., 1956-58, corp. controller, 1958-61, v.p., controller, 1961-64, v.p. fin., 1964-67, sr. v.p., 1967-69, exec. v.p., dir., 1969-72, pres., chief operating officer, 1972-76, chmn., chief exec. officer, 1976—; dir. Cleve. Trust Co., Cleve. Electric Illuminating Co., Midland-Ross Corp., Republic Steel Corp. Mem. bd. Fairview Gen. Hosp., Cleve. State U. Devel. Found.; trustee Dyke Coll. Served with AUS, 1942-45. Mem. Greater Cleve. Growth Assn. (dir.). Clubs: Pepper Pike (Ohio); OSU Presidents, Westwood Country; Clevelander, Cleve. Atheletic, The 50, Union, Laurel Valley (Cleve.); Duquesne (Pitts.); Firestone. Office: 11770 Berea Rd Cleveland OH 44111

HOLE, FRANK, anthropology educator; b. Oak Park, Ill, Nov. 13, 1931; s. Andrew Frank and Leta (Arnold) H.; m. Barbara Adkins, Aug. 20, 1954 (div. Sept. 1970); children: Steven, Robert; m. Bonnie Laird, Dec. 29, 1972; 1 son, Eric. B.A., Cornell Coll., Iowa, 1953; postgrad., Harvard U., fall 1957-58; M.A., U. Chgo., 1958, Ph.D., 1961. Asst. prof. anthropology Rice U., Houston, 1961-65, asso. prof., 1965-68, prof., 1968-79, chmn. dept. anthropology, 1974-79; prof. Yale U., New Haven, 1980—, chmn. dept. anthropology, 1980-83; dir. archeol. projects, Iran, 1961, 63, 65, 68-69, 73; archeologist Smithsonian Instn. project, Oaxaca, Mexico, summer 1966; research asso. U. Md. archeol. project, summer 1967. Author: (with Robert F. Heizer) An Introduction to Prehistoric Archeology, 1965, 69, 73, Spanish edit., 1969, Prehistoric Archeology: A Brief Introduction, 1977, Studies in the Archeological History of the Deluran Plain, 1977; editor: Am. Antiquity, 1974-78; Contbr. articles to profl. jours. Served with AUS, 1953-55. NSF fellow, 1959-60; U. Tehran (Iran), postdoctoral fellow, 1961-62; grantee, 1963-64, 65-66, 66, 68-70, 73-75. Fellow Am. Anthrop. Assn.; mem. Nat. Acad. Scis., Soc. Am. Archaeology, Soc. Profl. Archaeologists, AAAS, Prehistoric Soc. (Eng.), Sigma Xi. Office: Dept Anthropology Yale U New Haven CT 06520

HOLE, WILLIAM EDWARD, JR., manufacturing executive; b. Greenville, Ohio, July 2, 1927; s. William Edward and Dorothy (Coppock) H.; m. Gloria Beth Shiverdecker, June 24, 1951; children: William Jeffrey, Julie Ann. B.S. in Mech. Engring., U. Mich., 1951. With Am. Aggregates Corp., Greenville, 1951—, v.p., 1957-64, exec. v.p., 1964-69, pres., 1969—, also dir., mem. exec. com.; v.p., dir. Greenville Nat. Bank. Bd. dirs. Greenville Community Chest, 1955-57, chmn., 1981. Served with USAAF, 1945-46. Mem. Nat. Sand and Gravel Assn. (dir. 1964—, exec. com. 1965-75, v.p. 1970-71, pres. 1972-73), Ohio Sand and Gravel Assn. (dir. 1956—, pres. 1958-59), Ohio Mfrs. Assn. (dir. 1975—), Ohio C. of C. (dir. 1971—, v.p. 1979-83, chmn. 1983—), Greenville C. of C. (dir. 1962-69, pres. 1967). Republican. Congregationalist. Home: Box 122 Greenville OH 45331 Office: Drawer 160 Greenville OH 45331

HOLEN, HAROLD HAMPTON, educator; b. Big Timber, Mont., Feb. 25, 1935; s. Elias A. and Jimmie O. (Curtis) H.; m. Verna Brown, Dec. 23, 1962; children—Leslie, Hayley. B.S., Mont. State U., 1961, M.Ed., 1965, Ed.D., 1970. Author Haskins and Sells, Los Angeles, 1962; tchr. bus. Sweet Grass County High Sch., Big Timber, Mont., 1962-64; instr. Dawson Jr. Coll., 1964; prof. acctg. faculty Mont. State U., 1965—, dept. head, 1971—; cons. IRS, San Francisco, 1968. Contbr. to publs. in field. Served with AUS, 1955-58. Recipient leadership award Distributive Edn. Clubs Am., 1965. Mem. Am. Acctg. Assn. (membership com. 1972-74), Mont. C.P.A. Soc. (mem. govt. acctg. com. 1968-72), 1968-72), Phi Kappa Phi, Phi Delta Kappa, Pi Omega Pi. Republican. Lutheran. Club: Gallatein Sportsman. Home: 3416 W Babcock St Bozeman MT 59715

HOLGATE, JEANNE, painter, illustrator; b. London, Mar. 11, 1920; d. John Edward and Lucy Elizabeth Allen. Student pvt. schs., Eng.; Sec., Royal Coll. Art, London, 1952. Instr. in flower portraiture Longwood Gardens, 1968-71; lectr. on flower portraiture throughout U.S. Ofcl. artist, Royal Hort. Soc., London, 1954-66; exhibited in: Retrospective Show covering 20 yrs. of work at, Hunt Inst. for Bot. Documentation, Carnegie-Mellon U., Pitts., 1973, Flowers in Art, Brit. Mus., London, 1979; represented in permanent collections, Her Majesty Queen Elizabeth, London, The Queen Mother, London, Duke of Devonshire, Eng., Royal Hort. Soc., Brit. Mus., U. N.C., Hunt Inst. Bot. Documentation, also pvt. collections; works include: folios of prints Hybrid Orchids, Flowers of America; designer porcelain plate series, porcelain flower sculpture, Franklin Porcelain. Served with Women's RAF, 1942-45. Recipient awards, including Gold medals Royal Hort. Soc. (3). Primrose Cottage Houndscroft Stroud Gloucester England

HOLGUIN, ALFONSO HUDSON, physician, educator; b. El Paso, Tex., Apr. 3, 1931; s. Alfonso and Effie (Hudson) H.; m. Irby Hanna Spring, Sept. 12, 1954; children— Laura Marie, Mark Hudson, Theresa Lynn, Carol, Paul, Stephen. B.A., Tex. Western Coll., 1953; M.D., U. Tex., 1957; M.P.H., Harvard, 1964. Intern USPHS Hosp., Seattle, 1957-58; respiratory virus research, lab. br. USPHS, Berkeley, Calif., 1958-59, polio virus research, 1959-62, asst. to chief lab. br., 1962-63, asst. chief Tb br., 1964-65; chief Tb br. Communicable Disease Center, USPHS, Atlanta, 1965-69, dir. state and community service div., 1969-70, dir. tng. program, 1970-74; prof. epidemiology U. Tex. Sch. Pub. Health, Houston, 1974—. Author papers in field. Mem. AMA, Assn. Mil. Surgeons, U.S., Am. Pub. Health Assn., USPHS Commd. Officers Assn., Tau Kappa Epsilon, Phi Rho Sigma, Alpha Omega Alpha. Home: 12819 Queens Forest San Antonio TX 78230

HOLIDAY, HARRY, JR., steel company executive; b. Pitts., July 2, 1923; s. Harry and Charlotte Poe (Rutherford) H.; m. Kathlyn Collins Watson, Sept. 6, 1947; children: Edith Elizabeth, Harry III, Albert Logan II. B.S. in Metall. Engring. with honors, U. Mich., 1949. Spl. assignment metall. engring. adminstrn. Armco Steel Corp., Middletown, Ohio, 1949-55, asst. to supt. blast furnace, Hamilton, Ohio, 1955-57, supt. blast furnace, 1957-59, asst. gen. supt. steel plant, Middletown, 1959-64, gen. supt. steel plant, 1964-66, dir. raw materials, 1966-67, v.p. steel ops., 1967-69, exec. v.p. steel, 1969-74, pres., 1974-79, now chief exec. officer, also dir., chmn., 1982—; dir. Allis Chalmers, Reserve Mining Co., ASARCO, Nat. Cash Register. Pres. Middletown YMCA, 1955-58; pres. Moundbuilders Area council Boy Scouts Am., 1963-67. Served to capt. AUS, 1943-46. Mem. Am. Inst. Metall. Engrs. (recipient J.E. Johnson, Jr. Blast Furnace award), Am., Internat. iron and steel insts., Tau Beta Pi, Psi Upsilon. Office: Armco Inc 703 Curtis St Middletown OH 45042 *

HOLL, JOHN WILLIAM, educator; b. Danville, Ill., Feb. 20, 1928; s. William Benjamin and Anna Marie (Waldo) H.; m. Antoinette Fillhouer, Aug. 20, 1950; children—Jessica, Vanessa, Melissa, Cassandra, Alyssa, Nathan, Zachary. B.S. in M.E, U. Ill., 1949, M.S., 1949, Ph.D., Pa. State U., 1958. Research asst. in mech. engring. Engring. Experiment Sta. U. Ill., Urbana, 1949-51; research asso. Applied Research Lab. Pa. State U., 1951-54, 56-58, asst. prof. engring. research, 1958-59, asso. prof. aerospace engring., 1963-67, prof., 1967—; asso. prof. mech. engring. U. Nebr., Lincoln, 1959-63; cons. in field. Mem. Lincoln Symphony Orch., 1960-63, Nittany Valley Symphony Orch., State College, Pa., 1969—, State Coll. Mcpl. Band, 1977—; Trustee Unitarian Ch., Lincoln, 1961-62. Served with U.S. Army, 1955-56. Fellow ASME (R.T. Knapp award 1970, Melville medal 1970, Centennial medallion 1980); assoc. fellow AIAA; mem. Internat. Clarinet Soc., Amateur Chamber Music Players, Sigma Xi. Home: 1108 Mayberry Ln State College PA 16801 Office: Applied Research Laboratory PO Box 30 State College PA 16801

HOLLADAY, CHARLES EDWIN, state supt. edn.; b. Newton, Miss., July 12, 1918; s. Clarence O. and Gladys (Bounds) H.; m. Bess Edward, May 25, 1939; children—Charles E., Stephen E. B.A., Miss. Coll., 1946; M.A., Peabody Coll., 1949; Ed.D., U. Miss., 1969. Tchr. Duncan (Miss.) Pub. Schs., 1941-43, Enochs Jr. High Sch., Jackson, Miss., 1946-49; asst. prin. Central High Sch., Jackson, 1949-53, prin., 1953-58; supt. schs., Tupelo, Miss., 1958-76, state supt. edn. for, Miss., 1976—; Exec. sec. N.E. Miss. TV Council, 1961—; chmn. Miss. Accrediting Commn., 1963-65; ednl. auditor Fedn. project; developer ednl. mgmt. tng. program for adminstrs., N.E. Miss. Trustee Blue Mountain (Miss.) Coll. Served with USAAF, 1942-46. Recipient Merit award for outstanding ednl. program Miss. Econ. Council, 1966; named Ednl. Adminstr. of Yr. Miss. Assn. Ednl. Secs., 1979. Mem. NEA (PaceMaker award for Miss. 1965), Miss. Edn. Assn. (past pres. adult edn. div.), Tupelo Edn. Assn., Miss. Secondary Sch. Prins. Assn. (past pres.), Am., Miss. assns. schs. adminstrs., Mental Health Assn., Baptist (deacon), Phi Delta Kappa. Club: Rotary (past dir.). Home: 1211 Laurelwood Dr Clinton MS 39056 Office: State Supt Edn Sillers Office Bldg PO Box 771 Jackson MS 39205

HOLLADAY, HARLAN, educator, artist; b. Greenville, Mo., Dec. 10, 1925; s. Franklin and Mae (Croy) H.; m. Elsie Ruffena Calbert, Jan. 27, 1950; children—Joan Adrian, Carol Lisa, Jeffrey Carl. B.S. in Edn, S.E. Mo. State Coll., 1949; student, Washington U., St. Louis, 1947-49; M.A., U. Iowa, 1951; Ph.D., Cornell U., 1966. Tchr. art, dir. art Poplar Bluff (Mo) pub. schs., 1951-53; tchr. art Des Moines High Sch., 1953-55; instr., then asst. prof. art U. Nev., 1955-58; teaching asso. Cornell U., 1958-59; asst. prof. drawing Cornell U. State Coll. Agr., 1959-60; mem. faculty St. Lawrence U., Canton, N.Y., 1961—, prof. fine arts, 1966—, head dept. fine arts, 1966-71, Flint prof., 1967; tchr., artist-in-residence Am. Coll. Switzerland, Leysin, 1968-69. Paintings rep. several mus. and permanent collections. Mem. Canton Preservation Adv. Bd. Served with AUS, 1944-46. Recipient prizes in nat. and regional exhbns. Mem. AAUP, Coll. Art Assn. Soc. Archtl. Historians, St. Lawrence County Hist. Assn., Renaissance Soc. Am. Unitarian-Universalist Ch. Home: 23 Judson St Canton NY 13617

HOLLADAY, WENDELL GENE, physics educator; b. Huntingdon, Tenn., Aug. 23, 1925; s. Carlie Bertran and Josie (Crider) H.; m. Virginia Beatrice Mershon, Mar. 17, 1949; children: Frank Warren, Mark Wendell, Jane Mershon, Mary Joyce. B.A., Vanderbilt U., 1949, M.A., 1950; Ph.D., U. Wis., 1954. Alumni Research Found. fellow U. Wis., 1950-52, NSF fellow, 1952-54; vis. research asst. Brookhaven Nat. Lab., summer 1953; mem. faculty Vanderbilt U., 1954—, prof. physics., 1962—, provost, 1978-83, chmn. dept. physics and astronomy, 1965-69, dean Coll. Arts and Sci., 1969-75; vis. project asso. U. Wis., summer, 1955, vis. asso. prof., 1959-60; vis. research physicist U. Calif. Radiation Lab., summer 1956. Author: (with O. Oldenberg) Introduction to Atomic and Nuclear Physics, 4th edit, 1967; also articles. Mem. exec. com. Vanderbilt U. Employees Credit Union, 1963-66. Served with USNR, 1943-46. Fellow Am. Phys. Soc. (council S.E. sect. 1964-66, v.p. sec. 1966-67, pres. Southeastern sect. 1967-68), AAAS, Tenn. Acad. Sci. (treas. 1957-59, vis. scientist 1966-67); mem. AAUP (pres. chpt. 1963), Am. Assn. Physics Tchrs., Phi Beta Kappa, Sigma Xi. Unitarian (chmn. bd. dirs. 1963). Clubs: Old Oak; University (Nashville). Home: 1305 Hildreth Dr Nashville TN 37215

HOLLAENDER, ALEXANDER, biophysicist; b. Samter, Germany, Dec. 19, 1898; came to U.S., 1921, naturalized, 1927; s. Heymann and Doris (Rotholz) H.; m. Henrietta Wahlert, Oct. 10, 1925. A.B., U. Wis., 1929, M.A., 1930, Ph.D., 1931, D.Sc. honoris causa, 1969, U. Vt., 1959, U. Leeds, Eng., 1962, Marquette U., 1967; M.D. honoris cause, U. Chile Med. Sch., 1970; Prof. honoris causa, Fed. U. Rio de Janeiro. Asst. phys. chemistry U. Wis., 1929-31; NRC fellow in biol. scis., 1931-33; investigator Rockefeller Found., 1934; investigator charge radiation work NRC project, Wis., 1934-37; asso. biophysicist Washington Biophysics Inst., NIH, USPHS, 1937-38, biophysicist, 1938-41, sr. biophysicist, 1941-45, prin. biophysicist, 1945-46, head biophysicist, 1946-50; dir. biol. div. Oak Ridge Nat. Lab., 1946-66, sr. research adviser, 1967-73; prof. radiation biology U. Tenn., 1957-66; prof. biomed. scis. U. Tenn.-Oak Ridge Grad. Sch. Biomed. Scis., 1966—; dir. Archives Radiation Biology, U. Tenn., 1966—; Messenger lectr. Cornell U., 1962; cons. Oak Ridge Nat. Lab., Brookhaven Nat. Lab., Nat. Inst. for Environ. Health Scis., Nat. Cancer Inst., Plenum Pub. Co., EPA; organizer fgn. and domestic workshops and tng. courses in environ. mutagenesis and carcinogenesis. Civilian with AEC, OSRD, Office Surgeon Gen., USN; mem. com. radiation biology, mem. com. photobiology, div. biol. and agr., chmn. and mem. subcom. radiobiology, div. phs. scis. NRC. Editor: Radiation Biology (3 vols.), Vol. III, 1956, Radiation Protection and Recovery, 1960, Chemical Mutagens: Principles and Methods for their Detection, 7 vols, 1971-81, Genetic Engineering for Nitrogen Fixation, 1977, Limitations and Potentials for Biological Nitrogen Fixation in the Tropics, 1978, The Biosaline Concept: An Approach to the Utilization of Underexploited Resources, 1979, (with J.K. Setlow) Genetic Engineering: Principles and Methods, Vol. I, 1979, Vol. II, 1980, Vol. III, 1981, Vol. IV, 1982, (with Rains and Valentine) Genetic Engineering of Osmoregulation, 1980, (with others) Trends in the Biology of Fermentations for Fuels and Chemicals, 1981, Engineering of Microorganisms for Chemicals, 1981, (with R.A. Fleck) Genetic Toxicology: An Agricultural Perspective, 1982, (with others) Biological Basis of New Developments in Biotechnology, 1983, (with Kosuge and Meredith) Genetic Engineering of Plants: An Agricultural Perspective, 1983. Recipient AEC citation for outstanding service to atomic energy program, 1966, Finsen medal 5th Internat. Congress on Photobiology, 1968; E.M.S. award, 1975; decorated Order Merit Republic Italy, 1961. Fellow AAAS, Am. Acad. Arts and Sci., Indian Nat. Sci. Acad. (fgn.), Brazilian Acad. Sci. (fgn.); mem. Solar Energy Soc., Am. Physiol. Soc., Radiation Research Soc. (pres. 1954-55), Am. Soc. Cell Biology, Internat. Assn. Radiation Research (pres. 1962-66), Nat. Assn. de Photobiologie (pres. 1954-60, hon. pres. 1964, exec. com. 1960-66), Genetics Soc. Am. (citation 1979), Am. Soc. Naturalists (v.p. 1952-53), Soc. Gen. Physiologists, U.S. Nat. Acad. Scis. (award for environ. quality 1979), Am. Soc. Microbiology, Am. Physiol. Soc., Environ. Mutagen Soc. (pres. 1969-71), Internat. Environmental Mutagens Soc. (pres. 1973-77), Knoxville Acad. Medicine (hon.). Home: 2540 Massachusetts Ave NW Washington DC 20008

HOLLAND, ARTHUR JOHN, mayor; b. Trenton, N.J., Oct. 24, 1918; s. Joseph F. and Helen (Groh) H.; m. Elizabeth Anne Jackson, July 28, 1962; children: Cynthia, Elise, Christopher, Timothy, Matthew. Grad., St. Francis Coll., S.I.; A.B. in Social Studies, Rutgers U., 1954; M.A. in Pub. Adminstrn, Rutgers U., 1959. Research analyst Opinion Research Corp., Princeton, N.J., 1945-49; asso. dir. Princeton Research Service, 1949-51; dep. dir. Dept. Pub. Affairs, Trenton, 1951-52, Dept. Parks and Pub. Property, 1952-55; dir. Dept. Pub. Affairs, Trenton, 1955-62; acting city mgr., Passaic, N.J., 1967, mayor, City of Trenton, 1959-66, 70—; past cons. HUD; former cons. Nat. Inst. Pub. Affairs, Brookings Instn.; adj. research prof. Urban Studies Center, Rutgers U., 1966-70, lectr. polit. sci., 1967-72; lectr. program for adminstrs. Rider Coll., 1974—. Pres. Mercer County League Municipalities, 1956-57, 76; bd. govs. Del. Valley United Way, 1962-63, 73—, pub. div. chmn., 1954, 55, 63, 70-78, 80—; bd. dirs. Del.-Raritan Lung Assn., 1969-73, Social Service Council Greater Trenton, 1960-66, local chpt. ARC, 1953-68, 81, Trenton Social Service Exchange, 1951—; chmn. Trenton Social Service Exchange, 1959-62; hon. bd. mem. Mercer County Soc. Prevention Cruelty to Animals, 1950-62, publicity dir., 1952; bd. dirs., 1957-58, hon. bd. dirs., 1958-62; hon. mem. Trenton Assn. of Blind, 1957—; bd. dirs. Mercer County Assn. Mental Health, 1960-66; del. White House conf. To Fulfill These Rights, 1966; N.J. v.p. and bd. mem. Del. Valley Citizens Council for Clean Air; mem. bd. Del. Valley Citizens Transp. Com.; chmn., 1969-70, Human Relations Council Serving Greater Trenton Area, Delaware Valley Regional Planning Commn., 1975, 77; mem. Council for NE Econ. Action; mem. exec. com. Transp. Research Bd., Del.-Raritan Canal Commn.; bd. dirs. Urban League Met. Trenton, Inc., N.J. Social Welfare Council; past mem. bd. dirs. Social Welfare Research Found. N.J.; pres. N.J. Conf. Mayors, 1977; mem. adv. bd. U.S. Conf. Mayors, Nat. Conf. Dem. Mayors, 1980—; del. Democratic Nat. Conv., 1976. Recipient Young Man of Year Jr. C. of C., 1954; award for Interracial Justice Cath. Interracial Council N.Y., 1964; N.J. Americanization Conf. Citizenship award, 1964; Commendation for Meritorious Achievement Town Affiliation program Pres.'s People-to-People program; Brotherhood award Mercer County Conf. Christians and Jews; decorated knight Order Star of Solidarity, Italy). Mem. Nat. League of Cities (chmn. community facilities com., mem. exec. com., adv. council), N.J. League Municipalities (3d v.p.), Trenton Hist. Soc., NAACP, Am.-Hungarian Civic Assn., Trenton Cath. Alumni Assn. (pres. 1938-39), Ancient Order Hibernians, 1st Cath. Slovak Union, Regional Conf. Elected ofcls. (past pres., mem. exec. com. 1961-66). Clubs: K.C., Rutgers of Mercer County (N.J.) (v.p. 1955-56); Mercer County Social Welfare (treas. 1956-57). Home: 138 Mercer St Trenton NJ 08611 Office: City Hall Trenton NJ 08608

HOLLAND, CHARLES DONALD, chemical engineer, educator; b. Irdell County, N.C., Oct. 9, 1921; s. Charles Cyrus and Texie (Bess) H.; m. Eleanore Marie Williams, Aug. 22, 1945; children: Thomas P. Fowler, Nancy Lee, Charlotte Claire. B.S. in Chem. Engring, N.C. State Coll., 1943; M.S., Tex. A. and M. U., 1949, Ph.D., 1953. Registered profl. engr., Tex. Jr. engr. Burlington Mills Corp., 1947-48; mem. faculty Tex. A. and M. U., 1952—, prof. chem. engring., head dept., 1964—; cons. in field, 1960—. Author: Multicomponent Distillation, 1963, Unsteady State Processes with Applications in Multicomponent Distillation, 1966, Fundamentals and Modeling of Separation Processes—Adsorption, Distillation, Evaporation, and Extraction, 1975, Fundamentals of Chemical Reaction Engineering, 1979, Fundamentals of Multicomponent Distillation, 1981, Computer Methods for Solving Dynamic Separation Problems, 1983; also articles. Served to lt. USNR, 1943-46. Recipient award Former Students Assn., Tex. A. and M. U., 1955, Outstanding Prof. Coll. Engring. award, 1962. Fellow Am. Inst. Chem. Engrs. (Publ. award South Tex. sect. 1960, 65, 67); mem. Am. Soc. Engring Edn., Am. Chem. Soc., Am. Inst. Chemists, Tex. Soc. Profl. Engrs., Sigma Xi, Phi Kappa Phi, Phi Lambda Upsilon, Tau Beta Pi. Home: Box 1370 Route 5 College Station TX 77843

HOLLAND, DANIEL E., painter, ret. editorial cartoonist; b. Guthrie, Ky., Feb. 2, 1918; s. Oscar Carson and Mable (Beasley) H.; m. Allene Hyden, Sept. 5, 1942; 1 son, Daniel. Student, David Lipscomb Coll., 1936-38, Chgo. Acad. of Fine Arts, 1938-39. Instr. editorial cartooning Chgo. Acad. Fine Arts, 1946-74. Editorial cartoonist, Nashville Banner, 1939-41, Chgo. Tribune, 1945-50, 54-74; cartoonist, Washington Times-Herald, Washington, 1950-54; now watercolor painter. Served with USAAF, 1941-45; received wings, Aug. 5, 1942; dive-bomber, pursuit pilot, 1943; European Theatre; instr. combat tactics, 1944-45. Awarded Air medal with 4 oak leaf clusters; recipient Freedom Found. certificate of merit, 1949, also medals, 1950, 51, 68. Mem. Am. Legion. Republican. Home: 204 Rolling Fork Ct Nashville TN 37205

HOLLAND, DANIEL MARK, economics educator; b. N.Y.C., July 7, 1920; s. Abraham and Anna (Nydorf) H.; m. Jeanne A. Ormont, June 3, 1942; children—Laura, Jonathan, Andrew. B.A., Columbia U., 1941, Ph.D. in Econs., 1951. Instr. Columbia, 1946-51; staff mem. Nat. Bur. Econ. Research, 1951-72; assoc. prof. NYU, 1957-58, Sloan Sch., Mass. Inst. Tech., Cambridge, 1958-62, prof., 1962—. Author: Income

Tax Burden on Stockholders, 1958, Dividends Under the Income Tax, 1962, Private Pension Funds; Projected Growth, 1966; editor: Nat. Tax Jour., 1966—; contbr. to: The Nations Capital Needs: Three Studies, 1979; contbr. articles to profl. jours. Served with USNR, 1943-46. Mem. Am. Econ. Assn., Royal Econ. Soc., Nat. Tax Assn., Am. Fin. Assn. Home: 41 Turning Mill Rd Lexington MA 02173 Office: Sloan Sch Mass Inst Tech 50 Memorial Dr Cambridge MA 02139

HOLLAND, DAVID SCOTT, oil company executive; b. Havana, Ark., Mar. 26, 1931; s. William Lafayette and Mae Elizabeth (Scott) H.; m. Jacque Nell Hunter, July 11, 1952; children: David Scott, Terrence Hunter. Student, Hardin-Simmons U., 1949-51; B.S. in Geology, U. Tex., Austin, 1957. Geologist Marathon Oil Co., Midland, Tex., 1957-66; with Pennzoil Co., 1966—; v.p. Pennzoil Offshore Gas Operators, Inc., Houston, 1974-77; v.p., dir. Pennzoil La. and Tex. Offshore, Inc., Houston, 1974—, Pennzoil Producing Co., Pennzoil Oil & Gas, Inc., 1977—; sr. v.p. exploration Pennzoil Exploration & Prodn. Co., 1979-84, pres., chief exec. officer, 1984—. Contbr. papers to profl. lit. Active PTA, Boy Scouts Am., YMCA, Midland, 1957-68; bd. dirs. Christian Child Help Found., Sharpstown Sch. Served with USAF, 1951-54. Mem. Ind. Petroleum Assn. Am., Am. Assn. Petroleum Geologists (continuing edn. com.), Am. Petroleum Inst., West Tex. Geol. Soc., Houston Geophys. Soc., Houston Geol. Soc., Permian Basin Soc. Exploration Geophysicists, Western Gas and Oil Assn., Assn. Citizens Polit. Action Com., Atlantic Council (China policy com.). Clubs: Univ. of Houston, Petroleum of Houston and Lafayette. Home: 2914 Ann Arbor St Houston TX 77063 Office: Pennzoil Co PO Box 2967 Houston TX 77252

HOLLAND, DOROTHY WINIFRED, food company executive; b. Tiskilwa, Ill., Mar. 10, 1919; d. Daniel Joseph and Mary Ellen (McCarthy) H. B.S., Western Ill. U., 1942, H.H.D. hon., 1984. Tchr. home econs. Sandwich High Sch., Ill., 1942-46; with Marshall Field & Co., Chgo., 1946-47; lectr. Nat. Livestock & Meat Bd., Chgo., 1947-50; home economist Kraft, Inc., Chgo., 1950-57, dir. Kraft Kitchens, 1957-70, v.p. consumer affairs, 1970-84. Dir. Sr. Ctrs. Met. Chgo.; trustee Mary Crest Coll., Davenport, Iowa; mem. Art Inst. Chgo., Chgo. Hist. Soc., Chgo. Lyric Opera, Chgo. Symphony Orch. Named Old Master Purdue U., 1974; recipient Kraft Merit award Kraft, Inc., 1962, Outstanding Service award Ill. Vocat. Home Econs. Tchrs. Assn., 1969; named Disting. Alumna Western Ill. U., 1983. Mem. Grocery Mfrs. Am. (chmn. consumer affairs com.), Am. Home Econs. Assn. (pres. bd. trustees), Confrerie de la Chaine de Rotisseurs (officer), Dames d'Escoffier, Confrerie des Vignerons de St. Vincent, Home Economists in Bus. Roman Catholic. Home: 1310 Ritchie Ct Chicago IL 60610 Office: Kraft Inc Kraft Ct Glenview IL 60025

HOLLAND, EUGENE, JR., lumber company executive; b. Lincoln, Nebr., Dec. 13, 1922; s. Eugene and Louise (Bedwell) H.; m. Martha Randall, May 15, 1948; children: Diane Holland Drewry, Randall, Mary susan Boyd, Jean, Robert Lawrence. A.B., Princeton U., 1944. V.p., dir. Holland Lumber Co.; dir. Continental Ill. Finance Corp. Chmn. Chgo. bus. div. Am. Cancer Soc., 1961; dir. Kenilworth United Fund, 1961-63, Commerce and Industry div. Crusade of Mercy, 1972; Bd. dirs. Evanston Hosp. Served with USNR, 1943-46. Clubs: Princeton, Chicago (Chgo.); Princeton (N.Y.C.); Glen View. Home: 416 Sheridan Rd Kenilworth IL 60043 Office: 231 S LaSalle St Chicago IL 60690

HOLLAND, HEINRICH DIETER, geochemist, educator; b. Mannheim, Germany, May 27, 1927; came to U.S., 1940, naturalized, 1948; s. Otto and Jeanette (Liebrecht) H.; m. Alice Tilghman Pusey, June 20, 1953; children: Henry Lawrence, Anne Liebrecht, John Pusey, Matthew Tilghman. B.A., Princeton, 1946; M.S., Columbia, 1948, Ph.D., 1952; M.A., Harvard, 1972. Mem. faculty Princeton, 1950-72, prof. geology, 1966-72; prof. geochemistry Harvard, 1972—; dir. Center for Earth and Planetary Scis., 1978-80; NSF postdoctoral fellow Oxford (Eng.) U., 1956-57; Fulbright lectr. Durham (Eng.) U., 1963-64; vis. prof. U. Hawaii, 1968-69, 81. Author: (with R.A. Rich, U. Petersen) Hydrothermal Uranium Deposits, 1977, The Chemistry of the Atmosphere and Oceans, 1978, The Chemical Evolution of the Atmosphere and Oceans, 1984; also articles on geochemistry, ore forming fluids, ocean atmosphere evolution. Pres. sch. bd., Rocky Hill, N.J., 1961-63, 67-68; mem. Winchester (Mass.) Sch. Com., 1977-80, vice chmn., 1978-80; mem. Winchester Town Meeting, 1977-80; chmn. No. N.J. chpt. Scientists and Engrs. for Johnson, 1964. Served with AUS, 1946-47. Recipient Humboldt prize, 1980; Guggenheim fellow, 1975-76. Fellow Geol. Soc. Am., Mineral. Soc. Am., Geochem. Soc. (v.p. 1969-70, pres. 1970-71), Am. Geophys. Union; mem. Nat. Acad. Scis., Am. Acad. Arts and Scis. Home: 14 Rangeley Rd Winchester MA 01890 Office: Dept Geol Scis Harvard Univ Cambridge MA 02138

HOLLAND, HOMER JAY, banker; b. Madison, Wis., Nov. 30, 1941; s. Homer Jay and Dorothy Mae (McCormick) H.; m. Penelope Jane Peck, June 15, 1963; children: Jay, Kristin. B.S., U.S. Mil. Acad., 1963; M.S., M.I.T., 1967; D.B.A., George Washington U., 1972. With First Nat. Bank Chgo., 1971-79, sr. v.p., head adminstv. dept., 1975-79; dep. chmn. Exchange Nat. Bank, Chgo., 1979-80, pres., 1980—. Bd. mgrs. YMCA Met. Chgo., 1978-80; bd. govs. Inst. European Studies, 1976—. Served to maj. U.S. Army, 1963-71; Vietnam. Decorated Bronze Star. Mem. Assn. Res. City Bankers, Econ. Club Chgo. Mem. United Ch. of Christ. Clubs: Standard (Chgo.); Hinsdale Golf. Home: 311 Bonnie Brae Hinsdale IL 60521 Office: 130 S LaSalle St Chicago IL 60603

HOLLAND, HUBERT BRIAN, lawyer; b. London, Eng., Mar. 28, 1904; came to U.S., 1915, naturalized, 1929; s. Charles Hubert and Lois Amy (Barber) H.; m. Gertrude Bancroft, Aug. 4, 1931 (dec. Dec. 1975); children: Alice Katharine, Charles Howard; m. Helen Buxton, Aug. 21, 1976. Student, Taft Sch., 1918-21; Ph.B., Yale, 1925; LL.B., Harvard U., 1928. Bar: Pa. 1929, Mass. 1935. Assoc. Williams, Brittain & Sinclair, Phila., 1928-30; atty. Dept. Justice, Washington, 1930-35, asst. atty. gen., U.S., 1953-56; asso. firm Ropes & Gray., Boston, 1935-42, partner, 1942-53, 56-76, of counsel, 1976—; lectr. Fed. Tax Inst. N.E., Inst. Fed. Taxation N.Y. U., 1950-51. Hon. trustee Kodaly Mus. Tng. Inst.; bd. dirs. Sharon (N.H.) Art Center. Fellow Am. Bar Found.; mem. Am. Law Inst., Am., Mass., Boston bar assns. Episcopalian. Home: 63 Pine St Peterborough NH 03458 Office: 225 Franklin St Boston MA 02110

HOLLAND, JAMES R., communications exec.; b. Savannah, Ga., Aug. 3, 1929; s. Francis Ross and Eleanor (Struck) H.; m. Paul Shepard, Feb. 14, 1959; children—Kristine, Carey, Jaime. A.B. in Journalism, U. Ga., 1954. Vice pres. advt. and public relations John Hancock Mut. Life Ins. Co., Boston, 1961-70; asst. postmaster gen. for communications U.S. Postal Service, Washington, 1970-73; dep. asst. sec. public affairs HEW, Washington, 1973-74, spl. asst. to sec., 1975-76; asst. pres. sec. to Pres. Ford, Washington, 1975-76; v.p. corp. affairs Miller Brewing Co., Milw., 1976-80; exec. v.p. corp. communications NBC, N.Y.C., 1980—. Served with USAF, 1950-52. Mem. Sigma Delta Chi. Home: 22 Oriole Ave Bronxville NY 10708 Office: NBC 30 Rockefeller Plaza New York NY 10022

HOLLAND, JEFFREY R., university president; b. St. George, Utah, Dec. 3, 1940; s. Frank D. and Alice (Bentley) H.; m. Patricia Terry, June 7, 1963; children: Matthew, Mary, David. B.S., Brigham Young U., 1965, M.A., 1966; M.Phil., Yale U., 1972, Ph.D., 1973. Dean religious instrn. Brigham Young U., 1974-76, pres., 1980—; commr. Latter Day Saints Ch. Ednl. System, 1976-80; dir. Deseret News Pub. Co., Comml. Security Bancorp., Salt Lake City. Bd. dirs. Intermountain Health Care, Inc., Salt Lake City, Polynesian Cultural Center, Laie, Hawaii. Mem. Am. Assn. Ind. Colls. and Univs. (dir.), Am. Assn. Pres.'s Ind. Colls. and Univs., Am. Council Edn., Phi Kappa Phi. Home: President's Home Brigham Young U Provo UT 84602 Office: D-346 ASB Brigham Young U Provo UT 84602

HOLLAND, JEROME HEARTWELL, relief organization official; b. Auburn, N.Y., Jan. 9, 1916; s. Robert Howard and Viola (Bagby) H.; m. Laura Mitchell; children: Jerome, Pamela, Lucy, Joseph. B.S., Cornell U., Ithaca, N.Y., 1939, M.S., 1941; Ph.D., U. Pa., 1950; L.H.D., Northeastern U., 1965, Hobart and William Smith Colls., 1965, Hamilton Coll., 1967, St. Paul's Coll., Lawrenceville, Va., 1978; Litt.D., Union Coll., 1966; LL.D., U. Cin., 1966, Colgate U., 1969, Washington U., St. Louis, 1970, Del. State Coll., 1970, Rider Coll., N.J., 1971, Washington and Lee U., 1971, Columbia U., 1972, Eastern Mich. State U., 1972, Va. Union U., 1973, U. Pa., 1973, Adelphi U., 1973, Lincoln U., 1973, Am. Internat. Coll., Mass., 1975, Villa Maria Coll., Erie, Pa., 1976, Tuskegee Inst., 1977, Morehouse Coll., 1979; D.Public Service, Ohio No. U., 1973. Pres. Del. State Coll., Dover, 1953-60, Hampton (Va.) Inst., 1960-70; U.S. ambassador to Sweden, 1970-72; chmn. bd. govs. ARC, since 1979—; dir. AT&T, Chrysler Corp., The Continental Corp., Culbro Corp., Gen. Foods Corp., Federated Dept. Stores, Inc., Mfrs. Hanover Corp., Union Carbide Corp., Pan Am. Bancshares, Inc., Zurn Industries, Inc. Author: Black Opportunity, 1969. Vice-chmn. N.E. region NCCJ, 1975; vice-chmn. N.Y. adv. bd. Salvation Army, 1974; trustee Inst. Internat. Edn., 1973; trustee emeritus Cornell U.; bd. dirs. United Negro Coll. Fund, 1976—, The Johnson Found., 1973—. Carnegie Corp. grantee, 1964; Danforth Found. grantee, 1968. Fellow Am. Acad. Arts and Scis.; mem. Nat. Geog. Soc. (dir.), Fgn. Policy Assn. (dir.), Am. Arbitration Assn. (dir.), N.Y. C. of C. and Industry (dir.), Econ. Devel. Council (dir.), Council Fgn. Relations (dir.). Clubs: Alfalfa, Century Assn. Home: 36 Warwick Rd Bronxville NY 10708 Office: care ARC 17th and D Sts NW Washington DC 20006

HOLLAND, JOHN BEN, clothing manufacturing company executive; b. Scottsville, Ky., Mar. 26, 1932; s. Elbridge Winfred and Lou May (Whitney) H.; m. Margaret Irene Pecor, Jan. 31, 1954; children: John Sandra, Robert. B.S. in Acctg., Bowling Green Bus. U., 1959. With Union Underwear Co., Inc., Bowling Green, Ky., 1961—, v.p.-adminstrn., 1972-74, vice chmn., 1975, chmn., chief exec. officer, 1976—; dir. Am. Nat. Bank, Bowling Green. Bd. dirs. Ky. Council Econ. Edn., Louisville, 1981—. Mem. Bowling Green-Warren County C. of C. (bd. dirs. 1981—). Office: Union Underwear Co Inc 1 Fruit of the Loom Dr Bowling Green KY 42101

HOLLAND, KEN, congressman; b. Gaffney, S.C., Nov. 24, 1934; s. James A. H.; m. Diane L. Martin, Nov. 24, 1976; children by previous marriage—Lamar, Amy, Beth. B.A., U. S.C., 1960, LL.B., 1963, J.D., 1970. Bar: S.C. bar. Practiced law, Camden, S.C.; mem. 94th-97th Congresses from 5th S.C. Dist. Legal counsel S.C. Democratic Party, also mem. exec. com. Served with AUS, 1952. Mem. Am., S.C. bar assns., S.C. Trial Lawyers Assn., S.C. Jaycees (past v.p.). Methodist. Club: Kiwanis. Office: Webster Chamberlain and Bean 1747 Pennsylvania Ave NW Washington DC 20515 *

HOLLAND, KENNETH JOHN, editor; b. Mpls., July 19, 1918; s. John Olaf and Olga Marie (Dahlberg) H.; m. Maurine M. Strom, Aug. 15, 1948; children: Laurence, Wesley. B.A. in Religion, Union Coll., Lincoln, Nebr., 1949; postgrad., Vanderbilt U. Div. Sch., 1964-69. Chemist Capitol Flour Mills, St. Paul, 1937-40; copy editor So. Pub. Assn., Nashville, 1949-51; asso. editor These Times, 1952-56, editor, from 1957, Washington, 1981—; ordained to ministry Seventh-day Adventist Ch., 1958; condr. editorial councils overseas, writers workshops, U.S. Author: books, the most recent being The Choice, 1977. Served with U.S. Army, 1941-43; Served with USAAF, 1943-45. Recipient Am. In God We Trust Family medal Family Found. Am., 1980. Mem. Asso. Ch. Press (award of merit 1976, 77, 78, 80), Ams. United for Separation Ch. and State, Religious Public Relations Council, Internat. Platform Assn. Republican. Club: Old Hickory Country (Nashville). Home: 13524 Wisteria Dr Germantown MD 20874 Office: 55 W Oak Ridge Dr Hagerstown MD 21740

HOLLAND, LYMAN FAITH, JR., lawyer; b. Mobile, June 17, 1931; s. Lyman Faith and Louise (Wisdom) H.; m. Leannah Louise Platt, Mar. 6, 1954; children: Lyman Faith III, Laura. B.S. in Bus. Adminstrn, U. Ala., 1953; LL.B., 1957. Bar: Ala. 1957. Asso. firm Hand, Arendall & Bedsole, Mobile, 1957-62; partner firm Hand, Ardendall, Bedsole, Greaves and Johnston, 1963—. Mem. Mobile Historic Devel. Com., 1965-69, v.p., 1967-68; bd. dirs. Mobile Azalea Trail, Inc., 1963-68, chmn. bd., 1963-65; bd. dirs. Mobile Mental Health Center, 1969-76, v.p., 1972, pres., chmn. bd., 1973; bd. dirs. Mobile chpt. ARC, vice chmn., 1975-77, exec. vice chmn., 1978-80, chmn., 1980-82; bd. dirs. Deep South council Girl Scouts U.S.A., 1965-71, Gordan Smith Center Inc., 1973, Bay Area Council on Alcoholism, 1973-76, Community Chest and, Council of Mobile County, Inc., 1977—, Greater Mobile Mental Health-Mental Retardation, 1975-81; pres. Greater Mobile Mental Health-Mental Retardation, 1975-77. Served to 1st lt. USAF, 1953-55; lt. col. Res.; ret. Mem. Am., Mobile County bar assns., Ala. State Bar (chmn. sect. corp., banking and bus. law 1978-80), Am. Coll. Probate Counsel, Ala. Law Inst. (council), Pi Kappa Alpha, Phi Delta Phi. Baptist (deacon; ch. trustee 1968-73, chmn. trustees 1971-73). Clubs: Lions, Athleston (Mobile); Country Club of Mobile, Bienville. Home: 717 Westmoreland Dr W Mobile AL 36609 Office: Box 123 Mobile AL 36601

HOLLAND, MICHAEL FRANCIS, investment co. exec.; b. Cleve., July 8, 1944; s. Joseph Thomas and Mary Louise Holl; m. Louise Grace, Aug. 20, 1966; children—Brian, Thomas, Joseph, Daniel, John, Michael Francis. A.B., Harvard U., 1966; M.B.A., Columbia U., 1968. With Morgan Guaranty Trust Co., N.Y.C., 1968-80, investment mgr., 1972-80, v.p., 1975-80; sr. v.p. investments Reliance Group, Inc., also Reliance Ins. Co., N.Y.C., 1980—; dir. J. Rothschild Internat. Investments (S.A.), Target Trust Mgrs., Ltd. Bd. dirs. New Canaan (Conn.) Boys Baseball, 1977-81; gen. gifts chmn. class of 1966 Harvard Coll. Fund. Clubs: New Canaan Field, Winter (New Canaan); N.Y. Athletic, Harvard of Fairfield County. Home: 79 Lake Wind Rd New Canaan CT 06840 Office: Park Ave Plaza New York NY 10055

HOLLAND, PARK, JR., lawyer; b. San Antonio, July 31, 1919; s. Park and Helen (Hotaling) H.; m. Carolyn Letitia Lively, Oct. 13, 1945; 1 son, Park III. Student, U. Md., 1938-39, Auburn U., 1939-41, George Washington U., 1941-42; LL.B. cum laude, Albany Law Sch. of Union U., 1944, J.D., 1968. Bar: N.Y. 1944, Okla. 1974, D.C. 1976. Asso. Woollard & Morris, Albany, 1944-45, Cravath, Swaine & Moore, N.Y.C., 1945-47; prin. atty. N.Y. State Banking Dept., 1947-50; atty. Cities Service Co., N.Y.C., 1950-63, asst. gen. counsel, 1963-67, sec., asst. gen. counsel, 1967-74, sec., asso. gen. counsel, 1974-83, also dir. and/or officer various subs.; practice law, 1983—; Adv. bd. Internat. and Comparative Law Center. Mem. Okla. Bar Assn., ABA. Home: 1120 E 24th Pl Tulsa OK 74114

HOLLAND, PAUL DELEVAL, lawyer; b. Los Angeles., Feb. 1, 1910; s. Christopher Franklin and Louise (Deleval) H.; m. Claudine Florence Atkins. Student, U. Calif., Los Angeles, 1928-31; A.B., U. So. Calif., 1933, J.D., 1934. Bar: Calif. 1934. Pvt. practice in, Los Angeles, 1934-42, Beverly Hills, 1945-70, Los Angeles, Century City, 1970—. Mem. Conf. Bd. Pensions, United Methodist Ch., 1968—; Pres. Calif. Epilepsy Soc., 1966-70; pres. Epilepsy Found. Am., 1973-75, chmn., 1975-76, chmn. emeritus, 1977—; v.p. Epi Hab U.S.A. Mem. Am. Arbitration Assn., Am. Judicature Soc., Am., Los Angeles County, Century City bar assns., Phi Gamma Delta, Delta Theta Phi. Democrat. Home: 12023 Monogram Ave Granada Hills CA 91344 Office: 1880 Century Park East Los Angeles CA 90067

HOLLAND, RICHARD G., JR., apparel co. exec.; b. Boston, Sept. 4, 1927; s. Richard and Ruth (McCarthy) H.; m. Mary D. Cronin, June 20, 1952; children—Denise, Cheryl, Richard, Michael, Tracy. B.S., Boston U., 1949. Auditor Commonwealth Mass., 1949-50; sales staff Internat. Harvester Co., 1950-51; v.p. merchandising William Carter Co., Needham Heights, Mass., 1968-73, pres., 1973—. Served with USCG, 1944-46. Roman Catholic. Club: Charles River Country. Home: 230 Forest St Needham MA 02192 Office: 963 Highland Ave Needham Heights MA 02194

HOLLAND, ROBERT CAMPBELL, anatomist, educator; b. Bushnell, Ill., Aug. 16, 1923; s. Harvey Howard and Lois Sarah (Campbell) H.; m. Nancy Jean Hallenbeck, 1982; children: Jonathan Robert, Heather Ann. B.S., U. Wis., 1948, M.S., 1949, Ph.D., 1955. Instr. Northwestern U. Dental Sch., 1949-51; asst. prof. anatomy U. N.D. Sch. Medicine, 1955-60; assoc. prof. U. Ark. Sch. Medicine, 1960-66; prof. chmn. dept. anatomy Mahidol U., Bangkok, Thailand, 1966-76; prof., chmn. dept. anatomy Morehouse Sch. Medicine, Atlanta, 1976—; mem. staff Rockefeller Found., 1966-76; vis. prof. UCLA Sch. Medicine, 1976. Author research pubs. on the brain. Served with M.C. U.S. Army, 1943-46. Fellow Wis. Alumni Research Found., 1951-54, Nat. Found. for Infantile Paralysis, 1957-58; NIH grantee, 1959—. Mem. Am. Assn. Anatomists, Am. Acad. Neurology, Soc. Exptl. Biology and Medicine, AAAS, Soc. Neurosci., Sigma Xi. Office: Morehouse Sch Medicine Atlanta GA 30310

HOLLAND, ROBERT CARL, economist; b. Tekamah, Nebr., Apr. 7, 1925; s. Carl Luther and Gretchen (Thompson) H.; m. DeEtte Harriet Hedlund, Sept. 7, 1947; children: Joan DeEtte, Holland Gelty, Nancy Gretchen, Timothy Robert. Student, U. Nebr., 1942-43, 46, U. Wis., 1943-44; B.S. in Fin., U. Pa., 1948; M.A. in Econs., U. Pa., 1949, Ph.D., 1959. Instr. money and banking U. Pa., 1948-49; with Fed. Res. Bank Chgo., 1949-61, v.p., 1959-61; with bd. govs. Fed. Res. System, 1961-76; mem. bd. govs. FRS, 1973-76, sec. of bd., 1968-71, exec. dir., 1971-73, sec. to fed. open market com., 1966-73; pres. Com. for Econ. Devel., Washington, 1976—. Mem. bd. overseers Wharton Sch., U. Pa.; mem. bd. pensions Luth. Ch. Am.; bd. visitors Sch. Bus. Adminstrn., Georgetown U.; bd. dirs. Bur. Econ. Research, Aid Assn. Lutherans. Served with AUS, 1943-45. Mem. Am. Econ. Assn., Am. Fin. Assn., Beta Theta Pi. Clubs: Cosmos (Washington); Univ. of N.Y. (N.Y.C.); Kenwood Country (Bethesda, Md.). Home: 5508 Cromwell Dr Bethesda MD 20816 Office: Com for Econ Devel 1700 K St NW Suite 700 Washington DC 20006

HOLLAND, ROBERT LEE, business administration educator, business executive; b. N.C., Jan. 18, 1930; s. R.A. and Kathleen Holl; m. Geraldine Gantt, Aug. 4, 1950; 1 son, Robert Lee. B.S., U. Tenn., 1951, M.S., 1956; Ph.D., Tex. A&M U., 1960. County agrl. agt., N.C., 1953-55; instr., coop. agt. Tex. A. and M. U., 1956-60; economist, then chief staff officer Dept. Agr., 1960-67; ops. research officer IRS, 1967-68; assoc. prof. quantitative methods, chmn. dept., assoc. dean Sch. Govt. and Bus. George Washington U., 1968-74, dean Coll. Gen. Studies, 1975-81, sabbatical leave, 1981-82, assoc. prof. bus. adminstrn., 1982—; gen. ptnr. Holland & Holland Cosmetics; pres. Excalibur Electronics Inc. Author papers in field. Served with AUS, 1951-53. Fellow Nat. Inst. Pub. Affairs (1966-67); Mem. Nat. Univ. Extension Assn., Assn. Continuing Higher Edn., Washington Ops. Research Council. Home: 929 Glyndon St SE Vienna VA 22180 Office: 401 Maple Ave E Vienna VA

HOLLAND, TAYLOR GRIFFITH, JR., utility company executive; b. Phila., Sept. 13, 1928; s. Taylor Griffith and Anne (Miles) H.; m. Cornelia Murray Goodloe, Feb. 3, 1951; children: Delia Adair, Cornelia Goodloe, Katherine, Taylor III. B.E., Vanderbilt U., 1950. With Nashville Gas Co., 1950-73, v.p. mktg., 1968-71, sr. v.p., 1971-73; exec. v.p. Mississippi Valley Gas Co., Jackson, Miss., 1973-74, pres., chief exec. officer, 1974-76; chmn. bd., pres., chief exec. officer, 1976—; pres., dir. J.I.D. Corp.; dir. First Nat. Bank. Vice pres. United Way of Capitol Area, Jackson, 1975-76, pres., 1977-78; bd. dirs., pres. Jackson Symphony, 1976; vice chmn. Miss. Arts Center-Planetarium Commn., Jackson, 1977-81, chmn., 1981—. Mem. Am. Gas Assn., So. Gas Assn. (chmn. elect), Tenn. Gas. Assn., ASME., Jackson C. of C. (1st v.p.). Republican. Episcopalian. Clubs: Jackson Country, Colonial Country, River Hills, Univ., Capital City Petroleum. Lodges: Masons; Shriners (Nashville). Home: 2560 Lake Circle Jackson MS 39211 Office: 711 W Capitol St Jackson MS 39203

HOLLAND, THOMAS POWELL, social work educator; b. Bartow, Fla., Aug. 19, 1942; s. Thomas Wesley and Dorothy Ann (Powell) H.; 1 dau., Kimberly. B.A. magna cum laude, Wheaton Coll., 1964; M.S.W., Fla. State U., 1966; Ph.D., Brandeis U., 1972. Instr. social work Mailman Center for Child Devel., U. Miami, 1966-69; asst. prof. Case Western Res. U., 1972-74, assoc. prof., 1974-77, prof., 1977—; sr. research assoc. Human Services Design Lab., 1972-74, dir., 1974-77; chmn. doctoral program, 1977—. Trustee Inst. Child Advocacy, Inc., Cleve., 1977—. Nat. Inst. Child Health and Human Devel. fellow, 1969-71. Mem. Acad. Cert. Social Workers, AAUP, Am. Sociol. Assn., Nat. Assn. Social Workers, Pi Gamma Mu. Home: 18407 Winslow Shaker Heights OH 44122 Office: School Applied Social Sciences Case Western Reserve Univ Cleveland OH 44106

HOLLAND, TOM, painter, educator; b. Seattle, June 15, 1936; m. Judy, 1958; children: Randolph, Brendon, Joel. Student, U. Calif.-Berkeley, 1954-56, Willamette U., Salem, Oreg., 1956-58, U. Calif.-Santa Barbara. Instr. San Francisco Art Inst., 1963-68, 1971-75; asst. prof. UCLA, 1968-70. Exhibited one-man shows, Catholic U., Santiago, Chile, 1960, Richmond Art Ctr., Calif., 1962, Laynon Gallery, Palo Alto, Calif., 1963, 64, 65, Hansen Fuller Gallery, 1965, 74, Nicholas Wilder Gallery, Los Angeles, 1965, 67, 69, 76, Ariz. State U., Tempe, 1968, Neuendorf Gallery, Cologne, Germany, 1970, Robert Elkon Gallery, N.Y.C., 1970, 71, Corcoran and Corcoran, Miami, 1972, Multiples, Los Angeles, Knoedler Contemporary Art, N.Y.C., 1973, 75, Watson de Nagy Gallery, Houston, 1977, Smith Anderson Gallery, Palo Alto, Calif., 1978, Droll Kolbert Gallery, N.Y.C., San Francisco Art Inst., 1979, Corcoran Gallery, Los Angeles, 1980, Charles Cowles Gallery, N.Y.C., 1981, Fuller Goldeen Gallery,

San Francisco, 1982, group shows, San Francisco Art Inst., 1963, 67, San Francisco Mus. Modern Art, 1964, 70, La Jolla Mus. Calif., 1965, Los Angeles County Mus., 1966, Phila. Soc. Arts Invitational, 1968, Corcoran Mus., Washington, 1969, Mus. Modern Art, N.Y.C., 1970, Whitney Mus. Contemporary Art, 1970, 78, Albright-Knox Art Gallery, Buffalo, 1971, Walker Art Ctr., Mpls., 1972, Mus. Modern Art, N.Y.C., Whitney Mus. Am. Art, N.Y.C., 1973, Corcoran Biennial, Washington, 1975, Richmond Art Ctr., 1976, Nat. Collection Fine Arts, Washington, 1977, Mus. Modern Art, N.Y.C., 1981, Calif. Inst. Tech., Pasadena, 1982; represented permanent collections, Oakland Mus. Calif., Stanford U., St. Louis City Mus., Larry Aldrich Mus., Ridgefield, Conn., Mus. Art, San Francisco, Mus. Modern Art, N.Y.C., Chgo. Art. Inst., Walker Art Ctr., Mpls., Guggenheim Mus., N.Y.C., Hirshhorn Mus., Washington, others. Grantee Nat. Endowment for Arts, 1975-76; Fulbright fellow, 1959-60; Guggenheim fellow, 1979. Office: San Francisco Art Inst 800 Chestnut St San Francisco CA 94188 *

HOLLAND, WILLIAM JEREMIAH, naval officer; b. Iowa City, Nov. 8, 1932; s. William J. and Elizabeth (Kellenberger) H.; m. Anne Daly, June 23, 1956; children: William P., Peter J., Margaret M., John J., Mary E., James B., Kathleen. B.S., U.S. Naval Acad., 1955; M.P.A., Harvard U., 1969. Commd. ensign U.S. Navy, 1955, rear admiral, 1981—; capt., dir. profl. devel. U.S. Naval Acad., Annapolis, Md., 1974-76; capt. Comdg. Submarine Squadron One, Pearl Harbor, Hawaii, 1976-78, Comdg. Submarine Sch., New London, Conn., 1978-81; rear admiral, dep. dir. ops. Joint Chiefs of Staff, Washington, 1981-82; rear admiral, dir. Strategic and Theater Nuclear Warfare, Washington, 1982-83; rear admiral Comdg. Submarine Group, San Diego, 1983—. Bd. dirs. Uniformed Services Benefit Assn., Kansas City, Mo., 1983—. Decorated Def. Superior Services medal, Legion of Merit with star, Meritorious Service medal with 2 stars. Mem. U.S. Naval Inst. Roman Catholic. Home: 154 N Sylvester Rd San Diego CA 92106 Office: Submarine Group Five Submarine Base San Diego CA 92106

HOLLAND, WILLIAM RAY, diversified heavy equipment manufacturing corporation executive; b. Ada, Okla., 1938. B.A., U. Denver, 1960, LL.B., 1962. Atty. Southwestern Bell Telephone co., 1964-66; ptnr. firm Bridges, Young, Matthew & Davis, 1966-73; v.p., gen. counsel AMCA Internat. Corp., 1973-76, sr. v.p. adminstrn., 1976-81, exec. v.p., 1981—, AMCA Internat., Ltd.; pres. Koehring Co., 1981—. Office: Koehring Co Inc 200 Executive Dr Brookfield WI 53055

HOLLANDER, CHARLES SIMCHE, physician; b. N.Y.C., Aug. 25, 1934; s. Bernard and Beatrice (Bobrowsky) H.; m. Joan Simon, Dec. 17, 1972; children: Ellen, Ruth, Barbara. A.B., Columbia U., 1955, M.D., 1959. Intern Bellevue Hosp., N.Y.C., 1959-60; research fellow in medicine Johns Hopkins U., Balt., 1960-62, 65-66; sr. resident Peter Bent Brigham Hosp., 1962-63; research assoc. metabolism br. Nat. Cancer Inst., NIH, 1963-65; asso. physician in medicine, chief endocrinology Rochester (N.Y.) Gen. Hosp.; asso. prof. medicine U. Rochester, 1966-69, N.Y. U. Med. Center, 1969-74, prof. medicine, 1974—, chief endocrine div., 1969—, dir. clin. research unit, 1969—; asst. in medicine Harvard Med. Sch., 1962-63; asst. physician in medicine Johns Hopkins Hosp., 1965-66; asso. physician Strong Meml. Hosp., Rochester, 1966-69; attending physician N.Y. U. Hosp., 1969—, Bellevue Hosp., 1969—; cons. Manhattan VA Hosp., 1969—; mem. Clin. Research Centers Study Sect., 1979-81, chmn., 1981-82; mem. metabolism panel Health Research Council, N.Y.C., 1969-75; ad hoc cons. Alcohol Abuse and Alcoholism and Drug Abuse, NIH, 1978, VA merit rev., 1978; chmn. workshop com. on advanced neuroendocrinology Div. Research Resources NIH, 1981; mem. alcohol biomed. research rev. com. Nat. Inst. Alcohol Abuse and Alcoholism, 1983—. Served with USPHS, 1963-65. Mem. A.C.P. (Council Specialized Socs.), Am. Soc. Clin. Investigation, Am. Fedn. Clin. Research, Harvey Soc., Endocrine Soc. (mem. manpower liaison com. 1981—, chmn. 1982-83), Am. Thyroid Assn. (bd. dirs. Program Dirs. Assn. 1979—, pres. 1980-81), AAUP, N.Y. Acad. Scis., Phi Beta Kappa, Phi Delta Epsilon. Democrat. Jewish. Club: Men's B'hai Jeshurin. Home: 411 W End Ave New York NY 10024 Office: 550 1st Ave New York NY 10016

HOLLANDER, EDWIN PAUL, psychologist, educator; b. Rochester, N.Y., Aug. 15, 1927; s. Victor and Lillian (Kravetz) H.; m. Patricia Ann Harrington, Apr. 18, 1959; 1 son, Peter Andrew. B.S., Western Res. U., 1948; M.A., Columbia U., 1950, Ph.D., 1952. Asst. prof. psychology Carnegie Inst. Tech., Pitts., 1954-58; asso. prof. psychology Washington U., St. Louis, 1958-60; asso. prof. internat. communication and social psychology Sch. Internat. Service, Am. U., Washington, 1960-62; prof. psychology SUNY-Buffalo, 1962—, provost social scis. and adminstrn., 1971-73, dir. social psychology grad. program, 1962-68, 73-76; study dir. Nat. Acad. Scis., 1979-80; vis. faculty U. Istanbul, Turkey, 1957-58, U. Wis., 1961, Inst. Am. Studies, Paris, 1966-67, Harvard U., 1969-70, Oxford (Eng.) U., 1973; cons. NSF, 1965-68, HEW, 1967-72, Nat. Acad. Scis., NRC, Space Sci. Bd., 1969-70; prin. investigator research projects Office Naval Research, 1955-69, 76-79, NIMH, 1962-64. Author: Leaders, Groups and Influence, 1964, Principles and Methods of Social Psychology, 1967, 4th edit., 1981, Leadership Dynamics, 1978; co-editor: Current Perspectives in Social Psychology, 1963, 4th edit., 1976, Classic Contributions to Social Psychology, 1972; mem. editorial bd.: Jour. Abnormal and Social Psychology, 1962-64, Jour. Personality Social Psychology, 1965-67, Brit. Jour. Social and Clin. Psychology, 1967-79; editorial bd.: Sociometry, 1969-72; asso. editor, 1971-72; editorial bd., asso. editor: Internat. Rev. Applied Psychology, 1975-79; contbr. articles to profl. jours., chpts. to books, papers at internat. congresses and profl. meetings. Served with AUS, 1946-47; from ensign to lt. USNR, 1951-54. Disting. Achievement award Psychol. Assn. Western N.Y., 1983; Fulbright fellow, Turkey, 1957-58; NIMH sr. fellow Tavistock Inst. Human Relations, London, 1966-67. Fellow Am. Psychol. Assn. (chmn. com. psychology nat. internat. affairs 1962-63, mem. council reps. 1965-66, 68-70, 79-81, 83-86, mem. bd. social and ethical responsibility for psychology 1975-78, mem. com. on internat. relations in psychology 1981-84, pres. div. gen. psychology 1980-81), AAAS (sec. psychology sect. 1974-78); mem. AAUP (pres. Carnegie Tech. chpt. 1956-57), Soc. Exptl. Social Psychology (chmn. exec. com. 1969-70), Eastern Psychol. Assn. (dir. 1983—), Soc. Psychol. Study Social Issues (council 1968-70), Internat. Assn. Applied Psychology (exec. com. 1975—, U.S. treas. 1980-82), Am. Assn. Univ. Adminstrs., Acad. Mgmt., Authors Guild, Sigma Xi, Omicron Delta Kappa, Psi Chi. Club: Cosmos (Washington). Office: Dept Psychology SUNY 4230 Ridge Lea Rd Buffalo NY 14226

HOLLANDER, JACK M(ARVIN), chemist, educator; b. Youngstown, Ohio, Apr. 13, 1927; s. Isadore M. and Adele E. (Feuer) H.; children—Judith, Jeffrey, Allan. B.Sc. in Chemistry, Ohio State U., 1948; Ph.D., U. Calif., Berkeley, 1951. Instr. chemistry U. Calif., Berkeley, 1951-53, prof. energy resources, 1980—; dir. Energy Inst., 1980—; mem. staff Lawrence Berkeley Lab., 1953-75, asso. dir. lab., head energy and environment div., 1973-75, asso. dir. lab. planning, 1978-80; exec. dir. Nat. Acad. Scis., 1975-78; chmn. bd. Internat. Inst. Energy and Human Ecology, Stockholm, 1977—. Author: Table of Isotopes, 6th edit, 1967; Editor: Ann. Rev. Energy, 1974—. Guggenheim fellow, 1958, 66. Mem. Fedn. Am. Scientists (council 1969-70), Am. Phys. Soc., Am. Chem. Soc., AAAS, World Acad. Arts and Scis. (hon.), Royal Swedish Acad. Sci. Office: Ohio State U Columbus OH 43210

HOLLANDER, JOHN, humanities educator, author; b. N.Y.C., Oct. 28, 1929; s. Franklin and Muriel (Kornfeld) H.; m. Anne Helen Loesser, June 15, 1953 (div. 1977); children: Martha, Elizabeth.; m. Natalie Charkow, Dec. 15, 1983. A.B., Columbia U., 1950, A.M., 1952; Ph.D., Ind. U., 1959; D.Litt. (hon.), Marietta Coll., 1982. Jr. fellow Soc. Fellows, Harvard, 1954-57; lectr. English Conn. Coll., New London, 1957-59; instr. English Yale, 1959-61; asst. prof. English, fellow Ezra Stiles Coll., 1961-64, asso. prof., 1964-66; prof. Hunter Coll., CCNY, 1966-77; prof. English, Yale U.; also fellow Silliman Coll., 1977—; vis. prof. Linguistic Inst., Ind. U., 1964; faculty Salzburg Seminar in Am. Studies, 1965; Christian Gauss seminarian Princeton, 1962. Editorial assoc. for poetry: Partisan Rev., 1959-65; mem. poetry bd., Wesleyan U. Press, 1959-62; Author: A Crackling of Thorns, 1958, The Untuning of the Sky, 1961, Movie-Going and Other Poems, 1962, Various Owls, 1963, Visions from the Ramble, 1965, The Quest of the Gole, 1966, Types of Shape, 1968, Images of Voice, 1970, The Night Mirror, 1971, Town and Country Matters, 1972, The Head of the Bed, 1973, Tales Told of the Fathers, 1975, Vision and Resonance, 1975, Reflections on Espionage, 1976, Spectral Emanations, 1978, In Place, 1978, Blue Wine, 1979, The Figure of Echo, 1981, Rhyme's Reason, 1981, Powers of Thirteen, 1983, (with Saul Steinberg) Dal Vero, 1983; editor: Poems of Ben Jonson, 1961, (with Harold Bloom) The Wind and the Rain, 1961, (with Anthony Hecht) Jiggery-Pokery, 1966, Poems of Our Moment, 1968, Modern Poetry: Essays in Criticism, 1968, American Short Stories Since 1945, 1968, (with Frank Kermode) The Oxford Anthology of English Literature, 1973, (with R.A. Brower and Helen Vendler) For I.A. Richards: Essays in His Honor, 1973, (with Irving Howe and David Bromwich) Literature as Experience, 1979; Contbg. editor: Harper's mag, 1969-71; Contbr. poems, articles various jours. Recipient Yale Younger Poets award, 1958; Poetry Chap Book award, 1962; award in lit. Nat. Inst. Arts and Letters, 1963; Levinson prize, 1974; Bollingen prize, 1983; Overseas fellow Churchill Coll., Cambridge (Eng.) U., 1967-68; sr. fellow Nat. Endowment for Humanities, 1973—; Guggenheim fellow, 1979-80. Fellow Acad. Am. Poets; mem. Nat. Inst. Arts and Letters, Am. Acad. Arts and Scis., English Inst., Phi Beta Kappa. Club: Century Assn. (N.Y.C.). Office: Dept English Yale U New Haven CT 06520

HOLLANDER, LORIN, pianist; b. N.Y.C., July 19, 1944; s. Max and Mary Louis (Yarbro) H. Student, Profl. Children's Sch., N.Y.C., 1960, Juilliard Coll. Music, 1964, also C. W. Post Coll., Brookville, N.Y. Debut, Carnegie Hall, N.Y.C., 1956; concerts on Bell Telephone Hour, at Carnegie Hall, also on NBC radio and TV, 1957; concert tours, U.S., 1959—, Europe, 1965—; recording artist for, RCA Victor. Youngest artist on Great Artist Series, 1956. Office: care ICM Artists Ltd 40 W 57th St New York NY 10019 *

HOLLANDER, MILTON BERNARD, corp. exec.; b. Bayonne, N.J., Nov. 29, 1928; s. Harry and Lena (Hutner) H.; m. Betty Ruth Grodberg, June 6, 1952; children—Eva Lynn, J. Steven, Aaron Phillip, Joel Daniel. B.S., Purdue U., 1951; M.S., Mass. Inst. Tech., 1953; Ph.D., Columbia, 1959. Dir. engrng. center Am. Machine & Foundry Co., Springdale, Conn., 1956-67; v.p. tech. Am.-Standard, Inc., N.Y.C., 1967-72; chmn. bd. Gulf & Western Invention Devel. Corp., N.Y.C., 1975—; v.p. tech. Gulf & Western Industries, Inc., N.Y.C., 1972—; dir. PolyGulf Corp., Bklyn., 1973—; cons. electronics lab. Columbia U., 1955-57. Author tech. papers temperature measurement, metal cutting, instrumentation. Com. chmn. local Boy Scouts Am. Served with C.E. AUS, 1946-48; Korea. Research fellow Mass. Inst. Tech., 1952-53; duPont research fellow Columbia U., 1955-57; research fellow Am. Soc. Tool and Mfg. Engrs., 1954-55; recipient Outstanding Alumnus award Purdue U., 1972. Mem. ASME, Am. Welding Soc., Indsl. Research Inst., Sigma Xi. Patentee in field. Office: 1 Gulf & Western Plaza New York NY 10023

HOLLANDER, MORTON JOSEPH, lawyer; b. N.Y.C., Mar. 5, 1913; s. Emanuel and Eve (Cohen) H.; m. Maxine Sittenfeld, Dec. 26, 1937; children: Nancy (Mrs. Leonard Kane), Susan (Mrs. James Sidel). B.S., N.Y. U., 1934; LL.B., Harvard, 1937. Bar: N.Y. 1937, Md. 1939. Since practiced in, Balt.; asso. firm Samuel H. Hoffberger; later mem. firm Hoffberger & Hollander, Gordon Feinblatt, Rothman, Hoffberger & Hollander, 1972; now counsel Gordon, Feinblatt, Rothman, Hottberger & Hollander; dir. Motor Freight Express, CPC, Inc., Keystone Realty Co., Mchts. Mortgage Co., Blum's Inc. Bd. dirs. Hoffberger Found. Mem. Md. Bar Assn. (past v.p.), Balt. City Bar Assn. (past v.p.). Clubs: Woodholme Country, Mchts. of Balt. Home: 7941 Longmeadow Rd Pikesville MD 21208 Office: Garrett Bldg Redwood and South Sts Baltimore MD 21202

HOLLANDER, RICHARD ISAAC, editor; b. N.Y.C., Apr. 6, 1912; s. Herman and Bertha (Gichner) H.; m. Helen Cornelia Eskesen, Mar. 7, 1953. Student, Georgetown U., Washington, 1928-30, George Washington U., 1931. Editorial staff Wash. Daily news, 1929—, editor, 1966—; lectr., inst. langs. and linguistics Sch. Fgn. Service, Georgetown U., also George Washington U. Compiler: History of the Psychological Warfare Division, Supreme Headquarters Allied Expeditionary Forces, 1945. Decorated Order Brit. Empire, 1945. Home: 3502 Macomb St NW Washington DC 20016 Office: 777 14th St NW Washington DC 20005

HOLLANDER, ROBERT B., JR., educator; b. N.Y.C., July 31, 1933; s. Robert B. and Laurene (McGookey) H.; m. Jean Haberman, Apr. 23, 1964; children: Cornelia Vanness, Robert B. III. A.B., Princeton U., 1955; Ph.D., Columbia U., 1962. Tchr. Latin and English Collegiate Sch., N.Y.C., 1955-57; instr. English Columbia Coll., N.Y.C., 1958-62; mem. faculty depts. comparative lit. and Romance langs. Princeton U., 1962—, prof. European lit., 1974—; mem. Nat. Council on the Humanities, 1974-80, vice chmn., 1978-80; mem. N.J. Com. for the Humanities, 1980—. Author: Allegory in Dante's Commedia, 1969, Boccaccio's Two Venuses, 1977, Studies in Dante, 1980, Il Virgilio dantesco, 1983. Trustee Nat. Humanities Ctr., 1981—. Guggenheim fellow, 1970-71; NEH fellow, 1974-75, 82-83. Mem. Dante Soc. Am. (mem. council 1976—, pres. 1980—), Am. Assn. Univ. Profs. of Italian (1st v.p. 1977-79), Am. Boccaccio Assn., MLA. Republican. Club: Cosmos (Washington). Office: 326 E Pyne St Princeton U Princeton NJ 08544

HOLLANDER, SAMUEL, economist; b. London, Apr. 6, 1937; s. Jacob and Rachel-Leah (Bornstein) H.; m. Perlette Keroub, July 20, 1959; children: Frances, Isaac. B.Sc. in Econs, London Sch. Econs., 1959; M.A., Princeton U., 1961, Ph.D., 1963. Asst. in instrn. Princeton U., 1962-63; asst. prof. econs. U. Toronto, Ont., Can., 1963-66, assoc. prof., 1966-70, prof., 1970—. Author: The Sources of Increased Efficiency, 1965, The Economics of Adam Smith, 1973, The Economics of David Ricardo, 1979. Guggenheim fellow, 1968-69; Killam sr. fellow, 1973-75. Fellow Royal Soc. Can.; mem. Am. Econ. Assn., Royal Econ. Soc., Can. Econ. Assn. Jewish. Home: 87 Searle Ave Downsview ON M3H 4A6 Canada Office: 150 Saint George St Toronto ON M5S 1A1 Canada

HOLLANDER, TOBY EDWARD, educational administrator; b. Queens, N.Y., June 21, 1931; s. David and Eve (Shroot) H.; m. Harriet Goldberg, June 14, 1953; children: Marc, Deborah. B.S. cum laude, NYU, 1952, M.B.A., 1953; Ph.D., U. Pitts., 1960. Instr. econs. U. Pitts., 1957-58; asst. prof. Duquesne U., 1958-59; prof. Baruch Coll., CUNY, 1963-67, dean, 1967-69, vice chancellor, 1969-71; dep. commr. higher edn. N.Y. State Edn. Dept., 1971-77; chancellor N.J. Dept. Higher Edn., Trenton, 1977—. Author books in field; contbr. articles to profl. jours. Ex officio mem. bd. govs. Rutgers U.; mem. Council of State Colls. State of N.J., mem. Council of County Colls.; trustee U. Medicine and Dentistry of N.J.; mem. N.J. State Bd. Med. Examiners. Served with U.S. Army, 1953-55. Mem. State Higher Edn. Exec. Officers Assn. (pres. 1977-78), Nat. Center for Higher Edn. Mgmt. Systems, Edn. Commn. of the States, Am. Council on Edn., Assn. Governing Bds. of Univs. and Colls. Home: 74 Wilson Rd Princeton NJ 08540 Office: 225 W State St Trenton NJ 08625

HOLLANDS, JOHN HENRY, electronics company executive; b. North Hornell, N.Y., Mar. 14, 1929; s. Henry Ward and Marion Eloise (Stanton) H.; m. Helen Louise Bearer, June 22, 1957; children—Wendy Lynn, Robert John, Kathryn Jean, Christine Elizabeth. A.B., Cornell U., 1951, M.B.A., 1952. With Westinghouse Electric Corp., 1954-65; gen. mgr. BSR (USA) Ltd., Blauvelt, N.Y., 1965-74, pres., chmn. bd., 1974-82, also dir.; pres. Sony Tapes Sales Co., 1982—; dir. BSR Can. Ltd., BSR (Japan) Ltd., Audio Dynamics Corp., dbx, Inc. Trustee St. Thomas Aquinas Coll., Sparkhill, N.Y., 1973-76, Rockland County (N.Y.) Center Arts, 1976. Served with USAF, 1952-54. Mem. Electronics Industry Assn. (gov.). Republican. Methodist. Home: 79 Edgewood Rd Allendale NJ 07401 Office: BSR (USA) Ltd Route 303 Blauvelt NY 10913

HOLLANS, IRBY NOAH, JR., association executive; b. Christiansburg, Va., Nov. 3, 1930; s. Irby Noah and Annie May (Lester) H.; m. Frances Jo Cox, June 21, 1957; children: Susan Frances, Carol Leigh, Irby Neil. B.S. in Gen. Bus. Adminstrn., Va. Poly. Inst. and State U., 1953. Mgr. promotion Sta. WRVA-Radio, Richmond, Va., 1956-64, editor bus. news, 1956-64; dir. travel devel. Va. State C. of C., 1964-70, asst. exec. dir., 1970-72; exec. dir. Optical Labs. Assn., Washington, 1972—; instr. bus. Va. Commonwealth U., Richmond, 1965-71. Mem. Dulles (Va.) Internat. Airport Devel. Commn., 1968-76; mem. Va. Nat. Capital Airports Acquisition Study Commn., 1968-76; bd. dirs. Va. Thanksgiving Festival Inc., 1965-70, Keep Va. Beautiful, Inc., 1965-73, Central Va. Ednl. TV, 1970-72, Va. Travel Coordinating Com., 1964-72. Served to maj. USAF, 1953-72; Korea. Recipient Service award Va. Profl. Photographers Assn., 1966; Nat. award Profl. Photographers Assn. Am., 1970. Mem. Am. Soc. Assn. Execs. (cert.), Va. Public Relations Conf., U.S. C. of C., Nat. Assn. Wholesaler-Distbrs.-Pros Group, Am. Nat. Standards Inst. (med. devices standards mgmt. bd. 1973—), Washington Soc. Assn. Execs., Va. C. of C., Alpha Kappa Psi, Pi Delta Epsilon. Home: 2804 Albany Ct Fairfax VA 22031 Office: 6935 Wisconsin Ave Suite 200 Chevy Chase MD 20815

HOLLASCH, RAYMOND G., financial executive; b. N.J., Feb. 20, 1935. B.S.B.A., Rutgers U., 1956. Audit mgr. Arthur Andersen & Co., N.Y.C., 1956-65; with Irving Trust Co., N.Y.C., 1965—, now sr. v.p. and auditor. Mem. Am. Inst. C.P.A.s, N.J. Soc. C.P.A.s. Office: Irving Trust Co One Wall St New York NY 10015

HOLLDOBLER, BERTHOLD KARL, zoologist, educator; b. Erling-Andechs, Germany, June 25, 1936; came to U.S., 1973; s. Karl and Maria (Russmann) H.; m. Friederike Probst, Feb. 9, 1980. Dr. rer. nat., U. Wurzburg, 1965; Dr. habil., U. Frankfurt a.M., 1969. Prof. zoology U. Frankfurt a.M., 1971-72; prof. biology Harvard U., Cambridge, Mass., 1973—, Alexander Agassiz prof. zoology, 1982—. Mem. Am. Acad. Sci., Deutsche Akademie der Naturforscher Leopoldina. Office: 26 Oxford St Cambridge MA 02138

HOLLEB, ARTHUR IRVING, surgeon; b. N.Y.C., Apr. 1, 1921; s. Simon and Kate (Liss) H.; m. Carolyn R. Oglesby, June 16, 1951; children—Susan Jane and David Gene (twins). A.B., Brown U., 1941; M.D., N.Y. U., 1944. Diplomate: Am. Bd. Surgery. Intern Queens Gen. Hosp., Jamaica, N.Y., 1944-45; resident tumor surgery and pathology Meadowbrook Hosp., Hempstead, N.Y., 1945-46, chief resident gen. surgery, 1948-50, asst. dir. tumor service, 1954-56; mem. staff Meml. Hosp., N.Y.C., 1950—, asso. chief med. officer, 1966-67, cons. breast service, surgery dept., 1968—; asso. vis. surg. James Ewing Hosp., 1966-67; mem. staff M.D. Anderson Hosp. and Tumor Inst., Houston, 1967-68, mem. research staff, 1967-68, cons. breast cancer study sect., 1968—; sr. v.p. med. affairs and research, chief med. officer Am. Cancer Soc., N.Y.C., 1968—; from instr. to clin. asso. prof. surgery Cornell U. Med. Coll., 1965-67; asso. clinician Sloan-Kettering Inst., 1961-67; asso. prof. surgery U. Tex. M.D. Anderson Hosp. and Tumor Inst., 1967-68, asso. dir. edn., 1967-68; James Ewing Meml. lectr. Soc. Surg. Oncology, 1980; Wendell Scott Meml. lectr. Am. Coll. Radiology, 1978; mem. evaluation panel, sr. clin. traineeships in surgery, cancer control br. USPHS, 1965-68; mem. cancer control adv. com., diagnostic research adv. group and therapy com. Nat. Cancer Inst., NIH, 1972—. Editor in chief: Jour. CA; editorial adv. bd.: Am. Jour. Preventive Medicine. Served with USNR, 1946-48. Recipient W. W. Keen Disting. Service award Brown U., 1977. Mem. Am. Assn. Cancer Edn., Am. Assn. Cancer Research, AMA, Am. Cancer Soc. (dir. N.Y.C. 1964-67), A.C.S., Am. Radium Soc. (v.p. 1969-70), Assn. Am. Med. Colls., Assn. Hosp. Dirs. Med. Edn. (chmn. surg. edn. com. 1965-67), Harris County Med. Soc., Am. Soc. Clin. Oncology, James Ewing Soc. (pres. 1972-73), N.Y. Acad. Medicine, N.Y. County Med. Soc., N.Y. Acad. Scis., N.Y. Cancer Soc. (pres. 1971), N.Y. Surg. Soc. Clubs: Brown, Marco Polo (N.Y.C.). Home: 3 Highridge Rd Larchmont NY 10538 Office: 777 3d Ave New York NY 10017

HOLLEN, DONALD EDWARD, utility co. exec.; b. Buckhannon, W.Va., July 19, 1922; s. Cecil Edwin and Leona Dove (Cutright) H.; m. Betty Lee Baumgartner, Aug. 23, 1947; children—Donald Edward, II, Terri Lee. B.S. in Forestry, W.Va. U., 1949; grad., Advanced Mgmt. Program, Harvard U., 1968. Asst. extension forester W.Va. U., 1949-51; buyer, forester Kimball-Tyler Cooperage Co., Buckhannon, 1951-53; with Monongahela Power Co., Fairmont, W.Va., 1953—, now pres.; dir. City Nat. Bank, Fairmont. Campaign chmn. United Way, 1967, pres., 1977; bd. dirs. Found. Ind. Colls.; trustee Alderson-Broaddus Coll. Served with inf. U.S. Army, 1940-45. Decorated Silver Star, Purple Heart. Mem. Soc. Am. Foresters, Public Utilities Assn. of Virginias (exec. com., pres. 1977), W.Va. Research League, Edison Electric Inst., Ohio Electric Utility Inst., W.Va. C. of C. (dir.). Baptist. Club: Kiwanis (pres. club 1967-68). Office: 1310 Fairmont Ave Fairmont WV 26554

HOLLENBERG, MARTIN JAMES, university dean, anatomy educator; b. Winnipeg, Man., Can., June 30,1934; s. Abraham and Minnie (Pitkowski) H.; m. Vivian Tannis, June 18, 1959; children: Andrew, Lesley. M.D., U. Man., 1958, B.Sc., 1958; M.Sc., Wayne State U., 1964, Ph.D., 1965. Intern U. Man., 1958-59; trainee in surgery and anatomy U. Minn., 1959-65, Wayne State U., 1959-65; asst. prof. anatomy U. Western Ont., London, 1965-68, assoc. prof., 1968-71, prof., 1978—, dean of medicine, 1978—; prof. anatomy U. B.C.,

Vancouver, 1971-75, hon. profl. ophthalmology, 1972-75; prof., head morphological sci. U. Calgary, Alta., 1975-78; dir. J.P. Roberts Research Inst., London, Ont., Can., 1983—. Contbr. articles on ultrastructure of eye to profl. jours. Fellow Royal Coll. Physicians Can.; mem. Can. Assn. Anatomists (pres. 1979-81), Am. Assn. Anatomists, Can. Med. Assn., Ont. Med. Assn., Council Ont. Faculities of Medicine (chmn. 1983). Office: U Western Ont London ON Canada N6A 5C1

HOLLENBERG, MORLEY DONALD, research physician, educator; b. Winnipeg, Man., Can., July 2, 1942; s. Jacob and Esther (Gorsey) H.; m. Joan Leslie, Aug. 15, 1965; children: Elisa Michelle, Daniel Benjamin. B.Sc., U. Man., 1963, M.Sc., 1964; D.Phil. (Rhodes scholar), Oxford U., (Eng.), 1967; M.D., Johns Hopkins U., 1972. Med. intern Johns Hopkins Hosp., Balt., 1971-72; postdoctoral fellow dept. pharmacology and exptl. thereapeutics Johns Hopkins Sch. Medicine, 1972-73, asst. prof. dept. pharmacology and exptl. thereapeutics, 1973-79, instr. dept. medicine, 1974-75, asst. prof. dept. medicine, 1975-79; prof., chmn. dept. pharmacology and therapeutics U. Calgary, Alta./Can., 1979—; investigator Howard Hughes Med. Inst., 1974-79. Contbr. articles to profl. jours. Recipient Undergrad. Research award Johns Hopkins Med. Soc., 1971, Upjohn award for clin. proficiency Johns Hopkins Sch. Medicine; Med. Research Council Can. fellow, 1972-73. Mem. Am. Fedn. Clin. Research, Am. Soc. for Pharmacology and Exptl. Theapeutics, Am. Soc. Clin. Investigation, Can. Soc. Clin. Investigation. Office: Dept Pharmacology U Calgary 3330 Hospital Dr Calgary AB Canada T2N 4N1

HOLLENSHEAD, DAVID SMITH, banker; b. Needmore, Pa., Apr. 1, 1926; s. David and Blanche C. (Smith) H.; m. Raymeta L. Chaffee, Dec. 22, 1945; children: Karen Lee, Kathy Lynn. B.S.S., Hagerstown (Md.) Bus. Coll., 1943; B.A., Dickinson Coll., 1948; student, Wharton Sch., U. Pa., 1948-50, Northwestern U., 1956-57. With Fed. Res. Bank Phila., 1948-50; with York Bank & Trust Co., Pa., 1950—, exec. v.p., 1958-75, pres., 1975-84, chmn. bd., 1980-84, chmn. bd., chief exec. officer, 1984—, also dir.; pres., dir. Dickinson Life Ins. Co., 1982—; vice chmn. bd., dir. Continental Bancorp, Inc., Phila., 1983—; dir. York County Indsl. Devel. Corp., Small Enterprise Devel. Corp. (Sedco), El-Ge Potato Chip Co., Inc., Farmers Fire Ins. Co. Bd. dirs. Laurel Fish and Game Assn., Better York. Served with AUS, 1944-46; ETO. Recipient Recognition award for role in preparation of 1965 Pa. Banking Code. Mem. York Area C. of C., Sigma Chi. Clubs: Country of York, Lafayette (past pres.), Sertoma (past pres. York). Home: 49 Jolo Way York PA 17403 Office: 107 W Market St York PA 17405

HOLLERBACH, SERGE, artist; b. Pushkin, Russia, Nov. 1, 1923; came to U.S., 1949, naturalized, 1955; s. Lew and Ludmila (Agapov) H. Ed., Acad. Fine Arts, Munich, Germany, Art Students League. Tchr. art. Exhibited in group shows, Drawings, U.S.A., 1961, Met. Mus. Art, N.Y.C., 1966, Childe Hassam Fund Exhbn., Am. Acad. Arts and Letters, 1968; works represented in ann. exhbns., N.A.D., Am. Watercolor Soc., Audubon Artists, Nat. Arts Club; painter; designer; book illustrator. Recipient Gold medal Nat. Arts Club, 1963; prize N.A.D., 1965; Adolph and Clara Obrig prize, 1971, 76; Silver medal Am. Watercolor Soc., 1978; Gold medal Am. Watercolor Soc., 1983; medal and purchase Butler Inst. Am. Art, 1977; also numerous purchase awards and prizes. Mem. NAD; Mem. Am. Watercolor Soc., Audubon Artists, Nat. Soc. Painters in Casein, Allied Artists Am. Home: 304 W 75th St New York NY 10023

HOLLERITH, RICHARD, JR., industrial designer, consultant; b. Phila., Oct. 4, 1926; s. Richard and Mary (Spencer) H.; m. Joan Doughty Moore, Nov. 1951 (div. Oct. 1976); children: Nancy, Richard, John, Susan; m. Rosemarie Wittel, May 21, 1983 (div.). B.A., Darmouth Coll., 1947; diploma in indsl. design, Phila. Coll., 1951. Designer Parcher & Falk, Phila., 1951-54; indsl. designer Raymond Spilman, N.Y.C., 1954-56; dir. indsl. design Monroe/Litton Industries, West Orange, N.J., 1956-66; account mgr. Henry Dreyfuss Assocs., N.Y.C., 1966-68; owner Indsl. Design Cons., Montville, N.J., 1968—; co-founder I/O Devices, Inc., Montville, 1969—; bd. dirs. Nat. Ctr. Barrier Free Environment, Washington, 1981—. Contbg. editor: Indsl. Design Mag., 1978—; patentee in field. Bd. dirs., pres. West Essex Rehab. Ctr., Montclair, N.J., 1974—; mem. Pres.' Com. on Employment of Handicapped, 1966—. Nat. Endowment for Art fellow, 1976, 78. Fellow Indsl. Designers Soc. Am. (chmn. N.Y. chpt. 1965-66, v.p., dir. 1967-72, prof. 1977-80, Bronze Apple award N.Y. chpt. 1976, editor jour.); mem. Human Factor Soc., Soc. Plastic Engrs., Soc. Indsl. Design (v.p., bd. dirs. internat. council Brussels 1973-77). Office: Indsl Design Consultant 11 Skyline Dr Box 576 Montville NJ 07045

HOLLERMAN, CHARLES EDWARD, pediatrician; b. Turtle Creek, Pa., Apr. 22, 1929; s. Harry R. and Lena F. H.; m. Catharine, Aug. 22, 1953; children—James, Karen, Jeffrey, Pamela. B.S. in Chemistry, Allegheny Coll., 1951; M.D., Cornell U., 1955. Lic., Pa., N.Y., D.C., Va., S.D. Intern York County (Pa.) Hosp., 1955-56; resident U.S. Navy Sch. Aviation Medicine, Pensacola, Fla., 1957; pediatric resident Children's Hosp., Buffalo, 1960-62; fellow in clin. nephrology SUNY, 1964-65; asst. prof. pediatrics Georgetown U., 1966-69, asso. prof., 1969-74, prof., 1974-75, U. S.D., Vermillion, 1975-82, asst. dean clin. services, 1976-77, acting dean, exec. dean, 1977-79, dean, 1979-82, v.p. health affairs, 1979-82; chmn. dept. pediatrics Mercy Hosp., Pitts., 1982—; dir. Renal Clinic Comprehensive Care Clinic McKennan hosp., Sioux Falls, S.D., 1979-82. Author: Pediatric Nephrology-Medical Outline Series, 1979; contbr. in field. Served with USN, 1956-59. Mem. Am. Acad. Pediatrics, Am. Soc. Nephrology, AMA, Am. Soc. Internat. Soc. Nephrology, Pa. State Med. Assn., Phi Beta Kappa. Home: 1236 Wightman St Pittsburgh PA 15217 Office: Dept Pediatrics Mercy Hosp 1400 Locust St Pittsburgh PA 15219

HOLLETT, BYRON PIERCE, lawyer; b. Indpls., Sept. 28, 1914; s. John Everett and Katherine (Sullivan) H.; m. Joan Piel Metzger, Sept. 11, 1940 (div. 1974); children: Joan K., Byron Pierce; m. Frances L. Dawson, 1974. A.B., Wabash Coll., 1936, LL.D. (hon.), 1974; J.D., Harvard U., 1939. Bar: Ind. 1939. Partner firm Baker & Daniels, Indpls., 1951—; dir. Am. Fletcher Nat. Bank, Am. Fletcher Corp.; Lilly Endowment, Inc. Trustee Clowes Fund, Ind. Hist. Soc., Crown Hill Cemetery, United Fund Greater Indpls., Western Golf Assn.; gov. James Whitcomb Riley Hosp. Children; chmn. bd. trustees Wabash Coll.; mem. bus. and profl. friends Com. Nat. Center State Cts., Ind. Acad. Served with USNR, 1942-45. Decorated Bronze Star. Mem. Sigma Chi. Episcopalian (chancellor Diocese Indpls. 1964-78). Clubs: Woodstock, Skyline. Home: 3802 Springfield Overlook Indianapolis IN 46234 Office: Fletcher Trust Bldg Indianapolis IN 46204

HOLLEY, EDWARD GAILON, university dean, librarian; b. Pulaski, Tenn., Nov. 26, 1927; s. Abe Brown and Maxie Elizabeth (Bass) H.; m. Robbie Lee Gault, June 19, 1954; children: Gailon Boyd, Edward Jens, Beth Alison Holley, Amy Holley Spitler. B.A. magna cum laude, David Lipscomb Coll., Nashville, 1949; M.A., George Peabody Coll., 1951; Ph.D., U. Ill., 1961. Asst. librarian David Lipscomb Coll., 1949-51; mem. staff U. Ill., 1951-62, librarian edn., philosophy and psychology library, 1957-62; dir. libraries U. Houston, 1962-72; dean Sch. Library Sci., U. N.C. at Chapel Hill, 1972—; vis. lectr. U. Wis., Madison, summer, 1968; vis. prof. N. Tex. State U., summer, 1970; Mem. adv. council library resources U.S. Office Edn., 1968-71; cons. various libraries Tex., Ill., S.C. bds. higher edn., Nat. Endowment for Humanities. Author: Charles Evans, American Bibliographer, 1963, Raking the Historic Coals, 1967, (with Don Hendricks) Resources of Texas Libraries, 1968, ALA at 100, 1976, Resources of South Carolina Libraries, 1976; Co-author: The Library Services and Construction Act, 1983; Author also articles. Trustee Disciples of Christ Hist. Soc., 1973—; mem. governing bd. U. N.C. Press, 1975—. Served to lt. (s.g.) USNR, 1953-56. CLR fellow, 1971. Mem. ALA (Scarecrow Press award 1964, Melvil Dewey medal 1983, chmn. pub. bd. 1972-73, pres. 1974-75), Tex. Library Assn. (pres. 1971), Southeastern Library Assn., N.C. Library Assn., Assn. Coll. and Research Librarians (editor Monographs 1969-72), AAUP, Phi Kappa Phi, Kappa Delta Pi, Beta Phi Mu. (v.p. 1983-84). Democrat. Mem. Ch. of Christ. Address: 1508 Ephesus Church Rd Chapel Hill NC 27514

HOLLEY, FRANK EDWARD, banker, educator; b. Urbana, Ill., Nov. 24, 1919; s. Charles Elmer and Viola Esther (Wolfe) H.; m. Florence Esther Blekking, June 7, 1941; children: Douglas Edwin, Esther Annette (Mrs. Geoffrey L. Greene), David Russell. B.S. with high honors, U. Ill., 1940. With Eastman Kodak Co., 1940-53, asst. credit mgr., 1951-53; with Marine Midland Bank-Rochester (formerly Union Trust Co.), 1953-76, comptroller, 1954-62, exec. v.p., 1962-68, dir., chmn. exec. com., 1968-73, chmn. bd., chief exec. officer, 1973-76; distinguished lectr. econs. and fin. Rochester Inst. Tech., 1976—; mem. faculty Grad. Sch. Credit and Fin. Mgmt., Dartmouth, summers 1955, 57-59, 65-69. Contbr. chpts. to books. Past pres. Rochester Civic Music Assn.; past chmn. trustees Rochester Area Ednl. TV Assn.; Bd. dirs., past pres. Rochester Gen. Hosp.; trustee Genesee Valley Group Health Assn., Rochester Philharmonic Orch. Fund. Served to lt. (j.g.) USNR, 1943-46. Home: 1 Elmbrook Dr Pittsford NY 14534

HOLLEY, HOWARD LAMAR, physician, educator; b. Marion, Ala., July 14, 1914; s. Warren Alton and Lula (Fretwell) H.; m. Martha Holcomb, Sept. 7, 1946; children: Dan, Nancy, Warren, Howard, Jane. B.S., U. S.C., 1935; M.D., Med. Coll. S.C., 1941. Mem. faculty U. Ala. Med. Sch., 1947—, prof. internal medicine, 1959—; dir. Tumor Clinic, 1953-66, dir. div. rheumatology, 1955-70, distinguished faculty lectr., 1969, Anna Lois Waters prof. medicine in rheumatology, 1970—; hon. curator Reynolds Med. History Library, 1976; Chmn. arthritis tng. grants com. Nat. Inst. Arthritis, 1964-65. Author: (with Allen E. Hussar) Antibiotics and Antibiotic Therapy, A Clinical Manual, 1954, (with others) Potassium Metabolism in Health and Disease, 1955, A Continual Remembrance: Letters From Sir William Osler to his Friend, Ned Milburn, 1865-1919, 1968, A History of Medicine in Alabama, 1982; Contbr. articles profl. jours. Recipient Seale Harris Research award, 1962; Distinguished Service award Ala. chpt. Arthritis Found., 1968; Distinguished Internist's award Ala. Soc. Internal Medicine, 1973; Distinguished Alumnus award Med. U. S.C., 1974. Fellow A.C.P. (master, gov. Ala. 1966-72); mem. So. Soc. Clin. Investigation, Am. Rheumatism Assn., AMA, So. Med. Assn. (Disting. Service award 1980), Am. Fedn. Clin. Research, Med. Assn. Ala. (Jerome Cochran Meml. lectr. 1977), Sigma Xi. Home: 4016 Old Leeds Circle Birmingham AL 35213 *In striving to achieve the goals for my life, the following quotation gave me some words to live by, "One man with courage constitutes a majority."*

HOLLEY, IRVING BRINTON, JR., historian, educator; b. Hartford, Conn., Feb. 8, 1919; s. Irving B. and Mary L. (Sharp) H.; m. Janet Carlson, Oct. 9, 1945; children: Janet Turner Holley Wegner, Jean Carlson Holley Schmidt, Susan Sharp. B.A. cum laude, Amherst Coll., 1940; M.A. (Brooker scholar), Yale U., 1942, Ph.D., 1947; student, Oxford U., summer, 1937. Instr. dept. history Duke U., Durham, N.C., 1947-51, asst. prof., 1952-54, asso. prof., 1955-61, prof., 1962—; vis. prof. U.S. Mil. Acad., 1974-75, Nat. Def. U., 1978-79; cons. to Army Research Office, 1963-73; mem. U.S. Commn. on Mil. History, 1974—; occasional lectr. Army War Coll., USAF Acad., Infantry Sch., Air War Coll., Command and Gen. Staff Coll.; chmn. adv. com. on history Sec. Air Force, 1970-79; mem. adv. com. on history NASA, 1974—. Author: Ideas and Weapons, 1953, Buying Aircraft, 1964, Development of Aircraft Gun Turrets in the AAF, 1917-1944, Evolution of the Liaison Type Airplane, 1917-1944, 1946, An Enduring Challenge: The Problem of Air Force Doctrine, 1974, General John M. Palmer, Citizen Soldiers, and the Army of a Democracy, 1982; contbr. articles on mil. history to scholarly publs.; editor: The Transfer of Ideas: Historical Essays, 1968. Trustee Air Force Hist. Found., 1973—, chmn. program com., 1979—. Served with USAAF, 1942-47; to maj. gen. USAFR, 1947-81. Decorated D.S.M., Legion of Merit; recipient Outstanding Civilian Service to the Army medal, 1975, Exceptional Civilian Service to the Air Force medal., 1979. Fellow AIAA (asso.); mem. Am. Hist. Assn., Orgn. Am. Historians, Soc. History of Tech., Am. Mil. Inst., Inter-Univ. Seminar, Phi Delta Theta. Episcopalian. Home: 2506 Wrightwood Ave Durham NC 27705 Office: Dept History Duke Univ Durham NC 27706

HOLLEY, LAWRENCE ALVIN, labor union official; b. Elkhart, Ind., Nov. 7, 1924; s. Olin Coet and Carrie (Erwin) H.; m. Joyce Reed, Mar. 5, 1946; 1 dau., Claudia Joyce. Student public schs., Elkhart. Bus. rep. Vancouver (Wash.) Aluminum Trades Council, 1951-57; pres. Wash. State Card and Label Council, 1952-57; internat. rep. Aluminum Workers Internat. Union, St. Louis, 1957-65, wage engr., 1965, research and ednl. dir., 1967-75, dir. Region 5, Vancouver, Wash., 1975-77, pres., St. Louis, 1977—; v.p. Union Label and Service Trades Dept. AFL-CIO, 1980—, exec. bd. Maritime Trades Dept., 1981—. Served with U.S. Army, 1943-46; PTO. Decorated Bronze Star with oak leaf cluster. Democrat. Clubs: Am. Legion, Voyageur 4o/8, Order Eagles. Office: 3362 Hollenberg Dr Bridgeton MO 63044

HOLLEY, ROBERT WILLIAM, educator, scientist; b. Urbana, Ill., Jan. 28, 1922; s. Charles E. and Viola (Wolfe) H.; m. Ann Dworkin, Mar. 3, 1945; 1 son, Frederick. A.B., U. Ill., 1942; Ph.D., Cornell U., 1947. Am. Chem. Soc. fellow State Coll. Wash., 1947-48; asst. prof., then asso. prof. organic chemistry N.Y. State Agr. Expt. Sta., Cornell U., 1948-57; research chemist plant, soil and nutrition lab. U.S. Dept. Agr., Cornell U., 1957-64; prof. biochemistry Cornell U., 1964-69, chmn. dept. biochemistry, 1965-66; resident fellow Salk Inst. Biol. Studies, La Jolla, Calif., 1968—; mem. biochemistry study sect. NIH, 1962-66; vis. fellow Salk Inst. Biol. Studies; vis. prof. Scripps Clinic and Research Found., La Jolla, 1966-67. Recipient Distinguished Service award U.S. Dept. Agr., 1965, Albert Lasker award basic med. research, 1965; U.S. Steel Found. award in molecular biology Nat. Acad. Scis., 1967; Nobel prize for medicine and physiology, 1968; Guggenheim fellow Calif. Inst. Tech., 1955-56. Fellow AAAS; mem. Am. Acad. Arts and Scis., Am. Soc. Biol. Chemists, Am. Chem. Soc., Nat. Acad. Scis., Phi Beta Kappa, Sigma Xi. Home: 7381 Rue Michael La Jolla CA 92037 Office: PO Box 85800 San Diego CA 92138

HOLLIDAY, BARBARA MIRIAM BROOKS GREGG, journalist; b. Little River, Kans., Aug. 28, 1917; d. Ray and Nina Blanche (Cook) Brooks; m. Robert Breckenridge Holliday, Mar. 6, 1937 (dec.); children: Nina (Mrs. Tom Petersen), Robert Gregg, Mindy (Mrs. James Dow), Susan (Mrs. Fred Mabry). A.A., Christian Coll., 1937; B.J., U. Mo., 1939, M.A., 1967. Feature writer Columbia (Mo.) Tribune News Co., 1958-60; writer Detroit Free Press, Knight Newspapers, Inc., 1960—, asso. mag. editor, 1966-69, asst. Sunday editor, 1969, feature, book page editor, 1970-80, book editor, 1980—. Mem. bd. alumni publs., U. Mo., 1968—; Contbr. articles to popular mags. Recipient 1st pl. feature series Mo. Press Women, 1959, 60, award Nat. Press Women, 1960, Mich. A.P., 1963. Mem. Nat. Book Critics Circle, Sigma Delta Chi (exec. bd. Detroit 1971-78). Club: Detroit Press. Office: Detroit Free Press 321 W Lafayette St Detroit MI 48231

HOLLIDAY, POLLY DEAN, actress; b. Jasper, Ala., July 2, 1937; d. Ernest Sullivan and Velma Mabell (Cain) H. B.Music Edn., Ala. State Women's Coll., (now U. Montevallo), 1959; postgrad., Fla. State U., 1960; D.H.L. hon., Mt. St. Mary's Coll., 1982. Tchr. music Sarasota (Fla.) public schs., 1961. Appeared with, Asolo Theatre Repertory Co., Sarasota, 1962-72; appeared in: Off Broadway, Broadway show All Over Town, 1975; appeared as Flo on: CBS-TV series Alice, 1976-80, Flo, 1981; appeared in TV movies: The Shady Hill Kidnapping, 1981, All the Way Home, 1981, Missing Children, 1982, A Gift of Love, 1983. Recipient Golden Globe award for best supporting actress on TV series, 1978, 79. Episcopalian. Office: care Richard Dickens & Co 5550 Wilshire Blvd Suite 306 Los Angeles CA 90036

HOLLIEN, HARRY FRANCIS, scientist, educator; b. Brockton, Mass., July 16, 1926; s. Henry Gregory and Alice Bernice (Coolidge) H.; m. Patricia Ann Milanowski, Aug. 26, 1969; children: Karen Ann, Kevin Amory, Keith Alan, Brian Christopher, Stephanie Ann, Christine Ann. B.S., Boston U., 1949, M.Ed., 1951; M.A., U. Iowa, 1953, Ph.D., 1955. Asst. prof. Baylor U., 1955-58, U. Wichita, 1958-62; asso. prof. speech U. Fla., Gainesville, 1962-68, prof., 1968—, prof. linguistics, 1976—, prof. criminal justice, 1979—, asso. dir. communication scis. lab., 1962-68, dir., 1968-75, Inst. Advanced Study of Communication Processes, 1975—; vis. prof. Inst. Telecommunications and Acoustics, Wroclaw Tech. U., Poland, 1974; adj. prof. Juilliard Sch. Music, N.Y.C., 1973—; research asso. Gould Research Lab., 1958; vis. scientist Speech Transmission Lab., Royal Inst. Tech., Stockholm, 1970; fencing coach U. Iowa, 1953-55; mem. communication sci. study sect. NIH, 1963-67; field reviewer NSF, 1965—; mem. neurobiology merit rev. bd. VA, 1969-74, field reviewer, 1975—; pres. Hollien Assocs., 1966—; cons. in field. Assoc. editor: Jour. Speech and Hearing Research, 1967-69; editor: The Phonetician, 1975—; mem. editorial bd.: Jour. Communication Disorders, 1980—, Jour. Research in Singing, 1980-83, Jour. Phonetics, 1982—; contbr. numerous articles to profl. jours. Chmn. bd. Unitarian Fellowship, Waco, Tex., 1956-58; bd. dirs. Wildlife Retirement Village. Served with USN, 1944-46; Served with USNR, 1946-75. Recipient Garcia/Sandoz prize Internat. Assn. Logopedics and Phoniatrics, 1971, Gould award Wm. and Harrett Gould Found., 1975, Gutzmann medal Union European Phonatrists and Internat. Assn. Logopedics and Phoniatrics, 1980; NIH career fellow, 1965-70. Fellow Am. Speech and Hearing Assn., Acoustical Soc. Am., Internat. Soc. Phonetic Scis. (sec.-gen. 1975—, exec. v.p. 1983—), Am. Acad. Forensic Sci.; mem. Am. Assn. Phonetic Scis. (pres. 1973-75, editor 1976-79, exec. com. 1979—), Acad. for Forensic Application of Communication Scis. (editor 1975-80, exec. com. 1976—, mem. sci. council 1975-76), World Congress of Phoneticians (mem. permanent council), Voice Found. (sci.bd.), AAAS, N.Y. Acad. Sci., Fla. Acad. Scis., Undersea Med. Assn., Underwater Assn., S.E. Conf. Linguistics. Republican. Home: 229 SW 43d Terr Gainesville FL 32607 Office: Inst Advanced Study of Communication Processes Univ of Fla Gainesville FL 32611

HOLLIES, NORMAN ROBERT STANLEY, textile chemist, educator; b. Edmonton, Alta., Can., Oct. 18, 1922; s. Robert Talbot and Jessie Sutherland (McArthur) H.; m. Sheila Margaret Brigit Mercer, May 31, 1947; children—Brian Christopher, Robert Mercer, Kenneth Norman, Richard Ernest, David Ian. B.Sc. with honors, U. Alta., 1944; Ph.D., McGill U., 1947. Research chemist NRC Can., 1946-47; research asso. Harvard Med. Sch., Boston, 1947-50; project mgr., group leader Harris Research Labs., Washington, 1951-76; prin. scientist Gillette Research Inst., Rockville, Md., 1977-80; prof. dept. textiles and consumer econs. U. Md., College Park, 1981—; chmn. Gordon Conf. Fiber Sci., 1981. Author: (with L. Fourt) Clothing Comfort and Function, 1970, (with R. F. Goldman) Clothing Comfort, 1977. Served with Chem. Warfare Service, Can. Army, 1944-47. Canadian Industries Ltd. grad. fellow, 1944-47. Mem. Am. Phys. Soc., Am. Chem. Soc., Fiber Soc. (pres. 1980), Am. Vacuum Soc., Internat. Microscopical Soc., AAAS, Washington Acad. Sci., N.Y. Acad. Sci. Republican. Club: Cosmos. Home: 9823 Singleton Dr Bethesda MD 20817 Office: 2100 Marie Mount Dept Textiles and Cons U Md College Park MD 20742

HOLLIMAN, EARL, actor; b. Delhi, La., Sept. 11, 1928. Ed., U. So. Calif., Pasadena Playhouse. Appeared in: numerous films including Broken Lance, 1954, I Die a Thousand Times, 1955, Giant, 1956, Gunfight at the OK Corral, 1957, The Rainmaker, 1956, Trooper Hook, 1957, Last Train from Gun Hill, 1959, Armoured Command, 1961, The Sons of Katie Elder, 1965, Covenant with Death, 1967, The Power, 1968, Anzio, 1968, Smoke, 1969; TV movies include Tribes, 1970, Cannon, 1971; appeared in: TV series Hotel de Paree, 1959-60, Wide Country, 1962-63, Police Woman, 1974-78; other TV appearances include Ironside, Playhouse 90, Kraft Theatre, F.B.I., Medical Center, The Rookies; appeared in: TV movies Alexander: The Other Side of Down, 1977, The Solitary Man, 1979; stage appearances include A Streetcar Named Desire. Served with USN. Recipient Golden Globe award Hollywood Fgn. Press Assn. Mem. Actors and Others for Animals (pres.), Acad. Motion Picture Arts and Scis., AFTRA. *

HOLLIMAN, JOE MILTON, lawyer; b. Bartlesville, Okla., Oct. 13, 1921; s. John M. and Prudie (Smith) H.; m. Jean Felt, July 29, 1944; children—Janice Holliman Stanfield, John Howard, Joanna Holliman Potts. B.A., Okla. State U., 1943; LL.B., Okla. U., 1946. Bar: Okla. bar 1946. Since practiced in, Tulsa; mem. firm Holliman, Langholz, Runnels & Dorwart.; Pres., dir. Holarud, Inc., Hickory Oil Corp., Diamond Leasing Inc.; v.p., dir. Bryan Industries Inc., Geophys. Research Corp., Indel-Davis, Inc., Skinner Bros. Co., Inc., Indel-Davis Pte Ltd., Singapore, Indel-Davis Equipment S.A., Brussels, Indel-Davis Ltd., Hong Kong, So. Spltys. Corp.; dir. Utica Nat. Bank & Trust Co. Pres. Howard E. Felt Found.; past chmn. bd. advisers Tulsa Salvation Army. Mem. Am., Okla., Tulsa County bar assns. Methodist. Clubs: Tulsa (past pres.), Southern Hills Country (Tulsa); Eldorado Country (Indian Wells, Calif.). Home: 2716 S Birmingham Pl Tulsa OK 74114 Office: Suite 700 Holarud Bldg 10 E 3d St Tulsa OK 74103

HOLLINGS, ERNEST FREDERICK, U.S. senator; b. Charleston, S.C., Jan. 1, 1922; s. Adolph G. and Wilhlemine D. (Meyer) H.; m. Rita Liddy, Aug. 21, 1971; children by previous marriage—Michael Milhous, Helen Hayne, Patricia Salley, Ernest Frederick III. B.A., The Citadel, 1942; LL.B., U. S.C., 1947. Bar: S.C. bar 1947. Mem. S.C. Ho. of Reps., 1948-54, speaker pro tem, 1951-54; lt. gov. of, S.C., 1955-59, gov. of, 1959-63, practiced in, Charleston, 1963-66, U.S. senator, State of S.C., 1966—; Mem. Hoover Comm. on Intelligence Activities, 1954-55; mem. President's Adv. Comm. on Intergovernmental Relations, 1959-63. Mem. exec. council Lutheran Ch. Am.; Trustee Newberry Coll. Named one of Ten Outstanding Young Men U.S. Junior C. of C., 1954. Mem. Assn. Citadel Men, Hibernian Soc., Phi Delta Phi. Democrat. Lutheran. Club: Sertoma (Charleston). Office: Room 115 Russell Office Bldg Washington DC 20510

HOLLINGSWORTH, GERALD EUGENE, lawyer; b. Goose Creek, Tex., Aug. 15, 1923; s. Olan Atticus and Ava (Hillyer) H.; m. Eileen Roberts, June 6, 1945 (div. 1966); children: Louise Carpino, Michael

Hollingsworth; m. Marie L. McMahon, Aug. 31, 1976. A.A., George Washington U., 1948, LL.B., 1950. Bar: D.C. 1950. Counsel Office Gen. Counsel, Dept. Navy, Washington, 1950-57; sr. staff counsel RCA Corp., Camden, N.J., 1957-73; v.p., gen. counsel Random House, Inc., N.Y.C., 1973—. Served with USN, 1941-46; PTO. Democrat. Home: 5 Rutledge Ct East Brunswick NJ 08816 Office: Random House Inc 201 E 50th St New York NY 10022

HOLLINGSWORTH, JACK WARING, computer science educator; b. South Haven, Kans., Mar. 3, 1924; s. Virgil Braxton and Ethel (Waring) H.; m. Nancy Lee Harris, Sept. 14, 1950; children: Joel, Priscilla, Seth (dec.). B.S. in Engring. Physics, U. Kans., 1948, B.A., 1949; M.S., U. Wis., 1951, Ph.D., 1954. Teaching asst. U. Kans., 1947-49, U. Wis., 1949-50, computing asst., 1950-54; gen. sci. aide U.S. Naval Ordnance Lab., 1950; mathematician Gen. Electric Co., 1954-57; mem. faculty Rensselaer Poly. Inst., 1957-79, prof. math., 1961-79, supr. computer lab., 1957-70, chmn. interdisciplinary com. computer sci., 1967-73; prof. Sch. Computer Sci. and Tech., Rochester (N.Y.) Inst. Tech., 1979—, dir., 1980-82; Mem. Bd. Coop. Ednl. Services, Saratoga-Warren Counties, 1970-79. Served to 1st lt. USAAF, 1943-45. Decorated D.F.C., Air medal with 4 oak leaf clusters, Purple Heart. Mem. Assn. Computing Machinery (treas. spl. interest group of univ. computing centers 1964-70), Am. Math. Soc., Soc. Indsl. and Applied Math., Math. Assn. Am., Sigma Xi, Tau Beta Pi, Omicron Delta Kappa, Kappa Eta Kappa. Mem. Reformed Ch. (elder). Club: Mason. Home: 55 Crestview Dr Pittsford NY 14534 Office: Sch Computer Sci and Tech Rochester Inst Tech Rochester NY 14623

HOLLINGSWORTH, ROBERT EDGAR, nuclear cons.; b. Dawson, Ga., Sept. 23, 1918; s. John Cullen and Lillie (Christie) H.; m. Florence Beatrice Krieg, May 13, 1945; children—John Krieg, Joni Louise; m. Margaret Camille Jacob, July 14, 1960; children—Robert Edgar, Barbara Camille, William Lee, Bradford Damion. A.B., Columbia, 1939, postgrad., 1939-40, 46-47, Rosenwald fellow, 1946-47. Mem. staff AEC, 1947-74, asst. gen. mgr. for adminstrn., 1956-59, dep. gen. mgr., 1959-64, gen. mgr., 1964-74; mgr. comml. devel. Bechtel Corp., 1974-75, mgr. personnel, 1975-77; nuclear cons., 1977—. Trustee Golden Gate U., San Francisco, 1975-80. Served to lt. col. AUS, 1942-46. Recipient Arthur S. Flemming award, 1957; Distinguished Fed. Civilian Service award, 1966; Distinguished Service award AEC, 1969; Nat. Civil Service League award, 1973; Sigma Chi award, 1973. Clubs: Bankers, World Trade (San Francisco). Home and Office: 118 Northcreek Circle Walnut Creek CA 94598

HOLLINGSWORTH, SAMUEL HAWKINS, JR., bassist; b. Birmingham, Ala., June 29, 1922; s. Samuel Hawkins and Bennie Louise (Brown) H.; m. Patricia Ann Patton, Apr. 1, 1957 (div.); children—Priscilla P., Samuel Hawkins III; m. Elizabeth Mary Malezi, Dec. 31, 1974. Student, Juilliard Sch. Music, N.Y.C., 1940-42, George Peabody Coll. Tchrs., Nashville, 1953-54. Solo double bassist, Nashville Symphony Orch., 1946-65, Chamber Symphony, Phila., 1966-68, Dallas Symphony Orch., 1968-70, Pitts. Symphony Orch., 1970—. Mem. governing bd. dirs. Nashville Symphony Orch., 1958-61; chmn. Dallas Symphony Orch. Players, 1969-70. Home: 4403 Centre Ave Pittsburgh PA 15213 Office: Heinz Hall Pittsburgh PA 15222

HOLLINGTON, RICHARD RINGS, JR., lawyer; b. Findlay, Ohio, Nov. 12, 1932; s. Richard Rings and Annette (Kirk) H.; m. Sal;ly Stecher, Apr. 4, 1959; children: Florence A., Julie A., Richard R. III. Peter S. B.A., Williams Coll., 1954; J.D., Harvard U., 1957. Bar: Ohio 1957. Spl. counsel Ohio Atty. Gen., Cleve., 1963-70; ptnr. Marshman, Hornbeck & Hollington, Cleve., 1958-67, McDonald, Hopkins, Hardy & Hollington, 1967-69; law dir. City of Cleve., 1971-72; ptnr. Baker & Hostetler, Cleve., 1969-71, 73—; dir. Ohio Bank & Savs. Co. Mem. Ohio Gen. Assembly, 1967-70; mem. exec. com. Ohio Republican fin. Com., 1971—, Cuyahoga County Rep. Orgn., 1968—; mem. Cuyahoga County Rep. Central Com., 1962-66; trustee Greater Cleve. Hosp. Assn., 1976-82, Cleve. Mus. Natural History, 1969-81, Cleve. Zool. Soc., 1970—, N.E. Ohio Regional Sewer Dist., 1972-73, Cuyahoga County Hosp. Found., 1968-73, Greater Cleve. Growth Corp., 1972, Ohio Municiple League, 1972, others. Mem. ABA, Ohio Bar Assn., Cuyahoga Bar Assn., Greater Cleve. Bar Assn., Law Dirs. Assn., Court of Nisi Prius. Clubs: Union, Tavern, Rowfant, Cleve. Athletic (Cleve.); The Country (Pepper Pike); Roaring Gap (N.C.). Home: 20020 Marchmont Rd Shaker Heights OH 44122 Office: 3200 National City Ctr. Cleveland OH 44114

HOLLINSHEAD, ARIEL CAHILL, research oncologist; b. Allentown, Pa., Aug. 24, 1929; d. Earl Darnell and Gertrude Loretta (Cahill) H.; m. Montgomery K. Hyun, Sept. 27, 1958; children—William C., Christopher C. Student, Swarthmore Coll., 1947-48; A.B., Ohio U., 1951, D.Sc. (hon.), 1977; M.A., George Washington U., 1955, Ph.D., 1957. Asst. prof., fellow in virology Baylor U. Med. Center, 1958-59; asst. prof. pharmacology George Washington Med. Center, 1959-61, asst. prof. medicine, 1961-64, asso. prof. medicine, head lab. virus and cancer research, 1964-73, prof. medicine, dir. lab. for virus and cancer research, 1974—; cons. in field. Contbr. numerous articles to profl. jours. Named Med. Woman of Yr. Joint Bd. Am. Med. Colls., 1975-76; decorated Star of Europe. Fellow Washington Acad. Sci., Am. Acad. Microbiology, AAAS; mem. N.Y. Acad. Sci., Am. Acad. Microbiology, Grad. Women in Sci., Internat. Soc. Preventive Oncology, Nat. Soc. Exptl. Biology and Medicine, Am. Soc. Microbiology, Am. Assn. Cancer Research, Am. Assn. Immunologists, Am. Soc. Clin. Oncology, Internat. Assn. Study Lung Cancer, Internat. Union Against Cancer. Clubs: Kenwood Country, Blue Ridge Mountain Country. Home: 3637 Van Ness St NW Washington DC 20008 Office: Dept Medicine George Washington Univ 2300 Eye St NW Washington DC 20037 *The Latin phrase "Carpe diem", meaning seize the day, or, guard the moment, has always meant a great deal to me. The negative scientific data, carefully recorded, of one day may be the most important serendipitous data for a future observation of another day . . . so each day and each set of experiments must be done well and faithfully recorded.*

HOLLIS, CHARLES CARROLL, literature educator; b. Needham, Mass., Oct. 27, 1911; s. Stanley Meredith and Agnes (Carroll) H.; m. Alice Willard, Sept. 19, 1936; children—Charles C., Joseph W., Michael S. Ph.B., Marquette U., 1935; M.A., U. Wis., 1937; Ph.D., U. Mich., 1954. Grad. fellow English St. Louis U., 1937-38; mem. faculty U. Detroit, 1938-61, prof. English, 1957-61, chmn. dept., 1959-61; manuscript specialist in Am. cultural history Library Congress, Washington, 1961-63; prof. Am. lit. U. N.C. at Chapel Hill, 1963—, chmn. dept. English, 1966-71. Author: Language and Style in Leaves of Grass, 1983; also sects. in books. Literary Criticism of Orestes Brownson; Editorial bd.: Fresco, 1957-61, U. Detroit Press, 1959-61. Supr. Dept. Parks and Recreation, City Detroit, summers 1945-55; Precinct del. Democratic Party, 1955-61; exec. bd. 15th Dist. Ofcl. Dem. Orgn., 1957-61. Mem. Founders Soc. Detroit Inst. Arts., Cath. Renascence Soc. (dir. 1960), Am. Studies Assn. (pres. Mich. 1957), Mich. Acad. Arts, Scis. and Letters (chmn. lang. and lit. 1955), AAUP (pres. local chpt. 1969-70), Coll. English Assn., English Inst., South Atlantic Modern Lang. Assn., Modern Humanities Research Assn., Modern Lang. Assn., Nat. Council Tchrs. English, Manuscript Soc., South Atlantic Assn. Depts. English (exec. bd. 1968-70), South Atlantic Grad. English (pres. 1970). Home: 104 Glendale Dr Chapel Hill NC 27514

HOLLIS, EVERETT LOFTUS, lawyer; b. Wilkes-Barre, Pa., Dec. 6, 1914; s. Frank E. and Mary C. (Loftus) H.; m. Marion Jennings, June 21, 1941; children—Nicholas, Mary, Benjamin; m. Jane Scholl Farrell, Apr. 17, 1974. B.S., U. Ill., 1936; LL.B., Harvard, 1939. Bar: Mass. bar 1939, N.Y. bar 1954, Ill. bar 1966, D.C. bar 1970. Law clk. to Justice H. T. Lummus, Mass. Supreme Jud. Ct., 1940; pvt. law practice, Boston, 1941; atty. OPA, 1941-43; with AEC, 1947-52, gen. counsel, 1951-52; formerly gen. corp. counsel Gen. Electric Co., N.Y.C.; now sr. partner firm Mayer, Brown and Platt (attys.), Chgo. and; Washington; exec. dir. Commn. on Founds. and Pvt. Philanthropy.; Mem. Pres.'s Com. on Contract Compliance; mem. Nat. Commn. on Med. Profl. Liability. Co-author: Federal Conflict of Interest Laws, 1960. Bd. dirs. Chgo. Better Bus. Bur. Served as lt. USNR, 1943-46. Mem. Internat., Fed., Am., Ill., Chgo., N.Y.C. bar assns., Am. Law Inst., Chgo. Council Fgn. Relations, Beta Gamma Sigma. Clubs: Univ., Met. (Chgo.); Harvard (N.Y.C.). Home: 1448 N Lake Shore Dr Chicago IL 60610 Office: 231 S LaSalle St Chicago IL 60604 also 888 17th St NW Washington DC 20006

HOLLIS, HOWELL, lawyer; b. Columbus, Ga., Dec. 8, 1919; s. Howell and Aylmer (Illges) H.; m. Janet Bowers, Dec. 6, 1941; children: Howell III, Mary Jane. B.S. in Commerce, U. Ga., 1940; student, Law Sch., 1941. Bar: Ga. 1941. Mem. firms Young & Hollis, Columbus, 1945-60, Foley, Chappell, Hollis & Schloth, 1960-69, Hatcher, Stubbs, Land, Hollis & Rothschild, 1969—; Chmn. bd. dirs. Nat. Bank & Trust Co. Columbus; dir. various indsl., financial corps. Pres. St. Francis Hosp., 1950-80; Chmn. jud. coms. Ga. Senate and Ho. Reps., 1948-60. Served to lt. col. USAAF, 1941-45. Mem. Ga. Bar Assn. (pres. 1956-57). Home: 951 Overlook Ave Columbus GA 31906 Office: PO Box 2707 Columbus GA 31902

HOLLIS, MARK D., state ofcl.; b. Buena Vista, Ga., Sept. 24, 1908; s. Mark Dexter and Ann (Tharpe) H.; m. Virginia Dare Houchens, Aug. 10, 1927; children—Mark Dexter, Virginia Ann. B.S. in C.E, U. Ga., 1931, C.E., 1938; D.Sc., U. Fla., 1956. Typhus fever research and investigations, Ala., Va., Washington; asso. with USPHS and Rockefeller Found., 1931-34; state engr. of, N.D., 1934-39, research and investigations in stream pollution, 1939-41; commd. capt., regular corps USPHS, 1941; officer charge Pub. Health Service Communicable Disease Center, Atlanta, 1942-47; exec. officer Office of Surgeon Gen., 1947; asst. surgeon gen. with rank of maj. gen., 1951-61; dep. chief Bur. State Services, 1952-54; chief san. engring. officer, 1954-61; chief engr., dir. environ. health programs WHO, Geneva, Switzerland, 1961-73; vice chmn. Fla. State Environ. Regulatory Commn., 1974—. Mem. Am. Water Works Assn., Water Pollution Control Fedn. (pres. 1960), Nat. Malaria Soc. (pres. 1946-47), Am. Pub. Health Assn., ASCE, Conf. State San. Engrs., Nat. Acad. Engring. Baptist. Club: Cosmos (Washington). Home: 411 Lone Palm Dr Lakeland FL 33801

HOLLIS, REGINALD, bishop; b. England, July 18, 1932; emigrated to Can., 1954; s. Jesse Farndon and Edith Ellen (Lee) H.; m. Marcia Crombie, Sept. 7, 1957; children—Martin, Hilda, Aidan. B.A., Cambridge (Eng.) U., 1954, M.A., 1958; B.D., McGill U., Montreal, 1956; D.D. (hon.), U. South, 1977, Montreal Diocesan Theol. Coll., 1975. Ordained deacon Anglican Ch., 1956, priest, 1956; chaplain Montreal Diocesan Theol. Coll.; also chaplain to Anglican students McGill U., 1956-60; asst. St. Matthias Parish, Westmont, Que., 1960-63; incumbent St. Barnabas Ch., Roxboro, Que., 1963-66, rector, 1966-71, Christ Ch., Beaurepaire, Que., 1971-74; dir. parish and diocesan services Diocese Montreal, 1974-75, bishop, 1975—. Home: 3630 Mountain St Montreal PQ H3G 2A8 Canada Office: 1444 Union Ave Montreal PQ H3A 2B8 Canada

HOLLISTER, CHARLES DAVIS, oceanographer; b. Santa Barbara, Calif., Mar. 18, 1936; s. Clinton B. and Amelia Phipps (Davis) H. (Danelius); m. Jalien Green, Feb. 8, 1958; children: Robin Jalien Hall, David Hellyer. B.S., Oreg. State U., 1960; Ph.D., Columbia U., 1967. Asst. scientist Woods Hole (Mass.) Oceanographic Inst., 1967-72, assoc. scientist, 1972-79, sr. scientist, 1979—, dean, 1979—; cons. Sandia Labs., Albuquerque, 1979—, AT & T, N.Y.C., 1982—; project dir. High Energy Bethnic Boundary Layer Expt., Woods Hole, Mass., 1979—. Author: (with Bryce C. Hagen) Face of Deep, 1971; contbr. articles to profl. jours. Served with U.S. Army, 1955-57. Recipient Oliver La Gorce Gold medal Nat. Geog. Soc., 1967. Fellow AAAS, Geol. Soc. Am.; mem. Am. Geophys. Union (sec. oceanography sect. 1980-82, chmn. edn. and human resources com. 1982—), Seabed Working Group (chief scientist), N.Y. Acad. Scis. Home: 108 Woods Hole Rd Falmouth MA 02541

HOLLISTER, CHARLES WARREN, history educator, author; b. Los Angeles, Nov. 2, 1930; s. Nathan and Carrie (Cushman) H.; m. Edith Elizabeth Muller, Apr. 12, 1952; children: Charles Warren (dec.), Lawrence Gregory, Robert Cushman. A.B., Harvard U., 1951; M.A., UCLA, 1957, Ph.D., 1958. Lectr. Griffith Planetarium, Los Angeles, 1956-58; mem. faculty U. Calif., Santa Barbara, 1958—, prof. history, 1964—, chmn. dept., 1967-70; vis. asst. prof. Stanford U., 1962-63; vis. research fellow Merton Coll., Oxford (Eng.) U., 1965-66; vis. fellow Australian Nat. U., 1978; lectr. Oxford U., 1965, Cambridge (Eng.) U., 1966, U. Ghent, Netherlands, 1966, U. Leyden, 1966, U. Utrecht, 1966, U. Bologna, Italy, 1967, U. Melbourne, Australia, 1978, U. Sydney, 1978, U. Auckland, New Zealand, 1978. Author: Anglo-Saxon Military Institutions, 1962, Medieval Europe, 5th edit, 1982, The Military Organization of Norman England, 1965, The Making of England, 4th edit, 1982, Roots of the Western Tradition, 4th edit, 1982, The Impact of the Norman Conquest, 1969, The Twelfth-Century Renaissance, 1969, (with Judith Pike) The Moons of Meer, 1969, Odysseus to Columbus, 1974, (with others) Medieval Europe: A Short Sourcebook, 1982. Served to 2d lt. USAF, 1951-53. Recipient Triennial Book prize Conf. Brit. Studies, 1963, E Harris Harbison award for disting. teaching Princeton, 1966, Walter D. Love meml. prize, 1981. Fellow Royal Hist. Soc., Medieval Acad. of Am., Medieval Acad. Ireland; mem. Pacific Coast Conf. Brit. Studies (pres. 1968-70), Conf. Brit. Studies (exec. council 1968-70, pres.-elect 1983—), Am. Hist. Assn. (exec. council Pacific Coast br. 1968-71, v.p. for teaching 1974-76, chmn. program com. 1984), Medieval Assn. Pacific (exec. council 1971-73). Home: 4592 Via Clarice Santa Barbara CA 93111

HOLLISTER, IRENE, association executive; b. Detroit, June 14, 1920; d. Leo R. and Alice (Boehn) McLean; m. Paul Hollister, June 27, 1951. B.B.A., U. Toledo, 1942. Employment mgr. Gimbel Bros., N.Y.C., 1946-50, Bonwit Teller, 1950-51; personnel rep. Research Inst. Am., N.Y.C., 1952-58; exec. sec. Assn. Computing Machinery, N.Y.C, 1960-83, dir. found. corp. relations, N.Y.C., 1983—. Club: Town Hall (N.Y.C.). Office: Assn for Computing Machinery 11 W 42d St New York NY 10036

HOLLISTER, JOHN BAKER, iron company executive; b. Cin., July 25, 1925; s. John B. H.; m. Ruth Elizabeth Boyle; 4 children. B.A., Yale U., 1949. Asst. mgr. sales Cleve.-Cliffs Iron, 1951-63, sr. v.p., 1973—; v.p. Fed. Lime & Stone, Cleve., 1964-73, Fed. Ore. & Mineral, 1964-73. Mem. Hunting Valley council, Cleve.; trustee Health Hill Hosp., Cleve., Hiram House Camp, Cleve. Served to sgt. inf. U.S. Army, 1943-45; ETO. Office: Cleve-Cliffs Iron Co 14th Floor Huntington Bldg Cleveland OH 44115

HOLLISTER, WILLIAM GRAY, psychiatrist; b. Lincoln, Nebr., July 21, 1915; s. Vernon Leo and Lela Gretchen (Pilcher) H.; m. Frances Flora Scudder, Mar. 23, 1940; children—David W., Robert Michael, Alan Scudder, Frances Virginia. A.B. in Anthropology, U. Nebr., 1937, B.S. in Psychology, 1940, M.D., 1941; M.P.H. (Rockefeller fellow), Johns Hopkins U., 1947; postgrad., Washington Psychoanalytic Inst., 1958-65. Diplomate: Am. Bd. Psychiatry and Neurology, Am. Bd. Preventive Medicine. Intern Grady Hosp., Atlanta, 1941-42; resident in psychiatry Bishop Clarkson Meml. Hosp., Omaha, 1942-43, USPHS Hosp., Fort Worth, 1947-49; supr. venereal disease control Miss. Bd. Health, Jackson, 1943-46; psychiat. cons. Region IV USPHS, Atlanta, 1949-56; nat. sch. mental health cons. NIMH, Bethesda, Md., 1956-61, chief br. community research and services, 1962-65; prof. psychiatry, dir. community psychiatry U. N.C., Chapel Hill, 1965-80, prof. emeritus, 1980—; cons. in occupational psychiatry IBM, Research Triangle Park, N.C., 1965—; nat. mental health chmn. Nat. Congress PTA, 1958-62, 65-69. Author: Experiences in Rural Mental Health, 1974; editor: (with E. M. Bower) Behavior Science Frontiers of Education, 1967. Served with USPHS, 1943-65. Fellow Am. Psychiat. Assn., Am. Public Health Assn. (Disting. Service medal 1964); mem. AMA. Unitarian. Home: 2008 N Lakeshore Dr Chapel Hill NC 27514 Office: Room 252 Bldg 208H U NC Sch Medicine Chapel Hill NC 27514

HOLLOMAN, JOHN LAWRENCE SULLIVAN, JR., physician; b. Washington, Nov. 22, 1919; s. John Lawrence Sullivan and Rosa Victoria (Jones) H.; m. Patricia Ann Tatje, May 11, 1969; children: Charlotte W., Paul S., Karin E., Laura A., Ellen V. B.S. in Chemistry, Va. Union U., 1940, D.Sc. (hon.), 1983; M.D., U. Mich., 1943. Rotating intern Harlem Hosp., N.Y.C., 1943-44, resident in internal medicine, 1947-48, mem. med. staff, various dates, 1982—; pvt. practice medicine, N.Y.C., 1948—; med. dir. Riverton Labs., N.Y.C., 1947-74, H.I.P. Multiphasic Health Testing Center, 1970-72; med. staff Sydenham Hosp., N.Y.C., 1950-58; asst. med. dir. Diagnostic Labs., N.Y.C., 1969-74; asst. v.p. Health Ins. Plan Greater N.Y., 1972-74; pres., dir., chief exec. officer N.Y.C. Health and Hosps. Corp., 1974-77; med. dir. William F. Ryan Community Health Ctr., 1981—; med. cons. H. Lassitter, Inc., 1971-74; asso. vis. physician Logan Hosp., N.Y.C., 1965-79; clin. prof. adminstrv. medicine NYU, 1974-78; instr. urban health New Sch. Social Research, N.Y.C.; vis. prof. health adminstrn. U. N.C., Chapel Hill, 1977-78; lectr. numerous univs.; chmn. Health Manpower Devel. Program, 1972—; mem. profl. staff ways and means subcom. U.S. Congress, 1979-80; regional med. officer region II FDA, Dept. Health and Human Services, 1981. Mem. Mayor's Emergency Control Bd., 1974-77; bd. dirs. Am. Com. on Africa, Group Health, Inc., Consumers Assembly N.Y., Nat. Sharecroppers Fund, Nat. Planned Parenthood, N.Y. Epilepsy Found., 1969-75, Community Health, Inc., Blue Haven Farm, 1969-77, Harlem Drug Fighters, Inc., 1969-77, Sex Info. and Edn. Council U.S., Inc., 1968-78; pres., trustee Va. Union U., Richmond, 1962-82; trustee State U. N.Y.; mem. adv. com. N.Y. State Health Planning Commn., Community Council Greater N.Y. Health Task Force, 1968-78; health adv. resources com. N.Y. Dept. Correctional Services, 1970-75. Served with M.C. AUS, 1944-46. Recipient Haven Emerson award Pub. Health Assn., 1972, Ernst P. Boas award for advancement social medicine, 1975, Frederick Douglas award N.Y. Urban League, 1975; elected mem. Inst. Medicine, Nat. Acad. Scis., 1972. Fellow Am. Pub. Health Assn. (mem. adv. com. Mound Bayou bd. monitors 1972-75); mem. AMA, Nat. Med. Assn. (pres. 1966-67, award for pub. service in medicine and pub. health 1975), Student Nat. Med. Assn. (adv. bd.), Student Am. Med. Assn. (adv. bd.), Physicians Forum (nat. chmn. 1970-71), Am. Cancer Soc. (dir. N.Y.C. div. 1971—), Pub. Health Assn. N.Y.C. (dir. 1971-77), Am. Hosp. Assn. (dir. 1974-78), N.Y. State Hosp. Assn. (dir. 1974-78), Group Health Assn., Am., N.Y. Acad. Medicine, Herman Biggs Soc. Home: 27-40 Ericsson St East Elmhurst NY 11369 *The good life in America requires health care to be the right of all. It is the obligation of our society to provide health care because good health is fundamental to life. . .before liberty and the pursuit of happiness.*

HOLLOMON, JOHN HERBERT, educator; b. Norfolk, Va., Mar. 12, 1919; s. John Herbert and Pearl (Twiford); m. Margaret Knox Wheeler, Aug. 12, 1941 (dec.); children—Jonathan Bradford, James Martin, Duncan Twiford, Elizabeth Wheeler Vrugtman, Peter Heinz Richter; m. Nancy Elizabeth Gade, Dec. 27, 1970. Grad., Augusta Mil. Acad., Ft. Defiance, Va., 1936; B.S., M.I.T., 1940, Sc.D., 1946; hon. doctorates, Worcester Poly. Inst., 1964, Mich. Tech. U., 1965, Rensselaer Poly. Inst., 1966, Carnegie-Mellon U., 1967, Northwestern U., U. Akron, 1967. Instr. Harvard U. Grad. Sch. Engring., 1941-42; research asso. Gen. Electric Research Lab., Gen. Electric Co., 1946-49, asst. mgr. metallurgy research dept., 1949-52, mgr. metallurgy and ceramics research dept., 1952-60, gen. mgr., 1960-62; asst. sec. for sci. and tech. Dept. Commerce, 1962-67; also acting under sec.; pres. U. Okla., 1967-70; cons. to pres. and to provost M.I.T., 1970-72; dir. Center Policy Alternatives, 1972—, 1st Japan Steel Industry prof., 1975—; adj. prof. Rensselaer Poly. Inst., 1950-62; dir. Bell & Howell Corp.; cons. Pres.'s Sci. Adv. Com.; also chmn. Atmospheric Scis. Com., 1963-67; Mem. Commerce Tech. Adv. Bd., 1962-67. Author: (with Leonard Jaffe) Ferrous Metallurgical Design, 1947; Contbr. articles to profl. jours. Served as maj. AUS, 1942-46; chief phys. metallurgy sect.; Watertown (Mass.) Arsenal. Decorated Legion of Merit; recipient Rossiter W. Raymond award AIME, 1946, Alfred Nobel prize Combined Engring. Socs., 1947, Rosenhain medal Brit. Inst. Metals, 1958. Fellow Am. Phys. Soc., Am. Inst. Chemists, AAAS; mem. Soc. for History of Tech., Am. Acad. Arts and Scis., Am. Soc. Metals (trustee 1957), Royal Swedish Acad. Engring. Sci. (fgn.), Mid-Am. State Univs. (pres. 1969), Acta Metallurgica (sec.-treas.), Nat. Acad. Engring. (a founder), Nat. Planning Assn. (bus. adv. council), Sigma Xi, Kappa Sigma. Clubs: Harvard (Boston); Cosmos (Washington). Address: 121 Carlton St Brookline MA 02146

HOLLON, WILLIAM EUGENE, educator, author, historian; b. Commerce, Tex., May 28, 1913; s. Samuel Horace and Myrtle (Payne) H.; m. Francis Elizabeth Cross, May 10, 1941; 1 dau., Susan Jean. B.A., E. Tex. State Coll., Commerce, 1934; M.A., U. Tex., 1937, Ph.D., 1942. Tchr. pub. schs., Tex., 1934-40; prof. history, instr. Ground Sch., Schreiner Inst., Kerrville, Tex., 1942-45; mem. faculty U. Okla., 1945-67, prof. history, 1956-67; curator history Stovall Mus. Natural History and Scis., 1947-67; research prof. history U. Toledo, 1967-68, Ohio regents prof. Am. history, 1968-78, prof. emeritus, 1978—; vis. prof. U. N.Mex., summer 1959, Cath. U., Lima, Peru, 1958, U. Mont., summer 1965; dir. seminar on Am. West Huntington Library, summer 1978, U. N.Mex., summer 1979. Author: The Lost Pathfinder: Zebulon Montgomery Pike, 1949, History of Pre-Flight Training in the USAAF, 1917-52, 1953, Beyond the Cross Timbers: The Travels of Randolph B. Marcy, 1955, William Bollaert's Texas, 1956, (with Berthrong and Owings) Outline History of the United States, 2 vols., 1957, The Southwest Old and New, 1961 (Merit award Assn. State and Local Hist. Societies, Theta Sigma Phi), The Great American Desert, 1966, (with LeRoy Hafen) Western America, 1970, Violence on the American Frontier; Another Look, 1974, The Movie Cowboy, 1981; also articles, book revs. Fellow Newberry Library, 1953, Am. Philos. Soc., 1947, 50, 64, Huntington Library, 1969, 72, 77; Fulbright and Smith-Mundt fellow, to Peru, 1958, to Spain, 1966-67; recipient Distinguished Alumni award E. Tex. State U., 1971. Mem. Orgn. Am. Historians, Southwestern Ariz. Hist. Assn., Western Hist. Assn. (pres. 1966-67), Great Plains Hist. Assn. (editorial bd.), Ohio Hist. Assn. Democrat. Home: Route 7 Box 109WH Santa Fe NM 87501 *Although it sounds self-righteous, my greatest satisfaction in life has been derived* *from encouragement and objective criticism of the work of graduate students interested in historical research, writing, and teaching. Their subsequent achievements have also been mine. And each time one expresses a desire to repay a favor done or assistance given, I remind the individual of the comment made many years ago by my former professor and good friend, the late Walter Prescott Webb: "The only way you can repay me is for you to pass it on some day to your own students".*

HOLLORAN, THOMAS EDWARD, financial services company executive; b. Mpls., Sept. 27, 1929; s. Edward Francis and Florence G. (Loftus) H.; m. Patricia M. Holloran, June 26, 1954; children: Mary Patricia, Anne Florence. B.S., U. Minn., 1951, J.D., 1955. Bar: Minn. 1955, Fed. 1955. Partner firm Wheeler and Fredrikson, Mpls., 1955-67; exec. v.p. Medtronic, Inc., Mpls., 1967-73, pres., 1973-75; chmn., pres. Inter-Regional Fin. Group, Inc., Mpls., 1975—; dir. Am. Hoist & Derrick Co., St. Paul, Donovan Cos. Inc., Flexsteel Industries, Inc., Dubuque, Iowa, Inter-Regional Fin. Group, Inc., Medtronic, Inc., MTS Systems Corp., Mpls. Spl. judge Mcpl. Ct. of Shorewood, Excelsior, Tonka Bay, Greenwood and Deephaven, Minn., 1961-65; Mayor, City of Shorewood, 1971-74; chmn. Urban Coalition, Mpls., 1977-78, City of Mpls. Task Force on Tech., 1983—; mem. Mpls.-St. Paul Met. Airports Commn., 1974-82, vice chmn., 1976-82; bd. trustees Coll. St. Scholastica, 1971-81, chmn., 1979-81; trustee Coll. St. Thomas, U. Minn. Found., 1983—, Bush Found., 1982—, Mpls. Children's Health Ctr., 1983—; pres. Upper M.W. Council, Mpls., 1979-81; bd. dirs. InterStudy, Excelsior., Minn. Press Council, 1982—. Served with USN, 1952-54; Korea. Mem. Am. Bar Assn. Roman Catholic.

HOLLOWAY, ALBERT WESTON, govt. ofcl.; b. York County, Va., Nov. 4, 1918; s. John P. and Octavia (Weston) H.; m. Ethel Hilsman Edmondson, Mar. 19, 1950; 1 dau., Judith Warren. Student, William and Mary Coll., 1937, Harvard U. Bus. Sch., 1958. Mgr. Gen. Adjustment Bur., Albany, Ga., 1948-50, Nashville, 1950-51; treas. Engring. and Equipment Co., 1951-56, pres., gen. mgr., 1956—, Engring. and Equipment Co. Fla., Panama City; dir. Citizens and So. Bank of Albany. Mem. Ga. Ho. of Reps., 1957-58, Ga. Senate, 1963—; pres. pro tempore Ga. Senate, 1975—; Bd. dirs. Goodwill Industries. Served as pilot USAF, 1942-45. Decorated D.F.C., Air Medal and others. Mem. So. Wholesalers Assn., Ga. Wholesalers Assn., Am. Supply Assn., Ga. C. of C. (past pres.), Am. Legion, VFW. Democrat. Episcopalian. Clubs: Rotary, Elks, Moose. Office: PO Box 588 Albany GA 31702

HOLLOWAY, BRUCE KEENER, former air force officer; b. Knoxville, Tenn., Sept. 1, 1912; s. Frank P. and Elizabeth (Keener) H.; m. Frances Purdy, Oct. 14, 1944; children: Candace, Taylor, Amy. Student, U. Tenn., 1930-31; B.S., U.S. Mil. Acad., 1937, Calif. Inst. Tech., 1941; grad., Nat. War Coll., 1951. Commd. 2d lt. USAAF, 1937; advanced through grades to gen. USAF, 1965; comdr. fighter aviation 14th Air Force, China Theater, 1942-43, 1st Fighter Group, March AFB, Calif., 1946; various staff assignments Air Def. Command, 1947-50; dep. dir. requirements Hdqrs. USAF, 1951-55; dep. comdr. 9th Air Force, Shaw AFB, S.C., 1955-57, 12th Air Force, Waco, Tex., 1957-59; dir. requirements USAF; also dir. mil. liaison com. USAF, AEC, 1959-61; dep. comdr. in chief U.S. Strike Command, MacDill AFB, Fla., 1961-65; comdr. in chief U.S. Air Forces in Europe, 1965-66; vice chief of staff (Dept. Air Force), 1966-68; comdr. in chief SAC, Offutt AFB, Nebr., 1968-72; ret., 1972; acting asso. adminstr. for aeronautics and space tech. NASA, Washington, 1973-74; cons. aerospace industry, 1974—; pres. U.S. Strategic Inst., 1974-75, 82—; dir. Sierra Research Corp., 1979—. Trustee N.Y. Inst. Tech., 1972—, Nova U., 1974—. Decorated D.S.M., Silver Star, D.F.C., Legion of Merit, Air medal; Order Sacred Tripod, China; also other fgn. decorations. Mem. Def. Preparedness Assn., 14th Air Force Assn., Ret. Officers Assn., Order Daedalians, Phi Gamma Delta. Presbyn. Home: 5124 Belleville Ave Orlando FL 32812 Office: 20 Memorial Dr Cambridge MA 02142

HOLLOWAY, CHARLES ARTHUR, educator, university administrator; b. Whittier, Calif., May 28, 1936; s. Heber H. and Theodora S. (Stephens) H.; m. Christina Ahlm, July 11, 1959; children: Deborah, Susan, Stuart. B.S.E.E. with honors, U. Calif.-Berkeley, 1959; M.S., UCLA, 1963, Ph.D. with distinction in Engring., 1969. Sr. engr. Bechtel Corp., San Francisco, 1964-65; teaching fellow UCLA, 1965-66; asst. prof. to prof. Stanford (Calif.) U., 1968—, Herbert Hoover prof. pub. and pvt. mgmt., 1980—, dean acad. affairs Grad. Sch. Bus.; dir. Cardio Data, SBA Corp., Tioga Press. Authors: Decision Making Under Uncertainty: Models and Choices, 1979. Mem. adv. bd. GSA; bd. dirs. Rickover Found., League to Save Redwoods. Fellow Ford Found., 1966-68. Mem. Inst. Mgmt. Sci., Ops. Research Soc. Am. Home: 730 Santa Maria Ave Stanford CA 94305 Office: Stanford U Grad Sch Bus Stanford CA 94305

HOLLOWAY, DAVID, baritone; b. Grandview, Mo., Nov. 12, 1942; s. Milton and Elta Mae H.; 1 son by 1st marriage, Devin; m. Deborah L. Seabury, May 25, 1975; children—Robin, Bliss. Mus.B. in Voice, U. Kans., 1964, Mus.M., 1966; student, Luigi Ricci, Rome, 1971-72. Participant apprentice program, Santa Fe Opera, 1966-67, Western Opera Theatre, 1970, Met. Opera Studio, 1970, 71; appeared with opera cos., Kansas City (Mo.) Lyric Opera, Santa Fe Opera, Chgo. Lyric Opera, Boston Opera, Met. Opera, N.Y.C. Opera, Nat. Arts Center, Ottawa, Ont., Can., Houston Grand Opera, Dallas Civic Opera, Cin. Opera, Ft. Worth Opera; made European debut with, Hamburg State Opera, 1980; mem., Deutsche Oper am Rhein, Dusseldorf, W. Ger., 1981— (Winner San Francisco Opera Auditions 1968), Deutsche Oper am Rhein, Dusseldorf, W. Ger. (recipient Hi/Fi/Mus. Am. award Tanglewood Music Festival 1971). Martha Baird Rockefeller grantee, 1970; Nat. Opera Inst. grantee, 1971, 72. Office: care Columbia Artists Mgmt Inc 165 W 57th St New York NY 10019

HOLLOWAY, EDGAR AUSTIN, diversified bus. exec.; b. Anguilla, Miss., Mar. 29, 1925; s. Tom W. and Lillie (Martin) H.; m. Bettye Jo Marmor, Oct. 3, 1947; 1 dau., Janis Lynn (Mrs. Fichlie). B.S., U. Louisville, 1947. C.P.A., Ohio, Miss., Ky., Ariz. Accountant Haskins & Sells, Louisville, 1947-49, Cin., 1957-59; C.P.A. Coopers & Lybrand, Louisville, 1949-51; asst. treas. Diamond Crystal Salt Co., St. Clair, Mich., 1951-57; controller Diamond Internat. Corp., 1959-66; corp. controller Cudahy Co., Phoenix, 1966-68, v.p., controller, 1968-72, The Clorox Co., Oakland, Calif., 1972-73, v.p. fin., 1973-79; v.p. fin., treas. Three Phoenix Co., Ariz., 1979—. City treas., Jeffersontown (Ky.), 1943-47; bd. dirs. YMCA. Served to lt. (j.g.) USNR, 1954-57. Mem. Am. Arbitration Assn., Fin. Execs. Inst. (nat. dir. Western area 1978-79, sec. San Francisco chpt. 1977, treas. 1978, 2d v.p. 1979, dir. Ariz. chpt. 1980-81), Am. Inst. C.P.A.'s. Clubs: Orinda (Calif.); Country (fin. com. 1977-78), Rotary.). Home: 6532 N 60th St Scottsdale AZ 85253 Office: 21639 N 14th Ave Phoenix AZ 85027

HOLLOWAY, HILIARY HAMILTON, banker, lawyer; b. Durham, N.C., Mar. 7, 1928; s. Joseph Sim and Zelma (Slade) H.; m. Beatrice Gwen Larkin, Dec. 21, 1951; children: Hiliary H., Janis L. B.S.C., N.C. Central U., 1949; Ed.M., Temple U., 1956, J.D., 1964. Bar: Pa. 1965. Bus. mgr. St. Augustine's Coll., Raleigh, N.C., 1950-53; nat. exec. dir. Kappa Alpha Psi, Phila., 1953-65; mem. firm Hazell & Bowser, Phila., 1965-68; asst. counsel Fed. Res. Bank, Phila., 1968-72, v.p., gen. counsel, 1972-82, sr. v.p., gen. counsel, 1982—; arbitrator Am. Arbitration Assn. Chmn. bd. trustees N.C. Central U., 1981—; vice chmn. Met. YMCA, Phila., 1973—; trustee Lankenau Hosp., Phila., 1978—; bd. dirs. Phila. Mus. Art, 1980—. Recipient Disting. Community Service award Chapel of Four Chaplains, Phila., 1975, Martin Luther King award Educator's Roundtable, Phila., 1977, Laurel Wreath award Kappa Alpha Psi, Detroit, 1982. Mem. ABA, Phila. Bar Assn., Nat. Bar Assn., Fed. Bar Assn. Office: Fed Res Bank Phila 100 N 6th St Philadelphia PA 19106

HOLLOWAY, JAMES YOUNG, philosophy and religion educator, editor, author; b. Pensacola, Fla., Aug. 28, 1927; s. James Lavert and Amy Cecilia (Young) H.; m. Nancy Kay Attaway, June 14, 1959; children: Kay Louisa, James William, Joseph Patrick. B.A., Vanderbilt U., 1951, M.A., B.D., 1954; Ph.D., Yale U., 1961; student, U. Basel, Switzerland, 1957-58. Asst. prof. polit. sci. United Coll. Man., Can., 1959-60; asst. prof. Christian ethics Mercer U., Macon, Ga., 1961-64; asst. prof. polit. sci. St. Andrew's Presbyn. Coll., Laurinburg, N.C., 1964-65; assoc. prof. philosophy and religion Berea Coll., Ky., 1965—, McGaw prof., 1976—; cons. So. Regional Council, Atlanta, 1964. Author: (with W.D. Campbell) Up to Out Steeples in Politics, 1970, The Failure and the Hope, 1972, And the Criminals with Him. . . ., 1973; editor: Introducing Jacques Ellul, Callings, 1970. Bd. dirs. Council So. Mountains, Berea, 1966-69. Served to sgt. U.S. Army, 1946-47; PTO. Recipient Young award in Polit. Sci. Vanderbilt U., 1951, Tillett award in Theology Vanderbilt U., 1953; Yale U. scholar, 1954-56; Lilly scholar, 1958. Mem. Am. Polit. Sci. Assn., AAUP. Club: Tuttle Soc. (Berea) (capt. 1981—). Home: Davis Hollow Rd Berea KY 40403 Office: Berea Coll Sta Box 2307 Berea KY 40404

HOLLOWAY, JEROME KNIGHT, educator, ret. fgn. service officer; b. Phila., May 8, 1923; s. Jerome Knight and Emily Margaret (Ennis) H.; m. Gertrud Harms, Apr. 16, 1953 (dec. Jan. 1976); children—Jerome Knight III, Karen M., Nicholas H. A.B., Cath. U., 1947; M.A., U. Mich., 1959; lang. student, Tokyo, Japan, 1958-60; fellow, Harvard, 1968-69. Joined U.S. Fgn. Service, 1947, ret., 1975; 3d sec., Rangoon, Burma, 1947-49, vice-consul, Shanghai, China, 1949-50, Bremen, Germany, 1950-52, consul, Hong Kong, 1952-57, 2d sec., Tokyo, 1960-61; assigned State Dept., Washington, 1961-64, 69-70; 1st sec., Stockholm, Sweden, 1964-65, counselor, 1965-68, consul gen., Osaka-Kobe, Japan, 1970-74; state dept. adviser to pres. U.S. Naval War Coll., Newport, R.I., 1974-75, prof. strategy, 1976—. Served to lt. (j.g.) USNR, 1942-46. Mem. U.S. Naval Inst., Assn. Asian Studies. Home: 3 Cypress St Newport RI 02840 Office: Naval War Coll Newport RI 02840

HOLLOWAY, JOHN THOMAS, physicist; b. Cape Girardeau, Mo., June 19, 1922; s. Herbert Henry and Addie Mae (Cahill) H.; m. Kay Vickers, Nov. 11, 1965; children—Linda, Kim. A.B., Millikin U., Decatur, Ill., 1943; Ph.D., Iowa State U., 1957. With nuclear physics br. Office Naval Research, Washington, 1946-53, head br., 1951-52; research asst. Ames (Iowa) Lab., AEC, 1954-57; with Office Dir. Def. Research and Engring., Washington, 1958-61, dep. dir., 1959-61; with NASA, 1961-68, dep. dir. grants and research contracts, 1961-67, chief advanced programs and tech., space applications div., 1967-68; dir. Nat. Hwy. Safety Research Center, Dept. Transp., 1968-69; v.p. research Ins. Inst. Hwy. Safety, 1969-72; asso. dir. ops. Interdisciplinary Communications Program, Smithsonian Instn., 1972-77, program mgr. internat. program population analysis, 1972-77, research and devel. cons. in hwy. safety, biomed. electronics, energy conservation, 1977-78; sr. staff officer bd. on radioactive waste mgmt. Nat. Acad. Scis.-NRC, 1978—; dir. Interdisciplinary Communications Assos., Inc.; mem. conf. com. Nat. Conf. Advancement Research, 1971-75. Author papers in field; adviser documentary films. Served with USNR, 1944-46. Mem. Am. Phys. Soc., Philos. Soc. Washington, Sigma Xi. Clubs: Cosmos (Washington); Army-Navy Country (Arlington, Va.). Home: 2220 Cathedral Ave NW Washington DC 20008

HOLLOWAY, JOSEPH WESLEY, lawyer; b. Berne, Ind., July 26, 1930; s. Glenn and Wilma Jean (Timmons) H.; m. Janet Ann Brady, Apr. 12, 1953; children—Michael, Mary Lee. B.S., Purdue U., 1955; LL.B., Ind. U., 1958. Bar: Ind. bar 1958. Patent atty. Cutler-Hammer Co., Milw., 1958-59, Schmiedeskamp, Robertson (attys.), Quincy, Ill., 1959-66; corp. sec., chief legal counsel Gardner-Denver Co., Dallas, 1966-77, sr. corp. atty., 1977-79, patent atty., 1979—; dir. H & M Farms, Inc. Served with USN, 1951-54. Mem. Ind., Ill., Wis. bar assns., Phi Delta Phi. Republican. Methodist. Home: Box 175 R3 Liberty IL 62347 Office: PO Box 109 Quincy IL 62301

HOLLOWAY, LEONARD LEVEINE, foundation executive; b. Ada, Okla., Mar. 23, 1923; s. Leonard L. and Mamie (Burroughs) H.; m. Betty Gould, May 29, 1944; children: Shalia Kay, Jamie Lynn. B.A., Okla. Bapt. U., 1948; M.A., U. Okla., 1949, M.S., 1950, D.D. (hon.), 1958. Mem. faculty Tex. Women's U., 1950-51, Wayland Coll., 1951-52; dir. pub. relations Tex. Bapt. Gen. Conv., 1953-59; v.p. H.E. Butt Found., Corpus Christi, Tex., 1959-61, mem. exec. staff, 1970—; v.p., prof. New Orleans Bapt. Theol. Sem., also So. Bapt. Theol. Sem., 1961-66; pres. Mary Hardin-Baylor Coll., 1966-68, U. Corpus Christi, 1968-69; part-time pub. relations and mgmt. cons., 1958-66; dir. Nat. Bank Commerce, Kerrville, Tex.; Bd. dirs., past pres. Bapt. Pub. Relations Assn.; adminstrv. dir. H.E. Butt Found. Camps, Laity Lodge Found. and; C.M.I.; community relations adviser Peace Corps; mem. President's Com. Refugee Placement. Author: Encounter with God, 1972; also booklets, articles. Bd. dirs. Christian Men, Inc., local ARC, Conf. S.w. Founds., Gulf Coast council Boy Scouts Am.; chmn. bd. devel. Tex. Bapt. Children's Home. Served with USAAF, 1941-45, 52-53; lt. col. Res. (ret.) USAAF. Decorated D.F.C., Air medal with clusters. Home: 803 Bow Ln Kerrville TX 78028

HOLLOWAY, PAUL FAYETTE, aerospace exec.; b. Hampton, Va., June 7, 1938; s. Eldridge Manning and Minnie Powell H.; m. Barbara Jane Menetch, June 23, 1956; children—Paul Manning (dec.), Eric Scott. B.S., Va. Poly. Inst. and State U., 1960; postgrad., U. Va., 1961, Coll. William and Mary, 1962-63. With NASA Langley Research Center, Hampton, Va., 1960—, aerospace technologist, 1960-69, mem. space shuttle task group, 1969—, chief space systems div., 1972-75; acting dep. asso. adminstr. Office Aeronautics and Space Tech., 1977, dir. for space, 1975—. Asso. editor: Jour Spacecraft and Rockets, 1972-77; editor-in-chief, 1978-80; contbr. articles in field to profl. jours. Mem. Poquoson Planning Commn.; v.p. local PTA; active Boy Scouts Am. Recipient Outstanding Leadership medal NASA, 1980, Exceptional Service medal, 1981; Presdl. Rank award for meritorious exec., 1981. Asso. fellow AIAA; mem. Fed. Exec. Inst. Alumni Assn., Sigma Gamma Tau, Phi Kappa Phi. Methodist. Home: 16 N Westover Dr Poquoson VA 23662 Office: Mailstop 107 1/2 Langley Research Center Hampton VA 23665

HOLLOWAY, RALPH LESLIE, JR., anthropologist; b. Phila., Feb. 6, 1935; s. Ralph L. and Marguerite (Grugan) H.; children: Marguerite Yvonne, Eric Ralph, Benjamin Thomas. B.S., U. N.Mex., 1959; Ph.D., U. Calif., Berkeley, 1964. Asst. prof. anthropology Columbia U., N.Y.C., 1964-69, asso. prof., 1969-72, prof., 1973—, chmn. dept., 1979-81; adj. prof. New Sch. for Social Research, N.Y.C., 1972—. Editor: Primate Aggression, Territoriality and Zenophobia: A Comparative Perspective, 1974; Contbr. articles to profl. jours. Guggenheim fellow, 1974-75; NIMH fellow, 1964; NSF grantee, 1969—. Fellow AAAS, N.Y. Acad. Sci.; mem. Am. Anthrop. Assn., Am. Assn. Phys. Anthropology, Soc. Study of Social Biology, Internat. Soc. Research on Aggression, Internat. Primatological Soc., Sigma Xi, Phi Kappa Phi, Sigma Gamma Epsilon. Office: Dept Anthropology U New York NY 10027 *Always try to know and question your own biases.*

HOLLOWAY, ROBERT J., business educator; b. Walker, Iowa, Sept. 13, 1921; s. John Theron and Mabel Marie (Condon) H.; m. Lois Anita Ita, Jan. 13, 1945; children: Steven Robert, Anne Louise, Bruce Ita. B.S.C., U. Iowa, 1943; M.B.A., Stanford U., 1948, Ph.D., 1952. Prof. bus. environment and mktg. U. Minn., Mpls., 1950—, chmn. dept. bus. adminstrn., 1957-59; vis. prof. U. Philippines, 1955-56, Doshisha U., Kyoto, Japan, 1978-79, Keio U., Tokyo, 1979, 83. Co-author: Marketing in a Changing Environment; Co-editor: The Environment of Marketing Behavior. Mem. Am. Mktg. Assn. (pres. 1967-68). Home: 2208 Folwell St Saint Paul MN

HOLLOWAY, ROBERT ROSS, archaeologist, educator; b. Newton, Mass., Aug. 15, 1934; s. Charles Thomas II and Mildred Evelyn (Guthrie) H.; m. Nancy Jane Degenhardt, May 21, 1960; children: Anne Lovelace, Susannah Porter. A.B. summa cum laude, Amherst Coll., 1956, L.H.D., 1976; A.M., U. Pa., 1957; M.A., Ph.D., Princeton U., 1960, Brown U., 1967. Asst. prof. U. N.C., Chapel Hill, 1963-64; mem. faculty Brown U., 1964—, prof. archaeology, 1970—; del., dir. Center for Classical Archaelogy and Art, 1978—; cons. curator ancient art Mus. Art, R.I. Sch. Design, 1971—; Del. Centro Internat. di Studi Numismatici, Naples, Italy, 1973—, pres., 1980—. Author: The Thirteen-Months Coinage of Hieronymos of Syracuse, 1969, Satrianum, 1970, Buccino, 1973, A View of Greek Art, 1973, Influences and Styles in the Late Archaic and Early Classical Greek Sculpture of Sicily and Magna Graecia, 1975, Art and Coinage in Magna Graecia, 1978; co-author: Terina, 1983; Editor catalogue of classical collection, Mus. Art, R.I. Sch. Design, 1965. Grantee Am. Philos. Soc., 1962, Nat. Endowment for Humanities, 1972, 80, 82, 83; fellow Am. Council Learned Socs., 1969; Nat. Endowment for Humanities sr. fellow, 1977. Fellow Am. Numismatic Soc., Am. Acad. Rome; mem. Assn. Field Archaeology (pres. 1975-77), Archaeol. Inst. Am., Phi Beta Kappa; corr. mem. German Archaeol. Inst., Soc. Art Historians, Rome. Clubs: Bristol Yacht, Providence Art. Home: 185 Elmgrove Ave Providence RI 02906

HOLLOWAY, STERLING PRICE, actor, recording artist; b. Cedartown, Ga.; s. Sterling Price and Rebecca deHaven (Boothby) H.; 1 son, Richard Hargrove. Student, Am. Acad. Dramatic Art, 1921-23. Appeared in numerous stage plays, motion pictures, radio and television programs, 1925—; motion pictures include Won Ton Ton, Dog Who Saved Hollywood; radio and TV appearances include Baileys of Balboa; numerous others; voice of Winnie-the-Pooh for, Disney Prodns., 1971—; voice documentary Jungle Book, 1983; voice numerous TV commercials; Rec. artist, art lectr.; artist-in-residence, U. Calif., Irvine, 1971-72. Bd. dirs. Art Mus. Served with AUS, World War II. Recipient Grammy award for best childrens record, 1975; nominee, 1976; Americana award Cyprus Coll., 1978; bronze award, 1981. Mem. Nat. Acad. Recording Arts and Scis. Office: 137 N Sycamore Ave Los Angeles CA 90036 also 484 W 43d St New York NY 10036

HOLLOWAY, WILLIAM JIMMERSON, educator; b. Smithfield, Va., May 6, 1917; s. Arnett Jimmerson and Lucy Pernell (White) H.; m. Julia Naomi Edmundson, June 17, 1944; children: Wendell, Arnett, Lynn. B.S. with honors, Hampton Inst., 1940; M.A., U. Mich., 1946; Ed.D., U. Ill., 1961; postgrad., Harvard U., 1950. Prin. Union Sch., Hampton, Va., 1946-47; dean students Savannah State Coll., 1947-55; prin. Ligon High Sch., Raleigh, N.C., 1956-57; counselor N.C. Central U., Durham, 1959-61; supt. Va. State Sch., Hampton, 1961-65; edn. program officer U.S. Office Edn., Washington, 1965-70; vice provost Ohio State U., Columbus, 1970-78, prof. edn., 1970-82, prof. emeritus, 1982—; dir. Nigerian edn. program, Ohio State U., 1980-82; pres. Internat. Ednl. and Service Inst., Inc., Raleigh, N.C., 1981—. Editorial bd.: Negro Ednl. Rev, 1972. Trustee Freedoms Found., 1974, St. Augustines Coll., 1968-77. Recipient Freedoms Found. medal, 1954; Superior Accomplishment award HEW, 1968; Disting. Alumni award Hampton Inst., 1970; award Nat. Press Inst., 1972; Outstanding Citizen award Ohio Gen. Assembly, 1978; Outstanding Achievement award Ohio State U., 1978; Disting. Service award Ohio State U., 1984; Community Leadership award Capital U., 1978; Nat. Disting. Service award United Negro Coll. Fund, 1979; Excellence in Internat. Edn. award Govt. of Nigeria; Disting. Career award Negro Ednl. Rev., 1984; Harvard Far Eastern Studies fellow, 1956. Mem. Am. Assn. Higher Edn., Am. Personnel and Guidance Assn., Alpha Kappa Delta, Phi Delta Kappa, Kappa Delta Pi. Democrat. Presbyterian (elder). Clubs: Lions (pres. 1975); Cosmos (Washington)). Home: 7109 Tanbark Way Raleigh NC 27609 *As an educator I have worked to develop sensitivity to the needs, hopes, and aspirations of all people, particularly those at the bottom of the socio-economic ladder. With youth and adults I have labored to kindle sparks of brotherhood leading to harmony. I feel that our survival on this planet is linked with our capacity to use cultural differences in creative and constructive ways.*

HOLLOWAY, WILLIAM, JR., Judge U.S. Ct. Appeals 10th Circuit, Oklahoma City. Office: US Ct of Appeals 10th Circuit PO Box 1767 Oklahoma City OK 73101 *

HOLLY, EDWIN E., motion picture production company executive; b. Elizabethton, Tenn., Oct. 3, 1926; s. Earl H. and Rada C. (Jordan) H.; m. Patricia R. Motschman, Oct. 2, 1976; children: Patrice Katz, Amy Lowe. B.S., U. Tenn., 1949. C.P.A. Staff auditor Lybrand, Ross Bros. & Montgomery (C.P.A.s), N.Y.C., 1949-52; asst. corp. controller CBS, N.Y.C., 1952-54; v.p. adminstrn. and fin. Desilu Prodns. Inc., Hollywood, Calif., 1954-67; v.p. studio facilities Paramount Pictures Corp., Hollywood, 1967-69; dir. fin. William Morris Agy., Beverly Hills, Calif., 1969-75; pres. First Artists Prodn. Co., Ltd., Sherman Oaks, Calif., 1975-83; cons. entertainment industry, 1983—. Served with U.S. Army, 1944-46. Mem. Calif. Soc. C.P.A.s. Office: 29204 Village 29 Camarillo CA 93010

HOLM, CELESTE, actress; b. N.Y.C., Apr. 29, 1919; d. Theodor and Jean (Parke) H. Ed., Univ. Sch. for Girls, Chgo., Lycée Victor Durui, Paris, Francis Parker Sch., Chgo. Appeared on Broadway in role of Mary L. in the: Pulitzer prize play The Time of Your Life, 1939; opposite George M. Cohan in: The Return of the Vagabond, 1940; in: My Fair Ladies, 1941; Broadway and on tour in Papa Is All, 1941-42, The Damask Cheek, 1942-43; first musical comedy role Ado Annie, in: Oklahoma, 1943-44; then starred in: Bloomer Girl, 1944; made: supper club appearance in La Vie Parisienne, 1943, Persian Rm., Plaza Hotel, N.Y.C., 1944, 45, 53, 54, 55, 57, 59; U.S.O. entertainer, ETO, Aug.-Nov. 1945; appeared in: film Three Little Girls in Blue, 1946; starred in: films Come to the Stable, 1948, Everybody Does It, 1949, Champagne for Caesar, All About Eve, 1950, The Tender Trap, 1955, High Society, 1956; starred on stage in: Broadway comedy hit Affairs of State, Sept. 1950-June 1951; for Dept. State recreated original role in: Oklahoma, Berlin Arts Festival, Germany, 1951; starred in: revival of Anna Christie (Eugene O'Neill), N.Y.C. Center Theatre, January 1952; appeared: on Broadway in The King and I, 1952, Third Best Sport, 1958, Invitation to a March, 1960-61; off Broadway in: A Month in the Country, 1963; condr.: radio program People at the UN, WNBC radio sta., N.Y.C., 3 yrs; toured U.S. in: program Theatre-in-Concert, 1963, 64; toured, 8 Middle Eastern and European countries for, State Dept., 1966; appeared as fairy godmother in: color TV spl.

Cinderella, 1965, 66, 67; starred TV presentations, 1966; star, dir.: Affairs of State, Pasadena Playhouse, 1967; starred as Mame in, Nat. Co., 1967, 68; appeared in: movies Doctor You've Got to be Kidding, 1966, Tom Sawyer, 1972, Secret Files of J. Edgar Hoover, 1976, Bittersweet Love, 1976; on Broadway in: Candida, 1970, Habeas Corpus, 1975-76; (Received Motion Picture Academy award for best performance by an actress in a supporting role for 1947 for picture, Gentlemen's Agreement, nominated for Acad. Award for work in Come to the Stable 1950, and again for work in All About Eve, Performer of Year, Variety Clubs Am. 1966, Sarah Siddens award for role in Mame.). Mem. governing bd. U.S. Com. for UNICEF; mem. bd. Nat. Assn. Mental Health Bd. Coll. and Career Cons.; v.p. Arts and Bus. Council.; mem. Nat. Council Arts, 1982—. Woman of Year award Alliance Francaise. Made 21,000 mile tour U.S. Army Air Bases entertaining mil. personnel, 1949. Address: care Lionel Larner 850 7th Ave New York NY 10019 *

HOLM, DONALD SUTHERLAND, JR., university official, business management educator; b. Highland Park, Mich., Oct. 1, 1920; s. D. S. and Louise (Hemeyer) H.; m. Marilynn Ruth Lamb, June 8, 1951; children: Donald Sutherland, Elizabeth Lamb. A.B., 1941; M.B.A., Harvard U., 1947; M.A., Ind. U., 1950, Ph.D. (fellow), 1952. Asst. prof. bus. mgmt. U. Mo., Columbia, 1950-53, assoc. prof., 1953-58, prof., 1958—, chmn. dept. bus. mgmt., 1962-65, coordinator M.B.A. program, 1964-65, chmn. dept. mgmt., 1965-69, dir. grad. programs in bus., 1965-70, acting asst. v.p. fin., 1972-73, asst. v.p., asst. treas., 1973-77, treas. and asst. v.p., 1977—; cons. Dept. Labor, 1960, Comptroller and Budget Dir. Mo., 1962, Hawthorn Co., New Haven, Mo., 1963-64, Mo. State Library, 1962-63, M.F.A. Oil Co., Columbia, 1964-65, OEO, 1966-67, Mo. Dept. Revenue, 1967, Boone County Hosp., 1968, 73, Am. Coll. Hosp. Adminstrs., 1968-71, Mo. Hwy. Commn., 1956—, Mo. Savs. and Loan League, 1972; dir. Bank of Steele, (Mo.). Author books on labor and unemployment; contbr. articles on mgmt. to profl. publs. Mem. Mo. Com. on Econ. Devel., 1960-61; chmn. Columbia Personnel Adv. Bd., 1963-72; mem. Task Force on Personnel Adminstrn., Mo. Reorgn. Commn., 1970-71; chmn. Mo. Gov.'s Adv. Council on Employment Security, 1962-65. Served to lt. comdr. USNR, 1942-46. Recipient Outstanding Achievement award in aerospace edn. USAF, 1970; Ford Found. fellow, 1960. Mem. Acad. Mgmt., U.S. Navy League (dir. 1967-70), Central Assn. Coll. and Univ. Bus. Officers, Nat. Assn. Coll. and Univ. Bus. Officers, Mcpl. Fin. Officers Assn., Beta Gamma Sigma. Clubs: Columbia Country (treas., gov. 1966-71); Harvard (N.Y.C.); Mo. Athletic. Home: 106 W Ridgeley Rd Columbia MO 65201 Office: 215 K University Hall Columbia MO 65211

HOLM, GERALD LANGE, consumer finance company executive; b. Sept. 6, 1938; s. Walter William and Elizabeth (Lange) H.; m. Marjorie Louise Miller, July 2, 1960 (div. Dec. 1977); children: Charlotte, Melinda; m. Susan Gail Yeck, Apr. 14, 1978; 1 son, Nicholas. B.S., Tex. Tech. U., 1961, M.S., 1962. Data processing dir. Boeing Co., Huntsville, Ala., 1962-71; sr. mgr. Beneficial Data Processing, Morristown, N.J., 1971-73, v.p., 1973-74, pres., 1974-79; exec. v.p. Beneficial Mgmt., Peapack, N.J., 1979-81, mem. exec. com.; vice chmn. Beneficial Corp., Wilmington, Del., 1981—; dir. Beneficiial Corp., Wilmington, Del.; mem. exec. com. Beneficial Corp., Wilmington, Del.; dir. Western Auto Supply, Kansas City, Mo.; chmn. bd. Beneficial Leasing Group, N.Y.C. Office: Beneficial Corp 1100 Carr Rd Wilmington DE 19899

HOLM, HANYA, choreographer, dancer, dance educator; b. Worms-am-Rhine, Germany; came to U.S., 1931, naturalized, 1939; d. Valentin and Marie (Moerschel) Eckert; (married and) (div.); 1 son, Klaus Holm. Ed. pvt. schs., Germany; student of music, Hoch Conservatory and Dalcroze Inst., Frankfurt-am- Main; grad., Dalcroze Inst., Hellerau; dance diploma, Mary Wigman Central Inst., Dresden, Germany; D.F.A. (hon.), Colo. Coll., 1960, Adelphi U., 1969. Chief instr., co-dir. Wigman Inst., Dresden, 10 yrs; dir. dance dept. Mus. Theatre Acad., N.Y.C., 1962—; dir. own sch., N.Y.C., until 1968; dir. summer sessions in dance Colo. Coll., 1941-83; mem. staff Alwin Nikolais/Murray Louis Dance Theatre Lab., N.Y.C., 1972—, Juilliard Sch., 1975—; tchr., lectr. Bretton Coll., Eng., 1979. Mem. original, Wigman Co.; performer, dance dir., choreographer, Europe, until 1931; under auspices Sol Hurok, founder, dir., N.Y. Wigman Sch. Dance, 1931, which later became Hanya Holm Sch. Dance; began Am. concert career, 1936; major prodns. Trend, 1937 (N.Y. Times award from John Martin as best dance composition of year), Metropolitan Daily, 1938, Tragic Exodus, 1938 (Dance Mag. award for best group choreography in modern dance); in work with theatre; choreographer: Eccentricities of Davey Crockett, 1948, Kiss Me, Kate (Cole Porter), 1948 (best choreographer N.Y. Drama Critics award), Eng. prodn., 1951, Out of this World (C. Porter), 1950, My Darlin Aida, 1952; choreographer, dir.: The Golden Apple, 1954 (Critics Circle citation best musical); Reuben- Reuben, 1955; staged: dances for re-make of film Vagabond King, 1956; choreography and mus. numbers My Fair Lady, 1955-56 (Tony nominee), Israeli prodn., 1964, Where's Charley, My Fair Lady; English prodns., 1958; choreography and mus. numbers Camelot, 1960; Christine, 1960-61, Anya, 1965; staged dances: television show Pinocchio, 1957; choreographer: Dinner with the President, 1963, Metropolitan Daily; 1st dance prodn. on TV, 1939; dir., choreographer: world premiere opera The Ballad of Baby Doe, Central City, Colo. opera house, 1956; appeared on: Am. Cancer Soc. series Tactic, NBC, 1959; dir., choreographer: opera Orpheus and Euridice (Gluck), Vancouver Internat. Festival, 1959. Recipient Capezio award, 1978, award Fedn. Jewish Philanthropies, 1959, Colo. Centennial award and Gov.'s award, 1973, 74, Heritage Honor award Nat. Dance Assn., 1976, award and medal of distinction in fine arts City of Colorado Springs, 1978, Samuel H. Scripps Am. Dance Festival award, 1984; subject of film Hanya Holm, Portrait of an Artist/Teacher, 1983; Samuel H. Scripps Am. Dance Festival award, 1984. Mem. Am. Arbitration Assn. (nat. panel arbitrators), Soc. Stage Dirs. and Choreographers (v.p.). Pioneer Labanotation for copyright on dance scores musicals Kiss Me, Kate, 1948, My Darlin' Aida, 1952, My Fair Lady, 1956. Address: care Elsa Rainer 145 W 12th St New York NY 10011

HOLM, JEANNE MARJORIE, author, consultant, government official, former air force officer; b. Portland, Oreg., June 23, 1921; d. John E. and Marjorie (Hammond) H. B.A., Lewis and Clark Coll., 1956. Commd. 2d lt. U.S. Army, 1943; transferred to USAF, 1948, advanced through grades to maj. gen., 1973; chief manpower and mgmt. Hdqrs. Allied Air Forces So. Europe, Naples, Italy, 1957-61; congl. liaison officer, directorate manpower and orgn. Hdqrs USAF, Washington, 1961-65; dir. Women in the Air Force, 1965-73, Sec. Air Force Personnel Council, Washington, 1973-75; ret., 1975; cons. Def. Manpower Commn., Washington, 1975, undersec. air force, 1979—; spl. asst. to Pres., 1976-77; advisor U.S. Life Ins. Co., Washington; lectr. on manpower and women in mil. Author: Women in the Military: An Unfinished Revolution, 1982; Contbr. articles to profl. jours. Mem. internat. bd. govs. USO; bd. dirs. Nat. Def. U. Found.; bd. visitors Def. Equal Opportunity Mgmt. Inst., Orlando, Fla.; adv. com. women vets. VA, Washington; adv. com. USCG Acad. Decorated D.S.M. with oak leaf cluster, Legion of Merit, medal for Human Action (Berlin Airlift), Nat. Def. Service medal with Bronze Star; recipient Distinguished Achievement award Alumni Assn. Lewis and Clark Coll.; Eugene Zuckert Leadership award Arnold Air Soc.; citation of honor Air Force Assn.; named Woman of Year in Govt. and Diplomacy Ladies Home Jour., 1975. Mem. Air Force Assn., Ret. Officers Assn., Exec. Women in Govt. (founder, 1st chmn.). Home: 2707 Thyme Dr Edgewater MD 21037

HOLM, RICHARD HADLEY, chemist, educator; b. Boston, Sept. 24, 1933; m. Florence L. Jacintho, June 8, 1958; children—Sharon, Eric, Christian, Marg. B.S., U. Mass., 1955; Ph.D., Mass. Inst. Tech., 1959. Instr., then asst. prof. chemistry Harvard U., 1959-65, prof., 1980—; asso. prof. U. Wis., 1965-67; prof. chemistry Mass. Inst. Tech., 1967-75, Stanford U., 1975-80. Sloan Found. fellow, 1964-67. Mem. Am. Acad. Arts and Scis., Nat. Acad. Scis., Am. Chem. Soc., Chem. Soc. London. Home: 40 Temple St Belmont MA 02138 Office: Chemistry Dept Harvard Univ Cambridge MA 02138

HOLM, RICHARD WILLIAM, educator, biologist; b. Dallas, June 2, 1925; s. Clyde William and Beryle (Joyce) H. A.B., Washington U., St. Louis, 1946, A.M., 1948, Ph.D., 1950. Instr. botany Washington U., 1948; herbarium botanist U. Calif. at Berkeley, 1948-49; mem. faculty Stanford, 1949—, prof. biol. scis., 1965—, dir. div. systematic biology, 1961-71, dir. undergrad. studies biol. scis., 1972-74; cons. editor McGraw Hill Book Co. Contbr. articles to profl. jours., books on evolution, population biology, and botany.; Editor: Evolution, 1964-66. Fellow AAAS; mem. Phi Beta Kappa, Sigma Xi.

HOLMAN, ARTHUR STEARNS, artist; b. Bartlesville, Okla., Oct. 25, 1926; s. Newton Davis and Barbara (Hendry) H. B.F.A., U. N.Mex., 1951; postgrad., Hans Hofmann Sch., 1951, Calif. Sch. Fine Arts, San Francisco, 1953. One-man shows include, Esther Robles Gallery, Los Angeles, 1960, David Cole Gallery, San Francisco, 1962, 80, De Young Mus., San Francisco, 1963, San Francisco Mus., Gumps Gallery, San Francisco, 1964, 65, 66, 69, Marin Civic Center Gallery, 1970, William Sawyer Gallery, San Francisco, 1971, 73, 74, 76, John Bolles Gallery, Santa Rosa, Calif., 1982, group exhbns. include, Oakland Mus., 1959, San Francisco Mus., 1960, 76, Downey Mus., Los Angeles, 1961, 50 Calif. Artists, Whitney Mus., N.Y.C., Walker Art Center, Albright-Knox Gallery, Des Moines Art Center, 1962, U.N.C. Annual, 1965, Smithsonian Instn., Washington, 1977; represented in permanent collections, San Francisco Mus., Oakland Mus., Stanford U., Fine Art Mus. San Francisco, Eureka Coll., Achenbach Found. Served with USAAF, 1945-46. Address: Box 72 Lagunitas CA 94938

HOLMAN, BUD GEORGE, lawyer; b. N.Y.C., June 30, 1929; s. Harry and Fannie Abrams (Bass) H.; m. Kathleen Barbara McLean, Sept. 1, 1961; children: Jennifer Jean, Wayne George. B.B.A., CCNY, 1950; LL.B., Yale U., 1956. Bar: N.Y. 1956, Conn. 1979, D.C. 1982. Law sec. to judge N.Y. Ct. Appeals, 1956-58; practice in, N.Y.C., 1958—; partner firm Kelley Drye & Warren (and predecessors), 1965—; chmn. bd., pres. Sixty Sutton Corp.; pres., dir. Sutton Area Assn., Inc., Militia Assn. N.Y. Inc., 1976-77; dir. Containair Systems Corp., Cargo Packers, Inc., Air Cargo Packers, Inc., G.K. Heller Corp., Dynamic Appliance Sales & Service Corp.; lectr. Practising Law Inst., Wage Price Inst., Young Pres. Orgn. Editor: The Bar, 1949-50, Yale Law Jour., 1955-56. Trustee U.S. Naval Acad. Found.; bd. dirs. USO Met. N.Y., Soldiers, Sailors and Airman's Club. Served to lt. (j.g.) USNR, 1952-55; Korea; capt. Res. Mem. Naval Res. Assn. (pres. 3d naval dist. chpts. 1973-75, nat. adv. council 1975—), Army and Navy Union, Naval Order U.S. (recorder), Mil. Order World Wars (dir. N.Y. chpt.), Navy League (dir. N.Y. council), Beta Gamma Sigma. Democrat. Presbyn. Clubs: Yale (N.Y.C.); North Fork Country. Home: Park Ave Mattituck NY 11952 Office: 350 Park Ave New York NY 10022

HOLMAN, CHARLES RICHARDSON, chemical company executive; b. Norwood, Mass., Aug. 5, 1915; s. Charles F. and Emma (Richardson) H.; m. Priscilla Denison, June 24, 1939 (dec. Mar. 11, 1982); children: Charles Richardson, Donald B. and David W. (twins); m. Lucille Wesley, June 9, 1983. B.S., MIT, 1936, M.S., 1937. Chem. engr. exptl. sta. E. I. duPont Co., Wilmington, Del., 1937-38; research engr. Columbia-So. Corp. (subsidiary Pitts. Plate Glass Co.), Barberton, Ohio, 1938-41; with Pitts. Plate Glass Co., 1945-68, successively devel. engr., Milw., mgr. plastics prodn., Springdale, Pa., asst. gen. mgr., Newark, gen. mgr., East Point, Ga., 1945-58, chief process engr., Pitts., 1958-59, gen. mgr., Springdale, 1959-61, v.p. mfg. coatings and resins div., 1961-68; v.p., tech. asst. to chmn. bd. Reichhold Chems., Inc., White Plains, N.Y., 1969-71, v.p. corporate operations and Eastern region, dir., mem. exec. com., 1971-73; chmn. bd. Holman Co., 1972-78; chmn. bd., pres. Holco Enterprises Inc., 1979—; sr. project mgr. Crawford & Russell, Stamford, Conn., 1974—. Bd. dirs. Fulton County unit Am. Cancer Soc. Served from 2d lt. to maj. AUS, 1941-45; lt. col. Ga. Gov.'s staff. Fellow Am. Inst. Chemists; mem. East Point C. of C. (v.p., dir. 1956-58), Am. Chem. Soc., Am. Inst. Chem. Engrs., Pitts. Soc. Paint Tech., Paint, Varnish and Lacquer Assn. Methodist. Club: Kiwanis. Home: 96 Studio Rd Stamford CT 06903 Office: Crawford & Russell 17 Amelia Pl Stamford CT 06902

HOLMAN, CRANSTON WILLIAM, surgeon; b. Pasadena, Calif., Jan. 5, 1907; s. Frank Henry and Carolyn (Fieth) H.; m. Marion Nicholas, Sept. 17, 1928; children—Eric Williamson, Martha. A.B., Stanford, 1927, M.D., 1931. Diplomate: Am. Bd. Surgery, Am. Bd. Thoracic Surgery. Asst. resident surgeon Cin. Gen. Hosp., 1931-32, N.Y. Hosp., N.Y.C., 1932-35, resident surgeon, 1935-36, attending surgeon, 1953—, cons. in surgery, 1975; research fellow surgery Cornell U. Med. Coll., 1937, asso. surgery, 1938, asst. prof. surgery, 1938-48, asso. prof. clin. surgery, 1946-58, prof. clin. surgery, 1958—; cons. Hosp. for Spl. Surgery, 1955—; vis. surgeon Bellevue Hosp., 1949—, dir. 2d surg. div., 1951-62, cons., 1962—; cons. surgeon VA Hosp., Montrose, N.Y., 1950—, North Shore Hosp., Manhasset, N.Y., 1954—. Author: (with Drs. George J. Heuer, William Cooper) Treatment of Peptic Ulcer, 1944; Contbr. profl. jours.; Editor: (with Dr. Carl Muschenheim) Bronchopulmonary Diseases and Related Disorders, 1972. Served to col., M.C. AUS, 1942-46. Decorated Bronze Star. Mem. Soc. U. Surgeons, A.C.S., AMA, N.Y. Acad. Medicine, Am. Assn. Thoracic Surgery, N.Y. Surg. Soc. (pres. 1960), N.Y. Med. and Surg. Soc., Royal Soc. Medicine London (affiliate), Am. Surg. Assn., Soc. Clin. Surgery, Internat. Soc. Surgery, AAAS, Am. Thoracic Soc., N.Y. Heart Assn., Societa Triveneta di Chirurgia (hon.; Padova, Italy), Inter-Soc. Cytology Council, N.Y. Soc. for Thoracic Surgery (pres. 1964), N.Y. Gastroent. Assn., N.Y. Cancer Soc., Southwestern Ont. Surg. Assn. (hon.). Club: Century Assn. (N.Y.C.). Home: 200 E 66th St New York City NY 10021 Office: 862 Fifth Ave New York City NY 10021

HOLMAN, DONALD REID, lawyer; b. Astoria, Oreg., Jan. 30, 1930; s. Donald Reuben and Hattie Laveda (Card) H.; m. Susan Muncy Morris, Aug. 31, 1956; children: Donald Reid, Laura Morris, Holman O'Brien, Douglas Edward. B.A., U. Wash.-Seattle, 1951, J.D., 1958; postgrad., U. Oreg.-Eugene, 1955-57. Bar: Oreg. Assoc. Miller, Nash, Wiener, Hager & Carlsen, Portland, 1958-63, ptnr., 1963—; dir., corp. sec. La-Pacific Corp., Portland, 1972—, Dependable-Fordath, Inc., Sherwood, Oreg., 1982—, EBI Ins. Co., Portland, 1981—; corp. sec. EBI Cos., San Jose, Calif., 1978—. Served to lt. (j.g.) USN, 1951-55; capt. JAGC USNR, 1977—. Mem. Am. Soc. Corp. Secs. (mem. adv. com. northwest region 1983—), Order of Coif, Phi Delta Phi. Republican. Mormon. Clubs: Arlington, Multnomah Athletic (trustee 1982—), The Racquet (dir. 1981—, pres. 1983—); Waverly Country (Portland)). Home: 8040 SW Broadmoor Terr Portland OR 97225 Office: Miller Nash Wiener Hager & Carlsen 111 SW 5th Ave Portland OR 97204

HOLMAN, FRANCIS EDWARDS, judge; b. Salt Lake City, Sept. 13, 1915; s. Frank E. and Carrol (Edwards) H.; m. Eloise Dorothy Ferguson, July 5, 1941; children—Virginia Carrol, Frank Wyatt, Wendy. A.B., Stanford, 1936; B.A. in Jurisprudence, Oxford (Eng.) U., 1938, M.A., 1943; J.D., Harvard, 1940. Bar: Wash. bar 1941. Law clk. U.S. Ct. Appeals, Washington, 1940-41; practiced in, Seattle, 1941-73; judge Superior Ct. State of Wash., 1973—; Mayor, City of Lake Forest Park, Wash., 1961-67; mem. Wash. Ho. of Reps., 1st Dist., 1967-69, Wash. Senate, 1969-73; Mem. Council Municipality Met. Seattle, 1965-67; mem. Wash. Uniform Law Commn., 1967—, Wash. Jud. Council, 1967-73, 75-81; chmn. Wash. Pub. Disclosure Commn., 1973. Mem. vis. com. Coll. Edn., U. Wash., 1965—; chmn. Carman Scholarship Com., Seattle; bd. dirs. Shoreline Sch. Dist., 1956-65, pres., 1958-59, 63-64; trustee Northwest Hosp., Seattle, 1969-73. Served to capt. AUS, 1941-46, 51-52. Mem. Am., Wash., Seattle, King County bar assns., World Assn. Judges, Am. Judicature Soc., King County Sch. Dirs. Assn. (pres. 1956-65), Theta Delta Chi. Presbyterian. Club: Elk. Home: 200 W Highland Dr Seattle WA 98119 Office: King County Courthouse Seattle WA 98104

HOLMAN, G.W., JR., heavy construction company executive; b. 1929. Student, Pa. State U. Plant engr. Phila. Coke Co., 1952-54; designer Catalytic Constrn. Co., 1954-56; with Kaiser Engrs., Inc., Oakland, Calif., 1956—, v.p., 1974-77, 1977-81, exec. v.p., 1981—. Office: Kaiser Engrs Inc 300 Lakeside Dr Box 23210 Oakland CA 94623 *

HOLMAN, HARLAND EUGENE, mfg. co. exec.; b. Waupaca, Wis., Oct. 4, 1914; s. Clair R. and Elizabeth (Anderson) H.; m. Evelyn June Hooper, Dec. 24, 1940; children—John H., June Elizabeth (Mrs. Jon D. Huss), Catherine Ellen (Mrs. Michael J. Moore). B.A., U. Wis., 1936. C.P.A., Wis., Calif. Auditor Gen. Mills, Inc., 1936-42; v.p. finance Aviation Maintence Corp., Van Nuys, Calif., 1946-48; studio mgr. Warner Bros. Pictures, Inc., 1948-70; v.p. fin., treas. A.J. Industries, Inc., Los Angeles, 1970—; dir. Western Costume Corp., Warner Bros. Cosmetics Inc., Warner Bros. Records, Inc., Central Casting Corp. Served to lt. comdr. USNR, 1942-46; rear adm. Res. Decorated commendation USMC; recipient Civilian commendation Vice Pres. U.S., 1967; Minuteman award Treasury Dept., 1967. Mem. Assn. Motion Picture and TV Producers (dir.), Am. Inst. C.P.A.'s, Calif. Soc. C.P.A.'s, Navy League, Phi Beta Kappa. Presbyterian (elder). Home: 5011 Hayvenhurst Ave Encino CA 91436 Office: 11454 San Vicente Blvd Los Angeles CA 90049

HOLMAN, JACK PHILIP, engineering educator; b. Dallas, July 11, 1934; s. John Henry and Bessie Marie (Blew) H.; m. Katherine Karin Knowles, June 4, 1964; children: Blake Knowles, Bevin Winters. B.S. in Mech. Engring, So. Meth. U., 1955, M.S., 1956; Ph.D., Okla. State U., 1958. Asso. prof. mech. engring. So. Meth. U., Dallas, 1960-66; prof., dir. Thermal and Fluid Scis. Center, 1966—, prof., chmn. dept. civil and mech. engring., 1973—, asst. provost, 1978—; Dir. Delta P, Inc. Author: Heat Transfer, 5th edit, 1981, Experimental Methods for Engineers, 4th edit., 1984, Thermodynamics, 3d edit, 1980. Served with USAF, 1958-60. Recipient Excellence in Engring. Teaching award Gen. Dynamics Corp., 1970; named Outstanding Faculty mem. So. Meth. U., 1961, 65, 69, 71, 75, 77, 83. Mem. ASME, Am. Soc. Engring. Edn. (chmn. mech. engring. div. 1970, George Westinghouse award 1972). Methodist. Research and publs. on acoustic effects on heat transfer, fluidization, droplets, boiling, vortex flow and radiation. Home: 11407 Crest Brook Dr Dallas TX 75230

HOLMAN, J(OHN) LEONARD, manufacturing corporation executive; b. Moose Jaw, Sask., Can., Aug. 30, 1929; s. Charles Claude and Lillian Kathleen (Haw) H.; m. Julia Pauline Benfield, July 18, 1953; children: Nancy Jane, Sally Joan. B.S. in Civil Engring., U. Alta., 1953. Pres. Consol. Concrete Ltd., Calgary, Alta., Can., 1969-72; dir. pres. BACM Industries Ltd., Calgary, 1972-76; exec. v.p. Genstar Corp., Calgary, 1976-79, San Francisco, 1980—, dir. several subs. cos.; bd. dirs., officer several nat. trade assns. Mem. Assn. profl. Engrs. Alta. Lodge: Rotary. Home: 445 Darrell Rd Hillsborough CA 94010 Office: Genstar Corp 4 Embarcadero Suite 3800 San Francisco CA 94111

HOLMAN, KERMIT LAYTON, chemical engineer; b. Morris, Minn., Nov. 16, 1935; s. Melvin Martinous and Jennie Ethel (Erickson) H.; m. Audrey Mae Redwing, Nov. 21, 1959; children: Erik, Jennifer, Peter. Student, St. Olaf Coll., 1953-54; B.S., U. N.D., 1957; M.S., U. Idaho, 1961; Ph.D., Iowa State U., 1964. Tape devel. engr. 3M Co., St. Paul, 1957-60; sr. chem. engr. Dow Chem. Co., Golden, Colo., 1964-65; mem. faculty dept. chem. engring. N.Mex. State U., Las Cruces, 1965-76, prof., 1976—; prof., chmn. dept. chem. engring. U. Idaho, Moscow, 1976-81; tech. asso. Weyerhaeuser Co., Tacoma, 1981—; cons. in field. Fellow Am. Inst. Chemists; mem. Am. Inst. Chem. Engrs., Sigma Xi, Tau Beta Pi. Republican. Lutheran. Home: 31619 37th Ave SW Federal Way WA 98003 Office: Weyerhaeuser Co Weyerhaeuser Tech Center WTC 1B25A Tacoma WA 98477

HOLMAN, M. CARL, urban coalition executive; b. Minter City, Miss., June 27, 1919; s. Moses and Mamie (Durham) H.; m. Mariella Ama, Dec. 22, 1945; children: Kwasi, Kwami, Kinshasha. A.B. magna cum laude, Lincoln U., 1942; M.A., U. Chgo., 1944; M.F.A., Yale U., 1954; hon. doctorate, Lincoln U., 1978, Adelphi U., 1982. Assoc. prof. English and humanities Clark Coll., Atlanta, 1948-62; editor Atlanta Inquirer, 1960-62; dep. dir. U.S. Commn. Civil Rights, 1968-71; Pres. Nat. Urban Coalition, Washington, 1971—. Mem. Atlanta Council on Human Relations, 1958-62, Atlanta Student Adult Liaison Commn., 1960-62; press and publicity chmn. Atlanta NAACP, 1955-60; mem. exec. com. D.C. Bd. Higher Edn., 1968-72; bd. dirs. Ind. Sector, Jobs for Ams.' Grads., Nat. Rural Center, Manpower Research Devel. Corp., Full Employment Action Council, Minority Contractors' Assistance Project; commr. Pres.'s Commn. for Nat. Agenda for Eighties; sec.-treas. Black Leadership Forum; co-convenor Nat. Com. on Concerns of Blacks and Hispanics; co-chmn. Nat. Com. for Urban Recreation; founder TransAfrica.; Bd. dirs., v.p. Field Found.; bd. dirs. Nat. Low Income Housing Coalition, Nat. Endowment for Humanities. Fiske Poetry prize U. Chgo., 1944; Blevins Davis Playwriting award Yale U., 1954; Recipient Pub. Affairs Reporting award Am. Polit. Sci. Assn., 1962, Disting. Service award Nat. Newspaper Pubs. Assn., 1973, Nat. Conf. Social Welfare, 1981; citation for pub. service U. Chgo. Alumni Assn., 1977; Equal Opportunity Day award Nat. Urban League, 1981; Social Responsibility award Opportunities Industrialization Ctrs., 1983; Outstanding Alumni award; Whitney fellow, 1952-54. Mem. Omega Psi Phi. Home: 1221 4th St SW Washington DC 20024 Office: 1201 Connecticut Ave NW Washington DC 20036

HOLMAN, RALPH THEODORE, educator, biochemist; b. Mpls., Mar. 4, 1918; s. Alfred Theodore and May (Nilson) H.; m. Karla Calais, Mar. 26, 1943; 1 son, Nils Teodor Calais. A.A., Bethel Jr. Coll., 1937; B.S., U. Minn., 1939, Ph.D., 1944; M.S., Rutgers U., 1941. Instr. U. Minn., 1944-46, asso. prof. physiol. chemistry, 1951-56; prof. Hormel Inst., 1956—, dir. inst., 1975—; prof. biochemistry Mayo Med. Sch., 1977—; asso. prof. Tex. A. and M. U., 1948-51; Mem. adv. bd. Deuel Conf. Lipids, 1958—, chmn., 1972; mem. nutrition study sect. NIH, 1960-63; mem. com. fats Food and Nutrition Bd., Nat. Acad.

Scis.-NRC, 1956-62; pres. Golden Jubilee Congress on Essential Fatty Acids and Prostoglandins, 1980. Editor: (with W.O. Lundberg and T. Malkin) Progress in the Chemistry of Fats and Other Lipids, vols. 1-6, 1951-63; sole editor, vols. 7-16, 1963—; assoc. editor: Lipids, 1966-74; editor, 1974—; editorial bd.: Jour. Lipid Research, 1959-61, Jour. Nutrition, 1962-66, Jour. Parenteral and Enteral Nutrition, 1977-82, Jour. Lab. and Clin. Medicine, 1979—. Pres. Mower County Council Chs., 1954-58. Recipient Fachini medal Italian Oil Chemistry Soc., 1974; NRC fellow Med. Nobel Inst., Stockholm, Sweden, 1946-47; Am. Scandinavian Found. fellow U. Uppsala, Sweden, 1947; spl. fellow NIH, U. Gothenburg, Sweden, 1962. Mem. Am. Soc. Biol. Chemists, Am. Inst. Nutrition (Borden award 1966), Am. Oil Chemists Soc. (gov. bd. 1968-70, sec. 1972, v.p. 1973, pres. 1974, Bailey award 1972, award in lipid chemistry 1978), Soc. Exptl. Biology and Medicine, Nat. Acad. Scis., Hormel Found., Am. Orchid Soc., Sigma Xi. Democrat. Conglist. Research, over 300 publs. on spectrophotometric studies fat oxidation, isolation and characterization lipoxidase, displacement chromatography lipids, biochem. characterization essential fatty acid deficiency; established nutritional requirements essential fatty acids; research on metabolism polyunsaturated fatty acids, relationship of essential fatty acid abnormalities to diseases in humans, near-infrared spectra lipids, mass spectrometry lipids; analysis of odors; fragrance and taxonomy; developed methods for lipid analysis, quantitative chem. taxonomy magnolia and orchids based on floral odor, effect of double bond structure upon metabolism of unsaturated acids, effect of partially hydrogenated fats upon nutrition and metabolism of essential fatty acids. Home: 1403 2d Ave SW Austin MN 55912 Office: Hormel Inst U Minn Austin MN 55912

HOLMBERG, ALBERT WILLIAM, JR., publishing co. exec.; b. Orange, N.J., Sept. 18, 1923; s. Albert William and Margaret (Flanagan) H.; m. Dorothy McCollum, Oct. 27, 1945 (div. Apr. 1972); children—Jeanne (Mrs. Fletcher J. Johnson, Jr.), Margaret D. (Mrs. Roy D. Duckworth III), Ellen T.; m. Ruth Sulzberger Golden, May 26, 1972. B.S. in Bus. Adminstrn, Lehigh U., 1947. With N.Y. Times, 1947-70, circulation mgr., 1964-70; pres., gen. mgr. Chattanooga Times, 1970—; pres., dir. Times Pub. Co. Served to 1st lt. USAAF, World War II. Clubs: Rotary, Mountain City (Chattanooga). Home: 1108 Cumberland Rd Chattanooga TN 37419 Office: 117 E 10th St Chattanooga TN 37401

HOLMBERG, RUTH SULZBERGER, publishing company executive; b. N.Y.C., Mar. 12, 1921; d. Arthur Hays and Iphigene (Ochs) Sulzberger; children: Stephen A.O., Michael D., Lynn Iphigene Dolnick, Arthur Sulzberger; m. Albert William Holmberg, Jr., 1972. A.B., Smith Coll., 1943. Vice pres. Chattanooga Times Co., 1956-65, pub., 1965—, dir., 1961—; dir. N.Y. Times Co. Trustee U. Chattanooga Found.; chmn. Hunter Mus. Art.; bd. dirs. Reading is Fundamental; chmn. So. Ctr. for Internat. Studies. Mem. So. Newspaper Pubs. Assn. (officer); Sustaining mem. Jr. League; mem. Sigma Delta Chi. Home: 1108 Cumberland Rd Chattanooga TN 37419 Office: 117 E 10th St Chattanooga TN 37401

HOLME, THOMAS TIMINGS, industrial engineering educator; b. Frankford, Pa., Mar. 12, 1913; s. Justus Rockwell and Margaret (Mitchell) H.; m. Marjory Evans Walton, July 7, 1936; children: Judith Walton Holme Harrell, Thomas Timings, Penelope Walton. B.S., Lehigh U., 1935, M.S., 1940, I.E. (profl.), 1948; M.A. (hon.), Yale U., 1950; Dr. Engring., Lehigh U., 1970. Registered profl. engr., Pa., Conn. Indsl. engr. E. I. duPont de Nemours & Co., Wilmington, Del. and; Fairfield, Conn., 1935-37; asst. prof. mech. engring. Lehigh U., Bethlehem, Pa., 1937-41, asso. prof. indsl. engring., 1946-49, prof. indsl. engring., head dept. and dir. curriculum, 1949-50; prof. of indsl. engring., dept. adminstrv. sci. Yale U., 1950-73, emeritus prof., 1973—, chmn. dept., dir. grad. studies, 1954-63; fellow Trumbull Coll.; cons. U.S. Army Ordnance Corps, 1952-53, 56-57, Hughes Aircraft, 1959, 61-62, Hamilton Standard div. United Aircraft, 1963; nat. exec. sec. Sigma Xi, 1953-69, nat. exec. dir., 1969-81, exec. dir. emeritus, 1981—; Dir. Henry G. Thompson Co. Bd. dirs. Yale Coop., New Haven, exec. com., 1951-72; mem. Yale-Industry Com. of New Haven. With Ordnance Dept. U.S. Army, 1941-46; asst. works mgr., 1941-42; Springfield Armory; asst. works mgr., July 1942-Mar. 1944; E.T.O.; officer in charge engring., 1944-46; Springfield Armory; disch. rank of lt. col.; lt. col. Ordnance Res., 1946-53. Recipient U.S. Army Citation medal, Ordnance Certificate of Commendation, Legion of Merit. Fellow AAAS; mem. Am. Inst. Indsl. Engrs., Am. Soc. Engring. Edn., Newcomen Soc., Sigma Xi, Tau Beta Pi, Pi Tau Sigma, Pi Gamma Mu. Club: Fripp Island Beach and Golf. Home: 773 Marlin Dr Fripp Island SC 29920 Office: 345 Whitney Ave New Haven CT 06511

HOLMEN, (GEORGE) ROBERT, advertising agency executive; b. N.Y.C., May 3, 1933; s. George E. and Katherine J. (Smith) H.; m. Barbara Ann Jordan, Aug. 22, 1959; children: Britt Ann, Robert C., Mark E., Brigitte Ann. B.S., Holy Cross Coll., 1955; M.B.A., Dartmouth Coll., 1960. Account exec. Benton & Bowles, Inc., N.Y.C., 1960-64; with William Esty Co., Inc., N.Y.C., 1964-75, sr. v.p., mgmt. supr., 1970-75; exec. v.p., gen. mgr. McCann Erickson, Inc., N.Y.C., 1975-79; exec. v.p., chief operating officer Backer & Spielvogel, Inc., N.Y.C., 1979—. Trustee Canterbury Sch., New Milford, Conn. Served with USAF, 1955-58. Republican. Roman Catholic. Clubs: Whipporwill (Armonk, N.Y.); Milw. Athletic, Stratton Mountain Country. Office: Backer & Spielvogel Inc 11 W 42d St New York NY 10036

HOLMER, EDWIN CARL, petrochemical company executive; b. Oyster Bay, N.Y., Feb. 4, 1921; s. Edwin Carl and Agnes (Anderson) H. B.Ch.E., Renssalaer Poly. Inst., 1942. Chem. engr. Standard Oil of N.J., Linden, 1942-45, various engring. positions, 1945-56; asst. dir. chem. research Standard Oil Devel. Co., 1956-59; mgr. prodn. div. Jersey Prodn. Research Co., Tulsa, 1959-61, pres., 1961-64, Exxon Prodn. Research Co., Houston, 1964-66; sr. v.p. Exxon Chem. Co., N.Y.C., 1966-68, dir., 1966-68, exec. v.p., 1968-74; v.p. Exxon Corp., 1968—; exec. v.p. Esso Middle East, N.Y.C., 1974-76; pres. Exxon Chem. Co., Darien, Conn., 1976—; dir. Nat. Starch & Chem. Corp., Bridewater, N.J. Mem. Soc. Chem. Industry (exec. com. 1980-81, hon. treas. 1981-82, hon. sec. 1982-83, vice chmn. 1983—), Chem. Mfrs. Assn. (dir. 1981-82, vice chmn. 1982-83, chmn. exec. com. 1983—), Internat. Exec. Service Corp. (council 1982-83, bd. dirs. 1983—), Tau Beta Pi. Republican. Club: Country of Darien. Office: 9 Old Kings Hwy S Darien CT 06840

HOLMER, PAUL LEROY, philosophy educator; b. Mpls., Nov. 14, 1916; s. Paul Emmanuel and Elsie (Johnson) H.; m. Phyllis June Schulberg, Oct. 18, 1944; children: Paul L., Linnea K., Jonathan. B.A., U. Minn., 1940, M.A., 1941; student, U. Chgo., 1940; Ph.D., Yale U., 1945; L.H.D., U. N.D., 1960; LL.D., Norwich U., 1964, St. Olaf Coll., 1969, North Park Coll., 1966. Instr. philosophy Gustavus Adolphus Coll., 1944, Yale U., 1944-46; mem. faculty U. Minn., 1946-60, prof., 1955-60; prof. theology Yale U., 1960—, Noah Porter prof. philos. theology, 1981—; vis. prof. Northwestern U., summer 1952, Chgo. Lutheran Sem., 1953, Dartmouth Coll., 1958, Sacramento State Coll., summer 1959, Moorhead State Coll., 1963, Macalester Coll., 1967, U. Calif., 1969-70, Princeton Sem., 1976; lectr. Oxford U., 1967; vis. lectr. Frankfurt-am-Main U., Germany, summer 1954; vis. fellow Internat. Coll., Beirut, 1973; Drushal disting. service prof. Coll. of Wooster, 1979. Editor: Kierkegaard's Edifying Discourses, 2d edit, 1958, Philosophy and the Common Life, 1960, Theology and the Scientific Study of Religion, Vol. 1, 1961, Faith, Doubt and Certainty, 1964, C.S. Lewis, The Shape of His Faith and Thought, 1976, The Grammar of Faith, 1978, Making Sense Christianity, 1984; editorial bd.: Christian Scholar, 1955-61, Dialogue, 1960—. Treas. bd. Christian higher edn. Augustana Luth. Ch., 1954-60; mem. bd. coll. edn. Luth. Ch. Am., 1964—; Mem. adv. bd. Danforth Found., 1956—. Fulbright research prof., Denmark, 1953-54; Guggenheim fellow Oxford U., 1964-65. Mem. Am. Philos. Assn., Am. Theol. Soc., Am. Metaphys. Soc., Mind Assn. Home: 43 Swarthmore St Hamden CT 06514 Office: Yale Univ New Haven CT 06504

HOLMES, ALBERT WILLIAM, JR., physician; b. Chgo., Feb. 3, 1932; s. Albert William and Eleanor Muir H.; m. Lois Ann Geiger, Sept. 4, 1954; children—Nancy, William, Elizabeth, Robert. Student, U. Chgo., 1947-49; B.A., Knox Coll., 1952; M.D., Western Res. U., 1956. Intern Presbyn. Hosp., Chgo., 1956-57; resident Presbyn.-St. Luke's Hosp., Chgo., 1957-59, 61-62; dir. sect. hepatology Rush-Presbyn.-St. Luke's Med. Center, Chgo., 1966-75, asso. chmn. dept. medicine, 1972-75, acting v.p. research affairs, 1973-74; prof., chmn. dept. internal medicine Tex. Tech. U., Lubbock, 1975—; instr. U. Ill., Chgo., 1961-62, asso. prof., 1963-65, 1966-68, prof. medicine, 1968-70; prof. medicine and microbiology Rush Med. Coll., Chgo., 1971-75; acting dean Rush Grad. Coll., 1973-74. Contbr. articles in field to profl. jours. Served with U.S. Army, 1959-61. Recipient Alumni Achievement award Knox Coll., 1976; NIH spl. fellow, 1963-66. Fellow A.C.P.; mem. Am. Assn. Study Liver Diseases, Am. Assn. Immunologists, Assn. Profs. Medicine, Central Soc. Clin. Research, Alpha Omega Alpha. Presbyterian. Club: Econ. (Chgo.). Home: 3813 66th St Lubbock TX 79413 Office: Tex Tech U Health Scis Center Lubbock TX 79430

HOLMES, ALLEN CORNELIUS, lawyer; b. Bethel, Ohio, May 27, 1920. A.B., U. Cin., 1941; J.D., U. Mich., 1944. Bar: Ohio 1944, U.S. Supreme Ct. 1964. Asso. Jones, Day, Reavis & Pogue, Cleve., 1944-54, partner, 1954-74, mng. partner, 1975—, nat. mng. partner, 1977—; dir. Diamond Shamrock Corp., Nat. City Bank, Nat. City Corp., Sherwin-Williams Co. Contbr. articles to profl. jours. Chmn. bd. trustees, exec. com. Case Western Res. U., 1983—; chmn. bd. dirs., exec. com. Greater Cleve. Growth Assn., 1983—; v.p., trustee United Way Services, WVIZ-TV; trustee Cleve. Inst. Art, Cleve. Mus. Arts Assn., Cleve. Scholarship Program, Univ. Circle Inc.; bd. dirs. Kaiser Found. Hosps. Mem. ABA (past chmn. FTC com. antitrust sect., chmn. antitrust sect. council), Ohio Bar Assn., Cleve. Bar Assn., Assn. Bar City N.Y., Am. Law Inst. Clubs: Union, 50, Clevelander (Cleve.); Chagrin Valley Hunt, Tavern, Pepper Pike Country; Metropolitan (Washington); Links (N.Y.C.). Home: 2 Bratenahl Pl Bratenahl OH 44108 Office: 1700 Huntington Bldg Cleveland OH 44115

HOLMES, ANN HITCHCOCK, journalist; b. El Paso, Apr. 25, 1922; d. Frederick E. and Joy (Crutchfield) H. Student, Whitworth Coll., 1940, So. Coll. Fine Arts, 1944. With Houston Chronicle, 1942—, fine arts editor, 1948—. Mem. Houston Art Commn., 1965-74; mem. fine arts adv. council U. Tex., Austin, 1967—. Recipient Ogden Reid Found. award for study of arts in Europe, 1953; Guggenheim fellow, 1960-61; recipient Ford Found. award, 1965, John G. Flowers award archtl. writing Tex. Soc. Architects, 1972, 74, 77, 80. Mem. Am. Theater Critics Assn. (exec. com. 1975-80). Home: 10807 Beinhorn Rd Houston TX 77024 Office: Houston Chronicle 801 Texas Ave Houston TX 77002

HOLMES, ARTHUR FRANK, educator; b. Dover, Eng., Mar. 15, 1924; came to U.S., 1947, naturalized, 1961; s. Frank Austwick and Annie (Fairs) H.; m. Alice Caroline Henderson, June 25, 1949; children—Paul, Mark. A.B., Wheaton Coll., 1950, M.A., 1952; Ph.D., Northwestern U., 1957. Instr. Bible, philosophy Wheaton (Ill.) Coll., 1951-56, asst. prof. Bible, philosophy, 1956-60, asso. prof. philosophy, 1960-64, prof. philosophy, 1964—, chmn. dept., 1968—; dir. Inst. Advanced Christian Studies, 1976-80, 82—. Author: Christianity and Philosophy, 1960, Christian Philosophy in the Twentieth Century, 1969, Faith Seeks Understanding, 1971, The Idea of a Christian College, 1975, All Truth is God's Truth, 1977, Contours of a World - View, 1983; Editor: War and Christian Ethics, 1975; Contbg. editor: The Reformed Jour, 1970—. Served with RAF, 1942-47. Mem. Am. Philos. Assn., Soc. Christian Philosophers. Home: 911 N Washington St Wheaton IL 60187

HOLMES, BERT OTIS E., JR., newspaperman; b. Milan, Tenn., Sept. 20, 1921; s. Otis E. and Mary (Lassiter) H.; m. Marian Bush, June 10, 1942 (dec. Nov. 1964); children—Bert Otis E., Richard Bush; m. Helen Hankins, July 24, 1965; children—Chris, David. A.A., Magnolia A. and M. Jr. Coll., 1940; B.S., So. Meth. U., 1942. Employed with Dallas Times Herald, 1946—, successively copy reader, makeup editor, state editor, city staff reporter, city editor, 1946-56, news editor, 1956-60, asst. mng. editor, 1960-64, exec. editor, 1964-65, asso. editor, 1965—. Pres. Family Service Agy., 1963-68, Tex. United Community Services, 1970-72; bd. dirs. Dallas United Fund, Dallas Community Council. Served with AUS, 1942-46; PTO. Mem. Dallas Assembly, Sigma Delta Chi, Dallas Press Club (pres. 1957, 78-79). Methodist. Home: 4515 W Lawther Dr Dallas TX 75214 Office: Herald Square Dallas TX 75201

HOLMES, BROOX GARRETT, lawyer; b. Mobile, Ala., Nov. 15, 1932; s. Williams Coghlan and Philomene (Boogaerts) H.; m. Laura Claire Hays, Feb. 21, 1955; children: Broox Garrett, Dupree Hays, Williams Coghlan II. B.A., U. Ala., 1954, J.D., 1960. Bar: Ala. bar 1960. Since practiced in, Mobile; mem. firm Armbrecht, Jackson, DeMouy, Crowe, Holmes & Reeves, 1960—. Trustee St. Paul's Episcopal Sch., chmn. bd., 1980-83. Served to capt. USMCR, 1954-58. Fellow Am. Coll. Trial Lawyers; mem. Am., Ala., Mobile bar assns., Nat. Assn. R.R. Trial Counsel, Internat. Assn. Ins. Counsel, Am. Law Inst., Ala. Law Inst., Ala. Def. Lawyers (pres. 1977-78), Delta Kappa Epsilon, Phi Delta Phi. Episcopalian (vestryman). Clubs: Mobile Country (pres. 1983-1984), Lakewood, Mobile Touchdown, Athelstan (Mobile); Internat. Trade. Home: 609 Fairfax Rd E Mobile AL 36608 Office: Merchants Bank Bldg Mobile AL 36601

HOLMES, CHARLES HARVEY, ins. co. exec.; b. Rochester, N.Y., Apr. 5, 1918; s. William Harvey and Lillian L. (Popp) H.; m. Mary Celestine Phelan, Nov. 3, 1943; children—Jane Elizabeth Pendleton, Mary Ann, Peter Charles, William Harvey. B.A., U. Toronto, 1940, M.A., 1946. With Phoenix Mut. Life Ins. Co., Hartford, Conn., 1947—, controller, 1966—, 2d v.p., 1979—; treas. Phoenix Equity Planning Corp., 1968—, Phoenix Fund, Inc., 1970-78; Phoenix Capital Fund, Inc., 1970-78. Treas. Phoenix Fed. Credit Union, 1957-66, St. Mary's Fed. Credit Union, Simsbury, Conn., 1956—. Served to capt. USAAF, 1941-46; lt. col. Res. ret. Fellow Life Mgmt. Inst. Club: K.C. Home: 21 Northfield Rd Simsbury CT 06070 Office: 1 American Row Hartford CT 06115

HOLMES, COLGATE FREDERICK, hotel executive; b. Passaic, N.J., Aug. 21, 1935; s. Colgate and Orva Della (Gough) H.; m. Elizabeth Ann Troughton, June 6, 1959; 1 dau., Elizabeth Colgate. B.S., Cornell U., Ithaca, N.Y., 1956; postgrad. in fin. and mktg., Harvard U. Sch. Bus., 1958-59. Chgo. sales rep., asst. dir. catering Palmer House, Hilton Hotels, 1956-58; dir. food and beverage Caribe Hilton, Hilton Internat. Co., San Juan, P.R., 1963-64; gen. mgr. V.I. Hilton, St. Thomas, 1964-66, regional dir., Philippines, Guam, Australia; gen. mgr. Manila Hilton, Philippines, 1966-70, regional dir. S.Am.; gen. mgr. Sao Paulo Hilton, Brazil, 1970-71; mgr. conv. and group sales InterContinental Hotels, 1959-60, corp. dir. sales, N.Y.C., 1960-62; exec. asst. mgr. Hotel Indonesia, Djakarta, 1962-63; gen. mgr. Ala Moana Hotel, Americana Hotels, 1972-73; regional v.p., gen. mgr. Hyatt Regency-Chgo., Hyatt Corp., 1973-79; exec. v.p. Hyatt Internat. Corp., 1979-81, pres., 1981-82, Ritz-Carlton Hotel Co., 1982—; lectr. modern hotel ops. and food and beverage Sch. Hotel Adminstrn., Cornell U.; lectr. Philippine Inst. Hotel Mgmt.; bd. dirs. Better Bus. Bur. Chgo.; bd. dirs., mem. exec. com. Chgo. Conv. and Tourism Bur. Adv. bd.: Hotel & Motel Mgmt. Mag. Mem. Chaine des Rotisseurs, Cornell Soc. Hotelmen, Am. Hotel Assn., Chgo. Hotel Assn. (dir.), V.I. Hotel Assn. (v.p. 1965-66), Chgo. Hotel-Motel Assn. (pres. 1979), Hotel and Restaurant Assn. Philippines (v.p. 1968-69), Skal Club Internat., Am. Soc. Travel Agts., Alpha Chi Rho. Clubs: Manila Yacht; University Yacht (Atlanta); Atletico de São Paulo. Address: 3414 Peachtree Rd NE Atlanta GA 30326

HOLMES, DARRELL, ednl. center pres.; b. Angola, Ind., May 28, 1921; s. G.W. and Catharine (Conrad) H.; m. Eleonore Hohmann, Nov. 20, 1943; children—Kip Lee, Jeffrey, Lynn Ellen, Mary Ann. B.A., Ohio State U., 1941, M.A., 1948, Ph.D., 1950. Research asst. bur. ednl. research Ohio State U., 1949-50; asst. prof. Muskigum Coll., New Concord, Ohio, 1950-52, San Diego State Coll., 1952-54, asso. prof., 1955-58, exec. dean, 1958-64; pres. U. No. Colo., Greeley, 1964-71, East Stroudsburg (Pa.) State Coll., 1971-80, Internat. Center Ednl. Services, 1981—; Pres. Southwestern Research Assos., Inc., 1957-64; dir. First Nat. Bank, Greeley, Colo. Contbr. articles to profl. jours. Mem. Commn. Internat. Edn., 1969—; mem. nat. adv. com. Air Force ROTC, to sec. air force, 1965-69. Served from pvt. to 2d lt., C.E. AUS, 1942-45. Mem. Am. Council Edn. (dir. 1967—), AAAS, Am. Statis. Assn., Am. Edn. Research Assn., Am. Assn. State Colls. and Univs. (dir. 1967—, pres. 1971-72), Pa. Assn. Colls. and Univs. (dir. 1973—, v.p. 1976, pres. 1977). Club: Rotarian (dir.). Home: 7936 June Lake Dr San Diego CA 92119 *Until excellence is confronted, mediocrity is master. . .The search is a lifetime; this thought, the North Star.*

HOLMES, DYER BRAINERD, corporation executive; b. N.Y.C., May 24, 1921; s. Marcellus B. and Theodora (Pomeroy) H.; m. Roberta M. Donohue. B.S. in Elec. Engring. (McMullen scholar), Cornell U., 1943; postgrad., Bowdoin Coll., M.I.T., 1943-44; hon. degrees, U. N.Mex., 1963, Worcester Poly. Inst., 1978. Registered profl. engr., N.J. Design engr. Western Electric Co.; also mem. tech. staff Bell Labs., 1945-53; gen. mgr. maj. def. systems div., 1961; project mgr. Navy Talos land based missile system devel., 1954-57, Air Force Atlas launch control and checkout equipment devel., 1957, USAF ballistic missile early warning system, 1958-61; dep. asso. adminstr. manned space flight NASA, 1961-63; sr. v.p., dir. Raytheon Co., Lexington, Mass., 1963-69, exec. v.p., 1969-75, pres., 1975—, dir., 1969—; dir. Wyman-Gordon Co., Worcester, Mass., Bank of Boston Corp. (and subsidiary), Kaman Corp., Bloomfield, Conn.; chmn. bd. Beech Aircraft Corp. (subs. Raytheon Co.). Author articles, papers in field. Mem. corp. Northeastern U. Served with USNR, 1942-45. Recipient Outstanding Leadership medal NASA; Paul T. Johns award Arnold Air Soc. Fellow IEEE, AIAA; mem. Nat. Acad. Engring., Aerospace Industries Assn. U.S. (exec. com.), Am. Def. Preparedness Assn. (dir.), Nat. Security Indsl. Assn. (trustee), Navy League, Tau Beta Pi, Eta Kappa Nu. Clubs: Nat. Space, Metropolitan (Washington); Algonquin (Boston). Initiated, developed first precision rec. transmission measuring set, other test equipment; participated devel. long distance coaxial telephone and TV systems, RCA, 1953-61. Office: Raytheon Co 141 Spring St Lexington MA 02173

HOLMES, FRANCIS WILLIAM, plant pathologist; b. Yonkers, N.Y., May 21, 1929; m. Helen M. Bequaert, June 7, 1953; children: Peter, Sarah, Joseph. A.B. in Botany and Zoology, 1950; Ph.D. in Plant Pathology, Cornell U., 1954. Asst. prof. shade tree labs. U. Mass., Amherst, 1954-61, asso. prof., 1961-70, prof., 1970—, dir. shade tree labs., 1973—; NSF sr. postdoctoral fellow U. Utrecht, Baarn, Netherlands, 1962-63. Incorporator, treas. Amherst Human Relations Council, 1968-70; active Boy Scouts Am., 1942-60; librarian New Eng. Quaker Research Library, 1965—. Recipient public service award Nat. Arbor Day Found., 1980; Environ. Merit award EPA, 1980; Fulbright travel grantee, 1962-63, 70-71. Mem. Am. Assn. Bot. Gardens and Arboreta, Mycol. Soc. Am., Am. Phytopath. Soc., Can. Phytopath. Soc., Netherlands Soc. Plant Pathology, Internat. Soc. Plant Pathology, Internat. Soc. Arboriculture (gov., treas. New Eng. chpt., chmn. research com. 1979—, author award 1980), Royal Dutch Bot. Soc. (corr.), Mass. Tree Wardens and Foresters Assn. (advisor), Mass. Forest and Park Assn., Mass. Arborists Assn. (hon.), Am. Soc. Cons. Arborists, Am. Philatelic Soc., Sigma Xi. Quaker. Home: 24 Berkshire Terr Amherst MA 01002 Office: Shade Tree Labs U Mass Amherst MA 01003

HOLMES, FRED GILLESPIE, sugar co. exec.; b. Grand Junction, Colo., Aug. 29, 1913; s. Fred G. and Agnes Arnett (Whitley) H.; m. Alma Jeanne Sager, Nov. 11, 1946 (dec. 1971); children—Charles F., Winifred F.; m. Isabelle Davenport Truscott, 1973. B.S. in Bus, U. Colo., 1939. With Garden City Co., Kans., 1932-39; with Great Western Sugar Co., Denver, 1939-78, labor commr., 1948-61, v.p. agrl. adminstrn., 1961-71, dir. adminstrn., 1971-76, bd. dirs., 1969-71; v.p. No. Ohio Sugar Co., 1962-71; pres. Gt. Western Employment Agy., Inc., 1969—. Mem. exec. com. Nat. Council Agrl. Employers, Washington, 1964-78. Mem. Am. Soc. Sugar Beet Technologists, Delta Tau Delta. Home: 3435 E Virginia Ave Denver CO 80209 Office: Great Western Sugar Co Sugar Bldg Denver CO 80217

HOLMES, FREDERIC LAWRENCE, medical history educator; b. Cin., Feb. 6, 1932; m. Harriet Holmes, 1959; 3 children. B.S., MIT, 1954; M.A., Harvard U., 1958, Ph.D., 1962. Asst. prof. history of sci. MIT, 1962-64; asst. prof. to assoc. prof. Yale U., New Haven, 1964-72; prof., chmn. history of medicine dept., master Jonathan Edwards Coll., 1979—; prof. history of sci., chmn. dept. history of medicine and sci. U. Western Ont., 1972-79. Author: Claude Barhard and Animal Chemistry, 1974; contbr. articles to profl. jours. Research grantee NIH, 1963-67, NSF, 1968-70, Can. Council, 1973-74. Mem. History of Sci. Soc., Am. Assn. History Medicine, Can. Soc. Hist. and Philos. Sci. Office: Jonathan Edwards Coll Yale U New Haven CT 06520 *

HOLMES, GEORGE WASHINGTON, III, educator; b. Alamance County, N.C., Feb. 22, 1919; s. George Washington and Fannie (Thompson) H.; m. Mary Maxine Templeton, July 9, 1949; children—Leonard George, Mary Elizabeth. A.B., High Point (N.C.) Coll., 1939; M.A., U. N.C., 1947, Ph.D., 1951; postgrad., Columbia Tchrs. Coll., 1951-52. High sch. tchr., Mayodan, N.C., 1939-42, High Point, 1946, high sch. prin., Asheboro, N.C., 1947-49; dir. research Am. Sch. Pub. Corp., N.Y.C., 1951-52; ednl. asso. Jay C. Van Nuys Architects, Sommerville, N.J., 1952-54; asst. supt. schs., Roanoke, Va., 1954-58; mem. faculty U. Va., Charlottesville, 1958—, prof. edn., 1962—, chmn. dept. adminstrn. and supervision, 1967-72; cons. sch. plant planning. Exec. sec. Va. Sch. Bds. Assn., 1958—. Contbr. articles to ednl. jours. Served with USMC, 1942-45. Outstanding Service award, 1978. Mem. Council Ednl. Facility Planners, Am., Va. assns. sch. adminstrs., Phi Delta Kappa (Distinguished Service award 1969). Methodist. Home: 238 Stribling Ave Charlottesville VA 22903

HOLMES, HARRY EDWARD, hotel executive; b. Abilene, Tex., Dec. 5, 1925; s. Harry and Rita (Simmons) H.; m. Gayle Walter, Sept. 1, 1957; children: Marshall Walter, Hilary, Gay. A.B., U. Calif.-Berkeley, 1950. Mgr. San Ysidro Ranch, Santa Barbara, Calif., 1953-57, Santa Barbara Biltmore, 1957-59, Clift Hotel, San Francisco, 1959-60; v.p. Allied Properties, San Francisco, 1960-62; pres. Am. Convalescent Hosps., San Francisco, 1963-65; v.p., dir. Janss Corp., Thousand Oaks, Calif., 1965-67; pres., gen. mgr. Sun Valley Co., Sun Valley, Idaho, 1967-72; pres., dir., chief exec. officer Pebble Beach Co. (Calif.), 1973—; pres. Aspen Skiing Co., 1982—. Served with USAAF, 1944-45. Decorated Air medal with 4 oak leaf clusters, Purple Heart. Address: Pebble Beach Corp PO Box 1098 Pebble Beach CA 93953

HOLMES, HENRY ALLEN, foreign service officer; b. Bucharest, Rumania, Jan. 31, 1933; s. Julius Cecil and Henrietta (Allen) H.; m. Marilyn Janet Strauss, July 25, 1959; children: Katherine Anne, Gerald Allen. A.B., Princeton U., 1954; certificat d'etudes politiques (Woodrow Wilson fellow), U. Paris, 1958. Intelligence research analyst Dept. State, 1958-59, commd. fgn. service officer, 1959; assigned to Am. embassy, Yaounde, Cameroun, 1959-61, Dept. State, Washington, 1961-63, 67-70, Am. embassy, Rome, 1963-67; counselor polit. affairs Am. Embassy, Paris, 1970-74; sr. exec. Seminar in Fgn. Policy, Washington, 1974-75; assigned as dir. Office NATO and Atlantic polit. mil. affairs Bur. European Affairs, Washington, 1975-77; dep. chief of mission U.S. embassy, Rome, 1977-79; prin. dep. asst. sec. state for European affairs, Washington, 1979-82, ambassador to Portugal, 1982—. Served as capt. USMCR, 1954-57. Mem. Am. Fgn. Service Assn., Council Fgn. Relations. Episcopalian. Club: Met. (Washington). Home: 5027 Sedgwick St NW Washington DC 20016 Office: US Embassy Avenida Das Forcas Armadas 1098 Lisbon Code X Lisbon Portugal

HOLMES, JAMES, company executive; b. Eng., Oct. 24, 1919; s. David T. and Emily (Hill) H.; m. Mildred Alice Deans, July 14, 1943; children: David Caird, Barbara Mary. B.Sc. in Econs, U. London 1949. With Can. Pacific Ltd., Montreal, Que., Can., 1949-70, sr. research economist, 1960-61, spl. asst. fin. dept., 1961-63, asst. treas., 1963, treas., 1964-69, dir. fin. planning, 1969-70; dir. fin. Falconbridge Nickel Mines Ltd., Toronto, Ont., Can., 1970, v.p. fin., 1971-76, Falconbridge Dominicana (C por A), 1970-76; chmn. bd., chief exec. officer Electrohome Ltd., Kitchener, Ont., 1977-80, dir., 1977-81; chmn. bd., dir. Central Ont. TV Ltd., 1977-80; chmn. bd., chief exec. officer Homeware Industries Ltd., Homeware Ltd., 1980-82; pres. Holmes and Co., Toronto, 1983—; dir. Ronyx Corp. Ltd., Vulcan Indsl. Packaging Ltd., Gen. Aluminium Forgings Inc., Mothe's Pizza Parlours Ltd. Served with RAF, 1940-46. Mem. Am. Mgmt. Assn. (fin. council), Can. Mfrs. Assn. (dir. 1980—). Home: 149 Suffolk Ave Oakville ON L6J 2L5 Canada L6J 2L5 Office: 3300 Bloor St W Suite 550 Toronto ON Canada M8X 2X2

HOLMES, JAMES MURRAY, educator, chemist; b. Doaktown, N.B., Can., Sept. 30, 1919; s. Akeley and Elsie (Murray) H.; m. Helen Hargrave Hill, Sept. 6, 1946; children—Janet (dec.), John, Jean. B.Sc., U. N.B., 1940; M.A., U. Western Ont., 1942; Ph.D., McGill U., 1944. Sessional lectr. McGill U., 1946-48; lectr. Carleton U., 1948-49, asst. prof., 1949-53, asso. prof., 1953-61, prof. chemistry, 1961—, chmn. dept., 1957-73. Mem. Ont. Com. Univ. Affairs, 1972-74; bd. govs. Carleton U., 1972-81. Served with Can. Army, 1944-46. Beaverbook Scholar, 1936-40. Fellow Chem. Inst. Can. (Chem. Edn. award 1973); mem. Ont. Confedn. U. Faculty Assn. (chmn. exec. mem. 1966-69), Can. Assn. U. Tchrs. (exec. com. 1971-72), Am. Chem. Soc., Royal Chem. Soc. (Eng.), Sigma Xi. Club: Ottawa Hunt and Golf. Home: 60 Grove Ave Ottawa ON K1S 3A8 Canada

HOLMES, JAY THORPE, lawyer; b. Waukesha, Wis., Aug. 4, 1942; s. Oliver Wendell and Lillian (Thorpe) H.; m. Karen E. Johnston, Sept. 9, 1962; children: Jayne, Jay Daniel, Susan. B.A. in History, U. Alaska, 1964; J.D., U. Wis., 1967. Corp. atty. Cargill, Inc., Mpls., 1967-71; gen. counsel A. E. Staley Mfg. Co., Decatur, Ill., 1971-81; v.p., gen. counsel, sec. Bausch & Lomb Inc., Rochester, N.Y., 1981—. Bd. dirs. various civic/charitable orgns. Served with ROTC. Mem. Am. Bar Assn., N.Y. Bar Assn., Monroe County Bar Assn. Presbyterian. Office: Bausch & Lomb Inc 1 Lincoln Sq PO Box 54 Rochester NY 14601

HOLMES, JOHN CLELLON, author; b. Holyoke, Mass., Mar. 12, 1926; s. John McClellan and Elizabeth (Emmons) H.; m. Shirley Anise Allen, Sept. 9, 1953. Student, Columbia U., 1943, 45-46, New Sch. Social Research, 1949-50. Lectr. Yale U., 1959; vis. lectr. writers workshop State U. Iowa, 1963-64; writer in residence U. Ark., 1966; vis. prof. Bowling Green State U., 1968, Brown U., 1971-72; asso. prof. U. Ark., 1976-80, prof., 1980—. Author: Go, 1952, The Horn, 1958, Get Home Free, 1964, Nothing More To Declare, 1967, The Bowling Green Poems, 1977, Death Drag: Selected Poems, 1979, Visitor, 1981; Contbr. to popular mags. Served with Hosp. Corps USNR, 1944-45. Recipient Playboy mag. award for best article, 1964, 71, 73; John Clellon Holmes Collection award Boston U., 1966; Guggenheim fellow, 1976. Home: Box 75 Old Saybrook CT 06475 *As a writer, one lives day to day with the search for the specific truth of a character, a situation, or a moment in time. As a sometime-teacher, I have found that young people, even in these disruptive times, unfailingly respond to candor and encouragement, and will excell themselves when the uniqueness of their personalities is acknowledged. As a man, I am a pacifist by nature, who views violence and fanaticism of any stripe as the enemies of life. As I have gotten older, I have found that a warm-hearted skepticism towards existence is the surest road to maturity.*

HOLMES, JOHN RICHARD, educator, physicist; b. Chula Vista, Calif., Sept. 24, 1917; s. Robert and Mary Elizabeth (Burns) H.; m. Louise Murphy, 1951; children—Susan Diana, Ronald John, Sandra Kathleen. A.B. in Physics, U. Calif. at Berkeley, 1938, M.A., 1941, Ph.D., 1942. With radiation lab. U. Calif. at Berkeley, 1942-45; mem. faculty physics U. So. Calif., Los Angeles, 1945-63, prof., 1954-63, chmn. dept. physics, 1956-62; prof. U. Hawaii, 1963—, chmn. physics dept., 1963-72; Fulbright lectr. U. Madrid, Spain, 1962-63; cons. Autonetics Corp., Anaheim, Calif., Douglas Aircraft, Santa Monica, Calif., Electro-Optical Systems, Pasadena, Calif.; lectr., Edwards AFB, Loyola U., Los Angeles; UNESCO cons., Argentina, 1970. Fellow Am. Phys. Soc., Optical Soc. Am.; mem. AAAS. Office: Dept Physics and Astronomy U Hawaii Honolulu HI 96822

HOLMES, JOHN WENDELL, institute executive; b. London, Ont., Can., June 18, 1910. B.A., U. Western Ont., London, 1932, LL.D., 1973; M.A., U. Toronto, Ont., 1933; postgrad., U. London, 1938-40; LL.D. (hon.), U. N.B., 1975, U. Waterloo, 1976, York U., 1981, St. Lawrence and Carleton U., 1983, D.C.L., Acadia U., Wolfville, N.S., 1977; D.Litt., U. Windsor, 1980. With Can. Inst. Internat. Affairs, Toronto, 1940-43, 60—; with Can. Dept. External Affairs, 1943-53, served in, London, Moscow, N.Y.C.; under sec. state for external affairs, 1953-60; Claude T. Bissell vis. prof. Can.-U.S. relations U. Toronto, 1980-81; York U.; vis. prof. modern Commonwealth history U. Leeds, Eng., 1979; mem. advisory bd. on disarmament studies UN. Author: The Better Part of Valour, 1970, Canada: A Middle-Aged Power, 1976, The Shaping of Peace, Vol. 1, 1979 Vol. 2, 1982. Decorated Order Can.; Carnegie Endowment fellow, 1969. Fellow Royal Soc. Can.; mem. Internat. Peace Acad. (dir.). Home: 36 Castle Frank Rd Toronto ON Canada M4W 2Z7 Office: Can Inst Internat Affairs 15 King's Coll Circle Toronto ON Canada M5S 2V9

HOLMES, KENNETH HOWARD, lawyer; b. St. Paul, June 13, 1936; s. John Turner and Beatrice Carolina (Johnson) H.; m. Karen Ruth Seeger, Aug. 6, 1960; children: J. Scott, Mark, Michael. B.S. in Law, U. Minn., 1958, LL.B. magna cum laude, 1960. Bar: Minn. 1960, N.Y. 1962, U.S. Supreme Ct. 1969. Assoc. Dewey, Ballantine, Bushby, Palmer & Wood, N.Y.C., 1961-69, ptnr., 1969—. Mem. ABA, N.Y. State Bar Assn., Assn. Bar City N.Y., Order of Coif. Home: 864 Hillside Ave Westfield NJ 07092 Office: Dewey Ballantine Bushby Palmer & Wood 140 Broadway New York NY 10005

HOLMES, LARRY, philosophy educator; b. Kalamazoo, July 17, 1919; s. Carl Benton and Ruth (Miller) H.; m. Genevieve Lechevalier, June 14, 1951; children: Christopher, Sarah Louise, Peter. B.A., U. Iowa, 1940, M.A., 1941; M.A., Harvard U., 1949, Ph.D., 1962. Instr. philosophy Conn. Wesleyan U., 1949-51; fgn. affairs officer U.S. ACDA, 1961-63; asso. prof. philosophy SUNY-New Paltz, 1963-64, prof., 1965—, chmn. dept. philosophy, 1969-73, dir. philosophy program in Paris, 1971-74; v.p. Acad. Year Abroad, Inc., 1974. Mem., chmn. Planning and Zoning Commn., Vienna, Va., 1959-63. Served with AUS, 1943-46. Am. Council Learned Socs. fellow, 1942-43. Mem. Am. Philos. Assn., AAUP, Charles S. Peirce Soc. Episcopalian. Club: Harvard of Cape Cod. Home: 55 Bank St Harwich Port MA 02646

HOLMES, LARRY, profl. boxer; b. Cuthbert, Ga., Nov. 3, 1949; s. John and Flossie H.; children—Listy, Lisa. Ed. public schs. Formerly worked in car wash, quarry, rug mill, foundry, profl. boxer, 1973—. Heavyweight champion World Boxing Council, 1978—. Won 19 of 22 amateur fights. Office: care Holmes Enterprises Inc 704 Alpha Bldg Easton PA 18042 *

HOLMES, MALCOLM HERBERT, telecommunications company executive; b. London, Nov. 11, 1934; U.S., 1975; s. Harold and Gladys H.; m. Veronica Menezes, June 26, 1982. Grad., Scotland, 1956. Pres. Jamaica Telephone, Kingston, 1970-75; v.p. eastern region Continental Telephone, Washington, 1975-79, v.p. fin., Atlanta, 1979-82; exec. v.p. fin. Continental Telecom. Inc., Atlanta, 1982-83, exec. v.p. ops., 1983—. Mem. Fin. Execs. Inst., Brit. Inst. Mgmt., Inst. Chartered Accts. Scotland. Home: 120 Laurel Dr Atlanta GA 30342 Office: Continental Telecom Inc 245 Perimeter Center Pkwy Atlanta GA 30346

HOLMES, MARJORIE ROSE, author; b. Storm Lake, Iowa; d. Samuel Arthur and Rosa (Griffith) H.; m. Lynn Mighell, Apr. 9, 1932; children—Marjorie Mighell Croner, Mark, Mallory, Melanie Mighell Dimopoulos; m. George Schmieler, July 4, 1981. Student, Buena Vista Coll., 1927-29, D.Litt. (hon.), 1976; B.A., Cornell Coll., 1931. Tchr. writing Cath. U., 1964-65, U. Md., 1967-68; mem. staff Georgetown Writers Conf., 1959-81. Free-lance writer: short stories, articles, verse for mags. including Reader's Digest; weekly columnist: Love and Laughter, Washington Evening Star, 1959-75; monthly columnist: Woman's Day, 1971-77; Author: World By the Tail, 1943, Ten O'Clock Scholar, 1946, Saturday Night, 1959, Cherry Blossom Princess, 1960, Follow Your Dream, 1961, Love is a Hopscotch Thing, 1963, Senior Trip, 1962, Love and Laughter, 1967, I've Got to Talk to Somebody, God, 1969, Writing the Creative Article, 1969, Who Am I, God?, 1971, To Treasure Our Days, 1971, Two from Galilee, 1972, Nobody Else Will Listen, 1973, You and I and Yesterday, 1973, As Tall as My Heart, 1974, How Can I Find You God?, 1975, Beauty in Your Own Back Yard, 1976, Hold Me Up a Little Longer, Lord, 1977, Lord, Let Me Love, 1978, God and Vitamins, 1980, To Help You Through the Hurting, 1983; contbg. editor: Guideposts, 1977—; bd. dirs.: The Writer, 1975—. Bd. dirs. Found. Christian Living, 1975—. Recipient Honor Iowans award Buena Vista Coll., 1966, Alumni Achievement award Cornell Coll., 1963, Woman of Achievement award Nat. Fedn. Press Women, 1972; award Freedom Found. at Valley Forge, 1977. Mem. Am. Newspaper Women's Club, Va. Press Women, Washington Nat. Press Club, Children's Book Guild, Delta Phi Beta. Home: 637 E McMurray Rd McMurray PA 15317 *Talent imposes 2 responsibilities: To use it. And to use it for good.*

HOLMES, MAX JACOB, publishing co. exec.; b. Koenigshutte, Poland, Nov. 25, 1926; s. Chaim and Miriam (Rosenbaum) Hochzeit; m. Mala Rosenwasser, Feb. 10, 1949; children—Miriam, Hannah Babette. Student. U. Erlangen; B.B.A., CCNY, 1960. Asst. Walter J. Johnson, Inc., 1953-60; v.p. Maxwell, Meier & Holmes, 1960-61; pres. Internat. U. Booksellers, N.Y.C., 1962—, Holmes & Meier Pubs. Inc., 1969—. Trustee Union Orthodox Jewish Congregations, Fifth Ave. Synagogue. Mem. ALA, Med. Library Assn., Antiquarian, Booksellers Assn., Assn. Am. Publishers. Home: 630 Park Ave New York NY 10021 Office: 30 Irving Pl New York NY 10003

HOLMES, MELVIN ALMONT, insurance company executive; b. West New York, N.J., Jan. 2, 1919; s. Edward L. and Sarah J. (Brown) H.; m. Clare G. White, May 30, 1943; children: Clare Ann, Karen, Joan, Patricia, Catherine, Donald, Jacqueline. Student in bus. adminstrn., NYU; L.H.D. (hon.), Coll. of Ins., 1976. C.P.C.U., 1955. With Frank B. Hall & Co., Inc., Briarcliff Manor, N.Y., 1937-84, asst. mgr. liability dept., 1945-52, asst. v.p., 1952-56, v.p., 1956-68, chief exec. officer, pres., 1968-73, vice chmn., 1973-79, cons., dir., 1979-84; Chmn. bd. trustees Coll. of Ins., 1974-76. Hon. trustee Valley Hosp., Ridgewood, N.J. Served to capt. C.E., U.S. Army, 1941-46. Recipient Good Scout award Boy Scouts Am., 1975; Free Enterprise award Ins. Fedn. N.Y., 1975. Mem. Nat. Assn. Ins. Brokers (past pres.), Ins. Soc. N.Y., Soc. C.P.C.U.s (Eugene A. Toale Meml. award 1976), Ins. Inst. Am., Am. Inst. Property and Liability Underwriters Inc. (past trustee), Ins. Fedn. N.Y. (past pres.). Clubs: Ridgewood (N.J.); Country, Tequesta Country. Home: 275 Beach Rd Tequesta FL 33458 Office: 549 Pleasantville Rd Briarcliff Manor NY 10510

HOLMES, MELVIN CHARLES, lawyer; b. Chgo., Oct. 17, 1927; s. Carl O. and Marceleta (Gross) H.; m. Carol Thomas Boberg, June 16, 1951; children: Keith, Claire, Sarah, Anne. B.A., Carleton Coll., 1948; J.D., U. Mich., 1951. Bar: Ill. 1951. With firm Schumacher, Gilmore, Van Ness & Stern, Chgo., 1951-56; with AMSTED Industries, Inc., Chgo., 1956—, asst. sec., 1959-73, sec., corp. counsel, 1973-81; ptnr. firm Davis & Holmes, Woodstock, Ill, 1981—. Contbr. articles to legal jours. Mem. ABA, Ill. Bar Assn. (past chmn. corp. law dept. coms.), McHenry Bar Assn., Chgo. Bar Assn. (past chmn. corp. law dept. coms.). Clubs: Legal, Law, Univ. (Chgo.); Turnberry Country, Bagatelle. Home: 24 Marryat Rd Trout Valley Cary IL 60013 Office: 666 Russel Ct Suite 105 Woodstock IL 60098

HOLMES, NICHOLAS HANSON, JR., architect, archeologist; b. Chgo., Dec. 10, 1924; s. Nicholas Hanson and Emilie Perret (Clark) H.; m. Nancy Neiswender, Jan. 19, 1952; children: Nicholas Hanson, Mary Emilie Holmes Acklen, Andrew Harris. B.Arch., Auburn U., 1949; postgrad., Royal Danish Art Acad., Copenhagen, 1949-50. Partner Holmes & Holmes Architects, Mobile, Ala., 1954-57; ptnr. Holmes & Geer (Architect-Engr.), Mobile, 1960-74; practice architecture, Mobile, 1957-60, 74—; ptnr. Holmes & Holmes, Architects; mem. Mobile Archtl. Rev. Bd., 1962-71, 73—, Ala. Hist. Commn., 1966-72. Restoration architect: Ala. Capitol, 1977—, Barton Acad, Mobile, 1968, City Hall Complex, Mobile. Served with U.S. Army, 1943-46. Recipient Disting. Service award Ala. Hist. Commn., 1972. Fellow AIA (chmn. com. hist. resources 1972); mem. Soc. Profl. Archeologists., Am. Soc. Interior Designers. Episcopalian. Home: 22 S Lafayette St Mobile AL 36604 Office: 257 N Conception St Mobile AL 36602

HOLMES, PRESTON TURNER, banking executive; b. Richmond, Va., July 9, 1927; s. Raymond T. and Alma T. H.; m. Rachel Elizabeth Moore, Aug. 11, 1951; children: Mark Baldwin, Nancy Lynne, Scott Kendall. Grad., Am. Inst. Banking, 1951, Stonier Sch. Banking, 1953. Successively asst. cashier, asst. sec., asst. v.p., v.p., v.p. and cashier State Planters Bank, Richmond, 1952-67, sr. v.p., cashier, 1967-68; sr. v.p. United Va. Bankshares Inc., Richmond, 1968, Adminstrv. v.p., 1968, exec. v.p., 1970—; pres. United Va. Bank Service Corp., Richmond, 1968-70; dir. Buckhorn Coal Co., Richmond Cedar Works Mfg. Co., SDG Corp. Served with U.S. Army, 1945-46. Methodist. Home: 7800 Hopkins Rd Richmond VA 23234 Office: PO Box 26665 900 E Main St Richmond VA 23219

HOLMES, REED M., clergyman, former religious organization administrator; b. Mansfield, Wash., June 17, 1917; s. Lawrence Earl and Emma Virginia (Reed) H.; m. Dorothy Lois Carter, Aug. 3, 1943; children: David, Carol (Mrs. Leslie T. Flowers), Joy Holmes Soper, Jewell (Mrs. Andrew Bolton), Lawrence. A.A., Graceland Coll., 1937; B.A., State U. Iowa, 1939; M.A., Calif. State Coll., Los Angeles, 1959; postgrad., U. Wash., 1939-40, Boston U., 1948, U. Iowa, 1967-70; postgrad., Haifa U., 1983. Ordained to ministry Reorganized Ch. of Jesus Christ of Latter Day Saints, 1940; missionary, So. New Eng. and Maine, 1940-42, pastor, Attleboro, Mass., 1942-44, Boston, 1945-48, dist. pres., So. New Eng., 1942-48, ordained apostle, 1948; gen. dir. religious edn. World Hdqrs., Independence, Mo., 1948-54; field dir., Southwest states and Alaska, 1954-59, Australia, N.Z., French Polynesia, 1959-64, dir. communications and program services div., 1964-73, assoc. dir. field ministries, 1973-74, presiding patriarch, 1974-82; founder, chmn. bd. View Pax Mondiale, 1982. Author: Seek This Christ, 1952, Israel-Land of Zion, 1978, The Patriarchs, 1978, Kendra, 1979, The Forerunners, 1981, The Church in Israel, 1983; co-author: editor: Exploring the Faith, 1970; Contbg. editor: Saint's Herald, 1964-74. Chmn. Human Rights Commn., Independence, 1971, 72, Independence Personnel Com., 1974-76; bd. dirs. Restoration Trail Found., 1970-76. Hon. fellow Harry S. Truman Library Inst., 1974—. Mem. John Whitmer Hist. Assn., Maine Hist. Soc., Internat. Platform Assn., Jackson County Hist. Soc. Democrat. Home: 36A Sandy River Beach Jonesport ME 04649

HOLMES, RICHARD HUGH MORRIS, investment mgmt. exec.; b. Olean, N.Y., Dec. 11, 1925; s. Gerald Hugh and Caroline Elizabeth (Morris) H.; m. Dorothy Theone Minnich, Sept. 7, 1944; children—Richard Edward Griffin, James Stuart. Student, Brown U., 1942-43. Office mgr. Red Star Transit Co., Detroit, 1947-55; data processor Nat. Dairy Products Co., Detroit, 1955-58; asst. to controller Am. Sugar Co., San Francisco, 1958-66; with Am. Express Investment Mgmt. Co., San Francisco, 1966-75, pres., 1974-75; v.p. Capital Research & Mgmt. Co., San Francisco, 1975—; pres. Am. Balanced Fund, Inc., Growth Fund Am., Inc., Income Fund Am., Inc., Endowments, Inc., Bond Portfolio for Endowments, Inc. Served to capt. RAF, 1943-46. Mem. Investment Co. Inst., Mensa. Republican. Club: Los Angeles Athletic. Home: 580 Laurent Rd Hillsborough CA 94010 Office: 2 Embarcadero Center Suite 2320 San Francisco CA 94111

HOLMES, RICHARD WINN, state supreme ct. justice; b. Wichita, Kans., Feb. 23, 1923; s. Winn Earl and Sidney (Clapp) H.; m. Gwen Sand, Aug. 19, 1950; children—Robert W., David K. B.S., Kans. State U., 1950; J.D., Washburn U., 1953. Bar: Kans. bar 1953, U.S. Dist. Ct. bar 1953. Practice law, Wichita, Kans., 1953-77; judge Wichita Mcpl. Ct., 1959-61; instr. bus. law Wichita State U., 1959-60; justice Kans. Supreme Ct., 1977—. Served with USNR, 1943-46. Mem. Kans., Topeka, Wichita bar assns., N.Am. Judges Assn. (founder, bd. govs. 1980—). Home: 2535 Granthurst Ave Topeka KS 66611 Office: Kansas Judicial Center Topeka KS 66612

HOLMES, ROBERT BIGELOW, business exec.; b. Melrose, Mass., Dec. 21, 1931; s. Charles Wendell and Ruth Esther (Hudson) H.; 1 son, Peter Morgan. A.B., Harvard U., 1953. Trust officer New Eng. Mchts. Nat. Bank, Boston, 1953-63; with Lazard Freres & Co., N.Y.C., 1964-76, gen. partner, 1972-76; exec. v.p. Ticor, Los Angeles, 1977-78, pres., 1979-80; pres., chief exec. officer Aristar, Inc., Coral Gables, Fla., 1981—. Mem. Inst. Chartered Fin. Analysts.

HOLMES, ROBERT EDWARD, justice Ohio Supreme Ct.; b. Columbus, Ohio, Nov. 14, 1922; s. Harry Barclay and Nora Jane (Birney) H.; m. Jean Wren; children—Robert Edward, Hamilton Barclay. A.B., Ohio U., 1943, LL.B., 1949. Bar: Ohio bar. Practiced law, 1949-69; mem. Ohio Ho. of Reps., 1960-69; judge 10th Dist. Ct. Appeals, Columbus, 1969-78; justice Ohio Supreme Ct., Columbus, 1979—. Pres. Columbus Area Internat. Program, Council Internat. Programs; founder Columbus Community Camp; bd. dirs. Boy Scouts Am., Salvation Army, Pilot Dogs, Inc. Served with USN, 1944-46. Mem. Columbus Bar Assn., Ohio Bar Assn., Am. Bar Assn. Republican. Office: Supreme Ct Ohio 30 E Broad St Columbus OH 43215 *

HOLMES, ROBERT LAWRENCE, philosophy educator; b. Watertown, NY, Dec. 28, 1935; s. Augustus Spencer and Rhoda (Lawrenece) H.; children: Suzanne, Rebecca, Timothy Robert. A.B., Harvard Coll., 1957; M.A., U. Mich., 1959, Ph.D., 1961. Instr. U. Tex., 1961-62; asst. prof. U. Rochester, N.Y., 1962-66, assoc. prof., 1966-71, prof. philosophy, 1971—. Co-author: Philosophic Inquiry, 1968. Chmn. New Democratic Coalition, Rochester area, 1969; candidate Liberal Pary Ho. of Reps., 1968; exec. com. Am. Friends Service Com., upper N.Y. State, 1979—. Grantee-in-aid Am. Council Learned Socs., 1964; fellow ctr. for Advanced Study U. Ill., 1970-71; Nat. Humanities Inst. fellow Yale U., 1976-77; Fulbright lectr. U. Moscow, 1983. Mem. Am. Philos. Assn., Soc. for Philosophy and Pub. Policy, Soc. for Advancement of Am. Philosophy, Concerned Philosophers. Home: 12 Buckingham St Rochester NY 14607 Office: Dept Philosophy Univ Rochester Rochester NY 14627

HOLMES, ROBERT WILLIAM, university dean; b. Somerville, Mass., Jan. 9. 1929; s. Theodore Ewen and Marie (Kilduff) H.; m. Grace Feener, Oct. 11, 1951; children—Robert William, Elizabeth Grayce. Mus. B., Boston U., 1953, A.M., 1955, Ph.D., 1960. Asst. librarian music ref. div. Boston Pub. Library, 1956-58; chief librarian, instr. music history and theory Boston U. Sch. Fine and Applied Arts, 1958-60; asst. prof. music history Oakland U., 1960-62, asso. dean, 1962-63; asst. dir. Univ. Center Adult Edn., Detroit, 1963-64, dir., 1964-66; adj. asso. prof. musicology grad. div. Music Sch., Wayne State U., 1964-66; prof. music history, chmn. music dept. Western Mich. U., Kalamazoo, 1966-72, dean Coll. Fine Arts, 1972-80; exec. dir. Idyllwild campus U. So. Calif., 1980-82; dean Coll. Arts and Architecture, dir. Univ. Arts Services, prof. musicology Pa. State U., 1982—; chmn. 1st Mich. Congress on Arts. Pianist; program annotator, Gardner Museum, Boston, 1957-62, Detroit Symphony Orch., 1965-81, Los Angeles Chamber Orch., 1981—; Editor: The Arts in Michigan, A Ten-Year Projection, 1976. Bd. dirs. Kalamazoo Civic Auditorium, 1971-78, v.p., 1976-77, pres., 1977-78; bd. dirs. Mich. Orch. Assn., 1972-74; mem. adv. bd. Internat. Inst. Advanced Musical

Studies, 1971-74. Mem. Adult Edn. Assn. Mich. (chmn. coll.-univ. sect.), Internat. Council Fine Arts Deans (chmn. faculty exchange com. 1975-76, steering com. 1976—), Mich. Acad. Sci., Arts and Letters (vice chmn. fine arts sect. 1969-72, chmn. 1972-73), Nat. Symposium Music Adult Edn., Mich. Council on Arts (chmn. music com. 1967-70, exec. com. 1971, vice chmn. council 1973-78), Am. Musicol. Soc., Sinfonia (life alumni mem.), Pi Kappa Lambda., Phi Kappa Phi. Home: 2615 Acacia Dr State College PA 16801 Office: 111 Arts Bldg University Park PA 16802

HOLMES, ROSS ROBERT, mfg. co. exec.; b. Martins Ferry, Ohio, June 13, 1921; s. Ross F. and Eloise Anna (Helling) H.; m. Doris May Evens, Jan. 8, 1945; 1 son, Thomas Evens. B.S. in Metall. Engring, Carnegie Mellon U., 1942. Process engr. Delco Moraine div. Gen. Motors Corp., 1942-56; sect. supr. Ford Motor Co., 1956-59; v.p. mktg. Hoeganaes Corp., Riverton, N.J., 1959—. Served with USN, 1945-46. Mem. Am. Soc. Metals, Am. Powder Metallurgy Inst., Am. Welding Soc., Soc. Automotive Engrs. Lutheran. Club: Masons. Home: 68 Westbrook Dr Moorestown NJ 08057 Office: Taylors Ln and River Rd Riverton NJ 08077

HOLMES, THOMAS A., machinery mfg. co. exec.; b. Wilmington, Mass., Sept. 12, 1923; s. John Thomas and Marion (Burtt) H.; m. Joan Merritt, March 15, 1952; children-Nanne, Susan, John, Bruce. B.S.M.E., Mo. Sch. Mines, 1950; postgrad., Harvard Bus. Sch., 1969. With Ingersoll-Rand Co., Woodcliff Lake, N.J., 1950—, chmn., chief exec. officer, dir.; dir. Newmont Mining Corp., N.Y.C. Bd. dirs. Nat. Energy Found., N.Y.C; trustee Lafayette Coll., Easton, Pa. Served with USNR, 1943-46. Mem. Am. Inst. Mining Engrs., Mining and Metall. Soc. Am., Am. Mining Congress (dir.), Compressed Air and Gas Inst. (dir.). Club: Mining. Home: 445 Round Hill Rd Greenwich CT 06830 Office: 200 Chestnut Ridge Rd Woodcliff Lake NJ 07675

HOLMES, THOMAS HALL, psychiatrist; b. Goldsboro, N.C., Sept. 20, 1918; s. Thomas Hall and Elizabeth (Stephenson) H.; m. Janet Lawrence, Dec. 29, 1942; children—Thomas Stephenson, Janet, Eleanor Scott, Elizabeth Lawrence. A.B., U. N.C., 1939; M.D., Cornell U., 1943. Intern in medicine N.Y. Hosp., N.Y.C., 1943-44, resident in psychiatry, 1944; research in neurology Bellevue Hosp., N.Y.C., 1944; Hofheimer research fellow psychosomatic medicine N.Y. Hosp.-Cornell U. Med. Center, 1947-49; provisional asst. physician outpatient dept. N.Y. Hosp.; also clin. asst. vis. psychiatrist and neurologist Bellevue Hosp., 1948-49; mem. faculty U. Wash. Sch. Medicine, Seattle, 1949—, prof. psychiatry, 1958—; attending physician Harborview Med. Center, 1949—, Univ. Hosp., 1959—; attending staff Seattle VA Hosp., 1951—; hon. cons. psychiatrist Royal Prince Alfred Hosp., Sydney, Australia, 1971—. Co-author: The Nose, 1950; contbr. to med. jours. Served to maj. M.C. AUS, 1944-46. Mem. AAAS, Am. Psychiat. Assn., Am. Psychosomatic Soc., Am. Public Health Assn., Assn. Am. Med. Colls., N.Y. Acad. Scis., Wash. Med. Assn., King County Med. Soc., N. Pacific Soc. Neurology and Psychiatry, Am. Sociol. Soc., Assn. Research in Nervous and Mental Diseases, Psychiat. Research Soc., Western Soc. Clin. Research. Home: 3023 NE 180th St Seattle WA 98155 Office: Dept Psychiatry RP-10 U Wash Med Sch Seattle WA 98195

HOLMES, VERNON HARRISON, insurance company executive; b. Milford, Ill., Dec. 21, 1920; s. Harry and Alma (Schiewe) H.; m. Ruth Dewey, Oct. 24, 1943; children: Sharon Klabon, Charisse Holmes. B.Ed., Western Ill. U., 1943; grad., Inst. Mgmt., Northwestern U., 1965, Advanced Mgmt. Program, Harvard U., 1977. With Sentry Ins. Co., Stevens Point, Wis., 1946—, exec. v.p. adminstrv. services; pres., dir. Sentry Corp.; pres., dir. Sentry Found.; dir. Patriot Gen. Life Ins. Co., Patroit Gen. Ins. Co., Dairyland Ins. Co., Gt. S.W. Fire Ins. Co., Sentry Indemnity Co., Sentry Ins. A Mut. Co., Sentry Life Assurance Co., Citizens Nat. Bank, Stevens Point. Bd. dirs. St. Michael's Hosp., Stevens Point, Western Ill. U. Found.; past pres. Trinity Luth. Ch., Stevens Point. Served with USAAF, 1943-46. Mem. Stevens Point Area C. of C. (pres.); Mem. Soc. Preservation and Encouragement of Barber Shop Quartet Singing in Am. (past pres. Stevens Point). Club: Stevens Point Country (past v.p., dir.). Office: 1800 N Point Dr Stevens Point WI 54481

HOLMES, WILLIAM JAMES, college president; s. William J. and Libbie (Stodola) H.; m. Joanne Prokop, Sept. 8, 1951; children: Mary, Ann, Sara. B.A., Iowa State U., 1951, Ph.D. in Engring., 1962; postgrad., Ohio U., 1960, 62. Instr. engring. Iowa State U., 1955-58; with Ohio U., 1958-70, asst. prof., 1962-65, assoc. prof., 1965-70; pres. Simmons Coll., Boston, 1970—; dir. NDEA Inst. Engring., 1967. Contbr. articles to profl. jours. Served to capt. USAAF, 1945-49. Fellow Am. Council Edn. Program Acad. Administrn., 1968-69. Mem. MLA. Office: Office of the Pres Simmons Coll 300 The Fenway Boston MA 02115 *

HOLMGREN, HARRY D., physicist, educator; b. Mpls., Apr. 21, 1928; s. Harry W. and Myrtle (Dahl) H.; m. Monika Konig; children: Diane, Bruce, Cheryl, Cynthia. B.Physics, U. Minn., 1949, M.A., 1950, Ph.D., 1954. Physicist U.S. Naval Research Lab., Washington, 1954-61; mem. faculty U. Md., College Park, 1961—, prof. physics, astronomy, dir. Cyclotron Lab., 1965-78; pres. Southeastern Univs. Research Assn., Inc., 1980—; cons. to govt., industry and acad. instns. for nuclear sci. research and facilities and med. facilities. Recipient Edward O. Hulburt award U.S. Naval Research Lab., 1960, Arthur S. Flemming award Jr. C. of C. Washington, 1961. Fellow Am. Phys. Soc., Phi Beta Kappa, Sigma Psi. Club: Cosmos. Research, numerous publs. on nuclear sci., basic structure of nuclei of atoms and processes by which nuclear particles interact with atomic nuclei, nuclear instrumentation, accelerators for nuclear research and med. applications. Home: 3044-3 R St NW Washington DC 20007

HOLMGREN, LATON EARLE, clergyman; b. Mpls., Feb. 20, 1915; s. Frank Albert and Freda Ida (Lindahl) H. Student, U. Minn., 1934-35; A.B. cum laude, Asbury Coll., 1936; M. Div. summa cum laude, Drew U., 1941; postgrad., Edinburgh (Scotland) U., 1947; D.D., Ill. Wesleyan U., 1956, Asbury Theol. Sem., 1972. Ordained to ministry United Methodist Ch., 1942; asso. minister Calvary Meth. Ch., East Orange, N.J., 1940-42, Christ Ch. Meth., N.Y.C., 1943-48; minister Tokyo (Japan) Union Ch., 1949-52; lectr. internat. dept. Tokyo U. Commerce, 1950-52; adviser Japanese Fgn. Office, Tokyo, 1951; sec. for Asia Am. Bible Soc., N.Y.C., 1952-54, exec. sec., 1954-62, gen. sec., rec. sec., 1963-78, cons., 1978—; mem. exec. com. United Bible Socs., Stuttgart, Germany, 1957-78, chmn., 1963-72, spl. cons., 1978—. Trustee Asbury Theol. Sem. Recipient Gutenberg award, 1975; Disting. Alumni award Asbury Coll., 1981; Baron von Canstein award, 1982. Mem. Japan Soc. Club: Union League. Home: 322 W 57 St New York NY 10019 Office: 1865 Broadway New York NY 10023

HOLMGREN, MARVIN EDWARD, educator; b. Plainview, Tex., Mar. 20, 1918; s. Albin Edward and Mabel Christina (Landholm) H.; m. Joyce Lorraine Lachelt, Oct. 25, 1940; children: Charles Allan, Susan Jane, Lindsay Ann. B.S., St. Cloud (Minn.) State Tchrs. Coll., 1940; M.A., U. Minn., 1946, Ph.D., 1949. Tchr. Ogilvie (Minn.) High Sch., 1940-41, Rush City (Minn.) High Sch., 1941-43; research asst. U. Minn., 1947, teaching asst., 1948-49, lectr., 1950; asso. prof. edn. St. Cloud State Coll., 1949-56, dir. Bur. Research, 1950-63, dean Sch. of Grad. Studies, 1953-65, prof. edn., 1956-72, prof. ednl. administrn., 1972-81, prof. emeritus, 1981—, dean of acad. adminstrn., 1965-67, v.p. acad. affairs, 1967-72; dir. Central Minn. Ednl. Coop. Service Unit, 1979-81; Participant, recorder Midwest Invitational Conf. Coop. Research, 1955-61; mem. Minn. Sch. Financial Accounting Com., 1949-52; treas. bd. edn. Sartell (Minn.) Pub. Sch., 1961-64; mem. Minn. Adv. Com. on Tchr. Edn., 1965-68; Mem. inservice tng. com. synod Minn. United Presbyn. Ch., 1955-61; commnr. 170th Gen. Assembly United Presbyn. Ch., 1958; chmn. com. ch. extension Presbytery St., 1961-67, vice moderator, 1966-67. Author: (with others) Religious Activities in Public Colleges, 1959, Preparatory Programs for Elementary School Teachers, 1961. Bd. dirs. Westminster Found. Minn. Served with USNR, 1943-46. Mem. NEA, Minn. Edn. Assn., Am. Ednl. Research Assn., Am., Minn. assns. sch. adminstrs., Assn. Sch. Bus. Ofcls. (sch. fin. com.), Council Ednl. Facility Planners, Minn. Assn. Sch. Bus. Ofcls., Nat. Council on Measurment in Edn., Minn. Sch. Bds. Assn., Nat. Soc. Study Edn., St. Cloud C. of C., Kappa Delta Pi (pres. St. Cloud 1939-40), Phi Delta Kappa (pres. Epsilon Theta chpt. 1961). Club: St. Cloud Sertoma (v.p. 1960). Home: 608 N 1st St Sartell MN 56377

HOLMGREN, ROBERT BRUCE, magazine editor; b. Chgo., Apr. 26, 1920; s. Henry Robert and Madeline (McCrodan) H.; m. Jean Lois Greig, Nov. 16, 1952; children—Carolyn Greig, James Bruce. Student, Principia Coll.; B.A., Northwestern U., 1942; J.D., Chgo.-Kent Coll. Law, 1949. Bar: Ill. bar 1950. Mem. staff Chgo. Crime Commn., 1944-45, 46-48; asst. editor Howard Publishing Co., Chgo., 1945-46; successively research editor, exec. editor, editorial dir. packaging publs. Haywood Pub. Co., Chgo., 1949-55; chief editor Packaging Engring. mag., Chgo., 1955-83, editorial dir., 1983—. Author: Primary Police Functions, 1960. Mem. Evanston (Ill.) Police Res., 1945-51, chief, 1950-51; counsel Ill. Fire Chiefs Assn., 1951—; supt. Lake Bluff (Ill.) Police Res., 1952-54; mem. Evanston (Ill.) Police Res., 1945-51; Mem. planning com. Chgo.-Kent Inst. Criminal Justice, 1967-69; mem. exec. com. Packaging Edn. Found., 1978-80, chmn. grants com., 1978-81, chmn. selections com., 1983-84, Bd. dirs. Served with AUS, 1943-44. Named Packaging Man of Year Mich. State U., 1961; recipient award Nat. Inst. Packaging, Handling and Logistics Engrs., 1979; Friend of Extension award U. Wis., 1979. Fellow Packaging Inst. U.S.A. (profl. award 1981); mem. Am. Bar Assn., Ill. State Bar Assn., Soc. Packaging and Handling Engrs., Internat. Packaging Press Orgn., Chgo.-Kent Alumni Assn. (pres. 1970-71), Phi Delta Phi. Republican. Christian Scientist. Club: Mich. Shores. Home: 449 Sunset Rd Winnetka IL 60093 Office: 1350 E Touhy Ave Des Plaines IL 60018

HOLMGREN, THEODORE J., food company executive; b. N.Y.C., May 2, 1927; s. Oscar F. and Madeline (Thompson) H.; m. Miriam Brady, June 3, 1950; children: Miriam Jane (Mrs. James C. McCrea III), Barbara Lynn (Mrs. Benjamin Fowler), Theodore Douglas. A.B., Brown U., 1949; M.B.A., Harvard U., 1955. Asst. Donald Deskey, Indsl. Designer, 1955-60; dir. design services Gen. Foods Corp., White Plains, N.Y., 1960-62, corp. new products mgr., 1962-65, sr. product mgr., 1965-68; sr. cons. mktg. Peat, Marwick, Mitchell & Co., N.Y.C., 1968; v.p. mktg. Curtice-Burns, Inc., Rochester, N.Y., 1968—, sec., 1974—. Pres. Community Council Chs. Irvington, Ardsley, Dobbs Ferry, Hastings, and Hartsdale, N.Y., 1961-63; trustee Orphan Asylum Soc. City N.Y., 1962-68, Curtice-Burns Charitable Found., 1970—; mem. corp. bd. United Way of Greater Rochester.; life assoc. Pres.'s Soc. U. Rochester. Served to lt. (j.g.) USNR, 1951-53. Mem. Alpha Delta Pi. Clubs: Harvard Bus. Sch. (Rochester); U. Rochester Faculty. Home: 16 Esternay Ln Pittsford NY 14534 Office: 1 Lincoln 1st Sq Rochester NY 14602

HOLMQUEST, DONALD LEE, physician, astronaut, lawyer; b. Dallas, Apr. 7, 1939; s. Sidney Browder and Lillie Mae (Waite) H.; m. Ann Nixon James, Oct. 24, 1972. B.S. in Elec. Engring, So. Meth. U., 1962; M.D., Baylor U., 1967, Ph.D. in Physiology, 1968; J.D., U. Houston, 1980. Student engr. Ling-Temco-Vought, Dallas, 1958-61; electronics engr. Tex. Instruments, Inc., Dallas, 1962; intern Meth. Hosp., Houston, 1967-68; pilot tng. USAF, Williams AFB, Ariz., 1968-69; scientist-astronaut NASA, Houston, 1967-73; research asso. Mass. Inst. Tech., 1968-70; asst. prof. radiology and physiology Baylor Coll. Medicine, 1970-73; dir. nuclear medicine Eisenhower Med. Center, Palm Desert, Calif., 1973-74; asso. dean medicine, asso. prof. Tex. A. and M. U., 1974-76; dir. nuclear medicine Navasota (Tex.) Med. Center, 1976—, Med. Arts Hosp., Houston, 1977—; asso. firm Wood Lucksinger & Epstein, Houston, 1980—. Contbr. articles to med. jours. Mem. Soc. Nuclear Medicine, Am. Coll. Nuclear Physicians, Tex. Bar Assn., Am. Fighter Pilots Assns., Sigma Xi, Alpha Omega Alpha, Sigma Tau. Home: 3721 Tangley Rd Houston TX 77005

HOLMQUIST, CARL OREAL, aeronautical engineer, former naval officer; b. Salt Lake City, Nov. 18, 1919; s. Carl John and Hazel (Reeder) H.; m. Lavina Millsaps Ervin, Mar. 7, 1948; children: Kurt E., Derek E., Kristen, Gunnar E. B.S. in Aero. Engring., U.S. Naval Acad., 1942, U.S. Naval Postgrad. Sch., 1950; Aero. Engr., Cal. Inst. Tech., 1951, Ph.D., 1953. Commd. ensign U.S. Navy, 1942; advanced through grades to rear adm., asst. to Sec. Navy, Washington, 1958-61; chief naval research, Arlington, Va., 1970-73; dir. materials and mfg. tech. Convair div. Gen. Dynamics; vis. tchr. U. Md., 1954-56. Contbr. articles to profl. jours. Assoc. fellow AIAA; mem. Naval Hist. Soc. Home: 6478 Avenida Wilfredo La Jolla CA 92037

HOLMQUIST, WALTER RICHARD, research chemist, molecular evolutionist; b. Kansas City, Mo., Dec. 23, 1934; s. Walter Theodore and Elsie Wilburnia (Seitz) H.; m. Ann Marie Hofer, Sept.8, 1968; children: Laura Marie, Jon Aron. B.S., Washington and Lee U., 1957, Calif. Inst. Tech., 1961; Ph.D. in Chemistry, Calif. Inst. Tech., 1966. Lectr. organic chemistry and biochemistry U. Ife, Ibadan, Nigeria, 1966-68; research fellow in biology Harvard U., 1968-70; asst. research chemist Space Scis. Lab., U. Calif.-Berkeley, 1970-74, assoc. research chemist, 1974-80, research chemist, 1980—; exec. mem. Com. Space research Interdisciplinary Sci. Commn. on Life Scis. Related to Space, 1982—. Editor: Life Sciences and Space Research, 1976-82; mem. editorial bd.: Adv. Space Research, Jour. Molecular Evolution, BioSystems. Grantee Nat. Heart and Lung Inst., 1971-73, NSF, 1977-81, 83—. Mem. AAAS, AM. Chem. Soc., Am. Soc. Biol. Chemists., N.Y. Acad. Scis., Calif. Acad. Scis., Soc. for Study Evolution, Phi Beta Kappa, Sigma Xi. Home and Office: 760 Mesa Way Richmond CA 94805

HOLMQUIST, WILLIAM AXEL, lawyer; b. Waukegan, Ill., Apr. 15, 1923; s. Axel H. and Maybelle (Olsen) H. Student, Eureka Coll., 1942; B.A., Northwestern U., 1947, J.D., 1950. Bar: Ill. 1950. Asso. George G. McGaughey, Waukegan, 1950-52, Snyder, Clarke & Dalziel, 1952-54; partner Snyder, Clarke, Dalziel, Holmquist & Johnson, Waukegan, 1954-80; resident partner Wildman, Harrold, Allen & Dixon, Waukegan, 1981-84, William A. Holmquist, 1984—; city atty., Zion, Ill., 1954-59, spl. asst. atty. gen., Ill., 1963-64; dir. Deerfield (Ill.) State Bank, 1977-79; Pub. mem. Jud. Adv. Council Ill., 1961-68. Served as 2d lt. USAAF, 1942-45. Fellow Am. Coll. Trial Lawyers; mem. ABA, Ill. Bar Assn., Chgo. Bar Assn., Lake County Bar Assn. (pres. 1969), Internat. Soc. Barristers, Am. Bd. Trial Advs., Soc. Trial Lawyers, Lambda Chi Alpha, Phi Alpha Delta. Episcopalian. Club: Swedish Glee (Waukegan). Home: 920 Vose Dr Apt 312 Gurnee IL 60031 Office: 9 S County St Waukegan IL 60085

HOLOHAN, WILLIAM ANDREW, state chief justice; b. Tucson, June 1, 1928; s. Andrew S. and Dorothy L. (Bennett) H.; m. Kathryn Dewey, Dec. 12, 1953; 4 children. LL.B., U. Ariz., 1950. Bar: Ariz. 1950. Asst. U.S. atty., 1953-60; judge Superior Ct., 1963-72; justice Ariz. Supreme Ct., Phoenix, 1972—, chief justice, 1982—. Served with U.S. Army, 1950-53. Decorated Bronze Star medal. Office: Ariz Supreme Ct 217 South-West Wing Phoenix AZ 85007

HOLONYAK, NICK, JR., electrical engineering educator; b. Ziegler, Ill., Nov. 3, 1928; s. Nick and Anna (Rosoha) H.; m. Katherine R.A. Jerger, Oct. 8, 1955. B.S., U. Ill., 1950, M.S., 1951, Ph.D. (Tex. Instruments fellow), 1954. Mem. tech. staff Bell Telephone Labs., Murray Hill, N.J., 1954-55; physicist, unit mgr., mgr. advanced semiconductor lab. Gen. Electric Co., Syracuse, N.Y., 1957-63; prof. elec. engring. and materials research lab. U. Ill., Urbana, 1963—; mem. Center Advanced Study, 1977—; series editor Prentice-Hall, Inc., 1962—; cons. Monsanto Co., 1964—, Nat. Electronics Co., 1963-70, Skil Corp., 1967, GTE Labs. Tech. Adv. Council, 1973. Author: (with others) Semiconductor Controlled Rectifiers, 1964. Served with U.S. Army, 1955-57. Recipient Cordiner award Gen. Electric Co., 1962, John Scott medal City of Phila., 1975, GaAs Conf. award, 1976. Fellow Am. Phys. Soc., IEEE (Morris Liebmann prize 1973, Jack A. Morton award 1981); mem. Electrochem. Soc. (Solid State Sci. and Tech. award 1983), Math. Assn. Am., AAAS, Nat. Acad. Engring. Home: 2212 Fletcher St Urbana IL 61801 Office: Dept Elec Engring U Ill Urbana IL 61801

HOLOWENKO, ALFRED RICHARD, mech. engr.; b. Boston, Dec. 10, 1916; s. Adam Joseph and Nellie (Krause) H.; m. Virginia Verner Irwin, June 16, 1944; children—Richard Irwin, Robbin Diane. A.B. cum laude, Harvard U., 1938, M.S., 1939. Registered profl. engr., Tex. Mech. engr. Westinghouse Electric Corp., East Pittsburgh, Pa., 1939-42; asst. prof. mech. engring. U. Pitts., 1942-44; instr. Rice Inst., Houston, 1944-46; prof. mech. engring. Purdue U., West Lafayette, Ind., 1946—; cons. Author: Dynamics of Machinery, 1955, (with Hall and Laughlin) Theory and Problems of Machine Design, 1961. Recipient Harry L. Solberg Best Tchr. award Sch. Mech. Engring., Purdue U., 1975. Mem. Am. Soc. Engring. Edn., ASME, Pi Tau Sigma (hon.). Home: 300 Chippewa St West Lafayette IN 47906 Office: Sch Mech Engring Purdue U West Lafayette IN 47907

HOLQUIST, JAMES MICHAEL, Russian literature educator; b. Rockford, Ill., Dec. 20, 1935; s. Leonard and Billye Alberta (Applebye) H.; m. Lydia Landis, July 30, 1960 (div. Dec. 1972); children: Peter Isaac, Benjamin Michael, Joshua Applebye; m. Katerina Clark, Apr. 15, 1974; children: Nicholas Manning, Sebastian. B.A. with highest honors, U. Ill., 1963; Ph.D., Yale U., 1968. Asst. prof. Yale U., New Haven, 1968-72, assoc. prof., 1972-75; assoc. prof., dept. chmn. U. Tex., Austin, 1976-78, prof., 1978-80; prof. Slavic langs. and lit. dept., chmn. Ind. U., Bloomington, 1981—; Tory disting. vis. prof. U. Alta., 1983. Author: (with Kernan and Brooks) Man and His Fictions, 1973, Dostoevsky and the Novel, 1977; editor: (co-translator) The Dialogic Imagination: Four Essays by M.M. Bakhtin, 1981; editor-in-chief: Tex. Slavic Studies, 1980; co-editor: Ind. Soviet Studies, 1982; editorial bd.: Yearbook of Comparative and Gen. Lit., 1982, Slavic Rev., 1983; mem. adv. bd., PMLA. Served with U.S. Army, 1958-61. Rockefeller Humanities fellow, 1983; vis. scholar Phi Beta Kappa, 1984-85; fellow Soviet Acad. Scis., 1983; grantee NEH, 1979; Morse fellow Yale U., 1970. Mem. Am. Assn. Advancement Slavic Studies, Internat. Bakhtin Soc. (editor newsletter 1982—), Internat. Dostoevsky Soc., MLA, Am. Assn. Tchrs. Slavic and East European Langs. Democrat. Club: Grotesques (New Haven). Home: 1248 E Wylie St Bloomington IN 47401 Office: Slavic Langs and Lits Dept Ind U Ballantine Hall 502 Bloomington IN 47405

HOLROYD, LOUIS VINCENT, educator; b. Vancouver, C., Can., Jan. 22, 1925; came to U.S., 1950; s. Ernest George and Lalita Ann (Eva) H.; m. Helene Marie Laberge, May 20, 1950; children—Barbara Jane, John Edward, George Walter, Suzanne Marie. B.A., U. B.C., 1945, M.A., 1947; Ph.D., U. Notre Dame, 1950. Mem. faculty U. Mo., 1950—, prof. physics, 1965—, chmn. dept., 1956-74, safety coordinator, 1978—. Author: Physics Laboratory Manual, 1965. Mem. Columbia Cath. Sch. Bd., 1973-75; commr. Great Rivers council Boy Scouts Am., 1967—; pres. Parish Council, 1969-72; v.p. Columbia Cath. Sch. Bd., 1970-72; chmn. Mo. Legis. Hazardous Waste Task Force, 1981-82. Served to 2d lt., Signal Corps Canadian Army, 1944-45. Recipient Centennial of Sci. award U. Notre Dame, 1966. Mem. Am. Inst. Physics, Am. Assn. Physics Tchrs., Mo. Catholic Conf., Sigma Xi. Home: 400 Blair Ct Columbia MO 65201

HOLSCHUH, JOHN DAVID, judge; b. Ironton, Ohio, Oct. 12, 1926; s. Edward A. and Helen (Ebert) H.; m. Carol Stouder, Aug. 13, 1927; 1 son, John David. B.A., Miami U., 1948; J.D., U. Cin., 1951. Bar: Ohio bar 1951. Law clk. U.S. Dist. Ct. judge, 1952-54; mem. firm Alexander, Ebinger, Holschuh, Fisher & McAlister, Columbus, Ohio, 1954-80; judge U.S. Dist. Ct. for so. dist. Ohio, 1980—; adj. prof. law Coll. Law, Ohio State U., 1970; Chmn. bd. commrs. on character and fitness Supreme Ct. of Ohio. Pres. bd. dirs. Neighborhood House, 1969-70. Fellow Am. Coll. Trial Lawyers; mem. Nat. Assn. R.R. Trial Counsel (exec. com.), Order of Coif, Phi Beta Kappa, Omicron Delta Kappa. Home: 2630 Charing Rd Columbus OH 43221 Office: 85 Marconi Blvd Columbus OH 43215

HOLSEN, ROBERT CHARLES, accountant; b. Manitowoc, Wis., Nov. 10, 1913; s. Herman J. and Lilly (Krumm) H.; m. Constance Weber, Nov. 18, 1938; children: Robert Charles, Catherine Jane. Ph.B., U. Wis., 1938. C.P.A., Wis. Staff accountant Ernst & Ernst, Chgo., 1938-56, partner, 1956-62, 1962-76, cons., 1976—. Served to lt. comdr. USNR, 1944-46. Mem. Am. Inst. C.P.A.s (com. on auditing procedure, spl. com. on quality control, spl. com. on equity funding), Ohio Soc. C.P.A.s. Club: Masons. Home: 182 Valley Forge Nashville TN 37205 Office: 2000 One Commerce Pl Nashville TN 37239

HOLSHOUSER, DON FRANKLIN, educator; b. Dwight, Kans., Mar. 23, 1920; s. John Frederick and Lillian (Nordeen) H.; m. Marion Delores Stankus, May 19, 1943; children—Judy (Mrs. Hernan Tizon), Donna (Mrs. William Stinson), Eric. B.S., Kans. State Coll., 1942; M.S., U. Ill., 1950, Ph.D., 1958. Devel. engr. RCA, Lancaster, Pa., 1942-46; research asso. elec. engring. dept. U. Ill., Urbana, 1946-51, asst. prof., 1951-58, research dir., 1958—, prof., 1965—; cons. Hallicrafters Co., 1961-66. Recipient Air Force research grants, 1959-71. Fellow AAAS; mem. IEEE, Sigma Xi, Eta Kappa Nu, Sigma Tau. Home: Rural Route 5 Two Lights Rd Cape Elizabeth ME 04107

HOLSINGER, GEORGE ROBERT, JR., journalism educator; b. Youngstown, Ohio, May 1, 1925; s. George R. and Saidee (Gibson) H.; m. Linda J. Thompson, Jan. 11, 1973; children: Sarah Anne, Paul, Sue, Lise, Jonathan. B.S., Ohio State U., 1947, M.A., 1948, Ph.D., 1952. News dir. sta. WOSU Radio, Ohio State U., 1951-52, asst. program supr., 1952-56; program dir. WOSU-TV, 1956-58; asst. dean Coll. Arts and Scis., Ohio State U., 1958-61, dean part-time and continuing edn., 1961-66, exec. asst. to the pres., 1966-68, asst. v.p. acad. affairs, 1968-69, sec. univ. faculty and faculty council, 1961-68, prof., 1979—, acting dir., 1978-79. Mem. bd. edn., Worthington, Ohio, 1960-70; chmn. citizens adv. com. on adult edn. Ohio Bd. Edn.; Trustee Blue Cross of Central Ohio. Mem. Am. Film Inst., Assn. for Edn. in Journalism, Assn. for Popular Culture, Sigma Delta Chi,

Sigma Phi Epsilon. Roman Catholic. Home: 3535 Chowning Ct Columbus OH 43220

HOLSINGER, WAYNE TOWNSEND, retail chain executive; b. Trafford, Pa., Apr. 9, 1931; s. John Calvin and Cora Irene (Brethauer) H.; m. Marilyn Kay Wynn, May 25, 1957; 1 dau., Deborah Kay. B.S. in Edn., U. S.W. Mo., 1958. With Sears, Roebuck & Co., 1956—, v.p. women's apparel and accessories, 1976-81, v.p. wearing apparel, 1981—. Dir. Chgo. Boys Club, 1968-80. Served with USN, 1950-54. Mem. Men's Fashion Assn., Father's Day Council. Republican. Mem. Ch. of Christ. Home: 9 Hunt Club Ln Oakbrook IL 60521 Office: Sears Tower Chicago IL 60684

HOLSTEAD, JOHN BURNHAM, lawyer; b. Dallas, Mar. 5, 1938; s. J.B. and Maurice (Cook) H.; m. Marilyn Morris, Mar. 4, 1940; children: Will, Rand, Scott. B.A., La. Inst. Tech., 1959; LL.B., U. Tex.-Austin, 1962. Bar: Tex. 1962, U.S. Dist. Ct. (so. dist.) Tex. 1973, U.S. Dist. Ct. (no. dist.) Tex. 1965, Ala. 1969, Colo. 1981, U.S. Ct. Apls. (5th cir.) 1969, U.S. Ct. Apls. (10th cir.) 1981. Briefing clk. Tex. Sup. Ct., 1962-63; assoc. Culton, Morgan, Britain & White, Amarillo, Tex., 1963-65, Vinson & Elkins, Houston, 1965-72, ptnr., 1972—; speaker civil litigation and bus. disputes. Mem. ABA, Tex. Bar Assn., Houston Bar Assn. Episcopalian. Clubs: Ramada, River Oaks Country. Office: 3228 First City Tower Houston TX 77002

HOLSTEIN, PETER LAWRENCE, financier; b. Hartford, Conn., Aug. 31, 1942; s. Harold William and Ruth H.; m. Harriet Higdon, Sept. 7, 1968; children: Victoria, Alexander, Nicholas, Catherine. Diplome, U. Geneva, 1962. Assoc. Hallgarten & Co., N.Y.C., 1965-68; gen. partner Frederick & Co., N.Y.C., 1968-72; sr. v.p. Fiduciary Trust Co., N.Y.C., 1972-82; pres. Holstein & Co., 1983—. Served with U.S. Army, 1963-65. Fellow Fin. Analysts Fedn., N.Y. Soc. Security Analysts, Internat. Assn. Energy Economists, Oil Analysts Group of N.Y.; Mem. Nat. Assn. Petroleum Investment Analysts (dir.). Home: 353 Dendke Ridge New Canaan CT 06840 Office: Three Landmark Sq Stamford CT 06901

HOLSTEIN, THEODORE DAVID, physics educator; b. N.Y.C., Sept. 18, 1915; s. Samuel and Ethel (Stein) H.; m. Beverlee Ruth Roth, Aug. 31, 1945; children: Lonna Beth Holstein Smith, Stuart Alexander. B.S. cum laude, N.Y. U., 1935; M.S., Columbia U., 1936; Ph.D., NYU, 1940. Instr. CCNY, 1940; research physicist Westinghouse Research Lab., Pitts., 1941-60; prof. U. Pitts., 1960-65, UCLA, 1965—. Author articles on solid-state theory. Fellow Am. Acad. Arts and Scis.; mem. Nat. Acad. Sci., Am. Phys. Soc. Jewish. Office: UCLA Dept Physics Los Angeles CA 90024 *

HOLSTEIN, WILLIAM KURT, business administration educator; b. Stamford, Conn., Nov. 19, 1936; s. Kurt Edward and Doris Christiana (Werner) H.; m. Audrey Louise Bedford, Aug. 15, 1959; children: Kurt Edward II, William Kurt Jr., Catherine Louise. B.Chem. Engring., Rensselaer Poly. Inst., Troy, N.Y., 1958; M.S. in Indsl. Mgmt, Purdue U., 1959; Ph.D. in Econs, Purdue U., 1964. Instr., then asst. prof. indsl. mgmt. Purdue U., 1959-64; asst. prof., then asso. prof. Harvard U. Grad. Sch. Bus. Adminstrn., 1964-72; prof., dean Sch. Bus., SUNY, Albany, 1972-81, prof., 1981—; vis. prof. IMEDE, Lausanne, Switzerland, 1983-84; dir. exec. devel. programs in Singapore, Taiwan and Central Am., 1969—, cons. to industry. Co-author: Production Planning and Control, 1963, Casebooks in Production Management, 1968; author articles in field. Trustee Upsala Coll., 1969-72; mem. accreditation com., editorial adv. com., visitation teams Am. Assembly of Collegiate Schs. of Bus., 1972—; mem. exec. com. Middle Atlantic Assn. Schs. Bus. Adminstrn., 1976-81, pres., 1980; bd. dirs. Albany Symphony Orch., 1976—, Parson's Child and Family Center, Albany, 1977—; now v.p. and treas. Parson's Child and Family Center; chmn. Metro 2000 Project, 1979; mem. com. on computer-aided mfg. Nat. Acad. Scis., 1980—. Mem. Inst. Mgmt. Scis., Am. Prodn. and Inventory Control Soc., Delta Sigma Pi, Beta Gamma Sigma. Lutheran. Home: 10 Chestnut Hill N Loudonville NY 12211 Office: Sch Business State Univ NY at Albany Albany NY 12222

HOLSTI, KALEVI JACQUE, political scientist, educator; b. Geneva, Apr. 25, 1935; s. Rudolf Woldemar and Liisa Anniki (Franssila) H.; m. Mina E. Machado, June 24, 1972; children: Liisa, Matthew, Karina. B.A., Stanford U., 1956, M.A., 1958, Ph.D., 1961. Mem. faculty U. B.C., Vancouver, 1961—, now prof. polit. sci., head dept.; vis. prof. McGill U., Montreal, Que., 1972-73, Kyoto (Japan) U., 1977, Hebrew U., Jerusalem, 1978; vis. fellow Australian Nat. U., 1983; cons. in field. Author: International Politics: A Framework for Analysis, 4th edit, 1982, Why Nations Realign, 1982; Editor: Internat. Studies Quar, 1970-75; co-editor: Can. Jour. Polit. Sci, 1978-81. Fulbright scholar, 1959-60; Can. Council leave fellow, 1967, 72, 78. Fellow Royal Soc. Can.; Mem. Internat. Studies Assn., Can. Polit. Sci. Assn., World Assn. Internat. Relations. Office: Dept Polit Sci U BC Vancouver Canada V6T 1W5

HOLSTI, OLE RUDOLF, political scientist, educator; b. Geneva, Aug. 7, 1933; U.S., 1940, naturalized, 1954; s. Rudolf Waldemar and Liisa (Franssila) H.; m. Ann Wood, Sept. 20, 1953; children: Eric Lynn, Maija. B.A. with highest honors, Stanford U., 1954, Ph.D., 1962; M.A.T., Wesleyan U., Middletown, Conn., 1956. Asst. prof. Stanford U., 1962-67; asso. prof. U. B.C., Vancouver, Can., 1967-71, prof., 1971-74; George V. Allen prof. polit. sci. Duke U., 1974—, chmn. dept. polit. sci., 1977—; fellow Center for Advanced Study in Behavioral Scis., Stanford, Calif., 1972-73. Author: Enemies in Politics, 1967, Analysis of Communication Content, 1969, Content Analysis for Social Sciences and Humanities, 1969, Crisis, Escalation, War, 1972, Unity and Disintegration in International Alliances, 1973, Vietnam, Consensus and the Belief Systems of American Leaders, 1977, Change in the International System, 1980, American Leadership in World Affairs: Vietnam and the Breakdown of Consensus, 1984; contbg. author: numerous books including International Crises, 1972, Political Science Annual, 1975, Thought and Action in Foreign Policy, 1975, The Behavior of Nations, 1976, World Politics, 1976; editor: Internat. Studies Quar., 1970-75; contbr. numerous articles to profl. jours. Served with AUS, 1956-58. Gen. Electric Found. Research fellow, 1960-61; Haynes Found. Research fellow, 1961-62; Can. Council grantee, 1970-71; Ford Found. Research fellow, 1972-73; NSF grantee, 1975-77, 79-81, 83-85; Guggenheim fellow, 1981—. Mem. Internat. Studies Assn. (pres. region 1969-70, 75-77, pres. 1979-80), Internat. Inst. Strategic Studies, Am. Polit. Sci. Assn. (council 1982—), Can. Polit. Sci. Assn., Western Polit. Sci. Assn. (Best Dissertation award 1964), Phi Beta Kappa. Clubs: Duke Faculty, Duke Master Runners, Carolina Godiva Track, Fleet Feet Running. Home: 608 Croom Ct Chapel Hill NC 27514

HOLSTROM, CARLETON ARTHUR, financial executive; b. Appleton, Wis., Aug. 18, 1935; s. Carl W. and Nettie O. (Casterton) H.; m. Evan Grant Cameron, June 29, 1957 (div. 1977); children: Christina, Marcia, Cynthia; m. Marianne Blanche Saks, Sept. 30, 1978. B.S., U. Wis., 1957; M.A., Rutgers U., 1962. Asst. v.p. Irving Trust Co., N.Y.C., 1962-66, Bank of Commonwealth, Detroit, 1966-69, Bear, Stearns & Co., N.Y.C., 1969-73; ptnr. Bear, Stearns & Co, N.Y.C., 1973—. Bd. overseers Rutgers U. Found., New Brunswick, 1975—; trustees New Lincoln Sch., N.Y.C. Served to lt. USNR, 1957-61. Clubs: Ht. Casino (Bklyn.); Plandome Country (Manhasset, N.Y.). Home: 420 E 54th St New York NY 10222 Office: Bear Stearns & Co 55 Water St New York NY 10041

HOLT, CHARLES CARTER, economist, educator; b. Jennings, La., May 21, 1921; s. Milton Carter and Edith Grey (Pope) H.; children: Kathryn Wendy, Dorothea Susan, Steven Anthony. B.S., MIT, 1944, M.S. in Elec. Engring., 1944; M.A., U. Chgo., 1950, Ph.D. in Econs., 1955. Automatic control engr. MIT Servomechanisms Lab, 1943-47; sr. research fellow econs. dept. and Grad. Sch. Indsl. Adminstrn., Carnegie Inst. Tech., 1951-53, asst. prof., 1953-56, asso. prof., 1956-61; vis. mem. London Sch. Econs., 1958-60; prof. econs. U. Wis., 1961-68; chmn. Social Systems Research Inst., 1965-68; dir., sr. research economist Inflation and Unemployment Research Urban Inst., Washington, 1968-77; prof. mgmt. dept., dir. Bur. Bus. Research, U. Tex., Austin, 1977—; cons. Brookings Instn.; mem. rev. panel NSF; advisor Com. for Econ. Devel., 1975—. Author: (with F. Modigliani, John F. Muth, Herbert A. Simon) Planning, Production, Inventories and Work Force, 1960, (with others) Program STIMULATE, A User's Programmer's Manual, 1965, The Unemployment-Inflation Dilemma: A Manpower Solution, 1971; contbr. articles to profl. jours. Ford Found. grantee, 1958-60. Fellow Econometric Soc.; mem. Am. Econ. Assn., Inst. Mgmt. Sci., Assn. Computing Machinery, Indsl. Relations Research Assn., Sigma Xi. Unitarian. Home: PO Box 5748 Austin TX 78763 Office: Dept Mgmt Univ Tex Austin TX 78712

HOLT, DAVID EARL, librarian; b. Magna, Utah, May, 17, 1928; s. William Renold and Jenny (Kerr) H.; m. Mary Elizabeth Black, Apr. 30, 1955; children—Helen Lorraine, Jane Elizabeth, David Renold (dec.), Steven Earl. Student, U. Utah, 1946-47, 52-54, 58-59; B.A., Brigham Young U., 1957, M.A., 1958; M.S., Emory U., 1963. Library dir. Hayner Pub. Library, Alton, Ill., 1963-65; dir. libraries Waco-McLennan County Library, Waco, Tex., 1965-67; dir. Austin (Tex.) Pub. Library, 1967—; book editor Austin Am.-Statesman, 1967-69; staff Library/U.S.A. Exhibit, Fed. Pavilion, New York Worlds Fair, 1965; tchr. library adminstrn. Baylor U., 1966; columnist Waco Herald-Tribune, 1967. Trombonist, Sonny Dunham Orch., Tony Pastor Orch., Glenn Gray Orch., Gene Krupa Orch., Tex Beneke Orch., 1947-52; trombonist, arranger, Tommy Dorsey Orch., 1954-55; Editor: Waco Rotary Club Bull, 1966-67; Contbr. articles profl. jours. Mem. Am., Tex., S.W. library assns. Mem. Ch. of Jesus Christ of Latter-day Saints. Club: Rotarian. Address: 1802 Forest Trail Austin TX 78703

HOLT, DONALD DALE, editor; b. Chgo., Mar. 31, 1936; s. Edward Joseph and Elsie Edith (Matthies) H.; m. Lolita Saranne Larson, Aug. 15, 1959; children: Lisa, Bradley, Dawn, Courtney. B.A., Wheaton (Ill.) Coll., 1957; postgrad., U. Chgo., 1960-61, Roosevelt U., 1963-64. Reporter, asso. editor Press Publs., Elmhurst, Ill., 1958-61; reporter Chgo. Daily News, 1961-64; corr. Newsweek mag., N.Y.C., 1964-66, Chgo. Bur. chief, 1966-71, news editor, 1971-75, mng. editor internat. edit., 1975-77, sr. editor, 1977-79; bd. editors Fortune mag., 1979-81, internat. editor, 1981—. Author: The Justice Machine, 1972. Served as 1st lt. AUS, 1958. Recipient Robert F. Kennedy Journalism award, 1971, Gavel award Am. Bar Assn., 1972, Page One award New York Newspaper Guild, 1972. Office: Time and Life Bldg Rockefeller Center New York NY 10020

HOLT, DONALD EDWARD, JR., business executive; b. Waterloo, Iowa, July 30, 1945; s. Donald E. and Lucille P. (Queroli) H.; m. Julie A. Coats, Apr. 20, 1968; children: Carolyn, Suzanne, Elizabeth. B.S., Creighton U., 1967. Supervising sr. accountant Peat, Marwick, Mitchell & Co., Omaha, 1969-73; asst. controller Fairmont Foods Co., Omaha, 1973-75; controller (Abbotts Dairies div.), Phila., 1975-77, adminstrv. asst. dairy group, Des Plaines, Ill., 1977-78, dir. planning, 1978-79, v.p., gen. mgr., 1979-83; v.p. fin./controller Pennbrook Corp., Phila., 1983—; Trustee Dairy Pension and Welfare Funds. Served with U.S. Army, 1967-69. Mem. Am. Inst. C.P.A.s, Nebr. Soc. C.P.A.s. Home: 684 Franklin Place Mount Laurel NJ 08054 Office: Pennbrook Corp Darien St and Pattison Ave Philadelphia PA 19148

HOLT, DOUGLAS EUGENE, business executive, mechanical engineer; b. Milw., Aug. 12, 1924; s. Frank E. and Eleanor (Hansen) H.; m. Carol J. Filter, July 10, 1948; children: Barbara L. Holt Pomorski, Carol Ann. B.S.M.E. with honors, U. Wis., 1949; postgrad., U. Wis.-Milw., 1950-60. Registered prof. engr., Wis., 1954. Design engr. The Heil Co., Milw., 1949-54; chief engr. Indsl. Engring. Inst., Milw., 1954-56; engr., chief engr., dir. engring. Harnischfeger Corp., Milw., 1956-58, v.p. indsl. div., 1968-73, gen. mgr. handling systems, 1973-81, sr. v.p., 1981—. Patentee in field. Served to 1st lt. USAAF, 1943-45; ETO. Decorated D.F.C., Air Medal with 3 oak leaf clusters. Mem. Pi Tau Sigma, Tau Beta Pi. Office: Harnischfeger Corp 13400 Bishops Ln Brookfield WI 53005

HOLT, IVAN LEE, JR., former judge; b. Marshall, Mo., May 4, 1913; s. Ivan Lee and Leland (Burks) H.; m. Mary Edwards Depping, Dec. 26, 1945; children: Mary Diana Holt Hoxie, Janet Mildred Depping Holt Resnik, Ivan Lee III. Student, Princeton U., 1931-34; A.B., U. Chgo., 1935, J.D., 1937; LL.D., McKendree Coll., 1962; D.C.L., Central Meth. Coll., 1983. Bar: Mo. 1937. Asso. Marion C. Early, St. Louis, 1937-40; asst. circuit atty., City of St. Louis, 1940-42; asst. prof. law Washington U. Law Sch., St. Louis, 1947-48; asso. Jones, Hocker, Gladney & Grand, St. Louis, 1948-49; judge 22d Circuit Mo., 1949-83; spl. judge Supreme Ct. Mo., Mo. Ct. Appeals Eastern Dist.; mem. faculty Nat. Coll. State Trial Judges, 1967-70; mem. council judges Nat. Council on Crime and Delinquency, 1953-74, exec. com., 1970-73, chmn., 1973-74; mem. Nat. Conf. State Trial Judges, 1967-84, Mo. Commn. on Retirement, Removal and Discipline, 1972-82; mem. vis. com. Law Sch., U. Chgo., 1975-78; mem. Am. Judicature Soc., 1952-83, dir., 1962-64. Contbr. articles profl. publs. Bd. dirs. Barnes Hosp., Goodwill Industries, 1952-82, Mo. Hist. Soc., 1972-78, Methodist Children's Home Mo., 1948-74; pres. Methodist Children's Home Mo., 1952-62. Served from lt. (j.g.) to comdr. USNR, 1942-46. Fellow Inst. Jud. Adminstrn., 1966-70. Mem. Mo. Bar Assn. (del. 1957-64, 67-70), ABA (council sect. jud. adminstrn. 1955-62, chmn. jud. adminstrn. 1962-63, ho. of dels. 1963-66, mem. spl. coms. standards criminal justice and standards jud. conduct), St. Louis Bar Assn., Mo. Bar, Lawyers Assn. St. Louis (life), Am. Law Inst. (life), Law Library Assn. (mem. bd. 1962-72, pres. 1972-82), SR, Sigma Alpha Epsilon, Phi Delta Phi. Democrat. Methodist (jud. council 1956-60). Clubs: Univ., Pike County Country, Masons. Home: Box 165 Route 1 Louisiana MO 63353

HOLT, JOHN B., theologian; b. Abilene, Tex., June 15, 1915; s. Holl and Emma Cleora (Morriset) H.; m. Margaret Ann Buster, Feb. 14, 1940; children: John Michael, Stephen Lee, Paul Holland. B.S., McMurry Coll., 1937, D.D. (hon.), 1954; postgrad., U. Tex., 1938-39, U. Chgo., 1958; M.Th., So. Meth. U., 1945; D.D. (hon.), Paul Quinn Coll., 1962. Youth dir. Central Tex. Conf., United Meth. Ch., 1941-43; ordained to ministry United Meth. Ch., 1944; exec. sec. (Bd. Edn.), 1944-46; assoc. pastor Austin Ave. Meth. Ch., Waco, Tex., 1946-48; pastor Knox Ch., Manila, 1948-58; assoc. dean Perkins Sch. Theology, So. Meth. U., Dallas, 1958-82; sec. Gen. Conf. United Meth. Ch., 1973—. Author: Our Methodist Heritage, 1952, A Study Guide for the Book of Acts, 1956, Financial Aid for Seminarians, 1966; Editor: Perkins Perspective, 1958-72; Contbr. articles to mags. and jours. Trustee Mary Johnston Hosp., Union Theol. Sem., Am. Bible Soc., Philippine Christian Coll. Clubs: Kiwanis, Masons. Home: 3420 Centenary Dr Dallas TX 75225 Office: Perkins Sch Theology So Meth U Dallas TX 75222 *I never cease to marvel at the physical, spiritual and emotional possibilities offered in human life. To work and serve and love and play in a spirit of gratitude to the Infinite Power behind it all adds zest and meaning.*

HOLT, LEON CONRAD, JR., business executive, lawyer; b. Reading, Pa., June 19, 1925; s. Leon Conrad and Elizabeth (Bright) H.; m. June M. Weidner, June 30, 1947; children: Deborah Holt Weil, Richard W. B.S. cum laude in Metall. Engring, Lehigh U., 1948; LL.B., U. Pa., 1951. Bar: N.Y. 1952. With firm Mudge, Stern Williams & Tucker (attys.), N.Y.C., 1951-53; atty. Am. Oil Co. (and predecessor co.), N.Y.C., 1953-57; gen. atty. Air Products & Chems., Inc., Allentown, Pa., 1957-61, v.p., 1961-76, v.p. adminstrn., 1976-78, gen. counsel, 1961-78, vice chmn. bd., chief adminstrv. officer, 1978—, also dir., mem. exec., finance, pub. policy coms.; dir. VF Corp. Vice chmn. Lehigh Centennial Fund, 1964-65; chmn. Allentown Bd. Ethics, 1970-74; bd. dirs. Lehigh County United Fund, 1971—, mem. exec. com., 1971-74, campaign chmn., 1972; Bd. dirs. Allentown YMCA, 1965-69, trustee, 1972-79; trustee Allentown Art Mus., Com. Econ. Devel.; mem. Allentown Sch. Dist. Authority; mem. exec. com. Machinery and Allied Products Inst.; mem. adv. bd. U. Pa. Inst. Law and Econs.; trustee Dorothy Rider Pool Health Care Trust. Served to lt. (j.g.) USNR, 1943-46. Mem. Allentown C. of C. (gov. 1965-68), ABA, Assn. Bar N.Y.C., Pa. Soc., Tunkhannock Creek Assn., Alpha Tau Omega. Republican. Episcopalian. Club: Lehigh Country (Allentown) (bd. govs. 1970-77). Home: 3003 Parkway Blvd Allentown PA 18104 Pocono Lake Preserve PA 18348 Office: PO Box 538 Allentown PA 18105

HOLT, LLOYD EUGENE, foundation executive; b. Mitchell, Ind., Nov. 13, 1928; s. Samuel Eugene and Evelyn Juanita (Prow) H.; m. Cornelia Ann Polasky, Jan. 1, 1974; children: Jennifer Lynn, Lisa Ann. B.S. in Acctg, Ind. U., 1956. Portfolio mgr. Upjohn Co., Kalamazoo, 1956-69; treas., v.p. for fin. W.K. Kellogg Found., Battle Creek, Mich., 1969—. Dir. Franklin Community Hosp., Vicksburg, Mich. Served with U.S. Army, 1950-52. Mem. Nat. Assn. Accts., Council on Founds., Inc., Battle Creek C. of C. Club: Rotary (pres. Battle Creek). Office: 400 North Ave Battle Creek MI 49016

HOLT, MARJORIE SEWELL, congresswoman; b. Birmingham, Ala., Sept. 17, 1920; d. Edward Rol and Juanita (Felts) Sewell; m. Duncan McKay Holt, Dec. 26, 1946; children: Rachel (Mrs. Kenneth Hall Tschantre), Edward, Victoria (Mrs. James Lee Stauffer). Grad., Jacksonville U., 1945; J.D., U. Fla., 1949. Bar: Fla. 1949, Md. 1962. Practiced in, Annapolis, Md., 1962; clk. Anne Arundel County Circuit Ct., Annapolis, 1966-72; mem. 93d-98th congresses from 4th Dist. of Md.; mem. armed services com.; vice chmn. Office Tech. Assessment, 1977; chmn. Republican Study com., 1975-76; Supr. elections Anne Arundel County, 1963-65; del. to Rep. Nat. Conv., 1968, 76. Co-author: Case Against The Reckless Congress, 1976, Can You Afford This House, 1978. Recipient; Distinguished Alumna award U. Fla., 1975. Mem. Am., Md., Anne Arundel bar assns., Phi Kappa Phi, Phi Delta Delta. Presbyterian (elder 1959). Office: 2412 Rayburn House Office Bldg Washington DC 20515 *

HOLT, NANCY LOUISE, artist; b. Worcester, Mass., Apr. 5, 1938; d. Ernest Milton and E. Louise (Jellicoe) H.; m. Robert I. Smithson, June 8, 1963 (dec. 1973). B.S., Jackson Coll., Tufts U., 1960. Vis. artist U. R.I., U. Mont.; lectr., Priceton., N.Y. Author: Ransacked, 1980; One-woman shows, Art Gallery, U. Mont., 1972, Art Center, U. R.I., Kingston, LoGiudice Gallery, N.Y.C., 1973, Bykert Gallery, N.Y.C., 1974, Walter Kelly Gallery, Chgo., Franklin Furnace, N.Y., 1977, Whitney Mus. Young Am. Filmmakers Series, N.Y.C., John Weber Gallery, N.Y.C., 1979, 82; sculpture commns. include Inside Out, Washington, 1980, Star-Crossed, Miami U., Oxford, Ohio, 1979-81, Wild Spot, Ann. Ring, Saginaw, Mich., 1981, Catch Basin, Toronto, Ont., Can., 1982, Sole Source, Dublin, Ireland, 1983, Time Span, Laguna Gloria Art Mus., Austin, Tex.; films include Swamp, 1971, Pine Barrens, 1975, Sun Tunnels, 1978. CAPS grantee, 1975, 78; Guggenheim fellow, 1978; Nat. Endowment for Arts fellow, 1975, 78; WNET Artist in Residence grantee, 1977; Beard's Fund Inc., grantee, 1977. Home: 799 Greenwich St New York NY 10014

HOLT, PATRICIA LESTER, book review editor; b. Corona del Mar, Calif., Jan. 18, 1944; d. George William and Leah Beryl (Lester) H. B.A., U. Oreg., 1965. Publicity mgr. Houghton Mifflin Co., N.Y.C. and Boston, 1969-71; sr. editor San Francisco Book Co., San Francisco, 1971-77; western corr. Publishers Weekly, N.Y.C., 1977-82; book rev. editor San Francisco Chronicle, 1982—. Named Woman of Yr. Women's Nat. Book Assn., San Franisco chpt., 1982; recipient Ann. Hilly award No. Calif. Publs. Assn., 1983. Office: San Francisco Chronicle 901 Mission St San Francisco CA 94119

HOLT, PETER ROLF, physician, educator; b. Berlin, Sept. 8, 1930; s. Arthur and Ruth H.; m. Joyce Weil, May 15, 1979; children: Rachel Janna, Enid Harper, Shawn David, Tamara Naomi. B.Sc., U. London, 1949, M.B., B.S. with honors, 1954. Intern London Hosp., 1954-55; asst. resident in medicine St. Luke's Hosp. Center, N.Y.C., 1957-59; tng. fellow in medicine Mass. Gen. Hosp., Boston, 1959-61; chief gastroenterology med. Service St. Luke's Hosp. Center, N.Y.C., 1961—, attending physician, 1971—; assoc. attending physician Presbyn. Hosp., N.Y.C., 1976—; research collaborator Brookhaven Nat. Lab., Upton, N.Y., 1973-79; mem. faculty dept. medicine Coll. Physicians and Surgeons, Columbia U., N.Y.C., 1961—, prof., 1975—; mem. Bio-engring. Inst., Columbia U., 1975—, Inst. Human Nutrition, 1978—; mem. 12th work group on clin. research Nat. Commn. on Digestive Disease, 1977-79; mem. nat. sci. adv. com., nat. rev. com. Nat. Found. for Ileitis and Colitis, 1976—. Contbr. chpts. to books, articles to med. jours. Served to maj. Brit. Royal Army M.C., 1955-57. NIH grantee.; Recipient William H. Rorer award in Gastroenterology, 1965. Fellow A.C.P. (gov.'s com. 1978—); mem. N.Y. Gastroent. Soc. (pres. 1971-72), Am. Gastroent. Assn. (chmn. com. research 1973-74, chmn. com. on aging, mem. admissions com.), Intersoc. Com. Clin. Investigation in Digestive Disease (chmn. 1975-79), Am. Assn. Study of Liver Diseases, AAAS, Am. Fedn. Clin. Research, Am. Physiol. Soc., Am. Soc. Clin. Investigation, Am. Soc. Clin. Nutrition, Am. Soc. Parenteral and Enteral Nutrition, Eastern Gut Club, N.Y. Acad. Scis., N.Y.C. Lipid Research Club, Harvey Soc., St. George's Soc. Office: St Luke's Roosevelt Hosp Center 114th St and Amsterdam Ave New York NY 10025

HOLT, RALPH MANNING, JR., hosiery mill executive; b. Burlington, N.C., Sept. 7, 1931; s. Ralph Manning and Margaret (McElwee) H.; m. Eda Luciana Contiguglia, June 3, 1957; children: Ralph Manning III, Margaret Berrena, John Anthony, Michael McElwee. B.S., Davidson Coll., 1953; postgrad., Harvard Bus. Sch., 1956-57. With Holt Hosiery Mills, Inc., Burlington, 1957—, v.p., 1958-66, treas., 1959—, exec. v.p., 1966-67, pres., 1967—; v.p., treas. Holt Hosiery Corp., N.Y.C., 1959-69; dir., sec.-treas. Carolina Paper Box Co., Burlington, 1964—; dir., treas. Packrite Packaging Inc., High Point, N.C., 1974—; dir. Leath, McCarthy & Maynard, Sun Tex Corp., High Point, Burlington div. Wachovia Bank & Trust Co., N.A. Bd. dirs. Burlington United Way, YMCA, Burlington, Burlington Day Sch.; mem. pres.'s bd. advisers Elon Coll.; pres. Cherokee council Boy Scouts Am., 1975-76; chmn. bd. trustees Meml. Hosp., Burlington; past trustee St. Andrews Coll., Laurinburg, N.C.; bd. visitors

Davidson Coll. Served to lt. (j.g.) USNR, 1953-55. Mem. Nat. Assn. Hosiery Mfrs. (dir. 1978—, treas. 1979—, mem., 1st v.p. 1983-84, chmn. 1984-85); Mem. Beta Theta Pi. Club: N.Y. Athletic. Office: Box 819 Burlington NC 27215

HOLT, ROBERT LEROI, educator; b. Dixie, Ga., Jan. 1, 1920; s. John Gordon and Willie (Grimes) H.; m. Claire Rebecca Hardin, June 3, 1943; children—James Lawrence, Claire Rebecca, Susan Elaine. A.A., Mars Hill (N.C.) Jr. Coll., 1941; A.B., Wake Forest Coll., 1943, M.A., 1946; Ph.D., Duke, 1951. Ordained to ministry Bapt. Ch., 1942; minister various chs., 1941-50; dir. religious activities East Carolina U., Greenville, N.C., 1950-53, registrar, dir. admissions, 1958-60, dean, 1960-64, v.p., dean of univ., 1964-76, vice chancellor for adminstrn. and planning, 1976-79, prof. philosophy, 1979—; v.p. Mars Hill Jr. Coll., 1953-58; exec. com. N.C. Coll. Conf., 1961; mem. com. on colls. So. Assn., 1964-69, chmn. com. on standards and reports, 1965-69; mem. N.C. Adv. Council Civil Rights, 1966-71; chmn. com. standards and membership N.C. Assn. Colls and Univs., 1966-67, mem. adminstrv. com., 1967-70; mem. N.C. Adv. Council on Tchr. Edn. and Profl. Standards, 1961-75, chmn., 1972, N.C. Evaluation Com. Tchr. Edn., 1970-76; mem. Nat. Com. on Emeriti, 1971—, Citizens Awareness Com., 1969-70. Pres. United Fund, Madison County, 1957-58; pres. bd. dirs. Greenville Bicentennial; trustee Wake Forest U., 1965-68; adv. council N.C. Community Coll., 1963-77. Named Man of Year Civitan Club, Madison County, 1958. Mem. Assn. Acad. Deans N.C. Colls., N.C. Edn. Assn., NEA, Phi Delta Kappa, Pi Omega Pi (hon.), Phi Kappa Phi. Baptist (deacon). Clubs: Mars Hill Civitan (dir. 1957), Greenville Rotary (dir. 1960), Kiwanis.). Home: 1711 Knollwood Dr Greenville NC 27834

HOLT, SMITH LEWIS, JR., university administrator, chemistry educator; b. Ponca City, Okla., Dec. 8, 1938; s. Smith Lewis and Esther (Doepel) H.; m. Elizabeth Catherine Manners, Aug. 24, 1964; children: Alexandra, Smith Lewis. B.Sc., Northwestern U., 1961; Ph.D., Brown U., 1965. Asst. prof. Poly. Inst. Bklyn., 1966-69; assoc. prof. chemistry U. Wyo., Laramie, 1969-74, prof., 1974-78; prof., head chemistry dept. U. Ga., Athens, 1978-80; dean arts and scis. Okla. State U., Stillwater, 1980—. Editor: Solid State Chemistry: A Contemporary Overview, 1980, Inorganic Reactions in Organized Media, 1982, Inorganic Syntheses-V22, 1983; contbr. articles to profl. jours. Fulbright fellow U. Bordeaux, 1975. Mem. Am. Chem. Soc., AAAS, Sigma Xi. Home: 2807 Fox Ledge Ln Stillwater OK 74074 Office: Okla State U 201 LSE Stillwater OK 74078

HOLT, STEPHEN S., astrophysicist; b. N.Y.C., May 17, 1940; s. Aaron J. and Faye E. (Schwartz) H.; m. Carol Ann Weissman, June 3, 1961; children: Peter David, Eric Lawrence, Laura Kimberly. B.S., N.Y. U., 1961, Ph.D. in Physics, 1966. Instr. physics N.Y. U., 1964-66; astrophysicist Goddard Space Flight Center, Greenbelt, Md., 1966—; chief high energy astrophysics NASA Hdqrs., 1980-81; dir. Lab. for High Energy Astrophysics Goddard Space Flight Ctr., Greenbelt, Md., 1983—; lectr. physics U. Md., 1967—. Contbr. articles to profl. jours. Recipient medal for exceptional sci. achievement NASA, 1977, 80. Mem. Am. Phys. Soc., Am. Astron. Soc., Sigma Xi, Tau Beta Pi, Sigma Pi Sigma. Home: 1207 Mimosa Ln Silver Spring MD 20904 Office: Code 660 Goddard Space Flight Center Greenbelt MD 20771 *The most important intrinsic requisites for success in experimental science are probably imagination and diligence. Very few individuals possess these in sufficient quantities to dominate the extrinsic variables which shape their careers in research, however. I consider myself fortunate to have been able to capitalize on whatever talent I possess by having my research interests aligned with funding priorities, and by being blessed with the cooperation of unselfish and stimulating colleagues.*

HOLT, VICTORIA, author. Books include Mistress of Mellyn, 1960, Kirkland Revels, 1962, Bride of Pendorric, 1963, Legend of the Seventh Virgin, 1965, Menfreya In the Morning, 1966, The King of the Castle, 1967, The Queen's Confession, 1968, Shivering Sands, 1969, The Secret Woman, 1970, Shadow of the Lynx, 1971, On the Night of the Seventh Moon, 1972, The Curse of the Kings, 1973, The House of a Thousand Lanterns, 1974, Lord of the Far Island, 1975, Pride of the Peacock, 1976, The Devil on Horseback, 1977, My Enemy the Queen, 1978, The Spring of the Tiger, 1979, The Mask of the Enchantress, 1980, The Judas Kiss, 1981, The Demon Lover, 1982, The Time of the Hunters Moon, 1983. Address: care Doubleday & Co Garden City NY 11530

HOLT, (WILLIAM) KERMIT, journalist; b. Clarksburg, W.Va., Oct. 26, 1916; s. William Tilford and Emelyne (Gregory) H.; m. Gisela Marie Leers, May 7, 1941; children—William Henry, Heidi Marie Holt Gendusa. A.B., Salem (W.Va.) Coll., 1938; M.S. in Journalism, Northwestern U., 1939. Reporter Clarksburg Exponent, 1937-38; police and cts. reporter City News Bur., Chgo., 1939; night editor Milw. bur. AP, 1940; gen. assignments reporter, then fgn. corr. Chgo. Tribune, 1940-42, 46-49, copy editor, slot man, 1949-55, asst. makeup editor, 1955-60, travel editor, 1960-81. Served to 1st lt. USMCR, 1942-46. Decorated Purple Heart; recipient Mark Twain Travel Writing and Editing awards, 1960, 62, 63, Pacific Area Travel Assn. award best newspaper articles on Pacific countries, 1962, 65, 70, 71, 73, 77, Trans World Airlines Travel Writing award, 1965, 68, Edward Scott Beck award, 1970, Strebig-Dobben Meml. award, 1970, George Hedman award, 1967, 1st prize Am. category Am. Epress Travel Writers' Competition, 1981-82; named Salem Coll. Alumnus of yr., 1963, Disting. West Virginian, 1971. Mem. Soc. Am. Travel Writers (pres. 1966-67, chmn. bd. 1968-69), Marine Corps Combat Corrs. Assn., Soc. Profl. Journalists, Sigma Delta Chi. Republican. Clubs: Press (Chgo.) (gov. 1965-76, pres. 1975); Headline (Chgo.)). Home and Office: 227 Parkview Rd Glenview IL 60025

HOLTER, DON WENDELL, retired bishop; b. Lincoln, Kans., Mar. 24, 1905; s. Henry O. and Lenna (Mater) H.; m. Isabelle Elliott, June 20, 1931; children: Phyllis (Mrs. Robert Dunn), Martha (Mrs. Robert Hudson), Heather (Mrs. Lee Ellis). B.A., Baker U., 1927, D.D., 1948; postgrad., Harvard U., 1928; B.D., Garrett Theol. Sem., 1930; Ph.D., U. Chgo., 1934; LL.D., Dakota Wesleyan U., 1969; D.D., St. Paul Sch. Theology, 1973. Ordained elder Methodist Ch., 1934; asst. minister Euclid Meth. Ch., Oak Park, Ill., 1930-34; missionary in, Philippines, 1935-45; minister Central Ch., Manila, 1935-40; prof. Union Theol. Sem., Manila, 1935-40, pres., 1940-45; minister Hamline Meth. Ch., St. Paul, 1946-49; prof. Garrett Theol. Sem., 1949-58; pres. St. Paul Sch. Theology, 1958-72; bishop Nebr. area United Meth. Ch., 1972-76; Del. Internat. Missionary Conf., India and Near East, 1938; spl. study mission, Africa, 1958; rep. Gen. Bd. Missions Meth. Ch. in consultation in, Philippines, 1967; chmn. commn. ministry United Meth. Ch., 1968-70, mem. gen. bd. higher edn. and ministry, since 1972, chmn. div. ordained ministry, 1972-76, del. gen. and jurisdictional confs., 1964, 66, 68, 70, 72. Author: Fire on the Prairie, Methodism in the History of Kansas, 1969, Flames on the Plains, A History of United Methodism in Nebraska, 1983; also articles. Trustee St. Paul Sch. Theology. Home: 7725 Briar Dr Prairie Village KS 66208

HOLTER, MARVIN ROSENKRANTZ, research and development executive, physicist; b. Fairport, N.Y., July 4, 1922; s. Frank Marcus and Florence (Zonnevylle) H.; m. Frances Elizabeth Jenkins, July 15, 1955; children: Christine E., Ann F. B.S. in Physics, U. Mich., 1949, M.S. in Math., 1951, 1958. Prof. remote sensing U. Mich., Ann Arbor, 1968-70, head infrared lab., 1964-70; dep. dir. Willow Run lab. U. Mich., Ann Arbor, 1972-73; div. chief earth obs. div. NASA Johnson Space Ctr., Houston, 1970-72; exec. v.p. Environ. Research Inst. Mich., Ann Arbor, 1973—; invited lectr. univs. Stockholm, Upsalla, Lund, Sweden, 1969; mem. USAF Sci. Adv. Bd., 1963-79; mem. com. on remote sensing programs for earth resources surveys Nat. Acad. Sci.-NRC, 1973-77; mem. U.S.A.-USSR Working Group on Remote Sensing, 1971-77. Co-author: Fundamentals of Infrared Technology, 1962, Remote Sensing, 1970; editorial bd.: Remote Sensing of Environ., 1968-75. Recipient Exceptional Civilian Service award USAF, 1979, Sci. Achievement award NASA, 1973; co-recipient William T. Pecore award Dept. Interior, 1976, Interpretation award Am. Soc. Photogrammetry, 1969. Mem. Explorers Club, Sigma Xi. Club: Cosmos (Washington). Home: 493 Orchard Hill Dr Ann Arbor MI 48103 Office: Environ Research Inst Mich Box 8618 Ann Arbor MI 48107

HOLTERMANN, E. LOUIS, JR., publisher; b. N.Y.C., Dec. 28, 1927; s. E. Louis and Hilda Louise (Syska) H.; m. Jane Holland, May 5, 1951; children—Kim, Keith L. B.S., Columbia U., 1950, M.S., 1955. Salesman Nat. Sugar Refining Co., N.Y.C., 1952-58, Outdoor Advt., Inc., 1958-61; with Glamour mag., Conde Nast Publs., Inc., N.Y.C., 1961—, advt. dir., 1970-75, publisher, 1975—; Pres. Bronxville (N.Y.) schs. PTA, 1970-71. Served with AUS, 1950-52. Mem. Phi Gamma Delta. Club: Bronxville Field (gov. 1964-69). Home: 3 Legget Rd Bronxville NY 10708 Office: 350 Madison Ave New York City NY 10017

HOLTKAMP, DORSEY EMIL, medical research scientist; b. New Knoxville, Ohio, May 28, 1919; s. Emil H. and Caroline E. (Meckstroth) H.; m. Marianne Church Johnson, Mar. 20, 1942 (dec. 1956); 1 son, Kurt Lee; m. Marie P. Bahm Roberts, Dec. 20, 1957 (dec. 1982); stepchildren: Charles Timothy Roberts, Michael John Roberts; m. Phyllis Laurence Bradfield, Sept. 1, 1984. Student, Ohio State U., 1937-39; A.B., U. Colo., 1945, M.S., 1949, Ph.D., 1951; student, Med. Sch., 2 1/2 yrs. Teaching asst. in biochemistry, research asst. in biology U. Colo., 1945-46; univ. fellow U. Colo. Sch. Medicine, 1946, asst. in biochemistry, 1947-48, research fellow in biochemistry, 1948-51; sr. research scientist biochemistry sect. Smith, Kline & French Labs., Phila., 1951-57, endocrine-metabolic group leader, 1957-58; head endocrinology dept. Merrell-Nat. Labs. div. Richardson-Merrell, Inc., Cin., 1958-70, group dir. endocrine clin. research, med. research dept., 1970-81; group dir. med. research dept. Merrell Dow Pharms. subs. Dow Chem. Co., Cin., 1981—. Contbr. articles to profl. jours., sci. publs. Fellow AAAS, Am. Inst. Chemists; mem. Am. Soc. Clin. Pharm. and Therapeutics, Endocrine Soc., Am. Fertility Soc., Am. Chem. Soc., Am. Soc. Pharmacology and Exptl. Therapeutics, N.Y. Acad. Sci., Ohio Acad Sci., Soc. Exptl. Biology and Medicine, Reticuloendothelial Soc., Am. Inst. Biol. Scis., AMA (affiliate), Sigma Xi, Nu Sigma Nu. Republican. Presbyterian. Research on various phases endocrinology, pharmacology, tumor metabolism, fertility-sterility control, biochemistry, teratology, inflammation, nutrition; research and devel. on new drugs. Patentee in field. Home: 130 S Liberty-Keuter Rd Lebanon Oh 45036 Office: Merrell Dow Pharms 2110 E Galbraith Rd Cincinnati OH 45215

HOLTMAN, WILLIAM J., railroad company executive; b. 1921; married. Grad. in Metall. Engring., Colo. Sch. Mines, 1943, Met.E., 1947. With The Denver and Rio Grande Western R.R. Co., 1958—, chief mech. officer, to 1966, div. supt., 1966-68, v.p. exec. dept., 1968-69, exec. v.p., gen. mgr., 1969-76, pres., chief operating officer, 1976-78, pres., chief exec. officer, 1978—, dir.; pres., dir. Rio Grande Industries, Inc.; dir. 1st Nat. Bank of Denver. Served to 1st lt. USAAF, 1943-46. Office: Denver and Rio Grande Western Railroad Co 1515 Araphoe St Park Central Bldg Denver CO 80202 *

HOLTON, A. LINWOOD, JR., lawyer; b. Big Stone Gap, Va., Sept. 21, 1923; s. Abner Linwood and Edith (Van Gorder) H.; m. Virginia Harrison Rogers, Jan. 10, 1953; children—Virginia Tayloe, Anne Bright, A. Linwood III, Dwight Carter. B.A., Washington and Lee U., 1944; LL.B., Harvard, 1949; LL.D., Washington and Lee U., 1971, Va. State Coll., 1971, Coll. William and Mary, 1973, Va. Union U., 1972. Partner firm Eggleston, Holton, Butler and Glenn, Roanoke, Va., 1954-69; gov., Va., 1970-74, asst. sec. state for congl. relations, 1974-75; partner firm Hogan & Hartson, Washington, 1975-78; v.p., gen. counsel Am. Council Life Ins., Washington, 1978—. Past chmn. Roanoke City Republican Com.; vice chmn. Va. Rep. Central Com., 1960-69; mem. exec. com. Nat. Gov's Conf., 1972-73; del. Rep. Nat. Conv., 1960, 68, 72; Rep. candidate for Va. Ho. of Dels., 1955, 57; Rep. candidate for gov., 1965; one of six original members Nat. Nixon for Pres. Com., 1967; regional coordinator Nixon for Pres. Com., 1968; chmn. So. Growth Policy Bd., 1972-73, So. Regional Edn. Bd., 1972-73; bd. dirs. Wolf Trap Found., 1973-80; pres. Supreme Ct. Hist. Soc., 1980—; chmn. Burket Miller Center Public Affairs, U. Va., 1979—. Served with USNR, World War II. Mem. ABA, Va. Bar Assn. (past v.p.), Roanoke Bar Assn. (past dir.), D.C. Bar Assn., Va. State Bar, Omicron Delta Kappa. Presbyterian (elder, Sunday sch. tchr.). Home: 6010 Claiborne Dr McLean VA 22101 Office: 1850 K St NW Washington DC 20006

HOLTON, GERALD, physicist, historian of science; b. Berlin, Germany, May 23, 1922; s. Emanuel and Regina (Rossmann) H.; m. Nina Rossfort, Sept. 12, 1947; children: Thomas, Stephan. Nat. certificate elec. engring., Sch. Tech., Oxford, Eng., 1940; B.A., Wesleyan U., 1941, M.A., 1942, D.H.L. (hon.), 1981; M.A., Harvard, 1946, Ph.D., 1948; D.Sc. (hon.), Grinnell Coll., 1967, Kenyon Coll., 1977, Bates Coll., 1979; LL.D. (hon.), Duke U., 1981. Instr. Wesleyan U., 1941-42, Brown U., 1942-43; staff, officers radar course and OSRD Harvard, 1943-45, various faculty positions, 1945—; Mallinckrodt prof. physics and prof. history of sci.; exchange prof. Harvard-Leningrad U., 1962; vis. mem. Inst. Advanced Study, Princeton, 1964; fellow Center Advanced Study in Behavioral Scis., Stanford, 1975-76; vis. prof. M.I.T., 1976—; Herbert Spencer lectr. Oxford U., 1979; Jefferson lectr., 1981, John Simon Guggenheim fellow, 1980-81; mem. com. scholarly communications with People's Republic of China, Nat. Acad. Scis., 1970-71; mem. U.S. Nat. Commn. on UNESCO, 1975-80, Council of Scholars, Library of Congress, 1980—, U.S. Nat. Commn. on Excellence in Edn., 1981—. Author: Introduction to Concepts and Theories in Physical Science, 2d edit, 1973, (with D.H.D. Roller) Foundations of Modern Physical Science, 1958, Science and the Modern Mind, 1958, Science and Culture, 1965, (with others) The Project Physics Course, 1970, 75, 81, The 20th Century Sciences: Studies in Intellectual Biography, 1971, Thematic Origins of Scientific Thought: Kepler to Einstein, 1973, The Scientific Imagination: Case Studies, 1978, (with others) Limits of Scientific Inquiry, 1979, Albert Einstein, Historical and Cultural Perspectives, 1982; Editor-in-chief: Daedalus, 1958-61; contbr. articles to profl. jours. Trustee Wesleyan U., Boston Mus. Sci., Sci. Service. Recipient Robert A. Millikan medal, 1967; Gran-Premio Internat. Rome Documentary Film Festival for The World of Enrico Fermi, 1971; Oersted medal, 1980. Fellow AAAS (dir. 1967-71, George Sarton meml. lectr. 1962), Am. Acad. Arts and Sci. (editor 1957-63, mem. exec. bd. 1970-78), Am. Phys. Soc. (chmn. N.E. sect. 1962-63), Académie Internationale d'Histoire des Scis. (v.p. 1981—); mem. Am. Inst. Physics (governing bd. 1968-74), Am. Assn. Physics Tchrs. (commn. coll. physics 1960-64), History Sci. Soc. (council 1959-61, 63-65, pres. 1982—), Fedn. Am. Scientists, Phi Beta Kappa, Sigma Xi. Club: Cosmos. Home: 14 Trotting Horse Dr Lexington MA 02173 Office: Jefferson Phys Lab Harvard U Cambridge MA 02138

HOLTON, HARRY HUTCHINSON, chem. co. exec.; b. Montreal, Que., Can., Nov. 2, 1944; s. Harry Sirett and Margaret Denelda (Hutchinson) H.; m. Mary Lou Althea Hickson, May 18, 1968; children—Tara Lee, Danica Lynn. B.Sc. with honors in Chemistry, U. Windsor, Ont., Can., 1967, Ph.D., 1971. Postdoctoral fellow McMaster U., Hamilton, Ont., 1971-73; with CIL Inc., 1973—, market devel. mgr., 1977-79, research group mgr., Mississauga, Ont., 1979—. Contbr. articles to profl. jours. Med. Research Council fellow, 1971-73; recipient Marcus Wallenberg prize Wallenberg Found., Sweden, 1981. Mem. TAPPI, Can. Pulp and Paper Assn., Chem. Inst. Can., Am. Chem. Soc. Patentee in field. Home: 201 Weldon Ave Oakville ON L6K 2H9 Canada Office: 2101 Hadwen Rd Mississauga ON L5K 2L3 Canada *There is nothing easier than being honest. It simplifies decisions, improves communications and friendships, and unclutters the memory as you only need remember what you believe is correct, not what you might have said. What success I have had is due in large measure to this philosophy. As a scientist it is essential; as a member of society it is highly valuable.*

HOLTON, JAMES LEO, govt. exec.; b. Reading, Pa., Mar. 17, 1921; s. Leo A. and Bessie (Gallagher) H.; m. Ruth A. Homan, Sept. 9, 1949; children—Anne L., Robert M. Student, Albright Coll., 1942. Telegraph editor, news editor Reading Times, 1939-42; day editor AP, Pitts., 1946-50; writer NBC News, 1953-60, news editor, 1960-62, producer news spls., 1962-72, v.p. radio news, 1972-81; dir. public affairs Fed. Emergency Mgmt. Agy., Washington, 1981—; Vice chmn. Nat. Industry Adv. Com. for Emergency Broadcast Service. Served with U.S. Army, 1942-46, 50-53. Decorated Bronze Star. Mem. Radio-TV News Dirs. Assn., Sigma Delta Chi. Roman Catholic. Home: 8028 Old Falls Rd McLean VA 22101 Office: 500 C St SW Washington DC 20472

HOLTON, RAYMOND WILLIAM, botanist, educator; b. Riverside, Calif., Apr. 30, 1929; s. Homer Hopkins and H. Charlotte (Hall) H.; children: Betsey Diane, Nancy Joann, William Louis, Thomas Raymond. B.A., Pomona Coll., 1951; M.S., U. Mich., 1954, Ph.D., 1958. Instr. botany U. Mich.-Flint Coll., 1957-59, asst. prof., 1959-61; research asso. U. Tex., 1961-62, USPHS trainee, 1962-63; asst. prof. botany U. Tenn., 1963-64, asso. prof., acting head botany, 1964-65, prof., head botany, 1965-72, 73—; sr. Fulbright lectr. dept. botany U. Durham, Eng., 1972-73. Mem. Bot. Soc. Am., Am. Soc. Plant Physiologists, Phycol. Soc. Am., Internat., Brit. phycol. socs., AAAS. Physiol. and biochem. research on plants, particularly cyanobacteria. Home: 4619 Sunflower Rd Knoxville TN 37919 Office: Dept Botany U Tenn Knoxville TN 37996

HOLTON, RICHARD HENRY, educator; b. Columbus, Ohio, Mar. 17, 1926; s. Caryl Ames and Celia (Cathcart) H.; m. Constance Elizabeth Minzey, June 7, 1947; children: Melissa Louise, Jane Margaret, Timothy Hammond. B.S. in Bus. Adminstrn, Miami U., Oxford, Ohio, 1947; M.A. in Econs, Ohio State U., 1948; Ph.D., Harvard, 1952. Field research dir. Social Sci. Research Center, U. P.R., 1951-52; asst. prof. econs. Ohio State U., 1953, Harvard U., 1953-57; asso. prof. bus. adminstrn. U. Calif., Berkeley, 1957-61, prof., 1961—, dean, 1967-75; dir. Inst. Bus. and Econ. Research, 1959-61, on leave, 1961-65; spl. asst. for econ. affairs to sec. commerce, 1962-63, asst. sec. commerce for econ. affairs, 1963-65; dean Am. faculty Dalian Inst. Tech., Nat. Center Mgmt. Devel., People's Republic of China, 1981, 82; dir. Ata Bates Corp.; Trustee Northwestern Mut. Life Ins. Co., Milw. Author: (with J.K. Galbraith) Marketing Efficiency in Puerto Rico, 1955, (with R.E. Caves) The Canadian Economy, 1959; Editor: (with S.P. Sethi) Management of the Multinationals—Policies, Operations and Research, 1974. Chmn. Pres.'s Consumer Adv. Council, 1965-66; Trustee Mills Coll., Oakland, Calif. Fulbright research grantee U. Naples, Italy, 1961-62. Mem. Am. Econ. Assn., World Affairs Council No. Calif. (trustee), Phi Beta Kappa, Omicron Delta Kappa, Beta Theta Pi. Democrat. Unitarian. Home: 87 Southampton Ave Berkeley CA 94707

HOLTON, ROBERT PAGE, publishing company executive; b. St. Paul, Jan. 18, 1938; s. Robert Henry and Grace (Page) H.; m. Sandra Janice Heyl, July 16, 1960. B.S. in Indsl. Distbn., Clarkson Coll., 1960. Asst. editor Indsl. Distbn., McGraw-Hill, N.Y.C., 1960-61, dist. mgr., Chgo., 1963-65, McGraw-Hill-Textile World, Phila., 1965-71, McGraw-Hill-Chem. Engring., Pitts., 1971-76, mktg. service dir., N.Y.C., 1976-81; sr. v.p., pub. Simmons-Boardman, N.Y.C., 1981—. Contbr. articles to profl. jours. Mem. exec. bd. Fairfield County council Boy Scouts Am., 1979-83. Recipient Order of Merit Boy Scouts Am., 1969, Silver Beaver Boy Scouts Am., 1975. Mem. Bus. Profl. Adverisers Assn. (dir. 1975-76), Soc. Naval Architects and Marine Engrs. Clubs: Whitehall, Propeller (N.Y.C.). Office: Simmons Boardman Publishing Co. 345 Hudson St New York NY 10014

HOLTON, THOMAS LELAND, accountant; b. Prairie Hill, Tex., July 8, 1925; s. Homer and Esther (Rasco) H.; m. Maxine Swearengin, Apr. 7, 1946; children: Dana Ann, Thomas L. B.B.A., Baylor U., 1949, M.A., 1950. With Eaton & Huddle, 1950-58, mng. partner, until 1958; with Peat, Marwick, Mitchell & Co., 1958—; mng. partner Midwest Area partner, Chgo., 1959-68, chmn., chief exec., N.Y.C., 1979—; bd. dirs. Coalition Service, Industries, Inc., 1982—; mem. President's Adv. Com. on Trade Negotiations, 1980—; treas., mem. nat. adv. council Congl. award, 1982—. Served with U.S. Navy. Mem. Am. Inst. C.P.A.s (chmn. com. on auditing procedure 1969-72, chmn. com. on SEC regulations 1974-77, v.p. 1982—, dir., mem. council 1982—). Clubs: Economic, Links, Board Room (N.Y.C.); Burning Tree (Greenwich, Conn.); Blind Brook (Port Chester, N.Y.); Skokie Country (Ill.); Lost Tree (Fla.). Home: 108 Perkins Rd Greenwich CT 06830 Office: 345 Park Ave New York NY 10022

HOLTON, WILLIAM COFFEEN, electrical engineering executive; b. Washington, July 24, 1930; s. William B. and Esther (Coffeen) H.; m. Mary Schaeffer, Aug. 5, 1953; children: Elizabeth, William, Sarah Anne. B.S. in Physics, U. N.C., 1952, Ph.D., U. Ill., 1960. Mem. tech. staff Corp. Research Lab. Tex. Instruments, Dallas, 1960-65, mgr. Quantum Electronics, 1965-72, dir. Advanced Components Lab., 1972-78, dir. research and devel. Semiconductor Group, 1978-82, mgr. strategic planning, 1982—. Lt. (j.g.) USN, 1952-54. Union Carbide fellow, 1959. Fellow IEEE (mem. gov. bd. Electron. Device Soc. 1975-80, chmn. internat. electron device meeting 1975); mem. Am. Phys. Soc., AAAS. Presbyterian. Club: Rush Creek Yacht (Dallas). Home: 12106 Shiremont Dr Dallas TX 75230 Office: Tex Instruments Inc PO Box 225012 MS72 Dallas TX 75265

HOLTZ, EDGAR WOLFE, lawyer; b. Clarksburg, W.Va., Jan. 18, 1922; s. Dennis Drummond and Oleta (Wolfe) H.; m. Alberta Lee Brinkley, May 6, 1944; children: Diana Hilary, Heidi Johanna. B.A., Denison U., 1943; J.D., U. Cin., 1949. Bar: Ohio 1949, U.S. Supreme Ct. 1957, D.C. 1961. Assoc. firm Matthews & Matthews, Cin., 1949-53; asst. dean Chase Law Sch., Cin., 1952-55; asst. solicitor City of Cin., 1950-55; asst. chief office of opinions and rev. FCC, Washington, 1955-56, dep. gen. counsel, 1956-60; mem. firm Hogan & Hartson, Washington, 1960—. Trustee Denison U., Granville, Ohio, 1974—. Served to 1st lt. USAAF, 1943-45. Decorated D.F.C., Air medal with 2 clusters. Fellow Am. Bar Found.; mem. Am. Bar Assn. (standing com.

on gavel awards), Ohio Bar Assn., D.C. Bar Assn., Fed. Communications Bar Assn. (pres. 1977-78), Am. Judicature Soc., Newcomen Soc. N. Am., Nat. Communications Club. Republican. Methodist. Clubs: Metropolitan, George Town, International (Washington). Office: Hogan & Hartson 815 Connecticut Ave NW Washington DC 20006

HOLTZ, LOUIS LEO, football coach; b. Fallansbee, W.Va., Jan. 6, 1937; m. Beth Barcus, July 22, 1961; children—Luanne, Skip, Kevin Richard, Elizabeth. B.A., Kent State U., 1959; M.A., U. Iowa, 1961. Asst. football coach U. Iowa, Coll. William and Mary, U. Conn., U. S.C., Ohio State U.; head football coach Coll. William and Mary, 1969-71, N.C. State U., 1972-75; coach N.Y. Jets, 1976—; head football coach U. Ark., Fayetteville, 1977—. Author: Kitchen Quarterback. Named NCAA Dist. Coach of Year, 1973, Nat. Coach of Year Football Writers, Sporting News, 1977; S.W. Conf. Coach of Year AP, UPI, 1979. Roman Catholic. Home: 1209 Canterbury Fayetteville AR 72701 Office: Univ of Minnesota Football Office Minneapolis MN 55455

HOLTZ, SIDNEY, publishing company executive; b. N.Y.C., Mar. 24, 1925; s. Jacob and Rose (Cholmar) H.; m. Florence Fogel, Sept. 6, 1952; children: Jeffrey, Clifford, Linda. B.S., LIU, 1949; M.S., NYU, 1950; B.P.A. (hon.), Brooks Inst., 1973. Tchr. pub. schs., N.Y.C., 1951-53; advt. sales rep. N.Y. Herald Tribune, 1953-58; with Ziff-Davis Pub. Co., N.Y.C., 1958—; mem. sales staff Popular Photography, 1958-60, advt. dir., 1960-67, asso. pub., 1967-68, pub., 1968—, corporate v.p., 1972—. Served with U.S. Army, 1943-46. Named to Internat. Photography Hall of Fame. Mem. Internat. Center Photography, Photog. Art and Sci. Found., Photographic Mfrs. and Distributors Assn., Internat. Photog. Council. Club: Dellwood Country. Home: 206 Palisade Ave Dobbs Ferry NY 10522 Office: One Park Ave New York NY 10016

HOLTZCLAW, BENJAMIN CLARK, former educator; b. Perry, Ga., July 28, 1894; s. Benjamin Clark and Cornelia Goode (Smith) H.; m. Merle Marie Wood, Sept. 12, 1922; 1 dau., Alnita (Dyall). A.B., Mercer U., 1914, Oxford U., Eng., 1917, A.M., 1920; Ph.D., Cornell U., 1923. Faculty modern langs. Mercer U., Macon, Ga., 1919-21, prof. philosophy, 1926-29, dean, 1927-29, 1928-29; instr. Greek Cornell U., 1921-23, asst. prof., 1923-25; asst. prof. philosophy N.Y. U., 1925-26; prof. philosophy U. Richmond, Va., 1929-65; chmn. Faculty Personnel Com., 1932-42, dean, 1939-65, 1942-45. Contbr. articles to profl. jours. Served as 2d lt., 317th F.A., 81st Div. U.S. Army, 1917-19; Served as 2d lt., 317th F.A., 81st Div. A.E.F., 1918-19. Mem. Am. Philol. Assn., Am. Philos. Assn., So. Soc. for Philosophy and Psychology, Phi Beta Kappa, Phi Kappa Phi, Psi Upsilon, Omicron Delta Kappa, Kappa Alpha. Baptist. Home: 1900 Lauderdale Dr E-118 Richmond VA 23233

HOLTZCLAW, HENRY FULLER, JR., university dean, chemist; b. Stillwater, Okla., July 30, 1921; s. Henry Fuller and Euna (Smith) H.; m. Dorothy Louise Robbins, June 4, 1949 (dec. Aug. 1963); children: Jane Louise, Sara Jean; m. Ida Jean Davis, Nov. 24, 1968. A.B., U. Kans., 1942; M.S., U. Ill., 1946, Ph.D. (Univ. fellow), 1947. Chemist, Manhattan project Tenn. Eastman Corp., 1944-45; asst. instr. chemistry and math. U. Kans., 1942-43; asst. in chemistry U. Ill., 1943-44, 45-46, vis. lectr., summers 1951-52; instr. chemistry U. Nebr., Lincoln, 1947-49, asst. prof., 1949-52, assoC. prof., 1952-58, prof., 1958-67, Regents Found. prof., 1967—, dean grad. studies, 1976—; guest prof. U. Konstanz, W.Ger., 1973-74; mem. Grad. Record Exam. Bd., 1982—; mem. policy council, exec. com., research com. Test of English as Fgn. Lang., 1982—, chmn. research com., 1983—; mem. com. on testing Assn. Grad. Schs., 1982—; mem. nominating com. Council of Grad. Schs., 1982—. Author: (with W.H. Nebergall and F.C. Schmidt) General Chemistry, 1963, (with Nebergall and W.R. Robinson) rev. edit., 1980; College Chemistry with Qualitative Analysis, 1963, rev. edit., 1980, (with J.H. Meiser and F.K. Ault) Problems and Solutions for General Chemistry and College Chemistry, 2d edit., 1980; editorial bd.: Inorganic Syntheses, 1953—, v.p., 1969-70, sec.-treas., 1971-81; pres.-elect, 1981—; editor-in-chief vol. VIII, 1966; contbr. articles to research jours. Fellow AAAS; mem. Am. Chem. Soc. (nat. com. on coms. 1974-81, nat. com. on nominations and elections 1982—), AAAS, AAUP, Sigma Xi, Phi Lambda Upsilon, Alpha Chi Sigma, Pi Mu Epsilon, Alpha Kappa Psi. Presbyterian. Club: Kiwanis. Home: 7140 S Hampton Rd Lincoln NE 68506 Office: 412 Adminstrn Bldg U Nebr-Lincoln Lincoln NE 68588-0434

HOLTZER, ALFRED MELVIN, educator; b. Bklyn., Feb. 22, 1929; s. Abraham and Miriam (Brecher) H.; m. Joanne Rappaport, Feb. 6, 1954 (dec. Nov. 1967); children—Esther Rachel, Dan Robert; m. Marilyn Frances Emerson, June 24, 1969. A.B., Washington U., St. Louis, 1950; Ph.D., Harvard, 1954. Instr. chemistry Yale, 1954-57; asst. prof. chemistry Washington U., 1957-59, asso. prof., 1959-65, prof., 1965—. Mem. Am. Chem. Soc., Am. Soc. Biol. Chemists. Home: 6636 Pershing Ave St Louis MO 63130

HOLTZMAN, GARY YALE, retail executive; b. N.Y.C., Aug. 7, 1936; s. Abram and Pearl (Kashetsky) H.; m. Alice A. Lang, Sept. 5, 1958; children: Bruce, Sheri, Michele. B.B.A., CCNY, 1958. Exec. v.p. control and ops. Jordan Marsh Co., Miami, Fla., 1980—. Bd. dirs. Dade County Safety Council, Miami, 1978—, Jewish Community Ctr. So. Fla., Miami, 1983—, Fla. Bus. Roundtable, Miami, 1975-80; bd. advisers Opportunities Industrialization Ctr., Miami, 1982—; pres. Michael Ann Russell Jewish Community Ctr., Miami, 1984—; mem. Temple Adath Yeshurun, Miami, Fla. Retail Fedn., Tallahassee, Fla. Jewish Fedn., United Way of Dade County. Served to lt. U.S. Army, 1958-59; served to capt. USAR, 1958-65. Recipient Americanism award Anti-Defamation League, 1983, Adath Yeshurun Man of Yr. award, 1978. Mem. Greater Miami C. of C. Democrat. Home: 851 NE 182d St North Miami FL 33162 Office: Jordan Marsh Co 1501 Biscayne Blvd Miami FL 33132

HOLTZMAN, JEROME, journalist, publisher; b. Chgo., July 12, 1926; s. Samuel and Dorothy (Sloan) H.; m. Marilyn Genevieve Ryan, Apr. 2, 1949; children: Alice, Arlene, Catherine, Janet, Merrill. Student, Northwestern U., 1947, U. Chgo., 1953-54. With Chgo. Sun-Times, 1943-81, baseball writer, 1957-81; chief baseball writer Chgo. Tribune, 1981—; corr. Sporting News, weekly, 1958-79, columnist, 1958-79; founder, pres. Holtzman Press, Inc., Evanston, Ill., 1980—. Author: (books) No Cheering in the Press Box, 1974, Fielder's Choice, 1979, (with Tom Gorman) Three and Two, 1979; contbr.: numerous articles on baseball to old Saturday Evening Post; sports adv., Ency. Brit.; ann. contbr.: Official Baseball Guide, 1967-79. Served with USMC, 1944-46. Recipient Stick of Type award Chgo. Newspaper Guild, 1961, 69, 76. Office: care Chgo Tribune 441 N Michigan Ave Chicago IL 60611

HOLTZMAN, RICHARD EDWARD, hotel executive; b. Millersburg, Pa., Oct. 18, 1919; s. Lester Gilbert and Esther Zinn (Hess) H.; m. Janet Akin, Jan. 2, 1943; children: Sondra, Richard A., Cynthia. B.S. in Hotel Adminstrn, Cornell U., 1941. Dir. sales Pick Hotels Corp., Chgo., 1950-55; mgr. Greenbrier Hotel, White Sulphur Springs, W.Va., 1955-60; pres., gen. mgr. Sheraton Hawaii Corp.; mgrs. Royal Hawaiian, Moana, Surfrider, Princess Kaiuloni and Maui hotels, 1960-66; pres. Rockresorts, Inc., N.Y.C., 1966—; dir. Can. Life Assurance Co. of N.Y. Vice pres. Hawaii Visitors Bur., 1961-66; mem. Hawaii Bd. Planning and Econ. Devel., 1964; Bd. dirs. Hawaii chpt. A.R.C., 1963-66. Served with USAAF, World War II. Decorated Air medal, D.F.C. Mem. Hawaii Hotel Assn. (past pres.), Am. Hotel Assn. (sec. 1972—), W.Va. Hotel Assn. (pres. 1958), So. Hotel Assn. (pres. 1960), Am. Hotel and Motel Assn. (treas. 1974, v.p. 1975, pres. 1976), Cornell Soc. Hotelmen (pres. 1967), Honolulu C. of C. (dir.). Home: 128 Wellesley Dr New Canaan CT 06840 Office: 30 Rockefeller Plaza New York NY 10020

HOLTZMAN, WAYNE HAROLD, psychologist, educator; b. Chgo., Jan. 16, 1923; s. Harold Hoover and Lillian (Manny) H.; m. Joan King, Aug. 23, 1947; children: Wayne Harold, James K., Scott E., Karl H. B.S., Northwestern U., 1944, M.S., 1947; Ph.D., Stanford, 1950; L.H.D. (hon.), Southwestern U., 1980. Asst. prof. psychology U. Tex., Austin, 1949-53, asso. prof., 1953-59, prof., 1959—; dean Coll. Edn., 1964-70, prof. psychology and edn., 1965—; asso. dir. Hogg Found. Mental Health, 1955-64, pres., 1970—; Dir. Social Sci. Research Council, 1957-63, Centro de Investigationes Sociales, Mex., 1960—; cons. USAF, also mem. sci. adv. bd., 1969-71; mem. com. basic research com. NRC, 1968-71; mem. behavioral sci. study sect. USPHS, 1957-59, mental health study sect., 1960, chmn. personality and cognition research rev. com., 1968-72; research adv. panel Social Security Adminstrn., 1961-62. Author: (with B. M. Moore) Tomorrow's Parents, 1964, Computer Assisted Instruction Testing and Guidance, 1971, (with R. Diaz-Guerrero and J. Swartz) Personality Development in Two Cultures, 1975, Introduction to Psychology, 1978; Editor: Jour. Ednl. Psychology, 1966-72. Trustee Ednl. Testing Service, Princeton, 1972-74; dir. Sci. Research Assos., 1975—; bd. dirs. Southwest Ednl. Devel. Lab., pres., 1974-75; mem. adv. com. computing activities NSF, 1970-73; mem. computer sci. and engring. bd. Nat. Acad. Scis., 1971-73, chmn. panel on selection and placement of mentally retarded students, 1979—; chmn. interdisciplinary cluster on social and behavioral devel. Pres.'s Biomed. Research Panel, 1975-76; bd. dirs. Found.'s Fund for Research in Psychiatry, 1973-77, chmn., 1976-77; dir. Conf. of S.W. Found., 1976—, pres., 1978-79; trustee Ednl. Testing Service, 1977-80, J.W. and Cornelia Scarborough Found., 1977-82, Center for Applied Linguistics, 1978-80, Salado Inst. Humanities, 1980—, Population Inst., 1979—, Menninger Found., 1982—, Population Resource Center, 1980—; mem. nat. adv. mental health council Alcohol, Drug Abuse, and Mental Health Adminstrn., 1978-81; mem. acad. info. systems adv. council IBM, 1982—. Served from ensign to lt. (j.g.) USNR, 1944-46. Faculty Research fellow Social Sci. Research Council, 1953-54, Center Advanced Study Behavioral Scis., 1962-63. Fellow Am. Psychol. Assn.; mem. Tex. Psychol. Assn. (pres. 1957), S.W. Psychol. Assn. (pres. 1958), Am. Statis. Assn., AAAS, Interam. Soc. Psychology (pres. 1966-67), Am. Ednl. Research Assn., Internat. Union Psychol. Scis. (sec.-gen. 1972—), Philos. Soc. Tex. (pres. 1982-83), Sigma Xi. Methodist. Home: 3300 Foothill Dr Austin TX 78731

HOLYOKE, THOMAS CAMPBELL, mathematics educator; b. Milw., June 9, 1922; s. Sydney Archibald and Mary (Gibbs) H.; m. Leona Evadene Garber, Sept. 7, 1947; children: Linda (Mrs. John Odell), Kitty (Mrs. Peter Jensen), Andrew Garber. B.A. in Mech. Engring. magna cum laude, Harvard, 1943; Ph.D. in Math, Ohio State U., 1950; postgrad. in physics, U. Calif. at Berkeley, 1957-58. Engr. Curtiss-Wright Co., 1943-44; instr. Ohio State U., Columbus, 1949-50; asst. prof. Northwestern U., 1950-55, Miami U., Oxford, Ohio, 1955-58; prof. Antioch Coll., Yellow Springs, Ohio, 1958—, dir. Sci. Inst., 1969-72, assoc. acad. dean, 1977-80; vis. mathematician Wright-Patterson AFB, Ohio, 1956; vis. prof. Coll. of Wooster, 1980-81; mem. faculty, adminstrn. various NSF Insts., 1957-62; Fulbright-Hays lectr. Mindanao State U., Philippines, 1964-65, Ford Found. cons., project leader, 1967-69; Fulbright-Hays lectr. Chancellor Coll., Malawi, 1975-77. Author: (with others) Foundations of College Mathematics, 1971; editor: Foundations of Mathematics, 1969; bd. dirs.: Antioch Rev, 1972-75, 78—; book rev. editor (with others), 1981—. Chmn. Yellow Springs Community Council, 1963; Mem. Yellow Springs Village Council, 1973-75; Bd. dirs. ACLU, Yellow Springs, 1963, 71-72 Bd. dirs. ACLU, Ohio, 1963, 71-72, Yellow Springs Credit Union, 1963. Served with USNR, 1944-46. Northwestern faculty fellow, 1952; NSF sci. faculty fellow, 1957-58. Fellow Ohio Acad. Sci. (v.p. 1963); mem. Sigma Xi, Phi Beta Kappa, Pi Mu Epsilon. Home: 608 S High St Yellow Springs OH 45387

HOLZ, HAROLD A., chem. and plastics mfg. co. exec.; b. N.Y.C., June 26, 1925; s. Herman A. and Genevieve (Murphy) H.; m. Joanne Axtell, Oct. 3, 1953; children—Gretchen, Timothy. B.S., Stevens Inst. Tech., 1946, M.E., 1947. Tech. rep. Union Carbide Corp., N.Y.C., 1947-49, Hartford, Conn., 1949-52, St. Louis, 1952-58, asst. regional mgr., Chgo., 1958-64, regional mgr., 1964-65, account exec., N.Y.C., 1965—. Served with USNR, 1943-46. Mem. Soc. Plastics Engrs. (distinguished mem., pres. 1975—), Plastics Pioneers Assn. (bd. govs. 1981—). Clubs: Chappaqua (N.Y.); Swim and Tennis. Home: 35 Ridge Rd Chappaqua NY 10514 Office: 1 University Plaza Hackensack NJ 07601

HOLZ, HARRY GEORGE, lawyer; b. Milw., Sept. 13, 1934; s. Harry Carl and Emma Louise (Hinz) H.; m. Nancy L. Heiser, May 12, 1962; children: Pamela Gretchen, Bradley Eric, Erika Lynn. B.S., Marquette U., 1956, LL.B., 1958; LL.M., Northwestern U., 1960. Bar: Wis. 1958, Ill. 1960. Teaching fellow Northwestern U. Sch. Law, 1958-59; assoc. Sidley & Austin, Chgo., 1960; ptnr. Quarles & Brady, Milw., 1961—; lectr. law of securities regulation U. Wis. Law Sch., 1971-74, Marquette U. Sch. Law, 1976-81; faculty Wis. State Bar Advanced Tng. Seminars Program on Antitrust Law, 1975-82; bd. dirs., lectr. continuing edn. programs Corp. Practice Inst., Inc., 1977-78. Bd. visitors Marquette U. Sch. Law, 1978. Served to capt. C.E. U.S. Army, 1960-67. Mem. ABA, State Bar Wis. (chmn. dir. corps., banking and bus. law sect. 1978-79, dir. 1978—), Milw. Bar Assn., Bar Assn. 7th Fed. Circuit, Woolsack Soc. Marquette U. Sch. Law, Beta Gamma Sigma. Lutheran. Clubs: Milw. Athletic, Western Racquet. Office: Quarles & Brady 780 N Water St Milwaukee WI 53202

HOLZER, EDWIN, advertising executive; b. 1933. Mus.B., Yale U., 1954, Mus.M., 1955; postgrad., Ind. U., 1956. Acct. exec. Benton & Bowles Inc., N.Y.C., 1959-62; account supr. William Esty Co., N.Y.C., 1962-66, Grey Advt. Inc., 1966-68, mgmt. supr., 1968-70, exec. v.p., 1970-73; chief operating officer Grey-North Inc., Chgo., 1970-73, pres., chief exec. officer, 1973—. Office: Grey-North Inc. Merchandise Mart Chicago IL 60654

HOLZER, HANS, author; b. Vienna, Austria, Jan. 26, 1920; s. Leo and Marta (Stransky) H.; m. Catherine Countess Buxhoeveden, Sept. 29, 1962; children—Nadine, Alexandra. Student, U. Vienna, Columbia U.; Ph.D., London. Prof. parapsychology N.Y. Inst. Tech.; pres. Aspera Ad Astra, Inc. (film prodn. co.), N.Y.C.; own radio program Sta. WMCA, 1974; research dir. N.Y. Com. for Investigation Paranormal Occurrences; lectr. Writer-producer documentaries on psychic subjects; writer/producer: In Search of, NBC, 1976-77; TV personality; composer and; lyricist.; Author: 81 books including ESP and You; Contbr. to mags. and newspapers. Mem. AAAS, N.Y. Acad. Scis., Archaeol. Inst. Am., ASCAP, N.Y. Hist. Soc. Address: 140 Riverside Dr New York NY 10024

HOLZMAN, ALBERT GEORGE, industrial engineer, educator; b. Johnstown, Pa., Oct. 28, 1921; s. Albert James and Eulalia Marie (Haberkorn) H.; m. Joan P. Michalowski, Nov. 5, 1945; children: Thomas, Richard, Judi, Jacqueline, David. B.S. in Indsl. Engring., U. Pitts., 1949, M.S., 1954, Ph.D., 1958. Registered profl. engr., Pa. Indsl. analyst Bethlehem Steel Corp., Johnstown, 1949-51; asst. prof. indsl. engring. U. Pitts., 1951-53, assoc. prof., 1953-58, prof., 1958—, chmn. dept. indsl. engring., 1966—; cons. Westinghouse Electric Corp., Pitts., 1971-75, H.B. Maynard & Co., 1982—; air. On-Line Systems, Inc., Pitts., 1968-79. Author: (with others) Matrices and Mathematical Programming, 1963; editor: Operations Research Support Methods, 1979, Mathematical Programming, 1981, (with others) Encyclopedia of Computer Science, 16 vols., 1981. Served as 1st lt. USAAF, 1942-45; ETO. Fellow Inst. Indsl. Engrs. (dir. accreditation 1982—); mem. Ops. Research Soc. Am., Am. Soc. Engring. Edn., Omega Rho (sec. 1979-83). Republican. Roman Catholic. Home: 1812 President Dr Glenshaw PA 15116 Office: Univ Pittsburgh 1048 Benedum Hall Pittsburgh PA 15261

HOLZMAN, D. KEITH, record company executive; b. N.Y.C., Mar. 22, 1936; s. Jacob Easton and Minnette Cathryn (Sternberger) H.; m. Jo Susan Handelman, Nov. 16, 1971; children—Susanne Carla, Lucas Jon, Rebecca Leigh. B.A., Oberlin (Ohio) Coll., 1957; M.F.A., Boston U., 1959. Asst. to gen. mgr. and stage mgr. N.Y.C. Light Opera, 1959, 62-64; dir. prodn. Elektra Records, N.Y.C., 1964-70; v.p. prodn. and mfg. Elektra/Asylum/Nonesuch Records, Los Angeles, 1970-81, sr. v.p. prodn. and mfg., 1981—; dir. Nonesuch Records, 1980—. Served with AUS, 1960-62. Mem. Audio Engring. Soc., Nat. Acad. Rec. Arts and Scis., Assn. Classical Music (dir.). Office: 9229 Sunset Blvd Los Angeles CA 90069

HOLZMAN, FRANKLYN DUNN, economics educator; b. Bklyn., Dec. 31, 1918; s. Abraham and Mollie (Mandel) H.; m. Mathilda Sara Wiesman, Dec. 14, 1946; children—Thomas Ludwig, David Carl, Miriam Alexandra. B.A., U. N.C., 1940; M.A., Harvard, 1948, Ph.D., 1952. Economist Dept. Treasury, 1947-48, cons., 1949-52; research fellow Russian Research Center, Harvard, 1949-52, research asso., 1961—; prof. econs. U. Wash., 1952-61, Tufts U.; mem. faculty Fletcher Sch. Law and Diplomacy, 1961—; vis. prof. U. Calif. at, Los Angeles, 1956, Stanford, 1957, Columbia, 1962, Mass. Inst. Tech., 1963; Cons. U.S. Dept. Treasury, 1950, 51, UN, 1963-64, U.S. ACDA, 1964-73, Joint Econ. Com. U.S. Congress, 1959, 73, 81, U.S. Commn. on Trade and Investment Policy, 1971, U.S. Dept. Commerce, 1972, 75-78; Stockholm Internat. Peace Research Inst., 1978. Author: Soviet Taxation: The Fiscal and Monetary Problems of a Planned Economy, 1955, Foreign Trade under Central Planning, 1974, Financial Checks on Soviet Defense Expenditures, 1975, International Trade Under Communism-Politics and Economics, 1976, Soviet Economy: Past, Present and Future, 1982. Served to staff sgt. USAAF, 1942-45. Mem. Am. Econ. Assn., Am. Assn. Advancement of Slavic Studies (exec. com. 1964-65), Am. Assn. Study of Soviet-Type Economies (exec. com. 1966-67), Econometric Soc., Assn. for Comparative Econ. Studies (pres. 1976-77). Home: 33 Peacock Farm Rd Lexington MA 02173

HOLZMAN, MALCOLM, architect; b. Newark, Sept. 26, 1940; s. Herman and Bertha (Rachmiel) H.; m. Jean Drake Stover, Nov. 30, 1968 (div. 1980); 1 son, Maxwell. B.Arch., Pratt Inst., 1963. Registered architect, N.Y. Architect Hugh Hardy & Assocs., N.Y.C., 1964-67; architect, ptnr. Hardy Holzman Pfeiffer Assocs., N.Y.C., 1967—; Eschweiler prof. architecture and urban design grad. student U. Wis., Milw., 1977, 78; Davenport vis. prof. Yale U., New Haven, 1976. Author: (with Hardy/Pfeiffer) Reusing Railroad Stations, 1974; archtl. works include, Hult Ctr. for Performing Arts, Eugene, Oreg., 1982, The Joyce Theater, N.Y.C., Madison Civic Ctr., Wis., 1980, Best Products Corp. Hdqrs., Richmond, Va., 1979, St. Louis Art Mus., 1977, Cooper-Hewitt Mus., N.Y.C., 1976, others. Trustee Amon Carter Mus., 1981—. Recipient AIA honor award, 1983, Firm of the Yr. award, 1981, Brunner prize Nat. Inst. Arts and Letters, 1974. Fellow AIA; mem. Archtl. League. Office: Hardy Holzman Pfeiffer Assocs 257 Park Ave S New York NY 10010

HOLZMAN, PHILIP SEIDMAN, psychologist, educator; b. N.Y.C., May 2, 1922; s. Barnet and Natalie (Seidman) H.; m. Hannah Abarbanell, Sept. 18, 1946; children: Natalie Kay, Carl David, Paul Benjamin. B.A., CCNY, 1943; Ph.D., U. Kans., 1952; postgrad., Topeka Inst. for Psychoanalysis, 1949-54. Diplomate: Am. Bd. Examiners Profl. Psychology. Psychology intern Topeka VA Hosp., 1946-49; psychologist Topeka State Hosp., 1949-51, cons., 1951-58; psychologist Menninger Found., Topeka, 1949-68, dir. research tng., 1963-68; tng. and supervising psychoanalyst Topeka Inst. for Psychoanalysis, 1964-68; prof. psychiatry and psychology U. Chgo., 1968-77; tng. and supervising psychoanalyst Chgo. Inst. for Psychoanalysis, 1968-77; prof. psychology dept. psychology and social relations Harvard U., 1977—; prof. dept. psychiatry Med. Sch., 1977—; chief sect. psychology Labs. for Psychiat. Research, McLean Hosp., Belmont, Mass., 1977—; tng. and supervising psychoanalyst Boston Psychoanalytic Soc. and Inst., 1977—; vis. prof. U. Minn., 1965, U. Kans., 1966, Boston U., 1973, Jefferson Med. Coll., 1981; Mem. small grants com. NIMH, 1960-64, clin. projects research rev. com., 1964-68, clin. program projects research rev. com., 1970-74, treatment devel. and assessment rev. com., 1982—; cons. Ill. State Psychiat. Inst., 1970-77. Author: (with others) Cognitive Control, 1959, Psychoanalysis and Psychopathology, 1970, (with Karl Menninger) The Theory of Psychoanalytic Technique, rev. edit, 1973; Editor: (with Merton M. Gill) Psychology Versus Metapsychology, 1975, (with Mary Hollis Johnston) Assessing Schizophrenic Thinking, 1979; bd. editors: Psychol. Issues, 1968—, Contemporary Psychology, 1969-76, Bull. of Menninger Clinic, 1961—; also Psychoanalysis and Contemporary Thought; asst. editor: Jour. Am. Psychoanalytic Assn, 1973-76, Jour. Psychiat. Research; contbr. articles to profl. jours. Mem. Topeka Mayor's Com. on Human Relations, 1963-68; trustee Menninger Found., 1979—; chmn. bd. dirs. Founds.' Fund for Research in Psychiatry; mem. adv. coms. on classification of mental disorders WHO. Served with AUS, 1943-46. Recipient Career Scientist award NIMH, 1974-77. Fellow Am. Psychol. Assn., Am. Acad. Arts and Scis., AAAS; mem. Am. Psychoanalytic Assn., Boston Psychoanalytic Soc., Am. Psychosomatic Soc., Am. Psychopath. Assn., Sigma Xi. Office: William James Hall Harvard U Cambridge MA 02138

HOLZMAN, ROBERT STUART, tax consultant; b. Paterson, N.J., Nov. 18, 1907; s. Samuel and Lillian (Hamburger) H.; m. Eleanore Grushlaw, May 27, 1938. B.S., U. Pa., 1929; A.M., N.Y. U., 1947, Ph.D., 1953. Tax cons., lectr. fin. N.Y. U. Grad. Sch. Bus. Adminstrn., 1946-53, prof. taxation, 1953-73, dir. univ. budget, 1958-63; prof. accounting U. Conn., 1973-74, 76-80; dir. Standard Security Life Ins. Co., N.Y. Author: Corporate Reorganizations: Their Federal Tax Status, 1948, Guide to Pension and Profit-sharing Plans, 1953, rev., 1969, Stormy Ben Butler, 1954, General Baseball Doubleday, 1955, The Romance of Fire Fighting, 1956, The Tax on Accumulated Earnings, 1956, Arm's Length Transactions, 1958, Sound Business Purpose, 1958, Federal Income Taxation, 1960, The Taxpayer's Problem of Proof, 1962, Tax Basis for Managerial Decisions, 1965, Tax-Free Reorganizations, 1967, Holzman on Estate Planning, 1967, Federal Taxation of Capital Assets, 1969, Tax Free Reorganizations After the Tax Reform Act of 1969, 1970, Dun & Bradstreet's Handbook of Executive Tax Management, 1974, Accountant's and Treasurer's Complete Guide to the Accumulated Earnings Tax, 1974, Take It Off!, 1984, Tax-Free Organizations After the Pension Reform

Act of 1974, 1976, Adapt or Perish, 1976, New Tax Traps and New Opportunities, 1975, The Complete Book of Estate Planning, 1978, Landmark Tax Cases, 1979, Business Tax Traps, 1979, A Survival Kit for Taxpayers, 1979, Encyclopedia of Estate Planning, 1983, Estate Planning—The New Golden Opportunities, 1983; editor: Tax Practitioners Library, 15 vols, 1956-62; co-editor: Big Business Methods for the Small Business, 1952; Contbg. editor: Boardroom Reports; Editorial bd.: Taxation for Accountants; estate planning editor: Bottom Line Personal; Contbr. articles to profl. publs. Past pres. Fed. Tax Forum, Civil War Round Table, N.Y.C. Mem. Am. Hist. Assn., Fin. Execs. Inst., Estate Planners Council N.Y.C., Beta Alpha Psi, Beta Gamma Sigma. Club: N.Y. Univ. Home: Carlyle Rd Candlewood Vista Danbury CT 06810 Office: PO Box 1013 Danbury CT 06810

HOLZNER, BURKART, sociologist, educator; b. Tilsit, Ger., Apr. 28, 1931; came to U.S., 1957, naturalized, 1965; s. Hans Otto and Brigitte (Prenzel) H.; m. Leslie Salmon-Cox; children by previous marriage: Steven, Daniel, Claire. Student, U. Munich, 1949-52, 53-54, U. Wis., 1952-53, postgrad., 1957-59; Diplom Psychologe, U. Bonn, 1957, Ph.D., 1958. Grad. asst., acting instr. U. Wis., 1958-60; asst. prof. U. Pitts., 1960-63, assoc. prof., 1963-65, prof., chmn. sociology dept., 1966-80, dir. bd. visitors field staff Learning Research and Devel. Center, 1964-66, 71-78, dir. Univ. Center for Internat. Studies, 1980—, also mem. policy planning com. Univ. Ctr. Social and Urban Research, also sr. research assoc.; assoc. sociologist, assoc. dir. Social Sci. Research Inst., U. Hawaii, 1965-66; vis. prof. sociology, dir. Social Research Centre, Chinese U., Hong Kong, 1969-70; vis. prof. U. Augsburg, 1977, Chinese Acad. Social Scis., Beijing, 1979, 80,; cons. Nat. Inst. Edn., Westinghouse Electric Corp.; mem. exec. com. Pa. Council for Internat. Edn., 1980—, chmn., 1983. Author: Amerikanische und deutsche Psychologie, 1958, Völkerpsychologie, 1960, Reality Construction in Society, rev. edit, 1972, (with John Marx) Knowledge Application: The Knowledge System in Society, 1979; editor: Knowledge: Creation-Diffusion, Utilization, 1982; co-editor: (with Roland Robertson) Identity and Authority, Explorations in the Theory of Society, 1980, (with Jiri Nehnevajsa) Organizing for Social Research, 1981, (with Zdenek Suda) Directions of Change: Modernization Theory, Research and Reality, 1981. Mem. dist. export council U.S. Dept. Commerce. Mem. Am. Sociol. Assn., North Central (Sociol. Assn.), Pa. Sociol. Assn., Sozialwissenschaftlicher Studienkreis für Internationale Probleme, Internat. Soc. for Comparative Study of Civilizations (mem. U.S. council, v.p. 1977-79). Home: 6534 Bartlett St Pittsburgh PA 15217

HOLZWARTH, JAMES CARL, metallurgical engineer, industrial research administrator; b. Ft. Wayne, Ind., June 20, 1924; s. Carl George and Gladys Margaret (Streicher) H.; m. Niki Naomi Koopman, Nov. 12, 1945; children: Gregory, Michael, Karen. B.S. in Metall. Engring, Purdue U., 1945, M.S., 1948. Instr. in metallurgy Purdue U., 1947-48; with Gen. Motors Research Labs., Warren, Mich., 1948—, head dept. metall. engring., 1969-73, tech. dir. labs., 1973-82, dir. programs and plans, 1982—. Contbr. articles to profl. jours. Served to ensign USNR, 1943-45. Recipient Disting. Engring. Alumnus award Purdue U., 1974. Fellow Am. Soc. Metals (trustee 1978-80); mem. Soc. Automotive Engrs., AAAS, Engring. Soc. Detroit, Sigma Xi. Patentee in field. Office: Gen Motors Research Labs Gen Motors Tech Center Warren MI 48090

HOMBURGER, FREDDY, physician, scientist, artist; b. St. Gall, Switzerland, Feb. 8, 1916; came to U.S., 1941, naturalized, 1952; s. Ludwig and Cécile (Gaille) H.; m. Regina Thürlimann, Nov. 8, 1939. Student, U. Vienna, Austria, 1936-37; M.D., U. Geneva, Switzerland, 1941. Diplomate: Nat. Bd. Med. Examiners., Am. Bd. Toxicology. Research fellow, intern pathology Yale Med. Sch. and New Haven Hosps., 1941-43; intern, research fellow in medicine Harvard Med. Sch., Thorndike Meml. Lab., Boston City Hosp., 1943-45; fellow in medicine Meml. Hosp., N.Y.C., 1946-48; chief clin. investigation Sloan-Kettering Inst. Cancer Research, N.Y.C., 1945-48; instr. medicine Cornell U. Med. Coll., 1946-48, research prof. medicine, 1948-57; dir. cancer research and control unit Tufts U. Sch. Medicine, Boston, 1948-57; mem. courtesy staff Mt. Desert Island Hosp., Bar Harbor, Maine, 1955-73, Eastern Meml. Hosp., Ellsworth, Maine, 1957-60; sci. asso. Jackson Lab., Bar Harbor, 1951-60; research prof. oncology, div. basic scis. Sch. Grad. Dentistry, Boston U., 1973—; research prof. pathology Sch. Medicine, 1974—; mem. sci. staff Mallory Inst. Pathology, Boston City Hosp., 1979—; mem. Grad. Sch. Faculty Boston U., 1981—; Mem. corp. Gesell Inst. Child Devel., 1960-78; chmn. adv. com. Am. Students U. Geneva; pres., dir. Bio-Research Inst., Inc., 1957—, Bio-Research Cons., Inc., 1957—; pres. Trenton Exptl. Lab. Animal Co., Bar Harbor, 1969-81; treas., dir. Cambridge Coordinating Com. Drugs, 1972-74; hon. consul of Switzerland in, Boston, 1964—; neutral mem. mixed med. commn. War Dept., 1944-46. Author: The Medical Care of the Aged and Chronically Ill, 3d edit, 1973, The Biological Basis of Cancer Management, 1957; also numerous sci. papers.; Editor: The Physiopathology of Cancer, 3d edit, 1974-76, Progress in Experimental Tumor Research, vols. I-XXVII, 1960—; sr. editor: Symposia on Research Advances Applied to Medical Practice, Current Concepts in Toxicology; Exhibited paintings one-man shows, N.Y.C., Paris, Zurich, Geneva, Boston. Mem. overseers com. to visit Harvard, 1965-71, 76—; bd. dirs. Cambridge Soc. Early Music, 1970; trustee Opera Co., Boston, 1967—; chmn. Friends Busch-Reisinger Mus., 1974—; visitor paintings Boston Mus. Fine Arts, 1974—; mem. adv. bd. Lachaise Found. Fellow AAAS, N.Y. Acad. Scis. (ednl. adv. com. 1967); mem. Nat. Hypertension Assn. (nat. adv. council 1978—), AMA, Endocrine Soc., Am. Assn. Cancer Research, Am. Fedn. Clin. Research, N.Y. Acad. Medicine, Soc. Exptl. Biology and Medicine, Am. Writers Assn., Am. Assn. Pathologists, Soc. Toxicology, Am. Soc. Pharmacology and Exptl. Therapeutics, Royal Soc. Health, Brit. Soc. Toxicology, Soc. Pharmacological and Environ. Pathologists, Soc. Study Reproduction, Endocrine Soc., Am. Assn. Lab. Animal Scis., New Eng. Soc. Pathologists, Acad. Toxicological Scis., Cambridge C. of C. (dir. 1969-73), Sigma Xi. Clubs: Harvard (Boston); Yale (N.Y.C.); Cosmos (Washington). Home: 759 High St Dedham MA 02026 also Trenton ME 04605 Office: 9 Commercial Ave Cambridge MA 02141

HOMBURGER, WALTER FRITZ, symphony manager; b. Karlsruhe, Germany, Jan. 22, 1924; emigrated to Can., 1940, naturalized, 1951; m. Victor and Marianne (Bredig) H.; m. Emmy Schmid, June 23, 1961; children: Michael Victor, Lisa Marie. Student, Can. schs. Artists mgr., 1947; mgr. Nat. Ballet Can., 1951-55; mng. dir. Toronto Symphony, 1962—. Served with Can. Army, World War II. Club: Variety. Home: 278 Heath St E Toronto ON M4T 1T4 Canada

HOMER, WILLIAM INNES, educator, author; b. Merion, Pa., Nov. 8, 1929; s. Austin and Evelyn (Innes) H.; m. Virginia D. Keller, Aug. 14, 1954; 1 son, Stacy Innes. A.B., Princeton U., 1951; postgrad., N.Y.U., 1952-53; M.A., Harvard U., 1954; Ph.D. (Sachs Traveling Research fellow 1957-58), 1961. Instr. dept. art and archeology Princeton, 1955-59, lectr., 1959-61, asst. prof., 1961-64; assoc. prof. history of art Cornell U., 1964-66; prof. U. Del., Newark, 1966—, chmn. dept. art history, 1966-81; dir. index of dissertations and theses in Am. art Archives of Am. Art, Washington; vis. fellow Princeton U., 1972-73; assoc. fellow Center for Advanced Studies, Nat. Gallery of Art, 1980-81; Mem. Del. Arts Council, 1969-70, New Castle County Beautification Bd., 1967-70; adv. screening com. (overseas) Fulbright-Hays Fellowship Awards, 1970-72, chmn., 1971-72; mem. sr. fellowship panel Nat. Endowment for Humanities, 1970; mem. exhbn. com. Del. Art Mus., 1968-73, chmn. accessions com., 1974-78. Author: Seurat and the Science of Painting, 1964, Robert Henri and His Circle, 1969, Alfred Stieglitz and the American Avant-Garde, 1977, The Photographs of Gertrude Käsebier, 1979, Alfred Stieglitz and the Photo-Secession, 1983; editorial bd.: Am. Art Jour, 1970—, Winterthur Portfolio, 1978-80; contbr. articles to profl. jours. Mem. adv. com. Am. Studies Inst., Lincoln U., 1967-76; adv. council Dunlap Soc., 1975—; mem. corp. Mus. Art, Ogunquit, Maine, 1958—; chmn. West Side Larger Parish Scholarship Fund, 1973-75; regional adv. com. Archives Am. Art, 1979—; mem. bd. New Pictorialist Soc., 1981—. Council of Humanities fellow Princeton U., 1962-63; Am. Council Learned Socs. fellow, 1964-65; Guggenheim fellow, 1972-73; Nat. Endowment for Humanities fellow, 1980-81. Fellow Royal Soc. Arts (London); mem. Coll. Art Assn. Am., Am. Photog. Hist. Soc., Wilmington Soc. Fine Arts, Pictorial Photographers Am., Royal Photog. Soc., Phi Kappa Phi. Clubs: Princeton; (N.Y.C.); Nat. Arts. Home: 15 Dickinson Ln Wilmington DE 19807 Office: Dept Art History U Del Newark DE 19716

HOMGREN, EDWIN SURL, library adminstrator; b. Rock Springs, Wyo., June 13, 1934; s. Edwin Segurd and Helen Maurine (Larson) Holmgren; m. Priscilla A. Talbot, Dec. 27, 1959; children: Maurine Edna, Philip Edwin. A.B. in English, Stanford U., 1955; M.S., U. Ill., 1956. Cert. librarian, N.Y. Reference asst. Gary Pub. Libary, Ind., 1956-57; asst. dir., acting dir. Summit Free Pub. Library, N.J., 1957-60; library cons. Charles M. Upham Assoc., Inc., Bangkok, Thailand, 1960-62; asst. dir. New Orleans Pub. Library, 1962-65; asst. dir. for gen. adminstrn. and tech. services Rochester Pub. Library, N.Y., 1965-70; dir. The Branch Libraries, N.Y. Pub. Library, N.Y.C., 1971—; voting mem. Blue Cross-Blue Shield, N.Y.C., 1979—. Trustee Metro, N.Y.C., 1976—, Intershare, N.Y.C., 1980—; mem. com. Lincoln Center Edn. Council, N.Y.C., 1970—. Served to lt. (j.g.) USN, 1944-46; PTO. Mem. ALA, N.Y. Library Assn., Spl. Libraries Assn., Thai Library Assn., Am. Assn. Museums, Am. Soc. Pub. Adminstrn., Phi Beta Kappa, Beta Phi Mu. Home: 3333 J Henry Hudson Pdwy Riverdale NY 10463 Office: 455 Fifth Ave New York NY 10016

HOMJAK, JOHN, JR., hospital administrator; b. Ambridge, Pa., Dec. 5, 1933; s. John and Helen (Panek) H.; m. Dale Marea Carter, June 9, 1966; children: Kara Marie, Kendra Lee. B.S. in Pharmacy, Duquesne U., 1958; M.H.A., St. Louis U., 1960; LL.B., LaSalle Extension U., Chgo., 1966. Asst. hosp. adminstr. Aramco Med. Dept., Dhahran, Saudi Arabia, 1962-69; exec. adminstr. Burde Rehab. Ctr., White Plains, N.Y., 1969-70; assoc. adminstr. Timken Mercy Med. Ctr., Canton, Ohio, 1970-74; assoc. exec. adminstr. King Faisal Spl. Hosp., Riyadh, Saudi Arabia, 1974-75; pres., chief exec. officer Hawkes Hosp. of Mt. Carmel, Columbus, Ohio, 1975-83; mem. chief exec. officers council Holy Cross Health System, South Bend, Ind., 1979-83; mem. appeals com. Blue Cross, Columbus, 1981-82, chmn. dist. council, 1982-83; chmn. adminstrv. council Coalition for Cost Effective Health Care, Columbus, 1983—. Mem. Ohio Health and Med. Leaders People-to-People Del. to Peoples Repub. China Ohio State Health Dept. Served with AUS, 1954-55. Mem. Am. Coll. Hosp. Adminstrs. Home: 5056 Sharon Hill Dr Worthington OH 43085 Office: Hawkes Hosp of Mt Carmel 793 W State St Columbus OH 43222

HOMME, ROBERT ONAN, diplomat; b. Duluth, Minn., May 19, 1940; s. Olaf Anderson and Evelyn (Boucher) H.; m. Anelena Munoz, Dec. 18, 1964; children: Natalie, Marisa, Karina. B.A., Carleton Coll., 1962. Comm. fgn. service officer Dept. State, Washington, 1962, vice consul, Ciudad Juarez, Mexico, 1963-65, Calif., Colombia, 1965-67, spl. asst. to under sec., 1968-69, polit. officer, Rome, 1969-73, Panama, 1973-75; dept. European affairs (Dept. State), 1975-81; consul gen. Am. consulate gen., Strasbourg, France, 1981—. Mem. European Circle, Am. Fgn. Service Assn., Consular Corps of Strasbourg. Lutheran. Office: Am Consulate Gen 15 Avenue D'Alsacs 67082 Strasbourg France

HOMMES, FRITS AUKUSTINUS, biology educator; b. Bellingwolde, Netherlands, May 28, 1934; came to U.S., 1979; s. Aukustinus and Anje (Wester) H.; m. Grietje Renes, June 14, 1958; children: Peter, Anneliek. M.Sc. in Chemistry, U. Gronigen, Netherlands, 1958; Ph.D., U. Nijmegen, Netherlands, 1961. Research asst. dept. biochemistry U. Nijmegen, 1959-61; instr. U. NiJmegen, 1963-66; postdoctroal fellow dept. biochemistry and biophysics U. Pa., Phila., 1961-63; head lab. dept. pediatrics U. Groningen, 1966-72, assoc. prof., 1972-79; prof. dept. cell and molecular biology Med. Coll. Ga., Augusta, 1979—, dir. biochem. genetics lab., 1980—; cons. genetic diseases Dutch Health Council, 1974-79; chmn. Dutch Bioenergetics Study Group, 1975-77. Author: Inborn Errors of Metabolism, 1973, Normal and Pathological Development of Energy Metakbolism, 1975, Models for the Study of Inborn Errors of Metabolism, 1979; mem. editorial bd.: Nutrition and Metabolism, 1975—; contbr. articles to profl. jours.; patentee. Chmn. Groningen chpt. Round Table, 1970-71, No. Dist., Netherlands, 1973-75; mem. nat. bd. Nol Dist., Netherlands, 1974-75. Fulbright fellow, 1961-63. Mem. European Soc. Pediatric Research, Soc. Study of Inborn Errors of Metabolism, Soc. Inherited Metabolic Disease, Am. Soc. Human Genetics, AAAS, N.Y. Acad. Sci., Am. Soc. Biol. Chemists. Roman Catholic. Lodge: Rotary. Home: 793 Brookfield Pkwy Augusta GA 30907 Office: Dept Cell and Molecular Biology Med Coll Ga Augusta GA 30912

HOMSEY, SAMUEL, architect, artist; b. Boston, Aug. 29, 1904; s. Elias Samuel and Margaret (Sabbag) H.; m. Victorine duPont, Apr. 27, 1929; children—Coleman duPont, Eldon duPont. B.S., M.S., MIT, 1926. Practicing architect, 1926—. Contbr. articles to Archtl. Forum.; archtl. projects include Am. Embassy, Tehran, Iran. Bd. dirs. Wilmington Acad. Art, 1941-42. Served as comdr., Office Research and Inventions USNR; lt. comdr. Bur. Aeros. Recipient prize for instl. bldgs. Pitts. Glass Inst., 1938; diploma of merit for design of Cambridge Yacht Club Md. Soc. of Architects, 1940; 1st prize Del. Ann. 1st Oil Show Wilmington Soc. Fine Arts; two 1st prizes Del. Ann. Water Color Show. A.N.A. Fellow AIA (v.p.); mem. NAD (academician), Am., Phila. watercolor socs., Am. Water Color Soc., Confrerie Des Chevaliers du Tastevin. Republican. Club: Century Assn. Home: 1800 Wawaset St Wilmington DE 19806 Office: 2003 N Scott St Wilmington DE 19806

HOMSEY, VICTORINE DU PONT (MRS. SAMUEL E. HOMSEY), architect; b. Grosse Pointe Farms, Mich., Nov. 27, 1900; d. Antoin Bidermann and Ethel (Clark) duPont; m. Samuel E. Homsey, Apr. 27, 1929; children—Coleman duPont, Eldon duPont. A.B., Wellesley Coll., 1923; M.Arch., Cambridge (Mass.) Sch. Architecture, 1925. Practice as architect, 1926—; mem. archtl. firm Victorine and Samuel Homsey. Contbr.: Guide to Modern Architecture; major works include Am. Embassy, Tehran, Iran. Mem. exec. com. Greater Wilmington Devel. Council; mem. adv. bd. Historic Am. Bldgs. Survey; mem. Commn. Fine Arts, Washington, 1976—. Recipient 1st prize instl. architecture for Children's Beach House (Lewes, Del.) Pitts. Glass Inst.; regional, state awards for Cambridge Yacht Club Md. Soc. Architects; hon. mention award for design Stubbs Elementary Sch., Wilmington, Del., Sch. Exec. mag. Fellow AIA; mem. NAD (asso.), Colonial Dames. Episcopalian. Club: Wilmington Garden. (Del.). Home: 1800 Wawaset St Wilmington DE 19806 Office: 2003 N Scott St Wilmington DE 19806

HONAN, WILLIAM HOLMES, journalist; b. N.Y.C., May 11, 1930; s. William Francis and Annette (Neudecker) H.; m. Nancy Burton, June 22, 1975; children: Bradley, Daniel, Edith. B.A., Oberlin (Ohio) Coll., 1952; M.A., U. Va., 1955. Editor The Villager (weekly newspaper), N.Y.C., 1957-60; asst. editor New Yorker mag., 1960-64; freelance writer nat. mags., 1964-68; asso. editor Newsweek, 1969; asst. editor N.Y. Times mag., 1969-70, travel editor, 1970-72, 73-74, arts and leisure editor, 1974-82, culture editor, 1982—; mng. editor Saturday Rev., 1972-73. Author: Greenwich Village Guide, 1959, Ted Kennedy: Profile of a Survivor, 1972; pamphlet Another La Guardia, 1960; also numerous articles. Served with AUS, 1956-57. Office: NY Times 229 W 43d St New York NY 10036

HONDERICH, BELAND HUGH, publisher; b. Kitchener, Ont., Can., Nov. 25, 1918; s. John William and Rae Laura (Armstrong) H.; m. Florence Irene Wilkinson, Oct. 1943; John Allen, Mary Elizabeth, David Beland; m. Agnes Janet Hutchinson (Oct. 1969). Ed., pub. schs., Baden, Ont.; LL.D., York U., 1976, Wilfrid Laurier U., 1977. Reporter Toronto Star Ltd., Ont., 1943-45, fin. editor, 1945-55; editor in chief Daily Star and Star Weekly, 1955-66, pres., pub., 1966-76, chmn. bd., pub., 1976—, chmn. pres., 1977—. Address: Torstar Corp 1 Yonge St Toronto ON Canada M5E 1E6 *

HONEMANN, DANIEL HENRY, lawyer; b. Balt., Oct. 20, 1929; s. Henry Letcher and Maude Elizabeth (Wilson) H.; m. Rose Ann Clark, Mar. 23, 1974; children by previous marriage: Deborah, Dori, Daniel, Donna. A.B., Western Md. Coll., Westminster, 1951; LL.B., U. Md., 1956. Bar: Md. 1956. Since practiced in, Balt.; partner firm Clapp, Somerville, Honemann & Beach, 1962—; asst. U.S. atty. Dist. Md., 1960-61. Served to 1st lt. inf. AUS, 1951-53. Decorated Bronze Star, Combat Inf. badge. Fellow Am. Coll. Probate Counsel, Md. Bar Found.; mem. ABA (ho. of dels. 1978-80), Md. Bar Assn. (sec. 1977-84, bd. govs. 1975-84), Balt. Bar Assn. Home: 2318 Harcroft Rd Timonium MD 21093 Office: 1700 First Nat Bank Bldg Baltimore MD 21202

HONEY, RICHARD CHURCHILL, electrical engineer; b. Portland, Oreg., Mar. 9, 1924; s. John Kohnen and Margaret Fargo (Larrison) H.; m. Helen Waugaman, June 8, 1952 (div. Feb. 1980); children: Leslie, Steven, Laura, Janine. B.S., Calif. Inst. Tech., 1945; E.E., Stanford U., 1950, Ph.D., 1953. Research asst. Stanford U., 1948-52; sr. research engr. microwave group Stanford Research Inst., 1952-60; tech. program coordinator Electromagnetic Techniques Lab., 1960-64, lab. dir., 1964-70, staff scientist, 1970—; dir. ILC Tech.; mem. Army Sci. Bd., 1978—. Contbr. articles to books, encyc., profl. jours. Served with USN, 1943-46. Fellow IEEE, Optical Soc. Am.; mem. Optical Soc. No. Calif., Sigma Xi. Club: Palo Alto Yacht. Patentee in field. Office: 333 Ravenswood Menlo Park CA 94025 *

HONEY, RICHARD DAVID, educator; b. Millcreek Twp., Pa., Dec. 24, 1927; s. Bennett Vincent and Eleanor Violet (Will) H. A.B., Transylvania Coll., 1957; Ph.D., U. Chgo., 1962. Prof. psychology, clin. psychologist Transylvania U., Lexington, Ky., 1964—; Sr. psychologist Psychiat. Inst., Municipal Ct., Chgo., 1961, prin. psychologist, 1962-64; Clin. cons. VA Hosp. Served with AUS, 1952-54; Korea. Woodrow Wilson fellow; Danforth fellow. Mem. Ky., Am. psychol. assns., Am. Psychology-Law Soc., Soc. Values in Higher Edn., Sigma Xi, Phi Kappa Tau, Lampas Circle of Omicron Delta Kappa. Home: 545 Mt Tabor Rd Lexington KY 40502 *The ideal that always eludes me while constantly challenging me, is daily learning to strive to become an open channel for the love of God.*

HONEYCUTT, GEORGE LEONARD, photographer; b. High Point, N.C., Jan. 5, 1936; s. Leonard Franklin and Pearl (Reynolds) H.; m. Sandra Spencer, Mar. 29, 1955; children: George Keith, Stephen Kurt, Kevin Spencer. Student, Sch. Modern Photgraophy, N.Y.C., 1954. Photographer Charlotte (N.C.) News, 1959-62; Staff photographer Houston Chronicle, 1963, dir. photography, 1963—. Served with AUS, 1955-57. Recipient awards AP, UP, Headliners; 4-time winner Profl. Football Hall of Fame. Mem. Nat. Press Photographers Assn. (named Nat. Newspaper Photographer of Yr. 1962). Methodist. Office: 801 Texas Ave Houston TX 77002

HONG, HOWARD VINCENT, library administrator, philosophy educator; b. Wolford, N.D., Oct. 19, 1912. B.A., St. Olaf Coll., 1934; postgrad., Wash. State Coll., 1934-35; Ph.D., U. Minn., 1938; postgrad., U. Copenhagen, 1938-39; D.Litt. (hon.), McGill U., Montreal, 1977, D.D., Trinity Sem., Columbus, Ohio, 1983. With English dept. Wash. State Coll., 1934-35; with Brit. Mus., 1937; mem. faculty dept. philosophy St. Olaf Coll., Northfield, Minn., 1938—, asst. prof. philosophy, 1940-42, assoc. prof., 1942-47, prof., 1947-78, chmn. Ford Found. self-study com., 1955-56, dir. Kierkegaard Library, 1972—; vis. lectr. U. Minn., 1955; mem. Nat. Lutheran Council Scholarship and Grant Rev. Bd., 1958-66; lectr. Holden Village, Washington, 1963-70; mem. Minn. Colls. Grant Rev. Bd., 1970. Author: books most recent This World and the Church, 1955; editor, contbg. author: Christian Faith and the Liberal Arts, 1960; co-editor, translator: (with Edna H. Hong) works by Gregor Malantschuk, numerous works by Soren Kierkegaard, Soren Kierkegaard's Journals and Papers, Vol. 1, 1968 (Nat. Book award for transl. 1968), Soren Kierkegaard's Journals and Papers, Vol. 11, 1970, Soren Kirkegaard's Jornals and Papers, Vol. 111-1V, 1975, Soren Kierkegaard's Journals and Papers, V-V11, 1978, The Controversial Kierkegaard (Gregor Malatschuk), 1980, The Sickness unto Death (Soren Kierkegaard), 1980, The Corsaair Affair (Soren Kierkegaard), 1981, Fear and Trembling-Repetition, 1983; gen. editor: Kierkegaard's Writings, 1972—. Field sec. War Prisoners Aid, U.S., Scandinavia and Germany, 1943-46; sr. rep. Service to Refugees, Luth. World Fedn., Germany and Austria, 1947-49; sr. field officer refugee div. World Council Chs., Germany, 1947-48. Decorated Order of Dannebrog Denmark; fellow Am.-Scandinavian Found.-Denmark, 1938-39, Am. Council Learned Socs., 1952-53, Rockefeller Found., 1959; sr. research fellow Fulbright Commn., 1959-60, 64; sr. fellow NEH, 1970-71; grante NEH, 1972-73; publ. grantee Carlsberg Found., 1974; editing-translating grantee NEH, 1978-84. Office: Keirkegaard Library St Olaf Coll Northfield MN 55057

HONG, RICHARD, physician, educator; b. Danville, Ill., Jan. 10, 1929; s. William and Louise (See) H.; m. Marion Shaw Taylor, May 31, 1952; children—Susan, Steven, Andrew, Laura. B.S., U. Ill., 1949, M.D., 1953. Intern Cook County Hosp., Chgo., 1953-54; resident Children's Hosp., Cin., 1957-60; research asso. immunology dept. pediatrics Coll. Medicine, U. Cin., 1957-65; asst. prof. pediatrics U. Minn., 1965-67, prof., 1967-69; prof. pediatrics U. Wis. Med. Sch., Madison, 1969—, asso. dean, 1971—. Served with USAF, 1954-57. Mem. Soc. Pediatric Research, Am. Assn. Immunologists, Am. Soc. Clin. Investigation, Phi Beta Kappa, Phi Kappa Phi. Home: 201 Saratoga Circle Madison WI 53705

HONG, SE JUNE, computer engineer; b. Seoul, May 5, 1944; U.S., 1965; s. Eo Kil and Oak Soon (Sohn) H.; m. Karen Fay McCully, Aug. 31, 1968; 1 dau., Kessely Corea. B.S. in Elec. Engring., Seoul Nat. U., 1965, M.S., U. Ill., 1967, Ph.D, Seoul Nat. U., 1969. Staff engr.

Systems Devel. Lab., IBM, Poughkeepsie, NY, 1969-73, adv. engr., 1973-78, sr. engr., 1978; mem. research staff T.J. Watson Research Ctr.,IBM, Yorktown Heights, NY, 1978-81; mgr. T.J. Watson Research Ctr., IBM, Yorktown Heights, NY, 1981-82, sr. mgr., 1982—; vis. prof. Korea Advanced Inst. Sci. and Tech., Seoul, 1980. Author: Converstaional English, 1963; contbr. articles to profl. jours.; patentee in field. Bd. dirs. Mid-Hudson Arts and Sci. ctr., Poughkeepsie, NY, 1972-78, Dutchess County United Way, Poughkeepsie, NY, 1972-74, Dutchess County Family Counseling Service, Poughkeepsie, NY, 1973-78. Recipient Disting. Service award NY State Jaycees, 1976. Fellow IEEE (disting. visitor 1972-75); mem. Assn. Computing Machinery, Math. Assn. Am., Am. Assn. Artificial Intelligence, Assn. Computational Linguistics, Korean Scientists and Engrs. in Am., Sigma Xi. Democrat. Methodist. Home: 1374 White Hill Rd Yorktown Heights NY 10598 Office: TJ Watson Research Ctr IBM PO Box 218 Yorktown Heights NY 10598

HONG, TANY S., state attorney general; b. Makawao, Maui, Hawaii, Feb. 24, 1931; m. Naomi Hong; 3 children. B.A. in Econs., U. Hawaii, 1956; J.D., U. Gonzaga, 1967. Salesman, supr. Honolulu Gas Co., 1952-62; dep. atty. gen. State of Hawaii, Honolulu, 1967-78, atty. gen., 1981—, dir. dept. regulatory agys., 1978-81. Served with U.S. Army, 1949-52. Mem. Hawaii Bar Assn. Office: Atty Gen of Hawaii 405 State Capitol Honolulu HI 96813 *

HONIG, EDWIN, comparative literature educator, poet; b. N.Y.C., Sept. 3, 1919; s. Abraham David and Jane (Freundlich) H.; m. Charlotte Gilchrist, Apr. 1, 1940 (dec. 1963); m. Margot S. Dennes, Dec. 15, 1963 (div. 1978); children: Daniel D., Jeremy D. A.B., U. Wis., 1941, A.M., 1947; M.A. (hon.), Brown U., 1958. Instr. English Purdue U., 1942-43, N.Y.U. and Ill. Inst. Tech., 1946-47, U. N.Mex., 1947-48, Claremont Coll., summer 1949; instr. English Harvard U., 1949-52, Briggs-Copeland asst. prof. English, 1952-57; mem. faculty Brown U., 1957—, prof. English, 1960—, chmn. dept., 1967, prof. comparative lit., 1962—; vis. prof. U. Calif. at Davis, 1964-65; Mellon prof. Boston U. intersession, 1977; dir. Copper Beech Press. Author: Garcia Lorca, rev. edit, 1963; poems The Moral Circus, 1955; criticism Dark Conceit: The Making of Allegory, 1959; poems The Gazabos: 41 Poems, 1960, Survivals, 1964, Spring Journal: Poems, 1968, Four Springs, 1972, Shake a Spear With Me, John Berryman, 1974, At Sixes, 1974; criticism Calderon and The Seizures of Honor, 1972; play/ libretto Calisto and Melibea, 1972; poems The Affinities of Orpheus, 1976, Selected Poems (1955-1976), 1979, Interrupted Praise, 1983; stories Foibles and Fables of an Abstract Man, 1979; (with Jean Zaleski) art book Cow/Lines, 1982; plays Ends of the World and Other Plays, 1983; translations Calderon: 4 Plays, 1961, Cervantes' Interludes, 1964, Calderon's Life Is A Dream, 1970, Fernando Pessoa's Selected Poems, 1971, Garcia Lorca's Divan and Other Writings, 1974; (with Oscar Williams) anthologies The Mentor Book of Major American Poets, 1961, The Major Metaphysical Poets, 1968, Spenser, 1968; Produced plays, Cambridge, Mass., The Widow, 1953, N.Y.C., Washington and Denver, The Phantom Lady, 1964, Stanford Summer Festival, Calisto and Melibea, 1966, BBC Radio, London, Life Is A Dream, 1970; prod. opera, Davis, Calif., Calisto and Melibea, 1979. Recipient Golden Rose award New Eng. Poetry Club, 1961; grantee Nat. Acad. Arts and Letters, 1966; Poetry prize Sat. Rev., 1956; Phi Beta Kappa poet Brown U., 1961, 82; Guggenheim fellow, 1948, 62; Amy Lowell traveling poetry fellow, 1968; R.I. Gov.'s award for excellence in arts, 1970; Nat. Endowment for Humanities fellow for ind. study, 1975; grantee, 1977-80; Nat. Endowment for Arts fellow in creative writing, 1977; fellow in opera libretto, 1979; recipient Nat. Endowment for arts PEN fiction project award, 1983. Office: Brown Univ Box 1852 Providence RI 02912 *Being young and old at the same time; having little concern for past accomplishments, great concern for new possibilities; distrusting all dogmas; valuing friendship and solitude; becoming yourself through others; honoring trees, bridges, natural skies, water and fire as friends; taking air freely and escaping finally into it.*

HONIG, GEORGE RAYMOND, pediatrician, educator; b. Chgo., May 5, 1936; s. Joseph C. and Raymonde S. (Moses) H.; m. Karen R. Jacobson, Dec. 18, 1960; children: Sharon, Debra., Robert. B.S. in Liberal Arts and Scis, U. Ill., Urbana, 1958, 1959, M.D., 1961, M.S. in Pharmacology, 1961; Ph.D. in Biochemistry, George Washington U., 1966. Diplomate: Am. Bd. Pediatrics, Nat. Bd. Med. Examiners. Intern Johns Hopkins Hosp., 1961-62, asst. resident in pediatrics, 1962-63, fellow in pediatrics, 1961-63; fellow in pediatric hematology U. Ill., 1966-68; research asso. Nat. Cancer Inst., NIH, 1963-66; asst. prof. pediatrics U. Ill., 1968-69, asso. prof., 1969-74, prof., 1974-75; prof. pediatrics Northwestern U., 1975—; attending physician U. Ill., 1968-75, dir. pediatric hematology service, 1972-75; attending physician hematology Children's Meml. Hosp., 1975-83, dir. div. hematology, 1975-83; prof., head dept. pediatrics U. Ill. Coll. Medicine, 1984—. Contbr. numerous articles to profl. jours. Served as commd. officer USPHS, 1963-66. Mem. Am. Acad. Pediatrics, Am. Assn. Cancer Research, AAUP, Am. Soc. Biol. Chemists, Am. Soc. Hematology, Midwest Soc. Pediatric Research, Soc. Pediatric Research, Alpha Omega Alpha. Office: 840 S Wood St Chicago IL 60612

HONIG, LAWRENCE EDWARD, retail executive; b. Spartanburg, S.C., Jan. 19, 1948; s. O. Charles and Jean Gates (Davis) H.; m. Ellen Stokes, Aug. 7, 1971; children: Charles Edward, Ellenor Jackson. B.A., Washington and Lee U., 1970, B.S., 1970; M.A., U. Tex.-Austin, 1972; M.B.A., Harvard U., 1975. Assoc. Loeb, Rhoades & Co., N.Y.C., 1972-73; prin. McKinsey & Co., Chgo., 1975-82; exec. v.p. May Dept. Stores Co., St. Louis, 1982—. Author: John Henry Brown, 1972. Served to capt. U.S. Army, 1971-72. Home: 8 Ridgewood Rd Saint Louis MO 63124 Office: May Dept Stores Co 611 Olive St Saint Louis MO 63101

HONIG, MARVIN IRA, advt. agy. exec.; b. N.Y.C., Jan. 23, 1936; s. Sidney and Rose (Kahn) H.; m. Ellen Strasberg, Jan. 24, 1970; children—Katherine Rose, Jo Sidney. B.A., U. Louisville, 1957. Writer greeting cards Am. Greetings Corp., Cleve., 1961-63; advt. copywriter firm Campbell Ewald, Detroit, 1963-64, Doyle, Dane Bernbach Inc., N.Y.C., 1964-74, creative dir., 1974—. Served to 1st lt. USAF, 1958-60. Recipient 1st place award Advt. Club N.Y., 1970, Copy Club N.Y., 1970; Clio award Am. TV Comml. Festival, 1965, 69, 70, 73. Home: 15 Brookdale Ln Chappaqua NY 10514 Office: Doyle Dane Bernbach Inc 437 Madison Ave New York City NY 10036

HONIG, MERVIN, artist, art conservator; b. N.Y.C., Dec. 25, 1920; s. Joseph and Frances (Flaum) H.; m. Rhoda Sherbell, Apr. 28, 1956; 1 dau., Susan. Student with, Francis Criss, Amadee Ozenfant, Hans Hofmann; B.A., Bklyn. Coll., 1973; postgrad., Hofstra U., 1974—. Apprentice Bklyn. Mus., 1956-58, Keck Studio, 1956-58; asst. Mus. Modern Art, 1958; lectr. conservation of paintings Hofstra U., 1972—, Channel 21, L.I., N.Y., 1976-77; mem. faculty New Sch., 1975—. Exhibited one-man shows at, Kingsworthy Art Gallery, N.Y.C., 1961, County Art Gallery, Westbury, N.Y., 1963-65, Grace Gallery, N.Y.C., Community Coll., 1968, Westbury Meml. Pub. Library, 1969, Frank Rehn Gallery, N.Y.C., 1970, Nassau Community Coll., 1971, New Sch. Assos., N.Y.C., 1978, Bergen Mus. Art and Sci., Paramus, N.J., 1984, retrospective exhbn., Nat. Art Mus. of Sport, N.Y.C., 1977-78; exhibited in group shows at, Met. Mus. Art, 1944, Carnegie Inst., 1945, Los Angeles County Mus., Wm. Rockhil Nelson Gallery, Kansas City, Whitney Mus. Artists Ann., 1949, Bklyn. Mus., 1960, Nat. Acad. Galleries, 1963, 77, 78, 79, 80, 81, 82, 83, Wadsworth Atheneum, Conn. Acad. Fine Arts, 1965-66, Soc. 4 Arts, 1965, Jersey City Mus. Ann. Exhbn., 1966, Locust Valley Art Show (1st prize), Am. Vets. Soc. (Meml. Gold medal), Purdue U., Butler Inst. Am. Art, Youngstown, Ohio, 1967, 69, Nat. Art Mus. Sport, N.Y.C., 1968, 69, Audubon Artists Ann., 1968-70, 74-78, 79-80, 81, 82, 83, 84, Spectrum Gallery, N.Y.C., 1977, Queens Mus., 1978, Port Washington Library, L.I. Artists, C.W. Post Art Gallery, 1981, The Eye on Sport, CUNY, N.Y.C., 1983, Islip Art Mus., Pensacola (Fla.) Mus. Art, 1982, Owenboro (Ky.) Mus. Fine Art, Phila. Coll. Art, 1984; represented in permanent collections, Okla. Mus. Art, Oklahoma City, Colby Coll. Art Mus., Met. Mus. Art, N.Y.C., Okla. Mus. Art, Emily Lowe Gallery, Hofstra U., Colby Coll. Art Mus., Met. Mus. Art, Hofstra U., Nassau County Mus., Siena Hts. Coll., William Benton Mus. Art, also pvt. collections; Author papers on art conservation. Bd. advisors Nassau County Mus., 1978; trustee Nat. Art Mus. Sport, 1978. Recipient Bronze medal, hon. mention Am. Vets. Soc. Artists, 1968, also Gold medal; award of excellence Mainstream '70, Grover M. Hermann Arts Center, 1970; prize Knickerbocker Artists, 1978; Samuel Morton Meml. award Audubon Artists, 1983; others. Mem. Internat. Inst. Conservation Historic and Artistic Works, Coll. Art Assn. Am., Audubon Artists N.Y. (corr. sec. N.Y.C. 1977), Nat. Acad. (asso.), L.I. Hist. Soc., Allied Artists Am. (dir. oil, v.p. 1980—), Nassau Council Contemporary Art (sec. 1973-74). Address: 64 Jane Ct Westbury NY 11590 *The purpose of living for me is to realize one's potential with all the energy and dedication necessary to accomplish this personal goal, while one's goal should contribute positively to the benefit of human existence on a social level.*

HONIG, ORIE CHARLES, business executive; b. Dallas, Sept. 24, 1918; s. Orie Charles and May (Pendley) H.; m. Jean Davis, Feb. 5, 1944; children: Lawrence E., Philip C., Susan R. Student, So. Meth. U., 1935-39; B.B.A., U. Tex., 1940; M.B.A., Harvard U., 1943. Co-founder, chmn. bd., pres. Allied Security Ins. Co., Spartanburg, S.C., Charlotte, N.C., 1947-63; (merged with United Family Life Ins. Co., 1963); pres., dir. United Family Life Ins. Co., Atlanta, 1964-65; co-founder, exec. v.p., mem. exec. com., dir. Enstar Corp. (formerly Alaska Interstate Co.), Houston, 1966—, now pres., also chmn. bd., chief exec. officer; dir. Va. Internat. Corp., Staunton. Served to capt. AUS, 1943-46. Mem. Soc. Indsl. Engrs., Delta Chi. Clubs: Houston Harvard, River Oaks, Petroleum. Home: 10 S Briar Hollow Ln 65 Houston TX 77027 Office: The Galleria 2200 Post Oak Tower Bldg Houston TX 77056

HONIGBERG, BRONISLAW MARK, zoology educator; b. Warsaw, Poland, May 14, 1920; came to U.S., 1941, naturalized, 1948; s. Zachary Z. and Mary (Laks) H.; m. Rhoda Springer, Feb. 7, 1948; children: Paul Mark, Martin Philip. A.B., U. Calif., Berkeley, 1943, M.A., 1946, Ph.D. (A. Rosenberg research fellow 1949-50), 1950. Instr. to prof. zoology U. Mass., Amherst, 1950—, chancellor's medalist, lectr., 1975, faculty fellow, 1981-82; asst. prof. Columbia U., summer 1954; research asso. in pathobiology Sch. Hygiene, Johns Hopkins U., 1958-59; asst. prof. Harvard U., summer 1959; guest investigator lab. parasitic diseases Nat. Inst. Allergy and Infectious Diseases, NIH, 1965-66; guest investigator, hon. fellow Centre for Tropical Veterinary Medicine, U. Edinburgh, 1973-74; dir. tng. grants NIH, 1973—; mem. Internat. Commn. Protozoology, 1965—, tropical medicine parasitology study sect. NIH, 1973-77; v.p., chmn. sci. program V, Internat. Congress Protozoology, 1977; v.p. Internat. Symposiumon Trichomoniasis, Bialystok, Poland, 1981. Editor: Jour. Protozoology, 1971-80; asso. editor: Trans. Am. Micros. Soc., 1966-71; editor N.Am.,: Zeitschrift für Parasitenkunde, 1974—; bd. reviewers: Acta Tropica, 1977-82; contbr. articles to profl. jours. Trustee Am. Type Culture Collection, 1966-72, mem. exec. com., 1971-72. Recipient Gold medal for human trichomoniasis studies Med. Faculty Comenius U., Bratislava, Czechoslovakia, 1977; Alexander von Humboldt Found. sr. scientist award, 1982; NIH research grantee, 1955—; USPHS spl. research fellow, 1965-66, 73-74. Fellow AAAS, N.Y. Acad. Sci., Royal Soc. Tropical Medicine and Hygiene; mem. Soc. belge de Médicine Tropicale (corr.), Deutsche Gesellschaft für Parasitologie (corr.), Am. Soc. Zoologists, Am. Soc. Parasitologists, Soc. Protozoologists (pres. 1965-66, hon.), Am. Micros. Soc. (pres. 1964-65), Am. Soc. Tropical Medicine and Hygiene, Biol. Stain Commn., Soc. Systematic Zoology, Phi Beta Kappa, Sigma Xi, Phi Kappa Phi. Home: 95 Red Gate Ln Amherst MA 01002 Office: Zoology Dept Morrill Sci Center Univ Mass Amherst MA 01003

HONKALA, FRED SAUL, geologist, educator; b. Concord, N.H., Nov. 30, 1919; s. Walter and Anna Louise (Tolvanen) H.; m. Rose Marie Fraher, Mar. 15, 1951; children—Eric Ethan, Lisa Louise, Karl Frederick. B.S., U. N.H., 1940; M.A., U. Mo., 1942; Ph.D. (Rackham fellow 1947-48), U. Mich., 1949. Geologist U.S Geol. Survey, summers 1948-52; mem. faculty geology dept. U. Mont., 1948-50, asst. prof., 1950-55, asso. prof., 1955-57, prof. geology, 1957-68, chmn. dept., 1956-64, dean, dir., 1964-68; pres. Yankton (S.D.) Coll., 1970-72; dean faculty St. Mary's Coll. of Md., St Mary's, 1972-74; exec. dir. Am. Geol. Inst., 1974-78; rep. geol. cons. U.S. Senate Select Com. on Indian Affairs, Washington, 1979—; geologist Va. Div. Mineral Resources, Charlottesville, 1981—; cons. to NRC, U.S. Com. on Geology, 1974-78; dir. Adv. Sci. Edn. Program, NSF, 1968-70; with Shell Oil Co., summers 1954-57; mem. staff NSF Insts., U. Mont., summers 1958-59; dir. NSF gen. sci. program Mont. secondary sch. sci. and math. tchrs., 1959-60; vis. prof. geologic field sta. and NSF Insts. Ind. U., 1960-63; mem. gen. tech. adv. com. Office Coal Research, Dept. Interior, 1966-70; chmn. exec. com. Rocky Mountain Sci. Council, 1967-68; mem. U.S. com. Internat. Geologic Correlation Program. Pub.: Geotimes, 1974-78. Served to capt., C.E. AUS, 1942-46. Fellow Geol. Soc. Am. (sec. Rocky Mountain sect. 1958-59, mem. publs. com. 1974-78), Sigma Xi; mem. Am. Assn. Petroleum Geologists, AAAS, Pi Kappa Alpha. Episcopalian. Home: 215 S Alfred St Alexandria VA 22314 Office: Va Div Mineral Resources PO Box 3667 Charlottesville VA 22903

HONNOLD, JOHN OTIS, JR., legal educator; b. Kansas, Ill., Dec. 5, 1915; s. John Otis and Louretta (Wright) H.; m. Annamarie Kunz, June 26, 1939; children: Carol Honnold Davidon, Heidi Honnold Spencer, Edward. B.A., U. Ill., 1936; J.D., Harvard U., 1939. Bar: N.Y. 1940, Pa. 1953, U.S. Supreme Ct 1953. Atty. firm Wright, Gordon, Zachry & Parlin, N.Y.C., 1939-41, SEC, 1941; chief ct. rev. br. OPA, 1942-46; mem. faculty U. Pa. Law Sch., 1946-69, 74—, prof. law, 1952-69, 74—; Arthur Goodhart prof. sci. and law. U. Cambridge, 1982-83; chief internat. trade law br. UN; sec. UN Commn. on Internat. Trade Law, 1969-74; mem. faculty law sessions Salzburg (Austria) Seminar Am. Studies, 1960, chmn., 1963, 66; chief counsel Miss. Office, Lawyer's Com. for Civil Rights under Law, 1965; U.S. del., mem. drafting com. diplomatic conf. preparing uniform law for internat. sales of goods, The Hague, Holland, 1964; U.S. del UN Commn. Internat. Trade Law, 1969, 77; U.S. del. diplomatic confs. Conv. Carriage of Goods by Sea, Hamburg, 1978, Contracts for Internat. Sale of Goods, Vienna, 1980. Author: Sales and Sales Financing, 4th edit, 1976, Credit Transactions and Consumer Protection, 1976, The Life of the Law, 1964, (with E.L. Barrett, Jr. and P.W. Bruton) Cases and Materials on Constitutional Law, 3d edit, 1968, (with E. Allen Farnsworth) Commercial Law, 3d edit, 1976, Unification of the Law Governing International Sales of Goods, 1966, Uniform Law for International Sales under the 1980 UN Convention, 1982; also articles.; Bd. editors: Am. Jour. Comparative Law, 1959-70, 76—. Guggenheim fellow, 1958; Fulbright sr. research scholar U. Paris, 1958. Mem. Am., Phila. bar assns., Phi Beta Kappa, Phi Kappa Phi., Soc. of Friends. Democrat. Home: 524 Rutgers Ave Swarthmore PA 19081 Office: Law Sch U Pa 34th and Chestnut Sts Philadelphia PA 19104

HOOBLER, SIBLEY WORTH, medical educator; b. N.Y.C., Apr. 30, 1911; s. Bert Raymond and Madge (Sibley) H.; m. Catherine Oppmann, Nov. 11, 1976; children by previous marriage—Raymond, Patricia. A.B., Princeton, 1933; Sc.D., Johns Hopkins, 1937, M.D., 1938. Mem. faculty U. Mich. Med. Sch., 1945-76, prof. internal medicine, 1959-76; clin. prof. internal medicine Western Res. U. Med. Sch.; also adj. staff Cleve. Clinic Found., 1976—. Author: Hypertensive Diseases, 1959, also articles. Served to capt. M.C. AUS, 1942-46. Fellow ACP; mem. Am. Heart Assn. (chmn. high blood pressure council 1963-64), Soc. Exptl. Biology and Medicine, Am. Physiol. Soc., Central Soc. Clin. Research, Am. Soc. Clin Investigation, Am. Soc. Clin. Pharmacology and Therapeutics. Home: 13515 Shaker Blvd Cleveland OH 44120

HOOD, CHARLES HARVEY, foundation administrator, former dairy company executive; b. Brookline, Mass., Feb. 5, 1929; s. Harvey Perley and Barbara Ellen (Churchill) H.; m. Judith Deitrich, Sept. 9, 1961; 1 son, Harvey P. (dec.). Grad., Phillips Andover Acad., 1947; B.A., Dartmouth, 1951; M.B.A., Harvard, 1953. With H.P. Hood Inc., Boston, 1956-80, asst. treas., clk., 1962-66, treas., 1966-78, also dir., to 1980; treas. Charles H. Hood Found., 1966—, pres., 1974—; dir. State St. Bank & Trust Co., Boston. Trustee Joslin Diabetes Found., 1965—, treas., 1979—; trustee Children's Hosp. Med. Center, 1969—, Lesley Coll., Cambridge, Mass., 1968—; chmn. corp. Lesley Coll., Cambridge, Mass., 1983—; corp. mem. N.E. Deaconess Hosp., 1966—, Cardigan Mountain Sch., Canaan, N.H., 1966—, Mus. of Sci., 1974—; overseer Boys' Club Boston, 1964—, bd. dirs., 1976—; treas. Boston Study Group. Served with USNR, 1953-56. Clubs: Country (Brookline); Essex County, Manchester Yacht (Manchester); Commercial, Treasurers', Treasurers' (pres. 1979-80), Merchants (Boston)). Home: 395 Warren St Brookline MA 02146 Office: 500 Rutherford Ave Boston MA 02129

HOOD, EDWARD EXUM, JR., elec. mfg. co. exec.; b. Boonville, N.C., Sept. 15, 1930; s. Edward Exum and Nellie (Triplett) H.; m. Kay Transou, Dec. 30, 1950; children—Lisa Kay, Molly Ann. M.S. in Nuclear Engring, N.C. State U., 1953. Registered profl. engr., Ariz. Powerplant design engr. Gen. Electric Co., 1957-62, mgr. supersonic transport engine project, 1962-67, v.p., gen. mgr. comml. engine div., 1968—, v.p., group exec. internat. group, 1972-73, v.p., group exec., power generation group, 1973-77, sr. v.p., sector exec. tech. systems and materials sector, 1977—, vice-chmn., 1979—. Served with USAF, 1952-56. Fellow Am. Inst. Aeros. and Astronautics (asso.); mem. Nat. Acad. Engring., Aerospace Industries Assn. (chmn. 1981). Home: Woods End Rd New Canaan CT 06840 Office: Gen Electric Co Fairfield CT 06431

HOOD, JOHN JOSEPH, consulting entomologist; b. Cranston, R.I., July 7, 1924; s. James and Mary Ann (Willocks) H.; m. Beatrice Linke, June 18, 1949; children: Keith G., Glenn K., Betsy A. B.S., U. R.I., 1949; M.S., U. Del., 1951. R.I. State entomologist, 1952; with Ciba-Geigy Agrl. Chems. Co. (and predecessor), 1953-77, v.p., 1967-77; agrl. cons., Escoheag, R.I., 1977—; pres. Agrl. Research Inst., Washington, 1978-80; chmn. adv. council Coll. Resource Devel., U. R.I., 1977—; bd. dirs. Council Agrl. Sci. and Tech., 1978-80. Served with USAAF, 1943-46; lt. col. USAFR, ret. Mem. Am. Phytopath. Soc., Am. Registry Profl. Entomologists, Entomol. Soc. Am., Res. Officers Assn., Air Force Assn. Methodist. Patentee triazine herbicide formulations. Address: Woody Hill Rd Escoheag RI 02821

HOOD, LEROY EDWARD, biologist; b. Missoula, Mont., Oct. 10, 1938; s. Thomas Edward and Myrtle Evylan (Wadsworth) H.; m. Valerie Anne Logan, Dec. 14, 1963; children: Eran William, Marqui Leigh Jennifer. B.S., Calif. Inst. Tech., 1960, Ph.D. in Biochemistry, 1968; M.D., Johns Hopkins U., 1964. Med. officer USPHS, 1967-70; sr. investigator Nat. Cancer Inst., 1967-70; asst. prof. biology Calif. Inst. Tech., Pasadena, 1970-73, asso. prof., 1973-75, prof., 1975—, Bowles prof. biology, 1977—, chmn. div. biology, 1980—. Author: (with others) Biochemistry, a Problems Approach, 1974, Molecular Biology of Eukaryotic Cells, 1975, Immunology, 1978, Essential Concepts of Immunology, 1978. Mem. Am. Assn. Immunologists, Am. Assn. Sci., Nat. Acad. Scis., Am. Acad. Arts and Scis., Sigma Xi. Home: 1453 E California Blvd Pasadena CA 91106 Office: Div Biology Calif Inst Tech Pasadena CA 91125

HOOD, ROBIN LEE, photographer; b. Chattanooga, Sept. 22, 1944; s. James Lee and Betty Jean (Grandin) H.; m. Peggy Jean Jones, Sept. 10, 1970; children: Farrar Blakely Riding, Nicole Irene Grandin. Student, U. Tenn. at Chattanooga, 1962-66. Served as enlisted man U.S. Army, 1967, commd. 2d lt., 1969, advanced through grades to 1st lt., 1970; info. officer (1st Air Cav. Div.), S.Vietnam, 1970-71, resigned, 1971; with Chattanooga News-Free Press, 1971—, chief color photographer, 1977—; dir. photography, State of Tenn., 1980, freelance photographer, 1983—. Author: book color photographs The Tennesseans, A People and their Land, 1981. Decorated Bronze Star, Combat Air medal; recipient Pulitzer prize for feature photography, 1977. Office: State Capitol Nashville TN 37219

HOOD, THOMAS RICHARD, artist, graphic designer, educator; b. Phila., July 13, 1910; s. Thomas Richard and Anne Lovering (Grubb) H. Student, U. Pa., 1929-30; B.F.A. in Advt. Design, Phila. Mus. Coll. Art, 1953. Prof., design coordinator, exhbn. dir. Phila. Coll. Art; dir. Pa. Art Program, 1940-42, Pa. War Services Program, 1943. Exhibited nationally, 1936—; represented in permanent collections, Phila. Mus., Carnegie Library, Phila. Public Library, N.Y. Public Library, Library of Congress, Phila. Mus. Natural History, Mus. Modern Art, N.Y.C., Bryn Mawr Coll., Yale U., Nat. Portrait Gallery, Smithsonian Instn., also pvt. collections. Served with AUS, 1943-45. Recipient over 60 awards, including Phila. Print Club, 1937, 48, Western Pa. Prints, 1940, Soldier Art, 1945, 1st prize Times Herald Exhbn., Washington, 1945, Franklin medal, 1959 (2), 69, 70, award Del. Valley Graphic Arts, 1971, Silver and Bronze medals Art Dirs. Gold medal, 1966, 69, 73, Silver medal, 1971, 73, Neographics Gold, Silver and Bronze medals, 1973, Nat. Graphic Arts Design award, U.S. and Can., 1968, (2) 70, Disting. Design award Phila. Coll. Art, 1971, Andy award of Merit, 1973, Neographics Gold Medal, 1976; named to Wisdom Hall of Fame in Edn., 1975. Fellow Internat. Inst. Arts and Letters (life); mem. Am. Color Print Soc. (pres. 1956), Artist Decoys, The Authors, Phila. Art Alliance (chmn. print com. 1977-81), Mus. Modern Art, Phila. Print Club. Club: Peale. Home: 1452 E Cheltenham Ave Philadelphia PA 19124 Office: Phila Coll Art Broad and Spruce Sts Philadelphia PA 19102 *My interest in art developed at a very early age. By my twelfth year I was making prints, dry points and etchings on copper plates. During the depression years, serving as an administrator of art programs for the government, and later teaching, matured and enriched my understanding of art. In time my conceptions have become concerned with abstraction and the primordial forces which are a part of world growth and order. I have enjoyed my life very much and hope for more time for the further development of my art.*

HOOD, WILLIAM BOYD, JR., cardiologist, reseacher; b. Sylacauga, Ala., Mar. 25, 1932; s. William Boyd and Katherine Elizabeth (Anderson) H.; m. Katherine Candace Todd, May 5, 1972; 1 son, Jefferson Boyce. B.S. summa cum laude, Davidson Coll., 1954; M.D., Harvard U., 1958. Intern Peter Bent Brigham Hosp., Boston, 1958-59, resident in internal medicine, 1959-60, 62-63; from asst. prof. to assoc. prof. medicine Harvard U., 1967-71; from assoc. prof. to prof. medicine Boston U., 1971-82; chief cardiology Boston City Hosp., 1973-82; prof. medicine U. Rochester (N.Y.), 1982—; head cardiology unit Strong Meml. Hosp., Rochester, 1982—; cons. NIH, 1975—. Mem. editorial bd.: New Eng. Jour. Medicine, 1974-81, Circulation, 1980—, Circulation Research, 1982—; contbr. articles, revs. and editorials on cardiovascular physiology to profl. jours., chpts. to books. Served to capt. USAF, 1963-65. Research grantee NIH, 1971—; grantee Am. Heart Assn., 1971-76. Fellow ACP; mem. Am. Soc. Clin. Investigation, Assn. Am. Physicians, Am. Heart Assn., Am. Physiol. Soc., Phi Beta Kappa, Alpha Omega Alpha. Office: Cardiology Unit Box 679 Rochester Med Ctr 601 Elmwood Ave Rochester NY 14642

HOOD, WILLIAM CLARENCE, international banking official; b. Yarmouth, N.S., Can., Sept. 13, 1921; s. Percy Alexander and Vida Barr (Webster) H.; m. Alville Mary Lennox, June 4, 1948; children—Ronald Douglas, Nancy Anne. B.A. with honors, Mt. Allison U., 1941; M.A. in Econs, U. Toronto, 1943, Ph.D., 1948. Meteorologist RCAF, 1941-43; instr. econs. U. Sask., Saskatoon, 1944-46; prof. econs. U. Toronto, 1946-64; adviser Bank of Can., Ottawa, Ont., 1964-69; asst. dep. minister of fin., 1970-74, asso. dep. minister of fin., 1975-79, dep. minister, 1979; econ. counselor, dir. research IMF, Washington, 1980—; research asso. Cowles Commn. for Research in Econs., U. Chgo., 1949-50; asst. dir. research Royal Commn. on Can.'s Econ. Prospects, 1955-56; head UNESCO ednl. and econ. study mission, Sierra Leone, W. Africa, 1961; dir. research Can. Royal Commn. on Banking and Fin., 1961-63. Author: (with T.C. Koopmans) Studies in Econometric Method, 1953, (with A.D. Scott) Output Labour and Capital in the Canadian Economy, 1958, Financing of Economic Activity in Canada, 1959. Fellow Royal Soc. Can., Econometric Soc.; mem. Can. Econs. Assn. (pres. 1969-70), Am. Econs. Assn., Am. Statis. Assn., Royal Econs. Soc. Home: 9513 Liberty Tree Ln Vienna VA 22180 Office: Internat Monetary Fund 700 19th St NW Washington DC 20431

HOOGENBOOM, ARI ARTHUR, historian, educator; b. Richmond Hill, N.Y., Nov. 28, 1927; s. Ari and Clara (Behn) H.; m. Olive Gwendoline Youngberg, Aug. 28, 1949; children—Lynn Cordelia, Ari Arthur, Jan Margaret. B.A., Atlantic Union Coll., 1949; M.A., Columbia, 1951, Ph.D., 1958. Lectr. Columbia, 1955-56; from instr. to asst. prof. U. Tex., El Paso, 1956-58; Mem. faculty Pa. State U., 1958-68, prof., 1966-68, Bklyn. Coll., 1968—, chmn. dept. history, 1968-74; vis. lectr. U. Wis.-Milw., summer 1960; vis. asso. prof. U. Oreg., summer 1965. Author: Outlawing the Spoils: A History of the Civil Service Reform Movement, 1865-1883, 1961, (with William S. Sachs) The Enterprising Colonials: Society on the Eve of the Revolution, 1965, (with Philip S. Klein) A History of Pennsylvania, 2d edit, 1980, (with Olive Hoogenboom) A History of the ICC: From Panacea to Palliative, 1976; Editor: Spoilsmen and Reformers, 1964, The Gilded Age, 1967, An Interdisciplinary Approach to American History, 2 vols, 1973, (with Abraham S. Eisenstadt and Hans L. Trefousse) Before Watergate: Problems of Corruption in American Society, 1978. Pres. Central Pa. chpt. Am. Assn. UN, 1963-64. Guggenheim fellow, 1965-66. Mem. Am. Hist. Assn., Pa. Hist. Assn. (past sec.), N.Y. Hist. Soc., Orgn. Am. Historians. Democrat. Unitarian. Home: 1451 E 21st St Brooklyn NY 11210

HOOK, EDWARD WATSON, JR., physician, educator; b. Sumter, S.C., Aug. 10, 1924; s. Edward and Theola (Brogdon) H.; m. Jessie Dale Thurecht, June 14, 1949; children: Edward Watson III, Susan Dale, Margaret Jane, Robert Randall. B.S., Wofford Coll., Spartanburg, S.C., 1943; student, Yale U., 1943-44; M.D., Emory U., 1949. Diplomate: Am. Bd. Internal Medicine (mem. 1979—). Intern Univ. Hosps., Mpls., 1949-50; jr. asst. resident in medicine Grady Meml. Hosp., Atlanta, 1950-51, sr. asst. resident, 1953-54, chief resident, 1954-55; fellow dept. medicine Emory U. Sch. Medicine, Grady Meml. Hosp., 1955-56; practice medicine, specializing in internal medicine and infectious diseases, Charlottesville, Va., 1969—; instr. medicine Johns Hopkins Sch. Medicine, Balt., 1956-58, asst. prof., 1958-59; asso. prof. medicine Cornell U. Med. Coll., 1959-64, prof., 1964-69, vice chmn. dept. medicine, 1969; asso. attending physician N.Y. Hosp., 1959-64, attending physician, 1964-69, mem. med. bd., 1967-69; prof. honorario U. Bahia Sch. Medicine, Salvadore, Brazil, 1966; prof., chmn. dept. medicine U. Va. Sch. Medicine, Charlottesville, 1969—; physician-in-chief U. Va. Hosp., 1969—. Contbr. articles profl. jours.; Editor: Antimicrobial Agents and Chemotherapy, 1972-81; editorial bd.: Am. Jour. Medicine, 1974-80. Pres. Va. Partners of Americas, 1974-76; bd. dirs. Robert Wood Johnson Clin. Scholars Program, 1976—, chmn. bd., 1978—. Served with M.C. AUS, 1943-46, 51-53. Fellow A.C.P. (gov. for Va. 1975-79, council subsplty. socs. 1977-78, council med. splty. socs. 1976-82, residency rev. com. for internal medicine 1977—, regent 1980—); mem. Am. Fedn. Clin. Research, Am. Thoracic Soc., AMA, Albemarle County Med. Soc., Soc. for Exptl. Biology and Medicine, Am., So. socs. clin. investigation, Johns Hopkins Med. and Surg. Assn., Royal Soc. Tropical Medicine and Hygiene, Am. Assn. Immunologists, Am. Clin. and Climatology Assn. (council 1979—), N.Y. Med. and Surg. Assn., Infectious Diseases Soc. Am. (pres. 1975-76), Assn. Profs. Medicine (council 1977-83, pres. 1981-82), Assn. Am. Physicians, Council Med. Splty. Socs., Internat. Coll. Tropical Medicine, Sigma Xi, Alpha Omega Alpha. Home: 1203 Hilltop Rd Charlottesville VA 22903 Office: Sch of Medicine Box 466 U Va Charlottesville VA 22908

HOOK, EUGENE RAY, executive recruiter, retired insurance executive; b. South Milwaukee, Wis., May 30, 1919; s. Ray Alvin and Rena Angie (Roberts) H.; m. Mary-Louise Gehan, Mar. 4, 1946; children: James Rawson, Priscilla Ann. Ph.B., U. Wis., 1943. Agt. Provident Mut. Life Ins. Co., N.Y.C., 1949-50, supr., mgr., Westfield, N.J., 1952-63, sr. v.p., Phila., 1964-82; agt. Aetna Life & Casualty Co., Newark, 1951-52; pres. Eugene R. Hook and Assocs., Inc., Exec. Recruiting. Councilman Plainfield, N.J., Plainfield, N.J., 1951-53. Served to lt. USNR, 1941-46; PTO. Republican. Presbyterian. Clubs: Merion Golf (Ardmore, Pa.); Sawgrass Country, Tournament Players (Ponte Vedra Beach, Fla.). Home: 45 Village Walk Ponte Vedra Beach FL 32082

HOOK, HAROLD SWANSON, insurance company executive; b. Kansas City, Mo., Oct. 10, 1931; s. Ralph C. and Ruby (Swanson) H.; m. Joanne T. Hunt, Feb. 19, 1955; children: Karen Anne, Thomas W., Randall T. B.B.A., U. Mo., 1953, M.A., 1954; grad., So. Meth. U. Inst. Ins. Marketing, 1957; postgrad., N.Y. U., 1967-70; LL.D. (hon.), U. Mo., 1983, Westminster Coll., 1983. C.L.U. Faculty U. Mo. Sch. Bus., 1953-54; asst. to pres. Nat. Fidelity Life Ins. Co., Kansas City, Mo., 1957-60, dir., 1959-66, adminstrv. v.p., 1960-61, exec. v.p., investment com., 1961-62, pres., exec. com., 1962-66; sr. v.p. U.S. Life Ins. Co., N.Y.C., 1966-67, dir., 1967-70, exec. v.p., mem. exec. com., 1967-68, pres., 1968-70; pres., mem. bd., exec. com. Calif.-Western States Life Ins. Co., Sacramento, 1970-75, chmn., 1975-79, sr. chmn., 1979—; pres. Am. Gen. Corp., Houston, 1975-81, chmn., chief exec. officer, 1978—, mem. exec. com., 1975—, dir., 1972—; founder, pres. Main Event Mgmt. Corp., Sacramento, 1970—; dir. Panhandle Eastern Corp., Houston, Continental Airlines Corp., Tex. Commerce Bancshares, Inc., United Telecommunications, Inc., Kansas City, Mo. Trustee, chmn. fin. com. Baylor Coll. Medicine, Houston; Trustee Am. Coll., Bryn Mawr, Pa.; mem. council of overseers Jesse H. Jones Grad. Sch. Adminstrn., Rice U., Houston; bd. dirs. Tex. Research League, Houston Symphony, Soc. for Performing Arts, Houston., Business Arts Fund, Houston Area Research Ctr. Served to lt. USNR, 1954-57. Recipient Citation of Merit, U. Mo. alumni award, 1965; Faculty-Alumni award U. Mo., 1978; Silver Beaver award Boy Scouts Am., 1974; Distinguished Eagle Scout award, 1976; named Man of Year Delta Sigma Pi, 1969, Chief Exec. Officer award Fin. World Mag., 1979, 82, 84, Outstanding Chief Exec. Officer in Multiline Ins. Industry Wall St. Transcript, 1981, 83. Fellow Life Mgmt. Inst.; mem. Philos. Soc. Tex., Houston C. of C. (chmn. 1983-84), Beta Gamma Sigma Dirs. Table (nat. honoree 1984). Presbyterian. Clubs: Forum (bd. govs.), University, River Oaks Country, Petroleum, Ramada, Heritage (Houston); Economic (N.Y.C.); Morris County Golf (Morristown, N.J.); Mission Hills Country (Kansas City); Eldorado Country (Indian Wells, Calif.). Lodge: Rotary. Home: 2204 Troon Rd Houston TX 77019 Office: 2727 Allen Pkwy Houston TX 77019

HOOK, JOHN BURNEY, investment co. exec.; b. Franklin, Ind., Sept. 6, 1928; s. Burney S. and Elsie C. (Hubbard) H.; m. Georgia Delis, Feb. 8, 1958; children—David, Deborah. B.S., Ind. U., 1956, M.B.A., 1957. C.P.A. Store mgr. Goodman-Jester, Inc., Franklin, Ind., 1949-50; auditor Ernst & Ernst, Indpls., 1953-56; financial analyst Eli Lilly & Co., Indpls., 1957-59; gen. partner Ball, Burge & Kraus, Cleve., 1966-70; pres., dir. Cuyahoga Mgmt. Corp., 1966—; dir. Robinson-Ransbottom Pottery Co., 1964—. Mem. Cleve. Soc. Security Analysts, Am. Inst. C.P.A.'s, Am. Inst. Chartered Financial Analysts. Republican. Methodist. Clubs: Cleveland Athletic; Bear Creek Golf (Hilton Head Island, S.C.); Lakewood Country. Home: 435 Bates Dr Bay Village OH 44140 also 423 Plantation Club Hilton Head Island SC Office: Prescott Ball & Turben Cleveland OH 44115

HOOK, RALPH CLIFFORD, JR., educator; b. Kansas City, Mo., May 2, 1923; s. Ralph Clifford and Ruby (Swanson) H.; m. Joyce Fink, Jan. 20, 1946; children—Ralph Clifford III, John Gregory. B.A., U. Mo., 1947, M.A., 1948; Ph.D., U. Tex., 1954. Instr. U. Mo., 1947-48; asst. prof. Tex. A&M U., 1948-51; lectr. U. Tex., 1951-52; co-owner, mgr. Hook Buick Co., also Hook Truck & Tractor Co., Lee's Summit, Mo., 1952-58; assoc. prof. U. Kansas City, 1953-58; dir. Bur. Bus. Research and Services, Ariz. State U., 1958-66, prof. mktg., 1960-68; dean Coll. Bus. Adminstrn., U. Hawaii, 1968-74, prof. bus. adminstrn., 1974—; vis. Disting. prof. N.E. La. U., 1979; dir. Hook Bros. Farm, Hilo Coast Processing Co. Ltd., Pan Pacific Inst. Ocean Scis.; Mem. Nat. Def. Exec. Res., Dept. Commerce. Author: (with others) The Management Primer, 1972, Life Style Analysis, 1979; Contbr.: monograph series Western Bus. Roundup; Founder, moderator: Western Bus. Roundup radio series, 1958-68. Bd. dirs. Jr. Achievement Hawaii. Served to 1st lt. F.A. AUS, 1943-46; col. Res. Recipient alumni citation of merit U. Mo. Coll. Bus. and Pub. Adminstrn., 1969; Distinguished Service award Nat. Def. Transp. Assn., 1977; named to Faculty Hall Fame Ariz. State U. Coll. Bus. Assn., 1977. Fellow Internat. Council for Small Bus. (pres. 1963); mem. Hawaii World Trade Assn. (pres. 1973-74), Am. Marketing Assn. (v.p. 1965-67, pres. Central Ariz. chpt. 1960-61), Western Assn. Collegiate Schs. Bus. (pres. 1972-73), Sales and Mktg. Execs. Internat., Acad. Internat. Bus., Nat. Def. Transp. Assn. (Hawaii v.p. 1978—), Newcomen Soc. N. Am., Beta Gamma Sigma, Omicron Delta Kappa, Beta Theta Pi, Delta Sigma Pi (gold council). Methodist. Club: Rotarian. Home: 311 Ohua Ave Apt 11D Honolulu HI 96815 Office: Coll Bus Adminstrn U Hawaii Honolulu HI 96822

HOOK, SIDNEY, philosopher, educator; b. N.Y.C., Dec. 20, 1902; s. Isaac and Jennie (Halpern) H.; m. Carrie Katz, Mar. 31, 1924; 1 son, John Bertrand; m. Ann Zinken, May 25, 1935; children: Ernest Benjamin, Susan Ann. B.S., CCNY, 1923; M.A., Columbia U., 1926, Ph.D., 1927, L.H.D., 1960; LL.D., univs. Maine, Calif., Fla., Hebrew Union, Utah, Vt., Rockford Coll. Tchr. N.Y.C. pub. schs., 1923-28; lectr. Columbia, summer session, 1927, 30; instr. philosophy Washington Sq. Coll., N.Y. U., 1927-32, asst. prof., 1932-34, asso. prof., chmn. dept. philosophy, 1934-39, prof., 1939-69, emeritus, 1969—; head all-univ. dept. philosophy N.Y. U., 1948-69; chmn. Washington Sq. Coll. Arts and Scis., until 1969; sr. research fellow Hoover Instn. War, Revolution and Peace, Stanford, Calif.; vis. prof. Harvard U., 1961, U. Calif., San Diego, 1975; regents prof. U. Calif. at Santa Barbara, 1966. Author: books including Education for Modern Man, 2d edit, 1963, Heresy, Yes-Conspiracy, No, 1953, The Ambiguous Legacy: Marx and the Marxists, 1955, Common Sense and the Fifth Amendment, 1957, Political Power and Personal Freedom, 1959, The Quest for Being, 1961, The Paradoxes of Freedom, 1962, The Place of Religion in A Free Society, 1968, Academic Freedom and Academic Anarchy, 1970, Education and the Taming of Power, 1973, Pragmatism and the Tragic Senses of Life, 1974, Revolution, Reform and Social Justice, 1975, Philosophy and Public Policy, 1980, Marxism and Beyond, 1983; Contbr. articles to philos. jours.; Editor: American Philosophers at Work: The Current Philosophic Scene, 1956, Determinism and Freedom in An Age of Modern Science, The Idea of a Modern University; others. Organizer Conf. on Methods in Philosophy and Sci., Conf. on Sci. Spirit and Dem. Faith, Am. Com. for Cultural Freedom, Congress for Cultural Freedoms, Univ. Centers for Rational Alternatives, N.Y. U. Inst. Philosophy; pres., treas. John Dewey Found. Guggenheim fellow, 1928-29, 61-62. Fellow Am. Acad. Arts and Scis., Am. Acad. Edn.; mem. Am. Philos. Assn. (pres. eastern div. 1959), Nat. Endowment for Humanities (council 1972-78), League for Indsl. Democracy (v.p.), John Dewey Soc. Address: Hoover Instn Stanford CA 94305 *It is better to be a live jackal than a dead lion - for jackals, not men. Men who have the moral courage to fight intelligently for freedom have the best prospects of avoiding the fate both of live jackals and dead lions. Survival is not the be-all and end-all of a life worthy of man. Sometimes the worst thing we can know about a man is that he has survived. Those who say life is worth living at any cost have already written for themselves an epitaph of infamy, for there is no cause and no person they will not betray to stay alive. Man's vocation should be the use of the arts of intelligence in behalf of human freedom.*

HOOK, WALTER, artist; b. Missoula, Mont., Apr. 25, 1919; s. Herman and Elvira (Puskala) H.; m. Margaret Eloise Theime, June 5, 1943; children: Janet Gray, Gollen Beth. B.A., U. Mont., 1942; M.A., U. N.Mex., 1950. Tech. illustrator Sandia Base, Albuquerque, 1950-53, Gen. Electric, Richland, Wash., 1953-54; art. tchr. Missoula County High Sch., Mont., 1954-55; prof. art U. Mont., Missoula, 1955-77; freelance artist, Missoula, 1977—. Exhibited numerous one-man shows, 1979. Western State Arts Found. fellow, 1976. Mem. NAD (assoc.), Nat. Watercolor Soc., Artist's Equity. Address: 514 Westview Missoula MT 59803

HOOKE, ALBERT BEARDSLY, banker; b. Rome, N.Y., June 17, 1919; m. Priscilla Platt; children: Helen, Carolyn, A. William, Richard. B.A., Hamilton Coll., Clinton, N.Y., 1941; M.B.A., Columbia U., 1948. Exec. trainee Revere Copper, Rome, N.Y., 1941-42; trainee to asst. auditor Security Trust Co., Rochester, N.Y., 1948-51; with Community Savs. Bank, Rochester, 1951—, pres., chief exec. officer. Trustee, treas., mem. exec. com. Rochester Mus. Arts and Scis., 1970-78; chmn. bd. trustees Greater Rochester YMCA, 1981-83; trustee Rochester Area Downtown Devel., 1980—. Served to lt. USN, 1942-46. Mem. Savs. Banks Assn. N.Y. State (pres. 1976-77), Nat. Assn. Mut. Savs. Banks (chmn. 1980-81), Rochester C. of C. (trustee 1980—). Presbyterian. Club: Country of Rochester (dir. 1959-62). Lodge: Masons. Home: 40 Branford Rd Rochester NY 14618 Office: Community Savs Bank 235 E Main St Rochester NY 14604

HOOKER, DAN, electrical distribution company executive; b. Barre, Vt., June 25, 1936; s. Neale W. and Cleora M. H.; m. Betty Ann Aylward, June 21, 1958; children: Kaye, Scott, Dana, Gregory, Bethanie. B.S. in Elec. Engring, Norwich U., 1958. With Gen. Electric Co.; mgr. market planning Gen. Electric Supply Co., Phila.; regional mgr. H.K. Porter Co., Inc.; pres. Tidewater Supply Co., Huntington, W.Va.; now mgr. bus. improvement projects ITT Royal Electric Co., Pawtucket, R.I. Served with AUS, 1958. Mem. Am. Mgmt. Assn., Nat. Elec. Contractors Assn., Nat. Assn. Elec. Distbrs. Home: 70 Water Way Barrington RI 02806 Office: 95 Grand Ave Pawtucket RI 02802

HOOKER, JOHN LEE, singer, guitarist; b. Clarkdale, Miss., Aug. 22, 1917; m. Martella Hooker, 1943; 4 children. Sang in spiritual groups at age of 14; then studied guitar under, Will Moore; toured extensively across, N.Am., 1951—, Europe and U.K., 1961—; appeared at, Newport Folk Festival, 1959, 60, 63, Newport Jazz Festival, 1964, Am. Folk Blues Festival, 1964, 65, 68, Ann Arbor Blues Festival, 1969, 70, 73, 74; appeared, Carnegie Hall, 1971; TV appearances include Midnight Special, 1971, Don Kirsher's Rock Concert, 1978; film appearance The Blues Brothers, 1980; writer: numerous blues songs including She's Long, She's Tall, Boom Boom, Bookie Chillen, others; rec. artist for, Riverside, Vee-Jay, Modern records; also recorded under names, John Lee Booker, Birmington Sam, Texas Slim, Johnny Williams.; numerous blues songs including (Recipient Best Blues Album award Jazz and Pop mag. 1968, 69, Blues Hall of Fame award Ebony mag. 1975). Recipient Folk Heritage award Smithsonian Institution, 1983. Address: care Rosebud Agy PO Box 210103 San Francisco CA 94121 *Blues is the root of all music, jazz, spirituals, pop, rock, all of it. . .a good blues singer can really tell the story of my life, your life, everybody's life; it's got something in there to fit everybody, what everybody's been through. . .that's what I live for. . .I love playing for the people.*

HOOKER, MICHAEL KENNETH, college president; b. Richlands, Va., Aug. 24, 1945; s. Aaron Kenneth and Margaret (Smith) H.; m. Anna Hostettler, Dec. 22, 1966; 1 dau., Alexandra Christine. B.A., U. N.C., 1969; M.A., U. Mass., 1972, Ph.D., 1973. Asst. prof. Harvard U., Cambridge, Mass., 1973-75; asst. prof. philosophy Johns Hopkins U., Balt., 1975-77, asst. dean, 1977-78, assoc. dean, 1978-80, dean, 1980-82; pres. Bennington (Vt.) Coll., 1982—; chmn. biotech. adv. com. Office Tech. Assessment, Washington, 1981—; bd. dirs. Inst. Med. Research, Bennington, Vt., 1982—. Contbr. articles to philosophy jours.; editor: Descartes, 1978, Leibniz, 1982. Bd. dirs. various civic groups. Recipient Homewood award John Hopkins U., 1980; Woodrow Wilson fellow, 1972-73; Harvard U. faculty research fellow, 1974. Mem. Leibniz Soc. (bd. dirs. 1979-83), Internat. Berkeley Soc. (v.p. 1978-79), Am. Philos. Assn. Soc. (chmn. com., bd. officers 1977-82). Office: Bennington Coll Bennington VT 05201

HOOKER, ROGER WOLCOTT, JR., consumer products company executive; b. Niagara Falls, N.Y., May 14, 1941; s. Roger Wolcott and Grace (Garden) H.; m. Joan Folinsbee Wiggins, Jan. 18, 1975; children: Katherine Folinsbee, Sarah Wiggins. A.B., Princeton U., 1963; LL.B., Columbia U., 1967. Bar: N.Y. 1968. Asso. firm Webster & Sheffield, N.Y.C., 1967-70; counsel N.Y. State Commn. Elem. and Secondary Edn., 1970-72; dep. sec. to gov. N.Y. State; also dir. Washington office N.Y. State, 1972-73; dep. dir. Commn. Critical Choices, N.Y.C., 1974; asst. for Congl. affairs to Vice Pres. Nelson A. Rockefeller, 1975; asst. sec. U.S. Dept. Transp., 1976; v.p., gen. counsel, sec. GrandMet USA, Inc., Montvale, N.J., 1977—; also dir. Liggett Group Inc.; dir. Old Virginia Brick Co., Salem. Mem. ABA, Am. Soc. Corp. Secs., Assn. Bar City N.Y. Republican. Club: Univ. (N.Y.C.). Office: 100 Paragon Dr Montvale NJ 07645

HOOKER, VAN DORN, architect, educator, artist, consultant; b. Carthage, Tex., Sept. 22, 1921; s. Van Dorn and Anne (Wylie) H.; m. Marjorie Mead, June 14, 1947; children: Ann, Van Dorn III, John Hardy. Student, Coll. of Marshall, Tex., 1938-40; B.Arch., U. Tex., 1947; postgrad., U. Calif.-Berkeley, 1950-51. Registered architect, N.Mex., Tex. Architect, ptnr. McHugh & Hooker-Bradley P. Kidder & Assocs., Santa Fe, 1956-63; univ. architect U. N.Mex., Albuquerque, 1963—, mem. faculty, 1971—; cons. on campus planning and historic preservation and restoration. Designer numerous bldgs.; one-man show, Bradywine Gallery, Albuquerque, 1973, group shows include, Mus. of N.Mex., 1963, 1979; represented permanent collections, Mus. N.Mex.; contbr. articles to various publs. Trustee Albuquerque Acad., 1972-82. Fellow AIA (pres. Albuquerque chpt. 1961, silver medal Western Mountain region 1980); mem. N.Mex. Soc. Architects (pres. 1973), Assn. Univ. Architects (pres. 1971), Soc. Archtl. Historians. Lodge: Kiwanis. Office: PO Box 18 University Sta Albuquerque MN 87131 *When I recieved the Silver Medal from the Western Mountain Region, AIA, I made the following statement relative to my work at the University of New Mexico: "Now that many of the trees we planted are maturing, and some of the long-range intentions are apparent. I hope that this campus can demostrate some of the values of architecture and planning and that those who use it will remember when later they hire architects and make environmental decisions. Most of all, I hope this campus gives them a rich memory to keep as long as they live."*

HOOKS, BENJAMIN LAWSON, assn. exec.; b. Memphis; m. Frances; 1 dau. Student, LeMoyne Coll., Memphis, 1941-43, Howard U., 1943-44; J.D., DePaul U., Chgo., 1948; LL.D. (hon.), Howard U., 1975, Wilberforce U., 1976, Central State U., 1976. Bar: Tenn. bar 1948. Individual practice law, Memphis, 1949-65, 68-72, asst. pub. defender, 1961-64; judge Div. IV Criminal Ct. of Shelby County, 1966-68; ordained to ministry Baptist Ch., 1956; pastor Middle Bapt. Ch., Memphis, 1956-64, Greater New Mt. Moriah Bapt. Ch., Detroit, 1964-72; co-founder, v.p., dir. Mut. Fed. Savs. & Loan Assn., Memphis, 1955-69; mem. FCC, Washington, 1972-78; exec. dir. NAACP, N.Y.C., 1977—. Producer, host: television program Conversations in Black and White; co-producer: Forty Percent Speaks; panelist: What Is Your Faith. Bd. dirs. So. Christian Leadership Conf., Tenn. Council on Human Relations, Memphis and Shelby Human Relations Com. Served with AUS, World War II. Mem. ABA, Nat. Bar Assn. (jud. council), Tenn. Bar Assn. Office: NAACP 1790 Broadway New York NY 10019 *

HOOKS, WILLIAM GARY, geologist, educator; b. Asheville, N.C., Oct. 4, 1927; s. John Brantley and Virginia Evelyn (Fortune) H.; m. Peggy Raye Lucas, Dec. 27, 1951; children: William Gary, Deborah, Judson David, Stephen Borden. B.S., U. N.C., 1950, M.S., 1953, Ph.D., 1961. Asst. prof. dept. geology and geography U. Ala., 1954-61, asso. prof., 1961-67, prof., 1968—, chmn. dept., 1969-77, acting chmn. dept., 1981-82; geol. cons., 1955—. Mem. Geol. Soc. Am. (vice chmn. Southeastern sect.), Soc. Econ. Paleontologists and Mineralogists, Ala. Geol. Soc. (pres. 1966), Am. Assn. Petroleum Geologists, Phi Beta Kappa, Sigma Xi, Sigma Gamma Epsilon. Home: 3414 Kensington Ct Tuscaloosa AL 35405 Office: Box 1945 Dept Geology U Ala University AL 35486

HOOKSTRATTEN, EDWARD GREGORY, lawyer; b. Whittier, Calif., June 12, 1932; s. E.G. and Winona (Hewitt) H. B.S., U. So. Calif., 1953; LL.B., Southwestern U., Los Angeles, 1957. Bar: Calif. 1958, U.S. Supreme Ct. 1974. Individual practice law, Beverly Hills, Calif., 1960—; pres. Broadcast Artists, Ltd.; dir. Nat. Athletic Health Inst., Los Angeles Rams Football Co.; Mem. Dist. Attys. Adv. Council, 1965—. Commr. bd. adminstrn. Los Angeles Retirement System, 1970-71; commr. Los Angeles Dept. Pub. Utilities and Transp., 1971-73, v.p., 1973; commr. Los Angeles Dept. Recreation and Parks, 1973-75, v.p., 1974; commr. State of Calif. Motion Picture Council; life mem. So. Calif. Assos.; bd. dirs. U. So. Calif. Assos., Los Angeles Police Meml. Found. Mem. Los Angeles County Bar Assn., Beverly Hills Bar Assn. Clubs: Bel Air Country (Los Angeles); The Beach (Santa Monica, Calif.); Beverly Hills Tennis. Office: 9012 Beverly Blvd Los Angeles CA 90048

HOOLE, WILLIAM STANLEY, librarian, author; b. Darlington, S.C., May 16, 1903; s. William Brunson and Mary Eva (Powers) H.; m. Martha Anne Sanders, Aug. 7, 1931 (dec. May 1960); children: Martha DuBose, Elizabeth Stanley; m. Addie Shirley Coleman, May 31, 1970. A.B., Wofford Coll., 1924, A.M., 1931, Litt.D., 1954; Ph.D., Duke U., 1934; B.S. in L.S, North Tex. U., 1943; student, Columbia U., 1927, U. S.C., 1929, U. Chgo. Grad. Library Sch., summers 1935, 36, 38, 39; LL.D., U. Ala., 1975; D.Hum., Francis Marion Coll., 1980. Tchr. Spartanburg (S.C.) High Sch., 1924-25, Darlington High Sch., 1927-31; teaching fellow Duke U., 1931-34; asst. prof. English Birmingham (Ala.) So. Coll., 1934-35, librarian, 1935-37, Baylor U., Waco, Tex., 1937-39; dir. libraries North Tex. State U., 1939-44; dean libraries U. Ala., Tuscaloosa, 1944-71, prof. librarianship, 1971-73, dean emeritus, 1973—; library cons. So. Assn. Schs. and Colls., 1942-60, mem. commn. instns. higher learning, 1948-50; research cons. U.S. Ho. of Reps. subcom. on spl. edn., 1957-58; cons. U.S. Office Edn., 1959-60, Pres.'s Nat. Commn. on Libraries, 1967, U.S. Dept. Commerce, 1968, also various govt. agys., coms. Editor: North Texas Regional Union List of Serials, 1943, Classified List of Reference Books and Periodicals for the College Library, rev, 1957, Seven Months in the Rebel States, 1863, 1958, Reconstruction in West Alabama, 1959, A Visit to the Confederate States of America in 1863, 1962, And Still We Conquer, 1968, The Logs of the C.S.S. Alabama and C.SS. Tuscaloosa, 1972, (with Marie B. Bingham) Catalogue of Yucatan Collection in University of Alabama Libraries, 1973, (with Addie S. Hoole) A History of Madison County, Ala., 1732-1840, 1976, Confederate Foreign Agent: The European Diary of Major Edward C. Anderson, 1976, (with Addie S. Hoole) A History of Tuscaloosa, Ala., 1816-1880, 1977, Florida Territory in 1844: The Diary of Master Edward C. Anderson, USN, 1977, (with A. S. Hoole) Early History of N.E. Ala, 1979, Early History of Montgomery, 1979, History of Tuscaloosa, Ala., 1816-1949, 1980, Cherokee Indians of Georgia, 1980, A Rebel Spy in Yankeeland, 1981, History of the 14th Regiment Alabama Volunteers, 1983, History of the 47th Alabama Infantry Regiment, 1983, The Pee Dee Light Artillery, C.S.A., 1983; Author: Charleston Periodicals, 1936, Sam Slick in Texas, 1945, The Ante-Bellum Charleston Theatre, 1946, Let the People Read, 1946, A Library for Lauderdale, Alias Simon Suggs: The Life and Times of Johnson Jones Hooper, 1952, The James Boys Rode South, 1955, Vizetelly Covers the Confederacy, 1957, The Alabama Tories, 1862-65, 1960, Four Years in the Confederate Navy, 1964, Lawley Covers the Confederacy, 1964, According to Hoole, 1973, Ode to a Druid Oak, 1979, The Birmingham Horrors, 1979, Peedee Epiphany, 1981, Saga of Rube Burrows, 1981, Margaret Ellen O'Brien, 1981, Martha Young: Alabama's Foremost Folklorist, 1982, Alabama's Golden Literary Era, 1983, John Witherspoon Du Bose: A Neglected Southern Historian, 1983, History of Shockley's Alabama Escort Company, 1983; co-author: Mississippi Study of Higher Education, 1945, Studies of Higher Education in the South, 1947, A Study of Stillman Institute, 1947; Editor: The Alabama Rev, 1948-67, The Southeastern Librarian, 1951-52; assoc. editor: South Atlantic MLA Bull., 1947-52, Confederate Centennial Studies, 1956-65; Contbr. articles to scholarly, profl. and popular publs., including Grolier Ency. Recipient Lit. award Ala. Library Assn., 1958; Fulbright research fellow, U.K., 1956-57. Mem. Ala. Hist. Assn., Phi Beta Kappa, Phi Alpha Theta, Pi Tau Chi, Kappa Phi Kappa, PiKappa Phi. Methodist. Home: 39 University Circle Tuscaloosa AL 35401

HOOLEY, JAMES ROBERT, oral and maxillofacial surgeon, educator, university dean; b. Stillwater, Minn., Nov. 5, 1932; s. Robert Joseph and Dorothy Agnes (Goss) H.; m. Margaret Ann Sullivan, Aug. 22, 1959; children: Michael, Mary, Grace, Thomas. D.D.S., St. Louis U., 1957; postgrad., New York Med. Coll., 1957-59; certificate in oral surgery, U. Pa., 1960. Diplomate: Am. Bd. Oral and Maxillofacial Surgery. Practice dentistry, specializing in oral and maxillofacial surgery, Seattle, 1963—; instr. dept. oral and maxillofacial surgery U. Wash. Sch. Dentistry, 1963-65; chief U. Wash. Hosp. Dental Service, 1964-72, asst. dean, 1966-71, asso. prof., 1968-72, prof., chmn. dept., 1972-80; dean Sch. Dentistry, UCLA, 1981—; chmn. dept. oral and maxillofacial surgery Harvard U. Program in Health Systems Mgmt., 1978. Author: Hospital Dentistry, 1970, A Self-Instructional Guide to Oral Surgery in General Dentistry, 1978, Hospital Dental Practice, 1979; Sect. editor: Jour. of Oral Surgery, 1972-76. Democratic precinct committeeman 43d Dist., Seattle, 1979. Served to capt. U.S. Army, 1960-62; to capt. Dental Corps USN Res., 1963—. Mem. Am. Dental Assn., Wash. Dental Assn., Seattle-King County Dental Assn., Internat. Assn. Oral Surgeons, Calif. Dental Assn., Western Dental Soc., Brit. Assn. Oral Surgeons, N.W. Soc. Oral Surgeons, Am. Assn. Oral and Maxillofacial Surgeons, European Assn. Maxillo-facial Surgeons. Roman Catholic. Office: Sch Dentistry UCLA Los Angeles CA 90024

HOOLEY, JOSEPH GILBERT, chemist; b. Vancouver, C., Can., Sept. 26, 1914; s. Joseph Stringfellow and Cecelia Mary (Frisby) H.; m. Agnes Schroeder, Sept. 16, 1939. B.A., U. B.C., Vancouver, 1934, M.A., 1936; Ph.D., M.I.T., 1939. Research chemist Corning Glass Co., Corning, N.Y., 1939-42; asst. prof. chemistry U. B.C., 1942-47; asso. prof., 1947-52, prof., 1952—, chmn. dept., 1950-54; vis. prof. Can. Atomic Energy, 1947-48, Imperial Coll., London, U.K., 1959-60. Contbr. numerous articles on graphite intercalation to profl. publs., 1955—. Fellow Chem. Inst. Can.; mem. Am. Carbon Soc. (Pettinos award 1979), Am. Phys. Soc. Patentee glass compositions. Home: 4769 W 7th Ave Vancouver BC V6T 1C7 Canada Office: Chemistry Dept U BC Vancouver BC V6T 1W5 Canada

HOOPER, ARTHUR WILLIAM, association executive; b. Lynn, Mass., June 22, 1919; s. George Joseph and Mildred Mary (Devlin) H.; m. Mary Penny, Aug. 15, 1942; children: Arthur W., James David, Kenneth W. B.A., Columbia U., 1943. Editor McGraw-Hill Pub. Co., N.Y.C., 1945-55; exec. dir. Nat. Assn. Elec. Distbrs., Stamford, Conn., 1955—; dir. Nat. Edn. Found.; trustee Nat. Assn. Wholesalers. Served to lt. (j.g.) USCG, 1942-45; Phillipines. Home: 21 Prides Crossing New Canaan CT 06840 Office: National Association Electrical Distributors 600 Summer St Stamford CT 06901

HOOPER, BAYARD, editor; b. Southampton, L.I., N.Y., July 3, 1928; s. Roger F. and Justine V.R. (Barber) H.; m. Dorothy L. Peck, Feb. 16, 1952 (div. 1973); children—David B., Carolyn L., Robert C.; m. Mary Anne McCarthy, Apr. 13, 1973; 1 dau., Elizabeth Sheridan. A.B. cum laude, Harvard, 1950. With Life mag. Time, Inc., 1951-70, reporter, 1951-54, corr., bur. chief, 1954-60, writer, sr. editor, 1960-70; sr. editor Discover mag. Time Inc.; v.p. Louis Harris & Assos., 1970-73; editorial dir. Modern Medicine Publs., and; Harcourt Brace Jovanovich Health Care Publs., Mpls., 1973-78; exec. editor Esquire mag., N.Y.C., 1978-79; founding editor, editorial dir. Prime Time mag., N.Y.C., 1979-82. Home: Madison St Sag Harbor NY 11968 Office: Time & Life Bldg Rockefeller Center New York NY 10020

HOOPER, BLAKE HOWARD, mfg. co. exec.; b. Chgo., Oct. 20, 1922; s. William Dane and Helen (McLernon) H.; m. Frances Eleanor Barnes, Aug. 17, 1944; children—Kathy Ellen (Mrs. Volkert Hans Goebel), David Blake. B.S. in Chem. Engring, Ill. Inst. Tech., 1944. Chem. engr. Darling & Co., Chgo., 1946-50; tech. sales and service mgr. indsl. gases Chemetron, 1950-55; gen. mgr. Wilson Martin div. Wilson & Co., Phila., 1955-67, v.p., 1967-68; pres., chief exec. officer, dir. Wilson Pharm. & Chem. Corp., Chgo., 1968-73; chmn. bd., pres., chief exec. officer, dir. Morgan Adhesives Co., Stow, Ohio, 1973—; dir. Mactac Europe, Brussels, Mactac Can., Brampton, Ont.; chmn. bd. Accraply, Inc., Mpls., 1977—; Vice pres., mem. bd., exec. com. Chem. Industries Council-Midwest, 1972. Mem. Cherry Hill Twp. (N.J.) Zoning Bd., 1965. Served to lt. comdr. USNR, 1943-46; mem. Res (ret.). Mem. Am. Oil Chemists Soc., Fatty Acid Producers Council, Delta Tau Delta. Clubs: Walden Country, Silver Lake Country, Turtle Creek Golf. Home: 415-44 Hill Dr Aurora OH 44202 Office: 4560 Darrow Rd Stow OH 44224

HOOPER, EDITH FERRY, mus. trustee; b. Detroit, Nov. 30, 1909; d. Dexter Mason and Jeannette (Hawkins) Ferry, Jr.; m. Arthur Upshur Hooper, June 22, 1945; children—Jeannette Hooper Williams, Kate Hooper Gorman, Queene Ferry. B.A., Vassar Coll., 1932. Asst. indsl. design dept. Mus. Modern Art, N.Y.C., 1939-40; clk. U.S. Procurement Office, Detroit, 1941; asst. Roeper City and Country Sch., Detroit, 1944; Trustee Balt. Mus. Art, 1957—, pres. bd., 1973-75. Trustee Goucher Coll., Towson, Md., 1970-73; pres. bd. trustees Bryn Mawr Sch., Balt., 1965-71; chmn. bldg. com. Lower Sch., 1971-73; pres. D.M. Ferry, Jr. Trustee Corp. (found.), 1973—; bd. dirs. Friends of Art Gallery Vassar Coll., 1974-76. Clubs: Cosmopolitan (N.Y.C.); Hamilton St. (Balt.). Address: 1100 Copper Hill Rd Baltimore MD 21209 *The basic principle of my life has been to benefit, to the greatest extent I am able physically and financially, the communities in which I live and in which I am interested. The pleasures of involvement and progress in each field, especially art and education, have been completely rewarding.*

HOOPER, EMMET THURMAN, JR., biologist, educator; b. Phoenix, Aug. 19, 1911; s. Emmet Thurman and Frances Jewell (McDonald) H.; m. Helen Winifred Bacon, Feb. 19, 1936; children: Alan Bacon, Nicholas Kim. Student, San Diego State Coll., 1929-32; A.B., U. Calif.-Berkeley, 1933, A.M., 1936, Ph.D., 1939. Research asst. Mus. Vertebrate Zoology, U. Calif.-Berkeley, 1934-36, teaching asst. zoology, 1936-38; asst. prof. zoology U. Mich., 1946-52, asso. prof., 1952-58, prof., 1958-79, curator mammals, 1956-79, prof., curator emeritus, 1979—; project leader, sea otter research U.S. Fish and Wildlife Service, 1979—; program dir. NSF, Washington, 1964-65; chmn. biology faculty Orgn. Tropical Studies, 1967-70. Author tech. reports on evolution, ecology, systematics vertebrate animals. Served to capt. USAAF, 1943-46. Mem. Biol. Soc. Washington, Soc. Study Evolution, Am. Soc. Mammalogists (corr. sec. 1941-46, v.p. 1958-62, pres. 1962-64, hon. mem. 1976), Am. Inst. Biol. Scis., Wildlife Soc., Assn. Tropical Biology, Australian Mammal Soc., AAAS, Sci. Research Club (U. Mich.), Sigma Xi. Sci. expdns. N.Am. Home: 911 Balboa Ave Capitola CA 95010 Office: Coastal Marine Studies Applied Scis Bldg U Calif Santa Cruz CA 95064

HOOPER, FREDERICK RICHARD, ret. headmaster; b. San Francisco, July 31, 1908; s. John Franklin and May (Frisbee) H.; m. Grace Fletcher Read, June 24, 1937; 1 son, Robert Moore. A.B., Pomona Coll., 1933; postgrad., Claremont Grad. Sch., 1933-34. Master Webb Sch. of Calif., Claremont, 1933-62, head math. dept., 1939-1962, dir. studies, 1955-62, mem. faculty exec. com., 1957-62, headmaster, 1962-73, emeritus, 1973—. Troop committeeman Old Baldy council Boy Scouts Am., 1953-56. Mem. Calif. Assn. Ind. Schs. (head math. sect. 1958-62, treas. 1964-70), Am. Philatelic Soc., S.A.R., John More Assn., Headmasters Assn., First Century Families Calif., Cum Laude Soc., Phi Delta Kappa. Conglist. Clubs: Rotarian., Newport Beach Tennis, Bear Valley Gang Pomona Valley; California (Los Angeles). Home: PO Box 155 Corona Del Mar CA 92625

HOOPER, GILMAN STANLEY, chemist; b. Danvers, Mass., Mar. 18, 1909; s. George D. and Mary P. (Elliott) H.; m. Virginia L. Keyes, May 17, 1935; 1 son, George Gilman. B.S., Colby Coll., 1929; M.S., Brown U., 1930, Ph.D., 1933. Successively research chemist, research supr., asst. research dir., tech. supt., mgr. tech. service E.I. du Pont de Nemours & Co., 1934-49; with Indsl. Rayon Corp., Cleve., 1949-60; research mgr., 1951-57, dir. research, 1957, v.p. charge research, 1958-60; dir. research and devel., fiber devel. dept. Hercules Powder Co., 1960-63; v.p. Deering Milliken Research Corp., Spartanburg, S.C., 1963-71; exec. dir. Charles Lea Center for Rehab. and Spl. Edn., 1971-78; fin. officer E.T.V. Endowment of S.C., 1978—. Past pres., bd. dirs. United Cerebral Palsy Assn. Cuyahoga County, Ohio; bd. dirs. Spartanburg United Fund, Spartanburg County United Cerebral Palsy Assn., Spartanburg County Retarded Children's Assn., Council for Spartanburg County, Salvation Army; chmn. Spartanburg County Bd. for Mental Retardation and Devel. Disabilities; chmn. bd. Charles Lea Center Handicapped Children. Mem. Am. Chem. Soc., Am. Assn. Textile Tech., Phi Beta Kappa, Sigma Xi, Kappa Delta Rho. Home: 19 Springdale Ln Spartanburg SC 29302 Office: 1029 Woodburn Rd Spartanburg SC 29302

HOOPER, HENRY OLCOTT, university administrator, physicist; b. Washington, Mar. 9, 1935; s. Olcott Lorin and Eleanor (Drew) H.; m. Donna Faulkingham, June 10, 1956; children: Deborah, Bruce, Katherine, Michael, Andrew. B.S. in Engring. Physics, U. Maine, 1956; M.S. in Physics, Brown U., 1959, Ph.D., 1961. Asst. prof. Brown U., Providence, 1961-64; asst. prof. physics Wayne State U., Detroit, 1964-66, assoc. prof., 1966-70, prof., 1970-73; prof., chmn. dept. physics U. Maine, Orono, 1973-76, dean Grad. Sch., 1977-80; assoc. v.p. acad. affairs, dean grad. Coll. No. Ariz. U., Flagstaff, 1981—; con. NASA, Huntsville, Ala., 1967-68; mem. rev. panel div. ednl. programs Argonne Nat. Lab., Ill., 1982-84. Author: College Physical Science, 3d edit., 1974, Physics and the Physical Perspective, 1977; editor: Conf. Procs. Amorphous Magnetism, 1973. Fellow Am. Phys. Soc.; mem. Am. Assn. Physics Tchrs., AAAS, Am. Ceramic Soc. Home: 3230 Meadowbrook Flagstaff AZ 86001 Office: No Ariz U PO Box 4085 Flagstaff AZ 86011

HOOPER, IAN (JOHN DEREK GLASS), advt. agy. exec.; b. London, Sept. 8, 1941; U.S., 1979; s. John Desmond Glass and Moira Elizabeth (White) H. Student, Coll. Distributive Trades, 1960-62, 65-67, Harvard U., 1979. With S. H. Benson, London, 1960-62, Nairobi, Kenya, 1962-64, London, 1965-67; account exec. McCann-Erickson Advt., London, 1967-68; account supr., 1968-72, account dir., 1972-76, group account dir., 1976-79, sr. v.p., mgmt. rep., N.Y.C., 1979—. Mem. Inst. Practitioners in Advt., Advt. Assn. U.K. Home: 1049 Park Ave New York NY 10028 Office: 485 Lexington Ave New York NY 10017

HOOPER, JOHN ALLEN, banker; b. Danbury, Conn., Dec. 9, 1922; s. Kenneth Malcolm and Grace Lillian (Jardon) H.; m. Susanne Leona Sipperly, Nov. 27, 1948; children: Judith Elaine, John Nash. B.B.A., U. Mich., 1947, M.B.A., 1948. Sr. v.p. Chase Manhattan Bank, N.Y.C., 1948-71, exec. v.p., 1972—, mem. mgmt. com., 1975—, vice-chmn. bd., 1983—; chmn. bd., chief exec. officer Bank of the Commonwealth, Detroit, 1971-72; dir. Stone & Webster, Inc. Served with AUS, 1943-46. Decorated Army Commendation medal; named Man of Year, Inst. Human Relations, 1974. Mem. Assn. Res. City Bankers. Clubs: Patterson (Fairfield, Conn.); Laurel Valley (Ligonier, Pa.); Wilderness Country (Naples, Fla.). Home: 22 Silverbrook Rd Westport CT 06880 Office: 1 Chase Manhattan Plaza New York NY 10005

HOOPER, JOHN WILLIAM, economics educator; b. Laona, Wis., Nov. 6, 1926; s. Frank Arnold and Myldred (Barlement) H.; m. Eva Salmang, Aug. 14, 1959; children: Ellen Myldred, Carol Ann, Joan Claire. B.A. in Econs, Stanford, 1950, Ph.D., 1961; postgrad., U. Wash., 1950-51. Research economist Rand Corp., 1958-59; assoc. prof. econs. Yale U., 1959-66; prof. econs. U. Calif. at San Diego, 1966—, chmn. dept., 1967—; vis. prof. indsl. mgmt. U. Petroleum and Minerals, Dhahran, Saudi Arabia, 1977-79; sr. fellow Nat. U. Singapore, 1982-83; asst. dir. Cowles Found. Research Econs., 1961-64. Served with USNR, 1944-46. Fulbright scholar, 1957-58; sr. fellow Social Sci. Research Council, 1964-65; Ford Found. faculty research fellow, 1971-72. Mem. Am. Econ. Assn., Econometric Soc., Royal Econ. Soc. Home: 5878 Soledad Rd La Jolla CA 92037 Office: Dept Econs B-003 U Calif San Diego CA 92093

HOOPES, JANET LOUISE, educator, psychologist; b. Phila., Mar. 5, 1923; d. Raymond Talmage and Pearl H. (Jacobs) H. A.B., Bryn Mawr Coll., 1944, Ph.D., 1965; M.Clin. Psychology, U. Mich., 1948. Jr. psychologist Rochester (N.Y.) Guidance Center, 1948-51; psychologist Children's Aid Soc. Pa., Phila., 1951-58, chief psychologist, 1958-70; prof. edn. and child devel. Bryn Mawr (Pa.) Coll., 1970—. Author: An Infant Rating Scale: Its Validation and Usefulness, 1967, A Follow-Up Study of Adoptions: The Functioning of the Children, 1970, Prediction in Child Development: A Longitudinal Study of Adoptive and Non-Adoptive Families-The Delaware Family Study. Served as ensign Med. Service Corps, USNR, 1944-46. Mem. Am., Pa. psychol. assns. Presbyterian (elder 1967—). Home: 173 Marlyn Rd Lansdowne PA 19050 Office: West House Bryn Mawr Coll Bryn Mawr PA 19010

HOOPES, JOHN AUSTIN, civil and environmental engineering educator, consultant; b. Berkeley, Calif., Mar. 29, 1936; s. Harry Paul and Alice Jane (Nikirk) H.; m. Janet Irene Holden, July 25, 1959; children: Elizabeth Jane, Wesley John, Thomas Holden. B.S., U. Calif.-Berkeley, 1958, M.S., 1960; Ph.D., MIT, 1965. Asst. prof. U. Wis., Madison, 1964-68, assoc. prof., 1968-72, prof. civil and environ. engring., 1972—; sr. engr. Bechtel Civil and Minerals Inc., San Francisco, 1980-81; cons. to industry, state agys. Contbr. numerous tech. articles to sci. jours. Leader Four Lakes council Boy Scouts Am. Served to 2d lt. Transp. Corps U.S. Army, 1958-59. NATO sr. sci. fellow, summer 1970. Mem. ASCE (J. Waldo Smith hydraulic research fellow 1961, Walter L. Huber Civil Engring. Research prize 1972, Karl Emil Hilgard prize 1972), Am. Geophys. Union, Internat. Assn. Gt. Lakes Research, AAUP. Home: 1133 Edgehill Dr Madison WI 53705 Office: Civil and Environ Engring Dept U Wis 1261 Engring Bldg Madison WI 53706

HOOPES, LORENZO NEVILLE, former retailing executive; b. Brigham City, Utah, Nov. 5, 1913; s. Jesse W. and Matilda (Eastman) H.; m. Stella Bobbie Sorensen, Apr. 9, 1938; children: David Craig, Janet. Student, Weber Coll., 1931-33, U. Utah, 1934-35; LL.D. (hon.), U. Utah, 1975; grad., Advanced Mgmt. Program, Harvard, 1952; M.B.A., Pepperdine U., 1976; H.H.D. (hon.), Okla. Christian Coll., 1977. Engaged in coop. marketing agrl. commodities, 1935-40, operator egg shell processing plants, Idaho, Calif., 1941-46, installed, supervised 25 egg processing plants in, U.S., 1946-49, 15 fluid milk plants, 1949-53, exec. asst. to sec. of agr., 1953-54; exec. asst. to co. mgr. and plant ops. mgr. Lucerne Milk Co. div. Safeway Stores, Inc., 1949-59, mgr. dairy and egg div., 1959-67; v.p., mgr., supply ops. Safeway Stores, Inc., Oakland, Calif., 1963-71, sr. v.p., 1972-79, also dir. Pres. Eng. Bristol Mission, 1979-82; Pres. Oakland Bd. Edn., 1959-77; bd. dirs. United Bay Area Crusade; chmn. Found. for Am. Agr., 1976-79; vice chmn. Farm Found., 1976—; mem. nat. adv. council U. Utah, 1970—; chmn. nat. adv. council Grad. Sch. Mgmt., Brigham Young U., 1976-79; pres. Coordinating Council for Higher Edn., State Calif., 1973-74. Recipient Jesse Knight Indsl. Citizenship award Brigham Young U., 1974. Mem. Nat. Dairy Council (chmn., sec., dir. 1959-79), United Dairy Industries Assn. (founding dir. 1970-78). Mem. Ch. of Jesus Christ of Latter-day Saints (bishop, stake pres., mission pres., counselor to temple pres.). Lodge: Rotary. Home: 45 Mott Pl Oakland CA 94619

HOOPES, TOWNSEND WALTER, association executive; b. Duluth, Minn., Apr. 28, 1922; s. Henry Townsend and Andrea Edna (Mortrued) H.; m. Ann Merrifield, Oct. 17, 1964; 1 dau., Andrea; children by previous marriage: Townsend Walter III, Peter Schmidt; stepchildren: Marsha, Cecily, Briggs, Thomas. Grad., Phillips Acad., Andover, Mass., 1940; A.B. in Econs, Yale, 1944. Editorial writer Buffalo Evening News, 1946; asst. to chmn. com. armed services Ho. of Reps., Washington, 1947-48, asst. to sec. def., 1948-53, dep. asst. sec. def. internat. security affairs, 1965-66, prin. dep. asst. sec. def. internat. security affairs, 1966-67, undersec. air force, 1967-69; asst. to pres. Spencer Chem. Co., 1953-55; asso. J.H. Whitney & Co., 1955-57; partner firm Cresap, McCormick & Paget, 1958-64, v.p., dir. Washington office, 1969-71; also corporate dir.; pres. Assn. Am. Publishers, Washington and N.Y.C., 1973—; dir. Talley Industries, Inc., Phoenix.; Cons. orgn. Nat. Security Council, 1954, Dept. State, Dept. Def., 1957; sec. mil. panel Rockefeller Bros. Fund Spl. Studies Project, 1957-58; cons. Pres.'s Com. U.S. Information Activities Abroad, 1960. Author: The Limits of Intervention, 1969, The Devil and John Foster Dulles, 1973; co-author: Eye Power, 1979; Contbr. articles to profl. jours. Served with USMC, 1943-46. Fellow Woodrow Wilson Internat. Center Scholars, 1971-73. Mem. Council Fgn. Relations. Clubs: Yale, The Links, Century (N.Y.C.); Chevy Chase (Md.); 1925 F St (Washington). Home: 5039 Lowell St NW Washington DC 20016 Office: 2005 Massachusetts Ave NW Washington DC 20036

HOOPMAN, HAROLD DEWAINE, oil co. exec.; b. Lucas, Kans., July 22, 1920; s. Ira William and Mary B. (Dorman) H.; m. Eleanor Gessner, July 6, 1946; children: Judith Kristin Hoopman Hains, David W., Michael J. B.S. in Mech. Engring., U. Wyo., 1942; grad., Advanced Mgmt. Program, Harvard U., 1964; LL.D. (hon.), Marietta Coll., 1979, L.H.D., Eastern Ill. U., 1982. Exptl. test engr. Wright Aero. Co., Patterson, N.J., 1942-43; with Marathon Oil Co., 1946—, resident mgr., Guatemala, 1957-62, v.p. internat. div., 1962-67, asst. to pres., 1967-68, v.p. prodn., 1968-69, v.p. mktg. in U.S., Findlay, Ohio, 1969-72, pres., dir., 1972—, chief exec. officer, 1975—; vice-chmn. oil, gas and related resources U.S. Steel Corp., 1983—, also dir.; dir. 1st Nat. Bank, Findlay., PNC Fin. Corp., Pitts. Nat. Bank. Contbr. articles to profl. jours. Served with USNR, 1943-46. Mem. Am. Petroleum Inst. (dir.), Soc. Petroleum Engrs. of AIME, Nat. Petroleum Council. Lutheran. Club: Findlay Country. Office: 539 S Main St Findlay OH 45840

HOOVEN, FREDERICK JOHNSON, mech. engr.; b. Dayton, Ohio, Mar. 5, 1905; s. Claude Caldwell and Elizabeth (Johnson) H.; m.

Martha Galloway Kennedy, Apr. 28, 1928; children—John, Peter, Michael, Martha Hooven Richardson. S.B., M.I.T., 1927. Engr. DayFan Radio, 1925; jr. engr. Gen. Motors Research, 1927-28; engr. Dayton Rubber Mfg. Co., 1929-30, Am. Loth Corp., 1932; civilian aero. engr. USAAC, Dayton, 1930-31; chief engr. Radio Products Co., 1933-34; v.p., chief engr. Radio Products div. Bendix Aviation, 1935-37; cons. product devel., Dayton, 1938-56; with Ford Motor Co., Dearborn, Mich., 1956-67, dir. research planning, 1963-65, spl. cons. to gen. mgr. Ford div., 1966-67; adj. prof. engring. Thayer Sch. Engring., Dartmouth Coll., 1967-75, prof. engring., 1975—; cons. in field; vis. lectr. Antioch Coll., 1938-56; vol. research asso. in psychophysiology Fels Inst. for Human Devel., Yellow Springs, Ohio, 1946-56; Mem. ednl. council M.I.T., 1958-67, mem. vis. com. dept. mech. engring., 1959-65, mem. devel. com., 1961-68; mem. tech. adv. bd. Dept. Commerce, 1969-72. Contbr. articles to profl. jours. Mem. Oakwood (Ohio) Bd. Edn., 1949-56; trustee Antioch Coll., 1952-64, Miami Valley Hosp., Dayton, 1952-56, Charles F. Kettering Found., Dayton, 1959-77, Hitchcock Meml. Hosp., Hanover, N.H., 1968-75, Hitchcock Found., Hanover, 1968-73. Mem. AAAS, Dartmouth Soc. Engrs., Dayton Engrs. Club (Deeds Kettering Meml. award 1968), Exptl. Aircraft Assn., Fedn. Am. Scientists, Nat. Acad. Engring., Sigma Xi. Patentee aircraft radio direction-finders, receivers, navigation, blind-landing and guidance systems, automotive and aircraft high-energy and high-frequency ignition systems and components, electronic computing, control, measurement and switching systems, others. Home: Elm St Norwich VT 05055 Office: Thayer Sch Engring Dartmouth Coll Hanover NH 03755 *I have made the discovery that although one can never become young again in a field in which he has spent his life, he can in a very real sense become young again in a new field, especially in a field that is itself young.*

HOOVER, CHARLES M., appliance corporation executive; b. Okla., 1920. Ed., Okla. State U., 1942. Gen. sales mgr. Marquette Corp., 1942-60; with Roper Corp., Kankakee, Ill., 1960—, chmn. bd., chief exec. officer, 1967—, also dir.; chmn. bd., pres., chief exec. officer Roper Sales Corp.; pres. Eastern Products Corp. Office: 1906 W Court St Kankakee IL 60901 *

HOOVER, DWIGHT WESLEY, history educator; b. Oskaloosa, Iowa, Sept. 15, 1926; s. Homer Samuel and Ruth (Hull) H.; children: Polly Ruth, Sara Adeline, Elizabeth Anne. A.B., William Penn Coll., 1948; M.A. (T. Wistar Brown fellow), Haverford Coll., 1949; Ph.D., State U. Iowa, 1953. Prof., head social sci. dept. Bethune-Cookman Coll., Daytona Beach, Fla., 1953-55, 58; asst. prof. gen. studies dept. Kans. State U., 1958-59; mem. faculty Ball State U., Muncie, Ind., 1959—, asso. prof. history, 1963-67, prof., 1967—, dir. Ctr. Middletown Studies, 1981—; sr. cons. Middletown Film Project, 1977-81. Author: Understanding Negro History, 1968, Henry James, Sr. and the Religion of Community, 1969, A Teacher's Guide to American Urban History, 1971, The Red and the Black, 1976, Cities: A Multimedia Bibliography, 1976, A Pictorial History of Indiana, 1980; co-author: American Society in the 20th Century, 1972; contbg. author: All Faithful People; co-editor: Conspectus on History, 1975, 76, 77, 78, 79, 80, 81. Served to lt. USNR, 1955-58; Japan. Mem. AAUP, Am. Hist. Assn., Orgn. Am. Historians, Pi Gamma Mu, Phi Alpha Theta., Soc. Friends. Republican. Home: 705 N Forest Muncie IN 47304

HOOVER, FRANCIS LOUIS, gemologist, jewelry designer, appraiser fine arts and gems, educator, writer; b. Sherman, Tex., Mar. 12, 1913; s. Guy F. and Marie Louise Elizabeth (Louis) H.; m. Lucille Eddlemen, Sept. 1, 1935; 1 son, Jon Julien. B.S. (scholarship 1930-33), N. Tex. State U., 1933; M.A. (scholarship 1934-35), Columbia, 1935; Ed.D., N.Y. U., 1942; student, Art Students League, Sch. Social Research. Co-dir. LaSalle Art Gallery, N.Y.C., 1934-36; art dir. Carden Pvt. Sch., N.Y.C., 1934-36; free lance package designer, N.Y.C., 1934-36; asst. prof. art N. Tex. State U., 1936-40, Eastern Ill. U., 1941-44; prof. art Ill. State U., Normal, 1944-72, chmn. dept., 1944-69; dir. Internat. Collection Child Art, Research Center Ewing Mus. of Nations, 1970—, distinguished prof. and dir. univ. museums and galleries, 1970-72; editor Arts and Activities mag., 1951-66, Davis Publs., Inc., Worcester, Mass., 1966-70; publs. editor Art Resource Publs., Normal, 1964-66; dir. Fairway Gallery Art, Bloomington, Ill., 1962-67, Hoover Graphite Products; sponsor biennial exhbns. Am. Child Art, 1955, 57, 59, 61. Rep. exhbns. in, N.Y. Ill., Tex., 1935—; Author: Guide for Teaching Art Activities in the Classroom, 1956, Art Activities for the Very Young, 1961; filmstrip Art and Activities in the Classroom, 1955, African Art, 1974; also numerous articles.; Editor: Young Printmakers II. Bd. dirs. Art Edn. Found., 1956-66. Recipient Merit award editorial excellence, 6th ann. editorial competition Indsl. Marketing. Assn., 1954. Mem. Nat. Art Edn. Assn. (exec. council 1959-61), Ill. Art Edn. Assn. (pres. 1951), Western Arts Assn. (pres. 1949), NEA, Ill. Edn. Assn., AAUP, Am. Appraisers Assn., Delta Phi Delta, Phi Delta Kappa. Travel in Middle and S. Am. to study archaeol. sites; research on Cuna Indians. Donor Hoover Collection Pre-Columbian Ceramics to Ill. State U., Normal, 1972; Hoover collection Cuna art to Smithsonian Instn., 1976, other items from Hoover art collections to Phila. Mus. Art, Cleve. Mus. Art, Art Inst. Chgo., Field Mus. Natural History, Honolulu Acad. Fine Arts, Harvard U. Peabody Mus. Home: 1770 Avenida del Mundo 1405 Coronado CA 92118

HOOVER, HELEN D. (MRS. ADRIAN E. HOOVER), author; b. Greenfield, Ohio, Jan. 20, 1910; d. Thomas Franklin and Hannah (Gomersall) Blackburn; m. Adrian Everett Hoover, Feb. 13, 1937. Student, Ohio U., 1927-29, DePaul U., U. Chgo., 1943-49. Addressograph operator D-J Novelties Co., Chgo., 1930; proofreader Audit Bur. Circulations, Chgo., 1931-43; chemist Pitts. Testing Lab., Chgo., 1943-45; prodn. metallurgist Ahlberg Bearing Co., Chgo., 1945-48; research metallurgist Internat. Harvester Co., Chgo., 1948-54; free-lance writer gen., nature and juvenile mags., Minn., N.Mex. and Wyo., 1954—. Author: The Long-Shadowed Forest, 1963, The Gift of the Deer, 1966, Animals at My Doorstep, 1966, Great Wolf and the Good Woodsman, 1967, A Place in the Woods, 1969, Animals Near and Far, 1970, The Years of the Forest, 1973. Recipient Ann. Achievement award Metal Treating Inst., 1959; Blue Flame Ecology Salute, 1973; Zia award N.Mex. Press Women, 1973; Bklyn. Art Books for Children citation, 1976, 78; medal of Merit, Ohio U. Alumni Assn., 1979. Mem. Authors Guild, M.B.L.S., Nat. Cat Protection Soc., Life for God's Stray Animals, Wilderness Soc., Defenders of Wildlife, Greenpeace, Defenders of Animal Rights, Nature Conservancy, Animal Protection Inst., Friends of the Sea Otter, Internat. Fund Animal Welfare, Com. Preservation of Tule Elk, Humane Soc. U.S., Soc. Animal Protective Legislation, Howl, Inc., Internat. Council Bird Preservation, Internat. Union for Conservation of Nature, World Wildlife Fund, Soc. Animal Rights, Cousteau Soc., North Shore Animal League., Living Free Animal Sanctuary. Patentee agrl. implement disks. Office: Brandt and Brandt 1501 Broadway New York NY 10036

HOOVER, HERBERT WILLIAM, JR., business executive; b. 1918; 1941; m. Carl Good, 1941; children: Herbert William III, Elizabeth Lacey. A.B., Rollins Coll., 1941; LL.D. (hon.), Mt. Union Coll., 1959. Sales exec. Hoover Co., North Canton, Ohio, 1941-43, dir. pub. relations, 1945-48, asst. v.p., 1948-52, v.p. field sales, 1952-53, exec. v.p., 1953-54, pres., 1954—; dir. Hoover Co., Ltd., Can., 1952, pres., 1954; dir. Hoover, Ltd., Eng., 1954, chmn., 1956; dir., pres. Hoover, Inc., Panama, 1955, Hoover (Am. Latina) S.A., 1955, Hoover Mexicana S.A. de C.V., Mexico, 1955; dir. Hoover Co., pres., chmn., 1959-66, Hoover Indsl. y Comercial S.A., Colombia, 1960; pres., dir. Hoover Worldwide Corp., N.Y.C., 1960; dir. S.A. Hoover, France, 1965. Past regional vice chmn. U.S. Com. for UN, 1965; chmn. endowment com. Miami Heart Inst.; active YMCA, Council on Fgn. Relations; trustee emeritus U. Miami. Served with U.S. Army, 1943-45. Decorated chevalier French Legion of Honour, chevalier du Tasteviv. Mem. N.Y. Sales Execs. Club, Am. Soc. French Legion of Honour. Clubs: Key Largo Anglers (Fla.); New York Yacht; Rolling Rock (Ligonier, Pa.); Travelers of Paris; Indian Creek Country (Fla.). Address: 70 Park Dr 4 Bal Harbour FL 33154

HOOVER, JOHN ELWOOD, consultant, writer, former army officer; b. Timberville, Va., Apr. 28, 1924; s. Saylor Cornelius and Ruby Mae (Brill) H.; m. Mary Jo Cox, May 17, 1953; children—Mary Kathryn Yelverton, Holly Bullock. Student, Bridgewater (Va.) Coll., 1941-43, Amherst (Mass.) Coll., 1943-44; B.S., U.S. Mil. Acad., 1947; M.A., Georgetown U., 1955; postgrad., Columbia U., 1955-56, U.S. Army Command and Gen. Staff Coll., Ft. Leavenworth, Kans., 1958-59, U.S. Army War Coll., Carlisle Barracks, Pa., 1962-63. Commd. 2d lt. U.S. Army, 1947, advanced through grades to maj. gen., 1971; with (24th Inf. Div.), Japan and, Korea, 1948-51, Ft. Gordon, Ga., 1951-53, faculty dept. social scis., 1955-58, comdr., Germany, 1959-60; chief signal plans Hdqrs. U.S. Army Europe, Germany, 1961-62; with Office Asst. Sec. Def. for Internat. Security Affairs, Washington, 1963-66; chief communications plans (Hdqrs. Pacific Command), Hawaii, 1966-69, comdr., Vietnam, 1969-70; exec. officer, then dir. communications systems, then dep. asst. chief of staff for communication-electronics Hdqrs. Dept. Army, Washington, 1970-73; dep. comdg. gen. U.S. Army Communications Command, Ft. Huachuca, Ariz., 1973-74; dir. Joint Tactical Communications Office, Office Sec. Def., Ft. Monmouth, N.J., 1974-78; ret., 1978. Decorated D.S.M., Legion of Merit with oak leaf cluster, Bronze Star medal with oak leaf cluster, Meritorious Service medal, Air medal with oak leaf cluster, Joint Service Commendation medal, Army Commendation medal; Armed Forces Honor medal; Staff Service medal, Republic Vietnam; Vietnam Gallantry Cross with palm; Order Mil. Merit, Republic of Korea). Mem. Armed Forces Communications-Electronics Assn., Assn. U.S. Army, Assn. Grads. U.S. Mil. Acad., Nat. Audubon Soc., Nat. Wildlife Fedn., Signal Corps Assn. Office: 834 Wimbledon Dr Augusta GA 30909

HOOVER, LINN, geologist; b. Balt., Apr. 13, 1923; s. Z. Linn and Harriet (Beall) H.; m. Joan Patricia Williams, Jan. 31, 1953; children—Peter Linn, Hilary Joan. A.B., U. N.C., 1948; M.A., U. Mich., 1951; Ph.D., U. Calif. at Berkeley, 1959. Geologist U.S. Geol. Survey, 1948-60; exec. sec. div. earth scis. Nat. Acad. Sci., Washington, 1960-63; exec. dir. Am. Geol. Inst., Washington, 1963-74; dep. chief, office of energy resources U.S. Geol. Survey, Reston, Va., 1974-82, chief internat. sci. programs, 1982—; mem., sec. U.S. Nat. Com. on Geology, 1976—; del. Internat. Geol. Congress, Sydney, Australia, 1976, Paris, 1980. Served with AUS, 1943-45. Recipient Parker Meml. medal Am. Inst. Profl. Geologists, 1975. Fellow Geol. Soc. Am.; mem. Am. Assn. Petroleum Geologists, Am. Geophys. Union. Club: Cosmos (Washington). Home: 6902 Oakridge Ave Chevy Chase MD 20815 Office: US Geol Survey Reston VA 22092

HOOVER, ROBERT B., lumber company executive; b. Fresno, Calif., 1916. A.B., Stanford U., 1937, M.B.A., 1939. Partner Al Hoover Co., 1940-63; v.p. sales Pacific Lumber Co., San Francisco, 1963-71, sec., 1965-69, exec. v.p., 1971-73, pres., 1973-80, chief exec. officer, 1973-82, chmn. bd., 1980—, also dir.; pres., dir. Sangre de Cristo Timber Co., Yosuba Farm Co.; dir. Pacific Gas & Electric Co., Thermol Dynamics Co. Served to lt. (j.g.) USN, 1944-46. Office: Pacific Lumber Co PO Box 7406 San Francisco CA 94120 *

HOOVER, ROLAND ARMITAGE, publisher; b. Buffalo, Jan. 14, 1929; s. John Frank and Constance (More) H.; m. Cynthia Lee Adams, July 14, 1962; children: Sarah Adams, Emily Armitage. B.S., Yale U., 1949. Mgmt. trainee Cleve. Electric Illuminating Co., 1949-50; graphic designer studio of Hubert Leckie, Washington, 1955-56; supr. tech. reports Atomic Energy div. Allis-Chalmers Mfg. Co., Washington, 1956-63; editor-in-charge Publs. Office, Research and Engring. Support div. Inst. for Def. Analyses, 1963-65; exec. editor Brookings Instn., Washington, 1965-67, dir. publs., 1967—; propr. pvt. press, free lance typographer, 1958—. Served from ensign to lt. (j.g.) USNR, 1951-53. Mem. Am. Inst. Graphic Arts (pres. Washington chpt. 1965-66), Am. Printing History Assn., Soc. Scholarly Pub., Washington Book Pubs., Sigma Xi, Tau Beta Pi. Democrat. Episcopalian. Home: 7938 W Beach Dr NW Washington DC 20012 Office: 1775 Massachusetts Ave NW Washington DC 20036

HOOVER, WILLIAM RAY, computer service co. exec.; b. Bingham, Utah, Jan. 2, 1930; s. Edwin Daniel and Myrtle Tennessee (McConnell) H.; m. Sara Elaine Anderson, Oct. 4; children—Scott, Robert, Michael, James, Charles. B.S., M.S., U. Utah. Sect. chief Jet Propulsion Lab., Pasadena, Calif., 1954-64; v.p. Computer Scis. Corp., El Segundo, Calif., 1964-69, pres., 1969—, chmn. bd., 1972—. Home: 28965 Palos Verdes Dr E Rancho Palos Verdes CA 90274 Office: 650 N Sepulveda Blvd El Segundo CA 90245

HOPE, BOB, stage, radio, film, TV actor/comedian; b. Eltham, Eng., May 29, 1903; m. Dolores Reade, Feb. 19, 1934; children—Linda, Anthony, Kelly, Nora. Ed. pub. schs., Cleve; D.F.A. (hon.), Brown U., Jacksonville (Fla.) U., L.H.D., Quincy (Ill.) Coll., Georgetown U., So. Meth. U., Ohio State U., Ind. U., John Carroll U., U. Nev., Monmouth Coll., Whittier Coll., Pa. Mil. Coll., Miami U., Oxford, Ohio, U. Cin., Calif. State Colls., Mercy Coll., N.J., Coll. of Desert, Baldwin-Wallace Coll., LL.D., U. Wyo., Northwestern U., St. Bonaventure U., Pace Coll., Pepperdine U., U. Scranton, Western State U., Calif., H.H.D., Ohio Dominican Coll., Bowling Green U., Santa Clara U., Fla. So. Coll., Wilberforce U., Northwood Inst., Mich., Norwich U., Bethel Coll., Tenn., Utah State U., St. Anselm's Coll., N.H.; D. Internat. Relations, Salem Coll.; D.Pub. Service (hon.), St. Ambrose Coll., D. Humane Service, Drury Coll., D.Humane Humor, Benedictine Coll., Kans., D.Performing Arts, Dakota Wesleyan U., Litt.D., Gonzaga U. Began in vaudeville; and has also appeared on stage; now in motion pictures, TV, radio.; Has appeared in: stage Ballyhoo, 1932, Roberta, 1933, Ziegfeld Follies, 1935, Red Hot and Blue, 1936; motion pictures College Swing, 1938, Give Me a Sailor, 1938, Thanks for the Memory, 1938, Never Say Die, 1939, Some Like It Hot, The 1939, Cat and the Canary, 1939, The Road to Singapore, 1940, The Ghostbreakers, 1940, Caught in the Draft, 1941, Nothing But the Truth, 1941, Road to Zanzibar, 1941, Louisiana Purchase, 1941, Road to Morocco, 1942, My Favorite Blonde, 1942, Star Spangled Rhythm, 1942, They Got Me Covered, 1943, Let's Face It, 1943, The Princess and the Pirate, 1944, The Road to Utopia, 1945, Monsieur Beaucaire, 1946, My Favorite Brunette, 1947, Where There's Life, 1947, Road to Rio, 1948, Paleface, 1948, Sorrowful Jones, 1949, The Great Lover, 1949, Fancy Pants, 1950, Lemon Drop Kid, 1951, My Favorite Spy, 1951, Son of Paleface, 1952, Road to Bali, 1953, Off Limits, 1953, Here Come the Girls, 1953, Casanova's Big Night, 1954, 7 Little Foys, 1955, That Certain Feeling, 1956, Iron Petticoat, 1956, Beau James, 1957, Paris Holiday, 1958, Alias Jesse James, 1959, The Facts of Life, 1960, Bachelor in Paradise, 1961, Road to Hong Kong, 1962, Critic's Choice, 1963, Call Me Bwana, 1963, A Global Affair, 1964, I'll Take Sweden, 1965, Boy, Did I Get the Wrong Number, 1966, Eight on the Lam, 1967, The Private Navy of Sargeant O'Farrell, 1968, How to Commit Marriage, 1969, Cancel My Reservation, 1972; TV variety shows, 1950—; (4 spl. Acad. awards, Emmy award, Peoples Choice award 3 times as best male entertainer 1975-76); Author: They Got Me Covered, 1941, I Never Left Home, 1944, So This is Peace, 1946, Have Tux, Will Travel, 1954, I Owe Russia $1200, 1963, Five Women I Love, 1966, The Last Christmas Show, 1974, Road To Hollywood, 1977. Decorated hon. comdr. Order of Brit. Empire; recipient Congressional Gold medal Pres. Kennedy; Medal of Freedom Pres. Johnson; People to People award Pres. Eisenhower; Peabody award; Jean Hersholdt Humanitarian award; Criss award; Distinguished Service medals from all branches of Armed Forces; Poor Richard award; numerous others; fellow Westminster Choir Coll., N.J.). Entertained Service Forces, overseas and U.S., 1941. Office: 10000 Riverside Dr Suite 3 North Hollywood CA 91602 *

HOPE, CLARENCE CALDWELL, JR., banker, state official; b. Charlotte, N.C., Feb. 5, 1920; s. Clarence Caldwell and Margaret Boyd (Kidd) H.; m. Mae D. Duckworth, Feb. 5, 1944; children: Stephen Douglas, Clarence Caldwell III, Joan Jennings. Diploma, Mars Hill Coll., 1941; B.S., Wake Forest Coll., 1943, Harvard Grad. Sch. Bus. Adminstrn., 1944, Rutgers U. Grad. Sch. Banking, 1953, 56. With Esso Standard Oil Co., 1946-47; with First Union Nat. Bank N.C., Charlotte, 1947—, successively br. mgr., mgr. credit dept., asst. cashier, asst. v.p., v.p., Dilworth, sr. v.p., 1956-60, exec. v.p., 1960-77, vice chmn. bd., 1977—, also dir., sec. bd.; sec. commerce State of N.C., 1983—; exec. v.p., dir. 1st Union Corp. Bd. dirs., past pres. Mecklenburg County chpt. ARC, also mem. Southeastern area adv. council, fund vice chmn. for N.C.; mem. social planning council United Appeal; pres. Central Charlotte Assn.; chmn. N.C. Symphony Soc., Inc.; chmn. bd. trustees Wake Forest U.; trustee Pub. Library Charlotte and Mecklenburg Counties; vice-chmn. N.C. Bapt. Hosp.; trustee Annuity Bd. So. Bapt. Conv.; dean for bankers Southwestern Grad. Sch. Banking, So. Meth. U. Served to lt. USNR, World War II. Mem. Am. Bankers Assn. (mem. governing council, govt. relations council, adminstrv. com.; chmn. com. cooperation with bank regulatory agys., pres. 1979-80), N.C. Bankers Assn. (chmn. legis. com.), Assn. Registered Bank Holding Cos. (chmn. govt. relations com.), U. S. C. of C. (pub. affairs com.), Charlotte Mchts. Assn. (treas., dir., pres., chmn. finance com.), Bankpac (nat. chmn.), Charlotte C. of C., Robert Morris Assos. (past pres. Carolina-Virginias chpt.), Newcomen Soc., Wake Forest U., Central Charlotte Assn. (past pres.), Omicron Delta Kappa, Sigma Phi Epsilon. Baptist. Clubs: Charlotte Execs., Harvard, Myers Park Country, City (Charlotte, N.C.); Army-Navy (Washington). Home: 3807 Pomfret Ln Charlotte NC 28211 Office: 301 S Tryon St Charlotte NC 28288

HOPE, GARLAND HOWARD, lawyer, retired judge; b. Payne, Okla., July 18, 1911; s. Lawrence and Alabama (Anderson) H.; m. Willie Juanita Chandler, Apr. 18, 1942; children: Garland Howard Jr., Marilyn Sue (Mrs. Donald C. Fronterhouse), John David. B.S., U. Okla., 1937, J.D., 1942; postgrad., Nat. Coll. of Judiciary, 1970, 72. Bar: Okla. 1942. Chief clk. James Stewart Corp., Kansas City, Kans., 1942-43; pvt. practice law, Oklahoma City and Pauls Valley, Okla., 1946-53, county judge, Garvin County, Okla., 1953-57, 59-69, pvt. practice law, Maysville, Okla., 1957-58, dist. judge, Garfield County, Okla., 1969-74, rancher, cattle raiser. Active Enid YMCA, Boy Scouts Am. Served with AUS, 1943-45. Mem. Am., Okla. bar assns., County Judges Assn. (pres. 1962-63), County Officers Assn. (pres. 1967), Juvenile Judges Assn., Am. Legion (past vice comdr. Okla. dept.). Democrat. Baptist. Clubs: Masons, Shriners. Home: Route 3 Box 4 Pauls Valley OK 73075 Office: Pauls Valley OK 73075

HOPE, QUENTIN MANNING, educator; b. Stamford, Conn., Jan. 25, 1923; s. Frank Radford and Blanche (Lovett) H.; m. Nathalie Weaver, May 22, 1944; children—Kenneth, Geoffrey, Persis. B.A., Harvard, 1942, M.A., 1946; Ph.D., Columbia, 1956. Tchr. French Los Alamos Ranch Sch., 1942; tchr. Elisabeth Irwin High Sch., 1946-51; Cutting traveling fellow, Paris, 1952-53; instr. Wesleyan U., Middletown, Conn., 1953-56; asst. prof. Ind. U., Bloomington, 1956-61, asso. prof., 1961-66, prof., 1966—, chmn. dept. French and Italian, 1965-77; Postdoctoral Fulbright fellow, Paris, 1962-63; chmn. grad. record exam. com. Ednl. Testing Service, 1972—; pres. Assn. Depts. Fgn. Langs., 1976. Author: Saint-Evremond, the honnête homme as Critic, 1962, Spoken French in Review, 1963, Reading French for Comprehension, 1965; Contbr. articles to profl. jours. Served with Am. Field Service, 1943-45. Mem. Modern Lang. Assn., Am. Assn. Tchrs. French, Phi Beta Kappa. Home: 910 S Highland Ave Bloomington IN 47401

HOPE, SAMUEL HOWARD, association executive; b. Ownesboro, Ky., Nov. 5, 1946; s. James Russell and Lorraine (Jones) H.; m. Judy Bucher, June 24, 1978. B.Mus., Eastman Sch. Music, Rochester, N.Y., 1967; M.Music Arts, Yale U., 1970; pupil of, Nadia Boulanger, France, 1966, 67. Dean, composer-in-residence Atlanta Boy Choir Sch. Music, 1970-73, trustee, 1973—; vis. instr. Lee Coll., Cleveland, Tenn., 1973-74; exec. dir. music alumni, asso. dir. grad. profl. programs Campaign for Yale Yale U., 1974-75; exec. dir. Nat. Assn. Schs. Music, Nat. Assn. Schs. Art and Design, Reston, Va., 1975—, Joint Commn. on Dance and Theatre Accreditation, 1978-83; exec. sec. Nat. Assn. Schs. Theatre, 1980—; exec. dir. Higher Edn. Acts Data Services, 1981—, Nat. Assn. Schs. Dance, 1981—; chmn. assembly of specialized accrediting bodies Council on Postsecondary Accreditation, 1979-82; bd. dirs. Council Specialized Accrediting Agys., 1978-81, sec.-treas., 1979-81; mem. com. recognition Council Postsecondary Accreditation, 1984—. Composer: Piano Sonata I, 1968, II, 1971; motet Solus Ad Victimam Procedis, Domine, 1970, Blessed Be Thou Lord, 1976, Trio for Oboe, Cello and Piano, 1970, Cantata I, 1973, Cantata II, 1975, II, 1975, String Quartet I, 1981, Symphonia: Psalm 145, 1982. Chmn. govt. relations com. Nat. Music Council, 1976-79, bd. dirs., 1978-84; mem. exec. com. Am. Soc. Univ. Composers, 1977-83; nat. alumni council Eastman Sch. Music, 1975-78, chmn., 1976-77; bd. dirs. Am. Music Conf., 1978-82. Recipient Composition prize Yale U., 1968, 69, 70. Mem. Am. Music Center, Coll. Music Soc., Music Educators Nat. Conf., Am. Inst. Graphic Artists, Music Tchrs. Nat. Assn., Am. Theatre Assn., Assn. Classical Music (dir. 1983—). Episcopalian. Club: Yale (N.Y.C. and Washington). Home: 10717 Rosehaven St Fairfax VA 22030 Office: 11250 Roger Bacon Dr Suite 5 Reston VA 22090

HOPE, WILLIAM DUANE, zoologist, curator; b. Fort Collins, Colo., June 7, 1935; s. William Earl and Lois Howe (Burnett) H.; m. Colleen Bryan, Dec. 23, 1956 (div.); children: Pamella Kay, Karen Gail, Linda Michelle. B.S., Colo. State U., 1957, M.S., 1960; Ph.D., U. Calif., Davis, 1965. Systematic zoologist. dept. invertebrate zoology Nat. Mus. Natural History, Smithsonian Instn., Washington, 1964—, curator, 1969—, chmn. dept., 1976-81. Contbr. articles to profl. jours. Program chmn. No. Fairfax Audubon Soc. Mem. Am. Micros. Soc., Biol. Soc. Washington, Soc. Nematologists, Soc. Systematic Zoology, Internat. Assn. Meiobenthologists. Republican. Office: Nat Mus Natural History Smithsonian Instn Washington DC 20560

HOPF, WILLIAM HERBERT, manufacturing company executive; b. Natick, Mass., May 7, 1936; s. William M. and Janet (Herbert) H.; m. Sandra Jean Godbolt; 1 son, James Fredrik. B.S. in Mech. Engring., Worcester Poly. Inst., 1958, M.S., 1969. Registered profl. engr., Mass. Product engr. Gen. Electric, Lynn, Mass., 1958-64; chief engr.

Jamesbury Corp., Worcester, Mass., 1964-74; mgr. research and engring. Irvington Moore Co., Jacksonville, Fla., 1974-76; v.p., gen. mgr. Walworth Co., King of Prussia, Pa., 1976-80, Cooper Industries, Oklahoma City, 1980—. Served to 1st lt. U.S. Army, 1958-62. Named Valve Man of Yr. Valve Mfrs. Assn., 1979. Mem. Oklahoma City C. of C. (chmn. mfg. and service council). Republican. Baptist. *My career path compass has been Philippians 4:80·*

HOPFIELD, JOHN JOSEPH, biophysicist, educator; b. Chgo., July 15, 1933; s. John Joseph and Helen (Staff) H.; m. Cornelia Fuller, June 30, 1954; children—Alison, Jessica, Natalie. A.B., Swarthmore Coll., 1954; Ph.D., Cornell U., 1958. Mem. tech. staff Bell Telephone Labs., 1958-60, 73—; vis. research physicist Ecole Normale Superieure, Paris, France, 1960-61; asst. prof., then asso. prof. physics U. Calif. at Berkeley, 1961-64; prof. physics Princeton U., 1964-80, Eugene Higgins prof. physics, 1978-80; Dickinson prof. chemistry and biology Calif. Inst. Tech., Pasadena, 1980—. Guggenheim fellow, 1969. Fellow Am. Phys. Soc. (Oliver E. Buckley prize 1968); mem. Nat. Acad. Scis., Am. Acad. Arts and Scis., Neuroscis. Research Program, Phi Beta Kappa, Sigma Xi. Home: 1728 San Pasqual St Pasadena CA 91106

HOPKIN, JOHNS WILSON, SR., biology educator; b. Darlington, Md., Apr. 1, 1933; s. Johns Wilson and Margaret (Robinson) H.; m. Margaret Lowry, 1955; 1 son, Johns Wilson. B.S., Haverford Coll., 1955; Ph.D., Rockefeller U., 1960. Asst. prof. Harvard U., Cambridge, Mass., 1960-66; assoc. prof. Washington U., St. Louis, 1966-69, prof. biology, 1969—, chmn. dept., 1966-75; sci. dir. Painter Hopkins Pubs., Sausalito, Calif., 1977-80; pres. bd. dirs. The Learning Center, St. Louis, 1983—; cons. editor Addison-Wesley Pubs., Reading, Mass., 1962-77. Co-author: Twenty-Six Afternoons of Biology, 1962, Understanding Biology, 1983. Mem. Phi Beta Kappa, Sigma Xi. Home: 30 KingsburyPl Saint Louis MO 63112 Office: Biology Dept Washington U Saint Louis MO 63130

HOPKIN, THOMAS ROBERT, technical management executive; b. Putman County, Mo., July 6, 1926; s. George Robert and Oleva Elizabeth (Abel) H.; m. Charlise Wittwer Byers, Aug. 28, 1948; children: Lucy Carol, Lisa Byers, Robin Lea. B.S., U. Mo.-Columbia, 1948, M.A., 1949, Ph.D., 1951. Dir. research-devel. Spencer Chem. Co., Merriam, Kans., 165-68; v.p. Gulf research and devel. Gulf Oil Co., Harmarville, Pa., 1970-72, pres., 1972-75; v.p. research Lubrizol Corp., Wickliffe, Ohio, 1981-83, v.p. reseach-devel., 1983—. Patentee in field, 1979; contbr. articles to profl. jours., 1979. Mem. Am. Chem. Soc., Corp. Assocs. of Am. Chem. Soc., Indsl. Research Inst., Am. Mgmt. Assn. Office: 29400 Lakeland Ave Wickliffe OH 44092

HOPKINS, ALBERT LAFAYETTE, JR., engineer; b. Chgo., May 6, 1931; s. Albert Lafayette and Florence Jameson (Odil) H.; m. Bess House, June 21, 1952 (div. Jan. 1971); children: Albert Lafayette III, Thomas W.H., James A., Sarah B.; m. Ellen Berger, Mar. 18, 1971 (div. Apr. 1980); m. Lynne Zaccaria, Aug. 9, 1980; children—Albert Lafayette III, Thomas W.H., James A., Sarah B. A.B., Harvard, 1953, A.M., 1954, Ph.D., 1957. Instr. control systems engring. Harvard, 1957-60; with instrumentation lab. Mass. Inst. Tech., Cambridge, 1960-70, dep. asso. dir., 1967-69, asso. dir., 1969-70, asso. prof. aeros and astronautics, 1970-76; with C.S. Draper Lab., Cambridge, 1976-81; co-founder, pres. ITP Computer, Inc., Cambridge, 1981—. Mem. IEEE Computer Soc. (1st v.p. 1973, chmn. tech. com. on fault-tolerant computing 1979-81), AAAS, AIAA (Info. Systems award 1977), Tech. Com. Computer Systems, Sigma Xi. Co-designer Apollo guidance computer, 1961-65. Home: 25 Fifer Ln Lexington MA 02173

HOPKINS, ANTHONY, actor; b. Port Talbot, S. Wales, U.K., Dec. 31, 1937; s. Richard Arthur and Muriel Annie (Yeats) H.; m. Petronella, 1968 (div. 1972); 1 dau.; m. Jennifer Lynton, 1973. Student, Royal Acad. Dramatic Art, 1961-63, Cardiff Coll. Drama. Made: London stage debut in Julius Caesar, 1964; mem., Nat. Theatre Co., 1966-73; appearing in: Juno and the Paycock, 1966, A Flea in Her Ear, 1966, The Dance of Death, 1967, Three Sisters, 1967, As You Like It, 1967, The Architect & the Emperor of Assyria, 1971, A Woman Killed with Kindness, 1971, Coriolanus, 1971, Macbeth, 1972, The Taming of the Shrew, 1972; in: Equus, N.Y.C., 1974-75, Los Angeles, 1977, The Tempest, Los Angeles, 1979; films include The Lion in Winter, 1968, The Looking Glass War, 1970, When Eight Bells Toll, 1971, Young Winston, 1972, A Doll's House, 1973, The Girl from Petrovka, 1974, Juggernaut, 1974, A Bridge Too Far, 1977, Audrey Rose, 1977, International Velvet, 1977, Magic, 1978, The Elephant Man, 1979, A Change of Seasons, 1980; featured in: BBC-TV series War and Peace, 1972; TV shows The Lindbergh Kidnapping Case, 1976 (Emmy award), Dark Victory, Voyage of the Mayflower, 1979, The Bunker, 1980, The Acts of Peter and Paul, 1980, Othello, BBC, 1981, Little Eyolf, BBC, 1981 (Recipient Best TV Actor award Soc. Film and TV Arts 1973), BBC (Best Actor award N.Y. Drama Desk 1975), BBC (Outer Critics Circle award 1975), BBC (Am. Authors and Celebrities Forum award 1975), BBC (Los Angeles Drama Critics award 1977). Office: care Creative Artists Agy 1888 Century Park E Suite 1400 Los Angeles CA 90067

HOPKINS, CARL EDWARD, educator; b. Seattle, Aug. 23, 1912; s. Raymond Allen and Ethel Maude (Packard) H.; m. Florence Claire Walters, Oct. 20, 1962. A.B. summa cum laude, Dartmouth, 1933; A.M., Harvard, 1935, Ph.D., 1948; M.P.H., Johns Hopkins, 1957. Chief statistician Kaiser Co., Inc., 1941-45; econ. analyst UNRRA China Mission, 1945-49; asso. prof. pub. health U. Oreg. Med. Sch., 1949-60; prof. pub. health U. Calif., Los Angeles, 1964-80, prof. emeritus, 1980—, chmn., asso. dean, 1971-74; asso. prof. public health U. So. Calif., 1961-64; Spl. cons. Calif. Dept. Health, NIH, So. Permanente (Kaiser) Health Plan. Author: Health Insurance Plans: Promise and Performance, 1975; Contbr. articles to profl. jours. Spl. fellow USPHS, 1956-57. Fellow Am. Pub. Health Assn., Am. Statis. Assn.; mem. Biometric Soc. (pres. Western N.Am. region 1968), Health Info. Soc. (pres. 1969), Phi Beta Kappa, Sigma Xi. Home: 2155 Linda Flora Dr Los Angeles CA 90077

HOPKINS, DONALD ROSWELL, public health service physician; b. Miami, Fla., Sept. 25, 1941; s. Joseph Leonard and Iva (Major) H.; m. Ernestine Mathis, June 24, 1967. B.S., Morehouse Coll., 1962; M.D., U. Chgo., 1966; M.P.H., Harvard U., 1970. Intern San Francisco Gen. Hosp., 1966-67; resident U. Chgo. Hosps., 1970-72; med. officer program planning and evaluation Ctrs. for Disease Control, Atlanta, 1972-74, dep. chief environ. health service div., 1974, asst. dir. ops., 1977-80, asst. dir. internat. health, 1980—; asst. prof. tropical pub. health Harvard U., Boston, 1974-77; chmn., advisor on internat. health research Dr. Peter Bourne, White House, Washington, 1978; mem. U.S. del. World Health Assembly, Geneva, Switzerland, 1977-78, 80-83; mem. global adv. group on immunization WHO, Geneva, 1978-79, mem. steering com. epidemiology working group, 1980—. Author: Princes and Peasants-Smallpox in History, 1983. Recipient Commd. Corps Meritorious Service medal USPHS, 1982, Joseph Mountin Lecture award Ctrs. for Disease Control, 1981, Order of Bifurcated Needle WHO, 1977. Mem. Am. Soc. Tropical Medicine and Hygiene, Internat. Epidemiology Assn., Am. Assn. for History of Medicine, Phi Beta Kappa. Democrat. Episcopalian. Office: Ctrs for Disease Control 1600 Clifton Rd NE Atlanta GA 30303

HOPKINS, ERNEST LOYD, physician; b. Birmingham, Ala., Aug. 14, 1930; s. Clay and Ada (Feidls) H.; m. Lillie B. Blanks, Apr. 24, 1959; children—Ernest C., Loyd Byron, William E. B.S., Morehouse Coll., 1952; M.D., Howard U., 1957; L.H.D., Monrovia Coll., 1962. Diplomate: Am. Bd. Ob-Gyn. Intern Freedmen's Hosp., Washington, 1957-58, resident, 1958-62, Western Res. U., Cleve., 1961-62; asst. prof. obstetrics, gynecology and physiology Howard U. Coll. Medicine, Washington, 1965-69, asso. prof. ob-gyn, 1969-73, prof., 1973—, dir. maternal and fetal medicine, dept. ob-gyn, 1976—, dir. audiovisual aids sect., 1967—; USPHS spl. fellow Western Res. U., Universidad de la Republica, Uruguay, 1963-65; mem. staffs Providence Hosp., Cafritz Meml. Hosp., Washington Hosp. Center, Hadley Meml. Hosp., Columbia Hosp. for Women, Freedmen's Hosp. Patron Met. Police Boys' Clubs, 1965—, Mt. Pleasant Civic Assn. Decorated knight Humane Order of Star of African Redemption, Liberia. Mem. AMA, Nat. Med. Assn., Am. Coll. Obstetricians and Gynecologists, Am. Fertility Soc., Am. Heart Assn., AAAS, Med. Soc. D.C. (mem. exec. com. ob-gyn sect. 1966—). Home: 9351 Mellenbrook Rd Columbia MD 21043 Office: 5501 16th St NW Washington DC 20011 *The simple, direct, and honest approach to problem-solving provides the key to success.*

HOPKINS, EVERETT HAROLD, educator; b. Linville, Ohio, Oct. 25, 1912; s. John F. and Clara May (Dillon) H.; m. Bernice Brubaker, June 15, 1939; children—Jay Everett, David Harold, Richard Alan. B.S., Wittenberg U., 1934, LL.D., 1958; M.A., U. Pa., 1935; student, U. Minn., summers, 1939, 41, 48. Asst. dir. personnel and instr. psychology Wittenberg U., Springfield, Ohio, 1935-37; freshman adviser, instr. psychology Miami U., Oxford, Ohio, 1937-40; asst. prof. psychology, dir. asso. in arts program, 1940-42; asst. to pres. Wash. State U., 1946, dean students, 1947, acad. v.p., 1947-51; asso. dean faculties Washington U., St. Louis, 1951-52, asst. to chancellor, 1952-54, vice chancellor, 1954-61; v.p. instnl. advancement, asst. provost Duke, 1961-63, v.p. planning and instl. studies, 1963-67, prof. higher edn., 1961—; on leave as pres. Nat. Lab. for Higher Edn., 1967-72; Cons. higher edn. U.S. Office Edn. and to individual colls. and univs.; Mem. tech. adv. com. on regional higher edn. to 11 western govs., 1949-51; chmn. Wash. state survey com. on higher edn., 1949-51; mem. exec. com. Nat. Conf. Mblzn. Edn., 1950-51; mem. council advisers to U.S. commr. edn., 1950-52. Contbr. ednl. jours. Trustee Learning Inst. N.C., 1964-76; bd. dirs. Council Ednl. Devel. and Research, 1970-72; mem. accreditation com. N.C. Community Coll., 1978-80; bd. dirs. Internat. Assn. Torch Clubs, 1977—, pres., 1981-82. Served to lt. comdr. USNR, 1942-46; dir. personnel U.S. Naval Tng. Center, 1942-45; Farragut, Idaho; officer in charge West Coast Naval Classification Centers, 1945-46. Recipient Outstanding Achievement award in pub. relations for higher edn. Am. Coll. Pub. Relations Assn., 1958. Mem. Am. Coll. Pub. Relations Assn. (trustee 1961-64, chmn. devel. sect. 1958-59), Nat. Soc. Study Edn., NEA, Am. Psychol. Assn., Am. Coll. Personnel Assn. (pres. 1950-53), Am. Assn. Higher Edn., Am. Acad. Polit. and Social Sci., Am. Edn. Research Assn., Assn. for Study Higher Edn., World Future Soc., Crimson Circle, Kappa Phi Kappa, Phi Delta Kappa, Psi Chi, Alpha Tau Omega, Phi Kappa Phi, Phi Eta Sigma, Kappa Delta Pi, Omicron Delta Kappa. Methodist. Home: 1520 Pinecrest Rd Durham NC 27705

HOPKINS, FRANK ALBERT, manufacturing executive; b. East Providence, R.I., May 7, 1926; s. Frank Albert and Marian Elizabeth (Stevenson) H.; m. Lois E. O'Connor, Jan. 9, 1947; children: Leslee, Frank Albert, Stephen Cameron, Charles Kevin, Hiedee Joan. A.B., Brown U., 1949; postgrad., La. State U. With Uniroyal, Inc., N.Y.C., 1951-70, gen. mgr. chem. div., 1963-65, corp. v.p., 1965-70; exec. v.p. N.Am. Philips Corp., N.Y.C., 1970—. Mem. Nat. Agrl. Assn. (past dir.), Mfg. Chemists Assn. (asso. dir.). Clubs: N.Y. Athletic, Winged Foot Golf. Office: NAm Philips Corp 100 E 42d St New York NY 10017 *

HOPKINS, GEORGE EDGAR, insurance executive; b. Providence, June 3, 1924; s. Edgar Arnold and Ernestine Anna (Reis) H.; m. Mildred Mary Murray, Aug. 27, 1945; children: Stephen, Dale, Leslie, George Edgar. Student, Dartmouth Coll., 1946. With Mass. Mut. Life Ins. Co., Springfield, 1948—, sr. v.p., 1975-81, exec. v.p., 1981—; corporator Community Bank. Bd. dirs. Western Mass. Health Planning Council; past pres. Springfield YMCA; corporator Baystate Med. Center. Served with USAAF, 1942-45. Decorated Air medal with three oak leaf clusters. Home: 296 Ardsley Rd Longmeadow MA 01106 Office: 1295 State St Springfield MA 01111

HOPKINS, GEORGE MATHEWS MARKS, lawyer, business executive; b. Houston, June 9, 1923; s. C. Allen and Agnes Cary (Marks) H.; m. Betty Miller McLean, Aug. 21, 1954; children: Laura McLean, Edith Cary. Student, Ga. Sch. Tech., 1943-44; B.S. in Chem. Engring, Ala. Poly. Inst., 1944; LL.B., J.D., U. Ala., 1949; postgrad., George Washington U., 1949-50. Bar: Ala. 1949, Ga. 1954; Registered profl. engr., Ga.; registered patent lawyer, U.S., Can.; qualified deep-sea diver. Instr. math. U. Ala., 1947-49; assoc. firm A. Yates Dowell, Washington, 1949-50, Edward T. Newton, Atlanta, 1950-62; asst. dir. research, legal counsel Auburn (Ala.) Research Found., 1954-55; partner firm Newton, Hopkins and Ormsby (and predecessor), Atlanta, 1962—; spl. asst. atty. gen., State of Ga., 1978; chmn. bd. Southeastern Carpet Mills, Inc., Chatsworth, Ga., 1962-77, Thomas-Daniel & Assocs., Inc., 1981—, Eastern Carpet Mills, Inc., 1983—; dir. Xepol Inc. Served as lt., navigator, Submarine Service USNR, 1944-46, 50-51. Mem. ABA, Ga. Bar Assn. (chmn. sect. patents 1970-71), Atlanta Bar Assn., Am. Intellectual Property Law Assn., Am. Soc. Profl. Engrs., Submarine Vets. World War II (pres. Ga. chpt. 1977-78), Phi Delta Phi, Sigma Alpha Epsilon. Episcopalian. Clubs: Nat. Lawyers (Washington); Atlanta Lawyers, Univ. Yacht, Phoenix Soc., Cherokee Town and Country, Atlanta City. Home: 795 Old Post Rd NW Atlanta GA 30328 Office: Newton Hopkins & Ormsby 10th floor Equitable Bldg 100 Peachtree St Atlanta GA 30303

HOPKINS, HENRY TYLER, museum adminstr.; b. Idaho Falls, Idaho, Aug. 14, 1928; s. Talcott Thompson and Zoe (Erbe) H.; m. Jo Anne Bybee, Sept. 1, 1954 (div. Oct. 1968); children—Victoria Anne, John Thomas, Christopher Tyler; m. Jan Butterfield, July 1, 1972. B.A., Sch. of Art Inst., Chgo., 1952, M.A., 1955; postgrad., UCLA, 1957-60. Curator exhbns., publs. Los Angeles County Mus. of Art, Los Angeles, 1960-68; dir. Fort Worth Art Mus., 1968-74, San Francisco Mus. of Modern Art, 1974—; lectr. art history, extension U. Calif. at Los Angeles, 1958-68; instr. Tex. Christian U., Fort Worth, 1968-74; dir. U.S. representation Venice (Italy) Bienniel, 1970; dir. art presentation Festival of Two Worlds, Spoleto, Italy, 1970; co-commr. U.S. representation XVI São Paulo (Brazil) Biennale, 1981; cons. Nat. Endowment for Arts, mem. mus. panel, 1979—, chmn., 1981; cons., mem. mus. panel Nat. Endowment for Humanities, 1976. Contbr. numerous articles to profl. jours., also numerous mus. publs. Served with AUS, 1952-54. Decorated knight Order Leopold II, Belgium). Mem. Assn. Art Mus. Dirs., Coll. Art Assn., Am. Assn. Museums, Western Assn. Art Museums (pres. 1977-78). Home: 735 21st Ave San Francisco CA 94121 Office: San Francisco Mus of Art Van Ness Ave at McAllister St San Francisco CA 94102

HOPKINS, JAMES WALLACE, international agency executive; b. Pitts., Aug. 16, 1931; s. James Wallace and Josephine (Fresh) H.; m. Sara Payne Hynson, June 24, 1955; children—James, John, Robert, Lelia, Emily; m. Elisabeth de Lesparda, Oct. 11, 1975. B.A., Yale U., 1953; LL.B., Harvard U., 1959. Asso. firm Davis Polk & Wardwell, N.Y.C., 1959-67, partner, 1967-74; dep. legal adviser Dept. State, 1974-75; dep. exec. dir. Internat. Energy Agy., Paris, 1975—. Trustee Am. Coll. Paris, Am. Sch. Paris, Am. Library, Paris. Served with USN, 1953-56. Mem. Internat. Bar Assn., Bar Assn. City N.Y. Clubs: Metropolitan (Washington); Yale (N.Y.C.). Office: 2 rue Andre-Pascal Cedex Paris 5775 France *

HOPKINS, JEANNETTE ETHEL, book publisher, editor; b. Camden, N.J., Dec. 7, 1922; d. Carleton Roper and Gladys Eugenia (Hull) H. B.A., Vassar Coll., 1944; M.S., Columbia Sch. Journalism, 1945. Asst. to Sunday editor New Haven Register, 1945-46; reporter Providence Evening Bull., 1946-50, Oklahoma City Times, 1950-51; sr. editor Beacon Press, Boston, 1951-56, Harcourt Brace, N.Y.C., 1956-64; sr. editor, v.p. Harper & Row, N.Y.C., 1964-73; sr. editor Met. Applied Research Ctr., N.Y.C., 1973-80, cons. editor, 1973-80; dir. Wesleyan Univ. Press, Middletown, Conn., 1980—; faculty Wesleyan U., Middletown, Conn., 1981—. Author: Books That Will Not Burn, 1952, 14 Journeys to Unitarianism, 1951, (with Kenneth B. Clark) Relevant War Against Poverty, 1968. Mem. council Inst. Religion in an Age of Sci., 1960-64; bd. dirs. ACLU, 1970-80; mem. Commn. on Appraisal, 1976-78; bd. dirs. Am. for Democratic Action, 1963-64. Recipient Alumni award Columbia Sch. Journalism, 1980; Louise Hart Van Leon fellow Vassar Coll., 1944. Mem. Authors Guild, PEN. Democrat. Unitarian. Club: Vassar (Hartford, Conn.). Home: 329 Washington Terr Middletown CT 06457 Office: Wesleyan U Press 110 Mt Vernon St Middletown CT 06457

HOPKINS, KEVIN RANDALL, government official; b. Kansas City, Mo., Dec. 9, 1954; s. Aubrey Marion and Betty Sue (Burton) H.; m. Susan Lynn Sansum, June 24, 1978. B.A., William Jewell Coll., 1976; postgrad., U. Mo., 1976-77, UCLA, 1977-78. Pres. Chrysler & Jason Pub. Co., Kansas City, Mo., 1975-77; instr. econs. U. Mo., Columbia, 1976-77; research analyst Citizens for the Republic, Los Angeles, 1977-79; sr. policy analyst Reagan for Pres. Campaign, 1979-80; spl. asst. to Pres. Reagan White House, 1981—, dir. Office Policy Info., 1982—. Author: Comprehensible Economics, 1976. Republican. Office: Office Policy Info White House Washington DC 20500

HOPKINS, LARRY J., congressman; b. Detroit, Oct. 25, 1933; m. Carolyn Pennebaker; children: Shae, Tara, Joshua. Student, Murray State U., 1951-53. Stockbroker J.J.B. Hilliard and W.L. Lyons, Lexington, Ky., 1978; clk., Fayette (Ky.) County, 1969; mem. Ky. Ho. of Reps., 1972-78, Ky. Senate, 1978, 96th-98th congresses from 6th Ky. Dist. Chmn. Spl. Olympics, 1973. Served with USMC, 1954-56. Named Legislator of the Year, 1974, 76, 78. Mem. Am. Legion. Republican. Methodist. Clubs: Kiwanis, Masons, Pyramid, Shriners. Office: 331 Cannon House Office Bldg Washington DC 20515 *

HOPKINS, SAMUEL, investment banker; b. Highland, Md., Oct. 18, 1913; s. Samuel Harold and Roberta (Smith) H.; m. Winifred Holt Bloodgood, Oct. 15, 1938 (dec. Oct. 1954); children: Samuel, Henry; m. Anne E. Dankmeyer, Oct. 21, 1955; children: Robert, Frederick. B.S., Johns Hopkins U., 1934; LL.B., U. Md., 1938. With Fidelity & Deposit Co. of Md., 1934-69, asst. to treas., 1934-50, asst. treas., 1950-54, sec., 1954-67, v.p., sec., dir., 1967-69; dir., mem. trust com. Equitable Trust Co., Balt., 1967-81; sec., dir. Md. Life Ins. Co., 1963-69; gen. partner Alex. Brown & Sons (investment bankers), Balt., 1970-75, ltd. partner, 1976—. Mem. adv. com. housing for elderly U.S. Housing and Finance Agy., 1956-60; mem. Balt. Bd. Recreation and Parks, 1965-77, pres., 1965-67, 74-77, v.p., 1968-74; Republican candidate for Congress, 1952; mem. Md. Ho. of Dels., 1950-54; Rep. candidate for mayor, Balt., 1955; del. Rep. Nat. Conv., 1976; trustee Balt. Mus. Art, Peale Mus.; vice-chmn. bd. trustees Sheppard and Enoch Pratt Hosp.; trustee, v.p. State Colls. Md., 1963-70. Served from ensign to lt. USNR, 1942-45. Mem. ABA, Balt. Security Analysts Soc., Md. Hist. Soc. (treas. 1956-69, pres. 1970-75, trustee), Inst. Chartered Security Analysts. Episcopalian. Home: 45 Warrenton Rd Baltimore MD 21210 Office: Alex Brown & Sons 135 E Baltimore St Baltimore MD 21202

HOPKINS, SHIRLEY KNIGHT, actress; b. Goessel, Kans., July 5, 1936; d. Noel Johnson and Virginia Enola (Webster) Knight; m. John Hopkins; children: Kate, Sophie. Ed., Phillips U., Enid, Okla., Wichita (Kans.) U.; D.F.A. (hon.), Lake Forest Coll.; student, Lee Strasberg. Profl. actress: films The Dark at the Top of the Stairs, 1959, Sweet Bird of Youth, 1962, The Group, 1964, Petulia, 1967, The Film Dutchman, 1966, The Rain People, 1969, Endless Love, 1981; actress: Broadway plays including The Three Sisters, 1965, Kennedy's Children, 1975 (Tony award 1975), Losing Time (John Hopkins), 1979, Happy End (Weill-Brecht), 1977, Sophocles' Antigone, Eng., 1971, Economic Necessity, by John Hopkins, 1972, A Landscape of the Body (John Guare), 1977 (Joseph Jefferson award 1977), Creve Coeur (Tennesse Williams), 1978; TV spls. The Lie, by Ingmar Bergman, 1973, The Country Girl, by Clifford Odets, 1974, Friendly Persuasion, by Jessamyn West, 1974, Walk Into the Dark and That Quiet Earth, by John Hopkins, Some Distant Shadow, by John Hopkins, 1973; leider recital debut, Spoleto Festival, 1978 (Named best actress Venice Film Festival 1969), Spoleto Festival (nominated for Acad. award as best actress 1961, 62), Spoleto Festival (named Best Actress for A Streetcar Named Desire, N.J. Drama Critics 1977), Spoleto Festival (recipient Drama Critics award 1977).

HOPKINS, THOMAS ARSCOTT, lawyer; b. Clevel., June 29, 1931; s. Albert T. and Georgine Arscott (Robinson) H.; m. Ann Elizabeth White, Sept. 23, 1962; children: Ingrid O., Matthew W., Hannah R., Helen A. B.A., Yale U., 1953; LL.B., Harvard U., 1960. Bar: Ohio 1960, N.Y. 1961. Assoc. White & Case, N.Y.C., 1960-71, ptnr., 1972—, resident ptnr., Brussels, 1976-79. Mem. ABA, N.Y. State Bar Assn., Assn. Bar City N.Y. Office: White & Case 14 Wall St New York NY 10005

HOPKINS, THOMAS GENE, retail company executive; b. Lebanon, Ind., Sept. 29, 1932; s. Lloyd T. and Eunice A. (Budd) H.; m. Jeanett A. Bengert, June 12, 1955; children: T. Eric, Mark J. B.S., Ind. U., 1954, D. Bus. Adminstrn., 1966; M.B.A., U. Louisville, 1962. Various fin. positions Gen. Electric Co., Louisville, 1954-62; asst. prof. mgmt. U. Tex., Austin, 1965-67; dir. edn. and orgn. devel. Corning Glass Work, N.Y., 1967-78; v.p., dir. personnel Limited Stores, Inc., Columbus, Ohio, 1978-82, exec. v.p. orgn. devel., 1982—. Served to 2d lt. U.S. Army, 1955. Mem. Acad. Mgmt., Beta Gamma Sigma. Home: 5747 Strathmore Ln Dublin OH 43017 Office: Limited Inc 1 Limited Pkwy Columbus OH 43213

HOPKINS, THOMAS MATTHEWS, former naval officer; b. Balt., Feb. 3, 1927; s. John Howard and Grace Marie (Martin) H.; m. Marjorie Kendall Leonard, Apr. 8, 1950; children: Margaret, Karen, Annette. B.S. in Mech. Engring, Cornell U., 1948; naval engr. degree, M.I.T., 1955. Commd. ensign U.S. Navy, 1948, advanced through grades to rear adm., 1977; project officer, submarines Bur. Ships and subsequently Naval Ship Systems Command, 1964-68; force maintenance officer U.S. Submarine Force, U.S. Atlantic Fleet, 1968-71; project mgr. Naval Sea Systems Command, Attack Submarine (SSN) Acquisition Project, 1972-76; fleet maintenance officer U.S. Atlantic Fleet, 1977-80; dep. comdr. for ship systems Naval Sea Systems Command, Washington, 1980-82, ret., 1982; exec. cons. Harbridge House, Inc., Washington, 1982—, U.S. Maritime Adminstrn., 1982—. Decorated Meritorious Service medal (2), Legion of Merit. Mem. Am. Soc. Naval Engrs., Soc. Naval Architects and

Marine Engrs., ASTM (F-25 com. on shipbuilding), Sigma Xi. Episcopalian. Home: 1113 Carper St McLean VA 22101 Office: Harbridge House 1300 Pennsylvania Ave Suite 1200 Washington DC 20004

HOPLEY, DAVID PHILIP, agricultural machinery company executive; b. Ill., Nov. 7, 1932; s. Philip and Verda (Jones) H.; m. Eleanor Julia Knolt, Dec. 22, 1956; children: Cheryl, Sara, Julie, Susan. B.A., Augustana Coll., 1954. C.P.A., Ill. Auditor Arthur Andersen & Co., Chgo., 1954-59; v.p. John Deere & Co., Moline, Ill., 1959—; dir. Am. Trust Co., Dubuque, Iowa, 1978—. Bd. dirs. Augustana Coll., Rock Island, Ill., 1981—. Served with U.S. Army, 1954-56. Republican. Lutheran. Home: 5190 Center Ct Bettendorf IA 52722 Office: Deere & Co John Deere Rd Moline IL 61201

HOPP, RALPH H., librarian, educator; b. Cook, Nebr., Oct. 24, 1915; s. Charles and Caroline (Mannschreck) H.; m. Dorothy Gade, June 8, 1941; children: Caroline (dec.), Thomas, Susan. Student, Peru (Nebr.) State Tchrs. Coll., 1934-35, 37-38; B.S. in Chem. Engring, U. Nebr., 1943; M.S., U. Ill., 1950, Ph.D., 1956. Tchr., Douglas, Nebr., 1935-37; reserve and engring. librarian U. Nebr., Lincoln, 1940-43, agr. and sci.-tech. librarian, 1951-53; process chemist Martin-Nebr. Co., Omaha, 1943; research fellow Mellon Inst. Indsl. Research, Pitts., 1943-44; research editor Bituminous Coal Research, Inc., Pitts., 1944-45; research librarian Battelle Meml. Inst., Columbus, 1946-49; prof., univ. librarian U. Minn., Mpls., 1953-70, dir. libraries, 1971-76, prof. library devel., 1976-78, dir. Inst. Tech. Libraries, 1978-82, prof. emeritus, 1982—; pres. Universal Serials and Books Exchange, 1980; vis. prof. U. Denver, summer 1958; cons. library bldgs., orgn. and adminstrn. Author: Enjoying the Active Life After Fifty, 1979; columnist: Adventure Travel, 1979—. Fulbright lectr. U. Ankara, 1962-63. Mem. Assn. Research Libraries (pres. 1974-75), Am., Minn., Turkish library assns., AAUP, Beta Phi Mu. Home: 1341 Keston St Saint Paul MN 55108

HOPP, WILLIAM BEECHER, educator; b. Terre Haute, Ind., Sept. 4, 1917; s. William Henry and Kathryn Elsie (Beecher) H.; m. Eva Helen Cook, June 3, 1949; 1 son, William Beecher. B.S., Ind. State Tchrs. Coll., 1939; M.S., Purdue U., 1941, Ph.D., 1953. Instr. biology Purdue U., 1946-47; asst. prof. zoology Eastern Ky. State Coll., Richmond, 1947-55; faculty Ind. State U., 1955- -, prof. zoology, 1961—, chmn. sci. div., 1961-68; weekly radio program, 1957—, TV program, 1959—. Contbr. articles to profl. jours. Bd. dirs. Terre Haute Humane Soc., 1964-67. Mem. Wabash Valley Audubon Soc. (pres. 1962-63), Am. Soc. Parasitologists, Am. Soc. Ichthyologists and Herpetologists, Ind. Acad. Sci. (pres. 1973), AAAS, Am. Inst. Biol. Scis., AAUP, Sigma Xi, Kappa Delta Pi. Home: 335 S Brown Ave Terre Haute IN 47803

HOPPE, ARTHUR WATTERSON, journalist; b. Honolulu, Apr. 23, 1925; s. Arthur S. and Margaret (Watterson) H.; m. Gloria Nichols, Apr. 27, 1946; children—Leslie, Andrea, Arthur N., Prentiss. B.A. cum laude, Harvard, 1949. Mem. staff San Francisco Chronicle, 1949—, reporter, 1950-60, columnist, 1960—. Author: Love Everybody Crusade, 1960, Dreamboat, 1962, The Perfect Solution to Absolutely Everything, 1968, Mr. Nixon and My Other Problems, 1971, Miss Lollipop and the Doom Machine, 1973, The Tiddling Tennis Theorem, 1977. Served with USNR, 1942-46.

HOPPE, PETER CHRISTIAN, biologist, geneticist; b. Long Beach, Calif., Feb. 16, 1942; s. John Calvin and Venetia Bodell (Mortensen) H.; m. Linda Lee Peters, June 14, 1963; children—Tina Christine, Kirk Christian, Todd Christopher. B.S., Calif. State Poly. U., 1964; M.S., Kans. State U., 1966, Ph.D., 1968. Asso. staff scientist The Jackson Lab., Bar Harbor, Maine, 1970-73, staff scientist, 1973-81, sr. staff scientist, 1981—; vis. prof. U. Geneva, 1979-80. Asso. editor: Gamete Research, 1981—; contbr. articles in field to profl. jours. Named Disting. Alumnus Calif. State Poly. U., 1981; Am. Cancer Soc. Eleanor Roosevelt fellow, 1979-80. Mem. Soc. Study Reproduction, Am. Assn. Tissue Banks. Office: The Jackson Lab Bar Harbor ME 04609

HOPPER, DAVID HENRY, theologian; b. Cranford, N.J., July 31, 1927; s. Orion Cornelius and Julia Margaret (Weitzel) H.; m. Nancy Ann Nelson, June 10, 1967; children: Sara Elizabeth, Kathryn Ann, Rachel Suzanne. B.A., Yale Coll., 1950; B.D., Princeton Theol. Sem., 1953, Th.D., 1959; postgrad., Friedrich-Wilhelms Univeristat, Bonn, W. Ger., 1953-54. Asst. prof. religion Macalester Coll., St. Paul, 1959-67, chmn., 1969-78, 82—, asso. prof., 1967-73, James Wallace prof. religion, 1973—; vis. prof. Lane Coll., Jackson, Tenn., 1966. Author: Tillich: A Theological Portrait, 1968, A Dissent on Bonhoeffer, 1975. Served with U.S. Navy, 1945-46. Recipient Thomas Jefferson award Macalester Coll., 1978, award in religion N.J. Author's, 1968. Mem. Am. Acad. Religion, Internat. Bonhoeffer Soc., AAUP. Presbyterian. Home: 1757 Lincoln Ave Saint Paul MN 55105 Office: Dept Religious Studies Macalester Coll Saint Paul MN 55105 *Over the course of my life, I have found that perseverence in the good, the persistent affirmation of equality and justice, may not yield all the happiness we desire, but without the self-regard they also build, the quest for happiness becomes increasingly empty.*

HOPPER, DENNIS, actor, writer, photographer, film director; b. Dodge City, Kans., May 17, 1936. Ed., San Diego pub. schs. Numerous TV appearances include Loretta Young Show, 1954; appeared in: films Rebel Without a Cause, 1955, I Died A Thousand Times, 1955, Giant, 1956, Story of Mankind, Gunfight at the O.K. Corral, 1957, Night Tide, Key Witness, From Hell to Texas, 1958, Glory Stompers, 1959, The Trip, 1961, The Sons of Katie Elder, 1962, Hang 'Em High, 1966, Cool Hand Luke, 1967, True Grit, 1968, The American Dreamer, 1971, Kid Blue, 1973, The Sky is Falling, 1975, James Dean—The First American Teenager, Mad Dog Morgan, Tracks, 1976, American Friend, 1978, Apocalypse Now, 1979, King of the Mountain, Human Highway, 1981; numerous others; actor, writer, dir.: films Easy Rider, 1969, The Last Movie, 1971; actor, dir.: Out of the Blue, 1980; exhibited photographs at, Fort Worth Art Mus., Denver Art Mus., Wichita Art Mus., Cochran Art Mus., Spileto Mus. Recipient award as best new dir. Cannes Film Festival, 1969; Best Film award Venice Film Festival, 1971, Cannes Film Festival, 1980. Address: Box 1889 Taos NM 87571

HOPPER, WALTER EVERETT, lawyer; b. Houghton, Mich., Oct. 29, 1915; s. Walter E. and Maude (Crum) H.; m. Jeannette Ross, Aug. 23, 1941 (dec. 1947); 1 dau., Nancy Cameron Hopper Marcouci; m. Diana Kerensky, Sept. 24, 1958; 1 stepdau., Nicole Sudrow Hopper Neilan. A.B., Cornell U., 1937, J.D., 1939. Bar: N.Y. 1939, D.C. 1959, U.S. Supreme Ct. 1959. Practice in, Ithaca, 1939-42, N.Y.C., 1946—; chmn., chief exec. officer Fort Amsterdam Corp., 1973-81; dir. Davis Brake Beam Co., O'Brien Securities Mgmt., Inc., J.H. Securities Corp. Chmn. trustees Loyal Legion Found.; trustee Inst. on Man and Science, 1969-71, Signal Hill Ednl. Center; bd. dirs. U.S. Flag Found. Served from 1st lt. to lt. col. inf. AUS, World War II; ETO; col. U.S. Army Res.; ret. Decorated Army Commendation medal with oak leaf cluster; N.Y. State Conspicious Service Cross with Maltese Cross; Order Ruben Dario, Nicaragua; comdr. Order Orange-Nassau, Netherlands; Order St. John of Jerusalem. Mem. Internat. Assn. Protection Indsl. Property (exec. com. Am. group 1958-71), Internat. Fiscal Assn., Nat. Fgn. Trade Council (mem. coms.), Internat. C. of C. (U.S. council 1949-71, mem. coms.), Am. Arbitration Assn. (panelist), U.S. Trademark Assn. (past v.p., dir., chmn. internat. com.), UN Assn. (dir. N.Y. chpt. 1964-66), Holland Soc. (pres. 1966-71), Loyal Legion (comdr.-in-chief 1964-67), Assn. Bar City N.Y., Res. Officers Assn. (pres. N.Y. State 1949), Confrerie des Chevaliers du Tastevin, Pilgrims, Soc. War 1812, Founders and Patriots of Am., Mayflower Descs., Soc. Colonial Wars, St. Nicholas Soc. (pres. 1982—), S.R., Huguenot Soc. Am. (pres. 1972-75), Mil. Order Fgn. Wars, Soc. of Cincinnati. Clubs: Explorers, University, Leash (N.Y.C.); Metropolitan, Army-Navy (Washington). Home: 715 Park Ave New York NY 10021 *The key to success in human endeavor is determination.*

HOPPER, WILBERT HILL, oil company executive; b. Ottawa, Ont., Can., Mar. 14, 1933; s. Wilbert Clayton and Eva (Hill) H.; m. Patricia Marguerite Walker, Aug. 12, 1957; children: Sean Wilbert, Christopher Mark. B.Sc. in Geology, Am. U.; M.B.A., U. Western Ont. Petroleum geologist Imperial Oil Co. Ltd., 1955-57; petroleum economist Foster Assos. Ltd., 1959-61; sr. energy economist Nat. Energy Bd., Ottawa, 1961-64; sr. petroleum cons. Arthur D. Little & Co., Cambridge, Mass., 1964-73; sr. adv. energy policy, then asst. dep. minister energy policy Dept. Energy, Mines and Resources, Ottawa, 1973-76; pres. Petro-Can. Ltd., Calgary, Alta., 1976-78, chief exec. officer, 1976—, chmn., 1979—; dir. Panarctic Oils Ltd., Syncrude Can. Ltd., Polar Gas Project Ltd., Westcoast Transmission Co. Ltd.; bd. dirs. Can.-China Trade Council; chmn. com. internat. oil markets Internat. Energy Agy., Paris. Mem. Can. Econ. Assn., Can. Soc. Petroleum Geologists, Can. Inst. Mining and Metallurgy, Am. Econ. Assn., Am. Soc. Petroleum Geologists, Soc. Petroleum Engrs. Clubs: Rideau, Ranchmen's, Calgary Petroleum, Le Cercle Univ. d'Ottawa. 2083 Chalmers Rd Ottawa ON Canada Office: 407 2d St SW Calgary AB T2P 3E3 Canada

HOPPIN, CHARLES SWORDS, lawyer; b. N.Y.C., Sept. 4, 1931; s. Frederic Gallatin and May (Swords) H.; m. Mariana Field, Dec. 29, 1962 (div. Oct. 17, 1980); children: David Field, Ashley Gallatin; m. Nancy Dewey, Nov. 29, 1980; 1 dau., Margaret Barringer. A.B., Harvard U., 1953; LL.B., Columbia U., 1959. Bar: Calif. 1960, N.Y. 1964. Law clk. Supreme Ct. Calif., San Francisco, 1959-60; assoc. Colley, Crowley, Gaither, Godward, Castro & Huddleston, San Francisco, 1960-63, Davis Polk & Wardwell, N.Y.C., 1963-68, ptnr., 1968—; dir. Nashua Corp. Editor, author: articles Columbia Law Rev. Trustee Robert Coll., Istanbul. Named to Sailing Hall of Fame Intercollegiate Yacht Racing Assn., 1956; Nat. Intercollegiate champion Intercollegiate Yacht Racing Assn., 1952-53. Mem. ABA, Assn. Bar City of N.Y., N.Y. State Bar Assn. Home: 262 Central Park W New York NY 10024 Office: David Polk & Wardwell 1 Chase Manhattan Plaza New York NY 10005

HOPPING, LOUIS MELBERT, lawyer; b. Havana, Ill., May 31, 1900; s. Oliver Perry and Nannie Elizabeth (Yates) H.; m. Helen Irene Boutwell, Nov. 27, 1924; children—Eleanor Jean Hopping MacDonald (dec.), Helen Irene Hopping Johnson (dec.), George Boutwell, William Yates. Pre-med. and pre-law student, U. Ill., 1919-23; A.B., George Washington U., 1925, LL.B., 1927. Bar: Mich. bar 1932, also U.S. Supreme Ct 1932. With various companies, Ill., also, Washington, to 1924; sec. to mng. editor Washington Herald, 1924-26; sec. Congressman Clarence McLeod, 1926-31; asst. U.S. atty., 1931-45; with firm Fitsgerald, Walker, Conley & Hopping, Detroit, 1945—; magistrate 35th Mich. Dist. Ct., 1976—; Pres. Identity Registry, Inc. Author: History of Hopping Family in England and Genealogy of John Hopping in America. Mem. Northville Library Commn.; dir. Detroit Amateur Baseball Fedn.; pres. Mackenzie Meml. Assn.; founder, pres. Fed. Grand Jurors Assn.; mem. nat. awards jury Freedoms Found., Valley Forge, 1963. Served with USNRF, 1918-22. Named Distinguished Alumnus George Washington U., 1965, Japanese-Am. Soc. award. Mem. Inter-Am. Bar Assn. (del. cons. 1949—), ABA, Fed. Bar Assn. (chmn. ad hoc com. to make naturalization process more meaningful), Detroit Bar Assn., Detroit Bd. Commerce, State Bar Mich., George Washington Law Assn., Am. Soc. Internat. Law, Am. Judicature Soc., Mich. Hort. Soc. (trustee), Nat., Mich., Plymouth hist. socs., Plymouth Symphony Soc., Bradford Compact, Smithsonian Assos., Gen. Soc. Mayflower Descs. Republican. Christian Scientist. Clubs: Civitan (pres. Detroit 1946-47, lt. gov. Great Lakes dist. 1949-50), Civitan (gov. 1950-51), Civitan (internat. sgt.-at-arms 1950-51), Civitan (internat. judge adv. 1951-52), Civitan (trustee internat. found., internat. pres. 1963-64), Civitan (exec. bd. 1964-65). Home: 18165 Jamestown Circle Northville MI 48167 Office: Penobscot Bldg Detroit MI 48226

HOPPING, RICHARD LEE, college president; b. Dayton, Ohio, July 26, 1928; s. Lavon Lee and Dorothy Marie (Anderson) H.; m. Patricia Louise Vance, June 30, 1951; children: Ronald, Debra, Jerrold. Student, Chaffey Coll., 1947-48, U. Dayton, 1948-49, Sinclair Coll., 1948-49; B.S., So. Coll. Optometry, 1952, O.D., 1952, D.O.S. (hon.), 1972. Practice optometry, Dayton, Ohio, 1953-73; pres. So. Calif. Coll. Optometry, 1973—; cons. in field; chmn. adv. research council Am. Optometric Found., 1976-83. Contbr. numerous articles on vision and health care to profl. publs. Vice pres. Orange County (Calif.) council Boy Scouts Am., 1977-79; mem. Council Assocs. of Red Cross, North Orange County Service Center, 1978—. Named Optimist of Yr. Dayton View Optimists, 1956, Outstanding Young Man of Yr. Dayton C. of C., 1960. Fellow Am. Acad. Optometry (chmn. sect. on primary care optometry 1973-79, chmn. awards com. 1981—), Am. Pub. Health Assn.; mem. Am. Optometric Assn. (pres. 1971-72, chmn. task force on practical enhancement 1982—), Calif. Optometric Assn. (hon. life 1974—, jud. council), Assn. Ind. Calif. Colls. and Univs. (trustee 1973—), Optometric Extension Programs Found. (hon. life), Assn. Schs. and Colls. of Optometry (pres. 1983—), Ohio Optometric Assn. (pres. 1964-65, Optometrist of Yr. 1962, hon. life), Nat. Acads. Practice in Optometry (vice chmn., mem. at large 1973—). Office: 2001 Associated Rd Fullerton CA 92631

HOPPLE, RICHARD VAN TROMP, JR., advertising executive; b. Cin., Mar. 20, 1947; s. Richard Van Tromp and Marie (Mitchell) H.; m. Patricia Spalt, July 16, 1972; children: Peter Van Tromp, Richard Halstead. B.S., Northwestern U., 1969. Acct. exec. Dancer-Fitzgerald-Sample, N.Y.C., 1969-72; sr. v.p. Benton & Bowles, Inc., N.Y.C., 1972—. Bd. dirs. Wilton United Way, Conn., ct79. Club: Racquet and Tennis (N.Y.C.). Office: Benton & Bowles Inc 909 3d Ave New York NY 10022

HOPPONEN, RAYMOND ELLWOOD, pharmacist, univ. dean; b. New York Mills, Minn., July 6, 1921; s. Victor William and Hilma Lydia (Ruonakoski) H.; m. Mary Helen Robinson, Sept. 4, 1955; children—Lisa, Andrew, Susan. B.S., U. Minn., 1943, Ph.D., 1950; postgrad., U. Wis., 1962-63. Asst. prof., asso. prof., prof. U. Kans., 1950-64, asst. dean, 1964-66; dean pharmacy S.D. State U., Brookings, 1966—. Contbr. to: Handbook of Non-Prescription Drugs, 1st-7th edits, 1967—. Mem. Brookings Area Betterment Com., 1975-77, 79—; bd. dirs. Dakota affiliate Am. Heart Assn. Served with M.C. AUS, 1943-46. Recipient hon. mention Ebert prize in pharm. research, 1953; NIH Career Devel. fellow, 1962. Mem. Am. Pharm. Assn., Acad. Pharm. Scis., Am. Assn. Colls Pharmacy (exec. com., sec. council of deans), S.D. Pharm. Assn., Rho Chi (nat. pres. 1972-74). Democrat. Methodist. Club: Kiwanis. Home: 132 Teton Ln Brookings SD 57006 Office: SD State U Brookings SD 57007

HOPPS, HOPE ELIZABETH BYRNE, microbiologist; b. Warwick, R.I., June 15, 1926; d. William Stephen and Genevieve (Carbary) Byrne; m. George L. Hopps, Jan. 1, 1952. B.S., U. R.I., 1947; M.S., U. Md., 1950. Microbiologist, Walter Reed Army Inst. Research, Washington, 1951-56; research microbiologist Nat. Inst. Allergy and Infectious Diseases, NIH, Bethesda, Md., 1956-60; chief immunology sect. div. biologics standards Lab. of Viral Immunology, NIH, 1960-71; asst. to dir. bur. biologics FDA, Bethesda, 1972-81; asst. dir. program devel. and ops. Nat. Ctr. Drugs and Biologics, FDA, Rockville, Md., 1982—. Contbr. articles to profl. jours. Bd. dirs. W. Alton Jones Cell Sci. Center. Fellow Washington Acad. Sci.; mem. Am. Assn. Immunologists, Am. Soc. Microbiologists, Tissue Culture Assn. (exec. bd. 1974, v.p. 1976—), AAAS (mem. biol. scis. com. 1972—), N.Y. Acad. Sci., Grad. Women in Sci. (nat. pres. 1973). Home: 1762 Overlook Dr Silver Spring MD 20903 Office: Nat Ctr. Drugs and Biologics FDA 5600 Fishers Ln Rockville MD 20852

HOPPS, HOWARD CARL, pathologist, educator; b. Schenectady, Aug. 14, 1914; s. Carl Walter and Alice Clara (Janzer) H.; m. Ellen Clare Connellee, June 3, 1937; children—Christopher R., David C., Susan L.; m. Hilda M. Pinkelman, Apr. 20, 1968. B.S., U. Okla., 1935, M.D. with honors, 1937; Ph.D., U. Chgo., 1970. Diplomate: pathologic anatomy and forensic pathology Am. Bd. Pathology; certified Am. Bd. Legal Medicine. Intern Evanston Hosp., 1937-39; asst. pathology U. Chgo., 1940, instr., 1941-43, asst. prof., 1943-44; prof., chmn. dept. U. Okla., 1944-56, U. Tex. Med. Br., Galveston, 1957-63; chief div. geog. pathology Armed Forces Inst. Pathology, Washington, 1964-70; Curators' prof. pathology U. Mo., Columbia, 1970—; Cons. NIH, 1954-64, NSF, 1960-61, Am. Cancer Soc., 1958-72, Nat. Acad. Scis., 1970-75; clin. prof. pathology U. Md., 1964-70; mem. pathology test com. Nat. Bd. Med. Examiners, 1956-59; Fulbright vis. prof. Otago U., Dunedin, New Zealand, 1955-56; vis. prof. Northwestern U. Sch. Medicine, 1963, Temple U. Sch. Medicine, 1967-70; cons. geog. pathology NASA, 1969-71; cons. water resouces div. U.S. Geol. Survey, 1979—; mem. subcom. geochem. environment related to health and disease Nat. Acad. Sci., co-chmn., 1971-75; registrar Am. Registry Geog. Pathology, 1964-70; cons. Internat. Atomic Energy Agy., 1977. Author: Principles of Pathology, 1959, 2d edit., 1964, Computerized Mapping of Disease and Environmental Data, 1968; Editor: Internat. Pathology, 1965-70; Contbr. articles med. jours., sci. publs., also chpts. in books. Recipient Howard Taylor Ricketts prize for research, 1942; Distinguished Service award Med. Alumni Assn. U. Chgo., 1970; certificate Distinguished Service AFIP, 1971; Meritorious Civilian Service decoration Dept. U.S. Army, 1971. Mem. Am. Soc. Clin. Pathology, Am. Assn. Pathologists, Am. Assn. Cancer Research, Am. Soc. Exptl. Pathology, Am. Assn. Immunology, Internat. Acad. Pathology, Soc. Exptl. Biology and Medicine (chmn. southwestern sect. 1955-56), Internat. Soc. Biometeorology, Am. Soc. Tropical Medicine and Hygiene, Am. Meteorol. Soc., Soc. for Environ. Geochemistry and Health (sec.-treas. 1971-78, pres. 1979-80), N.Y. Acad. Scis., Mo. Acad. Sci. (v.p. 1975-76, pres. 1976-77), Sigma Xi, Phi Kappa Phi, Alpha Omega Alpha, Phi Zeta, Alpha Kappa Alpha. Home: 606 Longfellow Ln Columbia MO 65201

HOPPS, SIDNEY BRYCE, lawyer; b. Yale, Mich., May 10, 1934; s. Sidney J. and Betty E. (Bryce) H.; m. Ilene P. Morgan, June 20, 1953; children: Paulette, Tracy, Erin. B.A., U. Mich., 1957, J.D., 1960. Bar: Ohio 1960. Ptnr. Squire, Sanders & Dempsey, Cleve., 1960—. Mem. Ohio Bar Assn., Greater Cleve. Bar Assn., Phi Beta Kappa, Phi Kappa Phi. Home: 5580 Sleepy Hollow Rd Valley City OH 44280 Office: Squire Sanders & Dempsey 1800 Huntington Bldg Cleveland OH 44115

HOPSON, DAN, law educator, educational administrator; b. Phillipsburg, Kans., Sept. 23, 1930; s. Daniel Ashton and Ruth (Whitaker) H.; m. Phyllis Ann Gray, Nov. 23, 1956; children: Daniel Gray, Christopher Paul, Bruce Edward. Student, La. State U., 1947-48; A.B., U. Kans., 1951, LL.B., 1953; LL.M., Yale U., 1954; postgrad., Cambridge U., 1954-55. Bar: Kans. 1953. Asst. prof. law U. Kans., Lawrence, 1955-59, assoc. prof., 1959-63, prof., 1963-67; research assoc. Yale U., New Haven, 1959-60; prof.law Ind. U., Bloomington, 1967-80, assoc. dean faculties, 1974-789; dean prof. law So. Ill. U., Carbondale, 1980—; arbitrator Am. Arbitration Assn. and Fed. Mediation and Conciliation Service, 1963—. Author: (with Quintin Johnstone) Lawyers and Their Work, 1967; contbr. articles to law jours. Mem. ABA, Ill. Bar Assn., Jackson County Bar Assn., Council Juvenile Ct. Judges (assoc.), Order of the Coif, Phi Beta Kappa, Pi Sigma Alpha, Phi Alpha Delta, Phi Delta Theta. Episcopalian. Home: Rural Route Brush Hill Carbondale IL 62901 Office: Sch of Law So Ill U Carbondale IL 62901

HORADAM, WEYMAN WILSON, former banker; b. Yoakum, Tex., May 25, 1916; s. Frank A. and Verna (Willemin) H.; m. Lucile Simonton, July 12, 1952; children: Diana Louise, William Warren. B.B.A., U. Tex., 1941. With RFC, Houston, 1946-52; with Bank of Southwest, N.A., Houston, 1952-81, sr. v.p., cashier, 1979-81. Served to capt. USAAF, 1942-46. Mem. Robert Morris Assos., Beta Gamma Sigma, Beta Alpha Psi. Home: 20534 Manette St Katy TX 77450

HORAN, HAROLD EUGENE, diplomat; b. Houston, June 16, 1927; s. Eugene F. and Bessie (Bain) H.; m. Bonnie McLeroy, Aug. 25, 1950; children: Elizabeth, Tessa, James. Student, Rice U., 1944-45, U. Paris, 1950-51; B.B.A., U. Houston, 1950, J.D., 1953. Bar: Tex. 1953. Asst. county atty., Harris County, Tex., 1953-54; atty. FTC, Washington, 1954-57; fgn. service officer U.S. Dept. State, from 1957, U.S. ambassador to, Lilongwe, Malawi, Africa, 1978-80, dep. asst. sec. state, 1980—; sr. advisor for, Africa, Nat. Security Council, 1973-76. Served with USAAF, 1945-46. Recipient Bates Legal Scholar award, 1953; Meritorious Service award FTC, 1955, Dept. State, 1968. Mem. Am. Fgn. Service Assn., Fed. Bar Assn., Tex. Bar Assn. Methodist. Home: 230 South Carolina Ave SE Washington DC 20003

HORAN, HUME ALEXANDER, ambassador; b. Washington, Aug. 13, 1934; s. Harold and Margaret Robinson (Hume) H.; m. Nancy Jane Reinert, Apr. 2, 1960; children: Alexander Hume, Margaret Robinson, Jonathan Theodore. A.B. cum laude, Harvard U., 1958, A.M., 1963. Fgn. service officer Dept. State, 1960—; 3d sec. Am. embassy, Baghdad, Iraq, 1960-62, attache, Beirut, Lebanon, 1963-64, polit. officer, 2d sec., Baida, Libya, 1964-66; personnel officer Dept. State, 1966-67, desk officer, Libya, 1967-69; 1st sec., chief polit. sec. Am. Embassy, Amman, Jordan, 1970-72, minister, counselor, Jidda, Saudi Arabia, 1972-77; mem. sr. seminar Dept. State, Washington, 1977-78; dep. asst. sec. State Bur. Consular Affairs, 1978-80; ambassador to United Republic of Cameroon and Republic of Equatorial Guinea, 1980-83, ambassador to Democratic Republic of Sudan, 1983—. Served with U.S. Army, 1954-56. Presbyterian. Office: American Embassy APO New York NY 09668

HORAN, JAMES EDWARD, chemical company executive; b. Chgo., May 20, 1928; s. Lawrence James and Louise (Schevors) H.; m. Barbara Patch, Jan. 27, 1953; children: Julia, James, Michael. B.S., St. Procopius Coll., 1950; Ph.D., Pa. State U., 1955. Chemist Amoco Chem. Corp., Chgo., 1955-83; v.p. Amoco Chems. Corp., 1977—. Mem. Am. Chem. Soc., AAAS. Roman Catholic. Home: 249 Montclair Ave Glen Ellen IL 60137 Office: Amoco Chems Corp 200 E Randolph Dr Chgo IL 60601

HORAN, JOHN J., pharmaceutical company executive; b. S.I., N.Y., July 9, 1920; s. Michael T. and Alice (Kelly) H.; m. Julie Fitzgerald, Jan. 2, 1945; children—Mary Alice, Thomas, Jack, David. A.B., Manhattan Coll., 1940; LL.B., Columbia, 1946. Bar: N.Y. bar 1946. With firm Nims, Verdi & Martin, N.Y.C., 1946-52; atty. Merck & Co., Inc., 1952-55, counsel, 1955-57; dir. pub. relations Merck & Co., 1957-61, exec. dir. research adminstrn., research labs., 1961-62, dir. corp. planning, 1962-63; exec. v.p. mktg. Merck Sharp & Dohme, 1963-67; exec. v.p., gen. mgr., 1967-69, pres., 1969-72, corp. sr. v.p., 1972-74, exec. v.p., 1974-75, pres., chief operating officer, 1975-76, chmn., chief exec. officer, 1976—, also dir.; dir. NCR Corp., Gen. Motors Corp., J.P. Morgan & Co. Inc., Morgan Guaranty Trust; bd. mgrs. Beneficial Mut. Savs. Bank, 1971-74. Bd. dirs. Mgmt. Sci. Center of Wharton Sch. of U. Pa., 1971-78, Am. Found. Pharm. Edn., 1968-83, Manhattan Coll. Council Planning and Devel.; trustee Thomas Jefferson U. and Med. Coll., 1971-74; mem. nat. bd. United Negro Coll. Fund, 1978—; mem. O.I.C. Nat. Indsl. Adv. Council. Served to lt. USNR, 1942-46. Mem. Pharm. Mfrs. Assn. (chmn. bd. 1979-80), Bus. Council, Council on Fgn. Relations, Bus. Roundtable. Office: Merck & Co Inc Rahway NJ 07065

HORAN, JUSTIN THOMAS, association executive; b. Manchester, N.H., Feb. 6, 61927; s. Richard and Helen (Lenihan) H.; m. Helen Raymah Cook, Mar. 20, 1952; children: Catherine Helen, Carol Ann, Justin Thomas, Steven Edward, Daniel Kevin, Mark Gregory, Virginia Louise, Paul David. B.S., U. N.H., 1950; postgrad., Yale U., 1958, Syracuse U., 1961, Mich. State U., 1964. Asst. v.p. Manchester C. of C., 1955-57; exec. v.p. Newton (Mass.) C. of C., 1957-66, Greater Lawrence (Mass.) C. of C., 1966-69; pres. Greater Waterbury (Conn.) C. of C., 1969-75, Greater Pitts. C. of C., 1975—; chmn. bd. regents Inst. Orgn. Mgmt., 1966—. Contbr. articles to profl. publs. Met. chmn. Western Conn., Nat. Alliance Businessmen, 1973-75; mem. Mayor's Com. on Econ. Devel., Pitts., 1976—; trustee LaRoche Coll., Pitts.; mem. corp. North Hills Passavant Hosp., Pitts. Served to capt. U.S. Army Res., 1950-59. Mem. Am. C. of C. Execs. (dir., vice chmn. 1981-82, chmn. 1983-84), New Eng. Assn. C. of C. Execs. (past pres.), Mass. Assn. C. of C. Execs. (past pres.). Clubs: Duquesne, Allegheny (Pitts.). Home: 103 Camden Ct Pittsburgh PA 15237 Office: 411 7th Ave Pittsburgh PA 15219

HORAN, LEO GALLASPY, physician, educator; b. New Augusta, Miss., Sept. 17, 1925; s. Leo and Kate B. (Gallaspy) H.; m. Nancy Carolyn Flowers, July 23, 1966; children: David, Tracey, Paige. B.S., Tulane U., 1947, M.D., 1949. Intern Salt Lake County Gen. Hosp., Salt Lake City, 1949-50; resident in medicine Charity Hosp., New Orleans, 1952-56; asst. prof. medicine Tulane U., New Orleans, 1958-61; asso. prof. medicine U. Tenn., Memphis, 1961-67; prof. medicine Med. Coll. Ga., Augusta, 1967-73; prof., chmn. dept. medicine U. Louisville, 1973-82; prof. medicine Eastern Va. Med. Sch., Norfolk, 1983—; chief med. service VA Hosp., Augusta, Ga., 1967-73, Louisville Gen. Hosp., 1973-82; assoc. chief of staff for research VA Med. Ctr., Hampton, Va., 1983—. Mem. editorial bd.: Jour. Electrocardiology, 1968—; Contbr. articles to profl. jours. Served with USNR, 1950-52. USPHS grantee, 1965—; Am. Heart Assn. grantee, 1963-66. Fellow A.C.P., Am. Coll. Cardiology, Am. Coll. Chest Physicians; mem. Am. Soc. Clin. Investigation, Central Soc. Clin. Research, Assn. Profs. Medicine, Assn. Am. Physicians. Democrat. Presbyterian. Address: Box 5477 Hampton VA 23667

HORCHOW, S(AMUEL) ROGER, mail order executive; b. Cin., July 3, 1928; s. Reuben and Beatrice (Schwartz) H.; m. Carolyn Pfeifer, Dec. 29, 1960; children: Regen, Elizabeth, Sally. B.A., Yale U., 1950. Buyer Foley's, Houston, 1953-60; v.p. Neiman-Marcus, Dallas, 1960-68, 69-71; pres. Design Research, Cambridge, Mass., 1968-69, Kenton Collection, Dallas, 1971-73; chmn. Georg Jensen, Inc., N.Y.C., 1971-73, Horchow Collection, Dallas, 1973—; dir. Tenexalo Corp, Passport Internat. Author: Elephants in Your Mailbox, 1979, Living in Style, 1981. Bd. dirs. Dallas Mus. Fine Arts, Am. Inst. Public Service, Hockaday Sch., Nat. Trust Hist. Preservation, World Wildlife Fund U.S., Nat. Asthma and Allergy Found.; bd. dirs. Circle 10 council Boy Scouts Am.; bd. dirs. Better Bus. Bur. Dallas. Served to 1st lt., security U.S. Army, 1950-53. Clubs: Yale of N.Y.C., Nantucket Yacht. Home: 5722 Chatham Rd Dallas TX 75225 Office: 4435 Simonton Rd Dallas TX 75240

HORECKER, BERNARD LEONARD, biochemist; b. Chgo., Oct. 31, 1914; s. Paul and Bessie (Bornstein) H.; m. Frances Goldstein, July 12, 1936; children: Doris Colgate, Marilyn Diamond, Linda Lally. B.S., U. Chgo., 1936, Ph.D., 1939; Laureate honoris causa in Biol. Scis., U. Urbino (Italy), 1982. Research asso. chemistry U. Chgo., 1939-40; examiner U.S. Civil Service Commn., 1940-41; biochemist USPHS, NIH, Bethesda, Md., 1941-59; chief lab. of biochemistry and metabolism Nat. Inst. Arthritis and Metabolic Disease, 1956-59; professorial lectr. enzyme chemistry George Washington U., 1950-57; guest research-worker Pasteur Inst., Paris, France, 1957-58; prof. microbiology, chmn. dept. N.Y. U. Coll. Medicine, 1959-63; prof. molecular biology, chmn. dept. Albert Einstein Coll. Medicine, 1963-72, assoc. dean for sci. affairs, 1971-72; mem. Roche Inst. Molecular Biology, Nutley, N.J., 1972-84, head Lab. Molecular Enzymology,, 1977-84; adj. prof. Cornell U. Med. Coll., 1972-84, prof. bio chemistry, dean Grad. Sch. Med. Scis., 1984—; vis. prof. Albert Einstein Coll. Medicine, 1972-84; vis. prof. biochemistry U. Calif., 1954, U. Parana, Brazil, 1960, 63; vis. lectr. U. Ill., 1956; Ciba lectr. Rutgers U., 1962; Phillips lectr. Haverford Coll., 1965; vis. prof. Kyoto (Japan) U., 1967; vis. prof. biochemistry and molecular biology Cornell U., 1965; vis. prof. U. Ferrara, Italy; Reilly lectr. Notre Dame U., 1969; vis. lectr. U. Rotterdam, 1970; prof. honoris causa Fed. U. Parana, Curitiba, Brazil, 1981—; mem. sci. adv. bd. Roche Inst. Molecular Biology, Nutley, N.J., 1967-72, chmn., 1971-72; dir. Academic Press, Inc., 1968-73; mem. Research Career Award com. Nat. Inst. Gen. Med. Scis., 1966-70; mem. personnel com. Am. Cancer Soc., 1968-72, mem. sci. adv. com. for biochemistry and chem. carcinogenesis, 1974-78; mem. biology div. adv. com. Oak Ridge Nat. Lab., 1976-80; mem. Med. Scientist Tng. Program Sect. NIH, 1970—. Editor: Biochem. and Biophys. Research Communications, 1959—, Current Topics in Cellular Regulation, 1969—, Archives Biochemistry and Biophysics, 1960-68; chmn. editorial bd.: Archives of Biochemistry and Biophysics, 1968—; contbr. articles to sci. publs. Recipient Paul Lewis Labs. award in enzyme chemistry, 1952; Superior Accomplishment award Fed. Security Agy., 1952; Rockefeller Pub. Service award, 1957; Hillebrand prize Am. Chem. Soc., 1954; award in biol. scis. Washington Acad. Sci., 1954; Fulbright Travel award, 1963; Commonwealth Fund fellow, 1967. Fellow AAAS, Am. Acad. Arts and Scis.; mem. Am. Chem. Soc. (vice chmn. div. biol. chemistry 1975-76, chmn. 1976—), Biochem. Soc. (Eng.), Swiss Biochem. Soc. (hon. mem.), Spanish Biochem. Soc., hon. mem.), Japanese Biochem. Soc. (hon. mem.), Hellenic Biochem. and Biophys. Soc. (hon. mem.), Am. Soc. Biol. Chemists (pres. 1967-68, chmn. editorial com. 1962-63, Merck award 1981, Neuberg medal 1981), Nat. Acad. Scis., Harvey Soc. (v.p. 1969-70, pres. 1970-71), Brazilian Acad. Sci. (hon.), PanAm. Assn. Biochem. Socs. (vice chmn. 1971, chmn. 1972, mem. exec. com. 1971-78), Instituto de Investigaciones Citologicas (corr.), Phi Beta Kappa, Sigma Xi. Office: Cornell U Med Coll 1300 York Ave New York NY 10021

HORENSTEIN, SIMON, physician; b. Providence, Sept. 8, 1924; s. I.I. and Etta H.; m. Joan Gunville, June 12, 1948; children: Joshua, Deborah, Jonathan. Student, Brown U., 1941-43, U. Detroit, 1943, Ohio State U., 1944; B.S., U. Ill. Coll. Medicine, 1946, M.D., 1948. Teaching fellow, asso. neurology Harvard Med. Sch., Boston, 1950-62; asst. prof. Western Res. U., Cleve., 1962-66, asso. prof., 1966-70; prof., chmn. dept. neurology St. Louis U., 1970—; dir. neurology St. Louis Univ. Hosp., 1970—; chief neurology service St. Louis VA Hosp., 1972—. Editorial bd.: Jour. Chronic Disease, 1975—, Brain and Lang., 1973—, Archives of Neurology, 1976-81. Served with U.S. Army, 1943-46; with USN, 1951-53. Fellow Am. Acad. Neurology, Am. Neurol. Assn., ACP; mem. Soc. Neurosci., Assn. Research in Nervous and Mental Disease, Am. EEG Soc., Sigma Xi. Office: 456 N New Ballas Rd Saint Louis MO 63141

HORGAN, JAMES DONALD, biomed. engr.; b. Grand Rapids, Mich., May 21, 1922; s. James T. and Nona M. (Van Camp) H.; m. Rose Marie Rhora, Sept. 6, 1945; children—Kathleen, Daniel. B.E.E., Marquette U., 1946, M.S., 1951; Ph.D., U. Wis., 1957. Mem. staff Radiation Lab. Mass. Inst. Tech., 1942-45; mem. faculty Marquette U., 1946—, prof. elec. engring., 1958—, chmn. dept., 1956-61, biomed. engring. research, 1961—, prof. engring. in medicine, 1968. Fellow IEEE; mem. Am. Soc. Engring. Edn., Sigma Xi, Eta Kappa Nu, Tau Beta Pi, Triangle. Roman Catholic. Spl. research computer simulation of human physiol. systems. Home: 1530 Longwood St Elm Grove WI 53122 Office: Marguette U Milwaukee WI 53233

HORGAN, JOHN JOSEPH, JR., fin. exec.; b. Worcester, Mass., July 26, 1925; s. John Joseph and Catherine M. (Burke) H.; m. Catherine E. O'Neil, Sept. 11, 1948; children—Kathleen, Patricia, Jean, Daniel, Mary, Peter, Christine, Timothy, Tara. A.B., Harvard U., 1949; M.B.A., Columbia U., 1950. Asst. treas. Chase Manhattan Bank, N.Y.C., 1950-55; v.p. Peoples Trust Co., Hackensack, N.J., 1955-59; exec. v.p., cashier N.J. Nat. Bank, 1959-72; pres., dir. Haverhill Nat. Bank, Mass., 1972-78; fin. cons., 1978-79; mgr. fin. Mass. Bay Transp. Authority, 1979—; lectr. Fairleigh Dickinson U. Chmn. Renewal Adv. Commn., Trenton, 1965-69; vice chmn., treas. Mercer County Improvement Authority.; Pres., bd. dirs. Trenton Community Found., 1969-72; bd. dirs. Merrimack Valley United Fund, 1972-78, pres., 1978. Served with AUS, 1943-46. Mem. Haverhill C. of C. (v.p. 1977—). Clubs: Serra, Haverhill Golf and Country, Harvard, Rotary. Home: 374 Putnam Ave Cotuit MA 02635

HORGAN, PAUL, author, educator; b. Buffalo, Aug. 1, 1903; s. Edward Daniel and Rose Marie (Rohr) H. Student, N.Mex. Mil. Inst., 1919-23; Litt.D., Wesleyan U., 1956, So. Meth. U., 1957, Notre Dame U., 1958, Boston Coll., 1958, N.Mex. State U., 1962, Coll. Holy Cross, 1963, U. N.Mex., 1963, Fairfield U., 1964, St. Mary's Coll., 1976, Yale U., 1977; D.H.L., Canisius Coll., 1960, Georgetown U., 1962; Litt.D., D'Youville Coll., 1965, Pace U., 1968, Loyola Coll., Balt., 1968, Lincoln Coll., 1968, St. Bonaventure U., 1970, Cath. U., 1973; L.H.D., LaSalle Coll., 1971. Prodn. staff Eastman Theatre, Rochester, N.Y., 1923-26; librarian N.Mex. Mil. Inst., Roswell, 1926-42, asst. to pres., 1947-49; sr. fellow Center Advanced Studies, Wesleyan U., Middletown, Conn., 1959-61, dir., 1962-67, sr. fellow in letters, 1967-68, adj. prof. English, 1967-71, prof. emeritus, 1971—, author in residence, 1971—; lectr. Grad. Sch. Letters, U. Iowa, Feb.-June 1946; lectr. English, Yale U., 1969; hon. trustee Aspen Inst. Humanistic Studies, scholar in residence, 1968, 70, 71, 73; mem. nat. adv. bd. Center for the Book, Library of Congress, 1978—. Author: Men of Arms, 1931, The Fault of Angels, 1933 (Harper prize), No Quarter Given, 1935, Main Line West, 1936, From the Royal City, 1936, The Return of the Weed, 1936, A Lamp on the Plains, 1937, New Mexico's Own Chronicle, (with Maurice Garland Fulton), 1937, Far from Cibola, 1938, Figures in a Landscape, 1940, The Habit of Empire, 1941, A Tree on the Plains, an American Opera (music by Ernst Bacon 1942), Yours, A. Lincoln; (novel) The Common Heart, 1942; (novella) The Devil in the Desert, 1952, One Red Rose for Christmas, 1952; (history) Great River: The Rio Grande in North American History (Pulitzer prize, Bancroft prize, Tex. Inst. Letters award, 1954); (fiction) Humble Powers, 1954; (novella) The Saintmaker's Christmas Eve, 1955; (history) The Centuries of Santa Fe, 1956; (novel) Give Me Possession, 1957; (film narration) Rome Eternal, 1959; (novel) A Distant Trumpet, 1960; (biography) Citizen of New Salem, 1961; (collected novels) Mountain Standard Time, 1962; (history) Conquistadors in North American History, 1963; (juvenile) Toby and the Nighttime, 1962; (novel) Things as They Are, 1964; (poetry) Songs after Lincoln, 1965; (biography) Peter Hurd: A Portrait Sketch from Life, 1965; (novel) Memories of the Future, 1966; (short stories) The Peach Stone, 1967; (novel) Everything To Live For, 1968; (history) The Heroic Triad, 1970; (novel) Whitewater, 1970; (criticism) Maurice Baring Restored, 1970; (biography) Encounters with Stravinsky, 1972; (criticism) Approaches to Writing, 1973; (biography) Lamy of Santa Fe, His Life and Times (Pulitzer prize, Tex. Inst. Letters award, 1975); (novel) The Thin Mountain Air, 1977; (biography) Josiah Gregg and His Vision of the Early West, 1979; (novel) Mexico Bay, 1982; contbr. articles, fiction to mags. Chmn. bd. Santa Fe Opera, 1958-69, mem., 1969—; mem. adv. bd. John Simon Guggenheim Found., 1963-69; pres. bd. dirs. Roswell Mus., 1948-55; mem. bd. Roswell Pub. Library, 1958-62, hon. mem., 1962—; hon. life fellow Sch. Am. Research; fellow Pierpont Morgan Library, 1974—, mem. council, 1975-79, 82-83, life fellow, 1977—; trustee Assos. Yale U. Library, 1976-79; bd. dirs. Witter Bynner Found., 1972-79; founding trustee Lincoln County (N.Mex.) Heritage Trust, 1976—. Served from capt. to lt. col. AUS, 1942-46; recalled temp. active duty gen. staff Dept. Army, 1952; Washington. Created knight of St. Gregory, 1957; Guggenheim fellow, 1947-48, 58; Hoyt fellow Saybrook Coll., Yale U., 1965; asso. fellow Saybrook Coll., 1966—; Decorated Legion of Merit; recipient Tex. Inst. Letters awards, 1955, 71, 76; Campion award of Catholic Book Club, 1957; Cath. Book award Cath. Press Assn., 1965, 68; Laetare medal U. Notre Dame, 1976; Bronze medal Smithsonian Instn., 1980; medal Nat. Portrait Gallery, 1981; Baldwin medal Wesleyan U., 1982; Roswell Mus. addition named after him; N.Mex. Mil. Inst. library named after him. Fellow Am., Conn. acads. arts and scis.; past mem. Nat. Council Humanities; mem. Am. Cath. Hist. Assn. (pres. 1960), Am. Antiquarian Soc., Wesleyan Writers Conf. (adv. bd.), Nat. Inst. Arts and Letters, Phi Beta Kappa (orator 1973, hon. Alpha of Conn. chpt.), Soc. Am. Historians. Roman Catholic. Clubs: Yale, Century (N.Y.C.); Athenaeum (London, Eng.). Address: Wesleyan U Middletown CT 06457

HORGER, EDGAR OLIN, III, physician, educator; b. Eutawville, S.C., May 30, 1937; s. Edgar Olin Jr. and Frances Durant (Jordan) H.; m. Polly Jo Collins, May 29, 1960; children: Edgar Olin IV, David Collins, Patricia Bowen. B.S., Furman U., 1959; M.D., Med. Coll. S.C., 1962. Intern Med. U. Hosp., Charleston, S.C., 1962-63, resident in Ob-Gyn, 1963-67; NIH fellow U. Pitts., 1967-68, asst. prof. Ob-Gyn, 1968-69, Med. U. S.C., Charleston, 1969-71, asso. prof., 1971-76, prof., 1976—, prof. radiology, 1978—. Contbr. articles to profl. jours. Served to capt. AUS, 1963-66. Mem. AMA, S.C. Med. Assn., Am. Coll. Ob-Gyn, South Central Ob-Gyn Soc., South Atlantic Assn. Ob-Gyn (exec. com. 1983-85), So. Perinatal Assn. (dir. Mid-Atlantic region 1974-76), Soc. Perinatal Obstetricians (dir. 1977-78), Am. Assn. Ob-Gyn, Am. Gynecologic Soc., Alpha Omega Alpha. Club: Charleston Tennis. Home: 712 Angus Ct Mount Pleasant SC 29464 Office: Med Univ Hosp Charleston SC 29425

HORII, HOWARD NOBUO, architect, educator; b. Hermosa Beach, Calif., Jan. 4, 1923; s. Riki-Matsu and Konobu (Okita) H.; m. 1st; children: Steven C., Kenneth T.; m. 2d Paula Embree, June 11, 1975; 1 dau., Jane. B.A. in Architecture, Pratt Inst., Bklyn., 1958; cert. architecture, The Cooper Union, N.Y.C., 1954. Lic. architect, N.J. Designer The Grad Partnership, Newark, 1958-68, sr. assoc., 1968-74, ptnr. design, 1974-79, ptnr. interior design, 1979—; adj. prof. Pratt Inst., 1962—. Contbr. articles to profl. jours. Recipient numerous design. Fellow AIA (pres. Newark-Suburban chpt. 1975). Buddhist. Home: 63 E 9th St Apt 14K New York NY 10003 Office: The Grad Partnership Gateway One Newark NJ 07102

HORKEY, WILLIAM RICHARD, diversified oil company executive; b. Tulsa, Apr. 22, 1925; s. William Edward and Clara Doris (Rice) H.; m. Barbara Jeanne Williamson, Oct. 18, 1952; children: Elaine Gail, Edward Richard, Ellen Beth. B.A., State U. Iowa, 1947; LL.B., U. Okla., 1950; grad., Advanced Mgmt. Program, Harvard U., 1962. Bar: Okla. 1950. With Gulf Oil Corp., 1950-51, Skelly Oil Co., 1951-55, Helmerich & Payne, Inc., Tulsa, 1955—, sec., legal counsel, 1957-64, v.p., 1960-64, exec. v.p., 1964—, also dir.; v.p., dir. Helmerich & Payne Internat. Drilling Co., Helmerich & Payne Coal Co.; dir. Atwood Oceanics, Inc. Vice chmn. of oil div. of Tulsa Community Chest, 1964-69; chmn. met. div. Tulsa United Way, 1975-78, bd. dirs., 1978—; mem. bd. mgmt. S.E. Tulsa YMCA, 1963—, vice chmn., 1969-70, chmn., 1970-72; bd. mgmt. Met. Tulsa YMCA, 1970—, pres., 1972-73; bd. dirs. Tulsa chpt. ARC, North Tulsa Ambulatory Health Care, Inc., 1976—; trustee Tulsa Med. Edn. Found., Tulsa Emergency Med. Authority, 1977—; chmn. Tulsa Emergency Med. Authority, 1981; mem. med. adv. com. on indigent care Okla. Dept. Human Services. Served to 2d lt. USAAF, 1943-45. Mem. Am., Okla., Tulsa County bar assns., Am. Judicature Soc., Order of Coif, Phi Delta Phi, Phi Delta Theta. Presbyn. (deacon and elder). Clubs: Tulsa, So. Hills Country, Mid-Continent Harvard AMP (Tulsa) (pres. 1969-75). Home: 5686 S Evanston St Tulsa OK 74105 Office: 1579 E 21st St Tulsa OK 74114

HORMAN, ELIZABETH, artist; b. N.Y.C.; d. Morris and Carrie (Friendlich) Lazar; m. Edmund Charles Horman, Feb. 3, 1939; 1 son, Charles. A.B., Barnard Coll.; student, Art Students League, Nat. Acad. Design, Grand Central Art Sch. High sch. tchr., N.Y.C., 3 yrs; tchr. art Lenox Hill Settlement House, 1953-56. Freelance fashion artist, mural painter, book illustrator, 1952-79; artist, Henry O'Brien Advt., 1953-56, one-man exhbns. include, Radio City, N.Y.C., 1953, Casa de Portugal, N.Y.C., 1970, Barbizon Gallery, N.Y.C., 1969, 70, Chester (Vt.) Guild, 1968, So. Vt. Guild, Manchester, 1969, 225 Fifth Ave., N.Y.C., 1955, Roosevelt Center, N.Y.C., 1957, Edward Frisch Gallery, N.Y.C., 1978, one-woman TV shows, 1969, 77; exhibited in group shows, Nat. Assn. Women Artists, throughout U.S.; rep. permanent collections, throughout U.S. Recipient prize Pen and Brush Club, 1965, 67. Mem. Nat. Assn. Women Artists (pres. 1976-79, medal of honor 1979), Artists Equity (v.p. N.Y. chpt.), Barnard Coll. Alumnae Assn., Nat. Arts Club, Pen and Brush Club. Christian Scientist.

HORMATS, ROBERT DAVID, economist, investment banker; b. Balt., Apr. 13, 1943; s. Saul and Ruth H. B.A., Tufts U., 1965; M.A., Fletcher Sch. Law and Diplomacy, 1976, 1967, Ph.D., 1970. Research asst. Fletcher Sch. of Law and Diplomacy, 1968-69; research asso. Univ. Coll., Dar-es-Salaam, Tanzania, 1967-68; staff mem. internat. econ. affairs Nat. Security Council, 1969-73, sr. staff mem., 1974-77; sr. dep. asst. sec. for econ. and bus. affairs Dept. State, 1977-79; ambassador and dep. U.S. trade rep., 1979-81, asst. sec. state for econ. and bus. affairs, 1981-83; v.p. internat. corp. fin. Goldman Sachs and Co., 1982—; dir. Goldman Sachs Internat., 1982—; guest scholar Brookings Instn., 1973-74; cons. to Commn. on Critical Choices for Ams., 1973-74; vis. lectr. Princeton U., 1983; bd. dirs. Atlantic Council Overseas Devel. Council. Shell Oil Co. fellow, 1967-68; Council on Fgn. Relations fellow, 1973-74; Recipient Arthur Flemming award, 1978. Mem. Council Fgn. Relations. Home: 4715 Crescent St Chevy Chase MD 20816 Home: 500 E 83rd St New York NY 10028 Office: Goldman Sachs and Company 85 Broad St New York NY 10004

HORN, CARL, JR., utility executive; b. Rutherfordton, N.C., Oct. 21, 1921; s. Carl and Freda Wagner (Warden) H.; m. Frances Alice Emmet, Feb. 7, 1948 (dec. 1966); children: Carl III, Claire, Katherine, Thomas E.; m. Virginia Grey Johnston, Oct. 27, 1967. A.B., Duke U., 1942, LL.B., 1947. Bar: N.C. 1947. Practiced in, Charlotte, until 1953; asst. gen. counsel Duke Power Co., Charlotte, 1954-59, gen. counsel, 1959-63, v.p., gen. counsel, 1963-66, v.p. finance, gen. counsel, 1966-69, exec. v.p., gen. counsel, 1970-71, pres., chief exec. officer, 1971-76, chmn. bd., chief exec. officer, 1976-82; dir. United Telecommunications, Inc., Kansas City, Kans., Carolina Freight Corp., Cherryville, N.C.; exec. in residence Coll. Bus. Adminstrn., U. N.C., Charlotte, 1982—. Bd. dirs. Charlotte Meml. Hosp., N.C. Research Triangle Found.; trustee S.C. Found. Ind. Colls., Ind. Coll. Fund N.C.; chmn. N.C. Bd. Community Colls., 1980—. Served to capt. AUS, 1942-46; PTO; mem. N.C. N.G., 1953-54. Mem. Am., N.C. bar assns., Edison Electric Inst. (chmn. legal com. 1967—), Duke U. Law Alumni Assn. (pres. 1961), Newcomen Soc. N.Am., Order of Coif. Presbyterian (elder). Home: 2111 Wendover Rd Charlotte NC 28211

HORN, CAROL ELLEN, fashion designer; b. N.Y.C., June 12, 1936; d. Ely and Luba H. Student, Boston U., 1954-56, Columbia U. Sch. Fine Arts, 1956-58. Head designer Benson & Partners-Outlander Co., N.Y.C., 1968-72, Carol Horn Co., div. Malcolm Starr Inc., 1972-74; partner, head designer Carol Horn's Habitat, N.Y.C., 1974—; critic Fashion Inst. Tech., N.Y.C.; guest designer Shenkar Coll. Fashion and Textiles, Tel Aviv. Recipient Coty Fashion award, 1975, Wool Knit award Women's Knitwear Assn., 1975. Democrat. Jewish. Office: Carol Horn Designs Ltd 575 7th Ave New York NY 10018 *

HORN, CHRISTIAN FRIEDRICH, chemical company executive; b. Dresden, Germany, Dec. 23, 1927; came to U.S., 1954, naturalized, 1959; s. Otto Hugo and Elsa H.; m. Christa Winkler, Feb. 13, 1954; 1 dau., Sabrina. M.S., Technische Hochschule, Dresden, 1951, Ph.D., 1958. Research scientist German Acad. Sci., Berlin, 1951-53; research scientist Farbwerke Hoechst, Germany, 1953-54; research mgr. Union Carbide, N.Y.C., 1954-65; pres. Polymer Tech. Inc., N.Y.C., 1965-74; mem. bd. mgmt. Zimmer A.G., Frankfurt, Ger., 1971-73; v.p. W.R. Grace & Co., N.Y.C., 1974-81, sr. v.p., 1981—; dir. AWI, Microtest Systems, Inc., Anicon, Inc. Served with German Army, 1944-45. Decorated Iron Cross. Mem. Am. Chem. Soc., German Chem. Soc. Lutheran. Club: Princeton. Patentee in field. Home: 101 Dingletown Rd Greenwich CT 06830 Office: 1114 Ave of Americas New York NY 10036

HORN, FRANCIS HENRY, educator; b. Toledo, Nov. 18, 1908; s. Henry Frederick and Orpha Ford (Bennett) H.; m. Xenia Beliavsky, June 8, 1935; children—Michael Serge, Barbara Ann Horn Schaefer, Elizabeth Marie Horn Roberts. A.B., Dartmouth, 1930; M.A., U. Va., 1934, Yale U., 1942; Ph.D. (Sterling fellow 1946-47), Yale U., 1949; LL.D., U. Hartford, 1955, Providence Coll., 1959, Dickinson Coll., 1961; D.H.L., So. Ill. U., 1958, Ricker Coll., 1963, U. Nev., Las Vegas, 1969, Molloy Coll., 1971, Mt. St. Mary Coll., 1973, Pratt Inst., 1974, Albertus Magnus Coll., 1974, U. New Haven, 1974, Am. Coll. in Greece, 1978; D.C.L., Pace U., 1961; Litt.D., Ohio No. U., 1961, Kon Kuk U., Korea, 1973; D.Sc. Edn., Bryant Coll., 1961; Pd.D., R.I. Coll., 1962; LL.D., Brown U., 1963, U. N.H., 1964, Defiance Coll., 1966, U. Maine, 1967, D'Youville Coll., 1968, Wagner Coll., 1969, U.R.I., 1969; Ed.D., Western New Eng. Coll., 1966; H.H.D., Windham Coll., 1965; Ph.D. (hon.), China Acad., Taiwan, 1973. Instr. English and history

Am. U. in Cairo, Egypt, 1930-33; asst. dean Jr. Coll. of Commerce (now Quinnipiac Coll.), New Haven, 1936-37, acting dean, 1937-38, dean, 1938-42; asst. dean Biarritz Am. U., France, 1945-46; editor reports coop. study Lincoln (Nebr.) schs., 1946-47; dean eve. div., dir. summer session, asso. prof. edn. Johns Hopkins, 1947-51, acting chmn. dept. edn., 1951, vis. prof. edn., 1952-53; exec. sec. Am. Assn. Higher Edn., 1951-53; pres. Pratt Inst., Bklyn., 1953-57; vis. disting. prof. higher edn. So. Ill. U., 1957-58; pres. U. R.I., 1958-67, pres. emeritus, 1979; pres. Commn. on Ind. Colls. and Univ., State of N.Y., 1967-71, Albertus Magnus Coll., New Haven, 1971-74, pres. emeritus, 1974; exec. v.p. Wagner Coll., Staten Island, N.Y., 1974-77; pres. Am. Coll. of Switzerland, Leysin, 1977-79; v.p., dir. Brit. campus New Eng. Coll., Sussex, Eng., 1980-81; disting. vis. scholar, adviser to pres. Tunghai U., Taichung, Taiwan, 1982—. Author: Challenge and Perspective in Higher Education, 1971; Editor: College and University Bull, 1951-53, Current Issues in Higher Edn, 1952, 53, Literary Masterpieces of the Western World, 1953, Twenty Five Years in the Wide, Wide World, 1955, Go Forth, Be Strong, 1978; Contbr.: ednl. Jours. N.Y. Times Book Rev. Vice chmn. bd. Theta Delta Chi Ednl. Found.; dir. Near East Found.; counselor United Bd. Christian Higher Edn. Asia, past chmn. bd. trustees; mem. nat. adv. council Center for Study Presidency, past sec.-treas.; trustee U. R.I. Found., Calcusearch, Inc.; bd. dirs. Culinary Coll. of Washington; bd. fellows Am. Grad. Sch. Internat. Mgmt.; mem. Nat. Com. Middle East Understanding. Served from 1st lt. to lt. col. AUS, 1942-46. Decorated Legion of Merit, Army Commendation medal with cluster; recipient medal for distinguished pub. service U.S. Navy, 1967, outstanding civilian service award U.S. Army, 1967; Named to R.I. Heritage Hall of Fame, 1967, U. R.I. Hall of Fame, 1976. Mem. NEA, Phi Beta Kappa, Pi Sigma Alpha, Phi Delta Kappa, Phi Kappa Phi, Omicron Delta Kappa, Theta Delta Chi, Delta Sigma Pi, Alpha Delta Sigma. Conglist. Home: 42 Upper College Rd Kingston RI 02881

HORN, GERALD ANTHONY, artist; b. Detroit, Aug. 10, 1941; s. Anthony Paul and Lola Marie (Sturm) H. Student, Detroit Soc. Arts & Crafts, 1961-63, Highland Park Coll., 1968; B.F.A., Wayne State U., 1971; M.A., Hunter Coll., 1973. Art program dir. 12th St. Project, 1967-68; tchr. Detroit Inst. Arts, 1968-69; tech. asst. graphics dept. Hunter Coll., 1972-73. One-man shows, O.K. Harris Gallery, 1974, 75, 77, 80, 81, Jackie Feiginson Gallery, Detroit, 1981; exhibited group shows, Rosa Esman Gallery, N.Y.C., 1973, Neilson Gallery, Boston, 1974, Art Mus. South Tex., Corpus Christie, 1976, Kilcawley Center Art Gallery, Youngstown (Ohio) U., 1977, The Aldrich Mus., 1978, Orgn. Ind. Artists, N.Y.C., North Tex. State U., Denton, 1979, Erickson Gallery, N.Y.C., 1980, Md. Inst., Balt., 1981, Root Art Ctr., Hamilton Coll., Clinton, N.Y., I.C.A. Mus., London, 1982. Address: 115 W Broadway New York NY 10013

HORN, JOHN STEPHEN, university president; b. Gilroy, Calif., May 31, 1931; s. John Stephen and Isabelle (McCaffrey) H.; m. Mini Moore, Sept. 4, 1954; children: Marcia Horn Yavitz, Stephen. A.B. with great distinction, Stanford U., 1953, Ph.D., 1958; M.P.A. Administrn. fellow, Harvard U., 1955. Adminstrv. asst. U.S. Sec. Labor James P. Mitchell, 1959-60; legis. asst. U.S. Senator Thomas H. Kuchel, 1960-66; sr. fellow Brookings Inst., 1966-69; dean grad. studies and research Am. U., 1969-70; vice chmn. U.S. Commn. Civil Rights, 1969-80, commr., 1980—; pres. Calif. State U.-Long Beach, 1970—; fellow Harvard U. Inst. Politics, 1966-67. Author: The Cabinet and Congress, 1960, Unused Power: The Work of the Senate Committee on Appropriations, 1970, (with Edmund Beard) Congressional Ethics: The View from the House, 1975. Bd. dirs. Nat. Inst. Corrections, Inst. Internat. Edn.; mem. Long Beach Promotion Commn.; vice-chmn. Calif. Republican League. Congl. fellow Am. Polit. Sci. Assn., 1958-59. Mem. Am. Assn. State Colls. and Univs. (chmn. com. fed. relations), Calif. Scholarship Fedn. (chpt. pres.), Stanford Alumni Assn. (pres. 1976-77), Stanford Assocs., Phi Beta Kappa, Pi Sigma Alpha. Office: 1250 Bellflower Blvd Long Beach CA 90840

HORN, MARTIN LOUIS, JR., restaurateur; b. N.Y.C., Mar. 12, 1927; s. Martin Louis and Kathryn (Albert) H.; m. Leone L. Behrendt, June 18, 1949; 1 dau., Leone Susan. Student, Seton Hall U., 1946-47; B.S., Cornell U., 1950; LL.D., Northwood Inst., 1971. Pres., Pals Cabin Restaurant, West Orange, N.J., 1951-82, Mayfair Farms Restaurant, 1951-82, Pals Pancake Houses, 1961-79, Longhorn Restaurants, 1968-72, Horn Family Restaurants, 1971—, Post and Paddock Restaurant, Miami Beach, Fla., 1974-77, Bay Harbor Hotel and Club, Miami Beach, 1974-77. Served with USNR, 1945-46. Named to Hall of Fame, Hospitality mag., 1968. Mem. Nat. Restaurant Assn. (past pres.), N.J. Restaurant Assn. (past pres.), Am. Hotel-Motel Assn. (dir.), Cornell Soc. Hotelmen, Sigma Nu. Clubs: N.Y. Athletic; Jockey (Miami, Fla.); Ocean Reef (Key Largo, Fla.); Baltusrol Golf (Springfield, N.J.); Surf (Miami Beach, Fla.). Home: 1538 Laguna Dr Point Pleasant NJ 08742 Office: 265 Prospect Ave West Orange NJ 07052

HORN, MARTIN ROBERT, patent lawyer; b. N.Y.C., May 12, 1928; s. Isidor and Dora (Braver) H.; m. Rita Wenig, June 20, 1954; children: Leslie, Brian, Michael. B.S. in Elec. Engring, U. Calif. at Berkeley, 1951; J.D., UCLA, 1954. Bar: Calif. 1955. Patent atty. trainee J.B. Rea Co., Santa Monica, 1954; patent atty. Hughes Aircraft Co., Culver City, Calif., 1954-56; practiced law, Los Angeles, 1955—; partner Spensley, Horn, Jubas & Lubitz, Los Angeles, 1956—; instr. patent law UCLA, 1973; lectr. in field. Vice pres. Carthay Circle Home Owners, 1971-73, bd. dirs., 1970-73. Served with AUS, 1946-47. Mem. UCLA Law Alumni Assn. (pres. 1965), Century City Bar Assn. (pres. 1978). Home: 6136 Barrows Dr Los Angeles CA 90048 Office: 1880 Century Park E Suite 500 Los Angeles CA 90067

HORN, MILTON, sculptor; b. Kiev, Russia, Sept. 1, 1906; came to U.S., 1913, naturalized, 1917; s. Pinchos and Bessie (Komar) H.; m. Estelle Oxenhorn, Sept. 1, 1928 (dec. May 1975). Student, Copley Soc. Sculpture Classes, Boston, 1921-23; with, Henry H. Kitson, sculptor, Boston, 1921-23, Beaux Arts Inst. Design, N.Y.C., 1923-27; D.F.A. (hon.), Olivet Coll., 1976. Artist-in-residence, prof. art Olivet Coll., 1939-49. Exhibited in one-man shows, New Eng. Soc. Contemporary Art, Boston, 1931, Bklyn. Mus., 1932, Guild Art Gallery, N.Y.C., 1936, Wayne U., Detroit, 1941, U. Mich., Ann Arbor, Layton Art Gallery, Milw., 1942, Kalamazoo Inst. Arts, 1947; exhibited in group shows, including, Fairmount Park Art Assn., Phila., 1949, Whitney Mus. Am. Art, Met. Mus. Art, N.Y.C., 1951, Art Inst. Chgo., 1950, 51, Nat. Inst. Arts and Letters, N.Y.C., 1953, 54, 77; represented in permanent collections, including, Nat. Acad. Design, N.Y.C., Brookgreen Gardens, S.C., Nat. Mus. Am. Art, Washington; works include Moses Before the Burning Bush, Temple B'Nai Israel, Charleston, W.Va., 1960, Hymn to Water, Filtration Plant, Chgo., 1965, Man Wrests from Earth Matter and Energy, Nat. Bank Commerce, Charleston, 1969; Contbr. articles to various publs. Recipient citation of honor AIA Centennial Conv., 1957. Fellow Nat. Sculpture Soc. (Henry Hering Meml. medal 1972); mem. Nat. Acad. Design (academician), Sculptors Guild, Coll. Art Assn. Am. Jewish. Home and Office: 1932 N Lincoln Ave Chicago IL 60614 *Great sculpture has always been mythopeic. The sculptural image, like the verbal, comes out of the union between the mythopoet and the community, out of the roots of their common spiritual needs and experiences. This is the cause of its nature and the source of its style. In its highest sense it is never a soliloquy.*

HORN, MYRON KAY, petroleum geologist, administrator; b. Miami, Fla., Jan. 28, 1930; s. Harry I. and Sykes K. (Kaplan) H.; m. Barbara DeCasseres Rothschild, Apr. 9, 1955; children: Lisa, Marc, Nina. B.S., U. Colo., 1952; M.S., U. Houston, 1958; Ph.D., Rice U., 1964. Sr. research geologist Pure Oil Co., Crystal Lake, Ill., 1960-64; group leader geophys. research Cities Service Co., Tulsa, 1964-65, mgr. geol. research, 1965-70, dir. exploration and prodn. research, 1970-83, dir. applied research and tech. ops., 1983—; mem. U.S. sci. adv. com. Joint Oceanographic Inst., 1983—. Contbr. articles to profl. jours. Served to lt. (j.g.) U.S. Navy, 1952-55. Mem. Am. Assn. Petroleum Geologists (editor 1979—, exec. com.), Soc. Petroleum Engrs. Club: Petroleum (Tulsa). Home: 5919 S Gary Pl Tulsa OK 74105 Office: PO Box 3908 Tulsa OK 74102

HORN, PAUL JOSEPH, musician; b. N.Y.C., Mar. 17, 1930; s. Jack L. and Frances (Sper) H.; m. Tryntje; children: Marlen L., Robin F. Mus.B., Oberlin Conservatory Music, 1952; Mus.M. (fellow), Manhattan Sch. Music, 1952; student, Acad. Meditation, Himalayas, India, 1967, 68. Tchr. system transcendental meditation UCLA (also at Berkeley and centers throughout U.S. and Can.); Mem. Sauter-Finigan Band, 1956-57, Chico Hamilton Quintet, 1957-58, NBC Staff Orch., Hollywood, Calif., 1960; free-lance studio work, 1960-66; formed Paul Horn Quintet, 1959, Golden Flute Records, 1982. Rec. artist for, Dot, World Pacific, HiFi, Columbia, RCA Victor records; producer, artist, Epic Records; concerts throughout U.S. and Europe, 1957—; tours to People's Republic China, 1978, 81; concert tour of USSR, 1983; guest speaker, performer jazz clinics at numerous univs., 1961—; producer: TV documentary Paul Horn in China; (Recipient 5 Grammy nominations 1966, 2 Grammy awards 1966), motion picture appearances; guest TV performer; star: TV series The Paul Horn Show; made solo flute recs. in, Taj Mahal, (Inside), 1968; in, Gizeh pyramids, (Inside the Great Pyramid), Mushroom Records, 1976. Bd. dirs. Victoria Symphony Orch., Performing Rights Orgn. Can. Served with AUS, 1953-56. Also awards from Jazz Polls, Downbeat mag., Playboy mag. Address: PO Box 6193 Sta C Victoria BC V8P 5L5 Canada

HORN, ROBERT MILTON, stockbroker, investment banker; b. Davenport, Iowa, Oct. 26, 1931; s. Ralph W. and Dorothy L. (Pfeiff) H.; m. Katharine Horn, July 2, 1960 (div.); children: Michael R., Pamela M. Student, U. Iowa, 1954; B.S., Grinnell Coll., 1953. Stockbroker Dean Witter, Los Angeles, 1963-69; ptnr., stockbroker Crowell, Weedon, Newport Beach, Calif., 1969—. Served to lt. (j.g.) USN, 1954-57. Republican. Club: Racquet of Irvine. Home: 1 Silverbreeze Irvine CA 92714 Office: Crowell Weedon & Co 567 San Nicolas Dr Newport Beach Ca 92660

HORN, ROGER ALAN, mathematician, educator; b. Macon, Ga., Jan. 19, 1942; s. Woodrow A. and Betty L. (McClure) H.; m. Susan H. Dadakis, July 24, 1965; children—Ceres, Corinne, Howard. B.A. with distinction (Nat. Merit scholar), Cornell U., 1963; M.S., Stanford, 1964, Ph.D. (NSF fellow), 1967. Asst. prof. math. U. Santa Clara, Calif., 1967-68; asst. prof. Johns Hopkins U., 1968-71, asso. prof., 1972-75, prof., 1975—, chmn. dept. math. scis., 1972-79; asso. prof. U. Md., Balt., 1971-72; pres., dir. QC inc, Balt., 1975—. Contbr. articles to profl. jours. Alfred P. Sloan fellow, 1975-78; NSF grantee, 1968—. Mem. Am. Math. Soc., Math. Assn. Am., Soc. Indsl. and Applied Math., Phi Beta Kappa, Sigma Xi. Office: Dept Math Scis Johns Hopkins U Baltimore MD 21218

HORN, STEPHEN, university president; b. Gilroy, Calif., May 31, 1931; s. John Stephen and Isabelle (McCaffrey) H.; m. Nini Moore, Sept. 4, 1954; children: Marcia Karen Horn Yavitz, John Stephen. A.B. with great distinction, Stanford, 1953, postgrad., 1953-54, 55-56, Ph.D. in Polit. Sci, 1958; M.Pub. Administrn., Harvard, 1955. Congl. fellow, 1958-59, adminstrv. asst. to sec. labor, Washington, 1959-60; legislative asst. to U.S. Senator Thomas H. Kuchel, 1960-66; sr. fellow The Brookings Instn., 1966-69; dean grad. studies and research Am. U., 1969-70; pres. Calif. State U., Long Beach, 1970—; sr. cons., host The Govt. Story on TV, The Election Game (radio series), 1967-69. Author: The Cabinet and Congress, 1960, Unused Power: The Work of the Senate Committee on Appropriations, 1970, (with Edmund Beard) Congressional Ethics: The View from the House, 1975. Mem. urban studies fellowship adv. bd. Dept. Housing and Urban Devel., 1969-70, chmn., 1969; vice-chmn. U.S. Commn. Civil Rights, 1969-80, mem., 1980-82; mem. Pres.-elect Nixon's Task Force on Orgn. Exec. Br., 1968; mem. law enforcement edn. program, adv. commn. law enforcement assistance adminstrn. Dept. Justice, 1969-71; Co-founder Western U.S. Com. Arts and Scis. for Eisenhower, 1956; Bd. dirs. Nat. Inst. Corrections, Inst. Internat. Edn.; Fellow John F. Kennedy Inst. Politics, Harvard U., 1966-67. Mem. Stanford Assos., Stanford Alumni Assn. (pres. 1976-77), Phi Beta Kappa, Pi Sigma Alpha. Republican. Club: El Capitan Eating (Stanford). Home: 3944 Pine Ave Long Beach CA 90807

HORN, THOMAS CARL, ret. banker; b. Hay Springs, Nebr., Aug. 30, 1916; s. Carl Swift and Minnie (Sage) H.; m. Bernicia Jane Ellis, June 14, 1942; children—Christie Jane, Scott Ellis. Student, Chadron State Tchrs. Coll., 1934-35, Chilocothe Bus. Coll., 1935; B.Sc. magna cum laude in Bus. Adminstrn, U. Nebr., 1941, Air Command and Staff Sch., 1948; grad., Sch. Banking U. Wis., 1953, Air War Coll., 1957. Office mgr. Horn & Morgan, Inc., 1946-48; exec. v.p. 1st Nat. Bank, Hay Springs, 1948-56; bank specialist Burroughs Corp., St. Louis, 1957-59, Omaha, 1959-60; v.p. Security Nat. Bank, Sioux City, Iowa, 1960-63, sr. v.p., 1963-67, exec. v.p., 1967-76, also dir.; Pres. Security Nat. Corp., Sioux City, 1969-76; sec.-treas., dir. Midco Inc., Sioux City, 1965-76; vice chmn., dir. Security Bank & Trust, Alamogordo, N.Mex., 1976-81; dir. Northwestern State Bank, Orange City, Iowa, Iowa Bus. Devel. Credit Corp., Des Moines. Mem. exec. com., dir. Central City Bus. Devel. Com., 1964-71; bd. dirs. United Way, 1967—, Woodbury County Tax Conf., 1970—, Sioux City Art Center, 1965-68, Briar Cliff Coll., Sioux City, Rivercade Assn., Sioux City; treas., bd. dirs. Siouxland Community Blood Bank. Served with USAAF, 1941-46; Served with USAF, 1956-57; col. Res. Decorated D.F.C., Air medal with 4 oak leaf clusters, Purple Heart, others. Mem. Iowa Bankers Assn. (chmn. corr. bankers com. 1967-68, legis. com. 1970—), Sioux City Bankers Assn. (pres. 1963, 67, 71), C. of C. (mil. affairs com. 1968—), Sigma Chi (pres. 1941-42, treas. 1940-41), Beta Gamma Sigma. Republican. Presbyn. (deacon 1962-63; trustee 1965-68, 72—). Clubs: Mason (Shriner), Lion (dir. Sioux City Club 1969-71), mem. Order Eastern Star., Sioux City Country (dir. 1969-71). Home: 1511 Rockwood Alamogordo NM 88310 *Opportunity and success are the direct result of established objectives and hard work, done with a purpose, liberally interwoven with dedication, truth, honesty, education, self-reliance, understanding and freedom; with respect and helpfulness towards others.*

HORN, THOMAS D., education educator; b. Iowa City, Iowa, June 26, 1918; s. Ernest and Madeline (Darrough) H.; m. Grace Ellen Adams, Aug. 2, 1941; 1 dau., Diane. B.A., State U. Iowa, 1940, M.A., 1946, Ph.D., 1947; student, Cambrdige U., Eng., 1945. Tchr. pub. schs., Denver, 1940-42, River Forest, Ill., 1942-43; asst. prof. U. No. Iowa, 1947-51; assoc. prof. curriculum and instrn. Coll. Edn. U. Tex., Austin, 1951-59, prof., 1959—, chmn. dept., 1962-73; vis. lectr. U. Pitts., summer 1949, Harvard U., summer 1959, U. Mich., 1963; dir. USOE Project, 1964-65, Bi-Cultural Sect., Coll. Edn. Research and Devel. Ctr., 1965-67, San Antonio Lang. Research Project, 1967-68, Lang. Research Project, 1968—. Contbr. articles to profl. jours; co-author, cons. spelling and reading textbooks, instrnl. films; editor research monographs, book. Mem. Tex. commn. Services to Children and Youth, 1972-82, chmn., 1973-75, vice chmn., 1978-79. Served with U.S. Army, 1943-46; to capt. USAFR, 1950-55. Mem. Am. Ednl. Research Assn. Tchr. Edn. (exec. bd. 1953-59, pres. 1957-58), Tex. Assn. for Student Teaching (pres. 1952-53), Internat. Reading Assn. (Spl. Service award 1979), Nat. Conf. on Research in English (exec. bd. 1957-60, nat. pres. 1958-59), Nat. Council Tchrs. English (dir. elem. sect. 1965-68), NEA, Nat. Soc. Study Edn., Phi Delta Kappa, Phi Kappa Phi, Phi Gamma Delta. Home: 5302 Ridge Oak Dr Austin TX 78731 Office: Dept Curriculum and Instrn U Tex Austin TX 78712

HORNBACK, CLYDE V., energy development company executive; b. Humble, Tex., Aug. 14, 1928; s. William A. and Ida A. (Koinm) H.; m. Frances R. Collins, Apr. 12, 1952; children: Kay F., Joan Y., Donna J. Hornback Aurich. B.S. in Petroleum Engring., U. Tex., 1952; grad. exec. program in bus. adminstrn., Columbia U., 1968, Harvard U., 1979. Petroleum engr. S.W. div. Sun Oil Co., 1952-58; with Venezuelan Sun Oil Co., 1958-72, resident mgr., Maracaibo, 1965-70; v.p., gen. mgr., Maracaibo, 1970-72; ops. mgr. Region I, Internat. Sun Oil Co., Phila., 1972, dir. corp. materials mgmt., 1972-74, mgr. refineries Product Group, 1974-75, v.p. human resources and communications services, 1975-77; pres. Sunoco Energy Devel. Co., Dallas, 1977—. Mem. Nat. Caol Assn. (bd. dirs.). Methodist. Home: 7218 Dye Dr Dallas TX 75248 Office: 12700 Park Central Pl Suite 1500 Dallas TX 75251

HORNBACK, JOSEPH HOPE, educator; b. Nevada, Mo., Apr. 20, 1910; s. Joseph Thomas and Geordia (Munn) H. A.B., Central Coll., 1932; M.A., Harvard, 1933; Ph.D., U. Ill., 1952; postgrad., U. Chgo., 1933-34, 41-42, 46-49. Tchr. math. Calumet City (Ill.) High Sch., 1934-37, U. Chgo. Lab Sch., 1937-42; asst. prof. math. U. Ala., 1952-57, asso. prof., 1957-63, prof., 1963-80, prof. emeritus, 1980—; vis. scientist to high schs. for Ala. Acad. Sci. Chmn. gen. bd. 1st Christian Ch., Tuscaloosa, Ala., 1974-76; mem. world outreach com. Christian Chs. of Ala., 1973-75. Served as lt. USNR, 1942-46. Mem. Am. Math. Soc., Math. Assn. Am., Sigma Xi, Phi Kappa Phi. Club: Mason. Home: Bent Tree Apt 145 900 Hargrove Rd Tuscaloosa AL 35401 Office: Dept Math U Ala University AL 35486

HORNBEAK, HAROLD LANCASTER, architect; b. Springfield, Mo., May 5, 1913; s. Harold Leslie and Flora Miller (Silsby) H.; m. Margaret Anne Getchell, Dec. 31, 1948. Student, DePauw U., 1931-34; B.S., Washington U., St. Louis, 1948; M.S., Tex. A&M U., 1955. Ops. agt. Eastern Airlines, Jacksonville, Fla., 1939-40, St. Louis, 1940-41; engr. McDonnell Aircraft Corp., St. Louis, 1941-43, 45-46, 48-49; asst. prof. architecture Tex. A&M U., 1949-55; asso. prof. architecture U. Ill., Urbana, 1955-62, prof., 1962—; dir. architecture overseas program, Versailles, France, 1969-72. Served with inf. U.S. Army, 1944-46. Decorated Purple Heart. Mem. Am. Soc. Engring. Edn. (chmn. div. archtl. engring. 1964-66), Am. Legion, SAR, Sigma Xi (asso.), Tau Beta Pi Assn. Episcopalian. Office: 312 Architecture U Ill Urbana IL 61801 *The few honors and awards which I've received have not come by seeking them, but as a by-product of doing the best I could on the task at hand.*

HORNBEIN, PHILIP, JR., lawyer; b. Denver, Nov. 15, 1915; s. Philip and Flora (Anfenger) H.; m. Anne Ashkinazy, July 20, 1967. B.A., U. Colo., 1937, LL.B., 1939. Bar: Colo. bar 1939. Partner firm Hornbein & Hornbein, Denver, 1946-74, Hornbein, MacDonald & Fattor, 1974—; mem. Colo. Supreme Ct. Nominating Commn., 1972-78. Served with U.S. Army, 1942-45. Fellow Am. Coll. Trial Lawyers; mem. Am. Law Inst., Am. Bar Assn. Democrat. Jewish. Home: 255 Dexter St Denver CO 80220 Office: 1600 Broadway Denver CO 80202

HORNBEIN, THOMAS F., physician; b. St. Louis, 1930. M.D., Washington U., St. Louis, 1956. Diplomate: Am. Bd. Anesthesiology. Intern King County Hosp., Seattle, 1956-57; resident in anesthesiology Washington U. Hosp., 1957-59, research fellow in respiratory physiology, 1959-61; asst. in anesthesiology Barnes Hosp., St. Louis, 1960-61; asst. prof. anesthesiology U. Wash., 1963-67, asso. prof., 1967-70, prof. anesthesiology, 1970—, prof. physiology and biophysics, 1970—, vice chmn. dept. anesthesiology, 1972-74, chmn. dept., 1978—. Served to lt. comdr. USNR, 1961-63. Office: U Wash Sch of Medicine RN-10 Seattle WA 98195

HORNBEIN, VICTOR, architect; b. Denver, Oct. 26, 1913; s. Samuel and Rose (Frumess) H.; m. Ruth Kriesler, Mar. 20, 1947; children: Victoria Ann, Peter. Student, Atelier Denver, Beaux-Arts Inst. Design, 1930-35. Practice as Victor Hornbein, architect, 1940-60; with firm Victor Hornbein and Edward D. White, Jr., Denver, 1960-76, partner, 1960-76; prin. Victor Hornbein & Assos., Denver, 1976-80; partner Victor Hornbein & John James, 1980-82; prin. Victor Hornbein, Architect, 1982—; vis. lectr. U. Denver, 1949-52, U. Colo., 1958-59, 68, 75, mem. design rev. bd., 1969-73; design adv. panel region 8 Gen. Services Adminstrn., 1967-70. Major works include: conservatory and edn. bldg. Denver Bot. Gardens, 1966-71; Major works include: Porter Library, Colo. Women's Coll., Denver, 1962, Bethesda Hosp., Denver, 1970, René Spitz Children's div. Ft. Logan Mental Health Center, Denver, 1965, housing for elderly, 1973, Sanctuary Wellshire Presbyn. Ch., 1980, Orchid and Bromeliad House, Denver Bot. Gardens, 1980. Pres. Met. Council Community Services, 1957; bd. advisors Wright-Ingraham Inst., 1972—, trustee, 1974—, chmn. bd. trustees, 1975-82. Served with AUS, 1942-45. Decorated Bronze Star. Fellow AIA (pres. Colo. Central chpt. 1971). Home: 266 Jackson St Denver CO 80206 Office: 90 Madison St Denver CO 80206

HORNBLOWER, RALPH, JR., stock broker, investment banker; b. Boston, Feb. 1, 1919; s. Ralph and Eleanor (Greenwood) H.; m. Priscilla Alder Blumer, Feb. 9, 1944 (dec. Feb. 1960); children: Rosalie (Mrs. Catlin), Ralph III, Paul Skinner, Priscilla; m. Phoebe Mary Blumer, Oct. 12, 1960; children: John Greenwood, David Maitland, James Wainwright. Student, Milton Acad., 1934-37; B.S., Harvard U., 1941. Mem. N.Y. Stock Exchange., N.Y. Futures Exchange. Bd. dirs. Greenwich Boys Club Assn., Henry Hornblower Fund, Inc. Clubs: Owl (Cambridge, Mass.); Round Hill (Greenwich); Edgartown (Mass.) Golf; Squibnocket Associates (Chilmark, Mass.). Home: 10 Pine Ridge Rd Greenwich CT 06830

HORNBRUCH, FREDERICK WILLIAM, JR., corporation consultant; b. Roselle, N.J., July 14, 1913; s. Frederick William and Elsa M. (Becker) H.; m. Helen Novak, Apr. 10, 1936; children: Frederick William III, Harlan Richard. M.E., Stevens Inst. Tech., 1934. Engr. Weston Elec. Instrument Corp., Newark, 1934-40, Falstrom Co., Passaic, N.J., 1940-41; indsl. engr. Bendix Aviation Corp., Phila., 1941-43; prodn. mgr. Columbia Machine Works, Bklyn., 1943-44; chief engr., dir. Rath & Strong, Inc., Boston, 1944-57; v.p. Landers, Frary & Clark, Inc., New Britain, Conn., 1957-59, Atlas Corp., N.Y.C., 1959-64, dir., 1962-64; pres., dir. Titeflex, Inc., Springfield, Mass., 1960-64, Internat. Air, Inc., N.Y.C., 1962; chmn. bd. Metronics Corp., Santa Monica, Calif., 1960-64; v.p. Calumet & Hecla, Inc., Chgo., gen. mgr., 1964-68; v.p. Aero-Chatillon Corp., N.Y.C., 1968-69; v.p. adminstrn. Macrodyne-Chatillon Corp., N.Y.C., 1969; organizer cons. bus., Barrington Hills, Ill., 1970—. Author: (with Bruce, Chadruc) Practical Planning and Scheduling, 1950, Raising Productivity, 1977; Contbr. to: Handbook Bus. Administrn, 1967;

contbr., mem. adv. bd.: Handbook Modern Manufacturing Management, 1967-68. Mem. ASME, Soc. Advancement Mgmt., Newcomen Soc., Tau Beta Pi, Pi Delta Epsilon, Phi Sigma Kappa. Presbyn. Clubs: Engineers (N.Y.C.); Barrington Hills Country. Patentee instrument for synchronizing aircraft engines. Address: Rural Route 2 Three Lakes Rd Barrington Hills IL 60010 *Constructive creativity and high productivity are the source of lasting achievements for both individuals and nations. Real wealth is measured by the capacity to produce and enjoy worthwhile ideas and things. Thinking is work. Producing is work. The world is a big and wonderful place. There's room and resources for everyone. Our goal, then, must be to bring all people of the world to believe in working for betterment.*

HORNBY, LESLEY (TWIGGY), singer, actress; b. London, Eng., Sept. 19, 1949; d. William Norman and Helen (Reeman) H.; m. Michael Whitney; 1 dau., Carly. Student, Brondesbury and Kilburn Grammar Sch., 1960-66. Model, 1966-76; dir., mgr. Twiggy Enterprises Ltd., 1966—. Starred in: movies The Boy Friend, 1971, W, There Goes the Bride; recs. Here I Go Again, Twiggy, Get the Name Right; author: Twiggy: An Autobiography, 1975 *

HORNBY, WILLIAM HARRY, newspaperman; b. Kalispell, Mont., July 14, 1923; s. Lloyd G. and Margaret E. (Miller) H.; children: Margaret (dec.), Megan, Melinda, John, Mary Catherine. A.B. in Humanities, Stanford U., 1944, M.A. in Journalism, 1947; postgrad., U. London, Eng., 1949-50. Reporter, copyreader San Francisco News, 1947-48; reporter A.P., San Francisco, 1949; research asst. Hoover Library, Stanford, 1949-50; info. officer ECA, Paris and The Hague, 1950-52; asst. gen. mgr. Kalispell Lumber Co., 1953-56, partner, 1955-62; reporter Great Falls (Mont.) Tribune, 1957; copy-desk chief, editorial writer Denver Post, 1957-60, mng. editor, 1960-70, exec. editor, v.p., 1970-77, editor, v.p., 1977-82, sr. editor, 1982—; v.p. Yellowstone Newspapers, Inc., Livingston, Mont. Bd. dirs. Buffalo Bill Meml. Assn., Colo. Hist. Found. Mem. Am. Soc. Newspaper Editors (past pres.), Sigma Delta Chi, Sigma Nu. Republican. Episcopalian. Clubs: Denver, Univ., Denver Country. Lodge: Elks. Office: Denver Post 650 15th St Denver CO 80201

HORNE, CHARLES FRANCIS, III, naval officer; b. San Diego, Mar. 22, 1931; s. Charles Frederick and Evelyn (Tuttle) H.; m. Flora Eustice, Jan. 29, 1955; children: Charles F., Carolyn Helene. B.S., U.S. Naval Acad., 1952; M.S., George Washington U., 1968. Commd. 2d lt. U.S. Navy, 1952; rear admiral U.S Navy, 1979; comdg. officer U.S.S. Robison, San Diego, 1970-71; mil. asst. to asst. sec. intelligence U.S. Navy, Washington, 1971-75; comdg. officer U.S.S. Puget Sound, Norfolk, Va., 1975-77; comdr. Destroyer Squadron num 225, Norfolk, Va., 1977-78, Destroyer Squadron num 10, 1978-79, Mine Warfare Command, Charleston, S.C., 1979—. Decorated Dist. Service medal, Legion of Merit (3), Bronze Star, Meritorious Service medal. Mem. Naval Inst. Procs. Episcopalian. Home: Quarters B Naval Sta Charleston SC 29408 Office: Commander Mine Warfare Comman Naval Sta Charleston SC 29408

HORNE, DAVID HAMILTON, publisher; b. Worcester, Mass., Oct. 26, 1912; s. Ralph Hamilton and Harriet (Scott) H.; m. Elinor McCullough Clark, Nov. 6, 1948; children: Susan Hamilton, Beverly Palmer, Shirley Scott. A.B. magna cum laude with honors in English, Clark U., 1942; M.A., U. Mo., 1947; Ph.D., Yale U., 1950. Instr. English U. Mo., 1942-43, 46-47; instr. English Yale, 1950-52, univ. series editor, 1958-65; fellow Timothy Dwight Coll., 1962-65; with Yale U. Press, 1954-65, exec. editor, 1961-65; asst. dir. Harvard U. Press, 1966-67, assoc. dir., 1967-72; dir. U. Press of New Eng., 1972-79; pres., treas. Horne Assocs., Inc., Hanover, N.H., 1960—. Author: The Life and Minor Works of George Peele, 1952; Editor: (Shakespeare) The Tempest, 1955. Mem. Phi Beta Kappa. Home and Office: PO Box 246 West Lebanon NH 03784

HORNE, HARRY JAMES, Canadian foreign service officer; b. Shaunavon, Sask., Can., Oct. 8, 1916; s. Bernard James and Rose Catherine (Bourque) H.; m. Betty Jean Lewter, Aug. 25, 1979; children: Christopher Anthony, Mary Elizabeth. B.Comm., U. B.C., 1942; M.B.A., U. Toronto, 1947. Joined Can. Fgn. Service; served as trade commr., Norway, Sweden, Peru, Pakistan, Chgo., Ger., consul gen., Australia, Atlanta, San Francisco. Contbr. articles to profl. jours. Served with Can. Army, 1942-46. Mem. Trade Commr. Service Career Fgn. Ser. Officers. Address: Route 7 Box 33D Murfreesboro TN 37130

HORNE, HOMA JUDSON, banker; b. Live Oak, Fla., June 1, 1921; s. Homa Judson and Ruth Valroice (Cook) H.; m. Vivian Maxine Barnett, Sept. 20, 1946; children: Yvonne, Keith, Nancy, Connie. B.S. in Bus. Adminstrn., U. Fla., 1949. Mgr. acctg. div. Gulf Life Ins. Co., 1953-64, staff asst., 1965-69; acctg. officer Fla. Nat. Bank, Jacksonville, 1969-71, comptroller, 1972-83; tchr. accounting Am. Inst. Banking. Treas. Arlingwood Civic Assn., 1969. Served with USNR, 1942-45. Mem. Fin. Execs. Inst. Baptist (treas. 1964-66, 73-80 gen. supt. Sunday sch. 1967-69). Home: 1441 Arlingwood Ave Jacksonville FL 32211 Office: 214 Hogan St Jacksonville FL 33202

HORNE, JOHN E., insurance company executive; b. Clayton, Ala., Mar. 4, 1908; s. John Eli and Cornelia (Thomas) H.; m. Ruth F. Kleinman, July 27, 1938; children: Linda (Mrs. Richard Clark), Susan (Mrs. James K. Ewart). Normal certificate, Troy State U., 1928; A.B. with honors, U. Ala., 1933; M.A. (fellow in history 1933-35), U. Ala., 1941, LL.D., 1970, Troy State U., 1982. Tchr., Pike County, Ala., 1925-26, Columbiana, Ala., 1928-31; rep. Macmillan Pub. Co., 1935-39, Row, Peterson Pub. Co., 1939-42, 46; adminstrv. asst. to Senator John J. Sparkman of Ala., 1947-51, 53-61; adminstr. Small Def. Plants Adminstrn., 1951-53; staff dir. Democratic Senatorial Campaign Com., 1954; asst. campaign mgr. to Adlai E. Stevenson, 1956; exec. dir. Nat. Citizens Com. Kennedy-Johnson, 1960; adminstr. Small Bus. Adminstrn., 1961-63; mem. Fed. Home Loan Bank Bd., 1963-68; chmn., 1965-68; pres. Investors Mortage Ins. Co., 1969-70, chmn., 1970-78; pres. John E. Horne Assos., 1979—; dir. Continental Investment Corp., Boston, Tiger IMI, Midwest Fed. Savs. & Loan Assn., Mpls.; mem. adv. com. FNMA; mem. adv. council Fed. Home Loan Bank Bd.; Disting. vis. prof. Troy State U., 1978—, Adams-Bibby Chair Free Enterprise, 1983—. Pres. Pi Kappa Alpha Meml. Found., 1967-69; trustee Coop. Housing Found., 1976—, Nat. Small Bus. Assn., 1979—; treas. Nat. Housing Conf., 1978—. Served from lt. (j.g.) to lt. (s.g.) USNR, 1943-46; capt. Res.; ret.). Recipient Letter of Commendation for meritorious Navy service, Outstanding D.C. Alumnus award U. Ala., 1965, Outstanding Troy State U. Alumnus award, 1967; named one of 50 outstanding contbrs. to better housing in Am. Nat. Housing Conf., 1981. Mem. Fla. Jr. C. of C., Am. Legion, SCV, VFW, Newcomen Soc., Ala. Hist. Soc., Phi Beta Kappa, Omicron Delta Kappa, Phi Delta Kappa, Kappa Delta Pi, Pi Kappa Alpha (chmn. nat. conv. 1958, chmn. distinguished achievement award com. 1961-62, distinguished achievement award 1966, nat. treas. 1966-68, chosen among 200 most famous alumni 1976). Episcopalian. Clubs: Nat. Press, Nat. Capital Democratic (dir.), Congl. Staff, Post Mortem, Burro; Internat., Metropolitan (Washington); Algonquin (Boston); Elks. Home: 415 Crown View Dr Alexandria VA 22314

HORNE, L. DONALD, business executive; b. N.Y.C., Feb. 20, 1933; s. Louis and Florence (Arnett) H.; m. Cathleen Marie Hackett, Feb. 17, 1935; children: Patricia, William, Kimberly, Bradley. B.B.A., Pace U., 1955. Budget dir. Hudson Pulp and Paper Co., 1958-63; v.p. fin. P. Ballantine & Sons, Newark, 1963-69; group controller Litton Industries, N.Y.C., 1969-70; v.p. fin. The Mennan Co., Morristown, N.J., 1970-72, sr. v.p. adminstrn. and fin., 1972-75, pres. internat., 1975-77, pres., 1977-81, chmn. bd., chief exec. officer, 1981—; dir. Mohawk Data Scis., Parsippany, N.J., Cosmetic, Toiletry and Frangrance Assn., Washington. Trustee Pace U., N.Y.C., 1981—, Morris Mus. Arts and Scis., Morristown, 1980—; chmn. Morris County C. of C., 1977—; mem. corp. Moristown Meml. Hosp., 1971—. Named Alumni of Yr. Pace U., 1980. Mem. Fin. Execs. Inst., N.Y. State Soc. C.P.A.s. Club: Morris Country Golf. Office: The Mennan Co Hanover Ave Morristown NJ 07960

HORNE, LENA, singer; b. Bklyn., June 30, 1917; m. Lennie Hayton, Dec. 1947 (dec. 1971). Dancer, Cotton Club, 1934; toured, recorded with, Noble Sissle Orch., 1935-36; with, Charlie Barnet's Band, 1940-41; became cafe soc. singer; starred in: motion pictures Cabin in the Sky, Stormy Weather, Death of a Gunfighter, Thousands Cheer, I Dood It, Swing Fever, Broadway Rhythm, Two Girls and a Sailor, Ziegfield Follies, Panama Hattie, Till the Clouds Roll By, Words & Music, Duchess of Idaho, Meet Me in Las Vegas; others; singer popular music; TV appearances include spl. Harry and Lena, 1970; theatrical appearances in Dance with Your Gods, Blackbird; Author: (with Richard Schickel) Lena, 1965. Address: 1200 S Arlington Ave Los Angeles CA 90024 *

HORNE, MARILYN, mezzo-soprano, soprano; b. Bradford, Pa.; m. Henry Lewis; 1 child. Ed., U. So. Calif.; Mus.D., Rutgers U., 1970, Jersey City State Coll.; D.Litt., St. Peter's Coll. Operatic debut as Hata in: The Bartered Bride, Los Angeles Guild Opera; La Scala debut in: Oepidus Rex, 1969; Met. Opera debut as Adalgisa in: Norma, 1970; other roles include Rosina in: Barber of Seville; Cleonte in: The Siege of Corinth; Isabella in: L'Italiana in Algieri; Carmen at, Met. Opera, 1972-73; Laura in: Harvest, Chgo. Lyric Opera; other appearances include, Venice Festival (invitation Igor Stravinsky), San Francisco Opera (Marie in Wozzeck), Am. Opera Soc., N.Y.C., for several seasons; including roles in Iphigenie en Tauride, Semiramide), Vancouver Opera (Adalgisa in Norma), Philharmonic Hall, N.Y.C., Paris, Dallas, Houston, Covent Garden, London, (in Wozzeck); appeared as Italiana: La Scala, 1975, ann. recital at, Carnegie Hall, European tour with husband for, Dept. State, 1963; rec. artist for, London, Columbia and RCA records. Leading exponent florid vocal style. Address: care Columbia Artists Mgmt Inc 165 W 57th St New York NY 10019 *

HORNER, B. ELIZABETH, biologist; b. Merchantville, N.J., Apr. 29, 1916; d. Larson and Bessie Coles (Collins) H. B.S., Douglass Coll., 1938; M.A., Smith Coll., 1940; Ph.D. (Horace H. Rackham fellow), U. Mich., 1948. Instr. dept. zoology Smith Coll., 1940-44, 46-48, asst. prof. zoology, 1948-57, asso. prof., 1957-63, prof., 1963-70, Myra M. Sampson prof. biol. scis., 1970—; mem. various adv. coms. for conservation edn., Mass., N.H., Nev. AAUW fellow, 1954-55; USPHS and NSF grants. Fellow AAAS; mem. Am. Soc. Mammalogists (life), Australian Mammal Soc. (council 1963-64), Animal Behavior Soc., Soc. Study Evolution, Sigma Xi (pres. Smith Coll. chpt. 1965-66). Quaker. Research, publs. on ecol., behavioral and anat. aspects of small mammals of N. Am. and Australia. Office: Smith Coll Northampton MA 01063

HORNER, HARRY, art director, designer performing arts; b. Vienna, Austria, July 24, 1910; came to U.S., 1935, naturalized, 1940; s. Felix and Gisela (Kohn) H.; m. Betty Arnold Pfaelzer, Sept. 22, 1938 (dec.); m. Joan Frankel, 1952; children: James, Christopher, Tony. Archtl. engring. degree, U. Vienna, 1932; grad., Max Reinhardt Sem., State Acad. Theater, 1932. Pres. Enterprises Films Can., 1964—; mng. dir. Anglo Enterprise Films, London, 1966. Designer numerous Broadway plays and musicals; designer pageants for, N.Y.C. R.R., Cleve., 1937, N.Y. World's Fair, 1939-40; prodns. designed for Broadway include Eternal Road, 1936, World We Make, Lady in the Dark (mus.), The World of Christopher Blake, 1947, Joy to the World, Me and Molly, 1948, Herod, Family Portrait, Star and Garter; prodns. designed for motion pictures include Our Town, 1940, A Double Life, The Heiress, 1948 (Acad. award), Separate Tables, Born Yesterday, Wonderful Country, The Hustler (Acad. award), They Shoot Horses, Don't They?, 1969 (Acad. award nominee), Who is Harry Kellerman, 1970, Lady Sings the Blues, 1971, Up the Sandbox, 1972, Black Bird, 1974, Harry and Walter Are Going To New York, 1975, Audrey Rose, 1976, The Driver, 1977, Moment by Moment, 1978; motion picture dir., 20th Century Fox Films, 1951—; pictures directed include The Jazz Singer, 1980; operas designed and directed include Dialogues of the Carmelites, 1957, David, 1956, Magic Flute for Met. Opera, 1956; also operas for, Vancouver (B.C., Can.) Festivals, San Francisco Opera, others; producer, dir.: TV series Royal Canadian Mounted Police; also dir.: Gunsmoke. Served with USAAF, 1943-45. Recipient award for best moving picture script on a peace theme League of Nations, 1932. Mem. Screen Dirs. Guild, United Scenic Artist Union, Soc. Motion Picture Art Dirs., Acad. Motion Picture Arts and Scis., Canadian Dirs. Guild. Jewish. Home: 728 Brooktree Rd Pacific Palisades CA 90272

HORNER, JACK HENRY, transporation company executive; b. Blaine Lake, Sask., Can., July 20, 1927; s. Ralph Byron and May (MacArthur) H.; m. Leola Margaret Funnell, Apr. 11, 1950; children: Blaine, Craig, Brent. Ed., Univ. Alta. Can. Mem. Parliament of Can., Ottawa, Ont., 1958-79; minister without portfolio Govt. Can., Ottawa, 1977, minister of industry, trade and commerce, 1977-79; chmn. House of Commons Transport Com., Ottawa, 1972-74, Can. Nat. Rys., Montreal, Que., 1982—; dir. Can. Nat. Rys., Montreal, Que., 1980-82. Author: My Own Brand, 1979. Liberal. United Ch. of Canada. Office: Can Nat Rys 935 Lagauchetier St W Montreal PQ Canada H3C 3N4

HORNER, JAMES M., univ. pres.; b. Phillipsburg, Mo., Feb. 26, 1935; s. Cecil Edgar and Linnie Ann (McCoy) H.; m. Evelyn Jane Thieme, June 22, 1957; children—Steven Richard, Karen Elizabeth. B.S., U. Ala., 1961, M.A., 1962, Ph.D., 1964. Asso. sr. research mathematician Gen. Motors, Warren, Mich., 1964-65; asst. prof. math. U. Ala., Huntsville, 1965-67, asso. prof., 1967-72, prof., 1972-75, chmn. dept., 1966-68, 70-72, dean of faculty, 1972-75; v.p., provost Ill. State U., Normal, 1975-79; pres. Central Mo. State U., Warrensburg, 1979—; dir., cons. Intertech Research Services, Inc., Huntsville, 1968-70; cons. Northrop Space Labs., Huntsville, 1966-67. Served with U.S. Army, 1958-60. NDEA fellow, 1961-64. Mem. Math. Assn. Am. Office: Office of Pres Central Mo State U Warrensburg MO 64093

HORNER, JOHN EDWARD, college president; b. Passaic, N.J., Dec. 12, 1921; s. William Joseph and Cardera Estelle (Bissell) H.; m. Anne Catherine Evans, Aug. 16, 1952; children—Joanne, Jeffrey, Heather, Scott. A.B. cum laude, Drew U., 1943, LL.D. (hon.), 1971; M.A., Columbia, 1947; Ph.D., Ohio State U., 1955; Litt.D. (hon.), Morehead State U., 1975, LL.D., Ind. U., 1978, Wabash Coll., 1978, Ind. State U., 1979; L.H.D., Ill. Coll., 1980. Tchr. Latin, English, coach Morristown (N.J.) High Sch., 1945-49, Fulbright exchange tchr. and scholar, Latin, English, coach, London, Eng., 1949-50; instr. Latin, English Drew U., 1950-52; asst. prof., dir. athletics and coach Kans. Wesleyan U., 1952-53, asst. to pres., 1953-54; instr., adminstrv. asst. Ohio State U., 1954-56; asst. to pres. U. Omaha, 1956-58, asst. to pres., dean, 1957-58; pres. Hanover Coll., 1958—; Mem. survey com. higher edn. in, Nebr., 1957; mem. commn. on research and service, cons., examiner North Central Assn. Colls. and Secondary Schs.; participant leadership tng. project North Central Assn., 1957-58; exec. bd. of commn. colls. and univs.; mem. commn. on students and faculty Assn. Am. Colls.; bd. dirs. Ind. Colls. and Univs. Ind., sec. Council Ind. Colls., 1981—; mem. nat. com. Nat. Congress Ch.-Related Colls. and Univs.; mem. Gov.'s Task Force on Guaranteed Student Loan Secondary Market. Contbr. articles profl. jours. Mem. Ind. Library and Hist. Bd., pres., 1974; mem. Nat. Presbyn. Scholarship Com.; v.p. Historic Madison, Inc.; mem. Adv. Council on the Centennial History of Ind. Gen. Assembly, 1976; chmn. Ind. Student Assistance Commn., 1977. Named Sagamore of Wabash by Gov. Ind.; Ky. Col. Mem. Ind. State Scholarship Commn., Ind. Conf. Higher Edn. (pres. 1965-66), Ind. Assn. Ch.-Related and Ind. Colls. (pres. 1962-63), Classical Assn. Middle West and South, Am. Assn. Presidents of Ind. Colls. and Univs. (dir., treas. 1973, pres. 1978—), Assn. Higher Edn., Commn. Acad. Freedom and Tenure, AIM (fellow pres.'s council), Presbyn. Coll. Union (pres.), Asso. Colls. Ind. (pres. 1968), Newcomen Soc., Phi Delta Kappa. Presbyn. (ruling elder; mem. task force on edn. Synod Lincoln Trails). Clubs: University (N.Y.C.); Columbia, Rotary. Address: Hanover Coll Hanover IN 47243

HORNER, LORENZO DAVID, III, banker, author, historian; b. Lynchburg, Va., Dec. 13, 1934; s. Lorenzo David, Jr. and Katherine (Byers) H.; m. Jayne Bond, Sept. 10, 1955; children—Valerie Jayne, Victoria Lynn, Julie Bond. B.A., U. Va., 1956; Grad. degree, Stonier Grad. Sch. Banking, Rutgers U., 1967. With Bank of Va., Richmond, 1959-74, exec. v.p., 1969-74; pres. Bank of Central Va., Lynchburg, 1966-68; pres., chief exec. officer, chmn. bd. Southeast First Nat. Bank Maitland, Fla., 1974-75; chmn. Southeast Bank East Orange, Orlando, Fla., 1974-77; pres., chief exec. officer S.E. Nat. Bank of Orlando, 1974-77; cons., dir. ComBank, Winter Park, Fla., 1977-78; pres., chief exec. officer Gulf States Fast Foods, Inc. (Arthur Treacher's Fish & Chips), Orlando, 1977-78, Fla. Food Industries, Inc. (Popeye's Famous Fried Chicken), Winter Park, 1977—. Author: Shipwrecks, Skin Divers and Sunken Gold, 1965, Better Scuba Diving for Boys, 1966, The Blockade Runners, 1968, The Treasure Galleons, 1971. Bd. dirs., pres. Central Fla. YMCA; treas., trustee Edgewood Boys Ranch. Served with USNR, 1956-58. Mem. Am. Banking Assn. (state v.p.), Va. Bankers Assn. (past pres. young bankers sect.), Va. Skin Divers Assn. (past pres.). Club: Explorers (N.Y.). Home: 121 Variety Tree Circle Altamonte Springs FL 32701 Office: 2131 Lee Rd Winter Park FL 32789

HORNER, MATINA SOURETIS, college president; b. Boston, July 28, 1939; d. Demetre John and Christine (Antonopoulos) Souretis; m. Joseph L. Horner, June 25, 1961; children: Tia Andrea, John, Christopher. A.B. cum laude, Bryn Mawr Coll., 1961; M.S., U. Mich., 1963, Ph.D., 1968; LL.D., Dickinson Coll., 1973, Mt. Holyoke Coll., 1973, U. Pa., 1975, Smith Coll., 1979, Wheaton Coll., 1979; L.H.D. (hon.), U. Mass., 1973, Tufts U., 1976, U. Hartford, 1980. Teaching fellow U. Mich., Ann Arbor, 1962-66, lectr. motivation personality, 1968-69; lectr. social relations Harvard U., 1969-70, asst. prof. clin. psychology dept. social relations, 1970-72, asso. prof. psychology and social relations, 1972—; also cons. univ. health services; pres. Radcliffe Coll., 1972—; mem. council advisors Catalyst, 1976—; mem. nat. panel to study declining test scores Coll. Entrance Exam. Bd., 1976-77; dir. Time, Inc., Fed. Res. Bank Boston. Contbr. psychol. articles on motivation to profl. jours. Mem. adv. council NSF, 1977—, chmn., 1980—; trustee Groton Sch., 1977, Twentieth Century Fund, 1973—; bd. scholars Higher Edn. Research Inst.; bd. dirs. Population Inst., 1977-80, Women's Research and Edn. Inst., 1979—; chmn. research com. Women's Research and Edn. Inst., 1982—; hon. bd. dirs. Mass. Children's Lobby; mem. President's Commn. for Nat. Agenda for 1980s, 1979-80; mem. exec. com., chmn. Task Force on Quality Am. Life in '80s, 1979-80; mem. adv. com. Women's Leadership Conf. on Nat. Security, 1982—. Mem. UN Assn. (nat. policy panel to study U.S.-China relations 1978-79), Nat. Inst. Social Scis., Phi Beta Kappa, Phi Delta Kappa, Phi Kappa Phi. Office: Office of Pres Radcliffe College 10 Garden St Cambridge MA 02138

HORNER, RICHARD ELMER, electronics company executive; b. Wrenshall, Minn., Oct. 24, 1917; s. Marion Chester and Maude Nancy (Eckert) H.; m. Jean Margaret Hodgson, June 21, 1941; children—Richard James, Judith Rae. B.S. in Aero. Engring, U. Minn., 1940; M.S., Princeton U., 1947; postgrad., Ohio State U., 1948. Commd. 2d lt. USAAF, 1940, advanced through grades to col., 1948; comdr. (86th Bomb Squadron), MTO, 1942-43, dir. flight test engring., Wright Field, 1944-45, 47-49, tech. dir., 1950-55, dep. asst. sec. air force, 1955-57, asst. sec. air force for research and devel., 1957-59; asso. adminstr. NASA, 1959-60; sr. v.p. tech. Northrop Corp., Beverly Hills, Calif., 1960-70; pres. E.F. Johnson Co., Waseca, Minn., 1970-82, chmn., 1980—; dir. 1st Nat. Bank Waseca, Northrop, Los Angeles, Medtronic Inc., Mpls., Western Union, Upper Saddle River, N.J. Trustee Fuller Theol. Sem., Pasadena, Calif. Decorated Silver Star, Air medal with clusters. Fellow Am. Inst. Aeros. and Astronautics (past pres.), Am. Astronautical Soc.; mem. Electronic Industries Assn. (gov.). Congregationalist. Home: 905 11th St NE Waseca MN 56093 Office: E F Johnson Co 299 10th Ave SW Waseca MN 56093

HORNER, ROBERT DAVID, construction company executive; b. Chgo., Jan. 1, 1947; s. Robert Thomas and Doris Ruth (Schech) H.; m. Judith L. Moberg, Aug. 19, 1967; 1 son, William Thomas. B.B.A. with highest distinction, Northwestern U., 1971; M.B.A., NYU, 1975. Ops. mgr., cash mgr. Weeden & Co., Chgo. and N.Y.C., 1968-74; sr. cons. Touche Ross & Co., Detroit, 1974-76; v.p. fin. and adminstrn. Herman Transport, Omaha, 1976-78; v.p. fin., treas. Pulte Home Corp., West Bloomfield, Mich., 1978-80; corp. v.p., pres., gen. mgr. Ill. div. Pulte Home Corp., Hoffman Estates, Ill., 1980-82, corp. sr. v.p. fin. services, 1982—; chmn. bd. ICM Mortgage Corp., Denver, 1983—. Mem. leadership com. Boy Scouts Am., 1976-78; mem. Lutheran Schs. of Omaha Planning Study Group, 1976-77; bd. elders St. Matthew's Luth. Ch. Mem. Am. Mgmt. Assn., Homebuilders Assn. Greater Chgo. (bd. govs.), Young Pres. Orgn. Republican. Clubs: John Evans (Northwestern U.); Northwestern (Chgo.). Home: 5454 S Emporia Ct Englewood CO 80111 Office: 4380 S Syracuse Suite 200 Denver CO 80237

HORNER, THOMAS HARVEY, banker; b. Cleve., Mar. 29, 1928; s. William Wattles and Caroline Clagett H.; m. Virginia Hopkins Jackson, Sept. 15, 1956. B.A., Denison U., 1950; B.B.A., Western Res. U., 1954. Loan officer Central Nat. Bank, Cleve., 1955-63; asst. v.p. Marine Midland Trust Co., Mohawk Valley, Utica, N.Y., 1963-67; v.p. Union Commerce Bank, Cleve., 1967-70; v.p., chief loan officer, dir. Peoples-Mchts. Trust Co., Canton, Ohio, 1970-75; pres., chief exec. officer, dir. Dime Bank, Canton, 1975-77; sr. v.p. Central Trust Co. Northeastern Ohio NA, Canton, 1977—; dir. Gt. Lake Bancshares, Inc. Trustee Canton Art Inst., 1975—, pres., 1979; trustee E. Central Ohio chpt. Am. Heart Assn., 1974, trustee Ohio affiliate, 1976. Served with U.S. Army, 1950-52. Mem. Robert Morris Assos. (pres. No. Ohio chpt. 1973-74), Am. Inst. Banking (grad. cert. 1959), Am. Bankers Assn. (cert. comml. lender). Episcopalian. Clubs: Chagrin Valley Hunt, Congress Lake, Canton. Office: 101 Central Plaza S Canton OH 44702

HORNER, WILLIAM HARRY, biochemist; b. Kenmore, N.Y., Sept. 30, 1923; s. William Lawrence and Margaret Miller (Forsythe) H.; m. June Ellen Hottel, Jan. 3, 1962; children: Tina, Theodore, Philip, Ellen. Student, Muskingum Coll., 1941-43; M.D., Case Western Res. U., 1947; Ph.D., Cornell U., 1952. Intern Allegheny Gen. Hosp., Pitts., 1947-48; USPHS fellow Cornell U. Med. Coll., N.Y., 1949-51; asst. prof. dept. biochemistry State U. N.Y. Downstate Med. Center, Bklyn., 1952-56, asso. prof., 1956-59; dir. clin. chemistry labs. Georgetown U. Hosp., 1959-60; asso. prof. dept. biochemistry Schs. Medicine and Dentistry Georgetown U., Washington, 1959-61, prof., 1961—, chmn.dept. biochemistry, 1960-81. Contbr. articles to profl. jours. Served with U.S. Army, 1943-46; served to capt. U.S. Army, 1952-54. USPHS grantee, 1959-78, 80-83. Fellow AAAS; mem. Am. Soc. Biol. Chemists, Am. Chem. Soc., Harvey Soc., N.Y. Acad. Scis., Assn. Am. Med. Coll., Sigma Xi. Republican. Home: 5308 Westpath Way Bethesda MD 20816 Office: Georgetown U 3900 Reservoir Rd NW Washington DC 20007

HORNGREN, CHARLES THOMAS, accounting educator; b. Milw., Oct. 28, 1926; s. William Einar and Grace Kathryn (Manning) H.; m. Joan Estelle Knickelbine, Sept. 6, 1952; children: Scott, Mary, Susan, Catherine. B.S., Marquette U., 1949, D.B.A. (hon.), 1976; M.B.A., Harvard U., 1952; Ph.D., U. Chgo., 1955. C.P.A., Wis. Instr. U. Chgo., 1952-54, asst. prof., 1954-55, Marquette U., Milw., 1955-56; assoc. prof. U. Wis.-Milw., 1956-59, U. Chgo., 1959-63, prof., 1963-65; prof. dept. acctg. Stanford (Calif.) U., 1965—; dir. Am. Bldg. Maintenance Industries, San Francisco. Author: Cost Accounting, 5th edit, 1982, Introduction to Management Accounting, 6th edit, 1984, C.P.A. Problems and Approaches to Solutions (two vols.) 5th edit, 1979, Introduction to Financial Accounting, 2d edit., 1984; editor: Prentice-Hall Acctg. Series. Served with AUS, 1944-46. Recipient Alumni Merit award Marquette U., 1973, Edmund W. Littlefield professorship Stanford U., 1973. Mem. Am. Acctg. Assn. (dir. research 1964-66, pres. 1976-77, Outstanding Acctg. Educator award 1973), Am. Inst. C.P.A.s (acctg. prins. bd. 1968-73, council 1978-81), Calif. Soc. C.P.A.s (Faculty Excellence award 1975), Nat. Assn. Accts., Financial Acctg. Standards Bd. (adv. council). Home: 757 Tolman Dr Stanford CA 94305

HORNICK, RICHARD BERNARD, physician; b. Johnstown, Pa., Jan. 27, 1929; s. Paul Steve and Gertrude (Cowan) H.; m. Adele Free, July 3, 1954 (div.); children: Douglas, Thomas, Marcie, Blaine; m. Susan Finnegan. A.B., Johns Hopkins U., 1951, M.D., 1955. Diplomate: Am. Bd. Internal Medicine. Intern Johns Hopkins Hosp., Balt., 1955-56, resident in medicine, 1956-57; mem. faculty U. Md. Med. Sch., 1959-78, head infectious diseases, 1963-78; prof., chmn. dept. medicine U. Rochester, N.Y., 1979—; cons. WHO. Contbr. articles to med. jours. Served with U.S. Army, 1957-59. Fellow ACP (bd. govs., regent); mem. Am. Soc. Microbiology, Am. Fedn. Clin. Research, Am. Soc. Clin. Investigation, Am. Clin. and Climatol. Assn., Assn. Am. Physicians, Infectious Disease Soc. Am. Home: 3350 Elmwood Ave Rochester NY 14610 Office: Strong Meml Hosp 601 Elmwood Ave Rochester NY 14642

HORNIG, DONALD FREDERICK, scientist; b. Milw., Mar. 17, 1920; s. Chester Arthur and Emma (Knuth) H.; m. Lilli Schwenk, July 17, 1943; children: Joanna, Ellen, Christopher, Leslie. B.S., Harvard U., 1940, Ph.D., 1943; LL.D., Temple U., 1964, Boston Coll., 1966, Dartmouth Coll., 1974; D.H.L., Yeshiva U., 1965; D.Sc., U. Notre Dame, 1965, U. Md., 1965, Rensselaer Poly. Inst., 1965, Ripon Coll., 1966, Widener Coll., 1967, U. Wis., 1967, U. Puget Sound, 1968, Syracuse U., 1968, Princeton U., 1969, Seoul Nat. U., Korea, 1973, U. Pa., 1975, Lycoming Coll., 1980; D.Eng., Worcester Poly. Inst., 1967. Research asso. Woods Hole (Mass.) Oceanographic Instn., 1943-44; scientist, group leader Los Alamos Lab., 1944-46; asst. prof. chemistry Brown U., 1946-49, asso. prof., 1949-51, prof., 1951-57; dir. Metcalf Research Lab., 1949- 57, asso. dean grad. sch., 1952-53, acting dean, 1953-54; vis. prof. Princeton U., 1957, prof. chemistry, 1957-64, chmn. dept., 1958-64, Donner prof. sci., 1959-66; spl. asst. sci. and tech. to Pres. U.S., 1964-69; dir. Office Sci. and Tech., 1964-69; chmn. Fed. Council Sci. and Tech., 1964-69; v.p., dir. Eastman Kodak Co., 1969-70; prof. chemistry U. Rochester, 1969-70; pres. Brown U., Providence, 1970-76; hon. research asso. in applied physics Harvard U., 1976-77, prof. chemistry in pub. health, dir. Interdisciplinary Programs in Health, 1977—, Alfred North Whitehead prof. chemistry (public health), 1981—; dir. Upjohn Co., Westinghouse Electric Corp.; Mem. Pres.'s Sci. Adv. Com., 1960-69, chmn., 1964-69, Project Metcalf, Office of Naval Research, 1951-52. Author articles sci. jours. Bd. overseers Harvard U., 1964-70; bd. dirs. Overseas Devel. Council, 1969-75; trustee George Eastman House, 1969-71, Manpower Inst., 1969-76. Decorated Disting. Civilian Service medal, Korea; Guggenheim fellow, 1954-55; Fulbright fellow, 1954-55; recipient Charles Lathrop Parsons award Am. Chem. Soc., 1967, Engring. Centennial award, 1967, Mellon Inst. award, 1968. Fellow Am. Phys. Soc., Am. Acad. Arts and Scis.; mem. Nat. Acad. Scis., Am. Chem. Soc., AAAS, Am. Philos. Soc., Romanian Acad. (fgn.), Sigma Xi. Home: 16 Longfellow Park Cambridge MA 02138

HORNIG, JAMES FREDERICK, educator; b. Milw., Feb. 22, 1929; s. Herbert E. and Edna (Hennig) H.; m. Evalyn Ortelt, Nov. 1, 1952; children—David, Douglas, Linda. B.A., Harvard, 1950; Ph.D., U. Wis., 1954. Chemist E.I. duPont de Nemours & Co., 1956-58; asst. prof. U. Cal. at Riverside, 1958-62; prof. chemistry Dartmouth Coll., 1962—, Albert Bradley Third Century prof., 1975—, asso. dean faculty, dean grad. studies, 1964-75, chmn. environ. studies program, 1976—. Mem. Am. Chem. Soc., Am. Phys. Soc. Home: 10 Occom Ridge St Hanover NH 03755

HORNIK, HENRY, French educator; b. Chorostkow, Poland, Jan. 5, 1927; came to U.S., 1939, naturalized, 1944; s. Harry and Cilli (Huss) H. B.A. (Mayor's scholar), U. Pa., 1949, M.A. (G.L. Harrison scholar), 1951, Ph.D. in French, 1955; postgrad. (Fulbright scholar), U. Sorbonne, 1952-53. Instr. Haverford (Pa.) Coll., 1953-56, Hunter Coll., CUNY, 1956-57; asst. prof. MIT, Cambridge, 1957-59, Johns Hopkins U., Balt., 1960-62; asso. prof. dept. Romance langs. Queens Coll., CUNY, Flushing, 1964-68, prof. French and comparative lit., 1964—; founder, exec. officer Ph.D. in French, 1968-72, dep. exec. officer, 1972-80. Author: Jean Lemaire de Belges, Le Temple d'Honneur et de Vertus, 1957, Three Interpretations of the French Renaissance, 1960, Rabelais and Idealism, 1969, Montaigne and Idealism, 1973, The Philosophical Hermetica, 1975, Studies in French Renaissance Theory and Idealism, 1980, also articles on Renaissance lit. Served with AUS, 1945-46. Mem. AAUP, MLA, Renaissance Soc. Am., Am. Assn. Tchrs. French, Phi Beta Kappa. Jewish. Home: 150-38B Union Turnpike Flushing NY 11367 Office: Dept Romance Languages Queens College Flushing NY 11367

HORNING, MARJORIE GROOTHIUS, pharmacologist, researcher; b. Detroit, Aug. 23, 1917; d. Herman and Nina Jane (Potter) Groothuis; m. Evan C. Horning, Sept. 26, 1942. B.A., Goucher Coll., Balt., 1938; M.S., U. Mich.-Ann Arbor, 1940, Ph.D., 1943; D.Sc. hon., Goucher Coll., 1977. Research chemist Nat. Heart Inst., NIH, Bethesda, Md., 1951-61; research assoc. prof. biochemistry Baylor Coll. Medicine, Houston, 1961-63, assoc. prof., 1963-69, prof., 1969—; mem. Pharmacology-Toxicology Program Project Com., NIH, 1972-76, Bd. Sci. Counselors Nat. Toxicology Program, Research Triangle Park, N.C., 1979-83. Editor: (with J.R. Mitchell) Drug Metabolism and Drug Toxicity, 1984; mem. adv. editorial bd.: Trends in Pharmacol. Scis., 1979—; contbr. articles to profl. jours. Trustee Mus. Fine Arts, Houston, 1975-80, 82—. Recipient Warner-Lambert award Am. Assn. Clin. Chemists, 1976, Founders award Chem. Industry Inst. Toxicology, 1979; mem. Alumnae Athena award U. Mich., 1980. Fellow AAAS; mem. Am. Soc. Pharmacology and Exptl. Therapeutics (sec.-treas. 1981-82, pres. 1984-85), Am. Chem. Soc. (councillor 1974-83, Garvan medal 1977). Home: 11610 Starwood Dr Houston TX 77024 Office: Baylor Coll Medicine 1 Baylor Plaza Houston TX 77030

HORNING, ROSS CHARLES, JR., history educator; b. Watertown, S.D., Oct. 10, 1920; s. Ross Charles and Harriett (Meaghan) H. B.A., Augustana Coll., 1948; M.A., George Washington U., 1952; Ph.D. (Sanders fellow), 1958; postgrad. Russian, Inst. Langs. and Linguistics, Georgetown U., 1952-53. Instr. Wis. State U., Eau Claire, 1958-59; asst. prof. St. John's U., Collegeville, Minn., 1959-64; asso. prof. Russian history and internat. affairs Creighton U., 1964-68, prof., 1968—, pres. faculty, 1984—, also chmn. athletic bd. Mem. council Nebr. com. for humanities Nat. Endowment Humanities. Served with USAAF, 1943-46. Recipient Disting. Faculty Service award Creighton U., 1982; Fulbright scholar, India, summer 1967. Mem. AAAS, Am. Assn. Advancement Slavic Studies, Am. Hist. Assn., Am. Soc. Internat. Law, AAUP, Orgn. Am. Historians, Conf. Slavic and European Studies, Am. Com. for Irish Studies, Assn. Profl. Baseball Players, Omaha Urban League, Joslyn Liberal Arts Soc., S.W. Am. Assn. Advancement Slavic Studies, Western Social Sci. Assn., Am. Fgn. Service Assn., Canadian History Assn., Assn. Canadian Studies in U.S. (exec. council), Assn. Asian Studies, Omaha Symphony Assn., Assn. Canadienne de Sci. Politique, Internat. Law Assn., World Peace Through Law Center, Center for Study of Presidency, Am. Br. Fgn. Service Club (Washington), Nebr. Arts Council, Asia Soc., Opera/Omaha, Fulbright Alumni Assn., Omaha Press Club, Alpha Sigma Nu. Home: 4955 Cuming St Omaha NE 68132

HORNS, HOWARD LOWELL, physician; b. Buffalo, N.D., July 11, 1912; s. Otto and Crystal Belle (Sherwin) H.; m. Edith Marie Frostenson, Sept. 22, 1940; children—James S., Susan M. Horns Kolstad, William H. B.A., U. Minn., 1940, B.S., 1942, M.B., 1943, M.D., 1944. Intern U. Minn. Hosp.; resident in internal medicine; mem. faculty U. Minn. Med. Sch., 1947—, asst. dean, 1949-55, clin. prof. medicine, 1955—; staff physician Nicollet Clinic, Mpls., 1955—; pres. Minn. Bd. Med. Examiners, 1970, Fedn. State Med. Bds. U.S., 1974-75; mem. Nat. Bd. Med. Examiners, 1975—, Liaison Com. Continuing Med. Edn., 1975—. Contbr. articles to med. jours. Bd. dirs. Eitel Hosp., Mpls., 1956—. Served with M.C. AUS, 1953-55. Fellow A.C.P. (gov. 1970-74); mem. AMA, Minn., Mpls. socs. internal medicine, Alpha Omega Alpha. Unitarian. Home: 100 Melbourne Ave SE Minneapolis MN 55414 Office: 2001 Blaisdell Ave Minneapolis MN 55404

HORNSBY, ROGER ALLEN, classics educator; b. Nye, Wis., Aug. 8, 1926; s. Huntley and Lucile (James) Burton; m. Jessie Lynn Gillespie, June 8, 1960. A.B. magna cum laude, Adelbert Coll. Western Res. U., 1949; A.M., Princeton U., 1951, Ph.D., 1952. Instr. U. Iowa, Iowa City, 1954-59, asst. prof., 1959-62, asso. prof., 1962-67, prof. classics, 1967—, chmn. dept., 1966-81; chief reader advance placment Latin IV Ednl. Testing Service, 1965-69. Author: Reading Latin Poetry, 1967, Patterns of Action in the Aeneid, 1970; Contbr. articles on Latin poetry to profl. jours. Mem. council Am. Acad. in Rome, 1974. Served with AUS, 1952-54. Old Gold Research fellow, 1963. Fellow Am. Council Learned Socs.; mem. Am. Philol. Assn. (dir. 1974-77), Classical Assn. Middle W. and S. (pres. 1968-69), Archeol. Inst. Am. (pres. Iowa chpt. 1966-67), Am. Numis. Soc. (council 1973—, 2d 1984—), Am. Council Learned Socs. (del. 1984—). Home: 306 Montclair Park 201 1st Ave N Iowa City IA 52240

HORNUNG, PAUL ANDREW, sports editor; b. New Bavaria, Ohio, July 18, 1917; s. Andrew Jacob and Gertrude (Wolfe) H.; m. Cornelia I. Marshall, Sept. 21, 1940. Student, Ohio State U., 1935-39. Sports editor Ohio State U. Student Lantern, 1938-39; asso. editor Sundial, 1938-39; sports editor Columbus (Ohio) Dispatch, 1956-80; asso. editor Street and Smith Ann. Yearbook of Coll. Football, N.Y., 1960—; Ohio rep. Heisman Trophy Com., 1956—. Mem. Football Writers Am. (dir.), Sigma Delta Chi. Club: Agonis. Home: 3995 Mountview Rd Columbus OH 43221 Office: 34 S 3d St Columbus OH 43216

HORNYAK, EUGENE AUGUSTINE, bishop; b. Kucura, Backa, Yugoslavia, Oct. 7, 1919; emigrated to U.S., 1948, naturalized, 1955; emigrated to Eng., 1961; s. Peter and Juliana (Findrik) H. Ph.B., Pontifical U., Rome, 1941, S.T.D., 1947; J.C.B., Gregorian U., Rome, 1947. Ordained priest Roman Catholic Ch. (Byzantine-Ukranian rite), 1945; asst. priest, Struthers and Warren, Ohio, 1948-49; adminstr. St. Michael's Ch., Newton Falls, Ohio, 1949-50; prof. moral theology, canon law, liturgy, also spiritual dir. Sts. Cyril and Methodius Byzantine Seminary, Pitts., 1950-55; spiritual dir. St. Basil's Ukrainian Minor Seminary, Stamford, Conn., 1958-61; entered Order St. Basil the Great, Can., 1956-57; master novices, also superior St. Josaphat's Monastery, Glen Cove, L.I., 1961; apptd. titular bishop, Hermonthis; also aux. to Cardinal Godfrey (for Ukrainian Catholics in Eng. and Wales), London, 1961-63; bishop-apostolic exarch for Ukrainian Catholics in Eng. and Wales, 1963—, for Ukrainians in Scotland, 1968—; Mem. Cath. hierarchy, Eng., Wales, Scotland; mem. Ukrainian Cath. hierarchy in free world, Pontifical Commn. of Eastern Code of Canon Law, Rome, 1977—; consultor Sacred Congregation for Eastern Cath. Chs., Rome, 1978—; suffragan bishop to Met. See Westminster, London. Home and Office: 22 Binney St London England W1Y 1YN *Our earthly life comes, grows and fades away; it has God's support, it has its aims and its destiny. As a Christian, a monk and a Catholic bishop, I am endeavouring to attain those aims, reach that destiny, and be instrumental in helping and guiding my fellowmen to do likewise, according to the teachings and example of Christ, God incarnate, as faithfully transmitted to us by his Church.*

HOROVITZ, ISRAEL ARTHUR, playwright; b. Wakefield, Mass., Mar. 31, 1939; s. Julius Charles and Hazel (Solberg) H.; m. Doris Keefe, Dec. 25, 1959 (div. 1977); children—Rachael Keefe, Matthew Keefe, Adam Keefe; m. Gillian Adams, July, 1981. Fellow, Royal Acad. Dramatic Art, London, 1961-63; postgrad. in English, City U. N.Y., 1972-77, M.A., Coll. City N.Y., 1977. Am. playwright-in-resident Royal Shakespeare Co., London, 1965; lectr., 1961—; Fanny Hurst prof. theatre arts Brandeis U., 1974-75; artistic dir. N.Y. Playwrights Lab., 1977—, Gloucester (Mass.) Stage Co., 1980—. Author: The Comeback, 1958, The Death of Bernard the Believer, 1960, This Play is About Me, 1961, The Hanging of Emanuel, 1962, Jump, 1962, Hop and Skip, 1963, The Killer Dove, 1963, The Indian Wants the Bronx, 1964-66, It's Called the Sugar Plum, 1965, Line, 1967, Rats, 1967, The Honest-to-God Schnozzola, 1968, Chiaroscuro (or Morning), 1968, The World's Greatest Play, 1968, First Season; collection of plays, 1968, Leader, 1969, Morning, Noon and Night, (with others), 1969, Acrobats, 1971, Play for Germs; TV Dr. Hero, 1972, Shooting Gallery, 1972, The Wakefield Plays; 7-play cycle The Alfred Trilogy: Part 1-Alfred the Great, Part 2-Our Father's Failing, Part 3-Alfred Dies, 1972-77, The Quannapowitt Quartet: Part 1-Hopscotch, Part 2-The 75th, Part 3-Stage Directions, Part 4-Spared, 1971-79; Cappella; novel, 1973; Uncle Snake, 1975, The Great Labor Day Classic, 1979, The Primary English Class, 1975, The Bottom, 1975-76, Mackerel, 1977, Sunday Runners in the Rain, 1979-80, Nobody Loves Me; novella, 1975; play The Reason We Eat, 1976; adaption Ionesco's l'homme aux Valises: Man with Bags, 1977; adaptation from Melville's Bartleby, The Scrivener, 1978; The Former One-On-One Basketball Champion; teleplay Today I Am A Fountain Pen, 1977, A Rosen by Any Other Name, 1979, The Chopin Playoffs, 1978; play The Good Parts, 1979—; teleplay adaptation from Mailer's The Deer Park, 1979-80; adaptation from Dickens Scrooge and Marley, 1980-81; play Park Your Car in the Harvard Yard, 1980-83, The Widow's Blind Date, 1984; film Park Your Car in the Harvard Yard, 1983-84, Fast Eddie, 1980, The Strawberry Statement, 1971, Author! Author!, 1982, Fell, 1982-83, Berta, 1982-83; other films, TV.; Contbr. to nat. mags, plays translated, pub. and performed in more than 20 langs. Recipient Vernon Rice award, 1967-68, Drama Desk award, 1967-68, Jersey Jour. best play award, 1968, Obie award, 1967-68, 68-69, French Critics prize, 1974; Christopher award, 1975; Emmy award, 1975; Rockefeller fellow, 1968-69; Nat. Endowment for Arts fellow, 1974; Fulbright fellow, 1975-76; Guggenheim fellow, 1977-78. Mem. Actors Studio, New Dramatists Com., Eugene O'Neill Found., Authors' League Am. (exec. council). Nationally ranked masters track and road runner. Office: Writers and Artists Agy 160 W 56th St New York NY 10019 Ziegler-Diskant Agy 9255 Sunset Blvd Los Angeles CA 90069

HOROWITZ, BERNARD, furniture company executive; b. N.Y.C., May 20, 1924; s. Isadore and Celia (Kaisch) H.; m. Zelda Hope Jaspan, June 16, 1951; children: Elizabeth, Andrew, Edward, Jessica. B.A., Temple U., 1949. Salesman Futorian Corp., Chgo., 1952-64, regional mgr., 1964-68, v.p. sales, 1972-78, exec. v.p., 1978—; v.p. Barcalounger Co., Chgo., 1968-72. Served with USN, 1943-46. Home: 1154 Lincoln Ave S Highland Park IL 60035 Office: Futorian Corp 666 Lake Shore Dr Chgo IL 60611

HOROWITZ, CHARLES, lawyer; b. Bklyn., Jan. 5, 1905; s. Harry and Fanny (Mirkin) H.; m. Diana Glickman, Mar. 23, 1930; children—Caroline Ann, Elinor Louise. A.B. magna cum laude, U. Wash., 1925, LL.B. summa cum laude, 1927; B.A. (Rhodes scholar) with 1st class honors, Oxford (Eng.) U., 1929, M.A., 1952. Bar: Wash. bar 1927. Asso. Preston, Thorgrimson & Turner (now Preston, Thorgrimson, Ellis & Holman), Seattle, 1929-33, mem. firm, 1933-69, of counsel, 1980—; judge div. 1 Wash. Ct. Appeals, 1969-75, acting chief judge, 1969-70, chief judge, 1971-72; justice Supreme Ct. Wash., 1975-80; lectr. law U. Wash., 1932-33, 39, 45; mem. Jud. Council, 1971-72, vice chmn., 1976-80; Mem. Nat. Conf. Commrs. on Uniform State Laws, mem. spl. probate com., 1962-72, co-chmn., 1968-72; chmn. bd. Judiciary Edn., 1980; mem. Wash. Uniform Legislation Commn., 1960—, chmn., 1966—; chmn. joint editorial bd. Uniform Probate Code, 1970—. Co-editor: Washington Appellate Practice Handbook, 1980. Chmn. bd. N.W. Meml. Hosp. Assn., 1957-59, pres., 1959-61; trustee Wash. Commn. for Humanities, Fred Hutchinson Cancer Research Center; bd. dirs., v.p., sec. Saul Haas Found. Served with USCGR, World War II. Recipient Gonzaga Law medal, 1981. Fellow Am. Coll. Probate Counsel (hon.), Am. Bar Found.; mem. Am. Judicature Soc. (life; dir. 1973-76), Am. Law Inst., ABA, Wash. State Bar Assn. (Spl. Honor award 1980), Seattle Bar Assn. (pres. 1957-58), Order of Barristers (nat. mem.), Phi Beta Kappa (Disting. Service award 1978), Order of Coif. Home: 3923 NE 38th St Seattle WA 98105 Office: IBM Bldg Seattle WA 19101

HOROWITZ, DANIEL L., former foreign service officer; b. Newark, Oct. 7, 1916; s. Samuel and Anna (Litwin) H.; m. Loucele August, May 26, 1940; children: Paul August, Sanda Margaret. B.A., NYU, 1936, M.A., 1940; Littauer fellow, Harvard Sch. Pub. Adminstrn., 1941-42, Ph.D., 1963. Research analyst NLRB, 1936-37; research investigator N.Y. State Dept. Labor, 1937-38; labor relations examiner N.Y. State Labor Relations Bd., 1939-41; lectr. indsl. relations Harvard, also Radcliffe Coll., 1942-43; cons., chmn. disputes panels Nat. War Labor Bd., 1943; labor attache Am. embassy, Santiago, Chile, 1943-46; asst. chief div. internat. labor, social and health affairs Dept. State, 1946-50; labor adviser Bur. European Affairs, 1951-56; adviser U.S. del. UNECOSOC, 1948, 49; research asso. (resident in Italy) Harvard U., 1950-51, 54-55; labor attache, 1st sec., consul Am. embassy, Paris, 1956-60; labor attache, 1st sec., New Delhi, 1960-62; assigned to Nat. War Coll., 1962-63; counselor polit. affairs, The Hague, Netherlands, 1963-65; diplomat-in-residence U. Kans., 1965-66; coordinator, faculty mem. Nat. Inter-Departmental Seminar, 1966-69; dean acad. relations Fgn. Service Inst., State Dept., 1969-71; spl. asst. to sec. state, coordinator internat. labor affairs State Dept. and; dir. Office Labor Affairs, AID, 1971-73; Am. consul gen., Naples, Italy, 1973-75; counselor to cabinet com. on ILO, 1975-77, U.S. rep. to governing body, 1976—; spl. asst. to sec. labor for ILO affairs, 1976-77; U.S. del. to ILO confs., 1971, 72, chmn. U.S. del., 76, 77; del. Inter-Am. Labor Ministers Conf., 1972. Author: The Italian Labor Movement, 1963. Mem. Am. Fgn. Service Assn., Phi Beta Kappa. Home: 5217 Nahant St Bethesda MD 20816

HOROWITZ, DAVID CHARLES, consumer commentator, newspaper columnist; b. N.Y.C., June 30, 1937; s. Max Leo and Dorothy (Lippman) H.; m. Suzanne E. McCambridge, 1973; 2 daus. B.A., Bradley U., 1959; M.S.J., Northwestern U., 1960; CBS fellow, Columbia U., 1962-63. Editor-in-chief Tazewell County (Ill.) Newspaper, 1956; reporter Peoria (Ill.) Jour. Star, 1957-60, Lerner Newspapers and Chgo. City News Bur., 1959-60; newscaster KCCI Radio-TV, Des Moines, 1960-62; newswriter-producer ABC Radio Network, N.Y.C., 1963; far east corr. NBC News, 1963-64; pub. affairs dir. WMCA, N.Y.C., 1964-66; corr., edn. editor, consumer commentator NBC News, Los Angeles, 1966—; syndicated columnist Des Moines Register and Tribune Syndicate; creator, host, exec. producer syndicated TV show Fight Back!, 1978; dir. Ridgedale Farms Horse Breeding Ranch. Author: Fight Back and Don't Get Ripped Off, 1979. Patron Los Angeles County Art Mus.; bd. dirs. Nat. Broadcast Editorial Conf., Am. Cancer Soc.; bd. advisers Los Angeles Jewish Home for Aged, Calif. div. Am. Cancer Soc.; adv. bd. Am. Heart Assn. Los Angeles County, UCLA Publs.; adv. bd. to Los Angeles County Dist. Atty.; bd. dirs. City of Hope. Served with USNR, 1954-62. Recipient Los Angeles City and County citation for public service, 1979, 80, 81, 82, 83, Calif. State Legislature pub. service citation, 1980, 81, 82, 83; Spirit of Life award City of Hope, 1979; Disting. Alumnus award Bradley U., 1983; Chief U.S. Postal Insp.'s award, 1981; Emmy award for consumer reporting, 1974, 76, 77, 81, 82, 83. Mem. Acad. TV Arts and Scis., Internat. Radio-TV Soc., Radio-TV News Dirs. Assn., The Guardians, Alpha Epsilon Pi, Sigma Delta Chi, Phi Delta Kappa. Clubs: Friars, Overseas Press Am. (N.Y.C.). Home: PO Box 49740 Los Angeles CA 90049 *Life is full of compromise, but to compromise principle is to give up your self-respect. I don't want anyone to take me for a sucker, and I don't like to see anyone else taken, either. A lot of things are unfair in life. It's tough; that's the way it is. But, by heaven, if you can do something about it, do it*

HOROWITZ, DAVID H., communications company executive; b. N.Y.C., Sept. 11, 1928; s. Abraham and Florence (Bob) H.; m. Susan Welch, Aug. 9, 1980; children: Marilyn, Roger, Diana, Justin, Adam. A.B., Columbia, 1948, LL.B., 1950. Bar: N.Y. 1950. Asso.-in-law Columbia Law Sch., 1950-51; law clk. Judge Stanley H. Fuld, N.Y. Ct. Appeals, 1951-52; partner firm Schwartz & Frohlich, N.Y.C., 1952-63; with Screen Gems, Inc., N.Y.C., 1963-68, v.p., gen. counsel, 1966-68; v.p., sec., gen. counsel Columbia Pictures Industries, Inc., N.Y.C.,

1968-73; with Warner Communications Inc., 1973—, sr. v.p., 1973-74, exec. v.p., 1974-76, mem. Office of Pres., 1976—, co-chief operating officer, 1981—; adj. prof. telecommunications N.Y. U., 1979—; mem. faculty N.Y. Law Sch., 1961-62. Bd. visitors Columbia Law Sch., 1981—; mem. Met. Opera Assn., 1983—. Office: 75 Rockefeller Plaza New York NY 10019

HOROWITZ, DAVID JOEL, author; b. N.Y.C., Jan. 10, 1939; s. Philip and Blanche (Brown) H.; m. Elissa Krauthamer, June 14, 1959; children: Jonathan, Sarah, Benjamin, Anne. A.B., Columbia U., 1959; M.A., U. Calif.-Berkeley, 1961. Editor Ramparts mag., Berkeley, 1969-74. Author: Student, 1962, Free World Colossus, 1965, Empire and Revolution, 1969, Shakespeare-An Existential View, 1965, Fate of Midas, 1973; co-author: The Rockefellers: An American Dynasty, 1976, The First Frontier, 1979, The Kennedys: An American Drama, 1984; contbg. editor: Calif. Mag. Address: 9005 Cynthia #314 Los Angeles CA 90069

HOROWITZ, DON ROY, instrument co. exec.; b. Pitts., Mar. 12, 1930; s. Samuel and Clara (Aberman) H.; m. Carole Spiegel, Jan. 29, 1960; children—Cindy, Thomas. B.S., U. Pitts., 1952. Editor Pitts. Spectator mag., 1951-52; writer Fairchild Publs., 1952-53; pub. relations dir. Dubin. Feldman & Kahn. Inc., 1955-58; pres. Carlton Advt., Pitts., 1959-71, Corp. Communications Counselors, 1962-71, Defensive Instruments, Inc., Tulsa, 1968-74, v.p., 1974-77; pres. Mut. Advt. Agy. Network, Mpls., 1969-70, Homehelp Unlimited, Inc., Pitts., 1969-73, Flashguard, Inc., 1971-76, Showrooms-On-Wheels, Inc., 1976-77; v.p. Normda Industries, Inc., San Diego, 1969-72, Ednl. Crime Prevention Programs, Inc., Pitts., 1974-77, Plantscape, Inc., Pitts. and Cleve., 1977—. Served with AUS, 1953-55. Mem. Pitts. Advt. Club, Sales-Marketing Execs., Pi Lambda Phi. Clubs: Press, Westmoreland (Pitts.). Home: 5464 Darlington Rd Pittsburgh PA 15217 Office: 3801 Liberty Ave Pittsburgh PA 15201

HOROWITZ, FRANCES DEGEN, university official, psychology educator; b. Bronx, N.Y., May 5. 1932; d. Irving and Elaine (Moinester) Degen; m. Floyd Ross Horowitz, June 23, 1953; children: Jason Degen, Benjamin Meyer. B.A., Antioch Coll., 1954; Ed.M. (Ford Found. fellow), Goucher Coll., 1954; Ph.D., U. Iowa, 1959. Tchr. elem. sch., Iowa City, 1954-56; grad. research asst. Iowa Child Welfare Station, U. Iowa, 1956-59; asst. prof. psychology So. Oreg. Coll., Ashland, 1959-61; guest research asso. Bur. Child Research, U. Kans., summer, 1960, Parsons (Kans.) State Hosp. and Tng. Center, summer 1960; asst. prof. home econs. U. Kans., Lawrence, 1961-62, USPHS research fellow, 1962-63, asso. prof. dept. human devel. and family life, 1964-69, prof., 1969-75, chmn. dept. human devel. and family life, 1969-75, research asso., 1964-75, asso. dean, 1975-78, vice chancellor research, grad. studies and public service, also dean grad. sch., 1978—; dir. Infant Research Lab., 1964—; vis. prof. dept. psychology Tel Aviv U., Israel, 1973-74; guest researcher dept. pediatrics Kaplan Hosp., Rehovot, Israel, 1973-74; vis. lectr. dept. psychology Hebrew U., Jerusalem, 1976, cons. research programs in early edn., 1980—; pres. Center for Research, Inc., Lawrence, 1978—; cons. to OSE, 1971, U.S. Office Edn., 1969-73, NIMH, 1979; cons. to early infant stimulation program, Caracas, Venezuela, 1976, lectr. on infant devel. and day care to local and regional community groups, 1966—; mem. adv. com. Carolina Inst. on Early Edn. of the Handicapped, 1978—; reviewer NSF, 1978—; mem. U. Kans. del. to People's Republic of China, 1980; guest lectr. various profl. groups, univs., 1964—. Contbr. numerous articles on child behavior and devel. to profl. jours.; editorial bd.: Jour. Developmental Psychology, 1969-75, Early Childhood Education Quar, 1974—, Developmental Rev, 1981—; editor: Monographs of Soc. for Research in Child Development, 1976—. Bd. dirs. Community Children's Center, 1965-68, Douglas County Vis. Nurse Assn., 1968-69. Recipient Trustees award medal Cherry Lawn Sch., Conn., 1971; elected to Women's Hall of Fame U. Kans., 1974; OEO grantee, 1965-69; fellow Ctr. for Advanced Studies in Behavioral Scis., Stanford U., 1983-84. Fellow Am. Psychol. Assn. (pres. div. devel. psychology 1977-78); mem. Soc. for Research in Child Devel., Am. Assn. on Mental Deficiency, AAAS, N.Central Accrediting Assn. (mem. bd. commrs. 1977—), Sigma Xi. Jewish. Home: 505 Ohio St Lawrence KS 66044 Office: Research Grad Studies and Public Service Univ of Kansas Lawrence KS 66045

HOROWITZ, GEDALE BOB, investment banker; b. N.Y.C., June 13, 1932; s. Abraham and Florence (Bob) H.; m. Barbara Silver, Aug. 17, 1958; children: Ruth Ellen, Seth Robert. A.B., Columbia U., 1953, J.D., 1955. Bar: N.Y. 1956. With Salomon Bros., N.Y.C., 1955-67, gen. ptnr., 1967-81, mem. exec. com., 1976-81, mng. dir., mem. exec. com., 1981—; exec. v.p., dir. Phibro-Salomon, Inc., N.Y.C., 1981—. Trustee Barnard Coll., 1976—, L.I. Jewish Hosp., 1982—, Citizens Budget Commn., N.Y.C., 1982—. Served with U.S. Army, 1956-58. Mem. Pub. Securities Assn. (chmn. 1978-79), Mcpl. Securities Rulemaking Bd. (chmn. 1977-78), Mcpl. Bond Club N.Y. (pres. 1982-83). Office: Salomon Bros Inc 1 New York Plaza New York NY 10004

HOROWITZ, HAROLD, architect; b. Chgo., Sept. 6, 1927; s. Samuel and Anna (Miller) H.; m. Clara Marie Stastny, Sept. 1, 1950. B.A. in Architecture, Ill. Inst. Tech., 1950; M.Arch., Mass. Inst. Tech., 1951. Registered architect, N.J., Md. Research architect Bldg. Research Labs., S.W. Research Inst., Princeton, N.J., 1953-55; tech. dir. Bldg. Research Inst., Nat. Acad. Scis.-NRC, Washington, 1955-63; supervisory architect NSF, Washington, 1963-75, program mgr. div. advanced tech. applications, 1972, program mgr., div. advanced energy research and tech., 1973-75; program mgr. div. solar research Energy Research and Devel. Agy., 1975; dir. research Nat. Endowment for Arts, 1975—; mem. UNESCO Working Group on Cultural Stats., 1979—; lectr., cons. in field. Served with AUS, 1946-48. Recipient nat. and internat. awards. Mem. AIA (mem. research com. 1965-70). Home: 4 Barkwood Ct Rockville MD 20853 Office: Nat Endowment Arts Washington DC 20506

HOROWITZ, HERBERT EUGENE, foreign service officer; b. Bklyn., July 10, 1930; s. Max and Jean (Pomerantz) H.; m. Lenore Joan Glasser, Jan. 6, 1963; children: Jason, Richard. B.A., Bklyn. Coll., 1952; M.A., Columbia U., 1964, Fletcher Sch. Law, 1965; diploma, Nat. War Coll., 1972. Econ. officer Am. Embassy, Taipei, Taiwan, 1957-62; chief China econ. unit U.S. Consulate Gen., Hong Kong, 1965-69; chief comml. and econ. sect. U.S. Liaison Office, Beijing, 1973-75; dir. Office for Research, Dept, State, Washington, 1975-78, Econ. Policy Office East-West, Dept. Treasury, 1979-80; consul gen. U.S. Consulate Gen., Sydney, Australia, 1981—. Mem. Assn. Asian Studies, Am. Fgn. Service Assn. Club: Am. Nat. (Sydney, Australia). Home: 86 Darling Point Rd Darling Point (Sydney) New South WalesAustralia 2027 Office: American Consulate General Box 51 APO San Francisco CA 96209

HOROWITZ, IRVING LOUIS, educator, sociologist; b. N.Y.C., Sept. 25, 1929; s. Louis and Esther (Tepper) H.; m. Ruth Lenore Horowitz, 1950 (div. 1964); children: Carl Frederick, David Dennis. B.S.S., CCNY, 1951; M.A., Columbia U., 1952; Ph.D., Buenos Aires (Argentina) U., 1957; postgrad. fellow, Brandeis U., 1958-59. Asst. prof. sociology Bard Coll., 1960; assoc. prof. social theory Buenos Aires U., 1955-58; chmn. dept. sociology Hobart and William Smith Colls., 1960-63; assoc. prof., then prof. sociology Washington U., St. Louis, 1963-69; chmn. dept. sociology Livingston Coll., Rutgers U., 1969-73; prof. sociology grad. faculty Rutgers U., 1969—, Hannah Arendt prof. social and polit. theory, 1979—; vis. prof. sociology U. Caracas, Venezuela, 1957, Buenos Aires U., 1959, 61, 63, SUNY, Buffalo, 1960, Syracuse U., 1961, U. Rochester, fall 1962, U. Calif., Davis, 1966, U. Wis., Madison, 1967, Stanford U., 1968-69, Am. U., 1972, Queen's U., Can., 1973, Princeton U., 1976; vis. lectr. London Sch. Econs. and Polit. Sci., 1962; Prin. investigator for numerous sci. and research projects. Author: Idea of War and Peace in Contemporary Philosophy, 1957, Philosophy, Science and the Sociology of Knowledge, 1960, Radicalism and the Revolt Against Reason: The Social Theories of Georges Sorel, 2d edit, 1968, The War Game; Studies of the New Civilian Militarists, 1963, Historia y Elementos de la Sociologia del Connocimento, 1963, The New Sociology: Essays in Social Science and Social Values in Honor of C. Wright Mills, 1964, Revolution in Brazil: Politics and Society in a Developing Nation, 1964, The Rise and Fall of Project Camelot, 1967, rev. edit., 1976, Three Worlds of Development: The Theory and Practice of International Stratification, 1966, rev. edit., 1972, Professing Sociology: The Life Cycle of a Social Science, 1963, Latin American Radicalism: A Documentary Report on Nationalist and Left Movements, 1969, Sociological Self-Images, 1969, The Knowledge Factory: Student Power and Academic Politics in America, 1970, Masses in Latin America, 1970, Cuban Communism, 1970, 4th edit., 1979, Foundations of Political Sociology, 1972, Social Science and Public Policy in the United States, 1975, Ideology and Utopia in the United States, 1977, Dialogues on American Politics, 1979, Taking Lives: Genocide and State Power, 1979, Beyond Empire and Revolution, 1982, C. Wright Mills: An American Utopian, 1983; pres., editor-in-chief: Transaction/SOCIETY. Fellow AAAS; Mem. AAUP, Am. Polit. Sci. Assn., Am. Sociol. Assn., Authors Guild, Centre Internat. pour le Devel. (a founder), Center for Study The Presidency, Council Fgn. Relations, Internat. Studies Assn., Latin Am. Studies Assn., Internat. Soc. Polit. Psychology (founder), Council on Fgn. Relations, Soc. Internat. Devel., Soc. Study Social Problems (chmn. awards com. 1964-66). Home: Route 206, 1247 State Rd Bawenburg Rd/Rocky Hill Intersection Princeton NJ 08540

HOROWITZ, LEWIS JAY, stock exchange executive; b. N.Y.C., Feb. 13, 1935; s. Jack and Ethel Lahn (Wartur) H.; children: Jay B., Stephen G.; m. Jo-Ann Yacker, Jan. 13, 1983. B.A., Brown U., 1956. Ptnr. Bernard, Berk & Co., N.Y.C., 1958-65; specialist Phelan, Silver, Vesce & Barry, 1965-82; pres., chief exec. officer N.Y. Futures Exchange, 1983—. Bd. dirs. Jewish Bd. Guardians, 1970-78; pres. Ramapo Anchorage Camp, Rhinebeck, N.Y., 1973-78. Mem. Nat. Futures Assn., N.Y. Stock Exchange. Home: 40 E 88th St New York NY 10128 Office: New York Futures Exchange 20 Broad St New York NY 10005

HOROWITZ, MORRIS A., economist; b. Newark, Nov. 19, 1919; s. Samuel and Anna (Litwin) H.; m. Jean Ginsburg, July 12, 1941; children—Ruth, Joel. B.A. in Econs, N.Y. U., 1940, Ph.D., Harvard U., 1954. Mem. faculty Northeastern U., 1956—, prof. econs., chmn. dept., 1959—; ad hoc labor arbitrator, manpower cons. Home: 5 Riedesel Ave Cambridge MA 02138 Office: Northeastern U Boston MA 02115

HOROWITZ, MYER, college administrator; b. Montreal, Que., Can., Dec. 1932; s. Philip H. and Fanny Cotler (Horowitz); m. Barbara Rosen, Oct. 3, 1956; children: Carol Anne, Deborah Ellen. B.A., Sir George William U., 1956; M.Ed., U. Alta., 1959; Ed.D., Stanford U., 1965; LL.D., McGill U., 1979, Concordia U., 1982. Research and teaching asst. Stanford U.; tchr. elem. and high schs. Protestant Sch. Bd. of Greater Montreal, 1952-60; lectr. edn. McGill U., 1960-62, asst. prof., 1963-65, assoc. prof., 1965-67, asst. to dir., 1964-65, prof., 1967-69, asst. dean, 1965-69; prof., chmn. dept. elem. edn. U. Alta, 1969; dean edn. U. Alta., 1972-75, v.p. academics, 1975-79; pres. McGill U., 1975-79; chmn. Canadian Com. on Early Childhood; dir. Tanzania Edn. project. Contbr. articles to profl. jours. and mags. Chmn. adv. com. Study of Mental Retardation, U. Alta. Fellow Can. Coll. Tchrs. (pres. Edmonton chpt.); mem. Province Assn. Protestant Tchrs. Que., Alta. Tchrs. Assn. (pres. early childhood edn. council). Jewish. Office: Univ Alta Edmonton AV Canada T6G 2E1

HOROWITZ, NORMAN HAROLD, educator, biologist; b. Pitts., Mar. 19, 1915; s. Joseph L. and Jeanette (Miller) H.; m. Pearl Shykin, June 16, 1939; children—Joel Lawrence, Elizabeth Anne. B.S., U. Pitts., 1936; Ph.D., Calif. Inst. Tech., 1939, research fellow biochemistry, 1940-42, sr. research fellow, 1946; NRC fellow, Stanford, 1939-40, research asso., 1942-46. Teaching fellow biology Calif. Inst. Tech., Pasadena, 1936-39, asso. prof. biology, 1947-53, prof. biology, 1953—, chmn. dept., 1977-80; chief bio sci. sect. Jet Propulsion Lab., Pasadena, 1965-70; cons. NASA; mem., experimenter Viking Mars Biology Team, 1976-77. Editorial bd.: Jour. Biol. Chemistry, 1959-64; Contbr. articles tech. jours. Fulbright and Guggenheim fellow U. Paris, 1954-55. Mem. Am. Soc. Biol. Chemists, Genetics Soc. Am., AAAS, Nat. Acad. Scis., Am. Acad. Arts and Scis., Phi Beta Kappa. Home: 2495 Brigden Rd Pasadena CA 91104

HOROWITZ, PAUL, physicist; b. N.Y.C., Dec. 28, 1942; s. Harry and Ruth (Levy) H.; m. Carol Jan Grodzins, Apr. 28, 1973; children: Misha, Jacob. A.B. summa cum laude, Harvard U., 1965, Ph.D. in Physics (NSF fellow 1966-67, Harvard Soc. Fellows jr. fellow 1967-70), 1970. Asst. prof. physics Harvard U., 1970-73, asso. prof., 1973-74, prof., 1974—; cons. electronic design. Author: (with W. Hill) The Art of Electronics, 1980, (with I. Robinson) Laboratory Manual for The Art of Electronics, 1981. Frederick Sheldon travelling fellow, 1965-66; Alfred P. Sloan fellow, 1971-73. Research in optical timing on Crab Nebula pulsar, searches for new pulsars, devel. of synchrotron radiation facility and scanning x-ray microscope, devel. of scanning proton microprobe in atmospheric environment, radiofrequency searches for extraterrestrial intelligence. Home: 19 Fair Oaks Dr Lexington MA 02173 Office: Lyman Lab of Physics Harvard U Cambridge MA 02138

HOROWITZ, RAYMOND JACK, lawyer; b. N.Y.C., May 7, 1916; s. Israel S. and Sadye (Freiman) H.; m. Margaret Goldenberg, Sept. 22, 1940; 1 dau., Judith. A.B., Columbia U., 1936, LL.B., 1939. Bar: N.Y. 1939. Practiced in, N.Y.C., 1939-41, asst. corp. counsel, City of N.Y., 1941-43; asso. Meyer, Wallach & Silverson, N.Y.C., 1943-46; partner McGoldrick, Dannett, Horowitz & Golub (and predecessors), N.Y.C., 1946-69; mem. firm Graubard, Moskowitz, McGoldrick, Dannett & Horowitz, 1969—; Vice pres., gen. counsel Allied Maintenance Corp.; dir. Vista Resources, Inc., Ogden Corp.; cons. Nat. Housing Agy, 1946-47, Office Housing Expediter, 1947, Temporary State Housing Rent Commn., 1950-51. Author: (with others) Building Regulation in New York City, 1944. Chmn. trustees' vis. com. on Am. paintings and sculpture Met. Mus. Art. Mem. Assn. Bar City N.Y., N.Y. County Lawyers Assn., Phi Beta Kappa. Clubs: Century Assn., Wings (N.Y.C.). Home: 930 Fifth Ave New York NY 10021 Office: 345 Park Ave New York NY 10154

HOROWITZ, RICHARD SAMUEL, timpanist; b. N.Y.C., Feb. 3, 1924; s. Joseph A. and Mollie Anna (Glass) H.; m. Bernice Sylvia Isbit, Jan. 25, 1944; children—Mark David, Robert Neil. Student, Bklyn. Coll., 1940-43, Juilliard Sch. Music. With Chautauqua Symphony Orch., 1942, Worcester Festival Orch., 1942, City Center Symphony and Opera Orch., 1946, N.Y. Philharm. at Lewisohn Stadium; prin. timpanist Met. Opera Orchs., N.Y.C., 1946—; mem. faculty N.Y. State U., Purchase, Bronx Community Coll. Served with USAAF, 1943-46. Jewish. Club: Masons. Office: Met Opera Lincoln Center Plaza New York NY 10023

HOROWITZ, SIDNEY, corporation executive; b. Loch Sheldrake, N.Y., Nov. 21, 1920; s. Abraham and Jennie H.; m. Grace Fern Nelson, June 27, 1948; children: Richard Andrew, Joanne Patricia. B.B.A., St. Johns U., 1942. With Horowitz Bros., Inc., L.I., N.Y., 1945-61, pres., 1954-61; chmn. bd., chief exec. officer P & F Industries, Inc., Great Neck, N.Y., 1961—, also dir.; partner Crossways Indsl. Park; dir. Verit Industries; partner Internat. Plaza East. Pres. Grace and Sidney Horowitz Found.; bd. govs. Albert Einstein Coll. Medicine. Served to 1st lt. USAAF, 1943-45. Decorated Air medal with 7 oak leaf clusters, D.F.C. Club: Fresh Meadow (Great Neck, N.Y.). Office: 111 Great Neck Rd Great Neck NY 11021

HOROWITZ, STEVE, restaurant supply company executive; b. Los Angeles, May 29, 1930; s. Sam and Sylvia (Newworth) H.; m. Elaine Franklin, Mar. 30, 1958; children: Erin, Deanna. B.A. in Polit. Sci., UCLA, 1958. Salesman Interstate Restaurant Supply Co., Los Angeles, 1958-60, sales supr., 1960-63, sales mgr., 1963-68, v.p. sales and mktg., 1968-72, pres., 1972—; chmn. adv. bd. Instl. Distbn. Mag., N.Y.C., 1978—; mem. dist. bd. James River Co., N.J., 1980—. Chmn. fund div. United Jewish Welfare Fund, Los Angeles, 1979-82. Recipient Humanitarian award Westwood Shrine, Los Angeles, 1980; named Citizen of Week Sta. KFI, Los Angeles, 1983; honored United Jewish Welfare Fund, Los Angeles, 1983. Mem. Los Angeles C. of C. Club: Los Angeles Athletic. Office: Interstate Restaurant Supply Co Inc 901 E 31st St Los Angeles CA 90011

HOROWITZ, VLADIMIR, pianist; b. Kiev, Russia, Oct. 1, 1904; s. Samuel and Sophia (Bodik) H.; m. Wanda Toscanini, Dec. 21, 1933; 1 dau., Sonia (dec.). Ed., Kiev Conservatory; study under, Felix Blumenfeld, Sergei Tarnowsky. Made first appearance at age 17, Kiev, Russia; made debut, Europe, 1925; made debut in U.S. with, N.Y. Philharmonic, Jan. 1928; made concert tours of U.S., 1928—. Recipient 19 Grammy awards for best classical performance, instrumental soloist or soloists Nat. Acad. Rec. Arts and Scis., 1966-81, Best Classical Performance/Instrumental Soloist for Kreisleriana Ministry Edn. Japanese Govt., 1971, Acad. Award/Classic Best Instrumental Soloist, Rec. Geijutsu, 1971, Best Performance Award-Classic Instrumental Soloist CBS/SONY, 1970, Prix Mondial du Disque for Kreisleriana, 1971, Gold Medal Royal Philharm. Soc., 1972, Grand Prix des Discophiles, 1966. Address: care Columbia Artists Mgmt 165 W 57 St New York NY 10019

HORR, WILLIAM HENRY, lawyer; b. Portsmouth, Ohio, Sept. 23, 1914; s. Charles Chick and Effie (Amberg) H.; m. Marjorie Bell Marshall, Aug. 31, 1940; children—Robert W., Thomas M., Catherine, James C., Elizabeth. A.B., Ohio Wesleyan U., 1936; J.D., U. Cin., 1939. Bar: Ohio bar 1939. Practice in, Portsmouth, 1939-42, 45—; atty. Skelton, Kahl, Horr, Marshall & Burton, 1939-42, 45-78; spl. agt. FBI, Louisville, Indpls., Newark, 1942-45; substitute judge Municipal Ct., Portsmouth, 1955-80; gen. counsel Ohio Wesleyan U., 1966-70. Mem. Portsmouth Bd. Edn., 1947- 60; pres. Portsmouth YMCA.; Trustee Ohio U. Portsmouth Br., Shawnee State Coll., 1955-80, Ohio Wesleyan U., 1953-68; chmn. bd. Hill View Retirement Center, 1973—. Recipient Distinguished Service award Portsmouth Jr. C. of C., 1947. Mem. Ohio Bar Assn. (past mem. exec. com.), Portsmouth Bar Assn. (past pres.), Phi Delta Phi, Phi Kappa Psi, Omicron Delta Kappa. Republican. Methodist. Clubs: Rotary, Elks. Home: 1119 23d St Portsmouth OH 45662 Office: 428 Masonic Bldg Portsmouth OH 45662

HORRELL, KAREN HOLLEY, insurance company executive; b. Augusta, Ga., July 10, 1952; d. Dudley Cronelius and Eleanor (Shouppe) Holley; m. Jack E. Horrell, Aug. 14, 1976. B.S., Berry Coll., 1974; J.D., Emory U., 1976. Bar: Ohio 1977, Ga. 1977. Corp. counsel Great Am. Ins. Co., Cin., 1977-80, v.p., gen. counsel, sec., 1981—; counsel Am. Fin. Corp., Cin., 1980-81; gen. counsel numerous subsidiaries Great Ins. Co.; sec., asst. sec. numerous other fin. and ins. cos. Account mgr. United Appeal Corp. Campaign, 1983. Mem. ABA, Ohio Bar Assn., Cin. Bar Assn. (admissions com. 1978—), Am. Corp. Counsel Assn. Democrat. Presbyterian. Club: Cin. Bus. Profl. Women's (bd. dirs.) (1981-82). Home: 3733 Vineyard Pl Cincinnati OH 45226 Office: Great Am Ins Co 580 Walnut St Cincinnati OH 45202

HORRIGAN, ALFRED FREDERIC, clergyman; b. Wilmington, Del., Dec. 9, 1914; s. William James and Anna (Kienle) H. Student, St. Joseph Coll., Collegeville, Ind., 1928-34; B.A., St. Meinrad (Ind.) Sem., 1940; M.A., Cath. U. Am., 1942, Ph.D., 1944; LL.D., Belmont Abbey Coll., 1961, St. Joseph's Coll., 1966, U. San Diego, 1971, Bellarmine Coll., 1975, Centre Coll., 1976. Ordained priest Roman Catholic Ch., 1940; asst. pastor, Louisville, 1940-41, 44-49; head dept. philosophy Nazareth Coll., Louisville; also part-time prof. philosophy Ursuline Coll., U. Louisville, 1944-49; editor The Record (newspaper), 1946-49; first pres. Bellarmine Coll., Louisville, 1949-72, chmn. bd., 1972-73; exec. asst. to Archbishop of, Louisville, 1973; exec. dir. Commn. on Peace and Justice, Archdiocese Louisville, 1974-75; pastor St. James Ch., Louisville, 1976—. Author: Metaphysics as a Principle of Order in the University Curriculum, 1944; Editor: Roots of a Catholic College, 1955. Chmn. Louisville-Jefferson County Commn. on Human Relations, 1965-68. Mem. English Speaking Union. Club: Filson. Home: 1826 Edenside Ave Louisville KY 40204

HORRIGAN, EDWARD A., JR., tobacco company executive; b. N.Y.C., Sept. 23, 1929; s. Edward A. and Margaret V. (Kells) H.; m. Elizabeth R. Herperger, June 27, 1953; children: Ellen, Christopher, Gordon, Brian. B.S. in Bus. Adminstrn, U. Conn., 1950; grad., Advanced Mgmt. Program, Harvard U., 1965. Sales mgr. Procter & Gamble Co., N.Y.C., 1954-58; gen. mgr. Ebonite Co., Boston, 1958-61; div. v.p. T.J. Lipton Inc., 1961-73; chmn. bd., pres. Buckingham Corp., N.Y.C., 1973-78; chmn. bd., chief exec. officer R.J. Reynolds Tobacco Internat., Inc., Winston-Salem, N.C., 1978-80; chmn. bd., pres., chief exec. officer R. J. Reynolds Tobacco Co., Winston-Salem, 1980—; exec. v.p. R.J. Reynolds Industries, Inc., 1981-84, pres., chief operating officer, 1984—. Served as officer, inf. U.S. Army, 1950-54. Decorated Silver Star, Purple Heart, Combat Inf. badge, Parachute badge. Mem. Knights of Malta. Clubs: Old Town Country, Vintage. Home: 2815 Bartram Rd Winston-Salem NC 27106 Office: World Hdqrs Bldg Reynolds Blvd Winston-Salem NC 27102

HORROCKS, NORMAN, educator; b. Manchester, Eng., Oct. 18, 1927; s. Edward Henry and Annie (Barnes) H.; m. Sandra Sherriff, Feb. 3, 1967; children: Julie Carol, Carl Scott, Gina Louise, Anne Patricia, Sarah Helen. F.L.A., Sch. Librarianship, Manchester, 1950; B.A., U. Western Australia, 1960; M.L.S., U. Pitts., 1961, Ph.D., 1971. Asst. librarian Manchester pub. libraries, 1943-45, 50-53; librarian Brit. Council, Cyprus, 1954-55; tech. librarian State Library Western Australia, 1956-61; teaching fellow U. Pitts., 1963-64, instr., 1964-69, asst. prof., 1969-71; assoc. prof. Sch. Library Service, Dalhousie U., 1971-73, prof., 1973—, dir. sch., 1972—, dean Faculty Adminstrv. Studies, 1983—; vis. lectr. Perth Tech. Coll., 1961-63; extension lectr. Pa. State Library, 1966-70; vis. lectr. U. Hawaii, 1969; chmn. Overseas Book Centre, Halifax, 1980-83; mem. adv. bd. sci. and tech. info. NRC Can., 1980—; mem. adv. bd. com. on bibliog. services Nat. Library

Can., 1980—; mem. promotion and distbn. council Can. Council. Editor: North Western Newsletter, 1952-53, Jour. Edn. for Librarianship, 1971-76; asso. editor: Govt. Publ. Rev., 1973-81; contbr. articles to profl. jours. Bd. visitors Pratt Inst. Served with Brit. Army, 1945-48. Recipient W.H. Brown prize, 1950, Merit award Atlantic Provinces Library Assn., 1979, Disting. Alumnus award U. Pitts., 1982. Mem. ALA (council 1972-81, 83—, exec. bd. 1977-81, various coms.), Can. Library Assn. (2d v.p. 1978-80, various coms.), Halifax Library Assn., Can. Council Library Schs. (chmn. 1974-76), Assn. Library and Info. Sci. Edn. (v.p., pres. elect), Assn. Am. Library Schs. (chmn. editorial bd. 1971-76), Beta Phi Mu. Home: 14 Cleveland Crescent Dartmouth NS B3A 2L6 Canada Office: Sch Library Service Dalhousie U Halifax NS B3H 4H8 Canada

HORSBRUGH, PATRICK, architect, educator; b. Belfast, No. Ireland, June 21, 1920; came to U.S., 1960; s. Charles Bethune and Marion Rose (McQueen) H. Diploma with honors, Archtl. Assn. Sch. Architecture, 1949; diploma city planning, U. London, 1951. With Raglan, Squire and Partners, London, 1956-57; vis. critic Harvard Grad. Sch. Design, 1956; with depts. architecture, planning and landscape architecture univs. Ill., N.C., 1957-58; dep. dir., then dir. Hamilton-Wentworth Planning Area Bd., Hamilton, Ont., Can., 1958-60; vis. prof. architecture U. Nebr., 1960-65, U. Tex., 1965-67; prof. architecture U. Notre Dame, 1967—, dir. grad. program environic studies, 1970-80; chmn. bd. Environic Found. Internat. Inc., Notre Dame, Ind.; cons. environ. and planning issues, ednl. and design practices. Designer: High Paddington Project, London, Eng., 1951; co-designer: New Barbican Com. Project, London, 1954; Author: High Buildings in the United Kingdom, 1952, Pittsburgh Perceived, The Form, Features and Feasibilities of the Prodigious City, 1963; Editor: The Texas Conference on Our Environmental Crisis, 1966. Co-chmn. Internat. Earth Day, 1978; v.p. Channel Tunnel Assn. Served with Royal Arty., 1938-41; Served with RAF, 1941-46. Bernard Webb fellow Academica Britannica, Rome, 1950; B.Y. Morrison Meml. lectr. U.S. Dept. Agr., 1969. Fellow Royal Soc. Arts, AIA, Royal Geog. Soc., Brit. Interplanetary Soc.; mem. Royal Inst. Brit. Architects, Royal Town Planning Inst., Can. Inst. Planners, AIA, Am. Planning Assn., Ancient Monument Soc., Soc. Indsl. Archaeology, Soc. Protection Ancient Bldgs., Georgian Group, Nat. Trust (Gt. Britain), Nat. Trust for Historic Preservation, Am. Soc. Landscape Architects (hon.), Am. Inst. Interior Designers. (hon.). Office: Environic Found Internat PO Box 88 Notre Dame IN 46556-1088

HORSELL, MARY KAY, assn. exec.; b. Roundup, Mont., Nov. 3, 1917; d. Guy Elmer and Mary Catherine (Raridan) Smith; m. Arthur Howard Horsell, June 26, 1937; children—Barbara Horsell Koon, Mary Ann Horsell Boyette, Arthur Howard. B.S., Fresno (Calif.) State U., 1939. Owner, operator Food Merchandising Service, Oakland, Calif., 1954—; chmn. bd. Oakland Diocesan Council Cath. Women, 1962-64, program chmn., 1964-65, v.p., program chmn., 1965-66, pres., 1967-69; parliamentarian, Diocesan rep. Ch. Women United Bd., 1969-71, ways and means chmn., 1971-73; province dir. San Francisco Archdiocesan Council Cath. Women, 1973-75; pres. Nat. Council Cath. Women, Washington, 1975—; U.S. rep. from Nat. Council Cath. Women to World Union Cath. Women's Orgns., 1979—; mem. Commn. for Women in Ch., Oakland Diocese, 1978—; mem. exec. bd. Women in Community Service, Washington, 1979—; bd. dirs. World Union Cath. Women's Orgns., 1979—; Mem. central com. San Francisco Bay council Girl Scouts U.S.A., 1947-55; diocesan bd. mem., health chmn., program chmn., legis. chmn. Parent Tchrs. Groups, 1949-54; pres. East Bay Pres.'s Council, 1954-56, archdiocesan pres., 1958-60; pres. Oakland Diocese, 1962-64, St. Jarlath's Mothers Club, 1946-48, Bishop O'Dowd High Sch. Mothers Club, 1956-58; co-organizer Children's Vision Center of East Bay, 1957, pres., 1971-74, East Bay Motion Picture and TV Council, 1964-66; organizer Vol. Tchr. Assistance Program for elementary schs. in Oakland Diocese, 1965; bd. dirs. Met. Horseman's Assn., 1963-75, now v.p., Past Pres.'s trophy, 1975; vol. counselor juvenile delinquents awaiting trial, 1967—; sec. Fedn. Motion Picture Councils, Inc., 1975-77. Editor: Newsreel, Fedn. Motion Picture Councils, 1973-75. Recipient Pro Ecclesia Et Pontifice, 1964, Life membership East Bay Pres.'s Council Parent Tchrs. Groups, 1964; named Oakland Mother of Year, 1970. Club: Zonta Internat. Home: 11590 Circle Way Dublin CA 94566 Office: 1312 Massachusetts Ave NW Washington DC 20005 *It has been my conviction that I was most fortunate to have been born in America. It is my hope that each day I can lend a helping hand to someone who needs it. I hope my record of work indicates my love and deep concern for my fellow man.*

HORSEY, HENRY RIDGELY, state supreme court judge; b. Lewes, Del., Oct. 18, 1924; s. Harold W. and Philippa (Ridgely) H.; m. Ann M. Baker, May 19, 1979; children: Robert Wolfe, Josephine Elizabeth; children by previous marriage: Henry Ridgely, Edmond P.V., Alexandra Therese, Philippa Ridgely, Randall Revell. A.B., Harvard Coll., 1949, LL.B., 1952. Bar: Del. With firm Berl, Potter & Anderson, Wilmington, Del., 1952-62, Wilmington Trust Co., 1962-65; individual practice law, Dover, Del., 1965-69; mem. firm Morris, James, Hitchens & Williams, Wilmington, 1969-78; justice Supreme Ct. of Del., Dover, 1978—. Served with inf. AUS, 1943-46. Office: Supreme Ct Bldg 57 The Green Dover DE 19901

HORSEY, WILLIAM GRANT, corporation executive; b. Buffalo, Oct. 17, 1915; s. J. William and Clara (Banford) H.; m. Eleanor Mae Child, Feb. 17, 1940; 1 dau., Susan Horsey Dees. B.Comm., McGill U., 1938. Route salesman Standard Brands Ltd., Toronto, Ont., Can., 1938; jr. audit clk. McDonald Currie & Co., Montreal, Que., Can., 1938, sr. audit clk., 1941; asst. to dist. mgr. Dominion Stores Ltd., Halifax, 1939-40; treas. Apte Canning Sales Corp., Tampa, Fla., 1946-50; pres. J. William Horsey Corp., Plant City, Fla., 1950-55, Shirriff-Horsey Corp. Ltd., Toronto, 1955-57, Salada Foods Ltd. (formerly Salada-Shirriff-Horsey Ltd.), Don Mills, Ont., Salada Foods Inc. (formerly Salada-Shirriff-Horsey Inc.), Woburn, Mass., 1957-64; chmn. bd. Salada Foods Ltd., Salada Foods Inc., 1964-67; pres. Wilgran Corp. Ltd., Toronto, 1962—; chmn. bd. DRG Inc., Toronto; dir. Nat. Trust Co. Ltd., Gage Research Inst., Toronto. Trustee Toronto Western Hosp.; Employee Retirement Plan for Can. Employees of Reliance Ins. Cos., J. William Horsey Found., Toronto. Served to lt. Can. Army, 1943-46. Mem. Theta Delta Chi. Presbyterian. Clubs: Granite (Toronto); Toronto Club, Tampa Yacht and Country; University (Tampa). Home: 70 Cluny Dr Toronto ON Canada M4W 2R3 Home: 15910 Gulf Blvd Redington Beach FL 33708 Office: 261 Bowes Rd Unit 1 Concord ON Canada L4K 1H8

HORSFORD, HOWARD CLARKE, English educator; b. Montezuma, Iowa, Nov. 26, 1921; s. Forrest Fair and Clara Mary (Johnston) H. B.A. magna cum laude, Ripon (Wis.) Coll., 1943; M.A., Princeton U., 1951, Ph.D., 1952. Instr. math. Ripon Coll., 1946-48; instr., then asst. prof. English Princeton U., 1951-60, Bicentennial preceptor, 1957-60; vis. lectr. Bryn Mawr (Pa.) Coll., 1957-58; mem. faculty U. Rochester, N.Y., 1960—, prof. English, 1966—; vis. prof. Bread Loaf (Vt.) Sch. English, summers 1960, 61, 63, 64. Editor: Melville's Journal of a Visit to Europe and the Levant, 1856-1857, 1955, Oxford Anthology of English Poetry, 2d edit, 1956. Edn. adv. President's Com. Hungarian Refugee Relief, 1957. Served with Signal Corps AUS, 1943-46. Decorated Commendation medal. Mem. MLA, Melville Soc. (pres. 1957), Phi Beta Kappa. Democrat. Office: Dept English U Rochester Rochester NY 14627

HORSKY, CHARLES ANTONE, lawyer; b. Helena, Mont., Mar. 22, 1910; s. Antone J. and Marguerite (Bowden) H.; m. Barbara Egleston, Oct. 2, 1936; children: Margaret Ellen, Antone (dec.). A.B., U. Wash., 1931; LL.B., Harvard, 1934. Bar: N.Y. bar 1935, D.C. bar 1938. Clk. to Judge A.N. Hand, N.Y.C., 1934-35; atty. Solicitor Gen. Office, 1935-37, 38-39; mem. Covington & Burling, Washington, 1937-38, 39-62, 67—; advisor to Pres. for Nat. Capital Affairs, 1962-67; lectr. U. Va. Law Sch., 1956-62, 68—, 1969, 73, 80; dir. Am. Indian Nat. Bank.; Chmn. D.C. Bd. Higher Edn., 1967-70; dir. Atty. Gen.'s Com. Bankruptcy Adminstrn., 1934-40; mem. Nat. Bankruptcy Conf., 1945-62, 67-74, chmn., 1954-62, 74—; asso. in charge Washington office Office Chief of Counsel for War Crimes, 1945-47, asst. prosecutor, Nurnberg, Germany, 1948; mem. D.C. Jud. Planning Com. Author: The Washington Lawyer, 1952. Pres. Washington Housing Assn., 1955-62; mem. Commrs. Planning Adv. Council, chmn., 1960-62; Trustee Woodrow Wilson Internat. Center for Scholars, 1969-72, E. and A. Meyer Found. (pres. 1970-73, chmn. bd. 1973-81); trustee Fed. City Council, 1975—; bd. dirs. Nat. Bldg. Mus., 1980—; chmn. Council for Ct. Excellence, 1982—, Montgomery County Citizens Housing Adv. Com.; mem. nat. adv. council ACLU; chmn. Nat. Arbitration Panel, 1984—. Named D.C. Lawyer of Yr., 1980. Fellow Am. Acad. Arts and Scis., Am. Coll. Trial Lawyers; mem. ABA (state del. 1978—), Fed. Bar Assn., D.C. Bar Assn. (dir. 1972-78), Am. Judicature Soc. (Herbert Harley award 1984), Am. Law Inst., Assn. Bar City N.Y., Selden Soc., Order of Grizzly, Salzburg Seminar Alumni Assn. (pres. 1979—), Phi Beta Kappa, Pi Sigma Alpha. Clubs: Cosmos, Harvard, Nat. Lawyers, Metropolitan (Washington). Home: 1227 Pinecrest Circle Silver Spring MD 20910 Office: 1201 Pennsylvania Ave NW PO Box 7566 Washington DC 20044

HORSLEY, ANDREW BURT, educator; b. Brigham City, Utah, Nov. 23, 1918; s. William Clements and Adella (Burt) H.; m. Faye McBride, Sept. 18, 1940; children—Dee, Raymon, Christine, Linda, John. A.B., Brigham Young U., 1945, M.A., 1954; Ph.D., U. Muenster, Germany, 1956. Prin. piute Latter-day Saints Sem., 1945-46; prin. Cedar City Sem., 1946-53; supr. sem. tchr. tng. Brigham Young U., Provo, Utah, 1953-54, asst. prof., asso. prof., prof. philosophy and religion, 1956—, also mem. high council.; Mem. Mountain Plains Philos. Conf. Asso. editor: Greenwood Press Ency. Am. Instns; contbr. articles to profl. jours. Republican. Mem. Ch. of Jesus Christ of Latter-day Saints (past mem. high council, bishop). Club: Kiwanis. Home: 260 East 400 North Provo UT 84601

HORSLEY, JACK EVERETT, lawyer; b. Sioux City, Iowa, Dec. 12, 1915; s. Charles E. and Edith V. (Timms) H.; m. Sallie Kelley, June 12, 1939 (dec.); children: Pamela, Charles Edward; m. Bertha J. Newland, Feb. 24, 1950 (dec.); m. Mary Jane Moran, Jan. 20, 1973; 1 dau., Sharon. A.B., U. Ill., 1937, LL.B., 1939, J.D., 1965. Bar: Ill. 1939. Since practiced in Mattoon, Ill.; sr. counsel Craig & Craig (attys. for Ill. Central Gulf R.R. Co., C. & E.I. R.R. Co., Penn Central R.R. Co., Internat. Harvester Co., others); specialist in defensive trial work; vice chmn., dir. Central Nat. Bank, 1976—; mem. lawyers adv. council U. Ill. Law Forum, 1960-63; lectr. Practising Law Inst., N.Y.C., 1967-73, Ct. Practice Inst., Chgo., 1974—, U. Mich. Coll. Law Inst. Continuing Legal Edn., 1968; vis. lectr. Orange County (Fla.) Med. Soc., 1975, San Diego Med. Soc., 1970, U. S.C., 1976, Duquesne Coll., 1970; chmn. rev. com. Ill. Supreme Ct. Disciplinary Commn., 1973-76. Narrator: Poetry Interludes, Sta. WLBH-FM; author: Trial Lawyer's Manual, 1967, Voir Dire Examinations and Opening Statements, 1968, Current Development in Products Liability Law, 1969, Illinois Civil Practice and Procedure, 1970, The Medical Expert Witness, 1973, The Doctor and the Law, 1975, The Doctor and Family Law, 1975, The Doctor and Business Law, 1976, The Doctor and Medical Law, 1977, 2d edit. Testifying in Court, 1983, Anatomy of a Medical Malpractice Case, 1984; contbr. articles to profl. jours.; cons., contbr.: Med. Econs., 1969—; legal cons.: Mast-Head, 1972—; contbr.: RN Mag., 1976—; sect. on use of texts in evidence, Matthew Bender Co., 1980. Pres. bd. edn. Sch. Dist. 100, 1946-48; bd. dirs. Moore Heart Research Fund, 1969—. Served to lt. col. A.C., JAGD U.S. Army, 1942-46. Fellow Am. Coll. Trial Lawyers; mem. ABA, Ill. Bar Assn. (exec. council ins. law 1961-63, lectr. law course for attys. 1962, 64, 65, Disting. Service award 1982-83), Coles-Cumberland Bar Assn. (v.p. 1968-69, pres. 1969-70, chmn. com. jud. inquiry 1976—), Am. Arbitration Assn. (nat. panel arbitrators), U. Ill. Law Alumni Assn. (pres. 1966-67), Ill. Def. Counsel Assn. (pres. 1967-68), Soc. Trial Lawyers (chmn. profl. activities 1960-61), Adelphic Debating, Assn. Ins. Attys., Internat. Assn. Ins. Counsel, Am. Judicature Soc., Appellate Lawyers Assn., Scribes, Delta Phi (exec. com. Alumni Assn. 1960-61), Sigma Delta Kappa. Republican. Lodge: Masons (32°). Home: 50 Elm Ridge Mattoon IL 61938 Office: 1807 Broadway Mattoon IL 61938 *Success comes from careful preparation and study and these must be coupled with hard work. Anticipation of future obligations and careful advance work looking to handling them properly are essential. Knowledge is a paramount aspect; knowledge is power. But without understanding and sympathy it is nothing. Above all, one must know that it's possible to believe in a cause firmly and still lose with dignity or, equally important, to win with humility.*

HORSMAN, REGINALD, history educator; b. Leeds, Eng., Oct. 24, 1931; came to U.S., 1954, naturalized, 1965; s. Alfred William and Elizabeth (Thompson) H.; m. Lenore Lynde McNabb, Sept. 3, 1955; children: John, Janine, Mara. B.A., U. Birmingham, Eng., 1952, M.A., 1955; Ph.D., Ind. U., 1958. Mem. faculty U. Wis.-Milw., 1958—, prof. history, 1964-73, distinguished prof., 1973—, chmn. dept., 1970-72. Author: The Causes of the War of 1812, 1962, Matthew Elliott: British Indian Agent, 1964, Expansion and American Indian Policy, 1967, The War of 1812, 1969, The Frontier in the Formative Years, 1970, Napoleon's Europe: The New America, 1970, Race and Manifest Destiny: The Origins of American Racial Anglo-Saxonism, 1981. Recipient Kiekhofer teaching award U. Wis., 1961; Guggenheim fellow, 1965-66. Mem. Am. Hist. Assn., Orgn. Am. Historians, Soc. for Historians Early Am. Republic, Phi Beta Kappa (hon.), Phi Kappa Phi (hon.), Phi Eta Sigma (hon.), Phi Alpha Theta. Home: 3548 N Hackett Ave Milwaukee WI 53211

HORST, BRUCE EVERETT, mfg. co. exec.; b. Three Rivers, Mich., Feb. 17, 1921; s. Walter and Genevieve (Turner) H.; m. Patricia Kranish, Oct. 4, 1969; children—Michael, Diane, Mark. B.S. in Bus. and Engring. Adminstrn, Mass. Inst. Tech., 1943. With Barber-Colman Co., Rockford, Ill., 1946—, pres., 1965-75, vice chmn. bd., 1975-76; pres. Mid-States Screw Corp., 1976—, Redin Corp., 1979—. Bd. dirs. Rockford YMCA, 1964—, pres., 1965-67. Served to 1st lt. USAAF, 1943-45. Decorated Air medal. Clubs: Rotary; Forest Hills Country (Rockford) (past sec.). Home: 2625 Harlem Blvd Rockford IL 61103 Office: 1817 18th Ave Rockford IL 61108

HORSTMANN, DOROTHY MILLICENT, physician, educator; b. Spokane, Wash., July 2, 1911; d. Henry J. and Anna (Hunold) H. A.B., U. Calif., 1936, M.D., 1940; D.Sc. (hon.), Smith Coll., 1961, M.A., Yale, 1961, Dr. Med. Scis., Women's Med. Coll. of Pa., 1963. Intern San Francisco City and County Hosp., 1939-40, asst. resident medicine, 1940-41, Vanderbilt U. Hosp., 1941-42; Commonwealth Fund fellow, sect. preventive medicine Sch. Medicine, Yale U., New Haven, 1942-43, instr. preventive medicine, 1943-44, 45-47, asst. prof., 1948- 52, asso. prof., 1952-56, asso. prof. preventive medicine and pediatrics, 1956-61, prof. epidemiology and pediatrics, 1961—, John Rodman Paul prof. epidemiology, prof. emeritus, 1982—; instr. medicine U. Calif., 1944-45. Recipient Albert Coll. award, 1953; Gt. Heart award Variety Club Phila., 1968; Modern Medicine award, 1974; James D. Bruce award ACP, 1975; Thorvald Madsen award State Secum Inst. (Denmark), 1977; Maxwell Finland award Infectious Disease Soc.-Am., 1978; Disting. Alumni award U. Calif. Med. Sch., 1979; NIH fellow Nat. Inst. Med. Research, London, 1947-48. Master A.C.P.; hon. asso. fellow Am. Acad. Pediatrics; mem. Am. Soc. Clin. Investigation, Am. Epidemiol. Soc., Am. Pediatric Soc., Am. Soc. Virology (council 1983-84), Assn. Am. Physicians, Infectious Diseases Soc. Am. (pres. 1974-75), Am. Assn. Immunologists, Soc. Epidemiologic Research, Pan Am. Med. Assn., Internat. Epidemiol. Assn., Royal Soc. Medicine (hon. mem. sect. epidemiology and preventive medicine), Nat. Acad. Scis., Conn. Acad. Sci. and Engring., European Assn. Against Virus Diseases., South African Soc. Pathologists. Home: 11 Autumn St New Haven CT 06511

HORSTMANN, JAMES DOUGLAS, college official; b. Davenport, Iowa, Oct. 2, 1933; s. Leonard A. and Agnes A. (Erhke) H.; m. Carol H. Griffiths, Sept. 8, 1956; children: Kent, Karen, Diane. B.A., Augustana Coll., 1955. C.P.A., Ill., Wis. Staff acct., auditor Arthur Andersen & Co., Chgo., 1955-61; v.p., controller Harry S. Manchester, Inc., Madison, Wis., 1961-65; sr. v.p. fin., treas. H. C. Prange Co., Sheboygan, Wis., 1965-83, also dir.; dir. planned giving Augustana Coll., Rock Island, Ill., 1983—; chmn. Wis. Mchts. Fedn.; dir. First Wis. Nat. Bank, Fond du Lac. Chmn. Sheboygan County (Wis.) Republican Party, 1969-70; vice chmn. Wis. 6th Congl. Dist., 1972-73; del. Nat. Rep. Conv., 1976; campaign chmn. Sheboygan United Way, 1977, treas., 1973-75, v.p., 1975-78, pres., 1978-79; bd. dirs. Public Expenditure Survey Wis., 1981-83; v.p. Sheboygan Arts Found., 1973-75; v.p., bd. dirs. Sheboygan Retirement Home. Served with USN, 1955-57. Recipient Outstanding Service award Augustana Coll., 1979. Mem. Wis. Inst. C.P.A.s, Sheboygan County Assn. C.P.A.s, Fin. Execs. Inst. (dir.), Quad-City Estate Planning Council, Augustana Coll. Alumni Assn. (pres. 1970-71). Lutheran. Clubs: Econ. of Sheboygan (pres. 1976-77), Kiwanis.). Home: 1245 36th Ave Rock Island IL 61201 Office: Augustana College 639 38th St Rock Island IL 61201

HORSTMYER, KENNETH LEROY, photog. developing co. exec.; b. Scotia, N.Y., Nov. 13, 1921; s. Albert William and Elizabeth May (Buhrmaster) H.; m. Madeleine Mary Slaughter, Apr. 14, 1950; children—Kendra Sally, Linda Cheryl, Jeffrey Lee, Andrew William. B.S., Miami U., Ohio, 1947; grad., Advanced Mgmt. Program, Columbia U., 1958. Dir. new market devel. Union Carbide Corp., N.Y.C., 1960-63; exec. v.p. Quality Cts. Motels, Inc., Daytona Beach, Fla., 1963-66; cons., 1966-67; pres. frozen foods div. W.R. Grace & Co., N.Y.C., 1967-70; exec. v.p. Burger King Corp., Miami, Fla., 1970-79; pres. Bonanza Internat., Inc., Dallas, 1978-79, Arthur Treachers Seafood, Inc., Phila., 1980, Photo Quick Am., Inc., Randolph, Mass., 1981—. Served with USNR, 1943-47. Mem. Am. Mgmt. Assn., Am. Mktg. Assn. Office: 27 Pacella Park Dr Randolph MA 02368

HORTE, VERNON L., energy consultant; b. Kingman, Alta., Can., July 12, 1925; s. Thor and Marit (Haugen) H.; m. Thelma Margaret Boness, Feb. 18, 1950; children: Joan Thelma, Robert Vernon, Douglas Boness. B.Sc. in Chem., Engring, U. Alta., 1949. Registered profl. engr., Alta., Tex. Gas engr. Oil and Gas Conservation Bd., Alta., 1949-52; petroleum engring. cons. De Goyler and MacNaughton, Dallas, 1952-57; with TransCan. Pipelines Ltd., 1957—, pres., dir., 1968-72; pres. Canadian Arctic Gas Study Ltd., 1972-77, V.L. Horte Assos. Ltd., Calgary, Alta., 1977—; dir. Nat. Trust Co.; dir Pan Can. Petroleum Ltd., Pro Gas Ltd.; dir. Gen. Accident Assurance Co. of Can., Can. Utilities Ltd., Morgan Hydrocarbons Inc., Precambrian Shield Resources Ltd. Served with RCAF, 1943-45. Mem. Can. Gas Assn., AIME, Can. Inst. Mining and Metallurgy, Can. Soc. Petroleum Geologists. Home: 305-3204 Rideau Pl S W Calgary AB Canada T2S 1Z2

HORTEN, CARL FRANK, textile mfg. co. exec.; b. Fort Lauderdale, Fla., Aug. 19, 1914; s. Joseph Frederick and Phyllis (Gregory) H.; m. Alice Jeannette Yereance, June 8, 1940; children—Bruce Carl, Lynn Alice, Heather Belle. B.S., Geneva Coll., 1936; M.B.A., Harvard, 1938; grad. exec. program, U. N.C., 1959. Sales corr. L. Sonneborn Sons, 1938-40; asst. controller Nashua Mfg. Co., 1940-47; controller Textron So., Inc., 1947-49; with Springs Mills, Inc., Ft. Mill, S.C., 1949—, v.p., 1964-66, treas., 1967—, exec. v.p., 1966—, sec., 1969, also dir.; chmn. bd. Lancaster Internat. Sales Corp., S.C.; treas., dir. Boundsgreen Co. Ltd., Bermuda; dir. Carolina Carpet Co., Daralon Textile Mfg. Corp., Jakarta, Indonesia. Served to lt. (j.g.) USNR, 1943-46. Home: PO Box 396 Fort Mill SC 29715 Office: Springs Mills Inc Fort Mill SC 29715

HORTON, AARON WESLEY, chemistry educator; b. Detroit, June 13, 1919; s. Aaron and Ethel May (Plant) H.; m. Margaret Virginia Cole, Jan. 31, 1941; children: Margaret (Mrs. Roger Alan Young), Joyce (Mrs. Frank Butler Hammond), Glenn David, John Wesley, Daniel Timothy. B.Sc., Yale U., 1940, M.Sc. (Univ. fellow), 1947, Ph.D. in Chemistry, 1948; postgrad., U. Mich., 1940-41, U. Pa., 1946. Sr. research chemist Socony-Vacuum Labs., 1941-43, 45-46; research engr. Franklin Inst. Research and Devel. Lab., 1948; asst. prof. indsl. health Kettering Lab., U. Cin., 1948-49, asso. prof., 1949-62, prof., 1962-63, vis. prof., 1963-66; prof. biochemistry, environ. medicine U. Oreg. Med. Sch., Portland, 1962-76, acting head div. environ. medicine, 1969-72, prof. biochemistry, pub. health and preventive medicine, 1976—, chief sect. chem. biology and oncology, 1976—; vis. prof. Institut National de la Santé et de la Recherche Médicale, Hôpital Debrousse, Lyon, France, 1972; Indsl. cons. toxicological problems, 1950—; dir. research project carcinogenicity of petroleum Am. Petroleum Inst., 1949-59; mem. adv. com. lung cancer research Am. Cancer Soc., 1955-56; mem. com. safety mineral oil adjuvants FDA, 1965-67. Contbr. articles to profl. jours. Served with USAAF, 1943-45. Mem. Am. Chem. Soc., Phi Beta Kappa, Sigma Xi. Research in chem. carcinogenesis and biophys. mechanisms thereof. Patentee in field. Home: 1525 Maple St Lake Oswego OR 97034 *Mental and physical tone require regular stimulation. When life offers alternatives, choose the challenges. Blend the activities in which success comes easily with some that tax you to the limit. Climb the mountain because you're there.*

HORTON, BERNARD FRANCIS, newspaper editor; b. Peabody, Kans., May 26, 1916; s. Frank H. and Lula Elizabeth (Stovall) H.; m. Betty Mildred Wessels, Dec. 20, 1938; 1 son, Gary Francis. B.A., U. Wyo., 1938. Owner, editor, pub. Chugwater News (handset weekly), Wyo., 1938-42; editor No. Wyo. Daily News, Worland, 1942-43, Rawlins (Wyo.) Daily Times, 1946-49; asst. news editor Wyo. Eagle, Cheyenne, 1949-52, news editor, 1952-54, mng. editor, 1955-62, editor, 1962-82, columnist, cons., 1982—; columnist Political and Otherwise.; mng. editor Pacific Stars and Stripes, 1946. Served with AUS, 1943-46; chief pub. relations sect. 97th Inf. Div.; ETO. Mem. Wyo. Press Assn. (pres. 1971—). Home: 3618 Dover Rd Cheyenne WY 82001 Office: 110 E 17th St: Cheyenne WY 82001

HORTON, CLAUDE WENDELL, physicist, educator; b. Cherryvale, Kans., Sept. 23, 1915; s. Roy Wesley and Marie (Terwilleger) H.; m. Louise Walthall, Nov. 23, 1938; children: Claude Wendell, Margaret Elaine. B.A. with honors in Physics, Rice Inst., 1935, M.A. in Physics, 1936; postgrad., Princeton U., 1937-38; Ph.D. in Physics, U. Tex., 1948. Asst. seismologist Shell Oil Co., 1936-37, party chief field crew, 1938-43; research asso. underwater sound lab. Harvard, 1943-45;

research physicist def. research lab. U. Tex., Austin, 1945—, prof. physics, 1953—, acting chmn. dept., 1956-57, chmn. dept., 1957-62, prof. geology, 1965—; Mem. corp. Woods Hole (Mass.) Oceanographic Instn., 1966—. Assoc. editor: Underwater Sound, Jour. Acoustical Soc. Am., 1982—. Fellow Acoustical Soc. Am. (Pioneers of Underwater Acoustics medal 1980), Am. Phys. Soc.; mem. AAAS, Am. Geophys. Union, Soc. Exploration Geophysicists. Home: Rt 1 Box 592 Granger TX 76530

HORTON, FRANK, congressman; b. Cuero, Tex., Dec. 12, 1919; s. Frank J. and Mary (Hathcox) H.; m. Nancy Richmond, Dec. 14, 1980; children by previous marriage: Frank Jefferson III, Steven William. B.A., La. State U., 1941; LL.B., Cornell U., 1947. Bar: N.Y. 1947. Assoc. Johnson, Reif & Mullan (and predecessor firm), Rochester, N.Y., 1947-52, ptnr., 1952-69; mem. 88th-98th congresses from 29th Dist. N.Y.; ranking minority mem. com. govt. ops., mem. congressional travel and tourism caucus, mem. ad hoc com. on energy, vice chmn. select com. on profl. sports, N.Y. rep. Republican com. on coms., mem. select com. on coms., dean N.Y. Rep. Congressional Del., 1981; congressional adv. Pres.'s Com. for Nat. Agenda for the 80's, Pres.'s Com. on Federalism, 1981; Participant U.S.-Can. Interparliamentary Conf., Ottawa, Ont., 1969, Washington, 1973; chmn. Commn. on Fed. Paperwork; co-chmn. Northeast-Midwest Econ. Advancement Coalition. Co-author: How to End the Draft, 1967, A Study of Urban Education in America, 1968. Mem. exec. com. Seneca dist. Otetiana council Boy Scouts Am., 1955—; pres. Rochester Community Baseball, Inc., 1957-62; councilman-at-large Rochester City Council, 1955-61; v.p. 18th Ward Men's Republican Club, 1957. Served to maj. AUS, 1941-46. Mem. ABA, N.Y. Bar Assn., Monroe County Bar Assn. (sec. 1953-57), Fedn. Bar Assns. Western N.Y. (pres. 1956-57), Res. Officers Assn. (past pres.), VFW, Am. Legion, Order Coif. Presbyterian (elder, former trustee). Lodges: Masons (33 deg.); Shriners. Office: 2229 Rayburn Bldg Washington DC 20515

HORTON, FRANK ELBA, university official, geography educator; b. Chgo., Aug. 19, 1939; s. Elba Earl and Mae Pauline (Prohaska) H.; m. Nancy Yocom, Aug. 26, 1960; children: Kimberly, Pamela, Amy, Kelly. B.A., Western Ill. U., 1963; M.S., Northwestern U., 1964, Ph.D., 1966. Faculty U. Iowa, Iowa City, 1966-75, prof. geography, 1966-75; dir. Inst. Urban and Regional Research, 1968-72, dean advanced studies, 1972-75; v.p. acad. affairs, research So. Ill. U., Carbondale, 1975-80; prof. geography and urban affairs, chancellor U. Wis., Milw., 1980—; dir. First Wis. Nat. Bank of Milw. Author, editor: (with B.J.L. Berry) Geographic Perspectives on Urban Systems - With Integrated Readings, 1970, Urban Environmental Management - Planning for Pollution Control, 1974; editor: Geographical Perspectives on Contemporary Urban Problems, 1973; editorial adv. bd.: Transportation, 1971-78. Co-chmn. Goals for Milw. 2000, 1981—, Greater Milw. Com., 1980; bd. govs. Am. Heart Assn., Wis., 1980—. Served with AUS, 1957-60. Mem. AAAS (nat. council 1976-78), Assn. Am. Geographers, Nat. Hwy Research Soc. Club: Rotary Milw. Home: 4430 N Lake Dr Milwaukee WI 53211 Office: U Wis-Milw PO Box 413 Milwaukee WI 53201

HORTON, GARY J., advertising agency executive; b. Grand Rapids, Mich., Dec. 9, 1940; s. J. William and Ruth Elizabeth (Tenckinck) H.; m. Karen Mae Eberhardt, Apr. 2, 1966; children: Matthew J., Melissa S. A.A., Grand Rapids Jr. Coll., 1960; B.A., Mich. State U., 1962. With Gen. Motors-Fisher Body, Detroit, 1962-67; v.p., creative dir. Leo Burnett Co., Chgo., 1967-79; sr. v.p., mng. dir. concepts Young & Rubicam, N.Y.C., 1979-82; exec. v.p., dir. creative services D'Arcy-MacManus & Masius, Chgo., 1982—. Office: D'Arcy-MacManus & Masius 200 E Randolph St Chicago IL 60601

HORTON, HORACE ROBERT, biochemistry educator; b. St. Louis, Aug. 26, 1935; s. Horace Reade and Martha Elizabeth (Gorg) H.; m. Roberta Alanne Geehan, Jan. 31, 1959; Robert Reade, Michael Edward, Richard Ashley, Rebecca Alanne. B.S., Mo. Sch. Mines and Metallurgy, 1956; M.S., U. Mo., 1958, Ph.D., 1962. Nat. Acad. Sci. fellow Brookhaven Nat. Lab., Upton, N.Y., 1961-62, research assoc., 1962-64; asst. prof. chemistry and biochemistry N.C. State U., Raleigh, 1964-67, assoc. prof. biochemistry, 1967-72, prof., 1972-81, Alumni Disting. prof., 1979-82, William Neal Reynolds Disting. prof., 1981—; vis. prof. biochemistry Lund U., Sweden, 1974. Contbr. articles to profl. jours. Bd. dirs. Wake Blood Plan, 1980—. Danforth assoc., 1968; NSF fellow, 1959-61; grantee NIH, 1966-72, 82—, NSF, 1972-80. Mem. Am. Soc. Biol. Chemists, Am. Chem. Soc. (juror, Kenneth A. Spencer award 1980-82), AAUP, N.C. State Acad. Outstanding Tchrs. (exec. bd. 1980-82), Sigma Xi, Phi Kappa Phi. Presbyterian. Office: NC State U PO Box 5050 Raleigh NC 27650

HORTON, HOWARD LEAVITT, musician, author; b. Hingham, Mass., June 13, 1904; s. Ervin S. and Ellen (Leavitt) H.; m. Zillah Louise Schurman, Aug. 24, 1925; children—Howard Leavitt Richard, Guinevere Ellen (Mrs. Donald C. Baker). Student, Boston U., 1946-47, Harvard Extension Sch., 1945-47, Emerson Coll. Evening Sch., 1948. With Boston Mus. Fine Arts, 1937-67, ret. as head. Organist, 1st Baptist Ch., Hingham, 1920; pioneer pianist for silent movies; profl. musician, 1923—; organist, Cape Cod nightclubs and S.W., 1925-33, Windjammer Restaurant, Wareham, Mass., 1972—; also pianist; organist, K.T. Lodge, New Bedford, 1973-74; watercolor artist works exhibited in libraries.; Author: poems Treatise on Mysticism, 1942, Hingham the Beautiful, 1944, Aspects of a New England Town, 1945, The South Shore Sketch Book, Glimpses of the South Shore; history, 1948, Biography of William Hudson Jr. of Hingham, 1964, Maritime History of Hingham, Massachusetts, 1969, Whalers-Clippers and Coasters of Hingham, 1971; also articles, short stories and radio scripts.; Composer: for piano My Waterloo; Author-pub.: New Eng. Chronicle. Mem. Democratic Nat. Com., 1944-81; del. Dem. Nat. Conv., 1944, 46; pres.'s club Nat. Dem. Party, 1976-81; mem. People for the American Way, 1981—. Served as cpl. Signal Corps AUS, 1942-43. Recipient Medal for 50 Years Entertainer Community Services, 1976; Hon. fellow Harry S. Truman Library. Mem. Am. Fedn. Musicians (life mem. local 155), Internat. Platform Assn., Nat. Trust for Historic Preservation, Mass. Soc. Founders and Patriots Am., SAR, Smithsonian Instn., Nat. Writers Club, Authors League Am., Nat. Assn. Leavitt Families (v.p. emeritus; life), Bourne-Wareham Art Assn., Internat. Mark Twain Assn. (hon. life), Intercontinental Biog. Assn. U.K., Hingham Hist. Soc., Hingham Library Assn., Pugwash Hist. Soc. N.S., Quincy Hist. Soc., Mass. Soc. Mayflower Descs., Mil. Order Loyal Legion U.S. Episcopalian. Club: Mason (Shriner). Began playing piano at age 3. Home: 8 Head of Bay Rd Buzzards Bay MA 02532

HORTON, JACK KING, utilities executive; b. Stanton, Nebr., June 27, 1916; s. Virgil L. and Edna L. (King) H.; m. Betty Lou Magee, July 15, 1937; children: Judy, Sally, Harold. A.B., Stanford U., 1936; LL.B., Oakland Coll. Law, 1941. Bar: Calif. 1941. Treasury dept. Shell Oil Co., 1937-42; pvt. law practice, San Francisco, 1942-43; atty. Standard Oil Co., 1943-44; sec., legal counsel Coast Counties Gas & Electric Co., 1944-51, pres., 1951-54; v.p. Pacific Gas & Electric Co., San Francisco, 1954-59; pres. So. Calif. Edison Co., 1959-68, chief exec. officer, 1965—, chmn. bd., 1968-80, chmn. exec. com., 1980—; dir. First Interstate Bank of Calif., Pacific Mut. Life Ins., Lockheed Aircraft Corp., First Interstate Bancorp. Trustee U. So. Calif., Nat. Indsl. Conf. Bd. Mem. State Bar Calif., Tax Found. (trustee), Bus. Council. Clubs: Pacific Union, Bohemian, California, Los Angeles Country, Cypress Point. Office: 2244 Walnut Grove Ave Rosemead CA 91770

HORTON, JAMES BAWDEN, magazine executive; b. St. Louis, May 22, 1930; s. Byrne Joseph and Dorothy Elizabeth (Bawden) H.; m. Ines Kirsimagi, July 13, 1957; children: Elizabeth, Jennifer, Christiana. A.B., Columbia U., 1950; M.B.A., N.Y. U., 1960. Salesman Wall St. Jour., Am. Home, 1950-56; asst. to pres. Curtis Pub. Co., 1957-62; print media dir. Young & Rubicam, 1963-66; pub. Atlas, 1966-68; v.p., gen. mgr., pub. Psychology Today, Intellectual Digest, Del Mar, Calif., 1968-74; gen. mgr. Nat. Observer, N.Y.C., 1974-76; group v.p. bus. affairs Playboy, Chgo., 1976-78; pres., pub., chief exec. officer Working Woman mag., N.Y.C., 1978-83; pres., chief exec. officer HAL Publs., Inc., N.Y.C., 1978—; pub. SUCCESS mag., N.Y.C., 1984—; lectr. NYU, 1970-83, asst. adj. prof., 1984—. Recipient Significant Sig award, 1981. Mem. Mag. Pubs. Assn., Vets. Corps Arty., Sigma Chi. Clubs: Univ., Ex-mems. Squadron A. Home: 235 E 62d St New York NY 10021 Office: Working Woman Mag 342 Madison Ave New York NY 10173

HORTON, JAMES WRIGHT, lawyer; b. Belton, S.C., Dec. 24, 1919; s. John Aiken and Emmae (Tate) H.; m. Eunice Rice, Nov. 20, 1948; children—James Wright, Max Rice, Rex Rice. B.A., Furman U., 1942; J.D., Harvard, 1948. Bar: S.C. bar 1948. Partner Nettles & Horton, 1948-52, Rainey, Fant & Horton, 1952-70, Horton, Drawdy, Marchbanks, Ashmore, Chapman & Brown, 1970-78, Horton, Drawdy, Hagins, Ward & Johnson, 1978; all Greenville, S.C. Pres. United Fund Greenville County, 1959; mem. Greenville County Sch. Trustees, 1964-70, vice chmn., 1969; pres. Greenville Family and Children's Service, 1954-55, 68-70; bd. dirs. Salvation Army, 1969—, treas., 1970-71; bd. dirs. Family and Children's Service, Greenville Mental Health Clinic, 1956-59, Greater Greenville Community Found., 1981. Served with USMCR, 1942-46. Decorated Silver Star. Mem. Greenville County Bar Assn. (pres. 1981). Baptist (deacon 1964-69, 71-72). Home: 2 Osceola Dr Greenville SC 29605 Office: 307 Pettigru St Greenville SC 29602

HORTON, JARED C., corporation executive; b. Greenwich, Conn., Oct. 8, 1924; s. Frederic Jared and Marcelene (Churchill) H.; m. Pauline Elizabeth Finn, June 14, 1947; children: Janette Elizabeth Horton Hall, Cynthia Joan, Allison Jane, Juliana Ruth. Student, Yale U., 1942; grad., Packard Jr. Coll., 1948. With PM Industries, Stamford, Conn., 1948-54; with Alleghany Corp., N.Y.C., 1954—, treas., 1956—, sec., 1959-61, 63—, v.p., 1967—. Served to 1st lt. AUS, 1942-46. Mem. Am. Soc. Corporate Secs. Episcopalian. Home: Coachlamp Ln Greenwich CT 06830 Office: 350 Park Ave Plaza New York NY 10055

HORTON, JOHN ALDEN, advertising executive; b. Providence, Jan. 11, 1920; s. Elmer Stuart and Margaret (Metcalf) H.; m. Marilyn Easton, Sept. 5, 1942; children: John Alden, Whitney Easton, Gay. B.S., U. Pa., 1941. Founder Horton, Church & Goff Inc., Providence, 1954, pres., treas., 1954-81, chmn., chief exec. officer, 1976-81; now chmn., chief exec. officer Creamer Inc./New Eng.; dir. Citizens Trust Co., Providence, Colonial Linen Systems Inc., Pawtucket, R.I., Providence Mut. Fire Ins. Co. Pres. Narragansett council Boy Scouts Am., 1966-68; civilian aide to Sec. Army; trustee R.I. Sch. Design, 1967-74, R.I. Indsl. Found. Served to 1st lt. USAAF, 1942-46. Named man of year Providence Advt. Club, 1965. Clubs: Turks Head, Hope, Providence Art, Barrington Yacht, Rotary (pres. Providence 1965-66). Home: 18 Stone Tower Ln Barrington RI 02806 Office: 800 Turks Head Bldg Providence RI 02903

HORTON, JOHN TOD, engineering company executive; b. Chgo., May 2, 1928; s. Horace Babcock and Phyllis (Fay) H.; m. Helene Arvanitidi, Jan. 8, 1959; children: Horace H., John M. Ph.B., U. Chgo., 1946; B.Civil Engring., Rensselaer Poly. Inst., 1952, M.S., 1953. Instr. Rensselaer Poly. Inst., 1952-53; with Chgo. Bridge & Iron Co., 1955—, mgr. spl. designs and estimates, 1959- 60, v.p. research, 1961-66, exec. v.p., 1966-68, pres., 1968-69, now dir.; pres. Horton Maritime Explorations Ltd., Vancouver, B.C., Can.; dir. H.P.D. Inc., Glen Ellyn, Ill., Pref. Utilities Mfg. Corp., Danbury, Conn., Beverly Bank, Chgo., Scolite Corp., Troy, N.Y. Trustee Rensselaer Poly. Inst. Mem. Am. Phys. Soc., ASCE, ASME, Sigma Xi, Chi Epsilon, Tau Beta Pi. Office: PO Box 1 Troy NY 12181

HORTON, ODELL, federal judge; b. Bolivar, Tenn., May 13, 1929; s. Odell and Rosa H.; m. Evie L. Randolph, Sept. 13, 1953; children: Odell, Christopher. A.B., Morehouse Coll., 1951; cert., U.S. Navy Sch. Journalism, 1952; J.D., Howard U., 1956; H.H.D. (hon.), Miss. Indsl. Coll., 1969. Bar: Tenn. bar 1956. Individual practice law, Memphis, 1957-62; asst. U.S. atty. Western Dist. Tenn., Memphis, 1962-67; dir. div. hosp. and health services, City of Memphis, 1968; judge Criminal Ct. Shelby County, Memphis, 1969-70; pres. LeMoyne-Owen Coll., Memphis, 1970-74; commentator Sta. WREC-TV (CBS), Memphis, 1972-74; judge U.S. Dist. Ct. Western Dist. Tenn., 1980—. Bd. mgrs. Methodist Hosp., Memphis, 1969-79; bd. dirs. Family Service of Memphis, United Negro Coll. Fund, N.Y.C., 1970-74; trustee Mt. Pisgah Christian Methodist Episcopal Ch., Memphis, after 1957. Served with USMC, 1951-53. Recipient Disting. Alumni award Howard U., 1969; Bill of Rights award West Tenn. chpt. ACLU, 1970; Disting. Service award Mallory Knights Charitable Orgn., 1970, Smothers Chapel C.M.E. Ch., 1971; Outstanding Citizen award Frontiers Internat., 1969; Ralph E. Bunche Humanitarian award Boy Scouts Am., 1972; Outstanding Educator and Judge award Salem-Gilfield Bapt. Ch., 1973; Spl. Tribute award A.M.E. Ch., 1974; United Negro Coll. Fund award, 1974; Humanities award Citizens Com. Council of Memphis, 1969; Shelby County Penal Farm award, 1974; Disting. Service award LeMoyne-Owen Coll., 1974, Lane Coll., 1977; Dedicated Community Service award Christian Meth. Episc. Ch., 1979. Mem. Am. Bar Assn., Nat. Bar Assn., NAACP. Home: 2183 S Parkway East Memphis TN 38114 Office: Fed Bldg and US Courthouse 167 N Main St Room 957 Memphis TN 38103

HORTON, PAUL BRADFIELD, lawyer; b. Dallas, Oct. 19, 1920; s. Frank Barrett and Hazel Lillian (Bradfield) H.; m. Susan Jeanne Diggle, May 19, 1949; children: Bradfield Ragland, Bruce Ragsdale. B.A., U. Tex., Austin, 1943, student Law Sch., 1941-43; LL.B., So. Methodist U., 1947. Bar: Tex. 1946. Since practiced in Dallas; partner firm McCall, Parkhurst & Horton, 1951—; lectr. mcpl. bond law and pub. finance S.W. Legal Found.; draftor Tex. mcpl. bonds legislation, 1963-83. Mem. Gov.'s Com. Tex. Edn. Code, 1967-69. Served to lt. USNR, 1943-46. Mem. Am., Dallas bar assns., Nat. Water Resources Assn., Tex. Water Conservation Assn., Mcpl. Finance Officers Assn., The Barristers, Delta Theta Phi, Beta Theta Pi. Clubs: Dallas Country, City, Tower, Chaparral, 2001 (Dallas); Austin. Home: 5039 Seneca Dr Dallas TX 75209 Office: 900 Diamond Shamrock Tower Dallas TX 75201

HORTON, ROBERT CARLTON, mining executive, geologist; b. Tonopah, Nev., July 25, 1926; s. Frank Elijah and Eathel Margaret (Miller) H.; m. Beverly Jean Burhans, Dec. 5, 1952; children: Debra, Robin, Cindy. B.S., U. Nev., 1949, Geol. Engr., 1966. Registered profl. geol. engr., Nev. Assoc. dir. Nev. Bur. Mines, Reno, 1956-66; cons., Reno, 1966-76; dir. geology div. Bendix Field Engring Corp. (Grand Junction), Colo., 1976-81; dir. U.S. Bur. Mines, Washington, 1981—; mem. Nev. Gov.'s Mining Adv. Com., 1966-72. Author: Barite Deposits of Nevada, 1962, Fluorspar Deposits of Nevada, 1963, History of Nevada Mining, 1963. Republican candidate for Congress from Nev., 1958. Served to lt. USNR, 1944-46, 53-56; PTO. Kennecott scholar, 1948; named Engr. of Yr. Reno chpt. Nat. Soc. Profl. Engrs., 1967. Mem. AIME (subsect. chmn. Reno 1962-63), Soc. Econ. Geologists, Mining and Metall. Soc. Am. Methodist. Office: US Bur of Mines 2401 E St NW Washington DC 20241

HORTON, THOMAS EDWARD, JR., educator; b. Houston, Jan. 12, 1935; s. Thomas Edward and Minnie Tolula (Sloan) H.; m. Bobbie Jean Newcomb, June 8, 1963; children—Holly Anne, Thomas Edward. B.S., U. Tex., 1957, Ph.D., 1964; M.S. (Caterpillar research fellow), Stanford U., 1958. Jr. mech. engr. Shell Devel. Co., Houston, 1957-58; teaching asst., research asst., research scientist U. Tex., Austin, 1959-62; research engr. Jet Propulsion Lab. Calif. Inst. Tech., Pasadena, 1962, sr. research engr., 1963-66; asso. prof. mech. engring., research engr. U. Miss., 1966-71, prof., research engr., 1971—; dir. U.S. Army Laser Sci. Lab., Redstone Arsenal, Ala., 1975-76; cons. Army Research Office, Jet Propulsion Lab., Marathon Oil Co., Shell Devel. Co., Exxon, Chevron, Mobil, Gulf. Contbr. articles to profl. jours. Asso. fellow AIAA (mem. tech. coms.); mem. ASME (mem. tech. coms.), Am. Phys. Soc., Am. Soc. Engring. Edn. (research award Southeastern sect. 1971), Sigma Xi (pres. local chpt.), Tau Beta Pi (student adviser), Pi Tau Sigma, Phi Eta Sigma. Republican. Methodist. Patentee in field. Home: 209 St Andrews Circle Oxford MS 38655 Office: U Miss University MS 38677

HORVAT, JOHN JAMES, educator; b. Detroit, Nov. 26, 1933; s. Paul and Emily Theresa (Jarvis) H.; m. Nancy Marie Fogt, Dec. 19, 1953; children: Diana Louise, Jason Brent. B.S. (Pres.'s scholar), Ohio State U., 1959, M.A., 1962, Ph.D., 1968. Adminstr. Columbus (Ohio) Pub. Schs., 1960-64; research assoc. Univ. Council for Ednl. Adminstrn., Columbus, 1964-66; exec. officer Nat. Inst. for Study Ednl. Change, Bloomington, Ind., 1966-69; assoc. dean Sch. Edn., Ind. U., 1969-73; prof. edn. Coll. Edn., N. Tex. State U., Denton, 1973—, dean, 1973-76; vis. prof. Boston U., 1968; vis. Distinguished prof. U. Vt., 1970. Author: Professional Negotiations in Education, 1967; Contbr. articles to profl. jours. Served with USNR, 1952-56. U.S. Office Edn. research grantee, 1970-71. Mem. Am. Assn. Sch. Adminstrs., AAUP, Am. Ednl. Research Assn., Am. Mensa, Denton C. of C., Phi Delta Kappa. Democrat. Lutheran. Lodge: Rotary. Office: North Tex State U Box 13396 Denton TX 76203

HORVATH, CSABA, chemical engineering educator, researcher; b. Szolnok, Hungary, Jan. 25, 1930; came to U.S., 1963; s. Gyula and Roza (Lanyi) H.; m. Valeria Bianca, May 14, 1963; children: Donatella, Katalin. Diploma in Chem. Engring., U. Tech. Scis., Budapest, Hungary, 1952; Ph.D., J.W. Goethe U., Frankfurt-am-Main, W.Ger., 1963; M.A. hon., Yale U., 1979. Asst. in chem. tech. U. Tech. Scis., Budapest, 1952-56; chem. engr. Hoechst AG, Frankfurt am Main, 1956-61; research fellow Harvard U., Cambridge, Mass., 1963-64; assoc. prof. Yale U., New Haven, 1970-79; prof. chem. engring. Sch. Medicine Yale U., New Haven, 1979—; cons. various indsl. orgns. Co-author: Introduction to Separation Science, 1973; editor: Series High Performance Liquid Chromatography, 1981—; contbr. research papers to publs.; mem.editorial bds. 5 sic. periodicals. Recipient S. Dal Nogare award Delaware Valley Chromatography Forum, 1978, M. Tswett award Acad. Scis. USSR, 1979, Humboldt sr. U.S. scientist award Humboldt Found., W.Ger., 1982. Mem. Am. Inst. Chem. Engrs., Am. Chem. Soc. (nat. chromatography award 1983), Inst. Food Technologists, DECHEMA, Sigma Xi. Home: 69 Pine Crest Rd Orange CT 06477 Office: Yale U 9 Hillhouse Ave New Haven CT 06540

HORVATH, IAN, dancer, choreographer; b. Cleve., June 3, 1946; s. Ernie W. and Helen Elizabeth (Nagy) H. Student, Sch. Performing Arts, N.Y.C., 1963. Guest tchr. Nat. Assn. Regional Ballet, Am. Ballet Theatre; adj. prof. Cleve. State U., 1976. Appeared in: summer stock in Musicarnival, 1962; dancer: Broadway musicals Here's Love, 1963, Sweet Charity, 1966; Ed Sullivan Show, 1963, Dean Martin Show, 1966; soloist, Joffrey Ballet, N.Y.C., 1964; dancer, Am. Ballet Theatre Corps de Ballet, 1967-69; soloist, 1969-74; founder, Cleve. Dance Center, 1974; founding artistic dir., Cleve. Ballet, 1976-84; Cons., Cleve. Ballet, 1984—. Mem. Actors Equity Assn., AFTRA, Am. Guild Musical Artists, Screen Actors Guild, Am. Assn. Dance Cos. Democrat. Office: Cleve Ballet 1375 Euclid Ave Cleveland OH 44115 *

HORVATH, RONALD JOSEPH, community college director; b. N.Y.C., Feb. 15, 1939; s. Joseph J. and Helen S. H.; m. Gladys Ann Albright, Aug. 25, 1962; children: Timothy J., Anne T. B.S., Kutztown (Pa.) State Coll., 1960, M.Ed., 1966; Ed.D., Lehigh U., Bethlehem, Pa., 1973. High sch. English tchr., 1960-67; v.p. planning and devel., div. chmn., dean arts and scis. Lehigh County Community Coll., Schnecksville, Pa., 1967-73; v.p. acad. affairs, then acting pres. Broome Community Coll., Binghamton, N.Y., 1973-75; dir. Jefferson Community Coll., Louisville, 1975—; cons. in field. Author guidebook, reports in field. Served with USAR, 1960-67. Named Ky. Col., 1976, Disting. Citizen of Louisville, 1977. Mem. Am. Assn. Higher Edn., Phi Delta Kappa. Democrat. Presbyterian. Club: Conversation (Louisville). Home: 1705 Sutherland Dr Louisville KY 40205 Office: 109 E Broadway Louisville KY 40202

HORVITZ, DANIEL GOODMAN, statistician, educator; b. New Bedford, Mass., Mar. 4, 1921; s. Jacob A. and Lillian J. (Cohen) H.; m. Shirley Gordon, Sept. 30, 1945; children—Gary Alan, Paul Fisher, Barbara Ann. B.S., Mass. State Coll., 1943; Ph.D., Iowa State U., 1953. Asst. prof. biostats. Sch. Public Health, U. Pitts., 1951-53; asso. prof. exptl. stats. N.C. State U., Raleigh, 1953-56; statis. dir. A.J. Wood Research Corp., Phila., 1956-60; vis. prof. stats. U. Rangoon, Burma, 1960-62; sampling sect. head Research Triangle Inst., Research Triangle Park, N.C., 1962-66, dep. dir. stats. research div., 1966-71; dir. Center for Population Research and Services, 1971-73, v.p. statis. scis. group, 1974—; prof. biostats. Sch. Public Health, U. N.C., Chapel Hill, 1973-74, adj. prof., 1974—; chmn. panel on stats. for family assistance and related programs, com. on nat. stats. NRC, 1980—. Contbr. articles to profl. jours. Served with U.S. Army, 1943-46. Fellow AAAS, Am. Statis. Assn. (adv. com. to Bur. Census 1970-71, 80—, chmn. social stats sect. 1975, chmn. survey research methods sect. 1981); mem. Am. Public Health Assn., Internat. Assn. Survey Statisticians (council 1983-86), Internat. Statis. Inst. (program chmn. 1983), Population Assn. Am., Sigma Xi, Phi Kappa Phi. Jewish. Home: 3115 Eton Rd Raleigh NC 27608 Office: PO Box 12194 Research Triangle Park NC 27709

HORVITZ, WAYNE LOUIS, mediator-arbitrator, labor-management consultant; b. Chgo., Oct. 8, 1920; s. Aaron and Gertrude Jeannette (Wayne) H.; m. Ann Battie, Aug. 16, 1945; children—William Wayne, Lee Marc, Wayne Barrow, Philip Robert. A.B., Columbia U., 1942; M.S. (Sloan fellow), M.I.T., 1953. Personnel and labor relations exec. Gen. Cable Corp., N.Y.C., 1947-57; partner Western Mgmt. Cons., Inc., Phoenix, 1957-60; asst. prof. mgmt. Ariz. State U., 1957-60; labor-mgmt. arbitrator, Phoenix, 1957-60; v.p. indsl. relations Matson Nav. Co., San Francisco, 1960-67, v.p., Washington, 1967-69; arbitrator, cons. on labor and pub. affairs, 1969-77; dir. Fed. Mediation and Conciliation Service, 1977-80; partner Horvitz & Schmert, 1981—; public mem., vice chmn., chmn. food industry tripartite wage and salary com. Cost of Living Council, 1973-74; chmn.

Joint Labor Mgmt. Com. Retail Food Industry, 1974-77; mem. Nat. Commn. on Productivity and Quality of Working Life, 1974-77. Served with AUS, 1942-46. Mem. Indsl. Relations Research Assn. Clubs: Internat., Federal City (Washington). Home: 4821 Linnean Ave NW Washington DC 20008 Office: Washington DC

HORWICH, GEORGE, economist, educator; b. Detroit, July 23, 1924; s. Charles and Rose (Katzman) H.; m. Geraldine Lessans, Dec. 27, 1953; children: Ellen Beth, Karen Louise, Robert Lloyd, Susan Jean. Student, Wayne State U., 1942-43, 46, Ind. U., 1943-44; A.M., U. Chgo., 1951, Ph.D., 1954. Lectr. econs. Ind. U. Extension Centers, Gar and Calumet, 1949-52; instr. econs. Ind U., Bloomington, 1952-55; research assoc. Nat. Bur. Econ. Research, N.Y.C., 1955-56; asst. prof. to prof. econs. Purdue U., West Lafayette, Ind., 1956—, chmn. econs. dept. policy com., 1974-78, Burton D. Morgan prof. pvt. enterprise Krannert Grad. Sch. Mgmt., 1981—; sr. research assoc. Brookings Instn., Washington, 1958-62; sr. economist U.S. Dept. Energy, Washington, 1978-80; mem. U.S. Treasury Cons. Group, Washington, 1969; cons. Fed. Res. Bank, Chgo., 1971-72; vis. prof. econs. U. Calif.-San Diego, 1971-72; staff mem. Ind. Council Econ. Edn., West Lafayette, 1974—, Ctr. Pub. Policy and Pub. Adminstrn., Purdue U., 1977—; advisor Econ. Inst. Research and Edn., Boulder, Colo., 1977—; cons. U.S. Dept. Energy, 1980—. Author: Money, Capital and Prices, 1964, (with others) Costs and Benfits of a Protective Tariff on Refined Petroleum Products After Crude Oil Decontrol, 1980, Energy: An Economic Analysis, 1983; editor: Monetary Process and Policy, 1967, (with P.A. Samuelson) Trade, Stability, and Macroeconomics, 1974, (with J.P. Quirk) Essays in Comtemporary Fields in Economics, 1981, (with E.J. Mitchell) Policies for Coping with Oil-Supply Disruptions, 1982, Energy Use in Transportation Contingency Planning, 1983; contbr. articles to profl. jours. Served with U.S. Army, 1943-46; ETO. NSF grantee. Mem. Internat. Assn. Energy Economists, Am. Econ. Assn., Acad. Ind. Scholars, Midwest Econs. Assn., Phila. Soc. Home: 120 Seminole Dr West Lafayette IN 47906 Office: Dept Econs Purdue U Krannert Grad Sch Mgmt West Lafayette IN 47907

HORWITT, MAX KENNETH, biochemist, educator; b. N.Y.C., Mar. 21, 1908; s. Harry and Bessie (Kenitz) H.; m. Frances Levine, 1933 (dec.); children: Ruth Ann Horwitt Singer, Mary Louise Horwitt Goldman; m. Mildred Gad Weitzman, Jan. 1, 1974. B.A., Dartmouth Coll., 1930; Ph.D., Yale U., 1935. Diplomate: Am. Bd. Nutrition, Am. Bd. Clin. Chemistry. Research fellow physiol. chemistry Yale U., 1935-37, lab. asst., 1932-34, asst., 1934-35; dir. biochem. research lab. Elgin (Ill.) State Hosp., 1937-59, L.B. Mendel Research Lab., 1960-68, dir. research, 1966-68; asso. dept. biol. chemistry U. Ill. Coll. Medicine, Chgo., 1940-43, asst. prof., 1943-51, asso. prof., 1951-62, prof., from 1962; prof. dept. biochemistry St. Louis U. Sch. Medicine, 1968-76, prof. emeritus, 1976—, cons. in nutrition div. endocrinology dept. internal medicine, 1976—, chmn. univ. instl. rev. bd., 1981-82; acting dir. div. research services Ill. Dept. Mental Health, Chgo., 1967-68; cons. human nutrition Rush Med. Sch., Chgo., 1967-83, vis. prof. dept. internal medicine, 1979-82; mem. expert group on Vitamin E WHO, 1981-82; field dir. Anemia and Malnutrition Research Center, Chiang Mai Med. Sch., Thailand, 1968-69; cons., 1976—. Contbr. numerous articles on clin. nutrition, biochemistry and psychopharmacology to profl. publs.; editorial bd.: Jour. Nutrition, 1967-71; co-editor: Am. Jour. Clin. Nutrition, 1974. Pres. Kneseth Israel Congregation, Elgin, 1965. Recipient Osborne and Mendal award Am. Inst. Nutrition, 1961. Fellow AAAS, N.Y. Acad. Scis., Am. Inst. Chemists, Gerontol. Soc.; mem. Am. Soc. Biol. Chemists, Am. Soc. Clin. Nutrition, NRC (food and nutrition bd. 1980—, com. dietary allowances), Soc. Exptl. Biology and Medicine, Soc. Biol. Psychiatry, Assn. Vitamin Chemists, Am. Chem. Soc. Office: St Louis Univ Sch Medicine 1402 S Grand Blvd Saint Louis MO 63104

HORWITT, WILL, sculptor; b. N.Y.C., Jan. 8, 1934. Student, Art Inst. Chgo., 1952-54. One-man exhbns. include, Stephen Radich Gallery, N.Y.C., 1963, 65, 67, Lee Ault & Co., N.Y.C., 1972, 74, 77, 79, Vanderwoude Tananbaum, N.Y.C., 1983, numerous group shows, including, Open Air Mus. Sculpture, Antwerp, Belgium, 1971, Whitney Mus. Am. Art, N.Y.C., 1973, Mus. Art, Ogunquit, Maine, Tanglewood, Lenox, Mass., Van Dam Park, Paramus, N.J., 1974, Gruenebaum Gallery, Ltd., N.Y.C., 1975, Keene (N.H.) State Coll., SUNY, Purchase, 1976, Indpls. Mus. Art, Weathespoon Art Gallery, N.C., 1982, U. N.C., Greensboro, 1982; represented in permanent collections, Indpls. Mus. Art, Boston Mus. Fine Arts, Wadsworth Arheneum, Hartford, Conn., Yale U. Art Gallery, Smith Coll. Mus. Art, Guggenheim Mus., Amherst Coll., Cornell U., Collection N.Y. State, Stephens Coll., Columbia, Mo., Chase Manhattan Bank, N.Y.C., Tokyo, Rome, Geneva, State U. N.Y. at Purchase, Albright Knox Art Gallery, Buffalo., Nelson A. Rockefeller Collection, Nat. Trust for Historic Preservation. Guggenheim fellow, 1965; grantee Louis Comfort Tiffany Found., 1968-69, Hereward Lester Cooke Found., 1979. Address: 60 Beach St New York NY 10013

HORWITZ, DONALD PAUL, restaurant chain executive; b. Chgo., Feb. 5, 1936; s. Theodore J. and Lillian H. (Shlensky) H.; m. Judith Robin, Aug. 23, 1964; children—Terry Robin, Linda Diane, Gail Elizabeth. B.S., Northwestern U., 1957; J.D., Yale U., 1960. Bar: Ill. bar 1961, D.C. bar 1961, U.S. Supreme Ct 1966; C.P.A., Ill. With atty.'s gen. honors program Dept. Justice, 1961-63; atty. firm Gottlieb & Schwartz, Chgo., 1963-66; with Arthur Young & Co. (C.P.A.'s), Chgo., 1966-72, ptnr., 1971-72; exec. v.p., sec., dir. McDonald's Corp., Oak Brook, Ill., 1972—; dir. CML Labs.; lectr. Grad. Sch. Commerce, DePaul U., Chgo. Contbr. articles to profl. jours. Mem. caucus nominating com. Village of Glencoe, Ill., 1975-78; bd. dirs. Chgo. Med. Sch./U. Health Scis., Recordings for Blind, Anti-Defamation League., Highland Park Hosp. Mem. Am., Ill., Chgo. bar assns., Am. Inst. C.P.A.'s, Ill. Soc. C.P.A.'s. Club: Briarwood Country (pres., dir.). Address: 1 McDonald's Plaza Oak Brook IL 60521

HORWITZ, IRWIN D., otolaryngologist, educator; b. Chgo., Mar. 31, 1920; s. Sol and Belle (Stern) H.; m. Isabel Morwitz, July 23, 1944; children—Steven, Judd, Clare. B.S., U. Ill., 1941, M.D., 1943. Intern Cook County Hosp., Chgo., 1944; resident Ill. Eye and Ear Infirmary, Chgo., 1946-48; practice otolaryngology, Chgo., 1948—; clin. prof., head div. otolaryngology Chgo. Med. Sch., 1969; prof. Rush Med. Sch., 1976—; chief div. otolaryngology Mt. Sinai Hosp., 1969—, pres. med. staff, 1969—. Contbr. articles profl. jours. Served to capt., M.C. AUS, 1944-46. Fellow A.C.S.; mem. AMA, Chgo. Otol. and Laryngol. Assn., Am. Acad. Ophthalmology and Otolaryngology, Ill., Chgo. med. socs. Home: 6431 N Knox St Lincolnwood IL 60646 Office: 55 E Washington St Chicago IL 60602

HORWITZ, MARTIN, lawyer; b. Bklyn., Nov. 3, 1920; s. Ernest and Betty (Weinstein) H.; m. Caryl Krieger, June 13, 1945; children—William Eric, Lauren. Student, Bklyn. Coll., 1942; LL.B., Harvard, 1948. Bar: Mass. bar 1948, N.Y. bar 1950. Gen. counsel UV Industries, Inc. (formerly U.S. Smelting Refining and Mining Co.), 1964-70, chmn. bd., 1965-70, pres., chief exec. officer, 1970-76, chmn. bd., chief exec. officer, 1976—; dir. Alaska Gold Co., Arava Exploration Co., Fed. Pacific Electric Co., Fed. Pioneer Ltd., Mueller Brass Co., Richmond-Eureka Mining Co., Ruby Hill Mining Co., U.S. Fuel Co., Ussram Exploration Co., U.S.S. Lead Refinery, Inc., Wash. Mining Co., White Knob Mining Co. Served to 1st lt., inf. AUS, World War II. Mem. Am. Mining Congress, County Lawyers Assn. N.Y. Clubs: City, Copper (N.Y.C.). Office: 437 Madison Ave New York NY 10022 *

HORWITZ, MORTON J., law educator; b. 1938. A.B., CCNY, 1959, Ph.D., 1964; LL.B., Harvard U., 1967. Bar: Mass. 1970. Law clk. to judge U.S. Ct. Appeals D.C. Cir., 1967-68; Charles Warren fellow Harvard U., 1968-70, asst. prof. law, 1970-74, prof., 1974—. Author: The Transformation of American Law, 1780-1860, 1977. Mem. Selden Soc., Am. Soc. Legal History. Office: Harvard U Law Sch Cambridge MA 02138 *

HORWITZ, ORVILLE, physician; b. Strafford, Pa., Nov. 20, 1909; s. George Quintard and Marian (Newhall) H.; m. Nataline B. Dulles, Sept. 15, 1934; children: Marian Newhall Horwitz Parmenter, George Dulles, Jonathan. B.S., Harvard U., 1932; M.D., Johns Hopkins U., 1936; M.A. (hon.), U. Pa., 1971. Diplomate: Am. Bd. Internal Medicine. Intern Pa. Hosp., 1938-40, chief med. resident, 1940-41, fellow in cardiology, 1942; mem. faculty U. Pa. Med. Sch., 1941—, prof. medicine, 1970—, prof. pharmacology, 1973—; chief vascular clinic Hosp. U. Pa., 1966-69, chmn. com. patient care, 1973-75; cons. NASA, 1946-69; founder, since pres. Found. Vascular Hypertension Research., 1971. Author: Cardiac and Vascular Diseases, 1971; also articles.; Co-editor: Index of Suspicion in Treatable Diseases, 1975. Served to lt. comdr., M.C. USNR, 1942-46. Grantee NIH, 1950-81. Fellow A.C.P. (dir. courses 1972, 76, asso. editor bull. 1950-56); mem. Am. Coll. Cardiology (dir. course 1976), Am. Physiol. Soc., Microcirculatory Conf., Am. Clin. and Climatol. Assn. (v.p. 1982-83), Am. Heart Assn. (chmn. council circulation 1966-68, chmn. sci. councils 1973-75), Shakespeare Soc. Phila. Democrat. Episcopalian. Clubs: Phila., Sons of Copper Beaches, Faculty U. Pa., Athenaeum (Phila.); Gulph Mills Golf (dir. 1965-66). Home: 267 St Joseph's Way Philadelphia PA 19106 Office: 829 Spruce St Philadelphia PA 19107 *In the past half century technology has far outdistanced philosophy and good will. The bomb, the box, the machine, and the pill are each responsible for a revolution of their own. Only by understanding themselves and others will we be able to deal with scientific advances of such magnitudes.*

HORWITZ, PAUL, physicist; b. N.Y.C., Dec. 4, 1938; s. Louis David and Sylvia Helen (Laibman) H.; m. Eleanor Catherine Jahoda, Aug. 15, 1964; children: Gregory Douglas Lee, Catherine Helen, Laura Elizabeth. A.B. (Gen. Motors Corp. scholar), Harvard U., 1960; M.S., Columbia U., 1963; Ph.D., NYU, 1967. Research asso. Cornell U., Ithaca, N.Y., 1967-69, U. Oreg., Eugene, 1969-71; prin. research scientist Avco Everett Research Lab., Everett, Mass., 1971-79; sr. scientist Bolt, Baranek & Newman, Inc., Cambridge, Mass., 1979—; research fellow Center for Policy Alternatives, M.I.T., 1978-79. Contbr. articles to profl. jours. Mem. Sch. Com., Concord, Mass., chmn., Concord, Mass., 1983. Recipient Founders' Day award N.Y. U., 1969; Am. Phys. Soc. Congl. fellow, 1975-76. Mem. Am. Phys. Soc. (vice chmn. forum on physics and society 1978, chmn. 1979), AAAS, Fedn. Am. Scientists. Home: 32 Riverside Ave Concord MA 01742 Office: 10 Moulton St Cambridge MA 02138

HORWITZ, ROBERT HENRY, political science educator; b. El Paso, Tex., Sept. 3, 1923; s. David and Louise (Mendelsohn) H.; m. Noreen Margaret Surti, Jan. 1948; children: Susheila Louise, David D. B.A., Amherst Coll., 1949; M.A., U. Hawaii, 1950; Ph.D., U. Chgo., 1954. Asst. prof., researcher U. Hawaii, 1948-51; research asst. com. for study citizenship edn. U. Chgo., 1953-55; from asst. prof. to prof. polit. sci. Mich. State U., East Lansing, 1956-66; prof. polit. sci., chmn. dept. Kenyon Coll., Gambier, Ohio, 1966—, dir. Pub. Affairs Conf. Ctr., 1976-78. Co-author: John Locke's Questions Concerning the Law of Nature, 1981; editor: The Moral Foundations of the American Republic, 1977; contbr. articles to profl. jours. Served with AUS, 1942-46; ETO, PTO. Decorated Bronze Star, Combat Inf. badge; fellow Emil Schwartzhaupt Found., 1953-55, Rockefeller Found., 1959, Ford Found., 1956-58; NEH fellow, 1973-76. Mem. AAUP, Am. Polit. Sci. Assn., Am. Soc. Polit. and Legal Philosophy. Jewish. Home: 214 Kokosing Dr Gamier OH 43022 Office: Dept Polit Sci Kenyon Coll Gambier OH 43022

HOSAGE, DANIEL ANDREW, computer mfg. co. exec.; b. Wilkes-Barre, Pa., Aug. 18, 1932; s. Andrew H. and Julie B. (Socchnick) H.; m. Elizabeth Kokolus, Nov. 25, 1954; children—Brent, Daniel Andrew, Mark, Betsy. A.B., Muhlenberg Coll., 1954. With IBM, 1954-69, product program mgr., White Plains, N.Y., 1965-69; v.p. mktg. and program mgmt. REI, Dallas, 1970-71; v.p., group exec. ofvice systems group Datapoint Corp., San Antonio, 1979—. Author articles in field. Bd. dirs., v.p. San Antonio Chamber Players, 1980—. Office: 9725 Datapoint Dr San Antonio TX 78284

HOSBACH, HOWARD DANIEL, publishing company executive; b. North Bergen, N.J., Mar. 9, 1931; s. Howard D. and Marjorie V. (Hoffer) H.; m. Eugenia Elizabeth Paracka, Apr. 10, 1954; children: Susan Hosbach Murray, Cynthia Hosbach Miezeiewski, Beth Ann, Alyssa. B.S., Fairleigh Dickinson U., 1953, M.B.A., 1967. Advt. mgr. McGraw-Hill Book Co., N.Y.C., 1958-62, dir. mktg., 1962-66, gen. mgr. dealer and library sales, 1966-69; group v.p. Standard & Poor's Corp., N.Y.C., 1970-73, exec. v.p., chief operating officer, 1973-80, pres., chief exec. officer, 1981—, dir., 1970—; chmn. Standard & Poor's Computstat Services, Inc., Denver; dir. Standard & Poor's Internat. S.A., Belgium, Standard & Poor's Securities, Inc., N.Y.C. Vice chmn. devel. council Fairleigh Dickinson U.; trustee Peirce Jr. Coll.; chmn. Assn. for Help Retarded Children, 1983—; mem. Governing Bds. of Univs. and Colls., 1983—. Served with AUS, 1953-55. Recipeint Alumni medal for disting. service Fairleigh Dickinson U. Trustees. Roman Catholic. Home: 104 Green Way Allendale NJ 07401 Office: 25 Broadway New York NY 10004

HOSEA, ADDISON, bishop; b. Pikeville, N.C., Sept. 11, 1914; s. Addison and Alma Eugenia (Bowden) H.; m. Jane Eubank Marston, June 24, 1944; children: Nancy Jane, Addison III, Anne Cameron. A.B., Atlantic Christian Coll., 1938; M.Div., U. South, 1949, D.D., 1970; D.D., Episcopal Theol. Sem., Ky., 1968; postgrad., Union Theol. Sem., 1948, Duke, 1950-53; D.D., Episcopal Theol. Sem., Ky., 1968. Tchr. pub. schs., Wayne County, N.C., 1932-34, Currituck County, N.C., 1938-41; ordained to ministry Episcopal Ch.; as deacon, 1948, priest, 1949; priest-in-charge St. Gabriel's, Faison, N.C., 1949-51; rector St. Paul's, Clinton, N.C., 1949-54, St. John's, Versailles, Ky., 1954-70; bishop coadjutor Diocese of Lexington, Ky., 1970; 4th bishop of, Lexington, 1971—; prof. N.T. lang. and lit. Episcopal Theol. Sem., Ky., 1954-59, 65-70; mem. exec. council Diocese East Carolina, 1951-54, Diocese Lexington, 1954-70, examining chaplain, 1964-70; canon Cathedral St. George the Martyr, Crystal, Ky., 1964-70; Mem. standing com. Diocese Lexington, 1957-58, 60-64; dep. Gen. Conv., 1955, 58, 64, 67, 69. Trustee U. South, 1949-54, 70—. Served to capt. AUS, 1941-46. Mem. Soc. Bibl. Lit. Home: 536 Sayre Ave Lexington KY 40508 Office: 530 Sayre Ave Lexington KY 40508

HOSEY, RICHARD FREDRICK, oil company executive; b. San Angelo, Tex., July 24, 1944; s. K. Richard and Jean J. (Baer) H.; m. Barbara J. Mullins, June 3, 1978; children: Ross F., Amanda J. B.A., Tex. Christian U., 1966; J.D., So. Meth. U., 1969. Bar: Tex. Contracts analyst SIP, Inc., Houston, 1969-71; assoc. firm Mounger & Whittington, Houston, 1971-72; v.p., corp. counsel Research Fuels, Inc., Houston, 1972-76; asst. gen. counsel Conroy, Inc., San Antonio, 1976-79; corp. sec., atty. Commonwealth Oil & Refining Co., San Antonio, 1979-82; v.p., gen. counsel, sec. Harkins & Co., Alice, Tex., 1982—. Mem. ABA, Am. Soc. Corp. Secs., Tex Bar Assn. Club: Kiwanis. Home: 1309 Arcadia Dr Alice TX 78332 Office: 1000 Harkins Ave Alice TX 78332

HOSIE, WILLIAM CARLTON, walnut growers company executive; b. Stockton, Calif., June 25, 1936; s. Fred A. and Janet (Russell) H.; m. Sherryl Rasmussen, Jan. 12, 1963; children: Shaen Case, Erin Frick. B.S., U. Calif.-Davis, 1960. Field rep. Flotill Inc., Stockton, Calif., 1960-61; orchardist Hosie Ranch Inc., Linden, Calif., 1961-83; chmn. bd. dirs. Diamond Walnut Growers Inc., Stockton, Calif., 1981—; advisor U. Calif. Extension-Stockton, 1975—, Calif. Farm Bur., Sacramento, 1976—, Farmer and Mchts. Bank, Linden, 1979; dir. Walnut Mktg. Bd., San Mateo, Calif., 1981—. Pres. Stockton East Water Dist., 1969-79. Served with AUS, 1958-59. Mem. Stockton C. of C. Republican. Club: Rotary Internat. Home: PO Box 226 Linden CA 95236 Office: Diamond Walnut Growers Inc 1050 S Diamond St Stockton CA 95201

HOSKING, ROBERT LEROY, broadcasting exec.; b. Ramsey, N.J., Nov. 9, 1931; s. Charles E. and Luella (Bartholf) H.; m. Valentina Kopach, Sept. 8, 1957; children—Deborah, Patricia, Wesley. B.A., Gettysburg Coll., 1953; M.B.A., U. Mich., 1958. Mgmt. trainee CBS, Inc., 1958-59; account exec. WCBS, 1959-63; gen. sales mgr. WCBS radio, 1963-70; v.p., gen. mgr. Sta.-WCBS-TV, N.Y.C., 1970-74, Sta.-WCAU-TV, Phila., 1974-78; v.p. affiliate relations CBS TV Network, N.Y.C., 1978-81; pres. CBS Radio, N.Y.C., 1981—; bd. dirs. Radio Advt. Bur., Advt. Council. Served with USN, 1953-56. Named Outstanding Alumnus Gettysburg Coll., 1981. Presbyterian. Clubs: N.Y. Athletic, Hartwood. Office: CBS Radio 51 W 52d St New York NY 10019

HOSKINS, CHARLES ROSS, banker; b. Sneedville., Tenn., June 26, 1941; s. Clyde Ross and Cecile Mildred (Darnell) H.; m. Jo Ann Smith, Mar. 24, 1963; children: Ashley Arden, Charles Ross. B.S., U. Tenn., 1963; grad., Program Mgmt. Devel., Harvard U., 1971. Exec. v.p. Citizens & So. Nat. Bank, Atlanta, 1963-78; sr. v.p. Bancohio Corp., Columbus, 1978-83; exec. v.p. Fla. Nat. Bank, Jacksonville, 1983—. Mem. exec. bd., sustaining membership chmn. Atlanta Area council Boy Scouts Am., 1973-74; mem. Manpower Area Planning Commn., 1972-73; mem. steering com. Am. Inst. Banking; chmn. Devel. Com. Greater Columbus; mem. Leadership Atlanta, 1975-76; chmn. personnel com., bd. deacons 2d Ponce de Leon Baptist Ch.; trustee Franklin U., Columbus U.S.A. Assn. Served with AUS, 1967. Named one of Outstanding Young People of Atlanta, 1974. Mem. Bank Adminstrn. Inst. (human resource commn.), Nat. Alliance Businessmen (adv. bd.), Am. Soc. Personnel Adminstrs., U. Tenn. Alumni Atlanta (pres.), Am. Bankers Assn. (chmn. bank personnel div.; dir.), Delta Tau Delta. Clubs: Cherokee Town and Country, Rotary, Scioto Country, Columbus Athletic. Home: 4964 Prince Edward Rd. Jacksonville FL 32210 Office: 214 Hogan St Jacksonville FL 32202

HOSKINS, JOHN H., urologist, educator; b. Breckenridge, Minn., Mar. 18, 1934; s. James H. and Ruth (Johanson) H.; m. Nancy Weih, Aug. 3, 1957; children: William, James, Laura, Sarah. B.A. in History, U. Iowa, 1956; B.S. in Medicine, U. S.D., 1959; M.D., Temple U., 1961. Diplomate: Am. Bd. Urology. Practice medicine specializing in urology, Sioux Falls, 1966—; head sect. urology U.S.D. Sch. Medicine, Vermillon, 1977—. Maj. M.C. U.S. Army, 1967-69; Vietnam. Fellow ACS; mem. AMA, Am. Urol. Assn., Univ. Urol. Forum, Am. Fertility Soc. Republican. Methodist. Clubs: Deans (U. S.D.); Rotary (Sioux Falls). Office: Urology Specialists Chartered 1200 S Euclid Suite 312 Sioux Falls SD 57105

HOSKINS, JOHN RICHARD, mining engineering educator; b. Brewster, Wash., June 9, 1919; s. Joseph Henry and Frieda (Bloss) H.; m. Artys Leora Colton, Jan. 1, 1979; children: William N., Gretchen M., DeEtte. B.S., U. Idaho, 1947; Ph.D., Va. Poly. Inst., 1962; postgrad., U. Utah. Registered profl. engr., Alaska, Colo. From instr. to asst. prof. mining engring. U. Alaska-Juneau, 1952-57; NSF faculty fellow U. Utah, 1957-62, Va. Poly. Inst., 1958-59; prof. mining engring. U. Idaho, 1967—; developer, grader profl. engring. exams Idaho and U.S., 1968-82. Inventor high strength concrete; author: Mineral Industry Costs, 1981; contbr. chpt. to book. Bd. dirs. Moscow Christian Sci. Soc., 1980—; chmn. bd. Millcreek, Salt Lake City, 1964-67. Served with USNR, 1941-45. Recipient Starters N.W. Mining Assn., 1981. Mem. Soc. Mining Engrs. of AIME, Am. Soc. Engring. Edn. (exec. bd. 1974-76). Home: 745 Brent Dr Moscow ID 83843 Office: University of Idaho Mining and Metallurgy Dept Moscow ID 83843

HOSKINS, RICHARD JEROLD, lawyer; b. Ft. Smith, Ark., June 19, 1945; s. Walter Jerold and Emma Gladys (Gaither) H.; children: Stephen Weston, Philip Richard. B.A., U. Kans., 1967; J.D., Northwestern U., 1970. Bar: N.Y. 1971, Ill. 1976, U.S. Supreme Ct. 1982. Assoc. Davis Polk & Wardwell, N.Y.C., 1970-73; asst. U.S. atty., So. Dist. N.Y., 1973-76; assoc. Schiff Hardin & Waite, Chgo., 1976-77, ptnr., 1978—; lectr. U. Va. Law Sch., 1980—. Contbr. article to profl. jours. Mem. Chgo. Crime Commn.; bd. dirs. Garfield-Austin Community Legal Ctr.; mem. vis. com. U. Chgo. Div. Sch. Mem. ABA, Ill. Bar Assn., Chgo. Bar Assn., Chgo. Council Lawyers, assn. Bar City N.Y., Chgo. Council Fgn. Relations, Am. Arbitration asns. (nat. panel arbitrators). Clubs: Univ., Met. (Chgo.). Office: 7200 Sears Tower Chicago IL 60606

HOSKINS, TOM, department store executive; b. O'Donnell, Tex., May 27, 1944; s. Jack and Billie (Brandon) H.; m. Janice Stewart Clayton, Aug. 21, 1963; children: Laurie Carol, Julia Elizabeth. B.B.A., Tex. Tech. U., 1966. Exec. v.p. Dunlap Co., Ft. Worth, 1962—; pres. Stripling & Cox, Ft. Worth, 1978—. Home: 2314 Wakeforest Ct Arlington TX 76019 Office: Dunlap Co 200 Greenleaf St Ft. Worth TX 76107

HOSLER, CHARLES LUTHER, JR., meteorologist, educator, university dean; b. Honey Brook, Pa., June 3, 1924; s. Charles Luther and Miriam Deichley (Stauffer) H.; m. Gladys Cheesbrough, 1947 (div.); children:Sharon Elizabeth, David Charles, Lynn Rebecca, Peter William; m. Anna R. Stahel, 1971. Student, Bucknell U., 1943-44, Mass. Inst. Tech., 1944-45; B.S., Pa. State U., 1947, M.S., 1948, Ph.D., 1951. Faculty Pa. State U., University Park, 1948—, prof. meteorology, 1960—, head dept., 1961-65, dean, 1965—; Hydrographer Pa. Dept. Forests and Waters, 1949-59; meteorol. cons., 1950—, vis. prof. colls., lectr. civic and profl. groups; condr. daily TV weather program, 1957-67; spl. research microphysics of clouds; adv. com. on meteorology EPA; chmn. storm fury adv. panel Nat. Acad. Scis.; mem. nat. adv. com. on oceans and atmosphere., mem., chmn. bd. trustees Univ. Corp. for Atmospheric Research, Boulder, Colo., 1981—. Contbr. articles to profl. jours. Served to lt. (j.g.) USNR, 1943-46; lt. comdr. Res. Fellow Am. Meteorol. Soc. (councilor, pres. 1976); mem. Nat. Acad. Engring., Am. Geophys. Union (award outstanding paper hydrology 1955), ASCE (weather modification com.), Am. Chem. Soc. (regional lectr. 1971-72), AAUP (v.p. Pa. State U. 1961), AAAS, Sigma Xi (pres. Pa. State U. 1958, nat. lectr. 1972), Tau Beta Pi, Sigma Gamma Epsilon. Home: 1229 Smithfield Circle State College PA 16801 Office: Earth and Mineral Scis Pa State U University Park PA 16802

HOSLER, RUSSELL JOHN, ret. educator; b. DuPont, Ohio, Apr. 2, 1906; s. John Henry and Etta (Spitznaugle) H.; m. Hilda Elizabeth Weible, Dec. 25, 1927 (div. Oct. 1966); children—Philip Eugene, Helen Hosler Daggett, Russell John; m. Mary Margaret O'Connell, Aug. 23, 1968. A.B., Defiance Coll., 1932; M.A., Toledo U., 1941; Ed.D., Ind. U., 1946. Tchr. high sch., Montpelier, Ohio, 1927-34, Fostoria, Ohio, 1934-38, Libbey High Sch., Toledo, 1938-42; asst. prof. commerce Ind. U., 1942-46; faculty U. Wis., Madison, 1946—, prof., 1953-76, emeritus, 1976—, chmn. dept. edn., 1955-59. Co-author: Gregg Shorthand for Colleges, rev. edit, 1958, 65, 73, Gregg Transcription for Colleges, 1959, rev. edit., 1966, 75, Programmed Gregg Shorthand, 1969, Personal Typing, 1979; contbr. articles to profl. profl. mags. Recipient John Robert Gregg award, 1966. Mem. Nat. Bus. Edn. Assn. (pres. 1968-69), Nat. Bus. Tchrs. Assn. (pres. 1955), Nat. Assn. Bus. Tchr. Edn. (pres. 1959-61). Home: Rt 1Hwy KK Milton WI 53563

HOSOKAWA, WILLIAM K., editor; b. Seattle, Jan. 30, 1915; s. Setsugo and Kimiyo (Omura) H.; m. Alice Tokuko Miyake, Aug. 28, 1938; children: Michael, Susan Hosokawa Boatright, Peter, Christie Hosokawa Harveson. B.A., U. Wash., 1937. Mng. editor Singapore Herald, 1939-40; writer Far Eastern Rev., Shanghai, China, 1940-41; editor Heart Mountain (Wyo.) Sentinel, 1942-43; copy editor Des Moines Register, 1943-46; with Denver Post, 1946-83, war corr., 1950; editor Empire mag., 1950-57, exec. news editor, 1957-58, asst. mng. editor, 1958-60, Sunday editor, 1960-62, asso. editor, 1963-77, editor editorial page, 1977-83, columnist, 1983—; Pulitzer prize journalism juror, 1969, 70, 75, 76, 81; lectr. journalism U. No. Colo., 1973-75, U. Colo., 1974, 76. Author: Nisei: The Quiet Americans, 1969, The Two Worlds of Jim Yoshida, 1972, Thunder in the Rockies, 1976, 35 Years in the Frying Pan, 1978, (with Robert W. Wilson) East to America, 1980, JACL in Quest of Justice, 1982. Del. Japanese-Am. Assembly, 1972, Japanese-Am. Bilateral Meeting, Internat. Press Inst., 1972, 73, 75, 79, 81; Bd. dirs. Kidney Found., Rocky Mountain Region, Colo. People to People Corp. Recipient Disting. Achievement award Japanese Am. Citizens League, 1952; Nisei of Biennium, 1958; Western Heritage award Cowboy Hall of Fame, 1966; Outstanding Colo. Journalist award U. Colo., 1967; Outstanding Journalist award Colo. Soc. Profl. Journalists, 1976; hon. consul-gen. Japan for Colo., 1975—. Mem. Am. Assn. Sunday and Feature Editors (pres. 1956), Am. Soc. Newspaper Editors Nat. Conf. Editorial Writers, Sigma Delta Chi. Home: 140 S Upham Ct Denver CO 80226 Office: 650 15th St Denver CO 80202

HOSPERS, JOHN, philosophy educator; b. Pella, Iowa, June 9, 1918; s. John G. and Dena (Verhey) H. B.A., Central Coll., 1939, D.Litt., 1962; M.A., State U. Iowa, 1941; Ph.D., Columbia U., 1944. Instr., Columbia U., 1946-48; asst. prof., asso. prof. U. Minn., 1948-56; prof. Bklyn. Coll., 1956-66, Calif. State Coll., Los Angeles, 1966-68; prof. philosophy U. So. Calif. Sch. Philosophy, Los Angeles, 1968—; Fulbright research scholar U. London, 1954-55; vis. prof. UCLA, 1960-61, 64. Author: Meaning and Truth in the Arts, 1946, (with W. Sellars) Readings in Ethical Theory, 1970, Introduction to Philosophical Analysis, 1967, Human Conduct, 1961, rev. edit., 1982, Readings in Introductory Philosophical Analysis, 1968, Introductory Readings in Aesthetics, 1969, Artistic Expression, 1971, Libertarianism, a Political Philosophy for Tomorrow, 1971, Understanding the Arts, 1982. Mem. Am. Philos. Assn., Am. Soc. Aesthetics (pres.), Mind Assn. Home: 8229 Lookout Mountain Ave Los Angeles CA 90046

HOSPODOR, ANDREW THOMAS, electronics executive; b. Endicott, N.Y., Jan. 30, 1937; s. Andrew and Verna (Yurick) H.; m. Rose Marie Pitarra, June 28, 1958; children: Andrew D., Sarah E., Peter J. B.S.M.E., Cornell U., 1960; M.S.M.E., Lehigh U., 1963, M.B.A., 1967. Product specialist Air Products Inc., Emmaus, Pa., 1960-66; mgr. RCA Corp., Camden, N.J., 1966-77, dir. mktg., Burlington, Mass., 1977-79, program mgr. command and control, 1979-81, dir. v.p., gen. mgr., 1981—. Mem. Assn. U.S. Army, Air Force Assn., Navy League U.S., Am. Def. Preparedness Assn., AIAA. Home: 224 Chestnut St West Newton MA 02165 Office: PO Box 588 Burlington MA 01803

HOSTAGE, G. MICHAEL, corporate executive; b. N.Y.C., 1933; married. B.S. in Econs., Cornell U., 1954. Dist mgr. Procter & Gamble, 1955-63; corp. exec. v.p. Marriott Co., 1963-79; pres., chief exec. officer ITT Continental Baking Co., Rye, N.Y., 1979-81, Howard Johnson Co., 1982—. Office: Howard Johnson Co One Howard Johnson Plaza Boston MA 02125

HOSTERMAN, FRED O., mfg. co. exec.; b. Millheim, Pa., Mar. 16, 1916; s. Fred O. and Barbara (Winegardner) H.; m. Carol Henry, Nov. 7, 1958; 1 dau., Lynn Ann Hosterman; children by previous marriage—Barbara, Jane, Fred O. III. Student aero. engring., Bellefonte (Pa.) Sch. Aero., 1934; B.S. in Aero. Engring, Parks Air Coll., East St. Louis, Ill., 1936. From design engr. to design specialist Lockheed Aircraft Corp., 1936-51; with Weston Hydraulics div. Borg-Warner Corp., Van Nuys, Cal., 1951-70, pres., gen. mgr., 1959-61, pres., chief exec. officer, 1961-70; v.p., operations mgr. Hydraulic Research div. Textron Inc.; Mem. aircraft adv. com. to asst. sec. def. for research and devel., 1954-57. Adv. editor: Applied Hydraulics mag, 1949-51; Author papers in field. Recipient Alumni Merit award St. Louis U., 1959. Mem. Soc. Automotive Engrs. (chmn. So. Calif. sect. 1950-51, v.p. aircraft sect. 1956, chmn. tech. com. A-6A 1948-57), Am. Ordnance Assn., Van Nuys C. of C. Home: 7563 Bobby Boyar Ave Canoga Park CA 91304 Office: 25200 W Rye Canyon Rd Valencia CA 91355

HOSTETTLER, STEPHEN JOHN, naval officer; b. Evansville, Ind., Aug. 23, 1931; s. Ernest Hoffman and Frances Reitz (Bays) H.; m. Lucy Ann Ingalls, June 10, 1953; children: Kathryn Ann, Stephen John. B.S., U.S. Naval Acad., 1953; M.S.E.E., U.S. Naval Postgrad. Sch., 1960; P.M.D., Harvard Bus. Sch., 1969. Commd. ensign USN; advanced through grades to rear adm.; comdr. USS Halsey CG 23 USN; program mgr. Medium Range Missile Systems, Naval Sea Systems Command, 1974-76, comdr. U.S. Naval Forces, Korea; sr. mem. Mil. Armistice Commn., UN Command, Korea, 1979-81; dir. surface combat systems div. Office Chief Naval Ops., Navy Dept., Washington, 1981-82; dir. Joint Cruise Missile Office Navy Dept., Washington, 1982—. Decorated Bronze Star medal., Def. Superior Service medal. Office: Joint Cruise Missles Project Navy Dept Washington DC 20360

HOSTLER, CHARLES WARREN, financial executive; b. Chgo., Dec. 12, 1919; s. Sidney Marvin and Catherine (Marshall) H.; 1 son, Charles Warren, Jr. B.A., U. Calif. at Los Angeles, 1942; M.A., Am. U., Beirut, Lebanon, 1955, Georgetown U., 1950, Ph.D., 1956. Commd. 2d lt. U.S. Air Force, 1942, advanced through grades to col., 1963; ret., 1963; dir. internat. ops. McDonnell Douglas Corp., Middle East, N.Africa, Beirut, 1965-67, mgr. internat. ops., Paris, 1963-65, mgr. internat. mktg., missiles and space, 1967-69; pres. Hostler Investment Co., Newport Beach, Calif., 1969-74; chmn. bd. Irvine (Calif.) Nat. Bank, 1972-74; dir. Wynn's Internat., Inc., Fullerton, Calif., 1971-74; dep. asst. sec. for internat. commerce, dir. Bur. Internat. Commerce, U.S. Dept. Commerce, Washington, 1974-76; regional v.p. Mid-East and Africa, E-Systems Inc., Dallas, 1976-77; now pres. Pacific SW Capital Corp., San Diego; adj. prof. Sch. Internat. Service, Am. U., Washington, 1955-63. Author: Turkism and the Soviets, 1957; Contbr. articles to econ., comml. and mil. jours. Chmn. Calif. Contractors State License Bd., 1973-79, San Diego County Local Agy. Formation Commn., 1979—. Decorated Legion of Merit. Mem. Am. Polit. Sci. Assn., Am. Ordnance Assn., Middle East Inst. (bd. govs. 1962-80). Home: PO Box 9976 San Diego CA 92109 Office: 9580 Black Mountain Rd Suite H San Diego CA 92126

HOTCHKISS, EUGENE, III, college president; b. Berwyn, Ill., Apr. 1, 1928; s. Eugene and Jeanette (Kennan) H.; m. Suzanne Ellen Troxell, Nov. 17, 1962; 1 dau., Ellen Sinclair. A.B., Dartmouth Coll., 1950; Ph.D., Cornell U., 1960; LL.D. (hon.), Ill. Coll., 1976. Asst. to dean Dartmouth Coll., 1953-54, asst. dean, 1954-55, asso. dean, 1958-60; asst. dean Cornell U., Ithaca, N.Y., 1955-58; dean students, lectr. history Harvey Mudd Coll., Claremont, Calif., 1960-63, dean coll., 1962-68; exec. dean Chatham Coll., Pitts., 1968-70; pres. Lake Forest (Ill.) Coll., 1970—; mem. exec. com. Associated Colls. Ill., 1981—, Fedn. Independent Ill. Colls. and Univs.; chmn. Presbyn. Coll. Union, Asso. Colls. Midwest. Bd. dirs. Ind. Coll. Fund Am., 1981—. Served to lt. (j.g.) USNR, 1950-53. Mem. Phi Beta Kappa, Phi Kappa Phi, Chi Phi. Office: Lake Forest Cole Lake Forest IL 60045

HOTCHKISS, GERALD GODFREY, publisher; b. New Haven, Sept. 22, 1930; s. Gerald Godfrey and Ann (Macgowan) H.; m. Patricia Vollmer, May 23, 1959; children: Jane Chandler, Julia Anne, Samuel Stuart. B.S. in Applied Econs, Yale, 1952. European promotion dir. Life mag. Time, Inc., 1958-61; asst. dir. internat. edits. Newsweek, 1962-65; advt. dir. Eastern Airlines, N.Y.C., 1966-67; travel mgr. Look mag. Cowles Communication, Inc., N.Y.C., 1967-72; pres. Ziff-Davis mag. sales network Ziff-Davis Pub. Co., N.Y.C., 1972-74, pub., v.p. Psychology Today div., 1974-83; pub. Goldhirsh Group, N.Y.C., 1983—; dir. Criminal Justice Publs., Inc. Served to capt. USMCR, 1952-55. Decorated Presdl. Commendation medal. Mem. Mag. Pubs. Assn. (mktg. com.). Clubs: Yale (N.Y.C.); Bedford Golf and Tennis, Amateur Ski N.Y. (dir.). Office: 342 Madison Ave Suite 1224-1228 New York NY 10173 *

HOTCHKISS, ROBERT SHERMAN, urologist; b. Jamestown, N.Y., 1903; m. Olivia Naly, 1937 (dec.); children: Roberta (dec.), Fredrica, Sherman. M.D., U. Mich., 1928. Diplomate: Am. Bd. Urology. Intern Royal Victoria Hosp., Montreal, Que., Can., 1928-29; intern Bellevue Hosp., N.Y.C., 1929-31, resident in urology, 1930-31; emeritus prof., chmn. dept. urology N.Y. U. Sch. Medicine. Served with USNR, 1942-46. Recipient Lasker award Planned Parenthood Fedn. Am., 1945; 10th Ferdinand C. Valentine Lecture and award N.Y. Acad. Medicine, 1971; William P. Burpeau award and medal N.J. Acad. Medicine, 1974. Mem. Assn. Genito-Urinary Surgeons (pres. 1975), AMA, Am. Urol. Assn., Am. Fertility Soc. (pres. 1965), Bellevue Alumni Assn. (pres.), Phi Rho Sigma. Home: PO Box 96 Candlewood Isle New Fairfield CT 06810 Office: 566 1st Ave New York NY 10016

HOTCHKISS, ROLLIN DOUGLAS, biochemist, educator; b. South Britain, Conn., Sept. 8, 1911; s. Charles Leverett and Eva (Platt) H.; m. Shirley Dawson, June 24, 1933 (div. 1967); children: Paul, Cynthia; m. Magda Gabor, May 19, 1967. B.S., Yale U., 1932, Ph.D. (Loomis fellow), 1935, Sc.D., 1962; Sc.D. (hon.), U. Paris-Sud, 1980. Mem. staff Rockefeller U., N.Y.C., 1935—, prof., 1955-82, prof. emeritus, 1982—; research prof. biology SUNY-Albany, 1982—; Rockefeller Found. fellow Carlsberg Lab., Copenhagen, 1937-38; vis. prof. MIT, 1957-58; Dyer lectr. NIH, 1962; vis. prof. dept. genetics U. Calif., Berkeley, 1968; fellow-commoner Corpus Christi Coll., Cambridge (Eng.) U., 1970; scholar-in-residence Fogarty Internat. Center, 1971-72; vis. prof. dept. biology U. Utah, Salt Lake City, 1972, 73; Griffith lectr. Soc. Gen. Microbiology, 1974; vis. prof. U. Paris-Sud, Orsay, 1975, 79; Raine vis. prof. dept. microbiology U. Western Australia, Perth, 1980. Contbr. articles to profl. publs. Recipient Comml. Solvents award in antibiotics, 1954. Mem. Am. Soc. Cell Biology (councilor 1962-64), Harvey Soc. (pres. 1958-59), Am. Soc. Biol. Chemists, Am. Acad. Arts and Scis., Nat. Acad. Sci., Genetics Soc. Am. (pres. 1972), Am. Chem. Soc., AAAS, Am. Soc. Naturalists (v.p. 1965), Hungarian Acad. Scis. (hon.), Sigma Xi. Research immunochemistry bacterial polysaccharides, 1935-37, protein chemistry, 1937-39, (with R.J. Dubos) devel. and purification, chem. study, antibiotics gramicidin and tyrocidine, 1939-43, bacterial metabolism and physiology, peptide synthesis, 1944-47, genetic biochemistry deoxyribonucleic acids, 1947—, developed genetic transformation bacteria to drug resistance and sensitivity, 1951, polarity and heterozygosity in nucleic acid, 1962—, specificity of exonucleases, 1961—, fusion of bacterial protoplasts, 1975. Home: PO Box 278 Chester MA 01011 Office: SUNY Dept Biology Albany NY 12222

HOTCHKISS, WESLEY AKIN, clergyman, educator; b. Spooner, Wis., Jan. 26, 1919; s. Fay W. and Codie L. (Akin) H.; m. Mary Ellen Fink, Sept. 16, 1941; 1 dau., Tannia Larkin. B.A., Northland Coll., Wis., 1944, Th.D., 1958; M.S., U. Chgo., 1948, Ph.D., 1950; D.D., Yankton Coll., 1956; LL.D., Pacific U., 1965; L.H.D., Ill. Coll., 1979, Talladega Coll., 1981, Hawaii Loa, 1983; Litt.D., Ripon Coll., 1982. Ordained to ministry Congl. Ch., 1944; research asso. Chgo. Theol. Sem., 1947-49; research dir. Greater Cin. Council Chs., 1949-50, United Ch. Bd., 1950-55, sec., 1955-58, gen. sec. for higher edn., 1958-62. Trustee Affiliate Artists, Inc. Served as chaplain AUS, 1945-47. Fellow Assn. Am. Geographers; mem. AAAS, Am. Sociol. Assn., Religious Research Assn. Home: 420 McKinley Terr Centerport NY 11721 Office: 132 W 31 St New York NY 10001

HOTCHKISS, WINCHESTER FITCH, investment banker; b. N.Y.C., Jan. 24, 1928; s. Horace Leslie and Alta Jane (Fitch) H.; m. Jane Hutchinson Ellsworth, June 10, 1955; children: Winchester Fitch, Leslie Ellsworth, Mary Stevens. Student, Yale, 1952. Advt. mgr. Intercontinental Hotels Corp., N.Y.C., 1957-59; employed various investment banking firms, 1959—; with Stone & Webster Securities Corp., N.Y.C., 1967-75, v.p., 1969—. Mem. promotion com. Citizens for Eisenhower, 1956; mem. N.J. Republican Fin. Com., 1976—; trustee Westminster Sch., Simsbury, Conn.; v.p. Morristown Meml. Hosp., 1976—. Served with AUS, 1946-48; ETO. Mem. Securities Industry Assn. (mem. syndicate com. 1971). Clubs: Bond, River (gov. 1972—), River (N.Y.C.) (sec. 1978—); Somerset Hills (N.J.) Country (gov., sec. 1974, pres. 1983—. Home: 451 Claremont Rd Bernardsville NJ 07924 Office: 100 Madison Ave Morristown NJ 07960

HOTCHNER, AARON EDWARD, author; b. St. Louis, June 28, 1920; s. Samuel and Sally (Rossman) H.; m. Ursula; children: Timothy, Holly, Tracy. A.B., LL.B., Washington U., St. Louis, 1941. Bar: Mo. bar 1941. Practiced law in, St. Louis, 1941-42; articles editor Cosmopolitan mag., 1948-50. Free lance writer: short stories and articles in various mags. including Sat. Eve. Post, Esquire, Readers Digest, 1950—; TV playwright: Playhouse 90, 1958-60; adapted: major Hemingway works for TV including For Whom The Bell Tolls, 1958, The Killers, 1959; writer: screenplay Adventures of a Young Man, 1961; Author: The Dangerous American, 1958, Papa Hemingway: A Personal Memoir, 1966, Treasure, 1970, King of the Hill, 1972, Looking for Miracles, 1974, Doris Day, 1976, Sophia, Living and Loving, 1979, The Man Who Lived at the Ritz, 1981; plays The Short Happy Life, 1961, The White House, 1964, The Hemingway Hero, 1967, Do You Take This Man?, 1970, Sweet Prince, 1980. Served to maj. USAAF, 1942-46; NATOUSA. Mem. Mo. Bar Assn., Writers Guild Am., Dramatists Guild, P.E.N. Address: 14 Hillandale Rd Westport CT 06880

HOTTELET, RICHARD CURT, fgn. corr.; b. N.Y.C., Sept. 22, 1917; s. Richard and Antonie (Heck) H.; m. Ann Delafield, Jan. 21, 1942; children—Antonia Jane, Richard Peter. B.A., Bklyn. Coll., 1937; student, Friedrich-Wilhelms U., Berlin, Germany, 1937-38. Fgn. corr. United Press, 1938-42, OWI, London, 1942-44; war and fgn. corr. CBS, London, Moscow, Berlin and Bonn, 1944-56, CBS News, N.Y.C., 1956-60, UN corr., 1960—. Recipient Bklyn. Coll. award, 1957. Mem. Assn. Radio News Analysts, Council on Fgn. Relations, Century Assn. Home: Wilton CT 06897 Office: 530 W 57th St New York NY 10019

HOTZ, HENRY PALMER, physicist; b. Fayetteville, Ark., Oct. 17, 1925; s. Henry Gustav and Stella (Palmer) H.; m. Marie Brase, Aug. 22, 1952; children: Henry Brase, Mary Palmer, Martha Marie. B.S., U. Ark., 1948; Ph.D., Washington U., St. Louis, 1953. Asst. prof. physics Auburn U., Ala., 1953-58, Okla. State U., Stillwater, 1958-64; assoc. prof. Marietta Coll., Ohio, 1964-66; physicist, scientist-in-residence U.S. Naval Radiol. Def. Lab., San Francisco, 1966-67; assoc. prof. U. Mo., Rolla, 1967-71; physicist Qanta Metrix div. Finnigan Corp., Sunnyvale, Calif., 1971-74; sr. scientist Nuclear Equipment Corp., San Carlos, Calif., 1971-74, Envirotech Measurement Systems, Palo Alto, Calif., 1979-82, Dohrmann div. Xertex Corp., Santa Clara, Calif., 1982—. Cons. USAF, 1958-62. Served with USNR, 1944-46. Mem. AAUP (sec. chpt. 1959-64), Am. Phys. Soc., Am. Assn. Physics Tchrs., AAAS, Phi Beta Kappa, Sigma Xi, Sigma Pi Sigma, Pi Mu Epsilon, Sigma Nu. Methodist. Lodge: Masons. Home: 290 Stilt Ct Foster City CA 94404 Office: 3240 Scott Blvd Santa Clara CA 95050

HOTZ, ROBERT BERGMANN, editor, publisher; b. Milw., May 29, 1914; s. Harry Phillip and Emma (Bergmann) H.; m. Joan Willison, Nov. 18, 1944; children: George, Michael, Robert Lee, Harry II. B.S., Northwestern U., 1936. Reporter, Paris edit. N.Y. Herald Tribune, 1936-37; reporter, editor Milw. Jour., 1938-41; news editor McGraw-Hill Pub. Co., Washington, 1946-49; dir. pub. relations Pratt & Whitney Aircraft, Hartford, Conn., 1950-52; editor Aviation Week and Space Tech. mag., N.Y.C., 1953-80, pub., 1976-80; editor Space Tech. Internat., 1958-80; editorial cons. McGraw-Hill, Inc., 1980—. Author: With General Chennault, the Story of the Flying Tigers, 1943, Pratt and Whitney Aircraft Story, 1950, Both Sides of Suez, 1975, The Promise of the Space Age, 1980; editor: Way of a Fighter, Memoirs of Claire Lee Chennault, 1949. Mem. gen. adv. com. ACDA, 1982—. Served from 2d lt. to maj. USAAF, 1942-46. Decorated Air medal with oak leaf cluster; recipient Airpower award Air Force Assn., 1958; Paul Tissandier diploma Fedn. Aeronautique Internationale, 1958; Press award Nat. Space Club, 1965; Strebig and Ball trophies Aviation/Space Writers Assn., 1972; Pub. Service award Am. Astronautical Soc., 1974; Lauren D. Lyman award Aviation/Space Writers Assn., 1974; 11th Crain award Am. Bus. Press Assn., 1978; Meritorious Service award Nat. Bus. Aircraft Assn., 1981. Mem. 14th Air Force Assn., White House Corr. Assn., Royal Aero. Soc. (companion), AIAA (Pendray Aerospace Lit. award 1981). Clubs: Nat. Press, Caterpillar, Aero. (Washington); RAF (London); Explorers (N.Y.C.). Home: Rams Horn Farm 9702 Mt Tabor Rd Middletown MD 21769 Office: 1777 Kent St Suite 710 Arlington VA 22209

HOTZE, CHARLES WAYNE, publisher, printer; b. Moline, Ill., Feb. 19, 1919; s. Charles Edmund and Nellie (Gibbs) H.; m. Hazel Ann Tebbens, Dec. 20, 1956; children: Karen Ann, Carla Ann. B.A., U. Ill., 1941. Pres., chmn. bd. Fowle Printing Co., Milw., 1953-55; pub. Clin. Medicine, Northfield, Ill., 1954—; pres. Med. Digest, Inc. and; pub. Med. Digest, 1955—; pres. C.W. Hotze Bldg. Corp., 1956—, C.W. Hotze, Inc., 1957—, Med. Newsletter, 1958—, Pediatrics Digest, Inc., 1962—, Psychiatry Digest, 1962—, Dermatology Digest, 1963—, Obstetrics-Gynecology Digest, 1964—, Urology Digest, 1964—, Cardiology Digest, 1966; all Northfield; pres. Med. Communications, Inc., 1968—; chmn. bd. Lake County Press, Inc., Waukegan, Ill., 1971-78; pub. O.R.L. Digest, 1971—, Ophthalmology Digest, 1971—, Orthopedics Digest, 1973—, Pharmacy Digest, 1978—, Vet. Digest, 1978—, Radiology Digest, 1979—, Anesthesiology Digest, 1981—. Served to 1st lt. AUS, 1942-45. Mem. Soc. Acad. Achievement, Am. Med. Writers Assn., Pharm. Advt. Club, Midwest Pharm. Advt. Club, SAR, Mayflower Soc., Psi Upsilon. Club: Sunset Ridge (Northbrook, Ill.). Home: 1950 Sunset Ridge Rd Northbrook IL 60062 also 305 E 40th St New York NY 10016 Office: 444 Frontage Rd Northfield IL 60063

HOU, CHI MING, educator; b. Hopei, China, Dec. 3, 1924; s. H.T. and S.C. (Tien) H.; m. Irene Liu, June 20, 1953; children-Donald, William, Victor. LL.B., Fu Jen U., 1945; M.A., U. Oreg., 1949; Ph.D., Columbia, 1954. Faculty Colgate U., Hamilton, N.Y., 1956—, Charles A. Dana prof. econs., 1968—, chmn. dept., 1972-80, dir., 1980—; research prof. Brookings Instn., 1965-66; research fellow Chinese econ. studies Harvard, 1959-62; Fulbright lectr. econs., Taiwan, 1970-71. Author: Foreign Investment and Economic Development in China 1840-1937, 1965; Contbr. articles profl. jours. Mem. Am. Econ. Assn., Assn. Asian Studies. Address: 39 Maple Ave Hamilton NY 13346

HOUBOLT, JOHN CORNELIUS, physicist; b. Altoona, Iowa, Apr. 10, 1919; s. John H. and Hendreika (Van Ingen) H.; m. Mary Morris, June 14, 1949; children: Mary Cornelia, Joanna, Julie. B.S., U. Ill., 1940, M.S., 1942; Ph.D., Swiss Fed. Inst. Tech., Zurich, 1958, hon. doctorate, 1975. Bridge engr. I.C. R.R., 1940; city engr., Waukegan, Ill., 1941; aero. research scientist NASA, Hampton, Va., 1942-49; asso. chief dynamic loads div. NACA-NASA, 1949-62; chief theoretical mechanics div. NASA, 1962-63; chief scientist Langley Research Center, Hampton, Va., 1976—; sr. v.p., dir. Aero Research Asso. Princeton Inc., N.J., 1963-76; instr. grad. extension div. U. Va., 1944—, Va. Poly. Inst., 1958—; exchange scientist Royal Aircraft Establishment, Eng., 1949; dir. Doweave, Inc., Walker-Gordon Labs.; Mem. Air Force Scientific Adv. Bd. Asso. editor: Jour. Spacecraft and Rockets. Recipient Rockefeller Pub. Service award, 1956; NASA Exceptional Sci. Achievement award, 1963; AIAA Structures, Structural Dynamics and Materials award, 1967; U. Ill. Disting. Civil Engring. Alumni award, 1969; U. Ill. Illini Achievement award, 1970; NASA Space Act award, 1983. Hon. fellow AIAA (v.p. tech., Dryden Research Lecture award 1972). Research, numerous reports in aeros., aeroelasticity, structures, atmosphere turbulence, space flight and landing. Home: 51 Winsterfax Williamsburg VA 23185 Office: Langley Research Center NASA Hampton VA 23665

HOUBRICK, RICHARD STEPHEN, malacologist, research institution administrator; b. Trenton, N.J., Mar. 16, 1937; s. Stephen J. and Barbara Anna (Krebs) H. B.A. cum laude, St. Bernard Coll., 1959; postgrad., St. Leo Theol. Sem., 1960-64; M.S. in Zoology, U. Miami, Fla., 1967; Ph.D. in Biology, U. South Fla., 1971. Instr. zoology St. Leo Coll., 1964-65, 67-68; teaching asst. U. South Fla., 1967-69; supr. benthic sect. Oceanographic Sorting Center, Smithsonian Instn., Washington, 1971-76; curator div. mollusks Nat. Mus. Natural History, 1977—; AEC grantee, research scientist Mid Pacific Marine Lab., 1970, 75; instr. U.S. Dept. Agr. Grad. Sch., 1972—. Orgn. Tropical Studies Inc. grantee, 1965; NSF grantee, 1968, summer 1970; recipient Scholar award U. South Fla., 1970, award for grad. research Sigma Xi, 1971. Mem. Am. Malacological Union, Calif. Malacozool. Soc., Smithsonian Instn. Senate of Scientists, Malacological Soc. London (Eng.). Home: 721 3d St SW Washington DC 20024 Office: Smithsonian Instn Nat Mus Natural History Div Mollusks Washington DC 20560

HOUCHIN, LLOYD KENNETH, air force officer; b. Osceola, Ark., Nov. 14, 1935; s. Lloyd Stanley and Edna Lucy (Sielbeck) H.; m. Mary Kathryn Mitchell, May 25, 1956; children: Ramona Lynne, Mitchell Lloyd. B.S. in Edn., So. Ill. U., 1956; M.S. in Pub. Adminstrn., George Washington U., 1968. Commd. to lt. U.S. Air Force, 1956, advanced through grades to col., 1973—, jet fighter pilot, 1956-71, curriculum mgr. Air Force Air Command and Staff Coll., Maxwell AFB, Ala., 1971-75, sr. controller HDQ Strategic Air Commond, Offutt AFB, Nebr., 1975-78, ops. dir., vice comdr. Strategic Missele Wing, Whiteman AFB, Mo., 1978-82; prof. aerospace studies U. Ill., Urbana, 1982—; dir. Computerized System to Teach Planning of Air Force Ops., Fast Stick II, 1975. Research dir., editor: Battle for the Skies Over North Vietnam, 1976. Republican. Office: AFROTC Det 190 223 Armory Bldg 505 E Armory Champaign IL 61820 *As a member of the bureaucracies that are an absolute necessity in today's complex management environment, I have always striven to develop and operate processes that benefit the pople the bureaucracy serves. Persons and processes that serve the bureaucracy but not the subject population are a gross hindrance to social and economic processes and personal accomplishment.*

HOUCK, CHARLES WESTON, U.S. dist. judge; b. Florence, S.C., Apr. 16, 1933; s. William Stokes and Charlotte Barnwell (Weston) H.; m. Wana Kaye Hutchinson, Mar. 28, 1980; children: Charles Weston, Charlotte Elizabeth. Grad., U. N.C., 1954; LL.B., U. S.C., 1956. Bar: S.C. Pvt. practice, Florence, 1958-79; partner firm Houck, Clarke & Johnson, 1971-79; U.S. dist. judge Dist. S.C., Florence, 1979—. Mem. S.C. Ho. of Reps., 1963-66; chmn. Florence City-County Bldg. Commn., 1968-76. Served with AUS, 1957-58. Mem. ABA, S.C. Bar Assn. Episcopalian. Office: McMillan Fed Bldg PO Box 2260 W Evans St Florence SC 29503 *

HOUCK, JOHN BURTON, lawyer; b. Mt. Clemens, Mich., Apr. 6, 1928; s. William Alfred and Louis Ann (Macey) H.; m. Wanda Jean Wright, Feb. 4, 1950; children: Lisa Karen, William Wright, Katherine Jane. A.B., U. Mich., 1949, M.A. in Econs., 1951, J.D., 1953. Bar: N.Y. 1955, Mich. 1957, Ohio 1960, Calif. 1979. Assoc. Milbank, Tween, Hope & Hadley, N.Y.C., 1953-56; asst. sec. Ford Motor Co., Darborn, Mich., 1956-59; assoc. Jones, Day, Reavis & Pogue, Cleve., 1959-63, ptnr., 1963—, Los Angeles, 1981—. Contbr. articles to profl. jours. Mem. ABA (Council, sect. internat. law and practice), State Bar of Calif., Ohio State Bar Assn., State Bar Mich., Los Angeles County Bar Assn. (exec. com. sect. internat. law), Am. Law Inst., Greater Cleve. Internat. Lawyers Group (chmn. 1980-81), Order of Coif. Clubs: Riveria Tennis (Los Angeles); Clevelander (Cleve.). Home: 3985 Mandeville Canyon Rd Los Angeles CA 90049 Office: Jones Day Reavis & Pogue 2029 Century Park E Suite 3600 Los Angeles CA 90067

HOUCK, JOHN CANDEE, research facility administrator, biochemist; b. N.Y.C., Feb. 19, 1931; s. John Walter and Marjorie (Candee) H.; m. Charlotte DeHesse, Oct. 8, 1967; children: Leslie, Mary, John, Eric, Alexander, Emily. B.A., Columbia Coll., 1953; M.Sc., Western U., London, Ont., Can., 1956. Sr. research fellow surg. research lab. Georgetown U. Sch., 1957-58, dir. lab. surg. research and metabolism, 1958-60, asst. prof. biochemistry, 1958-60, professorial lectr., 1967-76; prof. pediatrics George Washington U. Sch. Medicine, 1969-71, prof. child health and devel., 1971-76; vis. prof. dept. biochemistry Univ. Coll., London, 1979—; dir. biochem. research lab. Children's Hosp., Washington, 1959-76; sci. dir. Research Found., 1969-76; dir. Virginia Mason Research Center, Seattle, 1976-82; pres. Endorphin Inc., 1982—, Immunogenics Corp., 1982—. Author: (with B. Forscher) Chemical Biology of Inflammation, 1968, Immunopathology of Inflammation, 1971, Chalones: Concepts and Current Researches, 1973, (with A. Bertelli) Inflammation Biochemistry and Drug Interaction, 1969, (with W. Daugherty) Chalones: A Tissue-Specific Approach to Mitotic Control, 1974, Chalones, 1976; contbr. numerous articles to profl. publs.; editor-in-chief: INFLO, 1967-78; asso. editor: Inflammation, 1975—; co-editor: Tissue Reactions, 1978—. Recipient A. Cressy Morrison award N.Y. Acad. Scis., 1962, Research award Am. Dermatol. Assn., 1965; NRC Can. research fellow, 1953-56. Fellow AAAS; mem. Am. Soc. Biol. Chemists, Am. Soc. Exptl. Pathology, Soc. Pediatric Research, Arthritis and Rheumatism Assn., Soc. Exptl. Biology and Medicine, Assn. Advancement Aging Research.; Mem. United Ch. Clubs: Cosmos (Washington); Seattle Yacht. Home: 5100 Latimer Pl NE Seattle WA 98105 Office: Immunogenics Corp 1000 Seneca St Seattle WA 98101

HOUCK, JOHN ROLAND, clergyman; b. Balt., Apr. 15, 1923; s. Walter Webb and Wilhelmina Anna (Pfaff) H.; m. Minerva Arline Wiessinger, Nov. 28, 1947; children—John Roland, James Michael, David Walter, Paul Harold. B.A. cum laude, Capital U., Columbus, Ohio, 1947, D.D. (hon.), 1976; B.D., Evang. Lutheran Sem., Columbus, 1950. Ordained to ministry Am. Luth. Ch., 1950; pastor St. Michael Luth. Ch., Perry Hill, Md., 1950-60; regional dir. bd. Am. missions Am. Luth. Ch., Washington, 1960-67, dir., Mpls., 1970-73, dir. div. service and mission in Am., 1974-79; asso. exec. sec. div. mission service Luth. Council U.S.A., N.Y.C., 1967-70, gen. sec., 1979—. Democrat. Home: 372 Fifth Ave Apt 4L New York NY 10018 Office: 360 Park Ave S New York NY 10010

HOUDEK, MARGARET ANNE (PEGGY DUNLAP HOUDEK), inn mgr., profl. singer; b. Santa Cruz, Calif., Oct. 21, 1936; d. William Henry and Edythe Mae (George) Hocking, Jr.; m. Newell Benjamin Dunlap, Apr. 2, 1960 (div. 1965); m. Richard G. Houdek, Aug. 3, 1974. A.A., Santa Rosa Jr. Coll., 1956; student, San Francisco Conservatory of Music, 1961-64. Adminstrv. asst. Consultants, Inc., 1964-69; fund drive coordinator San Francisco Opera, 1969-74; mng. editor Performing Arts Mag., Beverly Hills, Calif., 1974-80; co-owner, mgr. Walker House (Historic New Eng. Inn), Lenox, Mass., 1980—; mem. San Francisco Symphony Chorus, 1973-74, N.Y.C. Opera Chorus, 1975-80; soloist opera, ch. and synagogues. Photographer works pub., Los Angeles Times. Democrat. Christian Scientist. Home and office: 74 Walker St Lenox MA 01240

HOUGH, GEORGE ANTHONY, III, journalism educator; b. New Bedford, Mass., Nov. 15, 1920; s. George Anthony and Clara (Sharpe) H.; m. Mary Lu Slack, Oct. 20, 1943; 1 dau., Mary Patricia. B.A., U. Wis., 1943; M.A., Mich. State U., 1958, Ph.D., 1965. Reporter Falmouth (Mass.) Enterprise, Detroit Free Press, Madison (Wis.) State Jour.; editor, pub. Vernon County Censor, 1950-55; mng. editor Grant County Ind., 1955-57; from asst. prof. to prof. journalism Mich. State U., 1957-79, chmn., 1975-79; prof., head news-editorial sequence Henry W. Grady Sch. Journalism and Mass Communications, U. Ga., Athens, 1979-83, prof., 1983—. Author: News Writing, 1975, Structures of Modification in Contemporary American English, 1971. Served with USNR, 1943-46. Decorated Navy and Marine Corps medal. Mem. Assn. Edn. in Journalism, Am. Name Soc., Am. Dialect Soc., Sigma Delta Chi. Episcopalian. Office: Sch Journalism U Ga Athens GA 30602

HOUGH, HUGH FREDERICK, journalist; b. Sandwich, Ill., Apr. 15, 1924; s. Forrest Everett and Lila M. (Legner) H.; m. Ellen Marie Wesemann, Sept. 8, 1948; children—Hollis Ann Hough Bahnsen, Heidi Ann Hough, Peter Clark, Christopher Hugh. B.S., U. Ill., 1951. Sports editor Dixon (Ill.) Evening Telegraph, 1951-52; reporter, rewriteman Chgo. Sun-Times, 1952—, columnist, 1974—. Served with USAAF, 1943-45. Decorated Air medal.; Recipient Stick-o-Type awards Chgo. Newspaper Guild, 1960, 65, 66, award for prison reform stories John Howard Assn., 1961, Marshall Field award for outstanding editorial contbn. to Chgo. Sun-Times, 1969, Newswriting award Ill. Asso. Press, 1974, Pulitzer prize for gen. local reporting, 1974. Home: 747 N Catherine Ave La Grange Park IL 60525 Office: 401 N Wabash Ave Chicago IL 60611

HOUGH, RICHARD T., chemical company executive; b. Evanston, Ill., Nov. 5, 1923; s. William J. and Helen (Trevellyan) H.; m. Nancy Rambeau, Nov. 4, 1944; children: Hough Folley, William R., David R., Janet H. Student, Cornell U., 1942-43; B.A., Lake Forest Coll., 1948. With Chemcentral Corp., Chgo., 1948—, pres., 1965—, chmn. bd., 1975—, dir., 1954—. Served with USAAF, 1943-46. Mem. Am. Chem. Soc., Paint Varnish and Lacquer Assn. Republican. Club: Indian Hill Country (Winnetka, Ill.). Office: 7050 W 71st St Chicago IL 60638

HOUGHTON, ALAN NOURSE, educator, association executive; b. Hartford, Conn., Jan. 17, 1924; m. Elizabeth T. Jones, Mar. 30, 1946; children—Alan Nourse, Elizabeth Boardman, John Barnard, Suzanne Tolles. A.B. cum laude, Harvard, 1946, A.M., 1951; postgrad., Columbia, 1951, U. Conn., 1961, 62-63. Faculty Groton (Mass.) Sch., 1946-51; chmn. classics dept. Loomis Sch., Windsor, Conn., 1951-55; headmaster Pine Point Sch., Stonington, 1955-67, Renbrook Sch., West Hartford, 1967-73; exec. dir. Conn. Assn. Ind. Schs., 1974—. Mem. Sch. Bldg. Com., Lyme, Conn., 1959, Zoning Bd. Appeals, 1959-61, Zoning and Planning Commn., 1963-65, Bd. Finance, 1971-75, Lyme Democratic Town Com., 1957-63; Trustee Blair Acad., Blairstown, N.J., Pine Point Sch., Stonington, Conn., Renbrook Sch., Country Sch., Madison, Conn.; corporator Hartford Hosp. Served to 1st lt. USAAF, 1943-45. Decorated D.F.C., Air medal with three oak leaf clusters; Houghton Wing named for him at Pine Point Sch. Mem. Conn. Assn. Ind. Schs. (tchr. edn. and profl. standards rep. 1963-66, v.p., pres.), Classical Assn. New Eng., Sigma Alpha Epsilon, Phi Delta Kappa, Pi Eta. Congregationalist. Club: Mile Creek Beach (bd. govs. 1958-73). Home: 26 Sylvan Rd Madison CT 06443 Office: Box 1310 Madison CT 06443

HOUGHTON, ARTHUR AMORY, JR., corporation official; b. Corning, N.Y., Dec. 12, 1906; s. Arthur Amory and Mabel (Hollister) H.; m. Nina Rodale, May 22, 1973; children by previous marriage: Jane Olmsted (Mrs. Chalmer J. Carothers, Jr.), Sylvia Bigelow (Mrs. Richard G. Garrett), Arthur Amory III, Hollister Douglas (Mrs. William D. Haggard III). Student, St. Paul's Sch., Concord, N.H., 1920-25, Harvard, 1925-29; L.H.D., Lehigh U., 1950, U. Md., 1963; LL.D., U. Rochester, 1952, Alfred U., 1954, Wesleyan U., 1963, Salisbury Coll., 1976; Litt.D., Wash. Coll., 1953, Hofstra Coll., 1956, Trinity Coll., 1955, Beaver Coll., 1957, St. John's U., 1966; D.Sc., Hobart and William Smith Colls., 1958, Bucknell U., 1968; D.F.A., Washington and Jefferson Coll., 1971, MacMurray Coll., 1971. With mfg. dept. Corning Glass Works, 1929, treas. dept., 1929-30, asst. to pres., 1930-32, v.p., 1935-42; now life dir.; curator rare books Library of Congress, 1940-42; pres. Steuben Glass, N.Y.C., 1933-72, chmn., 1972-78; former dir. N.Y. Life Ins. Co., U.S. Steel Corp., U.S. Trust Co. of N.Y.; Vice pres. Corning Mus. of Glass. Trustee emeritus Pierpont Morgan Library; chmn. Am. Trust Brit. Library; past chmn. Inst. Internat. Edn.; chmn. Wye Inst.; past chmn. Philharmonic-Symphony Soc. N.Y., Lincoln Center Performing Arts; former overseer Harvard U.; trustee emeritus, past pres., past chmn. Met. Mus. Art; hon. trustee N.Y. Pub. Library; former dir. Am. Council Learned Socs.; former trustee Rockefeller Found.; hon. trustee, past chmn. Parsons Sch. Design; former trustee, chmn. emeritus Cooper Union; hon. curator Keats Collection, Harvard U.; hon. trustee Inst. Contemporary Art, Boston, Balt. Mus. Art. Served from capt. to lt. col. USAAF, 1942-45. Decorated officer Legion Honor, France; knight Order St. John of Jeruselem; comdr. l'Ordre des Arts et des Lettres (France); recipient Michael Friedsam medal in indsl. art; Gertrude Vanderbilt Whitney award Skowhegan Sch. Fellow Royal Coll. Art (sr.), Royal Soc. Arts; mem. English-Speaking Union U.S. (past pres.), Council Fgn. Relations. Episcopalian. Clubs: Century, Union, Harvard, Knickerbocker, Grolier (N.Y.C.). Home: Wye Plantation Queenstown MD 21658

HOUGHTON, CHARLES NORRIS, stage director, author, educator; b. Indpls., Dec. 26, 1909; s. Charles D. Mansfield and Grace (Norris) H. A.B., Princeton, 1931; D.F.A. (hon.), Denison U., 1959, H.H.D., U. Louisville, 1983. Lectr. drama, dir. dramatics Princeton, 1941-42; guest prof. drama Smith Coll., 1947; lectr. comparative lit. Columbia, 1948-54; producer, dir. television CBS, 1951-52; adj. prof. drama Barnard Coll., 1954-58; co-mng. dir. Phoenix Theatre, N.Y.C., 1953-63; adj. prof. drama, guest dir. Exptl. Theatre, Vassar Coll., 1959-60; prof. drama, dir. Exptl. Theatre, 1962-67; dean div. theatre arts State U. N.Y. Coll., Purchase, 1967-75, prof., 1967-80; bd. dirs. Theatre, Inc., N.Y.C., 1946-73; Berg. vis. prof. English N.Y. U., 1976, 80-81; Bingham prof. humanities U. Louisville, 1979. Stage mgr. on, Broadway, 1933-37; stage designer: Broadway prodns. Whiteoaks, 1937-38, Dame Nature, Waltz in Goosestep, Good Hunting, 1939-40, The Sleeping Prince, 1956; art dir., St. Louis Mcpl. Opera, 1939-40; dir., Elitch's Gardens Theatre, Denver, 1948-49, Macbeth, 1947, 82, Clutterbuck, 1949, Billy Budd, 1951, Julius Caesar, 1982, Misalliance, 1983; Author: Moscow Rehearsals, 1936, Advance from Broadway, 1941, But Not Forgotten, 1951, Return Engagement, 1962, The Exploding Stage, 1972; Editor: Masterpieces of Continental Drama, 3 vols, 1963, Great Russian Short Stories, 1958, Great Russian Drama, 1960; Asso. editor: Theatre Arts Mag, 1945-48; Contbr. to nat. theatrical mags. Pres. Am. Council Arts in Edn., 1973-75; vice chmn. panel Am. Council on Arts in Edn., 1975-77; v.p. Arts, Edn. and Americans, Inc. Guggenheim fellow, 1934, 35, 60-61. Fellow Am. Acad. Arts and Scis., Am. Theatre Assn.; mem. Nat. Council Chs. Christ (chmn. adv. com. on drama 1954-57), Nat. Theatre Conf. (pres. 1968-69), Am. Council Arts in Edn. (pres. 1973-75), Inst. Advanced Studies in Theatre Arts (mem. adv. council), Phi Beta Kappa. Clubs: Century, Coffee House (N.Y.C.). Home: 11 E 9th St New York NY 10003

HOUGHTON, DAVID DREW, meteorologist; b. Phila., Apr. 26, 1938; s. Willard Fairchild and Sara Nancy (Holmes) H.; m. Barbara Flora Coan, June 22, 1963; children: Eric Brian, Karen Jeanette, Steven Andrew. B.S., Pa. State U., 1959; M.S., U. Wash., 1961, Ph.D., 1963. Research scientist Nat. Center Atmospheric Research, Boulder, Colo., 1963-68; exchange scientist USSR Acad. Scis., Moscow, 1966; vis. scientist Courant Inst. Math. Scis., N.Y.C., 1966; asst. prof. dept. meteorology U. Wis., Madison, 1968-69, asso. prof., 1969-72, prof., 1972—, chmn. dept., 1976-79; scientist Internat. Sci. and Mgmt. Group for Global Atmospheric Research Program, Bracknell, Eng., 1972-73; lectr. Nanjing U., People's Republic of China, 1980. Contbr. articles to profl. jours.; editor-in-chief: Handbook of Applied Meteorology. Vice chmn. Planning Commn., Town of Dunn, Wis., 1977-81. NSF fellow, 1960-63. Fellow Am. Meteorol. Soc.; mem. AAAS, Phi Beta Kappa, Sigma Xi, Phi Kappa Phi. Quaker. Office: Dept Meteorology U Wis Madison WI 53706

HOUGHTON, JAMES RICHARDSON, glass manufacturing company executive; b. Corning, N.Y., Apr. 6, 1936; s. Amory and Laura (Richardson) H.; m. May Tuckerman Kinnicutt, June 30, 1962; children—James DeKay, Nina Bayard. A.B., Harvard U., 1958, M.B.A., 1962. With Goldman, Sachs & Co., N.Y.C., 1959-61; with Corning Glass Works, 1962—, v.p., gen. mgr. consumer products div., 1968-71, vice chmn. bd., dir., chmn. exec. com., 1971-83, chmn. bd., chief exec. officer, 1983—; v.p., European area mgr. Corning Glass Internat., Zurich, Switzerland and; Brussels, Belgium, 1964-68; dir. Corning Internat. Corp., Met. Life Ins. Co., J. P. Morgan Co. Inc., Dow Corning Corp., CBS, Inc. Trustee U.S. Council Internat. Bus.; Mem. Bus. Com. for Arts, N.Y.C., Council on Fgn. Relations.; Trustee Corning Glass Works Found., Corning Museum Glass, Pierpont Morgan Library, N.Y.C., Met. Mus. Art; dir. emeritus Fay Sch., Southboro, Mass. Served with AUS, 1959-60. Episcopalian. Clubs: Corning Country; River, Harvard, University, Links (N.Y.C.); Brookline (Mass.) Country; Tarratine (Dark Harbor, Maine); Augusta (Ga.) Nat. Golf; Rolling Rock (Ligonier, Pa.). Home: The Field Spencer Hill Rd RD 2 Corning NY 14830 Office: Corning Glass Works Corning NY 14831

HOUGHTON, KATHARINE, actress; b. Hartford, Conn., Mar. 10, 1945; d. Ellsworth Strong and Marion (Hepburn) Grant. B.A., Sarah Lawrence Coll., Bronxville, N.Y., 1965. Tchr., actress Summer Program sponsored by Theatre Devel. Fund at U. Colo.; Founding mem. Pilgrim Repertory Co. (Shakespeare touring co. sponsored by Ky. Arts Commn.), 1971-72, S.C. Arts Commn., 1972, Miss. Arts Commn., 1973, Conn. Arts Commn., St. Joseph Coll., 1974. Debut on: Broadway stage in A Very Rich Woman, 1965; appeared in: stage plays Charley's Aunt, New Orleans Repertory, 1966, The Front Page, Broadway, 1969, A Scent of Flowers (Theatre World award), Off Broadway, 1969, Misalliance, Hartford Stage Co., 1970, The Taming of the Shrew, Actors Theatre, Louisville, 1970, Ring Aroung the Moon, Hartford Stage Co., 1971, Major Barbara, The Glass Menagerie, Actors Theatre of Louisville, 1971, Suddenly Last Summer, Ivanhoe, Chgo., 1973, The Prodigal Daughter, Kennedy Center, Washington, 1973, The Rainmaker, Ind. Repertory Co., 1975, Spiders Web, Atlanta, 1977, Hedda Gabler, Nashville, 1978, Dear Liar, Dayton, Ohio, 1978, 13 Rue de L'Amour, Ind. Repertory Co., 1978, Antigone, Nashville, 1979, Uncle Vanya, Acad. Festival Theatre, Lake Forest, 1979, Forty Carats, Radford U. Theatre, Va., 1979, A Doll's House, St. Edward's U. Theatre, Tex., 1979, The Sea Gull, Pitts. Public Theatre, 1979, The Glass Menagerie, Pa. Stage Co., 1980, Taming of the Shrew, Pa. State Festival, 1980, Terra Nova, Actors Theatre of Louisville, 1980, The Streets of New York, various theatres, New Eng., The Merchant of Venice, South Coast Repertory, Costa Mesa, Calif., 1981, A Touch of the Poet, Yale Repertory Theatre, 1983; motion pictures include Guess Who's Coming to Dinner, 1967, The Gardener, 1972, Eyes of the Amaryllis, 1981; TV series The Adams Chronicles; appeared on: TV in The Color of Friendship, 1981; on tour in: Sabrina Fair, 1975, The Mousetrap, Arms and the Man, Dear Liar, 1976; appeared in: Spider's Web, Theatre of Stars, Atlanta, 1977; To True to Be Good, Acad. Festival Theatre, Lake Forest, Ill., 1977, Spingold Theatre, Waltham, Mass., Annenberg Center, Phila.; Co-author: Two Beastly Tales, 1975; author: (play) To Heaven in a Swing, 1982, Merlin, 1984.

HOUGHTON, ROBERT BIGELOW, diplomat; b. Boston, Apr. 4, 1921; s. Robert B. and Helen Marion H.; m. Lois Chapman, Oct. 13, 1950; children: Worthington C., Robert B., Gill W., Richard H., Eleni. A.B., Harvard U., 1942. Commd. fgn. service officer Dept. State, 1945; served in, Nairobi, Kenya, Jerusalem, Damascus, Syria, London, Beirut, Istanbul, Turkey, Beirut; consul gen. U.S. Consulate, Istanbul; dir. Office Multinat. Force and Observer Affairs Dept. State, Washington D.C., until 1983; was mem. Fulbright Commn. Bd. dirs. Adm. Bristol Hosp. Recipient Meritorious Service award Dept. State, 1977, John Jacob Rogers award, 1983. Mem. Middle East Inst. Club: Harvard Varsity. Office: 3416 Legation St NW Washington DC 20015

HOUGHTON, WOODSON PLYER, lawyer; b. Washington, Apr. 19, 1893; s. Harry Sherman and Alice Virginia (Ballentine) H.; m. Geta Triester, July 21, 1933. B.A., Washington and Lee U., 1915; LL.B., Georgetown U., 1918. Bar: D.C. bar 1918. Asst. sec. 2d Pan Am. Sci. Congress, 1916-17; since practiced in, Washington; mem. firm Ellis, Houghton and Ellis, 1919- 68, sr. partner, 1948-68; prof. law Nat. U. Law Sch., 1923-26; formerly mem. bd. Mut. Protection Fire Ins. Co., Norfolk and Washington Steamboat Co. Pres. Family Service Assn. (Asso. Charities); mem. bd. Family Welfare Assn. Am., Council Social Agys., Community Chest, D.C.; bd. govs. Nantucket Boys Club. Served as 1st lt. judge adv. gen. corps. U.S. Army., 1918-19; asst. port judge adv.; Port Embarkation, Newport News. Va. Mem. Am., D.C. bar assns., DuPont Circle Citizens Assn., Sheridan-Kalorama Neighborhood Council, S.A.R., Barristers, Sigma Chi, Phi Delta Phi, Omicron Delta Kappa. Clubs: Nantucket Yacht, Sankaty Head Golf, Metropolitan, Chevy Chase, 1925 F Street (gov.), Pacific, Wharf Rat. Home: 2337 California St NW Washington DC 20008 Office: 815 Connecticut Ave NW Washington DC 20006

HOUK, ALLEN RAMSEY, corporate executive; b. Denison, Tex., July 29, 1935; s. Clyde L. and Dalton A. (Ramsey) H.; m. Gale Sinnott, Oct. 23, 1965; children: Brett Alan, Keith Ramsey, Michael Jay. Student, Jacksonville (Fla.) Jr. Coll., 1954-55; B.A. in History, U. Fla., 1957; grad., La. State U. Banking Sch. of South, 1969. Mgmt. intern Bank New Orleans, 1958, credit mgr., 1958-63, asst. cashier, 1963-65, asst. v.p., 1965-67, v.p. comml. loans, 1967-70; v.p., mgr. met. and regional div. First Nat. Bank Commerce, New Orleans, 1970, sr. v.p. met. and regional div., 1970-71, exec. v.p., 1971-74; v.p. First Commerce Corp., 1971-73; pres., dir. First Commerce Financial Corp., 1971-73; v.p. First Commerce Real Estate Corp., 1971-74; pres. First Commerce Realty Investors, 1973-74, trustee, 1973-75; exec. v.p., dir. So. Nat. Bank, Houston, 1974-75, pres., 1975-78; pres., dir. Capital Nat. Bank, Houston, 1978-81, Diversified Group, Inc., 1981—; dir. Brookhollow Nat. Bank, Houston.; mem. faculty Banking Sch. of South, La. State U., 1969—, Miss. Sch. Banking, U. Miss., Oxford, 1976—. Past bd. dirs. Cancer Assn. Greater New Orleans, New Orleans chpt. ARC, Jr. Achievement Greater New Orleans; past bd. Boys Club Greater New Orleans; adv. trustee Houston United Fund, 1978; bd. dirs., mem. public edn. com. Am. Cancer Soc.; bd. elders Grace Presbyn. Ch., 1976—; adv. bd. Houston Symphony Orch., 1979—; trustee Mo. Ranch Presbyn. Retreat, 1983—. Named Outstanding Young Man in New Orleans Jaycees New Orleans, 1966; recipient Distinguished Service award, 1966. Mem. Blue Key (hon. life). Home: 12103 Maple Rock Dr Houston TX 77077 Office: Diversified Group Inc 9990 Richmond Suite 106 Houston TX 77042

HOUK, JAMES CHARLES, physiologist, educator; b. Northville, Mich., June 3, 1939; s. James Charles and Elowene Elsie (Tower) H.; m. Antoinette, Dec. 28, 1963; children—Philip Adler, Nadia Rosella, Peter Charles. B.S. in Elec. Engring, Mich. Technol. U., 1961; M.S., M.I.T., 1963; Ph.D. in Physiology, Harvard U., 1966. Research asso. Sch. Medicine, San Juan, P.R., summers 1962, 64; postdoctoral fellow Faculte de Medecine, Toulose, France, 1966-67, Harvard U. Med. Sch., 1967-68, instr., 1967-69, asst. prof. physiology, 1969-73; lectr. dept. elec. engring. M.I.T., 1971-73; assoc. prof. physiology Johns Hopkins U. Sch. Medicine, 1973-78; adj. assoc. prof. physiology U. N.C., 1975; Nathan Smith Davis prof., chmn. dept. physiology Northwestern U. Sch. Medicine and Dentistry, Chgo., 1978, prof. engring. sci. Technol. Inst., dir. behavioral neurosci. tng. program, 1979—, dir. tng. program in neural control, 1983—; mem. neurology B study sect. NIH, 1978-82. Contbr. to: Med. Physiology, 14th edit, 1980, Handbook of Physiology, Motor Control, 1981. Mem. IEEE,

AAAS, Am. Physiol. Soc., Soc. for Neuroscience, Sigma Xi, Tau Beta Pi, Eta Kappa Nu, Phi Kappa Phi. Home: 2900 Lincoln St Evanston IL 60201 Office: Northwestern U Med Center Dept Physiology Ward 5-319 303 E Chicago Ave Chicago IL 60611

HOUK, JOHN LOUIS, educator; b. Albuquerque, July 22, 1920; s. Goulding Heaton and Alma (Maier) H.; m. Martha Ann Coultrap, Apr. 2, 1949; children—Mia Catherine, John David. B.A., U. So. Calif., 1948, M.F.S., 1955, Ph.D., 1966. Asso. prof. Am. U., 1956-57; dean Coll. Letters, Arts and Scis. U. Guam, 1967-69, Sch. Bus. and Econs., Humboldt State U., 1969; dep. state dean acad. planning Calif. State Univs. and Colls., 1969-71; prof. polit. sci. Calif. State U., Los Angeles, 1971—, dean acad. planning, 1971-80; Mem. steering com. So. Calif., Conf. Internat. Studies. Author: Working with Peoples in Developing Areas, 1965, The Soviet Propaganda Program, 1951, (with others) Tensions within the Soviet Union, 1951, others. Served with USAAC, 1942-45. Decorated Bronze Star, Air medal with 6 oak leaf clusters.; Haynesfellow, 1956. Mem. Am. Polit. Sci. Assn., Western Polit. Sci. Assn., Acad. Polit. Sci., Am. Assn. Higher Edn., Assn. Gen. and Liberal Studies, Delta Phi Epsilon, Pi Sigma Alpha. Home: 6531 Elmhurst Dr Tujunga CA 91042 Office: Calif State U 5151 State University Dr Los Angeles CA 90032

HOUK, RALPH GEORGE, professional baseball manager; b. Lawrence, Kans., Aug. 9, 1919; s. George and Emma (Walters) H.; m. Bette Porter, June 3, 1948; children: Donna, Richard, Robert. Grad., Lawrence High Sch. With N.Y. Yankees orgn., 1939-73, player, 1947-54, coach, 1953, 54, 58, 59, 60, field mgr., 1961-63, 66-73, gen. mgr., 1963-66, v.p., 1965-66; field mgr. Detroit Tigers, 1974-78, cons., 1978-81; field mgr. Boston Red Sox, 1981—. Served to capt. AUS, World War II. Named Maj. League Mgr. of Yr., 1961. Lodge: Elks. Office: care Boston Red Sox Fenway Park 24 Yawkey Way Boston MA 02215 *

HOULE, CYRIL ORVIN, educator; b. Sarasota, Fla., Mar. 26, 1913; s. John Louis and Annie Mae (Hescock) H.; m. Bettie Eckhardt Totten, May 15, 1947; 1 son, David. A.B., U. Fla., 1934, M.A., 1934; Ph.D., U. Chgo., 1940; Fulbright fellow, U.K., 1950-51; D.H.L., Rutgers U., DePaul U., N.Y. U., Roosevelt U.; LL.D., Fla. State U., Syracuse U. Instr. U. Chgo., 1939-42, asst. prof., 1942-45, asso. prof., dean, 1945-52, prof., 1952-78, prof. emeritus, 1978—; vis. instr. U. Calif., 1940; Knapp vis. prof. U. Wis., Milw., 1960; vis. sr. research specialist Oxford U., 1968; sr. program cons. W.K. Kellogg Found., 1976—; dir. UNESCO seminar, Sweden, 1950; mem. Nat. Adv. Council on Extension and Continuing Edn. Author or co-author: Adult Education, 1937, Armed Services and Adult Education, 1947, Libraries in Adult and Fundamental Education, 1951, The University, the Citizen, and World Affairs, 1956, The Effective Board, 1960, The Inquiring Mind, 1961, Continuing Your Education, 1964, The Design of Education, 1972, The External Degree, 1973, Continuing Learning in the Professions, 1980; also articles in profl. jours. Recipient Tolley medal Syracuse U., 1966; Outstanding Achievement award Assn. Evening Colls., 1967, Nat. Assn. of Public Sch. Adult Educators, 1968. Mem. Nat. Acad. Edn., Phi Beta Kappa, Delta Tau Delta. Clubs: University, Quadrangle (Chgo.). Home: 5510 Woodlawn Ave Chicago IL 60637

HOULE, GUY, telecommunications executive; b. Montreal, Que., Can., Apr. 6, 1935; s. Lucien and Jeanne (Morin) H.; m. Celine Bienvenu, Dec. 24, 1960; children: Sylvie, Jean, Marie-Josee, Christine. B.A. summa cum laude, Coll. Ste-Marie, 1955; LL.B. magna cum laude, U. Montreal, 1958; postgrad., McGill U., 1959. Bar: Que. 1959. Practice law, Montreal, 1959-61; legal counsel Royal Commn. Inquiry on Edn., 1961-66; sec., legal adv. Gen. Investment Corp. Que. (and subs.'s), 1964-67; asst. v.p. law, then gen. counsel Bell Can., Montreal, 1967-80; corp. sec. Bell Can. Enterprises, Inc., 1983—; dir. Bell Can.-Internat. Mgmt. Research and Cons. Ltd., Tele Direct (Can.) Ltd., Capital Telephone Co. Ltd., Telebec Ltd., N. Am. Telegraph Co. Ltd., Ronalds-Federated Ltd. Bd. dirs. Que. Soc. Disabled Children, 1963—; chmn. Can. Student Exchange Program and Que. Student Intra-Exchange Program, Inc., 1980—; mcpl. judge, St. Bruno de Montarville, 1967—. Mem. Can. Bar Assn., Bar Province Que., Internat. Law Assn., Am. Bar Assn. (asso.), Am. Soc. Corp. Secs., Assn. Can. Gen. Counsel (emeritus mem., past pres.), Can. C. of C., St. Bruno C. of C., Montreal Bd. Trade. Roman Catholic. Clubs: St. Denis, Richelieu Valley Golf and Country, Ville Marie Squash. Home: 1895 de la Duchesse St Bruno PQ J3V 3M1 Canada Office: 1050 Beaver Hall Hill Montreal PQ Canada H2Z 1S4

HOULE, JOSEPH E., educator; b. Hartford, Conn., Oct. 11, 1930; s. Joseph E. and Rena (Cyr) H.; m. Constance Deschamps, June 19, 1954; children—Marie, Joseph, Celia, Elizabeth, Amy, Bernice. A.B., Cath. U. Am., 1952, M.A., 1954, Ph.D., 1959. From instr. to asso. prof. math. Georgetown U., 1953-62; asso. prof. Seton Hall U., 1962-63; prof. math. Pace U., N.Y.C., 1963—, chmn. dept., 1963-70, dean, 1971—. Danforth asso., 1968—. Fellow N.Y. Acad. Scis. (chmn. div. math. 1968-69); mem. Math. Assn. Am., Phi Beta Kappa, Sigma Xi. Roman Catholic. Home: 227 Garfield Pl South Orange NJ 07079 Office: Pace Univ Plaza New York City NY 10038

HOULT, PETER JOHN, tobacco company executive; b. Sheffield, Yorkshire, Eng., Dec. 7, 1943; came to U.S., 1983; s. Ralph Pickard and Phoebe Euniceon (Simony) H.; m. Linda Gwendoline Hill, July 28, 1962; children: Jacquelyn Ruth, Michael Andrew. B.A. with honors in Psychology, U. Reading, Berkshire, Eng., 1965. Psychologist Unilever Co., London, 1965-68; internat. research dir. Schlackman Orgn., London, 1968-72, R.J. Reynolds Tobacco Internat., Geneva, 1972-76, mktg. dir., gen. mgr., Hong Kong, 1976-79; mktg. v.p., exec. v.p. RJR Macdonald Tobacco Co., Toronto, Ont., Can., 1979-83; v.p. internat. mktg. R.J. Reynolds Tobacco Internat., Winston-Salem, N.C., 1983—. Co-author: Leading Cases in Market Research, 1969. Mem. Ch. of Eng. Office: RJ Reynolds Tobacco Internat. 4th & Main Sts. Winston-Salem NC 27102

HOULTON, LOYCE J., artistic director, choreographer; b. Proctor, Minn., June 13, 1926; d. Andrew and Ragna M. Johnson; m. William H. Houlton, July 28, 1950; children: Laif, Joel, Lise, Andrew. B.A., Carleton Coll., 1946, Hum.D. (hon.), 1981; M.A., NYU, 1950. Mem. dance adv. panel Minn. State Arts Council, 1972-75. Artistic dir., Minn. Dance Theatre, Mpls., 1962—; choreographer for, Berlin Deutsche Oper Ballet, Washington Ballet, Dayton (Ohio) Ballet, Louisville Ballet, Pacific N.W. Ballet, Pa. Ballet, Pauline Koner Dance Consert, N.Y.C., Tulsa Ballet Co.; subject of film Loyce. Recipient Plaudit award Nat. Dance Assn., 1980; Minn. State Arts Bd. choreographic fellow, 1978-79; Nat. Endowment for Arts Class A choreographic grantee. Mem. Nat. Assn. Regional Ballet (pres. Mid-States region 1972-73, dir. 1975—). Office: 528 Hennepin Ave Minneapolis MN 55403

HOUNSHELL, CHARLES DAVID, political science educator; b. Rural Retreat, Va., Dec. 19, 1920; s. David Washington and Florence Earhart (Brown) H.; m. Elizabeth Jane Yoak, Oct. 9, 1944; children: Jeffrey David (dec.), William Douglas, Elizabeth Anne. A.B., Emory and Henry Coll., 1942, LL.D., 1968; Ph.D., U. Va., 1950; Ford Faculty fellow, Princeton, 1953-54. Instr. polit. sci. U. Va., 1948-50; mem. faculty Emory U., 1950-66, asso. prof. polit. sci., 1955-66, asso. dean, 1960-66; dean Newcomb Coll.; prof. polit. sci. Tulane U., New Orleans, 1966-69; pres. Birmingham-So. Coll., Birmingham, Ala., 1969-71; spl. asst. to pres., prof. polit. sci. U. Ala., 1971-72; vice chancellor adminstrn. U. N.C. at Greensboro, 1972-80, prof., 1972—; Chmn. region VI Woodrow Wilson Nat. Fellowship Found., 1957-66, nat. rep., 1962-63, mem. nat. com., 1966-67, chmn. region XII, 1967-69; sec.-treas., editor proc. So. Univ. Conf., 1971-77; panelist Nat. Endowment for Humanities, 1976, 78. Author: The Legislative Process in Virginia, 1951; Book rev. editor: Jour. Politics, 1960-62. Served to lt. USNR, 1942-46; capt. Res. Philip Francis du Pont sr. fellow, 1947-48; research fellow, 1948; summer research scholar Duke Commonwealth Studies Center, 1957; research grantee Emory U. Research Com., 1952, 55, 60, U. Center in Ga., 1955. Sr. fellow Acad. for Ednl. Devel.; mem. Am. Polit. Sci. Assn., So. Polit. Sci. Assn. (exec. council 1954-57, v.p. 1957), Phi Beta Kappa, Omicron Delta Kappa. Democrat. Methodist. Home: 3906 Watauga Dr Greensboro NC 27410

HOUNTRAS, PETER TIMOTHY, educator; b. Memphis, Dec. 7, 1927; s. Timothy John and Ethel (Trakas) H.; m. Helen Madias, Nov. 21, 1954; children: John, Dean. B.S. cum laude, U. Toledo, 1946; M.A., U. Mich., 1951, Ph.D., 1955. Instr. U. Mich., 1954-57; asst. prof. psychology and edn. U. Pitts., 1957-59, asso. prof., 1959-61; asso. prof. ednl. psychology, guidance and counseling Northwestern U., Evanston, Ill., 1961-66; prof. counseling and guidance, chmn. dept. U. N.D., Grand Forks, 1966-70; dean of counseling services Eastern Mich. U., Ypsilanti, 1970—, adj. prof. psychology, 1972—; cons. psychologist, 1957—; Regional counseling and testing cons. Bur. Employment Security, U.S. Dept. Labor, 1966—; cons. to U.S. Office of Edn., 1967—. Author: Mental Hygiene, 1961, Manifest Anxiety and Achievement, 1970; Contbr. articles profl. jours. Recipient Distinguished Service Citation Gov. N.D., 1969. Fellow Am. Psychol. Assn.; mem. Am. Personnel and Guidance Assn., Ill., Midwestern psychol. assns., Assn. Counselor Educators and Suprs., N.D. Guidance and Personnel Assn., Nat. Soc. Study Edn., Psychologists Interested in Advancement Psychotherapy, Am. Ednl. Research Assn., A.A.U.P., Mich. Psychol. Assn., Sigma Xi, Psi Chi, Phi Kappa Phi, Phi Delta Kappa, Kappa Delta Pi. Presbyn. (elder). Club: Rotarian. Home: 24907 Woodridge End Farmington Hills MI 48018

HOURANI, GEORGE FADLO, philosophy educator; b. Manchester, Eng., June 3, 1913; came to U.S., 1950, naturalized, 1956; s. Fadlo and Sumaya (Racy) H.; m. Celeste Habib, June 15, 1940. B.A., Oxford (Eng.) U., 1936; Ph.D., Princeton U., 1939. Lectr. classics and philosophy Govt. Arab Coll., Jerusalem, Palestine, 1939-48; prof. Islamic history and philosophy U. Mich., 1950-67; prof. philosophy SUNY, Buffalo, 1967-83, Disting. prof., 1982-83, prof. emeritus, 1983—, chmn. dept. philosophy, 1976-80; vis. prof. philosophy UCLA, 1979. Author: Arab Seafaring in the Indian Ocean in Ancient and Early Medieval Times, 1951, Ethical Value, 1956, Ibn Rushd: (Averroes): Kitab fasl al-maqal, 1959, Averroes on the Harmony of Religion and Philosophy, 1961, Islamic Rationalism-The Ethics of 'Abd al-Jabbar, 1971; Editor: Essays on Islamic Philosophy and Science, 1975; Mem. editorial bd.: State U. N.Y. Press, 1972-77. Ford Found. area research fellow, 1956-57; Guggenheim fellow, 1963-64. Mem. Am. Oriental Soc. (asso. editor jour. 1964-70, pres. 1978-79), Am. Philos. Assn., Middle East Inst., Royal Inst. Philosophy (London), Middle East Studies Assn. (pres. 1968). Home: 105 Troy Del Way Williamsville NY 14221 Office: Dept Philosophy State U NY at Buffalo Amherst NY 14260

HOURTOULE, GILBERT OTTO, educator, polit. scientist; b. Newark, June 25, 1924; s. Gilbert and Georgiana (Schumm) H. A.B., Montclair State Coll., 1947; M.A., Stanford, 1948; Ph.D., Pa. State U., 1953. Instr. Montclair State Coll., 1949-51; asst. prof. Lafayette Coll., Easton, Pa., 1953-61, asst. dean coll., 1958-61; asso. prof., asst. to pres. Montclair State Coll., 1961-63, prof., 1968—, chmn. dept. polit. sci., 1968-72, dep. chmn. dept., 1981—; cons. U.S. Commn. Govt. Security, 1956. Contbr. profl. jours. Served with USAAF, 1943-46. Mem. Am. Polit. Sci. Assn., Am. Acad. Polit. and Social Sci., N.J. Polit. Sci. Assn., N.J. Fedn. Tchrs., Pi Sigma Alpha, Pi Gamma Mu, Kappa Delta Pi. Republican. Episcopalian. Club: Mason. Office: Montclair State Coll Upper Montclair NJ 07043

HOUSE, ARTHUR STEPHEN, speech scientist; b. N.Y.C., May 1, 1921; 2 children. B.S., CCNY, 1942; M.A., U. Denver, 1948; Ph.D. in Speech, U. Ill., 1951. Instr. speech sci. U. Ill., Champaign-Urbana, 1951-52; research assoc. Control Systems Lab., 1952-53; mem. staff speech communication Acoustics Lab., M.I.T., 1953-57, 1959-64; assoc. prof. audiology and speech pathology Syracuse U., 1957-59; prof. audiology and speech sci. Purdue U., Lafayette, Ind., 1964-71; staff mem. Communications Research div. Inst. Def. Analyses, Princeton, N.J., 1971—; Mem. com. on hearing, bioacoustics and biomechanics Nat. Acad. Sci.-NRC, 1965-66, 68-73. Served to s/sgt. AUS, 1942-46. Fellow Am. Speech and Hearing Assn., Acoustical Soc. Am., N.Y. Acad. Scis., AAAS. Address: Inst for Defense Analyses Princeton NJ 08540

HOUSE, CHARLES STAVER, judge; b. Manchester, Conn., Apr. 24, 1908; s. Herbert Bissell and Sophia (Staver) H.; m. Virginia Mabel Brown, Aug. 5, 1938; children: Carolyn, Arthur, Elizabeth. Grad., Williston Acad., 1926; A.B., Harvard U., 1930, LL.B., 1933; LL.D., Suffolk U., 1975. Bar: Conn. 1933. Ptnr. Day, Berry & Howard, Hartford, Conn., 1936-53; judge Conn. Superior Ct., 1953-65; assoc. justice Conn. Supreme Ct., 1965-71, chief justice, 1971-78, state trial referee, 1978—; chmn. bd. Heritage Savs. & Loan Assn.; vice chmn. Conn. Jud. Council, 1964-65, chmn., 1965-71, Jud. Rev. Council, 1970-71; vice chmn. Nat. Adv. Com. on Criminal Justice Standards and Goals, 1975-76; chmn. Nat. Conf. Chief Justices, 1975-76. Chmn. Manchester Bd. Edn., 1943-53; Rep. Conn. Gen. Assembly, 1939, state senator, 1947, 49; Republican leader Senate, chmn. legislative council, 1949; asst. state's atty., 1942-46; legal adviser Gov. Lodge, 1951-53; Hon. trustee Manchester Meml. Hosp. Fellow Am. Bar Found.; mem. Am., Conn. bar assns. Congregationalist. Lodge: Masons. Office: Drawer D Sta A Hartford CT 06106

HOUSE, FRANK OWEN, legal educator, retired air force officer; b. Birmingham, Ala., Sept. 15, 1927; s. Frank Macon and Irene (Love) H.; m. Joan Marie Zierak, June 14, 1952 (dec.); 1 son, John Macon. J.D. cum laude, St. Louis U., 1957; LL.M., George Washington U., 1964. Bar: Mo. 1957, U.S. Ct. Mil. Appeals 1957, U.S. Supreme Ct. 1962. Commd. 2d lt. USAAF, 1946; advanced through grades to brig. gen. USAF, 1972, dep. dir. civil law, Europe, 1957-60; spl. asst. and exec. to judge adv. gen., 1960-65, staff judge adv., Randolph AFB, Tex., 1966-68, Alaskan Air Command and Alaskan Command, 1968-70; dir. civil law USAF, Washington, 1970-73, Pacific Air Forces, 1973-76, ret.; assoc. prof. law Cumberland Sch. Law, Samford U. Decorated DSM, Legion of Merit with oak leaf cluster; Bronze Star; Commendation medal with 3 oak leaf clusters.

HOUSE, ROBERT WILLIAM, educator; b. Bristow, Okla., Nov. 28, 1920; s. Richard Morton and Elizabeth (Swartz) H.; m. Esther Jean Hawkins, June 5, 1943 (dec. Oct. 1977); children: R. Edmund, Richard M., Russell L., Kathryn M.; m. Mary Elaine Thornton Wallace, Mar. 12, 1979. B.F.A., Okla. State U., 1941; Mus.M., Eastman Sch. Music, 1942; Ed.D., U. Ill., 1954. Asst. prof. band, cello, wind instruments Nebr. State Coll., Kearney, 1946-55; prof. orch., cello and music edn., chmn. music dept. U. Minn., Duluth, 1955-67; dir. Sch. Music, So. Ill. U., Carbondale, 1967-76; head music dept. East Tex. State U., 1976—; cons. Ednl. Testing Service, 1962-66. Prin. cellist, Duluth Symphony, 1955-67; Author: (with Charles Leonhard) Foundations and Principles of Music Education, 1959, rev., 1972, Instrumental Music for Today's Schools, 1965, Administration in Music Education, 1973; Mem. editorial bd.: Jour. of Research in Music Edn, 1958-70; mng. editor: The Ill. Music Educator, 1975-76. Served with AUS, 1942-46; ETO. Mem. Nat. Assn. Schs. Music (panel evaluators 1966-76, chmn. com. on tchr. edn. in music 1963-67, chmn. com. on ethics 1970-72, com. on research and publs. 1973-75, chmn. com. nominations 1980-81), Music Educators Research Council (nat. chmn. 1958-60), Music Educators Nat. Conf. (mem. publs. planning com. 1972-82, chmn. 1976-82, pres.-elect North Central div. 1974-76, mem. com. for advancement music edn. 1976-80), Am. String Tchrs. Assn. (sec. Tex. unit 1978-80). Home: Rural Route 2 Box 93 Commerce TX 75428

HOUSE, ROY C., retired hospital executive; b. West Liberty, Ohio, July 11, 1917; s. Thomas C. and Myrtle (McLel) H.; m. Elizabeth M. Fritschle, Sept. 11, 1942; children: David R., Janet Sue. A.B., Evansville (Ind.) Coll., 1939; M.S. in Hosp. Adminstrn., Northwestern U., 1949; D.Health Services (hon.), Southwestern Coll., 1978. Asst. mgr. comml. foods div. Igleheart div. Gen. Foods Corp., Evansville, Ind., 1939-47; resident in adminstrn. Meth. Hosp., Indpls., 1948-49; asst. adminstr. Samuel Merritt Hosp., Oakland, Calif., 1949-50; adminstr. Warm Springs Found. Hosp. Crippled Children, Gonzales, Tex., 1950-54, Marion (Ind.) Gen. Hosp., 1954-57; exec. v.p., chief exec. officer Wesley Med. Center, Wichita, Kans., 1957-72, pres., 1972-81, pres. emeritus, 1981—; preceptor, lectr. Northwestern U., 1958-62, Washington U., St. Louis, 1962-83, Trinity U., San Antonio, 1978-83; pres. Austin (Tex.) Hosp. Council, 1953, East Ind. Hosp. Council, 1956, Hosp. Council Met. Wichita, 1960, Kans. Blue Cross Plan, 1965-66, mem. exec. bd., 1959-66, mem. exec. com., 1963-66, treas., 1964, pres., 1965; mem. Gov. Kans. Adv. Council Regional Med. Programs, 1965-75, chmn., 1972-74; charter mem., co-founder, sec. bd. dirs., mem. exec. com. Voluntary Hosps. Am., 1977-82; treas. Wesley Research Found., 1960-82. Recipient Laura Jackson award outstanding grad. hosp. adminstrn. Northwestern U., 1970. Fellow Am. Coll. Hosp. Adminstrs. (regent for Kans. 1966-69, dist. gov. 1971-72); mem. Am. Hosp. Assn. (ho. dels. 1971-78, trustee 1978-82), Kans. Hosp. Assn. (pres. 1968-69), Tau Kappa Alpha, Pi Gamma Mu, Alpha Delta Mu, Alpha Kappa Psi (hon.). Clubs: Rotary, Masons, Shriners. Home: 132 Morningside Wichita KS 67218 1301 Leisure World Mesa AZ 85206

HOUSEL, JERRY WINTERS, lawyer; b. Cripple Creek, Colo., Aug. 9, 1912; s. James Robert and Emma (Winters) H.; m. Mary Elaine Bever, July 8, 1941; children: James Robert, Jerry Laine, John Ora, Peter Elliott. B.A., U. Wyo., 1935, J.D., 1936; Ph.D., Am. U., 1941. Bar: Wyo. 1936. Practice in, Laramie, 1936; teaching fellow Am. U. Grad. Sch., 1937; asst. to U.S. Senator Schwartz, 1937-40; atty. FTC, 1941, War Relocation Authority, 1942; practiced in, Cody, Wyo., 1946—; past pres., mem. Wyo. Bd. Law Examiners, 1956-70; adv. dir. First Wyo. Bank, Cody. Mem. Cody City Council, 1950. Served with USNR, 1943-46. Mem. Wyo. State Bar (pres. 1964), Cody C. of C. (pres. 1952), Am. Legion (comdr. Cody post 1951), ABA (ho. of dels. 1965-67, 75—), Park County Bar Assn. (pres. 1950), Am. Judicature Soc. (dir. 1967). Home: 1500 11th St Cody WY 82414 Office: 1203 Sheridan Ave Cody WY 82414

HOUSEMAN, JOHN, producer, dir., actor; b. Bucarest, Rumania, Sept. 22, 1902; s. Georges and May (Davies) H.; m. Joan Courtney, Dec. 1950; children—John Michael, Charles Sebastian. Student, Clifton Coll., Eng.; Dr.Arts (hon.), Temple U., 1973—. Co-founder, pres. Mercury Theatre, 1937-39; v.p. David O. Selznick Prodns., 1941; chief overseas radio program bur. OWI, 1942-43; producer Paramount Pictures, 1943-46, RKO, 1947-49, Metro-Goldwyn-Mayer, 1950-56, CBS-TV, 1956-59; asso. prof. English drama Vassar Coll., 1937-38; lectr. New Sch. for Social Research, Barnard Coll., others; Regents lectr. U. Calif. at Los Angeles, 1960; head drama div. Juilliard Sch., 1968-76; Cockefair chair U. Mo., Kansas City, 1971-72; vis. prof. for performing arts U. S.C., 1977; pres. Martha Graham Center, 1972-73. Theatre dir.: plays Four Saints in Three Acts, 1934, Panic, 1935, Valley Forge, 1935, Hamlet, 1936, Liberty Jones, 1939, Lutesong, 1947, King Lear, 1951, Corioianus, 1953, The Country Girl, 1972, Don Juan in Hell, 1973, Clarence Darrow, 1974; producer: Negro Macbeth, 1935, Dr. Faustus, 1937, The Cradle Will Rock, 1937, Julius Caesar, 1937, Shoemaker's Holiday, 1938, Native Son, 1940, King Lear, 1964; dir.: operas The Devil and Daniel Webster, 1939, Othello, 1963, Tosca, 1965, 74, The Mines of Sulphur, 1968, Antigone, 1970, The Losers, 1971, Byron, 1972, Macbeth, 1973; artistic dir., Am. Shakespeare Festival, 1956-59, Profl. Theatre Group of U. Calif. at Los Angeles Extension, 1959-63, City Center Acting Co., 1972-75, Acting Co., 1975—; producing dir., A.P.A. Repertory Co., 1967-69, Phoenix Theatre, 1969-70; dir. drama div., Juilliard Sch., N.Y.C., 1967-76; producer motion pictures, The Unseen, Miss Suzie Slagle's, 1944, The Blue Dahlia, 1945, They Live by Night, 1946, Letter from an Unknown Woman, 1947, The Bad and the Beautiful, 1952, Julius Caesar, 1953, Executive Suite, 1954, The Cobweb, 1955, Lust for Life, 1956, All Fall Down, 1961, Two Weeks in Another Town, 1962, The Dancer's World, Three by Martha Graham, also (for U.S. Govt.) Tuesday in November, 1944, Voyage to America, 1964; actor: films The Paper Chase, 1974, Rollerball, 1975, Three Days of the Condor, 1975, St. Ives, 1976, The Cheap Detective, 1977; TV shows Fear on Trial, 1975, Truman at Potsdam, 1976, Six Characters in Search of an Author, 1976, The Displaced Person, 1976, Washington, 1977, Aspen, 1977, The French Atlantic Affair, 1979; starred in: TV series Paper Chase, 1978; exec. producer: TV Seven Lively Arts, 1957, Playhouse 90, 1958-59, The Great Adventure, 1963; radio editor: Mercury Theatre of the Air; writer: Helen Hayes Theatre; (Recipient Acad. award best supporting actor The Paper Chase 1974); Author: Run-through, a memoir, 1972, Front and Center, 1979. Mem. Author's League, Writers Guild, Screen Producers Guild, Actor's Equity, Screen Actors Guild, Nat. Theatre Conf. (pres. 1970-71), Internat. Theatre Inst. U.S. (v.p. 1968-70). Clubs: Century Assn., Players (N.Y.C.). Address: Artists Agy 190 N Canon Dr Beverly Hills CA 90210 *

HOUSER, DOUGLAS GUY, lawyer; b. Oregon City, Oreg., July 11, 1935; s. Roy B. and Shirley (Knight) H.; m. Lucy Anne Latham, Sept. 1, 1961; children: Brooks Bonham, Bradley Knight, Anne Elizabeth. B.A., Willamette U., 1957; J.D., Stanford, 1960. Bar: Oreg. 1960. Practice in Portland, 1961—; partner Bullivant, Wright, Leedy, Johnson, Pendergrass & Hoffman, 1965—; Chmn. com. on continuing legal edn. Oreg. State Bar, 1969-70, chmn. com. jud. adminstrn., 1975, bd. bar examiners, 1970-72, mem. bd. bar govs., 1977-80, treas., 1979-80; judge protem Circuit Ct.; asst. sec., dir. Nike, Inc.; lectr. Contbr. articles to profl. publs. Legal adviser Portland Sch. Dist. 1 Race and Edn. Com., 1963-64; mem. Eagle bd. Columbia-Pacific council Boy Scouts Am., 1962-70; chmn. lawyers sect. Multnomah County United Good Neighbors, 1970—; Past v.p., treas., bd. dirs. Waverley Children's Home; trustee Willamette U.; bd. visitors Stanford U. Sch. Law, 1977—; chmn. Oreg. State Jud. Fitness Commn., 1980—. Recipient certificate of appreciation Sch. Dist. 1 for work on race and edn. legal subcom., 1964. Fellow Am. Bar Found.; mem. ABA. (chmn. publs. com. 1980, council tort and ins. practice sect. 1981—), Oreg. Bar Assn. (plaque of appreciation 1969), Multnomah County Bar Assn. (chmn. com. continuing legal edn. 1977), Nat. Assn. R.R. Trial Counsel, Oreg. Assn. Def. Counsel (dir. 1972—, pres. 1976-77), Def. Research Inst., Fedn. Ins. Counsel (v.p.), Am. Judicature Soc.,

Internat. Assn. Ins. Counsel, Stanford Law Soc. Oreg. (pres.), Portland C. of C., Willamette U. Alumni Assn. (pres. 1972-74), Beta Theta Pi, Phi Delta Phi, Omicron Delta Kappa, Pi Gamma Mu. Republican. Episcopalian (trustee Diocese Oreg. 1972-75, sr. warden). Clubs: Waverly Country., Arlington. Home: 11710 SW Summerville Portland OR 97219 Office: 121 Salmon St Willamette Center Portland OR 97204

HOUSER, HAROLD BYRON, epidemiologist; b. North Liberty, Ind., Nov. 22, 1921; s. Edgar Allen and Gladys Chloe (Stillson) H.; m. Clara Jane Goin, Sept. 18, 1944; children: Cristene, Edgar, John, Susan, James. A.B., Ind. U., 1942, M.D., 1944. Intern U.S. Marine Hosp., New Orleans, 1944-45; resident Crile VA Hosp., Cleve., 1947-49; research fellow in preventive medicine Case Western Res. U., Cleve., 1949-52, asst. prof. medicine and community health, 1958-64, assoc. prof., 1965—, prof. epidemiology, 1974—, chmn. dept. biometry, 1975—; cons. in field; Trustee Cleve. PPRO; pres. Inst. Advancement Computer Use in Nutrition. Contbr. numerous articles to profl. jours. Served with U.S. Army, 1945-47, 49-52. Recipient Group Lasker award Am. Pub. Health Assn., 1954, Disting. Civilian award Dept. Def., 1973. Fellow Am. Coll. Preventive Medicine, Infectious Diseases Soc.; mem. Am. Epidemiol. Soc., Central Soc. Clin. Research, Acad. Medicine. Home: 2330 Delaware Dr Cleveland Heights OH 44106 Office: 2040 Adelbert Rd Cleveland OH 44106

HOUSER, JAMES HOWELL, chem. co. exec.; b. Milroy, Pa., Sept. 28, 1931; s. J. Lester and A. Adaleena (Treaster) H.; m. Sara Alice Graybill, July 25, 1956; children—James H., Patricia L., David B. B.S. in Chemistry, Dickinson Coll., 1953; M.S. in Indsl. Adminstrn, Carnegie-Mellon U., 1959. Sales rep. Koppers Co., Inc., 1959-63; sales rep. Pennwalt Corp., 1963-66, regional sales mgr., Phila., 1966-69, product mgr., 1969-73, dept. mgr., 1973-81, pres., 1981—. Chmn. United Way, 1978-80. Served with U.S. Navy, 1953-56. Republican. Presbyterian. Club: Whitford Country. Home: 1210 Karen Ln West Chester PA 19380 Office: 3 Parkway St Philadelphia PA 19102

HOUSER, ROBERT NORMAN, insurance company executive; b. Bloomfield, Iowa, Sept. 21, 1919; s. Charles B. and Venna C. (Bartholomew) H.; m. Doris V. Miller, Dec. 18, 1943; children: Theodore Alan, Judith Eileen, James Robert. B.A. summa cum laude, U. Iowa, 1947. With Bankers Life Co., 1936-38, 40-43, 47—, asst. actuary, 1953-60, asso. actuary, 1960-63, 2d v.p., actuary, 1963-68, v.p., actuary, 1968-71, v.p., chief actuary, 1971-72, sr. v.p., chief actuary, 1972-73, pres., 1973-75, pres., chief exec. officer, from 1975, now chmn., chief exec. officer; chmn. bd., pres. BLC Growth & Income Funds, BLC Fund, Inc.; chmn. bd. BLC Equity Mgmt. Co., BLC Equity Services Corp.; dir. BLC Ins. Co. Bd. dirs. Drake U., Mercy Hosp., United Way Greater Des Moines; bd. govs. Iowa Coll. Found. Served to 1st lt. USAAF, 1943-45; Served to 1st lt. USAF, 1951-52. Decorated D.F.C., Air medals. Fellow Soc. Actuaries; mem. Greater Des Moines C. of C. (dir.), Am. Council Life Ins. (dir.), Health Ins. Assn. Am. (dir.). Home: 2412 48th St Des Moines IA 50310 Office: 711 High St Des Moines IA 50307 *

HOUSER, WILLIAM DOUGLAS, satellite telecommunications company executive, former naval officer; b. Atlanta, Nov. 11, 1921; s. Harry M. and Berenice (Horton) H.; m. Betty Lou Worrall, Mar 11, 1946; children: Cynthia L., Gayle L., Francie L. B.S., U.S. Naval Acad., 1941; postgrad., U. Md., 1949-50, U.S. Naval War Coll., 1958-59, Harvard Bus. Sch., 1963; M.S., George Washington U., 1968. Commd. ensign USN., 1941, advanced through grades to vice adm., 1972; comdr. fighter squadron (Korean War and aircraft carrier U.S.S. Constellation in), Viet Nam, 1966, mil. asst. to sec. def., 1962-63; mem. joint staff Joint Chiefs of Staff, 1960-62, 67-68; dir. aviation plans and requirements USN, Washington, 1968-70; comdr. (Carrier Div. Two, U.S. Atlantic and Mediterranean Fleets), 1970-72, dep. chief naval ops. (air warfare), Washington, 1972-76; dir. satellite interconnection for pub. TV and radio Corp. for Public Broadcasting, Washington, 1976-79; dir. spl. projects Communications Satellite Corp., Washington, 1979—; asst. v.p. Comsat Gen. Corp., Washington, 1980, v.p., 1981—. Decorated D.S.M. with gold star, Legion of Merit with three gold stars, Bronze Star, Air Medal with gold star. Methodist. Home: 2430 Ft Scott Dr Arlington VA 22202 Office: 950 L'Enfant Plaza SW Washington DC 20024

HOUSEWORTH, RICHARD COURT, banker; b. Harveyville, Kans., Jan. 18, 1928; s. Court Henry and Mabel (Lynch) H.; m. Laura Louise Jennings, Nov. 1, 1952; children: Louise, Lucile, Court. B.S., U. Kans., 1950. Mgmt. trainee Lawrence Nat. Bank, Kans., 1951-52; pres. 1st Nat. Bank, Harveyville, 1952-55; exec. v.p. Ariz. Bank, Phoenix, 1955—; mem. fin. adv. com. Am. Mining Congress. Past pres. Better Bus. Bur., Tucson; past chmn. bd. Pacific Coast Banking Sch. U. Wash.; past pres. Barrow Neurol. Inst. of St. Joseph's Hosp.; bd. dirs., sec., treas., mem. exec. com. Valley of the Sun United Way. Served with U.S. Army, 1946-48. Recipient 1st Disting. Service award Scottsdale Jaycees, 1962. Mem. Robert Morris Assocs. (dir., past pres. Ariz. chpt., dir. loan mgmt. seminar), Ariz. C. of C. (1st pres., dir.), Tucson C. of C. (past pres.), Am. Inst. Banking (past pres. Maricopa chpt.), Ariz. Bankers Assn. (1st v.p.), Ariz. Acad., Urban League of Phoenix (chmn.), Phi Delta Theta. Republican. Episcopalian. Clubs: Paradise Valley Country (Scottsdale, Ariz.); Phoenix Country. Home: 2201 N Central Ave Phoenix AZ 85004 Office: 101 N 1st Ave Phoenix AZ 85003

HOUSEWRIGHT, RILEY DEE, microbiologist, society executive; b. Wylie, Tex., Oct. 17, 1913; s. Jick and Lillie (Townsend) H.; m. Marjory Bryant, June 10, 1939 (dec. July 1962); 1 son, Kim Bryant; m. Artemis Skevakis Jegart, Aug. 1969. B.S., North Tex. State Coll., 1934; M.A., U. Tex., 1938; Ph.D., U. Chgo., 1944; postgrad., Cambridge (Eng.) U., 1950. Diplomate: Am. Bd. Microbiology. Pub. sch. tchr., Tex., 1934-36; instr. S.W. Tex. State Coll., also in, San Marcos, Tex., 1937-41; chief microbial physiology and chemotherapy br., Ft. Detrick, Md., 1946-50, dep. chief, chief med. bacteriology div., 1950-56; sci. dir. U.S. Army Biol. Labs., 1956-70; v.p., sci. dir. Microbiol. Assos. Inc., Bethesda, Md., 1970-75; prin. staff officer Nat. Acad. Sci.-NRC, Washington, 1975-81; exec. dir. Am. Soc. for Microbiology, Washington, 1981—; mem. adv. com. to sci. dir. Inst. Microbiology, Rutgers U., 1959-67; mem. panel on regulatory biology NSF, 1967-70; cons. Office Edn., Dept. Health, Edn. and Welfare, 1973—; sr. cons. Leonard Wood Found., 1975—; cons. pharm. and food industry, 1970—. Author books, articles; editor: Bacteriol. Proc, 1957-59; editor-in-chief, ASM News, 1981—. Pres. Am. Soc. Microbiology Found., 1973—; bd. assos. Hood Coll., Frederick, Md., 1969-80; trustee Am. Type Culture Collection, 1973-81, Frederick Meml. Hosp., 1977-83. Served to lt. (j.g.) USNR, 1944-46; capt. Res. ret. U. Chgo. fellow, 1941-42; John and Mary E. Markle fellow, 1942-43; scholarship Am. Mgmt. Assn., 1957; recipient U.S. Patent awards, 1959; Meritorious Civilian Service award Dept. Army, 1962, 64; Distinguished Alumni citation N. Tex. State U., 1965; Exceptional Civilian Service award Dept. of Army, 1968. Fellow Am. Acad. Microbiology, A.A.A.S., N.Y. Acad. Scis.; mem. Am. Soc. Microbiology (hon. mem., pres. 1965-66, Barnett E. Cohen award Md. br. 1967), Soc. Gen. Microbiology (Eng.), Soc. Exptl. Biology and Medicine, Research Soc. Am., Sigma Xi, Phi Delta Kappa, Gamma Alpha. Club: Cosmos (Washington). Home: 147 Fairview Ave Frederick MD 21701 Office: 1913 I St NW Washington DC 20006

HOUSEWRIGHT, WILEY LEE, educator; b. Wylie, Tex., Oct. 17, 1913; s. Jick and Lillie (Townsend) H.; m. Lucilla Elizabeth Gumm, Dec. 27, 1939. B.S., N. Tex. State U., 1934; M.A., Columbia, 1938; Ed.D., N.Y. U., 1943. Dir. music pub. schs., Tex., N.Y., 1934-41; lectr. music N.Y. U., 1942-43; asst. prof. U. Tex., 1946-47; faculty Fla. State U., Tallahassee, 1947—, prof. music, 1948-79, prof. emeritus, 1980—, Disting. prof., 1961-62, dean, 1966-79; vis. summer prof. U. Mich., 1960, U. Ind., 1955; Fulbright scholar, Japan, 1956-57; Mem. U.S. nat. com. for UNESCO, 1958; music adv. panel internat. cultural presentations program State Dept., 1958-79. Editor: Birchard Music Series, vols. I-VI, 1962; chmn. editorial bd.: Music Educators Jour, 1957-66; editorial asso.: Jour. Research Music Edn, 1953-62; choral music rev. editor, 1955-57. Adv. bd. humanities and arts Ford Found., 1958—. Served to 1st lt. AUS, 1943-46. Decorated Distinguished Service citation; recipient Distinguished Alumni citation No. Tex. State U., 1967; Ford Found. grantee, 1966-68. Mem. Music Educators Nat. Conf. (pres. 1968-70), Am. Musicological Soc., Music Tchrs. Nat. Assn., Internat. Soc. Music Edn., Music Library Assn., Sonneck Soc., Am. Choral Dirs. Assn., Pi Kappa Lambda, Phi Delta Kappa, Phi Mu Alpha, Lambda Chi Alpha, Omicron Delta Kappa, Kappa Kappa Psi. Clubs: Rotary, Capital City Country, Govs. Home: 515 South Ride Tallahassee FL 32303

HOUSKA, CHARLES ROBERT, educator; b. Cleve., May 16, 1927; s. Charles and Anna (Gehrke) H.; m. Mary Frances Dittmer, Aug. 15, 1953; children—Catherine Mary, Robert Bradford, Susan Sanford. S.B. in Physics, Mass. Inst. Tech., 1951, S.M. in Metallurgy, 1954, Sc.D., 1957. Mem. research staff dept. physics Mass. Inst. Tech., 1951-52, dept. metallurgy, 1957-59; mem. research staff Union Carbide Research Inst., Tarrytown, N.Y., 1959-63; asso. prof. Va. Poly. Inst. and State U. at Blacksburg, 1963-65, prof., 1965-69, prof., head metals and ceramic engring., 1969-71, prof. materials engring., 1971—. Contbr. articles profl. jours. Served with USNR, 1945-46. Mem. Am. Inst. Mining, Metall. and Petroleum Engrs., Am. Crystallographic Assn., Sigma Xi, Alpha Sigma Mu. Home: 2301 Spring Hollow Lane NW Blacksburg VA 24060

HOUSMAN, ARTHUR LLOYD, educator; b. Missoula, Mont., June 8, 1928; s. Robert Lloyd and Mary Chaddock (Webster) H.; m. Cathryn Elizabeth Puckett, Feb. 28, 1953 (div.); children—Donna Lynn, Mary Cathryn, Lisa Ann; m. Cigdem Fatma Selisik, May 1, 1974. Student, Wesleyan U., 1946-47; B.A., DePauw U., 1950; M.A., State U. Iowa, 1951, Ph.D., 1956. Mem. faculty State Coll., St. Cloud, Minn., 1956-62, prof., chmn. speech and dramatic art, 1959-62; prof., chmn. theatre dept. Ohio State U., Columbus, 1968-71; prof., chmn. dept. dramatic art U. N.C. at Chapel Hill, 1971—. Served to 1st lt. AUS, 1951-54. Recipient specialist grants State Dept., Ankara, Istanbul, Turkey, 1965, 69. Mem. N.C. Theatre Conf., Nat. Theatre Conf., Am. Theatre Assn. Home: 408 Coolidge St Chapel Hill NC 27514 *I try to teach and to learn; to seek life and an understanding of the balance between the wisdom of age and the energy of youth.*

HOUSMAN, STEVEN A., stockbroker; b. Los Angeles, Feb. 23, 1945; s. Phillip and Lee H.; m. Carol Oliver, May 2, 1976 (div. May 1979); 1 dau., Stacey Oliver. Stockbroker, account exec. DuPont-Glore-Forgan, Sherman Oaks, Calif., 1966-74; ptnr. Crowell Weedon Co., Encino, Calif., 1974—. Jewish. Office: Crowell Weedon & Co 16130 Ventura Blvd Encino CA 91436

HOUSTON, ALFRED DEARBORN, energy company executive; b. Quincy, Mass., Aug. 14, 1940; s. Alfred Dearborn and Merriland Curry (Westwood) H.; m. Patricia Selko, Oct. 23, 1965; children—Melissa, Sherriden. B.S. in Econs, U. Pa., 1962; Advanced Mgmt. Program, Harvard U. With New Eng. Electric System (and subsidiaries), 1962—; v.p. corp. fin. New Eng. Energy Co., New Eng. Power Service Co., 1975-76, v.p., 1979—; v.p., dist. mgr. Narragansett Electric Co., Providence, 1976-77, v.p., treas., 1977-83; treas. New Eng. Electric System, New Eng. Electric Transmission Corp., Mass. Electric, Granite State Electric Co., New Eng. Power Co., 1983—. Active United Way So. New Eng., 1976-78. Club: U. Pa. (Boston) (past pres., trustee). Address: New Eng Electric System 25 Research Dr Westborough MA 01581

HOUSTON, E. JAMES, JR., financial consultant; b. Highland Park, Mich., Sept. 25, 1939; s. Ernest James and Frieda Mary (Milligan) H.; m. Ann Draper, Dec. 16, 1961; children: James Lee, Jay Douglas. B.S. in Finance, Wayne State U., 1964, M.B.A., 1967. Asst. v.p. Bank of the Commonwealth, Detroit, 1957-69; v.p. Birmingham Bloomfield Bank, Mich., 1969-70, pres., 1970-71; exec. v.p. Fidelity Bank Mich., Birmingham, 1971; pres. Houston & Assos., Inc., Birmingham, 1971—, Houston Funding, Inc., Houston Mgmt. Corp.; chmn. bd., pres. Xylem Corp.; sec. Hacht Sales & Mktg., Ltd., Farmington Hills, Mich.; lectr. fin. Wayne State U. Sch. Bus. Adminstrn., Detroit, 1971—; dir. Sutherland Leather & Felt Co., Inc., Troy, Mich. Active Bloomfield Hills Hockey Assn.; pres. pro tem Village of Bingham Farms Village Council; chmn. Southfield Twp. Citizens' Com.; v.p. Hickory Hollow Homeowners Assn.; trustee Southeastern Oakland County Water Authority; mem. Community House Assn., Birmingham; bd. dirs. CATV, Birmingham YMCA; mem. parents council Brookside Sch., Cranbrook, Mich.; pres. Brookside Sch. Dads Club; mem. Cranbrook Arena Com. Mem. Birmingham-Bloomfield C. of C., Greater Detroit C. of C. Republican. Presbyterian. Clubs: Wayne State Univ. Alumni, Rotary. Office: 9 Hickory Hollow Birmingham MI 48010

HOUSTON, HOWARD EDWIN, retired government official; b. Ryan, Iowa, Nov. 2, 1910; s. Frederick L. and Ida (Woodard) H.; m. Frances Gregory Crawford, Sept. 9, 1939; children: Frederick Woodard, Molly Crawford. A.B., Columbia, 1932. Dir. Bradley Home, Meriden, Conn., 1935-54; commr. pub. welfare State Conn., 1953-54; dep. dir. U.S. tech. cooperation mission to, India, 1955-56, minister dir., 1957-59; dir. AID/Korea; econ. counselor Am. embassy, Seoul, Korea, 1970-71; minister, dir. AID mission to, India, 1971-73; v.p. for devel. Overseas Pvt. Investment Corp., Washington, from 1975, also cons.; Dir. Meriden Trust & Safe Deposit Co., Central Bank for Savs., Meriden. Chmn. Gov.'s Com. on Med. Edn., 1952; v.p. World Edn., 1964; Mayor, Meriden, 1948-51, 62-63; mem. Meriden Charter Revision Commn., 1975, Conn. Republican Central Com., 1960-66; del. Conn. Constl. Conv., 1965; Former bd. dirs. Meriden Hosp.; mem. corp. Marine Biol. Lab., Woods Hole, Mass.; former trustee Colby Jr. Coll., New London, N.H. Served to 1st lt. AUS, 1943-46; PTO. Decorated Order of Civil Merit, South Korea; recipient Superior Honor award AID, 1974. Mem. Asia Soc. (chmn. India com. 1961), Inst. Social Scis., Washington Inst. Fgn. Affairs, Mil. Order World Wars, Psi Upsilon (past pres. Lambda chpt.). Episcopalian. Clubs: Rotary (Conn.); Nat. Press. Home: 2500 Virginia Ave NW Washington DC 20037 also Meriden CT 06450

HOUSTON, IVAN JAMES, ins. co. exec.; b. Los Angeles, June 15, 1925; s. Norman Oliver and Doris Talbot (Young) H.; m. Philippa Elizabeth Jones, July 15, 1946; children—Pamela, Kathleen (Mrs. Lawrence Johnson), Ivan Abbott. B.S., U. Calif. at Berkeley, 1948; postgrad., U. Man., 1948-49. With Golden State Mut. Life Ins. Co., Los Angeles, 1948—, v.p., actuary, 1962-66, sr. v.p., actuary, 1966-70, pres., chief exec. officer, 1970-77, chmn., pres., 1977-80, chmn., chief exec. officer, 1980—; dir. First Interstate Bank Calif., Pacific Indemnity Co., Pacific Telephone Co., Metromedia Inc., Kaiser Aluminum & Chem. Corp. Mem. Los Angeles World Affairs Council, 1970—; chmn. central region United Way, Inc., Los Angeles, 1973-75, corp. bd. dirs., 1973-80, v.p., 1973-75; bd. dirs. Los Angeles Urban League, pres., 1977—; bd. dirs. M & M Assn.; bd. fellows Claremont U. Center, 1972-80; bd. regents Loyola Marymount U., 1972-75, 79—. Served with inf. AUS, 1944-45. Decorated Purple Heart, Bronze Star, Combat Infantryman's badge. Fellow Life Office Mgmt. Inst.; mem. Am. Acad. Actuaries, Am. Soc. Pension Actuaries, Internat. Actuarial Assn., Los Angeles Actuarial Club, Conf. Actuaries in Pub. Practice (asso.), Am. Council Life Ins. (dir.), Life Office Mgmt. Assn. (dir., mem. exec. com. 1972-75, chmn. 1979), Calif. C. of C. (dir.), Los Angeles Area C. of C. (dir.), Town Hall, Kappa Alpha Psi, Sigma Psi Phi. Roman Catholic. Club: Cosmos (Los Angeles). Home: 5111 Holt Ave Los Angeles CA 90056 Office: 1999 W Adams Blvd Los Angeles CA 90018

HOUSTON, JOHN ALBERT, educator; b. Spokane, Dec. 24, 1914; s. John Alexander and Ethel (Robinson) H.; m. Marjorie Anne Robinson, Aug. 14, 1939 (dec. Sept. 1968); children—Alexandra Louise (Mrs. Lee Benham), John Alexander II, Ann Celeste; m. Pollyanna Turner, Nov. 1, 1969. A.B. in Econs, Stanford, 1936, M.A. in Internat. Relations, 1947; Ph.D. in polit. sci, U. Mich., 1951. Ins. broker Johnson & Higgins, San Francisco, 1936-37; case aide Calif. Relief Adminstrn., 1938-40; asst., then asso. prof. polit. sci. U. Miss., 1949-54; faculty Knox Coll., Galesburg, Ill., 1954—, prof. polit. sci., 1957-80, prof. emeritus, 1980—, Philip Sydney Post disting. prof., 1961-80; Sec.-treas. Midwest Collegiate Athletic Conf., 1961-67. Author: Latin America in the United Nations, 1956, Book; rev. editor: Midwest Jour. Polit. Sci, 1962-65. Mem. Galesburg Planning Commn., 1956-57. Served to lt. comdr. USNR, 1941-45. Social Sci. Research Council fellow, 1956. Mem. Am. Polit. Sci. Assn., Midwest Conf. Polit. Scientists, Omicron Delta Kappa, Pi Sigma Alpha, Scabbard and Blade, Sigma Alpha Epsilon. Home: 50 Deerfield Rd Hilton Head Island SC 29928

HOUSTON, JOHN COATES, JR., bus. cons.; b. Paterson, N.J., Jan. 17, 1909; s. John Coates and Elizabeth (Sullivan) H.; m. Elizabeth Ellis, Feb. 25, 1929. Student, Phillips Andover Acad., 1923-27, Yale, 1927-29. With Fed. Water Service Corp. (and subsidiary cos.), Rochester, N.Y., Chester, Pa., 1930-31, Buffalo, 1931-37; treas. R.P. Adams Co., Inc., Buffalo, 1937-42; dir. Program Controls Bur., WPB, Washington, 1942-45; com. of Civilian Prodn. Adminstrn., Washington, 1946-47; chmn. nat. prodn. urgency com. World War II; mem. com. on plans and policies of reconversion period; v.p. Stacom Industries, Inc., L.I., N.Y., 1948-50; staff asst. to pres. The White House, Washington, 1950-51; exec. vice chmn. Munitions Bd., 1952-53; adviser on mil. procurement Hoover Commn. on Fed. Govt. Orgn., 1954-55; indsl. cons., 1955-60; pres. Frederick Electronics Corp., Md., 1960-71; cons., 1972—. Home: 101 Valencia Cove Hawthorne-at-Leesburg Leesburg FL 32748

HOUSTON, PEYTON HOGE, environmental systems company executive, poet; b. Cin., Dec. 20, 1910; s. George Harrison and Mary Stuart (Hoge) H.; m. Priscilla Moore, Nov. 26, 1942 (div. Jan. 1959); stepchildren: Robert, Russell Stewart; m. Parrish Beaumont Cummings, May 22, 1959; stepchildren: Joseph P. Dobson, Michael Dobson, Laura Parrish Dobson. A.B., Princeton U., 1932. Free lance writer, 1934-41; with Houston & Jolles (mgmt. cons.), N.Y.C., 1941-49, exec. asst., 1941-43, v.p., 1946-49; with The Equity Corp. (and successor Wheelabrator-Frye now part of The Signal Cos., Inc.), N.Y.C. and Hampton, N.H., 1950—, asst. to pres., 1950-59, v.p., 1959-66; sr. v.p., dir. Gen. United Life Ins. Co. (subs. Equity Corp.), Des Moines, 1967-71; corp. sec. Wheelabrator-Frye, Inc., 1971-81, sec., dir. various subsidiaries. Author: Sonnet Variations, 1962, Occasions in a World, 1969, For the Remarkable Animals, 1970, The Changes, 1977, Arguments of Idea, 1980; editor: The Garden Prospect, Selected Poems by Peter Yates, 1980. Mem. Phi Beta Kappa. Club: Princeton (N.Y.C.). Home: Indian Chase Dr Greenwich CT 06830 Office: Liberty Ln Hampton NH 03842

HOUSTON, RALPH HUBERT, educator; b. Lewisville, Tex., June 17, 1910; s. Moses Walter and Pearl (Stover) H.; m. Francys McNew, Dec. 25, 1933; 1 dau., Susan (Mrs. William G. Reid). B.A., North Tex. State U., 1930; M.A., U. Tex., 1934, Ph.D., 1946. Tchr. Big Spring (Tex.) pub. schs., 1930-36; asst. prof. English Southwest Tex. State U., 1937-41, asso. prof., 1941-46, prof., 1946—, chmn. dept. English, 1958-65, dean, 1965-70. Served to maj., 1942-46; USAAF; Served to maj. USAF, 1950-52. Mem. Modern Language Assn., Am. Assn. U. Profs. Tex. Conf. Coll. Teachers of English (pres. 1967), Tex. Folklore Soc. (pres. 1971). Episcopalian. Home: 217 W Wood St San Marcos TX 78666

HOUSTOUN, LAWRENCE ORSON, JR., development consultant; b. Glen Ridge, N.J., Mar. 13, 1929; s. Lawrence Orson and Almeda Flemming H.; m. Bonise Feather, Apr. 17, 1976; children—Alexandra Taylor, Kate Cross. A.B., Lafayette Coll., 1952; postgrad., Princeton U., 1971; M.C.R.P., Catholic U. Am., 1980. Dir. N.J. Rehab. Commn., 1955-59; mem. N.J. Commn. on Aging, 1956-61; dir. exptl. manpower programs Dept. Labor, Washington, 1962-64; dir. program devel. U.S. Model Cities Adminstrn., 1967-72; asst. to sec. Commerce, Washington, 1977-80, sec. HUD, 1980-81; pres. Atlantic Corp.; mem. faculty George Washington U., 1973-79. Served to 1st lt. U.S. Army, 1952-54. Mem. Am. Inst. Cert. Planners, Am. Planning Assn. Democrat. Clubs: Princeton (Washington); Royal Commonwealth Soc.

HOUTCHENS, BARNARD, lawyer; b. Johnstown, Colo., Aug. 5, 1911; s. Everet Harrison and Evelyn Mary (Barnard) H.; m. Margaret Belle Colvin, Dec. 28, 1940; children: John Barnard, Marilyn (dec.). B.A., U. Nebr., 1933, LL.B., 1935; LL.D., U. No. Colo. at Greeley, 1963. Bar: Colo. 1935. Practiced in, Greeley, 1935—, city atty., 1941-47, 49-50; Pres. bd. dirs. United Bank, Greeley, chmn. bd., 1972-82; dir. Noffsinger Mfg. Co., Miner & Miner Cons. Engrs., Inc., Geriatrics, Inc., all Greeley; Mem. bar com. Colo. Bd. Law Examiners, 1947-81, chmn., 1968-81. Trustee State Colls., Colo., 1948-65, pres. bd., 1964-65; nat. sec.-treas. Assn. Gov. Bds. State Univs. and Allied Instns., 1960-62; bd. dirs. U. No. Colo. Found., 1975-79, pres., 1978-79. Fellow Am. Coll. Trial Lawyers; mem. ABA, Colo. Bar Assn., Weld County Bar Assn. (pres. 1946-47), Greeley Jr. C. of C., Greeley C. of C. (pres. 1951-52), Blue Key, Sigma Chi. Clubs: Rotary, Elks (past exalted ruler Greeley), Masons.). Home: 1020 48th Ave Greeley CO 80631 Office: 1007 9th Ave Greeley CO 80631

HOUTCHENS, ROBERT AUSTIN, JR., chemist; b. Denver, Mar. 31, 1953; s. Robert A. and Lorna G. (Smyth) H.; m. Cynthia Susan Barth, July 24, 1953. B.S. in Engring. Sci., Colo. State U., 1975; Ph.D., 1980. Grad. research asst. biochemistry dept. Colo. State U., Ft. Collins, 1976-80; sr. research chemist Dow Chem. Co., Midland, Mich., 1980—. Contbr. articles on biochemistry to profl. jours. Fellow Moettcher Found. Mem. Am. Chem. Soc., AAAS, Sigma Xi, Tau Beta Pi. Home: 2008 Laurel Ln Midland MI 48640

HOUTS, MARSHALL WILSON, author, editor, lawyer; b. Chattanooga, June 28, 1919; s. Thomas Jefferson and Mary (Alexander) H.; m. Mary O. Dealy, Apr. 27, 1946; children: Virginia, Kathy, Marsha, Patty, Tom, Cindy, Tim. A.A., Brevard Jr. Coll., 1937; B.S. in Law, U. Minn., 1941, J.D., 1941. Bar: Tenn. 1940, Minn. 1946,

U.S. Supreme Ct. 1967. Spl. agt. FBI, Washington, Brazil, Havana, Boston, 1941-44; partner Palmer & Houts, Pipestone, Minn., 1946-51; mcpl. judge, Pipestone, 1947-51; gen. counsel Erle Stanley Gardner's Ct. of Last Resort, Los Angeles, 1951-60; prof. law UCLA, 1954, Mich. State U., East Lansing, 1955-57; adj. prof. Pepperdine U. Law Sch., 1972—; clin. prof. forensic pathology Calif. Coll. Medicine, U. Calif., Irvine, 1972—; cons. police depts. Creator, editor: TRAUMA, 1959—; Author: Houts: Lawyer's Guide to Medical Proof, 3 vols., 1967, From Gun to Gavel, 1954, From Evidence to Proof, 1956, The Rules of Evidence, 1956, From Arrest to Release, 1958, Courtroom Medicine, 1958, Courtroom Medicine: Death, 3 vols., 1964, Photographic Misrepresentation, 1965, Where Death Delights, 1967, They Asked for Death, 1970, Proving Medical Diagnosis and Prognosis, 13 vols., 1970, Cyclopedia of Sudden, Violent and Unexpained Death, 1970, King's X: Common Law and the Death of Sir Harry Oakes, 1972, Art of Advocacy: Appeals; Art of Advocacy: Cross Examination of Medical Experts; Courtroom Toxicology, 6 vols., 1981. Served with OSS, 1944-46; CBI. Decorated Bronze Arrowhead. Address: 313 Emerald Bay Laguna Beach CA 92651 *Bureaucracy is no longer a problem-solving format for any ill. If a defect can't be cured at the local level, it can't be cured at all.*

HOVDE, CARL FREDERICK, educator; b. Meadville, Pa., Oct. 11, 1926; s. Bryn J. and Therese (Arneson) H.; m. Jane Hale Norris, Aug. 29, 1960; children—Katherine Hale, Sarah Therese, Peter Bryn. B.A., Columbia, 1950; M.A., Princeton, 1954; Ph.D., 1956. Instr. English Ohio State U., 1955-58; vis. lectr. U. Muenster, W. Germany, 1958-60; mem. faculty Columbia, N.Y.C., 1960- -, asso. prof. English, 1964-69, prof. English, 1969—, dean coll., 1968-72; vis. prof. U. Guanabara, Brazil, 1964. Served with AUS, 1944-46. Home: 460 Riverside Dr New York City NY 10027

HOVDE, DONALD INGVALD, government official; b. Madison, Wis., Mar. 6, 1931; s. Ingvald and Joseffa (Anderson) H.; m. Virginia E. Bothun, Feb. 20, 1954; children: Steven, Jane, James, Eric, Kirsten. B.B.A., U. Wis., 1953. Owner, pres. Hovde Realty, Inc., Madison, 1955—; pres. 122 Bldg. Corp., Madison, 1955—; under sec. U.S. Dept. HUD, Washington, 1981-83; mem. Fed. Home Loan Bank Bd., Washington, 1983—. Organizer Central Madison Council, 1971-81; dir. Meth. Hosp. Found., Madison, 1970-79, gen. chmn. fund raising dr., 1974-75; regional chmn. for Ind., Ill., Wis., Republican Party of Wis., 1980. Served to capt. U.S. Army, 1953-59. Named Realtor of Yr. Madison Bd. Realtors, 1967; Wis. Realtor of Yr., 1976. Mem. Nat. Assn. Realtors (pres. 1979), Madison C. of C. (pres. 1969), Madison Bd. Realtors (pres. 1962), Wis. Realtors Assn. (pres. 1975), Madison Found. for the Arts.

HOVDESVEN, ARNE, lawyer; b. Hagerstown, Md., May 17, 1928; s. E. Arne and Florence (Lesher) H.; m. Joan Tubbs, Dec. 2, 1956; children: Steven, Eric, Susan. B.A., North Tex. State Coll., Denton, 1947; J.D., U. Mich., Ann Arbor, 1956. Indsl. relations specialist Allis-Chalmers Mfg. Co., Milw., 1947-50; assoc. Shearman & Sterling, N.Y.C., 1956-65, ptrn., 1965—. 1st. lt. U.S. Army, 1950-53. Mem. ABA, N.Y. State Bar Assn. (vice chmn. bus. banking and corp. law sect. 1983—), Assn. Bar City N.Y. Lutheran. Clubs: Sleepy Hollow Country (Scarborough, N.Y.); Recess (N.Y.C.). Home: 680 Long Hill Rd W Braircliff Manor NY 10510 Office: Shearman & Sterling 53 Wall St New York NY 10005

HOVERSTEN, PHILIP EVERARD, publishing executive; b. Chgo., Oct. 3, 1947; s. Moris T. and Anne S. (Richardson) H.; m. Alison A. Hubby, May 31, 1975; children: Tiffany, Schuyler. B.A. in Econs., Colo. Coll., 1970; M.B.A., U. Pa., 1972. Asso. mergers and acquisitions Goldman Sachs & Co., N.Y.C., 1973-74; asso. mgmt. cons. Booz, Allen & Hamilton, Inc., N.Y.C., 1974-75; with Great A&P Tea Co., Inc., Montvale, N.J., 1975-81, sr. v.p. fin., treas., 1980-81; v.p., chief fin. officer MacMillan, Inc., N.Y.C., 1982—. Clubs: Racquet and Tennis (N.Y.C.); Nat. Golf Links of Am. (Southampton, N.Y.); Rockaway Hunting. Home: 520 E 86th St New York NY 10028 Office: 866 3d Ave New York NY 10022

HOVET, THOMAS, JR., educator, polit. scientist; b. Helena, Mont., Feb. 4, 1923; s. Thomas and Elizabeth (Strauss) H.; m. Erica Steinleitner, Sept. 6, 1957; children—Lisa, Heather. B.A., U. Wash., 1948; M.A., N.Y. U., 1949; Ph.D., Victoria Univ. Coll., U. New Zealand, 1954. Employment interviewer Wash. Dept. Employment Security, 1949; dist. crew leader Census Bur., 1950; research asso. Internat. Studies Group, Brookings Instn., 1951-53; instr. govt. N.Y. U., 1953-54; asst. prof. govt. Miami U., Oxford, Ohio, 1954-56; mem. faculty, N.Y. U., 1956-66, prof., 1962-66; prof. polit. sci. U. Oreg., Eugene, 1966—, head dept., 1968-7O; cons. State Dept., 1966. Author: Legislative History and Subject Analysis-Documents of the United Nations Conference on International Organization, Vol. XXI, in English, 1956, Vol. XXII, in French, 1956, (with Waldo Chamberlin and Richard H. Swift) Chronology of the United Nations, 1959, Bloc Politics in the United Nations, 1960, (with Waldo Chamberlin) A Chronology and Fact Book of the United Nations, 1941-1961, 1961, (with others) A Guide to the Use of United Nations Documents, 1962, Africa in the United Nations, 1963, (with Waldo Chamberlin and Erica Hovet) Chronology and Fact Book of the United Nations, (1941-64, 1964), (with others) Primacy of Politics in Africa, 1966, (with Waldo Chamberlin and Erica Hovet) Chronology and Fact Book of the United Nations, 1941-69, 1970, (with David J. Finlay) 7304: International Relations on the Planet Earth, 1975, (with Waldo Chamberlin and Erica Hovet) Chronology and Fact Book of the United Nations, 1941-76, 1976, (with Erica Hovet) Chronology and Fact Book of the United Nations, 1941-1979; Editor: (with Waldo Chamberlin and Richard N. Swift) Annual Review of the United Nations, 1959, 1960. Vice pres. UN Assn. Oreg., 1968-79; v.p. Taraknath Das Found., 1957-78, mem. adv. com., 1978—; rep. ACLU to UN, 1962-66; Chmn. Lane County (Oreg.) Democratic Party, 1968-69; chmn. 4th Congl. Dist. Dem. Party Oreg., 1968; Bd. dirs. Internat. League Rights of Man, 1964-66. Served with AUS, 1942-46. Fulbright scholar, 1950-51; recipient Ersted award distinguished teaching U. Oreg., 1968; Danforth Asso., 1964-66. Mem. Western Am., Internat. polit. sci. assns., Am., Indian socs. internat. law, Internat. Studies Assn., African Studies assn. Home: 95181 Hwy 101 Yachats OR 97498

HOVEY, JUSTUS ALLAN, JR., political scientist; b. Cambridge, Mass., May 13, 1922; s. Justus Allan and Lois Eugenia (Clark) H.; m. Peggy Streit, 1983; 1 dau., Anne Elisabeth Hovey Brandolini. A.B. magna cum laude, Swarthmore Coll., 1948; cert., Institut Universitaire de Hautes Etudes Internationales, 1948; M.A., Columbia U., 1950, Ph.D., 1965. Intern, Office Sec. Gen. UN, 1949; study dir. Council Fgn. Relations, N.Y.C., 1952; exec. dir. Am. Com. United Europe, N.Y.C., Paris, 1952-60; Washington rep. Olin Corp., 1960-68; Washington dir. Allen & Murden, Inc., 1965-68; v.p., sec. Radio Free Europe (Free Europe, Inc.), N.Y.C., 1968-76; internat. relations specialist GAO, Washington, 1976—; adj. assoc. prof. Manhattan Community Coll., CUNY, 1969-72, Queens Coll., 1973-75; Bd. dirs. Atlantic Council of U.S., Washington, Ontario Owners, Inc., English in Action, N.Y.C., 1973-76. Author: The Superparliaments, 1966, various GAO reports Atlantic Council, also policy papers.; editor: Toward a Consensus on Military Service, 1982; contbr. articles to profl. jours. Served to 1st lt., inf. AUS, 1943-46. Mem. N. Y. Council Fgn. Relations, Acad. Polit. Sci., Am. Acad. Polit. and Social Sci., Internat. Studies Assn., Phi Beta Kappa. Club: Nat. Press (Washington). Home: 2853 Ontario Rd NW Washington DC 20009 Office: GAO Washington DC 20548

HOVEY, RICHARD BENNETT, author, educator; b. Cin., July 28, 1917; s. George B. and Kathryn (Bennett) H.; m. Marcia L. Johnson, Aug. 20, 1955 (div.); 1 son, Daniel R. Student, Columbia U., 1935-36; A.B., U. Cin., 1942; M.A., Harvard U., 1943, Ph.D., 1950. Instr. U. Cin., 1943-46, U. Pa., 1949-55; asst. prof. Western Md. Coll., Westminster, 1955-57, asso. prof., 1957-60, U. Md., 1960-68, prof., 1968—. Author: John Jay Chapman; an American Mind, 1959, Hemingway; the Inward Terrain, 1968; Adv. editor: Hartford Studies in Literature; reviewer: Modern Age; Contbr. to books, also articles in field to popular and tech. mags. Ford Found. fellow, 1951-52. Mem. Nat. Council Tchrs. of English, Coll. English Assn. (pres. Middle Atlantic 1958-59), Phi Beta Kappa (pres. Md. chpt. 1971-72). Unitarian. Club: Harvard (Washington). Home: 10201 Grosvenor Pl Rockville MD 20852

HOVGARD, CARL, former publisher; b. Parsons, Kans., Oct. 1O, 1905; s. Christopher and Gyda (Holm) H.; m. Viga Matcass, Jan. 19, 1968. A.B., Coll. Emporia, 1928; LL.D., Parsons U., 1940. Founder Research Inst. Am., N.Y.C., 1935, pres., 1935-67; engaged in oil exploration and prodn., hdqrs., Abilene, Tex.; partner Nat. Law Press, N.Y.C., 1940-67, Hovgard-Johnson Oil Co., Abilene, Tex., 1953—; owner Worthree Mines (tungsten), Kingman, Ariz., 1953-60, Nevins Shipyard, City Island, N.Y., 1954-59; chmn. bd. Carefree Founders, Inc., 1971-74; pres. Hovgard Trust Co., 1972-78. Trustee Parsons Coll., 1948-64; pres. Hovgard Oil Trust, 1980—. Republican. Methodist. Clubs: Union League (past pres.), N.Y. Yacht, Wings (N.Y.C.); Am. Yacht (Rye, N.Y.) (commodore 1957-58); Cruising of Am.; Royal Swedish Yacht (Stockholm); Royal Ocean Racing (London, Eng.); Royal Norwegian Yacht (Oslo); Royal Danish Yacht. Comml. pilot with instrument rating; Class B winner Bermuda Yacht Race, 1954; skipper Yacht Circe 1955 Trans-Atlantic race, 1966 Trans-Atlantic race Bermuda to Denmark. Home: 2675 Ribera Rd Carmel CA 93923

HOVHANESS, ALAN, composer; b. Somerville, Mass., Mar. 8, 1911; s. Haroutioun and Madeleine (Scott) Hovhaness C. Student, New Eng. Conservatory Music, 1932-34; Mus.D. (hon.), U. Rochester, 1958, Bates Coll. Condr. concerts of original orchestral music, Symphony Hall, Boston, 1946, Carnegie Hall, N.Y.C., 1947; Composer: concertos Lousadzak, 1944, Elibris, 1944, Tzaikerk, 1945, no. 1, Arevakal, 1951, Khaldis, 1952, no. 6, 1953, Talin, 1953, no. 7, 1953, Hanna; ballet, 1953; cantatas Avak the Healer, 1946, 30th Ode of Solomon, 1947, Vartan Symphony, 1950, Easter Cantata, 1953, Shepherd of Israel, 1953, Glory to God, 1954; ballet Ardent Song, 1954; symphony Vision from High Rock, 1954, Symphony no. 15, Silver Pilgrimage, Symphony no. 16; for strings and Korean harp Symphony no. 19 Vishnu; commd., N.Y. Philharmonic, 1967, Symphony no. 22 City of Light, 1971; incidental music for play The Flowering Peach, 1955, Magnificat, 1958; opera Burning House; dance-opera Lady of Light, 1969, And God Created Great Whales, 1970; oratorio The Way of Jesus, 1974, Symphony 26, 1975, Revelations of Saint Paul, 1983; opera Pericles, 1975, Tale of the Sun Goddess Going into the Stone House, 1979; Symphonies 27, 28, 29, 30, 1976, String Quartet No. 5, 1976, Symphonies 31, 32, 33, 1977, Symphonies 34-39, 1978; opera Symphonies 40-52, 1979-83; music for, NBC-TV films, Assignment India, Southeast Asia. Guggenheim fellow (2); Fulbright research scholar to, India; Rockefeller grantee for mus. research in, Japan, 1962-63; Recipient awards Nat. Arts and Letters, Fromm Music Found. Address: care CF Peters Corp 373 Park Ave S New York NY 10016 *Music to bring power of healing from celestial mountains*

HOVIN, ARNE WILLIAM, agronomist, educator; b. Norway, Dec. 30, 1922; came to U.S., 1952, naturalized, 1957; s. Einar Lauritz and Aslaug H.; m. Carol Helen Frink, Oct. 24, 1953; children: Randi Ann, Leif Erik. B.S., Agrl. U. of Norway, 1949; Ph.D., UCLA, 1957. Research geneticist USDA Regional Pasture Research Lab., University Park, Pa., 1958-64; investigation leader Forage Br., Beltsville, Md., 1964-69; prof. agronomy and plant genetics U. Minn., St. Paul, 1969-81; asso. dir. Mont. Agrl. Expt. Sta., Bozeman, 1981—; chmn. Nat. Grass Variety Rev. Bd., 1968-69; sec. Grass Breeders Work Planning Conf., 1973-75, v.p., 1975-77, pres., 1977-79; sec., chmn. Regional Tech. Coms. on Forage Crop Breeding. Contbr.: chpts. to Turfgrass Science, 1969, Hybridization of Crop Plants, 1980; sci. articles to profl. jours. Served with Norwegian N.G., 1943-46. Mellon-King travel grantee, Australia, 1970; Fulbright-Hays sr. research scholar, Norway, 1978. Mem. Am. Forage and Grassland Council (Merit cert. 1975), Am. Soc. Agronomy, Crop Sci. Soc. Am., Sigma Xi, Alpha Zeta, Gamma Sigma Delta. Office: Agrl Expt Sta Mont State U Bozeman MT 59717

HOVING, JANE PICKENS, civic worker; b. Macon, Ga.; m. William C. Langley (dec.); 1 dau., Marcella Langley McCormack; m. Walter Hoving; Sept. 30, 1977. Grad., Curtis Inst. Music, Phila., Juilliard Sch. Music, N.Y.C. Now civic worker; a founder United Cerebral Palsy Assns.; one of chief organizers of ann. telethon; v.p. N.Y. Heart Assn.; pres., chmn. Greater N.Y. adv. bd. Salvation Army; former chmn. all domestic ops., mem. exec. com. ACTION, Washington.; Bd. dirs., sec. Cerebral Palsy Research and Ednl. Found.; bd. dirs. Metromedia Inc., Com. for Prevention of Child Abuse, Animal Med Center N.Y., U.S.O., Walter Hoving Home for Seriously Troubled Girls.; founder, pres. Tune In Inc. Former singer, actress; appeared on: daily Jane Pickens Show, NBC Radio, weekly Jane Pickens Show with NBC Symphony Orch, weekly Pickens Show for, ABC-TV; former mem.: weekly Pickens Sisters; starred in: musical Regina, 1949. Recipient Disting. Vol. Service award Mrs. Lyndon B. Johnson, 1968; award Fedn. Jewish Philanthropies N.Y.; achievement award Albert Einstein Coll. Medicine; Humanitarian award United Cerebral Palsy; Meritorious award Govt. of Mex.; USO Woman of Yr. award, 1980; Gold medal Nat. Inst. Social Scis.; numerous others. Home: 635 Park Ave New York NY 10021

HOVING, JOHN HANNES FORESTER, consulting firm executive; b. N.Y.C., July 18, 1923; s. Hannes and Mary Alma (Gilbert) H.; m. Anne Fisher Spiers, Feb. 1, 1958; children: Christopher, Karen Anne, Katherine Jean. B.A. in History, U. Chgo., 1947. Radio news editor, reporter Milw. Jour., also Capital Times, Madison, Wis., 1947-51; asst. to chmn. Democratic Nat. Com., 1952-54; exec. positions Kefauver, Johnson, Humphrey, Sanford presdl. campaigns; asst. to presdl. asst. for trade policy 1962; v.p. exec. action Air Transp. Assn. Am., Washington, 1956-64; propr. cons. firm, Washington, 1964-72; sr. v.p. Federated Dept. Stores, Inc., Cin., 1972-82; pres. The Hoving Group (cons. firm), Washington, 1982—. Former bd. dirs. Pub. Affairs Council; mem. vestry Christ Episcopal Ch., Cin.; bd. dirs. Am. Council Young Polit. Leaders., Partnerships Data Net, Fashion Inst. of Design Merchandising; dep. chmn. for planning Democratic Nat. Com. Served with AUS, 1943-46. Decorated Purple Heart. Mem. Am. Assn. Polit. Cons. Democrat. Clubs: Met., Nat. Press, Nat. Capital Dem. (Washington); Queen City (Cin.); Lotos, Sky (N.Y.C.). Home: 4831 Albemarle St NW Washington DC 20016 Office: 2550 M St NW Washington DC 20037

HOVING, THOMAS, magazine editor, museum and cultural affairs consultant, author; b. N.Y.C., Jan. 15, 1931; s. Walter and Mary (Osgood Field) H.; m. Nancy Melissa Bell, Oct. 3, 1953; 1 dau., Petrea Bell. B.A., Princeton U., 1953, M.F.A., 1958, Ph.D., 1959, H.H.D. (hon.), 1968, L.H.D., Hofstra U., 1966, LL.D., Pratt Inst., 1967, D.F.A., N.Y. U., 1968, Litt.D., Middlebury Coll., 1968. Staff Medieval Met. Mus. Art and The Cloisters, 1959-65, curator, 1965-66; commr. parks, N.Y.C., 1966-67; adminstr. Dept. Recreation and Cultural Affairs, 1967; dir. Met. Mus. Art, 1967-77; pres. Hoving Assocs., Inc.; museum and cultural affairs cons. firm Hoving Assos., Inc., N.Y.C., 1977—; arts and entertainment corr. ABC-TV show 20/20, 1978-84; editor Connoisseur mag., 1981—; dir. IBM World Trade Corp., Ams./Far East, Manhattan Industries, Inc. Author: Guide to the Cloisters, 1964, The Chase, The Capture, 1975, Two Worlds of Andrew Wyeth, Kuerners and Olsons; exhbn. catalogue, 1976, Two World of Andrew Wyeth: A Conversation with Andrew Wyeth, 1978, Tutankhamun, The Untold Story, 1978, King of the Confessors, 1981; contbr. articles on art, parks and recreation to profl. publs., mags. and newspapers. Former trustee Inst. Fine Arts N.Y. U. Served as lt. USMC, 1953-55. Decorated knight Legion of Honor, France; recipient Bronze medal Citizens Budget Com., 1966; Cue mag. award, 1966; Disting. Achievement award Advt. Club Am., 1966; Disting. Contbn. award Park Assn. N.Y.C., 1967; Elsie de Wolfe award Am. Inst. Interior Designers, 1967; Woodrow Wilson award Princeton U., 1977. Mem. AIA (hon.). Office: Hoving Assos Inc 150 E 73d St New York NY 10021

HOVING, WALTER, retail executive; b. Stockholm, Sweden, Dec. 2, 1897; s. Johannes and Helga (Adamsen) H.; m. Mary Osgood Field, Nov. 4, 1924; children: Petrea Field, Thomas Pearsall; m. Pauline V. Rogers, Apr. 30, 1937; m. Jane P. Langley, Sept. 30, 1977. Ph.B., Brown U., 1920, Ph.D., 1976; L.H.D., L.I. U., 1966; LL.D., Pratt Inst., 1966. With R.H. Macy & Co., N.Y. C., 1924-32, v.p., 1928-32, Montgomery Ward & Co., 1932-36, dir., 1934-36; pres. Lord & Taylor, N.Y.C., 1936-45, Hoving Corp., 1946-60, Bonwit Teller, Inc., 1950-60; chmn. bd. Tiffany & Co., N.Y.C., 1955—. Author: Your Career in Business, 1940, The Distribution Revolution, 1960. Chmn. organizing com. U.S.O., pres., 1940, chmn. bd., 1941-48; chmn. bd. U.S.O. Camp Shows, 1941-48; pres. Salvation Army Assn. N.Y., 1939-60; chmn. drive Salvation Army Citizens Appeal, 1939; nat. chmn. United Negro Coll. Fund, 1944; chmn. N.Y.C. Anti-Sales Tax Com., 1943, 63; asst. campaign mgr. nat. Republican presdl. campaign, 1944. Served with USNR, 1918-19. Recipient D.S.C., Salvation Army, 1942; decorated chevalier Legion of Honor (France); Order of Merit (Italy); M. Freedman gold medal N.Y. Archtl. League, 1967; award Am. Assembly Collegiate Bus. Schs., 1974; named Churchman of the Yr., Religious Heritage Am., 1974. Mem. Commerce and Industry Assn. N.Y. (pres. 1948-50), Fifth Ave. Assn. (pres. 1939-45, chmn. bd. 1946-52), Nat. Inst. Social Scis. (pres. 1953-56), Assn. Alumni Brown U. (pres. 1939-40), Delta Kappa Epsilon. Episcopalian (sr. warden). Clubs: Mason (32 deg.), Cammarian (Brown U.); Racquet and Tennis, River (N.Y.C.); Brook. Home: 635 Park Ave New York NY 10021 Office: 635 Park Ave New York NY 10021

HOVNANIAN, ARMEN, retail chain and direct mail executive; b. Akron, Ohio, Feb. 6, 1930; s. Aram and Marmar (Avedisian) H.; m. Suzanne C. Roberts, May 18, 1973; 1 son, Michael. B.S. in Pharmacy, Detroit Inst. Tech., 1951. With Cunningham Drug Stores, Inc., Detroit, 1948-78, store mgr., 1954-63, dist. mgr., 1963-67, dir. store ops., Mich., 1967-69, v.p. store ops., v.p. corp. store ops., 1969-70, dir., 1970-78, sr. v.p. corp. ops., 1971-77, sr. v.p. mktg., 1977-78; exec. v.p., ptnr. Living Distbrs., Inc., Walled Lake, Mich., 1978-82; exec. v.p., gen. mgr. Citrin Corp., Romulus, Mich., 1983—; dir. Jackson Nat. Life Ins. Co. Served with AUS, 1951-53. Mem. Kappa Psi. Mem. Armenian Apostolic Ch. (trustee). Home: 31001 Applewood Ln Farmington Hills MI 48018 Office: 28001 Citrin Dr Romulus MI 48174

HOVNANIAN, H. PHILIP, medical science research company executive; b. Aleppo, Syria, Dec. 17, 1920; s. Philip and Rosa (Jebejian) H.; m. Siran Norian, June 10, 1948; children: Rosemary Janice, Joan Anita, John Philip. B.S., Am. U., Beirut, 1942, postgrad., 1945-47; postgrad., Brown U., 1947-49; M.S., State Coll., Boston, 1951; Ph.D., U. Beverly Hills, Calif. Registered profl. engr., N.Y., Mass. Prin. investigator, research grant Nat. Heart Inst., NIH; faculty dept. physics Am. U., Beirut, 1942-47, Brown U., 1947-49; sr. engr. Western Electric Co., Haverhill, Mass., 1951-52; asst. chief engr. Calidyne Co., Winchester, Mass., 1952-53; sr. physicist, project head, asst. research dir. Boston Electronics div. Norden-Ketay Corp., 1953-56; partner, research and devel. dir. physics Neutronics Research Co., Waltham, Mass., 1956-58; sr. staff scientist Avco Corp., 1958, mgr. med. sci. dept., 1959-66; mgr. lunar biosci. NASA, Washington, 1966-67; mgr. biomed. engring. and biophysics Kollsman Instrument Corp., Syosset, N.Y., 1967-68; v.p., dir. biomed. products Cavitron Corp. and Cooper Med. Corp., 1969—; dir. Donti Instruments Inc., Milab, Inc.; guest lectr. biomed. engring. Northeastern U., MIT-Harvard Study Group on Biomed. Engring.; research asso. in surg. research Lahey Clin. Found.; mem. workshop interaction between industry and biomed. engring. Nat. Acad. Engring.; mem. ob-gyn. devices panel, former mem. panel on ear, nose and throat devices and dental devices FDA. Contbr. tech. papers to profl. jours. Fellow Inst. Physics (Brit.), Phys. Soc. (Brit.); mem. Optical Soc. Am., Am. Inst. Physics, IEEE (sr. mem., profl. group biomed. electronics), Internat. Fedn. Med. Electronics, Biomed. Engring. Soc., Research Soc. Am., Internat. Microscopy Assn., Am. Inst. Ultrasound in Medicine, Am. Soc. Laser Medicine and Surgery, Am. Soc. Microbiology, N.Y. Acad. Scis., AAAS, Assn. for Advancement Med. Instrumentation, Am. Dental Trade Assn. (com. on dental materials and devices), Am. Inst. Biol. Scis., Sigma Xi. Congregationalist (chmn. bd. trustees, moderator). Club: Masons. Patentee in field. Home: 3902 Manhattan College Pkwy Riverdale NY 10471 Office: Cooper Lasersonics PO Box 10133 Stamford CT 06904

HOVORKA, FRANK, educator; b. Cernikovice, Czechoslovakia, Aug. 5, 1897; came to U.S., 1913, naturalized, 1923; s. Frank and Anna (Pavlova) H.; m. Sophie Paul Nickel, June 12, 1926 (dec. 1979); m. Dorothy Humel, July 9, 1982. A.B., Iowa State Tchrs. Coll., 1922; M.S., U. Ill., 1923, Ph.D., 1925. Mem. faculty Case Western Res. U., Cleve., 1925—, prof. chemistry, 1942-54, dir. chem. labs., 1942-58, chmn. dept. chemistry, 1950-58, 62-64, Hurlbut prof. chemistry, 1954-68, prof. emeritus, cons. dept., 1968—, univ. fellow, 1973; research research asso. Argonne Nat. Lab., 1954-62; Western Res. U. rep. council sponsoring instns. Asso. Midwest Univs., 1947-58, dir., 1958-62. Contbr. articles phys. chemistry, electrochemistry, ultrasonics to profl. jours. Bd. dirs. Judson Park, Cleveland Heights, 1974. Recipient Disting. Tchrs. award Mfg. Chemists Assn., 1963; Alumni Achievement award State Coll. Iowa, 1964; Disting. Service award Cleve. Tech. Socs. Council, 1969. Fellow AAAS, Electrochem. Soc., Soc. Chem. Industry (Gt. Britain); mem. U.S. Capitol Hist. Soc.; Fellow Chem. Soc. London; mem. Am. Chem. Soc., Faraday Soc. (Eng.), AAUP, NEA, Cleve. Mus. Arts Assn., Cleve. Council World Affairs, Sigma Xi, Phi Lambda Upsilon, Pi Mu Epsilon, Epsilon Chi, Alpha Chi Sigma. Republican. Club: Cleve. Skating. Home: 2764 Landon Rd Shaker Heights OH 44122 Office: Dept Chemistry Case Western Res U Cleveland OH 44106

HOVSEPIAN, VATCHE, clergyman; b. Beirut, Lebanon, June 11, 1930; s. Krikor and Ovsanna (Tchakerian) H. Diploma, Armenian Theol. Sem., Lebanon, 1951; postgrad., Coll. Resurrection, York, Eng., 1953-54, U. Edinburgh, Scotland, 1954-56; B.Div., New Brunswick Theol. Sem., 1960. Ordained priest Armenian Apostolic Ch., 1951; instr. Armenian Theol. Sem., Lebanon; priest Holy Cross Ch., Union

City, N.J., 1956-67; bishop of, Can., 1967-71, elevated to archbishop, 1976; primate of Armenian Ch. of Western Diocese, Hollywood, Calif., 1971—. Mem. Nat. Council of Chs. (past mem. central bd.). Clubs: Riviera Country (Pacific Palisades, Calif.); Knights of Vartan. Address: 1201 N Vine St Hollywood CA 90038 *

HOWALT, FREDERICK HARVEY, JR., chem. mfg. co. exec.; b. Boston, Nov. 12, 1926; s. F. Harvey and Gertrude (French) H.; children—Janeila, Heather, Fredrika, Harvey. B.S., Boston U., 1947, LL.B., 1951. Pres. Textile Rubber & Chem. Co., Inc., Dalton, Ga., 1951—; dir. Fidelity Fed. Savs. & Loan Assn., Clark Equipment Co. Served with USAAF, World War II. Office: Textile Rubber & Chem Co Tiarco Dr SW Dalton GA 30720

HOWAR, BARBARA DEARING, TV corr., columnist; b. Nashville, Sept. 27, 1934; d. Charles Oscar and Mary Elizabeth (O'Connell) Dearing; (div.)children—Bader Elizabeth, Edward Dearing. Grad., Holton-Arms Jr. Coll. Columnist, Washington Post, New Yorker mag.; hostess: TV show Panorama; former CBS-TV news corr.; hostess: TV program Who's Who, 1976-77; author: Making Ends Meet. Mem. AFTRA, P.E.N. Democrat. Office: care Stein and Day Scarborough House Briarcliff Manor NY 10510 *

HOWARD, ARTHUR ELLSWORTH DICK, legal educator; b. Richmond, Va., July 5, 1933; s. Thomas Landon and Marie Antoinette (Dick) H. B.A., U. Richmond, 1954; LL.B., U. Va., 1961; B.A. with honors, Oxford U., 1960, M.A., 1965; LL.D., James Madison U., 1983. Bar: Va., D.C. 1961. Asso. Covington & Burling, Washington, 1961-62; law clk. to Supreme Ct. Justice Hugo L. Black, Washington, 1962-64; asso. prof. law U. Va., Charlottesville, 1964-67, prof., 1967-76, White Burkett Miller prof. law and public affairs, 1976—, asso. dean, 1967-69; Counsel sessions Gen. Assembly Va., 1969, 70; cons. Subcom. on Constl. Rights, U.S. Senate Judiciary Com., 1975—. Author: Commentaries on the Constitution of Virginia, 2 vols, 1974 (Phi Beta Kappa prize), The Road from Runnymede: Magna Carta and Constitutionalism in America, 1968, (with Baker and Derr) Church, State, and Politics, 1982; bd. editors: The American Oxonian, 1968—, The Wilson Quar, 1977—. Exec. dir. Va. Commn. on Constl. Revision, 1968-69; mem. Va. Ind. Bicentennial Commn., 1966—; vice chmn. Magna Carta Commn. Va., 1965-66, Va. sec. Rhodes Scholarship Trust, 1970—; counselor to gov. of Va., 1982—. Served with AUS, 1954-56. Recipient Disting. Prof. award U. Va., 1981; Fellow Woodrow Wilson Internat. Center for Scholars, Smithsonian Instn., Washington, 1974-75, 76-77; fellow Center for Advanced Studies, U. Va., 1970-71, 76-77, 82-83; Rhodes scholar Oxford U., 1958-60. Mem. Va. Bar Assn. (v.p. 1970-71), Va. Acad. Laureates (chmn. 1981—). Episcopalian. Clubs: Cosmos (Washington); Oxford and Cambridge (London, Eng.). Home: 627 Park St Charlottesville VA 22901

HOWARD, BION BRADBURY, business administration educator; b. Paris, France, Oct. 28, 1912; came to U.S., 1914; s. Bion B. and Lucile (Jones) H.; m. Lita Dickerson, Dec. 24, 1940; children—Bion Dickerson, Julia. Ph.B., U. Chgo., 1933; M.B.A., Northwestern U., 1940, Ph.D., 1950. Asst. buyer Montgomery Ward & Co., 1933-36; lectr. Northwestern U. Grad. Sch. Mgmt., Evanston, Ill., 1947-50, asst. prof., 1950-51, asso. prof., 1951-56, prof., 1956—, Nathan and Mary Sharp prof. finance, 1962—; vis. prof. Stanford Grad. Sch. Bus. Adminstrn., 1954-55, U. Va., 1971-72, U. Cape Town Grad. Sch. Bus., 1973, 75; Dir. Mathers Fund, United Wirecraft Co., Chgo.; Economist, price exec. consumer durable goods br. OPA, Washington, 1942-46; div. economist, asso. div. dir. consumer durable goods div. OPS, Washington, 1951. Author: (with Miller Upton) Introduction to Business Finance, 1953; Co-author: Managerial Problems in Finance, 1964, The Individual Marriage and the Family, 1967; Contbr. articles to profl. publs. Mem. Am. Finance Assn. (dir. 1959-60, pres. 1962), Fin. Mgmt. Assn., Investment Analysts Soc. Chgo., Inst. Chartered Fin. Analysts, Phi Beta Kappa, Beta Gamma Sigma, Delta Kappa Epsilon. Club: Univ. (Chgo.). Home: Rt 2 Box 82 Lexington VA 24450

HOWARD, CARL, lawyer; b. Chgo., July 23, 1920; m. Kathleen A. Costello, May 10, 1953; 1 son, Carl Michael. A.B., DePauw U., 1942; J.D., Hastings Coll. Law U. Calif., San Francisco, 1949. Bar: Calif. bar 1951. Supervising dep. corps. commr. Dept. Corps. State of Calif., 1951-69; supervisory asst., asst. house counsel Fed. Home Loan Bank of San Francisco, 1970-75; dir., legal counsel Home Fed. Savs. and Loan Assn., San Francisco, 1977—; asso. firm Kerner, Colangelo & Imlay, San Francisco, 1976—; lectr. evening div. U. San Francisco, 1967-70. Served to lt. USNR, 1942-46. Mem. State Bar Calif. (chmn. disciplinary com. San Francisco 1970-72, chmn. client security fund No. Dist. Com. 1972-76), San Francisco Bar Assn., Am. Bar Assn., Delta Chi. Home: 2450 Quintara St San Francisco CA 94166 Office: 114 Sansome St San Francisco CA 94104

HOWARD, CHARLES, chemist, educator; b. Evanston, Ill., Apr. 2, 1919; s. Marion Boyd and Mary (McLafferty) H.; m. Dorothy M. Thompson, July 16, 1945; children—John Charles, Robert William, Margaret Anne. B.S., U. Wis., 1940, Ph.D., 1943. Chemist Oscar Mayer & Co., Madison, Wis., 1941-46, acting chief chemist, 1946-50; dir. product control Arbogast & Bastian, Inc., Allentown, Pa., 1951-54; asst. plant supt. Valleydale Packers, Inc., Salem, Va., 1955-60; supt. Roegelein Provision Co., San Antonio, 1960-61; mem. faculty dept. chemistry San Antonio Coll., 1961-73, prof., to 1973, chmn. dept., 1967-73; prof. chemistry U. Tex., San Antonio, 1973—. Author works in field. Served with U.S. Navy, 1944-45. Office: U of Tex San Antonio TX 78285

HOWARD, DAGGETT HORTON, lawyer; b. N.Y.C., Mar. 20, 1917; s. Chester Augustus and Olive Ree (Daggett) H.; m. Patricia McClellan Exton, Sept. 1950; children: Daggett Horton, Jeffrey, David, Patricia. B.A. magna cum laude, Yale U., 1938, J.D., 1941. Bar: N.Y. 1942, D.C. 1961. Legal staff Root, Clark, Buckner & Ballantine, N.Y.C., 1941-43, Lend Lease Adminstrn., Fgn. Econ. Adminstrn., 1943-44; exec. asst. to spl. counsel to Pres. White House, 1945; legal adviser Fgn. Econ. Adminstrn., also Dept. State, 1945-47; internat. atty., asst. chief internat. and rules div. CAB, 1947-52; asso. gen. counsel Dept. Air Force, 1952-56, dep. gen. counsel, 1956-58; gen. counsel FAA, 1958-62; partner Cox, Langford & Brown, Washington, 1962-66, Howard, Poe & Bastian, 1966-83, Howard & Law, 1983—. Bd. editors: Yale Law Jour. Past mem. policy com. Daniel and Florence Guggenheim Aviation Safety Center; corp. mem. Children's Hosp. D.C. Recipient Exceptional Civilian Service award Dept. Air Force, 1958; Disting. Service award FAA, 1962. Mem. Yale Law Sch. Assn. Washington, Corbey Ct., Fed., Am. bar assns., Phi Beta Kappa, Alpha Sigma Phi. Clubs: Yale, Metropolitan, Nat. Capital Democratic (Washington); Chevy Chase. Home: 4554 Klingle St NW Washington DC 20016 Office: 1701 Pennsylvania Ave NW Washington DC 20006

HOWARD, DAVID, ballet school administrator; b. London, Eng., June 14, 1937; came to U.S., 1966; s. Walter and Dorothy (Fell) Edwards. Grad., Arts Ednl. Sch., London, 1955. Mem. faculty Sch. Ballet, Harkness House for Ballet Arts, N.Y.C., 1966—; prin. tchr. Harkness Ballet Co., N.Y.C., 1967—; dir. Sch. Ballet Harkness House for Ballet Arts, N.Y.C., 1969—; founder David Howard Sch. Ballet, N.Y.C., 1977; Am. adjudicator 1st Internat. Ballet Competition, Miss., 1979; co-dir., co-founder Northeastern Ballet Summer Sch., Bard Coll., 1979; asso. artistic dir. Catskill Ballet Theatre, 1980; adviser Sch. Performing Arts, Champaign, Ill.; adviser dance dept. Va. Intermont Coll. Prin. dancer, London Palladium, 1955-57; with, Royal Ballet Eng., 1957-63; soloist, 1958-63, Nat. Ballet Can., 1963-64; appeared in: musical Little Me, London, 1964-66; collaborator double album ballet music, 1981; Choreographer: Rachmaninoff Suite, 1971, Divertissement D'Adam, 1971, Rossini Variations, 1973, Designs in Shades of Baroque, 1974, Fantasy, 1980; teaching record albums include David Howard in Class; rec. video tapes. Recipient Dance Master of Am. ann. award, 1983. Mem. Nat. Assn. Regional Ballet (dir., pres.), Royal Acad. Dancing, London Actors Equity (Adeline Genee Silver medal for male dancers 1954), Brit. Actors Equity, Internat. Platform Assn. Home: 401 West End Ave New York NY 10024 Office: 36 W 62d St New York NY 10023 *I have followed with great enthusiasm the growth of dance in the United States and want to dedicate myself to the development of ballet training in American and bring it to a higher level. I have devoted my time and effort to The National Association for Regional Ballet which reflects and contributes to the ever increasing size of ballet audiences across America. With this happening, no longer will the dancers who are developed each year have to seek employment within the long established European system of state supported ballet houses.*

HOWARD, DAVID E., photographer; b. N.Y.C., Jan. 25, 1948; s. John C. and Florence (Martino) H. Student, Ohio U., 1969-71; B.F.A., San Francisco Art Inst., M.F.A., 1974. Comml. photographer, Athens, Ohio, 1969-71; tchr. photography San Francisco Center for Visual Studies, 1971-74, visual artist in photography, 1975—, dir., 1975—. Author: Photography for Visual Communicators; Objective Reality, 1972, Realities, 1976, Perspectives, 1978; one-man shows include, Images Gallery, N.Y.C., U. Calif. Extension, John Bolles Gallery, San Francisco, San Francisco Art Inst., Ohio U., Athens, Thomas J. Crowe Gallery, Los Angeles, Madison (Wis.) Art Center, Fourth Street Gallery, N.Y.C., Intersection Gallery, San Francisco, Third Eye Gallery, N.Y.C., Center for Visual Studies, San Francisco, numerous group shows, latest being, Art Commn. Gallery, San Francisco, DeYoung Mus., San Francisco, Oakland (Calif.) Mus., Palace of Fine Arts, San Francisco, Camera Work, Los Angeles, Erie (Pa.) Art Ctr., various art festivals, San Francisco, San Francisco Art Inst.; represented in permanent collections, Mus. Modern Art, N.Y.C., Oakland (Calif.) Mus., San Francisco Mus. Modern Art, City of San Francisco, De Saisset Art Gallery, Santa Clara, Calif. Recipient San Francisco Art Festival award. Home: 49 Rivoli St San Francisco CA 94117 Office: 405 Clayton St San Francisco CA 94117

HOWARD, DONALD ROY, educator, author; b. St. Louis, Sept. 18, 1927; s. Albert and Emily (Johnson) H. A.B. summa cum laude, Tufts U., 1950; M.A., Rutgers U., 1951; Ph.D., U. Fla., 1954. Mem. faculty Ohio State U., 1955-63, U. Calif., Riverside, 1963-66, UCLA, 1966-67; prof. English Johns Hopkins U., Balt., 1967-77, Caroline Donovan prof. English, 1974-77; prof. English Stanford U., 1977—. Author: The Three Temptations: Medieval Man in Search of the World, 1966, (with C.K. Zacher) Critical Studies of Sir Gawain and the Green Knight, 1968, (with James Dean) Chaucer, Canterbury Tales, A Selection, 1969, Chaucer, Troilus and Criseyde and Selected Short Poems, 1976, The Idea of the Canterbury Tales, 1976, (with M. W. Bloomfield, B.-G. Guyot, T. Kabealo) Incipits of Latin Works on the Virtues and Vices, 1979, Writers and Pilgrims: Medieval Pilgrimage Narratives and Their Posterity, 1980; also articles.; Mem. editorial bd.: Speculum, 1969-77, ELH (English Literary History); adv. bd.: PMLA, 1973-78, Assays. Served with USNR, 1945-46. Recipient Melville Cain award, 1977; Fulbright research fellow, Italy, 1959-60; Am. Council Learned Socs. fellow, 1963-64; Guggenheim fellow, 1969-70; NEH fellow, 1978-79. Mem. New Chaucer Soc. (trustee), MLA (del. assembly 1970-74), Medieval Acad. (councillor 1969-73), Internat. Assn. Univ. Profs. English, Phi Beta Kappa. Address: English Dept Stanford U Stanford CA 94305

HOWARD, GENE CLAUDE, state senator, lawyer; b. Perry, Okla., Sept. 26, 1926; s. Joe W. and Nell L. (Brown) H.; m. Belva J. Prestidge, Dec. 28, 1979; children: Jean Ann Howard Peterson, Joe Ted, Belinda Janice. LL.B., U. Okla., 1951. Bar: Okla. 1950, U.S. Supreme Ct., U.S. Ct. Mil. Appeals. Partner firm Gene C. Howard and Assos., Tulsa; mem. Okla. Ho. of Reps., 1958-62, Okla. Senate, 1964—, pres. pro tem, 1974-81; trustee Phila. Mortgage Trust; mem. exec. com. Council State Govts., 1976-82. Pres. Okla. Jr. Democrats, 1954; del. Dem. Nat. Conv., 1964; mem. So. Growth Policy Bd., 1972-76. Served to lt. col. USAAF, 1944-46; Served to lt. col. USAF, 1961-62. Mem. Okla. Bar Assn., Tulsa County Bar Assn. (Outstanding Young Atty. 1953), Phi Delta Phi. Mem. Christian Ch. (Disciples of Christ). Office: 2642 E 21st St Tulsa OK 74114

HOWARD, GEORGE SALLADÉ, music consultant, educator; b. Reamstown, Pa., Feb. 24, 1903; s. Hayden H. and Florence (Salladé) H.; m. Sadako Takenouchi, Apr. 5, 1957. Mus.B. with honors, Ithaca Coll., 1925; A.B., Ohio Wesleyan U., 1929; Mus.B., Chgo. Conservatory Music, 1934, Mus.M., 1935, Mus.D., 1939; M.A., N.Y. U., 1936; Mus. D. (hon.), Ithaca Coll. Dean Ernest Williams Sch. Music, Bklyn., 1935-36; dir. music, condr. bands Pa. State Tchrs. Coll., 1936-39; dir. bands, orch. and chorus sch., dir. music in extension Pa. State Coll., 1939-42; commd. capt. U.S. Army, 1942; advanced through grades to col. USAF, 1951; organizer, condr. music programs, Greenland, Iceland, Newfoundland, 1942-43; comdg. officer, condr. Ofcl. Army Air Forces Band, Washington, 1944; chief music and radio br. AAF Hdqrs., 1946; established, organized AAF Band Sch., 1946; chief bands and music USAF, condr., 1947, USAF Band on tour, U.S., Can., Eng., Scotland, Wales, Ireland, Germany, Austria, Norway, Denmark, Libya, Iceland, Azores, Japan, Korea, P.I., Cambodia, others; condr. command performances Buckingham Palace, Royal Palace of Cambodia, The White House; ret. USAF, 1963; distinguished prof. music Troy (Ala.) State U., 1974—; vis. prof., dir. wind ensemble U. Houston, 1977; music cons. (rank of insp.) Met. Police Dept., Washington, 1973—; condr. Met. Police Band, Washington, 1963-73, Air Force Village Voices, San Antonio, 1977—; guest condr. Goldman Band, 1961-75, hon. life mem., 1973; hon. comdr. Tokyo (Japan) Youth Symphony Orch., Tex. Longhorn Band U. Tex., 1975. Clarinetist, Patrick Conway Band, 1922-27; soloist, 1927-29; condr., Ohio Wesleyan U. Band, 1925-29; dir. music, condr., Moosehart Band, 1929-35; Author: Ten Minute Self-Instructor for Pocket Instruments, 1943, The Big Serenade, 1961; Composer: Niece of Uncle Sam, 1944, American Doughboy, 1945, My Missouri, 1945, General Spaatz March, 1947, The Red Feather; theme song, Community Chest, Official March of the Washington Evening Star, Official March of the Central Canada Exhibition, Official March Pacific Nat. Exhbn, Vancouver, B.C., Alfalfa Club March, Cougar's Victory, Bachelors of the Sky, others. Chmn. John Philip Sousa Meml., Kennedy Center for the Performing Arts, Washington. Decorated Legion of Merit with cluster, U.S.; Guarde Republique medal; comdr. Order of Nonsaraphon, Cambodia, Star of the Order, gold medal Sudler Found.; recipient Gold record for furthering Japanese-Am. relations thru music Nippon-Columbia Co., 1962; named to Hall of Fame for Disting. Band Condrs. Mem. ASCAP, Nat. Assn. Composers and Condrs. (citation for contbn. Am. music), Am. Bandmasters Assn. (hon. life), Tex. Bandmasters Assn. (pres. 1956-57), Nat. Band Assn. (pres. 1970-74), Phi Mu Alpha, Pi Kappa Lambda, Phi Kappa Tau, Kappa Kappa Psi, Phi Beta Mu. Club: Alfalfa (Washington). Address: Air Force Village 4917 Ravenswood Dr San Antonio TX 78227 *I attribute my present success in life to establishing an overall goal at an early age; a goal which was limited only by the scope of dreams and pursued by means of pragmatic methods.*

HOWARD, GEORGE, JR., U.S. dist. judge; b. Pine Bluff, Ark., May 13, 1924. Student, Lincoln U., 1951; B.S., U. Ark., J.D., 1954; LL.D., 1976. Bar: Ark. bar 1953, U.S. Supreme Ct. bar 1959. Pvt. practice law, Pine Bluff, 1953-57; spl. asso. justice Ark. Supreme Ct., 1976, asso. justice, 1977; U.S. dist. judge, Eastern dist., Little Rock, 1980—; Mem. Ark. Claims Commn., 1969-77; chmn. Ark. adv. com. Civil Rights Commn. Mem. Am. Bar Assn., Ark. Bar Assn., Jefferson County Bar Assn. (pres.). Baptist. Office: PO Box 349 Little Rock AR 72203 *

HOWARD, GERALD KENNETH, lawyer; b. East Orange, N.J., Nov. 3, 1934; s. Harold Kenneth and Gertrude Cecilia (Thornton) H.; children: Gerald Kenneth, Megan Lynn, Jon Devin. B.B.A., St. Bonaventure U., 1956; LL.B., St. John's U., Bklyn., 1960; LL.M., NYU, 1972. Bar: N.Y. 1960, N.J. 1972. Corp. tax mgr. Merck & Co., Rahway, N.J., 1968-73; dir. taxes Gould Inc., Chgo., 1973-75; v.p., tax counsel Sperry Corp., N.Y.C., 1975—. Served as lt. U.S. Army, 1957-64. Mem. Tax Execs. Inst., Machinery and Allied Products Inst. (tax council), Tax Soc. NYU, ABA, N.J. Bar Assn. Home: 97 Remington Rd Manhasset NY 11030 Office: Sperry Corp 1290 Ave of Americas New York NY 10104

HOWARD, HARRY CLAY, lawyer; b. Rockwood, Tenn., May 1, 1929; s. Harry Clay and Julia Roe (Cannon) H.; m. Mary Helen Harrison, June 12, 1951; children—Helen Howard Porter, Anne H. B.A. magna cum laude, Vanderbilt U., 1951; LL.B., Emory U., 1955. Bar: Ga. bar 1955. Since practiced in, Atlanta; sr. partner firm King & Spalding, 1960—; dir. Holder Constrn. Co.; mem. council Emory U. Law Sch., 1975—, chmn., 1976-77. Trustee Wesley Homes, Inc., Atlanta, 1967—, chmn., 1981—; past trustee Oglethorpe U., Lovett Sch.; bd. dirs. Central Atlanta Progress, Inc., 1981—. Served with USMC, 1951-53; Korea. Mem. Am. Bar Assn., State Bar Ga., Am. Law Inst., Atlanta Bar Assn., Lawyers Club Atlanta, Phi Beta Kappa, Omicron Delta Kappa. Methodist. Clubs: Piedmont Driving, Commerce. Office: 2500 Trust Co Tower Atlanta GA 30303

HOWARD, HARRY NICHOLAS, history educator; b. Excelsior Springs, Mo., Feb. 19, 1902; s. Alpheus M. and Lois A. (Foster) H.; m. Virginia Faye Brubaker, Aug. 13, 1932; children: Robert Wendell, Norman Foster. A.B., William Jewell Coll., 1924; A.M. (Gregory fellow), U. Mo., 1927; Ph.D., U. Calif., Berkeley, 1930. Research asst. Eastern European history U. Calif., 1928-29; asst. prof. history U. Okla., 1929-30, Miami U., 1930-37, asso. prof., 1937-40, prof., 1940-42; vis. prof. several univs., summers 1930-41; with Dept. of State, 1942-62, head East European unit Div. Territorial Studies, 1942-45, expert on internat. orgn., 1945-46, chief Near East Research br. Office Near Eastern and African Affairs, 1946-47, adviser div. Greek, Turkish and Iranian Affairs, 1947-49, adviser U.S. dels., cons. investigation concerning Greek frontier incidents, 1949-56; spl. UN com. on Balkans; UN adviser Bur. Near East, South Asian, African Affairs, 1949-56; acting U.S. rep. adv. commn. for Palestine refugees UN Relief and Works Agy., 1956-62, spl. asst. to commr. gen., 1962-63; prof. Middle East studies Am. U. Sch. Internat. Service, Washington, 1963-68, adj. prof. Middle East studies, 1968—; Vis. prof. internat. relations Columbia, 1955; program chmn. Nr. East and N. Africa area studies Fgn. Service Inst., Dept. State, summer 1966, 71-73, faculty adviser, 1967-68; lectr. Middle East U.S. Army War Coll., Carlisle, Pa., 1971-72; hon. fellow Harry S. Truman Library Inst.; Bd. govs. Middle East Inst., 1963-79, emeritus, 1979—; bd. dirs. Am. Near East Refugee Aid, 1968-79. Author: numerous books in field internat. politics, dealing primarily with Balkan and Middle East area including The King-Crane Commission An American Inquiry in the Middle East, 1963; Turkey, the Straits and U.S. Policy, 1974, The Partition of Turkey, 1913-23; Contbr. to: Ency. Brit., Ency. Americana; Asso. editor: Middle East Jour, 1963-68; book rev. editor, 1968-80; advisor, 1980—; Contbr. numerous articles to profl. jours. Recipient Citation of Achievement William Jewell Coll., 1947; Distinguished Alumni award Pi Kappa Delta; decorated comdr. Royal Order Phoenix, Greece). Mem. nat., state, local profl. assns. Home: 6508 Greentree Rd Bradley Hills Grove Bethesda MD 20817

HOWARD, HILDEGARDE (MRS. HENRY ANSON WYLDE), paleontologist; b. Washington, Apr. 3, 1901; d. Clifford and Hattie Sterling (Case) H.; m. Henry Anson Wylde, Feb. 6, 1930. A.B., U. Calif., 1924, A.M., 1926, Ph.D., 1928. Asst. in zoology UCLA, 1924-25, teaching fellow paleontology, 1925-26, research fellow zoology, 1927-28; research asst. Natural History Mus. of Los Angeles County, 1924-25, 28, avian paleontologist, 1929-38, curator avian paleontology, 1939-51, chief curator sci. div., 1951-61, research assoc., 1961-74, chief curator emeritus, 1974—; research asso. avian paleontology Santa Barbara Mus. Natural History, 1956—, Western Speleological Inst., 1958-74. Author monographs in field, 1927—; including: Avian Census of Individual Pits at Rancho La Brea, 1962, Fossil Birds from the Anza-Borrego Desert, 1963, Fossil Anseriformes, 1964, 2d edit., 1973, Pliocene Birds from Chihuahua, Mexico, 1966, Tertiary Birds from Laguna Hills, Orange County, California, 1968, Avian Fossils from three Pleistocene Sites in Central Mexico, 1969, A Review of the Extinct Genus, Mancalla, 1970, Pliocene Avian Remains from Baja California, 1971, Postcranial Elements of the Extinct Condor Breagyps clarki, 1974, A New Species of Flightless Auk from the Miocene of California, 1976, Late Miocene Marine Birds from Orange County, California, 1978, Fossil Birds from Tertiary Marine Beds at Oceanside, San Diego County, California, 1980; Editor: Los Angeles County Mus. Contbns. in Sci., 1957-61; Contbr.: articles to sci. jours. and to Ency. Paleontology. Recipient hon. Festschrift Natural History Mus. of Los Angeles County, 1980; John Simon Guggenheim Found. fellow, 1962-63. Fellow Geol. Soc. Am., Am. Ornithol. Union (Brewster Meml. award in ornithology 1953), AAAS, So. Calif. acad. sci. (pres. 1957-59), Calif. acad. sci.; mem. Cooper Ornithol. Soc. (hon. life), Soc. Vertebrate Paleontology (hon. life), Phi Beta Kappa, Sigma Xi, Phi Sigma. Club: Soroptimists. Home: 2045-Q Via Mariposa E Laguna Hills CA 92653 Office: Natural History Museum of Los Angeles County 900 Exposition Blvd Los Angeles CA 90007

HOWARD, HOWARD K., airline executive; b. Paterson, N.J., 1927. With Riddle Airlines, 1956-59, Robert Hewitt Accos. Inc., 1959-62; corp. v.p., pres. internat. airlines Overseas Holdings Inc., 1963-67; pres. Saturn Airways, 1967-76; exec. v.p., chief operating officer, div. Transamerica Airlines Inc., Oakland, Calif., 1976-83, pres., dir., 1983—. Office: Transamerica Airlines Inc 7901 Oakport St Box 2504 Oakland CA 94614 *

HOWARD, J. WOODFORD, JR., educator; b. Ashland, Ky., July 5, 1931; s. J. Woodford and Florence Alberta (Stephens) H.; m. Valerie Hope Barclay, Apr. 10, 1960; 1 dau., Elaine Hope. B.A. summa cum laude, Duke U., 1952; M.P.A., Princeton U., 1954, M.A., 1955, Ph.D., 1959. Instr. Lafayette Coll., Easton, Pa., 1958-59, asst. prof., 1959-62, Duke U., 1962-66, assoc. prof., 1966-67, Johns Hopkins U., 1967-69, prof. polit. sci., 1969-75, Thomas P. Stran prof., 1975—, chmn. dept., 1973-75. Author: Mr. Justice Murphy: A Political Biography, 1968, Courts of Appeals in the Federal Judicial System, 1981 (cert. merit ABA 1982); Mem. editorial bd.: Law and Soc. Rev, 1975-76, 78-82, Am. Polit. Sci. Rev., 1977-81, Jour. Politics, 1979—; contbr. articles to profl. jours. Served to lt. USAF, 1955-57. Merle Smith-Van Sanfoord fellow, 1953-54; Procter fellow Princeton U., 1957-58; Carnegie fellow law and polit. sci. Harvard Law Sch., 1961-62; Ford Found. faculty research fellow, 1968-69; recipient Outstanding Tchr. awards Lafayette Coll., 1960, Duke U., 1965-66, Johns Hopkins U., 1969, 70. Mem. Am., So., Internat. polit. sci. assns., Am. Judicature Soc., Am. Soc. Legal History, Law and Society Assn., Supreme Ct. Hist. Soc., Phi Beta Kappa, Omicron Delta Kappa. Club: Princeton (N.Y.C.). Office: Dept Polit Sci Johns Hopkins U Baltimore MD 21218

HOWARD, JACK, union exec.; b. Santa Ana, Calif., Aug. 26, 1924; s. Floyd Willie and Inez (Cooley) H.; m. Margaret Anne McKinnon, Aug. 25, 1950; children—Marc, Anne. A.B., U. Calif. at Berkeley, 1948; M.A., U. Calif. at Los Angeles, 1952. Reporter Springfield (Ohio) Daily News, 1949-51; labor editor San Francisco Chronicle, 1952-60; chief investigator govt. information subcom. U.S. Ho. of Reps., 1960-63; spl. asst. to undersec. of Labor, 1963-64; adminstr. Neighborhood Youth Corps, 1964-66, Bur. of Work Programs, 1966-67; exec. asst. to sec. Labor, 1968; v.p. Ednl. Scis. Programs, Inc., N.Y.C., 1969-71; sec.-treas., cons. William Benton Found., N.Y.C., 1971-80; asst. to pub. Ency. Brit., N.Y.C., 1971-73; asst. dir. Twentieth Century Fund, N.Y.C., 1974-76; asst. to pres. Am. Fedn. State, County and Municipal Employees AFL-CIO, 1976—; internat. v.p. Am. Newspaper Guild-AFL-CIO, 1957-60. Served with AUS, 1943-46. Congl. fellow Am. Polit. Sci. Assn., 1957-58; Recipient Distinguished Service award Dept. Labor, 1965. Mem. ACLU, Sigma Delta Chi. Clubs: Fed. City, Nat. Press (Washington). Home: 219 5th NE Washington DC 20002 Office: 1625 L St NW Washington DC 20036

HOWARD, JACK ROHE, newspaperman; b. N.Y.C., Aug. 31, 1910; s. Roy Wilson and Margaret (Rohe) H.; m. Barbara Balfe, Apr. 5, 1934 (dec. 1962); children: Pamela, Michael; m. Eleanor Sallee Harris, 1964. A.B., Yale U., 1932. Reporter Japan Advertiser, Tokyo, Shanghai (China) Evening Post and Mercury, 1932-33; reporter Indpls. Times, 1933-34; asst. telegraph editor, telegraph editor and news editor Washington Daily News, 1935; with program dept. Sta. WNOX, Knoxville, Tenn.; also Washington and N.Y.C. offices Continental Radio Co. (now Scripps-Howard Broadcasting Co.), 1936-39; asst. exec. editor Scripps-Howard Newspapers, 1939-42, 1945-48, gen. editorial mgr., 1948-75, pres., dir., mem. exec. com., 1953-75, chmn. exec. com., 1976—; pres., dir., chmn. exec. com. Scripps-Howard Broadcasting Co., 1937-42, 45-74, chmn. bd., mem. exec. com., 1974—; chmn. East Side adv. bd. Chem. Bank N.Y.; Mem. adv. bd. U.S. Post Office, 1955-61. Trustee Village of Centre Island, Oyster Bay, N.Y., 1977—, Soc. for Rehab. of Facially Disfigured, Inc., 1979—; bd. dirs. Wildlife Preservation Trust Internat., MacArthur Meml. Found., Boys' Clubs Am. Commd. lt. (j.g.) USNR, 1942; active duty, 1943; Washington; sea duty, 1944-45; PTO; now lt. comdr. USNR; ret. Fellow Inst. Jud. Adminstrn.; mem. Am. Soc. Newspaper Editors, Am. Newspaper Pubs. Assn. (dir. 1964-72), Inter Am. Press Assn. (pres. 1965-66, mem. adv. council), Phillips Exeter Alumni Assn. (pres. 1958-60), Beta Theta Pi, Sigma Delta Chi. Clubs: Dutch Treat, River, Pilgrims (N.Y.C.); Bohemian (San Francisco); Seawanhaka Corinthian Yacht (Oyster Bay, N.Y.). Address: 200 Park Ave New York NY 10166

HOWARD, JAMES J., congressman; b. Irvington, N.J., July 24, 1927; s. George P. and Bernice M. H.; m. Marlene Vetrano; children: Kathleen Howard Tjunin, Lenore Howard Buchanan, Marie. B.A., St. Bonaventure U., 1952; M.Ed., Rutgers U., 1958; LL.D. (hon.), Monmouth Coll., 1977; LL.D.(hon.), St. Bonaventure U., 1979; LL.D. (hon.), Georgian Court Coll., 1983. Tchr., acting prin. Wall Twp. (N.J.) Sch. System, 1954-64; mem. 89th-98th congresses 3d Dist. N.J.; chmn. com. public works and transp.; mem. Franklin Delano Roosevelt Meml. Commn., Nat. Transp. Policy Study Commn. Served with USN, World War II. Mem. NEA, N.J. Edn. Assn. (del. assembly), Monmouth County Edn. Assn. (past pres.). Democrat. Address: 2245 Rayburn House Office Bldg Washington DC 20515

HOWARD, JAMES JOHN, utility company executive; b. Granville, Iowa, June 22, 1942; s. Leonard C. and Marie A. H.; m. Cheryl A. Andersen, June 26, 1976. B.S., U. S.D., 1964. With Iowa Public Service Co., Sioux City, 1964—, asst. treas., 1973-77, asst. sec., 1974-81, treas., 1977—, asst. controller, 1979-81. Bd. dirs. Jr. Achievement, 1973—. Served with USAR, 1966-72. Republican. Roman Catholic. Home: Rural Route 1 Box 190A Hinton IA 51024 Office: Box 778 Sioux City IA 51102

HOWARD, JAMES MERRIAM, JR., educational association executive, writer; b. Morristown, N.J., Feb. 9, 1922; s. James Merriam and Gertrude Laura (Hunter) H.; m. Sarah Seymour, Sept. 25, 1942 (dec. 1945); 1 son, James Merriam III; m. Selena Tatlock, Nov. 19, 1949; children: Alida Babcock Howard Woods, Mary Carrington Howard Conklin, Eleanor Tatlock. Grad., Morristown Sch., 1938; student, All Saints Sch., Bloxham, Eng., 1938-39; B.A. in History, Yale U., 1943, M.A., Harvard U., 1952; Litt.D., Lafayette Coll., 1965. Reader in history Yale U., 1942; faculty Lawrenceville (N.J.) Sch., 1945-64; master Cleve. House, 1952-54; headmaster Blair Acad., Blairstown, N.J., 1954-76; editor Basic Edn., Washington, 1976-83; sr. staff assoc. Council for Basic Edn., 1983—. Author: (with Clifton Fadiman) Empty Pages: A Search for Writing Competence in School and Society; author: (with Thomas C. Mendenall) Making History Come Alive, Writing to Learn; contbr. articles to profl. jours. Served to 1st lt. USMCR, 1942-45; maj. Res. (ret.). Mem. Headmasters Assn., Phi Beta Kappa. Home: 229 Cornell Rd Westport MA 02790

HOWARD, JAMES WEBB, investment banker, lawyer; b. Evansville, Ind., Sept. 17, 1925; s. Joseph R. and Velma (Cobb) H.; m. Phyllis Jean Brandt, Dec. 27, 1948; children: Sheila Rae, Sharon Kae. B.S. in Mech. Engring, Purdue U., 1949; postgrad., Akron (Ohio) Law Sch., 1950-51, Cleve. Marshall Law Sch., 1951-52; M.B.A., Western Res. U., 1962; J.D., Western State Coll. Law, 1976. Registered profl. engr., Ind., Ohio. Jr. project engr. Firestone Tire & Rubber Co., Akron, 1949-50; gen. foreman Cadillac Motor Car div. Gen. Motors Corp., 1950-53; mgmt. cons. M.K. Sheppard & Co., Cleve., 1953-56; plant mgr. Lewis Welding & Engring. Corp., Ohio, 1956-58; underwriter The Ohio Co., Columbus, 1959; chmn. Growth Capital, Inc., Chgo., 1960—; pres. Meister Brau, Inc., Chgo., 1965-73, Growth SBIC, Inc., Home Mart, San Diego; sec., dir. Creative Mgmt. Group, Inc.; pres., dir. Indsl. Med. Corp.; dir. Bus. Mart, others. Co-chmn. Chgo. com. Ill. Sesquicentennial Com., 1968. Served with AUS, 1943-46. Decorated Bronze Star, Parachutist badge, Combat Inf. badge. Mem. ASME, Nat. Assn. Small Bus. Investment Companies (past pres.), Am. Mgmt. Assn., ABA, State Bar Calif., Nat. Assn. Realtors, Calif. Assn. Realtors, San Diego Bd. Realtors, Grad. Bus. Alumni Assn. Western Res. U. (past gov.), Tau Kappa Epsilon, Pi Tau Sigma, Beta Gamma Sigma. Methodist. Club: Masons. Home: PO Box A-80427 San Diego CA 92138 Office: 701 B St Suite 1300 San Diego CA 92101

HOWARD, JANE TEMPLE, author; b. Springfield, Ill., May 4, 1935; d. Robert Pickrell and Eleanor Grace (Nee) H. A.B., U. Mich., 1956; D.Litt. hon., Grinnell Coll., 1979, D.H.L., Hamline U., 1984. Editorial trainee Time, Inc., 1956-58; reporter Life mag., 1959-61, asst. editor, 1962-68, staff writer, 1969-72, contract writer, 1972-73; vis. lectr. U. Iowa Writers Workshop, 1974, U. Ga. Sch. Journalism, 1975, Yale U., 1976, SUNY-Albany, 1978; mem. nat. adv. bd. Library of Congress Ctr. for the Book, 1979. Author: Please Touch: A Guided Tour of the Human Potential Movement, 1970, A Different Woman, 1973, Margaret Mead: A Life, 1984, Families, 1978; contbr. artilces to popular mags. Recipient Non-Fiction Chgo. Found. for Lit., 1974; fellow Mac Dowell Colony, 1973, 76, 80. Address: 54 Riverside Dr New York NY 10024

HOWARD, JOHN ADDISON, former college president, institute executive; b. Evanston, Ill., Aug. 10, 1921; s. Hubert Elmer and Edith (Sackett) H.; m. Janette Marie Nobis, Aug. 11, 1951; children: Marie Starr, Steven Lamson, Martha Nobis, Katherine Louise. Student, Princeton U., 1939-42; B.S., Northwestern U., 1947, M.A., 1949, Ph.D., 1962; LL.D., Grove City Coll., 1972, Brigham Young U., 1976, Rockford Coll., 1980. Instr. French Palos Verdas Coll., Rolling Hills, Calif., 1947-49, dean students, 1949-51, v.p., 1950-51, pres., 1951-55; exec. vice chmn. Pres.'s Com. on Govt. Contracts, 1956-57; pres. Rockford (Ill.) Coll., 1960-77; dir. Rockford Coll. Inst., 1977-80; pres. The Rockford Inst., 1980—. Contbg. author: Dilemmas Facing the Nation, 1979. Mem. U.S. Commn. on Marijuana and Drug Abuse, 1971-73, Pres.'s Task Force on Priorities in Higher Edn., 1969-70; Bd. dirs. Farmington Trust, Brit.; pres. Ingersoll Found., 1983—. Served to 1st lt. AUS, 1942-45. Decorated Silver Star with oak leaf cluster, Purple Heart with oak leaf cluster.; Recipient Horatio Alger award, 1967; Educator of Yr. Religious Heritage Am., 1980. Mem. Am. Assn. Presidents Ind. Colls. and Univs. (pres. 1969-72), Phila. Soc. (pres. 1979-81), Mt. Pelerin Soc., Phi Beta Kappa (hon.). Clubs: Rotarian., Rockford Country; Princeton (N.Y.C.); University (Chgo.); Bohemian (San Francisco). Home: 2431 Rock Terr Rockford IL 61103

HOWARD, JOHN ARNOLD, marketing educator; b. Georgetown, Ill., June 21, 1915; s. Fred and Edith Mildred (Saylor) H.; m. Lynn Horstman, June 17, 1950; children: Jeffrey Sumner, Peter Hamilton. Student, Blackburn Coll., 1937-39; B.S., U. Ill., 1939, M.S., 1941; Ph.D., Harvard U., 1952. Asst. prof. U. Ill., 1948-50; asso. prof. U. Chgo., 1950-58; prof. U. Pitts., 1958-63; prof. mktg. Columbia U., N.Y.C., 1963—, George E. Warren prof., 1975. Author: Marketing Management, 1957, Marketing: Executive and Buyer Behavior, 1963, Marketing Theory, 1965, The Theory of Consumer Behavior, 1969, Consumer Behavior: Application of Theory, 1977. Served in U.S. Army, 1942-46. Decorated Bronze Star medal; recipient P.D. Converse award Columbia U., 1976; Ford Found. commn., 1960-62. Fellow Assn. Consumer Research; mem. Am. Mktg. Assn. Home: Sawmill Terr Greenwich CT 06830 Office: Columbia U New York NY 10027

HOWARD, JOHN BRIGHAM, lawyer, foundation executive; b. Edgewood, Pa., June 9, 1912; s. Lemuel Frederic and Anna (Kimm) H.; m. Dorothy Koch, June 5, 1937 (dec. Oct. 1966); children: Elizabeth K., Frederic K., Theodore B., Catherine M.; m. Margaret Betz, Sept. 12, 1970. B.S. summa cum laude, Harvard U., 1933, Ph.D., 1936; postgrad., Calif. Inst. Tech., 1933-34; J.D. cum laude, U. Chgo., 1942. Bar: Ill., D.C., Supreme Ct. bars. Jr. Harvard Soc. Fellows, 1936-39; asst. legal adviser Dept. State, 1946-47; adviser U.S. delegation to U.N. Atomic Energy Commn., 1946; counselor Am. Mission Aid to Greece, 1947, dep. chief, 1948; cons. Congl. relations ECA, 1948-49; special asst. to sec. of state, 1949-50; regional planning adviser Nr. East, S. Asia, Africa affairs Dept. State, 1950-51; dep. dir., dir. div. overseas activities Ford Found., 1952-54, dir. internat. tng. and research, 1955-67; pres., trustee Internat. Legal Center, 1967-77; trustee Internat. Center for Law in Devel., 1978—. Contbr. articles to profl. jours. Mem. Council on Fgn. Relations, Am. Soc. Internat. Law, Phi Beta Kappa, Phi Delta Phi. Club: University. Home: 86 Edgemont Rd Scarsdale NY 10583 Office: 777 UN Plaza New York NY 10017

HOWARD, JOHN LINDSAY, lawyer, forest industry company executive; b. Drumheller, Alta., Can., Nov. 18, 1931; s. Lindsay Lee and Nancy (Martin) H.; m. Jeanette Huguenin, Nov. 21, 1969. B.Comm., U. B.C., 1959, LL.B., 1961; LL.M., Harvard U., 1968; postgrad., McGill U., Montreal, Can., 1967. Bar: B.C. 1962, Que. 1967, Fed. Queen's Counsel 1977. Mem. Brahans, Dickerson & Howard, Vancouver, B.C., 1962-67, Tansey, de Grandpre, Montreal, 1968-71; asst. dep. minister Fed. Dept. Consumer and Corp. Affairs, Ottawa, Ont., 1971-79; sr. v.p. law and corp. affairs MacMillan Bloedel Ltd., Vancouver, 1979—; head Can. del. U.S.-Can. bilateral bankruptcy treaty, Ottawa, 1978. Co-author: Proposals for a New Corporation Law for Canada, 1971, Proposals for a Securities Market Law for Canada, 1979. Mem. Can. Bar Assn., Assn. Can. Gen. Counsel, Can. CLub, Can. Inst. Chartered Accts. (chmn. acctg. research adv. bd. 1983). Home: 1955 W Ave Apt 214 Vancouver BC Canada V6M 1B6 Office: MacMillan Bloadel Ltd 1075 W Georgia St Vancouver BC Canada V6E 3R9

HOWARD, JOHN STUART, advertising agency executive; b. N.Y.C., July 6, 1934; s. John Whittelsey Power and Mary (Stuart) H.; m. Karen Peterson, Feb. 13, 1960; children: John W., Katherine P. B.A., Yale U., 1955. Account exec. Benton & Bowles, N.Y.C., 1955-56, 57-60; with Ted Bates & Co. Inc., N.Y.C., 1960—, sr. v.p., 1968-79, exec. v.p., 1979-82, dir., 1972-81; sr. v.p. Foote, Cone & Belding, N.Y.C., 1982—. Clubs: Union, Maidstone, Devon Yacht. Home: 101 E 69th St New York NY 10021 Office: 101 Park Ave New York NY 10178

HOWARD, JOHN TASKER, city planner; b. Paris, June 7, 1911; s. Rossiter and Alice (Woodbury) H.; m. Eleanor M. Robb, Dec. 26, 1940; children: John T., Jr., Margaret Alice. Student, Antioch Coll., 1928-31; B.F.A., Yale U., 1934; B.Arch., M.I.T., 1935, M.C.P., 1936; traveling fellow in regional planning, 1936-37. Research asst. N.E. Regional Planning Commn., Boston, 1935-36; city planner Regional Assn. of Cleve., 1937-42; lectr. in city planning Western Res. U., 1939-49; planning dir. Cleve. City Planning Commn., 1942-49; city planning cons., Boston, Cleve., Hartford, Los Angeles, San Francisco Bay Area, Washington and other U.S. cities and towns, 1949—; partner Adams, Howard & Greeley, 1949-63, Adams, Howard & Oppermann, 1964-69; asso. prof. city planning Mass. Inst. Tech., 1949-57, prof., 1957-73, prof. emeritus, 1973—, head dept. city and regional planning, 1957-70. Mem. exec. com. Hwy. Research Bd., 1962-68; bd. consultants Eno Found. for Transp., 1962-72, 74-77, Gloucester Capital Improvement Adv. Bd., 1972-80; bd. dirs. Downtown Devel. Commn., 1974—, chmn., 1980—; corporator Addison Gilbert Hosp., 1978—, trustee, 1980—. Hon. asso. Cleve. chpt. AIA; recipient Yale medal distinction in Arts, 1959. Mem. Assn. Collegiate Schs. of Planning (pres. 1960), Am. Soc. Planning Ofcls. (dir. 1947-50, medal award 1975), Am. Inst. Planners (pres. 1954-56, distinguished service award 1963), Ohio Planning Conf. (pres. 1948, 60th Anniversary Spl. award 1979). Home and office: 741 Washington St Annisquam MA 01930

HOWARD, JOSEPH CLEMENS, judge; b. Des Moines, Dec. 9, 1922; m. Gwendolyn Mae London, Dec. 1954; 1 son. B.A., U. Iowa, 1950; LL.B., Drake U., 1955, M.A., 1957, J.D., 1968; postgrad., Washington and Lee U., Northwestern U. Law Sch., U. Nev., Morgan State Coll., 1972. Bar: Md. Probation officer Supreme Bench Balt. City, 1958-60; mem. firm Howard and Hargrove, 1960-64; asst. state's atty., 1964-66, chief of trial sect., 1966-67, asst. city solicitor, 1967-68; spl. cons. dept. edn.; asso. judge Supreme Bench of Balt. City, 1968-79; vis. prof. Grad. Sch. Nat. Coll. State Trial Judges, U. Nev., Reno, 1971; vis. lectr. Johns Hopkins U., Balt., 1971, 73; vis. prof. Nat. Coll. Dist. Attys., U. Houston, 1973; vis. lectr. Morgan State U., 1973-77; chief judge criminal ct. Supreme Bench of Balt. City, 1975-76; cons. communications dept. Nat. League Cities, 1978, Nat. Center for State Cts., 1978; chmn. exec. com. Md. Jud. Conf., 1977-78; judge U.S. Dist. Ct., Dist. Md., 1979—. Contbr. articles to legal jours. Mem. Mayor's Task Force on Community Relations, Balt.; chmn. Mayor's Task Force Juvenile Delinquency, Balt.; bd. govs. Antioch Coll. Sch. Law, 1976-79; mem. Nat. Com. Black Elected Ofcls., 1972; mem. bd. govs. Citizens Planning and Housing Assn.; bd. dirs. Legal Aid Bur., Nat. Bar Found.; trustee Antioch Coll., 1974-75. Served with U.S. Army, 1944-47; PTO. Recipient Afro-Am. award, 1968; Police Community Relations award, 1971; Walter P. Carter award, 1971; Kappa Alpha Psi Achievement award, 1973; Benjamin Banneker Public Affairs award, 1975; Bicentennial Jud. award Black Am. Law Students Assn., 1976; Delta Sigma Theta Jud. award, 1977; Henry McNeill Turner Soc. award Bethel A.M.E. Ch., 1978; Man of Year award Nat. Assn. Negro Bus. and Profl. Women's Clubs, 1979; Women Behind the Community award, 1979; Spl. Jud. Service award Herbert M. Frisby Hist. Soc., 1980. Mem. ABA, Nat. Bar Assn., World Assn. Judges, Monumental City Bar Assn., Phi Alpha Delta. Office: Suite 540 US Courthouse 101 W Lombard St Baltimore MD 21201 *

HOWARD, JOSEPH HARVEY, librarian; b. Olustee, Okla., Jan. 15, 1931; s. William Lester and Letitia Browder (Dickey) H.; m. Patricia Shaughnessy Schiebel, Apr. 10, 1980. B.Music Edn., U. Okla., 1952, M.L.S., 1957. Assoc. dir. pub. services U. Colo. Library, Boulder, 1960-63; vol. Peace Corps, Kuala Lumpur, Malaysia, 1963-65; head catalog dept. Washington U., St. Louis, 1956-67; asst. chief descriptive cataloging div. Library of Congress, Washington, 1967-68, chief, 1968-72, chief serial record div., 1972-75, asst. dir. (cataloging) processing dept., 1975-76, asst. librarian for processing services, 1976-83; dir. Nat. Agrl. Library, 1983—. Author: Malay Manuscripts—A Bibliographical Guide, 1966. Served with AUS, 1952-54. Mem. ALA. Home: 336 M St SW Washington DC 20024 Office: Nat Agrl Library Beltsville MO 20705

HOWARD, KENNETH JOSEPH, JR., actor; b. El Centro, Calif., Mar. 28, 1944; s. Kenneth Joseph and Martha Carey (McDonald) H.; m. Margo. A.B., Amherst Coll., 1966; postgrad., Yale Sch. Drama, 1966-68. Broadway debut in: Promises, Promises, 1968-69; appeared in: 1776, 1969 (Theatre World award); co-starred in: Otto Preminger film Tell Me That You Love Me, Junie Moon, 1970; appeared in: film 1776, 1972, Child's Play, 1970 (Tony award); starring role: Equus, Chgo., 1976-77; starred in: TV series Adam's Rib, 1973, The Manhunter, 1974-75, The White Shadow, 1978-81, It's Not Easy, 1983—. Office: care Creative Artists Agy Inc 1888 Century Park E Suite 1400 Los Angeles CA 90067

HOWARD, KINGSTON LEE, management services company executive; b. Hartford, Conn., Aug. 25, 1929; s. Raymond Herbert and Lucille (Dunn) H.; m. Jean Murphy, Feb. 11, 1956; children: Kingston Lee, Deborah Lynn. B.A., Trinity Coll., Hartford, 1953; M.B.A., Harvard U., 1955. Vice pres., gen. mgr. Brigham's, Inc., Cambridge, Mass., 1955-67; asst. to pres., coordinator internat. devel. Howard Johnson Co., N.Y.C., 1967-69; founder, pres. Internat. Mgmt. Services Co., Lexington, Mass., 1969-73, 74-77, 78—; pres., dir. Days Inn Am., Inc., Atlanta, 1973-77. Chmn. Lexington Bicentennial Com., 1970-73; mem. Lexington Republican Town Com., 1962-68. Served with AUS, 1950-52. Mem. Am. Hotel and Motel Assn. (cert. hotel adminstr.), Nat. Restaurant Assn. Republican. Episcopalian. Clubs: Harvard (N.Y.C.); Peachtree (Atlanta); Masons (Lexington). Home and office: 226 Commonwealth Ave Boston MA 02116

HOWARD, LAWRENCE CABOT, international affairs educator; b. Des Moines, Apr. 26, 1925; s. Charles P. and L. Maude (Lewis) H.; m. Elizabeth Fitzgerald, Feb. 14, 1953; children: Jane, Susan, Laura. B.A., Drake U., 1949; M.A., Wayne U., 1950; Ph.D., Harvard, 1956. Instr., then asst. prof. Hofstra U., 1956-58; asst. prof. Brandeis U., Waltham, Mass., 1958-63; asso. dir. Peace Corps, Philippines, 1961-63, Center on Innovation, N.Y. State Dept. Edn., 1964; dir. Inst. Human Relations, U. Wis., Milw., 1964-67; v.p. Danforth Found., 1967-69; prof. pub. and internat. affairs, dean Grad. Sch. Pub. and Internat. Affairs, U. Pitts., 1969-73, prof. pub. and internat. affairs, 1973—; Fulbright prof. U. Maiduguri, Nigeria, 1981-82; Cons. U.S. Office Edn., State Dept. Bur. External Researchs; mem. research and adv. bd. Com. Econ. Devel., 1973—; mem. Commn. on Operation of House, Commonwealth of Pa.; mem. nat. adv. commn. Tchrs. Corps., 1967-69; mem. Pitts. World Affairs Council, 1969—, Pitts. History and Landmarks Found.; mem. exec. council Nat. Assn. Schs. Pub. Affairs Adminstrn., 1971-73, Am. Soc. Pub. Adminstrn., 1972—. Co-author: Public Administration: Balancing Power and Accountability; contbr. articles to profl. jours. Trustee Church Soc. for Coll. Work, Drake U., St. Augustine Coll., Episc. Ch. Home Bd., Harvard Grad. Soc. for Advancement of Study and Research; vestryman Calvary Episcopal Ch., Pitts.; mem. standing com. on ecumenical relations. Episcopal Diocese Pitts. Served with AUS, 1943-45. Named Man of Year Alpha Phi Alpha, 1949. Mem. Am. Soc. Public Adminstrn. (pres. Conf. Minority Public Adminstrs.), Phi Beta Kappa. Home: 919 College Ave Pittsburgh PA 15232

HOWARD, LEE MILTON, physician; b. India, Nov. 9, 1922; s. John A. and Grace Mary (Lemen) H.; m. Maxwell C. Croft, June 22, 1946; children: Regan Ellis, Christine Baker, Kirk Anderson, Gene Reid. B.Sc., Baylor U., 1945; M.D., Johns Hopkins U., 1947, M.P.H., 1958, Dr.P.H., 1959. Diplomate: Am. Bd. Preventive Medicine. Med. and surg. resident Church Home Hosp., Balt., 1947-50; mem. med. staff Clough Meml. Hosp., Ongole, Andhra, India, 1950-53; dir. Victoria Meml. Hosp., Warangal, Andhra, India, 1953-56; physician Med. Care Clinic, Johns Hopkins Hosp., 1957; U.S. adviser on malaria, Philippines, 1960-62; U.S. regional malaria adviser Far East AID, 1962-64; chief malaria br. health div. AID, Washington, 1964-66; dep. dir. health service Office Tech. Coop. and Research, 1966-67, dir., 1967, Office Health, Devel. Support Bur., 1967-80; mem. expert co. on malaria WHO, 1966-79, chmn. com., 1970, adviser parasitic diseases, 1970; mem. U.S. del. World Health Assembly, 1969—, WHO cons. on resource moblzn., 1979-81; AID devel. fellow, 1979-80; vis. asso. prof. parasitology Inst. Hygiene, U. Philippines, 1960—; vis. lectr. Johns Hopkins U. Sch. Public Health, Harvard Sch. Public Health; vis. fellow Inst. Devel. Studies, U. Sussex, 1979; mem. U.S. del., PAHO directing council; chief office resource mblzn. PAHO, 1981—; sec., mem. exec. com. Gorgas Meml. Inst., 1972; mem. U.S. Sr. Exec. Service. Research fellow, U.S. Armed Forces Epidemiological Bd., 1958-59; recipient Superior Honor award AID, 1974. Fellow Am. Pub. Health Assn., Royal Soc. Tropical Medicine and Hygiene; mem. Am. Soc. Tropical Medicine and Hygiene, Philippine Pub. Health Assn., Nat. Council Internat. Health (charter mem.). Home: 621 Goldsborough Dr Rockville MD 20850 Office: Pan Am. Health Orgn. Washington DC 20037

HOWARD, MELVIN, duplication equipment manufacturing company executive; b. Boston, Jan. 5, 1935; s. John M. and Molly (Sagar) H.; m. Beverly Ruth Kahan, June 9, 1957; children: Brian David, Marjorie Lyn. B.A., U. Mass., 1957; M.B.A., Columbia U., 1959. Fin. exec. Ford Motor Co., Dearborn, Mich., 1959-67; v.p. adminstrn. Shoe Corps. of Am., Columbus, Ohio, 1967-70; asst. controller Bus. Products group Xerox Corp., Rochester, N.Y., 1970-72; v.p. fin. Bus. Devel. group Xerox Corp., 1972-74, sr. v.p., sr. staff officer, 1974-75, corp. v.p., controller, 1975-77, corp. v.p. fin., 1977-78, sr. corp. v.p. fin., 1978-81, sr. v.p., chief fin. officer, 1981-84, exec. v.p., pres. fin. services, 1984—; chmn. Xerox Credit Corp.; dir. Xerox Corp., LMH Fund Ltd., Crum and Forster, Inc., Van Kampen Merritt, Inc., Gould Pumps, Inc. Served to 1st lt. AUS, 1957. Mem. Fin. Execs.

Inst., Planning Execs. Inst., Am. Mgmt. Assn., Conf. Bd. Council Fin. Execs., Beta Gamma Sigma. Club: Birchwood Country. Home: 42 Red Coat Rd Westport CT 06880 Office: Xerox Corp High Ridge Park Stamford CT 06904

HOWARD, M(OSES) WILLIAM, JR., clergyman; b. Americus, Ga., Mar. 3, 1946; s. M. William and Laura (Turner) H.; m. Barbara Jean Wright, July 11, 1970; children: Matthew Weldon, Adam Turner. B.A., Morehouse Coll., 1968; M.Div., Princeton U., 1972; D.D., Miles Coll., 1979, Central Coll., 1980. Ordained to ministry Am. Baptist Ch., 1974; exec. dir. Black Council, Ref. Ch. in Am., N.Y.C., 1972—; bd. dirs. Nat. Conf. Black Churchmen, 1975-80; moderator Commn. of World Council Chs. Program to Combat Racism, 1976-78; bd. dirs. Nat. Media Found.; pres. Nat. Council Chs., 1979-81; condr. Christmas services for hostages Am. embassy, Tehran, 1979; chmn. UN Seminar on Bank Loans to South Africa, Zurich, 1981. Researcher: Born to Rebel - Autobiography of Benjamin Elijah Mays, 1967; editor: monthly newsletter Black Caucus RCA, 1973—; pub., producer ann. lectureship, 1975—. Active YMCA; trustee Trenton State Coll., 1981-82, Nat. Urban League; bd. dirs. Children's Def. Fund, The Independent Sector; founding mem. People for Am. Way. Recipient Disting. Service award as chmn. Commn. on Justice, Liberation and Human Fulfillment; Decorated comdr. Order Knights of Holy Sepulchre. Mem. NAACP, Sigma Pi Phi. Office: 18th FL 475 Riverside Dr New York NY 10027 *Perhaps the greatest challenge to humanity today is to see that our moral and ethical development catches up, and keeps pace, with our advances in technology.*

HOWARD, PAUL NOBLE, JR., construction company executive; b. Raleigh, N.C., Dec. 23, 1922; s. Paul Noble and Lucy Pauline (Sugg) H.; m. Julia Frances Ross, Apr. 26, 1952; children: Katherine H., Paul Noble, III, David Ross. B.C.E., N.C. State U., 1944; grad. exec. program, U. N.C., 1965. Founder, pres. Howard Constrn. Co., Greensboro, N.C., 1950-72; founder, co-v.p. Guilford Equipment Co., Greensboro, 1953-78; founder, pres. Paul N. Howard Co. (merged with Howard Constn. Co. 1972), Greensboro, 1963-78, chmn. bd., 1979—; pres., treas., founder Howard Corp., Greensboro, 1968-78, dir., 1979—; mem. Greensboro bd. dirs. N.C. Nat. Bank.; mem. N.C. Dist. Export Council U.S. Dept. Commerce; trustee Moses H. Cone Meml. Hosp. Mem. Greensboro-High Point Airport Authority, 1968-76, sec., 1970-76; vice chmn. bd. mgmt. Central YMCA, Greensboro, 1974; mem. Greensboro Sports Council. Served with U.S. Army, 1944-46. Named Outstanding Engrng. Alumnus N.C. State U., Raleigh, 1979; recipient Significant Sig award Sigma Chi, 1981; Greensboro Bus. Leaders Hall of Fame award Jr. Achievement, 1981. Mem. Associated Gen. Contractors Am. (pres. Carolinas br. 1970, nat. pres. 1979), Cons. Constructors Council Am., Am. Inst. Constructors, ASCE, N.C. Soc. Engrs., Greensboro C. of C. (dir.), N.C. State U. Alumni Assn. (pres. 1977-78), Phi Kappa Phi. Presbyterian. Clubs: Rotary, Greensboro Country (Greensboro); City (dir.). Home: 908 Country Club Dr Greensboro NC 27408 Office: PO Box 9846 Greensboro NC 27429

HOWARD, RICHARD (JOSEPH HOWARD), author; b. Cleve., Oct. 13, 1929. B.A., Columbia U., 1951; postgrad., Sorbonne, Paris, 1952-53. Pres. PEN-Am. Center, 1977-79. Author: poetry Quantities, 1962, The Damages, 1967, Untitled Subjects, 1969, Findings, 1971, Two-Part Inventions, 1974, Fellow Feelings, 1976, Misgivings, 1979; criticism Alone With America, 1969, Preferences, 1974; lit. reviewer various mags.; poetry editor: New Am. Review; translator works from French. Recipient Pulitzer prize, 1970; Guggenheim fellow, 1966-67; fellow Morse Coll., Yale U.; Nat. Inst. Arts grantee, 1970. Address: 23 Waverly Pl New York NY 10003 *

HOWARD, RICHARD TURNER, construction company executive; b. Rock Hill, S.C., Jan. 3, 1935; s. Paul Noble and Pauline (Sugg) H.; children: Richard Turner, James Fowles, George Anderson. B.S., U. S.C., 1957. Vice-pres. Howard Constrn. Co., 1957-72; exec. v.p. Paul N. Howard Co., Greensboro, N.C., 1972-77, pres., chief exec. officer, 1977—; mng. dir. Howard Internat., Howard of Saudi Arabia; dir. Geneva Corp. Bd. dirs. Greensboro C. of C., 1972-78, Greensboro Devel. Corp., Green Hill Art Gallery.; trustee U.N.C, Greensboro, NCCJ; bd. visitors Guilford Coll. Served with U.S. Army, 1957. Republican. Episcopalian. Clubs: Greensboro Country, Palm Bay. Home: Rt 1 Box 296 High Point NC 27260 Office: 201 N Elm St Greensboro NC 27420

HOWARD, ROBERT BRUCE, medical educator, editor; b. St. Paul, Dec. 25, 1920; s. Willard Samuel and Edna (Bole) H.; m. Lorraine Leavitt, Mar. 21, 1942; children: Gregory, David, Carol, Irene, Bradley. B.A., U. Minn., 1942, M.B., 1944, M.D., 1945, Ph.D. in Medicine, 1952. Faculty U. Minn., Mpls., 1948—, instr. medicine, asst. prof., asso. prof., dir. continuation med. edn., asso. dean med. scis., 1948-58, dean med. scis., 1958-70, prof. medicine, 1958-82, clin. prof., 1982—; prof. medicine, dir. med. edn. U. Teaching and Research Unit, Abbott-Northwestern Hosp., 1971-82. Cons. editor: Postgraduate Medicine, 1972-82; editor-in-chief, 1982—. Trustee, past sec.-treas. Minn. Med. Found. Fellow ACP; mem. Assn. Am. Med. Colls. (chmn. 1970, Disting. Service Mem. 1974), Am., Minn. med. assns., Am. Med. Writers Assn., Minn. Acad. Medicine, Minn., Mpls. socs. internal medicine, Phi Beta Kappa, Alpha Omega Alpha. Home: 3535 Bryant Ave S 514 Minneapolis MN 55408 Office: 4530 W 77th St Suite 350 Minneapolis MN 55435

HOWARD, ROBERT M., food products manufacturing company executive; b. 1923; married. B.S. in Engrng., U. Minn., 1947. With Internat. Multifoods Corp., Mpls., 1947—, dir. engrng. and milling, 1957-63, regional prodn. mgr. U.S. flour milling div., 1963-69, v.p. and gen. mgr. indsl. foods div., 1969-83, exec. v.p., 1981—. Served with USNR, 1944-46. Office: Internat Multifoods Corp 733 Marquette Ave 1200 Multifoods Bldg Minneapolis MN 55402 *

HOWARD, ROBERT MILLER, former college president; b. Charlotte, N.C., Aug. 14, 1919; s. John Mark and Clemmie (Long) H.; m. Agnes Isenhour, Nov. 25, 1941 (dec.); children: Susan, Molly, Roberta, Robert Jr.; m. Edith Humphey, Oct. 9, 1971. A.B., Wake Forest U., 1940, M.A., 1950; Ed.D., U. N.C., 1972. Tchr. Bethany Union Sch., Rockingham, N.C., 1940-41; tchr. and adminstr. Gastonia City Schs., N.C., 1941-54; rep. Pilot Life Ins. Co., Gastonia, 1954-61; adminstr. Gastonia City Schs., 1961-66; dean evening affairs Gaston Coll., Dallas, N.C., 1966-72, dean instrn., 1972-79, pres., 1979-81, Belmont Abbey Coll., N.C., 1981-82. Trustee Gaston Coll., 1963-66; mem. city council Gastonia, 1957-63. Served with USAAF, 1943-45. Mem. NEA, N.C. Assn. Educators, Gamma Beta Phi, Delta Kappa Gamma. Democrat. Presbyterian.

HOWARD, ROBERT STAPLES, newspaper publisher; b. Wheaton, Minn., Oct. 23, 1924; s. Earl Eaton and Helen Elizabeth (Staples) H.; m. Lillian Irene Crabtree, Sept. 2, 1945; children: Thomas, Andrea, William, David. Student, U. Minn., 1942, 45. Pres. Howard Publs. (20 daily newspapers, TV, cable TV). Served as pvt. AUS, 1942-43; 2d lt. USAAF, 1944-45. Home: PO Box 1337 Rancho Santa Fe CA 92067 Office: PO Box 570 Oceanside CA 92054

HOWARD, ROBERT THORNTON, broadcasting company executive; b. Red Bank, N.J., June 18, 1927; s. Harold Kenneth and Gertrude (Thornton) H.; m. Joan Alice Volkman, June 26, 1949; children—Barbara Jo, Robert Thornton, Gregory Lyon, Brian Devlin. Student, U. Va., Columbia U.; D.H.L., St. John's U., 1974. With NBC-TV Network, 1947—; nat. sales mgr. Sta. WNBC-TV, N.Y.C., 1963-64, sta. mgr., 1964-66; gen. mgr. Sta. KNBC, Los Angeles, 1966-73, v.p. adminstrn. and ops., N.Y.C., 1973-74; pres. NBC-TV Network, N.Y.C., 1974—; v.p. NBC, 1966-74, dir., exec. v.p., 1974—; v.p., gen. mgr. Sta. WNBC-TV, N.Y.C., 1978—; pres., chief operating officer Citicom Corp., 1980—. Bd. dirs. Ind. Coll. Funds of Am., Urban League; mem. exec. bd. Greater N.Y. council Boy Scouts Am.; pres. So. Calif. Visitors Council; mem. Gov.'s Flood Relief Task Force. Served with U.S. Marine Corps, World War II. Mem. Nat. Acad. TV Arts and Scis. (pres. internat. council 1976). Clubs: Manhasset Bay Yacht, Calif. Yacht. Office: 10 Willets Rd Old Westbury NY 11568

HOWARD, RON, actor; b. Duncan, Okla., Mar. 1; s. Rance and Jean H.; m. Cheryl Alley, June 7, 1975. Student, U. So. Calif., Los Angeles Valley Coll. Film appearances The Journey, 1959, Five Minutes to Live, 1959, Music Man, 1962, The Courtship of Eddie's Father, 1963, Village of the Giants, 1965, Wild Country, 1971, Mother's Day, American Graffiti, The Spikes Gang, 1974, Eat My Dust, 1976, The Shootist, 1976, More American Graffiti, 1979, Leo and Loree; dir., co-author, star: film Grand Theft Auto, 1977; regular: TV series The Andy Griffith Show, 1960-68, The Smith Family, 1971-72, Happy Days, 1974—; other TV appearances include New Breed, Wonderful World of Disney, Gentle Ben, Laverne and Shirley, Twilight Zone, Danny Kaye, Fugitive, Dennis the Menace, Bonanza, Five Fingers, Gunsmoke, The F.B.I., 11th Hour; exec. producer, co-author, dir.: TV movie Cotton Candy, 1978; appeared in: TV film Act of Love, 1980; dir.: Skyward, 1981. Mem. AFTRA, SAG, Acad. Motion Picture Arts and Scis. Office: care Talent Mgmt Internat 9110 Sunset Blvd Los Angeles CA 90069 *

HOWARD, SAMUEL FRANCIS, JR., lawyer; b. Chattanooga, May 16, 1918; s. Samuel Francis and Louise (Patterson) H. B.A., Mich. State U., 1941; J.D., Columbia U., 1949. Bar: N.Y. 1949. Assoc. in law Columbia U. Law Sch., 1949-52; with Kelley Krye & Warren and predecessor firms, N.Y.C., 1952—; dir. Guinness-Harp Corp. Author: History of the School of Law, Columbia U., 1955; editor: Columbia Law Rev., 1947-49. Served to sgt., arty. U.S. Army, 1941-45. Decorated Bronze Star; recipient Charles Bathgate Beck prize Columbia Law Sch., 1947. Mem. ABA, N.Y. State Bar Assn., N.Y. County Lawyers Assn., Assn. Bar City N.Y., Am. Judicatures Soc., Selden Soc., Am. Soc. Legal History, Baker Street Irregulars. Democrat. Episcopalian. Club: Met. Opera (N.Y.C.). Home: 9 Cranberry St Brooklyn NY 11201 Office: 101 Park Ave New York NY 10178

HOWARD, SANDY, motion picture producer; b. N.Y.C., Aug. 1, 1927; d. George and Victoria (Ampolsk) Sokoloff. Student, Fla. So. Coll. Prin. Sandy Howard Prodns., Los Angeles, 1947—. Producer: over 50 TV series and over 20 motion pictures including The Island of Dr. Moreau, 1977, The Silent Flute, 1978; Savage Harvest, 1981, Vice Squad, 1982. Recipient numerous TV awards. Mem. Dirs. Guild Am., Writers Guild Am. Office: Sandy Howard Prodns 9336 Washington Blvd Culver City CA 90230 *

HOWARD, THEODORE WALTER, mutual fund corporation executive; b. Estherville, Iowa, July 18, 1942; s. Walter Moody and June (Solem) H.; m. Maxine Nora Donstad, July 30, 1966; children: Denise Marjorie, Douglas Walter. A.A., Estherville Jr. Coll., 1962; B.B.A., U. Iowa, 1964. Tax auditor Wis. Dept. Revenue, Madison, 1964-66; tax acct. Ladish Co., Cudahy, Wis., 1966-68, Teledyne Inc., Los Angeles, 1968-69; tax mgr. Computing & Software Inc., Los Angeles, 1969-71, Waddell & Reed, Inc., Kansas City, Mo., 1971-75; treas. United Group of Mut. Funds, Kansas City, Mo., 1975—. Mem. Tax Execs. Inst., Am. Contract Bridge League (dir. Kansas City 1982—). Republican. Lutheran. Home: 4824 N Kensington Circle Kansas City MO 64119 Office: Waddell & Reed Services Co PO Box 1343 2400 Pershing Kansas City MO 64141

HOWARD, THOMAS BAILEY, JR., constrn. materials co. exec.; b. Meridian, Miss., July 31, 1928; s. Thomas Bailey and Lucille Elizabeth (Mackey) H.; m. Mary Francis Stubbs, June 6, 1953; children—Mary Elizabeth, Thomas R., William S., Laura Francis. B.S. in Indsl. Engrng, Ga. Inst. Tech., 1953; postgrad., Harvard U., 1962. With Vulcan Materials Co., Chgo., 1957-69, v.p., 1968-69, Gifford-Hill & Co., Inc., Atlanta, 1969-75, exec. v.p., 1976-77, pres., Dallas, 1977—, also dir.; dir. Overhead Door Corp., Lennox Industries. Mem. adv. council Dallas Community Chest Trust Fund, U. Tex., Dallas; mem. adv. com. Leadership Dallas. Served to 1st lt. U.S. Army, 1953-55. Mem. Am. Concrete Pipe Assn. (dir. 1973-75, 77—), Prestressed Concrete Inst. (dir. 1973-74), Am. Inst. Indsl. Engrs., Am. Mgmt. Assn., Dallas C. of C. (dir.). Roman Catholic. Clubs: Capital City (Atlanta); Dallas Country, City (Dallas). Home: 4415 Fairfax St Dallas TX 75205 Office: 8435 Stemmons Freeway Dallas TX 75247

HOWARD, WILLIAM ALLEN, physician; b. New Orleans, July 12, 1912; s. A. Allen and Ellie Kate (Elgin) H.; m. Marion McAlpine Rowcliffe, Sept. 5, 1947; children—Marion McNeill, Alison Rowcliffe, William Rowcliffe. M.D., Tulane U., 1934. Intern, asst. resident U. Ia. Hosp., 1934-36; asst. resident pediatrics Strong Meml. Hosp.; chief resident pediatrics Childrens Hosp. of D.C., 1937-38; teaching fellow Georgetown U. Med. Sch., 1938-39; practice medicine, specializing in pediatrics and allergy, Washington, 1939—; instr., asst. prof., prof. pediatrics George Washington U. Med. Sch., 1946-67, chmn. dept., 1959-67, clin. prof. pediatrics, 1967—; sr. attending staff in pediatrics Childrens Hosp. D.C., 1950-78, chief of allergy, 1960-78, emeritus chief allergy, 1978—, sr. adv. staff, 1978—, also bd. dirs., trustee. Contbr. articles profl. jours. Past chmn., cons. Am. Bd. Allergy and Immunology, 1972, 73; Chmn. sub bd. Pediatric Allergy, 1967-71. Served to lt. col. AUS, 1942-46. Decorated Legion of Merit. Fellow Am. Acad. Pediatrics (chmn. dist. III, mem. exec. bd. 1970-76), Am. Acad. Allergy (past v.p.), Am. Pediatric Soc., So. Soc. for Pediatric Research; mem. D.C. Med. Soc., Soc. Med. Cons. to Armed Forces (past pres.), Phi Chi, Alpha Omega Alpha, Pi Kappa Phi. Clubs: Metropolitan (Washington); Chevy Chase. Home: 3714 Cardiff Ct Chevy Chase MD 20015 Office: 3301 New Mexico Ave NW Washington DC 20016

HOWARD, WILLIAM GATES, JR., electronics company executive; b. Boston, Nov. 6, 1941; s. William Gates and Mary Louise (Creager) H.; m. Kathleen Louretta Shipp, June 4, 1983. B.E.E., Cornell U., 1964, M.S., 1965; Ph.D., U. Calif.-Berkeley, 1967. Asst. prof. dept. elec. engrng. and computer scis. U. Calif.-Berkeley, 1967-69; group ops. mgr. Motorola Semicondr. Group, Mesa, Ariz., 1969-76; v.p., dir. tech. and planning Motorola Semicondr. Sector, Phoenix, 1976-83; v.p., dir. research and devel. Motorola Inc., Schaumburg, Ill., 1983—; chmn. U.S. Dept. Commerce Semicondr. Tech. Adv. Com., 1978-83, Dept. Def. Adv. Group on Electron Devices, 1982—; mem. study com. on tech. and implications of VLSI, Nat. Acad. Scis., 1980. Author: (with D.J. Hamilton) Basic Intergrated Circuit Engineering, 1976; patentee (with J.B. Cecil) improved reference current source, ladder termination circuit, three terminal zener diode. Fellow IEEE (vice-chmn. circuits and sytems soc. 1976-78); mem. AAAS; MEM. Phi Kappa Phi; mem. Sigma Xi, Eta Kappa Nu, Tau Beta Pi. Office: Motorola Inc 1303 E Algonquin Rd Schaumburg IL 60196

HOWARD, WILLIAM JACK, consultant; b. Kimball, Neb., Aug. 25, 1922; s. Carl G. and Agnes (Forsling) H.; m. Georgia S. Holt, June 26, 1946; children: Melissa, Andrew Jay. B.S. in Mech. Engrng., N.Mex. State U., 1946; postgrad., U. N.Mex., 1947-50; hon. doctorate, N.Mex. State U., 1982. With engrng. div. Sandia base Los Alamos Sci. Lab., 1946-56; with Sandia Livermore (Calif.) Lab., 1956-63; chmn. liaison com. AEC, asst. to sec. def. for atomic energy, 1963-66; v.p. Sandia Corp., Albuquerque, 1966-73, exec. v.p., 1973-82; cons., 1982—; U.S. del. SALT, Geneva, 1976. Recipient Disting. Pub. Service medal Dept. Def., 1966, Disting. Alumnus award N.Mex. State U., 1970, Disting. Asso. award ERDA, 1976, U.S. Dept. Energy, 1982; decorated Purple Heart, Bronze Star. Mem. Nat. Acad. Engrng. Home and Office: 920 McDuffie Circle Albuquerque NM 87110

HOWARD, WILLIAM REED, airline executive; b. Wheatland, Wyo., May 26, 1922; s. Albert Thompkins and Antha Jane (Taylor) H.; m. Lusadel Moore (dec.); children—Thomas Morton, David Patrick, William Reed. A.B., George Washington U., 1952; LL.B., 1956. Assoc. firm Gambrell, Russell & Forbes, Atlanta, 1955-67; v.p. Eastern Airlines, N.Y.C., 1967-71, sr. v.p., Miami, Fla., 1971-78; sr. v.p. and asst. to pres. Piedmont Airlines, Winston-Salem, N.C., 1978-80, exec. v.p., 1980-81, pres., chief operating officer, dir., 1981-83, pres., chief exec. officer, 1983—; chmn. bd. subs. Air Service, Inc., 1983—, Aviation Supply Corp., 1983—; dir. Wachovia Bank & Trust Co. Bd. dirs. United Way Forsyth County, 1979-81. Served to capt. USAAF, 1942-46. Recipient George Washington U. Alumni Achievement award, 1984. Mem. Greater Winston-Salem C. of C. (dir. 1981-82), Air Transp. Assn. Am. (dir. 1983—). Office: Piedmont Airlines Winston-Salem NC 27156

HOWARD, WILLIE THOMAS, JR., univ. dean; b. Ailey, Ga., Oct. 15, 1928; s. Willie Thomas and Delia Minor (Gaffney) H.; m. Hazeline Watkins, May 26, 1952; children—Beverly Jean, Terry Kathleen, Wayne Thomas. B.S., N.C. A. and T. State U., 1953; M.Ed., U. Ill., 1956, advanced grad. certificate, 1958; Ed.D., Am. U., 1969. Counselor, psychologist, then dir. Office Research Projects and Grants, Morgan State U., Balt., 1958-70; asso. prof., chmn. dept. counseling, adminstrn., adult edn. and student personnel services Howard U., 1970-73, prof. edn., coordinator grad. program counseling, 1973-76, prof., 1976—, dean, 1976—, mem. nat. adv. bd., 1976—; lectr. Trinity Coll., Washington; cons. in field. Author papers in field. Served with USAAF, 1947-49; Served with AUS, 1953-55; Korea. Title III grantee, 1966-70; grantee D.C. Manpower Adminstrn.-U.S. Dept. Labor, 1971-75; scholar Am. Council Edn., 1976. Mem. Am. Ednl. Research Assn., Am. Personnel and Guidance Assn., Md. Psychol. Assn., Nat. Employment Counselors Assn., Assn. Study Afro Am. Life and History, Res. Officers Assn. (past chpt. v.p.), Phi Delta Kappa, past chpt. pres.). Democrat. Methodist. Club: Masons. Home: 8815 Saunders Ln Lanham MD 20801 Office: Sch Edn Howard Univ Washington DC 20059 *It has always been my belief that life is plentiful for those who are willing to believe, work hard, and persevere.*

HOWARD, WINSTON STANLEY, lawyer; b. Des Moines, Oct. 15, 1907; s. William Shadrick and Amanda (Sandstrom) H.; m. Marguerite Blair, June 7, 1933; children—Alan Blair, Joan. Student, U. Nebr., 1925-26; J.D. cum laude, U. Wyo., 1930. Bar: Wyo. bar 1930, Colo. bar 1935. Practice in, Big Horn County, Wyo., 1931-35, Denver, 1935—; partner firm Sherman & Howard, 1939—; co-organizer, former chmn. bd. Continental Nat. Bank, Englewood, Colo.; co-organizer Boulevard Nat. Bank, Denver; dir. various bus. corps. Mem. nat. council, Denver adv. bd. Salvation Army; chmn. Colo. Women's Coll.; bd. dirs. Denver Symphony Assn., Nat. Western Stock Show Assn.; former chmn. trustees Swedish Med. Center. Served from lt. to lt. comdr. USNR, 1944-46. Recipient Others award Salvation Army, 1962, 73, Distinguished Alumni award U. Wyo., 1967. Mem. ABA., Colo. Bar Assn. (past gov.), Denver Bar Assn., Denver, Englewood chambers commerce, Sigma Nu, Delta Sigma Rho. Republican. Episcopalian (former vestryman, warden). Clubs: Denver, Kiwanis (past pres.), Mile High (Denver); Garden of the Gods (Colorado Springs, Colo.). Home: 4860 S Dahlia St Littleton CO 80120 Office: First of Denver Plaza Denver CO 80202

HOWARD-CARTER, THERESA, archaeologist; b. Millbrook, N.Y., May 15, 1929; d. Clarence K. and Ann (Warren) Howard; 1 dau., Laura Coffin (dec.). A.B., Syracuse U., 1950; M.A., U. Pa., 1954; Ph.D. in Classical and Near Eastern Archaeology, Bryn Mawr Coll, 1962. Head reprodns. dept. Univ. Mus., Phila., 1950-52, student asst. ethnology dept., 1953-55, research asst., 1960-62, research assoc., 1962-64, dir. Iraq excavations, 1964; teaching asst. Bryn Mawr. Coll., 1961-62, deptl. asst., 1962-63; ann. prof. Am. Sch. Oriental Research, Baghdad, 1965-66; vis. lectr. dept. Near Eastern studies Johns Hopkins U., Balt., 1969-71, asst. prof., 1971-75; Mem. staff U. Pa. Gordion Expdn., Polatli, Turkey, 1955, 57; dir. U. Pa. Phoenician excavations, Lepcis Magna, Homs, Libya, 1960, 61, Cyrenaican Coastal Survey, U. Pa., 1962; asst. dir. Bryn Mawr Coll. excavations Kara Tash, Elmali, Turkey, 1963; co-dir. Tell al-Rimah Expdn., No. Iraq, 1964-66; collaborator for Univ. Mus. with Soprentendenza alle Antichitá di Napoli at Pithecusa, Lacco Ameno, Ischia, 1965; field dir. Sybaris project of U. Pa. in, Calabria, Italy, 1968; dir. Johns Hopkins expdns. to Syrian Euphrates Valley, 1972-74, to Arab-Iranian Gulf, 1972-74; research assoc. Near East sect. Univ. Mus., Phila., 1966—, cons. scholar for Mesopotamia and Gulf, 1983—; chief adv. to Kuwait Nat. Mus., 1980—. Contbr. articles to profl. jours. Bd. dirs. Theatre of Living Arts, Phila., 1964-67, chmn. Women's com., 1964-65. Nat. Endowment for Humanities grantee, 1973, 74, 79. Fellow Mid East Studies Assn.; mem. Archaeol. Inst. Am., Am. Oriental Soc., Am. Sch. Oriental Research, Brit. Sch. Archaeology in Iraq, Egypt Exploration Soc., Middle East Inst. Home: Grubbs Mill RD 1 West Chester PA 19380 Office: U Pa Museum 33d and Spruce Sts Philadelphia PA 19104

HOWARD-FLANDERS, PAUL, educator; b. Bristol, Eng., June 30, 1919; s. Leonard Richard and Millicent (Franks) H-F.; m. June Daphne Cain, Sept. 23, 1950; children—Rob Stewart, Mark Richard. B.S., London U., Eng., 1940, Ph.D., 1956; M.A., Yale, 1964. With Med. Research Council exptl. radio-pathology unit Hammersmith Hosp., London, 1953-59; asso. prof. radiobiology Yale, New Haven, 1959-63, prof. radiobiology, molecular biophysics and biochemistry, 1963—. Contbr. articles profl. jours. Office: 404 JW Gibbs Lab-Yale Univ Box 6666 New Haven CT 06511

HOWARTH, THOMAS, govt. ofcl., tax cons.; b. Eng., June 2, 1921; came to U.S., 1926, naturalized, 1936; s. Frank and Mary Elizabeth (Conner) H.; m. Eleanor Louise King, Feb. 4, 1942; 1 son, Thomas King. B.C.S., Benjamin Franklin U., 1946, M.C.S., 1947. With Springfield Nat. Bank, Mass., 1939-42; C.P.A., Washington, 1946-57; sec., treas. Nat. Coal Assn., Washington; treas. Fuels Research Council, Inc., Washington, 1957-70, Coal Exporters Assn. U.S., Inc., 1959-70; asst. treas. Bituminous Coal Research, Inc., 1960-70; dir. govt. relations U.S. Ind. Telephone Assn., Washington, 1970-75; tax cons., Washington, 1976—; budget officer Select Com. on Assassinations, U.S. Ho. of Reps., 1976-79; mem. Fed. Home Loan Bank Bd., Washington, 1980—; instr. accounting Am. Inst. Banking, Washington, 1948-57. Served with USNR, 1942-45. Mem. Inst. Orgn. Mgmt. (chmn. bd. regents 1969-70), Am., D.C. insts. C.P.A.'s. Episcopalian (chmn. dept. finance Diocese Washington 1964-67, treas. 1969-73, parish treas., vestryman, sr. warden). Clubs: Mason (Shriner),

Burning Tree (Bethesda, Md.)). Home: 1505 Live Oak Dr Silver Spring MD 20910

HOWAT, JOHN KEITH, curator; b. Denver, Apr. 12, 1937; s. James Bowcott and Nancy Selden (Skinker) H.; m. Anne Hadley, Jan. 21, 1958; children: Karen Louise, Laura Anne. Grad., Phillips Exeter Acad., 1955; B.A., Harvard U., 1959, M.A., 1962; Ford fellow, N.Y. U. Inst. Fine Arts, 1965-66. Curator Hyde Collection, Glens Falls, N.Y., 1962-64; asst. curator dept. Am. paintings and sculpture Met. Mus. Art, N.Y.C., 1967-68, assoc. curator-in-charge, 1968-70, curator, 1970-81, chmn. depts. Am. art, 1981—; Mem. adv. com. archives Am. art Smithsonian Instn., 1969—. Author: exhbn. catalog John Frederick Kensett 1816-1872, 1968; co-author: 19th Century America: Paintings and Sculpture, 1970, The Hudson River and Its Painters, 1972. Chester Dale fellow Met. Mus. Art, 1966-67. Clubs: Union, Century Association (N.Y.C.). Home: 1100 Park Ave New York NY 10028 Office: Met Mus Art Fifth Ave and 82d St New York NY 10028

HOWE, BRUCE IVER, resources company executive; b. Dryden, Ont., Can., May 19, 1936; s. Norman I. and Laura A. (Locking) H.; m. Elsie Evelyn Ann Ferguson, Aug. 25, 1962; children—Karen, Norman, Kristina. B.Sc. in Chem. Engring, Queen's U., Kingston, Ont., 1958; grad. program mgmt. devel., Harvard U., 1961; LL.D. (hon.), Lakehead U., 1983. Profl. engr., B.C. With MacMillan Bloedel Ltd., Vancouver, B.C., Can., 1963-80, group v.p. pulp paper, 1971-77, sr. v.p. ops., 1977-79, exec. v.p. ops., 1979-80, pres. and chief operating officer, 1980; also dir.; now pres., chief exec. officer B.C. Resources Investment Corp.; chmn. Westar Mining Ltd.; dir. Bank of Montreal, B.C. Place. Contbr. numerous articles on pulp and paper to profl. jours. Bd. govs. Vancouver Aquarium; pres. Vancouver YMCA, 1978-79, bd. govs., 1981—; past pres. Men's Can. Club of Vancouver; pres. Young Conservatives B.C., 1967-68; trustee, mem. univ. council Queen's U. Recipient Insignia award City and Guilds at London Inst., 1968. Mem. Can. Pulp and Paper Assn. (C. Howard Smith medal 1959, Weldon Gold medal 1961), Assn. Profl. Engrs., Am. Mgmt. Assn., Instrument Soc. Am., Brit. Paper and Board Makers Assn. (Marsh prize), TAPPI, Australian Pulp and Paper Industry Tech. Assn. Clubs: Vancouver, Vancouver Lawn Tennis. Office: 1176 W Georgia St Vancouver BC V6E 4B9 Canada

HOWE, DANIEL WALKER, historian, educator; b. Ogden, Utah, Jan. 10, 1937; s. Maurice Langdon and Lucie (Walker) H.; m. Sandra Fay Shumway, Sept. 3, 1961; children: Rebecca, Christopher, Stephen. A.B. magna cum laude, Harvard U., 1959; M.A., Oxford (Eng.) U., 1965; Ph.D., U. Calif., Berkeley, 1966. From instr. to asso. prof. history and Am. studies Yale U., 1966-73; asso. prof. history UCLA, 1973-77, prof., 1977—, chmn. dept., 1983—. Author: The Unitarian Conscience, 1970, The American Whigs: An Anthology, 1973, Victorian America, 1976, The Political Culture of the American Whigs, 1979. Served to lt. U.S. Army, 1959-60. Kent fellow Danforth Found., 1964-66; Charles Warren Center for Studies in Am. History fellow, 1970-71; Nat. Endowment for Humanities fellow, 1975-76; Guggenheim fellow, 1984-85. Mem. Am. Hist. Assn., Orgn. Am. Historians, Am. Studies Assn., Soc. for Values in Higher Edn. Episcopalian. Home: 3814 Cody Rd Sherman Oaks CA 91403 Office: Dept History UCLA Los Angeles CA 90024

HOWE, FISHER, management consultant, former government official; b. Winnetka, Ill., May 17, 1914; s. Lawrence and Hester (Davis) H.; m. Deborah Froelicher, June 4, 1945; children: Elizabeth, Shippen. A.B., Harvard, 1935; student, Nat. War Coll., 1948. Salesman Coats & Clarks Thread Co., N.Y.C., 1935-40, Patons & Baldwins, Ltd., Yorkshire, Eng., 1936-37; mem. staff Office of Dir., OSS, Washington, London, Mediterranean, Far East, 1941-45; spl. asst. under sec. of state, econ. affairs, 1945-46; exec. sec. Bd. Fgn. Service, Dept. State, 1947, dep. spl. asst. to sec. state, 1948-56; exec. sec. Dept. State, 1956-58, counselor of embassy, Oslo, Norway, 1958-62, The Hague, Netherlands, 1962-65, mem. policy planning council, 1965-68; exec. dir., asst. dean Johns Hopkins U. Sch. Advanced Internat. Studies, 1968-72; dep. exec. dir. Commn. on Orgn. of Govt. for Conduct of Fgn. Policy, Washington, 1973-75; sec., gen. adv. com. Energy Research and Devel. Adminstrn., 1975-77; asst. to pres., dir. instl. relations Resources for the Future, Inc., 1978-82; v.p. David Lavender/David Rice & Assocs., 1982—. Author: Computer and Foreign Affairs, 1968. Trustee Fountain Valley Sch., Colorado Springs, Colo., Hospice Care of D.C., Bur. Rehab. Served as lt. USNR, 1943-44; overseas service. Club: Metropolitan (Washington). Home: 2015 48th St NW Washington DC 20007 Office: 1990 M St NW Suite 700 Washington DC 20036

HOWE, GORDON, former professional hockey player; b. Saskatoon, Sask., Can., Mar. 31, 1928; came to U.S., 1944; s. Albert Clarence and Katherine (Schultz) H.; m. Colleen Janet Joffa, Apr. 15, 1953; children: Marty Gordon, Mark Steven, Cathleen Jill, Murray Albert. Student pub. schs. Can. Profl. hockey player with Detroit Red Wings Hockey Club (Nat. Hockey League), 1944-73, also past v.p.; with Houston Aeros (World Hockey Assn.), 1971-73, New Eng. Whalers (World Hockey Assn.), Hartford, Conn., 1977-78; dir. player devel. Hartford Whalers, 1980-82, spl. asst. to chmn., mng. ptnr., 1982—; chmn. bd. Howe Internat. Mktg. Author: Gordie Howe, No. 9. Recipient Order of Can. medal, 1971; named Canada's Athlete of Year, 1963; holder Hart Meml. Trophy, Art Ross Trophy, Lester Patrick Trophy. Mem. Nat. League Hall of Fame, Mich. Sports Hall of Fame, Omaha Sports Hall of Fame. Conglist. 12 times Nat. Hockey League 1st All Star Team, 9 times Nat. Hockey League 2d All Star Team; named Most Valuable Player and to 1st All-Star Team World Hockey Assn., 1974. Address: care Hartford Whalers One Civic Center Plaza Hartford CT 06103 *

HOWE, GRAHAM LLOYD, photographer, curator; b. Sydney, N.S.W., Australia, Apr. 4, 1950; came to U.S., 1976; s. Raymond R. and Gwendoline B. (Ford) H.; m. Jacqueline Markham, July 1, 1978. Diploma in art and design, Prahran Coll. Advanced Edn., Melbourne, Australia, 1971; M.A., UCLA, 1978, M.F.A., 1979. Dir. Australian Centre for Photography, Sydney, 1974-75; curator Graham Nash Collection, Los Angeles, 1976—. Author: Paul Outerbridge, Jr.: Photographs, 1980; co-author: Paul Outerbridge, Jr.: A Singular Aesthetic, 1982; author: catalogue Paul Outerbridge, Jr., 1976; co-author: Two Views of Manzanar, 1978; editor: New Photography Australia-A Selective Survey, 1974, Aspects of Australian Photography, 1974, The Graham Nash Collection, 1978. Grantee NEA, 1982, Ford Found., 1978; UCLA Art Council scholar, 1977. Mem. Soc. for Photog. Edn. Home: 113 E Union St Pasadena CA 91103

HOWE, H. PHILIP, banker; b. Manhattan, Kans., July 3, 1932; s. Harold and Ruth Madeline (Riordan) H.; m. Margaret Virginia Griffith, June 1, 1957; children—David, Janet, Evan, Kathleen. B.S., Kans. State U., 1954. Vice pres., head installment loans Union Nat. Bank, Manhattan, 1960-68; pres. Kans. State Bank, Manhattan, 1969-73, chmn. bd., 1973—; pres. Griffith Oil Co., Manhattan, 1962-72, chmn. bd., 1972—; v.p. Manhattan Real Properties, Inc., 1963—, Kans. State Travel Agy., 1968—; pres. Master Med. Corp., 1974—. Trustee Kans. Endowment Assn., 1976—, St. Mary Hosp., 1975-76; pres. United Way Manhattan, 1975-76. Served with U.S. Army, 1957-59. Mem. Am. Bankers Assn., Kans. Bankers Assn., Kans. Oilmens Assn., Beta Theta Pi. Roman Catholic. Clubs: Manhattan Country, K.C. Home: 1707 Thomas Circle Manhattan KS 66502 Office: 1010 Westloop Manhattan KS 66502

HOWE, HAROLD, II, former foundation executive, educator; b. Hartford, Conn., Aug. 17, 1918; s. Arthur and Margaret Marshall (Armstrong) H.; m. Priscilla Foster Lamb, Sept. 4, 1940; children: Catherine Howe Puchtler, Merrill Howe Leavitt, Gordon Armstrong. B.A., Yale U., 1940; M.A. in History, Columbia U., 1947; postgrad., Harvard Grad. Sch. Edn., 1958-59, U. Cin., 1953-55; LL.D. (hon.), Adelphi U., 1966, U. St. Louis, 1967, U. Notre Dame, 1967, Princeton U., 1968, Hunter Coll., 1981, U. Hartford, 1982, CUNY, 1983. Tchr. history Darrow Sch., New Lebanon, N.Y., 1940-41, Phillips Acad., Andover, Mass., 1947-50; prin. jr. and sr. high schs., Andover, Mass., 1950-53; prin. Walnut Hills High Sch., Cin., 1953-57, Newton (Mass.) High Sch., 1957-60; supt. schs., Scarsdale, N.Y., 1960-64; dir. Learning Inst. N.C., 1964-65; U.S. Commr. of Edn., Washington, 19665-68; program advisor on edn. in India Ford Found., 1969-70, v.p. for edn., N.Y.C., 1971-81; sr. lectr. Harvard U. Grad. Sch. Edn., 1982—. Author: Picking Up the Options, 1968. Trustee Yale U., 1962-68; trustee Vassar Coll., Taft Sch., Coll. Entrance Exam. Bd., John Hay Whitney Found., 1973—; bd. dirs. Kennedy Center, Washington, 1967-68; mem. Commn. on Humanities, Am. Council Learned Socs., 1962-63, Nat. Council on Edn. Research, 1978—; chmn. Nat. Council on Edn. Research, 1980—; chmn. bd. Inst. Ednl. Leadership, 1982. Served with USNR, 1941-46. Recipient Gold medal for public service NYU, 1968. Mem. Cleve. Conf. Home: 404 Elm St Concord MA 01742 Office: Harvard U Grad Sch Edn Cambridge MA 02138

HOWE, HERBERT MARSHALL, educator; b. Bristol, R.I., Mar. 21, 1912; s. Wallis Eastburn and Mary Emily (Locke) H.; m. Evelyn Grace Mitchell, Sept. 6, 1941; children—Evelyn Mitchell, Herbert Marshall, Emily Judson. Grad., St. George's Sch., 1930; A.B., Harvard U., 1934; M.A., U. Wis., 1941, Ph.D., 1948. Tchr., Latin, biology Brooks Sch., North Andover, Mass., 1934-40; Latin, history Pomfret (Conn.) Sch., 1942-48; faculty U. Wis., Madison, 1948—, prof. classics, 1956—, chmn. dept., 1954-68; chmn. Integrated Liberal Studies, 1975-80. Author: (with P.L. MacKendrick) Classics in Translation, 1952, (with W.R. Agard) Medical Greek and Latin, 1955, rev. edit., 1971, Ancient Religion and the Early Church, 1968, rev. edit., 1974. Mem. Am. Philol. Assn., Am. Inst. Archaeology, Logos. Episcopalian. Home: 2011 Chadbourne Ave Madison WI 53705

HOWE, IRVING, author, historian, critic; b. N.Y.C., June 11, 1920; s. David and Nettie (Goldman) H.; m. Ilana Wiener; 2 children. Grad., Coll. City N.Y. Tchr. English Brandeis U., 1953-61, Stanford U., 1961-63; prof. English City U. N.Y. at Hunter Coll., 1963—, Distinguished prof., 1970—; Christian Gauss seminar chair prof. Princeton U., 1954. Author: Politics and the Novel: A World More Attractive, 1963, Steady Work, 1966, Thomas Hardy, 1967, The Decline of the New, 1969, The Critical Point, 1973, World of Our Fathers, 1976 (Nat. Book award); co-author: The Radical Papers, 1966; editor: periodical Essential Works of Socialism, 1971; co-editor: A Treasury of Yiddish Poetry, 1971; contbr. to: N.Y. Times Book Rev. Served with AUS, World War II. Recipient Longview Found. prize for lit. criticism; Nat. Inst. Arts and Letters award; Kenyon Rev. fellow for lit. criticism, 1953; Bollingen Found. fellow; Guggenheim fellow, 1971. Address: Dept English Hunter Coll New York City NY 10021

HOWE, JACK HOMER, speech communication educator; b. Clarence, Mo., Aug. 20, 1923; s. Warren D. and Goldie Sarah (Howe) H. B.A., Morningside Coll., 1947; LL.B., U. S.D., 1949, M.A., 1949; Ph.D., U. Nebr., 1954. Bar: S.D. 1949. Instr. Southwestern Coll., Kans., 1951-52; lectr. U. Nebr., 1952-54; asst. prof. then assoc. prof. Southwestern Coll., Winfield, Kans., 1954-59; asst. prof. U. Ariz., 1959-60; assoc. prof. Southwestern Coll., 1960-61; asst. prof. then assoc. prof. U. Ariz., 1961-64; vis. prof. U. Calif., Santa Barbara, summer 1964; prof. U. Ariz., 1964-66; vis. prof. Frostburg (Md.) State Coll., 1966-67; prof. Calif. State U., Long Beach, 1967—. Editor: Intercollegiate Speech Tournament Results, 1965—; calendar editor: Jour. of the Am. Forensic Assn, 1968—. Served with U.S. Army, 1943-45. Decorated Purple Heart; recipient Outstanding Service to U. Ariz. award, 1971; Disting. Coaching award U. Utah, 1979; Critic of Yr. award UCLA, 1984; Coach of Yr. award Sacramento City Coll., 1984. Mem. Speech Communication Assn., Am. Forensic Assn. (v.p. 1966-68), Western Forensic Assn. (pres. 1962-64), Pacific S.W. Collegiate Forensic Assn. (pres. 1974-75), Nat. Forensic Assn. (v.p. 1973-77), Western Speech Communication Assn., Cross-Exam. Debate Assn. (exec. sec. 1971-84, pres. 1984-85), Delta Sigma Rho-Tau Kappa Alpha (nat. treas. 1975-79, nat. pres. 1979-81, Disting. Service award 1981). Methodist. Home: 2125 E Ocean Blvd Apt 2F Long Beach CA 90803 Office: Dept Speech Communication Calif State U Long Beach CA 90840

HOWE, JOHN PERRY, educator, research consultant; b. Groton, N.Y., June 24, 1910; s. Mather Crain and Belle Gertrude (Smith) H.; m. Marilyn Leilani Evans, Dec. 27, 1941; children: Roger Evans, Susan Lee, Nancy Kathleen, John Alton. B.S., Hobart Coll., 1933; Ph.D. (Jesse Metcalf fellow 1935-36), Brown U., 1936. Instr. chemistry Ohio State U., 1936-38; asst. prof. phys. chemistry Brown U., 1938-42; research asso. metall. lab. Manhattan Dist., U. Chgo., 1942-44, asso. dir., gen. research and devel. nuclear reactors, 1945; mgr. metallurgy sect. Knolls Atomic Power Lab., Gen. Electric Co., 1945-52; research energy conversion and storage Gen. Electric Research Lab., 1952-53; sect. chief reactor materials Atomics Internat., 1953-57, dir. research dept., 1957-61; Ford prof. engring., dir. dept. engring. physics and materials sci., Coll. Engring., Cornell U., 1962-64, dir. dept. engring. physics, 1965-67; staff mem. Inst. for Def. Analyses, Arlington, Va., 1967-68; asst. lab. dir., chmn. metallurgy Gen. Atomic, Inc., 1968-69, tech. dir. advanced energy systems, 1969-75, asso. dir. research and devel., 1970-71, tech. dir.-materials, advanced systems devel., 1971-75; cons. Gen Atomic, Inc., 1975—, Office of Tech. Assessment, 1975-77; adj. prof. U. Calif. at San Diego, 1973—; mem. adv. com. on classification AEC, 1952-67, editorial adv. bd. reactor handbook, 1953-63, mem. adv. com. on reactor safety, 1961-63, mem. bd. atomic safety and licensing, 1965-68; adviser AEC delegation; also vice chmn. session radiation effects Geneva (Switzerland) Conf. Peaceful Uses of Atomic Energy, 1955; del., advisor, vice session chmn. 1st AEC Conf. on Peaceful Uses of Atomic Energy, Geneva, 1958; mem. chemistry adv. com. Air Force Office Sci. Research, 1957-64; cons. spl. com. fundamental research in connection study made for Air Force, Nat. Acad. Scis., 1957- 58; cons. materials adv. group Inst. Def. Analyses, 1960; mem. sci. adv. group Air Force Office Aerospace Research, 1963-71; vis. com. nuclear engring. div. Brookhaven Nat. Lab.; vis. com. solid state div. Oak Ridge Nat. Lab., 1963-67; cons. Gen. Atomic, 1975-81. Author: (with others) Energy Vol. 3, 1976; Editor: (with R. Smith) Beryllium Oxide: Proc. First Internat. Beryllium Oxide Conf., Australian Atomic Energy Establishment, Sydney, 1963, (with Dr. M. Finniston) Progress in Nuclear Energy, series V. vols. 1-4, 1955-62, (with R.W. Cahn, P. Lacombe) Jour. Nuclear Materials, 1958-66; editor: Annals Nuclear Energy, 1973-78; editorial adv. bd.: Progress in Solid State Chemistry, 1970—; exec. editor also articles. Mem. pub. services adv. com., San Diego County, 1975-78; mem. San Diego County Regional Energy Task Force. Fellow Am. Phys. Soc., AAAS, Am. Inst. Chemists, Am. Soc. for Metals; mem. Am. Chem. Soc., AIME, Inst. Metals, Archaeol. Inst. Am., Phi Beta Kappa, Sigma Xi. Office: U Calif San Diego Energy Center LaJolla CA 92037

HOWE, JONATHAN THOMAS, lawyer; b. Evanston, Ill., Dec. 16, 1940; s. Frederick King and Rosaelie Charlotte (Volz) H.; m. Lois Helene Braun, July 12, 1963; children: Heather C., Jonathan T., Sara E. B.A. with honors, Northwestern U., 1963; J.D. with distinction, Duke U., 1966. Bar: Ill. 1966, U.S. Dist. Ct. (no. dist.) Ill. 1966, U.S. Ct. Appeals (7th cir.) 1967, U.S. Tax Ct. 1968, U.S. Supreme Ct. 1970, U.S. Ct. Appeals (D.C. cir.) 1976, U.S. Dist. Ct. (D.C.) 1976, U.S. Ct. Appeals (9th cir.) 1980. Ptnr. Jenner & Block, Chgo., 1966—, sr. ptnr. in charge assn. and adminstrv. law dept., 1978—. Contbg. editor: Ill. Inst. for Continuing Legal Edn., 1973—, Sporting Goods Bus., 1977—, Meeting News, 1978—; contbr. articles to legal jours. Mem. Dist. 27 Bd. Edn., Northbrook, Ill., 1969—, sec., Northbrook, Ill., 1969-72, pres., Northbrook, Ill., 1973-84; chmn. bd. trustees Sch. Employee Benefit Trust, 1979—; founding bd. dirs., pres. Sch. Mgmt. Found. Ill., 1976—; mem. exec. com. Northfield Twp. Republican Orgn., 1967-71; bd. deacons. Village Presbyn. Ch. Northbrook, 1975-78, trustee, 1981—. Mem. ABA (antitrust sect., Nat. Inst. com., corp. banking and bus. law sect., sect. on litigation, adminstrv. law sect.; mem. internat. law com., continuing edn. com.), Ill. State Bar Assn. (antitrust sec., civil practice sect., sch. law sect., adminstrv. law sect.; co-editor Antitrust Newsletter 1968-70), Chgo. Bar Assn. (def. of prisoners com. 1966—, antitrust law com. 1971—, continuing edn. com. 1977—), Nat. Sch. Bds. Assn. (nat. bd. dirs. com. 1979—, exec. com. 1981-82, sec.-treas. 1983—, chmn. resolutions and policy com. 1979-80, chmn. task force on global edn. 1980-81, chmn. constrn. and bylaws com. 1981—, chmn. devel. com. 1982—), D.C. Bar Assn., Am. Judicature Soc., Ill. Assn. Sch. Bds. (pres. 1977-79, bd. dirs. 1971—), Am. Soc. Assn. Execs. (vice chmn. legal com. 1983), Order of Coif, Psi Upsilon. Clubs: Legal, Law, Mid-America, Barclay, Sunset Ridge Country, Chgo. Athletic. Home: 3845 Normandy Ln Northbrook IL 60062 Office: One IBM Plaza Suite 4200 Chicago IL 60611

HOWE, JONATHAN TRUMBULL, naval officer; b. San Diego, Aug. 24, 1935; s. Hamilton Wilcox and Margaret Washington (Backus) H.; m. Harriet Edith Mangrum, June 21, 1957; children: Richard, Jonathan, David, Katharine, Paul, Margaret. B.S., U.S. Naval Acad., 1957; M.A., Tufts U., 1968, 1969, Ph.D., 1969. Commd. ensign U.S. Navy, 1957, advanced through grades to rear adm., 1980; engr. officer U.S.S. Patrick Henry, 1963-67, mil. asst. to asst. to pres. for nat. security affairs, 1969-73, comdg. officer U.S.S. Berkeley, 1974, asst. to v.p. for nat. security affairs, 1975-76, comdr. Destroyer Squadron 31, 1977-78, chief of staff, comdr. 7th Fleet, 1979-80; dir. Politico-Mil. Policy Div., Dept. Navy, Washington, 1980-81, sr. mil. asst. to dep. sec. def., 1981-82; dir. polit. mil. affairs Dept. State, 1982—. Author: Multicrises-Sea Power and Global Politics in the Missile Age, 1970; contbr. numerous articles to profl. jours. Decorated Def. D.S.M., Navy D.S.M., Legion of Merit (2). Mem. U.S. Naval Inst., U.S. Naval Acad. Alumni Assn. Home: 3410 Barger Dr Falls Church VA 22044 Office: Dept State Washington DC

HOWE, LAWRENCE, lawyer, bus. exec.; b. Evanston, Ill., Nov. 16, 1921; s. Lawrence and Hester (Davis) H.; m. Ellen G. Vaughan, Feb. 22, 1943; children—James, Ellen, Eliza, Samuel. A.B., Harvard, 1942; J.D., U. Chgo., 1948. Bar: Ill. bar 1948. Asso. firm Pope & Ballard, Chgo., 1948-52; asso., then partner firm Vedder, Price, Kaufman & Kammholz, Chgo., 1952-66, 74-75; v.p., sec. Bell & Howell Co., Chgo., 1966-71, sr. v.p., dir., 1971-74; exec. v.p. fin. and law, gen. counsel Jewel Cos., Inc., Chgo., 1975-80, vice-chmn., dir., 1980—, also chief fin. officer, chief legal officer. Pres. Village of Winnetka, Ill., 1964-68. Served to lt. USNR, 1942-45. Home: 175 Chestnut St Winnetka IL 60093 Office: 5725 N East River Rd Chicago IL 60631

HOWE, RICHARD CUDDY, state supreme ct. justice; b. South Cottonwood, Utah, Jan. 20, 1924; s. Edward E. and Mildred (Cuddy) H.; m. Juanita Lyon, Aug. 30, 1949; children: Christine, Andrea, Bryant, Valerie, Jeffrey, Craig. B.S., U. Utah, 1945, J.D., 1948. Bar: Utah. Law clk. to Justice H. James Wolfe, Utah Supreme Ct., 1949-50; judge city ct., Murray, Utah, 1951, individual practice law, Murray, 1952-80; justice Utah Supreme Ct., 1980—. Mem. Utah Ho. of Reps., 1951-58, 69-72, Utah Senate, 1973-78. Named Outstanding Legislator Citizens' Conf. State Legislatures, 1972. Mem. Utah Bar Assn. Mormon. Office: 332 State Capitol Salt Lake City UT 84114 *

HOWE, RICHARD ESMOND, JR., educator, musician; b. Murray, Utah, Apr. 30, 1927; s. Richard Esmond and Louise (Hill) H.; m. Agnes Jensen, May 31, 1949; 1 dau., Mary Katherine. Student, U. Utah, 1946; B.S. in Music, Juilliard Sch. Music, 1951, M.S., 1952, U. Florence, Italy, 1952-53; D.Mus. Arts, Eastman Sch. Music, 1956. Mem. faculty Grinnell (Iowa) Coll., 1956-73, prof. music, 1963—, chmn. dept., 1959-62, 65-67, 70-72, chmn. div. humanities, 1971-72; dean San Francisco Conservatory Music, 1973—. Contbr. articles to mus. jours. Served with USNR, 1945-46. Fulbright grantee, Italy, 1952-53, 53-54. Spl. research keyboard music of Baldassare Gallupi. Home: 409 Countyview Dr Mill Valley CA 94941

HOWE, ROBERT HSI LIN, biotechnology consultant; b. Swatow, China, Jan. 2, 1922; came to U.S., 1948, naturalized, 1962; s. Zulin and Afia (Lin) H.; m. Jean Ma, Dec. 23, 1953; children: David J., Roberta C., Albert G. B.S., Meth. U., Soochow, China, 1943; B.C.E., St. John's U., Shanghai, China, 1945; M.S., Cornell U., 1949, M.C.E., 1950; Ph.D., Purdue U., 1955; Sc.D. in Environ. and Chem. Engring. Sci., World Open U., Calif., 1977. Diplomate Acad. Environ. Engrs. Lectr. chem. engring. and physics Meth. U., 1943-47; Meth. Ch. scholar Cornell U., 1948-50; fellow Ind. Dept. Conservation, Lafayette, 1950-52; san. engr. Eli Lilly & Co., Lafayette, 1952-55, project engr., 1955-63, sr. san. engr., 1963-65, research scientist, 1966-83; cons. advanced biotech., acting head Ctr. Advanced Biotech. Info. and Services,, West Lafayette, Ind., 1983—, environ. tech. services cons., 1970—; tech. advisor water project Dept. State, Washington, 1958-59; Fulbright-Hays lectr., prof. Istanbul Teknik U., 1965-66; prof.-advisor San. Engring. chair, 1966-72; prof., lectr. Istanbul U., 1966, Milan Poly. U.; spl. profl. lectr. Middle East Tech. U., 1966; lectr. Acad. Sinica, 1967; spl. lectr. U.S. Dept. Agr., NRDD, 1968; vis. prof. U. Notre Dame, 1973-74; research advisor Nat. Sci. Council, Republic of China, 1974-76, hon. advisor, 1976—, spl. chair prof., 1980. Author: Applied Chemistry for Wastes Treatment and Water Purification, vol. 1, 1966, vol. II, 1975.; contbr. numerous articles to sci. jours.; editor: Progress in Hazardous Chems. Handling and Disposal, vol. 1, 1970, vol. II, 1971, vol. III, 1972, vol. IV, 1976. Recipient Talbert-Abrams award for water research, 1958; William-Hatfield award for pollution control, 1970; Buswell-Porges award for health sci. achievement, 1972; Research Adv. Service medal and plaque Nat. Sci. Council, Republic China, 1976. Fellow Royal Soc. Health, Am. Pub. Health Assn., Inst. Advanced Sanitation Research (pres.-elect 1981—); mem. Am. Chem. Soc., Nat. Soc. Profl. Engrs., Am. Soc. Photogrammetry, Ind. Acad. Sci., Sigma Xi. Clubs: Kiwanis, Toastmasters (named Disting. Toastmaster 1978). Developer economical high-altitude aerial method for discovery and evaluation water resources, a biochem. method for degradation cyanides; patentee low-energy oxygenation method, membrane separation of antibiotics, ion-exchange separation of organics, membrane concentration of antibiotics and related material, several methods for wastes and water treatment; condr. pollution survey along Bosphorus Strait. Home: 106 Drury Ln West Lafayette IN 47906 Office: Lilly Rd Lafayette IN 47902 *I believe in human dignity, responsibility, and creativity through the maximum effort and work by the individual. Also, I believe in God. Through Him I gain wisdom and strength in my study, research and work. With God, I have* *trust and faith in my fellow men. I pray that all men shall work toward the betterment of this world and peace on earth.*

HOWE, ROBERT WILSON, educator; b. Klamath Falls, Oreg., July 9, 1932; s. Fred Phillip and Adelaide Alice H.; m. Alma Ann Felton, Mar. 1955; children—Jeanine Adele, Jeffrey Philip. B.A., Willamette U., 1954; M.S., Oreg. State U., 1960, Ed.D., 1964. Tchr., counselor Arlington (Wash.) public schs., 1955-60; inst. Oreg. State U., 1961-63; asst. prof. Ohio State U., 1963-66, asso. prof., 1967-70, prof., 1970—, chmn. dept. sci. and math edn., 1969-77; dir. ERIC Clearinghouse, 1969—; cons. fed. agys., schs., state govts. Author, co author books; edit. bd.: Jour. Sci. Edn, 1970—; contbr. articles to profl. journs. Sec., bd. trustees Center Sci. and Industry, Columbus, Ohio. NSF fellow, 1959, 60, 61; EPA grantee, 1977—. Fellow Ohio Acad. Sci.; mem. Nat. Sci. Tchrs. Assn., Am. Ednl. Research Assn., Assn. Educators Tchg. of Sci., Phi Delta Kappa, others. Methodist. Home: 283 Weydon Rd Worthington OH 43085 Office: 1200 Chambers Rd Columbus OH 43212

HOWE, ROGER EVANS, mathematician, educator; b. Chgo., May 23, 1945; s. John Perry and Marilyn Leilani (Evans) H.; m. Carolyn Rutter Read, Sept. 9, 1967; children—Nicholas Read, Katherine Joanna. B.A., Harvard, 1966; Ph.D., U. Calif., Berkeley, 1969. Asst. prof. mathematics State U. N.Y., Stony Brook, 1969-72, asso. prof., 1972-74; vis. mem. Inst. for Advanced Study, Princeton, N.J., 1971-72; gastprofessor U. Bonn, W. Ger., 1973-74; prof. Yale U., New Haven, 1974—; vis. prof. Oxford (Eng.) U., 1978. Mem. Am. Math. Soc., Math. Assn. Am. Home: 21 Middle Rd Hamden CT 06517 Office: Dept Mathematics Yale U New Haven CT 06520

HOWE, STANLEY MERRILL, mfg. co. exec.; b. Muscatine, Iowa, Feb. 5, 1924; s. Merrill Y. and Thelma F. (Corriel) H.; m. Helen Jensen, Mar. 29, 1953; children—Thomas, Janet, Steven, James. B.S., Iowa State U., 1946; M.B.A. (Gerard Swope fellow), Harvard U., 1948. Production engr. HON Industries, Muscatine, Iowa, 1948-54, v.p. production, 1954-61, exec. v.p., 1961-64, pres., 1964—, also dir.; chmn. bd. Holga Metal Products Corp., Murphy-Miller Co., Corry Jamestown Corp.; pres. Norman Bates, Inc., Prime-Mover Co. Trustee Iowa Wesleyan Coll.; chmn. Muscatine Community Health Found. Mem. NAM, Iowa Mfrs. Assn., Am. Mgmt. Assn. Methodist. Clubs: Rotary, Elks, 33. Home: 1124 Oakland Dr Muscatine IA 52761 Office: 414 E 3d St Muscatine IA 52761

HOWE, WALLACE BRADY, state geologist; b. Lexington, Mo., Aug. 5, 1926; s. Clayton B. and Daisie D. (Simmons) H.; m. Lola Spenny, Aug. 24, 1948; 1 dau., Sally. B.A. in Geology, U. Mo., 1947, M.A., 1948; Ph.D., U. Kans., 1954. Field asst. Nat. Geophys. Co., Big Piney, Wyo., summer, 1946; field asst. Mo. Geol. Survey, summer, 1947; asst. instr. geology U. Mo., Columbia, 1947-48; asst. geologist Kans. Geol. Survey, summers, 1948-50; asst. instr. geology U. Kans., Lawrence, 1948-51; geologist Mo. Geol. Survey, 1951-60, sr. geologist, 1960-65, asst. state geologist, 1965-71, state geologist, 1971—; dir. and state geologist Mo. Div. Geology and Land Survey, Rolla, 1974—. Contbr. articles to profl. jours. Fellow Geol. Soc. Am.; mem. AAAS, Am. Assn. Petroleum Geologists (rep. N. Central Div. 1968-70), Am. Inst. Profl. Geologists (pres. Mo. 1960, mem. nat. standing com. 1970—, nat. exec. com. 1970), Assn. Mo. Geologists (pres. 1960), Mo. Acad. Sci. (pres. 1977-78), Sigma Xi. Democrat. Club: Rotary. Home: PO Box 565 Hwy 63N Rolla MO 65401 Office: PO Box 250 111 Fairgrounds Rd Rolla MO 65401

HOWE, WESLEY JACKSON, medical supplies executive; b. Jersey City, June 7, 1921; s. Wesley Veith and Phyllis (Jackson) H.; m. Suzanne Rodrock, July 20, 1946; children: Marc Edward, Richard Douglas, Suzanne. M.E., Stevens Inst. Tech., Hoboken, N.J., 1943, M.S., 1953. With Becton, Dickinson and Co., Rutherford, N.J., 1949—, group v.p., then exec. v.p., 1970-72, pres., chief exec. officer, dir., 1972-1980, chmn. bd., chief exec. officer, dir., 1980—, pres., 1983—; dir. First Nat. State Bank N.J., First Nat. State Bancorp. Bd. govs. Hackensack Hosp.; trustee Stevens Inst. Tech.; chmn. Found. of Coll. Medicine and Dentistry N.J. Served to 1st lt. AUS, 1944-46, 51-52. Mem. N.J. C. of C. (dir.), Health Industry Mfrs. Assn. (dir., founding chmn.). Clubs: Arcola (N.J.) Country, Upper Montclair (N.J.) Country; University (N.Y.C.). Office: Becton Dickinson and Co Mack Center Dr Paramus NJ 07652 *

HOWELL, ALFRED HUNT, former banker; b. Wyoming, Ohio, July 17, 1912; s. Alfred Corey and Florence Alice (Hunt) H.; m. Ruth Rea, Sept. 17, 1938; children: Ann Parkinson (Mrs. A. Joseph Armstrong), Alfred Hunt, Henry Parish. A.B., Princeton U., 1934; M.A., M.Phil., Columbia U., 1978. With Bethlehem Shipbldg. Corp., Quincy, Mass., 1934-37; with Citibank (formerly First Nat. City Bank), N.Y.C., 1937-72. V.p., pres. YMCA Greater N.Y., 1963-66, now dir. and trustee; trustee Nat. Council YMCAs; chmn. trustees, exec. com. YMCAs of N.Y. State; trustee Frick Collection; trustee emeritus, treas. Am. U. Beirut; trustee Am. Ctr. for Oriental Research, Amman, Jordan; bd. dirs. Near East Coll. Assn., Cleveland H. Dodge Found. Served with USNR, 1942-45; ETO, PTO. Decorated Order of Cedars, Lebanon; Recipient Order of Red Triangle YMCA Greater N.Y., 1966. Mem. Am. Oriental Soc., Medieval Acad. Am. Presbyn. Clubs: Grolier (pres. 1968-72), Century Assn. (N.Y.C.)). Home: 4602 Palisade Ave Riverdale Bronx NY 10471

HOWELL, ALMONTE CHARLES, JR., musicologist; b. Richmond, Va., May 2, 1925; s. Almonte Charles and Sara B. (Holmes) H.; m. Kathryn Norman, Apr. 30, 1954; children: Douglas, Elizabeth. A.B. with highest honors in Music, U. N.C., 1946, Ph.D. in Musicology, 1953; M.A. in English, Harvard U., 1947. Asst. prof. Southwestern at Memphis, 1954-56; from asst. prof. to prof. musicology U. Ky., 1956-67; research prof. U. Ga., Athens, 1967—; organist First Baptist Ch., Athens, 1974-79. Editor: Five French Baroque Organ Masses, 1961, Nine 17th Century Organ Transcriptions from the Operas of Lully, 1963, Seis Fugas para Órgano y Clave por D. Juan Sesse, 1976, Early Keyboard Jour.; Contbr.: articles, revs. to profl. jours. and Grove's Dictionary of Music and Musicians. Fulbright student grantee, 1950-51; research grantee, 1961-62; Folger Library fellow, 1953-54. Mem. Am. Musicol. Soc. (chmn. South Central chpt. 1964-65, 67-68, 76-77, 82-83), Music Library Assn., 16th Century Studies Soc., Ga. Conservancy, Ga. Bot. Soc., Phi Beta Kappa, Pi Kappa Lambda, Phi Mu Alpha Sinfonia. Democrat. Lutheran. Club: Athens Torch. Home: 280 Duncan Springs Rd Athens GA 30606 Office: School of Music Univ Ga Athens GA 30602

HOWELL, ALVIN HAROLD, engr.; b. Sedgwick, Kans., Feb. 5, 1908; s. George Alfred and Gertrude (Johnson) H.; m. Helen Whitney, Sept. 7, 1934; children—Elizabeth, Alvin Harold, John Arthur, Gordon Howard. B.S., U. Kans., 1929; student, Union Coll., Schenectady, 1929-30; M.S., Mich. Coll. Mining and Tech., 1934; Sc.D., Mass. Inst. Tech., 1938. Registered profl. engr., Mass. Test engr. Gen. Electric Co., Schenectady, 1929-30; instr. Mich. Coll. Mining and Tech., 1931-34, research geophys. prospecting methods, summers 1931-34; research asso. Mass. Inst. Tech., 1939-40; vis. prof., adminstrv. officer Radar Sch., 1942-43; asst. prof. elec. engring. Tufts U., 1940-41, asso. prof., head dept., 1941-43, prof., head dept., dir. research dept. elec. engring., 1943-70; prof., dir. Balloon Astronomy Lab., 1970—; devel. rocket and balloon type instrumentation; dir. Doble Engring. Co., 1960—, v.p., 1961-63, chmn. exec. com., 1969—, chmn. bd., 1979—; Mem. NRC; cons. on tethered and free floating balloon systems Air Force Geophysics Lab. Author: (with others) Principles of Radar, 1944; Contbr. articles to profl. publs. Recipient Exceptional Service award USAF, 1955; Distinguished Service award Tufts U., 1973; Tufts Service citation Tufts U. Alumni Assn., 1974. Mem. IEEE, Am. Phys. Soc., AAAS, AAUP, Sci. Ballooning Assn. (v.p. 1975-78), Am. Soc. Engring. Edn., Sigma Xi, Eta Kappa Nu, Tau Beta Pi. Baptist. Developer balloon-borne telescope for tracking planets and stars and balloon-borne payload for precisely pointing at ground targets to permit radiometric and interferometric measurements at IR wave lengths. Home: 990 Massachusetts Ave Arlington MA 02174 Office Tufts U Medford MA 02155

HOWELL, ARTHUR, lawyer; b. Atlanta, Aug. 24, 1918; s. Arthur and Katharine (Mitchell) H.; m. Caroline Sherman, June 14, 1941; children: Arthur, Caroline, Eleanor, Richard, Peter, James; m. Janet Kerr Franchot, Dec. 16, 1972. A.B., Princeton U., 1939; J.D., Harvard U., 1942; LL.D. (hon.), Oglethorpe U., 1972. Bar: Ga. 1942. Assoc. Alston & Bird (name changed to Bird & Howell, 1945, then to Jones, Bird & Howell, 1959), 1942-45, ptnr., 1945—; dir., gen. counsel Atlantic Steel Co.; v.p., dir. Creomulsion Co.; dir. Alpha Fund, Inc., J/S Tech., Inc., Watkins Associated Industries Inc.; past pres. Atlanta Legal Aid Soc. Pres. Met. Atlanta Community Services, 1956, dir., 1953—; pres. Community Planning Council, 1961-63; gen. chmn. United Appeal, 1955; spl. atty. gen. State Ga., 1948-55; spl. counsel Univ. System Ga., State Sch. Bldg. Authorities, 1951-70; adv. com. Ga. Corp. Code, 1967—; chmn. Atlanta Adv. Com. Parks.; Trustee Princeton, 1964-68, Atlanta Speech Sch.; trustee, past chmn. Oglethorpe U.; trustee Morehouse Coll., Westminster Schs., Atlanta, Episcopal High Sch., Alexandria, Va., Inst. Internat. Edn. (exec. com. 1969-72). Named hon. alumnus Ga. Inst. Tech. Fellow Am. Coll. Probate Counsel (chmn. com. on profl. standards, regent 1984—); mem. Am. Law Inst., Am., Ga., Atlanta bar assns., Lawyers Club of Atlanta (past pres.), Am. Judicature Soc., Soc. Colonial Wars, Phi Beta Kappa. Presbyn. (elder, trustee). Clubs: Capital City, Piedmont Driving, Commerce, Homosassa Fishing; Nassau (Princeton, N.J.); Princeton (N.Y.C.). Home: 33 Ivy Ridge Atlanta GA 30342 Office: 1200 C & S Bank Bldg Atlanta GA 30335

HOWELL, BENJAMIN FRANKLIN, JR., geophysicist, educator; b. Princeton, N.J., June 12, 1917; s. Benjamin Franklin and Claire M. (Mead) H.; m. Constance M. Benson, June 30, 1943; children: Barbara Carolyn, Catherine Ann (dec.), Bonnie Andrea, James Benjamin. A.B., Princeton U., 1939; M.S., Calif. Inst. Tech., 1942, Ph. D., 1949. Research engr. div. war research U. Calif. at San Diego, 1942-45; geophysicist United Geophys. Co., 1946-49; faculty Pa. State U., 1949—, prof. geophysics, 1953—, head dept. geophysics and geochemistry, 1949-63, asst. dean, 1968-70, asso. dean, 1970-82, dean emeritus, 1982—; Chief cons. seismologist Vibratech Engring. Co., Hazleton, Pa., 1955-69. Author: Introduction to Geophysics, 1959, Earth and Universe, 1972; Editor: Contributions in Geophysics in Honor of Beno Gutenberg, 1958. Fellow Am. Geophys. Union (sec. sect. tectonophysics 1956-59, sect. seismology 1959-63), Geol. Soc. Am.; mem. soc. Exploration Geophysics, Seismol. Soc. Am. (pres. 1963-64), Pa. Acad. Scis., Phi Beta Kappa, Sigma Xi. Baptist. Home: 1143 Smithfield Circle State College PA 16801 Office: 439 Deike Bldg University Park PA 16802

HOWELL, CHARLES MAITLAND, dermatologist; b. Thomasville, N.C., Apr. 14, 1914; s. Cyrus Maitl and Lilly Mae (Ammons) H.; m. Betty Jane Myers, Feb. 12, 1949; children—Elizabeth Myers, Pamela Jane. B.S., Wake Forest U., Winston-Salem, N.C., 1935; M.D., U. Pa., 1937. Intern Charity Hosp., New Orleans, 1937-38; resident in medicine Burlington County Hosp., Mt. Holley, N.J., 1938-39; sch. physician Lawrenceville (N.J.) Sch., 1939-42; resident in pathology N.C. Baptist Hosp., Winston-Salem, 1947-48; resident in dermatology Columbia-Presbyn. Med. Center, N.Y.C., 1948-50; resident in allergy Roosevelt Hosp., N.Y.C., 1950-51; practice medicine specializing in dermatology, Winston-Salem, 1951—; mem. staff N.C. Bapt., Forsyth Meml. hosps.; mem. faculty Bowman Gray Sch. Medicine, Wake Forest U., 1951—, prof. dermatology, 1967—, head sect., 1962—. Served as officer M.C. AUS, 1942-46. Fellow Am. Acad. Dermatology, Am. Acad. Allergy; mem. N. Am. Clin. Dermatol. Soc., N.Y. Acad. Scis. Democrat. Baptist. Clubs: Old Town (Winston-Salem); Bermuda Run Country (Clemmons, N.C.). Home: 1100 Kent Rd E Winston-Salem NC 27104 Office: Bowman Gray Med Sch Winston-Salem NC 27103

HOWELL, DONALD EDWARD, leasing company executive; b. Davenport, Iowa, Apr. 23, 1936; s. Willis Edward and Lucille J. (Tomas) H.; m. Phyllis Ann Campeau, May 31, 1957; children: Debora Ann, Diana Lynn. B.B.A., Western Mich. U., 1959. Mgr. br. office Assocs. Investment Co., Flint, Mich., 1939-64; regional mgr. J.I. Case Credit Corp., Denver, 1964-68; br. mgr. I.D.S. Leasing Corp., Atlanta, 1968-72; v.p. UHion Investment Co., Atlanta, 1972; pres. NCNB Leasing Corp., Charlotte, N.C., 1973—, dir., Charlotte, NCNB Fin. Services Corp. Mem. Am. Assn. Equipment Lessors (bd. dirs. 1981-84, exec. com.). Republican. Club: Athletic (Charlotte). Home: 11000 Dickie Ross Rd Matthews NC 28105 Office: NCNB Leasing Corp One NCNB Plaza Charlotte NC 28255

HOWELL, ELSWORTH SEAMAN, publisher; b. N.Y.C., Dec. 4, 1915; s. Clarence Seaman and Josephine Polhemus (Weller) H.; m. Elizabeth Roper, July 27, 1940; children—Jean Elizabeth Howell Salembier, Maureen Anne Howell Mawicke. Student, N.Y. U., 1935-36. Asst. editor Book of Knowledge, 1934-36; editor L'Encyclopedie de la Jeunesse, 1936- 37; mgr. mail order sales Grolier Soc., Inc., N.Y.C., 1939-46, v.p., 1947-59; pres., dir. Grolier Enterprises, Inc., N.Y.C., 1960-66, chmn. bd., 1967-68, House of Grolier Ltd., London, 1966-73; v.p. Grolier Internat., 1966-69, exec. v.p., 1969-73; pres., dir. Howell Book House, Inc., 1961—; dir. Grolier Ednl. Corp., Grolier Soc. Ltd., London, 1966-73; v.p., dir. Franklin Watts, Inc.; sec., dir. Americana Interstate Corp.; v.p., dir. Grolier, Inc., 1960-73, mem. exec. com., 1966-73; columnist Popular Dogs mag., 1955-66; editor Internat. Ency. of Dogs.; Pres. Allwood Homeowners Assn., Darien, Conn., 1963-65. Author: (with D.H. Tuck) The New Complete English Setter, 1964, 72, 82. Trustee Dog Writers Ednl. Trust. Recipient award Direct Mail Advt. Assn., 1954; Gaines' Dogdom's Man of Year award, 1970. Mem. English Setter Assn. Am. (v.p., past pres.), Dog Writers Assn. Am. Clubs: Wee Burn Country (Darien); Am. Kennel (N.Y.C.) (del., judge); Dog Fanciers (pres., dir.), Westminster Kennel, Ox Ridge Kennel (gov., v.p.), Publishers Lunch.). Home: 6 Tinywood Rd Darien CT 06820 also 111 E 56th St New York NY 10022 Office: 230 Park Ave New York NY 10169

HOWELL, EVERETTE IRL, educator; b. Shelby, Miss., Jan. 4, 1914; s. Thomas Daniel and Helen Lundy (Eason) H.; m. Beverly Ione McLaurin, June 12, 1943; children—Everette Irl, Marcia Marie, Beverly Jeannine. B.A., Miss. Coll., 1936; M.S., Vanderbilt U., 1937; Ph.D., U. N.C., 1940. Prof. phys. sci. Belhaven Coll., 1940-48; head dept. physics Miss. State U., 1948-79, prof., 1948-79, prof. emeritus, 1979—; summer teaching physics dept. Vanderbilt U., 1946, U. Fla., 1947; summer research participant Oak Ridge Nat. Lab., 1950, 51. Contbr. articles to sci. publs. Mem. Am. Inst. Physics, Am. Phys. Soc., Am. Assn. Physics Tchrs., Miss. Acad. Scis., Sigma Xi, Phi Kappa Phi. Presbyn. (elder). Address: Drawer 567 Mississippi State MS 39762

HOWELL, GEORGE BEDELL, diversified company executive; b. Schenectady, Sept. 19, 1919; s. Jesse M. and Grace (Gerhaeusser) H.; m. Mary Barbara Crohurst, July 10, 1944; children: Raymond Gary, Terry Barbara, Janice Patricia, Nancy Jo, George Bedell. B.S. in Adminstrv. Engring. (N.Y. State and Univ. scholar), Cornell U., 1942. With Gen. Electric Co., 1946-59; v.p. mfg. Leece Neville Co., Cleve., 1959-61, Royal Electric Co., Pawtucket, R.I., 1961-62; dir. operations packaging equipment and product devel. Acme Steel Co. (merged with Interlake Steel Corp. 1965), 1962-64; v.p. adminstrv. service Interlake Steel Corp., Chgo., 1964-66, v.p. internat. div., also v.p. Acme Products div., 1966-70; chief exec. officer dir. Golconda Corp., Chgo., 1970-72; v.p. devel. Internat. Minerals & Chems. Corp., 1972-73, sr. v.p., pres. industry group, 1974-77, exec. v.p., 1977-81; pres., chief exec. officer Wurlitzer Co., 1982—; dir. Structural Concepts Corp., Wurlitzer Co., First Nat. Bank of Oakbrook, Atcor, Inc. Trustee Village of Oak Brook, Ill., 1965-73, pres., 1973-79; trustee Christ Ch., Oak Brook. Served to maj. AUS, 1942-46; ETO. Mem. Nat. Piano Mfrs. Assn., Am. Music Congress (dir.), McGraw Wildlife Fedn. Clubs: Chicago Athletic, Medinah Country; Ocean Reef (Fla.). Home: 5 Brighton Ln Oak Brook IL 60521 Office: 403 E Gurler Rd De Kalb IL 60115

HOWELL, JAMES EDWIN, economist; b. Sterling, Colo., Mar. 6, 1928; s. James William, Jr. and Lois (Brown) H.; m. Linda Leinbach, 1965; children: Kenneth E., William J., Jan E., Caitlyn B. B.A., Fresno State Coll., 1950; M.A., U. Ill., 1951; Ph.D., Yale U., 1955. Instr. econs. and stats. Yale U., 1954-56; mem. staff Ford Found., 1956-58, 62, cons., 1958-72; Theodore J. Kreps prof. econs. Stanford U., 1958—, asso. dean Grad. Sch. Bus., 1965-70, dir. Exec. Program, 1975-79; dir. gen. Internat. Inst. Mgmt. and Adminstrn., Berlin, 1970-72; dir. SIAMP, France, 1979-81; sometime prof., lectr. U. Hawaii, U. Calif.-Berkeley; cons., U.S. and Europe. Author or co-author: Higher Education for Business, 1959, Mathematical Analysis for Business Decisions, 1971, European Economics-East and West, 1967. Served with AUS, 1946-47. Ford Found. faculty fellow Harvard U., 1959-60; NSF sr. postdoctoral fellow London Sch. Econs., 1963-64. Club: University (N.Y.C.). Home: 274 Atherton Ave Atherton CA 94025 Office: Grad Sch Bus Stanford U Stanford CA 94305

HOWELL, JAMES THEODORE, medical consultant, internist; b. Ironton, Ohio, Dec. 15, 1919; s. Leonard G. and Fay (Henry) H.; m. Sarah Lee Dunn, May 26, 1951; 1 dau., Mary Lee. A.B., Miami U., 1941; M.D., U. Cin., 1944. Diplomate: Am. Bd. Internal Medicine. Intern, resident Henry Ford Hosp., Detroit, 1944; practice medicine, 1944-65, specializing in internal medicine, 1945-65; chief 7th Med. Service, Henry Ford Hosp., Detroit, 1950-65, exec. dir., 1965-69; prin., nat. dir. health and med. affairs Peat Marwick Mitchell & Co., Washington, 1969-80; dir. planning Med. Center, Georgetown U., 1981—. Contbr. articles to profl. jours. Mem. med. bd. Care Medico, 1973-80; trustee Medic Alert Found., Holton Arms Sch., Florence Crittenton Home; founder mem. Cath. Health Corp., Health and Fitness, Inc. Fellow A.C.P., Am. Coll. Hosp. Adminstrs.; mem. Council Med. Adminstrn. (pres. 1958), Assn. Hosp. Dirs. Med. Edn., Assn. Am. Med. Colls., Soc. Med. Adminstrs., Omicron Delta Kappa, Beta Theta Pi, Nu Sigma Nu. Presbyn. (trustee). Address: 2500 Cathedral Ave Washington DC 20016

HOWELL, JOHN FLOYD, insurance company executive; b. Mt. Juliet, Tenn., Dec. 24, 1932; s. Robert Lee and Rachel Mae (Draper) H.; m. Margaret Ann Herring, Dec. 27, 1955; children: John Floyd, Leigh Ann, Stephen Donelson. Student, Vanderbilt U., 1951-53; B.A., U. Iowa, 1955, postgrad., 1955-56. Actuarial asst. Nat. Life & Accident Ins. Co., Nashville, 1963-64, asst. actuary, 1964-65, 2d v.p., 1965-71, v.p., 1971-81, sr. v.p., 1981—; also dir.; enrolled actuary Joint Bd. for Enrollment of Actuaries and U.S. Depts. Labor and Treasury, 1976. Mem. Metro Employee Benefit Bd., Nashville, 1976-81. Fellow Soc. Actuaries; mem. Am. Acad. Actuaries. Methodist. Club: Richland Country (Nashville). Home: 201 Hillwood Dr Nashville TN 37205 Office: Am Gen Ctr Nat Life & Accident Ins Co Nashville TN 37250

HOWELL, JOHN MCDADE, university chancellor, political science educator; b. Five Points, Ala., Jan. 28, 1922; s. John William and Bettie Mae (Lee) H.; m. Gladys Evelyn David, Aug. 9, 1952; children: David Noble, Joseph Lee. A.B., U. Ala., 1948, M.A., 1949; Ph.D., Duke U., 1954. Instr. U. Idaho, 1950; instr. Randolph-Macon Woman's Coll., Lynchburg, Va., 1951-52, Duke U., 1952-53; asst. prof. Sweet Briar Coll., Lynchburg, 1953-54, Memphis State U., 1954-57; assoc. prof. E. Carolina U., Greenville, N.C., 1957-61, prof., 1961—, chmn. polit. sci. dept., 1963-66, dean Coll. Arts and Scis., 1966-69, dean Grad. Sch., 1969-73, provost, 1973-77, vice chancellor for acad. affairs, 1977-79, chancellor, 1982—. Author: (with others) Conflict of International Obligations and State Interests, 1972; Contbr.: chpts. to The International Law Standard and Commonwealth Developments, 1966, De Lege Pactorum, 1970; articles to profl. jours. Served with USAAF, 1942-45. Decorated Bronze Star medal. Mem. Phi Beta Kappa, Phi Kappa Phi, Pi Sigma Alpha. Home: 605 E 5th St Greenville NC 27834

HOWELL, JOHN STEPHEN, lawyer; b. San Francisco, Sept. 4, 1917; s. George Alfred and Jane Elinor (McInerny) H.; m. Marjorie Roberts, 1960; children: John Stephen, George A., Jane M., David G., Lisa M. A.B., Stanford U., 1938; LL.B., 1941. Bar: Calif. bar 1941. Asst. dist. atty., San Francisco, 1945-47; partner law firm Sedgwick, Detert, et al, San Francisco, 1949—; prof. criminal law San Francisco Law Sch., 1947-49. Served with USNR, 1941-45. Mem. San Francisco Bar Assn. (dir. 1954-56), State Bar of Calif., Am. Coll. Trial Lawyers. Democrat. Roman Catholic. Club: Commonwealth of Calif. Home: 101 18th Ave Santa Cruz CA 95062 Office: 111 Pine St San Francisco CA 94111

HOWELL, KENNETH KENNEDY, lawyer; b. San Pedro, Calif., Dec. 30, 1931; s. Newton Price and Elaine (Kennedy) H.; m. Ann Glasscock, Apr. 7, 1961; 1 son, Kenneth K. Jr.; m. Gail Sager, Apr. 13, 1972; children: Adam K., Katherine K. B.A., 1956; J.D., U. Chgo., 1959. Bar: N.Y. 1960, Ala. 1961, Ill. 1964, Calif. 1971. Assoc. Sullivan & Cromwell, N.Y.C., 1959-61, Moore, Thomas, Taliaferro, Forman & Burr, Birmingham, Ala., 1961-63, Isham, Lincoln & Deale, Chgo., 1963-68; exec. dir. Legal Assistance Found., Chgo., 1968-76; ptnr. Sidley & Austin, Los Angeles, 1976—; assoc. prof. U. Ala., Birmingham, 1962-63, U. Chgo., 1970-71. Mem. Chgo. Counsel Lawyers (dir. 1972-76), Chgo. Bar Assn., Order of Coif. Home: 476 18th St Santa Monica CA 90402 Office: Sidley & Austin 2049 C[illegible]tury Park E Los Angeles CA 90067

HOWELL, PAUL NEILSON, oil company execu[illegible]
Miss., Sept. 13, 1918; s. Posey N. and Eva Meredi[illegible]
Evelyn Marie Edmiston, June 7, 1947; childre[illegible]
W., David L., Bradley N. B.S. in Chem. En[illegible]
Esso Standard Oil Co., Baton Rouge, L[illegible]
Lines, Inc., New Orleans, 1953-55, Ho[illegible]
1955-69; chmn., chief exec. officer [illegible]
chmn. Howel Petroleum Corp., [illegible]
Bank, Houston. Chmn. South[illegible]
Tex. Med. Ctr. Served to c[illegible]
Mem. Tex. Mil. Inst. ([illegible]
Petroleum Refiners A[illegible]
Nat. Petroleum C[illegible]

Ramada. Home: 3632 Inverness Dr Houston TX 77019 Office: Howell Corp 1010 Lamar Suite 1800 Houston TX 77002

HOWELL, RALPH RODNEY, pediatrician, educator; b. Concord, N.C., June 10, 1931; s. Fred Lee and Grace Mary (Blackwelder) H.; m. Sarah Vosburg Esselstyn, Nov. 19, 1960; children: Grace Meyer, Elizabeth Eriksson, John Esselstyn. B.S., Davidson Coll., 1957; M.D., Duke U., 1957. Intern Duke U., 1957-58, resident in pediatrics, 1958-59, research fellow in pediatrics and medicine, 1959-60; clin. asso. and staff NIH, Bethesda, Md., 1960-64; asso. prof. pediatrics Johns Hopkins U., Balt., 1964-72; pediatrician-in-chief Hermann Hosp., Houston, 1972—, chmn. med. bd., 1972—; David Park prof., chmn. dept. pediatrics U. Tex. Med. Sch., Houston, 1972—; cons. pediatrics M.D. Anderson Hosp. and Tumor Inst.; mem. metabolism study sect. NIH, 1973-77; mem. nat. clin. adv. com. Nat. Found. March of Dimes, 1973-79; nat. med. adv. bd. Muscular Dystrophy Assn.; chmn. maternal and child health adv. com. NIH, 1983—. Author: (with G.H. Thomas) Selected Screening Tests for Genetic Metabolic Diseases, 1973; contbr. articles to profl. jours. Served to sr. surgeon USPHS, 1960-64. Fellow Am. Acad. Pediatrics (com. on genetics); mem. Am. Pediatric Soc., Soc. Pediatric Research, Houston Pediatric Soc. (pres. 1978-79), AMA, Tex. Med. Assn., Soc. Inborn Errors of Metabolism (pres. 1981), Pi Kappa Alpha. Club: Meml. Forest (Houston). Home: 11 Sandalwood Houston TX 77024 Office: Dept Pediatrics U Tex Med Sch at Houston 6431 Fannin St Houston TX 77025

HOWELL, ROBERT JAMES, educator; b. Salt Lake City, Sept. 13, 1925; s. Elmer Virgil and Stella Myrtle (Knight) H.; m. Mary Winnie Raiford, Aug. 16, 1946; children—Carol Ann, Peggy Lynne, Robert Bruce. Student, Wash. State U., 1944; B.A., U. Utah, 1948, M.A., 1949, Ph.D., 1951. Instr. psychology Fresno State Coll., 1951-52; faculty Brigham Young U., Provo, Utah, 1952—, prof. psychology, 1960—, chmn. dept., 1961-68, dir. clin. tng., 1968—; sr. psychologist Utah State Hosp., 1958-60, cons., dir. psychol. tng., 1960-61; cons. Utah State Prison, 1961—; staff psychologist Patton State Hosp., 1965-66; research specialist Center for Tng. in Community Psychiatry, Los Angeles, 1968-69; adminstrv. dir. Timpanogos Mental Health Center, Provo, 1973-74; mem. Am. Bd. Forensic Psychology, 1980—, corr. sec., 1980-81, pres., 1981-82. Served with USAAF, 1943-46. Fellow Am. Psychol. Assn., Utah Psychol. Assn. (pres. 1963-64); mem. Rocky Mountain Psychol. Assn., Sigma Xi, Phi Kappa Phi, Psi Chi. Home: 2761 North Iroquois Dr Provo UT 84604

HOWELL, ROBERT WAYNE, agronomy educator; b. Houlka, Miss., Nov. 26, 1916; s. Raleigh Wayne and Frances Ethel (Stacy) H.; m. Elizabeth Virginia Blair, Sept. 25, 1940; children: Jacqueline Howell Choate, Richard James, Wayne Davis. Student, George Washington U., 1934-37; B.S., Miss. Coll., 1949; M.S., U. Wis., 1951, Ph.D., 1952. Clk., adminstrv. asst. U.S. Dept. Agr., Washington, Cheyenne, Wyo., Ithaca, N.Y., 1934-43; bus. mgr. Pineapple Research Inst., Hawaii, 1947; plant physiologist U.S. Regional Lab., Urbana, Ill., 1952-65; leader soybean investigations U.S. Dept. Agr., Beltsville, Md., 1965, chief oilseed and indsl. crops research br., 1966-71; prof. agronomy U. Ill., Urbana, 1971—, chmn. dept., 1971-82. Editor: Crop Science, 1969-71. Served to capt. AUS, 1943-46. Recipient award of merit Am. Soybean Assn., 1972. Fellow Am. Soc. Agronomy, AAAS; mem. Crop Sci. Soc. Am., Am. Soc. Plant Physiologists, Am. Soybean Assn. (hon. life), Sigma Chi. Home: 2012 S Cottage Grove Urbana IL 61801

HOWELL, ROGER, JR., educator; b. Balt., July 3, 1936; s. Roger and Katherine (Clifford) H.; children—Tracy Walker, Ian Christopher. Jr. A.B. summa cum laude, Bowdoin Coll., 1958; B.A. (Rhodes scholar), St. Johns Coll., Oxford (Eng.) U., 1960, M.A., D.Phil., 1964; LL.D., Nasson Coll., Colby Coll., 1970; L.H.D., U. Maine, 1971; Litt.D., Bowdoin Coll., 1978. Instr. history Johns Hopkins, 1960-61; research fellow, tutor final honour sch. modern history St. John's Coll., Oxford U., 1961-64, jr. dean arts of coll., 1962-64; tutor history and polit. theory Oxford U. Internat. Grad. Summer Sch., 1962-63, W.E.A. lectr. delegacy extramural studies, 1963-64; faculty Bowdoin Coll., 1964—, prof. history, 1968—, chmn. dept., 1967-68, 82—, acting dean coll., 1968-69, pres., 1969-78; Vis. prof. U. Maine, 1968-69, mem. higher edn. planning commn., 1969-72; pres. WCBB (Colby-Bates-Bowdoin Ednl. Telecasting Corp.), 1969-71, 75-77; mem. internat. adv. com. Univ. Coll. at Buckingham, 1974—; Chmn. Maine Savs. Bond Com., 1972-78. Author: Newcastle upon Tyne and the Puritan Revolution, 1967, Sir Philip Sidney: The Shepherd Knight, 1968, The Constitutional and Intellectual Origins of the English Revolution, 1975, Cromwell, 1977, Monopoly on the Tyne, 1978, also articles.; Editor: Prescott: The Conquest of Mexico, Etc, 1966, British Studies Monitor, 1969-81; adv. editor, 1982—; co-editor: Erasmus, 1976-81; editorial bd.: Maine Hist. Soc. Quar., 1982—. Bd. dirs. Allagash Group, 1970-73, Coast Heritage Trust, 1970-73; bd. govs. Inst. European Studies, 1974-77; trustee Waynflete Sch., Portland, Maine, 1969-78, Regional Meml. Hosp., Brunswick, 1970-78, North Yarmouth Acad., 1981-83, Campion Sch., Athens, 1983—. Recipient Outstanding Young Man of Year award Maine Jaycees, 1970, New Eng. Jaycees, 1970. Fellow Royal Anthrop. Inst. Gt. Britain and Ireland, Royal Hist. Soc.; mem. Hist. Assn. Gt. Britain, Am. Hist. Assn., Past and Present Soc., Econ. History Soc., Soc. Antiquaries Newcastle, Stubbs Soc. (Oxford U.), Scottish History Soc., Soc. d'Etude du XVIIe siecle, Maine Hist. Soc. (adv. com. 1980-82, trustee 1982—), List and Index Soc. Gt. Britain (council 1980—), New Eng. Hist. Assn. (exec. com. 1981-83), Conf. Brit. Studies (exec. com. 1967-69, 78—), New Eng. Conf. Brit. Studies (exec. sec. 1967-69, hon. pres. 1969-70), Anglo-Am. Assos. (exec. com.), Renaissance Soc. Am., Am. Assn. Advt. Agys. Ednl. Found. (chmn. acad. adv. com. 1970-78, trustee 1970-78), Phi Beta Kappa. Clubs: St. Botolph (Boston); Hamilton Street (Balt.); Cumberland (Portland); United Univ., Royal Commonwealth Soc. (London); London Scottish Rugby, Oxford Union; Century (N.Y.). Home: 16 Cleaveland St Brunswick ME 04011 Office: Dept History Bowdoin Coll Brunswick ME 04011

HOWELL, RUSSELL G., transportation equipment company executive; b. Windsor, Ont., Can., 1924; married. Student, U. Nebr., 1944; grad., U. Detroit, 1949. With Fruehauf Fin. Co., 1955—, chmn. bd., 1981—; exec. v.p. financing affairs Fruehauf Corp., Detroit, 1980—, dir., McLouth Steel Corp. Mem. Am. Trucking Assn. (nat. acctg. and fin. council). Office: Fruehauf Corp 10900 Harper Ave Box 238 Detroit MI 48232

HOWELL, SIDNEY CHARLES, manufacturing corporation executive; b. Elizabeth, N.J., Apr. 6, 1923; s. William Charles and Mabel Irene (Schmidt) H.; m. Aileen Read, June 9, 1945; 1 dau., Wendy. B.S., MIT, 1949; M.Indsl. Mgmt., NYU, 1956. With Weatherhead Co., Cleve., 1956-66, 69-78, v.p. sales, 1962-66, sr. v.p. ops., 1969-74, exec. v.p., 1975-76, pres., 1976-78, also dir.; v.p. automotive mktg. Cummins Engine Co., Columbus, Ind., 1966-69; group v.p. Dana Corp., Toledo, 1978-80, sr. v.p., 1980-81, exec. v.p., 1981—; dir. Blue Cross Northwestern Ohio. Mem. adv. bd. Case Western Res U., Cleve., 1977-82. Served to 1st lt. USAAF, 1943-45; ETO. Decorated D.F.C., Air medal; Teagle Found. scholar, 1946-49. Mem. Soc. Automotive Engrs., Ohio C. of C. Presbyterian. Clubs: Inverness Country; Belmont Country (Toledo). Office: Dana Corp PO [illegible]000 Toledo OH 43697

[illegible]EN HAVILAND, utility executive; b. Bethlehem, [illegible]hard and Marion (Mekeel) H.; m. Ann E. Adams, June 19, 1954; children—Cathy, Susan, David, Thomas. B.S.E., Princeton U., 1954; M.S. in Indsl. Mgmt. (Sloan fellow), M.I.T., 1966. Registered profl. engr., Mich. Exec. v.p. Consumers Power Co., Jackson, Mich., 1980—. Served with USNR, 1954-56. Mem. Soc. Petroleum Engrs., Am. Assn. Petroleum Geologists, Atomic Indsl. Forum. Republican. Presbyterian. Home: 3923 Harwich Ln Jackson MI 49201 Office: 212 W Michigan Ave Jackson MI 49201

HOWELL, THOMAS, history and political science educator; b. Houston, Jan. 20, 1944; s. John Thomas and Hazel (Hall) H.; m. Donna Jo Walker, Aug. 14, 1971; 1 dau., Catherine Jewel. B.A., La. Coll., 1964; M.A., La. State U., 1966, Ph.D., 1971. Instr. La. State U., 1967-68, La. Coll., Pineville, 1968-70, asst. prof., 1970-72, assoc. prof., 1972-77, prof., 1977, chmn. dept. history and polit. sci., 1975—. Mem. La. Elections Intergrity Commn., 1980—, vice chmn., 1981; coordinator La. Civitan Youth Citizenship Seminar, 1975-76; commr. Gulf Coast Athletic Conf., 1981—; mem. NAIA Nat. Eligibility Commn., 1983—. Mellon summer fellow, 1981. Mem. La. Hist. Assn., So. Hist. Assn., S.W. Assn. Pre-Law Advisers, Orgn. Am. Historians, So. Bapt. Hist. Assn., Alpha Chi, Omicron Delta Epsilon. Baptist. Home: 216 Myrtle St Pineville LA 71360 Office: Dept History La Coll Pineville LA 71360

HOWELL, WILBUR SAMUEL, former educator; b. Wayne, N.Y., Apr. 22, 1904; s. Wood Augustus and Edna (Hanmer) H.; m. Charlotte Coombe, June 26, 1928 (dec. April 5, 1956); 1 son, Samuel Coombe; m. Cecilia Jonkman van Eerden, June 27, 1962. A.B., Cornell U., 1924, M.A., 1928, Ph.D., 1931; postgrad., U. Paris, 1928-29. Instr. public speaking Iowa State Coll., 1924-25, Washington U., 1925-27, Cornell U., 1929-30, Harvard, 1930-33; asst. prof. Dartmouth, 1933-34, Princeton, 1934-40, asso. prof., 1940-55, prof. rhetoric and oratory, 1955-72, emeritus, 1972—, acting chmn. dept. English, 1947, clerk univ. faculty, 1958-68; sr. fellow Council Humanities, 1966; vis. prof. Stanford U., summer 1958, U. Mo., summer 1978. Author: The Rhetoric of Alcuin and Charlemagne, 1941, Problems and Styles of Communication, 1945, Fenelon's Dialogues on Eloquence, 1951, Logic and Rhetoric in England: 1500-1700, 1956, Eighteenth-Century British Logic and Rhetoric, 1971 (James A. Winans Book prize, Golden Anniversary Book prize Speech Communication Assn. 1972), Poetics, Rhetoric and Logic, 1975 (Golden Anniversary Book Prize 1976), also articles and reviews profl. jours.; Editor-in-chief: quar. jour. Speech, 1954-56; Asso. editor: Papers of Thomas Jefferson, 1973—; Contbr.: Ency. Brit. Foreman Mercer County (N.J.) Grand Jury, 1944; mem. Princeton Police Res., 1941-45; instr. A.S.T.P., 1943-45. Guggenheim fellow, 1948-49, 57-58; Huntington Library fellow, 1951-52, 62-63. Mem. Modern Lang. Assn., Speech Communication Assn., Renaissance Soc. Am., A.A.U.P., N.J. Edn. Assn. (parliamentarian 1938, 41), Phi Beta Kappa, Delta Sigma Rho, Pi Kappa Phi. Democrat. Episcopalian. Club: Nassau. Home: 20 Armour Rd Princeton NJ 08540 *Rhetoric has been my chief scholarly interest since my undergraduate days at Cornell. Why? Because of its central importance. In its full sense, rhetoric is the study and use of the persuasive factors inhering in the subject matter, the organization, the style, and the oral or written presentation of nonfictional verbal discourse.*

HOWELL, WILLIAM KENNETH, manufacturing executive; b. Radford, Va., May 22, 1930; s. Elbert Franklin and Hattie Lou (Holiday) H.; m. Barbara Williams, Sept. 5, 1953; children: Dean, Spencer. B.A. in Bus. Adminstrn., U. Richmond, 1953. With Philip Morris Co., 1955—; with C.A. Tabacalera Nacional (Venezuelan affiliate), to 1967; regional v.p. Philip Morris Internat., Latin Am., 1967; corp. v.p. Philip Morris Inc., 1975—; pres., dir. Miller Brewing Co. subs., Milw., 1972—, also chief operating officer; 1st exec. in residence U. Richmond; dir. First Wis. Nat. Bank, Milw. Bd. dirs. St. Mary's Hosp., Milw., Boys' Club Milw., Jr. Achievement Southeastern Wis.; mem. Greater Milw. Com.; mem. adv. council U. Wis., Milw. Sch. Bus. Adminstrn. Served with USMC, 1953-55. Clubs: Milw. Country, University, Wis., Johns Island. Office: 3939 W Highland Blvd Milwaukee WI 53201 *

HOWELL, WILLIAM R., retail executive; b. 1936. B.B.A., U. Okla., 1958. With J.C. Penney Co., Inc., 1958—, st. mgr., Tulsa, 1968, dist. mgr., Dallas, 1969; dir. Treasury stores, 1971, div. v.p., dir. domestic devel., 1974, regional v.p., western regional mgr., 1976, sr. v.p., dir. mdse., mktg. and catalog, 1980, exec. v.p., from 1981, chmn., chief exec. officer, 1983—. Office: JC Penney Co Inc 1301 Ave of Americas New York NY 10019 *

HOWELL, WILLIAM SMILEY, educator; b. Center Twp., Rock Co., Wis., Apr. 13, 1914; s. William Owen and Cora Del Myra (Smlley) H.; m. Jessie Irene Walker, Apr. 23, 1935; children—Mark William, Craig Walker. Student, Beloit Coll., 1931-32; B.S., U. Wis., 1935, M.A., 1938, Ph.D., 1942. Instr. Lake Geneva (Wis.) High Sch., 1935-37; instr. speech, dir. debate U. S.D., 1938-40; civilian ednl. cons. Tech. Tng. Command, USAAF, Truax Field, Madison, Wis., 1942-45; asst. prof., dir. forensics U. Minn., 1945-49, asso. prof., dir. forensics, 1949-54, prof., chmn. dept. speech and theater arts, 1954-59, prof., asso. chmn. dept. speech, theater arts, 1959-64, prof. speech communication, 1964—; vis. prof. U. Hawaii, 1967. Author: (with Winston Brembeck) Persuasion, A Means of Social Control, 1952, 2d edit., 1976, (with Donald K. Smith) Discussion, 1956, (with David W. Thompson and Donald K. Smith) Speech-Debate-Drama, 1968, (with others) Interpersonal Communication in the Modern Organization, 1969, (with Ernest G. Bormann) Presentational Speaking for Business and the Professions, 1971, (with others) Interpersonal Communication in the Organization, 1982, The Empathic Communicator, 1982. Mem. AAUP, Speech Communication Assn. (pres. 1971), Central States Speech Assn., Delta Sigma Rho, Phi Kappa Phi, Gown-in-Town. Club: Campus (Mpls.). Home: 2546 39th Ave S Minneapolis MN 55406 *A turning point in my life came when I discovered that one must say what needs to be said, rather than seek approval.*

HOWER, FRANK BEARD, JR., banker; b. Louisville, Nov. 26, 1928; s. Frank Beard and Katharine (Coffman) H.; m. Virginia W. Barker, Dec. 30, 1954; children: Frank Beard III, William. A.B., Centre Coll., Danville, Ky., 1950. With Liberty Nat. Bank, Louisville, 1950—, exec. v.p., 1967-71, pres., 1971—, chmn. bd., chief exec. officer, 1973—, also dir.; dir. Falls City Industries, Inc., Louisville, Louisville br. Fed. Res. Bank St. Louis, J.V. Reed Co., Louisville; chmn. NKC, Inc., 1983-84. Trustee Ky. Blue Cross Blue Shield, Churchill Downs; chmn. regional adv. bd. Comptroller of Currency, 1976; Mem. Ky. Registry of Election Finance, 1966-70, Ky. Econ. Progress Commn., 1964-70; vice chmn. Ky.-Tenn. Export Council; gen. chmn. United Appeal, 1969; chmn. Greater Louisville Fund for the Arts, 1976; v.p. Louisville Philharm. Orch., 1974-75; Bd. dirs. Louisville Norton Children's Hosp., Regional Airport Authority of Louisville and Jefferson County; chmn. Louisville Devel. Com.; bd. overseers U. Louisville; trustee, chmn. Ky. Ind. Coll. Found.; trustee Centre Coll. Served as 2d lt. USMCR, 1951-52; Korea. Mem. Am., Ky. bankers assns., Robert Morris Assos., Assn. Res. City Bankers, Louisville C. of C. (pres. 1973). Republican. Presbyn. Clubs: Louisville Country, Pendennis, Wynn-Stay, River Valley (Louisville). Home: 399-A Mockingbird Valley Rd Louisville KY 40207 Office: 416 W Jefferson St Louisville KY 40202

HOWERTON, HERMAN HUGH, real estate executive, lawyer; b. Tulsa, Oct. 10, 1943; s. Albert Hugh and Cora Marie (West) H.; m. Jane Lois Axenfield, Aug. 30, 1970; children: Michael, Kimberly. B.A. summa cum laude, Fresno State Coll., 1965; LL.B. cum laude, Harvard U., 1968. Bar: Calif. 1969. Asso. McCuthen, Doyle, Brown & Enersen, San Francisco, 1968-72; sec., counsel Itel Corp., San Francisco, 1972-78, v.p. legal affairs, sec., 1978-79, v.p., gen. counsel, sec., 1979-80, v.p., asst. to chmn., 1980-83, dir. various subs. Mem. ABA, Calif. Bar Assn., Am. Soc. Corp. Secs. Club: University (San Francisco). Office: 555 California St San Francisco CA 94104

HOWES, BARBARA, author; b. N.Y.C., May 1, 1914; d. Osborne and Mildred (Cox) H.; m. William Jay Smith, Oct. 1, 1947 (div. June 1965); children: David E., Gregory Jay. B.A., Bennington Coll., 1937. Editor: Chimera quar, N.Y.C., 1943-47; author: poetry The Undersea Farmer, 1948, In the Cold Country, 1954, Light and Dark, 1959, Looking up at Leaves, 1966, The Blue Garden, 1972, A Private Signal: Poems New and Selected, 1977, Moving, 1980; Editor: 23 Modern Stories, 1963, From the Green Antilles: writings of the Caribbean, 1966, The Sea-Green Horse: short stories for young people, (with G.J. Smith), 1970, The Eye of the Heart: Stories from Latin America, 1973 (Christopher award); author: short stories The Road Commissioner and Other Stories, 1980. Guggenheim fellow, 1955; recipient Brandeis U. Creative Arts poetry grant, 1958, Nat. Inst. Arts and Letters lit. award, 1971, Golden Rose award New Eng. Poetry Soc., 1973; Christopher award, 1974; Bennington award for outstanding contbns. to poetry, 1980. Home: Brook House North Pownal VT 05260 *Talent is essential, of course, for writing poetry; and this is God-given; but the other base from which any art springs is simply hard, steady work. If one sits around waiting for the lightning of inspiration to strike, it will almost surely strike across the way, where another poet is laboring.*

HOWES, BENJAMIN DURWARD, III, retail jeweler; b. Los Angeles, Oct. 31, 1922; s. Durward and Maxine (Eccleston) H.; m. Cynthia Marble, May 25, 1951; children: Cynthia Marble, Dana Belinda, Melisa Sanborn (dec.), Durward IV, Mary Devin, Daryl Brett, Briant Davidson. Student, Stanford U., 1941-42; B.S. in Bus. Adminstrn, U. So. Calif., 1943. With B.D. Howes & Son (retail jewelers), Palm Springs, Pasadena, Pebble Beach, Santa Barbara, Newport Beach,, Calif., also Hawaii, 1946—, pres., 1957—, chmn. bd., 1981—; founder, vice chmn., dir. Brookside Savs. & Loan, Pasadena.; Chmn. bd. jewelery Industry Council, 1970-71. Pres. Pasadena-Altadena Community Chest, 1960, 61; trustee, exec. com. Republican Assos. Served to lt. (j.g.) USNR, World War II. Recipient Disting. Service award as Outstanding Young Man in Pasadena U.S. Jaycees, 1957. Mem. World Bus. Council, Young Presidents Orgn. (chmn. San Gabriel 1964-65), Chief Execs. Orgn., Retail Jewelers Am. (pres. 1963-65), Calif. Retail Jewelers Assn. (pres. 1950), Calif. Jr. C. of C. (v.p. 1949), Pasadena Jr. C. of C. (pres. 1951-52), Pasadena C. of C. (v.p.), Los Angeles Area C. of C. (dir., v.p. 1971), Los Angeles Breakfast Panel (founder, past pres.), Pasadena Tournament Roses Assn., U. So. Calif. Alumni Assn. (bd. govs.), Alpha Delta Sigma, Kappa Alpha. Republican. Episcopalian. Clubs: Rotarian (Pasadena) (pres. 1967-68, dir. Home: 1145 Oak Grove Ave San Marino CA 91108 Office: 336 S Lake Ave Pasadena CA 91101

HOWES, THOMAS PRINCE, manufacturing executive; b. Boston, June 16, 1934; s. Richard O. and Anna G. (Haley) H.; m. Roxana, Nov. 24, 1960; children: Thomas Seth, Bradford Ted, Scott Christopher. B.A. in Econs., Harvard U., 1956; M.B.A. in Fin., Columbia U., 1960. Gen. mgr. N.Am. Telecommunications Group, ITT, N.Y.C., 1963-73; pres. Seatrain Shipbldg. Corp., Bklyn., 1973-74; pres., chief exec. officer Esterline Corp., Darien, Conn., 1974—; mem. adv. bd. Mfrs. Hanover Trust Co. Served to capt. Arty. USAR, 1956-58. Mem. Pres. Assn., Young Pres. Assn. Office: 1120 Post Rd Darien CT 06820

HOWITT, ROBERT MELCAEF, portfolio manager; b. Rochester, N.Y., Dec. 6, 1943; s. Henry Backus and Helen Louise (Graham) H.; m. Joan Carol Summerhays, Sept. 2, 1964; children: Wendy, Kari. B.S. in Econs., U. Pa., 1965. Chartered fin. analyst. Owner, operator Howitt Enterprises, N.J., 1969-72; security analyst 1st Hallgarten & Co., N.Y.C., 1972-74; gen. ptnr., portfolio mgr., analyst 1st Manhattan Co., N.Y.C., 1974—. Contbr. articles to profl. jours. Mem. Instnl. Investor All-Am. team in pub. and broadcasting, 1975-81. Mem. Printing and Pub. Analysts Group (pres. 1976-77), Entertaining Ananlysts Group, N.Y. Soc. Security Analysts. Libertarian. Home: 50 Smith Rd Denville NJ 07834

HOWKINS, JOHN BLAIR, mining company executive; b. Falkirk, Stirlingshire, Scotland, Feb. 12, 1932; emigrated to Can., 1965; s. George and Jemina Maclaren (Brown) H.; m. Heather Ferguson Nicoll, Jan. 8, 1955; children: Blair Nicoll, John Alexander, Cecilia Anne. B.S. with honors, U. Edinburgh (Scotland), 1953, Ph.D., 1961. Registered profl. engr., Ont. Sr. geologist Anglo Am. Corp., Central Africa, 1965; chief geologist Hudson Bay Mining and Smelting, Ont., Can., 1965-68, v.p. exploration, 1968-76, sr. v.p., 1978-82, exec. v.p., 1982—; pres. Inspiration Consol. Copper, N.J., 1976-78; chmn., pres. Black Pine Mining Co., Phoenix; adv. dir. First Interstate Bank of Ariz., Phoenix, Inspiration Consol. Copper Co., Terra Chems. Internat. Inc., Sioux City, Iowa. Mem. Canadian Inst. Mining and Metallurgy, Assn. Profl. Engrs. Ont., AIME, Geol. Assn. Can. Office: PO Box 28 Toronto Dominion Centre Toronto ON Canada M5K 1B8

HOWLAND, BETH, actress; b. Boston, May 28; m. Michael J. Pollard (div.); 1 dau., Holly. Stage appearances include A Tribute to Stephen Sondheim, Bye Bye Birdie, Twelfth Night, George M!, The Rainmaker, Any Wednesday, A Taste of Honey; regular on: TV series Alice, CBS-TV, 1976—; appeared in: TV spl. You Can't Take It With You; other TV appearances include Love Boat, Mary Tyler Moore Show, Little House on the Prairie, The Rookies, Cannon, Eight is Enough.

HOWLAND, MURRAY SHIPLEY, JR., physician; b. Syracuse, N.Y., June 5, 1911; s. Murray Shipley and Margaret Merrill (Granger) H.; m. Mary Thompson Glover, Sept. 13, 1941; children—Barbara Glover, Joan Granger, Sally Shipley. Grad., The Nichols Sch., 1929; A.B., Yale, 1933; M.D., Harvard, 1937. Intern Buffalo Gen. Hosp., 1937-38; resident in internal medicine, gastro-enterology, 1938-39; now attending physician; resident in internal medicine, gastro-enterology Lahey Clinic, Boston, 1940-41; practice medicine specializing in internal medicine, Buffalo, 1942—; clin. prof. State U. N.Y. Sch. Medicine, Buffalo, 1968—; a founder Buffalo Med. Group, now sr. partner. Trustee Buffalo Sem. Served to maj. M.C. AUS, 1941-46; ETO. Mem. A.C.P., Acad. Medicine, A.M.A., Erie County Med. Soc. (exec. com. 1966), Alpha Omega Alpha. Democrat. Episcopalian (vestryman). Clubs: Tennis and Squash, Canoe (Buffalo). Home: 55 Rankin Rd Snyder NY 14226 Office: 85 High St Buffalo NY 14203

HOWLAND, RICHARD HENRY, educator; b. Grand Rapids, Mich., Mar. 27, 1925; s. Henry James and Wilma (Rauser) H.; m. Marilyn Ruth Michaels, June 14, 1957; children: Carol Dawn, Michael Richard, Richard James, Mark Richard, Douglas Richard, John Richard. A.B., U. Mich., 1949, Ph.D., 1964; M.S., Simmons Coll., 1950. Distributive edn. tchr. and coordinator, Grand Rapids, 1950-55; assoc. prof., head mktg. dept. Ferris State Coll., Big Rapids, Mich., 1955-64; prof. mktg. dept. No. Ill. U., DeKalb, 1964—, former chmn. dept.; founder, pres. MAP Retail Computer Systems, Inc. Co-author: Principles of Marketing, 1961; author: Salesmanship, 1972,

Merchandising Analysis and Planning, 1979. Served with USAAF, World War II. Decorated Presdl. citation, Air medal with 6 oak leaf clusters; recipient award for teaching excellence Coll. Bus., No. Ill. U., 1977, 79, 80, 83. Mem. World Inst. Profl. Selling (founder, pres.), Am. Inst. Retailing (founder, pres.), Am., So., Southwestern mktg. assns., Sales-Mktg. Execs. Internat., Midwest Bus. Adminstrn. Assn., Mich. Pine Growers Assn., Delta Sigma Pi (Delta Sig educator-of-year award 1970), Beta Gamma Sigma, Pi Sigma Epsilon. Republican. Congregationalist. Club: Toastmaster (past pres. Grand Rapids). Home: 364 Rolfe Rd DeKalb IL 60115 *What we achieve in life is determined mainly by planning, perseverance, and being positive minded.*

HOWLAND, RICHARD HUBBARD, architectural historian; b. Providence, Aug. 23, 1910; S. Carl Badger and Cora Augusta (Hubbard) H. A.B., Brown U., 1931; also hon. doctor's degree; A.M., Harvard U., 1933; Ph.D., Johns Hopkins U., 1946. Fellow Agora excavations, Athens, Greece, 1936-38; instr. Wellesley Coll., 1939-42; chief pictorial records sect. OSS, 1943-44; organizer dept. history art Johns Hopkins, 1947, chmn. dept., 1947-56; pres. Nat. Trust for Historic Preservation, 1956-60; chmn. dept. civil history Smithsonian Instn., Washington, 1960-67, spl. asst. to sec., 1968—; Trustee Am. Sch. Classical Studies, Athens; founding mem. Am. Com. Internat. Commn. Historic Sites and Monuments. Author: (with Eleanor Spencer) Architecture of Baltimore, 1954, Greek Lamps and Their Survivals, 1958. Trustee L.A.W. Found., Sotterley Found., Irish Georgian Soc., Evergreen Found., Soc. Preservation of Greek Heritage, Heritage Found. R.I., Hist. House Assn. Am., Archaeol. Inst. Am. Fellow Royal Soc. of the Arts; Mem. Fellows in Am. Studies, Soc. Archtl. Historians (founding mem.), Soc. Cincinnati (hon.), Md. Soc. Colonial Wars, Victorian Soc. in Am. (nat. pres.), Phi Gamma Delta. Clubs: Century Assn., Knickerbocker (N.Y.C.); 14 West Hamilton Street (Balt.); 1925 F Street, Cosmos, Arts (Washington). Home: 1516 33d St Washington DC 20007 Office: Smithsonian Instn Washington DC 20560

HOWLAND, ROGER ALLAN, savs. and loan assn. exec.; b. Chgo., Nov. 20, 1934; s. Joseph Gerard and Evelyn (Cooper) H.; m. Joyce Ann Wachter, Aug. 26, 1961; children—Scott A., David A. B.S., U. Wis., Madison, 1959; postgrad., DePaul U. Internal auditor Fed. Res. Bank Chgo., 1959-61; with First Fed. Savs. & Loan Assn., Chgo., 1961—, acctg. mgr., 1967-71, treas., 1971—, v.p., 1975—; pres. Austin Investment Club, 1960-65, First Fed. Credit Union, 1968-71. Co-author: Hedging With Financial Futures, 1980. Pres. Libertyville (Ill.) High Sch. Caucus, 1974; mem. Winnetka (Ill.) Caucus, 1977. Served with USAR, 1957. Mem. Fin. Mgrs. Soc. Savs. and Loans (cert. merit 1980). Club: Monroe. Home: 818 Foxdale St Winnetka IL 60093 Office: PO Box 4444 Chicago IL 60680

HOWLAND, WILLIAM GOLDWIN CARRINGTON, chief justice; b. Toronto, Ont., Can., Mar. 7, 1915; s. Goldwin William and Margaret (Carrington) H.; m. Margaret Patricia Greene, Aug. 20, 1966. B.A., U. Toronto, 1936; LL.B., Osgoode Hall Law Sch., 1939; LL.D., Queen's U., 1972, U. Toronto, 1981. Bar: called to bar, Ont 1939. Read law with Rowell, Reid, Wright & McMillan, 1936-39; practice in, Toronto, 1939-75; asso. firm McMillan & Binch, 1936-75, partner, 1948-75; justice of appeal Ct. Appeal, Supreme Ct. Ontario, Toronto, 1975-77; chief justice Ont., 1977—; bencher Law Soc. Upper Can., 1960, 65, life bencher, 1969—, treas. (head), 1968-70. Author: Special Lectures, Law Society of Upper Canada, 1951, (with Marriott) Practice in Mortgage Actions in Ontario, 1960. Nat. pres. UN Assn. in Can., 1959-60; Bd. govs. Upper Can. Coll., 1968-70, 77—; mem. senate York U., 1968; adv. council Toronto Symphony; trustee Wycliffe Coll. Served to capt. Canadian Army, 1942-45. Mem. Canadian Bar Assn., Fedn. Law Socs. of Can. (pres. 1973-74), Canadian Inst. Internat. Affairs, Univ. Coll. Alumni Assn. (past pres.), Delta Upsilon, Phi Delta Phi. Anglican. Home: 2 Bayview Wood Toronto ON M4N 1R7 Canada Office: Osgoode Hall Queen St W Toronto ON M5H 2N5 Canada

HOWLAND, WILLIAM STAPLETON, educator, anesthesiologist; b. Savannah, Ga., July 21, 1919; s. William and May (Stapleton) H.; m. Miriam Adams, Feb. 14, 1974; children by previous marriage: Karen, William Stapleton. B.S., Notre Dame U., 1941; M.D., Columbia, 1944. Surg. intern Grady Hosp., Atlanta, 1944-45, asst. resident urology, 1945-46; asst. resident anesthesiology Presbyn. Hosp., N.Y.C., 1948-50, asst. anesthesiologist, 1950-52, asso. staff anesthesiologist, 1952-53; staff anesthesiologist, chmn. dept. anesthesiology Meml. Hosp., N.Y.C., 1953—, dep. chief med. officer, 1967-81, dep. gen. dir., 1974-81; asst. prof. anesthesiology Columbia, 1953; asso. prof. surgery Sloan Kettering div. Cornell U. Med. Coll., N.Y.C., 1954-55, head exptl. surgery, 1967—, asso. prof. surgery, 1955-68, prof. anesthesiology, 1968—, chmn. dept. anesthesiology, 1953-79, chmn. dept. critical care, 1979—, v.p. for clin. affairs, 1977-81; mem. Sloan-Kettering Inst., 1976—; mem. panel on blood and blood products Bur. Biologics, FDA, 1975—. Contbr. articles profl. jours. Served to capt. M.C. AUS, 1946-48; chief urology sect. 121st Gen. Hosp., 1946-48; Bremerhaven, Germany. Mem. Nat. bd. Med. Examiners, Meml. Hosp. Med. Bd. (pres. 1966, 67, 68-69), Am. Soc. Anesthesiologists, N.Y. State Soc. Anesthesiologists (v.p. 1958, pres. 1966), N.Y. Acad. Medicine, N.Y. Acad. Sci. Home: 345 E 68th St New York NY 10021

HOWLETT, CAROLYN CHANCE, association executive, civic worker; b. Millville, N.J., Aug. 28, 1915; d. R. Robinson and Carolyn Davidson (Abbott) Chance; m. Duncan Howlett, Apr. 26, 1943; children—Margaret (Mrs. Richard Spencer Hasty), Albert Duncan, Richard Chance, Carolyn Abbott (Mrs. Stephen Korth). Cert., Grad. Inst. Internat. Studies, Geneva, 1934; A.B. magna cum laude, Mt. Holyoke Coll., 1935; J.D., Yale U., 1938; D.H.L., Meadville/Lombard Theol. Soc. U. Chgo., 1983. Bar: N.J. bar 1939, N.Y. bar 1942. Atty. Kellogg & Chance, Jersey City, 1938-40, Hines Rearick Dorr & Hammond, N.Y.C., 1942-43; Bd. dirs. Barney Neighborhood House, Washington, 1965-69, Western Maine Counseling Service, 1975-77, treas., 1976-77; mem. Area V Mental Health Bd., Maine, 1976-77; treas. Lovell (Maine) Library, 1981—, pres., 1982—; bd. dirs. No. Cumberland Meml. Hosp., 1982—. Mem. LWV (dir. Boston chpt. 1953-57), Unitarian Universalist Women's Fedn. (dir. 1965-67, 2d v.p. 1967-69, treas. 1969-71), Unitarian Universalist Assn. (mem. com. study ch. and state relations 1965-68, social responsibility and investment 1969, com. appraisal 1973-77, del. to world congresses 1972, 75, 78, 81), Soc. Promoting Theol. Edn., Capital Area UN Assn. (dir. 1962-69, sec. 1964-69), Leadership Conf. Civil Rights (dir. 1967-69), Washington Urban League (5 Year Service award 1967), Council Nat. Orgns. for Adult Edn., Internat. Assn. Liberal Religious Women (pres. 1969-78), Internat. Assn. Religious Freedom (exec. com. 1972-81, chmn. nominating com. 1974-75, pres. 1978-81), Mt. Holyoke Coll. Alumnae Clubs (dir. Boston chpt. 1953-57, sec. Washington chpt. 1962-64, chmn. Maine leadership fund dr. 1975-78), Phi Beta Kappa. Home: Eastman Hill Rd RR1 Box 13 Center Lovell ME 04016

HOWLETT, CAROLYN SVRLUGA, art educator; b. Berwyn, Ill., Jan. 1914; d. John and Josephine (Blazina) Svrluga; m. James Howlett, July 15, 1939. Student, U. Chgo., 1933-36; B.Art Edn., Art Inst. Chgo., 1937, M.Art Edn., 1952; M.A., Northwestern U., 1953. Art instr. Oak Park (Ill.) Public Schs., 1934-37; art dir. Libertyville High Sch., 1937-43; instr. design, crafts, weaving, edn. Sch. of Art Inst., Chgo., 1935-43, head jr. sch., 1944-54, head art edn. dept., 1943-63, prof. art edn., 1955-70, prof. emeritus, 1970—, assoc. dean, 1963-65; ednl. cons. fine arts design, art edn., also artist free-lance designer and lectr., 1934—; lectr. Chgo. Council on Fgn. Relations, 1974-78. Exhibited: paintings and photographs Pan Am. and Internat. exhibits, Chgo. Hist. Soc., Art Inst. Chgo., Findlay Galleries, Chgo., Riverside Mus., N.Y.C., Mus. Sci. and Industry, Chgo., Press Club, others.; Author: Art Education Bibliography, 1959; author: tchrs. guide Orientation to the Visual Arts, 1966, Art in Craftmaking, 1974; Contbr.: articles on handicraft and basketry World Book Ency, 1945, 59; chpt. in Childcraft Ency, 1949; also articles in art publs. Tech. cons. arts and skills war program ARC, 1943-45. Mem. Nat. Art Edn. Assn. (Spl. Recognition award 1981), Ill. Art Edn. Assn. (pres. 1962, outstanding service award 1976, honor award 1981), Am. Fedn. Arts, Arts Club (profl. mem. Chgo.). Studio: 336 Coonley Rd Riverside IL 60546

HOWLETT, PHILIP GERAD, publishing executive; b. Cin., Mar. 3, 1928; s. Grayle Wallace and Ruth (Temmel) H.; m. Jean Ann Flowers, Sept. 22, 1949; children: Leslie Ann, Hilary, Peter Cameron, Grayle Hamilton, Philip Dougal. B.S., Northwestern U., 1950. Advt. and pub. relations div. Wilson Sporting Goods Co., Chgo., 1950-56; account exec. McCann, Erickson, Chgo., 1956-58; sales rep. Life mag., Chgo., 1958-65; mgr. Fortune mag., N.Y.C., 1965-70; European pub. dir. Time mag., London, 1970-74; advt. sales dir. Sports Illustrated, N.Y.C., 1974-80, pub., from 1980; now sr. v.p. mags. Time, Inc., N.Y.C. Author: (with Frank Sedgman) Winning Tennis, 1954, (with Paul Richards) Modern Baseball Strategy, 1955. Dir. Anglo-Am. C. of C., London, 1972-74. Served with C.E., AUS, 1946-47. Mem. Pilgrims U.S. Republican. Roman Catholic. Clubs: Winged Foot Golf (Mamaroneck, N.Y.); St. George's Hill Golf, Sunningdale Golf (London); N.Y. Athletic (N.Y.C.). Office: Time Inc Time-Life Bldg New York NY 10020 *

HOWORTH, LUCY SOMERVILLE, lawyer; b. Greenville, Miss., July 1, 1895; d. Robert and Nellie (Nugent) Somerville; m. Joseph Marion Howorth, Feb. 16, 1928. A.B., Randolph-Macon Woman's Coll., 1916; postgrad., Columbia U., 1918; J.D. summa cum laude, U. Miss., 1922. Bar: Miss. 1922, U.S. Supreme Ct. 1934. Asst. in psychology Randolph-Macon Woman's Coll., 1916-17; gauge insp. Allied Bur. Air Prodn., N.Y.C., 1918; indsl. research nat. bd. YMCA, 1919-20; gen. practice law Howorth & Howorth, Cleveland, Greenville and Jackson, Miss., 1922-34; U.S. commr. So. Jud. Dist. Miss., 1927-31; assoc. mem. Bd. Vet. Appeals, Washington, 1934-43; legis. atty. VA, 1943-49; v.p., dir. VA Employees Credit Union, 1937-49; assoc. gen. counsel War Claims Commn., 1949-52, dep. gen. counsel, 1952-53, gen. counsel, 1953-54; ptnr. James Somerville & Assocs. (overseas trade and devel.), 1954—; atty. Commn. on Govt. Security, 1956-57; pvt. law practice, Cleveland, Miss., 1958—; mem. nat. bd. cons. Women's Archives, Radcliffe Coll.; mem. lay adv. com. study profl. nursing Carnegie Corp. N.Y., 1947-48; chmn. Miss. State Bd. Law Examiners, 1924-28; mem. Miss. State Legislature, 1932-36, chmn. com. pub. lands, 1932-36; treas. Com. for Econ. Survey Miss., 1928-30; mem. Research Commn. Miss., 1930-34. Editor: Fed. Bar Assn. News, 1944; assoc. editor: Fed. Bar Assn. Jour., 1943-44; editor: (with William M. Cash) My Dear Nellie-Civil War Letters (William L. Nugent), 1977; contbr. articles profl. jours. Keynote speaker White House Conf. on Women in Postwar Policy Making, 1944, at conf. on opening 81st Congress. Recipient Alumnae Achievement award Randolph-Macon Woman's Coll., 1981, Lifetime Achievement award Schlesinger Library of Radcliffe Coll., 1983. Mem. AAUW (nat. dir., 2d v.p. 1951-55, mem. found. 1960-63), Nat. Fedn. Bus. and Profl. Women's Clubs (nat. dir.; rep. to internat. 1939, chmn. internat. conf. 1946), Nat. Assn. Women Lawyers, Miss. Library Assn. (life), Miss. Hist. Soc. (dir. 1982—, Merit award 1983), DAR, Daus. Am. Colonists, Am. Legion Aux. (past sec. Miss. dept.), Assembly Women's Orgns. for Nat. Security (chmn. 1951-52), Phi Beta Kappa, Pi Gamma Mu, Phi Alpha Delta, Alpha Omicron Pi, Delta Kappa Gamma, Omicron Delta Kappa. Democrat (del. nat. conv., 1932). Methodist. Club: Soroptimist (Washington). Address: 515 S Victoria Ave Cleveland MS 38732

HOWORTH, M. BECKETT, orthopedic surgeon; b. West Point, Miss.; s. Benjamin M. and Willie Capel (Beckett) H.; m. Marjorie Maye Meehan. B.S., U. Miss., 1921; M.D., Washington U., 1925; Med.Sci.D., Columbia U., 1933. Intern Presbyn. Hosp., N.Y.C., 1925-27, attending surgeon fracture service, 1933; resident N.Y. Orthopedic Hosp., 1927-29, asst. attending surgeon, 1934-51; asso. vis. orthopedic surgeon Bellevue, 1951-80; cons. orthopedist Vanderbilt Clinic, N.Y.C., 1931-49, Roosevelt Hosp., 1935-80; asso. clin. prof. orthopedic surgery Columbia Coll. Phys. and Surg., 1936-51, lectr. orthopedic phys. and occupational therapy, 1944-50, lectr. nursing edn., 1938-50; clin. prof. orthopedics N.Y. U. Postgrad. Med. Sch., 1951-80; clin. prof. orthopedic surgery U. Miss. Med. Center, Jackson, 1981—; lectr. orthopedic surgery Yale U., 1959-70; cons. orthopedic surgeon Greenwich (Conn.) Hosp., 1949-52, chief orthopedic dept., 1952-76; cons. orthopedic surgeon No. Westchester Hosp., Mt. Kisco, N.Y., 1949-63, Stamford (Conn.) Hosp., 1959-80, Newington (Conn.) Children's Hosp.; Mem. adv. bd. Assn. Aid Crippled Children, 1946-55, Rehab. Center, Stamford, Conn., 1950-70. Author: Textbook of Orthopedics, 1952, Examination and Diagnosis of the Spine and Extremities, 1962, Injuries of the Spine, 1964, (with Fred Bender) Tennis Elbow, 1977, How to Cure Your Own Backache, 1984; Contbr. numerous articles to med. and nursing jours., consumer research publs., also articles on mountaineering. Fellow A.C.S.; mem. Assn. Bone and Joint Surgeons, Pan Pacific Surg. Assn. (v.p. orthopedics 1963-66), Internat. Orthopedic Assn. (sec. 1960—), Am. Orthopedic Assn. (v.p. 1962, pres. 1963), Eastern Orthopedic Assn., Can. Orthopedic Assn., Swiss Orthopedic Assn., New Zealand Orthopedic Assn., Japanese Orthopedic Assn. (hon. mem.), Internat. Soc. Orthopedics and Traumatology, Orthopedic Corr. Club, A.A.A.S., Am. Assn. Phys. Anthropology, A.M.A., Orthopedic Research Soc., Am. Acad. Orthopedic Surgeons, Interurban Orthopedic Club (sec. 1940-81), N.Y. Acad. Medicine, New Zealand Orthopedic Assn. (corr.), Orthopaedic Corr. Club; hon. mem. Turkish, Western Pacific, La., New Eng., South African, orthopedic assns., Latin-Am., Chilean, Guatemalan socs. orthopedics and traumatology, Alpha Omega Alpha, Phi Rho Sigma. Methodist. Clubs: Rotarian., Am. Alpine (N.Y.C.); Appalachian Mountain (Boston); Alpine of Canada (Banff); Sierra (San Francisco); Rhino (South Africa); Spectators. Home: 254 Eastbrooke Jackson MS 39216 Office: Dept Orthopedics U Miss Med Center Jackson MS 39216

HOWREY, EDWARD F., lawyer; b. Waterloo, Iowa, Sept. 6, 1903; s. Benjamin J. and Ada C. (McStay) H.; m. Jane Pickett Gould, Nov. 10, 1933. A.B., U. Iowa, 1925; J.D. with honors, George Washington U., 1927; LL.D. (hon.), George Washington U., 1980. Bar: D.C., Iowa bars 1927, Va 1938. With U.S. Dept. Justice, 1927-29; asso. Sanders, Childs, Bobb & Wescott, Washington, 1929-37; partner successor firm Sanders, Gravelle, Whitlock & Howrey, 1937-53; chmn. FTC, 1953-55; practice law, Washington, 1955—; partner Howrey & Simon. Fellow Am. Coll. Trial Lawyers, Am. Bar Found.; mem. Am. Soc. Internat. Law, Internat. Bar Assn., Am. Judicature Soc., Acad. of Polit. Sci., English Speaking Union, Am. Bar Assn., Phi Kappa Psi, Phi Delta Phi, Order of Coif. Republican. Episcopalian. Clubs: Metropolitan, Chevy Chase (Washington); Fairfax Hunt; Middleburg Tennis (Va.). Home: St Brides Farm Upperville VA 22176 Office: 1730 Pennsylvania Ave NW Washington DC 20006

HOWSAM, ROBERT BASIL, educator; b. Tessier, Sask., Can., Aug. 28, 1916; came to U.S., 1956; s. Luther Frank and Elva Myrtle (Sutton) H.; m. Muriel May Ford, June 22, 1945; children—Patricia Ellen, Marilyn Rose, Robert Gary, William Alan. B.E. magna cum laude, U. Sask., 1948, M.Ed., 1950, LL.D., 1977; Ed.D., U. Calif. at Berkeley, 1956. Elementary sch. tchr., 1936-47; vice prin. Saskatoon pub. schs., 1940-47; lectr. U. Sask., 1949-50, part-time, 1948-49, 51-56, prin. univ. demonstration sch., 1951-56; asst., then asso. prof. ednl. adminstrn. U. Calif. at Berkeley, 1956-60; prof. ednl. adminstrn., asso. dean grad. studies Coll. Edn., U. Rochester, 1960-66; prof. ednl. adminstrn. U. Houston, 1966-81, prof. tchr. edn., 1981—, dean, 1966-79; chmn. commn. on edn. for profession of teaching Am. Assn. Colls. Tchr. Edn., 1974-76; speaker, lectr. on tchr. edn. and sch. adminstrn. Served with RCAF, 1941-45. Mem. Am. Assn. Sch. Adminstrs., NEA, Nat. Soc. Study Edn., Phi Delta Kappa, Phi Kappa Phi, Kappa Delta Pi. Developer competency-based and other innovations in tchr. edn

HOWSAM, ROBERT LEE, professional baseball executive; b. Denver, Feb. 28, 1918; s. Lee W. and Mary (Creley) H.; m. Janet Johnson, Sept. 15, 1939; children: Edwin, Robert Lee. Student, U. Colo., 1936-38. Gen. mgr., pres. Denver Bears Baseball Club, 1947-60; pres. Denver Broncos Football Club, 1960-61, Howsam-Brown, Inc., Denver, 1961-63; asst. v.p. Westamerica Securities Co., Denver, 1963-64; became gen. mgr., dir. St. Louis Nat. League Baseball Club, 1964; v.p., gen. mgr. Cin. Reds, Inc., 1967-73, pres., chief exec. officer, 1973-77, vice-chmn., 1978—; mem. Mayor Denver Exec. Sports Com.; past bd. dirs., v.p. Am. Assn., Denver, Old Timers Baseball Assn., Denver. Chmn. Gov. Colo. Conf. on Met. and Urban Problems; past chmn. Colo. Planning Commn.; vice chmn. Commn. for Higher Edn., Colo.; chmn. Denver and Colo. Crusade for Freedom, 1952-53; past asso. U. Denver; past dir., v.p. Denver area council Boy Scouts Am.; past mem. bd. mgmt. Denver YMCA. Served with USNR, 1941-46. Decorated Legion of Honor DeMolay, 1955; recipient Minor Leaguer Exec. of Year award Sporting News, 1951, 56, award Nat. Jewish Hosp., 1973; named one of Colo.'s five Outstanding Young Men Colo. Jr. C. of C., 1951; Denver's Young Man of Year Jr. C. of C., 1952; Gold Nugget award Nugget Boosters Club, 1954; named to Colo. Sports Hall Fame, 1971; Exec. of Year Atlanta Braves 400 Club, 1972; Cin. Ambassador award Cin. Conv. and Visitors Bur., 1973; Maj. League Exec. of Year award Sporting News, 1973; Distinguished Merit award Alpha Sigma Phi, 1974. Mem. Am. Legion (past post comdr.). Clubs: Mason (33 deg., shriner), Rotarian, Elk., Denver Press (life), Denver Country, Denver Athletic, Executive (past pres.), Pinehurst Country, Rolling Hills Country (first ann. Personality and Sports award 1956 Denver); Cincinnati, Hyde Park Country, Queen City (Cin.). Office: 100 Riverfront Stadium Cincinnati OH 45202 *

HOWSE, ERNEST MARSHALL, columnist, author, former clergyman; b. Twillingate, Nfld., Can., Sept. 29, 1902; s. Charles and Elfreda (Palmer) H.; m. Esther Lilian Black, Sept. 17, 1932; children: Margery (Mrs. Raymond Dyer), David C. Napier, George Arthur. Student, Meth. Coll., St. John's, Nfld., 1919-20, Albert Coll., Belleville, Ont., Can., 1924-25, Dalhousie U., Halifax, N.S., 1929; B.A., Pine Hill Div. Hall, Halifax, 1931; S.T.M., Union Sem., N.Y., 1932; Ph.D. in History, U. Edinburgh, Scotland, 1934; D.D., United Coll., Man., 1948, Laurentian U., 1964, Pine Hill Div. Hall, 1966, Victoria U., Toronto, Ont., 1967; D. Litt., Nfld. Meml. U., 1965. Ordained to ministry United Ch. Can., 1931; pastor Beverly Hills (Calif.) Presbyn. Ch., 1934-35, Westminister United Ch., Winnipeg, Man., 1935-48, Bloor Street United Ch., Toronto, 1948-70; free lance journalist, weekly columnist Toronto Star, 1970—; Participant, newspaper corr. 1st Assembly World Council Chs., Amsterdam, Holland, 1948, 2d Assembly, Evanston, Ill., 1954, 3d Assembly, New Delhi, 1961; press rep. 4th Assembly, Uppsala, Sweden, 1968, 5th Assembly, Nairobi, Kenya, 1974; del. 1st Muslim-Christian convocation, Bhamdoun, Lebanon, 1954; Christian co-pres. Continuing Com. on Muslim-Christian Cooperation, 1955-64; pres. Toronto conf. United Ch. Can., 1961-62; moderator United Ch. Can., 1964-66; mem. Exec. World Meth. Council; Canadian del. 1st World Conf. Religion and Peace, Japan, 1970. Author: Our Prophetic Heritage, 1945, The Law and the Prophets, 1947, Saints in Politics, 1952, 2d edit., 1960, 3d edit., 1971, Story of the English Bible, 1952, Spiritual Values in Shakespeare, 1955, paperback edit., 1964, The Lively Oracles, 1956, People and Provocations, 1965; Autobiography Roses, 1982; also weekly feature articles syndicated in Canadian newspapers, articles in mags. and other periodicals. People and Provocations. Named hon. citizen, Seoul, Korea, 1965; recipient Award of Merit with medallion City of Toronto, 1980. Mem. Internat. Meth. Hist. Soc. (v.p. 1966). Clubs: Empire (dir., hon. chaplain. Home: 31 Eastbourne Ave Toronto ON M5P 2E8 Canada Baysville Lake of Bays ON Canada

HOWSE, ROBERT DAVIS, business executive; b. Chgo., Apr. 15, 1908; s. Richard George and Editha (Davis) H.; m. Eloise Smith, 1931; 1 dau., Judith Ann (Mrs. Onthank). A.B., Yale, 1930. With Agfa Ansco Corp., Binghamton, N.Y., 1930-33, Literary Digest (Detroit office), 1933-37, Melvyn J. Evans Co., Chgo., 1937-40; pres. Argus, Inc., Ann Arbor, 1940-49, Electro-Phys. Labs., Inc., Stamford, Conn., 1950-52; exec. v.p. Waterman Pen Co., Inc., Seymour, Conn., 1952-54, pres., dir., 1954-59; v.p. Sterling Precision Corp., N.Y.C., 1959-62; exec. v.p. Edward Weck & Co., Inc., Long Island City, 1963-66, pres., 1966-72, vice chmn. bd., 1972-73; vice chmn. Chronogram Corp., Greenwich, Conn., 1973—; pres. E.P.L. Realty Co., 1973-82; pres., dir. E.P.L. Services, 1982—; dir. Interrad Corp., Stamford, 1974-77, SVP Communications, Inc., 1983—. Republican. Clubs: Yale (N.Y.C.); Greenwich Country. Home: 20 Church St Greenwich CT 06830 Office: 283 Greenwich Ave Greenwich CT 06830

HOWSER, RICHARD ALTON, baseball manager; b. Miami, Fla., May 14, 1937. B.S. in Edn, Fla. State U. Baseball player Kansas City Athletics, 1961-63, Cleve. Indians, 1963-66, N.Y. Yankees, 1967-68; mem. Am. League All-Star team, 1961, 63; coach N.Y. Yankees, 1969-78, mgr., 1980; baseball coach Fla. State U., Talahassee, 1979; mgr. Kansas City Royals, 1981—. Office: Kansas City Royals Harry S Truman Sports Complex PO Box 1969 Kansas City MO 64141 *

HOWZE, JOSEPH LAWSON EDWARD, bishop; b. Daphne, Ala., Aug. 30, 1923; s. Albert Otis and Helen Artamesa (Lawson) H. B.S., Ala. State U., 1948; postgrad. in bus. mgmt., Phillips Coll., Gulfport, Miss., 1980; LL.D. (hon.), U. Portland, 1974, St. Bonaventure U., 1977, Manhattan Coll., N.Y.C., 1979, H.H.D., Sacred Heart Coll., Belmont, N.Y., 1977. Ordained priest Roman Catholic Ch., 1959; pastor chs., Charlotte, Southern Pines, Durham, Sanford, Asheville, all N.C., 1959-72, aux. bishop of, Miss., 1972-73, bishop, 1973-77, bishop of, Biloxi, 1977—. Trustee Xavier U., New Orleans; mem. Miss. Health Care Commn.; mem. adminstrv. bd. NCCB/USCC; mem. edn. com. USCC, mem. social devel. and world peace com.; liaison com. to Nat. Office of Black Catholics, NCCB.; bd. dirs. Biloxi Regional Med. Ctr. Democrat. Clubs: K.C., Knights of St. Peter Claver. Home: PO Box 1189 Biloxi MS 39533 Office: PO Box 1189 Biloxi MS 39533

HOXIE, RALPH GORDON, author, educational administrator; b. Waterloo, Iowa, Mar. 18, 1919; s. Charles Ray and Ada May (Little) H.; m. Louise Lobitz, Dec. 23, 1953. B.A., U. No. Iowa, 1940; M.A., U. Wis., 1941; Ph.D., Columbia, 1950; LL.D., Chung-ang U., 1965; Litt.D., D'Youville Coll., 1966; grad., Air War Coll., 1971. Roberts fellow Columbia, 1946-47, Roberts travelling fellow, 1947-48, asst. to provost, 1948-49; asst. prof. history, gen. editor Social Sci. Found.;

asst. to chancellor U. Denver, 1950-53; project asso. Columbia Bicentennial History, 1953-54; dean Coll. Liberal Arts and Scis., L.I. U., 1954-55; acting dean C. W. Post Coll., 1954-55, dean, 1955-60, provost, 1960-62, pres., 1962-68; chancellor L.I. U., 1964-68, cons., 1968-69; pres. Center for Study of Presidency, 1969—; Pub. mem. Fgn. Service Officer Selection Bd., U.S. Dept. State; vis. lectr. U. Ala., U. Calif., Irvine, Columbia U., U. Colo., Colo. State U., U. Wyo., Chapman Coll., U. No. Colo., Colo. Coll., Naval War Coll., Nat. Archives, Nat. War Coll., Oglethorpe U., U. Tex. at El Paso, U. Wis., Northwestern U.; Bd. govs. La Banque Continentale br. Franklin Nat. Bank. Author: John W. Burgess, American Scholar, 1950, Command Decision and the Presidency, 1977, (with others) A History of The Faculty of Political Science, Columbia University, 1955, Organizing and Staffing the Presidency, 1980; Editor: Frontiers for Freedom, 1952, The White House: Organization and Operations, 1971, Presdl. Studies Quar, 1971—, The Presidency of the 1970's, 1973, The Presidency and Information Policy, 1981, The Presidency and National Security Policy, 1984; Contbg. author: Freedom and Authority in Our Time, 1953, The Coattailless Landslide, 1974, Power and the Presidency, 1976, Popular Images of American Presidents, 1984, Rating Game in American Politics, 1984, Speaking Out: An Oral History of the American Past, 1984; Contbr. articles to profl. jours. and encys. Bd. dirs. United Fund L.I., Bklyn. Inst. Arts and Scis., Tibetan Found., L.I. Council Alcoholism, Bklyn. chpt. A.R.C. Greater N.Y.; chmn., pres. bd. dirs. Am. Friends Chung-ang U.; pres. Pub. Mems. Assn. Fgn. Service; trustee Kosciuszko Found. N.Y., Mackinac Coll., North Shore chpt. Am. Assn. UN, Downtown Bklyn. Assn., Council Higher Ednl. Instns. N.Y.C.; mem. adv. bd. L. I. Air Res. Center; mem. adv. council Robert A. Taft Inst. Govt.; sec. Nassau County Commn. on Govt. Revision; co-chmn. Nassau-Suffolk Conf. Christians and Jews; dir., pres. Great-N.Y. Council Fgn. Students; bd. govs. Human Resources Center. Served from pvt. to capt. USAAF, 1942-46; brig. gen. USAF ret. Decorated Meritorious Service medal, Legion of Merit, numerous other medals; recipient Distinguished Service medal City N.Y., 1966; Paderewski Found. Man of Yr. award, 1966; Eloy Alfaro Internat. Found. Republic Panama Man of Year award, 1966; Alumni Achievement award U. No. Iowa; decorated Korean Cultural medal. Fellow Am. Studies Assn. Met. N.Y.; mem. Am. Hist. Assn., Internat. Assn. Univ. Pres., Am. Polit. Sci. Assn., Acad. of Polit. Sci., Navy League, Air Force Assn., Res. Officers Assn. (pres. Mitchel chpt.), V.F.W., Am. Legion, L.I. Assn. (dir.), Am. Polar Soc., Kappa Delta Pi, Pi Gamma Mu, Alpha Sigma Lambda, Delta Sigma Pi, Gamma Theta Upsilon. Republican. Episcopalian. Clubs: Century Assn., Met., Columbia Univ. Faculty House (N.Y.C.); Met. (Washington); Bklyn., Montauk (Bklyn.); Old Westbury Golf and Country and Mill River (hon.). Home: 10 Laurel Cove Rd Oyster Bay Cove NY 11771 Office: 208 E 75th St New York NY 10021 *Each day I seek to ask how I can better serve my fellowman. Assuredly, in so serving others, ours will be the richest of dividends and life takes on an ever-fuller meaning.*

HOY, CYRUS HENRY, educator; b. St. Marys, W.Va., Feb. 26, 1926; s. Albert Pierce and Marie Dorothy (West) H. B.A., U. Va., 1950, M.A., 1951, Ph.D., 1954. Instr. English U. Va., 1954-56; asst. prof. Vanderbilt U., 1956-60, asso. prof., 1960-64; prof. English U. Rochester, N.Y., 1964-76, John B. Trevor prof. English and Comparative lit., 1976—. Author: The Hyacinth Room, an Investigation into the Nature of Comedy, Tragedy, and Tragicomedy, 1964; author: intro., notes and commentaries to The Dramatic Works of Thomas Dekker, 4 vols, 1980; Mem. editorial bd.: Shakespeare Quar, 1968—, Medieval and Renaissance Drama, 1980—; Gen. editor: Regents Renaissance Drama Series, 1964-76; co-editor Dramatic Works in the Beaumont and Fletcher Canon, Vol. 1, 1966, Vol. 2, 1970, Vol. 3, 1976, Vol. 4, 1979, Vol. 5, 1982, Vol. 6, 1984; Contbr. articles to profl. jours. Fulbright scholar, 1952-53; Guggenheim fellow, 1962-63. Mem. MLA, Malone Soc., Shakespeare Assn. Am. Democrat. Presbyterian. Home: 70 Oliver St Rochester NY 14607 Office: Dept Engish U Rochester Rochester NY 14627

HOY, HARRY EUGENE, educator, geographer; b. Lincoln, Nebr., June 10, 1908; s. Ernest W. and Melissa Ann (Wells) H.; m. Eldora C. Larsen, Aug. 14, 1930; children: Don Roger, Douglas Stuart. B.S., U. Nebr., 1929, A.M., 1933, Ph.D., 1940. Instr. U. Ill., 1937-40; asso. prof. Eastern Mich. U., Ypsilanti, 1940-42, 43-45; cartographer OSS, Washington, 1942-43; field technician, explorer, Amazon Basin, Peru and Brazil, 1943; asst. prof. Western Res. U., Cleve., 1945-46; asso. prof. U. Okla., Norman, 1946-48, prof. geography, 1948—, chmn. dept., 1948-56, cons. prof. dept. biostatistics and epidemiology, Oklahoma City; Vis. prof. geography U. Leicester, Eng., 1970; Fulbright lectr. U. Cai, Egypt, 1961-62; geog. research, Costa Rica, El Salvador, summer 1965; research contractor Office Q.M. Gen., 1949-52; asso. dir. Office Naval Research Project, Boreal Fringe, Arctic, 1952-54. Co-author social studies series.; Contbr. articles to profl. jours. Fellow Okla. Acad. Sci.; mem. Am. Polar Soc., Assn. Am. Geographers, Am. Geog. Soc., S.W. Social Sci. Assn., Sigma Xi. Methodist. Clubs: Explorers (N.Y.C.); Lions. Home: 5300 Winding Oaks Ln Norman OK 73071

HOY, JOHN CRAVEN, public adminstr.; b. Yonkers, N.Y., Dec. 5, 1933; s. John Edward and Francis (Craven) H.; children—Jill A., John Craven, Jenifer T., Joshua Benjamin Craven, Elizabeth Breckenridge. B.A., Wesleyan U., 1955, M.A., 1960; postgrad., U. Chgo., 1959-62, U. Pa., 1963. Tchr. St. Louis Country Day Sch., 1955-56; asst. dir. admissions Wesleyan U., Middletown, Conn., 1956-59, asst. to pres., dean admissions, 1964-68, dean for spl. acad. affairs, 1968-69; vice chancellor student affairs U. Calif. at Irvine, 1969-75, vice chancellor univ. and student affairs, 1976-78; pres., exec. dir. New Eng. Bd. Higher Edn., Wenham, Mass., 1978—; dir. devel. Morgan Park Acad., Chgo., 1959-60; dir. admissions Lake Forest (Ill.) Coll., 1960-62; dean admissions Swarthmore (Pa.) Coll., 1962-64; Mem. selection com. for scholarships Nat. Merit Corp., Fansteel Corp., Sperry & Hutchinson Corp. Author: Choosing a College, 1967; editor: The Effective President, 1976, Higher Education and the Economy of New England, 1981; mem. editorial bd.: The Ednl. Record; contbg. author: Handbook of College Adminstration, 1970; contbr. articles to profl. jours. Trustee African scholarship program of Am. univs., Nat. Scholarship Service and Fund for Negro Students; mem. Mass. Youth Council. Mem. Assn. Coll. Admissions Counselors (chmn. editorial bd., v.p. exec. bd.). Home: Cape Deer Farm Pepperell MA Offfice: New Eng Bd Higher Edn 68 Walnut Rd Wenham MA 01984

HOY, MARY CAMILLA, French linguist, educator; b. Clinton, S.C., Jan. 3, 1925; d. William Edwin and Mabel Elizabeth (George) H. A.B. magna cum laude, U. S.C., 1943, M.A., 1944; postgrad., U. Paris, 1946-47; Ph.D., Bryn Mawr Coll., 1954. Instr. French and Spanish Sweet Briar Coll., 1948-50, St. Mary's Coll., Raleigh, N.C., 1952-59; asst. prof. French Birmingham So. Coll. (Ala.), 1959-61, assoc. prof., 1961-66; assoc. prof. French East Carolina U., 1966-67; prof. French and Spanish, chmn. dept. fgn. langs Greensboro Coll. (N.C.), 1967-83, chmn. div. humanities, 1982—. French Govt. fellow, 1946-47; fellow Bryn Mawr Coll., 1944-46. Mem. Am. Modern Lang. Assn., S. Atlantic Modern Lang. Assn., Am. Assn. Tchrs. French, Am. Assn. Tchrs. Spanish and Portuguese (sec. N.C. chpt. 1982—), AAUW (corp. del. Greensboro Coll.), Cousteau Soc., Phi Beta Kappa, Alpha Chi. Republican. Episcopalian. Home: 2906 W Cornwallis Dr Greensboro NC 27408 Office: Greensboro Coll Greensboro NC 27420 *I inherited good health, adaptability and intellectual curiosity. I was born in a region rich in opportunities for achievement and joyful living. I have lived in an era in which the success of women—at least of some of us—may be recognized. Many good companions, both family and friends, have looked to the future with me; we have worked together in faith and hope.*

HOY, WILLIAM IVAN, religion educator; b. Grottoes, Va., Aug. 21, 1915; s. William I. and Ileta (Root) H.; m. Wilma J. Lambert, Apr. 29, 1945; children: Doris Lambert, Martha Virginia. Student, Lees-McRae Coll., 1933-34; B.A., Hampden-Sydney Coll., 1936; B.D., Union Theol. Sem., 1942; S.T.M., Bibl. Sem. N.Y., 1949; Ph.D., U. Edinburgh, 1952. Tchr. high sch., Va., 1936-39; interim pastor Asheboro (N.C.) Presbyn. Ch., 1948, 52-53; asst. prof. Bible Guilford Coll., 1947-48; asst. prof. religion U. Miami, 1953-57, asso. prof., 1957-63, prof., 1963—, chmn. dept. religion, 1958-79; Moderator Presbytery of Everglades, 1960-61, stated clk., 1968-73, 78-79; pres. Greater Miami Ministerial Assn., 1964, 80-82. Co-author: History of the Chaplains Corps, USN, Vol. 6; author articles and book revs. in various publs. Adv. mem. bd. dirs. Greater Miami Council Chs., 1964; mem. bd. Christian edn. Presbyn. Ch. U.S., 1969-73; mem. Gen. Assembly Mission Bd., 1978—; bd. dirs. Met. Fellowship Chs., v.p., 1972-73, exec. sec., 1974-76; mem. Task Force on World Hunger, 1 978-80; trustee Davidson Coll., 1975—. Served from ensign to lt. comdr. USNR, 1942-45; comdr. Res. Decorated Purple Heart. Mem. Soc. Bibl. Lit., Am. Acad. Religion, Am. Soc. Ch. History, Studiorum Novi Testamenti Societas, Scottish Ch. History Soc., Soc. for Sci. Study Religion, Religious Research Assn., Am. Oriental Soc., Res. Officers Assn. (past nat. chaplain, nat. councilman 1965-66, pres. Fla. dept. 1965-66, v.p. for navy dept. Fla.), Iron Arrow, Phi Kappa Phi, Omicron Delta Kappa (province dep., mem. gen. council 1971-76, Distinguished Service Key 1976), Lambda Chi Alpha, Alpha Psi Omega, Theta Delta, Omega. Club: Rotary (Tiger Bay). Home: 5881 SW 52d Terr Miami FL 33155 Office: PO Box 248348 Coral Gables FL 33124 *Life is of uncertain duration. It is too precious to waste.*

HOYEM, ANDREW LEWISON, publisher; b. Sioux Falls, S.D., Dec. 1, 1935; s. Albert Gustav and Ellen Anne (Lewison) H.; m. Sally Cameron Heimann, June 24, 1961 (div. 1964); m. Judith Bordin, Dec. 31, 1970. B.A., Pomona Coll., 1957. Ptnr. Auerhahn Press, San Francisco, 1961-64; owner Andrew Hoyem Printer, San Francisco, 1965-66; ptnr. Grabhorn-Hoyem, San Francisco, 1966-73; owner Arion Press, San Francisco, 1973-79, pres., 1979—. Author: book of poetry Articles, 1969; artist: book illustrations Flatland, 1980; designer: Moby-Dick, 1979. Lt. (j.g.) USN, 1957-60. Clubs: Bohemian, Grolier. Office: Arion Press 566 Commercial St San Francisco CA 94111

HOYER, DAVID RALPH, oil company executive; b. Phila., Aug. 12, 1931; s. Ralph W. and Clara Barton (Patterson) H.; children: David, Ann, Richard. B.S., U. Del., 1953. Vice pres. refining Gulf Oil Co., Houston, 1972-75, v.p. supply and transp., 1975; pres. Warren Petroleum Co. div. Gulf Oil Corp., Tulsa, 1976-77, Gulf Oil Co.- Internat., London, 1977-82, Warren Petroleum div. Gulf Oil Corp., Tulsa, 1983—. Methodist. Office: Warren Petroleum Co PO Box 1589 Tulsa OK 74102

HOYER, HARVEY CONRAD, clergyman, retired college president; b. Clay Co., S.D., July 21, 1907; s. Gust and Johannah (Norder) H.; m. E. Margaret Larson, Sept. 3, 1930; children: Gustav Adolph, Helen JoAnn, Ruth, Marcus Conrad, Bernard Eric. Student, U. S.D., 1925-28; A.B., Augustana Coll., 1931, D.D., 1950; B.D., Augustana Theol. Sem., 1936. Ordained to ministry Luth. Ch., 1936; grad. sch. tchr., S.D., 1926-29; prin. Mission Hill Sch., S.D., 1931-32; pastor Central Luth. Ch., Madison, Wis., 1936-40, Calvary Luth. Ch., Chgo., 1940-42; pres. Ill. Conf. Luther League, 1938-42; v.p. Augustana Synod Luther League, 1947-49; exec. sec. Div. Am. Missions, Nat. Luth. Council, 1942-60; asso. exec. sec. div. home missions Nat. Council Chs. of Christ in U.S.A., 1960-64, asso. exec. sec. dept. for councils of chs., 1965-70; asso. exec. dir. Commn. Regional and Local Ecumenicism, 1970-72; pres. Luther Coll., Teaneck, N.J., 1974-75. Author, co-author: books, pamphlets, latest Go Into all the World, 1951, Ministering to People-on-the-move, 1952, Mission Fields U.S.A, 1956, Heritage and Horizons in Home Missions, 1960, Ecumenopolis-USA, 1971; also articles.; Editor: Am. Missions Together, 1946-60, Redeeming the Time, 1949, Christ for the Moving Millions, 1955, Adventuring in American Missions, 1955, Church Planning for Mission in Today's World, 1967, Ecumenopolis, U.S.A, 1971, Aging and the Response of Faith, 1981. Organizer Luth. Ch.'s ministry to temp. def. communities, 1942, Nat. Luth. Council's dept. chmn. for Christian approach to Jewish people, 1946, Christian Ministry to Nat. Parks, Nat. Council of Chs., 1957-60; Chmn. Price County (Wis.) Commn. on Aging, 1978; chmn. adv. com. Area Agy. on Aging, 1977-78; chmn. adv. com. to Wis. Bur. on Aging, 1978—; chmn. personnel and fin. Wis. Coalition on Aging Groups, pres., 1979—. Mem. Assn. Council Secs. (v.p. 1964-65, editor Jour.). Office: CM Star Route Box 180 Phillips WI 54555

HOYER, STENY HAMILTON, congressman; b. N.Y.C., June 14, 1939; s. Steen T. and Jean Baldwin (Slade) H.; m. Judith Elaine Pickett, June 17, 1961; children: Susan, Stefany, Anne. B.S., U. Md., 1963; LL.B, Georgetown U., 1966. Bar: Md. 1966. Exec. asst. to U.S. senator, 1962-66; mem. Haislip & Yewell, Marlow Heights, Md., 1966-69, Hoyer & Fannon, District Heights, Md., 1969-81; individual practice, 1981—; mem. Md. Senate from Prince George's County, 1966-78; chmn. Prince George's County del.; mem. fin., joint budget and audit coms., 1968, chmn. joint commn. on intergovtl. cooperation, 1971; pres. Senate, 1975; mem. 98th Congress from 5th Md. Dist., 1976. Mem. Md. Bd. Higher Edn., 1978-81, Balt. Council Fgn. Relations. Mem. U. Md. Alumni Assn. (trustee), Phi Sigma Alpha, Omicron Delta Kappa, Delta Theta Phi, Sigma Chi. Home: 6621 Lacona St Berkshire MD 20747 Office: Room 1513 Longworth House Office Bldg Washington DC 20515

HOYER, VINCENT EDGAR, ins. co. exec.; b. Metuchen, N.J., Dec. 13, 1924; s. Waldemar R. and Nellie (Miller) H.; m. Doris E. Sprague, Aug. 21, 1948; children—Gary Vincent, Dwight Waldemar, Gregg Wilbur, Mark David, Kevin Sprague, Elizabeth Ann. B.S. magna cum laude, Rider Coll., 1948. With N.J. Mfrs. Ins. Co., Trenton, 1948—, asst. treas., 1956-62, v.p., 1963-66, pres., dir., 1966—; pres., dir. N.J. Reins. Co., Trenton; dir. N.J. Nat. Bank, Trenton, N.J. Nat. Corp., Trenton. Bd. dirs. Mercer Med. Center, Trenton; trustee Rider Coll., Lawrenceville, N.J. Served to 1st lt. USAAF, World War II. Office: Sullivan Way CN00128 West Trenton NJ 08628

HOYME, CHAD EARL, packaging company executive; b. Sioux Falls, S.D., Nov. 6, 1933; s. Knute Odell and Martha (Johnson) H.; m. Carolyn Ella Robson, June 21, 1958; children: Christopher, Beth, Amy, Tod. B.S. in Bus. Adminstrn., U. S.D., 1956. Acctg. mgr. Cargill Inc., Mpls., 1956-63; chief acct. Northwest Paper Co., Cloquet, Minn., 1963-65; budget dir. Potlatch Corp., Lewiston, Idaho, 1965-67, corp. controller, 1968-72, gen. mgr. folding carton operations, 1972-75; owner Morris Floral Co., Minn., 1975-78; gen. mgr. Consol. Packaging Corp., Clinton, Miss., 1978-82, v.p. paper converting group, 1982—; dir. Cinema 360, Inc., 1982—, Consol. Packaging Flint, Inc., 1982—. Chmn. Lewiston Bd. Edn., 1970-72; pres. Morris C. of C., 1978; Mem. Republican State Central Com. Idaho, 1968-72. Served to 2d lt. AUS, 1956. Lutheran. Clubs: Elks, Rotary. Home: 102 Cedar Cove Clinton MS 39056 Office: Clinton Indsl Park Clinton MS 39056

HOYT, CLARK FREELAND, journalist; b. Providence, Nov. 20, 1942; s. Charles Freeland and Maude Leslie (King) H.; m. Jane Ann Hauser, Sept. 30, 1967 (div. Jan. 1978). A.B., Columbia U., 1964. Research asst. to U.S. Senator, Washington, 1964-66; reporter Lakeland (Fla.) Ledger, 1966-68; politics writer Detroit Free Press, 1968-70; Washington corr. Miami Herald, 1970-73; nat. corr. Knight Newspapers, Washington, 1973-75, news editor Washington bur., 1975-77; bus. editor Detroit Free Press, 1977-79, conv. editor, 1979-80, asst. to exec. editor, 1980-81; mng. editor Wichita (Kans.) Eagle-Beacon, 1981—. Recipient Pulitzer prize nat. reporting, 1973. Mem. Nat. Press Club (fin. sec., bd. govs. 1975), AP Mng. Editors Assn., Am. Soc. Newspaper Editors. Club: Wichita. Home: 102 W 17 St Wichita KS 67203 Office: PO Box 820 Wichita KS 67201

HOYT, DAVID LEMIRE, musician; b. Edmonton, Alta., Can., Mar. 14, 1951; s. Martin and Corinne Marie (Lemire) H.; m. Janet Marie Scott, June 3, 1978. B.Mus., U. Alta., 1973. Lectr. horn U. Alta., 1975—. Hornist, Can. Opera Co., 1973, Royal Winnipeg Ballet, Hamilton Philharm. Orch., 1974—; prin. hornist, Edmonton Symphony Orch. Home: 12452 52d Ave Edmonton AB T6H OP4 Canada Office: Univ Alta Edmonton AB Canada

HOYT, F(RANK) RUSSELL, association executive; b. Lowell, Mass., Dec. 7, 1916; s. Frank Russell and Ethel (Rivet) H.; m. Helen Elizabeth Tallmadge, Jan. 24, 1945; children: Alan James, Deborah Hoyt Eckert. B.A., Oberlin Coll., 1939; cert., Yale U. Bur. Hwy. Traffic, 1941. Accredited airport exec. Traffic safety engr. Mass. Safety Council, Boston, 1941-42; airport and airline mgr. Pan Am. Grace Air Lines, Quito, Ecuador, 1948-50, LaPaz, Bolivia, 1950-52, sr. ops. supt., Chile, 1952-56, asst. to chief pilot, Miami, Fla., 1956-59; exec. v.p. Am. Assn. Airport Execs., Washington, 1960—; mem. (cons.) White House Com. on Aviation Noise Abatement, Washington, 1960; mem. NASA adv. com. Washington and Calif. Aviation Safety Reporting System, 1979-83; cons. Transport Can., Ottawa. Editor, adviser: Jour. Airport Mgmt. Served with USAAF, 1941-45. Recipient Disting. Service Achievement award FAA, 1983, NASA, 1980. Mem. Am. Assn. Airport Execs. Clubs: Nat. Aviation, Aero (Washington). Home: 682 Azalea Dr Rockville MD 20850 Office: Am Asssn Airport Execs 2301 M St NW Washington DC 20037

HOYT, HENRY HAMILTON, pharm. co. exec.; b. N.Y.C., June 28, 1895; s. Frank A. and Susan (Gardiner) H.; m. Anna Orcutt, June 1925; children—Henry Hamilton, Charles O., Suzanne K. Litt.B., Princeton U., 1917. Partner A.D. Strauss & Co., 1925-30; with Carter-Wallace, Inc. (formerly Carter Products, Inc.), N.Y.C., 1930—, dir., 1930—, pres., now chmn. exec. com.; hon. dir. Bank of N.Y. Hon. trustee Hosp. Center at Orange, N.J. Served as capt., 2d Div. U.S. Army, 1917-19; AEF. Clubs: University, Union League (N.Y.C.); Baltusrol Golf (Springfield, N.J.); Oyster Harbors (Osterville, Mass.); Lyford Cay (Nassau, Bahamas). Home: 41 Lake Rd Short Hills NJ 07078 Office: 767 Fifth Ave New York NY 10022

HOYT, HENRY HAMILTON, JR., drug and toiletry co. exec.; b. Orange, N.J., Aug. 10, 1927; s. Henry Hamilton and Anna Clark (Orcutt) H.; m. Muriel Virginia Christie, Feb. 5, 1960. A.B. cum laude, Princeton U., 1949. With Carter-Wallace Inc., N.Y.C., 1950—, vice chmn. bd., 1973-74, chmn. bd., chief exec. officer, 1975—, also dir.; dir. Frank W. Horner Ltd., 1962-74. Trustee Princeton Elm Club, 1959—, Overlook Hosp. Found., Summit, N.J., 1976—; bd. dirs., treas. Arthritis Found. of N.J., 1967-78; bd. dirs. Deafness Research Found., 1977—; trustee Pingry Sch., Hillside, N.J., 1970-78, pres. bd., 1972—; mem. at large Council for Univ. Resources, Princeton U., 1972—. Served with Transp. Corps U.S. Army, 1946-47. Mem. Cosmetic, Toiletry and Fragrance Assn. (dir. 1965—, treas. 1966-76), Pharm. Mfrs. Assn. (dir. 1971-75), Proprietary Assn. (dir. 1970—). Episcopalian. Clubs: Univ., Met., Princeton of N.Y.; Baltusrol Golf (Springfield, N.J.); Oyster Harbors (Osterville, Mass.). Office: 767 Fifth Ave New York NY 10022

HOYT, HERBERT AUSTIN AIKINS, TV producer; b. Buffalo, N.Y., June 20, 1937; s. John Davidson Hill and Amie Dean (Aikins) H. B.A., Yale U., 1960. Reporter Niagara Falls Gazette, 1963-64; producer, exec. producer WGBH Ednl. Found., Boston, 1965—; producer The Advocates, 1969-74, Reagan's New Federalism: Shift or Shaft?, 1983. Exec. producer: Zoom, 1974-75, In Search of the Real America, 1975-78; producer: Enterprise, 1981, Vietnam: A TV History, 1981-82. Club: Yale (N.Y.C.). Home: 43 Linnaean St Cambridge MA 02138 Office: WGBH 125 Western Ave Boston MA 02134

HOYT, JOHN ARTHUR, humane society executive; b. Marietta, Ohio, Mar. 30, 1932; s. Claremont Earl and Margaret Adeline (Hawkins) H.; m. Gertrude Ellen Mohnkern, June 7, 1957; children: Margaret Rose, Karen Elizabeth, Anne Christine, Julie Kay. B.A., Rio Grande Coll., 1954; M.Div., Colgate Rochester Div. Sch., 1958; D.D., Rio Grande Coll., 1968. Ordained to ministry Baptist Ch., 1957; pastor Allen Park (Mich.) Bapt. Ch., 1958-60, First Presbyn. Ch., Leroy, N.Y., 1960-64; sr. minister Drayton Ave. Presbyn. Ch., Ferndale, Mich., 1964-68, First Presbyn. Ch., Fort Wayne, Ind., 1968-70; pres. Humane Soc. U.S., Washington, 1970—; lectr., guest various radio and TV programs. Contbr. articles to profl. jours. Trustee Rio Grande (Ohio) Coll., 1979—. Recipient Disting. Alumnus award Rio Grande Coll. Mem. World Soc. Protection Animals (council; v.p.) (London). Home: 14670 Seneca Rd Germantown MD 20874 Office: 2100 L St NW Washington DC 20037

HOYT, KENNETH BOYD, educator; b. Cherokee, Iowa, July 13, 1924; s. Paul Fuller and Mary Helen (Tinker) H.; m. Phyllis June Howland, May 25, 1946; children: Andrew Paul, Roger Alan, Elinore Jane. B.S., U. Md., 1948; M.A., George Washington U., 1950; Ph.D., U. Minn., 1954; Ed.D. (hon.), Crete Coll., 1981. Tchr., counselor Northeast (Md.) High Sch., 1948-49; dir. guidance Westminster (Md.) High Sch., 1949-50; teaching asst. U. Minn., 1950-51, instr. ednl. psychology, 1951-54; asst. prof. U. Iowa, Iowa City, 1954-57, assoc. prof., 1957-60, prof. edn., 1961-69; dir. Splty. Oriented Student Research Program, prof. edn. U. Md., Silver Spring, 1969-74; dir. office career edn. U.S. Office Edn., 1974—; Cons. Ordnance Civilian Personnel Agy., 1954-60, Iowa Dept. Pub. Instrn., 1954-69, U.S. Dept. Labor, 1956-68, 65—, U.S. Office Edn., 1958—, Nat. Inst. Edn., 1973—. Author: (with L.A. Van Dyke) The Drop-Out Problem in Iowa High Schools, 1958, (with C.P. Froehlich) Guidance Testing, 1960, Selecting Employees for Developmental Opportunites and Guidance Services; Suggested Policies for Iowa Schools, 1963, Career Education: Contributions to an Evolving Concept, 1976, Career Education: Where It Is and Where It Is Going, 1981; co-author: Career Education: What It Is and How To Do It, 1972, Career Education and the Elementary School Teacher, 1973, Career Education in the Middle Junior High School, 1973, Career Education for Gifted and Talented Students, 1974, Career Education in the High School, 1977; Editor: Counselor Education and Supervision, 1961-65; Mem. editorial bd.: Personnel and Guidance Jour, 1960-63; Contbr. articles to profl. jours. Served with AUS, 1943-46. Mem. Am. Personnel and Guidance Assn. (pres. 1966-67), Nat. Vocat. Guidance, Am. Vocational Assn. (Outstanding Service award 1972), Assn. Counselor Edn. and Supervision (Disting. Service award 1965), Nat. Vocat. Guidance Assn. (Eminent Career award 1981), Am. Sch. Counselors Assn., Am. Ednl. Research Assn., Am. Psychol. Assn., Phi

Delta Kappa. Home: 311 Colesville Manor Dr Silver Spring MD 20904

HOYT, LESTER HAROLD, pathologist; b. Scranton, Iowa, Sept. 28, 1911; s. Delmer L. and Clara J. (Allen) H.; m. Esther L. Harding, Oct. 9, 1938; children: Judy Anne (Mrs. Ronald Taylor), Mary Jane (Mrs. Steven May), Joseph Delmer, Lois Jean (Mrs. Richard Lewis). A.B., Simpson Coll., 1933; M.D., State U. Ia., 1937; postgrad., Wayne State U., 1940-41, Ind. U., 1965, U. S.C., 1956-57, Purdue U., 1966. Diplomate: Am. Bd. Pathology. Intern Meth. Hosp., Madison, Wis., 1937-38, resident in pathology, 1938-40, Ford Hosp., Detroit, 1940-41; patholgist Oakdale (Iowa) Sanitorium, 1942-43; practice medicine specializing in pathology, Indpls., 1943—; dir. labs. Meth. Hosp., Indpls., 1943-45, 56-76, dir. continuing med. edn., 1977-81, cons. for med. data processing, 1982—; asst. clin. prof. clin. pathology Ind. U. Sch. Medicine, 1952-76. Contbr. articles to profl. jours. Bd. dirs. Blue Cross Ind., 1959-78. Fellow Am. Soc. Clin. Pathologists (sec.-treas. 1960-66), Coll. Am. Pathologists (a founder); mem. AMA, Ind. Med. Assn. (del. 1952-65, treas. 1967-72), Marion County Med. Soc., Ind. Assn. Pathologists (past pres.), Soc. Computer Medicine, Am. Assn. Blood Banks, Ind. Assn. Blood Banks (founder), Community Blood Bank Marion County (founder, dir., past pres.), Am. Cancer Soc. (past com. chmn. Ind. div.), Am. Soc. Human Genetics, Soc. Nuclear Medicine, Acad. Internat. Medicine, Sigma Xi, Epsilon Sigma, Beta Beta Beta, Phi Chi. Mem. Christian Ch. (elder). Club: Mason. Home: 6502 Landborough S Dr Indianapolis IN 46220 Office: 1604 N Capitol Ave Indianapolis IN 46202

HOYT, MARY FINCH, author, editor, media consultant, former government official; b. Calif.; married; 2 sons. Former free-lance mag. writer, speechwriter; formerly with Ladies' Home Journal mag.; info. officer Peace Corps; pres. sec. to Mrs. Edmund Muskie, 1968, Mrs. George McGovern, 1972; former partner McClure, Schultz and Hoyt (pub. relations); press sec. to Mrs. Rosalynn Carter and East Wing coordinator The White House, Washington, 1977-81. Author: American Women of the Space Age, 1966, (with Eleanor McGovern) Uphill: A Personal Story, 1974. Mem. Presdl. Commn., 1977. Democrat.

HOYT, NELLY SCHARGO (MRS. N. DEMING HOYT), history educator; b. Nicolaev, Russia, Jan. 15, 1920; came to U.S., 1941, naturalized, 1946; d. Simon S. and Vera (Rivkind) Schargo; m. N. Deming Hoyt, Sept. 7, 1946; children: Susan, Victor. Bacc. es Lettres, Musee de l'Homme, 1939, certificate Anthropologie, 1940; B.A., Smith Coll., 1943; M.A., Columbia U., 1944, Ph.D., 1946. Research analyst U.S. Mission to UN, 1946-48; cons. research in comtemporary cultures Columbia U. Mus. Natural History, 1949-53; prof. dept. history Smith Coll., 1949—, Achilles prof. history, 1974—, chmn. dept., 1977-79, dir. Jr. Yr. in Geneva program, 1983-84; exchange prof. Hamburg U. Hist. Seminar, spring 1982. Editor: Smith Coll. Studies in History, 1961—; Author: (with T. Cassirer) Selections From Diderot's Encyclopedia, 1965, History in the Encyclopédie, 2d edit, 1970, Study of Culture at a Distance, 1950; Contbr.: articles to profl. jours. Study of Culture at a Distance. Bd. dirs. Alumnae Assn., chmn. assn. edn. com., 1972—; cons. Mus. Fine Arts, Springfield, Mass., 1979-80. Mem. Société du Dixhuitième Siècle. Home: 89 Maynard Rd Northampton MA 01060

HOYT, ROBERT JOSEPH, pharm. co. exec.; b. Utica, N.Y., Jan. 21, 1934; s. Joseph Andrew and Helen (Burns) H.; m. Joan Beverly Farrell, 1957; children—Michelle, Michael, Lisa, Robert. B.S. in Indsl. and Labor Relations, Cornell U., 1958. With Ross Labs., Columbus, Ohio, 1958-71, sr. v.p., 1968-71; dir. comml. devel. Latin Am. Abbott Internat., 1971-75; dir. mktg. Searle Labs., 1975-76; pres. Bio Products, Inc., N.Y.C., 1976-78; pres., chief operating officer Ketchum & Co., Inc., N.Y.C., 1978—. Served with AUS, 1954-56. Mem. Nat. Assn. Wholesale Druggists, Nat. Assn. Pharm. Mfrs., Cornell U. Class Council, Pi Kappa Alpha. Roman Catholic. Club: Cornell (N.Y.C.). Office: 16 E 40th St New York NY 10016

HOYT, WILLIAM VERNOR, computer, data processing co. exec.; b. Norwalk, Conn., Feb. 17, 1937; s. Fred Fisher and Lois Grace (MacNeil) H.; m. Nancy Plater Hale, Aug. 17, 1963; children—William, Edward, Walter. B.S., Newark Coll. Engring., 1963; M.B.A., Harvard, 1964. Financial analyst Mobil Oil Corp., N.Y.C., 1965-69; treas. Mobil Chem. Co., N.Y.C., 1969-70; dir. Office Fgn. Direct Investments, Commerce Dept., Washington, 1970-73; v.p. finance Marsh & McLennan Cos. Inc., Corp., N.Y.C., 1973-76; also dir.; asst. to the treas. IBM, Armonk, N.Y., 1976-77; dir. IBM retirement funds, 1977—; professorial lectr. Am. U., 1972. Walter C. Teagle fellow, 1962-64; George Baker scholar Harvard, 1963-64. Mem. Tau Beta Pi. Republican. Episcopalian. Club: Harvard (N.Y.C.). Home: Walnut Ln Staatsburg NY 12580 Office: Old Orchard Rd Armonk NY 10504

HRDLICKA, RICHARD FRANKLIN, mfg. co. exec.; b. Prague, Czechoslovakia, Apr. 3, 1932; came to U.S., 1948, naturalized, 1954; s. Josef and Beatrice (Ryant) H.; m. Carol Knott, Dec. 21, 1958; children—Carla Jayne, David Ryant. B.A., Friends U., Wichita, Kans., 1952; LL.B., Washburn U., Topeka, 1955. Bar: Kans. bar 1955. Partner firm Speir, Stroberg & Sizemore, Newton, 1962-68; county atty., Harvey County, Kans., 1960-64; corp. counsel Hesston Corp., Kans., 1972-75, v.p., gen. counsel, sec., 1972-75, sr. v.p., gen. counsel, sec., dir., 1975—; dir. Midland Nat. Bank, Newton. Trustee Friends U. Kans. Public Employees Retirement System; bd. govs. Washburn U. Law Sch.; past pres. bd. edn. Unified Sch. Dist. 373, Newton; past mem. select com. sch. efficiency Kans. Ho. and Senate. Served with AUS, 1955-57. Mem. Am. Bar Assn., Am. Judicature Soc., Am. Soc. Corp. Secs., Kans. Bar Assn., Central Kans. Bar Assn. (past pres.), Harvey County Bar Assn. (past pres.), Newton C. of C. (past dir.). Episcopalian. Clubs: Newton Country, Wichita Racquet, Wichita. Address: 420 W Lincoln Blvd Hesston KS 67062

HRDLICKA, RICHARD ROY, construction company executive; b. Akron, Ohio, Nov. 24, 1935; s. William Frank and Anna (Wagner) H.; m. Lillian Jean Kulich, Jan. 10, 1959; children: Ann Marie, Cheryl Ann, Scott. B.S. in Bus. Adminstrn, Kent (Ohio) State U., 1957. Acct. Saalfield Pub. Co., Akron, 1957-62; treas. John G. Rhulin Constrn. Co., Akron, 1962—; v.p. The Ruhlin Co.; dir. Ruhlin Devel. Co., Sharon Mfg. Co., Midwest Power Inc., Vector Constructors Inc. Mem. Nat. Assn. Accts., Am. Mgmt. Assn. Republican. Roman Catholic. Home: 3340 Barrett St Akron OH 44313 Office: 3 Cascade Plaza Akron OH 44318

HRISKEVICH, MICHAEL EDWARD, oil and gas consultant; b. Timmins, Ont., Can., Mar. 7, 1926; s. Elio and Antonina I. (Pashkevich) H.; m. Mary Ann Ban, May 10, 1947; children: Michael, Brian, Brenda, Shirley. B.S., Queens U., 1947, M.S., 1949; Ph.D., Princeton U., 1952. Registered profl. engr., Alta. Exploration mgr. Banff Oil Ltd., Calgary, Alta., 1965-69, tech. coordinator, 1969-71; exploration mgr. Aquitaine Co. of Can., Ltd., Calgary, 1971-76, v.p. exploration, 1976-80, sr. v.p. exploration, 1980-81; sr. v.p. corp. affairs and spl. projects Canterra Energy Ltd., Calgary, 1981-83, ret., 1983; oil and gas cons., 1983—. Contbr. articles to profl. jours. Segsworth scholar, 1943; Major Rattray scholar, 1947; Research Council Can. grantee, 1948-49. Mem. Can. Soc. Petroleum Geologists (pres. 1969), Am. Assn. Petroleum Geologists, Geol. Soc. Am., Assn. Profl. Engrs., Geologists and Geophysicists of Alta., Sigma Xi. Roman Catholic. Clubs: Glenco, Earl Grey Golf. Home: 4103 14 A St SW Calgary AB Canada T2T 3Y3

HRONES, JOHN ANTHONY, engineering educator; b. Boston, Sept 28, 1912; s. Emil and Olga Victoria (Cech) H.; m. Margaret Baylis, June 17, 1938; children: Janet H. Roach, Stephen Baylis, Mary H. Parsons, John Anthony. S.B., MIT, 1934, S.M., 1936, Sc.D., 1942. Asst. factory mgr. Coldwell Lawnmower Co., Newburgh, N.Y., 1937-39; asst. mech. engring. dept. MIT, 1934-36, instr., 1936-37, 39-41, asst. prof., 1941-45, asso. prof., 1945-48, prof. mech. engring., 1948, head machine design div., 1946, dir. Dynamic Analysis and Control Lab., 1950; v.p. acad. affairs Case Inst. Tech., Cleve., 1957-67, provost, 1964-67; provost sci. and tech. Case-Western Res. U., 1967-76, provost emeritus, prof. engring., 1976—; cons. automatic control and machine design, 1939—; chmn. Univ. Circle Research Center Corp., 1967-73; pres. ChiCorp., 1967-68, chmn., 1967-77; research adv. com. AID, 1978-82. Author: (with Nelson) Analysis of the Four Bar Linkage, 1951; contbr. articles to engring. publs. Bd. dirs. Cleve. Mus. Nat. History; trustee Asian Inst. Tech.; pres. A.I.T. Found. Mem. Newcomen Soc., ASME, Am. Soc. Engring. Edn., Am. Acad. Arts and Scis., Inst. for Def. Analyses (trustee), Nat. Acad. Engring., Sigma Xi, Tau Beta Pi, Pi Tau Sigma. Club: Cleveland Skating (trustee 1970-73). Home: 9397 Midnight Pass Rd Apt 306 Sarasota FL 33581 Office: Case Western Res U Cleveland OH 44106

HRUBY, FRANK M., musician, critic, educator; b. Emporia, Kans., June 29, 1918; s. Frank and Eva (Ptacek) H.; m. Pollee Menoher Phipps, May 10, 1945; children: F. Michael, George P., David A., Faith P., Mark S. B.Mus., U. Rochester, 1940, M.Mus., 1941. Head composition and theory dept. Miss. So. Coll., 1946-48; chmn. music and humanities dept. Univ. Sch., Shaker Heights, O., 1948-70, humanities faculty, 1970-75; music critic, columnist Cleve. Press, 1956-82; pres. Exec. Rewrite, 1983—; music cons. Ednl. Research Council, Cleve., 1965-66; mem. Music Critics Assn., 1956—, summer inst. faculty, 1972, 73, 83; dir. faculty Opera Inst., 1973, rec. sec., 1975-77. Mus. dir. Cain Park Summer mus. comedy prodns., Cleveland Heights, O., 1946-56; condn., Singer's Club Cleve., 1956-65; Contbr. to: Musical Am, 1956-60, 74—; Composer: String Quartet, 1953; plays-with-music for children Freddie and His Fiddle, 1952, Hiccupping Princess, 1953, Emperor's New Clothes, 1954, Clarinet Quartet, For the Birds, 1956. Served to lt. USNR, 1942-45. Mem. Music Educators Nat. Conf. Home: 2350 Beachwood Blvd Cleveland OH 44122

HRUBY, NORBERT JOSEPH, college president; b. Cicero, Ill., Feb. 4, 1918; s. Thomas John and Marie Frances (Rychtik) H.; m. Dolores Marie Smith, June 19, 1943; children: Michael G., Monica M., Patricia A. Ph.B., Loyola U., Chgo., 1939, M.A., 1941, Ph.D., 1951; postgrad. drama, Yale, 1946-47. Instr. English Loyola U., Chgo., 1947-48; asst. dean Coll. Commerce, 1948-51, dir. pub. info., 1951-55; dir. radio and TV U. Chgo., 1955-58; asso. dean Univ. Coll., 1958-62; v.p. Mundelein Coll., Chgo., 1962-69; pres. Aquinas Coll., Grand Rapids, Mich., 1969—; Ednl. cons., dir. coll. self-studies, 1966-70; cons. communications Am. Mut. Ins. Alliance, 1960-70; co-planner in founding Chgo. Ednl. TV Assn. channel WTTW, 1951-54; asso. dir. Court Theatre, Chgo., 1957-62; pub. relations cons. Forest Preserve Dist., Cook County, Ill., 1958-62; mem. Nat. Adv. Council on Adult Edn., 1973-75; examiner North Central Assn. Colls. and Secondary Schs., 1972—. Dir.: Faustus, 1957, The Cenci, 1958, Francesca da Rimini, 1959, Six Characters in Search of an Author, 1961; producer, dir., author radio and TV series, Loyola U., U. Chgo., 1951-58; Author: Survival Kit for Invisible Colleges, 1973, 2d edit., 1980; contbr.: chpts. to New Directions series. Officer Grand Rapids Area Council Chs.; pres. Grand Rapids Area Center for Ecumenism, 1972-74; Bd. dirs. Grand Rapids Symphony, Grand Rapids Civic Theatre, 1973-74, Greater Grand Rapids Housing Corp., 1971-74. Served to capt. AUS, 1942-46. Recipient 5 nat. awards for network and syndicated radio series prodns. U. Chgo., 1956-58. Mem. Assn. Cath. Colls. and Univs. (bd. dirs. 1971-80, chmn. 1976-78), Nat. Assn. Ind. Colls. and Univs. (bd. dirs. 1983—), Blue Key, Alpha Sigma Nu, Pi Gamma Mu. Roman Catholic. Home: 245 Briarwood Ave SE Grand Rapids MI 49506

HRUSKA, ALAN J., lawyer; b. N.Y.C., July 9, 1933. B.A., Yale U., 1955, LL.B., 1958. Bar: N.Y. 1959, U.S. Supreme Ct. 1970. Asso. firm Cravath, Swaine & Moore, N.Y.C., 1958-67, partner, 1968—; chmn. planning and program com. 2d Circuit Jud. Conf., 1974-80; co-chmn. 2d Circuit Commn. Reduction of Burdens and Costs in Civil Litigation, 1977—; commr. N.Y. State Exec. Adv. Commn. on Adminstrn. of Justice, 1981-83. Mem. Am. Coll. Trial Lawyers, ABA, N.Y. State Bar Assn., Assn. Bar City N.Y. (sec. 1965-66), Fed. Bar Council (trustee 1976—, pres. elect 1983—), Inst. Jud. Adminstrn. (trustee 1978—, pres. 1982). Office: Cravath Swaine & Moore One Chase Manhattan Plaza New York NY 10005

HRUSKA, ROMAN LEE, lawyer, retired senator; b. David City, Nebr., Aug. 16, 1904; s. Joseph C. and Caroline (Dvorak) H.; m. Victoria Kuncl, Sept. 24, 1930; children: Roman Lee, Quentin, Jana. Student, U. Omaha, 1923-25, U. Chgo. Law Sch., 1927-28; J.D., Creighton U., 1929; LL.D. (hon.), Creighton U., 1958, Doane Coll., 1963, H.H.D., Coe Coll., 1964, L.H.D., U. Nebr., 1977. Bar: Nebr. bar 1929. Practiced in, Omaha, county commr., Douglas County, Nebr., 1944-52; mem. 83d Congress from 2d Nebr. Dist.; U.S. senator from Nebr., 1954-76, practice law, Omaha, 1976—; Mem. adv. com. Nebr. Bd. Control, 1947-52; mem. Nat. Commn. Reform Fed. Criminal Laws, 1967-71; chmn. Nat. Commn. Revision Fed Ct. Appellate System, 1972—. Regent U. Omaha, 1950-57. Mem. Nat. Assn. County Ofcls. (v.p.), Nebr. Assn. County Ofcls. (pres.), ABA, Nebr., Omaha bar assns. Clubs: Masons, Shriners, Kiwanis. Home: 2139 S 38th St Omaha NE 68105 Office: Omaha Bldg 1650 Farnam St Omaha NE 68102

HRYCAK, PETER, mechanical engineer, educator; b. Przemysl, Poland, July 8, 1923; came to U.S., 1949, naturalized, 1956; s. Eugene and Ludmyla (Dobrzanska) H.; m. Rea Meta Limberg, June 13, 1949; children: Michael Paul, Orest W.T., Alexandra Martha. Student, U. Tubingen, Germany, 1946-48; B.S. with high distinction, U. Minn., 1954, M.S., 1955, Ph.D., 1960. Registered profl. engr., N.J. Instr. U. Minn., Mpls., 1955-60; mem. tech. staff Bell Telephone Labs., Murray Hill, N.J., 1960-65; sr. project engr. Curtiss-Wright Corp., Woodridge, N.J., 1965; assoc. prof. mech. engring. N.J. Inst. Tech., 1965-68, prof., 1968—. Contbr. articles to profl. jours. NASA grantee, 1967-68; NSF grantee, 1982-84. Sr. mem. Inst. Environ. Scis.; mem. ASME, AIAA, Am. Soc. Engring. Edn., Ukrainian Engrs. Soc. Am. (pres. 1966-67), N.Y. Acad. Scis., Am. Geophys. Union, AAUP, Shevchenko Sci. Soc., Ukrainian Acad. Arts and Scis. in U.S.A., Pi Tau Sigma, Tau Beta Pi, Sigma Xi. Home: 19 Roselle Ave Cranford NJ 07016 Office: 323 Martin Luther King Blvd Newark NJ 07102 *Looking back over my professional career, it seems to me that there is no substitute for interest in, and curiosity for, new developments, and hard work to generate new ideas and to update oneself in the rapidly shifting environment of today. First comes, however, one's responsiblity to maintain one's body in good mental and physical health. This may be achieved through a life filled with physical activities and hobbies, but also through an ability to "take it easy" at times, to recover from life's strain and to contemplate. All that should be filled with feelings for social justice and awareness of one's social responsibility which, in itself, may temper and blunt the inevitable desires, conflicts, and frustrations of the highly competitive modern life. Last but not least is perhaps the ability to laugh at oneself and be able to see both sides of the story.*

HSI, DAVID CHING HENG, plant pathologist and geneticist, educator; b. Shanghai, China, May 17, 1928; came to U.S., 1948, naturalized, 1961; s. Yulin and Sue Jean (King) H.; m. Kathy S.W. Chiang, 1952; children: Andrew C., Steven D. B.S. in Agr, St. John's U., Shanghai, 1948; M.S., U. Ga., Athens, 1949; Ph.D. (grad. teaching asst. 1950), U. Minn., St. Paul, 1951. Postdoctoral fellow U.S. Cotton Field Sta., Sacaton, Ariz., 1951-52; mem. faculty N.Mex. State U., Las Cruces, 1952—, prof. plant pathology and genetics, 1968—; cons. AID, Pakistan, 1970; tech. exchange, People's Republic China, 1978, Republic China, 1979, 81, 82, Brazil and Argentina, 1980, South Africa, 1981, Australia, 1983, S. Africa, 1981; judge sr. botany N.Mex. Sci. and Engring. Fair, 1979, 80, 81, 83. Author research papers in field. Past bd. dirs., treas. Carver Pub. Library, Clovis, N.Mex.; elder, worship com. chmn., adult edn. com. chmn. First United Presbyn. Ch., Albuquerque, 1981, 82; mem. nat. adv. council discipleship and worship Gen. Assembly United Presbyn. Ch. U.S.A., 1978-81, mem. nat. theol. reflections working group, 1980-81; mem. bd. edn. Albuquerque Pub. Schs., 1982, sec. bd. edn., 1983, v.p., 1984; bd. dir. Middle Rio Grande Council Govts. Recipient Disting. Research award Coll. Agr. and Home Econs., N.Mex. State U., 1971. Fellow AAAS (hon.); mem. Internat. Soc. Plant Pathology, Am. Phytopath. Soc. (judge Internat. Sci. and Engring. Fair 1983), Nat. Sweet Potato Collaborators Group (chmn. sprout prodn. and root piece propagation com. 1982-84), Nat. Geog. Soc., Am. Peanut Research and Edn. Soc. (chmn. site selection com. 1981, award com., pres.-elect 1981, pres. 1981, 82), N.Mex. Acad. Sci. (chmn. membership com. 1980, pres. 1981, 82), N.Y. Acad. Sci., N.Mex. Chinese Assn. (pres. 1983-84), Sigma Xi (life). Club: Kiwanis Internat. (past pres. Clovis, past chmn. spl. program com. Albuquerque). Co-developer new crop cultivars. Home: 1611 Ridgecrest Dr SE Albuquerque NM 87108 Office: NMSU Agr Sci Ctr 1036 Miller St SW Los Lunas NM 87031 *In grateful appreciation of my God-given talents and opportunities, my privileged academic trainings in China and U.S.A., and my professional experience and associations with world-wide scientists, I shall continue to contribute to the scientific advancement and practice, and to promote human understanding and international cooperation for the betterment of mankind and for the glorification of my Creator.*

HSIAO, MU-YUE, computer company engineer; b. Hunan, China, July 17, 1933; came to U.S., 1958, naturalized, 1969; s. Li-Wu and Zen-Ching H.; m. Mona Y-chuan Shao, Sept. 1, 1962; children: Rita, Wendy, Eric. B.S., Taiwan U., 1956; M.S., U. Ill., 1946; Ph.D., U. Fla., 1967. Teaching asst. Taiwan U., 1958; jr., asso. and sr. asso. engr. IBM, 1960-65; teaching asso. U. Fla., 1965-67; adv. engr. IBM, 1967, sr. engr., 1969-79; sr. tech. staff, mgr. Poughkeepsie (N.Y.) Lab., 1979—. Author: Principles of Electronic Digital Computers, 1964, Error Detecting Logic for Digital Computers, 1968; contbr. articles to research jours. Served with Chinese Air Force, 1956-58. Recipient Outstanding Intention award IBM, 1972, 79, 83, Achievement award, 1968-77. Fellow IEEE; mem. AAAS, Eta Kappa Nu, Phi Kappa Phi. Patentee in field. Office: PO Box 390 Poughkeepsie NY 12602

HSIEH, JUI SHENG, mechanical engineer, educator; b. Chungking, China, Mar. 5, 1921; came to U.S., 1948, naturalized, 1961; s. Lang Hsuan and Yun Liang (Huang) H.; m. Mary Cheng-Lian Wang, Sept. 2, 1961; children: Lawrence Szeche, Esther Szeyu, Vivian Szelun. B.Engring., Wuhan (China) U., 1943; M.S. in Mech. Engring, U. Ky., 1950; Ph.D., Ohio State U., 1955. Registered profl. engr., N.J. Asst. prof. mech. engring. U. Bridgeport, 1955-57, assoc. prof., 1957-60, N.J. Inst. Tech., 1960-65, prof., 1965—. Author: Principles of Thermodynamics, 1975, Chinese edit., 1981. Mem. ASME, Am. Soc. Engring. Edn., Internat. Solar Energy Soc., Pi Mu Epsilon, Pi Tau Sigma. Home: 4 O'Connor Dr Belle Mead NJ 08502 Office: NJ Inst Tech 323 High St Newark NJ 07102

HSU, CHEN CHAO, chemist; b. Changhwa, Taiwan, June 29, 1940; came to U.S., 1967, naturalized, 1976; s. Shui Y. and Pin (Yang) H.; m. Nancy F. Lai, Jan. 13, 1966; children: Samuel, Sandra. B.S. in Chemistry, Nat. Taiwan Normal U., 1963; M.S. in Phys. Chemistry, Brigham Young U., 1969; Ph.D., U. Utah, 1972. Teaching asst. Brigham Young U., Provo, Utah, 1967-69; teaching and research asst. U. Utah, Salt Lake City, 1969-72; postdoctoral research assoc. U. Chgo., 1972-74; software engr. Bell & Howell, Pasadena, Calif., 1974-75; phys. chemist. Argonne Nat. Lab., (Ill.), 1975-82; research chemist Chem. Research Devel. Ctr., U.S. Army, Aberdeen Proving Ground, Md., 1982—; cons. in field. Contbr. articles to profl. jours. Pres. parent adv. com. Head Start Day Care Ctr., Salt Lake City, 1972; v.p. Taiwanese Credit Union Chgo., 1979-80, sec., 1980-81. Scholar Taiwan Provincial Govt., 1967-72. Mem. Am. Chem. Soc. (mem. com. profl. relations and status Chgo. sect. 1977-78), Electrochem. Soc., Soc. Applied Spectroscopy, N.Am. Taiwanese Profs. Assn., Taiwanese Assn. Am. (dir., pres. Greater Chgo. chpt. 1980-81), Sigma Xi. Club: Taiwanese Toastmasters. Home: 392 Ellsworth Pl Joppa MD 21085 Office: Research Div Chem Research and Devel Ctr Aberdeen Proving Ground MD 21010

HSU, CHING-YU, educator, philosopher, author; b. Liuyang, Hunan, China, Dec. 25, 1898; s. Shih-kang and Shu-yi (Li) H.; m. Anna Yuen-Chi Ting, June 1, 1935; children: Stephen, Margaret (Mrs. Bob Mirsky), Victor, Yin-po (Mrs. H. N. Ma), Yin-sho (Mrs. William Cheng), Yu-Kuan. Ed., Hunan Coll. Law, Changsha, 1917-21; postgrad., Oxford (Eng.) U., 1922-25. Prof. philosophy Kwan Hwa U., Shanghai, 1926-28; dep. dir. transl. bur. exam. Juan, Nanking, 1928-30; acting chmn. nat. com. planning Nationalist Gov. China, 1932-34; spl. adminstr., Hunan, 1938-44; research fellow Hongkong U., 1953-58; spl. lectr. philosophy Chunchi Coll., Hongkong, 1952-53, Chee-loo U. (Shantung Christian U.), Tsinan, China, 1946-48. Author: Philosophy of Love, 1921, Philosophy of Confucious, 1925, Philosophy of the Beautiful, 1925, Co-wealthism and the New Age, 1975, Problem of China, 1966. Mem. adv. bd. Am. Nat. Security Council, 1974—; Mem. Presdl. Task Force; state advisor U.S. Congl. Adv. Bd.; Commr. interior central polit. council, Kuomintang, Nanking, 1936-39. Mem. Internat. Sci. Soc. Shanghai (dir. 1937-39), Chinese Co-wealthist Soc. Hongkong (founder 1956), China Rebuilding Fedn. (cochmn. 1964—). Address: 21-20 21st St Long Island City NY 11105 *Trust in God, live in hope, act in determination and love, along with patience and constancy—these are the basic factors that helped me to overcome difficulties and to fulfill a part of my mission, though I have not yet paid the whole debt I owe to the world.*

HSU, FRANCIS LANG KWANG, anthropology educator, author, lectr.; b. Chuang Ho, China, Oct. 28, 1911; s. Chung-ting Hsu and Lee Shih; m. Vera Y.N. Tung, Apr. 26, 1943; children: Eileen Hsu-Balzer, Penalope Hsu-Prepuolenis. B.A., Shanghai U., 1933; Ph.D., U. London, 1940. Asst. prof. to prof. anthropology, sociology Nat. Yunnan U., Kunming, China, 1941-44; lectr. Columbia, 1944-45; acting asst. prof. Cornell U., 1945-47; successively asst. prof., asso. prof., prof. anthropology Northwestern U., Evanston, Ill., 1947-78, chmn. dept., 1957-75; prof., dir. Center for Cultural Studies in Edn., U. San Francisco, 1978—; field expdns. to, Shansi, North China, 1936, West Yunnan, Southwestern China, 1941-42, 1943, Hawaii, 1949-50, 69-70, India, 1955-57, Japan, 1964-65, Hong Kong, South Asia, 1975-76; Chinese labor cons. Bur. Labor Statistics, U.S. Dept. Labor, 1945; vis. prof. Kyoto U., 1964-65, U. Hawaii, 1969-70, Chinese U., Hong

Kong, 1975-76. Author: Under the Ancestors Shadow, 1948, 71, Religion, Science and Human Crises, 1952, Americans and Chinese, Two Ways of Life, 1953, Psychological Anthropology, 1961, 72, The Study of Literate Civilizations, 1969, Kinship and Culture, 1971, Clan, Caste and Club, 1963, Americans and Chinese, Purpose and Fulfillment in Great Civilizations, 1970, The Challenge of The American Dream: The Chinese in The United States, 1971, Iemoto: The Heart of Japan, 1975; co-author: China Day by Day, 1974, Americans and Chinese: Passage to Differences, 1981, Rugged Individualism Reconsidered; contbr., co-editor: Moving A Mountain: Culture Change in China, 1979, The Fabric of Chinese Society; Asso. editor: Jour. Comparative Family Studies; adv. editorial bd.: Internat. Jour. Social Psychiatry; Editor: Aspects of Culture and Personality, 1954; Contbr. articles to profl. publs. Viking Fund fellow, 1944-45; Wenner-Gren Found. grantee, 1949-50, 55-57, 66-70, 72-73, 75-76; Social Sci. Research Council fellow, 1949-50; Rockefeller Found. fellow, 1955-57; Carnegie Corp. grantee, 1964-65; sr. specialist East-West Center, 1969-70; sr. fellow, 1978-79. Fellow Am. Anthrop. Assn. (pres. elect 1976-77, pres. 1977-78). Home: 61 Milland Dr Mill Valley CA 94941 *To me the most precious things in life are wholesome human relations, not love of human substitutes such as dogs and things. The more we depend on and look for substitutes, the less we will see loyalty, friendship, compassion, and love among human beings.*

HSU, HSIUNG, engineering educator; b. Nantung, China, Jan. 24, 1920; came to U.S., 1945; s. Deh-Cheng H. and Chung-Yu (Yuan); m. Priscilla Sich, Sept. 24, 1955; children: Peter, Elaine, Doreen. B.S. in Elec. Engring., Nat. Wuhan U., 1941; S.M. in Engring., Harvard U., 1946; Ph.D. in Applied Science, Harvard U., 1949. Registered profl. engr., Ohio. Engr. Internat. Broadcasting Sta XGOY, China, 1941-45; engr. devel. Gen. Electric Co., Owensboro, Ky., 1950-53, engr. research, Syracuse, N.Y., 1953-61; assoc. prof. engring. Ohio State U., Columbus, 1962-66, prof., 1966—; cons. Westinghouse Research Lab., Pitts., summer 1976, Advanced Tech. Ctr. LTV Aerospace Corp., Dallas, summer 1975. Contbr. articles to profl. jours.; contbg. author: Amplifier Handbook, 1966. Gordon McKay scholar, 1948-49; Harvard U. teaching fellow, 1946-47; recipient Mershon Ohio State U., 1979. Sr. mem. IEEE; mem. Am Phys. Soc., Am. Soc. Physics Tchrs., Sigma Xi. Home: 777 Olde Settler Pl Columbus OH 43214 Office: Dept Elec Engring Ohio State 2015 Neil Ave Columbus OH 43210

HSU, IMMANUEL CHUNG YUEH, history educator; b. Shanghai, China, May 6, 1924; came to U.S., 1949, naturalized, 1962; s. Thomas K.S. and Mary (Loh) H.; m. Dolores Menstell, Apr. 14, 1962; 1 son, Vadim Menstell. B.A., Yenching U., China, 1946; M.A., U. Minn., 1950; Ph.D. (Harvard-Yenching fellow), Harvard U., 1954. Postdoctoral research fellow Harvard U., 1955-58; vis. asso. prof. history, vis. prof. Harvard Summer Sch., 1961, 64, 68, 75; asst. prof. history U. Calif. at Santa Barbara, 1959-60, asso. prof., 1960-65, prof., 1965—, chmn. history dept., 1970-72; faculty research lectr., 1971; mem. del. to Chinese Acad. Scis., Peking, Spring 1979, 80; vis. prof. Hamburg U., Germany, spring 1973; Fulbright lectr., 1973. Author: Intellectual Trends in the Ch'ing Period, 1959, China's Entrance into the Family of Nations, 1960, The Ili Crisis: A Study of Sino-Russian Diplomacy, 1871-1881, 1965, The Rise of Modern China, 1970, 2d edit., 1975, internat. edit., 1975-76, 3d edit., 1983 (Commonwealth Lit. prize of Calif. 1971); editor: Readings in Modern Chinese History, 1971; Editor: Late Ch'ing Foreign Relations, 1866-1905, in The Cambridge History of China, Vol. 11, 1980, China Without Mao, 1983. Guggenheim fellow, 1962-63; Nat. Acad. Scis. scholar to China, spring 1983. Mem. Am., Pacific hist. assns., Assn. Asian Studies, Assn. Ch'ing Studies. Office: Dept History U Calif Santa Barbara CA 93106

HSU, JOHN TSENG HSIN, music educator, cellist, gambist, barytonist; b. Swatow, China, Apr. 21, 1931; came to U.S., 1949, naturalized, 1961; s. Benjamin D. H. and Lucy (Ma) Zi; m. Martha Russell, July 31, 1968. Mus.B., New Eng. Conservatory Music, Boston, 1953, Mus.M., 1955, Mus.D. (hon.), 1971. Music faculty Cornell U., 1955—; prof., 1966-76, Old Dominion Found. prof. humanities and music, 1976—, chmn. dept. music, 1966-71; artist-faculty mem. Aston Magna Found. for Music, 1974—; artist-in-residence U. Calif., Davis, winter 1983; barytonist Haydn Baryton Trio, 1981—. Cellist, Amadé Trio, Ithaca, N.Y., 1955—; active as viola de gamba recitalist; toured, throughout Europe, Am.; Recorded by, Musical Heritage Soc., N.Y.C., Titanic Records, Cambridge, Mass., Disques Alpha, Brussels, Da Camera Schallplatten- edition, Mannheim, Germany. Fellow Cornell Soc. for Humanities, 1971-72; Hon. mem. Riemenschneider Bach Inst., 1971—. Mem. viola da gamba socs. Am. and Eng., Pi Kappa Lambda. Home: 601 Highland Rd Ithaca NY 14850

HSU, KONRAD CHANG, microbiologist, educator; b. Taichow, China, Aug. 28, 1901; came to U.S., 1922, naturalized, 1962; s. George Chien and Wu (Yu) H.; m. Katharine D. Hawley, Jan. 31, 1951; children: Victoria Ruffner, Theodora Du., Alicia Wohl, Konrad T., Adelina, Lydia Yu, Linda Wei. B.S., St. John's U., Shanghai, China, 1921; M.A., Columbia U., 1923, Ph.D., 1924. Mem. faculty Gt. China U., 1924-26; with Chinese Govt. Mil. and Civil Service, 1926-37; gen. mgr. Chan Haw & Co., 1937-46; v.p. Sino-Hawaiian Corp., 1946-49, Dakon Corp., Bangkok, Thailand, Hong Kong, N.Y.C., 1949-54; mem. faculty Coll. Physicians and Surgeons, Columbia U., N.Y.C., 1954—, prof. microbiology, 1969—; vis. prof. U. Rome, U. Bonn, 1966, Ulm (Germany) U., 1969, 73; vis. scientist Inst. Gustave Roussy, Villejuif, France, 1966, Sydney U., 1967. Author numerous publs. in field. Chmn. bd. dirs. Overseas Chinese Music and Art Center, N.Y.C. Mem. Soc. Exptl. Biology and Medicine, Am. Assn. Immunologists, Reticuloendothelial Soc., Harvey Soc., Am. Assn. Pathologists, N.Y. Acad. Scis., Sigma Xi. Club: Masons. Home: 24 Schreiber St Tappan NY 10983 Office: 630 W 168th St New York NY 10032 *Any contribution to science makes life immortal.*

HSU, ROGER Y. K., lawyer; b. Tientsin, China, Apr. 9, 1927; came to U.S., 1948, naturalized, 1962; s. Mary C. Hsu; m. Evangeline C. Chung, Aug. 12, 1950; children: Daphne, Jeffrey. B.S., St. John's U., Shanghai, China, 1948; M.S., U. Mass., 1951; Ph.D., Case Western Res. U., 1953, J.D., 1964. Bar: Ohio 1964. With Lubrizol Corp., Wickliffe, Ohio, 1952—, now sr. v.p. and gen. counsel; lectr. organic chemistry Cleve. State U. Mem. Am. Bar Assn., Am. Arbitration Assn., Union Internationale des Avocats, Sigma Xi. Home: 14445 Hartwell Novelty OH 44072 Office: 29400 Lakeland Blvd Wickliffe OH 44092

HSU, YU-CHIH, mammalian embryologist, educator, researcher. M.D., Keio U., Tokyo, 1947, D.M.Sc., 1957. Instr. Keio U., Tokyo, 1950-58; research assoc. Johns Hopkins U., Balt., 1958-60, asst. prof., 1962-67, assoc. prof., 1966-77, prof., 1977—; researcher in vitro culture of whole mouse embryos, 1969. Home: 2204 Midridge Rd Timonium MD 21093 Office: Johns Hopkins University 615 N Wolfe St Baltimore MD 21205

HSUEH, CHUN-TU, political science educator; b. Canton, China, Dec. 12, 1922; came to U.S., 1949, naturalized, 1960; m. Cordelia Teh-hua Huang, Dec. 13, 1952. Cert., China Sch. Jornalism, Hong Kong, 1939; LL.B., Chaoyang U., China, 1946, Raffles Coll., Singapore, 1946-49; M.A., Columbia U., 1953, Ph.D., 1958; hon. doctorate, U. San Martín de Porres, Lima, Peru, 1984. Research assoc. polit. sci. Stanford U., 1959-62; lectr. history U. Hong Kong, 1962-64; vis. assoc. prof. SUNY, Plattsburgh, 1964-65; assoc. prof. U. Md., College Park, 1965-68, prof. politics, 1968—; prof. Columbia U., summer 1969; sr. assoc. mem. St. Antony's Coll., Oxford U., 1969; vis. prof., acting dir. Free U. Berlin, 1970; prof. Harvard U., summer 1979, 84; chmn. Washington and S.E. Regional Seminar on China, 1974—, Asian Polit. Scientists Group in U.S.A., 1975—; mem. vis. com. dept. internat. relations Lehigh U., 1979-85. Author: Huang Hsing and the Chinese Revolution, 1961, Chinese edit., 1980; Editor, contbr.: Revolutionary Leaders of Modern China, 1971, French edit., 1973, Dimensions of China's Foreign Relations, 1977, Asian Political Scientists in North America: Professional and Ethnic Problems, 1977, China's Foreign Relations: New Perspectives, 1982, The Chinese Revolution of 1911: New Perspectives, 1984; co-translator: Traditional Government in Imperial China: A Critical Analysis, 1982. Mem. Nat. Bicentennial Ethnic-Racial Council, 1974-76; mem. adv. com. Md. Bicentennial Commn., 1975-76; mem. nat. exec. com. Caucus for New Polit. Sci., 1973-75; bd. dirs. Asia Mail, Alexandria, Va., 1978-82. Home: 2011 Gatewood Pl Silver Spring MD 20903 Office: Dept Govt and Politics U Md College Park MD 20742

HU, CHANG-TU, history and education educator; b. Zhengjiang, China, Nov. 18, 1921; came to U.S., 1949; s. Hsin-yu and Wan-yu (Miao) H.; m. Dorothy G. Young, Jan. 20, 1947 (dec. Mar. 1962); children: Christopher K., Frederick K.; m. Cynthia Yao, Nov. 10, 1966 (dec. Jan. 1980). B.A., Fudan U., Chungking, China, 1942; M.A., U. Wash.-Seattle, 1950, Ph.D., 1954. Research assoc. human relations area files Yale U., New Haven, 1954-57; assoc. prof. SUNY-New Paltz, 1957-59; vis. prof. Princeton U., 1960-61; dean Grad. Sch. Chinese U., Hong Kong, 1975-76; prof. history Tchrs. Coll. Columbia U., 1959—; vis. prof. Harvard U., 1968; China program dir. United Bd. for Christian Higher Edn. in Asia, N.Y.C., 1981—; dir. Ctr. for Edn. in Asia, N.Y.C., 1974-80. Author: China: Its People, Its Society, Its Culture, 1961, Chinese Education under Communism, 1974; author-editor: Aspects of Chinese Education, 1969. Bd. dirs. Nat. Com. on U.S.-China Relations, N.Y.C., 1975-79. Mem. Comparative Edn. Soc. (editor 1962-63), Am. Hist. Assn. Democrat. Home: 110 Riverside Dr New York NY 10024 Office: Tchrs Coll Columbus U. W 120th St New York NY 10027

HU, CHI YU, physicist, educator; b. Szchwan, China, Feb. 12, 1933; came to U.S., 1956, naturalized, 1974; s. T.C. and P.S. (Yang) H.; children—Marica, Mark, Albert, Han Chin. B.S., Nat. Taiwan U., 1955; Ph.D., M.I.T., 1962. Research asso. St. John's U., Jamaica, N.Y., 1962-63; asst. prof. physics Calif. State U., Long Beach, 1963-68, asso. prof., 1968-72, prof., 1972—. Contbr. articles to profl. jours. NSF summer fellow, 1965, 76; NSF research grantee, 1969-70; Calif. State U. Long Beach Found. grantee, 1965, 66, 70, 72. Mem. Am. Phys. Soc., AAUP, United Profs. Calif. Office: Calif State U Long Beach CA 90840

HU, SZE-TSEN, educator; b. Huchow, China, Oct. 9, 1914; came to U.S., 1949, naturalized, 1955; s. Hsiao Tang and Su Mei (Tang) H.; m. Shia Zong Wang, Mar. 14, 1948 (dec. 1962); children—Herman, Charlotte. B.Sc., Nat. Central U., China, 1938; Ph.D., U. Manchester, Eng., 1947, D.Sc., 1959. Mem. Inst. Advanced Study, Princeton, 1950-52; asso. prof. Tulane U., 1952- 55; prof. U. Ga., 1955-56, Wayne State U., 1956-60, U. Calif. at Los Angeles, 1960—; cons. Lockheed Aircraft Corp., 1959-64. Author: Homotopy Theory, 1959, Elements of General Topology, 1964, Theory of Retracts, 1965, Elements of Modern Algebra, 1965, Threshold Logic, 1965, Introduction to General Topology, 1966, Homology Theory, 1966, Introduction to Contemporary Mathematics, 1966, Elements of Real Analysis, 1967, Introduction to Homological Algebra, 1968, Cohomology Theory, 1968, Mathematical Theory of Switching Circuits and Automata, 1968, Elementary Functions and Coordinate Geometry, 1969, Differtiable Manifolds, 1969, Calculus, 1970, Linear Algebra with Differential Equations, 1971, also numerous articles. Mem. Am. Math. Soc., Math. Assn. Am., London Math. Soc., Soc. Math. de France, Soc. Math. de Belgique, Wiskundig Genootschap re Amsterdam, Sigma Xi. Home: 1076 Tellem Dr Pacific Palisades CA 90272 Office: Dept Math U Calif at Los Angeles Los Angeles CA 90024

HUANG, CHEN-JUNG, educator; b. Formosa, July 1, 1925; U.S., 1955; s. Tsung-Pang and Cha-Mou (Li) H.; m. Takako Kagetsu, Aug. 6, 1955; children—Helen, William, Grace. B.Sc., Nat. Taiwan U., 1949; Ph.D., U. Toronto, 1955. Prof. chem. engring. U. Houston, 1955—, chmn. dept., 1962-65, asso. dean, 1967-69, asso. dean faculties, asst. v.p., 1969-73; Fulbright prof., Taiwan, 1966. Dir. Pasadena Nat. Bank, Tex.; Vice pres. Houston-Taipei Sister City Soc., 1971-75. Mem. Am. Inst. Chem. Engrs. (recipient chpt. best publ. award 1959, 64, 66). Home: 2410 Drexel Dr Houston TX 77027

HUANG, EUGENE YUCHING, civil engr., educator; b. Changsha, China, Nov. 28, 1917; came to U.S., 1948, naturalized, 1962; s. Sam and Yi Yun (Chao) H.; m. Helen W. Woo, Aug. 20, 1955; children—Martha, Pearl, William, Mary, Priscilla, Stephen. M.S., U. Utah, 1950; D.Sc., U. Mich., 1954. Registered profl. engr., Ill., Mich. Asst. engr. Chinese Nat. Hwy. Adminstrn., 1941-45, asso. engr., 1945-48; research asst. Engring. Research Inst., U. Mich., 1953-54; research asst. prof. civil engring. U. Ill., Urbana, 1954-58, asso. prof., 1958-63; prof. transp. engring. Mich. Tech. U., Houghton, 1963—; cons. transp. systems design, soil mechanics, 1954—. Author: Overview of the American Transportation System, 1976; contbr. numerous articles on transp. design systems and research on materials for pavement to profl. jours. Recipient Faculty Research award Mich. Tech. U., 1967. Fellow ASCE; mem. Am. Soc. Engring. Edn., AAAS, Assn. Asphalt Paving Technologists, Inst. Mgmt. Sci., Am. Ry. Engring. Assn., ASTM, NRC (transp. research bd. 1954), Sigma Xi, Chi Epsilon, Tau Beta Pi, Phi Tau Phi. Episcopalian. Home: 400 Garnet St Houghton MI 49931 Office: Mich Tech U Houghton MI 49931

HUANG, FRANCIS FU-TSE, engineering educator; b. Hong Kong, Aug. 27, 1922; came to U.S., 1945, naturalized, 1960; s. Kwong Set and Chen-Ho (Yee) H.; m. Fung-Yuen Fung, Apr. 10, 1954; children: Raymond, Stanley. B.S., San Jose State Coll., 1951; M.S., Stanford U., 1952; profl. mech. engr., Columbia U., 1964. Design engr. M.W. Kellogg Co., N.Y.C., 1952-58; faculty San Jose (Calif.) State U., 1958—, asso. prof. mech. engring., 1962-67, prof., 1967—, chmn. dept., 1973-81; hon. prof. heat power engring. Taiyuan (China) Inst. Tech., 1981—. Author: Engineering Thermodynamics—Fundamentals and Applications, 1976. Served to capt. Chinese Army, 1943-45. NSF faculty fellow, 1962-64; Named Tau Beta Pi Outstanding Engring. Prof. of Year, 1967, 76; recipient Calif. State Coll. System Disting. Teaching award, 1968-69. Mem. ASME, AIAA, Am. Soc. Engring. Edn., AAAS, AAUP, N.Y. Acad. Scis. Home: 1259 Sierra Mar Dr San Jose CA 95118 Office: Dept Mech Engring San Jose State U San Jose CA 95192

HUANG, KEE CHANG, physician, educator; b. Canton, China, July 22, 1917; came to U.S., 1949, naturalized, 1962; s. Chun Yue and M. Lee H.; m. Shou-Shan Chang, Feb. 16, 1947; children—Kou Chu, Anna, Karen. B.S., M.D., Dr. Sun Yat-Sen U., Canton, 1940; Ph.D., Columbia U., 1953. Research fellow pharmacology NIH, China, 1940-46; instr. pharmacology Nat. Shanghai (China) Med. Sch., 1946-49; fellow Columbia U., 1949-53; research asso. U. Louisville, 1953-56, asst. prof., 1956-59, asso. prof., 1959-63, prof. pharmacology, 1963—; guest scientist Max Planck Inst. für Biophysik, Frankfurt, W.Ger., 1967-68. Contbr. articles to profl. jours.; Author: Outline of Pharmacology, 1971, 2d edit., 1974. Recipient Outstanding Basic Sci. Instr. award. U. Louisville, 1958, 59, 61, 63, 64, 65, 73, 74, 76; Commonwealth Fund Am. scholar, 1967; NIH spl. fellow, 1967-68; Sr. Fulbright scholar, 1979. Mem. Am. Physiol. Soc., Am. Soc. Pharmacology and Exptl. Therapeutics, Soc. Exptl. Biol. Medicine, Royal Soc. Medicine (London), Am. Soc. Nephrology, Sigma Xi. Home: 154 Forest Dr Jeffersonville IN 47130 Office: Dept Pharmacology U Louisville Louisville KY 40232

HUANG, KERSON, physics educator; b. Nan Ning, Kwangsi, China, Mar. 15, 1928; came to U.S., 1947; s. Horton T. and Shi (Ng) H.; m. Rosemary E. Verducci, May 19, 1979; m. Julia M. Sheng, June 16, 1956 (div. 1971); 1 dau., Kathryn Camille. S.B., 1950; Ph.D., 1953. Faculty mem. MIT, Cambridge, 1953-55, 57—; fellow Inst. for Advanced Study, Princeton, N.J., 1955-57; prof. physics MIT, Cambridge, 1966; cons. editor World Sci. Publ. (Singapore), 1981—. Author: Statistical Mechanics, 1963, Quarks, Leptons and Gauge Fields, 1982. Alfred E. Sloan Found. fellow, 1961, 62; Guggenheim Found. fellow, Geneva, 1962; sr. Fulbright scholar Council for Internat. Exchange of Scholars, Santiago, Chile; hon. prof. Fudan U., Shanghai, China, 1980. Fellow Am. Acad. Arts and Scis., Am. Phys. Soc. Office: Dept Physics Room 6-309 MIT 77 Massachusetts Ave Cambridge MA 02139

HUANG, PETER C. R., investment company executive; b. Shanghai, China, July 25, 1935; m. Nancy Stoddart; 1 dau., Deirdre. B.S. in Engring., Stanford U., 1956; M.B.A., Columbia U., 1960. Asst. v.p. Webb & Knapp, Inc., 1962-65, R.C. Watt, Inc., 1965-66; with City Investing Co., N.Y.C., 1966—, v.p., then exec. v.p., 1967-76, pres., 1976—, chief operating officer, 1979—. Clubs: Wall St., Creek. *

HUANG, PIEN CHIEN, biochemistry educator; b. Shanghai, China, July 13, 1931; came to U.S., 1955, naturalized, 1969; s. C. Hwa and H. (Tong) H.; m. Ru chih Chow, June 10, 1956; children: Suber S., Suzanne S. B.S., Nat. Taiwan U., 1953; M.S., Va. Tech. U., 1956; Ph.D., Ohio State U., 1960. Research fellow Calif. Inst. Tech., 1960-65; asst. prof. dept. biochemistry Johns Hopkins U., 1965, assoc. prof., to 1976, prof., 1976—. Editor: (with Cohen, Lillienfield) Genetic Issues in Public Health and Medicine; contbr. articles to profl. jours. Chmn. bd. Chinese Sch. Assn. USA, 1978—. NIH fellow. Mem. Am. Soc. Biol. Chemists, Genetics Soc. Am., Am. Soc. Biophysics, Soc. Cell Biology. Office: 615 N Wolfe St Baltimore MD 21205 *

HUBATA, JOSEPH ALLEN, physician; b. Chgo., Oct. 18, 1904; s. Joseph and Anna Barbara (Herda) H.; m. Onelia T. Magnabosco, Dec. 26, 1943; 1 dau., Kerry Celeste. A.B., Oberlin Coll., 1926; M.D., Ill. Coll. Medicine, 1932; hon. degree in med. research, U. Terroni, Italy. Intern Englewood Hosp., Chgo., 1932-33; pvt. practice, Chgo., 1933-46, 69—; indsl. med. staff Internat. Harvester Co., 1938-46; med. dir., indsl. Armour & Co., 1946-50; med. dir. Armour Pharm. Co., 1950-70; instr. dept. medicine Rush Med. Sch., 1935-37; med. staff Am., Englewood hosps., Chgo.; dir. Franklin Devel. Co. Trustee Valmora Sanitorium; bd. dirs. Evanston Concert Ballet Found. Maj., M.C. Ill. State Guard, 1941-46. Decorated chevalier Republic of Haiti, comdr. Order of Merit Toussaint Louverture, Haiti). Mem. A.M.A., Am. Heart Assn., Royal Soc. Indsl. Health and Hygiene, Ill. Med. Assn., Chgo. Med. Soc., Central States Soc. Indsl. Medicine and Surgery, Acad. Occupational Medicine. Home: 1500 Sheridan Rd Wilmette IL 60091 Office: Am Hosp 850 Irving Park Rd Chicago IL 60613

HUBAY, CHARLES ALFRED, surgeon, educator; b. Chagrin Falls, Ohio, Jan. 23, 1918; s. Stephan and Mary Elizbaeth (Szitar) H.; m. Gladyce E. Jones, Sept. 8, 1945; children: Charles Alfred, William C., Thomas A. A.B., Adelbert Coll., 1940; M.D., Western Res. U., 1943. Diplomate: Am. Bd. Surgery. Intern Univ. Hosps., Cleve., 1943-44, resident, 1946-50; practice medicine, specializing in surgery, Cleve., 1950—; prof. surgery Western Res. U., 1965—, dir. gen. surgery, 1965-80; asso. surgeon Highland View Hosp. Contbr. articles to profl. jours. Served with AUS, 1944-46; ETO. Mem. A.C.S., Am., Central surg. assns., Soc. Univ. Surgeons. Home: 33325 Woodleigh Dr Cleveland OH 44124 Office: 2065 Adelbert Rd Cleveland OH 44106

HUBBARD, CARROLL, JR., Congressman. Mem. 94th-98th Congresses from 1st Ky. Dist.; asso. whip 94th-97th Congresses from 1st Ky. Dist., 1977—. Office: 2182 Rayburn House Office Bldg Washington DC 20515

HUBBARD, DAVID ALLAN, clergyman, educator; b. Stockton, Calif., Apr. 8, 1928; s. John King and Helena (White) H.; m. Ruth Doyal, Aug. 12, 1949; 1 dau., Mary Ruth. B.A., Westmont Coll., Calif., 1949; B.D., Fuller Theol. Sem., Pasadena, Calif., 1952, Th.M., 1954; Ph.D., St. Andrews U., Scotland, 1957; D.D., John Brown U., 1975; L.H.D., Rockford Coll., 1975. Ordained to ministry Conservative Bapt. Assn., 1952; lectr. O.T. St. Andrews U., 1955-56; asst. prof. Bibl. studies Westmont Coll., 1957, chmn. dept. Bibl. studies and philosophy, 1958-63; interim pastor Montecito (Calif.) Community Ch., 1960-62; pres., prof. O.T. Fuller Theol. Sem., 1963—; exec. v.p. Fuller Evangelistic Assn., 1969—; Tyndale O.T. lectr., Cambridge, Eng., 1965, Soc. O.T. Studies lectr., London, 1971, lectr. numerous U.S. univs., 1973—. Speaker: internat. radio broadcast The Joyful Sound, 1969-80; Author: With Bands of Love, 1968, (with others) Is God Dead?, 1966, Is Life Really Worth Living?, 1969, What's God Been Doing All This Time?, 1970, What's New?, 1970, Does the Bible Really Work?, 1971, Psalms for All Seasons, 1971, Is The Family Here To Stay, 1971, The Practice of Prayer, 1972, Spanish edit., 1974, Chinese edit., 1979, How To Face Your Fears, 1972, The Holy Spirit in Today's World, 1973, Church—Who Needs It?, 1974, They Met Jesus, 1974, More Psalms for All Seasons, 1975, An Honest Search for a Righteous Life, 1975, Colossians Speaks to the Sickness of Our Time, 1976, Happiness: You Can Find the Secret, 1976, Beyond Futility, 1976, Chinese edit., 1982, Themes from the Minor Prophets, 1977, Strange Heroes, 1977, Galatians: Gospel of Freedom, 1977, Thessalonians: Life That's Radically Christian, 1977, Why Do I Have to Die?, 1978, How to Study the Bible, 1978, What We Evangelicals Believe, 1979, Book of James: Wisdom That Works, 1980, Right Living in a World Gone Wrong, 1981, German edit., 1982, Parables Jesus Told, 1981, (with Bush and LaSor) Old Testament Survey, 1982; contbg. editor: Eternity mag; editorial bd.: The Ministers' Permanent Library, 1976—; adv. bd.: Evang. Book Club, 1977—; contbr. articles to dictionaries, mags. Chmn. Pasadena Urban Coalition, 1968-71; Mem. Calif. Bd. Edn., 1972-75; bd. dirs. Nat. Campus Ministries, 1974-78. Mem. Am. Acad. Religion, Soc. Bibl. Lit., Assn. Theol. Schs. in U.S. and Can. (exec. com. 1972—, pres. 1976-78). Clubs: Rotary, Univ. (Pasadena). Office: 135 N Oakland Ave Pasadena CA 91101

HUBBARD, ELIZABETH, actress; b. N.Y.C., Dec. 22; d. Benjamin Alldritt and Elizabeth (Wright) H.; (div.) 1 son, Jeremy Danby Bennett. A.B. cum laude, Radcliffe Coll.; postgrad., Royal Acad. Dramatic Art, London. Leading role: NBC daytime TV serial The Doctors; actress: Broadway prodns. including Present Laughter, 1982; performer off-Broadway including: Boys from Syracuse; also regional and stock appearances; movie appearances include I Never Sang for my Father; The Bell Jar, 1978, 1979; Ordinary People, 1980; frequent guest TV talk shows. Recipient Clarence Derwent award for The Physicists, 1965; Emmy award for best actress in The Doctors, 1974; for best actress in First Ladies Diaries: Edith Bolling Wilson, 1976.

HUBBARD, FRANK MULDROW, construction company executive; b. Florence, S.C., Feb. 15, 1920; s. Francis Evans and Mildred (Muldrow) H.; m. Ruth Scorgie, Sept. 7, 1941; children: Leonard Evans, Ruth Converse Miller; 1 foster son, Eddie Mesa. Student, Clemson (S.C.) Coll., Rollins Coll., Winter Park, Fla.; LL.D. (hon.), Rollins Coll., Winter Park, Fla., 1981. Vice pres., then pres. Hubbard Constrn. Co., Orlando, Fla., 1939-64, chmn. bd., 1964-80, chmn. exec. com., 1980—. Chmn. Central 9 Corp.; chmn. bd. Sun Banks, Inc., 1982—; past chmn. Sun Bank College Park; dir. Electric Fuels Corp., Fla. Power Corp., Fla. Progress Corp., Sun Bank, N.A., Orlando, Fla. Rock Industries, Inc.; Pres., dir. Fla. Citrus Open Golf Tournament; past chmn. bd. trustees Rollins Coll.; trustee Eckerd Coll., Webber Coll.; bd. dirs. Am. Found. at Bok Tower Gardens; past trustee Trinity Preparatory Sch. Served to capt., C.E. AUS, World War II; ETO. Decorated Bronze Star; named Man of Year Orlando YMCA, 1964; Salesman of Year Sales and Mktg. Club, 1967; Hamilton Holt award Rollins Coll., 1980; Trinity Founder's award, 1980; Alumni Disting. Service award Clemson U., 1981; Frank Hubbard Scholarship established Engring. Coll., U. Central Fla., 1981. Mem. Fla. Engring. Soc. (Outstanding Service to Engring. Profession award 1975), World Bus. Council, Fla. Council 100, Fla. Crippled Children's Commn., Nat. Alliance Businessmen. Democrat. Presbyterian. Clubs: Country, Univ., Citrus (Orlando). Home: 9100 Hubbard Pl Orlando FL 32811 Office: 1911 Silver Star Rd Orlando FL 32854

HUBBARD, FREDERICK DEWAYNE, trumpeter; b. Indpls., Apr. 7, 1938. Player trumpet, fluegelhorn, piano; with, Montgomery Bros., Indpls.; then with, Sonny Rollins, Slide Hampton, J.J. Johnson, Quincy Jones; mem., Art Blakey's Jazz Messengers., 1961, tours of, Europe, Japan, Austria; appeared: Berlin Jazz Festival, 1965; played with, Quincy Jones in; soundtrack for film The Pawnbroker, 1964; rec. for, Atlantic Records, 1966-70, Columbia Records, 1974—; recorded: soundtracks for motion pictures Blowup, 1966, The Bus Is Coming, 1971, Shaft's Big Score, 1972; (Recipient Down Beat New Star award for trumpet 1961, Grammy award Best Jazz Performance 1972, Down Beat award for best trumpet 1973-76, winner Playboy Allstar Jazz Poll 1974-75); (with Blakey) Recs. include River, (with Coleman) Ah, (with Dolphy, Henderson) Blue Note; others; albums include Windjammer. Mem. All Stars V.S.O.P. Address: care Headliners Talent Agy 1401 Ave of Stars Los Angeles CA 90067 *

HUBBARD, HAROLD MEAD, research company executive; b. Beloit, Kans., Apr. 16, 1924; s. Clarence Richard and Elizabeth (Mead) H.; m. Doreen J. Wallace, Aug. 13, 1948 (div. 1975); children—Stuart W., David D.; m. Barbara Bell Czarnecki, May 9, 1976. B.S., U. Kans., 1948, Ph.D., 1951. Instr. chemistry U. Kans., Lawrence, 1949-51; research chemist, research mgr., lab. mgr. E. I. dUpont de Nemours & Co., Inc., Wilmington, Del., 1951-69; dir. phys. sci. Midwest Research Inst., Kansas City, Mo., 1970-75, v.p. research, 1976-78, sr. v.p. ops., 1979-82; exec. v.p., dir. Solar Energy Research Inst., 1982—; dir. Guaranty State Bank, Percy Kent Inc. Mem. adv. com. U. Kans. Sch. Engring.; trustee U. Kansas City. Served with U.S. Army, 1942-45. Mem. Mo. Acad. Sci. (councillor at large 1977—), Tech. Transfer Soc. (v.p. 1978—), Am. Chem. Soc., AAAS, World Future Soc., Sigma Xi, Delta Upsilon. Unitarian. Club: Rockhill Tennis. Home: 2605 Vivian St Lakewood CO 80215 Office: 1617 Cole Blvd Golden CO 80401

HUBBARD, HOWARD JAMES, bishop; b. Troy, N.Y., Oct. 31, 1938; s. Howard James and Elizabeth D. (Burke) H. B.A., St. Joseph's Sem., Yonkers, N.Y.; S.T.L., Gregorian U., Rome; D.D. (hon.), Siena Coll., 1977, L.H.D., Coll. St. Rose, 1977. Ordained priest Roman Catholic Ch., 1963; bishop of, Albany, N.Y., 1977—; parish priest St. Joseph's Ch., Schenectady, Cathedral Parish, Albany; asst. dir. Cath. Charities, Schenectady; chaplain Convent of the Sacred Heart, Kenwood, Albany; dir. Providence House, Albany; vicar gen. Diocese of Albany; dir. Cath. Interracial Council; coordinator Urban Apostolate. Pres. Urban League. Office: 465 State St Albany NY 12206 *

HUBBARD, JAMES MITCHELL, accounting firm executive; b. Montgomery, Ala., May 7, 1943; s. Lawrence Thornton and Mary Elizabeth (Crumpton) H.; m. Margaret Nadene Darden, Apr. 26, 1975. B.S. in Acctg, U. Ala., 1966, postgrad., 1978-80. Internal auditor Vanity Fair Mill, Monroeville, Ala., 1966-68; staff acct. Arthur Young & Co., Birmingham, Ala., Charlotte, N.C., 1968-72; controller Constrn., Fin., Mgmt. Corp., Charlottesville, Va., 1972-73; audit mgr., adminstrv. mgr., treas. Motion Industries, Inc., Birmingham, Ala., 1973-80, dir. corp. purchasing and distbn., 1980-83; ptnr. Snow & Stewart, C.P.A.s, 1983—. Mem. Am. Inst. C.P.A.s. Home: 3657 Brookwood Rd Birmingham AL 35223 Office: 741 Alton Rd Birmingham AL 35201

HUBBARD, JESSE DONALD, educator; b. nr. Sardinia, Ind., May 2, 1920; s. Jesse Wilmar and Emma Susan (Dieringer) H.; m. Dorothy Emma Drake, June 6, 1948; children—Richard, Joseph, Debra, Jean. A.B., DePauw U., 1943; M.D., Johns Hopkins, 1951. Intern, resident Union Meml Hosp., Balt., 1951-54; resident Ind. U. Med. Center, Indpls., 1954-56, mem. faculty, 1956—, prof. pathology, 1968—, also pathologist. Served with USAAF, 1943-46. Mem. A.M.A., Am. Soc. Clin. Pathologists. Home: 4330 Black Oak Dr Indianapolis IN 46208

HUBBARD, JOHN BARRY, lawyer, business consultant, retired banker; b. Sweetwater, Tex., Mar. 16, 1917; s. John Howard and Shirley (McCarty) H.; m. Virginia Marie Olsen, Dec. 10, 1943; children—Carol Ann (Mrs. Sam Houston Lane III), Virginia Sue Tarlton, Jean Ellen (Mrs. Jackie D. Warren), John Barry. B.B.A., U. Tex., 1939, LL.B., 1940. Formerly sr. v.p. Tex. Am. Bancshares, Inc., Ft. Worth; now ind. bus. cons. Treas., bd. dirs. various civic orgns. Mem. Tex., Tarrant County bar assns., Tex. Bankers Assn. (past pres. trust sect.). Mem. Christian Ch. Home: 6232 Genoa Rd Fort Worth TX 76116

HUBBARD, JOHN RANDOLPH, university president emeritus, history educator; b. Belton, Tex., Dec. 3, 1918; s. Louis Herman and Bertha (Altizer) H.; m. Lucille Luckett, Jan. 29, 1947 (div. Dec. 1983); children: Elisa, Melisse, Kristin. A.B., U. Tex., 1938, A.M., 1939, Ph.D., 1950; L.H.D., Hebrew Union Coll., Los Angeles, 1971, Westminster Coll., Fulton, Mo., 1977; LL.D., Sch. of Ozarks, 1973, U. So. Calif., 1980. Pvt. sec. to ICC commr., 1939-41; teaching fellow U. Tex., 1946-48; vis. asst. prof. Brit. history La. State U., 1948; asst. prof. European history Tulane U., 1949-52, asso. prof., 1953-58, prof., 1958-65; dean Newcomb Coll., 1953-65; vis. asst. prof. European history Yale, 1952-53; chief edn. adviser U.S. AID, India, 1965-69; v.p. for acad. affairs, provost U. So. Calif., Los Angeles, 1969-70, pres., 1970-80, pres. emeritus, 1980—, John R. Hubbard prof. Brit. history, 1980—; co-chmn. Indo-U.S. Subcommn. on Edn. and Culture, 1982—; dir. El Paso Co., U.S. Borax & Chem. Co., Los Angeles. Contbr.: articles and revs. to Jour. Modern History; other ednl. jours. Mem. bd. Tulane-Lyceum Assn., 1953-65, Isidore Newman Sch., 1953-65; mem. Region 12 selection com. Woodrow Wilson Fellowship Program, also chmn., 1955-65; mem. bd. U.S. Edn. Found., India; mem. Indian adv. bd. Women's Coll. Faculty Exchange program; pres. bd. Am. Internat. Sch., New Delhi; mem. So. Calif. adv. bd. Inst. Internat. Edn.; trustee Scholarships for Children of Am. Mil. Personnel; bd. dirs. Community TV So. Calif., Los Angeles. Served as an aviator in USN, 1941-46; flight instr. and patrol plane comdr.; Atlantic and Pacific fleets; lt. comdr. Res. Decorated D.F.C., Air medals (4); Chevalier des Palmes Academeques; Stella della Solidarietà Italiana, Italy; Order of Taj 3d degree, Iran; recipient Disting. Services to Higher Edn. in U.S. award Tulane U., New Orleans, 1976; Air U. award, 1976; Disting. Alumnus award U. Tex., Austin, 1978. Mem. Am., Miss. Valley hist. assns., So. Hist. Soc. (exec. council 1954-56), Anglo-Am. Hist. Soc., Assn. Ind. Calif. Colls. and Univs. (trustee), Am. Council Edn. (commn. on fed. relations 1975-77), Assn. Am. Univs. (council on fed. relations 1975-79), Orgn. Am. Historians, Conf. Brit. Studies, Am. Council Learned Socs., Phi Beta Kappa, Phi Delta Kappa, Alpha Kappa Psi, Delta Kappa Epsilon, Omicron Delta Kappa. Clubs: Royal Aero, Athenaeum (London); Los Angeles Country; California (Los Angeles); University (N.Y.C.); Cosmos (Washington). Home: 251 S Orange Grove Ave Pasadena CA 91105 Office: U So Calif University Park Los Angeles CA 90089 *The fear of false knowledge is the beginning of wisdom.*

HUBBARD, L. RON, writer, explorer, philosopher, humanitarian; b. Tilden, Nebr., Mar. 13, 1911; s. Harry Ross and Ledora May (Waterbury) H.; m. Mary Sue Whipp; children: Diana Meredith de Wolf, Mary Suzette Rochelle, Arthur Ronald Conway. Student, George Washington U., 1932, Princeton Sch. Govt., 1945. Writer aviation and travel articles, 1930—, explorer, 1934—; leader Caribbean Motion Picture Expdn., 1931, W.I. Minerals Survey Expdn., 1932, Alaskan Radio-Exptl. Expdn., 1940; organizer Hubbard Found. for pub. interests; founder Scientology, 1951; dir. internat. humanitarian orgns. including Dianetics and Scientology, 1952-66; resigned all directorships to devote full time to research, 1966, research and tech. for improved edn., 1964-71, research and internat. programs to resolve drug abuse, 1966—, exptl. works in music and photography, 1974—. Author: over 2000 works including Dianetics: The Modern Science of Mental Health, 1950, Science of Survival, 1951, The Fundamentals of Thought, 1956, Scientology: A New Slant on Life, 1966, Self Analysis, 1968, Dianetics Today, 1975, Battlefield Earth: A Saga of the Year 3000, 1982, The Way to Happiness, 1981; Contbr. articles to various publs. Recipient community service awards in U.S., Internat. Inst. Community Service awards; over 75 awards for musical creations; internat. recognition for photog. creations, 1975; Internat. Social Reform award, 1976; Ingrams West award, 1977; Nat. Life Achievement award Ill. Soc. Psychic Research, 1978; Internat. Profl. Assn. award, 1978; Saturn award for spl. achievement Acad. Sci. Fiction, Fantasy and Horror Films for book Battlefield Earth, 1984; numerous hon. citizenships and keys to cities in U.S. Address: PO Box 29550 Los Angeles CA 90029 also St Hill Manor East Grinstead Sussex England *The first principle of my own philosophy is that wisdom is meant for anyone who wishes to reach for it. It is the servant of the commoner and king alike and should never be regarded with awe. The second principle of my own philosophy is that wisdom must be capable of being applied. Learning locked in mildewed books is of little use to anyone and therefore of no value unless it can be used. The third principle is that any philosophic knowledge is valuable only if it is true or if it works. One should share what wisdom he has; one should help others to help themselves; and one should keep going despite heavy weather, for there is always a calm ahead.*

HUBBARD, PAUL STANCYL, JR., educator; b. St. Petersburg, Fla., July 15, 1931; s. Paul Stancyl and Lee (Wilkerson) H.; m. Carol Sylvia Martyn, June 8, 1957; children—Carol Lee, Philip Martyn. B.S. in Physics, U. Fla., 1953; A.M., Harvard, 1954, Ph.D., 1958. Asst. prof. physics U. N.C. at Chapel Hill, 1958-63, asso. prof., 1963-68, prof., 1968—, asso. dean, 1969-72. Contbr. articles on nuclear magnetic resonance and relaxation to profl. jours. Sloan research fellow, 1962-66; NSF sr. postdoctoral fellow Clarendon Lab., Oxford, Eng., 1964-65. Fellow Am. Phys. Soc.; mem. Am. Assn. Physics Tchrs., AAAS, Phi Beta Kappa, Sigma Xi. Home: 1710 Audubon Rd Chapel Hill NC 27514

HUBBARD, PETER E., aviation company executive; b. Milw., Dec. 13, 1941; m. Judy Glass, Sept. 7, 1968; children: Christopher, Hillary. B.A. in Econs., Princeton U., 1964. Ops. analyst Flying Tigers, Los Angeles, 1968-70, mgr. service planning, 1970-72, asst. corp. controller, 1972-74, dir. fin. plans and services, 1974-75, gen. mgr. charter programs, 1975-78, v.p. Midwest region, 1978-80, v.p. N. Am., 1980-81, sr. v.p. mktg. and sales, 1981—. Served to lt. USNR, 1965-68. Recipient Air Freight Man of Year Air Freight Motor Carriers Conf., 1983. Office: Flying Tigers 7401 World Way Los Angles CA 90009

HUBBARD, RANDALL DEE, manufacturing executive; b. Smith Center, Kans., June 13, 1935; s. Miner and Louise H.; m. Joan Dale McLain; children: Derrol, Bret, Shana. B.A., Butler Community Coll., Kans., 1956. Tchr., coach Kans. Jr. High Sch., Towanda, 1956-57; loan mgr. MFC Fin., Wichita, Kans., 1957-59; gen. mgr., v.p. Safelite Industies, Wichita, 1959-68; pres. Safelite Industries, Wichita, 1968-78; chmn. bd. AFG Industries, Inc., Kingsport, Tenn., 1978—. Mem. Tenn. Dist. Export Council, 1980-82, Gov.'s Ambassador Program, 1983. R. Dee Hubbard Hall, Wichita State U., named in his honor. Mem. Internat. Assn. Businessmen and Profls. Found (life, Outstanding Achievement award 1982). Office: AFG Industries 1400 Lincoln St Kingsport TN 37662

HUBBARD, ROBERT HAMILTON, art historian; b. Hamilton, Ont., Can., June 17, 1916; s. Charles Robert and Mary Elizabeth (Strattan) H. B.A., McMaster U., 1937; student, U. Paris, 1938, Royal Museums, Brussels, 1939; M.A., U. Wis., 1940, Ph.D., 1942; LL.D., Mt. Allison U., 1965. Mem. faculty U. Toronto, Ont., 1945-46; mem. staff Nat. Gallery Can., Ottawa, 1946-78, chief curator, 1954-78; adj. prof. art history Carleton U., Ottawa, 1974—; cultural adviser to Gov. Gen. of Can., 1978-81, hon. historian and archivist, 1981—. Author: Nat. Gallery of Can. Catalogues, 3 vols, 1957-60, An Anthology of Canadian Art, 1960, European Paintings in Canadian Collections, 2 vols, 1956-62, The Development of Canadian Art, 1963, Scholarship in Canada, 1968, Thomas Davies in Early Canada, 1972, Rideau Hall, an Illustrated History of Government House, Ottawa, 1977, also numerous mus. catalogues, exhbn. catalogues.; Contbr. articles to profl. jours. Appointed officer Order of Can., 1977; Léger fellow, 1981, 82; Jules and Gabrielle Léger fellow, 1981. Fellow Royal Soc. Can. (hon. sec. 1969-71, hon. librarian 1971—); mem. Acad. Humanities and Social Scis. (pres. 1976-77), Coll. Art Assn. Am. (past mem. council), Internat. Council Museums, Canadian Hist. Assn., Royal Can. Geog. Soc. Clubs: Athenaeum (London); Rideau (Ottawa). Home: 200 Rideau Terr Ottawa ON Canada K1M 0Z3 Office: Govt House Ottawa ON Canada K1A 0A1

HUBBARD, STANLEY EUGENE, broadcasting exec.; b. Redwing, Minn., June 26, 1897; s. Frank Valentine and Minnie (Ayre) H.; m. Mary Jane Rogers, July 21, 1979; children—Alice Hubbard Liptak, Stanley Stub. Student, St. Paul and Mpls. schs. Founder Ohio Valley Aero Transp. Co., 1919, Sta. WAMD, Mpls., 1923, Sta. KSTP, St. Paul-Mpls.; chmn. bd., chief exec. officer Hubbard Broadcasting Inc., St. Paul. Served with U.S. Army, World War I. Decorated cavaliere Order Crown Italy, 1935. Clubs: Indian Creek Country, LaGorce Country, Bal Harbour Beach and Yacht, Somerset Country, Town and Country, Minn., St. Paul Athletic, Mpls. 271 Bal Cross Dr Bal Harbour FL 33154 Office: 3415 University Ave Saint Paul MN 55114 *

HUBBARD, STANLEY STUB, television executive; b. St. Paul, May 28, 1933; s. Stanley Eugene and Didrikke A. (Stub) H.; m. Karen Elizabeth Holmen, June 13, 1959; children: Kathryn Elizabeth, Stanley Eugene, Virginia Anne, Robert Winston, Julia Didrikke. B.A., U. Minn., 1955. With KSTP-TV, St. Paul, 1950—, pres., 1967—, Fairlee Inc., U.S. Satellite Broadcasting Co., Inc.; past dir. 2d Northwestern Nat. Bank Mpls.; mem. NBC Affiliates Bd., 1967-70. Mem. Gov.'s Crime Commn., 1967-68; tech. adviser for Ramsey County Arena Commn., 1970; chmn. St. Croix Valley Youth Center, 1968—; trustee Hubbard Found.; bd. dirs. St. Paul Ramsey United Arts Council, U.S. Hockey Hall of Fame, Psychoanalytic Found. Minn., Midway Hosp. Found., U. Minn. Found., Guthrie Theatre. Mem. Minn. Broadcasters Assn., Young Presidents Orgn., Internat. Radio and TV Soc., Broadcast Pioneers., Mpls. C. of C. (dir.), St. Paul C. of C. (dir.). Clubs: Minneapolis, St. Paul Athletic; Minn., St. Croix Yacht (Stillwater, Minn.); Town and Country (St. Paul); St. Croix Sailing (Lakeland, Minn.); St. Petersburg (Fla.) Yacht., Bal Harbour, Indian Creek Country, Ocean Reef, Key Largo Anglers, Palm Bay. Home: Route 1 Lakeland MN 55043 Office: 3415 University Ave Saint Paul MN 55114

HUBBARD, WILLIAM BOGEL, JR., planetary sciences educator, consultant; b. Liberty, Tex., Nov. 14, 1940; s. William Bogel and Marie (Young) H.; m. Jean North Gilliland, June 8, 1963; children: Lynne Marie, Laurie North. B.A., Rice U., Houston, 1962; Ph.D., U. Calif.-Berkeley, 1967. Research fellow Calif. Inst. Tech., Pasadena, 1967-68; asst. prof. astronomy U. Tex.-Austin, 1968-72; assoc. prof. planetary scis. U. Ariz., Tucson, 1972-75, dir. Lunar and Planetary Lab., 1977-81, prof., 1975—; cons. Lawrence Livermore Nat. Lab., Calif., 1972—, NASA, 1970—. Contbr. articles to profl. jours.; assoc. editor: Icarus, 1980—. Exchange scientist USSR Nat. Acad. Sci., 1973. Mem. Am. Astron. Soc., Am. Geophys. Union, Internat. Astron. Union, Sigma Xi. Democrat. Episcopalian. Home: 2618 E Devon St Tucson AZ 85716 Office: Lunar and Planetary Lab U Ariz Tucson AZ 85721

HUBBARD, WILLIAM NEILL, JR., pharm. co. exec.; b. Fairmont, N.C., Oct. 15, 1919; s. William Neill and Mary Emma (Fenegan) H.; m. Elizabeth Terleski, Dec. 28, 1945; children—William Neill III, Michael J., Mary E., Elizabeth A., Susan E. A.B., Columbia, 1942; postgrad., U. N.C. Sch. Medicine; M.D., N.Y. U., 1944. Mem. house staff 3d med. div. Bellevue Hosp., N.Y.C., 1944-50; instr. medicine N.Y. U., 1950-53, asst. prof., 1953-59; asst. dean, then asso. dean N.Y. U. Coll. Medicine, 1951-59; dean U. Mich. Med. Sch., 1959-70, asso. prof. internal medicine, 1959-64, prof., 1964-70; dir. U. Mich. Med. Center, 1969-70; gen. mgr. pharm. div., v.p. Upjohn Co., 1970-72, exec. v.p., 1972-74, pres., 1974—, dir., 1968—; dir. 1st Am. Bank Corp., Hoover Universal Inc., Consumers Power; bd. dirs. Pharm. Mfrs. Assn., 1978-80, 81—, chmn. bd., 1980-81; cons. USPHS. Mem. Nat. Adv. Commn. on Libraries, 1966-68; med. adv. com. W.K. Kellogg Found., 1959-67, trustee, 1979—; mem. Gov.'s Adv. Com. on Edn. Health Care, 1965-69; trustee Bronson Meth. Hosp., 1970—; chmn. Gov.'s Action Com. on Corrections, 1972-73; mem. panel ednl. consultants Commn. on Edn. for Health Adminstrn., 1973-75; mem. com. on med. edn. Brown U., 1974-77; mem. nat. sci. bd. NSF, 1974-80, cons. to bd., 1980—; bd. dirs. Internat. Fertility Research Program, 1981—; mem. bd. sci. and tech. for internat. devel. Nat. Acad. Scis., 1978-80, Council on Sci. and Tech. for Devel., 1978—; bd. visitors in East Asian studies U. Mich., 1976—, bd. dirs. devel. council, 1979—; bd. overseers Morehouse Coll., 1976-81; bd. dirs. Nat. Med. Fellowships, Inc., 1973-75, Nat. Fund. Med. Edn., 1962-75; trustee Kalamazoo Coll., 1973-78, Columbia U., N.Y.C., 1981—; mem. bd. regents Nat. Library of Medicine, 1963-67, 72-76, chmn., 1965-67, 74-76, cons., 1976—; bd. dirs. Am. Near East Refugee Aid, 1977—; dir. devel. council U. Mich., 1979—; mem. population adv. panel Office of Technology Assessment, U.S. Congress, 1979-81. Fellow A.C.P.; mem. Inst. Medicine of Nat. Acad. Scis., Harvey Soc., N.Y. Acad. Medicine, Soc. Alumni Bellevue Hosp., Mich. Med. Soc. (council 1960-62), AMA, Kalamazoo Acad. Medicine, Am. Soc. Clin. Pharmacology and Therapeutics, Assn. Am. Med. Colls. (pres. 1966-67), Sigma Xi, Alpha Omega Alpha. Home: 1401 Lama Rd Kalamazoo MI 49008

HUBBELL, JAMES WINDSOR, JR., insurance company executive; b. Des Moines, Iowa, May 17, 1922; s. James Windsor and Harriet Amanda (Cox) H.; m. Helen Houx, June 8, 1946; children: James, Harriet, Frederick, Michael. Student, Harvard U., 1941-46. Dir. Equitable of Iowa Cos., Des Moines, 1961—, chmn. bd., 1976—; trustee F.M. Hubbell Estate, Des Moines, 1962—; pres. F.M. Hubbell Son & Co., Des Moines, 1975—. Dir. Episcopal Corp. Iowa, 1960—; trustee Simpson Coll., Indianola, Iowa, 1974—. Served with USN, 1943-45. Mem. Des Moines C. of C. (pres. 1972). Episcopalian. Clubs: Porcellian., Wakonda, Lost Tree. Office: 604 Locust St Des Moines IA 50306

HUBBELL, RICHARD WHITTAKER, news agency executive; b. Mt. Vernon, N.Y., Sept. 13, 1914; s. Rowland Southworth and Hildegarde May (Whittaker) H.; m. Kyra Alanova Deakin, May 31, 1941 (dec. 1965); m. June Cortelyou, Oct. 25, 1965. B.A., Wesleyan U., 1936; postgrad., Columbia U., 1936-38. Announcer WOR, WQXR, N.Y.C., 1937-39; dir. news CBS-TV, N.Y.C., 1939-43; prodn. mgr., TV cons. Crosley Broadcasting, Cin., 1944-47; TV officer U.S. Dept. State, N.Y.C., 1951-53; sales exec. DuMont TV, N.Y.C., 1954-55, Internat. News Service, 1957-58; founder, pres. World Wide Information Services, N.Y.C., 1958—. Author: 4000 Years of Television, 1942, Television Programming and Production, 1945, 50, 56; Contbr. articles to various publs. Mem. Alpha Delta Phi. Home: 360 1st Ave New York NY 10010 360 1st Ave New York NY 10010

HUBBELL, WAYNE LESTER, medical educator; b. Riverside, Calif., Mar. 24, 1943; s. Lester Glenn and Helyn Marie (Fischer) H.; m. Cheryl Alice McAfee, Jan. 6, 1965; 1 son, Paul Wayne. B.S., Oreg. State U., 1965; Ph.D., Stanford U., 1970. Postdoctoral fellow Stanford (Calif.) U., 1970; asst. prof. chemistry U. Calif., Berkeley, 1970-73, asso. prof., 1973-79, prof. chemistry, 1979-83; Jules Stein prof. ophthalmology Sch. Medicine and prof. chemistry UCLA, 1983—. Contbr. articles to various publs.; editorial bd.: Membrane Bichemistry, 1978—, Jour. Membrane Biology, 1983—. Recipient Dreyfus Found. Tchr.-Scholar award, 1975; Air Force Office Sci. Research-NRC postdoctoral fellow, 1969-70; Alfred P. Sloan Found. fellow, 1973-75. Mem. Am. Chem. Soc., Biophys. Soc. Home: 1668 Michael Ln Pacific Palisades CA 90272 Office: UCLA Sch Medicine Los Angeles CA 90024

HUBBEN, HERBERT, corporation executive; b. Krefeld, Germany, June 26, 1923; came to U.S., 1933; s. William and Maria (Feckes) H.; m. Jane Tupper, Juen 16, 1963; children: Henry, Julie, William, Anne, Catherine. B.A., Antioch Coll., 1948; M.A., Cornell U., 1950. Vice pres. staff services Corning Glass Internat., N.Y., 1966-74; v.p. mgmt. resources Eaton Corp., Cleve., 1974-80; pres. Eaton Yale Ltd., London, Ont., Can., Eaton Internat. Inc., Liberia, 1974-80; v.p. internat. Eaton Corp., Cleve., 1980—; dir. Nitta-Moore, Osaka, Japan, Eaton SAM, Monaco, Japan Fawick, Tokyo, Eaton Yale Ltd., London, Ont. Mem. bus. adv. council internat. Cuyahoga Community Coll., Cleve., 1983. Served with U.S. Army, 1943-46. Mem. Cleve. World Tade Assn. (pres.), Nat. Fgn. Trade Council (dir. 1980—), No. Ohio Dist. Export Council (chmn. 1981—). Clubs: Cleve. Skating,

Vermillion Yacht; University (N.Y.C.). Office: Eaton Corp 100 Erieview Plaza Cleveland OH 44114

HUBBERT, MARION KING, geologist, geophysicist; b. San Saba, Tex., Oct. 5, 1903; s. William Bee and Cora Virginia (Lee) H.; m. Miriam Graddy Berry, Nov. 11, 1938. Student, Weatherford Coll., 1921-23; B.S., U. Chgo., 1926, M.S., 1928, Ph.D., 1937; D.Sc. (hon.), Syracuse U., 1972, Ind. State U., 1980. Asst. geologist Amerada Petroleum Corp., Tulsa, summer 1926, 27-28; teaching asst. geology U. Chgo., 1928-30; instr. geophysics Columbia, 1930-40; geophysicist Ill. Geol. Survey, summers 1931-32, 35-37; assoc. geologist U.S. Geol. Survey, summer 1934; pvt. research, writing, 1940-41; sr. analyst Bd. Econ. Warfare, Washington, 1942-43; research geophysicist Shell Oil Co., Houston, 1943-45, assoc. dir. research, 1945-51, chief cons. gen. geology, 1951-55; cons. gen. geology Shell Devel. Co., 1956-64; vis. prof. geology and geophysics Stanford U., 1962-63, prof., 1963-68, prof. emeritus, 1968—; vis. prof. geography Johns Hopkins U., spring 1968; regents prof. U. Calif. at Berkeley, spring 1973, mem. adv. bd., 1974-77; research geophysicist U.S. Geol. Survey, 1964-76, cons., 1976—; mem. U.S. delegation UN Sci. Conf. Conservation and Utilization Resources, Lake Success, N.Y., 1949; mem. com. geophysics Nat. Research Council; adviser Office Naval Research, 1949-51; mem. com. Disposal Radioactive Waste Products, 1955-63; mem. Adv. Selection Com. for Allowing Grants under Fulbright Act, 1950-51; mem. vis. com. earth scis. Mass. Inst. Tech., 1958-60; mem. earth scis. adv. panel NSF, 1953-57, chmn., 1954-57; vis. lectr. M.I.T., 1959; regents lectr. UCLA, 1960; mem. com. natural resources Nat. Acad. Scis., 1961-62; chmn. div. earth scis. Nat. Acad. Scis.-NRC, 1963-65; nat. adv. bd. U. Nev. Desert Research Inst., 1967-73; mem. com. resources and man NRC, 1966-70. Author: The Theory of Groundwater Motion and Related Papers, U.S. Energy Resources, A Review as of 1972; co-author: Resources and Man, Structural Geology; Editor: Geophysics, 1947-49; assoc. editor: Jour. Geology, 1958-82, Bull. Am. Assn. Petroleum Geologists, 1955-74; Contbr. articles to profl. jours. Trustee, sec. Population Reference Bur., 1966-72; lectr. exec. seminars U.S. Civil Service, Office of Personnel Mgmt., 1971—; USIA lectr., Europe, 1975, 77. Recipient Lucas medal Am. Inst. Mining, Metall. and Petroleum Engrs., 1971; Rockefeller Pub. Service award, 1977; William Smith medal Geol. Soc. London, 1978; Elliott Cresson medal for outstanding work in field of geology Franklin Inst., Phila., 1981; Vetlesen gold medal and cash award Columbia U., 1981. Fellow Am. Acad. Arts and Scis., AAAS, Geol. Soc. Am. (Day medal 1954, Penrose medal 1973, council 1947-49, pres. 1962), Internat. Union Geol. Scis. (U.S. nat. com. 1961-64, com. on geosci. and man 1972-76); mem. Am. Assn. Petroleum Geologists (hon., Distinguished lectr. U.S. and Can. 1945, 52, 73-74), Am. Geophys. Union, Soc. Petroleum Engrs. (hon., Distinguished lectr. 1963-64), Soc. Exploration Geophysicists (hon., life), Canadian Soc. Petroleum Geologists (hon.), Nat. Acad. Scis., Sigma Xi, Gamma Alpha. Club: Cosmos (Washington). Home: 5208 Westwood Dr Bethesda MD 20816

HUBEL, DAVID HUNTER, educator, physiologist; b. Windsor, Ont., Can., Feb. 27, 1926; s. Jesse Hervey and Elsie (Hunter) H.; m. Shirley Ruth Izzard, June 20, 1953; children: Carl Andrew, Eric David, Paul Matthew. B.Sc., McGill U., 1947, M.D., 1951, D.Sc. (hon.), 1978, A.M., Harvard U., 1962. Intern Montreal Gen. Hosp., 1951-52; asst. resident neurology Montreal Neurol. Inst., 1952-53, fellow clin. neurophysiology, 1953-54; asst. resident neurology Johns Hopkins Hosp., 1954-55; sr. fellow neurol. scis. group Johns Hopkins U., 1958-59; faculty Harvard U. Med. Sch., 1959—, George Packer Berry prof. physiology, chmn. dept., 1967-68, George Packer Berry prof. neurobiology, 1968-82, John Franklin Enders univ. prof., 1982—; George H. Bishop lectr. exptl. neurology Washington U., St. Louis, 1964; Jessup lectr. biol. scis. Columbia, 1970; James Arthur lectr. Am. Mus. Natural History, 1972; Ferrier lectr. Royal Soc. London, 1972; Harvey lectr. Rockefeller U., 1976; Weizmann meml. lectr. Weizmann Inst. Sci., Rehovot, Israel, 1979. Served with AUS, 1955-58. Recipient Trustees Research to Prevent Blindness award, 1971; Lewis S. Rosenstiel award for disting. work in basic med. research, 1972; Karl Spencer Lashley prize Am. Philos. Soc., 1977; Louisa Gross Horwitz prize Columbia U., 1978; Dickson prize in Medicine U. Pitts., 1979; Ledlie prize Harvard U., 1980; Nobel prize, 1981; Sr. fellow Harvard Soc. Fellows, 1971—. Fellow Am. Acad. Arts and Scis.; mem. Nat. Acad. Sci., Am. Physiol. Soc. (Bowditch lectr. 1966), Deutsche Akademie der Naturforscher Leopoldina, Soc. for Neurosci. (Grass lecture 1976), Assn. for Research in Vision and Ophthalmology (Friedenwald award 1975), Johns Hopkins U. Soc. Scholars. Research brain mechanisms in vision; bd. syndics Harvard U. Press, 1979-83. Home: 98 Collins Rd Waban MA 02168 Office: 25 Shattuck St Boston MA 02115

HUBER, SISTER ALBERTA, college president; b. Rock Island, Ill., Feb. 12, 1917; d. Albert and Lydia (Hofer) H. B.A., Coll. St. Catherine, St. Paul, 1939; M.A., U. Minn., 1945; Ph.D., U. Notre Dame, 1954. Faculty Coll. St. Catherine, 1940—, prof. English, 1953—, chmn. dept., 1960-63, acad. dean, 1962-64, pres., 1964-79. Bd. dirs. Jr. Achievement, St. Paul, Minn. Opera Assn.; trustee St. Joseph's Hosp., St. Paul, 1971-80; pres. UN Assn. Minn., 1980-81. Decorated chevalier d'Ordre des Palmes Academiques.; recipient Outstanding Achievement award U. Minn. Alumni Assn., 1981. Mem. Phi Beta Kappa, Pi Gamma Mu. Office: 2004 Randolph Ave Saint Paul MN 55105

HUBER, DON LAWRENCE, publisher; b. Milw., Aug. 17, 1928; s. Wallace Fred and Florence (Bleck) H.; m. Joan Mac Monnies, June 23, 1951. Student, Carthage (Ill.) Coll., 1946-48; B.S. in English, Northwestern U., 1950. Sales exec. sta. WOR (radio), N.Y.C., 1957-58; gen. mgr. sta. KALE (radio), Pasco, Washington, 1958-60; mgr. advtg. Standard Rate & Data Service (pub. co.), N.Y.C., 1961-70. Pub.: mag. Computer Decisions, Hayden Pub. Co., Rochelle Park, N.J., 1970—. Served with USN, 1946-48. Mem. Sales Execs. N.Y., Navy League. Club: Northwestern University (N.Y.C.). Home: 24 Rolling Dr Brookville NY 11545 Office: 50 Essex St Rochelle Park NJ 07662

HUBER, GORDON FLOYD, franchise foodservice executive; b. Victoria, Ill., Jan. 19, 1921; s. Floyd Benjamin and Edna (Moak) H.; m. Betty Louise Terpening, Feb. 27, 1944; children: James Clay, Elizabeth Ann Huber Webster, Jay Gordon. B.A., Monmouth Coll., Ill., 1943; mgmt. course, Am. Mgmt. Assn., 1969-70. Local mgr. Intra-State Telephone Co., Galesburg, Ill., 1947-52; mgr. Capitol Dairy Queen, Inc., Galesburg, 1953-56; gen. mgr. Illini Dairy Queen, Inc., Springfield, Ill., 1957-62; exec. v.p. Internat. Dairy Queen, Inc., Mpls., 1962—; pres. Dairy Queen of Utah, Inc., Minnetonka, Minn., 1980—; dir. Diary Queen of Japan Co., Ltd., Tokyo. County chmn. Nat. Found. Infantile Paralysis, Galesburg, 1951; solicitor United Way Community Chest, Galesburg and Mpls., 1947-52, 72-73. Served to lt. (j.g.) USNR, 1942-46; PTO. Republican. Congregationalist. Clubs: Illini Country (Springfield); Wayzata Country (Minn.) (v.p. 1976). Home: 18400 Wintergreen Ct Minnetonka MN 55343 Office: International Dairy Queen 5701 Green Valley Dr Minneapolis MN 55437

HUBER, JOAN ALTHAUS, sociology educator; b. Bluffton, Ohio, Oct. 17, 1925; d. Lawrence Lester and Hallie Moser (Althaus) H.; m. William Form, Feb. 5, 1971; children—Nancy Rytina, Steven Rytina. B.A., Pa. State U., 1945; M.A., Western Mich. U., 1963; Ph.D., Mich. State U., 1967. Asst. prof. sociology U. Notre Dame, Ind., 1967-71; asst. prof. sociology U. Ill., Urbana-Champaign, 1971-73, assoc. prof., 1973-78, prof., 1978—, head dept., 1979—. Author: (with William Form) Income and Ideology, 1973; editor: (with Glenna Spitze) Sex Stratification, 1983, Changing Women in a Changing Society, 1973, (with Paul Chalfant) The Sociology of Poverty, 1974. NSF research awardee, 1978-81. Mem. Am. Sociol. Assn. (v.p. 1981-83), Sociologists for Women in Soc., Midwest Sociol. Soc. (pres. 1979-80). Home: 612 La Sell Dr Champaign IL 61820 Office: Dept Sociology 326 LH U Ill Urbana IL 61801

HUBER, MICHAEL W., petroleum company executive; b. 1926. With J.M. Huber Corp., Edison, N.J., 1944—, chief exec. officer, chmn. bd., pres., dir., 1957—. Address: JM Huber Corp Thornall St Edison NJ 08818 *

HUBER, RICHARD GREGORY, lawyer, educator; b. Indpls., June 29, 1919; s. Hugh Joseph and Laura Marie (Becker) H.; m. Katherine Elizabeth McDonald, June 21, 1950; children: Katherine, Richard, Mary, Elizabeth, Stephen, Mark. B.S., U.S. Naval Acad, 1942; J.D., U. Iowa, 1950; LL.M., Harvard U., 1951. Bar: Iowa 1950. Instr. law U. Iowa, 1950; assoc. prof. law U. S.C., 1952-54; assoc. prof. Tulane U., 1954-57, Boston Coll., 1957-59, prof., 1959—, dean, 1970—. Contbr. articles and book reviews to profl. jours. Trustee Mass. Continuing Legal Edn.; vice chmn. Mass. chpt. Multiple Sclerosis Soc. Served with USN, 1941-47, 51-52. Mem. ABA (del., mem. council legal edn., trustee law sch. admissions council), Mass. Bar Assn., Boston Bar Assn., Am. Bar. Found.; Mem. Soc. Am. Law Tchrs., Mass. Bar Found., Assn. Am. Law Schs., Council of Legal Edn. Opportunity (pres. 1975-79), Flaschner Jud. Inst., Am. Judicature Soc. Democrat. Roman Catholic. Club: Windsor. Home: 406 Woodward St Newton MA 02168 Office: 885 Centre St Newton MA 02159

HUBER, ROBERT FREDERICK, publisher, editor; b. Oak Park, Ill., Aug. 29, 1925; s. Freh Frederick and Mary Elmetta (Dowds) H.; m. Verna Beth Graham, June 18, 1950; children: Catherine Ellen, Donald Graham, Greg Frederick. Student, Baldwin-Wallace Coll., 1943-44, Cornell U., Ithaca, N.Y., 1944, Harvard U., 1945; B.S. in Physics and Math., Denison U., 1949; postgrad. in Engring., Cleve. State U., 1950-51. Spl. apprentice Warner & Swasey Co., Cleve., 1949-51, sales engr., 1951-52; editor Steel Mag., Penton Pub. Co., Cleve., 1952-69, Prodn. (bus. mag.); v.p. Bramson Prodn. Pub. Co., Inc., Bloomfield Hills, Mich., 1969—. Author: Machine Tool Buyers' Guide, 1954, Depreciation, Its Long and Shortcomings, 1956, Time to Speak Out, 1970, How Equipment is Really Bought, 1972, How Research Dollars Are Committed, 1972. Chmn. North Trails dist. Boy Scouts Am., 1973—. Served to lt. (j.g.) USNR, 1943-45; PTO. Recipient Indsl. Mktg. Journalism award Indsl. Mktg. mag., 1954; Jesse Neal award for editorial excellence Am. Bus. Press, 1980. Mem. Am. Soc. Bus. Press Editors, Numerical Control Soc. Am., Soc. Mfg. Engrs., Sigma Delta Chi. Congregationalist (chmn. com. world missions 1973-75). Home: 4581 Wagon Wheel Birmingham MI 48010 Office: Box 101 Bloomfield Hills MI 48013

HUBER, THOMAS MARTIN, container company executive; b. Highland, Ill., Nov. 4, 1919; s. Martin J. and Ida R. (Burke) H.; m. Martha A. Kaseberg, Aug. 15, 1942; children: Timothy B., Martha A. Huber Scavone. B.S., U. Ill., 1941; student, Northwestern U. Grad. Sch. Bus.-Inst. Internat. Mgmt., 1970. With Owens-Ill. Inc., 1946—, v.p., gen. mgr. Cuban ops., 1957-60, v.p. internat. div. for industry relations, area mgr., N. Am., Caribbean, Far East, 1960-61, v.p., gen. mgr. Belgian ops., 1961-65, v.p., gen. mgr. Venezuelan ops., 1965-68, v.p., gen. mgr. European ops., 1968-73, corp. v.p., gen. mgr. European div., Toledo, 1973-80, gen. mgr. worldwide bus. devel., 1980-81, sr. v.p., 1981—; pres. Kibmle Italiana (S.p.A.), Italy, 1968-80, Owens-Ill. Internat. S.A., Switzerland, 1968-80, Durobor S.A., Belgium, 1968-80; dir. United Glass Ltd., U.K., 1968—, Giralt Laporta, S.A., Spain, 1968—. Served to maj. C.E. AUS, 1941-45. Republican. Roman Catholic. Clubs: Belmont Country, Geneva Golf., Chapel Hill Country. Home: 10125 Ford Rd Perrysburg OH 43551 Office: Owens-Ill Inc One Seagate Toledo OH 43666

HUBER, WILLIAM H., JR., university dean; b. Harrisburg, Pa., Apr. 18, 1922; s. William H. and Sarah Catherine (Peace) H.; m. Sarah Hughes Douglass, Oct. 5, 1942; 1 dau., Sarah Kathryn. A.B., Ohio State U., J.D., 1947. Bar: Ohio, N.Mex. Former instr. U. N.Mex., Albuquerque, prof. bus. adminstrn., mgmt., 1960—, dir. Univ. Coll., 1957-71, dir. Counseling Center, 1965-71, acting dean Sch. Adminstrv. Scis., 1968-69, dean Univ. Coll., 1971—; Cons. on acad. planning. Author: (with R.K. Evans) The Business Venture in New Mexico, 1952; also monographs and articles. Mem. N.M. Bar Assn., Phi Kappa Phi, Alpha Kappa Psi, Blue Key. Club: Kiwanian. Home: 2811 Campus Blvd NE Albuquerque NM 87106

HUBERT, BERNARD, bishop; b. Beloeil, Que., Can., June 1, 1929. Ordained priest Roman Catholic Ch., 1953; bishop of, St. Jerome, 1971-77, coadjutor bishop of, Saint-Jean-de-Que., 1977—. Office: 740 Boul Ste Foy CP 40 Longueuil PQ J4K 4X8 Canada *

HUBERT, FRANK WILLIAM RENE, retired university chancellor; b. Milam County, Tex., June 2, 1915; s. Jonce Sherod and Lura Gertrude (White) H.; m. Mary Julia Glidden, June 15, 1940; children: Frank William Rene, Mary Katherine. B.A., U. Tex., 1938, M.A., 1946, Ph.D., 1950; LL.D., Baylor U., 1979. Dir. Lutcher Stark Boys, Inc., Orange, Tex., 1938-44; prin., dir. secondary edn. Stark Sr. High Sch., Orange, 1946-48; research fellow, curriculum and instrn. U. Tex., 1948-49; adminstrv. asst. Found. Sch. Program Act div. Tex. Auditor's Office, Austin, 1949-50, dir. div., 1949-50; dir. div. profl. standards, also div. tchr. edn. Tex. Edn. Agy., Austin, 1950-55; supt. schs. Orange Ind. Sch. Dist., 1955-59; dean Sch. Arts and Scis., Tex. A&M U., College Station, 1959-65, dean Coll. Liberal Arts, 1965-69, dean Coll. Edn., 1969-79, dir. basic div., 1959-60, chancellor, 1979—, chancellor emeritus, 1983—; exec. sec. Tex. Bd. Exam. Tchr. Edn., 1952-55; mem. com. 75 U. Tex.; pres. Tex. Conf. Tchr. Edn., 1959; mem. Nat. Council Accreditation Tchr. Edn., 1953-55; v.p. S.W. Ednl. Devel Corp., 1966-67, pres., 1967-68; dir. Republic Bank A&M, Blocker Energy Corp.; mem. Nat. Adv. Commn. on Mexican-Am. Edn., U.S. Office Edn., 1967-69; adv. council U.S. Command and Gen. Staff Coll., 1972-75; pres. Corp. Research and Engring. in Edn., 1969—; mem. bd. cons. Center for Research and Edn. Free Enterprise, 1977-80; mem. Tex. Adv. Com. Tech.-Vocat. Edn., 1978-80, Gov.'s Com. Pub. Edn., 1966-69. Mem. charter change commn., Orange, 1958. Served with AUS, 1944-46. Mem. NEA, Orange Edn. Assn. (pres. 1943-44), Assn. Tex. Colls. and Univs. (pres. 1965-66), Am., Tex. assns. sch. adminstrs., Am. Acad. Polit. and Social Sci., Tex. Tchrs. Assn. (chmn. com. tchr. edn. and profl. standards 1955-60), Sons Republic Tex., Phi Kappa Phi, Phi Delta Kappa, Kappa Delta Pi. Home: 2404 Morris Ln Bryan TX 77801 Office: Tex A & M U College Station TX 77843

HUBERT, RICHARD F. (DICK HUBERT), TV, film prodn. co. exec.; b. N.Y.C., June 30, 1938; s. Alexander and Rebecca (Tall) H.; m. Jeltje M. Schuringa, Dec. 1, 1962; children—Douglas Deryk, Darren Alexander. B.A., Amherst Coll., 1960; postgrad., U. Stockholm, 1960-61. Corr. internat. service Swedish Broadcasting Corp., 1960-61; sr. editor UPI, London, 1961-62; corr. Am. Forces Network France, 1962-64; producer, writer, reporter ABC-TV News, N.Y.C., 1964-68; exec. producer urban Am. unit Westinghouse Broadcasting Co., 1968-74; chmn. Gateway Prodns., Inc., N.Y.C., 1974—. Trustee Amherst Coll., 1978—. Served with U.S. Army, 1962-64. Recipient Peabody award, DuPont-Columbia award (2), Ohio State U. award, Robert F. Kennedy Meml. Journalism award. Mem. Nat. Assn. TV Program Execs., Writers Guild Am., Sigma Delta Chi. Office: 304 E 45th St New York NY 10017

HUBERTUS, KENNETH LEONARD, airline exec.; b. Oshkosh, Wis., Nov. 28, 1928; s. Joseph John and Mary Theresa (Paulus) H.; m. Gertrude Anita Pilian, Oct. 7, 1952; children—Mary, Keith, Mark, Michael, Kenneth R., John, Jeffrey, Karen, Gail. Regional mgr. sta. ops. North Central Airlines, Chgo., 1960-76, mgr., Mpls., 1976-78; v.p. ground service Republic Airlines, Mpls., 1978-79, sr. v.p. customer service, 1979—. Served with USN, 1944-48. Roman Catholic. Home: 401 Harold Dr Burnsville MN 55337 Office: 7500 Airline Dr Minneapolis MN 55450

HUBIAK, DANIEL, clergyman; b. Akron, Ohio, Dec. 29, 1926; s. Athanasius and Susan (Wanchishen) H.; m. Evelyn Martynuk, Sept. 16, 1951; children—Larice, Annice. B.S., Columbia U., 1952, St. Vladimir's Orthodox Theol. Sem., N.Y.C., 1956. Ordained priest Orthodox Ch. in Am., 1952; asst. pastor Holy Trinity Ch., Detroit, 1952-53; pastor St. Mary Ch., Marblehead, Ohio, 1953-55; asst. pastor Holy Transfiguration Ch., Bklyn., 1956-58; pastor Holy Trinity Ch., East Meadow, N.Y., 1958-70; treas. Orthodox Ch. Am., Syosset, N.Y., 1963-70, sec.-treas., 1970-73, chancellor, 1973—. Trustee St. Vladimir's Orthodox Theol. Sem., Crestwood, N.Y., St. Tikhon's Theol. Sem., South Canaan, Pa. Served with AUS, 1945-46. Office: PO Box 675 Syosset NY 11791

HUBLER, JAMES T(ERRENCE), lawyer; b. Portland, Oreg., Sept. 11, 1943; s. Elmer M. and Katherine A. (McGinty) H.; m. Marcia Sydney McCabe, June 26, 1965; children—Lisa, Mark, Nicholas. B.S., Portland State U., 1965; J.D. cum laude, Lewis and Clark Coll., 1972; grad., Advanced Mgmt. Program, Harvard Sch. Bus., 1980. Bar: Oreg. bar 1972; Registered profl. engr., Oreg. Engr. Hyster Co., Portland, Oreg., 1965-71, lawyer, 1971-73; mem. firm Tooze Kerr Marshall & Shenker, Portland, 1973-74; corp. counsel Freightliner Corp., Portland, 1974-77, v.p., corp. counsel, 1977-78, sr. v.p. indsl. relations, gen. counsel, sec., 1978—, also dir.; arbitrator Am. Arbitration Assn., 1972. Bd. dirs. Newman Found., Portland State U. Mem. Oreg. Bar Assn., Multnomah County Bar Assn., Am. Bar Assn., Delta Theta Phi. Democrat. Roman Catholic. Office: 4747 N Channel Ave Portland OR 97217

HUBLER, JULIUS, artist; b. Granite City, Ill., Dec. 11, 1919; s. Voyle and Marie (Lewedag) H.; m. Loretta Lanter, Apr. 26, 1943; children: Stuart Alden, Ann Marlowe McClure. B.S., S.E. Mo. U., 1943; M.A., Ed.D., Columbia U., 1951. Sci. tchr. Wibaux High Sch., Mont., 1942-43, Ashton Hight Sch., Idaho, 1943-45; art instr. CCNY, 1946-48; prof. art SUNY-Buffalo, 1948-82; freelance artist, Buffalo, 1982—, painter, graphic designer, sculptor, photographer. Mem. Western N.Y. Peace Ctr. State U. Iowa grad. scholar, 1944; Arthur W. Dow scholar Columbia U., 1947; disting. service awardee U. Buffalo, 1958. Mem. AAUP (dir., pres. N.Y. state chpt. 1956-60), Soc. Am. Graphic Artists (Warren Mack Meml. purchase award 1962), Nat. Acad. Design (Samuel F.B. Morse medal 1977, Anonymous prize 1980). Club: Buffalo Stamp. Address: 94 Danbury Ln Buffalo NY 14217 *One is in debt to an endless number of people living and dead. Many have paid a horrible price. Change and, hopefully progress, are rarely welcome. Products of imagination testify to the necessary sacrifice, dedication, strength and vision. It is not a matter of formal education but vigilant attention to life, beliefs and purposes.*

HUBLEY, FAITH ELLIOTT, film maker, animator; b. N.Y.C., Sept. 16, 1924; d. Irving and Sally Irene (Rosenblatt) Chestman; m. John K. Hubley, June 24, 1955; children: Mark, Ray, Emily, Georgia. Ed., Art Students League, N.Y.C. Partner Storyboard Prodn. Co. (now Hubley Studio Inc.), N.Y.C., 1955—; vis. lectr. Yale U. Sch. Art, 1972—. Film editor, script supr., music editor, N.Y.C. and Hollywood, Calif., 1943-55; films include Spectre of the Rose; music editor, 1946, Twelve Angry Men; script supr., 1957, WOW (Women of the World); producer and dir., 1975, Second Chance: Sea, 1976, also numerous animated films, 1955—. Recipient (with John Hubley) six Cine Golden Eagle awards, three Academy awards; two Cine Golden Eagle awards for own films. Mem. Acad. Motion Picture Arts and Scis., Art Students League (life), Motion Picture Film Editors. Office: Hubley Studio 355 E 50th St New York NY 10022 *

HUBLEY, JOHN, animator, film producer and director; b. Marinette, Wis., 1914; m. Faith Elliott; children: Georgia, Mark, Ray, Emily. Student, Art Center Sch., Los Angeles. With, Walt Disney Studios, from 1935; art dir.: films Rite of Spring sect. Fantasia; producer tng. films for, USAF, World War II; staff, United Prodns. Am.; dir.: films Robin Hoodlum, 1948, The Magic Fluke, 1949, Rooty-Toot-Toot, 1952, Ragtime Bear (introduced character Mr. Magoo), 1949; co-founder prodn. co., Storyboard, 1955; producer, animator (with wife), The Adventures of an, 1956, Tender Game, 1958, Moonbird, 1959, The Hole, 1963, The Hat, 1964, Tijuana Brass Double Feature, 1966, Windy Day, 1968, Of Men and Demons, 1969, Cockaboody, 1973, Voyage to Next, 1974, People People People, 1975, Everybody Rides the Carousel, 1975; worked on segments of: ednl. TV shows. Sesame St (Winner Acad. award 1960, 63, 67, CINE Golden Eagle 1966, 70, 72, many other awards.). Office: Hubley Studio Inc 355 E 50th St New York NY 10022 *

HUBLEY, REGINALD ALLEN, publisher; b. New Rochelle, N.Y., Aug. 21, 1928; s. Reginald McDonald and Eleanor Francis (Stock) H.; m. Karleen J. Smith, Apr. 7, 1979; children: Brandon, Caroline. B.S. in Commerce and Fin., Bucknell U., 1952. Salesman McGraw Hill Pub. Co., N.Y.C., N.J., 1952-54; dist. mgr. Elec. Constrn. and Maintenance, and Elec. Wholesaling publs., Cleve., 1954-59, sales mgr., N.Y.C., 1959-63, pub., 1963-69, Nucleonics Week, Nucleonics & Sci. Research, N.Y.C., 1966-69, Aviation Week and Space Tech., 1969—, Am. Machinist, 1976—; v.p. European ops. McGraw-Hill Pub. Co., London, 1979—. Served with USN, 1946-48; PTO. Mem. Internat. Fedn. Periodical Pubs. (exec. com.), Aviation Hall of Fame (bd. nominations 1971—). Republican. Baptist. Office: 34 Dover St London W1X 3RA England

HUBNER, ROBERT WILMORE, consultant, former business machines company executive; b. Seattle, Mar. 21, 1918; s. Robert G. and Thurza (Wilmore) H.; m. Katherine L. Huick, Apr. 4, 1942; children: Melissa, Robert Wilmore. Grad., U. Wash., 1941. With IBM, 1941-43, 43—, dir. recruitment, 1956, exec. asst. to exec. v.p., 1957, sales mgr. data processing div., 1957-59, exec. asst. to chmn. bd., 1959-61, dir. mktg., 1961-65, v.p. mktg., 1965-68, v.p., group exec., 1968-71, sr. v.p., mem. mgmt. com., 1972-78; now cons. in field; dir. Marine Midlands Bank, Inc., Buffalo, Africa Corp., FMC Corp., Baldwin Technology Corp., Stamford, S&S Corrugated Machinery Co., N.Y., Internat. Income Properties Ltd., Hong Kong Shanghai Banking Corp., Hong Kong. Mem. adv. bd. Grad. Sch. Bus., U. Wash.; vice chmn. South Street Seaport, N.Y.C. Served with AUS, 1943. Clubs: The Brook, N.Y. Yacht (N.Y.C.) (trustee); Wee Burn (Darien, Conn); Edgartown (Mass.) Yacht (vice commodore), Cruising of Am.). Home: Butler's Island Darien CT 06820 Office: IBM Armonk NY 10504

HUBSCHMAN, HENRY A., lawyer; b. Newark, N.J., Aug. 12, 1947; s. Morris and Esther (Weissman) H. B.A., Rutgers U., 1969; J.D., Harvard U., 1973, M.Public Policy, 1973. Bar: Mass. bar 1973, N.J. bar 1974, D.C. bar 1974. Law clk. to Judge Frank Murray, U.S. Dist. Ct., Boston, 1973-74; asso. firm Fried, Frank, Harris, Shriver & Kampelman, Washington, 1974-77, 79-80; partner, 1980—; exec. asst. to Sec. HUD, Washington, 1977-79; dir. Fed. Nat. Mortgage Assn., 1979—. Henry Rutgers scholar, 1969; Recipient Outstanding Achievement award HUD, 1978, HUD Sec.'s award for excellence, 1979. Mem. Am. Bar Assn., Phi Beta Kappa. Democrat. Jewish. Home: 4234 Embassy Park Dr NW Washington DC 20016 Office: 600 New Hampshire Ave NW Washington DC 20037

HUCK, JOHN LLOYD, Pharmaceutical company executive; b. Bklyn., July 17, 1922; s. John Lloyd and Adrienne (Warner) H.; m. Dorothy Bertha Foehr, Nov. 20, 1943; children: Lloyd E., Jeanne Huck Miller, Virginia A. B.S. in Chemistry, Pa. State U., 1946. Research chemist Hoffmann-LaRoche, Nutley, N.J., 1946, sales rep., 1948, dir. sales tng., 1951, asst. gen. sales mgr., 1955, dir. product devel., 1958; dir. mktg. Merck Sharp & Dohme Div., West Point, Pa., 1958; v.p. mktg. planning MSD div., 1966, v.p. sales and mktg., 1968, exec. v.p., 1969, exec. v.p., gen. mgr., 1972, pres., 1973; sr. v.p. Merck & Co., Rahway, N.J., 1975, exec. v.p., 1977, dir., 1977—, pres., chief operating officer, 1978—; dir. Amstar Corp., AMF Corp. Patentee (in field). Trustee Pa. State U., 1977—, Morristown Meml. Hosp., N.J., 1979—; bd. dirs. Pa. Research Corp., University Park, 1982—. Served to 1st lt. USAAF, 1942-46. Alumni fellow Coll. Medicine Pa. State U., 1980, Coll. of Sci., 1983. Republican. Presbyterian. Clubs: Morris Country, Economics. Home: Village Rd New Vernon NJ 07976 Office: PO Box 2000 Rahway NJ 07065

HUCK, JOHN WENZEL, retired association executive; b. Chgo., Nov. 1, 1916; s. Claude Alexander and Margaret Columbia (John) H.; m. Dorothy Elizabeth Montgomery, Oct. 10, 1942; children-Geoffrey James, Christopher Claude, Stuart Montgomery. Grad., Phillips Exeter Acad., 1934; A.B., Dartmouth Coll., 1938; M.A., Columbia U., 1940; postgrad., U. Chgo., 1940-41; L.H.D., Lincoln Coll., 1966. Dir. med. devel. U. Chgo., 1946-55; founder John W. Huck & Assocs., Chgo., 1955-60; exec. dir. Assoc. Colls. Ill., 1961-81. Sec. U. Chgo. Cancer Research Found., 1948-56; sec.-treas. Cancer Research Found., Inc., 1954-56; mem. citizens bd. Loyola U.; cons. v.p. Oscar Mayer Found., 1969—; pres. Opera Theatre of Ill. Served as capt. Ordnance AUS, 1941-46. Mem. Phi Sigma Kappa. Republican. Home: 26 W 8th St Hinsdale IL 60521

HUCK, LEONARD WILLIAM, banker; b. Sioux City, Iowa, Dec. 4, 1922; s. Jay Myles and Eula Lea (Pinkley) H.; m. Suzanne Lesher, July 26, 1947; children: Leonard William, Robert C., Wendy. B.A., DePauw U., 1944; postgrad., Southwestern Grad. Sch. Banking, 1965, Harvard U., 1944. Asst. mgr. Camelback Inn., Phoenix, 1946-50; summer resort mgr. St. Mary's Glacier Lodge, Idaho Springs, Colo., 1950; mgr. Ariz. Country Club, Phoenix, 1950-57; exec. v.p. Valley Nat. Bank, Phoenix, 1957-82, pres., chief adminstrv. officer, 1982—; faculty Assembly for Bank Dirs., 1968—; dir. Southwestern Grad. Sch. Banking, 1966—, dean for bankers, 1973-75. Pres. Phoenix and Valley of the Sun Conv. and Visitors Bur., 1975, dir., 1975-77; chmn. Maricopa County Heart Assn., 1967, Desert Found., 1966-71; mem. Fiesta Bowl Com., 1983; pres. Scottsdale (Ariz.) Boys Club, 1965, St. Luke's Hosp., 1972-74; bd. dirs., mem. exec. com. Blood Systems, Inc.; trustee, sec. Phoenix Art Mus., 1971; nat. co-chmn. YWCA Fund for the Future, 1983. Served with USN, 1942-46. Named Phoenix Man of Yr., 1978; recipient Torch of Liberty award Anti-Defamation League, 1983. Mem. Bank Mktg. Assn. (dir. 1976—, pres. 1981-82), Assn. Res. City Bankers, Phoenix C. of C. (pres. 1977, dir. 1974-79), Am. Inst. Banking, Ariz. Club Mgrs. Assn., Ariz. Hotel and Motel Assn., Ariz. Heart Assn. Episcopalian. Clubs: Valley of the Sun Kiwanis (pres. 1961), Scottsdale Dinner (pres. 1967), Paradise Valley Country (dir. 1974-77), Paradise Valley Country (sec. 1976), Kiva (pres. 1970, 71), Phoenix Thunderbirds (big chief 1964), Valley Field Riding and Polo (v.p. 1978-79). Home: 4854 Calle del Medio Phoenix AZ 85018 Office: PO Box 71 Phoenix AZ 85001

HUCKABA, CHARLES EDWIN, consulting engineer; b. Huntingdon, Tenn., Oct. 20, 1922; s. Oscar Franklin and Fannie (Austin) H.; m. Ann Coleman Dickerson, June 12, 1946; children—Charles David, Carol Ann. B.S., Vanderbilt U., 1944; M.S., Mass. Inst. Tech., 1947; Ph.D., U. Cin., 1953. Registered profl. engr., N.Y., Pa. Asso. prof. chem. engring. Lamar State Coll. Tech., 1952-55; asso. prof. chem. engring. U. Fla., 1955-63; prof., chmn. chem. engring. dept. Drexel Inst. Tech., 1963-67; vis. prof. chem. engring. Columbia, 1967-68, sr. research asso., 1968-69, prof. rehab. medicine, mem. at large Faculty Engring. and Applied Sci., 1969-74; head engring. chemistry and energetics sect. NSF, Washington, 1974-76; Andrew Carnegie prof. engring. The Cooper Union, 1976-77, dir. engring. program devel., 1977-80; pres. Charles Huckaba Assos., 1981—; adj. prof. dept. clin. engring. George Washington U. Med. Sch., 1974-78; pres. Med. Products Devel. Corp., Larchmont, N.Y., 1972-80; cons. shipbuilding div. Bethlehem Steel Co., 1952-56, Thermal Research & Engring. Corp., 1965-67, Foxboro Co., 1970-71; Year-In-Industry educator E.I. duPont de Nemours & Co., Inc., 1961-62. Recipient Distinguished Engring. Alumnus award U. Cin., 1971; Stephen L. Tyler award N.Y. sect. Am. Inst. Chem. Engrs., 1972. Fellow Am. Inst. Chemists, Am. Inst. Chem. Engrs.; mem. Am. Soc. Engring. Edn., Sigma Xi, Tau Beta Pi, Phi Lambda Upsilon. Home: Box 263 217 W 18th St New York NY 10011

HUCKABY, THOMAS JERALD, congressman; b. Hodge, La., July 19, 1941; s. Thomas Milton and Eva Huckaby T.; m. Suzanna Woodard, Dec. 21, 1962; children: Michelle, Clay. B.S., La. State U., 1963; M.B.A., Ga. State U., 1968. With Western Electric Co., 1963-73; owner, operator soybean farm, Ringgold, La., 1973—; mem. 95th-98th Congresses from La. Mem. La. Farm Bur., North La. Milk Producers Assn., La. Cattlemans Assn. Democrat. Methodist. Home: PO Box 544 Ringgold LA 71068 Office: 2444 Rayburn House Office Bldg Washington DC 20515

HUCKEL, HUBERT E., chemical corporation executive. Grad., U. Vienna Sch. Medicine, 1956; attended, NIH, Bethesda, Md. With Am. Hoechst Corp., 1965—, v.p. med. affairs pharm. subs., 1966-68, exec. v.p., then pres. subs., 1968-75, corp. group v.p. pharms., agrl. chems., Somerville, N.J., 1975-78, exec. v.p. pharms., agrl. chems., 1978—, exec. v.p. corp. human resources dept., corp. tng. dept. and adminstrn., dir., 1980—. Office: Am Hoechst Corp 1041 Route 201-206 N Box 2500 Somerville NJ 08876 *

HUCKER, CHARLES OSCAR, former educator, author; b. St. Louis, June 21, 1919; s. Edward Christian and Katie (Bond) H.; m. Myrl C. Henderson, Feb. 12, 1943. B.A. with high honors, U. Tex., 1941; Ph.D. with honors, U. Chgo., 1950; H.H.D. (hon.), Oakland U., 1974. Instr. U. Chgo., 1950-54, asst. prof., 1954-56; assoc. prof. U. Ariz., 1956-58, prof., 1958-61, Oakland U., Rochester, Mich., 1961-65; prof. Chinese and history U. Mich., Ann Arbor, 1965-83, Williams emeritus prof., 1984—, chmn. dept. Far Eastern langs. and lits., 1965-71; Cons. U.S. Office Edn., 1960, 65, 66, Ford Found., 1962-63; mem. com. on studies Chinese civilization, chmn. subcom. polit. instns. Am. Council Learned Socs., 1963-69; cons. or vis. lectr. various colls. and univs.; mem. del. of Ming-Ch'ing historians to China from Am. Acad. Sci., 1979. Author: Chinese History: A Bibliographic Review, 1958, The Traditional Chinese State In Ming Times, 1961, China: A Critical Bibliography, 1962, The Censorial System of Ming China, 1966, Some Approaches to China's Past, 1973, China's Imperial Past, 1975, China to 1850: A Short History, 1978, The Ming Dynasty: Its Origins and Evolving Institutions, 1978, A Dictionary of Official Titles in Imperial China, 1984, (with others) Chinese Thought and Institutions, 1957, Confucianism in Action, 1959, An Introduction to Chinese Civilization, 1973, Chinese Ways in Warfare, 1974, Dictionary of Ming Biography, 1976; Editor: Chinese Government in Ming Times: Seven Studies, 1969; Contbr.: articles to Ency. Americana, Ency. Brittanica; (with others) profl. jours. Served to maj. USAAC, 1942-46; PTO. Decorated Bronze Star; postdoctoral fellow Rockefeller Found., 1952-54; sr. fellow NEH, 1968-69. Mem. Assn. for Asian Studies (sec. 1966-68, dir. 1960-63), Am. Oriental Soc., Am. Hist. Assn., Phi Beta Kappa, Phi Alpha Theta. Home: 6781 E 4th St Tucson AZ 85710

HUCKINS, CHARLES ALBERT, botanist; b. Honolulu, July 4, 1941; s. Thomas Averill and Sue (Edwards) H.; m. Mathilde Germaine Demisay, Sept. 27, 1975. B.A. in Biology, Brown U., 1963; M.S. in Horticulture, Cornell U., 1967; Ph.D. in Botany, Cornell U., 1972. Curator tropical plants Mo. Bot. Garden, St. Louis, 1974-77, asst. chief horticulturist, 1977-78, chmn. indoor horticulture dept., 1978-79; dir. Desert Bot. Garden, Phoenix, 1979—; adj. asso. prof. dept. botany-microbiology Ariz. State U., 1980—; cons. S.I. Bot. Garden Assn., 1974-79; cons. hort. therapist Clove Lakes Nursing Home, S.I., 1974-79; cons. hort. taxonomist N.Y.C. Dept. Parks, 1973-74. Author: Flower and Fruit Keys to the Ornamental Crabapples Cultivated in the U.S, 1967, A Revision of the Sections of the Genus Malus Miller, 1972; Editor: Preliminary Directory of Living Plant Collections of North America, 1983. Served with USMC, 1963-69. Oxford (Eng.) U. research grantee; recipient Wm. Frederick Dreer award Cornell U. Mem. Am. Assn. Bot. Gardens and Arboreta (chmn. plant collections com.), Central Ariz. Museum Assn. (v.p., pres.), Ariz. Bot. Garden Assn. (founding), Ariz. Mus. Assn. (founding), Sigma Xi, Phi Kappa Phi, Pi Alpha Xi. Office: 1201 N Galvin Pkwy Phoenix AZ 85008 *

HUCKMAN, MICHAEL SAUL, neuroradiologist, educator; b. Newark, Aug. 20, 1936; s. Louis Fillmore and Mollie (Lehman) H.; m. Beverly Joy Blachman, Aug. 2, 1964; children: Andrew Garfield, Robert Steven. A.B., Princeton U., 1958; M.D., St. Louis U., 1962. Rotating intern, then resident in radiology Phila. Gen. Hosp., 1962-63, 65-58; fellow in neuroradiology Edward Mallinckrodt Inst. Radiology, Washington U., St. Louis, also univ. instr. radiology, 1968-70; mem. faculty Rush Med. Coll., Chgo., 1970—, prof. radiology, 1978—; dir. sect. neuroradiology Rush-Presbyn.-St. Luke's Med. Center, 1970—; mem. faculty Cook County Grad. Sch. Medicine, 1972—; cons. Nat. Center for Health Care Tech., 1980—, Mt. Sinai Hosp., Grant Hosp., Swedish Covenant Hosp. Mem. editorial bd.: Jour. Computer Assisted Tomography, 1976—, Radiographics, 1983—; contbr. articles to med. jours. Served with USNR, 1963-65. Spl. fellow Nat. Inst. Neurol. Diseases and Blindness, 1968-70. Fellow Am. Coll. Radiology; mem. AMA, Am. Soc. Neuroradiology (sec. 1980-83), Radiol. Soc. N.Am., Assn. Univ. Radiologists, Ill. Med. Soc., Ill. Radiol. Soc., Chgo. Med. Soc., Blockley Radiol. Soc., Sigma Xi, Phi Delta Epsilon. Jewish. Club: Princeton Alumni of Chgo. (trustee 1982-84). Home: 2410 Lincoln St Evanston IL 60201 Office: 1753 W Congress Pkwy Chicago IL 60612

HUCLES, HENRY BOYD, bishop; b. N.Y.C., Sept. 21, 1923; s. Henry Boyd and Alma Leola (Lewis) H.; m. Mamie Dalceda Adams, Sept. 18, 1948; children: Henry Boyd IV, Michael Edward. B.S., Va. Union U., Richmond, 1943; M.Div., Va. Sem., Alexandria, 1946, D.D. hon., 1976. Ordained priest Episcopal Ch., 1947; parish minister Grace Ch., Millers Tavern, Va., 1946-49; rector St. George's Ch., Bklyn., 1949-79; prison chaplian Dept. Corrections, Bklyn., 1954-74; archdeacon of Bklyn. Episcopal Diocese of L.I., Garden City, N.Y., 1976-81, suffragen bishop, 1981—; mem. Anglican Council N.Am. and Caribbean, 1982—; canon Cathedral of the Incarnation, Garden City. Vice-pres. Ch. Charity Found., Hempstead, N.Y., 1956—. Named Man of Yr. Kings County Med. Soc., Bklyn., 1965. Democrat. Clubs: Bklyn., Garden City Golf; Cherry Valley Golf (Garden City). Home: 152 Kilburn Rd Garden City NY 11530 Office: Episcopal Diocese of Long Island 36 Cathedral Ave Garden City NY 11530

HUDACHEK, JOHN WILLIAM, army officer; b. Cedar Rapids, Iowa, May 21, 1930; s. Lewis Edward and Agnes Loretta (Casey) H.; m. Ann Hamilton, Dec. 18, 1954; children: Mary, Michael, Teresa, Susan. Student, U. Iowa, 1948-50; B.S., U.S. Mil. Acad., 1954; M.S., Ga. Inst. Tech., 1962; postgrad., U.S. Army Command and Gen. Staff Coll., 1966-67, Dept. Def. Indsl. Coll. Armed Forces, 1972-73. Commd. officer U.S. Army, 1954, advanced through grades to maj. gen.; comdr. 2d Armored Cav. Regt., Germany, 1974-76; chief of staff 1st Armored Div., Germany, 1976-77; project mgr. Saudi Arabian N.G. Modernization Project, 1977-79; comdr. U.S. Army Computer Systems Command, Ft. Belvoir, Va., 1979-80; comdg. gen. U.S. Army 4th Inf. Div. (Mechanized), Ft. Carson, Colo., 1980-82; chief of staff 8th U.S. Army, Korea, 1982—. Decorated Bronze Star, Meritorious Service medal, Air medal, Army Commendation medal. Mem. Assn. Grads. U.S. Mil. Acad., Assn. U.S. Army, U.S. Armor Assn., U.S. Naval Inst. Roman Catholic. Office: C/S EUSA APO San Francisco CA 96301

HUDAK, THOMAS F(RANCIS), retail executive; b. Donora, Pa., Jan. 29, 1942; s. Thomas Joseph and Ann Marie (Petrus) H.; m. Dorothy Ann Palko, July 27, 1963; children: Diana Lynn, Debra Ann, Thomas David. B.S., St. Vincent Coll., 1963; M.B.A., Ohio State U., 1968. Bar: C.P.A., Ohio. Accountant Coopers & Lybrand, Columbus, Ohio, 1963-65; dept. mgr., data processing Western Electric Corp., Columbus, 1965-66; fin. controls mgr. Indsl. Nucleonics Co., Columbus, 1966-69; sr. v.p. fin., chief fin. officer G.C. Murphy Co., McKeesport, Pa., 1969—, chmn. bd., 1981—; treas. Mack Realty Co., McKeesport, Murphy Devel. Corp., Court House Village Co., Spotsylvania Realty Co.; dir., pres. Terry Farris Stores, Inc.; mem. adv. bd. Liberty Mut. Ins. Co. Bd. dirs., v.p. G.C. Murphy Co. Found. Mem. U.S. C. of C., Fin. Execs. Inst. (dir. Pitts. chpt.), Assn. Gen. Mdse. Chains, Am. Inst. C.P.A.s, Risk and Ins. Mgmt. Soc., Nat. Retail Mchts. Assn. (dir. fin. div.), Nat. Assn. Corp. Dirs. Office: 531 5th Ave McKeesport PA 15132

HUDDLESON, EDWIN EMMET, JR., lawyer; b. Oakland, Calif., Jan. 28, 1914; s. Edwin Emmet and Gertrude (Connahan) H.; m. Mary Taeusch, July 21, 1941; children—Michael Stephen (dec.), Edwin Emmet III, Mary Catherine. A.B., Stanford U., 1935; LL.B., Harvard, 1938. Bar: Calif. bar 1939. Law clk. to Judge A.N. Hand, 1938-39; atty. Office U.S. Solicitor Gen., 1939-40; law clk. to Justice Frank Murphy, 1940; dir. spl. projects staff Office Asst. Sec. Intelligence, State Dept., 1946; dep. gen. counsel AEC, 1947-48; mem. firm Cooley, Godward, Castro Huddleson & Tatum, San Francisco, 1949—; dir. Varian Assos., U.S. Leasing Internat., Inc.; trustee Aerospace Corp., 1960-75, 76—, Mitre Corp., Rand Corp. Pres.: Harvard Law Rev, 1937-38. Trustee Center for Advanced Study in Behavioral Scis., System Devel. Found. Served to lt. col. AUS, 1941-46; PTO. Decorated Legion of Merit; recipient Exceptional Service award USAF, 1975. Mem. Phi Beta Kappa. Home: 2201 Bywood Dr Oakland CA 94602 Office: Alcoa Bldg 1 Maritime Plaza San Francisco CA 94111

HUDDLESTON, DAVID WILLIAM, actor, producer; b. Vinton, Va., Sept. 17, 1930; s. Lewis Melvin and Ismay Hope (Dooley) H.; 1 son by previous marriage, David Michael. Student, Am. Acad. Dramatic Arts, 1957. Pres., owner Shama Prodns., Inc., The Huddleston Co., Huddleston Music Co. Appeared in: TV series Hizzoner, Tenafly, Petrocelli; appeared in: TV films, including Kate Bliss and the Ticker Tape Kid, Brian's Song, How the West Was Won, The Oregon Trail, Winner Take All; films, including Smoky and the Bandit II, Breakheart Pass, Capricorn One, The World's Greatest Lover; Songwriter: Home Town Blues, 1978, theme songs TV series. Served with USAF, 1950-54. Mem. Screen Actors Guild, AFTRA, Actors Equity Assn. Clubs: Players (N.Y.C.); Calif. Yacht (Los Angeles). Office: care David Shapira and Assos Inc 9100 Wilshire Blvd East Tower Suite 231 Beverly Hills CA 90210 *

HUDDLESTON, EUGENE LEE, American studies educator; b. Ironton, Ohio, Jan. 29, 1931; s. James Earl and Bernice (McClave) H.; m. Mary Lou Fishbeck, June 17, 1961; 1 son, John. A.B., Marshall U., 1953; M.A., Ohio U., 1956; Ph.D., Mich. State U., 1965. Asst. prof. Ind. State U., Terre Haute, 1962-66; asst. prof., assoc. prof. Mich. State U., East Lansing, 1966-77, prof. Am. thought and lang., 1977—. Author: (with Douglas A. Noverr) The Relationship of Literature and Painting: A Guide to Information Sources, 1978, (with A. Staufer, P. Shuster) C&O Power: Steam and Diesel Locomotives of the Chesapeake and Ohio Railway, 1900-1965, 1965, Thomas Jefferson: A Reference Guide, 1982, (with T.W. Dixon, Jr.) The Allegheny-Lima's Finest, 1983. Recipient Norman Foerster award, 1966. Mem. Popular Culture Assn., MLA (Am. lit. sect.), Chesapeake and Ohio Hist. Soc., Soc. for Study Midwestern Lit. Home: 3926 Raleigh Dr Okemos MI 48864 Office: Dept Am Thought and Lang Mich State U East Lansing MI 48824

HUDDLESTON, WALTER DARLINGTON, U.S. senator; b. nr. Burkesville, Ky., Apr. 15, 1926; s. Walter Franklin and Lottie (Russell) H.; m. Martha Jean Pearce, Dec. 20, 1947; children: Stephen Pearce, Philip Dee. A.B., U. Ky., 1949. Program-sports dir. WKCT, Bowling Green, Ky., 1949-52; gen. mgr. WIEL, Elizabethtown, Ky., 1952-72; U.S. senator from, Ky., 1973—; Dir. 1st Fed. Savs. & Loan Assn., Elizabethtown, Radio Sta. WLBN, Lebanon, Ky.; Mem. Ky. Senate, 1966-72, majority leader, 1970-72; Democratic Caucus chmn., 1968. Served with AUS, 1944-46. Mem. C. of C. (pres. 1959), Ky. Broadcasters Assn. (pres. 1958). Methodist. Club: Pendennis (Louisville). Office: 262 Dirksen Senate Office Bldg Washington DC 20510 *

HUDEC, ROBERT EMIL, lawyer, educator; b. Cleve., Dec. 23, 1934; s. Emil and Mary (Tomcho) H.; m. Marianne Miller, Sept. 8, 1956; children: Michael Robert, Katharine Wright. B.A., Kenyon Coll., 1956, LL.D. (hon.), 1979; M.A., Cambridge U., 1958; LL.B., Yale U., 1961. Bar: D.C. 1963, Minn. 1974. Law clk. to Mr. Justice Potter Stewart, U.S. Supreme Ct., 1961-63; asst. gen. counsel Office Spl. Rep. for Trade Negotiations, Exec. Offices, 1963-65; Rockefeller Found. research fellow, 1965-66; asso. prof. law Yale U. Law Sch., 1966-72; prof. law U. Minn. Law Sch., Mpls., 1972—. Author: The Gatt Legal System and World Trade Diplomacy, 1975; Contbr. articles to profl. jours. Mem. Am. Law Inst., Minn. Bar Assn., D.C. Bar Assn. Office: U Minn Law Sch Minneapolis MN 55455

HUDELSON, GEORGE DAVID, manufacturing company executive; b. Bedford, Ind., Nov. 16, 1920; s. William E. and Mabel C. (Bair) H.; m. Patricia L. Night, Mar. 6, 1958; children: David, Peter, Patricia. B.M.E., Purdue U., 1943; M.Sc., Ohio State U., 1951. Registered profl. engr., Ohio. Research engr. Wright Aero. Corp., 1943-44, NACA, 1944-47; asst. prof. mech. engring. Ohio State U., 1947-57; with Carrier Corp., 1957—, asso. dir. research, Syracuse, N.Y., 1970-72, v.p. engring. and dir. research, 1972—; mem. indsl. adv. com. Herrick Labs., Purdue U.; mem. audit and rev. com. Accreditation Bd. Engring. and Tech., 1980—; cons. air conditioning design. Charter mem. industry adv. com. to Coll. Engring., Syracuse U., 1981. Contbg. editor: Production Handbook, 2d edit, 1958—. Recipient Disting. Alumnus award Purdue U., 1977, Ohio State U., 1979. Fellow ASHRAE. Presbyterian. Club: Willowbank Yacht. Patentee air conditioning apparatus, thermoelectric module. Home: 1946 Chard Rd Cazenovia NY 13035 Office: Adminstrn and Research Center Carrier Corp Syracuse NY 13201

HUDIBURG, JOHN JUSTUS, JR., utility executive; b. Raleigh, N.C., Jan. 16, 1928; s. John Justus and Lucille (Pearson) H.; m. Joan Helen Adams, Apr. 24, 1954; children: Lee Ann, Carol Joan, John Justus, Mark Adams. B.S., Ga. Inst. Tech., 1951; grad., Advanced Mgmt. Program, Harvard U., 1972. Registered profl. engr., Fla. With Fla. Power & Light Co., Miami, 1951—, dir. mgr., 1969-71, v.p., 1971-72, exec. v.p., 1973-79, pres., 1979—; chmn. Fla. Electric Power Coordinating Group, 1983-84. Mem. Fla. Prison Industries Commn., 1977-79; chmn. West Palm Beach United Fund campaign, 1967; pres. United Fund Palm Beach County, 1968; v.p. Goodwill Industries, West Palm Beach, 1968. Served with USNR, 1946-47. Mem. IEEE (chpt. chmn. 1964), Nat. Soc. Profl. Engrs., Fla. Engring. Soc. Episcopalian. Clubs: Internat. (Washington); Bankers (Miami); Harvard Bus. Sch. So. Fla. (pres. 1976). Office: PO Box 529100 Miami FL 33152

HUDNALL, JACK PROWERS, psychology educator; b. La Junta, Colo., Oct. 31, 1925; s. Leonard Hyden and Alice (Parsons) H.; m. Irene F. Poe, 1948 (div.); children: Karen, Kathleen, Jack Prowers; m. Helen Anne Heath, 1964; stepchildren: Terry, Doreen, Jeanette Howard. Student, Southwestern U., Tex., 1944; B.A., Colo. Coll., 1947; B.Ed. (Univ. fellow), Wash. State U., 1950; M.A. (Coll. fellow), Tchrs. Coll., Columbia U., 1959, postgrad., 1963-64. Sch. psychologist Seattle Public Schs., 1949-51; tchr. psychology Edison Tech. Sch., Seattle, 1951-57; dean Hibbing Jr. Coll., 1959-63; dean adminstrn. Kingsborough Community Coll., 1964-66; founding pres. Bristol Community Coll., 1966-78, prof. psychology, 1978-81, pres. emeritus, 1981—; cons. instr., evaluator community colls. Pres. Greater Fall River (Mass.) Planning Council, 1967-71; bd. dirs. Battleship Mass. Meml. Com., Fall River, 1974—, Easter Seals Soc. Mass., 1971-77. Served with USMC, 1944-46. Council for Advancement Secondary Edn. grantee, 1955-56. Mem. C. of C. of Fall River (dir. 1971-75), Am. Assn. Community and Jr. Colls. (mem. commns.), Phi Beta Kappa. Democrat. Home: 35 Hemlock Point East Freetown MA 02717 Office: 777 Elsbree Fall St River MA 02720

HUDNALL, JARRETT, JR., educator, business exec., mktg. cons.; b. Rhome, Tex., Oct. 6, 1931; s. Jarrett and Katherine (Wilson) H.; m. Sarah Ruth Warren, Nov. 24, 1955; children—Jarrett Joseph, William Warren, Katherine Lee, Thomas Wilson. Student, Arlington State Coll., 1948-50; B.B.A., U. Tex., Austin, 1953, M.B.A., 1956; Ph.D., U. Ala., 1966. Lectr. U. Tex., 1955-56; asst. prof. Arlington State Coll., 1956-58; instr. U. Ala., 1958-61; asst. prof. La Tech. U., 1961-62, asso. prof. mktg., 1962-67, prof., head dept. bus., 1967-77; exec. Superior Supply Co., Inc., 1978—; cons. firms in chem. fertilizer, petroleum, farm equipment mfg., distbg. bus. Author: (with A.L. Seeyle) Compensation of Retail Department Store and Specialty Store Salesman in Major Texas Cities, 1957, Attitudes of Gulf Service Station Dealers Toward Minor Tuneup and Repair Work, 1963, An Economic Analysis of Income and Employment in a Four-State Deep South Region, 1950-1960, 1966. Served to lt. AUS, 1953-55. Gulf Oil

Corp. fellow, 1963. Mem. Am., So. marketing assns., S.W. Assn. Allied Disciplines, Am. Collegiate Retailing Assn., Sigma Iota Epsilon, Beta Gamma Sigma, Alpha Kappa Psi. Democrat. Baptist. Office: PO Box 7002 Shreveport LA 71107

HUDNER, PHILIP, lawyer, rancher; b. San Jose, Calif., Feb. 24, 1931; s. Paul Joseph and Mary E. (Dooling) H.; m. Carla Raven, Aug. 6, 1966; Children: Paul Theodor, Mary Carla, William Charles. B.A. with great distinction, Stanford U., 1952, LL.B., 1955. Bar: Calif. 1955. Assoc. Pillsbury, Madison & Sutro, San Francisco, 1958-70, ptnr., 1970—; rancher San Benito County, Calif., 1970—. Asst. editor: Stanford Law Rev., 1954-55; author articles on estate and trust law. Pres. Soc. Calif. Pioneers, 1976-78; bd. regents Coll. Notre Dame, Belmont, Calif., 1980-83, trustee, Belmont, Calif., 1983—; trustee San Francisco Performing Arts Ctr. Garage, 1976-80; trustee, sec. Louise M. Davies Found., 1974—; trustee James A. Folger and Jane C. Folger Found., 1976—; bd. dirs., sec.-treas. Drum Found., 1983—. Served with U.S. Army, 1956-58. Fellow Am. Bar Found.; mem. Internat. Acad. Estate and Trust Law (steering com. 1974-75, exec. council 1980—), Attys. Probate Assn. San Francisco (1st v.p.), Am. Coll. Probate Counsel, Phi Beta Kappa. Democrat. Roman Catholic. Clubs: Pacific Union, Lagunitas Country, Frontier Boys. Office: 225 Bush St San Francisco CA 94104

HUDNUT, ROBERT KILBORNE, clergyman; b. Cin., Jan. 7, 1934; s. William Herbert and Elizabeth (Kilborne) H.; m. Janet Lee Morlan; children by previous marriage—Heidi, Robert Kilborne, Heather, Matthew. B.A. with highest honors, Princeton, 1956; M.Div., Union Theol. Sem., N.Y.C., 1959. Ordained to ministry Presbyn. Ch., 1959; asst. minister Westminster Presbyn. Ch., Albany, N.Y., 1959-62; minister St. Luke Presbyn. Ch., Wayzata, Minn., 1962-73, Winnetka (Ill.) Presbyn. Ch., 1975—; exec. dir. Minn. Pub. Interest Research Group, 1973-75; Co-chmn. Minn. Joint Religious Legis. Coalition, 1970-75. Author: Surprised by God, 1967, A Sensitive Man and the Christ, 1971, A Thinking Man and the Christ, 1971, The Sleeping Giant: Arousing Church Power in America, 1971, An Active Man and the Christ, 1972, Arousing the Sleeping Giant: How to Organize Your Church for Action, 1973, Church Growth Is Not the Point, 1975, The Bootstrap Fallacy: What The Self-Help Books Don't Tell You, 1978. Pres. Greater Met. Fedn. Twin Cities, 1970-72; chmn. Citizens Adv. Com. on Interstate 394, 1971-75; nat. chmn. Presbyns. for Ch. Renewal, 1971; Chmn. Democratic Party 33d Senatorial Dist. Minn., 1970-72, Minnetonka Dem. Party, 1970-72; fusion candidate for mayor, Albany, 1961; Bd. dirs. Minn. Council Chs., 1964-70; trustee Princeton U., 1972-76, Asheville (N.C.) Sch., 1979—. Rockefeller fellow, 1956; named Outstanding Young Man, Minnetonka, 1967; recipient Distinguished Service award Minnetonka Tchrs. Assn., 1969. Mem. Phi Beta Kappa. Home: 1078 Elm St Winnetka IL 60093 Office: 1255 Willow Rd Winnetka IL 60093

HUDNUT, WILLIAM HERBERT, III, mayor; b. Cin., Oct. 17, 1932; s. William Herbert, Jr. and Elizabeth (Kilborne) H.; m. Susan G. Rice, Dec. 14, 1974; children from previous marriage: Michael Conger, Laura Anne, Timothy Norton, William Herbert IV, Theodore Beecher. B.A. magna cum laude, Princeton, 1954; M.Div. summa cum laude, Union Theol. Sem., N.Y.C., 1957; D.D., Hanover Coll., 1967, Wabash Coll., 1969; LL.D., Butler U., 1980, Anderson Coll., 1982, Franklin Coll., 1983; Litt.D., Ind. Central U., 1981. Ordained to ministry Presbyn. Ch., 1957; asst. minister Westminster Ch., Buffalo, 1957-60; pastor 1st Presbyn. Ch., Annapolis, Md., 1960-63; dir. Westminster Found., Annapolis, 1960-63; sr. minister 2d Presbyn. Ch., Indpls., 1963-72; mem. 93d Congress from Ind., 1973-74; dir. dept. community affairs Ind. Central U., Indpls., 1975; mayor, Indpls., 1976—; mem. Presdl. Adv. Com. on Federalism, 1981—. Editor: Union Sem. Quar. Rev, 1956-57; Contbr. sermons, articles to profl. publs. Mem. Bd. Pub. Safety, Indpls., 1970-71; Pres. Anne Arundel County Mental Health Assn., 1961-63; pres., bd. dirs. Marion County Mental Health Assn., 1966-68, Westminster Found., Purdue U., 1969-73; bd. dirs. Community Service Council Met. Indpls., 1964-68, Weekday Religious Edn., Marion County, 1964-69, Family Service Assn., 1966-72, Ind. Mental Health Assn., 1968-69, Flanner House, 1968-72; pres. trustees Darrow Sch., New Lebanon, N.Y., 1968-75; bd. dirs. Nat. League Cities, 1977—, pres. bd. dirs., 1981; bd. dirs. Ind. Assn. Cities and Towns, 1976—, pres. bd. dirs., 1979; mem. Intergovtl. Sci., Engring. and Tech. White House Adv. Panel, 1976-77, U.S. Conf. Mayors; adv. bd. Am. Fedn. Small Bus.; mem. New Coalition Welfare Reform Task Force, 1976-77; pres. Ind. Rep. Mayors' Assn., 1980; bd. dirs. Indpl. Center Adv. Research, 1976—, Humane Soc., 1983—. Mem. Phi Beta Kappa. Republican. Clubs: Indianapolis, Columbia, Sertoma, Kiwanis, Masons (33 deg.), Moose (Indpls.)). Office: 2501 City-County Bldg Indianapolis IN 46204 *Life is relationships, and whatever we can do to enlighten and strengthen each other, in the family circle, among our friends, in business, in society at large, will help. This requires ardor and self-surrender, faith, hope and humor.*

HUDNUT, WILLIAM HERBERT, JR., clergyman; b. Youngstown, Ohio, May 29, 1905; s. William Herbert and Harriet (Beecher) H.; m. Elizabeth Kilborne, Nov. 21, 1931; children: William Herbert III, Robert Kilborne, David Beecher, Stewart Skinner, Harriet Hudnut Halliday, Thomas Cushman. A.B., Princeton U., 1927, D.D., 1967; B.D., Union Theol. Sem., 1930; D.D., Blackburn Coll., 1940; LL.D., Huron Coll., 1960; L.H.D., Pikeville Coll., 1964. Dir. religion The Hill Sch., Pottstown, Pa., 1930-32; pastor Glendale Presbyn. Ch., Cin., 1932-40, 1st Presbyn. Ch., Springfield, Ill., 1940-46, 3d Presbyn. Ch., Rochester, N.Y., 1946-64; nat. chmn. Presbyn. 50 Million Fund, 1964-67; interim pastor Chevy Chase (Md.) Presbyn. Ch., 1967-69, 1st Presbyn. Ch., Evanston, Ill., 1970, Brick Ch., N.Y.C., 1970-72, 2d Presbyn. Ch., Indpls., 1972-74, 1st Presbyn. Ch., Phoenix, 1975-76, Hastings, Nebr., 1977, Brick Ch., N.Y.C., 1977-78, 1st Presbyn. Ch., Glens Falls, N.Y., 1978-80; Dir. McCormick Theol. Sem., Chgo., 1942-49. Pres. Westminster Found. N.Y., 1947-53; mem. nat. student com. YMCA, 1946-57; mem. Presbyn. U.S.A. Gen. Council, 1950-58, 64-67; Bd. dirs. Union Sem., N.Y., 1957-75; mem. bd. Nat. Missions Presbyn. Ch. U.S.A., 1962-64; trustee Ill. Coll., 1943-46, Wilson Coll., 1967-70. Clubs: Princeton (N.Y.C.); Rochester City (pres. 1952-53). Home: Windover North Creek NY 12853 *The guiding principle of my life is the belief that God's purpose is the transformation of the human race into the human family. He will never accomplish this for us but only through us, as we devote ourselves to His service. He needs our help. God the Creator wants each of us to live creatively.*

HUDON, EDWARD GERARD, librarian, lawyer, educator; b. Brunswick, Maine, Jan. 24, 1915; s. Edward Joseph and Martha Laura (Mathurin) H.; m. Blanche Bernier, Dec. 26, 1949. B.S., Bowdoin Coll., 1937, LL.D., 1977; LL.B., J.D., Georgetown U., 1947, LL.M., 1950; M.L.S., Cath. U. Am., 1956; S.J.D., George Washington U., 1962; Docteur en Droit, U. Laval, 1976. Bar: D.C. 1947, Maine 1955. Interviewer, Maine Unemployment Compensation Commn., 1937-41; with Library of Congress, 1941-42; asst. librarian U.S. Supreme Ct. Library, Washington, 1947-66, librarian, 1972-76; asst. U.S. atty. Dist. Maine, Portland, 1966-70; individual practice law, Brunswick, 1970—; asst. prof. law Laval U., Quebec, Que., Can., 1970-71, prof., 1976-78; adj. prof. U. Maine Law Sch., 1979-84; mem. Maine-Can. Legis. Adv. Commn., 1979-84. Author: Freedom of Speech and Press in America, 1963, The Library Facilities of the Supreme Court of the United States, 1957; editor: The Occasional Papers of Mr. Justice Burton, 1969. Pres. Maine State Soc., Washington, 1959-62. Served with AUS, 1942-46. Mem. Am., D.C., Maine, Cumberland County bar assns. Address: PO Box 117 Brunswick ME 04011

HUDSON, ANTHONY WEBSTER, govt. ofcl.; b. Durham, N.C., Mar. 23, 1937; s. Emanuel and Adele (Nixon) H.; m. Glenda Buchanan, Jan. 18, 1964; children—April Lynn, Verna Lea. Student, Rutgers U., 1954-59, Columbia, 1960-62, George Washington U., 1967—. Personnel mgmt. specialist U.S. Civil Service Commn., N.Y.C., 1962-65, tng. officer personnel div., Washington, 1966, tng. officer, 1967, coordinator, 1968-70, dir. personnel, 1970-74; dir. fed. E.E.O., 1974-77; staff dir. personnel Def. Logistics Agy., 1977—; instr. U.S. Dept. Agr. Grad. Sch. Contbr. to: Ency. of Edn, 1971. Trustee Govt. Services, Inc., Washington; Chmn. merit personnel bd. Md.-D.C. Park and Planning Commn., Silver Spring; mem. Fed. Personnel Mgmt. Career Bd.; sec./treas., bd. dirs. Worldwide Assurance for Employees of Public Agys. Served from 2d lt. to 1st lt., arty. U.S. Army, 1959-60. Recipient Spl. citation U.S. Civil Service Commn., 1969, William A. Jump Meml. award, 1970. Mem. Am. Soc. Tng. and Devel. (exec. bd., chmn. community services 1966-68), D.C. Sociol. Soc., Am. Personnel and Guidance Assn., Soc. Personnel Adminstrn. (exec. com. 1971—), Internat. Personnel Mgmt. Assn. (exec. council 1977), Am. Sociol. Assn. (employment com. 1971—), Am. Fgn. Service Assn., NAACP, Phi Sigma Delta. Congregationalist. Club: Rutgers (Washington). Home: 7309 Pinehurst Pkwy Chevy Chase MD 20815 Office: DLA-K Def Log Agency Cameron Sta Alexandria VA 22314

HUDSON, DONALD ELLIS, civil engineering educator; b. Alma, Mich., Feb. 25, 1916; s. Albert W. and Ruth (Ellis) H. B.S., Calif. Inst. Tech., 1938, M.S., 1939, Ph.D., 1942. Prof. mech. engring. and applied mechanics Calif. Inst. Tech., Pasadena, 1941-81, prof. emeritus, 1981—; prof. and chmn. dept. civil engring. U. So. Calif., Los Angeles, 1981—, Fred Champion prof. engring., 1982—. Author: (with G.W. Housner) Applied Mechanics, Statics and Dynamics, 1949-50. Fellow ASME; mem. ASCE, Am. Soc. for Engring. Edn., Soc. Exptl. Stress Analysis, Am. Geophys. Union, Seismol. Soc. Am. (past pres., editorial com.), Internat. Assn. Earthquake Engring. (pres. 1980—), Earthquake Engring. Research Inst., Nat. Acad. Engring. Office: California Institute of Technology Thomas Laboratory 104-44 Pasadena CA 91125

HUDSON, DONALD J., stock exchange executive; b. Vancouver, B.C., Canada, Sept. 26, 1930; s. John Richard and Olive Colville (McCreath) H.; m. Patricia Hockridge, Aug. 20,7 1954; children: Sharon Ann, Susan Patricia. B.A., U. B.C., 1952. Dir. sales devel. C.P. Air, Vancouver, 1953-64; sr. v.p. Pacific div. T. Eaton Co., Ltd., Vancouver, 1964-81; pres. Vancouver Stock Exchange, 1982—. Trustee St. Paul's Hosp., Vancouver. Clubs: Can. Club of Vancouver (pres. 1982, dir. 1983. Home: 4410 Angus Dr Vancouver BC Canada V6J 4J3 Office: Vancouver Stock Exchange 609 Granville St Vancouver BC Canada V7Y 1H1

HUDSON, FRANKLIN DONALD, diversified company executive; b. Asheville, N.C., July 21, 1933; s. Halbert Austin and Lillian Naomi (Cook) H.; m. Rosemary Wheatley, Dec. 1, 1956; children: Lawrence Jamison, Lauren Jean. B.E.E., Yale U., 1955; M.B.A., NYU, 1962; postgrad., Pace U., 1972-75. Sales rep. RCA, N.Y.C., 1959-62; Latin Am. gen. mgr. GTE Sylvania, P.R., 1962-68, dir. mktg., 1968-71; dir. Home Equipment div. Singer Co., N.Y.C., 1971-75; v.p. internat. Corometrics Med. Systems, Inc., Wallingford, Conn., 1975-78; v.p. planning and devel. Norlin Corp., White Plains, N.Y., 1978-81; founder, exec. v.p. Integrated Genetics, Inc., 1981—; adj. prof. NYU, Boston U.; former mem. faculty Yale U., Post Coll. Contbr. articles to mags. Mem. Yale U. Alumni Bd., 1965-68; mem. Conn. Republican Fin. Com., 1968-74; asst. dir. The Campaign for Yale, 1978. Served to capt. USAF, 1956-58. Mem. Russell Trust Assn., Boston Mus. Fine Arts, Boston Com. Fgn. Relations. Episcopalian. Clubs: Longwood Cricket; Harvard (Boston); Mory's (New Haven). Office: 31 New York Ave Framingham MA 01701

HUDSON, GEORGE ELBERT, retired research physicist; b. Pitts., Apr. 25, 1916; s. George Elbert, Jr. and Mary Jane (Wilson) H.; m. Olive Gallant, June 24, 1939 (div. Apr. 1979); children: George, Brian, Nancy. B.S., George Washington U., 1938; Sc.M., Brown U., 1940, Ph.D., 1942. Vis. prof. physics Georgetown U., 1943-44; asso. prof. physics N.Y. U., 1946-49, prof. physics, 1949-63; physicist Taylor Model Basin, U.S. Navy, 1942-46; dir. research Smyth Research Assos., 1956-57; cons. Naval Ordnance Lab., 1957-59, Brookhaven Nat. Lab., 1958-61, Woods Hole Oceanographic Instn., 1959-61, Avco Corp., 1961-62, Nat. Bur. Standards, 1962-63, asst. chief radio physics div., Boulder, Colo., 1963-67; cons. time and frequency div. Inst. Basic Standards, Nat. Bur. Standards, 1967-70; sr. research cons. Naval Ordnance Lab., 1970-80; Adj. prof. physics Denver U., 1965-69. Contbr. articles to physics and math. prof. publs. Fellow Am. Phys. Soc., A.A.A.S.; mem. Washington Philos. Soc. (pres. 1973-74), Sigma Xi, Sigma Pi Sigma, Delta Tau Delta. Club: Cosmos (Washington). Home: 29928 Mallard Dr Lake Morena Village Campo CA 92006

HUDSON, HAROLD JORDON, JR., insurance executive; b. Kansas City, Mo., Mar. 10, 1924; s. Harold Jordan and Fannie (Jenkins) H.; m. Patricia Louise Orr, Oct. 1, 1949. B.S., U. Mo., 1945, LL.B., 1948; grad., Advanced Mgmt. Program, Harvard U., 1968. Bar: Mo. 1948. Practiced in, Kansas City, until 1952; atty. Comml. Union Co., Kansas City, 1952-53, Cleve., 1953-56, Gen. Reins. Corp., N.Y.C., 1956-58, asst. sec., 1958-61, sec., 1961-62, v.p., 1963-68, sr. v.p., 1968-70, pres., 1970-71, 1971-72, chief exec. officer, 1971—, chmn., 1973—, also dir.; chmn. Reins. Assn. Am., 1975-76; dir. Gen. Reassurance Co., Inter-Reins. Corp., Zurich, Switzerland, Reins. Corp. of Austral-Asia, Sydney, Australia, Putnam Trust Co., Greenwich, Conn., U.S. Trust Co., N.Y.C., Gen. Signal Co.; bd. govs. N.Y. Ins. Exchange. Trustee Coll. of Ins.; Trustee Griffith Found. Mem. Mo. Bar, Phi Delta Phi, Kappa Alpha. Clubs: Brook (N.Y.C.); Indian Harbor Yacht, Greenwich Country (Greenwich, Conn.). Office: 600 Steamboat Rd Greenwich CT 06830

HUDSON, HARRIET DUFRESNE, banker, former educator; b. Kirby, Pa., July 14, 1912; d. William Mestrezat and Florence Ronald (Barclay) H. Student, Blackburn Coll., 1929-30, LL.D., 1957; A.B., Wellesley Coll., 1933; M.A., U. Chgo., 1936, Ph.D., 1950. Grader Harvard Grad. Sch. Bus. Adminstrn., 1937-39; instr. econs. and sociology Pine Manor Jr. Coll., 1939-42, Mt. Holyoke Coll., 1942-47; asst. prof. econs. U. Ill., Urbana, 1948-53; prof. econs., dean coll. Randolph-Macon Woman's Coll., Lynchburg, Va., 1953-75; provost, dean of coll. St. Mary's Coll., Md., St. Mary's City, 1975-78; lectr. U. Calif., Irvine, 1979-80; customer service rep. First Interstate Bank of Calif., 1981—; mem. com. on coll. teaching Am. Council on Edn., 1959-61, mem. commn. on ednl. credit, 1971-75; mem. com. on standards and reports So. Assn. Colls. and Schs., 1960-70, exec. council commn. on colls., 1971-74; bd. dirs. Tuition Exchange, 1957-68. Trustee The Common Fund, 1973-75, Coll. Entrance Exam. Bd., 1963-66; mem. bd. Va. Found. for Humanities and Pub. Policy, 1974-75. Mem. Indsl. Relations Research Assn., AAUW, Am. Assn. Higher Edn. (exec. com. 1959-61), Am. Conf. Acad. Deans (dir. 1973-75), Alliance Francaise, P.E.O. Presbyterian. Home: 3500-1G Bahia Blanca Laguna Hills CA 92653

HUDSON, HERBERT EDSON, JR., environ. engr.; b. Chgo., Sept. 21, 1910; s. Herbert Edson and Etta May (Dow) H.; m. Annabelle Woods, May 28, 1932; children—Herbert Edson, Kenneth Alan. Jr. B.S., U. Ill., 1931. San. engr. Chgo. Water Dept., 1931-41, designer, 1941-42, filtration engr., 1945-46; research asso. U. Ill., 1942-44; head engring. subdiv. Ill. Water Survey, 1946-55; asso. Hazen and Sawyer Engrs., Detroit, 1955-57, partner, 1957-71; pres. Water and Air Research, Inc., Gainesville, Fla., 1971—; adj. prof. U. Fla. Author: Water Clarification Processes, 1981. Served with C.E. U.S. Army, 1944-45. Recipient Water Resource, Water Quality Research award Am. Water Works Assn., 1966, Diven medal, 1967, Fuller award, 1943, Research award, 1976. Fellow ASCE, Am. Inst. Chemists; mem. Nat. Acad. Engring., Am. Acad. Environ. Engrs. (diplomate, pres. 1968-69), Am. Water Works Assn. (hon. mem., dir. 1961-73, chmn. water resources div. 1955-56, chmn. water quality div. 1961-62), Am. Geophys. Union, Asociacion Interamericana de Ingenaria Sanitaria, Sigma Xi, Tau Beta Pi. Unitarian. Office: PO Box 1121 Gainesville FL 32602

HUDSON, JACK GRAYDON, corporate controller; b. DeWitt, Ark., Jan. 27, 1931; s. Raymond C. and Anna (Morrow) H.; m. Ina Lee Wiles, July 29, 1956; children: Anne Marie, Christopher. B.S. in Acctg., Ark. State U., 1956, M.B.A., La. State U., 1958. Acctg. supr. The Kroger Co., Atlanta, 1959-61, div. acct., Ft. Wayne, Ind., 1962-63, div. controller, St. Louis, 1964-72, KFS controller, Cin., 1972-78, v.p., corp. controller, 1978—. Adv. cons. No. Ky. U. Bus. Sch., Highland Heights, 1981-83; bd. dirs. audit com. Anderson Meth. Ch., Cin., 1979-80. Mem. Fin. Execs. Inst., Food Mktg. Inst. Home: 778 Kingswood Ct Cincinnati OH 45230 Office: The Kroger Co 1014 Vine St Cincinnati OH 45202

HUDSON, JACK KENNETH, manufacturing company executive; b. Detroit, Apr. 27, 1922; s. Emmet and Etta (Hein) H.; m. Elizabeth Deanesly, June 12, 1954; children: Mark Deanesly, Anne Elizabeth. B.S., U. Mich., 1947, J.D., 1949. Bar: Mich. 1949, Ill. 1950. Ptnr. Campbell, Miller, Carrol & Paxton, Chgo., 1957-62; with Bell & Howell Co., Chgo., 1962—, sec. gen. counsel, 1976-83, sr. v.p. law, 1983—. Served in maj. USMCR, World War II. Mem. ABA, Ill. Bar Assn. Home: 619 S Park Ave Hinsdale IL 60521 Office: Bell & Howell Co 7100 McCormick Rd Chgo IL 60645

HUDSON, JACK WILLIAM, JR., biology educator; b. Denver, Oct. 30, 1926; s. Jack William and Louise (Hibbs) H.; m. Virginia Clare Petersen, Mar. 30, 1947; children: Christine Ann Hudson Earle, Connie Lou Hudson Harrington. Student, Stanford, 1943-45; B.A., Occidental Coll., 1948, M.A., 1950; Ph.D., UCLA, 1960. Instr. El Camino Coll., 1950-55; instr. Occidental Coll., 1955-59; vis. asst. prof. U. Calif., Los Angeles, 1961-62; asst. prof. Rice U., 1962-65, asso. prof., 1965-67, Cornell U., Ithaca, N.Y., 1967-70, prof., 1971-78, chmn. dept. ecology and systematics, 1969-74; prof. biology U. Ala., Birmingham, 1978—, chmn. dept., 1978-81; program dir. NSF, 1974-75; Cons. World Book Ency., NSF; vis. prof. Sch. Zoology, U. New South Wales, Australia, 1974, 78; NIH cardiovascular trainee, 1959-60. Contbr. articles to profl. jours. Served with AUS, 1945-46. Danforth Tchr. grantee, 1957-58; NSF and NIH grantee, 1963—; Allied Chem. & Dye fellow, 1953-54. Mem. Am. Physiol. Soc., Alpha Kappa Lambda. Home: 3705 Richelieu Dr Birmingham AL 35216

HUDSON, JAMES JACKSON, historian, university dean; b. Lavaca, Ark., Jan. 19, 1919; s. Randolph Ingram and Lillie White (Pruitt) H.; m. Mabel Elizabeth McDonald, Feb. 1, 1942; children: Karen, Deborah. B.A., U. Ark., 1948, M.A., 1949; Ph.D., U. Calif., Berkeley, 1952. Mem. faculty U. Ark., Fayetteville, 1952—, prof. history, 1965—, dean Grad. Sch., 1972—. Author: Hostile Skies: A Combat History of The American Air Service in World War I, 1968; asso. editor: Ark. Hist. Quar., 1960—. Served with USAAF, 1942-45. Decorated Air medal with 5 oak leaf clusters. Mem. Am. Hist. Assn., Orgn. Am. Historians, Am. Aviation Hist. Soc. (adv. bd. jour.), Air Force Hist. Found., Cross and Cockade Soc., Conf. Grad. Schs. U.S., Conf. So. Grad. Schs. (pres.). Presbyn. Club: Rotary. Home: 721 N Ashwood St Fayetteville AR 72701 Office: Univ Ark Fayetteville AR 72701

HUDSON, JERRY E., university president; b. Chattanooga, Mar. 3, 1938; s. Clarence E. and Laura (Campbell) H.; m. Myra Ann Jared, June 11, 1957; children: Judith, Laura, Janet, Angela. B.A., David Lipscomb Coll., 1959; M.A., Tulane U., 1961, Ph.D., 1965. Systems engr. IBM, Atlanta, 1961; prof. Coll. Arts and Scis., Pepperdine U., 1962-75, provost, dean, 1971-75; pres. Hamline U., St. Paul, 1975-80, Willamette U., Salem, Oreg., 1980—. Mem. Am. Hist. Assn., Phi Alpha Theta. Office: Office of Pres Willamette U 900 State St Salem OR 97301 *

HUDSON, JOHN ALLEN, librarian; b. Beaumont, Tex., May 14, 1927; s. Walter Byron and Bessie (Aman) H.; m. Genevieve Lynch, Jan. 3, 1948; 1 dau., Lourdes Marie. B.A., U. Tex. at Austin, 1951, M.A., 1954; M.L.S., Case Western Res. U., 1957. Librarian journalism and newspaper collection U. Tex. at Austin, 1951-54; state dir. library extension Tex. State Library, Austin, 1954-56; univ. librarian U. Tex. at Arlington, 1957—, dir. Ctr. Mesoam. Studies, 1982—, project dir. micro-filming of Yucatecan archives, 1976-83, project dir. preservation of archives of Honduras, 1981—. Author: (with George Wolfskill) All but the People: Franklin D. Roosevelt and His Critics, 1933-39, 1969. Trustee Arlington Pub. Library. Served with USNR, 1944-45. Mem. Am., Southwestern, Tex. library assns.; mem. Texas Council State Coll. Librarians (pres. 1968—), Mem. Am. Hist. Assn., Southwestern Social Sci. Assn. Home: 1400 Oxford St Arlington TX 76013

HUDSON, JOHN LESTER, chemical engineering educator; b. Chgo., Juen 19, 1937; s. John Jones and Linda Madeline (Panozzo) H.; m. Janette Glenore Catan, June 29, 1963; children: Ann, Barbara, Sarah. B.S., U. Ill., 1959; M.S. in Engring., Princeton U., 1960; Ph.D., Northwestern U., 1962. Registered profl. engr., Ill. Asst. prof. chm. engring. U. Ill.-Urbana, 1963-69, assoc. prof., 1969-75; prof., chmn. dept. chem. engring. U. Va., Charlottesville, 1975—; mgr. Ill. Div. Air Pollution Control, Springfield, 1974-75; cons. to various industires and govt. agys., 1966—. Contbr. articles to profl. jours.l. NSF fellow, 1962; Fulbright fellow, 1962-63, 82-83. Mem. Am. Inst. Chem. Engrs., Am. Chem. Soc., Air Pollution Control Assn. Home: 1920 Thomson Rd Charlottesville VA 22903 Office: Thornton Hall U Va Charlottesville VA 22901

HUDSON, JOHN STEPHEN, banker; b. Dothan, Ala., Oct. 1, 1936; s. Aubrey Jefferson and Marie Reynolds (Lingo) H.; m. JoAnn Howsman, Sept. 15, 1957; children: Bryan Stephen, Carrie Lucinda Hudson Kennedy, Joanna, John Aubrey. B.S.A., U. Fla., 1957. Various managerial positions So. Bell Telephone Co., Fla., 1957-72; successively sr. v.p., exec. v.p., vice chmn. bd. Flagship Banks, Inc., Miami Beach, Fla., 1972—, also dir.; chmn. bd., pres., chief exec. officer Flagship Nat. Bank of Miami; dir. Flagship Bank of West Palm Beach, Flagship First Nat. Bank of Boynton Beach, Flagship Nat. Bank of Palm Beach County, Sea Forth Corp., Flagship Factors Corp. Pres. bd. trustees Fla. Internat. U., 1977-78; chmn. Dade Found., 1981; trustee U. Miami, 1979—; treas. Orange Bowl Com., 1977, v.p., 1978, 79, pres.-elect, 1980, pres., 1981. Recipient Outstanding Young Exec. award Miami Jaycees, 1972. Mem. Fla. Bankers Assn., Assn. Fla. Bank Holding Cos., Greater Miami C. of C. (pres. 1973-74). Democrat. Lutheran. Clubs: Miami, Bath, Bankers, Riviera Country. *

HUDSON, JOSEPH LOWTHIAN, JR., foundation executive; b. Buffalo, July 4, 1931; s. Joseph L. and Elizabeth (Gilbert) H.; m. Jean Bent Wright, Aug. 9, 1952; children: Joseph L. IV, Jean Croy, Richard Webber, Louise Wright. B.A., Yale U., 1953; H.H.D. (hon.), Mich. State U., 1978, U. Detroit, 1983. Exec. trainee J.L. Hudson Co., Detroit, 1953-54, asst. to gen. mgr., 1956, v.p., asst. gen. mgr., 1957, v.p., gen. mgr., 1957-61, pres., 1961-72, chmn., chief exec. officer, 1972-81, ret., 1982, also dir.; vice chmn., dir. Dayton Hudson Corp., 1969-81; dir. NBD Bancorp., Detroit Edison Co., Mich. Bell Telephone Co., McCormick Oil & Gas Co., Nat. Intergroup, Inc.; past dir. Asso. Merchandising Corp. Chmn. Webber Founds.; Pres. Detroit Arts Commn.; v.p., past chmn. United Found.; trustee Detroit Med. Ctr.; vice chmn., past chmn. Harper-Grace Hosps.; bd. dirs. United Way Am., Detroit Renaissance, Inc.; bd. dirs., founding chmn. New Detroit, Inc. Served to 1st lt. AUS, 1954-56. Recipient Distinguished Service award-Outstanding Young Man of Yr. Detroit Jr. C. of C., 1960; Humanitarian award B'nai B'rith, 1970; recipient Builders of Detroit award Wayne State U., 1974, Nat. Human Relations award Greater Detroit Round Table Christians and Jews, 1981, William Booth statue Salvation Army, 1981, Disting. Network Service award Nat. Urban Coalition, 1983. Mem. Am. Retail Fedn. (chmn. 1981), Nat. Retail Fedn. (past dir.). Clubs: Country of Detroit, Detroit Athletic, Detroit, Grosse Pointe Club. Office: 333 W Fort St 11th Fl Detroit MI 48226

HUDSON, LEONARD DEAN, physician; b. Everett, Wash., May 7, 1938; s. Marshall W. and Blanche V. (Morgan) H.; m. Louise Eleanor Vik, Dec. 30, 1961; children: Sean Marshall, Sherry Elizabeth, Kevin Arthur. B.S., Wash. State U., Pullman, 1960; M.D., U. Wash., Seattle, 1964. Diplomate: Am. Bd. Internal Medicine (pulmonary disease). Intern Bellevue Hosp. Center, N.Y.C., 1964-65; resident in internal medicine N.Y. Hosp., 1965-66, U. Wash. Hosps., 1968-69; chief resident Harborview Med. Center, Seattle; also instr. U. Wash. Med. Sch., 1967-70; Am. Thoracic Soc. fellow in pulmonary diseases U. Colo. Med. Center, 1970-71, instr., then asst. prof. medicine, 1971-73; mem. faculty U. Wash. Med. Center, 1973—, asso. prof. medicine, 1976-82, prof., 1982—; chief div. respiratory diseases, med. dir. ICU Harborview Med. Center, 1976—; chmn. Tb adv. com. Wash. Dept. Social and Health Services. Author papers, revs. in field. Served with USPHS, 1966-68. Named Outstanding Resident, Harborview Med. Center. Fellow ACP, Am. Coll. Chest Physicians (state gov. 1980—, mem.), Am. Fedn. Clin. Research, Am. Thoracic Soc. (sec.-treas. 1983-84), Western Soc. Clin. Research, Wash. Lung Assn. (dir., Vol. Hall of Fame 1977), Wash. Thoracic Soc., Phi Beta Kappa. Democrat. Club: Seattle Flounders Soccer. Office: 325 9th Ave Seattle WA 98104

HUDSON, LEONARD HARLOW, contractor; b. Canmer, Ky., Oct. 27, 1915; s. Leonard Lee and Mary Byrd (Harlow) H.; m. Mary Louise Sutton, Sept. 13, 1938; children: James Leonard, Richard Frank. A.B., Western Ky. U., 1935, B.S. in Bus. Adminstrn, 1938; M.B.A., Northwestern U., 1939; J.D., U. Balt., 1951; postgrad. bus., Harvard U., 1958. Bar: Md.; C.P.A., Md. Tchr. math. Greensburg (Ky.) High Sch., 1936-37; instr. acctg. Coll. St. Thomas, St. Paul, 1939; examiner Civil Service Commn., Washington, 1940; agt., group chief IRS, Balt., 1941-51; with Baltimore Contractors, Inc., 1951-82, pres., 1977-81, vice chmn. bd., 1981-82. Trustee Constrn. Industry Advancement Program, Constrn. Workers Trust Fund, Ednl. Found. U. Balt., 1980—; mem. vis. bd. U. Balt., 1975—; mem. Forest Adv. Commn. Md., 1975—. Served with USNR, 1941-45. Mem. Am. Arbitration Soc., ABA, Am. Inst. C.P.A.s. Methodist. Clubs: Harvard; Univ. (Washington); Masons. Home: 58 Milburn Circle Pasadena MD 21122 Office: 711 S Central Ave Baltimore MD 21202

HUDSON, LESTER ALPHUS, JR., textile company executive; b. Sumter, S.C., June 27, 1939; s. Lester Alphus and Essie Laura (Jones) H.; m. Margaret Jane Curtis, June 16, 1962; children: Steven Wayne, Patrick Curtis. B.A., Furman U., 1961; M.B.A., U. S.C., 1965. Supt. weaving Judson Mills, Deering Milliken, Inc., 1965-70; with Dan River Inc., 1970—, pres., 1977-80, corp. sr. v.p., Danville, Va., 1980-81, pres., chief operating officer, 1981—; dir. First & Mchts. Nat. Bank. Bd. dirs. Danville United Way, 1978-80, campaign chmn., 1980-81; chmn. adminstrv. bd. Mt. Vernon United Methodist Ch., Danville, 1980—; bd. assos. Averett Coll., 1978—. Served to 1st lt. USAR, 1962-64. Mem. Young Pres. Orgn. (dir.), So. Indsl. Relations Conf. (dir.), Va. Mfrs. Assn. (dir.), Danville C. of C. (dir.). Clubs: Rotary (v.p. 1979-80), Young Men's, German (Danville). Office: PO Box 261 Danville VA 24541

HUDSON, MANLEY O., JR., lawyer; b. Boston, June 25, 1932; s. Manley O. and Janet (Aldrich) H.; m. Olivia d'Ormesson, July 1, 1971. A.B., Harvard U., 1953, LL.B., 1956. Bar: N.Y. 1964. Law clk. Justice Stanley Reed, U.S. Supreme Ct., Washington, 1956-57; assoc. Cleary, Gottlieb, Steen & Hamilton, Paris, Brussel, N.Y.C., 1958-68, ptnr., N.Y.C., London, Paris, 1968-83, London, 1983—. Contbr. articles to profl. jours. Mem. ABA, Am. Soc. Internat. Law, Assn. Bar City N.Y., N.Y. County Lawyers Assn., N.Y. State Bar Assn., Union Internationale des Avocats. Democrat. Clubs: Century Assn., Council Fgn. Relations; France-Am. Soc. (N.Y.C.). Office: Winchester House 77 London Wall London UK EC2

HUDSON, MARY, oil executive; b. Athens, Tex., Sept. 30, 1912; d. John Thurmond and Lou Allie (Dewberry) H.; m. Cecil Wayne Driver, Sept. 20, 1939; 1 dau., Joyce Driver Cady; m. Frank Bane Vandgrift, June 2, 1945. Extension student, U. Okla., U. Kans. Co-founder, 1932; since pres., chief exec. officer, chmn. bd. Hudson Oil Co., Kansas City, Kans.; pres., chief exec. officer Hudson Refining Co., 1977—; adv. com. Nat. Petroleum Council, 1976. Counsel Republic Colombia in Kansas City, 1959—; Hon. bd. dirs. Rockhurst Coll., Kansas City, Kans. Named Hon. Citizen of Kansas City (Mo.), 1971, Ky. col., 1964. Mem. Soc. Ind. Gasoline Marketers Am. (a founder, pres. 1965-68), Ind. Gasoline Marketeers Council (a founder), Women's Kansas City Assn. Internat. Relations and Trade (pres. 1971-74), Am. Royal Assn. (gov.), Counsular Corps Greater Kansas City (dean), Am. Petroleum Inst., Am. Petroleum Refiners Assn., 25 Year Club Petroleum Industry, DAR. Clubs: Kansas City; Lauderdale Yacht (Ft. Lauderdale, Fla.); Order Eastern Star. Office: Hudson Oil Co PO Box 907 Kansas City MO 64141 *

HUDSON, MILTON WILLARD, economist; b. N.Y.C., Oct. 17, 1927; s. Sydney and Blanche (Calder) H.; m. Hildegard Moser, Nov. 19, 1949; children—Robert S., James M. B.S., Columbia U., 1951; M.A., N.Y. U., 1954. With Morgan Guaranty Trust Co., N.Y.C., 1951-77, asso. economist, 1960-77, v.p., 1960-77; asst. to chmn. Fed. Res. Bd., Washington, 1977-78; sr. v.p., head econ. analysis dept. Morgan Guaranty Trust, N.Y.C., 1978—. Editor: The Morgan Guaranty Survey, 1965-77. Served in USAF, 1946-47. Mem. Internat. Conf. Comml. Bank Economists, Am. Econ. Assn., Am. Fin. Assn., Nat. Assn. Bus. Economists. Republican. Congregationalist. Clubs: Rockville Links, Sagamore Yacht. Office: 23 Wall St New York NY 10015 *

HUDSON, PHILLIP F., banker; b. Syracuse, N.Y., Oct. 5, 1936; s. Arthur and Florence H.; Jan. 16, 1960; children: Brian, Kathryn. B.A. in Psychology, Syracuse U., 1960. With Lincoln First Bank of Syracuse, 1964-74, sr. v.p. banking div., to 1974; sr. v.p. holding co., dir. mktg. and long range planning First Va. Bankshares, Falls Church, 1974-77; pres., chief exec. officer First Va. Bank of Tidewater, 1974-76; exec. v.p. retail banking group Am. Nat. Bank & Trust of N.J., Morristown, 1977-83; exec. v.p. consumer banking Horizon Bancorp, Morristown, 1983—; mem. faculty Stonier Grad. Sch. Banking. Served with U.S. Army, 1954-57, 61-63. Mem. Am. Bankers Assn. (exec. com. mktg. div.), Bank Mktg. Assn. Office: 334 Madison Ave Morristown NJ 07960 *

HUDSON, RALPH PERCY, physicist; b. Wellingborough, Eng., Oct. 14, 1924; came to U.S., 1949, naturalized, 1960; s. Harold and Ada (Jenkinson) H.; m. Nancy Brisby, July 9, 1947; children: Geoffrey R., Wendy E. B.A., Merton Coll., Oxford U., 1944, M.A., 1949, Ph.D., 1949. Sci. officer U.K. Ministry Supply, Birmingham, Eng., Montreal, Que. and Chalk River, Can., 1944-46; vis. lectr. Purdue U., 1949-50, asst. prof., 1950-51; with Nat. Bur. Standards, Washington, 1951-80, chief cryogenic physics sect., 1954-61, chief heat div., 1961-78; dep. dir. Center for Absolute Phys. Quantities, 1978-80; dir. publs. Internat. Bur. Weights and Measures, Sèvres, France, 1980—. Editor: Metrologia, 1980—. Mem. U.K. Home Guard, 1941-43, U.K. Atomic Energy Program, 1944-46. Recipient Silver and Gold medals Dept. Commerce, 1957; Samuel Wesley Stratton award Nat. Bur. Standards, 1964; Edward U. Condon award, 1976; Guggenheim fellow, 1960-61. Fellow Am. Phys. Soc., Franklin Inst. (John Price Wetherill medal 1962); mem. Philos. Soc. Washington (pres. 1974-75). Club: Cosmos (Washington). Spl. research on behavior of matter near absolute zero temperature. Home: 10201 Grosvenor Pl Rockville MD 20852 Office: Bureau International des Poids et Mesures Pavillon de Breteuil F-92310 Sèvres France

HUDSON, ROBERT, artist; b. Salt Lake City, Sept. 8, 1938. B.F.A., San Francisco Art Inst., 1962, M.F.A., 1963. Instr. San Francisco Art Inst., 1964-65, chmn. sculpture and ceramic depts., 1965-66, asst. prof., 1976—; asst. prof. art. U. Calif., Berkeley, 1966-73; guest lectr. Md. Inst. Art, 1974, Kansas City Art Inst., 1974; artist in residence U. Wis., Madison, 1974; vis. artist Fresno State U., Calif., 1974; guest lectr. U. Calif., Berkeley, 1975. One man shows, Richmond Art Ctr., Calif., 1961, Bolles Gallery, San Francisco, 1962, Lanyon Galleries, Palo Alto, Calif., 1964, Allan Frumkin Gallery, N.Y.C., 1963, 65, 72, 76, 78, 81, Allan Frumkin Gallery, Chgo., 1969, 71, 76, Fuller Goldeen Gallery, San Francisco, 1982, Miami Dade Community Coll., Miami, Fal., 1979, group shows, Bolles Gallery, San Francisco, 1962, 68, Kaiser Ctr. Sculpture Sch., Oakland, Calif., 1963, Allan Frumkin Gallery, Chgo., 1964, 67, World House Gallery, N.Y.C., 1966, Chgo. Art Inst., 1967, Whitney Mus. Am. Art, N.Y.C., Portland Art Mus., 1968, San Francisco Mus. Modern Art, Jocelyn Art Mus., Omaha, 1970, David Stuart Gallery, Los Angeles, 1972, Margo Leavin Gallery, Los Angeles, 1974, Huntsville Mus. Art, Ala., 1977, U. Tex., Central Wash. U., Ellensburg, 1979, Norton Gallery and Sch. Art, West Palm Beach, Fla., Hirshhorn Mus. And Sculpture Garden, Allan Frumkin Gallery, N.Y.C., 1982, Palm Springs Desert Mus., Calif.; represented permanent collections, San Francisco Mus. Modern Art, Mus. Modern Art, N.Y.C., Anchorage Fed. Bldg. Recipient Purchase prize San Francisco Art Festival, 1961, Nealie Sullivan San Francisco Art Inst., 1965; grantee Nat. Endowment for the Arts, 1972; Guggenheim Found. fellow, 1976. Office: 392 Eucalyptus Ave Cotati CA 94928

HUDSON, ROCK (ROY FITZGERALD), motion picture actor-producer; b. Winnetka, Ill., 1925; m. Phyllis Gates (div. 1958). Hon. Doctor Arts, Marietta (Ohio) Coll., 1957; ed. high sch., Winnetka. Motion picture debut in Fighter Squadron; others include Giant (Acad. award nomination), Something of Value, A Farewell to Arms, This Earth is Mine, Pillow Talk, Come September, Lover Come Back, The Spiral Road, A Gathering of Eagles, Send Me No Flowers, Strange Bedfellows, Blindfold, Seconds, Tobruk, Ice Station Zebra, A Fine Pair, Darling Lill, The Hornet's Nest, Pretty Maids All in a Row, Showdown, Embryo, Avalanche, The Mirror Crack'd; star: TV series McMillan, 1971-76; mini-series Wheels, 1977-78; other TV appearances include The Starmaker, 1981, World War 3, 1981, The Devlin Connection, 1982; appeared in: plays I Do! I Do!, 1974-75, John Brown's Body, 1976, Camelot, 1977, On the Twentieth Century, 1979. Christmas Seal chmn., 1970. Served with USNR, 1941-46. Recipient Look mag. award, 1956; Exhibitor Laurel awards, 1958-66; Bambi awards, Germany, 1958-65; Golden Globe award as world favorite film actor Hollywood Fgn. Corrs. Assn., 1958, 60-62; King David award, 1970. Address: care Creative Artists Agy 1888 Century Park E Suite 1400 Los Angeles CA 90067 *

HUDSON, ROY DAVAGE, pharm. co. exec.; b. Chattanooga, June 30, 1930; s. Roy and Everence (Wilkerson) H.; m. Constance Joan Taylor, Aug. 31, 1956; children—Hollye Lynne, David Kendall. B.S., Livingstone Coll., 1955; M.S., U. Mich., 1957, Ph.D., 1962; M.A., Brown U., 1968; LL.D., Lehigh U., 1974, Princeton, 1975. Prof. pharmacology U. Mich. Sch. Medicine, 1961-66; prof. med. sci. Brown U. Sch. Medicine, 1966-70, asso. dean grad. sch., 1966-69; pres. Hampton Inst., 1970-76; dir. research planning and coordination Parke, Davis Pharm. Co., Ann Arbor, Mich., 1976; v.p. research planning and coordination Warner Lambert/Park-Davis Pharm. Research Div., Ann Arbor, 1977-79; mgr. sci. liaison Upjohn Co., Kalamazoo, Mich., 1979-81; mgr. CNS diseases research, 1981—; dir. Parke-Davis & Co., United Va. Bank-Citizens and Marine, United Va. Bankshares, Chesapeake and Potomac Telephone Co. of Va. Contbr. articles to profl. jours., chpts. to books. Mem. screening com. Danforth Grad. Fellowships, 1962—; mem. adv. council Danforth Grad. Fellows program Danforth Found., 1972—; chmn. Va. Com. on Selection Rhodes Scholars, 1973; mem. Commn. on Fed. Relations, Am. Council on Edn., 1972—, bd. dirs., 1973—; mem. adv. council to dir. NIH, 1974—; Mem. R.I. Commn. Econ. Devel., 1967-69, R.I. Urban League scholarship com., 1966-70; mem. inst. policy commn. So. Regional Edn. Bd.; Bd. dirs. Afro-Am. Soc. Conn. Coll.; bd. dirs., v.p. Nat. Assn. Equal Opportunity in Higher Edn.; trustee Brown U., Livingstone Coll., Peninsula United Community Services. Served with USAF, 1948-52. Recipient Distinguished Alumni award Livingstone Coll.; Outstanding Civilian Service award U.S. Army.; Danforth Grad. fellow, 1955-61. Mem. Am. Soc. Pharmacology and Exptl. Therapeutics, Peninsula C. of C. (hon. dir.), NAACP (life), AAAS, N.Y. Acad. Scis., Sigma Xi, Phi Kappa Phi, Phi Sigma, Beta Kappa Chi, Kappa Delta Pi, Omega Psi Phi, Gamma Alpha, Kappa Delta Pi. Home: 2233 Aberdeen Dr Kalamazoo MI 49008 Office: Upjohn Co Pharm Research Div Kalamazoo MI 49001

HUDSON, WILLIAM HENRY, manufacuting company executive; b. Perry, Mo., July 9, 1930; s. Denver M. and Anna Jesse (Stillwell) H.; m. Patricia A. Yount, June 6, 1954; children: Anne, Mark, Carolyn. B.S., Carnegie Mellon U., 1952; grad. advanced mgmt. program, Harvard U., 1964. Exec. v.p. Sovirel S.A. subs. Corning Glass Works, N.Y., 1967-73, dir.; v.p. Corning Internat. Corp. subs. Corning Glass Works, 1973-75; v.p., gen. mgr. tech. producats div. Corning Glass Works, 1975-80, sr. v.p., gen. mgr. tech. products div., 1980-83, pres. commerce and industry group, 1983—. Bd. dirs. Corning Hosp., Am. Fgn. Christian Union, N.Y.C. Served to 1st. lt. U.S. Army, 1952-54; Korea. Home: 111 W Hill Terr Painted Post NY 14870 Office: Corning Glass Works HP-CB-09 Corning NY 14831

HUDSON, WILLIAM RUCKER, otolaryngologist; b. Charlotte, N.C., May 16, 1925; s. Esper V. and Margaret (Rucker) H.; m. Nancy McLean, June 21, 1947; children—Margaret, Anne, William Rucker. Premed. student, Emory U., 1947; M.D., Wake Forest U., 1951. Intern U. Tex. Med. Center, 1951-52; gen. practice medicine, Canton, N.C., 1952-57; resident in otolaryngology N.C. Bapt. Hosp., Winston Salem, 1957-60; NIH fellow Johns Hopkins Med. Sch., Balt., 1960-61; mem. faculty Duke U. Med. Center, Durham, N.C., 1961—, prof. otolaryngology, 1967—, chmn. dept., 1967—. Served with inf. AUS, World War II. Decorated Purple Heart, Combat Inf. badge. Mem. AMA, Am. Acad. Otolaryngology, Am. Council Otolaryngology, N.C. Med. Soc., Durham Orange County Med. Soc. Office: Duke U Med Center Durham NC 27710

HUDSON, WILLIAM THOMAS, govt. ofcl.; b. Chgo., Dec. 14, 1929; s. Cornelius and Mary (Palmer) H. B.S., Northwestern U., 1953; M.A. in Polit. Sci, U. Chgo., 1954. Claims authorizer Bur. Retirement and Survivors Ins., Social Security Adminstrn., Dept. Health, Edn. and Welfare, Chgo., 1956-63; employee devel. officer Hdqrs. Retirement and Survivors Ins., Balt., 1963-64, spl. asst. for EEO to dir. bur., 1964-65; contract operations specialist Bur. Health Ins., 1965-66; dep. EEO officer Office Sec. HEW, Washington, 1966-67; program mgr. Internal EEO Program, Office Sec., Dept. Transp., Washington, 1967-70; chief Office Civil Rights, USCG, Washington, 1970—; detailed to Pres.'s Com. on Equal Employment Opportunity, Washington, 1964-65; resource cons. Nat. Urban League Conv., 1970. Served with U.S. Army, 1954-56. Mem. Nat. Assn. Human Rights Workers, Phi Delta Kappa. Home: 1006 G St SE Washington DC 20003 Office: 2100 2d St SW Washington DC 20593

HUDSON, WINTHROP STILL, clergyman, educator; b. 1911; s. Grant Martin and Mildred (Gilchrist) H.; m. Mildred Lois Austin, June 23, 1934; children: Judith Ann, Susan Camille. B.A., Kalamazoo Coll., 1933, D.D., 1958; B.D., Colgate Rochester Divinity Sch., 1937; Ph.D., U. Chgo., 1940; D.D. (hon.), Franklin Coll., 1978, McMaster U., Hamilton, Ont., Can., 1982. Ordained to ministry Bapt. Ch., 1937; minister York (N.Y.) Ch., 1935-37, Normal Park Ch., Chgo., 1937-42; instr. Colgate Rochester Divinity Sch., 1942-44, adminstrv. asso., 1947-48, James B. Colgate prof. history of Christianity, 1948-77, Disting. Sem. prof., 1977-80; prof. history U. Rochester, 1970-77; asso. prof. U. Chgo., 1944-47; vis. scholar U. N.C., 1979-80, adj. prof., 1980—. Author: John Ponet-Advocate of Limited Monarchy, 1942, The Great Tradition of the American Churches, 1953, The Story of the Christian Church, 1958, Understanding of Roman Catholicism, 1959, American Protestantism, 1961, Religion in America, 1965, 3d rev. edit., 1981, Nationalism and Religion in America, 1970, Baptists in Transition, 1979, The Cambridge Connection and the Elizabethan Settlement, 1980; editor: Christian Leadership in a World Society, 1946, Henry Scougal's Life of God in the Soul of Man, 1948, Roger Williams Experiments of Spiritual Life and Health, 1951, Baptist Concepts of the Church, 1959; subject of work: In the Great Tradition, Essays in Honor of Winthrop S. Hudson on Pluralism, Voluntarism and Revivalism, 1982. Recipient Susan Colver Rosenberg award for meritorious research, 1940; Nat. Endowment for Humanities sr. fellow, 1975; named Alumnus of Yr. U. Chgo. Divinity Sch., 1981. Mem. Am. Soc. Ch. History (pres. 1948, sec. 1955-60), Am. Bapt. Hist. Soc. (pres. 1955-66), Am. Hist. Assn. Home: 78 Hayes Rd Chapel Hill NC 27514

HUDSON, YEAGER, philosophy educator, clergyman; b. Meridian, Miss., Aug. 14, 1931; s. William Ernest and Effie (Yeager) H.; m. Margaret Luoise Hight, car. 20, 1953; children: Paul Brinton, Gareth Yeager. A.B., Millsaps Coll., 1954; S.T.B., Boston U., 1958, Ph.D., 1965; M.A. (hon.), Colby Coll., 1977. Ordained to ministry United Methodist Ch., 1963. Instr. Colby Coll., 1959-65, asst. prof. philosophy, 1965-70, assoc. prof., 1970-77, prof., chmn. dept. philosophy, 1977—; Fulbright lectr. Ahnednager Coll., (India), 1967-68. Editor: Profile of a College, 1972. Mem. Am. Philos. Assn., Soc. Advancement Am. Philosophy, Am. Inst. Indian Studies (trustee 1980—). Office: Colby Coll Dept Philosophy and Religion Waterville ME 04901

HUDSPETH, CHALMERS MAC, lawyer, educator; b. Denton, Tex., Oct. 18, 1919; s. Junia Evans and Ethel Leonice (Burns) H.; m. Demaris Eleanor De Lange, Jan. 30, 1945; children: Albert James, Thomas Richard, Helen Demaris. B.A., Rice U., Houston, 1940; J.D., U. Tex., 1946. Bar: Tex. 1946. Practiced in, Houston, 1947—; mem. firm De Lange, Hudspeth and Pitman, 1950-68; sr. mem. firm De Lange, Hudspeth, Pitman & Katz, 1968—; asst. prof. law U. Tex. at Austin, 1946-47; lectr. govt. Rice U., 1947—; mem. council overseers Jesse H. Jones Grad. Sch. Adminstrn., 1979—, bd. govs., 1980—, trustee, 1982—; vis. prof. law U. Houston, 1950-52; Dir. Stewart Info. Services Corp., Stewart Title Guaranty Co. Author: Torts—A Baker's Dozen, 2d edit, 1976; Contbr. articles to profl. jours. Mem. bi-racial com. Houston Ind. Sch. Dist., 1955-56; trustee, v.p. Brown Found., 1983—. Served to lt. USNR, 1942-45. Fellow Am., Tex. bar founds., Am. Coll. Probate Counsel; mem. Am. Judicature Soc., Tex., Am. bar assns., State Bar Tex. (dir. 1966-68, v.p. 1968-69), Houston Philos. Soc. (pres. 1964-65), Houston Com. on Fgn. Relations (chmn. 1973-74), Petroleum Club of Houston, Chancellors, Order of Coif, Phi Delta Phi. Office: 2800 Summit Tower 11 Greenway Plaza Houston TX 77046

HUDSPETH, EMMETT LEROY, physicist, educator; b. Denton, Tex., Dec. 3, 1916; s. Junia Evans and Ethel Leonice (Burns) H.; m. Mary Alice Barnes, Dec. 2, 1944; children: John, Philip, Anne, Paul. A.B., Rice Inst., 1937, M.A., 1938, Ph.D., 1940. Fellow physics Rice Inst., 1937-40; fellow Bartol Research Found., 1940-41, asst. dir., 1946-50; staff mem. radiation lab. Mass. Inst. Tech., 1941-45; prof. physics U. Tex., Austin, 1950—; dir. Nuclear Physics Lab. (U. Tex.), 1950-72; cons. USN, 1943-45; adviser Sec. War, 1942; com. on Undersea Warfare, 1947-49; sci. adv. com. Radiobiol. Lab., U. Tex. and USAF, 1954-58. Contbr. articles to profl. jours. Republican nominee from Tex. 10th Dist. for U.S. Ho. of Reps., 1978. Fellow Am. Phys. Soc., A.A.A.S.; mem. Phi Beta Kappa, Sigma Xi. Research nuclear physics, disintegration of light elements, energy levels of nuclei and others. Home: 6104 Janey Dr Austin TX 78731

HUDSPETH, HARRY LEE, judge; b. Dallas, Dec. 28, 1935; s. Harry Ellis and Hattilee (Dudney) H.; m. Vicki Kathryn Round, Nov. 27, 1971; children—Melinda, Mary Kathryn. B.A., U. Tex., Austin, 1955, J.D., 1958. Bar: Tex. bar 1958. Trial atty. Dept. Justice, Washington, 1959-62; asst. U.S. atty. Western Dist. Tex., El Paso, 1962-69; mem. firm Peticolas, Luscombe & Stephens, El Paso, 1969-77; U.S. magistrate, El Paso, 1977-79; U.S. dist. judge Western Dist. Tex., El Paso, 1979—. Bd. dirs. Sun Carnival Assn., 1976, Met. YMCA El Paso, 1980—. Mem. U. Tex. Ex-students Assn. (exec. council 1980—), Am. Bar Assn., El Paso Bar Assn., Chancellors, Order Coif, Phi Beta Kappa. Democrat. Mem. Christian Ch. (Disciples of Christ.). Club: Kiwanis (pres. 1975). Home: 9337 Turrentine St El Paso TX 79925 Office: 433 US Courthouse El Paso TX 79901

HUEBNER, HARLAN PIERCE, lawyer; b. Los Angeles, Apr. 10, 1927; s. Herbert A. and Lorna (Pierce) H.; m. Joan Hoffman, Nov. 1, 1952; children—Jo-Ellan, Loring Ann, Elizabeth. B.S., U. So. Calif., 1950; J.D., Southwestern Law Sch., 1956. Bar: Calif. bar 1958. Mem. firm Huebner & Worrel, Los Angeles, 1958—. Chmn. Glendale Council Girl Scouts Fund Dirve, 1968; active fund drives YMCA; v.p., bd. dirs. Glendale Symphony Orch. Assn.; pres. bd. trustees Twelve Oaks Retirement Home, 1976-79. Served with C.I.C. AUS. Mem. State Bar Calif. (chmn. patent and trademark and copyright sect. 1974-75), Am. Bar Assn., Am. Patent Law Assn. (bd. govs. 1966-69), Am. Judicature Soc. Clubs: Rotarian (dir. Los Angeles Club 5 1967-69),

Mason (Shriner). Home: 1446 Virginia St Glendale CA 91202 Office: Huebner & Worrel 900 Wilshire Blvd Suite 1000 Los Angeles CA 90017

HUEBNER, JOHN STEPHEN, geologist; b. Bryn Mawr, Pa., Sept. 9, 1940; s. John Mudie and Elizabeth (Converse) H.; m. Emily Mayer Zug, June 16, 1962; children: Christopher Converse, Jeffrey Worrell. A.B. magna cum laude, Princeton U., 1962; Ph.D., Johns Hopkins U., 1967. Research geologist U.S. Geol. Survey, 1967—; cons. NASA, 1976-78; lectr. George Washington U., 1971; sec.-treas. Am. Geol. Inst., 1974-75. Asso. editor: Jour. Geophys. Research, 1977-79; Contbr. articles profl. jours. Pres. Wood Acres Citizens Assn., 1977-78. Fellow Mineral. Soc. Am. (recipient award 1978); mem. Geochem. Soc. (treas. 1972-75), Am. Geophys. Union, AAAS, Geol. Soc. Washington, Sigma Xi. Club: Cosmos (Washington). Home: 6102 Cromwell Dr Bethesda MD 20016 Office: 959 National Center Reston VA 22092

HUEBNER, ROBERT JOSEPH, med. research scientist; b. Cin., Feb. 23, 1914; s. Joseph Frederick and Philomena (Brickner) H.; m. Harriet Lee, Feb. 5, 1975; children by previous marriage—Elizabeth, Frances, Geraldine, James, Virginia, Roberta, Edward, Louise, Daniel. Student, Xavier U., 1932-35, U. Cin., 1937-38; M.D., St. Louis U., 1942; LL.D., U. Cin., 1965; D.Sc. (hon.), Edgecliff Coll., 1970, U. Parma, Italy, 1970, U. Leuven, 1973. Commd. jr. asst. surgeon USPHS, 1942, advanced through grades to med. dir., 1953; mil. duty Alaskan area USCG, 1943- 44; virus and rickettsial disease research NIH, 1944-56, chief virus sect., 1949-56; chief lab. infectious disease Nat. Inst. Allergy and Infectious Diseases, 1956-68; chief viral carcinogenesis br. Nat. Cancer Inst., Bethesda, Md., 1968—; Gehrman lectr. U. Ill., 1955, Eli Lilly lectr., 1957; Gudakunst lectr. U. Mich., 1958, Harvey lectr., 1960, Puckett lectr., 1960. Contbr. numerous articles to profl. jours. Recipient Bailey K. Ashford award, 1949; certificate merit St. Louis U., 1949; James D. Bruce Meml. award, 1964; Pasteur medal, 1965; Distinguished Service medal USPHS, 1966; Howard Taylor Ricketts award, 1968; Nat. medal Sci., 1969; Kimble award, 1970; Rockefeller award, 1970; Guido Lenghi award, 1971. Fellow Am. Pub. Health Assn., N.Y. Acad. Scis.; mem. Nat. Acad. Scis., A.A.A.S., Am. Assn. Immunologists, Am. Epidemiol. Soc., Fedn. Am. Socs. Exptl. Biology and Medicine, Wash. Acad. Sci. (award biol. scis. 1949), Internat. Union Against Cancer, Am. Acad. Microbiology, Am. Assn. Cancer Research, A.M.A., Md. Angus Assn. (pres. 1959-60), Sigma Xi, Alpha Omega Alpha. Home: 12100 Whippoorwill Ln Rockville MD 20852 Office: Lab Cellular and Molecular Biology Nat Cancer Inst Bethesda MD 20205

HUENEMANN, RUBEN HENRY, clergyman; b. Waukon, Iowa, Jan. 15, 1909; s. William and Mary (Hansmeier) H.; m. Clara James, Aug. 19, 1936; children: Robert Gilchrist, Ralph William, Carol Ruth, Grace Noel. A.B., Luther Coll., Decorah, Iowa, 1933; B.D., Mission House Sem., Plymouth, Wis., 1936; postgrad., Washington U., also Pacific Sch. Religion, Berkeley, Calif.; D.D., Franklin and Marshall Coll., 1954; LL.D., Heidelberg Coll., 1960. Tchr. rural schs., S.D., 1927-29; ordained to ministry Evang. and Ref. Ch., 1936; pastor St. Stephen's Ch., Juneau, Wis., 1936-38, Salem Ch., St. Louis, 1938-44, Zion Ch., Lodi, Calif., 1944-54, Grace Ch., Milw., 1954-58, Faith Ch., 1958-60; pres. United Theol. Sem. of Twin Cities, Mpls., 1960-70; conf. exec. Central Pacific Conf. United Ch. Christ, Portland, Oreg., 1970-76; interim sr. pastor St. Paul's United Ch. of Christ, St. Paul, 1976-77; pres. Calif. Synod Evang. and Ref. Ch., 1950-54; moderator Gen. Synod, Tiffin, Ohio, 1953; mem. theol. com. United Ch. Christ. Contbr. articles to denominational periodicals. Mem. Nat. Council Chs. (gen. bd. 1966-69). Address: 12705 SE River Rd Portland OR 97222

HUESCA PACHECO, ROSENDO, archbishop.; b. Ejutla, Mex., Mar. 1, 1932. Ordained priest Roman Cath. Ch., 1956; named bishop, 1970; archbishop of Puebla de los Angeles, 1977—. Address: Calle 2 Sur N 305 Puebla Mexico

HUESTIS, CHARLES BENJAMIN, educational administrator; b. Seattle, Jan. 27, 1920; s. Claude Erwin and Eloise Marie (Pettit) H.; m. Kathryn Alice Porter, Mar. 1, 1942; children: Stephen Porter, Jeffrey Charles, Robin Rebecca. Student, Griffin Murphy Coll., Seattle, 1938-39, U. Calif. Berkeley, 1946. With Seattle First Nat. Bank, 1941; acct. Rheem Mfg. Co., Richmond, Calif., 1946-51, chief acct. aircraft div., Downey, Calif., 1951-54, corp. comptroller, 1954-56; v.p., treas. Hall-Scott Inc., Berkeley, Calif., 1956; exec. v.p., dir., treas., 1956-57; adminstrv. cons. Overseas Nat. Airways, Oakland, Calif., 1957-58; controller El Segundo div., Hughes Aircraft Co., 1958-59, controller Tucson div., 1959, treas., dir. chmn. finance com., 1959-66, chmn. finance com., 1959-66, v.p., 1962-66; v.p., treas., dir. Am. Mt. Everest Expdn., 1963; v.p. bus. and finance Duke U., Durham, N.C., 1966-83, sr. v.p., 1983—; dir. Technomics, Inc., Falls Church, Va., 1966-76; chmn. bd. Sta. WDBS, 1970-76. Bd. dirs. Santa Barbara (Calif.) Research Center, 1959-66; bd. dirs., mem. exec. com. Research Triangle Found., Research Triangle Park, N.C.; trustee Research Triangle Inst., Research Triangle Park, 1967-79, Sierra Club Found., 1969-79; chmn. N.C. Nature Conservancy., 1979-83; climbing leader Duke-Gettysburg Expdn. to Kurdisan, 1982. Mem. Explorers Club, Am. Alpine Club. Home: 1803 Woodburn Rd Durham NC 28301 Office: Duke U: Durham NC 27706

HUETTNER, RICHARD ALFRED, lawyer; b. N.Y.C., Mar. 25, 1927; s. Alfred F. and Mary (Reilly) H.; m. Eunice Bizzell Dowd, Aug. 22, 1971; children from previous marriage: Jennifer Mary, Barbara Bryan. Marine Engrs. License, N.Y. State Maritime Acad., 1947; B.S., Yale U. Sch. Engring., 1949; J.D., U. Pa., 1952. Bar: D.C. 1952, N.Y. 1954, U.S. Ct. Mil. Appeals 1953, U.S. Ct. Claims 1961, U.S. Supreme Ct. 1969, U.S. Ct. Appeals (fed. cir.) 1982, also other fed. cts, registered to practice U.S. Patent Office 1957, Canadian Patent Office 1968. Engr. Jones & Laughlin Steel Corp., 1954-55; asso. atty. firm Kenyon & Kenyon, 1955-61, mem. firm, 1961—; specialist patent, trademark and copyright law. Trustee N.J. Shakespeare Festival, 1972-79, sec., 1977-79; trustee Overlook Hosp., Summit, N.J., 1978—, vice chmn. bd. trustees, 1980-82, chmn. bd. trustees, 1982—; trustee Overlook Found., 1981—; v.p. Colonial Symphony Orch., 1974-76, pres. bd. trustees, 1976-79, trustee, 1972-82; chmn. bd. overseers N.J. Consortium for Performing Arts, 1972-74; mem. Yale U. Council, 1978-81; dir. Yale Communications Bd., 1978-80; chmn. bd. trustees Center for Addictive Illnesses, Morristown, N.J., 1979-82; rep. Assn. Yale Alumni, 1975-80, chmn. com. undergrad. admissions, 1976-78, bd. govs., 1976-80, chmn. bd. govs., 1978-80; chmn. Yale Alumni Schs. Com. N.Y., 1972-78; asso. fellow Silliman Coll., Yale U., 1976—; dir. Yale U. Alumni Fund, 1978-81; bd. dirs. Overlook Health Systems, 1984—. Served from midshipman to lt. USNR, 1945-47, 52-54; cert. JAGC, 1953; Res. ret. Recipient Yale medal, 1983. Mem. Am., N.Y. State bar assns., Assn. Bar City N.Y., N.Y. Patent Law Assn. (chmn. com. meetings 1961-64, chmn. com. econ. matters 1966-69, 72-74), AAAS, N.Y. Acad. Scis., N.Y. County Lawyers Assn., Internat. Patent and Trademark Assn., Am. Judicature Soc., Yale Sci. and Engring. Assn. (v.p. 1973-75, pres. 1975-78, exec. bd. 1972—), Fed. Bar Council. Clubs: Yale (N.Y.C.); Yale of Central N.J. (trustee 1973—); (Convent, N.J.) (pres. 1975-77); Morris County Golf (Convent, N.J.); The Graduates (New Haven). Home: 150 Green Ave Madison NJ 07940 Office: One Broadway New York NY 10004

HUEY, MARY EVELYN BLAGG, university president; b. Wills Point, Tex., Jan. 19, 1922; d. Henry H. and Melissa E. (Manning) Blagg; m. Griffin B. Huey, Aug. 21, 1954; 1 son, Henry Griffin. B.S. in English and Music, Tex. Woman's U., 1942, M.A. (grad. scholar) in English Lit, 1943; So. Regional Tng. Program in Public Adminstrn. fellow, U. Ala., U. Tenn., U. Ky., 1945-46; M.A. in Public Adminstrn, U. Ky., 1947; Ph.D. in Polit. Sci, Duke U., 1954; postgrad., Harvard U., summer 1950, Baiko Jo Gakuin, (Luth. Coll. for Women), Shimonoseki, Japan, 1981. Instr. English dept. Tex. Woman's U., Denton, 1943-45; asst. dir. Bur. Public Adminstrn., U. Miss., Oxford, 1946-47; instr. dept. govt. N. Tex. State U., Denton, 1947-51, asst. prof., 1954-63, asso. prof., 1963-66, prof., 1966-71; prof. govt. Tex. Woman's U., 1971—, dean, 1971-76, pres., 1976—. Author: The Legislative Process: A Handbook for Mississippi Legislators, 1947; contbr. articles and book revs. to jours. in edn., social sci. and polit. sci. Pres. United Way Denton County, 1979-80; mem. Bd. Adjustment Denton, 1962-68, chmn., 1963-68; mem. City Charter Rev. Com., 1976; PTA pres. TWU Demonstration Sch., 1970-71; dist. pres. women's aux. Tex. Dental Assn., 1957-58, state parliamentarian, 1958-59; state Young Republican Club rep. to Nat. Conv., Chgo., 1952; charter pres. Denton County Rep. Women's Club, 1955-57; mem. Denton County steering com. for Reagan and Bush, 1980; ch. sch. tchr. First Presbyn. Ch., Denton, 1955-56, 61, 64, 66, 68, 70-71, ruling elder, 1973-75. Recipient Disting. Alumna award Tex. Woman's U., 1974, Otis Fowler award Denton C. of C., 1980; named Public Adminstr. of Year Am. Assn. Public Adminstrn., 1977. Mem. Am. Council Edn., Am. Polit. Sci. Assn., Council Grad. Schs. U.S. (program com. 1975-76), Assn. Tex. Colls. and Univs. (exec. bd. 1977-80), Nat. Acad. Public Adminstrn., Am. Assn. State Colls. and Univs. (participant ednl. mission to Israel 1980), Southwestern Polit. Sci. Assn., Southwestern Social Sci. Assn., AAUW (Outstanding Woman of Tex. award 1977, pres. Denton br. 1962-63, state conv. del. 1963, 69), Tex. Acad. Sci., Tex. Assn. Coll. Tchrs. (sec.-treas. chpt. 1958-59), Nat. Home Fashions League (alt. nat. dir. 1980-81), D.A.R., Daus. Republic of Tex., Colonial Dames Seventeenth Century, Nat. Geneal. Soc., So. Polit. Sci. Assn., So. Univ. Council, Fine Arts Soc. Tex. (pres. 1977-79), North Central Tex. Council Govts. (exec. bd. 1970-71), Denton C. of C. (dir. 1976—), Pi Sigma Alpha, Sigma Alpha Iota (nat. award 1979), Delta Kappa Gamma (Outstanding Contbns. to Edn. award 1978). Clubs: Ariel (chmn. lit. dept. 1971-73, 1st. v.p. 1971-73), Soroptimist Internat.). Home: 2801 Longfellow Ln Denton TX 76201 Office: PO Box 23925 Tex Woman's Univ Station Denton TX 76204

HUEY, STANTON ENNES, cons. civil engr.; b. Eureka, Mo., July 12, 1898; s. Frank S. and Carrie May (Markley) H.; m. Julia Frances Stubbs, June 26, 1929; children—Stanton Ennes, Palmer Stubbs, Francis Markley. B.S. in Civil Engring. with honors, Washington U., St. Louis, 1924. Asst. to E.C. McGee (cons. engrs.), Monroe, La., 1924-26; civil engr. and surveyor, Monroe, 1926-34; mem. La. Bd. State Engrs., New Orleans, 1934-40, chief state engr., 1940-41; chmn. S.E. Huey Co. (cons. engrs.), Monroe, 1941—. Contbr. profl. jours. Mem. Monroe Utilities Commn., 1956-58. Fellow Am. Cons. Engrs. Council; mem. ASCE (life), Am. Concrete Inst., Am. Congress Surveying and Mapping, Am. Water Works Assn., Sigma Xi, Tau Beta Pi. Democrat. Presbyterian. Clubs: Lotus, Bayou DeSiard Country. Home: 1910 Island Dr Monroe LA 71201 Office: 1309 Louisville Ave Monroe LA 71201

HUFBAUER, GARY CLYDE, economist, lawyer, educator; b. San Diego, Apr. 3, 1939; s. Clarence Clyde and Arabelle Maxwell (McKee) H.; m. Carolyn Revelle, June 25, 1961; children: Randall Clyde Revelle, Ellen Arabelle Scripps. A.B., Harvard U., 1960; Ph.D., King's Coll., Cambridge U., Eng., 1963; J.D., Georgetown U., 1980. Bar: D.C. bar 1980, Md. bar 1980. Mem. faculty dept. econs. U. N.Mex., 1963-74, prof., 1970-74; dir. internat. tax staff Dept. Treasury, Washington, 1974-77; dep. asst. Sec. Treasury, Internat. Trade and Investment Policy, 1977-80; mem. firm Chapman, Duff & Paul, Washington, 1980—; dep. dir. Internat. Law Inst., Georgetown Law Center, 1980-82; sr. fellow Inst. Internat. Econs., 1982—; mem. Harvard Devel. Adv. Service, Pakistan, 1967-69; vis. prof. Stockholm Sch. Econs., 1974, Cambridge U., 1973, Georgetown U., 1975, 80—. Author: Synthetic Materials and the Theory of International Trade, 1966, Overseas Manufacturing Investment and the Balance of Payments, 1968. Ford Found. fellow, 1966-67; Fulbright research scholar, 1973. Mem. Am. Econ. Assn., Nat. Economists Club, Internat. Fiscal Assn. Episcopalian. Clubs: Cosmos, Gibson Island, United Oxford and Cambridge Univ. Home: 3213 Farmington Dr Chevy Chase MD 20815 Office: Inst Internat Econs 11 Dupont Circle NW Washington DC 20036

HUFF, HENRY P., airline corporation executive; b. 1920. With Slick Airways Inc., 1947-64; exec. v.p. Transamerica Airlines Inc., Oakland, Calif., 1964-69, pres., 1969-76, pres., chief exec. officer, dir., 1976-83, chmn., chief exec. officer, 1983—. Office: Transamerica Airlines Inc 7901 Oakport St Box 2504 Oakland CA 94614

HUFF, JOHN ROSSMAN, oil drilling company executive; b. Oxford, Miss., Mar. 14, 1946; s. William Jennings and Frances (Rossman) H.; m. Karen Keohane; children: Christopher, Travis. Student, Rice U., 1966; B.C.E., Ga. Inst. Tech., 1968; P.M.D., Harvard U., 1977. Engr. Offshore Co., Houston, 1968-70; structural engr. Zapata Off-Shore Co., Houston, 1970-72; with Western Oceanic, Inc., 1972—, v.p.-tech. services, Houston, 1975-76, v.p.-sales, 1976-78, v.p.-ops., 1978-80, pres., 1980—. Bd. dirs. U.S. Coast Guard Acad. Found., 1982—; mem. Houston Ballet Ambassadors, 1981—, Republican campaign coms., Houston, 1982-83, Strake-Jesuit Bd., Houston, 1983; active community fin. drive Strake-Jesuit Bd., Houston, 1983. NSF grantee Ind. U., 1963; Nat. Coll. Athletic Assn. scholar, 1964-68. Mem. ASCE, Internat. Assn. Drilling Contractors (bd. dirs. 1978, v.p. offshore com. 1983-84). Clubs: Houston, Houston Petroleum. Office: Western Oceanic Inc 515 S Post Oak Blvd Suite 1200 Houston TX 77027

HUFF, KENNETH ROBERT, supermarket and drug chain executive; b. 1927. B.J., U. Mo., 1952. Vice pres. The Fleming Cos., Inc., 1953-73; v.p., gen. mgr. distbn. ctrs. Albertson's, Inc., Boise, Idaho, 1974-75, v.p. supply and distbn., 1975-76, sr. v.p. wholesale ops., 1976-77, sr. v.p. distbn. and mgf., 1977-79; exec. v.p. Albertson's Inc., Boise, Idaho, 1979—. Office: Albertsons Inc 250 Parkcenter Blvd Box 20 Boise ID 83726

HUFF, PAUL EMLYN, insurance executive; b. Oronoque, Kans., Nov. 22, 1916; s. Clarence Elmer and Myrtle Ella (Sherman) H.; m. Virginia Arnold, June 1, 1938; children: Philip A., Roger A. B.S. in Commerce cum laude, Kans. State U., 1938. With Nat. Farmers Union Ser. Corp., Denver, 1938-60, dir. fin., 1956-60; pres. Acad. Life Ins. Co., Colorado Springs, 1960-64; sr. v.p., treas. Nat. Farmers Union Ser. Corp. and ins. subsidiaries, Denver, 1964-82; sec. Nat. Farmers Union, Denver, 1982—; dir. Baldwin Enterprises, Inc., Paris St. Corp., CEBA Dealer Corp.; mem. temp. faculty Denver U. Bus. Sch. Bd. dirs. United Cerebral Palsy Assn. Denver, 1952-60, 64-81, also pres.; bd. dirs., treas. El Paso County Assn. Retarded Children, 1962-63; bd. dirs., pres. United Cerebral Palsy Assn. Colo., 1957-58; bd. dirs. Mile High United Fund Denver, 1955-56. Mem. Am. Mgmt. Assn., Ind. Acctg. and Statis. Assn. Democrat. Club: Denver Athletic. Home: 9120 E Jewell Circle Denver CO 80231 Office: 12025 E 45th Ave Denver CO 80251

HUFF, ROBERT B., mfg. co. exec.; b. Evanston, Ill., 1941. B.B.A., U. Hawaii, 1965; M.B.A., Harvard, 1968. With Bell & Howell Co., 1965—; v.p. subs. Calhoun Co., 1968, gen. mgr. video div., 1969, adminstrv. asst. to pres., 1970, asst. to pres., 1972, corporate v.p., dir. corporate planning, 1973, pres. consumer group, 1974, corporate v.p., pres. micro-imagery group, 1977, sr. v.p., 1978, exec. v.p., 1980, pres., chief operating officer, 1981—. Address: Bell & Howell Co 7100 McCormick Rd Chicago IL 60645

HUFF, STANLEY EUGENE, dermatologist; b. Bremen, Ind., June 5, 1918; s. Otho H. and Gertrude M. (Nufer) H.; m. Helen Leonard, Oct. 30, 1946; children: John, Margaret, Thomas, Stephen, Katherine, Mary. B.S., U. Notre Dame, 1940; M.D., Northwestern U., 1944; M.S. in Dermatology, U. Minn., 1949. Intern Wesley Meml. Hosp., Chgo., 1944; pvt. practice, Evanston, Ill., 1950—; mem. staff Evanston Hosp.; prof. clin. dermatology Northwestern U. Med. Sch. Vice pres. Evanston United Fund, 1960-62. Served with M.C. AUS, 1944-46. Mem. Am. Acad. Dermatology (pres. 1968), Am. Dermatol. Assn. (v.p. 1979-80), Soc. Investigative Dermatology, AMA, Evanston C. of C. Club: Kiwanis. Home: 75 Balmoral Ct Northfield IL 60093 Office: 636 Church St Evanston IL 60201

HUFFARD, JAY CHOATE, commodities sales company executive; b. Chgo., July 3, 1941; s. Paul Phillippi and Edith Eyre (Schippers) H.; m. Kirke Arnam Dyett, Aug. 17, 1968; children: Joshua Choate, Benjamin Hathaway, Julia Kirke. B.A., Yale U., 1964; M.B.A., Stanford U., 1966. With Donaldson Lufkin & Jenrette, Inc., N.Y.C., 1966—, sr. v.p. securities div., 1973-80, mng. dir. parent co., 1980—, exec. v.p., 1980-81; pres., chief exec. officer subs. ACLU Internat., Inc., White Plains, N.Y., 1981—; dir. U.S. Surg. Corp., Norwalk, Conn., 1971—, Howe Furniture Corp., Norwalk, 1978—. Mem. Investment Assn. N.Y. Republican. Episcopalian. Clubs: Bond of N.Y., Links, Yale; City Midday (N.Y.C.). Home: 528 North St Greenwich CT 06830 Office: ACLI Internat Inc 717 Westchester Ave White Plains NY 10604

HUFFER, DAN L., banker; b. Lima, Ohio, July 7, 1937; s. Harold E. and Margaret L. (Van Meter) H.; m. Phyllis J. Reiff, Dec. 31, 1957; children: Mark Edwin, Michelle Elaine. B.S. in Acctg., Ohio State U., 1961. C.P.A., Ohio. Audit mgr. Price Waterhouse & Co., Columbus, Ohio and Cleve., 1961-72; gen. auditor Borden, Inc., Columbus, 1972-73; exec. v.p. BancOhio Nat. Bank, Columbus, 1973—; sr. v.p., treas. BancOhio Corp., Columbus, 1973—. Treas., bd. dirs. Columbus Zool. Soc., 1973-76; pres. Phi Kappa Tau Found., 1983; trustee, treas. Franklin U. Mem. Fin. Execs. Inst. (dir. 1979-82), Treas.' Club, Am. Inst. C.P.A.s, Columbus C. of C. Republican. Lutheran. Clubs: Brookside Country; Univ. Athletic (Columbus); Hoover Yacht. Home: 4045 W Henderson Rd Columbus OH 43220 Office: BancOhio Corp 155 E Broad St Columbus OH 43220

HUFFINE, COY LEE, chemical engineer; b. Knoxville, Tenn., Apr. 2, 1924; s. Coy Mann and Inez Belle (Story) H.; m. Virginia Elizabeth Browne, Mar. 31, 1951; children: Jeremy Bennett, Lucinda Jane. B.S., U. Tenn., 1945, M.S., 1947; Ph.D., Columbia U., 1953. Prin. engr. Gen. Electric Co., Oak Ridge and Cin., 1951-59; research chemist Gen. Electric Research Lab., Schenectady, 1959-60; project mgr. devel. and mfg., space systems div. Avco Corp., Lowell, Mass., 1960-67; with IBM, Rochester, Minn., 1968—, mgr. component tech., info. systems div., 1980—. Served with USN, 1945-46. Mem. Am. Inst. Chem. Engrs., AIME, Nat. Inst. Ceramic Engrs., Am. Ceramic Soc., N.Y. Acad. Scis., Sigma Xi. Home: 2247 5th Ave NE Rochester MN 55904 Office: IBM Corp 3605 Hwy 52 N Rochester MN 55901

HUFFINGTON, ROY MICHAEL, geologist; b. Tomball, Tex., Oct. 4, 1917; s. Roy Mackey and Bertha (Michel) H.; m. Phyllis Gough, Oct. 26, 1945; children—R. Michael, Terry Lynn. B.S., So. Meth. U., 1938; M.A., Harvard U., 1941, Ph.D., 1942. Sr. geologist, div. exploration geologist Humble Oil and Refining Co., 1946-56; pres. Roy M. Huffington, Inc., Houston, 1956—. Contbr. articles to profl. jours. Dir. Houston Ballet Found.; vice chmn. Interferon Found. Served to lt. comdr. USNR, 1942-45. Decorated Bronze Star. Fellow Geol. Soc. Am., AAAS; mem. Assn. Petroleum Geologists, Ind. Petroleum Assn. Am., Am. Petroleum Inst., Tex. Ind. Producers and Royalty Owners Assn., Tex. Mid-Continent Oil and Gas Assn., Houston Geol. Soc., Am. Inst. Profl. Geologists, Geochem. Soc., Marine Tech. Soc., Natural Gas Men Houston, S.A.R. Republican. Presbyterian. Clubs: Houston Petroleum, Houston Club, Houston Country, Ramada, New Orleans Petroleum, Metropolitan. Office: InterFirst Plaza PO Box 4455 Houston TX 77210

HUFFMAN, BERNARD LESLIE, JR., physician, medical systems consultant; b. Brundidge, Ala., Feb. 24, 1929; s. Bernard Leslie and Polly Ann (Cortner) H.; m. Frances Lee Matthews, July 25, 1925 (div. 1973); children: B. Leslie, III, Debra Lynn, James Walter; m. 2d Carol Lynn Fonk, July 2, 1974. B.A., Vanderbilt U., 1951, M.D., 1954. Diplomate: Am. Bd. Family Practice (pres. 1982-83). Intern Tripler Army Hosp., Honolulu, 1954, Toledo Hosp., 1955-56; pvt. practice family medicine, Toledo, 1956-73, prv. practice family medicine, Maumee, Ohio, 1973—; mem. staff. Toledo Hosp.; mem. staff Med. Coll. Ohio, Toledo, St. Luke's Hosp., Maumee; chmn. dept. family practice Med. Coll. Ohio, Toledo, part-time, 1974-76; trustee Family Health found. Am., Kansas City, Mo., 1976-83. Editor: Ohio Acad. Family Physicians News, 1957-67; mem. patient edn. adv. bd.: Patient Care Mag., 1976—. Cubmaster Boy Scouts Am., Toledo, 1962-65, chmn. com., Grand Rapids, Ohio, 1965-68. Fellow Am. Acad. Family Physicians (pres. 1976-77); mem. Ohio Acad. Family Physicians (pres. 1967-68), AMA, Ohio State Med. Assn. Republican. Presbyterian. Clubs: Toledo; Kiawah Island (Charleston, S.C.). Lodges: Masons (32 deg.); Shriners. Home: Deepwater Farm Grand Rapids OH 43522

HUFFMAN, DELTON CLEON, JR., educator, assn. exec.; b. St. Louis, Feb. 18, 1943; s. Delton Cleon and Kathryn (Saegesser) H.; m. Judy Hill, Aug. 11, 1962; children—Kimberly Lea, Jeffrey Keith. B.S. in Pharmacy (Archer Drug Co. scholar), U. Ark., 1966; Ph.D., U. Miss., 1971. Pharmacist Crank Drug Co., Inc., Little Rock, 1966-67; asst. prof., dir. div. pharmacy adminstrn. U. Tenn. Coll. Pharmacy, Memphis, 1970-73, asso. prof., chmn. dept. pharmaceutics, 1973; exec. v.p. Am. Coll. Apothecaries, 1971—, also prof., chmn. dept. pharmacy, 1974—. Contbr. articles to profl. lit. Recipient Lederle Faculty award, 1971; NDEA fellow, 1967-70; Am. Found. for Pharm. Edn. fellow, 1967-70. Fellow Am. Coll. Apothecaries; mem. Am. Assn. Colls. Pharmacy, Am. Pharm Assn., Tenn. Pharm Assn., Okla. Pharm. Assn. (hon. mem.), Ark. Pharm. Assn. (hon. life mem.), Memphis Pharm. Soc., Shelby County Pharm. Soc., Am. Soc. Assn. Execs., AAAS, Kappa Psi, Rho Chi. Home: 5100 Blackwell Rd Memphis TN 38134 Office: 874 Union Ave Memphis TN 38163

HUFFMAN, GEORGE GARRETT, educator; b. Winterset, Iowa, Feb. 13, 1916; s. Walker Garrett and Leota Marie (Greenfield) H.; m. Jane Irene Avery, July 9, 1941; children—Randall Avery, Laurence Marshall, Janice Carol. B.A. with high distinction, U. Iowa, 1940, M.S., 1941; Ph.D. (Lydia Roberts fellow), Columbia U., 1945. Geologist Texaco, Inc., Corpus Christi, Tex., 1943-46; faculty U. Okla., Norman, 1946—, prof. geology, 1955—, adviser, seminar dir., 1966—; Geologist Okla. Geol. Survey, summers 1949—; vis. scholar Okla. Coll. Liberal Arts, 1967-68; cons. geologist Cities Service Co., 1957-63, Jet Oil, 1970. Author: Laboratory Syllabus in Physical Geology, 1955, 60,

Laboratory Syllabus in Historical Geology, 1955; 6 Okla. Geol. Survey bulls. and guidebooks Kan. Geol. Soc. Field Conf. guidebooks, 1960, 64. Recipient Outstanding Teaching award U. Okla., 1955; Lowden prize in geology. Fellow Geol. Soc. Am.; mem. Am. Assn. Petroleum Geologists, Phi Beta Kappa (pres. Okla. U. 1972-73), Sigma Xi (pres. Okla. U. 1958-59). Presbyn. (deacon 1954-57, trustee 1957-60, elder 1960-63). Clubs: Lion (pres. Norman 1968-69, zone chmn. 1969-70. Research in paleozoic stratigraphy and tectonics of Okla. Ozarks, subsurface geology of mid-continent region, cretaceous stratigraphy of So. Okla. Home: 1509 Sunset Dr Norman OK 73069

HUFFMAN, JAMES THOMAS WILLIAM, oil exploration company executive; b. Norman, Okla., Mar. 27, 1947; s. Thomas William and Dorlese M. (Hicks) H.; m. Donna L. Haile, Aug. 27, 1969; 1 dau., Laura Anne. B.B.A., Baylor U., 1970. C.P.A. Mgr. Arthur Andersen & Co., Houston, 1970-76; sr. mgr. Price, Waterhouse & Co., Denver, 1976-79; v.p. Credo Petroleum Corp., 1978-80, pres., 1980-81, chmn., chief exec. officer, 1981—, also dir.; dir. Huffman Heat Exchangers Inc. Mem. Am. Inst. C.P.A.s, Tex., Colo. socs. C.P.A.s, Petroleum Landman, Ind. Petroleum Assn. Am., Ind. Petroleum Assn. Mountain State, Petroleum Accts. Soc. Republican. Baptist. Home: 2100 Green Oaks Dr Littletown CO 80121 Office: 1860 Lincoln St Suite 1000 Denver CO 80295

HUFFMAN, WILLIAM CHARLES, univ. ofcl.; b. Columbus, Ohio, June 2, 1910; s. Charles Houston and Laura Elizabeth (Craig) H.; m. Virginia Lee Ryle, Aug. 9, 1941; children—Deborah Elizabeth, Cynthia Ann, Diana Lee. B.S., Ohio State U., 1931, M.A., 1941; postgrad., Miami U., 1938, U. Cin., 1939, Harvard Bus. Sch., 1944; Ph.D., Northwestern U., 1949. Tchr., coach high sch., Waynesville, Ohio, 1932-33, Danville, Ky., 1933-36, Holmes High Sch., Covington, Ky., 1936-42; faculty econs., mgmt. U. Louisville, 1947—, prof., 1965—, acting head econs. dept., summers 1950-51, dir. div. adult edn., 1952-57, dean summer session, 1955—, acting dean, 1955, dean, 1957-73; v.p. U. Louisville Found., 1973—. Mem. adv. com. Ky. Authority Ednl. Television, Ky. Title I Adv. Commn.; Mem. Louisville-Jefferson County Planning Commn., 1966-72. Served from pvt. to 1st lt. USAAF, 1942-46. Mem. Assn. Univ. Evening Colls. (pres. 1967-68), Soc. Univ. Patent Adminstrs., Nat. Assn. Colls. and U. Summer Sessions, Purchasing Mgmt. Assn. (former econ. adviser), Adult Edn. Assn. U.S. (state dir. membership, state coordinator pub. relations 1954-57), Sales Exec. Council Louisville, Advt. Club Louisville (past dir.), Louisville C. of C., Phi Kappa Tau, Phi Kappa Phi. Episcopalian (vestryman). Club: Rotarian. Home: 5314 Hempstead Rd Louisville KY 40207

HUFFSTETLER, PALMER EUGENE, transportation company executive, lawyer; b. Shelby, N.C., Dec. 21, 1937; s. Daniel S. and Ethel (Turner) H.; m. Mary Ann Beam, Aug. 9, 1958; children: Palmer Eugene, Ben Beam, Brian Tad. B.A., Wake Forest U., 1959, J.D., 1961. Bar: N.C. 1961. Practiced in Kings Mountain, N.C., 1961-62, Raleigh, N.C., 1962-64; with State Farm Ins. Co., Orlando, Fla., 1962; gen. legal counsel Carolina Freight Carriers Corp., Cherryville, N.C., 1964—, sec., 1969—, sr. v.p., 1981—, also dir. Chmn. Cherryville Zoning Bd. Adjustment, 1967-70; mem. N.C. Gasoline and Oil Insp. Bd., 1974-76; Class chmn. Wake Forest Coll. Fund, 1972-79, decade chmn., 1981-82; mem. governing body, chmn. adminstrv. com. So. Piedmont Health Systems Agy., 1975-77; mem. Cherryville Econ. Devel. Commn., 1982—. Mem. N.C. State Bar, ABA., N.C. Bar Assn. (corp. counsel com.), Am. Soc. Corp. Secs. Methodist (mem. adminstrv. bd. 1965-69, 71-72, chmn. adminstrv. bd. 1969-70, 79, trustee 1970—). Club: Rotarian (past pres.). Home: Roy Eaker Rd Cherryville NC 28021 Office: Carolina Freight Carriers Corp Cherryville NC 28021

HUFFT, J. ALLEN, computing company executive; b. Springfield, Mo., June 14, 1932; s. Martin J. and Bertin J. (Brashear) H.; m. M. Sue Hufft, Sept. 27, 1958; children: Cynthia Sue, Craig Allen. B.S. in Bus. Mgmt., Tulsa U., 1954. Office mgr. Coynco Products, Tulsa, 1956-60; acctg. mgr. Allstate Ins. Co., Dallas, 1960-68; pres. Wyly, Univ. Computing Corp., Dallas, 1968—; dir. Wyly Corp., Dallas, 1982—. Elder Redgeview Presbyn. Ch., Dallas, 1975-78, 80-83. Served with U.S. Army, 1954-75. Mem. Assn. Data Processing Service Orgns. (pres. software products bd. 1982-83). Republican. Office: Univ Computing Co UCC Tower-Exchange Park Dallas TX 75235

HUFSCHMIDT, MAYNARD MICHAEL, city planning educator; b. Catawba, Wis., Sept. 28, 1912; s. John Jacob and Emma Lena (Von Arx) H.; m. Elizabeth Louise Leake, July 5, 1941; children: Emily Ann, Mark Andrew. B.S., U. Ill., 1939; M.Public Adminstrn., Harvard U., 1955, D.Public Adminstrn., 1964. Planner Ill. State Planning Commn., Chgo., 1939-41; engr. U.S. Nat. Resources Planning Bd., Washington, 1941-43; budget examiner U.S. Bur. Budget, Washington, 1943-49; program staff mem. Office of Sec., Dept. Interior, Washington, 1949-55; research asso. Grad. Sch. Public Adminstrn., Harvard U., 1955-65; prof. depts. city and regional planning, environ. scis. and engring. U. N.C., Chapel Hill, 1965—; fellow Environ. and Policy Inst., East-West Center, Honolulu, 1979—; cons. U.S. Bur. Budget, 1961, Council Econ. Advisers, 1965-67, Nat. Acad. Scis., 1967, 69-70, Pan-Am. Health Orgn., 1967, 70, WHO, 1970, 71, 76, 77, Resources for Future, 1955, 56, 72-74. Author: (with Arthur Maass and others) Design of Water-Resource Systems, 1962, (with Myron B Fiering) Simulation Techniques for Design of Water-Resource Systems, 1966; Editor: Regional Planning—Challenge and Prospects, 1969; editor: (with Eric L. Hyman) Economic Approaches to Natural Resource and Environmental Quality Analysis, 1982, (with David E. James and others) Environment, Natural Systems and Development: An Economic Valuation Guide, 1983. Recipient Clemens Herschel award Boston Soc. Civil Engrs., 1959; NSF sr. postdoctoral research fellow, 1971. Club: Cosmos. Office: Environment and Policy Inst East-West Center 1777 East-West Rd Honolulu HI 96848

HUFSTEDLER, SETH MARTIN, lawyer; b. Dewar, Okla., Sept. 20, 1922; s. Seth Martin and Myrtle (Younts) H.; m. Shirley Ann Mount, Aug. 16, 1949; 1 son, Steven. B.A. magna cum laude, U. So. Calif., 1944; LL.B., Stanford U., 1949. Bar: Calif. 1950. Since practiced in, Los Angeles; asso. firm Lillick, Geary & McHose, 1950-51; with Charles E. Beardsley, 1951-53; partner Beardsley, Hufstedler & Kemble, 1953—. Sec. United Way Regional Planning Council, 1971-75; Co-chmn. Pub. Commn. County Govt., Los Angeles, 1975-76; trustee AEFC Pension Fund, 1978—; mem. Calif. Citizens Commn. on Tort Reform, 1976-77, Calif. Jud. Council, 1977-78; Bd. visitors Stanford Law School, chmn., 1972-73. Served to lt. (j.g.) USNR, 1943-46. Mem. Am. Bar Assn. (chmn. action commn. to reduce ct. costs and delay 1979-81), Los Angeles County Bar Assn. (trustee 1963-65, 66-70, pres. 1969-70, Shattuck Price award 1976), State Bar of Calif. (bd. govs. 1971-74, pres. 1973-74), Am. Bus. Trial Lawyers Assn. (bd. govs. 1973-76), Am. Judicature Soc., Am. Law Inst., Am. Coll. Trial Lawyers, Am. Bar Found. (bd. govs. 1975—, pres. 1982—), Chancery Club (pres. 1974-75), Order of the Coif, Phi Beta Kappa, Phi Kappa Phi, Delta Tau Delta. Democrat. Home: 720 Iverness Dr Flintridge CA 91011 Office: 611 W 6th St Los Angeles CA 90017

HUFSTEDLER, SHIRLEY MOUNT (MRS. SETH M. HUFSTEDLER), lawyer, former U.S. judge; b. Denver, Aug. 24, 1925; d. Earl Stanley and Eva (Von Behren) Mount; m. Seth Martin Hufstedler, Aug. 16, 1949; 1 son, Steven Mark. B.B.A., U. N.Mex., 1945, LL.D. (hon.), 1972; LL.B., Stanford U., 1949; LL.D. (hon.), U. Wyo., 1970, Gonzaga U., 1970, Occidental Coll., 1971, Tufts U., 1974, U. So. Calif., 1976, Georgetown U., 1976, U. Pa., 1976, Columbia U., 1977, U. Mich., 1979, Yale U., 1981, Rutgers U., 1981, Claremont U. Center, 1981, Smith Coll., 1982, Syracuse U., 1983, P.H.H., Hood Coll., 1981. Bar: Calif. 1950. Mem. firm Beardsley, Hufstedler & Kemble, Los Angeles, 1951-61; practiced in, Los Angeles, 1961; judge Superior Ct., County Los Angeles, 1961-66; justice Ct. Appeals 2d Dist., 1966-68; circuit judge U.S. Ct. Appeals 9th Circuit, 1968-79; sec. U.S. Dept. Edn., 1979-81; partner firm Hufstedler, Miller, Carlson & Beardsley, Los Angeles, 1981—; dir. Hewlett Packard Co., US West, Inc. Mem. staff: Stanford Law Rev, 1947-49; articles and book rev. editor, 1948-49. Trustee Calif. Inst. Tech., Occidental Coll., 1972—, Aspen Inst. for Humanistic Studies, Colonial Williamsburg Found., 1976—, Constl. Rights Found., 1978-80, Nat. Resources Def. Council, 1983—; bd. councilors U. So. Calif. Law Center. Named Woman of Year Ladies Home Jour., 1976; recipient UCLA medal, 1981. Mem. Am., Los Angeles bar assns., Town Hall, Am. Law Inst. (council 1974—), Am. Bar Found., Women Lawyers Assn. (pres. 1957-58), Am. Judicature Soc., Am. Law Inst., Council on Fgn. Relations, Order of Coif. Office: Hufstedler Miller Carlson and Beardsley 700 S Flower St 17th Floor Los Angeles CA 90017

HUG, ARTHUR, JR., banker; b. Far Rockaway, N.Y., Dec. 17, 1922; s. Arthur and Jennie (Blick) H.; m. Julia Fowler. B.B.A., Hofstra U., 1953. Vice pres. Security Nat. Bank, Huntington, N.Y., 1956-59; exec. v.p. Nat. Bank N.Am., West Hempstead, N.Y., 1959-68; pres. L.I. Trust Co., Garden City, N.Y., 1968-74, chmn. bd., pres., chief exec. officer, 1974-79, chmn. bd., chief exec. officer, 1979-83, chmn. bd., 1983—; chmn. bd., pres., chief exec. officer LITCO Bancorp. of N.Y., Inc., Garden City, 1974—. Mem. Banking and Monetary Policy Commn., U.S. Chamber of Commerce, 1965-69, N.Y. State Assembly Adv. Subcom. on Econ. Devel., 1970-72; Chmn. council SUNY, Old Westbury, 1971-74; mem. Nassau County (N.Y.) Reapportionment Commn., 1975; bd. dirs. Action Com. for L.I. Inc., 1978—. Served with USNR, 1942-46. Mem. N.Y. State Bankers Assn. (1st v.p. 1980—, mem. Advertising Com. 1979—, chmn. communications com., chmn. fed. affairs com.), Am. Bankers Assn. (governing council 1979—, N.Y. State coordinator savs. bond com. 1979—), Ind. Bankers Assn. N.Y. (exec. comm. 1978, Co-chmn. legislative comm., dir. 1974-75), L.I. Bankers Assn. (director 1968—, treas. 1968, v.p. 1969, pres. 1970). Office: 1401 Franklin Ave Garden City NY 11530

HUG, PROCTER RALPH, JR., judge; b. Reno, Mar. 11, 1931; s. Procter Ralph and Margaret (Beverly) H.; m. Barbara Van Meter, Apr. 4, 1954; children—Cheryl Ann, Procter James, Elyse Marie. B.S., U. Nev., 1953; LL.B., J.D., Stanford, 1958. Bar: Nev. bar 1958. With firm Woodburn, Wedge, Blakey, Folsom & Hug, Reno, 1963-77; U.S. judge 9th Circuit Ct. Appeals, Reno, 1977—; Chmn. Nev. State Bar Com. on Jury Inst.; dep. atty. gen., State of Nev.; v.p., dir. Nev. Tel. & Tel. Co., 1958-77. Vice pres. Young Democrats Nev., 1960-61; Chmn. bd. regents U. Nev.; bd. visitors Stanford Law Sch. Served to lt. USNR, 1953-55. Recipient Outstanding Alumnus award U. Nev., 1967. Mem. Am. Bar Assn. (gov. 1976—), Nat. Assn. Coll. and Univ. Attys. (past mem. exec. bd.), U. Nev. Alumni Assn. (past pres.), Stanford Law Soc. Nev. (pres.). Office: 601 Liberty Center 350 S Center St Reno NV 89501 *

HUG, RICHARD ERNEST, environmental company executive; b. Paterson, N.J., Jan. 11, 1935; s. Gustave T. and Nelly (Rutishauser) H.; m. Lois-Ann Schack, Sept. 1, 1956; children: Donald R., Cynthia A. B.S., Duke U., 1956, M.F., 1957. Engr. forest products div. Koppers Co., Inc., Pitts., 1957-62, tech. rep., 1962-66, tech. sales rep., 1966-68, area sales mgr., 1968-70, mgr. product devel., 1970-72, gen. mgr. laminated products, 1972-73, v.p., gen. mgr. environ. systems div., 1973-74, corp. v.p., 1973-83; pres., chief exec. officer, owner Environ. Elements Corp., Balt., 1983—; dir. Blue Cross Md., 1974—, mem. exec. and fin. coms., 1978—. Mem. exec. bd., v.p. Balt. Area council Boy Scouts Am., 1976—; bd. dirs. Nat. Aquarium, 1976—, United Way of Central Md., 1978—, Greater Balt. Com., 1978, Ind. Coll. Fund Md., 1978—; trustee Loyola Coll., Balt., 1979—; trustee, v.p. John F. Kennedy Inst., 1979—; commr. Health Resources Planning Commn. Md., 1982—; mem. Duke U. Pres's Assocs., 1981—. Mem. Young Pres. Orgn. (chmn. chpt. devel. 1977-78, chmn. edn. 1978, chpt. chmn. 1979-80), Forest Products Research Soc., Water and Wastewater Equipment Mfrs. Assn. (dir.), Indsl. Gas Cleaning Inst. (forward planning com. 1976—, govt. relations com. 1977—, dir. 1980-82), Engring. Soc. Balt., Md. C. of C. (dir., v.p. 1981—). Republican. Presbyterian. Club: Center (Balt.). Home: 247 Oak Ct Severna Park MD 21146 Office: Environ Elements Corp 3700 Koppers St Baltimore MD 21203

HUGE, HARRY, lawyer; b. Deshler, Nebr., Sept. 16, 1937; s. Arthur and Dorothy (Vor de Strasse) H.; m. Reba Kinne, July 2, 1960; 1 son, Theodore. A.B., Nebr. Wesleyan U., 1959; J.D., Georgetown U., 1963. Bar: Ill. 1963, D.C. 1965. Assoc. Chapman & Cutler, Chgo., 1963-65, Arnold & Porter, Washington, 1965-71, ptnr., 1971-76; sr. ptnr. Ragovin, Huge & Lenzner, Washington, 1976—; dir. DBA Systems, Inc., Melbourne, Fla., 1967-78, 81—, Huge Sales, Inc., Gatlinburg, Tenn., 1978—, Wayne-Gossard Corp., Chattanooga, 1983—, Unique Electronics, Inc., Orlando, Fla., 1982—; chmn., trustee United Mine Workers Health and Retirement Funds, 1973-78. Contbr. articles to legal jours. Pres. Voter Edn. Project, Atlanta, 1974-78; mem. Pres.'s Gen. Adv. Com. Arms. Control, 1977-81; bd. trustees Nebr. Wesleyan U., 1978—; mem. task force local govt. Greater Washington Research Ctr., 1981—. Served with U.S. Army, 1960; with USNG, 1960-65. Mem. ABA (co-chmn. legis. com. litigation sect.), D.C. Bar Assn. (bd. profl. responsibility 1976-81). Home: 628 Boyle Ln McLean VA 22102 Office: Ragovin Huge & Lenzner 1730 Rhode Island Ave NW Washington DC 20036

HUGEL, CHARLES EMIL, engineering company executive; b. Plainfield, N.J., Aug. 9, 1928; s. Charles Emil and Alice (Durr) H.; m. Cornelia Fischer, Apr. 11, 1953; children: Jeffrey, Christian. A.B., Lafayette Coll., 1951. With N.J. Bell Telephone Co., 1952-66, 70-73, gen. mgr. So. area, 1964-66, v.p. ops., 1970-73; gen. mgr. N.E. region Western Electric Co., Newark, 1966-70; v.p. ops. New Eng. Telephone Co., Boston, 1974-75; pres. Ohio Bell Telephone Co., Cleve., 1975-78; exec. v.p. AT&T, Basking Ridge, N.J., 1978-82; pres., chief operating officer, dir. Combustion Engring., Inc., Stamford, Conn., 1982-84, pres., chief exec. officer, dir., 1984—; dir. Eaton Corp., Midland-Ross Corp., Nabisco Brands, Inc.; United Jersey Banks. Trustee Lafayette Coll., Nat. Urban League; bd. dirs. Council for Fin. Aid to Edn. Served with U.S. Army, 1951-52. Clubs: Links (N.Y.C.); Bald Peak Colony, Baltusrol Golf; Blind Brook (N.Y.). Office: Combustion Engring Inc 900 Long Ridge Rd PO Box 9308 Stamford CT 06904 *

HUGGHINS, ERNEST JAY, educator; b. Bryan, Tex., Dec. 25, 1920; s. Ernest Clarence and Dua (Harris) H.; m. Mildred K. Shields, Aug. 12, 1952; children—Susan Jane, Arley Jay, Mildred Kay. B.A., Baylor U., 1943; M.S., Tex. A. and M. U., 1949; postgrad., U. Mich. Biol. Sta., Marine Biol. Lab., Woods Hole, Mass.; Ph.D. (NIH Research fellow), U. Ill., 1952. Faculty S.D. State U., Brookings, 1952—, prof. zoology, 1961—, head biology dept., 1981—; zoologist Agrl. Exptl. Sta., 1954—; vis. prof. U. Okla. Biol. Sta., 1960; Fulbright prof. Universidad Villareal, Lima, Peru, 1967; prof. Black Hills Natural Scis. Field Sta., summers 1972, 73; cons. 1st Internat. Congress Parasitology, Office Naval Research, Rome, Italy, 1964; participant NATO Advanced Study Inst. on Animal Learning, nr. Ulm, W.Ger., 1976; sabbatical to, Kenya, 1981. Pres., bd. dirs. Brookings Community-Univ. Concert Series, 1970-71; bd. dirs. Brookings United Charities, 1969-70. La. State U. Interam. fellow to, Caribbean and S.Am., 1963; NSF research grantee study fish parasites, S.Am., 1967-69. Fellow A.A.A.S. (council rep. 1967-74, life mem.); mem. Am. Soc. Parasitologists (council rep. from Midwestern Conf. Parasitologists 1964-67), Helminthological Soc. Washington, Am. Micros. Soc., Am. Soc. Zoologists, Am. Inst. Biol. Scis., Wildlife Soc., Wildlife Disease Assn., Am. Soc. Mammalogists, S.D. Acad. Sci. (pres. 1960-61), Sigma Xi, Phi Kappa Phi, Gamma Sigma Delta. United Methodist (adminstrv. bd. 1974—). Club: Kiwanian (bd. dirs. 1974-76). Research and publs. on parasites of fishes in S.Am. and U.S., including zoogeog. relationships, parasites of wildlife, pesticide residues in wildlife. Home: 1034 6th Ave Brookings SD 57006

HUGGINS, CHARLES, surgical educator; b. Halifax, N.S., Can., Sept. 22, 1901; s. Charles Edward and Bessie (Spencer) H.; m. Margaret Wellman, July 29, 1927; children: Charles Edward, Emily Wellman Fine. B.A., Acadia U., 1920, D.Sc., 1946; M.D., Harvard U., 1924; M.Sc., Yale, 1947; D.Sc., Washington U., St. Louis, 1950, Leeds U., 1953, Turin U., 1957, Trinity Coll., 1965, U. Wales, 1967, U. Mich., 1968, Med. Coll. Ohio, 1973, Gustavus Adolphus Coll., 1975, Wilmington (Ohio) Coll., U. Louisville; LL.D., U. Aberdeen, 1966, York U., Toronto, U. Calif. at Berkeley, 1968; D.P.S., George Washington U., 1967, Bologna U., 1964. Intern in surgery U. Mich., 1924-26, instr. surgery, 1926-27; with U. Chgo., 1927—, instr. surgery, 1927-29, asst. prof., 1929-33, asso. prof., 1933-36, prof. surgery, 1936—, dir. Ben May Lab. for Cancer Research, 1951-69, William B. Ogden Distinguished Service prof., 1962—; chancellor Acadia U., Wolfville, N.S., 1972-79; Macewen lectr. U. Glasgow, 1958, Ravdin lectr., 1974, Powell lectr., Lucy Wortham James lectr., 1975, Robert V. Day lectr., 1975, Cartwright lectr., 1975. Trustee Worcester Found. Exptl. Biology; bd. govs. Weizmann Inst. Sci., Rehovot, Israel, 1973—. Decorated Order Pour le Mérite, Germany; Order of The Sun, Peru).; Recipient Am. Urol. Assn. award for research on male genital tract, 1948; Francis Amory award for cancer research, 1948; AMA gold medals for research, 1936, 40, Société Internationale d'Urologie, 1948; Am. Cancer Soc. award, 1953; Bertner award M.D. Anderson Hosp., 1953; award Am. Pharm. Mfrs. Assn., 1953; gold medal Am. Assn. Genito Urinary Surgeons, 1955; Borden award Assn. Am. Med. Colls., 1955; FRCS (hon.), Edinburg, 1958, London, 1959; Comfort Crookshank award Middlesex Hosp., London, 1957; Charles Mickle fellow Toronto U., 1958; Cameron prize Edinburg U., 1958; Valentine prize N.Y. Acad. Medicine, 1962; Hunter award Am. Therapeutic Soc., 1962; Lasker award for med. research, 1963; gold medal for research Rudolf Virchow Soc., 1964; Laurea and award Am. Urol. Assn., 1966; gold medal in therapeutics Worshipful Soc. Apothecaries of London, 1966; Gairdner award, Toronto, 1966; Nobel prize for medicine, 1966; Chgo. Med. Soc. award, 1967; Centennial medal Acadia U., 1967; Hamilton award Ill. Med. Soc., 1967; Bigelow medal Boston Surg. Soc., 1967; Distinguished Service award Am. Soc. Abdominal Surgeons, 1972; Sheen award A.M.A., 1970. Fellow A.C.S. (hon.), Royal Coll. Surgeons Can. (hon.), Royal Soc. Edinburgh (hon.); mem. Am. Philos. Soc., Nat. Acad. Scis. (Charles L. Meyer award for cancer research 1943), Am. Assn. Cancer Research, Canadian Med. Assn. (hon.), Alpha Omega Alpha. Home: 5807 Dorchester Ave Chicago IL 60637 Office: 950 E 59th St Chicago IL 60637

HUGGINS, CHARLES EDWARD, surgeon, cryobiologist; b. Chgo., May 7, 1929; s. Charles Brenton and Margaret (Wellman) H.; m. Nancy Tienhaara, June 1, 1952; children: Elizabeth Ann, Margaret Ruth, Nancy Wellman, Charles Edward, Gordon Spencer. Ph.B., U. Chgo., 1947; M.D. cum laude, Harvard U., 1952. Diplomate: Am. Bd. Surgery, Am. Bd. Pathology (in immunohematology and blood banking). Surg. intern Mass. Gen. Hosp., 1952-53, surg. resident, 1953-60, asst. surgery, 1960-64, asst. surgeon, also asst. dir. blood bank and transfusion service, 1964-67, clin. dir. blood bank and transfusion service, 1968-73, chief surg. low temperture unit, 1969—, asso. vis. surgeon, 1968—, dir. blood transfusion service, 1973—; instr., then clin. asso. surgery Harvard Med. Sch., 1960-63, 64-68, asst. prof. surgery, 1968-69, asso. prof. surgery, 1969—. Bd. dirs. N.E. region ACS, 1980—. Served as lt. M.C., USNR, 1954-56. Moseley Traveling fellow, 1958-59; clin. fellow Am. Cancer Soc., 1959-60. Fellow ACS; mem. Soc. Cryobiology (gov. 1965-66, 77-78, pres. 1968), Internat. Soc. Blood Transfusion, Soc. Univ. Surgeons, AMA, Soc. Internat. de Chirurgie, Mass. Med. Soc., Am. Assn. Blood Banks (dir. 1976-78), Alpha Omega Alpha. Home: 4 Longfellow Pl Boston MA 02114 Office: Mass Gen Hosp Boston MA 02114

HUGGINS, HOMER DON, manufacturing company executive; b. Chgo., Nov. 22, 1918; s. Homer C. and Elizabeth (Jamison) H.; m. Eugenis McFadden, Aug. 20, 1943; children: Andrew, Brian, Laurel. B.S. in Engring., U. Ill., 1941. Registered profl. engr., Wis. Engr. Elec. Utilities Co., Chgo., 1941-42, Modine Mfg. Co., Racine, Wis., 1946-51, chief engr., 1951-63, v.p., dir. engrs., 1963-79, sr. v.p. tech. services, 1979—. Patentee heat exchangers. Mem. Racine Bd. Edn., 1958-71, pres., 1964-65. Served to sr. lt. USCG, 1942-46. Mem. Soc. Automotive Engrs. Republican. Christian Scientist. Home: 4526 Pleasant Ln Racine WI 53405 Office: Modine Mfg Co 1500 De Koven Ave Racine WI 53401

HUGGINS, NATHAN IRVIN, historian, educator; b. Chgo., Jan. 14, 1927; s. Winston J. and Marie (Warsaw) H.; m. Brenda C. Smith, July 18, 1971. A.B., U. Calif. at Berkeley, 1954, M.A., 1955; A.M., Harvard, 1959, Ph.D., 1962. Asst. prof. Calif. State Coll. at Long Beach, 1962-64, Lake Forest (Ill.) Coll., 1964-66; asst. prof., then asso. prof. U. Mass.-Boston, 1966-70; vis. prof. U. Calif., Berkeley, 1969-70; prof. history Columbia, 1970-80; W.E.B. DuBois prof. history and Afro-Am. studies, dir. W.E.B. DuBois Inst. Harvard U., 1980—; fellow Center Advanced Studies in Behavioral Scis., 1979-80; juror Nat. Endowment Humanities, Nat. Humanities Center.; mem. USIA panel on internat. ednl. exchange, 1982—. Author: Protestants Against Poverty, 1971, Harlem Renaissance, 1971, Black Odyssey, 1977, Slave and Citizen, The Life of Frederick Douglass, 1980; Co-editor: Key Issues of the Afro-American Experience, 1971; editor: Voices from Harlem Renaissance, 1976; editorial bd.: Jour. Ethnic History, Am. Hist. Rev., 1978-82. Pres. Museum Afro-Am. History, Boston, 1967-69; Bd. advisers Children's TV Workshop, 1970—; v.p. Howard Thurman Ednl. Trust, 1968—; mem. Smithsonian Council, 1973-82; bd. dirs. N.Y. Council for Humanities, Mass. Council for Humanities, Literary Classics of the U.S. Served with AUS, 1945-46. Guggenheim fellow, 1971-72; Ford Found. travel-study fellow, 1971-72; Fulbright-Hayes sr. lectr., 1974-75; Rockefeller Found. humanities fellow, 1983-84. Mem. Authors Guild, P.E.N., Am. Hist. Assn., Orgn. Am. Historians (exec. council), Assn. Study Negro Life, Am. Council Learned Socs., Am. Antiquarian Soc. Home: 7 Bryant St Cambridge MA 02138 *I find in the study of history the special discipline which forces me to consider peoples and ages, not my own, in their own terms; yet with an informed and critical eye, enhanced by modern analytical tools and the gift of hindsight. It is the most humane of disciplines, and in ways the most humbling. For one cannot ignore those historians of the future who will look back on us in the same way.*

HUGGINS, ROBERT A(LAN), materials science educator; b. Stanford, Calif., Mar. 26, 1929; s. Maurice Loyal and Dorothy Bates (Gettell) H.; m. Eleanor J. Mitchell, July 7, 1951; children: Alan, John, Mark. B.A., Amherst Coll., 1950; M.S., M.I.T., 1952, Sc.D., 1954. Instr. M.I.T., 1953-54; asst. prof. materials sci. Stanford U., 1954-58, asso. prof., 1958-62, prof., 1962—, dir., 1961-77; dir. div. materials scis. Advanced Research Projects Agy., 1968-70; chmn. solid state scis. com. Nat. Acad. Scis.-NRC; cons. in field. Contbr. numerous articles to profl. jours.; editor: Solid State Ionics, Ann. Rev. Materials Sci.; asso. editor: Materials Research Bull; mem. editorial bd.: Revue de Chimie Minerale, Progress in Solid State Chemistry, Semicondrs. and Insulators. NSF sr. postdoctoral fellow, Gottingen, Germany, 1965-66; Nat. champion Snipe Class Sailboats, 1963; winner Silver medal Pan-Am. Games, São Paulo, Brazil, 1963; recipient Alexander von Humboldt Sr. U.S. Scientist award Max Planck Institut fur Festkorperforschung, Stuttgart, Germany, 1978; Vincent Bendix award Am. Soc. Engring. Edn., 1978; Robert Lansing Hardy award AIME; research award Electrochem. Soc. Home: 824 San Francisco Ct Stanford CA 94305 Office: Dept Materials Sci and Engring Stanford U Stanford CA 94305

HUGGINS, ROLLIN CHARLES, JR., lawyer; b. Berwyn, Ill., Oct. 11, 1931; s. Rollin Charles and Helen (Smith) H.; m. Charlotte Harrison, Apr. 26, 1952; children: Cynthia C., Shirley A., John C. A.B., Knox Coll., 1953; LL.B., Harvard U., 1958. Bar: Ill. 1958. Since practiced in, Chgo.; partner Bell, Boyd & Lloyd; lectr. Inst. for Continuing Legal Edn., 1968-83. Served to 1st lt. AUS, 1954-56. Mem. Am., Ill., Chgo. bar assns., Legal Club Chgo., Law Club Chgo., Am. Coll. Probate Counsel, Fed. Tax Forum, Phi Beta Kappa, Beta Theta Pi. Clubs: Univ. (Chgo.); Mich. Shores. Home: 700 Greenwood Ave Wilmette IL 60091 Office: 3 First Nat Plaza Chicago IL 60602

HUGGINS, ROY, TV and film producer, writer; b. Litelle, Wash., July 18, 1914; m. Adele Mara. Ed., U. Calif., 1935-41. Spl. rep. U.S. Civil Service Commn., 1941-43; indsl. engr., 1943-46; v.p. 20th Century Fox TV, 1961, MCA Revue, 1963; pres. Public Arts, Inc. (prodn. co.), Universal City, Calif., 1968—. Creator, producer: TV series Run for Your Life, Maverick, The Fugitive; creator: series The Rockford Files, Colt 45, 77 Sunset Strip, City of Angels; exec. producer: TV series The Captains and the Kings, Alias Smith and Jones, Cod Million, Baretta, Toma, The Bold Ones, Run for Your Life; also dir.; exec. producer: TV movies Hazard's People, This is the West, The Story of Pretty Boy Floyd, The Invasion of Johnson County; producer: TV series Conflict, Cheyenne; wrote or collaborated on: screenplay for motion pictures including Hangman's Knot; Pushover, Fuller Brush Man, Good Humor Man, Sealed Cargo, Women in Hiding, Gun Fury, Hangman's Knot; producer: motion picture A Fever in the Blood; Author 3 novels; many stories for Sat. Eve. Post. Mem. Dirs. Guild Am. *

HUGGINS, SARA ESPE, educator; b. Denver, June 29, 1913; d. Paul Albert and Ethel (Benton) Espe; m. Russell Arno Huggins; children—James, George. A.B., Aurora Coll., 1934; M.S., U. Ill., 1936; Ph.D., Western Res. U., 1939. Instr. biology Paine Coll., 1946-47; faculty U. Houston, 1947—, prof. biology, 1953-78, prof. emeritus, 1978—, chmn. dept., 1952-64; vis. prof. biology dept. physiology Baylor Coll. Medicine, 1971—; vis. prof. U. Fed. de Peruamonco, 1979-80, 83; acting chmn. dept. biology Faculty Sci. Mahidol U., Bangkok, Thailand, 1972-73; Sr. postdoctoral fellow Baylor Coll. Medicine, 1967-69. Mem. Am. Physiol. Soc., Soc. for Exptl. Biology and Medicine, Sigma Xi, Phi Kappa Phi. Home: 4811 Palmetto St Bellaire TX 77401 Office: U Houston Houston TX 77004

HUGGINS, WILLIAM HERBERT, electrical engineering educator; b. Rupert, Idaho, Jan. 11, 1919; s. William John and Alafretta Evelyn (Roraback) H. B.S., Oreg. State Coll., 1941, M.S., 1942; Sc.D., Mass. Inst. Tech., 1953. Instr. elec. engring. Oreg. State Coll., 1942-44; spl. research asso. radio research lab. Harvard, 1944-46; supervising scientist Air Force Research Center, Cambridge, Mass., 1946-54; research asso. Mass. Inst. Tech., 1949-54; prof. elec. engring. Johns Hopkins, 1954—, chmn. dept., 1970-74; Cons. editor Addison-Wesley Pub. Co., 1957-60, Blaisdell Pub. Co., 1961-65; cons. Rand Corp., 1955-73. Recipient decoration for exceptional civilian service USAF, 1954; Browder J. Thomson Meml. prize Am. I.R.E., 1948; Lindback Found. award for distinguished teaching, 1961; Western Electric Fund award Am. Soc. Engring. Edn., 1965. Fellow IEEE (Edn. medal 1966), Acoustical Soc. Am., AAAS; mem. Nat. Acad. Engring., Phi Beta Kappa, Sigma Xi. Home: One E University Pkwy Unit 1005 Baltimore MD 21218

HUGHES, ALFRED CLIFTON, clergyman, educator; b. Boston, Dec. 2, 1932; s. Alfred Clifton and Ellen Cecelia (Hennessey) H. A.B., St. John's Sem. Coll., 1954; S.T.L., Gregorian U., Rome, 1958, S.T.D., 1961. Ordained priest, Roman Catholic Ch., 1957; ordained bishop, 1981. Asst. pastor St. Stephen's Parish, Farmington, Mass., 1958-59, Our Lady Help of Christians, Newton, Mass., 1961-62; lectr. St. John's Sem., Brighton, 1962-65, spiritual dir., 1965-81, rector, 1981—; aux. bishop Archdiocese of Boston, 1981—. Author: Preparation for Church Ministry, 1979; contbr. articles to profl. jours. Mellon and Davis Founds. grantee, 1976. Mem. Catholic Theol. Soc. Am. Office: St John's Sem 127 Lake St Brighton MA 02135

HUGHES, ALLEN, journalist; b. Brownsburg, Ind., Dec. 28, 1921; s. Maurice McKinley and Bess (Collyer) H.; m. Marian Nina Berklich, Mar. 28, 1964. Student, George Washington U., 1940-42; B.A., U. Mich., 1946, B.Mus., 1947; postgrad., N.Y. U., 1948-50. Lectr. music Toledo Mus. Art, 1946-47; asst. editor, critic Mus. Am., 1950-53; free-lance writer, Paris, France, 1953-55; music critic N.Y. Herald Tribune, 1955-60; mem. music faculty Bklyn. Coll., 1958-60; music critic N.Y. Times, 1960-61, asst. dance critic, 1961-62, dance critic, 1962-65, music critic, 1965—. Served to lt. (j.g.) USNR, 1943-46. Office: 229 W 43d St New York NY 10036

HUGHES, AUTHOR E., JR., university president; b. Hoopeston, Ill., Nov. 4, 1929; s. Author Ernest and Nora (Clevel) H.; m. Marjorie Ann Herman, Aug. 21, 1956; children: James Gregory, Timothy Charles, John Andrew, Susan Marie. B.S., Eastern Ill. U., 1951; M.A., No. Colo. U., 1954; Ph.D., U. Iowa, 1960. High sch. bus. tchr., 1951-54, coll. bus. tchr., 1954-66; dean No. Ariz. U. Coll. Bus., Flagstaff, 1966-69, v.p., provost, 1969-71; pres. U. San Diego, 1971—; Cons. in systems field. Co-author: Automated Data Processing, 1969. Bd. dirs. United Way; mem. Pres.'s Commn. on White House Fellowships. Recipient Disting. Alumnus award Eastern Ill. U., Regional Brotherhood award NCCJ. Mem. Nat. Assn. Ind. Colls. and Univs. (v.p.), Assn. Calif. Ind. Colls. and Univs. (pres.), San Diego C. of C. (dir.), Beta Gamma Sigma, Phi Kappa Phi, Phi Sigma Tau, Delta Pi Epsilon, Delta Sigma Pi. Club: Rotarian. Home: Casa de Alcala Univ San Diego San Diego CA 92110

HUGHES, BARNARD, actor; b. Bedford Hills, N.Y., July 16, 1915; s. Owen and Madge (Kiernan) H.; m. Helen Stenborg, Apr. 19, 1950; 2 children. Student, Manhattan Coll. (Emmy award.), Stage debut with, Shakespeare Fellowship Co. in, The Taming of the Shrew, N.Y.C., 1934; appeared in numerous plays including: Dolls House, Hogan's Goat, Uncle Vanya, A Delicate Balance, Advise and Consent, Much Ado About Nothing, The Good Doctor, All Over Town, The Will and the Way, Da (Antoinette Perry award as best actor 1978); appeared in: film appearances include Tron, Midnight Cowboy, Oh God!, Where's Poppa; TV film appearances include Guilty or Innocent: The Sam Sheppard Murder Case; star of: TV series Doc, 1975-76; other TV appearances include Kill Me If you Can; star: TV show Mr. Merlin, 1981—. Served with U.S. Army. Recipient St. Clair Bayfield award, 1973. Address: care Internat Creative Mgmt 40 W 57th St New York NY 10019

HUGHES, BLAKE, architectural institute administrator; b. N.Y.C., June 24, 1914; s. Ferdinand Holme and Ines (de Cordova) H.; m. Betty Jean Wolf, Aug. 26, 1951; children: Diane Elizabeth, Brian Blake. A.B. summa cum laude, Dartmouth Coll., 1936; degre de civilisation, Sorbonne U., Paris, France, 1935; postgrad., Columbia, 1936-37. Salesman Edward B. Smith & Co., Smith, Barney & Co. (investment bankers), N.Y.C., 1936-38; salesman N.Y. Life Ins. Co., N.Y.C., 1939-40; promotion mgr. Engring. News Record, Constrn. Methods McGraw-Hill Inc., N.Y.C., 1947-50; promotion mgr., dir. marketing Archtl. Record, F.W. Dodge Corp., N.Y.C., 1951-61; asso. pub. Archtl. Record, McGraw Hill Inc., 1961-68, pub., 1968-80; pres. Internat. Inst. for Architecture, Washington, 1981—; pub. Archtl. Record Books, 1970-80, House & Home, Mc-Graw-Hill, Inc., 1976-77; Dir. Nat. Home Improvement Council, 1976-77. Trustee Unity (Maine) Coll., 1965-75; pres. Internat. Archtl. Found., 1973-78, Internat. Inst. for Architecture, 1978—. Served to lt. USNR, 1940-45. Decorated Order of Fatherland War, Russia). Mem. Union Internat. Architectes (archtl. critics com. 1978-80), Appalachian Housing Inst. (dir.), Phi Beta Kappa, Delta Sigma Rho. Episcopalian (vestryman). Club: Dartmouth (N.Y.C.). Home: 51st Ave Isle of Palms SC 29451 Office: 1101 16th St NW Suite 500 Washington DC

HUGHES, CARL WILSON, physician; b. Eminence, Mo., June 29, 1914; s. Stephen Mitchel and Sarah (Ward) H.; m. Eleanor Naomi Hulseweh, June 13, 1943; children—Elaine Leslie, Debra Lenor. A.B., U. Mo., 1939; M.D., U. Tenn., 1944. Diplomate: Am. Bd. Surgery. Intern Bapt. Meml. Hosp., Memphis, 1944; resident John Gaston Hosp., Memphis, 1945-46; commd. 1st lt. M.C. U.S. Army, 1946, advanced through grades to maj. gen., 1970; asst. chief, later chief surg. service (57th Field Hosp.), Wurzburg, Germany, 1946-47, chief surg. service, Nurnberg, Germany, 1948-49; surg. resident Walter Reed Army Hosp., 1949-52; vascular surg. cons. 8th Army, mem. surg. research team U.S. Army, Korea, 1953; dir. div. surgery Walter Reed Army Inst. Research; chief peripheral vascular surgery Walter Reed Hosp., 1954-57; chief gen. surgery staff, later chief dept. surgery Tripler Gen. Hosp., Honolulu, 1957-61; chief dept. surgery Madigan Gen. Hosp., Tacoma, 1961-64, Letterman Gen. Hosp., San Francisco, 1964-65, Walter Reed Gen. Hosp., 1965-69, comdg. gen., 1969-71, Tripler Gen. Hosp.; chief surgeon U.S. Army, Pacific, 1971-74; dir. surg. service VA, Washington, 1974-79, dep. asst. chief med. dir. for profl. services, 1979-81, asst. chief med. dir. for profl. services, 1981—; cons. vascular surgery surgeon gen., 1965-71; clin. asso. prof. surgery U. Wash. Sch. Medicine, Seattle, 1962-64; asso. clin. prof. surgery George Washington U. Sch. Medicine, 1966-71. Author, co-author 2 books, numerous articles. Decorated D.S.M., Bronze Star; Legion of Merit with oak leaf cluster; comdr. Most Noble Order Crown Thailand; recipient Sir Henry Wellcome award, 1958; Arthur M. Shipley award, 1968; citation of merit U. Mo. Alumni Assn. and Sch. Medicine, 1970; Faculty-Alumni award U. Mo., 1973. Mem. A.C.S., Soc. Vascular Surgery, Am. Assn. Surgery Trauma, So., Am. surg. assns., Assn. Mil. Surgeons U.S. Home: 5423 Linden Ct Bethesda MD 20814 Office: Asst Chief Med Dir Profl Services VA Washington DC 20420

HUGHES, CHARLES CAMPBELL, educator; b. Salmon, Idaho, Jan. 26, 1929; s. Charles Frederick and Grace (Campbell) H.; m. Jane Ellen Murphy, Feb. 6, 1951 (div. July 1962); m. Patricia Diane Devereux, Aug. 8, 1964 (div. May 1969); m. Leslie Ann Medert, Mar. 7, 1970; children: John Charles Campbell, Calisse Marie. A.B. magna cum laude, Harvard Coll., 1951; M.A., Cornell U., 1953, Ph.D., 1957. Asso. dir., sr. research asso. Cornell Program in Social Psychiatry Cornell U., 1957-61; asst. prof. anthropology, dept. psychiatry Cornell U. Med. Coll., 1959-61; fellow Center for Advanced Study in Behavioral Scis., Stanford, Calif., 1961-62; dir. African Studies Center, Mich. State U., 1962-70, asso. prof., 1962-64, prof. anthropology, 1964-73, prof. anthropology and psychiatry, 1970-73; prof. anthropology, chmn. behavioral sci. div. dept. family and community medicine U. Utah Coll. Medicine, Salt Lake City, 1973-78, dir. grad. studies, 1979—; Mem. behavioral sci. test com. Nat. Bd. Med. Examiners, 1973-77. Author: An Eskimo Village in the Modern World, 1960, (with others) People of Cove and Woodlot, 1960, Psychiatric Disorder Among the Yoruba, 1963; editor: Eskimo Boyhood: An Autobiography in Psychosocial Perspective, 1974; Editor: Make Men of Them: Introductory Readings for Cultural Anthropology, 1972, (with others) Custom Made: Introductory Readings for Cultural Anthropology, 1975. Fellow Am. Anthrop. Assn., Soc. Applied Anthropology (pres. 1969-70), Am. Sociol. Assn., African Studies Assn., Arctic Inst. N.Am., AAAS; mem. Am. Ethnol. Soc., Assn. for Behavioral Sci. and Med. Edn. (dir. 1975-78, pres. 1979-80), Soc. for Med. Anthropology (pres. 1981-82), Phi Beta Kappa, Sigma Xi, Phi Kappa Phi. Home: 7453 Enchanted Hills Dr Salt Lake City UT 84121

HUGHES, CHARLES E., III, architect; b. N.Y.C., Mar. 14, 1915; s. Charles E., Jr. and Marjorie Bruce (Stuart) H.; m. Gladys Christine Lindseth, Nov. 19, 1949 (div. 1960); m. 2d Kimberly Jean Wiss, Dec. 19, 1964. B.A. magna cum laude, Brown U., 1937; M.Arch., Harvard U., 1940. Designer Caribbean Archtl.-Engring., N.Y.C., 1941-42, Skidmore Owings & Merrill, 1946-53, assoc. ptnr., 1953-60; prin. Charles E. Highes, AIA, N.Y.C., 1961-75; mng. Hughes, Cecil, Goodman, N.Y.C., 1975-82; prin. Charles E. Hughes, FAIA, N.Y.C., 1982—; designers Manufacturers Trust, N.Y.C., 1954, Citybank, Kennedy Airport, 1959; v.p. N.Y. Bldg. Congress, N.Y.C., 1979-80. Trustee Corp.-Brown U., Providence, from 1955, now trustee emeritus, Providence; pres. Mcpl. Arts Soc. N.Y., 1968-70; v.p. Fine Arts Fedn. N.Y., 1971-73. Served to lt. USNR, 1942-46; PTO. Decorated Battle Star (12). Fellow AIA (chpt. pres. 1978-79); mem. Soc. Archtl. Historians, Phi Beta Kappa, Alpha Delta Phi. Club: Brown of N.Y. (past pres.). Home: 311 E 50th St New York NY 10022 Office: Charles E Hughes FAIA Architects 330 E 59th St New York NY 10022

HUGHES, CHARLES JOSEPH ARTHUR, Canadian justice; b. Fredericton, N.B., Can., Mar. 2, 1909; s. James Austin and Mary Eveleen (McMahon) H.; m. Edith Barbara Atwater, Aug. 19, 1937; children: Richard Atwater, Charles David, Barbara Helen. B.A., U. N.B., 1930, LL.D. (hon.), 1974, St. Thomas U., 1972. Bar: Called to N.B. bar 1933, created queen's counsel 1952. Pvt. practice, St. Stephen, N.B., 1935-41; vice chmn. War Labour Bd. and Labour Relations Bd., 1942-53; partner firm Winslow, Hughes & Dickson, Fredericton, 1945-56, Hughes, Dickson, Cochrane and Stevenson, 1957-65; judge County Ct., 1965-68, Ct. of Appeal, N.B., 1968—; chief justice, N.B., 1972—; lectr. U. N.B. Sch. Law, 1966-68. Mem. Canadian Bar Assn. (v.p. N.B. chpt. 1964-65), N.B. Barristers Soc. (pres. 1962-64). Roman Catholic. Club: Garrison (Fredericton). Office: Justice Bldg Queen St Fredericton NB Canada E3B 1Z2 *

HUGHES, DANIEL THOMAS, anthropology educator; b. N.Y.C., Feb. 7, 1930; s. Thomas Joseph and Josephine (Rogers) H.; m. Violeta Cantos Peralta, June 20, 1969; 1 son, Eric. A.B., Bellarmine Coll., 1953, Licentiate in Philosophy, 1955, M.A. in Edn., 1956; S.T.B., Woodstock Coll., 1962; Ph.D., Cath. U. Am., 1967. Research assoc. Inst. Philippine Culture, Manila, 1967-68; asst. prof. dept. sociology and anthropology Ateneo de Manial, 1967-69; acting chmn. dept. Ateneo de Manila, 1968; research assoc. NRC-Nat. Acad. Sci., Washington, 1969-70; mem. faculty Ohio State U., Columbus, 1970—, prof., chmn. dept. anthropology, 1976—. Author: Political Conflict and Harmony on Ponape, 1970, (with Sherwood G. Lingenfelter) Political Development in Micronesia, 1974; editor: (with James A. Boutilier and Sharon W. Tiffany) Mission, Church and Sect in Oceania, 1978; contbr. articles to profl. jours. NIH grad. fellow, 1964-67; NIH research grantee, 1966; Nat. Endowment of Humanities research grantee, 1973; Ohio State U. research grantee, 1975, 83. Fellow Am. Anthrop. Assn., Assn. for Social Antropology in Oceania; assoc. Current Anthropology; mem. Assn. for Polit. and Legal Anthropology, Pacific Asian Studies Assn. Democrat. Roman Catholic. Home: 4322 Kenmont Pl Columbus OH 43220 Office: Dept Anthropology Ohio State U 124 W 17th St Columbus OH 43210

HUGHES, DONALD, textile company executive; b. 1929; married. Grad., Harvard U., 1955, M.B.A., 1957. Research assoc. Harvard Bus. Sch., 1957-59; with Burlington Industries, Inc., Greensboro, N.C., 1959—, mem. controllers staff, 1959-63, mgr. ops. research dept., 1963-66, asst. controller, 1966-70, sr. asst. controller, 1970-73; treas., controller Burlington Industries, Inc., Greensboro, N.C., 1975-76, v.p. fin., controller, 1976, now exec. v.p., chief fin. officer, mem. exec. fin. and mgmt. policy coms., dir. Served with USN, 1946-50. Office: Burlington Industries Inc 3330 W Friendly Ave Greensboro NC 27420

HUGHES, EARL MULFORD, farmer, seed co. exec.; b. Woodstock, Ill., Sept. 6, 1907; s. Earl Christopher and Mary Magdalene (Wiedrick) H.; m. Mildred Margaret Shuman, Feb. 20, 1932; children—Helen Shuman, Robert Christopher, Earl Mulford. B.S. in Agr, U. Ill., 1929; Ph.D., N.Y. State Coll. Agr. at Cornell U., 1938. Farm laborer, 1924-25, with father, Woodstock, 1929-34; asst. in marketing Cornell U., 1934-38; asst. prof. agrl. econs. U. Ill. Extension Coll. Agr., 1938-42; partner Hughes Seed Farms, 1942—; farmer, also fieldman Farm Mgmt. Service, 1942-43; farmer, Woodstock, 1944-55, cons. to sec. agr., 1954; adminstr. Commodity Stblzn. Service; exec. v.p. CCC, Washington, 1955-56, mem. adv. bd., 1957-61, chmn., 1957-61; chmn. bd. Hughes Hybrids Inc., 1967—; chmn. bd. 1st Nat. Bank of Woodstock, Ill., 1972-74; dir. Country Mut. Casualty Co., Country Life Ins. Co., 1948-54, Ill. Bell Telephone Co., 1960-77. Mem. sch. bd. Rural Community Consol. Sch. Dist. 10, Woodstock, 1946-55; mem. Woodstock Community High Sch. Bd., 1952-55, U. Ill. Found., Univ. Civil Service Merit Bd. Ill., 1963-69; Trustee Farm Found., Found. Am. Agr., Univs. Retirement System Ill.; trustee U. Ill., 1956-75, pres. bd. trustees, 1969-75. Recipient Distinguished Service award Ill. Soc. Farm Mgrs., Rural Appraisers, 1968; award of merit U. Ill. Coll. Agr., 1968; award for service to agr. and people State Ill. Ill. Extension Advisers Assn., U. Ill. Coll. Agr., 1970; D. Howard Doane award Am. Soc. Farm Managers and Rural Appraisers, 1971; U. Ill. Alumni Assn. Distinguished Service award, 1975; State Agr. Experiment Sta. Centennial Medallion, 1976; Hon. Master Farmer award Prairie Farmer, 1976. Mem. Am. Farm Bur. Fedn., Ill. Agrl. Assn. (chmn. pub. relations com. and legislative com. 1953-54), McHenry County Farm Bur., Ill. Found. Seeds Inc., Ill. Crop Improvement Assn., Am. Seed Trade Assn., Alpha Zeta, Gamma Sigma Delta, Phi Kappa Phi. Methodist. Club: Farmhouse. Address: 206 N Hughes Rd Woodstock IL 60098

HUGHES, EDWARD HUNTER, editor, writer; b. Ashland, Ky., Aug. 20, 1921; s. Paul Jones and Jessie Lee (Owens) H.; m. Mary J. Stanford, Jan. 15, 1955 (dec.); m. Penelope Maugham, Aug. 25, 1975. A.B., Centre Coll. Ky., 1943; M.A., Harvard, 1947. Reporter, Washington bur. Wall Street Jour., 1947-50, reporter, Europe, Middle East and Africa, 1950-53, fgn. editor, 1953-54; Africa bur. chief Time Inc., 1954-56, Germany and Eastern Europe bur. chief, 1956-59, writer, 1959-62, sr. editor, 1962-68, Middle East bur. chief, 1968-70. Served with AUS., 1944-45; ETO. Address: 18 Markham Sq London SW3 England

HUGHES, EDWARD JOHN, artist; b. North Vancouver, B.C., Feb. 17, 1913; s. Edward Samuel Daniell and Katherine Mary (McLean) H.; m. Fern Rosabell Irvine Smith, Feb. 10, 1940 (dec. 1974). Grad., Vancouver Sch. Art, 1933. Exhbns. include retrospective, Vancouver Art Gallery, 1967, Surrey Art Gallery, Art Gallery of Greater Victoria, Edmonton Art Gallery, Calgary Glenbow Gallery, 1983-85, Nat. Gallery Can., Beaverbrook Gallery, Fredericton; represented in permanent collections, Nat. Gallery Can., Ottawa, Art Gallery Ont., Toronto, Vancouver Art Gallery, Montreal Mus. Fine Art, Greater Victoria Art Gallery; ofcl. Army war artist, 1942-46. Served with Can. Army, 1939-46. Recipient Can. Council grants, 1958, 63, 67, 70. Mem. Royal Can. Acad. Arts. Presbyterian. Address: 2449 Heather St Duncan BC V9L 2Z6 Canada

HUGHES, EDWARD T., bishop; b. Landowne, Pa., Nov. 13, 1920. Student, St. Charles Sem., U. Pa. Ordained priest Roman Catholic Ch. 1947. Ordained titular bishop Segia and aux. bishop Phila., 1976—. Office: Our Lady of Fatima Ch 1 Fatima Dr Sceana PA 19018 *

HUGHES, EDWIN R(OSS), medical educator; b. Solano, N.Mex., May 27, 1928; s. Edwin Harrison and Fay (Ross) H.; m. Tiona Lucinda Smith, Sept. 8, 1948; children: Daniel Francis, Earl Rea, Edwin Marcus, Richard Harrison, Martina Fay, Thomas Michael, Malachy Irene. B.S., Eastern N.Mex. U., 1951, M.S., 1952; M.D., U. Utah, 1956. Resident pediatrics U. Minn. Hosp., 1956-57; research asso. Brookhaven Nat. Labs., Upton, N.Y., 1959-61; mem. faculty Med. Center, U. Ark., 1961—, prof. biochemistry and pediatrics, 1968-72; prof. W.Va. U. Med. Center, 1972-73; prof. pediatrics U. South Ala., Mobile, 1973—, prof. biochemistry, 1978—, dir. grad. program in basic med. scis., 1978—. Editor: Brennemann's Pediatrics, 1969. Served with U.S. Army, 1946-48. Career research award Nat. Inst. Arthritis and Metabolism, 1962-70. Mem. Soc. Pediatric Research, Am. Chem. Soc., Soc. Exptl. Pathology, Am. Pediatric Soc. Club: Mason. Research biochemistry of metal metabolism; endocrine research in children. Home: 4736 Wicker Way Mobile AL 36609 Office: U South Ala Coll Medicine Mobile AL 36688

HUGHES, ELINOR LAMBERT, drama editor, critic; b. Cambridge, Mass., Mar. 3, 1906; d. Hector James and Elinor (Lambert) H.; m. David D. Jacobus, July 14, 1957; stepchildren—David P. Jacobus, John H. Jacobus. Ed., Buckingham Sch., Cambridge, 1915-20, May Sch., Boston, 1920-23; A.B., Radcliffe Coll., 1927. Asst. in drama dept. Boston Herald-Traveler, 1929-34, drama and film editor and critic, 1934-66; lectr. on drama and film criticism. Author: Famous Stars of Filmdom (Men) and Famous Stars of Filmdom (Women), 1932, Passing Through to Broadway, 1948; Blank verse rev. of Shakespearean prodns. included in Best News Stories of 1937-38. Mem. Soc. Preservation N.E. Antiquities, Inst. Contemporary Art. Republican. Unitarian. Clubs: Women's City (Boston); Harvard (N.Y.C.). Home: 24 Academy Ln Bellport NY 11713 *I was fortunate in many respects: knowing from the age of 13 years what I wanted to do (work in the theater), parents who provided me with a first-rate education and a home where I could live before I was sufficiently established to support myself; having friends who opened doors for me that I could not have opened for myself; and employers who, if a bit doubtful that a 27-*

year old woman could head the drama department of a metropolitan newspaper, gave me the opportunity and later confirmed me.

HUGHES, EUGENE MORGAN, university president; b. Scottsbluff, Nebr., Apr. 3, 1934; s. Ruby Melvin and Hazel Marie (Griffith) H.; m. Caroline Mae Hartwig, Aug. 1, 1954; children: Deborah Kaye, Greg Eugene, Lisa Ann. Diploma, Neb. Western Coll., 1954; B.S. in Math. magna cum laude, Chadron State Coll., 1956, M.S., Kans. State U., 1958, Ph.D., George Peabody Coll. for Tchrs., Vanderbilt U., 1968. Grad. asst. dept. math. Kans. State U. at Manhattan, 1956-57; instr. math. Nebr. State Tchrs. Coll. at Chadron, 1957-58; asst. prof. math., head dept. Chadron State Coll., 1958-66, asso. prof., 1966-69, prof. math., 1969-70, dir. research, 1965-66, asst. to the pres., 1966-68, dean adminstrn., 1968-70; grad. asst. dept. math. George Peabody Coll. for Tchrs., Nashville, 1962-63, 64-65, asst. to undergrad. dean, 1964, asst. to pres., 1964-65; instr. Peabody Demonstration Sch., 1963-64; prof. math. No. Ariz. U., Flagstaff, 1970—, dean, 1970-71, provost univ. arts and sci. edn., 1971-72, acad. v.p., 1972-79, pres., 1979—; Cons. Nebr. Dept. Edn., 1966-70. Mem. staff bd. trustees Nebr. State Colls., Lincoln, 1969-70; co-dir. workshop tchr. edn. N.Central Assn., U. Minn., 1968-70; officer various fed. ednl. programs, Nebr. and Ariz., 1966—; mem. com. on grad. studies Am. Assn. State Colls. and Univs., 1979—, bd. dirs., mem. com. on accreditation, 1980—; mem. Ariz. Commn. Postsecondary Edn.; bd. fellows Am. Grad. Sch. Internat. Mgmt., 1980—; mem. Gov.'s Com. on Quality Edn.; Mem. Chadron Housing Authority, 1968-70; mem. adv. bd. United Bank of Ariz.; mem. Pres.'s Commn. NCAA; bd. dirs. Flagstaff Summer Festival, Ariz. Council on Humanities and Public Policy, Mus. No. Ariz., Grand Canyon council Boy Scouts Am. Recipient Disting. Service award Chadron State Coll., 1982; Ariz. Acad. NSF fellow, 1963, 64. Mem. Math. Assn. Am. (vis. lectr. secondary schs. western Nebr. 1962), Nat., Ariz. edn. assns., N.Central Assn. Colls and Secondary Schs. (co-ordinator 1968-72, cons.-evaluator 1977—), Nat. Council Tchrs. of Math, Flagstaff C. of C. (dir.), Blue Key, Pi Mu Epsilon, Phi Delta Kappa, Kappa Mu Epsilon, Phi Kappa Phi. Clubs: Masons, Elks, Rotary (past pres.). Office: Northern Ariz Univ Box 4092 Flagstaff AZ 86011

HUGHES, EVERETT CLARK, otolaryngology educator; b. Wadena, Minn., Nov. 22, 1904; s. Albert B. and Pearl Sylpha (Moses) H.; m. Ruth Scherer, Aug. 3, 1907; children: Mary Alice (Mrs. Donald P. Allen), Kathleen (Mrs. Frederick D. Barker III), Robert, Bruce, Randolph. B.A. in Chemistry, Carleton Coll., Northfield, Minn., 1927; Ph.D., Cornell U., 1930. Research chemist Standard Oil Co. (O.), Cleve., 1930-44, chief chem. and phys. research div., 1944-54, mgr. research div., 1954-60, v.p., 1960-69; research dir., clin. asst. prof. dept. otolaryngology Sch. Medicine U. So. Calif., Los Angeles, 1970—. Contbr. articles profl. jours. Fellow A.A.A.S., Am. Inst. Chemists (chem. Pioneer of 1971 award); mem. Am. Chem. Soc. (Morley award and medal 1974), Phi Beta Kappa, Sigma Xi, Alpha Chi Sigma. Patentee in field. Home: 1225 Charles St Pasadena CA 91103 Office: Sch Medicine U So Calif Hoffman Research Bldg 2025 Zonal Ave Los Angeles CA 90033

HUGHES, FRED, newspaper publisher; b. Grand Rapids, Mich., Aug. 16, 1915; s. Fred G. and Mary Jane (McKay) H.; m. Rebekah Blair, Jan. 2, 1942; children—Sallie E., Mary Jane. A.B., U. Mo., 1937, LL.B., 1939; postgrad., U. Wis., 1938-39. Bar: Mo. bar 1939. Practice of law, Joplin, 1939-41; spl. agt. FBI, 1941-46; asst. gen. mgr. Joplin Globe Pub. Co., 1946-58, gen. mgr., 1958-77, dir., 1959—, pres., 1964-79, chmn. bd., 1979—; sec.-treas., dir. Mid-Continent Telecasting, Inc. (KOAM-TV). Dir. First Community Bankcorp., First Nat. Bank, Joplin.; Pres. Joplin YMCA, 1959-61, Mo. Good Rds. Assn., 1964-66; vice chmn. Mo. State Reorgn. Commn., 1970-72; Bd. regents Mo. So. State Coll., 1964-78, pres., 1964-78; dir. Mo. Pub. Expenditure Survey, 1969—, pres., 1974-75. Mem. Am. Newspaper Pubs. Assn., Inland Daily Press Assn. (pres. 1965), Mo. C. of C. (dir. 1973-78), U. Mo. Alumni Assn. (dir. 1974-78, chmn. communications com. Mo. Alumnus 1974-78), Phi Delta Theta. Presbyn. Club: Rotarian (past pres.). Home: 2400 E 12 St Joplin MO 64801 Office: 117 E 4th St: Joplin MO 64801

HUGHES, HARRY ROE, gov. Md.; b. Easton, Md., Nov. 13, 1926; s. Jonathan Longfellow and Helen (Roe) H.; m. Patricia Ann Donoho, June 30, 1951; children—Ann Donoho, Elizabeth Roe. B.S., U. Md., 1949; student, Mt. St. Mary's Coll., 1944-45; LL.B., George Washington U., 1952. Bar: Md. bar 1952. Practiced in, Denton, 1952-71; partner firm Everngam & Hughes, Denton, Md., 1952-59; sec. Md. Dept. Transp., 1971-77; gov. State of Md., Annapolis, 1979—; Mem. Md. Ho. of Dels., 1955-58; mem. Md. Senate, 1959-70; majority floor leader, chmn. fin. com.; chmn. Md. Democratic State Com., 1969-70. Trustee Meml. Hosp., 1954-60. Served with A.C. USN, 1944-45. Mem. Md. Bar Assn., Caroline County (Md.) Bar Assn. Home: Government House Annapolis MD 21404 Office: Office of Gov State House Annapolis MD 21404

HUGHES, H(ENRY) STUART, historian, educator; b. N.Y.C., May 7, 1916; s. Charles Evans Jr. and Marjory (Stuart) H.; m. Suzanne Rufenacht, Dec. 28, 1949 (div. 1963); children: Sandra Latham, Kenneth Stuart; m. Judith B. Markham, Mar. 26, 1964; 1 son, David Markham. A.B. summa cum laude, Amherst Coll., 1937, L.H.D. (hon.), 1967; M.A., Harvard U., 1938, Ph.D., 1940. Instr. Brown U., 1940-41; chief div. research for Europe Dept. State, 1946-48; asst. prof. Harvard U., 1948-52, prof., 1957-69, Gurney prof. history polit. sci., 1969-75; prof. history U. Calif. at San Diego, 1975—; asso. prof. Stanford U., 1952-55, prof., head dept. history, 1955-56; vis. mem. Inst. Advanced Study, Princeton, N.J., 1950; Bacon exchange prof. U. Paris, 1967. Author: An Essay for Our Times, 1950, Oswald Spengler: A Critical Estimate, 1952, The United States and Italy, 1953, Consciousness and Society, 1958, Contemporary Europe: A History, 1961, An Approach to Peace, 1962, History as Art and as Science, 1964, The Obstructed Path, 1968, The Sea Change, 1975, Prisoners of Hope, 1983. Independent candidate for U.S. Senate, 1962; Co-chmn. Nat. Com. for a Sane Nuclear Policy, 1963-67, chmn., 1967-70. Served from pvt. F.A., to lt. col. OSS AUS, 1941-46. Decorated commendatore dell'Ordine della Corona D'Italia; cavaliere ufficiale al merito della Repubblica Italiana.; Guggenheim fellow, 1955, 58; Fellow Center Advanced Study Behavioral Scis., Stanford, 1957. Mem. Am. Hist. Assn., Soc. Italian Hist. Studies (past pres.), Am. Acad. Arts and Scis., Am. Com. on History 2d World War (founding chmn.), Istituto per la Storia del Risorgimento Italiano, Phi Beta Kappa. Address: 8531 Avenida de las Ondas La Jolla CA 92037

HUGHES, IVOR W., tobacco company executive; b. Porth, Eng., 1925. Student, Birmingham U., Oxford U. Chmn. bd., chief exec. officer Brown & Williamson Tobacco Corp., Louisville. Office: Brown & Williamson Tobacco Corp 1600 W Hill St Louisville KY 40232

HUGHES, JAMES A., business executive; b. N.Y.C., Dec. 19, 1912; s. James A. and Dawn (Eggleston) H.; m. Elizabeth Sherman, Feb. 2, 1940; children: Anne Sharon, James S., Harriette, Timothy. A.B., Dartmouth Coll., 1935; LL.B., Yale U., 1938. With Am. Ship Bldg. Co., 1940-44, Dresser Industries, 1944-48; v.p. Affiliated Gas Equipment, Inc., 1948-55, Diamond Alkali Co., 1955-60, exec. v.p., dir., 1960-63, vice chmn., 1963—; pres. Diamond Shamrock Corp., 1967-71, chmn. bd., 1971-75, chmn. fin. com., 1975-78; chmn. 1st Union Real Estate Equity and Mortgage Investments, Cleve., 1978—; Dir. 1st Union Realty Corp., Scott and Fetzer Co., N.Am. Coal Corp., Ameritrust Corp., Epsilon Data., Life Techs. Inc. Trustee Univ. Sch.; chmn. bd. trustees Cleve. Clinic Found. Mem. Delta Kappa Epsilon. Clubs: Union, Kirtland, Pepper Pike (Cleve.); Yale (N.Y.C.). Home: 2762 Center Rd Cleveland OH 44124 Office: Diamond Shamrock Bldg Cleveland OH 44114 also 55 Public Sq Cleveland OH 44113

HUGHES, JAMES JOHN, manufacturing company executive; b. Boston, Sept. 19, 1933; s. Cyril Anthony and Anna (Boles) H.; m. Sheila Smith, Aug. 11, 1962; children: Elizabeth M., Terrence L., Sara A. B.S., Suffolk U., 1959; student, Bentley Coll. Acctg., 1950-52. Dir. XCOR Internat., Inc., Chgo., 1970—, vice chmn., 1980—. Served with USMC, 1953-56. Home: 2105 Maple Rd Homewood IL 60430 Office: 330 S Wells St Chicago IL 60606

HUGHES, JAMES PAUL, physician; b. Wilkinsburg, Pa., Apr. 9, 1920; s. Paul S. and Sara C. (Coleman) H.; m. Adelaide C. Mitchell, June 21, 1944; 1 son, James Mitchell. B.S., U. Pitts., 1944, M.D., 1945; D. Indsl. Medicine, U. Cin., 1952. Diplomate: Am. Bd. Preventive Medicine. Intern St. Francis Hosp., Pitts., 1945-46; resident in pathology Univ. Hosps., Cleve., 1948-49; fellow in indsl. medicine Kettering Lab. U. Cin., 1949-51; physician The Tex. Co., 1951-52, The Ethyl Corp., Cin., 1952-57; chief Bur. Indsl. Health Dept. Health City of Cin., 1952-55; med. dir. Kaiser Aluminum & Chem. Corp., Oakland, Calif., 1957-82; sr. ptnr. Hughes-Lewis Assocs., Oakland, Calif., 1982—; asst. prof. indsl. medicine U. Cin., 1952-55; asso. prof. preventive medicine Ohio State U., 1955-57; exec. v.p., dir. Kaiser Found. Internat., 1967-76; project dir. U.S. Peace Corps Health projects, W. Africa, 1966-68, USAID med. relief project, Port Harcourt, Nigeria, 1970-72, Health Services on Bandama River project, Kossou, Ivory Coast, 1970-72; v.p. health sers. Kaiser Industries Corp., 1972-74; clin. assoc. prof. occupational medicine U. Calif., San Francisco, 1979—. Author: (with N.H. Proctor) Chemical Hazards of the Workplace, 1978. Chmn. com. for Industry Council Tropical Health Harvard U. Sch. Public Health, 1969-76. Served to capt. U.S. Army, 1946-48. Decorated officier de l'Ordre Nat. Ivoirien, Abidjan, 1972. Fellow ACP, Am. Occupational Med. Assn. (Health Achievement award 1972), Am. Acad. Occupational Medicine (past pres., Kehoe award 1982); mem. Inst. Medicine-Nat. Acad. Scis., Internat. Epidemiologic Assn., Am. Indsl. Hygiene Assn. Home: 124 Guilford Rd Piedmont CA 94611 Office: 1916 Broadway Oakland CA 94612

HUGHES, JOE KENNETH, beverage company executive; b. Leonard, Tex., 1927; s. Medford F. and Ina M. (Akins) H.; m. Betty Penry, Feb. 26, 1949; children: Timothy J., Mark D. Student, N. Tex. State Coll.; B.A., So. Meth. U., 1948. Writer, then asst. city editor Dallas Times Herald, 1948-53; mgr. Dallas office Harshe-Rotman, Inc. (pub. relations), 1953-55; account exec., v.p., mgr. Dallas office Grant Advt., Inc., 1956-64, exec. v.p., 1964-68; v.p. franchise Dr. Pepper Co., 1968-69, v.p. mktg. services, 1969-70, v.p. mktg., 1970-73, exec. v.p., 1973-84, pres., chief operating officer, 1984—, also dir.; dir. Dr. Pepper Bottling Co., Waco, Tex., Dallas, Fort Worth, San Antonio, Houston, Dr. Pepper Bottling Co. of So. Calif., Dr. Pepper Japan Co., DPB Co. of Corpus Christi, Albuquerque, Gulf Coast Bottling Co., N.C. Bottling Co., Sherry Lane Nat. Bank. Bd. dirs. Cotton Bowl Council, Dallas Summer Musicals. Mem. Assn. Broadcast Execs. Tex., Dallas Advt. League, Dallas Sales and Mktg. Execs., Sigma Delta Chi. Clubs: Dallas Press (charter, dir. 1952-53), Lakewood Country.). Home: 3420 Wentwood Dr Dallas TX 75225 Office: Dr Pepper Co PO Box 225086 Dallas TX 75265

HUGHES, JOHN, government agency administrator, journalist; b. Neath, South Wales, Apr. 28, 1930; came to U.S., 1954, naturalized, 1965; s. Evan John and Dellis (Williams) H.; m. Vera Elizabeth Pockman, Aug. 20, 1955; children: Wendy Elizabeth, Mark Evan. Grad., Stationers' and Newspapermakers' Sch., London, Eng., 1946; Nieman fellow, Harvard U., 1961-62; LL.D. (hon.), Colby Coll., 1978. Mem. staffs Natal Mercury, Durban, South Africa, 1946-49, 52-54, Daily Mirror, London News Agy., Reuters, London, Eng., 1949-52; with Christian Sci. Monitor, Boston, 1954-79, Africa corr., 1955-61, asst. fgn. editor, 1962-64, Far Eastern corr., 1964-70, mng. editor, 1970, editor, 1970-76, editor and mgr., 1976-79; dir., cons. News Jour. Co., Wilmington, Del., 1975-78; broadcaster Westinghouse Broadcasting Co., Boston, 1962-64, from Far East, 1964-70; pres., pub. Hughes Newspapers, Inc., Orleans, Mass., 1977-81; asso. dir. USIA, Washington, 1981-82; dir. Voice of Am., Washington, 1982; asst. sec. of state, spokesman Dept. State, Washington, 1982—; Mem. Pulitzer Prize Bd., 1975-81. Author: The New Face of Africa, 1961, Indonesian Upheaval, 1967. Recipient Pulitzer prize internat. reporting, 1967; Overseas Press Club award best daily newspaper reporting from abroad, 1970; Yankee Quill award Sigma Delta Chi, 1977. Mem. Am. Soc. Newspaper Editors (dir. 1972-80, pres. 1978-79). Clubs: Overseas Press (N.Y.C.); Hong Kong Country, Fgn. Corrs. Hong Kong; Harvard (Boston). Office: Dept of State 2201 C St NW Washington DC 20520

HUGHES, JOHN CHAMBERLAIN, lawyer; b. Ft. Pierre, S.D., May 22, 1915; s. Felan T. and Florence (Chamberlain) H.; m. Marjorie Anstey, Jan. 31, 1948; children: Mary Kay, Patricia Ann, Bridget. Teaching certificate, Eastern State Tchrs. Coll., Madison, S.D., 1935; LL.B., U. S.D., 1940. Bar: Alaska 1947. Practiced in, Kodiak, 1947-51, Anchorage, 1951—; mem. law firm Hughes, Thorsness, Gantz, Powell & Brundin (and predecessor firms), 1951—; Pres. Tri-Lex, Inc., Anchorage, 1960—; sec., dir. Pago Investment Co., Anchorage, 1958—; dir. People's Bank & Trust Co. Pres. Kodiak Ind. Sch. Dist., 1948-51; mem. Alaska Territorial Banking Bd., 1951-52, Anchorage Borough Sch. Dist., 1960-69; pres. Anchorage Borough Sch. Dist., 1964-65; mem. Alaska Draft Bd., 1959—; Bd. dirs. Alaska Sch. Bds. Assn., 1964-69, pres., 1967-69; mem. Anchorage Estate Planning Council, 1962—, past pres.; mem. Alaska Ednl. Broadcasting Commn.; bd. dirs. U. Alaska Found., 1974—, August F. Reetz Found., 1976—; pres. Alaska Found., 1982-83. Served with U.S. Mcht. Marine, 1943-45. Mem. Pioneers of Alaska. Republican. Roman Catholic. Clubs: Elk, Lion (pres. Anchorage 1961-62). Home: 3627 E 88th Ave Anchorage AK 99507 Office: 509 W 3d Ave Anchorage AK 99501

HUGHES, JOHN EDWARD, educator; b. Phila., Mar. 1, 1922; s. John Thomas and Ann Pauline (Garrity) H.; m. Gertrude Nash, Sept. 22, 1945 (dec. Oct. 1959); children—Mary Susan Wilson-Hughes, Irene A. Hughes Murdock, Jennifer Hughes Tomlin. B.A., Temple U., 1948; M.A., U. Pa., 1949, Ph.D., 1960. Instr. sociology U. Pa., 1949-53; asst. prof. sociology U. Notre Dame, 1953-61; asso. prof. Villanova U., 1961-67, prof., 1967—, chmn. dept., 1961—. Served with U.S. Army, 1943-45. Decorated Purple Heart. Fellow Am. Sociol. Soc.; mem. Am. Catholic Sociol. Soc. (pres. 1961), Pa. Sociol. Soc. (pres. 1968). Home: 1000 Conestoga Rd Rosemont PA 19010

HUGHES, JOHN FARRELL, finance company executive; b. Bridgeport, Conn., Aug. 12, 1946; s. John Hubbell and Alice Catherine (Farrell) H.; m. Patricia Nancy Wetzel, July 10, 1971; children: Michael John, Jonathan Wetzel. B.B.A., U. Notre Dame, 1968; M.B.A., U. Ga., 1973. Banking officer Commerce Union Bank, Nashville, 1974-75, asst. v.p., 1975-77, v.p., 1977-78; asst. tres. Assocs. Corp., Dallas, 1978-79, asst. v.p., asst. treas., 1979-80, v.p., asst. treas., 1980-81, v.p., treas., 1981-83, sr. v.p., treas., 1983—. Vice chmn. St. Paul Hosp. Found. Drive, Dallas, 1982. Lt. USN, 1968-72; Vietnam. Mem. Fin. Execs. Inst., U.S. Naval Inst. Roman Catholic. Office: Assocs Corp NAm PO Box 222822 Dallas TX 75222

HUGHES, JOHN LAWRENCE, publisher; b. N.Y.C., Mar. 13, 1925; s. John Chambers and Margaret (Kelly) H.; m. Rose Marie Pitman, Nov. 27, 1947; children: Alexandra, Timothy, Christopher, Ian. B.A., Yale U., 1948. Reporter Nassau Review Star, Rockville Centre, L.I., N.Y., 1949; asst. sr. editor Pocket Books, Inc., N.Y.C., 1949-59; v.p. Washington Sq. Press, 1958, William Morrow & Co., Inc., N.Y.C., 1960-65, pres., chief exec. officer, 1965—, also dir. Former trustee Unquowa Sch., Fairfield, Conn., Pequot Library, Southport, Conn., N. Country Sch., Lake Placid, N.Y., St. Paul's Sch., Concord, N.H.; mem. U.S. Helsinki Watch Com.; former mem. adv. bd. Sta. WNET, Public TV, N.Y.C.; trustee Fund for Free Expression, N.Y.C.; bd. govs. Yale U. Press, New Haven. Served to 1st lt. USMCR, 1943-46, 51. Office: 105 Madison Ave New York NY 10016

HUGHES, JOHN RUSSELL, educator, physician; b. DuBois, Pa., Dec. 19, 1928; s. John Henry and Alice (Cooper) H.; m. Mary Ann Dick, June 14, 1958; children: John Russell (dec.), Christopher Alan, Thomas Gregory, Cheryl Ann. A.B. summa cum laude, Franklin and Marshall Coll., 1950; B.A. with honors, Oxford (Eng.) U., 1952, M.A., 1955, D.M. hon., 1976; Ph.D., Harvard U., 1954; M.D., Northwestern U., 1975. Neurophysiologist, NIH, 1954-56; dir. electroencephalography dept. Meyer Hosp., SUNY, 1956-63; dir. div. lab. scis., including electroencephalography Northwestern U. Med. Center, 1963-77, prof. neurology, 1968—; dir. EEG and Epilepsy Clinic, U. Ill. Med. Center, 1977—; staff U. Ill. Hosp., Community Hosp., Geneva, Delnor Hosp., St. Charles; cons. Chgo. VA Westside Hosp., Downey VA Hosp., Mercyville and Copley Meml. Hosp., Aurora, Ill., others; participant debate on brain death BBC-TV. Author: Functional Organization of the Diencephalon, 1957, Atlas on Cerebral Death and Coma, 1976, EEG in Clinical Practice, 1982, EEG Evoked Potentials in Psychiatry and Behavioral Neurology, 1983. Recipient Alumni award Franklin and Marshall Coll., 1978. Mem. Am. Electroencephalography Soc. (treas. 1965-68), Eastern Electroencephalography Soc. (sec.-treas. 1961-64), Central Electroencephalography Soc., Chgo. Acad. Medicine, Am. Epilepsy Soc., Am. Physiol. Soc., Soc. Neuroscis., Am. Acad. Neurology, Phi Beta Kappa, Sigma Xi (lectr. 1960—). Research and numerous publs. on coding in central nervous system, new theory on neural mechanisms in olfaction, electro-clin. correlations in different types of epilepsy, organic aspects in juvenile delinquency. Home: 720 Roslyn Terrace Evanston IL 60201 Office: 912 S Wood St Chicago IL 60612 *Always be ahead of your colleagues in every endeavor by having done it before they do. Do what you must do now to leave time for innovation later.*

HUGHES, JONATHAN ROBERTS TYSON, economist, educator; b. Wenatchee, Wash., Apr. 23, 1928; s. Benjamin Bartholomew and Rachel Estella (Ward) H.; m. Mary Gray Stillwell, Dec. 19, 1953; children: Benjamin, Margaret, Charis. B.S., Utah State U., Logan, 1950; D. Phil., Oxford U., Eng., 1955. Economist Fed. Res. Bank N.Y., N.Y.C., 1955-56; asst. prof. Purdue U., West Lafayette, Ind., 1956-57, assoc. prof., West Lafayette, 1958-60, prof., 1960-66; vis. asst. prof. Columbia U., N.Y.C., 1957-58; prof. econs. Northwestern U., Evanston, Ill., 1966. Author: The Vital Few, 1966, Social Control in the Colonial Economy, 1976, The Governmental Habit, 1977, American Economic History, 1983. Rohdes scholar, 1952; Guggenheim fellow, 1962; Ford Faculty fellow, 1971; vis. fellow All Souls Coll. Oxford U., 1971. Mem. Econ. History Assn. (pres. 1980-81). Democrat. Home: 1016 Ridge Ave Evanston IL 60202 Office: Dept Econs Northwestern Univ Evanston IL 60202

HUGHES, JOSEPH D., lawyer; b. Dothan, Ala., June 20, 1910; s. Robert T. and Ora (Domingus) H.; m. Jane Blackistone, Nov. 29, 1934; children: Thomas Mifflin, Gordon, Gerard. B.S., Auburn U., 1931, LL.D., 1962; J.D. with highest honors, George Washington U., 1934; LL.M., Georgetown U., 1936; postgrad., Grad. Sch. Public Affairs, Am. U., 1937; LL.D. (hon.), Waynesburg Coll., 1956, L.H.D., Thiel Coll., 1970. Bar: D.C. 1934, Pa. 1950. With Dept. State, 1934-35, Dept. Treasury, 1936-37, Bur. Internal Revenue, 1937-40, Pitts. Plate Glass Co., 1940-46; gov., v.p. T. Mellon & Sons, Pitts., 1946-69; v.p. Richard K. Mellon and Sons, Pitts., 1970-71. Adminstrv. trustee Richard King Mellon Found., 1946-71; trustee Auburn U. Found., George Washington U., P.E. Theol. Sem. in Va.; bd. dirs. Western Pa. Hosp.; former pres. Nat. Wildlife Fedn. Endowment, Inc., Corp. for Pub. Broadcasting, Pa. Pub. TV Network; bd. visitors Tulane U. Served with AUS, 1942-46; chmn. Japanese-Am. Joint Bd., 1943-44; civilian aide to sec. of army, 1955-63; asst. adj. gen. Commonwealth Pa., 1963-69; brig. gen. Pa. N.G. Decorated Legion of Merit; recipient Distinguished Service medal State of Pa.; Alumni Achievement award George Washington U. Law Sch., 1965. Mem. Am. Law Inst., Order of Coif, Sigma Phi Epsilon, Phi Delta Phi. Republican. Episcopalian. Clubs: Duquesne (Pitts.); Metropolitan (Washington); Chevy Chase (Md.). Home: 1331 Bennington Ave Pittsburgh PA 15217 Office: 616 Oliver Bldg Pittsburgh PA 15222

HUGHES, KEITH WILLIAM, banking and finance company executive; b. Cleve., July 1, 1946; s. Delmar Vern and Margaret Virginia H.; m. Cheryl F. Hughes, Aug. 30, 1969; 1 dau., Amy. B.S., Miami U., Oxford, Ohio, 1968, M.B.A., 1969. Mktg. mgr. Continental Bank, Chgo., 1970-73; exec. v.p. broker/dealer subs. Assos. Corp., 1973-74, exec. v.p., dir., Dallas, 1981—; v.p. mktg. Northwestern Nat. Bank, 1974-76; sr. v.p. Crocker Bank, San Francisco, 1976-81. Mem. adv. bd. St. Matthews Episcopal Sch.; active Big Bros. Am.; bd. dirs. Dallas Opera; active Family Service Agy., San Mateo, Calif. Mem. Am. Bankers Assn., Bank Mktg. Assn., Calif. Bankers Assn., Consumers Bankers Assn., Nat. Consumer Fin. Assn. Clubs: Olympic (San Francisco); Los Colinas Country (Tex.); Quadrant (Dallas). Home: 5500 Chatham Hill Dallas TX 75220 Office: 250 Carpenter St Irving TX

HUGHES, KENNETH RUSSELL, lawyer; b. Newport, Ky., Feb. 3, 1925; s. Isaac Hugh and Martha (Becknell) H.; m. Ann B. Ollinger, June 18, 1949; children—Kenneth Russell, Sharon Ann, Mark Edward. B.B.A., U. Cin., 1949; J.D., Salmon P. Chase Law Sch., 1956. Bar: Ohio bar 1956; C.P.A., Ohio. Conferee appeals div. IRS, Cin., 1949-57; partner firm Freiberg, Katz & Hughes, Cin., 1957-65, Santen, Santen & Hughes Co. (L.P.A.), 1965—; instr. fed. taxation Salmon P. Chase Law Sch., 1962-68. Served with inf. U.S. Army, 1943-46. Mem. Am. Bar Assn., Ohio State Bar Assn., Cin. Bar Assn. Club: Bankers of Cin. Home: Gen Delivery Neville OH 45156 Office: Suite 916 105 E 4th St Cincinnati OH 45202

HUGHES, LLOYD LYNNELL, hospital administrator; b. Independence, Kans., Sept. 6, 1920; s. Lloyd Lowrey and Jess (O'Connell) H.; m. Isabel Neiswanger, June 28, 1947; children: Lucinda, Nancy, Melissa, David Lloyd. A.B., Washburn U., 1942, J.D., 1947; M.H.A., U. Minn., 1951. Bar: Kans. bar 1947. Asst. gen. counsel Kans. Corp. Commn., 1947-49; asst. dir. R.I. Hosp., 1951-56; supt. U. Wis. Hosp., 1957-60; dep. dir. R.I. Hosp., 1960-62, exec. dir., 1962-70, exec. v.p., 1970-73, pres., 1973—; asso. prof. hosp. adminstrn. U. Wis., 1958-60; clin. preceptor U. Minn. program hosp. adminstrn., 1958-60, 62—; Mem. R.I. Adv. Commn. on Heart Disease, Cancer and Stroke, 1969-75; rep. Council of Teaching Hosps. to Am. Assn. Med. Colls., 1969-72, 75-78; councillor accreditation council ambulatory health care Joint Commn. Accreditation Hosps., 1975-79. Trustee Tri-

State Regional Med. Program, 1972-77, St. Andrews Sch., Barrington, R.I., 1976—; trustee R.I. Health Services Inc., 1975—, chmn. bd., 1976-79; R.I. diocesan chmn. Episcopal Charities, 1976-77, trustee, 1978—; bd. mgrs. Bethany Home, Providence, 1969—; sr. warden St. John's ch., Barrington, R.I., 1983—. Served with AUS, 1943-46. Mem. Hosp. Assn. R.I. (pres. 1967-69, trustee 1969—), New Eng. Hosp. Assembly (trustee 1969-77, chmn. edn. council 1977-78, pres. 1981), Am. Coll. Hosp. Adminstrs., Am. Hosp. Assn. (del. 1971-73). Episcopalian. Home: 26 Melrose Ave Barrington RI 02806 Office: 593 Eddy St Providence RI 02903

HUGHES, LYNN NETTLETON, judge; b. Houston, Sept. 9, 1941; s. James Baker and Mary Alma (Nettleton) H.; m. Olive Allen, May 17, 1975; 1 dau., Lindsey Lea. B.A., U. Ala., 1963; J.D., U. Tex., 1968. Bar: Tex. 1966. Practiced in, Houston, 1966-79; judge 165th Dist. Ct. Tex., Houston, 1979-80, 189th Dist. Ct. Tex., 1981—; adj. prof. South Tex. Coll. Law, 1973—; Mem. adv. bd. Houston Jour. Internat. Law, 1981—; Tex. del. Nat. Conf. State Trial Judges, 1983-86; lectr. Tex. Coll. Judiciary, 1983. Trustee Rift Valley Research Mission, 1978—. Fellow Tex. Bar Found.; mem. Am., Houston bar assns., State Bar Tex., Am. Judicature Soc., Am. Soc. Legal History, Am. Anthrop. Assn., Phi Delta Phi. Episcopalian. Home: 609 Saddlewood Houston TX 77024 Office: 301 Fannin St Houston TX 77002

HUGHES, MARIJA MATICH, law librarian; b. Belgrade, Yugoslavia; came to U.S., 1960, naturalized, 1971; d. Zarija and Antonija (Hudowsky) Matich. B.A. in Music, Mokranjac, Belgrade, U. Belgrade and Calif. State U., 1967; M.L.S., U. Md., 1968; student, McGeorge Sch. Law, 1968-69. Counselor, gen. mgr. Career Counseling Service, Sacramento, Calif., 1962-64; sec. to mgr. Sacramento State Coll., 1965-66; student librarian "High John" program U. Md., Fairmont Heights, 1967-68; head reference library-faculty liasion librarian Hastings Coll. Law U. Calif., San Francisco, 1969-72; head law librarian Am. Tel. & Tel. Corp., Washington, 1972-73; chief law librarian Nat. Clearinghouse Library, U.S. Commn. on Civil Rights, Washington, 1973—; owner, pub. Hughes Press. Author, compiler: The Sexual Barrier, Legal and Econ. Aspects of Employment, 1970-73; Author, compiler: The Sexual Barrier: Legal, Medical, Economic and Social Aspects of Sex Discrimination, 1977; contbr. articles to profl. jours. Mem. Am. Assn. Law Libraries, ALA, Nat. Women's Polit. Caucus, Spl. Libraries Assn., Assn. Internat. Law Libraries, Washington Ind. Writers. Club: Gaslight. Home: 500 23d St NW Apt B-203 Washington DC 20037 Office: Nat Clearinghouse Library US Commn on Civil Rights 1121 Vermont Ave NW Washington DC 20425

HUGHES, MICHAELA KELLY, ballet dancer, actress; b. Morristown, N.J., Mar. 31, 1956; d. Joseph Francis and Mary Elizabeth (Coughlin) H. Scholarship student, Houston Ballet Acad., 1970-73; part-time scholarship student, Sch. Am. Ballet, 1971. Child actress with, Alley Theatre, Houston, 1969, 71; mem., Houston Ballet, 1974, Eliot Feld Ballet, N.Y.C., 1975—; prin. dancer, 1975-80; mem., Am. Ballet Theatre, 1980-81; appeared in: A Chorus Line, 1981; Broadway appearances: On Your Toes, 1982, Mame, 1983. Mem. Am. Guild Mus. Artists, Screen Actors Guild, Equity., AFTRA.

HUGHES, PAULA D., investment company executive; b. N.Y.C., Sept. 25, 1931; 1 dau., Catherine H. Benton. With Brown & Bigelow, N.Y.C., 1953-61; account exec. Shields & Co., N.Y.C., 1961-72; v.p. Thomson McKinnon Securities Inc., N.Y.C., 1972-78, 1st v.p., dir., 1979—; gov. U.S. Postal Service, 1980—; allied mem. N.Y. Stock Exchange; life trustee Carnegie-Mellon U., chmn. fin. com.; lectr.-instr. Personal Investment Mgmt., NYU; lectr. various schs. and colls.; lectr. Vassar Coll.; speaker New Sch., N.Y.C., panel mem. Wall St. Conf., 1979, 82, 83; bd. govs. Greenwich House, N.Y.C., 1961—. Featured cover articles, Fin. World, 1975, 78, articles in publs., Fortune mag., Wall St. Jour., Pitts. Press, Ariz. Republic, articles to publs., N.Y. Times, articles in publs., N.Y. Post, Indpls. Star; guest, Wall St. Week. Recipient AMITA Golden Lady award in Fin., 1975, Disting. Friend of U. award Carnegie-Mellon U., 1983; named Bus. Woman of Yr. Calif. Bus. Women, 1976. Mem. Women's Forum (dir. 1979-81), Sales Execs. Club N.Y. (treas. 1977-79, dir. 1977—), Fin. Women's Assn., Am. Arbitration Soc., Internat. Assn. Fin. Planners. Republican. Clubs: Duquesne (Pitts.); Shenorock Shore (Rye); Yale (N.Y.C.). Office: Thomson McKinnon Securities Inc 200 Park Ave New York NY 10166 *In one's personal, professional or philanthropic activities, caring is what it's all about.*

HUGHES, PETER JAMES, hospital administrator; b. Huntington, N.Y., Nov. 18, 1933; s. I.W. and Maude A. (Riddle) H.; m. Eileen M. Barry, June 9, 1956; children: Kevin, Craig, Jean. B.B.A. in Acctg., St. John's U., Jamiaca, N.Y., 1959. Sr. acct. Haskins & Sells, N.Y.C., 1958-63; exec. v.p. Meml. Sloan-Kettering Cancer Ctr., N.Y.C., 1981—, bd. dirs., 1981—; dir. Blue Cross (Blue Shield of Greater N.Y.), N.Y.C., 1981—. Mem. East Rockaway Bd. Edn., N.Y., 1970-78, East Rockaway Drug Abuse Commn., 1974-78. Served with USMC, 1952-55; Korea. Mem. Greater N.Y. Hosp. Assn. (bd. dirs. 1981—), Hosp. Soc. N.Y., Hosp. Adminstrs. Club N.Y. Home: Meml Sloan-Kettering Cancer Ctr 1275 York Ave New York NY 10021

HUGHES, PHILLIP SAMUEL, government official, social scientist; b. Chgo., Feb. 26, 1917; s. Arthur Samuel and Beulah (Blish) H.; m. Jean Evans, July 9, 1938 (dec.); children: Suzanne, Patricia, Michael (dec.), Shirley. B.A., U. Wash., 1938, postgrad. in sociology, 1940. With State of Wash., 1938-43, chief research and stats., dept. social security, 1942-43; sr. labor market analyst War Manpower Commn., Seattle, 1943-44; with VA, Seattle, 1946-49, chief research and stats., 1946-49; with U.S. Bur. Budget, 1949-69; dep. chief Office Legis. Reference, 1956-59, asst. dir. legis. reference, 1959-66, dep. dir. bur., 1966-69; acting pres. Nat. Inst. Pub. Affairs, 1970-71; sr. fellow Brookings Instn., 1971-72; dir. Office Fed. Elections, GAO, 1972-73, asst. controller gen., 1973-77; cons. Devel. and Resources Corp., 1977, Smithsonian Instn., 1977; asst. sec. Dept. Energy, 1977—; cons. Office Mgmt. and Budget, Ford Found., conservation orgns.; chmn. bd. trustees Beacon Press, 1972. Bd. dirs. YMCA Met. Washington, 1961—, treas., 1972-76. Served with USNR, 1944-45. Recipient Career Service Nat. Civil Service League, 1962, Disting. Service Bur. of Budget, 1965, Rockefeller Pub. Service, 1973. Mem. Am. Soc. Pub. Adminstrn. (nat. council), Nat. Acad. Pub. Adminstrn., Wilderness Soc., Potomac Appalachian Trail Club, Delta Upsilon. Unitarian (trustee 1970-71). Office: Smithsonian Inst Office of the Undersecretary 1000 Jefferson Dr SW Washington DC 20560

HUGHES, ROBERT EDWARD, research administrator; b. N.Y.C., May 24, 1924; s. Morgan J. and Patricia J. (Collins) H.; m. La Velma J. Thompson, June 5, 1954; 1 son, Jeffrey Lynn. B.S., Lehigh U., 1949; Ph.D., Cornell U., 1952. Research asst. Bakelite Corp., 1941-42, 46-47; instr. Cornell U., 1952-53; asst. prof. chemistry U. Pa., 1953-60, asso. prof., 1960-64, prof., 1964, Cornell U., 1964-74, dir. Materials Sci. Center, 1968-74; asst. dir. for nat. and internat. programs NSF, 1974, asst. dir. for astron., atmospheric, earth and ocean scis., 1975-76, acting asst. dir. for sci., tech. and internat. affairs, 1975-76, asso. program on sci., tech. and soc., 1977-80; prof. Cornell U., 1977-80; pres. Associated Univs. Inc., 1980—; vis. prof. Oxford U., 1979; cons. Rohm & Haas Co., 1956-74, Sun Oil Co., 1957-63, 77-80, Gen. Motors Corp., 1978-80, NSF, 1977-78; mem. research and devel. study group U.S. Commn. on Govt. Procurement, 1971-72; mem. solid state scis. com. NRC-Nat. Acad. Sci., 1967-74, chmn., 1971-73, mem. solid state scis. panel, 1961—, mem. nat. materials adv. bd., 1978-81; head U.S. del. 8th Antarctic Treaty Cons. Meeting, 1975. Editor: Jour. Solid State Chemistry, 1969-74; asso. editor: Materials Sci. and Engring, 1970-72; editorial adv. bd.: Jour. Polymer Sci., Polymer Physics and Polymer Chemistry, 1966-74, Jour. Nonmetals, 1970-72; Contbr. numerous research articles to sci. jours. Mem. nat. adv. bd. Am. U. Served with AUS, 1943-46. NSF Sr. fellow Cambridge U., 1967-68. Mem. Am. Chem. Soc., Am. Crystallographic Soc., Phi Beta Kappa, Sigma Xi. Home: 6213 Leeke Forest Ct Bethesda MD 20034

HUGHES, ROBERT HARRISON, association executive; b. Puunene, Hawaii, Mar. 23, 1917; s. Robert Edwin and Alice Thayer (Walker) H.; m. Nadine Jeannette Hegler, Aug. 24, 1940 (div. 1983); children: Robert Lawrence, Linton Alice, Carole Nadine.; m. Judith R. Gething, Jan. 28, 1983. B.Sc. in Sugar Tech, U. Hawaii, 1938. With Hawaiian Comml. & Sugar Co., 1939-65, sugar mill supt., 1951-63, prodn. mgr., 1963-65; v.p. tech. services C. Brewer & Co., Ltd., Honolulu, 1965-69, sr. v.p. Hawaiian ops., 1969-77, exec. v.p., 1977-80, dir. subs., 1966-80; pres. Hawaiian Sugar Planters Assn., Aiea, 1981—; dir. C. Brewer & Co. Ltd., Hilo Coast Processing Co., Olokele Sugar Co. Ltd. Bd. regents U. Hawaii, 1961-66; trustee Hawaii Conf. Found., 1966—, Hawaii Loa Coll., 1980—, U. Hawaii Found., 1963-65, 73-78; pres. U. Hawaii Found., 1967-68; bd. dirs. Hawaii Multi-Cultural Center, 1979-81; chmn. adv. bd. Cancer Center of Hawaii, 1979-81; pres. Hawaii conf. United Ch. of Christ, 1962-63. Mem. Hawaiian Sugar Planters Assn. (dir. 1972-80). Home: 7148 Kukii St Honolulu HI 96825 Office: PO Box 1057 Aiea HI 96701

HUGHES, ROBERT JOSEPH, shipping company executive; b. New Brunswick, N.J., Aug. 28, 1908; s. James Henry and Catherine (Craven) H.; m. Catherine Maurita Coan, May 20, 1938 (dec.); children: Catherine (Mrs. Thomas J. Lamb), Helen (Mrs. Lawrence D. Schuler), James J., Margaret Mary (dec.), Robert Joseph.; m. Velma R. Ragan, Sept. 24, 1982. Grad. high sch. Account exec. Rhoades Williams, N.Y.C., 1926-38; with James Hughes Inc. and Hughes Brothers, Inc., N.Y.C., 1938—, partner both, 1951—; pres. James Hughes, 1965—; sec.-treas. Hughes Brothers, 1961—; dir. Peoples Nat. Bank Central Jersey, Piscataway, N.Y. Harbor and Towing Assos., 1971-75, Ocean Burning, Inc., N.Y.C., Heavy Lift, Inc., New Orleans; chmn. Am. Waterways Operators, Inc., Washington, 1975-76, N.Y. Towboat & Harbor Carriers Assn., 1976-78. Bd. dirs. Middlesex County Coll. Scholarship Fund, 1965-78, trustee, 1964-69. Mem. Maritime Assn. N.Y. Roman Catholic. Clubs: K.C., Whitehall, Propeller (N.Y.C.); Raritan Valley Country (treas. 1972-73). Home: 1 Lincoln Pl Apt 13B North Brunswick NJ 08902 Office: 17 Battery Pl New York NY 10004

HUGHES, ROBERT STUDLEY FORREST, art critic; b. Sydney, Australia, July 28, 1938; s. Geoffrey Eyre Forrest and Margaret (Vidal) H.; 1 son, Danton Vidal. Student arts and architecture, Sydney U., 1956-61. Free-lance writer, to 1970; mem. staff Time mag., N.Y.C., 1970—, now sr. writer; lectr. on art. Writer, narrator numerous art documentaries, BBC-TV, 1974—; including Rubens, Bernini, The Shock of the New, BBC-TV; author: The Art of Australia, 1966, Heaven and Hell in Western Art, 1970. Office: Time Mag Room 2673 Time-Life Bldg Rockefeller Center New York NY 10020 *

HUGHES, SARAH TILGHMAN, judge; b. Balt., Aug. 2, 1896; d. James Cooke and Elizabeth (Haughton) Tilghman; m. George E. Hughes, Mar. 13, 1922. A.B., Goucher Coll., 1917, LL.D., 1950; LL.B., George Washington U., 1922, LL.D., 1977; LL.D., So. Meth. U., Ind. State U., 1967, Wesleyan Coll., 1969, Mary Hardin-Baylor Coll., 1974; L.H.D., Clarkson Coll., 1975. Bar: Tex. 1922. Tchr. Salem Acad. and Coll., Winston-Salem, N.C., 1917-19; police woman Met. Police Dept. Washington, 1919-22; practiced in, Dallas, 1922-35; mem. Tex. Legislature, 1931-35; judge 14th Dist. Ct. of Tex., 1935-61, U.S. Dist. Ct., No. Dist. Tex., 1961—, now sr. judge. Active Nat. Fedn. Bus. and Profl. Women's Clubs, 1931—, 1st. v.p., 1948-50, pres., 1950-52; v.p. Internat. Fedn. Bus. and Profl. Women, 1953-59; Past trustee Goucher Coll., Bishop Coll. Mem. State Bar of Tex., Am., Dallas bar assns., Am. Judicature Soc., Nat. Assn. Women Lawyers, AAUW, Phi Beta Kappa, Delta Sigma Rho, Kappa Beta Pi, Delta Gamma, Delta Kappa Gamma (hon.). Democrat. Episcopalian. Home: 3816 Normandy St Dallas TX 75205 Office: US Dist Court 1100 Commerce St Room 13E21 Dallas TX 75242 *

HUGHES, STANLEY JOHN, mycologist; b. Llanelli, S. Wales, Sept. 17, 1918; emigrated to Can., 1952, naturalized, 1967; s. John Thomas and Gertrude (Roberts) H.; m. Lyndell Anne Rutherford, Oct. 11, 1958; children—Robert Conway, Glenys Anne, David Stanley. B.Sc. with honors, U. Wales, Aberystwyth, 1941, M.Sc., 1943, D.Sc., 1954. Asst. to adv. mycologist Nat. Agrl. Advisory Ser. U. Wales, 1941-45; asst. mycologist Commonwealth Mycological Inst., Kew, Eng., 1945-52; mycologist Research br. Agr. Can. Central Exptl. Farm, Ottawa, Ont., 1952-58, sr. mycologist, 1958-62, prin. mycologist, 1962—; Sr. research fellow New Zealand Dept. Sci. and Indsl. Research, 1963; Exchange scientist Nat. Research Councils of Can. and Brazil, 1974. Contbr. articles in field to profl. jours. Recipient Jakob Eriksson Gold medal, 1969; George Lawson medal, 1981. Fellow Royal Soc. Can., Linnean Soc. London; mem. Mycological Soc. Am. (pres. 1975), British Mycological Soc., Internat. Mycological Assn. (v.p. 1977—). Mem. United Ch. of Can. (elder). Home: 360 Hamilton Ave Ottawa ON K1Y 1C5 Canada Office: Biosystematics Research Institute Central Experimental Farm Ottawa ON K1A 0C6 Canada

HUGHES, SUE MARGARET, librarian; b. Cleburne, Tex., Apr. 13; d. Chastain Wesley and Sue Willis (Payne) H. B.B.A., U. Tex., Austin, 1949; M.L.S., Tex. Woman's U., 1960, doctoral candidate, 1983—. Sec.-treas. pvt. corps., Waco, Tex., 1949-59; asst. in public services Baylor U. Library, Waco, 1960-64, acquisitions librarian, 1964-79, acting univ. librarian, summer 1979; librarian Moody Library, 1980—. Mem. AAUP, ALA, Southwestern Library Assn., Tex. Library Assn., AAUW, Delta Kappa Gamma, Beta Phi Mu, Beta Gamma Sigma. Methodist. Club: Altrusa. Office: Box 6307 Waco TX 76706

HUGHES, TED, poet, author; b. 1930; s. William Henry and Edith (Farrar) H.; m. Sylvia Plath, 1956 (dec. 1963); 2 children; m. Carol Orchard, 1970. Student, Pembroke Coll., Cambridge (Eng.) U. Author: The Hawk in the Rain, 1957, Lupercal, 1960; (children's poems) Meet My Folks, 1961, The Earth-Owl and Other Moon People, 1963; (children's stories) How the Whale Became, 1963; Wodwo, 1967, Poetry in the Making, 1967, The Iron Man, 1968, Crow Wakes, 1970, A Few Crows, 1970, Crow, 1971, Eat Crow, 1971, Shakespeare's Poems, 1971, Prometheus on His Crag, 1973, Spring, Summer, Autumn, Winter, 1974, Season Songs, 1975, Cave Birds, 1976, Moon-Whales & Other Poems, 1976, Gaudete, 1977, Remains of Elmet, 1979, Moortown, 1980, Under the North Star, 1981, New Selected Poems, 1982; editor: A Choice of Emily Dickinson's Verse, 1968, A Choice of Shakespeare's Verse, 1971; joint editor: Five American Poets, 1963, Selected Poems of Keith Douglas, 1964; contbr. poems to leading mags. Recipient 1st prize Guinness Poetry awards, 1958; Somerset Maugham award, 1960; Hawthornden prize, 1961; Premio Internazionale Taormina, 1973; Queen's medal for Poetry, 1974; Guggenheim fellow, 1959-60. Address: care Harper & Row 10 E 53d St New York NY 10022 *

HUGHES, TERRY T., publishing company executive; b. Auckland, N.Z., Feb. 23, 1941; came to U.S., 1980; s. William Edward and Lynette Caroline (Bridge) H.; m. Beverly Joy Lincoln, Jan. 12, 1966; children: Glenn Anthony, Amanda Lynette. Student, U. Auckland. Mng. dir. Ashton Scholastic, Auckland, 1962-80, Gosford, Australia, 1968-80; internat. v.p. Scholastic Inc., N.Y.C., 1980—, exec. v.p., 1981—, pres., Toronto, Ont., Can., 1980—; dir. Ashton Scholastic, Australia and N.Z., 1962—, Scholastic Publs., London, 1980—, Lesen und Freizet, Rauensburg, Germany, 1981—. Sec. Boystown Police and Citizens Club, Auckland, 1962-68. Fellow Australian Inst. Mgmt., Co. Dirs. Australia; mem. Australian Book Pubs. Assn. (v.p. 1976-80), Am. Assn. Pubs. (internat. exec. 1980—). Home: 61 Studio Rd Stamford CT 06903 Office: Scholastic Inc 730 Broadway New York NY 10003

HUGHES, THOMAS H., company executive; b. Muncie, Ind., Feb. 23, 1929; s. Ray Myers and Dorothy (Stewart) H.; m. Judy A. Manning, Aug. 26, 1956; children: Theodore M., Elizabeth. B.S., Ind. U., 1951. Dir. mktg. Zimmer, Inc., subs. Bristol Myers, Warsaw, Ind., 1964-67, 1967-68, v.p. mktg., 1968-71, exec. v.p., 1971-79, pres., 1979—; sr. v.p. Bristol Myers. Mem. Health Industries Mfrs. Assn. (dir. 1979-82, 83). Republican. Home: Rural Route 2 PO Box 242 Warsaw IN 46580 Office: Zimmer Inc PO Box 708 Warsaw IN 46580

HUGHES, THOMAS JOSEPH, naval officer; b. Bklyn., Oct. 14, 1926; s. Thomas Joseph and Margaret (Dennigan) H.; m. Hazel Martha Köblitz, Feb. 18, 1948; children—Thomas, Alexander, Kevin, Theresa, Kathleen, Patricia, Mark, Michael. B.S., Harvard U., 1946; M.S., U.S. Naval Postgrad. Sch., 1962. Commd. ensign U.S. Navy, 1946, advanced through grades to vice adm., 1983, service in Korea and Vietnam; comdr. Destroyer Squadron 36 Destroyer Squadron 36 (U.S. Navy), 1971-72; comdr. Service Group 2 Service Group 2 (U.S. Navy), Atlantic and Mediterranean, 1976—; pres. Navy Fed. Credit Union, 1975-76, bd. dirs., 1978—; bd. govs. Navy Mut. Aid Assn., 1976. Decorated Legion of Merit (5), Bronze Star, Joint Commendation medal (2); Cross of Gallantry with gold star, Vietnam). Mem. Sigma Xi. Roman Cath. Club: Lions. Home: Quarters DD US Naval Station Washington DC 20374 Office: DCNO (Logistics) (OP-04) Washington DC 20350

HUGHES, THOMAS JOSEPH, mechanical engineering educator, consultant; b. Bklyn., Aug. 3, 1943; s. Joseph Anthony and Mae (Bland) H.; m. Susan Elizabeth Weh, July 1, 1972; children: Emily Susan, Ian Thomas, Elizabeth Claire. B.M.E., Pratt Inst., Bklyn., 1965, M.M.E., 1967; M.A. in Math., U. Calif.-Berkeley, 1974; Ph.D. in Engring. Sci., U. Calif.-Berkeley, 1974. Mech. design engr. Grumman Aerospace, Bethpage, N.Y., 1965-66; research and devel. engr. Gen. Dynamics, Groton, Conn., 1967-69; lectr., asst. research engr. U. Calif.-Berkeley, 1975-76; assoc. prof. structural mechanics Calif. Inst. Tech., Pasadena, 1976-80; assoc. prof. mech. engring. Stanford U., Calif., 1980-82, prof., 1983—; cons. in field. Author: A Short Course in Fluid Mechanics, 1976, Mathematical Foundations of Elasticity, 1983; editor: Nonlinear Finite Element Analysis of Plate and Shells, 1981, Computational Methods in Transient Analysis, 1983, Jour. of Computer Methods in Applied Mechanics and Engring., 1980—; contbr. numerous articles to profl. jours. Fellow Am. Acad. Mechanics; mem. ASME (Melville medal 1979), ASCE (Huber prize 1978), AIAA, Soc. Engring. Sci., Sigma Xi, Phi Beta Kappa. Office: Stanford U Div Applied Mechanics Durand Bldg Stanford CA 94305

HUGHES, THOMAS LOWE, foundation executive; b. Mankato, Minn., Dec. 11, 1925; s. Evan Raymond and Alice (Lowe) H.; m. Jean Hurlburt Reiman, May 7, 1955; children: Thomas Evan, Allan Cameron. B.A. summa cum laude, Carleton Coll., 1947, L.H.D. (hon.), 1974; B.Phil. in Politics (Rhodes scholar), Balliol Coll., Oxford (Eng.) U., 1949; J.D., Yale U., 1952; student, U. Minn. Law Sch.; LL.D. (hon.), Washington Coll., 1973, Denison U., 1980, H.H.D., Washington and Jefferson Coll., 1979. Bar: Minn. 1952, U.S. Supreme Ct. 1960, U.S. Dist. Ct. D.C. 1968. Profl. staff mem. U.S. Senate Subcom. on Labor and Labor-Mgmt. Relations, Com. on Labor and Pub. Welfare, 1951-52; asso. prof. polit. sci. and internat. relations U. So. Calif., 1953, Trinity Coll., Tex., 1954, George Washington U., 1957-58; exec. sec. to gov. of Conn., 1954-55; legis. counsel Sen. Hubert Humphrey, 1955-58; adminstrv. asst. U.S. Rep. Chester Bowles, 1959-60; spl. asst. to under sec. state Dept. State, 1961, dep. dir. intelligence and research, 1961-63, dir. intelligence and research with rank of asst. sec. state, 1963-69; minister, dep. chief mission Am. embassy, London, 1969-70; planning and coordination staff Dept. State, 1970-71; pres., trustee Carnegie Endowment for Internat. Peace, 1971—; former chmn. nuclear proliferation and safeguards adv. panel Office Tech. Assessment, Congress U.S. Chmn. editorial bd.: Fgn. Policy Mag.; contbr. articles to nat. periodicals. Trustee, sec. German Marshall Fund U.S., 1972-82; trustee Civilian-Mil. Inst.; bd. dirs. Arms Control Assn.; mem. Trilateral Commn., 1973-83; former bd. govs. Ditchley Found., Eng.; vis. com. Center for Internat. Studies, Harvard U., 1971-76; bd. visitors Sch. Fgn. Service, Georgetown U.; mem. adv. council Woodrow Wilson Sch., Princeton U.; mem. adv. bd. Fundacion Luis Munoz Marin, San Juan, P.R.; chmn. U.S.-U.K. Bicentennial Fellowships Com. on Arts, 1975-78; trustee Social Sci. Found., U. Denver; mem. sponsoring com. Hubert H. Humphrey Inst. Pub. Affairs; staff dir. platform com. Democratic Nat. Conv., 1960. Served to maj. JAGC, USAF, 1952-54. Mem. N.Y. Council Fgn. Relations, Inst. Strategic Studies London (trustee Am. com.), Am. Assn. Rhodes Scholars, Am. Polit. Sci. Assn., Am. Soc. Internat. Law, ABA, Atlantic Council U.S., Am. Acad. Polit. and Social Sci. (trustee), Fgn. Policy Assn., Internat. Studies Assn., Washington Inst. Fgn. Affairs, Oxford-Cambridge Assn. Washington (former chmn.), UN Assn., Phi Beta Kappa, Phi Delta Phi. Episcopalian. Clubs: Mid-Atlantic (chmn.), Cosmos (Washington); Century (N.Y.C.); Oxford (Eng.) Union. Home: 5636 Western Ave Chevy Chase MD 20815 Office: 11 Dupont Circle NW Washington DC 20036

HUGHES, THOMAS PARKE, history educator; b. Richmond, Va., Sept. 13, 1923; s. Hunter Russell and Mary Bronaugh (Quisenberry) H.; m. Agatha Chipley, Aug. 7, 1948; children: Thomas P. (dec.), Agatha H., Lucian P. B.M.E., U. Va., 1947, Ph.D., 1953. Instr. U. Va., Charlottesville, 1951-54; asst. prof. history Sweet Briar (Va.) Coll., 1954-56; asso. prof. history Washington and Lee U., Lexington, Va., 1956-63, M.I.T., Cambridge, 1963-66; vis. asso. prof. history Johns Hopkins U., Balt., 1966-69; prof. history Inst. Tech., So. Meth. U., Dallas, 1969-73; mem. faculty U. Pa., Phila., 1973—, prof. history and sociology of sci., 1973—. Author: Elmer Sperry: Inventor and Engineer, 1971 (Dexter prize), Networks of Power: Electrification in Western Society, 1880-1930, 1983; Gen. editor: Studies in History of Technology. Served to lt. (j.g.) USN, 1943-46. Fulbright postdoctoral fellow, Germany, 1958-59; NSF fellow, 1975; Rockefeller Found. fellow, 1975; Council Learned Socs.-Smithsonian fellow, 1969; Social Sci. Research Council fellow, 1972. Mem. Soc. History of Tech. (pres. 1978-80), History of Sci. Soc. (council 1976-79), Am. Acad. Arts and Scis., Phi Beta Kappa. Club: Cosmos (Washington). Office: E F Smith Hall D6 U Pa Philadelphia PA 19104

HUGHES, VESTER THOMAS, JR., lawyer; b. San Angelo, Tex., May 24, 1928; s. Vester Thomas and Mary Ellen (Tisdale) H. Student, Baylor U., 1945-46; B.A. with distinction, Rice U., 1949; LL.B. cum laude, Harvard U., 1952. Bar: Tex. bar 1952. Law clk. U.S. Supreme Ct., 1952; asso. firm Jackson, Walker, Winstead, Cantwell & Miller (and predecessors), Dallas, 1955-58, partner, 1958-76; partner firm

Hughes & Hill (and predecessor), 1976—; dir. Exell Cattle Co., LX Cattle Co., Stewart Systems Inc., Murphy Oil Corp., Cook Data Services, Inc., Austin Industries, Inc., First Nat. Bank Mertzon; Tax counsel Communities Found. of Tex., Inc. Bd. dirs. Larry and Jane Harlan Found.; trustee Dallas Bapt. Coll., 1967-77; trustee, exec. com. Tex. Scottish Rite Hosp. for Crippled Children; bd. overseers vis. com. Harvard Law Sch., 1969-75. Served to lt. AUS, 1952-55. Mem. Am. Bar Assn. (council sect. taxation 1969-72), Am. Law Inst. (council 1966—), Phi Beta Kappa, Sigma Xi. Baptist. Clubs: Masons (33 deg.), Order Eastern Star.). Home: 1222 Commerce St Dallas TX 75202 Office: 1000 Mercantile Dallas Bldg Dallas TX 75201

HUGHES, WALTER THOMPSON, JR., physician; b. Cleveland, Tenn., May 16, 1930; s. Walter Thompson and Millie Hassentine (Collett) H.; m. Frances Jeannette Skinner, Nov. 27, 1957; children: Carla Lynne, Gregory Stephen, Christopher Blake. Student, Tenn. Poly. Inst., 1948-50; M.D., U. Tenn., 1954. Diplomate: Am. Bd. Pediatrics. Mem. faculty U. Louisville Med. Sch., 1960-69; prof. pediatrics and microbiology U. Tenn. Med. Sch., 1969-77; prof. pediatrics U. Tenn. Ctr. for Health Scis., 1981—; dir. div. infectious diseases, chmn. dept. child health scis. St. Jude Children's Research Hosp., Memphis, 1969-77, 81—; dir. div. infectious diseases Johns Hopkins U. Med. Sch., Balt., 1981, prof. pediatrics, 1977-81. Contbr. articles to med. jours. Served to capt. M.C. AUS, 1957-59. Fellow Am. Acad. Pediatrics; mem. Soc. Pediatric Research, Infectious Disease Soc. Am., Am. Pediatric Soc., Am. Soc. Microbiology. Methodist.

HUGHES, WILLIAM ANTHONY, bishop; b. Youngstown, Ohio, Sept. 23, 1921; s. James Francis and Anna Marie (Philbin) H. Degree, St. Charles Sem., Balt., St. Mary's Sem., Cleve.; M.A. in Edn, Notre Dame U., 1956. Ordained priest Roman Catholic Ch., 1946; pastor chs. in, Boardman and Massillon, Ohio, 1946-55; prin. Cardinal Mooney High Sch., Youngstown, 1956-65; supt. schs. Diocese of Youngstown, 1965-72, episcopal vicar of edn., 1972-73, vicar gen., 1973-74; aux. bishop, 1974-79, bishop of, Covington, Ky., 1979—. Address: 1140 Madison St PO Box 192 Covington KY 41012

HUGHES, WILLIAM FRANK, mechanical and electrical engineering educator; b. Ash, N.C., Oct. 20, 1930; s. Olan T. and Elma (Frink) H.; m. Jane Thomas, June 27, 1959 (div. 1971); children: Christopher T., Eric Olan; m. Sue Evans, Jan. 1, 1979. B.S., Carnegie Inst. Tech., 1952; M.S., 1953; Ph.D., 1955. NSF postdoctoral fellow Cambridge (Eng.) U., 1957-58; mem. faculty Carnegie-Mellon U., Pitts., 1955—, prof. mech. and elec. engring., 1966—, co-ordinator space scis. program, 1963—; Fulbright lectr. U. Sydney, Australia, 1963. Author: (with F.J. Young) Electromagnetodynamics of Fluids, 1966; also articles. Mem. Am. Soc. M.E., Am. Phys. Soc., Am. Geophys. Union, Soc. Automotive Engrs., Sigma Xi, Tau Beta Pi, Pi Tau Sigma, Phi Kappa Phi. Research in magneto-fluid mechanics, lubrication and friction, space scis., fluid mechanics. Home: RD 3 Cambridge Springs PA 16403

HUGHES, WILLIAM FRANKLIN, JR., ophthalmologist, emeritus educator; b. Indpls., Apr. 18, 1913; s. William F. and Alta (Rentschler) H.; m. Wanema Dickey, June 28, 1941 (dec. 1969); children: William Franklin III, Jacqueline Alter, Sarah Lee; m. Jane M. Stockdale, 1970. A.B., Amherst Coll., 1934; M.D., Johns Hopkins, 1938. Diplomate: Am. Bd. Ophthalmology (mem. 1968-80). Intern, asst. resident and resident in ophthalmology Johns Hopkins, 1938-44, asst. prof. ophthalmology, 1944-46, research work, 1941-46; pvt. practice in ophthalmology Ind. U. Sch. of Medicine, 1946-47; prof. ophthalmology U. Ill., 1947—, head dept., 1947-58; ophthalmologist-in-chief Research and Ednl. Hosps. and Ill. Eye and Ear Infirmary, 1947-58; chmn. dept. ophthalmology Presbyn.-St. Luke's Hosp., Chgo., 1956-79; prof. ophthalmology Rush Med. Coll., 1971-81, prof. emeritus, 1981—; past mem. ophthalmology com. NRC. Author: Office Management of Ocular Diseases, 1953; Mem. editorial bds.: Archives of Ophthalmology, 1951-62, 81—; editor: Year Book Ophthalmology, 1959-81; Contbr. articles on chem. burns of eyes, cataract extraction, beta irradiation, retinal detachment, corneal diseases and corneal transplantation. Mem. AMA, Assn. Research in Ophthalmology (trustee 1949-55), Am. Ophthal. Soc. (council 1971-76, pres. 1981), Chgo. Ophthal. Soc. (past pres.), Inst. of Med. Chgo., Billings Med. Club of Chgo. (pres. 1965), Sigma Xi, Alpha Kappa Kappa, Phi Kappa Psi. Club: University (Chgo.). Home: 4 Court of Mohawk Valley Lincolnshire IL 60015

HUGHES, WILLIAM JOHN, congressman; b. Salem, N.J., Oct. 17, 1932; s. William W. and Pauline H.; m. Nancy L. Gibson; children: Nancy Lynne, Barbara Ann, Tama Beth, William John. A.B., Rutgers U., 1955, J.D., 1958. Bar: N.J. 1959. Since practiced in, Ocean City; mem. firm Loveland, Hughes & Garrett; 1st asst. pros. atty., Cape May County, N.J., 1960-70; mem. 94th-98th Congresses from 2d N.J. Dist. Bd. dirs. Cape May County Drug Abuse Council, 1968—; bd. govs. Shore Meml. Hosp., Sommers Point, N.J., 1972-76. Mem. Ocean City Hist. Soc. (dir. 1972-76), Ocean City C. of C. (dir. 1960—). Clubs: Exchange of Ocean City (pres. 1965-66, Nat. Big E. award 1965), Masons (past master lodge). Home: 1019 Wesley Rd Ocean City NJ 08226 Office: 341 Cannon House Office Bldg Washington DC 20515

HUGHES, WILLIAM LEWIS, electrical engineer, educator; b. Rapid City, S.D., Dec. 2, 1926; s. Clarence William and Newell (Chase) H.; m. Stella Marie Platt, June 9, 1950; children: Elizabeth Helen, James Edward, Judith Lee, Michael George. B.S. in Elec. Engring, S.D. Sch. Mines and Tech., 1949; M.S., Iowa State U., 1950, Ph.D., 1952. Broadcast and TV engr., 1946-49; mem. faculty Iowa State U., 1949-60; prof. elec. engring., 1959-60; prof. elec. engring., head Sch. Elec. Engring., Okla. State U., Stillwater, 1960-76, Clark A. Dunn prof. engring., 1976—, dir. Engring. Energy Lab., 1976—; chmn. ad hoc com. Nat. Acad. Scis., 1976, 79, mem. bd. sci. and tech. in devel., 1983; chmn. Nat. Acad. Scis./Philippine Govt. del. to, Philippines, 1978, Indonesia, 1979; cons. industry and govt.; mem. indsl. com. TV frequency allocation studies FCC, 1957-59. Author: Nonlinear electrical Networks, 1960; also articles; co-author: Lines, Waves and Antennas, 1961, 2d edit., 1973. Served with USNR, World War II. Fellow IEEE; mem. Am. Soc. Engring. Edn., Sigma Xi, Sigma Tau, Tau Beta Pi, Eta Kappa Nu, Pi Mu Epsilon. Patentee nonlinear systems, color TV systems, direct energy conversions systems. Home: Rural Route 1 Box 133 AA Stillwater OK 74074

HUGHES, WILLIAM NOLIN, educator; b. Raymond, Wash., May 21, 1918; s. William Garfield and Rhea (Cheshire) H.; m. Diane Krueger, Aug. 23, 1953; children—Megan Rhea, Michael William, William Richard. B.A., U. Wash., 1941; M.A., Northwestern U., 1952, Ph.D., 1955. Staff writer, pub. relations Boeing Aircraft Co., Seattle, 1941-46; asst. to labor adviser U.S. Element, Allied Commn. for Austria and ECA, Vienna, 1946-50; instr. German U. Mich., 1955-60; asst. prof. German Columbia, 1960-63; asso. prof. German Mich. State U., East Lansing, 1963-65, prof. German, chmn. dept. German and Russian, 1965-75, asst. dean, 1975-79, prof. German, 1979—. Contbr. articles to profl. jours.; sect. head: German lit. MLA Bibliography, 1980—. Mem. MLA, Mich. Fgn. Lang. Assn. (past pres.), Internat. Arthur Schnitzler Gesellschaft, Thomas Mann Gesellschaft, Delta Phi Alpha. Home: 513 Ardson Rd East Lansing MI 48823

HUGHES, WILLIAM TAYLOR, physicist, educator; b. Vidor, Tex., Nov. 15, 1936; s. Clarence and Lura (Bunch) H.; m. Ann Greenway Montgomery, June 15, 1965; 1 son, Thomas Abbott. B.S., MA., Ind. U., 1960; Ph.D., Northwestern U., 1967. With Smithsonian Instn., Washington, 1958-59; sr. staff NASA Satellite Sta., Curacao, 1958-59; instr. U. Mo., Columbus, 1963-64; asst. prof. U. W.Va., Charleston, 1964-66; prof. physics and astronomy Bowdoin Coll., Brunswick, Maine, 1967—, head dept., 1972-76; tech. cons. Mem. Gov.'s Adv. Com. on Reactor Safety. Author: Microbiology, 1978, Aspects of Biophysics, 1979; articles. NASA fellow; grantee NSF, Am. Heart Assn., Hearst Found., Am. Cancer Soc. Fellow Royal Astron. Soc. Home: 8 McKeen St Brunswick ME 04011 Office: Bowdoin College Brunswick ME 04011

HUGHLETT, ROBERT BROOKS, dentist; b. Grand Junction, Colo., Apr. 16, 1918; s. Hugh Brooks and Fern (Fancher) H.; m. Doris Nelms, Sept. 10, 1939; children: Marjorie, James, Carolyn, Patricia, Pamela. Student, U. Tampa, 1936-38; D.D.S., U. Tenn., 1942. Dental cons. Ala. Health Dept., 1942-43; gen. practice dentistry, Tampa, Fla., 1946—; pres. Hillsborough County Dental Research Clinic, 1954; mem. Fla. Bd. Dental Examiners, 1952-56; pres. Hughlett & Garrett, Inc., Tampa, 1959; v.p. Fla. Dental Services, Inc., 1972—. Pres. Pemberton Creek, Inc.; gen. partner Pemberton Creek 1st Addition Ltd. Served to lt. USNR, 1943-46. Recipient Faculty medal U. Tenn., 1942. Fellow Am. Coll. Dentists, Internat. Coll. Dentists; mem. ADA, Fla. Dental Assn. (pres. 1971-72, chmn. council legislation 1956-69, Dentist of Year award 1965, Service award 1977), West Coast Dental Soc., Hillsborough County Dental Soc., Omicron Kappa Upsilon. Home: 1701 Park Circle Tampa FL 33610 Office: 5420 Florida Ave Tampa FL 33604

HUGHS, RICHARD EARL, university administrator; b. Rochester, N.Y., Jan. 2, 1936; s. Earl Leaman and Frances Rose H.; m. Gretchen Markwardt, Mar. 31, 1959; children—Mark Allen, Grant Evan. B.S. in Physics, U. Rochester, 1957; M.S. in Math, Purdue U., 1959, Ph.D., 1962. Systems analyst Sandia Corp., Albuquerque, 1962-64; asst. prof. Carleton Coll., 1964-66; pres. Math. Service Assos., Inc., Edwardsville, Ill., 1966-69; asso. prof. applied math. and info. systems So. Ill. U., 1966-69; sr. cons. Cresap, McCormick & Paget, Inc., 1968-70; assoc. dean Grad. Sch. Bus. Adminstrn., N.Y. U., 1970-77; dean Coll. Bus. Adminstrn., U. Nev., Reno, 1977—; dir. Sierra Pacific Power Co., Inc., Sierra Energy Co., Inc., Lands of Sierra, Inc.; bd. dirs. Nev. World Trade and Tourism Assn., Nev. Ins. Edn. Found., Nev. Council Econ. Edn.; mem. com. on edn. C. of C. and Industry N.Y.C., 1970-74; mem. adv. com. Medgar Evers Coll., City U. N.Y., 1971-74; NSF research fellow Purdue U., 1958-60. Mem. deferred compensation com., State of Nev., 1978—. Mem. Inst. Mgmt. Scis., Acad. Mgmt., Western Indsl. Nev., Nev. Fin. Soc. (pres. 1981—), Western Assn. Collegiate Schs. Bus. (dir.), Sigma Xi, Beta Gamma Sigma. Club: Rotary (Reno). Office: Coll Bus Adminstrn U Nev Reno NV 89557

HUGHS, ROBERT NATHANIEL, insurance company executive; b. Atlanta, Oct. 10, 1917; s. William Denson and Susan (Flynn) H.; m. Maria Dendy Maret, Sept. 13, 1947; children: Mariah Dency, Sara Susan, Robert III. Student, Emory U., 1935-36. Mgr. S.E. dept. Asso. Aviation Underwriters, Atlanta, 1946-49; sr. v.p., dir. No. Ins. Co., N.Y.C., 1949-66; v.p. Am. Home Assurance Co., N.Y.C., 1969-72; pres., dir. Nat. Union Fire Ins. Co., Pitts., 1969-72, Integrity Ins. Co. N.J., 1972-76; pres. Beaufort Ins. Agy., S.C., 1978—. Served to capt. USAAF, 1941-46. Home: 32 Wade Hampton Dr Beaufort SC 29902 Office: 501 Lady's Island Dr Beaufort SC 29902

HUGO, VICTOR JOSEPH, JR., army officer; b. Beverly, Mass., May 28, 1931; s. Victor Joseph and Helen Bernadette (Box) H.; m. Jean Carolyn Duff, Apr. 27, 1957; children: Elizabeth Jean, Victor III, Russell. B.S., U.S. Mil. Acad., 1954; M.S. in Internat. Affairs, George Washington U., 1966, U. So. Calif., 1978. Commd. 2d lt. U.S. Army, 1954, advanced through grades to maj. gen., served with, Asia, 1955-56, 62-65, 68-69, 79-81; staff Joint Chiefs Staff, 1966-68, Army Staff, 1970-81; dir. mgmt. Dept. Army, 1981-83; comdg. gen. 32d AADCOM, Europe, 1983—. Active youth athletics, including Amateur Hockey Assn. U.S. Decorated Leion of Merit, Bronze Star with oak leaf cluster, Air medal with oak leaf cluster, others. Mem. Assn. Grads. U.S. Mil. Acad., Alumni Assn. Naval War Coll., Alumni Assn. George Washington U., Alumni Assn. U. So. Calif. Roman Catholic. Office: CG 32d AADCOM APO New York NY 09175

HUGON, JEAN SYLVAIN, physician; b. Brussels, Feb. 5, 1927; s. Sylvain and Helene (Desmeth) H.; m. Elizabeth Renaud, Sept., 1962. M.D., U. Louvain. Physician, Foreami, Belgian Congo, 1951-58, head dept. ob-gyn, Leopoldville, Belgian Congo, 1958-60; staff dept. radiobiology Belgium Nuclear Center, Mol, Belgium, 1960-68; staff dept. pathology Med. Center, Sherbrooke, Que., Can., 1968-75; chmn. dept. anatomy and cell biology U. Sherbrooke, 1975—. Mem. Am. Assn. Anatomists, Can. Assn. Anatomists, N.Y. Acad. Sci., Am. Soc. Cell Biology, Société Française de Microscopie Electronique, Cell and Tissue Culture Soc. Office: Faculty of Medicine U Sherbrooke Sherbrooke J1H 5N4 Canada *

HUGSTAD, PAUL STEVEN, educator; b. Hutchinson, Minn., Sept. 20, 1943; s. Alfred John and Elsie Elizabeth (Longergan) H.; m. Wendelyn Kay Lindbeck, Aug. 22, 1970; children: Erik Steven, Jonathan Paul. B.A., St. Olaf Coll., 1965; M.B.A., U. Ariz., 1967; Ph.D., U. Wis., 1970. Research and teaching fellow U. Wis., 1967-70; asso. prof. bus. adminstrn. U. Alta., Edmonton, 1970-73, asso. prof., 1973-77; economist FDA, Washington; also vis. prof. Am. U., Washington, 1977-78; prof. bus. adminstrn. Calif. State U., Fullerton, 1978—. Author: The Business School in the 1980s, 1983; Contbr. articles on bus. and edn. to profl. jours. HEW Fed. faculty fellow, 1977. Mem. World Future Soc., Am. Council Consumer Interests, Am. Mktg. Assn., Assn. Consumer Research, Acad. Mktg. Scis., Am. Inst. Decision Scis. Republican. Lutheran. Office: Mktg Dept Calif State U Fullerton CA 92634

HUGUS, Z. ZIMMERMAN, JR., educator; b. Washington, Aug. 14, 1923; s. Z Zimmerman and Marguerite (Weaver) H.; m. Nancy Anne Regin, June 25, 1947; children—Carily, Z Zimmerman III, Richard Regin, Patricia Helen Hugus Dale. B.A., Williams Coll., 1943; Ph.D., U. Calif. at Berkeley, 1949. Research fellow, instr. U. Calif. at Berkeley, 1949-52; mem. faculty U. Minn., 1952-67; prof., chief inorganic chemistry, 1963-67; prof. N.C. State U., Raleigh, 1967—, head dept. chemistry, 1967-73. Served with USNR, 1944-46. Fellow AAAS; mem. Am. Chem. Soc., N.C. Acad. Sci., Phi Beta Kappa, Sigma Xi, Phi Lambda Upsilon, Phi Kappa Phi, Alpha Chi Sigma, Phi Delta Theta. Home: 1201 Glen Eden Dr Raleigh NC 27612

HUHN, HOWARD ARTHUR, engineering educator; b. Pitts., Dec. 6, 1940; s. Howard E. and Selma S. (Schulze) Kuhn; m. Beverly A. Burke, Dec.l 23, 1961; children: Jeffrey, Amy, David, Stephen. B.S., Carnegie-Mellon U., 1962, M.S., 1963, Ph.D., 1966. Registered profl. engr., Pa. Prof. engring. Drexel U., Phila., 1966-74, U. Pitts., 1975—; cons. engr. Deformation Control Tech., Pitts., 1980—. Editor: Powder Metallurgy Processing, 1978; inventor powder metallurgy forging. Pres. PTA, Gibsonia, Pa., 1976-77, Richland Athletic Assn., Gibsonia, 1977-79; mem. civic adv. com., Gibsonia, 1978-82. Mem. ASME, Am. Soc. for Metals, Am. Powder Metallurgy Inst. Republican. Methodist. Home: 5408 Peace Dr Gibsonia PA 15044 Office: Univ Pitts 848 Benedum Hall Pittsburgh PA 15261

HUIE, IRVING RAYMOND, constrn. co. exec.; b. Catskill, N.Y., Sept. 30, 1928; s. Irving V.A. and Irene G. (Gartl) H.; m. Patricia Cronin, Mar. 27, 1955; children—Michael, Barbara, Terence, Peter, James, Eileen, Patricia, Kevin. B.C.E., Rensellaer Poly. Inst., Troy, N.Y., 1950; postgrad., Northwestern U. From engr. to v.p. Petrini Corp., Framingham, Mass., 1959-81, sr. v.p. heavy constrn., 1981—, also dir. Served with C.E. AUS, 1950-53. Mem. ASCE, Am. Soc. Mil. Engrs. Democrat. Roman Catholic. *

HUIE, WILLIAM BRADFORD, author; b. Hartselle, Ala., Nov. 13, 1910; s. John Bradford and Margaret Lois (Brindley) H.; m. Ruth Puckett, Oct. 27, 1934 (dec.); m. Martha Hunt Robertson, July 16, 1977. A.B., U. Ala., 1930. Author: Mud on the Stars, 1942, The Fight for Air Power, 1942, Can Do: The Story of the Seabees, 1944, From Omaha to Okinawa, 1945, The Case Against the Admirals, 1946, The Revolt of Mamie Stover, 1951, The Execution of Private Slovik, 1954, The Crime of Ruby McCollum, 1956, Wolf Whistle, 1959, The Americanization of Emily, 1959, The Hero of Iwo Jima, 1960, Hotel Mamie Stover, 1963, The Hiroshima Pilot, 1964, Three Lives for Mississippi, 1965, The Klansman, 1967, He Slew the Dreamer, 1969, In the Hours of Night, 1975, A New Life to Live, 1978, It's Me, O Lord!, 1979, The Ray of Hope, 1984, To Live and Die in Dixie, 1985; also numerous mag. articles and stories. Mem. Phi Beta Kappa. Home: PO Box 248 Hartselle AL 35640

HUIE, WILLIAM ORR, legal educator; b. Arkadelphia, Ark., Sept. 15, 1911; s. Robert W., Jr. and Minnie Belle (Smith) H.; m. Hugh Mae Wolff, Aug. 27, 1935 (dec. Jan. 1970); m. Grace E. Bishop, June 10, 1972. B.A., Henderson (Ark.) State Tchrs. Coll., 1932; LL.B., U. Tex., 1935; S.J.D., Harvard U., 1953. Bar: Tex. 1935. Mem. faculty U. Tex. Law Sch., 1936—, prof. law, 1946—, Lang prof., 1965—; vis. prof. U. Calif.-Berkeley, summer 1956, UCLA, summer 1961, Harvard U., 1961-62; with firm Greenwood, Moody & Robertson, Austin, 1935-36; sr. atty. OPA, 1942-43. Contbr. articles to legal jours., also author casebooks. Served with USNR, 1943-46. Research fellow Harvard Law Sch., 1939-40. Mem. Chancellors, Order of Coif, Phi Delta Phi. Democrat. Methodist. Home: 3401 Barranca Circle Austin TX 78731 *A strong desire to do well whatever I undertake has been a primary motivating force in my life.*

HUIE, WILLIAM STELL, lawyer; b. College Park, Ga., Dec. 23, 1930; s. Wm. M. and Nannie Lou (Stell) H.; m. Madaline Johnson, June 26, 1953; children—Helen Claire, Sarah Fort. LL.B., Emory U., 1953. Bar: Ga. bar 1952. Since practiced in, Atlanta; partner firm Kutak Rock & Huie, 1978—; lectr. Emory U. Law Sch., 1957-60, 1959-68; dir. Am. Bus. Products, Inc. Chmn. bd. dirs. Ga. YMCA, 1967-70; chmn. bd. dirs. Atlanta Phi Delta Theta Alumni Club, pres., 1966; chmn. bd. visitors Emory U., 1980-81; trustee White House Preservation Fund, 1979-80; bd. dirs. Presbyn. Found., 1966-71, Westminster Schs. Served as 1st lt. Judge Adv. Gen. Corps AUS; Korea. Fellow Am. Bar Found.; mem. Nat. Conf. Bar Presidents (exec. council 1977-79), ABA, Ga. Bar Assn. (bd. govs., exec. com.; pres. 1975-76), Atlanta Bar Assn. (pres. 1968), Lawyers Club Atlanta, Am. Judicature Soc., Atlanta Lawyers Found., Bryan Soc., Atlanta Emory U. Alumni Club (past pres.), Atlanta C. of C. (past dir.), Phi Delta Theta, Phi Delta Phi, Omicron Delta Kappa. Presbyterian (elder, deacon). Home: 363 Manor Ridge Dr NW Atlanta GA 30305 Office: Standard Fed Bldg Atlanta GA 30303

HUITT, RALPH KINSLOE, educator; b. Corsicana, Tex., Jan. 8, 1913; s. John Delloyd and Birdie (Wright) H.; m. Winnie Mavis Smith, Jan. 8, 1938; children—Frank Smith, Cynthia Beth. A.B., Southwestern U., 1934, LL.D., 1972; Ph.D., U. Tex., 1950. Boys work sec. Beaumont (Tex.) YMCA, 1934-42; asst. prof. Lamar Coll., Beaumont, 1942-46; asst. prof. polit. sci. U. Wis., 1949-54, asso. prof., 1954-59, prof., 1959-65, 78—; legis. asst. to Sen. William Proxmire, 1958; asst. sec. for legislation U.S. Dept. HEW, Washington, 1965-69; guest scholar Brookings Instn., 1969; exec. dir. Nat. Assn. State Univs. and Land Grant Colls., Washington, 1970-78; vis. prof. U. Okla. Author: (with Robert L. Peabody) Congress: Two Decades of Analysis, 1969; Contbr. articles profl. jours. Mem. commn. on adminstrv. rev. U.S. Ho. of Reps., 1975-76. Served with USNR, 1943-46. Named distinguished alumnus Southwestern U., 1970; Fund for Advancement of Edn. fellow, 1953-54. Mem. Am. Polit. Sci. Assn. (exec. com. 1958-59, council 1957-59), Phi Delta Theta. Democrat. Methodist. Office: North Hall U Wis Madison WI 53706

HUIZENGA, JOHN ROBERT, nuclear chemist, educator; b. Fulton, Ill., Apr. 21, 1921; s. Harry M. and Josie B. (Brands) H.; m. Dorothy J. Koeze, Feb. 1, 1946; children—Linda J., Jann H., Robert J., Joel T. A.B., Calvin Coll., 1944; Ph.D., U. Ill., 1949. Lab. supr. Manhattan Wartime Project, Oak Ridge, 1944-46; instr. Calvin Coll., Grand Rapids, Mich., 1946-47; asso. scientist Argonne Nat. Lab., Chgo., 1949-57, sr. scientist, 1958-67; professorial lectr. chemistry U. Chgo., 1963-67; prof. chemistry and physics U. Rochester, 1967-78, Tracy H. Harris prof. chemistry and physics, 1978—, chmn. dept. chemistry, 1983—; vis. prof. Joliot-Curie Lab., U. Paris, 1964-65, Japan Soc. for Promotion of Sci., 1968; chmn. Nat. Acad. Sci.-NRC Com. on Nuclear Sci., 1974-77. Author: (with R. Vandenbosch) Nuclear Fission, 1973; Contbr. articles to profl. jours. Fulbright fellow, Netherlands, 1954-55; Guggenheim fellow, Paris, 1964-65, Berkeley, Calif., 1973, Munich, W.Ger., 1974, Copenhagen, 1974; recipient E.O. Lawrence award AEC, 1966; named Disting. Alumnus Calvin Coll., 1975. Fellow Am. Phys. Soc., AAAS; mem. Nat. Acad. Sci., Am. Chem. Soc. (award for nuclear applications in chemistry 1975), Phi Beta Kappa, Phi Kappa Phi, Sigma Xi. Home: 51 Huntington Meadow Rochester NY 14625 Office: Dept Chemistry U Rochester Rochester NY 14627

HUIZINGH, WILLIAM, educator; b. Grand Rapids, Mich., Jan. 6, 1919; s. John and Gertrude (Steenwyk) H.; m. Vera Marion Patron, June 7, 1948; m. Edith W. Krueger, Feb. 9, 1979. Student, Calvin Coll., 1935-38; B.S., U. Denver, 1952, M.B.A., 1954; Ph.D., U. Mich., 1963. Sec.-treas. Huizingh Furniture Co., Denver, 1945-56, pres., 1956-59; asst. prof. U. Denver, 1954-59; mem. faculty Ariz. State U., Tempe, 1959—, prof., 1965—, chmn. dept. acctg., 1964-69, dir., 1969-71, asso. dean, 1970-81. Author: Working Capital Classification, 1967; Contbg. editor: Accountants Handbook, 1970. Mem. Citizens Com. Auditing Recommendation for Ariz., Citizens' Com. Reorgn. of Finance Function Ariz. Served with USAAF, 1942-45. Decorated Bronze Star.; Ford Found. fellow, 1957-58; Arthur Andersen & Co. Found. fellow, 1962-63; recipient Merit cert. Nat. Assn. Accts., Merit medallion Beta Gamma Sigma. Mem. Am. Inst. C.P.A.'s, Am. Acctg. Assn., Am. Arbitration Assn. (nat. panel arbitrators), Beta Gamma Sigma, Beta Alpha Psi, Alpha Kappa Psi, Tau Kappa Epsilon. Club: Mason. Home: 615 E Concorda Dr Tempe AZ 85282

HULBERT, BRUCE WALKER, banker; b. Evanston, Ill., Feb. 5, 1937; s. Bruce Walker and Mary Alice (Utley) H.; m. Linnette Ott, June 19, 1963; children: Christina, Jennifer, William. B.S. in Bus., Northwestern U., 1961. With 1st Interstate Bank of Calif., Los Angeles and San Francisco, 1962-78, sr. v.p., regional adminstr., 1977-78; pres., chief exec. officer, dir. First Interstate Bank of Denver, 1978—. Mem. nat. bd. trustees, mem. exec. com., regional chmn. Inst. Internat. Edn., 1979—; adv. bd. Jr. League Denver, 1980—; trustee Denver Found., 1978—; bd. dirs. Lutheran Med. Center Found., Denver, 1979—, Denver Partnership, 1978—, Denver Civic Ventures, Inc., 1978—; chmn. Denver Civic Ventures, Inc., 1984—; bd. dirs. Denver Area council Boy Scouts Am., 1981—, Nat. Jewish Hosp./Nat. Asthma Center, 1982, AMC Cancer Research Center, 1984—; bd. dirs., treas. Mile High United Way, Denver, 1981—; bd. dirs., exec. com. NCCJ, 1983—. Mem. Am. Bankers Assn., Colo. Assn. Bank Holding Cos. (exec. com., dir.), Colo. Bankers Assn., Denver Clearing House Assn. (dir.), Denver C. of C. Republican. Clubs: Chevaliers du Tastevin, Cherry Hills Country, Denver, Denver Petroleum. Office: 633 17th St Denver CO 80220

HULBERT, MARSHALL BRANDT, emeritus educator; b. Oshkosh, Wis., May 23, 1905; s. Chester Cephas and Anna (Brandt) H.; m. Ruth Logan, July 12, 1944; 1 dau., Ann Logan. A.B., Lawrence Coll., 1926, Mus.B., 1932; M.A., Columbia, 1939; Ph.D., Northwestern U., 1948; student voice, Frank La Forge, N.Y.C. Tchr. social sci., Wausau, Wis., 1926-30; sec. Lawrence Conservatory Music, Appleton, Wis., 1932-43; asso. prof. music Lawrence U., Appleton, 1939, asst. dean, 1943-45, dir. admissions, 1945-58, dean administrn., 1948-54, dean coll., 1954-61, v.p., 1961-70, dir. fgn. studies, 1966-70, Mary Mortimer prof. liberal arts, 1965-80, emeritus, 1980—; cons. Asso. Colls. Midwest, 1970-74, dir. alumni relations, 1972-74. Bus. mgr. Lawrence European Tour, 1936; choral dir. First Presbyterian Ch., Neenah, Wis., 1938-60. Mem. AAUP, Assn. Coll. Admissions Counselors, Phi Beta Kappa, Phi Mu Alpha-Sinfonia, Pi Kappa Lambda, Phi Gamma Delta. Episcopalian. Home: 1699 Alcan Dr Menasha WI 54952

HULBERT, RICHARD WOODWARD, lawyer; b. Cambridge, Mass., Sept. 24, 1929; s. woodward Dennis and Clifford (Halliday) H.; m. Dorothy Marie Hanni, Apr. 21,1954; children: Jonathan, Ann, Laura, Mary. A.B., Harvard U., 1951, LL.B., 1955. Bar: D.C. 1955, N.Y. 1956. Assoc. law firm Cleary, Gottlieb, Steen & Hamilton, N.Y.C., 1956-65; ptnr. Gleary, Gottlieb, Steen & Hamilton, N.Y.C., 1966—; mng. ptnr. Cleary, Gottlieb, Steen & Hamilton, N.Y.C., 1979—. Trustee Bklyn. Bot. Garden, 1983—. Sheldon fellow in history Harvard U., 1951-52. Mem. ABA, N.Y. Bar Assn., Assn. Bar City N.Y., N.Y. County Lawyers Assn. Democrat. Clubs: India House, The Heights Casino. Home: 52 rud de Bourgogne Paris France 75007 Office: 41 Avenue de Friedland Paris France 75008

HULBERT, SAMUEL FOSTER, college president; b. Adams Center, N.Y., Apr. 12, 1936; s. Foster Daivd and Wilma May (Speakman) H.; m. Joy Elinor Husband, Sept. 3, 1960; children: Gergory, Samantha, Jeffrey. B.S. in Ceramic Engring., Alfred U., 1958, Ph.D., 1964. Registered profl. engr., La. Asst. varsity and freshman football coach Alfred U. (N.Y.), 1959-61; lab. instr. N.Y. State Coll. Ceramics, Alfred, 1958-59; instr. math and physics Alfred U., 1960-64; asst. prof. ceramic and metall. engring. Clemson U. (S.C.), 1964-68, head div. interdisciplinary studies, assoc. prof. materials and bioengring., 1968-71; assoc. dean engring research and interdisciplinary studies, prof. materials engring. and bioengring., dir. materials engring. and bioengring., 1970-73; prof. bioengring., dean Sch. Engring. Tulane U., New Orleans, 1973-76; pres.-designate spl. asst. to pres. Rose-Hulman Inst. Tech., Terre Haute, Ind., 1976, pres., 1976—. Mem. editorial bd.: Annals of Biomed. Enging., 1974, Jour. Biomed. Materials Research, 1970—, Jour. Internat. Soc. Artificial Organs, 1977—; contbr. articles in field of biomaterials and artificial organ design to profl. jours. Pres. Terre Haute Com. Area Progress, 1979; mem. exec. com. Wabash Valley chpt. Boy Scouts Am. Recipient medal Italian Soc. Orthopaedics, 1973, Delitala medal Instituto Ortopedico Rizzoli, 1973. Mem. Am. Soc. Artificial Internal. Organs, Biomed. Engring. Soc., Soc. Biomaterials (dir. 1974—, pres. 1975-76), Am. Ceramic Soc., Nat. Inst. Ceramic Engrs., Am. Soc. Engring. Edn., Assn. Advancement Med. Instrumentation, Ind. Colls. and Univ. Assn., Associated Colls. Ind., Ind. Conf. Higher Edn., Ind. Engring. Colls. (sec. treas. 1977—), Am. Assn. Presidents of Ind. Colls. and Univs., Vigo County Hist. Soc. (dir. 1979—), Keramos, Blue Key, Sigma Xi. Republican. Lodge: Rotary. Office: Office President Rose Hulman Inst Tech 5500 Wabash St Terre Haute IN 47803

HULBERT, WILLIAM GLEN, JR., electric utility executive; b. Everett, Wash., Jan. 22, 1917; s. William Glen and Mabel Katherine (Baker) H.; m. Jean Edwards, July 25, 1945; children: William Glen, III, Tanauan, David; m. Clare Mumford, Jan. 6, 1973. B.A., Stanford U., 1938; M.S., Inst. Paper Chemistry, Lawrece Coll., Appleton, Wis., 1940, Ph.D., 1942. With Champion Paper Co., 1942, William Hulbert Mill Co., 1946—; with Public Utility Dist. 1 Snohomish County, Wash., Everett, 1962—, mgr., chief exec. officer, 1966—, commr., 1962. Campaign chmn. United Way Snohomish County, 1969. Served with USNR, World War II. Mem. Am. Public Power Assn. (pres. 1975, Disting. Service award 1977), Puget Sound Electric League (Elec. Man of Year award 1976). Episcopalian. Clubs: Cascade, Everett Golf and Country, Everett Yacht, Elks. Office: PO Box 1107 Everett WA 98206

HULBURT, HUGH MCKINNEY, university dean, chemical engineer; b. Nashua, N.H., Oct. 27, 1917; s. Clarence Hellings and Alice (McKinney) H.; m. Ann Podlucky, June 30, 1940; children: Susan Hulburt Wadelton, Margery Ann Hulburt Held; m. Pauline Podlucky, Dec. 1, 1956; 1 son, William Hugh. B.A., Carroll Coll., Waukesha, Wis., 1938; M.S., U. Wis., 1940; Ph.D., 1942; Ph.D. NRC fellow chemistry, Princeton U., 1942-43. Sr. research chemist Shell Oil Co., 1943-44; instr. Hunter Coll., 1944-46; asst. prof., then asso. prof. chemistry and chem. engring. Cath. U. Am., 1946-51; supr. engr., then dir. research and devel. Chem. Constrn. Co., N.Y.C., 1951-56; with Am. Cyanamid Co., 1956-63, dir. phys. research, central research div., 1959-63; prof. chem. engring. Northwestern U., 1963—, chmn. dept., 1964-70, asso. dean Grad. Sch., 1975-80, asso. dean Technol. Inst., 1980-83; Reilley lectr. U. Notre Dame, 1967; vis. prof. Swiss Fed. Tech. Inst., 1971; cons. in field. Editor: IEC Process Design and Development, 1962—; contbr. articles to profl. jours. Mem. Am. Inst. Chem. Engrs. (inst. lectr. 1962), Am. Chem. Soc., Am. Phys. Soc., Royal Soc. Chemistry, Electrochem. Soc., Catalysis Club N.Y. (pres. 1962), Sigma Xi. Club: Economic (Chgo.). Home: 2028 Highland Ave Wilmette IL 60091 Office: Technol Inst Northwestern Univ Evanston IL 60201

HULET, ERVIN KENNETH, nuclear chemist; b. Baker, Oreg., May 7, 1926; s. Frank E. and Marjorie (Suiter) H.; m. Betty Jo Gardner, Sept. 10, 1949; children—Carri, Randall Gardner. B.S., Stanford U., 1949; Ph.D., U. Calif. at Berkeley, 1953. AEC grad. student Lawrence Radiation Lab., Berkeley, Calif., 1949-53, research chemist radiochemistry div., Livermore, 1953-66, group leader, 1966—. Served with USNR, 1944-46. Fulbright scholar, Norway. Co-discoverer Element 106. Home: PO Box 411 Diablo CA 94528 Office: Lawrence Livermore Nat Lab U Calif Livermore CA 94550

HULETT, STANLEY WILLIAM, government executive; b. San Francisco, July 31, 1938; s. Leo Stanley and Isabelle Francis (Walker) H.; m. Velma Jo Allen, Oct. 15, 1961 (dec. 1966); 1 son, Gregory (dec.); m. Mary Ann Minenna, June 15, 1968. A.A., Menlo Coll., 1958; B.A., Stanford U., 1960. Assoc. dir. Nat. Park Service, Washington, 1971-73; dep. dir. Bur. Outdoor Recreation, Dept. Interior, Washington, 1973-74; v.p. Am. Paper Inst., Washington, 1974-77; exec. v.p. Calif. Forest Protective Assn., Sacramento, 1977-81; asst. sec. Dept. Interior, San Francisco, 1981—. Vice chmn. Mendocino County Republican Central Com., Calif., 1967-69; chmn. Willits Sch. Bd., Calif., 1967-69. Mem. Mendocino County C. of C. (pres. 1968). Lodges: Willits Rotary (dir. 1968-69); Mason (master 1967). Home: 1455 Jefferson St San Francisco CA 94123 Office: Dept Interior Fort Mason Bldg Suite 201 San Francisco CA 94123

HULINGS, NORMAN MCDERMOTT, JR., energy co. exec.; b. Tulsa, Aug. 25, 1923; s. Norman McDermott and Mildred Lillian (Marr) H.; children—Sharon Lee, Lisa Marr. B.S. in Petroleum Prodn. Engring, U. Tulsa, 1949. Registered profl. engr., Okla. With Okla. Natural Gas Co., 1949-80, v.p. gas supply, Tulsa, 1970-73, sr. v.p., 1973-80; pres. ONEOK Energy Cos., Tulsa, 1980—; adv. com. engring. dept. Tulsa U. Bd. dirs. Tulsa chpt. ARC, Okla. Ind. Coll. Found. Served to lt. comdr. USNR, 1942-46. Named to Hall of Fame U. Tulsa, 1979. Mem. Am. Gas Assn. (award merit 1963), AIME, Ind. Petroleum Assn. Am., Interstate Natural Gas Assn., Interstate Oil Compact Commn., So. Gas Assn., Natural Gas Men Okla., Okla. Ind. Petroleum Assn., Tau Beta Pi. Clubs: Tulsa, So. Hills Country (Tulsa). Home: 7430 S Winston Ave Tulsa OK 74136 Office: PO Box 871 Tulsa OK 74102

HULKA, BARBARA SORENSON, epidemiology educator; b. Mpls., Mar. 1, 1931; d. Herbert Fritchof and Mable (Alquist) Sorenson; m. Jaroslav Fabian Hulka, Nov. 13, 1954; children: Carol Ann, Gregory Fabian, Bryan Herbert. B.S., Radcliffe Coll., 1952; J.D., Juilliard Sch. Music, 1954; M.D., Columbia U., 1959, M.P.A., 1961. Research asst. prof. U. Pitts., 1966-67; asst. prof. U. N.C., Chapel Hill, 1967-71, assoc. prof., 1972-76, prof., 1977—, chmn. dept. epidemiology, 1983—; adj. prof. medicine Duke U. Med. Ctr., Durham, N.C., 1982—; chmn. epidemiology and disease study sect. NIH, 1979-83; bd. sci. counselors Nat. Cancer Inst., 1980—; mem. Inst. of Medicine com. toxic shock syndrome Nat. Acad. Sci., 1981-82; mem. Sci. Rev. and Evaluation Bd. VA, 1983—. Contbr. articles to profl. jours., chpts. to books. Health Resources Adminstrn. grantee, 1975-77; tng. grantee in cancer epidemiology Nat. Cancer Inst., 1980—; Prostate Cancer grantee Nat. Cancer Inst., 1983—; travel study fellow WHO, 1978. Mem. Soc. Epidemiol. Research (pres. 1975-76, exec. com. 1973-77), Am. Pub. Health Assn. (governing council 1976-78, chmn. epidemiol. sect. 1976-77), Am. Epidemiol. Soc., N.C. Pub. Health Assn. (award for excellence, stats, and epidemiology sect. 1975), Delta Omega. Home: 2317 Honeysuckle Dr Chapel Hill NC 27514 Office: Sch Pub Health Univ North Carolina Rosenau Hall 201H Chapel Hill NC 27514

HULKA, JAROSLAV FABIAN, physician; b. N.Y.C., Sept. 29, 1930; s. Jaroslav Hugo and Milada (Touskova) H.; m. Barbara E. Sorenson, Nov. 13, 1954; children—Carol Ann, Gregory Fabian, Bryan Herbert. B.A., Harvard U., 1952; M.D., Columbia U., 1956. Diplomate: Am. Bd. Ob-Gyn. Intern Roosevelt Hosp., N.Y.C., 1956-57; resident Sloane Hosp. for Women, Columbia-Presbyn. Med. Center, N.Y.C., 1957-60; Josiah Macy, Jr. fellow Columbia-Presbyn. Med. Center, 1960-61; practice medicine specializing in Ob-Gyn, 1961—; asst. prof. Ob-Gyn U. Pitts. Sch. Medicine, 1961-66, asso. mem. grad. faculty, 1962-66, acting chmn. dept. Ob-Gyn, 1963-64; asso. prof. dept. Ob-Gyn Sch. Medicine, U. N.C., Chapel Hill, 1967-76, prof. dept. Ob-Gyn and dept. maternal and child health, 1976—. Asso. dir. Carolina Population Center, 1967-74. Fellow Am. Coll. Obstetricians and Gynecologists; mem. Soc. for Gynecol. Investigation, Am. Assn. Gynecol. Laparoscopists (pres. 1980), Am. Fertility Soc. Patentee in field. Home: 2317 Honeysuckle Rd Chapel Hill NC 27514 Office: Dept Ob-Gyn Memorial Hosp Chapel Hill NC 27514

HULL, ADDIS EMMET, lawyer; b. Zanesville, Ohio, Nov. 2, 1919; s. Addis E. and Lois (Barnett) H.; m. Patricia Hull Hunt, June 1, 1947. B.S.B.A., Ohio State U., 1941; LL.B., Northwestern U., 1946. Bar: Ill. 1947. Assoc. Jenner & Block, Chgo., 1946-56, ptnr., 1956—. Author: Illinois Tax and Estate Planning, 1972, Stock Purchase Agreements in Estate Planning, 1979. Served with CIC, U.S. Army, 1942-44; ETO. Mem. Chgo. Bar Assn., Ill. Bar Assn., ABA, Estate Planning Council Chgo. (pres. 1973). Club: Mid-Am. (Chgo.). Home: 1245 Somerset Dr Glenview IL 60025 Office: Jenner & Block One IBM Plaza Chicago IL 60611

HULL, CORDELL WILLIAM, business executive; b. Dayton, Ohio, Sept. 12, 1933; s. Murel George and Julia (Barton) H.; m. Susan G. Ruder, May 10, 1958; children: Bradford W., Pamela H., Andrew R. B.E., U. Dayton, 1956; M.S., MIT, 1957; J.D., Harvard U., 1962. Bar: Ohio 1962; Registered profl. engr., Mass. Atty. Taft, Stettinius & Hollister, Cin., 1962-64, C & I Girdler, 1964-66; gen. counsel, treas., pres. C&I Girdler, Internat., Brussels, 1966-70; v.p. Bechtel Overseas Corp., San Francisco, 1970-73; pres., dir. Am. Express Mcht. Bank, London, 1973-75; v.p., treas. Bechtel Corp. and Bechtel Power, San Francisco, 1975-80; pres. Bechtel Fin. Services, San Francisco, 1975-82; v.p., chief fin. officer Bechtel Group Inc., 1980—; dir. Bechtel Investments Inc., Sequoia Ventures, Inc., Bechtel prin. operating cos., Bechtel Financing Services. Contbr. articles to profl. jours. Bd. dirs. Near East Found.; mem. adv. bd. Technology in Society.; mem. adv. com. Am. Enterprise Inst. for Pub. Policy Research; trustee Crystal Springs and Uplands Schs. Served with C.E. U.S. Army, 1956. Mem. ABA, Ohio Bar Assn., Conf. Bd. (Council Fin. Execs.), Am. Soc. Macro-Engring. (dir.). Democrat. Clubs: Bankers, Knickerbocker, Pacific Union, Harvard. Office: Bechtel Group Inc 50 Beale St San Francisco CA 94105

HULL, HARRY, business consultant; b. Athens, Ga., Jan. 18, 1912; s. Harry and Anne (Burnett) H.; m. Louisa Catherine Adams Clement, Aug. 19, 1943. B.S., U.S. Naval Acad., 1932; student, Naval Postgrad. Sch., 1939-41; grad., Advanced Mgmt. Program, Harvard U., 1954. Commd. ensign U.S. Navy, 1932, advanced through grades to rear adm., 1961, ret., 1967; exec. dir. Internat. Bus. Center New Eng., Inc., Boston, 1967-80. Decorated Navy Cross. Episcopalian. Home: Uplands Highland Ave Manchester MA 01944

HULL, HARVARD LESLIE, corporate official; b. Holstein, Neb., Oct. 23, 1906; s. Joel Leslie and Caroline Evangeline (Larsen) H.; m. Alta Zera Jones, June 9, 1928; children: Gwen Alta Hull Quackenbush, Janet Barbara Hull Clark. A.B. with distinction, Nebr. Wesleyan U., 1927, D.Sci. (hon.), 1984; Ph.D. in Physics, Columbia U., 1933. Project engr. Sperry Gyroscope Co., Bklyn, 1933-35, research engr., 1935-40, dir. remote control devel., 1940-43; introduced new equipment Sperry Gyroscope Co., Ltd., Eng., 1934, 35-36; dir. process improvement electromagnetic process of separation Uranium 235 Tenn. Eastman Corp., Oak Ridge, 1943-46; asso. dir. Argonne Nat. Lab., Chgo., 1946-49, dir. remote control engring. devel., 1949-53; v.p. research and devel. div. Capehart-Farnsworth Co., Ft. Wayne, 1953-54; pres. Farnsworth Electronics Co., Co. (div. ITT), Ft. Wayne, 1954-56; v.p. Litton Industries, Beverly Hills, Calif., 1956-57; pres. Hull Assos., Chgo., 1957—; dir., pres. Chgo. Aerial Industries, Inc., Barrington, Ill., 1962-64, Internat. Tech. Corp., Western Springs, Ill.; dir. Central Research Labs., Inc.; Dir. research Aero-Space Inst., Chgo., chmn. bd., 1973—. Fellow AIAA (asso.); mem. IEEE (life), Am. Nuclear Soc. (cert. of appreciation 1978), AAAS, Am. Phys. Soc., Nat. Telemetering Conf. (chmn. 1956), Sigma Xi, Phi Kappa Phi, Theta Chi. Conglist. Club: Executives. Address: 5223 Caroline Ave Western Springs IL 60558

HULL, HERBERT MITCHELL, plant physiologist, educator; b. La Jolla, Calif., Aug. 19, 1919; s. Daniel Ray and Emma (Kammeyer) H.; m. Mary Randall Mattison, Mar. 4, 1950; children: Laurinda Lee, Daniel James. A.A., Pasadena City Coll., 1939; B.S., U. Calif., Berkeley, 1946; Ph.D., Calif. Inst. Tech., 1951. Research fellow Calif. Inst. Tech., 1949-52; plant physiologist U.S. Dept. Agr., Tucson, 1952-78; prof. watershed mgmt. U. Ariz., 1966—. Served with USAAF, 1941-46. Fellow AAAS; mem. Ariz. Acad. Sci., Am. Soc. Plant Physiologists, Bot. Soc. Am., Sigma Xi, Alpha Zeta, Delta Kappa Omicron. Presbyterian. Home: 4040 W Sweetwater Dr Tucson AZ 85745 Office: U Ariz 325 Biosciences E Tucson AZ 85721

HULL, J(AMES) RICHARD, lawyer, hopsital supply company executive; b. Keokuk, Iowa, Dec. 5, 1933; s. James Robert and Alberta Margaret (Bouseman) H.; m. Patricia M. Kiesner, June 14, 1958; children—Elizabeth Ann, James Robert, David Glenn. B.A., Ill. Wesleyan U., 1955; J.D., Northwestern U., 1958. With Honeggers & Co., Inc., Fairbury, Ill., 1959-65, v.p., sec., gen. counsel, 1959-65, dir., 1963-65; v.p., gen. counsel Am. Hosp. Supply Corp., Evanston, Ill., 1965—. Trustee Ill. Wesleyan U., Bloomington. Mem. Am. Bar Assn., Ill. Bar Assn., Fla. Bar Assn., Chgo. Bar Assn. (chmn. corp. law dept.), Am. Soc. Corp. Secs., Sigma Chi. Clubs: Legal, Exec. (Chgo.); Gator Creek Golf. Home: 2603 Oak Ave Northbrook IL 60062 Office: Am Hosp Supply Corp One American Plaza Evanston IL 60201 *Success will come to those who plan & rehearse. Set your goals, define your strategies & implement your tactics. Your goals must always determine & never justify the means toward achievement.*

HULL, JOAN CAROL, historical society executive, consultant; b. Newark, Apr. 13, 1932; d. Milton Otto and Mildred (Molitor) H. B.A., St. Lawrence U., 1954; M.A., Montclair State Coll., 1962; D.H.D. hon., Kean Coll., 1983. Tchr. history Butler High Sch., N.J., 1958-63; dir. edn. N.J. Hist. Soc., Newark, 1963-68, asst. dir., 1968-79, exec. dir., pres., 1979—; mem. N.J. Battleship Commn., Trenton, 1980. Author tchrs. manual, N.J.—Mirror on America, 1978. Recipient Alumni Bicentennial award Montclair State Coll., 1975, award N.J. Hist. Commn., Trenton, 1978. Mem. Am. Assn. State Local History (chairperson regional awards 1981—), League Hist. Socs. N.J. (pres. 1978-82), AAUW (1st v.p. Essex County chpt. 1975-79). Club: soroptomists (Newark) (pres. 1968-72). Office: NJ Hist Soc 230 Broadway Newark NJ 07104

HULL, JOHN DANIEL, JR., educator; b. Mountain Grove, Mo., Mar. 11, 1900; s. John Daniel and Nancy Susan (McQuitty) H.; m. Alene Oliver, Dec. 21, 1924; children: Nancy Susan (Mrs. Willis A. McCracken), John Daniel III. B.S., U. Mo., 1920; A.M., U. Chgo., 1923; Ph.D., Yale U., 1933; LL.D., Drury Coll., 1964. Prin. high sch., Mountain Grove., Mo., 1918-19, Sullivan, Ind., 1920-24, Springfield, Mo., 1924-41, Shortridge High Sch., Indpls., 1941-47; with U.S. Office Edn., 1947-64, chief secondary schs., 1952-55, dir. instrn. services, 1955-64; instr. Grad. Sch., Drury Coll., 1965-68; prof. ednl. adminstrn., summers, S.W. Mo. State Coll., Drury Coll., La. State U., U. Buffalo, Yale, U. Mo., N.Y. U., George Washington U., U. Wyo., Syracuse U.; Mem. high sch. curriculum com. Mo. Dept. Edn., 1937-41; curriculum com. Ind. Dept. Edn., 1943-47. Author: Organization and Direction of Extracurricular Activities, 1940, A Primer of Life Adjustment Education, 1949, Offerings and Enrollments in High School Subjects, (with Grace Wright), 1948-49, American High School Administrations, (with French and Dodds), 1951, rev., 1957, (with Austin and French), 1962; Editor: Why Do Boys and Girls Drop Out of School and What Can We Do About It, 1950, Vitalizing Secondary Education, 1951, Improving School Holding Power, 1951, A Look Ahead in Secondary Education, 1954, Teaching Fast and Slow Learners in High School, (with Arno Jewett), 1954; Contbr. to ednl. jours. Exec. sec. Nat. Commn. on Life Adjustment Edn. for Youth, 1947-53; cons. to Dependent Schs., U.S. Army in Europe, 1952-53; chmn. U.S. del. to Internat. Conf. Secondary Edn., Chile, 1955; Trustee Long Coll. for Women, Hanover Coll., 1944-47; chmn. Springfield chpt. A.R.C., 1968, 69, 71; treas. Greene County Humane Soc., 1968-71. Recipient Shattuck Sch. Centennial citation for service to secondary edn., 1958. Mem. Nat. Assn. Secondary Sch. Prins. (curriculum com. 1946-51, nat. com. for nat. council social studies 1941-45), Ind. State Mental Hygiene Soc. (exec. com. 1944-47), N.E.A., Headmasters Assn. (hon.), Phi Delta Kappa, Kappa Alpha. Presbyn. (elder). Clubs: University, Hickory Hills Country. Address: 2222 Inglewood Rd Springfield MO 65804

HULL, MCALLISTER HOBART, JR., university provost; b. Birmingham, Ala., Sept. 1, 1923; s. McAllister Hobart and Grace (Johnson) H.; m. Mary Muska, Mar. 23, 1946; children: John McAllister, Wendy Ann. B.S. with highest honors, Yale, 1948, Ph.D. in Physics, 1951. From instr. to asso. prof. physics Yale U., 1951-66; prof. physics, chmn. dept. Oreg. State U., 1966-69, State U. N.Y. at Buffalo, 1969-72, dean, 1972-74, dean. grad. and profl. edn., 1974-77; provost U. N.Mex., 1977—; adviser to supt. schs., Hamden, Conn., 1958-65. Author papers, books, chpts. in books, articles in encys. Bd. dirs. Western N.Y. Reactor Facility, 1970-72; trustee N.E. Radio Obs. Corp., 1971-77; pres. Western Regional Sci. Labs., 1977; chmn. tech. adv. com. N.Mex. Energy Research Inst., 1981-83, mem., 1983—. Served with AUS, 1943-46. Faculty fellow Yale U., 1964-65. Fellow Am. Phys. Soc.; mem. Am. Assn. Physics Tchrs. (chmn. Oreg. sect. 1967-68). Address: U New Mexico Office of Provost Albuquerque NM 87131 *Experience says that everyman is sometimes wise, no man is always wise. One must develop the willingness to listen for wisdom from whatever source, the judgment to identify it, the skill to use it: only in this way can one's talents, however modest or extensive, be optimally enhanced and the number of wasted efforts minimized.*

HULL, RAYMOND HORACE, writer, lecturer; b. Shaftesbury, Eng., Feb. 27, 1919; s. Edgar John and May (Coates) H. Ed. pub. schs. Laborer, folk-singer, saw operator, puppeteer and other miscellaneous jobs, 1937-65; pres. Raymond Hull Enterprises, Ltd., 1970—. Writer of articles, books, plays, poetry, song lyrics, radio and TV scripts; lectr. on non-fiction books, articles and playwriting.; Author: Profitable Playwriting, 1968, Writing for Money in Canada, 1969, Tales of a Pioneer Surveyor, 1970, Successful Public Speaking, 1971, (with Jack Sleight) Home Book of Smoke Cookery and Smoke Curing, 1971, How To Get What You Want, 1969, (with Laurence J. Peter) The Peter Principle, 1969, (with Stanley F. Anderson) The Art of Making Wine, 1968, The Art of Making Beer, 1971, (with Olga Ruskin) Gastown's Gassy Jack, 1971, Man's Best Fiend, 1972, (with Rose Naumann) The Off-Loom Weaving Book, 1973, (with G. and S. Soules) Vancouver's Past, 1974, (with S.F. Anderson) The Advanced Winemaker's Practical Guide, 1975, (with Ida Claire Larden) The Off-Wheel Pottery Book, 1975, (with Helmut J. Ruebsaat) The Male Climacteric, 1975, (with Anthony Gargrave) How to Win an Election, 1979, How to Write "How-To" Books and Articles, 1981, How to Write a Play, 1983. Pres. Gower Point Property Owners' Assn., 1969-71; v.p. Vancouver Center Progressive Conservative Assn., 1965-66. Mem. Canadian Authors Assn., Canadian Anti-Dog Soc. (pres.). Address: 1703-1200 Alberni St Vancouver BC V6E 1A6 Canada *What you talk about, you think about. What you think about, you bring about. Think clearly, with interest and with pleasure, and your thought must be realized. Make yourself what you desire to be, and you will attract the kind of friends you desire to have.*

HULL, ROBERT GLENN, financial administrator; b. Ottumwa, Iowa, Sept. 14, 1929; s. C. Glenn and DeElda L. (Davidson) H.; m. Donna Marie Hastriter, Jan. 26, 1951; children: Cynthia Ann Hull Williams, Steven Kent. B.A., Friends U., 1956; M.S., Emporia Kans. State U., 1966. With Nat. Coop. Refinery Assn., McPherson, Kans., 1957—, treas., comptroller, 1968-76, v.p. finance, 1976—; dir. Jayhawk Pipeline Corp., Agri-Petco Internat., Clear Creek Cos. Bd. dirs.

Central Coll., McPherson. Served with USAF, 1951-55. Mem. Fin. Exec's. Inst., Nat. Assn. Accountants for Coops., Am. Petroleum Inst. Republican. Methodist. Clubs: Petroleum, McPherson Country. Home: 417 S Grand St McPherson KS 67460 Office: PO Box 1167 McPherson KS 67460

HULL, ROBERT MARVIN (BOBBY HULL), former professional hockey player; b. Point Anne, Ont., Can., Jan. 3, 1939; s. Robert Edward and Lena (Cook) H.; m. Joanne Merriel McKay, Feb. 24, 1960; children: Bobby Abbott, Blake Anthony, Brett Andrew, Bart Alexander. Grad. high sch. Profl. hockey player, 1957-80; mem. Chgo. Black Hawks Profl. Hockey Team, 1957-72, Winnipeg (Man., Can.) Jets (World Hockey Assn.), 1972-79, Hartford Whalers, 1979-80; pres. Bobby Hull Enterprises, Toronto, Can., from 1966. Author: Hockey is My Game, 1967. Recipient Hart trophy, 1965, 66, Lester Patrick award, 1969, Art Ross trophy, 1960, 62, 66, City of Hope award, 1965, Lady Byng Meml. trophy, 1964-65; named Most Valuable Player World Hockey Assn., 1973, 75; also numerous other sports awards. Office: care Chgo Black Hawks 1800 W Madison St Chicago IL 60612 *

HULL, ROGER HAROLD, college president; b. N.Y.C., June 18, 1942; s. Max Harold and Magda Mary (Stern) H.; m. Anne Elizabeth Dyson, July 4, 1980. A.B. cum laude, Dartmouth Coll., 1964; LL.B., Yale U., 1967; LL.M., U. Va., 1972, S.J.D., 1974. Bar: N.Y. 1968. Assoc. firm White & Case, N.Y.C., 1967-71; spl. counsel to gov., Va., 1971-74; spl. asst. to chmn., dep. staff dir. Interagy. Task Force Law of Sea, NSC, 1974-76; v.p. devel. Syracuse (N.Y.) U., 1976-79, v.p. devel. and planning, 1979-81; pres. Beloit (Wis.) Coll., 1981—; mem. U.S. del. Law of Sea Conf., 1974-76; adj. prof. Syracuse U. Law Sch., 1976-81; Bd. visitors Coll. William and Mary, Williamsburg, Va., 1970-74; mem. public instns. task force Assn. Gov. Bds., 1975. Author: The Irish Triangle, 1976; co-author: Law and Vietnam, 1968. Mem. Am. Bar Assn., Young Pres.' Orgn., Am. Soc. Internat. Law., Council on Fgn. Relations. Clubs: Beloit Country; Univ. (Chgo.). Office: Beloit Coll Beloit WI 53511

HULL, SUZANNE WHITE, library administrator; b. Orange, N.J., Aug. 24, 1921; d. Gordon Stowe and Lillian (Siegling) White; m. George I. Hull, Feb. 20, 1943; children: George Gordon, James Rutledge, Anne Hull Staff. B.A. with honors, Swarthmore Coll., 1943; M.S. in L.S., U. So. Calif., 1967. Mem. staff Huntington Library, San Marino, Calif., 1969—, dir. Art Gallery and Bot. Gardens, 1972—. Author: Chaste, Silent and Obedient, Books for Women, 1475-1640, 1982. Charter pres. Portola Jr. High Sch. PTA, Los Angeles, 1960-62; pres. Children's Service League, Los Angeles, 1963-64, YWCA Los Angeles, 1967-69; mem. community adv. council Los Angeles Job Corps Center for Women, 1972-78; mem. alumni council Swarthmore Coll., 1959-62, 83—; hon. life mem. Calif. Congress Parents and Tchrs.; co-founder, bd. dirs. Friends of Los Angeles YWCA, 1968-73; bd. dirs. Pasadena Planned Parenthood Assn., 1978—. Mem. Monumental Brass Soc. (U.K.), Renaissance Soc., Brit. Studies Conf., Beta Phi Mu (chpt. dir. 1981—). Home: 1465 El Mirador Dr Pasadena CA 91103 Office: 1151 Oxford Rd San Marino CA 91108

HULL, TREAT CLARK, judge; b. Danbury, Conn., June 14, 1921; s. Treat Clark and Elizabeth (Schmidt) H.; m. Betty Jane Rosoff, Apr. 24, 1948; children: Treat Clark, Jonathan Cooper, Steven Dalton. B.A., Yale U., 1942; LL.B., Harvard U., 1948. Bar: Conn. Mem. firm Pinney, Hull, Payne & VanLenten, Danbury, 1948-73; mem. Conn. Senate, 1963-71; lt. gov., State of Conn., 1971-73; judge Superior Ct. Conn., 1973-83, Appellate Ct. Conn., 1983—. Served with USAAF, 1942-46. Mem. Conn., Danbury bar assns. Republican. Congregationalist. Home: 187 Kohanza St Danbury CT 06810 Office: Superior Ct of Conn Danbury CT 06810

HULL, WILLIAM FLOYD, JR., former museum director; b. Pomeroy, Wash., June 27, 1920; s. William Floyd and Margherita Sophia (Bose) H.; m. Carolyn Elizabeth Wose, July 19, 1947 (dec. 1977); children: Alfred Frederick (dec.), Margherita Elizabeth. B.A. in Romance Langs, Wash. State U., 1946. Mng. dir. G.R. Crocker & Co., Syracuse, N.Y., 1948-57; dir. Everson Mus. Art, Syracuse, 1957-61; asso. dir. N.Y. State Council Arts, 1961-66; exec. dir. Ky. Arts Commn., 1966-71; dir. Mus. Art, Pa. State U., 1971-83, emeritus dir., 1983—; mem. state-fed. panel Nat. Endowment Arts, 1973-77. Author: Danish Ceramic Design, 1981. Served with AUS, 1942-45. Mem. Am. Ceramic Circle. Office: Museum Art Pa State U University Park PA 16802

HULL, WILLIAM HENRY, publishing company executive; b. Boonville, Mo., Oct. 29, 1918; s. Aubrey Grant and Mary Ann (Moore) H.; m. Carol Louise Hanson, Aug. 16, 1943; children: Judith Lynn (Mrs. E.T. Lindberg), Pauline Ann (Mrs. Patrick Conn). A.B. in English and Art, Central Coll., Fayette, Mo., 1940, M.A., So. Meth. U., 1941. Chmn. English dept., humanities div. Kemper Mil. Sch., Boonville, 1941-46; prof. English Mankato (Minn.) State Coll., 1946-47; bus. mgr., pub. relations mgr. Postgrad. Medicine jour., McGraw-Hill, Inc., Mpls., 1948-68, mktg. services mgr., 1968-71, circulation mgr., 1971-77, The Physician and Sportsmedicine, 1973-77; dir. circulation, med. publs. McGraw-Hill Publs. Co., 1977-81; pres. Garden Pub. Co., Edina, Minn., 1981—; free-lance garden writer; mem. spl. task force Bus. Publs. Audit of Circulations, 1978, spl. auditing revision com., 1978; speaker ann. spring conf. Direct Mail Mktg. Assn., 1978. Author: Public Relations for the Pharmacist, 1955, Buying Fruits and Vegetables, 1957, Aunt Zettie's Wonderful Salve, 1981; Editor: The Garden Spray, 1966-70; Contbr. articles to profl. jours. Mem. Men's Garden Clubs Am., 1952—, pres., Mpls., 1958, nat. bd. dirs., 1956—, nat. v.p., 1961-63, nat. pres., 1964, chmn. adv. bd., 1965; pres. Midwest Mail Mktg. Assn., 1976-77. Recipient bronze medal Men's Garden Club Mpls., 1966; silver medal Men's Garden Clubs Am., 1966; Direct Mail Leader award Direct Mail Mktg. Assn. Am., 1973, 74; also certificate of excellence, 1978; Holes Direct Mail award Midwest Mail Mktg. Assn., 1975; award of recognition Interstate Postgrad. Med. Assn., 1977. Mem. Minn. Press Club (charter), Garden Writers Am., Mensa, Alpha Phi Omega, Pi Delta Epsilon. Club: Mason. Home and Office: 6833 Creston Rd Edina MN 55435

HULLEY, CLAIR MONTROSE, mechanical engineering educator; b. Cin., Mar. 6, 1925; s. Clair Montrose and Vera Veronica (Von Hagen) H. B.S., U. Cin., 1947, M.E., 1947. Instr. engring. graphics Coll. Engring., U. Cin., 1947-57, asst. prof., 1957-66, asso. prof., 1966-68, prof. in charge engring. graphics, 1968-76, prof., coordinator computer graphics, 1976—, prof. engring. and computer graphic sci., 1978-80, prof. mech.-indsl. engring., 1980-83, emeritus prof. engring. and computer graphics sci., 1983—, mem. faculty, eve. coll., 1946-70; Cons. tensgridity structures NASA; cons. computer graphics Gen. Electric Co., Detroit, Allis Chalmers, Cin., Tool Steel Gear & Pinion, Formica Corp. Author: Hulleytran2, 1967, Hulleytran3, 1968, Digital Plotter Revolution in UC, 1970, Computer Graphics Contouring, 1970, COGO with Graphical Output, 1973, Applied Matrix Methods in Computer Graphics, 1976, Polynomial Curve Fitting, 1978, Efficient Computer Programming, 1980, Bytes, Bits and Binary Bumping, 1981. Founder, 1st pres. Sycamore Twp. Civic Assn., 1960; Bd. govs. Sycamore-Symmes Civic Assn., 1972—, pres., 1968-69, v.p., 1970-71. Recipient teaching award for long and dedicated service U. Cin., 1983. Mem. ASME (life), Am. Assn. Engring. Edn. Home: 11560 Deerfield Rd Cincinnati OH 45242 *For greatest accomplishment, criticize not those you disagree, but rather assist and praise your friends. Economies, progress, and life in general seem to swing like a pendulum. Those who are somewhere in the middle of the road will find the pendulum in their area twice as often as either extreme.*

HULM, JOHN KENNETH, physicist; b. Southport, Eng., July 4, 1923; came to U.S., 1949, naturalized, 1957; s. James and Frances Elizabeth (Goodall) H.; m. Joan Audrey Beatrice Askham, Sept. 25, 1948; children—Clair Frances, Carol Anne, Cherie, Megan, John Allen. B.A. in Natural Scis, Gonville and Caius Coll., Cambridge (Eng.) U., 1943; M.S. in Physics, Cambridge (Eng.) U., 1948; Ph.D. (Dept. Sci. and Indsl. Research research fellow), Cambridge (Eng.) U., 1949. Union Carbide research fellow U. Chgo., 1949-51, asst. prof. physics, 1951-54; mem. staff Westinghouse Research Labs., 1954-74, 76—, dir. systems research, 1972-74, dir. chem. scis. div., 1976—, dir. corp. research, 1980—; sci. attache Am. Embassy, London, 1974-76. Served as officer RAF, 1943-46. Recipient John Price Wetherill medal Franklin Inst. Fellow Am. Phys. Soc. (Internat. prize for new materials 1979); mem. Nat. Acad. Engring., Pitts. Phys. Soc. (pres. 1962-63). Home: 5636 Woodmont St Pittsburgh PA 15217 Office: Westinghouse Research Labs Pittsburgh PA 15235

HULME, MILTON GEORGE, JR., manufacturing company executive; b. Pitts., Oct. 12, 1926; s. Milton George and Helen Beatrice (Clougherty) H.; m. Aura N. Raspaldo, Jan. 24, 1953; children: Milton George, Charles Alan, Leslie Caroline. B.S.E.E., MIT, 1950; postgrad., Harvard U. Bus. Sch., 1957. With Mine Safety Appliances Co., Pitts., 1950—, asst. to pres., 1962-66, v.p.-mktg., 1966-78, pres., chief exec. officer, 1978—; dir. Pitts. br. Fed. Res. Bank, Cleve., 1980—, chmn., 1981—; v.p. Glover & MacGregor, Inc., Pitts., 1950-81, pres., 1981—, dir., 1950—; chmn. bd. Thorofare Markets, Inc., 1975-80; dir. Pitts. Brewing Co., Reading & Bates Corp., Equitable Gas Co., Safety Equipment Inst., Koppers Co. Bd. dirs. United Way Allegheny County, 1979—, Sta. WQED Public TV, 1971—; bd. dirs. Pitts. Symphony Soc., 1981—; trustee Shadyside Hosp., 1966—, chmn. bd. trustees, 1979—; trustee Carnegie-Mellon U., Pitts., 1981—; past bd. dirs. Pitts. br. ARC, Pitts. Assn. for Improvement of the Poor, Western Pa. Safety Council.; Past Bd. dirs. Indsl. Health Found., 1973—. Served with USNR, 1944-45. Mem. Indsl. Safety Equipment Assn. (dir. 1975—, v.p. 1975-77, pres. 1977-79). Republican. Presbyterian. Clubs: Duquesne (dir. 1980—), Fox Chapel Golf, Laurel Valley Golf, Rolling Rock. Office: 600 Penn Center Blvd Pittsburgh PA 15235

HULS, HARRISON, wholesale and retail grocery company executive; b. 1923; married. With Hale-Halsell Co., Tulsa, 1953—, v.p., 1962-73, pres., 1973—. Office: Hale-Halsell Co Inc Box 51298 Tulsa OK 74151 *

HULSBOS, CORNIE LEONARD, civil engineering educator; b. Given, Iowa, Aug. 23, 1920; s. Neal and Elizabeth (Van Klaveran) H.; m. Elsie Marthe Hallas, June 21, 1945; children: Susan, Betty, David. B.S., Iowa State U., 1941, M.S., 1949, Ph.D., 1953. Registered profl. engr., Iowa. With Am. Bridge Co., 1941-46; mem. faculty Iowa State U., 1946-60, prof. civil engring., 1957-60; research prof. civil engring., chmn. structural concrete div. Fritz Engring. Lab., Lehigh U., 1960-65; prof. civil engring., chmn. dept. U. N.Mex., Albuquerque, 1965—; mem. com. concrete bridges Transp. Research Bd., 1962—, chmn., 1971-77, mem. com. field testing bridges, 1965-80. Fellow ASCE (sec. treas. Iowa sect. 1957-60, 1st v.p. Lehigh Valley sect. 1964-65, chmn. Albuquerque br. 1968-69), Am. Concrete Inst.; mem. Am. Soc. Engring. Edn., Sigma Xi, Tau Beta Pi, Phi Kappa Phi, Chi Epsilon, Pi Mu Epsilon. Home: 7608 Palo Duro Ave NE Albuquerque NM 87110

HULSE, FRANK WILSON, airline executive; b. North Augusta, S.C., Sept. 12, 1912; s. Frank Wilson and Vivian (Chastaine) H.; m. Mary Jemison Cobb, Apr. 11, 1940; children: Mary Cobb (Mrs. Frank M. Young), Frank Wilson IV. B.S., Ga. Inst. Tech., 1934. Comml. pilot, Augusta, Ga., 1927-34, asst. airport mgr., Augusta, 1934-35; sta. mgr. Delta Airlines, 1935-36; pres. So. Airways of Ga., 1936-43; founder, chmn. bd. So. Airways, Inc., Atlanta, 1943-77, 1949-79; vice chmn. Republic Airlines, Inc., Mpls., 1979—; past chmn. asso., local transport airlines; dir. Fuqua Industries, Asso. Distbrs.; Mem. Ala. Aviation Commn., 1939-40; mem. Chief Execs. Forum. Mem. bd. nominations Aviation Hall Fame. Decorated by Brit. Govt. for tng. RAF pilots, World War II. Mem. Birmingham C. of C., Am. Helicopter Soc., Ga. Tech. Nat. Alumni Assn. (trustee). Episcopalian. Clubs: Rotarian., Wings (N.Y.C.); Aviation (Washington). Office: 2112 11th Ave S Suite 440 Birmingham AL 35205

HULSE, JERRY, journalist; b. Grand Junction, Colo., Sept. 5, 1924; s. Leslie and Elena (Bates) H.; m. Helene Carr, Oct. 20, 1945; children: Richard, Robert. Grad., Los Angeles City Coll., 1947. Newspaper reporter San Fernando Valley Times, 1947-52; reporter Los Angeles Times, 1952—, travel editor, 1960—. Writer: syndicated travel column On The Go, 1961—; Author: Jody, 1976; author over 300 mag. articles. Served with USNR, World War II. Recipient Strebig-Dobben award for journalism excellence, 1972; Henry Burroughs Meml. writing award, 1973; 1st place award Aviation Space Writers Assn., 1975; Can. travel award, 1980; recipient Silver Pen award Mexico, 1982. Republican. Club: Los Angeles Press. Office: Los Angeles Times Times-Mirror Sq Los Angeles CA 90053

HULSE, STEWART HARDING, JR., educator, experimental psychologist; b. Elizabeth, N.J., Aug. 25, 1931; s. Stewart Harding and Katharine (Jones) H.; m. Nancy Huppertz, Aug. 14, 1954; children: Stephen, Jennifer, Melissa. A.B., Williams Coll., 1953; Sc.M., Brown U., 1955, Ph.D., 1957. Mem. faculty dept. psychology Johns Hopkins U., 1957—. Author: (with J. Deese) Psychology of Learning, 4th edit., 1975, 5th edit. (with Deese and Egeth), 1980; Author, editor: G. Stanley Hall: Essays in Honor of 100 Years of Psychological Research in America, 1985; cons. editor psychol. jours.; contbr. profl. jours.; author, editor: (with H. Fowler and W.K. Honig) Cognitive Processes in Animal Behavior, 1978; editor: Jour. Supplement Abstract Services; assoc. editor: Animal Learning and Behavior, 1976-82. Bd. dirs. Sch. Bd. Nominating Conv. Balt. County, 1968-70. NSF grantee. Fellow Am. Psychol. Assn., AAAS (mem. sect. J com.); mem. Psychonomic Soc., Eastern Psychol. Assn., Animal Behavior Soc., Pavlovian Soc., Acoustical Soc. Am., N.Y. Acad. Scis., Sigma Xi, Psi Upsilon. Club: Johns Hopkins (pres. 1974-78). Home: 715 Chapel Ridge Rd Lutherville MD 21093 Office: Dept Psychology Johns Hopkins Baltimore MD 21218

HULSEBOSCH, CHARLES JOSEPH, truck mfg. co. exec.; b. N.Y.C., Dec. 14, 1933; s. Albert J. and Marie (Gough) H.; m. Elizabeth Ferguson, July 6, 1957; children—Albert, Daniel, Joseph, Kristine, Thomas, Howard, John. A.B., Dartmouth, 1955; M.B.A., Amos Tuck Sch., 1956. Financial analyst Ford Motor Co., 1956-60; from budget mgr. to controller Renault, Inc., N.Y.C., 1960-63; with United Fruit Co., 1963-69, treas., 1967-69; v.p., treas. Libby, McNeill & Libby, 1969-74, v.p. fin., 1974-77; also dir.; v.p. fin., treas., dir., mem. exec. bd. Oshkosh Truck Corp., Wis., 1978—. Mem. Oshkosh City Council, 1981—; active Boy Scouts Am. Mem. Fin. Execs. Inst., Newcomen Soc., Zeta Psi. Republican. Roman Catholic. Club: Oshkosh Power Boat. Home: 2015 Menominee Dr Oshkosh WI 54901 Office: 2307 Oregon St Oshkosh WI 54901

HULSIZER, ROBERT INSLEE, JR., physicist, educator; b. East Orange, N.J., Nov. 25, 1919; s. Robert Inslee and Dorothy Joy (Price) H.; m. Bernice Lord, June 21, 1941 (div. July 1965); children—Stephen, Ann, Deborah, Cynthia; m. Carol K. Ascher, May 27, 1967. B.S., Bates Coll., 1940; M.A., Wesleyan U., Middletown, Conn., 1942; Ph.D., Mass. Inst. Tech., 1948. Staff mem. Radiation Lab., Mass. Inst. Tech., 1942-46, grad. research nature cosmic rays, 1946-49; research cosmic rays U. Ill., 1949-51, devel. computer control naval air def. situation, 1951-57, research low temperature physics, 1957-60; research elementary particle physics and computer aids to data analysis, 1960—; prof. physics Mass. Inst. Tech., 1964—, chmn. faculty, 1977-79; dir. Edn. Research Center, 1964-68; asso. prof. U. Paris, France, 1973-74; cons. Office Naval Research Center, 1957-59; Mem. steering com. Phys. Sci. Study Com., 1959-64; mem. Commn. Coll. Physics, 1960-66; chmn. panel selection fellowships in physics NSF, 1962-65. Author: (with David Lazarus) The World of Physics, 1972; Editor vol. 22: Electronic Time Measurements of Radiation Laboratory Technical Series, 1946. Fellow Am. Phys. Soc.; mem. Am. Assn. Physics Tchrs., AAUP. Home: 305 Memorial Dr Cambridge MA 02139

HULSMAN, CARL HENRY, mfg. co. exec.; b. Medina, O., Feb. 21, 1929; s. John Ernest and Louise (Kirstein) H.; m. Jane Gay Tripp, Sept. 4, 1954; children—John Charles, Ann Elizabeth, Jean Ellen. B.S. magna cum laude, Kent State U., 1955. Pub. accountant Walthall & Drake, Cleve., 1955-62; controller Work Wear Corp., Cleve., 1962—. Served with inf. U.S. Army, 1946-52. Mem. Ohio Soc. C.P.A.'s, Beta Gamma Sigma. Home: 21173 Endsley Ave Rocky River OH 44116 Office: 1768 E 25th St Cleveland OH 44114

HULSTON, JOHN KENTON, lawyer; b. Bona, Mo., Mar. 29, 1915; s. John Fred and Myrtle Rosa (King) H.; m. Ruth Amis Luster, Dec. 18, 1944; 1 son, John Luster. A.B., Drury Coll., Springfield, Mo., 1936; J.D., U. Mo., Columbia, 1941. Bar: Mo. bar 1941, U.S. Supreme Ct. bar 1949. Tchr. Ash Grove (Mo.) High Sch., 1936-38; individual practice law, Springfield, 1946—; sec., dir., v.p. Ozark Air Lines, St. Louis, 1971—; chmn. bd., pres. Bank of Ash Grove, 1959—, Citizens Home Bank, Greenfield, Mo., 1966—; co-founder, dir. Pioneer Oil Co., Ft. Worth, Tex., 1954-79, Reed Oil Co., Big Spring, Tex., 1951-68; vice chmn. Centerre Bank of Springfield, 1972—; operator Copperhead Hill farms (beef production), 1955—; instr. real estate law Drury Coll., 1948-64; vis. lectr. corp. law E.R. Breech Sch. Bus., 1953; chmn. Wilson's Creek Nat. Battlefield Commn., 1961-79, Mo. Civil War Commn., 1961-65, Springfield Charter Commn., 1977; vice chmn. Springfield Home Rule Charter Commn., 1953. Author: Daniel Boone's Sons in Missouri, 1947, West Point and Wilson's Creek-1861, 1955, An Ozark Boy's Story, 1971, An Ozark Lawyer's Story, 1976, Hulston on History, 1979, Col. John Trousdale Coffee, C.S.A., 1983, History of Bank of Ash Grove, 1883-1983, 1983. Trustee Springfield Public Library, 1955-69; trustee Lester E. Cox Med. Center, 1959—, pres., 1966, vice chmn., 1967; chmn. Greene County Democratic Party, 1947-49; introduced Pres. Harry S. Truman at 1st Whistle Stop Speech, Springfield, 1948; trustee Drury Coll., 1973—, State Hist. Soc. Mo., 1974—, U. Mo. Law Sch. Found., Columbia, 1981—; v.p. U. Mo. Law Sch. Found., 1982—; mem. Mo. Civil War Centennial Commn., 1961-65; co-founder Civil War Round Table of the Ozarks, 1948—; Presidential elector for, Mo., 1948; co-founder dir. Wilson's Creek Battlefield Found., 1952, Greene County Hist. Soc., 1960, Mus. of the Ozarks, 1974. Served to maj. U.S. Army, 1941-45. Recipient Springfield Young Man of Year award, 1950, Disting. Alumni award Drury Coll., 1974, Springfieldian of Year award, 1978, Ozark Heritage award, 1979, Spl. commendation Nat. Park Service, 1981. Mem. Am. Judicature Soc., Am. Acad. Hosp. Attys., Am. Bar Assn., Mo. Bar Assn., Greene County Bar Assn. (pres. 1973), Springfield C. of C. (pres. 1950, 51, 54), SAR, Order of Coif, Phi Delta Phi, Kappa Alpha Order. Democrat. Presbyterian. Clubs: Hickory Hills Country, University of Mo. Jefferson (trustee 1976-82), Masons (32 deg.), Shriners (potentate 1963), Jester.). Home: 1300 E Catalpa St Springfield MO 65804 Office: 2060 E Sunshine St Springfield MO 65808 *To me average is not all bad. Awareness of one's limitations often keys extraordinary accomplishments. Recognition of being average sometimes inspires sustained effort necessary to do excellent work, and is the spur to extra drive.*

HULSTRAND, DONALD MAYNARD, bishop; b. Parkers Prairie, Minn., Apr. 16, 1927; s. Aaron Emmanuel H. and Selma Avendla (Liljegren) Hultstrand; m. Marjorie Richter, June 11, 1948; children: Katherine Ann, Charles John. B.A. summa cum laude, Macalester Coll., 1950, B.D., Kenyon Coll., 1953; M.Div., Colgate-Rochester Theol. Sem., 1974. Ordained priest Episcopal Ch., 1953, consecrated bishop, 1982. Vicar St. John's Episcopal Ch., Worthington, Minn., 1953-57; rector Grace Meml. Ch., Wabasha, Minn., 1957-62, St. Mark's Episcopal Ch., Canton, Ohio, 1962-68, St. Paul's Episcopal Ch., Duluth, Minn., 1969-75; assoc. rector St. Andrew's Episcopal Ch., Kansas City, Mo., 1968-69; exec. dir. Anglican Fellowship of Prayer, 1975-79; rector Trinity Episcopal Ch., Greenley, Colo., 1979-82; bishop Episcopal Diocese of Springfield, Ill., 1982; exec. bd. Episcopal Radio (TV Found.), Atlanta, 1982—, Anglican Fellowship of Prayer, Winter Park, Fla., 1968—; adv. bd. Episcopal Boys' Homes, Salinas, Kans., 1983—; com. of execs. Ill. Conf. Chs., 1982—; mem. House of Bishops, 1982—, Minn. Standing Com., 1970-73; chmn. Minn. Examining Chaplains, 1954-61; chaplain Pewsaction Fellowships U.S.A., 1983—; advisor Diocesan Youth of Minn., 1956-60. Author: The Praying Church, 1978, And God Shall Wipe Away All Tears, 1968, Intercessory Prayer, 1972, Upper Room Dialogues, 1980. Bd. dirs. Sr. Citizens Housing, Duluth, 1972-75, St. Luke's Hosp., Duluth, 1969-75; pres. Low-Rent Housing Project, Greenley, 1979-82. Served with USNR, 1945-46. Recipient Disting. Service award Young Life Minn., 1974; named hon. canon Diocese of Ohio, Cleve., 1967. Mem. Pi Phi Epsilon. Lodge: Rotary. Office: Episcopal Diocese of Springfield 821 S 2d St Springfield IL 62704

HULSWIT, MARIUS JAN (MART HULSWIT), actor; b. Maracaibo, Venezuela, May 24, 1940; came to U.S., 1955, naturalized, 1963; s. Marius Jan Frederik and Margaretha (DeHeus) H.; m. Maria Gellner, June 17, 1961; children—Maria Christina, Jennifer Allison. Student, Hobart Coll., 1958-59, Am. Acad. Dramatic Arts, 1960-61. (Recipient Antoinette Perry Promising Personality award 1963, named 1 of 10 top actors daytime TV 1972, Best Actor Daytime TV 1978), Stage appearances, N.Y. Shakespeare Festival, N.Y.C., 1961-63, Romeo and Juliet, Richard II, 1961, Merchant of Venice, The Tempest, King Lear, Macbeth, 1962, 1963, Amazing Grace, 1967, Jeremy Troy, 1977, In Celebration, 1977; TV appearances Naked City, 1962, The Defenders, 1963, duPont Show, 1963, Route 66, The Nurses, The Defenders, Hercules, Combat, 1964, Coronet Blue, Dr. Kildare, Combat, The Seway, 1965, 12 O'Clock High, Flipper, Island of the Lost, 1966, The Desperate Hours, 1967, Directions '68, A Selective Matter, Mannix, 1968, The Guiding Light, 1969—, Primus, 1971; movie roles Come Spy With Me, 1966, A Lovely Way to Die, 1967, Loving, 1969, Doc, 1970. Trustee St. Michaels Montessori Sch., N.Y.C., Bermuda Biol. Sta. Mem. Am. Malacological Union, Screen Actors Guild, Actors Equity Assn., AFTRA. Club: N.Y. Shell (pres. 1970-72). Home: 680 West End Ave New York NY 10025 Office: care Press Relations CBS TV Network 51 W 52d St New York NY 10019 *

HULTBERG, JOHN, artist; b. Berkeley, Calif., Feb. 8, 1922; s. John Waldemar and Mabel Olive (Hammer) H.; m. Hilary Editha Blesh, June 9, 1948 (div. 1956); children: Carl Rudolph, Stephanie Maria; m.

Joyce Elbert, 1959 (div. 1960); m. Lynne Drexler, 1961. A.B., Fresno State Coll., 1943; student, Calif. Sch. Fine Arts, 1947-49, Art Students League, N.Y.C., 1949-51. Exhibited, San Francisco Mus. Art, 1947-49, Los Angeles Mus., 1949, New Talent show, Mus. Modern Art, 1952, one man shows, Korman Gallery, N.Y.C., 1953, Martha Jackson Gallery, N.Y.C., 1955, Corcoran Gallery, Washington, Butler Art Inst., Ohio, UN Exhibit, San Francisco, 1955, Galerie Rive Droit, Paris, 1954-55, Galerie Nina Dausset, Paris, 1954, Galeria Spazio, Rome, 1955, Mus. Modern Art, Rome, Guild Hall, East Hampton, N.Y., I.C.A., London, 1956, others; rep. in collections, Met. Mus. Art, Whitney Mus., Roy R. Neuburger, Edward Root, Michel Tapie.; author 5 books. Served as lt. (j.g.) USNR, 1943-46. Recipient prize San Francisco Mus. watercolor ann., 1948; prize San Francisco oil ann., 1941; hon. mention Los Angeles Centennial painting exhibit, 1949; 1st prize Corcoran Biennial Exhibit, Washington, 1955; prize Congress for Cultural Freedom Exhbn. for painters under 35, Europe, 1955; hon. mention Carnegie Internat. Ex-hon., 1955; Norman Harris medal at 65th ann. exhbn. Art Inst. Chgo.; Altman prize NAD, 1972; Shatlov award NAD, 1983; Albert Bender fellow, San Francisco, 1949; Guggenheim fellow, 1956; Nat. Endowment Arts grantee, 1981. Assoc. mem. NAD. Office: Martha Jackson Gallery 521 W 57th St New York NY 10021

HULTGREN, HERBERT NILS, physician, educator; b. Santa Rosa, Calif., Aug. 29, 1917; s. Adolf W. and Hilda (Hakanson) H.; m. Barbara Brooke, Aug. 7, 1948; children—Peter B., Bruce H., John B. Jr. certificate, Santa Rosa Jr. Coll., 1937; A.B., Stanford, 1939, M.D., 1942. Intern San Francisco Gen. Hosp., 1942-43; resident medicine Stanford Hosp., 1943-44, resident pathology, 1946-47; fellow cardiology Thorndike Meml. Lab., Boston, 1947-48; instr. medicine Stanford Med. Sch., 1948-51, asst. prof., 1951-55, asso. prof., 1955-67, prof., 1967—; chief cardiology Service Palo Alto VA Hosp., 1969—; Chmn. Subspeciality Bd. Cardiovascular Disease, 1972—; co-chmn. VA Coop. Study Surgery in Coronary Artery Disease, 1972—. Contbr. articles to profl. jours. Served from 1st lt. to capt., M.C. AUS, 1944-46; ETO. Markle scholar in med. sci., 1951-56. Mem. Western Soc. Clin. Research (pres.), Western Assn. Physicians (pres.), Assn. U. Cardiologists (pres.), Phi Beta Kappa. Home: 827 San Francisco Ct Stanford CA 94305 Office: Palo Alto VA Hosp Palo Alto CA 94304

HULTGREN, WARREN CURTIS, clergyman; b. Mpls., Dec. 16, 1920; s. David Clarence and Myrtle Elvina (Hansen) H.; m. Wanda Lee Wadsworth, Sept. 3, 1946; children—Landa Lee Mabry, Warren Curtis, Howard Madison. B.A., Hardin-Simmons U., 1947; B.D., Southwestern Baptist Theol. Sem., 1950; Ph.D., Calif. Grad. Sch. Theology, Golden Gate U., 1976; D.Div., U. Corpus Christi, 1954; D.Litt., Christian U., Los Angeles, 1975; Litt.D., Am. Christian U., 1976; L.H.D., William Jewell Coll., 1977, Hardin Simmons U., 1977; D.S.T., S.W. Bapt. U. Mo., 1982. Ordained to ministry Bapt. Ch., 1944; pastor in, Corpus Christi, 1950-55, Lake Charles, La., 1955-57, First Bapt. Ch., Tulsa, 1957—; v.p. So. Bapt. Conv., 1971-72; pres. Bapt. Gen. Conv. Okla., 1974-75; exec. com. Bapt. World Alliance. Trustee Okla. Bapt. U., Hillcrest Med. Center, Tulsa; chmn. bd. Dillon Family and Youth Services, Acute Care Psychiat. Hosp.; bd. dirs. Tulsa Council on Alcoholism. Recipient Nat. Humanitarian award Inst. Human Relations, N.Y.C., 1978; hon. prof. Myong Ji U., Seoul, Korea. Fellow Royal Geog. Soc. Gt. Britain; mem. Am. Assn. Marriage and Family Therapy, Tulsa Com. Fgn. Relations, Knights of Malta (chaplain), Am. Schs. Oriental Research. Club: Rotarian (Paul Harris fellow). Home: 3127 S Lewis St Tulsa OK 74105 Office: First Baptist Ch 4th at Cincinnati St Tulsa OK 74103

HULTMAN, CHARLES WILLIAM, economics educator; b. Oelwein, Iowa, Apr. 6, 1930; s. John William and Alma (Loeb) H.; m. Irene Oliver, June 7, 1957; children: Susan, Gregory. B.A., Upper Iowa U., 1952; M.A., Drake U., 1957; Ph.D., U. Iowa, 1960. Asst. prof. U. Ky. at Lexington, 1960-64, prof. econs., 1967—, chmn. dept., 1969-71, asso. dir., 1971-73, asso. dean for research, 1976—; vis. asso. prof. U. Calif., 1964-65. Author: International Finance, 1963, American Business and the Common Market, 1964, Problems of Economic Development, 1967, Ireland in the World Economy, 1969, (with M. Wasserman, R. Ware) International Economics, 1969, Comparison of Projected Unemployment Insurance Costs, 1973; Book rev. editor: Internat. Devel. Rev; mem. editorial adv. bd.: Sage Papers in Internat. Studies; acting editor: Jour. Growth and Change, 1979—. Chmn. Ky. Council of Econ. Advisors, 1976—; mem. So. Growth Policies Bd., 1976—. Served with AUS, 1952-55. Fulbright lectr., Ireland, 1967-68. Mem. Am. Econ. Assn., So. Econ. Assn., Midwest Econ. Assn., Eastern Econ. Assn. (exec. bd. 1980—). Lutheran. Home: 3341 Crown Crest Lexington KY 40502

HULTMAN, EVAN LEROY, lawyer; b. Albia, Iowa, July 15, 1925; s. Paul Norman and Laura (Cox) H.; m. Betty A. Hook, Oct. 14, 1944; children: Susan Jane, Stevan Kent, Heidi Ann. Student, Iowa State U., Ames, 1943, U. Ill., 1944; B.A. summa cum laude, U. Iowa-Iowa City, 1949; J.D. cum laude, U. Iowa-Iowa City, 1952; postgrad. exec. program, Harvard U., 1982. Bar: Iowa, U.S. Dist. Ct. Iowa. Atty gen. State of Iowa, Des Moines, 1960-64; sole practice, Waterloo, Iowa, 1964-69; U.S. atty. U.S. Dept. Justice, Sioux City, Iowa, 1969-77, spl. prosecutor, Waterloo, 1977-78, U.S. atty., Cedar Rapids, Iowa, 1982—; sole practice, Waterloo, 1978-82; atty. City of Waterloo, 1978-82; res. asst. to Judge Advocate Gen. of Army, Washington, 1974-76. Author: Eminent Domain in Iowa, 1962, Tax Manual: Prosecuting Attorneys, 1976. Pres. Wapsininicon and Winnebago council Boy Scouts Am., Waterloo, 1970-76. Capt. U.S. Army, 1943-46. Recipient Outstanding Service award Iowa Policemen's Assn., Hall of Leadership award U.S. Jaycees, Silver Beaver award Boy Scouts Am., 1968, Silver Antelope award Boy Scouts Am., 1977. Mem. Iowa Fed. Bar Assn. (pres. 1973-74), Iowa Bar Assn., Fed. Bar Assn. (1st v.p. 1981-82, pres. 1983—), Res. Officers Assn. (nat. pres. 1981-82), Sr. Army Res. Comdrs. Assn. (nat. pres. 1983), Phi Beta Kappa, Phil Beta Sigma, Omicron Delta Kappa, Delta Sigma Rho. Republican. Methodist. Home: 525 Martin Rd Waterloo IA 50701 Office: US Attys Office 101 1st St SE Cedar Rapids IA 52401

HULTQUIST, PAUL FREDRICK, educator, electrical engineer; b. Holdrege, Nebr., Mar. 24, 1920; s. Fred Oscar and Lalan Ragnhild (Swanberg) H.; m. Juanita Marie Tokheim, Apr. 7, 1946; children: Fredrick James, Ann Marie. Student, Bethany Coll., Lindsborg, Kans., 1940-41, Hastings Coll., 1943-44; B.A. cum laude, U. Colo., 1945; Ph.D. (AEC predoctoral fellow), U. Colo., 1954. Instr. applied math. U. Colo., Boulder, 1952-55, asst. prof., 1955-59, asso. prof., 1959-63, prof., asst. dean engring., Colorado Springs, 1965-71, prof. elec. engring., asso. dean, Denver, 1971, prof. elec. and computer engring., 1971—, prof. computer sci., 1982—, asso. dir. Univ. Computer Center, 1973-76; asso. research scientist Lockheed Missiles and Space Co., Palo Alto, Calif., 1956-57; sr. staff scientist Ball Bros. Research Corp., Boulder, 1963-65; cons. in field. Contbr. numerous articles, revs. to profl. publs. Trustee Bethphage Mission, Inc., Axtell, Nebr., 1966-76, 78—; chmn. Bethphage Mission, 1980—; trustee Bethpage Residential Ctrs., 1983—; mem. mgmt. com. div. parish services Luth. Ch. Am., 1972-78, 80—, chmn., 1982—; bd. dirs. Luth. Sch. Theology at Chgo., 1972-78, chmn., 1975-78; bd. dirs. Pacific Luth. Theol. Sem., Berkeley, 1981—. Mem. Assn. Computing Machinery, Soc. Indsl. and Applied Math., IEEE (sr.), Math. Assn. Am., Soc. Petroleum Engrs. of AIME, Soc. Computer Simulation (asso. editor Simulation), Phi Beta Kappa, Sigma Xi, Tau Beta Pi. Democrat. Home: 2615 Van Gordon Dr Lakewood CO 80215 Office: 1100 14th St Denver CO 80202

HUMBARD, REX EMANUEL, TV evangelist; b. Little Rock, Aug. 13, 1919; s. Alpha Emanuel and Martha Bell (Childers) H.; m. Maude Aimee Jones, Aug. 2, 1942; children—Rex Emanuel, Don Raymond, Aimee Elizabeth, Charles Raymond. D.D. (hon.), Trinity Coll., Dunedin, Fla., 1970, L.H.D., Oral Roberts U., Tulsa, 1973. Ordained to ministry Evang. Ch., 1943; evangelistic radio ministry, 1933—; founder, pastor Cathedral of Tomorrow, Akron, Ohio, 1952—, also chmn. bd. dirs.; worldwide evangelistic TV ministry, 1952—; chmn. bd. dirs. Rex Humbard Ministry in Can.; del. Congress on Evangelism, Lausanne, Switzerland, 1974. Author: Put God on Main Street, 1970, Miracles in My Life, 1971, The Third Dimension, 1972, Numerous spiritual periodicals, tracts and recordings. Office: 2700 State Rd Cuyahoga Falls OH 44223 *The main ingredients to my success have been an adherence to the principles of God and the ability to think big. When I decided that I would go on television and reach the world with the gospel, TV was in its infancy. It is only when we think big that we really test the resources of God.*

HUMBERSTONE, JOSEPH HOWARD, mgmt. cons.; b. Toledo, Oct. 25, 1909; s. Ernest Howard and Pauline (Gildemeister) H.; m. Mary Ida Thomas, Oct. 23, 1933 (dec. 1969); 1 dau., Susan; m. Betty Jane Duvall, 1969. B.Met.E., Ohio State U., 1931, D.Sc. (hon.), 1962. Devel. engr. Gen. Electric Co., 1932-38; with Arcrods Co., N.Y.C., 1939-61, Airco, Inc., Montvale, N.J., 1948-74, v.p., 1951-63, group v.p., dir., 1963-74; pres. Patent Mgmt., Inc., N.Y.C., 1974—, Satra Cons. Corp., 1974—; prin. Case & Co. Internat., Inc., N.Y.C., 1978—; dir. Nat. State Bank, Elizabeth, N.J. Mem. war metallurgy com. NRC, 1942-44. Mem. Am. Welding Soc. (pres. 1954-56), Am. Ordnance Assn., Nat. Security Indsl. Assn., Nat. C. of C. Clubs: Greenwich (Conn.) Country; Blind Brook (Port Chester, N.Y.); Duquesne (Pitts.). Office: Patent Mgmt Inc 919 3d Ave New York NY 10022

HUME, ALEXANDER BRITTON, journalist; b. Washington, June 22, 1943; s. George and Virginia Powell (Minnigerode) H.; m. Clare Jacobs Stoner, Feb. 10, 1965; children—Louis, Virginia, Alexander. B.A., U. Va., 1965. Reporter Hartford Times, 1965-66, UPI, 1967, Balt. Evening Sun, 1968; freelance reporter, Washington, 1969; reporter Jack Anderson column, Washington, 1970-72; cons. ABC News, Washington, 1973-76, correspondent, 1976—. Author: Death and the Mines, 1971, Inside Story, 1974. Washington Journalism Center fellow, spring 1969. Mem. Radio-TV Correspondents Assn. Episcopalian. Club: Chevy Chase. Home: 5409 Blackistone Rd Bethesda MD 20816 Office: 1717 DeSales St Washington DC 20036

HUME, DAVID DESJARDINS, headmaster; b. New Milford, Conn., Jan. 18, 1928; s. Nelson and May Eleanor (DesJardins) H.; m. Catherine Porter Lewis, Apr. 11, 1953; children: Christopher, Adam, Benjamin, Charity, Amity, Noah. B.A., Yale U., 1949; M.A., Columbia U., 1950. Research asst. Columbia Tchrs. Coll., N.Y.C., 1950-52; headmaster Saint David's Sch., N.Y.C., 1953—. Pres. Independent Sch. Orch., N.Y.C.; pres. More House, Yale U., 1971—; trustee Marymount Sch., N.Y.C., 1969—; bd. dirs. Nat. Assn. Ind. Schs., 1972-77; pres. N.Y. State Assn. Ind. Schs., 1977-78, now trustee and mem. commn. on accreditation. Served with USNR, 1945-46. Mem. Country Day Schs. Headmasters Assn. (pres. 1976-77), Elem. Sch. Heads Assn. (treas. 1973-78, pres. 1978-79). Club: Elizabethan (Yale). Address: 12 E 89th St New York NY 10028

HUME, DAVID LANG, international trade consultant; b. Brookings, S.D., May 21, 1914; s. Albert Nash and Ruth (Thomson) H.; m. Selina Best, Oct. 11, 1942. B.S., S.D. State U., 1936, D.Agr. (hon.), 1977; M.S., N.D. State U., 1940. Adminstrv. asst. to dean agr. and to dir. agrl. expt. sta. N.D. State U., Fargo, 1940-41; with Q.M. Market Center System, U.S. Armed Forces, Chgo., 1945-52; v.p., partner Frank A. Donnelly Corp. (food wholesalers), Chgo., 1952-55; with U.S. Dept. Agr., 1955-77, asst. adminstr. Fgn. Agrl. Service, Washington, 1962-67; agrl. attache Am. embassy, London, 1968-72, Tokyo, 1972-73; adminstr. Fgn. Agrl. Service U.S. Dept Agr., Washington, 1973-77; internat. trade cons., 1977—. Served to maj. AUS, 1941-45. Recipient Superior Service award USDA, 1971; Disting. Alumnus award S.D. State U., 1973; Disting. Service award Am. Agrl. Editors Assn., 1974. Mem. Am. Soc. Agrl. Cons. (dir.-at-large), Am. Soc. Agrl. Cons. Internat. (founder, bd. govs.), Alpha Gamma Rho. Clubs: Farmers (London); Tokyo; Internat. (Washington); Army Navy Country (Arlington, Va.). Address: 10615 Campana Dr Sun City AZ 85351

HUME, JAMES NAIRN PATTERSON, computer science educator; b. Bklyn., Mar. 17, 1923; s. James Smith and Jean Frances (Nairn) H.; m. Patricia Anne Molyneux, Aug. 8, 1953; children: Stephen, Philip, Harriet, Mark. B.A., U. Toronto, 1945, M.A., 1946, Ph.D., 1949. Instr. physics Rutgers U., 1950; asst. prof. physics U. Toronto, 1950-57, assoc. prof., 1957-63, prof. physics and computer sci., 1963—, assoc.dean Grad. Sch., 1968-72, chmn. computer sci. dept., 1975-80, master Massey Coll., 1981—. Author: High-Speed Data Processing, 1958, Physics in Two Volumes, 1974, Structured Programming Using PL-1, 1975; other programming books on Fortran, 1977; Fortran77, 1979, Pascal, 1980, UCSD Pascal, 1982, Pascal Under Unix, 1983, Apple Basic, 1983; ednl. TV shows, Films. Recipient awards for best adult and children's sci. TV programs State of Ohio, 1962, citation for best sci. edn. film Edison Found., 1962, Silver medal Sci. Inst. Rome, 1962, Silver Core award Internat. Fedn. for Info. Processing, 1974, Disting. Service Citation Am. Assn. Physics Tchrs., 1979, Can. Centennial medal, 1967. Mem. Am. Phys. Soc., Assn. for Computing Machinery, Can. Info. Processing Soc., Sigma Xi. Club: Arts and Letters (Toronto). Home: 4 Devonshire Pl Toronto ON Canada M5S 2E1 Office: Dept Computer Sci U Toronto Toronto ON Canada M5S 1A7

HUME, JOHN E.N., JR., newspaper editor; b. Schenectady, Sept. 10, 1915; s. John E. N. and Anna Cady (Smith) H.; m. Marion Stewart Hume, Apr. 15, 1939; 1 son, John E.N. III. B.S., U. Va., 1937; L.H.D., Union Coll., 1978. With Schenectady Gazette, corr., 1930-37, reporter and photographer, 1937-40, city editor, 1940-46, editor, 1946—; also pres. Daily Gazette Co. Mem. Am., N.Y. State socs. newspaper editors, N.Y. State Pubs. Assn., Am. Ordnance Assn., Schenectady C. of C. (dir. 1945), Beta Theta Pi. Republican. Episcopalian. Clubs: Masons., Mohawk, Mohawk Golf, Saratoga Reading Rooms. Home: 2029 Lexington Pkwy Schenectady NY 12309 Office: 332 State St Schenectady NY 12301

HUME, PAUL CHANDLER, music editor, music educator; b. Chgo., Dec. 13, 1915; s. Robert Woolsey and Katherine English (Rockwell) H.; m. Ruth Fox, Dec. 29, 1949; children: Paul, Michael, Ann, Peter. Ed., U. Chgo., 1937; D.Mus. (hon.), Thiel Coll., 1968, L.H.D., Rosary Coll., 1977, Georgetown U., 1979. Music editor Washington Post, 1946-82; prof. music, Georgetown U., 1950-77; vis. prof. music Yale U., 1975—; lectr. Author: Catholic Church Music, 1956, (with Mrs. Hume) The Lion of Poland, 1962, King of Song, 1964, Verdi, 1977; Co-editor: Hymnal of Christian Unity, 1964. Recipient Peabody award, 1978; Profl. Achievement award U. Chgo. Alumni Assn., 1978. Mem. Music Critics Assn. (exec. com. 1962-63). Club: Cosmos (Washington). Home: 3625 Tilden St NW Washington DC 20008

HUME, WARREN CHARLES, manufacturing executive; b. Chgo., June 14, 1916; s. Charles and Genevieve (Keller) H.; m. Augusta Yust, June 5, 1939; children: David, Nicholas, Christina. A.B., Rollins Coll., 1939, LL.D., 1970; M.B.A., Mich. State U., 1950; grad., Advanced Mgmt. Program, Harvard U., 1956. With IBM, 1939-81, div. v.p., regional mgr., Chgo., 1960-61, div. v.p., gen. mgr., White Plains, N.Y., 1961, pres. data processing div., White Plains, 1961-65, corp. v.p., group exec., 1965-67, sr. v.p., 1967-77, also mem. corp. mgmt. com.; chmn. bd. Atlantic Pacific Marine Corp.; dir. Interpace Corp., Thysen Bornemesa Netherlands, Maersk Lines Ltd., Moller S.S. Lines. Contbr. articles to profl. jours. Trustee Rollins Coll.; internat. adv. bd. Columbia U. Grad. Sch. Bus. Served with USNR, 1942-46; PTO. Mem. USSGA Am. Srs., Eastern Srs. Home: 75 Cowdin Rd Chappaqua NY 10514 Office Old Orchard Rd Armonk NY 10504

HUMELSINE, CARLISLE HUBBARD, foundation executive; b. Hagerstown, Md., Mar. 12, 1915; s. Charles Ellsworth and Anna Barbara (McNamee) H.; m. Mary Miller Speake, Aug. 16, 1941; children: Mary Carlisle Humelsine Norment, Barbara Anne Humelsine Harmon. A.B., U. Md., 1937, H.H.D. (hon.), 1974, LL.D., Coll. William and Mary, 1963, Hampden-Sydney Coll., 1970, L.H.D., Rutgers U., 1976. Editor publs., spl. asst. to pres. U. Md., 1937-41; exec. sec. U.S. Dept. State, 1947-50, asst. sec., dep. under-sec. state, 1953; exec. v.p. Colonial Williamsburg Found., 1953-58, pres., chief exec. officer, 1958-77, chmn. bd., chief exec. officer, 1977-80, chmn. bd., 1980—; dir. N.Y. Life Ins. Co., Grand Teton Lodge Co., Caneel Bay Plantation, Chesapeake & Potomac Telephone Co., United Va. Bankshares, Inc., Sleepy Hollow Restoration, Inc.; chmn. emeritus Nat. Trust for Hist. Preservation, 1980—. Trustee, v.p. Nat. Gallery Art; regent, chmn. exec. com. Smithsonian Instn.; bd. dirs. Nat. Geog. Soc.; trustee emeritus Mariners Mus. Served from lt. to col. U.S. Army, 1941-45. Decorated D.S.M., Bronze Star. Mem. Alpha Tau Omega, Omicron Delta Kappa, Pi Delta Epsilon. Democrat. Episcopalian. Clubs: Metropolitan (Washington); Commonwealth (Richmond). Home: Moody House Williamsburg VA 23185 Office: Colonial Williamsburg Found Williamsburg VA 23185

HUMENIK, MICHAEL, automobile co. exec.; b. Garfield, N.J., Nov. 10, 1924; s. Michael and Rose (Biliy) H.; m. Audrey Svahra, Sept. 5, 1948; children—Gwen, Michael, Edward. B.S., Alfred U., 1949; Sc.D. in Ceramics, M.I.T., 1952. Research asst. M.I.T., 1949-52; research engr. Ford Motor Co., Dearborn, Mich., 1952-54, supr. ceramic and powder metallurgy, 1954-62, mgr. ceramics and glass research, 1962-69, asst. dir. mfg. research, 1969-75, dir. plastics and surface processing lab., 1975-76, dir. mfg. processes lab. research, 1976—. Served with USAAF, 1943-45. Recipient Fellow Am. Ceramic Soc. (Ferro Enamels award 1952); mem. Am. Soc. Metals, AIME, Soc. Mfg. Engrs. (Progress award 1980). Home: 17097 Cambridge Ave Allen Park MI 48101 Office: 24500 Glendale Detroit MI 48239

HUMES, JAMES CALHOUN, lawyer, communications consultant, author; b. Williamsport, Pa., Oct. 31, 1934; s. Samuel Hamilton and Elenor Kathryn (Graham) H.; m. Dianne Stuart, July 25, 1957; children: Mary Stuart, Rachel Bailey. Student, Hill Sch., Stowe Sch., Eng., Williams Coll., 1953-55; A.B., George Washington U., 1959, J.D., 1962. Bar: Pa. 1963. Mem. Pa. Ho. of Reps., 1962-65; exec. dir. Phila. Bar Assn., 1967-69; presdl. asst. policy planning sect. White House, Washington, 1969-70; dir. Office Policy and Plans, U.S. Dept. State, 1970-72; cons. U.S. Dept. Treasury, Middle East, 1972—; presdl. asst. White House Staff; White House cons. to Pres. Ford, 1976-77; pres. Kingstree Communications, 1979-82; Woodrow Wilson fellow Smithsonian Instn., 1982-83; mem. U.S. Commn. UNESCO. Author: Sweet Dream, 1966, Instant Eloquence, 1973, Podium Humor, 1975, Roles Speakers Play, 1976, How to Get Invited to the White House, 1977, Speaker's Treasury of Anecdotes, 1977; Co-Author: Primary, 1980; Author: Winston Churchill: Speaker of the Century, 1980, Talk Your Way to the Top, 1980; editorial advisor: Pres. Ford's memoirs A Time to Heal. Mem. St. Nicholas Soc., N.Y., Pilgrims, St. Andrew's Soc., Phila., S.R., Colonial Soc. Pa., Sons Colonial Wars, Order of Magna Charta. Republican. Presbyterian. Clubs: Athenaeum; Union League, Cricket (Phila.); Brook (N.Y.). Home: 203 W Chestnut Hill Ave Philadelphia PA 19118

HUMES, JOHN P., lawyer, diplomat; b. N.Y.C., July 21, 1921; m. Jean Cooper Schmidlapp; 6 sons. Grad., St. Paul's Sch.; A.B., Woodrow Wilson Sch. Pub. and Internat. Affairs, Princeton U., 1943; LL.D., Fordham U., 1948, Marist Coll. Bar: N.Y. 1948. Assoc. firm Shearman & Sterling, N.Y.C., 1948-55; partner firm Humes, Andrews & Botzow, N.Y.C., 1956-69; ambassador to Austria, Vienna, 1969-75, ret., 1975. Author: Excerpts from the Vienna Diaries of Ambassador John Portner Humes. Vice chmn. founders council Inst. for Study Diplomacy, Georgetown U.; exec. com. Nassau County council Boy Scouts Am.; hon. trustee Fay Sch., Southborough, Mass., Kips Bay Boys' Club; trustee North Shore Wildlife Preserve, Episcopal Found. Edn. Diocese L.I., Nat. Art Mus. Sport, Salzburg (Austria) Seminar in Am. Studies, Am. Inst. Mus. Studies, Graz, Austria, St. Luke's-Roosevelt Hosp. (hon.); hon. trustee Portledge Sch., Locust Valley, N.Y.; bd. visitors Georgetown Sch. Fgn. Service, Washington; bd. dirs. Council Am. Ambassadors; founder, pres. Humes Found.; charter trustee Am.-Austrian Found.; treas. Reading Reform Found. Served with AUS, 1943-46; ETO. Decorated Great Golden Medal of Honor with sash Republic of Austria; Merito Navali, Austria; grand officier Chevaliers des Tastevins; N.Y. State squash racquets champion, 1950. Mem. Assn. Bar City N.Y., ABA, N.Y. State Bar Assns., Internat. Law Assn., English Speaking Union, St. George's Soc., World Affairs Council Phila. (adv. council), Soc. Colonial Wars, SR (Disting. Patriot award), Alumni Assn. St. Paul's Sch. (pres. 1964-66), Pres.'s Council, Am. Ditchley Found., U.S. Squash Racquets Assn. (pres. 1954-56), Pilgrims U.S., Delta Theta Phi. Republican. Episcopalian. Clubs: Brook, Down Town Assn. (trustee), N.Y. Yacht, Union (N.Y.C.); Piping Rock (Locust Valley, N.Y.); Seawanahaka Corinthian Yacht (Oyster Bay, N.Y.); Chevy Chase (Washington); Travellers (Paris, France); Masons, Jesters, Royal Cornwall Yacht (Eng.), Royal Norwegian Yacht.). Home: Frost Mill Rd Mill Neck NY 11765 Office: 708 3d Ave Suite 3505 New York NY 10017

HUMES, ROBERT ERNEST, pharmaceutical company executive; b. Erie, Pa., Sept. 30, 1943; s. Millard and Mildred Rosemary (Sabatino) H.; m. JoAnn Florence Malanka, May 29, 1965; children: Christine Marie, Robert Ernest Jr. B.A., St. John's U., 1967; M.B.A., NYU, 1974. With Met. Life Ins. Co., N.Y.C., 1961-67; asst. to v.p. sales U.S. Life Ins. Co., N.Y.C., 1967-68; supr. ins. Bristol Myers Co., N.Y.C., 1968-71; mgr. personnel planning Squibb Corp., N.Y.C., 1971-72, dir. personnel planning, 1972-75, exec. asst. to chmn., 1975-79, v.p. exec. asst. to chmn., N.Y.C., 1979-82, sr. v.p. human resources, Princeton, 1982—. Chmn. Mayor's Task Force on Pvt. Sector Intiatives, Lawrence Twp., N.J., 1982—. Mem. N.Y. Indsl. Relations Assn. (pres. 1981-83), Am. Soc. Personnel Adminstrn., Am. Pension Conf. (steering com. 1981-83). Home: 40 Htchinson Dr Port Monmouth NJ 07758 Office: Squibb Corp PO Box 4000 Princeton NJ 08540

HUMMEL, ARTHUR WILLIAM, JR., fgn. service officer; b. Fenchow, China, June 1, 1920; s. Arthur William and Ruth Emily (Bookwalter) H.; m. Betty L. Fristenberger, May 31, 1951; children—Timothy A., William A. Student, Antioch Coll., 1937-39. Coll. of Chinese Studies, Peking, 1940-41; M.A., U. Chgo., 1949. English tchr. Fu Jen Middle Sch., Peking, 1941; interned by Japanese, 1941-44, escaped, 1944; mem. Chinese guerrilla unit, 1944-45; liaison officer UNNRA, Tientsin, China, 1945-46; staff lectr. United Service to China, N.Y.C., 1946-47; intelligence analyst officer naval Intelligence, 1950; fgn. affairs officer Dept. of State, 1950-52; consul, dep. pub. affairs officer, Hong Kong, 1952, pub. affairs officer, 1953-55; attache, dep. pub. affairs officer Am. embassy, Tokyo, Japan, 1955-57, attache, pub. affairs officer, Rangoon, Burma, 1957-60; assigned Nat. War Coll., 1960-61; dep. dir. Voice of Am., 1961-63; dep. asst. U.S. sec. of state for cultural and ednl. affairs, 1963-65; dep. chief of mission Am. embassy, Taipei, Taiwan, 1965-68; Am. ambassador, Rangoon, Burma, 1968-71; dep. asst. sec. state for Far Eastern and Pacific affairs, 1971-75; ambassador to, Ethiopia, 1975-76; asst. sec. state for Far Eastern and Pacific Affairs, 1976-77; ambassador to, Pakistan, 1977-81, to, China, Beijing, 1981—. Recipient Arthur S. Fleming award, 1959. Mem. Far Eastern Assn., Phi Beta Kappa. Office: US Embassy 17 Guanghua Lu Beijing People's Republic of China

HUMMEL, CHARLES FREDERICK, museum official; b. Bklyn., Sept. 16, 1932; s. Charles Frederick and Helen (Yost) H.; m. Marlene Simons, Aug. 16, 1952; children: Mark, Jonathan, Laura, Jeffrey. B.A. magna cum laude, CCNY, 1953; M.A., U. Del., 1955. Curatorial asst. Henry Francis du Pont Winterthur Museum, Winterthur, Del., 1955-58, asst. curator, 1958-60, assoc. curator, 1960-67, curator, 1967-79, dep. dir. collections, 1979—; adj. asso. prof. art history U. Del., Newark, 1964—; v.p., chmn. grants-in-aid com. Early Am. Industries Assn.; mem. Nat. Inst. for Conservation, Washington, 1973—, v.p., 1979-83. Author: With Hammer in Hand, 1968; co-author: exhbn. catalogue The Pennsylvania Germans: A Celebration of their Arts, 1683-1850, 1982; Contbr. to: Brit. Ency. Am. Art, 1973, Winterthur Guide to American Chippendale Furniture, 1976. Pres. Northridge Civic Assn., Claymont, Del., 1961-63; pres. Greenville (Del.) PTA, 1972-74. Served with CIC AUS, 1956-58. Fellow Winterthur Program in Early Am. Culture, 1953-55. Mem. Am. Assn. Museums, Hajji Baba Soc. N.Y., Phi Beta Kappa, Phi Alpha Theta. Unitarian (v.p., trustee 1963-66). Office: Winterthur Museum Winterthur DE 19735

HUMMEL, FRED ERNEST, architect; b. Sheridan, Wyo., Jan. 10, 1927; s. Fred Edward and Glenna Ruth (Horton) H.; m. Sue Anne Estep, May 11, 1970; children: Jessica, Rebecca and Amber (triplets); children by previous marriage: Glenn, Mark, Shaun and Lindsay (twins). B.A., U. Calif., Berkeley, 1951. Pvt. practice architecture, Ventura, Calif., 1951-68, Sacramento, 1973—; the state architect, State of Calif., Sacramento, 1968-73; instr. architecture extension night courses U. Calif., Los Angeles, 1966-67, Davis, 1974; mem. adv. panel for archtl. services GSA, 1974; cons. State of Ark. Capitol Outlay Study, 1975; chmn. Calif. Bldg. Standards Coordination Council, 1970-71; ex-officio mem. Calif. Bldg. Standards Commn., 1969-73, Field Act Adv. Group, 1968-72; archtl. cons. Mich. Gov.'s Commn. on Architecture, 1972; mem. Calif. Gov.'s Earthquake Council, 1972-73, Calif. Affirmative Action Implementation Com., 1971-72, Calif. Ad Hoc Commn. on Energy Conservation, 1973, Capitol Mall Adv. Planning Com., 1970-71, Calif. Gov.'s Task Force on Capitol Outlay Projects, 1970-71; mem. adv. com. on environ. design and urban studies to Calif. Coordinating Council for Higher Edn., 1970-71; mem. adv. group on engring. and earthquake scis. to Calif. Joint Legis. Com. on Seismic Safety, 1972-73; mem. Commn. of the Californias, 1972-82; mem. adv. bd. Nat. Park System, 1981—; mem. Sacramento County Sheriff's Air Squadron, 1981. Served to 1st lt. inf. U.S. Army, 1945-47, 51; Korea. Recipient award of honor Chico State U., 1974, Hon. award Cons. Engrs. Assn. of Calif., 1969, presentation Ann. Architects and Engrs. Forum, Los Angeles, 1969, Calif. Senate and Assembly resolutions of commendation, 1973. Fellow AIA (pres., dir. Santa Barbara, Calif. chpt. 1962, dir. Calif. council 1961-63, mem. Calif. profl. practice com. 1969, mem. exec. com. Calif. council, state treas. 1961-62, AIA Disting. Service Citation Calif. council 1973, v.p. edn. Calif. council 1978, mem. nat. govtl. relations com. 1974-76, nat. capitol com. 1973-74, dir. Central Valley chtp. 1973-74, mem. nat. architects in govt. com. 1971-72, chmn. Calif. council architects in govt. com. 1970-73, mem. Calif. govt. relations com. 1964-67, dir. Ventura County chpt. 1964-66, mem. Calif. evaluation bd. 1964). Republican. Home: 5007 Sugar Ln Carmichael CA 95608 Office: 4652 Whitney Ave Sacramento CA 95821 *Work hard, be honest, take time to smell the flowers, and trust in God.*

HUMMEL, GENE MAYWOOD, bishop; b. Lancaster, Ohio, Nov. 12, 1926; s. Ivan Maywood and Anna Mildred (Black) H.; m. R. Jeannine Lane, June 17, 1950; children: Gregory L., G. Michael. Student, Miami U., Oxford, Ohio, 1944, Dartmouth Coll., 1944-45; B.S. in Agr, Ohio State U., 1949, Ohio State U., 1950. Supr. North Am. Aviation Inc., Columbus, Ohio, 1951-57; prodn. control chief Martin Co., Orlando, Fla., 1957-61; ordained to ministry Reorganized Ch. of Jesus Christ of Latter Day Saints, 1961; ministerial asst. to Center Stake bishop, Independence, Mo., 1961-63; bishop San Francisco Bay Stake, 1964-70, Hawaii, 1968-70, Center Stake, 1970-72; bishop, mem. Presiding Bishopric Internat. Ch., 1972—; pres., dir. Health Care Systems, Inc., 1983—; dir. Center Place Improvement Inc., Independence, Central Profl. Bldg., Inc., E.A. Smith Retirement Center, Inc., Central Devel. Assn., Inc.; dir., v.p. Systems Communication, Inc., Independence, 1975—. Bd. dirs., pres. Independence Sanitarium and Hosp., 1972—; Bd. dirs. Mound Grove Cemetery, Independence, 1970—. Served with USNR, 1944-45. Mem. Independence C. of C. (v.p., dir.). Club: Rotary. Office: Box 1059: 221 W Lexington St Independence MO 64051

HUMMEL, MARTIN HENRY, JR., advertising agency executive; b. Glen Ridge, N.J., May 7, 1927; s. Martin Henry and Florence (Lanken) H.; m. Evelyn Mayer, Sept. 19, 1953; children—Martin Henry III, Patricia Katherine. A.B., Cornell U., 1949. With Vick Chem. Co., 1949-50, J. Walter Thompson, 1950-51, Crowell-Collier Pub. Co., 1952-57; with Sullivan, Stauffer, Colwell and Bayles, Inc., N.Y.C., 1957—, exec. v.p., 1968—, also dir.; vice chmn., mng. dir. SSC & B-Lintas Internat., Ltd. Served with Stars and Stripes, World War II. Mem. Am. Assn. Advt. Agys. (chmn. internat. com.). Clubs: Cornell, Pinnacle, Marco Polo, Overseas Press (N.Y.C.); American (London). Home: 6 Capron Ln Upper Montclair NJ 07043 Office: One Dag Hammarskjold Plaza New York NY 10017

HUMMER, DAVID GRAYBILL, astrophysicist; b. Manheim, Pa., Nov. 4, 1934; s. John Herbert and Lillian (Graybill) H.; m. Janet Wood, Mar. 25, 1961; 1 son, Julius. B.S., Carnegie Inst. Tech., 1957, M.S., 1958; Ph.D. (Fulbright scholar), Univ. Coll. London, 1963. Physicist Gen. Atomic Corp., San Diego, 1958-59; research asst. Univ. Coll. London, 1961-63, lectr., 1964-66; vis. fellow Joint Inst. for Lab. Astrophysics, Boulder, Colo., 1963-64, chmn., 1973-74, 77-78; physicist Nat. Bur. of Standards and; fellow Joint Inst. for Lab. Astrophysics, 1966—; adj. prof. U. Colo., Boulder. Co-editor: Atoms in Astrophysics, 1983; Contbr. articles to profl. jours.; translator: books from Russian Planetary Nebulae (G.A. Gurzadyan), 1969, Transfer of Radiation in Spectral Lines (V.V. Ivanov), 1974, Theory of Ionization of Atoms by Electron Impact (R.K. Peterkop), 1977. Recipient cert. commendation Nat. Bur. Standards, 1969, Spl. Achievement award, 1973, 77; Arthur S. Flemming award Downtown Jaycees, Washington, 1974. Fellow AAAS; mem. Am. Phys. Soc., Am. Astron. Soc., Astron. Soc. Pacific, Royal Astron. Soc., Internat. Astron. Union., Soc. Indsl. and Applied Math. Home: Alder Ln Pine Brook Hills Boulder CO 80304 Office: Joint Inst Lab Astrophysics U Colo Boulder CO 80309

HUMPERDINCK, ENGELBERT (ARNOLD GEORGE DORSEY), singer; b. Madras, India, May 3, 1936; S. Mervyn and Olive Dorsey; m. Patricia Healey, 1963; children—Louise, Jason, Scott. Albums recorded include Release Me, A Man Without Love, The Last Waltz, Englebert Humperdinck, We Made It Happen, Another Place, Another Time, In Time, King of Hearts, After the Lovin', Don't You Love Me Any More, Golden Love, Miracles, Ultimate, Last of the Romantics; nightclub performer: TV series The Engelbert Humperdinck Show, 1970 (Recipient Georgie award for best singer Am. Guild Variety Artists 1978) *

HUMPHREY, ARTHUR EARL, university administrator; b. Moscow, Idaho, Nov. 9, 1927; s. Samuel Earl and Iris May (Rowe) H.; m. Sheila Claire Darwin, June 13, 1951; children: Andrea Lynn, Allyson Dawn. B.S. in Chem. Engring, U. Idaho, 1948, M.S., 1950, D.Sc. (hon.), 1974; Ph.D., Columbia U., 1953; M.S. in Food Tech, Mass. Inst. Tech., 1959. Mem. faculty U. Pa., Phila., 1953-80, prof. chem. engring., 1961-80, dir., 1962-72, dean, 1972-80; provost, v.p., prof. biochem. engring. Lehigh U., Bethlehem, Pa., 1980—; also co-dir. Center for Biotechnology Research; NSF sci. tchr. fellow Mass. Inst. Tech., 1957-58; Fulbright lectr. U. Tokyo, Japan, 1963, U. New South Wales, Australia, 1970; guest lectr. Inst. Biology, Czechoslovakian Acad. Sci., 1964, Tech. Inst., Budapest, 1966; I.I.T. Delhi, New Delhi, India, 1970, Tungai U., Taichung, Taiwan, 1968; cons. Merck Sharp & Dohme, 1957-63, Merck Chem. Co., 1963-64, 80—, Sun Oil Co., 1961-68, Bioferm, 1964-67, Cryotherm, 1966-67, Fermentation Design, 1967-74, E.R. Squibb, 1967-73, Air Products, 1971—. Author: ann. Fermentation Rev., 1960-64; author textbooks on biochem. engring.; Contbr. articles to profl. jours. Pres. Phila. Trail Club, 1960-61; councilor Appalachian Trail Conf., 1961-67; chmn. space sci. panel Nat. Acad. Sci.; co-chmn. 3d Internat. Fermentation Symposium; mem. engring. adv. bd. NSF; mem. single cell protein working group, protein adv. group WHO-FAO-UN; chmn. group on prodn. substances by microbial means U.S.-USSR Cooperation in Sci. and Tech. Recipient Outstanding Tchr. award U. Pa., 1959. Mem. Nat. Acad. Engring., Internat. Assn. Microbiol. Socs. (sec.-gen. econ. and applied microbiology), Nat. Acad. Engring., Am. Chem. Soc. (chmn. div. microbial. chem. and tech. 1967, Div. Disting. Service award 1979), Am. Inst. Chem. Engrs. (chmn. food and bioengring. div. 1972, Profl. Progress award 1972, Food and Bio-Engring award 1973, Inst. lectr. 1975), Franklin Inst., Japanese Soc. Fermentation Tech., Am. Soc. Microbiology, Sigma Xi, Sigma Tau. Clubs: Trail, Horse-Shoe Trail (Phila.); Appalachian Mountain (Boston). Office: Alumni Hall Lehigh U Bethlehem PA 18015 *I have found that in many things I do in today's world it is much better to be approximately correct than exactly wrong.*

HUMPHREY, EDWARD WILLIAM, surgeon, medical educator; b. Fargo, N.D., Dec. 6, 1926; s. Edward W. and Minnie (Ramstad) H.; m. Noreen Sander, Sept. 23, 1950; children—Katherine Lisa, Joan Karen. B.A., U. Minn., 1948, M.D., 1951, Ph.D. in Physiology, 1959. Mem. faculty U. Minn. Med. Sch., Mpls., 1958—, prof. surgery, 1965—; mem. staff VA Hosp., Mpls., 1958—, chief surg. service, 1962—. Mem. A.C.S., Minn. Surg. Soc., Am., Central surg. assns., Soc. Univ. Surgeons, Am. Physiol. Soc., Am. Soc. Cell Biology, Am. Assn. Thoracic Surgery, Soc. Internat. De Chirurgie, Soc. Exptl. Biology and Medicine, Sigma Xi, Alpha Omega Alpha. Research, publs. in field of cancer, pulmonary physiology, Biol. transport, thoracic surgery. Home: 9734 Russell Circle Minneapolis MN 55431 Office: VA Hosp 48th Ave and 54th St Minneapolis MN 55417

HUMPHREY, EDWIN MURRAY, retired rubber company executive; b. N.Y.C., Nov. 25, 1917; s. Edwin Cooper and Margaret Veronica (Murray) H.; m. Eleanor M. Jackson, July 19, 1969; children: Susan Diane, Cynthia Jane, Kathy Lynn; step-children: James B. Holden Jr., Leah Holden. Student, Fordham U., 1934-35, Harvard U., 1963. With The Goodyear Tire & Rubber Co., Newark, 1938-40, Akron, Ohio, 1940-74, v.p., 1977-79, exec. v.p., pres. gen. product div., 1979-81; with Goodyear Aerospace Corp., Akron, 1974-77, exec. v.p., chief operating officer, 1974-77. Bd. dirs. Greater Akron Music Assn., 1976-77, now pres. Served with USAAF, 1943-46. Mem. Aviation Distributors and Mfrs. Assn., Navy League U.S., Aircraft Industries Assn., Gen. Aviation Mfrs. Assn., Soc. of the Plastic Industry, Am. Legion. Club: Portage Country. Home: 526 N Portage Path Akron OH 44303

HUMPHREY, FRED A., physician; b. Broken Bow, Nebr., Mar. 16, 1896; s. A.R. and Nellie (Nightengale) H.; m. Violet Osborne, June 20, 1921; children: Betty Clee (Mrs. T.M. Snow), Robert N. B.Sc., U. Nebr., 1919, M.D., 1921. Practice medicine, Ft. Collins, Colo., 1922-77; former mem. staff Poudre Valley Meml. Hosp., Ft. Collins.; past dir. Poudre Valley Nat. Bank. Trustee Colo. Blue Shield, 1952-67. Mem. Am. Acad. Gen. Practice (v.p., exec. com. 1951), AMA (chmn. council on rural health 1959-63), Colo. Med. Soc. (pres. 1949-50), Larimer County Med. Soc. (pres. 1935), Woodward Gov.'s Co. (emeritus dir. 1971—), Am. Legion (past post comdr.). Clubs: Masons (32 deg.), Shriners, Elk (past exalted ruler). Home: 837 Juniper Ln Fort Collins CO 80526

HUMPHREY, GEORGE MAGOFFIN, II, mining company executive; b. Cleve., Mar. 19, 1942; s. Gilbert Watts and Louise (Ireland) H.; m. Marguerite Burton, June 19, 1964; children: Mary O., Sandra. B.A., Yale U., 1964; J.D., U. Mich., 1967. Bar: Ohio 1967. Sales rep. Hanna Mining Co., Cleve., 1970-72, European rep., 1972-77, sales rep., 1977-78, mgr. sales, 1978, v.p. sales, 1978-80, sr. v.p. fin., 1980-81, sr. v.p. sales, 1981—, dir., 1981—; dir. Bankers Trust N.Y. Corp. Trustee Hotchkiss Sch., Cleve. Mus. Art, Cleve. Mus. Natural History, Cleve. Scholarship Programs, Inc., Univ. Hosps. Cleve. Served to capt. USMC, 1967-70. Mem. Am. Iron and Steel Inst., AIME. Republican. Episcopalian. Clubs: Union (Cleve.); Duquesne (Pitts.). Home: 480 W Hill Dr Gates Mills OH 44040 Office: Hanna Mining Co 100 Erieview Plaza Cleveland OH 44114

HUMPHREY, GORDON JOHN, U.S. senator; b. Bristol, Conn., Oct. 9, 1940; s. Gordon H. and Regina H.; m. Patricia Green, July 14, 1978. Ed., George Washington U., U. Md. Ferry pilot, 1964-65; with Universal Air Transport Co., Detroit, 1966-67; pilot Allegheny Airlines, 1967-78; mem. U.S. Senate from N.H., 1979—. Coordinator, dir. N.H. Conservative Caucus, 1977-78. Served with USAF, 1958-62. Mem. Airline Pilots Assn. Republican. Baptist. Home: Chichester NH Office: US Senate Washington DC 20510

HUMPHREY, HUBERT HORATIO, III, Minnesota attorney general; b. Mpls., June 26, 1942; s. Hubert Horatio and Muriel (Buck) H.; m. Nancy Lee Humphrey, Aug. 14, 1963; children: Lori, Pam, Hubert Horatio. B.A. in Polit. Sci., Am. U., Washington, 1965; J.D., U. Minn., 1969. Bar: Minn. Sole practice law, 1970-82; mem. Minn. State Senate, 1972-82; atty. gen. State of Minn., St. Paul, 1983—. Bd. mgmt. Northwest br. YMCA; trustee Mpls. Soc. Fine Arts. Mem. ABA, Minn. Bar Assn., Citizens League, Hennepin County Bar Assn. Mem. Democratic-Farmer-Labor Party. Home: 8116 40th Ave N New Hope MN 55427 Office: 102 State Capitol St. Paul MN 55155

HUMPHREY, LUCIE KING, mem. Republican Nat. Com.; b. Mokelumne Hill, Cal., Feb. 23, 1911; d. Ralph Mower and Mabel (Plumb) King; m. Marvin Bender Humphrey, Sept. 14, 1932; children—Joseph, Barbara (Mrs. F.E. Redman), Sarah (Mrs. Robert H. White), Ellen (Mrs. Thomas F. Riley). A.B., U. Nev., 1931. Sch. tchr., 1931-32; mem. Nev. Fedn. Rep. Women, 1950—, pres., 1950-53, Reno Rep. Women's Club, 1963-67; mem. Rep. Nat. Com. for Nev., 1968-80; mem. exec. com. Rep. Nat. Com., 1974-80; mem. steering com. San Rafael Park, 1979—. Bd. dirs. Sierra Nev.-Reno council Girl Scouts U.S.A., 1944-66, pres., 1946-48; pres. Nev. Campus YWCA, mem. bd., 1950-51. Mem. Nev. Hist. Soc., Nev. Hort. Soc., Gamma Phi Beta (local alumnae pres. 1933, house corp. pres. 1958-60). Episcopalian. Club: Monday (Reno) (pres. 1946—). Home: 30 Suda Way Reno NV 89509

HUMPHREY, NEIL DARWIN, university president; b. Idaho Falls, Idaho, May 20, 1928; s. Clair Pierce and Freda (Hatfield) H.; m. Mary Pat Smith, Aug. 21, 1950; childern: Ann, Therese. B.A. in Polit. Sci., Idaho State U., 1950; M.S. in Govt. Mgmt., U. Denver, 1951; Ed.D., Brigham Young U., 1974. Exec. sec. Nev. Taxpayers Assn., 1955-59; budget dir., Nev., 1959-61; bus. mgr. U. Nev., 1961-64, v.p. fin., 1964-67, acting pres., 1967-68; chancellor U. Nev. System, 1968-77; pres. U. Alaska, 1977-78; v.p. for fin. affairs Youngstown (Ohio) State U., 1978-79, exec. v.p., 1979-84, pres., 1984—. Home: 230 Evergreen Drive Poland Village OH 44514 Office: Youngstown State U Youngstown OH 44555

HUMPHREY, PHILIP STRONG, educator; b. Hibbing, Minn., Feb. 26, 1926; s. Watts Sherman and Katharine Strong (Osborne) H.; m. Mary Louise Countryman, Jan. 1, 1946; children—Margaret Hubbard, Stephen Strong. B.A. cum laude, Amherst Coll., 1949; M.S., U. Mich., 1951, Ph.D., 1955. Asst. curator ornithology, asst. prof. zoology Yale U., 1957-62; curator div. birds Nat. Mus. Natural History, Smithsonian Instn., 1962-65, chmn. dept. vertebrate zoology, 1965-67; dir. Mus. Natural History; prof. systematics and ecology U. Kans., Lawrence, 1967—. Author: Birds of Isla Grande, 1970. Mem. bd. World Wildlife Fund, Pan Am. sect. Internat. Council Bird Preservation, 1959—. Served with USAAF, 1943-47. Guggenheim fellow, 1960-61. Fellow AAAS; mem. Am. Ornithologists Union, Wilson Ornithol. Soc., Cooper Ornithol. Soc., Soc. Systematic Zoology, Sigma Xi. Club: Rotary (Lawrence, Kans.). Home: 612 Louisiana St Lawrence KS 66044 Office: Mus Natural History U Kans Lawrence KS 66045

HUMPHREY, RICHARD SEARS, JR., advt. exec.; b. Boston, Dec. 22, 1925; s. Richard Sears and Marion VanBuren (Emmons) H.; m. Linda Dwyer Stroh, June 11, 1966; children—Joan F., Katherine V.I., Brooks S., Diana E., Wendy S., Richard Sears III. A.B., Harvard, 1947. With Reach McClinton & Co., 1958-69; pres. Boston co. Humphrey Browning MacDougall Inc., 1970-78, chmn., 1978—. Served with USNR, 1944-47, 51-53. Home: 450 Essex St Beverly MA 01915 Office: 1 Beacon St Boston MA 02108

HUMPHREY, ROBERT CLAYTON, banker; b. Moweaqua, Ill., July 12, 1918; s. Clayton E. and Zoe (Hudson) H.; m. Vivian Anderson, Mar. 15, 1941; children—Susan, Michael, Matthew. B.S. in Fin, U. Ill., 1940; postgrad., Northwestern U., 1940-42; grad., Rutgers U. Grad. Sch. Banking, 1954. Vice pres. Comml. Nat. Bank, Peoria, Ill., 1946-62; pres., dir. State Nat. Bank, Evanston, Ill., 1962—; dir., mem. fin. com. Washington Nat. Ins. Co.; dir. Washington Nat. Corp., Am. Colloid Co.; Bd. assos. Northwestern U., 1963—. Trustee Hibbard Spencer Bartlett REIT. Served to lt. USNR, 1943-46. Clubs: Rotarian., University (Evanston); Bankers, Economic (Chgo.); Westmoreland Country (Wilmette, Ill.). Home: 9401 Hamlin Ave Evanston IL 60203 Office: 1603 Orrington Ave Evanston IL 60204

HUMPHREY, WILLIAM ALBERT, mining company executive; b. Potrerillos, Chile, Jan. 12, 1927 (parents Am. citizens); s. Thomas Z. and Ethel K. (Kolbe) H.; m. Edna Lillian Joule, Dec. 20, 1947; children: Patricia Ann, Nancy Joule, Katherine Elisabeth, William Albert. B.S., U. Ariz., 1950. Registered mining engr., Ariz. From jr. engr. to supervisory positions Cananea Consol. Copper Co., Sonora, Mex., 1950-68, v.p., asst. gen. mgr., 1968-71, exec. v.p., gen. mgr., dir., 1971-75; v.p. planning Anaconda Butte Ops., Butte, Mont., 1975; v.p. ops. Newmont Mining Corp., N.Y.C., 1975-81; exec. v.p. ops., dir. Homestake Mining Co., San Francisco, 1981—; dir. Idarado Mining Co., 1975—. Mem. Colo. Forum, Denver, 1981—, Western Regional Conf., Salt Lake City, 1981-83. Served with USN; 1945-46. Mem. AIME, Am. Mining Congress, Tau Beta Pi. Republican. Clubs: Bankers, World Trade, Commonwealth. Home: 2469 Biltmore Dr Alamo CA 94507 Office: Homestake Mining Co 650 California St San Francisco CA 94108

HUMPHREY, WILLIAM GREY, textile co. exec.; b. Clark, N.C., July 1, 1922; s. Jay Lee and Rose (Pittman) H.; m. Maclyn Mackie, Aug. 30, 1950; children—MacLyn, Monta, William Grey. B.S. in Textiles, N.C. State Coll., 1952. With Deering Milliken, Inc., 1951—, pres. fine goods mfg. div., 1962—; v.p. Pacolet Industries, Inc., Pacolet Mills, S.C., 1962-63, exec. v.p., 1963- 64, pres., 1964—, also dir.; pres., dir. Cotton Blossom Corp., Spartanburg, S.C.; pres. Gayley Rico Co., P.R.; v.p. Gayley Wycombe Corp. (Pai); v.p., treas. Clemson Industries, Marietta, S.C.; v.p., treas., dir. Lockhart Power Co.; dir. Magnolia Industries, Inc., Piedmont Motor Lines, Inc., Deering Milliken Research Corp., Deering Milliken Service Corp., Peoples Nat. Bank, Greenville, S.C. Co-chmn. textile div. Greenville County United Fund Campaign, 1963. Mem. Am. Textile Mfrs. Inst., S.C. Textile Mfrs. Inst. (dir.). Baptist. Clubs: Poinsett, Green Valley Country (Greenville); Piedmont, Spartanburg Country (Spartanburg); Union League (N.Y.C.). Home: 1305 Pinecrest Rd Spartanburg SC 29302 Office: PO Box 1926: Spartanburg SC 29301

HUMPHREYS, DAVID JOHN, lawyer, trade assn. exec.; b. Scranton, Pa., Jan. 30, 1936; s. David Evan and Josephine Mary (Tarrant) H.; m. Laura Margaret Baker, Aug. 11, 1973; children—Cecelia, Katie, Mary Claire, Theresa, Monica, Douglas, Justin, Brian, Casey, Molly. B.A., St. Mary's U., 1959; J.D., Cath. U., 1963. Bar: Va. bar, Supreme Ct. U.S 1972. Salesman Kraft Foods Co., 1959-63; pvt. practice law, Washington; mem. firm Sorrell, Jones & Paulson, 1964-69, Paulson & Humphreys, 1969-79, Humphreys & Loftus, 1979—; Washington counsel Recreational Vehicle Inst., 1969-74; gen. counsel, asst. sec. Recreation Vehicle Industry Assn., 1974-79, pres., gen. counsel, 1979—; chmn. bd. Am. Recreation Coalition, 1979—; Mem. adv. bd. U.S. Congl. Travel and Tourism Caucus, 1980—; chmn. Task Force on User Fees, 1981—. Served with Air N.G., 1959. Recipient Paul Abel award, 1977. Mem. Bar Assn. D.C., Am. Bar Assn., Am. Trial Lawyers' Assn. Office: 14650 Lee Rd PO Box 204 Chantilly VA 22021 *

HUMPHREYS, JAMES W., former air force officer, surgeon, medical board executive; b. Fredericksburg, Va., May 28, 1915; s. James William and Josephine (Rooks) H.; m. Josephine Bailey, Aug. 18, 1943; children: Jean Elizabeth, Josephine III. B.S. in Chem. Engring, Va. Mil. Inst., 1935; M.D., Med. Coll. Va., 1939; M.S., U. Colo., 1951. Diplomate Am. Bd. Surgery (dir. 1971—). Intern, surg. resident Cin. Gen. Hosp.; surg. resident Fitzsimmons Gen. Hosp.; commd. 1st lt. M.C. U.S. Army, 1940; advanced through grades to maj. gen. USAF, 1965; comdr. USAF Hosp., Wright-Patterson AFB, O., 1957-60, Wilford Hall USAF Hosp., San Antonio, 1960-65; surgeon, chief med. spltys., dir. land-based med. recovery facilities Project Mercury, 1960-63; cons. bioastronautics Project Gemini, 1964-65; asst. dir. for pub. health U.S. AID, Vietnam, 1965-67; dir. space medicine Manned

Space Flight, Hdqrs. NASA, 1967-70, dir. life scis., 1970-71; retired, 1971; exec. dir., sec.-treas. Am. Bd. Surgery, Phila., 1971—; vis. prof. surgery Hahemann Med. Coll., Phila., 1976—; mem. Am. Bd. Med. Spltys., 1974—. Decorated D.S.M. with oak leaf cluster, Legion of Merit with oak leaf cluster, Air medal with oak leaf cluster, Airmans medal, U.S.; Order of Merit, Iran; Nat. Order Cross of Valor with palm; Medal of Honor; Mil. Civil Action medal, Vietnam; Order Sikathuna, Philippines; Missione Medico Gold medal, Milan, Italy; recipient NASA medal for exceptional sci. achievement; Boynton award Am. Astronautical Soc. Fellow ACS, Aerospace Med. Assn. (Bauer Founders award), Am., So. surg. assns.; mem. Assn. Mil. Surgeons U.S., Soc. Air Force Clin. Surgeons, Soc. Air Force Flight Surgeons, Soc. Med. Cons. to Armed Forces, Pan Am. Med. Assn., Southwestern Surg. Congress, U. Cin. Grad. Surg. Soc., Alpha Omega Alpha. Home: 1700 Parkway Apt 1212 Philadelphia PA 19103 Office: Am Bd Surgery 1617 John F Kennedy Blvd Philadelphia PA 19103

HUMPHREYS, KENNETH KING, engineer, educator, association executive; b. Pitts., Jan. 19, 1938; s. Meredith Harold and Olga (Adamitis) H.; m. Harriet Elizabeth Moss, May 6, 1961; children: Kenneth King, Keith Alan, Kevin James, Karen Elizabeth. B.S., Carnegie Inst. Tech., 1959, postgrad., 1961-62; postgrad., U. Pitts., 1965; M.S., W. Va. U., 1967. Registered profl. engr., Pa., W. Va.; cert. cost engr. Tech. asst. Applied Research Lab.-U.S. Steel Corp., 1959-60, tech. assoc., Monroeville, Pa., 1960-62; asst. technologist Applkied Research Lab.-U.S. Steel Corp., Universal, Pa., 1962-63; assoc. research engr. Applied Research Lab.-U.S. Steel Corp., Universal, Pa., 1963-65; cost engr. W. Va. U. Coal Research Bur., Morgantown, 1965-67, sr. staff and cost engr., 1967-71, asst. dir., 1971-81; asst. prof. Coll. Mineral and Energy Resources-W. Va., Morgantown, 1970-73; assoc. prof. Coll. Mineral and Energy Resources-W. Va. U., Morgantown, 1973-76, prof., 1976-82, adj. prof., 1982—, asst. to dean, 1971-77, chmn. minerals program, 1978-81; asst. dean acad. affairs Coll. Mineral and Eenergy Resources-W. Va. U., Morgantown, 1979-82; exec. dir. Am. Assn. Cost Engrs., 1971—; engring. cons. metallurgy and fuel tech., 1963-82. Author: Publs. Index, 1956-78, Basic Cost Engineering, 1981; co-author, co-editor: Basic Mathematics and Computer Applications for Goal Preparation and Mining, 1983; co-author, assoc. editor: Coal Preparation, 4th edit., 1979; co-author, editor: Project and Cost Engineers' Handbook, 1984; contbr. articles to profl. jours.; patentee in field. Leader Boy Scouts Am., Allegheny Trails and Mountaineer Area council, 1961—, dist. commr., Allegheny Trails and Mountaineer Area council, 1969-72, dist. tng. chmn., Allegheny Trails and Mountaineer Area council, 1972-74, chmn. council tng., Allegheny Trails and Mountaineer Area council, 1975-77, vice-chmn. leadership devel., Area 6, East Central Region, 1977-79; deacon First Presbyterian Ch., 1968-70, ruling elder, 1972-75, pres. congregation, 1975-77. Recipient Silver Beaver award Mountaineer Area Coiuncil Boy Scouts Am., 1973, award of merit Mountaineer Area Council Boy Scouts Am., 1969, Woodbadge award Mountaineer Area Council Boy Scouts Am., 1971, Het Schaap mit vijf Poten award Royal Netherlands Industries Fair, 1977; named Hon. West Virginian Gov. West Virginia, 1974. Fellow Assn. Cost Engrs. (U.K.); mem. Soc. Mexicana Ingenieria Economica y de Costos (Mex.), Soc. Mining Engrs., AIME, Am. Assn. Cost Engrs. (nat. chmn. 1969-71, named Mem. of Moment 1970, nat. dir. 1971, award recognition 1979, mng. editor, pub. Cost Engring. mag., co-editor trans. 1982, 83), Internat. Cost Engring. Council (sec.), Nat. Soc. Profl. Engrs., W. Va. Soc. Profl. Engrs. (bd dirs. 1971-76, v.p. 1980-81, pres. 1982-83), Morgantown Soc. Profl. Engrs. (pres. 1969-70, bd. dirs. 1970-76), Am. Assn. Engring. Socs. (bd. govs. 1979—), W. Va. Coal Mining Inst., Sigma Xi, Beta Theta Pi, Alpha Phi Omega. Democrat. Home: 305 Lebanon Ave Morgantown WV 26505 Office: 308 Monogahela Bldg Morgantown WV 26505 *I am often asked why I am so active in scouting and other volunteer organizations and what I get out of it. My answer is that there is no better way to serve God and there is no greater reward than a smile and a sincere 'thank you' from someone whose life you may have touched and affected for the better. No one needs a better reason.*

HUMPHREYS, LLOYD GIRTON, research psychologist, educator; b. Lorane, Oreg., Dec. 12, 1913; s. John Pryor H. and Gertrude (Stephenson) Hemphreys; m. Dorothy Jane Windes, Dec. 27, 1937; children: John Daniel, Michael Stephenson, Margaret Anne, Susane Jeanne. B.S., U. Oreg., 1935; M.A., Ind. U., 1936; Ph.D., Stanford U., 1938. Instr. Northwestern U., 1939-42, asst. prof., 1945-46; assoc. prof. U. Wash., 1946-48, Stanford U., Calif., 1948-51; research psychologist U.S. Air Force, San Antonio, 1951-57; prof. psychology U. Ill., Champaign-Urbana, 1957—, chmn. dept. psychology, 1959-69, acting dean Coll. Liberal Arts and Scis., 1979-80; asst. dir. sci. edn. NSF, 1970-71; mem. bd. human resource data and analyses NRC, 1974-77; mem. Commn. on Human Resources NSF, 1978-82, mem. Gov.'s Blue Ribbon Commn. on Occupatinal Licensing, 1977-78; bd. dirs. Am. Insts. for Research, 1978—; mem. expert com. on pediatric neurobehavioral evaluations EPA, 1983, cons. clean air sci. adv. com., sci. adv. bd., 1983. Served to capt. USAAF, 1942-45. Mem. AAAS (chmn. sect. I 1962-63, v.p. 1963, council 1974-77, chmn. sect. J 1979-80), Psychometric Soc. (pres. 1959-60), Psychonomic Soc. (chmn. governing bd. 1962-63), Soc. Exptl. Psychologists, Chairmen Grad. Tng. Depts. Psychology (chmn. 1962-66), Phi Beta Kappa, Sigma Xi, Beta Gamma Sigma, Phi Delta Kappa, Delta Upsilon. Home: RFD 1 Box 110 White Heath IL 61884 Office: Dept psychology U Ill Champaign IL 61820

HUMPHREYS, MABEL GWENETH, educator; b. Vancouver, C., Can., Oct. 22, 1911; came to U.S., 1932, naturalized, 1941; d. Richard and Mabel Jane (Thomas) H. B.A., U. B.C., 1932; A.M., Smith Coll., 1933; Ph.D., U. Chgo., 1935. Instr. math., physics Mt. St. Scholastica Coll., Atchison, Kan., 1935-36; instr. math. Newcomb Coll., Tulane U., New Orleans, 1936-41, asst. prof., 1941-49; asso. prof. math. Randolph-Macon Woman's Coll., 1949-50, prof., 1950—, chmn. dept., 1950-79, later Larew prof. math., Dana prof., 1973-80, Dana prof. emeritus, 1980—. Mem. Am. Math. Soc., Math. Assn. Am., Can. Math. Soc., Soc. for Indsl. and Applied Math., AAUP, AAUW, Sigma Xi. Address: 1824 Clayton Ave Lynchburg VA 24503

HUMPHREYS, ROBERT LEE, advertising agency executive; b. Burbank, Calif., Dec. 30, 1924; s. Robert E. and Nancy Lucille (Gum) H.; m. Marie Dorthea Wilkinson, May 10, 1951; children: Dina Lizette, Gia Monique. B.S. in Mktg., UCLA, 1947. Merchandising rep. Life mag., Los Angeles, 1947-48; promotion mgr. Fortune mag., N.Y.C., 1948-49; copywriter BBDO Internat., Los Angeles, 1950-51; v.p., account group mgr. Foote, Cone & Belding, Los Angeles, 1951-61; pres. Western div. Grey Advt., Inc., Los Angeles, 1962—, dir., 1965—; dir. William O'Neil Fund, Beverly Hills, Calif., 1965-70; lectr. in field. Founding pres. UCLA Chancellor's Assocs., 1967—; founding vice chmn. UCLA Found., 1967—; mem. president's circle Los Angeles County Mus. Art, 1983—; bd. dirs. Advt. Industry Emergency Fund, 1980—. Served to lt. (j.g.) USN, 1943-46. Mem. Town Hall, World Affairs Council, Hollywood Radio and TV Soc. (dir. 1976-82), Los Angeles Advt. Club (dir. 1974-76), Am. Advt. Fedn. (dir.), Phi Gamma Delta. Clubs: Bel Air Country, California (Los Angeles); Bankers (San Francisco). Home: 12830 Parkyrs St Los Angeles CA 90049 Office: 3435 Wilshire Blvd Los Angeles CA 90010

HUMPHREYS, ROBERT RUSSELL, lawyer; b. Eugene, Oreg., May 7, 1938; S. Russell Wallace and Roberta Lois (Bennett) H.; m. Natalia Dimitrievna Lucenko; children: Tatyana Roberta, Grigori Robert. B.A., U. Wash., 1959; LL.B., George Washington U., 1965. Bar: Va. 1965, D.C. 1966. Law clk. firm Barco, Cook & Patton, Washington, 1963-64, Keller & Heckman, 1964; mgr. pub. affairs services Air Transport Assn. Am., Washington, 1965-66; asst. to v.p. fed. affairs, 1966-71; spl. counsel com. on labor and human resources U.S. Senate, Washington, 1971-77; commr. Rehab. Services Adminstrn., HEW, Washington, 1977-80; mem. firm Hoffheimer & Johnson, Washington, 1980-83; ptnr. firm Humphreys & Mitchell, Washington, 1983—. Contbr. articles to jours. Incorporator, dir., treas., counsel Nat. Center for Barrier-Free Environment, 1975-77, 81—; del. Va. Democratic Conv., 1981; bd. dirs. Va. Spl. Olympics. Mem. D.C. Bar Assn., George Washington U. Law Alumni Assn., Va. State Bar, Phi Delta Phi. Principal Senate draftsman for Black Lung Benefits Act, 1972, Rehab. Act, 1973, Randolph-Sheppard Act Amendments, 1974, Black Lung Benefits Reform Act, 1977. Office: 1915 Eye St NW Suite 500 Washington DC 20006

HUMPHRIES, FREDERICK S., university president; b. Apalachicola, Fla., Dec. 26, 1935; m. Antoinette Humphries; children: Frederick S., Robin Tanya, Laurence Anthony. B.S. magna cum laude, Fla. A&M U., 1957; Ph.D. in Phys. Chemistry (fellow), U. Pitts., 1964. Pvt. tutor sci. and math., 1959-64; asst. prof. chemistry U. Minn., Mpls., 1966-67; asso. prof. chemistry Fla. A&M U., 1964-67, prof. chemistry, 1964-67, dir. 13 coll. curriculum program, 1967-68; dir. summer confs. Inst. for Services to Edn., 1968-74, dir. interdisciplinary program, 1973-74, dir. two-univs. grad. program in sci., 1973-74, v.p., 1970-74; pres. Tenn. State U., Nashville, 1974—; cons. to various colls. and univs.; mem. Bd. Grad. Advocates, Meharry Med. Coll., 1976; co-chmn. Reston's Black Focus, 1973. Contbr. articles on higher edn. to profl. publs. Chmn. Fairfax County Anti-Poverty Commn., 1972-74; bd. dirs. YMCA, from 1975. Served with U.S. Army, 1957-59. Recipient Disting. Service to Advancement of Edn. for Black Americans award Inst. for Services to Edn., Disting. Edn. and Adminstr.; Meritorious award Fla. A&M U.; Human Relations award Met. Human Relations Commn. Nashville, 1978. Mem. Am. Chem. Soc., Am. Assn. Higher Edn., AAUP, AAAS, NAACP, Nat. Assn. State Univs. and Land-Grant Colls., Alpha Kappa Mu (pres., award), Alpha Phi Alpha (Meritorious Service award). Office: Office of President Tenn State U 3500 Centennial Blvd Nashville TN 37203 *

HUMPHRIES, JACK WOOD, univ. adminstr.; b. Mabank, Tex., Sept. 9, 1936; s. Ode Robert and Lila (Wood) H.; m. Sharon Ann Ridenhour, Jan. 31, 1959; children—Jeffery Marshall, Joel Mark, Jonathan Maury. A.A., Henderson County Jr. Coll., 1956; B.A., Baylor U., 1958, M.A., 1962; Ph.D., Tex. A. and M. U., 1969. Tchr. LaVega High Sch., Waco, Tex., 1958-60; instr. history, chmn. dept. Alvin (Tex.) Jr. Coll., 1960-65; asst. dir. admissions, instr. history Sam Houston State U., Huntsville, Tex., 1965-66, dean, 1969-71, v.p. univ. affairs, 1971-78, v.p. acad. affairs, 1978—; adminstrv. asst. to dean Coll. Liberal Arts, Tex. A. and M. U., 1966-69. Editor: The Academic Administrator, 1967, 1968, Powers and Responsibilities in Academic Governance, 1969; contbr. articles to profl. jours. Mem. So. Conf. Deans and Acad. Vice Presidents (pres. 1980-81), Tex. (exec. com. 1973-78, pres. 1976-77), Student Personnel Assn., So., Tex. hist. assns., Tex. Assn. Coll. Tchrs., Phi Alpha Theta, Phi Delta Kappa, Phi Theta Kappa (Nat. Hall of Honor 1978). Baptist. Home: Box 2073 Shsu Station Huntsville TX 77341

HUMPHRIES, JOHN O'NEAL, physician, educator; b. Columbia, S.C., Oct. 22, 1931; s. Arthur Lee and Helen Elliott (O'Neal) H.; m. Mary Ellen Cregan, Mar. 13, 1954; children: Arthur Thomas, Ellen Cregan, John Elliott. B.S., Duke U., 1952; M.D., Johns Hopkins U., 1956. Diplomate: Am. Bd. Internal Medicine (mem. bd. subsplty. cardiovascular disease 1974-79). Intern Johns Hopkins Hosp., 1957; asst. resident Osler Med. Service, 1958-60, resident physician pvt. med. service, 1962-64, staff physician, 1962-79; research fellow in cardiology Johns Hopkins U. Med. Sch., 1956-57, 61-62, mem. faculty, 1964-79, Robert L. Levy prof. cardiology, 1975-79, prof. medicine, 1976-79; chmn. dept. O.B. Mayer Sr. and Jr. prof. medicine U. S.C. Sch. Medicine, 1979—, dean Sch. Medicine, 1983—; research fellow cardiology U. London, St. George's Hosp., 1960-61; cons., physician Union Meml., Good Samaritan, VA hosps., all Balt.; dir. heart sta. Johns Hopkins Hosp., 1969-75, dir. clin. programs, cardiology div., 1972-79. Contbr. articles to med. publs.; mem. editorial bd. various jours. Bd. dirs. Md. Ballet, Balt., 1975-78. Fellow ACP, Am. Coll. Cardiology (gov. for Md. 1973-76); mem. Am. Fedn. Clin. Research, Am. Heart Assn. (fellow council clin. cardiology; chmn. postgrad. edn. com., exec. com. 1972-75), Central Md. Heart Assn. (pres. 1972-73), Md. Heart Assn. (pres. 1976-77), Assn. U. Cardiologists, Am. Clin. and Climatol. Assn., Alpha Omega Alpha. Home: 402 Park Lake Rd Columbia SC 29204 Office: U SC Dept Medicine Richland Meml Hosp Columbia SC 29203

HUMPHRIES, KENNETH B., accountant; b. Rahway, N.J., Jan. 16, 1928; s. John Phillip and Mary Amy (Miller) H.; m. Juanita Jean Hemsel, May 27, 1950; children—Donald Scott, Amy Jane, Fred Henry. B.S. in Commerce, Rider Coll., 1951. C.P.A., Pa., N.J. Indsl. accountant Vikon Tile Corp., Washington, N.J., 1951-58; pub. accountant, Washington, 1958-66, C.P.A., 1966—; sec.-treas., dir. Ferguson Containers, Corrugated Products Corp., E.L. Baxter Co. Inc., J.D. Fegely, Inc. Mem. Washington Borough Bd. Edn., 1966-68. Served with AUS, 1945-47. Fellow Am. Inst. C.P.A.'s, N.J. Soc. C.P.A.'s, Pa. Inst. C.P.A.'s. Roman Catholic. Home and Office: 317 March St Easton PA 18042 *I have always tried, to the best of my ability, to give a little more than I expect in return, especially when working for compensation.*

HUMPHRY, JAMES, III, librarian; b. Springfield, Mass., July 21, 1916; s. James and Elizabeth Lucy (Ames) H.; m. Priscilla Eaton, Dec. 26, 1942; children: Susan (Mrs. Michael C. Fitch), Elizabeth Ames (Mrs. George J. Schnabel). A.B., Harvard U., 1939; M.S., Columbia U., 1941. Reference asst. N.Y. Pub. Library, 1939-41, 46, chief map div., 1946; librarian, prof. bibliography Colby Coll.; bus. mgr. Colby Coll. Press, 1947-57; chief librarian Met. Mus. Art, 1957-68; v.p. H.W. Wilson Co., Bronx, 1968-82, also dir., 1965-82; cons. Am. Heritage, 1965-68, John Wiley & Sons, 1966—; lectr. Columbia Sch. Library Service, 1967-68; prof. Pratt Inst., Bklyn., 1982; vis. assoc. prof. Grad. Sch. Library Studies, U. Hawaii, 1983; library cons. Council Advancement Small Colls., 1956; Coordinator Maine Library Assn. for ALA sponsored Library Services bill, 1948-49, 55-57; nat. bd. Library Presdl. Papers, 1967-69; adminstr. grants-in-aid program N.Y. State Council Arts, 1967-68. Compiler, Library of Edwin Arlington Robinson, 1950; Editor: (with Carl J. Weber) Fitzgerald's Rubaiyat, 1959; Contbr. articles to mags. and jours. Trustee, chmn. adv. com. Archives Am. Art, 1967—; mem. fine arts vis. com. Harvard U., 1967-73; mem. adv. council St. John's U. Congress for Librarians, 1963-67; bd. dirs. Huguenot YMCA; trustee N.Y. Met. Reference and Research Library Agy., 1967—. Served with AUS, 1942-46; as maj., 1951-54; lt. col. Res. Mem. ALA (councilor 1959-63, 67-69, chmn. com. on Wilson index reference services div. 1959-65, mem. subscription books com. 1963-66), Met. Mus. Art Employees Assn. (pres. 1961-63, gov. 1958-66), Res. Officers Assn. U.S., Maine Library Assn. (pres. 1955-56), Am. Assn. Museums (chmn. library group), Archons of Colophon (convener 1963-65), N.Y. Library Assn. (cons.), Spl. Libraries Assn. (chpt. vice chmn., chmn. mus. group 1962-64, N.Y. conf. chmn. 1967), Assn. Coll. and Research Libraries (pres., dir. 1966-69), Internat. Council Museums (corr.). Clubs: Grolier, N.Y. Library (council 1959-67), N.Y. Library (N.Y.C.) (pres. 1965-66). Home: 10 Ridge Rd New Rochelle NY 10804 Home: 1600 Ala Moana Blvd Honolulu HI 96815 Office: 950 University Ave Bronx NY 10452

HUMPHRY, JOHN AMES, pub. exec., librarian; b. Springfield, Mass., July 21 1916; s. James and Elizabeth (Ames) H.; m. Elizabeth Daniell, Sept. 13, 1941; children—Jonathan Ames, Keith Daniell. A.B. in Econs, Harvard U., 1939; postgrad., Grad. Sch. Arts and Scis., 1942-43; B.S. in L.S, Columbia U., 1941. Gen. asst. Harvard Coll. Library, 1939-40, 41-44; part-time gen. asst. N.Y. Pub. Library, 1940-41; field service cons. OSRD, Office Chief Naval Ops., 1944-46; dir. book processing Enoch Pratt Free Library, Balt., 1946-48; dir. City Library, Springfield, Mass., 1948-64; exec. dir. Springfield Library and Museums Assn., 1960-64; dir. Bklyn. Pub. Library, 1964-67; state librarian, asst. commr. libraries N.Y. State Dept. Edn., 1967-77; vis. lectr. Am. Internat. Coll., 1959-61; exec. dir. Forest Press, 1977—; Spl. cons. ops. evaluation group Office Chief Naval Ops., Dept. Def., 1951-53; asso. pub. library adminstrn. Simmons Coll. Sch. Library Sci., 1952-54; mem. Mass. Library Devel. Com., 1957-59, chmn., 1959; mem. Mass. Bd. Library Commrs., 1957-64; mem. edn. com. Citizens Action Commn. of Springfield, 1958-62; dir. Brown U. study to coordinate library service in R.I.; adv. bd. Springfield Motion Picture Council, 1950-64; mem. adv. council Springfield Coll. Community Tensions Center, 1958-63; sec.-treas. Phillips Lecture Fund Com., 1956-64; mem. adv. com. on sch. library standards N.Y. State Edn. Dept., 1966; adv. council Office Urban Library Research, Wayne State U. Incorporator United Fund Greater Springfield Inc.; adv. bd. Springfield Goodwill Industries; trustee N.Y. Met. Reference and Research Library Agy. Mem. ALA (chmn. membership com. 1958-64, councilor 1960-64), New Eng. Library Assn. (bd. 1953-54), Mass. Library Assn. (exec. bd. 1949-63, pres. 1957-58), N.Y Library Assn. (mem. legis. com. 1964), Assn. State Library Agencies (pres. 1968-69), Council Library Resources (dir.), UN Assn. (librarian's adv. council 1948-50), Am. Econ. Assn., New Eng. Hist. and Geneal. Soc., World Affairs Council Conn. Valley (past treas.). Clubs: Automobile, Western Mass. Library, Melvil Dui Chowder and Marching Assn., N.Y. Library, Archons of Colophon (N.Y.C.); Harvard (Springfield). Home: 2316 Rosendale Rd Schenectady NY 12309 Office: Forest Press 85 Watervliet Ave Albany NY 12206

HUMPHRYS, RICHARD, consultant; b. Jasmin, Sask., Can., Mar. 27, 1917; s. William and Olive Mary (Maher) H.; m. Wilma Kay Grant, Oct. 3, 1942. B.A., U. Man., 1937. Actuarial clk. Great West Life Assurance Co., Winnipeg, Man., Can., 1939-40; with Dept. of Ins., Govt. of Can., Ottawa, Ont., 1940-46; asst. actuary then asso. actuary Tchrs. Inst. and Annuity Assn., N.Y.C., 1946-48; chief actuary Dept. Inst., Govt. of Can., Ottawa, 1948-54, asst. supt. ins., 1954-64, supt. of ins., 1964-82; cons. actuary, 1982—. Fellow Soc. Actuaries (dir. 1970-73, 74-77, v.p. 1979-81), Can. Inst. Actuaries (pres. 1965-66); mem. Internat. Actuarial Assn. Club: Ottawa Hunt and Golf. Home and Office: 50 Rothwell Dr Ottawa ON Canada K1J 7G6

HUND, JAMES MADDEN, business educator; b. Detroit, Apr. 27 1922; s. Henry E. and Emma L. (Madden) H.; m. Nancy Ione Black, June 10, 1950 (dec. Apr. 1967); children: Marcia Ione, Gretchen Elizabeth; m. Barbara M. Roberts, June 6, 1969; stepchildren: Stewart R. Roberts III, Barbara Elaine Roberts. Student, Stanford U., 1940-41; A.B., Amherst Coll., 1943; M.A. in Econs, Princeton, 1952, Ph.D., 1954. Asso. with Reo Motors, Inc., 1946-50; mem. faculty Clark U., 1954-57, Emory U., 1957—, prof. bus. adminstrn., 1961—, dean, 1965-68; Mem. N.Y. Met. Regional Study, 1957-58. Author articles; contbr. books. Served as officer USNR, 1944-46. Mem. So. Mgmt. Assn., Acad. Mgmt., Chi Psi. Methodist. Home: 1535 Victoria Falls Dr NE Atlanta GA 30329

HUND, WILLIAM HARRISON, freight lines exec.; b. Madelia, Minn., July 22, 1934; s. Harrison Andrew and Fanny Eloise (Mullen) H.; m. Jessica Maria Grant, Aug. 22, 1959; children—Troy Harrison, Tamara Lynn. B.A., Mankato State Coll., 1960; M.B.A., Ind. U., 1961. C.P.A., Colo. Pub. accountant Peat, Marwick, Mitchell & Co., Denver, 1961-68; controller Frontier Airlines, Inc., Denver, 1968-71; sec., treas. Navajo Freight Lines, Inc., Denver, 1971-79; v.p., controller BN Transport, Inc., Denver, 1979—. Served with U.S. Army, 1955-57. Mem. Am. Inst. C.P.A.'s, Colo. Soc. C.P.A.'s. Home: 7439 Pomona Dr N Arvada CO 80003 Office: 6775 E Evans Ave Denver CO 80224

HUNDLEY, JOHN WALKER, foundation executive; b. Highstown, N.J., July 4, 1899; s. H. Rhodes and Mabel Parker (Lewis) H.; m. Eleanor Rothschild, Mar. 24, 1932; 1 dau., Sally Lewis (Mrs. Robert Alan Bear). Student, Cornell U., 1917-18; Ph.B., Denison U., 1919. Asst. service dir. Oneida Truck Co., Green Bay, Wis., 1919-21; salesman No. Bond & Mortgage Co., Green Bay, 1921-22; gen. mgr., advt. mgr. Secrets of Smartness-Corr. Sch. Course for Women, 1935-38; network announcer, producer-writer, asst. dir. broadcasts-short wave dept. CBS Radio, 1938-48; charge day-time programming, mgr. network program services, mgr. client relations-network operations, mgr. sales devel. prodn. sales, editor program practices CBS-TV, 1948-65; pres. John Walker Hundley Enterprises, cons., adv., services, N.Y.C., 1965-66; exec. dir. Belle W. Baruch Found., N.Y.C., 1966-69; v.p. Found. Adv. Services, Inc., 1970—; cons. Catalyst for Environmental Quality mag.; mem. environmental edn. adv. bd. Doubleday & Co., Inc. Baritone with, Am. Opera Co., 1922-23; appeared in 10 Broadway mus. prodns. Pres. Percy Williams Home; treas. Actors Fund Am. Recipient citations Nat. Assn. Mental Health, 1952, Nat. Conf. Christians and Jews, 1951, Crusade for Freedom, 1950, Community Chest Am., 1950, Muscular Dystrophy Assn. Am., 1959-61; Denison U. Alumni citation, 1955. Mem. Beta Theta Pi, Phi Mu Alpha, Sinfonia. Clubs: Lambs, Players, Coffee House (N.Y.C.). Home: 168 E 74th St New York NY 10021

HUNDLEY, NORRIS CECIL, JR., history educator; b. Houston, Oct. 26, 1935; s. Norris Cecil and Helen Marie (Mundine) H.; m. Carol Marie Beckquist, June 8, 1957; children: Wendy, Jacqueline. A.A., Mt. San Antonio Coll., 1956; A.B., Whittier Coll., 1958; Ph.D. (Univ. fellow), UCLA, 1963. Instr. U. Houston, 1963-64; asst. prof. Am. history UCLA, 1964-69, asso. prof., 1969-73, prof., 1973—, chmn. exec. com. Inst. Am. Cultures, 1977—; chmn. UCLA program on Mex., 1981—; mem. adv. com. Calif. water atlas project Calif. Office Planning and Research, 1977-79. Author: Dividing the Waters: A Century of Controversy Between the United States and Mexico, 1966, Water and the West: The Colorado River Compact and the Politics of Water in the American West, 1975; co-author: California, 1982; editor: The American Indian, 1974, the Chicano, 1975, The Asian American, 1976; co-editor: The American West: Frontier and Region, 1969, Golden State Series, 1978—; mng. editor: Pacific Hist. Rev, 1969—; bd. editors: Jour. San Diego History, 1970—; bd. editorial consultants, Calif. Hist. Soc., 1980—; contbr. articles to profl. jours. Recipient award of merit Calif. Hist. Soc., 1979; Am. Philos. Soc. grantee, 1964, 71; Ford Found. grantee, 1968-69; U. Calif. Water Resources Center grantee, 1969-72; Sourisseau Acad. grantee, 1972; U. Calif. Regents faculty fellow in humanities, 1975; Guggenheim fellow, 1978-79. Mem. Am. Hist. Assn. (exec. council Pacific Coast br. 1969—), Western History Assn. (Winther award 1973, 79), Orgn. Am. Historians. Home: 19020 Pacific Coast Hwy Malibu CA 90265 Office: Dept History U Calif Los Angeles CA 90024

HUNDT, PAUL ROBERT, diversified industry executive, lawyer; b. N.Y.C., May 22, 1939; s. Frederick William and Helen Marie (Leonard) H.; m. Rosemary McIsaac, Feb. 23, 1974; children: Frederick William, Douglas Edmund. B.A., U. Notre Dame, Ind., 1960; J.D., Columbua U., 1963. Bar: N.Y. 1964. Assoc. Lord Day & Lord, N.Y.C., 1966-68; atty. Crane Co., N.Y.C., 1968-71, asst. counsel, 1971-75, assoc. gen. counsel, 1975-76, gen. counsel, sec., 1976-80, v.p., gen. counsel, sec., 1980—. Served to capt. U.S. Army, 1963-65. Mem. ABA, N.Y. City Bar Assn., Columbia Law Sch. Alumni Assn. (sec. 1970-74, bd. dirs. 1974-78), Phi Delta Phi. Roman Catholic. Clubs: N.Y. Athletic, Appalachian Mountain. Home: 541 E 20th St New York NY 10010 Office: Crane Co 300 Park Ave New York NY 10022

HUNEKE, HAROLD VERNON, ret. educator; b. Arnett, Okla., Aug. 26, 1917; s. Albert H. and Mary E. (Vosburgh) H.; m. Pauline D. Haworth, Apr. 23, 1948; children—Nancy, Craig. A.B., Northwestern State Coll., Alva, Okla., 1936; M.A., U. Okla., 1941, Ph.D., 1957. Tchr. Lambert (Okla.) High Sch., 1936-39; chmn. math. dept. Northwestern State Coll., Alva, 1946-48; prof. math. U. Wichita, Kans., 1951-60; prof. math. and edn. U. Okla., Norman, 1960-81; Staff NSF, New Delhi, India, 1969-71. Served with USAAF, 1942-46. Mem. Math. Assn. Am. (pres. Okla.-Ark. sect. 1964-65), Nat. Council Tchrs. Math. (pres. Okla. sect. 1967-68), Mu Alpha Theta (nat. sec.-treas. 1962—), Sigma Xi. Club: Lion. Home: 517 S Flood St Norman OK 73069

HUNG, TIN-KAN, engineering educator, researcher; b. Nanking, Republic of China, June 12, 1936; came to U.S., 1961; s. Mao-Hsiang and Yu-Hwa (Cheng) H.; m. Shu-Nan Cho, Feb. 14, 1971; children: Chee-Hahn, Chee-Mings, Chee-Yuen. B.S., Taiwan Cheng-Kung U., Tainan, 1959; M.S., U. Ill., 1962; Ph.D., U. Iowa, 1966. Research assoc. U. Iowa, Iowa City, 1963-66, research engr., 1966-67; vis. assoc. prof. U. Ill.-Chgo., 1972; asst. prof., assoc. prof. Carnegie-Mellon U., Pitts., 1967-75; research prof. U. Pitts., 1975—; cons. NRC, Republic of China, 1978—. Mem. editorial bd.: Jour. Engring. Mechanics, 1974-80, 82, Jour. Hydraulics Research, 1980—; mem. publ. bd.: Internat. Jour. Sci. and Engring., 1983—; contbr. articles to profl. jours. Chmn. presdl. classroom program Pitts. chpt. Orgn. Chinese Americans, Inc., 1978—. Recipient award NRC, 1979; research grantee NSF, 1971-74, 78-80, NIH, 1976-84. Mem. Internat. Assn. Hydraulic Research, Soc. Neurosci., ASCE (W.L. Huber civil engring. research prize 1978), ASME, Urodynamic Soc., Sigma Xi, Chi Epsilon. Home: 3900 Glencoe Ct Murrysville PA 15668 Office: U Pitts 949 Benedum Engring Pittsburg PA 15261

HUNGATE, JOSEPH IRVIN, JR., social worker; b. Killarney, W.Va., Apr. 30, 1921; s. Joseph Irvin and Nellie (Lickliter) H.; m. Betty Lou Hatzenbuehler, Sept. 11, 1948; children: Ann Elisabeth Hungate Clabough, Joseph Irvin, III, Sue Carol. A.B. cum laude, Concord Coll., 1948; M.A., U. Chgo., 1950; Ph.D., U. Tex., 1963; postgrad., St. Louis U., 1948-49. Disaster rep. Chgo. chpt. ARC, 1950; chief psychiat. social work service Valley Forge Army Hosp., Phoenixville, Pa., 1951; psychiat. caseworker Fitzsimons Army Hosp., Denver, 1952-53; chief med. social work service, Ft. Jackson, S.C., 1953-55; class dir., social work specialist program Army Med. Sch., San Antonio, 1955-58; asso. prof. social work U. Tex., 1959-68; dean, prof. social work Coll. Social Work, U. S.C., Columbia, 1968-79, dean Coll. Allied Health Professions, 1973-75; clin. social worker S.C. Dept. Health, 1980-81; dir. social work unit S.C. State Hosp., Columbia, 1981—; teaching cons. Austin State Hosp., 1963-68, William S. Hall Psychiat. Inst., 1972, Kans. Social and Rehab. Service, 1974; spl. cons. tech. tng. div. Bur. Family Services, HEW, Washington, 1962-65; mem. profl. adv. com. S.C. Mental Health Assn., 1970-79; chmn. S.C. Gov.'s Com. on Criminal Justice, Crime and Delinquency, 1968-75; vice chmn., mem. S.C. Health Care Adv. Bd., 1974—; mem. S.C. Gov.'s Health and Welfare Council, 1969-71; chmn. S.C. Merit System Council, 1974-75; cons., faculty mem. multiregional tng. in mgmt. Social Service Adminstrn., HEW, 1974-75; mem. com. dependency and state services S.C. State Planning Office, 1976-78. Author: A Guide for Training Public Welfare Adminstrators, 1965; contbr. articles to profl. jours; sr. editor: Arete, 1971-79. Mem. Columbia council USO, 1970-83; pres. Arcadia Democratic Precinct, Columbia, 1974-76, exec. com., 1976-78. Served to 1st lt. USAAF, 1942-45; capt. M.S.C. U.S. Army, 1950-58. Decorated Air medal with 3 oak leaf clusters, Purple Heart. Home: 3433 Willow Ridge Rd Columbia SC 29206

HUNGATE, WILLIAM LEONARD, judge, former congressman; b. Benton, Ill., Dec. 14, 1922; s. Leonard Wathen and Maude Irene (Williams) H.; m. Dorothy N. Wilson, Apr. 13, 1944; children—William David, Margie Kay (Mrs. Branson L. Wood III). A.B., U. Mo., 1943; LL.B., Harvard, 1948; LL.D., Culver-Stockton Coll., Canton, Mo., 1968; J.D., Central Meth. Coll., Fayette, Mo., 1975. Bar: Mo. bar 1948, Ill. bar 1949, U.S. Supreme Ct 1960, D.C. bar 1967. Practiced in, Troy, Mo., 1948-68, St. Louis, 1977-79; sr. partner firm Hungate and Grewach, 1956-68; partner firm Thompson and Mitchell, St. Louis, 1977-79; judge U.S. Dist. Ct. Eastern Dist. Mo., 1979—; pros. atty., Lincoln County, Mo., 1951-55, spl. asst. atty. gen. of Mo., 1958-64; research adminstrn. criminal justice in U.S. Am. Bar Found., 1956; mem. 88th-94th congresses, 9th Dist. Mo.; mem. judiciary com., chmn. subcom. criminal justice, select com. on small bus., chmn. subcom. on activities of regulatory agys.; vis. prof. polit. sci. U. Mo., St. Louis; also composer. Trustee William Woods Coll.; chmn. small bus. adv. com. Treasury Dept., 1977; chmn. Mo. Gov.'s Commn. on Campaign Reform and Ofcl. Conduct, 1978—; mem. Adv. Com. on Criminal Rules, 1977—. Mem. Ill. Bar Assn., Fed. Bar Assn., ABA (nat. conf. of fed. trial judges exec. com. 1980—), Mo. Bar Assn., D.C. Bar Assn., Harvard Law Sch. Assn. Mo. (pres. 1962-64), ASCAP, Mo. Squires. Mem. Christian Ch. (chmn. bd. 1964). Clubs: Kiwanian (Troy) (pres. 1951, lt. gov. 1959. Home: 26 Chapel Hill Estates Town and Country MO 63131

HUNGERFORD, GERALD FRED, anatomist, educator; b. Anaheim, Calif., Feb. 14, 1923; s. Daniel W. and Ruby (Patterson) H.; m. Vanda Ramella, June 20, 1955; 1 son, Marc Wesley. A.B., U. Calif., Berkeley, 1944, M.A., 1947, Ph.D., 1951. Instr. anatomy U. Calif., Berkeley, 1951-52; instr. anatomy U. So. Calif. Med. Sch., 1952-53, asso. prof., 1958-61, prof., 1961—; asst. prof. anatomy George Washington U. Med. Sch., 1953-58; curator for So. Calif. State Dept. Health.; Mem. Western Colls. Accreditation Com., 1962; cons. in field. Contbr. articles to profl. jours. Served with USNR, 1943-46. Commonwealth fellow, 1965-66. Mem. Am. Assn. Anatomists, AAAS, Soc. Exptl. Biology and Medicine, Nat. Geog. Soc., Pasadena Art Mus., Sigma Xi. Democrat. Home: 701 W Bellefontaine St Pasadena CA 91105 Office: 2025 Zonal Ave Los Angeles CA 90033

HUNGERFORD, HERBERT EUGENE, nuclear engineering educator; b. Hartford, Conn., Oct. 3, 1918; s. Herbert Eugene and Doris (Emmons) H.; m. Edythe Lugene Green, Nov. 4, 1949. B.S. in Physics, Trinity Coll., Hartford, 1941, M.S., U. Ala., 1949; Ph.D. in Nuclear Engring., Purdue U., 1964; part-time grad. student, U. Tenn., 1951-55, Wayne State U., 1956-61. Tchr. sci. Brent Sch., Baguio, Philippines, 1941; tchr. math. Choate Sch., 1945-46; head physics dept. Marion Mil. Inst., 1946-48; grad. instr. U. Ala., 1948-49; physicist Oak Ridge Nat. Lab., 1950-55; shielding specialist, head shielding and health physics sect. Atomic Power Devel. Assos., 1955-62; research asso. Purdue U., 1963-64, asso. prof., 1964-68, prof. nuclear engring., 1968-83; prof. emeritus, 1983—; on leave Argonne Nat. Lab., 1977-78; cons. in field. Author chpts. in books, articles. Prisoner of War; 1941-45. Recipient Presdl. citation Kiwanis Internat., 1970. Mem. Am. Nuclear Soc. (sec. shielding and dosimetry div. 1960-62, div. vice chmn. 1969-70, div. chmn. 1970-71, mem. standards com. 1959—), Am. Phys. Soc., Lafayette Organ Soc. (pres. 1971-72), Amateur Organists Assn. Internat., Health Physics Soc., Am. Assn. Physics Tchrs., Am. Soc. Engring. Edn., Internat. Platform Assn., Sigma Xi, Sigma Pi Sigma. Episcopalian (vestryman 1965-68). Club: Kiwanis (dir.) (1966-68). Inventor lattice model stochastic radiation transp.; pioneer use of serpentine and calcium borate as high temperature shield materials. Home: 2104 4th Ct SE Vero Beach FL 32962 *As a small boy I had osteomyelitis, which left me crippled for life. I have had to overcome the pains of this physical handicap as well as the normal stresses of life to reach my goals. I think my struggle to get to a meaningful position in life can be symbolized by a picture taken of me several years later. I was a senior at Mount Hermon School on Senior's Day, determined to hike to the top of Mount Monadnock, along with all my classmates. I was not the first to the top, but I struggled and made it. The triumphant smile on my face as I was photographed there on the pinnacle reflects, I think, my determination all through life to achieve the best that life has to offer, and to make the most of my talents and opportunities, no matter what the difficulties were, and if I persisted long enough and hard enough I would attain my goals.*

HUNKINS, FRANCIS PETER, teacher educator; b. Cambridge, Mass., May 22, 1938; s. Franklin Preston and Marguerite Frances (Sullivan) H.; m. Doreen Betty Field, Dec. 28, 1963; children: Leah Denise, Francis Peter. B.S. in Edn, Salem State Coll., 1960; M.Ed., Boston U., 1963; Ph.D., Kent State U., 1966. Tchr. pub. schs., Gloucester, Mass., 1960-63; research asst. bur. ednl. research Kent State U., 1963-65; prof. edn. U. Wash., Seattle, 1966—; cons. in field. Author: Influence of Analysis and Evaluation Questions on Achievement and Critical Thinking in Sixth Grade Social Studies, 1968, Questioning Strategies and Techniques, 1972, Asking About the U.S.A. and its Neighbors, 1971, 2d edit., 1975, Social Studies for the Evolving Individual, 1973, Involving Students in Questioning, 1976, Curriculum Development Program for NW Educators in Egypt, 1978; main author: Review of Research in Social Studies Education, 1970-75, 1977, Curriculum Development: Program Improvement, 1980, Social Studies in the Elementary Schools, 1982; co-author: World Geography, People and Places, 1984; contbr. articles to profl. jours. Mem. Assn. for Supervision and Curriculum Devel., Am. Ednl. Research Assn., Nat. Council for the Social Studies, Nat. Soc. Study Edn., World Future Soc., Wash. Assn. for Supervision and Curriculum Devel., Phi Delta Kappa. Office: 115 Miller Hall University of Washington Seattle WA 98195 *One's life can never be described completely for it is in a state of continuous evolvement. A key principle of my life has been to raise questions about the totality of life and my place within it. Without the question, one has no experience. The question is the vehicle for advancing one's knowledge.*

HUNNICUTT, VIRGINIA GAYLE, actress; b. Ft. Worth, Feb. 6, 1947; d. Sam Lloyd and Mary Virginia (Dickerson) H.; m. Simon Jenkins, Sept. 1, 1978. B.A. with honors (Regents scholar), UCLA, 1966. Appeared in films: TV appearances Fall of Eagles; appeared in: plays The Philadelphia Story; others. Mem. Kappa Kappa Gamma. Methodist. Office: 8888 Olympic Blvd Beverly Hills CA 90211

HUNSAKER, HAROLD JEFF, engring. co. exec.; b. Portland, Oreg., July 23, 1927; s. Harold J. and Zena Alexandra (Seabrook) H.; m. Keonaona Mary Joan Shorett, June 30, 1950; children—Paige, Michelle, Erik, Antonie, Dana. B.S.L., U. Wash., Seattle, 1950, LL.B., 1952. Bar: Wash. bar 1952, Calif. bar 1964. Asst. atty. gen., State of Wash., 1953-56; asso. firm Allen, DeGarmo & Leedy, Seattle, 1956-59; counsel Kaiser Engrs., Inc., Richland, Wash., 1959-63, Oakland, Calif., 1963-75, v.p., chief counsel, sec., Oakland, 1975—. Asso. editor: Wash. Law Rev, 1951-52. Served with USNR, 1945-46. Mem. Wash. Bar Assn., Calif. Bar Assn., Delta Kappa Epsilon. Republican. Home: 1224 Upper Happy Valley Rd Lafayette CA 94549 Office: 300 Lakeside Dr PO Box 23210 Oakland CA 94623

HUNSBERGER, ISAAC MOYER, chemist, author; b. Quakertown, Pa., Aug. 3, 1921; s. A.F. and Eliza (Moyer) H.; m. Elizabeth Rita Ochnich, Mar. 19, 1944; children—Donald Moyer, Elizabeth Anne, Gretchen, Mark, Carol, Luke, Heidi. B.S., Lehigh U., 1943, M.S., 1946, Ph.D., 1948; AEC postdoctoral fellow organic chemistry, U. Ill., 1948-49. Asst., then asso. prof. chemistry Antioch Coll., 1949-55; asso. prof. Fordham U., 1955-60; head dept. chemistry U. Mass., 1960-61, dean, research prof. chemistry, 1961-69; program adviser edn. Ford Found., Pakistan, 1969-71; dean Coll. Arts and Scis., State U. N.Y. at Albany, 1971-73; provost U. Okla., Norman, 1973-75; free-lance writer, 1975-81; v.p. acad. affairs, dean of faculty Am. U. in Cairo (Egypt), 1981—; Mem. com. modern methods handling chem. information NRC, 1959-65. Author: (with others) Survey of Chemical Notation Systems, 1964, The Quintessential Dictionary, 1978; editor sect. 36: Chem. Abstracts, 1960-64; Contbr. articles to profl. jours. Served with USAAF, 1943-45. Decorated D.F.C., Air medal with 5 oak leaf clusters. Fellow AAAS, Am. Inst. Chemists, mem. Am. Chem. Soc., AAUP, Phi Beta Kappa, Pi Mu Epsilon, Phi Eta Sigma, Phi Lambda Upsilon. Spl. research chemistry sydnones, reactions sulfoxides and N-oxides, hydrogen bonding. Home: 18 E Pine St Emmaus PA 18049

HUNSUCKER, ROBERT DEAN, pipeline company executive; b. Winchester, Kans. Formerly chief operating officer, pres. Panhandle Eastern Corp., Houston, pres., chief exec. officer, 1983—; now vice chmn., chief exec. officer Panhandle Eastern Pipe Line Co., Trunkline Gas Co., Houston; dir. Gifford Hill Corp., Anadarko Prodn. Co., Century Refining Co., Dixilyn-Field Drilling Co., Nat. Helium Co. Office: Panhandle Eastern Corp 3000 Bissonnet Ave Houston TX 77251 *

HUNT, ALBERT BARKER, textile company executive; b. Santa Barbara, Calif., Jan. 22, 1910. Student, Stanford U., 1932, Harvard U. Sch. Bus. Adminstrn., 1934. Pres., treas. Rivett, Inc., Boston, until 1967; vice chmn. bd. Fieldcrest Mills Inc., Eden, N.C., 1981-83; chmn. bd. Amoskeag Co., Boston; dir. Westville Homes Inc., Fiduciary Trust Co., Suffolk Franklin Savs. Bank, Bangor & Aroostook R.R. Co., Fanny Farmer, Inc. Office: Amoskeag Co Suite 4500 Prudential Center Boston MA 02199

HUNT, ALFRED MORTIMER, aluminum company executive; b. Pitts., Apr. 2, 1919; s. Roy Arthur and Rachel McMasters (Miller) H. Grad., St. Paul's Sch., 1938; A.B., Yale U., 1942. With Massena (N.Y.) works Aluminum Co. Am., 1942-45, 1945-47, 1948, 1948-50, dir., 1949—, asst. sec., 1950-52, sec., 1952—, v.p., 1963—; also mem. retirement bds.; dir. Alcoa Properties, Inc., Allendale Mut. Ins. Co. Mem. Carnegie Hero Fund Commn.; mem. sponsoring com. Allegheny Conf. on Community Devel.; Trustee Carnegie Inst., also chmn. finance com.; trustee emeritus Duke U.; trustee Roy A. Hunt Found., Hunt Found., Helen Clay Frick Found.; bd. dirs., v.p. Pitts. Regional Planning Assn.; bd. dirs. Alcoa Found., Pitts. History and Landmarks Found., Bishop's Fund; vice chmn. fin. and endowment com. Ch. of the Ascension, Pitts. Recipient F. Ambrose Clark Meml. award in steeplechasing, 1977. Mem. Masters of Foxhounds Assn. Am., Nat. Steeplechase and Hunt Assn. (sr.), Am. Inst. Mining and Metall. Engrs. (jr.), Newcomen Soc. Eng., Engrs. Soc. Western Pa., Pa. Horse Breeders Assn., Pa. Soc., Am. Soc. Metals, Am. Soc. Corp. Secs., Pitts. Bibliophiles, Berzelius, Rolling Rock Hunt Racing Assn. (co-chmn.), Chi Psi. Episcopalian. Clubs: Pitts. Golf, Fox Chapel Golf, Rolling Rock (gov.), Duquesne, University, Allegheny Country, Harvard-Yale-Princeton (Pitts.); Brook, Yale (N.Y.C.); Chagrin Valley Hunt (Cleve.); Rolling Rock-Westmoreland Hunt (ex-master fox hounds). Home: 4875 Ellsworth Ave Pittsburgh PA 15213 Office: Alcoa Bldg Pittsburgh PA 15219

HUNT, BOBBY RAY, engineering researcher, consultant; b. McAlester, Okla., Aug. 24, 1941; s. George Clifford and Shirley Mason (Core) H.; m. Susan Elizabeth Caldwell, Aug. 19, 1965; children: Vicki Lynn, Lori Jean. B.Sc. in Aero. Engring., Wichita State U., 1964; M.S. in Elec. Engring., Okla State U., Stillwater, 1965; Ph.D. in Systems Engring., U. Ariz., Tucson, 1967. Mem. tech. staff Sandia Lab., Albuquerque, 1967-68; staff mem. group leader Los Alamos Nat. Lab., 1968-75; prof. elec. engring. U. Ariz., Tucson, 1975—; chief scientist Sci. Applications Inc., Tucson, 1981—; cons. in field; dir. Internat. Imaging Systems, Milpitas, Calif., 1981—. Author: (with H.C. Andrews) Digital Image Restoration, 1976. NDEA fellow, 1964; NASA fellow, 1966. Fellow IEEE, Optical Soc. Am. Home: 1031 E Chula Vista Rd Tucson AZ 85718 Office: Dept Elec Engring U. Ariz Tucson AZ 85721 *In college I saw and bought a stick-on decal which has been, since that time, my motto and philosophy of life. The slogan on the sticker was a definition of luck that includes the Capriciousness of Dame Fortune, but also the responsibility of the individual in taking care of his own life. I've tried to live by that solgan, imperfectly of course, and have found that to the extent I have lived by it, I've been lucky. To the extent I've not live by it, I've found no reason to curse my Bad Luck. The slogan on the decal said "Luck—when preparation meets opportunity."*

HUNT, BRYAN, sculptor; b. Terre Haute, Ind., June 7, 1947; s. Charles E. and Martha H. (Bourne). B.F.A., Otis Art Inst., Los Angeles, 1971. Numerous one-man shows sculpture including, Blum Helman Gallery, N.Y.C., 1977, 78, 79, 81, Greenberg Gallery, St. Louis, 1978, Daniel Weinberg Gallery, San Francisco, 1976-78, Bernard Jacobson Gallery, London, 1979, Galerie Bruno Bishofberger, Zurich, Switzerland, Margo Leabin Gallery, Los Angeles, 1980, Akron (Ohio) Art Inst., 1981, numerous group shows, 1976—, latest being, Mus. Modern Art, N.Y.C., 1979, Whitney Mus. Am. Art, N.Y.C., 1979, 81, Audrey Strohl Gallery, M.I.T., Cambridge, 1979, Brown U. Gallery, Providence, 1980, U. Mass., Amherst, San Francisco Mus. Modern Art, Thomas Segal Gallery, Boston, Venice (Italy) Biennale, Indpls. Mus. Art, Hamilton Gallery, N.Y.C., 1981, Contemporary Art Mus. Houston; represented in permanent collections, Whitney Mus. Am. Art, N.Y.C., Mus. Modern Art, N.Y.C., Solomon R. Guggenheim Mus., N.Y.C., Albright-Knox Art Gallery, Buffalo, Dallas Mus. Fine Art, Stedelijk Mus., Amsterdam, Holland, Lehmbruck Mus., W. Germany, San Francisco Mus. Art, Yale U. Art Gallery, New Haven, Vassar Coll. Art Gallery, Poughkeepsie, N.Y., Des Moines Art Centers. Address: 31 Great Jones St New York NY 10012

HUNT, CARLTON CUYLER, JR., physiologist, educator; b. Waterbury, Conn., Aug. 11, 1918; s. Carlton Cuyler and Adele F. (Weidemann) H.; m. Marion Hall, July 3, 1965. B.A., Columbia, 1939; M.D., Cornell U., 1942. Intern N.Y. Hosp., 1942-43, asst. resident, 1946; research fellow Cornell U., 1946-48, instr. physiology, 1948; sr. fellow NRC, 1948-52; asst. prof. Johns Hopkins, 1951-52; asso. Rockefeller Inst., 1952-55; prof. physiology Albert Einstein Coll. Medicine, 1955-57; prof. physiology, chmn. dept. U. Utah, 1957-64, Yale Sch. Medicine, 1964, 68; prof., head dept. physiology and biophysics Washington U. Sch. Medicine, St. Louis, 1967—; Hon. research asso. U. Coll., London, Eng., 1962-63; mem. adv. panel NSF, 1958-59, NIH, 1959-62. Served as med. officer AUS, 1943-46. Mem. Harvey Soc., Am. Physiol. Soc. Spl. research sensory receptors. Home: 8 Rue des Eaux Paris France 75016

HUNT, CHARLES BROWNLOW, JR., university dean, musician; b. Nashville, July 20, 1916; s. Charles Brownlow and Mary Agnes (Buquo) H.; m. Margaret Mitchell, Sept. 14, 1973; children: Charles Hunt III, Carol Vann. Student, Northwestern U., 1936; B.S., M.A., Peabody Coll., 1938; postgrad., Eastman Sch. Music, 1941; Ph.D., U. Cal. at Los Angeles, 1949. Mem. faculty Peabody Coll., 1940-74, prof. music, head div. music, 1955-63, dir., 1963-65, dean Grad. Sch., 1965-74; dean Coll. Communications and Fine Arts, So. Ill. U., Carbondale, 1974—; Chmn. com. membership Council Grad. Schs. U.S., 1970-73; chmn. exec. com. Nashville U. Center, 1973-74; mem. evaluation bd. Nat. Council for Accreditation Tchr. Edn., 1964-66, 72; mem. Fine Arts Commn. of Nat. Assn. State Univs. and Land Grant Colls., 1975-76. Band dir., U. Calif. at Los Angeles, 1947-49; prin. clarinetist, Nashville Symphony Orch., 1946-61. Pres. Nashville Symphony Assn., 1971-73; mem. lit. panel Ill. Arts Council, 1977-80. Served with USNR, 1945-46. Mem. Music Educators Nat. Conf., Nat. Assn. Schs. Music (commn. curricula 1958-60, pres. 1962-65, exec. com., hon. (life), Internat. Council Fine Arts Deans. Home: 503 N Division St Carterville IL 62918 Office: Coll of Communications and Fine Arts So Ill U Carbondale IL 62901

HUNT, DAVID FORD, lawyer; b. Ft. Worth, Apr. 7, 1931; s. John Greffrey and Bernice (Ford) H. B.S., North Tex. State U., 1954; J.D., Vanderbilt U., 1960. Bar: Tex. 1961. Law clk. to U.S. dist. judge No. Dist. Tex., 1960-62; practice in, Dallas, 1962—; partner firm Holloway & Hunt, 1967-70; individual practice, 1970-80; partner firm Jenkens & Gilchrist, 1980—; chmn. com. on admissions Dist. 6 Tex. State Bd. Law Examiners, 1978—. Contbr. articles to legal jours. Co-chmn. pollwatchers com. Dallas County Republican Com., 1964; Sec. R. Jackson Research Found., 1972—, Bootstrap Ranch, 1972-74; pres. So. Methodist U. Lambda Chi Edn. Found., 1972-76. Served with AUS, 1954-56. Mem. Am., Fed., Tex., Dallas bar assns., Vanderbilt U. Law Sch. Alumni Assn. (pres. Dallas 1972-75), Lambda Chi (chancellor 1966-68). Baptist. Clubs: Chaparral, Engineers (Dallas); Lancers. Home: Route 3 Box 225D Roanoke TX 76262 Office: 2200 InterFirst One Dallas TX 75202

HUNT, DAVID W., business executive; b. Cedar Rapids, Iowa, Aug. 27, 1938; s. N.C. H. and Ermengard O. (Hunt); m. Elizabeth Whiton, June 6, 1959; children: Blakely, Eric, Kevin. B.A., Coe Coll., 1960; M.S., MIT, 1976. Vice-pres. Latin Am. Eastman Kodak Co., Rochester, N.Y., 1979-81, v.p. Europe, 1981-83; pres. Mariner Properties Inc., Ft. Myers, Fla., 1983—. Home: 881 Lingren Blvd. Sanibel Island FL 33957 Office: Mariner Properties Inc. 12999 McGregor Blvd Fort Myers FL 33901

HUNT, DONALD R., librarian; b. Richmond, Ind., Nov. 5, 1921; s. Ronald Gilbert Hunt and Mildred Rorena (Lathrop) Warfield; m. Virginia Clark, June 24, 1947; children—Cynthia Hunt Hatch, Jeffrey, Kristin. B.A., U. Colo., 1950, M.S., 1951; postgrad., Stanford U., 1951-53; M.A.L.S., U. Mich., 1954. Reference librarian Wash. State U., Pullman, 1954-55, head reference, 1957-62, asst. librarian, head pub. service, 1962-65; asso. dir. libraries Oreg. State U., 1965-72; dir. library San Jose (Calif.) State U., 1972-76; dir. libraries U. Tenn., Knoxville, 1976—. Served with USNR, 1943-46. Mem. ALA, Southeastern, Tenn. library assns., AAUP, Phi Kappa Phi. Home: 5213 Hickory Hollow Rd Knoxville TN 37919 Office: Library U of Tenn Knoxville TN 37916

HUNT, DONNELL RAY, educator; b. Danville, Ind., Aug. 11, 1926; s. Ray Hadley and Sarah Leona (Booty) H.; m. Dorothea Marie May,

Sept. 2, 1951; children: David Carter, DeAnne Elizabeth. B.S., Purdue U., 1951; M.S., Iowa State U., 1954, Ph.D., 1958. Registered profl. engr., Ill. Instr. to assoc. prof. Iowa State U., Ames, 1951-60; assoc. prof. U. Ill., Urbana, 1960-68, prof. agrl. engring., 1968—; cons. in field. Author: Farm Power and Machinery Management, 8th edit., 1983, Farm Machinery Mechanisms, 1972. Served with U.S. Army, 1945-46. Fulbright awardee, Ireland, 1968-69. Fellow Am. Soc. Agrl. Engrs.; mem. Am. Soc. Engring. Edn. Republican. Presbyterian. Office: Dept Agrl Engineering Univ Ill 1304 W Pennsylvania St Urbana IL 61801

HUNT, DOUGLASS, university official; b. Winston-Salem, N.C., 1924; s. John Douglas and Kate Thelma (Harrell) H.; m. Mary Jane Havilah Abdill, 1952; children: Lloyd Abdill, John Douglass III, Amanda Caroline, Arthur Laurence. A.B., U. N.C., 1946; LL.B., Yale U., 1951. Bar: D.C. 1952, also U.S. Supreme Ct 1955. Asso. firm Gardner, Morrison and Rogers, Washington, 1951-61; spl. asst. to undersec. treasury, 1961-65, to sec. treasury, 1965-69; v.p. for finance Columbia U., 1969-71, dep. to pres. for govt. affairs, 1971-73; vice chancellor for adminstrn. U. N.C., Chapel Hill, 1973-80, affirmative action officer, 1973-81, spl. asst. to chancellor, 1980—; Mem. council on fed. relations Assn. Am. Univs., 1970-73. Mem. tax com. Am. Council on Edn., 1971—; chmn. com. taxation Nat. Assn. Coll. and Univ. Bus. Officers, 1972-73, mem., 1973-75; chmn. exec. com. council families Drew U., 1972-73; Chmn. Alexandria City Democratic Com., 1959-61. Served with AUS, 1946-48. Mem. Phi Beta Kappa. Home: 409 Westwood Dr Chapel Hill NC 27514

HUNT, EARL BUSBY, psychologist; b. San Francisco, Jan. 8, 1933; s. Robert Walter and Beryl (Busby) H.; m. Mary Lou Smith, Dec. 20, 1954; children—Robert, Susan, Alan, Steven. Student, Cornell, 1950-51; B.A., Stanford U., 1954; Ph.D., Yale U., 1960. Asst. prof. psychology Yale U., New Haven, 1960-61; sr. research asso. U. Calif. at Los Angeles, 1961-62; sr. lectr. computer sci. U. Sydney, Australia, 1962-65; asso. prof. U. Calif. at Los Angeles, 1965-66; prof. psychology U. Wash., Seattle, 1966—; cons. NIMH, 1972-76. Author 3 books; contbr. articles in field to profl. jours.; editor: Cognitive Psychology, 1974—. Served with USMC, 1954-57. Fellow AAAS, Am. Psychol. Assn.; mem. Psychonomic Soc., Psychometric Soc. Office: Psychology Dept U Wash Seattle WA 98195

HUNT, EARL GLADSTONE, JR., bishop, college president; b. Johnson City, Tenn., Sept. 14, 1918; s. Earl Gladstone and Tommie Mae (DeVault) H.; m. Mary Ann Kyker, June 15, 1943; 1 son, Earl Stephen. B.S., East Tenn. State, U., 1941; M.Div., Emory U., 1946, D.D., 1983; D.D., Tusculum Coll., 1956, Lambuth Coll., 1978; LL.D., U. Chattanooga, 1957; D.C.L., Emory and Henry Coll., 1965; D.D., Duke U., 1969; L.H.D., Belmont Abbey Coll., 1976, Fla. So. Coll., 1981. Ordained to ministry Methodist Ch., 1944; pastor Sardis Meth. Ch., Atlanta, 1942-44; asso. pastor Broad Street Meth. Ch., Kingsport, Tenn., 1944-45, Wesley Meml. Meth. Ch., Chattanooga, 1945-50, First Meth. Ch., Morristown, Tenn., 1950- 56; pres. Emory and Henry Coll., 1956-64; resident bishop Charlotte Area, United Meth. Ch., 1964-76, Nashville area, 1976-80, Fla. area, 1980—; Participant Meth. series Protestant Hour, nationwide broadcast, 1956; mem. Meth. Gen. Bd. Edn., 1956-68; bd. fellows Interpreters' House, Inc., 1967-78; del. Meth. Gen. Conf., 1956, 60, 64, S.E. Jurisdictional Conf., 1952, 56, 60, 64; chmn. gen. commn. family life United Meth. Ch., 1968-72, mem. gen. council ministries, 1972-80, chmn. bicentennial planning com., 1978-80; pres. Southeastern Jurisdictional Coll. Bishops, 1973, Southeastern Jurisdictional Conf. Council on Ministries, 1978-80; Gen. Bd. Higher Edn. and Ministry, 1980—; lectr. numerous religious and ednl. founds. Author: I Have Believed, 1980; Editor: Storms and Starlight, 1974; Contbr. numerous articles to scholarly jours., mags. Trustee Emory U., Fla. So. Coll., Bethune-Cookman Coll., Wesleyan Coll., Lake Junaluska United Meth. Assembly; keynote speaker World Meth. Conf., Dublin, 1976; exec. com. World Meth. Council, 1976—, chmn. N.Am. div., 1981—; mem. governing bd. Nat. Council Chs., 1968-84; mem. Com. One Hundred, Emory U. Named young man of year Morristown Jr. C. of C., 1952. Mem. Newcomen Soc., Blue Key, Pi Kappa Delta. Address: PO Box 1747 Lakeland FL 33802

HUNT, EFFIE NEVA, univ. adminstr., educator; b. Waverly, Ill., June 19, 1922; d. Abraham Luther and Fannie Ethel (Ritter) H. A.B., MacMurray Coll. for Women, 1944; M.A., U. Ill., 1945, Ph.D., 1950; postgrad., Columbia U., 1953, Univ. Coll., U. London, 1949-50. Key-punch operator U.S. Treasury, 1945; spl. librarian Harvard U., 1947, U. Pa., 1948; Instr. English U. Ill., 1950-51; librarian Library of Congress, Washington, 1951-52; asst. prof. English Mankato State Coll., 1952-59; prof. Radford Coll., 1959-63, chmn. dept. English, 1961-63; prof. Ind. State U., 1963—, dean, 1974—. Author articles in field. Fulbright grantee, 1949-50. Mem. AAUP, MLA, Nat. Council Tchrs. English, Am. Assn. Higher Edn., Audubon Soc. Home: 3325 Wabash Ave Terre Haute IN 47803 Office: Coll Arts and Scis Ind State U Terre Haute IN 47809

HUNT, E(VERETTE) HOWARD, JR., author, former government official; b. Hamburg, N.Y., Oct. 9, 1918; s. Everette Howard and Ethel Jean (Totterdale) H.; m. Dorothy L. Wetzel, Sept. 7, 1949 (dec.); children: Lisa Tiffany, Kevan Totterdale, Howard, David.; m. Laura E. Martin, 1977; children: Austin Dairing, Hollis. A.B., Brown U., 1940. War corr. Life mag., 1943; screen writer, 1947-48; attaché Am. embassy, Paris, France, 1948-49, Vienna, Austria, 1949-50, Mexico City, 1950-53; polit. officer Far East Command, Tokyo, Japan, 1954-56; 1st sec., consul, Montevideo, Uruguay, 1957-60; cons. Dept. Def., 1960-65; with Dept. State, Washington, 1968-70; v.p., dir. Robert R. Mullen & Co., Washington, 1970-72; cons. to Pres. U.S., 1971-72. Movie script writer, editor: March of Time, 1942-43; Author 56 books, 1942—; including The Gaza Intercept, 1981; Contbr. articles to fgn. affairs and polit. jours.; lectr. Served with USNR, 1940-42; to 1st lt. USAAF, 1943-46. Guggenheim fellow, 1946. Club: Army and Navy (Washington). Fed. prisoner, 1973-74, 75-77. Home: 1245 NE 85th St Miami FL 33138

HUNT, FRANK BOULDIN, architect; b. Morrill County, Nebr., July 19, 1915; s. Frank Neal and Silvia Sybil (Ball) H.; m. Isabel Jean Phillips, Sept. 6, 1950; m. Donna Henderson Thomas, Dec. 27, 1955. Student, U. Nebr., 1934-35, U. Calif., Berkeley, 1937-38. Draftsman and designer firms in Calif., 1938-42, 46-48; partner Kitchen and Hunt (Architects), San Francisco, 1948-62, pres., 1962-73, Hunt and Co. (Architects), San Francisco, 1973-75, dir., 1975-81; v.p., dir. Kennedy/Jenks Engrs., San Francisco, 1975—, Ecker Co., 1966—. Prin. works include library expansion, residence halls, Crocker Nuclear Lab. at U. Calif., Davis, 1954-65, facilities for, VIII Olympic Winter Games, Squaw Valley, Calif., 1956-60; cons.: U.S. Olympic Tng. Center, 1978-80; facilities for Pacific No. Region sales bldg, Eastman Kodak Co., San Francisco, 1956-58, water treatment plants, Marin County (Calif.) Municipal Water Dist., 1957-73; F.B. Hunt Residence, 1958-60; Mausoleums at, Mountain View Cemetery, Oakland, Calif., 1958-60, 74-76, 80—; Donner Animal Bioradiol. Lab, Lawrence Berkeley (Calif.) Lab, 1961-64, 76; music classroom bldg., Calif. State U., Hayward, 1963-66, Reno-Sparks (Nev.) Joint Water Pollution Control plant, 1965-67, 77—, San Francisco Bay Area Rapid Transit Dist. stas. at, N. Berkeley, Oakland West, S. Hayward, Union City, Fremont, 1965-73, Santa Clara County (Calif.) water treatment plants and related facilities, 1966-73, Maintenance and Ops. Center, United Air Lines, San Francisco Internat. Airport, 1969-72, 76—, Pacific No. Region distbn. center, Eastman Kodak Co., San Ramon, Calif., 1967-69, Kern County (Calif.) water treatment plant, 1973-76, San Francisco SW Pumping Sta, 1976-80, Central Marin San. Agy. Treatment Plant, San Rafael, Calif., 1980—. Served to lt. USNR, 1942-45. Recipient numerous design awards including archtl. models of Blyth Olmpic Arena, F.B. Hunt residence, related material at Mus. Calif., Oakland. Fellow AIA; mem. Constrn. Specifications Inst., Soc. Am. Mil. Engrs., Coll. Environ. Design Council, Phi Gamma Delta. Office: 20 Hawthorne St San Francisco CA 94105

HUNT, GEORGE NELSON, bishop; b. Louisville, Dec. 6, 1931; s. George N. and Jessie Mae (Alter) H.; m. Barbara Noel Plamp, June 18, 1955; children: Susan, Paul, David. B.A., U. South, Sewanee, Tenn., 1953; M.Div., Va. Theol. Sem., Alexandria, 1956; D.D., Yale U., 1980. Ordained to ministry Episcopal Ch., 1956; vicar Holy Trinity Ch., Gillette, Wyo., 1956-60; priest in charge St. John's Ch., Upton, Wyo., 1957-60, St. Francis Ch., Reno Junction, Wyo., 1959-60; asst. St. Paul's Ch., Oakland, Calif., 1960-62; rector St. Alban's Ch., Worland, Wyo., 1962-65, St. Anselm's Ch., Lafayette, Calif., 1965-70, St. Paul's Ch., Salinas, Calif., 1970-75; exec. officer Episcopal Diocese Calif., 1957-80; bishop Episcopal Diocese R.I., Providence, 1980—; mem. nat. council ministry, 1973-79. Episcopalian. Club: University (Providence, R.I.). Office: 275 N Main St Providence RI 02903 *

HUNT, GORDON, lawyer; b. Los Angeles, Oct. 26, 1934; s. Howard Wilson and Esther Nita (Dempsey) H.; m. Marie Ann Agosta, June 21, 1958; children—Marianne, Stephanie. B.A. in Polit. Sci, U. Calif., Los Angeles, 1956; J.D., U. So. Calif., 1959. Bar: Calif. bar 1960. Law clk. Appellate Dept., Superior Ct. Los Angeles County, 1959-60; mem. firm Behymer & Hoffman, Los Angeles, 1960-65; partner firm Behymer, Hoffman & Hunt, Los Angeles, 1965-68, Munns, Kofford, Hoffman, Hunt & Throckmorton, Pasadena, 1969—; lectr., author UCLA, 1971, 77, 80, 81. Contbr. articles to legal jours. ABA, Calif. Bar Assn. (del. Conv. 1964-69), Los Angeles County Bar Assn. (exec. com. real property sect. 1970-72, sec. 1972-73, chmn. 1976-77), Am. Arbitration Assn. (arbitrator). Republican. Methodist. Office: 199 N Lake Ave Pasadena CA 91101

HUNT, H(AROLD) KEITH, business management educator, consultant; b. Apr. 16, 1938; married; 8 children. B.S. in Mktg. and Mgmt., U. Utah, 1961, M.B.A., 1962; Ph.D. in Mktg., Northwestern U., 1972. Instr. Imperial Valley Coll., El Centro, Calif., 1962-64; teaching asst. Northwestern U., 1964-66, instr., 1966-67; asst. prof. bus. adminstrn. and journalism U. Iowa, 1967-73; cons., staff mem. Office Policy Planning and Evaluation, FTC, Washington, 1973-74; assoc. prof. bus. adminstrn. U. Wyo., Laramie, 1974-75; assoc. prof. bus. mgmt. Brigham Young U., Provo, Utah, 1975-78, prof., 1978—; speaker in field; participant, chmn. various workshops, seminars, meetings; research expert, cons., expert witness on consumer research FTC, 1974—; cons., expert witness div. drug advt. FDA, 1975—; cons., adv. on consumer research Consumer and Corp. Affairs Can., 1978—. Editor, co-editor: (with Frances Magrabi) procs. Interdisciplinary Consumer Research, 1980, (with Ralph Day) Refining Concepts and Measures of Consumer Satisfaction and Complaining Behavior, 1980; mem. editorial bd.: Jour. Consumer Affairs, 1977—, Jour. Consumer Research, 1982—, Jour. Advt., 1978—, Jour. Mktg. and Pub. Policy, 1983—. Recipient Maeser Research award Brigham Young U., 1981; scholar in residence adv. dept. U. Ill., 1979; vis. research scholar Coll. Home Econs., U. Ala., 1980; vis. research scholar dept. mktg. and transp. U. Tenn., 1981; NSF grantee, 1975-77. Mem. Assn. Consumer Research (chmn. 1977 conf. program com., chmn. arrangements 1978 conf., pres. 1979, nominations com. 1980, exec. sec. 1983—), Am. Acad. Advt. (chmn. govt. relations com. 1976—, editor Jour. Advt. 1978—, pres. 1982-83, exec. sec. 1983—), Am. Mktg. Assn. (co-chmn. fed. govt. liason com. 1975-77, track chmn. Macro Mktg. Track 1976 conf.), Am. Psychol. Assn., Am. Council on Consumer Interests, Beta Gamma Sigma, Kappa Tau Alpha, Omicron Delta Epsilon, Phi Kappa Phi. Home: 835 E High Country Dr Orem UT 84057 Office: Inst Bus Mgmt Brigham Young U 632 TNRB Provo UT 84602

HUNT, HOWARD FRANCIS, psychologist, educator; b. Morgantown, W.Va., May 29, 1918; s. Harrison R. and Jane (Fisher) H.; m. Ida Altman, Aug. 16, 1941; children: Carol Ann Hunt Stark, William H., Steven C., John H. A.B., Mich. State Coll., 1940; Ph.D., U. Minn., 1943. Diplomate: clin. psychology Am. Bd. Examiners Profl. Psychology. Instr. psychology U. Minn., 1943-44; asst. prof. psychology Stanford U., 1946-48; asso. prof. U. Chgo., 1948-54, prof., 1954, chmn. dept. psychology, 1955-62; chief psychiat. research (psychology) N.Y. State Psychiat. Inst., N.Y.C., 1962-77; prof. med. psychology Coll. Physicians and Surgeons, Columbia U., 1962-77; prof. psychology Columbia U., 1962-77; prof. psychology in psychiatry Cornell U. Med. Coll., N.Y.C., 1977—; attending psychologist N.Y. Hosp.-Cornell Med. Center, 1978—; fellow (Center for Advanced Study in Behavioral Sci.), 1959-60; chmn. psychopharmacology rev. com. NIMH, 1958-61, mem., 1971-74, mem. bd. sci. counselors, 1961-65; mem. brain scis. com. Nat. Acad. Sci.-NRC, 1974-78; mem. N.Y. State Health Adv. Council, 1975-78. Contbr. articles to profl. publs.; editorial bd.: Jour. Psychiatry and the Law; editorial adviser on psychology: Ency. Brit., 1957—; editor: Dorsey Press Psychology Series, 1959-75, Jour. Abnormal Psychology, 1964-70. Bd. dirs. Founds. Fund for Research in Psychiatry, 1963-66; v.p. bd. dirs. Children's Village, Dobbs Ferry, N.Y. Served from ensign to lt. (j.g.) USNR, 1944-46. Recipient Salmon medal in psychiatry, 1978. Fellow Am. Psychol. Assn., AAAS, N.Y. Acad. Scis.; mem. Am. Psychopath. Assn. (treas. 1964-65), Internat. Brain Research Orgn., Eastern Psychol. Assn., Sigma Xi, Phi Kappa Phi, Kappa Sigma; Mem. Soc. of Friends. Home: Ardsley Park Irvington-on-Hudson NY 10533 Office: NY Hospital/Cornell Med Center 21 Bloomingdale Rd White Plains NY 10605

HUNT, JACOB TATE, educator; b. Sweetwater, Tenn., Aug. 22, 1916; s. Samuel Lon and Grace Viola (Beals) H.; m. Harriet Elizabeth Durnell, June 17, 1944; 1 son, Steven Craig. B.A., Maryville (Tenn.) Coll., 1938; M.S., U. Tenn., 1941; Ph.D., U. Calif. at Berkeley, 1950; Ford Found. postdoctoral fellow, U. Ill., 1956-57. Tchr. pub. schs., Tenn., 1938-40, Wash., 1940-42; instr. U. Calif. at Berkeley, 1946-48; asst. prof. Western Res. U., 1948-51; asst., then asso. prof. U. N.C., 1951-57; prof. U. Ariz., 1957-64, U. Wash., 1964-68; prof. spl. edn., chmn. div. exceptional children U. Ga., 1968—; summer vis. prof. U. Wash., 1952, 63, 64, U. Ill., 1956, U. Colo., 1960, 61, U. Calif. at Berkeley, 1962; Mem. study commn. exceptional children Western Interstate Commn. Higher Edn., 1958-60; mem. Ga. Coordinating Com. Exceptional Children, 1969—; cons. Saguaro Sch. Asthmatic Children, United Cerebral Palsy Assn., HEW. Author: Mentally Retarded Children, 1969; Editor: High Sch. Jour, 1952-56, Rev. Edn. Research, 1965-69, Education and Training of the Mentally Retarded; asso. editor: Exceptional Children, Jour. Spl. Edn., Scientia Paedagogica Experimentalis, 1967—. Bd. dirs. Pima Assn. Mental Health, 1960-64. Served with USNR, 1942-45. Grantee edn. handicapped U.S. Office Edn., 1964-77. Mem. Am. Ednl. Research Assn. (exec. com. 1959-64, chmn. editorial com. 1965-69), Council Exceptional Children (bd. dirs. 1978-83, editorial com. 1978-83), Am. Psychol. Assn., Internat. Reading Assn., Phi Kappa Phi, Phi Delta Kappa. Presbyterian. Home: 105 Chinquapin Way Athens GA 30605

HUNT, JAMES BAXTER, JR., governor N.C.; b. Guilford County, N.C., May 16, 1937; s. James Baxter and Elsie (Brame) H.; m. Carolyn Joyce Leonard, Aug. 20, 1958; children: Rebecca Hunt Hawley, James Baxter III, Rachel Henderson, Elizabeth Brame. B.S. in Edn., N.C. State U., 1959, M.S. in Econs., 1962; J.D., U. N.C., 1964. Bar: N.C. 1964. Econ. adviser H.M. Govt. of Nepal for Ford Found., 1964-66; mem. law firm Kirby, Webb & Hunt, 1966-72; lt. gov. State of N.C., 1973-77, gov., 1977—; State pres. Young Democrats, 1968; chmn. Dem. Study Commn., 1968. Author: Acreage Controls and Poundage Controls, Their Effects on Most Profitable Practices for Flue-Cured Tobacco, 1964, Rally Around the Precinct, 1968. Recipient first ann. Harry S. Truman award Nat. Young Democrats Club, 1975; named Outstanding Young Man of Yr. Wilson Jr. C. of C., 1969. Mem. Nat. Govs. Assn. (chmn. task force on technol. innovation, mem. exec. com., chmn. edn. com. of the states and nat. task force on edn. for econ. growth 1982-83). Presbyterian. Office: Governor's Office State of NC Raleigh NC 27611 *

HUNT, JAMES CALVIN, physician, university chancellor; b. Lexington, N.C., Sept. 11, 1925; s. James Lee and Sarah Della (Frank) H.; m. Irene Kivett, Sept. 17, 1949; children—James Calvin, Michael S., Cynthia Irene. A.B., Catawba Coll., 1949; M.D., Bowman Gray Sch. Medicine, 1953; M.S., U. Minn., 1958. Intern N.C. Bapt. Hosp., Winston-Salem, 1953-54; resident, fellow Mayo Grad Sch. Medicine, Rochester, Minn., 1954-58; practice medicine, specializing in internal medicine (cardiovascular-renal diseases), Rochester, 1958-78; cons., instr. to asst. prof. dept. medicine Mayo Clinic and Mayo Med. Sch., 1958-63, asso. prof., chmn. div. nephrology, 1963-72, prof., chmn. dept. medicine, 1974-78; prof., asso. dean clin. ednl. programs Mayo Med. Sch., 1972-74; prof. medicine U. Tenn., Memphis, 1978—, dean, 1978-81, chancellor, 1981—; mem. Nat. Heart, Lung and Blood Adv. Council, NIH. Contbr. articles to med. jours. Pres. Nat. Kidney Found., 1973-76; bd. dirs. Kidney Found. Upper Midwest.; trustee Christian Bros. Coll., 1983. Served with USAAF, 1943-46; ETO. Recipient Disting. Service award Bowman Gray Sch. Medicine, Wake Forest U., 1975; Disting. Alumnus award Catawba Coll., 1974. Fellow A.C.P., Am. Coll. Cardiology, Am. Heart Assn. (council on circulation); mem. Internat., Am. socs. nephrology, Internat. Soc. Hypertension, Soc. Nuclear Medicine, Council for High Blood Pressure Research, Am. Soc. Internal Medicine, AMA, Am. Soc. Clin. Pharmacology and Therapeutics, Sigma Xi, Alpha Omega Alpha, Phi Rho Sigma. Home: 343 S Goodwyn Memphis TN 38111 Office: Center for Health Sciences U Tenn 62 S Dunlap St Memphis TN 38163

HUNT, JAMES ROBERT, librarian; b. West Brownsville, Pa., May 5, 1925; s. James Clarence and Jesse (Sharp) H.; m. Gloria Solli, June 26, 1954; children—Christopher James, Marya Madeline, Megan Maura, Shelagh Maureen, Matthew Becket, Deirdre Mór. Ph.B., U. Detroit, 1951, M.A. in Polit. Sci, 1955, U. Mich., 1959. Co-mgr. Madonna Book Shop, Detroit, 1951-56; bookmobile librarian Wayne County (Mich.) Library, 1956-57, adminstrv. asst. to librarian, 1958-60, head central services, 1960-62; asst. state librarian Mich. State Library, Lansing, 1962-64; state librarian, asst. supt. library services Hawaii Dept. Edn., Honolulu, 1964-70, acting dep. supt. edn., 1970-71, state librarian, 1971; dir. Pub. Library Cin. and Hamilton County, Ohio, 1971—; Mem. library tech. com. Lansing Community Coll.; chmn. Hawaii Gov's. Com. State Library Resources, 1964; adv. com. U. Hawaii Grad. Library Sch., 1962—; mem. Gov.'s Com. on Hawaiian Textbook Materials, 1971; mem. adv. com. Continuation of Library Planning and Evaluation Inst., Ohio State U., 1972-73; mem. State Bd. Library Examiners, 1971. Contbr. articles to profl. publs. Mem. A.L.A. (life mem.; v.p. Assn. State Library Agys. 1971-72, pres. 1972-73), Mich. Library Assn. (chmn. library adminstrn. sect. 1961-62), Hawaii Library Assn. (A.L.A. rep. 1964-68), Ohio Library Assn., Hawaiian Hist. Soc. (dir.), Friends of Library, Cin. Hist. Soc. (mem. bd. 1972), Mcdowell Soc., Am. Soc. Pub. Adminstrn. (sec. Honolulu chpt. 1966—). Office: 800 Vine St Cincinnati OH 45202

HUNT, JANET ELAINE, trust co. exec., lawyer; b. Boston, June 17, 1940; d. Edward C. and Helga V. (Johnson) H. A.B., Wellesley Coll., 1962; J.D., Harvard U., 1965. Bar: N.J. bar 1965. With Irving Trust Co., N.Y.C., 1965—, v.p. personal trust div., 1976, v.p., mgr. new bus. and estate and trust adminstrn., 1976-79, sr. v.p., mgr. personal trust div., 1979—; mem. com. on trust and estate gift plans Rockefeller U. Trustee Bentley Coll., 1981—. Mem. N.Y. State Bankers Assn., Am. Bar Assn., N.J. Bar Assn. Office: Irving Trust Co One Wall St New York NY 10015

HUNT, JOE HAROLD, utility company executive; b. Oakman, Okla., Dec. 20, 1925; s. Virgil and Anna M. H.; m. Adeanya Standridge, June 24, 1946; children: Bruce, David, Paul, Gregory. B.S.E.E., Okla. State U., 1949. Plant asst. Southwestern Bell Telephone Co., 1949, exec. v.p., St. Louis, 1978—; with Bell Telephone System, 1949—; v.p. S.W. Bell Telephone Co.; asst. v.p. AT&T; dir. Merc. Trust Co., Merc. Bancorp. Bd. dirs. Bapt. Hosp., Ranken Tech. Inst.; trustee Lindenwood Coll. Served with USN, 1944-46, 50-52. Mem. Eta Kappa Nu, Phi Kappa Phi, Pi Mu Epsilon, Sigma Tau. Baptist (deacon). Office: 1010 Pine St Saint Louis MO 63101

HUNT, JOHN CLINTON, biotechnology company executive; b. Muskogee, Okla., July 24, 1925; m. Chantal Pepin de Bonnerive; 4 children. A.B., Harvard U., 1948; postgrad., Sorbonne, 1948-49, U. Iowa, 1949-50. Tchr. Thomas Jefferson Sch., St. Louis, 1951-56; exec. dir. Congress for Cultural Freedom, Paris, 1956-68; exec. v.p. Salk Inst. Biol. Studies, La Jolla, Calif., 1968-70; dir. internat. projects Royaumont Found., Paris, 1970-73; v.p. Aspen Inst. Humanistic Studies, N.Y.C. and Aspen, 1973-76; v.p., sec. corp. U. Pa., 1976-77, assoc. dir., sec. corp., 1976-77, Inst. Advanced Study, Princeton, N.J., 1977-81; chmn., chief exec. officer BioTechnica Internat., Inc., Cambridge, Mass., 1981—. Author: Generations of Men, 1956 (prize Western Writers Assn. Am., nominee Nat. Book award), The Grey Horse Legacy, 1968 (Lit. Guild alt.); off-Broadway play Knights Errant, 1982. Served to 2d lt. USMC, 1943-46. Decorated Nat. Order of Merit (France). Clubs: Harvard, Century Assn. Home: 12 Concord Ave Apt 1 Cambridge MA 02138 Office: BioTechnica Internat Inc 85 Bolton St Cambridge MA 02140

HUNT, JOHN DAVID, banker; b. Worcester, Mass., May 2, 1925; s. John J. and Honorea B. (Tully) H.; m. Claire A. Sullivan, June 25, 1949; children: Barbara A., Kathryn R. A.B., Brown U., 1949; postgrad., Williams Coll. Sch. Banking, 1960; Advanced Mgmt. Program, Harvard U., 1973; D.B.A. (hon.), Anna Maria Coll., 1982. Accountant Harry W. Wallis & Co., Worcester, 1949-50; with Worcester County Nat. Bank, 1952—, asst. v.p., 1959-61, v.p., 1961-69, sr. v.p., 1969-73, exec. v.p., 1973-77, pres., 1977—, loan officer, 1961-65, chmn. loan rev. com., 1961—, sr. loan officer, 1965—, also dir.; dir. RSC Industries, Wornat Devel. Corp., Worcester County Nat. Bank, Worcester Bus. Devel. Corp., Wornat Leasing Corp., Worcester Capital Corp., Empire Group Inc., Wornat Ins. Agy. Inc., State Mut. Securities Inc., Worcester Bancorp. Inc.; instr. Am. Inst. Banking, 1957-60. Chmn. fund drive Greater Worcester United Appeal, 1972; Bd. dirs. United Cerebral Palsy Assn. Worcester County, 1957-67; Wooster Better Bus. Bur., 1964-69, Catholic Charities Worcester, 1971-75, United Way Worcester; corporator Hahnemann Hosp.; trustee Assumption Coll.; corporator St. Vincent Hosp.; mem. Worcester Redevel. Authority, 1983. Served to lt. USNR, 1943-47, 50-52.

Recipient Outstanding Young Man award Worcester County, 1961. Mem. Am. Inst. Banking, Robert Morris Assos. (bd. govs. 1966-71, pres. New Eng. chpt. 1969-70), Am. Bankers Assn. (governing council), Mass. Bankers Assn., bd. govs. (1974—, chmn. 1977), Alpha Delta Phi. Republican. Roman Catholic. Clubs: Economic of Worcester, Worcester County Brown, First Friday, Worcester, Worcester Country, Plaza. Home: 12 Paul Revere Rd Worcester MA 01609 Office: 446 Main St PO Box 529 Worcester MA 01608

HUNT, JOHN WESLEY, university dean; b. Tulsa, Jan. 19, 1927; s. John Wesley and Alta (Johnson) H.; m. Marjorie Louise Bowen, Aug. 8, 1951; children: Stuart Griggs, Susan Scott, Emily Johnson. B.A., U. Okla., 1949; student, U. Minn., 1947; Ph.D., U. Chgo., 1961. Asst. prof. English Earlham Coll., Richmond, Ind., 1956-62, asso. prof., 1962-66, prof., 1966-72, chmn. English dept., Bain-Swiggett prof. English lang. and lit., 1968-71, asso. acad. dean, 1971-72; dean Coll. Arts and Sci., prof. English, Lehigh U., Bethlehem, Pa., 1972—. Author: William Faulkner: Art in Theological Tension, 1965; Asst. editor, Bull. Ill. Soc. Med. Research, 1954-56; mem. editorial bd.: Quest, 1952-56, Earlham Rev, 1966-72; co-editor: Perspectives on a Cuckoo's Nest, 1977; Contbr. chpts. to books, articles to profl. jours. Served with USNR, 1944-46. Recipient Danforth Tchr. Study grant, 1960-61, E. Harris Harbison award for distinguished teaching Danforth Found., 1965, Carnegie Humanities Program grant, 1967-68; Ira Doan Distinguished Tchr. Travel award Earlham Coll., 1970; Ford Found. Humanities Devel. Fund grant, summers 1970, 71; U. Chgo. fellow, 1952-54; Kent fellow, 1952—; Lilly postdoctoral fellow Lilly Endowment, Inc., 1964-65. Fellow Soc. for Values in Higher Edn. (chmn. postdoctoral selection com. 1968-70); mem. Nat. Council Tchrs. English, Modern Lang. Assn., Ann. Conf. Modern Lit., Soc. for Study So. Lit., Gt. Lakes Colls. Assn. (acad. council 1967-72, exec. com. 1968-72, sec. 1968-71, dir. 1971-72), Am. Conf. Acad. Deans, Lawrence Henry Gipson Inst. for 18th Century Studies (council 1972—). Home: Box 432 Springtown PA 18081 Office: Lehigh U Maginnes Hall 9 Bethlehem PA 18015

HUNT, J(OSEPH) MCVICKER, psychologist, educator; b. Scottsbluff, Nebr., Mar. 19, 1906; s. Robert Sanford and Carrie Pearl (McVicker, nee Loughborough) H.; m. Esther Dahms, Dec. 25, 1929; children: Judith Ann, Carol Jean. A.B., U. Nebr., 1929, A.M., 1930, D.Sc. (hon.), 1967; Ph.D., Cornell U., 1933; Sc.D. (hon.), Brown U., 1958. Diplomate: (clin.) Am. Bd. Profl. Psychology. Tng. and research, 1929-36; from instr. to asso. prof. Brown U., 1936-46; research cons. Inst. Welfare Research, Community Service Soc. N.Y., 1944-46, dir., 1946-51; lectr. Columbia Tchrs. Coll., 1948-50; adj. prof. Grad. Sch., NYU, 1950-51; prof. psychology U. Ill., 1951-67, prof. psychology and edn., 1967-74, prof. emeritus, 1974—; cons. VA Hosp., Danville, Ill., 1953-74; dir. Coordination Center, Nat. Lab. Early Childhood Edn., 1967-68, mem. adv. bd., 1968-70; chmn. White House Task Force Child Devel., 1966-67; lectr. Internat. Congress on Early Edn., Tokyo and Kyoto, Japan, 1978, hon. chmn., Tel Aviv, 1980. Editor: Personality and the Behavior Disorders (2 vols.), 1944, Jour. Abnormal and Social Psychology, 1950-55, Human Intelligence, 1972; Author: (with L.S. Kogan) Measuring Results in Social Casework: A Manual on Judging Movement, 1950, (with Blenkner and Kogan) Testing Results in Social Casework: A Field Test of the Movement Scale, 1950, (with Kogan and Bartelme) A Follow-Up Study of the Results of Social Casework, 1953, Intelligence and Experience, 1961, The Challenge of Incompetence and Poverty, 1969, (with I.C. Uzgiris) Assessment in Infancy: Ordinal Scales of Psychological Development, 1975, Early Psychological Development and Experience, 1980; Contbr.: (with I.C. Uzgiris) articles and Early Psychological Development and Experience; contbr. papers to profl. lit. Trustee Am. Psychol. Found., 1952-59, pres., 1953-54, 58-59; trustee Elizabeth McCormick Meml. Fund, 1954-61, Rocky Ridge Music Center Found., 1963—; pres. Rocky Ridge Music Center Found., 1977—. Recipient awards Am. Personnel and Guidance Assn., 1950, 60, Research Career award NIMH, 1962-74, Disting. Scholar award Hofstra Coll., 1973, citation significant contbns. Am. Montessori Soc., 1974; Heinz Werner Meml. lectr. Clark U., 1976; M.E.M. O'Neal lecture award in developmental pediatrics U. Nebr. Med. Center, 1977; Gold Medal award Am. Psychol. Found., 1979. Fellow AAAS (mem. council 1968-70), Am. Acad. Psychotherapists, Am. Psychol. Assn. (mem. council 1946-54, 68-71, dir. 1949-53, 70-73, pres. 1951-52, pres. div. personality and social psychology 1950-51, pres. div. clin. psychology 1968-69, Disting. Contbns. award div. clin. psychology 1973, G. Stanley Hall award div. developmental psychology 1976); mem. AAUP, Am. Statis. Assn., Eastern Psychol. Assn. (pres. 1947-48), Midwestern Psychol. Assn., Am. Sociol. Assn., Soc. for Research in Child Devel., Sigma Xi, Psi Chi, Phi Kappa Psi. Unitarian. Home: 1807 Pleasant Circle Urbana IL 61801 Office: Dept of Psychology Univ of Ill 603 East Daniel St Champaign IL 61820

HUNT, LACY H., economist; b. El Paso, Tex., July 29, 1942; s. Andrew William and Elizabeth (Mullen) H.; m. Jean Evans, Sept. 3, 1966; children: Lacy H., Eugene Rees. B.A., U. South, 1964; M.B.A., U. Pa., 1966; Ph.D., Temple U., 1969. Sr. economist Fed. Res. of Dallas, 1969-73; v.p. Chase Econometrics, Phila., 1973-76; exec. v.p., economist Fidelity Bank, Phila., 1976-83; pres. CM&M Asset Mgmt. Co., Inc., Phila., 1983—. Author: Dynamics of Forecasting Financial Cycles, 1976. Recipient Cert. of Honor Temple U. Gen. Alumni Assn., 1983. Mem. Nat. Assn. Bus. Economists (Adolph C. Abramson award 1974), Am. Fin. Assn., Am. Econ. Assn., U.S. C. of C. Presbyterian. Home: 167 Vassar Circle Villanova PA 19085 Office: CM&M Asset Mgmt Co Inc 1613 Spruce St Philadelphia PA 19103

HUNT, LAMAR, profl. football team exec.; b. 1933; s. H. L. and Lyda (Baker) H.; m. Norma Hunt; children—Lamar, Sharon, Clark. Grad., So. Meth. U. Founder, owner Kansas City Chiefs, NFL, 1959—, pres., 1959-76, chmn., 1977-78; founder, pres. AFL, 1959; (became Am. Football Conf.-NFL 1970); pres. Am. Football Conf., 1970—; dir. Great Midwest Corp., Interstate Securities, Traders' Nat. Bank. Bd. dirs. Profl. Football Hall of Fame, Canton, Ohio. Named Salesman of Year Kansas City Advt. and Sales Execs. Club, 1963; Southwesterner of Year Tex. Sportswriters Assn., 1969. Address: care Kansas City Chiefs One Arrowhead Dr Kansas City MO 64129 *

HUNT, MARK ALAN, museum director; b. Topeka, May 21, 1949; s. Ira B. and Marjorie May (McConnell) H.; m. Cynthia E. Rush, Feb. 21, 1976; children: Alexander Rush, Alice Claire. B.A. magna cum laude, Washburn U., 1971; M.A., Cooperstown Grad. Programs, N.Y. State U. Coll., Oneonta, 1982. Dir. Plymouth (Mich.) Hist. Mus., 1976; curator exhibits Kans. Hist. Soc. Topeka, 1976, asst. dir. mus., 1976-79, dir. mus., 1979—; cons. Menninger Found., 1980, Nat. Endowment Humanities, 1974, 75, 77, 1978, Mus. Assessment Program. Contbr. articles to profl. jours. Wiseman scholar, 1967-68; Washburn scholar, 1968-71; Clark fellow, 1973-74. Mem. Am. Assn. State and Local History (state membership chmn.; cons.), Mountain Plains Mus. Assn. (mem. bd. 1977, Kans. rep.), Kans. Mus. Assn. (pres. 1978-80), Am. Assn. Museums, Kans. Hist. Soc., Kappa Sigma, Phi Kappa Phi. Methodist. Home: 1720 Willow Ave Topeka KS 66606 Office: 120 W 10th St Topeka KS 66612

HUNT, NELSON BUNKER, corporate exec.; b. 1926; (married). Grad., So. Meth. U. With Hunt Internat. Resources Corp., 1974—, now chmn. bd., dir.; active personal and family investments. Office: 3600 First Internat Bldg Dallas TX 75270 *

HUNT, RICHARD HOWARD, sculptor; b. Chgo., Sept. 12, 1935; s. Cleophus Howard and Etoria Inez (Henderson) H.; m. Betty Marjorie; 1 dau., Cecilia Elizabeth. Studied sculpture, Nelli Bar, 1950-53; student, U. Chgo., 1953-55; B.A.E., Art Inst. Chgo. Exhibited: Artists of Chgo. and Vicinity exhbn., 1955-56, 62d, 63d, 64th Am. exhbns. Art Inst. Chgo., 1971, Carnegie Internat. Pitts., 1958, Mus. Modern Art, N.Y.C., 1959, 71, one-man shows, Alan Gallery, N.Y.C., 1960, B.C. Holland Gallery, Chgo., 1963, Dorsky Gallery, N.Y.C., 1971; represented permanent collections, Mus. Modern Art, N.Y.C., Whitney Mus., N.Y.C., Albright Gallery, Buffalo, Art Inst. Chgo., Nat. Mus. Israel; exhibited, Alan Gallery, N.Y.C., 1956, 58, Houston Mus., 1957, Whitney Mus., 1958, Mus. Modern Art, N.Y.C., 1957, Mus. 20th Century Vienna, Austria; vis. artist, Yale U., 1964, Chovinard Art Sch., 1964-65. Served with U.S. Army. Recipient Frank G. Logan medal and prize, 1956, Pauline Palmer prize, 1957, James Nelson Raymond traveling fellowship, 1957, Logan medal and prize Artists of Chgo. and Vicinity show, 1961; Guggenheim fellow. Address: 1017 W Lill Ave Chgo IL 60614

HUNT, ROBERT CHESTER, construction company executive; b. Dayton, Ohio, 1923. Grad., Case Inst. Tech., 1942. With Huber Hunt & Nichols Inc., Indpls., 1947—, sec., 1950-51, gen. mgr., 1951-52, v.p., 1952-56, chmn. bd., pres., 1956, chmn. bd., dir.; dir. Am. Fletcher Nat. Bank. Office: Huber Hunt & Nichols Inc 2450 S Tibbs Ave Indianapolis IN 46206 *

HUNT, ROBERT M., newspaper publisher; b. Sault Ste. Marie, Mich., Feb. 7, 1928; m. Janice Sutter, 1953; 3 children. Ed., Mich. State U. With Chgo. Tribune Co., 1950-79; mgr. N.Y. advt. office gen. div., 1965-66, sales mgr. gen. div., 1966-67, gen. advt. mgr., 1967-69, asst. circulation dir., 1969-72, advt. dir., 1972, v.p., 1972-74, pres., gen. mgr., 1974-79, chief exec. officer, 1976-79; v.p. Tribune Co., 1974-79, dir., 1974—, mem. exec. com., 1975—; pres., pub., chief exec. officer N.Y. Daily News (div. N.Y. News Inc.), 1979—; dir. Met. Sunday Newspapers, Inc., Newspaper Advt. Bur., N.Y.C. Partnership, Inc. Trustee Robert R. McCormick Charitable Trust; bd. dirs. Chgo. unit Am. Cancer Soc.; Citizen fellow Chgo. Inst. Medicine. Clubs: Tavern, Chicago (Chgo.); Sky, Metropolitan (N.Y.C.). Office: NY Daily News 220 E 42d St New York NY 10017

HUNT, ROBERT SHERWOOD, educator; b. Postville, Iowa, July 14, 1917; s. Gerald Winslow and Margaret (Sherwood) H.; m. Elaine Marie Hess, Aug. 18, 1948 (div.). A.B., Oberlin Coll., 1939; A.M., Harvard U., 1940; LL.B., Yale U., 1947; S.J.D. (Rockefeller fellow), U. Wis., 1952. Bar: Iowa bar 1948, Ill. bar 1951. From instr. to asst. prof. Coll. Law, U. Iowa, 1947-49; assoc. firm Schiff Hardin and Waite, Chgo., 1950-57, ptnr., 1957-66; prof. Sch. Law, U. Wash., Seattle, 1966—, assoc. dean, 1970-75; Dir. Security State Bank, Guttenberg, Ia., 1964-71. Author: Law and Locomotives: the Impact of the Railroad on Wisconsin Law in the 19th Century, 1958. Bd. dirs. Mary McDowell Settlement House, Chgo., 1962-66. Served to lt. comdr. USNR, 1940-46; PTO. Mem. Am. Vets. Com. (nat. vice chmn. 1955-56), Am. Bar Assn. Clubs: Corbey Court (New Haven); Cliff Dwellers (Chgo.). Home: 1415 38th Ave Seattle WA 98122

HUNT, ROGER SCHERMERHORN, hospital administrator; b. White Plains, N.Y., Mar. 7, 1943; s. Charles Howland and Mildred Russell (Schermerhorn) H.; m. Mary Adams Libby, June 19, 1965; children: Christina, David. B.A., DePauw U., 1965; M.B.A., George Washington U., 1968. Adminstrv. resident Lankenau Hosp., Phila., 1966-68; asst. adminstr. Hahnemann Med. Coll. and Hosp., Phila., 1968-71, hosp. dir., 1971-74, asso. v.p., hosp. adminstr., 1974-77; dir. Ind. U. Hosps., Indpls., 1977—; vice chmn. Alliance of Indpls. Hosps., 1978-80, chmn., 1981; v.p. Greater Indpls. Hosp. Dist., 1980-81, pres., 1982-83; mgr. bd. trustees, sec.-treas. Delaware Valley Hosp. Laundry, 1969-77; trustee Nat. Benefit Fund of Nat. Union Hosp. and Health Care Employees, 1973-77, Phila. Blood Center, 1972-74, United Hosp. Services, 1977—, pres., 1979-80; assoc. prof. hosp. adminstrn. Ind. U. Sch. Medicine, 1977—; Vice chmn. Pa. Emergency Health Services Council, 1975-77; pres. Chester County Emergency Med. Service Council, 1971-77. V.p. Wayne Area Jr. C. of C., 1969-70, pres., 1970-71, state dir., 1971-72. Fellow Am. Coll. Hosp. Adminstrs. (Postgrad. tng. award 1968); mem. Am. Hosp. Assn., Ind. Hosp. Assn. (bd. dirs. 1982—). Lodge: Rotary. Home: 744 Hawthorne Dr Carmel IN 46032 Office: Ind U Hosps 1100 W Michigan St Indianapolis IN 46202

HUNT, RONALD DUNCAN, pathologist, veterinarian, educator; b. Los Angeles, Oct. 9, 1935; s. Charles H. and Margaret (Duncan) H. B.S., U. Calif., Davis, 1957, D.V.M. with highest honors, 1959; student, UCLA, 1954-55. Research fellow pathology Harvard Med. Sch., 1963-64, research assoc. pathology, 1964-69, prin. assoc. pathology, 1969-72, assoc. prof. comparative pathology, 1972-77, prof. comparative pathology, 1977—; dir. Animal Resources Center Harvard Med. Sch., 1979—; affiliate pathologist Angell Meml. Animal Hosp., Boston, 1966-75; dir. New Eng. Regional Primate Research Center, Southborough, Mass., 1976—. Author: (with T.C. Jones) Veterinary Pathology, 1972, 5th edit., 1983, (with T.C. Jones and U. Mohr) Endocrine System; contbr. numerous articles on research in vet. pathology to profl. jours.; editorial bd.: Lab Animal Medicine, 1969—, Jour. Med. Primatology, 1977—, Internat. Life Scis. Inst, 1981—, Am. Jour. Vet. Research, 1978-80. Trustee Charles Louis Davis DVM Found., 1979—; exec. com. Tufts U. Sch. Vet. Medicine. Served with Vet. Corps U.S. Army, 1959-63. Mem. Am. Coll. Vet. Pathologists, AVMA, Internat. Acad. Pathology, Am. Soc. Exptl. Pathology, Am. Soc. Clin. Pathologists, Mass. Soc. Pathologists, Am. Assn. Lab. Animal Sci., New Eng. Soc. Pathologists, Internat. Primatological Soc., New Eng. Soc. Primatologists, N.Y. Acad. Scis. *Aside from customary reasons for advancement, I believe the factor of most importance to my career has been the ability to work as a member of a team, yet simultaneously remain independent and maintain broad vision, to pursue observations not necessarily related to primary objectives.*

HUNT, WENDELL ROGER, hospital adminstrator; b. Johnstown, Pa., June 30, 1937; s. Harvey Curtis and Velma (Bassett) H.; m. Carol Ann Rummel, May 3, 1958; children: Kerry Gar, Terri Sue. B.S., Pa. State U., 1959; M.Govt. Adminstrn., U. Pa., 1974. Bar: licensed tchr., Pa. Tchr. voc. agr. Saltsburg Joint Sch., Pa., 1959-60; asst. farm mgr. Selinsgrove Ctr., Pa., 1960-62, farm mgr., 1966-67, asst. bus. mgr. to bus. mgr., 1967-81; supt. adminstr. Mayview State Hosp., Bridgeville, Pa., 1981—; acting supt. Dixmont State Hosp., Sewickley, Pa., 1982—. Chmn. adminstrv. bd. Wesley Ch., Selinsgrove, Pa., 1972-74. Mem. Am. Health Planning Assn., Am. Coll. Hosp. Adminstrs., Wayne County Agr. Assn. (v.p. 1965-66). Republican. Methodist. Club: Kiwanis (pres. 1973-74). Lodge: Masons. Home: 126 Pennsylvania Ave Bridgeville PA 15017 Office: 1601 Mayview Rd Bridgeville PA 15017

HUNT, WILLIAM ALVIN, psychologist, educator; b. Hartford, Conn., Nov. 10, 1903; s. Alvin Ashbell and Mabel Stetson (Hodges) H.; m. Edna Reeve Bossen, June 15, 1929 (dec. Apr. 1959); m. Diana Bengston Theobald, Dec. 19, 1960 (div. Sept. 1978); 1 dau., Margit. A.B., Dartmouth, 1928; A.M., Harvard, 1929, Ph.D., 1931. Instr. Dartmouth, 1931-33; asst. prof. Conn. Coll. for Women, 1933-37; prof. Wheaton (Mass.) Coll., 1938-45; prof. psychology Northwestern U., 1945-67, chmn. dept. psychology, 1951-67; prof. psychology Loyola U., Chgo., 1967-74, prof. emeritus, 1974—; research scientist Learning Center, Am. U., 1974; cons. clin. psychol. Surgeon Gen. Army, VA, 1946—; cons. asst. sec. def., 1954—, Army Sci. Adv. Panel, 1956—; cons. clin. psychol. Surgeon Gen. Navy, 1958—; cons. Nat. Security Agy., 1962—, Nat. Heart, Lung and Blood Inst., 1975—. Asso. editor: Jour. Clin. Psychology, 1945—; Contbr. articles to profl. jours. Mem. research adv. com. Nat. Council on Alcoholism, 1974—. Served to comdr. USNR, World War II. Recipient Clin. Psychologist of Year award Ill. Psychol. Assn., 1973, Psychologist of Yr. award, 1978. Fellow Am. Psychol. Assn. (Outstanding Clin. award 1967, Disting. Contbns. award 1979, pres. div. clin. psychology 1954, pres. div. on teaching 1951), 1mem., Soc. Exptl. Psychology, Phi Beta Kappa, Sigma Xi, Alpha Delta Phi. Home: 6325 N Sheridan Rd Chicago IL 60660

HUNT, WILLIAM DUDLEY, JR., editor, architect; b. New Orleans, Mar. 23, 1922; s. William Dudley and Ruth (Lee) H.; m. Gwendolyn Pratt Munson, June 19, 1954; children: William Dudley III, Walter W., Ruth Lee, Stephen Clarendon Munson, Gwendolyn Munson, John Morgan. B.S., Jacksonville State U., 1949; B.Arch., Tulane U., 1957. Practice architecture William Dudley Hunt, Jr., New Orleans, Pensacola, Fla., N.Y.C., 1954-64; sr. editor Archtl. Record mag., N.Y.C., 1958-63; pub. A.I.A. Jour. mag., Washington, 1963-72; cons. editor archtl., related books McGraw-Hill, 1965-72; pub. dir. AIA, 1970-72, acting dep. exec. v.p., 1970-71; architecture editor John Wiley and Sons, Inc., 1972-82, cons. editor, 1983—; archtl. cons. to bldg. industry firms and assns.; asst. prof. Jacksonville State U., 1948-53; instr. Tulane U., 1953-58; Dir. Prod. Systems for Architects and Engrs., Inc., 1970-71; Del., publs. chmn. XI Pan Am. Congress Architects, 1965; commr. Pan Am. Fedn. Architects, 1972-73; Mem. Archtl. Rev. Bd., Rye, N.Y., 1963. Author: Contemporary Curtain Wall, 1958, Total Design, 1972, Encyclopedia of American Architecture, 1980, American Architecture: A Field Guide, 1984; author: The Enjoyment of Architecture, 1983; author, editor: Hotels, Motels, Restaurants and Bars, 1960, Hospitals, Health Centers and Clinics, 1961, Office Buildings, 1961, Comprehensive Architectural Services, 1965, Creative Control of Building Costs, 1967; contbr. to: Contemporary Architects, 1980, Ency. Internat., 1982, Ency. Americana, 1984; Am. editor: 2d internat. edit. Architects' Data, 1980; project dir.: 7th edit. Architectural Graphic Standards, 1981; contbr. articles to profl. jours. Served with USAAF, 1942-45; lt. col. Res.; ret. Recipient Dallas Mus. Fine Arts Furniture Design award, 1958; Merit award Am. Soc. Landscape Architects, 1980; Profl. and Scholarly Book award Assn. Am. Pubs., 1981; Outstanding Acad. Book award ALA, 1981. Fellow AIA; mem. Authors Guild, Authors League Am., Chi Phi, Tau Sigma Delta. Episcopalian. Home: River's Edge Route 4 Box 228-A Gloucester VA 23061 Office: Box 670 Gloucester VA 23061 also 605 3d Ave New York NY 10158

HUNT, WILLIAM EDWARD, neurosurgeon, educator; b. Columbus, Ohio, Nov. 26, 1921; s. William Willard and Marian Almina (Lerch) H.; m. Charlotte M. Curtis, June 15, 1972; children: William W., C. David, Virginia R. B.A. cum laude, Ohio State U., 1943, M.D. with honors, 1945. Bar: Diplomate Am. Bd. Neurol. Surgery. Rotating intern Phila. Gen. Hosp., 1945-46; asst. resident in gen. surgery White Cross Hosp., Columbus, 1948-49; asst. resident in neurosurgery Barnes Hosp., St. Louis, 1949-50, resident, 1951-52; fellow neurosurgery Washington U. Med. Sch., St. Louis, 1950-51; instr. neurosurgery, 1952-53; asst. anatomy Ohio State U. Med. Sch., 1945, mem. faculty, 1953—, prof. neurosurgery, dir. div. neurol. surgery, 1964—; mem. attending staff Ohio State U. Hosps.; cons. staff Children's, St. Anthony's hosps., both Columbus, USAF Med. Center, Wright-Patterson AFB, Ohio; affiliated teaching staff Riverside Methodist Hosp., Columbus; courtesy staff Mt. Carmel Hosp., Columbus; hon. staff Grant Hosp., Columbus. Author numerous papers in field. Served to capt. M.C. AUS, 1946-48. Grantee USPHS, Spinal Cord Injury Research Center, Bremer Fund, others. Mem. Pan Am. Med. Assn., Royal Soc. Medicine, Soc. Internat. Chirurgie, Am. Surg. Assn., World Fedn. Neurosurg. Soc., Internat. Assn. Study of Pain, Congress Neurol. Surgeons (v.p. 1967), Neurosurg. Soc. Am. (pres. 1979), Am. Assn. Neurol. Surgeons (chmn. coms., v.p. 1983), Soc. Neurol. Surgeons (pres. 1979-80), Assn. Brain Tumor Research (med. adv. com.), Am. Acad. Neurol. Surgeons, A.C.S., AMA, Soc. Neurosci., Interurban Neurosurg. Soc., Ohio State Neurosurg. Soc. (pres. 1961, 78), Ohio State Med. Assn. (del. 1968-69), Acad. Medicine Columbus and Franklin County (chmn. public relations com. 1975), Central Ohio Neuropsychiat. Assn., Phi Beta Kappa, Alpha Omega Alpha, Sigma Xi. Episcopalian. Office: 410 W 10th Ave Room N907 Columbus OH 43210

HUNTEN, DONALD MOUNT, planetary scientist, educator; b. Montreal, Que., Can., Mar. 1, 1925; came to U.S., 1963, naturalized, 1980; s. Kenneth William and Winnifred Binnmore (Mount) H.; m. Isobel Ann Rubenstein, Dec. 28, 1949; children: Keith Atherton, Mark Ross. B.Sc., U. Western Ont., 1946; Ph.D., McGill U., 1950. From research asso. to prof. physics U. Sask. (Can.), Saskatoon, 1950-63; physicist Kitt Peak Nat. Obs., Tucson, 1963-77; sci. adv. to asso. adminstr. for space sci. NASA, Washington, 1976-77; prof. planetary scis. U. Ariz., Tucson, 1977—; cons. NASA, 1964—. Author: Introduction to Electronics, 1964; contbr. articles to profl. jours. Recipient Public Service medal NASA, 1977, medal for exceptional sci. achievement, 1980. Mem. Am. Phys. Soc., Can. Assn. Physicists (editor 1961-63), Am. Geophys. Union, Am. Astron. Soc. (chmn. div. planetary scis. 1977), Internat. Astron. Union, Internat. Union Geodesy and Geophysics, Internat. Assn. Geomagnetism and Aeronomy, AAAS, Nat. Acad. Scis., Explorers Club. Club: Cosmos (Washington). Home: 10 Calle Corta Tucson AZ 85716 Office: Dept Planetary Scis U Ariz Tucson AZ 85721

HUNTER, ALLAN OAKLEY, lawyer, fin. co. exec.; b. Los Angeles, June 15, 1916; s. Henry A. and Janet S. (Oakley) H.; m. Loberta Geene Taylor, Jan. 15, 1949; children—Genella Hunter Williamson, Janet Hunter Donini, John Henry, Allan Oakley. A.B., Calif. State U., Fresno, 1937; J.D., U. Calif., Berkeley, 1940. Bar: Calif. bar. Spl. agt. FBI, 1940-44; individual practice law, Calif., 1946-50, 58-70; mem. Congress from 12th Calif. Dist.; gen. counsel U.S. Housing and Home Fin. Agy., 1955-57; pres., chmn. bd. Fed. Nat. Mortgage Assn., Washington, 1970-80, chief exec. officer, 1980—; Chmn. Calif. State Commn. on Housing and Community Devel.; mem. policy adv. bd. M.I.T. and Harvard Joint Center for Urban Studies, Cambridge, Mass., 1971-81. Served with USN, 1944-46; ETO. Mem. Sigma Chi. Republican.

HUNTER, BYNUM MERRITT, lawyer; b. Greensboro, N.C., June 13, 1925; s. Hill McIver and Annie (Merritt) H.; m. Ann Fulenwider, June 22, 1957 (div. 1968); children: Ann Shirley, Mary Parker; m. Mary Lane Yancey, Aug. 7, 1969 (div. 1978); m. Mary Bonneau McElveen, June 13, 1980; 1 son, Bynum. A.B., U. N.C., 1945, J.D., 1949. Bar: N.C. 1949. Since practiced in Greensboro; partner Smith, Moore, Smith, Schell & Hunter. Served with USNR, 1943-46, 51-53. Fellow Am. Coll. Trial Lawyers, Am. Bar Found.; mem. Internat. Assn. Ins. Counsel, Am. Judicature Soc., Am., Greensboro (pres. 1965-66) bar assns), Zeta Psi, Phi Delta Phi. Club: Rotary. Home: 710 Sunset Dr Greensboro NC 27408 Office: NCNB Bldg Greensboro NC 27402

HUNTER, CELIA MARGARET, newspaper and magazine columnist; b. Arlington, Wash., Jan. 13, 1919; d. Ira Russ and Bessie Margaret (Ashmun) H. B.A. in Botany, U. Alaska, 1964. Comml. pilot, flight instr., 1945—; mem. Women's Air Force Service Pilots, 1943-45; travel rep. Arctic Alaska Travel Service, Fairbanks, 1947, 49; tour condr. Arctic Alaska Tours and Wien Airlines, 1949-51; builder, operator Camp Denali, 1952-75; exec. sec. Alaska Conservation Soc., Fairbanks, 1960-72; commr. Fed.-State Land Use Planning Commn. for Alaska, 1972-79; chmn. Alaska Conservation Found.; mem. gov. council Wilderness Soc., Washington, 1969-76, pres., 1976-77, exec. dir., 1977-78; Alaska newspaper and mag. columnist. Mem. Alaska liaison Am. Friends Service Com., Seattle. Mem. Friends of Earth, Sierra Club. Home: Backwoods Trail Star Route 20972 Fairbanks AK 99701 *I find life a continual opening of new avenues of thought and action. The passage of years tallies up new experiences, new friends, new ideas, and the acquiring of new skills. It is a constant challenge to become the best that one is capable of being, always looking forward while still savoring the past.*

HUNTER, CHARLES DAVID, retail company executive; b. Alameda, Calif., Dec. 3, 1929; s. Adin Wesley and Bertha Anna (Mayer) H.; m. Alice Betty Trinski, Nov. 6, 1954 (dec. 1970); children: Jeffrey Paul, Karen Sue, Brian David, Robert Stephen; m. Joy Ann Morris, Jan. 12, 1973. A.A., Modesto Jr. Coll., 1949; B.S., U. Calif.-Berkeley, 1951. Staff auditor, mgr. Arthur Andersen & Co., Chgo., 1955-66; asst. controller Walgreen Co., Chgo., 1967-69, controller, 1969-71, v.p. adminstrn., 1971-78, exec. v.p., 1978—. Served to lt. USNR, 1952-55. Mem. Financial Execs. Inst., Am. Inst. C.P.A.s, Ill. Soc. C.P.A.s, Chgo. Retail Financial Execs. Assn. (pres. 1971-72). Home: 1589 S Garden St Palatine IL 60067 Office: 200 Wilmot Rd Deerfield IL 60015

HUNTER, DAVID ROMEYN, charitable foundation executive; b. Evanston, Ill., May 17, 1916; s. Joel Dubois and Beatrice (Wigmore) H.; m. Barbara Avallon, Dec. 18, 1954; children: Steven L. Moss, Daniel A. Moss (stepsons). Student, U. Colo., 1934-36; B.A., U. Calif. at Berkeley, 1938; M.A., U. Chgo., 1940. Cons. Am. Pub. Welfare Assn., 1940; asst. dir. Dallas Pub. Welfare Dept., 1941-42; exec. asst. to regional adminstr. OPA, Dallas, 1942-44, exec. asst. to adminstr., Washington, 1947; with UN Relief and Rehab. Adminstrn., Egypt, Cyprus and Italy, 1944-46; chief welfare sect. Berlin Sector, U.S. Mil. Govt., Germany; chief legislative rev. br., democratization br. U.S. Zone, 1947-49; program officer for Latin Am., resident rep. UNICEF, Mexico, 1950-59; program officer Pub. Affairs Program, Ford Found., 1959-63; exec. dir. Stern Fund, N.Y.C., 1964—, Ottinger Found., 1972—. Author: The Slums: Challenge and Response, 1964. Trustee Found. for Nat. Progress, World Policy Inst. Office: 370 Lexington Ave New York NY 10017

HUNTER, DAVID WITTMER, security brokerage executive; b. Pitts., Aug. 11, 1928; s. Frank H. and Josephine (Wittmer) H.; m. Mary Louise Clark, July 26, 1952; children: Peter C., Susan E., David Wittmer. B.A. cum laude, Amherst Coll., 1950; M.B.A., Harvard U., 1952. Ptnr., McKelvy & Co., 1954-69; exec. v.p. Parker/Hunter, Inc., 1969-71, pres., 1971—, chmn., chief exec. officer, 1978-83, chmn. bd., 1983—; dir. Lockhart Iron & Steel, Pitts., Fidelity Guard Services, Inc., Kiene Diesel Accessories, Addison, Ill., Consumer Credit Counseling Service Western Pa., 1968-75. Pres. Richland Youth Found., 1968-72; Bd. dirs. Better Bus. Bur., 1967-74, Pitts. Pub. Theater; bd. dirs. Pitts.-Allegheny County chpt. A.R.C., chmn., 1973-76; trustee, vice chmn. Shady Side Acad., 1965-75; bd. dirs. Minority Capital Found., West Penn AAA; corp. bd. dirs. North Hills Passavant Hosp. Served with AUS, 1952-54. Recipient Yale Aurelian award, 1946. Mem. Investment Bankers Assn. (pres. Western Pa. group 1970, chmn. Mid-Atlantic group 1972), Securities Industry Assn. (gov. 1973—, exec. com. 1975—, chmn. brokerage div. 1975, dir., vice chmn. bd. dirs. 1976, chmn. bd. dirs. 1977, chmn. governing council 1978, trustee econ. edn. 1978—), Newcomen Soc., Chi Psi. Republican. Presbyn. Clubs: Bond, Harvard-Yale-Princeton, Harvard Business School (Pitts.); Lunch, University, Butler Country, Rolling Rock. Home: Lookout Farm Hardt Rd Gibsonia PA 15044 Office: Parker/Hunter Inc 4000 US US Steel Bldg Pittsburgh PA 15219

HUNTER, DONALD H., justice Ind. Supreme Ct.; b. Anderson, Ind., Oct. 21, 1911; s. Carl Edward and Mary (Samuels) H.; m. Violet K. Oemler, Oct. 11, 1941; children—Jean Ellen (Mrs. John E. Stillions), Samuel E. LL.B., Lincoln U., 1937. Bar: Ind. bar 1941. Dep. atty. gen., Indpls., 1943, 46-47; hearing examiner Ind. Pub. Service Commn., 1948; asso. practice law Mr. Carl S. Willard, LaGrange, Ind.; judge LaGrange Circuit Ct., 1948-62; jud. mem. Statewide Com. for Revision of Adoption Laws, 1950-52, Adv. Com. on Probation and Parole for Ind. Citizens Council, 1953-55; judge Appellate Ct. Ind., 1963-66; then presiding justice, mem. Constnl. Revision Commn., 1967—; chief justice Ind. Supreme Ct., 1967-74, asso. justice, 1974—. Mem. Ind. Council of Freedoms Found. at Valley Forge; advancement chmn. Boy Scouts Am. Served with AUS, 1943-46. Decorated Bronze Star medal, Purple Heart medal; named a Sagamore of the Wabash Gov. Ind., 1976. Mem. Am., Ind. State, Indpls., Madison County bar assns., Am. Legion, V.F.W., Phi Delta Phi, Phi Alpha Delta, Tau Kappa Epsilon. Republican. Methodist. Club: Mason. Home: 1719 Costello Dr Anderson IN 46011 Office: 304 State House Indianapolis IN 46204

HUNTER, DORIAN, interior designer, educator; b. Sacramento, May 18, 1932; d. Paul Eyerly and Ramona Estelle (Haley) H. A.A., Stephens Coll., 1952; B.F.A., U. So. Calif., 1954; M.A., Mills Coll., 1956. Instr. art, Oakland, Calif., 1956-57, interior designer, Anaheim, Calif., 1957-60, Santa Ana, Calif., 1960-62; founder, pres. Dorian Hunter Interiors, Inc., Fullerton, Calif., 1962—; dir. Dorian Hunter Art Gallery, Fullerton, 1963-69; lectr. environ. design Calif. State U., Fullerton, 1970-74, 79-81, assoc. prof. environ. design, 1982—; instr. comml. interior design, program cons. Orange Coast Coll., 1976-77; mem. adv. bd. certificate program in environ. and interior design U. Calif., Irvine, 1977-81; mem. search com. for dean Sch. Architecture and Fine Arts, U. So. Calif., 1974-75, bd. councilors, 1976-78; mem. adv. com. art dept. Orange Coast Coll., 1974-75; mem. council Nat. Council for Interior Design Qualification, 1981-84. Contbr. articles to profl. publs. Bd. dirs. Cultural Groups Found. of No. Orange County, 1966-69. Recipient nat. design award for dental offices, Fountain Valley, Calif., 1969; Alumni Achievement award Stephens Coll., 1970. Fellow Am. Soc. Interior Designers (nat. com. fellows 1976, 78), Am. Inst. Interior Designers (pres. Orange County area chpt. 1967-68, nat. v.p. 1968-69, mem. exec. bd., nat. bd. govs. 1968-72); mem. Fullerton C. of C. (Distinguished Service award 1966), Archtl. Guild (U. So. Calif.) (pres. 1973-74), Art Alliance (Calif. State U. at Fullerton) (dir. 1969-71, chmn. bus. and arts com. 1975-76), League Women Voters (fin. adviser Fullerton 1966, 67). Home: 400 E Virginia Rd Fullerton CA 92631 Office: 607 E Chapman Ave Fullerton CA 92631

HUNTER, DUNCAN LEE, Congressman; b. Riverside, Calif., May 31, 1948; m. Lynne Layh, 1973; children: Robert Samuel, Duncan Duane. Student, U. Mont., U. Calif.-Santa Barbara; J.D., Western State U., 1976. Bar: Calif. 1976. Practiced in San Diego; mem. 97th Congress from 42d Dist. Calif., 98th Congress from 45th Dist. Calif. Served with U.S. Army, 1969-71; Vietnam. Decorated Air medal, Bronze Star. Mem. Navy League. Republican. Baptist.

HUNTER, E. ALLAN, electric utility executive; b. Grantsville, Utah, May 27, 1914; s. James Austin and Francis (Fraser) H.; m. Helen Spindler, July 12, 1941; children: Edward Allan, James Scott. B.S. in Elec. Engring., U. Utah, 1937; postgrad., U. Mich., 1955. Registered profl. engr., Utah. With Utah Power and Light Co., Salt Lake City, 1937—, various positions including asst. to pres., comml. mgr., 1937-62, v.p., 1963-68, asst. gen. mgr., dir., 1966-68, pres., chief exec. officer, 1969-79, chmn. bd., 1979—; pres., dir. Western Colo. Power Co., 1969-74; pres. WEST Assos., 1970-72; dir. First Security Corp., ZCMI.; Mem. Utah Nuclear Energy Commn., 1970-73; mem. industry adv. com. Def. Electric Power Adminstrn., 1975-77; mem. electric utilities com. Fed. Energy Adminstrn., 1975-77; mem. Western Regional Council, Gov.'s Mineral Lease Fund Adv. Com.; bd. dirs. Utah Bus. Devel. Corp., Nat. Assn. Electric Cos., 1974-77. Mem. adv. council Weber State U. Sch. Bus. and Econs., 1967-71, Brigham Young U., 1969-71; mem. nat. bd. advisors U. Utah Coll. Bus., 1976—; campaign chmn., dir. Utah United Funds, 1968-69; Trustee, treas. Utah Blue Cross, 1969-74; trustee Utah Found.; bd. dirs. Ballet West, 1969-74, Utah Symphony.; Utah state chmn. Nat. Com. Employer Support of Guard and Res., 1984. Served from 1st lt to maj. AUS, 1942-46; ETO. Decorated Bronze Star, Purple Heart; named Utah Outstanding Engr. in Industry, 1968. Mem. Utah N.G. Hon. Cols. Assn., Salt Lake Area C. of C. (pres. 1971-72, bd. govs.), Edison Electric Inst. (dir. 1974-77), Nat. Soc. Profl. Engrs. (past pres. local chpt.), Utah Mfrs. Assn. (dir. 1963-70, Mfr. of Year award 1971), N.W. Electric Light and Power Assn. (past dir.), N.A.M. (former dir. Utah), Nat. Elec. Contractors Assn. (citation 1974), High Temperature Reactor Devel. Assn. (trustee 1970-73), U. Utah Alumni Assn. Emeritus Club. Mem. Ch. Jesus Christ of Latter-day Saints. Clubs: Rotarian., Alta, Timpanogos, Salt Lake Country. Home: 4234 Neptune Dr Salt Lake City UT 84117 Office: 1407 W North Temple St PO Box 899 Salt Lake City UT 84110

HUNTER, EDGAR HAYES, architect; b. Hanover, N.H., Aug. 1, 1914; s. Edgar Hayes and Edna H. (Hill) H.; m. Margaret Greenough King, May 8, 1943; children: Christopher King, Margaret Greenough. Grad., Deerfield Acad., 1933; B.A., Dartmouth Coll., 1938, M.A., 1955; M.Arch., Harvard U., 1941. Instr. naval architecture Mass. Inst. Tech., 1941-42; underwater gear design Boston, N.Y. navy yards, 1942-45; partner E.H. & M.K. Hunter (architects-planners), Hanover, N.H., 1945-66; v.p., dir. Raleigh (N.C.) office Lyles, Bissett, Carlisle & Wolff, Columbia, S.C., 1966-69; partner E.H. & M.K. Hunter (architects-planners), Raleigh, 1969—; v.p. Cricket Corp., Winston-Salem, N.C., 1970—; prof. architecture Dartmouth, 1946-66; lectr. N.C. State U., 1968-69; archtl. cons. N.C. Higher Edn. Facilities Commn., 1969-70, mem. adv. council, 1968—; chmn. publ. com; N.C. Architect, 1969—. Exhibited in, Munich, Germany, 1958, traveling exhibit U.S. colls. and museums, 1963-66; Important works include Out Patient Clinic, N.H. State Hosp, 1954, Toll Collectors Sta. and Canopies, Everett and Spaulding turnpikes, N.H., 1955, Lutheran Ch, Hanover, 1962, Arts Center and Sci. Bldg., Colby Jr. Coll, New London, N.H., 1962, Stratton Mountain Site Planning, Vt., 1961, Loon Mountain Ski Area, Lincoln, N.H., 1966, dormitory, Conn. Coll. for Women, New London, 1964, classroom bldg. and dormitories, Bridgton Acad., Maine, 1965, apts. and classroom bldg., Dartmouth Coll., 1958, N.C. State Fair planning, 1970, Sugar Mountain land planning, 1969, Campus Plan for, N.C. Central U., 1971, relocatables, Cricket Corp., 1970; student Internat. Meditation Soc. at Santa Barbara campus, 1972, Happy Inns, N.C. and S.C., Crafts Pavillion at N.C. State Fairgrounds, 1974, Hunter's Creek Townhouses, Raleigh, 1983; Co-author: The Indoor Garden: Design Construction, and Furnishing, 1978; Illustrator: Own Kitchen and Garden Survival Book, 1978. Mem. Hanover Town Planning Commn., 1964-66; Bd. dirs. Downtown Housing Improvement Corp., Raleigh, 1974—, Raleigh Chamber Music Guild, Raleigh Children's Theatre. Recipient Progressive Architecture award, 1946, 47; award N.H. State Office Bldg. competition, 1950. Mem. A.I.A. (pres. Raleigh 1973, dir. N.C. chpt. 1973), Newcomen Soc., N.C. Land Use Congress. Presbyterian. Home: 3808 Tall Tree Pl Raleigh NC 27607 Office: 2414 Wycliff Rd Raleigh NC 27607

HUNTER, EDWIN FORD, JR., U.S. judge; b. Alexandria, La., Feb. 18, 1911; s. Edwin Ford and Amelia (French) H.; m. Shirley Kidd, Nov. 9, 1941; children—Edwin Kidd, Janin, Kelley. Student, La. State U., 1930-33; LL.B., George Washington U., 1938. Bar: La. bar 1938. Mem. firm Smith, Hunter, Risinger & Shuey, Shreveport, 1940-53; mem. La. Legislature, 1948-52; exec. counsel Gov. La., 1952; mem. La. State Mineral Bd., 1952; now sr. judge U.S. Dist. Ct., Western Dist. La., also mem. adv. com. on civil rules. Served as lt. USNR, 1942-45. Mem. Am. Bar Assn. (La. state chmn. jr. bar sect. 1945), Am. Legion (post comdr. 1945, judge adv. Dept. La. 1948), Sigma Chi. Roman Catholic. Home: 1000 Bayou Oaks Ln Lake Charles LA 70601 Office: PO Box 1337: Lake Charles LA 70601

HUNTER, ELMO BOLTON, U.S. judge; b. St. Louis, Oct. 23, 1915; s. David Riley and Della (Bolton) H.; m. Shirley Arnold, Apr. 5, 1952; 1 dau., Nancy Ann (Mrs. Ray Lee Hunt). A.B., U. Mo., 1936, LL.B., 1938; Cook Grad. fellow, U. Mich., 1941. Bar: Mo. bar 1938. Practiced in, Kansas City, 1938-51, sr. asst. city counselor, 1939-40; partner Sebree, Shook, Hardy and Hunter, 1945-51; state circuit judge, Mo., 1951-57, Mo. appellate judge, 1957-65, fed. dist. judge, 1965—; instr. law U. Mo., 1952-62. Contbr. articles to profl. jours. Mem. Bd. Police Commrs., 1949-51; Trustee Kansas City U., Sch. of Ozarks; fellow William Rockhill Nelson Gallery Art. Served to 1st lt., M.I. AUS, 1943-46. Recipient First Annual Law Day award U. Mo., 1964. Fellow ABA; mem. Fed., Mo. bar assns., Jud. Conf. U.S. (chmn. ct. adminstrn. com.), Am. Judicature Soc. (bd. govs., mem. exec. com., pres.), Acad. Mo. Squires, Order of Coif, Phi Beta Kappa, Phi Delta Phi. Presbyterian (elder). Home: 1234 W 68th Terr Kansas City MO 64113 Office: 811 Grand Ave Kansas City MO 64106

HUNTER, EVAN (ED MC BAIN), author; b. N.Y.C., Oct. 15, 1926; s. Charles F. and Marie (Coppola) Lombino; m. Anita Melnick, Oct. 17, 1949 (div.); children: Ted, Mark, Richard; m. Mary Vann Finley, June 1973; 1 stepdau., Amanda Eve Finley. Student, Cooper Union, 1943-44; B.A., Hunter Coll., 1950. Author: The Blackboard Jungle, 1954, Second Ending, 1956, Strangers When We Meet, 1958, A Matter of Conviction, 1959, The Remarkable Harry, 1960, The Wonderful Button, 1961, Mothers and Daughters, 1961, Happy New Year, Herbie, 1963, Buddwing, 1964, The Paper Dragon, 1966, A Horse's Head, 1967, Last Summer, 1968, Sons, 1969, Nobody Knew They Were There, 1971, Every Little Crook and Nanny, The Easter Man, 1972, Come Winter, 1973, Streets of Gold, 1974, The Chisholms, 1976, Me and Mr. Stenner, 1977, Walk Proud, 1979, Love, Dad, 1981, Far from the Sea, 1983, Lizzie, 1984; also mystery novels under pseudonym Ed McBain: The Pusher, Cop Hater, The Mugger, 1956; The Con Man, 1957, Killer's Choice, Killer's Payoff, Lady Killer, 1958, Killer's Wedge, 'Til Death, King's Ransom, 1959, Give the Boys a Great Big Hand, The Heckler, See Them Die, 1960, Lady, Lady, I Did It, 1961, The Empty Hours, Like Love, 1962, Ten Plus One, 1963, Ax, 1964, The Sentries, 1965, He Who Hesitates, Doll, 1965, Eighty Million Eyes, 1966, Fuzz, 1968, Shotgun, 1969, Jigsaw, 1970, Hail, Hail, the Gang's All Here, 1971, Sadie When She Died, Let's Hear It for the Deaf Man, 1972, Hail to the Chief, 1973, Bread, 1974, Where There's Smoke, 1975, Blood Relatives, 1975, So Long As You Both Shall Live, 1976, Long Time No See, 1977, Goldilocks, 1978, Calypso, 1979, Ghosts, 1980, Rumpelstiltskin, 1981, Heat, 1981; Beauty and the Beast, Ice, 1983, Jack and the Beanstalk, 1984, Lightning, 1984; writer screenplays: Strangers When We Meet, 1960; The Birds, 1962, Fuzz, 1972, Walk Proud, 1979; stage plays: The Easter Man, 1964; The Conjuror, 1969. Served with USNR, 31944-46. Named Lit. Father of Year, 1961; Profl. Achievement award Hunter Coll., 1981. Mem. Phi Beta Kappa. Address: care John Farquharson Ltd 250 W 57th St Suite 1914 New York NY 10019

HUNTER, FRANK HERBERT, broker; b. Pitts., Oct. 22, 1901; s. David Jr. and Elizabeth (Crow) H.; m. Josephine Wittmer, June 15, 1926; children: Barbara Josephine Hunter Moore (dec.), David Wittmer, Peter Crow. A.B., Amherst Coll., 1924; J.D., U. Pitts., 1927. Bar: Pa. 1927. Practice law, 1927-28, engaged in securities investment bus., 1929—; with McKelvy and Co., Pitts., 1932-69, partner, 1941-69; pres. Parker/Hunter, Inc., 1969-71, chmn. exec. com., 1971-73; bd. govs. N.Y. Stock Exchange, 1962-65. Mem. Investment Bankers Assn. Am. (past chmn. West Pa. group), Allegheny County Bar Assn., Nat. Assn. Securities Dealers (chmn. bd. govs. 1956). Republican. Presbyn. Clubs: Bond, Duquesne (Pitts.); Fox Chapel Golf. Home: Sherwood Oaks #214 100 Norman Dr Mars PA 16046 Office: 4000 US Steel Bldg 600 Grant St Pittsburgh PA 15219

HUNTER, GEORGE KIRKPATRICK, educator; b. Glasgow, Scotland, Oct. 7, 1920; s. Samuel George and Mary Scott (Currie) H.; m. Shelagh Kathleen Edmunds, Dec. 12, 1950; children—Mary Kathleen, Andrew George, Margaret Ruth. M.A., Glasgow U., 1942; D.Phil., Oxford (Eng.) U., 1950. Faculty U. Hull, Eng., 1948-55, U. Reading, 1955-58, U. Liverpool, 1958-64, U. Warwick, 1964-76, U. Rochester, N.Y., 1961, U. Calif., Berkeley, 1969; prof. English Yale U., New Haven, 1976—. Author: Shakespeare: the Later Comedies, 1962, John Lyly: the Humanist as Courtier, 1962, Dramatic Identities and Cultural Tradition, 1978. Served with Royal Navy, 1941-46. Guggenheim fellow, 1978-79. Fellow Am. Acad. Arts and Scis. Office: Linsly-Chittenden Hall Box 3545 Yale Sta New Haven CT 06520

HUNTER, HENRY HAMILTON, public relations and communications counsel; b. Pitts., Apr. 17, 1922; s. Henry Phipps and Marjorie (Hamilton) H.; m. Diane Webb, Feb. 7, 1959; children: Hyatt Hamilton, Alison Webb, Henry Hamilton. Student, Williams Coll., 1940-41; B.J., U. Mo., 1948. Asst. city editor Champaign (Ill.) News Gazette, 1949; editor Irving-Cloud Pub. Co., Cleve, 1950; asst. pub. relations dir. Ross Roy Inc., Detroit, 1950-51, Grant Advt., N.Y.C., 1951-54; with Olin Mathieson Chem. Corp., 1954-79, v.p. public relations and communications, 1967-79; public relations and communications counsel New Canaan, Conn., 1979—. Served with USMCR, 1941-45. Mem. Pub. Relations Soc. Am., Soaring Soc. Am., Theta Delta Chi, Kappa Tau Alpha, Sigma Delta Chi. Clubs: Country of New Canaan, N.Y. Yacht. Home and Office: 106 Gillies Ln West Norwalk CT 06854

HUNTER, HOWARD WILLIAM, church official, lawyer; b. Boise, Idaho, Nov. 14, 1907; s. John William and Nellie Marie (Rasmussen) H.; m. Clara May Jeffs, June 10, 1931; children: Howard William (dec.), John Jacob, Richard Allen. J.D. cum laude, Southwestern U., 1939. Bar: Calif. 1939. Engaged in banking, Calif., 1928-34, practiced law, Los Angeles, until 1959; mem. council of 12, Ch. Jesus Christ of Latter-day Saints, 1959—; dir. Beneficial Life Ins. Co., Salt Lake City, Watson Land Co., Los Angeles, Heber J. Grant & Co., First Security Corp., 1st Security Bank of Utah, Deseret Fed. Savs. and Loan Assn., Continental Western Life Ins. Co. Pres. Polynesian Cultural Center, Hawaii. Mem. Calif., Utah bar assns., Geneal. Soc. Utah (dir., past pres.). Home: 2833 Sherwood Dr Salt Lake City UT 84108 Office: 47 E South Temple Salt Lake City UT 84150

HUNTER, JACK CORBETT, banker; b. Youngstown, Ohio, Mar. 13, 1930; s. Charles E. and Margaret C. (Higgins) H.; m. Pauline Ann Pieton; children: Jonathan David, Jeannine Marie, Jo-Lynn, Jared Michael, Juliet Margaret. Degree, U. Denver; postgrad., Youngstown State U.; grad. degree, Kent State U. Instr. Youngstown State U.; asst. trust officer Mahoning Nat. Bank; ward councilman, 2 terms; mayor, City of Youngstown, 1970-77; v.p. Mahoning Nat. Bank, Youngstown, 1977—. Mem. Republican State Central Com. of Ohio; alt. del. Rep. Nat. Conv., 1968, del., 1976, 80; Trustee Youngstown U.; mem. Ohio Bd. Edn.-17th Dist. Served with USMC. Mem. Navy League, Phi Sigma Alpha. Home: 467 W Boston Ave Youngstown OH 44511 Office: Mahoning Nat Bank Youngstown OH 44503

HUNTER, JACK DUVAL, insurance holding company executive, lawyer; b. Elkhart, Ind., Jan. 14, 1937; s. William Stanley and Marjorie Irene (Upson) H.; m. Marsha Ann Goodsell, Nov. 14, 1958; children: Jason, Jon, Justin. B.B.A., U. Mich., 1959, LL.B., 1961. Bar: Mich. 1961, Ind. 1962. Atty. Lincoln Nat. Life Ins. Co., Ft. Wayne, Ind., 1961-64, asst. counsel, 1964-68, v.p., gen. counsel, 1975-79, sr. v.p., gen. counsel, 1979—; asst. gen. counsel, asst. sec. Lincoln Nat. Corp., Ft. Wayne, 1968-71, gen. counsel, 1971-72, v.p., gen. counsel, 1972-79, sr. v.p., gen. counsel, 1979—. Mem. ABA, Mich. Bar Assn., Ind. Bar Assn., Allen County Bar Assn., Assn. Life Ins. Counsel. (bd. govs.). Office: 1300 S Clinton St PO Box 1110 Fort Wayne IN 46801

HUNTER, JACQUELINE E.B., librarian; b. Toronto, Ont., Can.; d. James Lee and Bertha Rebecca (Lindsey) H. B.A., U. Toronto, 1949, B.L.S., 1959; M.A., U. B.C., 1973. Asst. librarian Nat. Gallery of Can., Ottawa, 1964-68, dep. librarian, 1971-79, chief librarian, 1980—. Mem. Can. Library Assn. Office: National Gallery of Canada 75 Albert St Ottawa ON Canada K1A 0M8

HUNTER, JAMES ALEXANDER, surgeon, educator; b. Cedar Rapids, Iowa, Aug. 30, 1928; s. James A. and Lenore A. H.; m. Charlotte Ann Brown, June 30, 1951; children—James A., Jennifer Augusta. B.S., U. Ill., 1952, M.D., 1954. Diplomate: Am. Bd. Surgery, Am. Bd. Thoracic Surgery. Intern U. Ill. Hosps., Chgo., 1954-55, resident in surgery, 1955-59; mem. faculty dept. surgery U. Ill., 1958—, asso. prof., 1960—; attending surgeon Presbyn.-St. Luke's Hosp., Chgo., 1970—; prof. cardiovascular surgery Rush Med. Coll., Chgo., 1970—; cons. cardiovascular surgery U.S. Navy, Great Lakes, Ill. Author med. textbooks; contbr. articles to profl. jours. Served with U.S. Army, 1946-47. Fellow A.C.S.; mem. AMA, Ill. State, Chgo. med. socs., Chgo. Surg. Soc., Internat. Cardiovascular Soc., Soc. Vascular Surgery, Central Surg. Soc., Midwest Surg. Soc., Chgo. Heart Assn., Am. Assn. Thoracic Surgery, Warren H. Cole Soc., Alpha Kappa Kappa, Alpha Omega Alpha. Home: 15 Old Hunt Rd Northbrook IL 60062 Office: 1725 W Harrison St Suite 850 Chicago IL 60612

HUNTER, (JAMES) GRAHAM, cartoonist, watercolorist, writer, advertising producer; b. LaGrange, Ill.; s. William Clarence and Rebecca (Faul) H.; m. Cornelia Isabel Seward. Student, Landon Sch. Cartooning, Cleve., Art Inst., Chgo., Art Instrn. Schs., Mpls. Formerly with Assoc. Editors' Syndicate, Chgo., Pub. Ledger Syndicate, Phila., McClure Syndicate, N.Y.C.; free-lance cartoonist, writer. Creator: Jolly Jingles strip, Chgo. Sunday Tribune and McClure Newspaper Syndicate, Motor Laffs, Motor mag., Biceps Brothers, Motor mag., Getting the Business, Motor mag., Sycamore Center cartoon feature, So. Agriculturalist and Farmer Stockman, Rhubarb Ridge cartoon feature, Curtis Pub. Co.; full-page bus. cartoons, Am. Bankers Assn.; Christmas ann. full-page cartoon feature Hometown Am., Only Yesterday, Augsburg. Pub. House, Mpls.; The Office Cat, Indse. Press Service; cartoon strip, Am. Farm Bur. Fedn.; watercolor covers Our Sunday Visitor; religious book illustrations, David C. Cook Pub. Co., Elgin, Ill., sch. bag art, Acme Brief Case Co., Christmas illus., Christian Life mag., color illus., The Lookout mag., editorial cartoons, NAM newspaper service; cartoon strip Bessie's Barnyard Banter, Milk

Marketer, Cleve.; cartoon feature for, Tobacco Inst., cartoon series for, ISSS Inc., BASF Wyandotte Corp.; cartoon series Sycamore Center, Country People, Milw.; children's monthly cartoon feature in, Marvel Comics, Electric Co. mag., illustrations for, Hoard's Dairyman mag., sales cartoons, Chock Full O'Nuts Corp., presentation cartoon series, Bob Hope Golf Classic, also advt. cartoons and copy, mag. cover drawings, light verse, prose humor,; specialist detailed busyscene drawings, automotive cartoons, humorous animal art; Work has appeared in numerous nat. mags., newspapers, and advt.; Represented permanent collections, FBI Cartoon Collection, Washington, Freedoms Found. Cartoon Collection, Valley Forge, Pa., Wayne State U. Cartoon Exhbn., Detroit, Peter Mayo Editorial Cartoon Collection, State Hist. Soc., Columbia, Mo.; Author: Cartoon Humor in Advertising, Doin's in Sycamore Center; author: Art Instr. Schs. Lesson: Creating the Busy Scene Cartoon. Recipient Distinguished Service citation U.S. Treasury Dept., George Washington Honor medal Freedoms Found., 1959, 62, Honor cert. Editorial Cartoon award, 1960, 61, 75, 76. Presbyterian. Home and studio: Lindenshade 42 Clonavor Rd Silver Spring Park West Orange NJ 07052 *An overlooked blessing in today's world is a good sense of humor.*

HUNTER, JAMES M., architect; b. Omaha, Nebr., Apr. 19, 1908; s. Edgar William and Ida L. (Bogue) H.; m. Madelyn J. Engleman, Feb. 5, 1937; children—John David, Janet Diane Hunter Powers. Student, Iowa State Coll., 1927-30; B. Arch., U. Ill., 1936. Registered architect, Colo., Wyo., Nebr. Practice architecture, 1940-76, cons., 1976—; firm James M. Hunter and Assos., Boulder, Colo., 1945-78; cons. architect, 1978—; planner, architect Colo. State U., Ft. Lewis Coll., Tarkio (Mo.) Coll., Regis Coll., Denver; architect in residence Am. Acad., Rome, 1963; vis. prof. architecture U. Colo.; Mem. adv. bd. Assn. Applied Solar Energy, U. Colo. Sch. Architecture; mem. pub. adv. panel on archtl. services GSA, 1965; chmn. archtl. jury HEW, 1966; profl. advisor to State Colo. in competition for Supreme Ct. and Heritage Bldgs. complex, 1975-76. Served as lt. (j.g.) USNR, World War II. Recipient award of merit AIA, 1955, regional awards, 1954, 55, 56, 57, 58, 60, 62, 65, 67; award N.Y. Archtl. League, 1954, 55; Church Archtl. Guild Am., 1956, 58. Fellow AIA (2d v.p. 1960-61, past nat. chmn. com. on edn., nat. chmn. com. on profession, regional dir. Rocky Mountain region 1964-67, past pres. Colo. chpt.), Am. Acad. in Rome; mem. Colo. Bd. Examiners of Architects (past pres.), Colo. Soc. Architects (past pres.). Club: Masons. Address: 1505 Mariposa Ave Boulder CO 80302

HUNTER, JAMES MEGARGEE, physician, educator; b. Merchantville, N.J., Apr. 5, 1924; s. Robert H. and Helen M. (Megargee) H.; m. Carolyn H. Lippincott, June 30, 1951 (dec. Feb. 1981); children: Gary, Kimberly, Jeffrey.; m. Joy Adams, Aug. 15, 1981; children: Vallerey, Lauren. B.S., Dickinson Coll., 1949; M.D., Jefferson Med. Coll., 1953. Diplomate: Am. Bd. Orthopedic Surgery. Intern Jefferson Med. Coll. Hosp., Phila., 1953-54; resident in gen. and orthopedic surgery Thomas Jefferson Univ. Hosp., 1954-58; fellow hand surgery Columbia Presbyn. Med. Center, 1959; now prof. orthopedic surgery Jefferson Med. Coll., Thomas Jefferson U., Phila.; chief hand surgery services Thomas Jefferson Univ. Hosp., Phila.; coordinator house staff edn.; also chief child amputee clinic Pa. Hosp. for Crippled Children, Elizabethtown; cons. in hand surgery Phila. Naval Hosp.; founder, pres. Hand Rehab. Center, Ltd., Phila.; cons. Valley Forge Gen. Hosp., Pa., 1963-73; orthpaedic surgery cons. Wills Eye Hosp., Phila. Contbr. numerous articles to profl. jours.; editor: Tendon Surgery in the Hand, 1975; Editor: Hand Rehabilitation, 1978. Served with AUS, 1943-46; ETO. Recipient commendation Valley Forge Gen. Hosp., 1973; NIH grantee, 1964, 66, 71-73; grantee to develop tendon implants and applications U.S. Army Research and Devel. Command, 1971-72, 73-76, 77-78. Mem. Am. Acad. Orthopedic Surgery, Am. Soc. Surgery of Hand, Am. Orthopedic Assn., Phila. Coll. Physicians, French Hand Soc., Société International de Chirurgie Orthopedique et de Traumatologie, Phi Kappa Psi, Nu Sigma Nu. Clubs: Union League (Phila.); Bachlor's Barge, Avalon Yacht (commodore 1977). Developed first artificial tendon. Home: 700 Hagysford Rd Narberth PA 19072 Office: 901 Walnut St Philadelphia PA 19107

HUNTER, J(AMES) PAUL, educator, literary critic; b. Jamestown, N.Y., June 29, 1934; s. Paul W. and Florence I. (Walmer) H.; m. Kathryn Montgomery, July 1, 1971; children: Debra, Lisa, Paul III, Anne. A.B., Ind. Central Coll., 1955; M.A., Miami U., Oxford, Ohio, 1957; Ph.D., Rice U., 1963. Instr., U. Fla., Gainesville, 1957-59, Williams Coll., Williamstown, Mass., 1962-64; asst. prof. U. Calif., Riverside, 1964-66; asso. prof. English Emory U., Atlanta, 1966-68, prof., 1968-80, chmn. dept. English, 1973-79; dean Coll. Arts and Sci.; prof. English U. Rochester, N.Y., 1981—. Author: The Reluctant Pilgrim, 1966, Occasional Form, 1975, Norton Introduction to Poetry, 2d edit., 1981, Norton Introduction to Literature, 3d edit., 1981. Guggenheim fellow, 1976-77. Mem. MLA, Am. Soc. 18th Century Studies (exec. bd.), Southeastern Am. Soc. for 18th Century Studies (pres. 1977-78), N.E. Am. Soc. for 18th Century Studies (pres. 1982-83). Home: 215 Melrose St Rochester NY 14619 Office: 325 Lattimore U Rochester Rochester NY 14627

HUNTER, JOHN HARNDEN, artist; b. Westmiddlesex, Pa., Sept. 26, 1934; s. John A. and Dorothea H.; children—Gregory Andrew, Christopher John. B.A., Pomona Coll., 1956; M.F.A., Claremont Grad. Sch., 1958. Prof. studio art San Jose (Calif.) State U., 1965—; adviser, critic textbooks Holt, Rinehart & Winston, N.Y.C., 1972-80; Bd. dirs. San Jose Mus. Art.; guest artist Tamarind Lithography Workshop, 1969, Lakeside Studios, Mich., 1978, 79. One-person show, Cannes Film Festival, 1966; exhibited in group shows, Basel Art Fair, Documenta VI, Kassel, Germany, Cologne Art Fair, Galerie Wolfgang Ketterer, Munich; represented in permanent collections, Nat. Gallery Art, Washington, Mus. Modern Art, N.Y.C., Norton Simon Mus. Art, Pasadena, U. Minn., Mpls., Scripps Coll., Morrison Library, U. Calif., Berkeley, Los Angeles County Mus. Art, Amon Carter Mus. Western Art, Fort Worth, Grunwald Graphic Arts Found, UCLA, others. Served with AUS, 1958-62. Fulbright fellow, Florence, Italy, 1963-64, 64-65. Office: Dept Art San Jose State U San Jose CA 95192

HUNTER, J(OHN) ROBERT, insurance consumer advocate; b. New Orleans, Nov. 20, 1936; s. J. Robert and Alberta M. (Cox) H.; m. Carole A. Means, Mar. 6, 1976; children—Laura Jeanne, James Douglas, John Robert, III. B.S., Clarkson Coll. Tech., 1958; grad. Program for Sr. Mgrs., Harvard U., 1976. Underwriter Atlantic Mut. Ins. Co., 1960-61; supervisory actuary Ins. Services Office, N.Y.C., 1961-67; asst. actuary Mut. Ins. Rating Bur., N.Y.C., 1967-71; chief actuary Fed. Ins. Adminstrn., HUD, Washington, 1971-74, acting adminstr., 1974-76, adminstr., 1976-77, dep. fed. ins. adminstr., 1977-80; founder, pres. Nat. Ins. Consumer Orgn., 1980—. Author: Taking the Bite Out of Insurance, 1980, Profitability and Investment Income in Property Casualty Insurance, 1983. Pres. Freeport (N.Y.) Community Chorale, 1970-71; pres., founder Rockville (Md.) Musical Theatre, 1974-75; vestryman Christ Ch., Alexandria, 1982-83. Recipient award for excellence Sec. HUD, 1977. Fellow Casualty Actuarial Soc.; mem. Am. Acad. Actuaries, Internat. Actuarial Assn. Home: 602 S Lee St Alexandria VA 22314 Office: 344 Commerce St Alexandria VA 22314

HUNTER, JOHN STUART, statistician, consultant; b. Holyoke, Mass., June 3, 1923; s. John and Irene (Robinson) H.; m. Edna Taylor Martz, Sept. 19, 1952; 1 dau., Jean Bartlett; m. T.J. Hirasuna, Aug. 13, 1977; children: William Mark, Anne Robinson. Ph.D. in Exptl. Stats., N.C. State U., 1954, M.S. in Engring. Math, 1949, B.S. in Elec. Engring, 1947. Staff statistician Am. Cyanamid Co., 1954-59; with Statis. Techniques Research Group, 1957-59, Math. Research Center, U. Wis., 1959-61; assoc. prof. Princeton, 1962-67; prof. engring. Princeton U., 1968-82, prof. emeritus, 1982—; statistician in residence U. Wis., 1967-68; lectr. Korean Standards Research Inst., 1979, Nat. Center: Indsl. Sci. and Tech. Mgmt. Devel., Dalian, People's Republic of China, 1981, 82; Mem. staff com. nat. statistics Nat. Acad. Scis., 1975-76, mem. com., 1976—, chmn. com. pres.'s of statis. socs., 1976-79; chmn. panel Nat. Bur. Standards, 1977-80. Author, cons., lectr. in field.; Founding editor: Technometrics, 1959-63. Served with AUS, 1942-46. Fellow Am. Statis. Assn., Am. Soc. Quality Control (Shewhart medal, 1971, Youden award 1977, Ott award 1979), AAAS (council mem. 1974-77, chmn. com. on fellows 1977); mem. Biometrics Soc., Inst. Math. Statistics, Am. Inst. Chem. Engrs., ASTM, Am. Soc. Indsl. Engrs., ASCE, Royal Statis. Soc., Internat. Statistics Inst. Episcopalian. Club: Cosmos. Home: 179 Longview Dr Princeton NJ 08540

HUNTER, JOHN TERRENCE, bank and commercial mortgage company executive; b. Charlestown, S.C., June 26, 1941; s. John E. and Earline W. H.; m. Mary Sneed, Feb. 11, 1963; children—John Terrence, Joseph Lee, Paige Nichole. B.S. in Econs, Middle Tenn. State U.; student various real estate courses and seminars, U. Ga., U. Nebr., U. Mo., Mich. State U. Real estate appraiser Metro Govt., Nashville, 1965-67; comml. loan officer Murphree Mortgage Co., 1967-69; with Commerce Union Bank, 1969—; exec. v.p.; pres., chief exec. officer TVB Mortgage Corp.; exec. v.p. Tennessee Valley Bancorp Inc., Nashville; pres. The Hunter Co., Nashville, 1982—; mem. Metro Bd. Equalization, Nashville. Mem. credit com. Roman Catholic Diocese of Nashville; trustee Middle Tenn. State U. Found.; bd. dirs. St. Mary's Retirement Community. Mem. Tenn. Mortgage Bankers Assn. (regional v.p. 1979), Nashville Mortgage Bankers Assn. (pres. 1976). Club: Nashville City. Office: 111 28th Ave S Nashville TN 37212

HUNTER, JOSEPH VINCENT, chemist, educator; b. Bklyn., June 12, 1925; s. John Joseph and Margaret (Horstmann) H.; m. Ann Marie Engels, June 8, 1957; children: John Gustav, Christopher William, Joseph Vincent, Margaret Ann, Suzanne Marie. B.S. cum laude, St. Johns U., 1947, M.S., 1949; postgrad., Bklyn. Poly. Inst., 1950, 51; Ph.D., Rutgers, The State U., 1962. Research chemist Nopco Chem. Co., 1952-55; mem. faculty Rutgers U., New Brunswick, N.J., 1955—, asso. prof. environ. sci., 1964-70, prof. environ. sci., 1970-83, prof. II, 1983—, dir. grad. program in environ. sci., 1979—, dep. chmn., 1981—; cons. water pollution abatement.; mem. N.J. Gov.'s Sci. Adv. Council, 1983—. Co-editor: Principles and Applications of Water Chemistry, 1967, Organic Compounds in Aquatic Environments, 1971; mem. editorial bd.: Environ. Letters; editorial adv. bd.: Environ. Energy Contents Monthly; contbr. articles to publs. Fellow Am. Inst. Chemists, Royal Soc. Health; mem. Am. Chem. Soc. (nat. speakers tour 1970, 71), Am. Water Works Assn., Water Pollution Control Fedn., Am. Public Health Assn., Water Resources Council of Rutgers, Sigma Xi. Patentee in organic chemistry. Home: 13 Patton Dr East Brunswick NJ 08816 Office: Rutgers U New Brunswick NJ 08903

HUNTER, KERMIT HOUSTON, univ. dean, writer; b. Hallsville, W.Va., Oct. 3, 1910; s. Otis John and Lillian Elizabeth Robinson (Farley) H. B.A., Ohio State U., 1931; M.A. in Theatre, U. N.C., 1949; Ph.D. in English Lit, U. N.C., 1955; D.Litt., Emory and Henry Coll., 1958; L.H.D., Okla. Christian Coll., 1971. Successively newspaper reporter C. of C. sec.; choir dir., organist, and piano study Juilliard Inst., 1931-40; bus. mgr. N.C. Symphony Orch., 1946; prof. drama Hollins Coll., Va., 1956-64; dean Meadows Sch. Arts, So. Methodist U., Dallas, 1964-76, writer in residence, 1976—; pres. Tex. So. News Printing Corp., Addison, Credille Pub. Co., Addison. Author, producer more than: 40 hist. dramas, especially Unto These Hills, 1950—. Served to lt. col. AUS, 1940-45. Decorated Legion of Merit. Home: 9151 Villa Park Circle Dallas TX 75225

HUNTER, KIM (JANET COLE), actress; b. Detroit, Nov. 12, 1922; d. Donald and Grace Mabel (Lind) Cole; m. William A. Baldwin, Feb. 11, 1944 (div. 1946); 1 dau., Kathryn Emmett; m. Robert Emmett, Dec. 20, 1951; 1 son, Sean Emmett. Ed. pub. schs.; student acting with, Charmine Lantaff Camine, 1938-40, Actors Studio. Lectr. High; Sch. for Performing Arts, N.Y.C., Friends Sem., 1961, S.D. U., 1965, Lehigh U., 1965, ANTA In-Tchrs.-Service, N.Y.C., 1965, High Sch. Music and Art, 1968, Brigham Young U., Provo, Utah, 1978. (Recipient Donaldson award for best supporting actress in A Streetcar Named Desire 1948, also on Variety N.Y. Critics Poll 1948, for film version 1952, winner Acad. award, LOOK award, Hollywood Fgn. Corrs. Golden Globe award, Emmy nominations for Baretta 1977, Edge of Night 1980); Author: Kim Hunter—Loose in The Kitchen, 1975; First stage appearance, 1939; played in stock, 1940-42; Broadway debut in A Streetcar Named Desire, 1947; appeared in: tour Two Blind Mice, 1950, Darkness at Noon, N.Y.C., 1951, The Chase, 1952, N.Y.C., They Knew What They Wanted, 1952, The Children's Hour; revival, N.Y.C., 1952, The Tender Trap, N.Y.C., 1954, Write Me a Murder, N.Y.C., 1961, Weekend, N.Y.C., 1968, The Penny Wars, N.Y.C., 1969; And, Miss Reardon Drinks a Little; tour, 1971-72, The Glass Menagerie, Atlanta, The Women, N.Y.C., 1973, In Praise of Love, 1975, The Lion in Winter, N.J., 1975, The Cherry Orchard, N.Y.C., 1976, The Chalk Garden, Pa., 1976, Elizabeth The Queen, Buffalo, 1977, Semmelweiss, Buffalo, 1977, The Belle of Amherst, N.J., 1978, The Little Foxes, Mass., 1980, To Grandmother's House We Go, N.Y.C., 1981, Another Part of the Forest, Seattle, 1981; frequent appearances summer stock and repertory theater, 1940—; appeared, Am. Shakespeare Festival, Stratford, Conn., 1961; film debut in: The Seventh Victim, 1943; other motion pictures include Tender Comrade, 1943, When Strangers Marry (re-released as Betrayed), 1944, You Came Along, 1945, A Canterbury Tale, 1949, Stairway to Heaven, 1946, A Streetcar Named Desire, 1951, Anything Can Happen, 1952, Deadline U.S.A, 1952, Storm Center, 1956, Bermuda Affair, 1957, The Young Stranger, 1957, Money, Women, and Guns, 1958, Lilith, 1964, Planet of the Apes, 1968, The Swimmer, 1968, Beneath the Planet of the Apes, 1970, Escape from the Planet of the Apes, 1971, Dark August, 1975; made TV debut on, Actors' Studio program, 1948; numerous TV appearances include Requeim for a Heavyweight, 1956, The Comedian, 1957, both on Playhouse 90, Give Us Barabbas on, Hallmark Hall of Fame, 1961, 63, 68, 69, Love, American Style, Colombo, Cannon, Night Gallery, Mission Impossible, The Magician, 1972-73, Marcus Welby, Hec Ramsey, Griff, Policy Story, Ironside, Med. Center, Bad Ronald, Born Innocent, 1974, Ellery Queen, 1975, Lucas Tanner, This Side of Innocence, Once an Eagle, Baretta, Gibbsville, Hunter, 1976, The Oregon Trail, 1977, Project: U.F.O., Stubby Pringle's Christmas, 1978, Backstairs at the White House, 1979, Specter on the Bridge, 1979, Edge of Night, 1979-80, F.D.R.'s Last Year, 1980, Skokie, 1981; rec. From Morning 'Til Night (and a Bag Full of Poems), RCA Victor, 1961, Come, Woo Me, Unified Audio Classics, 1964. Mem. Acad. Motion Picture Arts and Scis., ANTA, A.E.A. (council 1953-59), Screen Actors Guild, A.F.T.R.A. *Enjoy. If I don't like what I'm doing, it never works. That doesn't mean the pangs of creation don't exist—it only means I avoid like the plague anything I can't believe in, or might be ashamed of afterwards. It's also helped me to keep in mind a hand-me-down from my father- "It is first of all to be, then to know and to do, and only incidentally to have." All this doesn't necessarily add up to monetary "success"—but it does much for a personal satisfaction in work and in living.*

HUNTER, LEE, automotive equipment manufacturing company executive, inventor; b. St. Louis, Apr. 27, 1913; s. Lee and Ollie (Stark) H.; m. Jane Franklin Brauer, 1959; stepchildren: Arthur J. Brauer, Stephen F. Brauer. Ed., Westminster Coll., Fulton, Mo., Washington U., St. Louis; D.Sci. (hon.), Washington U., St. Louis, 1982, Westminster Coll., 1982. Draftsman, designer Herman Body Co., 1935-36; founder Lee Hunter Jr. Mfg. Co., 1936; pres. Hunter-Hartman Corp., 1937-42, Hunter Engring. Co., Bridgeton, Mo., 1947-55, chmn. bd., chief exec. officer, 1955—; pres. Hunter Aviation Co., 1955-60; hon. consul of, Belgium, St. Louis; adv. dir. St. Louis County Nat. Bank and County Nat. Bancorp. Trustee Washington U., St. Louis; bd. dirs. Jr. Achievement, West County YMCA; adv. trustee Westminster Coll., Fulton, Mo.; trustee Washington U., St. Louis; mem. St. Louis Consular Corps. Served to 1st lt. C.E. AUS, 1942-46. Recipient Alumni Achievement award Westminster Coll. Mem. Mo. C. of C., Phi Delta Theta. (Phi of Yr., Mo. chpt. 1980). Presbyterian (trustee). Clubs: St. Louis, Engineers (St. Louis); Bellerive Country, Racquet; Le Mirador (Switzerland). Inventor 1st rapid battery chargers; dynamic lever theory balancing; 1st on car mech. wheel balancer; 1st discharged battery analyzer; wheel alignment, automotive equipment, patentee. Home: Hunter Farms 13501 Ladue Rd Saint Louis County MO 63141 Office: Hunter Engring Co 11250 Hunter Dr Bridgeton MO 63044

HUNTER, LELAND CLAIR, JR., utility company executive; b. Phila., Feb. 22, 1925; s. Leland Clair and Lillian Mae E6(Failor) H.; m. Elva Joy Charlton, July 5, 1946; children: Charlton Lee, Steven Kent, Brian Scott, Donna Joy. B.S., Villanova U., 1948; postgrad., Columbia U., 1944-45; M.B.A., Fla. Research Inst., 1971; grad., Advanced Mgmt. Program, Harvard U., 1973. Test engr. Gen. Electric Co., Phila., 1949-50; with Fla. Power & Light Co., 1950—, v.p. indsl. relations, Miami, 1966-72, v.p. transmission and distbn., 1972-73, group v.p., 1973—, sr. v.p., 1978—; mem. spl. labor com. Sec. of Labor U.S., 1975-76; mem. Labor and Mgmt. Polit. Action Com. for Utility Industry, 1977, Gov.'s Adv. Council Productivity, 1981—. Vice chmn. adv. com. Dade County (Fla.) Sch. Bd., 1966; bd. govs. Gold Coast AAU, 1967-68; bd. dirs. Crime Commn. of Greater Miami, 1974—, Victoria Hosp.; dir. Pro-Fish of Fla.; Fla. Lawyers Prepaid Legal Services Inc. Crime Commn. of Greater Miami, 1980—; bd. advisors Stetson U.; mem. bus. adv. com. Brookings Instn., Washington; exec. v.p. Atlantic Gamefish Found. Served with USN, 1943-46. Recipient Key to City, Toledo and Coral Gables Fla.). Mem. Am. Soc. Tng. Dirs. (pres. local chpt. 1955-56). Clubs: Fla. Athletic (pres. 1962), Coral Gables (Fla.) Country; Univ. (Miami); (Jacksonville, Fla.). Home: 5577 SW 100 St Miami FL 33156 Office: PO Box 529100 Miami FL 33152

HUNTER, MARGARET KING, architect; b. Balt., May 13, 1919; d. Talmage Damron and Margaret Julie (Greenough) King; m. Edgar Hayes Hunter, May 8, 1943; children—Christopher King, Margaret Greenough. A.B., Wheaton Coll., 1941; postgrad., Smith Coll. Sch. Architecture, 1941-42, Harvard Grad. Sch. Design, 1942-45. Draftsman H.V. Lawrence, landscape architect, Mass., 1940, Antonin Raymond, architect, N.Y.C., 1942-43; designer Raymond Loewy, N.Y.C., 1943; partner E.H. & M.K. Hunter (architects-planners), Hanover, N.H., 1945-66, Raleigh, N.C., 1969—; owner Heritage Antiques, Raleigh, 1971—; writer Pencil Points, 1942-45; traveling exhibit of work, 1963-66; design instr. N.C. State U., 1968; lectr., writer architecture, conservation, 1945—. Author: Your Own Kitchen and Garden Survival Book, 1978, The Indoor Garden: Design, Construction, and Furnishing, 1978; Important works include Laconia (N.H.) State Sch. Dormitories, 1955, N.H. Toll Rd. Structures, 1955, Children's Study Home, N.H. State Hosp., 1954, apts. and classroom bldg., Dartmouth, 1960, House for Life mag., 1956, Colby Jr. Coll. Art Center and Sci. Bldg., New London, N.H., 1962; classroom bldg. Dormitories Bridgton (Me.) Acad, 1964, Loon Mountain Ski Area, Lincoln, N.H., 1966; dormitory, Conn. Coll., New London, 1965, twenty year campus plan, N.C. Central U., Durham, 1971, Student Internat. Meditation Soc. Acad., Santa Barbara, Calif., Clearwater Office Park, 1972, N.C. Central U. Law Sch., 1974, Hunter's Creek Townhouses, 1983. Chmn. Dance Com., Hanover, 1964-66; v.p. Culture Arts for Students, Raleigh, 1970; N.H. del. 1st Internat. Conf. Women Engrs. and Scientists, 1964; mem. edn. com. N.C. Land Use Congress, 1971, chmn. soils com., 1974, dir., 1976-78. Recipient Progressive Architecture Mag. award, 1946, 47; award N.H. State Office Bldg. Competition, 1950. Mem. AIA (chmn. pub. relations N.H. chpt. 1953-54), Soc. Women Engrs., Soil Conservation Soc., Constrn. Specifications Inst. Presbyterian. Club: Women's (Raleigh). Home: 3808 Tall Tree Pl Raleigh NC 27612 Office: 2414 Wycliff Rd Raleigh NC 27607

HUNTER, MICHAEL, publishing executive; b. Atlanta, Dec. 11, 1941; s. Joel H. and Eleanor Johnston; m. Katherine Garlick, Aug. 2, 1975. B.A. cum laude, Harvard U., 1964; postgrad., Columbia U., 1965-67. Dir. Spectum Books, Prentice-Hall Inc., Englewood Cliffs., N.J., 1974-80; pres. Gen. Pub. div. Prentice-Hall Inc., Englewood Cliffs., N.J., 1980—. Mem. Am. Assn. Pubs. (exec. council Gen. Pub. div.). Club: Universtiy (N.Y.C.). Home: 158 Old Winkle Point Rd Northport NY 11768 Office: Prentice-Hall Inc General Publishing Div Englewood Cliffs NJ 07632

HUNTER, MORGAN, lawyer; b. Ft. Worth, Mar. 9, 1923; s. A.D. and Shirley (Hammett) H.; m. Patricia Bell, Aug. 17, 1963; children: Marguerite Elizabeth, Colin Bowman, Valerie. B.B.A., U. Tex., 1943, LL.B., 1948. Bar: Tex. 1948; C.P.A., Tex. Accountant Arthur Andersen & Co., Houston, 1943-46; lectr. U. Tex., Austin, 1946-48; trial atty. U.S. Treasury Dept., Phila., 1949-51; partner McGinnis, Lochridge & Kilgore (attys.), Austin, 1951—; Dir. Columbia Sci. Industries Corp., Austin. Mem. Am., Travis County bar assns., State Bar Tex., Tex. Bar Found. Presbyn. Clubs: Headliners (Austin); Austin; Admirals (Austin). Home: 3500 Mt Bonnell Rd Austin TX 78731 Office: 900 Congress Ave 5th Floor Austin TX 78701

HUNTER, MORGAN VICTOR, marketing executive; b. Elk City, Okla., Mar. 18, 1929; s. Victor Earl and Willie Esther (Gunter) H.; m. Martha Veach Candell, Oct. 2, 1954; children: David Candell, Elizabeth Gay, Susan Jennifer. B.A., U. Okla., 1953. Advt. copy writer, account supr. Gen. Electric Co., Schenectady, 1953-57; with Procter & Gamble Co., 1957-75; v.p. coffee div., gen. mgr. Folger Coffee Co., Kansas City, Mo., 1971-75; sr. v.p., mem. exec. com. Am. Cyanamid Co., Wayne, N.J., 1975-77; pres., dir. R.J. Reynolds Tobacco Co., Winston-Salem, N.C., 1977-79, Scott Paper Co., Phila., 1979-80; mng. dir. mktg. group, chmn. MCA Advt., Mktg. Corp. Am., Westport, Conn., 1980—. Served with AUS, 1950-52; Korea. Decorated Bronze Star, Combat Inf. badge. Methodist. Office: Mktg Corp Am 285 Riverside Ave Westport CT 06880 Office: MCA Advt 405 Lexington Ave New York NY 10174

HUNTER, NORMAN L., art director; b. Eutaw, Ala., Aug. 28, 1932; s. Davis W. and Mary V. (Ray) H.; m. Claudia M.; children: Derek K., Marc C.; m. Claudia Hunter. Student, Art Inst. Detroit, 1948-49, Soc. Arts and Crafts Detroit, 1952-55, Art Inst. Chgo., 1955-57, EUCOM Mil. Sch. in Germany, 1951-52. With Johnson Pub. Co., Inc., Chgo., 1955—, art dir., since 1965—, 1973—; also co-chmn. art com., staff photographer. Designer: books The Shaping of Black America, Black Defenders of America, 1775-1973, Pictoral History of Black America, Black Power Gary Style, Black Society, 1976, Profiles of Black Mayors in America, DuBois: A Pictorial Biography, 1978, Wade in the Water, 1979, I Wouldn't Take Nothing for My Journey, 1981; others; designer for, Fashion Fair Cosmetics, Supreme Life Ins., WJPC Radio Sta. Served to sgt. AUS; Korea. Recipient Nat. Negro Press Assn. award photograph in Lyndon B. Johnson Library, 1973, Washington Art Dir. award, 1975, Chgo. Book Clinic award, 1977, CEBA award, 1978, 79, 80. Mem. Art Inst. Chgo., PUSH, NAACP. Office: 820 S Michigan Ave Chicago IL 60605 *Physical being of man is less important than his contributions to the world—what is left behind is of the essence. We are simply stepping stones for those who will follow. Everyday is a "beautiful" one and should be lived to the fullest. A day without a contribution to mankind is wasted.*

HUNTER, PAUL ROBINSON, architect; b. Buffalo, Ill., June 29, 1906; s. Guy Lester and Clara Charlotte (Robinson) H.; m. Helen Sabin Houston, Feb. 12, 1932; children—Paul Robinson, Frederic Houston, Helen Sabin (Mrs. F.S. Dutton, Jr.). Student, U. Calif., at Los Angeles, 1924-26, now grad. student in Indo-European studies; B.Arch., U. Pa., 1931. With archtl. offices Hunt & Chambers, Los Angeles, 1931-36, Roland E. Coate, 1936-39; partner Hunter and Reichardt, Los Angeles, 1939-42, Hunter and Benedict, 1957-66; pvt. practice, Los Angeles, 1942-56, 66-77; extension lectr. U. Calif., 1945, Coll. Arch., U. So. Calif., 1947. Author: (with Walter Reichardt) Residential Architecture in Southern California, 1939, Plastics in Building, 1946, also articles.; prin. works include Sch. Architecture at U. Calif. at Los Angeles, 1952, Aquatorium, City of Commerce, 1961, Monterey Park Hdqrs. Facilities, So. Counties Gas Co, 1963 (Recipient awards for design So. Calif. chpt. AIA, for horticulture bldgs. U. Calif. at Los Angeles 1946, nursery Childrens Home Soc. 1946, pre-sch. bldg. Berkeley Hall Sch. 1954, Christian Sci. Ch., Anaheim, Calif. 1957). Fellow AIA (pres. So. Calif. chpt. 1956); mem. Delta Upsilon, Tau Sigma Delta. Home: 4900 E Telegraph Rd Ventura CA 93003

HUNTER, PETER WILLIAM, advertising agency executive; b. Toronto, Ont., Can., July 26, 1930; s. Howard Wanless and Maple Elizabeth (Winterburn) H.; children: Geoffrey William, Elizabeth Hope. Degree in Commerce, Royal Mil. Coll. Can., 1953. Account exec. Foster Advt. Ltd., 1951-55; account exec. McConnell Eastman & Co. Ltd., Toronto, 1955-58; v.p. in charge Western Ont., London, 1958-60, v.p., account supr., Toronto, 1960-65; dir. Sta.; CJRT-FM; chmn., pres., dir. Signum Communications Ltd., Toronto, 1970-79, chmn., chief exec. officer, 1979—; dir. The Film House Group Inc., Audit Bur. Circulations. Chmn. Can. Liver Found.; bd. govs. York-Finch Gen. Hosp.; mem. reception com. Royal Agrl. Winter Fair. Served to lt. col. Gov. Gen.'s Horse Guards, 1952-67. Decorated Centennial medal, Can.; Can. Forces decoration. Mem. Am. Mktg. Assn., Inst. Canadian Advt., Royal Canadian Mil. Inst., Gov. Gen.'s Horse Guards Assn., Royal Canadian Armoured Corps Assn. (life), U. Toronto Schs. Alumni Assn. Clubs: Rosedale Golf, London, Empire, Canadian, Royal Mil. Coll. Home: Maple Ridge Farm Rural Route 2 Tottenham ON L0G 1W0 Canada Office: 234 Eglinton Ave E Toronto ON M4P 1K7 Canada

HUNTER, RICHARD EDWARD, physician; b. Worcester, Mass., May 30, 1919; s. William and Catherine (Powers) H.; m. Eleanor Louise Harrington, Sept. 10, 1944; children: Todd Wayne, Elayne Cheryl, Jill Elizabeth, Amy Louise. A.B., Clark U., 1941; M.D., Boston U., 1944. Diplomate Am. Bd. Ob-Gyn. Intern Worcester City Hosp., 1944-45; resident in gen. surgery Framingham (Mass.) Union Hosp., 1947; resident in ob-gyn Mercy Hosp., Balt., 1947-49; practice medicine specializing in ob-gyn, Worcester, 1949—; prof., chmn. dept. ob-gyn U. Mass., Worcester, 1976—. Contbr. articles to med. jours. Served with U.S. Army, 1945-47. Mem. Am. Coll. Ob-Gyn, ACS, New Eng. Assn. Gynecologic Oncologists, Soc. Gynecologic Oncology, Boston Obstetric Soc., New Eng. Cancer Soc. Republican. Home: 2 Monica Rd Worcester MA 01602 Office: 55 Lake Ave N Worcester MA 01605

HUNTER, ROBERT FRANK, manufacturing company executive; b. Chgo., Nov. 11, 1923; s. Roy and Ann Barbara (Sebek) H.; m. Patricia A. Heffernan, June 24, 1950; children: Mary W., Robert J., John D. B.S., U. Ill., 1950; postgrad., U. So. Calif., 1950-51, U. Chgo., 1963-64. Registered profl. engr., Ill., Mich., N.C., S.C. Design engr. Douglas Aircraft Co., Long Beach, Calif., 1950-51; gen. mgr. bearing div. Rex Chainbelt, Downers Grove, Ill., 1952-69; v.p., gen. mgr. Anchorpac div. Kysor Indsl. Corp., 1970-71; v.p., gen. mgr. aerospace div. Universal Oil Product, Bantam, Conn., 1971-74; v.p., dir. Thermoform Inc., Waukesha, Wis., 1974-76; mgr. Andrews Bearing div. Wheelabrator-Frye, Inc., Spartanburg, S.C., 1976-80; v.p., gen. mgr. Peter Zimmer of Am., Inc., Spartanburg, 1980; sales mgr. NTN Bearing Corp. Am., 1980—. Served with USMCR, 1943-46; PTO. Mem. Art Inst. Chgo. Club: Chgo. Athletic Assn. Home: 20 Big Oak Ln Riverwoods IL 60015 Office: 31 E Oakton St Des Plaines IL 60018 *1. Attempt to achieve more than set goals. 2. Be honest in all relationships. 3. Learn to relax at the proper time.*

HUNTER, ROBERT GRAMS, English educator; b. Milbank, S.D., Nov. 12, 1927; s. Donald Raymond and Esther (Grams) H.; m. Anne Ziesmer, Aug. 25, 1956; children: Timothy, Catherine. B.A., Harvard, 1949; M.A., Columbia, 1957, Ph.D., 1962. Instr. Robert Coll., Istanbul, Turkey, 1949-52; successively instr., asst. prof., asso. prof. Dartmouth, 1959-70; Kenan prof. English Vanderbilt U., Nashville, 1970-82; Frensley prof. English So. Meth. U., Dallas, 1982—. Author: Shakespeare and the Comedy of Forgiveness, 1965, Shakespeare and the Mystery of God's Judgments, 1976. Served with AUS, 1952-54. Home: 2925 Stanford St Dallas TX 75225 Office: English Dept So Meth U Dallas TX 75275

HUNTER, ROBERT P., government official; b. Bridgeport, Conn.; m. Marlene Hunter; 3 children. B.S. in Bus. Adminstrn., U. Conn., 1962; J.D., Vanderbilt U., 1965; LL.M. in Labor Law, NYU, 1966. Bar: Tenn., N.Y., U.S. Supreme Ct. Atty. NLRB, Buffalo and Cin., 1969-74; senatorial counsel, 1974-77; minority counsel subcom. alcoholism and drug abuse U.S. Senate, 1977-80, senatorial legis. dir., chief counsel, chief staff labor and human resources com., 1981; mem. NLRB, 1981—. Served to capt. USAF. Address: Office of Chmn NLRB 1717 Pennsylvania Ave NW Washington DC 20570 *

HUNTER, ROBERT TWEEDY, direct-sales company executive; b. Mt. Pleasant, Pa., June 10, 1934; s. Robert T. and Dorothy Jane (Connors) H.; m. Barbara Carol Rauschelbach, Aug. 24, 1957; children: Karen Ann, Robert Paul, Kristen, Ellen. B.S., Westminster Coll., 1956; M.S., Pa. State U., 1958. Research chemist Colgate Palmolive Co., Jersey City, 1958-64, research sect. head, Piscataway, N.J., 1964-70; research mgr. Amway Corp., Ada, Mich., 1970-72, research dir., 1972-76, exec. v.p., 1980—; exec. v.p. Nutrilite Products Inc., Buena Park, Calif., 1976-80, dir., Amcon Industries, First of Am. Bank, Grand Rapids. Contbr. articles on laundry detergents, fabric treatment to trade jours.; patentee in field. Gen. chmn. sustaining mems. Mich. Tchrs. council, Boy Scouts Am., 1983. Mem. Am. Chem. Soc., Am. Oil Chemists Soc. Republican. Lutheran. Club: Blythefield Country (Grand Rapids). Office: Amway Corp 7575 E Fulton ADA MI 49355

HUNTER, RODERICK OLIVER ALEXANDER, business exec.; b. Mather, Man., Can., Dec. 12, 1915; s. John Oliver and Ida (McLean) H.; m. Doris Audrey Moffat, Dec. 26, 1942; children—Roderick George, John David, Richard Craig. B.A., U. Man., 1937, LL.B., 1941; LL.D., U. Winnipeg. Bar: Called to Man. bar 1942. Mem. firm Parker, Parker, Hunter & Hamlin, Winnipeg, 1945-46; with Great-West Life Assurance Co., Winnipeg, 1946-71, sec., 1953-62, v.p., sec., 1962-71; also dir.; v.p. James Richardson & Sons, Ltd., Winnipeg, 1971-77; dir. Great-West Life Assurance Co. Dominion Textile Ltd., Investors Group Trust Co. Ltd., Investors Mut. Can. Ltd., Investors Growth Fund Can. Ltd., Investors Internat. Mut. Fund Ltd., Investors Japanese Growth Fund Ltd., Investors Dividend Fund Ltd., Provident Stock Fund Ltd. Campaign chmn. United Way Greater Winnipeg, 1966; mem. univ. grants commn. Province of Man., 1967-73; chmn. Man. CSC, 1978—; chancellor U. Winnipeg, 1978—. Served to lt. comdr. Royal Canadian Navy, 1941-45. Mem. U. Man. Alumni Assn. (past pres.), Assn. Life Ins. Counsel (past pres.), Man. Bar Assn., Man. Law Soc., Ducks Unltd. (chmn. Can. 1975-76). Mem. United Ch. Clubs: Manitoba, St. Charles Golf and Country. Home: 346 Oxford St Winnipeg MB R3M 3J7 Canada

HUNTER, ROSS, motion picture producer; b. Cleve., May 6, 1926; s. Isadore and Anna (Rosen) Fuss. M.A., Western Res. U. Sch. Tchr., Cleve., 1942-43. Actor for Columbia Pictures, 1944-47; producer plays, 1947-50; asst. producer, Universal Pictures, 1951-52; producer, 1953—; movies include Magnificent Obsession, Madame X, Thoroughly Modern Millie, 1967, Midnight Lace, Flower Drum Song, The Chalk Garden, Pillow Talk, Airport; TV movies include The Money Changers, A Family Upside Down, Suddenly, Love, The Best Place to Be. Address: 370 Trousdale Pl Beverly Hills CA 90210

HUNTER, SAM, art historian, educator; b. Springfield, Mass., Jan. 5, 1923; s. Morris and Lottie (Sherman) H.; m. Edys Merrill, July 22, 1954 (div. 1976); children: Emily C., Alexa J. A.B., Williams U., 1943; student, U. Florence, Italy, 1949-51. Art critic N.Y. Times, 1947-49; editor Harry N. Abrams, Inc., art books publisher, N.Y.C., 1952-53; lectr. Barnard Coll.; also asst. prof. UCLA, 1955-57; curator Mus. Modern Art, 1956-58; chief curator, acting dir. Mpls. Inst. Arts, 1958-60; dir. Rose Art Mus., Poses Inst. Art, Brandeis U., Waltham, Mass., 1960-65, asso. prof. art history dept., 1963-65; dir. Jewish Museum, N.Y.C., 1965-68; vis. prof. Cornell U., 1967-69; lectr. New Sch. Social Research, N.Y.C., 1967-68; Regent's prof., vis. critic U. Calif. at Riverside, 1968; vis. critic SUNY, 1968-69; prof. art and archeology Princeton U., 1969—, dir., 1978; Robert Sterling Clark vis. prof. Clark Art Inst. and Williams Coll., Williamstown, Mass., 1976; cons. NEH, 1978—; art cons. N.J. Nightly News, PBS-TV, 1978-79; dir. Am. Art, since 1950; (exhbn.), Seattle World's Fair, 1962; juror Internat. Art Jury 32d Venice Biennale, Italy, 1964; exec. dir. study visual arts in pub. higher edn. Bd. Higher Edn., Mass., 1968-69; dir. critic's choice program N.Y. State Council on Arts, 1968-69; v.p., editor-in-chief Harry N. Abrams, Inc (art pubs.), 1971-72, cons. editor, 1969—; dir. Monumenta outdoor sculpture exhbn., Newport, R.I.; mem. adv. bd. Modarco (S.A.), art investment group, London; lectr. contemporary Am. art USIA tour Japan, 1975; mem. spl. commn. art in state bldgs., State of Mich., 1976. Author: Jackson Pollock, 1956, Modern French Painting, 1956, Picasso: Cubism to the Present, 1957, David Smith, 1957, Piet Mondrian, 1958, Joan Miro: His Graphic Work, 1958, Modern American Painting and Sculpture, 1959, Hans Hofmann, 1963, Larry Rivers, 1969, New Art Around the World, 1966, American Art Since 1960, 1970, Josef Albers, 1971, American Art of the Twentieth Century, 1973, (with John Jacobus) rev. edit., 1974, Chryssa, 1974, Modern Art, from Post-Impressionism to the Present, 1976; catalog The Dada Surrealist Heritage, 1977, Kunst der Gegenwart, 1978, Isamu Noguchi, 1978, American Art, 1979; Art in Business, 1979, Twentieth Century Art, 1980; catalog Tony Smith, 1979, Seymour Lipton Sculpture, 1982, Aspects of Postmodernism, 1982; Contbr.: sect. on Am. painting to Art Since 1945, 1958, James Brooks, 1963, New Directions in American Painting, 1964. Mem. arts and humanities task force Carter-Mondale campaign, 1976. Served as lt. (j.g.) USNR, 1944-46. J.S. Guggenheim Meml. fellow, 1971-72. Mem. Coll. Art. Assn., Phi Beta Kappa. Home: 146 Mercer St Princeton NJ 08540 Office: McCormick Hall Princeton Univ Princeton NJ 08540

HUNTER, THOM HUGH, seminary administrator; b. Johnstown, Pa., Aug. 28, 1918; s. Thomas and Jeannie (McBlain) H.; m. Ruth Rinehart, Aug. 26, 1944; children—Jennifer Ruth, Hilary Anne, Hugh McBlain. B.A., Park Coll., 1942, LL.D., 1966; diploma, McCormick Theol. Sem., 1944; D.D. (hon.), Monmouth Coll., 1962. Ordained to ministry Presbyn. Ch., 1944; chaplain Cornell U., 1946-49, U. Ore., 1949-54, U. Tex. at Austin, 1954-57; dir. ch. relations McCormick Theol. Sem., Chgo., 1957-59, v.p., lectr. ch. and higher edn., 1959—; theol. edn. cons., dept. ministerial relations U.P. Ch. U.S.A.; Pres. Chgo. Faculties Union; mem. exec. bd. Assn. Chgo. Theol. Schs.; chaplain Scottish St. Andrew Soc. of Greater St. Louis, 1982; sec. Chgo. Theol. Inst.; commr. 195th Gen. Assembly, Presbyn. Ch. U.S.A., 1983. Served with USNR, 1944-46. Mem. Assn. Presbyn. U. Pastors (past pres.), Am. Soc. Ch. History (past pres.), N.W. Conf. Religion in Higher Edn. (past pres.), Council Theol. Edn., Park Coll. Alumni Assn. (past nat. pres.). Home: 20 Glenhave Dr Glendale MO 63122

HUNTER, THOMAS HARRISON, physician, educator; b. Chgo., Oct. 12, 1913; s. Edwin Llewellyn and Argyra (Harrison) H.; m. Anne E. Fulcher, Mar. 6, 1943; children: Charles, Elizabeth, William, Thomas, Peter. A.B. cum laude, Harvard U., 1935, M.D., 1940; Henry fellow, Cambridge (Eng.) U., 1935-38; L.H.D., Rush U., 1981. Intern, resident Presbyn. Hosp., N.Y.C., 1942-45, asst. physician, 1945-47; instr. medicine Columbia, 1945-47; asst. and asso. prof. medicine Washington U. Sch. Medicine, 1947-53, asst. dean, 1947-52, asso. dean, 1952-53; dean Sch. Medicine, U. Va., 1953-64, prof., 1953—, chancellor for med. affairs, 1965-70, v.p. med. affairs, 1970-71, Owen R. Cheatham prof. sci., dir. human biology and society program, 1971—; cons. USPHS; temporary staff mem. Rockefeller Found., 1962-63; fellow Center Advanced Studies in Behavioral Scis., Stanford, 1977-78; bd. overseers Harvard, 1956-62; mem. com. on med. edn. Brown U.; bd. overseers Sch. Medicine, Morehouse Coll.; mem. corp. vis. com. Sch. Medicine, Tufts U. Recipient Thomas Jefferson award, 1970; named Va. Cultural Laureat, 1981. Mem. Assn. Am. Physicians, Am. Clin. and Climatol. Soc., Am. Soc. Clin. Investigation, AAAS, AMA, Am. Acad. Arts and Scis., Assn. Am. Med. Colls. (pres. 1960, chmn. com. on internat. relations in med. edn.), Raven Soc., Phi Beta Kappa, Sigma Xi, Alpha Omega Alpha. Home: Big Oaks Keswick VA 22947 Office: Box 325 School of Medicine U Va Charlottesville VA 22908

HUNTER BLAIR, PAULINE CLARKE, author; b. Kirkby-in-Ashfield, Eng., May 19, 1921; d. Charles Leopold and Dorothy Kathleen (Milum) Clarke; m. Peter Hunter Blair, Feb., 1969. B.A. with honors, Somerville Coll., Oxford U., Eng. Free-lance writer, 1948—; lectr. Contbr., Eastern Daily Press; book reviewer, Times Lit. Supplement.; works include; under name Pauline Clarke: The Pekinese Princess, 1948, The Great Can, 1952, The White Elephant, 1952, Smith's Hoard, 1955, The Boy with the Erpingham Hood, 1956, Sandy the Sailor, 1956, James, the Policeman, 1957, James and the Robbers, 1959, Torolv the Fatherless, 1959, 2d edit., 1974, The Lord of the Castle, 1960, The Robin Hooders, 1960, James and the Smugglers, 1961, Keep the Pot Boiling, 1961, The Twelve and the Genii, 1962 (pub. in U.S. as The Return of the Twelves, 1963) (Library Assn. Carnegie medal 1962, Lewis Carroll Shelf award, Deutsche Jugend Buchpreis 1968), Silver Bells and Cockle Shells, 1962, James and the Black Van, 1963, Crowds of Creatures, 1964, The Bonfire Party, 1966, The Two Faces of Silenus, 1972; under pseudonym Helen Clare: Five Dolls in a House, 1953, Merlin's Magic, 1953, Bel, The Giant and Other Stories, 1956, Five Dolls and the Monkey, 1956, Five Dolls in the Snow, 1957, Five Dolls and Their Friends, 1959, Seven White Pebbles, 1960, Five Dolls and the Duke, 1963, The Cat and the Fiddle; and Other Stories from Bel, the Giant, 1968; also author short stories and plays for adults. Mem. Brit. Soc. Authors, Nat. Book League. Home: Church Farm House Bottisham Cambridge CB5 9BA England Office: c/o Curtis Brown Ltd 1 Craven Hill London W2 3EW England also c/o John Cushman Assos Inc 24 E 38th St New York NY 10016

HUNTHAUSEN, RAYMOND GERHARDT, archbishop; b. Anaconda, Mont., Aug. 21, 1921; s. Anthony Gerhardt and Edna (Tuchacherer) H. A.B., Carroll Coll., 1943, St. Edward's Sem., 1946; M.S., Notre Dame U., 1953; LL.D., DePaul U., 1960; postgrad. summers, St. Louis U., Catholic U., Fordham U. Ordained priest Roman Cath. Ch., 1946. Instr. chemistry Carroll Coll., 1946-57, football, basketball coach, 1953-57, pres., 1957-62; bishop Helena Diocese, Mont., 1962-75; archbishop of Seattle, 1975—. Mem. Am. Chem. Soc. Address: 907 Terry Ave Seattle WA 98104

HUNTING, CONSTANCE COULTER, publishing executive, author; b. Providence, Oct. 15, 1925; m. Robert Stilwell Hunting, Aug. 28, 1948; children: Robert Samuel Coulter, Miranda Hunting Goulden. B.A., Brown U., 1947; spl. student piano, New Eng. Conservatory, Boston, to 1950. Tchr. various univs.; propr. Puckerbrush Press, Orono, Maine; writer-in-residence U. Maine, Orono, 1979—; Co-ordinator NESPA in Maine, 1975-80; mem. lit. panel Maine Commn. on Arts and Humanities, 1975-80. Author: poetry collections After the Stravinsky Concert, 1969, Cimmerian, 1972, Beyond the Summerhouse, 1976, Nightwalk, 1980, Dream Cities, 1981; Collected Poems 1969-83, 1983; stories, criticisms, revs.; Editor: New Maine Writing Anthology, 1977, 79, Puckerbrush Rev, 1978—. Recipient Sesquicentennial Poetry prize, Ind., 1968; Ind. U. Writers prize poetry, 1970; named Woman of Yr. Maine Television, Press and Radio Women, 1972; fellow MacDowell Colony, 1973. Mem. Maine Writers and Pubs. Alliance (pres. 1978-79). Address: 76 Main St Orono ME 04473 *Survive. Work, And take joy when you can.*

HUNTING, DAVID DYER, mfg. co. exec.; b. Grand Rapids, Mich., Aug. 26, 1892; s. Edgar White and G. Grace (Dyer) H.; m. Mary Virginia Ives, May 25, 1925; children—David Dyer, Allen Ives, John Robert. B.A., U. Mich., 1914. With Steelcase Inc., Grand Rapids, 1914—, v.p. sales, 1922-60, vice chmn. bd., 1960—; dir. Stow-Davis Furniture Co. Past pres. East Grand Rapids Bd. Edn. Served to 1st lt. U.S. Army, World War I; Served to 1st lt. AEF; in France. Republican. Episcopalian. Clubs: Peninsular, Kent Country, University, Rotary, Masons. Address: 621 Lakeside Dr Grand Rapids MI 49506

HUNTINGTON, CHARLES ELLSWORTH, educator, biologist; b. Boston, Dec. 8, 1919; s. Ellsworth and Rachel (Brewer) H.; m. Louise Chapin Slater, Dec. 22, 1956; children—George Slocum, William Ellsworth, Katherine Chapin, Sarah Clarke. B.A., Yale, 1942, Ph.D., 1952. From instr. to prof. biology Bowdoin Coll., Brunswick, Maine, 1953—, chmn. dept., 1973-76; dir. Bowdoin Sci. Sta., Kent Island, Grand Manan, New Brunswick, 1953—; Mem. Harpswell Sch. Com., 1966-69; Bd. dirs. Maine Sch. Adminstrv. Dist. No. 75, 1969-74. Served with USNR, 1942-46. Guggenheim fellow, 1963-64. Mem. AAAS, Am. Inst. Biol. Sci., Soc. Study Evolution, Am., Brit. ornithologists unions, Wilson, Cooper ornithol. socs., Northeastern Bird-Banding Assn. (pres. 1962-67), Sigma Xi. Democrat. Unitarian. Home: RFD 2 Box 357 South Harpswell ME 04079 Office: Dept Biology Bowdoin Coll Brunswick ME 04011

HUNTINGTON, CURTIS EDWARD, insurance executive; b. Worcester, Mass., July 30, 1942; s. Everett Curtis and Margaret (Schwenzfeger) H. B.A., U. Mich., 1964, M. Actuarial Sci., 1965; J.D., Suffolk U., 1976. With New Eng. Mut. Life Ins. Co., Boston, 1965—, v.p., auditor, 1980—. Served with USPHS, 1965-67. Mem. Soc. Actuaries (vice gen. chmn. edn. and exam. com. 1983—), Am. Acad. Actuaries, Am. Coll. Life Underwriters, Internat. Actuarial Assn. Office: New Eng Mut Life Ins Co 501 Boylston St Boston MA 02117

HUNTINGTON, DAVID HANS, college president; b. Westford, N.Y., Mar. 19, 1926; s. Lowell S. and Meta C. (Juergensen) H.; m. Mary E. Cary, July 17, 1949; children: Scot L., Debra D. B.S., Cornell U., 1946, M.S., 1948, Ph.D., 1953. Asst. prof. agrl. engring. U. Maine Coll. Agr., 1953-56, asso. prof., 1957, asso. prof., asst. to dean, 1957-61, asst. dean, 1961-63, asso. dean, 1963-64; pres. A & T Coll., SUNY, Alfred, 1964—. Served to ensign USNR, 1944-47. Mem. N.Y. State Assn. Jr. Colls. (past pres.). Clubs: Wellsville Country (past pres.), Rotary). Home: 9 Reynolds St Alfred NY 14802

HUNTINGTON, DAVID MACK GOODE, foundation administrator; b. Millsboro, Del., Dec. 18, 1926; s. M. Paul St. Agnan and Lona Marie (Goode) H.; m. Mary Elizabeth Putman, Dec. 3, 1955; children: James Barrett, Sarah Phelps, Samuel Porter. A.B., Harvard U., 1949, Ed.M., 1954. Adminstrv. asst. customer relations Irving Trust Co., N.Y.C., 1949-52; supr., speech therapist Martin Hall, Bristol, R.I., 1952-55; asst. dir. Office Student Placement, Harvard U., 1955-59; dir. placement, asso. dean students Grad. Sch. Bus., U. Chgo., 1959-64, asso. dir. devel., 1965-67; dir. devel., asst. to dean div. biol. scis., exec. dir., sec. Cancer Research Found., 1967-69; dir., sec. Milw. Found., 1970—; sec. Faye McBeath Found., 1970—; adminstr. Walter and Olive Stiemke Found., 1970—; Incorporator Porter-Phelps-Huntington Found., Hadley, Mass. Served with AUS, 1945-46. Episcopalian. Clubs: University (Milw.); Harvard of Wis. Home: 4043 N Lake Dr Shorewood WI 53211 Office: 161 W Wisconsin Ave Suite 5146 Milwaukee WI 53203

HUNTINGTON, EARL LLOYD, natural resources company executive; b. Orangeville, Utah, Sept. 2, 1929; s. Lloyd S. and Hannah Annette (Cox) H.; m. Phyllis Ann Reed; children: Jane, Ann, Stephen. B.S., U. Utah, 1951, J.D., 1956; LL.M., Georgetown U., 1959. Bar: Utah bar 1956, D.C. 1959, N.Y. 1966. Trial atty. Dept. Justice, Washington, 1956-63; counsel Texasgulf Inc., N.Y.C., 1963-74, v.p., gen. counsel, 1974-81, sr. v.p., gen. counsel, 1981—, also dir.; dir. M&T Chems. Inc. Case note editor U. Utah Law Rev., 5-56. Served with U.S. Army, 1951-53. Mem. ABA; Mem. Fed. Bar Assn., Assn. Bar City N.Y., Westchester-Farfield Corp. Counsel Assn., Order of Coif, Phi Delta Phi, Beta Gamma Sigma. Clubs: Sky, Landmark; Country (Darien, Conn.). Home: 1 Maywood Ct Darien CT 06820 Office: Texasgulf Inc. High Ridge Park Stamford CT 06904

HUNTINGTON, HILLARD BELL, educator, physicist; b. Wilkes-Barre, Pa., Dec. 21, 1910; s. Frederick L. and Gertrude (Bell) H.; m. Ruth Smedley Wheeler, June 24, 1939; children: Frederic Wright, Hillard Griswold, David Champion. B.A., Princeton U., 1932, M.A., 1933, Ph.D., 1941; Dr. honoris causa, U. Nancy I, 1977. Teaching asst. U. Pa., 1941; physics instr. Washington U., 1941-42; staff mem. Radiation Lab., Mass. Inst. Tech., 1942-46; asst. prof. Rensselaer Poly.

Inst., Troy, N.Y., 1946-48, asso. prof., 1948-50, prof., 1950—, chmn. dept. physics, 1961-69; vis. prof. Yale U., 1960-61, Cornell U., 1968-69; liaison officer Office Naval Research, London, Eng., 1954-55. Fellow Am. Phys. Soc. (chmn. div. solid state physics 1966-67); mem. Fedn. Am. Scientists, Sigma Xi. Research in diffusion, electromigration, surface theory. Home: 219 Pinewoods Ave Troy NY 12180

HUNTINGTON, JAMES CANTINE, JR., equipment manufacturing company executive; b. Detroit, Mar. 21, 1928; s. James Cantine and Joanna (Donlon) H.; m. Bettyanne Hopkins, Sept. 21, 1973; children: James, Ann, Patricia, Carol, Judith, Amy. B.E.E., Cornell U., 1950. Mktg. exec. Harnischfeger Corp., Milw., 1953-62; cons., Milw., 1962-64; mgr. Colt Industries, Beloit, Wis., 1964-67; v.p., dir. Clark Equipment Co., Buchanan, Mich., 1967-76; sr. v.p. Am. Standard, Inc., 1976—; dir. Sealed Power Corp., Sullair Corp. Served with AUS, 1945-47, 50-53. Mem. Constrn. Industry Mfrs. Assn., Delta Kappa Epsilon, Tau Beta Pi, Eta Kappa Nu. Home: 613 Twin Pine Rd Pittsburgh PA 15215 Office: PO Box 67 Wilnerding PA 15148

HUNTINGTON, ROBERT HUBBARD, advertising agency executive; b. Sept. 28, 1937; s. Robert Hubbard and Katherine (Wolf) H.; m. Eleanor Huntington, Mar. 18, 1961; children—Robert Hubbard III, Thomas Andrew, Elizabeth. B.S., Cornell U., 1959; M.B.A., U. Pa., 1961. With Compton Advt., Inc., 1962—, account handling, 1962-69, asst. treas., 1969-75, treas., sr. v.p., 1975-78, exec. v.p., chief adminstrv. officer, 1978-80, exec. v.p., chief operating officer, 1980—. Served with U.S. Army, 1961. Clubs: University (N.Y.C.); Apawamis, Manursing Island (Rye, N.Y.); Skytop (Pa.). Office: 625 Madison Ave New York NY 10022 *

HUNTINGTON, SAMUEL PHILLIPS, political science educator; b. N.Y.C., Apr. 18, 1927; s. Richard T. and Dorothy S. (Phillips) H.; m. Nancy Alice Arkelyan, Sept. 8, 1957; children: Timothy Mayo, Nicholas Phillips. B.A., Yale, 1946; M.A., U. Chgo., 1948; Ph.D., Harvard U., 1951. Instr. govt. Harvard U., 1950-53, asst. prof. govt., 1953-58, prof., 1962—, Thomson prof. govt., 1967-81, Clarence Dillon prof. internat. affairs, 1981-82, Eaton prof. of sci. of govt., 1982—, chmn. dept., 1967-69, 70-71; research asso. def. policy Brookings Instn., Washington, 1952-53; faculty research fellow Social Sci. Research Council, N.Y.C., 1954-57; asst. dir. Inst. War and Peace Studies, Columbia, 1958-59, research asso., 1958-63, asso. dir., 1959-62, asso. prof. govt., 1959-62, Ford research prof., 1960-61; research asso. Center for Internat. Affairs, Harvard, 1963-64, mem. faculty, 1964—, exec. com., 1966—, asso. dir., 1973-78, acting dir., 1975-76, dir., 1978—; vis. fellow All Souls Coll., Oxford (Eng.) U., 1973; coordinator security planning Nat. Security Council, 1977-78; Cons. numerous govt. agys. Author: The Soldier and the State, 1957, The Common Defense, 1961, Political Order in Changing Societies, 1968, American Politics: The Promise of Democracy, 1981; co-author: Political Power: USA-USSR, 1964, The Crisis of Democracy, 1975, No Easy Choice: Political Participation in Developing Countries, 1976, Living with Nuclear Weapons, 1983; Editor: Changing Patterns of Military Politics, 1962; editor: The Strategic Imperative, 1982; co-editor: quar. Foreign Policy, 1970-77, Authoritarian Politics in Modern Society: The Dynamics of Established One-Party Systems, 1970; Contbr. articles to profl. jours. Chmn. Council on Vietnamese studies S.E. Asia Devel. Adv. Group, 1966-69; mem. Presdl. Task Force on Internat. Devel., 1969-70, Commn. on U.S.-Latin Am. Relations, 1974-76; trustee Internat. Devel. Found., 1969-76; bd. dirs. Frank Boas Found., 1980—. Served with AUS, 1946-47. Fellow Center for Advanced Study in Behavioral Scis., Stanford, 1969-70; Guggenheim fellow, 1972-73; Woodrow Wilson Ctr. fellow, 1983-84; Recipient Silver Pen award Jour. Fund, 1960. Fellow Am. Acad. Arts and Scis.; mem. Internat. Polit. Sci. Assn. (council 1973-75), Council Fgn. Relations, Internat. Inst. Strategic Studies, Am. Polit. Sci. Assn. (mem. council 1969-71). Home: 52 Brimmer St Boston MA 02108 Office: 1737 Cambridge St Cambridge MA 02138

HUNTINGTON, THOMAS FOSTER, corporation executive; b. Roselle, N.J., Apr. 14, 1920; s. Henry Strong and Edith Marguerite (Foster) H.; m. Pauline Herrick, Sept. 28, 1946; children: Ellen Foster Bryant, Louisa Boulton, Deborah Lawrence. B.S. in Mech. Engring. cum laude, Princeton U., 1942; M.B.A. with distinction, Harvard U., 1946-47. Engr. Pratt & Whitney Aircraft, 1942-45; plant supt., exec. asst. to pres., asst. div. gen. mgr. Personal Products Corp. div. Johnson & Johnson, Inc., 1947-57; prin. asso. Cresap, McCormick Paget, 1957-59; v.p., exec. asst. to pres. Trans World Airlines, Inc., N.Y.C., 1959-60, v.p. orgn. and procedures, 1961-63, v.p. spl. services div., 1963-68, v.p. sales and services, 1968-70; v.p. mfg. and merchandising CIT Financial Corp., N.Y.C., 1970-72; v.p. corporate devel. Nat. Kinney Corp., N.Y.C., 1972; pres. Holmes Protection, Inc., N.Y.C., 1973-77; chmn. bd. Kinney Safety Systems, 1973-75; pres., chief exec. officer Buffalo Color Corp., West Paterson, N.J., 1977-79; pres. Sterling Extruder Corp., South Plainfield, N.J., 1979-81; dir. ops. Space Transp. Co., Princeton, N.J., 1981—; dir. Pope, Evans & Robbins Inc. Trustee Robert Coll., Istanbul, Turkey, Near East Coll. Assn. Clubs: Princeton Charter, Carnegie Sailing, Nassau (Princeton, N.J.). Home: 73 Allison Rd Princeton NJ 08540

HUNTLEY, CHARLES WILLIAM, psychology educator; b. Schenectady, July 23, 1913; s. Charles Henry and Caroline Alice (Ritter) H.; m. Lee Hoffman, June 15, 1938; children: Deborah Lee, Elizabeth Meriwether. A.B., Union Coll., Schenectady, 1934; A.M., Ph.D., Harvard U., 1938. Instr. psychology Flora Stone Mather Coll., Western Res. U., Cleve., 1938-41; asst. prof. psychology Adelbert Coll., 1941-44, prof. psychology, 1944-47, dean coll., 1941-47, Union Coll., Schenectady, 1947-64, prof. psychology, 1947—, chmn. dept., 1962-78, sec. coll., 1964-79, provost, 1978-80; Armed Services rep. Western Res. U., 1942-44; trustee Middle States Assn. Colls. and Secondary Schs., 1978—; Bd. overseers Coll. of V.I., 1971—. Contbr. articles to jours. Fellow Am. Psychol. Assn.; mem. Phi Beta Kappa, Sigma Xi, Theta Delta Chi. Address: Union Coll Grounds Schenectady NY 12308

HUNTLEY, HARLAN HARRISON, textile company executive; b. Madison, Wis., Apr. 8, 1928; s. William E. and Ruth (Grose) H.; m. Marjorie Ann English, June 2, 1954; children: Ruth Ann, Kristen Sue, Scott Harlan. B.S. with honors, U. Wis., 1952, J.D., 1954. Bar: Wis. 1954, Va. 1959, Pa. 1963. Atty., asst. sec. TVA, Knoxville, Tenn., 1954-56; atty. Reynolds Metals Co., Richmond, Va., 1956-62; asst. gen. counsel Sealtest Foods div. Nat. Dairy Products Corp., N.Y.C., 1962-66; sr. atty. Am. Home Products Corp., N.Y.C., 1966-67; gen. counsel West Point Pepperell Inc., West Point, Ga., 1974-77; sec., assoc. gen. counsel Dan River, Inc., Danville, Va., 1967-74, v.p., gen. counsel, 1977—; dir. First & Mchts. Bank, Danville. Served with USN, 1946-47. Mem. ABA, Va. State Bar, Wis. State Bar, Phila. Bar Assn., Am. Soc. Corp. Secs., Artus, Order of Coif. Club: Danville Golf. Home: 142 Acorn Ln Danville VA 24541 Office: Dan River Inc 2291 Memorial Dr Danville VA 24541

HUNTLEY, JAMES ROBERT, government official, international affairs scholar and consultant; b. Tacoma, Wash., July 27, 1923; s. Wells and Laura H.; m. Colleen Grounds Smith, May 27, 1967; children by previous marriage: Mark, David, Virginia, Jean. B.A. magna cum laude in Econs., Sociology, U. Wash., 1948, postgrad. sociology and internat. relations (Carnegie fellow), 1948, 51; M.A. in Internat. Relations, Harvard U., 1956. Cons. Wash. Parks Recreation Commn., Olympia, 1949-51; exchange of persons officer U.S. Fgn. Service, Frankfurt, Nuremberg, Germany, 1952-54; dir. cultural center USIA, Hof/Saale, Germany, 1954-55; USIA postgrad. scholar Harvard U., 1955-56, asst. to Pres.'s coordinator for Hungarian relief, Washington, 1956; European regional affairs officer USIA, Washington, 1956-58; dep. pub. affairs officer U.S. Mission to European Communities, Brussels, 1958-60; mem. U.S. Delegation to Atlantic Congress, London, 1959; sec. organizing com. Atlantic Inst., Brussels and Milan, Italy, 1960, exec. sec. and co-founder, Paris, 1960-63, dir., Washington, 1963-65; founder, sec. Com. Atlantic Studies, 1963-65; sec. edn. com. NATO Parliamentarians Conf., Brussels, 1960-64; program asso., internat. affairs div. Ford Found., N.Y.C., 1965-67; sec. gen. Council Atlantic Colls., London, 1967-68; ind. writer, cons., lectr., internat. affairs, Guildford, Eng., 1968-74; founder, sec. Assn. Mid-Atlantic Clubs, 1970-74; founder, sec. gen. Standing Conf. Atlantic Orgns., 1972-74; research fellow, sr. adviser on internat. affairs Battelle Meml. Inst., Seattle, 1974-83; pres., chief exec. officer Atlantic Council of U.S., Washington, 1983—; European corr., environ. affairs Saturday Rev./World, 1972-74; Corrs. World Wide, London, 1970-74; European corr. Non-Profit Report, 1970-74. Author: (with W.R. Burgess) Europe and America - The Next Ten Years, 1970, The NATO Story, 1965, Man's Environment and the Atlantic Alliance, 1972, Uniting the Democracies, 1980; Contbr. articles to profl. jours. Bd. dirs. Internat. Standing Conf. Philanthropy, 1969-74, Fed. Union, Inc., 1976—, Seattle Com. Fgn. Relations, 1975-78, World Affairs Council of Seattle, 1975-83; founder, chmn. Coms. for a Community of Democracies, 1979—. Clubs: Rainier (Seattle); DACOR (Washington). Home: Waterwood 401 S Bay Ln Port Ludlow WA 98365 Office: Atlantic Council of US 1616 H St NW Washington DC 20006 *For a full life, embrace a worthy cause. Mine is the unity of the democracies. America's most precious asset is its free political system. It can be successfully defended only if we merge our force and our fortune with like-minded peoples. Like-mindedness is not simply a gift of history; it must be cultivated. My life's aim has been to forge consensus among the democracies as a prelude to the creation of a free, just, and durable world order.*

HUNTLEY, ROBERT CARSON, justice Idaho Supreme Court; b. Union City, Pa., Aug. 7, 1932; s. Robert Carson and Mildred (Kaltenmark) H.; m. Elfrieda Garvens, Feb. 11, 1955; children: Christopher F., Anthony R. B.S., U. Idaho, 1954, J.D., 1959. Bar: Idaho 1959. Ptnr. Racine, Huntley & Olson, Pocatello, Idaho, 1959-82; justice Idaho Supreme Ct., Boise, 1982—; mem. Idaho Jud. Council, 1967-81; bd. commrs. Idaho State Bar, 1982. Mem. Idaho Ho. of Reps., 1965-67, Pocatello City Council, 1962-64, Gov.'s Blue Ribbon Tax Com., 1978-79, Com. to Promote Funding for Edn., 1980, Pocatello Fin. Resources Com., 1980; chmn. Idaho Energy Resources Policy Bd., 1980-82. Served to capt. USNR, 1954-79. Mem. ABA, Idaho Bar Assn., Am. Bar Found., Idaho Trial Lawyers Assn., Assn. Trial Lawyers Am. Democrat. Unitarian. Lodge: Elks. Home: 604 San Felipe Way Boise ID 83702 Office: Idaho Supreme Court 451 W State St Boise ID 83702

HUNTLEY, ROBERT EDWARD ROYALL, educator; b. Winston-Salem, N.C., June 13, 1929; s. Benjamin F. and Elizabeth (Royall) H.; m. Evelyn Whitehurst, 1954; children—Martha, Catherine, Jane. B.A., Washington and Lee U., 1950, LL.B., 1957; LL.M., Harvard, 1962; LL.D., Randolph-Macon Coll., 1971, Wake Forest U., 1971; Litt.D., Coll. of Charleston, 1976. Bar: Va. bar 1957. Asso. firm Boothe, Dudley, Koontz and Boothe, Alexandria, Va., 1957-58; asst. prof. law Washington and Lee U., Lexington, Va., 1958-59, assoc. prof. law, 1959-64, prof. law, 1964—, dean Sch. Law, 1967-68, pres., 1968-83; Dir. Best Products Co., Inc., Philip Morris, Inc., Central Telephone & Utilities Corp.; dir. Piedmont Aviation; Dir. Shenandoah Life Ins. Co. Bd. dirs. George C. Marshall Research Found., 1969—; mem. Va. Bd. Edn., 1970-74; pres. Va. Found. for Ind. Colls., 1974-76, Council Ind. Colls. in Va., 1977-78; chmn. bd. trustees Union Theol. Sem., Richmond, Va., 1981—. Served with USN, 1950-53. Mem. Am., Va. bar assns., Phi Beta Kappa, Order of Coif, Omicron Delta Kappa. Home: 601 Ross Rd Lexington VA 24450

HUNTLEY, ROBERT ROSS, physician, educator; b. Wadesboro, N.C., Sept. 6, 1926; s. George W. and Louise (Ross) H.; m. Joan Cornoni, Apr. 10, 1976; children: Katherine, Robert, Julia, Elizabeth, Jeffress. B.S. in Chemistry, Davidson Coll., 1947; M.D., Bowman-Gray Sch. Medicine, 1951. Diplomate: Am. Bd. Preventive Medicine (trustee 1974-78), Am. Bd. Family Practice. Intern U. Mich. Hosp., Ann Arbor, 1951-53; resident, fellow N.C. Meml. Hosp., Chapel Hill, 1959-61; pvt. practice medicine, Warrenton, N.C., 1953-58; from instr. to asso. prof. medicine and preventive medicine U. N.C., Chapel Hill, 1959-68; asso. dir. Nat. Center for Health Services Research, HEW, 1968-70; prof., chmn. dept. community and family medicine Georgetown U., 1970—; pres. Georgetown U. Community Health Plan, Inc., 1972-80; cons. Robert Wood Johnson Found.; chmn. health care tech. study sect. HEW, 1978-82. Contbr. articles to profl. jours. Served with USN, 1945-46. Mem. Assn. Tchrs. Preventive Medicine, Soc. Tchrs. Family Medicine, D.C. Med. Soc., Am. Public Health Assn. Democrat. Methodist. Office: 3900 Reservoir Rd NW Washington DC 20007

HUNTRESS, KEITH GIBSON, emeritus humanities educator; b. South Portland, Maine, May 6, 1913; s. Frederick W. and Caroline (Lowell) H.; m. Ida E. Schaub, June 8, 1940; children: Deborah E. Huntress Adams, Jonathan K., Alison D. Huntress Rutledge, Margaret E. Huntress Avery, Bethany G. Huntress Vaughn. B.A., Wesleyan U., 4Middletown, Conn., 1935, M.A., 1936; Ph.D., U. Ill., 1942. Asst. underwriter Travelers Ins. Co., 1936-37; grad. asst. English Ill., 1937-41; instr. English Iowa State U., 1941-42, asst. prof., 1942-44, assoc. prof., 1944-46, prof., 1946-65, Disting. prof. sci. and humanities, 1965-80, prof. emeritus, 1980—. Author: Of Time and Truth, 1946, Analysis of Propaganda, 1949, Minimum Essentials for Good Writing, 1952, Ideas and Backgrounds, 1957, Murder of an American Prophet, 1960, Design for Reading, 2d edit, 1969, Narratives of Shipwrecks and Disasters, 1580-1860, 1974, A Checklist of Narratives of Shipwrecks and Disasters at Sea to 1860, 1979. Recipient Alumni award for teaching Wesleyan U., 1965. Mem. AAUP, Modern Lang. Assn., Iowa Coll. Conf. English, Phi Beta Kappa, Phi Kappa Phi (hon.), Phi Nu Theta. Home: 509 Ash Ave Ames IA 50010

HUNTSINGER, FRITZ ROY, former offshore equipment mfg. co. exec.; b. Oxnard, Calif., Feb. 28, 1935; s. Fritz and Mathilde (Ammen) H.; m. Nancy Rogers, Sept. 10, 1958; children—Susan, Elizabeth, Gretchen. B.A. in Econs, Stanford U., 1957. Prodn. analyst Melpar Inc., Alexandria, Va., 1957-58; prodn. mgr. Gray Tool Inc., Houston, 1958-60; sales mgr. Ventura Tool Co., Calif., 1960-66; mng. dir. Oilfield Tubular Service Ltd., London, 1966-68; exec. v.p. Vetco Inc., Ventura, 1969-73, pres., chief exec. officer, 1973-78; now pvt. investments. Trustee Hood Coll., Frederick, Md., St. Paul's Sch., Ventura, Community Meml. Hosp., Ventura; mem. president's bd. Pepperdine U., Malibu, Calif.; bd. dirs. Salvation Army, Ventura; Ventura council Boy Scouts Am., R.M. Pyles Boys Camp, Huntington Beach, Calif.; chmn. Benefactors Community Meml. Hosp. Served with AUS, 1953-54. Recipient award Boy Scouts Am., Boys Club, both Ventura). Mem. Am. Petroleum Inst., Nat. Ocean Industries Assn., NAM. Republican. Episcopalian. Club: Masons. Patentee in field. Address: 260 Maple Ct Suite 220 Ventura CA 93003

HUNTSMAN, STANLEY HOUSER, track coach; b. Scottdale, Pa., Mar. 20, 1932; s. James Owen and Frances Rebecca (Houser) H.; m. Sylvia K. Scalzi, Sept. 3, 1942; children: Stanley Stephen, Constance. A.B., Wabash Coll., 1954; M.S., Ohio U., 1956. Track coach Ohio U., Athens, 1956-71; track coach U. Tenn., Knoxville, 1971—; Coach N.C.A.A. champions-cross country, 1972, track and field, 1974; asst. coach track and field team U.S. Olympics, 1976, 80; head track coach U.S. World Cup Team, 1977; head track and field coach 1983 World Championships; chmn. men's track and field T.A.C. Named Outdoor Coach of Yr., 1983. Mem. U.S. Track Coaches Assn. (past pres., Outdoor Coach of Year 1974), U.S. Cross Country Coaches Assn. (Outdoor Coach of Year 1972), Phi Delta Theta. Club: Lions. Home: 5532 Timbercrest Trail Knoxville TN 37919

HUNTSMAN, WILLIAM DUANE, chemistry educator; b. Dart, Ohio, Mar. 1, 1925; s. Floyd Forrest and Leona Mae (Arnold) H.; m. Lizbeth Jane Phinney, July 2, 1949; children: William Floyd, Marilyn Jean, Lois Mae. B.S., Ohio U., 1947; Ph.D., Northwestern U., 1950. Research assoc. Northwestern U., Evanston, Ill., 1950-51; asst. prof. Ohio U., Athens, 1951-54, assoc. prof., 1954-61, prof., 1961-68, chmn. chem. dept., 1963-68, disting. prof. chemistry, 1968—. Served with USNR, 1944-46. Recipient Outstanding Tchr. award Ohio U., 1982. Mem. Am. Chem. Soc., Royal Inst. Chemistry, Sigma Xi, Phi Beta Kappa. Home: 48 Maplewood Dr Athens OH 45701 Office: Ohio U Chemistry Dept Athens OH 45701

HUNTZICKER, HARRY NOBLE, chemist, mfr.; b. Omaha, June 29, 1906; s. Albion Clinton and Annabelle (Noble) H.; m. Mildred Harriet Carlson, Aug. 14, 1934; children—Jon Noble, James Frederick. B.S., Macalester Coll., 1927; M.S., U. Wis., 1930, Ph.D., 1932. Sr. teaching asst. chemistry dept. U. Wis., 1930-32; tchr. high sch. chemistry, Rockford, Ill., 1932-35; with U.S. Gypsum Co., Chgo., 1935-56; research chemist, research supr. gypsum and lime products, tech. products mgr., prodn. mgr. lime plants, mgr. research and devel. labs., dir. research and devel., v.p. charge research and devel.; exec. v.p. Am.-Marietta Co., 1956-61, dir., 1961; v.p., dir. Martin Marietta Corp., 1961-66, pres. constrn. materials div., 1962-66; pres. Portland Cement Assn., Skokie, Ill., 1966-72; dir. Gen. Portland Inc., 1973-80, chmn. bd., 1975-80; Mem. bldg. research adv. bd. NRC, Nat. Acad. Scis., 1953; bd. govs. Bldg. Research Inst., 1954. Trustee Macalester Coll., St. Paul. Mem. Am. Standards Assn., Am. Chem. Soc., ASTM, Am. Soc. Engring. Edn., Am. Concrete Inst., Sigma Xi, Phi Lambda Upsilon, Alpha Chi Sigma. Republican. Presbyterian. Club: Westmoreland Country (Wilmette, Ill.). Patentee in field. Home: 9424 Monticello Ave Evanston IL 60203

HUNZEKER, HUBERT LA VON, educator; b. Pawnee City, Nebr., Nov. 12, 1920; s. Clyde F. and Lily (Branek) H.; m. Gladys Gloria Deters, Apr. 26, 1943; children—Mary Patrice, Lisa Elizabeth, James Hubert, Peter David. A.B., Peru State Coll., 1948; M.S., Iowa State Coll., 1950; Ph.D., U. Mich., 1969. Instr. math. Ohio U., 1950-52; asst. prof. DePauw U., 1953-57; asst. prof. math. U. Nebr., 1958-62; prof., head dept. math. U. Omaha, 1962-68, Mich. Technol. U., Houghton, 1968-71, prof. math., 1971—. Served with USN, 1941-43; Served with USNR, 1943-45. Mem. Am. Math. Soc., Math. Assn. Am., AAUP, Sigma Xi, Sigma Tau. Home: Canal Rd Box 244 Houghton MI 49931

HUNZIKER, ROBERT MCKEE, paper co. exec.; b. Paterson, N.J., Apr. 22, 1932; s. Walter Jacobus and Helen (McKee) H.; m. Joan DuBois, June 15, 1955; children—James D., William M., Hans B., Eric G. A.B. cum laude, Amherst Coll., 1954; LL.B., U. Mich., 1957. Bar: N.Y. State bar 1958, N.J. bar 1976. Asso. Shearman & Sterling, N.Y.C., 1957-64; gen. counsel, corporate sec. Riegel Paper Corp., N.Y.C., 1964-71; v.p. legal affairs Wheelabrator-Frye, Inc., N.Y.C., 1971-73; v.p. law, corporate sec. Union Camp Corp., Wayne, N.J., 1973-76; counsel White Papers Group, Internat. Paper Co., 1977—. Mem. Am., N.Y. State bar assns., Assn. Bar City N.Y., Delta Upsilon, Phi Delta Phi. Home: 2 Stoneleigh Park Westfield NJ 07090 Office: 77 W 45th St New York NY 10036

HUOT, GUY EUGENE, service organization executive; b. Ottawa, Ont., Can., Mar. 21, 1943; s. Eugene Joseph and Monique Marie (Duchesne) H. B.A., U. Ottawa, 1964. Spl. asst. to asst. under sec. state, Can., 1965-66; head music Can. Council Arts, 1966-73; music adminstr. Nat. Arts Centre, Ottawa, 1973-75; sec. gen. Canadian Music Council, Ottawa, 1976—; freelance music critic and writer. Spl. advisor bd. dirs. Ottawa Choral Soc. Editor: Musicanada, 1976—. Mem. Assn. Cultural Execs. (bd. dirs.), Internat. Soc. Contemporary Music (sec. Canadian sect. 1976—), Assn. Canadian Orchs. (sec. 1973-75), Interam. Music Council (1st v.p.), Espace Musique Soc. (v.p.). Home: 524 Clarence Ottawa ON K1N 5S2 Canada Office: 36 Elgin Ottawa ON K1P 5K5 Canada

HUPP, JACK SCOTT, insurance company executive; b. Seattle, Aug. 24, 1930; s. George R. and Audrey L. (Getchell) H.; m. Marilyn Rae Lashua, May 24, 1958; children: Heidi Rae, Heather Anne. B.A. in Sociology, U. Wash., Seattle, 1954; grad. exec. program, Stanford U., 1979. With Fireman's Fund Ins. Co., 1954—, v.p. sales, then v.p. mktg., 1974-77, sr. v.p. nationwide field ops., 1977-81, sr. v.p. nationwide field ops. and sales, 1981-82, exec. v.p. claims and ins. services, 1982—; v.p. Pacific Ins. and Surety Conf., 1981-82, also past pres.; pres. Western Ins. Info. Service, 1977. Sec., bd. dirs., past vice chmn. No. Calif. Presbyn. Homes, 1978-82. Served as officer USAR, 1948-79; ret. Mem. Res. Officers Assn., Assn. U.S. Army, Stanford U. Sch. Bus. Alumni Assn., U. Wash. Alumni Assn., Sigma Phi Epsilon. Clubs: Marin Country, Olympic, San Rafael Elks (San Francisco). Office: 777 San Marin Dr Novato CA 94998

HUPP, ROBERT PAUL, social services executive, clergyman; b. Wheeler County, Nebr., July 3, 1915; s. Ferdinand Martin and Anna Barbara (Funk) H. Student, St. Louis Prep. Sem.; M.A., Kenrick Sem., St. Louis, 1940; L.H.D. (hon.), U. Nebr., Omaha, 1977, Mt. St. Mary's Coll., 1980, LL.D., Cath. U. Am., 1980. Ordained priest Roman Catholic Ch., 1940; asst. pastor St. Bridget's Ch., Omaha, 1940-42; dir. Cath. Young Orgn., Archdiocese Omaha, 1946-50; chaplain Home of Good Shepherd, Omaha, 1946-50; pastor St. Mary's Ch., Wayne, Nebr., 1950-53; founding pastor Christ The King Parish, Omaha, 1953-73; vicar gen. Archdiocese Omaha, 1969-72; exec. dir. Father Flanagan's Boys' Home, Boys Town, Nebr., 1973—; U.S. del. 31st Gen. Assembly UN, 1976; chaplain Home of Good Shepherd (Girls Town), Omaha, Newman Club at Wayne (Nebr.) State Coll.; dept. chaplain Am. Legion; dir. Cath. Youth Orgn. Archdiocese Omaha. Served as chaplain USNR, 1943-46. Named hon. alumnus Creighton U., 1973, Man of Year U. Notre Dame, 1976, clergy knight Equestrian Order Holy Sepulchre Jerusalem, 1977; recipient Master Footprinter award, 1976. Life mem. Alpha Sigma Nu. Clubs: K.C. (life), Eagles (life), Elks.). Pioneer in devel. youth ednl. programs on drugs. Address: Father Flanagan's Boys' Home Boys Town NE 68010

HUPPER, JOHN ROSCOE, lawyer; b. N.Y.C., June 16, 1925; s. Roscoe Henderson and Dorothy Wallace (Healy) H.; m. Joyce Shirley McCoy, June 14, 1952; children: John Roscoe, Gail J., Craig W. A.B., Bowdoin Coll., 1949; LL.B., Harvard U., 1952. Bar: N.Y. 1954, U.S. Supreme Ct 1960. Assoc. Cravath, Swaine & Moore, N.Y.C., 1952-60, ptnr., 1961—. Overseer Bowdoin Coll., 1970-82, trustee, 1982—; trustee Allen-Stevenson Sch., 1968—; bd. dirs. Legal Aid Soc., N.Y.C., 1971-76, Travelers Aid Soc., N.Y., 1962-79. Served with U.S. Army,

1943-46. Fellow Am. Coll. Trail Lawyers; mem. Assn. Bar City N.Y., N.Y. County Lawyers Assn., N.Y. State Bar Assn., ABA. Republican. Clubs: Apawamis, Down Town, Univ., Union. Home: 105 E 67th St New York NY 10021 Office: Cravath Swaine & Moore 1 Chase Manhattan Plaza New York NY 10005

HURD, CARL BENTLY, hotel exec.; b. Cleve., Sept. 20, 1919; s. Carl Bently and Esther Louise (Waldron) H.; children—Richard, Carl. Student, Cleve. Coll., Western Res. U., 1937-42. Resident mgr. Marriott Motor Hotel, Washington, 1956-58; gen. mgr. George Washington Motor Lodges, Willow Grove, Pa., 1958-60, 62-63; v.p. Am. Motor Inns, Roanoke, Va., 1964-77; gen. mgr. Ramada O'Hare Inn, Des Plaines, Ill., 1977—. Chmn. bd. trustees Second Ch. of Christ, Scientist, Balt., 1971-72, first reader, 1976-77. Recipient Mayor's citation City of Balt., 1977. Mem. Ill. Hotel Assn. (dir. 1960-61, 77—), Greater Chgo. Hotel and Motel Assn. (dir.), Hotel Sales Mgmt. Assn., Am. Philatelic Assn. Democrat. Home and Office: 5400 astor lane rolling meadows IL 60008

HURD, CUTHBERT C., computer company executive, mathematician; b. Estherville, Iowa, Apr. 5, 1911; s. Harland Corwin and Olive Grace (Long) H.; m. Bettie Jane Mills, June 20, 1941; children: Steven, Diana, Susan, Elizabeth, Victoria. A.B., Drake U., 1932, LL.D., 1967; M.S., Iowa State Coll., 1934; Ph.D., U. Ill., 1936. Asst. prof. math. Mich. State Coll., 1936-42; dean Allegheny Coll., 1945-47; tech. research head Union Carbide & Carbon Corp., Oak Ridge, 1947-49; now cons.; dir. applied sci. dept. IBM, 1949-53, dir. applied sci. div., 1953-55, dir. electronic data processing machines, 1955-56, dir. automation research, 1956-60, dir. control systems, 1961-62; chmn. bd. Computer Usage Co., Inc., N.Y.C., 1962-74; chmn. Solar Energy Research, 1974-76, Cuthbert Hurd Assos., 1974, Picodyne Corp., 1978—, Quintus Computer Systems, 1984—; Mem. adv. com. Center Computer Scis. and Tech., Inst. Applied Tech., Nat. Bur. Standards; mem. computation com. NRC; chmn. computer sci. adv. com. Stanford U.; mem. adv. council to depts. econs. and sociology Princeton U. Trustee Drake U.; mem. devel. bd. Mass. Inst. Tech. Served as lt. comdr. USCGR, 1942-45. Fellow AAAS; mem. Inst. Mgmt. Scis. (past v.p., founder), Am. Math. Soc., Am. Meteorol. Soc., Biometric Soc., Am. Soc. Quality Control, Am. Statis. Assn., Assn. Computing Machinery (council), Econometric Soc., English Speaking Union, Indsl. Math. Soc., Inst. Math. Statistics, Math. Assn. Am. (com. on profl. opportunities), N.Y. Acad. Sci., Operations Research Soc. Am., Soc. Advancement Gen. Systems Theory, Soc. Indsl. and Applied Math., Phi Beta Kappa, Sigma Xi, Phi Kappa Phi. Clubs: University, Metropolitan, Univ. (N.Y.C.); Stanford Faculty. Address: 332 Westridge Dr Portola Valley CA 94025

HURD, J. NICHOLAS, banker; b. Boston, Dec. 10, 1942; m. Joan Hinton; children: Jennifer S., Marshall H. MacKenzie, P. MacKenzie. B.A. in Econs., Hobart Coll., 1965; postgrad. NYU Grad. Sch. Bus. Adminstrn., Stanford U. Bus. Sch. and Grad. Sch. Credit and Fin. Mgmt., summers 1971-73; grad. Advanced Mgmt. Program, Harvard U., 1979. Dist. mgr. Mfrs. Hanover Trust, N.Y.C., 1965, 74-77; sr. v.p. Hartford Nat. Bank, (Conn.), 1977-82; exec. v.p. Old Stone Bank, Old Stone Corp., Providence, 1982—. Bd. dirs. United Way Westchester County, (N.Y.), 1974-77, Jr. Achievement Central Conn., 1977-81, Hartford chpt. ARC, 1979-82; mem. exec. com. Hartford Stage Co., 1978-82. Mem. Am. Bankers Assn. (exec. com. corr. banking div. 1979-81). Clubs: R.I. Country (Barrington); University (Providence); Southport Yacht (West Southport, Mass.). Office: Old Stone Bank 150 S Main St Providence RI 02903

HURD, JAMES BRADDOCK, physician; b. Chgo., Mar. 29, 1921; s. Max Harold and Eunice (Braddock) H.; m. Jean Wescott, June 12, 1943; children: Barbara Wescott, Ann Braddock, Janet Darrow; m. Clare Lutes, July 6, 1974. A.B., Amherst Coll., 1942; M.D., Northwestern U., 1946; M.Sc. in Pathology, 1950. Intern Evanston (Ill.) Hosp., 1945-46; fellow pathology Cook County Hosp., Chgo., 1948-49, resident medicine, 1950-51; fellow medicine New Eng. Deaconess Hosp., Boston, 1949-50; pvt. practice, Chgo., 1951—; mem. sr. attending staff Chgo. Wesley Meml. Hosp. (name changed to Northwestern Meml. Hosp.), 1957—, chief med. service D, 1961-74, sec. staff, 1961-64, vice chief staff, 1964-66, chief staff, 1966-68; mem. faculty Northwestern U. Med. Sch., 1951—, asst. prof. internal medicine, 1965-71, asso. prof., 1971—. Served to capt. M.C. AUS, 1946-48. Mem. Am. Diabetes Assn. (dir. 1961—, chmn. com. affiliates 1963—, chmn. assembly affiliate dels. and state govs. 1961-63, v.p. 1968, pres. 1970-71), Diabetes Assn. Greater Chgo. (dir. 1952—, pres. 1959-61, chmn. camp. com. 1952—), A.M.A., Joslin Soc. Republican. Club: Glen View (Golf, Ill.). Home: 24199 N Hurdale Ln Barrington IL 60010 Office: 251 E Chicago Ave Chicago IL 60611

HURD, PETER, artist; b. Roswell, N.Mex., Feb. 22, 1904; s. Harold and Lucy Chew (Knight) H.; m. Henriette Wyeth, June 29, 1929; children: Peter Wyeth, Carol (Mrs. Peter W. Rogers), Michael. Student, U.S. Mil. Acad., 1921-23, Haverford Coll., 1923-24, Pa. Acad. Fine Arts, and under N.C. Wyeth, 1924-26; D. Fine Arts, Technol. Coll.; LL.D., N.M. State U., 1968. Mem. Nat. Fine Arts Commn., 1959-63. Represented in collections, Met. Mus., N.Y.C., Nat. Gallery, Edinburgh, Nat. Gallery, Rochester, Nat. Gallery, N.Y., Nat. Gallery, Wilmington, Nat. Gallery, Del., Nat. Gallery, Chgo., Nat. Gallery, Andover, Nat. Gallery, Mass., Nat. Gallery, Kansas City, Nat. Gallery, Bklyn., Nat. Gallery, Honolulu, Nat. Gallery, Roswell, Nat. Gallery, Mpls., Nat. Gallery, Dallas, Nat. Gallery, Newark, museums, Ft. Worth Club, 16 fresco panels in mus., Tex. Technol. Coll., fresco murals in, U.S. P.O., Big Spring, Tex., U.S. P.O., Alamogordo, N.Mex., mural panel, Prudential Ins. Co. Bldg., Houston; retrospective show, Amon Carter Mus., Ft. Worth, Legion of Honor, San Francisco, 1964-65, Phoenix Art Mus., 1983, Denver Art Mus.; Represented portrait, Pres. Johnson for White House Hist. Assn., now in permanent collection, Nat. Portrait Gallery, Washington; Book illustrator. With USAAF in, 1942; Eng.; U.S. Air Transport Command; S. Am., Africa, India, Arabia and Italy in 1944 as; war corr. for Life mag. Winner competition for 3 mural panels in U.S. Terminal Annex P.O., Dallas, 1938; awarded 1st prize 16th Internat. Watercolor Exhbn. Chgo. Art Inst., 1937; Elected asso. Nat. Acad., 1941; N.A., 1942. Mem. Assn. Grads. U.S. Mil. Acad., Wilmington Soc. Fine Arts, Am. Watercolor Soc. Club: Century Assn. (N.Y.C.). Home: Sentinel Ranch San Patricio NM 88348

HUREWITZ, J(ACOB) C(OLEMAN), political scientist, university administrator; b. Hartford, Conn., Nov. 11, 1914; s. Isaac S. and Ida (Aronson) H.; m. Miriam Freund, Mar. 29, 1946; children—Barbara Jean, Ruth Anne. B.A., Trinity Coll., Hartford, 1936; M.A., Columbia U., 1937, Ph.D., 1950. Sr. polit. analyst OSS, 1943-45, Dept. State, 1945-46; polit. adv. U.S. Cabinet Com. on Palestine, 1946; polit. affairs officer UN Secretariat, 1949-50; prof. Middle East polit. history Dropsie Coll., Phila., 1949-56; mem. faculty Grad. Sch. of Arts and Scis., Sch. Internat. Affairs, Columbia U., N.Y.C., 1950—, prof. govt., 1958—; dir. Middle East Inst., 1971—; vis. prof. polit. sci. Johns Hopkins Sch. Advanced Internat. Studies, 1956, Cornell U., 1970; cons. Carnegie Endowment for Internat. Peace, 1954, Rand Corp., 1962-71, Am. Council Learned Socs., 1963-64, Dept. State, 1966-71, Dept. Def., 1970-74, Stanford Research Inst., 1973-76, ABC News, 1979; founder, chmn. Univ. Seminar on the Middle East, Columbia U., 1971—; bd. research cons. Fgn. Policy Research Inst., Phila., 1972—, Inst. Fgn. Policy Analysts, Cambridge, Mass., 1976—; resident fellow Center for Advanced Studies in the Behavioral Scis., Stanford, Calif., 1962-63, Council on Fgn. Relations, N.Y.C., 1965-66; organizer, dir. internat. confs. on Middle East; participant Dartmouth Am.-Soviet Conf. XII, 1979. Author: The Struggle for Palestine, 1950, Middle East Dilemmas, 1953, Diplomacy in the Near and Middle East, 1956, Undergraduate Instruction on the Middle East in American Colleges and Universities, 1962, Middle East Politics: The Military Dimension, 1969, The Middle East and North Africa in World Politics: I, European Expansion 1535-1914, 1975, II, British-French Supremacy, 1914-1955, 1979; Editor and contbr.: Soviet-American Rivalry in the Middle East, 1969, Oil, the Arab-Israel Dispute and the Industrial World, 1976; Bd. editors: Middle East Jour, 1947-81, Orbis, 1974—, Terrorism, 1977-81. Mem. adv. panel on tech. transfer to Middle East Office of Tech. Assessment, 1982—. Served with U.S. Army, 1942. Social Sci. Research Council grantee, 1946-48; Ford Found. fellow, 1954; Guggenheim fellow, 1958-59; Am. Philos. Soc. grantee, 1960; Rockefeller Found. fellow, 1960-62; Ford Found. grantee, 1970; Exxon Edn. Found. grantee, 1981. Fellow Middle East Studies Assn. (founding fellow); mem. Am. Hist. Assn., Middle East Inst. Washington (gov. 1964—), Am. Polit. Sci. Assn., Acad. Polit. Sci., Council Fgn. Relations, Am. Inst. Iranian Studies (founding mem., 1st v.p. 1968-69), Internat. Inst. Strategic Studies, Inter-Univ. Seminar on Armed Forces and Soc. (founding mem.), Am. Research Center in Egypt (gov.), Phi Beta Kappa. Home: 445 Riverside Dr New York NY 10027 Office: Middle East Inst Columbia U New York NY 10027

HURLBERT, GORDON C., business executive; b. Raymond, S.D., 1924; married. B.M.E., Marquette U., 1946; M.B.A., Harvard U., 1955. With Westinghouse Electric Corp., 1946-83, gen. mgr. distbn. transformer div., 1955-62, gen. mgr. power transformation div., 1962-67, v.p. mfg., 1967-69, exec. v.p. power generation, 1969-74; pres. Power Systems Co. subs., Pitts., 1974-83; chmn., chief exec. officer GCH Mgmt. Services, Pitts., 1983—. Served to lt. (j.g.) USN, 1944-46. Office: GCH Mgmt Services Westinghouse Bldg Gateway Center Pittsburgh PA 15222

HURLBURT, WILBUR FRANKLIN, JR., electrical control equipment company executive; b. East Orange, N.J., June 16, 1913; s. Wilbur Franklin and Bertha Fullerton (Horst) Hurlburg; m. Jean F. Linzer, May 23, 1974; children: Margot E., Lindner, Michael H. Kline, Nancy Lee, Wilbur Franklyn. B.S., Newark Coll. Engring., 1935. With Automatic Switch Co., Florham Park, N.J., 1930—, gen. mgr., 1948-49, v.p., 1949-50, pres., 1951—, chmn., chief exec. officer, 1977—; dir. N.J. Mfrs. Ins. Co. Trustee Morristown Meml. Hosp., N.J. Mem. N.J. Bus and Industry Assn. (trustee), Nat. Elec. Mfrs. Assn. (bd. govs.), Fluid Control Inst. (past pres.), Nat. Fluid Power Assn., Air Conditioning and Refrigeration Inst., C. of C. Home: Spring Valley Rd Morristown NJ 07960 Office: Hanover Rd Florham Park NJ 07932

HURLBUT, CORNELIUS SEARLE, JR., mineralogist, retired educator; b. Springfield, Mass., June 06, 1906; s. Cornelius S. and Marion (Adams) H.; m. Anna Dawson, June 18, 1932 (dec. 1954); children: Cornelius Searle IV, Patricia Anne, Marcus Dawson; m. Margaret Richards Carver, 1956. A.B., Antioch Coll., 1929; A.M., Harvard, 1932, Ph.D., 1933. Instr. petrography Harvard, 1933-34, instr. mineralogy, 1935-40, asso. prof. mineralogy, 1941-53, prof. mineralogy, 1954-72, prof. emeritus, 1972—. Author: Minerals and How to Study Them, 1949, (with Henry E. Wenden) The Changing Science of Mineralogy, 1964, Minerals and Man, 1968, (with Cornelis Klein) Manual of Mineralogy, 1977, (with George S. Switzer) Gemology, 1979; editor: The Planet We Live On-An Illustrated Encyclopedia of the Earth Sciences, 1976. Fellow Geol. Soc. Am., Mineral. Soc. Am. (pres. 1963), Am. Acad. Arts and Scis., mem. Brit. Mineral Soc., Soc. Econ. Geologists, Geochem. Soc., Canadian Mineral Soc. Conglist. Home: 51 Clifton St Belmont MA 02178

HURLBUT, ROBERT ST. CLAIR, food company executive; b. Toronto, Ont., Can., June 10, 1924; s. St. Clair and Maude I. (Burleigh) H.; m. Anne Marilyn Moffat, May 2, 1953; children: Andrew, David. B. Commerce, U. Toronto, 1948; Barrister of Law, Osgoode Hall, 1951. Bar: Called to Ont. bar 1951. Mem. firm Daily, Thistle, Judson & McTaggart, Toronto, Ont., 1951-52; salesman to group mgr. Colgate Palmolive Co., Toronto, 1952-55; with Gen. Foods, Ltd., Toronto, 1956—, chmn., pres., 1967—; dir. No. Telecom Ltd., Hiram Walker Resources Ltd, Consumer's Gas Co., N.Am. Life Assurance Co., Rio Algom Ltd. Nat. bd. dirs. Jr. Achievement Can.; bd. govs. Olympic Trust Can.; bd. govs., mem. adv. council faculty of adminstrv. studies York U.; past bd. govs. Guelph U.; past bd. dirs. Orthopaedic & Arthritic Hosp; mem. Ont. Govt. Adv. Com. on Econ. Future, Ont. Govt. Adv. Com. on Quality of Working Life; sr. mem. Bus. Council on Nat. Issues.; adv. com. Can. Opera Co. Served to lt. Royal Can. Navy, 1943-45. Mem. Assn. Can. Advertisers (v.p. 1964-68), Grocery Products Mfrs. Can. (dir., past chmn.), Can. Mfrs. Assn. (adv. com.), Toronto Bd. Trade. Progressive Conservative. Anglican. Clubs: Granite, Rosedale Golf, National. Home: 3-3100 Bayview Ave Willowdale ON Canada M2N 5L3 Office: 95 Moatfield Dr Don Mills ON M3C 3J5 Canada

HURLBUTT, GUY GORDON, lawyer, educator; b. Augusta, Ga., Jan. 23, 1942; s. Guy Rodgers and Lydia (Vahovich) H.; m. Linda Faye, Apr. 11, 1970; children: Sara Frances, Lee Anthony. B.S. in Forestry, U. Ga., 1964; J.D., U. S.C., 1970; LL.M. with highest honors, George Washington U., 1974. Bar: S.C. 1971, Idaho 1975. Atty. U.S. Forest Service, Washington, 1971-72; fed. law clk. U.S. Cts., Greenville, S.C., 1972-74; chief dep. atty. gen. Atty. Gen. Idaho, Boise, 1975-78; assoc. Hurlbutt & Payne Chartered, Boise, 1978-81; U.S. atty. Dept. Justice, Boise, 1981—; adj. prof. Boise State U., 1978-79; affiliate por. U. Idaho, 1983—; mem. U.S. Atty. Gen.'s Econ. Crime Council, Washington, 1983—. Mem. Lincoln Day Banquet Com, Boise, 1977—; bd. dirs. Idaho City Hist. Soc., Idaho City, 1977-79; mem. fund raising com. YMCA, Boise, 1977-78; chmn. energy and legal coms. Leadership, Boise, 1979-81. Forestry scholar St. Regis Paper Co., 1963-64; recipient Freedom Found. award Valley Forge, 1969. Mem. Idaho State Bar (mem. com. 1982), S.C. Bar, Idaho Peace Officers Assn., Idaho Pros. Attys. Assn. Republican. Episcopalian. Home: 1301 S Owyhee St Boise ID 83705 Office: US Atty's Office Federal Bldg Room 693 550 W Fort St Box 037 Boise ID 83724

HURLEY, ALFRED FRANCIS, university administrator; b. Bklyn., Oct. 16, 1928; s. Patrick Francis and Margaret Teresa (Coakley) H.; m. Joanna Helen Leahy, Jan. 24, 1953; children: Alfred F., Thomas J., Mark P., Claire T., John K. B.A., St. John's U., 1950; M.A., Princeton U., 1958, Ph.D., 1961. Enlisted U.S. Air Force, 1950, commd. lt., 1952, advanced through grades to brig. gen., ret., 1980; v.p. adminstrv. affairs North Tex. State U., Denton, 1980-82, chancellor, 1982—; mem. adv. com. on USAF hist. program sec. USAF, Washington, 1982—. Author: Billy Mitchell, Crusader for Air Power, 1964, (rev. edit.) Billy Mitchell, Crusader for Air Power, 1975; editor: Air Power and Warfare, 1979. Decorated Legion of Merit (2); Guggenheim fellow, 1971-72; Smithsonian fellow, 1975-76. Mem. Am. Mil. Inst. (trustee 1973-78, 81—), U.S. Commn. Mil. History (trustee 1976-80), Air Force Hist. Found. (trustee 1980—), Orgn. Am. Historians, Am. Hist. Assn. Roman Catholic. Home: 828 Skylark Denton TX 76201 Office: N Tex State U Office of Chancellor Denton TX 76203

HURLEY, CHERYL JOYCE, publishing company executive; b. Pitts., Oct. 30, 1947; d. John and Violet Dernorsek; m. Kevin Hurley, July 27, 1974. Cert. de langue et de litt., Universite de Lyon, France, 1968; A.B., Ohio U., 1969; M.A., U. Mich., 1971. Research assoc. MLA, N.Y.C., 1972-74, dir. spl. programs, 1974-79; exec. dir. Literary Classics of U.S., N.Y.C., 1979—; cons. in field. Contbr. articles to profl. jours. Rackham fellow, 1969-70. Mem. Am. Studies Assn. (com. on publs. 1983—), Phi Beta Kappa, Alpha Lambda Delta, Phi Sigma Iota, Phi Kappa Phi. Home: 105 W 13th St New York NY 10028 Office: Literary Classics of US 14 E 60th St New York NY 10022

HURLEY, DANIEL FRANCIS, labor relations arbitrator; b. Hartford, Conn., Nov. 21, 1911; s. Daniel Cornelius and Catherine Mary (Cunningham) H.; m. Mary Lou Crescence De Wan, Feb. 27, 1943; children—Patricia Lee, Daniel Michael, Tarasia. Student, Trinity Coll., Hartford, Conn., 1929-30, Cleve. Coll. Western Res., 1947-48; LL.B., Northeastern U., 1954. Bar: Mass. bar 1954. Substitute clk. Hartford P.O., 1930-32; moulder Colt Patent Firearms Co., Hartford, 1935-36; labor relations adviser Am. Fedn. Actors, N.Y.C., 1936-39; commr. U.S. Conciliation Service, Dept. Labor, Washington, 1939-41, resident commr., Cleve., 1941-44, regional supr. for service, 1944-46, asst. regional dir., 1946-47; (entire service trans. to Fed. Mediation and Conciliation Service 1947), regional dir., Boston, 1948-54, commr., 1954-78, arbitrator in labor relations, 1978—; instr. Univ. Coll., Northeastern U., Boston. Contbr. articles to profl. jours. Recipient Cardinal Cushing award for excellence labor mgmt. as rep. of pub., 1967. Mem. Indsl. Relations Research Assn. (sec.-treas. Boston chpt. 1968-71), Boston (pres. 1971-72), Fed. bar assns. Roman Catholic. Clubs: K.C., University (Cleve.). Home: 2 Yorkshire Rd Dover MA 02030

HURLEY, FRANCIS T., archbishop; b. San Francisco, Jan. 12, 1927. Ed., St. Patrick Sem., Menlo Park, Calif., Catholic U. Am. Ordained priest Roman Cath. Ch., 1951; with NCWC, Washington, asst. sec., 1958-68; asso. sec. NCCB and USCC, 1968; consecrated bishop, 1970; titular bishop Daimlaig and aux. bishop Diocese of Juneau, Alaska, 1970-71, bishop of, Juneau, 1971-76; archbishop of, Anchorage, 1976—. Office: Chancery Office PO Box 2239 Anchorage AK 99510 *

HURLEY, GERARD FRANCIS, trade association executive; b. Washington, Oct. 9, 1935; s. Charles Thomas and Marguerite Mary (Curran) H.; m. Mary Docia Gilliam, Aug. 6, 1960; children: Jeanine, Diane. B.S., U. Md., 1959. Mgr. market research and promotion Blackburn & Co., Washington, 1960-63; mem. staff Am. Inst. (C.P.A.s), Washington, 1963-64; gen. mgr. Nat. Swimming Pool Inst., Washington, 1964-74; exec. dir. Nat. Club Assn., Washington, 1974—, Conf. of Pvt. Orgns., 1979—. Contbr. articles in field to trade jours. and consumer mags. Served with USNR, 1956-57. Mem. Am. Soc. Assn. Execs. (Mgmt. Achievement Merit award), Am. League Lobbyists, Greater Washington Soc. Assn. Execs. (chmn.-elect), Sommelier Soc. Republican. Roman Catholic. Clubs: Capitol Hill (bd. govs.), Nat. Assn. Execs.). Office: 1625 Eye St NW 609 Washington DC 20006

HURLEY, HARRY JAMES, JR., dermatologist; b. Phila., Oct. 10, 1926; s. Harry James and Margaret (McHenry) H.; m. Jeanne Florence Geiger, July 15, 1950; children: Susan, Harry James, III, Jeffrey, Marilyn, Nancy. Student, St. Joseph's Coll., Phila., 1943-45; M.D., Jefferson Med. Coll., Phila., 1949; D.Sc. in Medicine, U. Pa., 1958. Diplomate: Am. Bd. Dermatology (dir., examiner 1974-83, exec. com. 1978-79). Rotating intern Fitzgerald-Mercy Hosp., Darby, Pa., 1949-50; resident in Ob-Gyn, 1950-51; resident in dermatology and syphilogy U. Pa. Hosp., 1951-53; research fellow USPHS, 1955-56; mem. faculty U. Pa. Med. Sch., 1956-59, 62—, prof. clin. dermatology, 1978—; prof. dermatology, chief sect. Hahnemann Med. Coll., Phila., 1959-62, chief dermatol. sect. coll. hosp., 1959-62; chief dermatology Phila. Gen. Hosp., 1962-73; attending dermatologist U. Pa. Hosp., 1962—; chmn. adv. bd. Nat. Program Dermatology, 1974-75; pres. Dermatology Found., 1975-76; vice chmn. bd. dirs. Mut. Assn. Profl. Services, Pa. Mut. Life Ins. Co., 1980; cons., adv. in field. Contbr. numerous articles med. jours. Served to capt. M.C. USAR, 1953-55. Recipient Research Recognition award Phila. chpt. Nat. Cystic Fibrosis Found., 1959, Shaffrey award St. Joseph's U., Phila., 1980. Mem. Am. Acad. Dermatology (dir. 1972-75, chmn. council govt. liaison 1974-75), A.C.P. (chmn. self-assessment program sect. dermatology 1976), AMA (chmn. residency rev. com. 1979-82), Am. Dermatol. Assn. (dir. 1977-82, pres. 1983-84), A.C.P., Soc. Investigative Dermatology, Pa. Acad. Dermatology (pres. 1969-70), Pa. Med. Soc., Phila. Dermatol. Soc. (pres. 1970-71), Alpha Espilon Delta. Roman Catholic. Clubs: Overbrook Golf (Bryn Mawr, Pa.); Seaview Country (Absecon, N.J.). Home: 4119 Echo Valley Ln Newtown Square PA 19073 Office: 39 Copley Rd Upper Darby PA 19082

HURLEY, KATHY (KATHLEEN PATRICIA), playwright, actress; b. Plainfield, N.J., Apr. 1, 1947; d. James Francis and Gertrude Marie (Faucette) H. B.A., Ariz. State U., 1969; M.A., Ill. State U., 1971. Asst to editors Atheneum Pubs., N.Y.C., 1980—. Playwright The Alchemist's Book, 1969, Wander Darkling, 1974, The Forgotten Treasure, 1977, The Fading of Miss Dru, 1979, A Poet Against the World, 1982; performer, Pyramid Prodns., Greensboro, N.C., 1971-72, Pyramid Prodns., Atlanta, Tsa-La-Gi,Tahlequah, Okla., 1973, various off-off-Broadway and regional theatres, 1973—. NEA playwright in residency, N.Y.C., 1979; recipient Playwriting award Nat. Soc. Arts and Letters, Phoenix, 1971; Heckshire found. grantee, 1978; N.Y. Met. Short Play Festival grantee, 1979-80. Mem. Dramatists Guild, Broadcast Music's Musical Workshop, Actors Equity Assn., AFTRA. Democrat. Home: 484 W 3 St Apt 22P New York NY 10036

HURLEY, MARK JOSEPH, bishop; b. San Francisco, Dec. 13, 1919; s. Mark J. and Josephine (Keohane) H. Student, St. Joseph's Coll., Mountain VIew, Calif., 1939, St. Patrick's Sem., Menlo Park, Calif., 1944; postgrad., U. Calif. at Berkeley, 1943-45; Ph.D., Cath. U. Am., 1947; J.C.B., Lateran U., Rome, 1963; LL.D., U. Portland, 1971. Ordained priest Roman Catholic Ch., 1944; asst. supt. schs. Archdiocese, San Francisco, 1944-51; tchr. Serra High Sch., San Mateo, Calif., 1944; prin. Bishop O'Dowd High Sch., Oakland, Calif., 1951-58, Marin Cath. High Sch., Marin County, Calif., 1959-61; supt. schs. Diocese, Stockton, Calif., 1962-65, chancellor, diocesan counsultor, 1962-65; asst. chancellor Arcdiocese, San Francisco, 1965-67, vicar gen., 1967-69; titular bishop Thunusuda, aux. bishop, San Francisco, 1967-69; bishop, Santa Rosa, Cal., 1969—; pastor St. Francis Assisi Ch., San Francisco, 1967—; Prof. grad. schs. Loyola U., Balt., 1946, U. San Francisco, 1948, San Francisco Coll. Women, 1949, Dominican Coll., San Rafael, Calif., 1949, Cath. U. Am., 1954; Del. Conf. Psychiatry and Religion, San Francisco, 1957; mem. bd. Calif. Com. on Study Edn., 1955-60; del.-at-large Cal., White House Conf. on Youth, 1960; Cath. del., observer Nat. Council Chs., Columbus, Ohio, 1964; del. edn. conf. German and Am. educators, Nat. Cath. Edn. Assn., Munich, Germany, 1960; mem. commns. sems., univs. and schs. II Vatican Council, Rome, 1962-65; mem. commn. Christian formation U.S. Cath. Conf. Bishops, 1968; asst. archdiocesan coordinator Campaign on Taxation Schs. Calif., 1958, Rosary Crusade, 1961; adminstr. Cath. Sch. Purchasing Div., 1948-51, St. Eugene's Ch., Santa Rosa, Calif., 1959, St. John's Ch., San Francisco, 1961; mem. U.S. Bishops' Press Panel, Vatican Council, 1964-65, U.S. Bishops' Com. on Laity, 1964, U.S. Bishops' Com. Cath.-Jewish Relationships, 1965—, U.S. Bishops' Com. on Ecumenical and

Interreligious Affairs, 1970, Conf. Maj. Superiors of Men, 1970; chmn. citizens Com. for San Francisco State Coll., 1968—; mem. adminstrn. bd. Nat. Council Cath. Bishops, 1970, mem. nominating com., 1971; mem. Internat. Secretariat for Non-Believers, Vatican, 1973; chmn. Secretariat for Human Values, Nat. Conf. Cath. Bishops, Washington, 1975. Syndicated columnist, San Francisco Monitor, Sacramento Herald, Oakland Voice, Yakima (Wash.) Our Times, Guam Diocesan Press, 1949-66; TV speaker and panelist, 1956-67; Author: Church State Relationships in Education in California, 1948, Commentary on Declaration on Christian Education in Vatican II, 1966, Report on Education in Peru, 1965, The Church and Science, 1982. Trustee N.Am. Coll., Rome, 1970, Cath. U. Am., 1978—, Cath. Relief Services, 1979. Address: PO Box 1297 Santa Rosa CA 95402

HURLEY, MORRIS ELMER, JR., mgmt. cons.; b. Berkeley, Calif., Mar. 26, 1920; s. Morris Elmer and Alice Grace (Johnson) H.; m. Jeanne Marie Bassett, Jan. 31, 1943; children—Morris Elmer III, James, Richard, Steven, Robert. A.B., Harvard, 1941, M.B.A., 1943; Ph.D., Syracuse U., 1956. Asst. dean Coll. Bus. Adminstrn., Syracuse U., 1946-53, acting dean, 1953-54, dean, 1954-58, instr., 1945-48, asst. prof., 1948-53, asso. prof., 1953-57, prof., 1957-60, Istituto Direzionale ENI, San Donato Milanese, 1958, IPSOA Istituto Post-Universitairo Torino, Italy, 1959-61; cons. prof. IBM Exec. Sch. Blaricum, Holland, 1960-61; dir. Mgmt. Edn. Programs, Berkeley, 1961—; asso. economist with N.Y. dept. Commerce, 1948; research aide Study for the Ford Found., 1949; cons. IRS, 1957; Dir. WIZ Corp., Empire Casting Co. Author: Elements of Business Administration, 1953, Staff Notes, 1953, Economic Development Regionalism, 1956, Business Administration, 2d edit, 1960, Teaching Notes, 1960, Managing Human Endeavor, 1975. Mem. Syracuse city planning commn., 1957-58; Dir. Portsmouth (Va.) Community Chest, 1944-46, Frank S. Hiscock Legal Aid Soc., Syracuse, 1951-54. Served from ensign to lt. USNR, 1943-46; mem. Res. Mem. Am. Econ. Assn., Acad. Mgmt., Acad. Polit. and Social Sci., George F. Baker Scholars, Phi Beta Kappa, Beta Gamma Sigma, Pi Eta, Sigma Iota Epsilon, Alpha Kappa Psi. Home: 36 Greenbank Ave Piedmont CA 94611 Office: 3144 Claremont Ave Berkeley CA 94705

HURLEY, PATRICK MASON, geology educator; b. Hong Kong, China, Jan. 12. 1912; came to U.S., 1937, naturalized, 1943; s. F.C. Mason and Anne (Peacock) H.; m. Margaret Macurda, Aug. 9, 1941; children: David, Peter, Pamela. B.A., U. B.C., 1934, B.A.Sc., 1934; Ph.D., Mass. Inst. Tech., 1940. Geologist, mining engr., B.C., 1933-37; research assoc. M.I.T., 1940-42, asst. prof. geology, 1946-51, exec. officer geology dept., 1951—, prof., 1953—; Research asso. Nat. Def. Research Com., 1942-45; cons. mineral exploration and evaluation; research contracts AEC, Office Naval Research, NSF, NASA. Author: How Old is the Earth, 1959, Living With Nuclear Radiation, 1982; Contbr. articles to sci. jours. Fellow Geol. Soc. Am., Am. Acad. Sci., Am. Geophys. Union; mem. Am. Inst. Mining Engrs., Sigma Xi. Congregationalist. Home: South Seas West 280 Seaview Ct Marco Island FL 33937

HURLEY, ROBERT EMMET, banker; b. Mineola, N.Y., Nov. 13, 1937; s. Denis Michael and Alvina Margaret (Arnold) H.; m. Carol A. Cason, Jan. 23, 1960; children—Carol, Robert, Denise, James, John, Thomas. B.B.A., St. Francis Coll., Bklyn., 1960. C.P.A., N.Y. Staff auditor Lybrand, Ross Bros. & Montgomery, N.Y.C., 1960-63; gen. mgr. Exec. Health Examiners, N.Y.C., 1963-69; comptroller N.Am. Planning Corp., N.Y.C., 1969-70; mgr. Brown Bros. Harriman & Co., N.Y.C., 1970—; sec. Transatlantic Fund, Inc., 1978—; dir. Breezy Point Coop., Inc., 1977-80, pres., 1978-80. Treas. Our Lady of Lourdes Parents-Tchrs. League, 1969-70, pres., 1970-71; mem. Our Lady of Lourdes Sch. Bd., 1970-71; parish coordinator N.Y. Blood Program, 1971; mgr. Malverne (N.Y.) Jr. Baseball League, 1970-81; mem. fin. com. Our Lady of Lourdes Parish Council, 1977—, chmn., 1982—; Mem. exec. com. Ind. Party, Malverne, 1975—. Mem. Am., N.Y. insts. certified pub. accountants, Bank Adminstrn. Inst. (mem. chpt. exec. com. 1975-80). Home: 60 Wright Ave Malverne NY 11565 Office: Brown Bros Harriman & Co 59 Wall St New York NY 10005

HURLEY, ROBERT JOSEPH, lawyer; b. Chgo., May 21, 1932; s. Michael James and Dorothy E. (Pries) H.; m. Emily Hurley Costello, Sept. 14, 1957; children: Brenda, Nancy, Robert, Christopher, Michael, Matthew. B.S., St. Benedict's Coll., 1953; J.D., Loyola U., Chgo., 1962. Acct., auditor Shell Oil Co., Chgo., 1957-64; atty., N.Y., 1965-77, atty, Tulsa, 1965-77, atty., Chgo., 1965-77, Houston, 1965-77; sr. group counsel NL Industrial Inc., Houston, 1977-82; sr. v.p., gen. counsel NL Industries Inc., Houston, 1982—. Mem. adv. bd. Southwestern Legal Found., Richardson, Tex., 1982-83. Mem. Am. Corp. Counsel Assn., ABA, Ill. Bar Assn., Tex. Bar Assn., Ga. Bar Assn. Club: University. Home: 6202 Elmgrove St Spring TX 77379 Office: NL Industrial Inc 3000 N Belt E Houston TX 77032

HURLEY, ROBERT LANDON, JR., advertising agency executive; b. Pittsfield, Mass., Apr. 4, 1948; s. Robert L. and Elizabeth (Webster) H.; m. Cynthia Tillman, Sept. 26, 1977. B.A., Tufts U., 1970; M.B.A., Columbia U., 1975. Pres. Univ. Mktg. Corp., N.Y.C., 1971-74; account mgr. Compton Advt., N.Y.C., 1975, v.p., 1978, sr. v.p., Paris, 1980; sr. v.p., dir. bus. devel. N.Y.C., 1982—. Contbr. articles to profl. jours. Served with USAR, 1970-75. Clubs: Tuxedo (N.Y.); Raquet and Tennis (N.Y.C.). Home: Apt 4F 175 Riverside Dr New York NY 10024

HURLEY, SAMUEL CLAY, III, glass and plastic mfg. co. exec.; b. Peoria, Ill., Jan. 25, 1936; s. Samuel Clay, Jr. and Wilmina Marie (Loveless) H.; m. Jane Atkinson, Aug. 19, 1967; children—Samuel Clay, IV, Bruce Hilliard. A.B. in Econs, Brown U., 1958; M.B.A. in Finance, Northwestern U., 1960. Investment adviser Continental Ill. Nat. Bank, Chgo., 1960-62; asst. treas. Internat. Harvester Credit Corp., Chgo., 1964; mgr. bank relations Internat. Harvester Co., Chgo., 1969; asst. treas. Anchor Hocking Corp., Lancaster, Ohio, 1971-75, treas., 1975—. Mem. Fin. Execs. Inst. (com. on employee benefits, com. on corp. fin.), Lancaster C. of C., Fairfield Heritage Assn., Treas.'s Club Columbus, Smithsonian Instn., Soc. Internat. Treas.'s. Methodist. Club: Univ. (Columbus, Ohio). Home: 148 E Wheeling St Lancaster OH 43130 Office: 109 N Broad St Lancaster OH 43130

HURLEY, WILLARD LEE, banker; b. Gainesville, Ga., Aug. 1, 1926; s. Henry Lee and Cora (Laws) H.; m. Mary G. Bell, Apr. 27, 1957; children: Leslie Ann, Lee M. B.A., Huntingdon Coll., 1950; postgrad., Birmingham Sch. Law, 1960-65. Comptroller currency-nat. bank examiner, Washington, 1951-58; with First Ala. Bank (formerly Exchange Security Bank), Birmingham, Ala., 1958—, exec. v.p., 1970-72, pres., 1972—; vice chmn., chief operating officer First Ala. Banchares, 1982-84, chmn., chief exec. officer, 1984—. Served with AUS, 1944-47. Clubs: Rotarian., Birmingham Country, Downtown, The Club (Birmingham); Shoal Creek Country. Home: 3004 Brook Hollow Ln Birmingham AL 35243 Office: First Ala Bank PO Box 10247 Birmingham AL 35202

HURLEY, WILLIAM JOSEPH, lawyer, banker; b. Chgo., May 28, 1926; s. Ira William and Margaret Mary (Reilly) H.; m. Sheila Ann Sullivan, Dec. 28, 1957; children: Michael, Patrick, Anne, Kevin. Grad., U.S. Mcht. Marine Acad., 1947; J.D. cum laude, U. Notre Dame, 1953. Bar: Ill. 1953. Law clk. to judge Ill. Appellate Ct., 1954-55; practiced law, Chgo., 1955-67; counsel, asst. v.p. Talcott Bus. Finance, Chgo., 1968-73; v.p., gen. counsel Pioneer Bank & Trust Co., Chgo., 1974-78; sr. partner Hurley & Kallick, Ltd., Northbrook, Ill., 1978—; lectr. Ill. Inst. Continuing Legal Edn., 1972-78. Author: Sales and Financing Under Commercial Code, 1973, rev. edit., 1975; assoc. editor: Notre Dame Lawyer, 1952-53. Bd. dirs. Defenders of Fox River. Served to lt. USNR, 1953-54. Mem. Ill. Bar Assn., ABA, Bankers Club Chgo., Execs. Club Chgo. Democrat. Roman Catholic. Home: Route 3 Braeburn Rd Algonquin IL 60102 Office: 1200 Shermer Rd Suite 220 Northbrook IL 60062

HURLOCK, JAMES BICKFORD, lawyer; b. Chgo., Aug. 7, 1933; s. James Bickford and Elizabeth (Charls) H.; m. Margaret Lyn Holding, July 1, 1961; children: James Bickford, Burton Charls, Matthew Hunter. A.B., Princeton U., 1955; B.A., Oxford U., 1957, M.A., 1960; J.D., Harvard U., 1959. Bar: N.Y. 1960, U.S. Supreme Ct. 1967. Assoc. firm White & Case, N.Y.C., 1959-66, ptnr., 1967—; dir. Sea Co., Inc., N.Y.C., Sea Containers Ltd., Hamilton, Bermuda, First Bankcorp, Inc., New Haven, Altex Resources Ltd., Calgary, Alta., Can. Rhodes scholar, 1955. Mem. ABA, Assn. Bar City N.Y., N.Y. Bar Assn., Am. Law Inst., Am. Assn. Internat. Law. Republican. Episcopalian. Clubs: Links, River. Home: 46 Byram Dr Greenwich CT 06830 Office: 14 Wall St New York NY 10005

HURSON, MICHAEL, artist; b. Youngstown, Ohio, 1941. Student, Oxbough Summer Sch. Painting, Saugatuck, Mich., 1960-61, Yale U., 1962; B.F.A., Sch. Art Inst. Chgo., 1963. Exhibited in one-man shows, Michael Wyman Gallery, Chgo., 1972, Mus. Contemporary Art, Chgo., 1973, Mus. Modern Art, N.Y.C., 1974, Dart Gallery, Chgo., 1978, Daniel Weinberg Gallery, San Francisco, 1980, Paula Cooper Gallery, N.Y.C., 1982, group shows include, Art Inst. Chgo., 1961, 63, 64, 73, 75, 77, Met. Mus. Art, N.Y.C., 1974, 79, Guggenheim Mus., N.Y.C., 1977, Whitney Mus. Am. Art, N.Y.C., 1978, Renaissance Soc., U. Chgo., 1979, Mus. Contemporary Art, Chgo., 1979, 80, Mus. Boymans-van Beuningen, Rotterdam, Netherlands, 1980, Padiglione Contemporanea, Milan, Italy, Am. Pavilion, Venice, Italy, Mus. Modern Art, N.Y.C., 1981, 12 Duke St. Gallery, London, Paula Cooper Gallery, N.Y.C., 1981, 82, numerous other galleries U.S. and abroad; represented in permanent collections, Art Inst., Chgo., Met. Mus. Art, N.Y.C., Nat. Gallery of Australia, Canberra, Guggenheim Mus., N.Y.C., Whitney Mus. Am. Art, N.Y.C.; Subject of profl. publs. Recipient Joseph N. Eisendrath prize Art Inst. Chgo., 1963, Logan medal Art Inst. Chgo., 1964, Palmer prize, 1973; Vaklova award Mus. Contemporary Art, Chgo., 1980; George D. Brown traveling fellow, 1963; Nat. Endowment for Arts Individual Artist's Fellowship grantee, 1974-75. Office: care Paula Cooper Gallery 155 Wooster St New York NY 10012

HURST, JAMES WILLARD, legal educator; b. Rockford, Ill., Oct. 6, 1910; s. James Dominick and Mabel (Weinert) H.; m. Frances Wilson, Aug. 20, 1941; children: Thomas Robert, Mary Deborah. A.B., Williams Coll., 1932, LL.D., 1974; LL.B., Harvard U., 1935, research fellow, 1935-36; M.A., Cambridge (Eng.) U., 1967; LL.D., U. Fla., 1980, Ripon Coll., 1981. Bar: Ill. 1936, Wis. 1951. Law clk. Justice Brandeis, U.S. Supreme Ct., Oct. term, 1936; instr. law U. Wis., 1937-38, asst. prof., 1938-41, asso. prof., 1941-46, prof. law, 1946—; vis. prof summer sessions law schs. Northwestern, 1939, 40, Stanford, 1950, 62, U. Utah, 1952, U. Fla., 1978; Pitt prof. Am. history and instns. U. Cambridge, Eng., 1967-68, fellow Trinity Hall, 1967-68. Author: books pertaining to law including The Law Makers, 1950, Law and the Conditions of Freedom, 1956, Law and Social Process in U.S. History, 1960, Law and Economic Growth, 1964, Justice Holmes on Legal History, 1964, The Legitimacy of the Business Corporation, 1970, The Law of Treason in the United States, 1971, A Legal History of Money in the United States, 1973, Law and Social Order in the United States, 1977; Contbr. to: Supreme Court and Supreme Law, 1954, Law in American History (Fleming and Bailyn), 1971; also various law revs. Staff gen. counsel's office Bd. Econ. Warfare, 1942-43. Served to lt. USNR, 1943-46. Mem. Am. Philos. Soc., Wis. Hist. Soc., Am. Acad. Arts and Scis, Phi Beta Kappa, Phi Delta Phi, Order of Coif. Democrat. Conglist. Home: 3972 Plymouth Circle Madison WI 53705

HURST, JOHN WILLIS, cardiologist, educator; b. Cooper, Ky., Oct. 21, 1920; s. John M. and Verna (Bell) H.; m. Nelie Wiley, Dec. 20, 1942; children: John, Steve, Phil. B.S., U. Ga., 1941; M.D., Med. Coll. Ga., 1944. Diplomate: Am. Bd. Internal Medicine, Am. Bd. Cardiovascular Disease (chmn. subsplty. bd. cardiovascular disease 1967-70). Intern U. Hosp. Med. Coll. Ga., 1944-45, asst. resident, 1945-46; cardiac fellow Mass. Gen. Hosp., 1947-49; practice medicine, specializing in cardiology, Atlanta, 1949—; instr. cardiology Sch. Medicine Emory U., Atlanta, 1950-51, asso. in medicine, 1952-54, asst. prof., 1956-57, prof., chmn. dept. medicine, 1957—; chief of medicine Emory U. Hosp., 1980; head med. sect. Emory U. Clinic, 1980; regional cons. cardiology VA Hosp., Atlanta, 1951—; chief of medicine Grady Meml. Hosp., Atlanta, 1957—. Author: (with G.C. Woodson) Atlas of Spatial Vector Electrocardiography, 1952, Cardiac Resuscitation, 1960; Editor: (with N.K. Wenger) Electrocardiographic Interpretation, 1963, (with R.J. Myerburg) Introduction to Electrocardiography, 1973, Four Hats, 1970, (with H.K. Walker) The Problem-oriented System, 1972, (with R.C. Schlant) Advances in Electrocardiography, 1972, (with H.K. Walker, M.F. Woody) Applying the Problem-oriented System, 1973, The Heart, 1978, 5th edit., 1983; Mem. editorial bd.: Am. Heart Jour, 1964-70, Circulation, 1966, Am. Jour. Cardiology, 1968; editor: Mod. Conc. Cardiovasc, 1969; clinician, 1970; editor: Updates: The Heart, 1979-82, Clinical Essays on the Heart, 1983; editor-in-chief: Medicine for the Practicing Physician, 1983; Contbr. articles to med. jours. Mem. Presidents Com. on Heart Diseases, Cancer and Stroke, 1965—; mem. Nat. Adv. Heart and Lung Council, 1967-71. Served to capt. U.S. Army, 1946-47; comdr. USNR, 1954-55. Master A.C.P.; fellow Am. Coll. Cardiology; mem. AMA, Ga., Fulton County med. assns., Am. Heart Assn. (pres. 1971-72), Ga. Heart Assn. (past pres.), Am. Fedn. Clin. Research, Assn. Profs. Medicine, Assn. Am. Physicians, Assn. U. Cardiologists, So. Soc. Clin. Research, Am. Clin. and Climatological Assn., Paul D. White Soc. (pres. 1974), Alpha Omega Alpha. Address: 69 Butler St SE Atlanta GA 30303

HURST, KENNETH THURSTON, publisher; b. London, Apr. 3, 1923; U.S., 1947, naturalized, 1953; s. Ralph Thurston and Karen (Tottrup) H. Student pvt. schs. Account exec. Hutzler Advt. Agy., Dayton, Ohio, 1948-53; advt. and promotion mgr. McGraw-Hill Book Co., N.Y.C., 1953-58; advt. and publicity mgr. Hawthorn Books, Inc., N.Y.C., 1958-61; gen. mgr. Prentice-Hall of India Pvt. Ltd., New Delhi, 1961-63; v.p., gen. mgr. Prentice-Hall Internat., Inc., Englewood Cliffs, N.J., 1963-70, exec. v.p., 1970, now pres.; dir. Internat. Book Distbr., Ltd., Prentice-Hall S.E. Asia Ltd., Prentice-Hall India Ltd.; State Dept. adviser to, Brazil; adviser AID Mission to Turkey, 1964, Morocco, 1965; cons. U. N.C., U. Scranton, SUNY, Faculty Folio mag.; lectr. State Dept. Program Bur., NYU, Rockland Community Coll.; faculty ann. pubs. seminar; co-chmn. Internat. Sports Awards, 1982. Co-author: Books for National Growth, 1965, Indian Publishing Since Independence, 1980; contbr. articles to profl. jours. Trustee Valley Cottage Free Library; chmn. Rockland Spiritual Frontiers Fellowship., N.Y. Easter Seal drive, 1983. Served with Fleet Air Arm Royal Navy, 1942-47. Recipient Presdl. E award and E Star. Mem. Asia Soc., St. John's Old Boys' Assn., Assn. Am. Pubs. (chmn. internat. div., chmn. del. to India 1979, del. to Thailand 1981), Am. Mgmt. Assn., Inst. Bus. Planning, Mensa. Republican. Episcopalian. Clubs: Publishers, Rotary (dir.), Englewood (gov.). Home: Mountainview East 696 Sierra Vista Ln Valley Cottage NY 10989 Office: Prentice-Hall Inc Englewood Cliffs NJ 07632

HURST, LELAND LYLE, natural gas company executive; b. Mooreland, Okla., Oct. 16, 1930; s. Lewis Walter and Ellen Sarah (Riggs) H.; m. Karen Lee Lamkin, Jan. 24, 1969; children: Courtney Anne, Caroline Leigh. B.S. in Indsl. Engring., Okla. State U., 1952; M.S. in Petroleum Engring., U. Tulsa, 1958. Registered profl. engr., Okla. With Amoco Prodn. Co., 1958-80, engr., 1958-68, staff engr., Calgary, Alta., Can., 1968-70, div. engr. supr., Denver, 1970-73, area supt., Liberal, Kans., 1973-74, asst. div. engr., Denver, 1974-75, gas sales mgr., 1975-80; v.p. Amoco Gas Co., Houston, 1980-81, pres., 1981—. Served with Chem. Corps U.S. Army, 1953-55. Mem. Rocky Mountain Gas Men's Assn. (bd. dirs. 1977), Soc. Petroleum Engrs. (editorial com. 1953-55), Natural Gas Men of Houston-New Orleans. Republican. Clubs: Houston; Westlake (Houston). Office: Amoco Gas Co 501 Westlake Park Blvd Houston TX 77079

HURST, ROBERT JAY, securities company executive; b. N.Y.C., Nov. 5, 1945; s. Kurt and Jeanette (Sachs) H.; m. Fern Karesh, Dec. 13, 1970; children: Alexander, Amanda. B.A., Clark U., 1966; M.B.A., Wharton Grad. Sch. U. Pa., 1968. With investments banking div. Merrill Lynch, Pierce, Fenner& Smith, Inc., N.Y.C., 1969-74; v.p. Merrill Lynch, Pierce, Fenner & Smith, Inc., N.Y.C., 1974, Goldman, Sachs & Co., Inc., 1974-80; gen. ptnr. Sachs & Co., Inc., N.Y.C., 1980—. Bd. dirs. Henry Street Settlement, N.Y.C., 1982; trustee Clark U., 1983—, mem. adv. council Grad. Sch. Served with USAR, 1969-74. Mem. Securities Industry Assn., Investment Assn. N.Y. Jewish. Clubs: University (N.Y.C.); Union (Phila.). Office: Goldman Sachs & Co 85 Broad St New York NY 10004

HURST, VERNON JAMES, geologist, educator; b. Glenmore, Ga., July 18, 1923; s. Lonnie T. and Essie (Arnold) H.; m. Julia Corneil Wells, Nov. 5, 1950; children: Marc V., Karen Anne. Student, U. S.D., 1943; S.D., State Coll., 1944; B.S., U. Ga., 1951; M.S., Emory U., 1952; Ph.D., Johns Hopkins, 1954. Geol. cons., bldg. contractor, Alaska, 1946-50; geologist N.J. Zinc Co., 1951; geologist, chief mineralogist Ga. Dept. Mines, Mining and Geology, 1956-61; prof., head dept. geology U. Ga., Athens, 1961-69, chmn. phys. scis. div., 1966-69, research prof. geology, 1969—; cons. geologist, Alaska, Colombia, Panama, P.R., Honduras; pres Research Analysis, Inc.; Past mem. Environmental Scis. Panel, NSF; mem. marine resources adv com. Coastal Plains Regional Commn.; Trustee Coastal Plains Center for Marine Devel. Services; past chmn. bd. govs. Center for Research in Coll. Instrn. of Sci. and Math. Served with USAAF, 1943-46; ETO; Served with USAAF; PTO. Fellow Geol. Soc. Am. (past chmn. S.E. sect.), Mineral. Soc. Am.; mem. Ga. Acad. Sci. (past pres.), Soc. Econ. Geologists, Ga. Geol. Soc. (pres.), Clay Minerals Soc., Fine Particle Soc., Societe Francaise de Mineralogie et Cristallographie, Southeastern Assn. Spectrogrophers, Sigma Xi. Democrat. Presbyterian. Club: Kiwanian. Home: 445 Westview Dr Athens GA 30601

HURT, JAMES RIGGINS, English educator; b. Ashland, Ky., May 22, 1934; s. Joe and Martha Clay (Riggins) H.; m. Phyllis Tilton, June 5, 1958; children: Christopher, Ross, Matthew. A.B., U. Ky., 1956, M.A., 1957; Ph.D., Ind. U., 1965. Asst. prof. Ind. U., Kokomo, 1963-66; asst. prof. U. Ill., Urbana-Champaign, 1966-69, asso. prof., 1969-73, prof. English, 1973—. Author: Aelfric, 1972, Catiline's Dream, 1972, Film and Theatre, 1974; play Abraham Lincoln Walks at Midnight, 1980; co-editor: Literature of the Western World, 1984. Served with U.S. Army, 1957-59. Ill. Center Advanced Study fellow, 1979-80. Mem. Gt. Am. People Show, Ill. State Hist. Soc. Home: 1001 W William St Champaign IL 61820 Office: 325 English Bldg 608 S Wright St Urbana IL 61801

HURT, JOHN VINCENT, actor; b. Chesterfield, Eng., Jan. 22, 1940; s. Arhould Herbert and Phyllis (Massey) H. Student, Royal Acad. Dramatic Art, 1960-62. Plays include Chips with Everything, 1962, Hamp, 1964, Little Malcolm and His Struggle Against the Eunuchs, 1966, Man and Superman, 1969, The Caretaker, 1972, Travesties, 1974, The Shadow of a Gunman, 1978, Ostermans Week-End, 1982; Champions, 1983; film debut The Wild and the Willing, 1962; other films include A Man for All Seasons, 1966, Before Winter Comes, 1969, Mr. Forbush and the Penguins, 1971, Little Malcolm, 1974, The Disappearance, 1978, The Shout, 1978, Spectre, 1978, Alien, 1978, Midnight Express, 1978, Heaven's Gate, 1979, The Elephant Man, 1980, The Champions, 1983, The Hit, 1983; TV appearances include The Naked Civil Servant, 1974; appeared as Caligula in I Claudius, BBC, 1974; appeared in Crime and Punishment, BBC, 1979 (Emmy award 1976). Mem. Brit. Equity, Screen Actors Guild. Address: 60 Saint James's St London England SW1

HURT, WILLIAM, actor; b. Washington, Mar. 20, 1950; m. Mary Beth Hurt. Student, Tufts U., Juilliard Sch. Appeared with, Oreg. Shakespeare Festival prodn., Long Days Journey into Night, N.Y.C.; stage debut in: Henry V, 1976; other stage appearances include Mary Stuart, My Life, Ulysses in Traction, Lulu, Fifth of July, The Runner Stumbles, Hamlet, 'Hurlyburly''; films include Body Heat (Recipient Theater World award 1978), The Big Chill, Altered States, Eyewitness, Gorky Park. Office: care Kimble Parseghian Inc 9255 Sunset Blvd Suite 509 Los Angeles CA 90069 *

HURT, WILLIAM HOLMAN, investment management company executive; b. Los Angeles, Mar. 29, 1927; s. Holman G. and Mary E. (Ortloff) H.; m. Sheridan Ann Stephens, Aug. 10, 1950 (div. May. 1970); children—Kelley Anne Hurt Purnell, Kathleen Constance, Courtney Diana; m. Sarah Sherman, May 28, 1970. B.S. magna cum laude, U. So. Calif., 1949; M.B.A., Harvard U., 1951; postgrad., Wharton Sch. U. Pa., 1958-59. With Dean Witter & Co., Los Angeles, 1951-71, partner, 1959, sr. v.p., 1968-70, exec. v.p., dir., mem. exec. com., dir. marketing and research, 1969-71; vice chmn. bd., chmn. exec. com. Capital Research Co., 1972-77; chief exec. office Capital Group, Inc., Los Angeles, 1978-82; chmn. Capital Strategy Research, Inc., 1982—; mem. adv. com. Coldwell Banker Funds, 1978—; bd. councilors Grad. Sch. Bus. U. So. Calif., Los Angeles, 1978—. Served with USNR, 1945-46. Mem. Harvard Bus. Sch. Club So. Calif., Blue Key, Phi Kappa Phi, Beta Gamma Sigma, Kappa Alpha Order. Republican. Clubs: California, Los Angeles Athletic; New York Athletic, City Midday (N.Y.C.). Office: 333 S Hope St Los Angeles CA 90071

HURTEAU, GILLES DAVID, obstetrician, gynecologist, educator; b. Cornwall, Ont., Canada, Nov. 28, 1928; s. Joseph A. and Antoinette (St-Laurent) H.; m. Janine Anita Carriere, June 16, 1956; children: Michele, Jean, Louise, Pierre, Gilles Andre. B.A., U. Ottawa, 1951; M.D., C.M., McGill U., 1955. Licentiate, Med. Council Can., 1956; cert. in ob-gyn, 1961. Instr. and clin. asst. Yale U. Med. Sch., New Haven, 1961-62; asst. prof. U. Ottawa Med. Sch., Ont., 1963-66, assoc. prof., 1966, prof. and chmn. dept. ob-gyn, 1967-76, dean Sch. Medicine, 1976-78, dean Faculty Health Scis., 1978—. Editorial bd.: European Jour. Ob-Gyn and Reproductive Biology, 1970-78; contbr. articles to profl. jours., chpts to books. Mem. council Carleton Regional Dist. Health Council, Ottawa; mem. Joint Research Rev. Task Force, Ont. Council Health, Ont. Fellow Royal Coll. Physicians and Surgeons Can. (council 1970-78, v.p. 1976-78); mem. Council Ont. Faculties of Medicine. Club: Cercle Universitaire (Ottawa). Home: 1964 Norway Crescent Ottawa ON Canada K1H 5N7 Office: Sch Medicine U Ottawa 451 Smyth Rd Ottawa ON Canada K1H 8M5 *Ce que nons connaissons est per de chose; ce que nons ignorons est emmense.*

HURTIG, MEL, publisher; b. Edmonton, Alta., Can., June 24, 1932; s. Julius and Jennie H. LL.D. (hon.), York U., Toronto, 1980. Founder M.G. Hurtig Ltd. (booksellers), Edmonton, 1956, Hurtig Pubs., 1972, pres., 1972—; speaker.; Pres. Edmonton Art Gallery, 1963-65; mem. U. Alta. Senate, 1970-71; adv. to various Can. public interest groups and govt. agys.; founding mem. Com. for Ind. Can., 1970—, nat. chmn., 1973-75. Contbr. articles to newspapers, mags., chpts. to books; editorial bd.: Jour. Can. Studies. Named Can. Book Pub. of Year Can. Booksellers Assn., 1974, 81; decorated officer Order of Can. Mem. Can. Booksellers Assn. (chmn.). Club: Mayfair Golf and Country. Home: 9908 114 St Apt 1202 Edmonton AB Canada Office: 10560 105th St Edmonton AB Canada T5H 2W7

HURWITZ, CHARLES EDWIN, oil company executive; b. Kilgore, Tex., May 3, 1940; s. Hyman and Eva (Engler) H.; m. Barbara Raye Gollub, Feb. 24, 1963; children: Shawn Michael, David Alan. B.A., U. Okla., Norman, 1962. Chmn. bd., pres. Investam. Group, Inc., Houston, 1965-67, Summitt Mgmt. & Research Corp., 1967-70; chmn. bd. Summit Ins. Co. of N.Y., Houston, 1970-75; with MCO Holdings, Inc. (and predecessor), Los Angeles, 1978—, chmn. bd., chief exec. officer, 1980—; dir., 1978—; chmn. bd. Federated Reins. Corp.; chmn. bd., pres. Federated Devel. Co.; dir. MCO Resources, Inc. Co-chmn. Com. to Establish George Kozmetsky Centennial Chair in Grad. Sch. Bus., U. Tex., Austin, 1980—. Jewish. Office: 4801 Woodway St Suite 280E Houston TX 77056

HURWITZ, DAVID, physician, educator; b. Boston, Aug. 18, 1905; s. Max and Rose (Goldsmith) H.; m. Pearl Birnbaum, Sept. 9, 1928; children—R. Michael, Stephen J., Alfred L., Julie B. (Mrs. Michael Seelig). B.S. cum laude, Harvard, 1925, M.D., 1929. Diplomate: Am. Bd. Internal Medicine. Intern Boston City Hosp., 1929-31; resident U. Chgo. Clinics, 1931; practice medicine, specializing in internal medicine, Cambridge, Mass., 1934—; chief Diabetes Clinic, Boston City Hosp., 1950-71; chief div. medicine Mt. Auburn Hosp., Cambridge, 1951-71, dir. med. edn., 1963-71; vis. physician Harvard Med. Service, Boston City Hosp., 1956-71; chief diabetes service Boston City Hosp., 1956—; med. dir. Polaroid Corp., 1961-70; clin. prof. medicine Harvard Med. Sch., 1967-72, mem. admissions com., 1966-67; supt. Barnstable County Hosp., 1973-75; med. dir. Middlesex County Hosp., Waltham, Mass., 1978—; Mem. Recess Commn. To Study Establishment of Med. and Dental Sch., U. Mass., 1952-55. Author papers on diabetes. Mem. AMA, Mass., Middlesex South Dist. med. socs., Am. Diabetes Assn., New Eng. Diabetes Assn. (past pres.). Club: Aesculopian. Address: 5 Hedge Ln Falmouth MA 02540

HURWITZ, HENRY, JR., physicist; b. N.Y.C., Dec. 25, 1918; s. Henry and Ruth (Sapinsky) H.; m. Jean Klein, 1944 (div.); 1 son, Barry I.; m. Alma Rosenbaum, Apr. 15, 1951; children: Robin Elaine, Julia Lea, Wayne Mark. A.B., Cornell U., 1938; M.A., Harvard, 1939, Ph.D., 1941. Instr. physics Cornell U., 1941-44; research assoc. Los Alamos Sci. Lab., 1944-46, Knolls Atomic Power Lab. Gen. Electric Co., 1946-56; cons. physicist charge ANARPA, 1956; mgr. nucleonics and radiation sect. Research Lab., 1957-68; mgr. theory and systems br. Research and Devel. Center, 1968-72, physicist corporate research and devel., 1972—. Recipient AEC Ernest Orlando Lawrence award, 1961, Coolidge fellowship award Gen. Electric Corp. research and devel., 1975. Fellow Am. Phys. Soc., Am. Nuclear Soc. (chmn. Northeastern N.Y. sect. 1974-75), AAAS, N.Y. Acad. Scis.; sr. mem. IEEE; mem. Phi Beta Kappa, Sigma Xi, Tau Beta Pi. Office: Corporate Research and Devel Gen Electric Co PO Box 43 Schenectady NY 12301

HURWITZ, LAWRENCE NEAL, retail company executive, consultant; b. Austin, Tex., Mar. 21, 1939; s. John and Sarah Ruth (Blumenthal) H.; m. Kathleen O'Day, Feb. 1977; 1 dau., Kimberlee Colleen. Student, U. Tex., 1957-59; M.B.A. with distinction, Harvard, 1961. With research dept. Harvard, 1961-62; asst. to v.p. Atlantic Research Corp., 1962-65; comptroller TelAutograph Corp., 1965; dir. Gen. Artists Corp., 1965-69; pres. Sprayregen & Co., N.Y.C., 1969—; chmn. Country Junction, Inc., 1969—; vice chmn., mem. exec. com. Empire Life Ins. Co. Am.; dir., mem. exec. com. Old Town Corp., Stratton Group Ltd., Sayre & Fisher Co., Tech. Tape, Inc., DFI Communications Inc., Columbia Gen. Corp., Cal. Data Systems Corp.; dir. Indsl. Electronic Hardware Corp., Bloomfield Bldg. Industries, Inc., Apollo Industries, Inc., Aberdeen Petroleum Corp., Investors Book Club, Inc., Ling Fund, Am. Land Co., ific Nutrient & Chem. Corp., N. Lake Corp., Dataromen, Inc., Merada Industries, Inc., AK Electric Corp., Aerocon, Inc., Hallmark Communications, Inc., Detroit Gray Iron & Steel Foundries, Inc., Financial Tech., Inc., Wid's Films & Film Folks, Investors Preferred Life Ins. Co., Langdon Group, Inc., Essex Systems Corp., Chelsea Nat. Bank, Newport Chem. Industries, Inc. Contbr.: How to Invest in Letter Stock, 1970, Spin-Offs and Shells, 1971. Home: 4800 Ridge Oak Dr Austin TX 78731 Office: 412 Congress Ave Austin TX 78701

HUSA, KAREL, composer, condr., educator; b. Prague, Czechoslovakia, Aug. 7, 1921; came to U.S., 1954, naturalized, 1959; s. Karel and Bozena (Dongresova) H.; m. Simone Perault, Feb. 2, 1952; children—Catherine, Annette, Elizabeth, Caroline. Diploma summa cum laude, Conservatory and Acad. Music, Prague, 1945, 47; grad., Conservatoire de Paris, France, 1948; license for conducting, École Normale de Paris, 1947; D.Mus., Coe Coll., 1976. Condr. Prague Orch., 1945-46; guest condr. orchs. in, Hamburg, Brussels, Paris, Zurich, Suisse Romande, London, Manchester, Stockholm, Cin., Buffalo, N.Y.C., Boston, Rochester, N.Y., Balt., Syracuse, N.Y.; faculty Cornell U., Ithaca, N.Y., 1954—, prof. music, 1954—, dir. univ. symphony and chamber orchs., 1972—, Kappa Alpha prof. in music. Composer: Symphony, 1953, Fantasies for Orchestra, 1957, Divertimento for Brass, 1959, Poem for Viola and Orchestra, 1959, Elegy and Rondeau for Saxophone and Orchestra, 1961, Mosaiques for Orchestra, 1961, Fresque for Orchestra, rev, 1964, Sonatina for Piano, 1943, Sonatina Violin and Piano, 1945, Sonata for Piano, 1949, Evocations of Slovakia for Clarinet, Viola and Cello, 1951, Eight Duets for Piano, 1955, Twelve Moravian Songs, 1956, Poem for Viola and Piano, 1962, Serenade for Woodwind Quintet and Orchestra, 1963, Concerto for Brass Quintet and Orch, 1965, Two Preludes; flute, clarinet, bassoon, 1966, Music for Percussion, 1966, Concerto; alto saxophone, concert band, 1967, String Quartet No. 3, 1968 (Pulitzer prize 1969), Music for Prague; for Band, 1968, for Orch., 1969, Apotheosis of this Earth for Winds, 1970, for Orch. and Chorus, 1971, Concerto for Percussion and Winds, 1971, Two Sonnets from Michelangelo for Orch, 1971, Concerto for Trumphet and Wind Orch, 1973, Apotheosis of this Earth for Chorus and Orch, 1973, Sonata for Violin and Piano, 1972-73, The Steadfast Tin Soldier; for narrator and orch., 1974, Sonata for Piano, No. 2, 1975, Monodrama, ballet for orch, 1975, An American Te Deum; for mixed chorus, baritone solo, band and organ, 1976, for orch., 1978, also others, commns. from, UNESCO, Koussevitsky Found., Nat. Endowment for Arts, Friends of Music at Cornell, Fine Arts Found. Chgo., Butler U., Washington Music Soc., Coe Coll., also others.; Editor: French Barok Music: Reconstructions of old French Barok works by Lully and Delalande, 1961-68. Recipient prize Prague Acad. Arts, 1948, French Govt. award, 1946, 47, L. Boulanger award, 1952, Pulitzer prize in music, 1969; Guggenheim fellow, 1964-65. Life fellow Internat. Inst. Arts and Letters; mem. Am. Music Center (Yaddo fellow), Internat. Soc. Contemporary Music, French Soc. Composers, Am. Fedn. Musicians, Belgian Royal Acad. Arts and Scis. (asso.), Kappa Gamma Psi (hon.), Kappa Kappa Psi (hon.), Delta Omicron (hon.). Home: 333 The Parkway Ithaca NY 14850 *As long as there will be museums, concerts, orchestras, libraries, our works will be measured against the masterpieces of the past. For this reason, the search for technical perfection must continue even today, in addition to new ideas and contents. One cannot exist without the other.*

HUSAIN, TAQDIR, mathematics educator; b. Matiamau, India, July 16, 1929; emigrated to Can., 1961, naturalized, 1966; s. Abdul Razzaq and Mashooqa (Beg) Ali; m. Martha Tempelhof, Mar. 30, 1959; children: Asra, Ahmad, Masud. B.A., Muslim U., Aligarh, India, 1950, M.A., 1952; Ph.D., Syracuse U., 1960. Lectr. Muslim U., 1952-53, Forman Christian Coll., Lahore, Pakistan, 1955-57; instr. Syracuse (N.Y.) U., 1957-61; asst. prof. Ottawa (Ont., Can.) U., 1961-64; asso. prof. McMaster U., Hamilton, Ont., 1964-67, prof., chmn. dept. math., 1967—, chmn. dept. mathematical scis., 1979—. Author: Open Mapping and Closed Graph Theorems in Topological Vector Spaces, 1965, Introduction to Topological Groups, 1966, Topology and Maps, 1977, Barrelledness in Topological and Ordered Vector Spaces, 1978, Multiplicative Functionals on Topological Algebras, 1983; assoc. editor: Can. Jour. Math, 1979—; contbr. articles to profl. jours. Recipient Internat. prize Friedric Vieweg und Sohn Pub. House, Braunschweig, West Germany, 1963; Tata research fellow Tata Inst., Bombay, India, 1953-55. Mem. Am. Math. Assn., Am. Math. Soc., Canadian Math. Soc. (council 1969—).

HUSBY, DONALD EVANS, engineering company executive; b. Mpls., Nov. 30, 1927; s. Olaf and Elsie Louise (Hagen) H.; m. Beverly June Tilbury, Sept. 24, 1949. B.S., S.D. State U., 1952. Student engr., jr. asst., sr. engr., mgr. new products Westinghouse Electric Corp., Cleve., 1952-72; engring. mgr., v.p. engring. lighting div. Harvey Hubbell, Inc., Christiansburg, Va., 1972-76; pres. Elliptipar Inc., West Haven, Conn., 1976-78; fellow engr., mgr. engring. sect. Westinghouse Electric Corp., Vicksburg, Miss., 1978-82; engring. mgr. new products devel copper industries Crouse-Hinds LTG Products div Westinghouse Electric Corp, Vicksburg, Miss., 1982—; mem. indsl. adv. counsel Underwriters Labs. Contbr. articles to profl. jours. Served with USNR, 1945-47. Fellow Illuminating Engrs. Soc. (chmn., sec., dir.); mem. Internat. Municipal Signal Assn., Soc. Plastics Engrs., Nat. Elec. Mfrs. Assn., Am. Nat. Standards Inst., Am. Soc. Quality Control, Miss. Engring. Soc., D.C. Soc. Profl. Engrs., Designers Lighting Forum., Mensa Internat. Mem. Christian Ch. Club: Toastmasters Internat. Patentee in field. Home: 406 Elmwood Dr Vicksburg MS 39180 Office: PO Box 824 Vicksburg MS 39180

HUSHING, WILLIAM COLLINS, corp. exec.; b. St. Louis, Jan. 22, 1918; s. Sumner Kinney and Anne (Sandner) H.; m. Mary Hardy, Jan. 10, 1946; children—Druscilla, Rebecca Ann. B.S. in Elec. Engring, U.S. Naval Acad., 1939; M.S. in Naval Constrn. and Engring, Mass. Inst. Tech., 1944; student, Harvard Bus. Sch., 1962; D.Sc. (hon.), U. N.H., 1968. Commd. ensign U.S. Navy, 1939, advanced through grades to rear adm., 1967; aide, spl. asst. to chief (Bur. Ships), 1955-57; indsl. engr., comptroller U.S. Naval Shipyard, Mare Island, Calif., 1957-60; supr. shipbldg. U.S. Navy, Electric Boat div. Gen. Dynamics Corp., Groton, Conn., 1960-64; comdr. Naval Shipyard, Portsmouth, N.H., 1964-69; retired, 1969; exec. v.p. Bath Iron Works, 1969-70; pres. Forster Mfg. Co., Inc., 1970-72; mgmt. cons. Kensington Mgmt. Cons., Inc., Stamford, Conn., 1972-78; pres. Maine Multi-Power, Inc., Bath, 1979—. Decorated Navy Commendation medal, Legion of Merit with Star. Mem. Am. Soc. Naval Engrs., Soc. Naval Architects. Lutheran. Home: 1111 Washington St Bath ME 04530 Office: 37 Bowery St Bath ME 04530

HUSICK, CHARLES BERNARD, aircraft manufacturing executive; b. Bklyn., Jan. 10, 1933; s. Leo and Bess (Kaplan) H.; m. Babette A. Kraus, June 10, 1956; children: Lawrence, Bradley. B.E.E., Poly. Inst. Bklyn., 1954. Applications engr. Fischer & Porter Co., Hatboro, Pa., 1956-57; v.p. engring. Computer Systems, Inc., Monmouth, N.J., 1957-62; program mgr. Gemini Spacecraft, Sarasota, Fla., 1962-67; v.p., gen. mgr. Picker X-Ray Corp., Cleve., 1967-71; pres. Narco Avionics, Ft. Washington, Pa., 1971-77; sr. v.p. Cessna Aircraft Co., Wichita, Kans., 1977—. Served to lt. U.S. Army, 1954-56. Mem. Gen. Aviation Mfrs. Assn. (chmn.), Airplane Owners and Pilots Assn. Home: 109 Longford Wichita KS 67206 Office: PO Box 1521 Wichita KS 67201

HUSKEY, HARRY DOUGLAS, information and computer science educator; b. Whittier, N.C., Jan. 19, 1916; s. Cornelius and Myrtle (Cunningham) H.; m. Velma Elizabeth Roeth, Jan. 2, 1939; children: Carolyn, Roxanne, Harry Douglas, Linda. B.S., U. Idaho, 1937; student, Ohio U., 1937-38; M.A., Ohio State U., 1940, Ph.D., 1943. Temp. prin. sci. officer Nat. Phys. Labs., Eng., 1947; head machine devel. lab. Nat. Bur. Standards, 1948; asst. dir. Inst. Numerical Analysis, 1948-54; asso. dir. computation lab. Wayne U., Detroit, 1952-53; asso. prof. U. Calif. at Berkeley, 1954-58, prof., 1958-68, vice chmn. elec. engring., 1965-66; prof. info. and computer sci. U. Calif. at Santa Cruz, 1968—; dir. Computer Center, 1968-77, chmn. bd. info. sci., 1976-79, 82-83; vis. prof. Indian Inst. Tech., Kanpur; (Indo-Am. program), 1963-64, 71, Delhi U., 1971; cons. computer div. Bendix, 1954-63; vis. prof. M.I.T., 1966; mem. computer sci. panel NSF, Naval Research Adv. Com.; cons. on computers for developing countries UN, 1969-71; chmn. com. to advise Brazil on computer sci. edn. Nat. Acad. Sci., 1970-72; project coordinator UNESCO/Burma contract, 1973-79. Co-editor: Computer Handbook, 1962. Recipient Disting. Alumni award Idaho State U., 1978, Pioneer award IEEE Computer Soc., 1982; U.S. sr.scientist awardee Fulbright-Alexander von Humboldt Found., Mathematisches Institut der Tech. U. Munich, 1974-75. Fellow AAAS, IEEE (editorial bd., editor-in-chief computer group 1965-71), Brit. Computer Soc.; mem. Am. Math. Soc., Math. Assn. Am., Assn. Computing Machinery (pres. 1960-62), Am. Fedn. Info. Processing Socs. (governing bd. 1961-63), Sigma Xi. Designed SWAC computer, Bendix G-15 and G-20 computers. Home: 656 High St Santa Cruz CA 95060

HUSKINS, WILLIAM EVERETT, JR., airlines executive; b. Mpls., Feb. 10, 1925; s. William Everett and Bertha (Haukebo) H.; m. Shirley Eloise Larson, June 24, 1950; children: Deborah Lavonne, William Charles. B.Aero. Engring., U. Minn., 1945. Registered profl. engr., Minn. With N.W. Airlines, Inc., 1946-80; ops. mgr. Orient region, Tokyo, Japan, 1955-59, asst. to pres., 1959-61, v.p., 1961-67, v.p. communications and computer services, 1967-73, v.p. maintenance and engring., 1973-80; sr. v.p. engring. and maintenance Braniff Airways, Inc., 1980-81, exec. v.p. ops., 1981-83; sr. v.p. ops. services Eastern Airlines, 1983—. Mem. Beta Theta Pi, Tau Omega. Lodges: Masons; Order Eastern Star. Home: 6959 Sharpecroft Ct Miami Lakes FL 33148 Office: Eastern Airlines Inc Miami International Airport FL 33148

HUSKY, FERLIN, singer; b. Flat River, Mo., Dec. 3, 1927. WIth Sta.-KXLW, St. Louis; with Smiley Burnette; disc jockey, Bakersfield, Calif., 1949. Appearances include, Hometown Jamboree, Los Angeles, Grand Ole Opry, Sta.-WSM, Nashville; TV appearances include, Kraft TV Theatre, Ed Sullivan Show, Steven Allen Show, Rosemary Clooney Show, Alan Freed Show, Jubilee U.S.A., Tonight Show, Mike Douglas Show; appeared in: films Las Vegas Hillbillies; recordings for, Capitol Records, Four Star Records; songs recorded include: Country Music is Here to Stay; albums include: Best, Greatest Hits. Office: Buddy Lee Assos Inc 38 Music Square E-Suite 300 Nashville TN 37203 *

HUSOVSKY, IVAN, pharmaceutical company executive; b. Budapest, Hungary, Sept. 28, 1927; came to U.S., 1949, naturalized, 1954; s. Lewis and Gabriella (D'Elhoungne) H.; m. Joanna Lyon Parks, Sept. 29, 1956; children—Harold, Peter. A.B., U. Portland, Oreg., 1952; M.A., Notre Dame U., 1953; LL.B., Yale U., 1956. Bar: Conn. bar 1956, N.Y. State bar 1961. With firm Wiggin & Dana, New Haven, 1956-59; atty. Vick Chem. Co., N.Y.C., 1959-62; European counsel Richardson-MerrellInc., Paris, 1962-66, internat. counsel, N.Y.C., 1966-67; v.p. European area dir. Merrell Internat., N.Y.C., 1967-73; pres., gen. mgr. Merrell-Nat. Labs., Cin., 1973-80; sr. v.p., dir. Richardson-Vicks Inc., Wilton, Conn., 1981—; instr. U. Portland, 1952. Vice chmn. Gov. Conn.'s Com. for Hungarian Refugees, 1957; bd. dirs. Internat. House, Yale U., 1957-59. Mem. Am. Bar Assn., Pharm. Mfrs. Assn., Greater Cin. C. of C. (trustee 1979-80). Republican. Roman Catholic. Clubs: New Haven Lawn; Bankers, Yale, Wilton Riding (Cin.). Home: 56 Keelers' Ridge Rd Wilton CT 06897 Office: 10 Westport Rd Wilton CT 06897

HUSS, JACK LEWIS, manufacturing company executive; b. Muncie, Ind., June 16, 1931; s. Robert C. H. and Lois P. (Huss); m. Betty L. Godfrey, Oct. 14, 1950; children: Diane, Brian, Steven. Student, Tri-State Coll., 1949-51. Vice pres., div. gen. mgr. Crane Co., N.Y.C., 1951-75; pres. Hammond Valve Corp., (Ind.), 1975-78, ITT Grinnell Valve Co., Providence, 1978—. Mem. Valve Mfrs. Assn. (dir. Washington 1981-83). Republican. Methodist. Office: ITT Grinnell Valve Co Inc 260 W Exchange St Providence RI 02901

HUSSAR, DANIEL ALEXANDER, coll. dean; b. Phila., Feb. 12, 1941; s. Alexander and Anna (Nagel) H.; m. Suzanne Rose Fix, Aug. 26, 1967; children—Eric Fix, Christopher Nagel. B.S. in Pharmacy, Phila. Coll. Pharmacy and Sci., 1962, M.S., 1964, Ph.D., 1967. Mem. faculty Phila. Coll. Pharmacy and Sci., 1966—, prof. pharmacy, 1971—, dir. dept., 1971-75, Remington prof., dean faculty, 1975—; Fellow Am. Found. Pharm. Edn., 1962-64, NSF, 1964-66. Author articles, chpts. in books. Mem. Am. Pharm. Assn. (trustee 1977-80), Pa. Pharm. Assn. (pres. 1975-76), Am. Soc. Hosp. Pharmacists, Am. Coll. Apothecaries, Drug Info. Assn. (pres. 1977-78). Reformed Episcopalian. Home: 1 Boulder Creek Ln Newtown Square PA 19073 Office: Phila Coll Pharmacy and Sci 43d St and Kingsessing Mall Philadelphia PA 19104

HUSSEY, KEITH MORGAN, educator; b. Rock Island, Ill., Dec. 2, 1908; s. Ernest Samuel and Diana Hill (Stow) H.; m. Lillian Alberta Pepping, Dec. 26, 1937; children—Michael Keith, Patricia Ann. A.B., Augustana Coll., 1936; M.S., La. State U., 1939, Ph.D., 1940. Instr. U. Houston, 1940-42; asst. prof., asso. prof. Okla. U., 1945-49; faculty Iowa State U., Ames, 1949—, prof. geology, 1954-79, prof. emeritus, 1979—, head dept., 1961-74; spl. research micropaleontology of Gulf Coast (geomorphology and stratigraphy of), Colo., Wyo., Iowa, No. Alaska, N.Mex.; vis. geoscientist lectr. Am. Geol Inst., 1960-62; dir. Earth Sci. Tchr. Tng. Program, 1966-73. Asso. author: Handbook of Mathematical Calculations; Co-editor: Dictionary of Geological Terms, 1961; Contbr. articles to profl. jours. Served with USAAF, World War II. Recipient Outstanding Achievement award Augustana Coll., 1975; Faculty citation Iowa State U., 1978. Fellow Geol. Soc. Am., Iowa Acad. Sci., Arctic Inst. N.Am.; mem. Geol. Soc. Iowa (pres. 1967-68), Augustana Coll. Alumni (pres. 1972-73, dir.), Am. Assn. Petroleum Geologists (regional rep. 1967-69), Arctic Inst. N.Am., A.A.A.S., A.A.U.P., Wyo. Geol. Assn., Nat. Assn. Geology Tchrs. (pres. central sect. 1958), Sigma Xi, Phi Kappa Phi (pres. 1973-74). Home: 1910 Meadowlane Ave Ames IA 50010

HUSSEY, RUTH, actress; b. Providence, Oct. 30; d. George and Julia (Corbett) H.; m. C. Robert Longenecker, 1942; children: George R., John W., Mary Elizabeth. Ph.B., Brown U., D.F.A. (hon.), 1950; student, U. Mich. Appeared with Providence Players, 1933-35; Appeared with summer stock in Mich., 1934-35; on Broadway in State of the Union, 1945; motion pictures Madame X, 1937; The Women, 1939, Susan and God, 1940, The Philadelphia Story, 1940, H. M. Pulham, Esq., 1941, I Jane Doe, 1947, The Great Gatsby, 1948, Flight Command, 1940, The Uninvited, 1943, Louisa, 1950, Mr. Music, Woman of the North Country, Stars and Stripes Forever, The Lady Wants Mink, 1952, The Facts of Life, 1960, also, Joyful Hour; on Broadway in: Goodbye My Fancy, 1949; Appeared with also in TV films; star: TV shows Playrights and The Women; guest star series: Marcus Welby, 1971; guest star: series Jimmy Stewart Show, 1971, New Perry Mason Show, 1973, Robert Young Spl., 1973; co-star with: Facts of Life; motion picture, 1960. Recipient Acad. award nomination for Best Supporting Actress.

HUSSEY, WARD MACLEAN, government official, lawyer; b. Providence, Mar. 13, 1920; s. Charles Ward and Agnes (Shaw) H.; children—Thomas Ward, Carolyn Anne, Wendy Ellen. A.B., Harvard, 1940, LL.B., 1946; M.A., Columbia, 1944. Bar: D.C. bar. With Office of Legis. Counsel, U.S. Ho. of Reps., 79th to 98th Congresses, Washington, 1946—, dep. legis. counsel, 1970-72, legis. counsel, 1972—. Served with USNR, 1942-46. Home: 312 Princeton Blvd Alexandria VA 22314 Office: 136 Cannon House Office Bldg Washington DC 20515

HUSSEY, WILLIAM BERTRAND, retired foreign service officer; b. Bellingham, Wash., Oct. 23, 1915; s. Bertrand Brokaw and Ruth (Axtell) H.; m. Fredricka Bone, Dec. 31, 1940 (div. 1957); children: Christina, Pamela, Eva, William Bertrand, Peter; m. Piyachart Bunnag, May 20, 1959. B.S., Boston U., 1938; postgrad., UCLA, 1939-40, Naval War Coll., 1953-54. Asst. housing mgmt. supr. U.S. Housing Authority, 1941-42; chmn. London (Eng.) Liaison Group, also State Dept. rep., 1948-52; spl. State Dept. rep., Rome, 1949, Paris, 1950; chmn. regional conf., Dhahran, Saudi Arabia, 1949, chief civil-mil. relations sect., Munich, Germany, 1952-53, adminstrv. officer, Frankfurt, Germany, 1953-55, attache, Rangoon, Burma, 1955-56, consul, Chiengmai, Thailand, 1957-59; acting dep. chief plans and devel. staff Bur. Ednl. and Cultural Affairs, Dept. State, 1959-60, dep. chief cultural presentations div., 1960-61; mem. del. regional confs. in, Beirut, Lebanon and Kampala, Uganda, 1960; group leader Nat. Strategy Seminar, Asilomar, Calif., 1960; counselor of embassy, Lome, Republic of Togo, 1961-65, Blantyre, Malawi, 1965-66; chargé d'affaires Am. embassy, Maseru, Lesotho, 1966-67, Port Louis, Mauritius, 1967-68; UN rep., Western Pacific, Apia, Western Samoa, 1969-74, fgn. affairs cons., 1974—; del. UN Law of Sea Conf., 1975-80. Served with U.S. Mcht. Marine, 1930-33; served to lt. comdr. USN, 1942-48; ETO; PTO; capt. Res. Recipient Superior Service award Sec. of State, 1968. Address: 2576 Benedict Canyon Dr Beverly Hills CA 90210 *We must learn from mistakes. The measure is less the occasional stumble than how quickly and sharply the common cadence of our heritage is restored.*

HUSTED, JOHN EDWIN, geologist, educator; b. Lucasville, Ohio, Oct. 12, 1915; s. Edward Winthrop and Mary (Cary) H.; m. Kathryn Fay Stewart, June 18, 1942; children: Stewart Winthrop, Mary Husted

Hewett. B.S., Hampden-Sydney Coll., 1939; student, Va. Poly. Inst., summers 1938-40; M.A., U. Va., 1942; Ph.D., Fla. State U., 1970. Tchr. sci. Crewe (Va.) High Sch., 1938-40; chemist, geologist U.S. Geol. Survey, Washington, 1942-45; plant chemist Consol. Feldspar Corp., Erwin, Tenn., 1945-46; instr. geology and chemistry Washington and Lee U., 1946-48; geologist Humble Oil & Refining Co., Midland, Tex., 1948-49; chmn. geology dept. Trinity U., 1949-51; resident geologist Va. Iron, Coal & Coke Co., Roanoke, 1951-55; prin. geologist Batelle Meml. Inst., 1955-57; research scientist Ga. Inst. Tech., 1958-63, head mineral engring. group, 1960-66, asso. prof. geology, 1963-67, head mineral engring. br., 1966-72, research prof. geology, 1967-71, prof. geology, 1971-74; prof. mineral engring. Sch. Chem. Engring., 1974—, chmn. multidisciplinary com. for mineral engring., 1977—; acting dir. Ga. Mining and Mineral Resource Inst. (Coll. Engring.), 1978-80, dir., 1980—; mem. ad hoc list of visitors Accreditation and Engring. Council for Profl. Devel., 1968-70, Accreditation Bd. for Engring. and Tech., 1980-82; dep. dir. designate-minerals, CD Exec. Res. U.S. Dept. Interior, Emergency Minerals Adminstrn., Southeastern U.S., 1969-72; dir. designate Miscellaneous Non-Metals div., 1972—. Mem. editorial adv. bd., author: indsl. minerals sect. Mining Engring. Handbook, 1973; editorial bd. 4th and 5th edits.: Indsl. Minerals and Rocks. NSF Sci. Faculty fellow, 1966-67. Fellow Geol. Soc. Am.; mem. AIME (accreditation com. bd. edn. 1977—), Ga. Geol. Soc. (council 1961-62), Sigma Xi. Home: 2255 Brianwood Ct Decatur GA 30033 Office: Sch Chem Engring Ga Inst Tech Atlanta GA 30332 *Any successes that I have achieved have been from turning my life over to the Lord and seeking His guidance.*

HUSTED, RALPH WALDO, former utility executive; b. Martinsville, Ill., Apr. 2, 1911; s. Seth and Mary (Church) H.; m. Margaret Walden, Mar. 18, 1937; children: Catherine (Mrs. William R. Burleigh), David W. LL.B., Benjamin Harrison Law Sch., 1936. Bar: Ind. 1935. With Indpls. Power & Light Co., 1929—, sec., counsel, 1957-64, v.p. legal, sec., 1964-73, exec. v.p. adminstrn., 1973-74, pres., chief exec. officer, 1974-75, chmn. bd., chief exec. officer, 1975-76; dir. Security Savs. Assn., Indpls. Trustee Intercollegiate Studies Inst., Inc., Bryn Mawr, Pa., Liberty Fund, Indpls. Mem. Ind., Indpls., Am. bar assns. Home: 6230 Breamore Rd Indianapolis IN 46220 Office: 25 Monument Circle Indianapolis IN 46206

HUSTING, PETER MARDEN, advertising agency executive; b. Bronxville, N.Y., Mar. 28, 1935; s. Charles Ottomar and Jane Alice (Marden) H.; m. Carolyn Riddle, Mar. 26, 1960; children: Jennifer, Gretchen, Charles Ottomar. B.S., U. Wis., 1957; grad., Advanced Mgmt. Program, Harvard U., 1974. Sales rep. Crown Zellerbach Corp., 1958-59; with Leo Burnett Co., Chgo., 1959—, group v.p., 1979-82, exec. v.p., 1982—, also dir. Trustee Shedd Aquarium Soc., Chgo., 1980; bd. dirs. Chgo. Better Govt. Assn., 1976, Leadership Council Met. Open Communities, Chgo., 1980, Lyric Opera Guild, Chgo., 1971-78, Chgo. Forum, 1969-76. Served with AUS, 1958. Republican. Clubs: Indian Hill (Winnetka) (gov. 1976-79); Univ., Mid-Am. (Chgo.); Queen City (Cin.). Office: Leo Burnett Co Prudential Plaza Suite 1200 Chicago IL 60601

HUSTLER, JOHN GEORGE, newspaper financial executive; b. Toronto, Ont., Can., Apr. 15, 1945; s. Harry H. and Patricia M. (Kahn) H.; m. Sharon M. Crosby, June 18, 1983; 1 son, Damon. B.A., U. Western Ont., 1969. Controller Barrymore Carpet, Inc., Toronto, Ont., Can., 1976-80, The Globe and Mail, Toronto, 1980—. Home: 137A Wychcrest Ave Toronto ON Canada M6G 3Y3 Office: The Globe and Mail 444 Front St W Toronto ON Canada M5V 259

HUSTON, BEATRICE LOUISE, oil and gas co. exec.; b. Grantsburg, Wis., Dec. 26, 1932; d. Elvin and Fay Cynthia (Sybrant) H.; m. Gerald W. Huston, June 30, 1951 (dec.); 1 dau., Linda Sandell. Student, Minn. Sch. Bus., U. Minn. With Northwest Bus. Service, Mpls., 1950-51, Progressive Machine Co., Huntington Park, Calif., 1951-52; v.p. and corp. sec. Apache Corp., Mpls., 1954—. Bd. dirs. Mpls. Girls Clubs, Ebenezer Soc., Inc. Mem. Am. Soc. Corp. Secs., Minn. Women's Econ. Roundtable. Lutheran. Clubs: Zonta Internat., Woman's, Mpls. Athletic (Mpls.). Home: 8264 Xerxes Ave S Bloomington MN 55431 Office: 1700 Foshay Tower Minneapolis MN 55402

HUSTON, HARRIS HYDE, legal consultant; b. Pickaway County, Ohio, July 20, 1907; s. Edwin Minor and Lulu Beatrice (Hyde) H.; m. Hazel Frances Rollins, Dec. 18, 1948; children: Robert Hyde, Linda Rollins (Mrs. Glenn Cartaxo). A.B., Dartmouth Coll., 1929; LL.B., U. Dayton, 1933. Bar: Ohio 1933, D.C. 1970, U.S. Supreme Ct. Asso. Mattern & Sheridan (later Sheridan & Jenkins); later partner Jenkins & Huston, Dayton, Ohio, 1933-40; spl. agt. FBI, 1941-46; asso. dir. surveys and investigations, staff appropriations com. U.S. Ho. of Reps., 1947-48, dir. surveys and investigations, staff appropriations com., 1953-57; dir. tng. Office Spl. Investigations, insp. gen. Dept. Air Force, 1949- 52; spl. asst. to under-sec. for adminstrn. Dept. State, 1953, dep. adminstr. bur. security and consular affairs, 1957-60, acting adminstr., 1961; Am. consul gen., Curacao, Netherlands Antilles, 1962-69, legal cons., 1969—. Decorated comdr. Order Orange Nassau, Netherlands). Mem. Harvard Assos. Police Sci., Chi Phi. Clubs: Belle Haven Country, ABC (Alexandria, Va.); Nat. Aviation (Washington). Address: 619 29th Rd S Arlington VA 22202

HUSTON, JAMES ALVIN, historian, dean; b. Fairmount, Ind., Mar. 24, 1918; s. Alva Merrill and Nettie (Caskey) H.; m. Florence Ethel Webb, Dec. 29, 1946 (dec.); children: Nita Diane Huston Ultee James Webb.; m. Anne Clark Marshall, June 5, 1983. A.B. with honors, Ind. U., 1939, A.M., 1940; Ph.D., N.Y. U., 1947; postgrad, Oxford (Eng.) U., 1945, U. Fribourg, Switzerland, 1951. Mem. faculty Purdue U., 1946-72, prof. history, 1960-72; dean coll. Lynchburg (Va.) Coll., 1972—; Ernest J. King prof. maritime history Naval War Coll., 1959-60; vis. prof. fgn. affairs Nat. War Coll., 1966-67, 71-72; logistician U.S. Army Logistics Mgmt. Center, 1970; cons. Office Chief Mil. History, Dept. Army, 1948, 50. Author: Combat History of the 134th Infantry, 1948, Biography of a Battalion, 1950, Across the Face of France, 1963, 83, The Sinews of War, 1966, Out of the Blue: U.S. Army Airborne Operations in World War II, 1972, reprinted, 1982, One for All: The U.S. and International Logistics Through the Formative Period of NATO, 1983; Contbr. articles and revs. to profl. jours. Mem. exec. bd. Harrison Trails council Boy Scouts Am., 1965-71; pres. congregation Fed. Ch. West Lafayette, 1969-70; mem. bd. higher edn. Disciples of Christ, 1970-73. Served to capt. inf. AUS, 1942-46; ETO; to maj., 1951-53; col. Res. Decorated Bronze Star with oak leaf cluster; Penfield fellow N.Y. U., 1940-42; NATO fellow, 1964, 66. Mem. Am., So. hist. assns., Orgn. Am. Historians, Ind. Acad. Social Scis. (pres. 1966-67), Internat. Inst. Strategic Studies, Inst. World Affairs, Internat. Studies Assn., AAUP (pres. Purdue chpt. 1960-61), Lafayette Geog. Soc. (pres. 1958-59), Blue Key, Phi Beta Kappa (pres. Purdue chpt. 1970-71), Phi Delta Kappa, Omicron Delta Kappa, Alpha Phi Omega, Phi Eta Sigma, Acacia. Lodge: Rotary (pres. Lynchburg 1981-82). Home: 300 Langhorne Ln Lynchburg VA 24501

HUSTON, JOHN, writer, motion picture director; b. Nevada, Mo., Aug. 5, 1906; s. Walter and Rhea (Gore) H.; m. Evelyn Keyes, July 23, 1946; m. Enrica Soma, 1949 (dec. 1969); children: Walter Anthony, Anjelica; m. Celeste Shane, 1972 (div. 1975). L.H.D. (hon.), Monmouth Coll., West Long Branch, N.J., 1981. AT various times during early career became reporter, editor to picture mag.; artist (painter); writer; actor; became writer, Warner Bros. Studios, 1938; collaborator: The Amazing Dr. Clitterhouse, 1938, Juarez, 1939, Dr. Ehrlich's Magic Bullet, 1940, High Sierra, also Sergeant York, 1941; dir.: The Maltese Falcon, 1941, In This Our Life, 1942, Across the Pacific, 1942; writer and collaborator in: prodn. of screen play Three Strangers, 1945; dir.: Key Largo, 1948, The Treasure of Sierra Madre, 1949 (awards for dir., writer Acad. Motion Picture Arts and Sciences, also, New York Film Critics award, for best direction of year), Heaven Knows, Mr. Allison, Roots of Heaven, The Unforgiven, The Barbarian and the Geisha, The Misfits, Freud, The List of Adrian Messenger, Night of the Iguana, The Bible, Reflections in a Golden Eye, Casino Royale, Sinful Davey, A Walk with Love and Death, The Kremlin Letter, Fat City; Broadway play A Passenger to Bali, 1939, (collaborated in writing) In Time To Come (received N.Y. Drama Critics Circle award); Broadway prodn. of Jean Paul Sarte's play No Exit, 1945; opera The Mines of Sulphur, La Scala, 1966; producer-dir.: We Were Strangers, Horizon Films, which founded with S.P. Eagle; dir.: A Walk With Love and Death, 1969, The Kremlin Letter, 1970, Fat City, 1972, The Life and Times of Judge Roy Bean, 1972, The McIntosh Man, The Man Who Would Be King, 1975, Wise Blood, 1979, Escape to Victory, 1980, Annie, 1981; actor in: Battle for the Planet of the Apes, 1973, Chinatown, 1974, The Wind and the Lion, 1975, Hollywood on Trial, 1977, Winterkills, 1977; writer, dir., Metro-Goldwyn-Mayer, 1949—; assigned filming: World War II documentaries The Battle of San Pietro (Recipient One World award 1949, Screen Dirs. Guild award for the Asphalt Jungle 1950, named best dir. of the year for Moby Dick, New York Film Critics 1956, recipient award Nat. Bd. Rev. of Motion Pictures 1956, Silver Laurel award Screen Writers Guild 1963, Silver Dirs. Guild award for Night of the Iguana 1964, Martin Buber award, David di Donatello award for The Bible 1966, Motion Pictures Exhibitors' Internat. Laurel award for Reflections in a Golden Eye 1968); Author: autobiography John Huston—An Open Book, 1980. Served with U.S. Army, 1942-45; disch. with rank of maj. Recipient Am. Film Inst. Lifetime Achievement award, 1983. Address: care Paul Kohner Agy 9169 Sunset Blvd Los Angeles CA 90069

HUSTON, JOHN ALBERT, manufacturing company executive; b. Birmingham, Mich., May 4, 1920; s. Joseph Clark and Clara Amanda (Maynard) H.; m. Mary McClellan Barnhardt, Oct. 7, 1950; children—John A., Margaret G., James M. A.B., U. Mich., 1941, J.D., 1947. Bar: N.Y. 1948. With firm Chadbourne, Parke, Whiteside & Wolff (and predecessors), N.Y.C., 1947-59; with Sperry Gyroscope Co. (div. Sperry Corp.), N.Y.C., 1959-68, v.p. legal, 1963-68; asst. gen. counsel Sperry Corp., 1968-71, v.p. law, 1971-79, sr. v.p. law, 1979-81, sr. v.p., gen. counsel, 1981—. Trustee Devereux Found., 1974—, v.p., 1979—; bd. dirs. Charles E. Culpeper Found., 1978—, Mid. Atlantic Legal Found., 1979—, Lincoln Ctr. Inst., 1982—. Served with AUS, 1942-45. Mem. Am., Nassau County bar assns., Bar Assn. City N.Y., Phi Beta Kappa, Order of Coif. Clubs: N.Y. Athletic, N. Hempstead Country. Office: 1290 Ave of Americas New York NY 10104

HUSTON, JOHN LEWIS, educator; b. Lancaster, Ohio, Aug. 19, 1919; s. John Allen and Olive Blanche (Wilson) H.; m. Mary Margaret Lally, Sept. 12, 1964. A.B., Oberlin Coll., 1942; Ph.D., U. Calif. at Berkeley, 1946. Instr. chemistry Oreg. State U., Corvallis, 1946-49, asst. prof., 1949-52; mem. faculty Loyola U. at Chgo., 1952—, asso. prof., 1954-68, prof., 1968—; Cons. Argonne (Ill.) Nat. Lab., 1964—. Contbr. articles to profl. jours. AEC grantee, 1947-52, NSF grantee, 1953-58. Mem. Am. Chem. Soc., Phi Beta Kappa, Sigma Xi. Home: 4401 Keeney St Skokie IL 60076 Office: Dept Chemistry Loyola U Chicago IL 60626

HUSTON, JOHN WILSON, air force officer, historian; b. Pitts., Mar. 6, 1925; s. James Leslie and Kathryn Rachel (Ray) H.; m. Dorothy Winters Bampton, Aug. 27, 1960; children: Ann, John. B.A., Monmouth Coll., 1948; M.A., U. Pitts., 1950, Ph.D., 1957. Served as 1st lt. USAAF, 1943-45; advanced through grades to maj. gen. USAF Res., 1976; recalled to active duty as chief Office of Air Force History, Dept. Air Force, Washington, 1976—; lectr. history U. Pitts., 1949-56; prof. U.S. Naval Acad., Annapolis, 1956-76, chmn. dept. history, 1971-76; vis. prof. U. Rochester, 1964, Ball State U., 1965, 67, U. Md., 1969. Decorated D.S.M., D.F.C. with oak leaf cluster, Air medal with 3 oak leaf clusters, Joint Service Commendation medal, Air Force Commendation medal. Mem. Am. Hist. Assn., Orgn. Am. Historians, AAUP. Home: 115 E Lake Dr Annapolis MD 21403 Office: Hdqrs US Air Force AF/CVAH Bolling AFB Washington DC 20332

HUSTON, NORMAN EARL, nuclear engineering educator; b. Jefferson, Iowa, Jan. 24, 1919; s. Sherburn Sherwood and Helen Isadore (Briggs) H.; m. Mary Belle Felton, June 27, 1943; children—Norman Earl, Anne Marie (Mrs. Thomas Daniel Sigerstad), Susan Deane (Mrs. Alan Braddock). Student, Los Angeles City Coll., 1938-40; A.B., U. Calif. at Berkeley, 1943; Ph.D., U. So. Calif., 1952. Registered profl. engr., Wis., Calif. Physicist U. Calif. Radiation Lab., Berkeley, 1943-44; research engr., dir. dept. Atomics Internat. div. N.Am. Aviation Co., Los Angeles, 1950-65; sr. sci. adviser, asst. to v.p. Autonetics div., Anaheim, Calif., 1966; prof. nuclear engring., dir. Instrumentation Systems Center, U. Wis., Madison, 1966—; dir. Adv. Center for Med. Tech. and Systems, 1972-78; also dir. Ocean Engring. Labs., 1967-70, U. Wis.-NASA Biomed. Application Team, 1974-77; mem. subcom. of com. on interaction of engring. in biology and medicine Nat. Acad. Engring.; reviewer, cons. NSF, AID, project leader mission to Cairo, Mgmt. Lab. Instrn., 1976; project leader Egypt Sci. and Tech. Project, Nat. Research Center for AID and NSF, Cairo, 1977; UN expert on mission Singapore Inst. Standards and Indsl. Research, 1972; mem. NSF task force on instrumentation requirements to Nat. Research Centre, Egypt, 1974, NSF team mission to Cairo, Rome, workshops sci. intruments, 1975. Contbg. author: Summary of Reactor Design, 1955, Progress in Nuclear Energy, Series VI, Vol. 3, 1959; editor: Management Systems for Lab. Instrument Services, 1980; mem. editorial bd.: Jour. Internat. Measurement Confedn., 1982—; contbr. articles to profl. jours. Served to lt. (j.g.) USNR, 1944-47. Levi Strauss scholar, 1941-43. Fellow AAAS (council mem.), Instrument Soc. Am. (v.p. edn. and research 1971-72, v.p. publs. 1974-76, sec. 1977-78, pres. 1978-79), Inst. Measurement and Control; mem. Am. Nuclear Soc., Am. Soc. Engring. Edn., Am. Phys. Soc., Nat. Mgmt. Assn. (v.p. NAA Valley chpt., treas. 1958-59), Western Boys Baseball Assn. (pres. Woodland Hills 1959), Sigma Xi, Alpha Delta Sigma, Alpha Tau Omega. Club: Rotary (Madison). Patentee in field. Home: 4556 Winnequah Rd Monona WI 53716 Office: 1500 Johnson Dr Madison WI 53706

HUTCHENS, JOHN G., food company executive; b. High Point, N.C., Nov. 28, 1928; m. Jane Davis; children: John G., Julie, Jimmy, Cam. B.S., Davidson Coll., 1951; LL.B., U. N.C., 1954, J.D., 1970. Pres. Food World, Inc., Greensboro, N.C., 1974-82, chmn. bd., 1973-74, 82—; sec.-treas., dir. Westwood Devel. Co.; v.p., dir. United Roasters, Inc.; dir. Wachovia Bank & Trust Co. Mem. adv. devel. com. Salvation Army; chmn. orgn. and expansion com. Boy Scouts Am., High Point, 1965-66; mem., past dir. Guilford County Better Bus. Bur.; pres. U.S. Indsl. Council; chmn. Policy Statement Com., High Point Republican party, 1965, 6th Congl. dist., 1970-71; state chmn. Jim Gardner for Gov. Com.; mem. exec. com. Guildford County Rep. party, 1964-73; mem. state exec. com. and central com. N.C. Rep. party, 1970-74; dir. N.C. Conservation Union; N.C. fin. chmn. Citizens for Reagan, 1976-80; Southeastern fin. coordinator Regan for Pres., 1980; past deacon, treas., chmn. bd. dirs., elder Forest Hills Presbyn. Ch.; mem. Pres. Adv. Com. on Trade Negotiations, 1982—; civilian aide Sec. of Army, 1982—. Mem. Food Merchandisers Ednl. Council, Super Market Inst., Nat. Assn. Food Chains, ABA, N.C. Bar Assn., High Point Bar Assn., Winston-Salem C. of C., Greenboro C. of C., High Point Merchants Assn., High Point C. of C. (dir., past chmn. indsl. devel. com.). Office: Food World Inc 200 Distribution Dr Greensboro NC 27410

HUTCHENS, JOHN KENNEDY, journalist, editor; b. Chgo., Aug. 9, 1905; s. Martin Jay and Leila (Kennedy) H.; m. Katherine Regan Morris (dec.); children: Anne, Timothy; m. Marjorie Kohl Brophy (dec.); m. Ruth D. Brine. A.B., Hamilton Coll., 1926, Litt.D., 1951. Reporter, Daily Missoulian and Sentinel, Missoula, Mont., 1926-27; reporter, film critic, asst. drama editor N.Y. Evening Post, 1927-28; asst. editor Theatre Arts mag., 1928-29, drama critic, 1929-32; drama staff N.Y. Times, 1929-32, 34-38, radio editor, 1941-44; drama critic Boston Evening Transcript, 1938-41; asst. editor N.Y. Times Book Rev., 1944-46, editor, 1946-48; book news columnist, reviewer N.Y. Herald Tribune, 1948-56, daily book reviewer, 1956-63; mem. editorial bd. Book-of-the Month Club, 1963—. Author: One Man's Montana: An Informal Portrait of a State, 1964; editor: (anthology) The American Twenties: A Literary Panorama, 1952; (with George Oppenheimer) The Best in the World, 1973, The Gambler's Bedside Book, 1978. Mem. Authors Guild, Authors League Am. (council), Sigma Phi. Democrat. Clubs: Dutch Treat, The Players (N.Y.C.); Shenorock (Rye). Home: 100 Midland Ave Rye NY 10580 Office: Book-of-the-Month Club 485 Lexington Ave New York NY 10017

HUTCHENS, JOHN OLIVER, educator, physiologist; b. Noblesville, Ind., Nov. 8, 1914; s. Bernayse E. and Della M. (Moore) H.; m. Eleanore M. Mothersill, June 3, 1939; children: Margaret A., Judith M., Helen Louise. A.B., Butler U., 1936; Ph.D., Johns Hopkins U., 1939. Nat. research fellow biol. sci., dept. biol. chemistry Harvard Med. Sch., 1939-40; Johnston scholar biology Johns Hopkins U., 1940-41; instr. physiology U. Chgo., 1941, asst. prof. physiology, 1946, asso. prof., 1946-52, prof., 1952-73, chmn. dept., 1946-58, dir. toxicity lab., 1946-48, prof. pharmacology and physiology, asso. dir. toxicity lab., 1972-82, prof. emeritus, 1982—, dir., 1973-80; temp. sci. liaison officer Office Naval Research, London, 1954; cons.-examiner North Central Assn. Colls. and Secondary Schs., 1967—. Contbg. author: Handbook of Biochemistry, 1968. Mem. corp. Marine Biol. Lab. Served to maj., tech. dir. toxicol. research, med. div. AUS, 1945-46. Fellow AAAS, N.Y. Acad. Scis.; mem. Biochem. Soc. (Britain), Soc. Gen. Physiologists, AAUP, Chem. Warfare Assn., Am. Physiol. Soc., Soc. Exptl. Biology and Medicine, Phi Beta Kappa, Sigma Xi, Phi Kappa Phi, Gamma Alpha, Phi Eta Sigma, Blue Key. Methodist. Club: Quadrangle (Chgo.). Home: 5633 Drexel Ave Chicago IL 60637

HUTCHENS, TYRA THORNTON, physician, educator; b. Newberg, Oreg., Nov. 29, 1921; s. Fred G. and Bess (Adams) H.; m. Betty Lou Gardner, June 7, 1942; children: Tyra Richard, Robert Jay, Rebecca (Mrs. Mark Pearsall). B.S., U. Oreg., 1943, M.D., 1945. Diplomate: Am. Bd. Pathology, Am. Bd. Nuclear Medicine. Intern Minn. Gen. Hosp., Mpls., 1945-46; AEC postdoctoral research fellow Reed Coll., Med. Sch. U. Oreg., 1948-50; NIH postdoctoral research fellow Med. Sch. U. Oreg., 1951-53; mem. faculty Oreg. Health Scis. U., 1953—, prof., chmn. dept. clin. pathology, 1962—, prof. radiotherapy, 1963-71, allied health edn. coordinator, 1969-77; vis. lectr. radiobiology Reed Coll., 1955, 56. Mem. adv. bd. Oreg. Regional Med. Program, 1968-75; mem. statuatory radiation adv. com. Oreg. Bd. Health, 1957-69, chmn., 1967-69; founding trustee Am. Bd. Nuclear Medicine, 1971-77, 82-84, sec., 1973-75, 84—; voting rep. Am. Bd. Med. Specialties, 1973-78, chmn. com. long range planning, 1976-78; mem. sci. adv. bd. Armed Forces Inst. Pathology, 1978-83. Served to lt. (j.g.) M.C., USNR, 1946-48. Charter mem. Acad. Clin. Lab. Physicians and Scientists, Soc. Nuclear Medicine, Am. Coll. Nuclear Physicians; mem. Oreg. Pathologists Assn. (pres. 1968), Pacific N.W. Soc. Nuclear Medicine (pres. 1958), AMA, Coll. Am. Pathologists (bd. govs. 1967-74, pres. 1977-79, chmn. commn. on internat. affairs 1979-83, chmn. planning com. for 1987 World Congress Pathology), Am. Soc. Clin. Pathologists (bd. registry med. technologists 1967-71), World Assn. of Socs. of Pathology (mem. bur., chmn. commn. World Standards 1981—), Assn. Am. Med. Colls., AAAS, Phi Beta Kappa, Sigma Xi, Alpha Omega Alpha. Research, publs. radioactive carbon tracer studies of lipid metabolism, clin. radioisotope techniques. Home: 7821 SW 51st St Portland OR 97219

HUTCHEON, DUNCAN ELLIOT, pharmacologist; b. Kindersley, Sask., Can., June 21, 1922; s. Robert Scott and Anne McGibbon H.; m. Jean-Marie Kirkby, June 7, 1946; children—Robert Gordon, Jean-Marie, Marcia Louise, Megan McGibbon. M.D., U. Toronto, 1945; B.Sc. in Medicine, 1947; D.Phil., Oxford U., 1950. Diplomate: Am. Bd. Internal Medicine. Intern Toronto Gen. Hosp., 1945-46; resident Jersey City Med. Center, 1957-60; asso. prof. pharmacology U. Sask., 1950-53; sr. pharmacologist Pfizer Therapeutic Inst., Maywood, N.J., 1953-57; prof. pharmacology and medicine Coll. Medicine and Dentistry N.J., Newark, 1957—; mem. N.J. Drug Utilization Rev. Council, 1978—; chmn. Am. Bd. Clin. Pharmacology, Princeton, N.J., 1976—; pres., chief exec. officer Princeton Inst. Environ. Medicine, 1980—. Editor: Jour. Clin. Pharmacology, 1978—. Served with, M.C., Royal Can. Army; Served with, 1943-46. Nat. Research Council Can. fellow, 1948-50. Fellow Am. Coll. Clin. Pharmacology (Disting. Service award), A.C.P.; mem. Am. Soc. Pharmacology and Exptl. Therapeutics. Basic and clin. research on cardiovascular effects of drugs and indsl. chems. Home: 250 Harriot Ave Harrington Park NJ 07640 Office: 205 Nassau St Princeton NJ 08540

HUTCHERSON, BOBBY, jazz vibraphonist; b. Los Angeles, Jan. 27, 1941. Played with, Curtis Amy and Charles Lloyd, prior to 1961; asso. with, Blue Note sch. of experimentation; co-leader quintet with, Harold Land, 1969-71; solo performer, 1971—; performed with, Andrew Hill, Anthony Williams, Herbie Hancock, McCoy Tynes, Eric Dolphy; albums include Linger Lane, Dialogue, Happenings, Components, Stick-Up!, Total Eclipse, The View from Inside. Office: care Ms Management 130 E 31st St New York NY 10016 *

HUTCHESON, HAROLD LEO, educator; b. Castana, Iowa, Sept. 26, 1916; s. Leslie G. and Sadie (Moss) H.; m. Hazel Z. Moore, Dec. 11, 1943; children—Gayle Jolon, Rex Allison. B.A., Nebr. State Coll., 1948; M.A., U. Nebr., 1954, D.Ed., 1957. High sch. sci. tchr., Oakdale, Nebr., 1948-49, high prin., 1949-50, supt. schs., Atkinson, Nebr., 1951-55; instr. sch. adminstrn. U. Nebr., 1955-57; dir. tchr. edn. Nebr. State Coll., Peru, 1957-59; v.p. for devel. and services, dean Coll. Edn., U. Wis., Platteville, 1959-72, vice chancellor, 1972-76, prof., 1976—; Inaugurated project PITCH, program tng. tchrs. for culturally deprived children, 1963; planned coll. campus Richland Center, Wis., 1965; inaugurated Assn. for Excellence, 1971; mem. Wis. Sch. Health Council, 1965—, Wis. Vocat. Edn. Adv. Council, 1963—. Pres. city council, Peru, 1958; Exec. bd. Wis. PTA, 1965—; chmn. Platteville Community Chest, 1963; First pres. bd. dirs. Grant County (Wis.) Guidance Center, 1960-62; bd. dirs. U.S. Grant council Boy Scouts Am. Served as officer C.E. AUS, 1941-46. Recipient Patriotic Civilian Ser. citation U.S. Army, 1973. Mem. Council for Basic Edn., Assn. Wis. State Univ. Faculties, Phi Eta Sigma, Alpha Psi Omega, Phi Kappa Phi, Pi Gamma Mu, Pi Kappa Delta, Lambda Delta Lambda. Home: 455 Madison St Platteville WI 53818

HUTCHESON, JOSEPH CHAPPELL, III, lawyer; b. Houston, Jan. 5, 1907; s. Joseph Chappell and Anne Elizabeth (Weeden) H.; m. Mary Catherine Jacob, Feb. 18, 1933 (dec. Feb. 1980); m. Virginia McLeod Brelsford, June 12, 1982. Grad., Phillips Acad., 1924; B.A., U. Va., 1928; LL.B., U. Tex., 1931. Bar: Tex. 1931. Partner firm Baker & Botts (and predecessors), Houston, 1946—; Mem. chancellor's council U. Tex. System; chmn. bd. mgrs. Schlumberger Found., until 1981; mem. adv. bd. Duchesne Acad. Served to maj. AUS, 1942-46; ETO. Mem. Am. Law Inst., Am. Bar Assn., Mid-Continent Oil and Gas Assn., Order of Coif, Phi Delta Phi, Kappa Sigma. Home: 3601 Inverness Dr Houston TX 77019 Office: 3000 One Shell Plaza Houston TX 77002

HUTCHESON, THOMAS BARKSDALE, JR., educator; b. Christiansburg, Va., Nov. 4, 1926; s. Thomas Barksdale and Rosilie (Stockard) H.; m. Frances Elizabeth McEver, Jan. 16, 1954; children—Elizabeth McEver, Thomas Barksdale III, Joel Collier. B.S., Va. Poly. Inst., 1950; M.S., N.C. State U., 1952, Ph.D., 1956. Instr. agronomy N.C. State U., Raleigh, 1952-54; asst. prof. agronomy U. Ky., Lexington, 1956-59, asso. prof., 1959-64; prof. agronomy Va. Poly. Inst., Blacksburg, 1964-67, prof., head dept. agronomy, 1967—. Editorial bd.: Tobacco Science, 1969-72, Agronomy Jour, 1970-73, Soil Sci. Soc. Am. Proc, 1970-73. Served with AUS, 1945-46. Fellow Am. Soc. Agronomy, Soil Sci. Soc. Am.; mem. Sigma Xi, Alpha Zeta, Phi Kappa Phi, Epsilon Sigma Phi, Phi Sigma, Gamma Sigma Delta. Presbyterian (elder). Home: PO Box 398 Blacksburg VA 24060

HUTCHINGS, BRIAN LAMAR, biochemist, college dean; b. South Jordan, Utah, June 11, 1915; s. Joseph Nephi and Elizabeth Anne (Bird) H.; m. Ellen Anderson, Aug. 25, 1938; children: Robert L., Barbara A., Stephen B., David C. B.S., Brigham Young U., 1938; M.S., U. Wis., 1940, Ph.D., 1942. Research biochemist Lederle Labs., Am. Cyanamid Co., Pearl River, N.Y., 1942-46, head dept. biochem. research, 1947-50, asso. dir. chem. and biol. research, 1950-57, dir. biochem. research, 1958-65, sr. research fellow, 1965-68; prof., chmn. dept. biol. scis. Wright State U., Dayton, Ohio, 1968-72, dean Coll. Sci. and Engring., 1973—; cons. pharm. industry, 1969—. Contbr. articles to profl. jours. NIH grantee, 1969-76. Fellow N.Y. Acad. Sci., AAAS; mem. Soc. Exptl. Biology and Medicine, Am. Chem. Soc., Am. Soc. Microbiology, Am. Soc. Biol. Chemists, Sigma Xi. Mem. Ch. Jesus Christ Latter-day Saints. Home: 1402 Glen View Rd Yellow Springs OH 45387 Office: Wright State U Dayton OH 45435

HUTCHINGS, GEORGE HENRY, food company executive; b. Fort Worth, June 23, 1922; s. George H. and Emma (Harder) H.; m. Edith Van Gils, Mar. 23, 1946 (dec.); children: Mark Dennis, Lisa Ellen; m. Elizabeth T. Storey, Apr. 10, 1968. Student, Tex. A&M, 1940-42. Analyst mktg. research Frito Food Mfg., Dallas, 1946, mgr. mktg. research, Los Angeles, 1946-57, div. sales mgr., San Mateo, Calif., 1958-60, div. gen. mgr., 1961, v.p., 1961-62; v.p. for ops. Western zone, 1962—; pres. Nalley's, Inc., Tacoma, 1964, Nalley's div. W.R. Grace & Co., 1966—, Wash. Beverages, Inc., Tacoma, 1972-81; dir., mem. exec. com. Puget Sound Nat. Bank, Tacoma; cons., 1981—. Served to capt. USAAF, 1942-46. Decorated D.F.C., Air medal with 7 clusters. Mem. Tacoma C. of C. Presbyterian. Clubs: Tacoma, Tacoma Country and Golf, Tacoma Yacht. Lodge: Masons. Home: 11309 Clovercrest Dr SW Tacoma WA 98499 Office: 722 Commerce St Tacoma WA 98402
A man must know what he stands for before he can logically take a stand against anything.

HUTCHINS, CURTIS MARSHALL, business exec.; b. Boston, Apr. 23, 1907; Charles P. and Lena (Curtis) H.; m. Ruth Rich, Feb. 28, 1931; children—Hilda, Christopher, Hope. Student, Country Day Sch., Newton, Mass.; A.B., Williams Coll., 1928; forestry student, U. Maine, LL.D., 1951; M.S. (hon.), Colby Coll., 1949; L.H.D., Husson Coll., 1971. Pres. Dead River Co., Bangor, Maine, 1935-57, chmn., 1947—; pres. Bangor and Aroostook R.R. Co., 1948-57, chmn., 1952-58, 65, dir., 1952-58, 64-65; pres. St. Croix Paper Co., 1959-63; dir. Scott Paper Co., 1954-77, State St. Bank & Trust Co., Boston, 1954-78, Guilford Industries, Inc. (Maine), Bangor Punta Corp., 1964-79, Merrill Trust Co., Bangor, 1936-76. Mem. New Eng. Council, pres., 1954; dir. Assn. Am. R.R.'s, 1951-54; mem. Maine Environ. Improvement Commn., 1969-72; Mem. city council, Bangor, 1941-43, chmn., 1943; mem. Maine Legislature, 1943. Mem. U.S. C. of C. (dir., chmn. natural resources com. 1961-69), Phi Beta Kappa. Clubs: Penobscot Valley Country, Tarratine (Bangor); Union (Boston); Pinnacle (N.Y.C.). Home: 300 Kenduskeag Ave Bangor ME 04401 Office: 55 Broadway Bangor ME 04401

HUTCHINS, FRANK MCALLISTER, advertising executive; b. Rochester, N.Y., July 7, 1922; s. Francis Irving and Barbara Woodward (Arnold) H.; m. Jeanne Mathilda Bahn, Aug. 24, 1945; children: Katharine Arnold, Virginia Ann, Patricia Arms, Constance Anne. A.B., Dartmouth Coll., 1947, M.B.A., 1948. Editor-in-chief Dartmouth Yearbook, 1943; local advt. mgr. Dartmouth Daily Newspaper, 1946-47, bus. mgr., 1947-48; account exec. Hutchins Advt. Co., Inc., Rochester, 1948-50, v.p., gen. mgr., 1950, pres., treas., from 1951, chmn. bd., chief exec. officer, until 1971; chmn. exec. com. Hutchins/Darcy, Inc., 1971-75, chmn. bd., chief exec. officer, 1976-77; chmn., chief exec. officer Hutchins/Young & Rubicam Inc., Rochester, 1978—; dir. Dollinger Corp., Rochester, Sykes Datatronics Corp., Armotek Industries, Inc., Palmyra, N.J. Bd. dirs. Community Chest, Rochester, pres., 1974-75; bd. dirs. YMCA, Rochester, pres., 1969-71; trustee, mem. exec. com. Rochester Inst. Tech., chmn. bd., 1981—; trustee George Eastman House; mem. alumni council Dartmouth Coll., 1969-72. Served with OSS, AUS, 1943-45; as 2d lt. inf., 1945-46. Mem. Rochester C. of C. (pres. 1978), Rochester Advt. Council (chmn. bd. 1957), Rochester Conv. and Publicity Bur., Rochester Jr. C. of C. (pres. 1952-53), Nat. Sales Execs Club, Theta Delta Chi. Episcopalian (vestryman, sr. warden). Clubs: Dartmouth (pres. 1951-52), University, Rochester Country (pres. 1960-61), Rochester Country (Rochester) (bd. stewards 1973-76); Genesee Valley.). Home: 75 Indian Spring Ln Rochester NY 14618 Office: 400 Midtown Tower Rochester NY 14604

HUTCHINS, JOHN OSBORNE, insurance company executive; b. Roachdale, Ind., Feb. 19, 1920; s. Clarence Osborne and Pauline (Edwards) H.; m. Valeria Lorena Finch, Aug. 6, 1943; children: Stephen Edward, Toni Marie, Hutchins Kearns. Student, Ind. U., 1938-39. With United Farm Bur. Ins. Cos., 1941—, v.p. mktg., Indpls., 1963-65; mgr. Madison County agy., 1965-78, exec. v.p., chief exec. officer, 1978—; mem. adv. bd. Am. Agrl. Ins. Co. Served with AUS, 1942-45. Mem. Nat. Assn. Ind. Insurers, Assn. Indiana Life Ins. Cos. (dir.), Indiana Ins. Inst. (v.p.). Republican. Lodge: Masons. Home: Route 1 Box 35 Bainbridge IN 46105 Office: 130 E Washington St Indianapolis IN 46204

HUTCHINS, ROBERT MAYNARD, fund exec.; b. Bklyn., Jan. 17, 1899; s. William James and Anna Laura (Murch) H.; m. Maude Phelps McVeigh (div.); children—Frances Ratcliffe, Joanna Blessing, Clarissa Phelps; m. Mrs. Vesta Sutton Orlick. Student, Oberlin Coll., 1915-17; A.B., Yale, 1921, A.M. (hon.), 1922, LL.B., 1925; LL.D., W.Va. U., Lafayette Coll., Oberlin Coll., 1929, Williams Coll., 1930, Berea Coll., 1931, Harvard, 1936, Tulane U., 1938; hon. doctoral degrees, U. Copenhagen, 1946, U. Ill., 1947; LL.D., U. Frankfurt, 1948, U. Stockholm, 1949, Rollins Coll., 1950, U. Chgo., 1951, Colby Coll., 1956, U. Rochester, 1958, Lewis and Clark Coll., 1967; D.Litt., Georgetown U., 1964, Hebrew Union Coll., 1964. Master English, history Lake Placid (N.Y.) Sch., 1921-23; sec. Yale, 1923-27; lectr. Yale Law Sch., 1925-27, acting dean, 1927-28, dean, 1928-29, prof. law, 1927-29; pres. U. Chgo., 1929-45, chancellor, 1945-51; asso. dir. Ford Found., 1951-54; chief exec. officer Fund for Republic, 1954-74, Center for Study Democratic Instns., 1954-74, life fellow, 1974—, pres., 1975—, Fund for the Republic, 1975-79; dir. Ency. Brit., Inc., 1947-74, Ency. Brit. Films, Inc., 1947-74. Author: No Friendly Voice, 1936, The Higher Learning in America, 1936, Education for Freedom, 1943, St. Thomas and the World State, 1949, Morals, Religion and Higher Education, 1950, The Democratic Dilemma, Some Questions about Education in North America, The Great Conversation, 1951, The Conflict in Education, 1953, The University of Utopia, 1953, Freedom, Education and The Fund, 1956, Some Observations On American Education, 1956, The Learning Society, 1968, Dr. Zuckerkandl, 1968; Bd. editors: Ency. Brit, 1946-74. Served in ambulance service U.S. Army, 1917-19; Served in ambulance service Italian Army, 1918-19. Decorated Croce di Guerra, Italian, 1918; officer Legion, 1969; Honor, 1938; recipient Goethe medal, 1948; Aspen Founders award, 1960. Mem. Chgo. Bar Assn., Order of Coif, Phi Beta Kappa. Clubs: University, Tavern (Chgo.) (hon.). Address: care Public Affairs Press 419 New Jersey Ave SE Washington DC 20003 *

HUTCHINS, ROBERT SENGER, architect; b. Oakland, Calif., Dec. 13, 1907; s. Thomas Boyd and Alice Louise (Senger) H.; m. Evelyn Reed (Brooks), Oct. 12, 1934; children: Robert Ayer, Elizabeth O. Hutchins Bronnert. A.B., U. Calif., 1928; B.Arch., U. Pa., 1929, M.Arch., 1930. Lic. architect, N.Y., Conn., N.J. Apprentice Delano & Aldrich, N.Y.C., 1930-33; pvt. practice architecture, N.Y.C., 1933-37, Moore & Hutchins Partnership, 1937-72; ptnr. Hutchins, Evans & Lefferts, 1972-82; Dir. bldg. services USO, 1942-46; mem. Commn. on Ch. Bldg., Diocese N.Y., 1965—. Works include campus plans and numerous bldgs., Goucher Coll., Balt., N.Y.; specializing, SUNY, Harpur Coll., Binghamton; St. Lawrence U., Canton, N.Y., S.I. Community Coll., N.Y., St. Timothy's Sch., Balt., Cazenovia (N.Y.) Coll., also numerous other schs., colls., univs., chs., U.S. Battle Monuments Commn. permanent mil. cemetery, Carthage, North Africa, U.S. Ambassador's Residence, Dakar, Senegal, Village Hall, Garden City, N.Y., Community Ch., Glen Rock, N.J., Grad. Sch. Bus., Columbia U.; supervising architect, Vassar Coll., 1960—. Trustee St. Timothy's Sch., 1953-67, pres., 1956-60; trustee Mary I. Bassett Hosp., Cooperstown, Barnard Coll., 1955-76, Cathedral St. John the Divine, N.Y.C., 1964-70, St. Hilda's and St. Hugh's Sch., N.Y.C., 1976—; bd. dirs. Farmers Mus., Cooperstown; hon. trustee Met. Mus., N.Y.C., 1977—. Winner Goucher Coll. competition, 1938, Village Hall competition Garden City, N.Y., 1950. Fellow AIA (pres. N.Y. chpt. 1954-56, chmn. edn. com. 1966-68, chancellor coll. fellows 1974-75); mem. N.Y. State Hist. Assn. (trustee), NAD (mem. council 1974—, pres. 1977—), Mcpl. Art Soc. N.Y., Nat. Sculpture Soc. (allied profl. mem.), Order St. John of Jerusalem. Episcopalian. Club: Century Assn. (N.Y.C.). Home: 1220 Park Ave New York NY 10028 Office: 155 E 44th St New York NY 10017

HUTCHINSON, CHARLES SMITH, JR., book publisher; b. Topeka, Oct. 17, 1930; s. Charles S. and Cecil Marguerite (Weidenhamer) H.; m. Elizabeth Dunbar Hall, June 16, 1956; children: Amy Elizabeth, Todd Charles. B.A., Principia Coll., 1952. Editor-in-chief, sec., dir. Burgess Pub. Co., Mpls., 1955-65; editor-in-chief coll. and profl. books Reinhold Book Corp., N.Y.C., 1965-68, also dir.; editor-in-chief profl. and reference books Van Nostrand Reinhold Co., N.Y.C., 1968-70; pres., chmn. bd. Dowden, Hutchinson and Ross, Inc., Stroudsburg, Pa., 1970-78, v.p., sec., dir., 1978-80; v.p. Hutchinson Ross Pub. Co., 1980—; dir. Jacob Stroud Corp. Bd. dirs. Quiet Valley Hist. Farms Assn. Served with C.E., U.S. Army, 1952-55. Recipient NuJay award Mpls. Jaycees, 1957. Fellow Geol. Soc. Am., Am. Geophys. Union, Environ. Design Research Assn., Assn. Petroleum Geologists. Clubs: Kiwanis (treas. Stroudsburg chpt. 1977-78, v.p. 1978-80), Kiwanis (pres. 1980-81), Kiwanis (Disting. Pres. award 1981); Chemist's (N.Y.C.)). Home: HCR Box 54 Pocono Summit PA 18346

HUTCHINSON, DONALD STUART, electronics company executive; b. Keith, Scotland, Oct. 3, 1929; s. Thomas Edgar and Gladys Hogg (Jackson) H.; m. Heather, Aug. 13, 1960; children: David, Jennifer. Grad., Royal Naval Coll., Dartmouth, Eng., 1946, Greenwich, Eng., 1949; postgrad., Harvard U. Bus. Sch., 1957. Asst. prof. Institut pour L'Etudes des Methodes de Direction de l'Entreprise, Lausanne, Switzerland, 1957-58; asst. controller Polaroid, Cambridge, Mass., 1959-64; treas. Nat. Blank Book Co., Holyoke, Mass., 1964-70; v.p. adminstrn. Dennison Co., Framingham, Mass., 1971-78; chmn. bd., chief exec. officer Cramer Electronics, Newton, Mass., 1978-79; chmn. bd. Telelogic Inc., Cambridge, Mass., 1980—; chmn. fin. com. Dental Service Co of Mass. Served to lt. Brit. Royal Navy. Mem. Fin. Execs. Inst. Home: 15 Pendleton Rd Sudbury MA 01776 Office: 196 Broadway Cambridge MA 02139

HUTCHINSON, EDWARD PRINCE, educator, demographer, author; b. Auburn, Me., Jan. 3, 1906; s. Frederick William and Agnes (Prince) H.; m. Louise Forbes, Jan. 6, 1940 (dec. 1962); children—Joan, John. A.B., Bowdoin Coll., 1927, L.H.D., 1982; Ph.D., MIT, 1933; postdoctoral student, U. Stockholm, 1933-35, London Sch. Econs., 1935. Asst., instr. Harvard Sch. Pub. Health, 1929-32; fellow Social Sci. Research Council, 1933-35; instr. sociology Harvard, 1935-40; sr. research technician Nat. Resources Planning Bd., Exec. Office of Pres., 1942-43; supr. research Immigration and Naturalization Service, 1943-45; asso. prof., then prof. sociology U. Pa., 1945-76, prof. emeritus, 1976—; cons. Dept. Agr., Census Bur., UN, Dept. Justice, Dept. State. Author: (with K. A. Edin) Studies of Differential Fertility in Sweden, 1935, Guide to the Official Population Data and Vital Statistics of Sweden, 1943, Current Problems of Immigration Policy, 1949, Immigrants and Their Children, 1850-1950, 1956, The Population Debate, 1967, Legislative History of American Immigration Policy, 1981. Trustee Balch Inst., 1973—. Fellow Library of Congress, 1940; Guggenheim fellow, 1941-42, 56-57; Fulbright fellowship screening com. Com. Internat. Exchange of Persons, 1958-62; NSF fellowship panel Nat. Acad. Scis., 1959-65; vis. fellow Australian Nat. U., 1971-72. Mem. Am. Immigration and Citizenship Conf. (dir., chmn. research com.; editor Immigration Research Digest 1960-68), AAAS (sec. sect. social and econ. scis. 1936-44), Population Assn. Am. (past dir., treas., v.p.), Union Internationale pour l'Etude Scientifique de la Population, Phi Beta Kappa, Delta Upsilon. Home: 549 Beechtree Ln Strafford Wayne PO PA 19087 Office: Population Studies Center U Pa Philadelphia PA 19104

HUTCHINSON, EVERETT, lawyer; b. Hempstead, Tex., Jan. 2, 1915; s. Neely E. and Lida (Hosmer) H.; m. Elizabeth Stafford, Dec. 16, 1944; children: Stafford, Ann. B.B.A., U. Tex., 1939, LL.B., 1940. Bar: Tex. 1939, D.C. 1963. Practiced in, Hempstead and Austin, Tex., 1940-55, asst. atty. gen., Tex., 1949-51, 55; commr. ICC, Washington, 1955-65, chmn. commn., 1961; pres. Am. Bus. Assn., 1965-67; under-sec. transp., 1967-68; partner Fulbright & Jaworski, Washington, 1968-83, counsel, 1983—; Mem. council Adminstrv. Conf. U.S., 1961-62. Mem. Tex. Ho. of Reps., 1941-45; orgn. dir. Young Democratic Clubs of Tex., 1939-40. Served from apprentice seaman to lt. USNR, 1942-45; capt. JAGC, USNR (Ret.). Mem. ABA; Mem. D.C. Bar Assn.; mem. Fed. Bar Assn.; Mem. Motor Carrier Lawyers Assn., Nat. Def. Transp. Assn. (pres. 1975-77, chmn. bd. 1977-79), State Bar Tex., Friar Soc., Tex. Soc. Washington, Sigma Phi Epsilon. Episcopalian. Clubs: Metropolitan, Internat. (Washington); Houston Center (Houston); Pisces. Home: 5401 Albemarle St Bethesda MD 20816 Office: 1150 Connecticut Ave NW Suite 400 Washington DC 20036

HUTCHINSON, FRANKLIN, biophysicist; b. Bklyn., Feb. 29, 1920; s. Franklin and Marjorie (Rollhaus) H.; m. Edith Arnold Pringle, Sept. 16, 1944; children: Bruce, Franklin IV, Alexander, Mary Candace. B.S., Mass. Inst. Tech., 1942; Ph.D., Yale, 1948. With radiation lab. Mass. Inst. Tech., 1942-45; instr. radiology, biophysics Yale, 1948-51, asst. prof. physics, 1951-57, asso. prof. biophysics., 1957-60, prof., 1960—, chmn. dept. molecular biology, biophysics, 1960-63, chmn. dept. molecular biophysics, 1967-69, chmn. dept. molecular biophysics and biochemistry, 1973-76; Cons. radiation physics Yale-New Haven Hosp., Hartford Hosp.; chmn. biophysics tng. study sect. NIH, 1962-64. Guggenheim fellow King's Coll., London, 1963-64. Mem. A.A.A.S., Biophysics Soc., Am. Phys. Soc., Radiation Research Soc. Home: 45 Livingston St New Haven CT 06511

HUTCHINSON, FREDERICK EDWARD, organization executive; b. Atkinson, Maine, June 1, 1930; s. Malcolm Eugene and Gertrude (Sargeant) H.; m. Dione Kendall Williams, Sept. 6, 1952; children: Juliana, Karen. B.S., U. Maine, 1953, M.S., 1958; Ph.D., Pa. State U., 1966. Mem. faculty dept. plant and soil scis. U. Maine at Orono, 1953-72, prof. soil sci., 1967-72, chmn. dept., 1971-72, dean Coll. Life Scis. and Agr., dir. expt. sta., 1972-75, v.p. for research and pub. service, 1975-80, 81-82, acting v.p. acad. affairs, 1980-81; exec. dir. Bd. for Internat. Food and Agr. Devel., 1982—. Chmn. bldg. fund dr. U. Maine, 1973-75; mem. adv. bd. Maine Rural Environ. Conservation Program, 1974—; chmn. joint research com. AID, 1977-80. Served with AUS, 1948-49. Fellow Am. Inst. Chemists; fellow Soil Conservation Soc. Am.; mem. Am. Soc. Agronomy (Outstanding Tchr. award N.E. chpt. 1971); fellow Soil Conservation Soc.; mem. Soil Sci. Soc., Audubon Soc., Sigma Xi, Phi Kappa Phi, Alpha Zeta. Republican. Methodist (chmn. ch. bldg. com. 1967-73). Home: Apt 623 301 Staters Ln Alexandria VA

HUTCHINSON, IRA J., government executive, conservationist; b. Topeka, Sept. 15, 1926; s. Ira James and Alice Rosevelt (Jolly) Hutchison Fisher; m. Barbara Jean Revely, July 2, 1950 (div. 1963); children: Rhonda, Jay Scott; m. Patricia Arleen Miller, July 5, 1964; children: Kandl, Kerri, Angela. B.S., Kans. State U., 1950; M.S., Columbia U., 1965; LL.D., Barber-Scotia Coll., 1979. Recreation dir. Topeka State Hosp., 1950-63; dir. recreation-rehab. service Westside Regab. Ctr., N.Y.C., 1963-65; dir. recreation services St. Vincent Hosp., Harrison, N.Y., 1965-67; exec. sec. Nat. Recreation and Park Assn. and Nat. Therapeutic Recreation Soc., Washington, 1967-69; asst. dir. urban affairs exec. office Nat. Recreation and Parks Assn., Washington, 1969-70, asst. to pres., exec. office, 1970-72; chief community programs, Nat. Capital Region, Nat. Park Service Dept. Interior, Washington, 1972-73, supt. Nat. Capital Parks-East, 1973-77, supt. Gateway Nat. Recreation Area, Bklyn., 1977, dep. dir. Nat. Park Service, Washington, 1977-83, dir. Office Historically Black Coll. and Univ. Programs, 1983—; cons. in field, 1950-52, 62-63, 65-67. Contbr. chpts. to books, articles to profl. publs. Served with USN, 1944-46. Recipient award of appreciation Ga. Park and Recreation Soc., 1970, Calif. Park and Recreation Soc., 1973, Disting. Service award Nat. Therapeutic Recreation Soc., 1972, Spl. award Nat. council Nat. Recreation and Park Assn., 1974, Spl. Achievement award Nat. Capital Region Nat. Parks Service, 1977, EEO Achievement award Nat. Park Service, 1977, 83, Meritorious Service award, 1983, Community Service award Ft. Dupont Civic Assn., 1977, Nat. Disting Profl. award Nat. Recreation and Park Assn., 1979. Mem. Am. Acad. Park and Recreation Adminstrn., Nat. Recreation and Park Assn. (trustee 1976-77), Md. Park and Recreation Soc., D.C. Park and Recreation Soc., Nat. Therapeutic Recreation Soc. (pres. 1967-68), Colesville Civic Assn., Kappa Alpha Psi. Club: Spring Brook High Boosters (Silver Spring, Md.). Office: Dept Interior Office Historically Black Coll and Univ Programs 18th and C Sts NW Washington DC 20240

HUTCHINSON, J. EDWARD, former congressman; b. Fennville, Mich., Oct. 13, 1914; s. Marc C. and Wilna (Leland) H.; m. Janice Eleanor Caton, Sept. 19, 1959. A.B., U. Mich., 1936, J.D., 1938. Bar: Mich. bar 1938. Mem. Mich. Ho. of Reps. from Allegan County, 1946-50; Senate from 8th Senatorial Dist., 1951-60; del., v.p. Mich. Constl. Conv., 1961-62; mem. 88th-94th congresses from 4th Dist. of Mich. Served with AUS, 1941-46. Republican. Home: 2905 Gulf Shore Blvd N Naples FL 33940

HUTCHINSON, JOHN JOSEPH, physician; b. Urbana, Ill., Sept. 28, 1915; s. James and Suzanne (Drake) H.; m. Doris Sylvia Potter, June 14, 1940; children—James Potter, Sara Louise, Patricia Mae. A.B., U. Ill., 1936; M.D., Columbia U., 1940. Physician N.Y. Life Ins. Co., N.Y.C., 1946-48, asst. med. dir., 1948-54, asso. med. dir., 1954, med. dir., 1955-66, chief med. dir., 1966-70, v.p., 1970—. Served with M.C. U.S. Army, 1941-46. Mem. AMA, Assn. Life Ins. Med. Dirs. Am. (pres. 1977-78), Am. Life Ins. Assn. (med. sect.), Phi Beta Kappa. Home: 267 Cliff Ave Pelham NY 10803 Office: NY Life Ins Co 51 Madison Ave New York City NY 10010

HUTCHINSON, JOHN WOODSIDE, applied mechanics educator, consultant; b. Hartford, Conn., Apr. 10, 1939; s. John Woodside and Evelyn (Eastburn) H.; m. Helle Vilsen, Aug. 28, 1964; children: Leif, David, Robert. B.S., Lehigh U., 1960; M.S., Harvard U., 1961, Ph.D., 1963. Asst. prof. Harvard U., Cambridge, Mass., 1964-69, Gordon McKay prof. applied mathematics, 1969—; cons. to various industries; cons. Mobil Solar, Arthur D. Little, Gen. Electric, Westinghouse, U.S. Steel. Contbr. articles to profl. jours. Recipient award AAAS, 1973, Nat. Acad. Engring., 1983; Guggenheim Found. fellow, 1974. Fellow ASME; mem. ASTM (Irwin medal 1982). Home: 4 Mason St Lexington MA 02173

HUTCHINSON, MELVIN J., manufacturing company executive; b. Pontiac, Mich., 1918. Chmn. bd. Gittleman's, Inc. Trustee Gratiot Community Hosp. Mem. VFW, DAV, Am. Legion. Clubs: Masons, Elks. Home: 543 Fairlane Dr Alma MI 48801 Office: 612 E Superior St Alma MI 48801

HUTCHINSON, PEMBERTON, coal co. exec.; b. Charlotte, N.C., 1931. Grad., U. Va. Exec. v.p. Westmoreland Coal Co., Phila.; also pres. subs. Gen. Coal Co., 1979-81; pres., chief operating officer, dir. Westmoreland Coal Co., 1981—; dir. Burlington No., Inc., Teleflex, Inc., Girard Co. Office: Westmoreland Coal Co 2500 Fidelity Bldg Philadelphia PA 19109 *

HUTCHINSON, ROBERT EARL, convenience stores company executive; b. Weymouth, Mass., Feb. 2, 1924; s. Lester Miller and Gladys (Jermyn) H.; m. Flieda C. Gardner, Feb. 18, 1950; children: Larry K., Karen J. Served with U.S. Army, 1941-45; U.S. Air Force, 1947-64; ret., 1964; salesman Kraus Realty, Sunnymead, Calif., 1964-66; with Circle K Corp., Phoenix, 1966—, div. western region, 1975-76, pres. policy bd., 1976-79, pres., 1979—, also chief operating officer. Republican. Home: 1500 N Markdale Mesa AZ 85201 Office: Circle K Corp 4500 S 40th St Phoenix AZ 85036 *

HUTCHINSON, ROBERT L., food company executive; b. 1920. A.B., Principia Coll., 1942. With Curtice-Burns, Inc., 1946—, exec. v.p., 1976-82, pres., chief exec. officer, dir., 1982—. Served to 2d lt. U.S. Army, 1942-46. Address: Curtice Burns Inc 1 Lincoln First Sq Rochester NY 14603 *

HUTCHINSON, THOMAS CUTHBERT, environmental sciences educator; b. Sunderland, Eng., Feb. 18, 1939; emigrated to Can., 1967; s. Walter and Margaret Amelia (Bell) H.; s. Vivien Coyne, Sept. 8, 1961 (div. 1981); 1 dau., Sally Louise. B.S. with honors in Botany, Manschester (Eng.) U., 1960; Ph.D. in Ecology, Sheffield (Eng.) U., 1966. Sir James Knott fellow Newcastle (Eng.) U., 1964-67; asst. prof., then porf. environ. scis. Toronto U., 1967—; assoc. dir., then dir. Inst. Environ. Scis., U. Toronto, 1973-76; prof. faculty of forestry U. Toronto, 1978—, chmn. dept. botany, 1976-82. Editor: Heavy Metals in Environment, 1977; co-editor: Acid Rain Effects on Vegetation, 1980; contbr. articles to profl. jours. Fellow Explorers Club; mem. Am. Agronomy Soc., Can. Bot. Assn. (George Lawson medal 1982), Am. Ecol. Soc., Brit. Ecol. Soc. Arctic Inst. N. Am. Home: 37 Bulwer St Toronto ON Canada M5T 1A1 Office: Dept Botany U Toronto Toronto ON Canada M5S 1A1

HUTCHINSON, THOMAS EUGENE, biophysicist, educator; b. York County, S.C., Aug. 1, 1936; s. Eugene Hale and Miriam Stokes (Jackson) H.; m. Ora Colleen Ray, Aug. 30, 1959; children: Rachel, Thomas Eugene. B.S. in Physics, Clemson (S.C.) Coll., 1958, M.S., 1959; Ph.D., U. Va., 1963. Research scientist, then research specialist 3M Co., 1963-67; mem. faculty U. Minn., Mpls., 1967-76, prof. chem. engring., 1974-76; prof. chem. engring., asso. dir. tr. for Bioengring. U. Wash., Seattle, 1976-82, assoc. dean research Coll. Engring., 1981-82; William Stansfield Calcott prof. biomed. engring. and assoc. dean grad. programs U. Va., Charlottesville, 1982—; chmn. Center for Advanced Studies; fellow Clare Hall, Cambridge (Eng.) U., 1973; sr. research fellow natural philosophy Glasgow (Scotland) U., 1975—; adviser Minn. Pollution Control Agy., 1974; chmn. Gordon Conf. Thin Films, 1970, Battelle N.W., Battelle Conf. on Microanalysis of Biol. Systems, 1980; bd. dirs. High Voltage Electron Microscopy Labs. of NIH, 1972—. Author: Electron Microscopy, 1971; editor: Microprobe Analysis of Biological Systems, 1981; contbr. articles to profl. jours. Grantee AEC, 1967-76, NSF, 1971-82, NIH, 1971—. Mem. Am. Vacuum Soc. (dir. 1972-74), Electron Microscopy Soc. (chmn. Minn. chpt. 1973-74). Patentee in field. Address: A114 Thornton Hall Sch Engring and Applied Sci U Va Charlottesville VA 22901

HUTCHINSON, TRAVIS G., engineering company execuitive; b. N.Y.C., Sept. 12,1942; s. George A. and Helen (DeGeorge) H.; m. Margaret Ann Blakeslee, Dec. 26, 1964; children: David T., Peter B. B.S., Rutgers U., 1964; M.S., Newark Coll. Engring., 1967; M.B.A., NYU, 1971. With M. W. Kellog Co., N.Y.C., 1965-70; exec. sales engr. The Lumnus Co., Bloomfield, N.J., 1970-73, mgr. N. Am. sales, 1973-76, v.p. Western hemisphere sales, 1976-78; pres., dir. Lumnus Nederland B.V., Bloomfield, N.J., 1978-81; pres. The Lumnus Co., Bloomfield, N.J., 1981—; exec. v.p. Lummus Group Inc., Bloomfield, N.J., 1981—. Mem. Am. Inst. Chem. Engrs., Am. Mgmt. Assn. Office: The Lummnus Co 1515 Broad St Bloomfield NJ 07003 *My life has been one of movement. I have been Blessed by the good fourtune to work for and with people who have helped me understand and perform better. My family has tolerated the long days and absences better than one deserves.I've been very lucky!*

HUTCHINSON, WILLIAM BURKE, surgeon, research center director; b. Seattle, Sept. 6, 1909; s. Joseph Lambert and Nona Bernice (Burke) H.; m. Charlotte Rigdon, Mar. 25, 1939; children: Charlotte J. Hutchinson Reed, William B., John L., Stuatrt R., Mary Hutchinson Wiese. B.S., U. Wash., Seattle, 1931; M.D., McGill U., 1936; H.H.D., U. Seattle, 1982. Diplomate: Am. Bd. Surgery. Intern Balt. City Hosp., 1936-37; redisent lUnion Meml. Hosp., Balt., 1937-39; resident James Walker Meml. Hosp., Wilmington, N.C., 1939-40; surgeon Swedish Hosp. and Med. Ctr., Seattle, 1941—, Providence Hosp., 1941—, King County Harborview Hosp., 1941—; pres., founding dir. Pacific Northwest Research Found., Seattle, 1956, Fred Hutchinson Cancer Research Ctr., 1972—, dir. Surg. Cancer Cons. Service, 1982—; clin. prof. surgery U. Wash., 1974; pres. 13th Internat. Cancer Congress, 1978-82; mem. Yarborough com. for writing Nat. Cancer Act, 1970. Contbg. editor, 13th Internat. Cancer Congress. Recipient 1st Citizen of Seattle award, 1976, Alumnus Summa Laude Dignatus award U. Wash., 1983. Fellow ACS; mem. AMA, King County Med. Soc., Seattle Surg. Assn., North Pacific Surg. Assn., NRC, Am. Assn. Cancer Insts., Alpha Sigma Phi. Clubs: Men's University (Seattle); Seattle Golf and Country. Home: 7126-55th Ave So Seattle WA 98118

HUTCHINSON, WILLIAM DAVID, justice Pennsylvania Supreme Court; b. Minersville, Pa., June 20, 1932; s. Elmer E. and Elizabeth (Price) H.; m. Louise Meloney, 1957; children: Kathryn, William, Louise, Andrew. B.A. magna cum laude, Moravian Coll., 1954; J.D., Harvard U., 1957. Bar: Pa. Sole practice, Pottsville, Pa., 1958-62; asst. dist. atty. Schuylkill County, Pa., 1963-69, solicitor, 1969-71, Blue Mountain Sch. Dist., Cressona, Pa., 1968-82; assoc. justice Pa. Supreme Ct., Harrisburg, 1982—. Mem. Pa. Ho. of Reps., 1973-82, Blue Mountain Sch. Bd., 1963-66. Mem. ABA, Pa. Bar Assn., Am. Judicature Soc., Schuylkill County Bar Assn. (com. continuing legal edn.). Republican. Methodist. Office: Pennsylvania Supreme Court PO Box 1172 Harrisburg PA 17108 *

HUTCHINSON, WILLIAM RAYMOND, oil company executive; b. Londonberry, No. Ireland, Oct. 9, 1942; came to U.S., 1967; s. George Albert and Sarah Jane (Haire) H.; m. Jean Ruth Hershey, Aug. 10, 1968; children: Katherine, Elizabeth. B.A. in Econs. and Polit. Sci., Trinity Coll., Dublin, 1965; M.S. in Indsl. Engring. Mgmt., Cranfield Coll. Tech., Bedford, Eng., 1966; M.B.A., Harvard U., 1968; postgrad., Northwestern U., 1977-79. C.P.A., Ill. Fin. mgr. Standard Oil Co. (Ind.), Chgo., 1974-75, asst. treas., 1976, dir. acctg. policy, 1977-79, gen. mgr. info. service, 1981, treas., 1981—; v.p. planning and econs. Amoco Minerals Co., Englewood, Colo., 1979-81; dir. Standard Oil Co. subs., Chgo. Bank of Commerce; pres. Amoco Leasing Co., Chgo., 1981—, Amoco Credit Corp., 1981—. Recipient Sells cert of high distinction. Mem. Ill. C.P.A. Soc., Fin. Execs. Inst. Home: 362 Deepwood Rd Barrington Hills IL 60010 Office: Standard Oil Co. (Indiana) 200 E Randolph Dr Chicago IL 60601

HUTCHISON, CLYDE ALLEN, JR., chemistry educator; b. Alliance, Ohio, May 5, 1913; s. Clyde Allen and Bessie Gertrude (Bicksler) H.; m. Sarah Jane West, Dec. 29, 1937; children: Clyde Allen Hutchison III, Sarah Jane, Robert West. B.A., Cedarville Coll., 1933, Sc.D. hon., 1953; Ph.D., Ohio State U., 1937. NRC postdoctoral fellow Columbia U., N.Y.C., 1937-38, research assoc., 1938-39, SAM Labs., 1943-45; asst. prof. U. Buffalo, 1939-45; research assoc. Manhattan project U.Va., Charlottesville, 1942-43; mem. faculty U. Chgo., 1945—; asst. prof. chemistry Enrico Fermi Inst., Charlottesville, 1948-50, assoc. prof., 1950-54, prof., 1954-63, Carl William Eisendrath prof., 1963-69, Carl William Eisendrath Disting. Service prof., 1969-83, Carl William Eisendrath Disting. Service prof. emeritus, 1983—, chmn. dept. chemistry, 1959-62; mem. adv. panel in chemistry NSF, 1960-63; bd. dirs. Ohio State U. Research Found., Columbus, 1963-68; mem. chemistry research evaluation panel USAF Office Sci. Research, 1966-70; mem. adv. panel for inorganic materials div. Inst. Materials Research, Nat. Bur. Standards, 1968-70; mem. corp. vis. com. dept. chemistry MIT, Cambridge, 1971-72; mem. NRC Evaluation Panel for Phys. Chemistry, 1977-80; lectr. various orgns., 1959-82; cons. Los Alamos Sci. Lab., 1953-62, Argonne Nat. Lab., Ill., 1946-83; mem. adv. panel Brookhaven Nat. Lab., Brookhaven, N.Y., 1960-63, Oak Ridge Nat. Lab., 1963-66. Contbr. articles to various publs. Recipient Centennial Achievement award Ohio State U., 1970, Peter Debye award in phys. chemistry Am. Chem. Soc., 1972; Guggenheim fellow Oxford U., 1955-56, 72-73; named Eastman Prof. U. Oxford, 1981-82. Fellow Am. Acad. Scis., Am. Phys. Soc. (council 1967, div. chmn. 1965); mem. Nat. Acad. Scis., AAAS, Sigma Xi. Office: U Chgo 5735 S Ellis Ave Chicago IL 60637

HUTCHISON, DORRIS JEANNETTE, educator, microbiologist; b. Carrsville, Ky., Oct. 31, 1918; d. John W. and Maud (Short) H. B.S., Western Ky. State Coll., 1940; M.S., U. Ky., 1943; Ph.D., Rutgers U., 1949. Instr. Russell Sage Coll., 1942-44, Vassar Coll., 1944-46; research asst. Rutgers U., 1946-48, research asso., 1948-49; instr. Wellesley Coll., 1949-51; asst. Sloan-Kettering Inst., N.Y.C., 1951-56, asso., 1956-60, asso. mem., 1960-69, mem., 1969—, sect. head, 1956-72, acting chief div. exptl. chemotherapy, 1965-66, div. chief drug resistance, 1967-72, co-head lab. exptl. tumor therapy, 1973-74, lab. head drug resistance and cyto-regulation, 1973—, coordinator field edn., 1975-81; instr. Sloan-Kettering div. Cornell U. Grad. Sch. Med. Sci., N.Y.C., 1952-53; research asso. Sloan-Kettering Inst. div. Cornell U. Grad. Sch. Med. Sci., 1953-54, asst. prof., 1954-58, asso. prof. microbiology, 1958-70, prof. microbiology, 1970—, chmn. biology unit, 1968-74, asso. dir., 1974—; asso. dean Cornell U. Grad. Sch. Med. Sci., 1978—; asst. dean Cornell U. Grad. Sch., 1978—; Bd. dirs. Westchester div. Am. Cancer Soc., 1976—, exec. com., 1976—; project chmn. Target 5, 1977-80, v.p., 1979-81, pres., 1981—. Faculty fellow Vassar Coll., 1946; USPHS fellow, 1951-53; Philippe Found. fellow, Paris, 1959. Fellow N.Y. Acad. Sci., Am. Acad. Microbiology (charter), 3N.Y. Acad. Medicine (asso.); mem. AAAS, Am. Assn. Cancer Research, Harvey Soc., Genetics Soc. Am., Am. Inst. Nutrition, Am. Soc. for Microbiology (councilor N.Y.C. br. 1954-58, pres. N.Y.C. br. 1958-60, nat. councilor 1961-63, chmn. nat. meeting 1967, mem. pres.'s fellowship com. 1973-76, chmn. 1975-76), Soc. for Cryobiology, Am. Genetic Assn., Internat. Soc. Biochem. Pharmacology. Numerous publs. antibiotics and chems. effective in treatment of Tb and leukemia, reports on mechanisms explaining how leukemic cells become resistant to treatment; search for more effective antileukemia drugs. Home: Southgate Bronxville NY 10708 Office: Sloan-Kettering Inst 1275 York Ave New York NY 10021 *Achieving goals and providing support and guidance to others, who also wished to become contributors to the well-being of mankind, have been prime concerns to me. The slings and arrows during this time have been totally offset by the personal satisfaction felt as a result of our intangible and tangible achievements.*

HUTCHISON, JOSEPH CARSON, business executive; b. Cross Hill, S.C., Sept. 17, 1894; s. Joseph Carson and Bessie (Cauthen) H.; m. Annie Whitner, Oct. 7, 1919; children: Elise Whitner (Mrs. R.L. Cornell, Jr.), Helen (Mrs. T. E. Tucker). A.B., Wofford Coll., Spartanburg, S.C., 1915. High sch. tchr., Sanford, Fla., 1915-17; clk. Sanford Truck Growers, Inc., 1919, asst. sec.-treas., 1919-20, gen. mgr., sales mgr., 1920-35; propr. J. C. Hutchison & Co., Sanford, Fla., from 1935; chmn. bd. Chase & Co., Sanford, 1963-69, adv. dir., from 1969; Chmn. bd. Growers and Shippers League Fla., Orlando; chmn. exec. com. Fla. Celery Exchange, Orlando, 1961-74; chmn. adv. com. Fla. Celery Marketing Order, Orlando, 1962-74; dir. Fla. Fruit and Vegetable Assn., 1947-74, Fla. Sweet Corn Exchange, Zellwood (Fla.) Sweet Corn Exchange, Sugar Cane Growers Coop. Fla. Served from pvt. to 2d lt. F.A. U.S. Army, 1917-19; commd. 1st lt. Fla. N.G., 1921; advanced through grades to brig. gen., 1940; comdr. 62nd Inf. Brig.; called to active duty, 1940; asst. div. comdr. 31st Inf. Div., 1942-46; reverted to N.G. status, 1946; promoted to maj. gen., 1951; comdg. 48th Inf. Div.; Fla.-Ga. N.G.; ret. from mil. service as lt. gen. Fla. N.G., 1952. Decorated Silver Star, Legion of Merit, Bronze Star, Air medal, Florida Cross. Democrat. Clubs: Masons, Elks, Kiwanis, Rotary (hon.). Home: PO Box 906 Sanford FL 32771

HUTCHISON, STANLEY PHILIP, insurance company executive, lawyer; b. Joliet, Ill., Nov. 22, 1923; s. Stuart Philip and Verna (Kinzer) H.; m. Helen Jane Rush, July 25, 1945; children: Norman, Elizabeth. B.S., Northwestern U., 1947; LL.B., Kent Coll. Law, 1951. Bar: Ill. 1951. Legal asst. Washington Nat. Ins. Co., Evanston, 1947-51, asst. counsel, 1951-55, asst. gen. counsel, 1955-58, asso. gen. counsel, 1958-60, gen. counsel, 1960-63, v.p., gen. counsel, dir., 1963-66, exec. v.p., gen. counsel, dir., 1966-67, exec. v.p., gen. counsel, sec., dir., 1967-70, chmn. exec. com., 1970-73, vice chmn. bd., 1974-75, chmn. bd., chief exec. officer, 1976—; pres. Wash. Nat. Corp., 1970—, chief exec. officer, 1978—, chmn. bd., 1983—; dir. Anchor Nat. Life Ins. Co., Washington Nat. Life Ins. Co. N.Y., Anchor Nat. Financial Services, Inc., Washington Nat. Devel. Co. Served to lt. (j.g.) USNR, 1942-46. Mem. Ill. C. of C., Evanston C. of C. (pres. 1973-74), ABA, Ill. Bar Assn., Assn. Life Ins. Counsel, Am. Council Life Ins., dir. (1977-81), Ill. Life Ins. Council (dir. 1978—, pres. 1983—), Ins. Econs. Soc. Am. (dir. 1977—, chmn. 1981-82). Home: 830 Heather Ln Winnetka IL 60093 Office: 1630 Chicago Ave Evanston IL 60201

HUTCHISON, THEODORE MURTAGH, insurance executive; b. Iowa City, Iowa, May 19, 1932; s. Theodore Call and Helen Louise (Murtagh) H.; m. Susan K. Starman, July 30, 1954; children: Holly Hutchison Ardinger, Hilary Hutchison Wright, Theodore Thomas. B.A., U. Iowa, 1954, J.D., 1956; LL.M., U. Mich., 1958. Bar: Iowa 1956. Law clk. U.S. Ct. Appeals 8th Circuit, St. Louis, 1956-57; instr. law U. Mich., Ann Arbor, 1958-59; asst. prof. law Boston U., 1959-62, assoc. prof., 1962-63; atty., asst. counsel Bankers Life Co., Des. Moines, 1963-71, assoc. counsel, 1971-73, assoc. gen. counsel, 1973-77, v.p. counsel, corp. sec., 1977—. Mem. Des Moines Urban Renewal Bd., 1971-82, chmn., 1973-75, 80-82; bd. dirs. United Way, 1976-82, Iowa Law Sch. Found., 1974—, Hawley Found., 1980—. W.W. Cook fellow, 1957-58. Mem. ABA, Iowa Bar Assn., Polk County Bar Assn., Assn. Life Ins. Counsel, Iowa Supreme Ct. Commn. Continuing Legal Edn. (chmn. 1983—), Order of Coif. Republican. Presbyterian. Clubs: Des Moines; Prairie (Des Moines); Rotary. Home: 115 Glenview Dr Des Moines IA 50312 Office: Bankers Life Co 711 High St Des Moines IA 50307

HUTCHISON, THOMAS J., III, real estate executive; b. Indpls., Aug. 23, 1941; s. Thomas J. Jr. and Eleanor J. (Vesey) H.; m. Sharyl E. Nelson, Dec. 30, 1961 (div. 1978); children: Thomas J. IV, Shayle M.; m. Carolyn K. Kent, July 2; children: Catherine F., Andrew K. M.E., Purdue U., 1961; student, U. Md., 1962-64. Vice-pres. DYMO Industries, San Francisco, 1964-70; exec. v.p. NICO, Inc., Los Angeles, 1970-78; v.p., gen. mgr. Laub & Co., Los Angeles, 1978-79; pres. Murdock Devel. Co., Los Angeles, 1979—. Mem. Joffrey Ballet, Los Angeles County Mus. Art, Calif. State Republican Com. Recipient Humanitarian award Shrine Club, Los Angeles, 1982. Mem. Nat. Realty Com., Urban Land Inst., Bldg. Owners and Mgrs. Assn., West Los Angeles C. of C. Republican. Methodist. Clubs: Calif. Yacht, Regency (Los Angeles). Home: 434 S Rimpau Blvd Los Angeles CA 90020 Office: Murdock Development Co 10900 Wilshire Blvd Los Angeles CA 90024

HUTCHISON, VICTOR HOBBS, educator, biologist; b. Blakely, Ga., June 15, 1931; s. Joseph Victor and Veva (Hobbs) H.; m. Theresa Dokos, Dec. 14, 1952; children—Victoria Ann, John Christopher, David Michael, Kenneth Hobbs. B.S., N. Ga. Coll., 1952; M.A., Duke, 1956; Ph.D., 1959. Instr. Duke, 1957-58, faculty fellow, So. Fellowship Fund fellow, 1958-59; mem. faculty U. R.I., 1959-70, prof. biology, 1968-70; dir. Inst. Environ. Biology, 1966-70; prof., chmn. dept. zoology U. Okla., Norman, 1970-80, George Lynn Cross research prof. zoology, 1979—; research prof. U. Los Andes, Bogota, Colombia, 1965-66; prin. investigator Nat. Geog. Soc.-U. R.I. Herpetological Expdn. to Colombia, 1964-65. Contbr. articles to profl. jours., chpt. to books, taxonomic studies on amphibians and reptiles. Guggenheim fellow, 1965-66. Mem. AAAS, Am. Inst. Biol. Sci., Am. Soc. Icthyologists and Herpetologists, Am. Soc. Mammalogists, Am. Soc. Zoologists, Am. Physiol. Soc., Ecol. Soc. Am., Herpetologists League, Soc. Study Amphibians and Reptiles, Sigma Xi, Phi Sigma, Phi Kappa Phi. Club: Explorers. Research on animal-alga symbiosis, heat tolerances of lower vertebrates, effects of day-length on metabolism and temperature tolerance of lower vertebrates, physiol. lower vertebrates, physiol. ecology of amphibians and reptiles, respiration in amphibians. Home: 2010 Crestmont St Norman OK 73069 Office: Dept Zoology U Okla Norman OK 73109

HUTCHISON, WILLIAM FORREST, parasitologist, educator; b. Lakeland, Fla., Oct. 7, 1925; s. Chester Boyer and Verna Louise (Warren) H.; m. Nellie Niles Booth, June 5, 1951; children—Florence Niles, David Forrest, Martha Ellen, Rebecca Warren, Robert Chester. B.A., Emory U., 1949, M.S., 1952; Ph.D., Tulane U., 1958. Instr. parasitology Tulane U. Med. Sch., New Orleans, 1954-55; asst. prof. preventive medicine and clin. lab. sci. U. Miss. Sch. Medicine, Jackson, 1955-59, asso. prof., 1959-71, prof., 1971—; cons. Jackson VA Hosp., 1955—; parasitologist Univ. Hosp., Jackson, 1955-72. Contbr. articles to profl. jours. Served with U.S. Army, 1943-46; ETO. Decorated Purple Heart; named U. Miss. Med. Alumni Assn. Pre-Clin. Prof. of Yr., 1972, 81. Mem. Am. Soc. Parasitologists, Am. Soc. Tropical Medicine and Hygiene, Internat. Filariasis Assn., S.E. Assn. Parasitologists, Miss. Acad. Sci. (pres. 1972-73), Sigma Xi, Phi Sigma, Kappa Alpha Order. Presbyterian. Club: Jackson Yacht (commodore 1973). Home: 1910 Bellewood Rd Jackson MS 39211 Office: Dept Preventive Medicine U Miss Med Center 2500 N State St Jackson MS 39216

HUTCHISON, WILLIAM LEETE, oil and gas company executive; b. Dallas, May 20, 1932; s. George William and Ima (Leete) H.; m. Patsy Flo Pinson, Nov. 23, 1953; children: Gail, Bill, Katie, Chuck. Student, U. of South, 1950-51; B.A., So. Meth. U., 1955, LL.B., 1955. Bar: Tex. 1955. Practiced in, Dallas, 1955-57; with Tex. Oil & Gas Corp., Dallas, 1957—, exec. v.p., 1965-70, pres., 1970—, chief exec. officer, 1976—, chmn. bd., 1977—, also dir.; dir. InterFirst Bank Dallas, NA, Delhi Gas Pipeline Corp. Mem. Dallas Citizens Council; trustee So. Meth. U. Mem. Ind. Petroleum Assn. Am., Nat. Petroleum Council, Tex. Mid-Continent Oil and Gas Assn., State Bar Tex., Dallas Bar Assn., Am. Petroleum Inst. Presbyterian. Clubs: Dallas Petroleum, Dallas Country, Dallas Gun. Lodge: Masons. Office: 3100 Fidelity Union Tower Dallas TX 75201

HUTCHISON, WILLIAM ROBERT, history educator; b. San Francisco, May 21, 1930; s. Ralph Cooper and Harriet (Thompson) H.; m. Virginia Quay, Aug. 16, 1952; children: Joseph Cooper, Catherine Eaton, Margaret Sidney, Elizabeth Quay. B.A., Hamilton Coll., 1951, Oxford U., 1953, M.A., 1957; Ph.D., Yale U., 1956; M.A. (hon.), Harvard, 1968. Instr. history Hunter Coll., 1956-58; asso. prof. Am. studies Am. U., 1958-64, prof. history and Am. studies, 1964-68; Charles Warren prof. history of religion in Am. Harvard, 1968—; master Winthrop House, 1974-79; vis. asso. prof. history U. Wis., 1963-64. Author: The Transcendentalist Ministers, 1959, The Modernist Impulse in American Protestantism, 1976; Editor: American Protestant Thought, the Liberal Era, 1968; co-editor: Missionary Ideologies in the Imperialist Era, 1982; Contbr. articles to profl. Jours. Recipient Brewer prize Am. Soc. Ch. History, 1957; Guggenheim fellow, 1960-61; fellow Charles Warren Center for Studies in Am. history Harvard, 1966-67; Fulbright Sr. Research scholar Free U., Berlin, 1976; Fulbright Disting. lectr. in Am. history, India, summer 1981. Mem. Am. Hist. Assn., Orgn. Am. Historians, Am. Studies Assn., Am. Soc. Ch. History (pres. 1981), Unitarian Hist. Soc., Mass. Hist. Soc., Phi Beta Kappa. Democrat. Mem. Soc. of Friends. Home: 4 Ellery Sq Cambridge MA 02138

HUTH, DONALD EARL, fgn. corr.; b. Green Bay, Wis., May 28, 1915; s. Herman Albert and Ann (Klesges) H.; m. Anne Marie Kelly, Sept. 24, 1938; children—Dennis, Kathleen Marie. Ph.B., Marquette U. Reporter Milw. Sentinel, Milw. Jour., Waukesha (Wis.) Daily Freeman, Racine (Wis.) Jour.-Times, 1933-43; with A.P., 1943—, editor, Omaha, staff cable desk, N.Y.C.; war corr. CBI Theater, corr., Calcutta, Bombay, New Delhi, 1945-48, world desk editor, chief bur., Manila, P.I., war corr., Korea, and chief bur., Manila, 1952-57, chief bur., Singapore, 1958-59; chief Southeast Asian services, from 1959, exec. asst. world service div., until 1978; ret., 1978; Mem. publ. relations adv. com. Marquette U. Contbr.: chpt. on Nehru Men Who Make Your World. Recipient Byline award for outstanding reporting in Korea Marquette U., 1953; Alumni Merit award Marquette U. Alumni Assn., 1975. Mem. Fgn. Corrs. Assn. S.E. Asia (v.p. 1958-59). Clubs: Overseas Press of America, Overseas Press P.I. (v.p. 1952-55), Overseas Press P.I. (pres. 1956-57), Tokyo Correspondents (sec. 1951-52). Home: 17459 Plaza Animado Apt 131 San Diego CA 92128

HUTH, EDWARD JANAVEL, physician, editor; b. Phila., May 15, 1923; s. Edward Gaston and Suzanne Madeleine (Janavel) H.; m. Carol Elizabeth Monnik, Apr. 6, 1957; children—John Edward, James Janavel. B.A., Wesleyan U., Middletown, Conn., 1945; M.D., U. Pa., 1947. Diplomate: Am. Bd. Internal Medicine, Nat. Bd. Med. Examiners. Intern Hosp. of U. Pa., 1947-48, resident medicine, 1949-51, ward physician, 1951-61; mem. Diagnostic Clinic, 1959-61; postdoctoral fellow Life Ins. Med. Research Fund, 1952-53; spl. research fellow USPHS, Univ. Coll. Hosp., London, Eng., 1957-58; asst. instr. pharmacology Sch. Medicine, U. Pa., Phila., 1948-49, asso. in medicine, 1951-58, asst. prof. medicine, 1958-61; asso. prof. comparative medicine Sch. Vet. Medicine, 1963-68; adj. asst. prof. medicine Sch. Medicine, U. Pa., 1966-71, asso. prof. clin. medicine, 1971-74, adj. clin. prof. medicine, 1974-78, adj. prof. medicine dept. medicine Assoc. Faculty, 1978—; asst. prof. medicine Woman's Med. Coll., Phila., 1961-62, asso. prof., 1962-65; Chmn. com. on 4th edit. CBE Style Manual Council Biology Editors, 1971-78; mem. biomedical communications study sect. NIH, 1972-76; chmn. subcom. 10 of Com. Z39 Am. Nat. Standards Inst., 1974-77; mem. UNISIST Working Group on Primary Sources of Info., UNESCO, Paris, 1973-74; bd. regents Nat. Library Medicine, 1979-83. Asst. editor: Annals of Internal Medicine, 1960-63; asso. editor, 1963-71; editor, 1971—; Contbr. articles to profl. jours. Served with AUS, 1943-46. Fellow ACP, AAAS (council mem. 1968), Am. Med. Writers Assn. (pres. 1967-68); mem. Am. Assn. for History Medicine, Am. Fedn. for Clin. Research, AMA, Assn. Am. Med. Colls., Council Biology Editors (dir. 1970-75, chmn. 1973-74), European Life Sci. Editors, Coll. Physicians Phila., Phila. County Med. Soc., Phi Beta Kappa, Sigma Xi, Alpha Omega Alpha, Zeta Phi. Home: 1124 Morris Ave Bryn Mawr PA 19010 Office: 4200 Pine St Philadelphia PA 19104

HUTH, WILLIAM EDWARD, lawyer; b. South Bend, Ind., July 26, 1931; s. Edward Andrew and Margaret Mary (Emonds) H.; m. Mary Pamela Hall, Aug. 11, 1962; children: Katharine Louise, Alan Edward. B.S., U. Dayton, 1952; LL.B., Yale, 1957. Bar: N.Y. State 1958, Mich. 1962, Pa. bar 1975, U.S. Supreme Ct. bar 1972, Conn. bar 1978. Asso. firm Kelley, Drye, Newhall & Maginnes, N.Y.C., 1958-61; sr. atty. Chrysler Corp., Detroit, 1962-72; partner firm Ziegler, Dykhouse, Wise & Huth, Detroit, 1973-74; asso. gen. counsel Westinghouse Electric Corp., Pitts., 1974-76; asst. sec., asst. gen. counsel Combustion Engring., Inc., Stamford, Conn., 1976—; adj. prof. law Wayne State U., Detroit, 1969-74. Contbr. articles to profl. publs. Served to 1st lt. AUS, 1952-54. Mem. Wesfacca Bar Assn. (bd. dirs.), ABA, Conn. Bar Assn., Assn. Bar N.Y.C., Order of Coif. Roman Catholic. Clubs: Yale (N.Y.C.); Nat. Lawyers (Washington). Home: 8 Nickerson Ln Darien CT 06820 Office: Combustion Engring Inc 900 Long Ridge Rd Stamford CT 06902

HUTNER, SEYMOUR HERBERT, microbiologist, protozoologist; b. Bklyn., Oct. 28, 1911; s. Julius and Fannie (Zuckerman) H.; m. Reina Albagli, 1938 (dec. 1955); 1 son, Reed Albagli; m. Margarita Silva, Aug. 18, 1956. B.S., Coll. City N.Y., 1932; Ph.D., Cornell U., 1937; Sc.D. (hon.), St. Francis Coll., Bklyn., 1984. Research asso. dept. physics Mass. Inst. Tech., 1935-36; technician Labs. and Research Div., N.Y. State Health Dept., 1938-41; staff Haskins Labs., N.Y.C., 1941—; Haskins adj. prof. biology Pace U., 1970-77, prof. emeritus in residence, 1977—; vis. prof. Inst. Microbiology, U. Brazil, Rio de Janeiro, 1963-64, U. Ill., Urbana, 1967, U. Brazilia, 1970; adj. prof. Fordham U., N.Y.C., 1964-69; bus. mgr. Jour. Phycology, 1963-67; mem. botany com. N.Y. Bot. Garden, 1974-77; cons. research unit vector pathology U. Nfld. Editor: (with A. Lwoff) Biochemistry and Physiology of Protozoa, vol. 2, vol. 3, 1964; co-editor: (with M. Levandowsky) Biochemical Physiological Protozoology, 4 vols., 2d edit.; editorial bd.: Jour. Protozoology, 1953—; editor publs.: 5th Internat. Congress Protozoology, 1977. Fellow N.Y. Acad. Sci., Am. Acad. Microbiology; mem. Soc. Protozoologists (hon., pres. 1961-62, chmn. com. spl. publs. 1963—), Soc. Gen. Microbiology, Am. Soc. Microbiology, Mycol. Soc. Am., Phycological Soc. Am., Japanese Soc. Plant Physiology, Tissue Culture Assn., Am. Assn. for Cancer Research, Acad. Scis. Brazil (corr.). Home: 142 West End Ave New York NY 10023 Office: Haskins Labs Pace Univ 41 Park Row New York NY 10038

HUTSON, DAVID ALLEN, photographer; b. Brawley, Calif., Apr. 12, 1950; s. William A.F. and Nanette Eileen (Weaver) H. B.Jour., U. Mo., 1971. Advt. account exec. Martin Fromm & Assos., Kansas City, Mo., 1972; staff photographer Kansas City (Mo.) Star, 1973-77, picture editor, 1978-79; pres. David Hutson Prodn., Westwood, Kans., 1979—; dir. A Typesetter, Inc. Recipient medal of honor Long Beach Photojournalism Show, 1978, 3d place award Nikon Internat. Photo Competition, 1977. Mem. Nat. Press Photographers Assn. U.S.A., Am. Racing Press Assn., Am. Auto Racing Writers and Broadcasters Assn., Internat. Motorsport Photography Soc. U.K., Kappa Alpha Mu, Kappa Tau Alpha. Office: 8120 Juniper St Prairie Village KS 66208

HUTSON, DON D., insurance company executive; b. Tex., Apr. 28, 1936; m. Charlene J. Hutson; children: Karen, Donna. Student, U. Ark.-Little Rock, 1945-57, Loyola Coll., Balt., 1974-75. With Md. Casualty Co., Balt. Mem. Greater Balt. Com., U.S. Olympic Com. Office: Md Casualty Co 3910 Keswick Rd Baltimore MD 21211

HUTSON, FRANK ALFRED, JR., lawyer, retired communications company executive; b. N.Y.C., Feb. 24, 1917; s. Frank Alfred and Irene (Rigby) H.; m. Catherine Brent Halsey, Dec. 23, 1943; children: Catherine Wrenn (Mrs. John C. Boulton), William Halsey, Jean Rigby (Mrs. James C. Lister). B.A., Swarthmore Coll., 1937; LL.B., Yale U., 1940. Bar: N.Y. 1940, Mass. 1956. Atty. firm Winthrop, Stimson, Putnam & Roberts, N.Y.C., 1940-49; atty. Nat. Biscuit Co., N.Y.C., 1949-52; with AT&T, N.Y.C., 1952-56, 60-82, gen. atty., 1966-72, sec., gen. atty., 1972-82; of counsel Kraft & Hughes, Newark, 1982—; gen. solicitor New Eng. Tel. & Tel. Co., Boston, 1956-60; mem. industry adv. com. SEC, 1972—. Served to capt. AUS, 1941-45; ETO. Decorated Bronze Star; Croix de Guerre with palm and silver star, France. Mem. Am. Law Inst., Am., N.Y. State bar assns., Bar Assn. City N.Y., Am. Soc. Corp. Socs. (chmn. 1978-79), Phi Beta Kappa, Phi Kappa Psi. Episcopalian. Clubs: Montclair (N.J.) Golf; Sakonnet Golf (Little Compton, R.I.); University (N.Y.C.); Essex (Newark). Home: 56 Fellswood Dr Essex Fells NJ 07021 Office: 195 Broadway New York NY 10007

HUTSON, JEAN BLACKWELL (MRS. JOHN O. HUTSON), librarian; b. Summerfield, Fla., Sept. 7, 1914; d. Paul Douglass and Sarah Frances (Myers) Blackwell; m. John O. Hutson, June 3, 1950 (dec. 1957); 1 dau., Jean. Student, U. Mich., 1931-34; B.A., Barnard Coll., 1935; B.S., Columbia U., 1936; L.H.D. (hon.), King Meml. Coll., Columbia, S.C., 1977. Librarian N.Y. Pub. Library, 1936—; br. librarian Woodstock Br., 1948; curator Schomburg Collection, 1948-72; chief Schomburg Center for Research in Black Culture, 1972-80, asst. dir. collection mgmt. and devel., 1980—; Lectr. Coll. City N.Y., 1962-70, adj. asso. prof., 1970-73; asst. librarian U. Ghana, 1964-65; lectr. Columbia Tchrs. Coll., 1969. Vice pres. Harlem Cultural Council; sec. bd. dirs. Harlem Neighborhoods Assn.; Mem. Jack and Jill Found. Recipient Camp Minisink community service award, 1952, Who's Who award 7th Ave. Assn., 1954, various awards Assn. for Study Negro Life and History, 1955, 66, 71, Distinguished Service award Caucus of Black Legislators N.Y. State, 1971, Community Service award Kappa Omicrom chpt. Omega Psi Phi, 1976, Lewis-Schuyler-Wheatley Arts and Letters award Delta Sigma Theta, 1976. Mem. ALA, NAACP, Nat. Urban League Guild, Mcpl. Art Soc., African Studies Assn., Delta Sigma Theta. Home: 2255 Fifth Ave New York NY 10037 Office: 515 Lenox Ave at 135th St New York NY 10037

HUTT, PETER BARTON, lawyer; b. Buffalo, Nov. 16, 1934; s. Lester Ralph and Louise Rich (Fraser) H.; m. Eleanor Jane Zurn, Aug. 29, 1959; children: Katherine Zurn, Peter Barton, Sarah Henderson, Everett Fraser. B.A. magna cum laude, Yale U., 1956; LL.B., Harvard U., 1959; LL.M., N.Y. U., 1960. Bar: N.Y. 1959, D.C. 1961, U.S. Supreme Ct. 1967. Asso. firm Covington & Burling, Washington, 1960-68, partner, 1968-71; chief counsel FDA; asst. gen. counsel HEW, 1971-75; partner firm Covington & Burling, 1975—; dir. Am. Sterilizer Corp., Erie, Pa.; mem. adv. com. to dir. NIH, 1976-81; mem. com. on research tng. Nat. Acad. Sci., 1976-80; mem. adv. panel Scripps Clinic and Research Found., La Jolla, Calif., Ctr. for Advanced Studies, U. Va., Inst. for Health Policy Analysis, Georgetown U. Author: (with Patricia Wald) Dealing with Drug Abuse, 1972, (with Richard Merrill) Food and Drug Law, 1980; contbg. editor: Legal Times of Washington; mem. editorial bd. various jours. Bd. dirs. Sidwell Friends Sch., Washington, Legal Action Center, N.Y.C., Found. for Biomed. Research, N.Y.C.; mem. vis. com. Harvard Sch. Public Health. Recipient Disting. Service award HEW, 1974; Underwood-Prescott award Mass. Inst. Tech., 1977. Mem. Am. Bar Assn. (chmn. life scis. com., sect. on sci. and tech.), Inst. Medicine, Nat. Acad. Scis., Washington Lawyers Com. for Civil Rights Under Law. Democrat. Episcopalian. Home: 5325 Chamberlin Ave Chevy Chase MD 20015 Office: 1201 Pennsylvania Ave NW Washington DC 20044

HUTT, WILLIAM IAN DEWITT, actor, theatre producer; b. Toronto, Ont., Can., May 2, 1920; s. Edward Dewitt and Caroline Francis (Wood) H. B.A., Trinity Coll. U. Toronto, 1949; D.Litt. (hon.), U. Guelph, Ph.D., D.F.A., U. Ottawa; LL.D., U. Western Ont., 1981. Debut as actor with, Bracebridge Summer Stock Co., Ont., Can., 1949; mem., Canadian Players Co.; appearing as: Macbeth; mem., Stratford (Ont.) Shakespeare Festival Co., 1953—; appearing in: numerous roles including Froth in Measure for Measure, 1954; Ford in The Merry Wives of Windsor, 1956, Polonius in Hamlet, 1957, Worcester in Henry IV, part 1, 1958, Jacques in As You Like It, 1959, Prospero in The Tempest, 1962, 76, Banquo in Macbeth, 1962, Pandarus in Troilus and Cressida, 1963, Richard II in Richard II, 1964, Dorante in The Bourgeois Gentleman, 1964, Shallow in Falstaff, 1965, Chorus in Henry V, 1966; title role in: Tartuffe, 1968, Trigorin in The Seagull, 1968, Sir Epicure Mammon in The Alchemist, 1969, Volpone, 1971, King Lear, 1972; the king of: France in All's Well That Ends Well, 1977; also: Fool in King Lear; James Tyrone in: Long Day's Journey into Night; Dr. Dorn in the: also in The Visit; appeared in: Shrewsbury in Mary Stuart at, N.Y.C.'s Phoenix Theatre, 1957, Mr. Kolonaty in The Makropoulos Secret, 1957; Broadway play Tiny Alice, 1965, Saint Joan at, Lincoln Theatre, N.Y.C., 1967, The Sly Fox, Alliance Theatre Co., Atlanta; numerous Canadian TV programs including Beckett, 1970; documentary-drama series The National Dream, 1974, The First Night of Pygmalion, 1975; Canadian tour as Klestakov in The Government Inspector, 1967, Sir Epicure Mammon in The Alchemist, 1969; appeared as Caesar in: Caesar and Cleopatra, Eng.; appeared in: film The Fixer, Budapest, Hungary; starred in: The Wars, 1981; dir. plays at, Stratford (Can.) Festival, most recent being, As You Like It, 1972, A Month in the Country, 1973, Oscar Remembered, 1975, The Tempest, 1976; G. B. Shaw's St. Joan, Stratford, 1975; mem.: The Players, Gramercy Park, N.Y.C.; artistic dir., Theatre of London. Served to lt., World War II; ETO. Decorated companion of Order of Can., 1969; recipient Priz Anik; Tyrone Guthrie award, 1954. Address: 4 Waterloo St N Stratford ON N5A 5H4 Canada

HUTTENBACK, ROBERT ARTHUR, university chancellor; b. Frankfurt, Germany, Mar. 8, 1928; s. Otto Henry and Dorothy (Marcuse) H.; m. Freda Braginsky, July 12, 1954; 1 dau., Madeleine Alexandra. B.A., U. Calif. at Los Angeles, 1951, Ph.D., 1959; postgrad., Sch. Oriental and African Studies, U. London, Eng., 1956-57. Mem. faculty Calif. Inst. Tech., Pasadena, 1958-78, asst. prof., 1960-63, asso. prof., 1963-66, prof. history, 1966-78, master student houses, 1958-69, dean students, 1969-72, chmn. div. humanities and social scis., 1971-77; chancellor U. Calif., Santa Barbara, 1978—; cons. Jet Propulsion Lab., Pasadena, 1966-68. Author: British Relations with Sind, 1799-1843, An Anatomy of Imperialism, 1962, (with Leo Rose and Margaret Fisher) Himalayan Battleground-Sino-Indian Rivalry in Ladakh, 1963, The British Imperial Experience, 1966, Gandhi in South Africa, 1971, Racism and Empire, 1976. Served to 1st lt. U.S. Army, 1951-53. Mem. Assn. Asian Studies, Am. Hist. Assn. Home: 2661 Todos Santos Ln Santa Barbara CA 93105

HUTTER, DONALD STEPHEN, editor; b. London, Dec. 30, 1932; s. Stefan Severin and Catherine (Hutter) Fraenkel; m. Martha Corbett, Aug. 17, 1957; children: Anne Victoria, Stephanie Grace, Sarah Catherine. B.A., Princeton U., 1954. Editor Charles Scribner's Sons, N.Y.C., 1957-67; sr. editor Dial Press, N.Y.C., 1967-69, editor in chief, 1969-72; exec. editor Holt, Rinehart & Winston, N.Y.C., 1972-81, editor in chief, 1981-82; v.p., sr. editor Simon & Schuster, 1982—. Author: Abraham, 1947, Upright Hilda, 1967; Contbr.: short stories to Best American Short Stories, 1965; also mags., including Esquire. Served with F.A. AUS, 1955-57. Home: 154 White Oak Shade Rd New Canaan CT 06840 Office: 521 Fifth Ave New York NY 10017

HUTTER, JAMES RISQUE, lawyer; b. Spokane, Wash., Mar. 20, 1924; s. James R. and Esther (Nelson) H.; m. Patricia Ruth Dunlavy, Aug. 12, 1951; children: Bruce Dunlavy, Gail Anne, Dean James, Karl Nelson. B.S., UCLA, 1947; J.D., Stanford U., 1950. Bar: Calif. 1951, U.S. Supreme Ct. 1965. Assoc. Gibson, Dunn & Crutcher, Los Angeles and Beverly Hills, Calif., 1950-58, ptnr., 1959—; dir. Fifield Manors, Los Angeles, 1955—, v.p., 1964—. Bd. dirs., chmn. fin. com. Congl. Found. for Theol. Studies, Nat. Assn. Congl. Christian Chs., 1961-68; mem. San Marino City Planning Commn., Calif., 1968—, chmn., Calif., 1976—. Served to 1st. inf. AUS, 1943-46. Decorated Purple Heart. Mem. State Bar Calif. (com. on corps. 1973-76, exec. com. bus. law sect. 1976-78), ABA, Los Angeles County Bar Assn., Beverly Hills Bar Assn. (bd. govs. 1968-70), Am. Judicature Soc., Town Hall, Phi Delta Phi, Beta Gamma Sigma, Phi Kappa Psi. Clubs: Stock Exchange of Los Angeles, Valley Hunt. Home: 1400 Circle Dr San Marino CA 91108 Office: 333 S Grand Ave 48th Floor Los Angeles CA 90071

HUTTER, ROBERT VICTOR PAUL, physician, educator; b. Yonkers, N.Y., May 25, 1929; s. Jack and Anna H.; m. Ruth Lauterbach, Aug. 7, 1955; children—Andrew, Edie, Randi. B.A., Syracuse U., 1950; M.D., State U. N.Y. at Syracuse, 1954; M.A., Yale U., 1969. Diplomate: Am. Bd. Pathology. Intern Yale Med. Center, 1954-55, resident, 1955-56, Meml. Hosp. Cancer and Allied Diseases, N.Y.C., 1956-57, chief resident, 1957-58; practice medicine, specializing in pathology/oncology, 1958—; mem. staff Meml. Hosp. for Cancer and Allied Diseases, 1956-68; prof. pathology Yale Med. Sch., 1968-70; chief of pathology Yale-New Haven Med. Center, 1968-70; prof., chmn. dept. pathology Coll. Medicine and Dentistry N.J., Newark, 1970—; also Am. Cancer Soc. prof. clin. oncology; mem. staff Martland Med. Center N.J.; chmn. dept. pathology St. Barnabas Med. Center, Livingston, N.J., 1973—; adj. prof. pathology Columbia U. Coll. Physicians and Surgeons. Served with USNR, 1958-60. Am. Heart Assn. fellow, 1955-56; Am. Cancer Soc. fellow, 1956-57. Fellow Coll. Am. Pathologists, Am. Coll. Radiology (hon.); mem. Phi Beta Kappa, Alpha Omega Alpha. Home: 30 Surrey Ln Livingston NJ 07039 Office: St Barnabas Med Center Livingston NJ 07039

HUTTER, RUDOLF GUSTAV EMIL, educator; b. Berlin, Feb. 12, 1910; s. Georg and Marie (Hempt) H.; m. Ruth S. Fraenkel, Nov. 17, 1939; 1 dau., Barbara S. State exam., U. Berlin, 1936; Ph.D. in Physics, Stanford, 1944. Engr. Telefunken GmbH, Berlin, 1936-38; chief engr. Sta. KZIB, Manila, 1938-40; research asso. Stanford U., 1941-44; sr. engr.-asso. dir. research Sylvania Electric Products, Inc., N.Y., Calif., 1944-58, chief engr., 1958-64; prof. electrophysics Poly. Inst. Bklyn., 1964-75, adj. prof., 1975—; vis. McKay prof. U. Calif. at Berkeley, 1957-58; tech. adviser GTE Labs., Waltham, Mass., 1964—. Author: Beam and Wave Electronics in Microwave Tubes, 1960; Editor: C. Sussking Electronics Handbook, 1962, Focusing of Charged Particles, 1967, Advances in Image Pickup and Display, (B. Kazan), 1974; Contbr. articles to profl. jours. Fellow IEEE; mem. Research Soc. Am., Sigma Xi. Home: 445 E 80th St New York NY 10021

HUTTERER, FERENC, med. scientist; b. Budapest, Hungary, Jan. 27, 1929; s. David and Gisella (Herzog) H.; m. Maria Belle, Feb. 7, 1953; 1 son, Richard. M.D., U. Szeged, Hungary, 1953. Intern Univ. Hosp., Szeged; resident City Hosp., Szeged; dir. dept. chemistry Mt. Sinai Hosp., N.Y.C., 1965-75; prof. pathology Mt. Sinai Sch. Medicine, City U. N.Y., 1967-75; prof., chmn. dept. molecular pathobiology Northeastern Ohio U. Coll. Medicine, Rootstown, 1975—. Contbr. numerous chpts. to books, articles to profl. jours. Mem. Fedn. Am. Socs. Exptl. Biology, Am. Assn. Study of Liver Disease, AAAS. Home: 7539 Westlake Blvd Kent OH 44240 Office: 4209 State Rt 44 Rootstown OH 44272

HUTTO, EARL, congressman; b. Midland City, Ala., May 12, 1926; s. Lemmie and Mathis (Hutto); m. Nancy Myers, July 8, 1967; children: Lori, Amelia Ann. B.S., Troy State U., 1949. Tchr. Cottonwood (Ala.) High Sch., 1949-51; sports and program dir. Sta.-WDIG, Dothan, Ala., 1951-54; sports dir. Sta.-WEAR-TV, Pensacola, Fla., 1954-60; pres. Sta.-WPEX-FM, Pensacola, 1960-65; sports dir. Sta.-WSFA-TV, Montgomery, Ala., 1961-63; sports dir., state news editor Sta.-WJHG-TV, Panama City, Fla., 1963-74; mem. Fla. Ho. of Reps., 1972-78, 96th-98th Congresses from 1st Fla. Dist., 1978—; mem. Mcht. Marine and Fisheries com., Armed Services Com.; chmn. Tech. Transfer Panel, 1983. Adv. council Mary Mackin Sch. Retarded Children; bd. dirs. Apalachee Bend council Girl Scouts U.S.A., Fla. Easter Seal Soc.; chmn. state govt. div. United Way, 1976, 77; exec. bd. Gulf Coast council Boy Scouts Am.; adv. com. Haney Vocat.-Tech. Center; deacon 1st Baptist Ch., Panama City. Served with USN. Recipient State Leadership award Sunshine State Assn. for the Blind, 1973; Legislator of Yr. award Fla. Assn. Retarded Children, 1974; Woodmen of the World Conservation award, 1974; Conservationist of Yr. award Bay County Audubon Soc., 1975; Legis. award Fla. Assn. Community Colls., 1978. Mem. Christian Businessmen's Assn., Troy State U. Alumni Assn. Club: Civitan (dep. gov. Ala.-West Fla. dist. 1967-71). Office: 330 Cannon House Office Bldg Washington DC 20515

HUTTO, JAMES CALHOUN, city ofcl.; b. Florence, S.C., Jan. 7, 1931; s. James Samuel and Miriam Haynes (Calhoun) H.; m. Sarah Doylene Renfroe, Aug. 22, 1953 (div. 1975); children—Martha Haynes, James Calhoun; m. Eleanor Christine Bradshaw, Feb. 13, 1976. B.S. in Commerce, Citadel Mil. Coll. of S.C., 1953; diploma auditing, Sch. Bank Adminstrn., U. Wis., 1970. Certified internal auditor. Asst. br. mgr. C.I.T. Corp., N.Y.C., 1955-58; part owner Quality Tire Service, Inc., Orangeburg, S.C., 1958-61; auditor Am. Bank & Trust Co., Orangeburg, 1961-71; gen. auditor Br. Banking & Trust Co., Wilson, N.C., 1971-73; gen. auditor, v.p. Bank of N.C., Jacksonville, 1973-78; comptroller Humphrey Heating & Roofing Inc., Jacksonville, 1979-81; fin. dir. City of Jacksonville, 1981—; instr. Am. Inst. Banking. Served to 1st lt., arty. AUS, 1953-55. Mem. Bank Adminstrn. Inst. (dir. Columbia, S.C. chpt.), Am. Inst. Banking, Inst. Internal Auditors, Bank Adminstrn. Inst. Sch. Alumni Assn. Home: 4 Laran Rd Jacksonville NC 28540 Office: PO Box 128 Jacksonville NC 28540

HUTTON, ANN HAWKES, state ofcl.; b. Phila., Feb. 16, 1909; d. Thomas G. and Katharine (Gallagher) Hawkes; m. Leon John H. Hutton, Sept. 23, 1939 (dec.); 1 dau., Katharine Ann (Mrs. Charles E. Tweedy III). B.S. in Edn, U. Pa., 1931, J.D., 1934. Dir. advt. Wetherill Paint Co., Phila., Memphis, 1936-38, Caravel Films, N.Y.C., 1938-39; Dir. advt., v.p. Hutton Chevrolet Co., Riverside, N.J., 1949-70; mem. Washington Crossing Park Commn., 1939—, chmn., 1963—; Historian, authority Emanuel Leutze painting Washington Crossing the Delaware; past chmn., now mem. Bucks County Hist.-Tourist Commn., 1960—; commr. Am. Revolution Bicentennial Commn., 1969-73, vice-chmn. adv. council, 1973-76. Author: George Washington Crossed Here, 1948, House of Decision, 1956, Portrait of Patriotism, 1959, The Pennsylvanian, 1962; drama The Decision, 1963, The Year and Spirit of 76, 1972; script for documentary film Washington Crossing the Delaware, 1966; Composer: 1776 Suite From the Decision, 1970. Trustee, former chmn. bd., now mem. Historic Fallsington; chmn. bd. Washington Crossing Found.; pres. Hist. Found. Pa. Recipient Nat. Bicentennial medal, 1976; Recipient award of merit D.A.R., 1955; Achievement award Commonwealth Pa. for research and furnishing historic Thompson-Neely House, 1955; citation Nat. Camp, Patriotic Order Sons Am., 1959; award Am. Legion Phila., 1960; Freedom Leadership award Freedoms Found. at Valley Forge (1st woman to receive this award), 1960; award Pa. Soc. D.A.R., 1960; award Freedoms Found. for drama The Decision, 1964; Good Citizenship medal Phila.-Continental chpt. SAR, 1967; Exceptional Citizenship award Patriotic Order Sons Am., 1968; Disting. Alumni award Friend's Select Sch., Phila., 1976; Fame award Friendship Fete Phila. and Delaware Valley, 1982; named Distinguished Dau. Pa., 1958; medal of honor D.A.R., 1973; nat. award Nat. Soc. Daus. Founders and Patriots, 1976; Disting. Service award Bucks County Commrs., 1980. Mem. Disting. Daus. Pa. (v.p. 1976-79, pres. 1979-82), Chi Omega, Pi Lambda Theta. Clubs: Bristol Travel; Lost Tree (North Palm Beach, Fla.); Union League (Phila.) (asso.). Home: 6900 N Radcliffe St Bristol PA 19007 *My purpose in the restoration of the Thompson-Neely "House of Decision" at Washington Crossing Historic Park, Pa. and other historic landmarks, was to bring to life the events and the people who lived and visited there. Similarly the motivation for my books and plays was to dramatize the enduring leadership of the Father of our Country, George Washington.*

HUTTON, EDWARD LUKE, corporate executive; b. Bedford, Ind., May 5, 1919; s. Fred and Margaret (Drehobl) H.; m. Kathryn Jane Alexander, Dec. 22, 1942; children: Edward Alexander, Thomas Charles, Jane Clarke. B.S. with distinction, Ind. U., 1940, M.S., 1941. Dep. dir. Joint Export Import Agy. U.S.-U.K., Berlin, 1945-47; v.p. dir. World Commerce Corp., N.Y.C., 1948-51; asst. v.p. W.R. Grace & Co., N.Y.C., 1951-53; cons. internat. trade, finance, 1953-54; v.p., dir. New York & Cuba Mail S.S. Co., N.Y.C., 1954-61, fin. v.p., 1958-59; v.p. and group exec. W.R. Grace & Co., 1969-71; exec. v.p., gen. mgr. DuBois Chem. div. W.R. Grace & Co., 1964-68; pres. E. L. Hutton, Assos., Inc., 1954-69; pres., chief exec. officer Chemed Corp., 1971—; chmn. Omnicare; dir. Chemed Corp., W.R. Grace & Co., Am. States Ins. Co., Vestal Labs. Inc., Vestal Internat. Inc., Nurotoco, Inc., Roto-Rooter Corp., Du Bois Germany; dir., mem. exec. com. El Torito Restaurants, Herman's Sporting Goods Inc.; co-chmn. Pres.'s Pvt. Sector Survey on Cost Control, 1982—; mem. gov. bd. Acad. Freedom Fund AAUP, 1958—. Trustee Village Bronxville, 1965-68, Millikin U., 1973—. Served to 1st lt. AUS, 1943-46. Mem. Newcomen Soc., Directors' Table, Beta Gamma Sigma. Methodist. Clubs: Downtown Assn., Economics, University, Princeton (N.Y.C.); Queen City, Bankers (Cin.). Home: 6680 Miralake Dr Cincinnati OH 45243 also Harris Rd East Orleans MA 02643 Office: 1114 Ave of Americas New York NY 10036 also 1200 DuBois Tower Cincinnati OH 45202

HUTTON, JAMES MORGAN, III, investment banker; b. Detroit, Aug. 18, 1927; s. James Morgan, Jr. and Marianne (Wurlitzer) H.; m. Virginia Palfrey, Dec. 17, 1954; children—Marianne D. Hutton Felch, Sarah J., James P. Grad., Hill Sch., 1945, Dartmouth, 1950. Salesman New Eng. Mut. Life Ins. Co., 1950-51; with W.E. Hutton & Co., N.Y.C., 1951-74, partner, 1958-64, mng. partner, 1964-74, 1974, exec. v.p., 1974—; dir. Wurlitzer Co., Saxton Products Co. Served with USNR, 1945-46. Mem. Psi Upsilon. Clubs: Am. Yacht, Apawamis (Rye); Nantucket (Mass.) Yacht.). Home: 5 Platt Ln Rye NY 10580 Office: Thomson McKinnon Securities Inc 6 Barker Ave White Plains NY 10601

HUTTON, ROBERT FRANKLIN, marine biologist, govt. ofcl.; b. Red Lion, Pa., July 18, 1921; s. Carl Stiles and Mary C. (Jones) H.; m. Wanda Lou Haviland; children—Roberta Lou, Marilyn Diane. Student, Gettysburg Coll., summer 1947; B.S. cum laude, U. Miami, Fla., 1949, M.S., 1951; Ph.D., U. London, Eng., 1953. Research asst. U. Miami, 1949-50, research instr., 1951, asst. prof., 1954; biologist-in-charge, parasitologist Fla. Bd. Conservation Marine Lab., 1955-62; asst. dir., chief marine biologist Mass. Div. Marine Fisheries, 1963-65; exec. sec. Am. Fisheries Soc., Washington, 1965-72; asso. dir. Nat.

Marine Fisheries Service, Washington, 1972-75, recreational fisheries and conservation community coordinator, 1978—; spl. asst. state affairs NOAA, Dept. Commerce, 1975-78; Mem. Nat. Conservation Awards Selections Com., 1965-71, Atlantic States Marine Fisheries Commn., 1963-67, Gen. Thomas D. White Fish and Wildlife Conservation Award Selection Com., 1967, 68. Contbr. articles to profl. jours. Fulbright scholar, 1951-52, 52-53; recipient Gov. Mass. Conservation award, 1965. Fellow AAAS, Internat. Acad. Fishery Scientists; mem. Am. Fisheries Soc. (1st v.p. 1974, pres. 1976-77), Natural Resources Council Am. (treas. 1966-69), Am. Soc. Parasitologists, Helminthological Soc. Washington, Marine Biol. Assn. U.K. (life), Atlantic Fisheries Biologists, Outdoor Writers Assn. Am., New Eng. Fisheries Inst., Mass. Lobstermen's Assn., Fla. Acad Scis., Wildlife Soc., Sport Fishing Inst., Nat. Wildlife Fedn., Izaak Walton League, Mass. Inst. Biol. Scientists, Atlantic Estuarine Research Biologists, Beta Beta Beta. New larval trematode, Gigantobilharzia huttoni, named for him, 1953; new trematode, Neostictodora huttoni, named for him, 1959. Home: 4030 N Woodstock St Arlington VA 22207 Office: Room 430 Page Bldg 2 3300 Whitehaven St Washington DC 20235

HUTTON, ROBERT WILLIAM, cement company executive; b. Olympia, Wash., Apr. 28, 1921; s. George W. and Elsie (Doragh) H.; m. Charlotte Thompson, Feb. 4, 1944; children: Ann Christine, George Thompson. B.A., U. Wash., 1943; M.B.A., Stanford, 1948. Credit analyst Seattle First Nat. Bank, 1948-51; controller, treas. Gaasland Constrn. Co., 1951-54; gen. mgr. Bellingham Builders Supply Co., Wash., 1954-64; with Lone Star Industries Inc., 1964—, sr. v.p., 1969-73, exec. v.p., 1973-75, pres., chief exec. officer, 1975-78, vice-chmn., 1978—, dir., 1973—, pres., 1971-73. Vice pres. Seattle Symphony, 1967-68; commr. Whatcom County (Wash.) Pub. Utility. Served with AUS, 1943-46; PTO. Decorated Bronze Star. Episcopalian (vestryman 1958-65). Clubs: Seattle Golf, Seattle Yacht, Seattle Tennis, Wash. Athletic (Seattle); Am. Yacht (Rye, N.Y.); N.Y. Yacht; Belle Haven (Greenwich, Conn.). Office: 1 Greenwich Plaza Greenwich CT 06836

HUTTON, TIMOTHY, actor; b. Malibu, Calif., 1961; s. Jim and Maryline H. Appeared in: TV movie Zuma Beach, 1978, Best Place to Be, Baby Makes Six, Sultan and the Rock Star, Young Love, First Love, Friendly Fire, 1979; film Ordinary People, 1980, Taps, 1981, Daniel, 1983. Recipient Oscar for best actor, Ordinary People, 1980. Office: Internat Creative Mgmt 8899 Beverly Blvd Los Angeles CA 90048 *

HUTTON, WILLIAM, art historian; b. N.Y.C., Oct. 2, 1926; s. George V. D. and Ruth (Shafer) H.; m. Marjorie Mary Mattimoe, Dec. 29, 1956; children—William, Ruth K., Mary C., Eleanor A. B.A., Williams Coll., 1950; M.A., Harvard, 1952. Asst. curator Toledo Mus. Art, 1952-64; dir. Currier Gallery Art, Manchester, N.H., 1965-68; with dept. ceramics Victoria and Albert Mus., London, 1968-71; chief curator and sr. curator Toledo Mus. Art, 1971—. Editor: Toledo Mus. Art Am. Paintings, 1979, Toledo Mus. Art Mus. News. Served with AUS, 1945-46. Mem. Coll. Art Assn., Am. Assn. Museums. Episcopalian. Home: 4505 River Rd Toledo OH 43614

HUTZLER, ALBERT DAVID, JR., merchant; b. Baltimore County, Md., Mar. 1, 1916; s. Albert David and Gretchen (Hochschild) H.; m. Bernice Levy, Sept. 22, 1937; children—Elizabeth Ann Hutzler Friedman, Albert David, III, James Levy. Student, Friends Sch.; A.B., Johns Hopkins, 1937. Trainee R.H. Macy & Co., N.Y.C., 1937-38; with Hutzler Bros. Co., 1938-78, pres., gen. mgr., 1954-75, chmn. bd., 1975-78; ret., 1978. Dir., past pres. Com. for Downtown, Inc.; past mem. exec. com. Greater Balt. Com., Inc.; past mem. bd. dirs. United Fund Central Md., Inc.; bd. dirs. Asso. Jewish Charities and Welfare Fund, pres., 1967-69; trustee Johns Hopkins U.; pres. Hutzler Fund, Inc. Club: Center (Balt.). Home: 2066 N Ocean Blvd Boca Raton FL 33431 Office: Office Hutzler's Baltimore MD 21201

HUVOS, KORNEL, linguistics educator; b. Budapest, Hungary, Apr. 25, 1913; came to U.S., 1956, naturalized, 1961; s. Laszlo and Ilona (Vajda de Kunagota) Huvos de B.; m. Anna Maria Ledniczky, Mar. 25, 1945; 1 son, Christopher. Bachelier Lettres, U. Paris, 1931; J.S.D., Royal U. Budapest, 1938; Ph.D., U. Cin, 1965. French-German-Hungarian lexicographer Hungarian Acad. Scis., Budapest, 1947-56; news analyst Cin. Times Star, 1956-58; mem. faculty U. Cin., 1958—, Charles Phelps Taft prof. Romance langs and lits., 1975-82, head dept. Romance langs. and lits., 1977-81. Author: (with L. Clark Keating) Impressions d'Amerique: Les Etats-Unis dans la littérature francaise contemporaine, 1970, Cinq Mirages Américains: Les Etats-Unis dans l'oeuvre de Georges Duhamel, Jules Romains, André Maurois, Jacques Maritain et Simone de Beauvoir, 1972; contbr. articles to profl. jours. Decorated officer Nat. Order Acad. Palms (France); recipient George Rieveschl, Jr. award for Excellence in Scholarly Works, 1978; Woodrow Wilson fellow, 1959; U. Cin. Grad. Sch. fellow, 1979; Taft Meml. research grantee, 1969, 74, 78, 80, 82. Mem. South Atlantic MLA, Midwest MLA, MLA, Am. Assn. Tchrs. French, AAUP, Lit. Club Cin, Pi Delta Phi. Roman Catholic. Home: 1600 Thomson Heights Dr Cincinnati OH 45223 Office: Dept Romance Langs U Cin Cincinnati OH 45221

HUXTABLE, ADA LOUISE, architecture critic; b. N.Y.C.; d. Michael Louis and Leah (Rosenthal) Landman; m. L. Garth Huxtable. A.B. magna cum laude, Hunter Coll.; postgrad., Inst. Fine Arts, NYU; hon. degrees, Yale U., NYU, Washington U., U. Mass., Oberlin Coll., Miami U., R.I. Sch. Design, U. Pa., Radcliffe Coll., Oberlin Coll., Smith Coll., Skidmore Coll., Md. Inst., Mt. Holyoke Coll., Trinity Coll., LaSalle U., Pace Coll., Pratt Inst., Colgate U., Hamilton U., Williams Coll., Rutgers U., Finch Coll., Emerson Coll., C.W. Post Coll. at L.I. U., Cleve. State U., Bard Coll., Fordham U. Asst. curator architecture and design The Museum of Modern Art, N.Y.C., 1946-50; Fulbright fellow for advanced study in architecture and design, Italy, 1950, 52; free-lance writer, contbg. editor to Progressive Architecture and Art in America, 1950-63; architecture critic N.Y. Times, N.Y.C., 1963-82, mem. editorial bd., 1973-82; Cook lectr. in Am. instns. U. Mich., 1977; Hitchcock lect. U. Calif.-Berkeley, 1982; corp. vis. com. Harvard U. Grad. Sch. Design; mem. council Rockefeller U., Smithsonian Instn.; bd. dirs. N.Y. Landmarks Conservancy; mem. adv. bd. Urban Affairs Inst. NYU; mem. Ctr. Study Am. Architecture Columbia U. Author: Pier Luigi Nervi, 1960, Classic New York, 1964, Will They Ever Finish Bruckner Boulevard?, 1970, Kicked a Building Lately?, 1976. Recipient 1st Pulitzer prize for disting. criticism, 1970; Spl. award Nat. Trust for Historic Preservation, 1971; Archtl. Criticism medal AIA, 1969; medal for lit. Nat. Arts Club, 1971; Diamond Jubilee medallion City N.Y., 1973; Woman of Year award AAUW, 1974; Sec.'s award for conservation U.S. Dept. Interior, 1976; Thomas Jefferson medal U. Va., 1977; others.; Guggenheim fellow for studies in Am. architecture, 1958; MacArthur prize fellow, 1981. Fellow Am. Acad. Arts and Scis., N.Y. Inst. Humanities, Royal Inst. Brit. Architects (hon.); mem. Am. Acad. and Inst. Arts and Letters, AIA (hon.), Soc. Archtl. Historians. Office: 969 Park Ave New York NY 10028

HUYETT, DANIEL HENRY, III, judge; b. Reading, Pa., May 2, 1921; s. Daniel Henry, Jr. and Emma Alice (Moyer) H.; m. Mary Jane Hallford, Mar. 23, 1946; children: Cathy J. (Mrs. Tracy James Whitaker), Daniel B., Christina N. (Mrs. Harold G. Kelso III). A.B., U. Mich., 1942; J.D., U. Pa., 1948. Bar: Pa. 1949. Practiced in, Berks County, 1949-70, city solicitor, Reading, 1952-56; U.S. dist. judge Eastern Dist. Pa., Phila., 1970—; lectr. Fed. Jud. Center, Washington, 1977, 78, 79; instr. Atty. Gen. Advocacy Inst., 1978-83. Mem. Pa. Labor Relations Bd., 1966-68, Pa. Pub. Utility Commn., 1968-70. Served as 1st lt. USAAF, World War II; capt. USAF Res. Mem. Am., Pa., Berks County bar assns., Am. Judicature Soc., Supreme Ct. Hist. Soc., Am. Law Inst. Home: 403 Green Ln Greenfields Reading PA 19601 Office: 12614N US Courthouse Philadelphia PA 19106

HUYGENS, REMMERT WILLIAM, architect; b. Haarlem, Holland, Apr. 19, 1932; s. Willem and Antoinette (Bruynzeel) H. Student, Gymnazium, Alkmaar, 1951; dept. architecture, Amsterdam HTS, 1955. Registered architect, Mass. Pvt. practice architecture, 1960—; prin. Huygens and Dimella, Inc. (Architects and Planners), Boston, 1962—; guest lectr. Brockton (Mass.) Art Center, 1970, 71; mem. jury 1973 Homes for Better Living Awards Program, Am. Plywood Assn. Awards Program and; Mich. chpt. AIA; vis. critic Harvard U. Prin. works include: Longy Concert Hall Library, Cambridge, Mass., Riverview Office Tower, Cambridge, Mass., Interfaith Religious Center, Columbia, Md., Biogen Research Ctr., Geneva, N.H. Coll. Campus, Franklin Park Zoo, Boston, Cath. Med. Center, Manchester, N.H., Framingham (Mass.) Central Library, The Village of Loon Mountain, Lincoln, N.H., also residential projects and pvt. residences in, U.S., France, Switzerland and Holland; exhibited at, N.Y. Archtl. League, 1973, Mus. Modern Art, N.Y.C., 1979; works pub. in, U.S., Eng., Holland, Italy, Japan, France. Recipient Progressive Architecture Design award, 1966; citation, 2 hon. mentions AIA, 1969; 1st honor award, 1970; award of merit, 1979, 80; 1st award Plywood Design Awards Program, 1973; honor awards New Eng. regional council AIA, 1974, 1975, 76, 78; award of merit R.I. chpt., 1978; Abu-Dhabi Conf. Center award, 1975; numerous others. Mem. AIA (guest lectr. Ky. chpt. 1969, chmn. Ky. jury design award 1969, Vt. jury design awards 1975, jury mem. Homes for Better Living Awards 1981, Harleston Parker medal Boston chpt.), Boston Soc. Architects (mem. honors and awards com.). Club: New Bedford Yacht. Home: 125 Old Connecticut Path Wayland MA 01778 Office: 286 Congress St Boston MA 02110

HVIDSTON, COLBURN, III, photojournalist; b. Northwood, N.D., Apr. 25, 1939; s. Colburn and Margurite (Lyons) H.; m. Jacquelyn Dianne Brooks, June 20, 1961; children: Michael Colburn, Jennifer Marie, David Brooks. B.S. in Bus. Adminstrn, U. N.D., 1961. Photographer Grand Forks (N.D.) Herald, 1962-66; organizer Photo Service, U. N.D., Fargo, 1967, lectr. photojournalism, 1967-71; photo chief The Forum, Fargo, 1968—. Recipient Penney (Mo.) and Pix of Yr. photo awards, 1970, N.D. AP Picture of Yr. citation, 1970. Mem. Nat. Press Photographers Assn. (pres. 1982-83, Photo awards 1969, 71, Outstanding Bd. Mem. citation 1980). Home: 1225 2d St N Fargo ND 58102 Office: The Forum Box 2020 Fargo ND 58107

HYAMS, JOE, writer; b. Cambridge, Mass., June 6, 1923; s. Joseph Irving and Charlotte (Strauss) H.; m. Elke Sommer, Nov. 18, 1964. B.S., N.Y. U., 1948, M.A., 1949. Editor Reporter Publs., 1947-50; columnist N.Y. Herald Tribune, 1950-64. Author: (with Walter Wanger) My Life With Cleopatra, 1963, (with Maj. Riddle) A Weekend Gamblers Handbook, 1963, (with Edith Head) How To Dress for Success, 1966, (with Peter Sellers) Seller's Market, 1964, Bogie, 1966, A Field of Buttercups, 1968, (with Thomas Murton) Accomplices to the Crime, 1969, (with Tony Trabert) Winning Tactics for Weekend Tennis, 1972, Mislaid in Hollywood, 1973, (with Pancho Gonzales) Winning Tactics for Singles, 1973, (with Billie Jean King) Billie Jean King's Secrets of Winning Tennis, 1974, Bogart and Bacall: A Love Story, 1966, Inner Strength, 1977, The Pool, 1978, Zen in the Martial Arts, 1979, The Last Award, 1981, Playboy Guide to Self-Defense, 1981, Murder at the Academy Awards, 1983. Mem. Author's Guild, Am. Newspaper Guild. Clubs: Overseas Press (N.Y.C.); Savile (London). Address: care Saint Martin's Press Inc 175 Fifth Ave New York NY 10010

HYATT, DONALD BISHOP, TV and film producer-dir.; b. New Britain, Conn., Apr. 22, 1924; s. Isaac Robert and Emily (Cone) H.; m. Jeanne Hartnett, Mar. 14, 1959; children—Wendy, Christopher Robert. Grad., Taft Sch., 1943; B.A. summa cum laude, Dartmouth, 1950. Dir. Plymouth (N.H.) Slopes Ski Sch., 1946-48; instr. skiing Dartmouth, 1946-50; dir. spl. projects NBC-TV, from 1958; now ind. film producer-dir., TV cons.; vis. lectr. Yale U., 1980-81. Exec. producer: spl. projects programs including Wisdom series, 1958—, World of... series, 1961—; producer, dir. Project 20 programs, 1958—, The American Experience Bicentennial Series, 1973; producer dir., writer: ski film Hanover Hickory, 1950; Author: (with Richard Hanser) Meet Mr. Lincoln, 1960, The Coming of Christ, 1963, The Law and The Prophets, 1971. Pres. Linden Shore Dist., Branford, Conn. Served to 2d lt. USAAF, 1943-45. Recipient over 100 nat. and internat. awards for Projects 20 and spl. projects programs. Mem. Nat. Acad. TV Arts and Scis. (bd. govs.), Dirs. Guild Am. Conglist. Clubs: Dutch Treat (N.Y.C.); Pine Orchard Yacht and Country (commodore). Home: Linden Ave Indian Neck Branford CT 06405

HYATT, GERHARDT WILFRED, clergyman, college president; b. Melfort, Sask., Can., July 1, 1916; came to U.S., 1939, naturalized, 1945; s. Francis William and Mary Elizabeth (Faber) H.; m. Elda Rosa Mueller, Mar. 8, 1946; children: Ruth (Mrs. Robert Cornelius Heffron, Jr.), Matthew Leavenworth. Student, Concordia Coll., Edmonton, Alta., Can., 1935-39, Concordia Sem., St. Louis, 1939-44, D.D., 1969; M.A., George Washington U., 1964; L.D.H., Tarkio Coll., Mo., 1974. Ordained to ministry Lutheran Ch., 1944; pastor Our Savior Luth. Ch., Raleigh, N.C., 1944-45; commd. 1st lt. U.S. Army, 1945; advanced through grades to maj. gen.; with Office Dep. Chief of Staff, Army Gen. Staff, 1960-63; div. chaplain 3d Armoured Div. in Europe, dep. USAREUR chaplain, 1966-68; dir. personnel and ecclesiastical relations Office Chief of Chaplains, Washington, 1968-69; command chaplain U.S. Army Mil. Assistance Command, Vietnam, 1969-70; dep. chief of chaplains U.S. Army, Washington, 1970-71, chief of chaplains, 1971-75; pres. Concordia Coll., St. Paul, 1976-83; asst. to pres. Luth. Ch.-Mo. Synod, 1983—; established Grace Luth. Ch., Woodbridge, Va., 1959; v.p. Luth. Ch.-Mo. Synod. Decorated D.S.M., Legion of Merit, Bronze Star, Joint Service Commendation medal, Army Commendation medal with oak leaf cluster, Civil Actions Honor medal 1st class; Vietnam, Vietnamese Honor medal 1st class; recipient Four Chaplains award Alexander D. Goode-Ben Goldman Lodge, B'nai B'rith, 1969, Golden Rule award St. George Assn., N.Y.C. Police Dept., 1973. Mem. Mil. Order World Wars. Home: 9 Ridge Rd North Oaks MN 55110 Office: 1333 S Kirkwood Dr Saint Louis MO 63122

HYATT, JOEL Z., lawyer, management services services company executive; b. Cleve., May 6, 1950; s. David and Anna (B.) Zylberberg; m. Susan Metzenbaum, Aug. 24, 1975; 1 son, Jared Z. B.A., Dartmouth Coll., 1972; J.D., Yale U., 1975. Pres., chief exec. officer Hyatt Legal Services, Kansas City, Mo. Office: Hyatt Legal Services 4410 Main St Kansas City MO 64111

HYDE, DAVID ROWLEY, lawyer; b. Norwalk, Conn., Aug. 21, 1929; s. Thomas Arthur and Mary Julia (Sass) H.; m. Valerie Rosemary Worrall, Dec. 30, 1961; children: Meredith Ellen, Timothy Worrall. A.B., Yale U., 1951, LL.B., 1954. Bar: Conn. 1954, N.Y. 1956, U.S. Supreme Ct. 1969. Assoc. Cahill Gordon & Reindel, N.Y.C., 1954-59, 64-65, ptnr., 1966—; asst. U.S. atty. So. Dist. N.Y., 1959-63; chief civil div. U.S. Atty.'s Office, 1961-63. Home: 35 W 12th St New York NY 10011 Office: Cahill Gordon & Reindel 80 Pine St New York NY 10005

HYDE, DAYTON OGDEN, author; b. Marquette, Mich., Mar. 25, 1925; s. Frederick Walton and Rhoda (Williams) H.; m. Gerda Isenberg, Sept. 23, 1950; children—Dayton, Virginia, Marsha, John, Taylor. B.A., U. Calif. at Berkeley, 1950. Owner 6000-acre cattle ranch, So. Oreg., 1959—, lectr., conservationist, 1960. Also radio and TV guest articles and photographs appeared in nat. mags. and jours.; producer, star 1st Am. rodeos in, Europe.; Author: Sandy, 1968, Yamsi, 1971, Cranes in My Corral, 1971, The Last Free Man, 1973; Editor: Raising Wild Waterfowl in Captivity, 1973, Strange Companion, 1975 (Dutton Animal Book award). Bd. dirs. Defenders of Wildlife, Internat. Wild Waterfowl Assn. Served with U.S. Army, 1944-46; ETO. Constructed Hyde Lake, 400 acre refuge for wildlife, 1971-76; created Operation Stronghold, nationwide pvt. land wildlife stronghold network, 1980. Home: Yamsi Ranch Chiloquin OR 97624 *I've always enjoyed the discipline of hard work. America needs a return to the work ethic. Conservationwise we must realize that man, like any other species, is on his way somewhere, either advancing on the scale or retrogressing. We cannot continue to ignore the great natural laws, creating smarter and smarter coyotes, dumber and dumber people.*

HYDE, EARL K., chemist; b. Rossburn, Man., Can., Aug. 9, 1920; s. Howard Earl and Evelyn Stewart (Black) H.; m. Jean Babbitt, Jan. 1, 1949; children—Carol Anne, Wendy Jean, Charles Earl, Howard Alan. B.S. in Chemistry, U. Chgo., 1941, Ph.D., 1946. Research asso. in chemistry war research U. Chgo., 1942-44; research chemist Manhattan Project, 1944-46, Argonne (Ill.) Nat. Lab., 1946-49; staff chemist radiation lab. U. Calif., Berkeley, 1949-60; sr. scientist Lawrence Berkeley (Calif.) Lab., 1960-70, dep. head nuclear chemistry div., 1970-73, dep. lab. dir., 1973—; ofcl. del. 1st Geneva Conf. Peaceful Uses Atomic Energy, Geneva, 1955; chmn. Gordon Research Conf. Nuclear Chemistry, 1957. Co-author: The Nuclear Properties of the Heavy Elements, 3 vols, 1964; contbr. articles profl. jours. Fellow Am. Phys. Soc.; mem. Am. Chem. Soc. Office: Lawrence Berkeley Lab Univ Calif Berkeley CA 94720

HYDE, HENRY JOHN, congressman; b. Chgo., Apr. 18, 1924; s. Henry Clay and Monica (Kelly) H.; m. Jeanne Simpson, Nov. 8, 1947; children: Henry J., Robert, Laura, Anthony. Student, Duke U., 1943-44; B.S., Georgetown U., 1946; J.D., Loyola U., Chgo., 1949. Bar: Ill. Mem. Ill. Gen. Assembly, 1967-74, 97th-98th congresses from 6th Ill. Dist. Served with USN, 1944-46. Mem. Chgo. Bar Assn. Republican. Roman Catholic. Home: 1004 Argyle Ave Bensenville IL 60106 Office: 2104 Rayburn House Office Bldg Washington DC 20515 *

HYDE, JAMES NEVINS, lawyer; b. Chgo., Jan. 11, 1909; s. Charles Cheney and Mary (Tilton) H.; m. Margaret Wells, Nov. 30, 1935; children: Mary (Mrs. James H. Ottaway, Jr.), Margaret (Mrs. H. Denman Scott), James, Elizabeth (Mrs. Durward E. Littlefield), Andrea (Mrs. John F. Hagaman). A.B., Yale U., 1931; postgrad., Trinity Coll., Cambridge (Eng.) U., 1931-32; LL.B., Columbia U., 1935. Bar: N.Y. 1935. Asso. firm Miller, Owen, Otis & Bailly, N.Y.C., 1935-40; appellate practice with Nathan L. Miller, 1940-42; asst. to gen. counsel U.S. Steel Corp., 1942, with law dept., 1946-48; adviser, interim com. affairs U.S. Mission to UN, 1948-53; adviser Security Council and Gen. Affairs, 1949; dep. U.S. rep. interim com. Gen. Assembly, 1951; adviser U.S. del. 4th, 5th, 6th, 7th sessions Gen. Assembly; partner Gross & Hyde, N.Y.C., 1953-54, Hyde & de Vries, 1954-59; cons. internat. matters, 1959—; lectr. internat. law; law faculty Salzburg Seminar in Am. Studies, 1966; adj. prof. internat. law Fletcher Sch. Law and Diplomacy, 1973-78; Chmn. com. peaceful settlement disputes White House Conf. Internat. Coop., 1965; mem. curatorium Hague Acad. Internat. Law, 1968-74. Bd. editors: Am. Jour. Internat. Law, 1958-72, hon. mem., 1973—; contbr. articles to profl. jours. Served from lt. (j.g.) to lt. comdr. USNR, World War II; PTO. Mem. Am. Soc. Internat. Law (pres. 1963-64, hon. v.p.), Internat. Law Assn., Assn. Bar City N.Y. (chmn. fgn. law com. 1956-59). Home: Taunton Ln RD3 Newtown CT 06470

HYDE, JOSEPH R., III, wholesale food distribution executive; b. Memphis, Dec. 27, 1942; m. Judy Kendall; 3 children. B.S., U. N.C., 1965. With Malone & Hyde, Memphis, 1965—, pres., 1969—, chmn. bd. dirs., 1972—; dir. 1st Tenn. Bat. Bank, Fed. Express Corp., Browning-Ferris Industries, Inc. Bd. dirs. Hyde Found., Memphis U. Sch., Memphis Arts Council; chmn. bd. Leadership Memphis. Mem. Nat. Wholesale Grocers Assn. (dir.), Memphis C. of C. (dir.). Office: Malone & Hyde Inc 1991 Corporate Ave Memphis TN 38132

HYDE, LAURENCE EVELYN, artist, writer; b. London, June 6, 1914; emigrated to Can., 1926; s. Sydney Augustus and Lillian Mildred (Snelling) H.; m. Bettye Marguerite Bambridge, 1939; children: Anthony, Christopher. Film dir. Nat. Film Bd. Can., Ottawa, Ont., 1942-72; freelance writer children's books, film scripts. Recipient Film awards Cook Film Festival, Montreal Internat. Film Festival, Venice Biennale. Mem. Authors Guild Am., Ont. Soc. Artists. Home: 15 Crichton St Ottawa ON Canada K1M 2E3

HYDE, LAWRENCE HENRY, JR., manufacturing company executive; b. Cambridge, Mass., July 10, 1924; s. Lawrence Henry and Catherine I. (McMahon) H.; m. Lois A. Crehan, May 31, 1947; children—Abigail Ellen, Lawrence Henry III. A.B., Harvard U., 1946, M.B.A., 1947. With Ford Motor Co., 1947-65, dir. internat. purchasing office, 1960-62; v.p., gen. mgr. consumer products div. Philco Corp. div. Ford Motor Co., 1962-64; with Harris Corp., Cleve., 1965-73, dir. internat. ops., 1965-69, group v.p. internat., 1969-73; with Am. Motors Corp., Detroit, 1974—, v.p. internat., 1974-77, group v.p. cars and jeep Vehicles, 1977-79; group v.p. internat. and spl. vehicles ops. and pres. AM Gen. Corp., 1979-81, exec. v.p., 1982—. Trustee Am. U. in, Cairo. Office: 14250 Plymouth Rd Detroit MI 48232

HYDE, MARY MORLEY CRAPO (MRS. DONALD F. HYDE), author; b. Detroit, July 8, 1912; d. Stanford Tappan and Emma Caroline (Morley) Crapo; m. Donald Frizell Hyde, Sept. 16, 1939. A.B., Vassar Coll., 1934; M.A., Columbia U., 1936, Ph.D., 1947; D.Litt., Douglass Coll., 1964; Litt.D., Brown U., 1968, U. Birmingham, Eng., 1969; D.H.L., Union Coll., 1979. Mem. English dept. and library adv. councils Princeton, 1965—; mem. English dept. and libraries vis. coms. Harvard, 1966—. Author: Playwriting for Elizabethans, 1949; editor: (with E. L. McAdam and Donald Hyde) Johnson's Diaries, Prayers and Annals, 1958, Four Oaks Farm and Its Library, 1967, Impossible Friendship (Boswell and Mrs. Thrale), 1973, The Thrales of Streatham Park, 1977, Bernard Shaw and Alfred Douglas, A Correspondence, 1982; Mem. editorial coms.: Yale Works of Johnson, 1957, Private Papers of Boswell, 1966—. Trustee Pierpont Morgan Library, 1966—; trustee Johnson House, London, 1983; mem. council Friends of Columbia U. Libraries, 1954—; mem. humanities vis. com. U. Chgo., 1956—; trustee Yale Libraries Assos., 1970—, Am. Trust for Brit. Library, 1980. Decorated officer de l'Ordre de la Couronne, Belgium; Benjamin Franklin fellow Royal Soc. Arts, London. Mem. Am. Philos. Soc., Johnson Soc. (Lichfield, Eng.) (pres. 1957), Boswell Soc. (Auchinleck, Scotland) (pres. 1984), Hroswitha, Grolier Club (council 1979, v.p. 1982), Bibliog. Soc. Am., The

Johnsonians, Keats-Shelley Assn. Am. (dir. 1967—), N.Y. Hort. Soc., Association Internnationale de Bibliophilie (v.p. 1983), Phi Beta Kappa. Home: Four Oaks Farm 350 Burnt Mill Rd Somerville NJ 08876 Office: 20 Nassau St Princeton NJ 08540

HYDE, PAUL LITCHFIELD, banker; b. Cleve., July 7, 1932; s. Howard Linton and Katharine (Litchfield) H.; m. Sharon Lally Winger, July 12, 1958; children: Brinton, Nathan, Magreger. B.A., Amherst Coll., 1954; M.B.A., Harvard U., 1958. From trainee to v.p. Nat. City Bank, Cleve., 1958-76; pres. Bank One Dayton N.A., Dayton, Ohio, 1976—. Trustee USAF Mus., Dayton, 1980—, Mus. Natural History, Dayton, 1978—, Dayton Art Inst., 1977-83. Served to lt. USAF, 1954-56. Home: 2846 Turkey Foot Rd Bellbrook OH 45305 Office: Bank One Dayton NA Kettering Tower Dayton OH 45401

HYDE, ROBERT BURKE, JR., bus. exec.; b. Houston, Feb. 1, 1928; s. R. B. and Marian (Johnson) H.; m. Dorothy Gean Weempe, May 5, 1956; children—Julie Ann, Karen Kay. B.Ch.E., Tex. A. and M. U., 1949. Registered profl. engr., Tex. Sales and service engr. Dresser Industries, Inc., 1949; successively dist. mgr., chief service engr., mgr. engring. and mktg. services, mgr. research and engring., mgr. U.S. and Can. ops., exec. v.p. Magcobar, pres. oilfield products div., 1972-75, pres. oilfield products group, 1975-80, v.p. ops., 1980-81, sr. v.p. ops., 1981—; Met. chmn. Nat. Alliance Bus.; mem. public and polit. affairs com. Nat. Ocean Industries Assn. Mem. Petroleum Equipment Suppliers Assn. (exec. com.), Am. Petroleum Inst., AIME, others. Republican. Presbyterian. Clubs: Houston, Petroleum (Houston); Lakeside Country, Masons. Office: PO Box 6504 601 Jefferson St Houston TX 77005 *

HYDE, ROBERT PAUL, telecommunications executive; b. Cambridge, Mass., Jan. 15, 1930; s. Lawrence Henry and Catherine Isabel (McMahon) H.; m. Zay Dunphy, June 6, 1953; children: Ellen, Robert, Alison, Anne, William. A.B., Harvard U., 1951, M.B.A., 1955. From asst. to pres. to sales mgr. Carling Brewing Co., Cleve., 1955-63; v.p. mktg. Stroh Brewery Co., Detroit, 1963-70; pres. Rheingold Breweries, Inc., N.Y.C., 1970-73, Onondaga Products Corp., Syracuse, N.Y., 1975-81; exec. v.p. Western Union Telegraph Co., Upper Saddle River, N.J., 1980—. Served to capt. USMCR, 1951-53. Roman Catholic. Clubs: Harvard (Boston); Detroit Athletic, Country of Detroit, Cazenovia Country. Home: 48 N Island Ave Ramsey NJ 07446 Office: 1 Lake St Upper Saddle River NJ 07458

HYDE, STUART WALLACE, educator, author; b. Fresno, Calif., Aug. 8, 1923; s. Henry Jacob and Anna (Stuckert) H.; m. Allie Caroline Bargum, June 18, 1949; children: Stuart Wallace, John Christian, Allison Elizabeth Ann. Student, Fresno State Coll., 1941-42; B.A., UCLA, 1948; M.A., Stanford U., 1950, Ph.D., 1953. Instr. radio-TV Stanford, 1953-55; asst. prof. telecommunications U. So. Calif., 1955-58; asso. prof. radio-television-film San Francisco State Coll., 1958-63, prof., 1963—, chmn. dept., 1958-76, chair acad. senate, 1976-78. Author: Television and Radio Announcing, 4th edit, 1983; contbr. articles to profl. jours. Mem. community edn. com. San Quentin State Prison. Served to lt. (j.g.) USNR, 1943-46. Mem. Am. Council Better Broadcasts, Broadcast Edn. Assn., Calif. Tchrs. Assn., Calif. Coll. and Univ. Faculty Assn., Calif. State Employees Assn. Presbyn. (elder). Home: 586 Chapman Dr Corte Madera CA 94925 Office: 1600 Holloway Ave San Francisco CA 94132 *As a human being, I am a contributor to pollution, to overcrowding, and to all other problems of our day. It is, therefore, my responsibility to compensate for this by leaving my world a little bit better than I found it.*

HYDE, WALTER LEWIS, ednl. exec.; b. Mpls., May 30, 1919; s. Walter Lloyd and Edith (Drake) H.; m. Elizabeth Sanford, Aug. 14, 1941; children—Lee, Lewis, Benjamin, Elizabeth, Rebecca. S.B., Harvard, 1941, A.M., 1943, Ph.D., 1949. With Polaroid Corp., 1943-46, Baird Assos., 1947-50, Office Naval Research, 1950-53; asst. dir. research Am. Optical Co., Southbridge, Mass., 1953-60, dir. devel., 1960-63; prof. optics U. Rochester, 1963-68; dir. Inst. Optics, 1965-68; provost Univ. Heights Center, N.Y. U., 1968-72; exec. dir. Conn. Conf. Ind. Colls., 1972-79, Conn. State Tech. Colls., 1979—; sec., treas. Internat. Commn. Optics, 1966-69. Chmn. Woodstock Democratic Town Com., 1976. Mem. Optical Soc. Am. (pres. 1970), Nat. Assn. Ind. Colls. and Univs. (dir. 1976), Sigma Xi. Democrat. Unitarian. Home: Route 1 Box 371 Woodstock CT 06281

HYDE, WILLIAM L., JR., restaurant corporation executive; b. 1947; married. B.S., U. Southwestern La., 1970. With Chart House Inc., 1970—, mktg. coordinator, 1972-74, v.p., mktg., 1974-77, v.p. ops. hamburger div., 1977-80, exec. v.p., chief operating officer, Lafayette, Ind., 1980-81, pres., chief exec. officer hamburger div., dir., 1981-83, vice chmn., 1983—. Office: Chart House Inc 666 Jefferson St Layafette IN 70501 *

HYDE-WHITE, WILFRID, actor; b. Gloucestershire, Eng., May 12, 1903; s. Edward and Ethel Adelaide (Drought) Hyde-W.; m. Blanche Aitken, 1925; children: Michael, Punch, Juliet; m. Ethel Koreman, 1957. Diploma, Marlborough Coll., Wiltshire. Actor in plays and films, Eng. and U.S., 1922—; stage appearances include Beggar on Horseback, 1925, Rise Above It, It Depends What You Mean, Caesar and Cleopatra, Affairs of State, Hippo Dancing, The Reluctant Debutants, Not in the Book, Miss Pell is Missing, The Doctor's Dilemma, Lady Windermere's Fan, Meeting at Night, The Jockey Club Stakes, The Pleasure of His Company, Rolls Hyphen Royce; film appearances include Gaily, Gaily, Tarzan, the Ape Man, 1981, The Cat and the Canary, 1982, The Toy, 1982; also numerous others; TV appearances include series The Associates, 1979; series Buck Rogers in the 25th Century. Address: care Diamond Artists Ltd 119 W 57th St New York NY 10019 *

HYDOK, JOSEPH THOMAS, utility company executive; b. Nyack, N.Y., Sept. 23, 1928; s. Joseph Bernard and Mary Rose (McGovern) H.; m. Eleanor Patricia Bednar, May 3, 1952; children: Paul, Joanne Hydok Woolgar, Janice Hydok Maitre. B.S., L.I.U., 1950; M.B.A., CCNY, 1958. Jr. auditor Price Waterhouse, N.Y.C., 1947-50; with Con Edison, N.Y.C., 1950-78, 80—, v.p., 1969-78; sr. v.p., N.Y.C., 1980—. Dir. Mayor's Office of Operation, N.Y.C., 1978-80; mem. Mayor's Mgmt. Adv. Com., N.Y.C., 1978—; bd. dirs. Indsl. Home for Blind, Bklyn., 1981—; pres. Fulton Mall Improvement Assn., 1978—. Served to capt. U.S. Army, 1950-53; ETO. Named Man of Yr. YMCA, 1974, Alumnus of Yr. L.I.U., 1982; recipient Service award St. Patrick's Home for Aged, Bronx, N.Y., 1976, Kings County Am. Legion, N.Y., 1978. Mem. Am. Gas Assn. (bd. dirs. 1980—). Roman Catholic. Home: 80 Bocket Rd Pearl River NY 10965 Office: Consol Edison Co NY Inc 4 Irving Pl New York NY 10003

HYER, MARTHA (MRS. HAL WALLIS), actress; b. Ft. Worth, Aug. 10; d. Julien C. and Agnes (Barnhart) H.; m. Hal Wallis, Dec. 31, 1966. Student, Fairfax Hall Jr. Coll., 1943-45; B.A., Northwestern U., 1947. Featured in movies with, RKO Studios, Hollywood, Calif., 1950-55, Universal Studios, 1955-60; starred in: films, including Some Came Running, Carpetbaggers, Sons of Katie Elder, The Happening, The Chase, others. Mem. bd. trustees Mus. Natural History, Los Angeles, Eisenhower Med. Center, Palm Springs, Calif.; hon. pres. Blue Ribbon Group, Music Center of Los Angeles. Nominated for Acad. award, 1959. Mem. Pi Beta Phi. Office: 9200 Sunset Blvd Los Angeles CA 90069

HYLAND, DOUGLAS K.S., museum director; b. Salem, Mass., Oct. 7, 1949; s. Samuel F. and Patricia E. H.; m. Stephanie duP. Bredin, May 24, 1969 (div.); children: Samuel Irenee, Octavia duP.; m. Alice R. Merrill, Oct. 24, 1981. B.A., U. Pa., 1971; M.A., U. Del., 1975, Ph.D., 1980. Asst. prof. U. Kans., Lawrence, 1979-82; curator Spencer Mus., Lawrence, 1979-82; dir. Memphis Brooks Mus. Art, 1982—; assoc. prof. Southwestern U. at Memphis, 1983—. Editor: Catalogue of Sculpture, Spencer Mus., 1979, Catalogue Marius de Zayas, 1980, Catalogue Howard Pyle and the Wyeths, 1983. Mem. Am. Assn. Mus. Dirs., Coll. Art Assn., Am. Mus. Assn., Tenn. Mus. Assn., Memphis Mus. Assn. Home: 1905 Overton Park Memphis TN 38112 Office: Memphis Brooks Mus Art Overton Park Memphis TN 38112

HYLAND, EDWARD WILLIAM, cement co. exec.; b. New Haven, July 21, 1925; s. David J. and Charlotte V. (Griffin) H.; m. Melissa E. Twigg, Nov. 21, 1959; children—Paul, Charlotte, Sara, Thomas Hyland. B.A., Yale, 1949, LL.B., 1952. Bar: Conn. bar 1952, N.Y. bar 1953. With firm Brown, Wood, Fuller, Caldwell & Ivey, N.Y.C., 1952-58; atty. Lehigh Portland Cement Co., Allentown, Pa., 1959—, sec., 1960—, counsel, 1960-73, v.p., gen. counsel, 1973—. Mem. Am. Bar Assn., Am. Soc. Corporate Secs., Am. Arbitration Assn. Clubs: Livingston (bd. govs.), Lehigh Country (Allentown)). Home: 2802 Crest Ave S Allentown PA 18104 Office: 718 Hamilton Mall Allentown PA 18105

HYLAND, LAWRENCE A(VISON), industrial executive; b. N.S., Can., Aug. 26, 1897; came to U.S., 1909, naturalized, 1919; s. George F. and Harriette (Balcom) H.; m. Muriel Evans, May 7, 1943. D.Eng. (hon.), Lawrence Inst. Tech., 1954. Served to sgt. U.S. Army, 1917-1919; served with U.S. Navy, 1920-26; discharged as chief radioman; asst. radio engr. Naval Research Lab., Bellevue, D.C., 1926-32; v.p. Radio Research Co., Washington, 1932-37; with Bendix Aviation Corp., 1937-54; chmn. exec. com. Hughes Aircraft Co., Culver City, Calif., 1954—; cons. Pres.'s Sci. Adv. Commn.; cons. and mem. several adv. coms. to Dept. Def. Recipient medal for distinctive public service USN, 1950; Robert J. Collier award NASA, 1968; Gold medal award Armed Forces Communications and Electronics Assn., 1968; Founder's Gold medal IEEE, 1974; Howard R. Hughes Meml. award. Fellow IEEE (Pioneer award 1957); mem. Sci. Research Soc. Am., Am. Nuclear Soc. Clubs: Cosmos (Washington); Los Angeles Country. Office: Hughes Aircraft Co PO Box 1042 El Segundo CA 90245 *

HYLAND, RICHARD FRANCIS, JR., investment company executive; b. Phila., Mar. 22, 1937; s. Richard Francis and Jennie Margaret (Mooney) H.; m. Catherine J. Marlow, Jan. 25, 1980; children: Beth Ann, Kathleen Marie, Patricia. B.S. in Accounting, St. Joseph's Coll., Phila., 1959. C.P.A., Pa. Audit mgr. Coopers & Lybrand (C.P.A.'s), Phila., 1960-72; controller Vanguard Group of Investment Cos., Valley Forge, Pa., 1972-75, treas., 1975—. Served with U.S. Army, 1960-62. Mem. Am., Pa. Insts. C.P.A.'s. Home: 125 Weston Dr Cherry Hill NJ 08003 Office: PO Box 1100 Valley Forge PA 19482

HYLAND, ROBERT FRANCIS, JR., broadcasting executive; b. St. Louis; s. Robert Francis and Genevieve (Burks) H.; m. Martha A. Claiborne (dec.); m. Patricia Sowle; children: Robert Francis, III, William Claiborne, Matthew, Mary Genevieve. A.B., St. Louis U.; LL.D. (hon.), Lindenwood Colls. Regional v.p. CBS Radio; gen. mgr. Sta. KMOX and KHTR/FM, St. Louis, 1973—; dir. Centerre Bancorp., St. Louis Nat. Baseball Club, Inc., Wetterau, Inc. Numerous civic activities, including; chmn. bd. Lindenwood Colls.; pres. St. Louis Zool. Commn., Civic Progress, Mo. Commn. on Retirement, Removal and Discipline of Judges, 1971—; bd. dirs. Downtown St. Louis, Inc., chmn., 1980; chmn. bd. St. Anthony's Med. Center, St. Louis; past chmn. Regional Commerce and Growth Assn.; trustee St. Louis County Hist. Soc.; bd. dirs. CORO Found.; pres. St. Louis Sports Hall of Fame. Served as ensign USN, 1942-44. Decorated magistral knight Sovereign Mil. Order Malta, Vatican; recipient numerous awards, including St. Louis award, 1975; Honor award U. Mo., 1975; Abe Lincoln award So. Bapt. Radio-TV Commn., 1976; Silver Beaver award Boy Scouts Am., 1976; Brotherhood Through Sports award B'nai B'rith, 1973; Community Service award Negro History Week, 1972; Churchman of Yr. award Religious Heritage Am., 1980; named Outstanding Young Man of St. Louis C. of C. Met. St. Louis, 1955, to 10th Ann. Class of Mo. Acad. Squires, 1969. Mem. numerous orgns. including, Advt. Club Greater St. Louis (pres. 1962), Broadcast Pioneers, Cath. Actors Guild, Internat. Radio and TV Soc., Journalism Found. Met. St. Louis (hon. exec. com. 1973), Mo. Broadcasters Assn. (pres. 1962-63), Nat. Assn. Broadcasters (co-chmn. Mo. legis. liaison com.), NAACP (life), N.Am. Advisory for Vatican Radio, St. Louis Ednl. TV Commn., Unda-USA (Gabriel Personal Achievement award 1973), Variety Club St. Louis, Am. Mgmt. Assn., Am. Acad. Polit. Sci., Internat. Soc. Semantics. Roman Catholic. Clubs: Bellerive Country, Bogey Golf, Log Cabin, Media (founder, pres.), Mo. Athletic, Noonday, Racquet, St. Louis, St. Louis Stadium (founder, pres.), Univ. (hon. life). Home: 6 Bellerive Country Club Grounds Saint Louis MO 63141 Office: 1 Memorial Dr Saint Louis MO 63102

HYLAND, WILLIAM FRANCIS, lawyer; b. Burlington, N.J., July 30, 1923; s. Theodore J. and Margaret M. (Gallagher) H.; m. Joan E. Sharp, Apr. 20, 1946; children: William Francis, Nancy E. Hyland Wiley, Stephen J., Emma L. Hyland McCormack, Margaret M., Thomas M. B.S. in Econs, U. Pa., 1944, LL.B., 1949; D.H.L., Hahnemann Med. Sch. and Hosp., 1976. Bar: N.J. 1949, U.S. Supreme Ct. 1960. Mem. firm Riker, Danzig, Scherer and Hyland, Morristown, N.J.; atty. gen., N.J., 1974-78; gen. counsel, dir. Nat. Telephone Directory Corp.; dir. Fidelity Union Bank/1st Nat. State, Fidelity Union Bank/1st Nat. State Bancorp., Am. Water Works Co., Wilmington, Del. Mem. N.J. Gen. Assembly from Camden County, 1954-61, speaker of house, 1958; acting gov., N.J., 1958; chmn. N.J. Sports and Expn. Authority, 1978-82, commr., 1982-84; pres. N.J. Bd. Pub. Utility Commrs., also mem. cabinet govs. Meyner, Hughes, Byrne, N.J., 1961-68, 74-78; chmn. N.J. Atomic Energy Council, 1968-69, N.J. Commn. Investigation, 1969-71; co-chmn. Reapportionment Commn.; Chmn. Brazilian Mission Com., 1962-65; permanent del. Fed. Jud. Conf. 3d Circuit.; Del.-at-large Dem. Nat. Conv., 1964, del., 1968; sec., bd. dirs. Waterloo Found. for Arts, Inc.; Assoc. trustee U. Pa., 1960-74; trustee N.J. Symphony Orch., Drew U. Served as officer USNR, 1943-46; ETO, PTO. Decorated knight Order of St. Gregory (Pope Paul VI), 1964; recipient Distinguished Service award Camden County Jaycees, 1954, Outstanding Young Man in Govt. N.J. award N.J. Jaycees, 1958, Myrtle Wreath award Camden County So. N.J. region Hadassah, 1977, Pub. Service award Anti-Defamation League of B'nai B'rith, 1982; named Outstanding Citizen of N.J. Advt. Club. N.J., 1979. Mem. Camden County Bar Assn. (pres. 1959), Nat. Assn. R.R. and Utilities Commrs. (exec. com. 1965-68), Nat. Assn. Attys. Gen. (exec. com. 1975-78, v.p. 1976, pres. elect 1977-78), Phi Kappa Psi, ABA (Fellow N.J. chpt.), Essex County Bar Assn., Morris County Bar Assn. Home: 5 Ellyn Ct Convent Station NJ 07961 Office: Headquarters Plaza 11 Speedwell Avenue Morristown NJ 07960

HYLAND, WILLIAM LEROY, telecommunications and electronics company executive; b. Mt. Holley, N.J., Jan.18, 1939; s. William Adrien and Evelyn May (Rue) H.; m. Anne F. Engels, June 18, 1961; children: Laura Anne, Lynne Marie. B.S., Rutgers U., 1969. Broker Joseph M. Klein & Son, Livingston, N.J., 1961-64; asst. ins. mgr. C.I.T. Fin. Corp., N.Y.C., 1964-69; v.p. ins. GTE Corp., Stamford, Conn., 1969—; dir., pres. Telect Ins. Co., Hamilton, Bermuda, 1976—; dir. GTE Ins. Co., London, GTE Investment Mgmt., Stamford, Conn. Served with USN, 1956-59. Mem. Chartered property and Casualty Underwriters soc., Am. Pension Conf., Machinery and Allied Products Inst., Risk and Ins. Soc. Roman Catholic. Club: Yacht (Stamford, Conn.). Home: 186 Buena Vista Dr Ringwood NJ 07456 Office: GTE Corp 1 Stamford Forum Stamford CT 06904

HYLTON, HANNELORE MENKE, manufacturing executive; b. Duesseldorf, Ger., June 10, 1936; came to U.S., 1959, naturalized, 1977; d. Heinz and Margot (Frank) Menke; m. Richard E. Hylton, Aug. 23, 1974. Diploma, Bus. Coll., Duesseldorf, 1956, Alliance Française, Paris, 1956. Exec. sec. G.S. May Internat., Duesseldorf, 1957-59, Embassy of Pakistan, Washington, 1960, Nat. Indsl. Council, 1961-63; with Pubco Corp., McLean, Va., 1963—, v.p., 1970-79, exec. v.p., chief adminstrv. officer, 1979—, dir., 1971—. Club: Washington Golf and Country. Home: 700 W Washington St Highland Springs VA 23075 Office: 8300 Greensboro Dr McLean VA 22102

HYMAN, ALBERT LEWIS, physician; b. New Orleans, Nov. 10, 1923; s. David and Mary (Newstadt) H.; m. Neil Steiner, Mar. 27, 1964; 1 son, Albert Arthur. B.S., La. State U., 1943; M.D., 1945; postgrad., U. Cin., U. Paris, U. London, Eng. Diplomate: Am. Bd. Internal Medicine. Intern Charity Hosp., 1945-46, resident, 1947-49, sr. vis. physician, 1959-63; resident Cin. Gen. Hosp., 1946-47; instr. medicine La. State U., 1950-56, asst. prof. medicine, 1956-57; asst. prof., Tulane U, 1957-59, asso. prof., 1959-63, asso. prof. surgery, 1963-70, prof. research surgery in cardiology, 1970—, adj. prof. pharmacology, 1974—; dir. Cardiac Catheterization Lab., 1957—; sr. vis. physician Touro Hosp., Touro Infirmary, Hotel Dieu; chief cardiology Sara Mayo Hosp.; cons. in cardiology USPHS, New Orleans Crippled Children's Hosp., St. Tammany Parish Hosp., Covington La. area VA, Hotel Dieu Hosp., Mercy Hosp., East Jefferson Gen. Hosp., St. Charles Gen. Hosp.; electrocardiographer Metairie Hosp., 1959-64, Sara Mayo Hosp., Touro Infirmary, St. Tammany Hosp.; cons. cardiovascular disease New Orleans VA Hosp.; cons. cardiology Baton Rouge Gen. Hosp.; Barlow lectr. in medicine U. So. Calif., 1977; mem. internat. sci. com. IV Internat. Symposium on Pulmonary Circulation, Charles U., Prague. Contbr. articles to profl. jours. Recipient award for research of the Hadassah, 1980. Fellow ACP, Am. Coll. Chest Physicians, Am. Coll. Cardiology, Am. Fedn. Clin. Research; mem. Am. Heart Assn. (fellow council on circulation, mem. council on cardiopulmonary medicine, regional rep. council clin. cardiology, chmn. sci. com. of cardiopulmonary council 1981, chmn. cardiopulmonary council, bd. dirs.), La. Heart Assn. (v.p. 1974, Albert L. Hyman Ann. Research award), Am. Soc. Pharmacology and Exptl. Therapeutics, So. Soc. Clin. Investigation (chmn. membership com.), So. Med. Soc., Am. Physiol. Soc., N.Am. Soc. Pacing and Electrophysiology, N.Y. Acad. Scis., AAUP. Research in cardiopulmonary circulation. Home: 5550 Jacquelyn Ct New Orleans LA 70124 Office: 3601 Prytania St New Orleans LA 70115

HYMAN, ARTHUR, philosophy educator; b. Schwaebisch Hall, Germany, Apr. 10, 1921; came to U.S., 1936; s. Isac and Rosa (Weil) H; m. Ruth Salinger, Feb. 25, 1951; children: Jeremy Saul, Michael Samuel, Joseph Isaiah. B.A., St. Johns Coll., Md., 1944; M.A., Harvard U., 1947, Ph.D., 1953; M.H.L., Jewish Theol. Sem. Am., 1955. Instr. coll. dept. Jewish Theol. Sem., N.Y., 1950-55; rabbi, 1955; lectr., asst. prof. Dropsie Coll., Phila., 1955-61, acting dean students, 1958-61; assoc. prof. Yeshiva U., N.Y., 1961-67, prof., 1967-72, univ. prof., 1972—; Vis. prof. Hebrew U., Jerusalem, 1969-70, U. Calif., San Diego, 1977, Yale U., 1980; lectr. philosophy Columbia U., 1956-69, vis. prof., 1971—; Mem. commn. on religion in higher edn. Assn. Am. Colls., 1967-70. Editor: (with J.J. Walsh) Philosophy in the Middle Ages, 1967, 2d edit., 1983, (with S. Lieberman et al) Harry A. Wolfson Jubilee Volume, 1965, (with S. Lieberman) Salo W. Baron Jubilee Volume, 1974, Essays in Medieval Jewish and Islamic Philosophy, 1978; editor: Jewish philosophy div. Ency. Judaica, 1971; Contbr. articles on medieval Jewish and Islamic philosophy to profl. jours. Ford Found. fellow, 1951-52; Am. Philos. Soc. grantee, 1964; Nat. Endowment Humanities fellow, 1980-81. Fellow Am. Acad. Jewish Research (exec. com. 1970—, rec. sec. 1971-81); mem. Soc. Medieval and Renaissance Philosophy (pres. 1978-80), Am. Philos. Assn., Assn. Jewish Studies (dir. 1969-71), Conf. on Jewish Philosophy (chmn. 1967-72), Mediaeval Acad. Am., World Union Jewish Studies, Société Internationale pour l'Étude de la Philosophie Médiévale. Home: 845 West End Ave New York NY 10025

HYMAN, EARLE, actor, educator; b. Rocky Mount, N.C., Oct. 11, 1926; s. Zachariah and Maria Lilly (Plummer) H. Student, Bklyn. pub. schs. Roles include Rudolf in Anna Lucasta, N.Y.C., 1943-45; Mister Johnson in Mister Johnson, N.Y.C., 1956; Othello Am. Shakespeare Festival, Stratford, Conn., 1957; Oscar in The Lady from Dubuque, N.Y.C., 1980, James Tyrone in Lon Day's Journey Into Night, 1981; tchr. Herbert Berghof Sch. Acting, N.Y.C., 1957—; councilor Actors Equity Assn., 1956-71. Recipient award Theatre World, 1956, Actors Studio, 1980, Gry Statuette Husmodres Teater Forening, Oslo, Norway, 1965. Mem. Actors Equity Assn., Screen Actors Guild, AFTRA. Democrat. Episcopalian. Club: Players (N.Y.C.). Home: 109 Bank St New York NY 10014

HYMAN, EDWARD S., JR., economist; b. Mason, Tex., Apr. 8, 1945; s. Edward S. and Evelyn (Ward) H.; m. Caroline Howard; 1 dau., Prudence Howard. B.S. in Mech. Engring, U. Tex., Austin, 1967; M.S. in Mgmt, M.I.T., 1969. Econ. cons. Data Resources Inc., N.Y.C., 1969-72; sr. v.p., dir. Cyrus J. Lawrence, Inc., N.Y.C., 1972—. Named 1 Economist Institutional Investor Mag., 1980, 81, 82. Mem. Nat. Assn. Bus. Economists, N.Y. Soc. Security Analysts. Republican. Methodist. Home: 180 Gallows Hill Rd Redding CT 06875 Office: 115 Broadway Cyrus J Lawrence Inc New York NY 10006

HYMAN, HERBERT HIRAM, sociol. psychologist, educator; b. N.Y.C., Mar. 3, 1918; s. David Elihu and Gisella (Mautner) H.; m. Helen Raphael Kandel, Sept. 30, 1945; children—Lisa D., David K., Alex R. A.B. with honors, Columbia U., 1939, A.M., 1940, Ph.D., 1942. Social sci. analyst Dept. Agr., 1942; pub. opinion analyst OWI, 1942-44; dir. field surveys, morale div. U.S. Strategic Bomb Survey, 1944-45; research asso. Nat. Opinion Research Center, 1947-57; asst. prof. Bklyn. Coll., 1946-47; vis. prof. U. Calif., 1950, U. Oslo, Norway, 1950-51; prof. Columbia U., 1951-69, chmn. dept. sociology, 1965-68; fellow Center Advanced Studies, Wesleyan U., Middletown, Conn., 1968-69, prof. sociology, 1969-77, Crowell univ. prof., 1977—; vis. prof. U. Ankara, Turkey, 1957-58, U. Catania, Italy, 1976, Mass. Inst. Tech., 1976; program dir. Research Inst. Social Devel., UN, 1964-65. Author: Interviewing in Social Research, 1954, Survey Design and Analysis, 1955, Political Socialization, 1959, Applications of Methods of Evaluation, 1962, Readings in Reference Group Theory, 1968, Secondary Analysis of Sample Surveys, 1972, The Enduring Effects of Education, 1975, Education's Lasting Influence on Values, 1979. Recipient Fulbright award, Guggenheim award; spl. grantee Ford Found. Fellow Am. Psychol. Assn.; mem. Am. Assn. Pub. Opinion Research (past pres., Julian Woodward Meml. award), Sociol. Research Assn. (pres. 1974-75), Am. Sociol. Soc. (pres. methodology sect. 1962-63, social psychology sect. 1970-71), Soc. Psychol. Study Social Issues (exec. council), Sigma Xi. Address: 38 Woodside Ave Westport CT 06880 Office: Wesleyan Univ Middletown CT 06457

HYMAN, JEROME ELLIOT, lawyer; b. Rosedale, Miss., Dec. 26, 1923; s. Mose and Mary Ann (Sprecher) H.; m. Isabelle Miller, July 1, 1960. A.B., Coll. William and Mary, 1944; LL.B. magna cum laude, Harvard U., 1947. Bar: N.Y. State 1949, D.C. 1960. Mem. fgn. funds control staff Dept. Treasury, U.S. Mil. Govt., Frankfurt and Berlin, Germany, 1945-46; law clk. to judge U.S. Ct. Appeals, Boston, 1947-48; asso. firm Cleary, Gottlieb, Steen & Hamilton, N.Y.C., 1948-58, partner, 1959—; trustee, mem. exec. com. Practicing Law Inst., N.Y.C., 1972—; sr. v.p., gen. counsel Pan Am. World Airways, Inc., 1982—; v.p. Practicing Law Inst., 1979—. Bd. editors: Harvard U. Law Rev, 1945-47. Pres. Lexington Democratic Club, N.Y.C., 1956-58; counsel N.Y. Dem. Com. for Stevenson, 1956; del. various Dem. state and jud. convs.; alumni mem. Harvard Law Sch. Placement Com., 1976-79; trustee Lawyers' Com. for Civil Rights Under Law, 1981—. Fellow Am. Bar Found.; mem. Am. Bar Assn., Assn. Bar N.Y.C., Am. Law Inst., Am. Judicature Soc., New York County Lawyers Assn., Harvard Law Sch. Assn. N.Y. (trustee 1980—), Phi Beta Kappa. Clubs: Recess, Sky (N.Y.C.). Home: 1125 Park Ave New York NY 10028 Office: 1 State St Plaza New York NY 10004

HYMAN, MILTON, emeritus dental educator; b. N.Y.C., Apr. 1, 1905; s. Abraham and Bella (Langer) H.; m. Elsie Reiter, June 20, 1937; children: Leonard S., Deborah S. Student, CCNY, 1923-26; D.D.S., NYU, 1930. Mem. faculty Coll. Dentistry, NYU, 1930—, chmn. dept. oral diagnosis, 1943-73, prof., 1952-73, emeritus, 1973—, chmn. dept. oral diagnosis and roentgenology, 1954-73, asst. dir. Dental Assts. Tng. Program, 1961-67, dir. Tumor Clinic, 1962-73. Asst. editor: Dental Violet, NYU, 1929; editor-in-chief, 1930; faculty adviser, 1931-70; staff writer: N.Y. Jour. Dentistry, 1934-38; editorial staff: Jour. Am. Acad. Oral Medicine, 1972-83; Contbr. articles to textbooks, profl. jours. Mem. senate N.Y. U., 1966-70. Fellow Am. Acad. Oral Medicine (pres. 1969), Am. Coll. Dentists; mem. ADA (cons. Jour. 1976—), Bronx County Dental Soc. (dir. 1937-49, librarian 1941-44, v.p. 1945, editor bull. 1937-40), 1st Dist. Dental Soc. (dir. 1945-46, editor pathodontia sect. 1953, chmn. 1956), AAAS, Fedn. Am. Scientists, Orgn. Tchrs. Oral Diagnosis, A.A.U.P., N.Y. Acad. Scis., Am. Assn. Cancer Edn., Am. Assn. Dental Schs., Alumni Assn. City Coll. N.Y., Sci. Research Soc. Am., N.Y.U. Coll. Dentistry Alumni Assn., U.S. Power Squadron, Omicron Kappa Upsilon (pres. Omega chpt. 1959), Sigma Omega Psi (past pres. Alumni chpt.). Clubs: New York Univ., Woodmere Bay Yacht. Home: 86-20 Eton St Jamaica NY 11432 Office: 57 W 57th St New York City NY 10019

HYMAN, MILTON DAVID, lawyer; b. N.Y.C., Mar. 7, 1934; s. William and Lillian (Brimberg) H.; m. Nancy Young, Jan. 9, 1966; children: Jennifer, Karin, Rachel. B.A., Cornell U., 1955; LL.B., NYU, 1958. Bar: N.Y. 1959. Assoc. Matthew J. Tosti Esquire, Jamaica, N.Y., 1959-61; chief enforcement atty. SEC, Washington, 1961-69; dir. legal dept. Faulkner, Dawkins & Sullivan, N.Y.C., 1969-70; gen. ptnr. Bear Stearns & Co., N.Y.C., 1970—. Mem. Securities Industry Assn. (pres. Legal and Compliance Div. 1982). Office: Bear Stearns & Co 55 Water St New York NY 10041

HYMAN, MORTON PETER, shipping company executive; b. N.Y.C., Jan. 9, 1936; s. Irving S. and Dora (Pfeffer) H.; m. Chris Oliphant Stern, Mar. 18, 1979. B.A., Cornell U., 1956, LL.D. with distinction, 1959. Bar: N.Y. 1960. Assoc. firm Proskauer Rose Goetz & Mendelsohn, N.Y.C., 1959-63; officer, dir. Overseas Discount Corp., N.Y.C., 1963—, pres., 1983—; officer, dir. Overseas Shipholding Group, Inc., N.Y.C., 1969—, pres., 1971—. Bd. editors: Cornell Law Rev. Vice chmn. N.Y. State Health Planning Commn., 1977-78; mem. Public Health Council N.Y., 1971—, vice-chmn., 1977—; chmn. N.Y. State Health Care Capital Policy Adv. Com., 1982—; 1st v.p. bd. trustees Beth Israel Med. Center; trustee Mt. Sinai Med. Center; chmn. N.Y. State Joint Exec. and Legis. Task Force on Delivery of Health Care, 1977—, N.Y. State Joint Exec. and Legis. Com. on Residential Health Care Facilities, 1977—; bd. dirs. World Rehab. Fund, Inc., Jewish Bd. Family and Children's Services, Inc.; bd. mgrs. State Communities Aid Assn. Served as 2d lt. AUS, 1956-57. Mem. N.Y. Bar Assn., Order of Coif., Phi Kappa Phi. Republican. Jewish. Club: Harmonie (N.Y.C.). Home: 998 Fifth Ave New York NY 10028 Office: 1114 Ave of Americas New York NY 10036

HYMAN, MYRON A., entertainment company executive, lawyer; b. Phila., July 16, 1939; s. Martin and Helen (Goodman) H.; m. Carol E. Hyman, June 11, 1961; children: Eric, Scott, Shanna. A.B., Muhlenberg Coll., 1961; J.D., Villanova U., 1964. Bar: N.Y., Pa. Assoc. Goodis, Greenfield, Narin & Mann, Phila., 1964-69; div. counsel Gen. Electric Co., Phila., 1969-75; gen. counsel Gen. Learning Corp., Morristown, N.J., 1971-73; regional counsel Xerox Corp., Washington, 1975-77; assoc. gen. counsel CBS, Inc., N.Y.C., 1977-81; pres. MGM/UA Home Video, N.Y.C., 1981—. Mem. Pa. State Bar Assn., N.Y. State Bar Assn. Office: MGM/UA Home Video 1350 Ave of the Americas New York NY 10019

HYMAN, RALPH ALAN, journalist; b. Rochester, N.Y., Sept. 8, 1928; s. Harold M. and Sade (Rubens) H.; m. Norma Sheila Newman, June 19, 1955; 1 son, Daniel. B.A., U. Rochester, 1952. Sports writer Rochester Times-Union, 1952-58, exec. sports editor, 1958-70, mem. editorial dept., 1970—, copy editor, 1974—; Mem. sports com. A.P. Mng. Editors Report, 1964-66, 68; co-chmn. N.Y. State A.P. Sports Report, 1966. Bd. dirs. Town of Brighton Little League, 1978-79; active Otetiana council Boy Scouts Am., 1980—. Mem. Sigma Delta Chi. Home: 65 Beekman Pl Rochester NY 14620 Office: 55 Exchange St Rochester NY 14614

HYMAN, RICHARD JOSEPH, librarian, educator; b. Malden, Mass., Feb. 11, 1921; s. Meyer and Ida A. (Orlove) H. A.B. summa cum laude, Harvard U., 1942; B. Jewish Edn., Boston Hebrew Tchrs. Coll., 1942; M.B.A., Harvard U., 1948; M.S. with honors, Columbia Grad. Sch. Library Service, 1962, D.L.S., 1971. Statis. and market research analyst Ansco div. Gen. Analine and Film Corp., Binghamton, N.Y. and N.Y.C., 1949-50; adminstrv. asst. to regional sales mgr. Dayton Rubber Co., Ohio, 1950-51; asst. to v.p. sales Venus Pen and Pencil Corp., Hoboken, N.J. and N.Y.C., 1952-59; adminstrv. asst. to chmn. bd. Wolf, Block, Schorr and Solis-Cohen, Phila., 1959-60; asst. to librarian Queens Coll., CUNY, Flushing, 1962-63, asst. prof. library sci., 1968-71, asso. prof., 1972-80, prof., 1981—, chmn. dept. library sci., 1977-78, dir., 1979—; statis. and editorial cons. publs. in librarianship, 1966—. Author: Access to Library Collections, 1972, From Cutter to Marc: Access to the Unit Record, 1977, Analytical Access: History, Resources, Needs, 1978, Shelf Classification Research: Past, Present—Future?, 1980, Shelf Access in Libraries, 1982; contbr. articles on library resources and services to profl. pubs. Served with USN, 1942-46. Mem. ALA, Assn. Library and Info. Sci. Edn., Assn. Am. Library Schs., N.Y. Library Assn., Library Assn. of CUNY, Internat. Fedn. Library Assns. and Instns., AAUP, N.Y. Tech. Services Librarians, Beta Phi Mu, Phi Beta Kappa. Club: Archons of Colophon. Home: 300 W 109th St New York NY 10025 Office: Queens College Flushing NY 11367

HYMAN, SEYMOUR, capital and product devel. co. exec.; b. N.Y.C., June 19, 1927; s. Morris and Fannie (Baumwall) H.; m. Sandra Kammerman, Feb. 25, 1973. B.S., N.Y. State Maritime Coll., 1948; student, Bklyn. Poly. Inst., 1944-45, Columbia, 1949-51; M.S., N.Y. U., 1949. Chief mfg. engring. U.S. Naval Clothing Factory, Bklyn., 1950-51; chief indsl. engr. Peter Pan Mfg. Co., E. Newark, N.J., 1951-53; chief prodn. engr. Seampruf Inc., N.Y.C., 1953-54; founder, pres., chmn. bd. Herculite Protective Fabrics, Inc., N.Y.C., 1954-76; vice chmn. bd. Eckmar Corp., N.Y.C., 1969-75; co-founder pres., chmn. bd. Health-Chem. Corp., N.Y.C., 1971-76; pres. Delta Ventures Corp., N.Y.C., 1977—. Served with USNR, 1945-48. Mem. Soc. Plastic Engrs. Club: Mason (Shriner). Home: 425 E 58th St New York NY 10022 Office: 425 E 58th St New York NY 10022

HYMAN, SEYMOUR CHARLES, coll. pres.; b. N.Y.C., June 3, 1919; s. Jack and Rose (Bernhardt) H.; m. Charlotte Bank, June 26, 1943; children—Carol Joan, Judith Fay. B.Ch.E., CCNY, 1939; M.Sc., Va. Poly. Inst., 1940; Ph.D., Columbia U., 1950. Registered profl. engr., N.Y., N.J. Engr. Ashland Oil and Refining Co., Ky., 1940-42; prin. engr. Signal Corps Labs., Ft. Monmouth, N.J., 1942-47; dep. chancellor City U. N.Y., 1947-77; pres. William Paterson Coll. N.J., Wayne, 1977—; cons. Atomic Power Reactors, 1950-66. Mem. River Edge Regional Sch. Bd., 1960-61. Home: 48 Brandon Ave Wayne NJ 07470 Office: William Paterson Coll Wayne NJ 07470 *I have two guidelines. I have individual and final responsibility for everything I do or not do. I am proud to be identified with my work product.*

HYMES, DELL HATHAWAY, anthropologist, university dean; b. Portland, Oreg., June 7, 1927; s. Howard Hathaway and Dorothy (Bowman) H.; m. Virginia Margaret Dosch, Apr. 10, 1954; 1 adopted son, Robert Paul; children: Alison Bowman, Kenneth Dell; 1 stepdau., Vicki (Mrs. David Unruh). B.A., Reed Coll., 1950; M.A., Ind. U., 1953, Ph.D., 1955; postgrad., U. Calif. at Los Angeles, 1954-55. Instr., then asst. prof. Harvard, 1955-60; asso. prof., then prof. U. Calif. at Berkeley, 1960-65; prof. anthropology U. Pa., 1965-72, prof. folklore and linguistics, 1972—, prof. sociology, 1974—, prof. edn., 1975—, dean, 1975—; Bd. dirs. (Social Sci. Research Council), 1965-67, 69-70, 71-72, trustee, 1973-78. Author: Language in Culture and Society, 1964, The Use of Computers in Anthropology, 1965, Studies in Southwestern Ethnolinguistics, 1967, Pidginization and Creolization of Languages, 1971, Reinventing Anthropology, 1972, Foundations in Sociolinguistics, 1974, Studies in the History of Linguistics, 1974, Soziolinguistik, 1980, Language in Education, 1980, In Vain I Tried to Tell You, 1981, (with John Fought) American Structuralism, 1981; asso. editor: Jour. History Behavioral Scis, 1966—, Am. Jour. Sociology, 1977-80, Jour. Pragmatics, 1977—; contbg. editor: Alcheringa, 1973-80, Theory and Society, 1976—; editor: Language in Society, 1972—. Served with AUS, 1945-47. Fellow Center Advanced Study Behavioral Scis., 1957-58, Clare Hall, Cambridge, Eng., 1968-69; Guggenheim fellow, 1969; Nat. Endowment for Humanities sr. fellow, 1972-73. Fellow Soc. Applied Anthropology, Am. Folklore Soc. (pres. 1973-74); mem. Am. Anthrop. Assn. (exec. bd. 1968-70, pres. 1983), Linguistic Soc. Am. (exec. bd. 1967-69, pres. 1982), Am. Acad. Arts and Scis. (council 1979-80), Council on Anthropology and Edn. (pres. 1978). Home: 439 S 44th St Philadelphia PA 19104

HYMOFF, EDWARD, editor, author, news, broadcasting and publishing company executive; b. Boston, Oct. 12, 1924; s. Gustave and Gertrude E. (Kravetsky) H.; (div.)children: Jennifer K., Yves K. B.S. in Journalism, Boston U., 1949; M.A., Russian Inst., Columbia U., 1950. Reporter, city desk asst. N.Y. World Telegram and Sun, 1951; bur. chief, sr. war corr. in, Korea, Internat. News Service, 1952-53; news editor, mgr. NBC News, N.Y.C., 1954-58; spl. corr. CSB News, USSR, 1958-59; dir. news and pub. affairs radio sta. WMGM, N.Y.C., 1959; aero. sci. tech. and pub. policy accounts rep. Carl Byoir & Assos., N.Y.C., 1959-63; editorial dir. Vietnam Mil. Histories Pub. Co., Atlantic Highlands, N.J., Hong Kong, Vietnam, 1966-69; asso. editor THINK, IBM Corp., Armonk, N.Y., 1969-71; exec. editor NBC-TV News, 1974; dir. communications/pub. affairs Corp. for Pub. Broadcasting, 1977-80; mgr. editorial services Arthur D. Little, Inc., Cambridge, Mass., 1981—; dir. Universal Satellite Corp., 1981—; cons. USIA, 1957-58, Dept. Def., 1964-66, LWV Edn. Fund for Presdl. debates, 1980, Nat. Sci. Bd., NSF; TV documentaries and pub. affairs producer Nat. Ednl. TV Network, 1964-66; pub. relations cons. aerospace industries, 1963-66. Author: 10 books, including The Mission, 1964, The Kennedy Courage, 1965, International Troubleshooter for Peace, 1965, Guidance and Control of Spacecraft, 1966, 1st Marine Division in Vietnam, 1967, 1st Air Cavalry Division in Vietnam, 1967, 1st Marine Aircraft Wing in Vietnam, 1968, 4th Infantry Division in Vietnam, 1968, The OSS in World War II, 1972, Fire Prevention, Protection, Escape, 1984; author over 1000 mag. articles. Served with AUS, World War II. Recipient Non-Fiction Writing award Aviation/Space Writers Assn., 1965, 78, Distinguished Alumni Achievement award for journalism Boston U., 1966, Apollo Achievement award NASA, 1971. Mem. Internat. Inst. Strategic Studies, Inst. Conflict Mgmt. (trustee 1983—), Co. Mil. Historians, Authors Guild, Investigative Reporters and Editors, Writers Guild Am. East, Am. Soc. Journalists and Authors, Aviation/Space Writers Assn., Radio-TV News Dirs. Assn., U.S. Naval Inst., Veterans of the O.S.S. (exec. com. 1981—), Soc. Profl. Journalists, Sigma Delta Chi. Clubs: Overseas Press, Nat. Press, N.Y. Press. Home: PO Box 129 Belmont MA 02178 Office: Arthur D Little Inc Acorn Park Cambridge MA 02140

HYNE, JAMES BISSETT, university dean; b. Dundee, Scotland, Nov. 23, 1929; emigrated to Can., 1954, naturalized, 1969; s. William Simpson and Winifred Moore (Bissett) H.; m. Ada Leah Jacobson, Sept. 3, 1958. B.Sc., St. Andrews U., Scotland, 1951, Ph.D., 1954. Prof., head dept. chemistry U. Alta., Calgary, 1963-66; dean grad. studies, prof. chemistry U. Calgary, 1966—; dir. research Alta. Sulphur Research, Ltd., 1964—; cons. oil, gas and sulphur industries in, Can., U.S. and Gt. Britain; univ. rep. Can. Assn. Grad. Schs., Can. Assn. U. Research Adminstrs., Western Assn. Grad Schs., Western Can. Grad. Deans Com. Editor: Quar. Bull. of Alta. Sulphur Research, Ltd, 1964—; Contbr. articles on sulphur chemistry and tech. to profl. jours. Served with Can. Cameron Highlanders of Ottawa, 1954-58. Recipient Can. Centennial medal, 1967, R.S. Jane Meml. award for exceptional achievement in chem. engring. and indsl. chemistry, 1977; Queen Elizabeth II Jubilee medal, 1977; Alta. Achievement Excellence award, 1980. Mem. Can. Research Mgmt. Assn., Can. Soc. Chem. Engring., Can. Gas Processors Assn. (award of merit for contbns. to Can. natural gas industry in field sulphur prodn. 1974), Assn. Sci., Engring. and Technol. Community of Can., Internat. Assn. for Hydrogen Energy, Am. Chem. Soc., Chem. Soc., Chem. Inst. Can., Yale Chemists, Sigma Xi. Home: 312 Superior Ave SW Calgary AB T3C 2J2 Canada Office: Chemistry Dept U Calgary Calgary AB T2N 1N4 Canada

HYNEMAN, CHARLES S., emeritus political science educator; b. Gibson County, Ind., May 5, 1900; s. Willis Smith and Hattie (Ford) H.; m. Frances Virginia Tourner, Aug. 31, 1926; children: Richard Frank, Ruth Anne, Elizabeth Harriet. A.B., Ind. U., 1923, A.M., 1925; postgrad., U. Pa., 1925-26; Ph.D., U. Ill., 1929; L.H.D. (hon.), Ohio No. U., 1960, LL.D., Wabash Coll., 1971, Ind. U., 1980. High sch. tchr., univ. prof., 1923-41; prin. adminstrv. analyst U.S. Bur. Budget, 1942-43; chief tng. br. Mil. Govt. Div., Office Provost Marshal Gen., 1943-44; dir. Fgn. Broadcast Intelligence Service, FCC, 1944-45, asst. to chmn. commn., exec. officer, 1945-47; prof. polit. sci. Northwestern U., 1947-56; prof. govt. Ind. U., Bloomington, 1956-61, Distinguished Service prof. govt., 1961-71, prof. emeritus, 1971—; adj. scholar Am. Enterprise Inst. for Policy Research, Washington, 1971—; Fellow Woodrow Wilson Internat. Center Scholars, 1973-75; Mem. UN Monitoring Com., 1944-45, Social Sci. Research Council, 1944-47, NRC, 1963-65, Chgo. San. Dist. Civil Service Bd., 1952-56. Author: The First American Neutrality, 1935, Bureaucracy in a Democracy, 1950, The Study of Politics, 1959, The Supreme Court on Trial, 1963, Popular Government in America, 1968, (with C. Richard Hofstetter and Patrick F. O'Connor) Voting in Indiana, 1979; Editor: (with George W. Carey) A Second Federalist, 1967, (with Donald S. Lutz) American Political Writing During the Founding Era, 1760-1805, 1983; Contbr. articles to profl. jours. Mem. Am. Polit. Sci. Assn. (pres. 1961-62). Address: 2320 Fritz Dr Bloomington IN 47401

HYNES, CHARLES JOSEPH, lawyer; b. Bklyn., May 28, 1935; s. H.T. and Regina K. (Drew) H.; m. Patricia Pennisi, Oct. 19, 1963; children: Kevin, Sean, Patrick, Jeanne, Lisa. B.A. in English Lit, St. John's U., 1957, J.D., 1962. Bar: N.Y. 1962. Asst. dist. atty., trial bur., Kings County, N.Y., 1969, confidential asst. dist. atty., 1969-70, asst. dist. atty. in charge rackets bur., 1970-73, 1st asst. dist. atty., 1973-75, spl. prosecutor for nursing homes, health and social services, dep. atty. gen. for Medicaid fraud control, 1975-80, fire commr., N.Y.C., 1980-82; mem. Booth, Lipton & Lipton, N.Y.C., 1982—; Mem. Gov.'s Com. on Sentencing, 1979—; chmn. N.Y. State Jud. Screening Com., 2d Jud. Dept., 1983—. Served as 2d lt. USMC, 1957-58. Mem. Nat. Assn. Medicaid Fraud Control Units (past pres., mem. exec. bd.). Roman Catholic. Club: Lotos (N.Y.C.). Office: Booth Lipton & Lipton 405 Park Ave. New York NY 10022 *

HYNES, HUGH BERNARD NOEL, educator; b. Devizes, Eng., Dec. 20, 1917; s. Harry George Claude and Anna Minnie Lucy (Meyer) H.; m. Mary Elisabeth Hinks, Oct. 24, 1942; children—Richard Olding, Elisabeth Anne, Andrew John, Julian David. B.Sc., U. London, 1938, Ph.D., 1941, D.Sc., 1958. With Brit. Ministry Agr., 1941, Brit. Colonial Agrl. Ser., 1942-46; faculty U. Liverpool, Eng., 1947-64; prof. biology U. Waterloo, Ont., Can., 1964-83, prof. emeritus, 1983—; cons. in field. Author: The Ecology of Running Water; contbr. numerous articles to profl. jours. Decorated Can. Centennial medal. Fellow Royal Soc. Can., AAAS; mem. Am. Soc. Limnology and Oceanography, Brit. Ecol. Soc., Freshwater Biol. Assn., Internat. Assn. Gt. Lakes Research, Internat. Assn. Theoretical and Applied Limnology. Home: 127 Iroquois Pl Waterloo ON N2L 2S6 Canada Office: Dept Biology U Waterloo Waterloo ON N2L 3G1 Canada

HYNES, SAMUEL, educator, author; b. Chgo., Aug. 29, 1924; s. Samuel Lynn and Margaret (Turner) H.; m. Elizabeth Igleheart, July 28, 1944; children: Miranda, Joanna. B.A., U. Minn., 1947; M.A., Columbia U., 1948, Ph.D., 1956. Mem. faculty Swarthmore Coll., 1949-68, prof. English lit., 1965-68; prof. English Northwestern U., Evanston, Ill., 1968-76, Princeton U., 1976—, Woodrow Wilson prof. lit., 1978—. Author: The Pattern of Hardy's Poetry, 1961 (Explicator award 1962), William Golding, 1964, The Edwardian Turn of Mind, 1968, Edwardian Occasions, 1972, The Auden Generation, 1976; editor: Further Speculations by T.E. Hulme, 1955, The Author's Craft and Other Critical Writings of Arnold Bennett, 1968, Romance and Realism, 1970, Complete Poetical Works of Thomas Hardy, Vol. I, 1983. Served to maj. USMCR, 1943-46, 52-53. Decorated Air medal, D.F.C.; Fulbright fellow, 1953-54; Guggenheim fellow, 1959-60, 81-82; Bollingen fellow, 1964-65; Am. Council Learned Socs. fellow, 1969; Nat. Endowment for Humanities sr. fellow, 1973-74, 77-78. Fellow Royal Soc. Lit.; mem. English Inst., Phi Beta Kappa. Office: English Dept Princeton U Princeton NJ 08544

HYNNING, CLIFFORD J(AMES), lawyer, legal historian; b. Chgo., July 7, 1913; s. Peter Olav and Kirsti Knutsdatter (Raugstad) H.; 1 dau., Carol Hynning Smith. A.B. in Sociology, U. Chgo., 1934, Ph.D. in Political Sci., 1938; J.D., Kent Law Sch., 1934. Bar: Ill. 1934, D.C 1952. Tax analyst Temporary Nat. Econ. Com., 1938-40; fin. analyst, enforcement atty. Office Price Adminstrn., 1941-43; assigned as expert, in charge fin. interrogations leading Nazis War Dept., SHAEF and U.S. Control Council, Germany, 1945; prin. atty. internat. fin. Dept. Treasury, Washington, 1943-54; planner for Marshall Plan and NATO aid, 1948-54; treasury del. to secure exemptions from taxes for U.S. Mil. from NATO and Japan, 1952, individual practice law, Washington, 1954—; sec.-treas. Com. to Maintain a Prudent Def. Policy, 1968-69. Author: State Conservation of Resources, 1938, Taxation of Corporate Enterprise, 1941, Selected Financial Laws, Decrees and Regulations of Germany, 5 vols, 1945; Founding editor in chief: Am. Bar Assn. quar. Internat. Lawyer, 1965-68; contbr. articles to profl. jours. Mem. Am. Bar Assn. (del. to sec. of state's com. on pvt. internat. law 1965-69), Am. Law Inst., Am. Soc. Internat. Law, Phi Beta Kappa. Independent Democrat. Clubs: Cosmos, University. Home: Cosmos Club 2121 Massachusetts Ave NW Washington DC 20008 *Central to my interests have been the studies of the family of power and the abuses of power by monopolists, the Nazi and Communist elites and the contemporary usurpation of power by Presidents and courts.*

HYSLOP, DAVID JOHNSON, arts adminstr.; b. Schenectady, June 27, 1942; s. Moses McDickens and Annie (Johnson) H.; m. Sandra Wheeler, June 25, 1978; children—Kristopher Jae, Alexander; stepchildren—Marc Langhammer, Monica Langhammer. B.S. in Music Edn, Ithaca Coll., 1965. Elem. sch. vocal music supr., Elmira Heights, N.Y., 1965-66; mgr. Elmira Symphony Choral Soc., 1966; asst. mng. dir. Minn. Orch., Mpls., 1966-72; gen. mgr. Oreg. Symphony Orch., Portland, 1972-78; exec. dir. St. Louis Symphony Soc., 1978—. Trustee Nat. Com. on Symphony Orch. Support; bd. dirs. St. Louis Conservatory and Schs. for Arts, Portland State U., Chamber Music N.W.; lobbyist Com. for Arts in Mo. Martha Baird Rockefeller grantee, 1966. Mem. Am. Symphony Orch. League. Clubs: Mo. Athletic, Univ. (St. Louis). Home: 7131 Pershing Saint Louis MO 63130 Office: 718 N Grand St Saint Louis MO 63103

HYSON, CHARLES DAVID, economist; b. Hampstead, Md., Dec. 29, 1915; s. Harry Perry and Rose (Miller) H.; m. Winifred Chandler Prince, Sept. 7, 1946; children—David Prince, Pamela Chandler Hyson Martin, Christopher Perry. A.B., St. John's Coll., Annapolis, 1937; M.S., U. Md., 1939; M.A., Harvard, 1942, Ph.D., 1943. Agrl. economist FCA, 1939-40; staff Surplus Marketing Adminstrn., Washington, 1940-41; resident tutor, then sr. tutor Harvard, 1942-49, research asso., 1943-44, resident cons., 1943-49, instr. econs., 1946-48, asso. dir. marketing research program, 1948-49; regional economist, then chief prices and cost of living br. U.S. Bur. Labor Statistics, 1944-46; indsl. economist Fed. Res. Bank Boston, 1946-48; asst. econ. commr. ECA Mission to Norway, Oslo, 1949-50; trade specialist, staff spl. rep. in Europe, Paris, 1950; spl. asst. to chief of mission ECA, Mut. Security Agy., Lisbon, Portugal, 1950-52; dep. dir. U.S. Operations Mission to Portugal, Mut. Security Agy., FOA, ICA, 1952-55; spl. rep. to Portugal ICA, 1955-57, chief Western Europe div., Washington, 1957-59, chief European Div., 1959-60; assigned to Nat. War Coll., 1960-61; counsellor of embassy for econ. affairs Am. embassy, Lisbon, 1955-57; dep. asst. dir. for exec. staffing AID, Washington, 1961-62; adviser for econ. affairs Office Material Resources, AID, 1962-63; spl. asst. for econ. and trade affairs AID, 1963-74; cons. economist, 1975—; Dep. nat. coordinator, dep. exec. dir. Cabinet Com. Export Expansion, 1964; mem. White House Conf. on Internat. Coop., 1965. Contbr. numerous articles to econ. jours., books, also monographs. Decorated comdr. Order of Merit, Portugal. Fellow Royal Econ. Soc.; mem. Am. Fgn. Service Assn., Am. Acad. Polit. and Social Sci., Am. Econ. Assn., Am. Agrl. Econ. Assn., AAAS. Clubs: Harvard (Washington); Keene Valley (N.Y.) Country; Ausable

(St. Huberts, N.Y.); Adirondack Mountain. Address: 7407 Honeywell Ln Bethesda MD 20814

HYTCHE, WILLIAM PERCY, univ. chancellor; b. Porter, Okla., Nov. 28, 1927; s. Goldman and Bartha L. (Wallace) H.; m. Deloris Juanita Cole, Dec. 27, 1952; children—Pamelia Renee, Jaqueta Anita, William Percy. B.S., Langston U., 1950; M.S., Okla. State U., 1958, Ed.D., 1967. Tchr. math., Ponca City, Okla., 1952-60; asst. prof. math. Md. State Coll., Princess Anne, 1960-66, dean student affairs, 1968-70, 1970, asso. prof. math., 1970-71, head dept. math. and computer sci., dir., 1971-73, acting chmn. div. liberal studies, chmn., 1973-74, chmn. div. liberal studies, 1974-75, acting chancellor, 1975-76, chancellor, 1976—. Former pres. Men for Progress; bd. dirs. The Holly Center, Salisbury, Md. Served with AUS, 1950-52. Grantee NSF, 1957-58, 58, 60. Fellow Acad. Arts and Scis. (Okla. State U.); mem. Phi Sigma, Phi Delta Kappa, Alpha Phi Alpha. Methodist. Clubs: Helping Hands, Positive Relations. Home: 317 N Somerset Ave Princess Anne MD 21853 Office: Office of the Chancellor University of Maryland Eastern Shore Princess Anne MD 21853

HYTIER, ADRIENNE DORIS, French educator; d. Jean and Katharine Hytier M. B.A. summa cum laude, Barnard Coll., 1952; M.A., Columbia U., 1953, Ph.D., 1958. Instr. French Vassar Coll., 1959-61, asst. prof., 1961-66, assoc. prof., 1966-70, prof. French, Poughkeepsie, N.Y., 1970—, Lichtenstein Dale prof. French, 1974—; vis. assoc. prof. Columbia U., 1966, U. Calif., 1968-69. Editor: The 18th Century: A Current Bibliography/Two Years of French Foreign Policy: Vichy 1940-42, 1958, 2d edit., 1974, Les Dêêches diplomatiques du Comte de Gobineau en Perse, 1959, La Guerre, 1975; contbr. revs. and articles in field. Decorated chevalier des Palmes Academiques, 1974; fellow Guggenheim Found., 1967-68. Mem. MLA, Am. Soc. 18th Century Studies, North East Soc. for 18th Century Studies, Middle Atlantic Soc. 18th Century Studies, Internat. Soc. 18th Century Studies, Phi Beta Kappa. Home: 71 Raymond Ave Poughkeepsie NY 12601 Office: Vassar College Poughkeepsie NY 12601

IACOBELL, FRANK PETER, hospital administrator; b. Detroit, Oct. 29, 1937; s. Peter Herman and Josephine (Acierno) I.; m. Glenna Gaye Blevins, June 30, 1962; children: Angela J., Peter J. B.A., St. Bonaventure U., 1960; M.B.A., George Washington U., 1963. With Hutzel Hosp., Detroit, 1964—, v.p., dir., 1970-76, trustee, 1970—, exec. v.p., 1976-80, pres., 1980—, Hutzel Corp., 1981—; lectr. dept. mgmt. Wayne State U., 1966-71; dir., trustee Caymich Ins. Co., Grand Cayman Island, B.W.I., 1980—; dir. Mich. Hosp. Mut. Ins. Co. Trustee Detroit Med. Ctr., 1980—, Hutzel-Warren Hosp., 1982—; preceptor George Washington U., 1969—. Fellow Am. Coll. Hosp. Adminstrs.; mem. Am. Hosp. Assn., Detroit Execs. Assn. Republican. Roman Catholic. Clubs: Economic, Athletic, Golf (Detroit); Lost Lake Woods (Lincoln, Mich.). Home: 659 N Rosedale Grosse Pointe Woods MI 48236 Office: Hutzel Hosp 4707 Saint Antoine Blvd Detroit MI 48201

IACOCCA, LIDO ANTHONY (LEE IACOCCA), automotive manufacturing executive; b. Allentown, Pa., Oct. 15, 1924; s. Nicola and Antoinette (Perrotto) I; m. Mary McCleary, Sept. 29, 1956; children—Kathryn Lisa, Lia Antoinette. B.S., Lehigh U., 1945; M.E., Princeton U., 1946. With Ford Motor Co., Dearborn, Mich., 1946—, successively mem. field sales staff, various merchandising and tng. activities, asst. dirs. sales mgr., Phila.; dist. sales mgr., Washington, 1946-56, truck mktg. mgr. div. office, 1956-57, car mktg. mgr., 1957-60, vehicle market mgr., 1960; v.p. Ford Motor Co., gen. mgr., 1960-65, v.p. car and truck group, 1965-67, exec. v.p. of co., 1967-68, pres. of co., 1970-78, also pres.; pres., chief operating officer Chrysler Corp., Highland Park, Mich., 1978-79, chmn. bd., chief exec. officer, 1979—. Chmn. Statue of Liberty-Ellis Island Centennial Commn. Wallace Meml. fellow Princeton U. Mem. Tau Beta Pi. Club: Detroit Athletic. Office: Chrysler Corp 12000 Lynn Townsend Dr Highland Park MI 48288

IAKOVIDIS, SPYROS EUSTACE, archaeology educator; b. Athens, Aug. 28, 1923; U.S., 1977; s. Eustace and Electra (Lekkas) I.; m. Athina Kakouris, Sept. 15, 1968; 1 son, Alexander. U. Athens, 1946; Ph.D., 1962. With Greek Archaeol. Service, 1952-54; prof. archaeology U. Athens, 1970-74; vis. prof. U. Marburg, 1976-77, U. Heidelberg, 1977; prof. archaeology, chmn. grad. group classical archaeology U. Pa., Phila., 1979—. Author: Mycenaean Acropolis at Athens, 1962, Perati (3 vols. modern Greek), 1969-70, History of the Hellenic World, Period of Achaean Predominance, 1970, Mycenaean Citadels, 1973, Mykenische Wehrbauten, 1978, Guide to the Argolid, 1979, Perati (English), 1981, Late Helladic Citadels on Mainland Greece, 1983; contbr. articles to profl. jours. Served with Greek Nat. Guerilla Forces, 1944-45; Served with Greek Army, 1948-51. Brit. Acad. overseas vis. prof. grantee, 1976. Fellow Soc. Antiquaries London (hon.); mem. Archaeol. Soc. Athens, Greek Hist. and Ethnol. Soc., Soc. Promotion Hellenic Studies, Brit. Sch. Archaeology at Athens, Am. Inst. Archaeology, Inst. Advanced Study, Deutsches Archaologisches Institut, Société Prehistorique Française, Archaeol. Club. Christian Orthodox. Club: Faculty U. Pa. Home: 525 S 46th St Philadelphia PA 19143 Office: Univ Mus 33d and Spruce Sts Philadelphia PA 19104

IAKOVOS, ARCHBISHOP DEMETRIOS A. COUCOUZIS, clergyman; b. Imvros, Turkey, July 29, 1911; s. Athanasios and Maria Coucouzis. Grad., Theol. Sch. of Halki, Ecumenical Patriarchate, 1934; S.T.M., Harvard, 1945; D.D., Boston U., 1960, Bates Coll., 1970, Dubuque U., 1973, Assumption Coll., 1980; L.H.D., Franklin and Marshall Coll., 1961, Southeastern Mass. Tech. Inst., 1967, Am. Internat. Coll., 1972, Catholic U., 1974, Loyola Marymount U., 1979, Queen's Coll., 1982; LL.D., Brown U., 1964, Seton Hall U., 1968, Coll. of Holy Cross, 1966, Fordham U., 1966, Notre Dame U., 1979, N.Y. Law Sch., 1982, St. John's U., 1982; H.H.D., Suffolk U., 1967, Stonehill Coll., 1980; D.S.T., Berkeley Div. Sch., 1962, Gen. Theol. Sem., 1967, Thessalonica U., 1975; Lit.D., PMC Colls., 1971; others. Ordained deacon Greek Orthodox Ch., 1934, archdeacon, Met. Derkon, 1934-39, Greek Archdiocese; prof. Archdiocese Theol. Sch., Pomfret, Conn., 1939; ordained priest, 1940, parish priest, Hartford, Conn., 1940-41; preacher Holy Trinity Cathedral, N.Y.C., 1941-42; parish priest, St. Louis, 1942; dean Cathedral of Annunciation, Boston, 1942-54, Holy Cross Orthodox Theol. Sch., Brookline, Mass., 1954, now pres., bishop of, Melita, Malta, 1954-56; rep. Ecumenical Patriarchate, World Council Chs., Geneva, 1955-59, then co-pres. council, 1959-68; elevated to Metropolitan, 1956; archbishop, N. and S. Am., Holy Synod of Ecumenical Patriarchate, 1959—; Chmn. Standing Conf. Canonical Bishops in the Americas; mem. adv. bd., v.p. Religion in American Life. Author works in Greek, French, English, German. Pres. St. Basil's Acad., Garrison, N.Y.; chmn. trustees Hellenic Coll., Brookline; trustee Anatolia Coll., Salonika, Greece. Recipient Man of Yr. award B'nai B'rith, 1962, Nat. award NCCJ, 1962, Clergyman of the Yr. award Religious Heritage Am., 1970, Presdl. Citation as Disting. Am. in Voluntary Service, 1970, Man of Conscience award Appeal of Conscience Found., 1971, Presdl. Medal of Freedom, 1980, Interreligious award Religion in Am. Life, 1980, Clergyman of Yr. award N.Y.C. Council Churches, 1981. Mem. Am. Bible Soc. (bd. mgrs.). Address: 10 E 79th St New York City NY 10021

IAMMARINO, RICHARD MICHAEL, pathologist, educator; b. Cleve., Aug. 17, 1926; s. Salvatore Michael and Corinne (DePaul) I.; m. Therese Dolan, Aug. 9, 1952; children—Cynthia, Nancy, David, John. B.S., John Carroll U., 1949; M.D., Loyola U., Chgo., 1953. Intern St. Vincent Charity Hosp., Cleve., 1953-54; resident Crile VA Hosp., Cleve., 1954-56, U. Kans. Med. Center, Kansas City, 1956-58, Cleve. Met. Gen. Hosp., 1958-59; pathologist, dir. labs. St. Alexis Hosp., Cleve., 1959-63; instr. pathology U. Pitts., 1963-66, asst. prof., 1966-69, asso. prof., 1970-79; prof. pathology, dir. clin. labs. W.Va. U., 1979—; cons. pathology VA Hosp., Clarksburg, W.Va., 1981—; Pres. Morgantown (W.Va.) Hospice, Inc., 1981. Contbr. articles to profl. jours. Served with U.S. Navy, 1944-46. Am. Cancer Soc. grantee, 1965-67; Am. Heart Assn. grantee, 1978-79; NIH grantee, 1983-84. Fellow Coll. Am. Pathologists; Mem. Monongalia County Med. Soc., W.Va. Med. Soc., Electrophoresis Soc., Acad. Clin. Lab. Physicians and Scientists, Assn. Christian Therapists. Home: 348 Rotary St Morgantown WV 26505 Office: Clinical Labs West Virginia U Medical Center Morgantown WV 26505 *I have tried to live my life with a Christian perspective, mindful of the needs of my fellowman. Teaching and service as a physician and working for almost 20 years in medical education have provided a rich reward for me. I hope I have made an impact on young men and women, encouraging them to practice their profession mindful of human needs. What contributions I have made would not have been possible without the loving support given me by my wife, my parents, and my children.*

IAN, JANIS, singer, composer, song writer; b. N.Y.C., Apr. 7, 1951; d. Victor and Pearl Fink; m. Tino Sargo. Ed. to 10th grade. Rec. artist, 1966-69, 74—; albums recorded Janis Ian, 1966, For All the Seasons of Your Mind, 1967, The Secret Life of J. Eddy Fink, 1967, Who Really Cares, 1968, Stars, 1974, Between The Lines, 1975, Aftertones, 1975, Miracle Row, 1976, Janis Ian, 1979, Night Rains, Restless Eyes, 1981; arranger; scorer; guitar, piano player. (Recipient 1 Platinum, 2 Gold records, Grammy award for At 17 as best female popular vocal performance 1975); Author: poetry Who Really Cares, 1969; Songs written include At 17, Society's Child, Jesse. Office: care Magna Artists Corp 9200 Sunset Blvd Suite 1102 Los Angeles CA 90069 *

IANNI, FRANCIS ALPHONSE, state ofcl., former army officer; b. New Castle, Del., Aug. 2, 1931; s. Francisco and Mary (Marcozzi) I.; m. Ann Louise Wiggin, Apr. 16, 1955; children—Steven, Christina, Marisa, Jeanne, Marjorie. B.S., U.S. Mil. Acad., 1954; M.M.A. & S., U.S. Command and Gen. Staff Coll., 1963; M.A., U. Va., 1966. Served with U.S. N.G., 1945-50; commd. 2d lt., inf. U.S. Army, 1954, advanced through grades to maj. gen., 1977; ret., 1977, adj. gen., State of Del., Wilmington, 1977—. Decorated Silver Star, Def. Superior Service medal, Legion of Merit with oak leaf cluster, Bronze Star, D.F.C., Air medal. Mem. Assn. U.S. Army, N.G. Assn., VFW, Am. Legion. Roman Catholic. Home: 904 Delaware St New Castle DE 19720 Office: 9 Loockerman St Dover DE 19901

IANNI, FRANCIS ANTHONY, anthropologist, psychoanalyst, educator; b. Wilmington, Del., Mar. 29, 1926; s. Innocenzo and Rosa C. (Novellino) I.; m. Ursula Elizabeth Reuss, July 17, 1971; children: Juan, Anthony, Andrea. B.S. in Psychology, Pa. State U., 1949, M.A. in Anthropology, 1950, Ph.D., 1952; grad., N.Y. Psychoanalytic Inst., 1981. Cert. psychologist, N.Y. State. Instr. psychology and anthropology Russell Sage Coll., Troy, N.Y., 1952-53, asst. prof., 1954-55, asso. prof., 1955-56; asst. prof. Yale U., New Haven, 1956-57; prof. University Coll., Addis Ababa, Ethiopia, 1958-61; asso. commr. research HEW, Washington, 1961-65; prof. psychology dept. U. Florence, Italy, 1965; prof., dir. Horace Mann-Lincoln Inst., Columbia U., N.Y.C., 1965-80, prof., curator, Klingenstein fellow, 1965—; cons. med. psychology St. Luke's-Roosevelt Psychiat. Center, N.Y.C., 1977—; cons. to U.S. Dept. Edn., 1966—, U.S. Dept. Justice, 1974—. Author: American Social Legislation, 1955, Culture, System and Behavior, 1965, A Family Business, 1972, Black Mafia, 1974, Conflict and Change in Education, 1976, Cultural Relevance, 1973, The Crime Society, 1977. Mem. Mayor's Task Force on Organized Crime, N.Y.C., 1974-79; mem. Nat. Commn. on Criminal Justice Standards and Goals, 1974-75. Served with USN, 1943-46. Ford Found. fellow, 1951; Fulbright grantee, 1971, 74. Fellow Am. Sociol. Assn., Am. Anthrop. Assn., African Studies Assn.; mem. Am. Psychoanalytic Assn. (cert.), Am. Psychol. Assn., Am. Orthopsychiat. Assn., N.Y. Psychoanalytic Soc. Home: Villa L'Aquila Clover Rd Newfoundland NJ 07435 Office: PO Box 7 Teachers Coll Columbia Univ New York NY 10027

I'ANSON, LAWRENCE WARREN, ret. state chief justice; b. Portsmouth, Va., Apr. 21, 1907; s. James Thornton and Emma (Warren) I'A.; m. May Frances Tuttle, Aug. 5, 1933; children—Lawrence Warren, May Frances (Mrs. Peter McCrae Ramsey). A.B., Coll. William and Mary, 1928, LL.D., 1964; LL.B., U. Va., 1931; LL.D., Dickinson Law Sch., 1980. Bar: Va. bar 1931. Practiced in, Portsmouth, 1931-41, commonwealth's atty., 1938-41; judge Ct. of Hustings (now Circuit Ct.), 1941-58; justice Supreme Ct., Va., 1958-81, chief justice, 1974-81; mem. Jud. Council, 1948-70, chmn., 1974—; chmn. com. that prepared Handbook for Jurors used in all cts. of record in Va. Mem. Council of Higher Edn. of Va., 1956-59; chmn. Va. Ct. System Study Commn., 1968-71; sponsor Nat. Conf. on Judiciary, 1971; Pres. Beazley Found., Inc., Found. Boys Acad.; chmn. Conf. Chief Justices, 1979-80; pres. bd. Nat. Center for State Cts., 1979-80; chmn. State-Fed. Council. Trustee Eastern Va. Med. Sch. Found., 1970-79, Frederick Mil. Acad. Named First Citizen Portsmouth, 1946; recipient William and Mary Alumni medallion; U. Va. Sesquicentennial award, 1969; Lincoln Harley award Am. Judicature Soc., 1973; Disting. Service award Va. Trial Lawyers, 1973; Commonwealth award James Madison U., 1981. Fellow Am. Bar Found.; mem. ABA (com. to implement standards on jud. adminstrn. 1975-78), Va. Bar Assn. (chmn. jud. sect. 1949), Phi Beta Kappa (pres. chpt. 1981—), Order of Coif, Pi Kappa Alpha, Omicron Delta Kappa, Phi Alpha Delta. Democrat. Baptist (tchr. I'Anson Bible class 1933-65). Clubs: Harbor, Norfolk, Jesters, Nat. Sojourners, Mason (past dist. dep. Va.), Shriner, Kiwanian (past pres. Portsmouth), Moose, Elks. Home: 214 West Rd Portsmouth VA 23707

IAVICOLI, MARIO ANTHONY, lawyer; b. Camden, N.J., Aug. 11, 1939; s. Vito Anthony and Angelina Jessie (Marchionese) I.; m. Arlene V. LeDonne, July 6, 1963; children—Michelle, Denise, Laura. B.M.E., Drexel U., 1962; J.D., U. Pa., 1965. Bar: N.J. bar 1965. Asso. law firm Samuel P. Orlando, Camden, 1965-66, Ballen & Batoff, 1966-68; partner law firm Maressa, Console & Iavicoli, Berlin, N.J., 1968-72; first asst. prosecutor, Camden County, 1972-74, pvt. practice law, Pennsauken, N.J., 1974—; Counsel to speaker N.J. Gen. Assembly, 1970-72, N.J. Automobile Ins. Study Commn., 1970-74, Camden County Charter Study Commn., 1974, Camden County Republican party, 1974-76, N.J. Rep. party, 1976—. Author: No Fault and Comparative Negligence in New Jersey, 1973; Drafter: N.J.'s No Fault Law and other companion legislation, 1970-73. Chmn. Camden County Rep. Com., 1978—; Rep. state committeeman, 1976—; mem. Electoral Coll. from, N.J., 1976; solicitor Pennsauken Twp., 1975—; Vice pres. Haddonfield Home Sch. Assn., 1972-73; Bd. dirs. Drexel U. Class Endowment Fund; trustee Haddonfield Civic Assn. Named One of N.J.'s 5 Outstanding Young Men, 1974; recipient Ocean County Bar Assn. award, 1975. Mem. Camden County Jr. C. of C. (counsel 1967-68), Am., N.J., Camden County bar assns., Sons of Italy. Roman Catholic. Club: Rotarian. Home: 340 Marquis Rd Haddonfield NJ 08033 Office: 43 King's Hwy W Haddonfield NJ 08033

IBARRA, OSCAR HERERRA, computer science educator; b. Philippines, Sept. 29, 1941; came to U.S., 1963, naturalized, 1973; s. Higino Lugtu and Carmen Zaide (Herrera) I.; m. Naida Soriano, Sept. 14, 1968; children: Audra, Evelyn, Michael. B.S., U. Philippines, 1962; M.S., U. Calif., Berkeley, 1965, Ph.D., 1967. Instr. dept. elec. engring. U. Philippines, 1962-63, vis. prof. dept. engring. scis., 1975-76; research asst. dept. elec. engring. and computer sci. U. Calif., Berkeley, 1964-67, acting asst. prof., 1967-69; asst. prof. dept. computer sci. U. Minn., Mpls., 1969-73, asso. prof., 1973-78, prof., 1978—. Contbr. articles to profl. jours. NSF grantee, 1972—; Guggenheim fellow, 1984-85. Mem. Assn. Computing Machinery (spl. interest group for automata and computability theory), Soc. Indsl. and Applied Math. Home: 3616 Penrod Ln NE Minneapolis MN 55418 Office: Dept Computer Sci U Minn 136 Lind Hall 207 Church St SE Minneapolis MN 55455

IBELE, WARREN EDWARD, mechanical engineer, educator; b. New Orleans, Aug. 17, 1924; s. Emile Frank and May Hilda (Labarthe) I.; m. Mary Elizabeth Unumb, Sept. 3, 1947; children: Erik Warren, Gretchen Marie, Mark Adams, John Labarthe. B.S. in Mech. Engring, Tulane U., 1944; M.S., U. Minn., 1947, Ph.D., 1953. Asst. project engr. Pratt & Whitney Aircraft Corp., 1955-57; faculty U. Minn., 1947—, prof. engring., 1959—, assoc. dean, 1967-73, dean, 1975-83; Visitor curriculum accreditation Engrs. Council Profl. Devel.; mem. sect. SABER, Navy Bd. Ednl. Requirements, 1966-69. Author: (with N.A. Hall) Engineering Thermodynamics, 1960; also numerous articles.; Editor: Modern Developments in Heat Transfer, 1963. Served with U.S. Navy, 1944-46. Fellow ASME; mem. Am. Soc. Engring. Edn., Sigma Xi, Tau Beta Pi. Home: 1729 Logan Ave Minneapolis MN 55403

IBEN, ICKO, JR., astrophysicist, educator; b. Champaign, Ill., June 27, 1931; s. Icko and Kathryn (Tomlin) I.; m. Miriam Genevieve Fett, Jan. 28, 1956; children: Christine, Timothy, Benjamin, Thomas. B.A., Harvard, 1953; M.S., U. Ill., 1954, Ph.D., 1958. Asst. prof. physics Williams Coll., 1958-61; sr. research fellow in physics Calif. Inst. Tech., 1961-64; asso. prof. physics Mass. Inst. Tech., 1964-68, prof., 1968-72; vis. prof. astronomy Harvard, 1966, 68, 70; vis. fellow Joint Inst. for Lab. Astrophysics, U. Colo., 1971-72; vis. prof. astronomy and astrophysics U. Calif. at Santa Cruz, 1972; prof. astronomy and physics, head dept. astronomy U. Ill. at Urbana-Champaign, 1972—; vis. prof. physics and astronomy Inst. for Astronomy, U. Hawaii, 1977; mem. adv. panel, astronomy sect. NSF, 1972-75; mem. vis. com. Aura Observatories, 1979-82. Contbr. articles to profl. jours. Mem. Am. Astron. Soc. (councilor 1974-77). Home: 3910 Clubhouse Dr Champaign IL 61820 Office: Astronomy Bldg 1011 W Springfield Urbana IL 61801

IBERALL, ARTHUR SAUL, physicist, educator; b. N.Y.C., June 12, 1918; s. Benjamin and Anna (Katz) I.; m. Helene Rubenstein, Jan. 28, 1940; children—Eleanora Iberall Robbins, Pamela Iberall Rubin, Althea, Valerie Iberall Slate. B.S., CCNY, 1940, postgrad., 1940-41; postgrad., George Washington U., 1942-45; 183380hon. degree, Ohio State U., 1976. Gen. physicist Nat. Bur. Standards, Washington, 1941-53; research dir. ARO Equipment Corp., Cleve., 1953-54; chief physicist Rand Devel. Corp., Cleve., 1954-65; chief scientist, pres. Gen. Tech. Services, Inc., Upper Darby, Pa., 1965-81; vis. scholar UCLA, 1981—. Author: Toward a General Science of Viable Systems, 1972, On Pulsatile and Steady Arterial Flow, 1973, Physics of Membrane Transport, 1973, Bridges in Science—From Physics to Social Science, 1974, On Nature, Life, Mind and Society, 1976; editor: (with J. Reswick) Technical and Biological Problems of Control; A Cybernetic View, 1970, (with A. Guyton) Regulation and Control in Physiological Systems, 1973; assoc. editor: Am. Jour. Physiology, Integrative and Comparative Physiology, 1976—; contbr. tech. articles to profl. jours. Fellow ASME (chmn. auto. control div. 1973); mem. Am. Phys. Soc., N.Y. Acad. Scis., Biomed. Engring. Soc. (Alza Disting. lectr. 1975), Am. Cybernetic Soc., Microcirculation Soc., Instrument Soc. Am., Biophys. Soc., Sigma Xi. Democrat. Jewish. Club: Cosmos. Home: 4675 Willis Ave Sherman Oaks CA 91403 Office: UCLA 6417 Boelter Hall Los Angeles CA 90024 *Three things stand out—developing the integrity of self as a human being, learning how to participate in a good family life, and integrating, in a singular fashion, the thrust of a general physical science with all aspects of reality both personal and societal. The first two themes require no special note here. Many have mastered the rules. The third is worth an added comment. Consider the Enlightenment's claim of a unified science capable of dealing with nature, life, man, mind, and society. Would it not be worthy of a man's life pursuit? It is.*

IBERS, JAMES ARTHUR, chemist; b. Los Angeles, June 9, 1930; s. Max Charles and Esther (Imerman) I.; m. Joyce Audrey Henderson, June 10, 1951; children—Jill Tina, Arthur Alan. B.S., Calif. Inst. Tech., 1951, Ph.D., 1954. NSF post-doctoral fellow, Melbourne, Australia, 1954-55; chemist Shell Devel. Co., 1955-61, Brookhaven Nat. Lab., 1961-64; mem. faculty Northwestern U., 1964—, prof. chemistry, 1964. Mem. Am. Chem. Soc. (inorganic chemistry award 1979), Am. Crystallographic Assn. Home: 2657 Orrington Ave Evanston IL 60201 Office: Dept Chemistry Northwestern Univ Evanston IL 60201

IBRAHIM, MICHEL AYOUB, physician, epidemiologist; b. Egypt, Jan. 28, 1934; came to U.S., 1960, naturalized, 1965; s. Ayoub Joseph and Sara Farag I.; m. Betty Bullard, June 5, 1962; children: Daniel, Deborah, David, Peter. M.D., Cairo (Egypt) U. Med. Sch., 1957; M.P.H., U. N.C., Chapel Hill, 1961, Ph.D. in Epidemiology, 1964. Postdoctoral fellow U. N.C., Chapel Hill, 1960-64; asst. prof. Sch. Medicine, SUNY, Buffalo, 1964-68, asso. prof., 1968-71; dep. commr. Erie County Health Dept., Buffalo, 1968-71; asso. prof. dept. epidemiology Sch. Public Health, U. N.C., Chapel Hill, 1971-73, prof., 1973—, chmn. dept. epidemiology, 1976-82; dean Sch. Pub. Health U. N.C., 1982—; cons. NIH, WHO. Editor: The Case-Control Study, Jour. Chronic Disease 32, 1979. Fellow Am. Public Health Assn., Am. Heart Assn. (epidemiology council); mem. Internat. Epidemiol. Assn., Am. Epidemiol. Soc., Soc. Epidemiol. Research. Home: 509 Redbud Rd Chapel Hill NC 27514 Office: Rosenau Hall 201 H Univ of NC Chapel Hill NC 27514

ICE, RODNEY DEAN, radiopharm. scientist; b. Fort Lewis, Wash., Apr. 24, 1937; s. Shirley M. and Nellie R. I.; m. Joan Elizabeth McCullough, Mar. 21, 1958; children: Randal Dean, Rex Daryl, Ronald Dale. B.S., U. Wash., 1959; M.S., Purdue U., 1965, Ph.D., 1967. Owner, mgr. Rod's Tanglewilde Drugs, Olympia, Wash., 1959-65; radiol. health fellow Purdue U., 1964-67; asst. prof., asso. prof., radiation safety officer Temple U., Phila., 1967-71; prof., dir. radiopharm. services Coll. Pharmacy, U. Mich., Ann Arbor, 1971-76; dean, prof. Coll. Pharmacy, U. Okla., Oklahoma City, 1976-83. Contbr. aricles to profl. jours. Trustee Phila. Coll. Bible, 1970-80. Served with Army NG, 1953-63. Mem. AAAS, Am. Pharm. Assn., Soc. Nuclear Medicine, Am. Sci. Affiliation, Health Physics Soc., Okla. Pharm. Assn., Am. Bd. Health Physics. Baptist. Club: Gideons. Home: PO Box 3042 Edmond OK 73083 Office: 1313 Washington Ave Golden CO 804401

ICHINO, YOKO, ballarina; b. Los Angeles. Pupil of, Mia Slavenska. Mem., City Center Joffrey Ballet, N.Y.C., Stuttgart (W. Ger.) Ballet, 1975-76, Am. Ballet Theatre, 1977—; tchr. ballet, Munich, W. Ger.,

N.Y.C., Fla., Calif.; mem., Joffrey Ballet Sch.; guest work, including, Delacorte Theater, 2d World Ballet Festival, Japan, Internat. Festival, Munich, 7th Internat. Festival of Havana, Cuba; prin. roles include: Don Quixote, La Bayodere, The River, Swan Lake, Theme and Variations, Le Corsair, Sleeping Beauty. Recipient Bronze medal 3d Internat. Ballet Competition, Moscow, 1977. Address: Am Ballet Theatre 888 7th Ave New York NY 10019

ICHORD, RICHARD HOWARD, lawyer, former congressman; b. Licking, Mo., June 27, 1926; s. Richard Howard and Minda (Curtis) I.; m. Millicent Murphy Koch; children: Richard Howard, Pamela Lee, Kyle. B.S., Mo. U., 1949, J.D., 1952. Bar: Mo. 1952. Instr. bus. law U. Mo., 1950, 51; mem. firm Lay & Ichord, Houston, Mo., 1952-6O; city atty., Houston, 1952; mem. Mo. Ho. of Reps., 1953, speaker pro tem, 1957-58, speaker, 1959-60; mem. 87th-96th Congresses from 8th Mo. Dist.; pres. Washington Indsl. Team, Inc., 1980—; mem. firm Lathrop, Koontz, Righter, Clagett & Norquist, 1980-83. Served with A.C. USNR, 1944-46. Mem. VFW, Am. Legion, Houston C. of C. Democrat. Lodges: Masons; Odd Fellows. Office: 499 S Capitol St SW Suite 400 Washington DC 20003 *

IDLER, DAVID RICHARD, biochemist, marine scientist, educator; b. Winnipeg, Man., Can., Mar. 13, 1923; s. Ernest and Alice (Lydon) I.; m. Myrtle Mary Betteridge, Dec. 12, 1956; children: Louise, Mark. B.A., U. B.C., Can.), Vancouver, 1949, M.A., 1950; Ph.D., U. Wis., 1954. With Fisheries Research Bd. of Can., 1953-71; dir., investigator in charge of steroid biochemistry Halifax (N.S.) Lab., 1961-69, Atlantic regional dir. research, Halifax, 1969-71; dir. Marine Sci. Research Lab.; prof. biochemistry Meml. U. Nfld., Can., St. John's, 1971—. Editor: Steroids in Nonmammalian Vertebrates, 1972; editorial bd.: Steroids, 1963—, Gen. and Comparative Endocrinology, 1966-82, Endocrine Research Communications, 1974—, Can. Jour. Zoology, 1979—; mem. bd. corr. editors: Jour. Steroid Biochemistry. Served with RCAF, 1942-45. Decorated D.F.C. Fellow Royal Soc. Can.; mem. European Soc. Comparative Endocrinologists (founding), Can. Biochem. Soc., Am. Chem. Soc., AAAS, Am. Zool. Soc., Endocrine Soc., N.Y. Acad. Scis. Home: 44 Slattery Rd St John's NF A1A 1Z8 Canada Office: Marine Scis Research Lab Meml U Nfld St John's NF A1C 5S7 Canada

IDOL, JAMES DANIEL, JR., chemical company executive; b. Harrisonville, Mo., Aug. 7, 1928; s. James Daniel and Gladys Rosita (Lile) I.; m. Marilyn Thorn Randall, 1977. A.B., William Jewell Coll., 1949; M.S., Purdue U., 1952, Ph.D., 1955, D.Sc. (hon.), 1980. With Standard Oil Co., Ohio, 1955-77, research supr., 1965-68, research mgr., 1968-77; mgr. venture research Ashland Chem. Co., Columbus, Ohio, 1977-79, v.p., dir. corp. research and devel., 1979—; mem. adv. bd. NSF Presdl. Young Investigators Awards; cons. in field. Contbr. articles to profl. jours; mem. editorial bd. profl. jours. Mem. Cleve. Welfare Fedn. Recipient Modern Pioneer award Nat. Assn. Mfrs., 1965, Disting. Alumnus citation William Jewell Coll., 1971. Life fellow Am. Inst. Chemists (dir. 1981, Chem. Pioneer award 1968, Mems. and Fellows lectr. 1980); mem. Soc. Plastics Industry, Am. Chem. Soc. (Joseph P. Stewart Disting. Service award 1975, Creative Invention award 1975), Am. Inst. Chem. Engrs., Soc. Plastics Engrs., Indsl. Research Inst. (rep.), Plastics Pioneers Assn., Soc. Chem. Industry (Perkin medal 1979), Council Chem. Research (indsl. del.), Ind. Acad. Sci., AAAS., Sigma Xi, Alpha Chi Sigma, Theta Chi Delta, Kappa Mu Epsilon, Alpha Phi Omega, Phi Gamma Delta. Mem. Disciples of Christ Ch. Clubs: Cleve. Athletic, Worthington Hills Country, Masons, Shriners. Patentee in field. Home: 8008 Park Ridge Ct Worthington OH 43085 Office: PO Box 2219 Columbus OH 43216

IDRISS, IZZAT M., civil engineer, consultant; b. Damascus, Syria, Dec. 28, 1935; came to U.S., 1954, naturalized, 1970; s. Muhammad and Asma (Kanawaty) I.; m. Mariam Kanawati, July 29, 1961; children: Nizar, Nadania. B.C.E., Rensselaer Poly. Inst., 1958; M.S., Calif. Inst. Tech., 1959, postgrad., 1959-60; Ph.D., U. Calif.-Berkeley, 1966. With Dames & Moore, Los Angeles, N.Y.C., San Francisco, 1959-66, project mgr., 1963-66, sr. soils engr., San Francisco, 1968-69; asso. Woodward-Clyde Cons., San Francisco, 1969-74, prin., v.p., dir., 1974-82, mng. prin., v.p., dir., Los Angeles, 1982—; lectr. soil mechanics dept. civil engring. U. Calif.-Berkeley, 1967-68, asst. and asso. research engr., 1966-76; cons. to architect-engring. firms, 1966—; cons. nuclear reactor safety with respect to earthquake effects Govt. Italy, 1970-75; cons. IAEA, 1975—, UNESCO, Paris, 1981—; cons. prof. Stanford U., 1977—; cons. on seismic effects for earth and rockfill dams, nuclear plants, offshore platforms and other indsl. facilities, U.S., Latin Am., Europe, Middle East. Recipient Middlebrooks award ASCE, 1971, Walter L. Huber Engring. Research award, 1976, Croes medal, 1972, Norman medal, 1977; Indsl. Relations fellow Calif. Inst. Tech., 1959-60. Mem. Internat. Commn. on Large Dams (U.S. com.), ASCE, Earthquake Engring. Research Inst., Seismol. Soc. Am., Structural Engrs. Assn. So. Calif., Sigma Xi, Chi Epsilon (hon. mem. Rensselaer chpt.), Tau Beta Pi. Research and publs. on soil aspects of earthquake engring. Home: PO Box 677 South Laguna CA 92677 Office: 203 N Golden Circle Dr Santa Ana CA 92705

IDZERDA, STANLEY JOHN, educator, editor; b. N.Y.C., June 4, 1920; s. Hendrik and Therese (Miller) I.; m. Geraldine Ann Waters, Oct. 26, 1945; children—Ann, Geraldine, William, Christopher, Mary, James, Catherine. B.Naval Sci., U. Notre Dame, 1946; A.B., Baldwin-Wallace Coll., 1947; A.M., Western Res. U., 1950, Ph.D., 1951. Asst. prof. history Western Mich. Coll., 1951-52; mem. faculty Mich. State U., 1952-65, prof. history, 1958-65, dir., 1957-65; adj. prof. history, dean undergrad. studies Wesleyan U., Middletown, Conn., 1965-68; pres. Coll. St. Benedict, St. Joseph, Minn., until 1974; editor-in-chief Lafayette Papers, Cornell U., Ithaca, N.Y., 1974-79; prof. history Coll. St. Benedict, St. Joseph, Minn., 1979—; vis. lectr. history Yale Grad. Sch., 1966-67; distinguished vis. prof. No. Mich. U., 1967; Chmn. advanced placement com. Coll. Entrance Exam. Bd., 1965; regional asso. Am. Council Learned Socs., 1960-65, Fellow, 1950-51. Contbr. articles to profl. jours. Served with USNR, 1940-46. Decorated Purple Heart. Mem. Am., Am. Cath. hist. assns., Am. Soc. Aesthetics (trustee 1958-61), Soc. French Hist. Studies (pres. 1961-62). Home: PO Box 27 Saint Joseph MN 56374

IFFLAND, DON CHARLES, educator, chemist; b. Blissfield, Mich., Nov. 26, 1921; s. Fred C. and Letha (Lipp) I.; m. Mary Jane Sparks, Apr. 29, 1944; children—Diana, Charis. B.S., Adrian Coll., 1943; M.S., Purdue U., 1946, Ph.D., 1947. Asst. prof., then asso. prof. W.Va. U., 1947-56; asso. prof., then prof. Western Mich. U., Kalamazoo, 1956—, chmn. chemistry dept., 1968-78. Contbr. articles to profl. jours. Mem. Am. Chem. Soc., Am. Inst. Chemists, Sigma Xi. Home: 3430 Northview Dr Kalamazoo MI 49007

IGASAKI, MASAO, JR., utilities executive; b. Los Angeles, May 24, 1925; s. Masao and Aiko (Kamayatsu) I.; m. Grace Kushino, June 5, 1948; children: David, Paul. B.S. in Bus. Adminstrn., Northwestern U., 1949; M.B.A., U. Chgo., 1963. C.P.A., Ill. With Peoples Gas Light & Coke Co., Chgo., 1949—, auditor, 1966-69, asst. v.p., asst. controller, 1969-70, asst. v.p., 1970-76, asst. v.p., controller, 1976-77, v.p., controller, 1977-81, v.p., 1981—; v.p., controller Peoples Energy Corp., 1981—. Scoutmaster, Boy Scouts Am., 1964-67; trustee Mt. Sinai Hosp., Chgo. Served with AUS, 1944-46. Mem. Am. Inst. C.P.A.s, Ill. Soc. C.P.A.s, Assn. Commerce and Industry. Mem. United Ch. Christ. Clubs: Econ., Univ. (Chgo.). Home: 247 E Chestnut St Chicago IL 60611 Office: 122 S Michigan Ave Chicago IL 60603

IGGERS, GEORG GERSON, history educator; b. Hamburg, Germany, Dec. 7, 1926; came to U.S., 1938, naturalized, 1949; s. Alfred G. and Lizzie (Minden) I.; m. Wilma Abeles, Dec. 23, 1948; children: Jeremy, Daniel, Karl Jonathan. B.A., U. Richmond, 1944; A.M., U. Chgo., 1945, Ph.D., 1951; postgrad., New Sch. Social Research, 1945-46. Instr. U. Akron (Ohio), 1948-50; assoc. prof. Philander Smith Coll., Little Rock, 1950-57; from assoc. prof. to prof. Dillard U., New Orleans, 1957-63; assoc. prof. Roosevelt U., Chgo., 1963-65; prof. history SUNY, Buffalo, 1965—, disting. prof., 1978—, chmn., 1981—; vis. prof. U. Ark., Fayetteville, 1956-57, 64, U. Rochester, 1970-71; vis. assoc. prof. Tulane U., New Orleans, 1958-60, 63. Author: The Cult of Authority, 1958, The German Conception of History, 1968, New Directions in European Historiography, 1975; editor: (with Harold T. Parker) International Handbook of Historical Studies, 1979. Bd. dirs., counselor Draft and Mil. Counseling Ctr., Buffalo, 1967—; bd. dirs. Ark. Council Human Relations, Buffalo, 1965—; chmn. edn., exec. coms. NAACP, Little Rock, 1951-56, chmn. edn. com., New Orleans, 1957-63, bd. dirs, Buffalo, 1965—, chmn. edn. com., Buffalo, 1965-75, co-chmn. health com., Buffalo, 1979—. Fellow Guggenheim Found., 1960-61, Rockefeller Found., 1961-62, NEH, 1971-72, 78-79; hon. fellow Fulbright Commn., 1978-79. Mem. Internat. Commn. Historiography (v.p. 1980—), Am. Hist. Assn., French Hist. Soc., Conf. Group Central European History, Conf. Peace Research in History. Home: 100 Ivyhurst Rd Buffalo NY 14226 Office: Dept History SUNY Buffalo NY 14261

IGL, RICHARD FRANKLIN, lawyer; b. Klamath Falls, Oreg., Feb. 15, 1923; s. Englebert Matthew and Rose Ann (Haas) I.; m. Frances Marie Pytleski, Mar. 15, 1980. B.A., U. Oreg., 1947, M.A. with honors, 1948; J.D., Yale U., 1950. Bar: Calif. 1951, U.S. Supreme Ct. 1975, U.S. Tax Ct. 1975. Instr. polit. sci. Yale U., 1949-50; law clk. to judge U.S. Ct. Apppeals, N.Y. Circuit, 1950-51; asso. firm O'Melveny & Myers, Los Angeles, 1951-60, partner, 1960-63; pvt. practice, Beverly Hills, Calif., 1963—; judge pro tem Beverly Hills Municipal Ct., 1966; lectr. estate and tax planning course UCLA, 1963-64; lectr. Entertainment Law Inst., U. So. Calif., 1961; dir., sec.-treas. Crobsy Investment Corp., Los Angeles, 1960—; gen. counsel, dir. Seven-Up Bottling Co. Los Angeles, Inc., 1967-68. Bd. dirs., sec. Western Inst. for Cancer and Leukemia Research, Beverly Hills, 1963-68. Served to capt. AUS, 1942-46. Mem. ABA (del. 1969-72), Calif. Bar Assn., Los Angeles Bar Assn. (trustee 1970-71), Beverly Hills Bar Assn. (bd. govs. 1960-71, pres. 1968), Copyright Soc. Los Angeles (dir. 1964-66), Beverly Hills C. of C. (dir. 1977-78), Phi Beta Kappa. Home: 9800 Yoakum Dr Beverly Hills CA 90210 Office: 9720 Wilshire Blvd Beverly Hills CA 90212

IGLEHART, JOHN K., journalist; b. Milw., July 29, 1939; s. Marion McDonnal and Ruth (Gillen) I.; m. Mary Linda Dahlke, Dec. 26, 1964; children: Amy, David. B.S. in Journalism, U. Wis., 1961. With Milw. Sentinel, 1957-61; with AP, Chgo., 1962-68, night city editor, 1967-68; with Nat. Jour., Washington, 1969-79, contbg. editor., 1977-79; v.p. Kaiser Found. Health Plan, Inc., Washington, 1979-81; spl. corr. New Eng. Jour. Medicine, Washington, 1981—; editor Health Affairs, Millwood, Va. Contbr. articles to health and med. publs. Served with U.S. Army, 1962-68. Congressional fellow, 1968-69. Mem. Nat. Acad. Scis. Inst. of Medicine, Am. Polit. Sci. Assn. Home: 12008 River Rd Potomac MD 20854 Office: 4801 Massachusetts Ave NW Suite 650 Washington DC 20006

IGLESKI, THOMAS ROBERT, lawyer, ins. co. exec.; b. Chgo., June 16, 1934; s. William E. and Wanda M. I.; m. Arline Skowronski, Nov. 10, 1962; children—Mark, Laura. B.B.A., U. Notre Dame, 1955; J.D., De Paul U., 1962. Bar: Ill. bar 1962, U.S. Supreme Ct. bar 1968. Atty. CNA Ins. Cos., Chgo., 1962-68, corp. sec., asst. gen. counsel, 1972—, v.p., 1977—, corp. counsel subs., Chgo., 1968-72; dir. Gen. Finance Corp. Served with U.S. Army, 1956-58. Mem. Am., Ill., Chgo. bar assns., Am. Soc. Corp. Secs. Clubs: Calumet Country, Union League. Home: 19110 Pierce Ave Homewood IL 60430 Office: CNA Insurance Cos CNA Plaza Chicago IL 60685

IGLEWICZ, BORIS, statistician, educator; b. Omsk, USSR, Oct. 11, 1939; came to U.S., 1952, naturalized, 1959; s. Solomon and Faiga (Brucker) I.; m. Raja Brody, May 24, 1973; children—David, Alana. B.S., Wayne State U., 1962; M.A., 1963; Ph.D., Va. Poly. Inst., 1967. Instr. math. Mich. Tech. U., 1963-64; asst. prof. stats. Case Western Res. U., 1967-69; asso. prof. stats. Temple U., 1969-74, prof., 1974—, dir. Ph.D. program in stats., 1970-75, chmn. dept., 1978-82; v.p., dir. Meco Metals Corp., 1974. Author: (with J. Stoyle) An Introduction to Mathematical Reasoning, 1973; contbr. articles to profl. jours., chpts. to books. NIH fellow, 1964-67; advanced research fellow Harvard U., 1978. Mem. Am. Statis. Assn. (pres. Phila. chpt. 1981-83), Biometric Soc., Inst. Math. Stats., Sigma Xi, Pi Mu Epsilon, Beta Gamma Sigma. Home: 1912 Rolling Ln Cherry Hill NJ 08003 Office: Dept Stats Temple U Philadelphia PA 19122

IGNATIEFF, GEORGE, university chancellor; b. St. Petersburg, Russia, Dec. 16, 1913; s. Count Paul and Princess Natalie (Mestchersky) I.; m. Alison Grant, Nov. 17, 1945; children: Michael Grant, Andrew Grant. B.A., U. Toronto, 1936; M.A., New Coll., Oxford, Eng., 1938; LL.D. (hon.), Brock U., 1967, U. Toronto, 1968, U. Guelph, 1969, U. Sask., 1973, York U., 1975, Mt. Allison U., 1978, D.C.L., Bishop's U., 1973, D.Litt., U. Victoria Coll., 1977. Pvt. sec. to Rt. Hon. Vincent Massey High Commr. for Can., London, 1940-44; sec. Post Hostilities Planning Com., Ottawa, Ont., Can., 1944-45; diplomatic advisor to Gen. A.G.L. McNaughton UN AEC, 1945-46; advisor Can. Del. UN, 1946-47; alt. rep. UN Security Council, 1948-49; counsellor Can. Embassy, Washington, 1949-53; head def. Liason Div. Can. Dept. External Affairs, 1955-56; Can. ambassador to Yugoslavia, 1956-58; dep. to Hon. George Drew High Commr. Can. to U.K., 1959-60; asst. under-sec. State External Affairs, 1960-62; permanent Can. rep. NATO, 1963-65, UN Security Council, 1965-68, Disarmament Com., Geneva, 1968-71, European Office of UN, 1971-72; provost Trinity Coll., 1972-78; chmn. bd. trustees Nat. Mus. Can., 1973-78; gov. Heritage Can., 1978-80; pres. UN of Can., 1980-82; chancellor U. Toronto, 1980—. Home: 18 Palmerston Gardens Toronto ON Canada M6G 1V9 Office: Toronto 17 King's College Circle Toronto ON Canada M5S 1A1

IGNATIUS, PAUL ROBERT, assn. exec.; b. Los Angeles, Nov. 11, 1920; s. H. B. and Elisa (Jamgochian) I.; m. Nancy Sharpless Weiser, Dec. 20, 1947; children—David, Amy, Sarah, Alan. A.B., U. So. Calif., 1942; M.B.A., Harvard U., 1947. Instr. bus. adminstrn. Harvard Bus. Sch., 1947-50; v.p., dir. Harbridge House, Inc. (mgmt. cons.), Boston, 1950-61; asst. sec. army for installations and logistics, 1961-63, undersec., 1964, asst. sec. of def., 1964-67, sec. of navy, 1967-69; pres. The Washington Post, 69-71; exec. v.p. Air Transp. Assn., 1972, pres., chief exec. officer, 1972—. Bd. dirs. Nat. Symphony Orch.; bd. regents Georgetown U. Served with USNR, 1943-46. Recipient Distinguished Civilian Service award Dept. Army, 1962; Civilian Pub. Service award Dept. Navy, 1969; Distinguished Civilian Pub. Ser award Dept. Def., 1969. Mem. Phi Beta Kappa. Clubs: Chevy Chase (Md.); Metropolitan (Washington). Home: 3650 Fordham Rd Washington DC 20016 Office: 1709 New York Ave Washington DC 20006

IGNATOW, DAVID, poet; b. Bklyn., Feb. 7, 1914; s. Max and Yetta (Reinbach) I.; m. Rose Graubart, July 20, 1940; children: David, Yaedi. Ed. pub. schs., Bklyn. Assoc. editor Am. Scene mag., 1935-37; lit. arts editor N.Y. Analytic, 1937; editor Beloit (Wis.) Poetry Jour., 1949-59; poetry editor The Nation, 1962-63; guest editor, Chelsea, N.Y., 1962, co-editor, 1968; editor-at-large Am. Poetry Rev., 1973-76; instr. poetry workshop New Sch. Social Research, N.Y.C., 1964; vis. lectr. U. Ky., 1965-66; lectr. English, U. Kans., 1966—; vis. lectr. Vassar Coll., 1967-68; adj. prof. Southampton Coll. of L.I. U., 1967-68; also Columbia poet-in-residence York Coll., CUNY, 1969-84. Author: Poems, 1948, The Gentle Weight Lifter, 1955, Say Pardon, 1962, Figures of the Human, 1964, Earth Hard, Selected Poems, 1968, Rescue the Dead, 1968, Poems: 1934-69, 1970, Notebooks: 1934-1971, 1973; poems Facing The Tree, 1975, Selected Poems, 1975, Tread the Dark, 1978, Whisper to the Earth, 1981, Leaving the Door Open, 1984; prose Open Between Us, 1980. Recipient Nat. Inst. Arts and Letters award, 1964; Shelley Meml. award, 1966; CAP award, 1976; Bollingen award, 1977; Guggenheim fellow, 1965, 73; Rockefeller Found. grantee, 1968; Nat. Endowment for Arts grantee, 1970; Wallace Stevens fellow Yale U., 1977. Mem. Poetry Soc. Am. (pres. 1981—). Address: PO Box 1458 East Hampton NY 11937 *I think of writing, prose and poetry, as my means of making contact with others and through this contact giving others my thoughts on life and self. They will have to discover these thoughts for themselves in my writing, since it, for me, must conform to the standards I have set for myself as a writer of poetry, particularly—the imagination through language in league with life.*

IGNOFFO, CARLO MICHAEL, insect pathologist-virologist; b. Chicago Heights, Ill., Aug. 24, 1928; s. Joseph and Lucy (Sardo) I.; m. Florence F. Mielcarek, Sept. 3, 1949. B.S., No. Ill. U., 1950; M.S., U. Minn., 1954, Ph.D., 1957. Asst. prof. Iowa Wesleyan Coll., Mt. Pleasant, 1957-59; insect pathologist U.S. Dept. Agr., Brownsville, Tex., 1959-65; dir. entomology Internat. Minerals & Chems. Corp., Wasco, Calif. and Libertyville, Ill., 1965-71; lab. dir. U.S. Dept. Agr., Columbia, Mo., 1971—; prof. dept. entomology U. Mo., 1974—. Served with Chem. Corps U.S. Army, 1954-56. Mem. Internat. Orgn. Biol. Control (pres. 1974), AAAS, Am. Inst. Biol. Scis., Soc. Invertebrate Pathology (editorial bd. 1965-68, treas. 1968-70), Entomol. Soc. Am., Mo. Acad. Sci., C. of C. Isolated, commercialized 1st viral pesticide. Patentee in field. Office: PO Box A Research Park Columbia MO 65205

IGUSA, JUN-ICHI, educator, mathematician; b. Japan, Jan. 30, 1924; came to U.S., 1953; s. Shiro and Rui (Fukushima) I.; m. Yoshie Yamamoto, Oct. 7, 1948; children—Kiyoshi, Takeru, Mitsuru. Rigakushi, Tokyo Imperial U., 1945, Rigakuhakushi, 1953. Asst. prof. Kyoto (Japan) U., 1949-53; research asso. Harvard, 1953-55; mem. faculty Johns Hopkins, 1955—, prof. math., 1961—. Author: Theta Functions, 1972, Forms of Higher Degree, 1978; editor-in-chief: Am. Jour. Math. Mem. Math. Soc. Japan, Am. Math. Soc., Phi Beta Kappa. Home: 14209 Greencroft Ln Hunt Valley MD 21030 Office: Johns Hopkins Univ Baltimore MD 21218

IHARA, MICHIO, sculptor; b. Paris, France, Nov. 17, 1928; s. Usaburo and Shigeko (Shinkai) I.; m. Doreen Joyce Kaplan, July 7, 1966; 1 son, Akeo. B.F.A., Tokyo U., 1953; Fulbright fellow, MIT, 1961-62. Research asso. MIT, 1962-64; instr. Musashino U. Fine Arts, Tokyo, 1966-69. Exhibited in one man shows at, Kanegis Gallery, Boston, 1964, Tokyo Gallery, 1970, Staempfli Gallery, N.Y.C., 1977, 80, numerous group shows in Japan and U.S., 1957-74; important works include marble mural Chuo-koron Pub. Co, Tokyo, 1957; copper relief 275 Wyman St. Office Bldg, Waltham, Mass., 1963; altar canopy Josenji Temple, Tokyo, 1965; metal screen Imperial Theatre, Tokyo, 1966; relief Internat. Christian U, Tokyo, 1967, Fuji Film Co. Bldg, Tokyo, 1969; sculpture Internat. Sculptors Symposium, Osaka, 1970, Wellesley (Mass.) Office Park, 1973, Fitchburg (Mass.) Pub. Library; civic sculpture, Auckland, N.Z., 1977, Constellation Place, Balt., 1978; metal screen Rockefeller Center, N.Y.C., 1978, Neiman-Marcus, Beverly Hills, Calif., New World Hotel, Hong Kong, Pavilion Hotel, Singapore; wall sculpture S.E. Bank, Miami, 1983. JDR 3d Fund grantee, 1970-71; recipient award Mass. Council Arts and Humanities, 1974, Nat. Inst. Arts and Letters/Am. Acad. Arts and Letters award in art, 1973; Graham Found. fellow, 1963-64; MIT Center for Advanced Visual Studies fellow, 1970-73. Mem. Japan Artists Assn. Address: 63 Wood St Concord MA 01742

IHDE, AARON JOHN, history educator emeritus; b. Neenah, Wis., Dec. 31, 1909; s. John Lewis and Ella (Haase) I.; m. Olive Jane Tipler, June 14, 1933; children: Gretchen (Mrs. Hendrick Serrie), John. B.S., U. Wis., 1931, M.S., 1939, Ph.D., 1941. Chemist Blue Valley Creamery Co., Chgo., 1931-38; instr. chemistry Butler U., Indpls., 1941-42; mem. faculty U. Wis.-Madison, 1942—, prof. chemistry, integrated liberal studies and history of sci., 1958-80, emeritus prof., 1980—, chmn. dept. integrated liberal studies, 1963-70; Carnegie intern in gen. edn. Harvard, 1951-52; Mem. Wis. Food Standards Adv. Com., 1955-68, chmn., 1964-65. Author: The Physical Universe, 1963, Development of Modern Chemistry, 1964, 2d edit., 1984, Selected Readings in the History of Chemistry, 1965, (with others) Joseph Priestley, Scientist, Theologian, and Metaphysician, 1980. Recipient Dexter award history of chemistry div. Am. Chem. Soc., 1968. Mem. History of Sci. Soc., AAAS, Am. Chem. Soc., Wis. Acad. Scis., Arts and Letters (pres. 1963-64), Sigma Xi, Phi Lambda Upsilon. Democrat. Unitarian. Home: 2606 Marshall Pkwy Madison WI 53713

IHLE, JOHN LIVINGSTON, artist, educator; b. Chgo., Feb. 1, 1925; s. Chester and Martha Elizabeth I.; m. Marguerite Poeschel, July 30, 1955; children—Lars Eric, Jean Elaine. Student, U. Iowa, 1949; B.F.A., Ill. Wesleyan U., 1950; M.A., Bradley U., 1951. Prof. dept. art San Francisco State U., 1955—; vis. prof. art U. Alta., Edmonton, Can., 1968-69, Chgo. Art Inst., 1980. One-man exhbns. include, San Francisco Mus. Art, 1960, 66, 77, Achenbach Found. Graphic Art, 1962, Hansen Gallery, San Francisco, 1964, 68, group exhbns. include, Nat. Print Exhbn., Library of Congress, Nat. Print Invitationals, U. Ky., 1961, SUNY, 1968, U. Ill., 1970, Cin. Art Mus., 1973; represented in permanent collections, Library of Congress, Chgo. Art Inst., N.Y. Public Library, Calif. Palace of Legion of Honor, San Francisco, Nat. Gallery Art, Washington. Served with U.S. Army, 1943-46. Decorated Purple Heart.; Ford Found. grantee. Mem. Calif. Soc. Printmakers (past pres.), San Francisco Tapestry Workshop (chmn. bd.). Home: 49 Shell Rd Mill Valley CA 94941 Office: 49 Shell Rd Mill Valley CA 94941

IHRIG, JUDSON LA MOURE, chemist; b. Santa Maria, Calif., Nov. 5, 1925; s. Harry Karl and Luella (LaMoure) I.; m. Gwendolyn Adele Montz, July 22, 1950; children—Kristin, Neil Marshall. B.S., Haverford Coll., 1949; M.A., Princeton U., 1951, Ph.D., 1952. Asst. prof. chemistry U. Hawaii, 1952-58, asso. prof., 1958-72, prof., 1972—, dir. honors program, 1958-64, dir. liberal studies program, 1973-79, chmn. chemistry dept., 1981—; cons. chemistry local firms. Author publs. in field. Served with AUS, 1945-46. Mem. Am. Chem. Soc., AAUP, Phi Beta Kappa, Sigma Xi. Home: 386 Wailupe Circle Honolulu HI 96821 Office: 2545 The Mall Honolulu HI 96822

IKARD, FRANK NEVILLE, lawyer; b. Henrietta, Tex., Jan. 30, 1913; s. Lewis and Ena (Neville) I.; m. Jean Hunter, Oct. 15, 1940 (dec. Apr. 1970); children—Frank Neville, William Forsyth; m. Jayne Brumley, July 22, 1972. A.B., U. Tex., 1936, LL.B., 1936. Bar: Tex. bar 1936.

Mem. firm Bullington, Humphrey & Humphrey, Wichita Falls, 1937-47; judge 30th Jud. Dist. Ct., Wichita Falls, 1947-52; mem. 82d to 87th Congresses from 13th Tex. dist.; exec. v.p. Am. Petroleum Inst., 1961-63, pres., 1963-79; partner firm Danzansky, Dickey, Tydings, Quint & Gordon, Washington, 1979—; dir. Sheller-Globe Corp., Toledo, First Am. Bank, N.A., Washington, Consol. Petroleum Industries, Inc., Ind. Refinery Group, Inc.; Mem. natural gas adv. council Fed. Power Commn., 1964-70; mem. adv. bd. Center for Strategic Studies, Washington, 1966-69; mem. Nat. Petroleum Council, 1964—, Pres.'s Nat. Adv. Com. on Hwy. Beautification, 1966-68, Pres.'s Nat. Citizens Commn. on Internat. Cooperation, 1965-68, Pres.'s Industry-Govt. Spl. Task Force on Travel, 1966-68; mem. U.S. nat. conf. World Energy Congress, 1967-69, World Petroleum Congresses, 1963-70. Sec., trustee John F. Kennedy Center for Performing Arts, Washington; chmn. Meridian House Internat., Washington; vice chmn. bd. regents U. Tex. at Austin. Served with AUS, 1942-45. Mem. Am. Bar Assn., State Bar Tex., D.C. Bar, Ind. Petroleum Assn. Am., Japan-Am. Soc. Episcopalian. Clubs: Masons; Burning Tree (Chevy Chase, Md.); Carlton, City Tavern Assn., Internat., Met. (Washington); Hemisphere, Univ. (N.Y.C.). Home: 1801 Kalorama Sq NW Washington DC 20008 Office: 1120 Connecticut Ave NW Washington DC 20036

IKE, NOBUTAKA, educator; b. Seattle, June 6, 1916; s. Yasuji and Tsuya (Tanaka) I.; m. Tai Inui, Aug. 23, 1942; children—Linda Y., Brian Y. B.A., U. Wash., 1940, grad. student, 1940-41; Ph.D., Johns Hopkins, 1949. Instr. Japanese U.S. Naval Tng. Sch., U. Colo., 1942-46; lectr., Charles Peck fellow Johns Hopkins, 1948-49; curator Japanese collections Hoover Instn., Stanford, 1949-58; mem. faculty Stanford, 1958—, prof. polit. sci., 1963—, exec. head of dept., 1963-64; Rockefeller vis. prof. U. Philippines, 1968-69. Author: The Beginnings of Political Democracy in Japan, 1950, Japanese Politics, 1957, Japan's Decision for War, 1966, Japanese Politics: Patron-client Democracy, 1972, Japan: The New Superstate, 1973, A Theory of Japanese Democracy, 1978; asso. editor: Far Eastern Quar, 1950-55; Contbr. to: Major Governments of Asia, 2d edit, 1963. Recipient Demblzn. award Social Sci. Research Council, 1946-48; Ford fellow, 1953-55; Rockefeller fellow, 1964-65. Mem. Phi Beta Kappa, Pi Sigma Alpha. Home: 621 Alvarado Row Stanford CA 94305

IKE, REVEREND *See* **EIKERENKOETTER, FREDERICK JOSEPH, II**

IKEDA, TSUNEO, banker; b. Tokyo, Feb., 1934; s. Hideo I. and Kei (Arai) Nakamura; m. Kyoko Ikeda, Apr. 4, 1960; children: Naoki, Hiroki. B.A., Keio U., Tokyo, 1956. Various banking positions Mitsui Bank, Ltd., Tokyo, 1956-67; asst. mgr.Bombay br., India, 1967-69, asst. mgr.Internat. br., Tokyo, 1970-71, dep. gen. mgr. Los Angeles agy., 1971-75, dep. gen. mgr.Internat. div., Tokyo, 1976-81; sr. exec. v.p. Mitsui Mfrs. Bank, Los Angeles, 1981—, dir.; dir. Japan Bus. Assn. So. Calif., 1982. Mem. Internat. Bankers Assn., Keio U. Alumni Orgn. (pres. 1981). Clubs: Los Angeles Athletic; Riviera Country (Los Angeles). Office: Mitsui Mfrs Bank 515 S Figueroa St Los Angeles CA 90071

IKELER, HAROLD EDWIN, JR., banker; b. Lewisburg, Pa., Nov. 11, 1930; s. Harold Edwin and Geraldine (Lazarus) I.; m. Patricia A. Strine, June 28, 1952; children—R. Stephen, Thomas J., Robert A. B.A., U. Pa., 1952. Asst. examiner, examining officer Fed. Res. Bank, Phila., 1955-64; v.p., auditor Girard Trust Bank, Phila., now v.p. corp. trust div. Served to lt. (j.g.) USN, 1952-55. Mem. Am. Soc. Corp. Secs. (dir.), Stock Transfer Assn., Bank Adminstrn. Inst. Address: 252 Deer Run Media PA 19063

IKENBERRY, HENRY CEPHAS, JR., lawyer; b. Cloverdale, Va., Mar. 23, 1920; s. Henry Cephas and Bessie (Peters) I.; m. Margaret Sangster Henry, July 3, 1943; children: Anna Catherine Ikenberry Fawell, Mary Margaret Ikenberry Rauck. B.A., Bridgewater Coll., 1947; J.D., U. Va., 1947. Bar: Va. 1947, W.Va. 1948, D.C. 1948, U.S. Supreme Ct. 1954, U.S. Ct. Claims 1972. Asso. firm Steptoe & Johnson, Washington, 1947-49, 50-53, partner, 1953—; asst. counsel Gen. Aniline & Film Co., N.Y.C., 1949-50; mem. com. on unauthorized practice D.C. Ct. Appeals, 1972-76; dir. 1st Am. Bank, N.A., Washington. Ruling elder Chevy Chase Presbyn. Ch., Washington, 1970-72; trustee Mary Baldwin Coll., Staunton, Va. Served to lt. comdr. USNR, 1941-46; ETO, PTO. Recipient Alumni citation Bridgewater Coll., 1960; named Ky. col., 1973. Mem. Am., Va. bar assns., Bar Assn. D.C. (chmn. com. on corp. law 1960-61, com. comml. bus. law 1969-72), Am. Judicature Soc., Raven Soc., Am. Legion, Newcomen Soc. N.Am., Order Coif, Phi Delta Phi, Tau Kappa Alpha. Clubs: Metropolitan, International (Washington); Chevy Chase (Md.); Farmington Country (Charlottesville, Va.). Home: 3725 Cardiff Rd Chevy Chase MD 20015 also Pine Lodge Box 205 Route 1 Miles River Neck Easton MD Office: 1250 Connecticut Ave Washington DC 20036

IKENBERRY, STANLEY OLIVER, university president; b. Lamar, Colo., Mar. 3, 1935; s. Oliver Samuel and Margaret (Moulton) I.; m. Judith Ellen Life, Aug. 24, 1958; children: David Lawrence, Steven Oliver, John Paul. B.A., Shepherd Coll., Shepherdstown, W.Va., 1956; M.A., Mich. State U., 1957, Ph.D., 1960; LL.D., Millikin U. Grad. adviser men's residence halls Mich. State U., 1956-58; instr. Office Evaluation Services, 1958-60, instr. instl. research, 1960-62; asst. to provost for instl. research, asst. prof. edn. W.Va., U., 1962-65, dean, 1965-69; prof., asso. dir. Center Study Higher Edn., Pa. State U., 1969-71; sr. v.p., 1971-79; pres. U. Ill., Urbana, 1979—; mem. rehab. adv. com. Rehab. Sers. Adminstrn., HEW, Washington, 1966-70; dir. Franklin Life Ins. Co., Springfield, Ill., Pfizer, Inc. Contbr. articles to profl. jours. Pres. bd. Appalachia Edn. Lab., 1965-69; co-chmn. Ill. Gov.'s Commn. on Sci. and Tech., 1982—; trustee Carnegie Found. for Advancement Teaching. Named hon. alumnus Pa. State U. Mem. Am. Ednl. Research Assn. (dir.), Am. Assn. Higher Edn. (dir., chmn. planning com. for Nat. Conf. Higher Edn. 1975), Am. Assn. Instl. Research, Nat. Soc. Study Edn. Home: 711 W Florida Urbana IL 61801 Office: Office of Pres U Ill Urbana IL 61801

IKLE, FRANK WILLIAM, Educator; b. Zurich, Switzerland, Jan. 18, 1921; s. Martin W. and Helen (Prichystal) I.; m. Maurine Barnes, May 4, 1944; children—Martin, Maurice, Matthew. B.A., U. Calif. at Berkeley, 1941, Ph.D., 1953. Instr. Reed Coll., 1950-54; Carnegie fellow Harvard, 1951-52; Fulbright prof. U. Philippines, 1955-56; asso. prof. Miami U., Oxford, Ohio, 1957-63; prof. history, chmn. dept. U. N.Mex., 1963—; vis. prof. U. Hong Kong, 1975. Author: German-Japanese Relations, 1936-40, 1957, (with others) A History of Asia, 1963; also articles. Chmn. N.Mex. Humanities Council. Served to lt. comdr. USNR, 1942-46. Mem. Am. Hist. Assn., Assn. Asian Studies, AAUP. Home: 508 Chamiso Ln NW Albuquerque NM 87107

IKLE, FRED CHARLES, govt. ofcl.; b. Samaden, Switzerland, Aug. 21, 1924; s. Fritz A. and Hedwig M. (Huber) I.; m. Doris Eisemann, Dec. 23, 1959; children—Judith, Miriam. M.A. in Social Sci, U. Chgo., 1948, Ph.D. in Sociology, 1950. Research asso. Columbia Bur. Applied Social Research, 1950-54; mem. social sci. dept. Rand Corp., Santa Monica, Calif., 1955-61, head social sci. dept., 1968-73; research asso. Harvard Center for Internat. Affairs, 1962-63; prof. polit. sci. Mass. Inst. Tech., 1964-67; dir. U.S. ACDA, Washington, 1973-77; chmn. Conservation Mgmt. Corp., 1978-81; pres. Transat Energy Corp., 1978-81; under-sec. for policy Dept. Def., Washington, 1981—; Cons. Dept. State, 1966-73, Los Alamos Sci. Lab., 1977-81; co-chmn. Calif. Arms Control and Fgn. Policy Seminar, 1972-73; bd. dirs. Internat. Peace Acad., 1977-81, European-Am. Inst. for Security Research, 1977-81, Hudson Inst., 1979-81. Author: The Social Impact of Bomb Destruction, 1958, How Nations Negotiate, 1964, Every War Must End, 1971. Rockefeller Found. fellow, 1953, 60; recipient Disting. Public Service award U.S. Dept. Def. Mem. Internat. Inst. Strategic Studies, Am. Council Fgn. Relations. Republican. Clubs: Metropolitan, Capitol Hill (Washington). Home: 7010 Glenbrook Rd Bethesda MD 20814

ILAQUA, SALVATORE S., financial executive; b. Montreal, Que., Can., Mar. 4, 1936; s. Salvatore and Concetta (Mascitelli) I.; m. Marie Yvonne Ghislaine Beaudoin, Sept. 24, 1960; children: Marie Ann Caroline, John Eric. Student, Sir George Williams U., 1953-54, 63-64. With Toronto Dominion Bank, Montreal, Que., Can., 1953-63; v.p., treas. IAC Ltd., Toronto, Ont., Can., 1963-81; v.p., dir. Niagara Realty of Can. Ltd., Toronto, 1978-81, Niagara Fin. Co. Ltd., 1978-81; exec. v.p. fin. and investments Continental Bank Can., 1981—; v.p., dir. Continental Bank Fin. Corp., Continental Bank Mortgage Corp., Continental Bank Leasing Corp., Continental Bank Capital Corp., Continental Bank Realty Corp., 1981—. Clubs: Cambridge, York Downs Golf Country. Home: 18 Shaughnessy Blvd Willowdale ON M2J 1H5 Canada Office: Continental Place 130 Adelaide St W Toronto ON M5H 3R2 Canada

ILCHMAN, ALICE STONE, college president, former government official; b. Cin., Apr. 18, 1935; d. Donald Crawford and Alice Kathryn (Biermann) Stone; m. Warren Frederick Ilchman, June 11, 1960; children: Frederick Andrew Crawford, Alice Sarah Crawford. B.A., Mt. Holyoke Coll., 1957; M.P.A., Maxwell Sch. Citizenship, Syracuse U., 1958; Ph.D., London Sch. Econs., 1965. Asst. to pres., mem. faculty Berkshire Community Coll., 1961-64; asst. research polit. scientist Inst. Govtl. Studies, U. Calif. at Berkeley, 1966, lectr., program dir., 1966-68, 69-70, dir., India, 1968-69, lectr., asst. prof., dir., 1971-73; prof. econs. and edn., dean Wellesley (Mass.) Coll., 1973-78; asst. sec. ednl. and cultural affairs Dept. State, 1978; asso. dir. ednl. and cultural affairs Internat. Communication Agy., 1978-81; advisor to sec. Smithsonian Instn., 1981; pres. Sarah Lawrence Coll., Bronxville, N.Y., 1981—; intern, asst. to Sen. John F. Kennedy, 1957; seminar leader, dir. Peace Corps Tng. Program for India, 1965-66; nat. com. Fulbright-Hays award for South Asia, 1972-73; chmn. com. on women's employment Nat. Acad. Scis. Author: The New Men of Knowledge and the New States, 1968, (with W.F. Ilchman) Education and Employment in India, The Policy Nexus, 1976. Trustee Mt. Holyoke Coll., Mass. Found. for Humanities and Pub. Policy, 1974-77, East-West Center, Honolulu., Expt. in Internat. Living, Youth for Understanding. Mem. Nat. Acad. Public Adminstrn., Am. Soc. Public Adminstrn., Assn. Asian Studies, Council Fgn. Relations. Clubs: Cosmopolitan (N.Y.C.); Bronxville Field (N.Y.). Home: 935 Kimball Ave Bronxville NY 10708 Office: Sarah Lawrence Coll Bronxville NY 10708

ILCHMAN, WARREN FREDERICK, university provost, political science educator; b. Denver, Sept. 6, 1933; s. Frederick Warren and Imogene (Trovinger) I.; m. Alice Crawford Stone, June 11, 1960; children: Frederick Andrew Crawford, Alice Sarah Crawford. B.A., Brown U., 1955; Ph.D., U. Cambridge, Eng., 1959. Asst. prof. Williams Coll., also Center Devel. Econs., Williamstown, Mass., 1960-64; from asst. prof. to prof. polit. sci. U. Calif., Berkeley, 1965-73, dir. Center South and Southeast Asian Studies, 1970-73; vis. prof., research assoc. Center Population Studies, Harvard U., 1973-74; prof. polit. sci. and econs., dean arts and scis. and Grad. Sch., Boston U., 1974-76; program adviser internat. div. Ford Found., N.Y.C., 1976-80; v.p. for research and grad. studies SUNY, Albany, 1980-83, provost Nelson A. Rockefeller Coll. Pub. Affairs and Policy, 1983—, dir. Rockefeller Inst. Govt., 1983—. Author: Professional Diplomacy in the U.S. 1961, New Men of Knowledge and the Developing Nations, 1966, Professionals as Agents of Change, 1968, The Political Economy of Change, 1969 (translated into French, Spanish, Japanese, Hindi and Arabic), Political Economy of Development, 1972, Comparative Public Administration and The Conventional Wisdom, 1973, Policy Sciences and Population, 1975, Education and Employment: The Policy Nexus, 1976. Marshall scholar, U.K.; Recipient Harbison prize Danforth Found., 1969. Mem. Am. Soc. Pub. Adminstrn. (Burchfield award 1965), Asia Soc., Am. Polit. Sci. Assn., Assn. Asian Studies, Phi Beta Kappa. Episcopalian. Clubs: Cosmos (Washington); St. Botolph (Boston); University (N.Y.C.); Bronxville Field, Church. Home: 935 Kimball Ave Bronxville NY 10708 Office: Rockefeller Inst Govt 411 State St Albany NY 12203

ILIE, PAUL, educator; b. Bklyn., Oct. 11, 1932; s. Abraham and Dora (Smilovitz) I.; m. Marie-Laure Bouscaren, Feb. 28, 1969. B.A., Bklyn. Coll., 1954; M.A., Brown U., 1956, Ph.D., 1959. Mem. faculty U. Mich., Ann Arbor, 1959-82, prof. Spanish and comparative lit., 1968-82, U. So. Calif., Los Angeles, 1982—; guest prof. Hebrew U., Jerusalem, 1970, UCLA, 1980. Author: La novelística de Camilo J. Cela, 1963, 3d enlarged edit., 1978, The Surrealist Mode in Spanish Literature, 1968, Unamuno: An Existential View of Self and Society, 1967, Documents of the Spanish Vanguard, 1969, Los Surrealistas españoles, 1972, Literature and Inner Exile, 1972, 2d edit., 1982; also articles in profl. jours.; adv. editor: Hispanic Rev., 1969—, Jour. Spanish Studies, 1973-80, Eighteenth-Century Studies, 1975-77. Rackham fellow, 1960, 66, 71, 76; Guggenheim fellow, 1965-66; Am. Council Learned Socs. fellow, 1969-70; Nat. Endowment Humanities fellow, 1978. Mem. MLA (chmn. Spanish exec. com. 1969-73, European lit. relations 1980-82, 18th-century comparative lit. 1981—), Am. Assn. Tchrs. Spanish and Portuguese, AAUP, Am. Comparative Lit. Assn., Am. Soc. 18th Century Studies. Home: 1241 Kolle Ave South Pasadena CA 91030

ILIESCU, NICOLAE, educator; b. Romania, May 21, 1919; came to U.S., 1952; s. Marin and Iulia (Lupescu) I.; m. Esther Gheta, Apr. 26, 1953; children—Rodica P., Doina A. D.Letters, U. Padua, Italy, 1947; A.M., Harvard, 1956, Ph.D. in Romance Langs. and Lit, 1958. Instr. Italian Harvard, 1958-59, asst. prof., 1959-62, asso. prof. Romance langs. and lit., 1962-68, prof., 1968—. Author: Da Manzoni a Nievo-considerazioni sul romanzo italiano, 1959, Il 'canzoniere' petrarchesco e Sant'Agostino, 1962 (Premio Della Cultura Pres. Council of Ministers Italy 1964); Contbr. articles to lit. jours. Recipient medaglia della cultura Italian Govt., 1964. Mem. Dante Soc. Am., Mediaeval Acad. Am., Renaissance Soc. Am., Modern Lang. Assn., Societas Academica Daco-Romana (Rome), Am. Assn. Tchrs. Italian. Home: Deerhaven Rd Lincoln MA 01773 Office: Boylston Hall Harvard U Cambridge MA 02138

ILIFF, WARREN JOLIDON, zoo administrator; b. Madison, Wis., Nov. 5, 1936; s. Warren Jolidon and Wilma Marie (Lowenstein) I.; m. Ghislaine de Brouchoven de Bergeyck, Feb. 13, 1970. A.B., Harvard U., 1958. Helicopter pilot, crop duster, Central Am., 1962-66; dir. planning Air Transport Assn., Washington, 1966-67; spl. asst. to dir. Nat. Zoo, Washington, 1967-71; exec. dir. Friends of Nat. Zoo, 1971-73; asst. dir. Nat. Zoo, 1973-75; dir. Washington Park Zoo, Portland, Oreg., 1975—. Trustee Catlin Gabel Sch., 1982—; bd. dirs. Greater Portland Conv. and Visitors Assn., 1982—. Served with USMC, 1958-62. Mem. Am. Assn. Zool. Parks and Aquariums (chmn. ethics com. 1978-81), Internat. Union Dirs. Zool. Gard. Home: 01865 SW Palatine Hill Rd Portland OR 97219 Office: 4001 S W Canyon Rd Portland OR 97221

ILITCH, MICHAEL, professional sports team executive. Owner Detroit Red Wings Hockey Team. Office: Detroit Red Wings 600 Civic Center Dr Detroit MI 48226§

ILLICH, IVAN, educator; b. Vienna, Austria, Sept. 4, 1926; s. Peter and Ellen (Regenstreif) I. Lic.U. Philos., Gregorian U., Rome, 1945, Lic.U. Theology, 1950; Dr.Fac.Phil., U. Salzburg, 1951. Ordained priest Roman Catholic Ch., 1951; parish priest among Puerto Ricans, N.Y.C., 1951-56; v.p. U. Santa Maria, Ponce, P.R., 1956-60; staff lectr. dept. polit. sci. Fordham U., N.Y.C., 1960-76; researcher Center Intercultural Documentation, Cuernavaca, Mexico, 1961—, pres. bd., 1963-68, mem., 1968—; Guest prof. U. Kassel, (W.Ger.), 1979-81; Mem. Berlin Inst. Advanced Study, 1981-82; Disting. guest prof. U. Calif.-Berkeley, 1982; Guest prof. U. Marburg, (W.Ger.), 1983-84. Author: Celebration of Awareness, Deschooling Society, Tools for Conviviality, Energy and Equity, Medical Nemesis, Towards a History of Needs, (with others) The Right to Useful Unemployment, Shadow Work, Gender. Mem. Council Higher Edn., Commonwealth of P.R., 1959-61. Office: Apdo Postal 479 Cuernavaca 62000 Morelos Mexico

ILLIG, CARL, lawyer; b. Houston, Sept. 10, 1909; s. Carl and Olive (Kirlicks) I.; m. Lillian Elizabeth Horlock, Apr. 27, 1933; children: Elaine (Mrs. Franklin B. Davis), Carol (Mrs. Simeon T. Lake III), Dale. B.A., Rice Inst., 1930; LL.B., U. Tex., 1933; grad., Advanced Mgmt. Program, Harvard U., 1959. Bar: Tex. 1933. Practiced in, Galveston, Tex., 1933-34, Houston, 1967—; partner Illig, Brill and Dewitt, 1969-70; with Humble Oil & Refining Co., 1934-67, assoc. gen. counsel, 1961-67. Mem. Tex. Coordinating Water Com., 1960; mem. Gov. Tex. Statewide Water Com., 1961-62; chmn. budget com., trustee Houston-Harris County United Fund, 1957-58; chmn. Houston Community Council, 1960; mem. Tex. Water Devel. Bd., 1971-76; Trustee Rocky Mountain Mineral Law Found., 1965-66; bd. govs. Rice U., 1970-74, gov. adviser, 1974—; mem. Harvard Bus. Sch. Alumni Council, 1966-69. Mem. ABA (chmn. sect. natural resources law 1964-65, mem. ho. of dels. 1966-68), Tex. Bar Assn. (chmn. sect. corp. banking and bus. law 1959-60), Houston Bar Assn., State Bar Tex., Houston Philos. Soc., Assn. Rice Alumni (pres. 1952-53), Houston C. of C. (chmn. water supply and conservation com. 1969-70), Phi Beta Kappa. Club: Houston Country. Home: 5327 Doliver Dr Houston TX 77056 Office: 3636 Westheimer Houston TX 77056

ILLIG, JAMES MICHAEL, A.R.C. exec.; b. Erie, Pa., Mar. 6, 1913; s. William C. and Teresa A. (Messler) I.; m. Mary Elizabeth Moorhead, Sept. 1, 1936; children—Patricia Diane (Mrs. James A. Joy), Sally Louise (Mrs. Carl J. Santolli), Rosemary Elizabeth (Mrs. John L. Irons). B.S., U.S. Mil. Acad., 1936; M.B.A., Harvard, 1948; grad., Inf. Sch., 1939, Command and Gen. Staff Coll., 1943, Armed Forces Staff Coll., 1946, Indsl. Coll. Armed Forces, 1955, Advanced Mgmt. Program. Harvard, 1961. Commd. 2d lt. inf. U.S. Army, 1936, advanced through grades to brig. gen., 1961; air Q.M. (391st Hdqrs. Anti-Submarine Command), 1941- 43, fiscal dir., 1943-46, chief supply and procurement, 1948-51; chief programs and budget Army Gen. Staff (G-4), Dept. Army, 1951-55; chief staff U.S. Mil. Acad., 1955-57; comdg. officer U.S. Army Base Command, Hawaii, 1957-59; dir. financial operations Army Gen. Staff (logistics), Dept. Army, 1959-61; spl. asst. to dep. chief staff for logistics Army Gen. Staff, Dept. Army, 1961-62; comptroller Continental Army Command, Ft. Monroe, Va., 1961-65; ret., 1965; comptroller Am. Nat. Red Cross, 1965—. Decorated D.S.M., Legion of Merit with oak leaf cluster, Medal for Humane Action, Berlin Airlift device. Mem. Assn. Grads. U.S. Mil. Acad., Harvard Alumni Assn., Am. Soc. Mil. Comptrollers, Def. Supply assn., Indsl. Coll. Armed Forces Alumni Assn., Army Athletic Assn., Assn. U.S. Army. Clubs: Rotarian., Army and Navy Country (Arlington, Va.); Army and Navy, Washington Athletic, Harvard Business School (Washington). Home: 1428 Laburnum St Chesterbrook Woods McLean VA 22101 Office: Nat Hdqrs Am Nat Red Cross Washington DC 20006

ILTIS, HUGH HELLMUT, plant taxonomist and evolutionist, educator; b. Brno, Czechoslovakia, Apr. 7, 1925; came to U.S., 1939, naturalized, 1944; s. Hugo and Anne (Liebscher) I.; m. Grace Schaffel, Dec. 20, 1951 (div. Mar. 1958); children: Frank S., Michael George; m. Carolyn Merchant, Aug. 4, 1961 (div. June 1970); children: David Hugh, John Paul. B.A., U. Tenn., 1948; M.A., Washington U., St. Louis and Mo. Bot. Garden, 1950; Ph.D. (Univ. fellow), St. Louis and Mo. Bot. Garden, 1952. Research asst. Mo. Bot. Garden, 1948-52; asst. prof. botany U. Ark., 1952-55; mem. faculty U. Wis.-Madison, 1955—, prof., 1967—, curator univ. herbarium, 1955-68, dir. univ. herbarium, 1969—; vis. prof. U. Va. Biol. Sta., 1959; expdns. to, Costa Rica, 1949, Peru, 1962-63, Mexico, 1960, 71, 77, 78, 79, 80, 81, 82, Guatemala, 1976, Ecuador, 1977, USSR, 1979; mem. adv. bd. Flora N.Am., 1970—, Gov. Wis. Commn. State Forests, 1972-73. Author articles flora of Wis., Capparidaceae, biogeography, evolution of maize, human ecology, especially innate responses to, and needs for, natural beauty and diversity, preservation of biota. Served with AUS, 1944-46. Recipient Biology award U. Tenn., 1948. Mem. AAAS, Am. Inst. Biol. Scis., Bot. Soc. Am., Am. Soc. Plant Taxonomists, Internat. Assn. Plant Taxonomy, Soc. Study Evolution, Ecol. Soc. Am., Wis. Acad. Arts, Sci. and Letters, Forum for Corr.-Internat. Center Integrative Studies, Nature Conservancy (dir. Wis. chpt., Nat. award 1963), Wilderness Soc., Sierra Club, Nat. Parks Assn., Citizens Natural Resources Assn. Wis., Natural Resource Def. Assn., Environ. Def. Fund, Common Cause, Friends of Earth, Zero Population Growth, Sigma Xi, Phi Kappa Phi. Home: 2784 Marshall Pkwy Madison WI 53713 *If we are to remain healthy and sane, we must concern ourselves with the concept of an Optimum Human Environment, one which must include large portions of the wild and natural environment which shaped our bodies and souls through natural selection over the past millions of years. Hence, only in the preservation of nature, of the world's ecosystems and its species, and in a clear comprehension of evolution, can we find the foundations for a meaningful new ethic that will insure a livable world for our children.*

ILTIS, JOHN FREDERIC, advertising and public relations company executive; b. Chgo., Dec. 14, 1940; s. Frederic and Alice Henrietta (Nachan) I.; m. Gillian Ann Cane, Nov. 20, 1976; children: Claire Alexandra, Annika Leigh. Student, Lincoln Coll., 1962; A.A., Bradley U., 1964. Advt. and pub. relations asst. Balaban & Katz Theatres, Chgo., 1965-68; midwest dir. advt and pub. relations Universal Pictures, Chgo., 1968-69, field ops. dir., N.Y.C., 1969-70; owner, operator film prodn. and mktg. co., London, 1971-73; pres. John Iltis Assocs., entertainment, advt. and pub. relations, Chgo., 1973—; instr. pub. relations Columbia Coll., Chgo. Mem. adv. bd. DePaul, Goodman Sch. Drama; bd. dirs. Lawyers for Creative Arts, Chgo., Variety Club Ill. Served with U.S. Army, 1964. Mem. Publicity Club Chgo., Chgo. TV Acad., Publicists Guild. Home: 3844 Kenmore Ave Chicago IL 60613 Office: John Iltis Assocs 666 N Lake Shore Dr Chicago IL 60611

ILUTOVICH, LEON, organization executive; b. Odessa, Russia; s. Jacob and Leah (Plotycher) I.; m. Rebekka Landau. Ed., Law Sch., Warsaw (Poland) U. Exec. dir., nat. sec. Zionist Orgn. Am., exec. vice chmn., 1978—; mem. actions com. World Zionist Orgn.; del. to Zionist congresses; exec. bd. World Union Gen. Zionists; trustee United Israel Appeal; mem. nat. bd. Am. Zionist Fedn.; mem. Am. Conf. on Soviet Jewry, also; Pres.'s Conf. of Major Am. Jewish Orgns. Mem. editorial bd.: Am. Zionist mag. Mem. Jewish Book Council Am., Am. Arbitration Assn. (nat. panel), Hebrew Lang. and Culture Assn., Jewish Agy. Assembly.

IMAGAWA, DAVID TADASHI, virologist, educator; b. Isleton, Calif., Mar. 24, 1922; s. Kumahichi and Katsuyo (Nego) I.; m. Aiko Asaki, Sept. 3, 1955; children—David Kevin, Karen Kay. A.A., Sacramento Jr. Coll., 1942; B.A., Macalester Coll., 1944; M.S., U. Minn., 1946, Ph.D., 1950. Diplomate: Am. Bd. Microbiology. Instr. bacteriology and immunology U. Minn., Mpls., 1950-52; mem. faculty U. Calif. at Los Angeles, 1952—, prof. pediatrics and microbiology-immunology, 1969—; dir. pediatric research labs. Harbor Gen. Hosp., Torrance, Calif., 1966-76, co-dir., 1976—; cons. virology Long Beach VA Hosp., 1955-62, Hyland Labs., Los Angeles, 1964—; spl. cons. research Seifuen Hosp., Amagasaki, Japan, 1969—. Contbr. to profl. jours. Commonwealth fellow, 1964; research grantee Am. Cancer Soc., USPHS, HEW, Nat. Multiple Sclerosis Soc. Mem. Am. Soc. Microbiology, Am. Assn. Cancer Research, Soc. Exptl. Biology and Medicine, Am. Assn. Pathologists, Sigma Xi. Presbyterian (deacon). Research in virology, measles distemper rinderpest viruses complex, tumor viruses, distemper and measles viruses as model for persistent virus infections. Home: 6213 Moongate Dr Rancho Palos Verdes CA 90274 Office: Dept Pediatrics Harbor-UCLA Med Center UCLA Med Sch Torrance CA 90509

IMBRIE, ANDREW WELSH, composer; b. N.Y.C., Apr. 6, 1921; s. Andrew C. and Dorothy (Welsh) I.; m. Barbara Cushing, Jan. 31, 1953; children: Andrew, John (dec.). A.B., Princeton U., 1942; M.A., U. Calif.-Berkeley, 1947. Instr. music U. Calif.-Berkeley, 1947, 49-51, asst. prof., 1951, assoc. prof., 1957-60; prof. U. Calif., Berkeley, 1960—. Compositions include 3 symphonies, 4 string quartets, trios, sonatas, songs, orchestral and choral works, Angle of Repose (opera), 2 piano concerti, concerti for violin, cello, and flute; Dance-cantata Prometheus Bound. Bd. dirs. Koussevitzky Found.; bd. govs. San Francisco Symphony. Recipient Circle award N.Y. Music Critics, 1943-44; Alice M. Ditson fellow Columbia U., 1946-47; fellow Am. Acad. in Rome, 1947-49; grantee Nat. Inst. Arts and Letters, 1950; Guggenheim fellow, 1953-54, 60-61; merit award Boston Symphony Orch., 1955; creative arts award Brandeis U., 1958; Naumburg award, 1960; grantee Nat. Found. on Arts and Humanities; composer in residence Am. Acad. Rome, 1967-68; recipient Walter Hinrichsen award Columbia U., 1971. Mem. Nat. Inst. Arts and Letters, Am. Acad. Arts and Scis., Phi Beta Kappa. Club: Bohemian (San Francisco). Home: 2625 Rose St Berkeley CA 94708

IMESCH, JOSEPH LEOPOLD, bishop; b. Grosse Pointe Farms, Mich., June 21, 1931; s. Dionys and Margaret (Margelisch) I. B.S., Sacred Heart Sem., 1953; student, N.Am. Coll., Rome, 1953-57; S.T.L., Gregorian U., Rome, 1957. Ordained priest Roman Catholic Ch., 1956; sec. to Cardinal Dearden, 1959-71; pastor Our Lady of Sorrows Ch., Farmington, Mich., 1971-77; aux. bishop of, Detroit, 1973-79, asst. bishop, N.W. Region, 1977-79, bishop of, Joliet, Ill., 1979—. Office: Chancery 425 Summit St Joliet IL 60435

IMHOFF, WALTER FRANCIS, investment banker; b. Denver, Aug. 7, 1931; s. Walter Peter and Frances Marie (Barkhausen) I.; m. Georgia Ruth Stewart, June 16, 1973; children: Stacy, Randy, Theresa, Michael, Robert. B.S. in Bus. Adminstrn, Regis Coll., Denver, 1955. Asst. v.p. Coughlin & Co., Denver, 1955-60; pres., chief exec. officer Hanifen, Imhoff & Samford, Inc., Denver, 1960—; guest lectr. U. Colo., 1976. Trustee Regis Coll., 1975-81, treas., 1976-79, vice chmn., 1981, chmn., 1982—; bd. dirs. NCCJ, 1980—. Served with USAF, 1950-51; Korea. Named Outstanding Alumnus Regis Coll., 1970. Mem. Bond Club Denver (pres. 1965), Colo. Municipal Bond Dealers Assn. (pres. 1973), Mid-Continent Securities Industry Assn. (dir. 1972-74), Nat. Assn. Security Dealers, Securities Industry Assn., Pub. Securities Assn. (dir. 1972-75), Alpha Kappa Psi. Republican. Roman Catholic. Club: Denver (pres. 1981—). Home: 10432 E Ida Pl Englewood CO 80111 Office: 1125 17th St Suite 1700 Denver CO 80202

IMIG, DAVID GREGG, assn. exec.; b. Normal, Ill., July 25, 1939; s. Donald John and Margaret Winifred (Gregg) I.; m. Carol Janet Rowley, June 18, 1961; children—Douglas R., Mark D., Scott R., Jennifer C. B.A., U. Ill., 1961, M.A., 1964, Ph.D., 1969. Tchr. Nyakato Secondary Sch., Bukoba, Tanganyika, 1961-63; edn. officer AID mission to, Sierra Leone, 1966-68, devel. officer mission to, Liberia, 1968-70; dir. govtl. relations Am. Assn. Colls. Tchr. Edn., Washington, 1970-80, exec. dir., 1980—; Mem. adv. com. Tchr. Corps, 1978-81; mem. Joint Council Econ. Edn., 1980—, Nat. Council for Accreditation Tchr. Edn. Coordinating Bd., 1980—. Contbr. articles to various publs. Tchrs. for East Africa fellow Tchrs. Coll., Columbia U., 1961; Inst. Edn. (London) fellow, 1961; Makerere U. (Kampala) fellow, 1961. Mem. Am. Ednl. Research Assn., Phi Delta Kappa, Kappa Delta Pi. Home: 9 Cape Anne Ct Gaithersburg MD 20760 Office: 1 Dupont Circle Washington DC 20036

IMMEL, VINCENT CLARE, law educator; b. Gibsonburg, Ohio, Mar. 15, 1920; s. Joseph C. and Rosa F. (Bauer) I. Student, U. Toledo, 1937-38; B.S., Bowling Green State U., 1941; J.D., U. Mich., 1948. Bar: Ohio 1949, U.S. Supreme Ct. 1960, Mo. 1962. Mem. faculty Ohio No. U. Law Sch., 1948-58, prof. law, 1957-58; mem. faculty St. Louis U. Law Sch., 1958—, asso. prof. law, 1958-61, prof. law, 1961—, asst. dean, 1959-62, dean, 1962-69; vis. prof. law U. Ga., 1979-80, U. Liverpool (Eng.), 1982-83. Contbr. articles to legal jours. Mem. exec. com. St. Louis Civil Liberties Com.; bd. dirs. Little Symphony Assn., Legal Aid Soc. City and County St. Louis, St. Louis Symphony Soc. Served to lt. AUS, 1942-46. Decorated Bronze Star. Mem. Am., Ohio, Mo. bar assns., Am. Judicature Soc., Bar Assn. St. Louis, Am. Law Inst., Phi Beta Kappa, Phi Alpha Delta, Phi Kappa Theta, Kappa Mu Epsilon, Kappa Delta Pi, Pi Kappa Delta. Club: K.C. Home: 4475 W Pine St Saint Louis MO 63108

IMPARATO, ANTHONY MICHAEL, vascular surgeon; b. N.Y.C., July 29, 1922; s. Silverio and Olga (Santilli) I.; m. Agatha Maria Petriccione, Dec. 19, 1943; children: Maria April, Karen Elsa Imparato Cotton. A.B., Columbia U., 1943; M.D., NYU, 1946. Diplomate: Am. Bd. Surgery. Intern U.S. Naval Hosp., Bklyn., 1946-47; fellow in anatomy N.Y. U. Med. Sch., 1949-50; successively intern, asst. resident in surgery, resident, chief resident in surgery N.Y. U. Med. Center, 1950-56, mem. faculty, 1956—, prof. surgery, dir. div. vascular surgery, 1975—; cons. Norwalk (Conn.) Hosp., Patterson (N.J.) Gen. Hosp., Manhattan VA Hosp. Author articles in field, chpts. in textbooks. Served as officer M.C. USNR, 46-49, 50. Grantee USPHS, 1976-81. Fellow A.C.S., Am. Coll. Cardiology, Am. Coll. Angiology; mem. Am. Heart Assn. (fellow Stroke Council), Am. Surg. Assn., Soc. for Vascular Surgery (pres.-elect 1984-85), Internat. Cardiovascular Soc., Soc. Clin. Vascular Surgery, Soc. Angiologia Uruguay, Soc. Internat. Chirurgie, N.Y. Regional Vascular Soc. (a founder), N.Am. Soc. Pacing and Electrophysiology (a founder), James IV Assn. Surgeons (dir., treas.), Alpha Omega Alpha. Home: 870 UN Plaza New York NY 10017 Office: NYU faculty practice area 530 1st Ave New York NY 10016

IMPELLIZZERI, IRENE HELEN, coll. dean; b. Bklyn.; d. Joseph and Lucy (Colson) Macroe. B.S., N.Y. U., 1941; M.A., Columbia, 1942; Ph.D., Fordham U., 1958. Tchr. pub. schs., N.Y.C., 1942-59; prof. ednl. psychology Bklyn. Coll., 1961—, asso. dean dept. edn., 1968-71, dean, 1971—; psychologist Hearing and Speech Clinic, Manhattan Eye and Ear Hosp., 1955-58. Contbr. articles to profl. jours. Research coordinator N.Y.C. Bd. Edn., 1959-65, research cons., 1960-61. Mem. Am. Psychol. Assn., N.Y. State Psychol. Assn., Bklyn. Psychol. Assn. (exec. com., sec. 1959-64), Am. Personnel and Guidance Assn., N.Y.C. Personnel and Guidance Assn. (trustee 1963-67), N.Y. State Counselors Assn., Doctorate Assn. N.Y. Educators, AAUP, Am. Catholic Psychol. Assn., Nat. Cath. Guidance Conf., N.Y. Acad. Sci., Am. Ednl. Research Assn., Nat. Council on Measurement in Edn., Assn. for Measurement and Evaluation in Guidance. Home: 205 Clinton Ave Brooklyn NY 11205

IMPERATO, PASCAL JAMES, physician, health administrator, author, medical educator; b. N.Y.C., Jan. 13, 1937; s. James Anthony and Madalynne Marguerite (Insante) I.; m. Eleanor Anne Maiella, June 4, 1977; children: Alison Medalynne, Gavin Humbert. B.S., St. John's U., 1958, D.Sc. (hon.), 1977; M.D., SUNY, 1962; M.P.H. and Tropical Medicine, Tulane U., 1966. Diplomate: Am. Bd. Preventive Medicine, Nat. Bd. Med. Examiners. Assn. Am. Med. Colls.; Fgn. fellow, Kenya, Tanzania, Uganda, 1961; intern dept. internal medicine L.I. Coll. Hosp., 1962-63, resident dept. medicine, 1963-65; N.Y. Acad. Medicine fgn. research fellow Tulane Univ.-U. del Valle, Cali, Colombia, 1965; Glorney Raisebeck fellow Tulane U., New Orleans, 1965-66; med. epidemiologist smallpox eradication-measles control program USPHS, Mali, 1966-72; dir. Bur. Infectious Disease Control, N.Y.C. Dept. Health, 1972-74, prin. epidemiologist, dir. immunization program, 1972-74, 1st dep. commr., 1974-77, dir. residency tng. program, 1974-77; chmn. N.Y.C. Swine Influenza Immunization Task Force, 1976-77; med. cons. Africa Bur., AID, 1974; commr. health, N.Y.C., 1977-78; chmn. N.Y.C. Bd. Health, 1977-78; chmn. bd. N.Y.C. Health and Hosps. Corp., 1977-78; chmn. exec. com. N.Y.C. Health Systems Agy., 1977-78; acting health services adminstr., N.Y.C., 1977-78; clin. instr. dept. medicine Cornell U. Med. Coll., N.Y.C., 1972-74, asst. clin. prof., 1974-78, asst. prof. dept. pub. health, 1974-77, asso. clin. prof., 1977-78, adj. prof., 1979—; asso. prof. dept. preventive medicine and community health SUNY Downstate Med. Center, 1974-77, lectr., 1977-78, prof. and chmn., 1978—; mem. staff N.Y. Hosp., L.I. Coll. Hosp., 1973—, State Univ. Hosp., 1978—, Kings County Hosp., 1978—; lectr. dept. community medicine Mt. Sinai Sch. Medicine, City U. N.Y., 1974—; cons. N.Y. State Edn. Dept., 1982—. Author: Doctor in The Land of the Lion, 1964, (with Osa Johnson) Last Adventure, 1966, Bwana Doctor, 1967, The Treatment and Control of Infectious Diseases in Man, 1974, The Cultural Heritage of Africa, 1974, A Wind in Africa, 1975, What To Do About the Flu, 1976, African Folk Medicine, 1977, Historical Dictionary of Mali, 1977, Dogon Cliff Dwellers: The Art of Mali's Mountain People, 1978, Medical Detective, 1979, (with wife) Mali: A Handbook of Historical Statistics, 1982, The Administration of a Public Health Agency, 1983, Buffoons, Queens and Wooden Horsemen, 1983; contbr. articles to profl. jours.; cons. editor: N.Y. State Jour. Medicine, 1983—; dep. editor; (editorial bd.) Explorers Jour., 1979—. Bd. dirs. Public Health Research Inst., 1977-78, Community Council Greater N.Y., 1977-78, Med. Health and Research Assn., 1977-78, N.Y. Heart Assn., 1983—, Greater N.Y. Hosp. Assn., Milton Helpern Library Legal Medicine, 1977—; trustee Martin and Osa Johnson Safari Mus.; mem. adv. bd. Physicians for Social Responsibility, 1983—. Served to lt. comdr. USPHS, 1966-69. Recipient Meritorious Honor award and medal Dept. State, 1971, AID award, 1970; Outstanding Alumnus award Tulane U., 1978, Delta Omega; Nat. Merit award, 1978; Frank Babbot award SUNY, 1980. Fellow A.C.P., Royal Soc. Tropical Medicine and Hygiene, Royal African Soc., N.Y. Acad. Medicine, Am. Coll. Preventive Medicine; mem. Am. Soc. Tropical Medicine and Hygiene, Am. Coll. Epidemiology, N.Y. Soc. Tropical Medicine, Kings County Med. Soc., Tanzania Soc., Med. Soc. State N.Y., East African Wildlife Soc., African Studies Assn., Author's Guild, Explorers Club, Delta Omega, Alpha Omega Alpha. Roman Catholic. Office: 450 Clarkson Ave Brooklyn NY 11203

INALCIK, HALIL, historian, educator; b. Istanbul, Turkey, May 26, 1916; came to U.S., 1972; s. Seyit Osman and Bahriye I.; m. Sevkiye, Jan. 18, 1945; 1 dau., Gunhan. Ph.D., U. Ankara, 1942. Prof. history U. Ankara, 1943-72; prof. Ottoman history U. Chgo., 1972—; vis. prof. Turkish history Columbia U., 1953-54, Princeton U., 1967-68; dir. studies Ecole des Hautes Etudes, Paris, 1983; co-chmn. 1st. Internat. Congress on Social and Econ. History of Turkey, 1977. Author: Tanzimat Reforms and the Bulgarian Question, 1943, Studies on the Region of Mehmed the Conquerer, 1954, The Ottoman Empire in the Classical Age: 1300-1600, 1973, The Ottoman Empire: Conquest, Organization and Economy, 1978; co-editor: Archivum Ottomanicum, 1969—. Pres. Internat. Assn. S.E. European Assn., 1971-74. Served with Turkish Army, 1943-46. Fellow Rockefeller Found., 1956; Social Sci. Research fellow, 1975. Fellow Royal Asiatic Soc. (Eng. hon.); mem. Am. Acad. Arts and Scis., Am. Hist. Soc., Tirkish Hist. Soc., Royal Hist. Soc. (corr. mem.), Hist. Soc. Am., Am. Oriental Soc., Am. Acad. Polit. and Social Sci. Home: 5000 East End Ave Chicago IL 60615 Office: U Chicago Dept History 5801 S Ellis Ave Chicago IL 60637

INBAU, FRED EDWARD, lawyer; b. New Orleans, Mar. 27, 1909; s. Fred and Pauline (Boos) I.; m. Ruth L. Major, Sept. 21, 1935 (dec.); children: William Robert, Louise; m. Jane Hanchett Schoenewald, June 27, 1964. B.S., Tulane U., 1930, LL.B., 1932; LL.M., Northwestern U., 1933. Practiced law, since 1934; research asst. Sci. Crime Detection Lab., Northwestern U. Sch. Law, 1933-36; asst. prof. law Northwestern U. Sch. Law, 1936-38; dir. Chgo. Police Sci. Crime Detection Lab., 1938-41; trial atty. firm Lord, Bissell and Kadyk, 1941-45; prof. law Northwestern U., 1945—, John Henry Wigmore prof. law, 1974-78, emeritus, 1978—; Pres. Am. Acad. Forensic Scis., 1955-56, Ill. Acad. Criminology, 1951-52, Americans for Effective Law Enforcement, 1966-79, chmn., 1979-82, bd. dirs., 1982—. Author: Criminal Interrogation and Confessions, 2d edit., 1967, Criminal Law for the Police, 1969, Criminal Law for the Layman, 1970, 2d edit., 1977, Scientific Police Investigation, 1972, Medical Jurisprudence, 1971, Evidence Law for Police, 1972, Scientific Evidence in Criminal Cases, 2d edit., 1978, Cases and Comments on Criminal Law, 3d edit., 1983, Cases and Comments on Criminal Procedure, 1974, 2d edit., 1980, Criminal Law and Its Adminstration, 4th edit., 1979, Truth and Deception: The Polygraph (Lie-Detector) Technique, 2d edit., 1977; editor-in-chief: Jour. Criminal Law, Criminology, and Police Sci., 1967-70, Jour. Police Sci. and Adminstrn., 1973-77. Republican. Home: 40 E Oak St Chicago IL 60611

INCE, EUGENE ST. CLAIR, JR., retired naval officer; b. Goshen, Ind., Oct. 18, 1926; s. Eugene St. Clair and Jaye Louise (Green) I.; m. Jean Marion Gregory, June 8, 1949; children: Jaye Marion, Julie Harwood, John Hottel, Janet Helen, Ann Gregory. B.S., U.S. Naval Acad., 1949; M.A., George Washington U., 1964. Commd. ensign U.S. Navy, 1949, advanced through grades to rear adm., 1976; designated naval aviator, 1951, spl. duty officer cryptology, 1960; comdr. U.S. Naval Security Group, 1978-80; ret., 1980; disting. vis. prof. Ohio U., 1982. Decorated Air medal, Naval Commendation medal, Joint Services Commendation medal, Legion of Merit. Home: St Clair House SR3 Box 144 Madison VA 22727

INCH, MORRIS ALTON, theology educator; b. Wytopitlock, Maine, Oct. 21, 1925; s. Clarence Sherwin and Blanche (Mix) I.; m. Joan Parker, Dec. 16, 1950; children—Deborah, Lois, Thomas, Joel, Mark. A.B., Houghton Coll., 1949; M. Div., Gordon Div. Sch., 1951; Ph.D., Boston U., 1955. Ordained to ministry Baptist Ch., 1951; pastor South Boston Bapt. Ch., 1951-55, Union Sq. Bapt. Ch., Somerville, Mass., 1955-61; prof., dean students, dean of coll. Gordon Coll., Wenham, Mass., 1955-62; prof., chmn. dept. Biblical, religious and archeol. studies Wheaton (Ill.) Coll., 1962—. Author: Psychology in the Psalms, 1969, Christianity Without Walls, 1972, Paced by God, 1973, Celebrating Jesus as Lord, 1974, Understanding Bible Prophecy, 1977, The Evangelical Challenge, 1978, My Servant Job, 1979, Doing Theology Across Cultures, 1982; editor: (with Samuel Schultz) Interpreting the Word of God, 1976, (with C. Hassell Bullock) The Literature and Meaning of Scripture, 1981, (with Ronald Youngblood) The Living and Active Word of God, 1983; contbr. articles to profl. jours. Served with USAAF, 1943-46. Named Sr. Tchr. of Year Wheaton Coll., 1971. Mem. Coll. Theology Soc., Evang. and Theol. Soc. Republican. Home: 201 W Lincoln St Wheaton IL 60187 *Life consists for me in practising an openness to God, an availability to others and for their ministry to me. In these relationships I rely on the sustaining grace of Jesus Christ.*

INCROPERA, FRANK PAUL, mechanical engineering educator; b. Lawrence, Mass., May 12, 1939; s. James Frank and Ann Laura (Leone) I.; m. Andrea Jeanne Eastman, Sept. 2, 1960; children: Terri Ann, Donna Renee, Shaunna Jeanne. S.B. in Mech. Engring, M.I.T., 1961; M.S., Stanford U., 1962, Ph.D., 1966. Jr. engr. Barry Controls Corp., Watertown, Mass., 1959; thermodynamics engr. Aerojet Gen. Corp., Azusa, Calif., 1961; heat transfer specialist Lockheed Missiles and Space Co., Sunnyvale, Calif., 1962-64; mem. faculty Purdue U., 1966—, prof. mech. engring., 1973—; cons. in field. Author: Introduction to Molecular Structure and Thermodynamics, 1974, Fundamentals of Heat Transfer, 1981; also articles. Recipient Solberg Teaching award Purdue U., 1973, 77, Potter Teaching award, 1973. Mem. ASME, Am. Soc. Engring. Edn. (Ralph C. Roe award 1982, George Westinghouse award 1983), AAAS. Inventor bloodless surg. scalpel. Office: Sch Mech Engring Purdue U West Lafayette IN 47907

INDERFURTH, KARL FREDERICK, news correspondent; b. Charlotte, N.C., Sept. 29, 1946; s. Karl Henry and Frances (Seawell) I.; m. Meredith Roosa, May 21, 1977; children: Jean Scott, Ashley Ann. B.A., U. N.C., 1968; M.A., Princeton U., 1975. Mem. profl. staff intelligence com. U.S. Senate, Washington, 1975-77, dep. staff dir. fgn. relations com., 1979-81; spl. asst. to Dr. zbigniew Brzezinski Nat. Security Council White House, Washington, 1977-79; corr. ABCNews, Washington, 1981—. Fulbright scholar Stratchclyde U., Glasgow, Scotland, 1973. Mem. Internat. Inst. Strategic Studies, Am. Polit. Sci. Assn. Hoe: 3548 N Delaware St Arlington VA 22207 Office: ABC News 1717 DeSales St Washington DC 22207

INDIANA, ROBERT, artist; b. New Castle, Ind., Sept. 13, 1928. Student, John Herron Sch. Art, 1945-46, Munson-Williams-Proctor Inst., 1947-48, Skowhegan Sch. of Painting and Sculpture, summer 1953; B.F.A., Chgo. Art Inst., 1953, U. Edinburgh, Scotland, 1953-54; D.F.A. (hon.), Franklin and Marshall Coll., 1970, U. Ind., 1977. Exhbns. include, Mus. Modern Art, 1961, 63, Dallas Mus. Contemporary Arts, 1962, San Francisco Mus. Art, Art Inst. Chgo., 1963, Beaverbrook Art Gallery, Fredericton, N.B., Tate Gallery, London, Eng., 1963-64, Washington Gallery Modern Art, 1963, Whitney Mus., Guggenheim Mus., Albright-Knox Art Gallery, Buffalo, Am. Cultural Center, Paris, France, Gemeente Mus., The Hague, Netherlands, 1964, U. Ill. at Champaign, 1965, Worcester (Mass.) Art Mus., White House Festival Arts, Stedelijk Mus., Amsterdam, Wurttembergischer Kunstverein, Stuttgart, U. St. Thomas, Houston, Smithsonian Instn., 6th Biennale San Marino, Carnegie Inst., Royal Dublin Soc., Documenta IV, Germany, Whitney Mus. Am. Art, 1975, Corcoran Gallery, San Francisco Mus. Art, Fine Arts Gallery San Diego, 1976, Dallas Mus. Fine Arts, Josly Art Mus., Omaha, Greenville (S.C.) County Mus., 1977, Va. Mus. Fine Arts, Lafayette (La.) Natural History Mus. and Planetarium, numerous others., one-man shows at, Stable Gallery, N.Y.C., 1962, 64, 66, Rolf Nelson Gallery, Los Angeles, 1965, Stedelijk van Abbemuseum, Eindhoven, Holland, Mus. Haus Lange, Krefeld, Germany, Galerie Schmela, Dusseldorf, Germany, 1966, Wurttembergisher Kunstverein, Stuttgart, Germany, Inst. Contemporary Art U. Pa., 1968, McNay Inst., San Antonio, Herron Art Mus., Indpls., U. Tex., 1977, Santa Fe Mus., 1976, Indpls. Mus. Art, 1977, Osuna Gallery, Washington, 1981, Art Ctr., Waco, Tex., 1982, William A. Farnsworth Library and Art Mus., Rockland, Maine, others; designer: sets and costumes The Mother of Us All; executed mural for, N.Y. State Bldg., N.Y. World's Fair, 1964-65; represented in permanent collections, Mus. Modern Art, Whitney Mus., Finch Coll., N.Y.C., Albright-Knox Gallery Art, Larry Aldrich Mus., Ridgefield, Conn., Balt. Mus. Art, Detroit Inst. Arts, Walker Art Center, Mpls., Rose Art Mus. of Brandeis U., Sheldon Meml. Art Gallery of U. Neb., Washington Gallery Modern Art, Stedelijk Mus., Amsterdam, Holland, Stedelijk van Abbemuseum, Eindhoven, Holland, Von der Heydt Mus., Wuppertal, Germany, Mus. Hans Lange, Krefeld, Germany, Art Gallery of Toronto, Carnegie Inst., Krannert Art Mus., U. Ill., Los Angeles County Mus., Mich. U. Mus. Art, Inst. Contemporary Art, U.Pa., numerous others.; Artist-in-residence, Center Contemporary Art, Aspen, Colo., 1968. Served with USAAF, 1946-49. Decorated Medal of Merit; Albert A. List Found. grantee for inaugural poster of N.Y. State Theatre, Lincoln Ctr., 1964; Brown Travelling fellow Art Inst. Chgo., 1953; honored by Gov. Ind., 1973. Mem. Delta Phi Delta (pres. Zeta chpt. 1951-52). Address: care Multiples Inc 24 W 57th St New York NY 10019 *

INDIK, BERNARD PAUL, social work educator; b. Phila., Apr. 30, 1932; s. Jacob Joseph and Ida F. (Kaplan) I.; m. Harriet Sandra Simberloff, June 26, 1955; children: Joyce Janet, Martin Karl, Jay Joseph, Debra Ruth, William Aaron. B.S., U. Pa., 1954, M.B.A., 1955; textile engrng. cert., Phila. Textile Inst., 1955; A.M., U. Mich., 1959, Ph.D., 1961. Asst. mgr. Textured Yarn Co., Phila., 1955; asst. study dir. Survey Research Center, U. Mich., 1957-60, study dir., 1961; asst. research specialist Rutgers U., New Brunswick, N.J., 1961-65, asso. research specialist research program psychology dept. and Inst. Mgmt., 1965-68, prof. social work, 1)68—, Disting. prof. social work, 1978—; cons. Pres.'s Commn. on Civil Disorders, 1967-68, Gov.'s Commn. Report for Action, 1968, Dept. Labor and Industry N.J., 1965, 74-76. Author: (with G. Sternlieb) The Ecology of Welfare, 1973, (with R. Beauregard) A Human Service Labor Market: Developmental Disabilities, 1979; editor: (with F.K. Berrien) People, Groups and Organizations, 1968; contbr. articles and book revs. to profl. jours., chpts. to books. Mem. exec. bd. South Brunswick Community Council, 1967-68, exec. sec., 1968-69; mem. exec. bd. South Brunswick Citizens for Johnson, 1964; trustee South Brunswick Twp. Library, 1965-70, treas., 1970; mem. South Brunswick Twp. Planning Bd., 1976—, chmn., 1979-82; mem. long range planning com. United Way of Central Jersey, 1976—, trustee, v.p., 1978-79; South Brunswick Twp. rep. Middlesex County Housing and Community Devel. Commn., 1976—. Served with U.S. Army, 1955-57. Recipient Community Appreciation award United Way Central Jersey, 1976, 82; Mayor's Appreciation award South Brunswick, 1976; Small Community

Mayors of N.J. award, 1980. Fellow Am. Psychol. Assn., Soc. Psychol. Study Social Issues; mem. Council on Social Work Edn., Nat. Assn. Social Workers, Am. Acad. Polit. and Social Scis., Soc. Gen. Systems Research, Eastern Psychol. Assn. Democrat. Jewish. Club: Willows Swim (Kendall Park, N.J.) (trustee 1976). Home: 32 Kendall Rd Kendall Park NJ 08824 Office: Grad Sch Social Work Rutgers U 536 George St New Brunswick NJ 08903

INEZ, COLETTE, poet; b. Brussels, June 23, 1931; U.S., 1939, naturalized, 1952; m. Saul A. Stadtmauer, July 26, 1964. B.A., Hunter Coll., 1961. Tchr. English as second lang. NYU, 1962-63; tchr. gen. studies Nat. Acad. Ballet, N.Y.C., 1963-64; tchr. anti-poverty programs Fed. Title III, pub. schs., N.Y.C., 1964-70; instr. poetry workshop New Sch., N.Y.C., 1974—; Beck lectr. Denison U., 1974; lectr. poetry workshop SUNY, Stony Brook, 1975-76; vis. prof. Hunter Coll., 1979-80; poetry reviewer Parnassus mag. Readings Library Congress, 1973, Lamont Library, Harvard U., 1973; Poet-in-residence Kalamazoo Coll., 1976, 78, 81; poetry readings, seminars U.S. colls. and univs. Author: The Woman Who Loved Worms, 1972, Alive and Taking Names, 1977, Eight Minutes from the Sun, 1983; poetry in major anthologies and nat. and internat. lit. jours., 1960—. Recipient Book award Great Lakes Colls. Assn., 1972, Kreymborg award Poetry Soc. Am., 1975, Reedy Meml. award, 1972, Osgood Warren award Poetry Soc. New Eng., 1967, Nat. League Pen Women award, 1962, N.Y. State Creative Artists Pub. Service award, 1975; Nat. Endowment Arts fellow, 1974; Rockefeller Found. fellow, 1980; YADDO fellow, 1980. Mem. Poetry Soc. Am. (dir. 1977-80), PEN. Home: 5 W 86th St New York NY 10024

INGALL, DAVID, pediatrician; b. Boston, May 12, 1930; s. Louis and Sarah I.; m. Carol Ingall; children: Bettina, Lewis, Seth, David Hoffman, Cynthia Hoffman, Michael Hoffman. A.B., Boston U., 1952, A.M., 1953, M.D., 1957. Diplomate: Am. Bd. Pediatrics, Nat. Bd. Med. Examiners. Acting dir. dept. pediatrics Boston City Hosp., 1965-66, 70-72, asst. surgeon dept. ob-gyn, 1967-72; acting chmn. dept. pediatrics Boston U., 1970-71; chmn. dept. pediatrics Evanston (Ill.) Hosp., 1972—. Fellow Am. Acad. Pediatrics. Office: 2650 Ridge St Evanston IL 60201

INGALLS, DANIEL HENRY HOLMES, educator; b. N.Y.C., May 4, 1916; s. Fay and Rachel (Holmes) I.; m. Phyllis Sarah Day, June 27, 1936; children—Sarah (Mrs. Gary Daughn), Rachel Holmes, Daniel Henry Holmes. A.B., Harvard, 1936, M.A., 1938. Jr. fellow Soc. Fellows Harvard, 1938-42, 46-48, asst. prof. Sanskrit and Indian studies, 1948-52, asso. prof., 1952-56, Wales prof. Sanskrit, 1956—, editor, 1956—; Dir. Va. Hot Springs, Inc., 1946-57, pres., 1957-63, chmn. bd., 1963—. Author: An Introduction to Navva-Nyaya Logic, 1951, An Anthology of Sanskrit Court Poetry, 1965. Trustee Harvard-Yenching Inst. Served to capt. AUS, 1944-46. Mem. Am. Oriental Soc. (past pres.), Am. Philos. Soc., Am. Acad. Scis. Home: The Yard Hot Springs VA 24445

INGALLS, ROBERT LYNN, physicist, educator; b. Spokane, Wash., June 15, 1934; s. Keith Irving and Ruth Louise (Strauss) I.; m. Liisa Vasama, Jan. 28, 1961; children: Karen Liisa, Johnanna Louise, David Robert. B.S., U. Wash., 1956; M.S., Carnegie Inst. Tech., 1960, Ph.D., 1962. Instr. physics Carnegie Inst. Tech., 1961-63; research asso. U. Ill., 1963-65, research asso. prof., 1965-66; asst. prof. U. Wash., Seattle, 1966-69, asso. prof., 1969-74, prof. physics, 1974—; vis. scholar State U. Groningen, Netherlands, 1972-73. Bassoonist, Seattle Symphony Orch., 1952-57; Contbr. articles on solid state and high pressure physics, Mossbauer effect and X-ray absorption to profl. jours., books and encys. AEC contract, 1967-77; NSF grantee, 1976-83; Dept. Energy grantee, 1983—. Mem. Am. Phys. Soc., Fedn. Am. Scientists, Sigma Xi, Sigma Phi Epsilon, Zeta Mu Tau. Office: Physics Dept U Wash Seattle WA 98195

INGBAR, SIDNEY HAROLD, physician, educator; b. Denver, Feb. 12, 1925; s. David Harry and Belle (Friedl) I.; m. Mary Lee Gimbel Mack, May 28, 1950; children: David Harry, Eric Edward, Jonathan Clarence. Student, UCLA, 1941-43; M.D. magna cum laude (fellow), Harvard U., 1947. Practice medicine, specializing in endocrinology, Boston, 1949-72; mem. faculty Harvard Med. Sch., 1955-72, William B. Castle prof. medicine, 1969-72; program dir. Harvard Clin. Research Center, Boston City Hosp., from 1962, physician-in-charge, from 1963; asso. dir. Thorndike Meml. Lab., 1963-72; prof. medicine, asso. dean U. Calif.-San Francisco, 1972-74; prof. medicine Harvard U., 1974—; also dir. Thorndike Labs, Beth Israel Hosp., Boston, 1974—; Cons. Newton-Wellesley Hosp., from 1957, Mass. Soldiers Home, Chelsea, from 1964; Mem. Surgeon Gen. Adv. Com. Gen. Medicine, chmn. subcom. endocrinology and metabolism, 1963-70; mem. medicine test com. Nat. Bd. Med. Examiners, 1967-70; mem. endocrinology study sect. NIH, 1966-70, chmn., 1971-73; mem. bd. sci. counselors Nat. Inst. Arthritis, Metabolism and Digestive Diseases, 1973-75, mem. advanced exam. com. endocrinology and metabolism, 1973-75, chmn., 1975-77; sr. med. investigator VA, 1973—; mem. med. adv. bd. Nat. Hormone and Pituitary Program, 1982—. Mem. editorial bd.: Endocrinology, 1957-67, New Eng. Jour. Medicine, 1967-70, Jour. Clin. Investigation, 1968-72; editor-in-chief: Med. Grand Rounds, 1981—; editorial adv. com.: Jour. Endocrinologic Investigation, 1983—; contbr. articles profl. jours. Recipient Maimonides award Boston Med. Soc., 1947. Mem. Assn. Am. Physicians, Am. Fedn. Clin. Research, Am. Soc. Clin. Investigation (councillor 1967-70), Am. Thyroid Assn (pres. 1976-77, councillor 1972-75, Warner-Chilcott disting. lectr. 1978), Endocrine Soc. (Ernest Oppenheimer award 1965, councillor 1971-75, Disting. Leadership award 1979), Am. Physiol. Soc., Soc. Exptl. Biology and Medicine, Sigma Xi, Alpha Omega Alpha. Home: 305 Dudley St Brookline MA 02146 Office: Beth Israel Hosp Boston MA 02215

INGE, MILTON THOMAS, english educator; b. Newport News, Va., Mar. 18, 1936; s. Clyde Elmo and Bernice Lucille (Jackson) I.; m. Tonette Long Bond, 1982; 1 son, Scott Thomas; 1 stepson, Michael Gordon Bond. B.A., Randolph-Macon Coll., 1959; M.A., Vanderbilt U., 1960, Ph.D., 1964. Instr. English Vanderbilt U., 1962-64; asst. prof. Am. thought and lang. Mich. State U., 1964-68, assoc. prof., 1968-69; assoc. prof. English Va. Commonwealth U., Richmond, 1969-73, prof., 1973-80, chmn. dept. English, 1974-80; prof., chmn. dept. English Clemson U., S.C., 1980-83; resident scholar in Am. studies USIA, Washington, 1982-84; Blackwell prof. humanities Randolph-Macon Coll., Ashland, Va., 1984—; reader English Composition Test Coll. Entrance Exam. Bd., 1967, 69, 77, 80. Author: (with T.D. Young) Donald Davidson: Essay and Bibliography, 1965, Donald Davidson, 1971; editor: Sut Lovingood's Yarns, 1966, High Times and Hard Times, 1967, Agrarianism in American Literature, 1969, A.B. Longstreet, 1969, Faulkner: A Rose for Emily, 1970, Wm. Byrd of Westover, 1970, Studies in Light in August, 1971, Frontier Humorists: Critical Views, 1975, Ellen Glasgow: Centennial Essays, 1976, Black American Writers: Bibliographic Essays, 2 vols., 1978, Handbook of American Popular Culture, Vol. 1, 1978, Handbook of American Popular Culture, Vol. II, 1980, Handbook of American Popular Culture, Vol. III, 1981, Bartleby the Inscrutable, 1979, Concise Histories of American Popular Culture, 1982, James Branch Carell: Centennial Essays, 1983, American Women Writers: Bibliographical Essays, 1983, A Nineteenth Century American Reader, 1984, Huck Finn Among the Critics: A Centennial Selection, 1984, Resources for American Literary Study, 1971-79, American Humor: An Interdisciplinary Newsletter, 1974-79; gen. editor: Research Guides in English, Am. Critical Tradition series, Bio-Bibliographics in Popular Culture; book reviewer: Nashville Tenneseean, Richmond Times-Dispatch, Menomonee Falls Gazette. Bd. dirs. Friends of Richmond Pub. Libary, San Francisco Acad. Comic Art. Fulbright-Hays grantee, 1967-68, 71, 79; grantee Am. Philos. Soc., 1970, Mich. State U., 1965, 66, 68, Clemson U., 1981; So. Fellowship Fund fellow, 1959-62. Mem. MLA (del. assembly 1976-78, chmn. elections com. 1980), Am. Studies Assn., Popular Culture Assn., Am. Humor Studies Assn. (pres. 1978), Soc. Study So. Lit. (exec. council 1971-73, 78-80), Soc. Study Midwestern Lit., Melville Soc., Thoreau Fellowship, Ellen Glasgow Soc. (exec. council 1974-84), Mus. Cartoon Art (nominating com. Hall of Fame 1975—), Am. Assn. Tchrs. Spanish and Portuguese, Phi Beta Kappa, omicron Delta Kappa, Pi Delta Epsilon, Lambda Chi Alpha. Club: Va. Writers. Office: Randolph-Macon College Ashland VA 23005

INGELS, MARTY, theatrical agent, TV and motion picture production executive; b. Bklyn., Mar. 9, 1936; s. Jacob and Minnie (Crown) Ingerman; m. Jean Maire Frassinelli, Aug. 3, 1960 (div. 1969); m. Shirley Jones, 1977. Ed., Erasmus High Sch., 1951-53, Forest Hills High Sch., 1953-55. Founder Ingels Inc., 1975—; formed Stoneypoint Prodns., 1981; TV and motion picture producer, U.S. and abroad. Star: Dickens and Fenster series, ABC-TV, 1964; co-star: Pruitts of Southampton, 1968-69; films include Armored Command, 1962, Horizontal Lieutenant, 1965, Busy Body, 1967, Ladies Man, 1966, If It's Tuesday This Must Be Belgium, 1970, Wild and Wonderful, 1965, Guide for a Married Man, 1968; numerous TV appearances. Active various charity drives. Address: Ingels Inc 8322 Beverly Blvd Hollywood CA 90048 *The life of the comedian became too painful to me - too little control over your own destiny - too much of your guts at stake too many times for too many people you don't even know. So, I decided to do what I really do best - arrange things - anywhere, for anyone, anytime, for anything - circumventing the tangled relay system which has made the expedition of any project a frustrating agony.*

INGERSOLL, ALFRED CAJORI, human resources executive; b. Madison, Wis., June 8, 1920; s. Leonard R. and Helen (Flint) I.; m. Elizabeth R. McNamara, Feb. 22, 1946; 1 son, John Thomas. B.C.E., U. Wis., 1942, M.C.E., 1948, Ph.D., 1950; fluid mechanics symposium, U. Mich., summer 1947. Diplomate: Am. Acad. Environ. Engrs. Mem. tech. staff lab. Linde Air Products Co., Tonawanda, N.Y., 1942-46; instr. civil engring. U. Wis., 1946-49, project asst. engring. expt. sta., 1949-50; from instr. to asso. prof. civil engring. Calif. Inst. Tech., 1950-60; guest prof. applied mechanics Bengal Engring. Coll., U. Calcutta, India, 1954-55; dean Sch. Engring., U. So. Calif., 1960-70; asso. dean continuing edn. Sch. Engring. and Applied Sci., UCLA, 1970-82; mgr. human resource devel. Bechtel Operating Services Corp., San Francisco, 1982—; also dir. continuing edn. in engring. and math. UCLA Extension; cons. U.S. Naval Ordnance Test Sta., 1958, Albert C. Martin & Assos., 1970; v.p. Calif. Engring. Found., 1975-79, pres., 1979-82, dir., 1982—, Birtcher Corp., Los Angeles; res. sr. san. engr. USPHS; monthly columnist Engring. Edn.; mem. adv. com. Air Force Inst. Tech., 1970-73. Author: (with R.L. Daugherty) Fluid Mechanics with Engineering Applications, 5th edit, 1954, Heat Conduction with Applications in Engineering and Geology, 1954; series editor civil engring. books, Marcel Dekker, Inc.; contbr. numerous articles to engring. and ednl. publs. Mem. Los Angeles Citizens Adv. Com. on Rapid Transit, 1973-74; chmn. adv. panel on auto emission standards Calif. Assembly Com. Transp. and Commerce, 1968; Bd. visitors U. Santa Clara Engring. Sch., 1973-74. Named Educator of Year Soc. Mfg. Engrs., 1972. Fellow ASCE (pres. Los Angeles sect. 1970-71, Rudolph Hering medal for paper 1957, Daniel W. Mead prize student essay in ethics 1942, Edmund Friedman Profl. Recognition award 1969, mem. exec. com. edn. div. 1978—), Inst. Advancement Engring. (pres. 1970-72, pres. coll. fellows 1974-76, Merit award 1977); fellow Am. Soc. Engring. Edn. (chmn. Pacific S.W. sect. 1961-62, mem., v.p. West sects. 1966-68, chmn. relations with industry div. 1964-65, chmn. com. on deans insts. 1963-65, projects bd. 1970-73), Nat. Soc. Profl. Engrs. (chmn. com. pub. relations 1970-72, pres. ednl. found. 1973-77, trustee 1978—, v.p. Western region 1977-79, chmn. publs. com. 1979-81, continuing profl. devel. com. 1981-83, Engrs. Week 1982), Calif. Soc. Profl. Engrs. (pres. Los Angeles chpt. 1963-65, v.p. So. region 1965-66, nat. dir. 1968-77, 79—, Edn. Achievement award 1974, Profl. Achievement award 1977), Ams. for Energy Independence, Soc. for History Tech., Order of Engr., Sigma Xi, Chi Epsilon (pres. 1956-58), Tau Beta Pi, Phi Kappa Phi, Pi Tau Sigma, Phi Eta Sigma. Presbyterian. Clubs: Rotary, Pacific Palisades. Home: 102 Estates Dr Orinda CA 94563 Office: PO Box 3965 San Francisco CA 94119 *I have devoted my principal energies to advancing the engineering profession in which I have made my living, in earlier years through technical publications and in later years through promoting ethical conduct of engineers and in extending the benefits of engineering education to practicing professionals. The rewards of these endeavors have been in seeing former students and associates advanced to positions of responsibility and gain, perhaps because of what they have learned from me.*

INGERSOLL, JOHN SHEPHARD, utility holding company executive; b. Chgo., Oct. 18, 1928; s. Harold Gay and Florence (Shephard) I.; m. Patricia Kearse, June 25, 1955; children: John Shephard, Stephen Reid, Gaylord Kearse. Chmn. bd., pres., chief exec. officer La. Gen. Services Inc., Harvey; adj. prof. Tulane U. Grad. Sch. Bus., New Orleans. Bd. dirs. Econ. Devel. Council, New Orleans. Served to lt. U.S. Army, 1951-53. Republican. Episcopalian. Home: 1145 N Greenbay Rd Lake Forest IL 60045 Office: PO Box 433 Harvey LA 70059

INGERSOLL, PAUL MILLS, banker; b. Phila., Apr. 13, 1928; s. John H.W. and Frances Paul (Mills) I.; m. Eleanor S. Koehler, Oct. 6, 1951; children: Eleanor Ingersoll Sylvestro, Rita W., Frances M. B.A., Princeton U., 1950. With Provident Nat. Bank, Phila., 1963-78, v.p. adminstrn. and exec. mgmt., 1969, sr. v.p. retail banking div., 1969-73, pres., chief adminstrv. officer, 1973-78; pres., dir. Beaver Mgmt. Corp.; dir. Mut. Assurance Co.; Mid-Atlantic rep. Christie's Fine Art Auctioneers & Appraisers. Trustee Drexel U., William Penn Found. Served as 1st lt. AUS, 1950-52. Recipient Human Relations award Am. Jewish Com., 1973. Republican. Episcopalian. Clubs: Phila., Merion Cricket, State in Schuylkill. Office: 638 Morris Ave Bryn Mawr PA 19010

INGERSOLL, RALPH MCALLISTER, editor, author, publisher; b. New Haven, Dec. 8, 1900; s. Colin Macrae and Theresa (McAllister) I.; m. Mary Elizabeth Carden, 1925 (div. 1935); m. Elaine Brown Keiffer, Aug. 9, 1945 (dec. Apr. 1948); children: Ralph McAllister II, Ian Macrae; m. Mary Hill Doolittle, Nov. 25, 1948 (div. 1963); 1 adopted son, Brooks; m. Thelma Bradford, 1964. Student, Hotchkiss Sch., Lakeville, Conn., 1917-18; B.S., Yale, 1921; postgrad., Columbia, 1922. Mining engr.; reporter New Yorker mag., 1925, mng. editor, 1925-30; asso. editor Fortune, 1930, mng. editor, 1930-35; v.p., gen. mgr. Time, Inc. (pub. Time, Life, Fortune and Archtl. Forum, sponsoring radio and cinema prodns. "The March of Time), 1935-38; pub. Time mag., 1937-39; organizer, financier co. to publish PM (N.Y. daily evening newspaper), 1939-40; pres. R.J. Co., Inc., 1948-59, Gen. Pubs., Inc. (newspaper mgmt.), 1959-75, Ingersolls Publs. Co., 1975—. Author: In and Under Mexico, 1924, Report on England, 1940, America Is Worth Fighting For, 1941, Action on All Fronts, 1941, The Battle is the Payoff, 1944, Top Secret, 1946, The Great Ones, 1948, Wine of Violence, 1951, Point of Departure, 1961. Served from pvt. Engr. Amphibian Command to lt. col. Gen. Staff Corps AUS, 1943-45. Decorated Legion of Merit; officer Order of the Crown, Belgium). Episcopalian. Club: Brook (N.Y.C.). Home: Cornwall Bridge CT 06754 Office: Ingersoll Publs Co Sharon CT 06069

INGHRAM, MARK GORDON, educator, physicist; b. Livingston, Mont., Nov. 13, 1919; s. Mark Gordon and Luella Gallagher (McNay) I.; m. Evelyn Mae Dyckman, May 12, 1946; children: Cheryl Ann, Mark Gordon III. B.A., Olivet Coll., 1939; Ph.D., U. Chgo., 1947. Physicist, Manhattan Project, 1942-45; sr. physicist Argonne Nat. Lab., 1945-47; mem. faculty U. Chgo., 1947—, successively instr., asst. prof., asso. prof., prof., Samuel K. Allison Disting. Service prof. physics, 1969—, chmn. dept. physics, 1959-70, acting dir. Inst. for Study of Metals, 1960-61, asso. dean div. of phys. scis., 1964-71, master Phys. Sci. Coll. div., 1981—, asso. dean div. phys. sci., 1981—, asso. dean Coll., 1981—; mem. com. nuclear geophysics Nat. Acad. Sci., 1953-60, mem. com. sci. and pub. policy, 1966-69, mem. com. on exploration of moon and planets, 1958-61. Asso. editor: Jour. Chem. Physics, 1957-60; editorial bd.: Rev. Sci. Instruments, 1958-61; author articles in sci. jours. Fellow Am. Phys. Soc., Am. Acad. Arts and Scis.; mem. Nat. Acad. Scis. (J. Lawrence Smith medal 1957), AAAS. Home: 1534 E 59th St Chicago IL 60637

INGLE, JOHN IDE, dental educator; b. Colville, Wash., Jan. 19, 1919; s. John James and Jessie Belle (Ide) I.; m. Joyce Ledgerwood, July 11, 1940; children: John Geoffrey, Leslie Ide, Schuyler Neal. Student, Wash. State U., 1936-38; D.D.S., Northwestern U., 1942; M.S.D., U. Mich., 1948. Diplomate: Am. Bd. Endodontics, Am. Bd. Periodontology. Asst. Northwestern U., 1942-43; asst. prof. endodontics and periodontology Sch. Dentistry, U. Wash., 1948-51, asso. prof., 1951-59, prof., 1959-64, exec. officer dept., 1956-64; dean Sch. Dentistry, U. So. Calif., Los Angeles, 1964-72; dir. div. internat. health, sr. profl. asso. Inst. Medicine Nat. Acad. Scis., 1973-78; pres. Palm Springs Seminars, 1978; sr. lectr. UCLA, 1979; vis. lectr. Loma Linda U., 1983; attending staff exec. com. Los Angeles County/U. So. Calif. Med. Center, 1964-72; Cons. Nat. Bd. Dental Examiners, 1964—; endodontics, asst. surgeon gen. U.S. Army, 1969—, Nat. Naval Med. Center, 1973; mem. adv. com. dental health Office Sec. HEW, 1970—; mem. rev. com. on dental edn. NIH, 1970; mem. adv. panel on nat. health ins. U.S. Ho. of Reps. Ways and Means Com., 1975. Author: (with others) Endodontics, 1965, 2d edit. (with E.E. Beveridge), 1976, (with A.L. Ogilvie) An Atlas of Pulpal and Periapical Biology, 1965; editor: (with P. Blair) International Dental Care Delivery Systems, 1978. Bd. dirs. Los Angeles United Way Crusade, 1967-69. Served with Dental Corps AUS, 1943-46. Recipient Northwestern U. Alumni Merit award, 1966. Fellow AAAS, Internat., Am. colls. dentists; mem. Internat. Assn. Dental Research, Am. Assn. Endodontists (past pres.), Am. Acad. Periodontology, Am. Dental Assn. (cons. dental therapeutics), Los Angeles Dental Soc. (sec. 1968-71), Am. Assn. Dental Schs., Alpha Omega (hon. mem.). Club: Cosmos (Washington). Home: 2323 Oak Crest Dr S Palm Springs CA 92262

INGLIS, ANDREW FRANKLIN, consultant; b. Van, Mich., Mar. 17, 1920; s. David and Katherine (Smith) I.; m. Marie Adam, Sept. 5, 1942; children: David, Richard, Elizabeth, Andrew Franklin. B.S., Haverford (Pa.) Coll., 1941; postgrad., U. Chgo., 1941-42. Registered profl. engr., D.C. Clk. Eastman Kodak Stores, Detroit, 1940; lab. technician Eastman Kodak Co., Chgo., 1941-43; instr. U. Chgo., 1942; engr. Naval Research Lab., Washington, 1942-43, McIntosh & Inglis, 1946-49; engr., partner, 1949-53; div. v.p., gen. mgr. comml. communications systems div. RCA, Camden, N.J., 1953-77; pres. RCA Am. Communications Inc., Princeton, N.J., 1977-83, vice chmn., Princeton, 1983; v.p. RCA, 1981-83; cons., 1983—. Served with USNR, 1943-46. Club: Radio Club Am. (N.Y.C.). Home and office: 741 Stone House Rd Moorestown NJ 08057

INGLIS, DAVID RITTENHOUSE, physicist; b. Detroit, Oct. 10, 1905; s. William and Carolyn Clay (Rittenhouse) I.; m. Dorothy Rosalind Kerr, Mar. 26, 1934; 1 son, John Lockwood. A.B., Amherst Coll., 1928, D.Sc. (honoris causa), 1963, U. Mich., 1931, U. Ill., 1974; student, U. Afloat, U. Heidelberg, Germany. Instr. Ohio State U., 1931-34, asst. prof., 1934; research asso. U. Leipsig, Fed. Inst. Tech., Zurich, 1932-33; asst. prof. U. Pitts., 1934-37, Princeton U., 1937-38; asso. Johns Hopkins U., 1938-41, asso. prof., 1941-49; sr. physicist Argonne Nat. Lab., 1949-69; prof. physics U. Mass., 1969-75, prof. emeritus, 1975—; physicist OSRD, 1942, Ballistics Research Lab., Aberdeen Proving Ground, 1943; with theoretical div. Los Alamos Sci. Lab., 1943-46; vis. prof. U. Calif. at Berkeley, 1955-56, U. Grenoble, France, 1964; physicist European Orgn. Nuclear Research, Geneva, 1957-58; professorial lectr. U. Chgo., 1965-68. Author: Dynamic Principles of Mechanics, 1949, Nuclear Energy: Its Physics and Its Social Challenge, 1972, Wind Power and Other Energy Options, 1978; contbr. articles to profl. jours. Fellow Am. Phys. Soc. (Leo Szilard award for physics in pub. interest 1974), Fedn. Am. Scientists (chmn. 1959-60), Phi Beta Kappa, Sigma Xi, Alpha Delta Phi. Home: 15 Maplewood Dr Amherst MA 01002 *I could permit myself to follow the fascination of science as a career only with the rationalization that in the long run it does people good. Since having participated in the early nuclear technology, I am horrified by the harm it could do and believe that all decisions, be they on choice of political leaders, foreign policy, military and negotiation stance, energy problems or population trends, should be aimed at assuring that nuclear war shall not occur.*

INGLIS, THOMAS HERBERT, insurance company executive; b. Kincardine, Ont., Can., Apr. 1, 1928; s. John Malcolm and Helen Mary (Stevens) I.; m. Lena Veronica Leguard, Sept. 14, 1954; children: Helen, Jane, Thomas, Nancy, John. B.Commerce, U. Toronto, 1950. With N.Am. Life Assurance Co., Toronto, 1950—, asst. treas., 1961-66, asso. treas., 1966-68, treas., 1968-71, v.p., treas., 1971-74, v.p. fin., 1974-76, sr. v.p., 1976—; chmn. bd. Edgecombe Investment Services, Ltd., Edgecombe Properties Ltd., Edgecombe Realty Ltd.; dir. Innocan Investments Ltd., Cadillac Fairview Corp. Mem. Met. Toronto Bd. Trade. Clubs: Albany (Toronto) (dir.); Tamarack Island Fishing and Shooting (Stokes Bay, Ont.) (dir.); Lambton Golf and Country.). Home: 45 Montgomery Rd Toronto ON Canada M8X 1Z8 Office: 105 Adelaide St W Toronto ON Canada M5H 1R1

INGOLD, KEITH USHERWOOD, educator, chemist; b. Leeds, Eng., May 31, 1929; s. Christopher Kelk and Edith (Usherwood) I.; m. Carmen Cairine Hodgkin, Apr. 7, 1956; children: Christopher Frank, John Hilary, Diana Hilda. B.Sc. with honors in Chemistry, Univ. Coll., London, 1949; D.Phil., Oxford (Eng.) U., 1951. Postdoctoral fellow Nat. Research Council Can., 1951-53, research officer, 1955-77, asso. dir. chemistry, 1977—; postdoctoral fellow U. B.C., 1953-55; vis. scientist Chevron Research Co., Richmond, Calif., 1966, Univ. Coll., London, 1969, 72, Ford Motor Co., 1971, Esso Research and Engring. Co., Linden, N.J., 1973, U. Western Ont., 1975, Iowa State U., 1975, U. Bologna, Italy, 1975, U. Adelaide, Australia, 1979, U. Grenoble, France, 1983. Recipient Can. Silver Jubilee medal, 1977; Carnegie fellow U. St. Andrews, Scotland, 1977; vis. fellow Japan Soc. for Promotion Sci., 1982; fellow Italian Nat. Research Council, 1983. Fellow Royal Soc. Can. (treas. 1979-82, Centennial medal 1982), Royal Soc. (London), Chem. Inst. Can. (medal 1981, Syntex award for phys.

organic chemistry 1983); mem. Am. Chem. Soc. (award petroleum chemistry 1968), Chem. Soc. (award kinetics and mechanism 1978) (London). Research papers in free radical chemistry. Home: Box 712 Rural Route 5 Ottawa ON Canada Office: Nat Research Council Can Ottawa ON Canada

INGPEN, JOAN MARY EILEEN, opera assn. exec.; b. London, Eng., Jan. 3, 1916; d. John Hamilton and Daisy Grace (Howe) Williams. Licentiate, Royal Acad. Music, London, 1934; Asso., Royal Coll. Music, London, 1935. Artists mgr. Ingpen & Williams, Ltd., 1946-62; controller of opera planning Royal Opera House, Covent Garden, 1962-71; artistic adminstr. L'Opera de Paris, 1971-77; artistic adminstrn. dir. Met. Opera Assn., N.Y.C., 1978-81, asst. mgr., 1981—. Office: Met Opera Assn Lincoln Center New York NY 10023 *My guiding principles have always been the old-fashioned ones of hard work, integrity towards both those who work for me and those for whom I work and, I hope, a humanity in dealing with others especially the performers with whom most of my working life has been spent.*

INGRAHAM, EDWARD CLARKE, JR., foreign service officer; b. Mineola, N.Y., Feb. 2, 1922; s. Edward Clarke and Dorothy Hathaway (Sutton) I.; m. Susan Hartman, Jan. 25, 1947; children: John Edward, James William, Elizabeth Ann Ingraham Reed. B.A., Dartmouth Coll., 1943; postgrad., Cornell U., 1957-58. Editorial asst. Moody's Investors Service, N.Y.C., 1946-47; joined U.S. Fgn. Service, 1947; vice consul, Cochabamba, Bolivia, 1947-48, 3d sec. embassy, La Paz, Bolivia, 1948-50, vice consul, Hong Kong, 1950-51, Perth, Australia, 1951-54, consul, Madras, India, 1954-56, 2d sec. embassy, Djakarta, Indonesia, 1958-60; officer charge Australia-New Zealand affairs State Dept., 1961-62, officer charge Indonesian affairs, 1962-65; assigned Nat. War Coll., 1965-66; chief of embassy polit. sect., Rangoon, Burma, 1966-69; dep. dir. research and analysis for East Asia, State Dept., 1969-71; polit. counselor embassy, Islamabad, Pakistan, 1971-74; dir. Office of Indonesian, Malaysian and Singapore Affairs, State Dept., Washington, 1974-77; dep. chief mission Am. embassy, Singapore, 1977-79; diplomat in residence Lake Forest (Ill.) Coll., 1979-80; freedom of info. advisor U.S. Dept. State, 1980—; mem. U.S. del. ANZUS council meeting, Canberra, Australia, 1962, Intergovtl. Group on Indonesia, Amsterdam, Netherlands, 1975, 77. Served with USAAF, 1943-45; ETO. Mem. Am. Fgn. Service Assn. Address: 7700 Sebago Rd Bethesda MD 20817

INGRAHAM, JOE MCDONALD, U.S. circuit judge; b. Pawnee County, Okla., July 5, 1903; s. Millard F. and Emma (Patton) I.; m. Laura Munson, Oct. 29, 1954. LL.B., Nat. U., 1927. Bar: Okla. and D.C. bars 1927, Tex. bar 1928. Practice in, Stroud, Okla., 1927-28, Ft. Worth, 1928-35, Houston, 1935-54; judge U.S. Dist. Ct. So. Dist. Tex., 1954-69, U.S. Ct. Appeals for 5th Circuit, 1969-73, sr. judge, 1973—; judge Temporary Emergency Ct. Appeals of U.S., 1976—. Served as officer USAAF, 1942-46. Mem. Am. Bar Assn., Houston Bar Assn., Tex. State Bar, Am. Judicature Soc., S.A.R. (pres. Tex. Soc. 1937-38, Good Citizenship award Tex. Soc. 1958), Am. Legion. Republican. Presbyterian. Home: 2016 Main St Apt 1602 Houston TX 77002 Office: US Courthouse Houston TX 77002

INGRAHAM, REX, dentist; b. Grand Junction, Colo., Mar. 25, 1914; s. Eugene F. and Mary Della (Mace) I.; m. Lola Vannorsdel, June 1941 (dec.); children—Ronald R., Eric D.; m. Lucille Brokenshire, Oct. 1963. A.A., Mesa Coll., 1934; D.D.S., B.S., U. So. Calif., 1941. Faculty U. So. Calif. Sch. Dentistry, 1941—, prof., head dept. operative dentistry, 1945-69, Distinguished prof., 1966—, chmn. div. occlusion, 1970-77, dir. restorative dept., 1974-79, asso. dean clin edn., 1975-77, dept. restorative dentistry, 1979—; dir. human factors research dept. U. So. Calif.; lectr., U.S., Can., Philippines, Japan, S.Am., Europe, Australia, Africa, China. Author: Manual on Physiology of Occlusion, Atlas of Cast Gold Procedures, Atlas of Gold fore and Rubber Dam Procedures; contbr. articles to profl. jours. Active Boy Scouts Am. Decorated grand chevalier Order des Chevaliers du Vieux Moulin Nestou, Cagnes, France; recipient Alumni award of merit U. So. Calif., 1975, Pierre Fouchard Acad. award, 1978; named to Sch. Dentistry Hall of Fame, 1976; Torch of Learning award Am. Friends of Hebrew U., 1977; John R. Callahan award, 1980; Thomas P. Hinman award, 1980; Internat. Dentist of Year award Acad. Dentistry Internat., 1983. Fellow Am. Coll. Dentists, Internat. Coll. Dentists, Acad. Gen. Dentistry; mem. Am. Acad. Restorative Dentistry, Am. Acad. Operative Dentistry, Am. Acad. Gold Foil operators, Am. Acad. Gen. Practice, ADA (life), Internat. Acad. Gnathology, So. Calif. Acad. Gen. Dentistry, Am. Study Club Paris, Fedn. Prosthodontic Orgns., Am. Acad. Craniomandibular Orthopedics, Alumni Assn. U. So. Calif., Sch. Dentistry (life), Jones Gold Foil Study Club (dir.), Calif., Idaho, Los Angeles dental socs., Scull and Dagger, Omicron Kappa Upsilon. Clubs: Golden Century (life), Lucky Trojans, Dental Assos. (life), Piscadents.). Home: 1612 Thompson Ave Glendale CA 91201 Office: 5400 Balboa Blvd Encino CA 91316

INGRAM, ALVIN JOHN, surgeon; b. Jackson, Tenn., Mar. 31, 1914; s. Alvin Hill and Margaret (Gallagher) I.; m. Catherine Davis, Feb. 7, 1943; children: Mildred Ingram Dyer, Catherine Ingram Doyle, Peggy Ingram Tagg. B.S., U. Tenn., 1939, M.D., 1939, M.S. in Orthopaedic Surgery, 1947. Diplomate: Am. Bd. Orthopaedic Surgery (dir. 1972-78, v.p. 1976, pres. 1976-78; mem. residency rev. commn. orthopedic surgery 1972-76, chmn. 1975-76). Intern Univ. Hosp., Ann Arbor, Mich., 1939-40, asst. resident surgery, 1940-41; fellow orthopaedic surgery Campbell Clinic, Memphis, 1941-42, 46-47, mem. staff, 1947—, dep. chief of staff, 1967-69, chief of staff, 1970-78, chief of staff emeritus, 1979—; pvt. practice orthopaedic surgery, Memphis, 1947—; med. dir. Crippled Children's Hosp., 1948-61, chief staff, 1961-70; med. dir. Les Passes Cerebral Palsy Treatment Center, 1953-56; med. adv. com. Memphis and W. Tenn. chpt. Nat. Found. Infantile Paralysis, 1947-57, chmn., 1947-55; med. adv. com. Shrine Sch. Crippled Children, 1947-56; med. adv. bd. Variety Club Convalescent Hosp., 1952-56; asso. prof. orthopaedic surgery U. Tenn. Coll. Medicine, 1960-71, prof., chmn. dept., 1971-79, prof. emeritus, 1979—; mem. staff Bapt. Meml. Hosp., exec. com. med. staff, 1969-70, chmn. orthopaedic dept., 1970-74, pres. med. staff, 1973; mem. staff St. Joseph Hosp.; cons. orthopedics Richards Med. Co., 1983—; mem. staff LeBonheur Children's Hosp. (trustee 1968-71); cons. staff Meth. Hosp. Program; chmn. 2d Tenn. Conf. Handicapped Children, 1958; chmn. med. div. United Fund Shelby County, 1961, mem. budget com., 1963-65; dir. at large Nat. Assn. Blue Shield Plans, 1965-70; mem. Gov. Tenn. Adv. Bd. Crippled Children's Service, 1961-77, chmn., 1967-77; mem. exec. com. Am. Bd. Med. Specialties, 1980-83; mem. Tenn. Bd. Med. Examiners, 1981—. Contbr. to books. Bd. dirs. Front St. Theatre, Memphis, 1963-64. Served to maj. M.C., AUS, 1942-46. Mem. Am. Acad. Orthopaedic Surgeons (chmn. program com. 1954, 71, mem. manpower com. 1974-81), Am. Orthopaedic Assn. (chmn. program com., pres. 1973), Central Orthopaedic Club (charter), Tenn. Orthopaedic Soc. (pres. 1963-64), Willis C. Campbell Club (pres. 1967), Internat. Soc. Orthopaedics and Traumatology, Am. Acad. Cerebral Palsy (chmn. program com. 1955, publs. com. 1957, exec. com. 1958, pres. 1958-59), ACS (mem. grad. edn. com. 1974-76), AMA (ho. of dels. 1961-64, trustee 1964-70, sec. treas. 1968-70, sec. bd. trustees 1968-70), So. Med. Assn., Tenn. Med. Assn., Memphis and Shelby County Med. Soc. (pres. 1962, bd. censors 1963-65, ho. of dels. 1965), Nat. Acad. Sci. Inst. Medicine (council 1972-75), Memphis Ind. Practice Assn. (med. dir. 1983—), U.S. C. of C. Methodist (ofcl. bd. 1952—, vice chmn. ofcl. bd. 1965, 66, 69, 70, chmn. 1971-72, gen. chmn. every mem. canvass 1955-57, 63, pres. men's club 1958, sec. stewardship 1964-65). Home: 190 Belle Meade Ln Memphis TN 38117 Office: Campbell Clinic 869 Madison Ave Memphis TN 38173

INGRAM, CONLEY, lawyer; b. Dublin, Ga., Sept. 27, 1930; s. George Conley and Nancy Averett (Whitehurst) I.; m. Sylvia Williams, July 26, 1952; children: Sylvia Lark, Nancy Randolph, George Conley. A.B., Emory U., 1949, LL.B., 1951. Bar: Ga. 1952. City atty., Smyrna, Ga., 1958-64, Kennesaw, Ga., 1964; judge Cobb County Juvenile Ct., 1960-64, Superior Ct., Cobb Jud. Circuit, 1964-68; asso. justice Supreme Ct. Ga., 1973-77; partner firm Alston, Miller and Gaines, Atlanta, 1977—. Vice-chmn. bd. trustees Agnes Scott Coll.; bd. visitors Emory U.; chmn. council Emory U. Law Sch. Served with AUS, 1952-54. Recipient Distinguished Service award Kennesaw Mountain Jaycees, 1961, Ga. Jaycees, 1961; Distinguished Citizen award City of Marietta, Ga., 1973; hon. life mem. Ga. PTA. Fellow Am. Bar Found., Internat. Soc. Barristers; mem. Am., Ga. bar assns., Lawyers Club Atlanta, Assn. Trial Lawyers Am., Old War Horse Lawyers Club, Am. Law Inst., Cobb County C. of C. (past pres., Pub. Service award 1970). Democrat. Methodist. Club: Commerce (Atlanta). Address: 540 Hickory Dr Marietta GA 30064

INGRAM, DENNY OUZTS, JR., laywer; b. Kirbyville, Tex., Mar. 23, 1929; s. Denny Ouzts and Grace Bertha (Smith) I.; m. Ann Elizabeth Rees, July 11, 1952; children: Scott Rees, Stuart Tillman. B.A., U. Tex., 1955, J.D. with honors, 1957. Bar: Tex. 1956, N.Mex. 1967, Utah 1968. Editor Kirbyville Banner, 1949-50; mem. Tex. Ho. of Reps., 1951-52; asso. Graves, Dougherty, Gee and Hearon (and predecessors), Austin, Tex., 1957, 59-60, partner, 1961-66; asst. prof. law U. Tex., 1957-59, U. N.Mex., 1966-67; prof. U. Utah, 1968-77; partner McGinnis, Lochridge, and Kilgore, Austin, 1977—; vis. prof. U. Calif., Davis, 1973-74, U. Tex., summers 1968, 75; lectr. in field. Contbr. numerous articles to law revs., chpts. to books; asso. note editor: Tex. Law Rev., 1956-57. Research dir. Utah Constn. Revision Com., 1969-71, 73-74. Served with U.S. Army, 1951-54. Fellow Am. Coll. Probate Counsel, Am. Coll. Tax Counsel, Tex. Bar Found.; mem. Am. Law Inst., Tex. Bar Assn., Utah Bar Assn., N.Mex. Bar Assn., ABA, Chancellors, Order of Coif, Phi Delta Phi. Democrat. Episcopalian. Home: 908 Bluebonnet Ln Austin TX 78704 Office: 900 Congress Ave 5th Floor Austin TX 78701

INGRAM, EDITH JACQUELINE, judge; b. nr. Sparta, Ga., Jan. 16, 1942; d. Robert T. and Katherine (Hunt) I. B.S. in Edn, Fort Valley (Ga.) State Coll., 1963. Tchr. Moore Elementary Sch., Griffin, Ga., 1963-67, Hancock Central Elementary Sch., Sparta, 1967-68; judge Hancock County Ct. of Ordinary, Sparta, 1969—; Mem. Sheriff's Retirement Assn. Ga., Ordinaries Retirement Ga. Mem. Hancock County Democratic Club, 1967—. Recipient Macedonia Inspirational Choir.-pres. plaque for outstanding courage NAACP, 1969; certificate of Merit Booker T. Washington Bus. Coll., 1971; award Augusta Opportunities Industrialization Center, 1974; named Woman of Year Mirror Newspaper, Augusta, Ga., 1973. Mem. Internat. Assn. Probate Judges, Nat. Assn. Probate Judges, Nat. Coll. Probate Judges, Am. Judicature Soc., NAACP, Fort Valley State Coll. Alumni Assn., Delta Sigma Theta. Baptist. Club: Hancock Womens. Home: 503 Augusta Rd Sparta GA 31087 Office: PO Box 151 Sparta GA 31087

INGRAM, GEORGE, JR., business executive; b. Montclair, N.J., Dec. 10, 1920; s. George and Frances Elizabeth (Watts) I.; m. Olive May Holtz, Feb. 15, 1947; children: Patricia (Mrs. S. K. Bone), George III (dec.), Sara, John. B.S., Yale U., 1942; M.S., Stevens Inst. Tech., 1948. Registered profl. indsl. engr., Pa. Indsl. engr. RCA, 1942-45; cons. mgmt. engr. Stevenson, Jordan & Harrison, Inc., N.Y.C., 1945-51; controller Riegel Paper Corp., 1951-57, Raytheon Co., Lexington, Mass., 1957-60, v.p., 1960-61, v.p. fin., 1961-63, sr. v.p., dir., 1963-68; sr. v.p. Champion Internat., Inc., N.Y.C., 1968-69, exec. v.p., 1969-72, dir., 1968-72; pres., chief exec. officer, dir. Reed-Ingram Corp., N.Y.C., 1972-77, cons., 1977-83; pres. Dionis Corp., Nantucket, Mass.; chmn. bd., dir. Deerfield Splty. Papers, Inc., 1973-77, Oneida Packaging Products, Inc., 1973-77, Canadian Glassine Co., Ltd., 1973-77; chmn., sec., dir. Arctos Corp., Quaker Hill, Conn.; pres., treas., dir. Fitchburg Engring. Corp., Mass.; dir. M/A Com, Inc., Burlington, Mass. Trustee Coll. of Wooster, Ohio. Mem. Fin. Execs. Inst. (past pres. Boston; past chmn. nat. com. securities and exchanges regulation), ASME, Phi Gamma Delta. Republican. Episcopalian. Club: Nantucket Yacht. Home and office: 26 Washing Pond Rd PO Box 36 Nantucket MA 02544

INGRAM, JAMES CARLTON, economist, educator; b. Roanoke, Ala., Jan. 11, 1922; s. John Henry and Isabelle (Shanks) I.; m. Alice Jane Graham, May 1, 1948; children: Deborah, Susan, Melissa. B.S., U. Ala., 1942; A.M., Stanford, 1947; Ph.D. (Social Sci. Research Council fellow), Cornell U., 1952. Research analyst Indsl. Indemnity Ins. Co., San Francisco, 1947-48; successively asst. prof., asso. prof., prof. econs. U. N.C., Chapel Hill, 1952—, dean, 1966-69; vis. mem. London Sch. Econs., 1963-64; vis. prof. Thammasat U., Bangkok, Thailand, 1969-71; guest scholar Brookings Instn., 1976. Author: Economic Change in Thailand Since 1850, rev. edit, 1971, Regional Payments Mechanisms, 1962, International Economic Problems, 1966, 3d edit., 1978, International Economics, 1983; Mng. editor: So. Econ. Jour, 1961-65. Served with AUS, 1942-46. Ford Found. fellow, 1963-64. Mem. Am. Econ. Assn., So. Econ. Assn. (mem. exec. com., pres. 1972-73). Home: 1012 Highland Woods Chapel Hill NC 27514

INGRAM, LAWRENCE LEE, newspaper publisher; b. San Antonio, Jan. 27, 1936; s. Louis Lee and Mary Francis (Brasted) I.; m. Joanne Kay MacDonald, June 29, 1962; children: Jill Stacy, Amy Sue, Elizabeth. B.S.M.E., U. Colo., 1964. Registered profl. engr., Colo. Chief supt. Armco Steel, Denver, 1956-58; engr. Army Ballistic Missile Agy., Red Stone Arsenal, Ala., 1958-60; sr. engring. technician Colo. Hwy. Dept., Denver, 1960-62; dir. planning Tech. Service Co., Denver, 1964-71; pres. Aquarius, Inc., Denver, 1971-77; v.p., dir. prodn. N.Y. Daily News, N.Y.C., 1977—. Served with U.S. Army, 1958-60. Republican. Presbyterian. Home: 79 Taconic Rd Millwood NY 10546 Office: New York Daily News 220 E 42d St New York NY 10017

INGRAM, ROBERT PALMER, investment company executive; b. Norfolk, Va., July 21, 1917; s. Robert Palmer and Margaret (Wible) I.; m. Mary Elizabeth Renfro, Sept. 30, 1949; children: Marsha Jill, Robert Palmer III. Student, Washington and Lee U., 1935-36, U. Pitts., 1936-37. Salesman Anchor Hocking Glass Corp., Grand Rapids, Mich., 1943-44, Kansas City, Mo., 1945-46; pres. Robert P. Ingram & Co., Kansas City, 1946—, Tracy Devel. Co., TenMain Center, Mo., 1963—, Ingram Investment Co., 1964—, Econo-Car Rental Co., 1971—, LaSalle Leasing Co., 1971—, Ind. Mag., 1983—, radio stas. KXTR and KBEA, Kansas City, Rigby Corp.; dir. Rubbermaid Inc., Am. Cable TV, Kansas City, Harzfelds Inc., Gilbert & Robinson Inc., Boatmen's Bank & Trust Co., Country Club Bank; met. chmn. Nat. Alliance of Businessmen, 1969. Mem. com. on capital requirements for pub. schs., Kansas City, 1969; chmn. fin. com. Jackson County Republican Party, 1966; trustee U. Mo., Kansas City, Midwest Research Inst.; bd. govs. Starlight Theatre Assn., Kansas City Philharm., Conservatory of Music; bd. dirs. Civic Council of Greater Kansas City. Mem. Kansas City C. of C. (past pres.), Downtown Inc. (pres. 1970-72), Am. Royal Assn. (bd. govs.). Clubs: Kansas City, Carriage (Kansas City). Home: 1055 W 56th Kansas City MO 64113 Office: 800 Argyle Bldg 306 E 12 St Kansas City MO 64106

INGRAM, ROLAND HARRISON, JR., physician, educator; b. Birmingham, Ala., Mar. 10, 1935; s. Roland Harrison and Florence (Emerson) I.; m. Marguerite Lewis Colville, June 25, 1961; 1 dau., Mary Elizabeth. B.S., U. Ala., 1957; M.D. cum laude, Yale U., 1960; M.A., Harvard U., 1980. Intern Peter Bent Brigham Hosp., Boston, 1960-61; resident Barnes Hosp., St. Louis, 1963, 64, Yale U. Med. Center, 1964-65; asst. prof. medicine Emory U. Sch. Medicine, 1968, asso. prof., 1968-70, prof. medicine, 1970-73; asso. prof. medicine Harvard Med. Sch., 1973-79; dir. respiratory div. Brigham and Women's Hosp., Boston, 1973—, Beth Israel Hosp., 1980—; Parker B. Francis prof. medicine Harvard Med. Sch., 1979—. Mem. editorial bds.: New England Jour. of Medicine, 1974-77, Jour. of Applied Physiology, 1978—, Am. Rev. of Respiratory Diseases, 1980—; contbr. numerous articles to profl. jours. Served with USPHS, 1961-63. Recipient Research Career Devel. award Nat. Heart and Lung Inst., 1968-73. Mem. Am. Soc. Clin. Investigation, Assn. Am. Physicians, Am. Coll. Physicians, Am. Physiol. Soc., Am. Thoracic Soc., Phi Beta Kappa, Alpha Omega Alpha. Home: 206 Waban Ave Waban MA 02168 Office: 75 Francis St Boston MA 02115

INGRAM, ROY LEE, geologist, educator; b. Mamers, N.C., Mar. 21, 1921; s. Byron Perry and Berlena (McLean) I.; m. Jacqueline Sparks, June 5, 1944; children—Keith Sparks, Karen Ann. B.S., U. N.C., 1941; M.S., U. Okla., 1943; Ph.D., U. Wis., 1948. Asst. prof. U. N.C., Chapel Hill, 1947-51, asso. prof., 1951-57, prof., 1957—, chmn. dept. geology, 1957-64, 74-79; Cons. geologist; mem. N.C. Earth Resources Council, 1974—. Contbr. articles to profl. jours. Served to capt. USAAF, 1943-46. Mem. Geol. Soc. Am. (pres. Southeastern sect. 1958), Nat. Assn. Geology Tchrs. (treas. 1965-68), Am. Assn. Petroleum Geologists, Am. Inst. Profl. Geologists, Clay Minerals Soc., Internat. Assn. Sedimentologists, Phi Beta Kappa. Home: 601 Oteys Rd Chapel Hill NC 27514 Office: Dept Geology U NC Chapel Hill NC 27514

INGRAM, SAM HARRIS, univ. pres.; b. Acton, Tenn., Jan. 31, 1928; s. J. Quinn and Lois (Abernathy) I.; m. Betty White; children—Sam W., Glenn D. B.S. in Social Sci, Bethel Coll., 1951; M.A., Memphis State Coll., 1953; Ed.D., U. Tenn., Knoxville, 1959. Elementary and high sch. prin., McNairy County, Tenn., 1949-57; supr. curriculum Tenn. Dept. Edn., 1959-62; asst. prof. edn. Memphis State U., 1962; chmn. edn. dept. Middle Tenn. State U., 1962-67, dean, 1967-69; pres. Motlow State Community Coll., 1969-75; commr. edn., State of Tenn., Nashville, 1975-79; pres. Middle Tenn. State U., Murfreesboro, 1979—. Trustee Bethel Coll. Served with USMCR. Mem. Nat., Tenn. edn. assns., Council Chief State Sch. Officers, Edn. Commn. States, Tenn. Assn. Supervision and Curriculum Devel., Tenn. Curriculum Com. (past pres.), Tenn. Profs. Ednl. Adminstrn. (past pres.). Home: 212 N Tennessee Blvd Murfreesboro TN 37132 Office: Middle Tenn State U Murfreesboro TN 37132

INGRAM, WILLIAM AUSTIN, federal judge; b. Jeffersonville, Ind., July 6, 1924; s. William Austin and Marion (Lane) I.; m. Barbara Brown Lender, Sept. 18, 1947; children: Mary Ingram Mac Calla, Claudia, Betsy Ingram Friebel. Student, Stanford U., 1947; LL.B., U. Louisville, 1950. Assoc., Littler, Coakley, Lauritzen & Ferdon, San Francisco, 1951-55; dep. dist. atty., Santa Clara (Calif.) County, 1955-57; mem. firm Rankin, O'Neal, Luckhardt & Center, San Jose, Calif., 1955-69; judge Municipal Ct., Palo Alto-Mountain View, Calif., 1969-71, Calif. Superior Ct., 1971-76, U.S. Dist. Ct. No. Dist. Calif., San Francisco, 1976—. Served with USMCR, 1943-46. Fellow Am. Coll. Trial Lawyers. Republican. Episcopalian. Home: 1211 College Ave Palo Alto CA 94306 Office: 280 S 1st St San Jose CA 95113

INGRAM, WILLIAM TRUITT, sanitary engineer, educator; b. Cleves, O., June 16, 1908; s. Frank and Grace Lillian (Truitt) I.; m. Margaret B. Nelson, 1932; children—Beryl (Mrs. Jon V. Nielsen), Judith (Mrs. John F. Nelson), John E., Diane F.; m. Filomena T. Lioy., Apr. 19, 1958. B.A., Stanford, 1930; M.P.H., Johns Hopkins, 1942. Diplomate: Am. Acad. Environ. Engrs. Office engr. Pacific Gas & Electric Co., San Francisco, 1930-32; recorder U.S. Coast and Geodetic Survey, 1932-33; regional surveyor, supr. Fed. and State Mosquito Control, So. Cal. region, 1933-34; asst. county dir. Cal. Relief Adminstrn., 1934; san. engr. San Joaquin Local Health Dist., 1935-41; regional water works adviser Cal. Bur. San Engring., 1942; asst. regional san. engr. Office Civil Def., 9th region USPHS, 1942-44; camp san. engr. War Refugee Camps Middle East, Brit. Army, USPHS, UNRRA, 1943-44; chief engr. health div. UNRRA, Jugoslav Mission, 1944-46; engring, field asso. Am. Pub. Health Assn., 1947-49; asso. prof. pub. health engring. N.Y. U. Coll. Engring., 1949-54, adj. prof., 1954-73, Poly. Inst. N.Y., 1973—; cons., 1947—; vis. prof. preventive med. div. Cornell U. Coll. Medicine, 1956-76; lectr. Columbia Sch. Pub. Health; owner Wm. T. Ingram. (cons. engr.); pres. Newing Labs., Inc.; Mem. Chmn. Engring. Found. Coordinating Com. Air Pollution Research, 1960-67. Author: The Proposed Sanitary Code- Part III, 1949; chmn. joint editorial bd.: Revision Glossary Water and Wastewater Control Engring., 1962-76; Contbr. to books, also articles to tech. jours.; mem. joint editorial bd.: Revision Glossary Water and Wastewater Control Engring., 1977-81. Recipient Kenneth Allen Meml. award., 1960, Milton T. Hill award, 1976. Fellow Am. Pub. Health Assn., A.A.A.S., Am. Soc. C.E. (chmn. research council air resource engring. 1961-73), Am. Soc. Testing and Materials (2d vice chmn. com. D-22 1973-77, award 1976); mem. Am. Soc. Engring. Edn., Am. Indsl. Hygiene Assn., Air Pollution Control Assn., Inter-Am. Assn. San. Engring., Am. Nat. Standards Inst. (chmn. Z-4 com. 1971-81), Conf. Municipal Pub. Health Engrs., Am. Water Works Assn., Malba Assn. (pres. 1970-72), Sigma Xi. Home: 7 North Dr Whitestone NY 11357 Office: Poly Inst NY 333 Jay St Brooklyn NY 11201 *The baselines of my life were probably influenced most by my father and grandfather. They taught me, sometimes quite forcefully, that dishonesty in thought or action was poor policy; that lying, stealing, and cheating were not acceptable; that I had no primal right to, in, on, or with another person's possessions. Perhaps the essence of that training is in the principle that I must earn any advancement to which I might aspire.*

INGWERSEN, MARTIN LEWIS, shipyard exec.; b. Sandusky, Ohio, Nov. 5, 1919; s. John Christian and Irene Catherine (Hinkey) I.; m. Blanche Robinson, Apr. 26, 1947; children—Brenda, Richard Charles, Martin Lewis. B.S., U. Notre Dame, 1941; postgrad., Western Res. U., 1941, Princeton U., 1943. Asst. to hull supt. Gt. Lakes Engring. Works, Ashtabula, Ohio, 1941-43, asst. supt., 1946-49; supt. Buffalo plant Am. Ship Bldg. Co., 1948-50, mgr. plant, Toledo, 1950-52, Lorain, Ohio, 1952-53, v.p. ops., 1954-58; also dir.; v.p., works mgr. Ingalls Shipbldg. Corp., Pascagoula, Miss., 1958-65, v.p. ops., 1965-67; pres. Md. Shipbldg. & Drydock Co., Balt., 1967-68; also dir.; exec. v.p. Lockheed Shipbldg. and Constrn. Co., Seattle, 1968-73, pres., 1973-76, exec. v.p. office of pres., 1976—, also trustee, 1973—; dir. Puget Sound Bridge & Dry Dock Co., Seattle, Colby Crane & Mfg. Inc., Seattle. Served to lt. USNR, 1943-46. Mem. Am. Bur. Shipping, Seattle C. of C., Western Shipbuilders Assn., Soc. Naval Architects and Marine Engrs., Am. Soc. Naval Engrs., Navy League, Nat. Security Indsl. Assn., Propeller Club U.S., Conf. Bd. Roman Catholic. Club: Notre Dame of Western Wash. Home: 4256 Crestwood Pl Mercer Island WA 98040 Office: 2929 16th Ave SW Seattle WA 98134

INHORN, STANLEY LEE, medical educator; b. Phila., Aug. 1, 1928; s. Charles and Nan (Ostrow) Einhorn; m. Shirley Gertrude Sherburne, Aug. 22, 1954; children—Lowell Frank, Marcia Claire, Roger Charles. B.S., Western Res. U., 1949; M.D., Columbia, 1953. Diplomate: Am.

Bd. Pathology, Nat. Bd. Med. Examiners. Intern U. Wis. Hosp., Madison, 1953-54, resident, 1956-60; mem. faculty Med. Sch. U. Wis., Madison, 1959—, prof. pathology and preventive medicine, 1969—, chmn. dept. pathology, 1978-81; asst. dir. Wis. Lab. Hygiene, Madison, 1960-66, dir., 1966-79, med. dir., 1979—; cons. medicare div. HEW, 1968-69, 73-74, Center Disease Control, 1968-79. Violinist, Madison Symphony Orch., 1967-74. Bd. dirs. Wis. div. Am. Cancer Soc., Wis. Youth Symphony Orch., 1974—. Served with M.C. USNR, 1954-56. Mem. Am. Soc. Clin. Pathologists, Am. Pub. Health Assn., Am. Soc. Cytology. Research in cytogenetics of congenital anomalies, diagnostic lab. practice. Home: 210 Ozark Trail Madison WI 53705

INLOW, EDGAR BURKE, emeritus political science educator; b. Forest Grove, Ore., Dec. 14, 1915; s. Harvey Edgar and Eva Lou (Skaggs) I.; m. Louise Maurer, Oct. 21, 1971; children by previous marriage: Rush, Morgan (Mrs. George Douglas), Gerd, Brand, Shane. A.B., Wash. State U., 1937; M.A., U. Calif., 1939; Ph.D., Johns Hopkins U., 1949; postgrad., Gen. Theol. Sem., N.Y.C., 1950. Instr. Princeton U., 1947-49; ordained to ministry Episcopal Ch., 1950; parish priest, 1950-57, non-stipendiary priest, 1957-81, ret., 1981; tng. officer Def. Dept., Washington, 1957-61; prof. polit. sci. U. Calgary, Alta., Can., 1961-81, chmn. dept., 1961-71, prof. emeritus, 1981—; Project dir. Royal Commn. Health Services Can., 1962-64; cons. Civil Service Commn. Can., 1963; vis. prof. Vanderbilt U., Nashville, 1964-65; lectr. McMaster U., Hamilton, Ont., 1968, St. Paul's U., Japan, 1954, U. Tehran, Iran, 1970, U. Pahlavi, 1970. Author: The Patent Grant, 1949, Studies in Canon Law, 1957, The Health Grant Program in Canada, 1963, The Divine Right of Persian Kings, 1967, ShahanShah, The Monarchy of Iran, 1979; contbr. profl. jours. Served with AUS, 1941-45. Recipient Appreciation certificate Def. Dept., 1961, citation His Imperial Majesty Iran, 1967. Fellow Social Sci. Research Council; mem. Can. Council, Brit. Inst. Persian Studies, SAR (nat. committeeman), Phi Beta Kappa. Address: 2340 Magnolia Blvd W Seattle WA 98199

INMAN, BOBBY RAY, electronics executive; b. Rhonesboro, Tex., Apr. 4, 1931; s. Herman H. and Mertie F. (Hinson) I.; m. Nancy Carolyn Russo, June 14, 1958; children: Thomas, William. B.A., U. Tex., 1950; grad., Nat. War Coll., 1972. Commd. ensign U.S. Navy, 1952, advanced through grades to adm., 1981; asst. naval attache, Stockholm, 1965-67, exec. asst., sr. aide to vice chief naval ops., Washington, 1972-73, asst. chief staff intelligence on staff comdr. in chief U.S. Pacific Fleet, 1973-74; dir. Naval intelligence Dept. Navy, Washington, 1974-76; vice dir. Def. Intelligence Agy., 1976-77; dir. Nat. Security Agy., Ft. Meade, Md., 1977-81; dep. dir. CIA, 1981-82; chmn., pres., chief exec. officer Microelectronics and Computer Tech. Corp., Austin, Tex., 1983—. Decorated Def. D.S.M., Navy D.S.M., Legion of Merit, Def. Superior Service medal, Meritorious Service medal, Nat. Security medal, Joint Services Commendation medal. Office: 9430 Research Blvd Austin TX 78759

INMAN, FRANKLIN POPE, JR., biochemist, educator; b. Hamlet, N.C., Aug. 2, 1937; s. Franklin P. and Aieleen (Shelton) I.; m. Barbara Jean Bullock, Aug. 30, 1959; children: Jody Lin, James Walter. A.B. in Chemistry, U. N.C., 1959, Ph.D., 1964. Research assoc. dept. microbiology U. Ill.-Urbana, 1964-66; asst. prof. microbiology U. Ga., Athens, 1966-70, asst. prof. biochemistry, 1966-70, asso. prof. biochemistry, 1970-75, asso. prof. microbiology, 1970-75, prof. biochemistry, 1975-77, prof. microbiology, 1975-77; vis. lectr. immunology Harvard Med. Sch., Boston, 1975-76; prof., chmn. dept. biochemistry East Tenn. State U., Quillen-Dishner Coll. Medicine, Johnson City, 1977—. Contbr. numerous articles on immunology and biochemistry to sci. jours.; editorial bd.: Infection and Immunity, 1977-79; gen. editor: Contemporary Topics in Immunochemistry, 1970-72, Contemporary Topics in Molecular Immunology, 1973—. Bd. dirs. Forest Heights Pool, 1968-72. Recipient M.G. Michael award U. Ga., 1969; Am. Cancer Soc. scholar, 1976; John M. Morehead scholar, 1955-59. Mem. Am. Soc. Microbiology, Am. Soc. Biol. Chemists, Am. Assn. Immunologists, Am. Chem. Soc., N.Y. Acad. Scis., Assn. Med. Sch. Depts. Biochemistry, Sigma Xi. Home: 707 Willmar St Johnson City TN 37601 Office: Dept Biochemistry Quillen-Dishner Coll Medicine PO Box 19930A East Tenn State Univ Johnson City TN 37614

INMAN, ROSS BANKS, educator; b. Adelaide, Soth Australia, Nov. 4, 1931; came to U.S., 1960, naturalized, 1981; s. Douglas Keith and Vera Olive (Abbottomey) I.; m. Beverly; children—Andrew, David, Colleen. B.Sc., U. Adelaide, 1956, 1957, Ph.D., 1960. Research fellow Stanford Med. Sch., 1960-65; sr. research fellow U. Adelaide, 1965-67; prof. dept. biochemistry U. Wis., Madison, 1967—. Contbr. articles to profl. jours. Grantee in field. Home: 3918 Priscilla Ln Madison WI 53706 Office: 1525 Linden Dr Madison WI 53705

INMAN, STUART K., professional basketball team executive; m. Elinor Inman; children: Nancy, Sandy, Janice, Carol, David. B.S., San Jose State U., 1950. Basketball coach San Jose State U., Calif., 1957-66; with Portland Trailblazers, NBA, Oreg., 1970—, now gen. mgr., Oreg. Office: Portland Trailblazers 700 NE Multnomah St Lloyd Bldg Suite 950 Portland OR 97232

INMAN, WILLIAM PETER, financial consultant; b. Cleve., June 29, 1936; s. James B. and Lillian (Frances) I.; m. Marlene Joyce Miller, Mar. 30, 1963; children: William Peter, Elizabeth, David. Student, Miami U., 1954-55; B.A., Ohio State U., 1958; J.D., Case Western Res. U., 1960, M.B.A., 1966. Bar: Ohio 1960. Tax accountant U.S. Steel Corp., Cleve., 1960-63; asso. trust counsel Central Nat. Bank of Cleve., 1963-66; atty. Sherwin-Williams Co., Cleve., 1966-67, tax counsel, 1967, mgr. tax dept., 1967-68, corporate dir. taxes, 1968-69, asst. sec., dir. taxes, 1969-71, sec., dir. taxes, 1971-75, v.p., sec., asst. treas., 1975-78, v.p., treas., chief fin. officer, 1978-80; v.p. fin., chief fin. officer RTE Corp., Waukesha, Wis., 1980-83; v.p. fin., chief fin. officer, gen. counsel S&B Industries, Inc., Houston, 1983-84; fin. cons., Houston, 1984—. Mem. Greater Cleve. Growth Assn., 1969—; Trustee Ohio Pub. Expenditure Council, 1969—, v.p., 1970-73, pres., 1973-75, chmn. bd., 1975-77. Mem. Am. Soc. Corporate Secs., Fin. Execs. Inst., Cleve. Treasurers Club, N.A.M., Ohio Mfrs. Assn., Am., Ohio, Greater Cleve. bar assns., Estate Planning Council of Cleve., Phi Delta Phi, Beta Gamma Sigma, Beta Alpha Psi. Home: 15806 Parksley Dr Houston TX 77059 Office: 1010 Lamar St Suite 350 Houston TX 77002

INNAURATO, ALBERT, playwright; b. Phila., June 2, 1947; s. Albert and Mary (Walker) I. B.F.A., Calif. Inst. Arts, Los Angeles, 1972; M.F.A., Yale U., 1975. Playwright in residence Playwright's Horizons, N.Y.C., 1983, Pub. Theatre, 1977, Circle Repertory Theatre, 1979. Author: plays Earthworms, 1974, Gemini, 1977 (Obie award 1977), The Transfiguration of Benno Blimpie, 1977 (Obie award), Passione, 1980. Guggenheim grantee, 1976; Rockefeller grantee, 1977. Mem. Dramatists Guild, Writers Guild Am. Home: 325 W 22d St New York NY 10011 Office: William Morris Agy-George Lane 1350 Ave of the Americas New York NY 10019

INNERST, PRESTON EUGENE, journalist; b. York, Pa., Apr. 1, 1927; s. Morgan C. and Edna L. I.; m. Carol Jean McCleary, Sept. 25, 1966; children: Robert, Carol, Preston Eugene, Christine. Ed., Gettysburg (Pa.) Coll. With Gazette and Daily, York, 1943-64, city editor, 1956, 60-64; with Phila. Inquirer, 1964-70, night city editor, 1968-70; with Phila. Bull., 1970-82, asst. mng. editor, 1977-78, mng. editor/night, 1978-82; asst. mng. editor Washington Times, 1982—. Served with USMC, 1945-46. Mem. AP Mng. Editors Assn., Pa. Soc. Newspaper Editors. Office: Washington Times 3600 New York Ave NE Washington DC 20002

INNES, JOHN PHYTHIAN, II, aircraft manufacturing company executive; b. Indpls., Feb. 26, 1934; s. John Phythian and Eleanor (Tilton) I.; m. Marianne Berger, Oct. 29, 1966; children: Valerie Alexandra, James Walker, John Phythian. B.A., William Coll., 1955; J.D., Temple U., 1971. Bar: Pa. 1971, N.Y. 1973; Airline transport rated pilot. Commd. ensign U.S. Navy, 1955, advanced through grades to lt. comdr., 1966; served in, Vietnam, ret., 1966; with U.S. Steel Co., 1966-68; atty. Asso. Aviation Underwriters, N.Y.C., 1971-73; asso. firm Speiser & Krause, N.Y.C., 1973-76; sec., gen. counsel Gulfstream Aero Corp., Savannah, Ga., 1976—; dir. Chatham Travel Corp. Mem. Weston (Conn.) Police Commn., 1974. Mem. Assn. Bar City N.Y., Am. Bar Assn., Gen. Aircraft Mfrs. Assn. Episcopalian. Club: Marshwood at the Landings. Home: 3 Barnwell Ln Savannah GA 31411 Office: PO Box 2206 Savannah GA 31402

INNIS, DONALD QUAYLE, educator, geographer; b. Toronto, Can., Apr. 21, 1924; came to U.S., 1963; s. Harold Adams and Mary (Quayle) I.; m. Janet Marion Graham, 1949 (div. 1966); children: Mary Graham, John William; m. Winifred Norton Huggins, 1969; 1 dau., Katherine Anne. B.A. with honors, U. Toronto, 1947; Ph.D., U. Calif. at Berkeley, 1959. Instr. U. Chgo., 1948-50, U. Western Ont., 1952-53; instr., then asst. prof. Queen's U., Kingston, Ont., 1953-63; mem. faculty State U. N.Y. at Geneseo, 1963—, prof. geography, chmn. dept., 1965—, chmn. faculty senate, 1974-75; Chmn. Kingston br. African Students Found., 1962-63. Author: Canada: A Geographic Study, 1966, 21 Days on Spacecraft Earth, 1983. Recipient Chancellor's award SUNY, 1979. Mem. Canadian Assn. Geographers, Assn. Am. Geographers, Am. Geog. Soc., United Univ. Profs. (pres. chpt. 1976-77). Research small farm agr. in Jamaica and India, also on radio and TV. Office: Dept Geography SUNY Geneseo NY 14454

INNIS, ROBERT CECIL, research pilot; b. Red Bluff, Calif., Dec. 9, 1926; s. Cecil Robert and Violet May (McEwen) I.; m. Joan Ann Powell, June 15, 1956; children—Robin Lynn, Robert Charles. Student, Coll. of Pacific, 1944-45; A.B., U. Calif., 1951. Aero. research pilot NACA, Ames Aero. Lab., Moffett Field, Calif., 1953-58; aerospace research scientist and pilot NASA, Ames Research Center, Moffett Field, Calif., 1958-64, chief flight ops., 1964—. Served with USNR, 1944-49, 52-53. Decorated Air medal (4); recipient Octave Chanute award Am. Inst. Aeros. and Astronautics, 1964. Fellow Soc. Exptl. Test Pilots. Home: 317 Montclair Dr Santa Clara CA 95051 Office: NASA Ames Research Center Moffett Field CA 94035

INNIS, ROY EMILE ALFREDO, organization official; b. St. Croix, V.I., June 6, 1934; s. Alexander and Georgianna (Thomas) I.; m. Doris Valdena Funnye, Feb. 13, 1965; children: Alexander, Cedric, Patricia, Corinne, Kwame Niger, Kimathi. Student, CCNY, 1953-58. Chem. technician Vick Chem. Co., 1961-63; research asst. cardiovascular research labs. Montefiore Hosp., 1963-67; mem. CORE, 1963—, edn. chmn. Harlem group, 1964-68, chmn., 1965-68, 2d nat. vice chmn., 1967-68, asso. nat. dir., 1968, nat. dir., 1968—; founder CORE Community Sch., Bronx, N.Y., 1977; exec. dir. Harlem Commonwealth Council, 1967-68; 1st ofcl. N.Am. del. Orgn. African Unity, Ethiopia, 1973, Uganda, 1975. Contbr.: chpt. to The Endless Crisis, 1973, Black Economic Development, 1970; pub.: Profiles in Black, 1976. Served with AUS, 1950-52. Research fellow Met. Applied Research Center, 1967. Home: 800 Riverside Dr New York NY 10032 Office: 1916 Park Ave New York NY 10037

INNS, GORDON ELLIS, telecommunications company executive; b. Wiarton, Ont., Can., Feb. 27, 1926; s. Thomas Henry and Eleanor (Ellis) I.; m. Mary Gwendolyn Dobbie, June 17, 1950; children: Rebecca, Susan, Sandra, Bruce, Gail, David. B.Applied Sci., U. Toronto, 1948. Chief engr. toll area Bell Canada, Montreal, Que., 1966-68, Ottawa, 1968-69, v.p. engring. and planning, Montreal, 1969-71, v.p. computer communications, 1971-74, exec. v.p. Ont. region, Toronto, 1974-80, exec. v.p. mktg., 1980-83; exec. v.p. planning Bell Canada Enterprises, Inc., 1983—; chmn. engring. com. Trans Canada Telephone System, 1966-69, mem. bd. mgmt., 1974-78, 80-83; dir. Bell No. Research, Ottawa; dir., chmn. Bell Communications Systems, Inc.; dir. Bell Can. Internat., Tele-Direct (Canada) Ltd., Nfld. Telephone Co.; mem. Toronto Bd. Trade. Bd. dirs. Jr. Achievement Can.; bd. govs. Ryerson Poly. Inst. Served with Can. Army, 1943-45. Recipient Engring. medal Council Assn. Profl. Engrs. Province Ont., 1977. Fellow Engring. Inst. Can.; mem. IEEE (sr.), Assn. Profl. Engrs. Ont. Anglican. Clubs: Toronto, Donalda, Canadian (Toronto). Home: 39 Longwood Dr Don Mills ON M3B 1T9 Canada Office: PO Box 188 First Canadian Pl 100 King St W Suite 6900 Toronto ON Canada M5X 1A6

INOUYE, DANIEL KEN, U.S. senator; b. Honolulu, Sept. 7, 1924; s. Hyotaro I. and Kame Imanaga; m. Margaret Shinobu Awamura, June 12, 1949; 1 son, Daniel Ken. A.B., U. Hawaii, 1950; J.D., George Washington U., 1952. Jr. asst. pub. prosecutor, Honolulu, 1953-54, practice of law, 1954—; majority leader Territorial Ho. of Reps., 1954-58, Senate, 1958-59; mem. 86th-87th U.S. congresses from, Hawaii, U.S. Senate from, 1963—; sec. Senate Democratic Conf.; mem. Dem. Policy Com., Dem. Steering Com., Senate Com. on Appropriations; ranking mem. subcom. fgn. ops., mem. Commerce Com.; ranking mem. subcom. mcht. marine and tourism, chmn. Select Com. on Intelligence, 1976-77, ranking mem. subcom. budget authorizations, 1979—; mem. Select Com. Indian Affairs, Select Com. on Presdl. Campaign Activities, 1973-74; Dir. Central Pacific Bank. Author: Journey to Washington. Active YMCA, Boy Scouts Am. Keynoter; temporary chmn. Dem. Nat. Conv., 1968, rules com. chmn., 1980. Served from pvt. to capt. AUS, 1943-47. Decorated D.S.C., Bronze Star, Purple Heart with cluster; named 1 of 10 Outstanding Young Men of Yr. U.S. Jr. C. of C., 1960; recipient Alumnus of Yr. award George Washington U., 1961; Splendid Am. award Thomas A. Dooley Found., 1967; Golden Plate award Am. Acad. Achievement, 1968. Mem. D.A.V. (past comdr. Hawaii), Honolulu C. of C., Am. Legion (Nat. Comdr.'s award 1973). Methodist. Clubs: Lion., 442d Veterans (Hawaii). Home: 469 Ena Rd Honolulu HI 96814 Office: 722 Hart Senate Office Bldg Washington DC 20510 *

INSKEEP, GORDON CHARLES, educator; b. Bellefontaine, Ohio, Feb. 9, 1922; s. Clair Allen and Alleen (Chapman) I.; m. Cora Glasner Ryerson, Dec. 29, 1951; children—Robert, Ann Elizabeth. B. Chem. Engring., Ohio State U., 1943; Ph.D., Columbia U., 1967. Registered profl. engr., Ohio; cert. compensation profl. Supr. Comml. Solvents Corp., Terre Haute, Ind., Peoria, Ill., 1944-50; asso. editor Chem. and Engring. News, Chgo., London and N.Y.C., 1950-56; asst. to pres. Processes Research, Inc., N.Y.C., 1956-58; dir. tech. planning St. Regis Paper Co., N.Y.C., 1959-68; dir. Center for Exec. Devel., Tempe, Ariz., 1968-69; asso. prof. mgmt. Ariz. State U., Tempe, 1969-74, prof., 1974—. Mem. Acad. Mgmt., Am. Compensation Assn., Am. Chem. Soc., Am. Inst. Chem. Engrs., Am. Mgmt. Assn., Phi Delta Theta, Beta Gamma Sigma, Tau Beta Pi. Club: Tempe Racquet and Swim. Home: 621 E Geneva Dr Tempe AZ 85282

INSKEEP, J. JERRY, JR., investment company executive. Pres. Columbia Daily Income Co., Portland, Oreg. Office: Columbia Daily Income Co 1301 SW Fifth Ave Box 1350 Portland OR 97207§

INSKEEP, RICHARD GUY, chemistry educator; b. E. Liberty, Ohio, Mar. 11, 1923; s. Guy Hamilton and Crete (Riley) I.; m. Margaret Anne Lynch, Dec. 28, 1951. B.A., Miami U., Oxford, Ohio, 1944; M.S., U. Ill., 1947, Ph.D., 1949. Research fellow U. Minn., 1949-51; instr. Brown U., 1951-53; asst. prof., then asso. prof. U. Vt., 1953-61; asso. prof. U. Hawaii, 1961-65, prof. chemistry, 1965—, chmn. dept., 1962-71; vis. prof. chemistry U. B.C., Can., 1974-75; vis. scholar Stanford U., 1982-83. Served with USNR, 1944-45. NSF sci. faculty fellow Tech. U. Denmark, 1958-59. Mem. Am. Chem. Soc. (chmn. Hawaii 1963-64, nat. councillor 1968-71, 75-78). Home: 1667 Kanalui St Honolulu HI 96816

INSKO, CHESTER ARTHUR, JR., psychologist; b. Augusta, Ky., June 20, 1935; s. Chester A. and Elizabeth A. (Matthews) I.; m. Verla Mae Clemens, Nov. 18, 1961; children: Erik K., Kurt B. A.B. in Philosophy, U. Calif.-Berkeley, 1957, Ph.D. in Psychology, 1963; M.A., Boston U., 1958. Tchr., research asst. dept. psychology U. Calif., Berkeley, 1958-62; asst. prof. psychology U. Hawaii, Honolulu, 1963-65, U. N.C., Chapel Hill, 1965-68, assoc. prof., 1968-72, prof., 1972—, dir. grad. studies, 1971-74, dir. social psychology program, 1974-75. Author: Theories of Attitude Change, 1967, (with D.W. Schoeninger) Introductory Statistics for the Behavioral Sciences, 1971; Workbook to Accompany Introductory Statistics for the Behavioral Sciences, 1971; Introductory Statistics for Psychology, 1977, (with J. Schopler) Expermental Social Psychology, 1972; contbr numerous articles to profl. jours. Fellow Am. Psychol. Assn.; mem. Soc. Exptl. Social Psychology. Democrat. Home: 610 Surry Rd Chapel Hill NC 27514 Office: U NC 309 Davie Hall Chapel Hill NC 27514

INSLER, STANLEY, educator; b. N.Y.C., June 23, 1937. A.B., Columbia Coll., 1957; postgrad., U. Tubingen, 1960-62; Ph.D., Yale U., 1963. Mem. faculty Grad. Sch., Yale U., 1963—, now prof. Sanskrit, chmn. dept. linguistics; cons. NEH. Contbr. numerous articles on ancient langs. and lits. of India and Iran to profl. publs. Recipient fellowships Ford Found., Woodrow Wilson Found., Yale U. Mem. Am. Oriental Soc. (treas.), Deutsche Morgenlandische Gesellschaft, Lingistic Soc. Am., Royal Asiatic Soc. Gt. Brit. and Ireland, Societe Asiatique. Office: 317 HGS Yale U New Haven CT 06520

INSLEY, WILL, artist; b. Indpls., Oct. 15, 1929; s. Francis Henry and Lois (Wishard) I. B.A., Amherst Coll., 1951; B.Arch., Harvard, 1955. Lectr. dept. art U. N.C., 1967-68; vis. critic Cornell U., 1969; instr. Sch. Visual Arts, N.Y.C., 1969—. One man shows, Amherst Coll., 1951, Stable Gallery, N.Y.C., 1965, 66, 67, 68, Oberlin (Ohio) Coll., 1967, Weatherspoon Gallery, U. N.C., Walker Art Center, Mpls., 1968, Albright-Knox Gallery, Buffalo, N.Y., Inst. Contemporary Art, U. Pa., 1969, John Gibson Comms., N.Y.C., Mus. Modern Art, N.Y.C., 1970, Paul Maenz, Cologne, Germany, 1972, Visual Arts Gallery, N.Y.C., Fischbach Gallery, 1973, 74, 76, Haus Lange Mus., Krefeld, Germany, 1973, Galerie and Edition Annemarie Verna, Zurich, 1974, 76, Wurttembergischer Kunstverein, Stuttgart, Germany, 1974, U. Wis.-Oshkosh, 1975, Ohio State U., Mus. Contemporary Art, Chgo., 1976, Max Protetch Gallery, N.Y.C., 1977, 80, 82, Protetch McIntosh Gallery, Washington, 1977, Galerie Orny, Munich, W.Ger., 1978; exhibited in group shows at, Daniels Gallery, N.Y.C., 1965, Tibor DeNagy Gallery, N.Y.C., Graham Gallery, N.Y.C., Inst. Contemporary Art, Chgo., Kornblee Gallery, N.Y.C., Indiana Artists, Washington, Whitney Mus., N.Y.C., 1965, 67, Grippi & Waddell Gallery, N.Y.C., 1966, Finch Coll., N.Y.C., 1966, 67, Park Pl. Gallery, N.Y.C., 1966, Riverside Mus., N.Y.C., Guggenheim Mus., N.Y.C., Eleanor Rigelhaupt Gallery, Boston, U. Ill., 1967, Mus. Mdse., Phila., Stadler Gallery, Paris, Richard Feigen Gallery, N.Y.C., Waddell Gallery, N.Y.C., Sixth Biennale, San Marino, Italy, Am. Watercolors, Washington, Weatherspoon Gallery, 1967, 68, Aldrich Mus., Ridgefield, Conn., 1968, 82, Des Moines Art Center, 1968, J.L. Hudson Gallery, Detroit, Univ. House, N.Y.C., Friedrich Gallery, Munich, Germany, Friedrich Gallery, New Delhi, India, U. P.R., Inst. Contemporary Art, U. Pa., 1969, 72, 75, 78, 83, John Gibson Commns., N.Y.C., 1969, 70, Ft. Worth Art Mus., 1969, Paula Cooper Gallery, N.Y.C., Leo Castelli Gallery, N.Y.C., Found Maeght, St. Paul de Vence, 1970, Winn Gallery, Austin, Tex., White Mus., Willard Gallery, N.Y.C., 1971, Internat. Art Fair, Berlin, N.Y. Cultural Center, 1972, Fischbach Gallery, 1973, Detroit Inst. Arts, N.Y. Cultural Center, 1974, Akron (Ohio) Inst., Michael Wyman Gallery, Chgo., John F. Kennedy Center, Washington, Mus. Modern Art, Skidmore Coll., 1975, Castelli-Sonnabend Galleries, N.Y.C., Mpls. Mus. Art, Art 6/75, Basle, Switzerland, U. Guelph (Ont.), Corcoran Gallery Art, Washington, 1976, Basle Art Fair, Phila. Coll. Art, Sewall Gallery Rice U., John Gibson Gallery, N.Y.C., Documenta 6, 1977, Neuberger Mus., SUNY-Purchase, 1978, U. N.C., Chapel Hill, 1979, Drawings/Struckres, Inst. Contemporary Art, Boston, 1980, Los Angeles Inst. Contemporary Art, Council Gt. Brit., Hayward Gallery, London, 1980, Rijksmuseum Kröller-Müller, Otterlo, Michael Rea Collection, McIntosh/Drysdale Gallery, Washington, 1980, Tyler Sch. Art Phila., 1981, Louisiana Mus. Modern Art, Denmark, Annemarie Verna, Zurich, 1983, Max Protetch Gallery, N.Y.C., Hirshhorn Mus. and Sculpture Garden, Washington, numerous others; artist in residence, Oberlin Coll., 1966. Served with AUS, 1955-57. Recipient award Nat. Found. on Arts and Humanities, 1967; Guggenheim fellow, 1969. Address: 231 Bowery New York NY 10002

INSOLIA, ANTHONY EDWARD, editor, publishing executive; b. Tuckahoe, N.Y., Feb. 7, 1926; s. Salvatore and Lena I.; m. Joyce Louise Spencer, Aug. 19, 1950; children: Anne Helene Smyers, Janet Spencer Ford, Robert Spencer. B.A., NYU, 1949. Reporter, Yonkers (N.Y.) Daily Times, 1949; Reporter Park Row News Service, N.Y.C., 1950-51, Stamford (Conn.) Advocate, 1951-55; with Newsday Inc., L.I., N.Y., 1955—, mng. editor, 1970-78, editor, sr. v.p., 1978—; juror Pulitzer Prize, 1981, 82. Served with U.S. Army, 1944-46. Recipient 1st Ann. Alumni Achievement award Journalism Dept, NYU, 1982. Mem. Am. Soc. Newspaper Editors, AP Mng. Editors Assn., Inter Am. Press Assn. (dir.), Overseas Press Club. Office: Newsday Long Island NY 11747

INSTONE, FRANK DONALD, food company executive; b. Chgo., May 5, 1919; s. Joseph and Marion I.; m. Margery Snyder, Jan. 1944; children: Diane Bartels, Donald, Debra. Student, Washington U., St. Louis, 1937-40. Regional sales mgr. Richard Scale Co., Cin., 1946-55; sales mgr. packing equipment div. St. Regis Paper Co., Chgo., 1955-57; various managerial and officer positions Toledo Scale Co., 1957-68, v.p., gen. mgr., dir., 1966; v.p. corp. devel. Seaway Food Town, Inc., Maumee, Ohio, 1968-71, exec. v.p., dir., 1971—; dir. U.S. Berkel, Inc. Bd. dirs. Better Bus. Bur., Am. Cancer Soc., Goodwill Industries, Toledo Employers Assn., Toledo Area Govtl. Research Assn., Boys Club Am.; vice chmn. Ohio Retail Council Mchts. Served with USAAF, 1940-45. Mem. Toledo Area C. of C. (dir.). Clubs: Sylvania (Ohio) Country, Toledo, Toledo Yacht, Brandywine Country; Catawba Island (Port Clinton, Ohio). Home: 3416 Corey Rd Toledo OH 43615 Office: 1020 Ford St Maumee OH 43537

INSTONE, JOHN CLIFFORD, manufacturing company executive; b. Phila., Mar. 5, 1924; s. John Leonard and Anna Lena I.; m. Mary Elizabeth Ketchell, Feb. 12, 1949; children: Linda Jane, John Clifford.

B.S. in Mech. Engring., Drexel U., Phila., 1947. Engr., Proctor Electric Co., Phila., 1947-49; mfg. engr. IRC, Phila., 1949-51; div. gen. mgr. Proctor-Silex Corp. (div. SCM Corp.), Phila. and Mt. Airy, N.C., 1951-60; with SGL Industries Inc., Haddonfield, N.J., 1960—, pres., chief exec. officer, 1979—; also dir.; chmn. bd. B&S Screw Machine Products Inc., Phila., 1979—, also dir.; chmn. bd. SGL Homalite Corp., Wilmington, Del., 1979—; pres., dir. SGL Auburn Sparkplug Co., 1979—; dir. numerous SGL subs. Served to 1st lt. AUS, 1943-45. Mem. Am. Mgmt. Assn. Clubs: Rotary, Elks. Patentee electro-mech. mounting device, elec. outlet strip. Home: 465 Pelham Rd Cherry Hill NJ 08034 Office: Three Greentree Ctr Suite 201 Marlton NJ 08053

IONESCO, EUGENE, playwright; b. Nov. 13, 1912; s. Eugene and Marie-Therese I.; m. Rodica Ionesco; 1 dau., Anne-Marie-Therese. License es Lettres, Agrege de Lettres. Formerly lectr., critic, Bucharest. Author: various works written in French (trans. into 40 langs., performed in those langs.), including The Lesson, 1951; The Chairs, 1952, The Bald Prima Donna, 1950, Amedee, 1954, Victims of Duty, 1957, The New Tenant, 1956, Le Rhinocéros, 1959, The Killer, 1962, L'Impromptu de l'Alma, 1962, Present Past-Past Present; autobiography Fragments of a Journal, 1967; A Stroll in the Air, 1962, the Picture, 1962, Chemises de Nuit, 1962, Le roi se meurt, 1963, La Soif et la Faim, 1964; ballet Le Jeune Homme à Marien, 1965; The Hermit, 1974; novel L'homme aux valises, le Formidable bordel at Macbett. Peste, 1967; Jeu de Massacre, 1970, Ce Formidable Bordel, 1973, La Vase, 1973; film Macbett, La soif et la faim; also short stories. Decorated chevalier legion of Honor; recipient Austrian prize for European literature, 1971, Jerusalem prize, 1973; Internat. Writers' fellow Welsh Arts Council, 1973. Mem. Acad. Francaise.

IONESCU TULCEA, CASSIUS, educator, research mathematician; b. Bucharest, Rumania, Oct. 14, 1923; naturalized, 1967; s. Ioan and Ana (Caselli) Ionescu T. M.S., U. Bucarest, 1946; Ph.D., Yale, 1959. Mem. faculty U. Bucarest, 1946-57, asso. prof., 1952-57; research asso. Yale, 1957-59, vis. lectr., 1959-61; asso. prof. U. Pa., 1961-64; prof. U. Ill., Urbana, 1964-66, Northwestern U., 1966—. Author: Hilbert Spaces (in Rumanian), 1956; author: A Book on Casino Craps, 1980; co-author, 1982, Probability Calculus (in Rumanian), 1956, Calculus, 1968, An Introduction to Calculus, 1969, Honors Calculus, 1970, Topics in the Theory of Liftings, 1969, Sets, 1971, Topology, 1971, A Book on Casino Gambling, 1976, A Book on Casino Blackjack, 1982. Recipient Asachi prize Rumanian Acad., 1957; research grantee U.S. Army, 1961—. Mem. Sigma Xi. Office: Lunt Bldg Northwestern U Evanston IL 60201

IORILLO, MARIO ANGELO, lawyer; b. Southington, Conn., July 6, 1939; s. John and Mary Louise (Riccio) I.; m. Barbara Ann Santago, Jan. 6, 1962; children—Jeffrey Mark, Nicole Andrea, Christopher Marc. B.A., Cornell U., 1961; J.D., Harvard, 1964. Bar: Calif. bar 1965. Practiced in, Los Angeles, 1967—, chief dep. dist. atty., Stanislaus County, Calif., 1965-66; partner firm Kinkle, Rodiger, Graf, Dewberry & Spriggs, Los Angeles, 1967-73, Stockdale, Peckham, Estes & Iorillo, 1974-81, Mario A. Iorillo, P.C., 1981—. Active Boy Scouts Am., PTA. Mem. Los Angeles, Am. bar assns., State Bar Calif., Assn. So. Calif. Def. Counsel, Alpha Tau Omega. Clubs: Riviera Country, Los Angeles Athletic. Home: 1400 Jonesboro Dr Los Angeles CA 90049 Office: 3250 Wilshire Blvd Los Angeles CA 90010

IORIO, JOHN ANTHONY, designer women's clothing; b. N.Y.C., Apr. 28, 1938; s. Vito Anthony and Mary (Lombardo) I.; 1 son, Marc Anthony. Designer, Devonbrook Ltd., 1957-68, Adolph Zelinka Co., 1968-70; prin., John Anthony Inc., N.Y.C., 1971—. Recipient Rex award, 1971, 72, 74; Coty award, 1972, 76. Office: 550 7th Ave New York NY 10019 *

IPAKTCHIAN, SIDNEY, banker; b. Iran, Apr. 17, 1933; naturalized, 1967; s. Fathali and Razieh I.; m. Marita R. Rantala, June 11, 1961; children: Christine E., Derek C. B.S., Brigham Young U., 1962. With Security Pacific Nat. Bank, Los Angeles, 1962—, regional v.p., 1974-77, sr. v.p., 1977-82, exec. v.p., 1982—, also div. adminstr. Mem. Am. Bankers Assn. Office: 333 S Hope St Los Angeles CA 90071

IPCAR, DAHLOV, illustrator, painter; b. Windsor, Vt., Nov. 12, 1917; d. William and Marguerite (Thompson) Zorach; m. Adolph Ipcar, Sept. 29, 1936; children: Robert William, Charles. Student, Oberlin Coll., 1933-34; L.H.D. (hon.), U. Maine, 1979, D.F.A., Colby Coll., 1980. Exhibited in one-man shows, Mus. Modern Art, N.Y.C., 1939, Bignou Gallery, N.Y.C., 1940, Passedoit Gallery, N.Y.C., 1943, Phila. Art Alliance, 1944, ACA Gallery, N.Y.C., 1946, Farnsworth Mus., Rockland, Maine, 1949, 56, 79, Wellons Gallery, N.Y.C., 1950, 52, Portland Art Mus., 1959, 63, 70, U. Maine, 1965, 67, 68, 69, 75, Bates Coll., Lewiston, Maine, 1966, 70, 78, Westbrook Coll., (Maine), 1966, Dalzell-Hatfield Galleries, Los Angeles, 1970, Unity (Maine) Coll., 1976, Colby Coll., Waterville, Maine, 1980, group shows, Carnegie Inst., Corcoran Biennial, Pa. and Detroit Ann., Art: USA, Boston Art Festival, Eastern States Exhibit, Silvermine Guild, Portland Art Festival, 5 paintings shown, 14 Outstanding Women Artists, Detroit Inst., 1943, Am. Acad. & Inst. Arts & Letters, 1980; represented in public collections, Met. Mus. Art, N.Y.C., Whitney Mus. Am. Art, N.Y.C., Newark Mus., Bklyn. Mus., Farleigh-Dickinson U., Colby Coll., Bates Coll., Westbrook Coll., U. Maine at Orono and Farmington; executed murals, U.S. P.O., LaFollette, Tenn. and Yukon, Okla., Patten Free Library, Bath, Maine, Sun Savs. and Loan Assn., Auburn, Maine, Kingsfield (Maine) Elem. Sch., Narragansett Elem. Sch., Gorham, Maine, Poland Community Sch. (Maine); Author, illustrator: children's books Animal Hide And Seek, 1947, One Horse Farm, 1950, World Full Of Horses, 1955, The Wonderful Egg, 1958, Ten Big Farms, 1958, Brown Cow Farm, 1959, I Like Animals, 1960, Deep Sea Farm, 1961, Stripes and Spots, 1961, Wild and Tame Animals, 1962, Lobsterman, 1962, Black and White, 1963, I Love My Anteater With An A, 1964, Calico Jungle, 1965, Horses of Long Ago, 1965, Bright Barnyard, 1966, The Song Of The Day Birds and The Night Birds, 1967, Whisperings And Other Things, 1967, Wild Whirlwind, 1968, The Cat At Night, 1969, The Marvelous Merry-Go-Round, 1970, Sir Addlepate And The Unicorn, 1971, The Cat Came Back, 1971, The Biggest Fish in the Sea, 1972, A Flood of Creatures, 1973, The Land of Flowers, 1974, Bug City, 1975, Hard Scrabble Harvest, 1976, Lost and Found, 1981; author: teen-age novels General Felice, 1967, The Warlock of Night, 1969, The Queen of Spells, 1973; adult novel A Dark Horn Blowing, 1978; illustrator: children's picture books The Little Fisherman, 1945, Just Like You, 1946, Good Work, 1958; contbr.: adult short stories to Argosy, Yankee Mag., Tex. Quar. Recipient Maine State award Maine Commn. Arts and Humanities, 1972, Clara A. Haas award Silvermine Guild, 1957, Juror Merit award, Bridgeton, 1973; Deborah Morton award Westbrook Coll., 1978. Subject of USIA film. Home: Star Route 2 Bath ME 04530 *I have lived most of my life on a Maine farm and love the serenity and natural beauty that surrounds me, but my art is done entirely from my imagination. I strive to create my own unique vision of the world. I have come to feel that the reality created by the artist is more important than actual reality.*

IPPEN, ERICH PETER, electrical engineering educator; b. Fountian Hill, Pa., Mar. 29, 1940; s. Authur Thomas and Elisabeth Anne (Wagenplatz) I.; m. Dorothea Ellen Swansen, Sept. 24, 1966; children: Erich Peter, Jason Timothy. S.B., MIT, 1962; M.S., U. Calif.-Berkeley, 1965, Ph.D., 1968. Mem. tech. staff Bell Labs., Holmdel, N.J., 1968-80; vis. prof. MIT, Cambridge, 1977-78, prof. elec. engring., 1980—; cons. Bell Labs., 1981—, Allied Corp., Mt. Bethel, N.J., 1982—. Contbr. articles to profl. jours.; patentee in field. Recipient Edward Longstreth medal Franklin Inst., 1982. Fellow Am. Acad. Arts and Scis., Optical Soc. Am. (R.W. Wood prize 1981), IEEE (Morris E. Leeds award 1983); mem. Am. Phys. Soc., Sigma Xi. Home: 156 School St Belmont MA 02178 Office: MIT 77 Massachusetts Ave Cambridge MA 02139

IPPOLITO, ANGELO, painter, educator; b. S. Arsenio, Italy, Nov. 9, 1922; came to U.S., 1932; s. Arsenio and Margherita (Episcopo) I.; m. Cynthia Hart Durfey, July 21, 1958; children—Jon Cooper, Michael Arsene. Student, Ozenfant Sch. Fine Arts, N.Y.C., 1946-47, Bklyn. Mus. Sch., 1948, Inst. Meschini, Rome, Italy, 1949-50. Tchr. Newark Sch. Fine and Indsl. Art, 1955, Cooper Union, 1956-59, 62-66, Sarah Lawrence Coll., 1957, U. Calif. at Berkeley, 1961-62, Stanford, summer 1961, Mich. State U., summers 1962-63, 65-66, full term, 1966-67, Queens Coll., 1963-64, Silver Mine (Conn.) Coll., 1963-64; prof. painting State U. N.Y., Binghamton, 1971—; vis. critic Yale, 1961. Artist in residence, Yale-Norfolk, Conn., 1957; artist-in-residence Ford Found. grant, Arnot Art Gallery, 1965, Besser Mus., Alpena, Mich., 1968; One-man exhbns. include, Galleria della Rotonda, Bergamo, Italy, 1950, Tanager Gallery, N.Y.C., 1954, 62, Bertha Schaefer Gallery, N.Y.C., 1956, 58, Massillon (Ohio) Mus., 1960, Canton (Ohio) Mus., Cleve. Art Inst., U. Calif. at Berkeley, 1961, H.C.E. Gallery, Provincetown, Mass., Mich. State U., 1962, Grace Borgenicht Gallery, N.Y.C., 1963-64, 67, 72, 75, 77, Arnot Art Gallery, Elmira, N.Y., 1965, Springfield (Ohio) Art Center, 1967, Besser Museum, Albion Coll., Western Mich. U., Grand Valley State Coll., Grand Rapids, Mich., 1971, two-man show, Bolles Gallery, San Francisco, 1962, retrospective exhbn., Univ. Art Gallery, State U. N.Y.-Binghamton, 1975, numerous group exhbns., throughout U.S. and Europe, 1950—, including Carnegie Inst., Pitts. Arts Council, London, Sao Paulo Bieñal, Brazil; represented in permanent collections, Whitney Mus. Am. Art, Munson-William-Proctor Inst., Utica, N.Y., Phillips Gallery, Washington, Massillon Gallery, Chrysler Mus., Sarah Lawrence Coll., Mich. State U., U. Mich., N.Y. U., Mus. Modern Art, N.Y.C., Montreal Trust Co., Can., C.I.T. Bldg., N.Y.C., N.Y. Hilton Collection, Milw. Mus., Norfolk (Va.) Mus. Arts and Scis., New Am. Library, Joseph Hirshhorn collection, U. Ky., Western Mich. U., Kalamazoo, Chase Manhattan Bank, Inst. Internat. Edn., Newberger Collection. Served with AUS, 1943-45. Recipient Tiffany Found. award for painting, 1980; Fulbright fellow, Florence, Italy, 1959. Home: Friendsville Stage Binghamton NY 13903 Office: State U NY at Binghamton Binghamton NY 13901

IPSEN, KENT FORREST, artist; b. Milw., Jan. 4, 1933; s. Victor August and Muriel (White) I.; m. Shyla Mae Fischer, Nov. 7, 1957; children: Vicki Lynn, Steven Jay, Lisa Ann, Laura Kay, Nina Beth. B.S., U. Wis., Milw., 1961, M.S., M.F.A., 1965. Asst. prof. art Mankato (Minn.) State Coll., 1965-68; asso. prof. Chgo. Art Inst., 1968-73; prof. art Sch. Art, Va. Commonwealth U., Richmond, 1973—. Glass sculptor, 1975—, group exhbns. include, Corning (N.Y.) Mus., Vatican Mus., 1978, Wausau (Wis.) Mus. Art, 1979; rep. permanent collections, Corning Mus. Glass, Toledo Mus. Art, Milw. Art Mus., Mus. Contemporary Crafts, N.Y.C., Chgo. Art Inst., Chrysler Mus. Served with AUS, 1954-56. Grantee Nat. Endowment Arts, 1975. Presbyterian. Office: 901 W Franklin St Richmond VA 23220

IQBAL, ZAFAR, biochemist, neurochemist; b. Lucknow, India, July 12, 1946; came to U.S., 1972, naturalized, 1979; s. Shujaat Ali I. and Salena (Begum) Siddiqui; m. Bernida Lucile Jasiewica, Nov. 27, 1974; m. C. Jameel, Jan. 18, 1979; 1 son, Shirin. B.S., Lucknow U., 1961, M.S., 1963, cert. proficiency in French, 1965; Ph.D., All India Inst. Med. Scis., New Dehli, 1971. Jr. research fellow Council Sci. and Indsl. Research, India, 1963-66, research fellow, 1967-68; research scholar Directorate Gen. Health Services, India, 1966-67; asst. research officer Indian Council Med. Research, 1968-71; research assoc. in physiology, investigator Ind. Y. Sch. Medicine, Indpls., 1972—; asst. prof. med. biophysics Ind. U. Sch. Medicine, Indpls., 1977-82, asst. prof. biochemistry, 1979-82; asst. prof. neurology Northwestern U. Sch. Medicine, Chgo., 1982—. Contbg. author: Macromolecules in Storage and Transfer of Biological Information, 1969, Macromolecules and Behavior, 1972, Growth and Development of the Brain, 1975, Mechanism, Regulation and Special Function of Protein Synthesis in the Brain, 1977, Peripheral Neuropathies, 1978, Neurochemistry and Clinical Neurology, 1980, Calcium-Binding Proteins, 1980, Axoplasmic Transport, 1981, Calcium and Cell Function, 1982; editor: Aloplasmic Transport; contbr. articles to profl. jours. Research grantee NIH, 1973-77, Muscular Dystrophy Assn. Am., 1975-77, Am. Cancer Soc., 1979-80, NSF, 1981, Juvenile Diabetes Found., 1981, Am. Diabetes Assn., 1980. Mem. Am. Physiol. Soc., Indian Acad. for Neuroscis., Soc. Biol. Chemists (India), Internat. Brain Research Orgn., Internat. Soc. Neurochemistry, Soc. for Neurosci., Am. Soc. Neurochemistry, AAAS, Ind. Acad. Sci. (chmn. cell biology 1982-83), N.Y. Acad. Scis., Biophys. Soc., Soc. Exptl. Biology and Medicine, Sigma Xi. Office: Med Sci Bldg VA Lakeside Med Ctr Chicago IL 60611

IRANI, RAY R., chemical company executive; b. Beirut, Lebanon, Jan. 15, 1935; came to U.S., 1953, naturalized, 1956; s. Rida and Naz I.; m. Joan D. French; children—Glenn R., Lilliam M., Martin R. B.S. in Chemistry, Am. U. Beirut, 1953; Ph.D. in Phys. Chemistry, U. So. Calif., 1957. Sr. research group leader Monsanto Co., 1957-67; assoc. dir. new products, then dir. research Diamond Shamrock Corp., 1967-73; with Olin Corp., 1973-83, pres. chems. group, 1978-80, corp. pres., dir., Stamford, Conn., 1980-83; exec. v.p. Occidental Petroleum, N.Y.C., 1983—; chmn., chief exec. officer Occidental Chem. Corp., N.Y.C., 1983—. Author. Mem. Soap and Detergent Assn. (dir.), Chem. Mfrs. Assn., Dirs. Ind. Research, Ind. Research Inst. Patentee in field. Office: Occidental Petroleum Corp 10889 Wilshire Blvd Los Angeles CA 90024

IRBY, RICHARD LOGAN, military institute superintendent; b. Blackstone, Va., Feb. 26, 1918; s. William Logan and Emma (Gray) I.; m. Anne Short, Feb. 14, 1942; children: Richard Logan, Debra Anne, William Steed. B.S., Va. Mil. Inst., 1939; grad., Cav. Sch., 1941, Armor Sch., 1948, Command and Gen. Staff Coll., 1954, Army War Coll., 1961; M.A., George Washington U., 1961; LL.D., Washington and Lee U., 1976. Commd. 2d lt. U.S. Army, 1939, advanced through grades to maj. gen., 1965; asst. prof. mil. sci. and tactics Va. Mil. Inst., 1948-50; br. chief G4, Gen. Hdqrs., Far East Command, 1950-51, comdg. officer 2d Bn., 5th Cav. Regt., Korea and Japan, 1951-52, comdg. officer 13th Tank Bn., 1st Armored Div., 1952-53, comdg. officer Combat Command A, 1953, instr. dept. II, Command and Gen. Staff Coll., 1954-57, dep. Tng. Div. G3, 7th U.S. Army, 1957-58, chief Tng. Div. G3, 7th U.S. Army, 1958, comdg. officer Div. Tng., 3d Armored Div., 1958-59, comdg. officer Combat Command A, 1959-60; dep. Material Coordination Div., ODCSOPS, Dept. Army, 1961-62, chief, 1962-63; asst. dir. Orgn. and Tng. Directorate, ODCSOPS and OACSFOR, 1963; planner U.S. Army Element, NATO mil. com. and standing group, 1963-64, asst. chief of staff, exec. officer to U.S. rep., 1964-65; dir. instrn. U.S. Army Armor Sch., 1965-66, dep. asst. comdt., dir. instrn., 1966-67; comdg. gen. Army Tng. Center, Armor, 1967; asst. div. comdr. Airmobile 1st Cav. Div., 1967-68, comdg. gen., 1968, asst. div. comdr., 1968-69; dep. comdg. gen. Army Tng. Center, Inf., Ft. Lewis, 1969, comdg. gen., Ft. Polk, 1969-70, Army Armor Center; comdt. Army Armor Sch., 1970-71; ret., 1971; supt. Va. Mil. Inst., 1971—. Tng. dir. Stonewall Jackson dist. Boys Scouts Am., 1949-50, council mem., Ft. Leavenworth, Kans., 1953-57; mem. Lincoln Trail dist., Ft. Knox, Ky., 1967; mem. exec. bd., mem. bd. counselors Old Ky. Home council, Ft. Knox, 1970—. Decorated D.S.M., Silver Star with oak leaf cluster, Legion of Merit with 3 oak leaf clusters, D.F.C., Bronze Star with V device and 2 oak leaf clusters, Air medal with V device and 54 oak leaf clusters, Joint Service Commendation medal, Army Commendation medal with 2 oak leaf clusters, Combat Inf. badge; Spl. Order of Yun Hui-Cloud and Banner with two clusters, Nationalist China; Nat. Order of Vietnam 5th Class; Gallantry Cross with palm; medal of Honor 1st Class; Mil. Merit Fourragere (Vietnam). Mem. Kappa Alpha. Democrat. Methodist. Address: 800 Bowyer Ln Lexington VA 24450

IRELAND, ANDY, congressman; b. Cin., Aug. 23, 1930; s. Ellsworth Frederick and Dorothy Marie (Poysell) I.; m. Nancy Haydock, Sept. 12, 1981; children: Debbie, Mimi, Drew, Dutch. B.A. in Indsl. Adminstrn, Yale Sch. Engring. Chmn. bd. Barnett Bank of Winter Haven, Cypress Gardens, Auburndale, Fla.; treas. Fla. Bankers Assn.; dir. Jacksonville (Fla.) br. Fed. Res. Bank Atlanta; Fla. state v.p. Am. Bankers Assn.; mem. 95th-97th Congresses from 8th Fla. Dist., 98th Congress from 10th Fla. dist.; public rep. UN, 1981. Mem. Winter Haven City Commn., 1966-68. Mem. Winter Haven Area C. of C. (past pres.), Fla. Soc. D.C. (pres.). Episcopalian. Clubs: Masons, Shriners, Jesters, Elks, Kiwanis, Moose. Office: 2446 Rayburn House Office Bldg Washington DC 20515 *

IRELAND, HERBERT ORIN, educator, engr.; b. Buckley, Ill., June 12, 1919; s. Harvey Glenn and Anna Estella (Perkinson) I.; m. Mary Leota Austin, Mar. 1, 1941; children—Orin Lee, Marin Fae, Jeanne Lu. B.S., U. Ill., 1941, M.S., 1947, Ph.D., 1955. Registered structural and profl. engr., Ill. From research asst. to prof. civil engring. U. Ill., Urbana, 1946-79, emeritus, 1979—; cons. soil mechanics and found. engring., 1946—; mem. U.S. Commn. Large Dams. Contbr.: sect. to Structural Engineering Handbook, 1968; also articles profl. jours. Served from 2d lt. to maj., C.E. AUS, 1941-46. Fellow Am. Soc. C.E., Geol. Soc. Am.; mem. Am. Ry. Engring. Assn., Nat. Council Soil Mechanics and Found. Engring., Sigma Xi, Tau Beta Pi, Chi Epsilon. Methodist. Home: Rural Route 1 Box 185C Gilman IL 60938 Office: Newmark Civil Engring Lab Urbana IL 61801

IRELAND, JAMES DUANE, coal company executive; b. Duluth, Minn., Dec. 1, 1913; s. James Duane and Elizabeth Clark (Ring) Ireland M.; m. Cornelia Wilmot Allen, Nov. 30, 1946; children: James Duane III, Lucy Elizabeth, Cornelia Seward (Mrs. Robert E. Hallinan), George Ring. Student, St. Paul's Sch., 1928-31, Kent Sch., 1931-33, Cornell U., 1933-36. With Hanna Coal Co., 1937-45; pres. Peters Creek Coal Co., Summersville, W.Va., 1947-60; chmn. bd. successor co. Peerless Eagle Coal Co. (became subsidiary St. Joe Minerals Corp. 1975), 1960—, hon. chmn., 1975—; pres., dir. Gauley Mountain Coal Co., 1957-70; chmn. bd. Bratenahl Devel. Corp., Cleve., 1959-70; dir., trustee 1st Union Realty Cleve., 1961—; dir., mem. exec. com. Cleve. Cliffs Iron Co., 1951—, chmn. exec. com., 1980—. Trustee Western Res. Hist. Soc., 1954—, Cleve. Inst. Music, 1954—, Garden Center Cleve., 1958— (hon.; past treas), Boy Scouts Am., 1962—, Cleve. Council of World Affairs, 1958-64, 70-73, 75-81, Cleve. Symphony Orch., 1958—, Cleve. Mus. Art (also mem. accessions com., fin. com.), Cleve. Council Independent Schs., 1967-74, Central Sch. Practical Nursing, University Circle Devel. Found. (also vice chmn. exec. com.), Univ. Hosps., 1971—; trustee Hawken Sch., 1959-75, life trustee, 1975—; trustee, exec. com. Holdon Arboretum; pres., 1972-75; trustee Greater Cleve. Asso. Found., 1962-72, Cleve. Found., 1971-72; trustee, fin. com., sec., vice chmn. exec. com. Cleve. Inst. Art, 1957—; pres. Elizabeth Ring Mather and William Gwinn Mather Fund, 1957—. Mem. Psi Upsilon. Episcopalian (vestryman). Clubs: Union, Chagrin Valley Hunt, Tavern, Kirtland (Cleve.). Home: 2513 Marlboro Rd Cleveland OH 44118 Office: 1558 Union Commerce Bldg Cleveland OH 44115 also

IRELAND, JILL (JILL DOROTHY IRELAND BRONSON), actress; b. London, Eng., Apr. 24, 1941; d. John Alfred and Dorothy Connoll (Eborn) Irel; m. Charles Dennis Bronson, Oct. 5, 1968; children: Paul, Jason, Valentine, Zuleika. Ed. pvt. schs., Eng. Appeared in: films Breakheart Pass, From Noon Till Three, The Valachi Papers, Wild Horses, The Mechanic, Love and Bullets, 1979, Death Wish II, 1982; appeared in: TV series Shane, 1966. Office: care Paul Kohner, Inc 9169 Sunset Blvd Los Angeles CA 90069 *

IRELAND, RALPH LEONARD, dentist, educator; b. Rock Port, Mo., Aug. 3, 1901; s. Leonard Alvin and Clara Agusta (Broughton) I.; m. Marion Ione Becker, June 27, 1935 (dec. Jan. 1972); 1 son, Robert Michael; m. Kathleen T. Von Gillern, Aug. 24, 1973. D.D.S., U. Neb., 1927, B.S., 1929, M.S., 1944. Diplomate: Am. Bd. Pedodontics (sec.-treas.). Practice dentistry, Lincoln, Neb., 1929-36; mem. faculty U. Neb. Coll. of Dentistry, 1936—, prof. pedodontics, 1939—, chmn. dept., 1939-58, dean, 1958-68, dean emeritus, 1968—, dir. postgrad. and grad. courses, 1948—; Cons., staff Children's Meml. Hosp. Omaha, 1949—; cons. VA Hosp., Omaha, Lincoln; spl. cons. USPHS, 1946—. Author: Dentistry for Children Lincoln State Dept. of Health, 1938, rev. edits., 1942, 48; Contbr. articles to profl. jours. Fellow Am. Coll. Dentists; mem. Lincoln Dist., ADA (chmn. nat. bd. dental examiners 1964-66), Neb. Dental Assn. (editor jour. 1972—), Am. Assn. Dental Schs. (pres. 1966), Neb. Soc. Dentistry for Children (past pres.), Am. Acad. Pedodontics (past pres.), Internat. Assn. Dental Research, Sigma Xi, Omicron Kappa Upsilon, Sigma Chi, Xi Psi Phi. Republican. Episcopalian. Home: 3280 S 31st St Lincoln NE 68502 Office: Coll of Dentistry U Neb Lincoln NE 68508

IRELL, LAWRENCE E(LLIOTT), lawyer; b. Boston, Mar. 23, 1912; s. Hyman and Bessie (Shain) I.; m. Elaine Smith, Mar. 26, 1939; children: Stephen Charles, Eugene Harvey, Lauren Catherine; m. Erin Edwards, Jan. 18, 1972. B.A., UCLA, 1932; LL.B., U. So. Calif., 1935; LL.M., Harvard U., 1936. Bar: Calif. 1936. Practiced in, Los Angeles, 1936—; partner firm Berger & Irell, Los Angeles, 1941-49, Irell & Manella, 1949—; lectr. Tax Inst., U. So. Calif., 1950, 55, 59, 61, 64, instr. Law Center, 1951-54; del. Ann. Ccnf. State Bar Dels., 1960, 62-68, 70-72, 74. Bd. dirs. Jewish Centers Assn. Los Angeles, 1943—, pres., 1956-59; bd. dirs. Nat. Jewish Welfare Bd., 1953-64, pres. Western Region, 1953-55; bd. dirs. Reiss-Davis Child Study Center, 1951-58, v.p., 1955-58; bd. dirs. Met. Recreation and Youth Services Planning Council, 1950-68, pres., 1963-66, mem. nat. exec. council, 1972-76, 80-82; vice chmn. exec. bd., chmn. fin. com. So. Calif. chpt. Am. Jewish Com., 1970-72, chmn. fgn. affairs com., 1972-73, mem. exec. bd., 1967-82, nat. trustee, 1973—; trustee Jewish Community Found. Los Angeles, 1964—, pres., 1967-69; chmn. West Area Professions div. United Fund, 1966-67; bd. dirs. Jewish Fedn. Council Greater Los Angeles, 1938-41, 48-54, 58-66, 63-73, 75—, mem. exec. com., 1977—, vice chmn. community relations com., 1970-75, v.p., 1965-67, 71-73, 77-79, pres., 1980-81, chmn. out-reach com., 1982—; chmn. budget and allocations com., 1963-64, chmn. planning dept., 1965-67, pres. jr. div., 1937-41; gen. chmn. 1977 campaign United Jewish Welfare Fund; bd. dirs. Council Jewish Fedns. and Welfare Funds, Inc., 1960-79, nat. v.p., 1967-70, 82—, chmn. Western region, 1966-79, chmn. resolutions com., 1969, 80—, mem. overseas services com., 1961—, chmn. com. on nat. agy. support, 1981, chmn. Shroder awards com., 1982—, mem. exec. com., 1981—; bd. dirs. Constl. Rights Found., 1969-73, mem. exec. com., 1970-73; mem. exec. com.

Lawyers Adv. Council, 1974—; trustee Hope for Hearing Research Found., 1959—; mem. exec. com., trustee UCLA, 1967—, gen. counsel, 1967-71, pres. bd. trustees, 1971-75, chmn. bd., 1975-78, chmn. grants and allocations com., 1978—; bd. dirs. UCLA Found. Charitable Fund, 1978-80, chmn. bd. dirs., 1978-80, v.p., 1980—; mem. steering com. Town Hall West, Los Angeles, 1968-69. Recipient Human Relations award Los Angeles chpt. Am. Jewish Com., 1978. Mem. Fed. Bar Assn., ABA, Los Angeles County Bar Assn. (trustee 1971-72), Beverly Hills Bar Assn. (gov. 1963-72, pres. 1969, chmn. taxation com. 1954-60), Jewish Publ. Soc. Am. (dir. 1980—), Harvard Law Sch. Assn. (nat. council 1964-65), UCLA Alumni Assn. (trustee 1972-75, Profl. Achievement award 1971, Edward A. Dickson Alumnus of Yr. Achievement award 1979), Soc. Order of Blue Shield. Office: 1800 Ave of Stars Suite 900 Los Angeles CA 90067

IRESON, WILLIAM GRANT, industrial engineering educator, author; b. N. Tazewell, Va., Dec. 23, 1915; s. Henry Frank and Hattie Grimm (Smith) I.; m. Mamie Gillespie, Dec. 26, 1938; children: William Randall, Robert Grant. B.S. in Indsl. Engring, Va. Poly. Inst., 1937, M.S., 1943. Indsl. engr. Wayne Mfg. Corp., Waynesboro, Va., 1937-41; from instr. to acting prof., acting head dept. indsl. engring. Va. Poly. Inst., 1941-48; prof. Ill. Inst. Tech., 1948-51, Stanford U., 1951—, chmn. dept. indsl. engring., 1952-75; cons. to govt. and industry. Author or co-author: Principles of Engineering Economy, 7th edit, 1983, Factory Planning and Plant Layout, 1952, Handbook of Industrial Engineering and Management, rev. edit, 1971, also tech. papers.; Editor: Reliability Handbook, 1966. Recipient Air Force scroll appreciation, 1958; Order of Civil Merit, Mongryeon medal for contbns. to higher edn. Govt. S. Korea, 1978. Fellow Am. Inst. Indsl. Engrs. (Frank and Lillian Gilbreth Indsl. Engring. award 1980), Am. Soc. Quality Control (Eugene L. Grant award for contbns. to quality control edn. 1976); mem. Am. Soc. Engring. Edn., Inst. Mgmt. Sci., Tau Beta Pi, Phi Kappa Phi, Alpha Pi Mu. Episcopalian. Engring edn. developer in underdeveloped countries. Home: 735 Alvarado Ct Stanford CA 94305

IRETON, JOHN FRANCIS, JR., food co. exec.; b. Balt., May 15, 1939; s. John Francis and Mary Frances (O'Neill) I.; m. Dorothy A. Minakowski, Nov. 23, 1961; children: Mary Catherine, Megan O'Neill, Amy O'Neill, Allison Brae, Elizabeth Anne. B.A., Loyola Coll., Balt., 1962. Sr. accountant Main Lafrentz & Co. (C.P.A.s), Balt., 1957-62; with Gino's Inc., King of Prussia, Pa., 1962—, exec. v.p., 1968—, also dir.; pres., chief exec. officer, dir. Am. Foodservice Corp.; dir. Merry-Go-Round Enterprises, Inc., Balt., Balt. Fed. Fin. F.S.A. Mem. Crime Commn. Phila. Mem. Fin. Execs. Inst., Am. Mgmt. Assn. Roman Catholic. Club: Whitford Country (Exton). Home: 339 Beaumont Rd Devon PA 19333 Office: 400 Drew Ct King of Prussia PA 19406

IREYS, ALICE RECKNAGEL, landscape architect; b. Bklyn., Apr. 24, 1911; d. Harold S. and Amy Rea (Estes) Recknagel; m. Henry Tillinghast Ireys III, Sept. 1, 1943 (dec. 1962); children: Catherine, Anne, Henry Tillinghast IV. Student, Cambridge Sch. Architecture and Landscape Architecture, 1931-34. Registered landscape architect, N.Y. Self-employed landscape architect, 1939—; instr. in landscape gardening Conn. Coll. for Women; lectr. at bot. gardes, garden clubs, judge flower shows. Author: How to Plan and Plant Your Own Property, 1967, Small Gardnes for City and Country, 1978; contbr. articles to garden mags. and other publs. Fellow Am. Soc. Landscape Architects. Democrat. Episcopalian. Home: 45 Willow St Brooklyn NY 11201

IRIGARAY, PEDRO JOSE, physician; b. Torreon Coah, Mex., Apr. 28, 1932; came to U.S., 1957, naturalized, 1968; s. Pedro and Maria Luisa (Gonzalez) I.; m. Eleanor M. Durham, Feb. 21, 1959; children: Nedda Teresa, Marcos Federico. B.S., Centro U. Mex., 1948; M.D., U. Nat. Autonoma de Mexico, 1955. Psychiat. tng. Duke Med. Center, 1959-62; mem. staff John Umstead Hosp., Butner, N.C., 1962-77, med. supt., 1968-77; chief psychiatry Mountain Home VA Center, Johson City, Tenn., 1977-80; clin. asst. prof. psychiatry Duke Med. Center, 1968-77; assoc. prof. psychiatry East Tenn. State U. Med. Coll., 1977-80; dir. adult admission unit John Umstead Hosp., 1983—; clin. prof. psychiatry U. N.C., 1980; clin. assoc. prof. psychiatry Duke Med. Ctr., 1983. Fellow Am. Psychiat. Assn.; mem. So. Psychiat. Assn., Tenn. Med. Soc., N.C. Psychiat. Assn. Home: 2920 Chapel Hill Rd Apt 100-A Durham NC 27707 Office: Dorothea Dix Hospital Raleigh NC 27611

IRION, ARTHUR LLOYD, educator, psychologist; b. Springfield, Mo., May 14, 1918; s. Theophil William Henry and Edith Grace (Ham) I.; m. Isabelle Virginia Cox, 1944; children: John, Millard, Janet. B.A., U. Mo., 1939; M.A., State U. Iowa, 1941, Ph.D., 1947. From instr. to assoc. prof. U. Ill., 1947-51; prof., chmn. dept. psychology Tulane U., 1951-68; prof. U. Mo.-St. Louis, 1968-80, prof. emeritus, 1980—; vis. prof. U. Colo., summer 1953, U. Mich., summers 1966, 67, U. Richmond, 1978; mem. Bd. La. Examiners of Psychologists, 1967-68. Author: (with John McGeoch) The Psychology of Human Learning, 1952; also numerous tech. articles and chpts.; Cons. editor: Jour. Exptl. Psychology, 1954-67, Perceptual and Motor Skills, 1952-80, Jour. Motor Behavior, 1969-80. Served with AUS, 1942-46. Fellow Am. Psychol. Assn., AAAS; mem. Psychonomic Soc., Mo. Psychol. Assn., So. Soc. Philosophy and Psychology (pres. 1981-82), Phi Beta Kappa, Sigma Xi. Home: 8411 Knollwood Dr Saint Louis MO 63121

IRIONS, CHARLES CARTER, trade association executive; b. Princeton, Ind., June 24, 1929; s. Charles Carter and Flora Ellen (Woods) I.; m. Ethel Mae Knox, Nov. 8, 1952; children: Leslie Jo, Jonathan Knox. Student, Trinity U., 1948-50; B.B.A., George Washington U., 1963-64; disting. grad., Air Command and Staff Coll., 1963-64; student, U. Ala., 1960-61; disting. grad., Air War Coll., 1970-71; M.B.A., Auburn U., 1971. Enlisted in USAF, 1947, advanced through grades to maj. gen., ret., 1981; vice comdr. (60th Mil. Airlift Wing), Travis AFB, Calif., 1973-74, comdr., Scott AFB, Ill., 1974-75, dep. chief staff ops., 1975-77; dir. transp. USAF, Pentagon, Washington, 1977-79; dir. strategic mobility Joint Chiefs of Staff, 1979-81; pres. Am. Movers Conf., Arlington, Va., 1981—; Mem. dean's adv. council Sch. Bus., Ind. U., 1979—. Decorated D.S.M., Legion of Merit, Meritorious Service medal, D.F.C.; recipient Disting. Service award Nat. Def. Transp. Assn., 1978-79. Mem. Am. Legion, VFW, Daedalians, Nat. Def. Transp. Assn., Am. Trucking Assn., Inc. Republican. Methodist. Clubs: Capital Hill, Democratic, Tantallon Country, Elk. Home: 108 Inverness Ln Tantallon MD 20744 Office: 400 Army Navy Dr PO Box 2303 Arlington VA 22202

IRISH, LEON EUGENE, lawyer; b. Superior, Wis., June 19, 1938; s. Edward Eugene and Phyllis Ione (Johnson) I.; m. Carolyn Tanner, Aug. 6, 1960; children: Stephen T., Jessica L., Thomas A., Emily A. B.A. in History, Stanford U., 1960; J.D., U. Mich., 1964; D.Phil in Law, Oxford (Eng.) U., 1973. Law clk. to Asso. Justice U.S. Supreme Ct. Byron R. White, 1967; cons. Office Fgn. Direct Investments, Dept. Commerce, 1967-68; spl. rep. sec. def. 7th session 3d UN Conf. Law of Sea; mem. firm Caplin & Drysdale, chartered, Washington, 1968—; partner Caplin & Drysdale, 1973—; adj. prof. Georgetown U. Law Center, 1975—; visitors com. U. Mich. Law Sch.; Bd. dirs., chmn. exec. com. Vols. Tech. Assistance. Contbr. articles to legal jours. Mem. Am. Law Inst., Am. Bar Assn., D.C. Bar Assn. Democrat. Episcopalian. Home: 3301 Highland Pl NW Washington DC 20008 Office: 1101 17th St NW Suite 1100 Washington DC 20036

IRIYE, AKIRA, historian, educator; b. Tokyo, Oct. 20, 1934; s. Keishiro and Naoko (Tsukamoto) I.; m. Mitsuko Maeda, May 14, 1960; children: Keiko, Masumi. B.A., Haverford Coll., 1957; Ph.D., Harvard U., 1961. Instr. in history Harvard U., 1961-64, lectr. in history, 1964-66; asst. prof. history U. Calif., Santa Cruz, 1966-68; asso. prof. U. Rochester, 1968-69, U. Chgo., 1969-71, prof., 1971—, disting. service prof., 1983—, chmn. dept. history, 1979—. Author: books, including After Imperialism, 1965, Across the Pacific, 1967, Pacific Estrangement, 1972, The Cold War in Asia, 1974, Power and Culture, 1981; editor: The Chinese and the Japanese, 1980. John Simon Guggenheim fellow, 1974-75. Mem. Am. Hist. Assn., Am. Acad. Arts and Scis., Orgn. Am. Historians, Soc. Historians Am. Fgn. Relations (pres. 1978). Office: Dept History U Chgo Chicago IL 60637

IRIZARRY-YUNQUE, CARLOS JUAN, judge; b. Sabana Grande, P.R., June 24, 1922; s. Luis Manuel and Isabel (Yunque) Irizarry-Y.; m. Lillian Busigo, Dec. 19, 1944; 1 dau., Lida Isis Irizarry Egele. B.A., U. P.R., 1943, LL.B., 1949. Bar: P.R. Supreme Ct 1949, U.S. Circuit Ct 1952, U.S. Supreme Ct 1962. Legal advisor Dept. of Agr. and Commerce of P.R., San Juan, 1949-50, P.R. Police Dept., 1950-53; asst. dist. atty., Ponce, P.R., 1953-56; prof. Law Faculty of Cath. U. of P.R., Ponce, 1966-73; asso. justice of Supreme Ct. of P.R., San Juan, 1973—. Served with U.S. Army, 1943-46, 50-52. Mem. Am., P.R., Inter Am. bar assns., Am. Legion, Phi Alpha Delta. Roman Catholic. Club: Lions. Home: 6 Joffre Apt 5B Condado San Juan PR 00907 Office: Supreme Ct Bldg San Juan PR 00903

IRMEN, T.L. SAM, grain merchandising company executive; b. Maumee, Ohio, Jan. 14, 1928; s. Stephen B. and Kathryn B. (Wendlekovsky) I.; m. Charlene Betty Gates, Nov. 26, 1949; children: Patrick, Jaine, Michael, Terence, JoDee, Elizabeth, Thomas. B.S. in Agr, Mich. State U., 1949. Gen. partner, mgr. grain group The Andersons, Maumee, 1947—; bd. dirs., past pres. Toledo Bd. Trade.; mem. adv. com. Fed. Grain Inspection Service. Mem. N.Am. Export Grain Assn., Grain Elevator and Processing Soc. (past pres.), Ohio Grain, Feed and Fertilizer Assn. (pres. 1982-83), Nat. Grain and Feed Assn. (v.p.), Terminal Elevator Grain Mchts. Assn. (pres. 1983-84), Maumee C. of C. (past v.p.). Roman Catholic. Home: 1741 S Holland-Sylvania Rd Maumee OH 45537 Office: PO Box 119 Maumee OH 43537

IRMINGER, EUGENE HERMAN, utilities executive; b. Boise, Idaho, Feb. 16, 1929; s. Carl Eugene and Clara (Hirsbrunner) I.; m. Beatrice Evelyn Lawrence, June 20, 1953; children: Charles W., Steven E., Betticlare. Student, Boise Jr. Coll., 1948-49; B.B.A. with honors, U. Wis., 1953. C.P.A., Ill. Auditor, Arthur Andersen & Co., Chgo., 1956-61, mgr. adminstrv. services, Indpls., 1961-66; comptroller Boise Cascade Corp., 1966-72; v.p. finance Permaneer Corp., St. Louis, 1972-73; controller Central Corp., Chgo., 1973-82, v.p., 1975-82, sr. v.p. fin., 1982—. Troop com. chmn. Boy Scouts Am., 1967-72; adviser Jr. Achievement, 1967-69; mem. businessmens' adv. council Sch. Bus., Idaho State U., 1969-72. Served from ensign to lt. (j.g.) USN, 1953-56. Mem. Nat. Assn. Accts. (pres. Boise chpt. 1968-69), Am. Inst. C.P.A.s, Ill. Soc. C.P.A.s, Fin. Execs. Inst. (pres. Nebr. chpt. 1975-76, nat. com. on corp. reporting 1969-71, nat. dir. 1978-81, area v.p., exec. com. 1982-83), U.S. Ind. Telephone Assn. (chmn. acctg. com. 1977—), Sigma Nu, Beta Alpha Psi. Republican. Methodist. Clubs: Nebraska, Courtier. Home: 1 W Onwentsia Rd Lake Forest IL 60045 Office: O'Hare Plaza 5725 E River Rd Chicago IL 60631

IRONS, GEORGE VERNON, educator; b. Demopolis, Ala., Aug. 7, 1902; s. Andrew George and Belle (Allen) I.; m. Irma Velma Wright, June 16, 1926; children—George Vernon, William Lee. A.B., U. Ala., 1924, M.A., 1925; postgrad., Emory U., 1929, U. N.C., 1928; Ph.D., Duke U., 1936, Ohio State U., 1952, Columbia U., 1957. Asst. prin. Perry County High Sch., Marion, Ala., 1925-27; master Darlington Sch. for Boys, Rome, Ga., 1927-31; asst. dept. history Duke U., 1931-33; prof. history and polit. sci. Samford U., Birmingham, Ala., 1933-45, chmn. dept., 1945-67, chmn. div. social scis., 1962-67, prof. history, 1945—; participant Danforth Found. Seminar on Higher Edn., Bronxville, N.Y., 1957, Ford Found. Seminar in Polit. Sci., Berea, Ky., 1960. Contbr. articles to profl. jours., programs to, Ala. Ednl. TV Network. Mem. Jefferson County Jud. Commn., 1950-52; mem. Civil War Centennial Commn. Ala., 1961-65, Home Service Council, ARC, 1947-50; asso. dir. Freedoms Found. Seminar, Valley Forge, Pa., 1968, 70, 72, trustee Birmingham area chpt.; bd. dirs. Birmingham Council Parents and Tchrs. Served from capt. to lt. col., A.A.A. AUS., 1941-45. Recipient George Washington Honor medal Freedoms Found., 1962, Honor Cert. of award, 1963; Disting. prof. award Samford Bd. Trustees, 1968; univ. grand marshall, 1969—; dedication univ. yearbook, 1941, 60, 69, 74; honoree George V. Irons Day, 1974; named to Ala. Sports Hall of Fame, 1978; nominee Rhodes Scholarship, 1924. Mem. So. Hist. Assn., Ala. Hist. Assn. (past mem. exec. com., past mem. editorial bd.), Baptist Hist. Assn., Birmingham-Jefferson Hist. Assn. (treas. 1980—, Ann. award in Local History 1981), John H. Forney Hist. Soc., Ala. Writers Conclave (treas., past v.p.), Ala. Guidance Assn., Ala. Acad. Sci. (past v.p.), Res. Officers Assn., Phi Beta Kappa, Phi Alpha Theta, Omicron Delta Kappa, Pi Gamma Mu, Kappa Phi Kappa, Phi Sigma Kappa, Phi Kappa Phi (past pres.). Home: 316 Gran Ave Birmingham AL 35209 *I have found that when encountering obstacles in the achievement of certain popular and well-publicized goals, I have been able to realize substantial attainment in other fields of action—areas less traversed and dramatized, yet offering rich opportunities for service and usefulness. Fundamental to my happiness and peace of mind is an assurance of God's love for me, and God's vital presence in all human affairs. Fear God and keep His commandments.*

IRONS, JEREMY JOHN, actor; b. Cowes, Eng., Sept. 19, 1948; s. Paul Dugan and Barbara Anne (Sharpe) I.; m. Sinead Moira Cusack, Mar. 28, 1978; 1 son, Samuel James. Theatrical roles include: John the Baptist in Godspell, 1973, Mick in the Caretaker, 1974, Petrucio in The Taming of the Shrew, 1975, Harry Thunder in Wild Oats, Royal Shakespeare Co., 1976,77, James Jameson in Rear Column, 1978, The Real Thing, 1984 (Tony award 1984); film roles: Nijinsky, 1979, The French Lieutenant's Woman, 1980-81, Betrayal, 1982, Moonlighting, 1982, The Wild Duck, 1983, Swann in Love, 1983; TV roles: Alex Hepburn in The Captian's Doll, 1982, Charles Ryder in Brideshead Revisited, 1980-81. Address: Hutton Mgmt 200 Fulham Rd London England SW10 9PN

IRONS, LESTER, lawyer; b. nr. Sullivan, Ind., May 14, 1908; s. Francis F. and Susie (McBride) I.; m. Lucy M. Carmony, June 16, 1935; children: David Lester, Martha Jane Irons MacKenzie. A.B., Ind. State U., 1929; J.D., U. Mich., 1935. Bar: Mo. 1936, Ind. 1937, N.Y. 1942. Legal dept. Gen. Am. Life Ins. Co., St. Louis, 1935-38; assoc. firm Roberts & Warren, Evansville, Ind., 1938-40; mem. legal dept. Shell Oil Co., St. Louis, N.Y.C., 1940-46; partner Barnes, Hickam, Pantzer & Boyd (now Barnes & Thornburg), Indpls, 1946—; dir. Lacy Diversified Industries, Inc., Indpls., Mut. Hosp. Ins. Inc. Editor: U. Mich. Law Rev, 1934-35. Bd. dirs. United Fund Greater Indpls., 1962-77, Ch. Fedn. Greater Indpls., 1954; mem. nat. council Camp Central Coll.; pres. Ind. Interch. Center Corp.; chmn. bd. trustees Ind. Central U. Recipient Gulick Nat. Camp Fire award, 1961; selected Meth. Man of Year Indpls. dist. Mem. Am., Ind., Indpls. bar assns., Bar Assn. 7th Circuit, Order of Coif, Kappa Delta Pi. Republican. Club: Kiwanis. Home: 8403 Overlook Pkwy Indianapolis IN 46260 Office: Mchts Bank Bldg Indianapolis IN 46204

IRRGANG, WILLIAM, manufacturing company executive; b. Germany, Sept. 27, 1907; came to U.S., 1928, naturalized, 1933; s. Theodor and Hedwig (Preyer) I.; m. Mildred Klapka, Aug. 8, 1934 (dec.); children: Rosemary, Dorothy Louise. E.E., State Tech. Sch., Cologne, Germany, 1928; Dr. Sc. (hon.), Lake Erie Coll., 1967. With Lincoln Electric Co., Cleve., 1929—, successively supr., methods engr., plant engr., dir. plant engring., bd. dirs., exec. v.p. mfg., pres. and gen. mgr., 1954-72, chmn. bd., chief exec. officer, 1972—; dir. Big 3 Industries, Houston. Trustee Lake Erie Coll., Euclid Gen. Hosp., Ednl. Research Council; exec. com. Cleve. Council World Affairs. Mem. AIM, Am. welding Soc., Cleve. Engring. Soc., Nat. Elec. Mfrs. Assn. (bd. govs., James H. McGraw award 1982). Baptist. Clubs: Fifty, Univ. (Cleve.). Office: 22801 St Clair Ave Cleveland OH 44117

IRRMANN, ROBERT HENRY, educator, historian; b. Chgo., Dec. 5, 1916; s. Henry Swissler and Lydia (Kringel) I. B.A., Beloit (Wis.) Coll., 1939, Hum.D. (hon.), 1983; M.A., Harvard U., 1940; Ph.D., Ind. U., 1945. Mem. faculty Denison U., 1945-48; mem. faculty Beloit Coll., 1948-80, prof. history, 1957-80, coll. archivist, 1953—, chmn. dept., 1960-79, prof. emeritus, 1980—; Mem. regional com. X Woodrow Wilson Nat. Fellowship Found., 1955-62; mem. bd. Danforth Assos., 1957-60; reader, interviewer Danforth Tchr. Grants, 1962-66. Contbr.: Essays in Modern European History, 1951. Chmn. Wis. Historic Preservation Rev. Bd., 1976-78. Faculty fellow Asso. Coll. of Midwest-Newberry Library Seminar in Humanities, 1966-67. Mem. Rock County Hist. Soc. (trustee), Beloit Hist. Soc. (pres. 1974-75), AAUP, Am. Hist. Assn., Mediaeval Acad. Am., Navy Records Soc., Soc. Nautical Research, State Hist. Soc. Wis. (mem. Old World Wis. com. 1971, curator 1971-82, curator emeritus, 2d v.p. 1979-82), Phi Beta Kappa, Omicron Delta Kappa, Sigma Alpha Epsilon. Democrat. Episcopalian. Home: 911 Emerson St Beloit WI 53511

IRSAY, ROBERT, professional football club executive, construction company executive; b. Chgo., Mar. 5, 1923; s. Charles J. and Elaine (Nyrtia) I.; m. Harriet Pogorzelski, July 12, 1946; children: Thomas, James. B.S.M.E., U. Ill., 1941. Pres. Robert Irsay Co., Skokie, IL, 1952-78, Colt Constrn. and Devel. Co., 1978—, Balt. Football Club, Inc., 1972—; dir. Mich. Ave. Nat. Bank, Chgo., 1970-76. Bd. dirs. Clearbrook Ctr. for Handicapped, Rolling Meadows, Ill., 1982-83, Troubled Children's Found., Hialeah, Fla., 1982-83. Served to lt. USMC, 1941-46; PTO.

IRSFELD, JAMES BALTHAZAR, JR., lawyer; b. Hollywood, Calif., Apr. 3, 1912; s. James Balthazar and Mary Vincentia (Hall) I.; m. Billie Marie Kreichter, June 26, 1937; children—Peter, Michael, Sally Ann (Mrs. R. J. Considine), John. A.B., Stanford, 1933; LL.B., U. So. Calif., Los Angeles, 1936. Bar: Calif. bar 1936. Partner firm Irsfeld, Irsfeld & Younger, Hollywood, 1936—. Editor: So. Calif. Law Rev, 1935-36. Mem. advisory bd. St. Joseph's Med. Center, Burbank, Calif., 1976—; trustee St. Joseph Med. Center Found., 1978—, chmn. Served to capt., inf. AUS, 1942-45. Mem. Hollywood C. of C. (pres. 1962-63), Order of Coif. Clubs: Kiwanian., Lakeside Golf of Hollywood (pres. 1975-76). Home: 4954 Mammoth Ave Sherman Oaks CA 91423 Office: 7060 Hollywood Blvd Hollywood CA 90028

IRVIN, ROBERT JOSEPH, rancher; b. Grand Island, Nebr., Oct. 13, 1920; s. Ray J. and Beulah (Brown) I.; m. Nancy Story Irvin, Nov. 27, 1944; children—Catherine H., Robert C. B.S. in Bus. Adminstrn, U. Nebr., 1943. Employment mgr. Inland Steel Co., East Chicago, Ind., 1950-53; dir. indsl. relations Kawneer Co., Niles, Mich., 1953-59; v.p. personnel and employee relations Inland Container Corp., 1959-69, v.p. staff services, 1969-71, v.p. staff and material services, 1971-73; chmn. bd. Rexford Paper Co., 1971-73; pres. Indpls. Ink & Chem. Co., 1971-73; owner Wind River Ranch, Estes Park, Colo., 1973—; lectr., cons., 1973—. Mem. Bd. Child Guidance Clinic Marion County, 1963-71, pres., 1966-68; pres. Carmel Clay Ednl. Found., 1966-70, Tehosa Valley Assn., 1979—; v.p. Carmel Clay Sch. Bldg. Corp., 1967—; mem. Greater Indpls. Progress Com., 1970-73; bd. dirs. Salvation Army, Indpls., 1962-73, Forward, Inc., 1967-73, Elizabeth Knutsson Hosp., 1978—. Served with inf. AUS, 1942-43. Mem. Am. Mgmt. Assn. (personnel planning council 1967-73), Estes Park C. of C. (dir. 1977—), Colo. Dude and Guest Ranch Assn. (pres. 1983). Address: Box 3410 Estes Park CO 80517

IRVIN, TINSLEY HOYT, insurance broker; b. Cornelia, Ga., May 30, 1933; s. Henry Hoyt and Annie Ruth (Ray) I.; m. Gail Lee Wood, June 4, 1955; children: Cynthia Gaye, Diane Gail. B.B.A., Ga. State U., 1955. With Alexander & Alexander, Inc., 1953—, v.p., mgr. Atlanta office, 1965-70, sr. v.p. S.E. region, 1970-78, chmn., chief exec. officer, 1982—; pres., chief operating officer Alexander & Alexander Services, Inc., N.Y.C., 1982—. Served with U.S. Army, 1956-58. Republican. Congregationalist. Home: 8 Deer Park Ct Greenwich CT 06830 Office: 1211 Ave of Americas New York NY 10036

IRVINE, FRANCIS SPRAGUE, lawyer; b. Okmulgee, Okla., May 27, 1923; s. Francis Sprague and Hazel (Beckett) I.; m. Betty Lee Sullivan, Sept. 3, 1949; children: Marilee, Robyn. B.A., Okla. State U., 1948; LL.B., Okla. U., 1950. Bar: Okla. 1950. Practiced in, Oklahoma City, 1950—, pvt. practice, 1950-57; mem. firm Kerr, Conn & Davis, 1957-63; partner firm Kerr, Irvine & Rhodes, 1963—. Served to 1st lt. AUS, 1943-46. Mem. Mineral Lawyers Group Oklahoma City, Oklahoma City Soc. Title Attys., Am., Okla., Oklahoma County bar assns., Oklahoma City C. of C. Christian Scientist. Club: Whitehall (Oklahoma City). Home: 1836 NW 56th Terr Oklahoma City OK 73118 Office: Fidelity Plaza Bldg Oklahoma City OK 73102

IRVINE, LOUVA ELIZABETH, artist, filmmaker, design cons.; b. N.Y.C., Jan. 3, 1939; d. Robert Urquhart and Louva Elizabeth (Goodrich) I. Student, Art Students League, 1960-61, Sch. Visual Arts, 1962-63; B.A., Hans Richter Film Inst., CCNY, 1967. Prodn. mgr., set and costume designer showcase and original prodns., 1965-68; cons. Exptl. Design unit Time-Life Inc., 1969-71, Community Makers Inc., N.Y.C., 1971-73, Group Creativity, 1973-76, Improv Olympic, 1979-83; project cons., mentor Pratt Inst., 1971-72; pres. Total Design Assocs., N.Y.C., 1976—; co-founder Women's Film Collective, 1972; coordinator film festival UN Internat. Year of Woman, 1975; producer, dir. Sta. CJOH-TV, Ottawa, Ont., Can., 1975; mem. faculty Sch. Arts Inst. Film and TV, N.Y. U., 1976; designer, instr. workshops Solomon R. Guggenheim Mus., 1971-73, mentor, 1979; cons. 2nd Internat. Festival Women's Films, 1976; cons., scriptwriter Corinthian Prodns., 1982. Creator over 200 exptl. film studies since 1966, including, Walk, Don't Run, Citywalk, Rain, Elegy for My Sister, Waterdance, Murray Hill Morning, Blue Moment (Cine Golden Eagle award 1977, in permanent collection Guggenheim Mus.), Circus; co-author: script Homeward Bound, 1973; cons.: The Birth Film, 1971; co-producer, dir., prodn. mgr., music: Three Lives, 1970-71; assoc. dir.: play Halleluiah Day, 1973; set designer: Bathtub, 1969; film design: Traveling Light, 1979; film coordinator, Women's Interart Center, 1972-73; script cons., prodn. mgr., set and costume designer: showcase and original prodns. No Place to Be Somebody (Pulitzer prize, Obie award 1965-68). Recipient Meyer Goldman award, 1977;

MacDowell Colony fellow, 1976, 77; Millay Colony fellow, 1978; artist-in-residence Nat. Endowment for Arts; grantee S.C. Arts Commn., 1975, Film Workshop of Westchester, 1975-76. Mem. Soc. Women in Film, Tape and TV (co-founder, v.p. 1975- 6), Assn. Ind. Video and Filmmakers (charter mem., chmn. exptl. film distbn. com. 1974—), Graphic Artist Guild. Office: PO Box 189 Murray Hill Station New York NY 10016

IRVINE, REED JOHN, media critic, corporation executive; b. Salt Lake City, Sept. 29, 1922; s. William John and Edna Jessup (May) I.; m. Kay Araki, Aug. 14, 1948; 1 son, Donald. A.B., U. Utah, 1942; postgrad., U. Colo., 1943-44, U. Wash., 1949; B.Litt., Oxford U., Eng., 1951. With Gen. Hdqrs. of Allied Occupation of Japan, Tokyo, 1946-48; economist bd. govs. Fed. Res. System, Washington, 1951-63, adviser internat. fin., 1963-77; chmn. bd. Accuracy in Media, Inc., Washington, 1971—; editor AIM Report; syndicated columnist, radio commentator. Author: Media Mischief aND Misdeeds, 1984. Dir. Council Def. of Freedom, Washington, 1970—. Served with USNR, 1943-46; PTO; to capt. USMCR, 1944-46. Recipient George Washington medal Freedom Found., 1980. Mem. Phi Beta Kappa. Mormon. Club: Nat. Press (Washington). Home: 11120 Nicholas Dr Silver Spring MD 20902

IRVINE, THOMAS FRANCIS, JR., mechanical engineering educator; b. Northmont, N.J., June 25, 1922; s. Thomas Francis and Marie (Boeggeman) I.; children by previous marriage: Laura, Kay, Phoebe, Jill, Sadi; m. Olga Zilboorg, July 28, 1966; children: Thomas, Tanya. B.S., Pa. State U., 1946; M.S., U. Minn., 1951, Ph.D., 1956. Research asso. Pa. State U., 1947-49; research asst. instr. U. Minn., 1950-56, asst. prof. mech. engring., 1956-58, asso. prof., 1958-59; prof. mech. engring. U. N.C., 1959-61; prof. engring., dean Coll. Engring., State U. N.Y. at Stony Brook, 1961-71, prof., 1971—; Cons. in heat transfer, 1954—; Mem. exec. bd. heat transfer div. ASME, 1964-68, chmn. exec. com., 1968-69; mem. orgn. com. Internat. Center Heat and Mass Transfer, 1966—, chmn., 1972-74, 82—. Editor: (with J. P. Hartnett) Advances in Heat Transfer, vols. I-XVI, 1964-83, Pergamon Unified Engineering Series, Heat Transfer Soviet Research, Heat Transfer Japanese Research, Fluid Mechanics-Soviet Research, Previews in Heat and Mass. Transfer, McGraw-Hill-Hemisphere Series in Thermal and Fluids Engineering, 1976-82; tech. editor: Jour. Heat Transfer, 1960-63; editorial adv. bd.: Internat. Jour. Heat and Mass Transfer, 1959—, Letters in Heat and Mass Transfer, 1974—; Contbr. articles to profl. jours. Served with AUS, 1942-46. Fellow ASME, AAAS; mem. AIAA, Am. Soc. Engring. Edn., Sigma Xi, Tau Beta Pi, Eta Kappa Nu, Sigma Tau, Theta Tau. Home: 9 Leatherstocking Ln Stony Brook NY 11790

IRVING, DONALD J., university dean; b. Arlington, Mass., May 3, 1933; m. Jewel P. Irving; children: Kevin William, Todd Lawrence. B.A., Mass. Coll. Art, 1955; M.A., Columbia U. Tchrs. Coll., 1956, Ed.D., 1963. Tchr. art White Plains (N.Y.) High Sch., 1958-60; instr. art SUNY-Oneonta, 1960-62; prof. art, dean Moore Coll. Art, Phila., 1963-67; chmn. art dept., dir. Peabody Mus. Art, George Peabody Coll. Tchrs., Nashville, 1967-69; dir. Sch. Art Inst., Chgo., 1969-82; dean Faculty Fine Arts U. Ariz., Tucson, 1982—; mem. U.S. del. Conf. Nat. Soc. Edn. Through Art, Prague, Czechoslovakia, 1966; cons. ednl. TV series Art Now, WRCV-TV, Phila. Author: Sculpture Material and Process, 1970; contbr. articles in field to profl. jours. Mem. Nat. Assn. Schs. Art (treas., dir. 1975-77), Nat. Assn. Land Grant Colls. and Univs. Arts Commn., Union Ind. Colls. Art (dir. 1972-82, chmn. 1980-82), Nat. Council Art Adminstrs. (dir.), Fedn. Ind. Ill. Colls. and Univs. (dir.), Nat. Art Edn. Assn. (officer Eastern region 1966-68), Eastern Arts Assn. (council 1964-66, mgr. conv. 1959-64), Nat. Council Arts in Edn., Internat. Soc. Edn. Through Art, Coll. Art Assn., Phi Delta Kappa. Home: 5810 E Paseo San Valentine Tucson AZ 85715 Office: Univ of Arizona Coll of Fine Arts Tucson AZ 85721

IRVING, EDWARD, geophysicist; b. Colne, Eng., May 27, 1927; s. George Edward and Nellie (Petty) I.; m. Sheila Ann Irwin, Sept. 23, 1957; children: Kathryn Jean, Susan Patricia, Martin Edward, George Andrew. B.A., Cambridge (Eng.) U., 1950, M.A., 1957, Sc.D., 1965; D.Sc. (hon.), Carleton U., 1979. Research fellow Australian Nat. U., Canberra, 1954-57, fellow, 1957-59, sr. fellow, 1959-64; sci. officer Can. Dept. Mines and Tech. Surveys, Ottawa, Ont., 1964-66; prof. geophysics U. Leeds, Eng., 1966-67; research scientist Can. Dept. Energy Mines and Resources, Ottawa, 1967-81, Sidney, B.C., 1981—; adj. prof. geology Carleton U., Ottawa. Author: Paleomagnetism, 1964; asso. editor: Tectonphysics, Physics of Earth and Planetary Interiors; contbr. articles on paleomagnetism and related geol. topics to profl. publs. Served with Brit. Army, 1945-48. Recipient Chestien Mica Gondwana medal Mining, Geol. and Metall. Inst. India, 1965. Fellow Royal Soc. Can., Royal Soc. (London), Am. Geophys. Union (Walter H. Bucher medal 1979), Royal Astron. Soc. (U.K.), Geol. Soc. Am., Geol. Assn. Can. (Logan medal 1975). Mem. United Ch. Can. Office: Pacific Geosci Ctr PO Box 6000 Sidney BC V8L 4B2 Canada

IRVING, EDWARD MUIR, corporate executive, chemical engineer; b. London, Ont., Canada, Sept. 6, 1928; came to U.S., 1947; s. Edward and Rose A. (McEwan) I.; m. Catherine Ann Aloia, June 14, 1953. B.S. in Chem. Engring., N.J. Inst. Tech., 1955. With Inmont Corp., 1947-83, on internat. assignment, 1963-70, in sr. mgmt. positions, Clifton, N.J., 1970-80, pres., chief exec. officer, Clifton, 1980-83; corp. officer United Techs. Corp., Hartford, Conn., 1982—; sr. v.p. Indsl. Group, United Techs. Corp., Hartford, 1983—. Mem. Am. Chem. Soc., Am. Inst. Chem. Engrs., Tau Beta Pi. Clubs: Ridgewood Country (Paramus, N.J.); Coldstream Country (Cin.); Royal Automobile (London); Moor Park Golf (Rickmansworth, Eng.); Hartford. Office: United Techs Corp Hartford CT 06101

IRVING, GEORGE STEVEN, actor; b. Springfield, Mass., Nov. 1, 1922; s. Abraham and Rebecca (Sack) Shelasky; m. Maria Karnilove, Oct. 17, 1948; children: Alexander, Katherine. Student, Leland Powers Sch. of Theatre, Boston, 1941. Actor (on Broadway) play, Oklahoma, 1943, Lady In The Dark, 1943, Call Me Mister, 1946, Along Fifth Avenue, 1949, Gentlemen Prefer Blondes, 1949, Two's Company, 1952, Me and Juliet, 1953, Can-Can, 1954, Bells Are Ringing, 1957, The Beggar's Opera, 1957, The Good Soup, 1957, Irma La Douce, 1960, Romulus, 1962, Bravo Giovanni, 1962, Seidman and Son, 1962, Tovarich, 1963, A Murder Among Us, 1964, Alfie, 1964, Anya, 1965, Galileo, 1967, The Happy Time, 1968, Promenade, 1969, Irene, 1973 (Tony award for best supporting actor 1973); On Your Toes, 1983; stock and touring prodns. Club: The Players (N.Y.C.). Office: care Actors Equity Assn 165 W 46th St New York NY 10036

IRVING, JACK HOWARD, planning executive; b. Cleve., Dec. 31, 1920; s. William M. and Lottie (Green) I.; m. Florence Friedman, Feb. 1, 1948; children: Paul Howard, Karen Joy, Michael William. B.S., Calif. Inst. Tech., 1942; M.A., Princeton, 1948, Ph.D. in Physics, 1965. Staff radiation lab. Mass. Inst. Tech., 1942-45; asst. physics Princeton, 1946-48; fellow chemistry Calif. Inst. Tech., 1948-49; head systems planning and analysis dept. research and devel. labs. Hughes Aircraft Co., 1949-54; head spl. devices dept. Ramo-Wooldridge Corp., 1954-55, head intelligence systems dept., 1955-56, spl. asst. to exec. v.p., 1956-57, spl. asst. to pres. space tech. labs., 1957-58; corp. staff sci. Thompson Ramo-Wooldridge, Inc., 1958-60; asst. dir. Advanced Systems Planning div. Space Tech. Labs., Inc., 1960; v.p., gen. mgr. systems research and planning div. Aerospace Corp., El Segundo, Calif., 1960-63, v.p. corp. planning, 1965-72, v.p., gen. mgr. environment and urban div., 1972-75; tech. cons. and product devel. Jack H. Irving Assos., Los Angeles, 1976—; aerospace vis. fellow Princeton, 1963-65; mem. com. on interplay of engring. with biology and medicine Nat. Acad. Engring., 1967-73; chmn., dir. Med. Systems Tech. Services, Inc., 1968-80; dir. Commuter Transp. Services Inc., 1974—, mem. exec. com., 1974-79, treas., 1975-78, chmn. audit com., 1979—. Prin. author: Fundamentals of Personal Rapid Transit, 1978; Contbr. articles to tech. publs. Asso. fellow Am. Inst. Aeros. and Astronautics; mem. Advanced Transit Assn., Am. Phys. Soc., Sigma Xi. Dir. study fire control systems, Minuteman ballistic missile, communication satellites, personal rapid transit. Home: 13202 Jonesboro Pl Los Angeles CA 90049

IRVING, JOHN STILES, JR., lawyer; b. Plainfield, N.J., Nov. 13, 1940; s. John S. and Muriel (McLaughlin) I.; m. Dianne Nutwell Irving, Jan. 20, 1968; children: John S., Dianne. A.B., Brown U., 1962; J.D., Georgetown U., 1965, LL.M., 1967. Bar: N.J. 1965, D.C. 1966, U.S. Supreme Ct. 1969. With NLRB, 1965-69, atty. appellate ct. br., 1967-69; spl. asst. to solicitor and exec. asst. to under sec. labor Dept. Labor, Washington, 1969-70; asso. gen. counsel NLRB, Washington, 1971-72, dep. gen. counsel, 1972-75, gen. counsel, 1975-79; partner Kirkland & Ellis, Washington, 1979—. Contbr. articles to profl. jours. Recipient Young Fed. Lawyers award Fed. Bar Assn., 1975; meritorious award William A. Jump Meml. Found., 1975. Mem. ABA, D.C. Bar Assn., N.J. Bar Assn., Fed. Bar Assn., NAM (chmn. labor law adv. com.). Office: 655 15th St NW Washington DC 20005

IRVING, JOHN WINSLOW, author; b. Exeter, N.H., Mar. 2, 1942; s. Colin F.N. and Frances (Winslow) I.; m. Shyla Leary, Aug. 20, 1964; children: Colin, Brendan. Student, U. Pitts., 1961-62, U. Vienna, 1963-64; B.A., U. N.H., 1965; M.F.A., U. Iowa, 1967. Asst. prof. English Mt. Holyoke Coll., 1967-72, 75-78; writer-in-residence U. Iowa, 1972-75; with Bread Loaf Writer's Conf., 1976. Author: novels, including Setting Free the Bears, 1969, The Water-Method Man, 1972, The 158-Pound Marriage, 1974, The World According to Garp, 1978, The Hotel New Hampshire, 1981; contbr.: short stories and articles to other publs. Rockefeller Found. grantee, 1971-72; Nat. Endowment for Arts fellow, 1974-75. Office: care Random House 201 E 50th St New York NY 10022 *

IRVING, MICHAEL HENRY, architect; b. N.Y.C., Aug. 2, 1923; s. E. duPont and Carolyn (Mann) I.; m. Flora Miller, June 7, 1947 (div. 1981); children: Michelle Mann, Duncan Duer, Macculloch Miller, Fiona; m. Patricia Luces, July 1981. B.A., Harvard U., 1945; M.Arch., Columbia U., 1953. With archtl. firms Harrison & Abramovitz, N.Y.C., 1953-54, Sherwood, Mills & Smith, Stamford, Conn., 1954-60; pvt. practice, Westport, Conn., 1961-63, N.Y.C., 1964-69, New Canaan, Conn., 1969—; now partner Irving & Jacob. Trustee Whitney Mus. Am. Art, Norwalk Hosp.; past trustee New Canaan County Sch.; bd. dirs. Stamford (Conn.) Museum and Nature Center. Served with USNR, 1943-46. Mem. AIA, Archtl. League N.Y., Am. Arbitration Assn. Home: Old Saugatuck Rd Norwalk CT 06855 Office: 50 Water St Norwalk CT 06854

IRVING, ROBERT AUGUSTINE, conductor, pianist; b. Winchester, Eng., Aug. 28, 1913; came to U.S., 1958; s. Robert Graham and Oriane (Tyndale) I. Scholar, Winchester (Eng.) Coll., 1926-32, Royal Coll. Music, 1934-36; B.A. (scholar), New Coll., Oxford (Eng.) U., 1935. Prof. piano Winchester Coll., 1936-40; assoc. condr. BBC Scottish Orch., 1945-48; mus. dir. Royal Ballet Eng., 1949-58, N.Y.C. Ballet, 1958—; vis. condr. numerous orchs., U.S. and Eng., 1951—. Rec. artist for, HMV, RCA Victor, EMI, Capitol, Angel, Kapp records.; Composer: (with K. Hepburn) As You Like It, 1949, Floodtide 1949, 1958; also scores for films. Served with Royal Arty., 1940-41; Served with RAF, 1941-45. Decorated D.F.C. with bar. Home: 160 West End Ave New York NY 10023 Office: New York City Ballet NY State Theatre Lincoln Center New York NY 10023

IRVING, THOMAS HERBERT, medical educator; b. Saxonburg, Pa., Oct. 19, 1931; s. Herbert W. and Helen (McClain) I.; m. Virginia E. Schar, Dec. 26, 1953; children—Constance, Jennifer, Andrew. B.A., Pa. State U., 1953; M.D., Hahnemann Med. Coll., 1961. Intern Hosp. U. Pa., 1961-62, resident, 1962-64; practice medicine specializing in anesthesiology, Wichita, Kans., 1964-65; asst. prof. anesthesiology Kans. U. Med. Center at Kansas City, 1965-67; prof. Bowman Gray Sch. Medicine, Winston-Salem, N.C., 1967-73; chmn. dept. anesthesiology Bowman Gray/Sch. Medicine, Winston-Salem, N.C., 1967-82; chief profl. services N.C. Bapt. Hosp., 1973—. Served with USNR, 1953-56. Mem. Am. Soc. Anesthesiologists. Home: 705 Glen Echo Trail Winston-Salem NC 27106

IRVIS, K. LEROY, state legislator; b. Saugerties, N.Y., Dec. 27, 1919; s. Francis H. and Harriet (Cantine) I.; m. Cathryn L. Edwards; children—Reginald Dorwin, Sherri Letitia. A.B. summa cum laude, N.Y. State Tchrs. Coll., 1938; M.A., SUNY, Albany, 1939; J.D. (Owens fellow), U. Pitts., 1954. Bar: Pa. bar 1954. Tchr. pub. schs., Balt., 1939-42; civilian attache aviation tng. div. War Dept., 1942-44; law clk. Judges Anne X. Alpern and Loran Lewis, Pitts., 1955-57; asst. dist. atty., Pitts., 1957-63; mem. Pa. Ho. of Reps., 1958—, minority caucus chmn., 1963-64, majority caucus chmn., 1965-66, minority whip, 1967-68, 73-74, majority leader, 1969-70, 71-72, 75-76, 77, speaker, 1977-78, 83-84, minority leader, 1979-83; treas. Joint State Govt. Commn. of Pa. Bd. dirs. Post-Gazette Dapper Dan Club, Pitts., Greater Pitts. Bus. Devel. Corp., WQED Pub. TV, United Black Front, Bidwell Cultural and Tng. Center, Tng., Employment and Manpower, Three Rivers Improvement and Devel. Corp., Community Action of Pitts.; trustee U. Pitts., Neighborhood Assistance Adv. Bd., Penn's S.W. Assn., Pitts., State Pub. Sch. Bldg. Authority, Pa. Higher Edn. Facilities Authority; mem. adv. com. U. Pitts. Med. Sch.; mem. Gen. State Authority, Harrisburg, Pa.; del. Dem. Nat. Conv., 1968, 72, 76, vice chmn. Pa. del., vice co-chmn. conv., 1980; mem. Dem. Nat. Com. Mem. NAACP, Pub. Defender Assn. Pitts. (hon. chmn.), Order of Coif, Phi Beta Kappa, Pi Gamma Mu, Phi Delta Phi. Home: 205 Tennyson Ave Pittsburgh PA 15213 Office: Main Capitol Bldg Harrisburg PA 17120

IRWIN, ARTHUR SAMUEL, tribology research cons.; b. South Bend, Ind., Oct. 31, 1912; s. Arthur Samuel and Martha Olive (Chesnutwood) I.; m. Irene Louise Ricketts, July 30, 1938; children—Charles F., Barbara Irwin Metcalfe, Arthur Samuel. B.S. in Engring. Mechs, U. Mich., Ann Arbor, 1935. Engr. Bendix Products div., South Bend, 1934-37, Marlin Rockwell Corp., Jamestown, N.Y., 1937-40, asst. chief engring., 1947-56, mgr. sales research, 1962-66; sr. devel. engr. Bell Aircraft Corp., Buffalo, 1940-46; project mgr. Lamiflex, Marlin Rockwell/TRW, Jamestown, 1966-68; dir. research and devel. Marlin Rockwell div. TRW, Inc., Jamestown, 1956-62, 68-77; tribology cons., 1977—; mem. subcom. on lubrication and wear NACA, 1955-58. Mem. Jamestown Airport Commn., 1962-66. Fellow Am. Soc. Lubrication Engrs.; fellow AIAA (asso.); mem. ASME, Jet Pioneers Assn., Am. Def. Preparedness Assn. Club: Masons. Patentee in field. Home: Driftwood RFD 1 Bemus Point NY 14712

IRWIN, GEORGE RANKIN, physicist, mechanical engineering educator; b. El Paso, Tex., Feb. 26, 1907; s. William Rankin and Mary (Ross) I.; m. Georgia Shearer, June 10, 1933; children: Joseph Ross, Mary Susan Irwin Gillett, Sarah Belle Irwin Lofgren, John Shearer. A.B., Knox Coll., 1930; M.S., U. Ill., 1933, Ph.D., 1937; D.Eng. (hon.), Lehigh U., 1977. Asso. prof. physics Knox Coll., 1935-36; fellow physics U. Ill., 1936-37; physicist U.S. Naval Research Lab., 1937-67; prof. mechanics Lehigh U., 1967-72; prof. mech. engring. U. Md., 1972—; vis. prof. U. Ill., 1961, 70; hon. lectr. Internat. Congress on Fracture, 1981. Contbr. articles to profl. jours. Recipient Navy Disting. Civilian Service award, 1947; Knox Coll. Alumni Assn. Achievement award, 1949; Navy Conrad award, 1969; Grand medal French Metall. Soc., 1976; Clamer award Franklin Inst., 1978; Md. Gov.'s citation, 1982. Fellow ASTM (Dudley medal 1960, hon. mem. 1974), Washington Acad. Sci.; mem. Washington Philos. Soc., Soc. Exptl. Stress Analysis (Murray lectr. 1973, Lazan award 1977), ASME (Thurston lectr. 1966, Nadai award 1977), Am. Soc. Metals (Sauveur award 1974), Nat. Acad. Engring. Pioneer devel. fracture mechanics. Home: 7306 Edmonston Ave College Park MD 20740

IRWIN, GLENN WARD, JR., physician, university official; b. Roachdale, Ind., July 18, 1920; s. Glenn Ward and Elsie (Browning) I.; m. Marianna Ashby; children: Ann Graybill Irwin Warden, William Browning, Elizabeth Ashby Irwin Schiffli. B.S., Ind. U., Bloomington, 1942, M.D., 1944. Diplomate: Am. Bd. Internal Medicine. Intern Meth. Hosp., Indpls., 1944-45; resident Ind. U. Med. Ctr., Indpls., 1945-46; mem. faculty Ind. U., Indpls., 1950—, prof. medicine, 1961—, dean Sch. Medicine, 1965-73, v.p., 1974—; chancellor Ind. U.-Purdue U., Indpls., 1973-74. Bd. dirs. United Way, Indpls., Am. Fund for Dental Health, Chgo., 1977—, Indpls. Ctr. Advanced Research, 1975—, Commn. for Downtown Indpls., Goodwill Industries of Central Ind., Indpls., Greater Indpls. Progress Com. Served to capt. U.S. Army, 1946-48. Named Disting. Alumnus Ind. U. Sch. Medicine, 1972, Sagamore of the Wabash Gov. of Ind., 1979. Fellow ACP (gov. for Ind. 1964-70); mem. Sigma Xi, Alpha Omega Alpha. Presbyterian (elder). Lodge: Masons. Home: 5801 Sunset Ln Indianapolis IN 46208 Office: Ind U-Purdue U 355 Lansing St Indianapolis IN 46202

IRWIN, GRAHAM WILKIE, history educator; b. Adelaide, Australia, Oct. 12, 1920; came to U.S., 1962; s. William Henry and Edith Nina (Morris) I.; m. Jane Nora Bayly, Sept. 20, 1956. B.A., U. Adelaide, 1946; Ph.D., U. Cambridge, Eng., 1953. Lectr. history U. Malaya, 1953-56, U. Sydney, 1956-57; sr. lectr. history Univ. Coll., Accra, Ghana, 1958-59, prof. history, head dept. history, 1960-63; assoc. prof. Columbia U., N.Y.C., 1963-65, prof., 1965—, dir. Inst. African Studies, 1974-83, assoc. dean Sch. Internat. and Pub. Affairs, 1983—. Author: Nineteenth-Century Borneo, 1955, Africans Abroad, 1977; editor: Harper Encyclopedia of the Modern World, 1970. Served with Australian Army, 1940-46. Mem. African Studies Assn. (acting sec. 1965-66), Hist. Soc. Ghana (past pres.), African Studies Assn. U.K., Am. Hist. Assn. Episcopalian. Home: 464 Riverside Dr New York NY 10027 Office: Sch Internat and Public Affairs Columbia U New York NY 10027

IRWIN, HALE S., golfer; b. Joplin, Mo., June 3, 1945; s. Hale S. and Mabel M. (Philipps) I.; m. Sally Jean Stahlhuth, Sept. 14, 1968; children: Becky, Steven. B.S. in Marketing, U. Colo., 1968. Touring profl. golfer, 1968—; tour dir. Profl. Golf Assn. Am., 1978-79, v.p., 1979. State chmn. Mo. Easter Seal campaign, 1977. Mem. Phi Gamma Delta. Republican. Presbyn. Tour victories include Heritage Classic, 1971, 73, U.S. Open, 1974, 79, Western Open, 1975, Atlanta Golf Classic, 1975, 77, Glen Campbell-Los Angeles, 1976, Fla. Citrus, 1976, Hall of Fame Classic, 1977, Hawaiian Open, 1981, Buick Open, 1981, Inverrary Classic, 1982, Meml. Tournament, 1983. Office: 2801 Stonington St Frontenac MD 63131 *

IRWIN, HELEN TRATHEN, university dean; b. Pottsville, Pa., June 11, 1939; d. Percy Wayne and Emma Elizabeth (Trathen) I. B.S.B.A., Cedar Crest Coll., 1961; postgrad. in library sci., Drexel U., 1970; J.D., Cardozo Sch. Law, Yeshiva U., 1983. Editorial asst. Sat. Evening Post, Curtis Pub. Co., Phila., 1961-62; asst. sales promotion Holiday Mag., 1962; exec. asst. to dir. Pacific Sci. Center, Seattle, 1963-64; exec. asst. Penjerdel project Ford Found., Phila., 1964-65; asst. editor, mgr. editorial prodn. Phila. Mag., 1965-70; mng. editor Boston Mag., 1970-72; dir. advt. World Tennis Mag. CBS Inc., N.Y.C., 1972-75; asso. pub., dir. advt. Am. Home Mag., Am. Home Pub. Co., N.Y.C., 1975-76; dir. advt. women Sports Mag., Charter Pub. Co., N.Y.C., 1976-77; pub. New Dawn mag., N.Am. Pub. Co., N.Y.C., 1977-78; mng. editor Viva mag. Penthouse Internat. Ltd., N.Y.C., 1978-79, Media People mag., Media Pub. Corp., 1979; asst. dean student affairs Cardozo Sch. Law, Yeshiva U., N.Y.C., 1983—. Mem. adv. bd. alumnae mag., Cedar Crest Coll., 1968-72. Mem. Alumnae Assn. Cedar Crest Coll. (dir. 1977-80). Episcopalian. Home: 132 E 35th St New York NY 10016 Office: Cardozo Sch Law 55 Fifth Ave New York NY 10003

IRWIN, JAMES BENSON, former astronaut, foundation executive, aeronautical engineer; b. Pitts., Mar. 17, 1930; s. James and Elsie (Strebel) I.; m. Mary Ellen Monroe, Sept. 4, 1959; children: Joy Carmel, Jill Cherie, James Benson, Jan Caron, Joe Chau. B.S., U.S. Naval Acad., 1951; M.S. in Aero. Engring, U. Mich., 1957, D. Astronautical Sci., 1971; D.Sc., William Jewell Coll., 1971, Samford U., 1972. Commd. 2d lt. USAF, 1951, advanced through grades to col., 1971; project officer, Wright Patterson AFB, 1957-60, test dir., Edwards AFB, Calif., 1961-63, test pilot, Edwards AFB, 1963-65, br. chief, Colorado Springs, Colo., 1965-66; astronaut NASA, 1966-72. Author: To Rule the Night, More Than Earthlings. Founder, pres. evang. found. High Flight, Colorado Springs, Colo., 1972. Decorated NASA Distinguished Service Medal, D.S.M. USAF, City N.Y. Gold Medal, UN Peace medal, City Chgo. Gold medal; order Leopold, Belgium; recipient David C. Schilling trophy, 1971, Kitty Hawk meml. award, 1971, Haley Astronautics award AIAA, 1972, John F. Kennedy trophy Arnold Air Soc., 1972, Freedoms Found. Washington medal, 1976, Nat. Citizenship award Mil. Chaplains Assn., 1978, others. Mem. Air Force Assn., Soc. Exptl. Test Pilots. Baptist. Mem. support crew Apollo 10; backup lunar module pilot Apollo 12; lunar module pilot Apollo 15 moon landing crew, July 30, 1971. Address: PO Box 1387 Colorado Springs CO 80901 *

IRWIN, JOHN DAVID, electrical engineering educator; b. Mpls., Aug. 9, 1939; s. Arthur Fowle and Virginia (Farnham) I.; m. Patricia Edith Watson, Aug. 26, 1961; children: Geri Marie, John David, Laura Lynne. B.E.E., Auburn U., Ala., 1961; M.S., U. Tenn., 1962, Ph.D., 1967. Registered profl. engr., Ala., Ga., Fla. Mem. tech. staff Bell Labs., Holmdel, N.J., 1967-68; supr. Bell Labs, Holmdel, N.J., 1968-69; asst. prof. elec. engring. Auburn U., 1969-72; assoc. prof. Bell Labs., 1972-73; assoc. prof., head dept. Auburn U., 1973-76, prof., head dept., 1976—; co-founder, dir. Insouth Microsystems, Inc., Auburn, 1978-83; pres. Southeastern Ctr. for Elec. Engring. Edn., Orlando, Fla., 1983-84. Author: (with Nagle and Carroll) Introduction to Computer Logic, 1975, Industrial Noise and Vibration Control, 1979, (with E.R. Graf) Basic Engineering Circuit Analysis, 1984. Fellow IEEE (editor jour. Indsl. Electronics 1982, recipient Cert. of Appreciation 1982). Roman Catholic. Home: 127 Eastwood St Auburn AL 36830 Office: Auburn Univ Auburn AL 36849

IRWIN, JOHN NICHOL, II, lawyer; b. Keokuk, Iowa, Dec. 31, 1913; s. John R. and Florence V. (Johnstone) I.; m. Jane Watson, June 2, 1949 (dec. Dec. 1970); children—Jane, John; m. Jane German Reimers, Sept. 30, 1976. Grad., Lawrenceville Sch., 1933; A.B., Princeton, 1937; B.A. in Jurisprudence, Balliol Coll., Oxford (Eng.) U.,

1939, M.A., 1944; LL.B., Fordham U., 1941; LL.D., Parsons Coll., 1960, Union Coll., Schenectady, 1963. Bar: N.Y. bar 1946. Asso. firm Davis, Polk, Wardell, Sunderland and Kiendl, N.Y.C., 1946-50; partner Patterson, Belknap & Webb, 1950-57, 61-70, 74-77, of counsel, 1977—; dep. asst. sec. def. for internat. security affairs Dept. Def., 1957-58; asst. sec. def. for internat. security affairs, 1958-61, under sec. of state, 1970-72, dep. sec. state, 1972-73, Ambassador to, France, 1973-74; Mem. internat. council Morgan Guaranty Trust Co. N.Y.; dir. IBM Corp.; adviser Joint Philippine-Am. Finance Commn., 1947. Trustee Lawrenceville Sch., N.Y. Zool. Soc., Met. Mus. Art; trustee emeritus Princeton U. Served from 1st lt. to col. AUS, 1941-46. Decorated Legion of Merit; comdr. Philippine Legion of Honor; comdr. Ordre des Arts et des Lettres; recipient medal of Freedom, 1961. Mem. Bar Assn. City N.Y., Am., Fed., N.Y. State bar assns., Council Fgn. Relations, Pilgrims of U.S. Presbyn (elder). Clubs: Country (New Canaan, Conn.); 1925 F Street, Metropolitan, Chevy Chase (Washington); Princeton, River, University, Century Assn., Links (N.Y.C.); Fishers Island (N.Y.) Country. Home: 848 Weed St New Canaan CT 06840

IRWIN, JOHN THOMAS, educator; b. Houston, Apr. 24, 1940; s. William Henry and Marguerite Harriet (Hunsaker) I.; m. Laura Elizabeth Scott, Sept. 23, 1978. B.A., U. St. Thomas, 1962; M.A., Rice U., Ph.D., 1970. Supr. public affairs library NASA Manned Spacecraft Center, Houston, 1966-7; asst. prof. English, Johns Hopkins U., 1970-74, chmn., prof. writing seminars, 1977—; Decker prof. in humanities John Hopkins U., 1984—; editor Ga. Rev., U. Ga., 1974-77. Author: Doubling and Incest/Repetition and Revenge, 1975, The Heisenberg Variations, 1976, American Hieroglyphics, 1980; editor: Johns Hopkins Press Fiction and Poetry series, 1978—; contbr. articles to jours. Served with USNR, 1963-66. Recipient John Gardner medal Rice U., 1970; Danforth fellow, 1962. Mem. MLA. Club: Tudor and Stuart. Home: 5313 Springlake Way Baltimore MD 21212 Office: Writing Seminars Gilman 135 Johns Hopkins U Baltimore MD 21218

IRWIN, JOHN WESLEY, publisher; b. Toronto, Ont., Can., July 11, 1937; s. John Coverdale Watson and Annie Elizabeth (Hiltz) I.; m. Marjorie Eleanor Gray, Dec. 16, 1961; children—John Joseph, Marjorie Elizabeth, Peter David Gordon, Andrew James Gray. B.A. with honours, U. Toronto, 1959. Tchr., 1959-60; with Book Soc. Can. Ltd. (ednl. books), Agincourt, Ont., 1960—, gen. mgr., 1967-71, pres., 1971—. Recipient Canadian Confedn. medal, 1967. Mem. Assn. Canadian Pubs. (treas. 1977), Canadian Edn. Assn., Can. Copyright Inst. (gov. 1970-77, 81—), Inter-Varsity Christian Fellowship Can. (dir. 1973—, chmn. 1979—). Baptist. Club: Peiromai (Toronto). Home: 81 Bayview Ridge Willowdale ON M2L 1E3 Canada Office: 4386 Sheppard Ave E Agincourt ON M1S 3B6 Canada

IRWIN, JOSEPH AUGUSTUS, banker; b. Cleve., Apr. 3, 1936; s. Joseph Tilden and Naomi Eleanor I.; m. Barbara Joan Clever, July 9, 1960; children: Linda, Donald, Phillip. B.A. magna cum laude, Dyke Coll., Cleve., 1960. C.P.A., Ohio. With IRS, Cleve., 1960-68; mgr. tax dept. Sherwin-Williams Co., Cleve., 1968-71; corp. tax dir. Burroughs Corp., Detroit, 1971-74; sr. v.p. Security Pacific Nat. Bank, Los Angeles, 1974—, Security Pacific Corp., 1981—. Served with AUS, 1955-58. Mem. Internat. Fiscal Assn., Tax Execs. Inst., Nat. Assn. Rev. Appraisers, Am. Inst. C.P.A.'s, Am. Bankers Assn., Calif. Bankers Assn., Ohio Soc. C.P.A.'s, Calif. Taxpayers Assn. (dir.), Los Angeles Internat. Tax Club. Clubs: Los Angeles Internat., Jonathan (Los Angeles).

IRWIN, JOSEPH JAMES, English language educator; b. Clinton, Iowa, Oct. 29, 1908; s. Joseph Glen and Elizabeth Margaret (Paul) I.; m. Laurentia Mae Donhowe, Dec. 25, 1937; children: Joseph Paul, Martha Elizabeth, James Donhowe. B.A., Grinnell Coll., 1931; M.A., State U. Iowa, 1934, Ph.D., 1942. Tchr. English, speech and journalism Buena Vista Coll., Storm Lake, Iowa, 1934-36; mem. faculty Albion (Mich.) Coll., 1937—, prof. English, 1947-74, prof. emeritus, 1974—, chmn. dept., 1949-71, chmn. div. lang., lit. and speech, 1952-59; dean Bay View (Mich.) Summer Coll. Liberal Arts, 1947-63; prof. English program liberal arts edn. for adults Mich. State U., 1957-60; tutor Albion-Marshall Literacy Council, 1982—. Author: M.G. (Monk) Lewis; Contbr. articles to religious and profl. publs. Trustee Bay View Assn., 1947-53. Mem. AAUP (council 1948-52), Mich. Coll. English Assn. (pres. 1949-50), Modern Lang. Assn., Nat. Council Tchrs. English, Nat. Collegiate Players, Theta Alpha Phi, Alpha Phi Gamma. Episcopalian (lic. lay reader, mem. diocesan commn. on aging). Home: 416 E Erie St Albion MI 49224

IRWIN, LEO HOWARD, U.S. judge; b. Stratford, N.C., Aug. 1, 1917; s. W. Carl and Mallie (Wilson) I.; m. Doris Mickelson; children: Sandra Lee, Lisa Ann, Patrice Camille, Leo Howard, Lori Denice. Student, U. N.C., 1935-38; A.B., George Washington U., 1940; LL.B., Georgetown U., 1947. Bar: N.C., D.C. 1947, U.S. Supreme Ct. 1963. With various govt. agys., 1938-42; atty. Gen. Counsel's Office, CAB, 1947-48; mem. profl. staff, minority counsel com. ways and means Ho. of Reps., 1949-55, chief counsel, 1955-68; judge U.S. Tax Ct., Washington, 1968—; Guest German Govt. on econ. study tour, 1964, Swedish and Danish govts., 1964; adj. prof. Georgetown U. Law Center Grad. Sch., evenings 1962-63. Served as officer USNR, 1942-46. Mem. Fed. Bar Assn. Home: 3812 24th Ave Temple Hills MD 20748 Office: US Tax Ct 400 2d St NW Washington DC 20217

IRWIN, PAT, federal judge; b. Leedey, Okla., June 12, 1921; s. Marvin J. and Ollie D. (Newton) I.; m. Margaret Boggs, Aug. 18, 1950; children: William, Margaret. Student, Southwestern State Coll., 1939-41; LL.B., U. Okla., 1949. Bar: Okla. 1949. County atty., Dewey County, 1949-50; sec. to commrs. land office Okla. Sch. Land Commn., 1955-58; justice Okla. Supreme Ct., 1959-83, chief justice, 1969-70, 81-82; judge U.S. Dist. Ct. (we. dist.) Okla., 1983—; presiding judge appellate div. Okla. Ct. on Judiciary, 1971-74; mem. exec. council Conf. Chief Justices, 1971-72. Mem. Okla. Senate, 1951-54. Served to capt. USMCR, 1942-46; PTO. Mem. Am. Legion, Delta Theta Phi. Democrat. Club: Masons. Home: 1325 Andover Ct Oklahoma City OK 73120 Office: US Courthouse Oklahoma City OK 73102

IRWIN, PHILIP DONNAN, lawyer; b. Madison, Wis., Sept. 6, 1933; s. Constant Louis and Isabel Dorothy (Elfving) I.; m. Jo Ann Haycraft, June 23, 1956; children: Jane Donnan, James Haycraft, Victoria Wisnom. B.A., U. Wyo., 1954; LL.B., Stanford U., 1957. Bar: Wyo. 1957, Calif. 1958. Assoc. O'Melveny & Myers, Los Angeles, 1957-65, ptnr., 1965—; mem. planning com. Inst. Fed. Taxation of U. So. Calif. Law Ctr., 1976—; speaker legal seminars. Contbr. articles legal jours. Trustee Mackenzie Found., Los Angeles, 1969—. Republican. Episcopalian. Club: California (Los Angeles). Office: O'Melveny & Myers 400 S Hope St Los Angeles CA 90071

IRWIN, RICHARD ARNOLD, paper manufacturing executive; b. Tara, Ont., Can., Apr. 5, 1909; s. Alexander J. and Amelia (Hassard) I.; m. Catherine Janet Moffat, Sept. 4, 1937; children: Richard, Judith, Catherine, Elizabeth. B.A.Sc., U. Toronto, 1931; LL.D., St. Thomas U. Chemist Ont. Dept. Health, 1931-33, Nat. Carbon Co., 1933-34; with Somerville Industries Ltd., 1934-57, dir. sales, 1944-45, gen. mgr., 1945-48, v.p., gen. mgr., 1948-53, pres., gen. mgr., 1953-57; pres. Eddy Paper Co., Ltd., Hull, Que., 1954-56; pres., mng. dir. E.B. Eddy Co., 1954-56; v.p. Bathurst Power and Paper Co., Ltd. (name changed to Bathurst Paper, Ltd. 1965), Montreal, 1957-59, dir., 1958, pres., 1959-67; pres., chief exec. officer, dir. Consol. Bathhurst Inc., 1967-70, chmn., 1970-77; dir. T.I.W. Industries Ltd., Rolland Paper Co., Ltd., Maritime Paper Products Ltd. Past pres. met. bd. YMCA. Mem. Can. Paper Box Mfrs. Assn. (pres. 1953-54), Canadian Pulp and Paper Assn. (chmn. exec. bd. 1964-65), Phi Delta Theta. Clubs: London Hunt and Country, London; National (Toronto); Mount Royal (Montreal). Home: 597 Cranbrook Rd London ON N6K 2Y4 Canada

IRWIN, RICHARD DORSEY, publisher; b. St. Joseph, Mo., Nov. 2, 1905; s. William Herbert and Ida Ferrell (Dorsey) I.; m. Anne Marie Thompson, Feb. 2, 1927; children: Jacqueline Marie Irwin Pipher, Richard Dorsey, Jr. Student U. Ill., 1924-27; LL.D. (hon.), Ball State U., 1970. Mgr. coll. dept. A.W. Shaw Co., 1928, McGraw-Hill Book Co., 1928-32; hon. chmn., founder Richard D. Irwin, Inc., Homewood, Ill., 1933—; hon. chmn. Dorsey Press, Learning Systems Co., Bus. Publs., Inc., Irwin-Dorsey Internat., Dow Jones-Irwin, Inc.; dir. 1st Nat. Bank of Harvey; cons. O.P.A., 1943. Mem. Dist. 161 Sch. Bd., Flossmoor, Ill., 1948-54; chmn. bd. Richard D. Irwin Found.; trustee U. Ill. Found., Glenwood Sch. for Boys. Richard D. Irwin Grad. Sch. Mgmt. of Am. Coll., Bryn Mawr, Pa. named for him. Mem. Am. Assn. Collegiate Schs. Bus., Am. Acctg. Assn., Am., Midwest, So. econ. assns., Am. Mktg. Assn., Midwest Bus. Adminstrn. Assn., Am. Bus. Law Assn., Profl. Golfers Assn. (nat. adv. com.), Alpha Kappa Psi, Omicron Delta Epsilon, Beta Gamma Sigma. Clubs: Olympia Fields (Ill.) Country, Flossmoor Country, Chicago Athletic Assn. Home: 1230 Braeburn Rd Flossmoor IL 60422 Office: 1818 Ridge Rd Homewood IL 60430

IRWIN, RICHARD LOREN, assn. exec.; b. Los Angeles, Dec. 8, 1924; s. Loren Wilson and Letty Elizabeth (Tate) I.; m. Martha Louise Sutton, Dec. 15, 1945; children—Martha Jean, Carol Ann. Student, Lockyear's Bus. Coll., 1942-43, 46-48. Cert. assn. exec. Am. Soc. Assn. Execs. Mgr. machine accounting U. O. Colson Co., Paris, Ill., 1949-55; founder Nat. Machine Accts. Assn. (now Data Processing Mgmt. Assn.), 1951, internat. pres., 1954-55, exec. sec., Paris, Ill., 1955-60; asst. adminstrv. dir. Am. Optometric Assn., St. Louis, 1960-62; exec. dir. Assn. Systems Mgmt., Cleve., 1962—. Served with USNR, 1943-46. Ky. col. Mem. Am. Soc. Assn. Execs., U.S. C. of C., Data Processing Mgmt. Assn. (life). Republican. Presbyterian. Clubs: Am. Legion, Masons, Shriners, Elks, Moose. Home: 156 Sunset Dr Berea OH 44017 Office: 24587 Bagley Rd Cleveland OH 44138

IRWIN, RICHARD WARREN, consulting company executive; b. Flushing, N.Y., Jan. 8, 1951; s. Warren Barker and Shelia (Hoskins) I. Student, East Carolina U., 1969-70. Announcer Sta. WEGO, Concord, N.C., 1965-68; prodn. mgr. Sta. WIXE, Monroe, N.C., 1968-69; program dir. Sta. WYCL, York, S.C., 1970-73; asst. program dir. Sta. WJAR, Providence, 1973-75; program dir. Sta. WFEC, WQXA, York, Harrisburg, Pa., 1975-76, Sta. KAFY, Bakersfield, Calif., 1976-78; ops. mgr. Sta. KROY AM-FM, Sacramento, 1978-82; cons. Gary Burns & Assocs., San Antonio, 1982—. Home: 216 Grace Ave Sacramento CA 95838 Office: 216 Grace Ave Sacramento CA 95838

IRWIN, ROBERT JAMES ARMSTRONG, JR., investment company executive; b. Buffalo, June 27, 1927; s. Robert J.A. and Dorothy (McLean) I.; m. Donna Henwood, Sept. 10, 1966; children: William Baird, Elaine Mitchell, Elizabeth Flora, Robert J.A. IV, Ronald Henwood, Derrick Millet. B.A., Colgate U., 1949; postgrad., U. Buffalo, 1949-50, Babson Inst. Finance, Wellesley, Mass., 1952-53. Exec. trainee Mfrs. & Traders Trust Co., Buffalo, 1950-52; registered rep. Doolittle & Co., Buffalo, 1953-58; with Marine Trust Co. Western N.Y., Buffalo, 1958-66, investment mgmt. officer, 1959-61, v.p. charge investment mgmt. dept., 1961-66; v.p. Marine Midland Banks, Inc., N.Y.C., 1966-69, sr. v.p., 1969-71; exec. v.p. Dreyfus-Marine Midland Mgmt. Corp., 1970-72; sr. exec. v.p. Niagara Share Corp., Buffalo, 1972-74, pres., 1974—; mem. N.Y. State Comptroller's investment adv. com. for N.Y. State Common Retirement Fund, 1979—; dir. Transatlantic Fund., Mfrs. & Traders Trust Co., First Empire State Corp. Bd. dirs. Boys Club Buffalo, Inc., 1953—, v.p., 1964-65; bd. dirs. Buffalo Med. Found., 1975—, Am. Scottish Found.; trustee Baird Found., 1965—, Buffalo Fine Arts Acad., Ridley Coll. Found., James H. Cummings Found., 1978—. Mem. Assn. Publicly Traded Investment Funds. Clubs: Buffalo, Saturn, Mid Day, Canoe (Buffalo); Royal Canadian Yacht (Toronto); University (N.Y.C.). Home: 101 Meadow Rd Buffalo NY 14216 Office: 70 Niagara St Buffalo NY 14202

IRWIN, ROBERT WALTER, artist; b. Long Beach, Calif., Sept. 12. 1928; s. Overton Ernest and Goldie Florence (Anderberg) I. Student, Otis Art Inst., 1948-50, Chouinard Art Inst., 1952-53; Doctorate in Art (hon.), San Francisco Coll. Art, 1979. Instr. Chouinard Art Inst., 1957-58, UCLA, 1962, U. Calif., Irvine, 1968-69; lectr. in field. Exhibited in one-man shows, Jewish Museum, N.Y.C., 1968, Mus. Modern Art, N.Y.C., 1970, Chgo. Mus. Contemporary Art, 1976, Walker Art Center, Mpls., Whitney Mus. Am. Art, N.Y.C., 1977, group shows include, Los Angeles County Mus. Art, 1967, Venice Biennale, 1976-80; represented in permanent collections, including, Art Inst. Chgo., San Francisco Mus., Mus. Modern Art, N.Y.C., Whitney Mus. Am. Art, Walker Art Center, Des Moines Art Center; site installations include, North Entrance, Dallas, Wellesley (Mass.) Coll., Civic Center, Seattle, Old Post Office, Washington, U. Calif., San Diego. Served with U.S. Army, 1946-48, 50-51. NEA fellow, 1968-69; Guggenheim fellow, 1975-76. Office: 328 S Beverly Dr Beverly Hills CA 90212

IRWIN, THEODORE, writer; b. N.Y.C., Sept. 17, 1907; s. Ira S. and Rebecca (Arlow) I.; m. Rita Reisman, June 13, 1931 (dec. Mar. 1962); children: Jed, Kenneth; m. Helen Ross, Apr. 12, 1964. B.S., N.Y. U., 1928. Newspaper reporter, feature writer, 1928-31, free lance mag. writer, novelist, 1931-39; mng. editor Cue mag., 1939-41; asso. editor Look mag., 1941-45; edit. dir. Farrell Pub. Co., 1945-52; editor Real mag., 1952-54; pres. Editorial Services, 1954-56; editor Mediguide, 1972. Author: Collusion, 1932, Strange Passage, 1935, Accident of Birth, 1937, Holland: Fantastic Land Below the Sea, 1961, Modern Birth Control, 1961, Better Health After Fifty, 1964, What Executives Should Know About Tension, 1965, Instant Shrink, 1971, Understanding and Overcoming Depression, 1973, Stop, Thief!, 1978; contbr. to nat. mag. Mem. Am. Soc. Journalists and Authors (pres. 1970), Authors Guild. Home: 250 E 73d St New York NY 10021

IRWIN, THOMAS BARTON, energy co. exec.; b. Marlin, Tex., Sept. 8, 1930; s. John Landon and Velma (Barton) I.; m. Dolores Ann Harris, Apr. 19, 1952; children—Todd Harris, Constance Jo, Jay Barton. B.B.A., U. Houston, 1956. With Panhandle Eastern Corp. (and subs.'s), 1955—; fin. v.p. Anadarko Prodn. Co., Houston, 1979-81, corp. sr. v.p. fin., 1981—, also dir. Sect. dir. Pony Baseball. Served with AUS, 1953-55. Mem. Am. Gas Assn., Fin. Execs. Inst., Ind. Natural Gas Assn. Am. Republican. Methodist. Clubs: Houston, Houston City. Office: PO Box 1642 Houston TX 77251 *

ISAAC, SOL MORTON, lawyer; b. Columbus, Ohio, Dec. 5, 1911; s. Arthur J. and Bella (Loewenstein) I.; m. Dorothy Durlacher, Dec. 18, 1936 (dec.); children: Beatrice, Frederick Morton, Thomas Durlacher. B.A., Yale U., 1933; LL.B., Harvard U., 1936. Bar: Ohio 1936. Since practiced in, Columbus; asso. firm James M. Butler, 1936-40, Butler & Isaac, 1940-47, Isaac, Postlewaite, O'Brian and Oman, 1950-72; sr. mem. firm Isaac & Isaac, 1972-76, Isaac, Graham & Nester, 1976-83, Isaac, Brant, Ledman and Becker, 1983—; Sec., dir. Diamond Milk Products, Inc., 1959-70; chmn. bd. Sunday Creek Coal Co., 1970-71. Bd. dirs. United Community Council Columbus and Franklin County, 1958—, pres., 1969-70; chmn. Gov.'s Survey Com. Mental Health, 1956-57; mem. Ohio Commn. Children and Youth, 1961-62; mem. council on intercultural edn. Columbus Sch. Bd., 1966-68; bd. Ohio Citizens Council for Health and Welfare; pres., 1956-59, Family Service Assn. Am., 1953-54; v.p. Nat. Social Welfare Assembly, 1958-60; co-chmn. Nat. Conf. Lawyers and Social Workers, 1961-67; Bd. dirs. Columbus Acad., 1947-65, v.p., 1948-59, disting. alumnus award, 1978; bd. dirs., exec. com. Riverside Meth. Hosp., 1965-81; bd. dirs. exec. com. Riverside Meth. Hosp. Found., 1983—; bd. dirs. Columbus Area Leadership Lab. Inc., 1974-81, pres., 1979-80; bd. dirs. Nat. Legal Aid and Defender Assn., 1958-60. Served from lt. (j.g.) to lt. USNR, 1943-46. Recipient Brotherhood award Temple Israel, Columbus, 1973, Nat. Guardian of the Menorah award B'nai B'rith, 1974, Mayor's Community Service medal, 1978; Life with Dignity award Heritage House, Columbus, 1980. Fellow Am. Bar Found., Am. Coll. Probate Counsel; mem. ABA (chmn. sect. family law 1960-61), Ohio Bar Assn. (Ohio Bar medal 1972), Columbus Bar Assn. (pres. 1952-53, Community Service award 1969), Nat. Conf. Social Welfare (pres. 1964-65). Home: 97 Bishop Sq Columbus OH 43209 Office: 250 E Broad St Columbus OH 43215

ISAAC, WALTER, psychologist, educator; b. Cleve., June 13, 1927; s. Walter Roy and Irene (Pillars) I.; m. Dorothy Jane Emerson, Oct. 14, 1949; children: Susan Irene, Walter Lon. B.S., Western Res. U., 1949; M.A., Ohio State U., 1950, Ph.D., 1953. Predoctoral fellow Sch. Aviation Medicine, U.S. Air Force, Austin, Tex., 1953; research instr. Sch. Medicine U. Wash., Seattle, 1954-56; asst. research psychologist Sch. Medicine UCLA, 1956-57; assst. prof. psychology Emory U., Atlanta, 1957-60, asso. prof., 1960-65, prof., 1965-68; prof. physiol. psychology U. Ga., Athens, 1968—. Served with USNR, 1945-46. NIMH grantee. Fellow AAAS; mem. Psychonomic Soc., So. Soc. for Philosophy and Psychology, Southeastern Psychol. Assn., Am. Assn. Lab. Animal Sci., Soc. Behavioral Medicine, Nat. Acad. Neuropsychologists, Internat. Neuropsychol. Soc. Home: 180 Chinquapin Way Athens GA 30605 Office: Dept Psychology U of Ga Athens GA 30602

ISAAC, WILLIAM H., investments executive; b. Jacksonville, Fla., Sept. 1, 1935; s. Nathan and Claire (Mannassee) I.; children: Lisa, Robin. A.A., U. Fla., 1955. With San Jose Manor, Inc. (developer), Miami, Fla., 1960-62; from project mgr. to sr. v.p. ITT Levitt & Sons, Inc., Lake Success, N.Y., 1963-71; pres. Arundel Corp., Balt., 1972-74, also dir., 1970-74; self-employed real estate cons., 1974—; dir. Century Nat. Bank; adviser to bd. P&F Industries, Inc. Mem. exec. bd. Balt. council Boy Scouts Am. Served with AUS, 1957-59. Clubs: Center, Engineers (Balt.); International (Washington). Home: 5 Darby Ct Bethesda MD 20817 Office: 1910 K St NW Suite 800 Washington DC 20006 *Problems may otherwise be defined as challenges and opportunities.*

ISAAC, WILLIAM MICHAEL, government official; b. Bryan, Ohio, Dec. 21, 1943; s. Charles R. and Ruth L. (Hallberg) I.; m. Carma Sue Dunbar, Aug. 15, 1965; children: David M., Stephanie A. B.S., Miami U.-Oxford, Ohio, 1966; J.D. summa cum laude, Ohio State U., 1969. Bar: Wis. 1969, Ky. 1974. Mem. firm. Foley & Lardner, Milw., 1969-74; v.p., gen. counsel, sec. First Ky. Nat. Corp., Louisville, 1974-78; chmn. FDIC, Washington, 1978—; mem. Depository Instns. Deregulation Com., 1981—, Bush Task Group, 1982—; chmn. Fed. Fin. Instns. Exam. Council, 1983—. Author: Bank Holding Companies: A Practical Guide to Bank Acquisitions and Mergers, 1972. Mem. nat. council Coll. Law, Ohio State U., Columbus, 1980—. Mem. ABA, Wis. Bar Assn., Ky. Bar Assn. Republican. Presbyterian. Home: 9514 Neuse Way Great Falls VA 22066 Office: FDIC 550 17th St NW Washington DC 20429

ISAACS, EDGAR E., ins. cons.; b. New Douglas, Ill., Aug. 27, 1912; s. Edgar Percy and Julia Eliza (Head) I.; m. Alice Elizabeth Ross, Oct. 8, 1938; 1 son, Robert Erle. Student, Washington U., St. Louis; pre-legal student, Benton Coll. Law, St. Louis, 1934-36; LL.B., City Coll. Law and Finance, St. Louis, 1941; C.P.C.U., 1951. With Aetna Casualty and Surety Co., 1930-43, Am. Asso. Ins. Companies, 1943-52; with Atlantic Companies, 1952-61, v.p., 1956-61; exec. v.p. Continental Casualty Co., Chgo., 1961-64; asst. U.S. mgr., dir. Zurich-Am. Ins. Group, 1964-71; spl. exec. cons. Am. Gen. Ins. Group, Balt.; v.p. Assurance Co. Am., Md. Casualty Co., No. Ins. Co., 1972-76; exec. v.p., chief operating officer Med. Mut. Liability Ins. Soc. Md., 1976-78; pres. RIB Corp. of Cambria, Phoenix, Md., 1978—. Home and Office: 2501 Garsden Ct-Cambria Phoenix MD 21131

ISAACS, GERALD WILLIAM, educator, agricultural engineer; b. Crawfordsville, Ind., Sept. 3, 1927; s. William Paul and Verna (Johnson) I.; m. Phyllis Joyce Seaton, Aug. 22, 1948; children: Joyce Irene (dec.), David Gerald, Donald Phillip, Joseph Lee (dec.), Susan Verna, Linda Kay. B.S., Purdue U., 1947, M.S., 1949; Ph.D., Mich. State U., 1954. Registered profl. engr., Ind. Instr. Purdue U., 1948-52, asst. prof., 1954-57, asso. prof., 1957-60, prof., 1960-64, head agrl. engring. dept., 1964-81; grad. research asst. Mich. State U., 1952-54; chmn. agrl. engring. dept. U. Fla., Gainesville, 1981—. Contbr. articles to profl. jours. Served with USNR, 1945-46. Fellow Am. Soc. Agrl. Engrs. (pres. 1982-83); mem. Am. Soc. Engring. Edn., Nat. Soc. Profl. Engrs., Sigma Xi, Pi Mu Epsilon, Alpha Epsilon, Phi Tau Sigma, Tau Beta Pi, Gamma Sigma Delta. Lutheran. Club: Rotarian. Home: 2221 NW 27th Terr Gainesville FL 32605 Office: Agrl Engring Dept U Fla Gainesville FL 32601

ISAACS, HAROLD ROBERT, writer; b. N.Y.C., Sept. 13, 1910; s. Robert and Sophie (Berlin) I.; m. Viola Robinson, Sept. 14, 1932; children: Arnold R., Deborah S. A.B., Columbia U., 1930. Reporter N.Y. Times, also Honolulu Advt., Shanghai Eve. Post and China Press, 1928-31; with Agence Havas, Shanghai and N.Y.C., 1931-40, CBS, N.Y.C. and Washington, 1940-43; war corr., CBI, assoc. editor Newsweek mag., Washington, also China, S.E. Asia and N.Y.C., 1943-50; research assoc. Center Internat. Studies, MIT, Cambridge, 1953-65, prof. polit. sci., 1965-76, prof. emeritus, 1976—. Author: The Tragedy of the Chinese Revolution, 1938, No Peace for Asia, 1947, Two-Thirds of the World, 1950, Scratches on Our Minds, American Images of China and India, 1958, Emergent Americans, a Report on Crossroads Africa, 1961, The New World of Negro Americans, 1963 (Anisfield-Wolf award 1964), India's Ex- Untouchables, 1965, American Jews in Israel, 1967, Idols of the Tribe: Group Identity and Political Change, 1975, Power and Identity: Tribalism in World Politics, 1979; Editor: Straw Sandals, Chinese Stories, 1918-33, 1974. Guggenheim fellow, 1950. Fellow Am. Acad. Arts and Scis. Home: 96 Farlow Rd Newton MA 02158

ISAACS, KENNETH L., banker; b. Scranton, Pa., June 18, 1904; s. Albert George and Anna Carpenter (Richards) I.; m. Helen Coolidge Adams, Mar. 10, 1949; children: Kenneth C.A., Anne Carpenter Richards Merwin. M.E., Lehigh U., 1925, LL.D., 1965; M.B.A., Harvard U., 1927. Buying dept. Nat. City Co., 1927-30; pvt. investment work, 1930-32; asst. to comptroller Cornell U. (specializing on endowment fund investments), 1932-36; with Mass. Investors Trust, 1936-69; formerly chmn., mem. investment mgmt. com. Mass. Investors Trust, Mass. Investors Growth Stock Fund, Inc.; former partner Mass. Financial Services; hon. trustee Suffolk-Franklin Savs.

Bank; hon. dir. So. Pacific Co., Phelps Dodge Corp., Gen. Pub. Utilities Corp. Hon. trustee Lehigh U. Republican. Episcopalian. Clubs: Somerset (Boston); Brook, Harvard, Knickerbocker (N.Y.C.). Home: 68 Beacon St Boston MA 02108 Office: 200 Berkeley St Boston MA 02116

ISAACS, LAWRENCE MARTIN, retail chain executive; b. Kingston, Pa., May 3, 1921; s. John Raymond and Ethel (Williams) I.; m. Louise Kresge, Aug. 24, 1946; children: Jane Louise Isaacs Lowe, John David, Thomas Lawrence, Mary Ellen. B.S., Susquehanna U., 1943; M.B.A., U. Pa., 1947. With Price Waterhouse & Co., 1947-58, Bethlehem Steel Corp., 1958-62; dir. auditing and data processing RCA, 1962-67, v.p., controller, 1967-71; exe. v.p., chief fin. officer Allis Chalmers Corp., 1971-76; exec. v.p., fin. Federated Dept. Stores Inc., Cin., 1976—. Bd. dirs. Susquehanna U. Served to lt. USN. Mem. Am. Inst. C.P.A.s, Fin. Execs. Inst., Nat. Assn. Accts. Office: 222 W 7th St Cincinnati OH 45202

ISAACS, NORMAN ELLIS, educator, editor; b. Manchester, Eng., Mar. 28, 1908; s. Rufus and Esther (Simon) I.; m. Dorothy Ritz, 1932 (dec. 1977); children: Roberta (Mathews), Stephen; m. Mildred L. Wade, 1979. With Indpls. Star, 1925; with Indpls. Times, 1926-43, mng. editor, 1936-43; editorial dir. Indpls. News, 1943-45; mng. editor St. Louis Star-Times, 1945-51, Louisville Times, 1951-61; v.p., exec. editor Courier-Jour. and Louisville Times, 1962-71; asso. dean, editor in residence Columbia U., 1971-80; pres., pub. News Jour. Co., Wilmington, Del., 1975-76; chmn. Nat. News Council, 1977-82; Hearst prof. communications Stanford U., 1982; editor-in-residence East-West Ctr., Honolulu, 1983-84; chmn. U. Calif. Commn. Campus Press, 1970; vice chmn. task force on govt. and press 20th Century Fund, 1971; pub. affairs mission Dept. State, to India, 1958, to Yugoslavia, 1959; adv. bd. Pulitzer Prizes; chmn. Champion awards for bus. writing Dartmouth Coll., 1978—; mem. selection com. Nieman Fellows; mem. adv. bd. Stanford Fellows; mem. selection bd. Edward Murrow Fellowship. Author: Ethics and Journalism, 1984. Pres. Louisville Philharm., 1956-66, Louisville Fund, 1958-59. Recipient William A. White award; So. Meth. U. medal; N.Y. State Editors award for career-long services; named to Ind. Journalism Hall of Fame, 1983. Mem. Internat. Press. Inst., Am. Soc. Newspaper Editors (pres. 1969-70), Council Fgn. Relations, AP Mng. Editors Assn. (pres. 1953), Sigma Delta Chi (chmn. com. to rev. press 1954, nat. chmn. ethics com. 1955-56). Clubs: Century Assn., Coffee House (N.Y.C.). Home and Office: 97 Judson Ave Dobbs Ferry NY 10522

ISAACS, REGINALD RODERIC, emeritus city planning educator; b. Winnipeg, Can., July 20, 1911; came to U.S., 1922, naturalized, 1944; s. Mark and Sophia (Rau) I.; m. Charlotte Aldes, Mar. 24, 1937; children: Merry Aldes, Mark Aldes, Henry Aldes. B. Arch., U. Minn., 1935; M.Arch., Harvard U., 1939; student, U. Chgo., 1947-50. Licensed architect, Nat. Council Archtl. Registration Bds., D.C., Ill., Mass. Architect housing, city planner, Washington, Mpls., Chgo., Phila., other cities, 1926-40; city planner Chgo. Plan Commn., Syracuse Plan Commn.; with various fed. agys., 1940-45; dir. planning staff Michael Reese Hosp., Chgo., 1945-53; cons. South Side Planning Bd., Chgo., 1946-53; Charles Dyer Norton prof. regional planning Harvard, 1953-78, Norton prof. emeritus, 1978—, chmn. dept. city and regional planning, 1953-64; cons. to P.R. Govt., 1956—, UN, 1960-62, V.I. Gov., 1961—, Gulf Regional Planning Comm., 1966—, Ford Found.; specialist U.S. State Dept., 1959; chmn. cons. Am. Council to Improve Our Neighborhoods, 1954-55; dir. met. area planning study Met. Housing and Planning Council of Chgo., 1955-56. Author: (with John Dyckman) Capital Requirements for Urban Development and Renewal, 1960, Walter Gropius, Der Mensch und Sein Werk, 1983; contbr. articles profl. publs.; exhbns., Mus. Modern Art, 1947, Chgo. Art Inst., 1936, 7th Pan-Am. Congress Architects, Havana, 1950. Mem. bd. overseers com. to visit Harvard Grad. Sch. Design, 1951-53. Fellow Royal Soc. Arts.; mem. Kuratorium, Bauhaus-Archiv (Berlin). Address: 221 Mount Auburn St Cambridge MA 02138

ISAACS, ROGER DAVID, public relations executive; b. Boston, Oct. 23, 1925; s. Raphael and Agnes (Wolfstein) I.; m. Joyce R. Wexler, Oct. 23, 1949; children: Jill, Jan. Student, U. Wis., 1943; A.B., Bard Coll., 1949. With Pub. Relations Bd., Inc., Chgo., 1948—, account supr., 1948-51, partner, 1951-60, exec. v.p., 1960-66, pres., 1966-75, chmn., pres., 1975—; dir. Creative Design Bd., Pub. Relations Network/Internat., Pub. Relations Sports Network, Careful Office Service. Bd. dirs. Jewish Family and Community Service, Chgo. Crime Commn., Sr. Centers Met. Chgo., Highland Park Hosp., Met. Crusade of Mercy, Suburban Fine Arts Center, Asthma and Allergy Found.; mem. exec. com. Anti-Defamation League Chgo., Spertus Coll. Judaica. Served with AUS, 1943-45. Decorated Purple Heart. Mem. Pub. Relations Soc. Am., Chgo. Assn. Commerce and Industry. Clubs: Birchwood, Monroe, Publicity (Chgo.). Home: 2661 Sheridan Rd Highland Park IL 60035 Office: 150 E Huron Chicago IL 60611

ISAACS, STEPHEN DAVID, television news producer; b. Indpls., Dec. 8, 1937; s. Norman Ellis and Dorothy (Ritz) I.; m. Diane Scharfeld, June 8, 1963; children: Deborah Alice, David Arthur, Sharon Diane. A.B., Harvard U., 1959. Successively copy editor, music critic, fin. editor Louisville Times, 1959-60; reporter, editor various Brit. publns., 1960-61; with Washington Post., 1961-77, met. editor, 1964-70, chief N.Y. bur., 1971-74, nat. corr., 1974-77; dir. Los Angeles Times-Washington Post News Service, 1977-78; editor Mpls. Star, 1978-82; producer CBS News, N.Y.C., 1982—. Author: Jews and American Politics, 1974, also articles. Mem. Authors Guild. Office: 524 W 57th St New York NY 10019

ISAACSON, GERALD SIDNEY, publishing company executive; b. St. Augustine, Fla., Jan. 30, 1927; s. Albert L. and Mildred E. (Wigers) I.; m. Ann Suitts, July 29, 1950; children: Jill (Mrs. Daniel Gianola), G. Todd, Kurt A., Margaret Mary, Peter E. B.A., Knox Coll., 1950. Salesman, asst. Midwest mgr. Harcourt, Brace, Jovanovich, Chgo., 1950-64; v.p. sales Silver Burdett Co., Morristown, N.J., 1964-67; sales mgr., pres. sch. div. Macmillan, Inc., N.Y.C., 1967-72; pres. Xerox Edn. Publs., Middletown, Conn., 1972-77; v.p. Esquire, Inc., N.Y.C., 1978-81, sr. v.p., 1981—; pres. Esquire Edn. Group, 1978—; dir. Allyn and Bacon, Inc. Served to 1st lt., inf. AUS, 1951-53. Decorated Bronze Star. Mem. Phi Gamma Delta. Conglist. Clubs: Pettipaug Yacht, Essex Yacht, Riverside Yacht. Home: 45 Willow Rd Riverside CT 06878 Office: 488 Madison Ave New York NY 10022

ISAACSON, JULIUS, labor union official. Pres. Internat. Union Allied Novelty & Prodn. Workers. Office: 147-149 E 26th St New York NY 10010§

ISAACSON, WILLIAM JAMES, lawyer; b. Chgo., Aug. 22, 1927; s. Oscar William and Helen Violet (Doyle) I.; m. Mary Alice Disch, May 11, 1957; children: William James, Margaret Anne, James Edward. B.S.C., Loyola U., Chgo., 1949; J.D., Northwestern U., 1952. Bar: Ill. 1952. Tax acct. Arthur Andersen & Co. (C.P.A.s), Chgo., 1952-54; pvt. practice, Chgo., 1954—; ptnr. Henehan, Donovan & Isaacson, Ltd., 1955—. Bd. govs. Thomas Aquinas Coll., 1979—; trustee Am. Conservatory of Music, 1982—; bd. dirs. Friends for Life, Inc., 1978-83, Nat. Pro-Lifepac, 1978—; bd. dirs., sec. Inst. Religious Life, 1975—; mem. adv. bd. Cath. Charities Chgo., 1979—; bd. dirs. Cath. Home Study Inst., 1983—; pres. Chgo. chpt. Cath. League Religious and Civil Rights, 1983—. Served with USNR, 1945-46. Mem. Am., Ill., Chgo. bar assns., Fellowship of Cath. Scholars. Republican. Roman Catholic. Clubs: Chgo. Athletic, Cliff Dwellers, Met. (Chgo.). Home: 11 E Alden Ln Lake Forest IL 60045 Office: 135 S LaSalle St Chicago IL 60603

ISAKOFF, SHELDON ERWIN, chem. engr.; b. Bklyn., May 25, 1925; s. Harry and Rebecca I.; m. Anita Ginsburg, Aug. 18, 1946; 1 son, Peter D. B.S., Columbia U., 1945, M.S., 1947, Ph.D., 1952. Guest fellow Brookhaven Nat. Lab., Upton, N.Y., 1949-50; with E.I. duPont de Nemours & Co., Inc., Wilmington, Del., 1951—, dir. engring. research and devel., 1975—; mem. Nat. Materials Adv. Bd., 1980—. Served with USNR, 1943-46. Fellow Am. Inst. Chem. Engrs. (past dir., Founders award 1980), AAAS; mem. Am. Chem. Soc., Nat. Acad. Engring., Sigma Xi, Tau Beta Pi, Phi Lambda Upsilon. Address: RD 1 Box 361 Chadds Ford PA 19317

ISARD, WALTER, economics educator; b. Phila., Apr. 19, 1919; m. Caroline Berliner, July, 1943; children: Peter, Susan, Toni, Michael, Scott A., Roberta J., Anni K., Arthur. A.B., Temple U., 1939; M.A., Harvard U., 1941, Ph.D., 1943; postgrad., U. Chgo., 1941-42; hon. degrees, Poznan Acad. Economics, 1976, Erasmus U., 1978, U. Karlsruhe, 1979, Umea U., 1980. Lectr., research asso. Harvard U., 1949-53, vis. prof., 1965-70; asso. prof. regional econs. M.I.T., 1953-56, asso. dir. sect. urban and regional studies, 1953-55, dir., 1955-56; prof. econs. U. Pa., Phila., 1956-79; past chmn. dept. regional sci., chmn. dept. peace sci.; prof. Cornell U., 1979—; vis. prof. regional sci. Yale U., 1960-61; pres. Regional Sci. Research Inst., 1957—; exec. sec. Peace Research Soc. (Internat.), 1955; cons. Resources for Future. Author: Atomic Power, An Economic and Social Analysis, 1952, Location and Space-Economy, 1956, Municipal Costs and Revenues, 1957, Methods of Regional Analysis, 1960, General Theory, 1969, Spatial Dynamics and Optimal Space-Time Development, 1979, Conflict Analysis and Practical Conflict Management, 1983; Editor: Regional Sci. Studies series. Fellow World Acad. Art and Sci. (pres. 1977-81), Am. Acad. Art and Sci.; mem. Regional Sci. Assn. (pres., Founders medal 1978), Am. Econ. Assn., Econometric Soc., Assn. Am. Geographers, Phi Beta Kappa. Home: 3218 Garrett Rd Drexel Hill PA 19026 Office: Uris Bldg 476 Cornell U Ithaca NY 14853

ISAUTIER, BERNARD FRANÇOIS, oil company executive; b. St.-Symphorien, Indre et Loire, France, Sept. 19, 1942; s. Francois and Genevieve (Roy) I.; m. Charlotte Isautier, July 22, 1968; children—Anne-Caroline, Armelle, Francois. Grad., Ecole Polytechnique, Paris, 1963, Ecole des Mines, Paris, 1966, Institute d'Etudes Politiques, Paris, 1968. Head dept. mining exploration French Ministry of Industry, Paris, 1970-73, adviser to minister of industry for energy and raw materials, 1973-75; gen. mgr. SEREPT (subs. Elf-Aquitaine Group), Tunis, Tunisia, 1976-78; pres. Aquitaine Co. of Can. Ltd., Calgary, Alta., 1978-81; pres., chief exec. officer Canterra Energy Ltd., Calgary, Alta., 1981—; chmn., dir. Cansulex Ltd. Bd. dirs., vice chmn. Sulphur Inst. Served to lt. Res. Army of France, 1961-64. Decorated chevalier de l'Ordre du Merite, France). Mem. Canadian Petroleum Assn. (dir.). Clubs: Calgary Petroleum., Ranchmen's, U. Calgary Chancellor's. Office: Canterra Energy Ltd 505-5th St SW Calgary AB T2P 2K7 Canada

ISAY, JANE FRANZBLAU, publisher; b. Cin., Aug. 24, 1939; d. Abraham Norman and Rose (Nadler) Franzblau; m. Richard A. Isay, July 26, 1964; children: David Avram, Joshua Daniel. A.B., Bryn Mawr (Pa.) Coll., 1961. First reader Harcourt, Brace Co., 1963; asst. editor, then asso. editor Yale U. Press, 1964-66, editor, then exec. editor, 1966-79; asso. publisher Basic Books Inc., N.Y.C., 1979, co-pub., exec. v.p., 1979-83; v.p., dir. electronic and tech. pub. Harper & Row, 1983—; bd. advisers pub. program N.Y. U.; mem. adv. bd. Wesleyan U. Press; mem. editorial com. Am. Scientist. Bd. dirs. Ezra Acad., New Haven, 1964-79; bd. dirs. Yale U. Friends of Hillel, 1965-68. Fellow Timothy Dwight Coll., Yale U., 1969—. Office: 10 E 53d St New York NY 10022

ISBAN, ROBERT CHARLES, bank executive, accountant; b. Endicott, N.Y., July 21, 1926; s. Charles S. and Gladys (Lawton) I.; m. Marjorie B. Davis, Jan. 31, 1948. B.S., Syracuse U., 1949; M.B.A., NYU, 1954; postgrad., Stonier Grad. Sch. Banking Rutgers U., 1961; A.M.P., Harvard U., 1969. C.P.A., N.Y. Acct. R.G. Rankin & Co., N.Y.C., 1949-55, Price Waterhouse, Washington, 1955-56; asst. controller Hanover Bank, N.Y.C., 1956-70; controller Mfrs. Hanover Trust, N.Y.C., 1970-77; chief fin officer, exec. v.p. Mgrs. Hanover Trust, N.Y.C., 1977—. Trustee St. Joseph's Coll., 1975. Mem. Bank Adminstrn. Inst. (chmn. elect 1983—), Fin. Exec. Inst. Republican. Roman Catholic. Office: Mfrs Hanover Trust Co 270 Park Ave New York NY 10017

ISBELL, HORACE SMITH, chemist; b. Denver, Nov. 13, 1898; s. Harvey G. and Mary E. (White) I.; m. May Davidson, June 26, 1930. B.S., U. Denver, 1920, M.S., 1923; Ph.D. (USPHS fellow), U. Md., 1926. Asst. chemist Am. Smelting & Refining Co., Pueblo, Colo., 1920-21, Bur. Animal Industry, Dept. Agr., Washington, 1923-25; research chemist, chief organic chemistry sect. Nat. Bur. Standards, Washington, 1927-68; senior research scientist Am. U., Washington, 1968—. Recipient meritorious award Dept. Commerce, 1950; Distinguished Alumni award U. Denver, 1953; issue Carbohydrate Research mag. dedicated in his honor, 1974. Mem. Washington, N.Y. acads. sci., Am. Chem. Soc. (Hillebrand award Washington sect. 1951, Hudson Honor award div. carbohydrate chemistry 1954, councilor 1946, 63-66, chmn. div. carbohydrate chemistry 1938, chmn. Washington sect. 1945), Chem. Soc. London (W.N. Haworth medal 1973), Sigma Xi, Phi Lambda Upsilon, Alpha Chi Sigma. Club: Cosmos (Washington). Patentee and researcher field of sugars, sugar derivatives, tritium-labeled carbohydrates. Home: 4704 Blagden Ave Washington DC 20011 Office: Chemistry Dept American Univ Washington DC 20016

ISBELL, ROBERT, banker; b. Anderson, S.C., Nov. 26, 1923; s. Henry Pope and Aileen Annette (Dixon) I.; m. Frances Griffin, Apr. 19, 1953; children: Lyn, Andrea, Eden. A.B. in Journalism, U. S.C., 1948; grad., Sch. Financial Pub. Relations, Northwestern U., 1965, Bank Marketing Grad. Sch., U. Wis., 1973. News editor Elkin (N.C.) Tribune, 1948-50; mng. editor Florence (S.C.) Morning News, 1950-53; pub. relations counsel Tobias & Co., Charleston, S.C., 1954-62; v.p. Bankers Trust of S.C., Columbia, 1963-68, sr. v.p., 1972-76, exec. v.p., 1976—; sr. v.p., adminstr. marketing S.C. Nat. Bank, Columbia, 1969-71; mem. faculty Sch. Banking of South, La. State U., summers, 1971-72. Pres. Carolina Carillon, 1968. Served with AUS, 1943-46; PTO. Recipient Silver medal Am. Advt. Fedn., 1966, Laurel award J.B. White Stores, 1969. Mem. Am. Advt. Fedn. (S.C. gov. 1966-67), Columbia Advt. Council (pres. 1966), Pub. Relations Soc. Am. (dir. S.C. chpt. 1969-72, pres. 1972). Episcopalian. Club: Summit (Columbia). Home: 81 Ridge Lake Dr Columbia SC 29209 Office: Bankers Trust Tower Columbia SC 29202

ISBIN, HERBERT STANFORD, chemical engineering educator; b. Seattle, Dec. 9, 1919; s. Isadore and Rose (Metzger) I.; m. Katherine Brudnoy, June 15, 1948; children: Ira Michael, Neil Walter, Sharon Gail, Rena Ann. B.S., U. Wash., 1940, M.S., 1941; postgrad., U. Minn., 1941-43; Sc.D., Mass. Inst. Tech., 1947. Chem. engr. Md. Research Labs., 1943-45; chem. engr. Gen. Electric Hanford Works, Richland, Wash., 1947-50; prof. dept. chem. engring. U. Minn., Mpls., 1950-83; ret., 1983; past mem. adv. com. on reactor safeguards Nuclear Regulatory Commn. Author: Introductory Nuclear Reactor Theory, 1963; Contbr. articles to profl. jours. Mem. Am. Inst. Chem. Engrs. (past chmn. nuclear engring. div.), Am. Nuclear Soc., Am. Chem. Soc., Am. Soc. Engring. Edn., AAAS. Home: 2815 Monterey Pkwy Minneapolis MN 55416

ISBISTER, JAMES DAVID, association executive; b. Mt. Clemens, Mich., Mar. 31, 1937; s. Russell Lowell and Clara (Wild) I.; m. Jenefir Diane Wilkinson, July 23, 1960; children: Wendy Jill, Kirstin Ann. B.A. cum laude, U. Mich., 1958; postgrad., Princeton, 1958-59; M.A. (scholar), George Washington U., 1966. Mgmt. intern Navy Dept. and NIH, Washington, 1960-61; mgmt. analyst NIH, Bethesda, Md., 1962-63; asst. to asst. sec. adminstrn. HEW, Washington, 1963-65; exec. officer Nat. Library Medicine, Bethesda, 1965-67, NIMH, Rockville, Md., 1967-70, dep. dir., 1970-73; vis. academic London Sch. Econs., 1973-74; dir. U.S. Alcohol, Drug Abuse and Mental Health Adminstrn., 1974-77; v.p. Orkand Corp., 1977-78; asso. dir. Internat. Communication Agy., 1978-80; exec. Washington rep. Blue Cross/Blue Shield Assns., 1980-82, sr. v.p., 1982—; chmn. Nat. Adv. Mental Health Council, 1974-75, Nat. Adv. Council on Alcohol Abuse and Alcoholism, 1974-75, Internat. Conf. on Prevention, 1976; v.p. U.S. Com. Study Internat. Health Care, 1972-74. Editorial adv. bd.: Mental Health Digest, 1970-72, Adminstrn. in Mental Health, 1972-75. Mem. budget com. Washington Met. Health and Welfare Council, 1965-70; bd. dirs. Bedford Springs Festival for the Performing Arts, 1983—. Served with USAF, 1959-60, 61-62. Recipient Ethyl Kilham Modern Lang award, 1954, U. Mich. Regents-Alumni Honor award, 1955, Oreon Scott prize, 1955, William A. Jump Found. Meritorious award for exemplary achievement in pub. adminstrn., 1966; Superior Service award HEW, 1959; Distinguished Service award, 1973; Arthur S. Flemming award, 1977. Mem. Am. Soc. Pub. Adminstrn., Am. Polit. Sci. Assn., Pi Sigma Alpha. Episcopalian. Home: 9521 Accord Dr Potomac MD 20854 Office: 1700 Pennsylvania Ave NW Washington DC

ISELE, ELIZABETH, editor, author; b. Ridgewood, N.J., Oct. 18, 1942; d. Walther Alfred and Elizabeth Lillian (Stillwell) Friedlaender; children: Karlin, Jordan, Erinn, Lauren. B.A., Mills Coll., 1964. Editor Harper and Row, N.Y.C., 1975-82; editorial dir. children's book Little, Brown & Co., Boston, 1982—; cons. Children's Book Council and ALA, Assn. Am. Pubs. and ALA. Author: Pooks: My Life with the Maestro, 1983. Bd. dirs. Child Care Coordinating com., Ridgewood, N.J., 1977-81 bd. dirs. Child Care Coordinating com., Bergen County, N.J., 1979-81; cons. Gov.'s com Status of Women, State of N.J., 1981. Mem. Soc. Children's Book Writers, Authors Guild, Internat. Reading Assn. Republican. Episcopalian. Club: Cohasset Sailing (Mass.). Home: 52 Smith Pl Cohasset MA 02025 Office: Little Brown & Co 34 Beacon St Boston MA 02106

ISEMAN, JOSEPH SEEMAN, lawyer; b. N.Y.C., May 29, 1916; s. Percy Reginald and Edith Helene (Seeman) I.; m. June Lorraine Bang, Dec. 10, 1966; children: Peter A., Frederick J., Ellen M.; stepchildren: Anne (Mrs. Robert Latzen), Susan E. Hamilton, William C. Hamilton. B.A. magna cum laude, Harvard U., 1937; LL.B., Yale U., 1941. Bar: N.Y. State 1941, D.C. 1970. Investigator, clk. Comml. Factors Corp., 1937-38; atty. WPB, 1941-42; mng. dir. Iranian Airways Corp., 1946; asso. Chadbourne, Wallace, Parke & Whiteside, N.Y.C., 1946-50, Paul, Weiss, Rifkind, Wharton & Garrison, 1950-53, partner, 1954—; counsel Charles F. Kettering Found.; dir. Gould Paper Corp. Author: A Perfect Sympathy, 1937; contbr. articles to profl. jours. Sec., bd. dirs. Acad. for Ednl. Devel., Scherman Found., Met. Assistance Corp.; trustee Bennington Coll., 1969-81, acting pres., 1976; mem. Rye (N.Y.) Zoning Bd. Appeals; vice chmn. bd. visitors Wake Forest U. Served to capt. USAAF, 1942-46. Woodrow Wilson vis. fellow Coll. William and Mary, 1977, Ripon Coll., 1979, Rollins Coll., 1980, De Pauw U., 1980, Fisk U., 1981, Albright Coll., 1982, Hood Coll, 1983. Mem. Am., N.Y. State, N.Y.C. bar assns., Phi Beta Kappa. Democrat. Clubs: Century Assn. (N.Y.C.); Coveleigh (Rye, N.Y.). Home: One Walden Ln Rye NY 10580 Office: 345 Park Ave New York NY 10154

ISENBERG, ABRAHAM CHARLES, shoe manufacturing company executive; b. Lynn, Mass., Feb. 24, 1914; s. Louis and Alice (Lown) I.; m. Thelma F. Sisenwine, Oct. 30, 1938; children: Gerald, Lee Carol, Edward. B.S., Wharton Sch., U. Pa., 1935. With Consol. Nat. Shoe Corp., Norwood, Mass., 1935—, exec. v.p., 1967-68, pres., 1968-72, chief exec. officer, 1968-72, chmn. bd., treas., 1972—; Vice chmn. shoe div. Greater Boston area Combined Jewish Philanthropies, 1968—. Bd. dirs. New Eng. Anti-Defamation League of B'nai B'rith.; paralegal vol. Palm Beach County Ct. System. Mem. Two Ten Assos. (dir. 1956—, v.p. 1969—), Am. Footwear Assn. (dir. 1968, regional v.p. 1970—), Am. Footwear Inst. (trustee 1970-74), Boston Boot and Shoe Club (exec. com. 1967—, v.p. 1969, pres. 1973), Beta Sigma Rho. Clubs: Hebrew Rehab. Ctr. Men's (dir. 1970-72, dir. 1970-72); B'nai B'rith (dir. 1979—). Home: 3450 S Ocean Blvd Palm Beach FL 33480 *I have found that being honest and ethical with those I associated with in business or community affairs was the most rewarding behavior I could follow. I realize that some who act entirely contrary to these principles appear to be very successful, but I would not want success on those terms.*

ISENBERG, HENRY DAVID, microbiology educator; b. Giessen, Germany, Mar. 9, 1922; came to U.S., 1937, naturalized, 1943; s. Gerson and Flora (Gruenebaum) I.; m. Lila S. Grossman, Feb. 15, 1948; children—Ina Pepi Isenberg Stein, Gerald Alan. B.S., CCNY, 1947; M.A., Bklyn. Coll., 1951; Ph.D., St. Johns U., 1959. Diplomate: Am. Bd. Med. Microbiology (chmn. 1976-79). Asst. dir. Angrist Labs., 1947-54; chief microbiology L.I. Jewish Hillside Med. Center, New Hyde Park, N.Y., 1954—; asst. clin. prof. orthopedic surgery State U. N.Y. Downstate Med. Center, Bklyn., 1963-68; assoc. clin. prof. orthopedic surgery, 1968-71, professorial lectr. orthopedic surgery, 1971—; prof. clin. pathology State U. N.Y. Health Sci. Center, Stony Brook, 1970—; clin. prof. microbiology and immunology U. South Fla. Sch. Medicine, 1982—. Editor: Jour. Clin. Microbiology, 1974-79; editor-in-chief, 1979—; editor: CRC Critical Revs. in Microbiology, 1978-81; editor-in-chief: CRC Forum in Bacteriology; sect. editor: Manual of Clin. Microbiology, 3d edit; editorial bd.: Applied Microbiology, 1969-74; Contbr. numerous articles to profl. jours. and books. Served with U.S. Army, 1943-45. Named Microbiologist of Yr. Lab World mag., 1978; recipient Kimble award, 1980. Fellow Am. Acad. Microbiology (bd. govs.), N.Y. Acad. Scis., Am. Inst. Chemists, Assn. Clin. Scientists, Infectious Diseases Soc. Am., N.Y. Acad. Medicine (asso.); mem. Am. Soc. Microbiology (Becton/Dickinson award 1979), Soc. Gen. Microbiology, Soc. Protozoology, Sigma Xi. Jewish. Patentee in field. Home: 269-22D Grand Central Pkwy Floral Park NY 11005 Office: Long Island Jewish Hillside Med Center New Hyde Park NY 11042

ISENBERG, PHILLIP L., state legislator; b. Gary, Ind., Feb. 25, 1939; s. Walter M. and Violet R. (Phillips) I.; m. Marilyn Y. Araki, July 13, 1963. B.A., Sacramento Coll., 1961; J.D., U. Calif., Berkeley, 1967. Bar: Calif. 1967. Exec. sec. com. legis. representation Calif. Senate, 1961; since practiced in, Sacramento; adminstrv. asst. to Calif. Assemblyman Willie L. Brown, Jr., 1967-69; chief cons. com. ways and means Calif. Assembly, 1971; mem. Sacramento City Council, 1971-75; mayor, City of Sacramento, 1975-82, mem., Calif. Assembly, 1983—. Mem. Calif., Sacramento County bar assns. Democrat. Office: State Capitol Sacramento CA 95814

ISENBERGH, MAX, lawyer, musician, educator; b. Albany, N.Y., Aug. 28, 1913; s. David William and Tess (Solomon) I.; m. Pearl Evans, Aug. 10, 1939; children: Tess, David William, Joseph. A.B., Cornell U., 1934; J.D., Harvard U., 1938, LL.M., 1939, A.M., 1942. Bar: N.Y. 1938, U.S. Supreme Ct. 1945, D.C. 1950. Fellow Harvard U. Law Sch., 1938-39; tutor U. Chgo. Law Sch., 1939-40; various govt. postitions, 1940-48; legal sec. to U.S. Supreme Ct. Justice Hugo Black, 1941-42; spl. asst. to atty. gen. U.S., 1944-48; counsel European ops. Am. Jewish Com., 1948-50; legal adviser Point Four Program, State Dept., 1950-51; gen. counsel Pres.'s Materials Policy Commn., 1951-52; dep. gen. counsel AEC, cons. internal affairs, 1952-56; spl. asst. for atomic energy Am. embassy, Paris, 1956-61; dep. asst. sec. of state for edn. and cultural affairs, 1961-62; chmn. U.S. del. to UNESCO Conf. on Protection Cultural Property, 1962; counsel to chmn. Communications Satellite Corp., 1962-63; prof. George Washington U. Sch. Law, 1963-65, U. Md. Law Sch., 1970—; vis. prof. U. Va. Law Sch., 1965-66, 68, 69, Yale U. Law Sch., 1966-67, Am. U. Law Sch., 1969-70, 72, 73—; cons. Peace Corps, 1966-67; mem. panel arbitrators Am. Arbitration Assn.; prof. law Salzburg Seminar Am. Studies, Austria, summer 1965; lectr., TV panelist on arts and law; cons. IAEA, Vienna, Austria, aslo European Nuclear Energy Agy., Paris; participated as del., adviser, ofcl. observer numerous internat. confs.; exec. com. 3d Inter-Am. Music Festival; lectr., TV panelist on arts, law, atomic engery, 1956—. Editor: Harvard Law Rev., 1937-38; author articles, book revs., music and art criticism; clarinetist concerts, in U.S. and Europe. Mem. D.C. Mayor's Task Force Arts and Humanities, 1978. Recipient Rockefeller Pub. Service award, 1954. Mem. Am. Law Inst., Am. Fedn. Musicians, Phi Beta Kappa, Pi Lambda Phi (past pres. chpt.). Club: Cosmos (Washington). Home: 2216 Massachusetts Ave NW Washington DC 20009 Office: 500 W Baltimore St Baltimore MD 21201 *

ISENBURGER, ERIC, artist; b. Frankfurt on Main, Germany, May 17, 1902; came to U.S., 1941, naturalized, 1949; s. Sally R. and Olga (Neurmond) I.; m. Jula Elenbogen, Dec. 10, 1927. Student, Art Sch., Frankfurt on Main. One-man shows, Gallery Gurlitt, Berlin, 1933, Gallery Modern, Stockholm, 1934-38, Gallery Wolfgang Gurlitt, Munich, Germany, 1962, Knoedler Galleries, N.Y.C., 1941, 43, 45, 47, 48, 50, 53, 55, Balt. Mus., 1943, DeYoung Meml. Mus., San Francisco, 1945, Springfield (Mass.) Mus., Colorado Springs Fine Arts Center, John Herron Art Inst., Indpls., 1946, others; represented in permanent collections, Wadsworth Atheneum, Hartford, Conn., Mus. Tel-Aviv, Israel, Ency. Britannica, Pa. Acad. Fine Arts, Mus. Modern Art, Pa. Acad. Fine Arts, Corcoran Gallery Art, Bezalel Mus. of Jerusalem, John Herron Art Inst., Indpls., M.H. de Young Mus., San Francisco, Miami U. Art Mus., Oxford, Ohio, AAAL, Laguna Beach Art Mus., NAD, Philharmonic Hall, Lincoln Center, others. Recipient prize NAD, 1945, Edwin Palmer Meml. prize, 1957, Henry Ward Ranger Fund purchase, 1957, 80; 3rd prize Carnegie Inst., 1947; Medal of Honor, Pepsi Cola Art competition, 1948; 1st prize and Corcoran gold medal Corcoran Gallery Art, 1949; Thomas Proctor Prize NAD, 1963; Salmagundi Club prize, 1966; Edwin Palmer Meml. prize NAD, 1970; Andrew Carnegie prize, 1972; Aldro T. Hibbard Meml. award, 1976; Florence Brevoort-Eickemeyer prize Columbia U., 1980. Mem. NAD (council 1964-67, officer 1975-80), Audubon Artists (award 1969, 78, 79, Jane Peterson medal and prize 1971, 78, Simex award 1979, Stefan Hirsch meml. award 1981, dir. painting 1979). Home: 140 E 56th St New York NY 10022

ISENHOUR, THOMAS LEE, chemistry educator; b. Statesville, N.C., Jan. 29, 1939; s. Harold Lee and Ruth Catherine (Peacock) I.; m. Linda Ann Adkins, June 11, 1960; children: Anastasia, Joseph Bradley. Ph.D., Cornell U., 1965. Asst. prof. chemistry U. Wash., 1965-69; assoc. prof. U. N.C., 1969-74, prof., 1974—, chmn. dept. chemistry, 1975-80; I.M. Kolthoff sr. fellow Hebrew U., 1980; dean of sci. Utah State U., Logan, 1984; program dir. for chem. analysis NSF, 1982-83. Author numerous books; contbr. articles to profl. jours. Mem. Am. Chem. Soc., Fedn. Analytical Chemistry and Spectroscopy Soc., Phi Beta Kappa, Sigma Xi, Alpha Chi Sigma. Home: 407 Clayton Chapel Hill NC 27514 Office: Utah State Univ Coll of Sci Logan UT 84322

ISHAM, SHEILA EATON, artist; b. N.Y.C., Dec. 19, 1927; d. Walter Bradley and Margaret (Burton) Eaton; m. Heyward Isham, June 9, 1950; children: Christopher Eaton, Ralph Heyward, Sandra Calhoun. B.A. cum laude, Bryn Mawr Coll., 1950; student, Berlin Acad. Fine Arts, 1950-54. Trustee Mus. Haitian Art, Port-au-Prince; dir. Ind. Curators Inc., N.Y.C. Executed: lithographs for I Ching Portfolio; also 4 lithographs for Portfolio Marakech; One-woman exhbns. include, Galerie Springer, Berlin, 1954, Bader Gallery, Washington, 1960, Smithsonian Instn., Washington, 1961, Nihonbashi Gallery, Tokyo, 1964, Byron Gallery, N.Y.C., 1966, Jefferson Pl. Gallery, Washington, 1968-70, French & Co., N.Y.C., 1970, Brockton (Mass.) Art Center, 1972, Am. Cultural Center, Paris, 1973, Fischbach Gallery, N.Y.C., Corcoran Gallery, Washington, 1974, Albright-Knox Gallery, Buffalo, 1974, 81, Addison Gallery Am. Art, Andover, Mass., 1975, Pyramid Gallery, Washington, 1976, Met. Mus. Miami, New Orleans Mus. Modern Art, also 12 Latin and S. Am. countries, 1976-77, Musée d'Art Haitian, Port-au-Prince, 1977, State Dept., Washington, 1978, 80, Palm Beach (Fla.) Gallery, 1978, Osuna Gallery, Washington, 1980, Nat. Mus. Am. Art, Smithsonian Instn., 1981, Hood Coll., Md., 1982, Addison Ripley Gallery, Washington, Phoenix II Gallery, Washington. Recipient joint award Library of Congress, Corcoran Gallery Art. Mem. Artists Equity, Women Artists Am., Assn. Crafts Haiti (dir.). Address: 1601 19th St NW Washington DC 20009 also Sagaponack NY 11962

ISHERWOOD, CHRISTOPHER, author; b. High Lane, Cheshire, Eng., Aug. 26, 1904; came to U.S., 1939, naturalized, 1946; s. Francis Edward and Kathleen (Machell-Smith) I. Student, Repton Sch., 1919-22, Corpus Christi Coll., Cambridge, 1924-25. Sec. to Music Soc. String Quartet, London, 1926-27; med. student U. London, 1927-28; pvt. tchr. English, Berlin, 1928-33, travelled in Europe and China, 1934-38; guest prof. modern English lit. Los Angeles State Coll. and U. Calif. at Santa Barbara, 1959-60; Regents prof. U. Calif. at Los Angeles, 1965, U. Calif. at Riverside, 1966. Scenario-writer for, M.G.M., Warner Bros. and other motion picture studios intermittently, 1939—; free-lance writer, 1926—; editor: mag. Vedanta and the West, Hollywood, 1943-44; (Recipient N.Y. Drama Critics Circle award, best musical, Cabaret (based on his stories) 1966-67, Brandeis medal for fiction 1975); Author: books including Prater Violet, 1945; novel The World in the Evening, 1954; Christopher and His Kind, 1976; autobiography My Guru and His Disciple, 1980; co-author: (with W.H. Auden) plays On the Frontier, 1938; translator: The Intimate Journals of Charles Baudelaire, 1947, (with Swami Prabhavananda) The Bhagavad-Gita, 1944, The CrestJewel of Discrimination, (with Swami Prabhavananda), 1947, How to Know God, (with Swami Prabhavananda), 1953; travel The Condor and the Cows, 1949; (adapted by John van Druten from stories) Stage play I Am A Camera (critics award 1951), Down There On A Visit, 1962, A Single Man, 1964, Ramakrishna and His Disciples, 1965, Exhumations, 1966, A Meeting by the River, 1967, (play adapted from novel with Don Bachardy 1972) Kathleen and Frank, 1971; Editor: with introduction, and several contbns. Vedanta for the Western World, 1945. Worked with Am. Friends Service Com. on refugee relief project, Haverford, Pa., 1941-42; Nat. adv. bd. trustees Inst. Study Human Resources. Mem. A.C.L.U., Wider Quaker Fellowship, Screenwriters Guild, Nat. Inst. Arts and Letters, Acad. Motion Picture Arts and Scis. Vedantist. Home: 145 Adelaide Dr Santa Monica CA 90402

ISHIZAKA, JIRO, banker; b. Shanghai, China, Dec. 22, 1927; s. Rokuro and Ayako I.; m. Masako Hirayama, Apr. 11, 1954. Grad., Faculty of Law, U. Tokyo, 1951. With Bank of Tokyo, 1951—, dir., 1977, mng. dir., 1980; chmn. bd. Bank of Tokyo Trust Co., 1980-82; resident mng. dir., regional exec. Bank of Tokyo Ltd., N.Y.C. Mem. Japanese C. of C. in N.Y. (dir.), Japan Soc. (dir.). Clubs: Nippon (dir. N.Y.C.); Canyon (Armonk, N.Y.); Morefar (Brewster, N.Y.); City Midday (N.Y.C.). Office: Bank of Tokyo 100 Broadway New York NY 10005

ISKO, IRVING DAVID, corporate executive; b. N.Y.C., Nov. 26, 1927; s. Harry and Rose (Lehman) I.; m. June Alter, June 7, 1959 (dec. July 1980); children—Laura, Steven; m. Kathe Jados Truschke, Aug. 28, 1981. B.A., Cornell U., 1947; LL.B., Harvard U., 1950. Bar: N.Y. bar 1950. Asso. firm Schlesinger & Berliner, N.Y.C., 1951-54; gen. practice law, N.Y.C., 1954-56; with Philipp Bros., Inc., 1956; v.p. minerals and chems. Philipp Corp., 1963; v.p. Engelhard Minerals & Chem. Corp., 1967—, sr. v.p., gen. counsel, 1972, exec. v.p., N.Y.C., 1976-79, dir., 1978—, dep. chmn. bd., mem. exec. com., 1979—; pres., chief exec. officer, dir. Engelhard Corp., 1981-84. Contbr. article to law jour. Chmn. Mendham Borough (N.J.) Zoning Bd., 1980; mem. fin. com. Newark Acad., 1979; mem. chemistry com. Lehigh U., 1980. Mem. ABA, Am. Arbitration Assn., N.J. C. of C. (dir.), Harvard U. Law Sch. Alumni Assn. Office: Morristown Morristown NJ

ISMAIL, YAHIA HASSAN, dentist, educator; b. Egypt, Jan. 1, 1938; came to U.S., 1961; s. Hassan Kareem and Horia (Soloman) I.; m. Launa Lutz, Sept. 5, 1968; children: Alan Kareem, Zane Ziad. D.D.S., Cairo U., 1959; M.S., U. Pitts., 1965, D.M.D., 1973, Ph.D., 1973. Instr. Dental Sch. Cairo U., 1959-62; asst. prof. prosthodontics U. Pitts., 1962-68, asso. prof., 1968-70, prof., 1970—; dir. Prosthodontic Clinic, 1970—, chmn. dept., 1973—; vis. prof., Paris and Marseille, France, Cairo and Alexandria, Egypt, Begazi, Libya; mem. staff VA Hosp., Montefior Hosp., Univ. Med. Center Hosp., St. Margaret's Hosp. Contbr. articles to profl. jours., textbooks. Bd. dirs. Ridgewood Civic Assn., 1969-73; cubmaster Allegheny Trails council Boy Scouts Am.; coach Youth Soccer League Allegheny County. Fellow Internat. Coll. Dentists; mem. ADA, Am. Coll. Dentists, Internat. Assn. Dentofacial Abnormalities (dir., sec.-treas. 1973-77), Internat. Congress Oral Implantologists, Am. Prosthodontic Soc. (internat. circuite courses humanities citation), Pa. Prosthodontic Assn. (pres.), Prosthodontic Soc. Western Pa. (past pres.), Dental Soc. Western Pa. (past br. pres., bd. dirs.), Am. Coll. Prosthedontists, Am. Assn. Dental Schs., Internat. Assn. Dental Research, Omicron Kappa Upsilon. Republican. Club: Univ. Office: Sch Dental Medicine U Pittsburgh PA 15261 *Talk about ideas and philosophies rather than other people.*

ISOM, LLOYD WARREN, life insurance company executive; b. Arkansas City, Kans., Feb. 9, 1928; s. Loyd Denver and Cora Louvina (Messner) I.; m. Marjorie Louise Ghramm, Aug. 30, 1950; children: Cynthia Louise, John Warren. B.S., Drake U., Des Moines, 1952. C.L.U. Asst. actuary Security Benefit Life Ins. Co., Topeka, 1952-54; asst. actuary, asst. sec. Midwest Life Ins. Co., Lincoln, Nebr., 1954-57; agt. Bankers Life Ins. Co., Omaha, 1957; cons., sr. cons., dir. spl. services Life Ins. Mktg. Research Assn., Hartford, Conn., 1957-62; v.p., asst. to pres. Piedmont So. Life Ins. Co., Atlanta, 1963-64; pres. First Security Group, Milw., 1965-68; v.p. mktg. Liberty Life Ins. Co., Greenville, S.C., 1968-71; pres., chief exec. officer Am. Health & Life Ins. Co., 1971-75; pres., chief exec. officer, dir. Pierce Nat. Life Ins. Co., Los Angeles, 1975-77; mgmt. cons., 1977-78; pres., dir. Continental Life & Accident Co., Boise, Idaho, 1978—, Ins. Mgmt. Inc., Boise, 1980-82; sr. v.p. adminstrn. Am. Gen. Corp., Houston, 1982—. Bd. dirs. Boise Jr. Achievement, Boise Philharm. Served with USN, 1946-48. Mem. Am. Soc. Pension Actuaries, Am. Coll. Life Underwriters. Republican. Methodist. Clubs: Houston, Rotary. Home: 201 Vanderpool Apt 28 Houston TX 77024 Office: PO Box 3247 Houston TX 77253

ISON, JAMES RATCLIFFE, psychology educator; b. Essex, Eng., June 10, 1935; came to U.S., 1948, naturalized, 1958; s. James Ratcliffe and Irene (Sixsmith) I.; m. Sherrill Lynn Smith, Feb. 1, 1958; children: Timothy Michael, Sarah Jo, Christopher James. B.A., U. Mich., 1956, Ph.D., 1960. Prof. psychology, radiation biology and biophysics U. Rochester, N.Y., 1962—, chmn. dept. psychology, 1979—; NIH research scientist Oxford U., 1970-71. Contbr. articles in field to profl. jour. Rackham fellow, 1960-61. Fellow Am. Psychol. Assn. (bd. sci. affairs); mem. Assn. Advancement Psychology (trustee), Soc. Neuroscience, Soc. Psychophysiology, Behavior Pharmacology Soc., Psychonomic Soc., Fedn. Behavioral, Psychol., and Cognitive Scis. (mem. council). Office: Psychology Building Department of Psychology University of Rochester Rochester NY 14627

ISRAEL, DAVID, journalist; b. N.Y.C., Mar. 17, 1951; s. Hyman and Edith Oringer I. B.S. in Journalism, Northwestern U., 1973. Reporter Chgo. Daily News, 1973-75; columnist Washington Star, 1975-78, Chgo. Tribune, 1978-81, Los Angeles Herald Examiner, 1981—; v.p., dir. Utica Blue Sox Baseball Club (N.Y.); pres. Big Prodns., Inc., Los Angeles. Mem. AFTRA, Writers Guild Am. Office: 1111 S Broadway Los Angeles CA 90015

ISRAEL, PETER, book publisher; b. N.Y.C., Aug. 1, 1933; s. J. Leon and Ruth L. (Lustbader) I.; m. Peg Streep, 1982; 1 son, Elie. B.A., Yale U., 1954. Dir. fgn. service Editions Albin Michel, Paris, 1973-77; pres. The Putnam Pub. Group, N.Y.C., 1978—, The Berkley Pub. Group, 1983—. Author: novels The Hen's House, 1969, Hush Money, 1974, The French Kiss, 1976, The Stiff Upper Lip, 1978. Mem. Assn. Am. Pubs. (dir.). Office: The Putnam Pub Group 200 Madison Ave New York NY 10016

ISRAEL, RICHARD JEROME, lawyer; b. Woonsocket, R.I., Dec. 9, 1930; s. Fred and Cecile Lena (Kantrowitz) I.; m. Lana Biller, Nov. 20, 1977; children—Susan Emily, Eric Steven, Karen Esta. A.B., Brown U., 1951; J.D., Yale, 1954. Bar: R.I. bar 1954. Chief R.I. Div. Workmen's Compensation, 1960-61; practice law, Woonsocket, 1954-71, asst. atty. gen., R.I., 1967-71, atty. gen., 1971-75; partner firm Levy, Goodman, Semonoff & Gorin, Providence, 1975—. Served to 1st lt. AUS, 1955-57. Mem. Am., R.I. bar assns., Am. Judicature Soc.; mem. B'nai B'rith. Republican. Jewish. Club: Mason. Home: 29 Greaton Dr Providence RI 02906 Office: 11 Park Row Providence RI 02903

ISRAEL, WERNER, physics educator; b. Berlin, Oct. 4, 1931; s. Arthur and Marie (Kappauf) I.; m. Inge Margulies, Jan. 26, 1958; 1 son, Mark Abraham. B.Sc., U. Cape Town, 1951, M.Sc., 1954; Ph.D., Trinity Coll., Dublin, 1960. Asst. prof. physics U. Alta., 1958-68, prof., 1968—; Sherman Fairchild Disting. scholar Calif. Inst. Tech., 1974-75; vis. prof. Dublin Inst. Advanced Studies, 1966-68, U. Cambridge, 1975-76, Institut Henri Poincare, 1976-77, U. Berne, 1980. Editor: Relativity, Astrophysics and Cosmology, 1973; co-editor: General Relativity, An Einstein Centenary Survey, 1979. Recipient Izaak Walton Killam Meml. Prize, 1984. Fellow Royal Soc. Can.; mem. Internat. Astron. Union, Can. Assn. Physicists (medal of Achievement in Physics 1981), Internat. Soc. Gen. Relativity and Gravitation. Jewish. Office: Physics Dept U Alberta Edmonton AB T6G 2J1 Canada *

ISRAELIEVITCH, JACQUES HERBERT, violinist, condr.; b. Cannes, France, May 6, 1948; came to U.S., 1965, naturalized, 1976; s. Isidore and Simone (David) I.; m. Gail Ivy Bass, Aug. 27, 1972. Performer's cert., Ind. U., 1968. Mem. faculty Am. Conservatory Music, Chgo., 1974-78; co-founder Camerata Soc. Chgo., 1974; artist in residence Webster Coll., 1978—. Harpist, Ind. U., 1967-72; asst. concertmaster, Chgo. Symphony Orch., 1972-78; concertmaster, St. Louis Symphony Orch., 1978—; solo appearances with orchs. and in recital, France, Spain, Portugal, Italy, Ger., U.S., Can.; founder, Chgo. Pops Orch., 1975. Recipient 1st prize Paris Conservatory Music, 1964; named winner Paganini Internat. Competition, Italy, 1965, Alumnus of Yr. Ind. U., 1973. Mem. Am. Fedn. Musicians, Soc. Am. Musicians. Club: Arts of Chgo. Office: St Louis Symphony Orch Powell Symphony Hall 718 N Grand Blvd Saint Louis MO 63103

ISRAELS, LYONEL GARRY, hematologist, medical educator; b. Regina, Sask., Can., July 31, 1926; s. Simon and Sarah (Girtle) I.; m. Esther Hornstein, June 3, 1950; children: Sara, Jared. B.A., U. Sask., 1946; M.D., U. Man., 1949, M.Sc., 1950. Intern Winnipeg Gen. Hosp., 1948-49; resident internal medicine and hematology Salt Lake County Hosp., 1950-52; fellow in hematology Kantonsspital, Zurich, 1952-53; dept. biochemistry U. Man., 1953-55, asst. prof. biochemistry, 1955-59, asst. prof. medicine, 1959-62, assoc. prof. medicine, 1962-66, prof. medicine, 1966—, Disting. prof., 1983—, acting head dept. medicine, 1977-79; dir. Man. Inst. Cell Biology, 1970-73; exec. dir. Man. Cancer Treatment and Research Found., 1973—; attending physician Health Sci. Centre; cons. in hematology Children's Centre, Municipal Hosps. Winnipeg; chmn. Man. Health Research Council, 1980—. Contbr. articles on biochem. and immunol. aspects of blood, blood forming organs and cancer to sci. jours. Mem. Am. Soc. Clinical Investigation, Can. Soc. Clinical Investigation (pres. 1968), Royal Coll. Physicians and Surgeons Can., Can. Hematol. Soc. (pres. 1972-74), Can. Oncol. Soc., Can. Med. Assn., Med. Research Council Can., Nat. Cancer Inst. Can. (pres. 1976-78). Home: 502 South Dr Winnipeg MB R3T 0B1 Canada Office: 700 Bannatyne Ave Winnipeg MB R3E 0V9 Canada

ISRAILI, ZAFAR HASAN, educator; b. Moradabad, India, July 2, 1934; came to U.S., 1961, naturalized, 1977; m. Siddiq Hasan and Zahida Khatun I.; m. Sally Jean Smith, Oct. 24, 1970; children—Shahnaz Joy, Taj Hasan, Rana Shereen. B.Sc., Aligarh M. U., 1951, M.Sc. (Merit scholar), 1953; Ph.D., U. Kans., 1968. Lectr. chemistry Aligarh M. U., 1953-54, sr. research scholar, 1954-57; research asst., jr. sci. officer AEC India, 1957-61; research asso. U. Kans., 1968-69; sr. research chemist Alza Corp., Lawrence, Kans., 1969-70; asst. prof. medicine and chemistry Emory U., Atlanta, 1970-75, asso. prof. chemistry, 1975-78, asso. prof. medicine, 1975—, prof. chemistry, 1978—; research pharmacologist Atlanta VA Med. Center, Decatur, 1979—; mem. sci. staff Grady Hosp., Atlanta, 1974—. Asso. editor: Drug Metabolism Revs, 1974—; editorial bd.: Drug Devel. Research, 1979—; contbr. numerous articles to profl. jours., chpts. to books. Merck Sharpe & Dohm grantee, 1977; NIH grantee, 1978-80, 80—; VA grantee, 1979—; recipient Asia Found. award, 1962. Mem. Am. Soc. Clin. Pharmacology and Therapeutics, Am. Soc. Pharmacology and Exptl. Therapeutics, Soc. Exptl. Biology and Medicine, Am. Assn. Cancer Research, Am. Aging Assn., Am. Chem. Soc., Chem. Soc. London, Sigma Xi, Rho Chi, Phi Lambda Upsilon. Moslem. Home: 3567 Cloudland Dr Stone Mountain GA 30083 Office: Medical Research Atlanta VA Medical Center 1670 Clairmont Rd Decatur GA 30033

ISSACKEDES, JORDAN, floor covering company executive; b. N.Y.C., Oct. 20, 1931; s. and Elizabeth (Zahariades) I.; m. Claire Milonas, Sept. 27, 1959; children: Anastasia, Helen, Nicholas. B.A., Iona Coll., 1953. Sr. auditor Lybrand, Ross Bros. & Montgomery, N.Y.C., 1953-60; with Gen. Felt Industries, Inc. and Okonite Co., Saddlebrook, N.J., 1960-70; pres., gen. mgr. floor covering div. Okonite Co., 1970-71; pres., chief exec. officer Gen. Felt Industries, Inc., Saddle Brook, N.J., 1971-74, pres., chief operating officer, from 1974, also dir.; now with C & J Zimmerman Corp., N.Y.C. Recipient Golden Torch of Hope award Floor Covering and Allied Industries div. City of Hope, 1972. Mem. Carpet Cushion Council, Chgo. Floor Covering Assn., Tax Execs. Inst. (N.J. chpt.). Clubs: Hackensack Golf, Metropolitan, Pennington. Home: 73 Merritt Dr Oradell NJ 07649 Office: C & J Zimmerman 260 W Broadway New York NY 10013 *

ISSARI, MOHAMMAD ALI, cinema educator, film producer; b. Esfahan, Iran, Aug. 13, 1924; s. Abbas Bek and Qamar (Soltan) I.; m. Joan Gura Aamodt, 1953; children: Scheherezade, Katayoun, Roxana. B.A., U. Tehran, Iran, 1963; M.A., U. So. Calif., 1968; Ph.D., 1979. Films officer Brit. Embassy, Brit. Council Joint Film Div., Tehran, 1944-50; asst. motion picture officer USIS, 1950-65; cons. to various Iranian Govt. ministries on film and TV devels., 1950-77; liaison officer Am. and Iranian govt. ofcls., 1950-65; prof. cinema Coll. Communication Arts and Scis. Mich. State U., East Lansing, 1969—, also dir. instructional film and multimedia prodn., 1969-78; film, public relations adviser to Iranian Oil Operating Cos. in, Iran, 1963-65; spl. cons. on edn. and instructional TV Saudi Arabian Ministry of Info., 1972; tchr. Persian lang. Iran-Am. Soc., Tehran, 1949-59. Producer, dir. over 1000 ednl., instructional and documentary films, 1956-78; freelance film reporter: Telenews, UPI, Iran, 1959-61; project dir., exec. producer: Ancient Iran Film Series, 1974-78; dir. film prodn. workshops, Cranbrook Inst., Detroit, 1973-74; Author: (with Doris A. Paul) A Picture of Persia, 1977, What Is Cinema Vérité?, 1979; contbr. articles on ednl. communication and audio-visual instruction to periodicals and profl. jours. Founder, exec. sec. Youth Orgn. of Iran, 1951-52; v.p. Rugby Football Fedn., Iran, 1952-53, pres., 1954-55. Recipient Cine Golden Eagle award, 1975, Meritorious Honor award USIA, 1965; decorated Order of Magnum Cap Ord: S.F. Danaie M. Sigillum, Denmark, 1960, Order of Cavalieres, Italy, 1958, Order of Oranje Nassau Queen Juliana of Holland, 1959, Orders of Kooshesh and Pas HIM Shah of Iran, 1951, 57, Order of Esteghlal King Hussein of Jordan, 1960, Order of Ordinis Sancti Silvestri Papae Pope John 23d, 1959. Mem. Anglo-Iranian Dramatic Soc. (dir. 1943-50), Mich. Film Assn. (cofounder 1972, dir. 1972-73), Middle East Studies Assn. N.Am., Soc. Motion Picture and TV Engrs., Assn. Ednl. Communication and Tech., Delta Kappa Alpha (v.p. 1967). Introduced audio-visual edn. in Iran, 1951; established first film festivals in Iran. Home: 4454 Seneca Dr Okemos MI 48864 *Man will achieve his goals through honesty, hard work and perseverence. The goals worth pursuing are in the service of mankind.*

ISSAWI, CHARLES PHILIP, educator, economist; b. Cairo, Egypt, Mar. 15, 1916; came to U.S., 1947, naturalized, 1957; s. Elias and Alexandra (Abouchar) I.; m. Janina M. Haftke, July 20, 1946. B.A., Magdalen Coll., Oxford (Eng.) U., 1937, M.A., 1944. With Egyptian Ministry Fin., 1937-38; chief research Nat. Bank Egypt, 1938-43; adj. prof. Am. U., Beirut, Lebanon, 1943-47; mem. Middle East unit, econ. dept. UN Secretariat, 1948-55; faculty Columbia U., 1955-75, prof. econs., 1961-75, dir., 1962-64; Bayard Dodge prof. Near Eastern Studies Princeton U., 1975—; Cons. FAO, 1955, UN, 1956, 70. Author: Egypt: an Economic and Social Analysis, 1947, An Arab Philosophy of History, 1950, Mushkilat Qaumiyya, 1959, Egypt in Revolution, 1963; co-author: The Economics of Middle Eastern Oil, 1962, The Economic History of Iran, 1971, Oil, the Middle East and the World, 1972, Issawi's Laws of Social Motion, 1973, The Economic History of Turkey, 1980, The Arab World's Legacy, 1981, The Economic History of the Middle East and North Africa, 1982; editor: The Economic History of the Middle East, 1800-1914, 1966. Guggenheim fellow, 1961, 68; Social Sci. Research Council fellow, 1962, 75. Fellow Middle East Inst. (bd. editors jour. 1958—); mem. Council Fgn. Relations, Am. Econ. Assn., Middle East Studies Assn. (v.p. 1968, pres. 1973, bd. editors jour. 1970-78), Econ. History Assn., Middle East Econ. Assn. (pres. 1978). Home: 97 Castle Howard Ct Princeton NJ 08540 Office: Dept Near Eastern Studies Princeton U Princeton NJ 08540

ISSEL, DAN, profl. basketball player; b. Batavia, Ill., Oct. 25, 1948. Grad., U. Ky., 1970. With Ky. Cols. (Am. Basketball Assn.), 1970-75, Denver Nuggets (Am. Basketball Assn.), 1975-76, 1976—; player Nat. Basketball Assn. All Star Game, 1977. Office: care Denver Nuggets McNichols Sport Arena 1635 Clay St Denver CO 80204 *

ISSELBACHER, KURT JULIUS, educator, physician; b. Wirges, Germany, Sept. 12, 1925; came to U.S., 1936, naturalized, 1945; s. Albert and Flori (Strauss) I.; m. Rhoda Solin, June 22, 1955; children: Lisa, Karen, Jody, Eric. A.B., Harvard U., 1946, M.D. cum laude, 1950. Intern, then resident Mass. Gen. Hosp., Boston, 1950-53; investigator NIH, 1953-56; chief gastrointestinal unit Mass. Gen. Hosp., 1957, chmn. com. research, 1967; prof. medicine Harvard Med. Sch., 1966—, chmn. exec. com. depts. medicine, 1968—, Mallinckrodt prof. medicine, 1972—, chmn. univ. cancer com., 1972—. Editor-in-chief: (Harrison) Principles of Internal Medicine, 1976. Fellow Am. Acad. Arts and Scis., ACP; mem. Nat. Acad. Scis., Assn. Am. Physicians (pres. 1977-78). Research in structure and function of intestinal cells, membrane changes in malignant cells and serologic tests for malignancy. Discovered cause of galactosemia as 1st definitely proven disease due to hereditary enzyme defect; elucidated mechanism of intestinal fat absorption and causes of fatty liver; described genetic disturbance of amino acid and lipid metabolism (isovaleric acidemia); discovered specific defect in mucosa of patients with ulcerative colitis developed new serologic tests for diagnosis of cancer and viral hepatitis. Home: 20 Nobscot Rd Newton Center MA 02159 Office: Mass Gen Hosp Boston MA 02114

ISTEL, JACQUES ANDRE, investment company executive; b. Paris, Jan. 28, 1929; U.S., 1940, naturalized, 1951; s. Andre and Yvonne Mathilde Cremieux I.; m. Felicia Juliana Lee, June 14, 1973; 1 dau. by previous marriage, Claudia Yvonne. A.B., Princeton, 1949. Stock analyst Andre Istel & Co., N.Y.C., 1950, 55; pres. Parachutes Inc., Orange, Mass., 1957—, Intramgmt. Inc., N.Y.C., 1962-80; chmn. Pilot Knob Corp., 1982—; pres. VI World Parachuting Championships, 1962; capt. U.S. Parachuting team, 1956, capt., team leader, 1958; chmn. Mass. Parachuting Commn., 1961-62; lifetime hon. pres. Internat. Parachuting Commn., Fedn. Aero. Internat., 1965—; chmn. Hall of Fame of Parachuting, 1973—; founder Nat. Collegiate Parachuting League, 1957. Contbr. articles to encys., profl. publs. Trustee Inst. for Man and Sci., 1975-82; bd. dirs. Marine Corps Scholarship Found., 1975—. Served with USMC, 1952-54; lt. col. Res. Recipient Leo Stevens award, 1958, Diplome Paul Tissandier, 1969. Mem. Nat. Aero. Assn. (dir. 1965-68), Marine Corps Res. Officers Assn. Clubs: Racquet and Tennis, Princeton (N.Y.C.). Holder world record, parachuting, 1961. Patentee in field. Co-leader Nat. Geog. Soc. Vilcabamba Expdn., 1964. Home: 1040 Fifth Ave New York NY 10028 also Felicity Bimini Bahamas Office: Skyworld Lake Elsinore CA 92330 Office: Box 1014 Wildomar CA 92395

ISTEL, YVES-ANDRE, investment banker; b. Paris, Feb. 8, 1936; U.S., 1940, naturalized, 1954; s. Andre and Yvonne (Cremieux) I.; m. Nancy Lazrus, Aug. 6, 1964; 1 dau., Andrea Yvonne; 1 son by previous marriage, John Francis. A.B., Princeton U., 1957. With research, corp. fin. and fgn. depts. White, Weld & Co., N.Y.C., 1958-63; with Kuhn, Loeb & Co., N.Y.C., 1964-77, gen. partner, 1966-77; mng. dir. successor co. Lehman Bros. Kuhn Loeb, Inc., N.Y.C., 1977—; dir. Gen. Security Assurance Corp., Unity Fire & Gen. Ins. Co., Urbaine Life Ins. Co., Tex. Oil & Gas Corp., Transatlantic Securities Co. of Hartford, Dreyfus Intercontinental Investment Fund, Soc. Anonyme Française de Reassurances, Soc. d'Investissement et de Gestion; mem. internat. adv. bd. Compagnie de Saint-Gobain; mem. adv. com. on internat. capital markets N.Y. Stock Exchange. Trustee, mem. exec. com. U.S. Council Internat. Bus.; vice chmn. adv. bd. N.Y. U. Inst. French Studies; bd. dirs. French—Am. Found.; exec. v.p. French-Am. C.oC. in the U.S. Decorated chevalier de l'Ordre des Arts et des Lettres. Mem. Council Fgn. Relations, N.Y. Chamber Commerce and Industry (fin. and currency coms.). Clubs: Madison Sq. Garden, Town, Tennis. Home: 920 Fifth Ave New York NY 10021 Office: 55 Water St New York NY 10041

ISTOMIN, EUGENE, concert pianist; b. N.Y.C., Nov. 26, 1925; s. George T. and Assia (Chavin) I. Grad., Profl. Children's Sch.; pupil, Kyriena Siloti, Rudolf Serkin; student, Mannes Sch., 1935-38, Curtis Inst. Music, 1939-43. Appeared maj. orchs., U.S. and abroad, including six-continent world tour; appeared annually with Pablo Casals at, Casals Festivals, 1950—; mem., Istomin, Stern, Rose trio; recordings for, Columbia Masterworks. Winner Phila. Youth Contest and Leventritt award, 1943. Office: care ICM Artists Ltd 40 W 57th St New York NY 10019 *

ISTOMIN, MARTA, performing arts adminstr.; b. P.R., Nov. 2, 1936; d. Aguiles and Angelica M. (Martinez) Montanez; m. Pablo Casals, Aug. 3, 1957 (dec. 1973); m. Eugene Istomin, Feb. 15, 1975. Student, Mannes Coll. Music, N.Y.C., 1950-54; Mus.D. (hon.), World U., P.R., 1972, L.H.D., Marymount Coll., 1975. Prof. cello Conservatory Music, San Juan, P.R., 1961-64; vis. prof. cello Curtis Inst., Phila., 1974-75; co-chmn. bd., music dir. Casals Festival, 1974-77; artistic dir. John F. Kennedy Center for Performing Arts, Washington, 1980—; dir. Harcourt Brace Jovanovich, Inc., N.Y.C., cons. Latin Am. ednl. projects. Trustee Marlboro Sch. Music and Festival, Marymount Sch., N.Y.C., World U. Recipient Puerto Rican Fedn. Women's Clubs award, 1967; award for cultural achievements City of San Juan, 1975; Nat. Conf. Puerto Rican Women award, 1975; Casita Maria medal for outstanding contbns. to culture, N.Y.C., 1978; named Outstanding Woman of Yr., P.R., 1975, Woman of Achievement Sta. WETA-TV, Washington, 1981. Roman Catholic. Office: John F Kennedy Center for Performing Arts Washington DC 20566

ITABASHI, HIDEO HENRY, neuropathologist, neurologist; b. Los Angeles, July 7, 1926; s. Masakichi and Mitsuko (Kobayashi) I.; m. Yoko Osawa, Feb. 3, 1952; children—Mark Masa, Helen Yoko. A.B., Boston U., 1949; postgrad., Yale U., 1949-50; M.D., Boston U., 1954. Diplomate: in neuropathology Am. Bd. Pathology. Intern U. Mich. Hosp., Ann Arbor, 1954-55, resident in neurology, 1955-58; asso. research neurologist U. Calif., San Francisco, 1958-60, asst. clin. prof., 1964-65; asst. neuropathologist Langley Porter Neuropsychiat. Inst., San Francisco, 1960-65; cons. Neuropathologist San Francisco Gen. Hosp., 1964-65; cons. neurologist Ypsilanti (Mich.) State Hosp., 1966-71; cons. neuropathology dept., chief med. examiner-coroner, Los Angeles County, 1977—; asst. prof. neurology U. Mich. Med. Sch., 1965-68, asst. prof. pathology, 1966-68; asso. prof. neurology, pathology, 1968-71, asso. prof.-in-residence, 1971-75; prof.-in-residence pathology and neurology UCLA, 1975—; cons. VA Hosp., Sepulveda, Calif., 1977—; Spl. fellow in neuropathology Nat. Inst. Neurol. Diseases and Blindness, 1958-60. Contbr. numerous articles on neurol. disorders to med jours. Mem. Am. Assn. Neuropathologists, Am. Acad. Neurology. Office: Dept Pathology Harbor-UCLA Med Center 1000 W Carson St Torrance CA 90509

ITKIN, MYLES ROBERT, car rental and leasing executive; b. N.Y.C., Nov. 26, 1947; s. Simon and Lea Sybil (Haerman) I.; m. Frances Rothenberg, Oct. 10, 1982. B.A., Cornell U., 1969; M.B.A., NYU, 1974. Asst. treas. Sperry Corp., N.Y.C., 1975-81; treas. Hertz Corp., N.Y.C., 1981-83, staff v.p., treas., 1983—. Home: 1130 Park Ave New York NY 10128 Office: Hertz Corp 660 Madison Ave New York NY 10121

ITO, SUSUMU, educator; b. Stockton, Calif., July 27, 1919; s. Sohei and Hisayo (Watanabe) I.; m. Minnie Tsuji, May 29, 1948; children—Linda, Daniel, Celia, Bruce. B.S., Fenn Coll., 1949; M.S., Western Res. U., 1951, Ph.D., 1954; M.A. (hon.), Harvard, 1968. Post-doctoral fellow Western Res. U., 1955-56; fellow Max Planck Inst., Wilhelmshaven, Germany, 1956; instr. Cornell U. Med. Sch., 1957-59; Harvard Med. Sch., 1960-63, asst. prof., 1963-66, asso. prof., 1966-68, prof. anatomy, 1968—. Served to 1st lt. AUS, 1941-46. Decorated Bronze Star medal. Mem. Am. Assn. Anatomists, Am. Soc. Cell Biologists, N.Y. Acad. Sci., Electron Microscope Soc. Am., Soc. Study Reproduction, Am. Soc. Gastroenterology. Home: 16 Stearns St Wellesley MA 02181 Office: 25 Shattuck St Boston MA 02115

ITOH, TAKEHIKO, banker; b. Tokyo, Apr. 16, 1932; U.S., 1981; s. Toshio I. and Toshiko I.; m. Sadako Itoh, May 13, 1966; 1 child, Masahiko. B.A., Keio U., Tokyo, 1956. Sr. investment officer Pvt. Investment Co., Tokyo, Singapore, Panama,Asia, 1969-73; sr. mng. dir. Kwong On Bank, Hong Kong, 1973-78; dep. gen. mgr.Shinbashi br., Fuji Bank, Tokyo, 1978-80; gen. mgr.Oji Br. Fuji Bank, Tokyo, 1980-81; pres. Fuji Bank & Trust Co., N.Y.C., 1981-83; dir., gen. mgr. Fuji Bank, Ltd., N.Y.C., 1983—; chmn. bd. Fuji Bank & Trust Co., N.Y.C., 1983—. Home: 900 Park Ave Apt 10E New York NY 10021 Office: Fuji Bank Ltd One World Trade Ctr Suite 6011 New York NY 10048

ITOH, TATSUO, engineering educator; b. Tokyo, May 5, 1940; s. Yohnosuke and Kimi (Okamoto) I.; m. Seiko Fukumori, June 16, 1969; children: Akihiro, Elko. B.S., Yokohama Nat. U., Japan, 1964, M.S., 1966; Ph.D., U. Ill., 1969. Registered prof. engr., Tex. Research assoc. U. Ill., Urbana, 1969-71, research asst. prof., 1971-76; sr. research engr. Stanford Research Inst., Menlo Park, Calif., 1976-77; assoc. prof. U. Ky., Lexington, 1977-78, U. Tex., Austin, 1978-81, prof., 1981—, Hayden head prof., 1983—; guest researcher AEG-Telefunken, Ulm, W. Ger., 1979; cons. Tex. Instruments, Dallas, 1979, Hughes Aircraft. Guest editor: Transactions, 1981; inventor millimeter-wave line, 1975, quasi-optical mixer, 1982. Recipient Engring. Found. faculty awards, 1980.81. Fellow IEEE; mem. Microwave Theory and Techniques Soc. (editor), Internat. Sci. Radio Union, Inst. Electronics and Communication Engrs. Home: 3801 Green Trails N Austin TX 78731 Office: U Texas Dept Electrical Engineering Austin TX 78712

ITSKOVITZ, HAROLD DAVID, physician; b. Phila., Mar. 10, 1929; s. Morris and Mary (Gordon) I.; m. Gilda Kauffman, Dec. 26, 1954; children—Ellen Grace, Joanne, Linda Kay. A.B., U. Pa., 1953, M.D., 1957. Intern Phila. Gen. Hosp., 1957-58; resident in internal medicine Western Res. U. Hosp., Cleve., 1958-60; fellow hypertension U. Pa. Med. Sch., 1960-61, instr., then asst. prof. medicine, 1961-68; mem. faculty Med. Coll. Wis., Milw., 1968-81, prof. medicine and pharmacology, 1972—, dir. hypertension sect., 1968-81; prof. medicine and pharmacology N.Y. Med. Coll., 1981—, also dir. div. clin. pharmacology and hypertension, 1981—; founder Milw. Blood Pressure Program, 1974, project dir., 1974-75; founder Nat. Conf. Hypertension Control; mem. council Wis. Blood Pressure Program, 1976-79. Author papers in field, chpts. in books. Served with AUS, 1950-52. Recipient Outstanding Achievement award Nat. Conf. High Blood Pressure Conf., 1980. Fellow A.C.P.; mem. Internat. Soc. Hypertension, AMA, Am. Soc. Pharmacology and Exptl. Therapeutics, Am. Heart Assn. (med. adv. bd. council high blood pressure research), Am. Soc. Clin. Investigation, Am. Soc. Nephrology, Central Soc. Clin. Research, Phi Beta Kappa, Alpha Omega Alpha. Office: Dept Medicine NY Med Coll Valhalla NY 10595

ITTLESON, H(ENRY) ANTHONY, corporation executive; b. June 23, 1937; s. Henry and Nancy (Strauss) I.; m. Marianne Sundby, Feb. 6, 1961; children: Henry Philip, Christina Bee, Stephanie. B.A., Brown U., 1960. Credit adminstr. C.I.T. Financial Corp., N.Y.C., 1961-68, v.p., 1968-70, asst. to pres., 1970-71, v.p. mktg., 1971-78, v.p. financing div., 1978-81, exec. v.p., 1981—, also dir., mem. exec. com.; dir. C.I.T. Corp./Leasing, C.I.T. Comml. Fin. Co., C.I.T. Fin. Services, C.I.T. Corp. Fin., N.Am. Ins. Co., Wm. Iselin, Meinhard Comml. Corp., Tuition Plan Inc. Trustee Brown U., Brooks Sch.; bd. dirs. Boys Club of N.Y.; chmn. Ittleson Found. Mem. Phi Gamma Delta. Clubs: Garden of the Gods (Colorado Springs, Colo.); Brown U., Regency Whist, Madison Square Garden (N.Y.C.); Meadow, Nat. Golf Links Am. (Southampton, N.Y.). Home: 812 Park Ave New York NY 10021 Office: 650 CIT Dr Livingston NJ 07039

ITTMANN, MARJORIE MCCULLOUGH, Girl Scout ofcl.; b. Cin., July 12, 1923; d. Robert Stedman and Mildred (Rogers) McCullough; m. Homer E. Lunken, Apr. 15, 1944 (dec. 1970); children: Karen (dec. 1982), Kathryn Lunken Summers, Margo Lunken Yesner; m. William McLeod Ittmann, Mar. 17, 1972. Student, U. Cin., 1941-43. Active Girls Scouts U.S.A., 1962—, chmn. conv. com., 1969, 72, del. world convs., 1969, 72, 75, 78, chmn. pub. relations com., 1963-66, mem. nat. exec. com., 1963-75, mem. nat. bd., 1962—, 4th v.p., 1966-69, 1st v.p., 1969-72, nat. pres., 1972-75, chmn. nat. adv. council, 1975—; vice chmn. world com. World Assn. Girl Guides and Girl Scouts, 1978—; vice chmn. world conf., Orleans, France, 1981. Regional dir. Assn. Jr. Leagues Am., 1958-60, nat. pres., 1960-62; mem. br. Jr. League Cin., 1944-58, Nat. Tng. Labs., 1963-66, Nat. Assembly for Social Policy and Devel., 1968-71; mem. exec. com. Council Nat. Orgns. for Children and Youth, 1960-62, 68-72; bd. dirs. United Way Am., 1962-67, sec., 1965-66, v.p., 1966-67; mem. policy com. Center Vol. Soc., 1971-72; bd. dirs. Coll. Prep. Sch., Cin., 1962-69, pres., 1964-69; bd. dirs. Cin. Speech and Hearing Center, 1955-66, v.p., 1958-62, pres., 1963-66, trustee emeritus, 1966—; mem. bd. Children's Theatre, Cin., 1948-58, pres., 1948-50; bd. dirs. Community Health and Welfare Council Cin., 1957-49, Hamilton County (Ohio) Research Found., 1963—, Cancer Family Care, Cin., 1971-72, Boys Clubs Greater Cin., Marjorie P. Lee Home for Aged, Music Hall Assn., Cin. Symphony Orch.; rec. sec. Beechwood Home for Incurables; mem. Ohio Citizens Council, 1956-58; mem. bd. 7th Presbyterian Ch., 1967-74, ruling elder, 1976—; sr. warden St. Martin's in the Field, Biddeford Pool, Maine. Home: 2353 Bedford Ave Cincinnati OH 45208

ITZKOWITZ, NORMAN, educator; b. N.Y.C., May 6, 1931; s. Jack and Gussie (Schmier) I.; m. Leonore Krauss, June 13, 1954; children: Jay Noah, Karen Lisa. B.A. magna cum laude, CCNY, 1953; M.A., Princeton U., 1956, Ph.D., 1959. Instr. depts. history and Oriental studies Princeton U., 1958-61, asst. prof. Oriental studies, 1961-66, assoc. prof. Near Eastern studies, 1966-73, prof., 1973—, master Wilson Coll., 1975—; vis. prof. CCNY, summer 1959, Tchrs. Coll., Columbia U., 1964, N.Y. U., 1969, 72, 74, Hebrew U., Jerusalem, 1970, U. B.C., summer 1971. Author: Mubadele: An Ottoman-Russian Exchange of Ambassadors, 1970, Ottoman Empire and Islamic Tradition, 1980. Ford Found. fellow, 1954-59; HEW, SSRC, Littauer Found. fellow, 1970, 74. Mem. Am. Hist. Assn., Am. Oriental Soc. Jewish. Office: 108 Jones Hall Princeton U Princeton NJ 08544 *The goal of life is to be a mensch, a decent human being.*

ITZLER, RONALD STEPHEN, lawyer; b. Bronx, N.Y., Apr. 17, 1937; s. David Henry and Caroline (Spielberg) I.; m. Ronnie Lubell, Dec. 4, 1969; children—Jason Lubell, Jane Lubell. B.S., N.Y. U., 1957; M.B.A., Cornell U., 1959, LL.B., 1960. Bar: N.Y. bar 1961. Since practiced in N.Y.C. specializing in debtor rehab.; partner firm Ballon, Stoll & Itzler, 1967—; lectr. Cornell U. Law Sch., N.Y. U. Law Sch.; sec., dir. Bakers Equipment/Winkler, Inc. Mem. Mayor Fort Lee (N.J.) Adv. Com., 1976; bd. govs., treas. Ned B. Frank Philanthropic League. Served with USAF, 1961. Named Man of Year sportswear div. Am. Jewish Com., 1976. Mem. Assn. Bar City N.Y., Bankruptcy Lawyers Bar Assn. (gov.). Clubs: Montammy (Alpine, N.J.) (exec. com., gov., v.p.); Friars, Le Club (N.Y.C.). Home: 770 Anderson Ave Cliffside Park NJ 07010 Office: 1450 Broadway New York NY 10036 *Every day of my life should be filled with the sweetness of satisfaction and occasionally seasoned with the bitters of disappointment, so that the good may be distinguished from the bad and fully enjoyed.*

IVAN, THOMAS NATHANIEL, professional hockey team executive; b. Toronto, Ont., Can., Jan. 31, 1911; came to U.S., 1945, naturalized, 1957; s. Nickolas T. and Vera (Paul) I.; m. Dorothy L. Gardner. Ed. pub. schs. Gen. mgr. Chgo. Blackhawk Hockey Team, Inc., 1955-77, v.p., asst. to pres., 1977—. Recipient Lester Patrick trophy, 1975; named to Hockey Hall of Fame, 1974. Clubs: Carlton, Tavern (Chgo.); St. Andrews (Delray Beach, Fla.). Office: Chgo Blackhawks Hockey Team Inc 1800 W Madison St Chicago IL 60612

IVANICKI, RONALD JOSEPH, publishing company financial executive; b. Passaic, N.J., Oct. 3, 1940; s. Joseph W. and Catherine (Koc) I.; m. Deanna Germanski; children: Ronald, Robert, David, Deanna. B.S. in Acctg., Fairleigh Dickenson U., 1965. Div. controller Curtiss-Wright Corp., East Paterson, N.J., 1961-71; group controller Gulf & Western Industries, N.Y.C., 1971-80; v.p. fin. planning and analysis Simon & Schuster, N.Y.C., 1980—. Dist. commr. Babe Ruth Baseball, Trenton, N.J., 1983; league pres. Colts Neck Babe Ruth Baseball, N.J.; bd. dirs. Colts Neck Sports Found., 1981—. Republican. Roman Catholic. Home: 37 Squire Terr Colts Neck NJ 07722 Office: Simon & Schuster 1230 Ave of the Americans New York NY 10020

IVANIER, ISIN, manufacturing company executive; b. Vijnita, Rumania, Apr. 9, 1906; s. Jacob and Perl (Weintraub) I.; m. Francia Herling; children: Paul, Sydney. Grad., Technion, Haifa, Israel, 1982. Chmn., dir. Ivaco, Inc., N.Y. Wire Mills Corp., S.W. Transport, Inc.; dir., pres. Infatool, Ltd.; dir. Atlantic Steel Co., Ingersoll Machine & Tool Co., Ltd., Niagara Lockport Industries, Inc., Niagara Lockport Industries Que., Inc., Capitol Wire and Fence Co., Inc. Clubs: Hebrew, Montefiore. Office: Ivaco Inc 770 Sherbrooke St West Place Mercantile Montreal PQ Canada H3A 1G1

IVANIER, PAUL, industrialist. Pres. IVACO, Inc. Office: 770 Rue Sherbrooke Quest Montreal PQ Canada H3A 1G1§

IVANS, WILLIAM STANLEY, electronics company executive; b. New Rochelle, N.Y., June 17, 1920; s. William S. and Marion (Schultz) I.; m. Rebecca Peck Llewellyn, May 18, 1962; children—Dennis Llewellyn, Denise Louise; stepchildren—Virginia Kay Liebner, Joan Renee Liebner. B.S. in Elec. Engring, Pa. State U., 1942. With Convair div. Gen. Dynamics Corp., San Diego, 1946-57; chief electronics engr., 1954-57; v.p. engring. Cohu Electronics, Inc. (name changed to Cohu, Inc. 1972), San Diego, 1957-65, pres., 1965—, chief exec. officer, 1968-83, dir., chmn. bd.; dir. GTI Corp.; U.S. rep. gliding com. Fedn. Aero Internat., 1960-65, 66—, v.p., 1974-76, pres., 1976—. Served as officer USAAF, 1942-46; ETO. Recipient Lilienthal medal, 1950. Mem. Soaring Soc. Am. (pres. 1963-64), Western Electronic Mfrs. Assn. (dir. 1960-61), Nat. Aero. Assn. (dir. 1963-64, v.p. 1965—). Home: 807 La Jolla Rancho Rd La Jolla CA 92037 Office: 5725 Kearny Villa Rd San Diego CA 92123

IVERSON, FRANCIS KENNETH, metals company executive; b. Downers Grove, Ill., Sept. 18, 1925; s. Norris Byron and Pearl Irene (Kelsey) I.; m. Martha Virginia Miller, Oct. 24, 1945; children—Claudia (Mrs. Wesley Watts Sturges), Marc Miller. Student, Northwestern U., 1943-44; B.S., Cornell U., 1946; M.S., Purdue U., 1947. Research physicist Internat. Harvester, Chgo., 1947-52; tech. dir. Illium Corp., Freeport, Ill., 1952-54; dir. marketing Cannon-Muskegon Corp., Mich., 1954-61; exec. v.p. Coast Metals, Little Ferry, N.J., 1961-62; v.p. Nucor Corp. (formerly Nuclear Corp. Am.), Charlotte, N.C., 1962-65, pres., chief exec. officer, dir., 1965—; dir. Southeastern Savs. & Loan Co., C.H. Heist Co., Cato Corp.; bd. mgrs. Wachovia Bank and Trust Co., Charlotte. Contbr. articles to profl. jours. Served to lt. (j.g.) USNR, 1943-46. Named Best Chief Exec. Officer in Steel Industry Wall St. Transcript, 1980. Mem. NAM (dir.), Steel Joist Inst., Am. Soc. Metals, AIME, Am. Foundrymens Soc. Clubs: Carmel Country, Quail Hollow Country, Charlotte City Old Providence Racket (Charlotte). Office: 4425 Randolph Rd Charlotte NC 28211

IVERSON, KENNETH EUGENE, mathematician, researcher; b. Camrose, Alta., Can., Dec. 17, 1920; s. Olaf and Stella Adeline (Hill) I.; m. Jean E. Nicholson, Aug. 31, 1946; children: Eric, Paul, Keith, Janet. B.A., Queen's U., Kingston, Ont., Can., 1950; A.M., Harvard U., 1951, Ph.D., 1954. Asst. prof. applied math. Harvard U., 1954-60; with IBM (Thomas J. Watson Research Center), Yorktown Heights, N.Y., 1960—, fellow research div., 1971—. Author: A Programming Language, 1962, Elementary Functions, 1966, Algebra: An Algorithmic Treatment, 1972, Elementary Analysis, 1976, Introduction to APL, 1984. Served with Can. Armed Forces, 1942-46. Recipient Turing award Assn. Computing Machines, 1979; Harry Goode award Am. Fedn. Info. Processing Socs., 1975. Office: IP Sharp Assocs 2 First Canadian Pl Suite 1900 Toronto ON M5H 1J8 Canada

IVERSON, ROBERT LESTER, textbook company executive; b. Oak Park, Ill., Jan. 2, 1936; s. Edward Webster and Elvira (Grashorn) I.; m. Michelle Ann Follett, Aug. 9, 1958; children: Heather, Robert Michael, Wendy Michelle. B.S. magna cum laude, Williams Coll., 1958; M.B.A. with honors, U. Mich., 1960. Mgr. trade dept. Follett's Mich. Book Store, Ann Arbor, 1958-60; asst. mgr. Follett's Book Inc., Chgo., 1960-63; mgr. mdse. and systems Follett Retail Stores, Chgo., 1963-68; treas. Follett Corp., Chgo., 1968-73, v.p. fin., treas., 1973-77, pres. Follett Retail Stores div., 1977-83, also dir.; pres. Coll. Book Stores Am., Inc., 1983—. Mem. budget com. Oak Park River Forest Community Chest, 1969, 70. Mem. Nat. Assn. Accts., Am. Mgmt. Assn., Am. Mus. Natural History (asso.), Am. Acctg. Assn., 100 Thousand Miler Club, Chgo. Dist. Tennis Assn. (treas. 1975-78), Phi Beta Kappa, Phi Kappa Phi, Beta Gamma Sigma. Clubs: River Forest Tennis, Salt Creek Tennis, Wimbledon Palos (pres.), Chgo. Dist. Tennis Assn. (v.p. 1979). Home: 1053 Laurie Ln Burr Ridge IL Office: 907 North Elm Hinsdale IL 60521 *Find your niche and fill it with honor.*

IVES, BURL (ICLE IVANHOE), singer, actor; b. Hunt, Ill., June 14, 1909; s. Frank and Cordella (White) I.; m. Dorothy Koster, Apr. 1971;

1 son, Alexander. Student, Eastern Ill. State Tchrs. Coll., 1927-30, N.Y. U., 1937-38. With CBS, 1940-42. Made Columbia concerts annual country-wide concert tour as solo concert artist presenting folksongs and ballads; appears on radio and TV; makes theatrical appearances, tours and; stars in own co., every summer, also world tours; participated in: film productions including Just You and Me, Kid, 1979, Earthbound, 1981; and numerous other motion pictures; appeared in: musical productions including Showboat; plays including Cat on a Hot Tin Roof; appeared on: TV program The Bold Ones, 1970-72; former recording artist, Columbia and Decca; now records for, MCA; hist. song series, Ency. Britannica. (Recipient Motion Picture Acad. award for The Big Country.); Author: autobiography Wayfaring Stranger, 1948, Burl Ives Song Book, 1953, Sailing on a Very Fine Day, 1955, Tales of America, 1954, Burl Ives' Book of Seas Songs, Burl Ives Book of Irish Song, Song in America, 1961, A Wayfaring Stranger's Notebook: Albad, The Oaf, 1966. Mem. Am. Fedn. TV and Radio Artists, Writers Guild, Am. Fedn. Musicians, Screen Actors Guild. Democrat. Travelled throughout 46 states as troubadour, collecting and singing Am. folk songs, memorizing about 500 of them. Office: care Beakel & Jennings Agy 427 N Canon Dr Suite 205 Beverly Hills CA 90210 *

IVES, COLTA FELLER, museum curator, educator; b. San Diego, Apr. 5, 1943; m. E. Garrison Ives, June 14, 1966; 1 dau., Lucy Barrett. B.A., Mills Coll., 1964; M.A., Columbia U., 1966. Staff Met. Mus. Art, N.Y.C., 1966-75, curator charge prints and photographs, 1975—; adj. prof. Columbia U., 1970—. Author: The Great Wave 1974, Art Libraries Assn. award, 1975, The Flight Into Egypt, 1972, (with others) The Painterly Print, 1980. Travel grantee Met. Mus. Art, 1970-73. Mem. Print Council Am. (exec. bd. 1975-77). Club: Grolier (N.Y.C.). Office: Metropolitan Museum of Art Fifth Ave at 82d St New York NY 10028

IVES, DAVID HOMER, biochemist, educator; b. Rockford, Ill., Apr. 6, 1933; s. W. Homer and Elizabeth (Bridgeland) I.; m. Jean Ellen Seldon, Aug. 19, 1956; children: Laura Jean, Eric Gregory. B.A., Cornell Coll., Mt. Vernon, Iowa, 1955; Ph.D., U. Minn., 1960. NIH postdoctoral fellow U. Wis., 1960-62; asst. prof. biochemistry Ohio State U., Columbus, 1961-67, asso. prof., 1967-69, prof., 1969—. NIH, NSF grantee. Mem. Am. Soc. Biol. Chemists, Am. Sci. Affiliation, Am. Chem. Soc. Presbyterian (elder 1964—). Research on mechanisms regulating enzymes of cell proliferation in various organisms. Home: 1580 Cardiff Rd Columbus OH 43221

IVES, DAVID OTIS, television executive; b. Salem, Mass., Apr. 21, 1919; s. Oscar Jackson and Elinor (Goodhue) I.; m. Cecilia Coale van Hollen, Dec. 12, 1953 (div.); children: David van Hollen, Stephen Goodhue; m. Patricia Exton Howard, June 28, 1980; stepchildren: Daggett H. Howard, Jeffrey E. Howard, David M. Howard, Patricia G. Howard. A.B., Harvard U., 1941, M.B.A., 1943; D.H.L. (hon.), Northeastern U., 1975; H.H.D. (hon.), Suffolk U., 1977. Reporter, Salem Evening News, 1947; reporter, desk editor Wall St. Jour., N.Y.C., Detroit and Washington, bur. chief, Boston, 1947-58; editorial writer Sta. WBZ-TV-AM, Boston, 1958-60; asst. gen. mgr., dir. devel., pres., vice-chmn. WGBH Ednl. Found., Boston, 1960—; vice chmn. bd. mgrs. Public Broadcasting Service, 1974-77; trustee, pres., chmn. exec. com. Eastern Ednl. TV Network, 1976—; dir. Provident Instn. for Savs. Pres., Fair Housing, Inc., Boston, 1967-71; v.p. Boston Community-Media Council, 1977-81; bd. dirs. Assoc. Harvard Alumni, 1974-77; trustee Wellesley Coll., 1973—; mem. overseers com. to vis. dept. visual and environ. studies Harvard U., 1974-80; bd. dirs. New Eng. chpt. Deafness Research Found., 1979—; bd. overseers Boston Symphony Orch., 1971-77, chmn., trustee, 1975-77; trustee, chmn. bd. Nat. Assn. Public TV Stas. Home: 371 Mount Auburn St Cambridge MA 02138 Office: WGBH 125 Western Ave Boston MA 02134

IVES, DERMOD, lawyer; b. London, Eng., Jan. 23, 1904; came to U.S., 1909, naturalized, 1928; s. Robert Franklin and Mildred (Card) I.; m. Kathleen Christy, May 17, 1928; children—Patricia (Mrs. Endicott Perry), Dermod. B.A., Columbia, 1925, J.D., 1928, M.A. in Internat. Law, 1928, LL.D. (hon.). Bar: N.Y. bar 1928. Since practiced in, N.Y.C.; partner firm Windels Marx Davies & Ives (and predecessors), 1938—; dir. R.B. Davis Investment Co., Davis Jephson Finance Co.; Chief counsel N.Y. Commn. to Revise Laws of Estates, 1961-67. Vice chancellor L.I. Diocese Episcopal Ch., 1954-70, chancellor, 1971-72, adv. eccles. ct., 1958-62, standing com., 1962-72; Trustee Oxhollow Found., Anne B. Lichtenstein Found., Episcopal Church Bldg. Fund, Jephson Ednl. Trusts No. 1 and No. 2, The Third Street Music School Settlement. Mem. ABA, N.Y. State Bar Assn., Nassau County Bar Assn. (pres. 1960-61), Assn. Bar City N.Y. Clubs: Stanwich (Greenwich, Conn.); University Glee, University. Home: 884 North St Greenwich CT 06830 Office: 51 W 51st St New York NY 10019

IVES, GEORGE SKINNER, arbitrator, former government official; b. Bklyn., Jan. 10, 1922; s. Irving McNeil and Elizabeth (Skinner) I.; m. Barbara K. Turner, Aug. 14, 1948; children: Elizabeth Ives Radice, Nancy Ives Gove. Student, Taft Sch., 1940; A.B., Dartmouth Coll., 1943; LL.B., Cornell U., 1949. Bar: D.C. 1959, N.Y. 1949. Practice in, Washington, 1959-69, N.Y.C., 1950-53; legal asst. to chmn. NLRB, 1949-50; asso. atty. Simpson, Thatcher & Bartlett, 1950-53; adminstrv. asst., legal counsel U.S. Senator Irving M. Ives, N.Y., 1953-58; pvt. practice law, labor arbitrator, Washington, 1959-69; chmn., mem. Nat. Mediation Bd., 1969-81; arbitrator, Sarasota, Fla., 1981—. Served to lt. USNR, 1943-46. Mem. Am., N.Y., D.C. bar assns., Nat. Acad. Arbitrators, Am. Arbitration Assn. Home and Office: 1411 Kimlira Ln Sarasota FL 33581

IVES, J. ATWOOD, corporation executive; b. Atlanta, May 1, 1936; s. Stephen Bradshaw and Ellen (Atwood) I.; m. Elizabeth Saalfield; children: Ian, Anna, Benjamin. B.A. in Econs., Yale U., 1959; M.B.A., Stanford U., 1961; A.M.P., Harvard U., 1975. C.P.A., Calif. Acct. Price, Waterhouse & Co., San Francisco, 1961-64; fin. analyst Textron, Inc., Providence, 1964-66; ptnr., v.p. Paine Webber Jackson & Curtis, 1966-74; exec. v.p., chief fin. officer, dir. Gen. Cinema Corp., Chestnut Hill, Mass., 1974—; gen. ptnr. Crane Ranch, Wisdom, Wyo., 1980—. Trustee Inst. Contemporary Art, Boston, 1980—, Buckingham, Browne & Nichols, Sch., Cambridge, Mass., 1983—. Served with U.S. Army, 1961-62. Recipient award Haskins and Sells Found., 1961. Mem. Fin. Execs. Inst., Treasurers Club. Home: One Bennington Rd Lexington MA 02173 Office: Gen Cinema Corp 27 Boylston St Chestnut Hill MA 02167

IVES, JOHN DAVID (JACK IVES), research executive, educator; b. Grimsby, Eng., Oct. 15, 1931; came to U.S., 1967; s. Harry and Ellen May (McKay) I.; m. Pauline Angela H. Cordingley, Sept. 11, 1954; children—Nadine Elizabeth, Anthony Ragnar, Colin Harry, Peter Robert. B.A. in Gen. Geography/Geology, U. Nottingham, 1952, 1953; Ph.D., McGill U., Montreal, Que., Can., 1956. Postdoctoral research asst. Arctic Inst. N.Am., 1956-57; dir. (Subarctic Research Lab.); asst. prof. geography dept. McGill U., 1957-60; asst. dir. geog. br. Canadian Fed. Dept. Mines and Tech. Surveys, chief div. phys. geography, 1960-64; dir. geog. br. Canadian Fed. Dept. Energy, Mines and Resources, Ottawa, Ont., 1964-67; dir. Inst. Arctic and Alpine Research; prof. geography U. Colo., Boulder, 1967-79; guest prof. U. Bern, Switzerland, 1976-77; chmn. internat. working group UNESCO Man and the Biosphere Project 6; chmn. IGU Commn. on Mountain Geoecology, 1972-80; prof. mountain geoecology U. Colo., Boulder, 1980; cons. Time/Life Books; mem. adv. com. program natural resources UN U., 1978—, Coordinator study group; chmn. Canadian Nat. Adv. Com. on Geog. Research, 1964-67; mem. subcom. snow and ice NRC of Can., 1964-67. Co-editor: Arctic and Alpine Environments, 1974; founder, chmn. editorial bd., editor bd.: Arctic and Alpine Research, 1967-81; contbr. articles to profl. jours. U. Colo. Council on Research and Creative Work grantee for Nunatak study in Arctic Norway, 1973; research grantee NASA, 1971-82, NSF, 1969-79; Guggenheim Meml. fellow, 1976-77. Fellow Geol. Soc. Am., Arctic Inst. N.Am. (bd. govs.); mem. Glaciological Soc., Internat. Mountain Soc. (founding pres. 1980, editor Mountain Research and Devel. quar. 1981). Home: 2360 Dennison Ln Boulder CO 80303 Office: U Colo Campus Box 260 Boulder CO 80309 *I find comfort in adhering to a personal optimism; even if we can only envisage a partial solution, or a tiny step forward, we must try. The world is worth trying for and we can best do this through working with our fellow men and women.*

IVES, MARGARET, psychologist; b. Detroit, Apr. 10, 1903; d. Augustus Wright and Julia Claire (Chandler) I. A.B., Vassar Coll., 1924; M.A., U. Mich., 1929, Ph.D. (Alumnae Council fellow 1932-33, Univ. fellow 1934-35), 1938. Diplomate: clin. psychology Am. Bd. Profl. Psychology. Psychologist Juvenile Ct. (Wayne County Clinic Child Study), Detroit, 1929-32, Henry Ford Hosp., 1935-42; staff psychologist, then dir. psychol. services St. Elizabeth's Hosp., Washington, 1943-72, asso. dir. psychology, 1972-73; exec. officer Am. Bd. Profl. Psychology, Washington, 1977-81; lectr. George Washington U., 1946-55, 56-70; chmn. rating panel psychologists CSC, 1956-66; mem. D.C. Bd. Psychologist Examiners, 1971-77; prof. adv. com. D.C. Mental Health Assn., 1977—; adv. com. D.C. State Mental Health Plan, 1980—. Recipient Superior Service award HEW, 1964, Harold M. Hildreth Meml. award pschologists in public service, 1974, Disting. Psychologist award Am. Bd. Forensic Psychology, 1980. Fellow Am. Psychol. Assn., AAAS, Internat. Council Psychologists; mem. AAUW, D.C. Psychol. Assn., Va. Psychol. Assn., Detroit Hist. Soc., Phi Beta Kappa, Sigma Xi. Unitarian. Home and Office: 302 Rucker Pl Alexandria VA 22301 *I have always wondered about how people thought and behaved and why. On my first entering college my father advised me to become acquainted whenever possible with people from different cultures and different parts of the world. This I tried to do with some success.*

IVES, PHILIP, architect; b. N.Y.C., Aug. 8, 1904; s. Kenneth and Edith (Appleton) I.; m. Sarah Manning Holter, Nov. 10, 1928; children—Elizabeth Ives Clark, Sarah Ives Scully, Philip Appleton. Student, Yale U., 1927. Designer, asso. Ewing & Allen and Leigh Hill French, Jr., 1927-32; practice architecture under firm name Philip Ives, N.Y.C., 1932—; sr. project planner FPHA, World War II. Important works include St. Barnabas Ch, Greenwich (award Ch. Archtl. Guild Am.), Corp. Research Lab, Sterling Forest, N.Y. (certificate of merit N.Y. State Assn. Architects), Quarry Knolls Housing, Greenwich (Honor award for design excellence Fed. Housing and Home Finance Agy.), Chapel of St. Jude, Georgetown, Washington (Honor award Guild for Religious Architecture), First Presbyn. Ch, New Canaan, Conn., Visitors' Reception Center Gunston Hall Plantation, Lorton, Va., guest suites, Colonial Williamsburg (Va.) Found.; Author, editor: The Nativity in Stained Glass, 1977. Bd. dirs. Yale Alumni Fund, 1950-55. Fellow AIA; asso. NAD; mem. Archtl. League N.Y., Guild for Religious Architecture (dir. 1976-77), Century Assn., Order St. John of Jerusalem (comdr.), Pilgrims of U.S., Psi Upsilon. Republican. Episcopalian (vestryman 1975-78). Club: Field (Greenwich, Conn.) (past pres.). Home: Parsonage Rd Greenwich CT 06830 Office: 65 E 55th St New York NY 10022

IVES, VICTOR MILO, radio and television executive; b. San Francisco, Aug. 17, 1935; s. Milo and Lucy Marion (Lumsden) I.; m. Carol Lee Holyfield; children: Matthew, Michelle, Melissa. Student, Chico State Coll., 1953-54. Program dir. KGEE, Bakersfield, Calif., 1960-61, KAIR, Tucson, 1961-63; ops. dir. Phila. UHF TV, 1959-60; v.p., gen. mgr. KWUN Radio, Concord, Calif., 1963-70; exec. programming specialist Golden West Broadcasters, Portland, Oreg., 1970-75; host TV show, Portland, 1972-75; program dir. Radio Sta. KEX, Portland, until 1975, Sta. KSFO, San Francisco, 1978; v.p., gen. mgr. Radio Sta. WTWR, Detroit, 1978-81, v.p., 1981-82; pres., owner Radio Sta. KMJK, Portland, Oreg., 1982—. Host weekly TV, KPIX, San Francisco, 1950-51; Contbr. articles to profl. jours. Bd. dirs. Diablo Scholarships, 1966-68, Lake Oswego Community Theatre, Portland Tb and Respiratory Disease Assn.; commr. Moraga (Calif.) Cable Vision Commn. Recipient award for best local news award, 1967-68; named Program Dir. of Year Billboard mag., 1974. Mem. Nat. Assn. Broadcasters (Oreg. co-chmn. 1971-72), Calif. Assn. Broadcast Editorial Dirs. (founding officer 1968), Oreg. Assn. Broadcasters, Concord C. of C. (1st v.p. 1966-69), Portland Ad Club. Home: 2650 SW Riven Dell Rd Lake Oswego OR 97034 Office: 9500 SW Barbur Blvd Portland OR 97219 *Ideas are fragile (yours and others). Nurture them with respect. Strive to think "out of the box." To do so broadens the horizon and increases the field of opportunity. Always try to act rather than react, look to your own creativity for stimuli instead of the accomplishments of others.*

IVEY, HENRY FRANKLIN, physicist; b. Augusta, Ga., June 16, 1921; s. Henry Franklin and Minnie Lee (Lively) I.; m. Sylvia Berg, July 18, 1948; children—Lisa Anne, Stephen David. A.B. summa cum laude, U. Ga., 1940; M.S. in Physics, 1941; Ph.D., M.I.T., 1944. Mem. staff radiation lab. M.I.T., 1942-45; with lamp div. Westinghouse Electric Corp., Bloomfield, N.J., 1947-63, mem. staff research and devel. center, Pitts., 1963—, adv. scientist tech. assessment, 1975—. Author: Electroluminescence and Related Effects, 1963. Recipient cert. of appreciation OSRD, 1945. Fellow IEEE; mem. Am. Phys. Soc., Optical Soc. Am., Soc. Info. Display, AAAS, Electrochem. Soc. (hon.), Internat. Assn. Jazz Record Collectors, Phi Beta Kappa, Sigma Xi, Phi Kappa Phi, Pi Mu Epsilon, Sigma Pi Sigma. Office: Westinghouse Research and Devel Center Pittsburgh PA 15235

IVEY, JAMES BURNETT, polit. cartoonist; b. Chattanooga, Apr. 19, 1925; s. Bernard Steele and Alise (Buford) I.; m. Ellen Shea, Aug. 29, 1947 (div. Jan. 1957); m. Evelyn Rogers., Jan. 12, 1957; children—Susan Ellen, Donald James. A.A., George Washington U., 1948; student, U. Louisville, 1943, Nat. Art Sch., Washington, 1948-50. Polit. cartoonist Washington Star, 1950-53, St. Petersburg (Fla.) Times, 1953-59, San Francisco Examiner, 1959-66; free-lance polit. cartoonist, 1966-69; with Orlando Sentinel-Star, 1970-77; curator Cartoon Mus., 1967—; adj. prof. U. Central Fla., 1978—. Artist: syndicated feature Thoughts of Man; Contbr. articles newspapers, jours. Bd. dirs. San Francisco Acad. Comic Art. Served with USNR, 1943-46. Reid fellow, 1959. Mem. Nat. Cartoonists Soc., Assn. Am. Editorial Cartoonists. Address: 561 Obispo Ave Orlando FL 32807

IVEY, JEAN EICHELBERGER, composer; b. Washington, July 3, 1923; d. Joseph S. and Elizabeth (Pieffer) Eichelberger. A.B magna cum laude, Trinity Coll., 1944; Mus. M. in Piano, Peabody Conservatory, 1946, Eastman Sch. Music, U. Rochester, 1956; Mus. D., U. Toronto, 1972. Founder, dir. electronic music studio Peabody Conservatory, John Hopkins U., Balt., 1969—, coordinator dept. composition, 1982—. Performer piano recitals, concert tours including own compositions, U.S., Mex., Europe; compositions Passacaglia for Chamber Orch., 1954, Sonata for Piano, 1957, 6 Inventions for 2 Violins, 1959, O Come Bless the Lord, Lord Hear My Parayer, 1960, Sonatina for Unaccompanied Clarinet, Dinsmoor Suite, 1963, Enter Three Witches, 1964, Pinball, 1965, Tribute: Martin Luther King, 1969, Terminus, 1970, 3 Songs of Night, 1971, Forms in Motion, 1972, Hera, Hung from the Sky, 1973, Testament of Eve, 1976, Solstice, 1977, Prospero, 1978, Sea-Change, 1979, The Birthmark (opera), 1982, Notes toward Time, 1984; music for films, TV; subject: TV documentary A Woman Is—A Composer; recorded on: Folkways, 1967, 73, Composers Records Inc., 1974; contbr.: Electronic Music a Listeners Guide, 1972; articles to musical publs. Recipient Peabody Conservatory Disting. Alumni award, 1975; Nat. Endowment Arts grantee, 1978, 83. Mem. Am. Soc. Univ. Composers (editor newsletter 1968-70), ASCAP, internat. Soc. Contemporary Music (dir. U.S. sect. 1972-75, 79—), Coll. Music. Soc. (council 1971-74), Phi Beta Kappa, Sigma Alpha Iota (composer-judge). Home: 320 W 90th St New York NY 10024 Office: Peabody Conservatory John Hopkins U Baltimore MD 21202 *I consider all the musical resources of the past and present as being at the composer's disposal, but always in the service of the effective communication of humanistic ideas and intuitive emotion.*

IVEY, RICHARD MACAULAY, lawyer; b. London, Ont., Can., Oct. 26, 1925; s. Richard Green and Jean (Macaulay) I.; m. Beryl Marcia Nurse, Aug. 6, 1949; children: Richard William, Jennifer Louise, Rosamond Ann, Susanne Elizabeth. B.A., U. Western Ont., 1947, LL.D. (hon.), 1979; LL.B., Osgoode Hall, 1950. Bar: created Queen's counsel 1963. Asso. Ivey, Livermore & Dowler, London, Ont., 1950-60, partner, 1960-64, Ivey & Dowler, London, 1964—; chmn. bd. Allpak Ltd., London, Livingston Internat. Inc., Ivex Corp.; dir. No. Life Assurance Co. Can., London, F.W. Woolworth Co. Ltd., Bank of Montreal, Livingston Internat., Inc., Dashwood Industries Ltd., Eaton Yale Ltd., Union Gas Ltd. Bd. dirs. World Wildlife Fund, Can.; hon. trustee Royal Ont. Mus.; trustee World Wildlife Fund (Internat.); chancellor U. Western Ont.; councillor Wildfowl Trust, U.K.; adv. bd. Theatre London, Sch. Bus. Adminstrn., U. Western Ont., Ridley Coll., St. Catharines, Ont., St. Joseph's Hosp., London, Ont.; pres. Richard Ivey Found., 1967, World Wildlife Fund (Can.). Clubs: London Hunt and Country, London, Toronto. Home: 990 Wellington St London ON N6A 3T2 Canada Office: 618 Richmond St London ON Canada N6A 5J9

IVEY, WILLIAM JAMES, foundation executive; b. Detroit, Sept. 6, 1944; s. William James and Grace Christine (Hammes) I.; m. Patricia A. Hall, Mar. 5, 1977 (div. 1982). B.A. in History, U. Mich., 1966; M.A. in Folklore and Ethnomuscicology, Ind. U., 1969. Cataloguer Ind. U. Archives Traditional Music, 1969-71; library dir. Country Music Found., Nashville, 1971, dir. found., 1971—; asso. prof. music Bklyn. Coll., 1979-80; chmn. folk music panel Nat. Endowment Arts, 1976-78; bd. visitors Mid-South humanities project Middle Tenn. State U., 1979-80; bd. dirs. Nashville Songwriters Assn., 1974-75; mem. music industry adv. panel Belmont Coll., 1975-79. Author articles in field, chpts. in books; editor: Jour. Country Music, 1972-75; exec. editor, 1977—; rec/ rev. editor: Western Folklore, 1976-78. Recipient Billboard Country Liner Notes of Year award, 1974; sr. research fellow Inst. Studies Am. Music, 1979-80. Mem. Nat. Acad. Rec. Arts and Scis. (trustee 1976-80, v.p. 1980-81, 83-84, nat. pres. 1981-83), Am. Folklore Soc., Assn. Rec. Sound Collections, Am. Assn. State and Local History, Internat. Soaring Soc. Am., Nashville Area C. of C. (chmn. music industry liason com. 1978-80). Office: 4 Music Sq E Nashville TN 37203

IVISON, DONALD ALEXANDER STUART, manufacturing company executive; b. Ottawa, Ont., Can., June 3, 1932; (married); 3 children. B.A. with honors in Polit. Economy, McMaster U., Hamilton, Ont., 1953; M.B.A., U. Western Ont., London, 1955. With Du Pont Can. Inc., 1955—, first asst. treas., Montreal, Que., 1973-75, v.p., treas., 1975-79, v.p., chief fin. officer, 1979-80, sr. v.p., after 1980; now with E.I. DuPont de Nemours and Co., Wilmington, Del. Mem. Fin. Execs. Inst. Can. Office: 1007 Market St Wilmington DE 19898

IVKOVICH, RONALD SAMUEL, food company executive; b. McKeesport, Pa., July 23, 1938; s. Samuel and Rose Marie (Kasunic) I.; m. Janice Murphy, June 15, 1963; children: Jill Michele, Cheryl Lynn, Kevin Ronald. B.S., Cornell U., 1961, M.S., 1962. Sales rep. Campbell Soup Co., Syracuse, N.Y., 1965-66, dist. sales supr., Boston, 1966-67, asst. mgr. food services systems, Camden, N.J., 1967-68; v.p. Food Service div. P & C Food Markets, Syracuse, 1968-75; corp. dir. purchasing I.U. Internat. Viands Corp., Charlotte, N.C., 1975-76; pres. I.U. Internat. Clark & Lewis Co., Jacksonville, Fla., 1976-78, Redi Froz, Inc. div. Scot Lad Foods, South Bend, Ind., 1978—; v.p. Simon Bros. Inc., South Bend, 1982—. Bd. dirs. Camp Milhouse. Served with AUS, 1962-64. Mem. Midwest Frozen Food Assn., Nat. Frozen Food Assn., Cornell Hotel Assn. Home: 52091 Farmington Square Rd Granger IN 46530 Office: 1901 N Bendix Dr South Bend IN 46619

IVORY, PETER B.C.B., medical administrator; b. St. Germans, Eng., Jan. 15, 1927; s. Charles A. and Kathleen H. (Bishop) I.; m. Eleanor Nelson, June 29, 1957 (dec.); children—Mark, Anne; m. Eve Ervin, Dec. 6, 1974; 1 dau., Celeste. M.D., U. London, Eng., 1954. Diplomate: Am. Bd. Psychiatry and Neurology. With Fla. Div. Mental Health, 1961—; clin. dir. Fla. State Hosp., Chattahoochee. Mem. Am. Psychiat. Assn. Home: PO Box 3193 Tallahassee FL 32315 Office: Fla State Hospital Chattahoochee FL 32324

IVRY, ALFRED LYON, educator; b. Bklyn., Jan. 14, 1935; s. Morris and Belle (Malamud) I.; m. Joann Saltzman, June 15, 1958; children: Rebecca, Jonathan, Sara Beth, Jessica. B.A., Bklyn. Coll., 1957; M.A., Brandeis U., 1958, Ph.D., 1963; D.Phil., Oxford (Eng.) U., 1971. From asst. prof. to assoc. prof. Cornell U., Ithaca, N.Y., 1967-74; prof. Ohio State U., Columbus, 1974-76; prof. Sch. Near Eastern and Judaic Studies Brandeis U., Waltham, Mass., 1976—, Walter S. Hilborn prof. Near Eastern and Judaic Studies, 1977—; co-chmn. Colloquium in Medieval Philosophy, Boston, 1977-81, 84—. Mem. editorial bd.: Univ. Press of New Eng., 1982, 84; editor: (translator) Al-Kindi's Metaphysics, 1974, Moses of Narbonne: Perfection of the Soul, 1977; lectr.: Brandeis Nat. Women's Com., 1976-82. Trustee Boston Hebrew Coll., 1981—. Fulbright fellow, 1963-65, 72, 1982-83; grantee NEH, 1978-79, 80-81. Mem. Am. Oriental Soc., Am Philos. Assn., Assn. for Jewish Studies (bd. dirs. 1971-74), Medieval Acad. Am., Soc. Medieval and Renaissance Philosophy. Jewish. Home: 154 Randlett Park West Newton MA 02165 Office: Philip W Lown Sch Near Eastern and Judaic Studies Brandeis U Waltham MA 02254

IVY, RICHARD JOHN, manufacturing company executive; b. N.Y.C., July 19, 1940; s. Richard Frank and Olga V. I.; m. Sherrill Ann Mackay, Aug. 3, 1968; children: Christopher Scott, Davin Clark, Brandon Todd, Andrew Mackay. B.A., U. Va., 1963; M.B.A., Fairleigh Dickinson U., 1968. Mgmt. analyst Continental Corp., N.Y.C., 1966-68, asst. to treas., 1968-70, GAF Corp., N.Y.C., 1970-73; treas. Barnes Group Inc., Bristol, Conn., 1973-82; exec. v.p., chief fin. officer Economy Electric Supply, Manchester, Conn., 1982—. Mem. Project Bus., Jr. Achievement, 1977-78; Mem. exec. com., vice chmn. fin. com. chmn. trust fund promotion com., mem. audit com., mem. investment com. and mem. nominating com. Long Rivers council Boy Scouts Am., all 1979—; coach Youth Soccer Inc., Simsbury, Conn., 1979—; active Farmington Valley YMCA Fund Dr., Simsbury, 1979. Served to 1st lt. USAF, 1963-65. Mem. Bristol C. of C., Tau Kappa Epsilon.

Republican. Presbyterian. Clubs: Blandford (Mass.); Chippanee Golf (Bristol). Home: 40 Laurel Ln Simsbury CT 06070 also Kibbe Point East Otis MA Office: 440 Oakland St Manchester CT 06040

IWAN, WILFRED DEAN, mechanical engineer; b. Pasadena, Calif., May 21, 1935; s. Wilfred August and Dorothy Anna Sarah (Glass) I.; m. Alta Joan Gish, Sept. 13, 1957; children: William Douglas, Robert Dean, Stephen Bruce. B.S., Calif. Inst. Tech., 1957, M.S., 1958, Ph.D., 1961. Asst. and asso. prof. mechanics U.S. Air Force Acad., 1961-64; asst., asso. and prof. applied mechanics Calif. Inst. Tech., 1964—, exec. officer for civil engring. and applied mechanics, 1980—; dir. Winter-Shay Assos.; cons. to industry; prin. investigator on various federally sponsored research projects. Contbr. articles to profl. jours.; editor: Applied Mechanics in Earthquake Engineering, 1974, Strong Motion Earthquake Instrument Arrays, 1978. Active Lake Ave Congregational Ch., Pasadena; trustee Westmont Coll. Served with USAF, 1961-64. Mem. ASME. Research in vibration dynamics, earthquake engring. Inventor in field. Office: Mail Code 104-44 Calif Inst Tech Pasadena CA 91125

IWASAKI, IWAO, engineering educator; b. Tokyo, Japan, Feb. 6, 1929; came to U.S., 1950; s. Kuramatsu and Ichiko (Ishihara) I.; m. Junko Ikegami, 1972. Student, U. Tokyo, 1948-50; B.S., U. Minn., 1951, M.S., 1953; Sc.D., Mass. Inst. Tech., 1957; D.Eng., Tohoku U., 1961. Asst. prof. U. Minn., Mpls., 1957-59, asso. prof., 1963-66, prof., 1966—; research engr. Nippon Steel Corp., Tokyo, 1959-63. Contbr. articles to profl. jours. Mem. AIME (Antoine M. Gaudin award 1982, Arthur F. Taggart award 1982), Mining Inst. Japan, Soc. Mining Engrs. (Disting. Mem.), Iron and Steel Inst. Japan, Electrochem. Soc. Japan, Sigma Xi, Tau Beta Pi. Home: 2208 S Rosewood Ln Saint Paul MN 55113

IWASAWA, KENKICHI, mathematician; b. Kiryu, Japan, Sept. 11, 1917; came to U.S., 1950; s. Zensuke and Katsu (Anzai) I.; m. Aiko Kaneko, Mar. 30, 1941; children—Kazuko (Mrs. Yasutaka Ihara), Takashi, Mariko (Mrs. Dennis R. Molodowitch). Dr. Sci., U. Tokyo, Japan, 1945. Asst. prof. U. Tokyo, 1949-52; asst. prof., asso. prof. then prof. Mass. Inst. Tech., 1952-67; prof. math. Princeton, 1967—. Mem. Am. Math. Soc. (Cole prize 1962). Home: 12 Newlin Rd Princeton NJ 08540

IX, ROBERT EDWARD, food company executive; b. Woodcliffe, N.J., Oct. 15, 1929; s. William Edward and Helen Elizabeth (Gorman) I.; m. Mildred Gilmore, June 27, 1959; children: Helen Adele, Alesia Gilmore, Robert Owens Gilmore, Julia Ryan, Christopher Prouty. A.B., Princeton U., 1951; M.B.A., Wharton Grad. Sch., U. Pa., 1956; LL.D. (hon.), Marymount Coll., 1978, Sacred Heart U., Conn., 1984. Mgmt. cons. Arthur D. Little Inc., Cambridge, Mass., 1956-63; mktg. dir. Browne-Vintners Co., Distillers Corp.-Seagrams Ltd., N.Y.C., 1963-66; v.p. mktg. Schweppes (USA) Ltd., N.Y.C., 1966-68, pres., 1968; pres., chief exec. officer Cadbury Schweppes Inc., Stamford, Conn., 1970-78; chmn., chief exec. officer Am. region Cadbury Schweppes P.L.C., 1976—; dir. Cadbury Schweppes P.L.C., London, N.E. Bancorp Inc., Union Trust Co., Loctite Corp., Chase Bag Co. Trustee Marymount Coll., also chmn.; trustee Greenwich (Conn.) Acad., Trinity Pawling Sch. (N.Y.); mem. adv. council N.Y. Med. Coll., Valhalla, N.Y. Served to lt. comdr. USNR, 1951-55. Decorated Knight Sovereign Mil. Order Malta. Mem. Young President's Orgn., World Bus. Council, Chief Execs. Forum, Southwestern Area Commerce and Industry Assn. Conn. (dir. 1970—, chmn. bd. 1976-77), Def. Orientation Conf. Assn. (dir.), Grocery Mfrs. Am. (dir. 1981—), U.S. Navy League (dir. Conn.). Roman Catholic. Clubs: Univ. (N.Y.C.); Belle Haven (Greenwich); Greenwich Country; Landmark (Stamford) (chmn. bd. govs.). Office: High Ridge Park Stamford CT 06905

IYENGAR, SRINIVASA, engr.; b. French Rocks, India, May 6, 1934; came to U.S., 1957, naturalized, 1968; s. Anantha and Rathnamma Char; m. Ruth Helen Yonan, Dec. 17, 1966; children—Sona, Jay. B.Civil Engring., U. Mysore, 1955; M.Civil Engring., India Inst. Sci., 1957; M.A. in Civil and Structural Engring, U. Ill., Urbana, 1959. Grad. research asst. U. Ill., 1957-60; with Skidmore, Owings & Merrill (architects engrs.), Chgo., 1960—, asso. partner, dir. structural engring., 1969-75, partner, chief structural engring., 1975—; lectr. U. Ill., Cornell U.; mem. Mayor of Chgo.'s Com. on Bldg. Codes. Author articles in field.; prin. projects include Sears Tower, Chgo., 22 Riverside Plaza, Chgo., Three First Nat. Plaza, Chgo., 60 State St, Boston, First Can. Centre, Calgary, Alta., Century Plaza, Houston, Irving Trust Center, N.Y.C. Mem. Am. Concrete Inst. (chmn. coms.), ASCE, Structural Stability Research Council, Am. Inst. Steel Constrn., Reinforced Concrete Research Council. Clubs: Met., Monroe. Office: 33 W Monroe St Chicago IL 60603

IZANT, ROBERT JAMES, JR., pediatric surgeon; b. Cleve., Feb 4, 1921; s. Robert James and Grace (Goulder) I.; m. Virginia Lincoln Root, Sept. 27, 1947; children: Jonathan G. II, Mary Root, Timothy Holman. A.B. cum laude, Amherst Coll., 1943; M.D., Western Res. U., 1946. Diplomate: Am. Bd. Surgery, Am. Bd. Pediatric Surgery. Resident in surgery U. Hosp., Cleve., 1946-52; resident in pediatric surgery Boston Children's Med. Center, 1952-55; asst. prof. pediatric surgery Ohio State U., 1955-58; prof., dir. divs. pediatric surgery Case Western Res.U., 1958—; dir. div. pediatric surgery Univ. Hosps. Cleve., Rainbow Babies and Children's Hosp.; also Cleve. Met. Gen. Hosp.; mem. adv. bd. Ohio State Services for Crippled Children, 1972—. Co-author: The Surgical Neonate; contbr. articles to profl. jours. Trustee Am. Cancer Soc. Served to lt. (j.g.) M.C. USNR, 1947-49. Fellow A.C.S., Am. Acad. Pediatrics; mem. Central Surg. Assn., Am. Assn. Surgery of Trauma, AMA, Ohio Med. Assn., Cleve. Surg. Soc. (pres. 1971-72), Cleve. Acad. Medcine (dir. 1971-74), Am. Trauma Soc. (founding mem.), Teratology Soc., Lilliputian Surg. Soc., No. Ohio Pediatric Soc., Brit. Assn. Pediatric Surgery, Pediatric Surgery Biology Club, Am. Pediatric Surg. Assn. (founding mem.), Western Res. U. Sch. Medicine Alumni Assn. (pres. 1961-62), Am. Burn Assn., Sigma Xi, Alpha Omega Alpha, Nu Sigma Nu, Delta Kappa Epsilon. Home: 2275 Harcourt Dr Cleveland Heights OH 44106 Office: RCB Hosp Univ Circle Cleveland OH 44106

IZARD, CARROLL ELLIS, psychology educator; b. Georgetown, Miss., Oct. 8, 1923; s. Willis Lee and Willie (Cliburn) I.; m. Barbara Sinquefield; children: Carroll Ellis, Camille Sinquefield, Ellen Ashley. B.A., Miss. Coll., 1943; B.D., Yale U., 1945; M.A., Syracuse U., 1951, Ph.D., 1952. Diplomate: Am. Bd. Examiners in Profl. Psychology. Research asso. Tulane U., 1952-54; research asso. Research Assos., Inc., Phila., 1954-55; specialist, individual devel. and human relations Gen. Electric Co., Lynn, Mass., 1955-56; asst. prof. psychology Vanderbilt U., Nashville, 1956-61, asso. prof., 1961-64, prof., 1964-76, dir., 1956-71, dir. clin. tng. program, 1962-67; Unidel prof. psychology U. Del., 1976—; asso. Ed Glaser and Assos.; cons. VA; mem. Tenn. Bd. Examiners in Psychology, 1962-66; sr. scientist Human Devel. Lab., J.F. Kennedy Center, Peabody Coll., Nashville. Author: The Face of Emotion (Elliot Meml. award Century Psychology Series 1969), Patterns of Emotions: A New Analysis of Anxiety and Depression, 1972, Human Emotions, 1977; editor: (with S.S. Tomkins) Affect, Cognition and Personality, 1965, Emotions in Personality and Psychopathology, 1979, Measuring Emotions in Infants and Children; contbr. articles to profl. jours. Served to lt. (j.g.) USNR, 1944-46. Fellow AAAS, Am. Psychol. Assn., Sigma Xi. Home: Chambers Rock Farm Landenberg PA Office: Dept Psychology U Del Newark DE 19711

IZENOUR, GEORGE CHARLES, educator; b. New Brighton, Pa., July 24, 1912; s. Charles S. and Wilhelmina (Freseman) I.; m. Hildegard Hilt, Sept. 7, 1937; 1 son, Steven. A.B., Wittenberg Coll., 1934, M.A., 1936, D.F.A. (hon.), 1960, M.A., Yale U., 1961. Lighting dir. fed. theatres in, Calif., 1938-39; with OSRD, 1943-46; mem. faculty Yale U., 1946-77, prof. theatre design and tech., 1960-77, dir. electromech. lab., 1946-77; theatre cons., 1958—. Author: Theater Design, 1977; contbr. to: Ency. Brit, 1975; contbg. editor: theater sect. Dictionary Architecture and Constrn, 1975. Fellow Rockefeller Found., 1939-43, 46-47; Ford Found. fellow, 1960-61; Guggenheim fellow, 1971-72; Recipient Rodgers and Hammerstein award theatre design, 1960; award for contbns. to art and tech. Am. theater U.S. Inst. for Theater Tech., 1975; Benjamin Franklin fellow Royal Soc., 1975; Honor award Am. Theater Assn., 1977; George Friedly Meml. award Theater Library Assn., 1978. Mem. AAAS, ANTA, IEEE, Acoustical Soc. Am., Conn. Acad. Arts and Scis., Nat. Council Acoustical Cons., U.S. Inst. Theater Tech., Am. Soc. Theater Cons., Archaeol. Inst. Am. Inventor lighting systems, rigging, lighting and computer controls for theatre and TV. Home: 16 Flying Point Rd Stony Creek CT 06405

IZENSTARK, JOSEPH LOUIS, physician, educator; b. Chgo., Mar. 29, 1919; s. Paul and Flora (Berger) I.; m. Elizabeth Kaplan, June 25, 1944; children: Susan Rebecca, John Kenneth, Florence Pauline. B.A., U. Calif., Berkeley, 1948, M.D., 1951. Diplomate: Am. Bd. Radiology, Am. Bd. Nuclear Medicine. Intern USPHS, Chgo., 1951-52; resident Kern Gen. Hosp., Bakersfield, Calif., 1952-53; resident in radiology Cedars of Lebanon Hosp., Los Angeles, 1955-56; chief radiology resident Los Angeles County Harbor Gen. Hosp., Torrance, Calif., 1957-58; practice medicine specializing in radiology, Inglewood, Calif., 1953-55, Bakersfield, 1971—; dir. radiology Imperial Hosp., Inglewood, 1959-60; asst. prof. radiology Tulane U., 1960-62, asso. prof., 1963; asso. prof. radiology Emory U., 1963-67, dir. nuclear medicine, 1963-67; prof. radiology U. So. Calif., 1969—; prof. health scis. Bakersfield State Coll., 1973—; chief nuclear medicine Cedars of Lebanon Hosp., 1968-71; med. dir. Bakersfield Meml. Hosp., 1983—; spl. cons. radiol. health USPHS, Calif. Bur. Radiol. Health, U.S. Army; mem. La. Atomic Energy Adv. Council; dir. nuclear medicine Crawford W. Long Meml. Hosp.; mem. USPHS Commn. on Radiation Exposure Evaluation. Author: Anatomy and Physiology for X-ray Technicians, 1961; contbr. articles to profl. jours. Fellow Am. Cancer Soc., Am. Coll. Radiology; mem. Soc. Nuclear Medicine (pres. So. Calif. chpt. 1976), So. Valley Radiol. Soc. (pres. 1975), Kern County Med. Soc. (pres. 1978). Home: 4007 Brae Burn Dr Bakersfield CA 93306 Office: 400 34th St Bakersfield CA 93301 *Set your goal in a definite clear outline taking each step one at a time, as if climbing a ladder. Think about your goals; don't talk about them. Concentrate your abilities, your studies, your friends while denying yourself luxuries. Make your own decisions; stick by them. Don't have regrets. Be honest, sincere, and dedicated without regard to time. Finally, don't give up the fight—stick to your goal.*

IZLAR, WILLIAM HENRY, JR., lawyer; b. Phila., Mar. 23, 1931; s. William Henry and Pauline Elizabeth (Bowden) I.; m. Donna Marie Hauck, Aug. 30, 1952; children: William Henry, Paul Roberts Poinsett, James King, Donna Marie. A.B., U. N.C., 1953; LL.B., U. Va., 1960. Bar: Ga. 1960. Asso. firm King and Spalding, Atlanta, 1960-64, mem. firm, 1965—; counsel to Gov.'s Commn. for Efficiency and Improvement in Govt., 1963-66; dir. Trust Co. of Ga. Assocs., 1974-80. Trustee Westminster Schs., Inc., 1976—; trustee St. Joseph's Hosp.; bd. visitors Emory U., 1975-81, pres., 1979-80; fin. council Atlanta Archdiocese, 1968—; trustee Village of St. Joseph's Inc., 1967-81, pres., 1977-78. Served to lt. (j.g.) USN, 1953-57. Mem. Am. Law Inst., Am. Judicature Soc. (past dir.), Am. Bar Assn., Atlanta Bar Assn., Lawyers Club Atlanta, Atlanta C. of C. (past dir.), Council on Fgn. Relations. Roman Catholic. Club: Piedmont Driving. Office: 2500 Trust Co Tower Atlanta GA 30303

IZUTSU, SATORU, academic administrator; b. Hawaii, Sept. 7, 1928; s. Ryozo and Iseno (Yamashita) I. B.A., U. Hawaii, 1950; profl. certificate, Columbia U., 1952, M.A., 1955; Ph.D., Case-Western Res. U., 1963. Tng. adminstr. Waimano Tng. Sch. and Hosp., Hawaii Dept. Health, 1961-64; planner Comprehensive Plan Mental Retardation, Honolulu Dept. Health, 1964-65; exec. officer Waimano Tng. Sch. and Hosp., 1965-68; dir. Regional Med. Program Hawaii, Pacific Basin, 1969-72, exec. dir., 1974-76; prof. internat. health dept. Sch. Public Health, U. Hawaii, 1976—; project dir. Regional Tng. Service Agy./Asia, 1979-82; fellow Am. Council on Edn., 1982-83; project coordinator, Thailand, Am. Public Health Assn., 1973-74; mem. Commn. Cert. Psychologists Hawaii, 1968-75. Mem. Hawaii Policy Adv. Bd. for Elderly Affairs. Served to 1st lt. AUS, 1952-53; col. Res. Ret.; moblzn. designee to chief Army Med. Specialist Corps, 1974-80. Mem. Am. Psychol. Assn., Am. Personnel and Guidance Assn., Am. Occupational Therapy Assn., Am. Assn. Mental Deficiency. Home: 1350 Ala Moana Blvd Honolulu HI 96814 *A wonder of life is that in each of us there is a quality unduplicated in any other person. Recognition and development of this uniqueness are reinforced by one's belief in self and nuturing from family and friends. The purpose of life, then, is to give one's unique talent toward the refinement and comfort of all who participate in the human adventure.*

JABARA, FRANCIS DWIGHT, educator; b. Cambridge, Kans., Oct. 13, 1924; s. Farris George and Helen (Hourany) J.; m. Geri Ablah, Dec. 30, 1956; children—Leesa, Lori, Harvey F.G. B.S., Okla. State U., 1948; M.B.A., Northwestern U., 1949, C.P.A., 1956. Faculty Wichita (Kans.) State U., 1949—, asso. prof. accounting, 1954-59, prof., 1959—, head dept., 1962-64, dean, 1964-71, Wichita Soc. Accountants Distinguished prof. bus., 1971—; dir. Center for Entrepreneurship, 1977—; dir. Lear Fan Ltd., AFG Industries, Union Nat. Bank. Mem. Gov. Kans. Adv. Bd. to Bd. Accountancy, 1962—; Trustee Wichita YMCA, Kans. Newman Coll. Mem. Am. Inst. C.P.A.s, Kans. Soc. C.P.A.s, Wichita C. of C., Wichita Sales and Mktg. Execs., Alpha Kappa Psi, Beta Alpha Psi, Phi Kappa Phi, Alpha Tau Omega. Republican. Mem. Greek Orthodox Ch. Club: Rotarian. Home: 35 Hampton Dr Wichita KS 67207

JABBOUR, ALAN ALBERT, folklorist, musicologist, cultural organization administrator; b. Jacksonville, Fla., June 21, 1942; s. Albert and Irma (Williams) J.; m. Karen Singer, Aug. 17, 1962; children: Rebecca, Aaron, Hannah. B.A. magna cum laude, U. Miami, Fla., 1963; M.A. (Duke scholar, Woodrow Wilson fellow, Danforth fellow), Duke U., 1966, Ph.D., 1968. Violinist with Miami Symphony Orch., 1959-63, U. Miami String Quartet, 1961-63; asst. prof. English and folklore UCLA, 1968-69; head archive of folk song Library of Congress, Washington, 1969-74; dir. folk arts program Nat. Endowment for Arts, Washington, 1974-76; dir. Am. Folklife Center, Library of Congress, Washington, 1976—; cons. folklore and folklife to govt. agys. and pvt. orgns., 1971—; adj. faculty U. Md. and George Washington U., 1971—. Performer: traditional fiddle music with Hollow Rock String Band, 1965-73; 3 LP recs., 1972-82; Contbr. articles and recordings on Am. folk music and folklore to scholarly publs.; editor: long playing record American Fiddle Tunes, 1971; contbg. researcher and author: The Hammons Family: A Study of a West Viginia Family's Traditions, 1973. Trustee Am. Folklife Center, 1976—; mem. Fla. Folklife Council, 1979-82. Mem. Am. Folklore Soc., Soc. Ethnomusicology. Home: 3107 Cathedral Ave NW Washington DC 20008 Office: Library of Congress Ten First St SE Washington DC 20540

JABLONSKI, EDWARD, author; b. Bay City, Mich., Mar. 1, 1922; s. Boleslau and Isabel (Skrypczak) J.; m. Edith Garson, Sept. 2, 1951; children: David, Carla, Emily. A.A., Bay City Jr. Coll., 1948; B.A., New Sch., N.Y., 1950; postgrad., Columbia U., 1950-51. Dir., March of Dimes, N.Y.C., 1951-59; freelance writer, 1959—. Author: The Gershwin Years, 1958, 73; (with L.D. Stewart) Harold Arlen: Happy With the Blues, 1961, George Gershwin, 1962, The Knighted Skies, 1964, Flying Fortress, 1965, Warriors With Wings, 1966, Ladybirds, 1968, Airwar, 4 vols., 1971-72, Atlantic Fever, 1972, Seawings, 1972, Double Strike, 1974, (with Lowell Thomas) Doolittle, 1976; contbr. to: Music in American Soc, 1976, A Pictorial History of the World War II Years, 1978, A Pictorial History of the World War I Years, 1979, Man with Wings, 1980, Encyclopedia of American Music, 1981, America in the Air War, 1982, A Pictorial History of the Middle East, 1983. Served with AUS, 1942-46; PTO. Decorated Bronze Battle Star. Mem. Am. Aviation Hist. Soc., Soc. World War I Historians. Home: 161 W 75th St New York NY 10023

JABLONSKI, WANDA MARY, publishing company executive; b. Czechoslovakia; came to U.S., 1938, naturalized, 1945; d. Eugene and Mary J. B.A., Cornell U., 1942; postgrad., Columbia U., 1943; L.H.D. (hon.), St. Lawrence U., 1978. Oil editor Jour. Commerce, N.Y.C., 1943-54; sr. editor Petroleum Week, McGraw-Hill, N.Y.C., 1954-61; founder, owner, editor, pub. Petroleum Intelligence Weekly, N.Y.C., 1961—. Contbr.: articles to other mags. Mem. Oxford Energy Policy Club, Council Fgn. Relations, Middle East Inst. Club: Nat. Press. Office: One Times Square Plaza New York NY 10036 25 E 86th St New York NY 10028

JACHE, ALBERT WILLIAM, chemistry educator, university official; b. Manchester, N.H., Nov. 5, 1924; s. William Frederick and Esther (Ruemely) J.; m. Lucy Ellen Hauslein, June 14, 1948; children: Ann Gail, Ellen Ruth, Philip William, Heidi Verena. B.S., U. N.H., 1948, M.S., 1950; Ph.D., U. Wash., 1952. Sr. chemist Air Reduction Co., Murray Hill, N.J., 1952-53; research asso. physics dept. Duke U., 1953-55; asst. prof. chemistry dept. Tex. A.&M. U., College Station, 1955-58, asso. prof., 1958-61; asso. research dir. Ozark Mahoning Co., Tulsa, 1961-64, cons., 1960-61; sr. research asso. Olin Mathieson Chem. Corp. (now Olin Corp.), New Haven, 1964-67, sect. mgr., 1965-67, cons., 1967-75; prof., chmn. chem. dept. Marquette U., Milw., 1967-72, dean Grad. Sch., 1972-77, prof. chemistry, 1972—, asso. acad. v.p. for health scis., 1974-77, asso. v.p.-acad. affairs, prof. chemistry, 1977—; program coordination com. Med. Center S.E. Wis.; lectr. U. Tulsa, 1963-64, New Haven Coll., 1967; cons. Allied Chem. Corp., 1977-78. Trustee. Milw. Sci. Ednl. Found.; pres. Milw. Sci. Ednl. Trust, 1973—; trustee Argonne Univs. Assn., 1977-80. Served with AUS, 1943-46. Mem. N.Y. Acad. Sci., AAAS, Am. Chem. Soc. (chmn. fluorine div. 1982), Sigma Xi. Home: 1616 Martha Washington Dr Wauwatosa WI 53213 Office: 615 N 11th St Milwaukee WI 53233

JACHNA, JOSEPH D., photographer, educator; b. Chgo., Sept. 12, 1935; m. Virginia Kemper, 1962; children: Timothy, Heidi, Jody. B.S. in Art Edn., Inst. Design, Ill. Inst. Tech., 1958, M.S. in Photography, 1961. Part-time photog. asst. Derwin Studio Darkroom, Chgo., 1953-54; photo-technician Eastman Kodak Labs., Chgo., 1954; photographer's asst. DeSort Studio, Chgo., 1956-58; free-lance photographer, Chgo., 1961—; instr. photography Inst. Design, Ill. Inst. Tech., Chgo., from 1969, U. Ill.-Chgo., from 1969, now prof., coordinator photography Sch. Art and Design. One-man shows, Art Inst. Chgo., 1961, one-man shows, St. Mary's Coll., Notre Dame, Ind., 1963, U. Ill.-Chgo., 1965,77, Lightfall Gallery Art Ctr., Evanston, Ill., 1970, U. Wis.-Milw., Ctr. for Photog. Studies, Louisville, 1974, Nikon Photog. Salon, Tokyo, Afterimage Gallery, Dallas, 1975, Visual Studies Workshop Gallery, Rochester, N.Y., 1979, Chgo. Ctr. for Contemporary Photography, 1980, Focus Gallery, San Francisco, 1981, Perihelion Gallery, Milw., exhibited in group shows including, Art Inst. Chgo., 1963, MIT, Cambridge, 1968, Walker Art Ctr., Mpls., 1973, Renaissance Soc. Gallery, U. Chgo., 1975, Mus. Contemporary Art, Chgo., 1977, Mus. Art R.I. Sch. Design, Providence, 1978, Carpenter Ctr. for Visual Arts, Harvard U., Cambridge, 1981; represented in permanent collections, Mus. Modern Art, N.Y.C.; represented in permanent collections, Internat. Mus. Photography, George Eastman House, Rochester, N.Y., MIT, Art Inst. Chgo., Mus. Contemporary Art, Chgo., Ctr. Photog. Studies, Louisville, Ctr. for Creative Photography, U. Ariz., Tucson. Ferguson Found. grantee, 1973; Nat. Endowment for Arts grantee, 1976; Ill. Arts Council, 1979; Guggenheim fellow, 1980. Office: Sch Art and Design U Ill-Circle PO Box 4348 Chicago IL 60680

JACK, HOMER ALEXANDER, church official; b. Rochester, N.Y., May 19, 1916; s. Alexander and Cecelia (Davis) J.; m. Ingeborg Kind, June 14, 1972; children: Alexander, Lucy Jack Williams. B.S., Cornell U., 1936, M.S., 1937, Ph.D., 1940; B.D., Meadville Theol. Sch., 1944, D.D., 1971. Ordained to ministry Unitarian Universalist Assn., 1949; minister Universalist Ch., Litchfield, Ill., 1942, Unitarian Ch., Lawrence, Kans., 1943; exec. dir. Chgo. Council Against Racial and Religious Discrimination, 1944-48; minister Unitarian Ch., Evanston, Ill., 1948-59; asso. dir. Am. Com. on Africa, 1959-60; exec. dir. Nat. Com. for Sane Nuclear Policy, 1960-64, mem. nat. bd., 1965—; chmn. Non-Govtl. Orgn. Com. on Disarmament, UN Hdqrs., 1973—; dir. Div. Social Responsibility, Unitarian Universalist Assn., 1964-70; sec.-gen. World Conf. Religion and Peace, N.Y.C., 1970—; pres. Unitarian Fellowship for Social Justice, 1949-50; vice chmn. Ill. div. ACLU, 1950-59. Editor: Wit and Wisdom of Gandhi, 1951, The Gandhi Reader, 1956, Religion and Peace, 1967, World Religion and World Peace, 1969, Religion for Peace, 1973, Disarmament Workbook: The UN Special Session and Beyond, 1978, World Religion/World Peace, 1979, Disarm—Or Die, 1983. Bd. dirs. Albert Schweitzer Fellowship, 1974—. Recipient Thomas H. Wright award City of Chgo., 1958. Home: 330 E 43d St New York NY 10017 Office: 777 UN Plaza New York NY 10017

JACK, NANCY RAYFORD, manufacturing company executive; b. Hughes Springs, Tex., June 23, 1939; d. Vernon Lacy and Virginia Ernestine (Turner) Rayford; m. Kermit E. Hundley, Dec. 19, 1979; 1 son by previous marriage: James Bradford Jack, III. C.B.A., Keller Grad. Sch. Mgmt., 1980; cert. in acctg, Harper Coll., 1972, Harper Coll., 1973. Sr. sec. Gould, Inc., Rolling Meadows, Ill., 1971-73, staff asst., 1973-74, asst. sec., 1974-77, corp. sec., 1977—; sec. numerous subs. Recipient cert. of leadership YWCA Met. Chgo., 1975. Mem. Am. Soc. Corp. Secs., Nat. Assn. Female Execs., Midwest Corp. Transfer Agts. Assn., Beta Sigma Phi. Republican. Club: Meadow. Home: 1040 Creekside Dr Wheaton IL 60187 Office: 10 Gould Center Rolling Meadows IL 60008

JACK, PETER STUART, mining co. exec.; b. Stewart, B.C., Can., Feb. 17, 1925; s. Peter Shannon and Mary Florence (Cameron) J.; m. June Amelia McKenzie, Sept. 3, 1949; children—Wendy, Brian, Eileen. B.Applied Sci. with honors in Mining Engring, U. B.C., Vancouver, 1950. Research metallurgist Britannia Mining and Smelting Co., Britannia Beach, B.C., 1950-53, metallurgist, 1953-56; with Potash Co. Am., 1956—, supt., Carlsbad, N.Mex., 1956-63, v.p., Saskatoon, Sask., Can., 1963-80, exec. v.p. Canadian ops., 1980-82; dir.

Mining Assn. Can.; mem. Canadian Nat. Adv. Com. on Mineral Industry. Mem. Canadian Inst. Mining and Metallurgy. Home: 3854 S Niagara Way Denver CO 80237 Office: Po Box 8789 Denver CO 80201

JACK, ROBERT THOMAS, manufacturing company executive; b. Punxsutawney, Pa., Dec. 17, 1926; s. Harry Thomas and Margaret Jane (Rowl) J.; m. Myrna Louise Depp, Aug. 10, 1951; children: Douglas, Steven, Daniel. B.S. in Econs, Thiel Coll., 1950. Credit adjuster Comml. Credit Corp., Indiana, Pa., 1950-51; credit mgr., then asst. treas. Nat. Mine Service Co., Indiana, 1951-71, treas., 1971—. Chmn. Indiana chpt. ARC, 1980; campaign chmn. United Way Indiana County, 1979, pres., 1981. Served with USNR, 1944-46. Mem. Nat. Assn. Credit Mgmt., Credit Assn. W. Pa. Republican. Clubs: Rotary, Masons, Elks, Indiana Country. Home: 615 Virginia Ave Indiana PA 15701 Office: PO Box 310 Indiana PA 15701

JACKAMONIS, EDWARD GEORGE, state agency administrator; b. New Britain, Conn., Oct. 19, 1939; s. Edward George and Sophie (Horosik) J.; m. Barbara Bastenbeck, Aug. 26, 1962; children: April Marie, Jason Scott. B.A. magna cum laude, Northeastern U., 1962; M.S., U. Wis., Madison, 1964. Project asst. Inst. Govtl. Affairs, Madison, 1962-64; teaching asst. polit. sci. U. Wis., 1964-65; instr. polit. sci., Waukesha, 1966-71; mem. Wis. Assembly, 1971-83, speaker pro tem, 1975-76, speaker of assembly, 1977-83; exec. dir. Wis. Housing Fin. Authority, Madison, 1983—. Chmn. La Follette for Gov. Com. Waukesha County, 1968; sec. Waukesha County Democratic Party, 1969; chmn. 9th Congressional Dist. Lindsay for Pres. Com., 1972; del. Wis. Dem. Conv., 1968-83; active Waukesha County Assn. for Retarded Citizens, Environ. Action League. Mem. Wis. Acad. Scis., Arts and Letters, Waukesha County Mental Health Assn., La Casa de Esperanza (Waukesha), Waukesha Women's Center, Smithsonian Assos., Pi Sigma Alpha, Phi Alpha Theta. Home: 6 N Harwood Circle Madison WI 53715 Office: 131 W Wilson St PO Box 1728 Madison WI 53701

JACKEL, LAWRENCE, publishing company executive; b. N.Y.C., July 25; s. Solomon and Sylvia (Fisher) J.; children: Kenneth Isaac, Molly Laurie. B.B.A., CCNY, 1961, M.B.A., 1966. Accountant Aviquipo, Inc., N.Y.C., 1961-62; fin. exec. Litton Industries, N.Y.C., 1962-68; group controller Alloys Unlimited, Inc., N.Y.C., 1968-69; v.p. fin. Litton Ednl. Pub., Inc., N.Y.C., 1969-72, sr. v.p., 1972-75, exec. v.p., 1975-76, pres., 1976-80; pres., owner TAB Books Inc., Blue Ridge Summit, Pa., 1980—; pres. Delmar Pubs. div., Albany, N.Y., 1973-80. Democrat. Jewish. Club: University. Home: 17411 Sunshine Trail Sabillasville MD 21780 Office: TAB Books Inc Blue Ridge Summit PA 17214

JACKENDOFF, NATHANIEL, finance educator; b. N.Y.C., Feb. 24, 1919; s. Harry and Bella (Brainin) J.; m. Elaine Muriel Flanders, Apr. 4, 1943; children: Ray Saul, Harry Alan, Samuel Jay. B.S.S., Coll. City N.Y., 1938; M.A., U. Ill., 1939, Ph.D., 1948. Asst. prof. econs. Washington and Jefferson Coll., 1948-50; asst. prof. to prof. fin. Temple U., 1950—; Dir. SBA Research Project, 1959-60; econ. cons. U.S. Naval War Coll., Newport, R.I., 1962. Author: The Use of Financial Ratios by Small Business, 1961, A Study of Published Industry Financial and Operating Ratios, 1962, Money, Flow of Funds and Economic Policy, 1968. Served to tech. sgt. USAAF, 1943-45. Fulbright research scholar, Spain, 1969. Mem. Am. Econ. Assn., Am. Fin. Assn., Acad. Internat. Bus. Jewish. Home: 2217 Panama St Philadelphia PA 19103

JACKER, CORINNE LITVIN, writer; b. Chgo., June 29, 1933; s. Thomas Henry and Theresa (Bellak) Litvin. Student, Stanford U., 1950-52; B.S., Northwestern U., 1954, M.A., 1955, postgrad., 1955-56. Editor Liberal Arts Press, 1959-60, MacMillan Co., 1960-63; story editor Sta.-WNET-TV, N.Y.C., 1969-71, CBS-TV, 1972-74; instr. playwrighting NYU, 1976-78; vis. prof. playwriting Yale U., 1979-81. Exec. story cons.: Best of Families, Sta. CTV, N.Y.C., 1975-77; head writer: Another World (TV daytime serial), 1981-82; author: books Man, Memory, and Machines, 1964 (N.Y. Public Library 50 Best Books of Yr. 1964), Window on the Unknown, 1966 (AAAS 50 Best Books of Yr. 1966), A Little History of Cocoa, 1966, The Black Flag of Anarchy, 1968 (Pubs. Weekly 25 Best Books of Yr. 1968), The Biological Revolution, 1971; playwright: The Scientific Method, 1970, Seditious Acts, 1970, Travellers, 1973, Breakfast, Lunch, & Dinner, 1975, Bits and Pieces, 1975 (Obie award 1975), Harry Outside, 1975 (Obie award 1975), Night Thoughts & Terminal, 1976, Other People's Tables, 1976, My Life, 1977, After the Season, 1978, Later, 1979, Domestic Issues, 1981, In Place, 1982; TV writer, including: 3 episodes Actors' Choice, NET, 1970 (Emmy citation 1970); Virginia Woolf: The Moment Whole, NET, 1972 (CINE Golden Eagle award 1972); story editor: 4 episode series Benjamin Franklin, CBS, 1974 (Emmy citation 1974); The Adams Chronicles, 1975, Loose Change, NBC, 1978; 4 episode series, NBC, 1978; Best of Families, NET, 1978, The Jilting of Granny Weatherall, NET, 1980; radio play Night Thoughts and Terminal BBC, 1978; Overdrawn at the Memory Bank, NET, 1983. Rockefeller Found. grantee, 1979-80. Mem. Dramatists Guild, Writers Guild Am. East, PEN. Home and Office: 110 W 86th St New York NY 10024

JACKMAN, H. N. R., transportation company executive. Chmn. Algoma Central Ry., Saulte Ste. Marie, Ont., Can. Office: Algoma Central Ry 165 University Ave Toronto ON Canada M5H 3B8§

JACKMAN, LLOYD MILES, educator; b. Goolwa, South Australia, Apr. 1, 1926; came to U.S., 1967; s. Charles Stuart and Florence Olive (Green) J.; m. Marie Alma Sandow, 1950; children—Richard Miles, Donald Charles, Andrew Thorpe. B.Sc., U. Adelaide, Australia, 1945, 1946, M.Sc., 1948, Ph.D., 1951. Asst. lectr. organic chemistry Imperial Coll., London, Eng., 1952, lectr., 1953; reader U. London, 1961-62; prof., head dept. organic chemistry U. Melbourne, Australia, 1962-67; prof. chemistry Pa. State U., 1967—. Author: Applications of NMR in Organic Chemistry. Beit fellow U. London, 1951-52; NSF sr. fgn. fellow, 1965; Guggenheim fellow, 1973-74; Humboldt awardee, W.Ger., 1977. Fellow Chem. Soc. London, Am. Chem. Soc., Royal Australian Chem. Inst.; mem. N.Y. Acad. Scis., Phi Lambda Upsilon. Home: 710 Glenn Rd State College PA 16803 Office: 152 Davey Lab University Park PA 16802

JACKSON, ALLEN KEITH, college president; b. Rocky Ford, Colo., July 22, 1932; s. Monford L. and Leliah Jean (Hipp) J.; m. Barbara May Hollard, June 13, 1954; children: Cary Vincent, Deborah Kay and Edward Keith (twins), Fredrick James. B.A., U. Denver, 1954; Fulbright fellow, Cambridge (Eng.) U., 1955; Th.M. (Elizabeth Iliff Warren fellow), Iliff Sch. Theology, 1958; Ph.D. (Honor fellow), Emory U., 1960. Meth. student minister, Erie, Colo., 1955-58; ordained elder Meth. Ch., 1958; instr. sociology Emory U., 1958-60; chaplain, asst. prof. religion and sociology Morningside Coll., Sioux City, Iowa, 1960-62, dean coll., 1962-67; pres. Huntingdon Coll., Montgomery, Ala., 1968—. Contbr. articles to profl. jours. Past pres. Montgomery Area United Appeal. Mem. Ala. Assn. Ind. Colls. and Univs. (pres. 1969-71), Ala. Council Advancement Pvt. Colls. (pres. 1975-81), Phi Beta Kappa, Omicron Delta Kappa, Beta Theta Pi. Club: Rotarian. Home: 1393 Woodley Rd Montgomery AL 36106 *Time and reflection persuade me that there is no greater devotion or faithfulness to God or man than to seek the truth and to tell the truth. Seeing and telling of the ironies and surprises of life adds zest to living.*

JACKSON, ANNE (WALLACH, ANNE JACKSON), actress; b. Pitts.; d. John Ivan and Stella Germaine (Murray) J.; m. Eli Wallach, Mar. 5, 1948; children: Peter, Roberta, Katherine. Grad. high sch. Profl. debut: Cherry Orchard; mem. Am. Repertory Co.; Broadway plays include: Summer and Smoke, Oh, Men! Oh, Women!, Middle of the Night, Major Barbara, Rhinoceros, Luv, Waltz of the Toreadors, Diary of Anne Frank, Twice Around the Park, Nest of the Woodgrouse; off-Broadway plays: Typists, The Tigers; film appearances include: So Young, So Bad, Secret Life of an American Wife, Dirty Dingus McGee, Lovers and Other Strangers, The Shining; TV appearances include: 84 Charing Cross Road, Private Battle; film appearances include: Family Man, Golda I and II. Recipient Obie award.

JACKSON, ARTHUR GREGG, lawyer; b. Phila., June 19, 1921; s. Arthur and Anna M. (Gregg) J.; m. Dorothy Kempton Hollis, June 26, 1943; children: Gail, Laura, Nancy, Sarah. B.S., Yale U., 1943; J.D., Harvard U., 1950. Bar: Pa. bar 1951. Asso. firm Mancill, Cooney, Semans & Hedges, Phila., 1953-60; partner MacCoy, Evans & Lewis, Phila., 1961-75, Montgomery, McCracken, Walker & Rhoads, 1976-79; v.p., gen. counsel, sec. SPS Technologies, Inc., Jenkintown, Pa., 1979—; dir. Mutual Fire Marine & Inland Ins. Co., Phila., 1979—, UMI Group, Inc., 1979—. Pres. Merion (Pa.) Community Assn., 1974-80, Merion (Pa.) Civic Assn., 1972-73; dir. Merion (Pa.) Bot. Soc., 1964—; trustee Friends Central Sch., 1972-80. Served with Signal Corps U.S. Army, 1943-46, 51-52. Mem. Am. Pa., Phila. bar assns., Soc. Friends. Republican. Club: Union League Phila. Office: SPS Technologies Inc PO Box 1000 Newtown PA 18940

JACKSON, ARTHUR LEE, textile company executive; b. King's Mountain, N.C., Jan. 6, 1927; s. Thompson Wood and Beulah (Fleming) J.; m. Dorothy Dodd, June 19, 1952; children: Laura Jackson Owens, Ellen, Ann Jackson Ullman, Amy. Student, Westminster Coll., 1944-45, Yale U., 1945-46; B.S., N.C. State U., 1948; postgrad., U. N.C., 1954. With Fieldcrest Mills, Inc., Eden, N.C., 1948—, exec. v.p., 1981—; dir. Fieldcrest Found., Eden., 1971—, Delaware Valley Wool Scouring Co., Phila.; mem. cooton and econ. affairs coms. Am. Textile Mfrs. Inst., Inc., Washington, 1983—. Chmn. bd. trustees Morehead Meml. Hosp., Eden, 1973. Served with USN, 1944-46. Mem. Nat. Cotton Council (del., dir.), N.C. Textile Mfrs. Assn. (pres. 1981-82, dir.), Ga. Textile Mfrs. Assn. Democrat. Presbyterian. Clubs: Meadow Greens Country (Eden); Union (N.Y.C.); Green Island Country; Big Eddy (Columbus, Ga.); Chatmoss Country (Martinsville, Va.); Capital City (Raleigh, N.C.). Office: Fieldcrest Mills Inc Eden NC 27288

JACKSON, BLYDEN, educator; b. Paducah, Ky., Oct. 12, 1910; s. George Washington and Julia Estelle (Reid) J.; m. Roberta Bowles, Aug. 2, 1958. A.B., Wilberforce U., 1930; A.M., U. Mich., 1938, Ph.D. (Rosenwald fellow 1947-49), 1952. Tchr. English, pub. schs., Louisville, 1934-45; asst., then assoc. prof. English Fisk U., 1945-54; prof. English, head dept. Southern U., 1954-62, dean Grad. Sch., 1962-69; prof. English U. N.C., 1969-81, assoc. dean, 1973-76, spl. asst. to dean, 1976-81; Spl. research criticism Negro lit. Author: The Waiting Years; co-author: Black Poetry in America; Asso. editor: CLA Bull; adv. editor: So. Lit. Jour; Contbr. articles to profl. jours. Mem. Coll. Lang Assn. (pres. 1957-59), Modern Lang. Assn. (chmn. 20th century lit. div. 1976), Nat. Council Tchrs. English (Distinguished lectr. 1970-71, chmn. coll. sect. 1971-73, trustee research found. 1975—), Coll. Lang. Assn. (v.p. 1954-56, pres. 1956-58), Speech Assn. Am., N.C. Tchrs. English, Alpha Phi Alpha. Home: 102 Laurel Hill Rd Chapel Hill NC 27514

JACKSON, BOBBY RAND, clergyman; b. Wilson, N.C., Dec. 14, 1931; s. Joel John and Bessie Francis (Mayo) J.; m. Martha Jane Ketteman, May 30, 1953; children: Stephen Rand, Philip Wayne. B.A., Free Will Baptist Bible Coll., Nashville, 1954; M.A., Bob Jones U., Greenville, S.C., 1955. Ordained to ministry Free Will Baptists Ch., 1951, evangelist, Nashville, 1955-83; asst. moderator Nat. Assn. Free Will Baptists, Nashville, 1972-77, moderator, 1978—, mem. exec. com., 1972—, chmn. exec. com., 1978—, presiding officer of gen. bd., Nashville, 1978—. Author: Messages That Matter, 1960, Six Steps to Successful Living, 1962, Awakening in the Wilderness, 1965, Beyond the Stars, 1966; soloist: record albums Softly and Tenderly, 1968, Then Sings My Soul, 1969, Fill My Cup, Lord, 1970, My God and I, 1978. Mem. Free Will Baptist Bible Coll. Alumni Assn., Bob Jones U. Alumni Assn. Home: 1412 E 14th St Greenville NC 27834

JACKSON, BRINTON, librarian; b. Kalispell, Mont., May 19, 1919; s. Samuel Brinton and Alta Pearl (Nicholson) J.; m. Evelyn Frances Manning, Aug. 1, 1952 (div. 1966). B.M.E., Mont. State U., 1943; M.A., Tchrs. Coll., Columbia U., 1961. Asst. prof. Western Mont. Coll. Edn., Dillon, 1948-65; circulation librarian Juilliard Sch., N.Y.C., 1965-79, librarian, 1979—. Home: 45 Riverside Dr Apt 4A New York NY 10024 Office: Juilliard Sch Lincoln Ctr New York NY 10023

JACKSON, CARMAULT BENJAMIN, JR., physician; b. Newton, Mass., Apr. 19, 1924; s. Carmault Benjamin and Mabel (Robbins) J.; children—Carmault Benjamin, III, Thomas J., Molly Ann. M.D., U. Pa., 1952. Intern Hosp. of U. Pa., 1952-53, resident, 1953-56; internal medicine specialist U.S. Air Force, NASA Space Task Group, 1958-61; practice medicine specializing in internal medicine, San Antonio, 1961-76; asso. dir., asso. prof. medicine M.D. Anderson Hosp. and Tumor Inst., Houston, 1977—; adminstr. Met. Gen. Hosp., San Antonio; med. adv. Southwestern Bell Telephone Co., San Antonio area, 1968-76; vice chmn. Tex. Health Coordinating Council; mem. exec. com. Tex. Inst. Med. Assessment. Served with U.S. Army, 1942-45; Served with USAF, 1956-61. Decorated Purple Heart with 2 oak leaf clusters, Legion of Merit. Mem. AMA, So. Med. Assn., Tex. Med. Assn., Tex. Soc. Internal Medicine, Am. Soc. Internal Medicine, Tex. Acad. Internal Medicine, Am. Occupational Medicine Assn., Bexar County (Tex.) Med. Soc., Inst. Medicine, Nat. Acad. Scis. Office: 1310 N McCullough Ave San Antonio TX 78212

JACKSON, CHARLES IAN, association executive; b. Keighley, Yorkshire, Eng., Feb. 11, 1935; s. Harry Sydney and Nellie (Crabtree) J.; m. Margaret Cochrane Storrie, July 10, 1963; 1 dau., Janet Clare Luoise. B.A., London U., 1956; M.S., McGill U., 1959, Ph.D., 1961. Lectr. in geography London Sch. Econ., 1959-69; head econ. geography sect. Can. Dept. Energy, Mines and Resources, Ottawa, Ont., 1969-71; dir. planning and priorities Ministry of State for Urban Affairs, Ottawa, Ont., Can., 1972-78; sr. econ. affairs officer UN Econ. Commn. Europe, Geneva, Switzerland, 1978-81; exec. dir. Sigma Xi, New Haven, Ct., 1981—; cons. water resources UN Econ. Commn. Europe, 1966-67; cons. German Marshall Fund. U.S., 1975-77, Ford Found., 1977. Translator tech. lit. from French; editor books in field; author articles on history, resource mgmt. and geography. Recipient Darton prize Royal Meteorol. Soc., 1962, Evan Durbin prize Inst. Econ. Affairs, 1964. Mem. Hakluyt Soc. (council 1967-69), Champlain Soc., Hudson's Bay Record Soc., Sigma Xi. Club: Quinnipiack (New Haven). Office: Sigma Xi 345 Whitney Ave New Haven CT 06511

JACKSON, CLARENCE EVERT, educator, engineer, consultant; b. Graceville, Minn., Sept. 4, 1906; s. Caleb Adin and Anna Emily (Johnson) J.; m. Anne Grace Scott, June 25, 1936; children—Sue Anne (Mrs. Ronald J. Sloan), William Evert, Jane Scott (Mrs. David Bruss). B.A. with honors, Carleton Coll., 1927; postgrad., George Washington U., 1932. Registered profl. engr., Ohio. Sci. instr., Hot Springs, S.D., 1927-30; jr. metallurgist Nat. Bur. Standards, Washington, 1930-37; asst. metallurgist U.S. Naval Gun Factory, Washington, 1937-38; head welding sect. Naval Research Lab., Washington, 1938-46; research metallurgist, head welding sect. metals research labs. Union Carbide Corp., Niagara Falls, N.Y., 1946-57; assoc. mgr., electric welding devel. Linde div., Newark, 1957-64; assoc. prof. welding engring. Ohio State U., Columbus, 1964-75, prof., 1975-77, prof. emeritus, 1977—; guest lectr. Australian Welding Inst., Sydney, 1961, Chem. Soc., U. Leeds, Eng., 1977; del. Internat. Inst. Welding, 1960—; conferee 1st and 2d World Metall. Congresses, Am. Soc. Metals; C.A. Adams lectr. sci. arc welding Am. Welding Soc. Editor: Arc Welding, 1958; Contbg. author: Modern Materials, 1960, Ency. Americana, 1962, Weldability of Steels, 1971; contbr. numerous tech. papers to profl. lit. Recipient Disting. Civilian Service award Sec. Navy; MacQuigg Outstanding Tchr. award, 1971; Alumni Achievement award Carleton Coll., 1981. Fellow Brit. Instn. Metallurgists, Brit. Inst. Welding (hon.); mem. Am. Welding Soc. (nat. pres. 1963-64, S.W. Miller gold medal, life, R.D. Thomas award 1976), Am. Soc. Metals (life), Am. Inst. Mining and Metall. Engrs., French Soc. Welding, Tau Beta Pi. Presbyn. (elder). Home: 866 Mission Hills Lane Worthington OH 43085 Office: 190 W 19th Ave Columbus OH 43210

JACKSON, CLAYTON LEROY, ins. co. exec.; b. Owen Sound, Ont., Can., Aug. 25, 1917; came to U.S., 1955; s. Chester C. and Edna (Green) J.; m. Eula E. Gardner, Aug. 20, 1946; children—Heather, Alan. B.A., U. Toronto, 1949. C.L.U. Asst. actuary Mut. Life of Can., Waterloo, Ont., 1953-55; asst. actuary United Life & Accident Ins. Co., Concord, N.H., 1955, actuary, 1955-58, v.p., 1958-65, actuary, 1958-69, sr. v.p., 1965-69; also dir.; v.p., actuary Am. Nat. Ins. Co., Galveston, Tex., 1969-70, sr. v.p., actuary, 1970—. Served with Canadian Army, 1943-46. Fellow Soc. Actuaries, Canadian Inst. Actuaries, Life Office Mgmt. Assn.; mem. Actuaries Club of Southwest, Am. Acad. Actuaries, Am. Risk and Ins. Assn., Internat. Actuarial Assn. Conglist. Home: 2946 Dominique Dr Galveston TX 77551 Office: One Moody Plaza Galveston TX 77550

JACKSON, CURTIS MAITLAND, metallurgical engineer; b. N.Y.C., Apr. 20, 1933; s. Maitland Shaw and Janet Haughs (Dunbar) J.; m. Cordelia Ann Shupe, July 6, 1957; children: Carol Elizabeth, David Curtis. B.S. in Metall. Engring., NYU, 1954; M.S., Ohio State U., Columbus, 1959, Ph.D. (Battelle staff fellow), 1966. Registered profl. engr., Ohio. Prin. metall. engr. Columbus div. Battelle Meml. Inst., 1954-61, project leader, 1961-67, asso. chief specialty alloys, 1967-77, asso. mgr. phys. and applied metallurgy, 1977—. Chmn. bd.: Wire Jour, 1976-77; dir., 1973-78; Contbr. tech. articles profl. jours. Mem. troop com. Boy Scouts Am., 1975—, asst. scoutmaster, 1978—; advisor Order of DeMolay, 1954-57, 78—; mem. ofcl. bd. Methodist Ch., 1957-66. Recipient IR-100 award Indsl. Research Mag., 1976, certificate of appreciation Soc. Mfg. Engrs., 1977, awards Order of DeMolay, 1978, 83. Mem. Wire Found. (dir. 1974—), Wire Assn. Internat. (v.p. 1973-76, pres. 1976-77, dir. 1970-78, Mordica Meml. award 1977, J. Edward Donnellan award 1978, Meritorious Tech. Paper award 1981), N.Y. U. Metall. Alumni Assn. (pres. 1966-68), Am. Inst. Mining, Metall. and Petroleum Engrs. (chmn. Ohio Valley sect. 1964-66, chmn. North Central region 1965-66), Am. Soc. Metals, Am. Vacuum Soc., NYU, Ohio State U. alumni assns., Sigma Xi, Alpha Sigma Mu, Phi Lambda Upsilon. Club: NYU. Research on metall. tech. Home: 1667 Barrington Rd Columbus OH 43221 Office: 505 King Ave Columbus OH 43201

JACKSON, D. BROOKS, newspaperman; b. Seattle, Dec. 13, 1941; s. Dean B. and Betty June (Lindsay) J.; m. Beverly Yvonne Wyckoff, Nov. 17, 1972; children—Courtney Ann, Mark David. B.S., Northwestern U., 1964; M.S., Syracuse (N.Y.) U., 1967. Reporter A.P., N.Y.C. and Washington, 1967-80, Wall Street Jour., 1980—. Served to lt. (j.g.) USNR, 1964-66; Vietnam. Recipient A.P. reporting performance award A.P. Mng. Editors Assn., 1974, 1st runner-up, 1976; Raymond Clapper award for Washington reporting, 1974; John Hancock award for bus. and fin. journalism, 1978. Home: 2812 Adams Mill Rd NW Washington DC 20009 Office: 1025 Connecticut Ave NW Washington DC 20036

JACKSON, DANIEL FRANCIS, scientist; b. Pitts., June 11, 1925; s. Daniel F. and Edna (Marzolf) J.; m. Bettina Bush, Dec. 15, 1951. B.S., U. Pitts., 1949, M.S., 1950; Ph.D., State U. N.Y. Coll. Forestry at Syracuse U., 1957. Lectr. U. Pitts., 1949-51; asst. prof. Coll. Steubenville, Ohio, 1951-52; engr. C.E. U.S. Army, Pitts. dist., 1952-53; asst. prof., then asso. prof. Western Mich. U., 1955-59; asso. prof. U. Louisville, 1959-63; prof. civil engring. Syracuse U., 1963-73; dir., prof. div. environ. and urban systems Sch. Tech., Fla. Internat. U., Miami, 1973-78; prof., dir. Inst. Environ. Studies La. State U., Baton Rouge, 1982—; dir. research Jim Rodgers Pools, Inc., 1978—; dir. C.C. Adams Center Ecol. Study, 1955-59; asso. dir. Potamological Inst., 1960-63; dir. 1st NATO sponsored Advanced Study Inst., U.S., summer 1962. Author: Algae and Man, 1963, Some Aquatic Resources of Onondaga County, 1964, Some Aspects of Mexomixis, 1967, Algae, Man, and Environment, 1968, Some Endangered and Exotic Species, 1978; filmstrip sets Environmental Pollution, 1969, Man in the Biosphere, 1971; also articles. Pres. Ky. Soc. Natural History, 1961-63; Bd. dirs. Mich. Conservation Clubs, 1955-57. Served with AUS, 1943-46; ETO. Recipient Rotary Internat. award as outstanding tchr. in, Ky., 1962; Outstanding Community Leader award for environ. improvement, Onondaga County, 1969. Mem. Internat. Limnological Soc., Freshwater Assn. Brit. Empire, Water Pollution Control Fedn., Air Pollution Control Assn., Ecol. Soc. Am., Brit. Ecol. Soc., Limnology and Oceanography Soc., Sigma Xi, Phi Sigma, Nu Sigma Nu, Beta Beta Beta. Home: 5461 N College Hill Dr Baton Rouge LA 70808

JACKSON, DAVID PINGREE, publishing company executive; b. N.Y.C., June 3, 1931; s. Harold Mitchell and Frederica Elise (Elwang) J.; m. Nancy Jo Intlehouse, Oct. 10, 1954; children: Matthew, Julia, Frederica. B.A. in Psychology, Brown U., 1956. Sales rep. Chem. Products Corp., East Providence, R.I., 1956-66; account exec. Horton, Church & Goff, Inc., Providence, 1966-67; pub. Nat. Fisherman, Camden, Maine, 1967-82, Fishing Gazette, Rockland, Maine, 1983—. Bd. dirs. Sch. Adminstrv. Dist. 28, Pine Tree Soc. Crippled Children and Adults; past pres. Coastal Workshop. Served with USMCR, 1950-54. Home: PO Box 834 High St Camden ME 04843

JACKSON, DEMPSTER MCKEE, naval officer; b. San Diego, Nov. 17, 1930; s. Riley Richmond and Ruth (Remington) J.; m. Mary-Lin Moore, June 27, 1955; children—David, Dennis, Riley, Demarie. B.S.E.E., U.S. Naval Acad., 1952, U.S. Naval Postgrad. Sch., 1963. Commd. ensign U.S. Navy, 1952, advanced through grades to rear adm., 1978; comdr. (USS King), 1970-71, head undersea surveillance div., 1972-74, mgr. undersea surveillance project, 1974-78, comdr. anti-submarine warfare systems project, 1978-79, asst. dep. comdr., Washington, 1979—. Decorated Bronze star, Legion of Merit, others. Mem. S.A.R., Soc. Mayflower Descs. Home: 1422 Carrington Ln Vienna VA 22180 Office: Naval Sea Systems Command Navy Dept Washington DC 20362

JACKSON, DENISE SUZANNE, ballet dancer; b. N.Y.C., Oct. 19, 1951; d. John Henry and Audrey Frances (Kepple) J. Grad., Profl. Children's Sch.; studied dance br., Royal Ballet Acad., 1961-63, Am.

Ballet Center, 1963. Dancer with N.Y.C. Opera, 1968-69; mem. Joffrey Ballet, N.Y.C., 1969—, prin. dancer. Tours, U.S., Eng., Russia, Spain; featured soloist TV programs on, PBS, Dance in America; series, Nureyev and The Joffrey Ballet, 1981, Conversations on the Dance with Agnes De Mille, 1980. Recipient award Profl. Children's Sch., 1977. Mem. AFTRA, Am. Guild Musical Artists. Home: One Nevada Plaza New York NY 10023 Office: care Joffrey Ballet 130 W 56th St New York NY 10019

JACKSON, DON MERRILL, lawyer; b. Kansas City, Mo., Oct. 24, 1913; s. Merrill Marion and Vera (Long) J.; m. Henryetta J. Boese, Sept. 2, 1933 (dec.); children: Don Merrill, Martha Jackson Layton, Janet Jackson Akin; m. Caryle Jean Martin, Nov. 22, 1956. Student, Harvard U., 1930-31; J.D., U. Mo., Kansas City, 1936. Bar: Mo. 1936, Mass. 1941, Ariz. 1983. Practice law, Kansas City, Mo., 1936—, Phoenix, 1984—; counsel firm Jackson & Bailey P.C., 1983—, Harrison & Lerch, P.C., Phoenix, 1984—; mem. Jud. Commn. Clay County, Mo., 1973-76; City councilman, Kansas City, 1951-59; chmn. Kansas City Personnel Bd., 1964-65, Kansas City Plan Commn., 1965-70, Citizens Assn. Kansas City, 1949-50. Contbg. author: textbook Trials, 1967. Served as lt. USNR, 1943-52. Fellow Am. Coll. Trial Lawyers, Internat. Acad. Trial Lawyers (dir. 1967-73, 76—, dean 1979), Internat. Soc. Barristers, Am. Bar Found., Am. Judicature Soc., Am. Coll. Legal Medicine; mem. ABA (chmn. sect. ins., negligence and compensation law 1971-72, sect. del. 1973-79, bd. govs. 1978-80), Kansas City Bar Assn., Mass. Bar Assn., Mo. Bar Assn., Ariz. Bar Assn., Internat. bar assn., Am. Soc. Hosp. Attys. Club: Kansas City. Home: 5726 Scottsdale Rd Scottsdale AZ 85253 Office: 800 Bryant Bldg 1102 Grand Ave Kansas City MO 64106 Office: 650 N 2d Ave Phoenix AZ 85004

JACKSON, DUDLEY PENNINGTON, physician; b. Roanoke, Va., Apr. 1, 1924; s. Waddie Pennington and Bessie Mae (Gills) J.; m. Ada Patricia Custer, May 15, 1948. Student, Randolph Macon Coll., 1941-43, Sc.D. (hon.), 1982; M.D. (Henry Strong Denison scholar), Johns Hopkins U., 1947. Diplomate: Am. Bd. Internal Medicine. Intern Johns Hopkins Hosp., 1947-48, asst. resident, 1948-49, 51-52, research fellow in hematology, 1952-54; mem. faculty Johns Hopkins U., Balt., 1954-72, prof. medicine, 1971-72, Med. Sch., Georgetown U., Washington, 1972—, chmn. dept., 1972-82; physician-in-chief Georgetown U. Hosp., 1972-82, physician, 1982—. Contbr. articles to med. jours. Served with USNR, 1949-51. John and Mary R. Markle scholar Johns Hopkins U., 1954-59. Fellow A.C.P.; mem. Am. Physiol. Soc., Am. Fedn. Clin. Research, Am. soc. Clin. Investigation, Am. Soc. Hemtology, Soc. Exptl. Biology and Medicine, Assn. Am. Physicians, Assn. Profs. Medicine, Med. Soc. D.C., AMA. Home: 6121 Trotter Rd Clarksville MD 21029 Office: Georgetown Univ Hosp 3800 Reservoir Rd NW Washington DC 20007

JACKSON, EDWIN SYDNEY, insurance company executive; b. Regina, Sask., Can., May 17, 1922; s. Edwin and Dorothy (Bell) J.; m. Nancy Joyce Stovel, May 19, 1948; children—Patricia, Barbara, Catherine. B.Commerce, U. Man., 1947. Mem. actuarial dept. Mfrs. Life Ins. Co., Toronto, Ont., Can., 1948-52, asst. actuary, 1952-56, actuary, 1956-64, actuarial v.p., 1964-69, sr. v.p., 1969-70, exec. v.p., dir., 1970-72, pres., 1972—; dir. Can. Trust Co. Fellow Soc. Actuaries, Can. Inst. Actuaries (pres. 1966-67), Can. Life Ins. Assn. (chmn. 1977-78); mem. Life Office Mgmt. Assn. (chmn. 1982-83). Mem. United Ch. Can. Clubs: Toronto, Granite, Rosedale. Home: 101 Stratford Crescent Toronto ON M4N 1C7 Canada Office: 200 Bloor St E Toronto ON M4W 1E5 Canada

JACKSON, ELMER JOSEPH, lawyer, oil and gas company executive; b. Fairmont, Nebr., Sept. 16, 1920; s. Elmer Ellsworth and Kathleen Johanna (Sullivan) J.; m. Mary Elinor Booth, Sept. 1, 1943; children: Mary K., Teresa G., Cecilia A., Jean A., Joseph E., James O., Elizabeth J. LL.B. cum laude, U. Nebr., 1947. Bar: Nebr. 1947, Colo. 1980. With Stanolind Oil & Gas Co., Tulsa, 1948-52, K N Energy, Inc. (formerly Kans.-Nebr. Natural Gas Co.), 1952-84; exec. v.p., gen. council, sec., dir. Midlands Energy Co., 1984—. Served with U.S. Army, 1942-46. Decorated Bronze Star, Air medal; knight St. Gregory. Mem. Colo. Bar Assn., Nebr. Bar Assn., Am. Assn. Corp. Counsel, Am. Judicature Soc., Fed. Energy Bar, Am. Soc. Corp. Secs. Republican. Roman Catholic. Club: K.C. Office: 143 Union St Lakewood CO 80228 also PO Box 15640 Lakewood CO 80215

JACKSON, ELMER MARTIN, JR., publishing executive; b. Hagerstown, Md., Mar. 9, 1906; s. Elmer Martin and Blanche Beatrice (Bower) J.; m. Mary W. A. Conard, Aug. 27, 1929 (div.); children: Elmer Martin III, Allen Conard, Pamela Conard; m. Doris C. Grace, Apr. 18, 1972. A.B., St. John's Coll., Annapolis, Md., 1926. Reporter, sports editor, city editor, Hagerstown and Annapolis, Md., 1920-30; editor Evening Capital and Md. Gazette, Annapolis, 1933-41; v.p., editor and gen. mgr. Evening Capital and Md. Gazette Newspapers, 1947-69; pres., pub. Anne Arundel Times, 1969—; owner-pub. Worcester Democrat, Pocomoke City, Md.; gen. mgr., editor Capital-Gazette News, also County News, 1961-69; pres. Carroll County Times, Westminster, Md., Jackson Printing, Inc., Annapolis and St. Michael's, Md., 1975—; owner Scott Book Center, Annapolis; dir. Md. Nat. Bank. Author: The Rat Tat, 1927, Annapolis, Three Centuries of Glamour, 1938; nature study The Baltimore Oriole; Maryland Symbols, 1964. Past pres. dist. and state press assns.; mem. evaluating commn. Instns. Higher Learning.; Mem. bd. Fed. Council State Govt., Chgo. Alderman, Annapolis, 1932-36; del. Md. Legislature, 1937-41; Pres. Anne Arundel Pub. Library Assn., 1945—, Fine Arts Festival Found.; chmn. Anne Arundel County Econ. Devel. Commn., State Capital Planning Commn.; pres. Md. Gov.'s Prayer Breakfast Soc., 1967-76. Served as comdr. USNR, 1941-47. Named hon. adm. U.S. Naval Acad., 1965; recipient Man of Year award Anne Arundel County, 1965. Mem. Am. Soc. Newspaper Editors, Newcomen Soc., Md. Hist. Soc. (dir.), Mil. Order World Wars (comdr.), SAR (pres.-elect Md. 1984), Polit. Sci. Club, Sigma Delta Chi. Democrat. Episcopalian. Clubs: Elk. Clubs: Annapolis Athletic (past pres.), Annapolitan (sec.-treas.), Thirteen, Annapolis Yacht, Annapolis Roads Golf and Beach, Naval Academy Officers, Naval Academy Golf, Naval Academy Beach, Young Democratic of Anne Arundel County (past pres.); Army-Navy (Washington); University, So. Md. Soc., Propeller. Home: 219 Claude St Wardour Annapolis MD 21401 Office: Anne Arundel Times Bldg 208-10 West St Annapolis MD 21401 Summer Home: Rousby Hall Lusby MD *Since my days as a cub reporter at a salary of $6 a week my unswerving philosophy has been: Don't humiliate people, help them up a hill because when you do you are closer to the top yourself. I have never upgraded myself by downgrading another person. To me lying is the greatest sin.*

JACKSON, ELMORE, political scientist; b. Marengo, Ohio, Apr. 9, 1910; s. John Wesley and Cora (Osborn) J.; m. Elisabeth Averill, Dec. 26, 1934; children: Karen J. Williams, Gail Elisabeth. B.A., George Fox Coll., Newberg, Oreg., 1931; M.Div., Yale U., (Tew prize 1932), 1934, Univ. fellow in Govt., 1935-36. Asst. sec. social-indsl. sect. Am. Friends Service Com., 1936-40, personnel dir., 1941-46, asst. exec. sec., 1946-48; cons. Palestine refugees UN, 1948; dir. Quaker Program UN, 1948-52, 53-57, 58-61; personal asst. UN Rep. India, Pakistan, 1952, personal asst., polit. officer, 1952-53, cons., 1953-54, spl. adviser, 1958; dir. Project Survey of Middle East, Am. Friends Service Com., 1957-58; lectr. internat. relations Haverford Coll., 1951-53; spl. asst. policy planning to asst. sec. state internat. orgn. affairs Dept. State, 1961-64, spl. asst. to asst. sec. state for internat. orgn. affairs, 1964-66, cons., 1966-69, mem. adv. com. on internat. orgns., 1972-74; adviser U.S. del. 16th-18th UN Gen. Assemblies; v.p. policy studies UN Assn. U.S.A., 1966-73; cons. Rockefeller Found., 1973-77; spl. adv. Aspen Inst. Humanistic Studies, 1978-82; editorial cons. W.W. Norton & Co., 1980—. Author: Meeting of Minds, 1952, Middle East Mission, 1983; contbr. articles to profl. jours. Mem. corp. Haverford Coll. Mem. Council Fgn. Relations. Clubs: Yale, Century Assn. Home: Pennswood Village J 213 Newtown PA 18940

JACKSON, EUGENE BERNARD, librarian; b. Frankfort, Ind., June 18, 1915; s. John Herman and Goldie Belle (Michael) J.; m. Ruth Lillian Whitlock, Aug. 6, 1941. B.S. with distinction, Purdue U., 1937, U. Ill., 1938, M.A., 1942. Asst. engring. library U. Ill., 1938-40; asst. charge newspaper div. U. Ill. Library, 1940-41; documents librarian U. Ala., 1941-42; with tech. dept. Detroit Pub. Library, 1942-46; chief reference library, Wright Field, Ohio; chief library sect. Central Air Documents Office, Dayton, Ohio, 1946-49; chief research information sect. Research and Devel. Command, Q.M.C., Washington, 1949-50; chief div. aero. intelligence NACA, 1950-52, chief div. research information, 1952-56; head library dept. research labs. Gen. Motors Corp., Warren, Mich., 1956-65, chmn. corp. com. tech. lit., 1959-65; dir. information retrieval and library services IBM Corp., Armonk, New York, 1965-71; Grad. Sch. Library Sci., library cons. in automation. U. Tex., Austin, 1971-72, prof. library sci., 1971—; v.p. Engring. Index, Inc., 1967-68, pres., 1968-73; also dir. Attendee Gordon Research Confs. on Sci. Information, N.H., 1964—; vis. summer lectr. U. Mich., 1965, U. Ill., 1968; mem. task force United Engring. Info. System, 1966; cons.; U.S. mem. documentation com., adv. group aero. research and devel. NATO, Paris, France, 1953-61, chmn., 1955-56, dep. chmn., chmn. elect., 1960-61; McBee lectr. Simmons Coll., Boston, 1956; ofcl. U.S. del. gen. assemblies Fedn. International de Documentation, Tokyo, 1967, The Hague, 1968, Buenos Aires, 1970, Budapest, 1972, chmn. U.S. nat. com., 1970-72. Author: (with Ruth L. Jackson) Industrial Information Systems, 1978; Editor: Special Librarianship, a New Reader, 1980; Contbr. articles to profl. jours., chpts. to books. Mem. tech. adv. com. Macomb County (Mich.) Planning Commn. Served with AUS, 1943-46. Mem. Spl. Libraries Assn. (pres. 1962-63), A.L.A., Am. Soc. Info. Scis., AIAA (sec. Mich. 1964-65), Assn. Records Mgrs. and Adminstrs. Protestant Episcopalian (vestryman, lic. lay reader). Home: 8512 Silver Ridge Dr Austin TX 78759

JACKSON, EUGENE WESLEY, publisher; b. Tulsa, Feb. 23, 1928; s. George Wesley and Ora (Cook) J.; m. Marie-Louise Vermeiren, Jan. 17, 1962; children: Susan Lynne, Geoffrey William. B.A. in Natural Scis., Okla. A. and M. Coll., 1950; postgrad., Tulsa U., 1953-54, Temple U., 1981—. Tech. writer Carter Oil Co., Tulsa, 1952-55; med. editor, writer med. jour. Smith Kline & French Labs., Phila., 1956-69; mng. editor Cons. mag., 1961-66, editor, 1966-69; chmn. bd. Intermed Communications Inc., Horsham, Pa., 1970—; pub. Nursing, 1971—, 70-78, Nursing Skillbook series, 1975—, Nursing Photobook series, 1979—, Nurses' Guide to Drugs, 1981; chmn. bd. Springhouse Fin. Corp.; partner Springhouse Book Co., Springhouse Realty Co.; dir. Ravenswood Publs., Ltd., U.K. Editor: Common Complaints, 1964; contbr. articles on health and horticulture to consumer mags., 1964-66. Served with M.C., AUS, 1950-52. Mem. Nat. League Nursing, Am. Mgmt. Assn., Am. Heart Assn., Soc. Publs. Designers, Beta Theta Pi. Baptist. Club: Manufacturers (Dresher, Pa.). Home: Meadowbrook PA 19046 Office: 1111 Bethlehem Pike Springhouse PA 19477 *The key to success is not necessarily high intelligence, special education, or family wealth. I've seen many Phi Beta Kappas and Mensa members who failed miserably—in work and life. And the world abounds with wealthy, heirs who achieved nothing whatsoever. Indeed, too much intelligence or education or wealth can handicap severely. What matters is pure old hard work, plus a reasonable amount of talent and much determination. Hard work can make dreams come true.*

JACKSON, EVERETT GEE, painter, illustrator; b. Mexia, Tex., Oct. 8, 1900; s. W.B. and Fanny (Eubank) J.; m. Eileen Dwyer, July 21, 1926; 1 dau., Jerry Gee Jackson Williamson. Student, Tex. A&M Coll., 1919-21, Art. Inst. Chgo., 1921-23; A.B., San Diego State Coll., 1929; A.M., U. So. Calif., 1934. Faculty Sul Ross State Tchrs. Coll., Alpine, Tex., 1929; prof. art San Diego State U., 1930-63; tchr. U. Costa Rica, 1962; painter, illustrator, 1926—; adv. bd. to pres. San Diego State U. Illustrator: Miller, Mexico Around Me, 1937, Louis Untermeyer, Paul Bunyan, 1945, Ugly Duckling; Popol Vuh, 1954, Conquest of Peru, 1956, American Chimney Sweeps, 1958, Ramona, Helen Hunt Jackson, 1960, Estudio de Evaluation de la Academia de Bellas Artes, Universidad de Costa Rica, 1963, American Indian Legends, 1971; exhbns. include, Instituto Nacional de Antropologia e Historia at El Museo del Carmen, San Angel, Mexico City, 1979, retrospective, San Diego Mus. Art, 1984. Recipient citation Ltd. Edits. Club. Mem. AAUP, Fine Arts Soc. San Diego (trustee; founding chmn. Latin-Am. arts com.), San Diego Mus. Art. Home: 1234 Franciscan Way San Diego CA 92116

JACKSON, FELIX, writer and producer; b. Hamburg, Germany, June 5, 1902; came to U.S., 1937, naturalized, 1940; s. Siegfried and Fanny (Bloemendal) Joachimson; m. Ilka Windish, Aug. 6, 1955; 1 son, Lawrence Felix. Student, U. Freiburg, Germany, 1920-23. Reporter, city-editor, drama and music critic, Berlin, 1923-27, asst. theatre mgr., 1927-30, freelance writer and playwright, 1930-33, Vienna and Budapest, 1933-37, writer for motion pictures, Hollywood, Calif., 1937-39; writer, producer Universal Pictures, Hollywood, 1939-47, Young & Rubicam (advt.), N.Y.C., 1947-48, exec. producer for TV, 1948-52; producer Studio One, CBS, N.Y.C., 1953-57, Nat. Telefilm Assos., Hollywood; also BBC, London, 1958-60; v.p. West Coast programming NBC, 1960-63, v.p. prodns., TV network, 1963-65; freelance author and producer, 1965—. Author: So Help Me God, 1955, Maestro, 1957 (trans. Swedish and Polish), Secrets of the Blood, 1980. Mem. Acad. Motion Picture Arts and Scis. Home: 4149 Murietta Ave Sherman Oaks CA 91423

JACKSON, FRANCIS CHARLES, physician, surgeon; b. Rutherford, N.J., Sept. 2, 1917; s. Frank Emil and Margaret Charlotte (Kuhn) J.; m. Joan Gloria Mortenson, Sept. 1, 1949; children: Geoffrey P., Bradford M., Gregory C., Donna E. B.A., Yale U., 1939; M.D., U. Va., 1943. Diplomate: Am. Bd. Surgery, Nat. Bd. Med. Examiners. Intern N.Y. Hosp.-Cornell Med. Center, 1944, asst. resident surgery, 1945, asst. resident surgery to 1st asst. chief resident surgeon, 1947-49, chief resident surgeon, 1950; practice medicine, specializing in gen. and vascular surgery, Pitts., 1952-70; cons., chief surgeon Arabian Am. Oil Co., Dhahran, Saudi Arabia, 1951; asst. chief surg. service VA Center, Togus, Maine, 1952; chief surg. service, dir. Gen. Surg. Residency Program, VA Hosp., Pitts., 1952-70; dir. surg. service VA Central Office, Washington, 1970-72, spl. asst. to chief med. dir. for emergency and disaster med. services, 1972-73, dir. emergency and disaster med. services staff, 1973-75; mem. cons. staff Presbyn.-Univ. Hosp., Pitts., 1959-70; asst. in surgery Sch. Medicine Cornell U., 1946-49, asst. in anatomy, 1946, instr. surgery, 1950; asst. prof. surgery Sch. Medicine U. Pitts., 1953-60, assoc. prof. surgery, 1961-65, prof. surgery, 1965-70, sec. exec. com. dept. surgery, 1964-70, also MEND coordinator, 1967-68; clin. prof. surgery Georgetown U. Sch. Medicine, also George Washington U. Sch. Medicine, 1970-75; chmn. dept. surgery Sch. Medicine, Tex. Tech U., Lubbock, 1975-80, prof. surgery, 1975—, assoc. dean clin. edn., 1980-82; cons. Carnegie-Mellon Inst., 1969-71, Westinghouse Electric Corp. (Health Systems), AVCO Corp.; Chmn. local com. VA Adj. Cancer Chemotherapy Study, 1957-70; chmn. exec. com. Operation Prep. Pitts. Annual Med.-CD Disaster Drill, 1958-60; mem. ad hoc com. disaster med. surveys, div. med., vice chmn. com. emergency med. services Nat. Acad. Scis.-NRC, 1964-74; mem. surg. drugs adv. com. FDA, 1971-75; mem. panel on physicians asst. CSC, 1971-73; cons. on emergency and disaster services USPHS, 1965-72; VA rep., alternate observer, nat. health resources adv. com. Office Preparedness, 1972-75; VA rep., mem. interdepartmental com. on emergency med. services HEW, 1974-75; mem. ad hoc com. on emergency med. services communications, interdepartmental adv. com. on radio communications Office Telecommunications Policy, 1973-75. Author: Role of Medicine in Emergency Preparedness, 1968, also articles in surg. jours., surg. exhibits. Trustee Peddie Sch., 1972-74. Served as lt. (j.g.) USNR, 1945-46; to lt. comdr., M.C., 1953-55. Recipient Pfizer award of merit U.S. CD Council, Mpls., 1960, Key to City Louisville, 1964; Billings Gold Medal award AMA, 1966. Fellow A.C.S. (past chmn. residents program com. Southwestern Pa. chpt.; chmn. subcom. disaster, surgery and communications of trauma com., mem. trauma com. 1966-78, exec. com. 1976-78, pres. Southwestern Pa. chpt. 1970, gov. 1970-74); mem. AMA (chmn. com. disaster med. care, mem. Council Nat. Security 1958-67), Pa. Med Soc. (chmn. commn. on emergency med. services), Allegheny County Med. Soc., Soc. Biol. Research U. Pitts. Sch. Medicine, Pitts. Surg. Soc., Am. Assn. Surgery of Trauma, So. Surg. Assn., Assn. VA Surgeons (founder mem.), Central Surg. Assn., So. Med. Assn., Soc. Surgery Alimentary Tract, Assn. Mil. Surgeons U.S. (Stitt award 1968), Pitts. Acad. Medicine (Man of Year award 1969), D.C. Med. Soc., Am. Surg. Assn., Société Internat. de Chirurgie, Tex. Surg. Soc., Tex. Med. Assn. (chmn. surg. sect. program com. 1981-82, mem. subcom. on accreditation of continuing med. edn. programs), Lubbock Surg. Soc., Lubbock-Crosby-Garza County Med. Soc., Assn. Surg. Dept. Chmn., Alpha Omega Alpha. Office: Tex Tech U Sch Medicine Dept Surgery Lubbock TX 79430

JACKSON, FRANCIS JOSEPH, research and development company executive; b. Providence, May 23, 1932; s. Francis Joseph and Mary Elizabeth (Ryan) J.; m. Mary Veronica Brennan, Sept. 1, 1956 (div. Mar. 1983); children: Mary Cecilia, Paul Francis, Thomas Edward.; m. Nancy M. McMahon, May 21, 1983. B.S. magna cum laude, Providence Coll., 1954; Sc.M., Brown U., 1957, Ph.D., 1960. Research asso. Brown U., 1959-60; sr. scientist Bolt Bernaek & Newman Inc., Cambridge, Mass., 1960-68, div. v.p., 1968-77, v.p., 1977-79; sr. v.p. Bolt Beranek & Newman Inc., 1979—; adj. prof. Cath. U., 1973-77. Contbr. articles to profl. jours. Fellow Acoustical Soc. Am.; mem. IEEE (sr.), Am. Inst. Physics, Sigma Xi, Delta Epsilon Sigma. Club: Cosmos (Washington). Home: 14A Plato Terr Winchester MA 01890 Office: 10 Moulton St Cambridge MA 02138

JACKSON, FREDERICK HERBERT, educational administrator; b. New Haven, May 16, 1919; s. Fred and Mary (Butler) J.; m. Eleanor Stearns Whittemore, May 2, 1942; children: Isabel S. Jackson Freeman, David L. A.B., Brown U., 1941, LL.D., 1968; A.M., U. Pa., 1948, Ph.D., 1950. Instr. Marietta Coll., 1948-49, asst. prof., 1949-50; instr. U. Ill., 1950-52, asst. prof., 1952-55; exec. asst. Carnegie Corp., N.Y.C., 1955-57, exec. asso., 1957-64; asst. exec. v.p. N.Y.U., 1964-66, v.p. humanities and social scis., 1966-67; pres. Clark U., Worcester, Mass., 1967-7O; dir. Com. on Instl. Cooperation Big Ten Univs. and U. Chgo., 1970-84; dir. Paul Revere Variable Annuity Ins. Co., Stewart Systems Corp. Author: Simeon Eben Baldwin, American Social Scientist, 1955. Mem. Rep. Town Meeting, Westport, Conn., 1957-59, 61-67; trustee U. Bridgeport, 1961-71, life trustee, 1971—; bd. dirs. Worcester Art Mus., 1968-70, Paul Revere Courier Fund, 1971-77, New Trier Citizen's League, 1983-84; acad. adv. com. Center for Study Democratic Instns., 1975-78. Served to 1st lt. USAAF, 1942-46. Mem. Am. Hist. Assn., AAUP, Am. Antiquarian Soc., Common Cause (vice chmn. Ill. 1975-77, 82-83), Phi Beta Kappa. Clubs: Century Assn., Cosmos, St. Botolph. Home: 4 Weld St Westboro MA 01581

JACKSON, GEORGE GEE, physician, educator; b. Provo, Utah, Oct. 5, 1920; s. Elvon L. and Adelia (Gee) J.; m. Amy Smith Cox, Sept. 4, 1943; children: Janet (Mrs. Bruce J. Hendricks), Sandra (Mrs. Kent Davis), Christopher G., Amy Adelia, John Gee. A.B., Brigham Young U., 1942; M.D., U. Utah, 1945. Diplomate: Am. Bd. Internal Medicine, Pan Am. Med. Assn. Intern Boston City Hosp. (Harvard), 1945-46, asst. resident, 1948-49, resident medicine, 1949-50, asst., 1950-51; concurrently teaching fellow medicine Harvard, 1948-49, research fellow, 1949-50, Milton fellow in medicine, 1950-51; asst. prof. medicine and preventive medicine U. Ill. Coll. Medicine, 1951-52; chief div. infectious diseases, attending physician U. Ill. Hosp., Chgo., 1951—, mem. grad. faculty microbiology, 1951—, asso. prof. medicine, 1953-59, prof. medicine, 1959—, Robert Wood Keeton prof. medicine, 1979—, chief med. service, 1975-76; spl. fellow Tropeninstitut, Hamburg, Germany, 1968-69; vis. prof. dept. med. microbiology London Hosp. Med. Coll., 1977-78; guest prof. Max von Pettenkofer Inst. für Medizinische Mikrobiolgie der Ludwig-Maximilians Universität, Munchen, W. Ger., 1978-79; U.S. sr. scientist Alexander von Humbolt Stiftung, Bonn, W. Ger., 1978; cons. infectious diseases West Side VA Hosp., 1968—; dep. dir. commn. acute respiratory diseases Armed Forces Epidemiol. Bd., 1970-72; mem. med. examining com. Ill. Dept. Registration and Edn., 1961-67; virology study sect. NIH, 1970-74; merit rev. bd. VA, 1967-75; chmn. collaboration program for vaccine devel. Nat. Inst. Allergies and Infectious Diseases, NIH, 1962-67, mem. bd. sci. counsellors, 1960-62; chief sci. cons. Merit Rev. Bd. Infectious Diseases, VA, 1972-75; adv. bd. Center for Health and Environ. Studies, Brigham Young U., 1973—; guest lectr. various univs. and profl. orgns. Bd. dirs. Nat. Found. for Infectious Diseases; bd. dirs., med. adv. bd. Schweppe Found., 1975—; bd. sci. advisors Merck Sharp & Dohme Research Labs., 1976-80; mem. med. adv. com. Merck Internat., 1977-83. Editor: Jour. Infectious Diseases; editorial bd.: Jour. Lab. and Clin. Medicine, 1966-71, Proc. Soc. Exptl. Biology and Medicine, 1970-74, Antibiotics and Chemotherapy, 1971—, Infectious Diseases Am, 1969—, Infection jour, 1977—; editorial bd., chmn.: Council for Interdisciplinary Communications in Medicine, 1970-74; fgn. editorial advisor: Jour. Antimicrobial Chemotherapy, 1977—; Contbr. articles to profl. jours. Served as lt. (j.g.) MC USNR, 1946-48; mem. Res., 1948-56. Fellow A.C.P.; mem. AAAS, Am. Assn. Immunologists, Am. Epidemiol. Soc., Assn. Am. Physicians, Central Soc. Clin. Research, Am. Soc. Virology, Infectious Diseases Soc. Am. (sec.-treas. 1967-71, pres. 1973-74, council 1974-75), Am. Fedn. Clin. Research (emeritus), Am. Soc. Clin. Investigation (emeritus), Am. Soc. Microbiology, Chgo. Immunology Assn., Soc. Consultants to Armed Forces, Soc. for Exptl. Biology and Medicine, Med. Alumni Assn. U. Utah Coll. Medicine, Sigma Xi, Alpha Omega Alpha. Home: 315 N Lincoln St Hinsdale IL 60521 Office: Univ Illinois Hosp 808 S Wood St Chicago IL 60612 Office: Dept of Med/ID P O Box 6998 Chicago IL 60680

JACKSON, GEORGE LYMAN, physician; b. Arlington, Mass., Dec. 17, 1923; s. William and Alice (Tenney) J.; m. Alyce Verne Yeager, Sept. 7, 1946; children: Scott Douglas, Carole Elizabeth, Diane Priscilla, Richard Lee. B.S. cum laude, Franklin and Marshall Coll., 1944; M.D., U. Pa., 1948. Diplomate: Am. Bd. Internal Medicine, Am. Bd. Nuclear Medicine. Intern Hosp. U. Pa., 1948-49, resident, 1949-52; practice medicine specializing in internal medicine, Harrisburg, Pa., 1952-63; dir. med. edn., acting med. dir. Harrisburg Hosp., 1963-68, dir. undergrad. fellowships, 1968-69, head sect. nuclear medicine,

1965-75, med. dir. dept. nuclear medicine, 1975—; asst. prof. medicine Hahnemann Med. Coll., 1963-68, asso. prof., 1968-70; clin. asso. prof. M.S. Hershey Med. Centre, Pa. State U., 1970-76, clin. prof., 1976—; dir. Harrisburg Hosp. Sch. Nuclear Medicine Tech.; adj. faculty Harrisburg Area Community Coll., Millersville State Coll.; cons., chmn. med. adv. com. Lebanon (Pa.) VA Hosp., 1968-75; nuclear medicine adv. Pa. Dept. Edn., Pa. Med. Soc., Pa. Blue Shield. Contbr. articles to profl. jours. Mem. Central Dauphin Sch. Bd., 1971-73; bd. dirs. Bethesda Mission, Harrisburg Hosp. Med. Edn. and Research Found. Served with USNR, 1942-45. Fellow ACP (govs. com. for coll. affairs 1969-76, gov. 1976-80), Soc. Nuclear Medicine, Am. Coll. Nuclear Physicians (bd. regents), Am. Coll. Nuclear Medicine; mem. Am. Thyroid Assn., Pa. Soc. Internal Medicine (past pres.; chmn. liaison com.), Pa. Coll. Nuclear Medicine (pres.), Joint Rev. Com. Nuclear Medicine Tech., Phi Beta Kappa, Alpha Omega Alpha. Presbyterian. Home: 22 N Baltimore St Dillsburg PA 17019 Office: Harrisburg Hosp S Front St Harrisburg PA 17101 *The efforts of my adult life have been directed primarily at three priorities—family, profession, church. Success in achieving any of these is a consequence of a combination of providence, help from others and personal attributes. Help from others involves, principally, my family (in its largest sense) and of these my wife is most important. She is a source of understanding, wise counsel, inspiration, support and balance. My associates help significantly by their dedication, industry and responsibility. Personal attributes are hard work, absolute honesty, religious belief, and a conviction that the only justification for my professional life is to help the sick patients whom I am privileged to serve.*

JACKSON, GEORGE WOODROW, psychiatrist; b. White House, Tenn., Feb. 3, 1914; s. Alfred Thomas and Myra (Barry) J.; m. Ruth Gray, June 12, 1934; children—George Barry, William Thomas, Robert Graylon. M.D., U. Tenn., 1937. Diplomate: Am. Bd. Psychiatry and Neurology. Intern USPHS Hosp., New Orleans, Wallace Sanitarium, Memphis, 1937-38; resident psychiatry Western State Hosp., Bolivar, Tenn., 1940-42, asst. supt., 1942; clin. dir., supt. Ark. State Hosp., Little Rock, 1946-51, supt., 1961-79; med. dir. Bd. Tex. State Hosps. and Spl. Schs., 1951-53; dir. instns. Kans. Dept. Social Welfare, Topeka, 1953-61. Bd. dirs. ARC. Served with M.C. AUS, 1942-46. Fellow Am. Psychiat. Assn. (life); mem. Ark., Garland County med. socs., Mid-Continent Psychiat. Assn. Address: Rt 4 Box 660 Hot Springs AR 71901

JACKSON, GERALD AUDRON, management consultant; b. Lexington, Tex., Jan. 3, 1916; s. Miles and Mary Ellen (Cameron) J.; m. Mary E. Byrne, Feb. 1, 1946; children—Elizabeth Byrne (Mrs. Fritz L. Connally), Joe Patrick. With shipbuilding div. U.S. Steel Co., 1940-44, Levingston Shipbuilding Co., Orange, Tex., 1944-45; asst. gen. mgr. Austin Transit Co., Tex., 1945-49; with Champion Papers Inc., Hamilton, Ohio, 1949-67, dir. adminstrv. services, 1959-62, v.p. of materials planning services, 1962-67, formerly v.p. spl. relations and v.p., dir. materials services, Chgo.; v.p. materials services U.S. Plywood-Champion Papers Inc. (now Champion Internat. Corp.), N.Y.C., 1967-69, pres., 1969-76, v.p. real estate div., 1973-76; also pres. Champion Realty Corp., 1973-76; pres. Jackson, Mundy and Hart, 1983—. Co-author purchasing manual of, Nat. Assn. Purchasing Agts., 1956. Vice pres., dir. Pasadena (Tex.) Rodeo and Livestock Assn., 1955-58; chmn. Indsl. Com. Alcoholism, 1957; mem. Water Pollution Control Adv. Bd., Dept. Interior, 1964-67, Nat. Adv. Com. Alcoholism, HEW, 1966-69; chmn. Tex. Commn. on Alcoholism, 1972; Bd. dirs. Nat. Council on Alcoholism, 1968-70. Mem. Nat. Assn. Purchasing Agts. (dir. Houston 1956), Ohio, Ill. chambers commerce. Clubs: Mason, Shriner, International (Chgo.); International (Washington); Headliners (Austin). Home: PO Box 558 Lexington TX 78947 Office: 8705 Katy Freeway Suite 204 Houston TX 77024 *It is most important that we become a party to—rather than a victim of—change.*

JACKSON, GLENDA, actress; b. Birkenhead, Cheshire, Eng., May 9, 1936; d. Harry and Joan J.; m. Roy Hodges (div.); 1 son, Daniel. Ed., West Kirby County Grammar Sch. for Girls. Made stage debut; as student in: Separate Tables, Worthing, Eng., 1957; first appeared on London (Eng.) stage at Arts as Ruby in: All Kinds of Men, 1957; appeared in: Hammersmith, 1962, The Idiot, 1963, Alfie, 1963; joined, Royal Shakespeare Co. and; appeared in exptl. Theatre of Cruelty season, L.A.M.D.A., 1964, Stratford season, 1965; played Princess of France in: Love's Labour's Lost; Ophelia in: Hamlet, at Aldwych; played Eva in: Puntila, 1965; reader in: The Investigation, 1965; appeared as Charlotte Corday in: Marat/Sade, 1965, and repeating performance in N.Y. debut at, Martin Beck, 1965 (Variety award as most promising actress); appeared in, U.S. at Aldwych, 1966; as Masha in: Three Sisters at Royal Ct, 1967; as Tamara Fanghorn in: Fanghorn at Fortune, 1967; as Katherine Winter in: Collaborators, 1973; as Solange in: The Maids, 1974; as Hedda Gabler, 1975; as Vittoria Corombona in: The White Devil, 1976; appeared on: stage in Rose, N.Y.C., London, 1980-81; appeared in numerous films, 1968—; including Women in Love (Acad. award for Best Actress 1970), Sunday, Bloody Sunday, The Music Lovers, Marat-Sade, Negatives, Mary Queen of Scots, Triple Echo (being reissued as Soldier in Skirts), The Nelson Affair, A Touch of Class (Acad. award for Best Actress 1973), The Maids, The Romantic Englishwoman, The Incredible Sarah, Nasty Habits, House Calls, Lost and Found, 1979, Health, 1980, Hopscotch, 1980, Stevie, 1981, The Return of the Soldier, 1982; also numerous TV appearances, 1960—; including series Elizabeth R. Office: care Robinson Luttrell & Assocs 141 El Camino Dr #110 Beverly Hills CA 90212 *

JACKSON, GRANBERRY, III, warehousing executive; b. Nashville, Aug. 25, 1945; s. Granberry and Henriette (Weaver) J.; m. Mary Lee Whitehead, Apr. 28, 1973; children: Kathryn Weaver, Irene Kent. B.A., Vanderbilt U., 1967. Investment analyst Nat. Life Ins. Co., Nashville, 1967-72, asst. treas., asst. v.p., 1972-75, 2d v.p., 1975-81; v.p., treas. NLT corp., Nashville, 1981-83, Ingram Industries Inc., 1983-84; with Ozburn-Hessey Storage Co., Nashville, 1984—. Bd. dirs. Downtown YMCA, Nashville, 1975-80, chmn., Nashville, 1979-80; participant Leadership Nashville, 1977-78; mem. Nashville Com. Fgn. Relations, 1975—. Served to sgt. U.S. Army, 1967-69; Vietnam. Mem. Nashville Soc. Chartered Fin. Analysts (pres. 1978-79), Young Exec. Council, Fin. Execs. Inst., Nat. Assn. Corp. Treas, Beta Theta Pi. Roman Catholic. Clubs: Belle Meade Country, Vandrbilt of Nashville (treas. 1981-82). Home: 1223 Chickering Rd Nashville TN 37215 Office: Ozburn Hessey Storage Co 402 Murfreesboro Rd Nashville TN 37210

JACKSON, HARRY ANDREW, artist; b. Chgo., Apr. 18, 1924; s. Harry and Ellen Grace J.; m. Valentina Moya Lear, Feb. 22, 1974; children: Matthew, Molly, Jesse, Luke, Chloe. Founder pvt. foundry, Camaiore, Italy, 1964—; founder Wyo. Foundry Studios, 1965—, Western Fine Arts Found., 1974—. Author: Lost Wax Bronze Casting, 1972; One man exhbns. include, Amon Carter Mus., Fort Worth, 1961, 68, Smithsonian Instn., Washington, 1964, Whitney Gallery Western Art, Cody, Wyo., Mont. Hist. Soc., Southwest Mus., Los Angeles, 1979, Mpls. Inst. Arts, 1982, Trailside Galleries, Jackson, Wyo.; represented in permanent collections, Am. Mus. to Gt. Britain, U.S. Dept State, Lyndon Baines Johnson Meml. Library, Nat. Cowboy Hall of Fame, Wyo. State Mus., Whitney Mus. Western Art, Buffalo Bill Hist. Center, Plains Indian Mus., Amon Carter Mus., Willarac Mus., Mont. Hist. Soc., others; commd. works include: mural, Fort Pitts Mus., Pitts., 10-foot Sacajawea polychrome bronze monument, Plains Indian Mus., Cody, Wyo. Served with USMC, 1942-45. Decorated Purple Heart; recipient gold medal Nat. Acad. Design, 1968; Best Cover Art of 1969 award for sculpture of John Wayne Am. Inst. Graphic Arts, 1969; Fulbright grantee, 1954. Fellow Am. Artists League, Nat. Acad. Western Art; Mem. Nat. Sculpture Soc. Club: Bohemian (San Francisco). Home: Sage Creek Cody WY 82414 Office: care Roxanne Herman Wyo Foundry Studios PO Box 2836 Cody WY 82414 23 E 26th St New York NY 10017

JACKSON, HAZEL BRILL, sculptor; b. Phila.; d. William Henry and Lizabeth Lee (Stone) J. Student, Friends Select Sch., Phila., Boston Mus. Sch. Fine Arts, Scuola Rosatti, Florence, Italy; with, Angelo Zanelli, Rome, Italy. Exhibited, Nat. Mus. Modern Art, Rome, Trieste and Florence, Royal Acad. Scotland, Nat. Acad. N.Y.C., Guild Boston Artists; represented museums pvt. collections, including, Brookgreen Garden, S.C., Newburgh Pub. Library, bronzes at, Wellesley, Vassar, Dartmouth colls., Springfield (Mass.) Art Mus. Recipient Ellen Spayer Meml. award Nat. Acad., 1945, 48, 60, 65; Allied Artists prize Smithsonian Instn., 1963; other awards. Fellow Nat. Sculpture Soc.; mem. N.A.D. (Young Meml. prize 1965), Guild Boston Artists, Soc. Animal Artists, Am. Artists Profl. League. Clubs: American Alpine, Italian Alpine. Home: Old Balmville Rd Newburgh NY 12550 *Life to me has always seemed to be a privilege and a challenge. Sometimes the challenge appears to be too powerful, too overwhelming when viewed through the whirling machinery of modern so-called progress with its speed and rush and roar... the soft brave music of privilege is drowned in the clatter and thunder of wars and strife. In the studio I find one can realize again that the challenge of life is also the privilege of life*

JACKSON, HERB, artist, educator; b. Raleigh, N.C., Aug. 16, 1945; s. Walter H. and Virginia (Rogers) J.; m. Laura Dudley Grosch, June 9, 1967; 2 children. B.A., Davidson Coll., 1967; M.F.A., U. N.C., 1970. Prof. art dept. Davidson (N.C.) Coll., 1969—, chmn. dept. art, 1977—; dir. Art Gallery, 1974—; mem. artist adv. bd. Mint Mus. Art, Charlotte, N.C., 1979—. One-man shows: include, Mint Mus. Art, Charlotte, 1973, U. Nev., Reno, Rahr Mus., Manitowoc, Wis., Jane Haslem Gallery, Washington, 1974, Nielsen Gallery, Boston, Impressions Gallery, Boston, 1975, 81, Hahn Gallery, Phila., 1976, Dryden Gallery, Charlotte, Van Straaten Gallery, Chgo., 1977, Frances Aronson Gallery, Atlanta, 1978, N.C. Mus. Art, Raleigh, 1979, Rowe Gallery, U. N.C., Charlotte, Southeastern Center for Contemporary Art, Winston-Salem, N.C., 1981, Phyllis Weil Gallery, N.Y.C., 1981, 83, Princeton Gallery Fine Art, 1982, 83, Oxford Gallery (Eng.), 1982, DBR Gallery, Cleve., 1983, 84, Mint Mus. Art, Charlotte, N.C., 1983, Springfield Mus. Art (Mo.), Asheville Mus. Art (N.C.), Nat. Acad. Scis., Washington, Cheekwood Art Ctr., Nashville, Reading Art Mus. (Pa.), 1984, Gulbenkian Found., Lisbon, Portugal, Huntsville Mus. Art (Ala.), numerous group shows, 1962—, latest being, Internat. Print Biennale, Bradford, Eng., 1979, Mint Mus., Charlotte, 1979, 81, Southeastern Center Contemporary Art, Winston-Salem, 1979, Internat. São Paulo (Brazil) Bienal, Spring Mills Ann. Competition, Lancaster, S.C., 1980, Weatherspoon Gallery, Greensboro, N.C., Impressions Gallery, Boston, Associated Am. Artists, Phila., one-man shows: include, Am. Acad. and Inst. Arts and Letters, N.Y.C., 1981, Bklyn. Mus. Art, World's Fair, Knoxville, Tenn., 1982, Davos, Switzerland, 1983; represented in permanent collections, Balt. Mus. Art, Phila. Mus. Art, Victoria and Albert Mus., London, Whitney Mus. Art, N.Y.C., Mpls. Inst. Arts, Nat. Acad. Sci., Washington, Indpls. Mus. Art, Bklyn. Mus., USIA, Japan, U. Wis., Sheboygan, Yale U., New Haven, Mus. Fine Arts, Boston, N.Y. Public Library, Library of Congress, Mint Mus., Charlotte, So. Ill. U., Edwardsville, Kalamazoo Inst. Arts, Mus. Fine Arts, Springfield, Mass., Utah Mus., Salt Lake City, U. Nebr., Lincoln, U. Calif., Riverside, Minn. Mus. Art, St. Paul, Brit. Mus., London, others. Mem. Coll. Art Assn., So. Graphics Council, Charlotte Artists Coalition (dir. 1980-81), Mecklenberg-Charlotte Arts and Sci. Council (dir. 1977-79), Southeastern Coll. Art Conf. Home: PO Box 2495 Davidson NC 28036 Office: Davidson College Davidson NC 28036 *The artist's integrity is all he truly has, after all the trends, fads, and movements have faded into history. I try to make art which will stand as a personal statement.*

JACKSON, ISAIAH, conductor; b. Richmond, Va., Jan. 22, 1945; s. Isaiah Allen and Alma Alverta (Norris) J.; m. Helen Tuntland, Aug. 6, 1977; children: Benjamin, Katharine. B.A. cum laude, Harvard U., 1966; M.A., Stanford U., 1967; M.S., Juilliard Sch. Music, 1969, D.M.A., 1973. Founder, condr. Juilliard String Ensemble, N.Y.C., 1970-71; asst. condr. Am. Symphony Orch., N.Y.C., 1970-71, Balt. Symphony Orch., 1971-73; assoc. condr. Rochester Philharmonic Orch., N.Y., 1973—; music dir. Flint Symphony Orch., Mich., 1982—; guest condr. N.Y. Philharmonic Orch., N.Y.C., 1978, Boston Pops Orch., 1983, Cleve. Ocrch., 1983, Detroit Symphony Orch., 1983. Recipient First Gov.'s award for arts in Va. Commonwealth Va., 1979. Office: Rochester Philharmonic Orch 108 East Ave Rochester NY 16404

JACKSON, JACQUELINE DOUGAN, educator, author; b. Beloit, Wis., May 3, 1928; d. Ronald Arthur and Vera Arlouine (Wardner) Dougan; m. Robert Sumner Jackson, June 17, 1950 (div. 1973); children—Damaris Lee, Megan Trever, Gillian Patricia, Jacqueline Elspeth. B.A., Beloit Coll., 1950, H.H.D., 1977; M.A., U. Mich., 1951; D.Litt., MacMurray Coll., 1976. Instr. English Kent (Ohio) State U., 1964-68; asso. prof. lit. Sangamon State U., Springfield, Ill., 1970—. Writer, presenter: radio shows The Author is You, U. Wis. WHA Sch. of Air, 1969—, Reading and Writing and Radio, WSSR, Springfield, Ill., 1975—; Author: Julie's Secret Sloth, 1953, The Taste of Spruce Gum (Notable Book award 1966), 1966 (Dorothy Canfield Fisher award 1967), Missing Melinda, 1967, Chicken Ten Thousand, 1968, Spring Song, 1969, The Orchestra Mice, 1970, The Endless Pavement, (with William Perlmutter), 1973, Turn Not Pale, Beloved Snail, 1974; author-illustrator: The Paleface Redskins, 1958, The Ghost Boat, 1969; illustrator: (Chad Walsh) Knock and Enter, 1953. Mem. Modern Lang. Assn., Children's Reading Round Table, Phi Beta Kappa. Episcopalian. Home: 816 N 5th St Springfield IL 62702

JACKSON, JACQUELYNE JOHNSON, sociology educator; b. Winston-Salem, N.C., Feb. 24, 1932; d. James Albert and Beulah Naomi (Crosby) Johnson; m. Frederick A.S. Clarke, Aug. 26, 1955 (div. 1959); m. Murphy Jackson, May 15, 1962; 1 dau., Viola Elizabeth. B.S., U. Wis., 1953, M.S., 1955; Ph.D., Ohio State U., 1960; postgrad., U. Colo., summer 1961, Duke U., 1966-68, U. N.C., 1977-78. Prof. So. U., Baton Rouge, 1959-62, Jackson (Miss.) State Coll., 1962-64, Howard U., Washington, 1964-66, 78—; asst. to asso. prof. med. sociology Duke U., Durham, N.C., 1968—; prof. sociology St. Augustine's Coll., Raleigh, N.C., 1969—; cons. and speaker on aging, families and public policies. Author: These Rights They Seek, 1962, Minorities and Aging, 1980, also numerous articles; editor: Aging Black Women, 1975, Jour. Minority Aging, 1975—. Exec. dir. Nat. Council on Black Aging, Inc., 1975—; mem. Nat. Council on Equality of Ednl. Opportunity, 1973-78; Life mem. Tuskegee (Ala.) Civic Assn.; Trustee Carver Research Found., Tuskegee Inst. Recipient Pres.'s award Assn. Homes for Aging, 1972, Black Women's award in edn. Clark Coll., 1975; Solomon Fuller award Am. Psychiat. Assn., 1978; award Ret. Mems. Div., Local 1199, Nat. Hosp. and Health Care Employees, 1983; Ford fellow, summer 1957; John Hay Whitney fellow, 1957-59; NSF fellow, 1961; NIH fellow, 1966-68. Mem. Am. Sociol. Assn. (editor Jour. Health and Social Behavior 1972-75), Assn. Social and Behavioral Scientists (pres. 1969-72, pres.'s service award 1973, W.E.B. Du Bois award 1980), AAAS, Nat. Council on Family Relations, Gerontol. Soc., So. Sociol. Soc. Democrat. Episcopalian. Home: PO Box 8522 Durham NC 27707

JACKSON, JAMES OTIS, newspaper editor; b. Santa Fe, Nov. 21, 1939; s. Otis Lafel and Katie Mae (MacDonald) J.; m. Linda Anne Chase, Sept. 5, 1964. B.S. in Journalism, Northwestern U., 1961; postgrad., Harvard U., 1972-73. Reporter U.P.I., Miami, 1965-67, N.Y.C., 1967-68, Prague, Czechoslovakia, 1968-69, Moscow, 1969-72; reporter Chgo. Tribune, 1973, mem. editorial bd., 1978—, dep. editor editorial page, 1983—; Moscow corr. Chgo. Tribune Press Service, 1974-76, London corr., 1976-78. Served to lt. (j.g.) USNR, 1962-65. Home: 2603 Hartzell St Evanston IL 60201 Office: 435 N Michigan Ave Chicago IL 60611

JACKSON, JAMES SIDNEY, educator; b. Detroit, July 30, 1944; s. Pete James and Johnnie Mae (Wilson) J. B.S., Mich. State U., 1966; M.A., U. Toledo, 1970; Ph.D., Wayne State U., 1972. Probation counselor Lucas County Juvenile Ct., Toledo, Ohio, 1967-68; teaching and research asst. Wayne State U., Detroit, 1968-71; asst. to asso. prof. psychology U. Mich., Ann Arbor, 1971—; faculty asso. Research Center for Group Dynamics, Inst. for Social Research, 1971—, Inst. Gerontology, 1976—; cons. Emergency Sch. Aid Project, 1973-74, Commn. on Equal Opportunity in Psychology, 1970, Project to Provide Psychol. Services to Head Start Programs, 1973-74; mem. com. on aging Nat. Acad. Scis. Editorial cons.: Jour. of Behavioral and Social Scientists; Contbr. articles to profl. jours. Bd. dirs. Pub. Commn. on Mental Health. Recipient Disting. Faculty Service award U. Mich., 1976; Urban Studies fellow Wayne State U., 1969-70; NSF fellow, 1969. Mem. Assn. Advancement of Psychology (trustee 1973—, chmn. 1978-80), Black Students Psychol. Assn. (nat. chmn. 1970-71), Assn. Black Psychologists (nat. chmn. 1972-73), Am. Psychol. Assn. (policy and planning bd.), Soc. Psychol. Study of Social Issues, World Future Soc., Assn. Behavioral and Social Scientists, Psi Chi, Alpha Phi Alpha. Home: 517 Fairview Circle Ypsilanti MI 48197 Office: 5271 Inst Social Research U Mich Ann Arbor MI 48106

JACKSON, JERRY DONALD, lawyer; b. Warren, Ark., Nov. 18, 1944; s. Olin and Lurline Ruth (Moore) J.; m. Sharon Harvie Ragan, Nov. 28, 1966; children: Michael Steele, John Brooks. LL.B., U. Ark., 1968. Bar: Ark. Atty. Ark. Dept. Ins., 1968; partner firm Spitberg, Mitchell & Hays, Little Rock, 1969-79; sr. v.p. Ark. Power & Light Co., Little Rock, 1979; now ptnr. Mitchell, Williams, Selig, Jackson & Tucker. Commr. Ark. Labor Bd., 1971-74, Ark. Public Service Commn., 1974-75. Served with USAR. Mem. Am. Bar Assn., Ark. Bar Assn., Pulaski County Bar Assn. Methodist. Office: First National Bldg Little Rock AR 72205

JACKSON, JESSE LOUIS, clergyman, civic leader; b. Greenville, S.C., Oct. 8, 1941; s. Charles Henry and Helen J.; m. Jacqueline Lavinia Brown, 1964; children: Santita, Jesse Louis, Jonathan Luther, Yusef DuBois, Jacqueline Lavinia. Student, U. Ill., 1959-60; B.A. in Sociology, A & T Coll. N.C., 1964; postgrad., Chgo. Theol. Sem.; D.D. (hon.), Chgo. Theol. Sem. Ordained to ministry Baptist Ch., 1968; founder (with others) Operation Breadbasket joint project So. Christian Leadership Conf./ Coordinating Council Community Orgns., Chgo., 1966, nat. dir., 1966-71; founder, exec. dir. Operation PUSH (People United to Serve Humanity), Chgo., 1971—; candidate for Democratic nomination for Pres. U.S., 1983-84. Active Black Coalition for United Community Action, 1969. Recipient Presdl. award Nat. Med. Assn., 1969; Humanitarian Father of Year award Nat. Father's Day Com., 1971. Address: 930 E 50th St Chicago IL 60615

JACKSON, JOE, musician, singer, songwriter; b. Eng. Student composition, Royal Acad. Music. Plays piano, saxophone and guitar. Albums include Look Sharp, 1979, I'm the Man, 1979, Beat Crazy, 1980, Jumpin' Jive, Night and Day. Office: care Press Relations A & M Records 1416 N La Brea Ave Hollywood CA 90028

JACKSON, JOHN ELLETT, lawyer; b. Palestine, Tex., Aug. 3, 1892; s. Alexander Ellett and Abby Frederick (Watts) J.; m. Mary Louise Allen, Dec. 29, 1917; children: Mary Allen (Mrs. H. Robert Corder), John E. Jr. LL.B., Georgetown U., 1916. Bar: Tex. bar 1914, La. bar 1920, U.S. Supreme Ct. bar 1928. Pvt. practice law, New Orleans, 1921—; Republican candidate for lt. gov. of La., 1928; chmn. Rep. State Central Com., La., 1929-34; Rep. nat. committeeman for La., 1934-52, mem. exec. com., 1951-52, sub-com. on South, 1950-52; chmn. La. delegation Rep. Nat. Convs., 1932, 36, 40, 44, 48. Former trustee Robert A. Taft Meml. Found., Inc. Decorated hon. officer and comdr. Order Brit. Empire. Mem. ABA, La. Bar Assn., New Orleans Bar Assn. (pres. 1936-37). Republican. Presbyn. Clubs: Mason (New Orleans) (K.T., Shriner); Pickwick, Stratford (New Orleans)). Home: 401 Metairie Rd Metairie LA 70005 Office: 1st Nat Bank of Commerce Bldg New Orleans LA 70112

JACKSON, JOHN HOWARD, lawyer; b. Kansas City, Mo., Apr. 6, 1932; s. Howard Clifford and Lucile (Deischer) J.; m. Joan Leland, Dec. 16, 1962; children—Jeanette, Lee Ann, Michelle. A.B., Princeton U., 1954; J.D., U. Mich., 1959. Bar: Wis. bar 1959, Mo. bar 1959, Calif. bar 1964, Mich. bar 1970. Practice in, Milw., 1959-61; asso. prof., prof. law U. Calif., 1961-66; prof. law U. Mich., 1966—; on leave) gen. counsel U.S. Office Spl. Trade Rep., 1973-74, acting deputy spl. rep. for trade, 1974; vis. prof. U. Brussels, 1975-76; Ford Found. cons. legal edn., vis. prof. U. Delhi, India, 1968-69; cons. U.S. Treasury Dept., U.S. Office Spl. Trade Reps, U.S. Senate Finance Com., 1978-79, UN Conf. Trade and Devel., 1980; vis. fellow Inst. Internat. Econs., Washington, 1983. Author: World Trade and the Law of GATT, 1969, Contract Law in Modern Society, 1973, 2d edit. (with Lee Bollinger), 1980, Legal Problems of International Economic Relations, 1977; contbr. articles to profl. jours.; bd. editors: Jour. World Trade Law. Served with M.I. U.S. Army, 1954-56. Rockefeller Found. fellow for study European community law, Brussels, 1975-76. Mem. ABA, Am. Soc. Internat. Law, Council Fgn. Relations, Phi Beta Kappa, Order of Coif. Home: 1 Heatheridge Ann Arbor MI 48104 Office: Sch Law U Mich Ann Arbor MI 48109

JACKSON, JOHN MATHEWS, food technologist; b. Chgo., July 9, 1908; s. William Hayden and Adeline (Mathews) J.; m. Elizabeth Burd, Jan. 31, 1931; children—Frances (Mrs. Harry A. Skevington), William, Lynette (Mrs. Thomas G. Colmey), Margaret (Mrs. Curtis C. Haan), Martha A. (Mrs. William J. Fisher III), Barbara J., Robert M. (dec.). B.S., U. Chgo., 1929, Ph.D., 1932. With Am. Can Co., 1932-63, asst. mgr., 1949-51, mgr. research div. lab., Maywood, Ill., 1952-55, research div. lab., Barrington, Ill., 1955-57, sect. mgr., 1957-63; dir. research Green Giant Co., Le Sueur, Minn., 1963-67, dir. tech. relations and packaging research, 1967-73, cons., 1974—; pres. research and devel. assos. Q.M. Food and Container Inst., 1962-63; mem. subcom. radiation preservation foods NRC, 1955-57; mem. food process rev. com. FDA, 1974—. Co-author: Fundamentals of Food Canning Technology, 1979. Trustee Village of Barrington, 1961-63. Mem. Inst. Food Technologists (pres. 1962-63), Am. Chem. Soc., Nat. Canners Assn. (com. sci. research 1965-72). Club: Masons. Home: PO Box 87 Lakeside MI 49116

JACKSON, JOHN NELSON, lawyer; b. Brownwood, Tex., Apr. 28, 1905; s. Charles Young and Kate Venable (Wood) J.; m. Sallie Bell Gaston, May 17, 1935; children: Gertrude Gaston (Mrs. Robert Bush Smither, Jr.), Sallie Bell Flippen (Mrs. Nowell E. Loop). Student, Howard Payne Coll., 1922-24; LL.B. with highest honors, U. Tex., 1927. Bar: Tex. 1927. Practiced law in, Ft. Worth, 1927-30; asso., later mem. firm, now of counsel Coke & Coke, Dallas, 1930—. Trustee Leland Fikes Found., Dallas Symphony Found.; mem. Dallas County Heritage Soc., chmn., 1978; hon. trustee Heard Mus.; trustee, past chmn. Friends of Dallas Public Library; bd. dirs. Goals for Dallas. Recipient Founders Cup award Dallas County Heritage Soc., 1976; United Way Voluntarism award, 1979; Dallas Hist. Soc. award, 1984. Fellow Am. Bar Found., Tex. Bar Found., Am. Coll. Probate Counsel; mem. Southwestern Legal Found. (former v.p., now hon. trustee), Internat. Bar Assn., ABA, Dallas Bar Assn. (pres. 1959), World Assn. Lawyers, State Bar Tex., Am. Soc. Internat. Law, Am. Judicature Soc., Mexican Acad. Internat. Law, Am. Law Inst., Internat. Acad. Estate and Trust Law, SAR, S.C.V., Mil. Order Stars and Bars, Chancellors, Order of Coif, Phi Gamma Delta, Phi Delta Phi, Pi Kappa Delta. Episcopalian. Clubs: Northwood, City, Idlewild, Petroleum., Shakespeare (hon.), Codrington (hon.). Lodge: Mason. Home: 7408 Greenbrier Dr Dallas TX 75225 Office: First Nat Bank Bldg Dallas TX 75202

JACKSON, JOHN TILLSON, corporate executive; b. Milw., May 13, 1921; s. John F. and Elizabeth (Tillson) J.; m. Suzanne Bartley, Apr. 1953; children: Suzanne, Jennifer, John Tillson. B.S. in Adminstrv. Engring, Cornell U., 1942. Jr. engr. George S. Armstrong & Co., Inc., N.Y.C., 1946-48, sr. engr., 1948-49, v.p., 1949, dir., 1951; asst. to pres. Fed. Telecommunication Labs., 1953-55, ITT, N.Y.C., 1956-57, asst. v.p., 1957-58, v.p., 1959-60, Remington Office Equipment div. Sperry Rand Corp., 1960-66, Gen. Waterworks Corp., Phila., 1966-68, IU Internat., 1968-69, sr. v.p., 1969-72, exec. v.p., chmn. exec. com., 1973-82, vice chmn., 1982-83; chmn. C. Brewer & Co., Ltd. subs., 1975-82; dir. Vanguard Group of Investment Cos., IU Internat.; dir. Del. Trust Co., Ballagh & Thrall, Inc., Bradford-White Corp., Geothermal Resources Internat., Inc. Vice chmn. Acad. Natural Sci., Phila. Served from 2d lt. to maj. AUS, 1942-46. Mem. ASME, Zeta Psi. Clubs: Phila., Gulph Mills Golf, Racquet, Merion Cricket, Merion Golf, Philadelphia; Union League, University (N.Y.C.). Home: 155 Rose Ln Haverford PA 19041 Office: 1500 Walnut St Philadelphia PA 19102

JACKSON, JOHN WYANT, business executive; b. Corpus Christi, May 25, 1944; s. Donald LeGrade Marion and McNulty (Jackson) Vincent; m. Susan Gager, Sept. 6, 1969; children: Alexandria C., Kimberly F., Donald M., Jennifer L. B.A., Yale U., 1967; M.B.A., INSEAD, Fontainbleau, France, 1971; diploma, Institut de Sci. Politique, Paris, 1966. Dir. new products MSDI, Ramway, N.J., 1975-76, dir., Harlem, Holland, 1976-77, Merck Sharp & Dohme Internat., Ramway, N.J., 1977-78; dir. med. products Far East Am. Cyanamid Co., Wayne, N.J., 1978-79; dir. med. products Americas and Far East Am. Cyananmid Co., Wayne, N.J., 1979-81; v.p. Americas and Far East Am. Cyanamid Co., Wayne, N.J., 1981—; dir. U.S. Pakistan Econ. Council, N.Y.C., 1981—, U.S.-ROC Econ. Council, Crystall Lake, Ill., 1982—. Treas. Am. Men's Club, Portugal, 1974-75; active Internat. Rotary, Holland, 1976-77. Served to 1st lt. USMCR, 1967-70. Decorated Navy Commendation medal, Purple Heart. Mem. Pharm. Mfrs. Assn. (chmn. Far East regional com. 1981-82). Republican. Episcopalian. Office: Cyanamid Ams-Far East One Cyanamid Plaza Wayne NJ 07470

JACKSON, JULIAN ELLIS, food company executive; b. Perry, Fla., Oct. 24, 1913; s. Eddie H. and Eva M. (Reid) J.; m. Laurana H. Filson, Oct. 6, 1956; children—Julian Ellis, Eddie King, Robert Allen, Victor Pharis, Julian Ellis IV, Lester Mitchell. Grad., Andrew Jackson High Sch., Jacksonville, Fla., 1931; D.Sc. (hon.), Jones Coll., 1982. With Great Atlantic & Pacific Stores, 1931-43; pres. Jax Meat Co., 1943-58, Jackson's Minit Markets, Inc., 1958-69, Julian Jackson Investment Co., 1955—, Lil' Champ Food Stores, Inc., 1971—; co-owner Jackson-Cowart Realty Co., 1955—; dir. Fla. Nat. Bank, Jacksonville, Arlington. Past pres. United Cerebral Palsy, Jacksonville; chmn. Jacksonville Boxing Commn., 1952-71; pres. Gator Bowl Assn., 1957, Fla. Baseball League, 1958-60; Bd. dirs. Palmdale Med. Center, Police Athletic League, Jacksonville, Jacksonville Marine Inst., Jones Coll., Jacksonville. Named Super Market Man of Year, 1960; recipient Top Mgmt. award Sales and Mktg. Execs. Jacksonville, 1968. Mem. Fla. Super Market Assn. (pres. 1950-59), Fraternal Order Police. Clubs: Mason, Shriner, Ponte Vedra, Univ. Country, River, University, Sportsman (Jacksonville). Home: 5473 Golf Course Dr Jacksonville FL 32211 Office: 9 Acme St Jacksonville FL 32211

JACKSON, KEITH MACKENZIE, television commentator, writer, producer; b. Carrollton, Ga., Oct. 18, 1928; s. and Lucille Polly Perdue Jackson Bragg; m. Turi Ann Johnsen, Aug. 2, 1952; children: Melanie Ann, Lindsey Keith, Christopher Keith. B.A. in Broadcast Journalism, Wash. State U., 1954. Sports and spl. events dir., asso. news dir. KOMO Radio-TV, Seattle, 1954-64; news corr. ABC Radio, 1964-69; sports dir. Radio Sta. KABC, 1971-74; sports commentator, writer, producer ABC-TV, N.Y.C., 1964—. Founding mem. vis. com. Wash. State U.; trustee Wash. State U. Found. Served with USMC, 1946-50. Recipient Disting. Alumnus award, 1978; Recipient Sylvania award, 1956, Headliners award, 1958, Golden Mike award So. Calif. News Dirs. Assn., 1972; named Nat. Sportscaster of Year, 1972-76, Seattle-Puget Sound Sportscaster of Decade, 1978; recipient Am. Legion Good Guy award, 1983. Mem. AFTRA, Screen Actors Guild, Alpha Tau Omega. Presbyterian. Clubs: Los Angeles Country, Bellingham Yacht. Office: ABC Sports 28th Floor 1330 Ave of Americas New York NY 10019 *All any society owes an individual is an opportunity, and the color of a person's skin will never tell you anything about their character nor their potential.*

JACKSON, KENNETH ARTHUR, physicist, researcher; b. Connaught, Ont., Can., Oct. 23, 1930; s. Arthur and Susanna (Vatcher) J.; m. Jacqueline Della Olyan, June 20, 1952 (div.); children: Stacy Margaret, Meredith Suzanne, Stuart Keith; m. Camilla M. Maruszewski, June 21, 1980. B.S., U. Toronto, 1952, M.S., 1953; Ph.D., Harvard, 1956. Postdoctoral fellow Harvard U., Cambridge, Mass., 1956-58, asst. prof. metallurgy, 1958-62; mem. tech. staff Bell Labs., Murray Hill, N.J., 1962-67, head material physics research dept., 1967-81, head optical materials research dept., 1981—; Lectr. Welch. Found., 1970; mem. research adv. panel Air Force Office Sci. Research, 1976—. Contbr. articles to profl. jours. Recipient Mathewson Gold medal AIME, 1966. Mem. AIME, Internat. Orgn. Crystal Growth (treas. 1978—), Am. Assn. Crystal Growth (pres. 1968-75), Materials Research Soc. (v.p. 1975-77, pres. 1977-78, council), Am. Soc. Metals, Am. Phys. Soc., AAAS, Engring. Council for Profl. Devel. (mem. council). Patentee in field. Home: 33 Bethune St New York NY 10014 Office: Bell Labs 600 Mountain Ave Murray Hill NJ 07974

JACKSON, LAIRD GRAY, physician; b. Seattle, Oct. 10, 1930. B.A., Pomona Coll., 1951; M.D., U. Cin., 1955. Diplomate: Am. Bd. Internat. Medicine. Rotating gen. intern Sacramento County (Calif.) Hosp., 1955-56; resident internal medicine Jefferson Med. Coll., Phila., 1959-61, NIH postdoctoral fellow med. oncology, 1961-62, instr. medicine, 1962-64, asso. in medicine, 1964-66, asst. prof. medicine, 1966-69, asso. prof. medicine, pediatrics, obstetrics and gynecology, dir. div. med. genetics, 1969-78, prof. pediatrics, medicine, obstetrics and gynecology, 1978—. Mem. editorial bd.: Repository of Human Chromosomal Variants. Served to capt. USAF, 1956-59. Leukemia Soc. scholar, 1965-70; Leukemia Soc. fellow, 1963-65. Fellow ACP; mem. Am. Soc. Human Genetics (mem. social issues com. 1976-80), Am. Assn. Cancer Research, Birth Defects Soc., Soc. Pediatric Research. Home and office: 1025 Walnut St Philadelphia PA 19107

JACKSON, LARRY ARTOPE, college president; b. Florence, S.C., Feb. 7, 1925; s. Arthur Edward and Rosa (Gilbert) J.; m. Barbara Atwood, June 27, 1953; children: Elizabeth Lynne Jackson Eble, Arthur Edward, Barbara Gilbert Jackson Allen, Charles Rhett. A.B., Wofford Coll., 1947, D.Litt. (hon.), 1976; M.Div., Union Theol. Sem., 1953; M.A., U. Pacific, 1973, D.D. (hon.), 1961. Ordained to ministry United Meth. Ch., 1953; minister chs., 1953-59; dir. Santiago (Chile) Coll., 1959-64; provost Callison Coll. of U. Pacific, Stockton, Calif., 1964-70; v.p. for adminstrn. U. Evansville, 1970-73; pres. Lander Coll., Greenwood, S.C., 1973—. Editor: Concerned South Carolineans, 1957—. Mem. Fulbright Commn. for Chile, 1961-64, Commn. on Black Colls. Related to the Meth. Ch., 1973-76. Served with USAAF, 1943-45; with Am. Friends Ser. Com., 1948-49. Decorated Air medal with 2 oak leaf clusters. Mem. Am. Assn. Higher Edn., Phi Delta Kappa, Pi Gamma Mu. Democrat. Lodges: Rotary. Home: 304 W Durst Ave Greenwood SC 29646 Office: Lander Coll Greenwood SC 29646 *Love is the law of life and it is by striving to live under the rule of this law that we find authenticity.*

JACKSON, LAURA (RIDING), writer; b. N.Y.C., Jan. 16, 1901; d. Nathaniel S. and Sarah (Edersheim) Reichenthal; m. Schuyler Brinckerhoff Jackson, June 20, 1941 (dec. 1968). Student, Cornell U., other univs. Mem. The Fugitives, mid 1920's; mng. partner Seizin Press, 1927-38. Collaborator, 1st author: A Survey of Modernist Poetry, 1927, A Pamphlet Against Anthologies, 1928; critical essays Contemporaries and Snobs, 1928, Anarchism Is Not Enough, 1928, Four Unposted Letters to Catherine, 1930; essays and poems Though Gently, 1930; essays and stories Experts Are Puzzled, 1930; under pseudonym Madeleine Vara: Convalescent Conversations, 1935; collected stories Progress of Stories, 1935, new edit., 1982; hist. novel A Trojan Ending, 1937, new edit., 1984; hist. stories Lives of Wives, 1939; (with Harry Kemp) The Left Heresy, 1939, Collected Poems from 9 preceding vols, 1938, Selected Poems: In Five Sets, 1973, The Telling, 1972, (with husband) Rational Meaning: A New Foundation for the Definition of Words, publ. delayed; also articles and pamphlets, 1925—; editor, contbr.: gen. criticism Epilogue, Vols. I-III, 1935-37; editor, commentator: The World and Ourselves, 1938; Selected Writings, Published, Unpublished, book issue, Chelsea 35, 1976, Collected Poems, new edit, 1980, Description of Life Story, 1980, Some Communications of Broad Reference, 1984. Recipient Fugitive poetry prize, 1925; appreciation grant Mark Rothko Found., 1971; Guggenheim fellow, 1973. Home: Box 35 Wabasso FL 32970 *My concerns as a writer have been and are centered to a sense of there being a fundamental relation between the success of human beings as such and their fidelity in using words to what the words mean. I believe that to practice such fidelity is to observe standards of truth to which one commits oneself in spirit in using words.*

JACKSON, LEE, artist; b. N.Y.C., Feb. 2, 1909; s. Harry and Charlotte (Tallis) J.; m. Adele Grapes, Apr. 11, 1950. Student, Art Students League; with, John Sloan, George Luks. Faculty Sch. for Art Studies, 1947-48, Coll. City N.Y., 1948-54. One man show, Babcock Galleries, 1941, 43, 58, works exhibited, Met. Mus. Art, Whitney Mus. Am. Art, Art. Inst. Chgo., U. Ill., Corcoran Galleries of Art, Va. Mus. Fine Art, Pa. Acad. Art, N.A.D., Mus. City N.Y., Butler Art Inst., Audubon Artists, Nat. Art Mus. Sport, Madison Sq. Garden, 1968, others; rep. permanent collections, Met. Mus. Art, N.Y.C., Corcoran Galleries Art, Washington, Los Angeles County Mus. Art, Athens (Ga.) Mus., Walker Art Center, Mpls., Norfolk (Va.) Art Mus., Syracuse U., Smithsonian Mus., Washington, others. Guggenheim fellow in painting, 1941; Recipient ann. purchase prize Nebr. Art Assn., 1946; spl. invitation prize Salmagundi Club, 1950; Thomas G. Clarke prize N.A.D., 1951; Sudler and Hennessey prize, 1955; Grumbacher prize, 1956, 64; prize for painting in oil N.A.D., 1961. Mem. Art Student's League, Audubon Artists Am., Artists Equity Assn., Am. Water Color Soc., Nat. Soc. Painters in Casein. Home: Strongs Ln Water Mill NY 11976

JACKSON, LEROY EUGENE, microbiologist, researcher; b. Austin, Tex., Nov. 24, 1933; s. Carl Edgar and Anna Belle (Walsh) J.; m. Carolyn Ruth Peterson, June 25, 1954; children: Shari, Cindy, Becky, Jared, LeAnn, Caryn, Jenny. B.S., Brigham Young U., 1955; M.S., U. Tex., 1961; Ph.D., U. Kans., 1967. Research asst. M.D. Anderson Hosp. and Tumor Inst., Houston, 1955-56; instr. Brigham Young U., Provo, 1957-58; microbiologist Midwest Research Inst., Kansas City, Mo., 1961-64; prof. and chmn. dept. microbiology Weber State Coll., Ogden, Utah, 1969—81; sr. lab. mgr. Staley Research Center, Decatur, Ill., 1981-82; ind. researcher Brigham Young U., Provo, Utah, 1982—; NIH postdoctoral fellow Scripps Clinic and Research Inst., La Jolla, Calif., 1967-68; NSF faculty participant Staley Research Center, Decatur, Ill., summers 1974, 75. Named Outstanding Natural Sci. Tchr. faculty Weber State Coll., 1976. Mem. Am. Soc. Microbiology., Mycol. Soc. Am. Mormon. Home: 1114 North 200 East Orem UT 84057 Office: Dept Botany and Range Sci Brigham Young U Provo UT 84602

JACKSON, LEWIS ALBERT, former university official; b. Angola, Ind., Dec. 29, 1912; s. Albert and Cora (Beverly) J.; m. Violet Burden, Sept. 17, 1938; children: Joyce Harlene, Robert Lewis. B.S., Marion (Ind.) Coll., 1939; M.A., Miami U., Oxford, Ohio, 1948; Ph.D., Ohio State U., 1950. Tchr. Grant County (Ind.) Pub. Schs., 1936-40; contractor-flight instr. Chgo. Sch. Aeros., 1940; dir. tng. div. aeros. Tuskegee Inst., 1940-46; tchr. Gary (Ind.) Pub. Schs., 1964; faculty Central State U., Wilberforce, Ohio, 1946-66, 67—, prof. edn., dir. student personnel, 1950-57, dean coll., 1957-60, v.p., dean adminstrn., 1961-66, acting pres., 1965-66, chmn. dept. ednl. adminstrn. and guidance, 1967-69, dir. grad. studies, 1969-70, pres. univ., 1970-72, asst. to pres., 1972-73; assoc. prof. dept. aviation Ohio State U., 1966-67; v.p. for adminstrn. Sinclair Community Coll., Dayton, Ohio, 1973-79; now self-employed in aviation and investments.; Mem. tech. edn. com. Ohio Bd. Regents, cons. to evaluate programs, summer 1968; chmn. aviation com. Dayton-Miami Valley Consortium Colls. and Univs., 1968; mem. home econs. com. Ohio Dept. Vocational Edn.; sch. survey team Lincoln Heights Sch. Dist., 1961; mem. examining teams N. Central Assn. Colls. and Secondary Schs., 1973—; evaluation bd. Nat. Council Accreditation Tchr. Edn., 1973—; mem. citizens adv. com. on aviation FAA, 1975-77. Editor sect. in: Jour. Human Relations, 1952-57. Recipient Disting. Alumnus award Marion Coll. Alumni Assn., 1983. Mem. Conf. Deans Edn. State Univs. Ohio (sec. 1959, chmn. 1960), NEA, Am. Indsl. Arts Assn., Ohio Ednl. Assn., AAUP, Beta Kappa Chi, Phi Delta Kappa. Home: 733 Silvers Dr Xenia OH 45385 *Parent and teacher influence; wife's influence; application of knowledge gained through reading and experience; insight, innovative ideas, positive outlook. I have been willing to change my life for the better and have a strong desire to find better ways of doing everything to the maximum advantage for everyone.*

JACKSON, LIONEL STEWART, newspaper exec.; b. New Haven, June 25, 1915; s. John Day and Rose (Herrick) J.; m. Patricia Woolsey, June 16, 1938; children—Suzanne (Mrs. John G. Cartier), Sheila (Mrs. John M. Bates Jr.), Lionel S. Jr. Grad., Kent Sch., 1933; ed., Yale, 1937. With New Haven Register, 1936—, co-pub., gen. mgr., 1956-71, pub., 1972—; pres. The Register Pub. Co., New Haven, 1972—, Jour.-Courier, 1972—; pub., editor-in-chief Jackson Newspapers, Inc., chmn. bd., chief exec. officer, 1981—. Hon. bd. dirs. New Haven Symphony, New Haven Boys' Club. Served to 1st lt. AUS, 1944-46. Mem. New Haven C. of C. (dir.). Clubs: Maidstone, Devon Yacht (East Hampton, L.I.); N.Y. Yacht (N.Y.C.); Delray (Fla.) Beach Yacht (vice-commodore); Ocean, Gulfstream Bath and Tennis (Fla.)). Home: 201 Kings Hwy North Haven CT 06473 Office: 40 Sargent Dr New Haven CT 06511

JACKSON, MARION LEROY, agronomist, soil scientist; b. Reynolds, Nebr., Nov. 30, 1914; s. Cleve L. and Belle Josephine (Hanson) J.; m. Chrystie Marie Bertramson, Sept. 2, 1937; children—Marjorie Lee, Virginia Lynn (Mrs. Bruce P. Conlon), Stanley Bertram, Douglas Mark. B.S. maxima cum laude with high distinction, U. Nebr., 1936, M.S., 1937, D.Sc. (hon.), 1974; Ph.D., U. Wis., 1939. Land classification aide U.S. Dept. Agr., Lincoln, Nebr., 1936-37; grad. research asst. U. Wis., Madison, 1937-39, postdoctoral fellow, 1939-41, instr., 1941-42, asst. prof., 1942-45, asso. prof., 1946-50, prof., 1950-74, Franklin Hiram King prof., 1974—; chemist Purdue U., 1945-46; vis. prof. Cornell U., 1959; disting. vis. prof. U. Wash., Seattle, 1973; mem. panel on disposition radioactive wastes Nat. Acad. Scis., 1976-77; lectr. U.S., Canadian govts., numerous univs. Author: Soil Chemical Analysis, 1958, Soil Chemical Analysis-Advanced Course, 1956, 2d edit., 1969; contbr. articles to profl. jours. Troop chmn. Four Lakes council Boy Scouts Am., 1965, scoutmaster, 1966. Recipient Soil Sci. Achievement award, 1958. Fellow Am. Soc. Agronomy, Soil Sci. Soc. Am. (past pres.), AAAS, Mineral Soc. Am.; mem. Clay Minerals Soc. (past pres., Disting. Mem. award 1977), Internat. Soc. Soil Sci., Mineral Soc. London, Phi Beta Kappa, Sigma Xi, Phi Lambda Upsilon (Freshman Chemistry award), Alpha Zeta, Gamma Sigma Delta, Pi Mu Epsilon. Home: 309 Ozark Trail Madison WI 53705 Office: 1525 Observatory Dr U Wis Madison WI 53706 *Persistent intense curiosity concerning the scientific interrelatedness of inanimate and living things in nature is important. Teaching (sharing) of facts and ideas with students and colleagues, particularly colleagues in seemingly remote but allied disciplines, permits fruitful research and discovery of underlying principles governing complex systems.*

JACKSON, MARK EVAN, clergyman, coll. pres.; b. Fargo, N.D., Oct. 31, 1928; s. Paul Rainey and Stella (Chappell) J.; m. Irene Ruth Reynolds, June 10, 1949; children—Sheryl, Paul, Laurie, Lynne. Student, Wheaton (Ill.) Coll., 1945-46, Baptist Bible Sem., Johnson City, N.Y., 1946-50; D.D., Cedarville (Ohio) Coll., 1976. Ordained to ministry Baptist Ch., 1950; asst. pastor Grace Bapt. Ch., Binghamton, N.Y., 1950-52; pastor First Bapt. Ch., Dedham, Mass., 1952-55, Calvary Bapt. Ch., Everett, Wash., 1955-63, Bethel Bapt. Ch., Kalamazoo, 1963-68, Calvary Bapt. Ch., Muskegon, Mich., 1968-75, Walnut Ridge Bapt. Ch., Waterloo, Iowa, 1975-79; pres. Bapt. Bible Coll., Clarks Summit, Pa., 1979—; trustee Assn. Baptists for World Evangelism, Cherry Hill, N.J.; past chmn. Council of Eighteen, Gen. Assn. Regular Bapt. Chs., Schaumburg, Ill.; past chmn. nat. council and exec. com. Fellowship Baptists for Home Missions, Elyria, Ohio; past chmn. bd. trustees Bapt. Bible Coll. Author: Ready, Set-Grow!, 1977. Republican. Home: 538 Venard Rd Clarks Summit PA 18411

JACKSON, MARY, actress; b. Milford, Mich., Nov. 22, 1910; d. Thomas E. and Lela (Stephens) J.; m. Griffing Bancroft, Jr., July 4, 1937. B.A., Western Mich. U., 1932. Appeared on: Broadway in Kiss and Tell, 1943-45, Eastward in Eden, 1947, The Flowering Cherry, 1950, The Trial of the Catonsville Nine, 1970; appeared in: West Coast presentations of Desk Set, 1956, Birthday Party, 1965, the Fifth of July, 1979; films Targets, 1966, Airport, 1970, Dick and Jane, 1977, Audrey Rose, 1977, Coming Home, 1978, Some Kind of Hero, 1981; appears as Miss Emily Baldwin on: TV series The Waltons, 1972—; appeared on numerous TV programs. Mem. Los Angeles adv. com. Actors Fund Am. Recipient Disting. Alumna award Western Mich. U., 1976. Mem. Acad. Motion Picture Arts and Scis., Acad. TV Arts and Scis., Actors Equity Assn. Democrat. Presbyterian. Office: care Writers and Artists 450 N Roxbury Beverly Hills CA 90210

JACKSON, MICHAEL JOHN, physiologist, educator; b. Walton-on-Thames, Eng., Apr. 12, 1938; came to U.S., 1967; s. Leslie William and Mable Maud (Rudd) J.; m. Beryl Ann Tidy, Aug. 20, 1960. B.Sc. with 1st class honors, U. London, 1963; Ph.D, U. Sheffield, Eng., 1966. Lectr. physiology U. Sheffield, Eng., 1965-67; asst. prof. George Washington U., Washington, 1967-71, asspc. prof., 1971-77, prof., 1977—; guest investigator Nat. Inst. Arthritis, Metabolism and Digestive Disease, NIH, 1975-76; cons. USPHS, NIH, 1978,81,83, VA, 1978-81. Assoc. editor, Am. Jour. Physiology; contbr. articles to profl. jours. Recipient NIAMDD Research Career Devel. award., 1972-77. Mem. Physiol. Soc. (London), Am. Physiol. Soc., Am. Gastroent. Assn., AAAS, Soc. Exptl. Biology and Medicine, Biophys. Soc. Home: 8601 Canima Spring Ct Springfield VA 22152 Office: 2300I St NW Washington DC 20037

JACKSON, MICHAEL JOSEPH, singer; b. Gary, Ind., Aug. 29, 1958; s. Joseph Walter and Katherine Esther (Scruse) J. Student pvt. sch. Lead singer, Jackson-Five (group now called Jacksons), 1969—; performer on numerous TV programs; recs. for, Epic Records; performed at: Queen Elizabeth's Silver Jubilee, May 1977; appeared in: film The Wiz, 1978; in: TV series The Jacksons, 1976-77; recs. include Off the Wall, 1979, Thriller (listed in Guiness Book of World Records as most successful LP in rec. history); narrated: E.T.: The Extra Terrestrial storybook, 1982. Recipient gold and platinum record awards. Address: care Ziffren Brittenham and Gullen 2049 Century Park E Suite 2350 Los Angeles CA 90067

JACKSON, MILES MERRILL, university dean; b. Richmond, Va., Apr. 28, 1929; s. Miles Merrill and Thelma Eugertha (Manning) J.; m. Bernice Olivia Roane, Jan. 7, 1954; children: Miles Merrill, Marsha, Muriel, Melia. Student, U. N.Mex., 1949-50; B.A. in English, Va. Union U., 1955; M.S. in L.S, Drexel U., 1956; postgrad., Ind. U., 1961, 64; Ph.D., Syracuse U., 1974. Br. librarian Free Library Phila., 1955-58; acting librarian C.P. Huntington Meml. Library, Hampton (Va.) Inst., 1958-59, librarian, 1959-63, asst. prof. library sci., 1958-62; territorial librarian Am. Samoa, 1962-64; chief librarian Trevor Arnett Library, Atlanta U., 1964-69; also lectr. Sch. Library Sci.; asso. prof. State U. N.Y., Geneseo, 1969-75; prof. U. Hawaii, 1975—; Fulbright lectr. U. Tehran, Iran, 1968, 69; library cons., Fiji, Samoa, Papua New Guinea, Micronesia. Editor: A Bibliography of Materials on Negro History and Culture for Young People, 1968, Comparative and International Librarianship, 1971, International Handbook of Contemporary Developments in Librarianship; founder, editor: Pacific Info. and Library Services Newsletter; contbr. articles to profl. jours.; Book reviewer. Served with USNR, 1945-48. Research grantee Am. Philos. Soc., 1966; Council on Library Resources fellow, 1970; Harold Lancour fgn. travel awardee Beta Phi Mu, 1976. Mem. ALA, Coll. Lang. Assn. (hon. mention poetry 1954, 2d prize award short story 1955). Democrat. Office: Grad Sch Library Studies U Hawaii Honolulu HI 96822

JACKSON, MILTON (BAGS JACKSON), jazz musician; b. Detroit, Jan. 1, 1923. Studied music, Mich. State U. Faculty Sch. of Jazz,

Lenox, Mass., 1957. With, Dizzie Gillespie, N.Y.C., 1945, piano and vibraharp, 1950-52; with, Howard McGhee, Tadd Dameron, Thelonious Monk, Woody Herman Band, 1949-50, Modern Jazz Quartet, 1953-74; on tour, Europe, 1957-58, concert, Town Hall, N.Y.C., 1958 (Recipient new star award Esquire mag. 1947), Town Hall, N.Y.C. (numerous Down Beat mag. awards.); Recordings include Plenty, Plenty Soul Ballads in Blues, Jacksonville, Opus de Jazz, New Sounds in Modern Music, Modern Jazz Quartet, Milt Jackson, Bags & Flute, Bags & Trane, 1961, Ballad Artistry, Big Band Bags, Complete Milt Jackson, Opus de Funk, Goodbye, Olinga, Sunflower, Impulse Years, Jazz 'n Samba, Milt Jackson Quintet, Statements, 1962, Big Four '75, Feelings, Live at the Museum of Modern Art, That's the Way, Soul Believer, 1978 *

JACKSON, NORMAN BRADBURY, temporary services executive; b. Detroit, Aug. 23, 1922; s. Fred and Ann (Bradbury) J.; m. Elizabeth May Christa, Mar. 3, 1945; children: Norman B., Gary Steven, Donald Edward, Thomas Frederich. B.A., Highland Park Jr. Coll., 1942; postgrad., U. Mich., 1947-49, U. Detroit, 1949-52. Salesman A.B. Dick Co., Detroit, 1946-49; dist. mgr. Gen. Motors, Detroit, 1950-57; sr. v.p. Kelly Services, Troy, Mich., 1958—. Bd. dirs. Arthritis Assn. Mich., 1970-80. Lt. (j.g.) USNR, 1943-46. Decorated Air medal. Republican. Clubs: Detroit Athletic; Birmingham Country (past bd. dirs.). Home: 774 Brookwood Walke Bloomfield Hills MI 48013 Office: Kelly Services 999 Big Beaver Rd Troy MI 48084

JACKSON, NYLE M., government agency administrator; b. Bradleyville, Mo., Mar. 27, 1914; s. James Richard and Emma (Huntsman) J.; m. Elaine Hutcheson, Sept. 4, 1938. B.A., Westminster Coll., 1935. Advt. mgr. for daily and weekly newspapers, Seymour, Ind., 1938-41; exec. sec. Rep. Earl Wilson of Ind., 1941-53; adminstrv. asst. Sen. William E. Jenner of Ind., 1953-59; spl. staff mem. for Sen. Homer E. Capehart of Ind., 1959; legislative asst. to Sen. Thruston B. Morton; chmn. Republican Nat. Com., 1959; exec. asst. to postmaster gen., 1959-61, asst. to exec. asst., 1961-63; asst. dir. customer relations div. Post Office Dept., Washington, 1963-68, exec. asst. to asst. postmaster gen., 1969; asst. to dep. counsel to Pres., White House Staff, 1969-70; mng. dir. ICC, Washington, 1970—. Del.-observer Intergovtl. Commn. European Migration, 1957; Asst. sgt.-at-arms Rep. Nat. Conv., 1956. Served to lt. USNR, World War II. Recipient Alumni Achievement award Westminster Coll., 1972. Mem. Am. Legion, VFW, Congl. Secs. Club, Orgn. Cabinet Assts., Senate Assts. Group, Internat. Platform Assn., Mil. Order of Carabao. Baptist. Club: Capitol Hill (Washington). Home: 4429 35th St NW Washington DC 20008 351 Boca Ciega Point Blvd N Madeira Beach FL 33708 Office: ICC Washington DC 20423

JACKSON, PATRICK JOHN, public relations executive; b. Grand Rapids, Mich., Sept. 5, 1932; s. Ira William and Edythe Jane (Minnema) J.; m. Isobel W. Parke, Oct. 4, 1974; children: Richard, Kevin, Pamela, Roberta, Jennie. Student, Kenyon Coll., 1950-53; M.Ed., Antioch U., 1979. Sports publicity dir. Kenyon Coll., 1951-52; reporter Grand Rapids Press, 1953-54; advt. dir. Beckley (W.Va.) newspapers Corp., 1954-55; v.p. Jackson, King & Griffith, Waynesboro, Va., 1956-59; account exec. Ruder & Finn, N.Y.C., 1958; sr. counsel, co-founder Jackson, Jackson & Wagner, Exeter, N.H., 1959—; editor PR Reporter, 1976—, Channels, 1982—; adj. prof. public relations Boston U. Sch. Public Communication, 1973-82. Editor: N.H. Conservation Directory, 1970—. Chmn. Strafford-Rockingham Regional Council, 1977-78; chmn. Southeastern N.H. Regional Planning Commn., 1976-77; mem. Gov.'s Com. on N.H. Future, 1978-79; co-founder, legis. agt. Environ. Coalition, 1972—; mem. Gov.'s Com. on Forest Resources, 1981-82; founder, lobbyist Statewide Program of Action to Conserve our Environment, 1968—; founder Environ. Found., 1975; dir. Granite State Public Radio; mng. trustee Richmond Realty Trust, 1973-82; trustee Antioch U., 1981—; chmn. N.H. Agr. Task Force; mem. steering com. First Amendment Congress, 1980—; convenor N.Am. Public Relations Council, 1980—; founder, chmn. Epping Planning Bd., 1967-72; pres. Seacoast Region Assn., 1978-82; bd. dirs. N.H. Social Welfare Council, 1982—. Recipient Communicator of Yr. award Glassboro State U., 1980. Mem. Public Relations Soc. Am. (pres. New Eng. chpt. 1974-75, nat. dir. 1976-77, nat. sec. 1978, nat. pres. elect 1979, pres. 1980, Lincoln award for public service 1978), Am. Assn. Pub. Opinion Research. Quaker. Home: Tributary Farm Epping NH 03042 Office: Dudley House 14 Front St Exeter NH 03833 *Despite all the fears that perception, not reality, is the watchword today, I have found unequivocably that this is not so. What we do speaks so loudly no one can even hear what we say.*

JACKSON, PETER VORIOUS, III, association executive; b. Butte, Mont., May 18, 1927; s. Peter V. and Besse Portia (McLean) J.; m. Johneta Pierce, Apr. 29, 1949; children: Ward, Michelle (Mrs. Jerry Vanhour), Johnathan. Student, Mont. State Coll., 1946-49. Wheat and cattle rancher, 1949—; mem. Mont. Ho. of Reps., 1971-72; chief Grass Conservation bur. Mont. Dept. Natural Resources, Helena, 1972-74; supr. Conservation Dist. Madison County, Ennis, Mont., from 1957; past exec. dir. Western Environ. Trade Assn., Helena.; exec. v.p. Soc. for Range Mgmt., Denver. Author: Montana Rangeland Resources Program, 1970. Mem. Madison County Fair Bd. Recipient Renner award Soc. Range Mgmt., 1971, Conservation award Mont. Wildlife Fedn., 1966. Mem. Nat. Assn. Conservation Dists. (dir.), Mont. Assn. Conservation Dists. (exec. v.p. 1974), Soc. Range Mgmt. (nat. pres.). Clubs: Mason, Elk. Home: Box 86 Harrison MT 59735 Office: 2301 Colonial Dr Helena MT 59601

JACKSON, PHILIP WESLEY, educator; b. Vineland, N.J., Dec. 2, 1928; s. Raymond and Estelle (Sword) J.; m. Josephine Dandrea, May 1, 1948; children: Nancy, David, Steven. B.S., N.J. State Coll., Glassboro, 1951; M.Ed., Temple U., 1952; Ph.D., Columbia U., 1954. Instr. Columbia Tchrs. Coll., summer 1954, Wayne U., 1954-55; faculty U. Chgo., 1955—, prof. edn., 1963-73, David Lee Shillinglaw Distinguished Service prof., 1973—, also dir., 1970-75, chmn. dept. edn., 1973-78, dean grad. sch. edn., 1973-75; cons. U.S. Office Edn., NSF.; Simon vis. prof. U. Manchester, Eng., 1968-69; vis. prof. Harvard U., summer 1972. Author: (with J.W. Getzels) Creativity and Intelligence, 1962, Life in Classrooms, 1968, The Teacher and the Machine, 1968; contbr. articles to profl. jours., monographs. Served with USNR, 1947-48. Recipient Disting. Alumnus award Glassboro State Coll., 1970; fellow Center Advanced Study Behavioral Scis., 1962-63, Center for Policy Study U. Chgo., 1973. Mem. Nat. Acad. Edn. (v.p. 1975-77), Social Sci. Research Council (dir.-at-large 1976-81). Home: 1357 E 56th St Chicago IL 60637

JACKSON, REGINALD MARTINEZ, baseball player; b. Wyncote, Pa., May 18, 1946; s. Martinez J.; m. Juanita. Student, Ariz. State U. Outfielder with Kansas City/Oakland Athletics, 1967-75, Balt. Orioles, 1976, N.Y. Yankees, 1977-81; outfielder, designated hitter Calif. Angels, 1982—; mem. Am. League All-Star Team, 1969, 71-75, 77-82. Author: (with Bill Libby) Reggie, 1975, (with Joel Cohen) Inside Hitting, 1975. Named Most Valuable Player Am. League, 1973, The Sporting News Major League Player of Year, 1973; Named to The Sporting News Am. League All-Star Team, 1969, 73, 75, 76, 80. Office: California Angels Anaheim Stadium 200 State College Blvd Anaheim CA 92806 *

JACKSON, REGINALD SHERMAN, public relations counselor; b. Newport, R.I., Dec. 25, 1910; s. Sherman Clinton and Gertrude (Miller) J.; m. Frances Holland, Jan. 20, 1941; 1 son, Reginald Sherman. Student, U. Toledo, 1929-34. Reporter Toledo News-Bee, 1937; pub. relations dir. Ohio N.G., 1939-40; account exec. Flournoy & Gibbs, Inc., Toledo, 1945-51, 53-63, v.p., 1963-75, treas., 1967-75; pub. relations dir. Atlas Tours & Travel Service, Inc., Toledo, 1975-78. Past trustee, v.p. Boys Club Toledo, Toledo-Lucas County Pub. Library; moderator Park Congl. Ch., 1959. Served from 1st lt. to lt. col. AUS, 1940-46; lt. col. Res., 1951-60. Decorated Bronze Star with 2 oak leaf clusters. Mem. Res. Officers Assn. (pres. Toledo 1949), Am. Legion (Toledo comdr. 1949-50), Pub. Relations Soc. Am. (pres. N.W. Ohio chpt. 1963, dir., nat. treas. 1972), Toledo Area C. of C. (trustee 1973-76), Toledo Council World Affairs (charter), Beta Gamma Sigma (hon.), Alpha Phi Gamma. Republican. Clubs: Masons, Rotary, U. Toledo Tower, Toledo, Toledo Press. Home: 3707 Richlawn Dr Toledo OH 43614

JACKSON, RICHARD GEORGE, advertising agency executive; b. N.Y.C., Apr. 28, 1940; s. Nicholas and Mary (Vaselina) J.; m. Sandra Thelma LeMere, June 4, 1966; children: Catherine Lynn, Patricia Anne. B.A., Coll. City N.Y., 1961. Creative supr. Wells Rich Greene Inc. (Advt.), N.Y.C., 1967-68; exec. v.p., creative dir. Calderhead Jackson Inc., N.Y.C., 1968-74, Gardner Advt., N.Y.C., St. Louis, 1975; exec. v.p. Morgan, Reitzfeld & Jackson, Inc., N.Y.C., 1976-77; pres., chief exec. officer Altschiller, Reitzfeld & Jackson, N.Y.C., 1977—; chief exec. officer Altschiller, Reitzfeld, Jackson & Solin/NCK, Inc., N.Y.C., 1981-82; pres., chief exec. officer Dick Jackson Inc., N.Y.C., 1982. Recipient gold, silver keys Copywriter's Club, 1970; Distinctive Merit awards Art Dirs. Show, 1970; Andy award, 1970, 78. Mem. Copy Club N.Y. (v.p. 1974-75, pres. 1976-77), N.Y. Advt. Club, One Show (dir.). Home: 35 E 85th St New York NY 10028

JACKSON, RICHARD MONTGOMERY, former airline executive; b. Jacksonville, Fla., Dec. 9, 1920; s. William Kenneth and Katharine (Mitchell) J.; m. Martha Eustis Turner, Sept. 12, 1942; children: Richard Montgomery, Susanne (Mrs. Jeffrey Miller), William Mitchell. B.Sc., Harvard, 1942. With Am. Airlines, Inc., 1945-58; asso. L.S. Rockefeller, 1958-60; with Seaboard World Airlines, Inc., Jamaica, N.Y., 1960-80, pres., chmn. bd., 1960-80; chmn. exec. com. Flying Tiger Line, Jamaica, N.Y., 1980-81; dir. Burlington No. Airfreight, Norstar Bank of Long Island. Trustee Village of Lloyd Harbor, N.Y., 1960-68; pres. Lloyd Harbor Sch. Bd., 1957-58; chmn. African WildlifeFound.; bd. govs. Huntington (N.Y.) Hosp., 1960-74. Served to lt. comdr. USNR, World War II. Clubs: Anglers of N.Y. (N.Y.); Island (Hobe Sound, Fla.); Wings, Explorers (N.Y.C.). Home: 273 Southdown Rd Lloyd Harbor Huntington NY 11743

JACKSON, ROBERT LAWRENCE, physician, educator; b. Clare, Mich., Nov. 30, 1909; s. Lawrence W. and Josephine L. (Cour) J.; m. Sara Elizabeth Soisson, Sept. 6, 1937; children—Ann, Mary, Sara, Kathryn, Margaret, Martha, Robert. B.S., U. Notre Dame, 1930; M.D., U. Mich., 1934. Intern U. Iowa, 1934-35, resident, 1935-37, instr., 1937-41, asso., 1941-43, asst. prof., 1943-46, asso. prof., 1946-51, prof. pediatrics, 1951-54; resident U. Rochester, 1936-37; prof., chmn. dept. pediatrics U. Mo., Columbia, 1954-79, prof. emeritus, 1979—; prof. pediatrics U. Kansas City, Kans., 1980—; guest lectr. Internat. Pediatric Congress, Zurich, Switzerland, 1950, Pan Am. Pediatric Congress, Sao Paulo, Brazil, 1954; vis. prof. pediatrics Am. U. Beirut, 1962-63; mem. NRC; cons. NIH. Mem. Am. Council Rheumatic Fever, Am. Diabetes Assn. (Banting medal 1969), AMA, Am. Pediatric Soc., Soc. Pediatric Research, Am. Acad. Pediatrics, Central Soc. Clin. Research. Am. Inst. Nutrition, Sigma Xi, Alpha Omega Alpha. Home: 4613 W 113 Terr Leawood KS 66211

JACKSON, ROBERT STREET, physician, public health ofcl.; b. N.Y.C., Mar. 27, 1943; m. Jayne Gosnell, Mar. 22, 1969; children—Jason Street, Jennifer Deane. B.A., Wesleyan U., 1964; M.D., Columbia U., 1968. Diplomate: Am. Bd. Pediatrics. Intern U. Va. Hosp., Charlottesville, 1968-69, sr. resident, 1970-71; resident Babies Hosp., N.Y.C., 1969-70; practice medicine specializing in preventive medicine and public health, 1971—; dir. Bur. Epidemiology, Va. State Dept. Health, 1973-76; acting dir. Bur. Preventive Med. Services, 1974-76, asst. commr. health, 1976-78, asst. state health commr., 1978-79; dir. Office of Health Protection and Environ. Mgmt., 1978-79; clin. asst. prof. U. Va. Sch. Medicine, 1974-79; commr. S.C. Dept. Health and Environ. Control, Columbia, 1979—; adj. prof. Sch. Public Health, U. S.C., 1979—, clin. prof. dept. preventive medicine and community health, 1979—. Contbr. chpts. on immunization to med. books; contbr. articles on infectious diseases to profl. jours. Served with Epidemic Intelligence Service USPHS, 1971-73. Recipient A. Clarke Slaymaker award Va. Environ. Health Assn., 1977, Outstanding Public Health Service award Va. Public Health Assn., 1976; Charles G. Jordan award So. br. Am. Public Health Assn., 1977. Mem. Am. Public Health Assn., Assn. State and Territorial Health Ofcls., Soc. Occupational and Environ. Health, Am. Acad. Pediatricians, S.C. Pediatric Soc., S.C. Med. Assn., Columbia Med. Soc. Methodist. Home: 5 Gill Creek Ct Columbia SC 29206 Office: 2600 Bull St Columbia SC 29201

JACKSON, ROY, educator; b. Manchester, Eng., Oct. 6, 1931; came to U.S., 1968; s. Harold and Ellen (Roscoe) J.; m. Susan Margaret Birch, Jan. 12, 1957; children: Fiona Susan, Andrew John. B.A., Cambridge (Eng.) U., 1954, M.A., 1959; D.Sc., U. Edinburgh, 1968. Engr. Imperial Chem. Industries, Billingham, Eng., 1955-61; lectr. U. Edinburgh, 1961-64, reader, 1964-68; prof. Rice U., Houston, 1968-73, A.J. Hartsook prof. chem. engring., 1973-77, chmn. chem. engring., 1976-77; prof. U. Houston, 1977-82, Princeton U., 1982—; cons. Shell Devel. Co., 1969—. Asso. editor: Jour. Optimization Theory and Applications; Contbr. articles profl. jours. Served with RAF, 1949-51. Mem. Am. Inst. Chem. Engrs., Instn. Chem. Engrs. (London), Sigma Xi, Tau Beta Pi. Home: 55 College Rd W Princeton NJ 08540

JACKSON, R(OY) GRAHAM, architect; b. Sherman, Tex., July 1, 1913; s. Watt J. and Lilly Thompson (Graham) J.; m. Reba Martin, Jan. 6, 1940 (dec. Oct. 1967); m. Violet Stephen Lawrence, May 1, 1971. B.S. in Architecture, Rice U., 1935. With R. Graham Jackson (architect), 1936-45; partner Jackson & Dill (architects), Houston, 1946-53, Wirtz, Calhoun, Tungate & Jackson (architects), 1953-65, Calhoun, Tungate & Jackson (architects), 1965-75, Calhoun, Tungate, Jackson & Dill, 1975-82, CTJ&D, 1983—; asst. prof. architecture U. Houston, part time 1947-51; vis. lectr., critic Rice U., 1963-67; mem. panel arbitrators Am. Arbitration Assn. Archtl. works include design Lyndon B. Johnson Spacecraft Center, NASA, Houston, Willford Hall Hosp, Lackland AFB, Tex., Ryon Engring. Bldg., Rice U, Houston, Hankammer Sch. Bus., Baylor U, communications bldg. Tex. Tech. U, Darnall Army Hosp, Ft. Hood, Tex., Burleson acad. quadrangle Baylor U, Waco, Tex., Bergstrom AFB Hosp, Austin, Tex., library and performing arts bldgs. Sam Houston State U, Huntsville, Tex., 2d Bapt. Ch, Houston, Vets. Hosp, Temple, Tex., Coll. Tech., U. Houston, master plan Buckner Children's Village, Beaumont, Tex., Westbury Bapt. Ch, Houston. Mem. founding com. Houston Baptist U.; mem. Rice U. Fund Council, Houston Mus. Fine Arts, Friends of Bayou Bend, Houston Symphony Soc. Fellow Constrn. Specifications Inst. (pres. Houston chpt. 1958-59, region dir. 1961-64, chmn. conv. program com. 1965), AIA (treas. Houston chpt. 1950, pres. 1959, mem. nat. adminstrv. office practice com. 1951-53, 67-73, 78-81); mem. Am. Mgmt. Assn., Am. Arbitration Assn. (panel of arbiters), Rice U. Alumni, Rice U. Assos., Houston Baptist U. Alumni Assn. (hon.), Houston C. of C. (edn. com. 1950-53). Baptist (deacon). Clubs: Houston, Rice U. Faculty. Home: 716 Chimney Rock Houston TX 77056 Office: 7011 Southwest Freeway Houston TX 77074 *I have always wanted to leave to succeeding generations a better world in which to live. Architecture as a profession has offered for me a wonderfully exciting opportunity to accomplish this through design of institutions for learning, healing and worship.*

JACKSON, ROY P(ETER), corporation executive; b. San Francisco, Nov. 19, 1919; m. Charlotte L.; children: Roy Peter, David M. A.B., Stanford U., 1941; student exec. devel. program, UCLA, 1957-58. Chief analytical engr. Northrop Corp., Hawthorne, Calif., 1953-57, v.p. and asst. gen. mgr. Space Labs., 1962-66, v.p., asst. gen. mgr. Aircraft, 1966-70, corp. v.p. program mgmt., 1973-80, v.p., gen. mgr., 1980-83, sr. v.p. ops., Century City, Calif., 1983—; assoc. adminstr. NASA, Washington, 1970-73. Scout exec. Boy Scouts Am., Los Angeles, 1981. Fellow AIAA; mem. Calif. Mfg. Assn. (bd. dirs. 1983), Nat. Security Industry Assn. (trustee 1983), Stanford Alumni Assn. (pres. 1964). Office: Northrop Corp 1800 Century Park E Los Angeles CA 90277

JACKSON, RUDOLPH ELLSWORTH, pediatrician, educator; b. Richmond, Va., May 31, 1935; s. Samuel and Jennie Sue (Williams) J.; m. Janice Diane Ayer, Dec. 26, 1980; children by previous marriage: Kimberley, Rudolph Ellsworth, Kelley. B.S., Morehouse Coll., Atlanta, 1957; M.D., Meharry Med. Coll., 1961. Asst. in hematology St. Jude Children's Research Hosp., Memphis, 1969-72; asst. prof. pediatrics Sch. Medicine, U. Tenn., Memphis, 1969-72; program coordinator Nat. Sickle Cell Disease Program, HEW; chief sickle cell disease br. Nat. Heart, Lung, Blood Inst.; NIH, Bethesda, Md., 1972-76; assoc. prof. pediatrics and child health, assoc. prof. oncology Howard U. Hosp., Washington, 1976-79; prof., chmn. dept. pediatrics Meharry Med. Coll., Nashville, 1979—; cons., mem. research coms. Nat. Heart, Lung, Blood Inst., Nat. Cancer Inst., NIH.; Chmn. health task force com. for lead elimination, Washington, 1978-79; mem. sickle cell disease adv. com. to Sec. HEW, 1971-72. Contbr. articles to profl. publs. Served with USN, 1962-67. Mem. AMA, Am. Acad. Pediatrics, Nat. Med. Assn., Assn. Med. Sch. Pediatric Dept. Chairmen, Sigma Xi, Alpha Omega Alpha. Democrat. *

JACKSON, RUTH AMELIA, museum curator; b. Paterson, N.J., June 28, 1912; d. Gerald Breck and Mary (Mackid) J. With Montreal Mus. Fine Arts, 1956—, registrar, 1959-78, curator decorative arts, 1972-80, hon. councillor, bd. govs., archival cons., 1980—. Author: Canada's Heritage of Silver, 1976. Mem. Can. Guild Crafts (dir.). Office: Montreal Mus Fine Arts 3500 ave du Musee Montreal PQ H3G 1K3 Canada

JACKSON, SARAH JEANETTE, sculptor, graphic artist, xerographer, bookmaker; b. Detroit, Nov. 13, 1924; emigrated to Can., 1956, naturalized, 1977; d. Louis and Rose (Blumstein) Sherman; m. Anthony Jackson, Aug., 1949; children: Timothy Lynn, Melanie Naomie. B.A., Wayne State U., 1942, M.A., 1944. Artist in residence Tech. U. N.S.; lectr. in field. Contbr. articles, reprints to newspapers, mags.; Subject of: film Sarah Jackson, Halifax, 1980; One-man shows, Apollinaire Gallery, London, Eng., 1951, New Vision Gallery, London, 1956, Arts Club, Montreal, Que., Can., Montreal Mus., 1957, Robertson Galleries, Ottawa, Ont., Can., 1959, Mt. St. Vincent U., Halifax, N.S., Can., 1967, 68, 81, Galerie Libre, Montreal, 1964, 66, 68, Zwicker's Gallery, Halifax, 1971, Gallery Danielli, Toronto, Ont., Can., 1974, 75, Gallerie Scollard, Toronto, 1976, Art Gallery, Tech. U. N.S., Coll., Halifax, Pa. State U., 1978, Gadatsy Gallery, Toronto, 1979, Pictura Mus., Sweden, 1984, numerous others, group shows include, Roberts Gallery, Toronto, 1959-62, Here and Now Gallery, Toronto, Dalhousie Art Gallery, 1969, Inventions Gallery, Halifax, Mt. St. Vincent U., Halifax, 1975, 81, Gadatsy Gallery, Toronto, 1975, 76-77, 78, Gallery Danielli, Toronto, 1975, St. Lawrence Center, Toronto, 1978, Loranger Gallery, Toronto, Win Gallery, Toronto, 1979, Mirrorings, women artists touring exhbn., Can., numerous others; represented in permanent collections, Hirshhorn Museum and Sculpture Gardens, Washington, Smithsonian Instn., Nat. Gallery Can., Montreal Mus. Fine Arts, Montreal Mus. Contemporary Art, Art Gallery Ont., McGill U., Thomas More Inst., Montreal, N.S. Dept. Recreation, Xerox Corp. Can., Toronto, also pvt. collections. Mem. Canadian Artists Representation. Home: 1411 Edward St Halifax NS B3H 3H5 Canada Office: Tech U NS PO Box 1000 Halifax NS B3J 2X4 Canada *Making art in book form has been preoccupying me since "79 because it has become an immediate means of making statements. I can control the final effects of images and contents which becomes a very personal way of communication in a human statement through art.*

JACKSON, STEPHEN KEITH, forest products corporation executive; b. Ellsworth, Kans., Dec. 3, 1939; s. Hobart and Helen Fransis (Herrick) J.; m. Martha Grace Rheem, June 9, 1961 (div. 1973); children: Michael, Mark; m. 2d Kathleen Ann Gillespie, July 1948; 1 son, Matthew. B.S., Oreg. State U., 1961. Account supr. McCann & Erickson, Portland, Oreg., 1963-72; mgr. advt. and sales promotion Pulp, Paper and Chem. div. Ga.-Pacific, Portland, 1972, gen. mktg. mgr. dist. div., 1972-75; sr. v.p., gen. mgr. McCann-Erickson, Portland, 1975-77; v.p. advt. and pub. relations Ga.-Pacific, Atlanta, 1977-83, v.p. bldg. products communication, 1983—; bd. dirs. Am. Forest Inst., 1980—, Am. Wood Council, 1980—; chmn. Forest Products Industries Communications Council, 1981-83. Bd. dirs. Atlanta Jr. Achievement, 1983. Served to 1st lt. U.S. Army, 1961-63. Republican. Clubs: Multnoma Athletic (Portland); Capitol City (Atlanta). Office: Ga-Pacific Corp 133 Peachtree St NE Atlanta GA 30303

JACKSON, THEODORE MARSHALL, oil company executive; b. Beaumont, Tex., Oct. 18, 1928; s. Robert and Mary Louise (Walter) J.; m. Maria Pierracou-Dobrowolska Countess de Wernicki de Vladis la Goda, June 19, 1954; 1 son, Mark Andrew. B.B.A. in Engring, U. Tex., Austin, 1951. Vice pres., sec.-treas. Purvin & Gertz, Inc., Dallas, 1955-71; v.p. treasury and strategic planning New Eng. Petroleum Corp., N.Y.C., 1971-75; v.p. fin. Crown Central Petroleum Corp., Balt., 1975—. Served to lt. USNR, 1952-55. Mem. Fin. Execs. Inst., Am. Mgmt. Assn., Am. Petroleum Inst., Beta Gamma Sigma, Delta Tau Delta. Republican. Methodist. Home: 8 Wythe Ct Glen Arm MD 21057 Office: 1 N Charles St Baltimore MD 21201

JACKSON, THOMAS SEARING, lawyer; b. Washington, Dec. 1, 1909; s. Thomas and Jeannette (Hutchins) J.; m. Elizabeth Jacobs, Nov. 29, 1933; children—Thomas Penfield, Jeffrey Andrew. A.B., George Washington U., 1933, LL.B., 1935. Bar: D.C. bar 1935, Md. bar 1941, U.S. Supreme Ct. bar 1949. With Dept. Commerce, U.S. Forest Service, 1927-35; of counsel Jackson & Campbell (and predecessors), Washington, 1935—. Mem. Bd. Edn. Montgomery County, Md., 1950-52, pres., 1952. Fellow Am. Coll. Trial Lawyers (bd. regents 1964-68, pres. found. 1969-75), Am. Bar Found.; mem. Am. Bar Assn., Am. Judicature Soc. (dir. 1970-71), Bar Assn. D.C. (pres. 1962-63). Clubs: Rehoboth Beach (Del.); Barristers, Lawyers, Chevy Chase (Washington). Home: PO Box 316 Bethany Beach DE 19930 Apt C-051 7200 3d Ave Sykesville MD 21784 Office: 1120 20th St NW Washington DC 20036

JACKSON, VICTOR LOUIS, naturalist; b. Thanh-Hoa, Tonkin, Viet Nam, July 2, 1933; s. Richmond Merrill and Hazel Irene (Peebles) J.; m. Lois Annetta Scott, Apr. 4, 1959; children: Nathan Ray, Sharon Ruth, Jackson Maxwell. B.S., Wheaton Coll., (Ill.), 1955. Sub-dist. ranger Natchez Trace Pkwy., Collinwood, Tenn., 1958-61; park naturalist Gt. Smoky Mountains Nat. Park, Gatlinburg, Tenn., 1961-63; chief park naturalist Organ Pipe Cactus Nat. Monument, Ajo., Ariz., 1963-66; asst. chief naturalist Grand Teton Nat. Park, Moose, Wyo., 1966-73; chief park naturalist Zion Nat. Park, Springdale, Utah, 1973—; assn. coordinator Zion Natural History Assn., Springdale, 1973—. Author, photographer: Discover Zion, 1978; editor: Plants of Zion, 1976, Zion Adventure Guide, 1978. Bd. dirs. So. Utah Folklife Festival, 1976—. Served to 1st lt. Signal Corps U.S. Army, 1955-57. Named Outstanding Interpreter of Yr. in Nat. Park Service Nat. Parks and Conservation Assn., 1982; recipient Freeman Tilden award, 1982. Republican. Baptist. Office: Zion National Park Utah State Route 9 Springdale UT 84767

JACKSON, WALTER HARRY, editor; b. Paterson, N.J., July 9, 1948; s. Walter Harry and Dorothy Edith (Walters) J. B.A., Franklin Pierce Coll., 1971. Newspaper reporter, asso. editor Matzner Publs., West Milford, N.J., 1971-72, mng. editor, Wayne, N.J., 1972-73, True Detective mag., N.Y.C., 1973-80; actor, model Filor Models, Inc., N.Y.C., 1980—; asst. mng. editor Show Bus. Newspaper, N.Y.C., 1981-81; assoc. editor Inst. Internat. Edn., N.Y.C., 1981—. Mem. N.J. Press Assn. Home: 9 Cottonwood Ct Stockholm NJ 07460 Office: 809 UN Plaza New York NY 10036

JACKSON, WILLIAM CALHOUN, JR. (DECKER JACKSON), investment banker; b. Celeste, Tex., Mar. 20, 1907; m. Sally Carolyn Harrington, May 28, 1928. Registered pharmacist, Danforth Sch. Pharmacy, 1928. Mem. comml. banking dept. First Nat. Bank, Plano, Tex., 1929-30; dir., chmn. bd. First Southwest Co., Dallas, 1946—; pres., dir. Antelope Oil Corp., 1950—, Provident Oil Co., 1954—. Chmn. bd. Municipal Adv. Council, Tex., 1956-57. Served as lt. comdr. USNR, 1945. Mem. Investment Bankers Assn. Am. (gov. 1954-55, v.p. 1955-57, pres. 1957-58). Clubs: Dallas, Dallas Country, Northwood, City, Chaparral (Dallas). Home: 5122 Shadywood Lane Dallas TX 75209 Office: Mercantile Dallas Bldg: Dallas TX 75201

JACKSON, WILLIAM DAVID, research executive; b. Edinburgh, Scotland, May 20, 1927; came to U.S., 1955, naturalized, 1968; s. Joseph and Margaret (Johnston) J.; children—Margaret Eleanor, David Foster. B.Sc., U. Glasgow, Scotland, 1947, Ph.D., 1960; postgrad., U. Strathclyde, Glasgow, 1948. Apprentice English Electric Co., Stafford, 1945-47; research asst. elec. engring. dept. U. Strathclyde, Glasgow, 1948-51; lectr. elec. engring. U. Manchester, Eng., 1951-55, 57-58; vis. lectr. dept. elec. engring. Mass. Inst. Tech., 1955-57, asst. prof., 1958-62, asso. prof., 1962-66, lectr. elec. engring., 1968-73; vis. prof. Tech. U., Berlin, Germany, 1966; prof. elec. engring., dept. energy engring. U. Ill., Chgo., 1966-67; prin. research scientist, dir. tech. edn. Avco-Everett Research Lab., Everett, Mass., 1967-72; prof. elec. engring. U. Tenn. Space Inst., Tullahoma, 1972-73; mgr. Electric Power Research Inst., Palo Alto, Calif., 1973-74; mgr. office coal research Interior Dept., Washington, 1974-75; dir. magnetohydrodynamic div. ERDA, Washington, 1975-77; dir. tech. analysis div. Office Energy Research, Dept. Energy, Washington, 1977-79; pres. Energy Cons., Inc., 1979—, HMJ Corp., 1982—; professorial lectr. George Washington U., 1979—; cons. numerous indsl. firms and govt. agys., 1948—; chmn. internat. magnetohydrodynamic liaison group Internat. Atomic Energy Agy./UNESCO, 1966—, chmn., 1969-74; coordinator coop. program magnetohydrodynamic power generation, U.S.-USSR, 1974-79, mem. numerous govt. and internat. coms. and panels. Editor: Electricity From MHD, 1968; editorial bd.: Internat. Jour. Elec. Engring. Edn, 1962-70. U.K. Fulbright scholar, 1955-57. Fellow Instn. Elec. Engrs. (U.K.) (past com. sec., chmn.), IEEE (sr.; sec.-treas. profl. group biomed. electronics Boston sect. 1962-63, energy devel. subcom. 1973—, congl. fellow 1984); mem. AIAA, AAUP, Am. Phys. Soc., AAAS, ASME (past chmn. energetics div.), Am. Soc. Engring. Edn., Sigma Xi. Home and office: 3509 McKinley St NW Washington DC 20015

JACKSON, WILLIAM ELDRED, lawyer; b. Jamestown, N.Y., July 19, 1919; s. Robert Houghwout and Irene Alice (Gerhardt) J.; m. Nancy Dabney Roosevelt, Sept. 24, 1944; children—Miranda, Melissa, Melanie, Melinda, Marina. B.A., Yale U., 1941; LL.B., Harvard U., 1944. Bar: N.Y. bar 1944, U.S. Supreme Ct. bar 1952, D.C. bar 1960. Asso. firm Milbank, Tweed, Hadley & McCloy, N.Y.C., 1947-54, partner, 1954—. Served to lt. (j.g.) USNR, 1944-46. Mem. Am. Coll. Trial Lawyers, Am. Soc. Internat. Law, Assn. Bar City N.Y. (sec. 1953-54), N.Y. State Bar Assn., Am. Bar Assn., Fed. Bar Council, Am. Judicature Soc., Council Fgn. Relations. Democrat. Episcopalian. Clubs: Century, Downtown, Pilgrims, River. On staff Nuremburg trials. Home: 530 E 87th St New York NY 10028 also Turkey Ln Cold Spring Harbor LI NY 11724 Office: One Chase Manhattan Plaza New York NY 10005

JACKSON, WILLIAM LLOYD, consumer products company executive; b. Lawrence, Mich., Oct. 15, 1927; s. C. Paul and Orpha B. (Cook) J.; m. Janet Marie Ingling, Aug. 27, 1949; children: Edward L., Charles P., Bruce A. B.B.A., U. Mich., 1950, M.B.A., 1951. Various mktg. positions Jell-O div. Gen. Foods Corp., White Plains, N.Y., 1953-66; v.p. mktg. to group v.p., dir. Chesebrough-Pond's Inc., Greenwich, Conn., 1967-78; pres. Wilkinson Match N.A., Greenwich, 1978-80, Duracell N. Am., Bethel, Conn., 1980-82, Duracell Inc., Bethel, 1982—; group v.p. Dart & Kraft Inc., Northbrook, Ill., 1982—; dir. Binney & Smith Inc., Easton, Pa. Served as cpl. U.S. Army, 1946-47; Japan. Office: Duracell Inc Berkshire Indsl Park Bethel CT 06801

JACKSON, WILLIAM MACLEOD, management consultant; b. New Rochelle, N.Y., Apr. 18, 1926; s. William and Florence (MacLeod) J.; m. Mary Stuart Otto, June 12, 1948; children: Stuart MacLeod, Frederick Elliott, Allen Proctor, Susan Elizabeth. Student, M.I.T., 1943-45; B.S., Princeton U., 1947. With Bonney Forge div. Bonney Forge & Foundry, Inc., Allentown, Pa., 1948-69, v.p., 1958-66, pres., 1966-69, also dir.; pres. Bonney Forge & Foundry (group of 8 divs., Gulf & Western Indsl. Products Co.), Allentown, 1969-74; v.p. Gulf & Western Energy Products Group, 1974-75; pres. William M. Jackson Assos., Inc., corp. acquisition cons., 1976—; chmn. bd., dir. Bonney Forge Internat., Ltd., Laird Forge Ltd., Barr Thompson & Co., Scotland, Jader, SrL, Bonney Forge Italia, Milan, 1962-69; dir. Bonney Forge Australia (Pty), Sidney, 1964-69; served Am. Nat. Standards Inst. com., 1958—; mem. Lehigh Valley adv. bd. Fidelity Bank, Phila., 1979-80; affiliated Corp. Finance Assocs.; mem. vice chmn. The Bus. Group. Mem., vice chmn. Allentown Comml. & Indsl. Devel. Authority, 1983—; Pres. Friends of the Library, 1966-68; pres. Allentown Public Library, 1976-80, bd. dirs., 1968-80; bd. assos. Cedar Crest Coll., 1976—, mem. exec. com., 1979-82; bd. assocs. Muhlenberg Coll., 1979—; trustee YWCA-Allentown, 1983, chmn., 1984. Served with USNR, 1944-46. Mem. ASME, Phi Gamma Delta. Presbyn. (trustee 1968-74). Clubs: Princeton (N.Y.C.); Lehigh Country (Allentown, Pa.) (tennis chmn. 1964-67, bd. govs. 1967-70. Patentee. Home: 910 N 27th St Allentown PA 18104 Office: 1425 Hamilton St Allentown PA 18102

JACKSON, WILLIAM PAUL, JR., lawyer; b. Bexar, Ala., July 7, 1938; s. William Paul and Evelyn Mabel (Goggans) J.; m. Barbara Anne Seignious, Sept. 30, 1966; children: Jennifer Anne, Susan Barrett, William Paul III. B.S. in Physics, U. Ala., 1960, J.D., 1963. Bar: Ala. 1963, D.C. 1969. Law clk. to judge Ala. Ct. Appeals, Montgomery, 1965; assoc. Bishop and Carlton, Birmingham, Ala., 1965-68, Todd, Dillon and Sullivan, Washington, 1968-70; founding ptnr. Jackson & Jessup. P.C., Washington and Arlington, Va., 1970-76; pres., sr. atty. Jackson & Jessup, P.C., Washington and Arlington, Va., 1976—; advisor Oren Harriss chair of transp. U. Ark., 1974—. Conbtr. articles to legal jours. Vice pres. McLean Hunt Homeowners Assn., Va., 1974, pres., Va., 1975-76; bd. dirs. McLean Citizens' Assn., 1976-78; pres. McLean Legal Action Fund, Inc., 1977-81. Served to 1st lt. Signal Corps U.S. Army, 1963-65. Recipient Pub. Service awards Am. Radio Relay League, 1958, Public Service awards Armed Forces Communications and Electronics Assn., 1963; Sigma Delta Kappa scholar, 1963. Mem. Birmingham Fedn. Communications, Arlington Fedn. Communications, Fed. Fedn. Communications, ABA, Ala. Bar Assn., Va. Bar Assn., D.C. Bar Assn., Transp. Lawyers Assn., Assn. Transp. Practitioners, Am. Judicature Soc., So. Traffic League (exec. sec. 1970—), Eastern Indsl. Traffic League (exec. sec. 1978—), Bench and Bar Legal Honor Soc. (pres. 1963). Presbyterian. Home: 7807 Foxhound Rd McLean VA 22101 Office: Jackson & Jessup PC 3426 N Washingto Blvd PO Box 1240 Arlington VA 22210

JACKSON, WILLIAM R., JR., steel company executive; b. 1938; married. B.S., Iowa Coll., 1959. With Pitts.-Des Moines Steel Co., Pitts., 1959—; sec., exec. v.p. Pitts.-Des Moines Steel Co, Pitts., 1982-83; pres., chief operating officer Pitts.-Des Moines Steel Co., Pitts., 1983—. Office: Pitts-Des Moines Steel Co Neville Island Pittsburgh PA 15225 *

JACKSON, WILLIAM RICHARD, steel co. exec.; b. Des Moines, May 25, 1908; s. William H. and Minnine (Long) J.; m. Lucilla Scribner, June 4, 1932; children—William Richard, Mary (Mrs. A. P. Denmark), Polly (Mrs. G.B. Townsend). Student, Ohio Wesleyan U., 1925-27; B.S. in Bus. Adminstrn, Mass. Inst. Tech., (1930). With Am. Bridge div. U.S. Steel Corp., 1930-36; with Pitts.-Des. Moines Steel Co., 1936—, sec.-treas., 1943-59, pres., 1959-71, chmn. bd., 1971—, also dir. Trustee Dollar Savs. Bank, Pitts.; Councilman Borough Sewickley Heights, Pa., 1958—; v.p., bd. dirs. Allegheny council Boy Scouts Am., 1961—. Mem. Am. Inst. Steel Constrn. Presbyn. (elder). Clubs: Duquesne (Pitts.); Allegheny Country (Sewickley). Office: Pitts-Des Moines Corp Neville Island Pittsburgh PA 15225

JACKSON, WILLIAM TURRENTINE, educator; b. Ruston, La., Apr. 5, 1915; s. Brice H. and Luther (Turrentine) J.; m. Barbara Kone, Nov. 28, 1942. A.B., Tex. Western Coll., 1935; A.M., U. Tex., 1936, Ph.D., 1940. Instr. history UCLA, 1940-41, Iowa State U., Ames, 1941-42, asst. prof., 1944-46, asso. prof., 1946-48; asst. prof. Am. history U. Chgo., 1948-51; dir. Am. civilization program, asst. prof. Am. history U. Calif. at Davis, 1951-53, asso. prof. history, 1953-56, prof., 1956—, chmn. dept., 1959-60; vis. prof. Mont. State U., 1941, univs. Mich., 1944, Wyo., 1945, 63, Minn., 1946, Tex., 1947, So. Calif., 1953, 56, Colo., 1961, San Francisco State Coll., 1962, Yale and R.I., 1964, NDEA History Inst., Chadron (Nebr.) State Coll., 1965, La. State U., 1967, U. Ariz., 1968, U. Alta., 1969, U. Nev., 1970, U. Hawaii, 1970, Colo. State U., 1973, Utah State U., 1975; Walter Prescott Webb lectr. U. Tex., 1976; U.S. Dept. State Disting. Am. Specialist lectr. in, Western Europe, 1978; USIA seminar dir. Falkenstein Seminar in Am. Studies, Germany, 1978; cons. hist. sect. Calif. Div. Parks and Recreation, Nat. Park Service, Wells Fargo Bank, U.S. Army Engrs., Tetra Tech, Inc., Teknekron, Inc., Sci. Applications, Inc.; cons. legal sect. Calif. Atty. Gen., N.Mex. State Engrs. Office; mem. Calif. Gov.'s History Commn.; dir. Nat. Endowment for Humanities Summer Seminar for Coll. Tchrs., 1976-77, 80; hist. cons. Seminar for Secondary Sch. Tchrs., 1983; adv. com. Sacramento Landmarks Commn.; Mem. coordinating bd. Calif. Water Resources Center, 1972-81; bd. dirs. Calif. Heritage Council, Calif. Council Humanities in Pub. Policy. Author: Wagon Roads West, 1942, 65 (awards Pacific Coast br. Am. Hist. Assn., Nat. Inst. Graphic Arts, N.Y.C.), When Grass Was King (Merit award Am. Assn. State and Local History 1956), Treasure Hill, 1963 (Merit award Am. Assn. State and Local History), Twenty Years on the Pacific Slope, 1965, The Enterprising Scot, 1968, Gold Rush Diary of a German Sailor, 1970, Lake Tahoe Water, 1972, Water Policy in Sacramento-San Joaquin Delta, 1977, also numerous hist. monographs and articles.; Bd. editors: Pacific Hist. Rev, 1961-64, 67-70, So. Calif. Quar, 1962—, Arizona and the West, 1968-73, Jour. San Diego History, 1975—, Red River Valley Hist. Rev. Served to ensign USNR, 1942-44. Fulbright research fellow, Scotland, 1949-50; Rockefeller Found. fellow Huntington Library, 1953; grantee Am. Philos. Soc., 1955, Social Sci. Research Council, 1956, Am. Hist. Research Center, 1955-56, NSF, 1968-73, Nat. Endowment for Humanities, 1969-70, Humanities Inst., U. Calif., 1971; Guggenheim fellow, 1957-58, 65; Huntington Library fellow, 1972; grantee Am. Council Learned Socs., 1972; recipient Disting. Teaching award Acad. Senate U. Calif. at Davis, 1973-74, Assoc. Students Disting. Teaching award, 1981. Fellow Calif. Hist. Soc.; mem. Western History Assn. (pres. 1976-77), Am. Hist. Assn. (adv. com. nat. archives 1983—), Orgn. Am. Historians (mem. com. preservation hist. sites 1960-68, mem. Pelzer award com. 1968-73, Billington Book Prize com. 1982—), AAUP, Phi Alpha Theta, Pi Sigma Alpha, Theta Xi. Democrat. Methodist. Club: Commonwealth. Home: 702 Miller Dr Davis CA 95616

JACKSON, WILLIAM VERNON, library science educator; b. Chgo., May 26, 1926; s. William Olof and Lillian (Scharenberg) J. B.A. summa cum laude, Northwestern U., 1945; M.A., Harvard U., 1948, Ph.D., 1952; M.S. in L.S, U. Ill., 1951; Diploma honoris causa, U. Central Venezuela, 1968. Tchr. York Community High Sch., Elmhurst, Ill., 1946-47; teaching fellow Harvard U., 1948-50; spl. recruit Library Congress, 1951-52; librarian, asst. prof. library sci. U. Ill., Urbana, 1952-58, asso. prof., 1958-62; asso. prof. Spanish and Portuguese U. Wis., Madion, 1963-65, faculty research fellow, summers, 1963, 64; prof. library sci., dir. internat. library information center U. Pitts., 1966-70; prof. library sci. George Peabody Coll. for Tchrs., 1970-76; prof. Spanish and Portuguese Vanderbilt U., 1970-76; prof. library sci. U. Tex. at Austin, 1976—; Vis. lectr. U. Minn. Library Sch., summers 1954-56, Columbia U. Sch. Library Service, summer 1960, Syracuse U. Sch. Library Sci., summer 1962, Simmons Coll. Sch. Library Sci., summer, 1974, 75, Coll. Librarianship, Aberystwyth, Wales, summer 1977, U. Zulia, Maracaibo, Venezuela, summer 1980, Rosary Coll. Library Sci., summers 1981-83; vis. prof. Inter-Am. Library Sch., U. Antioquia, Medellín, Colombia, 1960, 68, adviser internat. exec. council, 1961-63; cons. State Dept., 1956, 59, 61, 62, 67, 77, Regional AID Office for C. Am. and Panama, 1965-66, AID Mission to Brazil, 1967-72, AID Mission to Colombia, 1970-71, USIA, 1979, 80, OAS, 1970-71; Council Rectors Brazilian Univs., 1972; cons. research libraries N.Y. Pub. Library, 1965-70, Hispanic Found., Library Congress, Washington, 1964-65; Fulbright research scholar, France, 1956-57; Fulbright lectr. U. Córdoba (Argentina), 1958, adviser, 1970, U. San Marcos, Peru, 1962, 75; external examiner U. West Indies, Jamaica, 1974-78; cons. Bibliothèque Nationale, France, 1979, 81—. Author: Basic Library Techniques, 1955, A Handbook of American Library Resources, 1955, 2d edit., 1962, Studies in Library Resources, 1958, The Foundation Grants Program, 1959, The Libraries of the Associated Colleges of the Midwest, 1960, Aspects of Librarianship in Latin America, 1962, Library Guide for Brazilian Studies, 1964, The National Textbook Program and Libraries in Brazil, 1967, Resources of Research Libraries, 1969, Steps Toward the Future Development of a National Plan for Library Services in Colombia, 1971, Catalog of Brazilian Acquisitions of Library of Congress, 1964-74, 1977; Resources for Brazilian Studies at the Bibliothèque Nationale, 1980; Editor: U. Ill. Library Sch. Assn. News Letter, 1954-56, Assn. Coll. Research Libraries Monographs, 1961-66, Latin Am. Collections, 1974, Reference Publications in Latin American Studies, 1977—; Mem. editorial staff: Library Trends, 1958-62, Ency. Library and Information Sci, 1971—, Jour. Library History, 1976—; Contbr. articles to profl. jours. Mem. Am. (chmn. internat. relations round table 1965-66, trustee endowment funds 1977—), Ill. library assns., Assn. Am. Library Schs., Bibliog. Soc. Am., Assn. Coll. and Research Libraries, MLA, Am. Assn. Tchrs. Spanish and Portuguese, Theatre Library Assn., Conf. on Latin Am. History, Latin Am. Studies Assn., Sem. on Acquisition Latin Am. Library Materials (pres. 1977-78), Pitts. Bibliophiles, Assn. Caribbean Univ. and Research Libraries, Asociación Paceña de Bibliotecarios (hon.; La Paz, Bolivia), Phi Beta Kappa, Beta Phi Mu (pres. 1955-56), Phi Sigma Iota, Sigma Delta Pi (hon.), Phi Lambda Beta (hon.). Club: Harvard (Chgo.). Home: 196 W Kathleen Dr Park Ridge IL 60068 Office: Sch Library Sci U Tex Box 7576 Austin TX 78712

JACKSON, WILLIAM WARD, chem. co. exec.; b. Irvington, N.J., Apr. 19, 1913; s. William Henry and Edwina (Ward) J.; m. Rae M. Applegate, Jan. 1, 1943; 1 dau., Hollace D. (Mrs. Tullman). B.S. in Chem. Engring, Newark Coll. Engring., 1936. Prodn., sales positions Celanese Corp. Am. and affiliates, 1932-51; gen. mgr. indsl. chems. dept. Comml. Solvents Corp., N.Y.C., 1951-53, v.p. petrochem. div., 1953-54, v.p. mktg., 1954-72, v.p. mktg. services and purchasing, 1972-75; also dir.; v.p. IMC Chems. Group, 1975-78, corp. cons., 1978—; pres. Ward Jackson Assos., 1978—; pres., dir. Can Carb Ltd., Medicine Hat, Alta., 1975—; dir., mem. exec. com. N.W. Nitro Chem. Corp., 1959-71, Medicine Hat, Alta.; Mem. Aircraft Prodn. Bd., 1942-43; asst. to vice chmn. WPB, 1943-44, aircraft cons., 1943-44; Chmn. bd. Millburn-Short Hills chpt. ARC, 1956-59, dir., 1954-6O; bd. dirs. Animal Health Inst. Recipient Certificate of Achievement U.S. Army; Certificate of Service Dept. Commerce. Fellow Am. Inst. Chemists, Soc. Chem. Industry; mem. Am. Inst. Chem. Engrs., Mfg. Chemists Assn., Pharm. Mfg. Assn., Am. Chem. Soc., Fertilizer Inst. Sales Exec. Club, Newcomen Soc. N.Am., Am. Def. Preparedness Assn. (v.p., dir.), Inst. Food Technologists, Drug Chem. and Allied Trade Assn. (past pres., treas., dir., chmn. adv. council, exec. com.), Am. Ordnance Assn. (dir.), N.Y. Bd. Trade (past dir., exec. com.), Armed Forces Chem. Assn., past nat. dir., exec. com., v.p., past pres.). Clubs: Short Hills (N.J.); Union League, Racquet and Tennis, N.Y. Yacht, Canadian (N.Y.C.); Capitol Hill (Washington). Patentee in field. Home: 2 Brooklawn Short Hills NJ 07078 Office: 245 Park Ave New York NY 10017

JACOB, BERNARD MICHEL, architect; b. Paris, Nov. 7, 1930; U.S., 1950; s. Paul and Therese (Abase) J.; m. Rosamond Gale Tryon, Feb. 17, 1951; children: Clara, Paul. Diploma in architecture, Cooper Union, 1955; B.Arch., U. Minn., 1958. Sr. designer Ellerbe Assocs., St. Paul, 1958-63; head design Grover Diamond & Assocs., St. Paul, 1963-70; co-founder Team 70 Architects, St. Paul, 1970—, pres., 1977-83, Bernard Jacob Architects, Ltd., Mpls., 1983—; mem. constrn. panel Am. Arbitration Assn., 1973—; lectr. Sch. Architecture, U. Minn., Mpls., 1982—. Editor: Architecture Minn. Mag., Minn. Soc. Architects, 1970-80; archtl. criticism columnist, Mpls. Star and Tribune, 1980-83, Corporate Report Mag., 1983. Founding chmn. Heritage Preservation Commn., St. Paul; mem. St. Paul Planning Bd. Scholar Jerome Found., Mpls., 1980. Fellow AIA. Home: 935 Linwood Ave Saint Paul MN 55105 Office: Bernard Jacob Architects Ltd 55 S 8th St Minneapolis MN 55402

JACOB, CHARLES ELMER, political scientist, educator; b. Detroit, June 5, 1931; s. Charles Henry and Thelma (Church) J.; m. Gale Sypher, Dec. 23, 1961; children: Charles Whitney, Andrew Wylie, John Church. A.B., U. Mich., 1953, M.A., 1954; Ph.D., Cornell U., 1961. Instr. polit. sci. Vassar Coll., 1960-62, asst. prof., 1962-67; asso. prof. Rutgers U., 1967-75, prof., 1975—, chmn. dept. polit. sci., 1974-77. Author: Policy and Bureaucracy, 1966, Leadership in the New Deal, 1967, (with others) The Performance of American Government, 1972, Politics in New Jersey, 1975, 79, The Election of 1976, 1977, The Election of 1980, 1981; contbr. World Book Ency., revs. and articles to profl. jours. Served with U.S. Army, 1954-56. Mem. Am. Polit. Sci. Assn., AAUP. Lutheran. Home: 532 Bradford Ave Westfield NJ 07090 Office: Dept Political Science Rutgers Univ New Brunswick NJ 08903

JACOB, CHARLES WALDEMAR, mgmt. cons.; b. Hamilton, Ohio, Sept. 22, 1943; s. Charles W. and Nancy (Egbert) J.; m. Patricia Suzanne Charlton, June 28, 1969; children—Charles Waldermar, III, Christopher Charlton. B.A., Wesleyan U., Middletown, Conn., 1965; M.B.A., Harvard U., 1967. Mem. fin. staff Ford Motor Co., Dearborn, Mich., 1967-71; dir. fin. analysis corp. staff Rockwell Internat. Corp., El Segundo, Calif., 1971-72, asst. controller automotive ops., Troy, Mich., 1972-74; corp. controller Chemetron Corp., Chgo., 1974-77; v.p. fin., treas., dir. Flying Tiger Line, Inc., 1977-81; mng. prin. Cunningham, Jacob & Assos., Redondo Beach, Calif., 1981—; chmn. econs. and fin. council Air Transp. Assn., 1980. Mem. Fin. Execs. Inst., Econ. Club Chgo. Republican. Episcopalian. Home: 2728 The Strand Hermosa Beach CA 90254 Office: 835 Hopkins Way Suite 309 Redondo Beach CA 90277

JACOB, EMERSON DONALD, librarian; b. Canton, Ohio, Mar. 17, 1914; s. John and Cora Louise (Kneuss) J.; m. Doris Geiger, Sept. 29, 1940; 1 dau., Patricia Lou. A.B., Mt. Union Coll., 1939; B.S. in Library Sci, Western Res. U., 1942, Ph.D., 1961; M.A., Columbia, 1952; postgrad., U. Mich., 1956. Asst. librarian Mt. Union Coll., 1943-45; order librarian U. Md., 1945-48; acquisitions librarian Mich. State U., 1948-58; librarian Baldwin Wallace Coll., 1959-64, Calif. State Poly. Coll., 1964-65, N.Y. State U. Coll. at Fredonia, 1965-68, Rutgers U. at Newark, 1968-70, Capitol campus Pa. State U., Harrisburg, 1971—; Mem. librarians commn. Cleve. Commn. Higher Edn.; trustee Western N.Y. Library Resources Council. Mem. A.L.A., Am. Hist. Assn. Roman Catholic. Home: 2202 Rudy Rd Harrisburg PA 17104

JACOB, GUY ARTHUR, labor union official; b. Hull, Que., Can., Aug. 13, 1927; s. Arthur and Gabriel (Landry) J.; m. Yvette Letourneu, June 30, 1951 (div.); 1 son, Jean.; m. Fernande Fluet, Jan. 22, 1984. Student, U. Montreal. Pres. Montreal local 10107, Union of Can. Transport Employees, nat. pres., 1972—; 3d exec. v.p. Pub. Service Alliance Can., Ottawa, Ont., 1979-82, 1st exec. v.p., 1982—; dir. Que. Fedn. Labour. Office: 233 Gilmour St 11th Floor Ottawa ON K2P 0P1 Canada

JACOB, HARRY MYLES, management firm executive; b. Bloomfield, N.J., Mar. 19, 1913; s. Henry Martin and Edith (Myles) J.; m. Elsie Mary Medlicott, June 12, 1937; children: Reid M., Jere V. B.C.S., NYU, 1936. With Pogson, Peloubet & Co. (C.P.A.s), 1930-36, Inspiration Consol. Copper Co., N.Y.C., 1936-81, successively asst. sec. and treas., sec. and treas., v.p. and sec., 1936-57, dir., 1953-81, exec. v.p., 1958-59, pres., 1960-74, chmn. bd., chief exec. officer, 1973-78; dir. Lobex Mgmt. Ltd., 1981—; dir. Callahan Mining Corp. Mem. AIME, Mining and Metall. Soc. Am. Clubs: Mining, Clove Valley, Rod and Gun; Copper, Met. (N.Y.C.). Home: Box 140 RD 5 Flemington NJ 08822

JACOB, HARRY SAMUEL, physician; b. San Francisco, Apr. 6, 1933; s. Barney and Sayra Rae (Ludwig) Landsberg; m. Lila Ann Field, Jan. 23, 1954; children—Myles, Kenneth, Douglas. B.A., Reed Coll., Portland, Oreg., 1954; M.D. cum laude, Harvard U., 1958. Intern, then resident in medicine Boston City Hosp., 1958-60; fellow, instr. medicine Thorndike Lab., Harvard U. Med. Sch., 1960-65; asst. prof. medicine Tufts U. Med. Sch., 1965-68; prof. medicine, chief div. hematology U. Minn. Med. Sch., Mpls., 1968—; Bd. dirs. Children's Theatre Mpls. Author numerous papers in field; mem. editorial bds. profl. jours. Grantee NIH. Mem. Assn. Am. Physicians, Am. Soc. Clin. Investigation, Am. Fedn. Clin. Research, Central Soc. Clin. Research. Home: 30 Greenway Gables Minneapolis MN 55403 Office: Univ Minn Hosp Minneapolis MN 55455

JACOB, HENRY GEORGE, educator, mathmatician; b. New Haven, June 11, 1922; s. Henry George and Catherine (Blockhaus) J.; m. Gretchen Mary Asman, Feb. 26, 1944; children—Paula Louise, Philip Henry, Victoria Elaine. B.E., Yale, 1943, M.E., 1947, Ph.D., 1953. Mem. faculty La. State U., 1953-62; prof. math. U. Mass. at Amherst, 1962—; Vis. prof. Johns Hopkins, Balt., 1956-57, 69-70. Author: (with Duane Bailey) Linear Algebra, 1971. Served to lt. (j.g.) USNR, 1943-46. Mem. Math. Assn. Am., AAUP, Am. Math. Soc. Home: 51 Butterfield Terr Amherst MA 01002

JACOB, HERBERT, political science educator; b. Augsburg, Germany, Feb. 10, 1933; came to U.S., 1940, naturalized, 1946; s. Ernest I. and Annette (Loewenberg) J.; m. Lynn Susan Carp, Aug. 19, 1968; children: Joel Benjamin, David Samuel, Jenny Ellen, Michael Max. A.B., Harvard U., 1954; M.A., Yale U., 1955, Ph.D., 1960. Mem. faculty Tulane U., 1960-62; mem. faculty U. Wis.-Madison, 1962-69, prof., 1967-69; prof. polit. sci. Northwestern U., Evanston, Ill., 1969-84, chmn. dept., 1974-77; Hawkins disting. prof. polit. sci. U. Wis., Madison, 1984—; vis. prof. Johns Hopkins U., 1972; prin. investigator Govtl. Responses to Crime Project, 1978-81; vis. fellow Center for Sociolegal Research, Oxford U., 1981. Author: Justice in America, 4th rev. edit., 1984, Politics in the American States, 3d rev. edit, 1976, Debtors in Court, 1969, Urban Justice, 1973, Felony Justice, 1977, Crime and Justice in Urban America, 1979, Crime and Politics in American Cities, 1983, The Frustration of Policy, 1984. Mem. Human Relations Commn. Evanston, 1971-73. Served with AUS, 1955-57. Recipient Emil H. Steiger award U. Wis., 1964; NSF faculty fellow, 1967-68; fellow Ctr. for Advanced Studies in Behavioral Scis., 1973-74, Ctr. for Socio-legal Research, Oxford U., 1981. Mem. Law and Society Assn. (pres. 1981-83). Home: 3410 Lake Mendota Dr Madison WI 53705

JACOB, JOHN EDWARD, social service agency executive; b. Trout, La., Dec. 16, 1934; s. Emory and Claudia (Sadler) J.; m. Barbara Singleton, Mar. 28, 1959; 1 dau., Sheryl Renee. B.A., Howard U., 1957, M.S.W., 1963. Caseworker, then child welfare casework supr. Balt. Dept. Public Welfare, 1960-65; mem. staff Washington Urban League, 1965-70, acting exec. dir., 1968-70; dir. community orgn.-tng. Eastern region Nat. Urban League, 1970; exec. dir. San Diego Urban League, 1970-75; pres. Washington Urban League, 1975-79; exec. v.p. Nat. Urban League, N.Y.C., 1979-81, pres., 1982—; field work instr. Howard U. Sch. Social Work, 1963-65, lectr., 1967-69; cons., lectr. in field. Vice chmn. trustees Howard U., 1971—. Mem. jud. nominating commn. U.S. Dist. Ct. and U.S. Circuit Ct., D.C., 1978; bd. overseers U. Calif., San Diego, 1974-75. Served with AUS, 1957-58. Recipient Whitney M. Young Meml. award Washington Urban League, 1979, Public Service award United Black Fund Washington, 1979, Achievement award Eastern province Kappa Alpha Psi, 1976, Outstanding Community Service award Howard U. Sch. Social Work Alumni Assn., 1979. Mem. Nat. Assn. Social Workers, Acad. Cert. Social Workers. Democrat. Episcopalian. Office: 500 E 62d St New York NY 10021

JACOB, PAUL BERNARD, JR., electrical engineering educator; b. Columbus, Miss., June 9, 1922; s. Paul Bernard and Sarah Dorsey (Jamison) J.; m. Mildred Evelyn Hammack, Aug. 20, 1946; children: William Boswell, Paul Bernard, III. B.S. in Elec. Engring., Miss. State U., 1944; M.S., Northwestern U., 1948. Registered profl. engr., Miss. Engr., Tenn. Eastman Corp., Oak Ridge, 1944-46; mem. faculty Miss. State U., 1946—, prof. elec. engring., 1956—, asso. head dept., 1962—; cons. in field. Author articles on high voltage engring. Sr. mem. IEEE; mem. Power Engring. Soc. (chmn. coms.), Am. Soc. Engring. Edn., Sigma Xi, Tau Beta Pi, Eta Kappa Nu (dir. 1962-63, nat. v.p. 1982-83, nat. pres. 1983-84), Phi Kappa Phi, Sigma Alpha Epsilon (nat. pres. 1969-71, Disting. Service award 1975), Omicron Delta Kappa. Baptist. Club: Rotary (past pres. Starkville, Miss.). Home: PO Box 5252 Mississippi State MS 39762 Office: PO Drawer EE Mississippi State MS 39762

JACOB, PHILIP ERNEST, political science educator; b. Istanbul, Turkey, July 12, 1914; s. Ernest Otto and Sarah Orilla (Conard) J.; m. Betty Muther, Dec. 24, 1935; children: Sarah Elizabeth, Albert Kirk, Stephen Philip. B.A., Yale U., 1935; M.A., U. Pa., 1939; Ph.D., Princeton U., 1941. Sec. Am. Friends Service Com., Phila., 1936-38, 1941-45; tchr. polit. sci. Princeton, 1939-40, research radio propaganda, 1940-41; faculty internat. law and orgn., prof. polit. sci. U. Pa., Phila., 1945-71, dir. summer sch., also coll. collateral courses, 1950-57, dir. Internat. Studies Values in Politics, 1964-71; prof. polit. sci. U. Hawaii, Honolulu, 1970-80, prof. emeritus, 1980—; Lectr. polit. sci. Swarthmore (Pa.) Coll., 1946-55; co-dir. Ford Found. grant research on social values and pub. policy, 1960-65; sr. fellow East-West Center, 1969, 76-77, research assoc., 1977-78; co-investigator, U.S. rep. Multi-Nat. study of Automation and Indsl. workers, 1972—; internat. coordinator Multi-nat. Comparative Studies of Leadership, Participation and Local Govt. Performance, 1979—; dir. Stein Rokkan Internat. comparative Archive. Author: (with Childs, Whitton) Propaganda by Short Wave, 1942, (with M. Sibley) Conscription of Conscience, 1952, Changing Values in College, 1957, (with J. Flink) Values and Their Function in Decision-Making, 1962, (with others) The Integration of Political Communities, 1964, (with A. Atherton) The Dynamics of International Organization, 1965, 72, (with others) Values and the Active Community, 1971, The City in Comparative Perspective, 1977, Cross-National Comparative Survey Research, 1977, Bonds Without Bondage: Cultural Relations of the Future, 1978, Automation and Industrial Workers, 3 vols, 1980-83. Recipient Franklin D. Roosevelt Found. award, 1953. Fellow Nat. Council on Religion in Higher Edn.; mem. Internat. Studies Assn., AAUP, Phi Beta Kappa.; Mem. Soc. Friends. Home: 17 Aalapapa Pl Kailua HI 96734 Office: Polit Sci Dept U Hawaii Honolulu HI 96822 *As a conscientious objector, convinced that war and the preservation of humane values are incompatible, I have tried through scholarship, teaching and public service to strengthen bonds of international cooperation and the processes of peacemaking. In pioneering a new diplomacy of cross-national collaborative research with fellow social scientists from East and West, we have joined minds and resources across barriers of ideology and politics in a common exploration of how to better the human condition. What emerges is continuing conviction that people can shape their destinies—individuals do count.*

JACOB, PIERS ANTHONY DILLINGHAM, author; b. Oxford, Eng., Aug. 6, 1934; came to U.S., 1940, naturalized, 1958; m. Carol Marble, June 23, 1956. B.A., Goddard Coll., 1956; teaching cert., U. S. Fla., 1964. Formerly tchr. English, tech. writer. Author: Chthon, 1967, Omnivore, 1968, Macroscope, 1969, Battle Circle, 1978, Tarot Trilogy: Gods of Tarot, 1979, Vision of Tarot, 1980, Face of Tarot, 1980. Served with U.S. Army, 1957-59. Office: care Press Relations Berkley Pub Corp 200 Madison Ave New York NY 10016

JACOB, RICHARD JOSEPH, rubber and plastic manufacturing company executive; b. Detroit, July 25, 1919; s. Ben B. and Nettie (Byron) J.; m. Louise Marks, Apr. 2, 1949; children: Patricia Josephine, Arnold Marks. Student, Butler U., 1938-39, Miami U., 1940-41. Exec. with Mfg. Engring. Co., Detroit, 1945-46; exec. v.p., pres. Cadillac Plastics & Chem. Co., Detroit, 1945-65, dir., 1945—; exec. v.p. Dayco Corp., Dayton, Ohio, 1965-68, pres., 1968-73, chmn. bd., chief exec. officer, 1971—, also dir.; dir. Elder-Beerman Stores Corp., Dayton, FLa. Leasing & Capital Corp., Qartel Corp., Mich. Nat. Corp., Bloomfield Hills; Bank One, Dayton N.A.; Mem. adv. bd. Kettering (Ohio) Med. Center; bd. dirs. Rubber Mfrs. Assn. Hon. trustee Children's Med. Center; trustee Nat. Urban League; bd. overseers Hebrew Union Coll., Cin.; life mem. bd. dirs. Brandeis U. Mem. Dayton Area C. of C., Soc. Plastics Industry, Soc. Plastic Engrs. Clubs: Standard-City (past pres., dir. Detroit); Hundred (chmn.), Racquet, Miami Valley Skeet, Meadowbrook Country (Dayton); Renaissance (Detroit); Standard-City (Chgo.); Palm Beach (Fla.) Country; Ocean Reef (Key Largo, Fla.); Moraine Country (Kettering); Franklin Hills Country (Franklin, Mich.); Harmonie (N.Y.C.). Home: 333 Oakwood Ave Dayton OH 45409 Office: Dayco Corp Dayton OH 45401

JACOB, STANLEY WALLACE, surgeon, educator; b. Phila., 1924; s. Abraham and Belle (Shulman) J.; m. Marilyn Peters; 1 son, Stephen; m. Beverly Swarts; children—Jeffrey, Darren, Robert; m. Gail Brandis; 1 dau., Elyse. M.D. cum laude, Ohio State U., 1948. Diplomate: Am. Bd. Surgery. Intern Beth Israel Hosp., Boston, 1948-49, resident surgery, 1949-52, 54-56; chief resident surg. service Harvard Med. Sch., 1956-57, instr., 1958-59; asso. vis. surgeon Boston City Hosp., 1958-59; Kemper Found. research scholar A.C.S., 1957-60; asst. prof. surgery U. Oreg. Med. Sch., Portland, 1959-66, asso. prof., 1966—; Gerlinger prof. surgery Oreg. Health Scis. U., 1981—. Author: Structure and Function in Man, 5th edit, 1982, Laboratory Guide for Structure and Function in Man, 1982, Dimethyl Sulfoxide Basic Concepts, 1971, Biological Actions of DMSO, 1975; contbr. to: Ency. Brit. Served to capt. M.C. AUS, 1952-54; col. Res. ret. Recipient Gov.'s award Outstanding N.W. Scientist, 1965; 1st pl. German Sci. award, 1965; Markle scholar med. scis., 1960. Mem. Phi Beta Kappa, Sigma Xi, Alpha Omega Alpha. Co-discoverer therapeutic usefulness of dimethyl sulfoxide. Home: 1055 SW Westwood Ct Portland OR 97201 Office: Oreg Health Scis U Dept Surgery 3181 SW Sam Jackson Park Rd Portland OR 97201

JACOB, THOMAS BERNARD, plastic company executive; b. Salinas, Calif., June 5, 1934; s. Henry E. and Miriam F. J.; 2 children. B.S. in Bus. Adminstrn., Wayne State U., 1960. Br. mgr. Cadillac Plastic and Chem. Co., Toledo, Indpls., Boston, 1961-65, dist. mgr., Dallas and Chgo., 1966-72, v.p. field ops., 1972-76; exec. v.p. Cadillac Plastic Co., Detroit, 1976—; pres. Cadillac Plastic (Can.) Ltd., 1976—, Cadillac Plastic Co. Mich./Ohio; dir. Dayco Can. Ltd. Served with U.S. Army, 1955-57. Mem. Soc. Plastics Industry, Soc. Plastics Engrs., Nat. Assn. Plastic Distbrs. Clubs: Recess, Renaissance. Office: 26580 W Eight Mile Rd Southfield MI 48034

JACOBI, EILEEN M., univ. dean; b. Ireland, May 7, 1918; came to U.S., 1930, naturalized, 1941; d. Patrick and Marion (Mahon) Ahern; m. A. Francis Jacobi, Aug. 2, 1941 (dec. 1975); children—Francis, Virginia. Diploma nursing, Cumberland Hosp., 1940; B.S., Adelphi Coll., 1954, M.A., 1956; Ed.D., Columbia Tchrs. Coll., 1968. Charge nurse Queens Gen. Hosp., Jamaica, N.Y., 1941-43; pvt. duty nursing, N.Y. area, 1943-50; supervising nurse Creedmoor Inst. Psychobiol. Studies, Queens Village, N.Y., 1950-56; asst. prof. nursing Adelphi Coll., 1956-60, asso. prof., dean, 1960-66, prof., dean, 1960-68; asso. exec. dir. Am. Nurses Assn., 1969-70, exec. dir., 1970-76; prof., dean Coll. Nursing, U. Tex. at El Paso, 1976—; mem. survey team for survey med. and nursing edn. in, Iran, ICA, 1961; cons. to surgeon gen. U.S. Army, 1968-76, USN, 1975-76. Mem. Am. Nurses Assn., Nat.League Nursing, Am. Pub. Health Assn., L.I. Regional Hosp. Rev. and Planning Council, Am. Heart Assn., Kappa Delta Pi, Pi Lambda Theta, Sigma Theta Tau. Home: 9213 Lait Dr El Paso TX 79925

JACOBI, JOHN EDWARD, educator; b. Mansfield, Ohio, Feb. 4, 1907; s. Edward Walter and Josephine (Munhall) J.; m. Carrie Anna Baumann, Dec. 29, 1933; children—John Edward, Susan Jane Jacobi Sherman. B.A., Lehigh U., 1929; Ph.D., N.Y. U., 1933. Prof. sociology, dean Tusculum Coll., Greeneville, Tenn., 1941-46; prof. sociology Albright Coll., Reading, Pa., 1946-48, Lehigh U., Bethlehem, Pa., 1948-62; lectr. Boston Coll., 1965-68; prof. sociology State U. Coll., Oneonta, N.Y., 1968—, head dept., 1970-73; vis. prof. N.Y. U., summers 1946, 48, 49; dir. local area research and demonstration project Mass. Com. Children and Youth, 1962-68; co-dir. inter-disciplinary research team Lehigh U., 1957-60. Author: Meeting the Needs of Children and Youth in a Regional Area, 1968, Meeting the Needs of Children and Youth in an Urban Community, 1968, Meeting the Needs of Children and Youth in Massachusetts Communities, 1968, A Professor's Odyssey, 1976; Co-editor: An Introduction to the Social Sciences, 1954. Mem. nat. youth program com. YMCA, 1959-65. Rockefeller fellow, 1930-33. Mem. Am., Eastern sociol. socs., Pi Gamma Mu, Beta Gamma Sigma, Lambda Chi Alpha. Home: 6 Garden St Oneonta NY 13820

JACOBI, LOU, actor; b. Toronto, Ont., Can., Dec. 28, 1913; s. Joseph and Fay J.; m. Ruth Ludwin, July 15, 1957. Student, Jarvis Collegiate Sch., Toronto. Drama dir. Toronto YMHA, 1940. Theatrical appearances include The Rabbi and the Priest, 1924, Spring Thaw, 1949, Remains to be Seen, 1952, Pal Joey, 1954, The World of Shalom Aleichem, 1955, Into Thin Air, 1955, The Diary of Ann Frank, 1955, The Tenth Man, 1959, Come Blow Your Horn, 1961, Fade In—Fade Out, 1964, Don't Drink the Water, 1966, A Way of Life, 1969, Norman, Is That You?, Epstein, 1971, Eli, the Fanatic, 1971, Milliken Breakfast Show, 1972, The Sunshine Boys, 1974, Cheaters, 1978; motion picture appearances include A Kid for 2 Farthings, 1956, The Diary of Anne Frank, 1959, Song Without End, 1960, Irma La Douce, 1963, Everything You Always Wanted to Know About Sex But Were Afraid to Ask, 1972, Roseland, 1977, The Lucky Star, 1980, Arthur, 1981, Chu Chu and The Philly Flash, 1981, My Favorite Year, 1982, The Lucky Star, 1982; numerous radio and TV appearances, 1954—; including Ivan the Terrible, 1976, Rear Guard, 1976, Somerset, 1976. Address: care of William Morris Agy 1350 Ave of Americas New York NY 10019 *

JACOBS, ALAN MARTIN, physicist, educator; b. N.Y.C., Nov. 14, 1932; s. Samuel J. and Amelia M. (Ziegler) J.; m. Evelyn Lee Banner, Aug. 7, 1955 (dec. Jan. 1977); children: Frederick Ethen, Heidi Joelle; m. Sharon Lynn Auerbach, Oct. 14, 1978; children: Aaron Michael, Seth Joseph. B.Engring. Physics (John McMullen scholar, LeVerne Noyes scholar, Clevite scholar), Cornell U., Ithaca, N.Y., 1955; postgrad., Oak Ridge Sch. Reactor Tech., 1955-56; M.S., in Physics, Pa. State U., 1958, Ph.D., 1963. Research asso. nuclear reactor facility Pa. State U., 1956-63, mem. faculty, 1963—, prof. nuclear engring., 1968-80; prof. U. Fla., Gainesville, 1980—, chmn. dept. nuclear engring. scis., 1980-82; cons. to industry. Co-author: Basic Principles of Nuclear Science and Reactors, 1960. NSF sci. faculty fellow, 1960-61. Mem. Am. Nuclear Soc., Am. Assn. Physicists in Medicine, Health Physics, Soc., Am. Soc. Engring. Edn., Sigma Xi, Tau Beta Pi, Pi Mu Epsilon. Patentee dynamic radiography, control of radiation beams by vibrating media. Home: 2120 NW 20 St Gainesville FL 32605 Office: U Fla Gainesville FL 32611

JACOBS, ANDREW, JR., congressman; b. Indpls., Feb. 24, 1932; s. Andrew and Joyce Taylor (Wellborn) J.; m. Martha Elizabeth Keys. B.S., Ind. U., 1955, LL.B., 1958. Bar: Ind. Practiced in Indpls., 1958-65, 73-74; mem. 89th-92d congresses, 94th-97th congresses from 11th Dist. Ind., 98th Congress from 10th Dist. Ind.; Mem. Ind. Ho. of Reps., 1958-60. Served with USMC, 1950-52. Mem. Indpls. Bar Assn., Am. Legion. Democrat. Roman Catholic. Office: 1533 Longworth House Office Bldg Washington DC 20515 *

JACOBS, ARTHUR THEODORE, college administrator, labor arbitrator; b. Chgo., Aug. 19, 1912; s. Morris and Laura (Abraham) J.; m. Marcia Fox, Oct. 23, 1937; children: John, Jeffrey. B.A., U. Wis., 1934, M.A., 1935; Ph.D., U. Mich., 1951. Asst. chief statistician Pub. Welfare Dept., Indsl. Commn. Wis., Madison, 1935-38; research economist Social Sci. Research Council, Washington; instr. econs. U. Mich., 1939-40; economist Bur. Budget USES, War Manpower Commn., 1940-44; mgmt. cons. Labor Relations Asso., Inc., Chgo., 1944-45; dir. execs. labor service, editor Execs.' Labor Letter, Nat. Foremen's Inst., Inc., N.Y.C., New London, Conn., 1945-48; asso. exec. dir. N.Y. Assn. New Ams., N.Y.C., 1948-52; mgmt. cons. Fedn. Jewish Philanthropies, N.Y., 1952-53; exec. dir. Hebrew Immigrant Aid Soc., 1953-55; dir. adminstrn., adminstrv. sec. Union Am. Hebrew Congregations, N.Y.C., 1955-65; exec. v.p. Jewish Theol. Sem. Am., 1965-71; v.p. Ramapo Coll. N.J., Mahwah, 1972—; Labor arbitrator N.Y. N.J. bds mediation, Am.; Arbitration Assn., N.Y. State Public Employment Relations Bd., N.J. Public Employment Relations Commn., Fed. Mediation and Conciliation Service; impartial chmn. Local 169, Amalgamated Clothing and Textile Workers, Men's Washable Suits, Novelties and Sportswear Contractors Assn., Infant and Juvenile Mfrs. Assn.; mem. joint bd. Neckwear Workers and Mfrs. Assn., Shirt, Leisurewear, Robe, Glove and Rainwear Workers Union, Men's and Boy's Shirt and Leisurewear Assn.; former sec. Temple Service Agy.; Bd. dirs. Am. Immigration Conf.; bd. dirs., asst. sec. Rabbinical Pension Bd.; bd. dirs. Futura House Found., 1979—, pres., 1981—. Mem. Am. Econ. Assn., Indsl. Relations Research Assn., Assn. Jewish Book Pubs. (founder, 1st pres. 1962-65), Soc. Profls. in Dispute Resolution (charter), Ams. for Dem. Action (dir.). Home: Tamarac Trail Harrison NY 10528 Office: Ramapo Coll Mahwah NJ 07430

JACOBS, BRADFORD MCELDERRY, newspaper editor; b. Balt., Sept. 30, 1920; s. Joseph Streett and Sarah Hopkins (McElderry) J.; m. Molly Carter Bruce, May 10, 1952; children: Molly Bruce, Sarah Hopkins, Ann McElderry. B.A., Princeton U., 1942. With Balt. Sunpapers, 1946—, beginning as reporter, successively editorial writer, 1953-54, chief London (Eng.) bur., 1954-56, Washington corr., 1956-57, editorial writer, 1957-68, polit. columnist, 1962-68; editor The Evening Sun, 1968-80. Author: Thimbleriggers: The Law v. Governor Marvin Mandel, 1984. Served with AUS, 1942-46; ETO. Decorated Bronze Star; Croix de Guerre, France). Democrat. Clubs: Maryland, Green Spring Valley Hunt, Hamilton Street (Balt.); Jupiter Island (Hobe Sound, Fla.); Century (N.Y.C.). Home: Stevenson PO Baltimore County MD 21153 Office: Balt Sun Calvert and Centre Sts Baltimore MD 21203

JACOBS, BURLEIGH EDMUND, foundry executive; b. Milw., Feb. 3, 1920; s. Burleigh Edmund and Ora (Harmon) J.; m. Janet Eloise Grede, Nov. 1, 1942; children: Mary (Mrs. Merrill York), Bruce, Scott, William. B.A., U. Wis., 1942. Joined Grede Foundries, Inc., Milw., 1945; successively works mgr. Iron Mountain Foundry, 1947-49; works mgr. Milw. Steel Foundry, 1950-51, asst. sales mgr., 1952-57, asst. v.p., 1957-60, pres., 1960-73, chmn., chief exec. officer, 1973—; dir. Marshall & Ilsley Bank, Milw., Milsco Mfg. Co., Soo Line R.R. Co. Pres. bd. Met. Milw. YMCA, 1968-70; mem. Greater Milw. Com., 1969—; bd. dirs. Jr. Achievement, 1968-71, Better Bus. Bur. Served with USNR, 1942-45. Recipient Frederick A. Lorenz Meml. medal Steel Founders' Soc. Am., 1970; named Mktg. Man of Yr. Soc. Mfg. Engrs., Milw., 1980. Mem. Steel Founders' Soc. Am. (pres. 1966-69), Am. Foundrymen's Soc. (v.p. 1971-72, pres. 1972-73, Peter L. Simpson gold medal 1983), Cast Metals Fedn. (pres. 1974), Gray and Ductile Iron Founders' Soc. (Gold medal 1973). Conglist. (moderator 1962-64). Club: Bluemound Country (Wauwatosa, Wis.). Home: 14505 Juneau Blvd Elm Grove WI 53122 Office: 9898 W Blue Mound Rd Milwaukee WI 53226

JACOBS, C. BERNARD, banker; b. Davenport, Iowa, May 15, 1918; s. Henry Bernard and Ruth Alberta (Douglas) J.; m. Irene May Niesen, Mar. 17, 1939; children: Judith, Victoria, Rosemary, Mary Louise, Julie. B.S. in Commerce, Northwestern U., 1948; postgrad. in banking, U. Wis., 1955. V.p. Continental Ill. Nat. Bank, Chgo., 1959-64; exec. v.p. Nat. City Bank, Mpls., 1964-66, pres., 1966-69, chmn. bd., 1969—; pres., chief exec. officer Nat. City Bancorp, Mpls., 1982—; dir. Banks of Iowa, Inc., Des Moines, Dahlberg Elec. Inc., Mpls., Info. Dialogues Inc. Bd. dirs. Archdiocesan Cath. Charities, Mpls., 1975—, Downtown Council, Mpls., 1976—, St. Mary's Hosp., Mpls., 1976—. Clubs: Minikahda (Mpls.); Hozeltine Nat. (Chaska, Minn.) (pres. 1973-75); Quail Ridge Country (Boynton Beach, Fla.)). Office: Nat City Bancorp 75 S 5th St Minneapolis MN 55435

JACOBS, CHARLES EDWARD, JR., engineer, manufacturing company executive; b. Flushing, N.Y., May 19, 1927; s. Charles Edward and Alma P. (Nowack) J.; m. Margot H. Stainmuller, July 2, 1949; children: Christopher Edward, Clifford Charles, Megan Elise. B.E.E., Poly. Inst. Bklyn., 1951. Asst. dir. engring. Sylvania Electronics Systems, Needham, Mlass., 1951-68; with Raytheon Co., 1968—, mgr. PATRIOT Air Def. System, Bedford, Mass., 1974-78, corp. v.p., gen. mgr. missile systems div., 1978—. Served with USNR, 1945-46. Fellow Poly. Inst. N.Y.; Sr. mem. IEEE; mem. Am. Def. Preparedness Assn., Assn. U.S. Army, Navy League. Office: Raytheon Co Missile Systems Div Bedford MA 01730

JACOBS, CLYDE EDWARD, educator, author; b. Herington, Kans., Jan. 19, 1925; s. Harry Charles and Jessie Irene (Tarbill) J. A.B., U. Kans., 1946; postgrad., Inst. des Sciences Politiques, Paris, 1946-47; M.A., U. Mich., 1948, Ph.D., 1952. Faculty U. Calif. at Davis, 1952—, asso. prof. polit. sci., 1960-63, prof., 1963—, chmn. dept., 1960-66; acting dir. Inst. Govt. Affairs, 1961-62; stagiaire Conseil d'Etat, Paris, 1975-76. Author: Law Writers and the Courts, 1954, 75, Justice Frankfurter and Civil Liberties, 1961, 74, The Eleventh Amendment and Sovereign Immunity, 1972; co-author: California Government, 1966, 70, The Selective Service Act, 1967; contbr. articles to profl. jours. Mem. Davis Planning Commn., 1960-62, Yolo County Water Resources Bd., 1962-64; chmn. Davis Personnel Bd., 1966-72; councilman City of Davis, 1960-64. Mem. No. Calif. Polit. Sci. Assn. (pres. 1974-75), Phi Beta Kappa, Beta Theta Pi, Pi Sigma Alpha, Phi Kappa Phi, Delta Sigma Rho. Republican. Roman Catholic. Home: 2708 Cadiz St Davis CA 95616

JACOBS, DAVID, TV producer, author; b. Balt., Aug. 12, 1939; s. Melvin and Ruth (Levenson) J.; m. Diana Pietrocarli, Feb. 12, 1977;

children: Aaron Michael, Molly Sarah. B.F.A., Md. Inst. Art, 1961. Art articles editor: The Book of Knowledge, 1961-65; editor, writer: American Heritage Books, 1965-68; free lance writer, 1968-76; staff writer: TV The Blue Knight, 1976; story editor: Family, ABC, 1977-78; writer and ind. producer various projects for, CBS; writer, ind. producer, Lorimar Productions, Culver City, Calif.; prodns. include Dallas, 1977, Married: The First Year, 1978, Knots Landing, 1978, Secrets of Midland Heights, 1980; Author: Master Painters of the Renaissance, 1968, Master Builders of the Middle Ages, 1969, Constantinople, City on the Golden Horn, 1969, (with Anthony E. Neville) Bridges, Canals and Tunnels, 1969, Beethoven, 1970, An American Conscience, Woodrow Wilson's Fight for World Peace, 1973, Architecture, 1974, (with Sara Ann Friedman) Police: A Precinct at Work, 1975, Chaplin, The Movies and Charlie, 1975. Recipient Humanitas prize award, 1978. Mem. Writers Guild Am., Acad. TV Arts and Scis. Office: 10202 W Washington Blvd Culver City CA 90230

JACOBS, DAVID, sculptor, educator; b. Niagara Falls, N.Y., Mar. 1, 1932; s. John B. and Adell (Pruitt) J.; m. Georganne Clark, 1951 (div. 1969); children: Christine Ann, Kathryn Lee, David Theodore; m. Joan Berlingeri, 1969; 1 dau., Casimira Johanna. Student, So. Calif. Coll., 1949-51; A.A., Orange Coast Coll., 1953; A.B., Los Angeles State Coll., 1955, M.A., 1957. Tchr. W.F. Dexter Sch., Whittier, Calif., 1955-56; supr. crafts Ohio Union, Ohio State U., 1957-61; instr. Ohio State U. Sch. Art, 1961-62; instr. art dept. Hofstra U., 1962-66, asst. prof., 1966-71, asso. prof., 1971-78, prof., 1978—, chmn. dept. fine arts, 1982-85; instr. sculpture Jewish Center, Columbus, Ohio, 1959, Huntington (N.Y.) Twp. Art League, 1963-64, Marcusson Sch., Port Washington, N.Y., 1963-64. Exhibited in one man shows at, Los Angeles State Coll., 1957, Otterbein Coll., Ohio, 1958, Ohio State U., 1959, Barone Gallery, N.Y.C., 1961, Kornblee Gallery, N.Y.C., 1963-65, Emily Lowe Gallery, Hempstead, N.Y., 1964-67, Witte Mus., 1969, Colgate U., 1970, San Jose State Coll., Albion Coll., Cornell U., 1971, Vancouver (B.C., Can.) Art Gallery, 1973; works performing soft and hard, moving, sound sculpture, Wah Chang-Box Works Assyrian Air Fair, 1967, Sound at P.S.I, Inst. Art and Urban Resources, N.Y.C., 1979; represented in permanent collections, Assyrian embassy, Va. Mus., Otterbein Coll., Guggenheim Mus., Ohio State U., Raycom Industries, Valley Mall, Hagerstown, Md., also pvt. collections; designer: set decoration for A Farce, T. Griffith Prodns., Hollywood, Calif., 1955; producer: Three Artists, WOSU-TV, Columbus, 1958; designer: props Naked City, N.Y.C., 1963; sets and costumes Skin of Our Teeth, Hofstra Playhouse, 1982; Contbr. revs., reprodns. to periodicals. Address: 51 8th Ave Sea Cliff NY 11579

JACOBS, DAVID HAROLD, state trial referee; b. N.Y.C., Oct. 3, 1909; s. Samuel H. and Leah (Angel) J.; m. Fan Kaplan, June 15, 1939; children—Betsy Edith, Samuel Angel. A.B. cum laude, Clark U., 1930; LL.B., Yale, 1934; Ph.D., Pacific Western U., 1981; LL.D., U. New Haven, 1981. Bar: Conn. bar 1934. Since practiced in, Meriden; asst. and acting pros. atty. Meriden Police Ct., 1940-42; corp. counsel, City of Meriden, 1950-52; mem. faculty Boston U. Law Sch., 1939-42; judge Circuit Ct., Conn., 1959-75; chief judge, 1973-75; disting. vis. prof. law U. Ghana, 1971; Vice chmn. exec. com., mem. jud. rev. council Judges of Circuit Ct.; mem. Conn. Adult Probation judge Conn. Superior Ct., 1973-75, sr. judge, 1975-78; state trial referee State of Conn., 1979—; instr. Boston U. Law Sch., 1939-43; Commn, 1974-77. Editor: Conn. Bar Jour, 1947-53; sr. editor, 1971—; Contbr. articles to profl. jours. Field dir. A.R.C., 1943-44; Mem. Gubernatorial Med. Commn., 1950; bd. dirs. Meriden Public Library, 1979—. Mem. ABA (ho. of dels. 1956-58), Conn. Bar Assn. (pres. 1955-56), Meriden-Southington-Wallingford Bar Assn. (pres. 1952-53), New Haven County Bar Assns., Stair Soc. Scotland, Phi Beta Kappa. Home: 127 Lambert Av Meriden CT 06450 Office: Circuit Ct Bldg Meriden CT 06450

JACOBS, DONALD P., banking and finance educator; b. Chgo., June 22, 1927; s. David and Bertha (Nevod) J.; children: Elizabeth, Ann, David; m. Dinah Nemeroff, May 28, 1978. B.A., Roosevelt Coll., 1949; M.A., Columbia U., 1951, Ph.D., 1956. Mem. research staff Nat. Bur. Econ. Research, 1952-57; instr. Coll. City N.Y., 1955-57; mem. faculty to Morrison prof. fin. Northwestern U. Grad. Sch. Mgmt., 1970-78, chmn. dept., 1957—, dean, 1975—, Gaylord Freeman Disting. prof. banking, 1978—; participant Inst. Internat. Mgmt., Burgenstock, Switzerland, 1965—; formerly chmn. bd. dirs. Amtrak; dir. Commonwealth Edison, Hartmarx Corp., Union Oil Co., Swift Ind. Corp., Galaxy Carpet Mills, Inc.; co-dir. fin. studies Presdl. Commn. Fin. Structure and Regulation, 1970-71; sr. economist banking and currency com. U.S. Ho. of Reps., 1963-64; dir. Conf. Savs. and Residential Financing, 1967—. Editor proc.: Conf. Savs. and Residential Financing, 1967, 68, 69; contbr. articles to profl. jours. Served with USNR, 1945-46. Ford Found. fellow, 1959-60, 63-64. Mem. Am. Econ. Assn., Am. Statis. Assn., Am. Fin. Assn., Econometrics Soc., Inst. Mgmt. Sci. Home: 617 Milburn St Evanston IL 60201

JACOBS, DONALD PAUL, architect; b. Cleve., Aug. 8, 1942; s. Joseph William and Minnie Mae (Grieger) J.; m. Sharon Daugherty, Apr. 13, 1963. B.S., U. Cin., 1967. Draftsman Skidmore, Owings & Merrill, San Francisco, 1967-70; pvt. practice architecture The Sea Ranch, Calif., 1970—; Chmn. Sea Ranch Design Rev. Com. Mem. AIA. Republican. Office: 1000 Annapolis Rd PO Box 9 The Sea Ranch CA 95497

JACOBS, ELEANOR ALICE, clinical psychologist, educator; b. Royal Oak, Mich., Dec. 25, 1923; d. Roy Dana and Alice Ann (Keaton) J. B.A., U. Buffalo, 1949, M.A., 1952, Ph.D., 1955. Clin. psychologist VA Hosp., Buffalo, 1954—, EEO counelor, 1962-79, chief psychology service, 1979-83; clin. prof. SUNY, Buffalo, 1950—; speaker on psychology to community orgns. and clubs, 1952—; Mem. adult devel. and aging com. NICHD, HEW, 1971-75. Recipient Outstanding Superior Performance award Buffalo VA Hosp., 1958, Spl. Recognition award SUNY, Buffalo, 1971; W.L. McKnight award Miami Heart Inst., 1972; Adminstrs. commendation VA, 1974; Dirs. commendation VA Med. Center, Buffalo, 1978; Disting. Alumni award SUNY, Buffalo, 1983; named Woman of Yr. Bus. and Profl. Women's Clubs, Buffalo, 1973. Mem. Am. Psychol. Assn., Eastern Psychol. Assn., N.Y. State Psychol. Assn., Am. Group Psychotherapy Assn., Am. Soc. Group Psychotherapy and Psychodrama, Nat., Western, N.Y. leagues nursing, Psychol. Assn. Western N.Y. (Disting. Achievement award 1976), Group Psychotherapy Assn. Western N.Y., Undersea Med. Soc., Sigma Xi. Research, publs. on hyperbaric medicine, hyperoxygenation effect on cognitive functions in aged. Home: 221 Pleasant Ave N Ridgeway ON Canada LOS 1 NO

JACOBS, FRANCIS ALBIN, biochemist, educator; b. Mpls., Feb. 23, 1918; s. Anthony and Agnes Ann (Stejskal) J.; m. Dorothy Caldwell, June 5, 1953; children: Christopher, Gregory, Paula, Margaret, John. B.S., Regis Coll., Denver, 1939; postgrad, U. Denver, 1939-41; Ph.D., St. Louis U., 1949. Postdoctoral fellow Nat. Cancer Inst., Bethesda, Md., 1949-50; instr. physiol. chemistry U. Pitts. Sch. Medicine, 1951-52, asst. prof., 1952-54; asst. prof. biochemistry U. N.D. Sch. Medicine, Grand Forks, 1954-56, asso. prof., 1956-64, prof., 1964—; dir., research supr. Nat. Sci. Research Participation Program in Biochemistry, 1959-63; advisor directorate for sci. edn. NSF. Contbr. articles to profl. jours. Fellow AAAS, N.D. Acad. Sci. (editor 1967, 68); mem. Am. Soc. Biol. Chemists, Am. Inst. Nutrition, Soc. Exptl. Biology and Medicine, Am. Chem. Soc. (chmn. Red River valley sect. 1971), AAAS, AMA, Sigma Xi (pres. chpt. 1965-66, Faculty award for Outstanding Sci. Research 1982), Alpha Sigma Nu, Phi Lambda Upsilon. Home: 1525 Robertson Ct Grand Forks ND 58201 *Have faith in yourself and your creator; do what is right, and seek what is true.*

JACOBS, FREDERICK L., advt. exec.; b. N.Y.C., Nov. 23, 1921; s. Morris and Janet (Exler) J.; m. Gloria J. Solomon, Mar. 28, 1954; children—Nancy, Margery, Susan. B.B.A., CCNY, 1943; J.D., N.Y. Law Sch., 1952. Bar: N.Y. bar 1952. Accountant Baumgarten & Arum (C.P.A.'s), N.Y.C., 1945-48; spl. agt. IRS, N.Y.C., 1948-53; individual practice law and accounting, N.Y.C., 1953-66; exec. v.p. fin. and adminstrn., sec.-treas. Wells, Rich, Greene, Inc., N.Y.C., 1966-80, vice-chmn., 1980—; dir. Served with USAAF, 1943-45. Decorated Air medal. Mem. Am. Assn. Advt. Agencies (mem. com. fiscal control). Democrat. Jewish. Office: 767 Fifth Ave New York NY 10022 *

JACOBS, HARRY ALLAN, JR., investment firm executive; b. N.Y.C., June 28, 1921; s. Harry Allan and Elsie (Wolf) J.; m. Marie Stevens, Dec. 31, 1942; children: Nancy (Mrs. William F. Haneman, Jr.), Harry Allan III. B.A., Dartmouth, 1942. With Bache Group Inc., N.Y.C., 1946—, partner, 1956—, dir., 1966—, pres., 1968—, chief exec. officer, 1976, chmn., 1977—; trustee, chmn. finance com. Greenburgh Savs. Bank, Hawthorne, N.Y.; mem. downtown adv. com. Chase Manhattan Bank; bd. govs. N.Y. Stock Exchange, 1969-72. Trustee Paul Smith's Coll., Paul Smith, N.Y., Trudeau Inst., Lake Placid, N.Y. Served to 1st lt. USAAF, 1942-45. Mem. Bond Club N.Y. (past gov., sec.), Assn. Stock Exchange Firms (past com. chmn., mem. exec. com.), Investment Bankers Assn. (past gov., chmn. pub. relations com.), Investment Assn. N.Y. (past pres.). Clubs: Wall Street, N.Y. Stock Exchange Luncheon (N.Y.C.); Ardsley (N.Y.) Country; Lake Placid (N.Y.). Office: Bache Group Inc 100 Gold St New York NY 10038

JACOBS, HARVEY COLLINS, editor, writer; b. Trafalgar, Ind., Sept. 6, 1915; s. Ralph L. and Ruth Marie (Ragsdale) J.; m. Florence Giddings, Apr. 5, 1942 (div. 1979); children: Phillip, Kenneth; m. Charlene Clark, Aug. 7, 1980. A.B., Franklin (Ind.) Coll., 1938, Litt.D., 1974; M.A., Ind. U., 1949; Litt.D., Sussex Coll. Tech., Eng., 1973. Reporter, editorial writer and columnist Franklin Evening Star, 1937-44; dir. pub. relations Franklin Coll., 1941-49, head dept. journalism, 1949-55; asst. editor Rotarian mag., Evanston, Ill., 1955-56; head program div. Rotary Internat., 1956-58, undersec., 1958-63; founder, chmn. dept. journalism and mass communications N.Mex. State U., Las Cruces, 1963-74; dir. Center Broadcasting and Internat. Communications, 1970-74; editor Indpls. News, 1974—; also dir. Pulliam Fellowships Program; cons. in field. Author: Rotary: 50 Years of Service, 1955, Seven Paths to Peace, 1959, Adventure in Service, 1961, We Came Rejoicing, 1968; co-writer: This Great Land, 1983. Bd. dirs. Fine Arts Soc. Indpls., Indpls. United Way; trustee Franklin Coll. Recipient Distinguished Alumnus citation Franklin Coll., 1957; Nat. Headliner award U. Okla., 1970; Distinguished Service award N.Mex. Broadcasters Assn., 1971; Carl Towley award Journalism Edn. Assn., 1974; Golden Crown award Columbia U., 1975; Community Service award Hoosier Press Assn., 1976; Best Columnist award, 1975, 76, 80, 82. Fellow Pub. Relations Soc. Am.; mem. Assn. Edn. Journalism, Am. Soc. Newspaper Editors, Authors Guild, AP Mng. Editors Assn., Nat. Conf. Editorial Writers, Ind. Hist. Soc., Indpls. Press Club, Sigma Delta Chi. Mem. Disciples of Christ Ch. Clubs: Indpls., Athletic, Press, Rotary (Indpls.) (past dist. gov.). Home: 524 Leisure Ln Greenwood IN 46142 Office: 307 N Pennsylvania Ave Indianapolis IN 46204

JACOBS, HELEN HULL, writer; b. Globe, Ariz., Aug. 6, 1908; d. Roland Herbert and Eula (Hull) J. Student, U. Calif.-Berkeley, 1926-29, William and Mary Coll., 1942. Designer sports clothes, N.Y.C.; Author: (autobiography) Beyond the Game, 1936; Storm Against the Wind, 1944, Laurel for Judy; Gallery of Champions, 1949, Center Court, 1950, Judy, Tennis Ace, 1951, Proudly She Serves, 1953, Famous American Women Athletes, 1964, Better Physical Fitness for Girls, 1964, The Young Sportsman's Guide to Tennis, 1965, Courage To Conquer, 1967, The Tennis Machine, 1972, Famous Modern American Women Athletes, 1975, Beginner's Guide to Winning Tennis, 1975, The Savage Ally, 1977; contbr. articles to mags. Served as lt. USNR, 1943-46; W.R.; to comdr., 1952-54. Recipient Tennis Immortal award Tennis Writers Assn. Am., 1968; named to N. Calif. Tennis Hall of Fame, Nat. Tennis Hall of Fame, San Francisco Bay Area Sports Hall of Fame, U. Calif. Athletic Hall of Fame, Coll. William and Mary Athletic Hall of Fame. Hon. mem. All Eng. Lawn Tennis and Croquet Club, Internat. Lawn Tennis Club U.S., Eugene Field Soc., English Speaking Union (London), Nat. Geog. Soc., Mark Twain Soc.; mem. Kappa Alpha Theta, Jr. League Oakland-East Bay. Episcopalian. Clubs: Women's Athletic, San Francisco Press, California Writers, Berkeley Tennis; Women's Athletic (Oakland, Calif.); Nice (France) Tennis. Nat. jr. tennis champion, 1924-25; champion U.S. women's singles and doubles, 1932, singles champion, 1933, champion U.S. singles, doubles and mixed doubles, 1934; champion U.S. singles, doubles, 1935 (1st to win single championship 4 times successively); 6 times Wimbledon finalist; Wimbledon singles champion, 1936; mem. Am. Wightman Cup team for 13 successive years. Home: 26 Joanne Ln Weston CT 06883 *Never be willing to settle for second best, but keep achievement in proper perspective, and recognize that qualities of spirit have far greater value than personal accomplishments.*

JACOBS, HOWARD, distribution executive; b. N.Y.C., July 23, 1937; s. Milton J. and Hortense (Wilson) J.; m. Margaret Ellen Reitman, Aug. 1, 1963; children: Karen, Kristy. A.B., Washington and Lee U., 1958; M.B.A., Cornell U., 1960. Asst. to pres. Jonathan Logan, Inc., N.Y.C., 1960-65; exec. trainee Joseph E. Seagram, N.Y.C., 1965-66; sales supr. Reitman Industries, Caldwell, N.J., 1966—, mktg. mgr., 1976-78, pres., 1978—. Bd. dirs. East Orange Gen. Hosp., N.J., 1978—; trustee Am. Heart Assn., Glen Ridge, N.J., 1978—; bd. dirs. Wine and Spirits Wholesalers Am. 1st lt. U.S. Army, 1960-77. Club: Mountain Ridge Country (trustee) (1972-80). Home: 57 Mayhew Dr South Orange NJ 07079 Office: Galsworthy 10 Patton Dr West Cladwell NJ 07006

JACOBS, JAMES NAJEEB, supt. schs.; b. Tonawanda, N.Y., Mar. 4, 1930; s. Leo and Sofea (Johns) J.; m. Suzanne A. Hetzel, July 26, 1969; children—Lance, Thor, Lars. B.A. in Psychology, Mich. State U., 1951, M.A. in Guidance and Counseling, 1952, Ed.D. in Founds. of Edn, 1957. With Cin. Public Schs., 1954—, examiner, 1954-61, asso. dir. evaluation services, 1962-65, dir. program research and design, 1965-73, asst. supt. research and devel., 1973-76, supt. schs., 1976—; mem. com. research and devel. Coll. Bd.; tchr. Fletcher Elem. Sch., Tonawanda, 1951; Hughes Evening Sch., Cin., 1955; asso. prof. Coll. Edn. U. Cin., 1960; lectr. Miami U., Oxford, Ohio, 1960, Xavier U., Cin., 1960; vis. asst. prof. U. Md., 1960; adj. asso. prof. Ohio State U., 1971; counselor Boys' Reformatory Sch., N.Y., 1952; field agt. Mich. Dept. Vocat. Rehab., 1953; UNESCO cons. ednl. stats. Iraq Ministry of Edn., 1961-62; cons. U.S. Office of Edn., Nat. Inst. Edn., Tex. Ednl. Renewal Center, Lansing (Mich.) Public Schs., Ohio State Evaluation Center, others. Editorial bd.: Jour. Ednl. Measurement, 1972, Measurement and Evaluation in Guidance, 1969-76; editor: Jour. Program Research and Devel, Cin. Public Schs., 1972; contbr. numerous articles to profl. jours. Presenter/participant Urban Supts. Network, Nat. Inst. Edn., 1979—; Bd. dirs. Cin. Ednl. TV Found., Appalachia Ednl. Lab., Center Econ. Edn., Jr. Achievement Greater Cin.; mem. community adv. bd. Paul I. Hoxworth Blood Center; adv. council Miami U. Named Ohio PTA Educator of Yr., 1981; recipient Dan Tehan award March of Dimes, 1978. Mem. Am. Personnel and Guidance Assn., Ohio Assn. Supervision and Curriculum Devel. (research com.), Nat. Council Measurement in Edn., Am. Ednl. Research Assn. (large city research dirs.), Am. Assn. Sch. Adminstrs. (large city supts.). Republican. Presbyterian. Club: Cincinnatus Assn. Office: 230 E 9th St Cincinnati OH 45202 *

JACOBS, JANE, author; b. Scranton, Pa., May 4, 1916; d. John Decker and Bess Mary (Robison) Butzner; m. Robert Hyde Jacobs, Jr., May 27, 1944; children—James Kedzie, Edward Decker, Mary Hyde. Author: Downtown Is For People in The Exploding Metropolis, 1959, The Death and Life of Great American Cities, 1961, The Economy of Cities, 1969, The Question of Separatism, 1980. Address: care Random House 201 E 50th St New York NY 10022

JACOBS, JIM, actor, playwright; b. Chgo., Oct. 7, 1942; m. Diane Rita Gomez, June 5, 1965 (div. 1974); 1 dau., Kristine; m. Denise Nettleton, Apr. 29, 1978. Student, Chgo. City Coll. Appeared in: A Shot in the Dark, 1963, Taste of Honey, 1963, Come Blow Your Horn, 1964, Suddenly Last Summer, 1964, Five Finger Exercise, 1964, Look Back in Anger, 1965, Hello Out There, 1966, Tom Jones, 1966, Until the Monkey Comes, 1966, Picnic on Battlefield, 1967, Take Me Along, 1967, The Boy Friend, 1968, Flora, The Red Menace, 1968, Entertaining Mr. Sloane, 1969, The Serpent, 1969, Don't Drink the Water, 1970, Jimmy Shine, 1970, all Chgo., No Place to Be Somebody; nat. touring co., 1971, on Broadway, 1971, The Magnolia Club, Chgo., 1975, The Local Stigmatic, Chgo., 1976; dir.: The Ruffian on the Stair, Chgo., 1975, The Tiger, 1975; actor: film Medium Cool, 1969, Love in a Taxi, 1976, Equity Library Theatre Showcases, 1969—, TV series, Open All Night, 1982, TV commls., 1968—; Author, lyricist, composer: (with Warren Casey) Grease; Broadway musical and film, 1972; author: Island of Lost Coeds, 1979, (with Jim Weston) Bats in the Belfry, 1982. Mem. Dramatists Guild, Authors League Am., ASCAP, Actors Equity Assn., Screen Actors Guild., AFTRA. Address: c/o Internat Creative Mgmt 40 W 57th St New York NY 10019

JACOBS, JOHN CLAYTON, energy consultant, lawyer; b. Guymon, Okla., June 27, 1917; s. John Clayton and Patience (Goodlander) J.; m. Elinor Margaret Blanchard, June 20, 1942; children: Ann Clayton, Elizabeth Pelham. B.S., Ga. Inst. Tech., 1939; LL.B., Yale U., 1948. Bar: Tex. 1949. Process engr. Standard Oil Co. La., 1939-44; supervisory engr. Creole Petroleum Corp., 1944-46; with Heldt & O'Boyle, Dallas, 1948-51; pvt. practice, Dallas, 1951-53; exec. v.p., dir. Wilcox Trend Gathering System, Inc., Dallas, 1953—; v.p. Tex. Eastern Transmission Corp., Houston, 1955-66, sr. v.p., 1966-76, exec. v.p., 1976-78, vice-chmn., dir., 1978-80; dir. Interam. Oil Corp. Author: (with Leeston and Crichton) The Dynamic Natural Gas Industry, 1963. Chmn. bd. Tex. Bill Rights Found., 1972-74; bd. dirs. Intercultural Cooperation N.Am. Mem. Am. Inst. Chem. Engrs., Soc. Petroleum Engrs., Am. Petroleum Assn., ABA, Am. Gas Assn. (chmn. natural gas reserves com.), Colegio de Ingenieros de Venezuela, English Speaking Union (pres. Houston br. 1972-74, nat. bd. dirs. 1976-80), Inst. Petroleum Engrs., Inst. Gas Engrs., Beta Theta Pi, Omicron Delta Kappa, Phi Kappa Phi. Episcopalian. Clubs: River Oaks, Ramada, Petroleum (Houston) (pres. 1981); Bankers (Mexico City); Hurlingham (London, Eng.). Home: 4627 Banning St Houston TX 77027 Office: PO Box 2521 Houston TX 77252

JACOBS, JOHN HOWARD, association executive; b. Phila., June 7, 1925; s. Howard Elias and Elizabeth Pauline (Dresel) J.; m. Shirley Elizabeth Salini, Apr. 21, 1960. B.S. in Econs., N.Mex. State U., 1950. Adminstrv. officer U.S. Fgn. Service (NATO), London, Paris, 1951-53; gen. mgr. Vis-a-Pack Corp., Beverly, N.J., 1953-58; exec. dir. Red. Agy., City of Stockton, Calif., 1958-66, San Francisco Planning and Urban Research, 1966-81, San Francisco C of C, 1981—; pres. Pacific Region Nat. Assn. Housing and Redevel. Ofcls., Stockton, 1965-66, nat. bd. govs., San Francisco, 1966-70. Mem. San Francisco Mayor's Fiscal Adv. Com.; mem. adv. com. Golden Gate Nat. Recreation Area, San Francisco; trustee Fine Arts Mus. of San Francisco; bd. dirs. SPUR, San Francisco, San Francisco Devel. Fund. Served with AUS, 1943-45. Mem. Nat. Assn. Housing and Redevel. Ofcls., Lambda Alpha (dir.). Home: 2823 Octavia St San Francisco CA 94123 Office: San Francisco C of C 465 California St San Francisco CA 94104

JACOBS, JOSEPH DONOVAN, engineering firm executive; b. Motley, Minn., Dec. 24, 1908; s. Sherman William and Edith Mary (Donovan) J.; m. Virginia Mary O'Meara, Feb. 8, 1937; 1 son, John Michael. B.S. in Civil Engring, U. Minn., 1934. Civil engr., constrn. supr. Walsh Constrn. Co., N.Y.C. and San Francisco, 1934-54; chief engr. Kaiser-Walsh-Perini-Raymond, Australia, 1954-55; founder, sr. officer Jacobs Assos., San Francisco, 1955—; Chmn., U.S. nat. com. on tunnelling tech. Nat. Acad. Scis., 1977. Recipient Golden Beaver award for engring., 1980; Non-Mem. award Moles, 1981. Fellow ASCE, Instn. Engrs. Australia; mem. Nat. Acad. Engring., Am. Inst. Mining and Metall. Engrs., Nat. Soc. Profl. Engrs., World Trade Club San Francisco, Engrs. Club San Francisco, Delta Chi. Club: Corinthian Yacht (San Francisco). Inventor in field of mining and tunnel excavation. Home: 84 Almenar Dr Greenbrae CA 94904 Office: 500 Sansome St San Francisco CA 94111

JACOBS, JOSEPH JOHN, engineering company executive; b. June 13, 1916; s. Joseph and Afiffie (Forzley) J.; m. Violet Jabara, June 14, 1942; children: Margaret, Linda, Valerie. B.S. in Chem. Engring, Poly. Inst. N.Y., Bklyn., 1937, M.S., 1939, Ph.D., 1942. Registered profl. engr., N.Y., N.J., La., Calif. Chem. engr. Autoxygen, Inc., N.Y.C., 1939-42; sr. chem. engr. Merck & Co., Rahway, N.J., 1942-44; v.p., tech. dir. Chemurgic Corp., Richmond, Calif., 1944-47; pres. Jacobs Engring. Co., Pasadena, Calif., 1947-74; chmn. bd., chief exec. officer Jacobs Engring. Group, Inc., Pasadena, 1974—. Contbr. tech. articles to profl. jours. Area dir. United Way, 1978—; chmn. bd. trustees Poly. Inst. N.Y.; trustee Harvey Mudd Coll.; mem. adv. bd. St. Luke Hosp.; active Assocs. Calif. Inst. Tech. Recipient Herbert Hoover medal United Engring. Socs., 1983. Fellow Am. Inst. Chem. Engrs., Am. Inst. Chemists, Inst. for Advancement Engring.; mem. Am. Chem. Soc., AAAS, Los Angeles C. of C., Pasadena C. of C., Sigma Xi, Phi Lambda Upsilon. Clubs: Altadena Town and Country, California, Annandale Golf, Pauma Valley Country; Union League (N.Y.C.); (San Francisco). Office: 251 S Lake Ave Pasadena CA 91101

JACOBS, KLAUS KARL EWALD, banker; b. Munich, Germany, Mar. 9, 1934; came to U.S., 1968; s. Hermann and Therese (Hinlein) J.; m. Karin Heik, Oct. 28, 1961. Ed., Comml. Coll., Munich, 1952-54. With Deutsche Bank A.G., Germany, 1955-68; exec. asst. to chmn., 1957-64, mgr., 1964-68; pres. European-Am. Banking Corp., European Am. Bank & Trust Co., N.Y.C., 1968-78, Paramount Group, Inc., 1979—; mng. partner TASA, Inc., 1980—

JACOBS, LEON, medical research administrator; b. N.Y.C., Mar. 26, 1915; s. Samuel and Evelyn (Rosenthal) J.; m. Eva Eisenberg, Nov. 28, 1946; children: Jonathan H., Alice E., Abby M. B.A., Bklyn. Coll., 1935; M.A., George Washington U., 1938, Ph.D., 1947. Zoologist, protozoologist NIH, 1937-43, 46-59, chief Lab. Parasitic Diseases,

Bethesda, Md., 1959-64; acting sci. dir. Nat. Inst. Allergy and Infectious Diseases, Bethesda, 1965; sci. dir. Div. Biologics Standards, NIH, Bethesda, 1966-67, asso. dir. collaborative research, 1969-78; dir. Fogarty Internat. Center for Advanced Study in Health Scis., Bethesda, 1978-79; dep. asst. sec. for sci. HEW, Washington, 1967-69; sci. dir. Nat. Soc. Med. Research, Washington, 1981—; lectr. Johns Hopkins U., Case Western Res. U.; vis. prof. U. Ariz., 1979, 80, U. So. Fla., 1980—; bd. dirs. Gorgas Meml. Inst., 1967—, pres., 1983—; mem. WHO Expert Panel on Parasitic Diseases, 1969-79. Contbr. numerous chpts., articles on parasitic diseases, revs. to profl. publs. Served with U.S. Army, 1943-46. Recipient Arthur S. Flemming award U.S. Jr. C. of C., 1954, Biol. Sci. award Washington Acad. Sci, 1954, Disting. Alumnus award Bklyn. Coll., 1955, Barnet Cohen award Md. Soc. Bacteriology, 1956, Disting. Service medal USPHS, 1966, Superior Service award HEW, 1968; named Disting. Alumnus, Bklyn. Coll., 1955, George Washington U., 1967; Fulbright scholar, 1960-61; Guggenheim fellow, 1960-61. Mem. Am. Soc. Parasitologists (editor 1955-58, Henry B. Ward medal 1963, pres. 1978), Am. Soc. Tropical Medicine and Hygiene (v.p. 1970), Helminthological Soc. Washington (pres. 1950), Am. Assn. Immunologists, Soc. Protozoology, Tropical Medicine Soc. Washington (pres. 1971), AAAS, Sigma Xi. Club: George Washington U. Home: 3705 Morrison St NW Washington DC 20015 Office: Nat Soc Med Research 1029 Vermont Ave NW Washington DC 20005

JACOBS, MARK NEIL, financial services corporation executive, lawyer; b. Ogdensburg, N.Y., Apr. 2, 1946; s. Al Milton and Alma (Rothwein) J.; m. Susan Ruth Sadowsky, Aug. 17, 1968; children: Melanie Beth, Andrew Lawrence, Jonathan Alexander. B.A., Wagner Coll., 1967; J.D., N.Y. Law Sch., 1971. Bar: N.Y. Law clk. Goldman, Frier & Altesman, N.Y.C., 1971-72; trial atty. U.S. SEC, N.Y.C., 1972-75; supervisory trial atty., br. of enforcement, 1975-77; asst. gen. counsel Dreyfus Corp., N.Y.C., 1977-82, sec., assoc. gen. counsel, 1982—; sec. Dreyfus Third Century Fund, Ind., N.Y.C., 1977—, Dreyfus Growth Opportunity Fund, Inc., 1977—, Dreyfus Mgmt., Inc., 1977—, Dreyfus Life Ins. Co., 1982—, Daiwa Money Fund Inc., 1981—, Gen. Money Fund Inc., 1981—, Gen. Govt. Securities Money Market Fund, Inc., 1982—, L.F. Rothschild Earnings and Liquidity, Inc., N.Y.C., 1982—, Dreyfus Calif. Tax Exempt Bond Fund, Inc., Dreyfus Intermediate Tax Exempt Bond Fund, Inc., N.Y.C., 1983, others. Mem. ABA. Home: 297 Lupine Way Short Hills NJ 07078 Office: Dreyfus Corp 767 Fifth Ave New York NY 10153

JACOBS, MILTON, anthropologist; b. Braddock, Pa., Aug. 9, 1920; s. Charles and Sarah (Weiss) J.; m. Colette Benhaim, Dec. 10, 1944; children: Renee Jacobs Payne, David. B.A., George Washington U., 1948, M.A., 1950; Ph.D., Cath. U., 1956. Social sci. analyst U.S. Govt., 1950-60; prof. research Am. U., Washington, 1961-66; prof. anthropology State U. Coll., New Paltz, N.Y, 1966—, chmn. dept., 1968-74, pres. senate profl. assn. chpt., 1971-73, del. to coll. assembly; lectr. in anthropology Cath. U., 1954-57, CCNY, 1957-61, Georgetown U., 1963-64; vis. prof. U. Md., summer 1981. Contbr. articles to scholarly jours. Pres. New Paltz chpt. Union United Professions, 1980-82. Served with USAAF, 1942-45. Recipient Research award Washington chpt. Am. Mktg. Assn., 1957. Mem. N.Y. Acad. Scis., Soc. Applied Anthropology, Assn. Polit. and Legal Anthropology, Sigma Xi. Democrat. Home: PO Box 248 New Paltz NY 12561

JACOBS, MORRIS ELIAS, advt. exec.; b. Omaha, Aug. 7, 1896; s. Nathaniel Elias and Gertrude (Shafton) J.; m. Rae Sara Iseman, Sept. 15, 1927; 1 dau., Susie. Student, U. Mo., 1914-16; LL.D., Creighton U., 1954, St. Joseph's Coll., 1960. Reporter Des Moines Register-Tribune, 1917-18; reporter, feature writer Omaha Daily Bee, Omaha Daily News, 1918-20; cons. Bozell & Jacobs Advt. and Pub. Relations Agy., Omaha, 1922-80; dir. Omaha Downtown Parking Assn. Mem. exec. com. Omaha Indsl. Found., 1953—; pres. State Bd. Edn., 1955-57; active Boy Scouts Am.; chmn. Nat. Planning Com. for Coop. Electric Refrigeration Bur., 1931-33; mem. exec. com. Pub. Utilities Advt. Assn., 1932-36; co-chmn. initial gifts com. Jewish Philanthropies, 1939; mem., vice chmn. midwest region Am.-Jewish Joint Distbn. Com., 1940; mem. bd. electors Hall of Fame of Omaha U.; chmn. Jewish Philanthropies campaign for war relief and refugees, 1940; pres. W. Central States regional conf. Jewish Fedns. and Welfare Funds, 1941; del. Am. Jewish Conf., 1943; mem. nat. exec. com. Am. Jewish Com.; chmn. Com. of '52 Found.; Bd. dirs. Children's Meml. Hosp., Omaha Symphony Orch. Found.; nat. bd. dirs. United Service Orgn.; trustee Clarkson Hosp., St. Joseph Coll.; bd. dirs. Omaha YMCA, Nat. Conf. Christians and Jews; bd. regents Creighton U.; trustee chmn. 1954 Omaha Centennial Celebration, selected King Ak-Sar-Ben LX, 1954; nat. chmn. U. Mo. Sch. Journalism 50 year commemoration. Recipient B'nai B'rith Americanism citation, 1953; Beth Israel Synaby Neb. Wesleyan U., 1957. Mem. Am. Legion (life), Alpha Delta Sigma, Delta Sigma Chi, Zeta Beta Tau (asso.). Republican. Jewish (pres. temple 1940-41). Home: 1810 Avenida del Mundo Coronado CA 92118 *We must pay rent for the space we occupy on this earth, through service to the religion of our choice and to our community, state and country.*

JACOBS, NORMAN G(ABRIEL), sociologist, educator; b. N.Y.C., Feb. 28, 1924; s. Joseph and Beatrice (Esserman) J.; m. Margaret Alice Ayres, Aug. 20, 1956; children: Laurie, Charles. B.S., City Coll. N.Y., 1943; A.M., Harvard, 1950, Ph.D., 1951. Sociologist natural resources sect. SCAP, Tokyo, 1945-46; lectr. Taiwan Normal U., 1955-57; researcher Am. U., 1957-59; community devel. adviser AID, Shiraz, Iran, 1959-61; from asst. prof. to prof. sociology U. Kans., Lawrence, 1962-65; prof. sociology and Asian studies U. Ill., Urbana, 1965—; Fulbright prof., Thailand, 1965-66; sr. research scholar Korean Inst. Buddhist Studies, 1975; exchange prof. Keio U., Tokyo, 1968-69. Author: The Origin of Modern Capitalism and Eastern Asia, 1958, 81, Sociology of Development, 1966, Modernization without Development, 1972, also articles.; Co-author: Japanese Coinage, 1953, 72. Served with AUS, 1943-46. Life mem. Indian Sociol. Soc.; mem. Assn. Asian Studies, Pali Text Soc. Theravada Buddhist. Home: 312 S Willis St Champaign IL 61821 Office: Sociology Dept Univ Ill Urbana IL 61801

JACOBS, NORMAN JOSEPH, pub. co. exec.; b. Chgo., Oct. 28, 1932; s. Herman and Tillie (Chapman) J.; m. Jeri Kolber Rose, Jan. 2, 1977; 1 son, Barry Herman; children by previous marriage—Carey, Murray, Dale. B.S. in Mktg, U. Ill., 1954. Display salesman Chgo. Daily News, 1954-57; dist. mgr. Davidson Pub. Co., Chgo., 1957-62; v.p. Press-Tech, Inc., Evanston, Ill., 1962-69; pres. Century Pub. Co., Evanston, 1969—. Served with USNR, 1951-59. Mem. Alpha Delta Sigma, Tau Epsilon Phi. Jewish. Club: B'nai B'rith. Office: 1020 Church St Evanston IL 60201

JACOBS, RICHARD MATTHEW, dentist; b. Wloclawek, Poland, Oct. 31, 1924; s. Kuba Kopel and Irene (Spiro) Jakub; m. Ruth Federbusch, May 21, 1960; 1 son, Steven Kenneth. Dr. Med.Dent., Maximilian U., 1948; D.D.S., N.Y. U., 1952; M.P.H., U. Calif., 1961; Ph.D., Med. Coll. Va., 1964; M.S., U. Ill., 1965. Pvt. practice dentistry, N.Y.C., 1956-59, pub. health dentist, Nev., 1959-60; asso. prof., head dept. orthodontics U. B.C., 1965-66; asso. dean, prof. orthodontics, coordinator curriculum, head dept. oral biology U. Iowa, 1966-71, prof. orthodontics, 1971—; chmn. grad. and postgrad. sect. Am. Assn. Dental Schs., 1975-76; councilman group on engring. in medicine and biology IEEE, 1973-77. Served as 1st lt. AUS, 1953-55. Fellow Am. Coll. Dentists, Am. Pub. Health Assn., Sigma Xi; mem. Assn. Am. Med. Colls., ADA, Am. Assn. Anatomists, Teratology Soc., Internat. Assn. Dental Research, Am. Assn. Higher Edn. Club: Univ. Athletic (Iowa City). Research on teratol. studies cleft palate, effects of muscular activity on fetal devel., pressure sensitive devices for measuring muscular activity, cost effectiveness in edn., control in formal orgns. Home: 327 Ferson St Iowa City IA 52240

JACOBS, ROBERT, educator; b. Murphysboro, Ill., July 17, 1913; s. Arthur Clarence and Zylphia May (Porter) J.; m. Oma Lee Corgan, Aug. 13, 1939; children: Robert Corgan, Janice Lee, Lawrence James, Linda May (Mrs. Paul Wineberg). B.Ed., So. Ill. U., 1935; M.A., U. Ill., 1939; Ed.D., Wayne State U., 1949. Pub. sch. tchr., adminstr., Wood River, Ill., 1935-42; personnel staff Ford Motor Co., 1945-46; asst. instr. Wayne U., 1946-47; asst. dir. Ednl. Records Bur., N.Y.C., 1947-51; dir. counseling, prof. edn. Tex. A. and M. Coll., 1951-54; ednl. measurements adviser, dep. chief edn. div. U.S. Operations Mission to Ethiopia, FOA, 1954-56; regional edn. adviser S.E. Asia U.S. Operations Mission, Thailand, 1956-58; chief Far East program div. Office Edn., ICA, 1958-61; chief edn. div. Office Ednl. and Social Devel. AID, 1961-62; prof. edn., dean internat. service div. So. Ill. U., Carbondale, 1962-67, prof. emeritus, 1974—; regional edn. adviser Office Regional Devel. Affairs, Am. embassy, Bangkok, Thailand, 1967-74; cons. S.E. Asian Ministers of Edn. Orgn., Bangkok, 1974—; continuing cons. SEAMEO; ednl. cons., writer, lectr., 1974—; vis. prof., extension lectr. U. Ark., U. Ala., Rutgers U., U. Addis Ababa, George Washington U.; numerous surveys and evaluations edn. programs abroad, including, Korea, Cambodia, Syria, Nigeria, India, Congo, Chile, Colombia; mem. internat. adv. com. Ednl. Records Bur. Served with AUS, 1942-45. Recipient of meritorious service citation ICA, AID, 1959, meritorious honor award Dept. State, 1968. Mem. NEA, Nat. Soc. Study Edn., AARP, Phi Delta Kappa. Methodist. Home: PO Box 431 Murphysboro IL 62966

JACOBS, ROGER FRANCIS, librarian, educator, lawyer; b. Detroit, Jan. 1, 1937; s. Melvin Frank and Florence L. (Romine) J.; m. Alice Virginia Reckstin, Aug. 10, 1963; children: Stephen, Magdalene, Sarah. A.B., U. Detroit, 1962, J.D., 1970; M.L.S., U. Mich., 1964. Bar: Mich. 1970. Law librarian U. Detroit, 1962-67, U. Widsor, Ont., Can., 1967-73; prof. law, librarian So. Ill. U., Carbondale, 1973-77; librarian U.S. Supreme Ct. Library, Washington, 1978—. Co-author: Illinois Legal Research Sourcebook, 1977; compiler: Memorials of Supreme Court Justices, 1982. Served with USNR, 1954-58. Mem. Am. Assn. Law Libraries (exec. bd. 1976-79, pres. 1981-82), Can. Assn. Law Libraries (pres. 1971-73), Phi Alpha Theta. Office: US Supreme Court Library 1 1st St NW Washington DC 20543

JACOBS, ROSETTA, actress; b. Detroit, Jan. 22, 1932; m. Joseph Morgenstern, 1962; 1 child. Student, Los Angeles pub. sch. Acted in sch. plays; motion picture debut in Louisa; other motion pictures include Carrie, 1976, Tim, 1978; TV appearances include Skag; appeared: Broadway play Glass Menagerie, 1965; off-Broadway plays Rosemary and The Alligators, 1961 (Acad. award nominee for The Hustler 1962, Carrie 1976). Mem. Acad. Motion Picture Arts and Scis.

JACOBS, RUTH HARRIET, sociology educator; b. Boston, Nov. 15, 1924; d. Samuel J. Miller and Jane G. (Miller); m. Neal Jacobs, Aug. 1948 (div.); children: Eliha, Edith. B.S., Boston U, 1964; Ph.D, Brandeis U., 1969. Reporter, feature writer Herald-Traveler, Boston, 1943-49; tchr. Mass. Bay Community Coll., Northeastern U., 1961-69; mem. faculty, Boston U., 1969-82; prof. sociology Boston U., 1969-82; prof., chmn. dept. sociology Clark U., Worcester, Mass., 1982—; cons. in field. Author: Life after Youth; Female, Forty, What Next, 1979, Button, Button, Who Has the Button, 1983; co-author: Re-engagement in Later Life: Re-employment and Re-marriage, 1979; contbr. articles to profl. jours., chpts. to books. NIMH grantee, 1972-75; NSF postdoctoral fellow, 1977-78. Mem. Am. Sociol. Assn., Soc. Sci. Study Social Problems, Clin. Sociology Assn., Eastern Sociol. Assn., Mass. Sociol. Assn. (v.p. 1979), Boston Soc. Gerontol. Psychiatry. Jewish. Home: 75 High Ledge Ave Wellesley MA 02181 Office: Dept Sociology Clark U Worcester MA 01610

JACOBS, SOPHIA YARNALL, author, civic worker; b. Haverford, Pa., June 23, 1902; d. Charlton and Anna Brinton (Coxe) Yarnall; m. Reginald Robert Jacobs., Oct. 14, 1921 (div.); children—Denholm Muir, Charlton Yarnall (Mrs. Stowe Catlin Phelps). Student, Bryn Mawr Coll., 1919-21. Promotion mgr. Phila. Orch., 1942-45; Former bd. dirs. Am. Symphony Orch.; former mem. Urban League Greater N.Y., pres., 1956-60, chmn. bd., 1960-64; dir.; bd. dirs. The Africa Fund, 1969—; former bd. dirs. ACLU, Rachel Carson Trust for Living Environment; pres. Nat. Council of Women of U.S., 1960-65. Free lance writer: women's mags. including Parents, 1930—; Author: The Clark Inheritance, 1981. Clubs: Cosmopolitan, Women's City (N.Y.C.). Home: 11 E 73d St New York NY 10021

JACOBS, TRAVIS BEAL, historian, educator; b. N.Y.C., Apr. 22, 1936; s. Albert Charles and Loretta Field (Beal) J.; children: Travis Beal, Holmes Morison. A.B., Princeton U., 1958; M.A., Columbia U., 1960, Ph.D., 1971. Mem. faculty Middlebury Coll. (Vt.), 1965—, prof. history, 1978—, chmn. dept. history, 1976—. Co-editor: Navigating The Rapids, 1918, 1971, From the Papers of Adolf A. Berle, 1973, America and the Winter War, 1939-40, 1981. Cons. 20th Century Fund, 1972-73; bd. dirs. Psi Upsilon Found. Mem. Am. Hist. Assn., Orgn. Am. Historians, Soc. Historians Fgn. Relations, So. Hist. Assn., Vt. Hist. Assn. Episcopalian. Home: 21 Seminary St Middlebury VT 05753 Office: Middlebury Coll Middlebury VT 05753

JACOBS, WILBUR RIPLEY, historian, educator; b. Chgo.; Walter R. and Nona I. (Deutsch) J.; children: Shirley Elizabeth, Catherine Elaine, William Ripley. B.A., M.A., Ph.D., UCLA; postgrad. (John Martin Vincent scholar), Johns Hopkins U. Jr. instr. Johns Hopkins U., Balt.; instr. history Stanford U.; instr. Am. history U. Calif. at Santa Barbara, then asst. prof., assoc. prof., prof., dean of men, research lectr., 1956, chmn. dept. history, 1959-63; acad. asst. to pres. U. Calif. at Berkeley, 1964-65; mem. editorial bd. history panel U. Calif. Press, 1965-68; Vis. prof. Ind. U., U. Colo., UCLA, 1964, Claremont Grad. Sch., 1968; William L. Clements library lectr. U. Mich., 1967; U.S. State Dept. del. Cultural Exchange Program, Yugoslavia, 1965; Fulbright vis. prof. Australian Nat. U., 1969; lectr. U. Papua, New Guinea, 1969, Melbourne U., 1969; cons. Nat. Endowment for the Humanities, NSF, 1975—. Author: Wilderness Politics and Indian Gifts, 1966, The Historical World of Frederick Jackson Turner, 1968, Dispossessing the American Indian, 1972; also articles in Ency. Britannica and other reference works, scholarly jours., mags., newspapers.; Co-author: Turner, Bolton and Webb, 1979; Editor: Letters of Francis Parkman, 2 vols, 1960 (selected for J.F. Kennedy White Ho. collection of distinguished books), The Appalachian Indian Frontier, 1967, The Paxton Riots and the Frontier, 1967, Benjamin Franklin, Philosopher-Statesman or Materialist?, 1972, Frederick Jackson Turner's Legacy, 1977, Indians as Ecologists, 1980; Editorial bd.: Pacific Hist. Rev, 1966-70, American West mag, 1969—, Western Hist. Quar, 1969-74, Am. History and Life, 1969—, Am. Indian Quar, 1974-81, Environ. Rev, 1977—, The Public Historian, 1979—. Served with USAAF. Research grantee Rockefeller Found., 1949, Am. Philos. Soc., 1956, 69, Huntington Library, 1960, 64, 70, 79, Ford Found., 1962; research fellow NEH, 1983. Mem. Am. Hist. Assn. (council mem. Pacific Coast br., Pacific Coast prize 1947, v.p. Pacific Coast br. 1975, pres. 1976-77, mem. Beveridge and Dunning prize com. 1969-72, joint com. with Orgn. Am. Historians, Soc. Am. Archivists 1983), Orgn. Am. Historians, History Guild So. Calif. (mem. council Conf. for Peace Research in History 1966-72), Am. Soc. for Ethnohistory (exec. bd. 1966—, pres. elect 1978-79), Am. Soc. Environ. History (pres. 1978-80). Research on early Am. history, Am. frontier, native Am. Indian and environmental history, historiography. Office: Dept History U Calif Santa Barbara CA 93106 *I have always enjoyed university teaching, research, and writing—the life of a professor. I think one can be better when it is a pleasure to perform.*

JACOBS, WILLIAM BRUCE, biochemist; b. Lincoln, Nebr., May 3, 1938; s. Martin Alfred and Molly (Schmidt) J.; children by previous marriage—Bruce Alan, Jennifer Kay. Student, Hastings Coll., 1956-60, U. Nebr., 1960-61, Trinity U., San Antonio, 1962-63. Staff U.S. Air Force Sch. Aerospace Medicine, San Antonio, 1961-65; biochemist Midwest Research Inst., Kansas City, Mo., 1965-76, head sect. life scis. div. bio. scis., 1976—; water monitor Continuous Aqueous Monitor, 1972; air monitor Immobilized Enzyme Alarm, 1976; spot checker, portable air monitor Pesticide Monitor, 1977. Served with USAF, 1961-65. Mem. AAAS. Republican. Methodist. Club: Masons. Office: 425 Volker Blvd Kansas City MO 64110

JACOBS, WILLIAM PAUL, botanist, educator; b. Boston, May 25, 1919; s. Vincent H. and Elizabeth (Kennedy) J.; m. Jane Shaw, Mar. 12, 1949; children: Mark, Anne. A.B., Harvard U., 1942, Ph.D., 1946. Research assoc. biology Harvard U., 1946-47; jr. prize fellow Harvard Soc. Fellows, 1947-48; faculty Princeton, 1948—, prof. biology, 1962—, W.L. Schultz prof. biology, 1969; Mem. com. innovation lab. study Biol. Scis. Curriculum Study, 1959-64; vis. prof. U. Calif.-Berkeley, 1952, U. Oxford, 1962, U. Colo., 1972, U. Bristol (Eng.), 1980. Author: (with C.E. LaMotte) Regulation in Plants by Hormones, 1964, Plant Hormones and Plant Development, 1979; contbr.: articles to sci. publs. Plant Hormones and Plant Development. Served with M.C. AUS, 1942-44. Recipient Morrison prize N.Y. Acad. Scis., 1951; Lalor fellow, 1950-51; NSF sr. postdoctoral fellow, 1957; Sci. Faculty fellow, 1962; Guggenheim fellow, 1967; grantee Am. Cancer Soc., NSF, NASA, Office Naval Research, U.S. Army, Hoyt Found. Mem. Soc. Study Devel. and Growth (pres. 1960-61), Bot. Soc. Am. (Dimond prize 1974), Am., Soc. Plant Physiologists, Internat. Soc. Plant Morphologists, Internat. Phycological Soc., Soc. Exptl. Biology (Brit.). Home: 64 Maclean Circle Princeton NJ 08540 Office: Biology Dept Princeton U. Princeton NJ 08544

JACOBS, WINFRED OSCAR, telephone company executive; b. Joliet, Ill., Dec. 2, 1922; s. James Winfred and Helen (Brown) J.; m. Katherine Marie Kaiser, Sept. 15, 1946; children: Richard W., Robert E. B.A., U. Denver, 1946. Div. sales mgr. Mountain Bell Telephone, Phoenix, 1955-57, mktg. mgr., Salt Lake City, 1960-62, dir. long range planning, Denver, 1963-64, v.p., gen. mgr., Boise, Idaho, 1965-67, v.p. public relations, Denver, 1968-69, v.p. ops., 1970-78, exec. v.p., chief operating officer, 1979—, dir., 1970—; engr. AT&T, N.Y.C., 1957-59; dir. 1st Nat. Bank of Denver., 1st Interstate Bank of Denver. Chmn. Boise United Fund, 1967, Idaho Gov.'s Task Force on Edn., Boise, 1967; trustee Coll. of Idaho, Caldwell, 1966-77, Loretto Heights Coll., 1969—; bd. dirs. Met. Sci. Center, 1976—, Central City Opera Assn., 1977—, Inst. of Health, 1979—. Served with AUS, 1943-46; ETO. Mem. U. Denver Alumni Assn. (dir. 1968-71). Clubs: Denver Athletic, Denver; Rolling Hills Country (Golden, Colo.). Home: 15100 Foothill Rd Golden CO 80401 Office: 931 14th St Denver CO 80202

JACOBS, WOODROW COOPER, meteorologist, oceanographer; b. Pasadena, Calif., Sept. 11, 1908; s. William Rozel and Mabelle (Cooper) J.; m. Dorothy Cecelia Quinn, June 15, 1933; 1 dau., Marilyn Rozel (Mrs. Wilbur M. Ott). Student, Va. Mil. Inst., 1926-27; A.B., UCLA, 1930; Ph.D., 1948; M.S., U. So. Calif., 1934. With U.S. Weather Bur., San Diego, 1931-36, forecaster fruit-frost service, Pomona, Calif., 1936-41; research asso. Scripps Instn. Oceanography, also Carnegie Inst., 1937; chief civilian meteorologist Hdqrs. USAAF, 1941-46; head climatological branch U.S. Weather Bur., Washington, 1946-48; dir. climatology USAF Air Weather Service, Washington, 1948-60; phys. sci. specialist Library of Congress, 1960-61; dir. Nat. Oceanographic Data Center, 1961-67, World Data Center A, Oceanography, 1962-67; dir. environ. data service Environ. Sci. Service Adminstrn., Silver Spring, Md., 1967-70; sr. scientist Ocean Data Systems, Inc., Rockville, Md., 1971—; vis. prof. Mass. Inst. Tech., 1950, U. Chgo., 1956; lectr. meteorology and oceanography Dept. Agr. Grad. Sch., 1942-58; professorial lectr. George Washington U., 1957; USAF mem. two panels Research and Devel. Bd., Dept. Def., 1948-52; com. climatology joint meteorol. com. Joint Chiefs Staff, 1948-58; U.S. del. Internat. Meteorol. Orgn., Toronto, Can., 1947, pres. subcom. agrl. forecasts, 1947-50; mem. commn. climatology World Meteorol. Orgn., 1950-62, chmn. internat. com. exchange data, 1953-60; U.S. del. of Nat. Acad. Scis. to assembly Internat. Union Geodesy and Geophysics, Brussels, 1951, Rome, 1954, Toronto, 1957, Lucerne, 1967; mem. coms. NRC-NSF, 1948—; chmn. interagy. atmospheric scis. oceanography com. on air-sea research, 1963-64; com. on oceanography Smithsonian Instn., 1962-67; working group Intergovtl. Oceanographic Commn., UNESCO, 1962-67; panel mem. Interagy. Com. on Oceanography, 1961-67; adv. council Oceanic Research Inst. of San Diego, 1964—; adv. panel on sea-air interaction program Dept. Commerce, 1964-67; chmn. working group on air-sea inter actions World Meteorol. Orgn., UN, 1964-68; U.S. del. 2d Oceanographic Congress, Moscow, 1966; U.S. mem. Intergovernmental Oceanographic Commn. Com. on Ocean Stas., Paris, 1966; mem. data adv. panel Pres.'s Council on Marine Resources and Engring. Devel., 1967-69; mem. com. on radio frequency requirements for sci. research Nat. Acad. Sci., 1969-70; mem. com. biog. classification Internat. Assn. Phys. and Sci. Oceanography, 1968—; Dept. Commerce mem. Pres.'s Commn. Food from the Sea, 1968-69; adv. bd. Office Critcial Tables Fed. Council, 1968-69; U.S. del. planning com. Internat. Indian Ocean Expdn., Paris, 1964. Author: Energy Exchange Between Sea and Atmosphere, 1951, Meteorological Satellites, 1962; co-author: Arctic Meteorology, 1956; also numerous articles in field.; Editor: English edit. Oceanology, Acad. Sci. USSR for scripta technica, Inc, 1962-75; adv. bd.: Meteorol. and Geoastrophys. Abstracts, 1963—; asso. editor: four publs. Am. Meterol. Soc, 1946-70. Recipient Certificate of Appreciation USAAF, 1946; Distinguished Service award Dept. Commerce, 1970. Fellow Am. Geophys. Union (exec. com. 1947-61, council 1961, sec. sect. meteorology 1947-74, chmn. com. geophys. data), Am. Meterol. Soc. (council 1961-64, chmn. bd. certified cons. meteorologists 1960-62), Washington Acad. Sci.; mem. Internat. Platform Assn., Royal Meteorol. Soc., Md., N.Y. acads. scis., Marine Tech. Soc., Oceanographical Soc. Japan, AAAS, Am. Soc. Limnology and Oceanography, Archeol. Soc. Md., U.S. Navy League (Ormond Beach, Fla.), U.S. Naval Inst. (Annapolis, Md.), SAR, Blue Circle C (UCLA), Sigma Xi, Alpha Tau Omega, Alpha Kappa Psi, Blue Key. Methodist. Clubs: Shawnee Country (Winchester, Va.); Halifax Yacht (Daytona Beach, Fla.); Cosmos (Washington). Home: 6309 Bradley Blvd Bethesda MD 20817 234 Ocean Palm Dr Flagler Beach FL 32036 Office: 6000 Executive Blvd Rockville MD 20852 *The proudest moment of my life was when an inspection team reported that the federal agency of which I was director had the highest morale of any federal agency that they had reviewed in their 20 years. Success does not have to be achieved at the expense of others.*

JACOBSEN, ADOLF MARCELIUS BERGH, university administrator, former naval officer; b. Bklyn., June 29, 1926; s. Oscar B. and Paula (Vik) J.; m. Mary A. Tellefsen, May 23, 1948; children: Irene L., Beverly A. Grad., N.Y. Maritime Coll., 1946; B.T., Tex. State Tech. Inst., 1970; M.A., U.S. Internat. U., 1973, Ph.D., 1980. Marine engr. U.S. Mcht. Marines, 1946-54; commd. U.S. Navy, 1954, advanced through ranks to capt., 1971; logistics and material officer, San Diego, 1954-56, squadron engr., Newport, R.I. and Key West, Fla., 1956-58; moblzn. plans officer Bur. Naval Personnel, Washington, 1962-64; exec. officer USS Cambria, Norfolk, Va., 1969-70, comdg. officer Naval Res. Center, San Diego, 1970-73, asst. chief of staff for Naval Res. and Tng., 1973-74, comdr. Naval Res. Readiness Commd., Los Angeles, 1974-75, ret., 1975; v.p. univ. affairs Nat. U., San Diego, 1975—. Co-author: To Better Prepare Myself to Serve, 1974, The Perspective of Minority Reservists, 1974, The Pleased, The Perplexed and the Perturbed, 1974. Decorated Navy Commendation medal with combat "V; recipient Disting. Service citation Res. Officers Assn. U.S., 1972. Mem. Am. Soc. Tng. and Devel., Ret. Officers Assn., Navy League U.S., World Affairs Council. Clubs: Univ., Kona Kai, Sons of Norway. Home: 3236 Casa Bonita Dr Bonita CA 92002 Office: 4141 Camino del Rio S San Diego CA 92108 *

JACOBSEN, ARTHUR, department store executive; b. S.I., N.Y., Sept. 21, 1921; s. Alf and Jenny S. (Smith) J.; m. Elizabeth B. Sayford, May 12, 1951; children: Martha, Bruce. Student, N.Y. U., 1939-42; B.A., Princeton U., 1948. Asst. cashier First Nat. City Bank N.Y., 1939-55; with J.C. Penney Co., N.Y.C., 1955—, treas., 1957-69, v.p., dir. consumer fin. services, 1969—; chmn. bd. J.C. Penney Fin. Corp., 1964-69; chmn. bd., dir. J.C. Penney Ins. Cos., 1967—, J.C. Penney Casualty Ins. Co., 1973—; dir., chmn. audit com. Telecredit Inc., Los Angeles; dir. Pizza Inn Inc., Dallas; mem. Midtown adv. bd. Chem. Bank N.Y. Trust Co. Trustee, chmn. planning com. Morris Mus. Mem. Phi Beta Kappa. Home: 77 Midwood Terr Madison NJ 07940 Office: 1301 Ave of the Americas New York NY 10019

JACOBSEN, EDWARD HASTINGS, physicist; b. Elizabeth, N.J., Jan. 2, 1926; s. Edward H. and Marie (Thomas) J. B.S. in Physics, Mass. Inst. Tech., 1950; Ph.D., 1954. With Gen. Electric Research Lab., 1955-61; prof. physics U. Rochester, N.Y., 1961—. Postdoctoral Fulbright fellow, 1954-55; NIH Career Devel. fellow, 1966-68. Mem. Am. Phys. Soc., AAAS, Sigma Xi. Office: Physics Dept U Rochester Rochester NY 14627

JACOBSEN, HUGH NEWELL, architect; b. Grand Rapids, Mich., Mar. 11, 1929; s. John Edwall and Lucy Ellen (Newell) J.; m. Robin Kearney, Dec. 27, 1952; children: John Edwall, Matthew Christian, Simon Townsend. B.A., U. Md., 1951; B.Arch., Yale, 1955; cert., Archtl. Asso. Sch. Architecture, London, Eng., 1954; L.H.D. (hon.), Gettysburg Coll., 1974. Architect with Philip Johnson, New Canaan, Conn., 1955-57, Keyes, Lethbridge & Condon, Washington, 1957-58; prin. Hugh Newell Jacobsen, FAIA, Washington, 1958—; lectr. univs.; vis. prof. U. Cairo, Egypt, 1970. Editor: A Guide to the Architecture of Washington, D.C, 1965. Mem. joint com. Landmarks of Nat. Capital, after 1976, Com. of 100 of Fed. City; trustee Found. Preservation Historic Georgetown, Corcoran Gallery Art. Served with USAF, 1955-57. John Fitzgerald Kennedy Meml. fellow N.Z. Govt., 1971; recipient numerous awards for design Met. Washington Bd. Trade, Archtl. Record, Silver medal for excellence in design Clemson U., 1981. Fellow AIA (honor awards 1969, 74, 78, 80, homes for better living awards, others); mem. Tau Sigma Delta. Clubs: Cosmos (Washington); Century Assn., Yale (N.Y.C.). Home: 1352 28th St NW Washington DC 20007 Office: 2529 P St NW Washington DC 20007

JACOBSEN, JOHN CHARLES, oil company executive, lawyer; b. Detroit, Apr. 12, 1929; s. Edward Hastings and Marie (Thomas) J.; m. Frances Jane Dickey, Oct. 18, 1952; children: Scott Thomas, Kathleen Marie. B.A., Mich. State U., 1951; LL.B., Wayne State U., 1958. Bar: Mich. 1958. With Shell Oil Co., 1953—, asst. mgr. corp. econs., N.Y.C., 1958-60, successively fin. mgr. div. synthetic rubber, mgr. corp. accounting, 1960-70, asst. treas., Houston, 1970-75, treas., 1975-77, controller, 1977-82, v.p. fin., 1983—; dir. Shell Oil Co. subs. Mem. city planning bd., Cedar Grove, N.J., 1965-66; mem. acctg. adv. com. U. Tex. Served to 2d lt. AUS, 1951-53. Mem. Mich. Bar Assn., Fin. Execs. Inst. (com. on corp. reporting), Am. Petroleum Inst. (fin. com.), Lambda Chi Alpha. Republican. Presbyn. Club: River Plantation Country. Home: 143 Jeb Stuart Ln Conroe TX 77301 Office: 1 Shell Plaza PO Box 2463 Houston TX 77001

JACOBSEN, JOSEPHINE WINDER BOYLAN, author; b. Coburg, Ont., Can., Aug. 19, 1908; d. Joseph Edward and Octavis (Winder) Boylan; m. Eric Jacobsen, Mar. 17, 1932; 1 son, Erlend Ericsen. Grad., Roland Park Country Sch., 1926; L.H.D., Coll. Notre Dame Md., 1974, Goucher Coll., 1974. Critic; short story writer; lectr.; poetry cons. Library of Congress, 1971-73, hon. cons. in Am. letters, 1973—; v.p. PSA, 1979—. Author: The Human Climate, 1953, For the Unlost, 1948, The Animal Inside, 1966, (with William Mueller) The Testament of Samuel Beckett, 1968, Genet and Ionesco Playwrights of Silence, 1968, The Shade-Seller: New and Collected Poems, 1974, A Walk With Raschid and Other Stories, 1978 (Notable Books of 1978), The Chinese Insomniacs, New Poems, 1981; writing also included in Best American Short Stories, 1966, O'Henry Awards Prize Stories, 1967, 71, 73, 76, Fifty Years of the American Short Story, 1970, Best Poems of, 1961, 64, 68, 72, 73, 74, 75. Mem. panel D.C. Commn. of the Arts and Humanities, 1973; mem. women's com. Center Stage, Washington, 1972-73; mem. lit. panel Nat. Endowment for Arts, 1980—; mem. com. Millay Colony for Arts; bd. dirs. Nat. Council for Arts. Recipient Prairie Schooner Fiction award, 1974, Borestone Mountain Poetry award, 1976, Pushcart prize, 1980, 83, best poem of 1981 award Cath. Journalist Assn., award for service to lit. Am. Acad. and Inst. Arts and Letters, 1982; MacDowell Colony fellow; Yaddo fellow. Mem. PEN. Democrat. Roman Catholic. Home: Mountain View Rd Whitefield NH 03598

JACOBSEN, RICHARD T., mechanical engineering educator, thermodynamics researcher; b. Pocatello, Idaho, Nov. 12, 1941; s. Thorleif and Edith Emily (Gladwin) J.; m. Vicki Belle Hopkins, July 16, 1959 (div. Mar. 1973); children: Pamela Sue, Richard T., Eric Ernest; m. Bonnie Lee Stewart, Oct. 19, 1973; 1 son,Jay Michael; 1 Stepson, Erik David Lustig. B.S.M.E., U. Idaho, 1963, M.S.M.E., 1965; Ph.D. in Engring. Sci., Wash. State U., 1972. Registered profl. engr., Idaho. Instr. U. Idaho, 1964-66, asst. prof. mech. engring., 1966-72, assoc. prof., 1972-77, prof., 1977—, chmn. dept. mech. engring., 1980—, assoc. dir. Ctr. for applied Thermodynamic Studies, 1975—. Author: Nitrogen-International Thermodynamic Tables of the Fluid State-6, 1979; numerous reports on thermodynamics properties of fluids, 1971-83; contbr. articles to profl. jours. NSF sci. faculty fellow, 1968-69; NSF research and travel grantee, 1976-83; nat. Bur. Standards grantee, 1974-83. Mem. ASME (faculty advisor 1972-75, 78—), Soc. Automotive Engrs. (Ralph R. Teetor Edn. award, Detroit 1968), Sigma Xi, Tau Beta Pi. Mormon. Office: Dept Mech Engring U Idaho Gauss Engring Lab 202 Moscow ID 83843

JACOBSEN, ROBERT RAY, national park administrator; b. Omaha, Aug. 17, 1929; s. Ray William and Irma Anna (Svoboda) J.; m. Phelma Marie Karvakko, June 10, 1953; children: (adopted) Maile Chrinstine, Lisa Ann. B.S. in Forest Recreation, Colo. State U., Ft. Collins, 1951. Park ranger Crater Lake Nat. Park, Klamath, Oreg., 1954-55, Hawaii Volcanoes Nat. Park, Volcano, 1955-57, dist. park ranger, 1957-59, Olympic Nat. Park, Clearwater, Wash., 1959-62, Sequoia Nat. Park, Giant Forest, Calif., 1962-63; supt. Lehman Caves Nat. Monument, Baker, Nev., 1963-65, Chalmette Nat. Hist. Park, Arabi, La., 1965-67; new area keyman Nat. Park Service, Washington, 1967-69, chief br. of new areas, 1969-72; supt. Shenandoah Nat. Park, Luray, Va., 1972—. Served as 2d lt. USAF, 1951-53; Korea. Home: Route 2 Box 377 Luray VA 22835 Office: Shenandoah Nat Park Route 4 Box 292 Luray VA 22835

JACOBSEN, THOMAS HERBERT, banker; b. Chgo., Oct. 15, 1939; s. Herbert Rogde and Catharine (Ball) J.; m. Nancy Kay Ferree, Mar. 9, 1963. B.S., Lake Forest (Ill.) U., 1963; M.B.A., U. Chgo., 1968; grad., Advanced Mgmt. Program, Harvard U., 1979. From asst. cashier to v.p. computer ops. First Nat. Bank Chgo., 1966-76; v.p., then sr. v.p. Barnett Banks Fla., 1976-79, exec. v.p., chief fin. officer, Jacksonville, 1979-82, sr. exec. v.p., 1982-84, vice-chmn., dir., 1984—; lectr. Grad. Sch. Bus., U. North Fla. Chmn. bd. trustees North Fla. Multiple Sclerosis Soc. Mem. Am. Bankers Assn. Republican. Presbyterian. Clubs: Union League (Chgo.); Bob O'Link Golf (Highland Park, Ill.); Players (Ponte VedraBeach, Fla.); N Men's (Northwestern U.). Office: 100 Laura St Jacksonville FL 32202

JACOBSEN, THOMAS WARREN, educator, archeologist; b. Mankato, Minn., Mar. 18, 1935; s. Maurice and Effie (Jensen) J.; m. Kathryn Jane Anderson, Aug. 18, 1956 (dec. June 1978); children: Mark Thomas, Kirsten.; m. Susan K. Lehr, Aug. 1, 1981. B.A., St. Olaf Coll., 1957; M.A., U. Minn., 1960; postgrad., Am. Sch. Classical Studies, Athens, Greece, 1962-63; Ph.D., U. Pa., 1964. Asst. prof. classics, classical archeology Vanderbilt U., 1964-66; asst. prof. Ind. U., 1966-68, asso. prof., 1968-75, prof., 1975—, chmn. dept. classical studies, 1975-78, chmn. program in classical archaeology, 1970—; staff mem. excavations, Porto Cheli, Greece, 1962, 65, 66, field dir., 1967, dir. excavations at Franchthi Cave, Greece, 1967—, staff excavations, Kea, Greece, 1963; du Pont spl. research fellow Am. Sch. Classical Studies, Athens, 1980-81. Served with AUS, 1957. Fulbright scholar, Greece, 1962-63; Olivia James fellow Archeol. Inst. Am., Greece, 1968-69; Am. Council Learned Socs. fellow, 1973-74; NSF postdoctoral fellow, 1973-74; Am. Philos. Soc. grantee, 1973-74. Mem. Archeol. Inst. Am., Soc. for Am. Archaeology, Prehistoric Soc. (Eng.), Soc. Profl. Archaeologists, Ind. Classical Conf., Soc. for Preservation Greek Heritage, Brit. Inst. Archeology, Ankara Assn. Field Archaeology, AAAS, Am. Assn. Advancement of Humanities., AAUP. Lutheran. Home: 3712 Fenway Pl Bloomington IN 47401 Office: Dept Classical Studies and Program in Classical Archaeology Ind U Bloomington IN 47401

JACOBSOHN, DAVID HENRY, computer engr.; b. Washington, Jan. 16, 1925; s. Isadore Meyer and Mary (Shufro) J.; m. Sandra Lee Kamner, Aug. 28, 1951; children—Dori Evelyn, Lee Morris. Ph.B., U. Chgo., 1948, S.B. in Math, 1953. Asst. elec. engr. Argonne (Ill.) Nat. Lab., 1945-58, computer engr. applied math. div., 1961—, head computer engring. sect., 1966-71; sr. computer engr. Inst. for Computer Research, U. Chgo., 1958-61; lectr. Ill. Inst. Tech., Chgo., 1963-67; research Los Alamos Nat. Lab., summers 1969, 71. Mem. IEEE (sr.), Computer Soc. (governing bd. 1973-78), Inst. Certification Computer Profls. (founding mem. 1973), Sci. Research Soc. Am., Gamma Alpha. Research in computer arithmetic and logical orgn. Home: 5642 Harper Ave Chicago IL 60637 Office: 9700 S Cass Ave Argonne IL 60439

JACOBSOHN, PETER M.W.S., editor; b. Berlin, Sept. 3, 1916; U.S., 1948, naturalized, 1954; s. Siegfried and Edith Lotte (Schiffer) J.; m. Annette Margarete Wallach, June 18, 1947; 1 son, Nicholas. Student, Grunewald Gymnasium, Berlin, 1926-33; grad., Alpine Coll., Switzerland, 1934; student, Columbia U., 1951-52, Bklyn. Coll., 1958-62. Lit. asso., promotion mgr. New Leader Mag., N.Y.C., 1952-63; asso. editor W. W. Norton & Co., N.Y.C., 1963-65; editor, dir. promotion Atherton Press, N.Y.C., 1965-67; prin. editor Ency. Brit., Chgo., 1967-72; editor publs. Center Internat. Affairs, Harvard U., 1973-81; mgr. publs. Michael Reese Hosp. and Med. Ctr., Chgo., 1982—. Home: 420 W Aldine Ave Chicago IL 60657 Office: Michael Reese Hosp Lake Shore Dr at 31st St Chicago IL 60616

JACOBSON, ALAN DONALD, corp. exec.; b. Perth Amboy, N.J., Aug. 10, 1940; s. Lewis S. and Rose M. (Goldstein) J.; m. Nancy Reese Deinstein, Jan. 16, 1966; children—Julie Victoria, Matthew Arne. A.B. in Am. Studies, Cornell U., 1961; LL.B., Yale, 1964. Bar: Cal. bar. Asso. firm Gibson, Dunn & Crutcher, Los Angeles, 1965-69; with Whittaker Corp., Los Angeles, 1969—, gen. counsel, now sr. v.p., sec. Office: 10880 Wilshire Blvd Los Angeles CA 90024

JACOBSON, ALBERT HILLMAN, insurance broker; b. Chgo., Apr. 17, 1907; s. Harry E. and Ida (Klink) J.; m. Bette Wolf, June 30, 1935. Student, Northwestern U., John Marshall Law Sch., Central YMCA Coll., Chgo. Ins. broker, 1932—. Fifty eight year vet. Boy Scouts Am.; pres. Mid-West Region United Synagogue Am., 1966-68; vice chmn. adminstrv. com. Zionist Orgn. Chgo., 1967—, v.p. North dist., 1966, treas., 1969-83. Served with AUS, World War II. Mem. Chgo. Council Conservative Men's Clubs (past pres.), Nat. Fedn. Jewish Men's Clubs (nat. pres. 1952-54, hon. pres. midwest region), Am. Legion (past post comdr.), Alpha Gamma Pi (past chpt. chancellor). Jewish (past pres. congregation). Clubs: Lions (pres. Rogers Park 1969-70), Masons (master 1981-82), Shriners (Pres. Legion of Merit 1982-83), B'nai B'rith (past pres., sr. dep. for Ill. AZA 1937-43), Star Craft Ill. (pres. 1975), N. Shore Shrine (pres. 1975). Home: 8500 Skokie Blvd Skokie IL 60077 Office: 141 W Jackson Blvd Suite 3040 Chicago IL 60604

JACOBSON, ALBERT SIGFRIED, editor; b. Hudson, N.Y., May 22, 1931; s. Albert Sigfried and Anna Marie (Poleschner) J.; m. Caroline Marcia Freeman, June 24, 1961; children—Barry Freeman, Amy Sigrid. B.S., Rensselaer Poly. Inst., 1953; M.S., U. Ill., 1959. Research chemist Durez Plastics Co., LeRoy, N.Y., 1953-55; tchr. high sch. math. Pavilion (N.Y.) Central Sch., 1955-58, Newton (Mass.) High Sch., 1959-61; editor, sr. editor, mng. editor, exec. editor D.C. Heath & Co., Lexington, Mass., 1961—. Home: 17 Longfellow Rd Needham Heights MA 02194 Office: 125 Spring St Lexington MA 02173

JACOBSON, ALFRED THURL, petroleum exec.; b. Delta, Utah, Nov. 12, 1919; s. Joseph Alfred and Ella Adelia (Robison) J.; m. Virginia Lorraine LaCom, Apr. 7, 1942; children—Wendy Jean (Mrs. Higginbotham), Deborah Ann (Mrs. Wasden), Alfred Thurl. A.B. in Geology, U. Utah, 1940, M.A., 1941. With Amerada Petroleum Corp., N.Y.C., 1946-72, mgr. fgn. operations, 1960-61, v.p., 1961-62, sr. v.p., 1962-63, exec. v.p., 1963-67, pres., chief exec. officer, 1967-69; also dir.; pres., dir. Amerada Hess Corp., 1969-72, worldwide expln. adminstr., 1976-79, group v.p. exploration and prodn., 1980—; petroleum industry cons., 1972-76. Active Boy Scouts Am.; Former trustee Tulsa U. Served with F.A. AUS, 1941-46; ETO. Decorated Croix de Guerre, France). Mem. Am. Inst. Mining and Metall. Engrs., Am. Petroleum Inst., Am. Assn. Petroleum Geologists, Am. Inst. Profl. Geologists, Assn. Profl. Geol. Scientists, Phi Beta Kappa, Phi Kappa Phi. Mormon. Home: 358 Oxford Dr Short Hills NJ 07078

JACOBSON, ANTONE GARDNER, zoology educator; b. nr. Salt Lake City, May 22, 1929; s. Rufus Ingman and Marvell (Gardner) J.; m. Jacqueline James, July 26, 1962; children: Lauren, Eric. A.B., Harvard, 1951; Ph.D., Stanford U., 1955. Mem. faculty dept. zoology U. Tex. at Austin, 1957—, asso. prof., 1961-68, prof., 1968—; dir. Devel. and Reprodn. Research Center; instr. Marine Biol. Lab., Woods Hole, Mass., 1969-70; Cons. NIH, 1972—. Contbr. articles to profl. jours. Harvard Nat. scholar, 1947-51; Henry Newell Honors scholar, 1951-55; NIH grantee, 1958—. Mem. Internat. Soc. Developmental Biologists, Soc. Developmental Biology, Am. Soc. Zoologists, AAAS, Sigma Xi. Home: 201 Skyline Dr Austin TX 78746 Office: Dept Zoology Univ Tex Austin TX 78712

JACOBSON, DAN, writer; b. Johannesburg, South Africa, Mar. 7, 1929; s. Hyman Michael and Liebe (Melamed) J.; m. Margaret Pye, Feb. 13, 1954; children: Simon Orde, Matthew, Jessica. B.A., U. Witwatersrand, Johannesburg, 1949. Journalist and tchr., 1950-54, profl. writer, 1954—; fellow in creative writing Stanford U., 1956-57; vis. prof. English lit. Syracuse U., 1965-66; lectr. Univ. Coll., London, 1975-79; reader in English U. London, 1980—; vis. fellow Humanities Research Centre Australian Nat. U., 1981; vice chmn. lit. panel Arts Council Gt. Britain, 1972-74. Author: The Trap, 1955, A Dance in the Sun, 1956, Price of Diamonds, 1957, The Zulu and the Zeide, 1959, Evidence of Love, 1960, No Further West, 1961, The Beginners, 1966, Through The Wilderness, 1968, The Rape of Tamar, 1970, Inklings, 1973, The Wonder-Worker, 1974, The Confessions of Josef Baisz, 1978; author: The Story of the Stories, 1982. Recipient John Llewelyn Rhys award Nat. Book League, 1958; W. Somerset Maugham award Soc. Authors, 1964; H. H. Wingate award Jewish Chronicle, 1978. Address: care Am Heath & Co 40-42 William IV St London WC2 England

JACOBSON, DAVID, rabbi; b. Cin., Dec. 2, 1909; s. Abraham and Rebecca (Sereinsky) J.; m. Helen Gugenheim, Nov. 6, 1938; children: Elizabeth Anne, Dorothy Jean Jacobson Miller. A.B., U. Cin., 1931; Rabbi, Hebrew Union Coll., 1934, D.D., 1959; Ph.D., St. Catherine's Coll., U. Cambridge (Eng.), 1936; LL.D., Our Lady of Lake Coll., 1964. Instr. Hebrew Union Coll., 1933-34; rabbi West Central Liberal Congregation, London, 1934-36, Indpls. Hebrew Congregation, 1936-38, Temple Beth-El, San Antonio, 1938-76, emeritus, 1976—; rabbi Temple Mizpah, Abilene, Tex., 1981—; aux. chaplain, area mil. installations; chaplain Audie Murphy VA Hosp., 1973—; chmn. Rabbinical Placement Commn., 1973-78; chmn. discussion program KSAT-TV, 1956-80, KLRN-TV, 1983. Author: Social Background of the Old Testament, 1942, The Synagogue Through the Ages, 1958; contbr. articles to profl. and gen. publs.; also contbr. to: Universal Jewish Ency, 1939-43. Mem. Tex. Senate Com. Welfare Reform, 1970, Tex. State Ethics Commn., 1971, Tex. State Medicaid Task Force, 1977; mem. com. nursing homes Tex. Dept. Human Resources, 1978-80; pres. San Antonio Soc. Crippled Children and Adults, 1963-66, Goodwill Industries San Antonio, 1956-60, Bexar County chpt. Nat. Tb Assn., 1955-57, Community Welfare Council San Antonio, 1951-53, San Antonio Area Found., 1965-69, Research and Planning Council San Antonio, 1966-67, Tex. Social Welfare Assn., 1967-69, San Antonio Manpower Devel. Council, 1968-76, S.W. region Central Conf. Am. Rabbis, 1969-70, Multiple Sclerosis Soc. San Antonio, 1975-78, Nat. Conf. Social Welfare, 1976-77, Am. Inst. Character Edn., 1976-78, Prevent Blindness Soc., San Antonio, 1980-82; mediator San Antonio Printing Trades and Employers, 1968—; mem. nat. labor panel Am. Arbitration Assn., 1977—, Fed. Mediation and Conciliation Service, 1981—; commr. Housing Authority San Antonio, 1954-58; bd. dirs. Our Lady of Lake U., 1966-76, hon. bd. dirs., 1977—; also chmn. adv. bd. Worden Sch. Social Service of coll., 1958-67; founder U. Ind. Hillel Found., 1938, San Antonio Vis. Nurses Assn., 1952, Community Welfare Council San Antonio, 1944; bd. dirs. S.W. Tex. Meth. Hosp., 1956—, San Antonio Med. Found., 1962—, Alamo council Boy Scouts Am., 1950—, Children's Hosp. Found., 1964—, Keystone Sch., San Antonio, 1960-80, Ecumenical Center for Religion and Health, 1968—, Alamo chpt. Am. Cancer Soc., 1975-83, Hospice of St. Benedict's Hosp., 1977-81, Tex. Council Higher Edn., 1969—, Nat. Jewish Welfare Bd., 1964-72, Alamo chpt. Assn. U.S. Army, 1964-71, Hemis Fair, 1968; life mem. bd. Tex. United Community Services, 1970—; co-chmn. community relations council San Antonio Jewish Fedn., 1978-79; chmn. religion com. United San Antonio, 1980-81, vice chmn. public sector, 1981—; chmn. Bexar County Community Corrections Commn., 1979-81; mem. nat. bd. Goodwill Industries Am., 1965-78; bd. overseers Hebrew Union Coll.-Jewish Inst. Religion, 1966—, bd. govs., 1966-68; bd. govs. Commn. on Social Action of Reform Judaism, 1978—; mem. nat. bd. Nat. Council on Crime and Delinquency, 1972—, Florence G. Heller-Jewish Welfare Bd. Research Center, 1966-70; nat. council U.S.O., 1968—. Served as chaplain with USNR, 1944-46. Recipient Silver Beaver award Boy Scouts Am., 1958; Aristotle-Aquinas award Cath. Coll. Found. S.A., 1959; Golden Deeds award Exchange Club San Antonio, 1959; Keystone award Boys' Club Am., 1962; Lifetime Achievement award B'nai B'rith, 1964; Nat. Humanitarian award, 1975; Edgar Helms award Goodwill Industries, 1972; leadership award San Antonio Transcendental Meditation Soc., 1977; Shofar award, 1984; named Outstanding Jew NCCJ, 1961, Citizen of Year Sembradores de Amistad, 1971. Mem. Central Conf. Am. Rabbis (chmn. com. Judaism and health 1967-72, chmn. nominating com. 1979), Kallah of Tex. Rabbis (pres. 1950-51, chancellor-historian 1977—), Am. Social Health Assn. (dir. 1969-75), Tex. Congress Parents and Tchrs. (hon. life), Sigma Alpha Mu, Pi Tau Pi. Clubs: Rotary, B'nai B'rith (hon. chmn. 1974), Torch (pres. 1961), Argyle (San Antonio)). Home: 207 Beechwood Ln San Antonio TX 78216

JACOBSON, GAYNOR I., retired association executive; b. Buffalo, May 17, 1912; s. Morris and Rose (Fleishman) J.; m. Florence Stulberg, Feb. 22, 1937; children—Margot (Mrs. Harold Gotoff), Helen (Mrs. Murray Levin). B.A., U. Buffalo, 1937, certificate in social work, 1939, M.S.W., 1941. Exec. sec. Jewish Community Council, Rochester, N.Y., 1937-40; exec. dir. Jewish Family and Child Care, Rochester, 1938-44, Jewish Child Care Assn., Phila., 1950-51, Am. Technion Soc., 1951-53; country dir. Am. Joint Distbn. Com., Italy, 1944-45, Greece, 1945-46, Czechoslovakia, 1946-47, Hungary, 1947-50; dir. European and N. African ops. HIAS Inc., 1953-54, 61-66, dir. Latin Am. ops., 1955-61, exec. dir., 1966-68, exec. v.p., 1968-81, hon. exec. v.p., 1981—. Sculpture exhibited various galleries in, U.S. and Brazil. Bd. dirs. United Jewish Appeal Greater N.Y.; mem. Nat. Com. Plastic Arts Brazil. Recipient Independence citation and Silver pin State of Israel, 1973; decorated Nat. Order So. Cross, Brazil, 1979. Mem. Nat. Assn. Social Workers, Nat. Assn. Jewish Family and Children's Health Services. Home: 340 E 64th St New York NY 10021 Office: 200 Park Ave S New York NY 10003

JACOBSON, HAROLD GORDON, physician, educator; b. Cin., Oct. 12, 1912; s. Samuel and Regina (Dittman) J.; m. Ruth Enenstein, Aug. 10, 1941; children: Richard, Arthur. B.S., U. Cin., 1934, M.B., 1936, M.D., 1937. Diplomate: Am. Bd. Radiology (trustee 1971-82, chmn. written exams. com. in diagnostic radiology 1973-81, co-chmn. 1981—, treas. 1976-78, v.p. 1978-80, pres. 1980-82, mem. residency rev. com. 1976-82, vice-chmn. 1979-80, chmn. 1980—, exec. com. 1976—). Intern Los Angeles County Gen. Hosp., 1936-38; fellow in pathology Longview Hosp., Cin., 1938; resident Mt. Sinai Hosp., N.Y.C., 1939-41, Associated Hosps. U. Tex., 1941-42; asst. in radiology U. Tex., 1941-42; assoc. radiologist New Haven (Conn.) Hosp.; also instr. Yale U., 1952; asst. chief, asso. radiologist VA Hosp., Bronx, N.Y., 1946-50, chief radiology service, 1950-53, cons., 1958—; asst. clin. prof. N.Y. U., 1952-53, clin. prof., 1953-59, prof. clin. radiology, 1959-64; prof.

radiology Albert Einstein Coll. Medicine, 1964-71; prof., chmn. Albert Einstein Coll. Medicine of Montefiore Hosp. and Med. Center, N.Y.C., 1972—; dir. dept. roentgenology Hosp. for Spl. Surgery, N.Y.C., 1953-55; radiologist-in-chief Montefiore Hosp. and Med. Center, N.Y.C., 1955—; sr. cons. in radiology Nat. Bd. Med. Examiners, 1975—, mem. bd., 1979-83; vis. prof. radiology Inst. Orthopaedics, U. London, 1975—; vis. prof., lectr., U.S.A., Israel, Brazil, Finland.; named lectures include Felson Lecture, Carman Lecture, Baylin Lecture, Beeler Lecture, Freedman Lecture, Pfahler Lecture, Chamberlain Lecture, Evans Lecture, Sampson Lecture, Wolf Meml. Lecture, Caffey Lecture, Grubbe Lecture, Myron Melamed Lecture. Author: (with Clarence Schein, William Z. Stern) The Common Bile Duct, 1967, Neuroradiology Workshop, Vol. III, 1968, (with Ronald O. Murray) Radiology of Skeletal Disorders: Exercises in Diagnosis, 1971, 2d edit., 1977; co-author: Bone Disease Syllabus, 1972, 2d series, 1976, 3d series, 1980, Index for Roentgen Diagnosis, 3d edit, 1975; co-editor in chief: Jour. Internat. Skeletal Soc, 1976—; editorial bd.: Excerpta Medica, 1974—, Jour. AMA, 1979—; coordinator: topics in radiology Jour. AMA, 1977-79; editor, 1979—; mem. editorial bd. for radiology, 1979—; contbr. articles to profl. jours. Served as maj. M.C AUS, 1942-46. Recipient Gold medal Assn. Univ. Radiologists, 1982, Phi Lambda Kappa, 1983. Fellow Am. Coll. Radiology (councilor 1960—, bd. chancellors, chmn. com. on radiol. coding 1967—, mem. commn. on credentials 1968—, chmn. commn. on affairs Am. Inst. Radiology 1971—, co-chmn. com. on diagnostic coding index and thesaurus 1973—, Gold medal 1978), Royal Coll. Radiologists (London) (hon.); mem. N.Y. Roentgen Soc. (pres. 1959-60, historian 1967—), AMA, N.Y. State, N.Y. med. socs., Soc. of Chairmen Acad. Radiology Depts. (mem. exec. council 1972—, pres. 1973-74), Radiol. Soc. N.Am. (pres. 1966-67, mem. bd. censors 1968—, gold medal 1972), Am. Roentgen Ray Soc. (Cert. of Appreciation 1983), Royal Soc. Medicine (hon.), Internat. Skeletal Soc. (co-founder, pres. 1974-75, chmn., mem. exec. com. 1976—), Alpha Omega Alpha (Rigler lectr. 1964, 70, Crookshank lectr. London 1974, Holmes lectr. Boston 1974). Home: 3240 Henry Hudson Pkwy New York NY 10463

JACOBSON, HAROLD KARAN, political science educator, research; b. Detroit, June 28, 1929; s. Harold Kenneth and Maxine Anna (Miller) J.; m. Merelyn Jean Lindbloom, Aug. 25, 1951; children: Harold Knute, Eric Alfred, Kristoffer Olaf, Nils Karl. A.B., U. Mich., 1950; M.A., Yale U., 1952, Ph.D., 1955. Asst. prof. polit. sci. U. Houston, 1955-57; mem. faculty U. Mich., Ann Arbor, 1957—, assoc. prof., 1961-65, prof., 1965—, research scientist, 1977—, chmn. dept., 1972-77, acting chmn., 1981; vis. prof. Grad. Inst. Internat. Studies, U. Geneva, 1965-66, 70-71, 77-78; World Affairs Center fellow, 1959-60; vis. research scholar European Center Carnegie Endowment for Internat. Peace, Geneva, 1970-71. Author: The USSR and the UN's Economic and Social Activities, 1963, Networks of Interdependence, 1979, 84, (with Eric Stein) Diplomats, Scientists, and Politicians, 1966, (with R.W. Cox and others) The Anatomy of Influence, 1973, (with Dusan Sidjanski and others) The Emerging International Order, 1982; Editor: (with David A. Kay and others) Environmental Protection, 1983, America's Foreign Policy, 1960, 65, The Shaping of Foreign Policy, 1969; Editorial bd.: Internat. Orgn, 1968-76, 78—, Am. Jour. Internat. Law, 1979—, Internat. Studies Quar, 1980—, Jour. Conflict Resolution, 1961-72. Mem. U.S. Nat. Commn. for UNESCO, 1980—. Mem. UN Assn. U.S.A. (dir. 1980—), Internat. Studies Assn. (pres. Midwest div. 1969-70, nat. pres. 1982-83), Internat. Polit. Sci. Assn., Council Fgn. Relations, Detroit Com. Fgn. Relations, Internat. Polit. Sci. Assn., Am. Polit. Sci. Assn., Midwest Polit. Sci. Assn., AAAS, AAUP, Phi Beta Kappa, Phi Kappa Phi. Clubs: Cosmos (Washington); Yale (N.Y.C.); de la Fondation Universitaire (Brussels). Home: 2174 Delaware Dr Ann Arbor MI 48103

JACOBSON, HAROLD LELAND, lawyer; b. Chgo., Oct. 31, 1926; s. Oliver I. and Annabelle (Hershenson) J.; m. Nancee Jean Klein, Aug. 22, 1948; children: Reid, Gary. B.S., U. Ill., 1948; J.D., Loyolo U., Chgo., 1953. Mem. law firm Schatz Busch & Jacobson, Chgo., 1953-57; ptnr. Lord Bissell & Brooks, Chgo., 1958—; instr. John Marshall Law Sch., Chgo., 1967-70. Contbr. articles to profl. jours.; contbg. author: Ill. Inst. Continuing Legal Edn., 1980, 83. Served with U.S. Army, 1944-46. Fellow Am. Coll. Trial Lawyers; mem. Am. Bd. Trial Advocates, Fedn. Ins. Counsel, Soc. Trial Lawyers. Club: Union League. Office: Lord Bissell & Brook 115 S LaSalle St Chicago IL 60603

JACOBSON, HERBERT LAURENCE, diplomat, journalist; b. N.Y.C., Apr. 7, 1915; s. Benjamin Paul and Katherine (Laurence) J.; m. Baronessa Fiora Ravasini-Osti, May 29, 1949; children: Jesse, Julian. B.A. with honors, Columbia U., 1936; LL.D. (hon.), Wilfred Laurier U., Waterloo, Ont., Can., 1969. Radio-TV writer and producer, N.Y.C. and Chgo., 1937-41; dir.-gen. radio-TV network Free Terr. Trieste, 1946-52; head U.S.-German radio ops., W. Ger. and W. Berlin, 1953-55; info. officer Am. embassy, Rome, 1955-57; dir. fgn. bus. Mondadori Publns., Milan, Italy; also Squibb Pharms., Rome, 1958-60; So. European regional rep. Cotton Council Internat., Barcelona, Spain, Rome and St. Gall, Switzerland, 1960-64; dir.-gen. UN/GATT Internat. Trade Center, Geneva, 1964-79; adv. econ. and social affairs OAS, Washington, 1980—81; cons. UN, 1981—. Co-author: University on the Heights, 1969, A Century of College Humor, 1979; columnist: Columbia U. Forum, 1974-76; producer, author, dir.: film Aquila, 1950; contbr. articles mags., newspapers. Served with AUS, 1941-46. Recipient Gen. Staff Commendation. Mem. Phi Beta Kappa. Clubs: Nat. Press (Washington); Costa Rica Country. Home: Apartado 160 Escazu Costa Rica Office: UN ILANUD Apartado 10071 San Jose Costa Rica

JACOBSON, HERBERT LEONARD, electronics company executive; b. N.Y.C., Mar. 22, 1940; s. Divid and Lena (Goldberg) J.; m. Beverly Goldman, Nov. 23, 1961; children: Julie Ellen, Joel Howard. B.S. in E.E., U. R.I., 1961; LL.B., Bklyn. Law Sch., 1965; LL.M., NYU, 1970. Bar: N.Y. 1965, U.S. Patent and Trademark Office 1966, U.S. Supreme Ct. 1969, N.J. 1972. Planning engr. Am. Electric Power, N.Y.C., 1961-66; patent atty. RCA Corp., Princeton, N.J., 1966-74, counsel, N.Y.C., 1974-79, dir. licensing, 1979-83, staff v.p., 1983—. Exec. v.p. Reform Temple, East Burnswick (N.J.), 1983. Mem. N.J. State Bar Assn. Home: 42 Yorktown Rd East Brunswick NJ 08816 Office: RCA Corp PO Box 2023 Princeton NJ 08540

JACOBSON, HOWARD, classics educator; b. Bronx, N.Y., Aug. 21, 1940; s. David and Jeannette (Signer) J.; m. Elaine Z. Finkelstein, June 10, 1965; children: Michael Noam, Daniel Benjamin, Joel Avram, David Moses. B.A., Columbia U., 1962, Ph.D., 1967; M.A., U. Chgo., 1963. Instr. Greek and Latin Columbia U., 1966-68; asst. prof. classics U. Ill., 1968-73, assoc. prof., 1973-80, prof., 1980—; Lady Davis vis. prof. Hebrew U., Jerusalem, winter 1983; Lady Davis vis. prof. Hebrew U. Jerusalem, winter 1983. Author: Ovid's Heroides, 1974, The Exagoge of Ezekiel, 1983. Nat. Endowment for Humanities fellow, 1971-72. Mem. Am. Philol. Assn., Phi Beta Kappa. Jewish. Office: Dept Classics 4072 Foreign Languages Bldg 707 S Mathews St Urbana IL 61801

JACOBSON, ISHIER, utility executive; b. Worcester, Mass., June 21, 1922; s. Aaron and Mollie (Mallor) J.; m. Maria Bohm, Dec. 18, 1948; children: Joanna M., Jonathan B., Paula R. B.A., Clark U., 1946; M.S. in Mech. Engring, Harvard U., 1947, LL.B., 1951. Bar: Conn. bar. Asst. to pres., gen. counsel Connor Engring. Corp., Danbury, Conn., 1951-53; with Citizens Utilities Co., Stamford, Conn., 1954—, exec. v.p., 1970, pres., chief operating officer, 1970-81, pres., chief exec. officer, 1981—, also dir.; dir. subs. cos. Citizens Utilities Co. Served to lt. USNR, 1942-46. Home: 326 Four Brooks Rd Stamford CT 06903 Office: High Ridge Park Stamford CT 06905

JACOBSON, JAY J., lawyer; b. N.Y.C., Mar. 4, 1936; s. Seymour and Dorothy J.; m. Patricia Durand, Dec. 17, 1961; children: Jennifer, Daniel. B.A., Amherst Coll., 1956; LL.B., Columbia U., 1959. Bar: N.Y. Legis. asst. to Maureen Neuberger, 1960-62; sr. parliamentary counsel Govt. of Malawi, 1962-64; asso. firm Karelsen Karelson Lawrence & Nathan, 1965-66, Feldesman & D'Atri, 1966-69; v.p.-law, sec. Saxon Industries, Inc., N.Y.C., 1969-83; gen. counsel Nutri/System, Inc., 1983—. Mem. Assn. Bar City N.Y., N.Y. State Bar Assn., Am. Bar Assn. Office: Nutri/System Inc Old York and Rydal Rds Jenkintown PA 19046

JACOBSON, JOEL ROSS, state official; b. Newark, July 30, 1918; s. Herman and Gussie (Ross) J.; children—Howard Michael, Monica. B.S., N.Y. U., 1941; Litt.D. (hon.), Montclair (N.J.) State Coll., 1959; LL.D., Rutgers U., 1974. Exec. sec. Essex-W. Hudson (N.J.) CIO Council, 1949-54; exec. v.p. N.J. CIO Council, 1954-60; pres., 1960-61; 1st exec. v.p. N.J. AFL-CIO, 1961-68; pres. N.J. Indsl. Union Council, AFL-CIO, until 1968; dir. community affairs Region 9, UAW, Cranford, N.J., 1968-74; commr. N.J. Bd. Pub. Utility Commrs., 1974-76, pres., 1976-77; N.J. commr. Dept. Energy, 1977-81; commr. N.J. Casino Central Commn., 1981—; del. to White House Conf. Edn., 1955; mem. N.J. adv. com. to U.S. Civil Rights Commn., 1960—; mem. N.J. Health Planning Council, 1969—; lectr. labor and politics univs. including Rutgers, Yale, Princeton, Bklyn. Poly. Inst. Vice chmn. New Democratic Coalition, 1968-69; del. Dem. Nat. Conv., 1972; bd. govs. Rutgers U., 1959-74. Served to 2d lt. AUS, World War II. Decorated Bronze Arrowhead. Home: 2 Kendall Ave South Orange NJ 07079 Office: 3131 Princeton Pike Lawrenceville NJ 08625

JACOBSON, JOHN, food company executive; b. 1910. With Chgo.-Dressed Beef Co., 1933-65, Nat. Beef Packing Co., 1965-75; chmn. bd., chief exec. officer, dir. Idle Wild Foods, Inc., Worcester, Mass., 1975—. Address: Idle Wild Foods Inc 256 Franklin St Worcester MA 01604 *

JACOBSON, LEON ORRIS, physician; b. Sims, N.D., Dec. 16, 1911; s. John and R. Patrine (Johnson) J.; m. Elizabeth Benton, Mar. 18, 1938; children: Eric Paul, Judith Ann. B.S., N.D. State Coll., 1935, D.Sc. (hon.), 1966; M.D., U. Chgo., 1939; D.Sc., Acadia U., N.S., 1972. Intern U. Chgo., 1939-40, asst. resident medicine, 1940-41, asst. in medicine, 1941-42, instr., 1942-45, asst. prof., 1945-48, asso. dean, div. biol. scis., 1945-51, asso. prof., 1948-51, prof. medicine, 1951—, Joseph Regenstein prof. biol. and med. scis., 1965—, chmn. dept. medicine, 1961-65, dean div. biol. scis., 1966-75; head hematology sect. U. Chgo. Clinics, 1951-61; mem. Inst. Radiobiology and Biophysics, 1949-54; dir. Franklin McLean Meml. Research Inst., 1974-77; asso. dir. health Plutonium project Manhattan Dist., 1943-45, dir. health, 1945-46; dir. Argonne Cancer Research Hosp., U. Chgo., 1951-67; U.S. rep. 1st and 2d UN Conf. on Peaceful Uses Atomic Energy, Geneva, 1955, 58, WHO conf. Research Radiation Injury, 1959; cons. biology div. Argonne Nat. Lab.; mem. adv. com. on isotope distbn. AEC, 1952-56; mem. nat. adv. com. radiation USPHS, 1961, mem. com. radiation studies, cons. hematology study sect.; mem. com. cancer diagnosis and therapy NRC, 1949-55; mem. bd. sci. counselor Nat. Cancer Inst., 1963-67; mem. nat. adv. cancer council, nat. cancer adv. bd. NIH, 1968-72; chmn. sci. adv. bd. Council for Tobacco Research; lectr. Internat. Soc. Hematology and Internat. Congress Radiology, Eng., France, Norway, Sweden, 1950, 5th Internat. Cancer Congress, Paris, 1950, Internat. Soc. Hematology, Argentina, 1952, Paris, 1954, others. Author book on erythropoletin; contbr. chpts. on specialized items to various med. books, articles to med. jours.; Book editor: Perspectives in Biology and Medicine, 1979—. Recipient Janeway medal, 1953; Robert Roesler de Villiers award Leukemia Soc.; Borden award med. scis. Assn. Am. Med. Colls., 1962; Modern Med. and Am. Nuclear Soc. awards, 1963; John Phillips Meml. award, 1975; Theodore Roosevelt Rough Riders award State of N.D., 1977; Lincoln Laureate State of Ill., 1979; Kennecott lectr., 1963. Mem. A.C.P. (master), Am. Soc. Clin. Investigation, Assn. Am. Physicians, Soc. Exptl. Biology and Medicine, Central Soc. Clin. Research, Am. Assn. Cancer Research, Internat. Soc. Hematology, AMA, Nat. Acad. Sci., Central Clin. Research Club, AAAS, Radiation Research Soc., Am. Soc. Exptl. Pathology, Sigma Xi, Theta Chi, Nu Sigma Nu, Blue Key, Alpha Omega Alpha. Home: 5801 Dorchester Ave Chicago IL 60637 Office: 5841 S Maryland Chicago IL 60637

JACOBSON, LEONARD, architect; b. Phila., Mar. 7, 1921; s. David and Rose (Tollman) J.; m. Joan Katz, July 10, 1950; children: Eric, Daniel. B.Arch., U. Pa., 1942, M.Arch., 1947. Registered architect, N.Y., Mass. Staff architect various firms, N.Y.C., 1947-53; with I.M. Pei & Ptnrs., N.Y.C., 1953—, assoc. ptnr., 1968-79; ptnr. I.M. Pei. & Ptnrs., N.Y.C., 1980—. Served with AC U.S. Army, 1942-45; Africa, Middle East, India. Fellow AIA; mem. N.Y. chpt. AIA, Am. Arbitration Assn. Democrat. Jewish. Home: 794 Sleepy Hollow Rd Briarcliff Manor NY 10510 Office: I M Pei & Ptnrs 600 Madison Ave New York NY 10022 *My motivation was always to achieve something worthwhile, while participating in a field I enjoyed.*

JACOBSON, LEONARD I., psychologist, educator; b. Bklyn., Aug. 9, 1940; s. Harry L. and Violet (Natkin) J. A.B. cum laude, CUNY, 1961; Ph.D., SUNY-Buffalo, 1966. Research psychologist Children's Hosp., Buffalo, 1965-66; asst. prof. psycholgy U. Miami, Coral Gables, Fla., 1966-71, assoc. prof., 1971-76, prof., 1976—; adj. asst. prof. Guidance Ctr.-U. Miami, Coral Gables, 1969-70; prof. pediatrics U. Miami Sch. Medicine, 1980—; cons. Miami Mental Health Ctr., 1968-79, Sunland Tng. Ctr. at Miami, Opa-Locka, 1969-72, Camarillo State Hosp. (Calif.), 1970, Mailman Ctr. for Child Devel.-U. Miami Sch. Medicine, 1972-75, Maimi Lighthouse for the Blind, 1975—; mem. outcome study panel Dade-Monroe Mental Health Bd., 1980. Contbr. articles to profl. jours. USPHS clin. fellow, 1962-63; grantee NSF, 1966-68, NIHM, 1967-68, 1968, Soc. Psychol. Study Social Issues, 1969, NASA, 1969-71. Mem. Am. Psychol. Assn., Southeastern Psychol. Assn., Western Psychol. Assn., Fla. Psychol. Assn., AAAS, Assn. Advancement of Behavior Therapy, Am. Assn. Workers for the Blind, Soc. Research in Child Devel., Psychonomic Soc., Soc. Psychotherapy Research, Met. Dade County Com. for the Physically Handicapped, Sigma Xi, Psi Chi. Republican. Office: Dept Psychology U Miami Coral Gables FL 33124

JACOBSON, LESLIE SARI, biologist, college dean; b. N.Y.C., May 22, 1933; d. William and Gussie (Mintz) Goldberg; m. Homer Jacobson, Aug. 18, 1957; children: Guy Joseph, Ethan Samuel. B.S., Bklyn. Coll., 1954, M.A., 1955; postgrad., Columbia U., 1956, Calif. Inst. Tech., 1960; Ph.D., NYU, 1961. Instr. dept. biology Bklyn. Coll., 1954-57, fellow dept. chemistry, 1962-63, prof. health sci., 1974—; dean Sch. Gen. Studies and Continuing Higher Edn., 1974-80, Grad. Studies and Continuing Higher Edn., 1980-82; asst. prof. dept. nursing L.I. Coll. Hosp., 1958; asst. prof. biology L.I. U., Bklyn., 1963-66, asso. prof., 1967-71, prof. biology, 1971-74, dean Grad. Sch., 1973-74, 82—; nat. program chmn. Assn. Continuing Higher Edn., 1978, nat. bd. dirs., 1978-81, pres.-elect, 1980-81, pres., 1981-82; bd. dirs. Center for Labor and Mgmt., N.Y. Bd. dirs. Alpha Sigma Lambda Found. Recipient Founders Day award NYU, 1961; N.Y. Adult Edn. Council award, 1978. Mem. Sigma Xi, Alpha Sigma Lambda (nat. pres. 1978-80). Research, publs. in bacterial virology and endocrine physiology. Home: 642 E 26th St Brooklyn NY 11210

JACOBSON, M. HOWARD, food company executive; b. 1928. Pres. Idle Wild Foods, Inc., 1973-75, pres., treas., chief fin. officer, dir., 1975—. Address: Idle Wild Foods Inc 256 Franklin St Worcester MA 01604 *

JACOBSON, MARCUS, physiologist; b. Cape Town, South Africa, Apr. 2, 1930; s. Solly and Rosa (Javsitz) J.; m. Erika Wyler, Sept. 16, 1963 (dec. Dec. 1975); children—Vera, Lara; m. Geraldine Meerbott, Mar. 25, 1977; 1 son, Justin. B.Sc., U. Cape Town, 1951, M.B., Ch.B., 1956; Ph.D., U. Edinburgh, Scotland, 1960. Lectr. physiology Edinburgh U., 1960-65; asso. prof. Johns Hopkins U., 1965-69, prof. biophysics, 1969-73; prof. physiology and biophysics Med. Sch., U. Miami, Fla., 1973-77; prof., chmn. anatomy U. Utah Coll. Medicine, 1977—. Author: also research articles. Developmental Neurobiology. Address: U Utah Coll Medicine Salt Lake City UT 84132

JACOBSON, MELVIN JOSEPH, applied mathematician, acoustician, educator; b. Providence, Nov. 25, 1928; s. Charles and Rose (Chusmir) J.; m. Dorothy Troup, June 8, 1952; children—Deborah Lynn, Donald Bruce. A.B., Brown U., 1950; M.S., Carnegie Inst. Tech., 1952, Ph.D., 1954. Instr. Carnegie Inst. Tech., Pitts., 1953-54; mem. tech. staff Bell Telephone Labs., Whippany, N.J., 1954-56; asst. prof. math. Rensselaer Poly. Inst., Troy, N.Y., 1956-58, asso. prof., 1958-63, prof., 1963—; prin. investigator Office Naval Research Contracts, 1957—, NSF grant, 1962-67; vis. prof. Rosenstiel Sch. Marine and Atmospheric Scis., U. Miami, Fla., 1963-64, adj. prof., 1969-72; Cons. to industry. Contbr. articles to numerous publs. Fellow Acoustical Soc. Am.; mem. AAUP, Am. Math. Soc., Math. Assn. Am., Sigma Xi, Phi Kappa Phi, Pi Mu Epsilon. Home: 1 Lisa Ln Troy NY 12180

JACOBSON, MICHAEL FARRADAY, association administrator, consumer advocate; b. Chgo., July 29, 1943; s. Larry and Janet (Siegel) J. B.A., U. Chgo., 1965; postgrad., U. Calif.-San Diego, 1965-67; Ph.D., MIT, 1969. Research assoc. Salk Inst. for Biol. Studies, 1970-71; cons. Ralph Nader's Ctr. for Study of Responsive Law, 1970-71; co-founder, exec. dir. Ctr. for Sci. in the Pub. Interest, Washington, 1971—. Co-author: Nutrition Scoreboard, 1975, Eater's Digest, 1976, The Booze Merchants, 1983, Salt: The Brand Name Guide to Sodium, 1983, The Changing American Diet, 1983; co-editor: Food for People Not for Profit, 1975. Originator, nat. coordinator Food Day, 1975-77. Office: Ctr for Sci in the Pub Interest 1501 16th St NW Washington DC 20036

JACOBSON, NORMAN L., educational administrator, researcher; b. Eau Claire, Wis., Sept. 11, 1918; s. Frank R. and Elma E. (Baker) J.; m. Gertrude A. Neff, Aug. 24, 1943; children: Gary, Judy. B.S., U. Wis., 1940; M.S., Iowa State U., 1941, Ph.D., 1947. Asst. prof. animal sci. Iowa State U., Ames, 1947-49, assoc. prof., 1949-53, prof., 1953, Disting. prof. agr., 1963—, assoc. dean Grad. Coll., 1973—, assoc. v.p. research, 1979—. Contbr. articles to profl. jours., chpts. to books. Served to lt. USN, 1942-46; ETO, PTO. Fellow AAAS; mem. Am. Dairy Sci. Assn. (pres. 1972-73), Am. Feed Mfrs. Assn. (award 1955, Borden award 1960), Am. Soc. Animal Sci. (Morrison award 1970), Am. Inst. Nutrition. Republican. Presbyterian. Home: 339 Hickory Dr Ames IA 50010 Office: Iowa State U 201 Beardshear Hall Ames IA 50011

JACOBSON, ORVILLE WILLIAM, labor union ofcl.; b. Amery, Wis., May 31, 1921; s. Martin B. and Esther E. J.; m. Ruth E., 1943; 3 children. Student, Okla. A. and M. U., 1943, Superior (Wis.) Vocat. Sch., 1939-43. With Brotherhood of Ry. Carmen of U.S. and Can., 1940—; rec. sec. Local 811, 1946-52, local chmn., 1952-60, mem. gen. exec. bd., 1963-67, gen. v.p., 1967-71, asst. gen. pres., 1971, now gen. pres.; gen. chmn. Gt. No. Joint Protective Bd., 1962-67; chmn. bd. Labor Coop. Ednl. and Pub. Soc.; dir. Union Labor Life Ins. Co. Corp. sponsor Nat. Easter Seal Telethon. Served as cpl. USAF, 1942-46. Office: 4929 Main St Kansas City MO 64112

JACOBSON, PHILLIP LEE, architect, educator; b. Santa Monica, Calif., Aug. 27, 1928; s. Allen Wilhelm and Greta Percy (Rohde) J.; m. Effie Laurel Galbraith, Nov. 6, 1954; children: Rolf Wilhelm, Christina Lee, Erik Mackenzie. B. Archtl. Engring. with honors, Wash. State U., 1952; postgrad. (Fulbright scholar), U. Liverpool, Eng., 1952-53; M.Arch., Finnish Inst. Tech., Helsinki, 1969. Field supr. Gerald C. Field (Architect), 1950; designer, draftsman John Maloney (Architect), 1951, 53-55; designer, project mgr. Young, Richardson, Carleton & Detlie (Architects), 1955-56; designer, project architect John Carl Warnecke (Architect), San Francisco, Calif., 1956-58; partner, design dir., planning dir. The Richardson Assos., Seattle, 1958—; prof. architecture and urban design U. Wash., Seattle, 1962—; treas. TRA Internat.; pres. TRA Alaska Inc. Author: Housing and Industrialization in Finland, 1969, The Evolving Architectural Design Process, 1969; Contbr. articles to profl. jours.; Major archtl. works include Aerospace Research Lab, U. Wash., Seattle, 1969; McCarty Residence Hall, 1960, Highway Adminstrn. Bldg, Olympia, Wash., 1970, Sea-Tac Internat. Airport, 1972, Issaquah (Wash.) High Sch, 1962, State Office Bldg. 2, Olympia, 1976, Sealaska Corporate Hdqrs. Bldg, Juneau, Alaska, 1977, Group Health Hosp, Seattle, 1973, Metro Shelter Program, Seattle, 1977, N.W. Trek Wildlife Preserve, 1976, Rocky Reach/Rock Island Recreation Plan, 1974, master plan mouth of Columbia River, 1976, U. Wash. Biol. Sci. Bldg, 1981. Mem. Seattle Planning and Redevel. Council, 1959-69, v.p., 1966-67; mem. Seattle Landmark Preservation Bd., 1976-81; trustee Pilchuck Sch. Served with U.S. Army, 1946-47. Fulbright-Hays Sr. Research fellow, Finland, 1968-69; Recipient numerous awards for archtl. design. Fellow AIA (pres. Wash. state Council 1965, dir. Seattle chpt. 1970-73, sr. council 1970—); mem. Am. Inst. Cert. Planners, Phi Kappa Phi, Tau Beta Pi, Tau Sigma Delta, Scarab, Sigma Tau (outstanding alumnus 1967). Home: 3935 51st Ave NE Seattle WA 98105 Office: 215 Columbia St Seattle WA 98104

JACOBSON, PHYLLIS COLLEEN, educator; b. Idaho Falls, Idaho, Sept. 4, 1929; d. Lathen Wells and Eva Alta (McKay) J. B.S., Utah State U., 1953; M.S., 1954; Ph.D., U. Utah, 1970. Tchr. public schs., Jerome, Idaho, 1950-52, Las Vegas, 1954-57; mem. faculty Brigham Young U., Provo, Utah, 1957—, prof. phys. edn., 1975—, chmn. women's dept., 1970-80, chmn. dance dept., 1980—; mem. Gov.'s Phys. Fitness Adv. Council Utah, 1975; mem. coll. opportunity program San Juan Sch. Dist., 1970-75. Author: Fundamental Skills in Physical Education, 1970, Move It, Proven Exercise for Family Fitness, 1978, Hooked on Aerobics, for Total Body Fitness, 1982; creator, author: Hooked on Aerobics, PBS TV dance series. Chmn. phys. fitness, recreation and sports com. Ch. Jesus Christ of Latter-day Saints. Recipient Karl G. Maeser Disting. Faculty award Brigham Young U., 1978. Mem. Utah Assn. Phys. Edn., Health and Recreation (service award 1972, honor award 1973, pres. 1971-72), S.W. Dist. Assn. Health, Phys. Edn. and Recreation (dir. 1968-72), AAHPER, Western Soc. Phys. Edn. for Coll. Women, Phi Kappa Phi. Office: Brigham Young U Provo UT 84601

JACOBSON, RICHARD WILLIAM, stockbroker; b. Los Angeles, Oct. 26, 1937; s. Harold and Florence E. (Allen) J.; m. Mary Ann Smith, Sept. 15, 1962; children: Andrew, Susan, Cathy. B.A., Stanford U., 1959. Stockbroker, br. mgr. EI DuPont Walsto and Predecessor firms, Sherman Oaks, Calif., 1964-74; stockbroker, br. mgr., ptnr. Crowell Weedon & Co., Encino, Calif., 1974—. Served to lt. USNR, 1959-64. Republican. Home: 20472 Celtic St Chatsworth CA Office: 16130 Venture Blvd Encino CA 91436

JACOBSON, ROBERT, editor; b. Racine, Wis., July 28, 1940; s. Joseph and Frances (Barr) J. B.A. in English, U. Wis., 1962; postgrad. musicology, Columbia, 2-63. Asst. editor Musical Am., 1963; freelance editor, 1963-65; editor Lincoln Center program Sat. Rev., 1965-73, Opera News, N.Y.C., 1974—, Ballet News, 1979—; freelance music and dance critic Cue mag., 1973-76; freelance contbr. After Dark, 1969-79; contbg. editor L'Officiel, 1977-79, Ovation, 1980—. Author: Interviews with the World's Leading Musicians, 1974, Opera People, 1982; also numerous articles, record liner notes; broadcaster: Met. Opera broadcasts Met. Opera Live, also; syndicated program First Hearing; lectr. in field. Home: 100 Hudson St New York NY 10013 Office: 1865 Broadway New York NY 10023

JACOBSON, ROBERT MANFRED, hospital administrator; b. Chisholm, Minn., June 17, 1930; s. Clarence and Edna Jesse (Johnson) J.; m. Helen Syverson, Dec. 27, 1952; children—Mark, Daniel, Peter, Joanna, Deanna, Sarah. B.A. in Econs, St. Olaf Coll., 1952; M.H.A., U. Minn., 1954. Asst. adminstr. Lutheran Hosp., Fort Dodge, Iowa, 1957-63; adminstr. Deaconess Hosp., Grand Forks, N.D., 1963-70; mem. faculty U. N.D., 1968-79; exec. v.p. United Hosp., Grand Forks, 1971-76, pres., 1976—; mem. faculty U. Minn., 1971; clin. faculty Concordia Coll., 1969—; sec. Grand Forks Med. Park Corp., 1971—; mem. fin. com. North Star Mut. Ins., Ltd.; bd. dirs., mem. exec. com. Agassix Health Systems Agy. Bd. dirs. Upper Midwest Hosp. Conf., YMCA; bd. dirs., mem. plan devel. com. N.D. Health Coordinating Council, chmn., 1982-83; Tchr. Sunday Sch., Luth. Ch., 1959-62, 68-71; active Grand Forks Council on Alcoholism, 1965-69; pres. United Fund, 1967; chmn. citizens adv. com. to mayor, Grand Forks, 1968; bd. dirs. YMCA, 1981—. Served to lt USAF, 1954-57. Mem. Am. Hosp. Assn. (del.), N.D. Hosp. Assn. (dir., treas., v.p., pres.), Am. Assn. Hosp. Planning (dir.), Am. Coll. Hosp. Adminstrs., Nat. League Nursing (v.p. N.D.), Grand Forks C. of C. (v.p. 1978). Club: Rotary. Home: 1015 Reeves Dr Grand Forks ND 58201 Office: 1200 S Columbia Rd Grand Forks ND 58201

JACOBSON, RUTH ANNETTE KRAUSÉ, public relations counselor; b. Watertown, N.Y., June 30, 1925; d. Thomas M.R. and Ruth E. (Parmelee) Krausé; m.; 1 dau., Anne Heyliger Jacobson. Grad., Medill Sch. Journalism, Northwestern U., 1947; postgrad., U. Chgo. Guest editor Mademoiselle Mag., N.Y.C., 1945; with Howard G. Mayer & Assocs., Chgo., 1947-48; Midwest area rep. CARE, Inc., Chgo., 1948-50; account exec. Harshe-Rotman & Druck, Chgo., 1950-51; free-lance pub. relations counselor, 1955-57; pub. relations counselor Fleishman-Hillard, Inc., St. Louis, 1957-68, dir. spl. events, 1968—, sr. ptnr., 1971—. Chmn. pub. relations com. Mary Inst., Chatillon-DeMenil House Found.; sec. Greater St. Louis council Girl Scouts U.S.A., mem. pres.'s adv. cabinet; mem. community adv. bd. Sta. KWMU, U. Mo., St. Louis; bd. dirs. Downtown St. Louis, St. Louis Regional Commerce and Growth Assn., Jr. Achievement of Mississippi Valley, Inc., Miss Vanderschmidt's Secretarial Sch., St. Louis Conservatory and Schs. for Arts, also; mem. pub. relations com., bd. dirs. St. Louis Ambassadors; gov., chmn. pub. relations com. Winston Churchill Meml. and Library in U.S., Westminster Coll., Fulton, Mo. Mem. Women in Communications, St. Louis Forum, Mo. Hist. Soc., St. Louis Symphony Soc., Friends of City Art Mus., Nat. Trust for Historic Preservation, Assn. Churchill Fellows, Dance St. Louis. Episcopalian. Office: 1 Memorial Dr Saint Louis MO 63102 *

JACOBSON, SAUL P., business consultant; b. Los Angeles, Nov. 2, 1916; s. Alexander and Rosa (Breamer) J; children—Paul, Stephen; m. Karin Belling, 1969. B.S., Mass. Inst. Tech., 1938. Mech. engr. Bemis & Call Co., Springfield, Mass., 1938-39; indsl. engr., prodn. mgr. Sears, Roebuck & Co., Louisville, 1939-42; asst. chief mfg. engr. Fairchild Aircraft Co., Hagerstown, Md., 1942-43; with Brunswick Corp., Muskegon, Mich., Chgo., 1943-72, corporate officer, dir., 1951-71, pres. Bowling div., 1959-61, variously group v.p. bowling, sporting goods, boating, internat., def. products div., 1961-65, sr. v.p. bus. devel. and tech., 1965-71, ret.; bus. cons. various cos., 1972—; dir. Am. Store Equipment Co., Muskegon. Past pres. Santa Barbara (Calif.) Symphony Assn. Recipient Distinguished Service award U.S. Jr. C. of C., 1951. Mem. Am. Mgmt. Assn. Clubs: Masons, Shriners, Channel City, Santa Barbara, La Cumbre Golf and Country (Santa Barbara, Calif.). Home: 4642 Via Roblada Santa Barbara CA 93110

JACOBSON, SVERRE THEODORE, minister; b. Loreburn, Sask., Can., Sept. 20, 1922; s. Sverre and Aline Tomina (Joel) J.; m. Phyllis Lorraine Sylte, Sept. 14, 1948; children—Katherine Ann, Paul Theodore. B.A., U. Sask., 1946; B.D., Luther Theol. Sem., Sask., 1947, postgrad., 1952-53; Th.D., Princeton Theol. Sem., 1959. Ordained to ministry Evang. Lutheran Ch., Can.; pastor, Lomond, Alta., 1947-53; lectr. Luther Theol. Sem., Saskatoon, Sask., 1956-57; pastor, Torquay, Sask., 1958-63; asst. to pres. Evang. Luth. Ch. Can., Saskatoon, 1963-70, pres., 1970—. Home: 53 Moxon Crescent Saskatoon SK S7H 3B8 Canada Office: 247 1st Ave N Saskatoon SK S7K 4H5 Canada

JACOBSTEIN, J(OSEPH) MYRON, educator, librarian; b. Detroit, Jan. 27, 1920; s. Benjamin and Etta (Roberts) J.; m. Belle Lottman, Sept. 29, 1949; children—Ellen R., Bennett M. B.A., Wayne State U., 1946; M.S., Columbia, 1950; J.D., Chgo.-Kent Coll. Law, 1953. Cataloger U. Chgo. Library, 1950-51; librarian Cowles Commn. for Research in Econs., 1951-53; asst. law librarian U. Ill., 1953-55, Columbia, 1955-59; law librarian, prof. law U. Colo., Boulder, 1959-63, Stanford, 1963—. Author: (with R.M. Mersky) Fundamentals of Legal Research, 1981; Editor: Law Books in Print, 4 vols, 1976. Served with USAAF, 1942-45. Mem. Am. Assn. Law Libraries (pres. 1978—), Am. Soc. Info. Sci., Am. Soc. Internat. Law. Home: 19 Pearce Mitchell Pl Stanford CA 94305

JACOBUS, JOHN M., JR., educator, author, photographer; b. Poughkeepsie, N.Y., Sept. 15, 1927; s. John M. and Louise (Rayl) J.; m. Marion Langdon Townsend, Nov. 12, 1951; 1 dau., Jacqueline. A.B., Hamilton Coll., 1952; M.A., Yale U., 1954, Ph.D., 1956; A.M. (hon.), Dartmouth Coll., 1974. Prof. art and archtl. history Princeton U., 1956-60, U. Calif. at Berkeley, 1960-63, Ind. U., 1963-69, Dartmouth Coll., 1969—. Author: Philip Johnson, 1962, Twentieth Century Architecture, The Middle Years, 1967, Henri Matisse, 1973, (with Sam Hunter) American Art of the Twentieth Century, 1973, Modern Art, from Post-Impressionism to the Present, 1977. Guggenheim fellow, 1974-75. Home: 5 Hilltop Hanover NH 03755

JACOBY, A. JAMES, securities brokerage firm executive; b. N.Y.C., Jan. 8, 1939; s. D. Paul and Lillian (Jacobson) J.; m. Jayne Wachter, Apr. 16, 1961; children: Karen, Jill, Laurie. A.B., Cornell U., 1959; M.B.A., NYU, 1962. Gen. ptnr. Asiel & Co., N.Y.C., 1959—. Mem. Nat. Assn. Securities Dealers (vice chmn. 1983, chmn. nat. bus. conduct com. 1982). Club: Bond (N.Y.C.). Office: Asiel & Co 20 Broad St New York NY 10005

JACOBY, GEORGE ALONZO, former personnel executive; b. Pleasureville, Ky., May 13, 1904; s. George Alonzo and Sarah (Hieatt) J.; m. Ruth Burtner, Oct. 6, 1928; children: George Alonzo, John Burtner. A.B., Georgetown (Ky.) Coll., 1924, LL.D., 1958; M.S., Columbia, 1927. With Irving Trust Co., N.Y.C., 1925-40, asst. sec., 1929-37, asst. v.p., 1937-40; asst. personnel dir. Buick Motor div. Gen. Motors Corp., Flint, Mich., 1941-45; mem. labor relations staff Gen. Motors Corp., Detroit, 1945-46, dir. personnel services, 1946-56, dir. personnel relations, 1956-69; Pres. Mich. Safety Conf., 1954; dir. Nat. Safety Council, 1947-66; mem. Mich. Employment Security Adv. Council, 1947-60, Fed. Adv. Council Employment Security, 1952-54; exec. dir. Gen. Motors Com. Ednl. Grants and Scholarships, 1955-69. Regent Gen. Motors Inst., 1957-69; trustee Alma Coll., 1956-70; bd. govs. Inst. Indsl. Health, U. Mich., 1957-69. Recipient achievement award Georgetown Coll., 1963. Mem. Pi Kappa Alpha, Alpha Kappa Psi, Beta Gamma Sigma. Presbyn. Clubs: Orchard Lake Country, Recess (Detroit). Home: 233 Barden Rd Bloomfield Hills MI 48013

JACOBY, GEORGE V., electrical engineering consultant, technical advisor; b. Esztergom, Hungary, Feb. 26, 1918; came to U.S., 1950; s. Gabor and Gabriella (Prigl) J.; m. Paula B. Busa, Oct. 2, 1941 (div. 1958); 1 son, Charles G.; m. Andrea O. Oltay, Apr. 24, 1959 (div. 1972); m. Paula B. Busa, Feb. 1973. Dipl. Ing. Elec. Engring., Royal Hungarian U. Tech. Scis., Budapest, 1941, postgrad. in bus. adminstrn. and econs. Registered profl.engr., Pa. Design enhr. W.T. LaRose & Assocs., Troy, N.Y., 1950-53; research engr. Honeywell-Brown Instruments, Phila., 1953-58; devel. engr. RCA Electronic Data Processing, Camden, N.J., 1958-68; leader RCA Computer Systems, Marlboro, Mass., 1968-71; mgr. advanced rec. Sperry Univac-ISS, Blue Bell, Pa., and Santa Clara, Calif., 1971-83; sr. profl. cons. Magnetic Peripherals of Control Data Corp., Santa Clara, 1983—. Patentee in field. Recipient Outstanding Contbr. award ISS-Sperry Univac., Santa Clara, 1978, Invention award ISS-Sperry Univac., Santa Clara, 1980. Fellow IEEE. Roman Catholic. Home: 1315 Middleton Ct Los Altos CA 94022 Office: Magnetic Peripherals Inc of Control Data Corp 3333 Scott Blvd Santa Clara CA 95051

JACOBY, HENRY DONNAN, economist, educator; b. Dallas, June 25, 1935; s. Henry Harris and Margaret Cameron (Miller) J.; m. Martha Hughes Jacoby, Apr. 4, 1959; children—Daniel Donnan, Caroline Hughes. B.S. in Mech. Engring, U. Tex., Austin, 1957; Ph.D. in Econ, Harvard U., 1967. Systems analyst Tudor Engring. Co., San Francisco, 1959-61; economist Harvard Devel. Adv. Service, Argentina Project, 1963-65; asst. prof. dept. econs. Harvard U., Cambridge, Mass., 1965-69; assoc. prof. polit. economy John F. Kennedy Sch. Govt., 1969-73; prof. mgmt. MIT, Cambridge, 1973—; dir. Center for Energy Policy Research, 1978-83; vis. scholar London Bus. Sch., 1983-84; chmn. Mass. Gov.'s Emergency Energy Tech. Adv. Com., 1973-74; mem. Nat. Petroleum Council, 1975-83. Author: (with F.S. Brooman) Macroeconomics, 1970, (with R. Dorfman and H.A. Thomas, Jr.) Models for Managing Regional Water Quality, 1973, (with J.D. Steinbruner) Clearing The Air, 1973, Analysis of Investment in Electric Power, 1979, (with R. deLucia) Energy Planning for Developing Countries, 1982. Served with USN, 1957-59. Mem. Am. Econ. Assn., Tau Beta Pi. Democrat. Episcopalian. Office: MIT Sloan Sch of Mgmt 50 Memorial Dr Cambridge MA 02139

JACOBY, ROBERT BIRD, lawyer; b. Marion, Ohio, July 2, 1906; s. John Wilbur and Edna Leora (Bird) J.; m. Alice Helen Matthias, June 25, 1938; children—Robert Matthias, Richard Matthias. A.B., Ohio Wesleyan U., 1928; LL.B., Harvard, 1931. Bar: Ohio bar 1932, U.S. Dist. Ct. for D.C 1944, U.S. Supreme Ct 1945. Practiced law Jacoby and Jacoby, Marion, 1932; asso. Taft, Stettinius and Hollister, Cin., 1933-40; counsel Fed. Home Loan Bank of Cin., 1933-40; asso. gen. counsel Fed. Savs. and Loan Ins. Corp., Washington, 1941-46; dep. gov. Fed. Home Loan Bank System, 1946-47, became acting gov., Dec. 1947; with office chief counsel Bur. Internal Revenue, 1948-74; Lectr. Am. Savs. and Loan Inst., 1937-40. Co-author: Cyclopedia of Federal Savings and Loan Associations, 1939; Contbr. articles to savs. and loan pubs. Mem. Ohio State, Am., Fed. bar assns., Phi Gamma Delta. Democrat. Methodist. Club: Harvard (Washington). Home: 3806 47th St NW Washington DC 20016

JACOBY, ROBERT EAKIN, JR., advt. exec.; b. Union City, N.J., Mar. 26, 1928; s. Robert E. and Anna M. (Bach) J.; m. Monica Ann Flynn, Oct. 23, 1954; children—Debra Jean, Cynthia Marie, Patricia Ann, Laura Jayne. A.B. cum laude in Econs, Princeton, 1951. Econ. analyst Shell Oil Co., N.Y.C., 1951-52; v.p., account supr. Compton Advt. Agy., N.Y.C., 1952-62; sr. v.p., dir. Needham, Harper & Steers Advt., N.Y.C., 1963-65; v.p., account group head Ted Bates & Co., N.Y.C., 1962-63, pres., 1965—, also chmn., chief exec. officer. Served with AUS, 1946-47; Japan. Mem. Sales Execs. Club N.Y., Assn. Am. Advt. Agys., Phi Beta Kappa. Office: Ted Bates & Co 1515 Broadway New York NY *

JACOBY, SIDNEY BERNHARD, lawyer, educator; b. Berlin, Germany, Dec. 7, 1908; came to U.S., 1934, naturalized, 1939; s. Siegfried and Amanda J.; m. Elaine Heavenrich, Oct. 17, 1942; children—Evelyn, Anne Jacoby Atkins. Jur.D., Friedrich Wilhelm U., Berlin, Germany, 1933; LL.B., Columbia U., 1939. Bar: N.Y. 1940, D.C. 1958, Ohio 1970. Atty. U.S. R.R. Retirement Bd., 1940-45, U.S. Dept. Interior, 1945-47, Office of Chief of Counsel, Nuremberg, Germany, 1945-46, U.S. Dept. Justice, 1947-57; prof. law Georgetown U., Washington, 1957-68, Law Sch., Case Western Res. U., Cleve., 1968-76, John C. Hutchins prof. law, 1975; prof. law Cleveland-Marshall Coll. Law, Cleve. State U., 1976-81; lectr. Western Ont. Law Sch., London, fall 1977; counsel in proc. before World Ct., 1957, 58; adj. prof. Antioch Sch. Law, 1981. Author: (with David Schwartz) Government Litigation, 1963, (with John Steadman and David Schwartz) Litigation with the Federal Government, 1970, 2d edit., 1983, Ohio Civil Practice Under the Rules, 2 vols. with ann. supplements, 1970; Contbr. articles to legal publs. Recipient dedication Case Western Res. U. Law Rev., summer 1977. Mem. Am. Law Inst., Fed. Bar Assn. Jewish. Home: 3709 S George Mason Dr Falls Church VA 22041

JACOBY, WILLIAM JEROME, JR., physician; b. Mt. Carmel, Pa., Aug. 9, 1925; s. William Jerome and Florence Marie (White) J.; m. Joeann J. Powroznick, May 5, 1956; children—William Jerome, Teresa Marie. A.B., Emory U., 1946; M.D., Jefferson Med. Coll., Phila., 1950. Diplomate: Am. Bd. Internal Medicine. Intern Jefferson Med. Coll. Hosp., 1950-51, resident in internal medicine, 1951-52, 55-56, Am. Heart Assn. fellow, 1956-57; chmn. dept. medicine U.S. Naval hosps., Gt. Lakes, Ill., 1964-69, Phila., 1969-72; chmn. dept. medicine, dir. edn. and research Nat. Naval Med. Center, Bethesda, Md., 1972-75; comdg. officer Naval Regional Med. Center, Portsmouth, Va., 1975-78; dir. med. service VACO, Washington, 1978-80, dep. chief med. dir., 1980—; asso. clin. prof. Jefferson Med. Coll., 1969; prof. medicine George Washington U. Med. Sch., 1972, Eastern Va. Sch. Medicine, Norfolk, Va., 1976-78; adv. council Nat. Heart Lung Blood Inst., NIH, Emergency Med. Services. Contbr. articles to med. jours. Commd. lt. (j.g.) M.C. U.S. Navy, 1950; advanced through grades to rear adm., 1972. Decorated Legion of Merit, Meritorious Service medal. Fellow A.C.P.; mem. Assn. Mil. Surgeons (Founders medal 1974), Internat. Soc. Internal Medicine, Alpha Omega Alpha, Phi Beta Pi. Roman Catholic. Address: 8221 Windsor View Terr Potomac MD 20854

JACOLOW, JERALD JOSHUA, corporate executive; b. N.Y.C., Mar. 17, 1931; s. Henry and Eleanora (Varon) J.; m. Joan Grossman, Oct. 3, 1953 (div. Oct. 1966); children: Ellen Sue, Sandford; m. Joyce Siano, Nov. 19, 1966 (div. Nov. 1976). B.B.A., City Coll. N.Y., 1952. C.P.A., N.Y. Accountant J.J. Fried & Co., C.P.A.s, N.Y.C., 1952-55; accountant, auditor A.A. Miller & Co., C.P.A.s, 1956-58; gen. practice accounting, 1958-63; controller Ormont Drug & Chem. Co., Inc., Englewood, N.J., 1964-66, treas., v.p. finance, 1964-66, exec. v.p., dir., 1966-76, pres., chief operating officer, 1976-79, U.S. Products, Inc., 1979-80, chmn. bd., chief exec. officer, dir., 1980-82; pres., dir. Gold Leaf Pharmacal Co., Inc., 1965-79, Lawton Labs., Inc., 1965-79, A-G Pharmaceuticals, Inc., 1971-79; exec. v.p., dir. Yorktown Research, Inc., 1976-79; mgr. syndicate dept. Quantum Capital Group, Inc., Boca Raton, Fla.; with U.S. Products, Inc., Miami, Fla.; exec. dir. Bydand, Ltd.; dir. Natural Scis., Inc., Ormont Pharmaceuticals, Ltd.; pres., dir. Funds for Expansion, Ltd., N.Y.C., 1963-72, N.J., 1966-73; v.p., dir. Bedford-Acme Surg. Instrument Co., 1973-79, Fed. Pharmacal Corp., 1974-79, Pan Am. Pharm. Co., 1974-76, Amfre-Grant, Inc., 1973-79, Edcoa Inc., 1974-77. Mem. Mail Users Council Englewood, 1965-79. Mem. Am. Inst. C.P.A.s, N.Y. State Soc. C.P.A.s, N.Y. State Assn. Professions, Am. Mgmt. Assn. (pres.'s council), N.Y. Credit and Financial Mgmt. Assn., Nat. Assn. Pharm. Mfrs. (dir., mem. exec. council, treas., chmn. ins. com., pres. 1973-76, chmn. 1976-79), N.Y. Acad. Scis., Tau Delta Phi. Home: 8491 Gatehouse Rd Plantation FL 33324 Office: 7200 W Camino Real Suite 200 Boca Raton FL 33433

JACOX, RALPH FRANKLIN, educator, internist, rheumatologist; b. Alfred, N.Y., Oct. 30, 1913; s. John Woolworth and Ruby (Franklin) J.; m. Florence Stella Monaghan, June 30, 1940; children: Virginia Ann, Mark Franklin, Christine Louise. B.S., Alfred U.; M.D., U. Rochester, 1940. Am. Bd. Internal Medicine. Asst. in bacteriology Johns Hopkins Sch. Hygiene, Balt., 1940-41; instr. medicine U. Rochester Sch. Medicine and Dentistry (N.Y.), 1941-46, prof. medicine, 1963—; cons. in medicine Rochester Gen. Hosp. and Genessee Hosp., Rochester, 1958—; cons. in rheumatology Oxford U. (Eng.), 1969-70. Contbr. numerous articles to med. jours. Hon. trustee Alfred U., 1964-66. Served to capt. M.C. AUS, 1942-45; ETO. Mem. Heberden Soc. (Eng.), Am. Soc. Clin. Investigation, ACP. Republican. Home: 3 Livingston St Honeoye Falls NY 14472 Office: Rheumatology Unit Univ Rochester Sch Medicine and Dentistry 260 Crittenden Blvd Rochester NY 14642

JACQUES, ANDRE CHARLES, banker; b. Verviers, Belgium, July 27, 1921; s. Charles and Adrienne (Nalinne) J.; m. Ghislaine I. Ubaghs, May 4, 1949; children—Patrick, Manoele. License in Fin. and Econs. magna cum laude, Liege U., Belgium, 1943. With Banque Belge pour l'Etranger (Extreme-Orient), Hong Kong and Tientsin, China, 1947-51, Banque Belge et Internationale en Egypte, S.A., Cairo and Alexandria, Egypt, 1951-61, Belgian Am. Banking Corp., N.Y.C., 1961-68; vice chmn. bd. European Am. Bank, N.Y.C., 1968—; pres. Universitas, Ltd.; dir. Belgian Line, Inc.; adv. bd. Societe Generale de Belgique. Bd. dirs. Internat. Center N.Y., Belgian Am. Ednl. Found., Hoover Found., Brussels. Served with Belgian Army, World War II. Decorated Officer Order of the Crown, (Belgium)., Order of Leopold, (Belgium). Mem. Belgian Am. C. of C. in U.S. (bd. dirs.). Club: Creek (Locust Valley, N.Y.). Office: European American Bank 10 Hanover Sq New York NY 10015

JACQUES, MICHAEL LOUIS, art educator, artist printmaker; b. Barre, Vt., Apr. 12, 1945; s. Louis and Verna Netti (Fleck) J.; m. Rose Yesu, Aug. 1969 (div.); m. Karen Eckler, July 7, 1983; 1 stepson, Sebastian. B.F.A., Boston U., 1968. Assoc. prof. Emmanuel Coll., Boston, 1971—; artist-in-residence Va. Mus., Richmond, 1981-82, ABT Assocs. Inc., Cambridge, Mass., 1980-81; illustrator U.S. Army, Washington, 1969-71. Author and illustrator: Images of Age, 1981 (nominated Am. Book award 1982, award in graphic design DESI 1981, book cover award 1981, Book design award Art Dirs. Club Boston 1981, Jacket Design award 1981); work represented in permanent collections, Chrysler Mus., Va., in permanent collectioins, Decorova Mus., Mass., in permanent collections, Ho. of Reps., Washington, Phila. Mus., Peking Collection, Republic China, Springfield Mus. Fine Arts. Mem. Boston Printmakers (bd. dirs. 1982), Boston Visual Artists Union, Audubon Artists Assn., Acad. Artists Assn., Copley Soc.

JACQUET, HERVÉ MICHEL, mathematics educator; b. Oullins, Rhone, France, Aug. 4, 1939; came to U.S., 1967; s. Albert Vincent and Helene (Cagnard) J.; m. Yasuko Matsuoka, Apr. 23, 1969. Licence Agregation de Mathematiques, Ecole Normale Superieure, Paris, 1963; Ph.D. in Math., U. Paris, 1967. Researcher CRNS, Paris, 1963-69; mem. Inst. Advanced Studies, Princeton, N.J., 1967-69; assoc. prof. U. Md., College Park, 1969-70; assoc. prof. math. CUNY, 1970-73, prof., 1973-74, Columbia U., N.Y.C., 1974—; Peccot lectures Coll. de France, Paris, 1970. Recipient Prix Petit d'Ormoy Academie des Scis., 1979. Mem. Am. Math Assn., Academie des Scis. Office: Columbia U. New York NY 10027

JACQUIN, WILLIAM C., chamber of commerce executive; b. Peoria, Ill., Sept. 1, 1935; s. William C. and Katheryn J.; m. Deborah Young, Aug. 21, 1956; children: Susan, Gregg, Lisa. B.A. in Polit. Sci., Wabash (Ind.) Coll., 1957; postgrad., U. Ariz. Engaged in ins. bus., 1962—; So. regional dir. Ariz. C. of C., 1975, dir. govt. and polit. affairs, Phoenix, 1975—; mem. Ariz. Ho. of Reps., 1965-66, Ariz. Senate, pres., 1971-74, majority floor leader, 1969-70. Del. Republican Nat. Conv., 1972; mem. bd. advisers Ariz. Center Occupational Safety and Health; mem. White House Council Families; bd. dirs. Freedom Found.; mem. Ariz. Citizens Commn. Tax Reform and Sch. Fin., 1978-79. Recipient Outstanding Legis. Leader award Citizens Conf. State Legislatures, 1971. Mem. Ariz. Soc. Assn. Execs. (dir. 1980-81). Office: 1366 E Thomas Suite 202 Phoenix AZ 85014

JACUZZI, ALDO JOSEPH, pump co. exec.; b. Berkeley, Calif., Apr. 26, 1921; s. Joseph and Rena (Beggio) J.; m. Granuccia Maria Amadei, Apr. 26, 1942; children—Roy Aldo, Victor Steven, Rita Carol. Student, Armstrong Bus. Coll., Berkeley. With Jacuzzi Bros. Inc., 1939-80, v.p. purchasing, 1965-70, chmn. bd., 1970-80, dir. Can. expansion project, 1951-54, cons., 1980—; dir. Jacuzzi Mex. S.A., Jacuzzi Domestic Internat. Sales Corp. Active local Boy Scouts Am., Ark. Art Center, Salvation Army, Girl Scouts, United Way. Served with USNR, 1944-46. Mem. Ark. Hall of Fame. Mem. Ednl. Athletic Scholarship Assn., Ark. Auto Assn., Ark. Community Concert Assn., Little Rock C. of C., Leonardo da Vinci Soc., Sons of Italy. Democrat. Roman Catholic. Clubs: Little Rock, Capital. Office: 1 Financial Centre 650 Shackleford Rd Suite 401 Little Rock AR 72211

JADOT, JEAN LAMBERT OCTAVE, clergyman; b. Brussels, Belgium, Nov. 23, 1909; s. Lambert Paul and Gabrielle Marie (Flanneau) J. D.Philosophie Thomiste, U. Catholique Louvain, Belgium, 1930. Ordained priest Roman Catholic Ch., 1934, consecrated bishop, 1968; parish asst., 1934-39; nat. chaplain Jeunesse Etudiante Catholique, 1939-45; chaplain Ecole Royale Militaire, 1945-52; chief chaplain Force Publique Belgian Congo, 1952-60; nat. dir. Propagation of Faith for Belgium, 1960-68; apostolic pro nuncio in Thailand, also apostolic del. in, Laos, Malaysia and Singapore, 1968-71, apostolic pro nuncio in Cameroun and Gabon, also apostolic del. in, Equatorial Guinea, 1971-73, apostolic del. to, U.S., 1973-80;

permanent observer of Holy See to OAS, 1978—; pro pres. Secretariat for Non Christians at Vatican, 1980—; titular arch-bishop of, Zuri, 1968. Served as chaplain Belgian Army, 1945-52. Decorated Order Leopold. Address: The Vatican Rome Italy 00120

JAEDICKE, ROBERT K., accounting educator, university official; m. Marilyn Jaedicke; 4 children. B.B.A., U. Wash., 1952, M.B.A., 1953; Ph.D., U. Minn., 1957. Teaching fellow U. Wash., 1952-53; from instr. to asst. prof. U. Minn., 1953-58; asst. prof. Harvard U., Cambridge, Mass., 1958-61; faculty mem. Stanford U. Grad. Sch. Bus., Calif., 1961—, dir. Ph.D. program, 1965-68, apptd. Kimball prof. acctg., 1975—, assoc. dean for acad. affairs, 1969-81, acting dean Sch. Bus., 1979-80, dean, 1983—. Author: books including Managerial Accounting, Accounting Flows-Income, Funds, Cash; contbr. articles to profl. jours. Served with USAF, 1946-49. Mem. Am. Acctg. Assn. (former dir. research), Nat. Assn. Accts. Office: Office of Dean Stanford U Grad Sch Bus Stanford CA 94305 *

JAEGER, CARL GUSTAVE, magazine publisher; b. Bronxville, N.Y., Apr. 12, 1940; s. Gustave A. and Nancy E. (Gaines) J.; m. Helen Fordham Calhoun, July 27, 1968; children: Michael, Douglas. B.A., Dartmouth Coll., 1962. Mail order sales mgr. Time-Life Books, Time Inc., N.Y.C., 1969-74, dir. sales, 1974-76, exec. v.p., Alexandria, Va., 1976-81, pres., Alexandria, 1981-82; pub. Discover Mag., Time Inc., N.Y.C., 1982—; dir. Time-Life Books, Inc., Alexandria, 1976-82, Book-of-the-Month Club, N.Y.C., 1980-82, Inland Container Corp., Indpls., 1980-83. Served with U.S. Army, 1963. Mem. Assn. Am. Pubs. (chmn. direct mktg. book club div. 1979-81), Assn. Third Class Mail Users (dir. 1977-82), Mag. Pubs. Assn. Clubs: St. Andrews Golf (Hastings-on-Hudson, N.Y.); Washington Golf and Country (Arlington, Va.). Office: Discover Mag Time Inc 1271 Ave of Americas New York NY 10020

JAEGER, GEORGE WILLIAM, diplomat; b. Vienna, Austria, May 26, 1926; emigrated to U.S., 1940; s. Fredrick George and Emilie (Stachura) J.; m. Patricia Clark, Jan. 12, 1970; 1 dau., Christina. B.A., St. Vincent's Coll., Latrobe, Pa., 1948; M.A., Harvard U., 1951; student, Nat. War Coll., 1973-74. With State Dept., 1956—, polit. officer U.S. embassy, Bonn and West Berlin, 1965-70, staff dir. Pres.'s Adv. Com. on Disarmament, Washington, 1970-73, dep. polit. couselor U.S. embassy, Paris, 1975-78, consul gen. U.S. Consulate Gen., Quebec, 1979-83, polit. counselor U.S. embassy, Ottawa, Ont., Can., 1983—; occasional lectr. SUNY Can. Studies Ctr., Plattsburgh, Laval U., Quebec, 1982, 83. Served with AUS, 1944-46; ETO. Recipient Superior Honor awards Dept. State, 1979, 82. Mem. Am. Fgn. Service Assn., Nat. War Coll. Alumni Assn. Roman Catholic. Clubs: Garrison; Cercle Universitaire (Quebec). Home: 231 Park Rd Ottawa ON Canada KIM 0C9 Office: Dept State Mailroom Washington DC 20520 *To serve with integrity and courage.*

JAEGER, LEONARD HENRY, former public utility executive; b. Bklyn., Oct. 6, 1905; s. Leonard and Marie (Ziegler) J.; m. Mary Elizabeth Fallon, Dec. 15, 1951. Grad., Pace Coll., 1926; postgrad., N.Y. U., evenings 1926-30. Accountant Southeastern Power & Light Co., 1926-30; with Commonwealth & So. Corp., 1930-42, 46-49, asst. comptroller, 1948-49; treas. So. Co., Atlanta, 1949-70, v.p. finance, 1957-70, dir., 1966-70, adv. dir., 1970-75; exec. v.p. So. Co. Services, Inc., 1963-67, dir., vice chmn. bd., 1967-70. Served to capt. AUS, 1942-45. Mem. Fin. Execs. Inst., N.Y. Soc. Security Analysts, N.Y. U. Alumni Assn., Pace Alumni Assn., Edison Electric Inst. (mem., past chmn. investor relations com.). Republican. Lutheran. Home: PO Box 21495 Sarasota FL 33583

JAEGER, LESLIE GORDON, university administrator; b. Southport, Eng., Jan. 28, 1926; s. Henry M. and Beatrice A. (Highton) J.; m. Annie Sylvia Dyson, Apr. 3, 1948; children: Valerie Ann, Hilary Frances.; m. Kathleen Grant, July 24, 1981. B.A., Cambridge U., 1946, M.A., 1950; Ph.D., London U., 1955. With W.P. Thompson & Co., Liverpool, Eng., 1948-50, Renold Ltd., Manchester, Eng., 1950-52; mem. faculty Univ. Coll. of Khartoum, 1952-56; Univ. lectr. Cambridge (Eng.) U., 1956-62; prof. civil engring. and applied mechanics McGill U., Montreal, Que., Can., 1962-64, 66-70; Regius prof. engring. U. Edinburgh, Scotland, 1964-66; dean Coll. Engring., U. N.B., Fredericton, 1970-75, acting v.p., 1972-73; acad. v.p. Acadia U., Wolfville, N.S., Can., 1975-80; spl. asst. to pres. Tech. U. N.S., Halifax, 1980—; cons. structural engring. Expo '67, Rolls Royce Ltd., Adjeleian & Assos., Ottawa, and others. Author: (with A.W. Hendry) The Analysis of Grid Frameworks and Related Structures, 2d edit, 1968, Elementary Theory of Elastic Plates, 1962, Cartesian Tensors in Engineering Science, 1964; Contbr. numerous research papers to profl. jours. Mem. Cambridge City Council, 1961-62; mem. Nat. Council Liberal Party U.K., 1960-62; Bd. govs. Magdalene Coll., Cambridge, 1959-62. Served with Royal Navy, 1945-48. Recipient Telford premium Instn. Civil Engrs., 1959, Nat. Research Council Can. research grantee, 1962—, A.B. Sanderson award Can. Soc. Civil Engring., 1983. Fellow Royal Soc. Edinburgh, Instn. C.E. (London), Instn. Structural Engrs. (London), Instn. Mech. Engrs. (London); mem. Engring. Inst. Can. Clubs: Mason., Halifax (N.S.). Office: PO Box 1000 Halifax NS B3J 2X4 Canada

JAEGGI, KENNETH VINCENT, computer co. exec.; b. Rockville Centre, N.Y., Nov. 15, 1945; s. Kenneth Vincent and Gloria (Gross) J.; m. Dorothy McDonald, Sept. 17, 1966; children—Laura Kaye, H.K. Michael. B.S. in Bus. Adminstrn, Northwestern U., 1967; M.B.A., U. Chgo., 1977. With Zenith Radio Corp., 1971-80, controller, 1978-80, v.p., 1980; v.p., chief fin. officer Data Gen. Corp., Westboro, Mass., 1980—. Served with USN, 1967-71. Office: 4400 Computer Dr Westboro MA 01580

JAFFE, ANTHONY ROBERT, advt. agy. exec.; b. N.Y.C., Sept. 30, 1934; s. Louis A. and Pearl J.; m. Gwen Daner, Jan. 17, 1960; children—Thomas M., Elizabeth D. Grad., Horace Mann Sch., 1948-51; B.A., Brown U., 1955. Copy trainee Doyle-Dane-Bernbach Advt., N.Y.C., 1956-57; copywriter J. Walter Thompson Co., N.Y.C., 1957-60; v.p., copy supr. Dancer-Fitzgerald-Sample, N.Y.C., 1960-69; sr. v.p. William Esty Co. Inc., N.Y.C., 1970—. Songwriter, composer: Lemon Soul, 1969, Crystal Dawn, 1973. Served with AUS, 1957-63. Mem. Am. Soc. Composers and Publishers, Pi Lambda Phi. Home: 221 Hunting Ridge Rd Stamford CT 06903 Office: 100 E 42d St New York City NY 10017

JAFFE, ARTHUR MICHAEL, physicist, mathematician, educator; b. N.Y.C., Dec. 22, 1937; s. Henry and Clarisse J.; m. Nora Frances Crow, July 24, 1971. A.B., Princeton U., 1959, Ph.D., 1965; B.A., Cambridge U., 1961. Acting asst. prof. math. Stanford U., 1966-67; asst. prof. physics Harvard U., Cambridge, Mass., 1967-69, asso. prof., 1969-70, prof. physics, 1970-77, prof. math. physics, 1977—; research fellow Princeton U., 1965-66, Stanford Linear Accelerator Center, 1966-67; mem. Inst. for Advanced Study, 1967; vis. prof. Eidgenössische Technische Hochschule, Zurich, 1968; vis. prof. math. physics Princeton U., 1971; vis. prof. Rockefeller U., 1977. Author: Vortices and Monopoles, 1980, Quantum Physics, 1981; Asso. editor: Jour. Math. Physics, 1970-72; editorial council: Annals of Physics, 1975-77; asst. editor, 1977—; editor: Communications Math. Physics, 1976—; chief editor, 1979—; mem. adv. bd.: Letters in Math. Physics, 1975—; editor: Progress in Physics, 1979—, Selecta Mathematica Sovetica, 1980—; contbr. articles to profl. jours. Alfred P. Sloan Found. fellow, 1968-70; Guggenheim Found. fellow, 1977-78; award Math. and Phys. Scis., N.Y. Acad. Sci., 1979; Dannie Heineman prize for Math. Physics, 1980. Fellow Am. Phys. Soc., Am. Acad. Arts and Scis.; mem. Am. Math. Soc., AAAS, Internat. Assn. Math. Physics. Home: 27 Lancaster St Cambridge MA 02140

JAFFE, BERNARD MICHAEL, surgeon; b. N.Y.C.; s. Abner I. and Sylvia (Rothman) J.; m. Marlene Lambert, June 4, 1961; children: Mark Allen, Debra Lynn. B.A., U. Rochester, 1961; M.D., NYU, 1964. Asst. prof. surgery Washington U., St. Louis, 1971-75, asso. prof., 1975-77, prof., 1977-79; prof., chmn. dept. surgery SUNY, Downstate Med. Center, Bklyn., 1979—. Author: (with Behrman) Methods of Hormone Radioimmunoassay, 1980. Served to lt. col. USAF, 1972-74. James IV traveling surg. fellow. Mem. Assn. Acad. Surgery (pres. 1978-79), Soc. Univ. Surgeons (sec. 1979-82, pres. 1983-84), Am. Surg. Assn., Soc. Clin. Surgery, Surg. Biol. Club I (sec. 1982—), Am. Soc. Clin. Investigation, ACS, Phi Beta Kappa, Alpha Omega Alpha. Office: 450 Clarkson Ave Brooklyn NY 11203 *

JAFFE, DAVID, author, publisher; b. Slonim, Poland, Jan. 20, 1911; came to U.S., 1912, naturalized, 1921; s. Louis and Sadie (Arner) J.; m. Sylvia S. Turner, Nov. 8, 1942. B.A., Duke U., 1933, M.A., 1937. State editor Durham Morning Herald, (N.C.), 1938-41; mem. editorial staff U. N.C. Press, 1942-44; freelance editor N.Y.C., 1946-47; mem. editorial staff Ctr. for Mil. History, Washington, 1948-76, sr. editor, 1961-76; pub. Mardi Press, Arlington, Va., 1976—. Author: The Stormy Petrel and the Whale: Some Origins of Moby-Dick, 1976, Bartleby the Scrivener and Bleak House: Melvile's Debt to Dickens, 1981; contbr. articles to newspapers, profl. lit. jours. Mem. Melville Soc., Phi Beta Kappa. Home: 1913 S Quincy St Arlington VA 22204

JAFFE, FROHM FILMORE, lawyer; b. Chgo., May 4, 1918; s. Jacob Isadore and Goldie (Rabinowitz) J.; m. Mary Main, Nov. 7, 1942; children: Jo Anne, Jay. Student, Southwestern U., 1936-39; J.D., Pacific Coast U., 1940. Bar: Calif. 1945, U.S. Supreme Ct. 1964. Practiced law, Los Angeles, 1945—; partner Bernard & Jaffe, Los Angeles, 1947-74, Jaffe & Jaffe, 1975—; mem. Los Angeles Traffic Commn., 1947-68; Arbitrator Am. Arbitration Assn., 1968—; chmn. pro bono com. Superior Ct. Calif., County of Los Angeles, 1980-83. Served to capt. inf. AUS, 1942-45. Decorated Purple Heart, Croix de Guerre with Silver Star, Bronze Star with oak leaf cluster. Mem. Los Angeles County, ABA, Los Angeles Criminal Ct. Bar Assn. (charter mem.), Calif. Trial Lawyers Assn. Club: Mason (Shriner). Office: 6420 Wilshire Blvd Los Angeles CA 90048

JAFFE, HANS H., educator; b. Marburg, Germany, Apr. 17, 1919; came to U.S., 1940, naturalized, 1946; s. Gunther and Hedwig (Schlesinger) J.; m. Martha Ledbetter, Mar. 1946 (div. Jan. 1959); children—Charles, Charlotte, John. B.S., State U. Iowa, 1941; M.S., Purdue U., 1943; Ph.D., U. N.C., 1952. Phys. chemist U.S. Health Service, Balt., Chapel Hill, N.C., 1946-54; asst. prof. U. Cin., 1954-59, asso. prof., 1959-61; prof., 1961—, head dept. chemistry, 1966-71, 75-76. Author: Theory and Applications of Ultraviolet Spectroscopy, 1962, Symmetry in Chemistry, 1965, The Importance of Antibonding Orbitals, 1967, Symmetry Orbitals and Spectra, 1971; Contbr. articles to profl. jours. Served with AUS, 1943-46. Recipient Rievschl award U. Cin., 1982; Named Cin. Scientist of Year. Mem. Am. Chem. Soc. (Eminent Chemist Cin. sect. 1961), Am. Phys. Soc., AAAS, Tech. and Sci. Socs. Council Cin., Sigma Xi (1st Ann. Distinguished Research award U. Cin. chpt. 1961), Phi Lambda Upsilon. Home: 2069 Faywood Ave Cincinnati OH 45238

JAFFE, HAROLD, government official; b. Chgo., May 8, 1930; s. Harry and Mary (Ginsberg) J.; m. Mimi Ester Kranz, Feb. 4, 1951; children: David L., Deborah R., Sandra L. B.S. in Chemistry, U. Ill., 1951; Ph.D. in Nuclear Chemistry, U. Calif. at Berkeley, 1954. Research chemist Union Oil Co., 1954-55; mgr. gas cooled reactor program Aerojet Gen. Corp., 1956-60, mgr. applied tech. div., 1960-66, asst. to v.p. nuclear div., 1966-69, gen. mgr., 1969, asst. to pres., 1970; mgr. isotope flight systems Space Nuclear Systems div. AEC, Washington, 1970-75; tech. asst. to asst. adminstr. for nuclear energy ERDA, Washington, 1975-76; dep. dir. Office Internat. Tech. Cooperation, Dept. Energy, 1976-83; dep. asst. sec. for internat. affairs Dept. Energy, 1983—; dir. Idaho Nuclear Corp., 1968-70; Asst. prof. J.F. Kennedy U., Martinez, Calif., 1967-70. Recipient Exceptional Service medal NASA, 1974. Fellow Am. Inst. Chemists; mem. Am. Chem. Soc., Am. Nuclear Soc., Sigma Xi, Phi Kappa Phi, Phi Lambda Upsilon. Home: 10702 Great Arbor Dr Potomac MD 20854 Office: Dept Energy Washington DC 20585

JAFFE, JAN PAYNTER, advt. agy. exec.; b. Chgo., Sept. 23, 1944; d. Gilman Caldwell and Helen Jean (Hepner) Paynter; m. Harris S. Jaffe, June 19, 1965 (div. Aug. 1969). B.A., U. Chgo., 1964, M.B.A., 1966. Staff exec. devel. program Tatham-Laird & Kudner, Inc., Chgo., 1966-67, v.p., N.Y.C., 1968-73, Smith/Greenland Co., Inc., 1973, McCann-Erickson, Inc., 1973-79; sr. product mgr. Airwick Consumer Products div. Airwick Industries, Teterboro, N.J., 1979; sr. v.p. Backer & Spielvogel, N.Y.C., 1979—; cons. Vol. Urban Cons. Group, 1973—. Bd. dirs. League Sch., 1976-79, N.Y. Jazz Mus., 1976, Off-Off Broadway Alliance, 1976; chmn. bd. Encompass Theatre, 1976-79. Mem. Advt. Research Found. Home: Aspen 2 Village 2 New Hope PA 18938

JAFFE, LEO, motion picture executive; b. N.Y.C., Apr. 23, 1909; m. Anita. B.C.S., N.Y. U., 1931. Former pres., chief exec. officer and chmn. bd. Columbia Pictures Industries, Inc., now chmn. emeritus. Past Industry chmn. United Jewish Appeal, Federated Charities, NCCJ; bd. dirs. Will Rogers Meml. Hosp., San Juan Racing Assn., Beth Abraham Hosp. and, Home for Aged; hon. chmn. bd. trustees Nat. Found. March of Dimes, N.Y.C., trustee nat. bd. Decorated commandatore Italian Republic; Grande Ufficiale-Italy; recipient N.Y.C. medal honor (2).; Fellow Brandeis U.; fellow, mem. pres.'s council, life trustee N.Y.U. Sch. Bus. Adminstrn., Dean Madden Meml. award, 1977, Jean Hersholt Humanitarian award, 1978, Israel Prime Ministers' medal honor, 1978, U.S. medal honor Bond Sales dr. (2); Gold award NCCJ, 1981. Mem. Motion Picture Pioneers (dir., Man of Year award 1972), Motion Picture Assn. Am. (dir.), Delta Mu Delta, Alpha Phi Sigma, Alpha Sigma Phi. Clubs: Hampshire Country; City Athletic, Friars (N.Y.C.); Tamarisk Country (Rancho Mirage, Calif.). Home: 425 E 58 St New York NY 10022 Office: 711 Fifth Ave New York NY 10022

JAFFE, LEONARD SIGMUND, financial executive; b. Balt., Oct. 31, 1916; s. Benjamin I. and Anna J. (Berkow) J.; m. Marjorie Dorf, Apr. 24, 1941; children: Carol (Mrs. Frederick Levinger), Ellen (Mrs. Richard Perlman), Sue A. B.A., Johns Hopkins, 1937; M.B.A., Harvard, 1939. Corp. controller, div. controller, asst. plant mgr. Joseph E. Seagram, N.Y.C., 1942-58; v.p. finance, dir. Capehart Corp., N.Y.C., 1958-62; v.p. finance, sec.-treas. Rheingold Corp., N.Y.C., 1962-68; v.p. finance Work Wear Corp., Cleve., 1970-73; exec. v.p. finance, dir. Cook United, Inc., Cleve., 1974-77; pres. Marlen Corp. of Miami, 1978—, Corp. Fin. Assocs., Boca Raton, Fla., 1983—; instr. U. Louisville, 1946-47. Mem. nat. student alumni council Johns Hopkins U. Mem. Fin. Execs. Inst., Am. Accounting Assn., Nat. Inst. Accountants, Am. Soc. Corp. Secs. Clubs: Harvard (N.Y.C.); Oakwood (Cleve.); Harvard Business School, Clevelander; Birchwood Country (Westport, Conn.); Rotary. Home: 2664 NW 23 Way Boca Raton FL 33431 Office: NCNB Bldg Suite 107 150 E Palmetto Park Rd Boca Raton FL 33432

JAFFE, LIONEL FRANCIS, biology educator; b. Bklyn., Dec. 28, 1927; s. Bernard and Celia (Lesser) J.; m. Miriam E. Walther, June 14, 1949; children—Laurinda, Amanda, David. S.B., Harvard U., 1948; Ph.D. in Embryology, Calif. Inst. Tech., 1954. NRC-NSF fellow Hopkins Marine Sta., Pacific Grove, Calif., 1953-55; fellow marine biology Scripps Instn. Oceanography, La Jolla, Calif., 1955-56; asst. prof. biology Brandeis U., 1956-60; asst. prof., then asso. prof. U. Pa., 1960-67; prof. biology Purdue U., 1967-82; dir. Nat. Vibrating Probe Facility, Marine Biol. Lab., Woods Hole, Mass., 1982—; Tyler Meml. lectr. Calif. Inst. Tech., 1978; Jenkinson lectr. Oxford (Eng.) U., 1982. Editorial bd.: Jour. Cell Biology, 1981—. Grantee Office Naval Research, NSF, NIH. Mem. Am. Soc. Devel. Biology, Biophys. Soc., Soc. Gen. Physiologists, Cell Biology Soc. Inventor ultrasensitive vibrating probe for measuring natural elec. currents through living cells and organisms. Office: Marine Biol Lab Woods Holl MA 02543

JAFFE, MICHAEL, corporation executive; b. Bklyn., Apr. 18, 1940; s. Ben and Anne (Sterzer) J.; m. Janie Trencher, June 25, 1981; 1 dau., Jordana. B.A., Bkln. Coll., 1960; LL.B., Harvard U., 1963. Pres. Ampal-Am. Israel Corp., N.Y.C., 1981—. Office: Ampal-Am Israel Corp 10 Rockefeller Plaza New York NY 10020

JAFFE, MORRIS, supermarket company executive. Chmn. Handy-Andy, Inc. Office: Handy-Andy Inc PO Box 1161 San Antonio TX 78294§

JAFFE, NORA, artist; b. Urbana, Ohio, Feb. 25, 1928; d. Harry Jefferson and Margaret Elizabeth (McNab) Miller; m. Joseph Jaffe, Jan. 19, 1951; children: Lenore A., Kenneth A. One person shows, Village Art Center, N.Y.C., 1963, Sachs Gallery, N.Y.C., 1965, Gallery Lasson Modern Art, London, 1970, Open Studio Gallery, Rhinebeck, N.Y., 1978, Vasar Coll., Poughkeepsie, N.Y., 1979, Pastoral Gallery Art, Easthampton, N.Y., 1983; exhibited in group shows, Mus. Modern Art, N.Y.C., 1961, 64, Pa. Acad. Fine Arts, 1964, 67, 68, David Stuart Galleries, Los Angeles, 1969, Va. Mus. Fine Arts, Richmond, 1970, Orpheus Ascending, Stockbridge, Mass., 1971, New Sch. Art Centre, N.Y.C., 1973, Albin Ziegler Gallery, N.Y.C., Grad. Center CUNY, 1978; represented in permanent collection, Pa. Acad. Fine Arts, Phila., Finch Coll. Mus., N.Y.C., MacDowell Colony, Pan Am. Bldg., N.Y.C., Univ. Art Mus., U. Calif., Berkeley, Bklyn. Mus. MacDowell Colony resident, 1969, 70. Mem. N.Y. Artists Equity Assn. Home: 285 Central Park West New York NY 10024

JAFFE, PAUL LAWRENCE, lawyer; b. Phila., June 24, 1928; s. Albert L. and Elsie (Pelser) J.; m. Joan Helene Feldgoise, Mar. 13, 1955; children: Marc David, Richard Alan, Peter Edward. B.A., Dickinson Coll., 1947; J.D., U. Pa., 1950. Bar: Pa. Practice law, Phila.; sr. partner firm Mesirov, Gelman, Jaffe, Cramer and Jamieson (and predecessors), 1959—; Dir. Eanco, Inc. Trustee Fedn. Jewish Agencies Phila.; trustee Moss Rehab. Hosp., pres., 1977-80, chmn. bd., 1980—; trustee, mem. exec. com. Union Am. Hebrew Congregations. Mem. Am., Pa., Phila. bar assns. Jewish (pres. congregation 1974-77). Clubs: Locust, Racquet, Lawyers (Phila.); Loveladies Tennis. Home: 2301 Cherry St Philadelphia PA 19103 Office: 123 S Broad St Philadelphia PA 19109

JAFFE, ROBERT BENTON, obstetrician-gynecologist, reproductive endocrinologist; b. Detroit, Feb. 18, 1933; s. Jacob and Shirley (Robins) J.; m. Evelyn Grossman, Aug. 29, 1954; children: Glenn, Terri. M.S., U. Colo., 1966; M.D., U. Mich., 1957. Intern U. Colo. Med. Center, Denver, 1957-58, resident, 1959-63; asst. prof. Ob-Gyn. U. Mich. Med. Center, 1964-68, asso. prof., 1968-72, prof., 1972-74, dir. steroid research unit, 1964-74; prof. U. Calif., San Francisco, 1974—, also chmn. dept. Ob-Gyn and reproductive scis., dir., 1974—; mem. nat. adv. council, mem. human embryology and devel. study sect. Nat. Inst. Child Health and Human Devel.; bd. dirs. Population Resource Center. Author: Reproductive Endocrinology: Physiology, Pathophysiology and Clinical Management, 1978; contbr. numerous articles to profl. jours.; editorial bd.: Jour. Clin. Endocrinology and Metabolism, 1971—, Fertility and Sterility, 1972—, Obstetric and Gynecologic Survey, 1979—. Josiah Macy Found. faculty fellow, 1967-70, 81; USPHS postdoctoral fellow, 1958-59, 63-64; Rockefeller Found. grantee, 1974—; Andrew Mellon Found. grantee, 1978-81. Mem. Endocrine Soc., Soc. Gynecologic Investigation (pres. 1975-76), Perinatal Research Soc. (pres. 1973-74), Am. Coll. Obstetricians and Gynecologists (awards), Internat. Soc. Neuroendocrinology. Democrat. Jewish. Home: 90 Mount Tiburon Rd Tiburon CA 94920 Office: U Calif San Francisco 3d and Parnassus St M1490 San Francisco CA 94143

JAFFE, RONA, author; b. N.Y.C., June 12, 1932; d. Samuel and Diana (Ginsberg) J. B.A., Radcliffe Coll., 1951. Sec., N.Y.C., 1952; assoc. editor Fawcett Publs., N.Y.C., 1952-56. Author: The Best of Everything, 1958, Away From Home, 1960, The Last of the Wizards, 1961, Mr. Right is Dead, 1965, The Cherry in the Martini, 1966, The Fame Game, 1969, The Other Woman, 1972, Family Secrets, 1974, The Last Chance, 1976, Class Reunion, 1979, Mazes and Monsters, 1981. Office: care Ephraim London London Buttenwieser 875 3d Ave New York NY 10022

JAFFE, SHELDON MAYER, lawyer; b. Hartford, Conn., Nov. 21, 1934; s. Louis and Rose Carol (Cohen) J.; m. Nancy Linda Cornet, Sept. 4, 1974; children: Seth Lawrence, Jeremy Robert, Rebecca Jane. A.B., Yale U., 1956; LL.B., Harvard U., 1962. Bar: Calif. 1965, Conn. 1965, Mass. 1965. Mem. staff SEC, Los Angeles, 1962-63, Calif. Dept. Corps., 1964-65; practiced law, Los Angeles, 1966—; partner firm Jaffe and Orliss, Los Angeles, 1970-75, Williams, Jaffe & Stewart, Santa Monica, Calif., 1981-82; practicioner in securities field, 1975—. Author: Broker-Dealers and Securities Markets, 1977; also articles. Served with AUS, 1957-58. Mem. Los Angeles County, Century City, Am. bar assns., Assn. Bus. Trial Lawyers. Home: 1001 Wellesley Ave Los Angeles CA 90049 Office: 1888 Century Park E Los Angeles CA 90067

JAFFE, SIGMUND, educator, chemist; b. New Haven, Mar. 1, 1921; s. Morris and Rose (Blosveren) J.; m. Elaine Leventhal, Aug. 25, 1946; children—Matthew Lee, Paul Jonathan. A.B. with high distinction in Chemistry, Wesleyan U., Middletown, Conn., 1949; Ph.D., Iowa State U., 1953. Research in rare earths Ames (Iowa) Lab., 1949-53; research in carbides, metal and high temperature inorganic reactions, research labs. Air Reduction Corp., 1953-58; prof. chemistry Calif. State U. at Los Angeles, 1958—, chmn. dept., 1958-64; vis. prof. Queen Mary Coll., U. London, 1978-79; Research solid propellant fuel systems, 1958-60; photochemistry and gas phase kinetics Jet Propulsion Lab., Calif. Inst. Tech., Pasadena, Calif., 1960-64; NIH fellow Wiezmann Inst. Sci., Israel, 1964-65, vis. prof., 1971-72. Contbr. articles to profl. jours. Served with USNR, 1942-46. Named Outstanding prof. Calif. State U. at Los Angeles, 1973-74. Mem. Am. Chem. Soc., Sigma Xi, Phi Beta Kappa, Phi Lambda Upsilon, Phi Kappa Phi. Home: 420 S Madison Ave Pasadena CA 91101 Office: Dept Chemistry Calif State U Los Angeles CA 90032

JAFFE, STANLEY RICHARD, film producer; b. N.Y.C., July 31, 1940; s. Leo and Dora (Bressler) J.; children—Bobby, Betsy. B.S. in

Econs, Wharton Sch., U. Pa., 1962. With Seven Arts Asso. Corp., 1962-67, exec. asst. to pres., 1964; dir. E. Coast programming Seven Arts TV, 1963-64, dir. programming, 1965-67; exec. v.p., chief corp. officer Paramount Pictures Corp., 1969-70; pres. corp., also pres. Paramount TV, 1970-71; pres. Jaffilms, Inc., 1971; exec. v.p. worldwide prodn. Columbia Pictures Corp., 1975-76. Creator, writer, asso. producer: The Professionals, 1963; exec. producer series for syndication, 1965-67; cartoon series for syndication Johnny Cypher, 1965-67; producer: films Goodbye, Columbus, 1968, Bad Company, 1971, Bad News Bears, 1974, Kramer vs. Kramer, 1978 (Oscar award best picture Acad. Motion Picture Ars and Scis., Di Donatello award 1979), Taps, 1981; exec. producer: film Man on a Swing, 1973. Mem. Acad. Motion Picture Arts and Scis. Club: Variety (N.Y.C.)

JAFFEE, DWIGHT M., economist; b. Chgo., Feb. 7, 1943; s. Woodrow W. and Gertrude B. J.; m. Annette Williams, Aug. 16, 1964; children: Jonathan, Elizabeth. Student, Oberlin Coll., 1960; B.A., Northwestern U., 1964; Ph.D., M.I.T., 1968. Mem. faculty dept. econs. Princeton U., 1968—, prof., 1975—; cons. U.S. Treas., Fed. Res. System, Fed. Home Loan Bank Bd. Author: Credit Rationing and the Commercial Loan Market, 1971, Electronic Monetary Transfer Systems, 1976; Assoc. editor: Jour. Am. Fin. Assn, 1975—; assoc. editor: Housing Fin. Rev., 1982, Jour. Banking and Fin., 1982. Woodrow Wilson fellow, 1964; NSF grantee. Mem. Am. Econs. Assn., Am. Fin. Assn., Phi Beta Kappa. Office: Dept Econs Princeton U Princeton NJ 08540

JAFFEE, MICHAEL, musician; b. Bklyn., Apr. 21, 1938; s. Leo and Eva (Tzizes) J.; m. Kay Frances Cross, July 24, 1961. B.A., NYU, 1959, M.A., 1963. Musical dir., 1965—; faculty Henry St. Settlement Sch., Third St. Music Sch., 1962-64; instr. NYU, 1975-78, Dartmouth Coll., 1976; vis. judge Internat. Erwin Bodky Competition, Cambridge (Mass.) Soc. for Early Music, 1977, 79. Founder: early music ensemble Waverly Consort, N.Y.C., 1965—; guitarist lutenist orchs. and chamber ensembles including, N.Y.C. Opera Orch., Clarion Concert Soc., Bach Aria Group, Fine Arts String Quartet; rec. artist, Vanguard Rec. Soc., Columbia Records; arranger, conductor: mus. score ballet The Consort, Eliot Feld Co., 1974. Recipient Art Critics Circle award, Chile, 1978; award Stereo Rev., 1973, Record World, 1977. Mem. Am. Musicol. Soc., Chamber Mus. Am. (founding dir., 1st pres.), NYU Grad. Sch. Alumni Assn. (dir. 1980—). Office: 305 Riverside Dr New York NY 10025

JAFFEE, ROBERT ISAAC, research metallurgist; b. Chgo., July 11, 1917; s. Louis Robert and Sadie (Braidman) J.; m. Edna Elspeth Winram, June 2, 1945; children: William Louis, Michael David. B.S., Ill. Inst. Tech., 1939; S.M., Harvard U., 1940; Ph.D., U. Md., 1943. Lectr. U. Md., 1942; metallurgist Leeds & Northrup, Phila., 1943, U. Calif., 1944; with Battelle Meml. Inst., Columbus, Ohio, 1944-75, asso. mgr., 1960-64, sr. fellow, 1964-73, chief materials scientist, 1973-75; sr. tech. advisor Electric Power Research Inst., Palo Alto, Calif., 1975—; cons. prof. Stanford, 1975—; Mem. Nat. Material Adv. Bd., 1970-74; mem. Acta Metall. Bd. Govs., 1969-74, chmn., 1974—; cons. PSAC, 1966; chmn. NASA Adv. Com. Materials, 1966-71; mem. NATO-AGARD Structure and Materials Panel, 1961-63, 69—; Gillett lectr. ASTM, 1976. Author: The Science, Technology and Application of Titanium, 1970, Refractory Metals and Alloys III, Applied Aspects, 1966, Refractory Metals and Alloys IV, Research and Development, 1967, Phase Stability in Metals and Alloys, 1967, Dislocation Dynamics, 1968, Inelastic Behavior of Solids, 1969, Molecular Processes on Solid Surfaces, 1970, Critical Phenomena in Alloys, Magnets and Superconductors, 1971, Interatomic Potentials and Simulation of Lattice Defects, 1972, Defects and Transport in Oxides, 1973, Titanium Science and Technology, 1973, Physical Basis of Heterogeneous Catalysis, 1974, Fundamental Aspects of Structural Alloy Design, 1975, also articles. Fellow Inst. Metallurgists (London), Metall. Soc., Am. Inst. Metall. Engrs. (hon. mem.; pres. 1978), Am. Soc. Metals (Campbell lectr. 1977, James Douglas gold medal 1983); mem. Nat. Acad. Engring., Am. Phys. Soc., AAAS, Harvard Soc. Sci. and Engring., Sigma Xi, Tau Beta Pi, Phi Lambda Upsilon. Club: Stanford Golf. Research non-ferrous phys. metallurgy, particularly titanium and refractory metals. Patentee in field. Home: 3851 May Ct Palo Alto CA 94303 Office: 3412 Hillview Ave Palo Alto CA 94304

JAFFIN, CHARLES LEONARD, lawyer; b. N.Y.C., Feb. 27, 1928; s. Joseph M. and Rhoda (Abeloff) J.; m. Rosanna G. Webster, June 12, 1952; children: David W., Jonathan H., Rhoda E., Lora W., Katherine G. A.B., Princeton U., 1948; J.D., Columbia U., 1951. Bar: N.Y. 1951. Since practiced in, N.Y.C.; ptnr. Battle, Fowler, Jaffin & Kheel, 1960—; dir. Sterling Extruder Corp., Pamarco, Inc., Kepner-Tregoe, Inc., Ga. Synthetics, Inc. Bd. dirs. Found. for Research into Origin Man. Home: 522 Rosedale Rd Princeton NJ 08540 Office: 280 Park Ave New York NY 10017

JAFREE, SYED MOHAMMED JAWAID IQBAL *See* **GEOFFREY, IQBAL**

JAGEL, ROBERT CONDIT, chemical company executive; b. Syracuse, N.Y., Jan. 2, 1930; s. Robert Edward Condit and Margaret Enid (Doolittle) J.; m. Nancy Juergens, June 6, 1952; children: Karin, Mark Condit, Erik Abbott, Peter Hugh, Christopher Doolittle, Robin. A.B., Columbia Coll., 1951; B.S. in Chem. Engring., Columbia U., 1952. Vice pres. mfg. A.G. Internat. Chem. Co., Toyko, 1968-71; mgr. mfg. Amoco Chem. Corp., 1971-76; v.p. planning and adminstrn. Amoco Chem Corp, Chgo., 1981-82; v.p. mfg. and engring. Amoco Chem Corp., Chgo., 1982—; pres. China Am. Petro Chem. Co., Taipei, Taiwan, 1976-80; mng. dir. Amoco Chem. Belgium, Geel, 1980-81. Mem. Belgian-Am. Assn., Antwerp, Belguim, 1981-82; mem,. planning com. United Way Chgo., 1983. Served to lt. (j.g.) USN, 1952-55. Mem. Am. Chem. Soc., Am. Inst. Chem. Engrs., Soc. Chems. Industry, Am. C. of C. in Japan, Am. C. of C. in Republic of China, Am. C. of C. in Belgium (bd. dirs.), U.S Power Squardon. Republican. Christian Scientist. Club: Mid-Am. (Chgo.). Home: 429 N Garfield St Hinsdale IL 60521 Office: Amoco Chem Corp 200 E Randolph St Chicago IL 60601

JAGENDORF, ANDRE TRIDON, plant physiologist; b. N.Y.C., Oct. 21, 1926; s. Moritz Adolph and Sophie Sheba (Sokolsky) J.; m. Jean Elizabeth Whitenack, June 12, 1952; children—Suzanne E., Judith C., Daniel Z.S. B.A., Cornell U., 1948; Ph.D., Yale U., 1951. Merck postdoctoral fellow UCLA, 1951-53; from asst. prof. to prof. Johns Hopkins U., 1953-66; prof. plant physiology Cornell U., 1966—, Liberty H. Bailey prof. plant physiology, 1981—. Author papers, revs. in field. Recipient Outstanding Young Scientist award Md. Acad. Sci., 1961, Kettering Research award, 1963; Weizmann fellow, 1962. Fellow Am. Acad. Arts and Scis., AAAS; mem. Nat. Acad. Sci., Am. Soc. Plant Physiologists (pres. 1967, C.F. Kettering award in photosynthesis 1978), Am. Soc. Biol. Chemists, Am. Soc. Photobiology (councilor 1980), Soc. Gen. Physiologists, Am. Soc. Cell Biology, Japanese Soc. Plant Physiologists. Jewish. Office: Plant Biology Sect Plant Sci Bldg Cornell Univ Ithaca NY 14853

JAGGER, MICK (MICHAEL PHILIP JAGGER), rock performer; b. Dartford, Kent, Eng., July 26, 1943; s. Joe and Eva J.; m. Bianca Perez Morena de Macias, May 12, 1971 (div. Nov. 1979); 1 dau., Jade. Student, London Sch. Econs., 1962-64. Mem., lead singer, Rolling Stones, 1962—, tour of, Europe, 1970, 73, 76, U.S., 1969, 72, 75, 78, 81, Australia, 1973; Film appearances include Performance, 1969, Ned Kelly, 1970, Gimme Shelter, 1970, Sympathy for the Devil, 1970, Ladies and Gentlemen, The Rolling Stones, 1974, Let's Spend the Night Together, 1983; Composer: (with K. Richard) She's So Cold, Satisfaction, Brown Sugar, Honky Tonk Woman, Jumpin' Jack Flash, Sympathy for the Devil, Get Off My Cloud; albums include: December's Children, 1965, Aftermath, 1966, Between the Buttons, 1967, Flowers, 1967, Beggars Banquet, 1968, Let it Bleed, 1969, Through the Past Darkly, 1969, Sticky Fingers, 1971, Hot Rocks, 1972, It's Only Rock and Roll, 1974, Metamorphosis, 1975, Black and Blue, 1976, Love You Live, 1977, Some Girls, 1978, Emotional Rescue, 1980, Tatoo You, 1981, Still Life, 1982, Under Cover, 1983. Address: care Atlantic Records 75 Rockefeller Plaza New York NY 10019

JAGO, MARY, ballet dancer; b. Henfield, Eng., 1946. Grad., Royal Ballet Sch., Eng. Mem., Covent Garden Opera Ballet, 1965; mem., Nat. Ballet of Can., Toronto, Ont., 1966-84; soloist, 1968-70; prin. dancer, 1970-84; maj. roles include; Finger Fairy and Princess Aurora in: The Sleeping Beauty; The Sugar Plum Fairy in: The Nutcracker; Swanilda in: Coppelia; The Queen of the Wilis in: Giselle; Desdemona in: The Moor's Pavane; Swan Quen Odette und Odile: Swan Lake; the Lady in White in: Don Juan; Juliet in: Romeo and Juliet; Lise in: La Fille Mal Gardee. Office: care Nat Ballet of Can 157 King St E Tornoto ON M5C 1G9 Canada *

JAGODA, BARRY LIONEL, media adviser, communications consultant; b. Youngstown, Ohio, Feb. 5, 1944; s. Saul S. and Anne (Fradin) J. B.A., U. Tex., 1966; M.S., Columbia U., 1967. Writer, editor NBC News, Washington, N.Y.C., 1967-69; producer CBS News, N.Y.C., 1969-75; partner Houston, Ritz, Cohen, Jagoda, N.Y.C., 1975; TV advisor Jimmy Carter presdl. campaign, 1976; spl. asst. to the Pres., Washington, 1977-79, cons., 1979—; pres. Am. Info. Exchange, 1979—. (Recipient Emmy award as producer CBS news special, Watergate 1974) Ford Found. fellow, 1967. Mem. Sigma Delta Chi. Home: 1650 29th St NW Washington DC 20007 Office: 2130 H St NW Washington DC 20052

JAGOW, ELMER, coll. pres.; b. West Bend, Wis., Apr. 25, 1922; s. Bernard and Florence (Kurth) J.; m. Ellen Knief, Oct. 7, 1944; children—Kathryn (Mrs. William Mohrman), Allyson (Mrs. William Weir). B.S. in Edn, Concordia Tchrs. Coll., 1944; M.B.A., Northwestern U., 1955; L.H.D. (hon.), Christian Theol. Sem., 1968, LL.D., Ohio U., 1973. Asst. bus. mgr. Concordia Tchrs. Coll., River Forest, Ill., 1944-46, bus. mgr., 1946-56; mem. adminstrn. Knox Coll., Galesburg, Ill., 1956-66, treas., bus. mgr., 1961-64, v.p. finance, treas., 1964-66; pres. Hiram (Ohio) Coll., 1966—; dir. Acceleration Corp., Columbus, Huntington Nat. Bank, Kent, Ohio. Trustee Ohio Found. Ind. Colls., Robinson Meml. Hosp., Common Fund, N.Y.C. Mem. Assn. Ind. Colls. and Univs. Ohio, Am. Council Edn., N. Central Assn. Colls. (cons. examiner), Assn. Am. Colls., Ohio Coll. Assn., Garfield Soc. Clubs: Union (Cleve.); Pepper Pike (Ohio) Country; Univ. (N.Y.C.). Home: 11861 Garfield St Hiram OH 44234

JAHN, HELMUT, architect; b. Nuremberg, Germany, Jan. 1, 1940; came to U.S., 1966; s. Wilhelm Anton and Karolina (Wirth) J.; m. Deborah Ann Lampe, Dec. 31, 1970. Dipl. Ing.-Architect, Technische Hochschule, Munich, Germany, 1965; postgrad., Ill. Inst. Tech., 1966-67; D.F.A. (hon.), St. Mary's Coll., Notre Dame, Ind., 1979. With P.C. von Seidlein, Munich, 1965-66; with C.F. Murphy Assos., Chgo., 1967-81, exec. v.p., dir. planning and design, 1973-81; prin. Murphy/Jahn, 1981—. Prin. works include Kemper Arena, Kansas City, Mo., 1974, Auraria Learning Resources Center, Denver, 1975, Richmond (Va.) Courts Bldg, 1976, Kansas City (Mo.) Conv. Center, 1976, Maywood (Ill.) Courts Bldg, 1976, Michigan City (Ind.) Library, 1977, St. Mary's Coll. Athletic Facility, South Bend, Ind., 1977, Rust-Oleum Hdqrs, 1978, Xerox Centre, 1980, De La Garza Career Center, East Chicago, Ill., 1981, Area 2 Police Hdqrs, Chgo., 1981, First Bank Center, South Bend, Ind., 1981, Argonne (Ill.) Support Facility, 1981. Winner nat. competition for Minn. Capitol Expansion, 1977. Mem. AIA (Nat. Honor award for Kemper Arena 1975, St. Mary's Athletic Facility 1978, progressive architecture citation 1976-78, Chgo. chpt. award 1975-78). Roman Catholic. Clubs: Arts, Chgo. Athletic. Home: 2400 Lakeview Chicago IL 60614 Office: 224 S Michigan Ave Chicago IL 60604

JAHN, LAURENCE ROY, biologist, institute executive; b. Jefferson, Wis., June 24, 1926; s. Roy Johaan and Mabel Marie (Kothlow) J.; m. Helen Florence Faville, Sept. 5, 1947; children: Katharine Marie (Mrs. Ronald J. Cook), Richard Alan. B.S., U. Wis., 1949, M.S., 1958, Ph.D., 1965. Aquatic biologist Wis. Dept. Natural Resources, 1949-59; with Wildlife Mgmt. Inst., Washington, 1959—, v.p., 1971—; mem. waterfowl adv. com. U.S. Fish and Wildlife Service, 1968-76; mem. spl. adv. panel on water resources research Dept. Interior, 1971-73, chmn., 1973, mem. adv. com. on fish, wildlife and parks, 1975-77, mem. adv. com. on outer continental shelf environ. studies, 1975-77; mem. adv. com. on water data for public use and working group on river quality assessment U.S. Geol. Survey, 1972—; mem. wildlife adv. com. Dept. State, 1972-76; mem. adv. com. on natural resources conservation award Sec. Def., 1973, 76, 80; mem. adv. panel on tuna-porpoise Nat. Marine Fisheries Service, 1974; mem. environ. adv. bd. U.S. Army C.E., 1979—, chmn., 1983—; mem. marine fisheries adv. com. NOAA, 1982—; mem. bd. agr. and renewable resources Nat. Acad. Scis., 1980-83, mem. exec. bd., 1981-83. Author numerous articles in field.; Editor symposia procs. and books. Pres. Horicon (Wis.) Bd. Edn., 1965-67; bd. dirs. Citizens Com. on Natural Resources, 1970-78; mem. steering com. Nat. Watershed Congress, 1971—, chmn., 1977—; trustee N.Am. Wildlife Found., 1972—, sec.-treas., 1974—; chmn. program com. N.Am. Wildlife and Natural Resources Conf., 1972—; bd. dirs. Urban Wildlife Research Center, 1972-76. Served with USNR, 1944-46. Recipient certificate merit Nash Conservation Awards Program, 1953; resolution appreciation Miss. Flyway Council, 1970. Fellow AAAS; mem. Wildlife Soc. (pres. 1979, Trypensee-McPherson award 1984), Soil Conservation Soc. (commendation 1969), Am. Water Resources Assn. (interim dir. S. Atlantic dist. 1975), Natural Resources Council Am. (exec. com. 1976—, sec. 1978-81, vice chmn. 1981-83, chmn. 1983—), Nat. Audubon Soc., Wilderness Soc., Internat. Assn. Fish and Wildlife Agencies, Am. Forestry Assn., Nat. Wildlife Fedn., Wis. Acad. Scis., Arts and Letters, Am. Fisheries Soc., Washington Biologists' Field Club. Presbyn. Home: 2435 Riviera Dr Vienna VA 22180 Office: 1101 14th St NW Washington DC 20005

JAHN, ROBERT GEORGE, educator; b. Kearny, N.J., Apr. 1, 1930; s. George E. and Minnie (Holroyd) J.; m. Catherine Seibert, June 20, 1953; children—Eric George, Jill Ellen, Nina Marie, Dawn Anne. B.Sc. in Mech. Engring. with highest honors, Princeton U., 1951, M.A. in Physics, 1953, Ph.D., 1955. Teaching asst. Princeton U., 1953-55; instr. Lehigh U., Bethlehem, Pa., 1955-56, asst. prof., 1956-58; asst. prof. jet propulsion Calif. Inst. Tech., Pasadena, 1958-62; asst. prof. aero. engring. Princeton U., 1962-64, asso. prof., 1964-67, prof. aerospace scis., 1967—, dir. grad. studies aerospace and mech. scis. dept., 1968-71, dean. sch. engring. and applied sci., 1971—, exec. com. council univ. community, 1969-71, research bd., 1971—; Cons. editor Am. Scientist, 1966-70; mem. research adv. com. on fluid mechs. NASA, 1965-68, mem. research and tech. adv. subcom. on electrophysics, 1968-71, mem. research and tech. adv. com. on space propulsion and power, 1971-72; mem. com. on space propulsion and power NASA Research and Tech. Adv. Council, 1976-77, mem. space systems and tech. adv. com. nat. adv. council, 1978—; mem. ad hoc adv. com. minority engring. edn. Alfred P. Sloan Found., 1974-79; mem. com. edn. and employment women in sci. and engring. of commn. on human resources NRC, 1975-79. Author: Physics of Electric Propulsion, 1968; also contbr. articles in field. Trustee Asso. Univs., Inc., 1971—, chmn. bd., 1977-79; chmn. council on energy and environ. studies Princeton U., 1973—. Recipient Shuichi Kusaka Meml. prize in physics, 1951, Curtis W. McGraw Research award Am. Soc. for Engring. Edn., 1969. Fellow Am. Phys. Soc., Am. Inst. Aeros. and Astronautics (lectr. electric propulsion ednl. programs 1971—, electric propulsion tech. com. 1963-67, 71-74); mem. AAUP (asso.), Am. Soc. Engring. Edn., Phi Beta Kappa, Sigma Xi. Home: 60 Monroe Ln Princeton NJ 08540

JAHODA, FRITZ, musician; b. Vienna, Austria, May 23, 1909; came to U.S., 1939, naturalized, 1945; s. Karl and Betty (Probst) J.; m. Hedwig Kramer, Oct. 26, 1935 (dec. 1961); 1 dau., Eleanor (Mrs. Paul Horwitz). Student, U. Vienna, 1928-30. Free-lance pianist and chamber music player, 1928—, opera condr., Dusseldorf, Germany, 1930-33, Graz, Austria, 1934-38; faculty Converse (S.C.) Coll., 1939-40, Sarah Lawrence Coll., 1940-46; prof. City Coll., City U. N.Y., 1946-74, emeritus, 1974—, chmn. music dept., 1964-70. Mem.: N.Y. Trio, 1951-61; guest condr., State Opera Vienna, 1947, Radio Orch. Vienna, 1958. Home: 3530 Henry Hudson Pkwy New York City NY 10463 also Brooksville ME 04617

JAHSMAN, WILLIAM EDWARD, mechanical engineer; b. Detroit, May 13, 1926; s. William Edward and Eleanor Isabel (Blanchard) J.; m. Nona Marie Simi, June 20, 1949; children—William Edward, III, Hendrick Edwin, Amy Luise. B.Engring. Physics, Cornell U., 1951; M.S. in Engring. Mechanics, Stanford U., 1953, Ph.D., 1954. Research asso. Oak Ridge Nat. Lab., summer, 1950; engr. Boeing Airplane Co., Seattle, summer 1951, Gen. Electric Co. Knolls Atomic Power Lab., Schenectady, 1954-55, supr., 1955, mech. specialist, 1955-56; research scientist Lockheed Palo Alto Research Lab., Calif., 1956-61, staff scientist, 1961-64, mgr., 1964-65, cons. scientist, 1965-67; prof. mech. engring. U. Colo., Boulder, 1967—, chmn. dept. mech. engring., 1974-80; mgr. assembly quality assurance Intel Corp., Santa Clara, Calif., 1980—; lectr. dept. aeros. and astronautics Stanford U., 1961-67; liaison scientist Office Naval Research, London br., 1969-70; vis. prof. Oxford (Eng.) U., 1979. Contbr. numerous articles on solid and fluid mechanics to profl. jours. Served with USN, 1944-46. U. Colo. at Boulder Council on Research and Creative Work faculty fellow, 1979; NSF grantee, 1970-73, 73-76. Mem. ASME, Am. Soc. Engring. Edn., Am. Acad. Mechanics (charter), Assn. Chairmen Depts. Mechanics, U.S. Nat. Metric Assn. Home: 650 Georgia Ave Palo Alto CA 94306 Office: Dept C-256 Intel Corp 3065 Bowers Ave Santa Clara CA 95051

JAIN, PIYARE LAL, educator; b. Punjab, India, Dec. 11, 1921; came to U.S., 1950, naturalized, 1961; s. Labh Ch and Maya (Devi) J.; m. Sulakshana Dhawan, Feb. 15, 1966. B.A., Punjab U., 1944, M.A., 1948; Ph.D., Mich. State U., 1954. Research asso. chemistry dept. U. Minn., 1953-54; instr. physics dept. State U. N.Y., Buffalo, 1954-59, asst. prof., 1959-61, assoc. prof., 1961-67, prof., 1967—; research asso. U. Chgo., 1959-60, Lawrence Radiation Lab., Berkeley, Calif.; vis. prof., Bristol, Eng., 1961-62, U. Wash., Seattle, summer 1960; Fulbright vis. prof. Rajasthan U., India, 1965-66; Sci. adviser Am. embassy AID, New Delhi, India, summer 1966. Fellow Am. Phys. Soc. Research in solid state physics, electron and nuclear magnetic resonance, cosmic radiation and high energy physics, heavy ions physics. Home: 223 Surrey Run Williamsville NY 14221 Office: State U NY at Buffalo Buffalo NY 14260

JAIN, SAGAR CHAND, educator; b. India, May 13, 1930; s. Bihari Lal and Pisto (Devi) J.; m. Sushila Khare, Jan. 23, 1959; children—Dinesh, Monic. Ph.D., Cornell U., 1964. Asso. dir. Xavier Labor Relations Inst., Jamshedpur, India, 1952-53; head grad. program labor welfare Delhi U., 1954-64; asso. prof. Sch. Bus. Adminstrn., E. Tenn. State U., Johnson City, 1964-65; asst. prof. to asso. prof. U. N.C., Chapel Hill, 1965-71, prof. health adminstrn., chmn. dept., 1971—, Kenan prof., 1974-75; cons. World Bank, UNFPA, Ford Found., several fgn. govts. and univs. Author books, monographs, articles in field. Fellow Royal Soc. Health; mem. Am. Public Health Assn. (gov. 1977-79), Assn. Dirs. of Programs Health Adminstrn. in Schs. of Public Health (pres. 1971-74), Am. Mgmt. Assn., Am. Soc. Public Adminstrn., Am. Sociol. Assn., Population Assn. Am. Address: Dept Health Policy and Adminstrn Sch Public Health Univ NC 201-H Chapel Hill NC 27514

JAKAB, IRENE, physician; b. Oradea, Rumania; came to U.S., 1961, naturalized, 1966; d. Odon and Rosa A. (Riedl) J. M.D., Ferencz József U., Kolozsvar, Hungary, 1944; license in psychology, pedagogy, philosophy cum laude, Hungarian U., Cluj, Rumania, 1947; Ph.D. summa cum laude, Pazmany Peter U., Budapest, 1948; Dr.h.c., U. Besançon (France), 1982. Diplomate: Am. Bd. Psychiatry. Rotating intern in neurology and psychiatry Ferencz József U., 1943-44; resident in psychiatry Univ. Hosp., Kolozsvar, 1944-47, resident in neurology, 1947-50; resident internal medicine Univ. Hosp. for Internal Medicine, Pecs, Hungary, 1950-51; chief physician Univ. Hosp. for Neurology and Psychiatry, Pécs, 1951-59; staff neuropathol. research lab. Neurol. Univ. Clinic, Zurich, 1959-61; sect. chief Kans. Neurol. Inst., Topeka, 1961-63; dir. research and edn., 1966; resident psychiatry Topeka State Hosp., 1963-66; asst. psychiatrist McLean Hosp., Belmont, Mass., 1966-67, assoc. psychiatrist, 1967-74; prof. psychiatry U. Pitts. Med. Sch., 1974—, co-dir. med. student edn. in psychiatry, 1981—; dir. John Merck Program, 1974-81; mem. faculty dept. psychiatry Med. Sch., Pecs, 1951-59; asst. Univ. Hosp. Neurology, Zurich, 1959-61; asso. psychiatry Harvard U., Boston, 1966-69, asst. prof. psychiatry, 1969-74, lectr. psychiatry, 1974—; dir. planning John Fund Children's Treatment and Ednl. Center, 1970-81, program dir. grad course mental retardation, 1970-81, program dir. postgrad. course in mental retardation. Author: Dessins et Peintures des Aliénés, 1956, Zeichnungen und Gemälde der Geisteskranken, 1956; editor: Psychiatry and Art, Proc. 4th Internat. Colloquium of Psychopathology of Expression, 1968, Art Interpretation and Art Therapy, 1969, Conscious and Unconscious Expressive Art, 1971, Transcultural Aspects of Psychiatric Art, 1975; co-editor: Dynamische Psychiatrie, 1974; editorial bd.: Confinia Psychiatrica, 1975-81; editor-in-chief: Annales Medico-Psychologiques, 1959; reviewer: Acta Paedopsychiatrica, 1959; contbr. articles to profl. jours. Prinzhorn prize, 1967; Recipient 1st prize Gold award for sci. exhibit, 1980; Bronze Chris plaque Columbus Film Festival, 1980; Leadership award Am. Assn. on Mental Deficiency, 1980; Ernst Kris Silver award, 1981; Fellow Menninger Sch. Psychiatry, Topeka, 1963-66. Mem. AMA, Am. Psychol. Assn., Am. Psychiat. Assn., Société Medico Psychologique de Paris, Internat. Rorschach Soc., N.Y. Acad. Scis., Internat. Soc. Psychopathology of Expression (v.p. 1959—), Am. Soc. Psychopathology of Expression (chmn. 1965—), Internat. Soc. Child Psychiatry and Allied Professions, Deutschsprachige Gesellschaft für Psychopathologie des Ausdruckes (hon.), Deutschsprachige Gesellschaft fur Psychopathologie des Ausdrucks (Prinzhorn prize 1967). Home: 228 Parkman Ave Pittsburgh PA 15213 Office: 3811 O'Hara St Pittsburgh PA 15213

JAKES, JOHN WILLIAM, author; b. Chgo., Mar. 31, 1932; s. John Adrian and Bertha (Retz) J.; m. Rachel Ann Payne, June 15, 1951; children—Andrea, Ellen, John Michael, Victoria. A.B., DePauw U.,

1953, Litt.D. (hon.), 1977; M.A., Ohio State U., 1954; LL.D. (hon.), Wright State U., 1976. With advt. dept. Abbott Labs., 1954-60; with creative dept. various advt. agencies, 1960-69; creative dir. Dancer Fitzgerald Sample Co., Dayton, Ohio, 1969-70. Author: Am. Bicentennial Series: The Bastard, 1974, The Rebels, 1975, The Seekers, 1975, The Furies, 1976, The Titans, 1976, The Warriors, 1977, The Lawless, 1978, The Americans, 1980, North and South, 1982. Trustee DePauw U. Recipient Ohio Gov.'s award, 1977, ann. lit. award Friends of Rochester Pub. Library, 1983. Mem. Sci. Fiction Writers Am., Dramatists Guild, Authors Guild., PEN. Office: care Harcourt Brace Jovanovich Inc 757 3d Ave New York NY 10017

JAKES, WILLIAM CHESTER, JR., electrical engineer; b. Milw., May 15, 1922; s. William Chester and Eleanor (Knight) J.; m. Mary Elizabeth Bristle, Sept. 3, 1948; children: Robert, Elizabeth. B.S. in Elec. Engring, Northwestern U., 1944, M.S., 1947, Ph.D., 1949. With Bell Tel. Labs., Inc. (various locations), 1949—, head radio treansmission research dept., Holmdel, N.J., 1963-71; dir. Radio Transmission Lab., North Andover, Mass., 1971—; Mem. sci. adv. bd. Voice of Am., 1957-58. Contbr. articles to profl. jours. Served with USN, 1944-46. Ph.D. (hon.) Iowa Wesleyan U., 1961; recipient Alumni Merit award Northwestern U., 1962. Fellow IEEE (Paper award 1971); mem. Eta Kappa Nu, Pi Mu Epsilon. Patentee antennas and communications systems. Home: 58 Wild Rose Dr Andover MA 01810 Office: 1600 Osgood St North Andover MA 01845 *Intense dedication to physics and engineering with constant desire for understanding and intellectual honesty, plus the enjoyment of working with others, have been my guiding principles.*

JAKOBSEN, JAKOB KNUDSEN, mech. engr.; b. Bording Sogn, Denmark, Aug. 7, 1912; came to U.S., 1952, naturalized, 1958; s. Laust Peder and Inger Marie (Kristensen) J.; m. Eva Koch, Nov. 19, 1941; children—Marianne Gyrithe (Mrs. Earl C. Green), Peter Laust (dec. 1969), Claus Michael, Suzanne Elizabeth, Niels-Olaf Sejten, Lars Jakob. M.S. in Mech. Engring, Royal Tech. U. Denmark, 1941. Registered profl. engr., Mich., Calif. Mech. engr. Brown Boveri et Cie, Switzerland, 1941-43; project engr. Pub. Power Utilities of Copenhagen, Denmark, 1943-45; mech. engr. Burmeister & Wain, Copenhagen, 1945-52; gas turbine engr. Clark Bros. Co., Olean, N.Y., 1952-55; staff engr. automotive research Chrysler Corp., Detroit, 1955-60; sr. tech. specialist for research Rocketdyne, Canoga Park, Calif., 1960—; asst. prof. machine design Royal Tech. U. Denmark, 1941. Author: NASA monograph Rocket Engine Turbopump Inducers, 1971; Contbr. articles profl. jours. Mem. ASTM (com. for erosion by cavitation and impingement 1964—), ASME (chmn. steering com. San Fernardo Valley sect., recipient Melville Gold medal 1964), Soc. Automotive Engrs. (chmn. power plant activities), Am. Inst. Aeros. and Astronautics, Nat. Soc. Profl. Engrs., Danish Inst. Civil Engrs. Republican. Lutheran. Patentee compressor design, diesel engine turbosupercharger, pump diffusor. Home: 10531 Etiwanda Ave Northridge CA 91326 Office: Rocketdyne 6633 Canoga Ave Canoga Park CA 91304

JAKOBSON, MARK JOHN, educator; b. Carlyle, Mont., May 4, 1923; s. Hans M. and Bessie Mae (Fessenden) J.; m. Marguerite Elizabeth Thomsen, Aug. 17, 1945; children—Kristin Marie, Sandra Lynne. B.A., U. Mont., 1944, M.A., 1947; Ph.D. (Whiting fellow), U. Calif. at Berkeley, 1951. Physicist Lawrence Radiation Lab., 1951-52; instr. U. Wash., 1952-53; prof. U. Mont., Missoula, 1953—, chmn. physics and astronomy dept., 1969-73; mem. vis. staff Los Alamos Sci. Lab., 1963—. Bd. dirs. Luth. Found. Mont. Served to lt. (j.g.) USNR, 1944-46. Fellow Am. Phys. Soc.; mem. Sigma Xi, Phi Beta Kappa, Pi Mu Epsilon. Democrat. Lutheran. Home: 3000 Queen St Missoula MT 59801 *A dominant force in my life has been a commitment to the work ethic, a commitment that was nurtured by the Depression. As part of that work ethic I have tried to focus my entire being at any given time on a particular problem. I believe that characteristic, when present in a delineated effort, is what identifies the true professional.*

JAKOWATZ, CHARLES V., engineering educator; b. Kansas City, Kans., Feb. 6, 1920; s. Louis and Pauline (Steinmetz) J.; m. Robert Townley, June 27, 1947; children: Judy, Charles V. B.S. in Elec. Engring., Kans. State Coll., 1944, M.S., 1947; Ph.D., U. Ill., 1953. Registered profl. engr., Kans.; lic. amateur radio operator. Asst. prof. elec. engring. U. Ill., 1948-53; communications engr. research lab. Gen. Electric Co., 1953-63, liaison scientist, 1963-65; dean and prof. Coll. Engring., Wichita State U., 1965-79, prof. elec. engring., 1980—; adj. prof. Rensselaer Poly. Inst., 1956-65. Contbr. articles to profl. jours. Bd. dirs. Midwest Med. Research Inst. Served to lt. (j.g.) USNR, 1944-45. Recipient Disting. Elec. Engring. Alumnus award U. Ill., 1972; Disting. Service award Wichita State U., 1978, Coll. Engring., Kans. State U., 1982. Mem. IEEE, Math. Assn. Am., Am. Soc. Engring. Edn., Nat. Soc. Profl. Engrs., Kans. Engring. Soc., Sigma Xi, Tau Beta Pi, Phi Kappa Phi, Eta Kappa Nu, Phi Mu Epsilon, Sigma Tau. Patentee in field. Home: 533 N Broadmoor Ave Wichita KS 67206

JAKSTAS, ALFRED JOHN, museum conservator, consultant; b. Boston, Oct. 30, 1916; s. Walter John and Julia (Barkevich) J.; m. Valerie Jevaraus, Oct. 11, 1942; children: Janet, Julianne. A.B., Harvard U., 1938. Teaching fellow Harvard U., 1943-44; conservator Isabella Stewart Gardner Mus., 1943-61; conservator paintings Art Inst. Chgo., 1961-81; lectr., cons., 1981—; Cons. conservation Currier Gallery Art, Mus. Art, R.I. Sch. Design, Wadsworth Atheneum, Springfield Mus. Fine Arts, Notre Dame Gallery, various colls. Fellow Internat. Inst. Conservation Mus. Objects. Home: 10737 Welk Dr Sun City AZ 85373 Office: Art Inst Chgo Chicago IL 60603 *The spirit of man must be preserved, as individual bodies pass away.*

JAKUBAUSKAS, EDWARD BENEDICT, coll. pres.; b. Waterbury, Conn., Apr. 14, 1930; s. Constantine and Barbara (Narstis) J.; m. Ruth Friz, Aug. 29, 1959; children—Carol, Marilyn, Mark, Eric. B.A., U. Conn., 1952, M.A., 1954; Ph.D., U. Wis., 1961. Economist FPC, 1956, Dept. Labor, 1956-58; instr. U. Wis., 1961-62, asst. prof. econs., 1962-63, Iowa State U., 1963-65, asso. prof., 1965-66, prof., 1966-71; dean U. Wyo., 1971-76, prof. econs., 1971-79, v.p. acad. affairs, 1976-79; pres. SUNY, Geneseo, 1979—. Author: Manpower Economics, 1971. Served with U.S. Army, 1954-56. Mem. Am. Econ. Assn., Am. Assn. State Univs. and Colls. Democrat. Mem. United Chs. of Christ. Club: Rotary. Office: Erwin Adminstrn Bldg SUNY Geneseo NY 14454

JALLOW, RAYMOND, economist; b. Baghdad, Iraq, Oct. 10, 1930; came to U.S., 1953; s. Jawad M. and Naima (Hussain) J. B.A., U. Baghdad, 1951; M.A., U. So. Calif., 1956; Ph.D., UCLA, 1966. Supr. revenue dept. Iraqi Rys., Baghdad, 1947-52; auditor Robert Young, C.P.A., Pasadena, Calif., 1956-57; economist mgr. econ. research and planning dept. First Interstate Bank, Los Angeles, 1959-66, v.p., chief economist, 1966-70, sr. v.p., chief economist, dir. research and planning div., 1970-81; chief economist First Interstate Bancorp.; pres. Jallow Internat. Ltd., Los Angeles, 1981—; faculty mem. U. Calif. Extension, 1962-68; lectr. in U.S. and fgn. countries econs. and monetary fields; adv. to govts. and corps., Europe, Middle East, Far East; dir. Barrick Investment Ltd., Triad Am. Corp., ATV Systems, Inc., Midwestern Cos., Inc.; appears on major radio and TV networks including ABC, CBS, NBC, on econ. and fin. subjects. Contbr. over 100 articles to profl. jours., including ann. econ. forecast. Chmn. bd. U.S. OMEN, 1972; mem. new dimensions com. Calif. Lutheran Coll., bd. regents; mem. adv. bd. Calif. Poly. State U.; mem. 2200 plus 20 future research council U. So. Calif. Recipient merit awards from 25 bus. and philanthropic orgns. Mem. Am. Bankers Assn. (econ. adv. com.), Nat. Assn. Bus. Economists (founder, pres. So. Calif. chpt. 1968-69), Am. Statis. Assn., Am. Mgmt. Assn., Internat. C. of C. (monetary affairs com. U.S. council), U.S. Arab C. of C. (bd. dirs.), Seaver's Inst. (fin. com.), Blue Key, Beta Gamma Sigma. Subject documentary film developed by USIA as one of 5 most successful Arab-Ams. Home: 2530 Park Oak Ct Los Angeles CA 90068

JAMAIL, JOSEPH DAHR, JR., lawyer; b. Houston, Oct. 19, 1925; s. Joseph Dahr and Marie (Anton) J.; m. Lillie Mae Hage, Aug. 28, 1949; children: Joseph Dahr III, Randall Hage, Robert Lee. B.A., U. Tex., 1950, J.D., 1953. Bar: Tex. 1952. Since practiced in, Houston, asst. dist. atty., Harris County, Tex., 1954-55; prof. tort law U. Tex., 1981. Contbr. articles to profl. jours. Served to sgt. USMCR, 1943-46. Fellow Internat. Acad. Law and Sci., Internat. Soc. Barristers, Internat. Acad. Trial Lawyers, Am. Coll. Trial Lawyers, Inner Circle of Advocates; mem. Am., Houston bar assns., Houston Jr. Bar (dir. 1954-55, treas. 1955-56, v.p. 1956-57, pres. 1957-58), State Bar Tex. (chmn. grievance com. 1963, chmn. town hall task force 1973-74), Tex. Assn. Plaintiff Attys. (dir. 1961-63), Tex. Trial Lawyers Assn., Assn. Trial Lawyers Am., Am. Judicature Soc., Am. Bd. Trial Advocates, Lawyer-Pilot Bar Assn., Delta Theta Phi. Home: 5750 Indian Circle Houston TX 77057 Office: 3300 One Allen Center Houston TX 77002

JAMBOR, ROBERT VERNON, lawyer; b. Chgo., Aug. 29, 1936; s. Vernon C. and Anne M. (Kohout) J.; m. Arlene M. Gale, Nov. 9, 1957; children—Robyn, Cheryl, Steven. B.M.E., Gen. Motors Inst., Flint, Mich., 1958; J.D., John Marshall Law Sch., Chgo., 1963. Bar: Ill. bar 1963. Product engr. product devel. Electro-Motive div. Gen. Motors Corp., La Grange, Ill., 1958-63; asso. firm Marks & Clerk, Chgo., 1961-63; patent atty. Borg-Warner Corp., Chgo., 1964-69; partner firm Haight, Hofeldt, Davis & Jambor, Chgo., 1970—; instr. John Marshall Law Sch., 1963-73; arbitrator Am. Arbitration Assn., 1965. Mem. Am., Ill., 7th Circuit bar assns., Am. Patent Law Assn., Patent Law Assn. Chgo., Bohemian Lawyers Assn. Chgo. Club: Chgo. Athletic. Home: 6S622 Meadowbrook Ct Naperville IL 60540 Office: 55 E Monroe St Suite 3614 Chicago IL 60603

JAMES, ALBERT J., consumer goods company executive; b. Somers Point, N.J., Oct. 28, 1936; s. Leonard Robert and Helen (Ingersoll) J.; m. Louise A. Winkler-Prinz, Aug. 21, 1958; children: Elizabeth L., Catherine A. B.S. in Chem. Engring., U. Rochester, 1958. Vice pres Luck's Inc., Seagrove, N.C., 1968-75; dir. RJR Foods, Inc., Winston-Salem, 1975-78, sr. dir., 1978-80; v.p. PF&B Group, Del Monte, San Francisco, 1980-81; pres. Canadian Canners Ltd., Hamilton, On., 1981—; dir. Canadian Canners Ltd., 1981—, Aylmer Foods Warehousing, 1982—, St. Williams Preservers, 1982—. Mem. steering com. Nutrition Found. of Can., Toronto, Ont., 1982—; adv. council McMaster U., 1983—. Served to lt. USN, 1958-61. Mem. Can. Food Processors Assn. (dir. 1983—). Republican. Club: Hamilton, Burlington Golf and Country. Office: 44 Hughson St S Hamilton ON Canada L8N 3K6

JAMES, ALLIX BLEDSOE, emeritus university president; b. Marshall, Tex., Dec. 17, 1922; s. Samuel Horace and Tannie Etta (Judkins) J.; m. Sue Nickens, Feb. 14, 1945; children: Alvan Bosworth, Portia Veann. A.B., Va. Union U., 1944, M.Div., 1946; Th.M., Union Theol. Sem. Va., 1949, Th.D., 1957; postgrad., Boston U., summer 1951, Pa. State U., summer 1957; LL.D., U. Richmond, 1970; D.D., St. Paul's Coll., 1980. Ordained to ministry Bapt. Ch., 1942; moderator No. Neck Bapt. Assn., 1950-52; minister Union Zion Bapt. Ch., Gloucester, Va., 1944-53, Mt. Zion Bapt. Ch., Downings, Va., 1945-57, 3d Union Bapt. Ch., King William, Va., 1953-70; dean students Va. Union U., Richmond, 1950-57, dean, 1957-70, Henderson-Griffith prof. pastoral theology, v.p., 1960-70, pres., 1970-79, pres. emeritus, 1979—. Author: Calling a Pastor in a Baptist Church; Contbg. editor: The Continuing Quest, 1970. Pres. Va. Bd. Edn., 1980-82; Chmn. Richmond City Planning Commn., 1969-75; dir. Va. Electric and Power Co., Consol. Bank and Trust Co.; Mem. Commn. on Ch. Family Fin. Planning; mem. scholarship selection com. Philip Morris, Inc.; mem. Mayor's Commn. on Human Relations, 1963-65; pres. Norrell Sch. PTA, 1963-65; mem. exec. com. Central Va. Ednl. TV; mem. Richmond Independence Bicentennial Commn., Richmond Downtown Econ. and Devel. Commn.; co-chmn. Northside Community Assn., 1964-68; chmn. Univ. Center in Va.; mem. State Bd. Edn. Va., 1975—; Bd. dirs. Va. Inst. Pastoral Care, Task Force for Renewal Urban Strategy and Tng., Richmond chpt. ARC, 1974-75, Better Richmond, Inc., Richmond Downtown Devel. Unltd., Am. Council on Edn., 1970-72, Fund for Theol. Edn., 1970-72, Richmond Renaissance, Inc., Richmond Leadership; mem. adv. bd. Inst. for Bus. and Community Devel., U. Richmond; bd. fellows Interpreters House, Lake Janaluska, N.C.; Trustee Richmond Meml. Hosp. Nat. Assn. for Equal Opportunity in Edn. (v.p.); pres. Richmond Gold Bowl Sponsors, Inc. Recipient Distinguished Service award Links, Inc., 1971; named Citizen of Year Astoria Beneficial Club, 1971, Omega Psi Phi, 1972, Richmond Urban League, 1974. Mem. Clergy Assn. Richmond Area (pres.), Am. Assn. Theol. Schs. (pres. 1970-72), Am. Bapt. Conv. (pres. council on theol. edn. 1969-72), Bapt. Gen. Conv. Va. (mem. exec. bd.), Soc. for Advancement Continuing Edn. for Ministers (mem. exec. bd.), Greater Richmond C. of C. (dir.), NCCJ (co-chmn. Va.), Alpha Kappa Mu, Alpha Phi Alpha (Edn. Achievement award 1981), Sigma Pi Phi. Club: Kiwanis. Office: 1500 N Lombardy St Richmond VA 23220

JAMES, BENJAMIN DAVID, college dean; b. Plymouth, Pa., Aug. 10, 1912; s. David John and Jeanette (King) J.; m. Grace Davis Picton, Jan. 12, 1937; children: Benjamin David, J. Wesley; m. Elizabeth Flower Donahue, Jan. 19, 1980. A.B., Dickinson Coll., 1934; M.A., Bucknell U., 1936; Ph.D., U. Pa., 1962; LL.D., Dickinson Sch. Law, 1976. Tchr., coach Plymouth (Pa.) High Sch., 1934-41; instr. edn. and psychology, head football and track coach Dickinson Coll., Carlisle, Pa., 1941-44, prof. edn., chmn. dept. edn. and psychology, dean admissions, 1944-63, R.V.C. Watkins prof. psychology, 1957-78, dir. summer session, dean students, 1963-68, prof. psychology and edn., dean tchr. edn., 1968-78, also prof. edn., personal rep. of pres., 1978—; cons. to industry; chmn.-convenor Joint Com. Pa. Labor and Industry. Author: Graduate Study in the Liberal Arts College, 1962. Chmn. classified sect. United Fund; chmn. Pa. Adv. Com. for Employment Security, 1968—; mem. adv. com. Harrisburg Community Coll.; past chmn. Cumberland County Child Welfare Adv. Com.; trustee Kiskiminetas Springs Prep. Sch., Meth. Home for Children. Served to lt. USNR, 1944-46. Named Man of Yr., Exchange Club, 1979; Town-Coll. award Carlisle, 1980. Mem. Pa. Admissions Assn. (v.p.), Nat. Assn. Coll. Admissions Counselors (Pa. officer), Kappa Phi Kappa, Omicron Delta Kappa, Phi Kappa Psi. Club: Rotary (past pres.). Home: 355 Graham St Carlisle PA 17013

JAMES, BRIAN ROBERT, chemistry educator; b. Birmingham, Eng., Apr. 21, 1936; emigrated to Can., 1964, naturalized, 1974; s. Herbert Arthur and Frances Vera (Stride) J.; m. Mary Jane Thompson, Oct. 6, 1962; children: Jennifer Ann, Peter Edward, Sarah Elizabeth, Andrew Francis. B.A., Oxford (Eng.) U., 1958, M.A., 1960, D.Phil., 1960. Research fellow U. B.C., Vancouver, 1960-62, mem. faculty, 1964—, prof. chemistry, 1974—; sr. sci. officer U.K. Atomic Energy Authority, Harwell, Eng., 1962-64; NATO Summer Sch. lectr., 1974; mem. catalysis study group NATO, 1972; mem. chemistry grants com. NRC Can., 1973-77; grad. research fellowships com. Internat. Nickel Co., 1974-77; cons. in field. Author: Homogeneous Hydrogenation, 1973; also numerous papers.; editor: Homogeneous Hydrogenation in Organic Chemistry, 1976, Biological Aspects of Inorganic Chemistry, 1977; mem. editorial bds. profl. jours.; editor: Can. Jour. Chemistry, 1978—. Bursarship, Royal Soc., London, 1970; research grantee NRC Can., 1964—, NATO, 1976-78; Guggenheim fellow, 1983. Fellow Chem. Soc. London, Royal Soc. Can., Chem. Inst. Can. (Noranda lectr. 1975); mem. Am. Chem. Soc., N.Y. Acad. Scis., Wadham Coll. Soc. Home: 4010 Blenheim St Vancouver BC V6L 2Y9 Canada Office: Chemistry Dept Univ BC Vancouver BC V6T 1Y6 Canada

JAMES, CAROLYNE FAYE, mezzo-soprano; b. Wheatland, Wyo., Apr. 27, 1945; d. Ralph Everett and Gladys Charlotte (Johnson) J. Mus.B., U. Wyo., 1964; Mus.M., Ind. U., 1967. Asst. prof. voice U. Iowa, Iowa City, 1968-72. Debut in opera as Madame Flora in: The Medium, St. Paul Opera, 1971; also sang role with, Houston Grand Opera, 1972, Opera Theatre St. Louis, 1976, Augusta (Ga.) Opera Co.; N.Y.C. Opera debut as Baroness in: The Young Lord, 1973; N.Y.C. Opera debut as Widow Begbick in: Mahogonny, Opera Co. of Boston, 1973; created role Mother Rainey in: The Sweet Bye and Bye, 1973; Mrs. G. in: Captain Jinks, 1976; Mrs. Cratchit in: A Christmas Carol (Musgrave), 1979; created Mrs. Doc in world premiere of: A Quiet Place (Leonard Bernstein), Houston, 1983; debut, Chgo. Lyric Opera, 1983; numerous appearances with opera cos. throughout U.S. and fgn. countries including, Dallas Civic Opera, Cin. Opera Co., Netherlands Opera, Amsterdam, Florentine Opera; Rec. artist. Martha Baird Rockefeller grantee; Met.; Opera Assn. grantee; recipient Lillian Garabedian award Santa Fe Opera, 1967; Corbett Found. grantee, 1968; named Young Artist Nat. Fedn. Music Clubs, 1972. Office: 165 W 57 St New York NY 10019

JAMES, CHARLES FRANKLIN, JR., engineering educator; b. Des Arc, Mo., July 16, 1931; s. Charles Franklin and Beulah Frances (Kyte) J.; m. Mollie Keeler, May 18, 1974; children: Thomas Elisha, Matthew Jeremiah. B.S., Purdue U., 1958, M.S., 1960, Ph.D., 1963. Sr. indsl. engr. McDonnel Aircraft Co., 1963; asst. prof. U. R.I., 1963-66, prof., chmn. dept. indsl. engring., 1967-82, mem. Robotics Research Ctr., 1980-83; C. Paul Stocker prof. engring. Ohio U., Athens, 1982-83; dean Coll. Engring. and Applied Sci., U. Wis.-Milw., 1984—; assoc. prof. U. Mass.-Amherst, 1966-67; cons. Asian Productivity Orgn.; arbitrator Fed. Mediation and Conciliation Service, Am. Arbitration Assn. Contbr. articles to profl. jours. Served with USAF, 1951-55. Mem. Am. Statist. Assn., Am. Inst. Indsl. Engrs., Am. Soc. Engring. Edn., ASME, Soc. Mfg. Engrs., Am. Foundrymen's Soc. Office: Coll Engring Univ Wis PO Box 784 Milwaukee WI 53201

JAMES, DANIEL J., management consultant; b. Nokomis, Ill., Mar. 21, 1920; s. Daniel and Katie (Lauer) J.; m. Ann Wilder, June 12, 1954; children—Karen Ann, Debra Kay. B.E., Eastern Ill. State U., 1942; M.S., U. Ill., 1946, Ph.D., 1952; Dr. Pedagogy (hon.), Eastern Ill. U., 1958. Chief prodn. scheduling Taylor Instrument Co., Rochester, N.Y., 1946-47; instr. Flint (Mich.) Jr. Coll., 1947-48; asst. prof. Central Mich. Coll., Mt. Pleasant, 1948-50; asst. prof. Atlanta div. U. Ga., 1952-54; prof. marketing U. Ark., Fayetteville, 1954-57; adviser to Govt. of Chile, FAO, UN, 1957-58; program officer AID (formerly ICA), Seoul, Korea, 1959-62; internat. economist Bur. Econ. Affairs, State Dept., 1963; officer in charge politico-econ. affairs Office Near East-South Asian Affairs, 1963-64; econ.-sci. officer Am. embassy, Taipei, Tawian, 1964-69, polit.-econ., econ.-comml. officer Am. embassy, New Delhi, India, 1969-72; dep. dir., spl. projects officer Office of Security Assistance and Sales, Bur. Politico-Mil. Affairs, Dept. of State, 1972-78; polit. adviser hdqrs. U.S. Army Europe and 7th Army, Heidelberg, Germany, 1978-79, Office Internat. Security Ops., Bur. Politico-Mil. Affairs, Dept. State, Washington, 1979-80; v.p. Mgmt. Logistics Internat., Ltd., Arlington, Va., 1980—. Served to 1st lt. AUS, 1942-45. Home: 723 Lawton St McLean VA 22101 Office: 1401 Wilson Blvd Arlington VA 22209

JAMES, DAVID LEE, lawyer, service company executive; b. Chgo., Aug. 23, 1933; s. Roy L. and Ethel (Wells) J.; m. Sheila Feagley, May 26, 1962; children: Pamela, James, Winifred, Paul, Brian, Adam. A.B., Harvard U., 1955; J.D., U. Chgo., 1960; grad. exec. program, Stanford U., 1979. Bar: N.Y. 1961, N.J. 1968, Hawaii 1976. With law firms in, N.Y.C., 1960-67; asst. gen. counsel, asst. sec. Texasgulf Inc., N.Y.C., 1967-75; gen. counsel, sec. Dillingham Corp., San Francisco, 1975-77, v.p., gen. counsel, sec., 1977-84, v.p. legal affairs, sec., 1984—; hon. consul of Malaysia, hon. consul of Hawaii, 1977-84; adv. bd. Internat. and Comparative Law Center, Southwestern Legal Found., Dallas, 1976—; adv. com. Law of Sea Inst., Honolulu, 1977-84. Bd. dirs. Jr. Achievement Hawaii, 1976-84, Hawaii Opera Theatre, 1981-84, Friends of East-West Ctr., 1982-84, Library Assocs. U. Hawaii, 1983-84; mem. Morristown (N.J.) Bd. Edn., 1967-68. Served to lt. (j.g.) USNR, 1955-57. Mem. Am. Bar Assn., World Assn. Lawyers, Southwestern Legal Found. Clubs: Pacific (Honolulu); Stock Exchange (San Francisco). Office: Dillingham Corp Two Embarcadero Center San Francisco CA 94111

JAMES, DON, university football coach; m. Carol Hoobler; children: Jeff, Jill, Jeni. M.Ed., U. Kans., 1957. Grad. asst. U. Kans., 1956-57; tchr., coach Southwest Miami (Fla.) High Sch., 1957-59; asst. coach Fla. State U., 1959-66, U. Mich., 1966-68, U. Colo., 1968-70; head football coach Kent State U., 1971-74, U. Wash., Seattle, 1974—; coach North-South Shrine Game, Miami, 1973, Ohio Shrine Game, 1973, 74, Am. Bowl, 1976, East-West Shrine Game, San Francisco, 1979, Japan Bowl, 1979. Served with Transp. Corps U.S. Army; 1954-56. Named Coach of Yr. Mid Am. Conf., 1972, Ohio Coach of Yr. Coll. Football Coaches Assn., 1972, Coach of Week UPI, 1977, Nat. Coach of Yr. Am. Football Coaches Assn., 1978, Athlon Publs., 1981, Pre-Season Coach of Yr. Playboy Mag., 1982; U. Wash. Rose Bowl Champions, 1978, 82; U. Wash. Sun Bowl Champions, 1979; Pac-10 Champions, 1980, 81; Aloha Bowl Champions, 1982. Mem. Omega Delta Kappa. Lodge: Rotary. Office: U Wash 224 Graves Bldg Seattle WA 98105

JAMES, DOROTHY BUCKTON, political science educator; b. N.Y.C.; d. LaVerne and Eva Christian (Saunders) Buckton; m. Judson Lehman James, June 11, 1965; 1 dau., Christina Elise. B.A., Barnard Coll., 1959; M.A., Columbia U., 1961, Ph.D., 1966. Asst. prof. Hunter Coll., CUNY, 1962-68; asso. prof. Herbert Lehman Coll., CUNY, 1968-74; prof. polit. sci., head dept. Va. Poly. Inst. and State U., Blacksburg, 1974-80; dean Sch. Govt. and Public Adminstrn., Am. U., Washington, also prof. polit. sci., 1980—. Author: The Contemporary Presidency, 1974, Poverty, Politics and Change, 1972, Outside, Looking In, 1972, Analyzing Poverty Policy, 1975; editor several jours.; contbr. articles to profl. jours. Mem. Am. Polit. Sci. Assn. (exec. com.), Am. Soc. Public Adminstrn., Nat. Assn. Schs. Public Affairs and Adminstrn., Policy Studies Orgn. (pres.), So. Polit. Sci. Assn., Pi Sigma Alpha. Office: American U Sch Govt and Pub Adminstrn Washington DC 20016

JAMES, D(ORRIS) CLAYTON, educator; b. Winchester, Ky., Feb. 13, 1931; s. Dorris Clayton and Opal (Shetter) J.; m. Erlene Downs, June 2, 1953; children: Dorris Sherrod James Worley, Newell Edmund, Judith Erlene, Allie Brady. B.A. with honors, Southwestern at Memphis, 1953; B.D., Louisville Presbyn. Theol. Sem., 1956; postgrad., U. Cin., 1956-57; M.A., U. Tex. at Austin, 1959, Ph.D.,

1964. Ordained to ministry Presbyterian Ch. U.S., 1956; minister Union (Ky.) Presbyn. Ch., 1954-57, First Presbyn. Ch., Cameron, Tex., 1958-60; teaching asst. U. Tex., 1960-61; instr. history La. State U., Alexandria, 1961-64; asst. prof. Mankato (Minn.) State Coll., 1964-65; prof. Miss. State U., Mississippi State, 1965-77, Disting. prof. history, 1978—; mem. grad. council, 1972-75; Harold K. Johnson chair mil. history U.S. Army Mil. History Inst. and Army War Coll., 1979-80; John F. Morrison chair mil. history U.S. Army Command and Gen. Staff Coll., 1980-81; vis. prof. Miss. Valley State U., 1967-68, Smithsonian Inst., 1979; Harmon Meml. lectr. U.S. Air Force Acad., 1981; cons. BBC, Univ. Press Miss., Presidio Press, U. Pa. Press, Ind. U. Press, U.S. State Dept., Dept. Army. Head tech. adviser motion picture: Mac Arthur, Universal City Studios, 1976; Author: Antebellum Natchez, 1968, The Years of MacArthur, 1880-1941, vol. 1, 1970, 1941-45, vol. 2, 1975, South to Bataan, North to Mukden, 1971; contbg. author: Ency. Brit, 1974, Ency. Am. Biography, 1974, World Book Ency, 1981; Contbr. articles to profl. jours. Served to lt., S.G. USNR, 1956-62. Recipient Outstanding Teaching-Research award Miss. State U., 1972; Parshad fellow, 1949-53; Nat. Endowment for Humanities grantee, 1968; Miss. State U. Research grantee, 1968-79. Mem. Miss. State U. Soc. Disting. Profs. (chmn. 1974-75), Am., So. hist. assns., Orgn. Am. Historians, Am. Mil. Inst. (trustee), Soc. Historians Am. Fgn. Relations, Am. Com. on History of Second World War, Alpha Tau Omega, Phi Alpha Theta, Omicron Delta Kappa., Phi Kappa Phi. Home: 1702 Linden Circle Starkville MS 39759 Office: History Dept Miss State U Mississippi State MS 39762

JAMES, E. PENDLETON, govt. ofcl.; b. Washington, Ill., Oct. 23, 1929. B.A., U. Pacific, 1954. Personnel mgr. Aerojet-Gen. Corp., Sacramento, 1956-66; mem. staff Heidrick & Struggles, Los Angeles, 1966-71; dep. spl. asst. to Pres. Richard Nixon, Washington, 1971-73; pres. western ops. Russell Reynolds Assos., Los Angeles, 1974-77; pres., owner Pen James & Assos., Inc., Los Angeles, 1978-81; asst. to Pres. Reagan, Washington, 1981—.

JAMES, EDWIN CLARK, thoracic surgeon; b. Lordsburg, N.Mex., Sept. 8, 1932; s. Louis Reginald and Rose Etta (Brandt) J.; m. Carol Elizabeth Weech, Dec. 27, 1958; children—Edwin H., Jeffrey A., Gary M., Karla J., Sara L., Laura S. B.A., U. Oreg., 1958, M.D., 1962. Diplomate: Am. Bd. Surgery, Am. Bd. Thoracic Surgery. Served as enlisted man U.S. Army, 1949-55, commd., served as officer to, 1975; resident in gen. surgery, thoracic and cardiovascular surgery, 1965-71; chief of surgery, cons. Surgeon Eighth Army, U.S. Army Hosp., Seoul, Korea, 1971-72; chief of surgery, asst. chief thoracic surgery Valley Forge (Pa.) Army Hosp., 1972-73; chief thoracic surgery Madigan Army Med. Center, 1973-75; ret., 1975; asso. prof. surgery, chief vascular surgery W.Va. U. Med. Center, 1975-77; prof. surgery, chief thoracic surgery U. N.D. Sch. Medicine, Grand Forks, 1977—, prof., chmn. dept. surgery, 1980—; cons. VA hosps., Clarksburg, W.Va., 1975-77, Fargo, 1977—; active surg. staff United Hosp., Med. Center Rhab. Hosp.,, 1977—; active participant N.D. Outreach Med. Program, 1977—. Lectr.; speaker; contbr. articles to profl. publs.; author books. Served with Armed Forces; Korea. Decorated Legion of Merit. Fellow A.C.S.; mem. AMA, Soc. Thoracic Surgeons, Southeastern Surg. Congress, Assn. Acad. Surgery, So. Thoracic Surg. Assn., Internat. Cardiovascular Soc., Soc. Surg. Chairmen, Central Surg. Assn., Am. Assn. Thoracic Surgery. Mormon. Office: 501 Columbia Rd Grand Forks ND 58201 *

JAMES, FLOYD BENJAMINE, constrn. co. exec.; b. Gibsland, La., Jan. 24, 1907; s. Thomas L. and Maggie (Hodges) J.; m. Kathryn Ayres, June 12, 1928; children—Renna (Mrs. L.O. Burkhalter), Floyd Benjamine, John, Tom. B.A., U. Tenn., 1927. Sec., treas. Ruston (La.) Drilling Co., 1927-33; sec.-treas. T.L. James & Co., Ruston, 1933-44, pres., 1944-68, chmn. bd., 1968—. Trustee La. Meth. Children's Home. Recipient Silver Beaver Boy Scouts Am., 1955, Silver Antelope, 1961. Mem. Phi Kappa Phi, Sigma Chi. Methodist. Club: Kiwanian. Home: 1500 N Trenton St Ruston LA 71270 Office: PO Box O Ruston LA 71270

JAMES, FORREST DONALD, university president; b. Oklahoma City, Sept. 14, 1927; s. Forrest and Dorothy (Donaldson) J.; m. Gerti Hauser, Dec. 28, 1974; children—Kevin, Kurt. A.B. magna cum laude, Oklahoma City U., 1951; S.T.B., Boston U., 1954, Ph.D. (Lucinda Bidwell Beebee fellow), 1959; postgrad. (Rotary Found. fellow), U. Zurich, Switzerland, 1956-57. From instr. to asso. prof. Miami U., Oxford, Ohio, 1958-65, asst. dean arts and scis., 1961-64, acting dean arts and scis., 1964-65; v.p. acad. affairs U. R.I., Kingston, 1965-67, acting pres., 1967-68; pres. Central Conn. State U., New Britain, 1968—; corporator Savs. Bank New Britain. Mem. New Eng. Bd. Higher Edn.; mem. Conn. Edn. Council.; bd. dirs. Klingberg Family Ctr., New Britain Gen. Hosp. Served with USNR, 1945-48. Mem. Internat. Assn. Univ. Pres.'s (chmn. N. Am. council), Am. Assn. State Colls. and Univs. (internat. studies com.), Phi Mu Alpha Sinfonia, Phi Delta Kappa. Home: 10 Highwood Circle Avon CT 06001 Office: 1615 Stanley St New Britain CT 06050

JAMES, FRANCIS EDWARD, JR., investment counselor; b. Woodville, Miss., Jan. 5, 1931; s. Francis Edwin and Ruth (Phillips) J.; m. Iris Senn, Nov. 3, 1952; children: Francis III, Barry, David. B.S., La. State U., 1951; M.S., Rensselaer Poly. Inst., 1966, Ph.D., 1967. Commd. 2d lt. USAF, 1950, advanced through grades to col., 1972; prof. mgmt. and statistics, chmn. dept quantitative studies Air Force Inst. Tech., Wright Patterson AFB, 1967-71, dir. grad. edn. div. mgmt. programs, 1972-74; pres. James Investment Research, Inc., Xenia, Ohio, 1974—; investment counsel to Miami Citizens Bank, Ohio., State Bank Ohio; cons. math. modeling. Author: A Matrix Solution for the General Linear Regression Model; contbr. articles to profl. jours. Decorated Legion of Merit, D.F.C., Air medal, Joint Services Commendation medal, Meritorious Service medal; recipient Outstanding Acad. Achievement award Rensselaer Poly. Inst., 1965. Mem. Am. Statis. Assn., Mil. Ops. Research Soc., Am. Finance Assn., Investment Counsel Assn. Am., Mktg. Technicians Assn., Soc. Logistics Engring. (Eckles award 1973, tech. chmn.), Sigma Iota Epsilon, Epsilon Delta Sigma. Lodges: Masons; Rotary. Home: 2604 Lantz Rd Xenia OH 45385 Office: James Investment Research Inc Box 8 Alpha OH 45301 *To come up with an outstanding idea is brilliance. To put that idea into action is real genius.*

JAMES, FRED CALHOUN, bishop; b. Prosperity, S.C., Apr. 7, 1922; s. Edward and Rosa Lee J.; m. Theressa Gregg, Dec. 39, 1944. A.B., Allen U., 1943; M.Div., Howard U., 1947. Ordained to ministry African Methodist Episcopal Ch.; pastor Friendship A.M.E. Ch., Irmo, S.C., 1945; Bishop Meml. A.M.E. Ch., Columbia, S.C., 1946, Wayman A.M.E. Ch., Winnsboro, S.C., 1947-50, Chappelle Meml. A.M.E. Ch., Columbia, S.C., 1950-53, Mount Pisgah A.M.E. Ch., Sumter, S.C., 1953-72; elected 93d bishop A.M.E. Ch., Dallas, 1972—; dean Dickerson Theol. Sem., 1949-53; bishop in, Botswana, Lesotho, Swaziland, Mozambique, South Africa, Namibia, 1972-76, presiding bishop in, Ark. and Okla., 1976—; chmn. Commn. on Missions, A.M.E. Ch., 1976—; mem. World Conf. Ch. and Soc., Geneva, 1966, Nat. Council Chs. Christ, U.S.A., 1979—; hon. consul-gen. representing Lesotho, in, Ark. and Okla., 1979—; del. World Meth. Council, Honolulu, 1981; sec. A.M.E. Council of Bishops, 1981. Author social action bill, A.M.E. Ch., 1960. Pres. Sumter br. NAACP, 1959-72; chmn. Wateree Community Actions Agy., 1969-72; bd. dirs. Greater Little Rock Urban League; chmn. bd. Shorter Coll.; founder Mt. Pisgah Apts., Sumter, James Centre, Maseru, Lesotho. Mem. Nat. Interfaith Com., Fund for Open Soc. Democrat. Clubs: Odd Fellows, Masons, Shriners. Home: 6514 Sherry Dr Little Rock AR 72204 Office: 604 Locust St North Little Rock AR 72114

JAMES, GEORGE BARKER, II, forest products industry executive; b. Haverhill, Mass., May 25, 1937; s. Paul Withington and Ruth (Burns) J.; m. Beverly A. Burch, Sept. 22, 1962; children: Alexander, Christopher, Geoffrey, Matthew. A.B., Harvard U., 1959; M.B.A., Stanford U., 1962. Fiscal dir. E.G. & G. Inc., Bedford, Mass., 1963-67; financial exec. Am. Brands Inc., N.Y.C., 1967-69; v.p. Pepsico, Inc., N.Y.C., 1969-72; sr. v.p., chief fin. officer Arcata Corp., Menlo Park, Calif., 1972-82; exec. v.p. Crown Zellerback Corp., San Francisco, 1982—; dir. Pacific States Industries, Inc. Author: Industrial Development in the Ohio Valley, 1962. Mem. Andover (Mass.) Town Com., 1965-67; chmn. bd. dirs. Towle Trust Fund; trustee Nat. Corp. Fund for the Dance, Cate Sch.; v.p., trustee San Francisco Ballet Assn. Served with AUS, 1960-61. Mem. Newcomen Soc. N.Am., Fin. Execs. Inst. Clubs: Stock Exchange, Commonwealth Calif. (San Francisco); Menlo Circus (Atherton, Calif.); Harvard (Boston and N.Y.C.); Harvard Varsity (Cambridge, Mass.). Home: 215 Coleridge Ave Palo Alto CA 94301 Office: One Bush St San Francisco CA 94104

JAMES, HAMILTON EVANS, investment banking firm executive; b. Wyandotte, Mich., Feb. 3, 1951; s. Hamilton Renson and Waleska Bacon (Evans) J.; m. Anabel George Boyce, Aug. 25, 1973; 1 dau., Meredith Evans. B.A., Harvard U., 1973, M.B.A., 1975. Registered rep. N.Y. stock exchange. Assoc. Donaldson, Lufkin & Jenrette, N.Y.C., 1975-77, v.p., 1977-80, sr. v.p., 1980-82, sr. v.p., prin., 1982—; dir. Musser-Fiss Inc., Denver, 1977-80. Vice pres. DLJ Found., N.Y.C., 1979-81, chmn. bd., N.Y.C., 1981-82. John Harvard scholar, 1973; Banker scholar, 1975. Republican. Episcopalian. Clubs: River (N.Y.C.); Tuxedo (Tuxedo Park, N.Y.); Ad (Cambridge, Nass.) (pres. 1972-73). Office: Donaldson Lufkin & Jenrette 140 Broadway New York NY 10005

JAMES, HAROLD ARTHUR, lawyer; b. Youngstown, O., Oct. 4, 1903; s. Arthur and Welcome Minnie (Williams) J.; m. Alice Beaver McCann, Nov. 7, 1929; children: Franklin D. (dec.), Arthur F., Douglas H. Ph.B., Denison U., 1926; J.D., Ohio State U., 1929. Bar: Ohio bar 1929. Since practiced in, Toledo; partner Doyle, Lewis & Warner, 1937—; Chmn. cts. com. Toledo Bar Assn.-Regn. Ct. Rules, 1952-53; sec. Jobst Inst., Inc. Commr. Nat. Commn. Community Health Services, 1963-67; Trustee, v.p. Toledo YMCA, 1950—, pres., 1965-69, life trustee, 1973—; mem. Nat. council YMCA, 1968—; bd. dirs. Greater Toledo Community Chest, 1954-62, Toledo Council Social Agys., 1952-62; pres. Toledo Council Social Agys., 1958-59; trustee Greater Toledo Area C. of C., 1959-60, Ohio Bapt. Conv. Endowment Fund, 1954—, Ohio Council Chs. Found., 1961-69; bd. dirs., treas. Hosp. Planning Assn. Toledo, 1960-68; bd. dirs. Ohio Citizens Council Health and Welfare, 1957—, pres., 1961-63, hon. life mem., 1973—; chmn. Community Planning Adv. Council, 1961-67; bd. dirs. United Community Funds and Councils Am., 1961-69, v.p., 1963-69. Recipient Distinguished Service award Toledo Council Social Agys., 1963; alumni citation Denison U., 1966; Alumni Citizenship award Ohio State U., 1980. Mem. Am., Ohio, Toledo bar assns., Kappa Sigma, Phi Delta Phi. Republican. Baptist. Club: Toledo. Home: 4922 Courville Rd Toledo OH 43623 Office: Nat Bank Bldg Toledo OH 43604

JAMES, HENRY THOMAS, foundation executive; b. Ferryville, Wis., May 19, 1915; s. Harry T. and Alice (Morgan) J.; m. Vienna Lewis, June 6, 1939; children: Angelyn Alice (Mrs. Richard J. Grillo), Henry Thomas, Jennifer Lewis (Mrs. Timothy J. Regan), Mary Ellen, Elizabeth Elinor (Mrs. M. Kieran Folliard), Arthur Earl. B.S., Wis. State U., 1938; Ph.M., U. Wis., 1939; Ph.D., U. Chgo., 1958. High sch. tchr., Barron, Wis., 1939-42, supervising prin., Woodville, Wis., 1942-43; counselor U. Wis., Madison, 1946; supt. schs., Augusta, Wis., 1946-49, Whitewater, Wis., 1949-50, asst. supt. pub. instrn., Wis., 1950-54; lectr. U. Mich., 1954; asso. dir. Midwest Adminstrn. Center, asst. prof., asso. prof., dir. field services U. Chgo. Sch. Edn., 1954-58; prof. Stanford Sch. Edn., 1958-70, dean, 1966-70; pres. Spencer Found., Chgo., 1970—; cons. in field, 1954—, dir. studies sch. bds. and state sch. finance systems, 1954—; mem. N.Y. Fleischmann Commn., 1969-72, Presdl. Task Force on Edn., 1968, 80; adviser subcom. efficiency and innovation in edn. Com. Econ. Devel.; series editor various pub. cos. Sr. author: School Revenue Systems in Five States, 1961, Wealth, Expenditures and Decision-Making for Education, 1963, Determinants of Educational Expenditures in Large Cities of the United States, 1966, The New Cult of Efficiency and Education, 1969; Editor: Boardmanship, 1961; Editorial adv. bd.: Edn. and Urban Society, 1968—, Contemporary Edn. Rev., 1982—; Contbr. articles to profl. jours. Served to lt. USNR, 1943-46. Recipient Distinguished Service award Nat. Assn. State Bds. Edn., 1973; Viterbo Coll. award for service to higher edn., 1975. Mem. Am. Ednl. Research Assn. (chmn. nominating com. 1964-65, cons. editor jour. 1964-70, program chmn. 1968), Am. Assn. Sch. Adminstrs., AAAS, Nat. Acad. Edn., Univ. Council Ednl. Adminstrn., Chgo. Com., Council on Fgn. Relations, Phi Delta Kappa (bd. editorial cons. 1984—). Presbyn. Club: Century Assn. (N.Y.C.). Home: 175 E Delaware Pl Chicago IL 60611 Office: The Spencer Found 875 N Michigan Ave Chicago IL 60611

JAMES, HERBERT ISIDOR, chemist; b. St. Thomas, V.I., Mar. 30, 1933; s. Henry O. and Frances (Smith) J.; m. Christine M. Stolz, Nov. 29, 1962; children: Herbert Isidor, Robyn. B.S., Hampton Inst., 1955; M.A., Clark U., 1958, Ph.D., 1965. Instr. math. and sci. Hampton Inst., 1958-61, Exptl. Coll. of V.I., 1960-61; instr. math. Charlotte Amalie (V.I.) High Sch., 1960-61; research scientist Electric Storage Battery, Inc., 1965-76; scientist Xerox Corp., Webster, N.Y., 1976—; stock broker, financial planner, life ins. broker. Contbr. articles to profl. jours. Numerous activities Episcopal Ch. including; commr. Episcopal Restitution Fund. Commn.; vestryman, lay reader, del. to Diocesan Conv.; bd. dirs. Freedom Valley council Girl Scouts Am.; mem. exec. com. Bucks County council Boy Scouts Am. Recipient VIPAC award, 1965. Mem. Am. Chem. Soc., Electrochem. Soc., AAAS, Instrument Soc. Am., Beta Kappa Chi, Alpha Kappa Mu. Patentee in field. Home: 107 Panorama Trail Rochester NY 14625 Office: Xerox Corp 800 Phillips Rd Webster NY 14580

JAMES, HOWARD ANTHONY, JR., journalist, author; b. Iowa City, May 28, 1935; s. Howard Anthony and Catherine (Richey) J.; m. Dorothy Spear Fontaine, Aug. 25, 1956 (div. Apr. 1971); children: Paul Cooper, Heidi Sue; m. Judith Ray Vogel Munro, Jan. 1, 1972; 1 son, Jonathan Howard Chafee; stepchildren: Mark, Eric, Katherine, Stevenson. B.A., Mich. State U., 1958, LL.D., 1971. Radio and TV news reporter, 1955-60, pub. weekly newspaper, Mich., 1959; reporter Chgo. Tribune, 1960-63; city-state editor Morning Democrat, Davenport, Iowa, 1963-64; pub. relations dir. Chgo. met. dist. Montgomery Ward & Co., 1964; with Christian Sci. Monitor, 1964-70, Midwestern news bur. chief, 1965-70; pres. Howard James Co., Inc., Norway, Maine; editor, pub. Berlin (N.H.) Reporter, Rumford (Maine) Falls Times, Norway (Maine) Advertiser-Democrat; pres. James Newspapers, Inc., Oxford Hills Pub. Co., Somerset Reporter Co., Skowhegan, Maine, The Group; pub. The Irregular, North Conway, N.H.; lectr., cons. Author: Crisis in the Courts (Pulitzer prize nat. reporting 1968), 1968 (Sidney Hillman Found. award 1968), Children In Trouble: A National Scandal, 1970, The Little Victims, 1975; also film. Chmn. Forum 23 White House Conf. Children, 1970. Recipient Silver Gavel awards Am. Bar Assn., 1968, 70, Pub. Service award Am. Trial Lawyers' Assn., 1968; named Mich. Mental Health Man of Year, 1970. Mem. Maine Press Assn. (pres. 1980-81). Address: Crockett Ridge Rd Norway ME 04268

JAMES, HOWARD P., hotel chain executive; b. Estes Park, Colo., July 9, 1923; s. Howard P. and Edna (Cobb) J.; m. Margaret Von Wyl, Sept. 12, 1948; children: Kathy, Paul, Steven, Nancy. Student, Cornell U., 1941, 46; B.S. in Hotel Mgmt, U. Denver, 1948. Food and beverage dir. Hilton Hotel Corp., 1958-60; exec. v.p. Del E. Webb Hotel Corp., 1960-65; pres. Sahara—Nev. Corp., 1965-70; chmn., pres., chief exec. officer Sheraton Corp., Boston, 1970-83, chmn., chief exec. officer, 1983—. Past pres. Boulder Dam (Colo.) council Boy Scouts Am., mem. exec. bd. Boston council, 1970-71, 74—, pres., 1971-72, chmn., 1972-73; treas. Scout Forward Fund, 1973-74. Served with Armed Forces, World War II. Decorated D.F.C., Air Medal with oak leaf cluster. Mem. Am. Hotel and Motel Assn. (dir., adv. council). Office: Sheraton Corp 60 State St Boston MA 02109 *

JAMES, IRVING ARTHUR, lawyer; b. N.Y.C., Feb. 20, 1922; s. Samuel and Lillian Pearl (Budner) J.; m. Helene (dec.); children: Michael, Jeffrey. B.S., Coll. City N.Y., 1941; J.D., N.Y. U., 1947. Bar: N.Y. 1948. Partner firm Sommerfield & James, N.Y.C., 1957—; dir. Pickwick Orgn., Inc., Transvac Electronics Internat., Ltd., Vynamics, Inc., Photronics Corp.; pres., dir. Oyster Bay Indsl. Devel. Corp., 1966-77; adj. lectr. polit. sci. C.W. Post Coll., L.I., N.Y., 1968. Contbr. articles to newspapers. Pres. Jericho Pub. Library, 1970, trustee, 1965-70; chmn. Jericho div. United Jewish Appeal, 1969; bd. dirs. Jacob H. Schiff Center, Bronx, 1949-54; Commr. commerce and industry, Oyster Bay, L.I., N.Y., 1966-77; vice-chmn. Nassau County Liberal party, 1967—, vice-chmn. state law com. party, 1970—. Served to 1st lt. USAF, 1942-46; CBI, ETO. Named Man of Year Nassau County Liberal Party, 1972. Mem. Nassau County Bar Assn., Jewish War Veterans (N.Y. state vice-comdr. 1953), Tau Delta Phi. Jewish. Lodge: Masons. Office: 366 N Broadway Jericho NY 11753

JAMES, JOHN V., corporate executive; b. Plains Township, Pa., July 24, 1918; s. Stanley S. and Catherine N. (Jones) J.; m. Helen L. Brislin, June 25, 1949; 1 dau., Barbara Ann. Certificate in mgmt., U. Pa., 1948, B.S. in Econs, 1941; D. Bus. Adminstrn. (hon.), Hillsdale Coll., 1976, D. Commercial Sci., St. Bonaventure U., 1976. Office mgr., controller Carr Consol. Biscuit Co., Wilkes Barre, Pa., 1941-42; div. controller Corning Glass Works, 1948-56, mgr. budgets and procedures, 1956-57; asst. controller Dresser Industries, Inc., Dallas, 1957-58; v.p. finance subsidiary Clark Bros. Co., Olean, N.Y., 1958-60, controller parent co., 1960-65, v.p., 1962-65, group v.p. machinery, 1965-68, exec. v.p., 1968-69, pres., chief exec. officer, 1970-81; chmn. bd. Dresser Industries, Inc., 1976-83, now dir., chmn. exec. com. Served to capt. AUS, 1942-46. Mem. Financial Execs. Inst., Nat. Assn. Accountants (dir. 1960-62), Beta Gamma Sigma. Congregationalist. Clubs: Mason, Rotarian (pres. Corning 1957). Home: 7222 Azalea Ln Dallas TX 75230 Office: 2340 LTV Tower Dallas TX 75201

JAMES, JOSEPH B., political science educator; b. Clearwater, Fla., July 17, 1912; s. L.P. and Ilah J. (Miles) J.; m. Jacquelyn McWhite, June 8, 1937; children: Glenn Joseph, William Bruce. B.A.E., U. Fla., 1934, M.A., 1935; Ph.D., U. Ill., 1939. Instr. gen. extension div. U. Fla., 1935-36; asst. and fellow U. Ill., 1936-39; head dept. history and polit. sci. Williamsport Dickinson Jr. Coll., 1939-40, Union Coll., Ky., 1940-43; dean of faculty William Woods Coll., 1943-45; head dept. social studies Miss. State Coll. for Women, 1945-58; dean of coll. Wesleyan Coll., Macon, Ga., 1958-71, Callaway prof. polit. sci., 1971-80, prof. emeritus, 1980—; vis. prof. summer sessions U. Fla., U. Miss., Florence (Ala.) State Tchrs. Coll., Middle Tenn. State Coll. Author: The Framing of the Fourteenth Amendment, 1956, rev. edit., 1965, Ratification of the Fourteenth Amendment, 1984; contbr. to scholarly jours. and reference publs. Mem. So. Polit. Sci. Assn., Ga. Polit. Sci. Assn. (exec. council), Am. Acad. Polit. Sci., So. Hist. Assn., Assn. Coll. Honor Socs. (council), Phi Beta Kappa (past pres. Middle Ga. Grad. Assn.), Phi Kappa Phi (past pres. Wesleyan chpt.), Kappa Delta Pi, Kappa Phi Kappa, Pi Gamma Mu (nat. pres. emeritus, trustee). Methodist (adminstrv. bd.). Club: Rotary. Home: 3450 Osborne Pl Macon GA 31204 *Problems have added interest to life, which has seemed good even in times of severe testing. People, not things, have always been especially important to me. The beauties of nature, especially the sea, have the power to enchant and inspire me. Ideals are important to me. I have sought to reach them by practical means.*

JAMES, PATRICIA ANN, philosophy educator; b. Newberry, Mich., Mar. 17, 1933; d. Albert Michael and Antonette (Sholar) J.; m. James William Dickoff, July 3, 1970; 1 dau., Sara Dorn-Havlik-Dickov. Student, Mich. Coll. Mining Tech., 1951-53; B.S., U. Detroit, 1955; M.A., Yale U., 1958, Ph.D., 1962. Research asst. in philosophy and law Yale U., 1959-62, lectr. in philosophy, 1962-64, instr., 1964-65, asst. prof. philosophy, 1965-70; asso. prof. Kent (Ohio) State U., 1970-73, prof., 1973—; vis. prof. Sch. Nursing, Oreg. Health Scis. U., 1982-83. Fulbright fellow, Belgium, 1955-56. Office: Kent State University Dept of Philosophy Kent OH 44240

JAMES, P.D. (PHYLLIS DOROTHY JAMES WHITE), author; b. Oxford, Eng., Aug. 3, 1920; d. Sidney Victor and Dorothy May Amelia (Hone) J.; m. Ernest Connor Bantry White, 1941; children: Clare Bantry, Jane Bantry. Student Brit. schs. Adminstr. Nat. Health Service, 1949-68; prin. police dept., also criminal policy dept. Home Office, 1968-79. Author: Cover Her Face, 1962, A Mind to Murder, 1963, Unnatural Causes, 1967, Shroud for a Nightingale, 1971, An Unsuitable Job For a Woman, 1972, The Black Tower, 1975, Death of an Expert Witness, 1977, Innocent Blood, 1980, The Skull Beneath the Skin, 1982. Mem. Crime Writers Assn. (Silver Dagger award), Detection Club. Address: care Elaine Greene Ltd 31 Newington Green London England N16 9PU *

JAMES, REMBERT FAULKNER, newspaperman; b. Waxahachie, Tex., Oct. 14, 1905; s. Benjamin Franklin and Mae (Faulkner) J.; m. Catherine Moore Hodges, Aug. 11, 1934. Student, U. So. Calif., 1922-24, UCLA, 1927, U. Calif., Berkeley, 1942. Reporter Santa Monica (Calif.) Outlook, 1926; mng. editor Culver City (Calif.) Star-News, 1928-35; with AP (burs. Los Angeles, San Francisco, Moscow and Paris), 1936-48; gen. mgr., editor Copley News Service, San Diego, 1960-68, v.p. and editor, 1968-70. Mem. Sigma Delta Chi. Clubs: Nat. Press (Washington); Explorers, Overseas Press, Circumnavigators (N.Y.C.); Travelers Century. Home: 5578 Calumet Ave La Jolla CA 92037

JAMES, ROBERT CHARLES, bus. equipment mfg. co. exec.; b. Cleve., Jan. 15, 1943; s. Robert Gardner and Rhue Eleanor J.; m. Sally Ann Schaefer, June 19, 1965; 2 children. B.A., Wittenberg U., 1965; M.B.A., Ohio State U., 1971. With NCR Corp., Dayton, Ohio, 1971—, mgr. capital investment analysis, 1973-75, dir. fin. planning and analysis, 1975-77, treas., 1977-81, v.p. office systems div., 1981—; adj. prof. Wright State U. Bd. dirs. Children's Hosp., Dayton, 1977—. Served with USN, 1966-69. Mem. Fin. Execs. Inst. (dir. Dayton chpt.). Office: 1700 S Patterson Blvd Dayton OH 45479

JAMES, ROBERT CLARKE, mathematics educator, author; b. Bloomington, Ind., July 30, 1918; s. Glenn and Inez (Clarke) J.; m. Edith Maria Peterson, Oct. 28, 1945; children: Judith Marie (Mrs. Joseph Grounds), Linda Inez (Mrs. Gerald Anooshian), David Vernon, Robert Glenn. B.A., UCLA, 1940; Ph.D., Calif. Inst. Tech., 1947. Benjamin Pierce instr. math. Harvard, 1946-47; instr. math. U. Calif. at Berkeley, 1947-49, asst. prof., 1949-51; asso. prof. math. Haverford (Pa.) Coll., 1951-57; prof. math., chmn. dept. Harvey Mudd Coll., Claremont, Calif., 1957-67; prof. math. State U. N.Y., Albany, 1967-68; prof. math., chmn. dept. Claremont (Calif.) Grad. Sch., 1968-72, prof. math., 1972—; mem. Inst. Advanced Study, Princeton, N.J., 1962-63; fellow Inst. Advanced Studies, Jerusalem, 1976-77, Mittang-Leffler Inst., Djursholm, Sweden. Author: Mathematics Dictionary, 1942, rev. 1949, 59, 68, 76, University Mathematics, 1963, Advanced Calculus, 1966; Contbr. articles to profl. jours. Fellow AAAS; Mem. Am. Math. Soc., Math. Assn. Am., Soc. Indsl. and Applied Math., Fedn. Am. Scientists, Phi Beta Kappa, Sigma Xi. Mem. Soc. of Friends. Home: Trees and Bushes 18040 McCourtney Rd Grassvalley CA 95945 Office: Claremont Grad Sch Claremont CA 91711

JAMES, ROBERT LEO, advt. exec.; b. N.Y.C., Sept. 23; s. Leo Francis and Mildred Virginia (Schaffa) J.; m. Anne Krapp, Feb. 2, 1968; children: Robert Leo, Victoria, Jeffrey. A.B., Colgate U., 1958; M.B.A., Columbia, 1961. Field researcher Farm Jour., Inc., Cleve., 1956-57; salesman Procter and Gamble Co., Schenectady, 1958-59, office head sales mgr., Syracuse, N.Y., 1959-60; product mgr. household products, brand mktg. and new product devel. Colgate Palmolive Co., N.Y.C., 1961-64; account exec. Ogilvy and Mather, Inc., N.Y.C., 1964, account supr, 1965-66, v.p., account supr., 1967-69; sr. v.p., mgmt. service dir. Marschalk Co., Inc., N.Y.C., 1968, dir., 1969—, exec. v.p., 1970, gen. mgr., 1971, pres., 1974, chmn. bd., chief exec. officer, 1975-80; vice chmn. Interpub. Group of Cos., Inc., 1980—, also dir.; vice chmn. McCann-Erickson Worldwide, 1981—, also dir.; adj. asso. prof. mktg. Fordham U., 1968-69; dir. Broadlands Farm (thoroughbred horses.). Nat. service council Colgate U.; trustee Fordham Prep. Sch., 1977-83; bd. dirs. March of Dimes, N.Y.C. Mem. Young Pres.'s Orgn., Greenwich Power Squadron, Delta Kappa Epsilon. Clubs: Milbrook (Greenwich); N.Y. Yacht, Indian Harbor Yacht (dir.), NY40 Assn. (chmn.), Colgate U. Pres.'s.). Home: 68 W Brother Dr Greenwich CT 06830 Office: McCann-Erickson Worldwide 485 Lexington Ave New York NY 10017

JAMES, RONALD R., association executive; b. San Jose, Calif., June 11, 1928; s. William Ray and Mina (Pelton) J.; children: Lauron, Cynthia, William, Alexander. B.A., Stanford U. Vice pres., gen. mgr. James Transfer & Storage Co., San Jose, 1951-65; mayor City of San Jose, San Jose, 1966-71; pres., chief exec. officer San Jose C. of C., 1974—; dir. Calif. Auto Assn., San Jose Water Works. Pres. YMCA, San Jose, 1972-74. Republican. Baptist. Lodge: San Jose Rotary. Home: 552 Toyon Ave San Jose CA 95127 Office: San Jose C of C One Pasco de San Antonio PO Box 6178 San Jose CA 95113

JAMES, SIDNEY LORRAINE, television executive; b. St. Louis, Aug. 6, 1906; s. William Henry and Katherine (Wiese) J.; m. Agnes McCarthy, Oct. 21, 1932; children: Christopher, Timothy, Mary, Sidney. Student, Washington U., St. Louis. Mem. editorial staff St. Louis Post-Dispatch, 1928-36; nat. affairs writer Time mag., 1936-38; chief Time, Inc., Chgo., 1938-41, chief Western editorial operations, 1941-46, v.p. corp. mgmt., N.Y.C., 1965-67, v.p., Washington, 1967-70; asst. mng. editor Life mag., 1946-54; mng. editor Sports Illustrated, N.Y.C., 1954-60, pub., 1960-65; chmn. bd. Greater Washington Ednl. TV Assn. (WETA), Inc., 1970—; 1st vice chmn. bd. Pub. Broadcasting Service. Mem. President's Adv. Com. Youth Fitness; lay trustee Trinity Coll.; mem. Peabody Awards Bd. Mem. Def. Orientation Assn., Nat. Inst. Social Scis., U.S. Srs. Golf Assn. Clubs: American Yacht, Apawamis (Rye, N.Y.); New York Racquet and Tennis, Burning Tree; 1925 F Street, Nat. Press, The International (Washington). Home: 5499-3F Paseo Del Lago W Laguna Hills CA 92653

JAMES, SYDNEY VINCENT, educator; b. Chgo., Mar. 9, 1929; s. Sydney Vincent and Caroline Beatrice (Topping) J.; m. Jean Wooster Middleton, July 8, 1950; children—Samuel Wooster, Catherine Lyon. A.B. cum laude, Harvard, 1950, A.M., 1951, Ph.D., 1958. Instr. history Kent State U., 1956-58; asst. prof. Brown U., 1959-62, U. Oreg., 1962-65; asso. prof. U. Iowa, Iowa City, 1965-67, prof. history, 1967—, chmn. dept., 1970-74. Author: A People Among Peoples; Quaker Benevolence in Eighteenth-Century America, 1963, Colonial Rhode Island-A History, 1975; Contbr. articles to profl. jours. Grantee-in-aid Social Sci. Research Council, 1963, Center for Study History of Liberty in Am., 1963-64, Am. Council Learned Socs., 1964-65, Nat. Endowment for Humanities, 1972-74, Charles Warren Center for Studies in Am. History, Harvard U., 1979-80. Fellow R.I. Hist. Soc.; mem. Am. Hist. Assn., Orgn. Am. Historians, Colonial Soc. Mass., Internat. Commn. for History of Rep. and Parliamentary Instns. Home: 1101 Kirkwood Ave Iowa City IA 52240 Office: Dept History U Iowa Iowa City IA 52242 *Gradually I have learned the need to maintain respect for both elements in certain pairs of opposites, notably reason and reverie, daring and caution, tradition and iconoclasm, form and substance, detail and outline, insides and outsides, purpose and drift, snap judgments and considered opinions, precise questioning and wide-open receptivity. The middle road by itself is too narrow.*

JAMES, THOMAS NAUM, cardiologist, educator; b. Amory, Miss., Oct. 24, 1925; s. Naum and Kata J.; m. Gleaves Elizabeth Tynes, June 22, 1948; children—Thomas Mark, Terrence Fenner, Peter Naum. B.S., Tulane U., 1946, M.D., 1949. Diplomate: Am. Bd. Internal Medicine (mem. subsplty. bd. cardiovascular diseases 1972-78, bd. govs. 1982—). Intern Henry Ford Hosp., Detroit, 1949-50, resident in internal medicine and cardiology, 1950-53; practice medicine specializing in cardiology, Birmingham, Ala., 1968—; mem. staff Henry Ford Hosp., 1959-68, U. Ala. Hosps., 1968—; instr. medicine Tulane U., New Orleans, 1955-58, asst. prof., 1959; prof. medicine U. Ala. Med. Center, Birmingham, 1968—, prof. pathology, 1968-73, assoc. prof. physiology and biophysics, 1969-73, dir. Cardiovascular Research and Tng. Center, 1970-77, chmn. dept. medicine, 1973—, Mary Gertrude Waters prof. cardiology, 1976—; Disting. prof. of univ. U. Ala., 1981—; mem. adv. council Nat. Heart Lung and Blood Inst., 1975-79; mem. cardiology del. invited by Chinese Med. Assn. to, People's Republic of China, 1978. Author: Anatomy of the Coronary Arteries, 1961, The Etiology of Myocardial Infarction, 1963; Mem. editorial bd.: Circulation, 1966-83; mem. editorial bd.: Am. Jour. Cardiology, 1968-76; assoc. editor, 1976—; mem. editorial bd.: Am. Heart Jour, 1976-79; Contbr. articles on cardiovascular diseases to med. jours. Served as capt. M.C. U.S. Army, 1953-55. Mem. ACP (gov. Ala. 1975-79, master 1983), AMA, Am. Clin. and Climatological Assn., Assn. Am. Physicians, Am. Soc. Clin. Investigation, Assn. Univ. Cardiologists (pres. 1978-79), Am. Heart Assn. (pres. 1979-80), Am. Coll. Cardiology (v.p. 1970-71, trustee 1970-71, 76-81, First Disting. Scientist award 1982), Am. Soc. Pharmacology and Exptl. Therapeutics, Soc. Exptl. Biology of Medicine, Am. Coll. Chest Physicians, Central Soc. Clin. Research, So. Soc. Clin. Investigation, Am. Fedn. Clin. Research, Phi Beta Kappa, Sigma Xi, Omicron Delta Kappa, Ala. Acad. Honor, Alpha Omega Alpha, Alpha Tau Omega, Phi Chi. Presbyterian. Clubs: Cosmos, Mountain Brook. Office: Dept Medicine U Ala Med Center Birmingham AL 35294

JAMES, WILBUR ALBERT, wholesale food company executive; b. New Engle, Pa., June 3, 1923; s. Martin L. and Sarah (Todd) J.; m. Virginia Jones, Feb. 26, 1948; children: Linda Carol (Mrs. John Fetchen), Keith James, Virginia L. (Mrs. Lane Smail). Diploma, Robert Morris Coll., 1949. With Miss. Glass Co., Floreffe, Pa., 1941-43; auditor Pitts. Coal Co., Library, Pa., 1950-54; with Fox Grocery Co., Belle Vernon, Pa., 1954—, dir. finance, 1958-72, v.p. finance, 1972—, sec.-treas., 1961-72; v.p., dir. Webb Crawford Co., Athens, Ga., 1976-80; pres. MonVale Multiphasics Inc., 1984—; v.p., sec.-treas. Fox Fund, Inc. (formerly Fox Industries, Inc.); dir. Follow Co., Belle Vernon. Exec. com. Monongahela Valley Hosp., 1974—; Chmn. bd. New Eagle (Pa.) Sch. Dist. Authority, 1964; pres. bd. Monongahela Valley United Fund, 1971—; bd. dirs. Pa. Economy League, Washington, Pa.; active Boy Scouts Am., Boys Club; trustee Fox Ednl. Found.; trustee, sec. Monongahela Valley Hosp.; bd. dirs. Pi Hs. Baptist Assn. Served with USAAF, 1943-46; ETO (prisoner of war, Germany). Decorated Purple Heart.; Recipient Heritage award Robert Morris Coll., 1973. Mem. New Eagle Sportsmen Assn. (v.p. 1949-50). Baptist (chmn. bd. trustees 1955—, deacon). Home: 478 4th Ave New Eagle PA 15067 Office: Fox Industries Inc 400 Penn Center Blvd Pittsburgh PA 15235

JAMES, WILLIAM, mining company executive; b. Ottawa, Ont., Canada, Feb. 5, 1929; s. Fleming and Leanore (McEvoy) J.; m. Joanna Watson, Sept. 15, 1954; children: Paul, William, Anne, Mary, George, John. B.A., U. Toronto, 1954, M.A., 1954. With Falconbridge Ltd., Toronto, now pres., chief exec. officer, also chmn., 1982—. Mem. Mining Assn. Can. (dir.), Assn. Profl. Engrs. Ont. Clubs: Engineers, York. Office: Falconbridge Ltd PO Box 40 Commerce Ct W Toronto ON Canada M5L 1B4 *

JAMES, WILLIAM RAMSAY, cable television executive; b. South Bend, Ind., Oct. 6, 1933; s. William Stubbs and Rose (Ramsay) J.; m. Jane Mehrer, Dec. 29, 1955; children: William Harold, Martha Courtney Quay. B.S.M.E., Princeton U., 1955; M.B.A., Harvard U., 1960. C.P.A., Mich. Plant mgr. N. A. Woodworth Co., Ferndale, Mich., 1960-62; partner Touche Ross & Co., Detroit, 1962-69; v.p., gen. mgr. WJR, Detroit, 1969-80; pres. Cable div. Capital Cities Communications, Bloomfield Hills, Mich., 1980—; dir. Ferro Mfg. Corp., Southfield, Mich. Vice-chmn. bd. trustees Cranbrook Ednl. Community; bd. visitors Sch. Economy and Mgmt., Oakland U. Served to 1st lt. USAF, 1955-58. Mem. Am. Inst. C.P.A.'s, Mich. Assn. C.P.A.'s. Republican. Episcopalian. Clubs: Country (Bloomfield Hills, Mich.); Orchard Lake Country, Detroit. Office: 710 N Woodward St Bloomfield Hills MI 48013

JAMESON, DOROTHEA, sensory psychologist; b. Newton, Mass., Nov. 16, 1920; d. Robert and Josephine (Murray) J.; m. Leo M. Hurvich, Oct. 23, 1948. B.A., Wellesley Coll., 1942; M.A. (hon.), U. Pa., 1973. Research asst. Harvard, 1941-47; research psychologist Eastman Kodak Co., Rochester, N.Y., 1947-57; research scientist, N.Y. U., 1957-62; vis. scientist Venezuelan Inst. Sci. Research, 1965; research asso. to prof. Psychol. and Inst. Neurol. Scis., U. Pa., 1962-74; Univ. prof. U. Pa., 1975—; vis. prof. Center Visual Sci., U. Rochester, 1974, Columbia U., 1974-76; cons. in field. Mem. Nat. Acad. Sci.-NRC Commn. on Human Resources, 1977-80, chmn. com. on vision, 1980-81. Co-author: The Perception of Brightness and Darkness, 1966; co-author: (E. Hering) introduction and English translation Outlines of a Theory of the Light Sense, 1964; Co-editor, author: Visual Psychophysics: Handbook of Sensory Physiology, vol. VII/4, 1972; Contbr. articles to profl. jours. Recipient I.H. Godlove award Inter-Soc. Color Council, 1973; Alumnae Achievement award Wellesley Coll., 1974; fellow Center for Advanced Study in the Behavioral Scis., 1981-82. Mem. Soc. Exptl. Psychologists (Howard Crosby Warren medal 1971), Internat. Brain Research Orgn., Am. Psychol. Assn. (Distinguished Sci. Contbn. award 1972), Nat. Acad. Scis., Am. Acad. Arts and Scis., AAAS, Assn. Research in Vision and Ophthalmology, Biophys. Soc., Internat. Research Group Color Vision Deficiencies, Optical Soc. Am. (Tillyer medal 1982), Psychonomic Soc., Soc. Neurosci., Sigma Xi. Home: 286 St James Pl Philadelphia PA 19106 Office: 3815 Walnut St Philadelphia PA 19104

JAMESON, MICHAEL HAMILTON, classics educator; b. London, Eng., Oct. 15, 1924; s. Raymond Deloy and Rose (Perel) J.; m. Virginia Broyles, June 8, 1946; children: Nicholas Andrew, Anthony David, John Timothy, David Richmond. A.B., U. Chgo., 1942, Ph.D., 1949. Asst. prof. classical langs. and archaeology U. Mo., 1950-53; mem. faculty U. Pa., Phila., 1954-76, prof. classical studies, 1962-76, dean Grad. Sch. Arts and Scis., 1966-68, research asso. classical archaeology Univ. Mus., dir. Argolid Exploration Project, 1960—, dir. Ctr. Ancient History, 1968-76; prof. classics Stanford U., 1976—, Edward Clark Crossett prof. humanistic studies, 1977—; mng. com. Am. Sch. Classical Studies, Athens, Greece. Contbr. articles to profl. jours. Served to lt. USNR, 1943-46. Recipient citation teaching and research Pa. Dept. Pub. Instrn., 1963; Fulbright fellow, 1958; Am. Council Learned Socs. fellow, 1958, 76; Guggenheim fellow, 1965; sr. fellow NEH, 1971-72. Mem. Archaeol. Inst. Am., Am. Acad. Arts and Scis., Am. Acad. in Rome (sr. fellow classics 1958-59), Am. Philol. Soc. (pres. 1981). Home: 647 Glenbrook Dr Palo Alto CA 94306 Office: Dept Classics Stanford U Stanford CA 94305

JAMESON, SAMUEL WALTER, newspaperman, fgn. corr.; b. Pitts., Aug. 9, 1936; s. Vernon L. and Dorothy W. (Wilson) J. B.S., Northwestern U., 1958, M.S., 1959. Copyreader Chgo. Tribune, 1959-60, Tokyo bur. chief, 1963-71, Los Angeles Times, 1971—; Chmn. Fgn. Press Japan, 1971-72. Mem. Fulbright Commn. Japan, 1971-81. Served with AUS, 1960-62. Clubs: Fgn. Corrs. Japan (pres. 1973-74), Tokyo Lawn Tennis.). Office: Los Angeles Times Tokyo Bur Yomiuri Bldg 1-7-1 Otemachi Chiyoda-Ku Tokyo 100 Japan

JAMESON, WILLIAM JAMES, judge; b. Butte, Mont., Aug. 8, 1898; s. William J. and Annie J. (Roberts) J.; m. Mildred Lore, July 28, 1923; children: Mary Lucille (Mrs. Walker Honaker), William James, Jr. A.B., Mont. U., 1919, J.D., 1922, LL.D., 1952; LL.D., U. Man., Can., 1954, Rocky Mountain Coll., 1969; Dr. Laws, McGeorge Coll. Law, 1965. Bar: Mont. 1922. Assoc. Johnston, Coleman and Johnston, Billings, 1922-29; mem. Johnston, Coleman & Jameson, 1929-40, Coleman, Jameson & Lamey, 1940-57; judge U.S. Dist. Ct. for Mont., 1957-69, sr. judge, 1969—; judge Temporary Emergency Ct. Appeals, 1976—; Mem. S.A.T.C. Mem. Mont. Ho. of Reps., 1927-30; Sch. Bd. Trustee, Billings, 1930- 32; chmn. Yellowstone County chpt. A.R.C., 1931-45. Recipient Disting. Achievement award Law Sch., Gonzaga U., 1970. Fellow Am. Bar Found.; mem. ABA (bd. govs. 1943-46, assembly del. 1946-53, pres. 1953-54, pres. endowment 1961-63, chmn. sect. jud. adminstrn. 1963-64, chmn. spl. com. on adminstrn. criminal justice 1969-73, recipient gold medal 1973), Mont. Bar Assn. (pres. 1936- 37), Am. Law Inst. (mem. council 1956—), Am. Judicature Soc. (pres. 1956-58, Herbert Lincoln Harley award 1974), Am. Legion, Phi Delta Phi. Methodist. Lodges: Masons; Lion (dist. gov. 1941-42). Office: PO Box 2115 Fed Bldg-U S Courthouse Billings MT 59103

JAMIESON, DAVID DONALD, lawyer; b. Phila., Apr. 8, 1926; s. David and Emma L. (Matthews) J.; m. Nannette L. Detrick, Feb. 4, 1961; children—Heather Lee, David Douglas. B.S., U. Pa., 1947, LL.B., 1950; grad., Nat. Coll. State Trial Judges, 1966. Bar: Pa. bar 1950. Asso. firm Price & Propper, Phila., 1950-52; asst. U.S. atty. Eastern Dist. Pa., 1953-55; partner firm Richman, Price & Jamieson, Phila., 1955-63, Steinberg, Richman, Price & Steinbrook, 1963-65; pres. judge Ct. Common Pleas No. 9 Pa., 1965-70, Ct. Common Pleas, Phila., 1970-75; exec. v.p. First Pa. Bank, N.A., Phila., 1975-77; partner firm Mesirov, Gelman, Jaffe, Cramer & Jamieson, Phila., 1977—; dir. Mel Richman, Inc.; hon. consul of Netherlands in, Phila., 1976-79. Contbr. legal jours. Bd. dirs. Univ. City Sci. Center, Frankford Hosp., Gloria Dei Village; trustee LuLu Temple; chmn. Republican City Com. Served to capt. AUS, 1953-53. Recipient numerous awards for contbns. to justice system. Mem. ABA, Pa. Bar Assn. (chmn. jud. code commn.), Phila. Bar Assn. (gov.), Defenders Assn. Phila. (dir.). Lutheran. Club: Union League (Phila.). Home: Pine Rd and Kings Oak Ln Philadelphia PA 19115 Office: 15th Floor Fidelity Bldg Philadelphia PA 19109

JAMIESON, DONALD CAMPBELL, Canadian diplomat; b. St. John's, Nfld., Apr. 20, 1921; s. Charles and Isabelle (Bennett) J.; m. Barbara Elizabeth Oakley, Dec. 20, 1946; children: Donna, Heather, Roger, Debbie. Student, Prince of Wales Coll., St. John's; LL.D., Meml. U., 1970. Mem. Nfld. Legislature, 1979; leader Liberal Party in Nfld., 1979; leader of the opposition, 1979-80; mem. Can. House of Commons, 1966-70, 72-76; minister of def. prodn., 1968, minister of transport, 1969, minister of regional econ. expansion, 1972-75, minister of indsl. trade and commn., 1975-76, minister of external affairs, 1976-79, Can. high commr. to Britain, London, 1983—. Author: The Troubled Air, 1966. Mem. consultative com. on pvt. broadcasting Bd. Broadcast Govs.; com. on broadcasting Troika Com., 1963; past dir. broadcast news, past chmn. affiliates sect. network adv. com. CBC; past chmn. fin. campaign Can. Cancer Soc. Mem. Can. Assn. Broadcasters (pres. 1961-64). Liberal. Presbyterian. Club: City. Office: Canadian High Commission Macdonald House 1 Grosvenor Sq London England W1X 0AB *

JAMIESON, EDWARD LEO, magazine editor; b. Boston, Sept. 18, 1929; s. Leo and Estelle (Mullen) J.; m. Ann Booth, Sept. 1961. A.B., Boston U., 1951. Reporter Medford (Mass.) Daily Mercury, 1951-54; contbg. editor Time mag., 1955-58, asso. editor, 1958-63, sr. editor, 1963-69, asst. mng. editor, 1969-76, exec. editor, 1976—. Office: Time Mag Rockefeller Center New York NY 10020

JAMIESON, GRAHAM A., biochemist, organization official; b. Wellington, N.Z., Aug. 14, 1929; came to U.S., 1956; s. Andrew Wilson and Nan (Graham) J.; m. Barbara MacLachlan, Feb. 20, 1960; 1 son, Brian. B.Sc., U. Otago, 1949; M.Sc. (Sir George Grey scholar), U. N.Z., 1951; Ph.D. Lister Inst. Preventive Medicine, U. London, 1954, D.Sc., 1972. Research fellow dept. biochemistry Cornell U., N.Y.C., 1956; vis. scientist NIH, 1957-61, mem. exptl. hematology study com., 1978—; research biochemist Am. Nat. Red Cross, Bethesda, Md., 1961-64, asst. dir. research, 1964-69, dir. research, 1969-78, asso. dir. blood services, 1978—; lectr. biochemistry Georgetown U., Washington, 1961, professorial lectr., 1966-74, adj. prof., 1974—; Winzler Meml. lectr. U. Fla., 1975; mem. adv. com. on blood preservation and substitutes U.S. Army Med. Research and Devel. Command, 1980, chmn., 1981. Editor: (with T.J. Greenwalt) Red Cell Membrane-Structure and Function, 1969, Formation and Destruction of Blood Cells, 1970, Glycoproteins of Blood Cells and Plasma, 1971, The Human Red Cell In Vitro, 1974, Transmissible Disease and Blood Transfusion, 1975, Trace Components of Plasma-Isolation and Clinical Significance, 1976, The Granulocyte: Function and Clinical Utilization, 1977, The Blood Platelet in Transfusion Therapy, 1978, (with D.M. Robinson) Mammalian Cell Membranes, Vol. I, 1978—, Generalizations and Methodology, Vol. II, 1978—, The Diversity of Membranes, Vol. III, 1978—, Surface Membranes of Specific Cell Types, Vol. IV, 1978—, Membranes and Cellular Functions, Vol. V, 1978—, Responses of Plasma Membranes; Thrombosis Research, 1978—; (with Alice R. Scipio) Interaction of Platelets and Tumor Cells, 1982; contbr. articles to profl. jours. Mem. Am. Soc. Biol. Chemists, Am. Chem. Soc., Biochem. Soc. (London), AAAS, Internat. Soc. Thrombosis and Hemostatis (council 1979—), N.Y. Acad. Scis., Am. Heart Assn. (exec. com., council on thrombosis, exec. com.), Am. Soc. Hematology, Soc. Exptl. Biology and Medicine, Soc. for Complex Carbohydrates (exec. com.). Home: 5622 Johnson Ave Bethesda MD 20034 Office: 9312 Old Georgetown Rd Bethesda MD 20014

JAMIESON, HENRY LOUIS, financial executive; b. Ft. Wayne, Ind., Aug. 28, 1911; s. Henry L. and Helen May (Jones) J.; m. Georgia Marie Homsher, Dec. 23, 1935; children; Caroline Hagopian, Elizabeth Rothman, Edward B. A.B., George Washington U., 1936. Div. mgr. Investors Diversified Service, San Francisco, 1946-53; pres. H.L. Jamieson Inc., San Francisco, 1954-57, Hare's Ltd., N.Y.C., 1957-61; v.p., pres. King Merrit & Co., N.Y.C., 1961-63; chmn. bd. Trust Securities Corp., Boston, 1963-67, Winfield & Co., Inc., San Francisco, 1967-70; chmn. Franklin Family of Funds, San Mateo, Calif., 1970—. Served to lt. comdr. USNR, 1943-46. Republican. Clubs: Commonwealth (San Francisco); Peninsula Golf and Country (San Mateo). Office: Franklin Fund 155 Bovet Rd San Mateo CA 94402

JAMIESON, JOHN CHARLES, philologist, educator; b. Boston, June 30, 1933; s. George and Florence Ruth (Holt) J.; m. Cholhee In, Jan. 13, 1960; children: Ellen, Caroline. A.B., U. Calif., Berkeley, 1959, M.A., 1963, Ph.D., 1969. Asst. prof. Oriental langs. U. Calif., Berkeley, 1967-72, assoc. prof., 1972-78, prof., 1978—; dir. Stanford U. Inter-Univ. Program for Chinese Lang. Studies, 1969-70, Stanford-Berkeley Joint East Asia Lang. and Area Center, 1974—; mem. joint com. on Korean Studies Am. Council Learned Socs.-Social Sci. Research Council, 1974—, chmn., 1978—; mem. com. on scholarly communications with People's Republic of China Nat. Acad. Sci., mem. com. on advanced study in China, 1975—. Author: Elementary Chinese Companion, 1975; contbr. articles on Asian studies to profl. publs. Served with U.S. Army, 1952-55. Recipient Younger Humanist award Nat. Endowment Humanities, 1973; Fulbright fellow, 1959-61; Ford fellow, 1964-66. Mem. Assn. Asian Studies, Chosen Gakkai, Phi Beta Kappa. Club: Commonwealth. Office: Dept Oriental Langs U Calif Berkeley CA 94720 *

JAMIESON, JOHN KENNETH, oil field services company executive; b. Medicine Hat, Alta., Can., Aug. 28, 1910; s. John Locke and Kate Alberta (Herron) J.; m. Ethel May Burns, Dec. 23, 1937; children—John Burns, Anne Frances. B.S. in Civil Enging, M.I.T., 1931. With Brit. Am. Oil Co., Can., 1934-38; v.p. Imperial Oil Co. Ltd., Toronto, 1945-58; pres. Internat. Petroleum Co., Ltd., 1959-61; v.p. Exxon Co., U.S.A., Houston, 1961-62, exec. v.p., 1964-65, pres., 1965-69, chmn. bd., 1969-75, dir., 1964-1981; chmn. bd. Crutcher Resources Corp., Houston, 1977-82; dir. Equitable Life Assurance Soc. U.S., 1971—, Raychem Corp., 1977—; Chmn. Nat. Fgn. Trade Council; vice chmn. Center for Internat. Bus. Bd. visitors MDA Cancer Inst. Mem. Internat. C. of C., Houston C. of C., Am. Council on Germany, Council Fgn. Relations, Am. Petroleum Inst., Midcontinent Oil and Gas Assn., M.D. Anderson Cancer Inst. Episcopalian. Clubs: Houston Country, Augusta Nat. Golf, Ramada. Office: 1100 Milam Bldg Suite 4601 Houston TX 77002

JAMIESON, ROBERT JOHN, television journalist; b. Streator, Ill., Feb. 1, 1943; s. Robert Arthur and Evelyn (O'Neill) J.; married; children: Courtney, Maura. Student, Knox Coll., Galesburg, Ill., 1961-62, Bradley U., Peoria, Ill., 1962-65. Anchorman WMBD-TV, Peoria,

1967; anchorman, reporter KSD-TV, St. Louis, 1967-68; anchorman WBBM-TV, CBS, Chgo., 1968-71; reporter NBC News, N.Y.C., 1971-73, Midwest corr., 1973-76, White House corr., Washington, 1976-79, nat. corr., N.Y.C., 1979—. Served with USNR, 1964-66. Decorated AEF medal; recipient AP TV Reporting award, 1969, Pub. Service award Nat. Kidney Found., 1973. Mem. Radio-TV Corrs. Assn., White House Corrs. Assn., Sigma Delta Chi (award for pub. service reporting 1964). Club: Fed. City (Washington). Office: NBC News 30 Rockefeller Plaza New York NY 10020 *

JAMISON, JOHN AMBLER, circuit judge; b. nr. Florence, S.C., May 14, 1916; s. John Wilson and Elizabeth Ambler (Fleming) J.; m. Mildred Holley, Sept. 22, 1945. LL.B. cum laude, Cumberland U., Lebanon, Tenn., 1941; postgrad., George Washington U., 1943-44, also Indsl. Coll. Armed Forces, 1961; J.D., Samford U., 1969, LL.D., 1983. Bar: S.C. 1941, Va. 1942, U.S. Supreme Ct. 1945. Atty. Va. Div. Motor Vehicles, 1947-54; practiced law, Fredericksburg, Va., 1954-72; asso. judge Stafford and King George County Cts., also Fredericksburg Municipal Ct., 1956-72; judge 15th Jud. Circuit Va., 1972—, chief judge, 1976—; Counsel, dir. Nat. Bank Fredericksburg, 1958-73. Mem. adv. bd. Va. Gov.'s Hwy. Safety Commn., 1956-62, Cumberland Sch. Law; pres. Fredericksburg Rescue Squad, 1960-62, now hon. life mem.; chmn. bd. Fredericksburg Area Mental Hygiene Clinic, 1962-63; hon. chmn. Fredericksburg Area Bicentennial Commn., 1975-77; charter mem. Thomas Jefferson Inst. for Religious Freedom, 1975; bd. dirs. Rappahannock Area Devel. Commn., 1960-66. Served from ensign to comdr. USNR, 1941-46; comdg. officer Richmond Naval Res. Div., 1948-54; mem. Res., 1946-54; naval aide to govs. Va., 1954-72. Recipient award S.C. Confederate War Centennial Commn., 1965, Cross of Mil. Service UDC. Mem. ABA, Va. Bar Assn., S.C. Bar Assn., 15th Jud. Circuit Bar Assn. (pres. 1959-60, 69-70), Am. Judicature Soc., Am. Law Inst., Res. Officers Assn., Mil. Order World Wars, Naval Res. Assn., Nat. Soc. S.A.R., Am. Legion (post comdr. 1951-52), Cumberland Law Sch. Alumni Assn. (nat. pres. 1978-79, dean's council 1980—), Jud. Conf. Va., Cumberland Order Jurisprudence, Hon. Order Ky. Cols., Blue Key, Sigma Delta Kappa. Episcopalian (past vestryman, warden, lay reader). Lodges: Masons; Shriners; Jesters; Kiwanis. Home: 509 Hanover St Fredericksburg VA 22401 Office: PO Drawer 29 Fredericksburg VA 22404

JAMISON, JOHN CALLISON, business educator, investment banker; b. Lafayette, Ind., July 12, 1934; s. John Ruger and Sara (Callison) J.; m. Carol Ann Sansone, July 7, 1979; children: Kelly Elizabeth Loehr, Deborah Louise Loehr. B.S. in Indsl. Econs., Purdue U., 1956; M.B.A., Harvard U., 1961. Assoc. Goldman, Sachs & Co., N.Y.C., 1961-69, ptnr., 1969-82, ltd. ptnr., 1983—; dean Sch. Bus. Adminstrn. Coll. William and Mary, Williamsburg, Va., 1983—; dir. G. C. Murphy Co., McKeesport, Pa., Hershey Foods Corp., Pa., Cowles Broadcasting, Inc., Daytona Beach, Fla. Trustee Hurricane Island Outward Bound Sch., Rockland, Maine, 1977—; bd. govs. Purdue Found., West Lafayette, Ind., 1979-83; bd. dirs. Theatre Devel. Fund, N.Y.C., 1979-83. Served to lt. USN, 1956-59; PTO. Recipient Old Master award Purdue U., 1977, Sagamore of Wabash award Gov. of Ind., 1982. Mem. Beta Gamma Sigma. Republican. Episcopalian. Club: Ocean Reef (Keylargo, Fla.).

JAMISON, JUDITH, dancer; b. Phila., 1944; d. John J. Student, Fisk U., Phila. N.Y. dance debut in Agnes DeMille's "The Four Marys", 1965; dancer, Alvin Ailey Am. Dance Theater, N.Y.C., 1965-80; guest appearances with, Harkness Ballet, Am. Ballet Theatre, San Francisco Ballet, Dallas Ballet; starring role created for her in: Joseph's Legend (John Neumeier), Vienna Opera, Le Spectre de la Rose (Maurice Bejart), Brussels, Paris, N.Y.C.; star: Broadway show Sophisticated Ladies, 1980; now with, Maurice Hines Dance Sch., N.Y.C. Recipient Disting. Service award Mayor of N.Y.C., 1982, Harvard U., 1982, Key to City of N.Y., 1976. Subject of book Aspects of a Dancer. Address: care Alvin Ailey Am Dance Theater 1515 Broadway New York NY 10036

JAMISON, OLIVER MORTON, lawyer; b. Portland, Oreg., Aug. 1, 1916; s. Homer B. and Jean (Allison) J.; m. Margaret Ratcliffe, July 18, 1941; children—Stephen, Thomas, Daniel. A.B., Stanford, 1938, LL.B., 1941. Bar: Calif. bar 1941. Since practiced in, Fresno; partner firm Thomas, Snell, Jamison, Russell, Williamson & Asperger, 1941—; Lectr. taxation Calif. Bar Continuing Edn. Program, 1948, 51, 54, 64, Am. Law Inst., 1949, 50, 53, U. So. Calif. Inst. Fed. Taxation, 1961; mem. taxation adv. commn. Calif. Bar Legal Splzn. Bd., 1971-74; bd. govs. Calif. State Bar, 1976-79, v.p., 1979. Trustee Calif. State U., Fresno Found., 1973-78, Fresno Community Hosp., 1972-78. Served to capt. AUS, 1942-46. Mem. Am., Fresno County bar assns., Fresno County and City C. of C. (pres. 1960), State Bar Calif., Am. Law Inst., Am. Judicature Soc., Order of Coif, Phi Alpha Delta. Home: 4950 N Sunset Dr Fresno CA 93704 Office: Del Webb Bldg Fresno CA 93721

JAMISON, PHILIP, artist; b. Phila., July 3, 1925; s. Philip Duane and Daisy (McCadden) J.; m. Jane B. Gray, Oct. 11, 1950; children: Philip Duane III, Terry Jane, Linda B. Student, Phila. Mus. Sch. Art, 1946-50. Author: Capturing Nature in Watercolor, 1980; One man shows, Hirschl & Adler Galleries, N.Y.C., 1959, 63, 65, 67, 69, 71, 74, 76, 80, Sessler Gallery, Phila., 1963, 72, Duke U., 1969, Del. Art Mus., 1973, Janet Fleisher Gallery, Phila., 1977, Grand Gallery, Wilmington, Del., Whistler's Daughter Gallery, Basking Ridge, N.J., 1981, Newman Galleries, Bryn Mawr, Pa., 1982; represented in permanent collections, Pa. Acad. Fine Arts, NAD, Wilmington Soc. Fine Arts, U. Del., Boston Mus. Fine Arts, Nat. Air and Space Mus., Washington, Brandywine River Mus., Pa., others.; NASA artist for Apollo-Soyuz space launch, 1975. Served with USNR, 1943-46. Recipient Dawson medal Pa. Acad. Fine Arts, 1959, 77, Dana medal, 1961; first award Nat. Arts Club, N.Y.C., 1961; Lena A. Mason prize NAD, 1962; Samuel Finley Breese Morse medal NAD, 1969; Walter Biggs Meml. award NAD, 1982; William Church Osborn prize Am. Watercolor Soc., 1961, 79; Medal of Honor Knickerbocker Artists, N.Y.C., 1961; Bainbridge award Allied Artists Am., 1958, 60; first prize Wilmington Soc. Fine Arts, 1957, 59, 61; M.W. Zimmerman Meml. prize Phila. Watercolor Club, 1963; Gold medal honor Allied Artists Am., 1964; Childe Hassam Fund purchase prize AAAL, 1965; Lily Saportas award Am. Watercolor Soc., 1965; C.F.S. award, 1966; Edgar A. Whitney award, 1971; High Winds award, 1972; Whitney award, 1973; Ted Kautzky Meml. award, 1974; Ranger Fund purchase prize NAD, 1962; prize, 1967; Adolph and Clara Obrig award, 1974; Thornton Oakley Meml. prize Phila. Watercolor Club, 1967; gold medal Franklin Mint Gallery Am. Art, 1974; Merit award Nat. Watercolor Exhbn., Springfield (Ill.) Art Assn., 1979. Mem. Am. Watercolor Soc. (Mary S. Litt medal 1978, Larry Quackenbush Meml. award 1982), Phila. Water Color Club (Dawson Meml. prize 1977, George Gansworth Meml. prize 1981). Home: 104 Price St West Chester PA 19380 Studio: 104 Price St West Chester PA 19380

JAMISON, RICHARD MELVIN, virologist, educator; b. Rayne, La., Oct. 28, 1938; s. Melvin Linwood and Lina Katharine (Muller) J.; m. Diane E. Cella, Oct. 24, 1964; children: Richard Wilhelm, Diane Elizabeth, Bonny Alyssa. M.S. (USPHS fellow), Baylor U. Coll. Medicine, 1962, Ph.D., 1966. Diplomate: Am. Bd. Med. Microbiology (virology com. 1983—). Research asso. Oak Ridge Nat. Lab., 1966-67; asst. prof. U. Colo. Med. Center, Denver, 1967-70; virologist La. State U. Med. Center, Shreveport, 1970—, prof. microbiology and Immunology, 1978—; cons. Al Fateh U., Socialist People's Libyan Arab Jamahiri ya. Vice pres. Shreveport Civic Opera Assn., 1977-79. Mem. AAAS, Electron Microscopy Soc. Am., Am. Soc. Microbiology, Sigma Xi. Research in tumor viruses, host-virus interactions and picornaviruses. Home: 505 Stratford Shreveport LA 71105 Office: PO Box 33932 Shreveport LA 71130

JAMOUNEAU, WALTER COREY, aircraft co. exec.; b. Irvington, N.J., Sept. 21, 1912; s. Walter H. and E. Prudence (Corey) J.; m. Helen E. Hoey, June 22, 1934; children—W. Jeffry, William C. B.S. in Mech. Engring, Rutgers U., 1932. With Piper Aircraft Corp. (and predecessor), 1933-77, chief engr., 1936-77, sec., 1947-69, asst. sec., 1969-77, v.p. engring., 1969-73, v.p. product assurance, 1973-77; cons. Bangor Punta Corp., 1977—. Chmn. Lock Haven United Fund drive, 1961; mem. Lockhaven Sch. Bd., 1961-72; Chmn. finance com. Clinton County Republican Com., 1962-74; Trustee Lock Haven State Coll.; mem. adv. bd. Lock Haven Salvation Army; trustee Piper Found. Mem. Soc. Automotive Engrs., Inst. Aerospace Scis., Am. Soc. Corp. Secs., Rutgers Engring. Soc., Lambda Chi Alpha, Tau Beta Pi. Home: 708 N Front St Wormleysburg PA 17043

JAMPLIS, ROBERT WARREN, surgeon, medical foundation executive; b. Chgo., Apr. 1, 1920; s. Mark and Janet (McKenna) J.; m. Roberta Cecelia Prior, Sept. 5, 1947; children: Mark Prior, Elizabeth Ann Jamplis Halliday. B.S., U. Chgo., 1941, M.D., 1944; M.S., U. Minn., 1951. Diplomate: Am. Bd. Surgery, 1952, Am. Bd. Thoracic Surgery, 1953; Lic. physician, Calif., Minn., Ill. Asst. resident in surgery U. Chgo., 1946-47; fellow in thoracic surgery Mayo Clinic, Rochester, Minn., 1950-52; chief thoracic surgery Palo Alto (Calif.) Med. Clinic, 1958—, exec. dir., 1965-81; clin. prof. surgery Stanford U. Sch. Medicine, 1958—; dir. Coopers Labs., Inc.; mem. council SRI Internat.; vice-chmn. bd. TakeCare Corp.; charter mem., bd. regents Am. Coll. Physician Execs.; mem. staff Stanford Univ. Hosp., Santa Clara Valley Med. Center, San Jose, VA Hosp., Palo Alto, Sequoia Hosp., Redwood City, Calif., El Camino Hosp., Mountain View, Calif., Harold D. Chope Community Hosp., San Mateo, Calif.; pres., chief exec. officer Palo Alto Med. Found.; vice-chmn. Fedn. Western Clinics; mem. physician adv. com. Blue Cross Calif.; varsity football team physician Stanford U. Contbr. numerous articles to profl. jours.; author: (with G.A. Lillington) A Diagnostic Approach to Chest Diseases, 1965, 3d edit., 1984. Trustee Santa Barbara Med. Found. Clinic; pres. Calif. div. Am. Cancer Soc.; chmn. bd. Group Practice Polit. Area Com.; mem. athletic bd. Stanford U.; mem. cabinet U. Chgo.; bd. dirs. Herbert Hoover Boys' Club; past trustee No. Calif. Cancer Program; past bd. dirs. Core Communications in Health, Community Blood Res., others. Served to lt. USNR, 1944-46, 52-54. Recipient Alumni citation U. Chgo., 1968, Nat. Div. award Am. Cancer Soc., 1979, Med. Exec. award Am. Coll. Med. Group Adminstrs., 1981, Russel V. Lee award lectr. Am. Group Pratice Assn., 1982. Mem. Inst. Medicine of Nat. Acad. Scis., ACS, Am. Assn. Thoracic Surgery, Samson Thoracic Surg. Soc. (pres.), Western Surg. Assn., Pacific Coast Surg. Assn., San Francisco Surg. Soc. (past pres.), Portland Surg. Soc. (hon.), Doctors Mayo Soc., Am. Coll. Chest Physicians, Calif. Acad. Medicine, Am. Fedn. Clin. Research, Am. Group Practice Assn. (pres.), AMA, Calif. Med. Assn., Santa Clara County Med. Assn., Sigma Xi. Republican. Roman Catholic. Clubs: Bohemian, Commonwealth of California (San Francisco); Menlo Country (Woodside, (Calif.); Menlo Circus (Atherton, Calif.); Stanford (Calif.) Golf; Rancheros Visitadores (Santa Barbara, Calif.). Office: 400 Channing St Palo Alto CA 94301

JAMPOLIS, NEIL PETER, designer; b. Bklyn., Mar. 14, 1943; s. Samuel and Beatrice (Swenken) J.; m. Maritza Jane Reisman, July 24, 1971. B.F.A. in Stage Design, Art Inst. Chgo., 1965. Designer 10 prodns., Sante Fe Opera, 4 prodns., Netherlands Opera, Houston Grand Opera, 1 prodn., Met. Opera, Central City Opera, 4 prodns., St. Paul Opera, Opera Soc. Washington; designer: scene, costumes or lighting for many Broadway prodns. including Borstal Boy, 1969, In the Bar of a Tokyo Hotel, 1968, Butley, 1972, Crown Matrimonial, 1973, Sherlock Holmes, 1974, The Innocents, 1976, Otherwise Engaged, 1977; also Am. premieres of operas Die Jakobsleiter, 1968, Cardillac, 1967, Melusine, 1972; world premiere opera Spinoza, Amsterdam, 1971; set designer: The Brownsville Raid, 1977, also numerous others; lighting designer: Night and Day, 1979, Harold and Maude, 1980; lighting designer with, Cin. Playhouse, 1979-80, Man. Theatre Centre (Recipient Tony award for lighting Sherlock Holmes 1975). Mem. United Scenic Artists Am. Address: 130 W 57th St New York NY 10019 *

JAMRICH, JOHN XAVIER, retired university president; b. Muskegon Heights, Mich., June 12, 1920; s. John and Mary (Mudry) J.; m. June Ann Hrupka, June 26, 1944; children: June Ann, Marna Mary, Barbara Sue. Student, Milw. State Tchrs. Coll., 1939-40, Ripon Coll., 1940-42; B.S., U. Chgo., 1942-43; M.S., Marquette U., 1946-48; Ph.D., Northwestern U., 1951; L.H.D. (hon.), No. Mich. U., 1968. Instr. math. Marquette U., 1946-48; asst. instr. math. U. Wis., 1948-49; asst. dean men Northwestern U., 1949-51; dean students Coe Coll., Cedar Rapids, Iowa, 1951-55; dean faculty, prof. math. Doane Coll., Crete, Nebr., 1955-57; assoc. dir. Legis. Survey Higher Edn. in Mich., 1957-58; prof. higher edn., dir. Center for Study Higher Edn., Mich. State U., 1957-63, assoc. dean Coll. Edn., prof. higher edn., 1963-68; pres. No. Mich. U., 1968-83, adj. prof., 1983—; cons.-examiner N. Central Assn. Colls. and Secondary Schs., 1962—; cons. in field, 1959—; Ford Found. cons. for devel. U. Nigeria, 1964; cons. higher edn. Govt. of Thailand, 1967; dir. Lake Superior & Ishpeming R.R.; chmn. Nat. Adv. Council Fin. Aid to Students, 1975. Author numerous articles in field; co-author several books. Bd. dirs. Mich. Joint Council on Econ. Edn., 1977—; trustee Marquette (Mich.) Gen. Hosp.; bd. dirs. Bay Cliff Health Camp, Marquette; mem. Mich. Council for Arts, 1969-73. Served to capt. USAAF, 1942-46. Decorated Order Lion, Finland; recipient City of Peace award, Israel). Mem. Newcomen Soc. N.Am. Home: 2594 Woodhill Dr Box 287 Okemos MI 48864

JANAS, JOHN ALBERT, broadcast company executive; b. Providence, Sept. 8, 1941; s. Joseph and Lillian H. J.; children: Mark, Scott, Craig. A.B. in Econs, Boston Coll., 1963, J.D., 1966. Bar: R.I. 1966, Mass. 1971. Vice-pres. ops., gen. counsel XTRA, Inc., Boston, 1970-73; v.p. consumer products div. Allied Van Lines, Chgo., 1973-77; v.p. media group Rollins, Inc., Atlanta, 1977-83; pres., chief exec. officer Seashell, Inc., Atlanta, 1983—. Served with JAGC U.S. Army, 1966-70. Mem. R.I. Bar Assn., Mass. Bar Assn. Club: Atlanta Sporting. Home: 345 Yellowroot Ln Atlanta GA 30338 Office: 2215 Perimeter Park Suite 6 Atlanta GA 30341

JANATA, RUDOLPH, lawyer; b. Pitts., May 19, 1920; s. Rudolph and Jean (Baker) J.; m. Mary Jean McCally, Mar. 17, 1951; children: Jeffrey Ward, Julie Ellen, David Wells. A.B., U. Pitts., 1941; J.D., Harvard U., 1948. Bar: Ohio 1949. With firm Porter, Wright, Morris & Arthur, Columbus, 1949—. Contbg. author: Personal Injury Litigation in Ohio, 1965, Deposition Strategy, Law and Forms, 1981. Mem. exec. com., bd. dirs. Ohio Citizens Council, 1963-68; chmn. Ohio Com. on Crime and Delinquency, 1963-65; pres. Columbus Area Council Chs., 1958-60; bd. dirs. Columbus Met. YMCA, 1965—, pres., 1973-77; trustee Heidelberg Coll., 1965-75, vice chmn., 1967-74; trustee Ohio Legal Center Inst., 1971-75; chmn. bd. trustees, 1974-75; trustee Nat. Council on Crime and Delinquency, 1962-65; bd. dirs. Def. Research Inst., 1970-77, pres., 1974-75, chmn. bd. dirs., 1975-76. Served to maj. AUS, 1941-46. Recipient Distinguished Service award U.S. Jaycees, 1953. Fellow Am. Bar Found., Ohio State Bar Assn. Found.; mem. Harvard Law Sch. Alumni Assn. Ohio (pres. 1961-62), Harvard Law Sch. Assn. (nat. v.p. 1964-71), Am. Bar Assn., Columbus Bar Assn., Ohio State Bar Assn. (pres. 1972-73), Ohio Def. Assn. (pres. 1967-68), Internat. Assn. Ins. Counsel. Clubs: University (trustee 1961-64, 82—, v.p. 1964), Columbus Country, Crichton, Harvard, Zanesfield Rod and Gun (trustee 1969—), Zanesfield Rod and Gun (pres. 1980-82). Home: 6976 Clark State Rd Blacklick OH 43004 Office: 37 W Broad St Columbus OH 43215

JANDACEK, GEORGE WARREN, petroleum corporation executive; b. Chgo., Sept. 8, 1924; s. George Warren and Margaret (McCormick) J.; m. Patricia Franzen, Jan. 18, 1975; children by previous marriage: James, Jane Ann, Steven. B.S. in Chem. Engring., Northwestern U., 1949. With Universal Oil Products Co., 1949-52, Deep Rock Oil Co., 1952-53; chem. engr. Sunray DX Oil Co., Tulsa, Duncan, Okla., 1953-64, Corpus Christi, Okla.; refinery gen. mgr. Clark Oil & Refining Corp., Blue Island, Ill., 1964-65, v.p. refining, 1966-71, exec. v.p., 1971-74, pres., 1974-78, also dir.; v.p. refining group Tosco Corp., Los Angeles, 1978-79; pres., chief operating officer Crown Central Petroleum Corp., Balt., 1980—. Office: Crown Central Petroleum Corp 1 N Charles St Baltimore MD 21203

JANDL, HENRY ANTHONY, architect, educator; b. Spokane, July, 17, 1910; s. Paul and Marie (Zitterbart) J.; m. Gertrude Ward, June 4, 1940 (dec. 1976); children: Margaret M., H. Ward; m. Nancy Crater, Oct. 2, 1976. Student, Fontainebleau (France) Sch. Fine Arts, 1933; B.Arch., M.Arch., Carnegie Inst. Tech., 1935; M.F.A. in Architecture, Princeton U., 1937; postgrad., Ecole des Beaux Arts, Paris, 1937-39. Faculty Princeton, 1940-43, 45—, prof. architecture, 1957-75, prof. emeritus, 1975—, acting dir., 1964, exec. officer, 1968-74; plant engr. Corning Glass Works, N.Y., 1943-45; pvt. practice architecture, 1943—; Vis. critic U. Va., 1957; cons. architect; cons. on phys. facilities to comdg. gen., Fort Monmouth, N.J., 1966-67; archtl. cons. art and architecture com. Diocese of Trenton. Mem., vice chmn. bd. Environ. Design Rev. for Princeton Twp. John Stewardson fellow, 1933; Whitney Warren fellow, 1937; Recipient Princeton prize, 1935; honor award for design of Princeton Borough Hall N.J. chpt. AIA, 1966. Fellow AIA (pres. Capitol chpt. N.J. 1961-62, James River chpt. 1978—, Coll. of Fellows 1971—); mem. Assn. Collegiate Sch. Architecture, Assn. Princeton Grad. Alumni, Nat. Inst. Archtl. Edn., Alpha Rho Chi (medal for excellence 1935), Phi Kappa Phi, Tau Sigma Delta. Republican. Home: 4311 Coventry Rd Richmond VA 23221

JANDL, JAMES HARRIMAN, physician; b. Racine, Wis., 1925. M.D., Harvard, 1949. Diplomate: Am. Bd. Internal Medicine. Successively intern, asst. resident, research fellow, research asso., asst. physician, asso. physician, dir. Thorndike Meml. Lab.; asso. vis. physician, physician, dir. Harvard Med. unit Boston City Hosp., 1961—; physician Beth Israel Hosp., 1975—; mem. faculty Harvard Med. Sch., 1952—, asso. prof. medicine, 1964-68, prof. medicine, 1968—, George R. Minot prof. medicine, 1968—; vis. prof. Mass. Inst. Tech., 1973-74. Served with USNR, 1950-52. Mem. Am. Fedn. Clin. Research, Am. Soc. Clin. Investigation, Assn. Am. Physicians. Home: 816 Lowell Rd Concord MA 01742 Office: Harvard Med Sch 25 Shattuck St Bldg E-2 Boston MA 02115

JANELLI, DONALD ERNEST, surgeon; b. N.Y.C., Dec. 4, 1920; s. Ernest and Helen May (Pettengill) J.; m. Gloria Patricia Enge, Aug. 30, 1943; children: Jeffrey Donald, Chris Pettengill, Bruce Drury. B.A., Columbia, 1942; M.D., N.Y. Med. Coll., 1945; M.S. in Surgery, N.Y. U., 1953. Diplomate: Am. Bd. Surgery. Intern Jersey City Med. Center, 1945-46; resident Nassau Hosp., Mineola, N.Y., 1948-52; practice medicine, specializing in surgery, Williston Park, N.Y., 1952-70, Mineola, 1970—; chief surgery Nassau Hosp., 1970-79, emeritus chief, cons. in surgery, 1979—; prof. clin. surgery SUNY, Stony Brook, 1973—, exec. dep. for clin. affiliations, 1979—, exec. com. faculty senate, 1979—; cons. in surgery Nassau County (N.Y.) Med. Center, East Meadow, St. Francis Hosp., Roslyn, N.Y., VA Hosp., Northport, N.Y.; vis prof. U. Santo Tomas, Manila, 1975. Editorial bd.: Internat. Surgery, 1979—; contbr. numerous articles to profl. jours. Bd. dirs. L.I. div. Am. Cancer Soc., 1979-82. Served to capt. as flight surgeon M.C. USAAF, 1946-48. Fellow A.C.S. (liaison fellow N.Y. State Commn. on Cancer 1970—, dir. Bklyn. chpt. 1979—), Internat. Coll. Surgeons (internat. exec. council 1979-81, treas. internat. exec. com. 1981-83), Nassau Acad. Medicine (founding), Royal Soc. Medicine (London) (affiliate); mem. Nassau County, N.Y. State med. socs., Nassau Surg. Soc., AMA. Episcopalian. Club: The Creek. Home: The Creek Locust Valley NY 11560 Office: 222 Front St Mineola NY 11501

JANENSCH, PAUL, newspaper editor; b. Evanston, Ill., Nov. 26, 1938; s. Carl Paul and Ruth Ann (Enright) J.; m. Gail Alice Evans, Feb. 1, 1969; children—Laurel Ann, William Paul, Michael Fritz. A.B., Georgetown U., 1960; M.S. in Journalism, Columbia U., 1964. Salesman Procter & Gamble Co., Chgo., 1960-61; reporter City News Bur., Chgo., 1961-62, UPI, 1962-63; successively reporter, Washington corr., city editor Louisville Courier-Jour., 1964-72; publisher Pollution Abstracts, Inc., San Diego, 1972-75; mng. editor Phila. Daily News, 1975-76, Louisville Times, 1976-78, Louisville Courier-Jour., 1978-79; exec. editor Louisville Courier-Jour., also Louisville Times, 1979—. Mem. AP Mng. Editors Assn., Am. Soc. Newspaper Editors. Democrat. Roman Catholic. Office: 525 W Broadway Louisville KY 40202

JANES, G(EORGE) SARGENT, physicist; b. Bklyn., Apr. 12, 1927; s. Warham W. and George Sargent (Leubuscher) J.; m. Ann P. Brown, June 29, 1952; children: William, Thomas, Catherine, George, Susan. B.A., Cornell U., 1949; Ph.D., M.I.T., 1953. Mem. research staff nuclear sci. div. Indsl. Coop, M.I.T., 1953-56; prin. research scientist Avco Everett Research Lab., Everett, Mass., 1956-74, v.p. isotope research, 1974-82, dir. laser isotope research program, 1974-81, dir. liquid dye laser research, 1983—; v.p. research Jersey Nuclear Avco Isotopes, Inc.; mem. adv. com. M.I.T. Regional Laser Center, 1981—; assoc. Woods Hole Oceanographic Inst., 1983. Contbr. articles to profl. jours. Trustee Valley Pond Realty Trust, Lincoln, Mass. Fellow Am. Phys. Soc., AIAA (assoc.); mem. Sigma Xi. Club: Appalachian Mountain (past governing council). Patentee in field. Co-inventor atomic vapor laser isotope separation process for enrichment of uranium light water nuclear reactor fuel. Home: Conant Rd Lincoln MA 01773 Office: Avco Everett Research Lab 2385 Revere Beach Pkwy Everett MA 02149

JANESS, RONALD A., business executive; b. Chgo., May 24, 1946; s. C.O. and Geneviev (Mossman) J.; m. Tamara L. Janess, Apr. 22, 1972; children: Shannel, Matthew. A.A., Foothill Coll., 1968; B.S., Chico State U., 1969. Cert., secondary sch. tchr., Calif. Dist. mgr. CP Nat. Corp., Westwood, Calif., 1974, dir. telephone ops., San Francisco, 1975-79, assoc. v.p. adminstr., 1979, v.p. gas, Concord, Calif., 1980-82, exec. v.p., 1982—, now. pres. regulated ops. Served USAR, 1971-77. Mem. Am. Gas Assn., Pacific Central Gas Assn. Home: 566 Webster Dr Martinez CA 94553 Office: CP Nat Corp 1355 Willow Way Concord CA 94520

JANEWAY, ELIOT, economist; b. N.Y.C., Jan. 1, 1913; s. Meyer Joseph and Fanny (Siff) J.; m. Elizabeth Hall, Oct. 29, 1938;

children—Michael, William. Ed., Cornell, 1932; grad. student, London Sch. Econs. Bus. editor Time mag., N.Y.C.; adviser to editor-in-chief Time, Inc.; bus. trends cons. Newsweek mag.; econ. adviser numerous industries; pub. Janeway Letter; pres., dir. Janeway Pub. & Research Corp. Author: The Struggle for Survival, 1951, reissue, 1968, The Economics of Crisis, 1968, What Shall I Do With My Money?, 1970, You and Your Money, 1972, Musings on Money, 1976. Berkeley fellow Yale U. Address: 15 E 80th St New York NY 10021

JANEWAY, ELIZABETH HALL, author; b. Bklyn., Oct. 7, 1913; d. Charles H. and Jeannette F. (Searle) Hall; m. Eliot Janeway; children: Michael, William. Student, Swarthmore Coll.; A.B., Barnard Coll., 1935; Ph.D. in Lit. (hon.), Simpson Coll., Cedarcrest Coll., Villa Maria Coll.; L.H.D., Russell Sage Coll., 1981. Asso. fellow Yale. Author: The Walsh Girls, 1943, Daisy Kenyon, 1945, The Question of Gregory, 1949, The Vikings, 1951, Leaving Home, 1953, Early Days of the Automobile, 1956, The Third Choice, 1959, Angry Kate, 1963, Accident, 1964, Ivanov Seven, 1967, Man's World, Woman's Place, 1971, Between Myth and Morning: Women Awakening, 1974, Powers of the Weak, 1980, Cross Sections: From a Decade of Change, 1982; contbr. to: Comprehensive Textbook of Psychiatry, 2d edit, 1980, Harvard Guide to Contemporary American Writing, 1979, also short stories and critical writing in periodicals and newspapers. Trustee Barnard Coll. Recipient educator's award Delta Kappa Gamma, 1972; named Disting. Alumna Barnard Coll., 1979; recipient Medal of Distinction, 1981. Mem. Authors Guild (council), Authors League Am. (council), PEN, Phi Beta Kappa (hon.). Home: 15 E 80th St New York NY 10021

JANEWAY, MICHAEL CHARLES, editor; b. N.Y.C., May 31, 1940; s. Eliot and Elizabeth Ames (Hall) J.; m. Mary Struthers Pinkham, Dec. 18, 1965; children: Samuel Struthers, Mary Warwick. B.A., Harvard, 1962. Reporter Newsday, Garden City, N.Y., 1963; writer, editor Newsweek, N.Y.C., 1964; asso. editor The New Leader, 1965; editor The Atlantic, Boston, 1966-70, mng. editor, 1970-76, exec. editor, 1976-77; spl. asst. to Sec. State, Washington, 1977-78; editor Sunday mag. Boston Globe, 1978-81, asst. mng. editor, 1981-82, mng. editor, 1982—. Co-editor: Who We Are: An Atlantic Chronicle of the United States and Vietnam, 1969; Contbr. numerous articles, revs. to publs. Served with AUS, 1963-64. Shaw Travelling fellow Harvard, 1962-63. Mem. Phi Beta Kappa. Home: 21 Buckingham St Cambridge MA 02138 Office: Boston Globe Boston MA 02107

JANEWAY, RICHARD, medical college dean; b. Los Angeles, Feb. 12, 1933; s. VanZandt and Grace Eleanor (Bell) J.; m. Katherine Esmond Pillsbury, Dec. 23, 1955; children—Susan Kent, David VanZandt, Elizabeth Anne. A.B., Colgate U., 1954; M.D., U. Pa., 1958. Diplomate: Am. Bd. Psychiatry and Neurology. Intern Hosp. U. Pa., 1958-59; resident N.C. Baptist Hosp., Winston—Salem, 1963-66; practice medicine specializing in neurology, Winston-Salem, 1966—; mem. faculty Bowman Gray Sch. Medicine, Wake Forest U., Winston-Salem, 1966—, prof. neurology, 1971—, dir., 1969-71, dean Sch., 1971—; v.p. health affairs Wake Forest U., 1983—; dir. Forsyth Bank and Trust, 1973-83, mem. loan and investment com., 1973-82, chmn. personnel and compensation com., 1973-82, mem. exec. com., 1978-82; dir., chmn., mem. exec. com. So. Nat. Bank, Winston-Salem, 1982—; Mem. spl. task force on arteriosclerosis Nat. Heart and Lung Inst., 1971, joint com. for stroke facilities, 1969-72; mem. nat. adv. council regional med. programs HEW, 1974—; mem. N.C. Bd. Human Resources, 1975-77; Mem. adv. com. undergrad. med. evaluation Nat. Bd. Med. Examiners, 1974, chmn., 1979—, mem. at large, 1979—, mem. com. on coms., 1981—, mem. fin. com., 1981—; mem. N.C. Joint Conf. Com. on Med. Care, Inc., 1983—. Mem. personnel com. Winston-Salem/Forsyth County Bd. Edn., 1970-73, mem. policy com., 1970-73, chmn. policy com., 1972-73. Served to capt. USAF, 1959-63. USPHS fellow, 1956; Markle scholar, 1968-73. Fellow ACP, Am. Acad. Neurology; mem. Am. Neurol. Assn., Am. Heart Assn. (fellow council on stroke), AAAS, AMA, Assn. Am. Med. Colls. (council of deans adminstrv. bd. 1977—, exec. council 1977—, mem. liaison com. on grad. med. edn. 1978-80, accreditation council on grad. med. edn. 1981—, chmn. council of deans 1982-83, exec. com. 1982—), Am. Clin. and Climatol. Assn., Acad. Mgmt., Soc. Neurosci., Inst. Medicine of Nat. Acad. Scis., Phi Beta Kappa, Alpha Omega Alpha. Clubs: Rotary (dir. 1977-80, v.p. 1981-82), Rotary (pres. 1982-83), Rotary (chmn. nominating com. 1983-84), Cosmos). Home: 2815 Country Club Rd Winston-Salem NC 27104

JANGAARD, NORMAN OLAF, brewing company executive; b. Seattle, Oct. 11, 1941; s. Olaf Anders and Emilia (Pierog) J.; m. Brenda Lee Benson, June 30, 1963; children: Lisa Carol, Amanda Lee. A.B. in Life Scis., San Diego State Coll., 1962; Ph.D. in Biochemistry, UCLA, 1966; J.D., U. Denver, 1976. Bar: Colo. 1976. Research scientist Pfizer, Inc., Groton, Conn., 1966-68, Shell Devel. Co., Modesto, Calif., 1968-72; v.p. various engring. research and devel. Adolph Coors Co., Golden, Colo., 1972-82, v.p. prodn., 1982-83, v.p. biotech., 1983—; dir. Coors Food Products Co., Golden, 1979-82; mem. sci. adv. com. U.S. Brewers Assn., Washington, 1976-82. Contbr. articles on brewing to profl. jours. Active Wilderness Soc., Denver, 1982—; trustee Jefferson County Unit-Am. Cancer Soc., Denver, 1979-81. Mem. Am. Soc. Brewing Chemists, Muster Brewers Assn. Am., Inst. Food Technologists, Am. Chem. Soc., Am. Assn. Cereal Chemists, ABA, Denver C. of C. (participant leadership Denver 1979, mem. energy and environ. com. 1980-82), Phi Kappa Alpha. Republican. Lutheran. Home: 7647 Bear Mountain Littleton CO 80127 Office: Adolph Coors Co Dept 903 Golden CO 80401

JANICH, GEORGE PETER, ins. co. exec.; b. Long Beach, Calif., May 14, 1929; s. Peter Paul and Maria J.; m. Angelina Chernoff, Aug. 16, 1953; children—Michael, Steven, Gary. B.B.A., Woodbury Coll., Los Angeles. With claims dept. Travelers Ins. Co., Long Beach, 1956-59, Indsl. Indemnity Co., 1959-62; with Fremont Indemnity Co., Los Angeles, 1962—, now sr. v.p. claims. Served with AUS, 1952-54. Mem. Pacific Claim Execs. Assn. (pres. 1981), Assn. Calif. Ins. Cos. (chmn. workers compensation com. 1981), Calif. Workers Compensation Inst. (past chmn. claims com.). Office: 1709 W 8th St Los Angeles CA 90017

JANICKI, ROBERT STEPHEN, pharmaceutical company executive; b. Manette, Wash., Dec. 7, 1934; s. Stephen Walter and Elizabeth Caroline (Gorman) J.; m. I. Jane Betcher, Aug. 18, 1956; children: Robert, Beth, David. B.S., Grove City Coll., 1956; M.D., Temple U., 1961. Diplomate: Nat. Bd. Med. Examiners. Intern U.S. Naval Hosp., Phila., 1961-62, resident in occupational medicine, 1962-63; asso. dir. clin. research Dow Pharms., Indpls., 1966-68; asso. med. dir. Neisler div. Union Carbide Corp., Sterling Forest, N.Y., 1968-69; asso. med. dir. regulatory affairs Abbott Labs., North Chicago, Ill., 1969-70, dir. clin. research pharm. products div., 1970-71, v.p. med. affairs pharm. products div., 1971-79, v.p. research pharm. products div., 1979-83, corp. v.p. research and devel. Pharm. Products div., 1983—. Contbr. articles profl. to jours. Served to lt. comdr., M.C. USN, 1961-66. Mem. Marion County (Ind.) Med. Soc., Am. Soc. Clin. Pharmacology and Therapeutics, Inst. Medicine Chgo., Alpha Omega Alpha. Home: 801 Hawthorne Ln Libertyville IL 60048 Office: Abbott Laboratories Abbott Park North Chicago IL 60064

JANIS, ALLEN IRA, physics educator; b. Chgo., Sept. 11, 1930; s. David M. and Rosa (Ginsburg) J.; m. Phyllis Meyer, Sept. 6, 1953; children: Stuart, Wynne. B.S., Northwestern U., 1951; postgrad., Cornell U., Ithaca, N.Y., 1951-53; Ph.D., Syracuse U., 1957. Faculty U. Pitts., 1957—, asso. prof. physics, 1963-68, prof., 1968—, sr. research asso. Philos. Sci. Center, 1967-75, asso. dir. Philos. Sci. Center, 1975—. Mem. Fedn. Am. Scientists (sec. 1964-65), Am. Phys. Soc., Am. Assn. Physics Tchrs., AAAS, AAUP, Philosophy of Sci. Assn. Home: 425 Garden City Dr Monroeville PA 15146 Office: Dept Physics Univ Pitts Pittsburgh PA 15260

JANIS, BYRON, concert pianist; b. McKeeport, Pa., Mar. 24, 1928; s. Samuel and Hattie (Horelick) Yanks; m. June Dickson-Wright, Nov. 30, 1953 (div. Aug. 1965); 1 son, Stefan; m. Maria Cooper, Apr. 11, 1966. Pvt. student, Josef and Rosina Lhevinne, Adele Marcus and Vladimir Horowitz. Debut, Carnegie Hall, N.Y.C., 1948; European debut, Concertgebouw Orch., Amsterdam, 1952; represented U.S. at, Brussels World Fair, 1958; tours, N.Am. and S.Am., 1947—; 1st Am. sent in cultural exchange with USSR, 1960, 62; soloist major Am. orchs., 1948—; rec. artist, Mercury, R.C.A Victor, Phillips; TV film: A Portrait of Fredrick Chopin, 1975. Decorated chevalier L'Ordre Des Artes et Lettres, France; recipient Grand Prix du Disque, 1962; Harriet Cohen Internat. Music award; Beethoven medal, 1962. Mem. Friends of Chopin in Paris (pres.). Discoverer 2 unknown Chopin waltz manuscripts in Chateau Thoiry, France, 1968; uncovered 2 additional versions of same waltzes at Yale U., 1970. Address: care ICM Artists Ltd 40 W 57th St New York NY 10019

JANIS, CONRAD, actor, jazz musician, art dealer; b. N.Y.C., Feb. 11; s. Sidney and Harriet J.; m. Ronda Copland, Apr. 22, 1979 (div. Apr. 1982); children from previous marriage: Christopher, Carin. Appeared in: numerous Broadway plays including Junior Miss, 1942, Dark of the Moon, 1945, Time Out for Ginger, 1952, Visit to a Small Planet, 1957, Sunday in New York, 1961, Marathon '33, 1963, The Front Page, 1969, Same Time Next Year, 1975-76; films include Snafu, 1945, Margie, 1946, That Hagen Girl, 1947, Airport '75, The Buddy Holly Story, 1977, Roseland, 1977, Oh God, Oh God, 1979; appeared in: over 200 major network TV shows from Suspense, 1950 to St. Elsewhere, 1984; numerous TV movies; appears in: TV series Mork and Mindy in role of Frederick, 1978-82; leader jazz group, 1951—; appeared in major jazz clubs, throughout US, concerts at, N.Y. Carnegie Hall, Town Hall, Phila. Acad. Music and, TV shows; jazz trombonist with jazz artists, Roy Eldredge, Coleman Hawkins, Bud Freeman, Bobby Hackett, Hot Lips Page, Wild Bill Davison; leader, Beverly Hills Unlisted Jazz Band, 1978—, numerous recs. for many jazz labels; co-dir., Sidney Janis Gallery, N.Y.C. Recipient Theatre World award, 1952; named to Playboy Jazz Poll, 1960, 61; Silver Theatre award, 1950. Mem. Actors Equity Assn., Screen Actors Guild, AFTRA, Am. Fedn. Musicians. Club: Nautico (Bilbao, Spain).

JANIS, DONALD LEON, lawyer, former security company executive; b. New Britain, Conn., Dec. 25, 1931; s. Stanley and Nellie (Story) J; m. Ethel Mildred Smith, June 21, 1958; children: Stephen Smith, Timothy Hill, Peter Bartley. A.B., Boston U., 1953; M.A., U. Conn., 1958; J.D., U. Chgo., 1961. Bar: N.Y. 1961. Asso. firm Cravath, Swaine & Moore, N.Y.C., 1961-65; asst. gen. counsel Indian Head, Inc., N.Y.C., 1965-68; v.p. adminstrn. Informations Handling Services Inc., Englewood, Colo., 1968-70; exec. v.p., sec., gen. counsel Burns Internat. Security Services, Inc., Briarcliff Manor, N.Y., 1970-82, also dir., mem. exec. com.; dir. Seguridad Burns de Colombia S.A.; mng. dir. Burns Internat. Security Services (U.K.) Ltd., Willburns Assurance Co. Ltd., Bermuda. Coach Pickwick League Football.; mem. Parents' adv. council Hamilton Coll.; mem. nat. alumni council Boston U. Served with AUS, 1955-56. Named to Boston U. Collegium Disting. Alumni. Mem. Assn. Bar City N.Y. (mem. com. legal aid 1966-69, com. on corp. law depts. 1972-75), ABA, N.Y. State Bar Assns. (com. on SEC fin. and corp. law governance), Westchester County Bar Assn., Westchester-Fairfield County Lawyers Assn., Com. Nat. Securities Cos. (vice chmn. 1973, chmn. 1974), Am. Soc. Indsl. Security (vice chmn. pvt. security services council), N.E. Greenwich Assn. (pres., dir.), Nat. Council Investigation and Security Services (v.p., dir.-at-large), Am. Soc. Corp. Secs. Clubs: Greenwich Country (Conn.); University (N.Y.C.). Home: 150 Parsonage Rd Greenwich CT 06830

JANIS, IRVING LESTER, psychology educator; b. Buffalo, May 26, 1918; s. M. Martin and Etta (Goldstein) J.; m. Marjorie Graham, Sept. 5, 1939; children: Cathy Wheeler, Charlotte. B.S., U. Chgo., 1939; Ph.D. in Psychology, Columbia, 1948. Research asst., exptl. div. study war time communications Library of Congress, 1941; sr. social sci. analyst, spl. war policies unit Dept. Justice, 1941-43; research asso., spl. com. Social Sci. Research Council, 1945-46, research fellow, 1946-47; mem. faculty Yale, 1947—, prof. psychology, 1960—; Research cons. RAND Corp., 1948-74; mem. panel social psychol. research NSF, 1965-66; mem. com. disaster studies NRC-Nat. Acad. Scis., 1953-57; mem. Surgeon Gen.'s Sci. Adv. Com. on TV and Social Behavior, 1969-71. Author: Air War and Emotional Stress, 1951, (with Hovland and Kelley) Communication and Persuasion, 1953, Psychological Stress, 1958, (with others) Personality and Persuasibility, 1959, Stress and Frustration, 1971, Victims of Groupthink, 1972, (with L. Mann) Decision Making, 1977, (with D. Wheeler) A Practical Guide for Making Decisions, 1980, (with others) Counseling on Personal Decisions: Theory and Research on Short-term Helping Relationships, 1982; Group Think, 1983; author Stress, Attitudes and Decisions: Selected Papers (Centennial Psychology Series); Author also articles, chpts. in books.; Editor: Current Trends in Psychology: Readings from American Scientist, 1977; contbg. editor: Jour. Abnormal and Social Psychology, 1955-65; mem. editorial bd.: Jour. Exptl. Social Psychology, 1966-70, Am. Scientist, 1970-79, Jour. Behavioral Medicine, 1978—, Brit. Jour. Social Psychology, 1980—; chmn. editorial bd.: Jour. Conflict Resolution, 1972—. Served with AUS, 1943-45. Recipient Hofheimer prize Am. Psychiat. Assn., 1959; Socio-Psychol. prize AAAS, 1967; Fulbright Research fellow, 1957-58; Sr. Faculty fellow Yale, 1961-62, 69-70; Faculty Research fellow Social Sci. Research Council, 1961-62, 66-67; Guggenheim fellow, also fellow Center Advanced Study Behavioral Scis., 1973-74; research fellow Netherlands Inst. Advanced Studies, 1981-82. Fellow Am. Acad. Arts and Scis.; mem. Am. Psychol. Assn. (rep. on council AAAS 1965-70, Disting. Sci. Contbn. award 1981), AAAS (judge sociol-psychol. prize 1963-64). Home: 1205 Race Brook Rd Woodbridge CT 06525 Office: Dept Psychology Yale Univ 2 Hillhouse Ave New Haven CT 06510

JANIS, JAY, banker, savs. and loan assn. exec., former govt. ofcl.; b. Los Angeles, Dec. 22, 1932; s. Ernest and Diana (Friedman) J.; m. Juel Mendelsohn, 1954; children—Laura, Jeffrey. A.B. with high honors, Yale U., 1954. Partner, community developer Janis Corp. (named changed to MGIC-Janis Properties 1970) and related cos. in pvt. bldg. industry), South Fla., 1956-64, 69-75; with Dept. Commerce, Washington, 1964-66, exec. dir. nat. citizens' com., community relations service, 1964-65; dir. OEO, spl. asst. to under sec. Commerce, 1965-66; exec. asst. to sec. HUD, Washington, 1966-69, under sec., 1977-79; chmn. Fed. Home Loan Bank Bd., Washington, 1979-80; pres. Calif. Fed. Savs. and Loan Assn., Los Angeles, 1981—; sr. v.p. for mgmt. and bus. affairs U. Mass., 1976-77; former prin. housing adviser to gov. Fla.; former bd. dirs. Nat. Assn. Home Builders, Nat. Com. against Discrimination in Housing; former mediator labor disputes in constrn. industry. Past pres. bd. trustees Fla. Internat. Univ. Found., Miami. Served with Intelligence Corps U.S. Army, 1954-56

JANIS, SIDNEY, art dealer, author; b. Buffalo, July 8, 1896; s. Isaac and Celia (Cohn) J.; m. Harriet Grossman, Sept. 2, 1925; children: Conrad, Carroll. Student pub., tech. and aero. schs. Engaged in mfg., 1924-39, collector modern art, 1925—; owner Janis Gallery, N.Y.C., 1948—; Mem. adv. com. Mus. Modern Art, N.Y.C., 1933-48; mem. art panel IRS, Washington, 1975-76. Author: They Taught Themselves, 1942, Abstract and Surrealist Art in America, 1944, (with Harriet Janis) Picasso: Recent Years, 1946; also articles in art jours., 1941. Hon. trustee Mus. Modern Art N.Y., 1983—. Mem. Art Dealers Assn. Am. Donated Sidney and Harriet Janis collection 20th Century Art to Mus. Modern Art, N.Y.C., 1967, also Living Legend, N.Y. U. Sch. Social Work, 1979. Address: 110 W 57th St New York NY 10019

JANISCH, ANDREW, petroleum and natural gas co. exec.; b. Wallern, Austria, Nov. 7, 1931; emigrated to Can., 1934, naturalized, 1954; s. Joseph and Anna (Summer) J.; m. Jessie Patterson Dickson, Aug. 23, 1953; children—Stephen Alexander, Gregory Joseph, Mark Richard, Matthew Lawrence. B.Sc.C.E., U. Man., Can., 1953. With Can. Gulf Oil Co. (later Gulf Oil Can. Ltd.), 1953-74, mgr. prodn., Toronto, Ont., 1971-74; v.p., gen. mgr. Gulf Minerals Can. Ltd., Toronto, 1974-75, pres., 1975-77; sr. v.p. Petro-Can., Calgary, Alta., Can., 1977-79, pres., chief operating officer, 1979—, also dir.; dir. Panarctic Oils Ltd. Mem. Alta. Assn. Profl. Engrs. and Geologists, Alta.-N.W. Chamber of Mines, Soc. Petroleum Engrs., Am. Petroleum Inst., Calgary C. of C., Can. Inst. Mining and Metallurgy. Clubs: Engrs. (Toronto); Calgary Petroleum. *

JANKLOW, MORTON LLOYD, lawyer, literary agent; b. N.Y.C., May 30, 1930; s. Maurice and Lillian (Levantin) J.; m. Linda Mervyn LeRoy, Nov. 27, 1960; children: Angela LeRoy, Lucas Warner. A.B., Syracuse U., 1950; J.D., Columbia U., 1953. Bar: N.Y. 1953, D.C. 1959, U.S. Supreme Ct 1959. Sr. partner firm Janklow & Traum, N.Y.C., 1967—; chmn., chief exec. officer Morton L. Janklow Assocs., Inc. (lit. agy.), 1977—; Dir. Children's Television Workshop Prodns., Inc., N.Y.C.; dir., mem. finance com. McCaffrey & McCall, Inc., N.Y.C.; chmn. exec. com. Harvey Group, Inc., N.Y.C., 1968-71, Cable Funding Corp., 1971-73; mem. exec. com. Sloan Commn. Cable Communications, 1970-71; Andrew Wellington Cordier fellow Columbia U. Sch. Internat. Affairs; vis. lectr. Radcliffe Coll., Columbia Law Sch., NYU; bus. and fin. adv. bd. N.Y. U. Press and N.Y. U. Sch. Arts, 1977—. Bd. dirs., exec. com., devel. chmn. City Center Music and Drama, 1971-75; bd. dirs. Film Soc., Lincoln Center, 1972-75, Am. Cinematheque, 1971—; bd. govs. Jewish Mus., 1969-75; trustee Mr. and Mrs. Harry M. Warner Found., 1965—; mem. Council of Friends, Whitney Mus. Am. Art, 1973-82, also mem. com. on paintings and sculptures; adv. bd. Guggenheim Mus.; adv. council Sch. Arts, N.Y. U. Served with AUS, 1953-55. Mem. Assn. Bar City N.Y. (membership com. 1967—), N.Y. County Lawyers Assn., N.Y. State, Am., Fed. Communications bar assns., Am. Judicature Soc., Council on Fgn. Relations. Home: 32 E 64th St New York NY 10021 Office: 598 Madison Ave New York NY 10022

JANKLOW, WILLIAM JOHN, gov. S.D.; b. Chgo., Sept. 13, 1939; s. Arthur W. and LouElla Bernice (Gulbranson) J.; m. Mary Dean Thom, Sept. 3, 1960; children—Russell, Pam, Shonna. B.S.B.A., U. S.D., 1964, J.D., 1966. Bar: S.D. bar 1966, U.S. Supreme Ct. bar 1970. Staff atty. S.D. Legal Services, 1966-67, directing atty., chief officer, 1967-72; chief trial atty. S.D. Atty. Gen's Office, Pierre, 1973-74, atty. gen., 1975-78; gov., S.D., 1979—; lectr. in field. Bd. dirs. Nat. Legal Services Corp. Served with USMC, 1956-59. Recipient Nat. award for legal excellence and skill Nat. Legal Aid and Defenders Assn., 1968. Mem. Nat. Assn. Attys. Gen., Am., S.D. trial lawyers assns., Am. Judicature Soc. Republican. Lutheran. Office: State Capitol Bldg Pierre SD 57501

JANKOWSKI, GENE F., broadcasting executive; b. Buffalo, May 21, 1934; s. Walter and Mary (Talarczyk) J.; m. Sally Ritzenthaler, 1961; 4 children. B.S., Canisius Coll.; M. Communication Arts, Mich. State U., H.H.D. (hon.). Account exec. CBS Radio network sales, 1961-66; Eastern sales mgr. CBS Radio, 1966-69; account exec. CBS-TV network sales, 1969-70; gen. sales mgr. Sta. WCBS-TV, N.Y.C., 1970-71, dir. sales, 1971-73; v.p. sales CBS-TV stas., N.Y.C., 1973-74, v.p. fin. and planning, 1974-76; v.p., controller CBS Inc., 1976, v.p. adminstrn., 1977; exec. v.p. CBS Broadcast Group, 1977, pres., 1977—. Trustee Canisius Coll., Buffalo. Served with USN, 1955-58. Recipient Disting. Communications medal So. Baptist Radio and TV Commn., 1983. Mem. Nat. Acad. TV Arts and Scis., Internat. Radio and TV Execs. Soc., Am. Film Inst. (trustee). Office: 51 W 52d St New York NY 10019

JANKURA, DONALD EUGENE, hotel executive; b. Bridgeport, Conn., Dec. 20, 1929; s. Stephen and Susan (Dirga) J.; m. Elizabeth Deborah Joynt, June 20, 1952; children: Donald Eugene, Stephen J., Daria E., Diane E., Lynn M. B.A., Mich. State U., 1951. Asst. sales mgr. Pick Fort Shelby Hotel, Detroit, 1951-53; steward Dearborn Inn and Colonial Homes, Dearborn, Mich., 1953-54, sales mgr., 1954-60, resident mgr., 1960-62; gen. mgr. Stouffer's Northland Inn, Southfield, Mich., 1962-64; staff adv. Stouffer Motor Inns, Cleve., 1964-66, v.p., 1966-68, Asso. Inns & Restaurants Co. Am., Denver, 1968-76, exec. v.p., 1976-81, sr. v.p., 1981—; guest lectr. Mich. State U., 1964, Fla. Internat. U., 1968, Cornell U., 1983. Mem. Am. Hotel and Motel Assn. (dir. 1978-80, vice chmn. industry adv. council 1980-81, sec.-treas. 1985), Colo./Wyo. Hotel and Motel Assn., Hotel Sales Mgmt. Assn., Denver C. of C., Phi Kappa Tau. Episcopalian. Clubs: Pinery Country, Masons, Shriners. Home: 7445 Windlawn Way Parker CO 80134 Office: Asso Inns and Restaurants Co Am 4552 S Quebec St Denver CO 80237

JANNARONE, JOHN ROBERT, retired utility exec., former army officer; b. Newark, July 3, 1914; s. Charles and Concetta (Caruso) J.; m. Anna May Miller, Nov. 22, 1941; children: Jack Miller, Robert Neil, Richard Thomas, Dorothy Ann, Nancy May. Student, Montclair State Coll., 1932-34; B.S., U.S. Mil. Acad., 1938; M.S., Calif. Inst. Tech., 1951; C.E., Columbia U., 1962. Commd. 2d lt. C.E. U.S. Army, 1938, advanced through grades to brig. gen., 1965; comdg. officer 293d Engr. Combat Bn., 1943, asst. engr. 8th Army, 1944-45; spl. asst. to comdg. gen. Manhattan Project, 1945-47; dep. dist. engr., Los Angeles, 1951-52; dir. C.E. Ark.-White-Red River Basins Planning Office, 1952-55; chief program rev. and analysis sect. Office Chief Staff, 1956-57; asst. prof. physics U.S. Mil. Acad., West Point, N.Y., 1947-50, prof., 1957-65, dean acad. bd., 1965-73; v.p. Consol. Edison Co., N.Y.C., 1973—79. Decorated Legion of Merit, Bronze Star medal, D.S.M. Fellow ASCE; mem. Am. Soc. Engring. Edn., Regional Plan Assn. (dir.), Soc. Am. Mil. Engrs. Home: 22 Woodland Ave Ridgewood NJ 07450

JANNETTA, PETER JOSEPH, neurosurgeon; b. Phila., Apr. 5, 1932; s. Samuel and Frances (Alfano) J.; m. Ann Bowman, June 23, 1954; children: Susan, Carol, Joanne, Peter, Elizabeth, Samuel Michael. A.B., U. Pa., 1953, M.D., 1957. Diplomate: Am. Bd. Surgery, Am. Bd. Neurol. Surgery. Intern Hosp. U. Pa., 1957-58, resident in surgery, 1958-63; resident in neurosurgery, asso. UCLA Center for Health Scis., 1963-66; asst. instr. U. Pa., 1958-62, instr., 1960-63, instr. surgery, 1962-63; asso. prof., chmn. surgery La. State U., 1966-71, prof., chmn. surgery, 1971; prof. U. Pitts., 1971-76, Francis Sergeant Cheever Disting. prof., 1976—, chmn. dept. neurol. surgery, 1973—, dir. div. neurol. surgery, 1971-73; active staff Presbyn.-Univ. Hosp.,

Pitts., Children's Hosp. Pitts.; sr. attending staff Montefiore Hosp., Pitts.; sr. cons. VA Hosp., Pitts. Co-editor: The Cranial Nerves, 1981; Contbr. numerous articles to profl. jours. Mem. A.C.S., AMA, AAAS, Am. Surg. Assn., Allegheny County, Pa. med. socs., Assn. Academic Surgery, Am. Assn. Neurol. Surgeons, Congress Neurol. Surgeons, Fellowship Acad. Neurosurgeons, Internat. Assn. Study Pain, Internat. Soc. Pediatric Neurosurgery, Mid-Atlantic, Pa., Pitts. neurosurg. socs., N.Y. Acad. Scis., Pitts. Acad. Medicine, Pitts. Surg. Soc., Ravdin-Rhoads Surg. Soc., Research Soc. Neurol. Surgeons, Soc. Critical Care Medicine, Soc. Neurol. Surgeons, Soc. Neurosci., Soc. Neurosurg. Anesthesia and Neurol. Supportive Care. Home: 1269 Murray Hill Ave Pittsburgh PA 15217 Office: Dept Neurol Surgery U Pitts Pittsburgh PA 15261

JANNING, MARY BERNADETTE, nun, association executive; b. Custer City, Okla., May 20, 1917; d. Frank R. and Mary Elizabeth (Kreizenbeck) J. R.N., St. Francis Hosp. Sch. Nursing, Wichita, Kans., 1942; B.S. in Nursing Edn, Marquette U., 1951, M.S., 19S2; postgrad., George Washington U., 1972. Joined Sisters of Sorrowful Mother, 1935; asst. dir. St. Johns Sch. Nursing, Tulsa, 1952-56; dir. St. Francis Sch. Nursing, Wichita, 1956-65; provincial superior Tulsa Province, Sisters of Sorrowful Mother, 1965-70; asso. adminstr. St. Francis Hosp., Wichita, 1972-73, pres., chief exec. officer, dir., 1973-79; exec. dir. Franciscan Villa, Inc., Broken Arrow, Okla., 1979-80, Okla. Cath. Health Conf., 1980—. Author: Life of a Student Nurse, 1961. Chmn. bd. Kans. affiliate Am. Diabetes Assn., 1974; sec. bd. dirs. Midway Kans. chpt. ARC, 1974—, pres., 1979; chmn. Mid-Central Kans.; adv. bd. KBEZ Stereo 93, Tulsa, Okla., 1982-83. Recipient Twenty-Year Pin award ARC, 1962; Alumni Nurse of Year award St. Francis Sch. Nursing, 1972. Fellow Am. Coll. Hosp. Adminstrs.; mem. Am. Hosp. Assn., Kans. Hosp. Assn. (dir.), Catholic Hosp. Assn., Nat., Kans. leagues nursing, Kans. Hosp. Assn., Kans. Conf. Cath. Health Affairs (pres. 1977), Hosp. Council Met. Wichita, Wichita Hosp. Adminstrs. Office: 17600 E 51st St Broken Arrow OK 74012

JANOFSKY, LEONARD S., lawyer, assn. exec.; b. Los Angeles, Oct. 13, 1909; s. E. and Ida (Schwartz) J.; m. Nancy Nielson, Dec. 29, 1948; children—Annelies Irene Hartzell, John Stephen. B.A., Occidental Coll., 1931, LL.D., 1981; LL.B., Harvard, 1934; LL.D., Pepperdine U., 1979. Bar: Calif. bar 1934. Since practiced in, Los Angeles; sr. regional atty. NLRB, 21st Region Ariz. and So. Calif., 1935-36; spl. trial counsel eminent domain proceedings Housing Authority, City Los Angeles, 1950-54; partner firm Paul, Hastings, Janofsky & Walker, 1951—; U.S. State Dept. del. ILO Conf., Geneva, 1969, 70. Contbr. articles profl. jours. Trustee Occidental Coll., 1963—, chmn., 1969-72; mem. overseers com. to visit Harvard Law Sch., 1969-74; bd. visitors Stanford Law Sch., 1972-75. Served to lt. comdr. USNR, 1942-45. Recipient Gold Seal award for outstanding alumnus Occidental Coll., 1973; Medallion award St. Thomas More Law Honor Soc., Loyola U., 1977. Fellow Am. Bar Found., Am. Coll. Trial Lawyers; mem. Am. Law Inst., Internat. Bar Assn., Inter-Am. Bar Assn., ABA (chmn. spl. com. specialization 1970-71, dir. Am. Prepaid Legal Services Inst. 1974—, vice chmn. Commn. Med. Profl. Liability 1975—, ho. of dels. 1975—, chmn. council sect. labor relations law 1975-76, bd. govs. 1978—, pres. 1979-80), Calif. Bar Assn. (pres. 1972-73, gov. 1970-73, exec. com. law in a free soc. 1971-72, 73-77, mem. spl. adv. com. med. malpractice 1975), Los Angeles County Bar Assn. (pres. 1969-70, trustee 1967-69, Shattuck-Price award 1977), Nat. Conf. Bar Presidents (pres. 1973-74, mem. council 1970-75), Nat. Legal Aid and Defender Assn. (dir.), Am. Judicature Soc., Lawyers Club Los Angeles, Harvard Law Sch. Assn. (2d v.p. 1976-77), Phi Beta Kappa. Clubs: Chancery (Los Angeles); Rotary. Home: 661 Thayer Ave Los Angeles CA 90024 Office: 555 S Flower St Los Angeles CA 90071

JANOS, JOHN WILLIAM, chemical company executive; b. North Tarrytown, N.Y., Nov. 29, 1924; s. Leonard William and Mary (Kopel) J.; 1 son, Jeffrey. B.B.A., Iona Coll., 1956. Clk.-cost acct. Sonotone Corp., Elmsford, N.Y., 1946-57; cost acct., staff acct., asst. comptroller, comptroller Reichhold Chem., Inc., White Plains, N.Y., 1957-72, v.p. fin., 1972—. Mem. Henry H. Reichold Scholarship Com., 1972—. Served with USNR, 1943-46. Mem. Fin. Execs. Inst. Home: Pines Bridge Rd Ossining NY 10562 Office: 525 N Broadway White Plains NY 10602

JANOSIK, EDWARD GABRIEL, educator; b. Youngstown, O., Jan. 16, 1918; s. Gabriel John and Katrina (Javorsky) J.; m. Ellen Martin Hastings, Aug. 10, 1943; children—Susanne (Mrs. Charles McNally), Claire Louise (Mrs. John Griffin). B.S. in Edn, S.E. Mo. State Coll., 1939; postgrad., U. Mich., summers 1939, 40; M.A., U. Pa., 1947, Ph.D., 1951. Asst. prof. Washington Coll., Chestertown, Md., 1947-49; from instr. to asso. prof. U. Pa., Phila., 1951-67; prof. dept. polit. sci. State U. N.Y. at Geneseo, 1967—; Vis. lectr. Haverford Coll., 1949-50, 57, Franklin and Marshall Coll., 1950-51. Author: (with Edward Cooke) Pennsylvania Politics, 2d edit, 1964, (with Garold Thumm) Parties and the Governmental System, 1967, Constituency Labour Parties in Britain, 1968. Democratic candidate for Pa. Gen. Assembly, 1958; alternate del.-at- large Dem. Nat. Conv., 1960, alt. dist. del., 1976. Served to maj. AUS, 1940-46. Decorated Purple Heart. Mem. Am. Polit. Sci. Assn., Am. Assn. U. Profs. Home: 20 Candlewood Dr. Pittsford NY 14534

JANOVY, DAVID LEE, educator, gerontologist; b. Seward, Nebr., Nov. 10, 1934; s. Joseph F. and L. Gretchen (Hoagland) J.; m. Darlene Joan Murphy, Dec. 23, 1956; children: Lisa, Jennifer. B.A. in Edn., Wayne (Nebr.) State Coll., 1956; M.A., U. Nebr., 1962, Ph.D., 1967. From asst. to asso. prof. Ill. State U., 1964-68; faculty Mankato (Minn.) State Coll., 1968—, prof. sociology, dept. chmn., 1968-79, dir. gerontology program, 1979—. Mem. area adv. com. on aging; bd. dirs. Mankato Sr. Citizens Center.; Mem. planning div. Mankato United Fund. Served to 1st lt. USMCR, 1956-60. NSF grad. fellow, 1963-64; Fulbright-Hayes advanced research grantee, 1967; postdoctoral fellow Midwest Council Social Research in Aging, 1966-68. Mem. Am. Sociol. Assn., Gerontol. Soc., Midwest Sociol. Soc., Midwest Council Social Research in Aging, Omicron Delta Kappa. Club: Masons. Home: 106 Westwood Dr Mankato MN 56001

JANOWITZ, HENRY DAVID, physician, editor; b. Paterson, N.J., Mar. 23, 1915; s. Sam and Rose (Meyers) J.; m. Adeline R. Tintner, Oct. 31, 1942; children: Mary Rebecca, Anne Francis. B.A., Columbia U., 1935, M.D., 1939; M.S., U. Ill., 1949. Intern Mt. Sinai Hosp., N.Y.C., 1939-41, resident in medicine, 1947-48; practice medicine specializing in gastroenterology, N.Y.C., 1956—; head div. gastroenterology Mt. Sinai Hosp., 1958—, attending physician gastroenterology, 1961—, clin. prof. medicine, 1967—; mem. Am. Bd. Gastroenterology, 1966-70; chmn. program project com., div. arthritis and metabolism NIH, 1969-70. Author: (with D.A. Dreiling and C.V. Perrier) Pancreatic Inflammatory Disease, 1965; contbr. articles to profl. jours.; editorial bd.: Proceedings of Soc. for Exptl. Biology and Medicine, 1974—, Am. Jour. Physiol, 1970-74, Jour. Chronic Diseases, 1966—. Served to maj. U.S. Army, 1942-46. Recipient Jacobi medal Mt. Sinai Sch. Medicine, N.Y.C., 1974. Mem. Am. Soc. Clin. Investigation, Assn. Am. Physicians, Am. Phys. Soc., Am. Gastroent. Assn. (pres. 1972-73), N.Y. Gastroent. Assn. (pres. 1968-69). Home: 180 East End Ave New York City NY 10028 Office: 1075 Park Ave New York City NY 10028

JANS, JAMES PATRICK, educator; b. Detroit, Apr. 6, 1927; s. John Theodore and Lucile Ann (McKenna) J.; m. Barbara Smith, Aug. 26, 1950; children—Lita Helen, Philip James. A.B., U. Mich., 1949, M.A., 1950, Ph.D., 1954. Instr. Yale, 1954-56; asst. prof. math. Ohio State U., 1956-57; mem. faculty U. Wash., Seattle, 1957—, asso. prof., 1960-64, prof., 1964—. Author: Rings and Homology, 1964. Served with USAAC, 1945-46. Mem. Am. Assn. U. Profs., Am. Math. Soc., Math. Assn. Am., Phi Beta Kappa. Home: 17040 10th Ave NW Seattle WA 98177

JANSEN, ANGELA BING, artist; b. N.Y.C., Aug. 17, 1929; d. Lester and Jean Bing; m. Gunther Jansen, Mar. 8, 1956; children—Edmund, Douglas. B.A., Bklyn. Coll., 1951; M.A., N.Y. U., 1953; student, Bklyn. Mus. Art Sch., 1947-50, Atelier 17, N.Y.C., 1950-52. Tchr. art, public schs., N.Y.C., 1954—. One-man shows, Madison (Wis.) Art Center, 1977, Gimpel & Weitzenhoffer, N.Y.C., 1974, 78, group shows, Bklyn. Mus., 1950, 70, 76, Library of Congress, Washington, 1969, 71, Ljubijana Internat. Print Biennale, Yugoslavia, 1971, 73, 75, 77, Venice Biennale, 1972, Internat. Exhbn. Drawing, Rejeka, Yugoslavia (award), Internat. Print Biennale, Cracow, Poland, 1978; represented in permanent collections, Mus. Modern Art, N.Y.C., Met. Mus. Art, N.Y.C., Art Inst. Chgo., Tate Gallery, London. Nat. Endowment for Arts grantee, 1974-75.

JANSEN, G. THOMAS, dermatologist; b. Manitowoc, Wis., July 16, 1926; s. Gerald M. and Sarah (Grady) J.; m. Frances Bovick, Sept. 6, 1952; children: Mark, Kurt, Anne, Drew, Fran. B.S., U. Wis., Madison, 1948, M.D., 1950. Diplomate: Am. Bd. Dermatology. Intern Med. Coll. of Va., 1950-51; resident in dermatology U. Wis., 1953-54, U. Mich., 1954-56; practice medicine specializing in dermatology, Little Rock, 1956—; pres. Little Rock Dermatology Clinic, 1968—; mem. faculty U. Ark. Med. Center, 1956—, prof. dermatology, 1965—, chmn. dept., 1968; mem. staff Doctors Hosp., U. Ark. Hosp., St. Vincent Infirmary, Bapt. Hosp.; pres. Am. Dermatology Found., 1980-81. Served as officer M.C. USNR, 1951-54. Mem. Am. Acad. Dermatology (asst. sec.-treas. 1980-83, sec.-treas. 1983—), AMA, Soc. Investigative Dermatology, Am. Dermatol. Assn., Nat. Program Dermatology, Am. Coll. Chemosurgery, So. Med. Assn. (pres. 1976-77), Ark. Med. Soc., Ark. Dermatol. Soc., Pulaski County Med. Soc., Alpha Omega Alpha. Roman Catholic. Home: 6601 Pleasant Pl Little Rock AR 72205 Office: 4301 W Markham St Slot 576 Little Rock AR 72205

JANSEN, MARIUS BERTHUS, educator, historian; b. Vleuten, The Netherlands, Apr. 11, 1922; came to U.S., 1923, naturalized, 1937; s. Berthus and Gerarda Christina (Holscher) J.; m. Margaret Jean Hamilton, July 30, 1948; 1 dau., Maria Christine. A.B., Princeton U., 1943; M.A., Harvard U., 1948, Ph.D., 1950; Litt.D. (hon.), Middlebury Coll., 1976. Faculty U. Wash., 1950-59, prof. history, 1958-59, Princeton U., 1959—, dir. E. Asian studies program, 1962-68, chmn. East Asian studies dept., 1969-72; Exec. assoc. Internat. House Japan, 1960-61; mem. Council Fgn. Relations. Author: The Japanese and Sun Yat-sen, 1954, Sakamoto Ryoma and the Meiji Restoration, 1961, Japan and China: from War to Peace, 1894-1972, 1975, Japan and Its World: Two Centuries of Change, 1981, (with others) The Modernization of Japan and Russia, 1975; Editor: (with Harold C. Hinton) Major Topics on China and Japan: A Handbook for Teachers, 1957, (with J.W. Hall) Studies in the Institutional History of Early Modern Japan, 1968. Served with AUS, 1943-46. Fellow Am. Acad. Arts and Scis.; mem. Am. Hist. Assn., Assn. Asian Studies (pres. 1976-77). Home: 222 Mount Lucas Rd Princeton NJ 08540

JANSON, ANTHONY FREDERICK, museum curator; b. St. Louis, Mar. 30, 1943; s. Horst Woldemar and Dora Jane J.; m. Helen Patricia Brown, July 26, 1968; 1 dau., Jennifer. B.A., Columbia U., 1965; M.A., N.Y. U., 1972; Ph.D., Harvard U., 1975. Asst. prof. art SUNY, Buffalo, 1973-75, Coll. Charleston, S.C., 1975-78; sr. curator Indpls. Mus. Art, 1978—. Contbr. articles profl. publns. Served with AUS, 1968-71. Home: 4726 N Park Ave Indianapolis IN 46205 Office: 1200 W 38th St Indianapolis IN 46208

JANSON, JOSEPH BROR, II, editor; b. Kansas City, Mo., June 28, 1928; s. Joseph Bror and Stella Lee (Lemen) J.; m. Joyce Paula Andrick, Oct. 9, 1954; children—Kimberly, Leslie. A.B., William Jewell Coll., 1950; M.A., Vanderbilt U., 1952. With Travelers Ins. Co., Kansas City, Mo., 1954-58, Penn Mut. Life Ins. Co., Kansas City, 1958-60; sales rep., editor Holt, Rinehart & Winston, Inc., N.Y.C., 1960-66; editor W.W. Norton & Co., Inc., N.Y.C., 1966—, v.p., 1972—, also dir.; dir. Nat. Book Co., Inc., N.Y.C., Liveright, Inc. Served with USAF, 1952-54. Home: 66 Milton Rd Rye NY 10580 Office: 500 Fifth Ave New York City NY 10036

JANTZEN, CARL RAYMOND, sociology and anthropology educator; b. Beatrice, Nebr., Apr. 2, 1931; s. Jacob P. and Helen J.; Dec. 19, 1960; 1 son, Franz Matthew. B.A., Bethel Coll., 1957; M.A., Mich. State U., 1959. With Mackinac Island State Park Commn., summers, 1960-61; grad. asst. dept. sociology and anthropology Mich. State U., East Lansing, 1957-61, Inst. for Community Devel., 1961-63; mem. faculty Miami U., Oxford, Ohio, 1963—, now prof., chmn. dept. sociology and anthropology; lectr. Conrad Grebel Coll. of Waterloo U., summer, 1971. Fellow Am. Anthropol. Assn.; mem. Central States Anthropology Soc. (sec., treas., then pres.), Middle East Studies Assn., Am. Sociol. Assn. (asso.), Soc. Applied Anthropology. Episcopalian. Office: Dept of Sociology and Anthropology Miami Univ Oxford OH 45056

JANTZEN, J(OHN) MARC, educator; b. Hillsboro, Kans., July 30, 1908; s. John D. and Louise (Janzen) J.; m. Ruth Patton, June 9, 1935; children: John Marc, Myron Patton, Karen Louise. A.B., Bethel Coll., Newton, Kans., 1934; A.M., U. Kans., 1937, Ph.D., 1940. Elementary sch. tchr., Marion County, Kans., 1927-30, Hillsboro, Kan., 1930-31, high sch. tchr., 1934-36; instr. sch. edn. U. Kans., 1936-40; asst. prof. Sch. Edn., U. of Pacific, Stockton, Calif., 1940-42, asso. prof., 1942-44, prof., 1944-78, prof. emeritus, 1978—, also dean sch. edn., 1944-74, emeritus, 1974—, dir. summer sessions, 1940-72; condr. seminars; Past chmn. commn. equal opportunities in edn. Calif. Dept. Edn.; mem., chmn. Commn. Tchr. Edn. Calif. Tchrs. Assn., 1956-62; mem. Nat. Council for Accreditation Tchr. Edn., 1969-72. Bd. dirs. Ednl. Travel Inst., 1965—. Recipient Hon. Service award Calif. Congress of Parents and Tchrs., 1982; Paul Harris fellow Rotary Found., 1980. Mem. Am., Calif. edn. research assns., Calif. Council for Edn. Tchrs., Calif. Assn. of Colls. for Tchr. Edn. (sec.-treas. 1975—), N.E.A., Phi Delta Kappa. Methodist. Club: Rotary. Home: 117 W Euclid Ave Stockton CA 95204 *I maintain that my success in life is a result of multiple factors, among which the most important are a supportive home environment on a Kansas family farm; a wife who shared her husband's ambitions and supported him fully, often at considerable personal sacrifice; an attempt to serve others through a "power with" attitude rather than a "power over" struggle; and a conviction that one's life transcends the immediacy of the here and now.*

JANUARY, LEWIS EDWARD, physician, educator; b. Haswell, Colo., Nov. 14, 1910; s. Frank Puleng and Estella (Miller) J.; m. Virginia Eloise Taylor, Sept 13, 1941; children: Alan Frank, Craig Taylor. B.A., Colo. Coll., 1933, D.Sc. (hon.), 1966; M.D., U. Colo., 1937. Diplomate: Am. Bd. Internal Medicine. Successively intern, resident internal medicine, asst. physician U. Ia. Hosps., 1937-42; mem. faculty U. Iowa Coll. Medicine, 1946—, prof. medicine, 1953-81, emeritus prof., 1981—, asso. chmn. for clin. programs dept. medicine, 1973-81, spl. asst. to chmn., 1981—; also dir. cardiovascular tng. program; mem. staff, dir. heart sta. U. Iowa Hosp., Iowa City, 1946-79; mem. staff VA Hosp., Iowa City.; Mem. Inter-Soc. Commn. for Heart Disease Resources, 1968-71; vis. prof. Ein Shams U., Cairo, Egypt, 1972; mem. cardiovascular tng. com. Nat. Heart and Lung Inst., 1972-74; mem. heart adv. com. Joint Commn. on Accreditation of Hosps., 1974. Author articles in field.; Editorial bd.: Circulation, 1969-74, Am. Heart Jour, 1974-80. Bd. dirs. Community Health, 1966-67, Found. for Joffrey Ballet, 1979—. Served to lt. col., M.C. AUS, 1942-46. Recipient Honors Achievement award Angiology Research Found., 1965; Gold Heart award Am. Heart Assn., 1969; Silver and Gold award U. Colo. Sch. Medicine, 1971; Helen B. Taussig award, 1972; Whitaker Teaching award Iowa Med. Soc., 1977; Internat. Achievement award Am. Heart Assn., 1977; spl. citation for disting. service to internat. cardiology, 1978; Tchr. of Yr. award U. Iowa, 1981; Disting. Alumni award U. Iowa, 1983. Master A.C.P.; fellow Am. Coll. Cardiology, Council Clin. Cardiology (chmn. 1961-63); mem. AMA, Am. Clin. and Climatol. Assn. (council 1973-77), Am. Fedn. Clin. Research, Am. Heart Assn. (dir. 1955-71, pres. 1966-67, internat. program com. 1968-78), Iowa Heart Assn. (dir. 1948-52, heart fund chmn. 1963, pres. 1952-53), Assn. U. Cardiologists (council 1973-76), Am. Soc. Internal Medicine, AAUP, Central Soc. Clin. Research (council 1951-54), Central Clin. Research Club (pres. 1954), Iowa Clin. Med. Soc., Pan Am. Med. Soc. (life), Inter Am. Soc. Cardiology (dir. 1968-76), Internat. Cardiology Fedn. (v.p. 1970-78), Internat. Soc. and Fedn. Cardiology (exec. bd. 1976-78), Sigma Xi, Phi Delta Theta, Nu Sigma Nu, Alpha Omega Alpha. Club: University Athletic (Iowa City) (pres. 1961-64). Home: 3324 Hanover Ct Iowa City IA 52240

JANZOW, WALTER THEOPHILUS, coll. pres.; b. Ada, Minn., Dec. 18, 1918; s. Frederick William and Emma (Wiegner) J.; m. Frances Enae Snider, June 4, 1944; children—Fred, Frank, Kathleen, Daniel. Student, Concordia Coll., 1935-37; B.A., Concordia Sem., St. Louis, 1941, M. Div., 1944; M.A., So. Ill. U., 1957; Ph.D., Nebr. U., 1970; D.D. (hon.), Concordia Sem., Springfield, Ill., 1965. Ordained to ministry Lutheran Ch., Mo. Synod, 1944; pastor Zion Luth. Ch., Mavie, Minn., 1944-45, Immanuel Luth. Ch., McIntosh, Minn., 1945-51, Murphysboro, Ill., 1951-59; prof. sociology Concordia Tchrs. Coll., Seward, Nebr., 1959-63, pres., 1963-77, dir. coll. relations, 1977—; Pres. So. Ill. Dist. Luth. Ch. Mo. Synod, 1957-59. Editor: Issues in Christian Education, 1968-70, The Great Breakthrough, 1962; Contbr. articles to religious jours. Bd. dirs. State U. Nebr. Adv. Council, 1973-77. Mem. Am., Midwest Sociol. assns., Nebr. Assn. Ch. Colls. (pres. 1964-65), Nebr. Assn. Colls. and Univs. (pres. 1971-72), Soc. Sci. Study Religion, Luth. Acad. Scholarship, Luth. Human Relations Assn. Am. Club: Rotarian. Home: 520 Bader Ave Seward NE 68434 Office: 800 N Columbia St Seward NE 68434

JAQUA, JOHN CLAYTON, lawyer; b. Muncie, Ind., Apr. 23, 1919; s. John Clayton and Matilda (Over) J.; m. Mary Elizabeth Costantino; children: Nancy, Louise, David, Marilyn, Michael, Stephen. A.B., Cornell U., 1940; LL.B., Yale U., 1946. Bar: N.Y. 1946. Assoc. law firm Sullivan & Cromwell, N.Y.C., 1946-852, ptnr., 1953—; dir. La.-Pacific Corp., Portland, 1973-82; participant in many panels on corporate law. Editor-in-chief, Yale Law Jour., 1942. Served to capt. USMC, 1942-45. Mem. Yale Law Sch. Assn. (pres. 1973-75, exec. com. 1973), Yale Law Sch. Fund (chmn. 1961-63), Assn. Bar City N.Y. (mem. Fed. legis. com. 1954-56, securities regulations com. 1967-70), ABA (mem. law and acctg. com.), N.Y. State Bar Assn. Democrat. Clubs: Broad Street; Yale (N.Y.C.). Office: 250 Park Ave New York NY 10177

JAQUA, RICHARD ALLEN, pathologist; b. Fort Dodge, Iowa, Apr. 15, 1938; s. John Franklin and Esther Constance (Rossing) J.; m. Mary Joanne Stewart, Dec. 29, 1969. B.A. magna cum laude, Yale U., 1960; M.D., Harvard U., 1965. Diplomate: Am. Bd. Pathology, Am. Bd. Nuclear Medicine. Teaching fellow pathology Harvard Med. Sch., 1965-67; resident clin. pathology NIH, 1967-69; intern pathology Mass. Gen. Hosp., Boston, 1965-66; fellow tumor pathology Meml.-Sloane Kettering Cancer Center, N.Y.C., 1969-70; asst. prof. pathology U. S.D. Sch. Medicine, Vermillion, 1970-73, asso. prof., 1973-74, asso. prof., acting chmn. dept. lab. medicine, 1974-77, prof., chmn. dept. lab. medicine, 1977—, dir., 1979—; pathologist VA Hosp., Sioux Falls, S.D., 1978—; practice medicine specializing in anatomic and clin. pathology and nuclear medicine Lab. Clin. Medicine, Sioux Falls, 1970—. Served with USPHS, 1967-69. Recipient Outstanding Prof. awards U. S.D. Med. Students, 1971, 75, 77; VA grantee, 1980-82. Fellow Coll. Am. Pathologists, Am. Soc. Clin. Pathologists; mem. Electron Microscopy Soc. Am., Am. Assn. Cancer Edn., AAAS, Internat. Acad. Pathology, Soc. Nuclear Medicine, Sigma Xi, Alpha Omega Alpha. Home: Rural Route 3 Oak Valley Canton SD 57013 Office: 1212 S Euclid St Sioux Falls SD 57105

JAQUES, LOUIS BARKER, pharmacologist; b. Toronto, Ont., Can., July 10, 1911; s. Robert Herbert and Ann Bella (Shepherd) J.; m. Helen Evelyn Delane, May 15, 1937; 1 dau., Mary Jaques Hall. B.Sc., U. Toronto, 1933, M.A., 1935, Ph.D., 1941; D.Sc., U. Sask., 1974. Faculty U. Toronto, 1934-46; faculty U. Sask., Saskatoon, 1946—, prof. physiology, head physiology, pharmacology, 1946-71, W.S. Lindsay prof., 1972-79, emeritus prof. physiology, research assoc. dentistry, 1979—; ofcl. Can. rep. Council and Gen. Assembly Internat. Union Physiol. Scis., Leyden, 1962. Author: The Prayer Book Companion, 1963, Anticoagulant Therapy; Pharmacological Principles, 1965; also numerous articles. Fellow N.Y. Acad. Sci., Royal Soc. Arts, Royal Soc. Can., Internat. Soc. Hematology; mem. Am. Physiol. Soc., Am. Soc. Pharmacology and Exptl. Therapeutics. Research on metabolism and action of anticoagulant and related drugs basic to use of these compounds. Home: 682 University Dr Saskatoon SK S7N 0J2 Canada Office: Coll Dentistry U Sask 521 Health Sci Bldg Saskatoon SK S7N 0W0 Canada

JAQUES, THOMAS FRANCIS, librarian; b. Crowley, La., Dec. 25, 1938; s. Robert Edward and Frances (Broussard) J.; m. Trudy Sue Seidel, May 16, 1964; children: Michael Thomas, Christopher Seidel. B.B.A., U. Southwestern La., 1961; M.S., La. State U., 1969. Certified adminstrv. librarian, La. Asst. librarian Rapides Parish Library, Alexandria, La., 1969-73; asst. state librarian Miss. Library Commn., Jackson, Miss., 1973-75; state librarian La. State Library, Baton Rouge, 1975—. Mem. ALA, Southeastern, La. library assns., Chief Officers of State Library Agencies, Beta Phi Mu. Democrat. Episcopalian. Home: 12348 E Sheraton Ave Baton Rouge LA 70815 Office: Box 131 Baton Rouge LA 70821

JAQUETTE, JOHN JOSEPH, utility cons.; b. Phila., Aug. 30, 1918; s. William Alderman and Henrietta (Stratton) J.; m. Margaret Laura Leaf, Sept. 7, 1940; children—David L., Stratton C., Peter B. B.S., Haverford Coll., 1939; M.B.A., Harvard, 1941. Prodn. planner Armstrong Cork Co., Pa., 1941-42; customer service mgr. Sears, Roebuck & Co., Honolulu, 1946-48; mng. dir. Cardinal Services, Ltd., Honolulu, 1948-49; with Hawaiian Telephone Co., Honolulu, 1949-70, financial v.p., 1965-70, exec. v.p., 1962-65; sr. v.p. finance United Telecommunications, Inc., Kansas City, 1970-73, exec. v.p., 1973-74; chmn. bd. Asso. Utility Services, Inc., 1975—; dir. Intelect, Inc.; mem. Hawaii Manpower and Full Employment Commn., 1965-70; lectr. pub. utility econs. U. Hawaii, 1956-57. Contbr. articles profl. jours.

Del., com. chmn. Hawaii Constl. Conv., 1968. Served from ensign to lt. USNR, 1942-46. Mem. Fin. Execs. Inst. (pres. Hawaii chpt. 1967-68), Nat. Assn. Accountants (pres. Hawaii 1961-62), Phi Beta Kappa. Clubs: Rotary (Honolulu); Oahu (Hawaii); Country (bd. dirs. 1967-69), Bucks Harbor (Maine) Yacht; Island Country (Deer Isle, Maine). Home: 999 Wilder Ave Apt 1403 Honolulu HI 96822 Office: PO Box 4283 Honolulu HI 96813

JAQUIER, LLOYD L., diversified company executive. Exec. v.p. W.R. Grace & Co., N.Y.C. Office: W R Grace & Co 1114 Ave of Americas New York NY 10036§

JAQUITH, RICHARD HERBERT, educator, university official; b. Newton, Mass., Mar. 31, 1919; s. Milo W. and Helen F. (Evans) J.; m. E. Louise Bottum, Apr. 4, 1942; children: Nancy L., Richard L., David A., Robert E., Randall W. B.S., U. Mass., 1940, M.S., 1942; Ph.D., Mich. State U., 1955. Instr. chemistry U. Conn., 1942-47; asst. prof. Colby Coll., 1947-54; mem. faculty U. Md., 1954—, prof. chemistry, 1965—, asst. vice chancellor for acad. affairs, 1973—. Served with USNR, 1944-46, 50. Mem. Sigma Xi, Alpha Phi Omega, Omicron Delta Kappa. Home: 5807 Cherrywood Terr Greenbelt MD 20770 Office: Office Acad Affairs: Univ Md College Park MD 20742

JARAMILLO, MARI-LUCI, university administrator; b. Las Vegas, N.Mex., June 19, 1928. B.A., N.Mex. Highland U., 1955, M.A., 1959; Ph.D., U. N.Mex., 1970. Lang. arts cons. Las Vegas Sch. System, 1965-69; asst. dir. instructional services Minority Group Center, 1969-72; asso. prof., chmn. dept. elementary edn. U. N.Mex., 1972-75, coordinator Title VII tchr. tng., 1975-76, asso. prof. edn., 1976-77, prof., 1977, spl. asst. to pres., 1981—, assoc. dean Coll. Edn., 1982—; ambassador to Honduras, Tegucigalpa, 1977-80; dep. asst. sec. for inter-Am. affairs Dept. State, Washington, 1980-81. Contbr. articles to jours., chpts. to books. Mem. Nat. Assn. Bilingual Edn., Latin Am. Assn. Office: Coll Edn U NMex Albuquerque NM 87131

JARC, FRANK ROBERT, food company executive; b. Waukegan, Ill., Apr. 4, 1942; s. Frank Joseph and Edith Gertrude (Cankar) J.; m. Me Randy Jarc; 1 dau., Jennifer. B.S. in Indsl. Engring, U. Mich., 1964; M.B.A., Harvard U., 1967. Mgmt. trainee Mich. Bell Telephone Co., 1964; with regulatory proceedings dept. United Airlines, Chgo., 1966; fin. analyst Ford Motor Co., Dearborn, Mich., 1967, Freeport Minerals Co., N.Y.C., 1972-73; Fin. analyst Esmark, Inc., Chgo., 1973; controller subs. Swift Grocery Products Co., Chgo., 1973-75; fin. v.p. subs. Estech, Inc., Chgo., 1975-77; v.p. consumer products subs. ESTECH Gen. Chem. Co., Agrl. Chems. Corp., Chgo., 1977-80; sr. v.p., chief fin. officer Wilson Foods, Oklahoma City, 1980—. Served to capt. USAF, 1967-71. Mem. Evans Scholarship Alumni Assn., Golf Course Supts. Assn. Am. Club: Union League Chgo. Home: 3005 Broken Bow Edmond OK 73034 Office: 4545 Lincoln Blvd Oklahoma City OK

JARDETZKY, OLEG, scientist, educator; b. Yugoslavia, Feb. 11, 1929; came to U.S., 1949, naturalized, 1955; s. Wenceslas Sigismund and Tatiana (Taranovsky) J.; m. Erika Albensberg, July 21, 1975; children by previous marriage: Alexander, Theodore, Paul. B.A., Macalester Coll., 1950, D.Sc. (hon.), 1974; M.D., U. Minn., 1954, Ph.D. (Am. Heart Assn. fellow), 1956; postgrad., U. Cambridge, Eng., 1965-66; LL.D. (hon.), Calif. Western U., 1978. Research fellow U. Minn., 1954-56; NRC fellow Calif. Inst. Tech., 1956-57; asso. Harvard U., 1957-59, asst. prof. pharmacology, 1959-66; dir. biophysics and pharmacology Merck & Co., 1966-68, exec. dir., 1968-69; prof. Stanford U., 1969—, dir. Stanford Magnetic Resonance Lab., 1975—, dir. NMR Center, Sch. Medicine, 1983—; vis. fellow Merton Coll., Oxford (Eng.) U., 1976; cons., vis. prof., lectr. in field; chmn. Internat. Council on Magnetic Resonance in Biology, 1972-74. Contbr. articles to profl. jours.; mem. editorial bd.: Jour. Theoretical Biology, 1961—, Molecular Pharmacology, 1965-75, Jour. Medicinal Chemistry, 1970-78, Biochimica Biophypica Acta, 1970—, Revs. on Bioenergetics, 1972—, Biomembrane Revs., 1972-80. Recipient USPHS Career Devel. award, 1959-66, Kaiser award, 1973, Von Humboldt award, 1977; NSF grantee, 1957—; NIH grantee, 1957—; Am. Physiol. Soc. Travelling fellow, 1959. Mem. AAAS, Am. Chem. Soc., Am. Soc. Biol. Chemists, Assn. Advanced Tech. in Biomed. Scis. (pres. 1981—), Phi Beta Kappa, Sigma Xi, Alpha Omega Alpha. Home: 950 Casanueva St Stanford CA 94305 Office: Magnetic Resonance Center Sch Medicine Stanford U Stanford CA 94305

JARECKIE, STEPHEN BARLOW, museum curator; b. Orange, N.J., Feb. 18, 1929; s. Eugene Albert and Doris Condit (Brittin) J.; m. Gretchen Kinsman Fillmore, Aug. 10, 1959. B.A., Lehigh U., 1951; M.A., Syracuse U., 1961. Installation asst. Munson-Williams-Proctor Inst., Utica, N.Y., 1955-60, edn. asst., 1960-61; registrar Worcester Art Mus., Mass., 1961-83, asso. in photography, 1962-69, asso. curator photography, 1969-73, curator photography, 1973—. Contbr. alogue, pamphlets, articles to mus. lit. Served with AUS, 1951-53. Guest of Fed. Republic Germany to study W. German mus., 1967. Mem. New Eng. Mus. Assn., Internat. Mus. Photography (George Eastman House), U.S. Naval Inst. (asso.). Episcopalian. Built scale model original bldgs., grounds of Proctor Inst., 1957-60. Home: 47 Mount View Dr Holden MA 01520 Office: 55 Salisbury St Worcester MA 01608

JARETT, LEONARD, pathologist, diabetes researcher; b. Lubbock, Tex., Aug. 25, 1936; s. Hymen Jerome and Nellie M. (Bloomberg) J.; m. Arlene Kramer, June 10, 1962; children: Stacy, Douglas, Jennifer. B.A., Rice Inst., 1958; M.D., Washington U., St. Louis, 1962; M.A., U. Pa., 1982. Diplomate: Am. Bd. Pathology. Intern Barnes Hosp., St. Louis, 1962-63, resident, 1963-64; assoc. prof. pathology, head div. lab. medicine Washington U., St. Louis, 1969-73, prof., 1973-80; prof., chmn. dept. pathology and lab. medicine Hosp. of U. Pa., Phila., 1980—; dir. Central Diagnosis Lab., Barnes Hosp., St. Louis, 1969-79; mem., steering com. Nat. Diabetes Research Interchange, 1980-82; mem., sci. adv. bd. St. Jude's Childrens Research Hosp., 1980—; mem., med. sci. adv. com. Juvenile Diabetes Found., 1982—; mem., external adv. com. diabetes and endocrinology research Baylor Coll. Medicine, 1982—. Editor: Gradwohl's Clinical Laboratory Methods and Diagnosis, 1980; contbr. articles to profl. jours., chpts. to profl. books. Served with USPHS, 1964-66. Recipient Richard S. Brookings award Sch. Medicine Washington U., 1962, Sheard-Sanford award Am. Soc. Clin. Pathology, 1962, David Rubbough award Juvenile Diabetes Found., 1980, Super-Achiever award Phila. Juvenile Diabetes Found., 1982; John and Mary Markle scholar, 1967-72. Home: 1024 Great Springs Rd Rosemont PA 19010 Office: U Pa Sch Medicine 36th & Hamilton Walk Philadelphia PA 19104

JARMAN, JOSEPH, jazz musician; b. Pine Bluff, Ark., Sept. 14, 1937; s. Joseph and Eva (Robinson) J. Student, Chgo. City Jr. Coll., 1958-59, Chgo. Tchrs. Coll., 1958-59, Mil. Inst. Tech., 1959-60, U. Ariz., 1960-61, Am. Conservatory Music, 1966. Tchr. Goodman Sch. Music, 1964; lectr. U. Chgo., 1966; pvt. tchr., 1966—; lectr., dir. music and theatre workshop Circle Pine Center, Delton, Mich., summer 1968. Began performing with, Assn. Advancement Creative Musicians, 1965; appeared at, Harper Theatre, Chgo., neo-music theatre concert, Chgo., 1966; selected to, Detroit Jazz Conf., Wayne State U., 1967, environ. music concert, U. Chgo., 1967; joined, Art Ensemble of Chgo., 1969—, instruments include: saxaphone, bassoon, oboe, flute, clarinet, percussion; composer: Tribute to the Hard Core, 1965, Non-Cognitive Aspects of the City, 1966, Hollows Ecliptic, 1967, Imperfections in a Given Space, 1965, Indifferent Piece for Six, 1967; albums include Egwin (with Don Moye), Song For, Sunhound, Together Alone; composer others with, Art Ensemble of Chgo. Office: care Rasa Artists 144 W 27th St New York NY 10001 *

JARMIE, NELSON, physicist; b. Santa Monica, Calif., Mar. 24, 1928; s. Louis and Ruth (Wydman) J. B.S., Calif. Inst. Tech., 1948; Ph.D., U. Calif.-Berkeley, 1953. Staff mem. Los Alamos Sci. Lab., 1953—; vis. prof. U. Calif.-Santa Barbara, 1960; adj. prof. U. N.Mex., 1957-71; mem. adv. council Los Alamos Grad. Ctr., 1958—; participant Vis. Scientist Program, 1965-71. Contbr. numerous articles to sci. jours. and mags.; research in low energy nuclear physics, medium energy particle physics and astrophysics. Mem. Econ. Devel. Council Los Alamos County, N.Mex., 1968. Fellow Am. Phys. Soc., AAAS; mem. Am. Assn. Physics Tchrs., Sigma Xi, Tau Beta Pi. Office: Los Alamos Nat Lab Los Alamos NM 87545

JARMOLOW, KENNETH, aerospace industry executive; b. Lebanon, Conn., Sept. 15, 1924; s. Joseph Harry and Rose (Lubetsky) J.; m. Shirley S. Mendoza, Jan. 31, 1947; children—Elizabeth Dale, Janet Alice. B.S. in Aero. Engring, Mass. Inst. Tech., 1948; postgrad., Johns Hopkins U., 1951-52, 59. Aerodynamicist Glen L. Martin Co., Balt., 1948-57, chief staff, 1957-58, mgr. tech. devel., 1958-63; dir. Research Inst. for Advanced Studies, Martin Marietta Corp., Balt., 1963-74, corp. dir. research and devel., 1974-83, corp. v.p. research and devel., 1983—; head dept. aerospace engring. Drexel Inst. Tech., Balt., 1964-67; mem. research and tech. adv. com. NASA, 1970-77, mem. space systems and tech. adv. com., 1978—. Served to lt. USAAF, 1942-45. Asso. fellow AIAA, Md. Acad. Scis., Sigma Xi; mem. AAAS, Am. Astronautics Soc. Home: Old Court Rd Brooklandville MD 21022 Office: 1450 S Rolling Rd Baltimore MD 21227 *In the end, each of us will have little left to give and much to look back on. How much better to see our lives as having been lived to the fullest, in which we gave the best.*

JARNAGIN, RICHARD CALVIN, educator; b. Dallas, Aug. 26, 1930; s. Calvin Elgin and Dorothy Edris (Brown) J.; m. Patsy Sue Hatchel, June 20, 1958; children—Kurt Randall, Forest Neal. Student, N. Tex. Agrl. Coll., 1947-49; B.S., So. Meth. U., 1952; Ph.D., Yale U., 1958. Teaching fellow So. Meth. U., Dallas, 1952-53; research chemist, prof. U. N.C., Chapel Hill, 1958—; cons. P.R. Nuclear Center, 1965-66; vis. scientist Sandia Labs., 1978-79. Served with USAF, 1953-55. NSF fellow, 1957-58; profl. devel. award, 1978-79; J.S. Guggenheim fellow, 1967-68. Fellow Am. Phys. Soc.; mem. Am. Chem. Soc., N.Y. Acad. Sci., Sigma Xi. Home: 609 Caswell Rd Chapel Hill NC 27514 Office: Dept Chemistry 045A U NC Chapel Hill NC 27514

JARON, DOV, biomedical engineer, educator; b. Tel Aviv, Oct. 29, 1935; U.S., 1958, naturalized, 1972; s. Meir and Sara (Levit) Yarovsky; m. Brooke E. Boberg, Sept. 16, 1978; children: Shulamit, Tamara. B.S. magna cum laude, U. Denver, 1961; Ph.D., U. Pa., 1967. Sr. research asso. Maimonides Med. Center, Bklyn., 1967-70; dir. surg. research Sinai Hosp. of Detroit, 1970-73; asso. prof. elec. engring. U. R.I., Kingston, 1973-77, prof., 1977-79, coordinator biomed. engring., 1973-79; dir. Biomed. Engring. and Sci. Inst., Drexel U., Phila., 1979—, prof. elec. and computer engring., 1979—; vis. prof. elec. engring. Rutgers U., New Brunswick, N.J., 1968-73; adj. prof. biomed. engring. Wayne State U., 1971-73; adj. prof. physiology Temple U. Sch. Medicine, 1980—; adj. prof. radiology Jefferson Med. Coll., 1983—. Contbr. articles to sci. jours. NSF, NIH, Office Naval Research, pvt. founds. research grantee. Mem. Biomed. Engring. Soc., Am. Soc. Engring. Edn., Assn. Advancement Med. Instrumentation, Internat. Soc. Artificial Organs, Am. Soc. Artificial Internal Organs, Biophys. Soc., N.Y. Acad. Scis., IEEE, Am. Soc. for Engring. Edn., AAAS, AAUP, Sigma Xi, Tau Beta Pi, Eta Kappa Nu. Researcher in cardiac assist devices, cardiovascular modeling, biomed. instrumentation. Home: 122 Bethlehem Pike Philadelphia PA 19118 Office: Drexel U Philadelphia PA 19104

JAROS, DEAN, university dean; b. Racine, Wis., Aug. 23, 1938; s. Joseph and Emma (Kotas) J. B.A., Lawrence Coll., Appleton, Wis., 1960; M.A., Vanderbilt U., 1962, Ph.D., 1966. Asst. prof. polit. sci. Wayne State U., Detroit, 1963-66; from asst. prof. to prof. polit. sci. U. Ky., 1966-78, asso. dean, 1978-80; dean Grad. Sch., asso. provost grad. studies and research No. Ill. U., DeKalb, 1980—. Author: Socialization to Politics, 1973, Political Behavior: Choices and Perspectives, 1974, also articles.; Mem. editorial bds. profl. jours. Mem. Exptl. Aircraft Assn. Office: Colorado State Univ Grad Sch Fort Collins CO 80523

JARRARD, JERALD OSBORNE, food industry executive; b. Mt. Washington, Mo., Oct. 12, 1917; s. Frank Lewis and Mary Minerva (Osborne) J.; m. Deena Morgan, Sept. 29, 1978; children: Sharon Louise, Jerry Michael, Janeece Rene (Mrs. Anthony Swainey). Student, Kansas City Jr. Coll., 1935-36, 38-39; LL.B. magna cum laude, U. Mo., 1947. Bar: Mo. 1947. With Trans World Airlines, 1942-60, dir. labor relations, 1957-60; v.p. indsl. relations Eastern Airlines, 1960-63; v.p. personnel Am. Airlines, Inc., 1963, regional v.p. sales and services, N.Y., 1964-66, system v.p. sales and services, 1966-68; pres. Contract Food Services div. Marriott Corp., Washington, 1968-78, sr. corp. v.p., spl. asst. to pres., 1978—. Editor: U. Mo. Law Rev, 1944-46. Mem. Mo. Integrated Bar, Inst. Radio Engrs., Am. Soc. Travel Agts., Newcomen Soc. N. Am., Nat. Restaurant Assn., Nat. Rifle Assn., Sales Execs. Club, Phi Delta Phi. Methodist. Clubs: Pinnacle, Wings (N.Y.C.); Congressional (Washington); Isla del Sol (St. Petersburg, Fla.). Home and Office: 5700 Escondida Blvd Unit 304 Saint Petersburg FL 33715

JARRARD, LEONARD EVERETT, psychologist, educator; b. Waco, Tex., Oct. 23, 1930; s. Thomas Ivan and Lewis Everett (Lasswell) J.; m. Janet Grier Shoop, Aug. 16, 1958; children: Alice Grier, David Frazier, Hugh Everett. B.A., Baylor U., Waco, 1955; M.S., Carnegie Inst. Tech., Pitts., 1957, Ph.D., 1959. Asst. to asso. prof. psychology Washington and Lee U., 1959-66; asso. prof. to prof. psychology Carnegie-Mellon U., 1966-71; prof., head dept. psychology Washington and Lee U., Lexington, Va., 1971—; vis. lectr., prof. exptl. psychology U. Oxford, Eng., 1975-76; interim asso. prof. anatomy U. Fla., 1965-66. Editor: Cognitive Processes of Nonhuman Primates, 1971; cons. editor: Jour. Comparative and Physiol. Psychology, 1970-75. Served with USAF, 1952-54. Mem. AAAS, Am. Psychol. Assn., Soc. for Neurosci., Psychonomics Soc., Va. Acad. Sci., So. Soc. Philosophy and Psychology, Phi Beta Kappa, Sigma Xi. Home: PO Box 1067 Lexington VA 24450 Office: Dept Psychology Washington and Lee U Lexington VA 24450

JARRATT, MARY CLAIBORNE, government official; b. Clifton Forge, Va., Oct. 29, 1942; d. Robert Bell and Mary Louise (Wood) J. B.A., Mary Baldwin Coll., Staunton, Va., 1964; cert. bus., Katharine Gibbs Sch., Boston, 1965. Staff asst. com. on agr. U.S. Ho. of Reps., 1975-81; asst. sec. food and consumer services Dept. Agr., 1981—. Editor various legis. reports. Republican. Episcopalian. Home: 1046 N Royal St Alexandria VA 22314 Office: Dept Agr Washington DC 20250

JARREAU, AL, singer; b. Milw., Mar. 12, 1940. B.S. in Psychology, Ripon Coll., 1962, M.S., U. Iowa, 1964. Solo rec. artist, 1975—; recs. include We Got By, 1975, Glow, 1976, Look to the Rainbow, 1977, All Fly Home, 1978, This Time, 1980, Breaking Away, 1981 (Winner Readers Poll, Down Beat mag. 1977, 78, 79, Grammy award best jazz vocalist 1978, 79).

JARRETT, BEVERLY J., editor; b. Alexandria, La., Oct. 27, 1940; d. Emmett Davis and Virginia Lee (Eversull) J.; m. Carl Otis Penny, Apr. 7, 962 (div. 1971); children: Sarah Feliciana, Aimee Elizabeth; m. William Ward Mills, Aug. 19, 1979. B.A., La. Coll.-Pineville, 1961; M.A., La. State U.-Baton Rouge, 1966. Copywriter La. State U. Press, Baton Rouge, 1963-66, mng. editor, 1971—, exec. editor, assoc. dir., 1983—; instr. English N.C. Central U., Millsaps Coll., U. New Orleans. Episcopalian. Home: PO Box 712 Old River Rd Baton Rouge LA 70780 Office: La State Univ Press Baton Rouge LA 70892

JARRETT, JERRY VERNON, banker; b. Abilene, Tex., Oct. 31, 1931; s. Walter Elwood and Myrtle Elizabeth (Allen) J.; m. Martha Ann McCabe, June 13, 1953; children: Cynthia Ann, Charles Elwood, Christopher Allen, John Carlton. B.B.A., U. Okla., 1957; M.B.A., Harvard U., 1963. Gen. sales mgr. Tex. Coca-Cola Bottling Co., Abilene, 1957-61; exec. v.p. Marine Midland Bank, N.Y.C., 1963-73, Ameritrust Co., 1973-76, vice chmn., 1976-78, chmn., chief exec. officer, 1978—; chmn., chief exec. officer Ameritrust Corp. Co-author: Creative Collective Bargaining, 1964. Served with USAAF, 1950-54. Mem. Phi Gamma Delta. Home: 2751 Chesterton Rd Shaker Heights OH 44122 Office: 900 Euclid Ave Cleveland OH 44101

JARRETT, KEITH, pianist; b. Allentown, Pa., May 8, 1945. Ed., Berklee Sch. Music. Pianist with groups lead by, Art Blakey, 1965, Roland Kirk, Charles Lloyd, 1966-69, Miles Davis, 1970-71; soloist and leader of own groups, 1969—; albums include Survivor's Suite; also recorded with, Jack DeJohnette, Jan Garbarek, Charlie Haden, Dewey Redman. (Winner Readers Poll, Down Beat mag. 1974), Dewey Redman. (Critics Poll 1975); solo improvisation concert recs. include Köln Concert, Sun Bear Concerts; debut as concert soloist Phila. Orch.,, San Francisco Symphony, 1983. Office: care Vincent Ryan 135 W 16th St New York NY 10011 *

JARRETT, NOEL, chemical engineer; b. Long Eaton, Eng., Nov. 17, 1921; came to U.S., 1926, naturalized, 1946; s. John Richard and Lena Eliza (Hexter) J.; m. Violet E. Dipner, Sept. 24, 1949; children: Robert, Kenneth, James, Thomas. B.S. in Chem. Engring, U. Pitts., 1949, M.S., U. Mich., 1951. Lubrication sales engr. Freedom-Valvoline Co., Freedom, Pa., 1949-50; with Alcoa Labs., Aluminum Co. Am., 1951—, chief div. process metallurgy, 1969-81, asst. dir. metal prodn. labs., 1981-82, tech. dir. chem. engring., 1982—. Served with U.S. Army, 1942-45. Fellow Am. Soc. Metals; mem. Nat. Acad. Engrs., Am. Inst. Chem. Engrs., AIME, Electrochem. Soc., Sigma Xi. Episcopalian. Clubs: Masons, Elks. Patentee smelting and melting of aluminum. Home: 149 Jefferson Ave Lower Burrell PA 15068 Office: Alcoa Labs Alcoa Center PA 15069 *I have found that the one who performs the tasks immediately at hand so well that his work cannot be ignored will reap society's rewards without asking.*

JARRIEL, THOMAS EDWIN, correspondent; b. LaGrange, Ga., Dec. 29, 1934; s. William Lester and Ruth (Knight) J.; m. Joan Borgeson, Jan. 24, 1935; children: Michael, Stephen, Jeffrey. B.A., U. Houston, 1956. Corr. ABC News, Atlanta, 1965-68, Washington, 1968-69, ABC News White House, 1969-77, ABC News, Washington, 1977—; frequent contbr. ABC News TV show 20/20; also anchors ABC's World News Tonight, The Weekend Report and ABC News Brief. Recipient 3 Emmy awards, 1983. Office: ABC News 7 W 66th St New York NY 10023

JARROTT, CHARLES, film and TV director; b. London, June 16, 1927. Began career as asst. stage mgr. with, Arts Council of Gt. Britain Touring Co.; joined, Nottingham Repertory Theatre; as stage dir. and juvenile acting leader, 1949; joined new co. touring, Can., 1953; leading man, resident leading actor, Ottawa Theatre; dir. debut, CBC, 1957; resident dir.; dir.: Armchair Theatre, ABC-TV, London; films include Anne of a Thousand Days, Mary, Queen of Scots, The Amateur; TV shows Dr. Jekyll and Mr. Hyde, A Married Man; stage plays The Dutchman. Served with Brit. Navy. Office: care William Morris Agy 151 El Camino Beverly Hills CA 90212

JARVIE, CHARLES LAWRENCE, liquor industry executive; b. Washington, Nov. 10, 1936; s. Lawrence L. and Helen E. (Williams) J.; m. Janet K. Arps, Sept. 6, 1958; children: Douglas L., Lawrence E., Steven M., Wendy A. B.S., Cornell U., 1958, M.B.A., 1959. With Procter & Gamble Co., 1959-80, v.p. indsl. food div., 1976-77, v.p., gen. mgr. food products div., 1977-80; pres., chief operating officer Dr. Pepper Co., Dallas, 1980-83; pres. Fidelity Mktg. Corp., Boston, 1983—; pres., chief exec. officer Schenley Industries Inc., 1984—; dir. Tex. Commerce Bank Shares, Houston; rep. Inst. Shortening and Edible Oils, 1977-79; trustee Nutrition Found., 1977-79. Nat. com. bus. and public adminstrn. fund raising Cornell U., 1979-81; exec. com. Dan Beard council Boy Scouts Am., 1976-79; chmn. bus. fund raising campaign Hamilton County (Ohio) Republican Party, 1979; elder, deacon Mt. Washington United Presbyn. Ch., Cin., 1970-79. Clubs: Cornell (N.Y.C.); City, Lancers (Dallas). Office: 5523 E Mockingbird Ln Dallas TX 75206 PO Box 225086 Dallas TX 75265

JARVIK, LISSY F., psychiatrist; b. The Hague, Netherlands; m. Murray E. Jarvik, Dec. 19, 1954; children—Laurence A., Jeffrey G. A.B. cum laude, Hunter Coll., N.Y.C., 1946; M.A., Columbia U., 1947, Ph.D., 1950; M.D., Western Res. U., 1954. Diplomate: Am. Bd. Pediatrics. From research asst. to psychiatrist II N.Y. State Psychiat. Inst., N.Y.C., 1946-72; rotating intern Mt. Sinai Hosp., N.Y.C., 1954-55; resident in pediatrics Babies Hosp., Columbia-Presbyn. Med. Center, N.Y.C., 1955-56; fellow pediatrics Vanderbilt Clinic, N.Y.C., 1957-58, asst. attending, then attending psychiatrist, 1962-72; from research asso. to asso. prof. Columbia U. Coll. Phys. and Surg., 1956-72; chief psychogenetics unit Brentwood VA Hosp., Los Angeles, 1970—; vis. asso. prof. UCLA Med. Sch., 1970-71, prof. psychiatry, 1972—; M.S. McLeod vis. prof. U. Adelaide, Australia, 1981; vis. prof. Australian Postgrad. Fedn. Medicine, 1981; cons. in field, mem. numerous task forces. Mem. editorial bds. profl. jours.; author articles in field. Recipient R. Thornton Wilson award, 1967, Woman in Sci. award UCLA, 1981; named Woman of Achievement Women's Equality Day, 1980. Fellow AAAS, Gerontol. Soc., Am. Geriatric Soc. (a founder), Internat. Soc. Twin Studies, Am. Acad. Pediatrics, Am. Psychol. Assn. (div. pres.); mem. AMA, Am. Soc. Human Genetics, Environ. Mutagen Soc., Am. Eugenics Soc., Eastern Psychiat. Research Assn., Am. Psychopath. Assn., Am. Psychiat. Assn., Sigma Xi. *

JARVIK, MURRAY ELIAS, educator; b. N.Y.C., June 1, 1923; s. Jacob and Minnie (Haas) J.; m. Lissy, Dec. 19, 1954; children—Laurence Ariel, Jeffrey Gil. B.S., CCNY, 1944; M.A., UCLA, 1945; M.D., U. Calif., San Francisco, 1951, Ph.D., 1952. Research technician phys. chemistry Rockefeller Inst., N.Y.C., 1943-44; research asso. neurophysiology neurology dept. Mt. Sinai Hosp., 1953-55; research asso. psychopharmacology L.I. Biol. Assn., Cold Spring Harbor, N.Y., 1955-56; asst. prof. pharmacology Albert Einstein Coll. Medicine, 1956-60, asso. prof., 1960-68, prof., Sadie Danciger Distinguished scholar, 1968, prof. psychiatry, 1969-72; prof. psychiatry, pharmacology U. Calif. at Los Angeles, 1972—; chief psychopharmacology unit Brentwood VA Hosp., 1972—; Vis. asst.

prof. physiol. psychology U. Calif. at Berkeley, 1955; adj. asst. prof. N.Y. U., 1957; vis. physician Bellevue Hosp., N.Y.C., 1960; research scientist N.Y. U. Med. Center, 1936-65, sr. research scientist, 1965; mem. adv. com. on abuse of stimulant and depressant drugs Bur. Drug Abuse Control, FDA, 1966—; mem. adv. com. on tobacco habituation Am. Cancer Soc., 1967—. Mng. editor: Psychopharmacologia, 1966-71; editorial adv. bd.: Behavioral Biology. Recipient Career Scientist award Nat. Inst. Mental Health, 1971, 1971-72. Fellow AAAS, N.Y. Acad. Scis., Am. Psychol. Assn. (div. pres. 1966-68); mem. Am. Coll. Neuropsychopharmacology, Collegium Internatonale Neuro-Psychopharmacologium, Internat. Brain Research Orgn., Am. Psychopath. Assn., Phi Beta Kappa, Sigma Xi. Office: VA Medical Center Brentwood Los Angeles CA 90073 *A guiding principle in my life has been that psychiatry can and should be a science and not merely an art. The principles of validation and control should be applied to psychiatry just as they are to any other science. I have felt that psychopharmacology and the study of the brain are the pathways one must follow to learn more about behavior. To achieve this goal I have studied memory mechanisms in various species of animals and I have tried to understand how drugs can disrupt and reinforce behavior.*

JARVIK, ROBERT KOFFLER, artificial organ company executive physician; b. Midland, Mich., May 11, 1946; s. Norman Eugene and Edythe (Koffler) J.; m. Elaine Levin, Oct. 5, 1968; children: Tyler, Kate. B.A., Syracuse U., 1968, Dr. Sci. (hon.), 1983; M.A., NYU, 1971; M.D., U. Utah, 1976. Research asst. Div. Artificial Organs-U. Utah, Salt Lake City, 1971-76, asst. dir. exptl. labs., 1976-82; pres. Kolff Med., Salt Lake City, 1981—; asst. research prof. surgery U. Utah, 1979—. Sect. editor: Internat. Jour. Artificial Organs, 1979—; inventor repeating hemostatic clip instruments and cartridges, total artificial hearts powered by electrohydraulic energy; patentee in field. Named Inventor of Yr. Intellectual Property Owners, 1982, John W. Hyatt award Soc. Plastics Engrs., 1983, Golden Plate Am. Acad. Achievement, 1983, Gold Heart award Utah Heart Assn., 1983. Mem. Am. Soc. Artificial Internal Organs. Office: 825 N 300 W Salt Lake City UT 84103

JARVIS, DAVID, financial executive; b. Gillingham, Eng., Mar. 9, 1941; came to U.S., 1978; s. Harold and Phyllis Emma (Hart) J.; m. Williamina Colby, Feb. 9, 1963; children—Julian, Andrea, Nicola. Profl. Accts. Qualification - Asso., Maidstone Coll. Tech., 1960. Vice pres., controller Anderson Clayton & Co., Mexico, 1970-73, v.p., chief fin. officer, 1973-75, v.p. consumer products div., 1975-78; v.p. Latin Am./Pacific ops. Pillsbury Co., 1978-80, v.p. internat. bus. devel., 1980-81; sr. v.p. N.W. Bancorp., Mpls., 1981—, also v.p. subsidiaries. Bd. trustees Minn. Outward Bound Sch. Mem. Inst. Cost & Mgmt. Accts. U.K. Methodist. Clubs: N.W. Racquet, Wayzata Country., Minneapolis. Home: 1895 Foxridge Rd Long Lake MN 55356 Office: Northwest Corp 1200 Peavey Bldg Minneapolis MN 55480

JARVIS, FREDERICK H., insurance company executive; b. 1928. B.B.A., Upsala Coll., 1951. Pres. U.S. Fire Ins. Co., 1973—, chief exec. officer, chmn. bd., dir., 1978—; chmn., pres. chief exec. officer N. River Ins. Co., Internat. Ins. Co., Werchester Fire Ins. Co. Address: US Fire Ins Co 110 William St New York NY 10038 *

JARVIS, GRAHAM POWLEY, actor; b. Toronto, Ont., Can., Aug. 25, 1930; came to U.S., 1935; s. William Henry Reginald and Margaret Biddulph (Scatcherd) J.; m. Janet JoAnna Vaughan Rader, Oct. 24, 1970; children: Matthew Graham Reginald, Alexander Charles Rader. Student, Williams Coll., 1947-50, Am. Theatre Wing, N.Y.C., 1955-57. With, Barter Theatre of Va., summers, 1956-60; appeared in: Broadway shows, including The Best Man, 1960-61, The Investigation, 1966, Halfway Up the Tree, 1967, The Rocky Horror Show, 1975; off-Broadway show Adaptation-Next, 1969; films include The Out-of-Towners, 1969, A New Leaf, 1970, Cold Turkey, 1970, The Travelling Executioner, 1971, Middle Age Crazy, 1980, Silkwood, 1983, Deal of the Century, 1983; TV shows include Mary Hartman, Mary Hartman, 1976-77, Forever Fernwood, 1977-78; appeared as John Ehrlichman in: Blind Ambition, 1979. Office: care McCartt Oreck Barrett Lionel Larner Ltd 9200 Sunset Blvd Los Angeles CA 90069

JARVIS, HERBERT WOODHULL, manufacturing company executive; b. Greenwich, Conn., Mar. 9, 1925; s. Herbert W. and Harriett J. (Belmer) J.; m. June Reid, Jan. 2, 1947; children: Laurian Jarvis Cargill, Averill, Leslie Jarvis Abernathy, Suzanne. B.S. in Indsl. Adminstrn, Yale U., 1947; postgrad., Boston U. Grad. Sch. Bus. Mgmt., 1950. With USM Corp. (and successor Emhart Corp.), 1947-79, pres., 1968-79; exec. v.p. Sybron Corp. (diversified mfg. co.), Rochester, N.Y., 1980-81, pres., chief operating officer, 1981-83, pres., chief exec. officer, 1983—; dir. Berkshire Life Ins., Pittsfield, Mass., Shawmut Bank, Shawmut Corp., both Boston, Gen. CINGMA Corp. Trustee Rochester Inst. Tech., Eastman Dental Ctr. Served with A.C. USNR, 1943-45. Clubs: Oakhill Country, Genesee Valley (Rochester); Bald Peak (N.H.) Colony. Office: 1100 Midtown Tower Rochester NY 14604

JARVIS, JOSEPH BOYER, university administrator; b. Springville, Utah, June 1, 1923; s. Joseph Smith and Mildred (Boyer) J.; m. Patricia Ann Potts, Dec. 17, 1955; children: Seth N., Nathan Y., Mary Beth. Student, Harvard U., 1942; B.A., U. Ariz., 1947; M.A., Ariz. State U., 1950; Ph.D., Northwestern U., 1958. Instr. speech U. Ariz., 1950-52, Dartmouth Coll., 1954-55; asst. prof. U. Utah, 1956-63, asso. prof., 1963-68, prof. speech, 1968-72, prof. communication, 1972—, asst. dean Coll. Letters and Sci., 1958-60, asso. program dir. sta. KUED-TV, 1957-60, asst. to pres., 1962-64, adminstr. U. Utah Theatre, 1963-64, dean summer sch., 1962-67, dean admissions and registration, 1965-71, asso. v.p. acad. affairs, 1967—; Spl. asst. to U.S. Commr. Edn., Washington, 1961-62. Bd. dirs. Salt Lake City Pub. Library, 1976—, pres., 1978-80; bd. dirs. Youth Inc., Salt Lake City, 1969-77, chmn., 1970-71; vice chmn. Alberta Henry Edn. Found., 1973-80. Mem. Speech Communication Assn., Western Speech Communication Assn., UN Assn. Utah (v.p. 1978-80, pres. 1980-82), Phi Beta Kappa, Phi Kappa Phi. Home: 2357 Blaine Ave Salt Lake City UT 84108

JARVIS, MORRIS O., textile company executive; b. New Albany, Miss., Nov. 20, 1940; s. Robert Lafayette and Mary Loud (Sanford) J.; m. Sue Randolph, Dec. 20, 1959; children: Leigh Anne, Leslie. Student, Orange Bus. Coll., 1960, Ky. Sch. Mortuary Sci., 1965. Store mgr. Hancock Fabrics, Hurst, Tex., 1968-69, dist. mgr., Dallas, 1970-74; ops. mgr. Hancock Textile Co. Inc., Tupelo, Miss., 1974-76, mdse. mgr., 1976-77, dir. ops., 1977-80, pres., 1980—. Baptist. Office: Hancock Textile Co Inc N/S/W Main St Tupelo MS 38801

JARVIS, OSCAR T., JR., university official; b. May, Tex., July 21, 1930; s. Oscar T. and Cordya (Steel) J.; m. Retha Ganelle Nabors, May 28, 1960; children: David Mark, Lee Ann. B.S., Howard Payne U., 1951, M.Ed., 1959; Ed.D., U. Houston, 1962. Asst. county sch. supt., Brown County, Tex., 1956-59, tchr. pub. schs., Midland, Tex., 1959-60, Austin, Tex., 1960-61; asst. prof. edn. U. Ga., Athens, 1962-66, grad. faculty, 1964-70, asso. prof., 1966-70; prof. curriculum and instrn. U. Tex., El Paso, 1970-74, chmn. dept., 1970-72; prof. edn., dean Sch. Edn. U. Pacific, Stockton, Calif., 1974-83, acad. v.p., 1983—; cons. Inst. Ednl. Devel., N.Y.C., 1968. Author: (with H. Gentry, L. Stephens) Public School Business Administration and Finance: Effective Policies and Practices, 1969, (with Haskin R. Pounds) Organizing, Administering and Supervising the Elementary School, 1969, (with M.J. Rice) An Introduction to Elementary Education, 1972. Mem. Am. Assn. Sch. Adminstrs., Am. Ednl. Research Assn., AAUP, Phi Delta Kappa, Phi Kappa Phi. Office: Office of Acad Vice Pres Univ of Pacific Stockton CA 95211

JARVIS, RONALD DEAN, life insurance company executive; b. Maloy, Iowa, Mar. 2, 1937; s. James E. and Ruth S. (Balcom) J.; m. Mary Campanelli, Aug. 26, 1961; children: James M., Susan C., Elaine M. B.S., U. Conn., 1965; C.L.U., 1970. With Security-Conn. Life Ins. Co., 1965—, v.p., then sr. v.p., chief mktg. officer, Avon, Conn., 1970-78; pres., chief operating officer, 1978—, also dir. Bd. corporators St. Francis Hosp. and Med. Center, Hartford, Conn., Hartford (Conn.) Hosp.; mem. adv. bd. U. Conn.; bd. dirs. Inst. of Living. Recipient Outstanding Alumni award U. Conn., 1980. Mem. Nat. Assn. Life Underwriters, Am. Soc. C.L.U.s, U. Conn. Alumni Assn. Republican. Roman Catholic. Office: 20 Security Dr Avon CT 06001

JARVIS, TERRANCE CARLYLE, department store executive, consultant; b. Mobile, Ala., Mar. 26, 1943; s. Henry Milton and Ida Jo J.; m. Gabriela C. Rotter, Dec. 9, 1971; children: Erik C., Alexander C. B.S., U. Ala., 1968. Mgr. gen. mdse Gayfer's Dept. Store, Mobile, 1972; store mgr. Gayfer's Dept Store, Pensacola, Fla., 1972-73; mgr. gen. mdse Mercantile Stores, N.Y.C., 1974-76; pres., chief exec. officer Peoples Store, Tacoma, 1976, Lion Store, Toledo, 1976-78, Jones Store Co., Kansas City, Mo., 1978—; bd. dirs. Credit Bur., Kansas City, 1978—. Bd. dirs. local council Boy Scouts Am., 1979—; bd. dirs. Kansas City Arts Council, 1980—, Am. Cancer Soc., Kansas City chpt., 1980—; mem. Kansas City Civic Council, 1979—, Kansas City Downtown Council, 1980—. Mem. Young Pres. Orgn., Kansas City C. of C. Office: Jones Store Co 1201 Main Kansas City MO 64105 *I am forever grateful to God and to those with whom I came in contact early in my adult years. Through the example and kindness of others did I learn early. Success is the result of dedication, loyalty and ethusiasm, but true success is a calmness of mind. My continuing goals in life include offering the same assistance to others that I was so fortunate to receive, sharing family joys, building true friendships and experiencing frequent tranquility.*

JARVIS, WILLIAM ESMOND, Canadian government official; b. Gladstone, Man., Can., Dec. 10, 1931; s. Frederick Roberts and Dorothy Wells (Tuckwell) J.; children—Cheryl, Darrell, Dennis, Morgan. B.Sc., U. Man., 1950-55; M.Sc., Mich. State U., 1960. With Dept. Agr. Province of Man., Can., 1955-67, dept. minister, 1962-67; asst. dept. minister Govt. Can., Ottawa, Ont., 1967-75; coordinator grains group Dept. Industry Trade and Commerce, 1971-75, asso. minister, 1975-77; chief commr. Can. Wheat Bd., Winnipeg, Man., 1977—. Recipient U. Man. Alumni Assn. Jubilee award, 1981. Mem. Agrl. Inst. Can., Man. Inst. Agrologists. Mem. Ch. of Can. Home: 4 Neil Pl Winnipeg MB R3P 0T8 Canada Office: 423 Main St Winnipeg MB R3C 2P5 Canada

JASANOFF, JAY HAROLD, linguistics educator; b. Bklyn., June 12, 1942; s. Milton and Edith (Deutsch) J.; m. Shelia Sen, June 15, 1968; children: Alan, Maya. A.B., Harvard U., 1963; postgrad., U. Bonn., Germany, 1963-64; Ph.D., Harvard U., 1968. Asst. prof. U. Calif., Berkeley, 1969-70, Harvard U., 1970-75, assoc. prof., 1975-78; assoc. prof. linguistics Cornell U., 1978-81, prof., 1981—, chmn. dept., 1981—. Author: Stative and Middle in Indo-European, 1978. Fellow Am. Inst. Indian Studies, 1968-69. Mem. Linguistic Soc. Am., Societe de Linguistique de Paris, Philol. Soc., Innstrucker Sprachwissenschaftliche Gesellschaft, Phi Beta Kappa. Home: 115 Glen Pl Ithaca NY 14850 Office: Cornell Univ Ithaca NY 14853

JASEN, MATTHEW JOSEPH, state justice; b. Buffalo, Dec. 13, 1915; s. Joseph John and Celina (Perlinski) Jasinski; m. Anastasia Gawinski, Oct. 4, 1943 (dec. Aug. 1970); children: Peter M., Mark M., Christine (Mrs. David K. Mac Leod), Carol Ann, (Mrs. J. David Sampson); m. Gertrude O'Connor Travers, Mar. 25, 1972 (dec. Nov. 1972); m. Grace Yungbluth Frauenheim, Aug. 31, 1973. Student, Canisius Coll., 1936; LL.B., U. Buffalo, 1939; postgrad., Harvard U., 1944; LL.D. (hon.), Union U., 1980, N.Y. Law Sch., 1981. Bar: N.Y. 1940. Partner firm Beyer, Jasen & Boland, Buffalo, 1940-43; pres. U.S. Security Rev. Bd., Wurttemberg-Baden, Germany, 1945-46; judge U.S. Mil. Govt. Ct., Heidelberg, Germany, 1946-49; sr. partner firm Jasen, Manz, Johnson & Bayger, Buffalo, 1949-57; Supreme Ct. justice State N.Y. 8th Jud. Dist., 1957-67; sr. assoc. judge N.Y. State Ct. Appeals, Albany, 1968—. Contbr. articles to profl. jours. Mem. council U. Buffalo, 1963-66; trustee Canisius Coll. Chair of Polish Culture, also, Nottingham Acad. Served to capt. AUS, 1943-46; ETO. Fellow Hilbert Coll.; recipient Distinguished Alumnus award State U. N.Y. at Buffalo Sch. Law, 1969, also Alumni Assn., 1976, Canisius Coll., 1978. Mem. Nat. Conf. Appellate Judges, State U. N.Y. at Buffalo Law Sch. Alumni Assn. (pres. 1964-65), Am., N.Y. State, Erie County bar assns., Am. Law Inst., Am. Judicature Soc., Lawyers Club Buffalo (pres. 1961-62), Nat. Advocates Club, Profl. Businessmen's Assn. Western N.Y. (pres. 1952), Phi Alpha Delta, DiGamma Soc. Roman Catholic (mem. Bishop's Bd. Govs., Buffalo diocese 1951—). Clubs: K.C. (4 deg.), Wanakah Country.). Home: 26 Pine Terr Orchard Park NY 14127 Office: Court of Appeals Hall Albany NY 12207 also Court of Appeal Chambers Erie County Hall Buffalo NY 14202

JASINOWSKI, JERRY JOSEPH, economist; b. La Porte, Ind., Jan. 4, 1939. A.B., Ind. U., 1962; M.A., Columbia U., 1967. Fellow Ind. U., 1962; commd. 2d lt. U.S. Air Force, 1962, advanced through grades to capt., 1970; asst. prof. econs. U.S. Air Force Acad., 1970-72; mem. Joint Econ. Com., 1972-76; asst. sec. for policy Dept. Commerce, Washington, 1977-80; exec. v.p., chief economist NAM, Washington, 1980—. Contbr. articles to profl. publs. Mem. Democratic Platform Com., 1976; econ. issues coordinator Carter-Mondale Campaign, liaison coordinator Carter-Mondale transition, 1976-77. Office: Nat Assn Mfrs 1776 F St NW Washington DC 20006

JASKOT, JOHN JOSEPH, insurance company executive; b. Allentown, Pa., Dec. 5, 1921; s. George W. and Anna (Kuzma) J.; m. Joyce Ranck, May 25, 1946; children: Lisa Anne, Philip Ross. Student, Muhlenberg Coll., Allentown, 1947-49; J.D., George Washington U., 1951, LL.M., 1953. Bar: D.C. 1951. Sr. v.p., gen. counsel, corp. sec. United Services Life Ins. Co., Washington, 1953—; v.p., legal counsel, corp. sec. United Services Gen. Life Co., 1968—; v.p., legal counsel Gen. Services Life Ins. Co., Washington, 1975—; sec. Bankers Security Life Ins. Soc., 1982—, Provident Life Ins. Co., 1983—; dir. United Services Equities.; corp. sec. Provident Life Ins. Co., Bismarck, N.D. Served with USCGR, 1942-46; PTO. Mem. D.C. Bar Assn., ABA, Assn. Life Ins. Counsel, Nat. Lawyers Club. Home: 12505 Galway Dr Silver Spring MD 20904 Office: 1701 Pennsylvania Ave NW Washington DC 20006 *True success should only be measured by an individual's own assessment of his accomplishments.*

JASLOW, ROBERT IRWIN, physician, hosp. adminstr.; b. Reading, Pa., Apr. 27, 1923; s. Paul and Frances (Miller) J.; m. Edith Kay Supak, May 18, 1946; children—Ann Sharon, Alan Philip, Paula Sue. B.A., Lehigh U., 1943; M.D., Jefferson Med. Coll. Phila., 1947. Diplomate: Am. Bd. Pediatrics. Intern Jewish Hosp., Phila., 1947-48; resident Willard Parker Hosp. for Contagious Diseases, N.Y.C., 1948; pediatrics Jewish Hosp., Bklyn., 1949-50; practice medicine specializing in pediatrics, Chambersburg, Pa., 1953-60, adminstr. medicine, Northville, Mich., 1960-65, Washington, 1965-71, White Plains, N.Y., 1971-72, Fairfax, Va., 1972-74; clin. dir. Pennhurst State Sch. Annex No. 1 South Mountain, Pa., 1955-59; psychiat. clin. dir. Plymouth State Home and Tng. Sch., 1960-61, acting med. supt., 1961, med. supt., 1961-65; asso. pediatrician Children's Hosp., Detroit, 1964-65; chief Mental Retardation br. USPHS, Washington, 1965-67; dir. div. mental retardation Dept. Health, Edn. and Welfare, 1967-71; dir. Westchesster (N.Y.) State Sch., 1971-72, No. Va. Tng. Center for Mentally Retarded, Fairfax, 1972-74, Woodhaven Center, Phila., 1974-78; med. dir. New Lisbon (N.J.) State Sch., 1978—; instr. pediatrics Sch. Medicine, Wayne State U., 1961-64, clin. asst. prof., 1964-65; asso. prof. clin. pediatrics Georgetown U., 1966-70, prof. clin. pediatrics, 1970-71, 72-74; clin. prof. pediatrics Temple U., 1975-78, Camden br. Rutgers Med. Sch., 1978—; Faculty Sch. Edn. U. Mich., summer 1963, lectr. maternal and child health, 1963-65; cons. Nat. Inst. Child Health and Human Devel., HEW, 1963-65. Contbr. articles to profl. jours. Served to capt. AUS, 1951-53. Fellow Am. Acad. Pediatrics (past chmn. juvenile delinquency com. Mich. chpt.), Am. Assn. Mental Deficiency, Am. Pub. Health Assn.; mem. N.Y. Acad. Scis. Home: 10 Stafford Pl Yardley PA 19067 *Although I have been embroiled in the need for more money for more services, I cannot help feel that more can be done for the needs of people by the more creative use of resources presently available but not appreciated or utilized properly.*

JASMIN, CLAUDE, writer; b. Montreal, Que., Can., Nov. 10, 1930; s. Edouard and Germaine (Lefevre) J. Author TV serials, also, TV plays, theater, plays, movies; designer.; Author 12 novels, 12 TV dramas, essays, fiction, radio dramas. Recipient Prix Cercle du Livre de France, Prix France-Quevec and France-Can. Prix Wilderness-Anik, Prix Duvernay, Prix Dominion Drama Festival 63. Mem. Writers Union Que., Soc. Authors and Composer Can. Clubs: Seven, Le Groupe des Sept. Home: Box 24 Route No 1 Ste-Adele Jorilo PQ Canada Office: CBC Radio-Can 1400 Dorchester East Montreal PQ Canada

JASMIN, GAETAN, pathologist, educator; b. Montreal, Que., Can., Nov. 24, 1924; s. Horace and Antoinette (Piquette) J.; m. Suzanne Dupont, Oct. 18, 1952; children: Eve, Luc, Pierre. B.A., Coll. St. Laurent, 1945; M.D., U. Montreal, 1951, Ph.D., 1956. Intern Hotel Dieu, Montreal, 1950; asst. prof. exptl. medicine U. Montreal, 1952-55, prof., 1955—, chmn. dept. pathology, 1970-82; research assoc. Md. Research Council Can., 1958-69. Mem. Soc. Exptl. Biology and Medicine, Am. Physiol. Soc., Can. Soc. Clin. Investigation, Histochem. Soc., Muscular Dystrophy Assn. Can., Fedn. Can. Socs. Biology, Internat. Acad. Pathology, Royal Coll. Physicians and Surgeons Can. Home: 189 Glengarry St Montreal PQ H3R 1A3 Canada Office: Dept Pathology Faculty Medicine U Montreal PO Box 6128 Montreal PQ H3C 3J7 Canada

JASNOW, DAVID MICHAEL, physics educator; b. N.Y.C., Apr. 27, 1943; s. George and Muriel (Kaden) J.; m. Carol Ann Herrmann, June 10, 1964; children: Stephanie, Laine. A.B., Cornell U., 1964; Ph.D., U. Ill., 1969. Research assoc. chemistry Cornell U., Ithaca, N.Y., 1968-70; vis. scientist K.F.A. Julich, W. Germany, 1970-71; asst. prof. physics U. Pitts., 1971-75, assoc. prof., 1975-82, prof., 1982—. Contbr. numerous articles to profl. jours. Alfred P. Sloan Found. research fellow, 1973; NSF grantee, 1974—. Mem. Am. Phys. Soc., Phi Beta Kappa. Office: Dept Physics U Pitts Pittsburgh PA 15260

JASPEN, NATHAN, educational statistics educator; b. N.Y.C., Oct. 21, 1917; s. Jacob J. and Sarah (Kantor) J.; m. Helen G. Shulman, June 11, 1944; children: David, Robert, Sandra Hughes, Daniel, Richard. B.S., CCNY, 1942; M.A., George Washington U., 1944; Ph.D., Pa. State U., 1949. Occupational analyst USES, Washington, 1942-47; research fellow Pa. State U., 1947-49, asso. prof., 1949-52; dir. stats. automation Nat. League Nursing, N.Y.C., 1952-59; also cons.; asso. prof. N.Y. U., 1959-62, prof. ednl. stats., 1962-82, prof. emeritus, 1982—, chmn. dept. ednl. stats., 1963-80, chmn. dept. math., sci. and statis. edn., 1980-82; cons. Am. Public Health Assn., USPHS, Bd. Coop. Edn. Services, Westchester. Contbr. articles to profl. jours. Fellow AAAS, Am. Psychol. Assn.; mem. AAUP, Am. Ednl. Research Assn., Am. Statis. Assn., Assn. Computing Machinery, Inst. Math. Stats., Math. Assn. Am., Psychometric Soc., Sigma Xi, Pi Mu Epsilon. Home: 200 Winston Dr Cliffside Park NJ 07010

JASPER, DAVID WESTWATER, lawyer; b. Columbus, Ohio, Aug. 31, 1916; s. David W. and Charlotte (Evans) J.; m. Eleanor Frances Osborn, Aug. 2, 1941; children: Sara C., Mary H., David W., Kenneth O., Jasper. A.B., Kenyon Coll., 1938, LL.D., 1983; J.D., Northwestern U., 1941. Gen. atty. Carrier Corp., Syracuse, N.Y., 1953-59, v.p., gen. counsel, 1959-70, v.p. legal and tax adminstrn., 1970-72, sr. v.p., 1972-76. Trustee Onondaga Savs. Bank, 1959-79; Mem. adv. council N.Y. State Health Planning Commn., 1970-72; pres. Republican Citizens Com. Onondaga County, 1964; trustee emeritus Kenyon Coll. Mem. Am., N.Y. State bar assns., Phi Beta Kappa, Beta Theta Phi, Phi Alpha Delta. Club: Venice Yacht. Home: 126 Bayview Dr Nokomis FL 33555

JASPER, JAY RICHARD, advertising agency executive; b. New Rochelle, N.Y., May 5, 1937; s. David L. and Dorothy W. J. M.A., Brandeis U., 1959; postgrad., Yale U., 1959-60; summer student, Fashion Inst. Tech., Parson's Sch. Design. With Grey Advt., 1966-69; with Ogilvy & Mather, Inc., N.Y.C., 1969—; now sr. v.p., creative dir.; film adaptor-translator Ancinex S.A., Paris, 1960-64; Adviser Nat. Genetics Found., 1978—. Author screenplays. Recipient Clio awards, 1st Stephen Kelly award, Andy awards, Effie awards, Internat. Broadcast awards, 3 David Ogilvy awards; Fulbright grantee, 1961-63. Mem. Nat. Acad. TV Arts and Scis., Am. Film Inst. Office: 2 E 48th St New York NY 10017

JASPER, MARTIN THEOPHILUS, educator; b. Hazlehurst, Miss., Mar. 19, 1934; s. Thomas Theophilus and Alice Maie (Norton) J.; m. Mary Altha Ledbetter, Nov. 2, 1963; children—Nellie Rebecca, Alice Hesta, Martin Theophilus, Mary Margaret, William Richard. B.S., Miss. State U., 1955, M.S., 1962; postgrad., Stevens Inst. Tech., 1963; Ph.D., U. Ala., 1967. Registered profl. engr., Miss. Engr. Am. Cast Iron Pipe Co., Birmingham, Ala., 1955-56; plant metallurigist Vickers, Inc., Jackson, Miss., 1957-59; sr. design engr. missile div. Chrysler Corp., Huntsville, Ala., 1959-60; instr. mech. engring. Miss. State U., 1960-63, asst. prof., 1966-68, asso. prof., 1968-75, prof., 1975—. Contbr. articles to profl. jours. Served to 2d lt., M.S.C. AUS, 1956-57. NSF fellow, 1963-66. NASA fellow, 1963-66. Mem. ASME (chmn. Miss. sect. 1971-72), Soc. Mfg. Engrs. (chpt. chmn. 1969-70, chmn. nat. research edn. grants com. 1974-75), Am. Soc. Engring. Edn., Miss. Acad. Sci., N.Y. Acad. Sci., Sigma Xi, Pi Mu Epsilon, Tau Beta Pi, Pi Tau Sigma. Democrat. Baptist. Clubs: Masons, K.T., Shriners, Kiwanis. Research on fluid dynamics, combustion and incineration systems, design and analysis. Home: PO Box 155 Mississippi State MS 39762

JASPERSEN, FREDERICK ZARR, economist; b. Phila., Sept. 23, 1938; s. Frederick Franklin and Jean Lorraine (Zarr) J.; m. Margie C. Trainor, Oct. 10, 1965. B.A. in Internat. Relations, Dartmouth Coll., 1961; M.A. Peace Corps fellow, Ind. U., 1965; Ph.D. in Econs., Ind. U., 1969. Mem. Peace Corps, Colombia, 1961-63; teaching asst. fellow Ind. U., Bloomington, 1964-65; Harvard U. econ. advisor Ministry Fin., Chile, 1968-69; economist Standard Oil N.J., N.Y.C., 1969-70, Am. Embassy Brazil, 1970-71; sr. economist World Bank, Washington,

1971—; lectr. econs. Chile, Brazil, Ind. U. Contbr. author: World Development Report, 1981, Adjustment Experience and Growth Prospects of the Semi-Industrial Countries, 1981. V.p. Sidwell Friends Sch. Alumni Assn., 1978-80. Ford Found. Latin Am. teaching fellow Fletcher Sch., Tufts U., 1967-68. Mem. Am. Econ. Assn. Clubs: Dartmouth (Washington); Georgetown, U. Yates. Home: 5013 Randall Ln Washington DC 20816 Office: 1818 H St Washington DC 20433

JASPIN, ELLIOT GARY, newspaper reporter; b. Mineola, N.Y., May 26, 1946; s. Leon and Ethel Rica (Schoenfeld) J.; m. Janet Gail Thomas, Aug. 13, 1977; children: Jessica Megan, Katy Rebecca. B.A. in Econs, Colby Coll., Waterville, Maine, 1969. Reporter Kennebec Jour., Augusta, Maine, 1971-72; investigative reporter Pottsville (Pa.) Republican, 1972-74, 76-79; wire service editor Times News, Lehighton, Pa., 1974-76; investigative reporter Phila. Daily News, 1979—. Recipient Keystone Press award investigation reporting, 1974, 78, 79; Edward J. Meeman award, 1978; Silver Gavel award, 1979; Pulitzer prize spl. local reporting, 1979; AP Mng. Editors award, 1978, 79; U. Mo. Sch. Journalism award, 1978; others. Mem. Investigative Reporters and Editors Assn. Office: Providence Journal 75 Fountain St Providence RI 02902

JASSY, LIONEL SAMI, lawyer; b. Cairo, May 17, 1923; U.S., 1963, naturalized, 1968; s. Sami and Rachel (Mosseri) J.; m. Marlene DuFort, Sept. 10, 1969; children—Lucien, Loic. LL.B., Sorbonne, 1945; postgrad., N.Y. U. Law Sch., 1966. Bar: Egyptian bar 1945, N.Y. Bar 1968. Partner firm S & L Jassy, Cairo, 1949-64; with European Am. Bank, 1964—, v.p., 1969-76, sr. v.p., gen. counsel, N.Y.C., 1976—; chmn. bd. Gestam Inc.; dir. Artois Imports, Inc. Mem. Am. Bar Assn., N.Y. State Bar Assn., N.Y. Clearing House Assn., N.Y.C. Bar Assn., N.Y. State Bankers Assn. Club: India House (N.Y.C.). Home: 114 Arcadia Rd Allendale NJ 07401 Office: 10 Hanover Sq New York NY 10015

JASTROW, ROBERT, physicist; b. N.Y.C., Sept. 7, 1925; s. Abraham and Marie (Greenfield) J. A.B., Columbia, 1944, M.A., 1945, Ph.D., 1948; post-doctoral fellow, Leiden U., 1948-49, Princeton Inst. Advanced Study, 1949-50, 53, U. Calif. at Berkeley, 1950-53; D.Sc. (hon.), Manhattan Coll., 1980. Asst. prof. Yale, 1953-54; cons. nuclear physics U.S. Naval Research Lab., Washington, 1958-62; head theoretical div. Goddard Space Flight Center NASA, 1958-61, chmn. lunar exploration com., 1959-60, mem. com., 1960-62; dir. Goddard Inst. Space Studies, N.Y.C., 1961-81; adj. prof. geology Columbia, 1961-81, dir. Summer Inst. Space Physics, 1962-70, adj. prof. astronomy, 1977-82; adj. prof. earth sci. Dartmouth, 1973—. Author: The Evolution of Stars, Planets and Life, 1967, Astronomy: Fundamentals and Frontiers, 1972, Until the Sun Dies, 1977, God and the Astronomers, 1978, Red Giants-White Dwarfs, 1979, The Enchanted Loom, 1981; Editor: Exploration of Space, 1960; co-editor: Jour. Atmospheric Scis, 1962-74, The Origin of the Solar System, 1963, The Venus Atmosphere, 1969. Recipient Medal of Excellence Columbia, 1962, Grad. Faculties Alumni award, 1967; Arthur S. Flemming award, 1965; medal for exceptional sci. achievement NASA, 1968. Fellow Am. Geophys. Union, A.A.A.S., Am. Phys. Soc.; mem. Internat. Acad. Astronautics, Council Fgn. Relations, Leakey Found. Clubs: Cosmos, Explorers, Century. Home: 22 Riverside Dr New York NY 10023

JATRAS, STEPHEN JAMES, electronics company executive; b. Mckeesport, Pa., Apr. 7, 1926; s. Andrew and Verna (Filakowski) J.; children: Stephanie Ann, Andrew Anthony, Christopher Dale, Cindy Lou, Shawn James, Todd Charles. B.S. in Elec. Engring, Carnegie Inst. Tech., 1947; S.M., Mass. Inst. Tech., 1952; Sloan fellow, Stanford Grad. Sch. Bus, 1958. Dial systems engr. Stromberg Carlson Co., Rochester, N.Y., 1947-48; instr. elec. engring. U. Mass., 1948-50; research engr. Mass. Inst. Tech., 1950-52; v.p. chief engr. Midwestern Instruments Co., Tulsa, 1952-56; v.p., gen. mgr. Lockheed Electronics div. Lockheed Aircraft Corp., 1956-65; pres., dir. Telex Corp., Tulsa, from 1965, chief exec. officer, chmn. bd., 1981—; dir. D.G. O'Brien Inc., Fourth Nat. Bank. Chmn. bd. Tulsa YMCA; trustee Carnegie Mellon U.; adv. bd. Salvation Army, Indian Nations council Boy Scouts Am. Served with AUS, 1944-46. Mem. IEEE (sr.), Tulsa C. of C. (dir.), Sigma Xi, Tau Beta Pi. Office: Box 1526 Tulsa OK 74101

JAUCHEM, CLARENCE RALPH, government consultant; b. Akron, Ohio, Nov. 22, 1916; s. Edward B. and Mina (Rutteman) J.; m. Roberta M. Ohl, Jan. 9, 1942; children: Philip, James. B.S. in Bus Administrn, U. Akron, 1941; grad. auditing, Ohio State U., 1945-46. C.P.A., N.C. Cons. to sec. treasury Commonwealth P.R., 1955; asst. dir., policy staff comptroller gen., U.S., 1958; mem. profl. staff U.S. Congress, 1958-60; treas., dir. finance Pan Am. Union, 1961-64; dir. budget and finance systems staff, spl. asst. State Dept., 1964-65; dir. financial systems div. P.O. Dept., Washington, 1965-70; asst. controller for accounting U.S. Postal Service, Washington, 1970-72; lectr. Inst. Pub. Administrn., Kampala, Uganda, 1971; adviser to Ministry of Fin., Uganda, 1971; financial cons. to minister finance, Jamaica, W.I., 1972—; mem. panel fiscal experts IMF, 1974—; budget adviser to ministry finance Govt. of Jordan, 1974; fiscal adviser Ministry of Fin. and Planning, Govt. of Sri Lanka, 1977, Ministry of Planning, Govt. of Tanzania, 1979; acctg. adviser Govt. of Liberia, 1980, Govt. of Kenya, 1981-82; budget and acctg. cons. Govt. of Federated States of Micronesia, 1983. Bd. dirs. Pan Am. Devel. Found. Mem. Fed. Govt. Accountants Assn. (dir.). Methodist (asso. dist. lay leader Va. conf.). Home and Office: 7112 Capital View Dr McLean VA 22101

JAUDON, VALERIE, artist; b. Greenville, Miss., Aug. 6, 1945; d. Baize R. and Gladys E. (Hill) J.; m. Richard Kalina, Oct. 23, 1979. Student, Miss. State Coll. for Women, 1963-65, Memphis Acad. Art, 1965, U. of Americas, Mexico, 1966-67, St. Martins Sch. Art, London, 1968-69. One-woman shows of paintings include, Holly Solomon Gallery, N.Y.C., 1977-79, 81, Pa. Acad. Fine Arts, Phila., 1977, Galerie Bishofberger, Zurich, Switzerland, 1979, Galerie Hans Strelow, Dusseldorf, W. Ger., 1980, Corcoran Gallery, Los Angeles, 1981, Sidney Janis Gallery, N.Y.C., 1983, Quadrat Mus., Bottrop, W.Ger., Amerika Haus, Berlin, Dart Gallery, Chgo., numerous group shows, latest being, Mayor Gallery, London, 1979, Galerie Habermann, Cologne, Germany, Galerie Hans Strelow, Dusseldorf, Galerie Modern Art, Vienna, Austria, 1980, Mus. Modern Art, Oxford, Eng., Greenberg, Gallery, St. Louis, Ill. Wesleyan U., Bloomington, Ill., Sidney Janis Gallery, N.Y.C., St. Peters Ch., N.Y.C., San Francisco Art Inst., Mus. Modern Art, N.Y.C., SUNY, Plattsburgh, Leo Castelli Gallery, N.Y.C., Thomas Segal Gallery, Boston, Venice (Italy) Biennale, Nat. Gallery of Art, Washington, Hamilton Coll., Clinton, N.Y., 1981, Chgo. Art Inst.; numerous group shows, latest being, Mus. Fine Arts, Boston, 1982, Neuberger Mus., Purchase, N.Y., 1982, Hudson River Mus., Yonkers, N.Y., 1983, Berkshire Mus., Pittsfield, Mass., La Jolla Mus., Calif.; executed mural, Ins. Co. of N. Am., Phila., 1977; represented in permanent collection, Hirshhorn Mus., Washington. Recipient 1st prize award So. Contemporary Arts Festival, 1967, Art award Miss. Inst. Arts and Letters, 1981; N.Y. State CAPS grantee for graphics, 1980. Address: 139 Bowery St New York NY 10002

JAUMOT, FRANK EDWARD, JR., automobile parts manufacturing company executive; b. Charleston, W.Va., Aug. 3, 1923; s. Frank Edward and Fayetta Florence (Williams) J.; m. Jean Adelaide Hite, Sept. 7, 1947; children: Cherie Jeanne Jaumot Ratliff, Frank Edward. B.S. in Physics, Western Md. Coll., Westminster, 1947, D.Sc. (hon.), 1966; Ph.D. in Physics, U. Pa., 1951. Instr. physics U. Pa., 1950-52, vis. asso. prof. metallurgy, 1954-56; chief physics of metals sect. Franklin Inst. Labs., 1952-56; with Delco Radio div. Gen. Motors Corp., 1956-70, dir. research and engring., 1966-70, dir. research and engring. Delco Electronics div., Kokomo, Ind., 1970—; mem. nat. materials adv. bd. Nat. Acad. Sci. Author: A Bibliography of Diffusion of Gases, Liquids and Solids in Solids, 1958; contbr. to: Foundations of Future Electronics, 1961, Selected Papers on New Techniques for Energy Conversion, 1961, Advances in Electronics Vol. 17, 1962; also numerous papers. Past pres., life mem. bd. dirs. Kokomo YMCA, 1957—; pres., exec. bd. Sagamore council Boy Scouts Am., 1967—; treas. Kokomo Symphonic Soc., 1973-79; mem. long range planning com. of bd. trustees Western Md. Coll., 1975—; mem. microelectronics and fed. research programs coms. Ind. Bd. Sci. and Tech. Served with AUS, 1942-46. Recipient Alumni award Western Md. Coll., 1962. Mem. Am. Phys. Soc., IEEE, Soc. Automotive Engrs., Am. Assn. Physics Tchrs., Am. Inst. Physics, Am. Ordnance Assn., Armed Forces Communications and Electronics Assn., Kokomo Engring. Soc., Electronic Industries Assn. (past chmn., mem. exec. com. solid state products div.), Howard County C. of C., Sigma Xi. Republican. Methodist. Clubs: Kokomo Country, Rotary (past pres.), Elks (Kokomo)). Home: 505 Rue de Chateau Kokomo IN 46902 Office: PO Box 1104 M/S R232 Kokomo IN 46901

JAUNICH, ROBERT, II, computer company executive; b. Norristown, Pa., Feb. 18, 1940; s. Raymond M. and Florence Merrill (Messersmith) J.; m. Kathleen Magee, June 27, 1964; children: Robert Prescott, Peter Christian, William Matthew. B.A. in Econs, Wesleyan U., 1961; M.B.A. in Mktg, Wharton Grad. Sch., U. Pa., 1963. Brand mgr. Procter & Gamble Co., Cin., 1964-70; with Memorex Corp., Santa Clara, Calif., 1970-78, exec. v.p., 1971-78; sr. v.p. Consol. Foods Corp., Chgo., 1978-84, exec. v.p., 1981-82, pres., 1983; pres., chief exec. officer, dir. Osborne Computer Corp., Hayward, Calif., 1984—; dir. Maui Divers Hawaii, Ltd. Served with U.S. Army, 1961-62. Home: 69 Flood Circle Atherton CA 94025 Office: Osborne Computer Corp 26500 Corporate Ave Hayward CA 94545

JAVAN, ALI, educator, physicist; b. Tehran, Iran, Dec. 27, 1926; came to U.S., 1948, naturalized, 1963; s. Moosa and Jamileh (Azarbaghi) J.; m. Marjorie Browning, July 12, 1962; children: Maia Azar, Lila Hamideh. Student, Tehran U., 1947-48; Ph.D., Columbia U., 1954. Mem. research staff Bell Telephone Labs., Murray Hill, N.J., 1958-61; mem. faculty MIT, 1960—, prof. physics, 1964—, Francis Wright Davis prof., 1978—; founder, chmn. bd. Laser Sci., Inc., 1981—; cons. to industry and govt., 1960—. Recipient John and Fanny Hertz Found. award, 1964, Ballantine medal Franklin Inst., 1962, Sepas medal, Iran, 1971; Frederic Ives medal Optical Soc. Am., 1975; Outstanding Patent award N.J. Research and Devel. Council, 1977; U.S. Sr. Scientist award Humboldt Found., 1980; Guggenheim fellow, 1967. Fellow Am. Phys. Soc., Optical Soc. Am., Nat. Acad. Sci., Third World Acad. Scis. (assoc. founding fellow); mem. Am. Acad. Arts and Scis., Royal Acad. Sci. in Iran (hon.), Sigma Xi. Spl. research fundamental quantum electronics. Inventor first gas laser, 1960. Home: 12 Hawthorne St Cambridge MA 02138 Office: Mass Inst Tech Cambridge MA 02139

JAVID, MANUCHER J., neurosurgeon; b. Tehran, Iran, Jan. 11, 1922; came to U.S., 1944, naturalized, 1957; s. Asdolah and Touba (Ahdiyeh) J.; m. Lida Emma Fabbri, Oct. 19, 1951; children—Roxane, Daria, Jeffrey, Claudia. M.D., U. Ill., 1946. Diplomate: Am. Bd. Neurosurgery. Intern Augustana Hosp., Chgo., 1946-47, resident gen. surgery, 1947-48, resident neurosurgery, 1948-49; asst. in neuropathology Ill. Neuropsychiat. Inst., Chgo., 1948-49; fellow in neurosurgery Lahey Clinic, Boston, 1949; resident neurosurgery New Eng. Med. Center, Boston, 1950; clin. research fellow neurosurgery Mass. Gen. Hosp., Boston, 1950, asst. resident, 1951, sr. resident neurosurgery, 1952; teaching fellow in surgery Harvard, 1952; instr. Med. Sch. U. Wis., Madison, 1953-54, asst. prof., 1954-57, asso. prof., 1957-62, prof. neurosurgery, 1962, chmn. div. neurosurgery, 1963—; Cons. neurosurg VA Hosp., Madison, Mercy Hosp., Janesville, Wis., 1956—. Contbr. articles profl. jours. Mem. AMA, ACS, Soc. Neurol. Surgeons, Am. Assn. Neurol. Surgeons, AAAS, Am. Assn. Med. Colls., AAUP, Am. Trauma Soc., Pan Am. Med. Assn., Soc. for Neurosci., Central Neurosurg. Soc. (pres. 1964), N.Y. Acad. Scis., Xeiron, Sigma Xi, Phi Beta Pi. Mem. Baha'i Faith. Club: Rotarian. Introduced clin. use of urea for reduction intracranial and intraocular pressure. Home: 4750 Lafayette Dr Madison WI 53705 Office: Univ Wis Hosp and Clinics 600 Highland Ave Madison WI 53792 *Since I was a small child, I wanted to be a doctor and help the sick. As I grew older, the Baha'i Faith, served as a guideline to achieve this goal. Its teachings have helped me to appreciate the oneness of God, the oneness of religion, the oneness of humanity, and the sanctity of life.*

JAVITS, ERIC MOSES, lawyer; b. N.Y.C., May 24, 1931; s. Benjamin Abraham and Lily (Braxton) J.; m. Margaretha Espersson, May 24, 1979; children by previous marriage: Jocelyn Ingrid, Eric Moses. Student, Stanford U., 1948-49; A.B., Columbia U., 1952, J.D., 1955. Bar: N.Y. 1955, U.S. Supreme Ct. 1959. Temp. cons. Office Def. Moblzn., Washington, 1951; asso. firm Javits & Javits, N.Y.C., 1955-58, mem. firm, 1958-82; sr. ptnr. Javits Hinckley Rabin & Engler, 1982—; ind. gen. ptnr. ML Venture Ptnrs.; dir. Royal Palm Beach Colony Inc., Banco Central N.Y.; pres., dir. Fair Return League, Inc.; chmn. bd., dir. Euclid Equipment; spl. dep. to N.Y. Atty. Gen. Elections Frauds Bur., 1958-59; counsel N.Y. Senate Com. on Affairs of City N.Y., 1959. Author: SOS New York, 1961. Mem. N.Y.C. Mayor's Com. for N.Y. Shakespeare Festival, 1963-64; mem. N.Y. met. com. United World Federalists, 1964-65; mem. numerous charitable coms.; bd. govs. N.Y. Young Republican Club, 1955-58, v.p., 1957-58, bd. advisers, 1958-64; mem. exec. com. Jacob K. Javits campaigns, 1954—; mem. N.Y. Republican County Com., 1960-64; mem. exec. com. Nat. Republican Club, 1962-70; exec. sec. U.S. Paper Exporters Council, Inc., 1964-72; trustee, sec. Am. Health Found.; pres., bd. dirs. Shareowners Ednl. Found., Spanish Inst., N.Y.C.; bd. dirs. Nat. Com. Am. Fgn. Policy, Inc. Decorated Order of Isabella Catolica (Spain), 1981. Mem. Assn. Bar City N.Y., New York County Lawyers Assn., Am., N.Y. State bar assns., Nat. Inst. Social Scis., Am. Judicature Soc., World Peace Through Law Center (charter), Citizens Union, Phi Beta Kappa, Beta Theta Pi, Phi Alpha Delta, Nacoms. Jewish. Clubs: City Athletic, Town Tennis (N.Y.C.). Office: 1345 Ave of Americas New York NY 10105

JAVITS, JACOB KOPPEL, former U.S. senator, educator, lawyer; b. N.Y.C., May 18, 1904; s. Morris and Ida (Littman) J.; m. Marian Ann Borris, Nov. 30, 1947; children: Joy D., Joshua M., Carla I. LL.B., NYU, 1926; 37 hon. degrees. Bar: N.Y. 1927. Since practiced in N.Y.C.; trial lawyer; mem. 80th-83d congresses 21st N.Y. Dist.; atty. gen. New York, 1955-57; U.S. senator from N.Y., 1957-80; ranking minority mem. Labor and Human Resources Com., Joint Econ. Com., mem. Fgn. Relations Com., Govt. Affairs Com.; mem. firm Javits, Trubin, Sillcocks and Edelman, N.Y.C., 1958-71; of counsel Trubin, Sillcocks, Edleman & Knapp, 1981—; adj. prof. public affairs Columbia U., N.Y.C., 1981—; adj. prof. SUNY-Stony Brook, 1982—; chmn. No. Atlantic Assembly's Polit. Com., Com. of Nine, Parliamentarian's Com. for Less Developed Nations; U.S. del. to 25th anniversary UN Gen. Assembly, 1970; mem. Nat. Commn. Marijuana and Drug Abuse, 1971-73; lectr. on econ. and polit. subjects. Author: A Proposal to Amend the Anti-Trust Laws, 1939, Discrimination U.S.A, 1960, Order of Battle, A Republican's Call to Reason, 1964, Who Makes War, 1973, Javits: The Autobiography of a Public Man, 1981; series of articles on polit. philosophy for Rep. party, 1946. Commd. maj. U.S. Army, 1942; asst. to chief of ops. in C.W.S.; served in ETO and PTO, 1942-45; discharged as lt. col.; col. chem. warfare N.Y.N.G. Decorated Legion of Merit; awarded Presdl. medal of Freedom, 1983. Mem. Am. Legion, VFW, Amvets, Jewish War Vets., Am. Vets. Com. Republican. Jewish. Clubs: City Athletic, Harmonie (N.Y.); Capitol Hill (Washington).

JAWETZ, ERNEST, physician, educator; b. Vienna, Austria, June 9, 1916; came to U.S., 1939, naturalized, 1944; s. Karl and Angela (Goldhammer) J.; m. Mary Jean Morse, Oct. 29, 1954; children: Katherine, Steven, Michael, Anne. Student, U. Vienna, 1934-38; M.S., U. N.H., 1940; Ph.D., U. Calif. at San Francisco, 1942; M.D., Stanford, 1945. Intern Stanford Lane Hosp., San Francisco, 1945-46; sr. asst. surgeon USPHS, 1946-48; mem. faculty U. Calif. Med. Center, San Francisco, 1948—, prof. microbiology and medicine, lectr. pediatrics, 1953—, chmn. dept. microbiology, 1962-78; Cons. VA, 1952—; A. Wright lectr., London, Eng., 1952, McArthur lectr., Edinburgh, Scotland, 1952; Univ. lectr. U. London, 1962. Author: Review of Medical Microbiology, 16th edit, 1984; also numerous articles.; Mem. editorial bds. med. jours. Served with AUS, 1943-46. Mem. Am. Fedn. Clin. Research (chmn. Western sect. 1952), Western Soc. Clin. Research (pres. 1961), Am. Soc. Clin. Investigation, Western Assn. Physicians. Spl. research infectious diseases, chemotherapy, virology, immunology. Home: 19 Cushing Dr Mill Valley CA 94941 Office: Univ California Med Center San Francisco CA 94143

JAWORSKI, RONALD VINCENT, professional football player; b. Lackawanna, N.Y., Mar. 23, 1951. Student, Youngstown State U. Player Los Angeles Rams, 1973-77, Phila. Eagles, 1977—; ptnr. Ron Jaworski Sports Enterprises; mem. NFL Championship Game, 1980 season, Nat. Football All-Star Game, 1981. Office: Phila Eagles Veterans Stadium Philadelphia PA 19148 *

JAY, BURTON DEAN, insurance actuary; b. Sparta, Ill., Jan. 16, 1937; s. Everett Russell and Bertha (Halemeyer) R.; m. Eva May Eudy, Aug. 10, 1958; children—Cynthia Ann, Sylvia Ruth, Jon Russell. B.A. in Math, Ripon Coll., 1959. Actuarial student Northwestern Nat. Life Ins. Co., Mpls., summers 1953-55; exec. v.p., chief actuary United of Omaha Life Ins. Co., Omaha, 1962—. Served to 1st lt. AUS, 1959-62. Fellow Soc. Actuaries (chmn. part VI com. 1969-73, program com. 1975-80, chmn. 1980, gov. 1982, gov.); mem. Am. Acad. Actuaries (com. on life ins. financial reporting prins., chmn. 1980, dir. 1981), Life Ins. Mktg. Research Assn. (fin. mgmt. research com., chmn. com. 1977-78), Am. Council Life Ins (actuarial com. 1983). Methodist (adminstrv. bd.). Home: 3056 Armbrust Dr Omaha NE 68124 Office: United of Omaha Omaha Plaza Omaha NE 68175

JAY, ERIC GEORGE, educator; b. Colchester, Eng., Mar. 1, 1907; s. Henry and Maude (Lucking) J.; m. Margaret Webb, July 22, 1937; children—Christine (Mrs. Oskar Sykora), Susan (Mrs. Phillip Andersen), Peter. B.A., Leeds (Eng.) U., 1929, M.A., 1930; B.D., London (Eng.) U., 1937, M.Th., 1940, Ph.D., 1951; D.D. (hon.), Montreal Diocesan Theol. Coll., 1965, Trinity Coll., Toronto, 1975, United Theol. Coll., Montreal, 1976. Ordained to ministry Anglican Ch., 1931; asst. curate St. Augustine's Ch., Stockport, Cheshire, Eng., 1931-34; lectr. theology King's Coll., London, 1934-47; dean of Nassau, Bahamas, 1948-51; sr. chaplain to Archbishop of Canterbury, 1951-58; prin. Montreal Diocesan Theol. Coll., 1958-63; prof. hist. theology McGill U., Montreal, Que., Can., 1958-75, emeritus prof., 1977—, dean faculty div., 1963-70; canon Christ Ch., Montreal, 1960—. Author: The Existence of God, 1946, Origen's Treatise on Prayer, 1954, Friendship with God, 1958, New Testament Greek, An Introductory Grammar, 1958, Son of Man, Son of God, 1965, The Church: Its Changing Image Through Twenty Centuries, 1977. Served as chaplain RAF, 1940-45. Fellow King's Coll., 1949. Mem. Canadian Theol. Soc. (pres. 1965). Home: 570 Milton St Apt 15 Montreal PQ H2X 1W4 Canada

JAY, FRANK PETER, editor, educator; b. Bklyn., Feb. 12, 1922; s. Frank G. and Harriet Ann (Niffer) J.; m. Jayne Marie Charles, Aug. 15, 1947; children—Jennifer, Christopher, Alison, Angela, Jonathan, Melissa, Bryan, Nicole, Matthew. A.B., Fordham U., 1943; M.A., Columbia U., 1946. Mem. faculty Fordham U., 1946—, prof. English, 1948—; editor-in-chief reference books Funk & Wagnalls, N.Y.C., 1963-65, exec. editor, 1968-73; editor-in-chief reference books Reader's Digest, N.Y.C., 1965-66; dictionary editor-in-chief IEEE, 1975—; sec. com. terminology IEEE. Author: Jack: The Story of a Pretty Good Donkey, 1970, also articles, short stories; editor-in-chief: The New Internat. Year Book, 1963, 64, 65, Internat. Everyman's Ency., 20 vols, 1970. Served with USAAF, 1942-43. Mem. Kappa Delta Pi. Clubs: Overseas Press, Princeton (N.Y.C.); Village Bath (Manhasset, N.Y.). Home: 3 Huntington Rd Port Washington NY 11050

JAY, HERBERT LLOYD, mktg. exec.; b. N.Y.C., May 11, 1924; s. Louis Maurice and Bess (Schottenfeld) J.; m. Charlotte E. Masia, July 31, 1949; children—Adam Reid, Amy Louise. Student, Cornell U., 1942, 45, 46. Advt. mgr. Alexander Smith Inc., 1950-53; v.p., asst. to pres. Aldon Rug Mills. Inc., 1953-56; v.p. marketing Spectrum Fabrics Inc., N.Y.C., 1956-57; dir. advt. Mohasco Industries Inc., Amsterdam, N.Y., 1957-67; pres. Harold J. Siesel Co. Inc., N.Y.C., 1967-71; formed Herbert L. Jay Assos., Inc., 1971—; founder, pres. H.L. Jay Home Fashion Center, 1972—; co-founder Holsted, Inc., N.Y.C., 1981—; cons. Ethan Allen Inc., 1977—; corporator Norwalk Savs. Soc., 1978—. U.S. del. 1st Internat. Econ. Conf., Jerusalem, 1968; Active sch. coms., Dobbs Ferry and Irvington, N.Y., also, local Boy Scouts Am. Served with AUS, 1943-44. Mem. N.Y. Sales Promotion Execs. Club (charter), Advt. Club N.Y.C., Norwalk C. of C., Cornell Book and Bowl Soc. Home: 60 Lords Hwy Weston CT 06880 Office: 556 Main Ave Norwalk CT 06851 *Over the years, I have found that a business will always make more money when it learns to change its primary objective from the accumulation of wealth to providing its public with service.*

JAY, JAMES M(ONROE), educator; b. Fitzgerald, Ga., Sept. 12, 1927; s. John B. and Lizzie (Wells) J.; m. Patsie Phelps, June 5, 1959; children—Mark E., Alicia D., Byron R. A.B., Paine Coll., 1950; M.S., Ohio State U., 1953, Ph.D., 1956. Postdoctoral fellow Ohio State U., Columbus, 1956-57; from asst. prof. to prof. biology So. U., Baton Rouge, 1957-61; asst. prof. Wayne State U., Detroit, 1961-64, asso. prof., 1964-69, prof., 1969—; pres. Balamp Pub. Co., Detroit, 1971—. Author: Modern Food Microbiology, 1970, 2d edit., 1978, Negroes in Science: Natural Science Doctorates, 1876-1969, 1971; contbr. articles to profl. jours. Treas. Detroit Council Polit. Edn., 1971-74, 1st. v.p., 1975-77, pres., 1977-79; bd. dirs. Met. Hosp. Detroit, 1965-69, sec., 1968-69. Served with AUS, 1946-47. Recipient Probus award Wayne State U., 1969, Disting. Alumni award Paine Coll., 1979; Army Research Office grantee, 1978—; NIH grantee, 1957-72, 78—. Fellow Am. Public Health Assn.; mem. Am. Chem. Soc., Am. Soc. Microbiology, Inst. Food Technologists, Soc. Applied Bacteriology (U.K.), Sigma Xi. Home: 4205 Fullerton St Detroit MI 48238

JAY, LONNY JOSEPH, retail department store executive; b. Detroit, Apr. 1, 1942; s. Roman and Harriet (Hosner) J.; m. Becky A. Jay, Aug. 17, 1963; children: Michele, Debra, Laurie. B.S. in Acctg., U. Detroit., 1963, M.B.A. in Fin., 1965. Sr. v.p. May Dept. Stores Co., St. Louis, 1975-80, corp. controller, 1980-81; exec. v.p. adminstrn. May Co.-Calif., Los Angeles, 1981-83, vice chmn., 1983; chmn. Famous-Barr, St. Louis, 1983—. Bd. dirs. U. Santa, Clara, Calif., 1983—, Central City Assn., Los Angeles, 1983—, Visitors Conv. Bur., Los Angeles, 1983—; sect. chmn. United Way, Los Angeles, 1983—. Mem. Am. Mgmt. Assn. Office: Famous-Barr 601 Olive St Saint Louis MO 63101

JAYABALAN, VEMBLASERRY, nuclear medicine physician, radiologist; b. India, Apr. 3, 1937; came to U.S., 1970; s. Parameswara and Janakay (Amma) Menon; m. Vijayam Jayabalan, May 2, 1963; children: Koshore, Suresh. B.Sc., Madras Christian Coll., (India), 1955; M.B., B.S., Jipmer U., (India), 1961; Diploma in Med. Radioagnosis, U. Liverpool, (Eng.), 1967. Diplomate: Am. Bd. Radiology, Am. Bd. Nuclear Medicine. Intern Jipmer Hosp., Pondicherry, India, 1961-62; resident in cariology K.E.M. Hosp., Bombay, India, 1962-63; resident in radiology Mt. sinai Hosp., Chgo., 1970-72; fellow in nuclear medicine Michael Reese Hosp., Chgo., 1972-73; dir. nuclear medicine Hurley Med. Ctr., Flint, Mich., 1973—; asst. clin. prof. radiology Mich. State U. Fellow Internat. Coll. Physician; mem. Mich. Coll. Nuclear Medicine (mem. legis. com.), Genesee County Med. Soc. (mem. credential and membership com.), Mich. Med. Soc, Radiol. Soc. N.Am., Am. Coll. Nuclear Medicine, Am. Coll. Nuclear Physicians, Brit. Inst. Radiology, Royal Coll. Radiology, Soc. Nuclear Medicine (mem. program com. Central chpt.). Home: 5495 Florida Dr Swartz Creek MI 48473 Office: Hurley Med Ctr Flint MI 48502

JAYE, DAVID ROBERT, JR., hosp. adminstr.; b. Chgo., Aug. 15, 1930; s. David R. and Gertrude (Gibfried) J.; m. Mary Ann Scanlan, June 6, 1953; children—David, Jeffery, Kathleen. B.S., Loyola U. at Chgo., 1952; M.H.A., Northwestern U., 1954. Adminstrv. asst. Chgo. Wesley Meml. Hosp., 1953-54; asst. adminstr. Sharon (Pa.) Gen. Hosp., 1957-60, St. Joseph Hosp., Joliet, Ill., 1960-65; adminstr. Sacred Heart Hosp., Allentown, Pa., 1965-69; pres., chief exec. officer St. Joseph's Hosp., Marshfield, Wis., 1969—. Past pres. North Central Wis. Hosp. Council; mem. Wis. State Health Policy Council; bd. dirs. Wis. Blue Cross. Served as lt., Med. Service Corps USAF, 1954-57. Fellow Am. Coll. Hosp. Adminstrs. (council regents); mem. Am. Hosp. Assn. (council fed. relations), Cath. Hosp. Assn. (past trustee), Wis. Hosp. Assn. (past chmn. bd. trustees). Clubs: Rotary, Elks, K.C., Riveredge Country. Home: 1125 Ridge Rd Marshfield WI 54449 Office: 611 St Joseph Ave Marshfield WI 54449

JAYNE, BENJAMIN ANDERSON, educator; b. Enid, Okla., Oct. 10, 1928; s. Albert and Bertha Elizabeth (Anderson) J.; m. Betty Lu Bailey, Aug. 10, 1950; children—David N., Kristie A., Summer L. A.A., Boise Jr. Coll., 1949; B.S., U. Ida., 1952; M.F., Yale, 1953, Ph.D., 1955. Asst. prof. Yale, 1955-58; asso. prof. Wash. State U., 1959-62; sr. postdoctoral fellow U. Cal. at San Diego, 1963; prof. forestry N.C. State U., 1963-66, U. Wash., Seattle, 1966—, asso. dean, 1966-71, dir., 1971-76; dean Sch. Foresty and Environmental Studies Duke U., 1976—. Editor: Wood and Fiber, Jour. Soc. Wood Sci. and Tech, 1969-72. Mem. A.A.A.S., Soc. Wood Sci. and Tech. (pres. 1968), Soc. Am. Forestry, Sigma Xi, Xi Sigma Pi. Home: 2610 Sevier St Durham NC 27705 Office: Sch Forestry and Environmental Studies Duke U Durham NC 27706

JAYSON, LESTER SAMUEL, lawyer, educator; b. N.Y.C., Oct. 25, 1915; s. Morris and Mary (Gardner) J.; m. Evelyn Sylvia Lederer, Feb. 6, 1943; children: Diane Frankie, Jill Karen, Jayson Ladd. B.S.S. with spl. honors in History and Govt, Coll. City N.Y., 1936; J.D. (bd. student advisers), Harvard, 1939. Bar: N.Y. bar 1940, also D.C. bar, U.S. Supreme Ct 1940. With firm Oseas and Pepper, N.Y.C., 1939-40, Marshall, Bratter & Seligson, 1940-42; spl. asst. to atty. gen. U.S., 1942-50; trial atty. Dept. Justice, 1951-56, chief torts sect. civil div., 1957-60; sr. specialist Am. pub. law, chief Am. law div. Congl. Research Service, Library of Congress, 1960-62, dep. dir. service, 1962-66, dir., 1966-75; prof. law Potomac Sch. Law, 1975-81; Vice chmn. Interdeptl. Fed. Tort Claims Com., 1958-60; rep. Justice Dept. to legal div., air coordinating com. Internat. Civil Aviation Orgn., 1959-60; mem. com. exec. privilege Justice Dept., 1956-60; adv. statutory studies group Commn. Govt. Procurement, 1970-72; mem. adv. council Office Tech. Assessment, 1973-75; cons. govt. relations com. Nat. Assn. Theatre Owners, 1978-79. Author: Handling Federal Tort Claims: Judicial and Administrative Remedies, 1965-83; also articles.; Supervising editor: The Constitution of the United States of America-Analysis and Interpretation, 1964, 72. Mem. ABA, Fed. Bar Assn. (chmn., then vice chmn. fed. tort claims com. 1963-66, 70-74, chmn. 1967-68, mem. nat. council 1967-73), Am. Friends of Wilton Park, Assn. Trial Lawyers Am., Pi Sigma Alpha (hon.). Clubs: Cosmos, Harvard (Washington). Home: 7512 Newmarket Dr Bethesda MD 20817

JAZAYERY, MOHAMMAD ALI, foreign languages and literature educator; b. Shushtar, Iran, May 27, 1924; came to U.S., 1951; s. Mohammad Kazem and Batul J. J. Lic., U. Tehran, 1950; postgrad., U. Mich., 1953, Georgetown U., 1954; Ph.D., U. Tex., 1958. Tchr. English high sch., Ahvaz, Iran, 1950-51; teaching asst. in English U. Tex., Austin, 1953-54, instr., 1955-57, lectr., 1957-58, vis. assoc. prof. lingustics and English, 1962-65, assoc. prof. linguistics, 1965-68, prof., 1968-70, prof. Persian dept. Oriental and African Langs. and lit., 1970—; asst. dir. Ctr. for Middle Eastern Studies, 1966-73, dir., 1981—; acting chmn. dept., 1973, chmn., 1976—; linguistic researcher Am. Council Learned Socs., Washington, 1954-55; assoc. prof. English U. Tehran, 1958-59; lectr. Persian U. Mich., Ann Arbor, 1959-62; vis. prof. Johns Hopkins U. Sch. Internat. Studies, Washington, 1957, Harvard U., 1958, Utah State U., Logan, 1961, Princeton U., 1967, NYU, 1968, Portland State U.(Oreg.), 1972; translator Voice of Am, Washington, 1954,55,56; U.S. Office Edn. linguistic researcher in Persian U. Mich., 1959-62; dir. lang. tng. for Iran programs U.S. Peace Corps, Logan, Austin, 1962-65; cons. in field. Author: The Abuses of Our Society, 1947, (with Herbert H. Paper) English for Iranians, 1955, Writing System of Modern Persian, 1955, Elementary Lesson in Persian, 1968; translator: Farhangestan: La Academia Irania de la Lengua, 1979, Practical Psychology in Plain Language, vols. 1-7, 1949-50; editor: (with Peter Avery, massud farzan, H.H. Paper) Modern Persian Reader, vols. 1-3, 1963, (with Edgar C. Plome, Werner Winter) Linguistic and Literary Studies in Honor of Archibald A. Hill. vols. 1-4, 1978-79; bd. editors: Lit. East and West, 1970—; acting editor, 1974-75; contbr. articles to profl. jours., Iran, Europe, U.S. U. Tehran fellow, 1950; Fulbright fellow, 1951-52; grantee Am. Council Learned Socs., 1953, HEW, 1969-70. Mem. MLA, Am. Oriental Soc. (nominating com. 1965-67), Linguistic Soc. Am. (life), Nat. Council Tchrs. of English, Soc. Linguistica Europaea, Middle East Studies Assn. N. Am. (life mem., program com. 1968), Am. council on teaching of Fgn. Langs., Soc. Iranian Studies (council 1978-83), Tchrs. of English to Speakers of Other Langs. Moslem. Home: 705 Laurel Valley Rd Austin TX 78746 Office: Dept Oriental and African Langs and Lits U Tex Austin TX 78712

JEANLOZ, ROGER WILLIAM, biochemist, educator; b. Berne, Switzerland, Nov. 3, 1917; came to U.S., 1947, naturalized, 1953; s. William M. and Rose (Poisat) J.; m. Dorothea A.H. de Passavant, Dec. 20, 1945; children: Patrick Marc (dec.), Claude-André, Raymond François, Danielle Renée, Sylvie Anne. Baccalaureate, Coll. Geneva, Switzerland, 1936; Chem.E., U. Geneva, 1941, D.Sc., 1943; A.M. (hon.), Harvard, 1961, D.Sc., U. Paris, 1980. Research asso. U. Geneva, 1943-45, U. Basel, 1945-46; asst. U. Montreal, 1946-47; sr. research fellow NIH, 1947-48; sr. scientist Worcester Found. Exptl. Biology, 1948-51; asso. biochemist Mass. Gen. Hosp., Boston, 1951-61, biochemist, 1961—; research asso. Harvard Med. Sch., 1951-57, asso. organic chemistry, 1957-60, asst. prof. biol. chemistry, 1960-61, asso. prof., 1961-69, prof., 1969—; Mem. study sect. physiol. chemistry div. research grants NIH, 1964-68, 69-70; mem. physiol. chemistry B. research study com. Am. Heart Assn., 1971-74. Author: (with Balazs) The Amino Sugars, 4 vols, 1965, (with Gregory) Glycoconjugate Research, 2 vols, 1979; Editor: Carbohydrate Research; editorial bd.: Connective Tissue Research, Molecular Biology, Biochemistry and Biophysics; Contbr. articles to profl. jours. Recipient medal Société de Chimie Biologique de France, 1960, U. Liege, 1964, Prix Jaubert U. Geneva, 1973, Hudson prize Am. Chem. Soc., 1973; Stratton award Am. Friends & Switzerland, 1981; Alexander von Humboldt sr. scientist award, 1983; Guggenheim fellow, 1976-77. Mem. Am. Soc. Biol. Chemists, Am. Chem. Soc., Swiss Chem. Soc., Chem. Soc. (London), French Biochem. Soc., Soc. Complex Carbohydrates, Am. Rheumatism Assn. Home: 42 Ruthven Rd Newton MA 02158 Office: Mass Gen Hosp Fruit St Boston MA 02114

JEANNERET, MARSH, publisher; b. Toronto, Ont., Can., Feb. 9, 1917; s. Francois Charles Archile and Evelyn Frances (Geikie) J.; m. Beatrice Mellon, Dec. 31, 1938; children: David Kenneth, Keith Marsh. B.A. in Honour Law, U. Toronto, 1938; LL.D. (hon.), McGill U., Montreal, Que., Can., 1966, D.Litt., Meml. U., St. John's, Nfld., Can., 1977, D.U., Laval U., Que., 1978. Editor Copp Clark Co., Ltd., Toronto, 1938-53; dir. U. Toronto Press, 1953-77; pres. Can. Book Publishers' Council, 1968-69; mem. Ont. Royal Commn. on Book Pub., k1970-73. Author: The Story of Canada, 1946, Canada in North America, 1956; contbr. articles to profl. jours.; chmn. editorial bd.: Scholarly Pub, 1976-80. Decorated officer Order of Can., 1978. Mem. Assn. Canadian Pubs., Assn. Am. Univ. Presses (pres. 1970-71), Canadian Book Mfg. Assn., Graphic Arts Industries Assn. Can., Internat. Assn. Sch. Pubs. (pres. 1976-78), Canadian Copyright Inst. Mem. United Ch. Can. Club: Bd. of Trade (Toronto). Home and Office: Rural Route 1 King City ON L0G 1K0 Canada

JEANNERO, DOUGLAS M., food company executive; b. Canton, Ohio, Sept. 20, 1926; s. Russell K. and Pauline M. (Robertson) J.; m. Ann C. Peterson, June 24, 1950; children: Nan R., Susan T., Jane M. B.B.A., U. Mich., 1951, M.B.A., 1954. Financial analyst Ford Motor Co., Dearborn, Mich., 1951-53; with Gerber Products Co., Fremont, Mich., 1954—, successively fin. analyst, budget mgr., asst. to pres., v.p. finance; dir. Fremont Bank & Trust Co., Fremont Mut. Ins. Co. Bd. dirs., treas. Gerber Meml. Hosp.; trustee Fremont Area Found. Served with AUS, 1944-46. Mem. Fin. Execs. Inst. Congregationalist. Home: 429 Cherokee Dr Fremont MI 49412 Office: 445 State St Fremont MI 49412

JEANNIOT, PIERRE JEAN, airline executive; b. Montpellier, France, Apr. 9, 1933; emigrated to Can., 1947, naturalized, 1954; s. Gaston and Renee (Rameaux) J.; m. Marcia David, Apr. 28, 1979; children: Pierre, Michel, Lynn. B.Sc., Concordia U., Montreal, Que., 1957; postgrad., McGill U., Montreal. With Sperry Gyroscope, to 1955; with Air Can., 1955—, dir. systems adminstrn. and operational research, 1968-70, v.p. computer and systems services, 1970-71, head corp. planning office, 1971-76, v.p. Eastern region, exec. in charge subs. and associated cos., 1976-79, sr. v.p. mktg. and planning, 1979-80, exec. v.p., chief airline ops., 1980-82, exec. v.p., chief operating officer, 1982—; chmn. bd. La Revue du Commerce, 1979-83. Bd. dirs. U. Que., Montreal, chmn. bd., Montreal, 1972-77; chmn. bd. Foundation U. Que. Montreal, 1979—. Mem. Can. Operational Research Soc. (past nat. pres.), Can. Air Transport Assn. (v.p.), Montreal Traffic Club. Roman Catholic. Clubs: Saint-Denis, Mt. Stephen, Laval-sur-le-Lac. Office: Air Canada 1 Pl Ville Marie Montreal PQ Canada H3B 3P7

JEAVONS, NORMAN STONE, lawyer; b. Cleve., Apr. 18, 1930; s. William Norman and Mildred (Stone) J.; m. Kathleen Taze, Oct. 18, 1936; children: Kathleen Stone, Ann Lindsey. B.A., Dartmouth Coll., 1952; LL.B., Case Western Res. U., 1958. Bar: Ohio 1958. Atty. firm Baker & Hostetler, Cleve., 1958—, ptnr., 1968—. Trustee Laurel Sch., Shaker Hts., Ohio, 1980—, Beech Brook, Cleve., 1972—. Served to lt. j.g. USCG, 1952-55. Mem. ABA, Ohio Bar Assn., Cleve. Bar Assn., Order of Coif. Republican. Clubs: Univ. (Cleveland); Cleveland Racquet (Pepper Pike). Home: 22550 Shelburne Rd Shaker Heights OH 44122 Office: 3200 National City Center Cleveland OH 44114

JEBSEN, ROBERT HARRY, medical educator; b. Bklyn., Sept. 5, 1931; s. Henry O. and Frieda P. (Stockfish) J.; m. Joan H. Dannevig, Mar. 25, 1951; children: Eric, James, Lawrence; m. Rebecca Hendricks, Apr. 15, 1978. B.A., Bklyn. Coll., 1953; M.D., N.Y. State U. Downstate, 1956; M.Med. Sci., Ohio State U., 1960. Intern Harrisburg (Pa.) Hosp., 1956-57; resident Ohio State U., 1957-60; dir. dept. phys. medicine and rehab. St. Luke's Hosp., Cedar Rapids, Iowa, 1962-63; asst. prof., asso. prof. phys. medicine and rehab. U. Wash. Sch. Medicine, 1963-68; prof., dir. dept. phys. medicine and rehab. U. Cin. Coll. Medicine, 1968-74, clin. prof., 1974—; dir. dept. phys. medicine and rehab. Christ Hosp., Cin., 1974-77. Editorial bd.: Archives Phys. Medicine and Rehab, 1973-79; asso. editor, 1977-79. Served to capt. M.C. USAF, 1960-62. Nat. Found. Infantile Paralysis grantee, 1957-60. Mem. Am. Acad. Phys. Medicine and Rehab., Am. Congress Rehab. Medicine, Am. Assn. Electromyography and Electrodiagnosis (sec. treas. 1968-71, dir. 1968-76, pres. 1974-75), Assn. Acad. Physiatrists. Home: PO Box 149 Sunman IN 47041

JECK, ROBERT VAN HOUTEN, manufacturing company executive; b. Atlantic, Iowa, Oct. 8, 1931; s. George Van Houten and Gladys (Thomson) J.; m. Beverly Jean Braniff, July 9, 1955; children: Thomas, Tamara, Cynthia. B.S., Iowa State U., 1952; postgrad., London Sch. Econs., 1955-57; M.B.A., Wharton Sch., U. Pa., 1958; A.M.P., Harvard U. Bus. Sch., 1973. With E.I. Dupont de Nemours, Wilmington, Del., 1958-67; pres. div. Amerace Corp., Butler, N.Y., 1968-79, v.p. corp., 1972-79, group v.p. corp., 1972-79; with Worthington div. McGraw Edison Co, Basking Ridge, N.J.; pres., dir. Truck Safety Equipment Co., 1970-77. Served to lt. USN, 1953-57. Mem. Soc. Automotive Engrs., Motor and Equipment Mfrs. Assn. (chmn., bd. dirs. 1976-79), Soc. Plastics Engrs. Episcopalian. Clubs: Baltusrol (Springfield, N.J.); Iverness Country (Ill.); Seaview Country (Absecon, N.J.); Rockaway River Country (Denville, N.J.).

JEDEL, PETER HAROLD, investment executive; b. Bklyn., May 19, 1939; s. Joseph L. and Marjory (Zucker) J.; m. Elaine T. Binder, July 1, 1962; children: Marc, Lynn. B.A., Cornell U., 1960; M.B.A., NYU, 1962. Credit analyst Chem. Bank, 1960-63; fin. analyst Gen. Foods Co., 1963-65; sr. fin. analyst Zerox Co., Rochester, N.Y., 1965-68; mgr. strategic planning TWA, N.Y.C., 1968-69; investment banker Alan-Maged, N.Y.C., 1969-70; chief economist Cities Service Co., Tulsa, 1970-82; with Kidder Peabody Co. Inc., 1982—; chmn. adv. com. Tulsa Sch. Econs. Contbr. articles to profl. jours. Mem. Northwestern Okla. Econs. Adv. Com., Mayor's Budget Rev.; past bd. dirs. Tulsa Arts and Humanities Council, Cities Service Fed. Credit Union. Served with U.S. Army, 1962-63. Mem. UN Assn., Nat. Assn. Bus. Economists (council 1978-81), Tulsa Econs. Club (chmn., founder), Am. Econ. Assn. Home: 7308 E 68th Pl Tulsa OK 74133

JEDENOFF, GEORGE ALEXANDER, steel consultant; b. Petrosovodsk, Russia, July 5, 1917; came to U.S., 1923, naturalized, 1928; s. Alexander N. and Barbara Vacilivna (Sepiagina) J.; m. Barbara Jane Cull, Feb. 27, 1943; children: Nicholas, Nina. A.B. in Mech. Engring. magna cum laude, Stanford, 1940, M.B.A., 1942. Registered profl. engr., Calif. With U.S. Steel Corp., 1942-74, indsl. engr., Pittsburg, Calif., 1942-43, gen. foreman, 1946-52, asst. supt. sheet finishing, 1952-53, cold reduction, 1953-54, supt. cold reduction, 1954, asst. gen. supt., 1955-58, gen. supt., 1959, Utah, 1960-67, Gary, Ind., 1967-69, gen. mgr. heavy products, Pitts., 1969-70; v.p. (Western Steel ops.), 1970-73; pres., dir. USS Engrs. & Cons., Inc. (subsidiary), Pitts., 1974; pres., chief operating officer, dir. Kaiser Steel Corp., Oakland, Calif., 1974-77; dir. Kaiser Internat. Shipping Corp., Kaiser Resources Ltd. (Can.), Hamersley Holdings (Melbourne), Australia, Kaiser Industries, 1974-77; now cons. steel industry and gen. mgmt. Active Boy Scouts Am., 1960—; pres. Utah Valley United Fund, 1966, N.W. Ind., 1968; co-chmn. Urban Coalition, Gary, 1968; mem. health and med. com. Am. Bur. Med. Aid to China, 1974; Bd. dirs. Mercy Hosp., Gary, 1967-69; mem. adv. council Brigham Young U., 1965-73; bd. dirs. Keep Am. Beautiful; chmn. East Bay major gifts com. Stanford U., 1978. Served to lt. USNR, 1943-46. Recipient Jesse Knight Indsl. Citizenship award Brigham Young U., 1966; Disting. Service award Stanford Bus. Sch. Alumni Assn., 1978; named Man of Year Utah Harvard Club, 1967. Mem. Iron and Steel Soc. of AIME, Am. Iron and Steel Inst., Assn. Iron and Steel Engrs. (pres. 1977, now spl. advisor), Western Pa. Safety Council (exec. com. 1970-74), Engrs. Soc. Western Pa., Bituminous Coal Operators Assn. (dir. 1974-77), Am. Assn. Engring. Socs. (commn. internat. relations), Oakland C. of C. (dir. 1976-79), Ind. C. of C. (dir. 1967-69), Soc. Advancement Mgmt., Stanford U. Bus. Sch. Alumni Assn. (nat. pres. 1956-57), Phi Beta Kappa, Tau Beta Pi. Clubs: Duquesne (Pitts.); Alta (Salt Lake City); Claremont (Oakland); Pacific-Union (San Francisco). *My approach has been to develop meaningful objectives and to strive to achieve such objectives regardless of the obstacles encountered. However the relative importance of various goals must be constantly evaluated and priorities re-established. To pursue this, there must be a dedication to identify the truth (facts) and an acceptance of the attitude that there is always a better way. Through such actions there must be recognition of the rights, dignities and great potential of people. Inspiration and courage to pursue difficult objectives come from faith in the Almighty.*

JEFFAY, HENRY, medical educator; b. Bklyn., Feb. 9, 1927; s. Alexander and Dora (Soloman) J.; m. Ana Idalia Muniz, Feb. 9, 1957; children: Randall, Kevin, Jason, Stefanie, Susan. B.S., U. Wis., 1948, M.S., 1949, Ph.D., 1953. Instr. U. P.R. Sch. Medicine, 1955; research asso. U. Ill. Coll. Medicine, 1955, asst. prof. biochemistry, 1956, assoc. prof., 1961-67, prof., 1967—, asst. dean, 1970-77, dean, 1977-80; dir. basic med. scis. Rockford (Ill.) Sch. Medicine, 1974-76; cons. West Side VA Hosp., Chgo., Norwegian Am. Hosp.; dir. med. edn. Roosevelt Meml. Hosp., Chgo. Contbr. articles to profl. jours. Trustee Glen Ellyn Pub. Library (Ill.), 1970-76. Served with AUS, 1945-46. Recipient research award Chgo. Dental Soc., 1959. Mem. Am. Soc. Biol. Chemists, AAAS, Internat. Assn. Dental Research. Home: 354 Hawthorn St Glen Ellyn IL 60137 Office: 1853 W Polk St Chicago IL 60612

JEFFE, SIDNEY DAVID, automotive engineer; b. Chgo., May 6, 1927; s. J.I. J.; children: Robert A., Leslie A. B.S. with honors in Mech. Engring., Ill. Inst. Tech., 1950; M.S. with honors in Automotive Engring., Chrysler Inst. Engring., 1952; grad. program for execs., Carnegie-Mellon U., 1968. With Chrysler Corp., 1950-80, v.p. engring. and research, 1976-82; sr. v.p. ops. Sheller Globe Corp., Detroit, 1982—; exec. dir. Transp. Research Center Ohio, E. Liberty; prof. mech. engring. Ohio State U., 1980-82; sec.-treas. Transp. Research Bd. Ohio, 1980-82; mem. bd. Engring. Sch., Oakland U., 1977—; cons. in field. Author papers in field. Served with AUS, 1945-47. Fellow Engring. Soc. Detroit; mem. Soc. Automotive Engrs. (Russell Springer award 1957), Tau Beta Pi (Outstanding New Mem. award 1948), Pi Tau Sigma (Outstanding New Mem. award 1948). Unitarian. Clubs: Orchard Lake Country, Detroit Athletic. Home: 3673 Quail Hollow Bloomfield Hills MI 48013 Office: Sheller Globe Corp 1641 Porter St Detroit MI 48216

JEFFEE, SAUL, industrialist; b. Elizabeth, N.J., Mar. 30, 1918; s. Michael and Frieda (Copeland) J.; m. Beatrice Ball Kahn, Oct. 26, 1952; 1 dau., Gail Susan. Student, N.Y. U., Columbia. Pres., founder, chmn. bd. Movielab, Inc., 1934—; pres., chmn. bd. Movielab-Hollywood, Inc.; chmn. bd., chief exec. officer Movielab Video Services, Inc.; chmn. bd., pres. Movielab Theatre Service, Inc.; Vice chmn. Film Soc. Lincoln Center; patron Lincoln Center for Performing Arts.; Chmn. Am. tech. rep. U.S.-U.S.S.R. Cultural and Sci. Exchange Agreement, Russia, 1965; mem. N.Y.C. Mayor's Adv. Council for Motion Pictures; adv. bd. Cinema lodge B'nai B'rith. Author: Narcotics-An American Plan, 1966. Nat. adv. com. on scouting for handicapped Boy Scouts Am.; trustee United Jewish Appeal, Fedn. Jewish Philanthropies, Will Rogers Hosp. and Research Center; chmn. bd. trustees Lorge Sch., 1968-81. Fellow Soc. Motion Picture and TV Engrs. (treas.); mem. Assn. Cinema Labs. (pres. 1963), Motion Picture Pioneers, Acad. Motion Picture Arts and Scis., Nat. Acad. TV Arts and Scis., Max Steiner Music Soc. (life; chmn. life patron program), Variety Clubs Internat. (dir. N.Y.), Jewish Chataugua Soc. Clubs: City Athletic, Friars, Masons (Shriner, 32 deg.). Patentee motion picture equipment. Office: 619 W 54th St New York NY 10019

JEFFERDS, VINCENT HARRIS, film production company executive; b. Jersey City, Aug. 23, 1916; s. Jerome V. and Jenny J.; m. Jean Macbride, Dec. 8, 1946; children: Jean, Vincent, Jenny. B.A. in Journalism and Advt, Rutgers U., 1941. Asst. to pres., dir. Times Sq. Stores, N.Y.C., 1946-51; with Walt Disney Prodns., Burbank, Calif., 1951—, v.p. sales promotion, 1961-71, v.p. consumer products div., 1975-79, sr. v.p. mktg., 1980—. Served to capt. U.S. Army, 1942-46. Named World's Outstanding Licensing Marketer Nuremberg Toy Conf., 1968; recipient U.S. Licensing Mfrs. Assn. award, 1983; numerous awards for mktg. programs Procter & Gamble; others. Established Winnie the Pooh apparel program at Sears, Disney book clubs U.S. and abroad; creator Orange Bird animated character for Fla. Citrus Commn.

JEFFERIES, JOHN TREVOR, astrophysicist; b. Kellerberrin, Western Australia, Apr. 2, 1925; s. John and Vera (Healy) J.; m. Charmian Candy, Sept. 10, 1949; children: Stephen R., Helen C., Trevor R. B.Sc., U. Western Australia, 1947, D.Sc., 1961; M.A., Cambridge U., 1949. Research officer Commonwealth Sci. and Indsl. Research Orgn., Sydney, Australia, 1949-60; cons. to dir. Nat. Bur. Standards, Boulder, Colo., 1960-62; fellow Joint Inst. Lab. Astrophysics, Boulder, 1962-64; prof. physics and astronomy, dir. Inst. Astronomy, U. Hawaii, 1964-83; dir. Nat. Optical Astronomy Obs., 1983—; prof. Coll. de France, 1970, 77; bd. dirs. Associated Univs. for Research in Astronomy, 1976—. Author: Spectral Line Formation, 1967; Contbr. articles profl. jours. Guggenheim fellow, 1970. Fellow Royal Astron. Soc., AAAS; mem. Internat. Astron. Union (pres.

commn. X 1970-73), Am. Astron. Soc. (chmn. solar phys. div. 1971-72). Home: 6760 Placita Manzanita Tucson AZ 85718

JEFFERIES, MICHAEL JOHN, electrical engineer; b. London, Feb. 2, 1941; U.S., 1967; s. Charles William and Dorothy Eleanor (Bates) J.; m. Mary Ann Cenci, May 27, 1969; children: Carlyn, Kevin. B.Sc. in Elec. Engring., Nottingham U., 1963, Ph.D., 1967. With Gen. Electric Co., Schenectady, 1967—, mgr. cryogenics br. corp. research and devel., 1976-77, mgr. elec. systems and tech. lab., 1977-80, research and devel. mgr. engring. physics labs., 1980—. Contbr. articles to profl. jours. Mem. IEEE, Instn. Elec. Engrs. (U.K.). Home: 2171 Mountain View Ave Schenectady NY 12309 Office: Gen Electric Co PO Box 8 Schenectady NY 12301

JEFFERIES, ROBERT AARON, JR., furniture co. exec.; b. Richmond, Ind., June 30, 1941; s. Robert Aaron and Roberta June (Hart) J.; m. Sylvia Mae Gilmore, Apr. 16, 1962; children—David E., Michael S., Stephen R. A.B. with honors in Govt, Earlham Coll., Richmond, 1963; J.D. with distinction (Herman C. Krannert scholar 1963-65), Ind. U., 1966. Bar: Ohio bar 1966, Ind. bar 1966, Ill. bar 1970, Mo. bar 1970. Asso. firm Shumaker, Loop & Kendrick, Toledo, 1966-69; asst. gen. counsel, asst. sec. May Dept. Stores Co., St. Louis, 1969-77; v.p., gen. counsel, sec. Leggett & Platt, Inc., Carthage, Mo., 1977—. Contbr. articles to legal jours.; bd. editors law jour., Ind. U., 1965-66. Mem. Am. Bar Assn., Ind. Bar Assn., Ohio Bar Assn., Ill. Bar Assn., Mo. Bar Assn., St. Louis Bar Assn., Order of Coif. Office: PO Box 757 Carthage MO 64836

JEFFERS, DAVID MARSHALL, zoo manager; b. Richmond, Va., Nov. 20, 1953; s. Robert Savage and Joyce (Reiney) J.; m. Alexandria Fredric, Aug. 29, 1981; 1 son, Robert Fredric. B.A., U. N.C. With admissions dept. Davenport Coll., Grand Rapids, Mich., 1975-77; admissions dir. Princess Anne Bus. Coll., Virginia Beach, Va., 1977-78; ranger Kings Dominion, Doswell, Va., 1978-82, zoo mgr., 1982—. Football scholar, 1972. Office: Box 166 Doswell VA 23047

JEFFERS, DONALD E., insurance company executive; b. Louisville, Ill., Aug. 21, 1925; s. Byron V. and Alice B. (Burgess) J.; m. Marion D. Benna, Aug. 14, 1948 (dec.); 1 son, Derek; m. Janice C. Smith, Apr. 21, 1979. B.S. in Accountancy, U. Ill., 1948. C.P.A., Ill., D.C. Sr. accountant Coopers & Lybrand, C.P.A.s, N.Y.C. and Chgo., 1948-56; asst. v.p. Continental Casualty Co., Chgo., 1956-64; dep. comptroller First Nat. Bank Boston, 1965-67; exec. v.p., treas. Interstate Nat. Corp., Chgo., 1967-74, pres., chief exec. officer, 1974—, also dir.; sec., dir. Ill. Ins. Info. Service; chmn., dir. Interstate Ins. Group, Geo. F. Brown & Sons, Inc. Bd. dirs. Clarence Darrow Community Ctr. Served with inf. AUS, 1943-45. Decorated Purple Heart. Mem. Am. Inst. C.P.A.'s, Ill. Soc. C.P.A.'s. Clubs: Attic, Chicago, Westmoreland Country, Carlton, Economic, Mid-America, Executives (Chgo.). Office: 55 E Monroe St Chicago IL 60603

JEFFERS, JAMES R(ANDALL), economics educator, researcher, consultant; b. Cedar Rapids, Iowa, Apr. 8, 1938; s. Everett Floyd and Helen Lucile (Gregg) J.; m. Jill Ann Metcalf (div. Jan. 1980); m. 2d Rinko Ikeda, May 22, 1982. B.B.A., U. Iowa, 1960; Ph.D., Tulane U., 1966. Lectr. La. State U., 1963; asst. prof. econs. U. Iowa, Iowa City, 1963-67, assoc. prof., 1967-74, prof., 1974—; cons. in field; mem. Task Force on Econs. of Health Services U.S. C. of C., 1970; mem. research study sect. Nat. Ctr. for Health Services Research and Devel., HEW, 1977-78. Author: Health Manpower Resources: Patterns and Trends, 1971, Economic Issues: Korea Health Planning and Policy Formulation, 1976. Mem. Johnson County Regional Planning Commn., (Iowa), 1970-73. Recipient Edgar C. Hayhow award Am. coll. Hosp. Adminstrs., 1972, Disting. Research award Korea Devel. Inst., Seoul, 1976; Beta Gamma Sigma nat. def. fellow, 1960; grantee Ford Found., 1964. Mem. Am. Econ. Assn., Am. Pub. Health Assn. Republican. Home: 1339 E Davenport Iowa City IA 52240 Office: Dept Econs U Iowa Iowa City IA 52242

JEFFERS, MICHAEL BOGUE, lawyer; b. Wenatchee, Wash., July 10, 1940; s. Richard G. and Betty (Ball) J.; m. Suzanne Middleton, Aug. 14, 1977. B.A., U. Wash., 1962; LL.B., 1964; LL.M. in Taxation, NYU, 1970. Bar: Wash. 1964, N.Y. 1970. Partner Battle, Fowler, Jaffin & Kheel, N.Y.C., 1973—. Alumni trustee U. Wash., 1970-73. Served to capt. JAGC USAF, 1965-68. Mem. U. Wash. Alumni Assn. Greater N.Y. (pres. 1972—), Phi Gamma Delta. Home: 993 Park Ave Apt 8-B New York NY 10028 Office: 280 Park Ave New York NY 10017

JEFFERSON, ARTHUR, ednl. adminstr.; b. Ala., Dec. 1, 1938; (married); 2 children. B.S., Wayne State U., 1960, M.A. in Polit. Sci, 1963, Ed.D. in Curriculum Leadership, 1973. Asst. region supt. Detroit Public Schs., 1970-71, region supt., 1971-75, interim gen. supt., 1975, gen. supt. schs., 1975—. Mem. Nat., Mich. councils social studies, Assn. Supervision and Curriculum Devel., Am. Assn. Sch. Adminstrs., Mich. Assn. Supervision and Curriculum Devel., Council Basic Edn., Met. Detroit Soc. Black Ednl. Adminstrs., Nat. Alliance Black Sch. Educators, ACLU, NAACP, Wayne State U. Edn. Alumni Assn. (gov. 1968-71), Wayne State U. Alumni Assn. (trustee 1968-71), Phi Sigma Alpha. Home: 19445 Gloucester St Detroit MI 48203 Office: 5057 Woodward Ave Detroit MI 48202

JEFFERSON, EDWARD GRAHAM, chemical company executive; b. London, July 15, 1921; U.S., 1951, naturalized, 1957; s. Edward Hemmings and Margaret Agatha (Graham) J.; m. Naomi Nale Love, June 27, 1953; children: Edward Graham, Charles David, Peter Love (dec.), Andrew McKinley. Ph.D., King's Coll., U. London, 1951. With E.I. du Pont de Nemours & Co., Wilmington, Del., 1951—, asst. dir. Research & Devel. div., 1964-66, dir. Fluorocarbons div., 1966-69, asst. gen. mgr. plastics dept., 1969-70, asst. gen. mgr. explosives dept., 1970-72, asst. gen. mgr. polymer intermediates dept., 1972, v.p., gen. mgr. film dept., 1972-73, sr. v.p., mem. exec. com., dir., 1973-79, pres., chief operating officer, dir., 1980, chmn., chief exec. officer, 1981—; dir. AT&T, Chem. N.Y. Corp./Chem. Bank., Seagrams Co. Ltd., Conoco Inc. Mem. Bus. Com. for Arts; bd. dirs. Nat. Action Council for Minorities in Engring., 1980-83; trustee U. Del., U. Pa., U.S. Council Internat. Bus., Tuskegee Inst., Acad. Natural Sci., Winterthur Mus.; mem. Bus. Com. for Arts, Bus. Council; mem. vis. com. Med. Sch. and Sch. Dental Medicine Harvard U. Served to capt. Brit. Army, 1942-47. Fellow King's Coll., U. London.; Mem. Bus. Roundtable (policy com.), Am. Chem. Soc., Am. Inst. Chem. Engrs., Soc. Chem. Industry (Am. sect.), Conf. Bd. (vice chmn.), Dirs. of Indsl. Research. Episcopalian. Home: Greenville DE 19807 Office: 1007 Market St Wilmington DE 19898

JEFFERSON, JOHN LARRY, profl. football player; b. Dallas, Feb. 3, 1956. Student, Ariz. State U. With San Diego Chargers (NFL), 1978-81, Green Bay (Wis.) Packers, 1981—; player NFL All-Star Game, 1978, 79, 80. Office: care Green Bay Packers 1265 Lombardi Ave Green Bay WI 54303 *

JEFFERSON, PETER AUGUSTUS, architect; b. Wheeling, W.Va., Aug. 23, 1928; s. Joseph Seybold and Josephine Rosalie (Pollack) J.; m. Joan S. A. Lester, Dec. 19, 1967; children—Mark, Ann, Dale, Angelique, Dean. Student, Washington and Jefferson Coll., 1946-47, U. Mich., 1947-50. Archtl. draftsman, supr. Thomas Madden (Architect), Miami, Fla., 1954-57; archtl. draftsman, designer Alfred Browning Parker (Architect), Miami, 1957-59; prin. Peter Jefferson (Architect), Miami, 1959-67, Stuart, Fla., 1967—; founder Grove House, Miami; minister of design Republic of New Atlantis, Greater Antilles, 1967. Served with C.E. U.S. Army, 1952-54. Fellow AIA (award Fla. chpt.). Address: 407 Atlanta Ave Stuart FL 33494

JEFFERSON, THOMAS BRADLEY, mech. engr., educator; b. Urich, Mo., Nov. 25, 1924; s. Thomas Ulmont and Mary (Bradley) J.; m. Carolyn Chelf, Dec. 20, 1946; children—Thomas Calvin, Richard Kent, Terry Anne. B.S. in Mech. Engring, Kans. State U., 1949, M.S., U. Nebr., 1950; Ph.D., Purdue U., 1955. Registered profl. engr., Ark., Ind., Ill. Instr. mech. engring. U. Nebr., 1949-52; instr. mech. engring. Purdue U., 1952-55, asst. prof., 1955-58; prof. mech. engring., head dept. mech. engring. U. Ark., 1958-68, asso. dean engring., 1968-69; dean Sch. Engring. and Tech., So. Ill. U., Carbondale, 1969-78, prof. thermal and environ. engring., 1978—; ednl. cons. Allison div. Gen. Motors Co., 1956-57; summer faculty participant Boeing Co., Wichita, Kans., 1957; sr. engr., design engr. 1 Martin Co., Denver, summers 1958-64, 66-67. Served as pilot USAAF, 1943-46. Mem. ASME, Am. Soc. Engring. Edn., Nat. Soc. Profl. Engrs., Sigma Xi, Tau Beta Pi, Pi Tau Sigma, Sigma Tau, Omicron Delta Kappa, Phi Kappa Phi. Presbyn. (elder). Club: Rotarian. Home: 901 S Glenview Carbondale IL 62901

JEFFERY, ALEXANDER HALEY, insurance company executive, lawyer; b. London, Ont., Can., Jan. 29, 1909; s. James Edgar and Gertrude (Dumaresq) J.; m. Eulalie E. Murray, June 29, 1934; children: Alexander M., Judith E. (Nursey). Grad., U. Western Ont., 1931, Osgoode Hall, Toronto, 1934. Bar: Ont. bar 1934. Ind. practice law, London, 1934—; dep. chmn. bd. London Life Ins. Co.; pres., dir. Forest City Investment Ltd.; dir. London Realty Mgmt. & Rentals Ltd., London Winery, Ltd., Thames Valley Investment Co. Mem. Parliament for Constituency City of London, 1949-53. Mem. Am. Assn. Life Ins. Counsel, Can. Bar Assn. Anglican. Clubs: Mason (32 deg.), London Hunt and Country, London; Royal Canadian Yacht (Toronto); Windsor Yacht, Sarnia Yacht, Port Stanley Sailing Squadron, Great Lakes Cruising. Office: 174 King St PO Box 2095 London ON Canada N6A 4E1

JEFFERY, GEOFFREY MARRON, medical parasitologist; b. Dundee, N.Y., May 13, 1919; s. Joseph Ewart and Augusta (Knapp) J.; m. Jane Wicker, Aug. 16, 1941; children: Janet A. Harrison, Thomas W., Sarah V. Houghton, Susan E. Tosh. A.B., Hobart Coll., 1940; M.A., Syracuse U., 1942; Sc.D., Johns Hopkins U., 1944; M.P.H., Yale U., 1961. Biol. aide health and safety dept. TVA, 1944; commd. officer USPHS, 1944, scientist dir., 1960; tech. aid, cons. malaria control in war areas TVA, 1944-45; assigned div. lab. services Communicable Disease Center, 1945-46; charge br. lab. Communicable Disease Center, Sch. Tropical Medicine, San Juan, P.R., 1946-47; asst. prof. biology U. Bridgeport, Conn., 1947-48; charge Malaria Research Lab., NIH, Milledgeville, Ga., 1948-54; mem. staff Lab. Tropical Diseases-Lab. Parasite Chemotherapy, NIAID, NIH, Columbia, S.C., 1954-63, head sect. epidemiology, 1961-63; asst. chief Lab. Parasite Chemotherapy, NIAID, NIH, Bethesda, 1963-66, acting chief, 1966, chief, 1967-69, C.Am. Malaria Research Sta., San Salvador, El Salvador, 1969-74; asst. dir. Bur. Tropical Diseases, Center Disease Control, Atlanta, 1974-75; dir. vector biology and control div. Bur. Tropical Diseases, 1975-80; dir. vector biology and control div. Bur. Tropical Diseases Center for Infectious Diseases, Ctrs. for Disease Control, 1981—; asst. dir. div. parasitic diseases; Mem. expert adv. panel on malaria WHO, 1963—; asso. mem. commn. malaria Armed Forces Epidemiol. Bd., 1965-69, mem., 1969-73; Del. Internat. Congress Tropical Medicine and Malaria, Lisbon, 1958, Rio de Janeiro, 1963, Teheran, Iran, 1968, Internat. Congress Parasitology, Rome, Italy, 1964, Washington, 1969, Internat. Conf. on Protozoology, London, 1965, Latin Am. Congress Parasitology, Medellin, Colombia, 1973; mem. sci. group on chemotherapy of malaria WHO, Geneva, 1967, mem. sci. group on parasitology, Teheran, 1968; cons. on status of malaria in Africa AID, 1979; mem. sci. working group on applied field research in malaria WHO, Geneva, 1979, mem. steering com., 1981—; cons. on malaria U.S.-China Health Agreement, 1980; temporary advisor meetings WHO, Kuala Lumpur, 1981, Albuquerque, 1982. Contbr. numerous articles to sci. jours. tropical medicine and parasitology. Recipient Public Health Service Commendation medal, 1966, Dept. Army cert. of appreciation patriotic civilian service, 1973. Fellow Royal Soc. Tropical Medicine; mem. Am. Soc. Tropical Medicine and Hygiene (sec.-treas. 1961-67, v.p. 1971, pres. 1975, Bailey K. Ashford award 1959), Am. Soc. Parasitologists, Assn. Southeastern Biologists (editor bull. 1959-60, exec. com. 1962-66), Tropical Medicine Assn. Washington, Southeastern Soc. Parasitologists, S.C. Acad. Sci. (council 1960, 62, Jefferson award 1952, 56, 60), Commd. Officers Assn. USPHS, Sigma Xi, Kappa Sigma. Presbyn. Home: 1093 Blackshear Dr Decatur GA 30033 Office: Center Disease Control Atlanta GA 30333

JEFFERY, JOSEPH, lawyer; b. London, Ont., Can., Sept. 1, 1907; s. James Edgar and Gertrude (Dumaresq) J.; m. Nora Alicia Morris, Oct. 19, 1949; children: Elizabeth, Joseph, John, Alicia, Jennifer, Deborah. Grad., Osgoode Hall Law Sch., 1930, Ins. Inst., 1936; LL.D. (hon.), U. Western Ont., 1975. Bar: Ont. 1930. Since practiced in, London, Ont., created Queen's counsel, 1955; mem. firm Jeffery & Jeffery, 1930—, partner, 1958—; with London Life Ins. Co., 1930-83, chmn., chief exec. officer, until 1982, hon. chmn., dir., 1983; dir. Duffwell Realties Ltd., Lonvest Corp.; pres., dir. Covent Garden Bldg. Inc., Tobermory Islands Devel. Ltd., London Hunt Kennels, London Winery Ltd.; v.p., dir. Forest City Investment Ltd., London Realty Mgmt. & Rentals Ltd.; sec., dir. Lonwin Holdings Ltd.; treas., dir. Dunwell Holdings Ltd., Hagor Holdings Ltd., Thames Valley Investments, Ltd., Kilworth Holdings (London) Ltd.; sec.-treas., dir. London Broadcasters Ltd.; dir. Markborough Properties Ltd., Hiram Walker-Gooderham & Worts, Ltd., Hiram Walker Resources Ltd., Can. Enterprise Devel. Corp., Ltd., Trilon Fin. Corp. Mem. Can. bus. and industry adv. com. OECD.; Trustee YMCA, YWCA; past chmn. bd. London Health Council; bd. dirs. Can. Exec. Service Overseas, London Health Assn., Can. Com.; mem. adv. com. Sch. Bus. Adminstrn.; past chmn. bd. govs. U. Western Ont.; hon. v.p. London United Services Inst.; adv. bd. London Little Theatre; vice chmn., mem. hosp. adv. com., resources mem. London br. St. John Ambulance Assn., 1978—; chmn. Thames Valley Dist. Health Council, 1982-83; hon. v.p. Can. Arthritis and Rheumatism Soc.; mem. bd. mgmt., past pres., life mem. Victorian Order of Nurses for Can.; mem. adv. com. Royal Can. Naval Benevolent Fund, 1979—; mem. Ont.-Jamaica Partnership Found. Served to capt. Royal Canadian Navy, 1940-46; sec. Naval Intelligence Dept.; later mem., sec. Naval Bd. Can. Decorated Order Brit. Empire, Can. Decoration; named hon. col. London Service Bn. (ret.). Mem. John Howard Soc. of London and Middlesex (v.p.), Internat. C. of C. (former vice chmn. Can. council), Can. C. of C. (pres. 1960-61, mem. adv. com., mem. bd. dirs.), London C. of C. (pres. 1957-59), Ontario C. of C. (past pres.), Fedn. Commonwealth Chambers of Commerce (past chmn.), Canada-Israel Chamber Commerce and Industry (dir.), Canadian Inst. Internat. Affairs, UN Assn. (past pres. London br.), Can. Bar Assn. (council for Ont. 1956-57, v.p. Ont. 1958-59), Can. Legion (past pres. Vimy br.), Can. Council Christians and Jews (dir., exec. com., Human Relations award 1956), IEEE (life), Can. Inst. Public Affairs, IRE, Middlesex Law Assn., Ont. Bus. and Commerce Tchrs. Assn. (hon. past pres.), Travel Industry Assn. Can. (adv. council), Can. Inst. Internat. Affairs, Newcomen Soc. N. Am., Law Soc. Upper Can. Liberal. Anglican Ch. Clubs: Mason., London Hunt and Country Limited (joint master of foxhounds), London Baconian, London City Press, London (London); Toronto, Sarnia Yacht, Great Lakes Cruising; St. Denis (Montreal); Royal Can. Naval Sailing Assn.; of Rome (Can. Sect.). Home: Black Acre Pl Kains Rd Rural Route 3 London ON N6A 4B7 Canada Office: care Jeffery & Jeffery PO Box 2095 London 12 ON N6A 4E1 Canada

JEFFETT, FRANK ASBURY, oil company executive; b. Helena, Ark., Feb. 8, 1927; s. William Fletcher and Eufaula (Austin) J.; m. Nancy Pearce, Dec. 29, 1956; children: William Fletcher, Elizabeth Pearce. Student, U. Miss., 1949; B.S., U. Ark., 1950. Agy. Aetna Life, Helena, 1950; supr. Campbell Vinyard Agy., Little Rock, 1950-52; spl. rep. for agy. devel. in Ark. Fidelity & Deposit Co., Md., Memphis, 1952-54; reins. rep. Republic Nat. Life Ins. Co., Dallas, 1954, asst. v.p. rein. div., 1955, v.p., 1959, v.p., exec. asst. to sr. v.p., 1964, v.p. in charge reins. div., 1965-71, sr. v.p. reins. div., 1971-74, exec. v.p. in charge reins. div., 1974-81; pres. Atlas Energy Co., 1981—. Author: This Love of Hunting, 1972. Bd. dirs. Camp Grady Spruce YMCA, Dallas, 1958, Leukemia Soc. Am., 1970, Maureen Connolly Brinker Tennis Found., Inc., 1969—. Served with USAAF, World War II; ETO. Mem. Am. Council Life Insurers, Nat. Assn. Life Ins. Cos., Life Ins. Conf. Episcopalian. Clubs: Dallas Country, Tower, Laconia Hunting., Dallas Hunting and Fishing. Home: 5419 Wateka Dr Dallas TX 75209 Office: Majestic Resources Corp North Dallas Bank Bldg Suite 330 Dallas TX 75235 *Live each day and each week as if it might be our last, yet plan for a long-range future and treat your fellow men accordingly.*

JEFFORDS, JAMES MERRILL, congressman; b. Rutland, Vt., May 11, 1934; s. Olin Merrill and Marion (Hausman) J.; children: Leonard Olin, Laura Louise. B.S., Yale U., 1956; LL.B., Harvard U., 1962. Bar: Vt. 1962. Law clk. Judge Ernest Gibson, Vt. Dist., 1962; partner Bishop, Crowley & Jeffords, Rutland, 1963-66, Kinney, Carbine & Jeffords, 1967-68, Jeffords and Rice, 1973-74; atty. gen. State of Vt., 1969-73; mem. 94th-98th Congresses from Vt., mem. agr. com., edn. com., labor com., ranking Republican employment opportunities subcom., livestock, dairy and poultry subcom., chmn. environ. study conf., 1977-79, charter mem. solar coalition, 1976—. Town agt., Shrewsbury, 1964-68, zoning adminstr., Shrewsbury, 1966-68; mem. Jud. Selection Bd., 1967-68; chmn. Hwy. Dept. Investigating Com., 1968; Mem. Vt. Senate, 1967-68; bd. dirs. Nat. Sun Day, 1978. Served to capt. USNR, 1956—. Mem. Am., Vt., Rutland County bar assns., Am. Judicature Soc. (dir. 1973-75). Republican. Conglist. Club: Elk.

JEFFREY, KIRK, banker; b. Cedar Rapids, Iowa, Mar. 1, 1913; s. Ray E. and Katherine Graham (Kirk) J.; m. Virginia Hammond, Aug. 2, 1941; children: Kirk, Charles Dana, Mary Dana (Mrs. Kai Lee). A.B., U. Mo., 1934, J.D., 1937. Bar: Mo. 1937. Asso. firm Thompson, Mitchell, Thompson & Young, St. Louis, 1937-48; partner Todd & Jeffrey, St. Louis, Washington, 1948-50; v.p. Manchester Bank, St. Louis, 1952-60; Sr. v.p. Western Bank, San Francisco, 1961-63; organizing pres., chief exec. officer, dir. Stanford Bank, Palo Alto, Calif., 1963-71; sr. v.p. Union Bank, Los Angeles, 1971-75; regional v.p. 1st Nat. Bank of San Jose, Calif., 1975-77; pres. C.M. Capital Co., 1977—; dir. C.M. Techs., Tietex Corp. Bd. dirs. Stanford Hosp., 1968-72, pres., 1971-72. Served with AUS, 1942-46; as lt. col. USAF, 1950-52. Mem. Sigma Nu. Presbyn. Club: Palo Alto. Home: 2320 Byron St Palo Alto CA 94301 Office: 525 University Ave Palo Alto CA 94301

JEFFREY, LOUIS PAUL, pharmacy service administrator; b. Everett, Mass., Nov. 23, 1928; s. Samuel Francis and Pauline (D'Angelo) J.; m. Dorothy Ann Rowley, May 25, 1952; children: Paul Louis, Anne Dorothy, Michele Theresa. B.S., Mass. Coll. Pharmacy, 1953, M.S., 1955, Sc.D. in Pharmacy (hon.), 1979. With Mass. Gen. Hosp., Boston, 1943-54, resident, 1953-56; resident pharmacy Peter Bent Brigham Hosp., Boston, 1954; adminstrv. asst., dir. pharmacy and central supply Albany (N.Y.) Med. Center Hosp., 1954-66; dir. instl. and pharmacy relations Roche Labs. div. Hoffmann-LaRoche, Inc., Nutley, N.J., 1966-68; dir. pharmacy services R. I. Hosp., Providence, 1968—; clin. prof. pharmacy U. R.I., 1969-77; cons. in field. Contbr. articles to profl. jours. Bd. dirs. Albany County (N.Y.) Tb and Respiratory Disease Assn., 1960-66, exec. com., 1964-75; bd. dirs., exec. com. Am. Cancer Soc., Albany; bd. dirs. Northeastern N.Y. Speech Center, Albany, 1960-64; Chmn. Formulary Commn. of R.I., 1964-69; Trustee Mass. Coll. Pharmacy, 1964—. Served with USPHS. Named Outstanding Pharmacist of Yr. R.I. Pharm. Assn., 1976; recipient Cath. Pharmacist of Yr. award, 1980, A.H. Robins Bowl of Hygeia award, 1980, award Am. Soc. Hosp. Pharmacists Research and Edn. Found., 1981. Mem. Internat. Pharm. Fedn., Am. Soc. Hosp. Pharmacists (pres. 1962-63), Am. Pharm. Assn. (trustee 1974-75), Am. Coll. Apothecaries, Am. Assn. Colls. Pharmacy, Am. Inst. History Pharmacy, AAAS (chmn. sec. pharm. scis. 1964-65), AMA (assoc.), Nat. Cath. Pharmacists Guild, New Eng. Council Hosp. Pharmacists (pres. 1972-73), R. I. Soc. Hosp. Pharmacists, Hosp. Assn. R. I., Mass. Coll. Pharmacy Alumni Assn., Phi Delta Chi (Disting. Alumnus award Eta chpt. 1980), Rho Chi. Home: 19 Old Oak Dr Warwick RI 02886 Office: 593 Eddy St Providence RI 02902

JEFFREY, RICHARD CARL, educator; b. Boston, Aug. 5, 1926; s. Mark M. and Jane (Markovitz) J.; m. Edith Kelman, Jan. 2, 1955; children—Daniel, Pamela. Student, Boston U., 1943-44; M.A., U. Chgo., 1951; Ph.D., Princeton U., 1957. Logical designer computers MIT Digital Computer Lab. also Lincoln Lab., 1952-55; asst. prof. elec. engring. MIT, 1958-59; asst. prof. philosophy Stanford U., 1959-63; vis. mem. (Inst. for Advanced Study), 1963; assoc. prof. philosophy CCNY, 1964-67; prof. philosophy U. Pa., 1967-74, Princeton U., 1974—. Author: The Logic of Decision, 1965, 2nd edit., 1983, Formal Logic: Its Scope & Limits, 1967, 2d edit., 1981, (with George Boolos) Computability and Logic, 1974, 2d edit., 1981; editor: (with Rudolf Carnap) Studies in Inductive Logic and Probability, 1970, vol. 2, 1979. Served with USNR, 1944-46. Mem. Am. Philos. Assn., Assn. for Symbolic Logic, Philosophy of Sci. Assn. Home: 55 Patton Ave Princeton NJ 08540

JEFFREY, ROBERT CAMPBELL, university dean; b. San Antonio, Nov. 11, 1927; s. John George and Mary (Anderson) J.; m. Marjorie Louise Carspecken, Feb. 9, 1947 (div. 1973); children: Robert Campbell, Paula, Douglas, Nora, Margaret; m. Phillis Jane Hopkins Rienstra, Nov. 1, 1974. B.A., U. Iowa, 1949, M.A., 1950, Ph.D., 1957. Asst. prof. Cornell Coll., Mt. Vernon, Iowa, 1950-53; instr. U. Iowa, Iowa City, 1953-54; asst. prof. speech communication U. Va., Charlottesville, 1954-59; assoc. prof. Ind. U., Bloomington, 1959-68; prof., chmn. dept. U. Tex., Austin, 1968-69, dean Coll. Communication, 1979—; cons. Assn. Communication Adminstrn., Washington, 1976—. Co-author: Legislature Procedures in the General Assembly of the State of Indiana, 1969, Speech: A Text with Adapted Readings, 3d edit., 1980, Speech: A Basic Text, 2d edit., 1983. Parliamentarian Ind. Senate, Inpls., 1964-68; pres. Ind. U. Employees Fed. Credit Union, 1966-67; bd. dirs. Paramount Theatre, Austin, 1980—. Served with USNR, 1945-46; PTO. Recipient Allan Shivers Centennial Chair in Communication U. Tex., Austin, 1983. Mem. Nat. Speech Communication Assn. (exec. sec. 1960-63), Nat. Speech Commmunication Assn. (pres. 1973), Tex. Speech Communication Assn. (exec. sec. 1970-80, Outstanding Service award 1980), Assn. Communication Adminstrn. (pres. 1977); pres. Golden Key Nat. Honor Soc.; mem. Phi Kappa Phi. Democrat. Home: 2001 Robin

Hood Tr Austin TX 78703 Office: Coll Communication U Tex Austin TX 78712

JEFFREY, ROBERT GEORGE, JR., industrial company executive; b. Bronx, N.Y., Oct. 2, 1933; s. Robert George and Ethel Ruth (Roebuck) J.; m. Carolyn H. Endres, Dec. 5, 1959; children: Diana, Christine, Jennifer. B.B.A., Pace U., 1959; M.B.A., NYU, 1966. C.P.A., N.Y. Sr. accountant Haskins & Sells, N.Y.C., 1959-65; asst. mgr. corp. accounting Union Camp Corp., Wayne, N.J., 1965-66, asst. to comptroller, 1966-69, mgr. corp. accounting, 1969-70, dir. financial planning, 1970-72, corporate comptroller, 1972-79; exec. v.p. Huntington Mgmt. Corp., 1980-82; v.p. fin. Rudco Industries Inc., 1982—. Trustee Wayne Twp. Bd. Edn., 1975-78. Served with USAF, 1952-56. Mem. Am. Inst. C.P.A.s, N.Y. State Soc. C.P.A.s. Home: 29 Pelham Rd Wayne NJ 07470 Office: 30 W Century Rd Paramus NJ 07652

JEFFRIES, CARSON DUNNING, physicist, educator; b. Lake Charles, La., Mar. 20, 1922; s. Charles William and Yancey (Dunning) J.; m. Elizabeth Dyer, Sept. 15, 1945 (div. 1976); children: Andrew, Patricia. B.S., La. State U., 1943; Ph.D., Stanford U., 1951. Research assoc. Radio Research Lab., Harvard U., 1943-45; research asst. Stanford U., 1946-50; instr. Physikalisches Institut der Universitat, Zurich, Switzerland, 1951; mem. faculty U. Calif. at Berkeley, 1952—, prof., 1963—; dir. AEC (Office Naval Research projects in solid state physics), 1953—; faculty sr. scientist Lawrence Berkeley Lab., 1978—. Author: Dynamic Nuclear Orientation, 1963, Electron Hole Droplets in Semiconductors, 1983; Contbr. articles profl. jours.; Profl. sculptor. Sr. Postdoctoral fellow NSF, Oxford (Eng.) U., 1958, Harvard, 1965-66; Fulbright prof., France, 1959. Fellow Am. Phys. Soc., Am. Acad. Arts and Scis.; mem. Nat. Acad. Scis. Office: Le Conte Hall U Calif Berkeley CA 94720

JEFFRIES, GRAHAM HARRY, physician; b. Barmera, Australia, May 31, 1929; came to U.S., 1959, naturalized, 1965; s. Harry and Florence J.; m. Elizabeth T. Jones, June 25, 1955; children—David, Peter, Elizabeth, Robert. B.Med.Sci., Otago (N.Z.) U., 1950, M.B., Ch.B., 1953; D.Phil., Oxford (Eng.) U., 1955. House physician United Oxford Hosps., 1955-57, Hammersmith Hosp., Postgrad. Med. Sch., London, 1958; from research fellow to asso. prof. medicine Cornell U. Med. Coll., 1958-69; prof. medicine, chmn. dept. Pa. State U. Coll. Medicine, Hersey, 1969—. Rhodes scholar, 1953-55. Fellow A.C.P.; mem. Am. Gastroenterol. Assn., Am. Soc. Clin. Investigation. Presbyterian. Address: Hershey Med Center Hershey PA 17022

JEFFRIES, JAMES E., congressman; b. Detroit, June 1, 1925; m. Barbara Cray, 1947; children—James Thomas, Jeri Lee, Gregory Alan. Attended, Mich. State U. Mem. 96th-97th Congresses from 2d Kans. Dist.; mem. vets. affairs, public works, transp. coms.; mem. Am. Security Council; investment counselor. Bd. govs. Agr. Hall of Fame, Found. for Def. Analysis. Served to master sgt. AC U.S. Army, 1943-45. Mem. YMCA, Am. Legion. Republican. Presbyterian. Clubs: Masons, Shriners.

JEFFRIES, MCCHESNEY HILL, lawyer; b. Norfolk, Va., Jan. 3, 1922; s. McChesney Hill and Jessie Tait (Watt) J.; m. Alice Mitchell, July 19, 1952; children: McChesney Hill, Helen Elizabeth, Lewis Mitchell. A.B. cum laude, Davidson Coll., 1947, LL.B., Harvard U., 1950. Bar: Ga. 1950. Assoc. firm Moise, Post & Gardner, Atlanta, 1950-58, partner, 1958-62; partner firm Hansell & Post, Atlanta, 1962—; chmn., pres., dir. First Phoenix Fund; dir. R & R Mfg. Co., Withers Tool, Die & Mfg. Co., Inc., Octagon Properties, Inc. Trustee Presbyterian Home, Inc., Quitman, Ga., Hillside Cottages, Inc., Atlanta, Atlanta Lawyers Found., Inc.; chmn. Atlanta Speech Sch., Inc., 1981-82, Atlanta Found., Inc., 1980—; elder 1st Presbyn Ch., 1969-75, 77-81, 84—. Fellow Am. Bar Found.; Mem. Am. Law Inst. (348 com.), ABA, State Bar Ga. (chmn. corp. and banking sect. 1980-81, chmn. commn. on continuing lawyer competence 1982—), Atlanta Bar Assn., Lawyers Club Atlanta (pres. 1965-66), Phi Beta Kappa, Omicron Delta Kappa. Clubs: Piedmont Driving, Capital City (bd. govs. 1980-83). Home: 3051 Habersham Rd NW Atlanta GA 30305 Office: 3300 First Atlanta Tower Atlanta GA 30303

JEFFRIES, ROBERT ALAN, physicist; b. Indpls., Nov. 11, 1933; s. Seth Manes and Mary Elizabeth (Christman) J.; m. Kelly Grisso, June 5, 1954; children: Russell A., D. Craig. B.S., U. Okla., 1954, M.S., 1961, Ph.D., 1965. Project engr. Pontiac Motor div. Motors Corp., (Mich.), 1954-55; mem. staff Los Alamos Sci. Lab., 1957-76, group leader, 1976-77, asst. div. leader, 1977-79, program mgr. nat. security programs, 1979—. Chmn. Los Alamos County Econ. Devel. Council, 1967; bd. dirs. Los Alamos Cancer Clinic, 1977-80. Served with USAF, 1955-57. Mem. Am. Phys. Soc., Sigma Xi.

JEFFRIES, ROBERT JOSEPH, educator, business executive; b. Norwalk, Conn., Jan. 6, 1923; s. Charles William and Christine (Jacobsen) J.; m. Anna Darling Cumming, Oct. 13, 1945; children: Christine Darling, Bruce Cumming. B.S., U. Conn., 1944, M.S., 1946; D.Eng., Johns Hopkins, 1948. Engr. NACA, 1944-46; instr. Johns Hopkins U., 1946-48; research assoc. N.C. State Coll., 1948-49; assoc. prof. Mich. State U., 1949-54; tech. planning adviser Schlumberger Instrument Co., 1954-55; asst. to pres. Daystrom, Inc., 1955-57; pres., founder Data-Control System, Inc., 1957-66, chmn. bd., 1966-68; prof. U. Bridgeport, Conn., 1968-75; founder, dir. Ednl. & Tech. Cons., Inc., 1953—; prin. Van Dyck Assocs.; chmn. bd. Metraplex Corp.; dir. Evergreen Fund, Evergreen Total Return Fund; prin. Evergreen Ltd. Mktg. Fund; v.p., founder Found. Instrumentation Edn. and Research, 1958—; fellow-in-residence Edgar Cayce Found., Virginia Beach, Va., 1981—. Editor: Jour. Instrument Soc. Am, 1953-54; Author tech. papers. Trustee U. Bridgeport, Am. Unitarian Assn. Recipient Disting. Alumnus award U. Conn., John Hopkins U. Mem. Instrument Soc. Am. (pres. 1957-58), NRC, Assn. Research and Enlightenment (trustee), Conn. Commn. for Higher Edn. (vice chmn.), U. Conn. Engring. Alumni Assn. (pres. 1969-71), Sigma Xi, Tau Beta Pi, Eta Kappa Nu. Club: Cedar Point Yacht (Westport, Conn.). Home: 3946 Ocean Hills Ct Virginia Beach VA 23451 Office: Edgar Cayce Foundation 67th and Atlantic PO Box 595 Virginia Beach VA 23451

JEFFRIES, WILLIAM WORTHINGTON, museum director, archivist, historian; b. Mobile, Ala., July 23, 1914; s. Frank Mauzy and Gertrude (Worthington) J.; m. Mary Ruth Franklin, Aug. 31, 1940; children: John Worthington, Susan Jeffries Clinton, Gertrude Jeffries Parker, Margaret Jeffries McKee., Virginia Jeffries Oxford. A.B., Birmingham-So. Coll., 1935; M.A., Vanderbilt U., 1936, Ph.D., 1941. Teaching fellow Vanderbilt U., 1936-38, 40-41; instr. Birmingham-So. Coll., 1938-40; asst. prof. history U. Miss., 1941-42; officer instr. U.S. Naval Acad., 1942-46, asst. prof., 1946-48, assoc. prof., 1948-55, prof., 1955—, sr. prof. English, history and govt., 1955-70, archivist, 1970—, dir. Acad. Mus., 1973—. Co-author: American Sea Power since 1775, 1947, International Relations, 1955, 3d, rev. edit., 1960; editor, co-author: Geography and National Power, 1956, 4th, rev. edit., 1967; editor: Ann. Command History of U.S. Naval Acad, 1970—. Served with USNR, 1942-46. Mem. So. Hist. Assn., Middle Atlantic Regional Archives Conf., U.S. Naval Acad. Alumni Assn. (asso.), Sigma Alpha Epsilon, Omicron Delta Kappa, Pi Gamma Mu, Kappa Phi Kappa, Delta Phi Alpha. Democrat. Methodist. Home: 716 Melrose Ave Annapolis MD 21401 Office: US Naval Acad Annapolis MD 21402

JEFFRIS, RONALD DUANE, mfg. co. exec.; b. Gays, Ill., Aug. 30, 1937; s. Orval B. and Ola May (Henderson) J.; m. Myra Marie Edmonds, July 4, 1963. B.S., Eastern Ill. U., 1959; M.S., U. Ill., 1961. C.P.A., Ill., Okla. Auditor Arthur Andersen & Co., Chgo., 1961-66; mgr. adminstrn. and credit U.S.I. Farm Chems., Danville, Ill., 1966-68; dir. tech. accounting No. Ill. Gas Co., Aurora, 1968-73; controller Williams Cos., Tulsa, 1973—. Mem. Am. Inst. C.P.A.'s, Okla. Soc. C.P.A.'s. Home: 3622 E 66th Pl Tulsa OK 74136 Office: One Williams Center Tulsa OK 74172

JEGHERS, HAROLD JOSEPH, physician, educator; b. Jersey City, Sept. 26, 1904; s. Albert and Matilda (Gerckens) J.; m. Isabel J. Wile, June 21, 1935; children: Harold, Dee, Sanderson, Theodore. B.S., Rensselaer Poly. Inst., 1928; M.D., Western Res. U., 1932; D.Sc. (hon.), Georgetown U., 1975, Coll. Medicine and Dentistry of N.J., 1976. Intern 5th med. service Boston City Hosp., 1933-34, resident, 1935-37, physician-in-chief, 1943-46, cons. physician, 1946-66; instr. to asso. prof. medicine Boston U. Sch. Medicine, 1935-46; prof. and dir. dept. medicine Georgetown U. Sch. Medicine, 1946-56; prof., dir. dept. medicine N.J. Coll. Medicine and Dentistry, Jersey City, 1956-66, emeritus, 1966—; med. dir. St. Vincent Hosp., Worcester, Mass., 1966-78, emeritus, 1979—; prof. med. edn. Office Med. Edn. Research and Curriculum Devel., Northeastern Ohio Univs. Coll. Medicine, 1977—; cons. med. edn. St. Elizabeth Hosp., Youngstown, Ohio, 1977—, Cleve. Health Scis. Library, Case Western Res. U., 1979—, Cleve. Med. Library Assn., 1979—; prof. Tufts U., 1966-74; dir. med. ward service Jersey City Med. Center, 1958-66; dir. Tufts med. service Boston City Hosp., 1969-71; cons. medicine Georgetown U. Sch. Medicine, 1957-59; rep. from A.C.P. to div. med. scis. NRC, 1950-53. Author articles and sects. in books.; developer: Jeghers Med. Index Research Library. Recipient Laetare award Guild of St. Luke, Boston, 1958; Distinguished Alumni award Case Western Res. U. Sch. Medicine, 1974. Fellow A.C.P., Am. Soc. for Clin. Investigation; mem. A.M.A., Am. Fedn. for Clin. Research, So. Soc. for Clin. Research (v.p. 1948-49), Assn. Am. Physicians, Mass. Med. Soc., Sigma Xi. Home: PO Box 1063 Marshfield MA 02050 Office: 1044 Belmont Ave Youngstown OH 44501

JEHOREK, STEVEN SCOTT, communications executive; b. Evanston, Ill., Feb. 13, 1950; s. Hillard I. and Jeanne C. (Lewis) J.; m. Audrey E. Chap, Mar. 1, 1975. Ed., Northwestern U. Prodn. mgr., then bus. mgr. Field Newspaper Syndicate, Irvine, Calif., 1969-76, gen. mgr., 1976-78, v.p., gen. mgr., 1978-80, pres., chief exec. officer, 1980—. Mem. Am. Mgmt. Assn., Sigma Delta Chi. Club: Balboa Bay. Office: 1703 Kaiser St Irvine CA 92714

JEKELI, WALTER, educator; b. Wiesbaden, Germany, Feb. 23, 1925; came to U.S., 1962; s. Julius Michael and Gertrud (Kuhn) J.; m. Eva Ingeborg Kuhn, Apr. 15, 1952; children—Christoph, Klaus. M.A., Staatsexamen U. Marburg, 1955; Ph.D., Staatsexamen II, 1957. Instr. U. Marburg, 1953-55; tchr. Gymnasium, Marburg/Kassel, Germany, 1955-62; asst. prof. physics Clarkson Coll. Tech., Potsdam, N.Y., 1962-64, asso. prof., 1964-66; prof. physics State U. Coll. at Potsdam, 1966—, chmn. dept., 1967-76. Mem. Am., German phys. socs., Am. Assn. Physics Tchrs. Research theoretical physics, optical and microwave spectroscopy. Home: 16 Castle Dr Potsdam NY 13676

JELINEK, FREDERICK, electrical engineer; b. Prague, Czechoslovakia, Apr. 18, 1932; came to U.S., 1949, naturalized, 1955; s. William and Trudy (Kocmanek) J.; m. Milena Tobolova, Feb. 4, 1961; children—Hannah, William. B.S., MIT, 1956, M.S., 1958, Ph.D., 1962. Instr. MIT, Cambridge, 1959-62; lectr. Harvard U., Cambridge, 1962; asst. prof. Cornell U., Sch. Elec. Engring., Ithaca, N.Y., 1962-66, assoc. prof., 1966-72, prof., 1972-74; vis. scientist MIT, Lincoln Lab., 1964, 65, IBM, 1968-69; sr. mgr. continuous speech recognition IBM, T.J. Watson Research Center, Yorktown Heights, N.Y., 1972—. Author: Probabilistic Information Theory, 1968; contbr. articles to profl. jours. Chmn. Liberal Party, Ithaca, N.Y., 1970-72, mem. state exec. com., 1971-73. Recipient IEEE-Info. Theory Group best paper award, 1971. Fellow IEEE (pres. Info. Theory Group 1977, bd. govs. 1970-79, 81—). Office: IBM T J Watson Research Center PO Box 218 Yorktown Heights NY 10598

JELINEK, HANS, artist, educator; b. Vienna, Austria, Aug. 21, 1910; came to U.S., 1938, naturalized, 1943; s. Hermann and Paula (Stwertka) J.; m. Gertrude Stwertka. Grad., U. Vienna, 1933, Vienna Kunstgewerbeschule, 1933. Mem. art faculty New Sch. Social Research, 1945-57; asst. prof. art Coll. City N.Y., 1948-58, asso. prof., 1958-66, prof., 1966-79, prof. emeritus, 1979—; mem. faculty Nat. Acad. Sch. Fine Arts, 1973—. Represented in permanent collections, Met. Mus., Library of Congress, Cooper Union, Dartmouth, N.Y. Pub. Library, Nelson A. Rockefeller collection, many others, work exhibited, throughout U.S., one man shows, Va. Mus. Art, Smithsonian Instn., others. Awarded 1st prize Artists for Victory Nat. Graphic Art Exhbn.; Pennell prize Library Congress 3rd nat. print exhbn.; Tiffany award; others.; Academician NAD; Benjamin Franklin fellow Royal Soc. Arts, London. Address: 675 West End Ave New York NY 10025

JELINEK, JOHN PETER, educator; b. Omaha, May 16, 1916; s. Vaclav Francis and Frances (Holy) J. A.B., St. Louis U., 1939, M.A., 1943, S.T.L., 1949; Ph.D., Gregorian U., Rome, Italy, 1951. Joined Soc. of Jesus, 1934; ordained priest Roman Cath. Ch., 1947; instr. Latin and English Campion High Sch., Prairie du Chien, Wis., 1942-45; instr. philosophy Regis Coll., Denver, 1951-52, St. Louis U., 1952-55, asst. prof., 1955-59; mem. faculty Creighton U., 1959—, prof. philosophy, 1962—, chmn. dept. philosophy, 1962-67; summer vis. lectr. Rockhurst Coll., Kansas City, Mo., 1948, 52, Regis Coll., 1954. Contbr. articles to profl. jours. Mem. Am. Cath. Philos. Assn., Mountain-Plains Philos. Conf. Address: Creighton Univ Omaha NE 68178

JELINEK, JOSEF EMIL, dermatologist; b. Prague, Czechoslovakia, Feb. 12, 1928; came to U.S., 1958, naturalized, 1964; s. Frank and Olga (Frankl) J.; m. Vera Adrienne Schnitzer, June 19, 1960; children—David Frank, Paul William. M.B., B.S., U. London, 1951; postgrad., U. London Postgrad. Sch., 1956, N.Y. U., 1963—. Diplomate: Am. Bd. Dermatology. Intern, house surgeon in orthopedics St. Mary's Hosp., London, 1951-52; house physician in internal medicine Harold Wood Hosp., Essex, Eng., 1952, Princess Beatrice Hosp., London, 1955; registrar internal medicine Royal Victoria Hosp., Bournemouth, Eng., 1955-57, Dulwich Hosp., London, 1957-58; precepteeship in dermatology with Norman B. Kanof, N.Y.C., 1958-61; chief resident dermatology Bellevue Hosp., N.Y.C., 1962-63; chief resident Univ. Hosp., N.Y.C., 1963; cons. VA Hosp., N.Y.C., 1965—; asst. attending physician Bellevue Hosp., N.Y.C., 1965—; attending physician Univ. Hosp., N.Y.C., 1976—; clin. prof. dermatology N.Y. U. Sch. Medicine, N.Y.C., 1976—; practice medicine specializing in dermatology, N.Y.C., 1963—; cons. AMA Council on Drugs and the Dept. of Drugs, 1972. Contbr. articles to profl. jours, also chpts. to textbooks. Served to lt. RAF, 1952-54. Fellow ACP, Am. Acad. Dermatology; mem. Atlantic Dermatologic Conf. (past chmn.), Dermatologic Soc. Greater N.Y. (past pres.), N.Y. Acad. Medicine (past chmn.), Manhattan Dermatol. Soc. (past pres.). Office: 15 W 12th St New York NY 10011

JELINEK, ROBERT ALAN, advt. exec.; b. Phila., Mar. 13, 1929; s. Sydney and Isabel (Jans) J.; m. Diana Mary Carter, Sept. 11, 1965; children—Ian, Kate. A.B., U. Pa., 1950; J.D. cum laude, Harvard, 1953. Bar: N.Y. bar 1956. Asso. firm White & Case, N.Y.C., 1955-57; mem. legal dept. Young & Rubicam Inc., N.Y.C., 1957-60; with CBS TV, 1960-66, dir. bus. affairs, 1964-66; with Young & Rubicam Inc., 1966—, sr. v.p., dir., 1970—, gen. counsel, sec., 1973—, exec. v.p., 1980—. Pres. Young & Rubicam Found. Mem. Assn. Bar City N.Y. Clubs: Harvard, Pinnacle (N.Y.C.); Georgica Assn. (Wainscott, N.Y.). Home: 1 Lexington Ave New York NY 10010 Office: 285 Madison Ave New York NY 10017

JELKS, EDWARD BAKER, archeologist, educator; b. Macon, Ga., Sept. 10, 1922; s. Oliver Robinson and Lucille (Jarrett) J.; m. Juliet Elizabeth Christian, Aug. 12, 1944; 1 son. Edward Christian. B.A., U. Tex., 1948, M.A., 1951, Ph.D., 1965. Archeologist Smithsonian Instn., 1950-53, Nat. Park Service, 1953-58; research scientist U. Tex., Austin, 1958-65; assoc. prof. anthropology So. Meth. U., Dallas, 1965-68; prof. anthropology Ill. State U., Normal, 1968—; dir. Midwestern Archeol. Research Ctr., 1981—; active archeol. field research Tex., La., Ill., Va., Mo., Nfld., Micronesia. Co-author: Handbook of Texas Archeology, 1954, Trick Taking Potential, 1974, The Joachim De Brum House, Likiep, Marshall Islands, 1978; author: Archaelogical Explorations at Signal Hill, Newfoundland, 1973. Served with USN, 1942-44. Smithsonian Instn. research fellow, 1968. Fellow AAAS, Am. Anthropol. Assn.; mem. Tex. Archeol. Soc. (pres. 1957-58), Soc. Profl. Archeologists (pres. 1976-77), Soc. Hist. Archaeology (pres. 1968-69), Am. Soc. for Conservation Archaeology (v.p. 1975-76), Pan Am. Inst. Geography and History (chmn. archaeology work group 1982—), Soc. for Am. Archaeology, Assn. Field Archaeology, Archaeol. Inst. Am., Delta Chi. Home: 605 N School St Normal IL 61761 Office: 105 Edwards Hall Ill State Normal IL 61761

JELLIFFE, CHARLES GORDON, banker; b. Mansfield, Ohio, Nov. 28, 1914; s. Charles Mitchell and Florence (Findley) J.; m. Carolyn V. Wolf, Oct. 3, 1942; children: Charles Martin, Joyce Findley, John Bour, Jannell W. B.Sc., Ohio State U., 1937. Salesman Hawley Huller & Co. (investment securities), Cleve., 1937-40; with Columbus Coated Fabrics Corp., Ohio, 1940-64, pres., chmn. bd., 1961-64; pres. City Nat. Bank & Trust Co., Columbus, 1964-74; pres., chief exec. officer, dir. First Nat. Bank N.J., Totowa, 1974—; sec., treas., dir. First Banc Corp. of Ohio, Inc., Columbus; dir. Lumbermans Mut. Ins. Co., Mansfield. Bd. dirs. Columbus Downtown Area Commn., 1962—; trustee Columbus United Community Council, 1964-74, Columbus Gallery Fine Arts, 1963-74, Defiance (Ohio) Coll., 1961-72. Served to maj. AUS, 1941-46. Mem. Assn. Res. City Bankers, Columbus Area C. of C. (dir., treas.), Ohio State U. Alumni Assn. (pres.). Congregationalist (chmn. trustees). Clubs: Columbus (v.p., dir.), Golf, Columbus Athletic, Scioto Country (Columbus); Pinnacle, Univ. (N.Y.C.); Royal Poinciana Golf (Naples, Fla.); Naples Yacht (Fla.); Arcola Country (Paramus, N.J.). Home: 920 Cherokee Ln Franklin Lakes NJ 07417 Office: 515 Union Blvd Totowa NJ 07512

JELLIFFE, ROGER WOODHAM, cardiologist, clinical pharmacologist; b. Cleve., Feb. 18, 1929; s. Russell Wesley and Rowena (Woodham) J.; m. Joyce Miller, June 12, 1954; children: Susan, Amy, Betsy, Peter. A.B., Harvard U., 1950; M.D., Columbia U., 1954. Diplomate: Am. Bd. Internal Medicine, Am. Bd. Cardiovascular Disease. Intern Univ. Hosps., Cleve.; also jr. asst. resident in medicine; Nat. Found. Infantile Paralysis exptl. medicine fellow Case Western Res. U., Cleve., 1956-58; staff physician in medicine VA Hosp., Cleve., 1958-60, resident in medicine, 1960-61; instr. medicine U. So. Calif. Sch. Medicine, Los Angeles, 1961-63, asst. prof., 1963-67, asso. prof., 1967-76, prof. medicine, 1976—; cons. Dynamic Scis. Inc., Van Nuys, Calif., 1976—, Simes S.p.A., Milan, Italy, 1979—, IVAC Corp., San Diego, 1983—. Contbr. articles to profl. jours; cons. editor: Am. Jour. Medicine, 1972-78, Current Prescribing, 1974-79. Fellow A.C.P., Am. Coll. Cardiology, Am. Soc. Clin. Pharmacology and Therapeutics, Am. Coll. Clin. Pharmacology; mem. Am. Heart Assn. (fellow council on clin. cardiology). Maj. interest: optimal mgmt. of drug therapy; developer time-shared computer programs for mgmt. of drug therapy for hosps. Home: 825 S Madison Ave Pasadena CA 91106 Office: 2025 Zonal Ave Los Angeles CA 90033

JELLINEK, GEORGE, writer, broadcaster; b. Budapest, Hungary, Dec. 22, 1919; came to U.S., 1941, naturalized, 1943; s. Daniel and Jolan J.; m. Hedy Dicker, July 29, 1942; 1 dau., Nancy Berezin. Student, Lafayette Coll., Easton, Pa., 1943. Dir. program services SESAC, Inc., N.Y.C., 1955-64; rec. dir. Muzak Inc., N.Y.C., 1964-68; music dir. Sta WQXR, N.Y.C., 1968—; asst. prof. music NYU, 1976—. Author: Callas, Portrait of a Prima Donna, 1960; Author opera librettos: (music by Eugene Zador) The Magic Chair, 1966, The Scarlet Mill, 1968; contbg. editor: Stereo Rev., 1958—; contbr. articles to various mags. Served to 1st lt. M.I., U.S. Army, 1942-46. Recipient award for excellence in broadcasting Ohio State U., 1978; Major Armstrong Broadcast award, 1978; Oral Communication award L.I. U., 1979; Broadcast Media award San Francisco State U., 1983. Mem. ASCAP, AFTRA, Friends of Mozart (dir.). Office: Sta WQXR 229 W 43d St New York NY 10036

JELLINEK, ROGER, editor; b. Mexico City, Mexico, Jan. 16, 1938; s. Frank Louis Mark and Marguerite Lilla Donne (Lewis) J.; m. Margheria DiCenzo, Dec. 22, 1963; children—Andrew Mark, Claire. Student, Bryanston Sch., Dorset, Eng., 1951-56; M.A., Clare Coll., Cambridge (Eng.) U., 1961. Asso. editor Random House, 1963-64; editor Walker & Co., 1964-65, N.Y. Times Book Rev., 1966-70, dep. editor, 1970-73; editor-in-chief Times Books, Quadrangle/The N.Y. Times Book Co., 1974-78, sr. editor, 1978-81; pres. Clairemark, Ltd., Palisades, N.Y., 1981—. Served with Royal Marines, 1956-57; as 2d lt. Brit. Intelligence Corps, 1957-58. Mellon fellow Yale, 1961-63. Home: Snedens Landing NY 10964 Office: Washington Spring Rd Palisades NY 10964

JELLISON, RICHARD MARION, educator; b. Muncie, Ind., Dec. 26, 1924; s. Carl R. and Leora Melvina (Falkner) J.; m. Kathleen Elizabeth Frick, May 5, 1945; children—Richard G., Stephanie L., Leslie N. B.S., Ball State U., 1948; A.M., Ind. U., 1949, Ph.D., 1953. Instr. history Ind. U., 1952-56; instr. Mich. State U., 1956-58; asso. prof. Eastern Ill. U., 1958-62; prof. Miami U., Oxford, Ohio, 1962—, chmn. dept. history, 1971—; lectr. U. Berlin, 1966, U. Siena, Italy, 1968, Budapest, Hungary, 1974. Author: Society, Freedom and Conscience: The American Revolution in Virginia, Massachusetts and New York, 1976; contbr. articles to profl. jours. Served with U.S. Navy, 1942-44; PTO. Colonial Williamsburg summer research fellow, 1958-62. Mem. Am. Hist. Assn., Inst. Early American Culture, Am. Assn. History Medicine, Orgn. Am. Historians, Internat. Soc. History Medicine, Ohio Hist. Soc., Ind. Hist. Soc., S.C. Hist. Soc., AAUP (pres. Miami U. chpt. 1967). Office: Dept History Miami Univ Oxford OH 45056

JEMELIAN, JOHN NAZAR, merchant; b. N.Y.C., May 10, 1933; s. Nazar and Angel (Jizmejian) J.; m. Rose Melkonian, Nov. 22, 1958; children: Sheri, Lori, Brian, Joni. B.S., U. So. Calif., 1956. Mgr. audit staff Price Waterhouse & Co., Los Angeles, 1958-64; treas. The Akron, Los Angeles, 1964—, v.p. fin., 1976, exec. v.p., 1977-82; v.p., gen. mgr., dir. Acromil Corp., City of Industry, Calif., 1982—; dir. D.L. Engring.,

Inc.; Financial adviser African Enterprises, 1966-68. Bd. dirs. Pasadena Christian Sch., 1965-67, 69-70, treas., 1965-67; deacon Lake Ave. Congregational Ch., 1964-68, trustee, 1970-73, chmn. bd. trustees, 1972-73; bd. dirs. Forest Home Christian Conf. Center, 1972-75, 78—; chmn. bd. Media Ministries, Inc., 1975—, Donor Automation, 1975—; trustee Haigazian Coll., Beirut, 1974-78, Narramore Christian Found., 1976—, Met. Ministries, 1979-80; chmn. Christian Bus. Men's Com., 1979—, Sahag Mesiob Armenian Christian Sch., 1980—. Served with F.A. U.S. Army, 1956-58. Named Boss of Year Beverly Hills chpt. Nat. Secs. Assn., 1970. Mem. Am. Inst. C.P.A.s, Calif. Soc. C.P.A.s, Retail Controllers Assn. (dir. 1973-74), Delta Sigma Pi, Beta Alpha Psi, Beta Gamma Sigma. Clubs: Mason., Los Angeles Athletic, Toastmasters-Windjammers (Los Angeles) (pres. 1963). Home: 261 Sharon Rd Arcadia CA 91006 Office: 18421 Railroad St City of Industry CA 91744

JEMIAN, WARTAN ARMIN, materials engineering educator; b. Lynn, Mass., Dec. 31, 1925; s. Simon Calouso and Emmy Frieda (Kunzler) J.; m. Martha Alice Jackson, June 22, 1958; children: Robert A., Mary C., Rebecca A., Peter R. B.S. in Chemistry, U. Md., 1950; M.S. in Metallurgy, Rensselaer Poly. Inst., 1953, Ph.D., 1956. Registered profl. engr., Ala. Engr. Westinghouse Elec. Corp., Youngwood, Pa., 1955-58; sr. fellow Mellon Inst., Pitts., 1958-62; adj. prof. U. Pitts., 1956-62; research dir. Fansteel Metal Corp., North Chicago, Ill., 1962; prof. Auburn U. (Ala.), 1962—, chmn. materials engring., 1963-82; cons. Oak Ridge Nat. Lab., 1982—. Past pres. Auburn Chamber Music Soc., 1972-74; mem. Auburn Arts Assn., 1983—. Mem. Am. Soc. for Engring. Edn. (chmn. materials div. 1972-74, chmn. materials div. 1983-84), Am. Soc. for Metals (pres. elect Birmingham chpt.), Am. Welding Soc., AIME, ASTM, Soc. for Biomaterials, Sigma Xi. Lodge: Rotary (Auburn). Home: 350 Singleton St Auburn AL 36830 Office: Materials Engring Dept Auburn U Auburn AL 36849

JEN, FRANK CHIFENG, finance and management educator; b. Shanghai, China, May 15, 1931; came to U.S., 1957; s. Seybold E. and Susan (Lin) J.; m. Daisy Chi, Aug. 26, 1962; children: Amy K., Wendy K., Edward K. B.S., N. Central Coll., 1959; M.B.A., U. Wis., 1960, Ph.D., 1963. Asst. prof. finance SUNY, Buffalo, 1964-66, assoc. prof., 1966-68, prof., 1968—, Mfrs. & Traders Trust Co.'s prof. banking and finance, chmn. dept. finance, 1967-70, chmn. dept. operating analysis, 1970-77, dir. advanced comml. lending and credit analysis program, 1977—; vis. prof. Nat. Center for Indsl. Mgmt. Devel. at Dalian, China, 1980—. Asso. editor finance dept.: Management Science, 1970—, Jour. Financial and Quantitative Analysis, 1970-72. Mem. Inst. Mgmt. Scis., Am. Fin. Assn., Am. Econ. Assn., Fin. Execs. Inst., Pi Gamma Mu, Beta Gamma Sigma. Home: 287 Forestview Dr Williamsville NY 14221 Office: Sch Mgmt State U NY at Buffalo Buffalo NY 14214

JENCKS, CHRISTOPHER SANDYS, sociology educator; b. Balt., Oct. 22, 1936; s. Francis Haynes and Elizabeth (Pleasants) J. B.A., Harvard U., 1958, M.Ed., 1959; postgrad., London Sch. Econs., 1959-61; LL.D., Kalamazoo Coll., 1969; D.Litt., Columbia Coll., 1983. Asso. editor New Republic mag., 1961-63; fellow Inst. Policy Studies, Washington, 1963-67, Cambridge Policy Studies Inst., 1968-75; mem. faculty Harvard U., 1967-80, prof., 1973-80; prof. sociology and urban affairs Northwestern U., Evanston, Ill., 1980—. Author: (with David Riesman) The Academic Revolution, 1968, (with others) Inequality, 1972, Who Gets Ahead?, 1979. Guggenheim fellow, 1967-68, 82-83. Office: Northwestern U Evanston IL 60201

JENCKS, WILLIAM PLATT, educator, biochemist; b. Bar Harbor, Maine, Aug. 15, 1927; s. Gardner and Elinor (Melcher) J.; m. Miriam Ehrlich, June 3, 1950; children—Helen Esther, David Alan. Grad., St. Paul's Sch., Balt., 1944; student, Harvard, 1944-47, M.D., 1951. Intern Peter Bent Brigham Hosp., Boston, 1951-52; postdoctoral fellow Mass. Gen. Hosp., Boston, 1952-53, 55-56; postdoctoral fellow chemistry Harvard, 1956-57; mem. faculty Brandeis U., 1957—, prof. biochemistry, 1963—. Served as 1st lt., M.C. AUS, 1953-55. Mem. Am. Chem. Soc. (award biol. chemistry 1962), Am. Soc. Biol. Chemists, Am. Acad. Arts and Scis., AAAS, Nat. Acad. Scis., Alpha Omega Alpha. Home: 11 Revere St Lexington MA 02173 Office: Grad Dept Biochemistry Brandeis Univ Waltham MA 02254

JEND, WILLIAM, JR., telephone co. exec., physician; b. Detroit, Sept. 12, 1918; s. William James and Stella (Baur) J.; m. Norma Elizabeth Rowe, June 4, 1942; children—W. James, Henry Rowe, Patricia Elizabeth. A.B., Albion Coll., 1939; M.D., U. Mich., 1943; postgrad., Wayne State U., 1947-49. Diplomate: Am. Bd. Preventive Medicine. Intern Grace Hosp., Detroit, 1943; resident in medicine Jennings Meml. Hosp., Detroit, 1944, VA Hosp., Dearborn, Mich., 1947-49, also sr. physician in medicine, 1949-52; mem. med. staff Mich. Bell Telephone Co., Detroit, 1952—, asst. med. dir., 1953-54, med. dir., 1955—; instr. clin. medicine Wayne State U., 1949-52, clin. asst. prof. occupational and environmental health, 1966—; lectr. occupational medicine Med. Sch., U. Mich., 1962—. Mem. gen. planning com. United Community Services, 1957-70; tech. adviser Mich. Dept. Civil Service, 1969—; Bd. dirs. Am. Lung Assn. Southeastern Mich., 1960-70, World Med. Relief Orgn., 1965—, Mental Health Assn. in Mich., 1977—; trustee Mich. Cancer Found., 1974—. Served to maj. M.C. AUS, 1945-47. W.K. Kellogg Found. fellow, 1941. Fellow Am. Occupational Med. Assn. (pres. 1972), Am. Acad. Occupational Medicine, ACP, Am. Coll. Preventive Medicine; mem. AMA, Am. Public Health Assn., Am. Soc. Internal Medicine, Mich. Occupational Med. Assn. (pres. 1962), Mich. Med. Soc. (chmn. occupational health com. 1965-69), Wayne County Med. Soc. (chmn. occupational health com. 1961-63), Detroit Occupational Physicians Assn. (pres. 1977), Tau Kappa Epsilon, Phi Rho Sigma. Methodist. Home: 5255 Wing Lake Rd Bloomfield Hills MI 48013 Office: 444 Michigan Ave Detroit MI 48226

JENDEN, DONALD JAMES, educator, pharmacologist; b. Horsham, Sussex, Eng., Sept. 1, 1926; came to U.S., 1950, naturalized, 1958; s. William Herbert and Kathleen Mary (Harris) J.; m. Jean Ickeringill, Nov. 18, 1950; children: Patricia Mary, Peter D., Beverly J. B.Sc. in Physiology with 1st class honours (scholar 1944), Westminster Med. Sch., U. London, 1947; M.B., B.S. (Univ. gold medal 1950), U. London, 1950; D.Pharm. Sci. (hon.), U. Uppsala, Sweden, 1980. Demonstrator physiology and pharmacology U. London, 1947-50; lectr. pharmacology, then asst. prof. pharmacology U. Calif.-San Francisco, 1950-53; mem. faculty U. Calif.-Los Angeles, 1953—; prof. pharmacology UCLA, 1960—, prof. pharmacology and biomath., 1968—, chmn. dept. pharmacology, 1968—; hon. research asso. Univ. Coll., London., 1961-62. Contbr. articles in field. Served to lt. M.C., USNR, 1954-56. Fellow Am. Coll. Neuropsychopharmacology; mem. Am. Soc. Pharmacology and Exptl. Therapeutics, Am. Physiol. Soc., AAAS, Physiol. Soc. (London), Brit. Med. Assn., Soc. Neurosci., Am. Chem. Soc. (div. med. chemistry), Western Pharmacology Soc., Assn. for Med. Sch. Pharmacology, Am. Soc. Mass Spectrometry, Am. Soc. Neurochemistry, Internat. Union Pharmacology (sect. on toxicology), N.Y. Acad. Sci. Home: 3814 S Castlerock Rd Malibu CA 90265 Office: Sch Medicine Center Health Scis Univ California Los Angeles CA 90024

JENERICK, HOWARD PETER, scientist; b. Chgo., May 1923; s. Peter and Helen Agnes (Gavin) J.; m. Helen Catherine Pirhofer, June 14, 1947; children: Stephanie, Karen, Christopher. Student, Ill. Inst. Tech., 1941-42; Ph.B. with honors, U. Chgo., 1946, S.B., 1948, Ph.D., 1951. Instr., asst. prof. biology M.I.T., 1951-58; exec. sec. NIH, Bethesda, Md., 1958-60; asso. prof. Emory Med. Sch., Atlanta, 1960-64; br. chief, spl. asst. Nat. Inst. Gen. Med. Scis., NIH, 1965-76, chief, 1976—, now asst. dir. evaluation. Served with USNR, 1942-45. Decorated D.F.C., Air medal; USPHS fellow, 1950-51. Office: NIH Bethesda MD 20205

JENKIN, HOWARD MILTON, microbiologist; b. N.Y.C., May 1, 1925; s. Meyer and Rose J.; m. Beverly Mae Harms, Aug. 15, 1956; children: Keith A., Kristen M., Donna J. B.S. in Med. Bacteriology, U. Wis., 1949; Ph.D. in Microbiology, U. Chgo., 1960. NRC fellow, virus-rickettsial div. U.S. Biol. Lab., Ft. Detrick, Md., 1959-60, med. investigation div., 1961-62; research asst. prof., dept. preventive medicine U. Wash., 1962-66; with Naval Med. Research Unit 2, Taipei, Taiwan, 1963-66; assoc. prof. Med. Sch. and Hormel Inst., U. Minn., Mpls., Austin, 1966-71, prof., 1971—. Contbr. articles on normal and infected cell culture molecular biology, spirochetal, chlamydial, arboviral, herpes virus, pseudorabies research, lipid metabolic studies, cell transformation biochemistry to profl. jours. City councilman, Austin, 1974-78. NIH grantee, 1966-81; Office Naval Research grantee, 1971-78; USDA grantee, 1978-82. Mem. Am. Soc. Microbiology, Tissue Culture Assn., Soc. for Exptl. Biology and Medicine, Am. Venereal Disease Assn., Sigma Xi.

JENKINS, ALBION URBAN, JR., insurance company executive; b. Paterson, N.J., Oct. 4, 1922; s. Albion Urban and Lillian Rebecca (Taylor) J.; m. May Marguerite Willett, Jan. 24, 1946; 1 son, Richard. B.A., Wesleyan U., Middletown, Conn., 1947. With Prudential Ins. Co. Am., 1947—, v.p., Newark, 1977-78, sr. v.p. corp. services and bldgs. dept., 1978—. Chmn. task force for econ. devel. Nat. Urban League Commerce and Industry Council; mem. commerce and industry council Nat. Urban League; bd. overseers Met. Lithographers Assn.—NYU Ctr. Graphic Arts; chmn. steering com. North Jersey Constrn. Users Council.; chmn. bd. trustees Community Congl. Ch., Short Hills, N.J. Served to 1st lt. USAAF, 1943-46. Fellow Soc. Actuaries, Am. Acad. Actuaries. Club: Towanda Country. Office: Prudential Ins Co Am Prudential Plaza Newark NJ 07101

JENKINS, BENJAMIN LARRY, insurance company executive; b. Washington, Aug. 17, 1938; s. Benjamin Joseph and Ruth Elizabeth (deButts) J.; m. Catherine O. Hungerford, June 30, 1956; children: Lynne, Lisa, Larry, Laine, Lacy, Lexy. B.S., Mt. St. Mary's Coll., Emmitsburg, Md., 1960. C.L.U. Dist. agt. Peoples Life, Waldorf, Md., 1959-62; sales mgr. People Life, Waldorf, Md., 1962,65; mgr. Peoples Life, Waldorf, Md., 1965-69, supt. agys., Washington, 1969-71, v.p., 1971-74, sr. v.p., 1974-76, exec. v.p., 1976-77, pres., 1977-78, chmn. bd., pres., 1978-82; vice chmn. Monumental Life Ins. Co., Balt., 1982—; dir. Mercantile Bankshares, Balt., 1982—; vice chmn. Life Insurers Conf., Richmond, Va., 1982—. Trustee Balt. Mus. of Art, 1983-86. Mem. Am. Council Life Ins., Am. Soc. Chartered Life Underwriters, Nat. Assn. Life Underwriters, Life Insurers Conf. (vice chmn.). Republican. Roman Catholic. Home: 8530 Park Heights Ave Baltimore MD 21208 Office: Monumental Life Ins Co 20 E Chase St Baltimore MD 21202

JENKINS, BRUCE STERLING, fed. judge; b. Salt Lake City, May 27, 1927; s. Joseph and Bessie Pearl (Iverson) J.; m. Margaret Watkins, Sept. 19, 1952; children—Judith Margaret, David Bruce, Michael Glen, Carol Alice. B.A. with high honors, U. Utah, 1949, LL.B., 1952, J.D., 1952. Bar: Utah bar 1952, U.S. Dist. Ct. bar 1952, U.S. Supreme Ct. bar 1962, U.S. Circuit Ct. Appeals bar 1962. Individual practice law, Salt Lake City, 1952-59; asso. firm George McMillan, 1959-65; asst. atty. gen. State of Utah, 1952; dep. county atty., Salt Lake County, 1954-58; bankruptcy judge U.S. Dist. Ct., Dist. of Utah, 1965-78, U.S. dist. judge, 1978—. Research, publs. in field; contbr. essays to Law jours.; bd. editors: Utah Law Rev, 1951-52. Mem. Utah Senate, 1959-65, minority leader, 1963, pres. senate, 1965; vice chmn. commn. on orgn. exec. br. of Utah Govt., 1965-66; Mem. adv. com. Utah Tech. Coll., 1967-72; mem. instl. council Utah State U., 1976. Served with USN, 1945-46. Mem. Utah State Bar Assn., Salt Lake County Bar Assn., Am. Bar Assn., Fed. Bar Assn., Order of Coif, Phi Beta Kappa, Phi Kappa Phi, Phi Eta Sigma, Phi Sigma Alpha, Tau Kappa Alpha. Democrat. Mormon. Office: Room 235 US Courthouse 350 S Main St Salt Lake City UT 84101

JENKINS, DANIEL EDWARDS, JR., educator, physician; b. Omaha, July 19, 1916; s. Daniel Edwards and Anne (Finley) J.; m. Dora Solis, Aug. 1, 1942; children—Daniel Edwards III, Mark Schering, Tessa Ann. Student, Hampden-Sydney Coll., 1934; B.A., U. Tex., 1936, M.D., 1940. Intern, then resident U. Mich. Hosp., 1940-44; asst. prof. medicine U. Coll. Medicine, 1947—, prof. internal medicine, 1956—, chief sect. pulmonary diseases, 1947-74, chief sect. environ. medicine, 1974—; part-time pvt. practice, 1947—; chief pulmonary disease service Harris County Hosp. Dist., 1947-74; cons. VA, 1949-75. Author articles in field. Recipient So. Conf. award So. Tb Conf., 1967. Fellow A.C.P., Am. Coll. Chest Physicians (pres. So. chpt. 1958); mem. A.M.A., Am. Thoracic Soc. (pres. 1958-59), Am. Fedn. Clin. Research, Am. Clin. and Climatol. Assn., Am. Lung Assn. (dir. 1958-75, pres. 1967-68), Tex. Tb and Respiratory Disease Assn. (dir. 1949—, pres. 1966-67), Alpha Omega Alpha, Alpha Kappa Kappa. Home: 3550 Sun Valley Dr Houston TX 77025

JENKINS, DANIEL THOMAS, theologian, clergyman, educator; b. Merthry Tydfall, Wales, UK, June 9, 1914; s. Evan and Eleanor (Davies) J.; m. Agatha Helen Cree, Aug. 15, 1942; children: Simon David, Katharine Mary, Priscilla Frances, Caroline Helen, Thomas Cree. M.A., Edinburg U., Scotland, 1935, B.D., 1938, D.D. hon., 1964; B.A., Oxford U., 1939; D.D. hon., Knox Coll., Toronto, Ont., Can., 1957. Ordained minister, 1940. Minister, chaplain Congregational Ch., London, Eng., 1940-48; minster Congregation Ch., London, Eng., 1950-62; prof. U. Chgo., 1950-62; reader, chaplain U. Sussex, Brighton, Eng., 1963-73; minister United Reformed Ch., London, 1971-81; prof. Princeton Theol. Sem., N.J., 1981—; Lyman Breecher lectr. Yale U., New Haven, 1964; resident in religion Bryn Mawr Coll., Pa., 1971; vis. prof. Kings Coll., London, 1972-75; Warfield lectr., 1975. Author 20 books; The British: Their Identity and Their Religion, 1975, Christian Maturity and Christian Success, 1982. Bd. dirs. Nat. Council Acad. Awards, London, 1974-79; mem. Central religious adv. com. BBC, 1975-80; bd. dirs. World Council Chs. Commonwealth Fund fellow, N.Y.C., 1948-49; Nuffield Found. grantee, 1959-63. Club: Athenaeum (London). Home: 301 Willoughby House Barbican London UK EC2Y 8BL Office: Princeton Theological Seminary Princeton NJ 08542

JENKINS, DONALD JOHN, art association executive; b. Longview, Wash., May 3, 1931; s. John Peter and Louise Hazel (Pederson) J.; m. Mary Ella Bemis, June 29, 1956; children: Jennifer, Rebecca. B.A., U. Chgo., 1951, M.A., 1970. Museum asst. Portland (Oreg.) Art Mus., 1954, asst. curator, 1960-69, curator, 1974, dir., 1980—; assoc. curator Oriental art Art Inst. Chgo., 1969-74; dir. Portland Art Assn., 1975-80; mem. gallery adv. com. Asia House Gallery, N.Y.C.; mem. mus. subcom. U.S.-Japan Conf. Cultural and Ednl. Interchange, 1973-80; reviewer, div. public programs Nat. Endowment for Humanities, Washington, 1977-78; mem. Pittock Mansion adv. Commn., Portland Bur. Parks, 1975—, chmn., 1983—; mem. Portland Mall art steering com. Met. Arts Commn. Portland, 1976-78, ARTQUAKE steering com. Met. Arts Commn. Portland, 1977-78; co-chmn. N.W. Regional China Council, 1980—; mem. adv. com. U.S. Courthouse Renovation, 1981—; mem. pub. art selection com. Performing Arts Ctr., 1983—. Author: catalogs Ukiyo-E Prints and Paintings, The Primitive Period, 1680-1745, 1971, The Ledoux Heritage, The Collecting of Ukiyo-E Prints, 1973, Masterworks in Wood: China and Japan, 1976; Images of a Changing World: Japanese Prints of the 20th Century, 1983. Art Mus. Dirs. grantee Mus. Mgmt. Inst., U. Calif., Berkeley, summer 1979. Mem. Am. Assn. Mus., Assn. Art Mus. Dirs., Internat. Hajji Baba Soc., Soc. Japanese Arts and Crafts, Art Mus. Assn. Home: 16418 NW Rock Creek Rd Portland OR 97321 Office: Portland Art Assn 1219 SW Park Ave Portland OR 97205

JENKINS, EDGAR LANIER, congressman; b. Young Harris, Ga., Jan. 4, 1933; s. Charlie S. and Evia Mae (Souther) J.; m. Beni Jo Thomasson, Dec. 27, 1959; children: Janice Kristan and Amy Lynn. A.A., Young Harris Coll., 1951; LL.B., U. Ga., 1959. Bar: Ga. 1959. Partner firm Jenkins & Landrum, Jasper; asst. U.S. atty., Atlanta, 1962-64, county atty., sch. bd. atty., Pickens County, Ga., 1964-70; mem. 95th-98th Congresses, 9th Dist. Ga. Served with USCGR, 1952-55. Mem. Am. Bar Assn., State Bar Ga. Democrat. Baptist. Office: 217 Cannon House Office Bldg Washington DC 20515 *

JENKINS, FERGUSON ARTHUR, baseball player; b. Chatham, Ont., Can., Dec. 13, 1943. Pitcher Phila. Phillies (Nat. League), 1965-66, Chgo. Cubs (Nat. League), 1966-73, 82-83, Tex. Rangers (Am. League), Arlington, 1973-75, 78-81; pitcher Boston Red Sox (Am. League), 1975-77. Author: Inside Pitching, 1972. Named to Nat. League All-Star Team Sporting News, 1967, 71-72; named Nat. League Pitcher of Year, 1971; recipient Nat. League Cy Young Meml. award, 1971. Address: care Chicago Cubs Wrigley Field N Clark and Addison Sts Chicago IL 60613 *

JENKINS, GEORGE, stage designer, film art director; b. Balt., Nov. 19, 1911; s. Benjamin Wheeler and Jane (Clarke) J.; m. Phyllis Adams, May 6, 1955; 1 dau by previous marriage, Jane Jenkins Griffin; 1 stepdau., Alexandra Kirkland Marsh. Student, U. Pa., 1931. Cons. theatre U. Pa., Anenberg Theatre; designer, partner Sugar Mill Inn, St. Vincent, W.I., 1954—; mem. bd. theatre standards ANTA, 1954—. Set designer: Broadway prodns., including I Remember Mamma, 1944, Dark of the Moon, 1945, Lost in the Stars, 1949, Bell, Book and Candle, 1950, The Bad Seed, 1954, Happiest Millionaire, 1956, Miracle Worker, 1959, Wait Until Dark, 1966, Only Game in Town, 1968, Night Watch, 1972, SLT Fox, 1976; art dir.: films, including Best Years of Our Lives, 1946, Secret Life of Walter Mitty, 1948, Mickey One, 1965, Up the Down Staircase, 1966, Wait Until Dark, 1967, No Way to Treat a Lady, 1967, Subject Was Roses, 1968, Klute, 1970, 1776, 1971, The Paper Chase, 1972, Parallax View, 1973, Funny Lady, 1974, All the President's Men, 1977, Comes A Horseman, 1978, China Syndrome, 1978, Starting Over, 1979, The Postman Always Rings Twice, 1980, Roll Over, 1981, Sophie's Choice, 1982; TV programs, including Annie Get Your Gun, 1957, The Dollmaker, ABC-TV, 1983; art dir. in charge color, CBS-TV, 1953-54; (Recipient Donaldson award for I Remember Mamma, Billbd. Publs. 1946, Oscar award All the President's Men, Acad. Motion Picture Arts scis. 1977). Mem. Delta Phi. Office: 740 Kingman Ave Santa Monica CA 90402 also 124 E 72 St New York NY 10021

JENKINS, HAROLD RICHARD, library consultant; b. Pottstown, Pa., Aug. 23, 1918; s. Stanley Frederick and Flora (High) J.; m. Margaret Houston Leech, Nov. 1, 1957; children: M. Elizabeth, Richard H. B.A., Ursinus Coll., 1953; M.A. in L.S, U. Mich., 1956. Catalog librarian Washington and Lee U., Lexington, Va., 1956-58; dir. Kingsport (Tenn.) Pub. Library, 1958-59, Wise County (Va.) Regional Library, 1959-61, Pottstown Pub. Library, 1961-63, Lancaster County (Pa.) Library, 1963-74, Kansas City (Mo.) Pub. Library, 1974-83; 2d v.p. Pa. Library Assn., 1968; state chmn. Nat. Library Week, 1967. Author: Management of a Public Library, 1981; contbr. articles to profl. jours. Bd. dirs. Lancaster County Hist. Soc., 1972-73. 1Served with C.E. AUS, 1941-52. Mem. ALA, Mo. Library Assn. (pres. 1977-78), Beta Phi Mu, Pi Gamma Mu. Club: Rotarian.

JENKINS, IREDELL, educator; b. Blue Ridge Summit, Md., Aug. 12, 1909; s. James Iredell and Mary (Dobie) J.; m. Isabel Lawson Cook, Dec. 27, 1934; children—Anne (Mrs. Thomas R. Ball), Armistead Dobie. B.A., U. Va., 1933, M.A., 1934, Ph.D., 1937; student, U. Paris, France, 1935-36. From instr. to asso. prof. philosophy Tulane U., 1937-46; asst. philosophy Yale, 1946-49; prof. philosophy, chmn. dept. U. Ala., 1949—; vis. prof. Northwestern U., 1964-65. Author: Art and The Human Enterprise, 1958, Social Order and the Limits of Law: A Theoretical Essay, 1980, also numerous articles.; Mem. editorial bd.: So. Jour. Philosophy, Law and Soc. Rev. Research grantee Rockefeller Found., 1957-58, Am. Council Learned Socs., 1952-53, U. Chgo., 1959-60, NSF, 1975-76. Mem. Am. Philos. Assn., Metaphys. Soc. Am., Internat. Assn. Philosophy Law and Social Philosophy (pres. Am. sect.), Am. Soc. Aesthetics, Phi Beta Kappa. Home: 90 Brookhaven Tuscaloosa AL 35405

JENKINS, JAMES ALLISTER, mathematician, educator; b. Toronto, Ont., Can., Sept. 23, 1923; came to U.S., 1950, naturalized, 1956; s. James Thomas and Maude (Zuern) J. B.A., U. Toronto, 1944, M.A., 1945, postgrad., 1946; Ph.D., Harvard, 1948. Postdoctoral fellow Harvard U., 1948-49, Inst. for Advanced Study, 1949-50; asst. prof. math. Johns Hopkins U., 1950-54; asso. prof. U. Notre Dame, 1954-56, prof., 1956-59, Washington U., St. Louis, 1959—; Mem. Inst. Advanced Study, 1957-59, 61-62, 73-74, 80-81. Author: Univalent Functions and Conformal Mapping, 1965; Contbr. articles to profl. jours. Mem. Am., French, German math. socs. Home: 526 Purdue Ave Saint Louis MO 63130

JENKINS, JAMES MICHAEL, restaurant company executive; b. Los Angeles, Sept. 7, 1946; s. J.C. J. and Janet (Silver); m. Peggy Christine Mahony, Feb. 5, 1966 (div. May 1982); 1 dau., Cheryl; m. Joan Eileen Gloden, Aug. 8, 1983. Student, Calif. State U., 1964, 68-70; M.B.A., So. Methodist U., 1982. Mgmt. positions S&A Restaurant Corp., Dallas, 1970-79, exec. v.p., 1979-83, pres., 1983—, dir.; dir. ops. Gt. Earth Vitamins Inc., Irvine, Calif., 1979; regional v.p. Sambo's Restaurant Corp., Dallas, 1979; dir. Pace Fin. Mgmt. Inc.; mem. adv. bd. Genesis Venture Inc. Served with USAF, 1964-68. Mem. Am. Mgmt. Assn. Republican. Club: Toastmasters (Richardson, Tex.). Office: S&A Restaurant Corp 6606 LBJ Freeway Dallas TX 75240 *Do only what is exhilarating, or you will miss the true joys of living; challenge, commitment and love.*

JENKINS, JOHN SMITH, university dean, lawyer; b. Pittston, Pa., Dec. 11, 1932; s. Walter Hershel and Mildred (Lewis) J.; m. Marilyn Lewis, Aug. 23, 1958; 1 son, John Smith. B.A., Lafayette Coll., Easton, Pa., 1954; J.D. with honors, George Washington U., 1961; M.A., Am. U., 1967. Bar: Va. bar 1961. Commd. ensign USN, 1955, advanced through grades to rear admiral, 1978; stationed at naval communications sta., Pearl Harbor, Hawaii, 1955-56, duty on U.S.S. Rochester, 1956-57, with Bur. Naval Personnel, Washington, 1957-62, with Hdqrs. 1st Naval Dist., Boston, 1962-64, staff Office Navay JAG, 1964-65, staff Office Legis. Affairs, Washington, 1969-71, staff Office of Asst. Sec., 1971-73, spl. counsel to sec. Office of Asst. Sec., 1973-76, asst. civil law JAG, 1976-78, dep. JAG, 1978-80, JAG, 1980-82, asst.

dean Nat. Law Ctr., Washington, 1982—. Decorated Legion of Merit. Mem. Am., Fed., Va. bar assns. Episcopalian. Home: 5809 Helmsdale Ln Alexandria VA 22310 Office: Nat Law Ctr George Washington U 720 20th St NW Washington DC

JENKINS, KEMPTON BOYCE, foreign service officer; b. Jacksonville, Fla., June 8, 1926; s. Nelson Boyce and Margaret L. (West) J.; m. Lucy Cabell Crichton, July 19, 1975; children: Peter, Michael, Timothy, Greig Crichton, Ann Crichton. B.A., Bowling Green State U., 1948; M.A., George Washington U., 1950; M.P.A., Harvard U., 1958. Commd. fgn. service officer Dept. State, 1950; asst. dir. (USIA for Eastern Europe), 1968-73; dep. asst. sec. of State for Congressional Relations, 1973-78, Sec. of Commerce for East-West Trade, Dept. Commerce, Washington, 1978-80; pres. (US-USSR Trade and Econ. Council), Washington, 1980-81; v.p. for govt. affairs Armco Corp., 1981—; professorial lectr. Georgetown U. Served with USNR, 1944-46. Office: Armco 1747 Pennsylvania Ave NW Suite 702 Washington DC 20006

JENKINS, LEO WARREN, univ. chancellor; b. Succasunna, N.J., May 28, 1913; s. Warren Maylon and Cecila (McPeek) J.; m. Lillian Olga Jacobsen, Oct. 11, 1942; children—James, Jeffrey, Patricia, Sallie, Jack, Suzanne. B.S., Rutgers U., 1935; M.A., Columbia, 1937; postgrad., Duke, summer 1937; Ed.D., N.Y. U., 1941. Tchr. English and social studies Pleasantville (N.J.) High Sch., 1935-37; tchr. history, dean boys Somerville (N.J.) High Sch., 1937-41; supr. practice tchrs., mem. faculty Montclair (N.J.) State Tchrs. Coll., 1945-46; asst. higher edn. N.J. State Dept. Edn., Trenton, 1946-47; dean instrn., dir. summer sch. East Carolina Coll., Greenville, N.C., 1947-55, v.p., 1955-60, pres., 1960—; dir. Wachovia Bank & Trust Co., Carolina Tel. & Tel., Little Mint Food Services; spl. adv. to gov. N.C., 1978—; Mem. AEC, N.C. Atomic Energy Adv. Com., Gov.'s Com. for Pub. Schs., N.C. State Adv. Com. Ednl. Adminstrn.; cons. N.C. Edn. Commn.; advisor to dir., div. spl. edn. N.C. Dept. Edn. Resource-Use Edn. Commn.; ednl. chmn. N.C. Congress Parents and Tchrs.; mem. N.C. Sch. Survey Panel. Producer: Tar Heel Portraits, NBC. Chmn. Pitt County Polio Campaign, 1950; mem. N.C. Sports Hall of Fame, Nat. Commn. on Accrediting; chmn. N.C. Commn. Internat. Cooperation.; Bd. dirs. N.C. League for Crippled Children, N.C. Symphony Soc., N.C. Zool. Authority; trustee Louisburg Coll. Served as capt. USMCR, 1942-46; Guadalcanal, Guam, Iwo Jima. Decorated Bronze Star medal with oak leaf cluster.; Recipient Golden Deeds award Greenville Exchange, 1963, Citizen of Year award Greenville C. of C., 1967, N.C. Pub. Service award, 1977. Mem. NEA (dept. higher edn.), Am. Assn. Sch. Adminstrs., Internat. Assn. Univ. Presidents, N.C. Edn. Assn., Am. Legion, VFW, Greenville Jaycees (hon. life), Nat. Football Hall of Fame (dir. Triangle chpt.). Methodist (steward). Club: Kiwanian (dir.)

JENKINS, LEROY, jazz violinist, composer; b. Chgo., Mar. 11, 1932; m. Linda Jenkins; 1 dau., Chantille Kwintana. Student with, Walter Dyett, Chgo.; B.S., Fla. A&M U., 1961. Mem. Assn. for Advancement of Creative Musicians, Chgo., 1965-69; instr. Chgo. sch. system, 1965-69; instr. Chgo. Urban Poverty Corps, 1969. Formed (with Anthony Braxton and Leo Smith) trio, 1968; also played (with Arnette Coleman, Albert Ayler, Archief Shepp, Alice Coltraine, Cecil Taylor); formed, Revolutionary Ensemble, 1971-77; then formed (with Muhal Richard Abrams and Andrew Cyrille) trio; also performed (with Oliver Lake) duets; appeared in jazz festivals including, Ann Arbor, 1973, Newport Jazz Festival, 1974; albums include New Worlds Survival of America, Vietnam, Manhattan Cycles, The People's Republic, Creative Construction Company, Levels and Degrees, Space Minds. Nat. Endowment Arts grantee, 1973; Recipient Downbeat Critic's poll, 1974. Office: care Rasa Artists 144 W 27th St New York NY 10001 *

JENKINS, LLEWELLYN, banker; b. N.Y.C., Aug. 25, 1919; s. Thomas M. and Clare E. J.; m. Doris Mischanko, Sept. 12, 1947; children: Lynne, Thomas, Robert, David. B.S. in Econs., U. Pa.; postgrad., Stonier Grad. Sch. Banking, Rutgers U., Grad. Sch. Credit, Dartmouth Coll. With Central Hanover Bank, 1946-61, asst. v.p., 1956-60, v.p., 1961-69; sr. v.p. Mfrs. Hanover Trust Co., N.Y.C., 1969-73, exec. v.p., 1973-79, vice chmn., 1979-83; pres. Statue of Liberty-Ellis Island Found. Inc., 1983—; dir. Bucyrus-Erie Co., South Milwaukee, Wis. Author: Check List for Revolving Credit and Term Loans. Served to capt. inf. U.S. Army, World War II. Office: 101 Park Ave New York NY 10017 *

JENKINS, MARGARET LUDMILLA, choreographer, dancer; b. Berkeley, Calif., Dec. 1, 1942; d. Hyman David and Edith Arnstein J.; m. Albert J. Wax, Apr. 2, 1972; 1 dau., Leslie Marissa. Student, Juilliard Sch. Music, 1960-61, UCLA, 1961-63. Dancer Jack Moore Dance Co., N.Y.C., 1960, Al Huang Dance Co., 1961, Gus Solomons Jr. Dance Co., 1963-65; tchr. Merce Cunningham Sch., N.Y.C., 1965-70; asst. to Merce Cunningham, N.Y.C., Boston, Stockholm, La Rochelle, France, 1965-74; dancer Twyla Tharp Dance Co., 1965-67, Viola Farber Dance Co., 1967-70; tchr., Paris, London, Stockholm, 1967; artistic dir. Margaret Jenkins Dance Co., San Francisco, 1972—; panelist NEA, Nat. Endowment for Arts, 1977-80; vice-chmn. DANCE/USA. Choreographer: Videosongs, 1976, Copy, 1977, About The Space In Between, 1977, Into Three, 1978, Red Yellow Blue, 1978, No One But Whittington, 1978, Straight Words, 1979, Invisible Frames, 1979, Duets, 1980, Versions By Turns, 1980, Harp, 1981, Cortland Set, 1982, In the Round I, 1982, In the Round II, 1982. Guggenheim fellow, 1980; Nat. Endowment for Arts fellow, 1978-79, 80, 81. Mem. San Francisco Bay Area Dance Coalition., Am. Arts Alliance (trustee). Home: 3973 25th St San Francisco CA 94114 Office: 1590 15th St San Francisco CA 94103

JENKINS, ORVILLE WESLEY, religious administrator; b. Hico, Tex., Apr. 29, 1913; s. Daniel Wesley and Eva (Caldwell) J.; m. Louise Cantrell, June 29, 1939; children—Orville Wesley, Jannette (Mrs. John Calhoun), Jeanne (Mrs. David Hubbs). Student, Tex. Tech. U., 1929-34; B.A., Pasadena Coll., 1938, Nazarene Theol. Sem., 1946-47; D.D., Bethany Nazarene Coll., 1957. Ordained to ministry Ch. of Nazarene, 1939; pastor, Dinuba, Calif., 1938-42, Fresno, Calif., 1942-45, Topeka, 1945-47, Salem, Oreg., 1947-50, Kansas City, Mo., 1959-61; supt. West Tex. Dist. Ch. of Nazarene, 1950-59, Kansas City Dist., 1961-64; exec. sec. dept. home missions Ch. of Nazarene, Kansas City, 1946-68, gen. supt., 1968—. Trustee Bethany Nazarene Coll. Home: 2309 W 103d St Leawood KS 66206 Office: 6401 Paseo Kansas City MO 64131 *The Christian life has brought meaningful and purposeful existence and has led to a wonderful sense of fulfillment in living. It is a joy to follow the day-to-day excitement of this life.*

JENKINS, PAUL, painter; b. Kansas City, Mo., July 12, 1923; s. William Burris and Nadyne (Fellers) J.; (married); 1 dau., Hilarie Paula. Student, Art Students League, N.Y.C., 1948-52; Hum.D., 1973. Author: play Strike the Puma, 1966; also articles.; Producer: film The Ivory Knife, 1965 (award Venice Biennale 1966); Exhbns. include, Gimpel Weitzenhoffer Gallery, N.Y.C., Karl Flinker Gallery, Paris, Georges Fall Gallery, Paris, Gimpel Gallery, London, Eng.; rep. permanent collections, Mus. Modern Art, Whitney Mus., Guggenheim Mus., Corcoran Gallery, Tate Gallery, London, Musee D'Art Moderne, Paris, Centre Georges Pompidou, Paris, Stedelijk Mus., Amsterdam, Netherlands, Mus. Western Art, Tokyo. Served with USNR, 1943-45. Decorated Commandeur des Arts et Lettres, France; recipient Silver medal Corcoran Gallery Art, 1967. Subject of 2 biographies. Address: 831 Broadway New York NY 10003

JENKINS, ROBERT ELLSWORTH, JR., ecologist; b. Lewistown, Pa., Sept. 30, 1942; s. Robert Ellsworth and Ellen Magdalena (Wesner) J.; m. Diane Alyce St. Pierre, Nov. 4, 1964; children: Heather Elizabeth, Robert Ellsworth III. A.B., Rutgers U., 1964; Ph.D., Harvard U., 1970. Mem. staff Nature Conservancy, Washington, 1970—, v.p. sci. programs, 1972—; co-founder Center Applied Research in Environ. Scis., 1971; founder, dir. State Natural Heritage Programs, 1974—; Mem. Conservation sect. U.S. com. Internat. Biol. Program, 1970-75; mem. Fed. Com. Research Natural Areas, 1970—, U.S. Nat. Commn. for UNESCO, 1974-76; research asso. Smithsonian Instn., 1971-73; mem. bd. Rare Animal Relief Effort, 1974-76; mem. parks and preserves com. U.S./Soviet Environ. Protection Agreements; mem. adv. council Kai Moku Found., 1976-80; mem. natural areas com. U.S. Man and Biosphere Program, 1978—. Bd. dirs. Mass. Planned Parenthood League, 1970-73. Recipient Conservation award Am. Motors Corp., 1978; Henry Rutgers scholar, 1963-64; Richmond fellow, 1965-69; research fellow Orgn. Tropical Studies, 1966; Demographic fellow Population Council, 1969-70. Fellow AAAS (council 1972-73); mem. Am. Inst. Biol. Scis. (bd. govs. 1970—), Inst. for Conservation Biology (bd. dirs. 1984—), Ecol. Soc. Am., Soc. Study Evolution, Wildlife Soc., Internat. Assn. Ecology, Nature Conservancy, Zero Population Growth (founder, dir. Mass. 1969-70), Inst. Ecology. Home: RFD 1 Box 15 Warrenton VA 22186 Office: 1800 N Kent St Arlington VA 22209

JENKINS, ROBERT SPURGEON, management consultant; b. Wellston, Ohio, Oct. 24, 1921; s. Isaac Spurgeon and Carolyn (Burns) J.; m. Margaret Gene Kennard, Sept. 1, 1946; children: Deborah Gene and Priscilla Ann (twins), Roberta Kennard, Cynthia Carolyn. A.A., Rio Grande Coll., 1943; A.B., Denison U., 1946; M.A., Ohio State U., 1948, Ph.D., 1951. Capital investment analysis supr. Ford div. Ford Motor Co., 1952-55, exec. to exec. v.p., 1956-57, asst. orgn. and systems mgr., 1958-60, mktg. adminstrn. mgr., 1960-63, sales and mktg. mgmt. mgr., 1964-65; sr. dir. personnel Trans World Airlines, 1965-69; pres. R.S. Jenkins & Co. (Mgmt. Cons. and Exec. Search), 1970-71; sr. v.p., mng. partner, dir. Eastman & Beaudine, Inc. (Internat. Mgmt. Cons.), 1971—; Asst. dir. research Ohio Tax and Revenue Study Commn., 1951; prof. indsl. mgmt. Henry Ford Coll., 1958-63; lectr. Am. Mgmt. Assn., 1968-69; personnel cons. Peace Corps, Washington, 1970. Mem. Livonia (Mich.) Sch. Bd., 1957, Plymouth (Mich.) Sch. Bd., 1965; pres. Plymouth Symphony Soc., 1960-62; Mem. personnel bd. N.Y. Light House Assn., N.Y.C., 1968-70. Served with USAAF, 1943-46. Mem. Am. Econ. Assn., Am. Mgmt. Assn., Sigma Chi. Presbyterian (elder 1969-71). Clubs: Wee Burn Country (Darien, Conn.); Univ., Board Room, Wings (N.Y.C.); Landmark (Stamford, Conn.). Home: 21 Stephanie Ln Darien CT 06820 Office: 437 Madison Ave New York NY 10022

JENKINS, RUBEN LEE, chemical company executive; b. Beggs, Okla., Nov. 27, 1929; s. William Arnold and Myrtle (Kimble) J.; m. Sylvia Griffin, July 17, 1956; children: Amy, Kimble Lee, William Griffin. B.A., U. Okla., 1952, LL.B., 1956; LL.M., N.Y. U., 1959. Bar: Okla. 1956. Law clk. chief judge U.S. Dist. Ct. Western Dist. Okla., Oklahoma City, 1956; clk. U.S. Ct., 1956-58; research asst. internat. law N.Y. U., 1958-59; practiced in, Buenos Aires, Argentina, 1959-60; gen. counsel White Eagle Internat., Inc., Midland, Tex., 1960-65, exec. v.p., 1963-65, dir., 1961-65; v.p. corp. devel. Plough, Inc., Memphis, 1965-72, sr. v.p., 1972-73, exec. v.p., 1973-76, pres., 1976—, dir., 1970—; sr. v.p. Schering-Plough Corp., 1976-80, exec. v.p., 1980—, dir., 1971—, Nat. Bank Commerce; dir. Proprietary Assn., Washington, 1976—. Trustee Memphis U. Sch., 1978—; bd. dirs. Council on Family Health; bd. dirs. Chickasaw council Boy Scouts Am. Served to capt. USMC, 1952-54. Mem. ABA, Phi Delta Phi, Kappa Alpha. Presbyterian. Club: Union League (N.Y.C.). Home: Germantown TN 38138 Office: 3030 Jackson Ave Memphis TN 38151

JENKINS, SPEIGHT, opera director, writer; b. Dallas, Jan. 31, 1937; s. Speight and Sara (Baird) J.; m. Linda Ann Sands, Sept. 6, 1966; children: Linda Leonie, Speight. B.A., U. Tex.-Austin; LL.B., Columbia U. News and reports editor Opera News, N.Y.C., 1967-73; music critic N.Y. Post, N.Y.C., 1973-81; TV host Live form the Met, Met. Opera, N.Y.C., 1981-83; gen. dir. Seattle Opera, 1983—; classical music editor Record World, N.Y.C., 1973-81; contbg. editor Ovation Mag., N.Y.C., 1980—, Opera Quar., Los Angeles, 1982—. Served to capt. U.S. Army, 1961-66. Recipient Emmy award for Met. Opera telecase La Boheme TV Acad. Arts and Scis., 1982. Mem. Music Critics Assn., Phi Beta Kappa. Presbyterian. Home: 2125 First Ave Seattle WA 98121 Office: Seattle Opera PO Box 9278 Seattle WA 98101

JENKINS, THOMAS DAVID, petroleum company executive; b. Watervalley, Miss., Feb. 22, 1927; s. David Smith and Mattie Rozelle (Brooks) J.; m. Roberta Xandra Williams, Dec. 23, 1951; children: Robin Murray, Thomas David. B.B.A., U. Miss., 1950, LL.B., 1951, J.D., 1968. Bar: Miss. 1951. Landman California Co., 1951-54; landman Calif. Co., New Orleans, 1951-54; v.p. Cactus Petroleum Inc., Houston, 1954-60; vice president Permian Corp., Houston, 1960-70, pres., from 1970; pres., chief operating officer Occidental Oil & Gas Co., Houston, 1975—; exec. v.p. Occidental Petroleum Corp., Los Angeles, from 1972; now chmn., chief exec. officer Can. Occidental Petroleum Ltd.; dir. S.W. Bancshares, Inc. Served with USMC, 1944-47. Mem. Am. Petroleum Inst. Clubs: Houston, Riverbend Country, University. Office: Office of Chmn Can Occidental Petroleum Ltd 700 4th Ave SW Calgary AB Canada T2P 3J5 *

JENKINS, THOMAS LLEWELLYN, physics educator; b. Cambridge, Mass., July 16, 1927; s. Francis A. and Henrietta (Smith) J.; m. Glen Pierce, July 8, 1951; children: Gale F., Phillip P., Matthew A., Sarah E. B.A., Pomona Coll., 1950; Ph.D., Cornell U., 1956. Physicist Lawrence Radiation Lab., Livermore, Calif., 1955-60; faculty Case Western Res. U., Cleve., 1960—, prof. physics, 1968—. Sci. and Engring. Research Council fellow Southampton U., (Eng.), 1983. Mem. Am. Phys. Soc., AAAS, Phi Beta Kappa, Sigma Xi. Home: 869 Belwood Dr Highland Heights OH 44143 Office: Physics Dept Case Western Res Univ Cleveland OH 44106

JENKINS, WILLIAM ATWELL, univ. chancellor; b. Scranton, Pa., Nov. 18, 1922; s. William A. and Thelma (Atwell) J.; m. Gloria Hyam, Mar. 12, 1944 (div. Aug. 1974); m. Alice Carney, Nov. 1, 1974; children—William Arthur II, Darcy Ann. B.S. in Edn, N.Y.U., 1948; M.S., U. Ill., 1949, Ph.D., 1954. Mem. faculty U. Wis.-Milw., 1953-70, asso. dean, dir. tchr. edn. and grad. studies, 1963-70; vis. prof. edn. U. Hawaii, summer 1969; dean Sch. Edn., Portland (Oreg.) State U., 1970-74; v.p. Fla. Internat. U., Miami, 1974-78; vice chancellor for acad. affairs U. Colo., Denver, 1978-80; chancellor U. Mich.-Dearborn, 1980—; cons. in field. Co-author numerous texts, articles. Sec. Portland Devel. Commn., 1972-73, chmn., 1973-74. Served to 1st lt., C.E. AUS, 1943-46. Mem. Nat. Council Tchrs. English (pres. 1968-69), Nat. Conf. Research and English, Edn. Writers Assn., Wis., Ore. council tchrs. English, Phi Kappa Phi, Phi Delta Kappa, Kappa Delta Phi, Pi Lambda Theta. Home: 551 Golfcrest Dr Dearborn MI 48124

JENKINS, WILLIAM ROBERT, coll. dean; b. Hertford, NC., Sept. 12, 1927; s. William Herman and Dorothy Frances (Perrow) J.; m. Mary Frances Earhart, Aug. 18, 1951; children—William Brian, Robert Edward, Mary Ellen, Linda Elaine. B.S., William and Mary Coll., 1950; M.S., U. Va., 1952; Ph.D., U. Md., 1954. Asst. prof. biology U. Md., College Park, 1954-59; asso. prof. Rutgers U., New Bruswick, N.J., 1960-63, prof., 1963—, chmn. dept. biology, 1969-74; asso. dean Livingston Coll., 1974-77, dean, 1977—. Author: Nematology-Fundamentals and Recent Advances, 1960, Plant Nematology, 1967; contbr. articles to profl. jours. Pres., bd. edn. North Brunswick, 1965-68; bd. dirs., co-chmn. Hunterdon Somerset Jetport Assn., 1970-81; scoutmaster, mem. dist. council Boy Scouts Am., 1968-74. Served with USNR, 1945-47. Recipient Silver Beaver award Boy Scouts Am., 1974. Mem. Soc. Nematologists, Helminthological Soc. Washington, Council Colls. Arts and Scis., Assn. Adminstrs. Higher Edn., AAAS, Sigma Xi, Phi Kappa Phi. Home: RD 3 Box 285 Flemington NJ 08822 Office: Office Dean Livingston Coll Rutgers U New Brunswick NJ 08903

JENKINS, WILLIAM ROBERT, architect, university administrator; b. Des Moines, Jan. 14; s. Frank Lafette and Gladys Adel (Reach) J.; m. Mary Lou Forrester, June 14, 1947; children: Melena, Cassandra. B.Arch., U. Houston, 1951; M.Arch., Tex. A. and M. U., 1966. Now pres. William R. Jenkins Architects Corp., Houston; asst. prof. architecture U. Houston, 1956-60, asso. prof., 1960—, dean Coll. Architecture, 1968—. Co-investigator NSF/Solar Enery Project. Served with USN, 1942-46. Recipient design awards Tex. Soc. Architects, AIA, Contemporary Arts Soc., House and Home Mag., Progressive Architecture, Houston Ind. Sch. Dist., Houston Home and Garden. Fellow AIA; mem. Nat. Council Archtl. Registration Bds., Assn. Collegiate Sch. Architecture, Tex. Soc. Architects, Tex. Archtl. Found. (past sec.). Office: U Houston Coll Architecture Houston TX 77004 *

JENKINS, WILMER ATKINSON, II, chem. co. exec.; b. Chgo., Feb. 10, 1928; s. Wilmer Atkinson and Gertrude (Elmore) J.; m. June Barbara Bigelow, June 24, 1949; children—Bruce Bigelow, Andrew Magill, Judith Lee. B.A., Swarthmore (Pa.) Coll., 1949; Ph.D. in Chemistry, Calif. Inst. Tech., 1952. With E.I. duPont de Nemours & Co., Inc., Wilmington, Del., 1952—, mgr. plant tech., 1968-71, dir. research, 1970-76, dir. polyester and acrylics div., 1977-78, dir. flexible packaging div., 1978—. Author articles. Pres. Carrcroft Civic Assn., 1968-70; exec. com. High Sch. PTA, 1974. Mem. Phi Beta Kappa, Sigma Xi, Phi Delta Theta. Unitarian. Patentee in field. Home: 107 Baynard Blvd Wilmington DE 19803 Office: DuPont Co Wilmington DE 19899

JENKS, DOWNING BLAND, railroad executive; b. Portland, Oreg., Aug. 16, 1915; s. Charles O. and Della (Downing) J.; m. Louise Sweeney, Nov. 30, 1940; children: Downing Bland, Nancy Randolph. B.S., Yale, 1937. Chainman Spokane Portland & Seattle Ry., Portland, 1934-35; asst., engr. corps N.Y. div. Pa. R.R., 1937-38; roadmaster, div. engr., trainmaster various divs. G.N. Ry., 1938-47, div. supt., Spokane, Wash., 1947-48; gen. mgr. C.& E.I. R.R., Chgo., 1948-49, v.p., gen. mgr., 1949-50; asst. v.p. ops. Rock Island Lines, Chgo., 1950-51, v.p. operations, 1951-53, exec. v.p., dir., 1953-56, pres., 1956-61; dir., pres. M.P.R.R., St. Louis, 1961-72, chmn., 1972—, chief exec. officer, 1961-74, Mo. Pacific Corp., 1971-83, pres., 1971-74, chmn. bd., 1974-83; dir. Bankers Life Co. Nat. pres. Boy Scouts Am., 1977-80; trustee Northwestern U. Served from 1st lt. to lt. col. AUS, 1942-45; ETO. Mem. Tau Beta Pi. Office: 9900 Clayton Rd Saint Louis MO 63124

JENKS, GEORGE MERRITT, librarian; b. Purcell, Okla., Aug. 1, 1929; s. Darrell C. and Muriel Helena (Denison) J.; m. Zoya Elaine Hochstein, Mar. 2, 1957; children: Darrell Allan, Mark Denison, Andrew Leslie. B.A., U. Okla., 1949, M.A., 1951, M.L.S., 1959; postgrad., UCLA, 1954-56. Reports officer CIA, Washington, 1956-57; instr. fgn. langs. N.Mex. State U. at Las Cruces, 1957-58; librarian Queens Borough Pub. Library, Jamaica, N.Y., 1959-60; cataloger, head acquisitions librarian San Fernando Valley State Coll., Northridge, Calif., 1960-63; asst. and acting librarian U. Tasmania, Hobart, 1963-66; chief tech. services, asso. librarian, univ. librarian Bucknell U., Lewisburg, Pa., 1966-81, collection devel. librarian, 1981—; acting dir. Univ. Press, 1975—; Lectr. library sci. Immaculate Heart Coll., Los Angeles, 1961-62; lectr. in librarianship Hobart Tech. Coll., Tasmania, 1965; mem. Australian Adv. Council on Biliog. Services, 1965-66. Editor: Library Opinion, 1964; editorial bd.: Bucknell U. Press, 1970—. Served with USMC, 1951-53. Decorated Purple Heart.; Grantee Library Systems Inst., Rensselaer Poly. Inst., 1968; Fulbright-Hays sr. lectr. U. Coimbra (Portugal), 1976. Asso. Library Assn. Australia (pres. Tasmanian br. 1965); mem. Pa. Library Assn. (pres. West Br. chpt. 1969-71, state dir. 1974—), ALA (councilor 1972-74), ACLU (sec. N. Central Pa. chpt. 1969-71), Nat. Ry. Hist. Soc. (pres. Central Pa. chpt. 1974-75), Sigma Delta Pi, Beta Phi Mu. Democrat. Club: Kiwanian (pres. Lewisburg 1975—). Home: 202 N 2d St Lewisburg PA 17837

JENKS, GEORGE SCHUYLER, banker; b. Sydney, Australia, Mar. 11, 1927; s. Ernest Ellsworth and Dorothy (Tarbell) J.; m. Elizabeth Glover, Dec. 27; 1 son, Robert Schuyler. A.B., Cornell U.; ed., Rutgers U., U. Minn. With Spurlock & Wetzler, Holbrook, Ariz., 1943, Great Neck (N.Y.) Post Office, 1945, Savoy Plaza Hotel, N.Y.C., 1948; with Albuquerque Nat. Bank, 1950—, chmn. bd., chief exec. officer, 1974—; pres., chief exec. officer 1st N.Mex. Bankshare Corp. (name now Sunwest Fin. Services, Inc.), 1981—, also dir.; dir. Sunwest Bank, N.A., Roswell, N.Mex., Clovis, N.Mex., Denver br. Kansas City Fed. Res. Bank, Clovis Nat. Bank. Adv. council Robert L. Anderson Sch. Bus., U. N.Mex. Served with AUS, 1945-46. Mem. Am. Bankers Assn., Albuquerque C. of C. Clubs: Albuquerque Country, Petroleum, N.Mex. Boosters. Home: 3005 Colonnade Ct NW Albuquerque NM 87107 Office: 303 Roma Ave NW Albuquerque NM 87102

JENKS, HOMER SIMEON, editor; b. Waltham, Mass., Nov. 13, 1914; s. Willard Irving and Iva Mae (Shepardson) J.; m. Beryl Louise Clinton, Sept. 21, 1940 (dec. 1966); m. Moira Catherine O'Connor, Aug. 19, 1968; 1 dau., Jacqueline Moira. Student, Boston U., 1932-35. City editor Quincy (Mass.) Evening News, 1931-35; staff corr. United Press, Boston, N.Y.C., London, 1935-52; asso. editor Collier's, 1952-56, Newsweek, 1956-57; exec. news editor Boston Traveler, 1957-62, mng. editor, 1962-64; editor Sunday Herald Traveler, 1964-72; asst. mng. editor Boston Herald Am., 1972-73, asso. editor, 1976-82; mng. editor Sunday Herald Advertiser, 1973-76; Sunday editor Boston Herald, 1983—; lectr. Simmons Coll., 1977-82. Home: 777 Randolph Ave Milton MA 02186 Office: 300 Harrison Ave Boston MA 02106

JENKS, THOMAS ELIJAH, lawyer; b. Bronxville, N.Y., Apr. 5, 1910; s. Elijah and Anna (Robeson) J.; m. Janet Shares, Sept. 19, 1936 (dec.); children: Linda Ann (Mrs. Nils Swanson), Susan Shares (Mrs. Thomas J. Breen); m. Maurita Williams, Sept. 16, 1972. A.B., Williams Coll., 1931; LL.B., Columbia, 1934. Bar: N.Y. 1934, D.C. 1936. With Office Spl. Adviser Fgn. Trade, 1934-35; sec., asst. gen. counsel Export-Import Bank, 1935-36; with firm Alvord & Alvord, Washington, 1936-41, partner, 1942-50; partner firm Lee, Toomey & Kent, Washington, 1950—. Contbr. legal jours. Bd. dirs. Graydon Manor Psychiat. Ctr.; hon. trustee Miss Hall's Sch., Pittsfield, Mass. Mem. Am., D.C. bar assns., Internat. Fiscal Assn., Soc. Alumni Williams Coll. (planned giving com.), Phi Beta Kappa. Republican. Clubs: Chevy Chase (Md.); Nat. Lawyers, International, Capitol Hill

(Washington); Congressional Country (Md.). Home: 800 25th St NW Washington DC 20037 Office: 1200 18th St NW Washington DC 20036

JENNEKENS, JON HUBERT, nuclear engr.; b. Toronto, Ont., Can., Oct. 21, 1932; s. Hubert Joseph and Laura Cecelia (Thorvaldson) J.; m. Norah Margaret Magee, June 5, 1954; children—Sandra Ellen, Jon Darren, Jennifer Norah. Student, Royal Mil. Coll. Can., 1950-54; B.Sc. with honors, Queen's U., 1956. Nuclear ops. engr. Chalk River Nuclear Labs., 1958-62; sci. adviser Atomic Energy Control Bd., Ottawa, Ont., 1962-72, dir. licensing, 1972-78, dir. gen. ops., 1978, pres., 1978—. Served with Canadian Army, 1954-58. Mem. Assn. Profl. Engrs. Ont. Mem. Ch. of Can. Club: Canadian Progress. Office: 270 Albert St Ottawa ON K1P 5S9 Canada

JENNER, ALBERT ERNEST, JR., lawyer; b. Chgo., June 20, 1907; s. Albert E. and Elizabeth (Owens) J.; m. Nadine N., Mar. 19, 1932; 1 dau., Cynthia Lee. J.D., U. Ill., 1930, LL.D., 1979; LL.D., John Marshall Law Sch., 1962, Columbia Coll., 1974, U. Notre Dame, 1975, Northwestern U., 1975, William Mitchell Law Sch., 1975, U. Mich., 1976. Bar: Ill. 1930. Practiced in Chgo., 1930—; sr. partner firm Jenner & Block; counsel, dir. Gen. Dynamics Corp.; spl. asst. atty gen. Ill., 1956-65; counsel Ill. Budgetary Commn., 1956-57; prof. law Northwestern U., 1952-53; chmn. U.S. Supreme Ct. Adv. Com. on Fed. Rules of Evidence, 1965-75; Chmn. Ill. Commn. on Uniform State Laws, 1952-80; mem. Nat. Conf. Commrs. Uniform State Laws, 1952—, pres., 1969-71; mem. Adv. Com. Fed. Rules of Civil Procedure, U.S. Supreme Court, 1960-70, Nat. Conf. Bar Assn. Pres.'s U.S., 1950—, pres., 1952-53; mem. U.S. Loyalty Review Bd., 1952-53; mem. council U. Ill. Law Forum, 1948-51; sr. counsel Presdl. Commn. to Investigate the Assassination of President Kennedy (Warren Commn.), 1963-64; chief spl. counsel to minority Ho. of Reps. Judiciary Com. that conducted impeachment inquiry regarding Pres. Richard M. Nixon.; Law mem. Ill. Bd. Examiners Accountancy, 1948-51. Author and co-author: Illinois Civil Practice Act Annotated, 1933, Outline of Illinois Supreme Court and Appellate Court Procedure, 1935, Smith-Hurd Ill. Annotated Statutes, Volumes on Pleading, Evidence and Practice, 10 edits, 1933-84,, also Vols. on Uniform Marriage and Dissolution of Marriage; Mem. permanent editorial bd.: Uniform Commercial Code, 1961—; Contbr. to law revs. and legal publs. on various phases of practice, pleading, evidence, procedure and other legal subjects. Mem. Pres. Lyndon B. Johnson's Nat. Commn. on Causes and Prevention of Violence in U.S., 1968-69; sec. U.S. Navy Meml. Found.; trustee Evanston-Glenbrook Hosp. Arthritis Found., Cerebral Palsey Found., Northwestern U. Library Bd.; mem. presdl. adv. bd. Mus. Sci. and Industry. Recipient Distinguished Service award for outstanding pub. service Chgo. and Ill. Jr. C. of C., 1939, U. Ill. Disting. Alumni award, 1962, Disting. Civic Achievement award Am. Jewish Com., 1973, N.Y. U. Distinguished Citizen's award, 1975; named Chicagoan of Year Chgo. Press Club, 1975; laureate Lincoln Acad. of Ill. Fellow Am. Coll. Trial Lawyers (bd. regents, pres. 1958-59), Internat. Acad. Trial Lawyers, Am. Bar Found.; mem. Ill. Soc. Trial Lawyers, Nat. Assn. Def. lawyers in Criminal Cases, Inter-Am. Bar Assn., Internat. Bar Assn., Am. Bar Assn. (ho. of dels. 1948—, fellow Young Lawyers Sect., state del. 1975-78, chmn. standing com. on fed. judiciary 1965-68, chmn. sect. individual rights and responsibilities 1973-74, mem. council sect. legal edn. 1967-75, bd. govs. 1977-80), Ill. Bar Assn. (pres. 1949-50), Chgo. Bar Assn. (bd. dirs. 1934-49, sec. 1947-49), Assn. Bar City N.Y., Am. Judicature Soc. (pres. 1958-60), Am. Inst. Jud. Adminstrn., Nat. Lawyers Com. for Civil Rights Under Law (dir., nat. co-chmn. 1975-78), Bar Assn. U.S. Ct. Appeals 7th Circuit (bd. govs. 1955-60, Robert Maynard Hutchins Distinguished Service award 1976), Am. Law Inst., Chgo. Council Lawyers, NAACP Legal Def. Fund, Center for Study Dem. Instns. (dir. 1975-79), Order of Coif, Alpha Chi Rho, Phi Delta Phi. Republican. Clubs: Tavern, Midday, Skokie Country, Law, Legal, Chicago. Office: One IBM Plaza Chicago IL 60611

JENNER, BRUCE, athlete, sportscaster; b. Mt. Kisco, N.Y., Oct. 28, 1949; s. William and Ester J.; m. Chrystie Crownover (div.); m. Linda Thompson; 1 son, Brendan. Grad., Graceland Coll., Lamoni, Iowa, 1973. Mem. U.S. Olympic Team, Munich, 1972, Montreal, 1976; formed (with wife) 8618, Inc., 1976; lectr. at colls. and univs., bus. and indsl. convs. Entertainer, sports commentator, NBC-TV; Author: (with Philip Finch) Decathlon Challenge: Bruce Jenner's Story, 1977, Bruce Jenner's Guide to Family Fitness, 1978. Named Male Athlete of Year in AP Poll, 1976; recipient James E. Sullivan trophy as Outstanding Amateur Athlete of Year, 1976; Track and Field Performer of Year award Sport mag., 1976. Won Gold medal in decathlon, 1976 *

JENNER, RICHARD HOWARD, concrete pipe and steel mfg. co. exec.; b. Heuvelton, N.Y., Apr. 7, 1930; s. Charles Albert and and Etta Maria (Dewey) J. B.S., Ithaca Coll., 1951. Various adminstrv. positions Ameron, Inc., Monterey Park, Calif., 1957-70, sec.-treas., 1970-77, v.p., 1977—. Served with USN, 1951-55. Mem. Los Angeles Nat. Assn. Accountants, Risk and Ins. Mgmt. Soc. Club: Los Angeles Stock Exchange. Home: 700 S Lake Ave Pasadena CA 91106 Office: Ameron 4700 Ramona Blvd Monterey Park CA 91754

JENNESS, ROBERT, biochemist, educator; b. Rochester, N.H., Sept. 21, 1917; s. Myron I. and Ruth (Libby) J.; m. Katherine Ward, Aug. 30, 1940; children: Douglas F., Malcolm I., David R. B.S., U. N.H., 1938; M.S., U. Vt., 1940; Ph.D., U. Minn., 1944. With Vt. Agrl. Expt. Sta., 1938-40; mem. faculty U. Minn., 1940—, prof. biochemistry, 1953—. Author: (with Patton) Principles of Dairy Chemistry, 1959, (with Walstra) Dairy Chemistry and Physics, 1984; also numerous articles, revs. Fulbright scholar, The Netherlands, 1961-62. Fellow AAAS; mem. Am. Chem. Soc. (Borden award in dairy chemistry 1953), Am. Soc. Biol. Chemists, Am. Dairy Sci. Assn., Am. Soc. Mammalogists, Sigma Xi, Phi Kappa Phi, Phi Lambda Upsilon, Alpha Zeta., Gamma Sigma Delta. Research on structure and properties milk proteins in relation to species and genetic variation, immunology, denaturation, indsl. utilization, biosynthesis ascorbic acid by mammals. Home: 942 Oak Ridge Ave Saint Paul MN 55112

JENNEY, NEIL FRANKLIN, JR., artist, philosopher; b. Torrington, Conn., Nov. 6, 1945; s. Neil Franklin and Ruth Irene (Beyer) J. Farmhand, salesman, lifeguard, laborer, 1959-66, artist and philosopher, N.Y.C., 1966—; pres. Mcpl. Asthetic Consultations and Co., N.Y.C., 1984—; guest critic Yle U., New Haven, Conn., 1969, 83; cons. N.Y.C. Art Commn.-Transit Authority, 1980-83. Pub.: Baseball Action Shots Annual, 1982-84. Guggenheim fellow. Democrat. Office: Mcpl Asthetic Consultations 383 W Broadway New York NY 10012

JENNI, DONALD ALISON, zoology educator; b. Pueblo, Colo., June 20, 1932; s. George Luis and Genevieve Agnes (Cox) J.; m. Mary Anne Hovland, Aug. 16, 1956; children—Robert Walter, William George, Karen Elizabeth, Thomas Iver. B.S., Oreg. State U., 1953; M.S., Utah State U., 1955; Ph.D., U. Fla., 1961. Asst. prof. zoology U. Fla., 1961-62; asst. prof. Eastern Ill. U., 1962-64; vis. scientist U. Leiden, Netherlands, 1964-66; asso. prof. U. Mont., 1966-71, prof., 1971—, chmn. dept. zoology, 1972-75; vis. prof. Cornell U., 1975, U. Wash., 1979. Served with USAF, 1955-57. NIH fellow, 1964-66; NSF research grantee, 1970, 73, 74; NATO and NRC travel grantee, 1970-72; Crockett Club research grantee, 1981-83; Campfire Research Fund grantee, 1983—. Mem. Am. Ornithologists Union, Animal Behavior Soc., Ecol. Soc. Am., Assn. Tropical Biology, Am. Soc. Mammalogists, Wilson Ornithol. Soc., Cooper Ornithol. Soc., Am. Soc. Zoologists. Office: Dept Zoology U Mont Missoula MT 59812

JENNINGS, ALBERT RAY, educator; b. Grosvenor, Tex., Nov. 11, 1926; s. Albert M. and Alice P. (Ashcraft) J.; m. Gladys V. Sweeten, Oct. 2, 1944; children—Andrew Roman, Ann Sharon. B.S. summa cum laude in Geology, Hardin-Simmons U., 1958; M.S. in Geology, Tex. A. and M. U., 1960, Ph.D., 1964. Research asst. Tex. Engring. Expt. Sta., College Station, 1960-64; exploration geologist Mobil Oil Corp. (Houston div.), 1964-68; asst. prof. geology East Carolina U., Greenville, 1968, asso. prof., prof. geology, chmn. dept. geology, 1969-74; asso. prof. geology Hardin-Simmons U., Abilene, Tex., 1974—, head dept., 1976—; also ind. petroleum geologist. Served with USAF, 1951-55. Fellow Geol. Soc. Am.; mem. Am. Inst. Profl. Geol. Scientists, Am. Assn. Petroleum Geologists, Abilene Geol. Soc., Sigma Xi, Alpha Chi, Phi Kappa Phi. Home: 1725 Bel Air Abilene TX 79603

JENNINGS, ALSTON, lawyer; b. West Helena, Ark., Oct. 30, 1917; s. Earp Franklin and Irma (Alston) J.; m. Dorothy Buie Jones, June 12, 1943; children: Alston, Eugene Franklin, Ann Buie. A.B., Columbia U., 1938; J.D., Northwestern U., 1941. Bar: Ark. 1941. Practiced law, Little Rock, 1947—; spl. agt. intelligence unit Treasury Dept., 1946; asso. Wright, Harrison, Lindsey & Upton, 1949-51, mem., 1951-60, Wright, Lindsey, Jennings, Lester & Shults, 1960-65, Wright, Lindsey and Jennings, 1965—. Bd. dirs. Community Chest Greater Little Rock; mem. adv. bd. Salvation Army, Pulaski County. Served to lt. USNR, 1941-45. Fellow Am. Bar Found.; mem. ABA, Ark. Bar Assn., Pulaski County Bar Assn. (past pres.), Internat. Assn. Ins. Counsel (pres. 1972-73), Am. Coll. Trial Lawyers (regent 1975-79, treas. 1979-80, pres.-elect 1980-81, pres. 1981-82). Home: 5300 Sherwood Little Rock AR 72207 Office: 2200 Worthen Bank Bldg Little Rock AR 72201

JENNINGS, BOJAN HAMLIN, chemist, educator; b. Waukegan, Ill., Apr. 4, 1920; d. Frank M. and Gertrude E. (Miller) Hamlin; m. Addison Llewellyn Jennings, June 12, 1942; children: Hamlin Manson, Nora Lyn, Constance. A.B., Bryn Mawr Coll., 1941; M.A., Radcliffe Coll., 1943; Ph.D., Harvard U., 1955. Mem. faculty Wheaton Coll., Norton, Mass., 1944-46, 50—, A. Howard Meneely prof. chemistry, 1975-78. Research grantee NIH, Petroleum Research Fund, Research Corp., NSF. Mem. Am. Chem. Soc., N.Y. Acad. Scis. Home: Box 215 25 Priscilla Rd White Horse Beach Plymouth MA 02381 Office: Wheaton Coll Norton MA 02766

JENNINGS, BURGESS HILL, educator, mech. engr.; b. Balt., Sept. 12, 1903; s. Henry Hill and Martha (Burgess) J.; m. Etta M. Crout, Nov. 7, 1925; 1 son, Robert Burgess. B.E., Johns Hopkins, 1925; M.S., Lehigh U., 1928, M.A., 1935. Test engr. Consol. Gas & Electric Co., Balt., 1925; mem. faculty Lehigh U., 1926-40; prof. dept. mech. engring. Northwestern U., 1940—, chmn. dept., 1943-57, asso. dean, 1962-70; research investigator U.S. OSRD, 1942-45; dir. research labs. Am. Soc. Heating, Refrigerating and Air Conditioning Engrs., Cleve., 1957-60; cons. and gen. research and writing relating to refrigeration, air conditioning and energy usage, 1930—. Author: books and articles on engring., heating, air conditioning Heating and Air Conditioning, 1956, Environmental Engineering, 1970, The Thermal Environment, 1978; co-author: Gas Turbine Analysis and Practice, 1953, Air Conditioning and Refrigeration, 1958. Recipient Richards Meml. award in Mech. Engring., 1950; Merit award Chgo. Tech. Socs. Council, 1963; Worcester Reed Warner medal, 1972. Fellow ASHRAE (pres. 1948-49, F. Paul Anderson medal 1981); mem. ASME (hon.), Nat. Acad. Engring., Am. Soc. Lubricating Engrs. (v.p. 1947-50), Am. Soc. Engring. Edn., Internat. Inst. Refrigeration (v.p. 1958-67), Sigma Xi, Pi Tau Sigma (pres. 1948-50), Tau Beta Pi. Club: Michigan Shores (Wilmette, Ill.). Home: 1500 Sheridan Rd Wilmette IL 60091

JENNINGS, EDWARD HARRINGTON, university president; b. Mpls., Feb. 18, 1937; s. Edward G. and Ruth (Harrington) J.; m. Mary Eleanor Winget, Nov. 4, 1958; children: William F., Steven W. B.S., U. N.C., 1959; M.B.A., Western Res. U., 1963; Ph.D. (NDEA fellow 1966-69), U. Mich., 1969. Engr. Deering Milliken Co., Spartanburg, S.C., 1959-61, Merck & Co., West Point, Pa., 1963-65; mem. faculty U. Iowa, 1969-75, v.p. fin., 1975-79; vis. prof. U. Der es Salam, Tanzania, 1971-72; pres. U. Wyo., Laramie, 1979-81, Ohio State U., Columbus, 1981—. Co-author: Fundamentals of Investments, 1976; contbr. articles profl. jours. Mem. Am. Fin. Assn., Western Fin. Assn., Midwest Fin. Assn. Lutheran. Office: Ohio State Univ 190 N Oval Mall Columbus OH 43210

JENNINGS, EDWARD MORTON, JR., financial consultant; b. Winthrop, Mass., Nov. 24, 1906; s. Edward Morton and Grace W. (Waite) J.; m. Mary L. Sabine, July 14, 1934; children—Edward Morton III, Charles Sabine. Grad., Phillips Acad., Andover, Mass., 1924; B.S., Dartmouth, 1928; M.C.S., Amos Tuck Sch. Bus. Adminstrn., 1929, Stonier Grad. Sch. Banking, 1944. With First Nat. Bank Boston, 1929—, v.p., 1948-65, sr. v.p., 1965-71; dir. William Carter Co., Needham, Mass. Author: Bank Loans to Shoe Manufacturers, 1944. Trustee Trans-Lease Group.; Trustee Boston Symphony Orch. Home: 105 Lyman Rd Chestnut Hill MA 02167

JENNINGS, FRANK GERARD, editor; b. Bklyn., May 23, 1915; s. Gerard Thomas and Martha (Hirsch) J.; m. Gloria Miehling, Mar. 22, 1941. B.S., NYU, 1949, M.A., 1950. Tchr. composition, lit. and allied courses NYU, U. Denver, Walter Harvey Jr. Coll., N.Y.C., Yeshiva U., Columbia Tchrs. Coll., Dillard U., pub. high schs.; participant ednl. confs., book award juror; reading specialist; exec. dir. Library Club Am., 1956-65; editor-at-large Sat. Rev., 1959—; assoc. Lang. Arts Inst., Columbia U., 1956-57; cons. Horace Mann-Lincoln Inst. for Sch. Experimentation, Columbia Tchrs. Coll., 1957-58; dir. coll. relations Tchrs. Coll., 1969-70, sec. coll., 1970-76; editor Tchrs. Coll. Record, 1970-76; editorial cons. Harcourt, Brace & Co., 1957-64; sr. editor Harvard Classics, 1960-62; ednl. editor Crowell Collier Ednl. Corp., 1960-62; ednl. cons. New World Found., 1963-69; Cons. fed., state edn. agys. Mem. Com. on Study History C, Amherst Project. Author: This is Reading, 1965, also textbooks.; Contbr. articles to numerous mags., profl. jours. Pres. Initial Alphabet Found., Ednl. Planning Found.; bd. dirs. Scandinavian Seminar Found., 1971-76. Served with USAAF, 1942-45. Mem. Nat. Acad. Edn. (sec. com. on reading), Internat. Reading Assn. (pres. Manhattan chpt. 1960-61), Phi Delta Kappa, Kappa Delta Pi. Home and Office: 45 Horatio St New York NY 10014

JENNINGS, FRANK LAMONT, pathologist, educator; b. Mpls., Apr. 25, 1921; s. Frank L. and Helen (Germond) J.; m. Beverly K. Carlson, Dec. 15, 1948; children—Frank Lamont III, Kathryn Eleanor, Paul Ernest, Mark Oliver. A.B., Ind. U., 1942, M.D., 1947. Fellow U. Chgo. Hosps., 1947-51, intern, 1951-52; instr., then asst. prof. U. Chgo. Clinics, 1954-60; mem. faculty U. Tex. Med. Br., Galveston, 1960-77, prof. pathology, chmn. dept., 1963-75; prof., chmn. dept. pathology Wright State Sch. Medicine, 1977—; Sec. Gulf Coast Waste Disposal Authority, 1970-77. Bd. dirs. Tex. div. Am. Cancer Soc. Served with M.C. AUS, 1955-57. Mem. A.M.A., Am. Soc. Clin. Pathologists, Coll. Am. Pathology (bd. govs. 1975—), Am. Assn. Pathologists Bacteriologists, Internat. Acad. Pathology, Am. Soc. Exptl. Pathology, Am. Assn. Cancer Edn., Radiation Research Soc. Home: 7828 Braewood Trail Dayton OH 45459

JENNINGS, JESSE DAVID, anthropology educator; b. Oklahoma City, July 7, 1909; s. Daniel Wellman and Grace (Cruce) J.; m. Jane Noyes Chase, Sept. 7, 1935; children: Jesse David, Herbert Lee. B.A., Montezuma Coll., 1929; Ph.D., U. Chgo., 1943; D.Sc., U. Utah, 1980. Anthropologist Nat. Park Service, 1937-42, 45-48; mem. faculty U. Utah, 1948—, prof. anthropology, 1949-75, 81—, disting. research prof., 1970—, disting. prof. anthropology, 1975—; Mem. anthropology-psychology div. Nat. Acad. Sci.-NRC, 1954-56; vis. prof. anthropology Northwestern U., 1960, U. Minn., 1961, U. Hawaii, 1965, 67-68; lectr. summer inst. anthropology U. Colo., 1961, Fairmont Coll., 1962; lectr. semi-centennial symposium Am. archeology Rice U., 1962; Reynolds lectr. U. Utah, 1962, Leigh lectr., 1975; dir. Glen Canyon Archeol. Salvage Project, 1957-66, Utah Mus. Natural History, 1965-73; cons. instl. studies NSF, 1964-66. Author: (with A.V. Kidder and E.M. Shook) Excavations at Kaminal Juyu, Guatemala, 1946, (with E.A. Hoebel) Readings in Anthropology, 3d edit, 1972, The Archeology of the Plains: An Assessment, 1956, Danger Cave, 1957, also numerous articles, reports, papers.; Editor: (with Edward Norbeck) Prehistoric Man in the New World, 1964, (with Robert F. Spencer) Native Americans, 1965, 2d edit., 1977, Prehistory of North America, 1968, 2d edit., 1974, Warner Modular Publs. in Anthropology, 1972-74, (with others) Pacific Anthrop. Records No. 25, 1976, Ancient Native Americans, 1978, (with others) Prehistory of Utah and the Eastern Great Basin, 1978, Prehistory of Polynesia, 1979, Cowboy Cave, 1980, Bull Creek, 1981, Ancient North Americans, Ancient South Americans; editor for: N.Am., Atlas of Archaeology, Rainbird Reference Books, 1972. Served to comdr. USNR, 1942-45. Recipient Viking medal in archaeology Wenner Gren Found. Anthrop. Research, 1958. Mem. Nat. Acad. Sci., Soc. Am. Archaeology (editor bull. 1950-54, pres. 1959-58, Disting. Service award 1982), Am. Anthrop. Assn. (exec. bd. 1953-56), AAAS (nat. v.p., chmn. sect. H 1961, 69), Sigma Xi, Phi Kappa Phi. Home: Box 331-A River Route Siletz OR 97380

JENNINGS, JOSEPH ASHBY, banker; b. Richmond, Va., Aug. 12, 1920; s. Joseph Ashby and Leone (Bishop) J.; m. Anne Barrow Hatcher, Oct. 29, 1960; children: Joseph Ashby III, Ashby Anne. B.S., U. Richmond, 1949; grad. certificate, Stonier Grad. Sch. Banking, Rutgers U., 1952. With United Va. Bank, Richmond, 1949—, v.p., 1956-66, sr. v.p., 1966-67, exec. v.p., 1967-71, pres., 1971, chmn. bd., 1972—; also dir.; vice chmn. bd. United Va. Bankshares, Inc., 1972-75, pres., 1975-76, chief adminstrv. officer, 1972-76, chmn. bd., chief exec. officer, 1976—; dir. Life Ins. Co. Va., Investors Mortgage Ins. Co., Lawyers Title Ins. Co., Va. Life Ins. Co. of N.Y., United Va. Bankshares, Inc., Western Employers Ins. Co., Universal Leaf Tobacco Co. Trustee U. Richmond, Hollins Coll., Union Theol. Sem., Va. Found. Ind. Colls.; capital funds bd. United Givers Fund; mem. Va. Bus. Council, pres.'s council Old Dominion U. Served with USAAF, 1942-46. Mem. Fin. Analysts Fedn. (past exec. v.p., dir.), Assn. Res. City Bankers, Assn. Bank Holding Cos.; mem. Va. Bankers Assn.; Mem. Phi Beta Kappa, Omicron Delta Kappa, Phi Delta Theta, Beta Gamma Sigma. Presbyn. Office: 919 E Main St Richmond VA 23219

JENNINGS, JOSEPH LESLIE, textile executive; b. West Point, Ga., Dec. 20, 1937; s. Joseph Lester and Marie (Lanier) J.; m. Ann B. Martin, June 10, 1961; children: Joseph Leslie, John Martin, Clayton Lanier. B.S., U. Alta., 1961. With West Point Pepperell, Ga., 1964-71, plant mgr., LaGrange, Ga., 1971-74; v.p. Mt. Vernon Mills, Inc., Greenville, S.C., 1974-80, exec. v.p., 1980-82, pres., chief operating officer, 1982—; dir. Textile Hall Corp., Greenville. Bd. dirs. J.E. Sirrine Found., Clemson, S.C., 1981—, Am. Textile Mfg. Inst., 1983—, Christ Ch. Episcopal Sch., Greenville, 1983-84. Served to 1st lt. USMC, 1961-64. Mem. S.C. Textile Mfg. Assn. (pres. 1983-84). Home: 24 Sirrine Dr Greenville SC 29605 Office: Mt Vernon Mills Inc Daniel Bldg Suite 2400 Greenville SC 29602

JENNINGS, LEANDER WARREN, accountant; b. Dossville, Miss., Dec. 12, 1928; s. Samuel T. and Cora (Bell) J.; m. Billye Ruth Barnes, Aug. 13, 1950; 1 son, Darrell Lee. B.S. in Accounting, Tex. Christian U., 1957; M.B.A., U. Houston, 1962. V.P., controller A.L. Davis Stores, Fort Worth, 1959-62; with Peat, Marwick, Mitchell & Co., 1963—, partner-in-charge, Chgo., 1971-77, mng. partner, 1977, also mem. operating com. Bd. dirs. Chgo. Crime Commn., Chgo. Youth Centers, Protestant Found. Greater Chgo., Michael Reese Hosp. & Med. Center, Lyric Opera, Art Inst. Chgo., Chgo. Theol. Sem., Shakespeare Globe Theatre Center, London, U.S. Olympic Com. Served with USAF, 1951-55. Mem. Econs. Club Chgo., Execs. Club Chgo., Nat. Coll. Edn., Northwestern U. Assos., Chgo. Assn. Commerce and Industry (bd. dirs.), Am. Inst. C.P.A.s, Ill. C.P.A. Soc., Chgo. Council Fgn. Relations. Presbyterian. Clubs: Carlton, Chgo., Glen View, Univ., Favern, Old Elm, Westmorland Country, Racquet, Country of Fla. Home: 1110 N Lake Shore Dr Chicago IL 60611 Office: Peat Marwick Plaza 303 E Wacker Dr Chicago IL 60601

JENNINGS, LEE BYRON, educator; b. Willard, Ohio, May 3, 1927; s. Lee and Grace (Kime) J.; m. Margit Palmer, Apr. 23, 1978. B.A. in German, Ohio State U., 1949; M.A., U. Ill., 1951, Ph.D., 1955. Instr. U. Colo., Boulder, 1956, Harvard U., 1956-57; from instr. to asst. prof. UCLA, 1957-62; asso. prof. U. Tex., Austin, 1962-68; prof. German, U. Ill.-Chgo., 1968—; vis. prof. U. Marburg, W.Ger., summer 1965, U. Calif., Berkeley, summer 1961, UCLA, summer 1969. Author: The Ludicrous Demon: Aspects of the Grotesque in German Post-Romantic Prose, 1963, Justinus Kerners Weg nach Weinsberg, 1982; contbr. articles to profl. jours. Fulbright research grantee, W.Ger., 1954-55; Alexander von Humboldt Found. research fellow, 1965-67. Mem. MLA, Am. Assn. Tchrs. of German (pres. Tex. chpt. 1964), Phi Beta Kappa. Home: 708 N Kenilworth Ave Oak Park IL 60302 Office: Dept German U Ill Box 4348 Chicago IL 60680

JENNINGS, MADELYN PULVER, communications company executive; b. Saratoga Springs, N.Y., Nov. 23, 1934; d. George Joseph and Martha (Walsh) Pulver. B.A. in Bus. and Econs., Tex. Woman's U., 1956. Asst. mgr. pub. relation Slick Airways, Dallas, 1956-58; asst. dir. radio-TV promotion VIP Service, Inc., N.Y.C., 1958; asst. to pres. Smith, Dorian & Burman, Hartford, Conn., 1959; bus. mktg. planning Gen. Electric Co., Bridgeport, Conn., 1960-68, mgr. manpower planning, 1968-71, mgr. environ. support operation, 1973-73; v.p. human resources Standard Brands, Inc., N.Y.C., 1976-80; sr. v.p. personnel and admistrn. Gannett Co., Rochester, N.Y., 1980—. Trustee Russell Sage Coll., Gannett Found; mem. adv. bd. Clarkson Coll. Mem. Am. Soc. Personnel Adminstrn., Human Resources Roundtable, Sr. Personnel Execs. Forum, Human Resources Planning Soc., Newspaper Personnel Relations Assn., Sr. Personnel Execs. Roundtable, Conf. Bd. (adv. council mgmt. and personnel). Office: Gannett Co Inc. Lincoln Tower Rochester NY 14604

JENNINGS, MANSON VAN BUREN, coll pres.; b. Trenton, N.J., Oct. 24, 1916; s. Harold Manson and Mabel (Tuthill) J.; m. Deborah Hunt, Sept. 14, 1946; children—Susan Briggs, David Tuthill. A.B., Harvard, 1938; M.A., Columbia, 1939, Ph.D., 1949. Instr. Horace Mann Sch. Tchrs. Coll., Columbia, 1939-41, instr. social studies dept., 1946-49, asst. prof., 1949-54, asso. prof., 1954-58, prof. history, 1958-61; dean Cortland Coll., State U. N.Y., 1961-65, Adelphi U. Grad. Sch. Arts and Scis., Garden City, N.Y., 1965-71; pres. So. Conn. State Coll., New Haven, 1971-81, pres. emeritus, 1981—; ednl. cons. Current Affairs Films, 1956-75; social studies cons. Charles Scribner's Sons,

1960-62. Author: Development of the Modern Problems Course in the Senior High School, 1949; Contbr. articles to profl. jours. Served from pvt. to 1st lt. AUS, 1941-45. Mem. Nat. Council Social Studies (monthly contbr. Social Edn. 1952-59), AAUP. Office: 501 Crescent St New Haven CT 06515

JENNINGS, MYRON KENT, educator; b. Chowchilla, Calif., June 4, 1934; s. Talmadge Aldine and Ethel Lulabelle (Dodd) J.; m. Holly Lucille Phillips, Sept. 1, 1956; children: James Steven, Cynthia Diane, Larkin Kent. B.A. magna cum laude, U. Redlands, (Calif.), 1956; Ph.D., U. N.C., 1961. Research assoc. Brookings Instn., Washington, 1960-63; from asst. prof. to prof. polit. sci. U. Mich., Ann Arbor, 1963-82, adj. research scientist, 1982—; prof. polit. sci. U. Calif.-Santa Barbara, 1982—; vis. research assoc. U. Oreg., Eugene, 1969-70; vis. prof. U. Tilburg, (Netherlands), 1971-72, UCLA, 1980. Author: Community Influentials, 1964, (with others) The Political Character of Adolescence, 1974, Governing American Schools, 1974, Generations and Politics, 1981. Guggenheim fellow, 1977-78; fellow Ctr. for Advanced Studies in Behavioral Scis., 1977-78, Am. Acad. Arts and Scis., 1982. Mem. Am. Polit. Sci. Assn. (council 1976-77), Midwest Polit. Sci. Assn. (v.p. 1980-81), Western Polit. Sci. Assn., Internat. Soc. Polit. Psychology (council 1982-84), Phi Beta Kappa. Home: 492 Pacific Oaks Rd Goleta CA 93117 Office: Univ Calif Santa Barbara CA 93106

JENNINGS, PETER CHARLES, TV anchorman; b. Toronto, Ont., Can., July 29, 1938; s. Charles and Elizabeth (Osborne) J.; m. Kati Marton. Student, Trinity Coll. Sch., Port Hope, Ont., Carleton U., Ottawa, Ont.; LL.D., Rider (N.J.) Coll. With CBC, Montreal, Que., CJOH-TV, Ottawa; parliamentary corr., network anchorman Canadian TV, Ottawa; network anchorman, nat. corr. ABC News, N.Y.C., from 1964; London anchorman on World News Tonight, until 1983, anchorman, sr. editor, 1983—; also involved with prodn. numerous network documentaries. Mem. Internat. Radio and TV Soc. Club: Overseas Press. Office: care ABC Press Relations 1330 Ave of Americas New York NY 10019 *

JENNINGS, PETER RANDOLPH, tropical agriculturalist, rice breeder; b. Orange, N.J., Jan. 15, 1931; s. Alvin Randolph and Alice Louise (Fredericks) J.; m. Gloria Calderon, Aug. 20, 1970; 1 son, David. B.A., Drew U., 1953, Dr.Sc., 1970; M.S., Purdue U., 1955, Ph.D., 1957, Dr.Agr., 1971. Rice breeder, tropical agriculturalist Rockefeller Found., N.Y.C., 1957—. Contbr. numerous articles to various publs. Recipient John Cross award and medal City of Phila., 1969, Donald F. Jones medal Conn. Agr. Exptl. Sta., 1974, Colombia Minstry of Agr. Medal, 1976. Fellow Am. Soc. Agronomy; mem. Phi Beta Kappa. Home: The Rockefeller Found 1133 Ave of the Americas New York NY 10036

JENNINGS, RICHARD LOUIS, civil engineer, educator; b. Newark, July 28, 1933; s. Louis Alpheus and Florence Eva (Warnecke) J.; m. Jan Hayden Bush, Sept. 2, 1956; children—Sheryll, Gregory. Student, Marietta Coll., 1951-54; B.S. in Math, Ohio U., 1956, Ohio U., 1957, M.S., U. Ill., 1958, Ph.D., 1964. Constrn. supt. AT&T, White Plains, N.Y., 1955-56; prof. civil engring. U. Va., Charlottesville, 1963—; cons. in structural analysis and aerospace tech., nuclear reactor stress analysis; cons. earthquake analysis of nuclear reactor facilities; cons. to U.S. Army on mil. logistics. Contbr. articles on deflections of radio telescopes, cable-suspended structures, overloaded hwy. pavements and earthquakes to profl. publs. Pres. Charlottesville PTA Council, 1969-73; chmn. joint bd. Charlottesville-Albemarle Tech. Edn. Center, 1973-74; bd. dirs. Planned Parenthood Central Va., 1969-76, WVPT Ednl. TV, 1979-80, Piedmont Va. Community Coll., 1982—; bd. mgrs. Family Service Agy., Charlottesville, Va., 1982—, Va. Congress of Parents and Tchrs., 1970-72; mem. Charlottesville City Sch. Bd., 1972-81, vice chmn., 1974-76, chmn., 1976-81. NASA-ASEE fellow. Mem. ASCE, Va. Acad. Sci. (exec. com. 1977-80), Sigma Xi, Tau Beta Pi, Alpha Tau Omega. Democrat. Episcopalian. Home: 1607 Jamestown Dr Charlottesville VA 22901

JENNINGS, RICHARD WORMINGTON, law educator; b. Bois D'Arc, Mo., Oct. 19, 1907; s. William Thomas and Hattie (Wormington) J.; m. Elizabeth Robison, Aug. 10, 1935; children: Susan Elizabeth, Margaret Anne, William Thomas. A.B., Park Coll., Parkville, Mo., 1927, LL.D., 1975; M.A., U. Pa., 1934; J.D., U. Calif. at Berkeley, 1939. Bar: Calif. 1939. Tchr. high sch., Pinckneyville, Ill., 1927-30, Camden, N.J., 1930-33; asso. firm Jesse H. Steinhart, San Francisco, 1939-45, mem. firm, 1945-47; atty. OPA, 1942; lectr. law U. Calif. at Berkeley, 1940-42, prof., 1947—, James W. and Isabel Coffroth prof., 1955-75, emeritus, 1975—; Fulbright lectr. U. Tokyo, Japan, 1961; vis. prof. Cologne U., summer 1972; lectr. Salzburg Seminar Am. Studies, 1972; Cons. SEC, 1962. Author: (with Harold Marsh, Jr.) Securities Regulation-Cases and Materials, 1963, 5th edit., 1982, supplement, 1983, (with Richard M. Buxbaum) Corporations-Cases and Materials, 5th edit, 1979. Pres. Internat. Inst. San Francisco, 1949-51. Mem. Am., Calif. bar assns., Am. Law Inst., Am. Bar Found., Order Coif, Phi Beta Kappa. Presbyn. Home: 425 Vassar Ave Berkeley CA 94708

JENNINGS, ROBERT BURGESS, med. educator, exptl. pathologist; b. Balt., Dec. 14, 1926; s. Burgess Hill and Etta (Crout) J.; m. Linda Lee Sheffield, June 28, 1952; children—Carol L., Mary G., John B., Anne E., James R. B.S., Northwestern U., 1947, M.S., B.M., 1949, M.D., 1950. Diplomate: Am. Bd. Pathology in pathologic anatomy, 1954, in clin. pathology, 1955. Intern Passavant Meml. Hosp., Chgo., 1949-50, resident pathology, 1950-51; mem. faculty Northwestern U. Med. Sch., 1953-75, prof. pathology, 1963-75, Magerstadt prof. and chmn. pathology dept., 1969-75; chmn. dept. pathology Duke U. Med. Sch., 1975—, James B. Duke prof., 1980—; vis. scientist Middlesex Hosp. Med. Sch., London, Eng., 1961-62; cons. Baxter Labs., Morton Grove, Ill., 1957—, VA Research Hosp., Chgo.; mem. attending staff Northwestern Meml. Hosp., Chgo., 1969-75; Mem. pathology A study sect. USPHS, 1960-65; mem. clin. cardiology adv. com. NIH, 1976-80. Author research papers.; Editorial bd.: Lab. Investigation, 1967—, Archives of Pathology, 1970-80, Jour. Molecular and Cellular Cardiology, 1972—, Exptl. and Molecular Pathology, 1973—, Circulation Research, 1976—. Trustee Am. Bd. Pathology, 1976—. Served as lt. (j.g.) USNR, 1951-53. Markle scholar med. scis., 1958-63. Mem. Am. Assn. Pathologists, AMA, N.C. Med. Soc., Soc. Exptl. Biology and Medicine, Am. Soc. Cell Biology, Internat. Acad. Pathology, Internat. Soc. Heart Research (pres. 1978-80), Alpha Omega Alpha, Alpha Delta Phi, Nu Sigma Nu. Office: Duke U Med Center Dept Pathology Durham NC 27710

JENNINGS, W. CROFT, lawyer; b. Bishopville, S.C., Nov. 8, 1906; s. Larkin Hamilton (M.D.) and Maria Anne Lenud (Croft) J.; m. Elizabeth Bethune Brandon, Feb. 14, 1928; children: Anne M., W. Croft. B.S., U.S. Naval Acad., 1927; student, Harvard Law Sch., 1929-30; J.D., U. Mich., 1932. Bar: S.C. bar. Asso. Bulkley, Ledyard, Dickinson & Wright, Detroit, 1932-34; spl. asst. U.S. Atty. Gen., 1934-41; partner Roberts & Jennings, Columbia, S.C., 1946-56, Roberts, Jennings, Thomas & Lumpkin, 1956-62, Roberts, Jennings & Thomas, 1963—; counsel Dial, Jennings, Windham, Thomas & Roberts, 1976—; spl. lectr. fed. taxation U.S.C. Law Sch., 1946-54; mem. adv. group to U.S. Commr. Internal Revenue, 1962-63. Active local chpt. A.R.C., nat. bd. govs., 1954-60, vice chmn., 1959-60; bd. dirs. Joint Blood Council, Inc., 1958-62; mem. bd. Columbia Music Festival Assn., 1949-51; trustee Columbia Museum Art, 1964-70, pres., 1967-69; commr. Columbia Art Commn., 1970—, chmn., 1976-84, adv. council, 1984—; chancellor Episcopal Diocese Upper S.C., 1950-71, chancellor emeritus, 1971—; dep. Triennial Conv., P.E. Ch., 1958, 61 64, 67, 69, 70. Served as ensign USN, 1927-29; from lt. to capt. USNR, 1941-46; comdr. USNR Battalion, 1938-41; Washington; comdr. USNR Battalion, 1946-49; Columbia; rear adm., ret., 1953. Decorated Legion of Merit with combat distinguishing device, other decorations and theater ribbons. Mem. Am., S.C., Richland County bar assns., Am. Judicature Soc., Phi Delta Phi. Episcopalian (vestryman). Clubs: Pine Tree Hunt, Forest Lake, Palmetto (Columbia); Army Navy (Washington); Linville Golf (Linville, N.C.). Home: 610 Spring Lake Rd Columbia SC 29206 also Hickory Ln Linville Resorts Linville NC 28646 Office: Barringer Bldg Columbia SC 29201

JENNINGS, WAYLON, country musician; b. Littlefield, Tex., June 15, 1937; m. Jessi Colter; 4 children. Disc jockey, Littlefield and Lubbock, Tex.; with, Buddy Holly's band, 1958-59; formed own band: The Waylors; performed in nightclubs; rec. artist with, RCA, 1965—; albums include Ol' Waylon, Black on Black, It's Only Rock and Roll, Waylon and Co., Take it To the Limit, Waylon Live; rec. artist with many others; narrator: TV series The Dukes of Hazzard, 1979—. Office: care Regency Artists 920 Sunset Blvd Los Angeles CA 90012 *

JENNINGS, WILLIAM MITCHELL, lawyer; b. N.Y.C., Dec. 14, 1920; s. Harry B. and Nettie I. (Mitchell) J.; m. Elizabeth Hite, Oct. 16, 1943; children: William Mitchell, Jeffrey H., Eunice M., Elizabeth B., Priscilla H. A.B., Princeton U., 1941; J.D., Yale U., 1943. Bar: N.Y. 1945. Law clk. to presiding judge U.S. Cir. Ct. Appeals (2d cir.), N.Y.C., 1943-44; assoc. Simpson Thacher & Bartlett, N.Y.C., 1944-51; ptnr. Simpson Thacher & Barlett, N.Y.C., from 1952; now gen. ptnr. Bear Stearns & Co., N.Y.C.; pres., dir. N.Y. Rangers Inc.; adv. dir. Madison Sq. Garden Corp.; dir. Suburban porpane Gas Corp., Lee Nat. Corp., Warnaco Inc., Warnaco Can. Ltd. Gen. chmn. Thunderbird Golf Classics, 1963-65; bd. dirs. World Golf Hall of Fame; founder, gen. chmn. Westchester Golf Classic, 1967—; mem. nat. adv. com. Profl. Golfers' Assn. Am., Inst. Sports Medicine and Athletic Trauma; bd. govs. Nat. Hockey League, 1962—, chmn. bd. govs., 1968-70; pres. United Hosp., Port Chester, N.Y., 1959-69, chmn., Port Chester, N.Y., 1969-74, hon. chmn., Port Chester, N.Y., 1974—; trustee Rye Presbyterian Ch., N.Y. Recipient Lester Patrick trophy Nat. Hockey League, 1971, Disting. Service Met. Golf. Writers Assn., 1975, Gold Lee Met. Golf Writers Assn., 1977; elected to Hockey Hall of Fame, Toronto, 1975, Westchester Sports Hall of Fame, N.Y., 1979. Mem. N.Y. Bar Assn., N.Y.C. Bar Assn. Clubs: Apawamis (Rye, N.Y.); Country N.C. (Pinehurst); Links, Downtown Assn., Madison Sq. Garden (N.Y.C.); Blind Brook (Port Chester). Home: Byram Shore Rd Greenwich CT 06830 Office: Bear Stearns & Co 55 Water St New York NY 06830

JENRETTE, RICHARD HAMPTON, investment banker; b. Raleigh, N.C., Apr. 5, 1929; s. Joseph M. and Emma V. (Love) J.). B.A., U. N.C., 1951; M.B.A., Harvard U., 1957; Litt.D. (hon.), U. N.C. With Brown Bros. Harriman & Co., N.Y.C., 1957-59; with Donaldson, Lufkin & Jenrette, Inc., N.Y.C., 1959—, now chmn. bd., chief exec. officer; dir. Rose's Stores, News & Observer, Bus. Found. N.C. Chmn. Adv. Council Historic Preservation. Served to 2d lt. USAR, 1953-55. Mem. Securities Industry Assn. (dir., exec. com.), Inst. Chartered Fin. Analysts, N.Y. Soc. Security Analysts, Phi Beta Kappa. Democrat. Episcopalian. Clubs: University, Brook, City Midday, Harvard, Harvard Bus. Sch. (N.Y.C.); Carolina Yacht (Charleston, S.C.). Office: Donaldson Lufkin & Jenrette Inc 140 Broadway New York NY 10005 *

JENSEN, ADOLPH ROBERT, educator; b. Elmhurst, Ill., Apr. 14, 1915; s. Adolph George William and Marie (Diener) J.; m. Nelle B. Willams, Sept. 5, 1950; children—Robert, Margaret. B.S., Wheaton (Ill.) Coll., 1937; M.S., U. Ill., 1940, Ph.D., 1942; postgrad., Ohio U., summer 1959, Rensselaer Poly. Inst., summer 1962, Purdue U., summer 1970, Duke, summer 1971. Head analytical chemistry sect. Lewis Flight Propulsion Lab., NASA, Cleve., 1942-46; prof. chemistry Baldwin-Wallace Coll., Berea, Ohio, 1946—, chmn. dept. chemistry, 1956-71; vis. scientist Ohio Acad. Sci., 1960-64. Fellow AAAS; mem. Am. Chem. Soc., Ohio Acad. Sci. (v.p. chemistry sect. 1969-70), AAUP, Lutheran Acad. Scholarship, Sigma Xi, Phi Lambda Upsilon, Sigma Pi Sigma. Home: 25527 Butternut Ridge North Olmsted OH 44070 Office: Wilker Hall Baldwin-Wallace Coll Berea OH 44017

JENSEN, ARTHUR MILTON, college president; b. Chgo., Aug. 22, 1921; s. Hobart O. and Marie (Severson) J.; m. Marion McBride, May 26, 1945; children: Mary Ann, Arthur Ray, Patricia Lynn. B.S., Western Mich. U., 1949, M.A., 1953; Ed.D., UCLA, 1965. Dir. placement San Diego City Coll., 1959-63; adminstrv. and asst. dir. San Diego Evening Coll., 1963-66; chief jr. coll. bur. gen. edn. Calif. Dept. Edn., Sacramento, 1966-67; pres. San Bernardino Valley (Calif.) Coll., 1967—; Ednl. cons. in organizing and operating multi-campus jr. colls., 1964—; mem. jr. coll. sect. Accrediting Commn. for Western Schs. and Colls., 1966-67. Author: Adminstration of Multicampus Junior College Districts, 1965. Vice pres. Inland Empire council Boy Scouts Am., 1967—, pres.-elect, 1984; mem. adv. bd. Salvation Army, 1967—; active model city planning Conv. Cultural Community Center, 1967-72; pres. San Bernardino Symphony Assn., 1972-74; bd. dirs. Arrowhead United Way, 1974—, v.p., campaign dir., 1975-76. Served with USNR, 1943-46, 50-51; Korea; capt. Res. Kellogg fellow, 1962-64. Mem. Am. Assn. Jr. Colls., Calif. Jr. Coll. Assn., AAUP, Navy League (sec. 1971-73), Phi Delta Kappa. Club: Rotarian. Home: 1349 Pine Knoll Crest Redlands CA 92373 Office: 701 S Mt Vernon St San Bernardino CA 92403

JENSEN, ARTHUR ROBERT, educator; b. San Diego, Aug. 24, 1923; s. Arthur Alfred and Linda (Schachtmayer) J.; m. Barbara Jane DeLarme, May 6, 1960; 1 dau., Roberta Ann. B.A., U. Calif. at Berkeley, 1945; Ph.D., Columbia, 1956. Asst. med. psychology U. Md., 1955-56; research fellow Inst. Psychiatry, U. London, 1956-58; prof. ednl. psychology U. Calif. at Berkeley, 1958—. Author: Genetics and Education, 1972, Educability and Group Differences, 1973, Educational Differences, 1973, Bias in Mental Testing, 1979, Straight Talk about Mental Tests, 1981; Contbr. to profl. jours., books. Guggenheim fellow, 1964-65; fellow Center Advanced Study Behavioral Scis., 1966-67. Fellow Am. Psychol. Assn., Eugenics Soc., AAAS; mem. Am. Ednl. Research Assn. (v.p. 1968-70), Psychonomic Soc., Am. Soc. Human Genetics, Soc. for Social Biology, Behavior Genetics Assn., Psychometric Soc., Sigma Xi. Home: 30 Canyon View Dr Orinda CA 94563

JENSEN, ARTHUR SEIGFRIED, consulting engineering physicist; b. Trenton, N.J., Dec. 24, 1917; s. Emil Anthony and Emma Anna (Lund) J.; m. Lillian Elizabeth Reed, Aug. 9, 1941; children: Deane Ellsworth, Alan Forrest, Nancy Lorraine. B.S., U. Pa., 1938, M.S., 1939, Ph.D., 1941; diploma in advanced engring., Westinghouse Sch. Applied Sci., 1972, Westinghouse Sch. Applied Sci., 1977. Research physicist U.S. Naval Research Labs., Washington, 1941; research physicist RCA Labs., Princeton, N.J., 1945-57; mgr. spl. electron devices Westinghouse Electronic Tube Div., Balt., 1957-65; sr. adv. physicist Westinghouse Def. and Electronic Systems Center, Balt., 1965—; mem. Md. State Bd. Registration Profl. Engrs., 1979—, vice chmn., 1983; cons. Nat. Acad. Sci., 1970. Contbr. articles to profl. jours. Served to capt. USN, 1941-46, 46-63; Served to capt. Res., to 1977. Fellow IEEE (life), Washington Acad. Scis.; mem. AAAS, Res. Officers Assn., Ret. Officers Assn., Am. Phys. Soc., Am. Assn. Physics Tchrs., Soc. Photo-Optical Instrumentation Engrs., AIAA, Optical Soc. Am., N.Y. Acad. Scis., Md. Acad. Scis., Nat. Council Engring. Examiners (internat. relations com.), Infrared Info. Symposium, Sigma Xi, Pi Mu Epsilon, Kappa Phi Kappa. Club: U.S. Naval Acad. Officers and Faculty. Patentee in field. Home: 5602 Purlington Way Baltimore MD 21212 Office: Westinghouse Def and Electronic Systems Center Baltimore MD 21203 *The true miracle of creation is that fewer than thirty laws of nature suffice to determine the course of the universe since its beginning. While it is highly doubtful that an infinitely wise Creator would ever have had need to suspend any of these laws, yet the statistical nature of the Second Law of Thermodynamics and the Uncertainty Principle provides means for the Creator to influence our lives without violating any law, by affecting our thoughts and perceptions.*

JENSEN, BRUCE H., university administrator, consultant; b. Redmond, Utah, Dec. 24, 1931; s. Swen L. and Florence (Herbert) J.; married, Mar. 1, 1951 (div. 1972); children: Conne Lee, Bruce J., Jennifer; m. JoAnn J., May 7, 1974. A.A.S. in Engring., So. Utah State U., 1952; B.F.A., U. Utah, 1956, B. Arch., 1957. Lic. architect, Utah. Assoc. planner Salt Lake County Planning Commn., Salt Lake City, 1953-56; assoc. architect Lowell Parrish & Assocs., Salt Lake City, 1956-60; master planner New Coll. Campus, Orem, Utah; coordinator, master planner Utah State Bldg. Bd., Salt Lake City, 1973-75; architect, dir. facilities adminstrn. U. Utah, Salt Lake City, 1963-73, 75—; cons. campus planning and ednl. facilities. Author: Chronology of Book of Mormon, 1969; dir., author: U. Utah Master Plan, 1899-1981, 1981 (Am. Planners Assn. 1983); researcher, lectr. on ancient temples, 1980—. Active Utah State Bicentennial Fine Arts Programming Com., Bicentennial Civic Ctr. Expansion Com. Recipient Gov.'s Gold Key, Elimination of Handicapped Barriers, 1974, Aesthetic Conscience of U. Utah, 1973, awares of appreciation and metir Utah Tech. Coll., 1975-81. Fellow AIA (com. on architecture for edn. 1970—); mem. Utah Soc. AIA (pres.-elect 1984, award of merit 1982), Assn. Univ. Architects (disting. mem., pres. 1968-69), Council Ednl. Facilities Planners (devel. dir. 1981-82), AIA-Com. on Architecture for Edn. (liaison 1970-83), Phi Kappa Phi. Mormon. Club: Ft. Douglas Social. Home: 2062 Michigan Salt Lake City UT 84108 Office: Facilities Adminstrn Univ Utah Salt Lake City UT 84112

JENSEN, CLAYNE R., coll. adminstr.; b. Gunnison, Utah, Mar. 17, 1930; s. Alton H. and Arvilla R. J.; m. Elouise Henrie, Mar. 14, 1952; children—Craig, Mike, Blake, Chris. B.A., U. Utah, 1952, M.A., 1956; Ph.D., Ind. U., 1963. From instr. to asso. prof. phys. edn., coach Utah State U., 1956-64; asso. prof., coordinator coll. programs Brigham Young U., Provo, 1965-67, prof., 1968-74; asst. dean Coll. Phys. Edn., 1968-74, dean, 1974—; vis. prof. No. Ill. U., DeKalb, 1969. Author: Manual of Kinesiology, 1966, (with Garth Fisher) Scientific Basis of Athletic Conditioning, 1972, (with Vernom Barney, Cynthia Hirst) Conditioning Exercises to Improve Body Form and Function, 1972, (with Mary Bee Jensen) Square Dance, 1973, Folk Dance, 1972, (with Clarence Robison) Modern Track and Field Coaching Technique, 1974, Recreation and Leisure Time Careers, 1976, Winter Touring and Mountaineering, 1977, Leisure and Recreation in America—A Guide and Overview, 1977, (with Clark Thorstenson) Issues in Outdoor Recreation, 1977, (with Karl Tucker) Skiing, 1977, Outdoor Recreation in America, 1977, Applied Kinesiology, 1978, Administration of Physical Education and Athletic Program, 1981, Backpacking, 1981; contbr. articles to profl. jours. Exec. dir. Utah Inter-Agy. Council for Recreation and Parks, 1962-65; chmn. Nat. Conf. on Inter-Agy. Planning for Parks and Recreation, 1963-64. Served with USMC, 1953-55. Recipient Breitbrad Athletic Found. award, 1955; spl. citation for outstanding contbns. to recreation and park devel. State of Utah, 1965. Mem. Utah Recreation and Parks Assn. (exec. dir., gov. 1958-63), Utah Assn. Health, Phys. Edn., Recreation and Athletics (pres. 1970), AAHPER. Mormom. Home: 1900 Oak Ln Provo UT 84601 Office: Coll Phys Edn Brigham Young U Provo UT 84602 *As a professional educator I have long been devoted to the concept of helping people succeed and not causing them to fail. Success of each individual ought to be the principle objective of education. In my administrative role, I have tried to perpetuate an environment in which people are constantly encouraged and where there is opportunity for professional development and personal improvement.*

JENSEN, D. LOWELL, lawyer, government official; b. Brigham, Utah, June 3, 1928; s. Wendell and Elnore (Hatch) J.; m. Barbara Cowin, Apr. 20, 1951; children: Peter, Marcia, Thomas. A.B. in Econs, U. Calif.-Berkeley, 1949, LL.B., 1952. Bar: Calif. 1952. Dep. dist. atty., Alameda County, 1955-66, asst. dist. atty., 1966-69, dist. atty., 1969-81; asst. atty. gen. criminal div. Dept. Justice, Washington, 1981-83, assoc. atty. gen., 1983—; mem. Calif. Council on Criminal Justice, 1974-81; past pres. Calif. Dist. Atty.'s Assn. Served with U.S. Army, 1952-54. Fellow Am. Coll. Trial Lawyers; mem. Nat. Dist. Atty.'s Assn. (victim/witness commn. 1974-81), Boalt Hall Alumni Assn. (past pres.). Office: Main Justice Bldg 10th and Constitution Ave Washington DC 20530

JENSEN, DICK LEROY, lawyer; b. Audubon, Iowa, Oct. 25, 1930; s. A.B. and Bernice (Fancher) J.; m. Nancy Wilson, June 30, 1956; children—Charles F., Sarah R. LL.B., U. Iowa, 1954. Bar: Iowa bar 1954. Practice in, Audubon, Iowa, 1958-60; gen. counsel, sec. Walnut Grove Products, Co., Atlantic, Iowa, 1960-64; legal staff W.R. Grace & Co., Atlantic, 1964-66; gen. counsel, v.p., sec. Spencer Foods, Inc., Iowa, 1966-72, dir., 1968-72; lawyer with firm Dreher, Wilson, Adams & Jensen, Des Moines, 1972—. Notes and legis. editor: Iowa Law Rev, 1953-54. Pres. S.W. Iowa Mental Health Inst., 1964-66. Served to lt. USNR, 1955-58. Mem. Sigma Nu, Phi Delta Phi. Republican. Presbyn. Club: Mason. Home: 3901 River Oaks Dr Des Moines IA 50312 Office: Dreher Wilson Adams & Jensen Stephens Bldg Des Moines IA 50309

JENSEN, EJNER JACOB, English educator; b. Omaha, Jan. 28, 1937; s. Jacob Anker and Maynhild Marie (Sorensen) J.; m. Lineve Grace McKie, Dec. 27, 1959; children: Sten Anker, Maren Lineve. B.A., Carleton Coll., Northfield, Minn., 1959; M.A., Tulane U., 1960, Ph.D., 1965. Asst. prof. English Lit. U. Mich., Ann Arbor, 1964-70, assoc. prof., 1970-79, prof., 1979—, assoc. chmn., 1976-81. Author: John Marston, Dramatist, 1979. Elder First Presbyterian Ch., Ann Arbor, 1972-75. Henry Huntington Library fellow San Marino, Calif., 1969; recipient Matthews Underclass Teaching award U. Mich., 1982. Mem. MLA, Malone Soc., Renaissance Soc. Am. Democrat. Home: 1324 Brooklyn St Ann Arbor MI 48104 Office: U Mich Ann Arbor MI 48109

JENSEN, ELWOOD VERNON, biochemist; b. Fargo, N.D., Jan. 13, 1920; s. Eli A. and Vera (Morris) J.; m. Mary Welmoth Collette, June 17, 1941 (dec. Nov. 1982); children: Karen Collette, Thomas Eli. A.B., Wittenberg U., 1940, D.Sc. (hon.), 1963; Ph.D., U. Chgo., 1944; D.Sc. (hon.), Acadia U., 1976. Faculty U. Chgo., 1947—; assoc. prof. biochemistry Ben May Lab. Cancer Research, 1954-60, prof., 1960-63, Am. Cancer Soc. research prof. physiology, 1963-69; dir. Ben May Lab., 1969-82; med. dir. Ludwig Inst. Cancer Research, 1983—; prof. physiology Ben May Lab., 1969-73, 77—, prof. biophysics, 1973—, prof. biochemistry, 1980—; med. dir. Ludwig Inst. for Cancer

Research, 1983—; dir. Biomed. Center for Population Research, 1972-75; Vis. prof. Max-Planck-Inst. für Biochemie, Munich, Germany, 1958; chmn. endocrinology panel Cancer Chemotherapy Nat. Service Center, 1960-62; mem. chemotherapy rev. bd. Nat. Cancer Inst., 1960-62, bd. sci. counselors, 1969-72; mem. Nat. Adv. Council Child Health and Human Devel., 1976-80; mem. adv. com. biochemistry and chem. carcinogenesis Am. Cancer Soc., 1968-72, council for research and clin. investigation, 1974-77; mem. assembly life scis. NRC, 1975-78; mem. com. on sci., engring. and public policy Nat. Acad. Scis., 1981-82. Editorial bd.: Perspectives in Biology and Medicine, 1966—, Archives of Biochemistry and Biophysics, 1979—; editorial adv. bd.: Biochemistry, 1969-72, Life Scis, 1973-78, Breast Cancer Research and Treatment, 1980—; assoc. editor.: Jour. Steroid Biochemistry, 1974—; Contbr. articles to profl. jours. Guggenheim fellow, 1946-47; recipient D.R. Edwards medal, 1970, La Madonnina prize, 1973, G.H.A. Clowes award, 1975, Papanicolaou award, 1975, prix Roussel, 1976, Nat. award Am. Cancer Soc., 1976, Amory prize, 1977, Gregory Pincus Meml. award, 1978, Gairdner Found. award, 1979, Lucy Wortham James award, 1980, Charles F. Kettering prize, 1980, Nat. Acad. Clin. Biochemistry award, 1981, Pharmacia award, 1982, Hubert H. Humphrey award, 1983, Rolf Luft medal, 1983. Mem. Am. Acad. Arts and Scis., Am. Soc. Biol. Chemists, Am. Chem. Soc., Am. Assn. Cancer Research, Endocrine Soc. (pres. 1980-81), AAAS, Soc. Study Reprodn. Clubs: Chicago Literary, Cosmos. Home: Kanalweg 5a CH-8714 Feldbach Switzerland Office: Stadelhoferstrasse 22 CH-8001 Zurich Switzerland

JENSEN, ERIC FINN, lawyer, mfg. co. exec.; b. N.Y.C., Oct. 17, 1927; s. Olaf and Sigrid (Anderson) J.; m. Janet Stirling Clark, Aug. 26, 1950; children—Mari Nelms, Deborah Bowne, Eric David. B.S., Cornell, 1951; LL.B., Bklyn. Law Sch., 1956; grad., Advanced Mgmt. Program Harvard, 1968. Bar: N.Y. bar 1956. Since practiced in, N.Y.C.; arbitration atty. Bethlehem Steel Corp., 1951-61; mgr. labor relations ACF Industries, Inc., N.Y.C., 1961-64, dir. indsl. relations, 1964-65, v.p. indsl. relations, 1965-79, v.p. govt. and labor relations, 1979—; Chmn. adv. council Cornell Sch. Indsl. and Labor Relations. Served with AUS, 1946-47. Mem. Am. Bar Assn., Indsl. Relations Soc. (dir., past pres.), N.Y. Indsl. Relations Assn., Bklyn. Law Sch. Rev. Assn. Club: Cornell (N.Y.C.). Home: 15 Winslow Rd White Plains NY 10606 Office: 750 3d Ave New York NY 10017

JENSEN, GEORGE ALBERT, lawyer; b. St. Louis, June 27, 1929; s. Albert P. and Mary E. (Baker) J.; m. Martha Jean Collins, Sept. 10, 1949; children: Noncy, Georgia, Peter. A.B., Washington U., 1952, J.D., 1954. Bar: Mo. bar 1954. Since practiced in, St. Louis; mem. Peper, Martin, Jensen, Maichel & Hetlage (and predecessor firms), 1954—, partner, 1958—; Dir., gen. counsel Commerce Bank of Mound City; dir., mem. exec. com. NAVCO Corp., Nat. Gen. Ins. Co.; dir. A.G. Edwards & Sons, Inc.; A.G. Edwards, Inc. Contbr. articles to profl. jours. Trustee St. Louis U.; former trustee Nat. Urban League. Served with U.S. Army, 1946-48. Mem. Mo. Bar, Bar Assn. Met. St. Louis, Am. Bar Assn., Order of Coif, Phi Beta Kappa, Phi Delta Phi. Conglist. (deacon, trustee, moderator). Clubs: Noonday, University, Media (St. Louis). Home: 6 Forest Ridge Dr Clayton MO 63105 Office: 720 Olive St Saint Louis MO 63101

JENSEN, GRADY EDMONDS, assn. exec.; b. Pitts., Nov. 8, 1922; s. Claude Henry and Margaret (Edmonds) J.; m. Mary Margaret Wilber, July 5, 1952; children—Timothy Sage, Margaret Eliza, Caroline Grosvenor. B.A., Hobart Coll., Geneva, N.Y., 1943; M.B.A., U. Pa., 1949; cert., Stonier Grad. Sch. Banking, Rutgers U., 1967. Asst. to asst. treas. U. Pa., Phila., 1949-50; staff engr. Cresap, McCormick & Paget (mgmt. cons.), N.Y.C., 1950-55; bus. mgr. sta. WABC-TV, N.Y.C., 1955-56; asso. bus. mgr. N.Y. U., 1956-61; asst. budget dir. Eastern Air Lines, Inc., N.Y.C., 1961-62; asst. to v.p. bus. and fin. Columbia U., 1962-63; 2d v.p. corp. personnel and internat. dept. Chase Manhattan Bank, N.Y.C., 1963-70; dir. orgn. and mgmt. devel. Am. Express Co., N.Y.C., 1970-74; v.p. adminstrn., sec. Harwood Cos., Inc., N.Y.C., 1974-80; exec. adminstr. Assn. Bar City N.Y., 1981—. Mem. Scarsdale (N.Y.) Village Bd. Trustees, 1975-81, mayor, 1979-81. Served with USNR, 1943-45. Mem. Guild Book Workers, Am. Revolution Round Table N.Y., Naval Aviation Commandery, Tailhook Assn., Mensa, Westchester County Hist. Soc., Scarsdale Hist. Soc., Provincetown Hist. Soc., SAR, Soc. Mayflower Descs., N.Y. Geneal. and Biog. Soc. Clubs: Town (Scarsdale) (past pres.); Hobart (N.Y.) (past pres.); Grolier, Wings, U. Pa. (N.Y.C.). Home: 16 Ridgecrest W Scarsdale NY 10583 Office: 42 W 44th St New York NY 10036

JENSEN, HARLAN ELLSWORTH, veterinarian, educator; b. St. Ansgar, Iowa, Oct. 6, 1915; s. Bert and Mattie (Hansen) J.; m. Naomi Louise Geiger, June 7, 1941; children: Kendra Lee Jensen Belfi, Doris Eileen, Richard Harlan. D.V.M., Iowa State U., 1941; Ph.D., U. Mo., 1971. Diplomate: Charter diplomate Am. Coll. Vet. Ophthalmologists (v.p. 1970-72, pres. 1972-73). Vet. practice, Galesburg, Ill., 1941-46, small animal internship, New Brunswick, N.J., 1946-47, small animal practice, Cleve., 1947-58, San Diego, 1958-62, Houston, 1962-67; faculty U. Mo., Columbia, 1967—, chief opthalmology, prof. Vet. Sch., 1967-80, prof. emeritus Vet. Sch., 1980—, assoc. prof. ophthalmology Med. Sch., 1972-80, now cons. vet. opthalmology Med. Sch.; cons. in vet. ophthalmology to pharm. firms; guest lectr., prof. opthalmology U. Utrecht (Netherlands) Vet. Sch., 1973; tchr., lectr. various vet. meetings; condr. seminar World Congress Small Animal Medicine and Surgery, 1977. Author: Stereoscopic Atlas of Clinical Ophthalmology of Domestic Animals, 1971, Stereoscopic Atlas of Ophthalmic Surgery of Domestic Animals, 1974; co-author: Stereoscopic Atlas of Soft Tissue Surgery of Small Animals, 1973, Clinical Dermatology of Small Animals, 1974; contbr. articles to profl. jours. Recipient Gaines award AVMA, 1973. Mem. Am. Vet. Radiology Soc. (pres. 1956-57), Am. Vet. Ophthalmology Soc. (pres. 1960-62), Farm House Frat., Sigma Xi, Phi Kappa Phi, Phi Zeta, Gamma Sigma Delta. Lutheran. Clubs: Rotary (pres. Pacific Beach, Calif. 1960-62, pres. Columbia 1977-78. Inventor instrument for ear trimming in dogs, 1949, breathing apparatus, 1953; designed sound proof animal hosps.; developed 3-D study program for vet. ophthalmology, 1969. Home and Office: 6810 Overlook Dr Fort Myers FL 33907

JENSEN, HAROLD SHERWOOD, real estate executive; b. Detroit, Aug. 29, 1930; s. Harold Soren and Lyndon Elizabeth (Neddermeyer) J.; m. Dona Bernard, Apr. 26, 1958; children: Barbara, Lyndon, Susan, Karl. B.S. in Civil Engring. cum laude, Mich. Tech. U., 1952, D. Engring. (hon.), 1978; postgrad., Wayne State U., 1954; M.B.A., Harvard U., 1957. Chief survey party Brennan Constrn. Co., Detroit, 1955-56; asst. structural engr. Metcalf & Eddy, Boston, 1956-58; mgr. fin. and devel. Gilbane Bldg. Co., Providence, 1958-62; exec. v.p. Lumbermen's Co., Austin, Tex., 1962-66; asst. v.p. real estate Penn Central, Phila., 1967-69; group v.p. real estate I.C. Industries, Inc., Chgo., 1970-77; partner Met. Structures, 1977—; pres. Urban Land Inst., 1977-79; trustee Bay Colony Property Co.; dir. First Nat. Bank of Lake Forest (Ill.), Chgo. Bank Commerce. Served with C.E. AUS, 1952-54. Mem. Tau Beta Pi, Chi Epsilon, Theta Tau. Clubs: Tavern (Chgo.); Lake Forest Bath and Tennis. Home: 925 E Westminster Dr Lake Forest IL 60045 Office: 1 Illinois Center Chicago IL 60601

JENSEN, JAMES HERBERT, agriculturist; b. Madison, Nebr., June 16, 1906; s. Jens and Eda (Hansen) J.; m. Lucille Christopher, Nov. 2, 1931; children—James Michael, Karen (Mrs. J.A. Bailey), Stephen, Roger. B.Sc., U. Nebr., 1928, A.M., 1930; postgrad., Columbia, 1931-32; Ph.D., U. Wis., 1935; D.Sc., N.C. State U. Raleigh, 1966; LL.D., U. Nebr., 1966, Kasetsart U., Thailand, 1980. Asst. pathologist Tropical Plant Research Found., Baragua, Cuba, 1930-31; plant pathologist P.R. Agrl. Expt. Sta., 1935-37; asst. prof. plant pathology U. Nebr., 1937-45; plant pathologist N.C. Agrl. Expt. Sta., 1945-48; chief biology br., div. biology and medicine A.E.C., Washington, 1948-49; chmn. sub-com. Nat. Com. Radiation Protection, 1949-57; prof. and head plant pathology, faculty N.C. State Coll. A. and E., 1949-53, Reynolds prof., 1951-53; provost, prof. botany Iowa State U., 1953-61; pres. Oreg. State U., Corvallis, 1961-69, prof. botany and plant pathology on leave, 1969-71, pres. emeritus, prof. botany and plant pathology emeritus, 1971—; agr. project leader Rockefeller Found., Bangkok, Thailand, 1969-73; acting vice rector planning and devel. Kasetsart U., 1969-73; sr. agrl. research adviser Devel. & Research Corp., Tehran, Iran, 1973-74; cons. Rockefeller Found., World Bank, U.S. AID.; Mem. exec. com. Assn. State Univs. and Land-Grant Colls., 1962-64, pres., 1966-67, chmn., 1967-68; mem. Nat. Commn. on Accrediting, 1964-69; agrl. research planning com. U.S. Dept. Agr., 1964-66; chmn. pesticides residues com. Nat. Acad. Sci., 1964-65, chmn. persistent pesticides com., 1967-68; pres. Associated Midwest Univs., 1958-59, dir., 1959-65; mem. research adv. com. Boyce Thompson Inst., 1960-69; mem. policy adv. bd. Argonne Nat. Lab., 1961-67. Author: Refugee Settlement in the Dominican Republic, 1942, also articles on plant viruses and diseases of tropical plants, profl. publs. Fellow AAAS, Am. Phytopathol. Soc. (pres. 1954- 55); mem. Sigma Xi, Phi Kappa Phi. Home: PO Box 212 Green Valley AZ 85614

JENSEN, JAMES ROBERT, educator, dentist; b. Mpls., Mar. 17, 1922; s. Ernest William and Edith Ann (Norstedt) J.; m. Alvern Halverson, Mar. 24, 1945; children: Thomas, Mark, James, Elizabeth. B.A., U. Minn., 1944, D.D.S., 1946, M.S., 1950. Diplomate: Am. Bd. Endodontics. Teaching asst. U. Minn., 1948-50, asst. prof., 1950-53, asso. prof., 1953-57, prof., chmn. div. operative dentistry and endodontics, 1957-69, asst. dean acad. affairs, 1969-74, asso. dean acad. affairs, 1974—, prof., chmn. div. endodontics, 1969—; part time practice specializing endodontics; cons. endodontics VA Hosp., Mpls.; team leader operative dentistry and endodontics Project Vietnam of AID; cons. dental health Pan Am. Health Orgn., WHO; mem. staff Hennepin County Gen. Hosp., Univ. Hosp. of U. Minn.; postgrad. faculty Universidad Autonoma de Nueva Leon, Monterrey, Mexico. Author: (with Thomas P. Serene and Fernando Sanchez) Fundamentos Clinicos de Endodoncia, 1977, (with Thomas P. Serene) Fundamentals of Clinical Endodontics, 7th edit, 1977, Japanese edit, Effective Dental Assisting, 6th edit, 1982; Contbr.: articles to profl. jours. Effective Dental Assisting, 6th edit. Served with U.S. Army, 1943-44; as capt. Dental Corps, 1946-48; res. dental surgeon USPHS and Assn. Res. Officers. Fellow Am., Internat. colls. dentists; mem. Am., Minn. dental assns., Mpls. Dist. Dental Soc., Internat. Assn. Dental Research, Am. Assn. Endodontists. Home: 2167 N Rosewood Lane Saint Paul MN 55113 Office: Sch of Dentistry Univ Minnesota Minneapolis MN 55455

JENSEN, JOHN ERIC, broadcast exec.; b. Alhambra, Calif., July 10, 1943; s. John V. and Margaret C. (Crabtree) J. Student, Mt. San Antonio Coll., 1961-66. Field rep. Knoll Pharm. Co., San Francisco, 1967-68; sales mgr. Radio Sta. KREP, San Jose, Calif., 1968-71; gen. mgr. Radio Sta. KMPX, San Francisco, 1972—; cons. KPPC, 1973; v.p. Nat. Sci. Network, 1976—. Broadcast cons., Francis Ford Coppola Enterprises; radio producer, Coppola Studio's Hammett, 1980; writer, co-producer: Edgar Bergen's Command Performance, 1978, American Forces Television Command Performers, 1981; co-producer: Big Band special, An Evening with Elsa Lanchester, 1981; lectr., San Francisco State Broadcast Div.; Writer/producer: The Big Broadcast, 1975, Bing Crosby's Command Performance, 1975, Life Magazine Goes to War, 1977. Recipient certificate of merit San Francisco Bd. Suprs., 1975; Am. Revolution Bicentennial Commn. award, 1976; U.S. Navy Letter of Commendation, 1976. Mem. San Francisco Press Club (dir. 1977-79, v.p. 1979-80), San Francisco Broadcast Mgrs. Assn., No. Calif. Broadcasters Assn. Pacific Pioneer Broadcasters. Home: 1156 Arcadia Ave Arcadia CA 91006 Office: 1061 W Temple St Los Angeles CA 90012

JENSEN, JOHN LAWRENCE, advertising executive; b. Kansas City, Mo., Sept. 4, 1942; s. Hans and Pearl M. (Johnson) J.; m. Marla Del Wright, 1 dau. Jessica Marla. B.F.A., U. Kans. Med. Ctr., 1964; A.A., Kansas City Jr. Coll., 1962. Chief med. illustrator U. Kans. Med. Ctr., Kansas City, 1964-68; v.p., creative dir. Allmayer Advt., Inc., Kansas city, Mo., 1968-71; creative dir. Bernstein-Rein & Boasberg Advt., Inc., Kansas City, Mo., 1971-73; v.p., account supr. Christenson, Barclay & Shaw Advt., Inc., Kansas City, Mo., 1973-75; sr. v.p., creative dir. Barickman Advt., Kansas City, Mo., 1975-82; pres., chief operating officer Baarickman Advt. div. Doyle Dane Bernbach Advt., Inc., Kansas City, Mo., 1983-84; chief exec. officer Barickman Advt. div. Doyle Dane Bernbach Advt., Inc., Kansas City, Mo., 1984—; creative cons. Kans. Regional Med. Program, 1967-68. Bd. dirs. Westport Ballet, Kansas City, 1980. Served in USMC, 1966-72. Recipient Effie award Am. Mktg. Assn., 1980, 81, 82. Mem. Advt. Club Kansas City. Democrat. Unitarian. Clubs: Friends of Art, Kansas City (Kansas City, Mo.). Office: Barickman Advt 427 W 12th St Kansas City MO 64105

JENSEN, JULIE MAE, educator; b. Huthinson, Minn., Dec. 6, 1943; d. Axel M. and Mae A. (Hoodecheck) J. B.S., U. Minn., 1965, M.A., 1968, Ph.D., 1970. Tchr. Mpls. Pub. Schs., 1965-67; instr. U. Minn., 1967-70; mem. faculty U. Tex., Austin, 1970—, prof. edn., 1981—; vis. prof. U. Tenn., 1975, U. Minn., 1977, 83. Author: (with Fagan and Cooper) Measures for Research, (with Petty) Developing Children's Language, 1980; editor: Lang. Arts, 1976, 83; contbr. revs., articles, chpts. in books. Recipient award of excellence for profl. journalism Ednl. Press Assn. Am., 1982; NDEA fellow, 1967-70. Mem. Nat. Council Tchrs. of English (research award in teaching English 1970), Nat. Conf. Research in English. Office: 406 Edn Bldg U Tex Austin TX 78712

JENSEN, MICHAEL CHARLES, journalist, author; b. Chgo., Nov. 1, 1934; s. Stanley Charles and Billie Jane (Cooke) J.; m. Jane Rice Woodruff, July 23, 1960; children: Heidi, Michael Charles. A.B., Harvard Coll., 1956; M.S., Boston U., 1961. Reporter Boston Herald-Traveler, 1960-63, exec. fin. editor, 1963-64; editor Am. Metal Market, N.Y.C., 1965-69; reporter, editor N.Y. Times, N.Y.C., 1970-78; econ. affairs corr. NBC Network News, N.Y.C., 1978—. Author: The Financiers, 1976; contbg. author: Corporations and Their Critics, 1980; contbr.: articles to Saturday Rev., Harvard Bus. Rev. Mem. Westchester County (N.Y.) 4-H Program Com., 1975-79. Served to lt., j.g. USNR, 1957-60. Recipient Page One award Newspaper Guild N.Y., 1973; Deadline Club award N.Y.C. Profl. chpt. Sigma Delta Chi, 1976; Media awards for econ. understanding, 1980; Janus award for excellence in fin. broadcasting, 1981. Mem. Am. Soc. Bus. Press Editors (pres. N.Y. chpt. 1965-66), Am. Bus. Press (dir. 1967). Club: Harvard of N.Y. Office: 30 Rockefeller Plaza New York NY 10020

JENSEN, MICHAEL COLE, economics educator; b. Rochester, Minn., Nov. 30, 1939; s. Harold J. and Gertrude M. J.; children: Natalie Ann, Stephanie Kathrine. A.B., Macalester Coll., 1962; M.B.A., U. Chgo., 1964, Ph.D., 1968. Instr. Grad. Sch. Mgmt., Northwestern U., Evanston, Ill., 1967; asst. prof. U. Rochester, N.Y., 1967-71, assoc. prof., 1971-79, prof., dir. managerial econs. research center Grad. Sch. Mgmt., 1980—. Editor: Studies in the Theory of Capital Markets, 1972, Jour. Fin. Econs. Mem. Am. Econ. Assn., Western Econ. Assn. (exec. com.), Am. Fin. Assn. (bd. dirs.). Office: Univ Rochester Grad Sch Mgmt Rochester NY 14627

JENSEN, OLIVER ORMEROD, editor, writer; b. Ithaca, N.Y., Apr. 16, 1914; s. Gerard E. and Dorothea H. (Ormerod) J.; m. Alison Pfeiffer Hargrove, Feb. 21, 1970; stepchildren: Christopher, Stephen, Penelope. B.A., Yale U., 1936. With J. Walter Thompson Co., 1937-38; asst. mng. editor Judge mag., 1938-39; with Benton & Bowles, 1939-40; writer Life mag., 1940-41, 46-50, articles editor, mem. bd. editors, 1946-50; a founder Thorndike, Jensen & Parton, Inc. (publishers), 1950, Am. Heritage mag., 1954, mng. editor, 1954-59, editor, 1959-76, sr. editor, 1976-80, 83—; editorial bd. Horizon mag., 1958-76; v.p., dir. Am. Heritage Pub. Co., 1954-77, cons., 1977-80; pres. Conn. Valley R.R. Co., Essex, 1971-74, 76-80, chmn. bd., 1980—; chief div. prints and photographs Library of Congress, Washington, 1981-82. Author: Carrier War, 1945, The Revolt of American Women, 1952, reissued, 1971, A College Album, 1974, The American Heritage History of Railroads in America, 1975, America's Yesterdays, 1978; co-author: American Album, 1968; Editor: America and Russia, 1962, Great Crimes and Trials, 1974, Bruce Catton's America, 1979. Mem. Andover Alumni Council, 1962-65. Served from ensign to lt. USNR, 1942-45. Recipient James Gordon Bennett prize Yale, 1936. Mem. Am. Scenic and Historic Preservation Soc. (trustee), Am. Assn. State and Local History (mem. council 1957-76), Conn. Hist. Soc. (trustee), Soc. Am. Historians (dir.), Am. Antiquarian Soc., Phi Beta Kappa. Clubs: Yale (council 1974-77), Century (N.Y.C.); Acorn (Conn.). Address: PO Box 620 Old Saybrook CT 06475

JENSEN, REUBEN ROLLAND, former automotive company executive; b. Ainsworth, Nebr., Dec. 22, 1920; s. Jens Christian and Amy Caroline (Boyer) J.; m. Janet A. McCann, Oct. 19, 1974; children: Shannon (Mrs. Roger Santora), Bruce, Scott. Student, U. Nebr., 1938-41. With Gen. Motors Corp., Detroit, 1946; jr. engr. Hydra-Matic div. Gen. Motors Corp., 1965-67, gen. mgr., 1967-70, Allison div. Gen. Motors Corp., 1970-72, v.p., group exec., 1972-74, exec. v.p., 1974-84; Mem. adv. bd. Chem. Bank Internat., 1973—. Served with USNR, 1943-45. Recipient Silver Beaver, Disting. Eagle, Silver Buffalo, Boy Scouts Am., 1973. Mem. Assn. U.S. Army, Navy League U.S., Am. Ordnance Assn., Alpha Tau Omega. Clubs: Meadowbrook Country (Northville, Mich.); Quail Ridge Country, Pine Tree Country (Boynton Beach, Fla.). Lodge: Masons. Home: 10838 Tamarisk Boynton Beach FL 33436

JENSEN, ROBERT P., electronics company executive; b. Chgo., Dec. 29, 1925; s. Louis P. and Ellen (Goede) J.; m. Anne F. Burke, June 15, 1980; children—Erik P., Curtis R. B.S. in Mech. Engring, Iowa State Coll., Ames, 1948; postgrad., U. Mich., 1953-54; grad., advanced mgmt. program Harvard, 1965. Salesman, br. and dist. mgr., gen. sales mgr., operations mgr. Kaiser Aluminum & Chem. Sales, Inc., 1954-61, gen. mgr. bldg. products div., 1963-66, dir. bus. planning aluminum div., 1967; exec. v.p., gen. mgr. Olin Foil Packaging Corp. (subsidiary Olin Mathieson Chem. Corp.), 1961-63; v.p. aluminum group Howmet Corp., N.Y.C., 1967-68, exec. v.p., 1968-70, chief operating officer, dir., 1970, pres., chief exec. officer, 1971-72; also dir.; chief operating officer, pres., chief exec. officer, dir. Gen. Cable Corp. (now GK Technologies, Inc.), Greenwich, Conn., 1973—, chmn. bd., after 1978; now chmn., chief exec. officer EF Hutton LBO Inc.; dir. Conoco Inc., Irving Bank Corp., Irving Trust Co., Jostens, Inc., Sprague Electric Co., Arrow Electronics, Aerospace Corp. Trustee Council of Americas, Stamford Hosp.; mem. corp. Greenwich Hosp. Assn.; bd. dirs. Greenwich Boys' Club Assn., Nat. Multiple Sclerosis Soc. Served to lt. (j.g.) USNR, 1944-46. Mem. Aluminum Assn. (chmn.'s adv. council), U.S. Power Squadron. Clubs: Westchester Country (Rye, N.Y.); Board Room, Union League (N.Y.C.); Capitol Hill (Washington); Greenwich Country, Indian Harbor Yacht (Greenwich, Conn.); Landmark (Stamford, Conn.); La Cumbre Golf and Country (Santa Barbara, Calif.). Office: EF Hutton LBO Inc 8 E Figuero #230 Santa Barbara CA 93101

JENSEN, ROBERT TRYGVE, lawyer; b. Chgo., Sept. 16, 1922; s. James T. and Else (Uhlich) J.; m. Marjorie Rae Montgomery, Oct. 3, 1959 (div. June 1973); children: Robert Trygve, James Thomas, John Michael; m. Barbara Mae Wilson, Aug. 5, 1974. Student, U. N.C., 1943; LL.B., J.D., Northwestern U., 1949, B.S., 1949; LL.M., U. So. Calif., 1955. Bar: Calif. 1950. Asst. counsel Douglas Aircraft Co., Inc., 1950-52, 58-60, counsel El Segundo div., 1952-58; gen. counsel Aerospace Corp., El Segundo, 1960—, asst. sec., 1961-67, sec., 1967—. Founding mem. World Assn. Lawyers of World Peace Through Law Center. Served with AUS, 1942-46; PTO. Mem. Am., Beverly Hills, Fed. bar assns., Am. Arbitration Assn. (nat. panel arbitrator), Alpha Delta Phi, Phi Delta Phi. Home: 10610 Ashton Ave Los Angeles CA 90024 Office: 2350 E El Segundo Blvd El Segundo CA 90245

JENSEN, RUE L., animal pathologist, educator; b. Vermillion, Utah, Oct. 24, 1911; s. James Louis and Ella (Casto) J.; m. Millie Domgaard, May 19, 1942; children: Louis, Mary Ann Hagen. B.S., Utah State U., 1937, M.S., 1939; D.V.M., Colo. State U., 1942; Ph.D., U. Minn., 1953; D.V.Sc. (hon.), Kasetsart U., Thailand, 1965. Diplomate: Am. Coll. Vet. Pathologists. Instr., La. State U., 1942-43; mem. faculty Colo. State U., 1943—, successively asst. prof. pathology Coll. Vet. Medicine, asst. pathologist Expt. Sta., 1943-48, prof. pathology, also pathologist Expt. Sta., 1948—, dean Coll. Vet. Medicine, chief animal disease sect. Expt. Sta., 1957-66, dir. Agrl. Exptl. Sta., 1966-69, v.p. research, 1966-73, dir. diagnostic labs., 1973—; cons. pathologist Monfort of Colo., Inc., 1977—, U. Wyo., 1978—, Nielson Ranches, Cody, Wyo., 1983—; mem. U.S. Dept. Agr. del. vet. sci., USSR, 1958; Dept. Agr., Aid cons. U. Tehran, 1962; cons. Kasetsart U., Thailand, 1964; mem. Colo. Gov.'s Sci. Adv. Council, 1973-75. Research, publs. on diseases of cattle and sheep; author: (with D.R. Mackey) Diseases of Cattle, (with B.L. Swift) Diseases of Sheep. Active Boy Scouts Am.; pres. Colo. State U. Research Found., 1955; bd. advisers Charles L. Davis Found., 1972—. Ralston Research fellow, 1950; Mayo Found. fellow, 1950; recipient Service award Colo. State U., 1977, award Colo. Cattle Feeders Assn., 1982. Fellow AAAS; mem. Internat. Acad. Pathologists, AVMA (rep. Agrl. Research Inst. 1973—), Sigma Xi, Phi Kappa Phi. Home: 1712 W Vine Dr Fort Collins CO 80521

JENSEN, SAM, lawyer; b. Blair, Nebr., Oct. 30, 1935; s. Soren K. and Frances (Beck) J.; m. Marilyn Heck, June 28, 1959; children—Soren R., Eric, Dana. B.A., U. Nebr., 1957, J.D., 1961. Bar: Nebr. 1961. Mem. firm Smith Bros., Lexington, Nebr., 1961-63, Swarr, May, Smith and Andersen, Omaha, 1963-83, Erickson & Sederstrom, P.C., 1983—; v.p. bd. dirs. Omaha Public Power Dist., 1979-81; chmn. Nebr. Coordinating Commn. for Postsecondary Edn., 1976-78. Del. Nat. Republican Conv., 1960; mem. Nebr. Rep. Central Com., 1968-70, Regents Commn. Urban U., U. Nebr., Omaha; chmn. Task Force on Higher Edn. Recipient Disting. Service award U. Nebr., 1981. Mem. Omaha Bar Assn. (past exec. com.), Nebr. Bar Assn. (chmn. com. public relations 1973-76), Am. Bar Assn., U. Nebr. Alumni Assn. (pres. 1976-78), Beta Theta Pi, Phi Delta Phi. Clubs: Rotary, Omaha, Racquet. Office: One Merrill Lynch Plaza 10330 Regency Pkwy Dr Omaha NE 68114

JENSH, RONALD PAUL, anatomist, educator; b. N.Y.C., June 14, 1938; s. Werber G. and Dorothy (Hensle) J.; m. Ruth Eleanor Dobson, Aug. 18, 1962; children: Victoria Lynn, Elizabeth W. B.A., Bucknell U., 1960, M.A., 1962; Ph.D., Jefferson Med. Coll., 1966. Instr. in anatomy Thomas Jefferson U., Phila., 1966-68, assoc. in radiology, 1966-68, asst. prof. radiology and anatomy, 1968-74, assoc. prof. radiology and anatomy, 1974-82, prof., 1982—, head anatomy div. Coll. Allied Health Scis., 1975—, co-dir. pre-doctoral tng. program, 1971—; mem. staff Op. Concern Inc., Cherry Hill, N.J., 1970-72; cons. reproductive biology Bio-Search Inc., Argus Research Lab. Inc., Ortho Research Found. Contbr. articles to sci. jours. Mem. task force com. on communications S. Jersey Methodist Conf., 1974-80; chmn. Learning Resources Ctr., Haddonfield United Meth. Ch. (N.J.), 1976-79. Recipient Christian R. and Mary F. Lindback Found. Disting. Teaching award, 1973; NIH grantee. Mem. Am. Soc. Zoologists, N.Y. Acad. Scis., AAAS, Teratology Soc., Behavioral Teratology Soc., Am. Assn. Anatomists, Soc. Am. Mus. Natural History, Inst. Social Ethics and Life Scis., Sigma Xi, Psi Chi, Phi Sigma. Home: 230 E Park Ave Haddonfield NJ 08033 Office: 561 Jefferson Alumni Hall 1020 Locust St Philadelphia PA 19107

JENSIK, ROBERT JOSEPH, thoracic surgeon; b. Chgo., Sept. 15, 1915; s. William Paul and Marie Louise (Eck) J.; m. Florence M. Hassebrook, Oct. 25, 1941; children: Stephen Carl, Robert Ross. B.S., U. Ill., 1936, M.S., 1938, M.D., 1939. Intern Milw. County Gen. Hosp., 1938-39; resident in pathology U. Ill. Hosps., 1939-40, 42-44, resident in surgery, 1939-40, 48, St. Joseph's Hosp., Chgo., 1946-48; preceptorship Willard Van Hazel, 1944-47, 49-54; resident in Tb Rockford (Ill.) Mcpl. Tb Hosp., 1941-42; practice medicine specializing in thoracic surgery, Chgo., 1944—; pres. med. staff Rush-Presbyn.-St. Luke's Med. Center, 1981-83; clin. prof. U. Ill. Med. Sch., 1965—, Rush Med. Coll., 1969—; bd. dirs. Chgo. Lung Assn. Author articles in field. Mem. Internat. Assn. Study Lung Cancer, Am. Assn. Thoracic Surgery, Am. Coll. Chest Physicians, A.C.S., AMA, Soc. Thoracic Surgery, Warren H. Cole Soc., Chgo. Med. Soc., Chgo. Surg. Soc., Inst. Medicine Chgo., Chest Club. Club: Medinah Country. Home: 67 Briarwood Ln Oak Brook IL 60521 Office: 1725 W Harrison St Chicago IL 60612

JENSON, JON EBERDT, association executive; b. Madison, Wis., Aug. 1, 1934; s. Theodore Joel and Gertrude Beatrice (Edberdt) J.; m. Jeannette Marie Hasman, May 1, 1976; children: James, Peter. B.S., U. Wis., 1956; postgrad., Goethe U., Frankfort, W. Ger., 1956; diploma, U. Cologne, W. Ger., 1957. From staff rep. to dir. mktg. and tech. services Forging Industry Assn., Cleve., 1959-75; exec. v.p., sec. Am. Metal Stamping Assn., Cleve., 1975-80, pres., 1980—; exec. dir., sec. Forging Industry Ednl. and Research Found., Cleve., 1967-75; lectr. N.Y. U., 1973-75. Author: Forging Industry Handbook, 1966; editor: Metal Stamping mag, 1975—. Bd. regents Insts. Orgn. Mgmt., U.S. C. of C., 1977—, vice chmn., 1982, chmn., 1983; Mem. bd. regents Marycrest Sch., Independence, Ohio, 1979—. Served with USNR, 1958-59. Rotary Internat. fellow, 1956. Mem. Am. Soc. Assn. Execs., Cleve. Soc. Assn. Execs. Clubs: Capitol Hill, Cleve. Athletic. Home: 5700 Brookside Rd Independence OH 44131 Office: 27027 Chardon Rd Richmond Heights OH 44143

JENSON, PAUL GERHARD, coll. pres.; b. Milan, Minn., June 27, 1925; s. Canute T. and Emma (Rohne) J.; m. Elizabeth Ann Dybdal, Aug. 24, 1947; children—Thomas Dybdal, John Jacob, Paula Gay, Brian Dean, Richard Asle. B.A., Luther Coll., 1948; M.A., U. Minn., 1951, Ph.D., 1955. Research asst., teaching asst., jr. student personnel worker U. Minn., 1950-53; research asso. Bur. Instl. Research, 1961-62; instr., prof., chmn. dept. psychology Macalester Coll., St. Paul, 1953-64; asso. leadership tng. project N. Central Assn. Colls. and Secondary Schs., 1957-58, cons., examiner, 1958—, coordinator, dir., dir. workshops in higher edn. com. liberal arts edn., 1959-64; v.p. acad. affairs Temple Buell Coll., Denver, 1964-71; v.p. acad. affairs, dean faculty, prof. psychology Colby Coll., Waterville, Maine, 1971-80; pres. Thomas Coll., Waterville, 1980—. Served with USAAF, 1943-46. Research grantee U.S. Office Edn., 1964. Mem. Am. Psychol. Assn., Am. Conf. Acad. Deans (dir., chmn. 1979), Assn. Am. Colls. (dir.) Home: Webber Pond Rd Vassalboro ME 04989

JENSON, SHERMAN MILTON, insurance executive; b. Berthold, N.D., Jan. 15, 1920; s. Canute T. and Emma (Rohne) J.; m. Mary G. Blaul, Oct. 14, 1948; 1 dau., Jennifer Ann. B.A., Luther Coll., 1941; diploma bus. adminstrn., LaSalle U., 1948. Chemist, Solvay Process Co., Hopewell, Va., 1941-43; pharm. salesman Lakeside Labs., St. Paul, 1946-47; regional group mgr. Minn. Mut. Life Ins. Co., Chgo., 1947-55; v.p. group Am. United Life Ins. Co., Indpls., 1955-69; gen. mgr. group div. Bankers Life & Casualty Co., Chgo., 1969-73; pres., chief exec. officer, chmn. exec. com. Nat. Investors Life Ins. Co., Little Rock, 1973-83, pres. emeritus, 1983—; v.p. Baldwin United Corp.; dir., chmn. bd., pres. NOR Securities Co., 1975-83; dir., chmn. bd., pres., mem. exec. com. Nat. Investors Pension Ins. Co., 1978-83. Served with USNR, 1943-46. Clubs: Little Rock, Capital, Pleasant Valley Country. Home: 11900 Fairway Dr Little Rock AR 72212 Office: Nat Investors Life Bldg Little Rock AR 72201

JENSON, THEODORE JOEL, educator; b. New Richmond, Wis., Oct. 9, 1905; s. John Gabriel and Tilla (Johnson) J.; m. Gertrude Beatrice Eberdt, June 7, 1930; children: Jon Eberdt, Karen Ann (Mrs. Daniel M. Voecks). Diploma, Wis. State Coll., River Falls, 1926; Ph.B., U. Chgo., 1928; M.S., U. Wis., 1930, Ph.D., 1952. Student sec. YMCA, 1928-30; supervising prin. schs., Wis., 1930-34, supt. schs., Delavan, Wis., 1934-40, Fond du Lac, 1940-46, Shorewood, Wis., 1946-57; instr. Wis. State Coll., Milw., summers 1953-54; cons., adviser Internat. Edn. Service, Hesse, Germany, 1954; lectr. U. Wis., 1954, instr., summer 1955; prof. edn. Ohio State U., 1957-62, chmn. dept., 1962-65; prof. Coll. Edn. Bowling Green (Ohio) State U., 1965-73, dean, 1965-71, trustee prof., 1971-73, prof. emeritus, 1973—; also dir. Anderson Center for Personal Devel.; arbitor, cons., lectr., mediator, researcher, 1973—; prof. U. So. Calif., summer 1961. Co-author: Educational Administration: The Secondary School, 1961, Elementary School Administration, 1963, Practice and Theory in Educational Administration, 1963, also articles. Del. White House Conf. on Edn.; Active Boy Scouts Am. Recipient Distinguished Alumnus award U. Wis.-River Falls, 1974. Mem. Am. Assn. Sch. Adminstrs., Am. Ednl. Research Assn., NEA, Nat. Soc. Study Edn., Ohio Sch. Adminstrs., Wis. Sch. Adminstrs. (past pres.), Classroom Tchrs. Assn., NCCJ, Ohio, Wis. edn. assns., Am. Acad. Polit. and Social Sci., Columbus Schoolmasters Club, Ohio Council Advancement Ednl. Adminstrn. (chmn.), Kappa Delta Pi, Phi Kappa Phi, Phi Delta Kappa. Clubs: Rotarian., Conservation (Fond du Lac, Wis.). Edn. auditorium at Bowling Green State U. named in his honor, 1983. Home: 325 Palo Verde Dr Leesburg FL 32748 *Early in my life I was taught to be a problem solver rather than a problem maker. I have always enjoyed the challenge and opportunities to creatively arrive at solutions to problems. I have a strong conviction that humaneness and people should have top priority.*

JENTES, WILLIAM ROBERT, lawyer; b. Kalamazoo, Mich., Oct. 2, 1932; s. Tedrel Krantz and Gretchen Elizabeth (Hawk) J.; m. Janet Sue Oberg, Sept. 15, 1956; 1 dau., Justine Devereaux. A.B., U. Mich., 1953, J.D., 1956; postgrad., Universite de Grenoble, France, 1956-57. Bar: Ill. 1957. Assoc Kirkland & Ellis, Chgo., 1957-62, ptnr., 1962—, firm com., 1975—; lectr. U. Chgo. Law Sch., 1980—, numerous orgns. Trustee Orchestral Assn. Chgo., 1982, Latin Sch., Chgo., 1981—; v.p. Chgo. Opera Theater, 1980—; sustaining fellow Art Inst. Chgo., 1981—. Served with USN, 1953-55. Recipient Fulbright scholar Universite de Grenoble, 1956-57. Mem. ABA, Bar Assn. Seventh Cir., Econ. Club Chgo., Order of Coif, Phi Beta Kappa. Clubs: Saddle and Cycle, Mid-Am. Home: 1500 N Lake Shore Dr Apt 3-c Chicago Il 60610 Office: Kirkland & Ellis Suite 5800 200 E Randolph Il 60601

JENTZ, GAYLORD ADAIR, lawyer, educator; b. Beloit, Wis., Aug. 7, 1931; s. Merlyn Adair and Delva (Mullen) J.; m. JoAnn Mary Hornung, Aug. 6, 1955; children: Katherine Ann, Gary Adair, Loretta Ann, Rory Adair. B.A., U. Wis., 1953, J.D., 1957, M.B.A., 1958. Bar: Wis. 1957. Pvt. practice law, Madison, 1957-58; from instr. to asso. prof. bus. law U. Okla., 1958-65; vis. instr. to vis. prof. U. Wis. Law Sch., summers 1957-65; asso. prof. to prof. U. Tex., Austin, 1965-68, prof., 1968—, Herbert D. Kelleher prof. bus. law, 1982—, chmn. gen. bus. dept., 1968-74, 80—. Author: (with others) Business Law Text and Cases, 2d edit, 1968, Tex. Uniform Comml. Code, 1967, rev. edit., 1975, Business Law; Text and Cases, 1978, West's Business Law: Text and Cases, 2d edit., 1983; author: West's Business Law: Alternate UCC Comprehensive Edition, 1984; contbr. articles to profl. jours.; dep. editor: Social Sci. Quar, 1966-82; editorial staff: Am. Bus. Law Jour, 1967-69; editor in chief, 1969-74; adv. editor, 1974—. Served with AUS, 1953-55. Recipient Outstanding Tchr. award Tex. U. Coll. Bus., 1967, Jack G. Taylor Teaching Excellence award, 1971, Joe D. Beasley Grad. Teaching Excellence award, 1978, CBA Found. Adv. Council award, 1979, Grad. Bus. Council Outstanding Grad. Bus. Prof. award, 1980, James C. Scorboro Meml. award for outstanding Leadership in Banking Edn. Colo. Grad. Sch. Banking, 1983. Mem. Southwestern Fedn. Adminstrv. Disciplines (v.p. 1979-80, pres. 1980-81), Am. Arbitration Assn. (nat. panel 1966—), Am. Bus. Law Assn. (pres. 1971-72, Faculty award of excellence 1981), So. Bus. Law Assn. (pres. 1967), Tex. Assn. Coll. Tchrs. (pres. Austin chpt. 1967-68, exec. com. 1969-70, state pres. 1971-72), Wis. Bar Assn., Omicron Delta Kappa, Phi Kappa Phi. (pres. 1983-84). Home: 4106 North Hills Dr Austin TX 78731 Office: Coll Bus Adminstrn BEB600 Univ Texas Austin TX 78712 *I have always considered the primary goal of an academician to be the development of a student's mind. Although research and service are essential and complement this primary goal, the real essence of learning is the result of excellence in teaching. A good teacher must stimulate, encourage, give constructive criticism, and even pressure the student to develop his or her capabilities. Regardless of the difficulty imposed, fairness to all students commands respect, and respect in turn results in learning.*

JENZANO, ANTHONY FRANCIS, planetarium director; b. Phila., May 20, 1919; s. Joseph and Theresa (Monzo) J.; m. Myrtle E. Packer, Nov. 12, 1941; children: Anthony Francis, Carol. Grad., Marine Elec. Sch., Phila., 1942, USN Gun Fire Control Sch., 1943, USN Advanced Gun Fire Control Sch., 1943; student, Capitol Radio Engring. Inst., 1948-51. Head technician Fels Planetarium, Phila., 1946-49; chief technician Morehead Planetarium, U. N.C., 1949-51, mgr. planetarium, art galleries and sci. exhibit areas, 1951-60, planetarium dir., 1960-81; counselor U.S. and Can. Zeiss Planetarium, 1981—; engaged in complete dismantlement and reassembly Fels Zeiss Planetarium instrument, 1948, Morehead Zeiss Planetarium instrument, 1949, 59, Model VI, 1969; U.S. adviser to architect and contractors for London (Eng.) Planetarium, 1956-57; cons. Buhl Planetarium console, 1957, Atlanta Planetarium, 1968; Dir. Celestial Tng. Program for U.S. Mercury, Gemini, Apollo, Skylab, Apollo-Soyuz, and Space Shuttle Astronauts, 1960—. State dir. N.C. Sci. Fairs, 1961-63; Instnl. rep. Boy Scouts Am. Served with USNR, 1943-45. Recipient U.S. Astronaut Super Snoopy award for profl. excellence and support, 1974. Mem. Am. Assn. Mus., Assn. Astronomy Educators, Pacific Planetarium Assn., Southeastern Planetarium Assn., Great Lakes Planetarium Assn., N.C. Acad. Scis., Am. Astron. Soc. (asso.), Mid-Atlantic Planetarium Soc., Internat. Planetarium Soc., Planetarium Assn. Can. Home: 37 Oakwood Dr Chapel Hill NC 27514

JEPPESEN, MYRON ALTON, educator; b. Logan, Utah, Oct. 28, 1905; s. Charles R. and Matilda (Jensen) J.; m. Madeleine Caron, June 25, 1939; children—Martha (Mrs. Peter Meyer), Matilda (Mrs. John Newton), Mary (Mrs. Ryan Ostebo), Laura (Mrs. Daniel Stepner). B.S., U. Idaho, 1930; M.S., Pa. State U., 1932, Ph.D., 1936. Mem. faculty Bowdoin Coll., 1936—, prof. physics, 1948—, chmn. dept., 1964-72; lectr., vis. prof. Stanford, 1947-49; research fellow physics U. Calif. at Berkeley, 1956-57; cons. in field, 1954—; Asso. program dir. grad. fellowships NSF, 1963-64. Author articles optics, spectroscopy, solid state physics. Guggenheim fellow, 1956-57. Fellow AAAS, Am. Optical Soc., Am. Phys. Soc.; mem. Am. Assn. Physics Tchrs. Home: Sinclair ME 04779

JEPPSON, JAY HERALD, securities executive; b. Brigham, Utah, Aug. 21, 1926; s. Jay Carl and Zola (Call) J.; m. Lou Stoddard, Sept. 26, 1947; children: JoAnn, Barbara, David Jay. B.S., Brigham Young U., 1949, U. Idaho, 1955; postgrad., Fresno State Coll., 1966. Trust officer Bank of Am., 1955-66; v.p. Mich. Nat. Bank, 1966-70; v.p., sr. trust officer Zions 1st Nat. Bank, Salt Lake City, 1970-83, Twin Falls Bank & Trust, Twin Falls, Idaho, 1976-83, Alaska Nat. Bank, Anchorage, 1978-83; v.p., trust officer Bank of Calif., San Francisco, 1975-83; pres. Pacific Trading Co., Bountiful, Utah, 1983—; trust cons., 1976; dir. O.C. Tanner Co., Wycoff Co.; lectr. U. Utah; cons. Utah Fruit Growers. Author: Pyramid Lost, 1958. Park commr. Port Huron, Mich.) Twp., 1967-70; fin. advisor City of Bountiful. Served to lt. comdr. USNR, 1943-46, 51-53. Decorated Bronze Star, Meritorious Service medal. Mem. San Joaquin Trust Co. Assn., Utah Trust Assn. Am. (exec. com. trust div. 1973-74, 75-78), Utah (pres. trust div. 1974) Bankers Assn. Mem. Ch. of Jesus Christ of Latter-day Saints. Clubs: Port Huron Country; University (Salt Lake City). Home: 1693 Homalo Ct Anchorage AK 99504 Office: PO Box 61 Bountiful UT 84010

JEPSEN, ROGER WILLIAM, U.S. senator; b. Cedar Falls, Iowa, Dec. 23, 1928; s. Ernest and Esther (Sorensen) J.; m. Dee Ann Delaney, Sept. 26, 1958; children: Jeffrey, Ann, Craig, Linda, Deborah, Coy. B.S., Ariz. State U., 1950, M.A., 1953. Br. mgr. Conn. Gen. Life Ins. Co., Davenport, Iowa, 1956-72; exec. v.p. Agridustrial Electronics Co., Bettendorf, Iowa, 1973-76; pres. H.E.P. Mktg. Co., Davenport, 1976-78; mem. Iowa Senate, 1967-69; lt. gov., State of Iowa, 1969-73; mem. U.S. Senate from Iowa, 1979—; chmn. Nat. Orgn. Lt. Govs., 1971-72; instr. mktg. U. No. Iowa, 1955; Supr. Scott County, Iowa, 1962-66. Served with U.S. Army, 1946-47. Mem. Nat. Assn. Life Underwriters, Gen. Agts. and Mgrs. Assn., Assn. Mentally Retarded, Scott County Y (dir.), Res. Officers Assn. Republican. Clubs: Shriners, Moose, Jesters. Office: US Senate Washington DC 20510

JEPSON, HANS GODFREY, investment company executive; b. Spencer, W.Va., July 24, 1936; s. Hans G. and Juanita Imogene (Shears) J.; m. Barbara Gayle Keller, Dec. 3, 1966. A.B. magna cum laude, Princeton U., 1958. Exec. editor Arnold Bernhard & Co., N.Y.C., 1961-68; v.p., research dir. Dominick & Dominick, Inc., N.Y.C., 1968-70; dir., sr. v.p., research dir. Alliance Capital Mgmt. Corp., N.Y.C., 1970-76; exec. v.p., chief investment officer U.S. Trust Co. N.Y., N.Y.C., 1976-80; dir., pres. Valquest Assos., Inc., N.Y.C., 1980—; pres. Lafayette Enterprises, Inc., N.Y.C., 1983—; dir. PRN Holdings, Inc., United Newspapers, Inc., Kinderhill Corp., Ultrafin Internat. Corp. Bd. dirs. J. Aron Charitable Found., Bark Peking Found. Served to 2d lt. U.S. Army, 1958-59. Mem. Fin. Analysts Fedn., N.Y. Soc. Security Analysts. Clubs: Dial, Princeton (N.Y.C.). Home: 11 Fifth Ave New York NY 10003 Office: 126 E 56th St New York NY 10022

JERGER, EDWARD WILLIAM, university dean, mechanical engineer; b. Milw., Mar. 13, 1922; s. Nickolaus and Ann (Huber) J.; m. Dorothy Marie Post, Aug. 2, 1944 (dec. 1981); children: Betty Ann (Mrs. Frank Tinus), Barbara Lee (Mrs. Greg Guthrie); m. Elizabeth Cordiner Sweitzer, Mar. 27, 1982. B.S. in Mech. Engring, Marquette U., 1946; M.S., U. Wis., 1948; Ph.D., Iowa State U., 1951. Registered profl. engr., Iowa, Ind. Process engr. Wis. Malting Co., Manitowoc, 1946-47; asst. prof. mech. engring. Iowa State U., 1948-55; asso. prof. mech. engring. U. Notre Dame, 1955-61, prof., head mech. engring., 1961-68, asso. dean, 1968-82, prof. mech. engring., 1982—; cons. U. Madre De Maestra Santiago, Dominican Republic, 1965-71. Served with USAAF, 1943-46. Mem. ASME, Am. Soc. Engring. Edn., Nat. Soc. Profl. Engrs., Internat. Assn. Housing Sci. (dir.), Nat. Fire Protection Assn., Internat. Assn. Arson Investigators, Sigma Xi, Phi Kappa Phi, Pi Tau Sigma (nat. v.p. 1969-74, pres. 1974-78), Tau Beta Pi. Home: 16197 Barryknoll Way Granger IN 46530 35 Lawton Dr Hilton Head Island SC 29928 Office: College Engineering Univ Notre Dame Notre Dame IN 46556

JERISON, MEYER, educator; b. Bialystok, Poland, Nov. 28, 1922; came to U.S., 1929, naturalized, 1933; s. Elia Israel and Esther (Rasky) J.; m. Miriam Schwartz, Aug. 5, 1945; children—Michael, David. B.S., Coll. City N.Y., 1943; M.S., Brown U., 1947; Ph.D., U. Mich., 1950. Physicist NACA, 1944-46; lectr. Case Inst. Tech., 1945-46; research asso. U. Ill. at Urbana, 1949-51; research engr. Lockheed Aircraft Corp., 1952; asst. prof. Purdue U., 1951-56, asso. prof., 1956-60, prof., 1960—, chmn. div. math. scis., 1969-75. Author: (with Leonard Gillman) Rings of Continuous Functions, 1960. Mem. Am. Math. Soc. (editor bull 1980—), AAUP, Math. Assn. Am. (com. on undergrad. program in math. 1968-71, gov. 1981—), Phi Beta Kappa, Sigma Xi. Home: 147 Pathway Ln West Lafayette IN 47906

JERNIGAN, KENNETH, association executive; b. Detroit, Nov. 13, 1926; s. Jesse Clayton and Novella (Trail) J.; m. Anna Katherine Evans, Apr. 20, 1951. B.S., Tenn. Tech. U., 1948; M.A., George Peabody Coll. for Tchrs., 1949; H.H.D., Coe Coll., 1968; LL.D., Seton Hall U., 1974; H.H.D., Drake U., 1975. Tchr. Sch. for Blind, Nashville, 1949-53; mem. faculty Oakland (Calif.) Orientation Center for Blind, 1953-58; dir. Iowa Commn. for Blind, Des Moines, 1958-78; pres. Nat. Fedn. Blind, Des Moines, 1968—; exec. dir. Am. Brotherhood for Blind, 1978—. Recipient Capt. Charles W. Browne award to outstanding blind student in nation, 1949; Newel Perry award for greatest contribution to advancement of gen. welfare blind, 1960; Spl. award for work in rehab. of blind U.S. Pres., 1968. Mem. Internat. Platform Assn., Nat. Rehab. Assn. Home: 4206 Euclid Ave Baltimore MD 21229 Office: 1800 Johnson St Baltimore MD 21230

JEROME, ALBERT DAVID, broadcasting station executive; b. N.Y.C., July 9, 1942; s. Jerold Eli and Evelyn Pauline (Levy) J.; m. Michele Braverman, Nov. 1, 1980; children: Gregory A., Kenneth E., Zachary B. A.B., Cornell U., 1964; M.B.A., N.Y. U., 1966. With Am. Broadcasting Cos., Inc., 1966-68; account exec. Sta. WABC-TV, 1966-68, Sta. WCBS-TV, N.Y.C., 1968-69, automotive sales mgr., 1969-70, nat. sales mgr., 1970-71; Eastern sales mgr. Sta. WBBM-TV, Chgo., 1971-72; gen. sales mgr. Sta. WCAU-TV, 1972-74; with Nat. Broadcasting Co., 1974—; nat. sales mgr. Sta. WMAQ-TV, Chgo., 1975-76, dir. sales, 1976-77, sta. mgr., 1977-80; gen. mgr. Sta. WNBC-TV, N.Y.C., 1980-82; pres. NBC TV Stas. Div., N.Y.C., 1982—. Mem. Cornell U. Alumni Assn.

JEROME, FREDERICK LOUIS, public relations executive, journalist; b. N.Y.C., Feb. 10, 1939; s. Victor Jeremy and Alice Rose (Hamburger) J.; m. Jocelyn Beatrice Boyd, May 1, 1963; children: Rebecca, Mark, Daniel. B.A. magna cum laude, CCNY, 1960. Staff writer Wilmington Star-News (N.C.), 1961, Augusta Herald (Ga.), 1962, AP, San Francisco, 1967-71; assoc. editor Pub. Employees Press, N.Y.C., 1963; editorial asst. Newsweek mag., N.Y.C., 1964-66; pub. relations writer St. Lukes Hosp., N.Y.C., 1975; pub. info. dir. Scientists Inst. Pub. Info., N.Y.C., 1975—, dir. media resource service, 1980—; lectr. environ. health SUNY-Empire State Coll., 1975; adj. prof. grad. div. SUNY-Stony Brook, 1976; adj. prof. journalism N.Y.U.; prof. journalism Sch. Visual Arts; adj. prof. CUNY; mem. adv. bd. Ctr. Health Studies, 1973-74; mem. adv. com. occupational safety and health project U. Calif.-Berkeley, 1974; cons. Ctr. Biomed. Edn. CUNY, 1983—; chmn. task force on society at large NRC, 1984—. Author articles for profl. and gen. publs.; assoc. editor: Environment mag.; adv. bd.: Tech. Rev. Mem. Nat. Assn. Sci. Writers, Pub. Relations Soc. Am., AAAS, Phi Beta Kappa. Home: 230 W 79th St New York NY 10024 Office: 355 Lexington Ave New York NY 10017

JEROME, JAMES ALEXANDER, justice Federal Court Canada; b. Kingston, Ont., Can., Mar. 4, 1933; s. Joseph Leonard and Phyllis (Devlin) J.; m. Barry Karen Hodgins, June 7, 1958; children: Mary Louise, William Paul, James Leonard, Joseph Alexander, Megan Phyllis. B.A., U. Toronto, 1954; LL.B., Osgoode Hall, 1958. Bar: Ont. Mem. House of Commons for Sudbury, Ont., 1968—, speaker, 1974-79; parliamentary sec. to pres. Privy Council, 1970-76; Queen's Counsel, 1976-80; asso. chief justice Fed. Ct. Can., 1981—; mem. Queen's Privy Council for Can., 1981—. Pres. Sudbury Young Liberal Assn., 1960-65; alderman Sudbury City Council, from 1965; chmn. Heart Fund Drive Dist. of Sudbury, 1964; pres. Lo-Ellen Park Community Assn., 1962-65; treas. Sudbury Indsl. Commn., 1965-66. Mem. Commonwealth Parliamentary Assn. (pres. 1976—). Roman Catholic. Office: Room 88 Fed Ct Can Supreme Ct Can Bldg Ottawa ON K1A 0H9 Canada

JEROME, JOSEPH WALTER, mathematics educator; b. Phila., June 7, 1939; s. Joseph Walter and Hermena Josephine (Ostertag) J.; m. Doreen Jean Funk, Apr. 8, 1967; children: Jon, Peter. B.S. in Physics, St. Joseph's U., 1961; M.S., Purdue U., 1963, Ph.D., 1966. Vis. asst. prof. U. Wis., Madison, 1966-68; asst. prof. Case Western Res. U., Cleve., 1968-70; faculty Northwestern U., Evanston, Ill., 1970—, assoc. prof., 1972, prof. math., 1976—; vis. fellow Oxford (Eng.) U., 1974-75; vis. prof. U. Tex., Austin, 1978-79; cons. Bell Labs., N.J., 1981—, vis. scientist, 1982-83. Contbr. articles to jours.; author: (with S. Fisher) Springer Lecture Series Math. 479, 1975, Approximation of Nonlinear Evolution Systems, 1983. Brit. Sci. Council sr. vis. fellow Oxford, 1974-75; NSF research grantee, 1970—. Mem. Am. Math. Soc., Soc. for Indsl. and Applied Math. Roman Catholic. Home: 2080 Drury Ln Northfield IL 60093 Office: 2033 Sheridan Rd Evanston IL 60201

JEROME, NORGE WINIFRED, nutritionist, anthropologist; b. Grenada, W.I., Nov. 3, 1930; came to U.S., 1956, naturalized, 1973; d. McManus Israel and Evelyn Mary (Grant) J. B.S. magna cum laude, Howard U., 1960; M.S., U. Wis., 1962, Ph.D., 1967. Asst. prof. U. Kans. Med. Sch., 1967-72, asso. prof., 1972-78, prof., 1978—, dir. community nutrition div., 1981—; dir. ednl. resource centers U. Kans. Med. Center, 1974-77, head community nutrition labs., 1978—; cons. Children's TV Workshop, 1974-77; chairperson adv. bd. Teenage

Parents Center, 1971-75; mem. planning and budget council, children and family sers. United Community Services, 1971-80; mem. panel on nutrition edn. White House Conf. on Food, Nutrition and Health, 1969; mem. bd. dirs., health care com. Prime Health, 1976-79; bd. dirs. Council on Children, Media and Merchandising, Washington, 1977-80; mem. consumer edn. task force Mid-Am. Health Systems Agy., 1977-79; commr. N.Am. working group Commn. Anthropology Food and Food Habits, Internat. Union Anthrop. and Ethnol. Scis., 1979-80; chmn. com. nutritional anthropology Internat. Union Nutritional Scis., 1979-80; mem. lipid metabolism adv. com. NIH, 1978-80; mem. nat. adv. panel multi-media campaign to improve children's diet U.S. Dept. Agr., 1979—. Sr. author: Nutritional Anthropology, 1980; asso. editor: Jour. Nutrition Edn, 1971-77; adv. council, 1977-80; editor: Nutritional Anthropology Communicator, 1974-77; editorial adv. bd.: Med. Anthropology: Cross Cultural Studies in Health and Illness, 1976—; adv. bd.: Internat. Jour. Nutrition Planning, 1977—, Nutrition and Cancer: An Internat. Jour, 1978—, Jour. Nutrition and Behavior, 1981—; contbr. articles to profl. jours. Mem. com. man-food systems NRC, 1980—; Bd. dirs. Kansas City Urban League, 1969-77, Crittenton Center, Kansas City, Mo., 1979-80; mem. awards com. in nutrition edn. Met. Life Found., 1983—. Decorated Dau. Brit. Empire.; Recipient First Higuchi/Irvin Youngberg Research Achievement award U. Kans., 1982. Fellow Am. Anthrop. Assn. (chairperson com. on nutritional anthropology 1974-77, founder com. nutritional anthropology 1974), Soc. Applied Anthropology; mem. Am. Public Health Assn. (food and nutrition council 1975-78, governing council 1982—), Am. Inst. Nutrition, Am. Soc. Clin. Nutrition, Soc. Med. Anthropology, Am. Men and Women of Sci., Nat. Acad. Scis. (world food and nutrition study panel), N.Y. Acad. Scis., Inst. Food Technologists, Am. Dietetic Assn., Club of Rome (U.S. asso.). Home: 14402 W 68th St Shawnee KS 66216 Office: 39th St and Rainbow St Kansas City KS 66103 *Creative blending appears to have been the key for me—the melding of multiple traditions and styles, the melding of philosophies and strategies, and most importantly, the melding of ancient and modern thought and practices.*

JERRARD, RICHARD PATTERSON, educator; b. Evanston, Ill., July 23, 1925; s. Leigh Patterson and Lillian (Taylor) J.; m. Margot Leon Poritsky, June 23, 1951; children—Laura, Leigh, Robert. B.S., U. Wis., 1949, M.S., 1950; Ph.D., U. Mich., 1957. Devel. engr. Gen. Electric Co., Schenectady, 1950-54; instr. U. Mich., 1956-57; mathematician Bell Telephone Labs., Whippany, N.J., 1957-58; from asst. prof. to prof. math. U. Ill., Urbana, 1958—; Fellow U. Warwick (Eng.), 1965-66, 77, U. Cambridge, 1972-73. Served with USAAF, 1943-45. Prin. investigator for NSF grants for research in differential geometry, 1964-70. Mem. Am. Math. Soc., Math. Assn. Am., Sigma Xi. Home: 507 W Indiana St Urbana IL 61801

JERRITTS, STEPHEN G., computer company executive; b. New Brunswick, N.J., Sept. 14, 1925; s. Steve and Anna (Kovacs) J.; m. Audrey Virginia Smith, June 1948; children: Marsha Carol, Robert Stephen, Linda Ann; m. Ewa Elizabet Rydell-Vejlans, Nov. 5, 1966; 1 son, Carl Stephen. Student, Union Coll., 1943-44; B.M.E., Rensselaer Poly. Inst., 1947, M.S., 1948. With IBM, various locations, 1949-58, IBM World Trade, N.Y.C., 1958-67, Bull Gen. Electric div. Gen. Electric, France, 1967-70, merged into Honeywell Bull, 1970-74; v.p., mng. dir. Honeywell Info. Systems Ltd., London, 1974-76; group v.p. U.S. Info. Systems, Boston, 1977-80; pres., chief operating officer dir. Honeywell Info. Systems, Mpls., 1980-82; pres., chief operating officer, dir. Lee Data Corp., 1983—; dir. First Bank, Mpls. Bd. dirs. Guthrie Theatre, 1980, Charles Babbage Inst., 1980, Minn. Orch., 1982—; trustee Rensselaer Poly. Inst., 1980—. Served with USNR, 1943-46. Mem. Computer Bus. Equipment Mfrs. (dir. 1979-82), Assoc. Industries Mass. (dir. 1978-80). Club: Wellesley (Mass.) Country. Home: 2480 Lafayette Rd Wayzata MN 55391 Office: Honeywell Info Systems Inc Honeywell Plaza Minneapolis MN 55408

JERRY, ROBERT HOWARD, educator; b. Brazil, Ind., July 25, 1923; s. Floyd W. and Zetta (Hoffman) J.; m. Marjorie O. Collings, July 23, 1950; children: Robert Howard II, E. Clair. B.S., Ind. State U., 1949, M.S., 1951; Ed.D., Ind. U., 1963; postgrad., Colo. U., 1951. Tchr. elem. sch., Fowler, Ind., 1949-50, high sch., Delphi, Ind., 1951-57; prin. Covington (Ind.) High Sch., 1957-60; supt. Worthington (Ind.) Schs., 1961-63; mem. faculty Ind. State U., Terre Haute, 1963—, prof. edn., 1974—; Dep. state supt. public instrn., Ind., 1967-69. Co-author: Leagal Rights and Responsibilities of Indiana Teachers. Served with USNR, 1943-46. Mem. Am. Assn. Sch. Adminstrs., Nat. Assn. Secondary Sch. Prins., Blue Key, Theta Alpha Psi, Alpha Phi, Pi Gamma Mu, Phi Delta Kappa, Phi Delta Theta. Elder, Christian Ch. Clubs: Exchange (pres. 1973-74), Fathers (pres. 1972-73). Home: 2908 Crawford St Terre Haute IN 47803 *

JERVEY, HAROLD EDWARD, JR., association executive; b. Charleston, S.C., Dec. 3, 1920; s. Harold Edward and Stella (White) J.; m. Lillian Pearce Hair, July 13, 1946; children: Harold Edward, III, Nancy Middleton, Margaret Pearce, Harriett Beachum, Helen White, Charles Stewart, Lillian Hair. B.S., U. S.C., 1941; M.D., Med. U. S.C., 1949. Intern Greenville (S.C.) Gen. Hosp., 1949-50; house officer Bapt. Hosp., Columbia, S.C., 1951-54; gen. practice medicine, Columbia, 1951-74; acting head health facilities U. S.C., 1968-70, acting dir. health facility, 1975-77; asst. prof. Med. U. S.C., 1970-77; exec. dir.-sec. Fedn. State Med. Bd. U.S., Ft. Worth, 1978—; med. cons. S.C. Law Enforcement Agy., 1958-61, S.C. Vocat. Rehab. Dept., 1961-63, S.C. Indsl. Commn., 1963-68, S.C. Dept. Family Practice, 1971-74; med. adv. S.C. Gov. Health and Social Devel., 1973-75; vice-chmn. S.C. Bd. Med. Examiners, 1962-64; bd. dirs. Fedn. Assn. Health Regulatory Bds., 1977—; mem. adv. bd. Am. Bd. Med. Specialties, 1959-70; pres., chmn. bd. Ednl. Commn. Fgn. Med. Grads., 1978-80; past pres. Gen. Practitioners Club Central S.C., Columbia Med. Club. Author articles in field.; Contbg. editor: Med. Economics. Served to lt. comdr. USNR, World War II. Fellow Am. Acad. Family Practice; mem. AMA, Tex. Med. Assn., Tex. Acad. Family Practice, Tarrant County Med. Soc. Episcopalian. Office: 2630 West Freeway Suite 138 Fort Worth TX 76102

JERVIS, ROBERT, political science educator; b. N.Y.C., Apr. 30, 1940; s. Herman and Dorothy J.; m. Kathe Weil, June 19, 1967; children: Alexa, Lisa. B.A., Oberlin Coll., 1962; M.A., U. Calif., Berkeley, 1963, Ph.D., 1967. Asst. prof. govt. Harvard U., 1968-73, asso. prof., 1973-75; vis. asso. prof. polit. sci. Yale U., 1974-75; prof. polit. sci. UCLA, 1975-80, Columbia U., N.Y.C., 1980—; Lady Davis vis. prof. Hebrew U., Jerusalem, spring 1977. Author: Perception and Misperception in International Politics, The Madness beyond MAD; contbr. articles to profl. jours. Council Fgn. Relations fellow, 1970-71; Guggenheim fellow, 1978-79. Mem. Am. Polit. Sci. Assn., Internat. Studies Assn., AAAS. Democrat. Home: 1170 Fifth Ave New York NY 10029 Office: Dept Polit Sci Columbia U New York NY 10027

JERVIS, ROBERT E., chemistry educator; b. Toronto, Ont., Can., May 21, 1927; s. Bertram Charles and Mary Elizabeth (Gibbings) J.; m. Frances Jane (Jean) McCourt, Dec. 30, 1950; children: Ann K., Peter R. B.A., U. Toronto, 1949, M.A., 1950, Ph.D., 1952. Registered profl. engr., Ont. Research chemist Atomic Energy Can., Chalk River, 1952-58; prof. applied chemistry and chem. engring. U. Toronto, 1958—, dir. nuclear reactor, 1970—, asso. dean research faculty engring., 1974-78; vis. prof. radio chemistry U. Tokyo, 1965-66; vis. prof. Cambridge U., 1978, Nat. U. Malaysia, 1979; cons., dir. Chem. Engring. Research Cons., Ltd., Toronto. Co-author: Nuclear Methods of Crime Investigation; Contbr. profl. jours. Bd. dirs. Inter Varsity Christian Fellowship Can. Fellow Chem. Inst. Can., Indian Acad. Forensic Sci. (hon.), Royal Soc. Can. Home: 30 Chestergrove Crescent Agincourt ON M1W 1L4 Canada Office: Dept Chem Engring and Applied Chemistry U Toronto Toronto ON M5S 1A4 Canada *Applying science to community problems is of special interest to me because I see my science as a type of service. I am a religious man and like to think that my work is an expressive and integral part of my life of thought and faith.*

JESCHKE, CHANNING RENWICK, librarian; b. Buffalo, Dec. 28, 1927; s. William Marion and Vera Mabel (Voll) J.; m. Carol Louise Ahrens, June 24, 1955. B.A., Oberlin (Ohio) Coll., 1949; B.D., Yale U., 1952; Ph.D., U. Chgo., 1966; M.S., Columbia U., 1967. Ordained to ministry United Ch. Christ, 1952; chaplain, master Bible history Taft Sch., Watertown, Conn., 1952-55; minister N. Ill. synod Evang. and Ref. Ch., 1955-61; mem. library staff Union Theol. Sem., N.Y.C., 1961-66; asst. librarian, then librarian, also asst. prof., then asso. prof. theol. bibliography Berkeley Div. Sch., New Haven, 1966-71; librarian, asso. prof. Pitts Theology Library, Emory U., Atlanta, 1971-79, prof., 1979-83, Margaret A. Pitts prof., 1984—; program cons. higher edn. facilities program HEW. Assn. Schs. in U.S. and Can. study grantee, 1978-79. Author articles, revs., indexes, bibliographies. Mem. Am. Theol. Library Assn. (chmn. com. publ. 1974-75, dir. 1975-78), Meth. Librarians Fellowship, Hist. Soc. United Ch. Christ, Internat. Assn. Mission Studies. Home: 11 Prescott Walk NE Atlanta GA 30307 Office: Pitts Theology Library Emory U Atlanta GA 30322

JESINA, CARL LEE, drug store chain executive; b. Cedar Rapids, Iowa, Aug. 29, 1929; s. Frank and Faye (Sheldon) J.; m. Joan Atkinson, Dec. 27, 1957; children: Jenny Lee, Kenneth Frank. B.A. in Chemistry, U. Iowa, 1952, B.S. in Pharmacy, 1955; J.D., Georgetown U., 1960. Bar: Md. 1961, U.S. Supreme Ct. 1967; registered pharmacist, Iowa, Md., Ohio, Mich. Exec. v.p. Peoples Drug Stores, Inc., Washington, 1957-71; v.p., gen. counsel Superx Drug, Inc., Cin., 1971-75, Gray Drug Fair, Inc., Cleve., 1975—. Pres. Bd. Edn. Strongsville, Ohio, 1980—. Mem. ABA, Ohio Pharm. Assn. Republican. Home: 17631 Falling Leaves St Strongsville OH 44136 Office: Gray Drug Fair Inc 666 Euclid Ave Cleveland OH 44114

JESKE, HOWARD LEIGH, life insurance company executive; b. York, Nebr., Sept. 25, 1917; s. Charles W. and Sina (Hanna) J.; m. Bettyclaire Barton, Nov. 23, 1943; children: Vaughn C., Craig B., Lynn Ellen Jeske Braziel, Laurel Claire. A.B., Cornell Coll., Mt. Vernon, Iowa, 1940; LL.B., McGeorge Coll. Law, Sacramento, 1951. Bar: Calif. 1951. With Carnegie-Ill. Steel Corp., 1940-41; accountant Spreckels Sugar Co., Sacramento, 1946-51; practice law, Sacramento, 1952-53; with Calif.-Western States Life Ins. Co., Sacramento, 1954-82, v.p., gen. counsel, sec., 1968-79, dir., 1977-82, pres., chief exec. officer, 1979-82; pres., dir. Calif.-Western Securities Co., 1977-82; chmn. Nat. Pub. Service Ins. Co., Seattle, 1979-82; corp. cons. life ins., 1982—. Trustee, Sutter Community Hosps., Sacramento, 1983—. Served to capt. USAAF, 1942-45. Mem. Am., Calif. bar assns., Health Ins. Assn. Am. (dir. 1980-82). Republican. Club: Sutter (Sacramento). Home: 3421 E Curtis Park Dr Sacramento CA 95818

JESSE, MARY JANE, pediatric cardiologist, government administrator; b. Owensboro, Ky., Jan. 8, 1918; d. Joseph Preston and Ethel (May) J. A.B., Spalding Coll., 1939; M.D., Columbia U., 1959; D.Sc., Spalding Coll., 1980. With Young & Rubicam Advt., N.Y.C., 1947-54; faculty Columbia U. Coll. Physicians and Surgeons, 1960-70, U. Miami (Fla.) Sch. Medicine, from 1970; prin. investigator Specialized Center of Research in Atherosclerosis, Berenson prof. pediatric cardiology, 1973-76; dir. div. heart and vascular disease Nat. Heart, Lung and Blood Inst., NIH, Bethesda, Md., 1976-79; prof., vice chmn. dept. pediatrics and dept. medicine U. Miami, 1979—; v.p., exec. com. med. staff, pres.-elect U. Miami-Jackson Meml. Hosp. Med. Center.; mem. adv. bd. Cable Health Network. Contbr. numerous articles to med. publs. Fellow Am. Acad. Behavioural Sci.; mem. Am. Acad. Pediatrics, Am. Coll. Cardiology, Am. Pediatric Soc., Am. Heart Assn. (pres. 1982-83), Internat. Soc. and Fedn. Cardiologists (exec. com. council epidemiology). Democrat. Roman Catholic. Home: 1 Grove Isle Apt 205 Coconut Grove FL 33133 *Accept failure only as a stepping-stone to success. I have failed often, and have enjoyed many successes from those learning experiences. It continues to happen.*

JESSER, BENN WAINWRIGHT, engineering and construction company executive; b. N.Y.C., June 10, 1915; s. Edward Arthur and Vera Wainwright (Benn) J.; m. Alice Forster Abeel, July 3, 1939 (dec.); m. Dorothea Potter Coogan, Aug. 29, 1954 (div.); children: Wendy, Penny, Bonnie Benn, John, Dorothea.; m. Barbara Gill Jenter, June 6, 1982. B.S. in Chem. Engring, Princeton U., 1936, M.S., 1941. Control engr. du Pont Co., Gibbstown, N.J., 1936-38; instr. Princeton U., 1938-42; v.p. ops. M.W. Kellogg, N.Y.C./London, 1942-71; pres. Hoechst-Uhde Corp., Englewood Cliffs, N.J., 1971-80, chem. engring. cons., 1980—; dir. Rockware Internat., New Haven. Contbr. articles to profl. jours. Chmn. bd. trustees Stoneleigh Burnham Sch.; bd. dirs. council Girl Scouts U.S.A.; trustee Saddle River Country Day Sch. Mem. Am. Inst. Chem. Engrs., ASME, Princeton Engring. Assn. (com. engring. law), Princeton Alumni of No. N.J. (v.p.), Sigma Xi, Tau Beta Pi. Republican. Mem. Dutch Reformed Ch. Clubs: Forsgate Country, Nantucket Yacht, Fox Meadow Tennis, Shenorock Shore, Bedens Brook Country; Princeton (N.Y.C.). Home: 241 Polpis Rd PO Box 562 Nantucket MA 02554

JESSER, ROGER FRANKLIN, brewing company executive; b. Ft. Collins, Colo., Mar. 8, 1926; s. Frank H. and Frances (Blado) J.; m. Sarah Joanna Sunderland, June 16, 1956; children: Jan Karl, Robin Kay, Jesser Bull. B.S. in Civil Engring., Colo. State U., 1949. Lic. profl. engr., Colo., La., Va. Engr. U.S. Bur. Reclamation, Loveland, Colo., 1950-52, Western Engring. Co., Denver, 1952-54, Al Ryan Cons. Engr., 1954-55; engr. constrn. supr. Adolph Coors Co., Golden, Colo., 1955-76, v.p. constrn., 1976-81, v.p. engring. constrn., 1981—; dir. Lutheran Med. Ctr., Wheatridge, Colo., 1980—. Exec. com. Denvoys-Denver C. of C., 1982—. Served with U.S. Army, 1944-46. Mem. Nat. Soc. Profl. Engrs., Profl. Engrs. Colo. (treas. 1980-81, sec. 1981-82, v.p. 1982-83, pres. elect 1982-84). Republican. Lutheran. Home: 10390 W 74th Pl Arvada CO 80005 Office: Adolph Coors Co Golden CO 80401

JESSUP, JOE LEE, educator, management consultant; b. Cordele, Ga., June 23, 1913; s. Horace Andrew and Elizabeth (Wilson) J.; m. Genevieve Quirk Galloway, Aug. 29, 1946; 1 dau., Gail Elizabeth. B.S., U. Ala., 1936; M.B.A., Harvard U., 1941; LL.D., Chung-Ang U., Seoul, Korea, 1964. Sales rep. Proctor & Gamble, 1937-40; liaison officer bur. pub. relations U.S. War Dept., 1941; spl. asst. and exec. asst. Far Eastern div. and office exports Bd. Econ. Warfare, 1942-43; exec. officer, office deptl. adminstrn. Dept. State, 1946; exec. sec. adminstr.'s adv. council War Assets Adminstrn., 1946-48; v.p. sales Airken, Capitol & Service Co., 1948-49; asso. prof. bus. adminstrn. George Washington U., 1949, prof., 1952-77, prof. emeritus, 1977—, asst. dean Sch. Govt., 1951-60; pres. Jessup and Co., Ft. Lauderdale, Fla., 1957—; dir. Giant Foods, Inc., 1971-75, mem. audit com., 1974-75; dir. Hunter Assos. Labs., Inc., Fairfax, Va., 1964-70, exec. v.p., gen. mgr., 1967-69, mem. exec. com., 1966-69; coordinator air force resources mgmt. program, 1951-57; del. in edn. 10th Internat. Mgmt. Conf., Sao Paulo, Brazil, 1954, 11th Conf., Paris, 1957, 12th Conf., Sydney and Melbourne, Australia, 1960, 13th Conf., Rotterdam, Netherlands, 1966, 14th Conf., Tokyo, 1969, 15th Conf., Munich, Germany, 1972; mem. Md. Econ. Devel. Adv. Commn., 1973-75. Mem. nat. adv. council Center for Study Presidency, 1974; mem. Civil Service Commn., Arlington County, Va., 1952-54; trustee Tng. Within Industry Found., Summit, N.J., 1954-58. Served from 2d lt. to lt. col. AUS, 1941-46. Decorated Bronze Star; recipient cert. of appreciation Sec. of Air Force, 1957. Mem. Acad. Mgmt., Am. Mktg. Assn. Clubs: Harvard (N.Y.C.); Coral Ridge Yacht, Tower (Ft. Lauderdale). Home: 2801 NE 57th St Fort Lauderdale FL 33308

JESSUP, PAUL FREDERICK, investment advisor, financial analyst; b. Evanston, Ill., Apr. 16, 1939; s. Paul S. and Gertrude (Strohmaier) J.; m. Johanna A.M. Friesen, June 27, 1970; children: Christine Marieke, Paul Charles Friesen. B.S., Northwestern U., 1960, Ph.D., 1966; A.M., Harvard U., 1963; B.A., U. Oxford (Eng.), 1963, M.A., 1983. Economist com. banking and currency U.S. Ho. of Reps., Washington, 1963-64; faculty U. Minn., Mpls., 1967-82, prof. fin., 1973-82; with Jessup & Co., St. Paul, 1982—; dir. Coldstream Investments Ltd., Gerbill Inc., St. Anthony Park State Bank; Sabbatical prof. in residence Fed. Res. Bank, Mpls., 1973-74. Author: The Theory and Practice of Nonpar Banking, 1967, (with Roger B. Upson) Returns in Over-the-Counter Stock Markets, 1973, Competing for Stock Market Profits, 1974, Modern Bank Management: A Casebook, 1978, Modern Bank Management, 1980; editor: Innovations in Bank Management: Selected Readings, 1969; Contbr. articles to profl. jours. Treas. Cathedral Ch. of St. Mark; trustee Diocese of Minn., Episc. Ch. Mem. Midwest Fin. Assn. (past pres.). Clubs: Skylight (Mpls.); University (Chgo.). Home: 1478 Branston St Saint Paul MN 55108 Office: Jessup & Co 2301 Como Ave Saint Paul MN 55455

JESSUP, PHILIP CARYL, JR., lawyer, mining company executive; b. Utica, N.Y., Aug. 30, 1926; s. Philip C. and Lois K. (Kellogg) J.; m. Dorothy K. Kerr, Jan.15, 1951 (div.); children: Timothy, Nancy, Margaret; m. 2d Helen I. Ibbitson, Jan.24, 1969; stepchildren: Genevieve, Lucinda, Francesca, Alexander. B.A., Yale Coll., 1949, J.D., Harvard U., 1952. Bar: N.Y. 1954. Mem. Whitman, Ransom & Coulson, N.Y.C., 1952-58; legal officer Internat. Nickel Co., Inc., N.Y.C., 1958-63; gen. solicitor Internat. Inco Ltd., N.Y.C., 1963-68; chief legal officer, sec., dir. Inco Europe Ltd., London, 1968-72; pres., mng. dir. P.T. Internat. Nickel Indonesia, Jakarta, 1972-78; v.p., gen. counsel and sec. Inco Ltd., N.Y.C., 1978—, Toronto, Can., 1978—; dir. Biogen N.V., Geneva, 1981—, Indonesian Mining Assn., Jakarta, 1974-78; chmn. bd. Inco Gulf, E.C., Bahrain, 1980—. Trustee Obor, Inc., Clinton, Conn., 1978—; mem. Council on Fgn. Relations, N.Y.C., 1972—; pres. West Bklyn. Ind. Democrats, 1956-58. Served to staff sgt. C.E. U.S. Army, 1944-46. Mem. N.Y.C. Bar Assn., ABA, Am. Soc. Internat. Law. Democrat. Clubs: Century Assn., India House (N.Y.C.); Queens Club (London). Home: 1105 Park Ave New York NY 10128 Office: Inco Ltd 1 New York Plaza New York NY 10004 Office: Inco Ltd 1 First Canadian Pl Toronto Ont. Canada M5X 1C4

JESSUP, WARREN T., patent lawyer; b. Eureka, Calif., Aug. 1, 1916; s. Thurman W. and Amelia (Johnson) J.; m. Evelyn Via, Sept. 13, 1941; children: Thurman W., Paul H., Stephen T., Marilyn R. Jessup Huffman. B.S., U. So. Calif., 1937; J.D., George Washington U., 1942. Engr. Gen. Electric Co., 1937-38, patent dept., 1938-42; mem. patent div. USN, 1944-46; patent counsel 11th Naval Dist., 1946-50; mem. Huebner, Beehler, Worrel & Herzig, 1950-56; partner Herzig & Jessup, 1957-59; individual practice law, 1959-68; mem. firm Jessup & Beecher, Sherman Oaks, also, Los Angeles, 1968—; instr. patent law, grad. div. Law Sch., U. So. Calif.; instr. bus. law U. Calif. at Los Angeles. Author: Patent Guide for Navy Inventors, 1950; Contbr. to: Ency. of Patent Practice and Invention Mgmt. Chmn. citizens adv. com. Point Mugu State Park, 1973; mem. Ventura County Mental Health Adv. Bd., 1977—, chmn., 1979. Served from ensign to lt. comdr. USN, 1942-46; comdr. Res. Mem. Patent Law Assn. Los Angeles (pres. 1974-75), Nat. Soc. Profl. Engrs., Am. Patent Law Assn., Conejo Valley Hist. Soc. (dir. 1971-83), Order of Coif, Tau Beta Pi, Eta Kappa Nu, Phi Kappa Phi, Phi Delta Phi. Baptist. Home: Thousand Oaks CA 91360 Office: 875 Westlake Blvd Suite 205 Westlake Village CA 91361 *"Have no anxiety about anything; for all things work together for good to them that love God." Many times the limitations in human faith make it impossible to believe that. But it is true and will materialize whenever faith is strong enough to let God rule.*

JESTER, ROBERTS CHARLES, JR., engineering services company executive; b. Atlanta, July 12, 1917; s. Roberts Charles and Lynwood (Waters) J.; children: Rita (Mrs. Charles B. Jones, Jr.), Carol (Mrs. John M. Sisk, Jr.), Janelle (Mrs. Michael C. Patty). B.S., U. Ga., 1940; grad., Advanced Mgmt. Program, Harvard, 1957. Chief clk. Ga. R.R., 1936-40; project mgr. Mich. Design & Engring. Co., 1941-42; partner Allstate Engring. Co., Dayton, Ohio, 1943-45, pres., 1945—; pres., chief exec. officer Allstates Design & Devel. Co. Inc., Trenton, N.J., 1954—; dir. N.J. Nat. Bank. Bd. dirs., vice chmn. Greater Trenton Symphony Assn.; bd. dirs. George Washington council Boy Scouts Am.; bd. govs. Hamilton Hosp.; mem. lay adv. bd. St. Francis Hosp.; trustee YMCA, Trenton. Mem. Greater Trenton C. of C. (bd. dirs.), Trenton Coalition, Metro 49'ers. Republican. Presbyn. Clubs: Mason (Shriner, Jester), Engineers, Trenton Country (past pres.); Metropolitan (N.Y.C.); Pitts. Athletic; Little Egg Harbor Yacht (N.J.). Office: 367 Pennington Ave Trenton NJ 08608

JESTIN, HEIMWARTH B., coll. adminstr.; b. Montreal, Que., Can., Sept. 24, 1918; s. Emil Ernst and Rosa (Ege) J.; m. Catherine M. Townshend, Oct. 14, 1944; children—Loftus, Jennifer, Carolyn. B.S., Central Conn. State Coll., 1947; M.A., Yale, 1949, Ph.D., 1954. Head English dept., tchr. history Thomaston (Conn.) High Sch., 1947-50; prin. Canton High Sch., Collinsville, Conn., 1951-53; supt. schs., Canton, Conn., 1953-62; prof. philosophy and edn. Central Conn. State Coll., 1956-65, dean coll., 1965-67, v.p. acad. affairs, 1967—; prof. U. Hartford, 1961-63; Mem. Conn. Health and Ednl. Facilities Authority. Author: Critical Experiences During the Early Years of Superintendency, 1955, The Canton Evaluation Plan, 1960, Role of the Superintendent of Schools in Connecticut, 1967, Ecology Holds Key to Man's Destiny, 1969, Well-Educated Barbarians?, 1970, Higher Education Direction, 1971, Year Round Schooling Keyed to Modern Need, 1972, For a New State University System, 1977, They Know a Lot, But are They Educated?, 1977, Crucial Year for Higher Education, 1978, Enrollments Not Nose Diving, 1979, To Improve Higher Education, a Two-Tier University System, 1980, For a State University System, 1981; co-editor: The Connecticut Study of the Role of the Public School, 1960. Trustee Roaring Brook Nature Center; bd. mgrs., life mem. Conn. PTA. Served with AUS, 1941-46. Decorated Order Brit. Empire. Mem. Conn. Council Sch. Coll. Relations. Home: 180 Garden St Farmington CT 06032 Office: 1615 Stanley St New Britain CT 06050

JESURÚN, HAROLD MÉNDEZ, physician, educator; b. San Juan, P.R., Dec. 24, 1915; s. Willy and Esterlinda (Méndez) J.; m. Dolores López y Piñero, May 17, 1947; children: Carlos Antonio, John Alberto, Maria Celeste, Richard James. B.A., Columbia U., 1937; M.D., U. Mich., 1940. Diplomate: Am. Bd. Ob-Gyn. Intern, Kings County (N.Y.) Hosp., Bklyn., 1940-41; commd. 1st lt. M.C., U.S. Army, 1941, advanced through grades to col., 1959; area med. dir., Brit. Guiana, 1942-43, malariologist, New Guinea, 1943-44, chief provincial health officer, Taegu, Korea, 1945-46, exec. officer, chief cholera control officer, Korea, 1946; asst. resident Fitzsimmons Gen. Hosp., Denver, 1947-48; resident to chief sr. resident Brooke Gen. Hosp., San Antonio, 1948-50; asst. chief ob-gyn service, 1952-55; chief ob-gyn William Beaumont Gen. Hosp., El Paso, Tex., 1950-51, Percy Jones Gen. Hosp., Battle Creek, Mich., 1951-52, U.S. Army Hosp., Ft. Ord, Calif., 1952, Rodriguez Army Hosp., San Juan, 1955-58; chief ob-gyn, chief instr. ob-gyn Letterman Gen. Hosp., San Francisco, 1958-62; chief ob-gyn service, dep. comdr. U.S. Army 97th Gen. Hosp., Frankfurt, Germany, 1962-66; chief ob-gyn service, asst. chief profl. service Madigan Gen. Hosp., Tacoma, 1966-67, ret., 1967; program dir. ob-gyn St. Michael Hosp., Newark; and asso. clin. prof. N.J. Coll. Medicine and Dentistry, 1967-69; clin. dir. ob-gyn R.E. Thomason Gen. Hosp., El Paso, 1969-73; project dir. Family Planning, OEO, El Paso, 1970-73; clin. investigator Am. Women's Health Program, Temple U., 1972-73; prof. ob-gyn U. Tex.-Houston, 1973-81; clin. prof. ob-gyn Tex. Tech. U. Med. Sch., 1981—; asst. prof. obstetrics Baylor Med. Sch., 1954-55; ob-gyn cons. U.S. Army Europe, 1962-66; cons. 6th U.S. Army Area, San Francisco, 1958-62. Contbr. numerous articles to profl. jours. Bd. dirs., pres. El Paso chpt. Am. Cancer Soc., 1971-72, bd. dirs. Houston chpt., 1975. Decorated Bronze Star, Army Commendation medal, Legion of Merit; recipient Physician's Recognition award AMA, 1969. Fellow ACS, Am. Coll. Obstetricians and Gynecologists; mem. AAAS, Soc. Med. Cons. to Armed Forces, Houston Ob-Gyn Soc., Tex. Assn. Ob-Gyn, Am. Assn. Tropical Medicine and Hygiene, Bishop Alonso Manso Soc. (v.p. 1957-58), Assn. Mil. Surgeons, Harris County (Tex.) Med. Soc., Am. Med. Soc. Vienna (Austria) (life), Phi Rho Sigma (v.p. 1939-40). Home: 914 Sunset El Paso TX 79922 *There is no substitute for excellence.*

JETER, WAYBURN STEWART, educator, microbiologist; b. Cooper, Tex., Feb. 16, 1926; s. Joseph Plato and Beulah (Stewart) J.; m. Margaret Ann McDonald, May 30, 1947; children—Randall Mark, Monette Ann, Marcus Kent. B.S., U. Okla., 1948, M.S., 1949; Ph.D., U. Wis., 1950. Diplomate: Am. Bd. Microbiology. Mem. faculty U. Iowa, 1950-63, asso. prof., 1958-63; prof. microbiology U. Ariz., Tucson, 1963—, head dept. microbiology and med. tech., 1967—, dir. lab., 1976—, dir. med. tech. program, 1976-79; vis. prof. immunology and med. microbiology U. Fla., 1980. Contbr. articles profl. jours. Served with USNR, 1943-46. Fellow AAAS; mem. Am. Acad. Microbiology, Am. Assn. Immunologists, Am. Pub. Health Assn., Ariz. Acad. Sci., Am. Soc. Microbiology (mem. council 1975-77), Reticuloendothelial Soc., Soc. Exptl. Biology and Medicine, Sigma Xi. Democrat. Presbyn. Home: 4834 E Glenn St Tucson AZ 85712

JETTON, CLYDE THOMAS, teacher educator; b. St. James, Ark., Oct. 23, 1918; s. William Thomas and Laura Ellen (Greenway) J.; m. Dorothy Marie Chasteen, Nov. 30, 1944; 1 son, Ronald Clyde. B.A., Northeastern State Coll., 1939; M.A., Okla. State U., 1940; Ph.D., Tex. Tech. Coll., 1955. Tchr. elementary sch., Locust Grove, Okla., 1940; psychometrist Hardin-Simmons U., 1947-49; counselor VA, 1949-51, Sweetwater (Tex.) pub. schs., 1951-54; prof. edn. Hardin-Simmons U., Abilene, Tex., 1955-80, grad. dean, 1965-80; vis. prof. Colo. State U., 1957-59, George Peabody Coll., 1963; cons. mental retardation, psychol. testing, counseling. Served to maj. AUS, 1940-47. Decorated Bronze Star, Purple Heart. Mem. Am. Personnel and Guidance Assn., NEA, Tex. Tchrs. Assn., So. Assn. Counselor Educators and Suprs., Nat. Vocat. Guidance Assn., Phi Delta Kappa. Baptist. Clubs: Civitan (sec. 1963, dir. 1962—. Home: 720 Amherst Dr Abilene TX 79601 *Two traits which I have always esteemed highly are wisdom and understanding—and the greater of these is understanding. He who has a valid understanding of himself, his aspirations (and the reasons for these), his fellowmen, and God is not far from being a complete person.*

JETTON, GIRARD REUEL, JR., oil co. exec.; b. Washington, Feb. 19, 1924; s. Girard Reuel and Hallie (Grimes) J.; m. Mera Riddell, Sept. 4, 1948; children—Mera Elizabeth, Robert Girard, James Thomas. B.S. in Engring, George Washington U., 1945, B.A., 1947; J.D., Harvard U., 1950. Bar: D.C. bar 1951, Md. bar 1959, Ohio bar 1960. Elec. engr. in research, 1944-45, patent atty., Washington, 1950-51; atty. IRS, Washington, 1951-54; trial atty. Dept. Justice, 1954-55; atty., then partner firm McClure & McClure, Washington, 1955-60; with Marathon Oil Co., Findlay, Ohio, 1960—, asst. to chmn. bd., 1969-73, corp. sec., 1973—. Served with USNR, 1945-46. Mem. Am. Bar Assn., Fed. Bar Assn., Tax Execs. Inst., Am. Soc. Corp. Secs., Am. Petroleum Inst., Bar Assn. D.C., Ohio Bar Assn., Findlay/Hancock County Bar Assn. Episcopalian. Club: Met. (Washington). Home: 170 Orchard Ln Findlay OH 45840 Office: 539 S Main St Findlay OH 45840

JEUCK, JOHN EDWARD, business educator; b. Chgo., Oct. 17, 1916; s. John S. and Lila E. (Burke) J. A.B., U. Chgo., 1937, M.B.A., 1938, Ph.D., 1949; M.A. (hon.), Harvard U. Instr. marketing, dir. placement, sch. bus. Miami U., 1940-41; instr. marketing, sch. bus. U. Chgo., 1946-47, asst. prof., 1947-50, asso. prof. marketing, asso. dir. exec. program, 1950-52, prof. marketing, dean sch. bus., dir. exec. program, 1952-56; prof. bus. adminstrn. Harvard Grad. Sch Bus. Adminstrn., 1955-58; cons. in mgmt. edn. European Productivity Agy., 1956-57; bus. cons., 1950—; Robert Law prof. bus. adminstrn. U. Chgo., 1958—. Author: (with Boris Emmet) Catalogues and Counters, A History of Sears, Roebuck and Company, 1950; Co-editor: Readings in Market Organization and Price Policy, 1952; Editorial bd.: Jour. Marketing, 1951-61; Contbr. articles to profl. jours. Served as lt. USNR, 1942-46. Mem. Am. Econ. Assn., Am. Marketing Assn. (nat. award 1951), Beta Gamma Sigma. Roman Catholic. Clubs: Quadrangle, University, Economic, Tavern (Chgo.).

JEWELL, GEORGE HIRAM, lawyer; b. Fort Worth, Jan. 9, 1922; s. George Hiram and Vera (Lee) J.; m. Betty Elizabeth Jeffries, July 21, 1944; children: Susan Jewell Cannon, Robert V., Nancy Jewell Wommack. B.A., U. Tex., 1942, LL.B., 1950. Bar: Tex. 1950. Geophysicist Gulf Research and Devel. Corp., Harmarville, Pa., 1946-47; assoc. Baker & Botts, Houston, 1950-60, ptnr., 1960-70, sr. ptnr., 1970—; dir. Schlumberger Ltd., N.Y., Paris, S.W. Bancshares, Inc., Houston, Bank of S.W., Pogo Producing Co. Contbr. articles to profl. jours. Trustee Tex. Children's Hosp., Houston, 1977—, pres., Houston, 1982-83; bd. dirs. Schlumberger Found., N.Y.C., 1982—; mem. adv. council Coll. Natural Scis., U. Tex. Served to lt. USNR, 1943-46, 50-51. Fellow Am. Coll. Tax Counsel, Am. Bar Found.; mem. ABA, Order of Coif, Phi Delta Phi. Clubs: Houston Country, Coronado (pres. 1976-77). Home: 6051 Crab Orchard Ln Houston TX 77057 Office: Baker & Botts 3000 One Shell Plaza Houston TX 77002

JEWELL, ROBERT BURNETT, engineering company executive; b. Binghamton, N.Y., Mar. 20, 1906; s. Howard Clinton and Anne Bersina (Burnett) J.; m. Helen Louise Pflug, May 18, 1935; children—Robert William, Linda Louise. B.S. in Civil Engring, Lehigh U., 1928. Registered profl. engr., N.Y., Ky. Asst. engr. Friestedt Found. Co., N.Y.C., 1928-30; asst. engr. Port of N.Y. Authority, N.Y.C., 1930-39; with Mason & Hanger Co., 1939-43; resident engr. for constrn. Bklyn. Battery Tunnel, 1942-43; with Silas Mason Co., 1943-55; project mgr. Ft. Randall Tunnels, 1949-51, AEC Nev. Test Site, 1951-53; chief engr., co. rep. constr. Harvey Canal Tunnel, New Orleans, 1953-55; with Mason & Hanger-Silas Masons Co., Inc., 1955—, v.p., chief engr., Lexington, Ky., 1959-64, v.p. ops., 1964-75, exec. v.p., 1975-76, pres., 1976—; also dir.; chmn. bd. Mason Chamberlain Inc.; fellow U. Ky., 1972—; Van Meter fellow Lees Jr. Coll., 1979—, trustee, 1977. Recipient Disting. Service award Dept. Energy, 1981. Fellow ASCE; mem. AIAA, Nat. Soc. Profl. Engrs., The Moles, Beavers, Tau Beta Pi. Presbyterian. Clubs: Lexington Country, Lafayette, Keeneland, Rotary. Office: 200 W Vine St Lexington KY 40507

JEWELL, WILLIAM MACINTYRE, artist; b. Lawrence, Mass., Dec. 9, 1904; s. Ernest C. and Elizabeth Galbraith (MacIntyre) J.; m. Barbara Dailey, Sept. 6, 1939; children—Thomas N., Lydia R. A.B., Harvard, 1927, student archtl. sch., 1927-29. Instr. Boston U., 1934-46, asst. prof., 1946-50, asso. prof., 1950-54, prof. fine arts, 1955-70, prof. emeritus, 1970—, chmn. dept., 1955-68; faculty Harvard U. Extension, 1958-75. Designer Boston archtl. firms, 1929-31; designer residences, Mass., N.H., 1st one man show paintings, Doll & Richards Gallery, Boston, 1934, other local, nat. groups shows, 1934—; represented in permanent collections, Fogg Mus. Art, Farnsworth Mus., Rockland, Maine, DeCordova Mus., also pvt. collections, portraits at, Maine State House, Augusta, Putnam Lodge, Pomfret, Conn., others. Trustee Boston Arts Festival. Recipient Mitton gold medal and cash award N.E. Artists, 1941, 46, 47, 62; grant-in-aid Am. Council Learned Socs., 1960; award spring exhbn. Boston Water Color Soc., 1960. Fellow Am. Acad. Arts and Sci.; mem. Harvard Musical Assn., Harvard Glee Club Alumni Assn., Guild Boston Artists, Am. Water Color Soc., Colonial Soc. of Mass., Medieval Acad. (asst. editor Speculum 1956-62), AAUP, Coll. Art Assn., Harvard Grad. Sch. Design Assos., Phi Beta Kappa (hon.). Club: St Botolph. Home: 37 Dana St Cambridge MA 02138

JEWELL, WILLIAM SYLVESTER, engineering educator; b. Detroit, July 2, 1932; s. Loyd Vernon and Marion (Sylvester) J.; m. Elizabeth Gordon Wilson, July 7, 1956; children—Sarah, Thomas, Miriam, William Timothy. B.Engring. Physics, Cornell U., 1954; M.S. in Elec. Engring, MIT, 1955, Sc.D., 1958. Assoc. dir. mgmt. scis. div. Broadview Research Corp., Burlingame, Calif., 1958-60; asst. prof. dept. indsl. engring. and operations research U. Calif.-Berkeley, 1960-63, asso. prof., 1963-67, prof., 1967—, chmn. dept., 1967-69, 76-80; dir. Teknekron Industries, Inc., Berkeley, 1968—; cons. operations research problems, 1960—; guest prof. Eidgenössiches Technische Hochschule, Zurich, 1980-81. Contbr. articles to profl. jours. Fulbright research scholar, France, 1965; research scholar Internat. Inst. Applied Systems Analysis, Austria, 1974-75. Mem. Ops. Research Soc. Am., Inst. Mgmt. Scis., Am. Risk and Ins. Assn., Actuarial Assn. Netherlands, Assn. Swiss Actuaries, Internat. Actuarial Assn., Mensa, Triangle., Sigma Xi, Triangle. Home: 67 Loma Vista Orinda CA 94563 Office: U Cal Dept Indsl Engring and Operations Research Berkeley CA 94720

JEWETT, EDGAR BOARDMAN, III, graphic arts company executive, consultant; b. Buffalo, Apr. 7, 1928; s. Edgar Boardman, II and Helen Stowe (Barnard) J.; m. Frances Bass Appleton, Jan. 12, 1952; children: Edgar Boardman IV, Pamela Bass, Catherine Appleton. B.S., U. Buffalo, 1948; P.M.D., Harvard U., 1971. Vice pres. nat. sales J. W. Clement Co., Buffalo, 1954-69; v.p. mktg. Kingsport Press, Tenn., 1969-71; exec. v.p. ops. Arcata Graphics Corp., Los Angeles, 1971-73, pres., Menlo Park, Calif., 1973-74; v.p. Arcata Corp., Calif., 1973-82, group exec., 1974-82, sr. v.p., 1982, exec. v.p., chief operating officer, 1983; now with Ruffian Enterprises, Inc., Wilton, Conn. Bd. dirs. Graphic Arts Tech. Found., Pitts., 1981-85; pres. North Salem Bd. Edn., N.Y., 1956-62. Served with Med. Service Corps. USNR, 1952-54. Recipient Disting. Service award North Salem Sch. Bd., 1962, Am. Jewish Com., N.Y.C., 1980, William Caxton Human Relations award, 1980, Disting. Service award Printing Industry Am., 1978, 80. Mem. Conf. Bd. Maj. Printers (founder 1979, v.p. 1979-81, pres. 1978-79, Disting. Service award 1977, 79), Printing Industries Am. (bd. dirs. Arlington, Va. 1979-81), Am. Mgmt. Assn. (lectr., instr., Disting. Service award 1969). Republican. Episcopalian. Clubs: Sky (N.Y.C.); Landmark (Stamford, Conn.); Saugatuck Harbor Yacht. Home: 66 Drum Hill Rd Wilton CT 06897 Office: Ruffian Enterprises Inc 66 Drum Hill Rd Wilton CT 06897

JEWETT, EMELYN KNOWLAND, publishing company executive; b. Alameda, Calif., Apr. 24, 1928; d. William Fife and Helen Davis (Herrick) Knowland; m. Harold Woodward Jewett, Jr., Dec. 26, 1949; children: Emelyn Grace Jewett Carothers, Helen Estelle, Harold Woodward III. Ed., U. Calif. at Berkeley. Pres. Tribune Pub. Co., Oakland, Calif., 1974-77, dir., 1950-77; sr. v.p. Oakland Tribune, Inc., 1977—; dir. Downtown Realty Co., The Clorox Co., Kaiser Cement Co.; pres., dir. Oakland City Center Hotel Co., Inc., 1978—. Trustee Peralta Hosp., 1976—, United Way Bay Area, 1975-79, John F. Kennedy U., 1979—; bd. dirs., mem. exec. com., treas. Oakland Council Econ. Devel., 1976—; bd. dirs. Oakland Conv. and Visitors Bur., 1979—; trustee U. Calif. Alumnae Found., 1970-72. Mem. Jr. League Oakland (pres. 1967-68), Oakland C. of C. (dir. 1975—). Clubs: Women's Athletic, Claremont Country. Home: 3015 Burdeck Dr Oakland CA 94602 Office: Oakland Tribune 409 13th St Oakland CA 94612

JEWETT, FRANK BALDWIN, JR., mechanical engineer; b. N.Y.C., Apr. 4, 1917; s. Frank B. and Fannie (Frisble) J.; m. Edar von L. Fleming, Sept. 5, 1942; children: Frank Baldwin III, Robert F., Rebecca L., Edar F. B.S., Calif. Inst. Tech., 1938; M.B.A. magna cum laude, Harvard U., 1940. Registered profl. engr., Minn. Research asst. Harvard Bus. Sch., 1940-41; with Nat. Research Corp., 1941-47, v.p., mgr. vacuum engring. div., 1944-47; with Gen. Mills, Inc., 1947-55, dir. devel. and bus. adminstrn. research labs., also dir. aero. research labs., 1947-52, mng. dir. engring. research and devel., 1952-55; v.p., dir. Vitro Corp. Am., N.Y.C., 1956-58, exec. v.p., dir., 1959, pres., dir., 1959-69; pres. Tech. Audit Assos., Inc., 1969—. Mem. U.S. Olympic Yacht Team, 1936, Edina (Minn.) Sch. Bd., 1953-55; trustee Tabor Acad., Marion, Mass., 1954-74; hon. Rockford Coll., Ill.; mem. corp. Woods Hole Oceanographic Instn. Recipient certificate merit Crusade for Freedom, 1951. Mem. ASME (hon. life), N.Y. Acad. Scis., U.S. Yacht Racing Union (sr. judge). Clubs: Union League (N.Y.C.); Holmes Hole Sailing Assn., Vineyard Haven Yacht. Home and Office: 589 Oenoke Ridge New Canaan CT 06840

JEWETT, GEORGE FREDERICK, JR., forest products company executive; b. Spokane, Wash., Apr. 10, 1927; s. George Frederick and Mary Pelton (Cooper) J.; m. Lucille Winifred McIntyre, July 11, 1953; children: Mary Elizabeth, George Frederick III. B.A., Dartmouth Coll., 1950; M.B.A., Harvard U., 1952. Asst. sec., asst. treas. Potlatch Corp., 1955-62, v.p. adminstrn., 1962-68, corporate v.p. adminstrn., 1968-71, sr. v.p., 1972-77, vice chmn. bd. adminstrn., 1977-78, vice chmn., 1979—, also dir. Mem. San Francisco Com. of Asian Art and Culture; trustee Asia Found., San Francisco, Pacific Med. Center, San Francisco, Calif. Acad. Sci., Carnegie Instn. Washington; chmn. Asian Art Found., San Francisco. Clubs: St. Francis Yacht, Marin Yacht, N.Y. Yacht, Bohemian, Pacific Union., San Diego Yacht. Home: Skyland Way Ross CA 94957 Office: PO Box 3591 San Francisco CA 94119

JEWETT, JOHN GIBSON, univ. dean; b. Birmingham, Ala., Jan. 21, 1937; s. William Cornell and Margaret (Nowell) J.; m. Susan Rideout, Aug. 4, 1962; children—Elizabeth, Jennifer. A.B., Harvard, 1958; Ph.D., Mass. Inst. Tech., 1962. Postdoctoral research asso. Ind. U., Bloomington, 1962-64; asst. prof. chemistry Ohio U., Athens, 1964-68, asso. prof., 1968-72, prof. chemistry, 1972-77, dean, 1972-77; prof. chemistry, dean Coll. Arts and Scis., U. Vt., Burlington, 1977—. Recipient research grant NSF, 1965-72. Mem. Am. Chem. Soc. (research grant 1964-65), AAAS, AAUP, Sigma Xi, Phi Lambda Upsilon. Home: 1720 Dorset St South Burlington VT 05401 Office: U Vt Burlington VT 05401

JEWETT, JOHN RHODES, real estate executive; b. Indpls., Nov. 24, 1922; s. Chester Aten and Grace (Rhodes) J.; m. Marybelle Bramhall, June 12, 1946; children: John R., Jane B. B.A., DePauw U., 1944. Econ. research analyst Eli Lilly & Co., Indpls., 1946-48; with Pitman-Moore Co., Indpls., 1948-65, v.p., asst. to pres., 1959-65; with F.C. Tucker Co., Inc., Indpls., 1965—, sr. v.p., 1978—; pres. Market Sq. Arena, 1974-79, Ind. Pacers (profl. basketball team), 1977-79. Chmn. Marion County Heart Assn.; dir. Marion County Child Guidance Clinic, ARC; trustee Meth. Hosp., Indpls.; committeeman Republican Precinct. Served with AUS, 1943-46. Mem. Met. Indpls. Bd. Realtors, Ind. Assn. Realtors, Nat. Assn. Realtors, Indpls. C. of C. Clubs: Columbia, Meridian Hills Country, Kiwanis. Home: 5234 Graceland Indianapolis IN 46208 Office: Suite 2500 1 Indiana Sq Indianapolis IN 46204

JEWISON, NORMAN F., producer-director; b. Can. Student, Malvern Collegiate Inst., Toronto, Ont., Can., 1940-44; B.A., Victoria Coll., U. Toronto, 1950; LL.D., U. Western Ont., 1974. Dir. numerous TV shows; producer-dir.: spls. Judy Garland; pictures directed include In the Heat of The Night (Acad. award 1967); producer, dir.: And Justice for All; producer: Billy Two Hats; exec. producer: The Dogs of War, 1982. Named Dir. of Yr. Nat. Assn. Theatre Owners, 1982. Address: care William Morris Agy Inc 151 El Camino Beverly Hills CA 90212

JEWITT, DAVID WILLARD PENNOCK, banker; b. Cleve., Feb. 22, 1921; s. Homer Moore and Helen Katherine (Pennock) J.; m. Margaret Van Pelt Cool, Apr. 13, 1957; children: Andrea, Joel. B.A., Amherst Coll., 1943; Amherst Meml. fellow, Harvard, 1946-47; LL.D. (hon.), Fairfield U., 1980. With Irving Trust Co., N.Y.C., 1947-51, Chem. Bank, 1951-59; with Conn. Nat. Bank, Bridgeport, 1959—, exec. v.p., 1977—; dir. Inter-Ch. Residences, Inc., Thirty Thirty Park, Inc. Trustee Am. Seamen's Friend Soc., N.Y.C.; trustee Fairfield U., chmn. bd. trustees, 1972-78, trustee emeritus, 1980 (recipient medal of Merit), 1968; trustee Gaylord Hosp., Wallingford; pres. Oak Lawn Cemetery Assn., Fairfield; trustee Mystic Seaport Mus.; pres. Mystic Seaport Mus. subs. ops. Served to lt. USNR, 1943-46. Decorated comdr. Order Ruben Dario, Nicaragua. Mem. Theodore Gordon Flyfishers, Nat. Beagle Club, The Pilgrims, Ex-Mems. Assn. Squadron A, Soc. Colonial Wars, Beta Theta Pi. Episcopalian. Clubs: Fairfield Beach; Algonquin (Bridgeport); Graduate (New Haven); Anglers (N.Y.C.); Army and Navy (Washington); Farmington (Charlottesville); Royal Bermuda Yacht, Royal Swedish Yacht. Home: 1498 Bronson Rd Fairfield CT 06430 Office: 888 Main St Bridgeport CT 06602

JEWSON, RUTH HATHAWAY (MRS. VANCE JEWSON), association executive; b. Ellendale, N.D.; d. Floyd C. and Mabel (Hay) Hathaway; m. W. Vance Jewson, Mar. 19, 1938; children: Douglas, Meredith, Roberta, Dwight. Ph.D., U. Minn., 1978. Tchr. Avon-Grove Consol. High Sch., West Grove, Pa., 1935-37, Hudson (Wis.) High Sch., 1937-38, U. High Sch., Mpls., 1939-40; research asst. U. Minn., 1938-39; tchr. adult edn. Mpls. Pub. Schs., 1951-69; exec. officer Nat. Council Family Relations, 1956—; past mem. task force to study programs and program components leading to cert. for tchrs. in field family life edn. Minn. Dept. Edn.; past mem. adv. bd. sch. curriculum project Children's Home Soc. Minn. and Social Sci. Consortium, Boulder, Colo.; mem. Minn. Gov.'s Adv. Com. on Families, Gov.'s Com. on Stress and the Family, Gov.'s Com. on Work and the Family; mem. nat. task force White House Conf. on Families, 1980. Pres. bd., past sec. Minn. Council on Family Relations; past standards and personnel com. Mpls. YWCA; bd. dirs. Christian Children's Fund; past mem. bd. U. Minn. YWCA, Pillsbury Citizens Service Neighborhood House; past co-chmn. strengthening family life com. Gov.'s Council Children and Youth; past mem. task force White House Conf. on Aging.; pres. bd. dirs. Hennepin Ch. Counseling Ctr. Mem. Am. Home Econs. Assn. (resolutions com., nominating com.), Minn. Home Econs. Assn. (past v.p. and past sec.), U. Minn. Coll. Agr., Forestry and Home Econs. Alumni Assn. (bd. dirs. 1965-69), Twin City Home Economists in Homemaking (past pres.), Groves Conf. (program chairperson 1984), Mortar Bd., Phi Upsilon Omicron, Omicron Nu, Gamma Sigma Delta. Methodist. Home: 5515 E Oberlin Circle Minneapolis MN 55432 Office: Fairview Community Sch Ctr Suite 147 1910 West County Rd B Roseville MN 55113

JEX, VICTOR BIRD, chemist; b. Salt Lake City, Apr. 17, 1919; s. Heber Charles and Sarah Emeline (Bird) J.; m. Marva Tingey, May 24, 1946; children: Douglass Tingey, Janet Jex Hatt, Timothy Tingey. A.B., U. Utah, 1942, M.A., 1947; Ph.D., MIT, 1950. With Union Carbide Corp., 1950—, dir. devel. consumer products div., Tonawanda, N.Y., then Tarrytown, N.Y., 1962-72, dir. devel. home and automotive products div., Tarrytown, 1972-77, sr. research asso., 1977—. Mem. exec. bd., v.p. scouting Westchester-Putnam council Boy Scouts Am., 1970—; pres. N.Y. Stake Mormon Ch., 1975-78, Yorktown (N.Y.) Stake, 1978-83. Served with AUS, 1942-46. Decorated Bronze Star; Teaching fellow U. Utah, 1946-47; research asso. Mass. Inst. Tech., 1947-50. Mem. Am. Chem. Soc., AAAS, Sigma Xi, Alpha Chi Sigma. Club: Lochinvar. Patentee carbon functional silicones, 1958-70. Home: 29 Doris Dr Scarsdale NY 10583 Office: Union Carbide Tech Center Tarrytown NY 10591

JILER, WILLIAM LAURENCE, publisher; b. Bridgeport, Conn., Oct. 16, 1925; s. Jacob and Sarah J.; m. Jan Gardner, Oct. 14, 1956; children: Wendy Jo, James Paul. B.S., Bates Coll., Lewiston, Maine, 1948; postgrad., U. So. Calif., 1950. With E.R. Squibb & Co., New Brunswick, N.J., 1948-50; with Commodity Research Bur., Inc., N.Y.C., now Jersey City, 1950-64, 69—, pres., 1969—; with Standard & Poor's Corp., 1964-69, dir., 1964-69; mem. econ. adv. com. Commodity Futures Trading Commn., 1975-76. Author: How Charts Can Help You in the Stock Market, 1962; asso. editor: Commodity Year Book, 1951-80. Served to 2d lt. USAAF, 1943-45. Mem. Nat. Assn. Bus. Economists, Market Technicians Assn., N.Y. Soc. Security Analysts. Office: 75 Montgomery St Jersey City NJ 07302 *Find a need and fulfill it to the best of your ability.*

JIMENEZ, LUIS ALFONSO, JR., sculptor; b. El Paso, Tex., July 30, 1940; s. Luis Alfonso and Alicia (Franco) J.; 1 dau., Elisa Victoria. B.S. in Art and Architecture, U. Tex., Austin, 1964; postgrad., Ciudad U., Mexico City, 1964. Exhibited in one-man shows, including, Graham Gallery, N.Y.C., 1969-70, O.K. Harris Works of Art, N.Y.C., 1972-75, Contemporary Arts Mus., Houston, 1974, Mus. of N. Mex., Santa Fe, 1980, Frumkin Struve, Chgo., 1981, Adeliza's Candy Store Gallery, Folsom, Calif., 1983; exhibited in group shows, including, Nat. Mus. Am. Art, Washington, 1980, Albuquerque Mus., Edinburgh (Scotland) Festival, Walker Art Center, Mpls., U. Minn., Mpls., 1981; represented in permanent collections, Nat. Mus. Am. Art, Witte Mus., San Antonio, Long Beach (Calif.) Mus., New Orleans Mus. Art, Roswell (N. Mex.) Mus. and Art Center, Sheldon Meml. Gallery, Lincoln, Nebr., Art Inst. Chgo., others, also pvt. collections; works include Vaquero Sculpture, Moody Park, Houston, 1977; Nat. Endowment for Arts and City Housing Authority commn. 500 Buster sculpture, Fargo, N.D., 1977; Nat. Endowment for Arts commn. Art in

Pub. Places Southwest Pietà, City of Albuquerque, 1981; Nat. Endowment for Arts Steel Worker, La Salle Sta., Buffalo, N.Y.; Niagara Frontier Transp. Authority Commn. Recipient Steuben Glass award, 1972; Nat. Endowment for Arts fellow, 1977; Am. Acad. in Rome fellow, 1979; Am. Acad. Arts and Letters Hassam Fund award, 1977. Home: 1415 E Nevada El Paso TX 79902 Office: Box 175 Hondo NM 88336 *I am a traditional artist in the sense that I give form to my culture's icons. I work with folk sources; the popular culture and mythology, and a popular material; fiberglass, shiny finishes, metal flake, and at times with neon and illuminated. In the past the important icons were religious now they are secular.*

JINKS, ROBERT LARRY, newspaper editor; b. Mt. Pleasant, Tex., Jan. 26, 1929; s. Leon Carlton and Mary (Cunnyngham) J.; m. Anne Claire van Ravesteyn, May 8, 1971; children by previous marriage: Laura Beth, Daniel Carlton. B.J., U. Mo., 1950; M.S., Columbia, 1956. News editor Muskogee (Okla.) Times-Democrat, 1950-51; reporter Greensboro (N.C.) Daily News, 1953-55; reporter, city editor Charlotte (N.C) Observer, 1950-60; mem. staff Miami (Fla). Herald, 1960-77, mng. editor, 1966-72, exec. editor, 1972-77; editor, v.p. San Jose (Calif.) Mercury, San Jose (Calif.) News, 1977-80; sr. v.p./ editorial Knight-Ridder Corp., Miami, Fla., 1980—; pres. AP Mng. Editors, 1975-76, Fla. Press Assn., 1975. Served with AUS, 1951-53. Named to 50th anniversary honors list Columbia Grad. Sch. Journalism, 1963. Mem. Am. Soc. Newspaper Editors (dir. 1980-83). Unitarian.

JINKS, ROBERT LARRY, newspaper company executive; b. Mt. Pleasant, Tex., Jan. 26, 1929; s. Leon Carlton and Mary Jean (Cunnyngham) J.; m. Anne Claire Van Raveyston, May 8, 1971; children: Beau Backus, Laura Beth, Daniel Carlton. B.J., U. Mo., 1950; M.S. in Journalism, Columbia U., 1955. Mng. editor Miami Herald (Fla.), 1966-72, exec. editor, 1972-76; editor Mercury News, San Jose, Calif., 1977-80; v.p. news Knight-Ridder Newspapers, Miami, 1980-82, sr. v.p., 1983—. Mem. exec. com. Greater Miami United, 1982—; bd. dirs. Dade County chpt. ARC, Miami, 1982—. Served to 2d lt. U.S. Army, 1951-53. Recipient Pulitzer Traveling scholar, 1956, Alumni award Journalism Alumni Assn. Columbia U., 1982. Mem. AP Mng. Editors Assn. (pres. 1975-76), Am. Soc. Newspapers Editors (dir. 1980—), Fla. Soc. Newspaper Editors (pres. 1974-75). Democrat. Home: 5401 Banyan Dr Miami FL 33156 Office: Knight Ridder Newspapers Inc 1 Herald Plaza Miami Fl 33101

JOANIS, JOHN WESTON, insurance company executive; b. Hopewell, Va., June 13, 1918; s. Edmund W. and Emma Elvira (Westen) J.; m. Marian G. Sinrud, Aug. 16, 1945; children: Susan Kay, Mary Ellen, William John. LL.B., U. Wis., 1942; grad., Advanced Mgmt. Program, Harvard, 1950. Bar: Wis. 1943. Pvt. practice, Oshkosh, 1945-47; with Hardware Mut. Casualty Co. (now Sentry Ins. A Mut. Co.), Stevens Point, Wis., 1947—, asst. sec., 1948-52, sec., gen. counsel, 1952-56, v.p., gen. counsel, 1956-62, exec. v.p., 1962-66, pres., chief exec. officer, 1966-72, chmn. bd., chief exec. officer, 1972—, dir., 1960—; chmn. bd., chief exec. officer Sentry Life Ins. Co., 1967—, Sentry Corp., 1973—, dir., 1967—; chmn. bd., dir. Sentry Indemnity Co., 1978—, Dairyland Ins. Co., Scottsdale, Ariz., 1970—, Gt. S.W. Fire Ins. Co., Scottsdale, 1972—, Middlesex Ins. Co., Concord, Mass., 1974—, Sentry Investors Ins. Co., Concord, 1974—, Patriot Gen. Life Ins. Co., 1978—, Australian Casualty Co. Ltd., Australia, 1978—, Sentry Holdings Ltd., 1978—, Sentry Fin. Mgmt., Ltd., 1978—, Sentry Ins. (Australasia) Ltd., 1978—, Sentry Life Assurance Ltd., 1978—, Sentry Holdings (Antilles) N.V., 1978—, Sentry (Hong Kong) Ltd., 1978—, Sentry Holdings (PTE) Ltd., Singapore, 1978—, City of Westminster Assurance Co. Ltd., Eng., 1978—, City of Westminster Assurance Soc., Ltd., 1978—, Sentry Fin. Ltd., 1978—; chmn. bd., pres. Sentry Assurance Internat. Ltd., Bermuda, 1979—, Sentry Internat. Bond Fund Ltd., 1979—; dir. Sentry Investment Mgmt., Inc., Sentry Life Ins. Co. N.Y., Syracuse, A. E. Staley Mfg. Co., Decatur, Ill., 1st Nat. Bank, Stevens Point, Wis. Bd. dirs. Alliance Am. Insurers and Am. Insurers Hwy. Safety Alliance, 1966, Wis. Found. Ind. Colls., Inc.; mem. exec. com. Wis. Clergy Econ. Edn. Conf.; trustee Stevens Point YMCA, 1969—, past pres. bd. Served to capt. USAAF, 1942-45. Mem. Am., Wis., Portage County bar assns., Ins. Inst. Am. (trustee), Am. Inst. Property and Liability Underwriters (trustee), Internat. Assn. Ins. Counsel, Am. Legion,. Clubs: Elks, Rotary, Madison, Milw. Athletic; Marco Polo (N.Y.C.); Union League (Chgo.). Office: 1800 N Point Dr Stevens Point WI 54481

JOANNING, HAROLD T., life ins. co. exec.; b. Alton, Iowa, May 30, 1927. A.B., Claremont Men's Coll., 1954. With Pacific Mut. Life Ins. Co., 1944—, asst. v.p. adminstrn., 1964-65, treas., 1965—, v.p., controller, 1970-81, sr. v.p., fin. exec., 1981—. Mem. Fin. Execs. Inst. Office: Pacific Mut 700 Newport Center Dr Newport Beach CA 92660 also 3621 Sausalito Dr Newport Beach CA 92625

JOANOU, PHILLIP, advertising executive; b. Phoenix, June 5, 1933; s. Paul and Alice (Lukken) J.; m. Michelle Mason, Aug. 18, 1956; children: Janet, Phillip, Jennifer, Kathleen. B.S., U. Ariz., 1956. Exec. v.p. Galaxy Inc., Los Angeles, 1958-60; sr. account exec. Erwin Wasey Co., 1960-64; account supr. Dancer, Fitzgerald, Sample Co., Los Angeles, 1964-67; v.p. Grey Co., Los Angeles, 1966-68, Doyle, Dane & Bernbach Inc., 1968-71; exec. v.p., dir. Nov. Group, N.Y.C. and Washington, 1971-72; chmn., chief exec. officer, dir. Dailey & Assocs., Los Angeles, 1972—; instr. mktg. U. So. Calif., 1975-76, dir., 1976-77. Mem. Washington Com. to Re-elect Pres. Nixon, 1971-72; advisor Pres. Ford Election Com., 1976, Pres. Reagan Campaign, 1980; bd. dirs. Crippled Children's Soc., Crippled Children's Hosp., Los Angeles, 1980—; pres. La Canada Ednl. Found. Served to capt. USAR, 1957-58. Mem. Western States Advt. Assn. (dir. 1975—, pres. 1980-81), Am. Assn. Advt. Agencies (gov. 1980-81, bd. dirs. 1981-83), Mktg. Execs. Club, Los Angeles Advt. Club (dir.), World Affairs Council. Republican. Episcopalian. Club: Jonathon. Home: 5663 Bramblewood Rd La Canada CA 91011 Office: 3055 Wilshire Blvd Los Angeles CA 90010

JOBE, LARRY ALTON, accountant, auditor; b. Knox City, Tex., Jan. 12, 1940; s. Lloyd Alton and Georgia (Swift); m. Suzanne Marie Storch, Aug. 2, 1980; 1 dau., Jennifer Marie; children by previous marriage: Lorrie Aileen, Lezlie Amee, Lowell Alton, Lloyd Alan, Leland Austin, Llewyn. B.B.A., N. Tex. State U., 1961, postgrad., 1961-65. C.P.A., Tex., Ill., Iowa, D.C. Joined Alexander Grant & Co., Dallas, 1961, mgr., 1967-69, partner, 1968-69; asst. sec. commerce, Washington, 1969-72; v.p. finance Dart Industries, 1972-73; mng. partner, mem. exec. com. Alexander Grant & Co., Dallas, 1973—, S.W. regional mng. ptnr., 1983—; Mem. accounting adv. bd. N. Tex. State U., U. Tex.; dir. Dixico, Inc., Allied Bank of Dallas. Contbr. articles to profl. jours. Mem. Dallas Citizen's Council, Chief Execs. Roundtable; chmn. bd. Dallas Alliance for Minority Enterprise, Dallas Minority Bus. Center. Recipient Excellence in Accounting award Haskins & Sells Found., 1960, Outstanding Alumni award North Tex. State U., 1965, U.S. Interagency Audit Tng. award, 1970; Outstanding Service award; 1st Place Author's award Fed. Govt. Accountants Assn., 1970. Mem. Am. Inst. C.P.A.s, Tex. Soc. C.P.A.s, Fed. Govt. Accountants Assn., Dallas C. of C. (dir., vice chmn.), Blue Key, Phi Eta Sigma, Alpha Chi, Alpha Lambda Pi, Beta Alpha Psi. Office: One Dallas Centre Dallas TX 75201

JOBS, STEVEN PAUL, computer corporation executive; b. 1955; adopted s. Paul J. and Clara J. (Jobs). Student, Reed Coll. With Hewlett-Packard, Palo Alto, Calif.; designer video games Atari Inc., 1974; chmn. bd. Apple Computer Inc., Cupertino, Calif. Co-designer: (with Stephan Wozniak) Apple I Computer, 1976. Office: Apple Computer Inc 10260 Bandley Dr Cupertino CA 95014 *

JOBUSCH, FREDERICK HENRY, architect; b. Collinsville, Ill., Feb. 24, 1916; s. Frederick August and Edna Emelia (Emig) J.; m. Josephine Buckley Cook, 1, May 20, 1939; children: Lizette Christine, Georgia Jean, Anthony Jack. B.S. in Archtl. Engring., U. Ill., 1937. Registered profl. engr., Ariz.; registered architect, Ariz., N.Mex., Calif., C.Z. Structural designer, Ind., Ill. and Ariz., 1937-45; archtl. engr. James Macmillan, Tucson, 1946-47, Place & Place (Architects), 1947-48, Terry Atkinson, 1953-56; cons. structural engr., Tucson, 1948-53; prin., v.p. Friedman & Jobusch (Architects and Engrs., Inc.), Tucson, 1956-80; prin. Fred Henry Jobusch (Cons. Architect), 1980—; dir. Home Fed. Savs. & Loan Assn. Ariz.; chmn. Ariz. Bd. Tech. Registration for Architects and Engrs., 1955-56; mem. profl. adv. council Coll. Architecture, U. Ariz., 1958—. Important works include Chris-Town Shopping Center Mall, Phoenix, City Hall Tower, Tucson, Health Scis. Center, U. Ariz., Chemistry Bldg., U. Ariz., New U. Library, Marana (Ariz.) High Sch., Ariz. Bank Plaza Bldg., Tucson, Kino Community Hosp., Pima County. Chmn. Old Pueblo Redevel. Com., Tucson Planning and Zoning Commn., 1963-64; pres. bd. dirs. United Way, Tucson, 1964; mem. exec. bd. Catalina council Boy Scouts Am., 1967—, pres. bd., 1973-74; chmn. Catalina chpt. Nat. Eagle Scout Assn., 1975—; mem. exec. bd. St. Lukes In The Desert, Inc., 1967-80, pres., 1976-80; active Pres.'s Club and U. Ariz. Found., 1968—. Recipient Silver Beaver award Boy Scouts Am., 1975. Fellow AIA (pres. So. Ariz. chpt. 1956-57, 68, chmn. judiciary com. Western Mountain region 1966-69); mem. Ariz. Soc. Architects (pres. 1968), Ariz. Soc. Profl. Engrs. (pres. So. Ariz. chpt. 1952-53, Engr. of Year award 1964), Constrn. Specifications Inst. (pres. Tucson chpt. 1971), Structural Engrs. Assn. Ariz., Ariz. C. of C., Tucson C. of C. (chmn. Task Force for Old Town Devel. 1971-73), Am. Arbitration Assn. (arbitrator), U. Ill. Alumni Assn., Alpha Rho Chi. Clubs: Masons (32 deg.), KT, Shriners, Order Eastern Star, Downtown Tucson Sertoma, Old Pueblo. Home: 2650 N Bonanza Ave Tucson AZ 85749 Office: 2500 N Pantano Rd Suite 117 Tucson AZ 85715

JOCHUM, VERONICA, pianist; b. Berlin; d. Eugen and Maria (Montz) J.; m. Wilhelm V. von Moltke, Nov. 15, 1961. M.A. equivalent, Staatliche Musikhochschule, Munich, 1955, Concert Diploma, 1957; pvt. study with, Edwin Fischer, Josef Benvenuti, 1958-59, Rudolf Serkin, Phila., 1959-61. Faculty Settlement Sch. Music, Phila., 1959-61, New Eng. Conservatory Music, Boston, 1965—, Berkshire Music Center, Tanglewood, 1974. Recorded albums with, Deutsche Grammophon, Philips, Golden Crest.; Numerous tours, throughout N. and S. Am., Asia, Europe and, Africa; as soloist with world renowned orchs., including, Boston Symphony, Balt. Symphony, London Philharmonic, Los Angeles Chamber Orch., London Symphony, Mpls. Symphony, Berlin, Hamburg and Munich philharmonics, Mpls. Symphony, Bavarian and Bamberg symphonies, Munich Chamber Orch., radio orchs. of, Hamburg, Munich, and Frankfurt, Orch. Maggio Musicale, Florence, La Fenice Orch., Venice, RAI-Orch., Naples, Mozarteum Orch., Salzburg, Concertgebouw Orch., Amsterdam, The Hague Philharmonic, Venezuelan Symphony, Caracas, Jerusalem Symphony, others; appearances on radio and TV, recitals in more than 50 countries on 4 continents; participant, Marlboro Music Festival, 1959-60, Montreux Festival, Bregewz Festival; artist-in-residence, Eastern Music Festival, 1967-72, 78. Office: New England Conservatory of Music 290 Huntington Ave Boston MA 02115

JOCKUSCH, CARL GROOS, JR., educator; b. San Antonio, July 13, 1941; s. Carl Groos and Mary English (Dickson) J.; m. Elizabeth Ann Northrop, June 17, 1964; children—William, Elizabeth, Rebecca. Student, Vanderbilt U., 1959-60; B.A. with highest honors, Swarthmore Coll., 1963; Ph.D., M.I.T., 1966. Instr. Northeastern U., 1966-67; asst. prof. math. U. Ill., Urbana-Champaign, 1967-71, asso. prof., 1971-75, prof., 1975—. Contbr. articles to profl. jours.; Editor: Journal of Symbolic Logic, 1974-75. NSF research grantee. Mem. Assn. Symbolic Logic, Am. Math. Soc., Math. Assn. Am. Home: 704 McHenry St Urbana IL 61801 Office: Dept Math 1409 W Green St Univ Ill Urbana IL 61801

JOEL, BILLY (WILLIAM MARTIN JOEL), musician; b. Bronx, N.Y., May 9, 1949; s. Howard and Rosalind (Nyman) J. Popular rec. artist, 1972—; songs include Just the Way You Are, 1978 (Grammy award for record of yr., Grammy award for song of yr.), Honesty, 1979 (Grammy nomination for song of yr.); albums include Piano Man, Streetlife Serenade, Turnstiles, The Stranger, 52nd Street (Grammy awards for best album, best male vocal performance 1979), Glass Houses, 1980 (Grammy award for best rock male vocal performance, Am. Music award as album of yr.), Songs in the Attic, The Nylon Curtain, 1982 (Grammy nomination as album of yr.), An Innocent Man. Office: care Frank Mgmt Inc 375 N Broadway Jericho NY 11753

JOFFE, CHARLES, motion picture producer, comedy management executive; b. N.Y.C., July 16, 1929; s. Sid and Esther (Gordon) J.; m. Carol Shapiro; children: Suzanne, Nicole. B.S., Syracuse U. Ptnr. Rollins & Jaffe, N.Y.C. Producer: film Take the Money and Run, 1969, Don't Drink the Water, 1969, Love and Death, 1975, Everything You Always Wanted to Know About Sex But Were Afraid to Ask, 1972, Interiors, 1978, Manhattan, 1979; exec. producer: Bananas, 1971, Play It Again, Sam, 1972, Sleeper, 1973, The Front, 1976, Annie Hall, 1977 (Acad. award for best picture), Stardust Memories, 1980, Arthur, 1981, A Midsummer Night's Sex Comedy, 1982, Zelig, 1983; producer: Woody Allen TV spls. Mem. Acad. Motion Pictures, Am. Film Inst. Office: Rollins Joffe Morra & Brezner Paramount Studios 5555 Melrose Ave Los Angeles CA 90038

JOFFREY, ROBERT (ABDULLAH JAFFA BEY KHAN), ballet company director, choreographer, dancer; b. Seattle, Dec. 24, 1930; s. Dolha and Marie (Galetti) J. Student, Mary Ann Wells Sch. of Dance, Seattle, 1944-48, Cornish Sch. Music, Seattle, 1945-48, Sch. Am. Ballet, 1948; pupil, Alexandra Federova; student modern dance with, May O'Donnell, Gertrude Shurr, 1949-52. Mem. faculty High Sch. Performing Arts, N.Y.C., 1950-55; also Am. Ballet Theatre Sch.; founder ballet sch. Am. Ballet Center, 1953, dir. faculty, 1953-65; Pres. Ballet Am. Found.; bd. dirs. Found. Am. Dance. Resident choreographer, N.Y. City Center Opera, 1955-61; founder, 1956; since artistic dir., choreographer, The Joffrey Ballet (formerly Robert Joffrey Ballet Co.); co. toured, Near East for, State Dept., 1962-63; toured, Russia, 1963; performed at, White House, 1963, 65, ann. U.S. tours, 1956-64; organizer dance dept., Chautauqua, N.Y., 1959; choreographer, NBC-TV Opera, 1955, 57, 58; made debut as soloist with, Petit's Ballet de Paris; creator: ballets Remembrances. Recipient ann. award Nat. Acad. Dance Masters, Chgo., 1962; Dance mag. award, 1964; Dance Masters of Am. award, 1965; Ford Found. grant Robert Joffrey Ballet, 1964. Office: 434 6th Ave New York NY 10009 also 130 W 56th St New York NY 10019 *

JOHANNES, GEORGE ROBERT, manufacturing executive, accountant; b. N.Y.C., Dec. 19, 1938; s. George and Regina (Gensler) J.; m. Dorothe Elizabeth Redmond, Apr. 16, 1960; children: Robert, Linda. B.B.A., Manhattan Coll., N.Y.C., 1962; exec. program, Stanford U., 1981. C.P.A., N.Y. Gen. practice mgr. Coopers & Lybrand, N.Y.C., 1968-74; dir. acctg. Johns-Manville Service Corp., Denver, 1974-78; sr. dir. acctg. Manville Service Corp., Denver, 1978-82; sr. v.p. fin., chief fin. officer Manville Corp., Denver, 1982—. Served to sgt. U.S. Army, 1968. Mem. Am. Inst. C.P.A.s, Fin. Exec. Inst., N.Y. State Soc. C.P.A.s. Republican. Roman Catholic. Office: Manville Corp PO Box 5108 Denver CO 80217

JOHANNES, WILFRED CLEMENS, educator; b. Dyersville, Iowa, Jan. 19, 1924; s. William Frank and Zita (Langel) J. B.A., Loras Coll., 1945; M.A., Catholic U., 1951; Ph.D., U. Mich., 1963. Ordained priest Roman Catholic Ch., 1948; asst. dean students Loras Coll., Dubuque, Iowa, 1949-54, asso. prof. classical langs., 1963-69, prof., 1970—, chmn. dept., 1968—. Author: The People of Menander, 1963. Mem. Am. Philol. Assn., Classical Assn. Middle West and South, Assn. Internationale de Papyrologues. Address: First and Chestnut Sts Hopkinton IA 52237

JOHANNESEN, AUDREY, pianist; b. Regina, Sask., Can., Sept. 12, 1930; d. Victor and Dorothy (Chew) Johnston; m. Joseph J. Johannesen, May 10, 1958; children—Veronique, Joel, Grant. Student, Central Collegiate Regina, 1944-48; A.R.C.T., U. Toronto, Ont., Can., 1945; L.R.A.M., Royal Acad. Music, London, 1950, postgrad., 1950-53; postgrad., Conservatoire Royal, Brussels, 1953-58. Mem. faculty Shawnigan Summer Sch. Arts, 1971-72; tchr. piano; adjudicator in field. Accompanist for, Carlo Van Neste, violinist, Italy, 1954; rec. artist, Can. Broadcasting Co., 1962-76, Distinguished Artist Series; concert pianist on European tours, 1966, 76. Recipient McFarran Gold medal Royal Acad. Music, London, 1950; Henderson scholar, 1951-53; recipient Premier prix Conservatoire Royale, 1954, prix Van Kutsem, 1955. Mem. Am. Fedn. Musicians. Home: 1307 Nanton Ave Vancouver BC V6H 2C8 Canada

JOHANNSEN, CHRIS JAKOB, agronomist, educator, administrator; b. Randolph, Nebr., July 24, 1937; s. Jakob J. and Marie J. (Lorenzsen) J.; m. Joanne B. Rockwell, Aug. 16, 1959; children: Eric C., Peter J. B.S., U. Nebr.-Lincoln, 1959, M.S., 1961; Ph.D., Purdue U., 1969. Program leader Lab. for Applications of Remote Sensing, Purdue U., 1966-69; asst. prof. agronomy Purdue U., 1969-72; assoc. prof. agronomy U. Mo., Columbia, 1972-77, prof., 1977—; dir. Geographic Resources Ctr., U. Mo., Columbia, 1981—; vis. prof. U. Calif., Davis, 1980-81; cons. Lockheed Electronics, Houston, 1975-76, NOAA, Columbia, Mo., 1978-80, FAO UN, Nairobi, Kenya, 1983. Pres. council St. Andrew's Lutheran Ch., Columbia, 1975-77; asst. scout master Boy Scouts Am., Gt. Rivers council, Columbia, 1979—. Recipient Tech. Innovation Research award NASA, 1979, Disting. Service award Mo. Assn. Soil and Water Conservation Dists., 1982. Fellow Am. Soc. Agronomy, Soil Sci. Soc. Am. (pres. 1982-83); mem. World Assn. of Soil and Water. Home: 1318 Ridge Rd Columbus MO 65201 Office: Dept Agronomy U Mo 214 Waters Hall Columbia MO 65211

JOHANNSEN, ROBERT WALTER, history educator; b. Portland, Oreg., Aug. 22, 1925; s. Walter George and Hedwig Bertha (Flemming) J.; m. Lois Adele Calderwood, Mar. 19, 1949; children: Nancy Louise, Robert Douglas. B.A., Reed Coll., 1948; M.A., U. Wash., 1949, Ph.D., 1953; D.H.L. (hon.), Lincoln Coll., 1983. Instr. history U. Wash., 1953-54; asst. prof., then asso. prof. U. Kans., 1954-59; mem. faculty U. Ill., 1959—, prof. history, 1962—, J.G. Randall Distinguished prof. Am. history, 1973—, chmn. dept., 1963-67, 1968-69; vis. lectr. U. Wis., 1957; vis. assoc. prof. U. Oreg., summer 1960, Duke, summer 1962; vis. Coe prof. Stanford, summer 1970; vis. Disting. prof. Ariz. State U., 1979, La. State U., 1984. Author: Frontier Politics and the Sectional Conflict, 1955, The Union in Crisis, 1965, Democracy on Trial, 1966, Stephen A. Douglas, 1973 (Francis Parkman prize), also articles.; Editor: (with H.V. Jaffa) In the Name of the People, 1959, The Letters of Stephen A. Douglas, 1961. Served with F.A. AUS, 1944-46. Recipient Merit Award Am. Assn. State and Local History, 1962; Guggenheim fellow, 1967-68. Fellow Soc. Am. Historians; mem. Am. Hist. Assn. (recipient Koontz prize Pacific Coast br. 1953), So. Hist. Assn. (bd. editors 1966-70), Western Hist. Assn. (bd. editors 1974-78), Ill. Hist. Soc. (merit award 1973), Orgn. Am. Historians (Pelzer prize 1952, exec. bd. 1974-77), Am. Studies Assn. Home: 1019 W Union St Champaign IL 61820

JOHANSEN, EIVIND HERBERT, former army officer, corporate executive; b. Charleston, S.C., Mar. 7, 1927; s. Andrew and Ruth Lee (Thames) J.; m. Dolores E. Klockmann, June 9, 1950; children: Chris Allen, Jane Elizabeth. B.S., Tex. A & M U., 1950; M.S., George Washington U., 1968; postgrad., Harvard U., 1955, Army Command and Gen. Staff Coll., 1963, Naval War Coll., 1967, Advanced Mgmt. Program, U. Pitts., 1971. Quartermaster officer U.S. Army, 1950-79, advanced through grades to lt. gen., 1977; strategic planner Office Joint Chiefs of Staff, 1968-69, group comdr., 1969-70; army dir. distbn., 1970-72, dir. materiel, 1972-75; comdg. gen. Army Aviation Systems Command, St. Louis, 1975-77; army dep. chief staff for logistics, Washington, 1977-79, ret., 1979; exec. v.p., chief exec. officer Nat. Industries for Severely Handicapped, Inc., 1979—; mem. exec. council, chmn. mgmt. improvement com. Fed. Exec. Bd., St. Louis, 1975-77; bd. advs. Am. Def. Preparedness Assn., St. Louis, 1975-77, tech. and mgmt. adv. bd., Washington, 1977-79; chmn. Army Logistics Policy Council, 1977-79; bd. advs. Army Logistic Mgmt. Center, 1978-79, Army Mgmt. Engring. Sch., 1978-79. Contbr. articles to profl. jours. Mem. Pres.' Com. for Purchase from Blind and Other Severely Handicapped, Washington, 1973-74, chmn., 1975; mem. Pres.'s Com. on Employment of Handicapped; bd. dirs., chmn. ind. ops. com. Mo. Goodwill Industries, 1975-77; chmn. Jr. Achievement Youth Program, St. Louis, 1975-77; sponsor Air Explorer Post, Boy Scouts Am., St. Louis, 1975-77; bd. dirs. Q.M. Found., 1979-83. Decorated D.S.M., Legion of Merit with two oak leaf clusters, Bronze Star, numerous others. Mem. Assn. U.S. Army (bd. advisors St. Louis 1975-77), Am. Helicopter Soc., Army Aviation Assn. Am., Ret. Officers Assn., Nat. Rehab. Assn., Tex. A&M Alumni Assn. Washington (exec. bd. 1974, 78-79, pres. 1975), George Washington U. Alumni Assn., U. Pitts. Alumni Assn., Harvard U. Alumni Assn. Club: Toastmasters. Home: 6310 Windpatterns Trail Fairfax Station VA 22039

JOHANSEN, JULIAN ELLIOTT, mayor; b. Charleston, S.C., Mar. 17, 1923; s. Andrew and Ruth (Lee) J.; married; children: Bruce, Linda, Andrew. B.S. in Engring., U.S. Coast Guard Acad. Commd. ensign U.S Coast Gaurd, 1944, advanced through grades to rear admiral, 1973, comdg. officer air sta., San Juan, P.R., 1964-65, Port Angeles, Wash., 1965-68, San Diego, 1968-70, chief res., 1973-75, comdr. 5th Dist., 1975-78, ret., 1978; v.p. Citizens Trust Bank, Portsmouth, Va., 1979-80; mayor City of Portsmouth, 1980—. Campaign dir. Portsmouth United Fund, 1977, pres., 1978. Decorated Legion of Merit. Lodge: Rotary. Home: 3601 Templar Ct Portsmouth VA 23703 Office: PO Box 820 Portsmouth VA 23705

JOHANSON, DONALD CARL, physical anthropologist; b. Chgo., June 28, 1943; s. Carl Torsten and Sally Eugenia (Johnson) J.; m. Susan Whelan Johanson, May 16, 1981; children: Colleen, Matthew. B.A., U. Ill., 1966; M.A., U. Chgo., 1970, Ph.D., 1974; D.Sc. (hon.), John Carroll U., 1979. Mem. dept. phys. anthropology Cleve. Mus. Natural History, 1972-81, curator, 1974-81; With Inst. Human Origins, Berkeley, Calif., 1981—; adj. prof. Case Western Res. U.,

Kent State U.; host, narrator series Pub. Broadcasting Service, 1982; dir. Internat. Inst. for Study of Human Origins, Berkeley, Calif., 1981-82. Film producer: The First Family, 1981, Lucy in Disguise, 1982; Contbr. chpts. to books, articles to profl. jours. Recipient Jared Potter Kirtland award for outstanding sci. achievement Cleve. Mus. Natural History, 1979, Am. Book award, 1982; NSF, Nat. Geog. Soc., L.S.B. Leakey Found., Cleve. Found., George Gund Found. grantee. Fellow AAAS; mem. Am. Assn. Phys. Anthropologists, Internat. Assn. Dental Research, Current Anthropology, Internat. Assn. Human Biologists, Assn. Africanist Archaeologists, Soc. Vertebrate Paleontology, Soc. Study of Human Biology, Explorers Club, Societe de l'Anthropologie de Paris. Office: Inst Human Rights 2700 Bancroft Way Berkeley CA 94704

JOHANSON, PATRICIA MAUREEN, artist, architect, design consultant; b. N.Y.C., Sept. 8, 1940; d. Alvar Einar and Elizabeth (Deane) J.; m. E.C. Goossen; children: Alvar Deane, Gerrit Hull, Nathaniel James. Student, Bklyn. Mus. Art Sch., 1958, Art Students League, 1961; A.B., Bennington Coll., 1962; M.A., Hunter Coll., 1964; B.S., B.Arch., City Coll. Sch. Architecture, 1977. Vis. prof. art State U. N.Y., Albany, 1969; vis. artist Mass. Inst. Tech., 1974, Oberlin Coll., Ohio, 1974, Alfred U., N.Y., 1974; Southworth lectr. Colby Coll., Maine, 1981; cons. Mitchell-Giurgola Assos. (Architects), N.Y.C., also Phila., 1972—, N.Y. State Council on Arts, 1978. One-man shows, Tibor de Nagy Gallery, NYC, 1967, State U. N.Y. at Albany, 1969, Montclair (N.J.) State Coll., 1974, Rosa Esman Gallery, N.Y.C., 1978, 79, 81, 83, Dallas Mus. Fine Arts, 1982, retrospective, Bennington Coll., 1973, group shows, Hudson River Mus., Yonkers, N.Y., 1964, Bennington Coll., Stable Gallery, N.Y.C., 1966, Tibor de Nagy Gallery, N.Y.C., 1966, 68, Larry Aldrich Mus., Ridgefield, Conn., 1968, Mus. Modern Art, N.Y.C., Grand Palais, Paris, Kunsthaus Zurich, 1969, Tate Gallery, London, Vassar Coll., Finch Coll. Mus., 1971, Everson Mus., Syracuse, N.Y., Detroit Inst. Arts, 1973, Mass. Inst. Tech., 1974, Casa Thomas Jefferson, Brasilia, Brazil, 1975, Pa. Acad. Fine Arts, Phila., Greenwich (Conn.) Library Art Gallery, 1977, Bklyn. Mus., New Gallery Contemporary Art, Cleve., Cleve. State U., Cooper-Hewitt Mus., N.Y.C., 1978, Mus. Modern Art, N.Y.C., 1979, Newark Mus., Graham Gallery, N.Y.C., 1980, U. Mass., Amherst, Bklyn. Mus., Mus. Contemporary Art, Chgo., 1981, Sotheby-Parke Bernet, N.Y.C., 1980, Centro de Documentación de Arte Actual, Barcelona, Spain, 1980, 81, Galeria O'Patacón la Coruña, Spain, 1981, Rosa Esman Gallery, N.Y.C., Met. Mus. Art, N.Y.C., 1982, 83, Berkshire Mus., Pittsfield, Mass., 1982, numerous others; represented in permanent collections, Detroit Inst. Arts, Mus. Modern Art, Met. Mus. Art, N.Y.C., N.Y. State Council on Arts Film Collection, Syracuse, Storm King Art Center, Mountainville, N.Y., Crawford and Chester Sts. Park, Cleve., Bennington Coll., also pvt. collections; films The Art of the Real, USIA, 1968, Stephen Long, CBS-TV, 1968, Patricia Johanson: Cyrus Field, 1974, The City Project: Cleveland, 1977; works include sculpture, landscape sculpture, street furniture, pavement designs, site planning for, Consol. Edison Co., Yale U., Columbus East High Sch., Ind., House and Garden mag., Internat. Yr. of Child Commn., Fair Park, Dallas, Corning Preserve, Albany, N.Y., and others. (Recipient 1st Prize Environ. Design Competition, Monclair State Coll. 1974), and numerous others. (Internat. Womens Yr. award 1976), and others. (Gold medal Acad. Italia delle Arti, Parma 1979). Guggenheim fellow, 1970, 80; Nat. Endowment Arts fellow, 1975. Home: RFD 1 Buskirk NY 12028 Office: Rosa Esman Gallery 121 Spring St New York NY 10012 also Philippe Bonnafont Gallery 2200 Mason St San Francisco CA 94133

JOHANSON, SVEN LENNART, lawyer, insurance company executive; b. St. Paul, Nov. 21, 1931; s. Sven Nathaniel and Elsa Marie (Sandberg) J. B.S. in Bus, U. Colo., 1957; J.D., U. Denver, 1961. Bar: Colo. bar 1961, Ill. bar 1969. Atty. SEC, Washington, 1962-69; corp. sec., corp. counsel Kemper Group, Long Grove, Ill., 1969—. Bd. dirs. Mental Health Assn. Greater Chgo. Mem. Am., Chgo. bar assns., Am. Soc. Corp. Secs. (bd. dirs.). Office: Kemper Center Long Grove IL 60049

JOHN, DEWITT, editor; b. Safford, Ariz., Aug. 1, 1915; s. Franklin Howard and Frances (DeWitt) J.; m. Morley Marshall, Feb. 14, 1942; children: DeWitt, Jennifer John Strom. B.A., Principia Coll., Mo., 1936; M.A., U. Chgo., 1937; M.S., Columbia U., 1938. Editor editorial page St. Petersburg (Fla.) Times, 1938-39; mem. staff Christian Sci. Monitor, Boston, 1939-42, editor, 1964-70, mgr. C.S. coms. on publ., 1962-64, bd. dirs., 1970-80; editor Christian Sci. Jour., Sentinel and Heralds, 1981—. Author: The Christian Science Way of Life, 1962. Served with USNR, 1942-45. Decorated Bronze Star. Home: Old Concord Rd Lincoln MA 01773 Office: Christian Sci Center Boston MA 02115

JOHN, ELTON (REGINALD KENNETH DWIGHT), musician; b. Pinner, Middlesex, Eng., Mar. 25, 1947; s. Stanley and Sheila Eileen (Farebrother) Dwight. Student, Royal Acad. Music, London, 1959-64. Singer, songwriter, musician; began playing piano, 1951; joined group, Bluesology, 1965; appeared in: movie Tommy, 1975; toured America 10 times, 1970-76 (Recipient gold discs for all albums composed and performed); composer, performer: Empty Sky, 1969, Elton John, 1970, Tumbleweed Connection, 1971, Friends, 1971, 11.17.70, 1971, Madman Across the Water, 1971, Yellow Brick Road, Caribou, Captain Fantastic and the Brown Dirt Cowboy, 1975, Rock of the Westies, 1975, Here and There, 1976, Blue Moves, 1976, A Single Man, 1978, Victim of Love, 1979, 21 at 33, 1980, The Fox, 1981; composer, performer albums: Your Song, 1970, Crocodile Rock, 1972, Goodbye Yellow Brick Road, 1973, Bennie and the Jets, 1974, Don't Let The Sun Go Down On Me, 1974, Lucy in the Sky with Diamonds, 1974, Philadelphia Freedom, 1975, Someone Saved My Life Tonight, 1975, Island Girl, 1975, Don't Go Breaking My Heart, 1976, Ego, 1978, Part Time Love, 1978, Song for Guy, 1978, Are You Ready for Love, 1979, Little Jeannie, 1980, Nobody Wins, 1981, Jump Up, 1982, Too Low for Zero, 1983; composer, performer single records. Chmn. Watford Football Club, 1976—. 1st popular western singer to perform in USSR, 1979. Office: care John Reid Enterprises 125 Kensington High St London W8 5SN England *

JOHN, ERWIN ROY, neuroscientist; b. Brownsville, Pa., Aug. 14, 1924; s. Siegfried and Josephine (Kroh) J.; m. Miriam Garfin; children: Sarah A., Sheila P., Steven S., Martha S., Michael S., David J. Student, CCNY, 1944; B.S., U. Chgo., 1948, Ph.D., 1954. Sr. research technician Argonne Nat. Lab., 1946-51; from research fellow to research asso. U. Chgo., 1951-56; asso. research physiologist UCLA, 1956- 58; asso. prof. U. Rochester, 1959-60, prof., dir. center brain research, 1961-64; prof., dir. brain research lab. N.Y. Med. Coll., 1964-77; prof., dir. brain research lab. dept. psychiatry NYU Med. Center, 1977—. Served with AUS, 1943-46. Mem. Inter Brain Research Orgn., AAAS, Am. Physiol. Soc., Soc. Neurosci., Am. EEG Soc. Home: 930 Greacen Ln Mamaroneck NY 10543 Office: Dept Psychiatry NY U Med Center New York NY 10016

JOHN, FRITZ, educator, mathematician; b. Berlin, Germany, June 14, 1910; came to U.S., 1935, naturalized, 1941; s. Hermann and Hedwig (Buergel) Jacobsohn; m. Charlotte Woellmer; children—Thomas Franklin, Charles Frederic. Ph.D., Goettingen (Germany) U., 1933; student, Cambridge (Eng.) U., 1934-35. Asst., then asso. prof. U. Ky., 1935-42; mathematician Aberdeen Proving Grounds, 1942-45; prof. math. N.Y. U., 1946—; Courant prof. Courant Inst., 1976—; dir. Research Inst. Numerical Analysis, Nat. Bur. Standards, 1950-51; spl. research applied math., math. analysis; Sherman Fairchild disting. scholar Calif. Inst. Tech., 1979-80; Josioh Willard Gibbs lectr. Am. Math. Soc., 1975. Author: Plane Waves and Spherical Means, 1955, (with L. Bers and M.S. Schechter) Partial Differential Equations, 1964, (with R. Courant) Introduction to Calculus and Analysis, 1965, Partial Differential Equations, 1978. Recipient G.D. Birkhoff prize in Applied Math., 1973; Rockefeller fellow, 1935, 42; Fulbright lectr. Goettingen U., 1955; Guggenheim travel grantee, 1963; Sr. U.S. Scientist Humboldt award, W. Ger., 1980-81; Benjamin Franklin fellow Royal Soc. Arts. Mem. Nat. Acad. Scis., Am. Math. Soc., AAAS, Math. Assn. Am., Deutsche Akademie der Naturforscher Leopoldina, Sigma Xi. Office: Courant Inst New York Univ 251 Mercer St New York NY 10012

JOHN, JAMES EDWARD ALBERT, mechanical engineer, educator; b. Montreal, P.Q., Can., Nov. 6, 1933; s. Richard Rodda and Margaret Gwendolyn (Howard) J.; m. Constance Brandon Maxwell, Aug. 15, 1958; children—Elizabeth, James, Thomas, Constance. B.S. in Engring, Princeton U., 1955, M.S., 1957; Ph.D. in Mech. Engring, U. Md., 1963. Research engr. Airco, Murray Hill, N.J., 1956-59; instr. dept. mech. engring. U. Md., College Park, 1959-63, asst. prof., 1963-65, assoc. prof., 1965-69, prof., 1969-71; exec. dir. Com. on Motor Vehicle Emissions, Nat. Acad. Scis., Washington, 1971-72; prof., chmn. dept. mech. engring. U. Toledo, 1972-77, Ohio State U., Columbus, 1977-82; dean Sch. Engring. U. Mass., Amherst, 1983—. Author: Gas Dynamics, 1969, (with W. Haberman) Introduction to Fluid Mechanics, 1971, rev. edit., 1980, Engineering Thermodynamics, 1980. Mem. ASME, Soc. Automotive Engrs., Am. Soc. Engring. Edn. Home: 1405 Carriage Rd Powell OH 43065 Office: U Mass 201 Engring Bldg E Amherst MA 01003

JOHN, RALPH CANDLER, college president, educator; b. Prince Frederick, Md., Feb. 18, 1919; s. Byron Wilson and Gladys Bennett (Thomas) J.; m. Dorothy Corinne Prince, Aug. 17, 1943; children: Douglass Prince, Byron Wilson II, Alan Randall. B.A., Berea Coll., 1941; student, Duke U., 1941-43; S.T.B., Boston U., 1943, S.T.M., 1944; Ph.D., Am. U., 1950; L.H.D., Iowa Wesleyan U., 1968; Litt.D., Simpson Coll., 1972. Ordained to ministry United Methodist Ch., 1941; asso. minister Foundry Meth. Ch., Washington, 1945-49; chmn. dept. philosophy and religion Am. U., 1949-51, dean students, 1955-58, dean Coll. Arts and Scis., 1958-63, hon. lifetime prof. philosophy, 1963—; pres. Simpson Coll., Indianola, Iowa, 1963-72, Western Md. Coll., Westminster, 1972—; dir. mut. funds Bankers Life Co., Fair Lanes, Inc.; Chmn. adv. com. Washington Internat. Center, 1959-63; mem. commn. on instl. affairs Assn. Am. Colls. Del., World Meth. Conf., London, 1966; dir. Student Aid Internat., Inc., 1975—. Trustee Randolph-Macon Acad., 1959—. Served to capt. AUS, 1951-53; maj. Res. Recipient Alumni Recognition award Am. U., 1968, Disting. Alumnus award Boston U., 1969, Berea Coll., 1976. Mem. Am. Council on Edn. (commn. on edn. and internat. affairs 1959-63), Am. Philos. Assn., Am. Acad. Religion, Am. Acad. Polit. and Social Sci., Md. Ind. Coll. and Univ. Assn. (chmn. bd., exec. com.), Newcomen Soc. N.Am., Phi Beta Kappa, Phi Kappa Phi, Omicron Delta Kappa, Pi Gamma Mu, Pi Sigma Alpha. Clubs: Prairie (Des Moines); Center (Balt.); Cosmos (Washington); Ocean Pines.

JOHN, THOMAS EDWARD, JR., baseball player; b. Terre Haute, Ind., May 22, 1943; s. Thomas Edward and Ruth Kathryn (Wood) J.; m. Sally D. Simmons, July 13, 1970; 1 dau., Tamara Marie. Student, Ind. State U., 1961-64. Pitcher Cleve. Indians, 1963-65, Chgo. White Sox, 1965-71, Los Angeles Dodgers, 1972-78, N.Y. Yankees, 1979-82, Calif. Angels, 1982—; asst. baseball team Calif. State U., Fullerton. Author: The Tommy John Story, 1978; personal appearances in off season. Served with USAF, 1965-71. Mem. Fellowship of Christian Athletes., Alpha Tau Omega. Mem. Am. League All Star team, 1968, 79, Nat. League All Star team, 1978. Office: Calif Angels Anaheim Stadium 2000 State College Blvd Anaheim CA 92806 *

JOHNCOCK, GORDON WALTER, professional race car driver; b. Hastings, Mich., Aug. 5, 1936; s. Walter and Frances (Bennette) J.; children: Peggy, Wally, Patsy, Pamilee, Gordy. Student pub. schs., Hastings. Profl. race car driver, 1954—; driver U.S. Auto Club sprint cars, from 1963, U.S. Auto Club championship cars, 1964—. First place winner Indpls. 500 Race, 1973, 82; U.S. Auto Club champion, 1976. Home: 715 S Fall River Dr Coldwater MI 49036 Office: care CART 12626 US 12 Brooklyn MI 49230

JOHN PAUL II, HIS HOLINESS POPE (KAROL JOZEF WOJTYLA), b. Wadowice, Poland, May 18, 1920; s. Karol and Emilia (Kaczorowska) W. Student, Jagiellonian U., Krakow; studied in underground seminary, Krakow, during World War II; Doctorate in ethics, Pontifical Angelicum U., Rome, 1948, Catholic U. of Lublin, Poland; Dr. (hon.), J. Guttenberg U., Mainz, W. Ger., 1977. Ordained priest Roman Cath. Ch., 1946; prof. moral theology Jagiellonian U.; prof. ethics Cath. U. of Lublin, 1954-58, dir. ethics inst., 1956-58; aux. bishop of Krakow, 1958, archbishop of Krakow, 1964-78; great chancellor Pontifical Theol. Faculty, Krakow; created cardinal by Pope Paul VI, 1967; elected Pope, Oct. 16, 1978, installed, Oct. 22, 1978. Author of: books, poetry, plays, including The Goldsmith's Shop; Play Easter Vigil and Other Poems, 1979, Love & Responsibility, 1960, The Acting Person, 1969, Foundations of Renewal, 1972, Sign of Contradiction, 1976, Redemptor Hominis; Encyclical Redemptor Hominis, 1979; contbr. articles on philosophy, ethics and theology to jours. Address: Palazzo Apostolico Vatican City

JOHNPOLL, BERNARD KEITH, communications educator; b. N.Y.C., June 3, 1918; s. Israel Joseph and Ray (Elkin) J.; m. Lillian Kirtzman, Feb. 14, 1944; children: Janet Johnpoll Greenlee, Phyllis. A.B. magna cum laude, Boston U., 1959; A.M., Rutgers U., 1963; Ph.D., SUNY, 1966. Reporter, rewriter Post-Gazette, Pitts., 1946-51; copy editor news editor Boston Record Am., 1951-61; asst. prof. polit. sci. Hartwick Coll., 1963-65; vis. asst. prof. U. Sask., 1965-66; prof. polit. sci. SUNY-Albany, 1966-82; prof. communications Fla. Atlantic U., Boca Raton, 1982—. Writer-producer: ednl. TV series Prologue, Berkshire Prodns.; TV program American Diary, A Year to Remember; author: The Politics of Futility, 1967, Pacifist's Progress, 1970, The Impossible Dream, 1981; editor, contbr.: Polit. Sci., 1977—. NDEA, 1960-63; Nat. Council Jewish Culture fellow, 1963-65. Mem. Am. Polit. Sci. Assn., Soc. Propagation Judaism (trustee 1971—), Pi Sigma Alpha. Democrat. Jewish. Club: Workmen's Circle (Albany, N.Y.). Home: 3015 Ocean Blvd Highland Beach FL 33431 Office: Fla Atlantic U Dept Communications Boca Raton FL 33431

JOHNS, ALBERT CAMERON, polit. scientist; b. Rockford, Ill., Dec. 28, 1914; s. Robert Alexander and Jane Scott (Anderson) J.; m. Edna Gale, Aug. 23, 1941; children—Ronald Cameron, Janene Laurie, Pamela Gayle. A.A., Los Angeles City Coll., 1942; A.B., Chapman Coll., 1948; M.A., Claremont Grad. Sch., 1963, Ph.D., 1965. Reporter Pasadena (Calif.) Star News, 1950-52; dir. public relations Tournament Roses Assn., Pasadena, 1952-59; real estate editor, columnist Los Angeles Times, 1959-62; instr. govt. Redlands (Calif.) U., 1963-64; asst. prof. Chapman Coll., Orange, Calif., 1964, asso. prof., 1965-66; asso. prof. polit. sci. U. Nev., Las Vegas, 1967-75, prof., 1975-81; owner Al Johns Co., Pasadena, 1950—, West Covina, Calif., 1959—, Las Vegas, 1967—; asso. prof. Pa. State U., summer 1967; chmn. Clark County Urban Studies program U. Ariz., 1968; dir. labor seminar Four State Program, 1968. Author: Nevada Government and Politics, 1971, rev. edit., 1973, Governing Our Silver State, 1973, Nevada Politics, 1973, 3d edit., 1978; co-author: American Politics in Transition, 1977; Co-author: Rocky Mountain Urban Politics, 1971; Contbr. articles to profl. jours. Dir. public relations Miss Universe Pageant, Long Beach, Calif., 1955-58; field rep. 20th dist. Calif. for U.S. Ho. Reps., 1952-56; 1st v.p. So. Nev. Community Concert Assn. Served with AUS, 1942-46. Recipient Nat. Assn. Homebuilders Outstanding Service award as real estate editor, 1960, Real Estate Editors Excellence award, 1960; named Alumnus of Yr. Chapman Coll., 1960. Mem. So. Calif. Polit. Sci. Assn. (dir. 1965-67), Western Polit. Sci. Assn., Am. Polit. Sci. Assn., AAUP, Am. Acad. Polit. and Social Sci., Claremont Grad. Sch. Alumni Assn. (bd. dirs.), Pi Sigma Alpha. Home: 5433 Longridge Ave Las Vegas NV 89102

JOHNS, CHRISTOPHER GEORGE, photojournalist; b. Medford, Oreg., Apr. 15, 1951; s. George Arthur and Joanne Harriet (Utz) J.; m. Pamela Jean Formick, Sept. 11, 1976. B.S., Oreg. State U., 1974; postgrad., U. Minn. Sch. Journalism and Mass Communications, 1975. Staff photographer Albany (Oreg.) Democrat-Herald, 1973-74; teaching asst. U. Minn. Sch. Journalism, Mpls., 1974-75; staff photographer Topeka Capital-Jour., 1975-80, Seattle Times, 1980—. Named Photographer of Yr., Region 7 Nat. Press Photography Assn., 1977, 78, Newspaper Photographer of Yr. Pictures of Yr. Competition, 1978. Mem. Nat. Press Photographers Assn., Sigma Delta Chi. Office: PO Box 70 Seattle WA 98110

JOHNS, CLAUDE JACKSON, JR., librarian; b. Jacksonville, Fla., Aug. 28, 1930; s. Claude Jackson and Agnes (Dugger) J.; m. Rachel Ann Sutton, Sept. 1, 1956; children—Michael Raymond, Kenneth Patrick. B.S., Fla. State U., 1952, M.S., 1953; Ph.D., U. N.C., 1964; M.A., U. Denver, 1975. Commd. 2d lt. USAF, 1956, advanced through grades to lt. col., 1969; prof. polit. sci. USAF Acad., 1961-76, dir. libraries, 1969-76; ret., 1976; dean library services U. No. Colo., Greeley, 1976—; cons. libraries to Shah of Iran, 1975. Author: American Defense Policy, 2d edit, 1968, Handbook on Library Regulations, 1976, also articles. Decorated Legion of Merit, Commendation medal. Mem. Spl. Libraries Assn. (John Cotton Dana lectr. 1974-75), ALA (mem. council 1978—), Colo. Library Assn. (pres. 1977-78), Mountain Plains Library Assn., Colo. Alliance for Research Libraries (chmn. 1977-78), Am. Soc. Info. Sci., AAUP. Democrat. Episcopalian. Home: 29 Alles Dr Greeley CO 80631 Office: Michener Library Univ No Colo Greeley CO 80639

JOHNS, DON HERBERT, chemist; b. LaCrosse, Wis., June 30, 1925; s. Herbert D. and Lillian M. (Davis) J.; m. Elizabeth K. Jallings, July 21, 1945; children—Cheryl Lynn Sweazey, Donna Johns Dewitte. B.S., U. Wis., 1948, M.S., 1951, Ph.D., 1953. Jr. chemist Shell Oil Co., Deer Park, Tex., 1948-50; chemist Barrington (Ill.) Lab., Am. Can Co., 1953-56, supr., 1956-58; group leader Western Lab., San Francisco, 58-60; sect. mgr. Barrington Lab., 1960-62, asst. to dir. research and devel., N.Y.C., 1962-66, dir. research and devel., 1966-70, Princeton (N.J.) Research Center, 1970-79, Continental Can Co., 1979—; mem. adv. council Polymer Materials Program, Princeton U., 1975—. Mem. Fox River Grove (Ill.) Sch. Bd., 1956-58. Served with USAAF, 1943-45. Decorated Purple Heart, Air medal. Mem. Indsl. Research Inst. (dir.), NAM (tech. com.), AAAS, Am. Chem. Soc., Sigma Xi. Clubs: Masons; Nassau (Princeton). Home: 20 Eno Ln Westport CT 06800 Office: 51 Harbor Plaza Stamford CT 06904

JOHNS, HAROLD ELFORD, biophysicist; b. Chengtu, W. China, July 4, 1915; s. Alfred E. and Myrtle (Madge) J. (parents Canadian citizens); m. Sybil Hawkins, June 15, 1940; children: Gwyneth, Claire, Marilyn. B.A. in Physics with honors, McMaster U., Ont., Can., 1936, D.Sc. (hon.), 1968; M.A. in Physics, Toronto, 1937; Ph.D., Toronto, 1939; LL.D. (hon.), U. Sask., 1959, D.Sc., Carleton U., Ottawa, 1976, U. Western Ont., 1978. Lectr. physics U. Alta., Edmonton, 1939-45; lectr. radar to Navy personnel, 1939-45; ofcl. radiographer aircraft castings for Western Can., 1942-45; mem. faculty U. Sask., 1945-56, prof. physics, until 1956; physicist Sask. Cancer Commn., 1945-56; prof. physics U. Toronto, 1956-81, prof. med. biophysics, 1958-81, prof. emeritus, 1981—, head dept., 1962-71; prof. Inst. Med. Scis., 1968—; head physics div. Ont. Cancer Inst., Toronto, 1956-80; mem. Internat. Commn. Radiol. Units, 1952-65; mem. radiation study sect. NIH, 1961-66; bd. dirs. Nat. Cancer Inst. Can., 1954-58. Author: The Physics of Radiology, 1961, also articles. Decorated officer Order of Can.; named Saskatoon Citizen of Year, 1952; recipient Canadian Centennial award, 1968; Gairdner Internat. award, 1973; gold medal Am. Soc. for Therapeutic Radiologists, 1980; numerous others. Fellow Royal Soc. Can. (Henry Marshall Tory medal 1971, Coolidge award 1976), Am. Coll. Radiology (hon., Gold medal 1980); mem. Can. Assn. Radiologists, Canadian Assn. Med. Physicists, Canadian Assn. Physicists (medal 1965), Brit. Inst. Radiology (Roentgen award 1953), Am. Phys. Soc., Biophys. Soc., Am. Assn. Physicists in Medicine, Radiation Research Soc., Am. Radium Soc. Home: 4 Roxbury Rd Etobicoke ON M9C 2W2 Canada Office: Ont Cancer Inst Physics Div 500 Sherbourne St Toronto ON M4X 1K9 Canada

JOHNS, JASPER, artist; b. Augusta, Ga., May 15, 1930; s. Jasper and Jean (Riley) J. Student, U. S.C., 1947-48. One-man exhbns. include, Leo Castelli Gallery, N.Y.C., 1958, 60, 61, 63, 66, 68, 76, 81, Minami Gallery, Tokyo, 1965, 75, Galerie Rive Droite, Paris, 1959, 61, Galleria D'Arte Del Naviglio, Milan, Italy, 1959, Ileana Sonnabend, Paris, 1963, Columbia Mus. Art (S.C.), 1960, Jewish Mus., N.Y.C., 1964, White-chapel Gallery, London, Pasadena Mus. (Calif.), 1965, Smithsonian Instn. Nat. Collection Fine Arts, 1966, Arts Council Great Britain, 1974-75, Whitney Mus. Am. Art, 1977, Kunsthalle, Cologne, 1978, Centre Pompidou, Paris, Hayward Gallery, London, Seibu Mus., Tokyo, San Francisco Mus. Modern Art, Kunstmuseum, Basel, 1979; represented in permanent collections, Mus. Modern Art, Albright-Knox Art Gallery, Buffalo, Tate Gallery, London, Moderna Museet, Stockholm, Stedelijik Mus., Amsterdam, Holland, Whitney Mus., N.Y.C., Kunstmuseum, Basel, Centre Pompidou. Recipient 1st prize Print Biennale, Ljubljana, Yugoslavia, prize IX Sao Paulo (Brazil) Bienal. Mem. Nat. Inst. Arts and Letters. Address: care Leo Castelli Gallery 420 W Broadway New York NY 10012

JOHNS, JOHN EDWIN, university president; b. Ozart, Ala., Nov. 15, 1921; s. T.M. and Susie E. (Spires) J.; m. Martha Mauney, Aug. 23, 1947; children: John Edwin, Steven M., Marcus M. A.B., Furman U., 1947, LL.D., 1972; M.A., U. N.C., 1948, Ph.D., 1958; LL.D., Stetson U., 1971; Litt.D., William Jewell Coll., 1972; H.H.D., Rollins Coll., 1975. Prof. history Stetson U., DeLand, Fla., 1948-63, bus. mgr., 1963-68, v.p., 1968-70, pres., 1970-76, Furman U., Greenville, S.C., 1976—; dir. First Fed. Savs. & Loan Assn., Greenville; trustee Bert Fish Testamentary Trust. Author: Florida during the Civil War, 1963; contbr. to: Ency. Brit., 1960; contbr.: Jefferson Ency., 1970. Pres. United Fund; mem. Fla. Council of 100. Served to 1st lt. USAAF, 1942-46; ETO. Decorated D.F.C., Air medal with 4 oak leaf clusters, Purple Heart. Mem. Ind. Univs. and Colls. S.C. (chmn. pres.'s council), Greenville C. of C. (bd. dirs.). Baptist. Clubs: Green Valley Country, Poinsett. Lodges: Masons; Rotary. Home: 104 Kensington Rd Greenville SC 26909 Office: Furman U Office of President Greenville SC 29618

JOHNS, SAMUEL EARL, JR., oil service company executive; b. Brookville, Pa., Mar. 17, 1927; s. Samuel Earl and Alta Lynne

(Fonner) J.; m. Molly Margaret Helmheckel, July 6, 1952; children: Alan Ross, Samuel Earl III, Clyde William, Jo Allison. B.S., Clarion State U., 1950. Sta. mgr. Birdwell, Inc. (now div. Seismograph Service Corp.), Tulsa, 1952-58; sr. v.p. tech. Gearhart Industries, Inc., Fort Worth, 1958—; mem. mgmt. com. Devel. Geophysics, Denver, 1981—. Author: Basic Electric Log Manuel, 1955; contbr. articles to profl. jours.; patenete (in field). Served with USN, 1943-46. Republican. Club: Century II (Fort Worth). Office: Gearhart Industries Inc 1100 Everman Rd Fort Worth TX 76101 *The pennant winning baseball team wins a few more than it loses, and last place results from a few more losses than wins. Good fortune and bad befalls us in about equal doses. A decent mind, an extra effort or a touch of each often produces those few extra wins called Success.*

JOHNS, VARNER JAY, JR., med. educator; b. Denver, Jan. 27, 1921; s. Varner Jay and Ruby Charlene (Morrison) J.; m. Dorothy Mae Hippach, Dec. 7, 1944; children—Marcia Johns Hinshaw, Donna Johns Bennett, Varner Jay III. B.S., La Sierra Coll., 1944; M.D., Coll. Med. Evangelists, 1945. Diplomate: Nat. Bd. Med. Examiners, Am. Bd. Internal Medicine, Am. Bd. Cardiovascular Disease. Intern White Meml. Hosp., Los Angeles, 1944-45, resident, 1945-47; resident pathology Loma Linda (Calif.) U., 1947-48; head physician Los Angeles County Hosp., 1951; asso. dean Sch. Medicine Loma Linda U., 1951-54, chmn. dept. medicine, 1956-69, 80—, prof. medicine, 1957—, asso. dean continuing edn., 1975—; chief medicine service White Meml. Hosp., Los Angeles, 1956-62, 78-80, Loma Linda U. Hosp., 1964-69, 80—; physician in chief Los Angeles County Hosp., 1958-64; cons. Office Surgeon Gen., Dept. Army, 1956-67; vis. colleague Inst. Cardiology, London, 1962-63; hon. vis. physician Nat. Heart Hosp., London, 1962-63; cons. Jerry L. Pettis Meml. VA Hosp., Loma Linda, 1978—. Editorial bd.: Calif. Medicine, 1964-74; contbr. articles to profl. jours. Pres. bd. govs. Alumni Fedn. Loma Linda U., 1970-71; bd. dirs. Audio/Digest, 1975—. Served to maj. M.C. AUS, 1954-56. Fellow A.C.P. (gov. So. Calif. region II 1972-76), Am. Coll. Cardiology; mem. Los Angeles Acad., Medicine (governing bd. 1965-68, 74-79, treas. 1977-78, v.p. 1978-79, pres. 1979-80), San Bernardino County Heart Assn. (dir. 1966-72), Am. Heart Assn. (fellow council clin. cardiology), Western Assn. Physicians, Royal Soc. Medicine, Internat. Soc. Internal Medicine, Am. Fedn. Clin. Research, AMA, Calif. Med. Assn., Los Angeles Soc. Internal Medicine (pres. 1961-62), Inland Soc. Internal Medicine, Alpha Omega Alpha, San Bernardino County Med. Soc. (v.p. 1972-73, pres. 1974-75). Clubs: Torch (San Bernardino Valley, Calif.) (pres. 1971-72); Redlands Country (Calif.)). Home: 11565 Hillcrest Ct Loma Linda CA 92354 *Each new day needs to be approached with optimism and courage. There is a lifelong need to continue the quest for new knowledge, broader understanding and greater wisdom. Living and working can only be truly enjoyed in the context of a healthy, happy, well-balanced personal and family life.*

JOHNS, WILLIAM DAVIS, JR., educator, scientist; b. Waynesburg, Pa., Nov. 2, 1925; s. William Davis and Beatrice (VanKirk) J.; m. Mariana Paull, Aug. 28, 1948; children—Sydney Ann, Susan Helen, David William, Amy Matilda. B.A., Coll. Wooster, 1947; M.A., U. Ill., 1951, Ph.D., 1952. Spl. research asst. petrology Engring. Expt. Sta., U. Ill., 1949-52; research asst., then asst. prof. geology U. Ill., 1952-55; mem. faculty Washington U., St. Louis, 1955-69, prof. earth scis., 1964-69, chmn. dept., 1962-69; now with dept. geology U. Mo., Columbia. Recipient U.S. Scientist award U. Goettingen, Germany, 1976-77; Fulbright fellow U. Goettingen, Germany, 1959-60, U. Heidelberg, Germany, 1968-69. Fellow Geol. Soc. Am., Mineral. Soc. Am.; mem. Mineral. Soc. Great Britain and Ireland, Mineral. Soc. Can., Deutsches Mineralogisches Gesellschaft, Geochem. Soc., Phi Beta Kappa. Presbyn. (elder). Home: 2200 Yuma Dr Columbia MO 65201

JOHNSEN, GORDON NORMAN, hospital administrator; b. Concord, Mass., Sept. 18, 1926; s. Olaf Magnus and Esther Victoria (Johnsen) J.; m. Barbara Ann Haddon, July 7, 1951; children: Carrie, Paul, Victoria, Peter. B.B.A., U. Wis., 1950, M.S., 1953; M.H.A., U. Minn., 1955; grad., Advanced Mgmt. Program, Harvard, 1974. Asst. adminstr. Iowa Meth. Hosp., Des Moines, 1956-57; adminstr. Madison (Wis.) Gen. Hosp., 1958-75, pres., 1975—; asst. clin. prof. dept. preventive medicine U. Wis. Med. Sch., 1974—; Dir. Viking Ins. Co.; Chmn. Wis. Comprehensive Mental Health and Mental Retardation Planning Commn., 1963-65. Trustee Trinity Coll., Deerfield, Ill., 1979-83, Edgewood Coll., Madison, Wis. Served with USAAC, 1945-46. Recipient Merit award Tri-State Hosp. Assembly, 1970. Fellow Am. Coll. Hosp. Adminstrs.; mem. Wis. Hosp. Assn. (pres. 1968-69), Am. Hosp. Assn. (trustee 1974-77), Ygdrasil Lit. Soc. (pres. 1972-73). Methodist. Clubs: Rotarian., Madison, Blackhawk Country., Torske Klubben. Home: 1102 Willow Ln Madison WI 53705 Office: 202 S Park St Madison WI 53715

JOHNSEN, JOHN HERBERT, geologist, educator, geological consultant; b. S.I., N.Y., Aug. 19, 1923; s. John Hansen and Sigrid (Rueness) J.; m. Catherine Priscilla Brush, June 25, 1948; children—John Frederick, Catherine Sigrid and Cynthia Ellenor (twins). A.B., Syracuse U., 1947, M.S., 1948; Ph.D., Lehigh U., 1957. Geol. asst. Syracuse U., 1946-48; mining geologist N.J. Zinc Co., 1948-49; faculty Vassar Coll., 1951—, prof. geology, chmn. dept., 1964—; dir. summer inst. geology, 1961-64, 66-72; research geologist N.Y. State Geol. Survey, summers 1950-52, 54-58; Vis. prof. sci. camp U. Wyo., 1953; engring. geologist Bur. Phys. Research, N.Y. State Dept. Pub. Works, summer 1959; vis. prof. State U. Coll., New Paltz, N.Y., summer 1960, spring 1964, 65; geol. cons. Hudson River Valley Commn., 1965, Office Planning Coordination, 1966; Mem. radiol. team Dutchess County Civil Def., 1956—; cons. Central N.Y. Region Planning and Devel. Bd., 1969-70. Bd. dirs., exec. com. Dutchess County chpt. ARC, chmn., 1964-67; bd. dirs. Dutchess-Columbia County Tb, Respiratory Disease and Health Assn., 1971-74, Mid-Hudson Patterns for Progress, 1982—. Served to 1st lt. USAAF, 1942-46. Decorated Air medal with four clusters.; N.J. Zinc research fellow, 1949-51. Fellow Geol. Soc. Am.; mem. Paleontol. Soc., Soc. Econ. Paleontologists and Mineralogists, Am. Geophys. Union, Assn. Geology Tchrs., N.Y. State Geol. Assn. (pres. 1954-55, 75-76, dir. 1975-81), AAAS, Am. Assn. Profl. Geologists, Sigma Xi. Home: 46 Thornwood Dr Poughkeepsie NY 12603

JOHNSEN, RUSSELL HAROLD, educator, chemist; b. Chgo., Aug. 5, 1922; s. Harold Gunnar and Irene (Gaul) J.; m. Dorothy Ruth Pehta, Jan. 20, 1948; children: Peter B., Margaret A. B.S., U. Chgo., 1947; Ph.D., U. Wis., 1951. Research chemist Ninol Labs., Chgo., 1947-48; teaching asst. U. Wis., 1948-51; mem. faculty Fla. State U., Tallahassee, 1951—, prof. chemistry, 1961—, chmn. dept. phys. sci., 1951-65, sr. scientist Electron Van de Graaf program, 1958—, assoc. provost Coll. Arts and Scis., 1974-77, assoc. dean grad. studies and research, 1977—; cons. editor W.A. Benjamin, Inc., N.Y.C., 1961-68; Mem. adv. bd. Advances in Radiation Chemistry. Author: (with E.M. Grunwald) Atoms, Molecules and Chemical Change, 3d edit, 1971, (with G.R. Choppin) Introductory Chemistry, 1972; Bd. editors: Jour. Radiation Research Soc, 1966-72. Bd. govs. Center Research Instruction in Coll. Sci. and Math., 1966-71; bd. dirs. Radiation Chemistry Data Center, U. Notre Dame, 1973-79, chmn., 1977-79; bd. dirs. Gordon Research Conf., 1974-76; exec. bd. dirs. State U. System Press, 1978—. Served to 1st lt. USAAF, 1943-46. Fellow AAAS; mem. Am. Chem. Soc., Am. Phys. Soc., Radiation Research Soc. (councilor 1970-71), Am. Soc. Mass Spectrometry, Sigma Xi. Club: Apalachee Bay Yacht (past rear commodore). Research, publs. on chem. effects of ionizing radiation, with emphasis on primary reaction steps, reaction mechanisms of gaseous hydrocarbons and organic solids, electron spin resonance studies. Home: 1425 Devil's Dip Tallahassee FL 32308

JOHNSON, A. DEXTER, association executive; b. Manchester, Conn., Sept. 17, 1907; s. Aaron and Christine (Magnell) J.; m. Lois G. Stoller, July 15, 1957; children: Robert D., Dexter A. Ph.B., Brown U., 1930. With Eastman Kodak Co., 1934-72, advt. mgr., 1959-64, asst. v.p., 1960-72, dir. advt., 1964-72; dir. Eastman Savs. & Loan Assn.; Mem. Assn. Nat. Advertisers, 1962-72, dir., 1968-71; mem. Nat. Advt. Rev. Bd., 1971-72; Nat. Advt. Council coordinator Prisoner of War campaign, 1971-72; mem. Rochester Advt. Council, 1972—; pub. relations dir. new campus fund Rochester Inst. Tech., 1964-68, trustee, 1965-78; dir. Audit Bur. of Circulations, 1968-73. Bd. dirs. Point-of-Purchase Inst., 1956-60; trustee Harley Sch., Rochester, 1953-54. Clubs: Genesee Valley, Brown Univ (Rochester). Home: 4052 East Ave Rochester NY 14618 *Seek a field in which work is a pleasurable experience, studiously acquire a knowledge of it in depth, and develop a willingness to share it to achieve worthwhile objectives.*

JOHNSON, ALAN ARTHUR, physicist, educator; b. Beckenham, Eng., Aug. 18, 1930; came to U.S., 1962; s. Frederick W. and Dorothy (Tew) S.; m. Elizabeth Ann Banks, June 22, 1958; children—Stephen Graham, Michael Andrew, David Nicholas, Brian Philip, Susan Christine. B.Sc. with spl. honours in Physics, Reading (Eng.) U., 1952; M.A. in Physics, U. Toronto, 1954; Ph. D. in Metal Physics, U. London, Eng.; diplomate, Imperial Coll., London, 1960. Sci. officer Royal Naval Sci. Service, Eng., 1954-56; lectr. metallurgy Imperial Coll. Sci. and Tech., U. London, 1960-62; dir. research Materials Research Corp., Orangeburg, N.Y., 1963-65; prof. phys. metallurgy Bklyn. Poly. Inst., 1965-71, head dept. phys. and engring., metallurgy, 1967-71; prof. materials sci., chmn. dept. Wash. State U., 1971-75; dean Grad. Sch., U. Louisville, 1975-76, prof. materials sci., 1975—; cons. to govt. and industry, 1960—. Editor: Water Pollution in the Greater New York Area, 1971; Contbr. articles to profl. jours.; Editor in chief: Internat. Jour. Ocean Enging, 1968-75; asso. editor, 1975—. Mem. Am. Soc. Engring Edn., Am. Soc. Metals (nat. nominating com. 1980-81, chmn. Louisville chpt. 1981-82, chmn. metals engring. inst. com. 1982-83), AAAS, AAUP, Am. Inst. Mining and Metall. Engrs., Sigma Xi, Tau Beta Pi, Phi Kappa Phi. Office: Room 310B Ernst Hall U Louisville Louisville KY 40292

JOHNSON, ALBERT WESLEY, political science educator; b. Insinger, Sask., Can., Oct. 18, 1923; s. Thomas William and Louise Lillian (Croft) J.; m. Ruth Elinor Hardy, June 27, 1946; children: Andrew, Frances, Jane, Geoffrey. B.A., U. Sask., 1942; M.A., U. Toronto, Ont., Can., 1945; M.P.A. (Littauer fellow), Harvard U., 1950, Ph.D., 1963; LL.D. (hon.), U. Regina, 1977, U. Sask., 1978, Mt. Allison U., 1982. Dep. provincial treas. Govt. of Sask., Regina, 1952-64; asst. dep. minister fin. Govt. of Can., Ottawa, Ont., 1964-68, econ. adviser to prime minister on constn., 1968-70, sec. treasury bd., 1970-73, dep. minister nat. welfare, 1973-75; pres. CBC, Ottawa, 1975-82; Shelton-Clark fellow Queens U., 1982-83; prof. polit. sci. U. Toronto, 1983—. Contbr. articles to profl. publs.; editorial bd.: Can. Public Policy, 1974-75. Bd. dirs. Nat. Film Bd., 1970-82, U. Sask. Hosp., 1957-64; mem. Nat. Arts Centre, 1975-82; bd. govs. U. Sask., Saskatoon, 1952-63. Recipient Gold medal Profl. Inst. of Pub. Service of Can., 1975; decorated Order of Can. Mem. Ottawa Polit. Economy Assn. (pres. 1969-70), Inst. Public Adminstrn. Can. (pres. 1962-63, Vanier medal 1976, nat. council 1951-69), Can. Polit. Sci. Assn. (exec. council 1963-64). Mem. United Ch. of Can. Office: U. Toronto 100 St George St Toronto ON Canada M5S 1A1

JOHNSON, ALBERT WILLARD, ednl. adminstr.; b. Belvidere, Ill., July 29, 1926; s. Foster D. and Frida (Heinemann) J.; m. Susan G. Gemeroy, Nov. 15, 1970; children—David D., Peter A.; children by previous marriage—Mark A., Curtis N., Christopher S. B.S., Colo. A. and M. Coll., 1949; M.S., U. Colo., 1951, Ph.D., 1956. Research asst. U. Colo. Inst. Arctic and Alpine Research, 1951-56, instr. biology, 1955; instr., asst. prof., asso. prof. botany U. Alaska, 1956-62; research biologist U. Calif. at Los Angeles, 1962-64; asso. prof., prof. biology San Diego State U., 1964—, dean, 1969-79, acting v.p. acad. affairs, 1977-79, v.p. acad. affairs, 1979—. Mem. San Diego Quality of Life Bd., San Diego Environ. Appeals Bd.; Past pres. Citizens Coordinate for Century III, San Diego; bd. dirs. San Diego U. Found.; trustee San Diego Natural History Soc. Served with USAAF, 1945. Mem. AAAS (past exec. sec. Alaska div.), Ecol. Soc. Am., Soc. for Study Evolution, Sigma Xi. Home: 4363 Middlesex Dr San Diego CA 92116

JOHNSON, ALLEN HUGGINS, physician, educator; b. Columbia, S.C., May 25, 1937; s. Allen H. and Mae Elizabeth (Burgess) J.; m. Martha Davis Johnson, May 24, 1981; children: Allen H., Kathryn Ann, Brooks Burgess. B.S., U. S.C., 1958; M.D., Med. U. S.C., 1962. Diplomate: Am. Bd. Internal Medicine. Intern Med. U. S.C. Hosp., Charleston, 1962-63, asst. resident in medicine, 1965-67; USPHS research fellow dept. medicine Emory U. Sch. Medicine, Atlanta, 1967-69; asst. prof. medicine Med. U. S.C., Charleston, 1969-72, asst. prof. microbiology, 1970-72, assoc. prof. medicine and microbiology, 1972-78, prof. medicine, 1978—, acting chmn. dept., 1979-82, dir. gen. internal medicine div., 1978—, interim dean Coll. Medicine, 1983; chief med. service Charleston County Hosp., 1972-73; chief univ. med. service St. Francis Xavier Hosp., 1974-78. Contbr. articles to med. jours. Served to capt. M.C. U.S. Army, 1963-65. Fellow ACP (gov.); mem. Am. Soc. Internal Medicine, Charleston County Med. Soc., S.C. Med. Assn. Home: 725 Creekside Dr Mount Pleasant SC 29464 Office: 171 Ashley Ave Charleston SC 29403

JOHNSON, ALLEN LEROY, hospital administrator; b. Calmar, Alta, Can., Feb. 15, 1935; s. Lloyd Ferdinand and Lelia Myrtle (Graham) J.; m. Helen Joyce Weitzel, Oct. 6, 1956; children: Allen Donald, Paddy Lou, Sandy Lee. B.A., 1970; M.H.A., U. Minn., 1974. Area mgr. Triad Oil Co., Edmonton, Alta., 1959-62; personnel dir. Misericordia Hosp., Edmonton, 1962-65, Foothills Hosp., Calgary, Alta., 1965-70; cons. Alta. Govt., Edmonton, 1970-72; adminstr. Henry Ford Hosp., Detroit, 1973-79; pres. St. Vincent Med. Ctr., Toledo, 1979—; v.p., trustee Fairlane Health Services, Detroit, 1979—; dir. Blue Cross of N.W. Ohio, Toledo. Chmn. New Ctr. Area Council, Detroit, 1975-80; vice chmn. Community Services Div., United Way, Toledo, 1980—; bd. dirs. Toledo Area Govtl. Research Assn., 1982. Mem. Can. Coll. Health Services Execs., Am. Coll. Hosp. Adminstrs., Am. Pub. Health Assn., Hosp. Council N.W. Ohio (dir. 1979—), Cath. Conf. of Ohio, Ohio Hosp. Assn. (dir. 1981-84), Toledo Area C. of C. (dir. 1982—). Mormon. Club: Inverness. Home: 6958 Leicester St Toledo OH 43615 Office: St Vincent Hosp and Med Ctr 2213 Cherry St Toledo OH 43608 *To have contributed toward an improved health care system in America, therefore to improve health care of Americans is as personally rewarding as the accumulated salary and honors I have received.*

JOHNSON, ALTON CORNELIUS, educator; b. Argyle, Wis., Apr. 27, 1924; s. Herman A. and Cora E. (Hendrickson) J.; m. Virginia R. Kroener, Aug. 15, 1959; children: Vance, Brian. B.A., St. Olaf Coll., 1949; M.B.A., U. Wis., 1953, Ph.D., 1957. Partner Johnson Motor Service, Argyle, Wis., 1949-52; instr. U. Okla., Norman, 1953-55; asst. prof. U. Wis., Madison, 1957-62, asso. prof., 1962-65, prof., 1965—, chmn. dept. mgmt., 1966-72; cons. to industry and govt. Pres. Madison Area Assn. for Retarded Children, 1972-73. Co-author: Management of Hospitals; Contbr. articles, monographs. Earhart Found. fellow, 1956-57; research grantee Ford Found., 1960-63; U.S. Office Edn., 1965-66; U.S. Bur. Health Resources Devel., 1974—. Mem. Acad. Mgmt., Indsl. Relations Research Assn., Am. Soc. Personnel Adminstrs., Am. Mgmt. Assn., Gerontological Soc., Phi Kappa Phi. Lutheran (pres. ch. 1969. Home: 641 Chatham Terrace Madison WI 53711

JOHNSON, ALVIN CARL, banker; b. Chgo., Apr. 9, 1919; s. Alvin A. and Gertrude M. (Schau) J.; m. Eileen Myrtle Weise, May 25, 1946; children: Kristine Ann (Mrs. Mark E. Bean), Lisa Ellen (Mrs. J. Keith Cupples), Alvin Carl, Paul Andrew. Ed., Am. Inst. Banking, 1935-37, Sch. Commerce, Northwestern U., 1937-41, 46-47, Stonier Grad. Sch. Banking, 1958. With First Nat. Bank Chgo., 1935-78, v.p. charge div. I, from 1963, sr. v.p. charge corp. banking dept./indsl., to 1978; pres. Mgmt. and Fin. Services, Inc., Dallas, 1978-83; sr. v.p. Northpark Nat. Bank, Dallas, 1983—. Decorated knight Order of North Star, Sweden). Mem. Am. Petroleum Inst. Episcopalian (vestryman). Clubs: Oil Men's (Chgo.); Hinsdale Golf; Northwoods, Tower (Dallas). Home: 6905 Chevy Chase Dallas TX 75225 Office: 1300 Northpark Ctr Dallas TX 75225

JOHNSON, A(LYN) WILLIAM, ednl. and research adminstr.; b. Calgary, Alta, Can., Dec. 16, 1933; came to U.S., 1954, naturalized, 1981; s. Alyn C. and Irene (Johnston) J.; m. Joan Auger, July 26, 1956; children—Patricia, Nancy, Robert, Katherine. B.Sc., U. Alta., 1954; Ph.D., Cornell U., 1957. Research fellow Mellon Inst., Pitts., 1957-60; asst., then asso. prof. chemistry U. N.D., 1960-65; asso. prof., chmn. dept. chemistry U. Sask., 1965-67; dean Grad. Sch., prof. chemistry U. N.D., Grand Forks, 1967-75, 77—, dir. research and devel., 1967-75; dir. N.D. regional environ. assessment program N.D. Legis. Council, Bismarck, 1975-77. Author: Ylid Chemistry, 1966, also numerous articles and abstracts. Fellow Chem. Inst. Can., AAAS; mem. Am. Chem. Soc., N.D. Acad. Sci., Sigma Xi. Episcopalian. Clubs: Curling, Grand Forks Country (Grand Forks); Rotary. Home: 416 Terrace Dr Grand Forks ND 58201 Office: 416 Twamley Hall U ND Grand Forks ND 58202

JOHNSON, ANDREW EMERSON, III, headmaster; b. Monterey, Va., July 26, 1931; s. Andrew Emerson and Virginia (Miller) J.; m. Matilee Howard, Dec. 27, 1977; children: Rebecca, Andrew Emerson IV. B.S., Hampden-Sydney Coll., 1952, Litt.D., 1969; M.Ed., U. N.C. at Chapel Hill, 1959; Nat. Def. Edn. Act fellow, Williams Coll., 1967. Instr. math. Norfolk (Va.) Acad., 1952-56, head math. dept., instr. Bible, 1957-59, asst. headmaster, 1959-61; headmaster North Cross Sch., Roanoke, Va., 1961-69, Charlotte (N.C.) Country Day Sch., 1969-73; pres. Westminster Schs., Atlanta, 1973-76; pres., headmaster Shady Side Acad., Pitts., 1976—. Chmn. edn. govt. div. United Fund, 1967; mem. adv. com. Roanoke City Chaplain, 1967-69; Bd. dirs. Community Concert Series, Charlotte, Urban League of Pitts.; trustee Roanoke Fine Arts Center, 1967-69; chmn. Ind. Ednl. Services., Ednl. Records Bur. Mem. Nat. Assn. Prin. Schs. for Girls, Country Day Sch. Headmasters Assn., Pa. Assn. Ind. Schs. (pres.), Headmasters Assn., Omicron Delta Kappa. Presbyn. Clubs: Mason., Fox Chapel Golf, Duquesne. Address: 423 Fox Chapel Rd Pittsburgh PA 15238

JOHNSON, ARTE, comedian; b. Benton Harbor, Mich., Jan. 20, 1934; s. Abraham Lincoln and Edythe MacKenzie (Goldben) J.; m. Gisela von Busch, Aug. 15, 1968. B.A., M.A., U. Ill. Regular on: TV series Laugh-In, 1968-73; numerous other TV appearances; films include The Subterraneans, 1960, The Third Day, 1965, The President's Analyst, 1967, Twice in a Lifetime, 1974, Bud and Lou, 1978, Love at First Bite, 1979, The Sacketts, 1979, If Things Were Different, 1980, Detour by Terror, 1980. Office: care Richard Lawrence 301 N San Vicente Blvd Los Angeles CA 90048

JOHNSON, ARTHUR GILBERT, microbiology educator; b. Eveleth, Minn., Feb. 1, 1926; s. Arthur Gilbert and Selma (Niemi) J.; m. Mildred Louise Anderson, June 15, 1951; children: Susan, Sally, Gary, Peter. B.A., U. Minn., 1950, M.Sc., 1951; Ph.D., U. Md., 1955. Biochemist Walter Reed Army Inst. Research, Washington, 1952-55; asst. prof. U. Mich., 1956-62, asso. prof., 1962-66, prof. microbiology, 1966-78; prof., head dept. med. microbiology/immunology U. Minn. Sch. Medicine, Duluth, 1978—; Mem. nat. adv. dental research council NIH, 1972-75; mem. Nat. Bd. Med. Examiners, 1980—; mem. bacteriology and mycology study sect. NIH, 1983—; cons. microbology. Editor: Infection and Immunity, 1977—. Served with US Merchant Marine, 1943-46. Mem. Am. Soc. Immunologists, Am. Soc. Microbiology, Reticuloendothelial Soc., Soc. Exptl. Biology and Medicine. Research immunology. Home: 209 Rockridge Circle Duluth MN 55804

JOHNSON, ASHMORE CLARK, JR., oil company executive; b. Phila., Dec. 7, 1930; s. Ashmore Clark and Elsie (Carstens) J.; m. Myra Lee Wheeler, Dec. 2, 1967; 1 dau., Elyse Charlotte. B.A., Haverford Coll., 1952; M.B.A., U. Pa., 1954. Gen. sales mgr. Pyrofax Gas Corp., 1961-67; v.p. mktg. Union Tex. Petroleum div. Allied Chem. Corp., 1972-76, exec. v.p. div., 1976-77, pres. specialty chems. div., 1977-79, exec. v.p., Morristown, N.J., 1979-82; pres. Allied Chem. Co., 1982-83, Union Tex. Petroleum Corp., 1983—; dir. Dixie Pipeline Co. Republican. Episcopalian. Office: PO Box 2120 Houston TX 77252

JOHNSON, AVERY FISCHER, artist, educator, cartographer; b. Wheaton, Ill., Apr. 3, 1906; s. Nicholas L. and Faith (Fischer) J.; m. Nina Gertrude Ryder, Mar. 7, 1935; children: Sandra (Mrs. John E. Van Hoven, Jr.), Susan, Stephanie (Mrs. Thomas Easton). B.A., Wheaton Coll., 1928; grad., Sch. Art Inst. Chgo., 1933. Instr. Newark Sch. Fine and Indsl. Art, 1947-60, Montclair Art Mus., 1940-70. Illustrator: The Lamp, 1948, The Humble Way, 1949-50, Modern Manufacturing and Factory, 1967-71; illustrator children's books for, Random House, Longmans Green, E.P. Dutton, Alfred A. Knopf, Thomas Nelson & Sons, Grossett & Dunlap, Abingdon Press, 1939-61; Murals in U.S. post offices in, Marseilles, Ill., Liberty, Ind., Lake Village, Ark., Catonsville, Md., Bordentown, N.J., North Bergen, N.J.; represented in permanent collections, Newark Mus., Montclair, (N.J.) Mus., Philbrook Mus., Tulsa, Holyoke (Mass.) Mus., Library of Congress, U. Oreg. Library, numerous others, exhbns. include, Met. Mus., 1967, Met. Mus., Mexico City, 1968, 50 Yrs. Painting, Seton Hall U., 1982, numerous others. Civilian with OWI, 1944-45. Recipient awards Am. Watercolor Soc., Montclair Mus., N.J. Water Color Soc., numerous others A.N.A. Mem. Am., N.J. watercolor socs., Audubon Artists. Address: 38 Cooper Rd RFD Denville NJ 07834

JOHNSON, BELTON KLEBERG, rancher; b. Balt., Nov. 23, 1929; s. Henry Belton, Jr. and Sarah Spohn (Kleberg) J.; m. Patricia Lewis Zoch, Nov. 3, 1956; children—Belton Kleberg, Sarah Spohn Kleberg, Cecilia Lewis. B.S. in Agr., Animal Husbandry and Agrl. Econs, Cornell U., 1953; postgrad., Stanford U. Grad. Sch. Bus., 1957-58. Mgr. hdqrs. div. King Ranch, Kingsville, Tex., 1944-56; with exec. tng. program Bank of Am., San Francisco, 1957; rancher, La Pryor, Tex., 1957—; dir. Campbell Soup Co., AT&T, Tenneco, First City Bancorp. of Tex. Active Commn. on Critical Choices for Americans, 1973, Center for Inter-Am. Relations, 1974—; co-chmn. Republican Nat. Finance Com., 1979—. Served to 1st lt., arty. U.S. Army, 1953-55. Recipient Francisco de Miranda award, Venezuela, 1965. Mem. U.S. Meat Export Fedn. (adv. council 1978—), Tex. and Southwestern

Cattle Raisers Assn. (dir. 1962—), Santa Gertrudis Breeders Assn. (dir. 1971-80). Episcopalian. Clubs: Capitol Hill, River, Racquet and Tennis, Clove Valley Rod and Gun, San Antonio Country, Corpus Christi Yacht; Beach and Tennis (Pebble Beach, Calif.); Cypress Point, Kings Men, Order of Alamo, Links. 825 Contour Dr San Antonio TX 78212 Office: One Forum Suite 1400 8000 IH-10 West San Antonio TX 78230

JOHNSON, BEN *See* **JOHNSON, FRANCIS BENJAMIN**

JOHNSON, BENJAMIN EDGAR, clergyman; b. Sterling, Colo., Oct. 30, 1921; s. A. Judson and Elsie Lydia (Marks) J.; m. Kathryn May Pierret, Feb. 8, 1944; children: Lois Louise Johnson Van Hooser, Janet Elizabeth Johnson Bonstrom. B.A., Pasadena Coll., 1943, D.D., 1965. Ordained to ministry Ch. of Nazarene, 1943; pastor, Los Angeles, 1943-46, Whittier, Calif., 1946-58, Santa Ana, Calif., 1958-62, Upland, Calif., 1962-64; dist. sec. Ch. of Nazarene, 1950-64, gen. sec., Kansas City, Mo., 1964—; dir. Nazarene Pub. House, Central Am. Holding Corp., N.J. Hispanic Nazarene Corp. Editor of: Nazarene Manual, 1964, 68, 72, 76, 80, Quadrennial Denominational Jour, 1964, 68, 72, 76, 80. Trustee Pasadena Coll. Mem. Am. Soc. Assn. Execs., Mid Am. Soc. Assn. Execs. (pres.), Assn. Statisticians Am. Religious Bodies (pres.), Religious Conv. Mgrs. Assn. (pres.), A.I.M., Nat. Assn. Evangelicals, Christian Holiness Assn. Office: 6401 The Paseo Kansas City MO 64131

JOHNSON, BERNARD GROVER, engineering executive; b. Dallas, June 11, 1915; s. Grover Cleveland and Mae (Duggy) J.; m. Emma Theresa Lyons, Sept. 2, 1940; children: Bernard, Mary Yager, Rebecca Frazier, Jane Green, Susan Johnston, David, Mark, Stephen. B.S. in Elec. Engring., Tex. A&M U., 1937; cert., U.S. Army Command and Gen. Staff Sch., 1945. Registered profl. engr., Tex., 25 other states. Pres., chief exec. officer Bernard Johnson Inc., Houston, 1947—; chmn. bd. Grover Printing Co., Houston, 1970—, St. Edward's U., Austin, 1968-69, Bernard Johnson Builders, 1979—, Grover Automotive Inc., 1980. Vice chmn. bd. regents Tex. State U. System, Austin, 1969—; trustee S.W. Research Inst., San Antonio, 1983—; del. White House Conf. on Natural Beauty, 1963. Served with Signal Corps U.S. Army, 1942-46. Decorated Knight Comdr. of Holy Sepulchre Pope Paul VI. Mem. Am. Cons. Engrs. Council, Nat. Soc. Profl. Engrs., Am. Soc. Profl. Engrs., Houston C. of C. (dir. 1978). Roman Catholic. Clubs: River Oaks Country, Petroleum, Serra, Houston. Home: 5524 Sturbridge St Houston TX 77056 Office: Bernard Johnson Inc 5050 Westheimer St Houston TX 77056

JOHNSON, BERNARD THOMAS, cement and gypsum co. exec.; b. Toronto, Ont., Can., July 31, 1921; came to U.S., 1979; s. Reuben and Nellie Louise (Gallois) J.; m. Shirlie Marie Tait, May 5, 1979; children—Susan, Carol, Jane, Liane, Steven, Mark, James. B.A.Sc. in Chem. Engring, U. Toronto, 1943; postgrad. in mgmt., McGill U., Montreal, Que., Can., 1972-76. Profl. engr., Ont. Project engr. Genstar Ltd., Montreal, 1956-60, v.p., 1966-70, sr. v.p., 1970-72, exec. v.p., Montreal and San Francisco, 1976—; v.p. Genstar Chem. Ltd., Brockville, Ont., 1960-66, chmn., chief exec. officer, Montreal, 1970-76; dir. Nitrochem Inc., Nutrite Inc., R&K Distbrs. Inc. Mem. exec. council Can. C. of C., 1971-75, chmn. council, bd. dirs., 1976-78. Served with RCAF, 1943-45. Recipient Silver Jubilee medal. Mem. Chem. Inst. Can., Ont. Assn. Profl. Engrs. Clubs: Glenora (Edmonton, Alta., Can.); Peninsula Golf and Country, Engrs. Office: Suite 4000 4 Embarcadero Center San Francisco CA 94111

JOHNSON, BETSEY LEE, fashion designer; b. Hartford, Conn., Aug. 10, 1942; d. John Herman and Lena Virginia J.; m. John Cale, Apr. 4, 1966; 1 dau., Lulu; m. Jeffrey Olivier, Feb. 7, 1981. Student, Pratt Inst., N.Y.C., 1960-61; B.A., U. Syracuse, 1964. Editorial asst. Mademoiselle mag., 1964-65; ptnr., co-owner Betsey, Bunky & Nini, N.Y.C., 1969—. Prin. designer: Paraphernalia (owned by Puritan Fashions, Inc.), 1965-69; designer, Alvin Duskin Co., San Francisco, 1970; head designer: Alley Cat by Betsey Johnson, div. LeDamor, Inc., 1970-74; freelance designer for, Jr. Womens div. Butterick Pattern Co., 1971, Betsey Johnson's Kids Children Wear for new div, Shutterbug, Inc., 1974-77, Betsey Johnson for, Jeanette Maternities, Inc., 1974-75; designer first line womens clothing for, Gant Shirtmakers, Inc., 1974-75; Tric-Trac by Betsey Johnson, Womens Knitwear, 1974-76; childrens wear for Butterick's Home Sewing catalog, 1975—; head designer jr. sportswear co.: Star Ferry by Betsey Johnson and Michael Milea, 1975-77; owner, head designer, B.J., Inc.; designer wholesale co., N.Y.C., 1978; pres., treas., B.J. Vines, N.Y.C.; owner, Betsey Johnson store, N.Y.C., 1979— (Recipient Mademoiselle mag. Merit award 1970), Betsey Johnson store, N.Y.C. (Coty award 1971), Betsey Johnson store, N.Y.C. (2 Tommy Print awards 1971). Mem. Womens Forum. Office: 1441 Broadway New York NY 10018

JOHNSON, BOB, professional hockey coach. Coach Calgary Flames, N.H.L., Alta., Can. Office: care Calgary Flames PO Box 1540, Sta M Calgary AB Canada T2P 3B9§

JOHNSON, BOINE THEODORE, JR., medical instruments company executive, mayor; b. N.Y.C., Dec. 17, 1931; s. Boine Theodore and Emma (Hall) J.; m. A. Louise Jordan, Apr. 29, 1967; children—Boine Theodore III, Marc Ian, Jordan James, Jann Louise. B.A. cum laude, Williams Coll., 1953; M.B.A. with high distinction (Baker scholar), Harvard, 1958. Instr. Harvard Bus. Sch., 1958-59; asst. to dir. corporate planning AMF Corp., N.Y.C., 1959-62; mgr. mgmt. cons. div. Commonwealth Services Inc., N.Y.C., 1962-66; mgr. corporate planning Gen. Electric Co., 1966-68; sr. v.p. corporate devel., gen. mgr. chem. div. Technicon Corp., Tarrytown, N.Y., 1968-79; v.p. Perkin Elmer Corp., Norwalk, Conn., 1979-81; v.p., gen. mgr. Capintec, Inc., Montvale, N.J., 1981-82; pres. Voland Corp., Hawthorne, N.Y., 1982—; dir. Datamedic, Inc., Peoples Bank for Savs. of New Rochelle. Trustee, mayor Village of Scarsdale, N.Y., 1971-77; Bd. dirs. Music for Westchester Symphony Orch., Council for Arts in Westchester; bd. dirs., vice chmn. Westchester County Assn.; trustee United Fund, Tarrytown. Served to lt., C.E. USNR, 1953-56. Mem. Sci. Apparatus Makers Assn., Theta Delta Chi (trustee edn. found. 1968-72, pres. Founders' Corp. 1966—, pres. grand lodge 1969-71). Republican. Presbyn. Clubs: Harvard, Williams, Amateur Comedy (N.Y.C.); Town (Scarsdale). Home: 18 Fairview Rd Scarsdale NY 10583 Office: 5 Skyline Dr Hawthorne NY 10532

JOHNSON, BRUCE, mechanical engineering educator; b. Hawarden, Iowa, Sept. 4, 1932; s. York and Dorothy Ellen (DeBruce) J.; m. Dorothy Jane Rylander, Aug. 27, 1955; children: Sharon Lee, Kristen Kay. B.S. in Mech. Engring, Iowa State U., 1955; M.S. in Mech Engring, Purdue U., 1962, Ph.D., 1965. Instr. U.S. Naval Acad., Annapolis, 1957-59, asso. prof., 1964-70, prof., 1970—, project dir. model basin, 1968—, Naval Sea Systems Command prof. hydrodynamics, 1975—; dir. Hydromechanics Lab., 1976—; instr. Purdue U., 1959-64; chmn. 18th Am. Towing Tank Conf., 1977; U.S. rep. on info. Com. of Internat. Towing Tank Conf., 1975—. Author: (with T. Gillmer) Introduction to Naval Architecture, 1982; editor: (with B. Nehrling) Proc. of 18th Am. Towing Tank Conf, 1977; contbr. articles to profl. publs. Trustee Bauman Bible Telecasts, 1970—. Served with USN, 1955-59. Ford Found. grantee, 1962-64; recipient award for excellence in engring. teaching Western Electric Fund, 1971. Mem. ASME, Am. Soc. for Engring. Edn., Soc. Naval Architects and Marine Engrs., Am. Soc. Naval Engrs. (nat. scholarship chmn.). Methodist. Research in hydrodynamics and brain wave analysis. Home: 12600 Kilbourne Ln Bowie MD 20715 Office: Naval Systems Engring Dept US Naval Acad Annapolis MD 21402

JOHNSON, BRUCE, TV producer and writer; b. Oakland, Calif., July 7, 1939; s. Robert Steele and Edith Kristene (Pederson) J.; m. Kathleen Ross, Nov. 5, 1966; children—Jonathan Alan, Grant Fitzgerald. Student, Coll. City San Francisco, 1958-60; B.A., U. So. Calif., 1962. Producer and head writer: TV shows Gomer Pyle, 1967-68, Jim Nabors Hour, 1969-71, Arnie, 1971-72, The Little People, 1972-73, The New Temperature's Rising Show, 1973-74, Sierra, 1974-75, Excuse My French, in Can, 1975-76, Alice, 1976-77, Blansky's Beauties, 1977, Quark, 1977-78, Angie, 1978-79, Mork and Mindy, ABC, 1978—, also numerous movies of the week and pilots for TV.; (Recipient Best TV Show award for Mork and Mindy, People's Choice 1979, Photoplay award for best evening TV show 1979, Emmy nomination for Best Comedy Series 1979). Served with USAFR, 1962-68. Mem. Writers Guild Am.-West, Producers Guild Am., Caucus for Producers, Writers and Dirs. Office: Paramount Studios 5451 Marathon St Hollywood CA 90038

JOHNSON, BRUCE MARTIN, English educator; b. Chgo., Apr. 29, 1933; s. George A. and Elsie L. (Clausing) J.; m. Jean C. Kruger, June 29, 1957; 1 son, Abram. A.B., U. Chgo., 1952; B.A., Northwestern U., 1954, M.A., 1955, Ph.D., 1959. Instr. English U. Mich., 1958-62; asst. prof. English U. Rochester, N.Y., 1962-68, assoc. prof., 1968-76, prof., 1976—, chmn. dept. English, 1981-84. Author: Conrad's Models of Mind, 1971, True Correspondence: A Phenomenology of Thomas Hardy's Novels, 1983. Sr. fellow NEH, 1974-75; fellow Guggenheim Found., 1977-78. Mem. MLA, Assn. Depts. English. Democrat. Home: 16 Kirklees Rd Pittsford NY 14534 Office: Dept English Univ Rochester Rochester NY 14627

JOHNSON, C. BEDFORD, lawyer; b. Amarillo, Tex., Feb. 10, 1920; s. C. Bedford and Agnes (Huff) J.; m. Sarah Ann Barber, Jan. 5, 1946; children: Douglas Bedford, Scott William, Blair Martin. A.B. magna cum laude, Harvard U., 1940, LL.B., 1947. Bar: N.Y. With Shearman & Sterling, N.Y.C., 1947—, ptnr., 1956—. Mem. adv. com. on nat. bank manual revision: Comptroller of Currency, 1962-63. Served to capt. USMCR, 1942-46. Decorated Bronze Star medal, Purple Heart. Mem. ABA, N.Y. State Bar Assn., Assn. of Bar City of N.Y., Am. Judicature Soc. Episcopalian. Club: Harvard (N.Y.C.). Home: 180 E 79th St New York NY 10021 Office: Shearman & Sterling 153 E 53rd St New York NY 10022

JOHNSON, C. RAYMOND, JR., manufacturing company executive; b. Seattle, June 10, 1946; s. Clyde Raymond and Margaret (Edwards) J.; m. Karen Ann Long, Aug. 21, 1971; children: Steven Joseph, Joseph Allen, Thomas Daniel. Student, Central Wash. State Coll., 1965. Gen. mgr. S.S. Assocs., South Bend, Ind., 1973-78; v.p., gen. mgr. COA of Calif., Vacaville, 1978-79; pres. FAN Coach, LaGrange, Ind., 1979-81; exec. v.p. RV Group Coachmen Industries, Inc., Middlebury, Ind., 1981-83; pres. RV Group Coachmen Industries,Inc., Middlebury, Ind., 1983—; dir. COA Holding Co., Recreation World, Inc., Orlando, Fla., Ala. Leisure, Inc., Montgomery. Served with USN, 1967-69. Mem. Recreational Vehicle Industry Assn., Nat. Assn. Bus. Economists, Am. Mgmt. Assn., Elkhart (Ind.) C. of C. Republican. Methodist. Home: PO Box 1145 Middlebury IN 46540 Office: Coachman Industries Inc PO Box 30 Middlebury IN 46540 *The thought that has been most helpful in business and otherwise is this: "Be strong enough to be vulnerable." Have the courage to accept your imperfections without losing faith in your overall character or ability to perform. Failures, large or small, are bad only if you stop trying or stop believing in yorself. Bottom line. . .neither humility or leadership can stand alone and be succesful.*

JOHNSON, CAROL ROXANE, landscape architect; b. Elizabeth, N.J., Sept. 6, 1929; s. Harrison Brymer and Edith (Otto) J. B.A. in English, Wellesley Coll., 1951; M. in Landscape Architecture, Harvard U., 1957. Registered landscape architect, Mass., Va., Conn., Ohio, Maine, R.I. Landscape architect Bucks Country Parks Bd., Doylestown, Pa., 1955, Stephen Hopkins Assocs., Roxbury, Mass., 1956-57, John Blackwell, Planner, Boston, part-time 1957, Whitman & Howard, Inc., Wellesley, Mass., 1957-58, The Architects Collaborative, Cambridge, Mass., 1958-59; founder, pres. Carol R. Johnson & Assocs., Inc., Cambridge, 1959—; guest lectr. in field; instr. dept. landscape architecture Harvard U., 1982; instr. Dept. City and Regional Planning, 1966-73. Mem. Cambridge Hist. Soc., 1980. Recipient various landscape awards. Fellow Am. Soc. Landscape Architects (honor award 1982, Merit award 1980); mem. Boston Soc. Landscape Architects (cert. of recognition 1981, sec. 1972-74, examing bd. 1973), Am. Soc. Landscape Architects Profl. Practice Inst. Office: Carol R Johnson & Assocs Inc 15 Mt Auburn St Cambridge MA 02138

JOHNSON, CECIL AUGUST, lawyer; b. Stratford, Iowa, June 9, 1905; s. Franklin A. and Louise (Erickson) J.; m. Esther M. Nelson, June 30, 1926 (dec. Aug. 1959); children—Newell D., M. Nadyne, Franklin C., Richard A.; m. Harriet L. Paige, Sept. 1, 1960. Student, Iowa State Coll., 1922-23; LL.B., Southeastern U., 1936, M.P.L., 1938, B.S.C., 1939; LL.M., Columbus U., Washington, 1937; LL.D. (hon.), Midland Lutheran Coll., 1964. Bar: Iowa bar 1936, D.C. bar 1937, Ill. bar 1945, Nebr. bar 1950. Pvt. bus., Ames, Iowa, 1926-33; exec. asst. A.A.A., U.S. Dept. Agr., 1933-35, dir. commodity loans, 1935-38; sec. and asst. mgr. Fed. Crop Ins. Corp., Washington, 1938-42; directed reorgn. Office Civilian Def., Washington, 1942; asst. to gov. FCA, Kansas City, Mo., 1942-44; partner law firm Ekern, Meyers & Matthias, Chgo., 1944-51; mem. firm Barton & Johnson, Washington, 1951-66, Johnson & Hunter, Omaha, 1951-64, Johnson & Ilich, 1964-73, Johnson & Fike, 1973-77; individual practice law, Omaha, 1977—; gen. counsel C. A. Swanson & Sons, Omaha, 1951-55, Butter Nut Foods Co., 1955-64, Swanson Enterprises, Omaha, 1955-79; Dir. adv. bd. indsl. alcohol prodns., govt. alcohol plant, 1944-49; lay mem. Nat. Adv. Council for Neurol. Diseases and Blindness, USPHS, 1950-51. Co-author: Fed. Crop Ins. act and Nat. All Risk Crop Ins. program. Trustee Immanuel Med. Center; chmn. bd. trustees Lutheran Ch. Am. Found., 1963-71, U. Nebr. Found., Midland Luth. Coll.; bd. dirs. Am. Missions Luth. Ch. Am., mem. mgmt. com. office adminstrn. and finance; bd. dirs. Swedish Council in Am. Mem. Am., Iowa, Ill., Nebr., Chgo. bar assns., Am. Judicature Soc., Theta Chi. Democrat. Lutheran. Club: Mason. Home: 8717 Capitol Ave Omaha NE 68114 Office: 8717 Capitol Ave Omaha NE 68114 *How kind people have been—and the Lord especially—to bless me with much work, some sorrow, but mostly comfort and joy. The greatest ingredient for success is integrity—and to that there must be added courage, desire to work, and belief in our nation and the Lord.*

JOHNSON, CECIL EARL, educator; b. Sweetwater, Tex., Feb. 11, 1924; s. Asberry and Jewel Dicey (Headrick) J.; m. Ruth Wade, Aug. 26, 1950. B.A. cum laude, Baylor U., 1949, M.A., 1950; Ph.D. (Univ. fellow), U. Tex., Austin, 1954. Asst. prof. Tex. Technol. Coll., 1955-60; prof., chmn. dept. polit. sci. So. Meth. U., Dallas, 1960—, George Arnold prof. polit. sci., 1973—; research asso. Columbia, 1966-68; Wilton Park lectr. British Fgn. Office, 1976. Author: The Domestic Policies of the Castro Regime, 1961, Communist China and Latin America, 1959-1967, 1970, China and Latin America: New Ties and Tactics, 1972. Bd. dirs. Arnold Found., Houston. Served with USAAF, 1943-46. Named Outstanding Prof. So. Meth. U., 1964, 66, 73, Outstanding Alumnus Baylor U., 1976; Sr. fellow Research Inst. on Communist Affairs, Columbia, 1968. Mem. Am. Polit. Sci. Assn., Assn. for Asian Studies, Pi Sigma Alpha, Phi Alpha Theta, Alpha Chi. Democrat. Home: 6820 Leameadow Dr Dallas TX 75248 Office: So Meth U Dallas TX 75275

JOHNSON, CHARLES A., co. exec.; b. Santa Monica, Calif. B.A., Harvard U., M.B.A. With N.W. Internat. Bank, N.Y.C., Commodities Corp., Princeton, N.J.; dep. dir. fgn. treasury ops. ITT World Headquarters, N.Y.C., 1966-71; asso. treas. ITT Europe, Inc., Brussels, 1971-76; v.p., treas. ITT Corp., N.Y.C., 1976-81, corp. v.p., 1981—. Mem. Conf. Bd. Europe (fin. council). Club: Harvard of Belgium. Office: ITT World Headquarters 320 Park Ave New York NY 10022 *

JOHNSON, CHARLES BARTLETT, mutual fund executive; b. Montclair, N.J., Jan. 6, 1933; s. Rupert Harris and Florence (Endler) J.; m. Ann Demarest Lutes, Mar. 26, 1955; children: Charles E., Holly, Sarah, Gregory, William, Jennifer, Mary. B.A., Yale U., 1954. With R.H. Johnson & Co., N.Y.C., 1954-55; pres. Franklin Distbrs., Inc., N.Y.C., 1957—, Franklin Resources, Inc., 1969—; dir. Franklin Custodian Funds Inc., Gen. Host Corp., Franklin Option Fund, Franklin Money Fund, Research Equity Fund, Inc., Franklin Calif. Tax Free Income Fund, Research Capital Fund, Inc.; Bd. govs. Investment Co. Inst. Treas., bd. dirs. Hillsborough Schs. Found. Served to 1st lt. AUS, 1955-57. Clubs: Burlingame Country (Calif.); University (San Francisco). Home: 550 Eucalyptus Ave Hillsborough CA 94010 Office: 155 Bovet Rd San Mateo CA 94402

JOHNSON, CHARLES CHRISTOPHER, JR., consulting environmental engineer; b. Des Moines, Sept. 6, 1921; s. Charles C. and Haley Dale (Evans) J.; m. Betty Jean Tanner, Dec. 25, 1947; children: Charles Christopher III, Teresa Ilene. Student, Dowling Jr. Coll., Des Moines, 1941-42; B.S. in Civil Engring., Purdue U., 1947, M.S., 1957. Diplomate: Am. Acad. Environ. Engrs.; Registered profl. engr., D.C., Md. Commd. jr. grade officer USPHS, 1947, advanced through ranks to asst. surgeon gen., 1968; chief sanitation facilities constrn. br. Div. Indian Health, 1960-66, chief office environ. health, 1966-67; adminstr. consumer protection and environ. health service HEW, 1968-69, adminstr. environ. health service, 1970; asso. exec. dir. Am. Pub. Health Assn., Washington, 1970-72; asst. commr. health for environ. health N.Y.C. Health Dept., 1967-68; v.p. research and devel. Washington Tech. Inst., 1973-74; resident mgr. Malcolm Pirnie, Inc., Washington and Silver Spring, Md., 1974-77, v.p., 1977-79; founder, pres., chief exec. officer CC Johnson and Assocs., Inc. (environ. engrs.), 1979—; adj. assoc. prof. N.Y. U. Sch. Environmental Medicine, 1967-68; cons. Booz, Allen & Hamilton, N.Y.C., 1967. Contbr. articles to profl. jours. Bd. dirs. Urban Am., Nat. Cath. Found., Episcopal Ch. Am., Washington, Community Health, Inc.; mem. adv. council Sch. Engring. Stanford U., 1970-74; mem. Nat. Capitol Planning Commn., 1971-74; tech. adv. group for municipal waste water systems EPA, 1973-75; mem. adv. council Sch. Engring., Purdue U., 1972-75; Commn. on Edn. for Health Adminstrn., 1972-74; mem., chmn. Nat. Drinking Water Adv. Council, 1975-81; mem. Md. Drinking Water Adv. Council, 1975, Adv. Com. Water Data for Public Use, U.S. Geol. Survey-Dept. Interior, 1979-80. Served with USMCR, 1942-46. Recipient Meritorious Public Service award Gov. D.C., 1967; Distinguished Engring. Alumnus award Purdue U. Sch. Engring., 1969; Walter F. Snyder award Nat. San. Found.-Nat. Environ. Health Assn., 1977. Mem. Commd. Officers Assn., Am. Pub. Health Assn., Nat. Environ. Health Assn., Am. Waterworks Assn., Water Pollution Control Fedn. Home: 6705 Kenhill Rd Bethesda MD 20034 Office: 11510 Georgia Ave Silver Spring MD 20902

JOHNSON, CHARLES RAYMOND, editor; b. Williston, N.D., Sept. 16, 1925; s. Charles Andrew and Lena Mae (Quick) J.; m. Lillian Georgina Hilmo, Aug. 21, 1949 (div. 1977); children: Linda Jane, Eric Charles, Paul Andrew, Thomas Peter; m. Corrine Margaret Reuter Zarnik, Nov. 26, 1978. Student, Miss. Coll., 1944, MIT, 1944-45; B.Ph., U. N.D., 1948. Asst. sports editor Fargo (N.D.) Forum, 1948-52; sports writer Milw. Jour., 1952-58, asst. sports editor, 1958-68, sports editor, 1968-75, asst. news editor, 1975—, electronics systems editor, 1977-81, suburban news editor, 1981—; discussion leader AP Inst., Columbia, now Reston, Va., 1968—; instr. journalism Marquette U., 1979—, U. Wis., Milw., 1979—. Author: The Green Bay Packers, Pro Football's Pioneer Team, 1961, Greatest Packers of Them All, 1968. Chmn. nat. devel. fund U. N.D., 1975-76, mem. alumni bd., 1978—. Served with USNR, 1943-46. Mem. Wis. AP Sports Writers (pres. 1971), Milw. Press Club (pres. 1972-74). Lutheran (pres. ch. 1969, 75, 76). Home: 756 E Lexington Blvd Whitefish Bay WI 53217 Office: 333 W State St Milwaukee WI 53201

JOHNSON, CHARLES SIDNEY, JR., educator; b. Albany, Ga., Mar. 7, 1936; s. Charles Sidney and Mary Virginia (Reid) J.; m. Ellen Cook McFarland, Sept. 3, 1958; children—David Mason, Daniel Cook. B.S. in Chemistry, Ga. Inst. Tech., 1958; Ph.D. in Phys. Chemistry, Mass. Inst. Tech., 1961. Nat. Acad. Sci.-NRC postdoctoral fellow, instr. U. Ill., 1961-62; asst. prof. Yale, 1962-66, asso. prof., 1967; prof. chemistry U.N.C., 1967—. Author: Problems and Solutions in Quantum Chemistry and Physics, 1974; Editorial bd.: Jour. Magnetic Resonance, 1971—; Contbr. articles to profl. jours. NSF fellow, 1958-61; Yale Faculty fellow, 1966-67; Alfred P. Sloan fellow, 1966; J.S. Guggenheim Meml. fellow, 1972-73. Fellow Am. Phys. Soc.; mem. A.A.A.S., Phi Kappa Phi, Sigma Xi, Tau Beta Pi. Home: 1833 N Lake Shore Dr Chapel Hill NC 27514

JOHNSON, CHAUNCEY PAUL, banker; b. Detroit, Oct. 25, 1931; s. Chauncey Frederic and Lois Jean (Hon) J.; m. Anne Gayman, June 1949; children: Julianne, Deborah, Rebecca. Student, Denison U., 1949-51; B.S., Mich. State U., 1953. Account exec. Robert W. Baird, Milw., 1956-59; pres. Wis. Capital Corp., Milw., 1959-64, Reef Club Hotel, Ocho Rios, Jamaica, 1964-66, Maru Imports, Inc., 1959-66; sr. v.p., dir. Milw. Western Bank, 1967-70; pres. Growth Capital, Inc., Chgo., 1970-72; chmn. bd., chief exec. officer Colonial Bank & Trust Co., Chgo., 1972—; pres., chief exec. officer 1st Colonial Bankshares; chmn. bd. Bankers Tech., Colonial Group, Inc.; pres. Popo Agie Ranch Ltd., Lander, Wyo.; vice chmn. bd. Northwest Commerce Bank, Rosemont, Ill.; chmn. bd., chief exec. officer All Am. Bank, Chgo. Trustee Am. Field Service; mem. exec. bd. Chgo. area Boy Scouts Am. Served as 1st lt. USAF, 1953-56. Mem. Ill. Bankers Assn. (past pres. Chgo. dist.), Northside Bankers Assn. (past pres.), Belmont Central C. of C. (past pres.), Lambda Chi Alpha. Clubs: Ridgemore Country, Milw. Athletic, Union League. Office: 5850 W Belmont Ave Chicago IL 60634

JOHNSON, CLARKE COURTNEY, educator; b. Wisconsin Rapids, Wis., July 11, 1936; s. Julius J. and Esther (Larsen) Lohnson. B.S.E.E., U. Wis., 1958; M.S.I.M., Purdue U., 1962, Ph.D., 1972. Asst. prof., asst. dean U. Wis.-Milw., 1966-72; vis. prof. Boston U. Sch. Mgmt., 1973-75; assoc. prof., assoc. dean DePaul U. Coll. Commerce, Chgo., 1975-77; prof., dean Iona Coll. Sch. Bus., New Rochelle, N.Y., 1977-79; prof. fin. Pace U. Grad. Sch. Bus., N.Y.C., 1979—; cons. in field. Contbr. articles to profl. jours. Served with USAF, 1958-61. Mem. Am. Fin. Assn., Am. Econs. Assn., Fin. Mgmt. Assn., Eta Kappa Nu. Home: 222 W 23d St Apt 411 New York NY 10011 Office: 1 Pace Plaza W 415 New York NY 10038

JOHNSON, CLIFFORD HENRY, rubber company exeecutive; b. Mpls., Mar. 31, 1925; emigrated to Can., 1977; s. Henry J. and Ethel I. (Parsons) J.; m. Rose Herrmann, Aug. 28, 1949; children: Mary Johnson Eymann, Pamela Johnson Ehrlich, Clifford Henry. B.S.M.E., U. Wis., 1951. Prodn. squadron trainee Goodyear Tire & Rubber Co., Akron, Ohio, 1951-52; sales and mgmt. positions Godyear Tire & Rubber Co., various locations, 1952-72; mgr. automotive replacement products Goodyear Tire & Rubber Co., 1972-76, mgr. mktg. indsl. products, 1976-77; v.p. gen. products Goodyear Can., Inc., Toronto, Ont., 1977-79, v.p. tire sales, 1979-80, exec. v.p., 1980-81, pres., chief exec. officer, 1981—, dir., 1981—; dir. Seiberling Can. Inc., Toronto, Kelly-Springfield Can. Inc. Served to lt. USN, 1943-47; PTO. Mem. Rubber Assn. Can. (chmn. dir. 1983—), Toronto Bd. Trade. Clubs: Mississaugua Golf and Country (Toronto); Glen Abbey Golf (Oakville). Lodges: Masons; Shriners. Office: Goodyear Can Inc 21 Four Seasons Pl Islington ON Canada M9B 6G2

JOHNSON, CLIFFORD R., retail executive; b. Chgo., Aug. 19, 1923; m. Mitzi Delich, Sept. 9, 1949; children: Susan, Glenn, Jeanne, Robert. B.S., Northwestern U., 1947; postgrad., U. Chgo., 1963-64; grad., Advanced Mgmt. Program, Harvard U., 1973. With Jewel Cos., Inc., 1949—, exec. v.p., from 1973, now sr. v.p.; dir. Northwest Trust and Savs. Bank, Arlington Heights, Ill. Bd. dirs. Kellogg Sch. Mgmt., Northwestern U. Mem. Ill. Chamber Commerce and Industry (dir.), Urban Land Inst., Internat. Council Shopping Centers. Clubs: Mid-America, Economic (Chgo.). Home: 520 Banbury Rd Arlington Heights IL 60005 Office: O'Hare Plaza 5725 E River Rd Chicago IL 60631

JOHNSON, CORWIN WAGGONER, lawyer, educator; b. Hamlet, Ind., Oct. 5, 1917; s. Lonnie Edmund and Nora Lee (Drake) J.; m. July 24, 1942; children: Kent Edmund, Kirk Allan. B.A., U. Iowa, 1939, J.D., 1941; postgrad. (Sterling fellow), Yale U. Law Sch., 1941, 46. Bar: Iowa 1941, Calif. 1946, Tex. 1957. Spl. agt. FBI, Dept. Justice, 1942-46; instr. in law U. Iowa, 1946-47; asst. prof. law U. Tex., Austin, 1947-49, asso. prof., 1949-54, prof., 1954—. Author: (with J. E. Cribbet) Cases and Materials on Property, 1960, 4th, rev. edit., 1978; contbr. articles to law revs. Mem. Austin Planning Commn., 1954-56. Mem. Am. Law Inst., Tex. State Bar, AAUP, Order of Coif, Phi Beta Kappa. Democrat. Methodist. Home: 3425 Monte Vista Dr Austin TX 78731 Office: U Tex Law Sch 727 E 26th St Austin TX 78705

JOHNSON, CRAIG NORMAN, shipping company executive; b. Warren, Pa., Jan.8, 1942; s. Norman Andrew and Edice (Rieder) J.; m. Salley Van Dusen, May 23, 1969; children: Maria Pepper, Anna Sargent, Samantha Bennett. B.S., U. Pa.-Phila., 1963, M.B.A., 1968. Cert. mgmt. cons. Inst. Mgmt. Cons. Prin. William E. Hill & Co. Inc., N.Y.C., 1968-72; v.p. INA Properties, Phila., 1972-75; sr. prin. Hays Assocs., Phila., 1975-80; exec. v.p. Lavino Shipping Co., Phila., 1980—; dir. Phila. Maritime Exchange. Mem. Com. of Seventy, Phila., 1975—; bd. dirs. Springside Sch., Phila., 1982. Repubican. Episcopalian. Office: Lavino Shipping Co 3 Penn Ctr Plaza Philadelphia PA 19102

JOHNSON, CURTIS LEE, editor, writer; b. Mpls., May 26, 1928; s. Hjalmar N. and Gladys (Goring) J.; m. Jo Ann Lekwa, June 30, 1950 (div. 1974); children: Mark Alan, Paula Catherine; m. Rochelle Miller Hickey, Jan. 11, 1975 (div. 1980); m. Betty Axelrod Fox, Aug. 28, 1982. B.A., U. Iowa, 1951, M.A., 1952. Mag. and ency. editing and writing, Chgo., 1953-60, textbook and ednl. editing and writing, 1960-66; editor, pub. December mag., 1962—; free-lance editing and writing, 1966-72, 78—; mng. editor Aldine Pub. Co., 1972-73; v.p. St. Clair Press, 1973-77; sr. writer Bradford Exchange, 1978-81; mng. editor Regnery Gateway, 1981-82. Author: (with George Uskali) How to Restore Antique and Classic Cars, 1954; novels Hobbledehoy's Hero, 1959, Nobody's Perfect, 1973, Lace and a Bobbitt, 1976, The Morning Light, 1977, Song for Three Voices, 1984; Editor: (with Jarvis Thurston) Stories from the Literary Magazines, 1970, Best Little Magazine Fiction, 1970, (with Alvin Greenberg) Best Little Magazine Fiction, 1971, (with Jack Conroy) Writers in Revolt; essays The Forbidden Writings of Lee Wallek, 1978; also fiction, articles.; Cons. editor: Panache mag, 1967-76. Served with USN, 1946-48. Nat. Endowment Arts writing grantee, 1973, 81. Mem. Phi Beta Kappa, Phi Eta Sigma. Office: 309 Dato St Highland Park IL 60035

JOHNSON, CYRUS EDWIN, business executive; b. Alton, Ill., Feb. 18, 1929; s. Cyrus L. and Jennie C. (Keen) J.; m. Charlotte E. Johnson, Feb. 5, 1955; children: Julie M., Renee B. B.S., U. Ill., 1956, M.A., 1959. Dist. traffic mgr. Ill. Bell Telephone Co., Chgo., 1970-71, dist. comml. mgr., 1971-73; v.p. social action Gen. Mills, Inc., Mpls., 1973-78, v.p. dir. corp. personnel, 1978-80, v.p. human resource environment, 1980-81, v.p., dir. facilities and services, 1981—; dir. Ault, Inc., Mpls., Life-Span, Inc. Bd. dirs. United Way Mpls. Area, 1975—; active Nat. YMCA, 1973-79; mem. citizens adv. com. Mpls. Tech. Inst., 1981—; mem. deans adv. council Coll. Bus., U. Ill., Chgo., 1981—; past pres. Harvard U. Bus. Sch. Assn., Boston, 1978-79. Served with U.S. Army, 1950-52. Recipient Old Masters Program award Purdue U., 1975, Chgo. Defender Roundtable of Commerce award, 1963. Mem. Nat. Passenger Traffic Assn. Baptist. Lodges: Rotary; Masons. Home: 2040 Major Circle Golden Valley MN 55422 Office: Gen Mills Inc 9200 Wayzata Blvd Minneapolis MN 55440

JOHNSON, DANIEL, Canadian provincial official; b. Montreal, Que., Can., Dec. 24, 1944; s. Daniel and Reine (Gagne) J.; m. Jocelyne Pelchat, Sept. 9, 1967; children—Philippe, Stephanie. B.A., U. Montreal, 1963, LL.B., 1966; LL.M., London U., 1968, Ph.D., 1971; M.B.A., Harvard U., 1973. Bar: Called to Que. bar 1967. Sec. Power Corp. Can., Montreal, 1973-81; v.p. Power Corp. Can. Ltd., 1978-81; mem. Nat. Assembly Que., Quebec City, 1981—. Mem. Can. Bar Assn., Que. Bar Assn., Harvard U. Bus. Sch. Assn. Office: Room 288A Hotel du Parlement Quebec City PQ G1A 1A4 Canada

JOHNSON, DAVID ALFRED, hospital administrator; b. Gary, Ind., Sept. 9, 1929; s. George Kasper and Edla Marie (Gustafson) J.; m. Joyce Ann Graham, May 5, 1957; children: Keith, Lisa, Kevin, Lori. A.B. in Bus. Adminstrn, Augustana Coll., Rock Island, Ill., 1951; M.B.A., U. Chgo., 1954. Asst. dir. Miami Valley Hosp., Dayton, Ohio, 1955-62; asst. adminstr. Protestant Deaconess Hosp., Evansville, Ind., 1962-64; exec. dir., bd. dirs. Deaconess Hosp., Evansville, 1965—, pres., 1982—. Pres. Council for Health and Welfare Services, United Ch. of Christ, 1968-70; mem. Met. Evansville Progress Com., 1981—. Served with U.S. Army, 1951-53. Mem. Am. Protestant Hosp. Assn. (pres. 1972-73), Am. Hosp. Assn. (vice chmn. council nursing 1979-81, mem. ho. of dels. 1981—), Assembly of Hosp. Schs. Nursing (governing council 1974-76), Ind. Hosp. Assn. (chmn. 1976-77), So. Ind. Health Systems Agy. (pres. bd. dirs. 1975-77, dir. 1977-82), Assn. Community Cancer Centers (dir. 1975—, sec. 1976-77, treas. 1978, pres.-elect 1981, pres. 1982-83), Met. Evansville C. of C. (dir. 1970—, v.p. 1974-78). Methodist. Clubs: Masons, Scottish Rite, Shriners, Kiwanis. Home: 2411 E Chandler Ave Evansville IN 47714 Office: 600 Mary St Evansville IN 47747

JOHNSON, DAVID BUTLER, educator; b. Madison, Wis., July 24, 1918; s. Paul Browning and Helen Armine (Fay) J.; m. Marjorie Ann Kaun, Dec. 27, 1941; children—Timothy E., Deborah D., David D. B.A., Antioch Coll., 1942; M.S., U. Wis., 1948, Ph.D., 1955. Field examiner NLRB, Cin., 1946-47; chief contractor personnel br. div. orgn. and personnel U.S. AEC, Washington, 1950-57; asst. prof. U. Wis., Madison, 1957-59, asso. prof., 1959-63, prof., 1963—, chmn. dept. econs., 1965-68, dean internat. studies and programs, 1972-80; dir. Indsl. Relations Research Inst., 1977-79; Nat. Acad. Arbitrators, Soc. Internat. Devel. Served with AUS, 1942-45. Mem. Am. Econ. Assn., Am. Arbitration Assn., Indsl. Relations Research Assn. (nat. sec.-treas. 1962-73). Democrat. Unitarian. Home: 5806 Anchorage Ave Madison WI 53705

JOHNSON, DAVID GALE, economist, educator; b. Vinton, Iowa, July 10, 1916; s. Albert D. and Myra Jane (Reed) J.; m. Helen Wallace, Aug. 10, 1938; children: David Wallace, Kay Ann. B.S., Iowa State Coll., 1938, Ph.D., 1945; M.S., U. Wis., 1939; student, U. Chgo., 1939-41. Research asso. Iowa State Coll., 1941-42, asst. prof. econs., 1942-44; with dept. econs. U. Chgo., 1944—, beginning as research asso., successively asst. prof., asso. prof., 1944-54, prof., 1954—, asso. dean div. social scis., 1957-60, dean, 1960-70, chmn. dept. econs., 1971-75, 80—, acting dir. library, 1971-72, dir. Office Econ. Analysis, 1975-80, v.p., dean of faculties, 1975, provost, 1976-80; economist OPA, 1942, Dept. State, 1946, Dept. Army, 1948; mem. food adv. com. Office of Tech. Assessment, U.S. Congress, 1974-76; cons. TVA and Rand Corp., AID, 1962-68; pres. Nat. Opinion Research Center, 1962-75, 79—; agrl. adviser Office of Pres.'s Spl. Rep. for Trade Negotiations, 1963-64; mem. Pres.'s Nat. Adv. Commn. on Food and Fiber, 1965-67; adv. bd. Policy Planning Council State Dept., 1967-69, Nat. Commn. on Population Growth and the Am. Future, 1970-72; mem. steering com. Pres.'s Food and Nutrition Study, Nat. Acad. Scis., 1975-77. Author: Forward Prices for Agriculture, 1947, Agriculture and Trade: A Study of Inconsistent Policies, 1950, (with Robert Gustafson) Grain Yields and the American Food Supply, 1962, The Struggle Against World Hunger, 1967, World Agriculture in Disarray, 1973, World Food Problems and Prospects, 1975, (with Karen Brooks) Prospects for Soviet Agriculture in the 1980s, 1983. Bd. dirs. Wm. Benton Found., 1980—; pres. S.E. Chgo. Commn., 1980—. Fellow Am. Acad. Arts and Scis.; mem. Social Sci. Research Council (dir. 1953-56), Am. Econ. Assn., Am. Farm Econ. Assn. (pres. 1964-65), Phi Kappa Phi, Alpha Zeta. Address: 5617 S Kenwood Ave Chicago IL 60637

JOHNSON, DAVID LINCOLN, lawyer, insurance company executive; b. Boston, May 21, 1929; m. Agnes M. D'Aguiar, Oct. 8, 1967; children: David, Burr, Chris, Ture, Jennifer. B.A., U. Conn., 1950; LL.B., Boston U., 1954; LL.M., Northeastern U., 1956. Bar: Mass. 1954. Supr. group underwriting John Hancock Mut. Life Ins. Co., Boston, 1953-56; counsel George B. Buck, N.Y.C., 1956-65; asst. gen. counsel Factory Mut. System, Providence, 1965-71; gen. counsel Allendale Mut. Ins. Co., Johnston, R.I., 1971-77, v.p., gen. counsel, 1977-81, v.p., sec. gen. counsel, 1981—. Mem. Bd. of Reps., Stamford, Conn., 1960-63, minority leader, Stamford, Conn., 1960-63; mem. Rep. Town Com., Barrington, R.I., 1968—, mem. Bd. Tax Appeals, Barrington, R.I., 1972-75; trustee R.I. Council on Econ. Edn., Providence, 1983—. Mem. Fedn. Ins. Counsel, ABA, R.I. C. of C. Club: R.I. Country (Barrington). Home: 32 New Meadow Rd Barrington RI 02806 Office: Allendale Mut Ins Co 1301 Atwood Ave Johnston RI 02919

JOHNSON, DAVID LIVINGSTONE, emeritus electrical engineering educator; b. Gustavus, Ohio, Feb. 17, 1915; s. David Charles and Margaret (Delaney) J.; m. Eugenia Gibson McQuarie, Jan. 23, 1954. A.B., Berea Coll., 1936; M.A., State U. Iowa, 1938, B.S. in Elec. Engring, 1942; M.S., Okla. State U., 1950, Ph.D., 1957. Registered profl. engr., La., Okla. Instr. U.S. Naval Tng. Sch., Okla. State U., 1942-44; field engr. Airborne Coordinating Group, 1944-45; instr. Spartan Sch. Aeros., Tulsa, 1945-48; asst. prof. Okla. State U., 1948-55; prof., head dept. elec. engring. La. Tech. U., Ruston, 1955-80, prof. emeritus, 1980—. Mem. A.A.A.S., I.E.E.E., Am. Soc. Engring. Edn., Assn. Computing Machinery, Nat. Soc. Profl. Engrs., Am. Assn. U. Profs., Instrument Soc. Am., Sigma Xi, Eta Kappa Nu, Phi Kappa Phi, Pi Mu Epsilon, Upsilon Pi Epsilon, Tau Beta Pi. Home: 1604 Valley Dr Ruston LA 71270

JOHNSON, DAVID LYNN, materials scientist, educator; b. Provo, Utah, Apr. 2, 1934; s. David Elmer and Lucile (Maughan) J.; m. Rolla LaRae Page, June 26, 1959; children: Jeannette, David Page, Brice Aaron, Jeffrey Lynn, Karyn Rae. B.S., U. Utah, 1956, Ph.D., 1962. Mem. faculty dept. materials sci. and engring. Northwestern U., Evanston, Ill., 1962—, prof., 1971—, chmn. dept. materials scis. and engring., 1982—; cons. in field. Contbr. articles to profl. jours. NSF grantee, 1971-77, 79—. Fellow Am. Ceramic Soc. (chmn. basic sci. div. 1978-79, trustee 1980-81); mem. Metall. Soc., Internat. Inst. for Sci. of Sintering, AAAS, Sigma Xi, Alpha Sigma Mu, Phi Eta Sigma, Phi Kappa Phi, Theta Tau. Mormon. Office: Dept Materials Sci and Engring Northwestern U 2145 Sheridan Rd Evanston IL 60201 *Truth and reality are independent of man's perception of truth and reality. The nearer we approach truth, the clearer we perceive God, His majesty and glory. It is exciting to be involved in the scientific pursuit of truth, but it is far more so to live and work and to be with and grow with one's fair wife and children, through time and eternity. Herein lies the ultimate of truth and reality.*

JOHNSON, DAVID RALPH, bank holding company executive; b. Page, Nebr., Sept. 30, 1933; s. David M. and Bernice (Simmons) J.; m. Mary Fuelberth, July 8, 1955; children: Jill, Ann, Jane, Beth. B.S., Coll. Agr. U. Nebr., 1955, Colo. Grad. Sch. Banking U, Colo., 1964. Exec. v.p. Omaha Nat. Bank, 1958-74; pres., chief exec. officer Comml. Nat. Bank, Gand Island, Nebr., 1974-78; chmn., chief exec. officer, pres. First Wyo. Bancorp., Cheyenne, 1978—, also dir.; dir. First Wyo. Bank, Kemmerer, Jackson, Casper, Evanston, Lander. Served to capt. U.S. Army, 1955-61; U.S. and Germany. Democrat. Presbyterian. Office: First Wyo Bancorp 18th and Carey Cheyenne WY 82001

JOHNSON, DAVID SIMONDS, government official, meteorologist; b. Porterville, Calif., June 29, 1924; s. Frank David and Wanda (Simonds) J.; m. Margaret T. McFarland, Nov. 29, 1974. Student, U. Calif.-Berkeley, 1942-43, Reed Coll., 1943-44, Harvard U., 1945; A.B., UCLA, 1948, M.A., 1949. Meteorol. aide U.S. Weather Bur., Boise, Idaho, 1946-47; research asst. to asst. meteorologist UCLA, 1947-52; asso. meteorologist Pineapple Research Inst., Honolulu, 1952-56; with U.S. Weather Bur., 1956-65, dir. Nat. Weather Satellite Center, 1964-65; dir. Nat. Environ. Satellite Center, Environ. Sci. Services Adminstrn., Washington, 1965-70, Nat. Environ. Satellite Service, NOAA, 1970-80; asst. adminstr. for satellites NOAA, 1980-82; spl. asst. to pres. Univ. Corp. for Atmospheric Research, Washington, 1982—, also cons.; mem. working group II com. space research Internat. Council Sci. Unions, 1965-69; Mem. working group II com. space research working group VI, 1965-78, chmn. panel neutral atmosphere, 1966-69; mem. panel edn. and manpower com. atmospheric scis. Nat. Acad. Scis., 1967-69; mem. Gov. Md. Sci. Resources Adv. Bd., 1963-67; exec. com. panel on satellites World Meteorol. Organ., 1973-82, cons. to sec.-gen., 1982—. Co-author: Studies of the Structure of the Atmosphere over the Eastern Pacific Ocean in Summer, 1961. Served with USAAF, 1943-46. Recipient Gold medal Dept. Commerce, 1965; Exceptional Service medal NASA, 1966; award Nat. Civil Service League, 1974; William T. Pecora award, 1978; Presdl. Meritorious Exec. award, 1980. Fellow Am. Meterol. Soc. (pres. 1974, councilor 1963- 65, 68-70, 73-76, 81-83, exec. com. 1969-70, 73-75, 81-83, chmn. com. atmospheric measurements 1965-68, Brooks award 1982), AIAA (asso.), Am. Geophys. Union; mem. A.A.A.S., Internat. Acad. Astronautics (corr.), Am. Astronautics Soc. (Achievement award 1982), Sigma Xi. Mem. United Ch. Christ. Club: Cosmos (Washington). Home: 3061 Mimon Rd Annapolis MD 21403 Office: UCAR 2100 Pennsylvania Ave Washington DC 20037

JOHNSON, DAVID WOLCOTT, psychologist, educator; b. Muncie, Ind., Feb. 7, 1940; s. Roger Wildfield and Francis Elizabeth (Pierce) J.; m. Linda Mulholland, July 7, 1973; children: James, David, Catherine, Margaret, Jeremiah. B.S., Ball State U., 1962; M.A., Columbia U., 1964, Ed.D., 1966. Asst. prof. ednl. psychology U. Minn., Mpls., 1966-69, asso. prof., 1969-73, prof., 1973—; organizational cons., psychotherapist. Author: Social Psychology of Education, 1970, (with Goodwin Watson) Social Psychology: Issues and Insights, 1972, Reaching Out, 1972, 2d edit., 1981, Contemporary Social Psychology, 1973, (with Frank Johnson) Joining Together, 1975, 2d edit., 1982, (with Roger Johnson) Learning Together and Alone, 1975, Human Relations and Your Career, 1978, Educational Psychology, 1979, (with Dean Tjosvold) Productive Conflict Management, 1983, Circles of Learning, 1983; contbr. over 170 articles to profl. jours.; editor: Am. Ednl. Research Jour, 1981—. Bd. dirs. Walk-In Counseling Center, 1971-74. Recipient Gordon Allport award Soc. for Psychol. Study of Social Issues, 1981. Fellow Am. Psychol. Assn.; mem. Am. Sociol. Assn., Am. Ednl. Research Assn. Democrat. Home: 162 Windsor Ln New Brighton MN 55112 Office: 330 Burton Hall U Minn: Minneapolis MN 55455 *Success is a combination of focus, perseverance, and pain-endurance.*

JOHNSON, DEAN CONWAY, editor; b. Dodge Center, Minn., July 22, 1934; s. Roy William and Josie Priscilla (Hovl) J. A.B., St. Olaf Coll., 1956; A.M., Kans. U., 1962. Instr. English U. Cin., 1962-66, Miami U., Oxford, Ohio, 1966-67; salesman Houghton Mifflin Co., Boston, 1967-71, developmental editor, 1971, sponsoring editor, 1971-74, editor-in-chief, 1974-78, sr. editor, 1978—. Served with U.S. Army, 1957-60. Mem. Modern Lang. Assn., Speech Communication Assn., Phi Beta Kappa. Democrat. Lutheran. Home: 151 Tremont St Boston MA 02111 Office: 1 Beacon St Boston MA 02107

JOHNSON, DEANE FRANK, communications co. exec.; b. Des Moines, Sept. 2, 1918; s. Frank Joseph and Alma Odessa J.; m. Anne McDonnell, Nov. 9, 1968; 1 son, Deane Frank. A.B., Stanford, 1939, J.D., 1942. Bar: bar. Mem. firm O'Melveny & Myers, 1942-49, partner, 1949-81, mng. partner, 1977-81; pres. Warner Communications, Inc., N.Y.C., 1981—, also dir. Trustee Am. Film Inst., Calif. Inst. Tech. Mem. Am. Bar Assn., Order Coif. Episcopalian. Clubs: Los Angeles Country, Calif. (Los Angeles); The Links (N.Y.C.); Nat. Golf Links (Southampton, L.I.); Lyford Cay (Bahamas); Mt. Kenya Safari. Office: 75 Rockefeller Plaza New York NY 10019

JOHNSON, DENNIS, professional basketball player; b. San Pedro, Calif., Sept. 18, 1954. Student, Los Angeles Harbor Jr. Coll., Pepperdine U. Player Seattle Supersonics, NBA, 1976-80, Phoenix Suns, 1981-83, Boston Celtics, 1983—; player NBA All-Star Game, 1979, 80. Office: Boston Celtics North Sta Boston Garden Boston MA 02114 *

JOHNSON, DENNIS LESTER, consulting firm executive; b. Hampton, Iowa, Oct. 23, 1938; s. Royden Lester and Lorraine Anita (Rhoades) J.; m. Carolyn Louise Campbell, Aug. 18, 1963; children: Dené Lynn, Laurie Anne. B.A., Parsons Coll., 1960. Admissions officer, regional dir., dir. admissions counselors Parsons Coll., Fairfield, Iowa, 1960-67; pres., chmn. bd. Johnson Assocs., Inc., Glen Ellyn, Ill., 1967—; Speaker, lectr. in field. Columnist: Nation's Schools and Colls, 1974—; contbr. articles to profl. jours. Bd. dirs. DuPage Easter Seal Treatment Center, 1975-76, United Cerebral Palsy Greater Chgo., 1977—. Mem. Am. Assn. Higher Edn., Am. Personnel and Guidance Assn., Soc. Coll. and Univ. Planning, Am. Mktg. Assn. Presbyterian. Clubs: Oak Brook Bath and Tennis; Executives (Chgo.). Home: 1103 Fairview Ave Lombard IL 60148 Office: Suite 17 Bldg A 800 Roosevelt Rd Glen Ellyn IL 60137 *Change, if it is positive, is a reasonable and necessary goal. However, change is too often proper for the other person, organization, system, or group, and is threatening when it affects, or seems to relate to self. Truth, as a part of change, is the one ingredient that cannot, nor should not, be sacrificed if one is to be a change agent. Truth begins in the parental home and is the foundation for any truly successful individual. It cannot be compromised or misused without negative results.*

JOHNSON, DIANE LAIN, educator, critic; b. Moline, Ill., Apr. 28, 1934; d. Dolph Lain and Frances Eloise (Elder) Lain; m. John Frederic Murray, Nov. 9, 1969; children: Kevin, Darcy, Amanda, Simon Johnson. A.A., Stephens Coll., 1953; B.A., U. Utah, 1957; M.A., Ph.D., UCLA, 1968. Mem. faculty dept. English U. Calif., Davis, 1968—, now prof. English. Author: Fair Game, 1965, Loving Hands at Home, 1968, Burning, 1970, The Shadow Knows, 1975, Lying Low, 1978, Lesser Lives, 1972, Terrorists and Novelists, 1982, Dashiell Hammett, 1983. Woodrow Wilson grantee, 1967; AAUW fellow, 1968; Guggenheim Found. fellow, 1977-78; Nominee Nat. Book Awards, 1973, 79; recipient Rosenthal award Am. Acad. Arts and Letters, 1979. Mem. MLA, PEN.

JOHNSON, DONAL DABELL, agronomy educator; b. Rigby, Idaho, July 20, 1922; s. Alfred Tom and Jennie (Dabell) J.; m. Ruth Beardall, Aug. 22, 1945; children: Kemp B., Alfred Tom, Donal B. B.S., Brigham Young U., 1948; M.S., Cornell U., 1950, Ph.D., 1952. Pre-doctoral fellow AEC, 1952; mem. faculty Coll. Agr., Colo. State U., Ft. Collins, 1952—, prof., 1962—, assoc. dean, 1967, dean, 1968-83; coordinator agrl. devel. Colo. State U.-AID, Eastern Nigeria, 1964-68; dep. dir. Colo. Agrl. Expt. Sta., 1970-83; Mem. Western Regional Agrl. Planning Com., 1972-76, chmn. research implementation com., 1975-76. Trustee Consortium for Internat. Devel., 1973-83, chmn., 1976-79. Served with USAAF, 1943-47. Mem. AAAS, Am. Soc. Agronomy, Soil Sci. Soc. Am., Western Assn. Agrl. Expt. Sta. Dirs. (exec. com. 1976—, chmn. 1980-82), Gt. Plains Agrl. Council (exec. com. 1971, 76-77, chmn. 1977), Sigma Xi, Gamma Sigma Delta., Phi Kappa Phi, Alpha Zeta. Home: 1812 Orchard Pl Fort Collins CO 80521

JOHNSON, DONALD DODGE, JR., educator; b. Glen Ridge, N.J., Feb. 27, 1937; s. Donald Dodge and Lillian Moller (Gilbreth) J.; m. Martha Louise Niepold, Aug. 11, 1962; children—Donald Dodge III, Katherine Louise. A.B., Princeton U., 1959; M.A., U. N.C., 1964, Ph.D., 1970. Tchr. Milton (Mass.) Acad., 1959-61, Haverford (Pa.) Sch., 1961-62; asso. prof., asso. dean St. Lawrence U., Canton, N.Y., 1967-78; prof. English, provost DePauw U., Greencastle, Ind., 1978—; dir. Arthur R. Johnson Co. Recipient Wanamaker prize in English Lang. Mem. Omicron Delta Kappa. Office: Provost's Office DePauw U Greencastle IN 46135

JOHNSON, DONALD EDWARD, farm supply executive, former government official; b. Cedar Falls, Iowa, June 5, 1924; s. Chris E. and E. and Jacolyn (Johnson) Hansen; m. Mary Jean Suchomel, Oct. 13, 1947; children—Alan, David, Brian, Kevin, Julie, Kurt, Joan, Robert, Beth, Susan Carol. Student, Iowa State U., 1941-42, 46, Eastern Oreg. Coll. Edn., LaGrande, 1943; LL.D., Iowa Wesleyan Coll., 1971. Sec.-treas. Johnson Hatcheries Inc., West Branch, Iowa, 1947-61; pres. D.J. Services, Inc., 1961-69, 77—, West Branch Farm Supply, Inc., 1961-69,

77—; sec.-treas. S. J. Poultry Co., Inc., West Branch and Waterloo, 1956-69, 77—; v.p. ME-JON Fertilizers Inc., Oxford, Iowa, 1956-65; chmn. bd. Protein Blenders Inc., Iowa City, 1961-66; mem. adminstr. vets. affairs VA Central Office, Washington, 1969-74; dep. asst. sec. commerce for domestic and internat. bus., Washington, 1974-77, adminstrv. asst. to Sen. Roger Jepsen (Iowa), 1983—. Chmn. Iowa chpt. Crusade for Freedom, 1954, 57, U.S. Civil Rights Commn., 1958; Iowa adv. mem. U.S. Commn. Civil Rights, 1959-60; pres. West Branch Community PTA, 1960, West Branch Heritage Found., 1956-66; mem. Pres.'s Domestic Council, 1972; pres. Herbert Hoover Library Assn., 1977-83; Councilman, West Branch, 1948-49, 66-67. Served with inf. AUS, 1942-46; ETO; Served with inf. AUS; CBI. Decorated Bronze Star medal, Purple Heart; Croix d'Officer de la Reconnaissaince, Belgium, 1964; named Iowan of Year Iowa Radio and TV Broadcasters, 1965; recipient Gold Plate award Am. Acad. Achievement, 1971, Iron Mike award Marine Corps League. Mem. Am. Legion (comdr. Iowa 1952-53, mem. nat. exec. com. from Iowa 1957-61, nat. comdr. 1964-65), Iowa Feed and Grain Assn., Am. Feed Mfrs. Assn., West Branch C. of C. (pres. 1947-48). Republican. Roman Catholic (chmn. bldg. com. 1959). Home: 906 Emerald Dr Alexandria VA 22308 Office: Box 577 West Branch IA 52358 *My most critical judgment and thoughts on my life turn on how well I have served my family and my God.*

JOHNSON, DONALD MILTON, insurance executive; b. Los Angeles, Feb. 15, 1920; s. Oscar E. and Maude F. (Philips) J.; m. Marguerite Glaze, Feb. 14, 1942; children: Stephen, Thomas, Andrew, Kenneth. B.S., UCLA, 1941. Field rep. Aetna Casualty & Surety Co., Los Angeles, 1946-50, supt. agy. dept., 1950-55, mgr., 1956-60, gen. mgr., 1960-61, asst. v.p. exec. dept., Hartford, 1960-65; v.p. corp. services Aetna Life & Casualty Co., 1965-66, v.p. exec. dept., 1966-67, sr. v.p., 1968, exec. v.p. ins. ops., 1968, pres., dir., mem. exec. com., 1970-76; chmn. bd., chief exec. officer Indsl. Indemnity Co., San Francisco, 1976—; dir. Crum & Forster. Bd. dirs. Calif. Roundtable, St. Luke's Hosp.; trustee San Francisco Bay Area Council, City of Hope Pilot Med. Ctr., United Way of Bay Area; bd. dirs. Internat. Ins. Seminar, San Francisco Bay Area Council; bd. dirs., v.p. Calif. Workers' Compensation Inst. Served to maj. O.M.C. AUS, 1942-46. Mem. Am. Ins. Assn. (past chmn.), Health Ins. Assn. Am. (past chmn.), Nat. Assn. Casualty and Surety Execs. (past pres.), Ins. Inst. Am. (bd. govs.), Am. Inst. Property and Liability Underwriters (trustee), U.S. C. of C. (mem. policy com.), San Francisco C. of C. (dir., treas.). Congregationalist. Clubs: Pacific Union, Bankers (San Francisco). Office: Indsl Indemnity Co 255 California St San Francisco CA 94111

JOHNSON, DOROTHY GREENE, historian; b. Chgo., June 6, 1921; d. Louis and Mildred (Brody) Greenberg; m., June 14, 1947. B.A., U. Chgo., 1942, M.A., 1951, Ph.D., 1956. Propoganda analyst Office Coodinator Inter-Am. Affairs, Washington, 1942-43; field program officer in charge Central Am. and Caribbean cultural ctrs. U.S. Dept. State, 1944-47; lectr. Western civilization U. Chgo., 1957-67; historian-archivist, index editor Jane Addams papers U. Ill., Chgo., 1977—. Pres. Women's Scholarship Assn., Roosevelt U., Chgo., 1972-75, bd. dirs., v.p., Chgo., 1969-72. Honors scholar U. Chgo. Mem. Historians of Met. Chgo., Midwest Conf. Brit. Studies. Home: 5545 S Kimbark St Chicago IL 60637 Office: Hull House Univ Ill Chicago IL 60680

JOHNSON, DOUG, advertising and public relations executive; b. Watertown, N.Y., Aug. 16, 1919; s. H. Douglas and Clare (Lane) J.; m. Geraldine Evans, Aug. 11, 1943; children: Molly E., Faith D. Student pub. schs. Cert. bus. communicator Bus./Profl. Advt. Assn. Pres. Doug Johnson Assos. (pub. relations), Syracuse, N.Y., 1949-61, Barlow/Johnson, Inc. (advt. and pub. relations), Syracuse, 1961-80, Johnlow Corp., Fayetteville; chmn. bd. Nowak Barlow Johnson, Fayetteville, 1980-82; v.p. mktg. Edward Jay Co., Inc., Syracuse, 1982—; pres. Highbridge Properties; dir. Agway Life Ins. Co., Dewitt, N.Y., Agway Ins. Co., Dewitt, Key Bank of Central N.Y., Syracuse, Syracuse Baseball Club, Inc. Home sec. to congressman, 1949-65; Mem. pres.'s assos. LeMoyne Coll.; bd. dirs. Community Gen. Hosp. Syracuse, N.Y. State Coll. Forestry Found.; bd. dirs., pres. Boys Club N.Y. Served with AUS, 1941-45. Decorated Purple Heart with 3 oak leaf clusters. Mem. Public Relations Soc. Am. (accredited mem.), Am. Assn. Advt. Agys., Syracuse C. of C. (pres. 1968-69). Clubs: Century (gov.), Press (Syracuse)). Home: 10 Thornwood Ln Fayetteville NY 13066 Office: 905 Canal St Syracuse NY 13217

JOHNSON, DUANE FADINAND, librarian; b. Brookville, Kans., Oct. 26, 1940; s. Orlando F. and Alice Mae (Halsey) J.; m. Ann Lynn Dolloff, Sept. 15, 1963 (dec. 1978); 1 dau., Marcia Kay (dec.). A.B., Kans. Wesleyan U., 1964; M.S., Fla. State U., 1966. Asst. librarian Salina Pub. Library, Kans., 1966-68; dir. Great Bend Pub. Library (Central Kans. Library System), Kans., 1968-72, Hutchinson Pub. Library, 1972-82; state librarian Kans. State Library, Topeka, 1982—. Mem. Bd. Edn., U.S. Dist. 313, 1977-82; del. White House Conf. on Libraries, 1979. Mem. ALA (council), Kans. Library Assn. (pres. 1976), Mountain Plains Library Assn., Beta Phi Mu. Home: 2216 SE Burr St Topeka KS 66605 Office: Kans State Library State Capitol Topeka KS 66612

JOHNSON, EARL, JR., judge, author; b. Watertown, S.D., June 10, 1933; s. Earl Jerome and Doris Melissa (Schwartz) J.; m. Barbara Claire Yanow, Oct. 11, 1970; children: Kelly Ann, Earl Eric, Agaarn Yanovitch. B.A. in Econs., Northwestern U., 1955, LL.M., 1961; J.D., U. Chgo., 1960. Bar: Ill. 1960, 9th Circuit Ct. 1964, D.C. 1965, U.S. Supreme Ct. 1966, Calif. 1972. Trial atty., organized crime sect. Dept. Justice, Washington, Miami, Fla. and Las Vegas, Nev., 1961-64; dep. dir. Neighborhood Legal Services Project, 1964-65, OEO Legal Services Program, 1965-66, dir., 1966-68; vis. scholar Center for Study of Law and Soc., U. Calif., Berkeley, 1968-69; assoc. prof. U. So. Calif. Law Center, Los Angeles, 1969-75, prof. law, 1976-82, dir. Program Study Dispute Resolution Policy, Social Sci. Research Inst., 1975-82, dir. clin. programs Program Study Dispute Resolution Policy, Social Sci. Research Inst., 1970-73; assoc. justice Calif. Ct. Appeal, 1982—; co-dir. Access to Justice Project, European U. Inst., 1975-79; vis. scholar Inst. Comparative Law, U. Florence, Italy, 1973, 75; Robert H. Jackson lectr. Nat. Jud. Coll., 1980; adv. panel Legal Services Corp., 1976-80; legis. impact panel Nat. Acad. Scis., 1977-80; faculty Asian Workshop on Legal Services to Poor, 1974; mem. Internat. Legal Center, Legal Services in Developing Countries, 1972-75; Founder, bd. mem. Action for Legal Rights, 1971-74; pres., trustee Western Center on Law and Poverty, 1972-73, 76-80; v.p., chmn. exec com. Calif. Rural Legal Assistance Corp., 1973-74; exec. com. Nat. Sr. Citizens Law Center, 1980-82; sec. Nat. Resource Center for Consumers of Legal Services, 1974-82; mem. task force on dispute mgmt. Center for Public Resources, N.Y.C., 1981-82. Author: Justice and Reform: The Formative Years of the American Legal Services Program, 1974, 2d edit., 1978, Toward Equal Justice: A Comparative Study of Legal Aid in Modern Societies, 1975, Outside the Courts: A Survey of Diversion Alternatives in Civil Cases, 1977, Dispute Processing Strategies, 1978; editor: U. Chgo. Law Rev, 1960; contbr. articles to books and periodicals. Bd. dirs. Beverly Hills Bar Found., 1972-73; trustee Los Angeles Legal Aid Found., 1969-71; mem. Los Angeles County Regional Planning Commn., 1980-81; bd. visitors U. San Diego Law Sch., 1983—. Served with USNR, 1955-58. Recipient Dart award for acad. innovation U. So. Calif., 1971; Loren Miller Legal Services award Calif. State Bar, 1977; named So. Calif. Citizen of Week, 1978; Ford Found. fellow, 1960; Dept. State lectr., 1975; grantee Ford Found., Russell Sage Found., Law Enforcement Assistance Adminstrn., NSF. Mem. ABA (com. chmn. 1972-75, mem. spl. com. resolution minor disputes 1976—), Calif. Bar Assn., Los Angeles Bar Assn. (mem. neighborhood justice center com.), Law and Soc. Assn., Nat. Legal Aid and Defenders Assn. (dir. 1968-79), Am. Acad. Polit. and Social Sci., Lawand Society Assn., Calif. Judges Assn. (appellate cts. com. 1983—), Order of Coif. Democrat. Home: 1627 Monterey Hermosa Beach CA 90254 Office: State of Calif Ct Appeal 2d Appellate Dist 3580 Wilshire Blvd Los Angeles CA 90010 *I have profound faith in the power of ideas to shape American society and in the special significance of one fundamental concept—equal justice, in its full meaning.*

JOHNSON, EARL MORTIMER, hotel exec.; b. Chgo., May 2, 1908; s. Francis Royal and Hilda Louise (Rapp) J.; m. Dolores Wetzel, Jan, 18, 1936; children—Dianne Marie, Dennis Dolan, Dolores Michelle, Valerie Ann, Bruce Anthony, Francis Jerome. B.S., Northwestern U., 1932. Pres. Johnson Land & Timber Co., 1936—, Earl M. Johnson (realtors), 1945—; owner Johnson's Rustic Resort, all Houghton Lake, Mich., 1936—; Mem. exec. com. Mich. Indsl. Ambassadors. Pres. Mich. Tourist Council, 1953-54; Bd. dirs. Mich. Accident Fund. Served to lt. USNR, 1943-45. Recipient Disting. Citizen award Mich. Ho. of Reps., 1978; named Mich. Ambassador of Tourism Gov. Millikan, 1980; named to Hospitality Mag. Hall of Fame, 1957. Mem. Hotel Assn. Redbook Directory Corp. (dir.), Am. Hotel Assn. (resort com., hon. mem.), Mich. Hotel Assn. (past pres., hon. life dir.), Am. Hotel and Motel Assn. (cert. hotel adminstr., past pres., hon. life dir.), East Mich. Tourist Assn. (past pres.), Paul Bunyan Bd. Realtors (past pres.), Theta Xi. Clubs: Tavern (N.Y.C.); Chicago Culver, Executive (Chgo.). Address: Johnson's Rustic Resort Houghton Lake MI 48651 *Attempt always to employ management personnel who are smarter than you are. From them you will receive initiative, ideas, and suggestions which will help the efficiency and growth of your business.*

JOHNSON, EARLE BERTRAND, insurance executive; b. Otter Lake, Mich., May 3, 1914; s. Bert M. and Blanche (Sherman) J.; m. Frances Pierce, 1940 (dec.); children: Earle Bertrand, Victoria, Julia, Sheryl; m. Peggy Minch Rust, Apr. 30, 1972. B.S., U. Fla., 1937, J.D., 1940. With State Farm Ins. Cos., Bloomington, Ill., 1940—, regional agy. dir., 1958-60, regional v.p., 1960-65, v.p., sec. State Farm Mut. Automobile Ins. Co., 1965-80, dir., 1967—; also mem. exec. com.; sr. v.p., treas. State Farm County Mut. Ins. Co. Tex., 1965-80, treas., 1963-80; chmn. bd., mem. exec. com. State Farm Life Ins. Co., 1970—; v.p., mem. exec. com. State Farm Fire & Casualty Co., 1965-80, dir., 1965—, State Farm Investment Mgmt. Corp.; v.p., sec. State Farm Internat. Services, Inc., 1967—. Mem. Agy. Officers Round Table (exec. coms.), Am., Fla. bar assns., Soc. Former FBI Agts., Life Ins. Mktg. and Research Assn. (dir. 1975-78), Life Underwriter Tng. Council (trustee 1974-77), Phi Alpha Delta, Phi Kappa Tau. Home: 59 Country Club Pl Bloomington IL 61701 Office: One State Farm Plaza Bloomington IL 61701

JOHNSON, EARVIN (MAGIC JOHNSON), professional basketball player; b. Lansing, Mich., Aug. 14, 1959; s. Earvin and Christine J. Student, Mich. State U. Profl. basketball player Los Angeles Lakers, NBA, 1979—. Player NBA All-Star Game, 1980, 84. Office: care Los Angeles Lakers 3900 W Manchester Blvd PO Box 10 The Forum Inglewood CA 90306 *

JOHNSON, EDGAR FREDERICK, manufacturing company executive; b. Waseca, Minn., June 13, 1899; s. Charles John and Edna Sophia (Swanson) J.; m. Ethel Jones, July 28, 1923; children: Shirley Johnson Duley, Lois Johnson Chaffin. B.S. in E.E, U. Minn., 1921. Founder E.F. Johnson Co., Waseca, Minn., 1923, gen. mgr., 1923-53, pres., 1953-68, chmn. bd. dirs., 1968-78, founder dir., 1978-83; dir. Research, Inc., Mpls., 1950's; dir., treas. Waseca Savs. and Loan Assn., 1963-82. Trustee Gustavus Adolphus Coll., 1976—, First Congl. Ch., Midwest Research Inst., 1976-78, North Star Research Inst., 1967-78, Courage Found., 1976—; trustee Johnson Found., 1964-83, pres., 1975-83; trustee Operation Bootstrap Tanzania, 1963-80, pres., 1969; exec. council Minn. Hist. Soc., 1970—; mem. Bd. Edn. Waseca, 1932-50, pres., treas.; mem. Charter Commn. Waseca, 1963-71, pres., 1950-58. Served with U.S. Army, 1918. Recipient Outstanding Achievement award U. Minn., 1977, Bi-centennial gold medal King Karl Gustaf XVI of Sweden, 1976; named to Minn. Bus. Hall of Fame, 1977. Fellow Radio Club Am. (Sarnoff citation 1975); mem. IEEE (life). Republican. Clubs: Waseca Lions (pres. 1931), Waseca Lakeside (pres. 1948), Masons.). Home: 520 Ninth St NE Waseca MN 56093

JOHNSON, EDWARD A., manufacturing executive; b. Providence, R.I., June 6, 1917; s. Andrew J. and Tekla E. (Wilson) J.; m. Florence Skoog, Aug. 29, 1942; children: Bradford D., Pamela J. Johnson Bassett, Cynthia. B.S.M.E., U. R.I., 1940. Asst. to v.p. Proportioneers, Inc., Providence, R.I., 1940-48; v.p. mktg., dir. Barry Controls, Inc., Watertown, Mass., 1948-60; sr. v.p., vice chmn. bd., sec. Barry Wright Corp., Newton, Mass., 1960—. Mem. ASME, Engring. Soc. New Eng., Am. Mktg. Assn., Nat. Investor Relations Inst., Sales and Mktg. Execs. Greater Boston. Home: 4350 Shelldrake Ln Quail Ridge Boynton Beach FL 33436 Office: One Newton Exec Park Newton Lower Falls MA 02162

JOHNSON, EDWARD CHARLES, life insurance company executive, consultant; b. Ocean Springs, Miss., Mar. 10, 1922; s. James Charles and Mable (Tardy) J.; m. Jayne Matthews, June 24, 1949; children: Cathy Johnson Randall, Betty Johnson Snell, Debra Johnson Noble. Student public schs. C.L.U. With Mut. Benefit Life Ins. Co., 1953-83, gen. agt., Chgo., then v.p. agencies home office, Newark, 1973-79, sr. v.p. agencies, 1979-83; pres. Edward C. Johnson, Inc., 1983—; dir. MBL Life Assurance Corp. Served with AUS, 1940-41. Mem. Nat. Assn. Life Underwriters, Am. Soc. C.L.U.'s, Gen. Agts. and Mgrs. Conf. Democrat. Presbyterian. Clubs: Knickerbocker Country, Essex., Shriners. Office: 520 Broad St Newark NJ 07101

JOHNSON, EDWARD CROSBY, III, fin. co. exec.; b. Boston, June 29, 1930; s. Edward Crosby and Elsie (Livingston) J.; m. Elizabeth Bishop Hodges, Oct. 8, 1960; children—Abigail Pierrepont, Elizabeth Livingston, Edward Crosby. A.B., Harvard U., 1954. With Fidelity Mgmt. & Reseacch Corp., Boston, 1957—, pres., chief exec. officer, 1972-77; chmn. bd., chief exec. officer parent co. FMR Corp., 1977—. Trustee Mus. Fine Arts, Boston, 1971—; mem. council Mass. Hist. Soc., 1971-78, Essex Inst., 1967-78; bd. visitors Am. and New Eng. studies program Boston U., 1974—. Served with AUS, 1954-56. Mem. Am. Acad. Arts and Scis., Fin. Analysts Fedn. Office: 82 Devonshire St Boston MA 02109

JOHNSON, EDWARD ELEMUEL, psychologist, educator; b. Jamaica, B.W.I., July 25, 1926; U.S., 1941, naturalized, 1948; s. Edward and Mary Elizabeth (Blake) J.; m. Beverley Jean Morris, Jan. 26, 1955; children—Edward Elemuel, Lawrence Palmer, Robin Jeannine, Nathan Jerome, Cyril Ulric. B.S., Howard U., 1947, M.S., 1948; Ph.D., U. Colo., 1952. Asso. prof. psychology Grambling Coll., La., 1954-55; prof. So. U., Baton Rouge, 1955-60, prof., head dept. psychology, 1960—69, asso. dean univ., 1969-72, also dir.; clin. prof. La. State U. Sch. Medicine, New Orleans; dir. Exptl. Curriculum Devel. Program, United Bd. for Coll. Devel., 1972-74; clin. prof. psychiatry Emory U. Med. Sch., Atlanta, 1974; prof. psychiatry Coll. Medicine and Dentistry N.J.-Rutgers Med. Sch., Piscataway, N.J., 1974—; cons. collaborative child devel. project; cons. State Indsl. Sch. Scotlandville, La.; vocat. cons. HEW; mem. mental health adv. group Westinghouse Health Systems, 1978—; region II mental health coordinator Head Start Program, 1978—; mem. gen. research support rev. com. NIH, 1980—; Mem. acad. council Thomas A. Edison Coll. of N.J., 1978—. Served to 1st lt. AUS, 1951-53. Fellow AAAS; mem. Am. Psychol. Assn. (com. on adv. services for edn. and tng. 1968—), N.Y. Acad. Scis. (life), Sigma Xi. Club: Masons (33 deg.). Home: PO Box 597 East Brunswick NJ 08816

JOHNSON, EDWARD ROY, library director; b. Denver, Nov. 29, 1940; s. Burton Clifford and Bonnie Jean (Daughtry) J.; m. Benita Irene Hulbert, June 14, 1964; 1 son, Elliot Hulbert. B.A., U. Colo., 1964; M.A., U. Wis., 1966; Ph.D., 1974. Library asst. Univ. Colo., Boulder, 1964-65; ref. librarian Univ. Iowa, Iowa City, 1966-67, bus. librarian, 1967-69; asst. dean libraries Pa. State Univ., State College, 1972-79; dir. libraries North Tex. State Univ., Denton, 1979—. Author: (with Stuart H. Mann) Organization Development for Academic Libraries, 1980. Pres. Jewish Community Center, State College, 1977-79, Jewish Congregation, Denton, Tex., 1981—. Recipient U.S. Dept. Health, Edn., Welfare fellowship, 1969-72; Research grant Council Library Resources, 1977-78. Mem. Am. Library Assn., AAUP, Oral History Assn., Tex. Library Assn., Am. Philatelic Soc., Phi Alpha Theta, Beta Phi Mu. Clubs: Kiwanis, B'nai B'rith. Home: 529 Northridge St Denton TX 76201 Office: Willis Library North Tex State Univ Denton TX 76203

JOHNSON, EDWIN BARNER, mining company executive; b. Ishpeming, Mich., Oct. 21, 1923; s. Edwin William and Blanche (Carlson) J.; m. Lois Millman; children: Scott, Vicki Johnson Caneff, Marsha Johnson Nardi. B.S. in Metallurgy, Mich. Tech. U., Houghton, 1947. Chief metallurgist Cleveland-Cliffs Iron Co., Ishpeming, 1963-64, asst. mgr., 1964-66, mgr. Mich. mines, 1966-71, gen. mgr. mines, Cleve., 1971-73, v.p. ops., 1973-75, sr. v.p., 1975-83, pres., 1983—, also dir.; dir. Soc. Corp., Cleve., Soc. Nat. Bank, U.P. Grnerating Co., Houghton. Mem. Baldwin Wallace Bus. Adv. Council, Berea, Ohio, 1977; trustee Mich. Tech. Fund, Houghton, 1981; mem. Fairview Gen. Hosp., Cleve. Served with U.S. Army, 1942-45. Mem. Am. Iron and Steel Inst., Am. Iron Ore Assn., AIME, Can. Inst. Mining and Metallurgy, Mich. Mfg. Assn. (bd. dirs.). Republican. Presbyterian. Clubs: Union, Westwood Country. Office: Cleveland Cliffs Iron Co 1460 Union Commerce Bldg Cleveland OH 44115

JOHNSON, ELLIOTT AMOS, lawyer; b. Soldier, Iowa, Feb. 21, 1907; s. John C. and Sarah (Knutson) J.; m. Katherine Ryckman, Oct. 17, 1936; children: Nancy, Glenn, Karen. Ph.B., U. Chgo., 1928, J.D., 1931; student, Northwestern U., 1923-24, 34-36; LL.B., South Tex. Coll., 1937. Bar: Ill. 1931, Tex. 1937. Prin., coach Melvin (Iowa) High Sch., 1928-29; atty., Chgo., 1931-36; with Schlumberger Well Surveying Corp., Houston, 1936-68; formerly v.p. finance, treas., gen. counsel; former v.p. Schlumberger Tech. Corp.; partner Johnson, Wurzer & Westmoreland, Houston, 1968—. Councilman-at-large, city of Houston, 1945-47; Bd. Dirs Travelers Aid Soc., Houston, 1946-60, pres., 1958-60; bd. dirs. Profit Sharing Research Found., 1958-60, 69-72, South Tex. Coll. Law, 1951—; chmn. bd. South Tex. Jr. Coll., 1967-74; trustee U. Houston Found., 1965—, v.p., 1975-80, chmn. bd., 1980—; trustee Rosewood Gen. Hosp., 1964-76, pres., 1972-76. Mem. Profit Sharing Council Am. (dir. 1951-62, chmn. 1958-60), Am. Petroleum Inst. (dir. 1960-62), Petroleum Equipment Suppliers Assn. (dir. 1951—, pres. 1960-61), Houston Soc. Fin. Analysts (pres. 1957-58), Tax Research Assn. (pres. Houston 1952-53), Tex. Mfrs. Assn. (dir. 1956-59), Am., Tex., Houston bar assns., Phi Delta Theta, Alpha Kappa Psi. Presbyterian. Clubs: Houston, Houston Country. Lodges: Masons; Kiwanis (pres. 1964). Home: 2929 Buffalo Speedway Apt 1303 Houston TX 77098 Office: 2200 S Post Oak Blvd Suite 707 Houston TX 77056 *Be honorable in everything you do. You can't get ahead getting even! The sum of wisdom is this, Time is never lost that is devoted to work. True happiness lies not in possession or satiation but in achievement.*

JOHNSON, ELMER MARSHALL, reproductive toxicologist and teratologist; b. Midlothian, Ill., June 16, 1930; s. Burt and Gertrude Esther (Miller) J.; m. Sharon Ann Coyle, May 9, 1976; children—Mark Dee, Kim Lea, Erik Marshall, Lora Marlys. Student, U. Mex., 1948; diploma, Thornton Jr. Coll., 1950; B.S. (teaching asst.), Tex. A. and M. U., 1954, M.S., 1955; Ph.D. (teaching asst.), U. Calif., Berkeley, 1959. Research asst. U.S. Army Surgeon Gen./Tex. A. and M. U. Research Found., College Station, 1955; instr. anatomy and physiology Contra Costa Coll., San Pablo, Calif., 1958-59; instr. U. Fla. Coll. Medicine, Gainesville, 1960-61, asst. prof., 1961-65, asso. prof., 1965-68, prof., 1968-70, acting chmn. dept. anatomy, 1969-70; prof., chmn. dept. anatomy, prof. dept. developmental and cellular biology U. Calif., Irvine, 1970-72; prof., chmn. dept. anatomy, dir. Daniel Baugh Inst., Jefferson Med. Coll., Thomas Jefferson U., Phila., 1972—; chmn. bd. Argus Research Labs., Inc., Perkasie, Pa.; cons. Allied Chem. Co., Dow Chem. Co., Johnson & Johnson, Argus Research Labs., Public Utilities, EPA, U.S. Naval Hosp., Phila., Kirkland & Ellis, Esq., Hoffman-LaRoche, Merck, Inc., McGraw-Hill, Inc., Sterling-Winthrop Research Inst., Interagy. Regulatory Liaison Group, Nat. Acad. Scis., NRC, Columbia Nitrogen Co. Asso. editor: Teratology, 1974-81, Jour. Environ. Pathology and Toxicology, 1979—, Fundamental and Applied Toxicology, 1981—. Served to 2d lt. U.S. Army, 1959. USPHS predoctoral fellow, 1953-55; March of Dimes Nat. Found. research grantee, 1962-63; NIH research grantee, 1963—; Growth Soc. research grantee, 1972-74; NIH teratology predoctoral tng. grantee, 1955-59. Mem. AAAS, Teratology Soc., Am. Assn. Anatomists, Assn. Anatomy Chairmen, Genetic Toxicology Assn., Soc. Toxicology, Am. Coll. Toxicology, So. Soc. Anatomists, Mid Atlantic Reproduction and Teratology Assn., Sigma Xi. Republican. Unitarian. Office: 1020 Locust St Philadelphia PA 19107

JOHNSON, ELMER WILLIAM, automotive executive, lawyer; b. Denver, May 2, 1932; s. Elmer William and Lillian Marie (Nelson) J.; m. Constance Dorothy Mahon, June 18, 1955; children: Julianne Marie, Valerie Lynn, Garrett Douglas. B.A., Yale U., 1954; J.D., U. Chgo., 1957. Bar: Ill. 1957. Assoc. Kirkland & Ellis, Chgo., 1956-62, ptnr., 1962-71, mng. ptnr., 1971—; v.p., group exce. gen. counsel Gen. Motors Corp., Detroit, 1983—; gen. counsel Internat. Harvester, Chgo., 1982-83; spl. counsel to chmn. of regional holding co. for 5 midwestern Bell operating cos., Chgo., 1983; dir. Fed. Singal Corp., Oak Brook, Ill. Trustee U. Chgo., 1977—. Mem. Ill. State Bar Assn., ABA. Republican. Presbyterian. Clubs: Chgo. (exec. com. 1976-80), Chgo. Golf (pres. 1981-83). Office: Gen Motors Corp 3044 W Grand Blvd Detroit MI 48202

JOHNSON, ELVIS EUGENE, insurance company executive; b. Redford, Mo., Aug. 15, 1921; s. Edgar Elvis and Ollie Mae (Flowers) J.; m. Jean Alice Cain, Dec. 3, 1949; children: Patricia Ann, Karen Sue. B.S. in Bus. Adminstrn, Southwest Mo. State U., Springfield, 1949. With Am. Nat. Ins. Co., Galveston, Tex., 1951—, v.p. field ops., ordinary agy. dept., 1972-73, exec. v.p., dir., 1973-76, sr. exec. v.p., chief mktg. officer, dir., 1976-83, assoc. regional dir., Springfield, Mo., 1983—; pres., dir. Am. Nat. Life Ins. Co. of Tex.; dir. Am. Nat. Ins. Service Co., Springfield, Mo., Am. Nat. Property & Casualty Co., Springfield, Am. Nat. of Okla. Corp., Wilmington; chmn. bd., chief exec. officer Commonwealth Life & Accident Ins. Co., St. Louis; dir.

Securities Mgmt. & Research Corp., Galveston, Standard Life & Accident Ins. Co., Oklahoma City. Served with USAF, 1941-45. Decorated D.F.C. with 2 oak leaf clusters, Air medal with 4 oak leaf clusters, Purple Heart, Presdl. citation with oak leaf cluster. Mem. Nat., Tex. assns. life underwriters, Million Dollar Round Table (life), Am. Soc. Chartered Life Underwriters, Am. Council Life Ins., Alumni Assn. Southwest Mo. State Coll. (pres.). Democrat. Presbyterian. Clubs: Masons, Shriners, Galveston Country; Twin Oaks Country (Springfield). Office: PO Box 10405 Glenstone Sta Springfield MO 65804

JOHNSON, EMERY ALLEN, physician; b. Sioux Falls, S.D., Apr. 16, 1929; s. Emery Albert and Florence Emily J.; m. Nancy Mourning, June 19, 1954; children: Steven, Scott, Jennifer, Jill. B.S., Hamline U., 1951; M.D., U. Minn., 1954; M.P.H., U. Calif., Berkeley, 1964. Commd. med. officer USPHS, 1955-81, Indian health area dir., Billings, Mont., 1964-66, asst. and dep. dir. Indian Health Service, Rockville, Md., 1966-69, dir. Indian Health Service, 1969-81, asst. surgeon gen., 1969-81; cons. in pub. health and med. care adminstrn., 1981—; cons. Peace Corps, WHO, AID, Nat. Med. Center, Liberia; U.S. del. UNICEF Exec. Bd., 1978. Recipient Rockefeller Public Service award, 1979; Excellence in Public Service award Am. Acad. Pediatrics; medals USPHS. Mem. AMA, Am. Acad. Family Practice, Am. Public Health Assn. (chmn. health adminstrn. sect.).

JOHNSON, ERIC FOLKE, former assn. exec.; b. Oyster Bay, N.Y., Mar. 6, 1916; s. Johannes Stefanus and Anna Alida Jansson; m. Catherine Myers, Sept. 6, 1947. A.B., Antioch Coll., 1939. With Wilcox & Follett Co., Chgo., 1939-40; with Am. Water Works Assn., Denver, 1940-79, editor, dir. publs., 1946-47, asst. sec., 1947-67, dir. pub. relations, 1961-67, exec. dir., 1967-79, author monthly column, 1979-82; sec.-treas. Am. Water Works Assn. Research Found., 1967-79; exec. bd., hon. mem. Internat. Water Supply Assn.; editorial cons., 1979—. Treas. Pinehurst Village Condominium Assn., 1979-80, pres., 1981. Served with USMCR, 1943-46. Mem. Am. Water Works Assn. (hon., medal for outstanding service 1981), Brit. Water Works Assn. (hon.), Inst. Water Engrs. and Scientists (Eng.) (profl. asso., Friendship medal 1978), Am. Soc. Assn. Execs., Water Conditioning Assn. Internat. (hon.), Environ. Council. Home: 6350 W Mansfield Ave Apt 54 Denver CO 80235 *Success, I believe, must be measured not by level of accomplishment, but by the maximization of one's talents in achieving one's objectives without compromising one's own principles and those of the community. Earning a place in Who's Who, then, becomes less a measure of success than it is of high and community-approved objectives. I'm happy to be Who.*

JOHNSON, ERNEST FREDERICK, JR., chemical engineer, educator; b. Jamestown, N.Y., Apr. 4, 1918; s. Ernest Frederick and Esther Marie (Engstrom) J.; m. Marjorie Ruth McMullin, July 15, 1944; children: David S., Carolyn L. Doherty, Arthur B., Melissa A. B.S., Lehigh U., 1940; Ph.D., U. Pa., 1949. Research engr., tech. supr. synthetic organic chems. mfr. Barrett div. Allied Chem. Corp., Phila., 1940-46; asst. prof. dept. chem. engring. Princeton, 1948-54, asso. prof., 1954-59, prof., 1959—, acting chmn. dept. chem. engring., 1959-60, chmn., 1977-78, asso. dean faculty, 1962-66, assoc. Plasma Physics Lab., 1955—; cons. petroleum, chem., engring. food processing firms, 1949—; Dir. Autodynamics, Inc.; Mem. adv. bd. Indsl. and Engring. Chemistry, 1964-67. Author: Automatic Process Control, 1967; Contbr.: Advances in Chemical Engineering, 1958, Ency. Chemistry, Chemistry of Fusion Power Devel, 1972, also articles to sci. jours. Trustee Asso. Univs., Inc., 1962-68, chmn. exec. com., chmn. bd., 1965-67; trustee Westminster Found., 1973-79. Fellow AAAS, Am. Inst. Chemists, Am. Inst. Chem. Engrs. (exec. com. Central Jersey sect. 1972—); mem. Am. Chem. Soc. (exec. com. div. indsl. and engring. chemistry 1965-67, council 1976-78), Am. Soc. Engring. Edn., Princeton Engring. Assn. (sec.-treas. 1954-57, exec. com. 1954—), Am. Swedish Hist. Found., Sigma Xi, Tau Beta Pi, Phi Eta Sigma. Presbyn. (elder). Clubs: Adirondack Mountain, Tärnavrå Yacht. Home: 90 Lambert Dr Princeton NJ 08540 also Indian Point Rd Stonington ME 04681

JOHNSON, EUGENE WALTER, mathematician; b. El Paso, Tex., May 25, 1939; s. Walter Albert and Lillian Ann (Martinets) J.; m. Sandra Sue Gilbert, Oct. 16, 1959; 1 dau., Catherine Mary. Student, Riverside City Coll., 1958-60; B.A., U. Calif., Riverside, 1963, M.A., 1964, Ph.D., 1966. Asst. prof. Eastern N.Mex. State U., 1966; asst. prof. math. U. Iowa, Iowa City, 1966-70, asso. prof., 1970-75, prof., 1975—, chmn. dept., 1976-79. Contbr. articles to profl. jours. Mem. Am. Math. Soc. Democrat. Home: 3303 Lower West Branch Rd Iowa City IA 52240 Office: Dept Math Univ of Iowa Iowa City IA 52242

JOHNSON, EVERETT RAMON, coll. dean; b. Bklyn., Dec. 18, 1915; s. George and Margaret (Nelsen) J.; m. Lucy Anna Rossini, June 27, 1942; children—Thomas G., Lisa M., Aimee A. B.A., U. Ia., 1937; M.A., Harvard, 1940; Ph.D., U. Rochester, 1949; M.S. in Engring. (hon.), Stevens Inst. Tech., 1960. Scientist Brookhaven Nat. Lab., 1949-53; research engr. RCA Labs., 1953-54; prof. chemistry Stevens Inst. Tech., 1954-62; phys. sci. adminstr., div. research AEC, 1964-66; program mgr. Nat. Standrad Reference Data System, Nat. Bur. Standards, 1966; asso. dean U. Md. Coll. Engring., College Park, 1966—. Author: Chemistry and Physics of High Energy Reaction, 1969, Radiation Induced Decomposition of Inorganic Molecular Ions, 1970; Asso. editor: Jour. Chem. and Engring. Data, 1966—. Served to 1st lt. AUS, 1943-46. Mem. Radiation Research Soc., Am. Chem. Soc., Sigma Xi. Office: Coll Engring U Md College Park MD 20742

JOHNSON, F. ROSS, food products company executive; b. Winnipeg, Man., Can., Dec. 13, 1931; s. Frederick Hamilton and Caroline (Green) J.; m. Laurie Ann Graumann; children: Bruce, Neil. B.Comm., U. Man., 1952; M.B.A., U. Toronto, Ont., Can., 1956; LL.D. (hon.), St. Francis Xavier U., Antigonish, 1978, Meml. U. Nfld., 1980. Tchr. U. Toronto, 1962-64; dir. mktg. CGE, Toronto, 1964-66; mgr. mdse. T. Eaton Co., 1966-67; exec. v.p. GSW Ltd., 1967-71; pres. Standard Brands Ltd., Toronto, 1971, pres., chief exec. officer, 1972; v.p. Standard Brands, Inc., N.Y.C., 1973, sr. v.p., dir., 1974, pres., 1975-81, chief exec. officer, 1976-81, chmn., 1977-81, chmn., chief operating officer, 1981; pres., chief operating officer Nabisco Brands, Inc. (formerly Standard Brands, Inc. and Nabisco, Inc.), Parsippany, N.J., 1984—; dir. Wosk's Ltd., Vancouver, Bank of N.S., Toronto. Mem. adv. council Columbia U. Bus. Sch., N.Y.C.; chmn. bd. N.Y.C. chpt. Nat. Multiple Sclerosis Soc., 1980—. Served to lt., Ordance Corps Royal Can. Army. Mem. Grocery Mfrs. Assn. (dir.), Young Pres.'s Orgn., Phi Delta Theta (pres. 1951). Clubs: Mt. Bruno Country; Brook, The Links, Blind Brook, Econ. (N.Y.C.); Conn. Golf (Easton). Office: 625 Madison Ave New York NY 10022 Office: 7 Campus Dr Parsippany NJ 07054

JOHNSON, FALK SIMMONS, English educator; b. Wake Forest, N.C., Oct. 17, 1913; s. Walter Nathan and Eva (Coppedge) J.; m. Laura Frances Stark, June 11, 1940; children: Mark Hartman, Bruce Walter, Martha Frances. B.A., Wake Forest Coll., 1935, M.A., 1936; postgrad., Northwestern U., 1937-40; Ph.D., U. Chgo., 1956. Tchr. English, Campbell Coll., N.C., 1936-37; mem. pub. relations staff Northwestern U., 1937-38; tchr. English, Mars Hill Coll., 1938-40; instr. English, Northwestern U., 1945-49; mem. faculty U. Ill., Chgo., 1949—, prof. English, 1966-73, prof. linguistics, 1973—. Author: A Spelling Guide and Workbook, 1959, How To Organize What You Write, 1964, Improving What You Write, 1965, A Self-Improvement Guide to Spelling, 1965, Improving Your Spelling, 3d edit., 1979; editor: Bobbs-Merrill Series in Composition and Rhetoric; ednl. TV, 1958-60. Served as 1st lt. Signal Corps, AUS, 1942-45. Mem. Linguistic Soc. Am., Am. Dialect Soc. Home: 7624 Maple St Morton Grove IL 60053

JOHNSON, FERD, cartoonist; b. Spring Creek, Pa., Dec. 18, 1905; s. John F. and Bessie A. J.; m. Doris Lee White, Feb. 24, 1930; 1 son, Thomas. Student, Chgo. Acad. Fine Arts, 1923. Color artist, Chgo. Tribune, 1923; asst. to, Frank Willard (Moon Mullins), 1923-58; sports illustrator: Westbrook Pegler, 1925-30; cartoonist: Texas Slim; synicated, Chgo. Tribune-N.Y. News Syndicate, 1925-27, 40-58, Moon Mullins, 1958—; oil paintings represented in, various So. Calif. galleries. Mem. Nat. Cartoonist Soc., Comics Council.

JOHNSON, FRANCIS BENJAMIN (BEN JOHNSON), actor; b. Foraker, Okla., June 13, 1918; s. Benjamin John and Ollie (Workmon) J.; m. Carol Elaine Jones, Aug. 31, 1941. Student pub. sch. Rancher, Sylmar, Calif., 1966—. Film appearances include Rio Grande, 1950, Cheyenne Autumn, 1964, Hang Em High, 1968; co-star: films Fort Defiance, 1941, War Drums, 1957, Ten Who Dared, 1960, Undefeated, 1969, Will Penny, 1968, Wild Bunch, 1969, Getaway, 1972, Kid Blue, 1973, Fort Bowie, 1958, Train Robbers, 1972, Chisum, 1970, The Last Picture Show, 1971, Terror Train, 1980, The Hunter, 1980; star: Wagonmaster, 1950, Mighty Joe Young, 1949, Wild Stallion; other movies include One Eyed Jacks, 1961, Shane, 1953, Dillinger, 1973, Sugarland Express, 1974, Bite the Bullet, 1975, Hustle, 1975, Breakheart Pass, 1976, The Town that Dreaded Sundown, 1977, The Greatest, 1977, Grayeagle, 1978, The Swarm, 1978; numerous TV appearances; other movies include Ruckus, 1981, Tex, 1982, Soggy Bottom U.S.A., 1982; co-star: TV series the Monroes, 1966-67; TV movies of week Runaway, 1973, Locusts, 1974, The Savage Bees, 1976. Named Best Supporting Actor for film The Last Picture Show, 1972. Office: care Herb Tobias & Assos 1901 Ave of Stars Los Angeles CA 90067 *

JOHNSON, FRANCIS SEVERIN, physicist; b. Omak, Wash., July 20, 1918; s. Ralston Severin and Elizabeth (Gruenes) J.; m. Maurine Marie Green, Sept. 12, 1943; 1 dau., Sharan Kaye. B.Sc. with honors in Physics, U. Alta., Can., 1940; M.A. in Physics and Meteorology, UCLA, 1942; Ph.D. in Meteorology, UCLA, 1958. Head, high atmosphere research sect. U.S. Naval Research Lab., Washington, 1946-55; mgr. space physics research Lockheed Missiles & Space Co., 1955-62; head, atmospheric and space scis. div. S.W. Center Advanced Studies, Dallas, 1962-64, dir. earth and planetary scis. lab., 1964-69; acting pres. U. Tex. at Dallas, 1969-71; dir. Center for Advanced Studies, 1971-74, Cecil H. and Ida M. Green honors prof. natural sci., 1974—, exec. dean grad. studies and research, 1976-79; asst. dir. astron., atmosphere, earth and ocean scis. NSF, Washington, 1979-83; cons. ionospheric physics subcom., space scis. steering com. NASA, 1960-62, mem. planetary atmospheres subcom., space scis. steering com., 1962-67, chmn. lunar atmospheric measurements team. Apollo sci. planning teams, 1964-67; mem. adv. bd. Mars space missions, 1964-67, mem. lunar and planetary missions bd., 1967-71; mem. adv. panel atmospheric scis. NSF, 1962-67; mem. working group IV COSPAR, 1965-80, v.p., 1975-80; mem. Nat. Acad. Scis. panel adv. to central radio propagation lab. Nat. Bur. Standards, 1962-65; mem. panel weather and climate modification Nat. Acad. Scis., 1964-70; mem. adv. com. research to coordinating bd. Tex. Coll. and Univ. System, 1966-67; mem. space sci. bd. Nat. Acad. Scis., 1969-81, mem. geophysics research bd., 1971-77; mem. Nat. Acad. Scis. com. advisory to NOAA, 1966-71; mem. sci. advisory bd. USAF, 1968-79; mem. nat. adv. com. Oceans and Atmosphere, 1971-73; mem. Climate Research Bd., Nat. Acad. Scis., 1977-79; pres. Spl. Com. on Solar Terrestrial Physics, 1974-77. Author: Satellite Environment Handbook, 1965; also numerous articles. Served with USAAF, 1942-46. Decorated Bronze Star medal; recipient Henryk Arctowski award Nat. Acad. Scis., 1972; Exceptional Sci. Achievement medal NASA, 1973; Meritorious Civilian Service award USAF, 1979. Fellow Am. Geophys. Union (vice chmn. sect. geomagnetism and aeronomy 1964-68, pres. sect. solar planetary relationships 1970-72, John Adam Fleming award 1977), AAAS (council mem. 1968-72), Am. Meteorol. Soc. (councilor 1976-78), IEEE; asso. fellow AIAA (chmn. tech. com. space and atmospheric physics 1961-64, Space Sci. award 1966); mem. Am. Phys. Soc., Am. Astron. Soc., Internat. Assn. Geomagnetism and Aeronomy (exec. com. 1967-71), Internat. Union Radio Sci. (chmn. U.S. Commn. IV 1964-67, sec. U.S. nat. com. 1967-70, vice chmn. 1970-73, chmn. 1973-76), Internat. Union Geodesy and Geophysics (U.S. nat. com. 1973-76), Sigma Xi. Office: U Tex at Dallas PO Box 688 Richardson TX 75080

JOHNSON, FRANK MINIS, JR., federal judge; b. Winston County, Ala., Oct. 30, 1918; s. Frank M. and Alabama (Long) J.; m. Ruth Jenkins, Jan. 16, 1938; 1 son, James Curtis (dec.). Grad., Gulf Coast Mil. Acad., Gulfport, Miss., 1935, Massey Bus. Coll., Birmingham, 1937; LL.B., U. Ala., 1943; LL.D. (hon.), U. Ala., 1977, also LL.D., Notre Dame U., 1973, LL.D., Princeton U., 1974, Boston U., 1979, Yale U., 1980, J.D., St. Michael's Coll., 1975. Bar: Ala. 1943. Mem. firm Curtis, Maddox & Johnson, 1946-53; U.S. atty. No. Dist. Ala., 1953-55; U.S. dist. judge Middle Dist. Ala., 1955-79; U.S. judge Ct. Appeals for 11th Circuit, Montgomery, Ala., 1979—; mem. Temporary Emergency Ct. Appeals of U.S., 1972—; mem. rev. com. Jud. Conf., 1969-78, mem. jud. ethics com., 1978—; mem. Spl. Com. on Habeas Corpus, 1971-78. Served from pvt. to capt. inf. AUS, 1943-46. Decorated Purple Heart with oak leaf cluster, Bronze Star. Mem. Ala. Acad. Honor. Office: US Court House PO Box 35 Montgomery AL 36105 *

JOHNSON, FRANK STANLEY, JR., government official; b. N.Y.C., Dec. 24, 1930; s. Frank Stanley and Alice Claire (Stern) J.; m. Lavern Schlemeyer, Aug. 19, 1978; children: Kenneth F. (dec.), Scott D., Lisa Lam. B.S. in Mktg. with honors, Ind. U., Bloomington, 1955. Reporter, then edn. editor Newsday, Garden City, N.Y., 1955-59; asst. to pres. Daniel & Florence, also Solomon R. Guggenheim founds., N.Y.C., 1959-61; asst. dir., then dir. info. Sci. Research Assos., Inc., subs. IBM, Chgo., 1962-66; asst. to pres., dir. public affairs Rodman Job Corps Tng. Center subs. IBM, New Bedford, Mass., 1966-68; mgr. communications IBM Corp., Endicott, N.Y., 1968-69; v.p. Chgo. Bd. Trade, 1969-72; dir. public affairs U.S. Dept. Labor, Washington, 1972-73; dir. public affairs and advt. Gen. Dynamics, Inc., St. Louis, 1974-78; v.p. public affairs Revlon, Inc.; also pres. Revlon Found., Inc., N.Y.C., 1978-81; pres. Frank Johnson & Assocs. Ltd., 1981—; v.p. Newport News Shipbldg. & Dry Dock Co. (Va.), 1981-83; now dir. pub. affairs NASA; founder, 1st chmn. Internat. Grad. Achievement, Inc., 1960-63. Bd. dirs. Susquehango County (N.Y.) council Boy Scouts Am., 1968-69, St. Louis chpt. Nat. Multiple Sclerosis Soc., 1974-78, Acting Co., Inc., N.Y., 1980—82, Goodwill Industries Am., Washington, 1982—, Va. Opera Assn., Norfolk, 1982—; adv. bd. Adelphi Coll., Garden City, N.Y., 1957-59, Nat. Resources Council, Manhattanville Coll., Purchase, N.Y., 1980—; trustee Manhattanville Coll., Purchase, N.Y., 1982—; adv. bd. European Pub. Relations Roundtable, 1982—. Served with USM, 1950-53. Recipient Golden Trumpet award Publicity Club Chgo., 1969, Outstanding Shareholder Communications award Nat. Security Traders Assn., 1969; Best in Industry award Fin. World mag., 1975, 76, 2d best, 1962. Mem. Public Relations Soc. Am., Am. Mgmt. Assn., Aero. Inst. Am., AIAA, Pharm. Mfrs. Assn., Proprietary Assn., Cosmetic, Toiletries and Fragrance Assn., Edn. Writers Assn., Nat. Sci. Writers Assn., Issues Mgmt. Assn. Washington. Clubs: Capitol Hill, Nat. Press (Washington); Chgo. Press, Mid-Am., city (Chgo.); Overseas Press Am., Wings (N.Y.C.). Office: NASA Hdqrs 400 Maryland Ave Washington DC 20546

JOHNSON, FRANKLIN RIDGWAY, lawyer, financial executive; b. Boston, Mar. 23, 1912; s. Howard Franklin and Mary Helena (Morse) J.; m. Hope Gray Lord, June 1, 1940; children: Nathaniel, Samuel, Anne, Rebecca; m. Sarah Q. Shaw, Aug. 16, 1962. LL.B., Northeastern U., 1939; spl. student, Harvard U. Law Sch., 1941-42. Bar: Mass. 1939. Ptnr. Choate, Hall & Stewart, Boston, 1950-56; sr. officer, legal counsel Colonial Mgmt. Assocs., 1956-63, Eaton & Howard, Inc., 1963-65; sr. v.p., gen. counsel Keystone Custodian Funds, Inc., 1965-77; pres., dir. Keystone OTC Fund, Inc., Boston, 1974-77; of counsel Choate, Hall & Stewart, Boston, 1978-80; sole practice law, Boston, 1980-83; of counsel Edes's McNally, Inc., Concord, Mass., 1983—; trustee Middlesex Savs. Bank; dir., mem. audit com. Pioneer Fund, Pioneer II, Pioneer Three, Pioneer Bond Fund. Mem. Concord Bd. Selectmen, (Mass.), 1951-55; chmn. bd. Concord Bd. Selectment, (Mass.), 1953-55; mem. adv. com. Harvard Law Sch. Study State Securities Regulation, 1954-56. Mem. ABA, Nat. Assn. Securities Dealers (gov. 1971-73), Investment Co. Inst. (gov. 1959-62, 68-71). Republican. Episcopalian. Clubs: Harvard (Boston); Concord (Country). Home: 1717 Wedgewood Common Concord MA 01742 Office: 7 Main St Concord MA 01742

JOHNSON, FREDERICK CHARLES, naval officer; b. Keewatin, Minn., Sept. 3, 1925; s. Charles Albert and Carrie Marie (Stremel) J.; m. Holly Elizabeth Murphy, June 7, 1952; children: Holly Diane Johnson Mooney, Kandy Karen, Frederick C. B.S., U.S. Naval Acad., 1952; postgrad., U.S. Naval War Coll., 1963-64, U.S. Naval Post Grad. Sch., 1957-59, George Washington U., 1963-69. Enlisted U.S. Navy, 1943, commd. ensign, 1952, advanced through grades to rear adm., 1978; comdr. USS Gray, 1970-71; chief of staff Comdr. Carrier Group Five, 1975-77; dir. navy command and control planning and programming div. Navy Dept., Washington, from 1977; now comdr. Tng. Command Pacific, San Diego. Decorated Legion of Merit (2), Bronze Star (2). Lutheran. Office: Tng Command Pacific Dept Navy San Diego CA 92147

JOHNSON, FREDERICK WILLIAM, lieutenant governor Saskatchewan; b. Sedgetey, Staffordshire, Eng., Feb. 13, 1917; emigrated to Can., 1928; s. Edwin Priestley and Laura (Caddick) J.; m. Joyce Marilyn Laing, July 30, 1949; children: F. William, Royce L.C., Sheil F. B.A., U. Sask., 1947, LL.B., 1949. Justice Ct. of Queen's Bech, Saskatchewan, 1965-77; chief justice Ct. of Queen's Bench, Saskatchewan, 1977-83; lt. gov. Province of Sask., Regina, 1983—. Served to maj. Royal Can. Arty., 1941-46; Europe. Mem. Law Soc. Sask (bencher 1960-65). Mem. United Ch. of Can. Club: Assiiboia (Regina). Office: Govt House Regina SK Canda S4T 6N5

JOHNSON, GARY BERTRAM, semiconductor executive; b. Presque Isle, Maine, Feb. 12, 1942; s. Ernest Elwood and Shirley (Archer) J.; m. Faith Heather, Feb. 27, 1965. B.S., U. Conn., 1963, M.S., 1966; M.B.A., Ariz. State U., 1970. Prof. computer sci. U. Conn., Storrs., 1965-67; prof. bus. Ariz. State U., Phoenix, 1967-68; mgr. internat. mktg. Motorola Inc., Phoenix, 1968—; cons. in field. Mem. Am. Mgmt. Assn., Am. Mktg. Assn., Internat. Elec. Engring. Soc. Republican. Baptist. Home: 1956 E Redfield Rd Tempe AZ 85283 Office: Motorola Inc. 5005 E McDowell Phoenix AZ 85283

JOHNSON, GEORGE E., beauty care products manufacturing company executive; b. Richton, Miss., June 16, 1927; m. Joan Henderson; children: Eric, John, George E., Joan Marie. Student, Chgo. public schs.; D.B.A. (hon.), Xavier U., 1973, D.Humanities, Clark Coll., 1974, D.C.S., Coll. Holy Cross, 1975, LL.D., Babson Coll., 1976, Fisk U., 1977, Tuskegee Inst., 1978, Lake Forest Coll., 1979, D.H.L., Chgo. State U., 1977, Lemoyne-Owen Coll., 1979. With Fuller Products Co. (cosmetics mfrs.), Chgo., founder, 1954; since pres. Johnson Products Co., Inc., Chgo.; dir. Debbie's Sch. Beauty Culture; former chmn. Independence Bank Chgo.; dir. Commonwealth Edison Co., Met. Life Ins. Co. Pres. George E. Johnson Ednl. Fund, George E. Johnson Found.; mem. corp. Babson Coll.; exec. bd. Chgo. Area council Boy Scouts Am.; bd. govs. Chgo. Orchl. Assn.; trustee Chgo. Sunday Eve. Club, Northwestern U., Ravinia Festival Assn.; bd. dirs. Chgo. Urban League, Dearborn Park Corp., Lyric Opera Chgo., Nat. Asthma Center, Northwestern Meml. Hosp., Operation PUSH, Protestant Found. Greater Chgo.; mem. nat. adv. com. Interracial Council Bus. Opportunity; v.p. Jr. Achievement Chgo.; sponsoring com. NAACP Legal Def. Fund; mem. 100 Club Cook County. Recipient Humanitarian Service award Abraham Lincoln Center, 1972, Am. Black Achievement award Ebony mag., 1978, Public Service award Harvard Club Chgo. Mem. Sigma Pi Phi. Congregationalist. Clubs: Gurnham Yacht, Chgo. Yacht, Comml., Economic, Metropolitan, Mid-Am. (Chgo.); Carlton, PIPS Internat.; Runaway Bay Country (Jamaica); Tres Vidas En La Playa (Acapulco, Mex.); Jockey (Miami, Fla.); Le Mirador (Switzerland). Address: Johnson Products Co Inc 8522 S Lafayette Ave Chicago IL 60620 *

JOHNSON, GEORGE EDWARDS, economist; b. Boston, Jan. 31, 1940; s. George Philip and Ruth (Grimes) J.; m. Gloria Bogdan, Apr. 2, 1980. B.S., Babson Coll., 1960; M.A., U. Calif.-Berkeley, Ph.D., 1966. Research assoc. Princeton U., N.J., 1967-68; vix. fellow U. Nairobi, Kenya, 1970-71; dir. Office Evaluation U.S. Dept. Labor, Washington, 1973-74; prof. econs. U. Mich., Ann Arbor, 1966—. Contbr. articles to profl. jours. Office: Dept Econs U Mich Ann Arbor MI 48104

JOHNSON, GEORGE, JR., physician, educator; b. Wilmington, N.C., Apr. 6, 1926; s. George W. and Evelyn (Hill) J.; m. Marian Patterson Ritchie, July 1, 1950; children—Sally Hope, George William, David Ritchie, Robert Hill. B.S., U. N.C., 1948, certificate medicine, 1950; M.D., Cornell U., 1952. Intern, resident surgery N.Y. Hosp., 1952-59; pvt. surg. practice, 1959-62; asst. prof. to prof., chief div. vascular surgery, vice chmn. dept. surgery U. N.C., 1962—, Roscoe B.G. Cowper disting. prof. in surgery, 1973—; Mem. adv. com. N.C. Emergency Med. Services, chmn., 1977—. Contbr. chpts. to books, articles to profl. jours. Served to 1st lt. inf. AUS, 1944-46. Mem. Univ. Assn. Emergency Med. Services (pres. 1973), Am., So. surg. assns., A.C.S. (pres. N.C. chpt., gov. 1977, trauma com. 1974-81, exec. bd. trauma com. 1977-81), So. Univ. Surgeons, So. Assn. Vascular Surgery (sec.-treas. 1981—), Durham-Orange County Med. Soc. (pres. 1971), Halsted Soc. Club: Rotary. Home: 410 Westwood Dr Chapel Hill NC 27514

JOHNSON, GEORGE ROBERT, educator; b. Caledonia, N.Y., Aug. 2, 1917; s. Arthur E. and Mary J. (Sinclair) J.; m. Beatrice E. Caton, Nov. 7, 1942; children: Diane K., Jane A. Eiden, Rosemary E. Johnson Kurek, Martha L. Brinkman. B.S., Cornell U., 1939; M.S., Mich. State U., 1947, Ph.D., 1954. Tchr. Corfu-East Pembroke Central Sch., Corfu, N.Y., 1939-42; asst. agrl. country agt., St. Lawrence (N.Y.) County, 1942-43; instr. animal husbandry Cornell U., 1943-47, asst. prof., 1947-48, assoc. prof., 1948-55, Ohio State U., 1955-58, prof., chmn. dept. animal sci., 1958—. Mem. Am. Soc. Animal Sci.,

Sigma Xi, Alpha Zeta, Gamma Sigma Delta. Home: 251 Fairlawn Dr Columbus OH 43214

JOHNSON, GEORGE WILLIAM, univ. pres.; b. Jamestown, N.D., July 5, 1928; s. George Carl and Mathilde (Trautman) J.; m. Joanne Ferris, June 11, 1955; children—Robert Craig, William Garth. B.A., Jamestown Coll., 1950; M.A., Columbia U., 1953, Ph.D., 1960. Asst. chmn. dept. English Temple U., Phila., 1964-66, asso. dean liberal arts, 1966-67, chmn. dept. English, 1967-68, dean liberal arts, 1968-78; pres. George Mason U., Fairfax, Va., 1978—. Contbr. articles to scholarly jours. Served in U.S. Army, 1950-52. Mem. Am. Assn. State Colls. and Univs., Am. Council Edn. Roman Catholic. Home: 4520 Roberts Rd Fairfax VA 22030 Office: 4400 University Dr Fairfax VA 22030

JOHNSON, GERALD EDWIN, lawyer; b. Warren, Pa., Sept. 2, 1907; s. Albert Edwin and Selma C. (Nelson) J.; m. Gertrude Blomquist, Aug. 14, 1937; children: Christina, Paul L. A.B., Wittenberg U., 1929; J.D., Case Western Res. U., 1932. Bar: Ohio 1932. Since practiced in, Cleve.; partner firm Johnson and Umstead, 1969-75; of counsel Squire, Sanders & Dempsey, 1975—; chief rent atty. Cleve. area OPA, 1942-43. Pres. bd. trustees Albert Rees Davis Endowment Fund, 1960-70; trustee Alcoholism, Services Cleve., 1974-79, Ridgecliff Hosp. Fellow Am. Coll. Probate Counsel; mem. ABA, Ohio Bar Assn. (council dels.), Cleve. Bar Assn. (exec. com.), Court Nisi Prius (judge 1968-69), Ohio Bar Found., Am. Soc. Hosp. Attys., Order of Coif, Alpha Tau Omega (pres. 1958-62, treas. 1968-70), Phi Delta Phi, Tau Kappa Alpha. Clubs: Union, Singers (Cleve.) (pres. 1952). Home: 21 Edgewater Sq Lakewood OH 44107 Office: Union Commerce Bldg Cleveland OH 44115

JOHNSON, GIFFORD K., testing lab. executive; b. Santa Barbara, Calif., June 30, 1918; s. Elvin Morgan and Rosalie Dorothy (Schlagel) J.; m. Betty Jane Crockett, June 10, 1944; children: Craig, Dane, Janet. Student, Santa Monica (Calif.) City Coll., 1938-39, UCLA, 1940, Harvard Bus. Sch., 1944. With N.Am. Aviation, Inc., 1935-41; chief indsl. engr. Consol. Vultee Aircraft Corp., 1941-48; prodn. mgr. to pres. Chance Vought Aircraft Corp., 1950-61; pres., chief operating officer Ling-Temco-Vought, Inc., 1961-64; pres. S.W. Center Advanced Studies, 1965-69; pres., chief exec. officer Am. Biomed. Corp., 1969-78; exec. v.p. Nat. Health Labs., 1978-81; chmn., chief exec. officer Woodson-Tenent Labs. Inc., Dallas, 1981—. Mem. devel. bd. U. Tex., Dallas; v.p., trustee Excellence in Edn. Found.; pres. C.C. Young Meml. Home; bd. dirs. Tex. A&M Research Found. Mem. Am. Clin. Lab. Assn. (dir.), Navy League (life). Methodist (treas.). Clubs: Northwood Country; Salesmanship (Dallas). Home: 10555 Pagewood Dr Dallas TX 75230 Office: 10300 NC Expy Bldg 4 Suite 220 Dallas TX 75231 *We are what we make of ourselves in this free land. Not everyone will like me but hopefully will see me as an honest man.*

JOHNSON, GLEN R., investment banking executive; b. Lake Lillian, Minn., May 2, 1929; s. Oscar A. and Ruth (Anderson) J.; m. LaVonne Corley, Jan. 7, 1949; children—Vicki, David, Lori. Student, Gustavus Adolphus Coll., 1946-47, Minn. Sch. Bus., 1947-48. Founder Lake Lillian Crier, 1949, editor, pub., 1949-61; pub. Fishing and Boating News, 1959-61; dep. dir., area mgr. for Minn. U.S. Savs. Bonds, 1961-62, dir., Minn., 1962-67, nat. dir., 1967-69; v.p. Motivational Systems, Inc., N.Y.C., 1969-70; pres. Fund for U.S. Govt. Securities, Pitts., 1970—; pres. Money Market Mgmt., Inc., Trust for Short-Term U.S. Govt. Securities Inc., Federated Tax-free Income Fund, Inc., Federated Master Trust, Federated Money Market, Inc., Federated Tax-Free Trust, Money Market Trust, Trust for U.S. Treasury Obligations, Liquid Cash Trust. Pres. Weekly Press Assn., Kandiyohi County, Minn., 1957-59; Chmn. Kandiyohi County chpt. Minn. Mental Health Assn., 1960; Campaign mgr. 7th dist. Senator Hubert H. Humphrey, 1960; bd. dirs. Abraxas Found., 1978-79. Named Twin City Civil Service Employee of Year, 1965; recipient Certificate of Merit Treasury Dept., 1965, Distinguished Service award Lutheran Brotherhood, 1968. Mem. Nat. Soc. Financial Counseling (bd. govs.), Minn. Newspaper Assn. (hon.). Lutheran (sec. congregation 1954-56). Clubs: Minn. Press (charter), New York Athletic, Pitts. Athletic Assn., Rivers, Duquesne, Marco Island Country (Fla.), Longue Vue. Home: 5563 Northumberland Pittsburgh PA 15217 Office: 421 7th Ave Pittsburgh PA 15219

JOHNSON, GLENN ANDOR, steel company executive; b. Duluth, Minn., Oct. 29, 1925; s. Fred Henry and Edith Victoria (Nystrom) J.; m. Ann Marilyn Henrikson, May 19, 1951; children: Carol, Jeffrey, Ross, Nan. M.S., Harvard U., 1949, M. Engring., 1951. Registered profl. engr., Ohio, Ind. Indsl. hygiene engr. St. Joseph Lead Co., Monaca, Pa., 1951-54; with Inland Steel and subs., Chgo., Milw., 1954-61; div. chief engr. Republic Steel, union drawn div., Massillon, Ohio, 1961-73, dir. environ. control, Cleve., 1973-79, v.p. engring., 1979—. Mem. planning commn., Massillonm Ohio, 1967-73; chmn., mem. Better Schs. Better Massillon Com., 1970-73. Served with USCG, 1944-47. Mem. Am. Iron and Steel Inst., Assn. Iron and Steel Engrs., Nat. Soc. Profl. Engrs., Cleve. Engring. Soc., Greater Cleve. Growth Assn., Delta Omega. Methodist. Club: Harvard of Cleve. Lodge: Rotary. Home: 8058 Tanager Oval Brecksville OH 44141 Office: Republic Steel Corp 25 W Prospect Ave Cleveland OH 44101

JOHNSON, GLENN THOMPSON, judge; b. Washington, Ark., July 19, 1917; s. Floyd and Reola (Thompson) J.; m. Evelyn Freeman, June 27, 1948; children: Evelyn A., Glenn T. B.S., Wilberforce U., 1941; J.D., John Marshall Law Sch., 1949, LL.M., 1950; grad., Nat. Coll. State Trial Judges, 1971, Appellate Ct. Judges Seminar, N.Y. U., 1974; LL.D. (hon.), Ark. Bapt. Coll., 1978. Bar: Ill. 1950. Pvt. practice law, 1950-57, asst. atty. gen., Ill., 1957-63; sr. asst. atty. Met. San. Dist. Chgo., 1963-66; asso. judge Circuit Ct., Cook County, Chgo., 1966-68, judge, 1968-73; justice Ill. Appellate Ct., 1973—. Trustee John Marshall Law Sch. Served with AUS, 1942-46. Recipient merit award John Marshall Law Sch., 1970; Merit award Beatrice Caffrey Youth Service, 1976. Mem. Nat. Bar Assn. (merit award 1970), ABA, Ill. Bar Assn., Chgo. Bar Assn., Cook County Bar Assn. (awards 1967, 73, pres. 1964-66) bar assns), Am. Acad. Matrimonial Lawyers (gov.). Methodist. Home: 6133 S Evans Ave Chicago IL 60637 Office: Richard J Daley Ctr Chicago IL 60602

JOHNSON, GLENN WALTER, JR., manufacturing corporation executive; b. Albuquerque, May 24, 1921; s. Glenn Walter and Myrtle M. (Reynolds) J.; m. Harriet E. Schwindt, Oct. 26, 1970; children by previous marriage: Kristina, Mitzi A., Glenn Walter III. Grad. magna cum laude, Stanford U., 1947. Pilot Pan-Am. Airways, Miami, Fla., 1945-46; sales engr., regional sales mgr., plant mgr., gen. mgr., v.p. AGA div. Elastic Stop Nut Co., Elizabeth, N.J., 1947-59, exec. v.p. parent co., Union, N.J., 1967, pres., 1968; sr. v.p. Amerace Corp., N.Y.C., 1969-74, exec. v.p., 1974-83; pres. Aircast Inc., Summit, N.J., 1983—. Patentee in field. Served with USAAF, 1943-45. Decorated Air medal. Mem. Phi Beta Kappa, Phi Gamma Delta. Club: Baltusrol Golf (Springfield, N.J.). Home: 10 Friar Tuck Circle Summit NJ 07901 Office: Amerace Corp 555 Fifth Ave New York NY 10017

JOHNSON, GORDON EDWARD, pharmacology educator; b. Welland, Ont., Can., Sept. 21, 1934; s. Edward and Dorothy Lilly (Williams) J.; m. Mary-Jane Graham Bowles, Sept. 20, 1958; children: Dorothy, Ian, Warren, Louise, Edward, Rebecca. B.Sc. in Pharmacology, U. Toronto, 1957, M.A., 1959, Ph.D., 1961. Asst. prof. U. Toronto, 1963-66, asso. prof., 1966-71, prof., 1971-73; prof., head dept. pharmacology U. Sask., 1973—; vis. scientist Med. Research Council Can.; Chmn. drug quality assessment com. Sask. Prescription Drug Plan. Contbr. articles to profl. jours. Fellow Am. Coll. Clin. Pharmacology; mem. Am. Soc. Clin. Pharmacology, Am. Soc. Pharmacology and Exptl. Therapeutics, Can. Soc. Clin. Pharmacology., Pharm. Soc. Can. Home: RR 5 Saskatoon SK S7K 3J8 Canada Office: Dept Pharmacology U Sask SK S7N 0W0 Canada

JOHNSON, GRAHAM MADDEN, coll. dean; b. Commerce, Tex., Nov. 7, 1914; s. Ben Franklin and Nellie (Madden) J.; m. Norma Jane Hall, June 4, 1938; children—Claudia, Ethel, Robert. B.S., East Tex. State U., Commerce, 1935; M.B.A., U. Denver, 1941, Ph.D., 1954. Tchr. Henderson (Tex.) High Sch., 1936-40; instr. Kilgore Coll., 1941-43, chmn. dept. bus. adminstrn., 1945-47; prof. Lamar State Coll., 1955-56; prof., head dept. bus. adminstrn., dean Coll. Bus., East Tex. State U., 1968—. Served with AUS, 1943-45. Mem. Psi Chi, Delta Sigma Pi, Pi Omega Pi, Phi Delta Kappa, Beta Gamma Sigma, Omicron Delta Epsilon. Mem. Christian Ch. (elder 1948-73). Lion. Home: 2303 Mayo St Commerce TX 75428

JOHNSON, GRANT LESTER, lawyer, mfg. co. exec.; b. Virginia, Minn., Aug. 16, 1929; s. Ernest and Anna Elizabeth (Nordstrom) J.; m. Esther Linnea Nystrom, June 16, 1956; children—Karen Elisabeth, Elise Ann. A.B., Cornell U., 1951; LL.B., Harvard, 1957. Bar: Ohio bar 1958, Ill. bar 1972. Asso. Squire, Sanders & Dempsey, Cleve., 1957-58; atty. Pickands Mather & Co., Cleve., 1958-71, asso. gen. counsel, 1967, gen. counsel, 1968-71, sec., 1969-71; corporate counsel Interlake, Inc., Chgo., 1971-73, v.p. law, 1974-78, v.p. law and adminstrn., 1978—. Served as lt. (j.g.) USN, 1951-54. Mem. Am., Ill., Chgo. bar assns., Am. Iron and Steel Inst. Home: G-205 4 Oak Brook Club Dr Oak Brook IL 60521 Office: Commerce Plaza: 2015 Spring Rd Oak Brook IL 60521

JOHNSON, GUY, mathematics educator; b. Dallas, Mar. 11, 1922; s. Guy and Flossie Josephine (Posey) J.; m. Jean Elizabeth Steward, Sept. 5, 1942; children: Guy, Kenneth, Bonnie. Ph.D., Rice U., 1955. Instr. Rice U., Houston, 1954-56, asst. prof., 1956-61, assoc. prof., 1961-66; assoc. prof. math. Syracuse U., N.Y., 1966-69, prof., 1969—. Contbr. articles on math. to profl. jours. Served to capt. AUS, 1943-45; ETO. Recipient Sigma Xi research award, 1954, research award Syracuse U., 1972. Mem. Math. Assn. Am., Am. Math. Assn. Office: Dept Math Syracuse U Syracuse NY 13210

JOHNSON, H. ARVID, lawyer; b. Chgo., Aug. 21, 1936; s. Harold A. and Agnes B. (Lorenzen) J.; m. Janice Meeg Alison, Oct. 15, 1982; children: Susan Joy, Steven Lee. B.A., Northwestern U., 1958, J.D., 1961. Bar: Ill. 1961, U.S. Dist. Ct. (no. dist.) Ill. 1961, U.S. Ct. Mil. Appeals 1962, U.S. Supreme Ct. 1963, U.S. Ct. Appeals (7th cir.) 1965. Atty. Ross, Hardies & O'Keefe, Chgo., 1961-67; assoc. gen. counsel R.R. Donnelley & Sons, Chgo., 1967-71; gen. counsel, sec. Stanray Corp., Chgo., 1971-73; sr. v.p., gen. counsel Container Corp. Am., Chgo., 1973—; dir. T.R. Miller Mill Co., Brewton, Ala., Pioneer Paper Stock Co., Chgo., Calif. Container Corp.; bd. dirs. Ctr. Pub. Resources, 1982—. Contbr. articles to profl. jours. Served to capt. USAF, 1962-65. Northwestern U. scholar, 1956-58, 58-61; recipient Am. Jurisprudence award, 1960. Mem. ABA, Ill. Bar Assn., Chgo. Bar Assn., Am. Soc. Corp. Secs., Assn. Corp. Counsel, Northwestern U. Law Alumni Assn. (bd. dirs. 1982—). Republican. Presbyterian. Clubs: Law, Legal; University (Chgo.). Home: 269 Woodlawn Ave Winnetka IL 60093 Office: 1 First National Plaza Suite 5400 Chicago IL 60603

JOHNSON, HAL HAROLD GUSTAV, marketing educator; b. Saginaw, Mich., Apr. 30, 1915; s. Harold Hjalmar and Ruth W. (Broman) J.; m. Elizabeth Schreiner, June 15, 1940; children: Judith Lynn, David Schreiner, John Bradley. B.S., Beloit Coll., 1936, M.S., 1938; Ph.D., U. Wis., 1941. Instr. Beloit Coll., 1935-38; instr. U. Wis., 1938-41; organic chemist Comml. Solvents Corp., Inc., Terre Haute, Ind., 1941-45; asst. gen. mgr. Dykem Co., St. Louis, 1945-46; mgr. Organic div. Monsanto Co., St. Louis, 1946-49, asst. dir. gen. devel. dept., 1949-52, dir. research and devel., San Francisco, 1952-54, dir. gen. devel. dept. research and engring. div., 1954-57; dir. chem. and rubber div. Bus. and Def. Services Adminstrn., Dept. Commerce, Washington, 1957; v.p. Vick Chem. Co. (now known as Richardson-Vicks Co.), N.Y.C., 1957-59; cons. Hal Johnson Assocs., 1959-62, 66-69; v.p. mktg., dir. S.W. Potash Corp. div. Am. Metal Climax, 1962-66; dir. comml. devel. Borg-Warner Corp., 1969-71; prof. mktg. No. Ill. U., DeKalb, 1971—; vis. prof. U. Linkoping, (Sweden), 1977-78. Contbr. articles to sci. and mktg. jours. Trustee Beloit Coll. Mem. Am. Chem. Soc. (chmn. St. Louis sect.; chmn. chem. mktg. and econs. div.), Am. Mktg. Assn., Comml. Devel. Assn. (past pres.), Phi Beta Kappa, Sigma Xi, Sigma Alpha Epsilon, Gamma Alpha, Delta Sigma Pi, Beta Gamma Sigma, Pi Sigma Epsilon. Patentee in field. Home: 14 Roosevelt St Saint Charles IL 60174

JOHNSON, HAROLD EARL, chain dept. store exec.; b. Lincoln, Nebr., July 11, 1939; s. Earl W. and Evelyn Jean (Sipp) J.; m. Carol Louise Schmidt, Aug. 17, 1971; children—Andrew Brian, Daniel Earl. B.S., U. Nebr., 1961. From indsl. relations trainee to mgr. profl. employment Am. Can Co., 1961-68; dir. recruitment/devel. metal mining div. Kennecott Copper Corp., 1968-73; v.p. personnel Am. Medicorp Inc., 1973-75; v.p. employee relations. devel., then sr. v.p. employee relations and corp. adminstrn. INA Corp., 1975-79; sr. v.p. human resources Federated Dept. Stores, Inc., Cin., 1979—. Mem. personnel and public relations policy com. Bethesda Hosp. and Deaconess Assn., Cin. Mem. Am. Mgmt. Assn., U.S. C. of C., Conf. Board, Nat. Retail Mchts. Assn., Am. Retail Fedn., Human Resources Roundtable. Republican. Presbyterian. Clubs: University (N.Y.C.); Kenwood Country, Queen City (Cin.). Office: 7 W 7th St Cincinnati OH 45202

JOHNSON, HAROLD R., gerontology educator, dean; b. Windsor, Ont., Can., Jan. 9, 1926; m. Marion Johnson; children: Robert Harold, Karen Elizabeth, Alan Douglas. Student, Patterson Collegiate Inst., Windsor; B.A., U. Western Ont.; postgrad., Assumption Coll., Windsor; M.S.W., Wayne State U. Internat. rep. Internat. Union of United Brewery, Soft Drink and Distillery WorkersAm., 1951-57; exec. dir. Windsor Labor Com. on Human Rights, 1951-57; planning cons. United Community Services of Met. Detroit, 1957-61; assoc. dir. Neighborhood Services Orgn., Detroit, 1961-69; dir. Office of Youth Services, State of Mich., 1970; prof., co-dir. Inst. Gerontology, U. Mich.-Wayne State U.; prof. gerontology U. Mich. Sch. Social Work, Ann Arbor, 1980—, dean, 1981—; lactr. and cons. in field. Chmn. Blue Ribbon Citation com. Wayne County Bd. Suprs., Mich.; v.p., chmn. program com. Northeastern Wayne County Child Guidance Clinic; vice chmn. Mich. Commn. on Criminal Justice. Served with Royal Can. Armoured Corps, 1944-46. Mem. Assn. Gerontology in Higher Edn. (pres. 1979), Nat. Assn. Social Workers (past chmn. met. Detroit chpt.), Gerontol. Soc., Council on Social Work Edn., Acad. Cert. Social Workers, Assn. Black Social Workers. Office: Univ Mich Sch Social Work Ann Arbor MI 48109 *

JOHNSON, HAYNES BONNER, journalist; b. N.Y.C., July 9, 1931; s. Malcolm Malone and Ludie (Adams) J.; m. Julia Ann Erwin, Sept. 21, 1954 (div.); children—Katherine Adams, David Malone, Stephen Holmes, Sarah Brooks, Elizabeth Haynes. B.J., U. Mo., 1952; M.S., U. Wis., 1956. Reporter Wilmington (Del.) News-Jour., 1956- 57; with Washington Star, 1957-69; nat. corr. Washington Post, 1969-73, asst. mng. editor, 1973-77, columnist, 1977—; TV commentator NBC Today Show, Pub. Broadcasting Service Washington Week in Rev.; lectr. colls., univs. Author: Dusk at the Mountain, 1963, The Bay of Pigs, 1964, (with Bernard M. Gwertzman) Fulbright: the Dissenter, 1968, (with George C. Wilson) Army in Anguish, 1972, (with Nick Kotz) The Unions, 1972, (with Richard Harwood) Lyndon, 1973, The Working White House, 1975, In The Absence of Power, 1980; Editor: The Fall of a President, 1974. Served to 1st lt. AUS, 1952-55. Recipient Pub. Service prize and Grand award for reporting Washington Newspaper Guild, 1962, 68, Interpretive Reporting award, 1965, Nat. Reporting award, 1968; Pulitzer Prize for nat. reporting, 1966; Headliners award for nat. reporting, 1968; Sigma Delta Chi gen. reporting award, 1969; fellow in communications Duke U., 1973-74; Ferris prof. journalism Princeton, 1975, 78. Mem. Nat. Acad. Pub. Adminstrn. Clubs: Gridiron (Washington); Nassau (Princeton). Office: Washington Post 1150 15th St NW Washington DC 20071

JOHNSON, HENRY CLAY, lawyer; b. Canton, Ohio, Mar. 16, 1910; s. Henry Moore and Bertha (Burns) J.; m. Rosemary Fitzpatrick, 1945; children: Michael Clay, Peter H., Catherine J. Meffert, Anne J. Marchetta. A.B. magna cum laude, U. Notre Dame, 1932, LL.B., 1934; LL.M., Cath. U. Am., 1935. Bar: Ind. 1934, N.Y. State 1975. Practiced in, South Bend, Ind., 1934-35; counsel RFC, 1935-41; mem. law faculty Cath. U. Am., 1935-41; spl. asst. to pres. N.Y. Stock Exchange, 1941-42; v.p., gen. counsel Rubber Res. Co., 1942-45; dir., gen. counsel Rubber Devel. Co., 1943-45; v.p. War Damage Corp., 1942-45; exec. v.p., gen. counsel, dir. Royal-Globe Ins. Cos., 1945-65, pres. and chmn. bd., 1965-74, chmn., 1974-75; counsel McCarthy, Fingar, Donovan, Drazen & Smith, 1975—; dir., mem. exec. com., chmn. finance com. Med. Liability Mut. Ins. Co., 1976—; pres. Ins. Information Inst., 1964-65; chmn. Nat. Arbitration Panel for R.R. Industry, 1976-84. Mayor, city of Rye, N.Y., 1962-65; Mem. adv. council U. Notre Dame.; Chmn. bd. trustees United Hosp., Port Chester, N.Y., 1967-75; pres. N.Y. Foundling Hosp., 1979-82. Knight of Malta; Knight Holy Sepulcher. Mem. Am., N.Y. State, Westchester County bar assns. Roman Catholic. Clubs: University (N.Y.C.); Am. Yacht. Office: 175 Main St White Plains NY 10601

JOHNSON, HERBERT ALAN, history and law educator, lawyer; b. Jersey City, Jan. 10, 1934; s. Harry Oliver and Magdalena Gertrude (Diemer) J.; m. Barbara Arlene Balcerak, Sept. 24, 1955 (dec. Nov. 1980); children: Amanda Blair, Vanessa Paige.; m. Jane McCue, June 4, 1983. A.B., Columbia U., 1955, M.A., 1961, Ph.D. (Schiff fellow), 1965; LL.B., N.Y. Law Sch., 1960. Bar: N.Y. 1960, U.S. Supreme Ct 1965, D.C. 1967, S.C. 1983. Jr. clk. First Nat. City Bank of N.Y., N.Y.C., 1955; adminstrv. asst. Chase Manhattan Bank, N.Y.C., 1957-60; practiced in, N.Y.C., 1960-67; research asst. Papers of John Jay, Columbia U., 1961-63, asso. sem. on history of legal polit. thought, 1966-77, asso. sem. on early Am. history, 1967-77; lectr. Hunter Coll. City U. N.Y., 1964-65, asst. prof. history, 1965-67; asso. editor Papers of John Marshall, Inst. Early Am. History and Culture, Williamsburg, Va., 1967-70, co-editor, 1970-71, editor, 1971-77; prof. law and history U. S.C., 1977—; lectr. Coll. William and Mary, Williamsburg, 1967-77; Bostick vis. research prof. So. studies program U. S.C., 1976, 77; mem. com. research, publs. Heritage '76 Com. Am. Revolution Bicentennial Commn., 1972-73; Mem. bd. adjustments, appeals, Williamsburg, 1970-77; trustee Fund for Preservation of John Marshall House, 1972-74, Fund Coop. Editorial Research Am. Antiquarian Soc., 1972-76. Author: The Law Merchant and Negotiable Instruments in Colonial New York, 1664-1730, 1963, John Jay, 1745-1829, 1970, Imported Eighteenth-Century Law Treatises in American Libraries 1700-1799, 1978; co-author: Historical Courthouses of New York State-18th and 19th Century Halls of Justice Across the Empire State, 1977, Foundations of Power—John Marshall, 1801-15, vol. 2, History of theSupreme Court of the United States, 1981; editor: The Papers of John Marshall, Vol. 1, 1974, Vol. II, 1977, South Carolina Legal History, 1980; Contbr. articles to profl. jours. Served as 1st lt. USAF, 1955-57; col. Res., 1957—. Recipient William P. Lyons Masters' Essay award Loyola U., 1962; Am. Council Learned Socs. fellow, 1974-75; Inst. Humane Studies fellow, 1981. Mem. N.Y. State Hist. Assn. (lectr. Am. culture 1969, 75, Paul S. Kerr History prize 1970), Am. Hist. Assn. (Littleton-Griswold com. 1976-81, mem. interim com. Bicentennial era 1976-77), Selden Soc., Stair Soc., Osgoode Soc., Air Force Assn., Assn. Am. Law Schs. (chmn. legal history sect. 1979), Am. Soc. Legal History (pres. 1974-75, del. Am. Council Learned Socs. 1977-80), Swedish Colonial Soc., U. South Caroliniana Soc., Res. Officers Assn., English Speaking Union U.S. (pres. Columbia br. 1978-79). Office: Dept History Gambrell Hall Hall U SC Columbia SC 29208

JOHNSON, HERBERT FREDERICK, university administrator, librarian; b. St. Paul, Aug. 1, 1934; s. Herbert Oscar and Hazel Grace (Otto) J.; m. Delores Elaine Madson, Aug. 21, 1955; children: Steven F., Eric L., Kirsten M. B.A., U. Minn., 1957, M.A., 1959; M.A., Kursverksamheten Vid Lunds Universitet, Betyg, 1975. Librarian U.S. Govt., Washington, 1959-61; asst. bus. librarian Columbia U., 1961-64; head librarian, assoc. prof. Hamline U., 1964-71; librarian, prof. Oberlin Coll., 1971-78; librarian Oberlin Pub. Library, 1971-78; dir. libraries Emory U., 1978—, mem. faculty adv. com. Jimmy Carter Ctr. for Policy Studies, 1982—; lectr. U. Minn. Library Sch.; vis. prof. Atlanta U. Sch. Library Services, 1979; charter bd. Cooperating Libraries in Consortium, St. Paul, 1969-71; library adv. com. Minn. Higher Edn. Coordinating Commn., 1970-71; mem. com. input standards Ohio Coll. Library Center, 1972-73, chmn. com. patron input, 1973-75; chmn. Ohio Multitype Interlibrary Cooperation Com., Ohio State Library Bd., 1976-78; mem. adv. and steering com. Ohio Pre-White House Conf. on Library and Info. Services, 1977-78; chmn. librarians adv. com. Univ. Center, Atlanta, 1979-80; bd. dirs. Southeastern Library Network, 1980-83, chmn. bd. dirs., 1981-83; del. users council OCLC Online Computer Library Center, Inc., 1981-83. Contbr. articles to profl. jours. Mem. com. on internat. programs Nat. Student YMCA's, 1962-64; mem. Minn. Republican Task Force on Edn., 1966; pres., treas. Lord of Life Lutheran Ch., Lorain, Ohio, 1972-75; mem. Lorain Coop. Luth. Ministry Bd., 1976-78; v.p. St. Luke Luth. Ch., Atlanta, 1979-80, 81-82; bd. dirs. DeKalb (county, Ga.) Families in Action, 1979—; mem. adv. com. DeKalb/Rockdale counties of Met. Atlanta chpt. ARC, 1981—. Served with M.I. U.S. Army, 1958. Decorated Army Commendation medal, Meritorious Service medal; George Williams fellow, 1957; Council on Library Resources fellow, 1974-75; NSF grantee, 1967-71. Mem. ALA, Am. Soc. Info. Sci., Assn. Research Libraries (bd. dirs. 1983—), Am. Scandinavian Found., Am. Swedish Inst., Am. Swedish Hist. Found. and Mus., Ga. Library Assn., Southeastern Library Assn., Southeastern Library Network (dir. 1980-83), Atlanta Zool. Soc., Am. Swedish Hist. Soc., Common Cause, Minn. Library Sch. Alumni Assn. (chmn. 1967), Wildlife Preservation Trust, Nat. Trust Hist. Preservation, High Mus. Art, Beta Phi Mu. Lodges: Rotary (North DeKalb, Ga.) (sec. 1981-82, pres. elect 1983—). Office: Emory U RW Woodruff Library Atlanta GA 30322

JOHNSON, HOLLIS RALPH, astronomer; b. Tremonton, Utah, Dec. 2, 1928; s. Ellwood Lewis and Ida Martha (Hansen) J.; m. Grete Margit Leed, June 3, 1954; children: Carol Ann Johnson Watson, Wayne L., Lyle David, CharlotteJohnson Willian, Lise Marie, Richard L. B.A. in Physics, Brigham Young U., 1955, M.A., 1957; Ph.D. in Astrophysics, U. Colo., 1960. NSF postdoctoral fellow Paris Obs.,

1960-61; research asso. Yale U., 1961-63; asso. prof. astronomy Ind. U., 1963-67, prof., 1967—, chmn. dept. astronomy, 1978-82; Nat. Acad. Scis./NRC sr. fellow NASA Ames Research Ctr., 1982-83. Contbr. articles to profl. jours. Served with U.S. Army, 1951-53. Recipient Vis. Scientist award High Altitude Obs., Boulder, Colo., 1971-72. Mem. Internat. Astron. Union, Am. Astron. Soc., AAAS, AAUP, Sigma Xi. Mormon. Office: Astronomy Dept Swain W 319 Ind U Bloomington IN 47405

JOHNSON, HOMER FIELDS, educator, chem. engr.; b. Lynchburg, Va., Sept. 8, 1920; s. Homer Fields and May (Royall) J.; m. Virginia Lee Cain, May 17, 1947; children-Philip Royall, Richard Wesley, Lee Duncan, Jeffrey Alan. B.Chem. Engring., U. Va., 1942; M.Engring., Yale, 1944, D.Engring., 1946. Registered profl. engr. Grad. asst., instr. Yale, New Haven, Conn., 1942-45; chem. engr. Standard Oil Devel. Co., Linden, N.J., 1945-49; asst. prof. U. Tenn., Knoxville, 1949-51, asso. prof., 1951-58, prof., 1958—, head dept. chem., metall. and polymer engring., 1960—. Contbr. articles on mass transfer and drop phenomena and chem. engring. edn. to profl. jours. Fellow Am. Inst. Chem. Engrs. (chmn. Knoxville-Oak Ridge sect. 1955); mem. Am. Soc. Engring. Edn., AAUP (pres. U. Tenn., Knoxville chpt. 1977—), Raven Soc., Sigma Xi, Phi Kappa Phi, Alpha Chi Sigma, Tau Beta Pi. Presbyterian (elder). Home: 3612 Timberlake Rd Knoxville TN 37920

JOHNSON, HORACE RICHARD, electronics company executive; b. Jersey City, Apr. 26, 1926; s. Horace Adam and Grace (Lower) J.; m. Mary Louise Kleckner, July 29, 1950; children: Lucinda Louise, Karen Ann, Richard Adam, Russell Kleckner, David Thorp. B.E.E. with distinction, Cornell U., 1946, postgrad., 1947; Ph.D. in Physics, M.I.T., 1952. Mem. tech. staff Hughes Aircraft Co., 1952-57; co-founder Watkins-Johnson Co., Palo Alto, Calif., 1958, pres., 1967—; lectr. engring. UCLA, 1956-57, Stanford U., 1958-68; chmn. Los Angeles Profl. Group on Electron Devices, 1955-56; dir. WEMA, 1971-72, Vols. Internat. Tech. Assistance, 1971-73. Contbr. articles to profl. jours. Pres. Stanford Area council Boy Scouts Am., 1968-70, bd. mem., 1967-77; campaign chmn. Palo Alto-Stanford chpt. United Fund, 1967. Served with USNR, 1943-46. Research Lab. for Electronics fellow, 1947-51. Fellow IEEE; mem. Nat. Acad. Engring., NAM (dir. 1983—), Am. Phys. Soc., Newcomen Soc. N.Am., Sigma Xi, Eta Kappa Nu, Tau Beta Pi, Phi Kappa Phi, Gamma Alpha. Club: Commonwealth of Calif. Patentee in field. Office: 3333 Hillview Ave Palo Alto CA 94304

JOHNSON, HORTON ANTON, pathologist; b. Cheyenne, Wyo., Nov. 12, 1926; s. Horton Antonius and Katharine Mary (Tidball) J.; m. Caryl Abell Daly, Nov. 20, 1970; children by previous marriage: Katherine, Kristin, Margaret, Ann, Gregory, Marjorie. A.B., Colo. Coll., 1949; M.D., Columbia U., 1953. Diplomate: Am. Bd. Pathology. Intern Univ. Hosp., Ann Arbor, Mich., 1953-54, resident in pathology, 1954-57, Pondville Cancer Hosp., Walpole, Mass., 1957-58; scientist Brookhaven Nat. Lab., 1958-60, 63-70; asst. prof. pathology U. Utah, 1960-63; prof. pathology SUNY, Stony Brook, 1970-72, Ind. U., 1972-75; prof., chmn. dept. pathology Tulane U., New Orleans, 1975-84; prof. pathology Columbia U., N.Y.C., 1984—; dir. pathology St. Luke's-Roosevelt Hosp. Ctr., N.Y.C., 1984—. Served with USNR, 1944-46. Recipient Lederle Med. Faculty award, 1961. Fellow Coll. Am. Pathologists; mem. Am. Assn. Pathologists, Internat. Acad. Pathology, Biophys. Soc., Radiation Research Soc., N.Y. Acad. Scis., Assn. Pathology Chairmen, Assn. Clin. Scientists, Soc. Health and Human Values, Phi Beta Kappa, Alpha Omega Alpha. Research on radiation injury, aging, theoretical biology. Home: 250 Lincoln St Englewood NJ 07631 Office: 428 W 59th St New York NY 10019

JOHNSON, HOWARD EDWARD, advertising agency executive; b. Pontiac, Mich., Nov. 23, 1936; s. Howard Edward and Harriet (Van Hollenbeck) J.; m. Patricia Saghy, Nov. 18, 1961; children: Jody, Jeffrey, Mark. B.A. in English, Hillsdale Coll., Hillsdale, Mich., 1959. Account exec. MacManus, John, Adams, 1960-64, R.L. Polk, 1964-67; account supr. Wells, Rich, Greene, Detroit, 1967-72; v.p. Campbell-Ewald, Detroit, 1972-76, Kenyon & Eckhardt, 1976-77, Batten, Barton, Durstine & Osborn, 1977-79; pres. D'Arcy-MacManus & Masius, Chgo., 1979-80, chmn., 1980—, also mem. Mem. public affairs com. Field Museum Natural History, Chgo.; chief crusader Crusade of Mercy. Served with USAR, 1959-65. Mem. Adcraft Club Detroit, Chgo. Advt. Club (dir.). Republican. Roman Catholic. Clubs: Butterfield Country, University, Mid-Am., East Bank (Chgo.); Birmingham (Mich.); Athletic. Office: D'Arcy-MacManus & Masius 200 E Randolph Dr Chicago IL 60601 *

JOHNSON, HOWARD WESLEY, former university president, business executive; b. Chgo., July 2, 1922; s. Albert H. and Laura (Hansen) J.; m. Elizabeth J. Weed, Feb. 18, 1950; children: Stephen Andrew, Laura Ann, Bruce Howard. B.A., Central Coll., Chgo., 1943; M.A., U. Chgo., 1947; certificate, Glasgow (Scotland) U., 1946; recipient numerous hon. degrees. From asst. to assoc. prof., dir. mgmt. research U. Chgo., 1948-51, 53-55; asst. to v.p. personnel adminstrn. Gen. Mills, Inc., 1952-53; assoc. prof., dir. exec. programs, assoc. dean Sloan Sch. Mgmt., Mass. Inst. Tech., 1955-59, prof., dean, 1959-66; pres. Mass. Inst. Tech., 1966-71; chmn. corp., 1971-83, hon. chmn., 1983—; exec. v.p. Federated Dept. Stores, 1966; now dir.; chmn. Fed. Res. Bank Boston, 1968-69; dir. Hitchiner Mfg. Co., 1961-71, John Hancock Mut. Life Ins. Co., Champion Internat. Corp., E.I. duPont de Nemours & Co., Morgan Guaranty Trust Co.; trustee Putnam Funds, 1961-71; Mem. Pres.'s Adv. Com. on Labor-Mgmt. Policy, 1966-68; chmn. Environ. Studies Bd. Nat. Acad. Scis.-Nat. Acad. Engring., 1973-75; mem. sci. adv. com. Mass. Gen. Hosp., 1968-70; mem. Nat. Manpower Adv. Com., 1967-69, Nat. Commn. on Productivity, 1970-72; trustee Com. Econ. Devel., 1968-71, Wellesley Coll., Radcliffe Coll., 1973-79; hon. trustee Aspen Inst. for Humanistic Studies, Inst. Def. Analyses, 1971-79; mem. corp. Woods Hole (Mass.) Oceanographic Instn. Trustee WGBH Ednl. Found., 1966-71; mem. corp. Mus. Sci., Boston; overseer Boston Symphony Orch., 1968-72; mem.-at-large Boy Scouts Am.; pres. Boston Mus. Fine Arts, 1975-80, chmn. bd. overseers, 1980—. Served with AUS, 1943-46. Fellow Am. Acad. Arts and Scis., AAAS; mem. Council Fgn. Relations, Phi Gamma Delta. Clubs: Univ. (N.Y.C.); Somerset, Comml., Tavern, St. Botolph (Boston). Home: 100 Memorial Dr Cambridge MA 02142

JOHNSON, HUGH, publishing co. exec.; b. N.Y.C., Nov. 27, 1919; s. C. Haldane and Sophie (Sanders) J.; m. Anne I. Marco Vecchio, Sept. 25, 1965; children by previous marriage—Marion S., Virginia W., Douglas H. Grad., Lawrenceville Sch., 1939. With A.S. Barnes & Co., N.Y.C., 1945-58, v.p. sales, 1952-58; with Hammond, Inc., Maplewood, N.J., 1958—, v.p., 1962-68, exec. v.p., 1968—, dir., 1965—. Pres. South Orange (N.J.) Rescue Squad, 1958-60; Trustee Arlington (N.J.) Cemetery, 1960—. Served to 1st lt. inf. AUS, 1941-45; ETO. Mem. Assn. Am. Pubs. (program chmn. 1973), Pubs. Lunch Club (pres. 1974-75). Presbyn. Clubs: Seaview (Absecon, N.J.); Essex County Country (West Orange, N.J.); Coffee House (N.Y.C.). Home: 140 Hepburn Rd Clifton NJ 07012 Office: 515 Valley St Maplewood NJ 07040

JOHNSON, HUGH BAILEY, architect; b. South Bombay, N.Y., Mar. 12, 1904; s. Fenton Wesley and Florence Genevieve (Bailey) J.; m. Ida Rita Viale, Aug. 3, 1928; children—Hugh Bailey, David Wesley, Philip Anthony; m. Phyllis Walker Alexander, Jan. 12, 1968. B.Arch., Syracuse U., 1929. Mem. staff architect's office Bd. Edn. Rochester, N.Y., 1928-40; researcher and writer Am. Council Edn., Washington, 1940-42; mem. staff War Dept., 1942-45, Nat. Housing Agy., 1945-47; prin. Hugh Johnson Assos., Inc., Washington, 1947-78; pres. McGaughan & Johnson, P.C., 1978—. Bd. dirs. Arlington (Va.) Symphony Assn., 1956—, pres., 1956-62; mem. Arlington County Adv. Com. on Alt. Growth Policy, 1974-76, successor com., 1977-78. Fellow AIA (nat. govt. liaison com. 1963-70, chmn. 1963-64, mem. nat. regional devel. and natural resources com. 1970—, chmn. 1973-74); mem. Va. Soc. AIA (dir. 1976-77, chmn. land use and natural resources com. 1976-79). Democrat. Methodist. Patentee bldg. components. Home and office: 2830 N Westmoreland St Arlington VA 22213 *I believe that our American society depends upon the integrity of our professions, the influence of church, and unselfish participation of citizens in local government. My involvement in all three areas has not made me more successful in the usual sense, but it gives me great satisfaction.*

JOHNSON, IRVING STANLEY, pharmaceutical company executive, scientist; b. Grand Junction, Colo., June 30, 1925; s. Walter Glen and Frances Lucetta (Tuttle) J.; m. Alwyn Neville Ginther, Jan. 29, 1949; children: Rebecca Lyn, Bryan Glenn, Kirsten Shawn, Kevin Bruce. A.B., Washburn U., Topeka, 1948; Ph.D., U. Kans., 1953. With Lilly Research Labs., Indpls., 1953—, v.p. research, 1973—; mem. profl. edn. com. Am. Cancer Soc., 1972—; active in several areas of biol. research including cancer, virus, genetic engring.; cons. in field. Author articles in field; asso. editor: Cancer Research, 1974—; editorial bd.: Chemico-Biol. Interactions, 1968-73. Mem. edn. com. Indpls. Urban League, 1968-70; pres. Indpls. chpt. Am. Field Service Exchange Program, 1969-70; bd. dirs. Indpls. Ctr. Advanced Research. Served with USNR, 1943-46. Mem. AAAS, Am. Assn. Cancer Research, Am. Soc. Cell Biology (pub. policy com.), Environ. Mutagen Soc., Internat. Soc. Chemotherapy, Kans. Acad. Sci., N.Y. Acad. Scis., Soc. Exptl. Biology and Medicine, Sigma Xi, Phi Sigma. Episcopalian. Patentee in field. Office: 307 E McCarty St Indianapolis IN 46285

JOHNSON, J. DONALD, JR., environmental chemist, educator; b. Inglewood, Calif., Aug. 1, 1935; s. James Donald and Mary Katherine (Biggs) J.; m. Elizabeth Joanne Wolf, Sept. 2, 1955; children: Christopher Robert, Katherine Donna. B.S., U.C.L.A., 1957; Ph.D., U. N.C., 1962. Asst. prof. environ. scis. U. N.C., 1961-66, assoc. prof., 1966-71, prof., dir. program environ. chemistry and biology, dept. environ. scis. and engring., 1971-80; lectr. chemistry Wesleyan Coll., Rocky Mt., N.C., 1962-64; vis. prof. U. Gothenburg, Sweden, 1970-71; participant Nobel Symposium 20, Gothenburg, 1971; vis. scientist Swiss Water Lab., Zurich, 1982; cons. TVA, Nat. Sanitation Found. Author: Disinfection-Water and Wastewater, 1975. Am. Enka Research fellow, 1959-60; R. J. Reynolds Research fellow, 1960-61; EPA Spl. Postdoctoral fellow, 1970. Mem. Water Pollution Control Fedn., Am. Chem. Soc. (environ. chemistry div. exec. com.), Am. Water Works Assn. (chmn. standard methods com., task group on chlorine residual 1978—, chmn. disinfection research com. 1977—, mem. disinfection treatment com.), ASTM (D-19 com. on chlorine residual, com. on methods), Nat. Acad. Scis. (safe drinking water com. on disinfection), Sigma Xi (treas. 1974-76). Club: Mason. Home: 720 Bradley Rd Chapel Hill NC 27514

JOHNSON, JACK THOMAS, educator; b. Burlington, Iowa, July 16, 1915; s. James H. and Emily L. (Holihan) J.; m. Lavelda Hall, Mar. 10, 1976. B.A., State U. Iowa, 1935, M.A., 1936, Ph.D., 1938. Asst. in instrn. State U. Iowa, 1936-40, instr. polit. sci., 1940-42, asst. prof., 1942-47, asso. prof., 1947-51; asst. adminstr. tng. and edn. Office FCDA, 1951-53; provost Hofstra Coll., 1953-57, v.p., 1957-62; vis. prof. polit. sci. N.M. Western Coll., 1962-63; dir. Bur. Govt. Research, Ind. State U., 1964-65; asso. dir. Inst. Higher Edn., Tchrs. Coll., Columbia, 1965-68; asso. dean arts and scis. Ind. State U., 1968-70, dir. spl. gen. edn. projects, 1974-75, prof. polit. sci., 1975—. Author: A Railroad to the Sea, 1939, Peter A. Dey, 1939, A Handbook for Iowa Mayors, 1943, Iowa Government, 1951, The Changing Mission of Home Economics, 1968; Contbr. profl. jours. Served to ensign USNR, 1944-46. Rockefeller Found. fellow, 1946. Mem. Phi Beta Kappa, Pi Gamma Mu, Omicron Delta Kappa, Alpha Tau Omega, Pi Delta Epsilon, Sigma Kappa Alpha. Home: 1901 N 7th St Terre Haute IN 47804

JOHNSON, JAMES DOUGLAS (JIM), lawyer; b. Crossett, Ark., Aug. 20, 1924; s. Thomas William and Maudie Myrtle (Long) J.; m. Virginia Morris, Dec. 21, 1947; children: Mark Douglas, John David and Joseph Daniel (twins). LL.B., Cumberland U., 1947. Bar: Ark. 1948. Practice in, Crosset, 1948-58; assoc. justice Supreme Ct. Ark., 1958-66; practice law, Little Rock, 1966—; Ark. Senate 22d Senatorial Dist., 1950-54. Served with USMCR, World War II. Mem. Ark. Jud. Council, Lamda Chi Alpha. Republican. Christian Scientist. Club: Mason (32 deg., Shriner). Home: Route 3 Box 945 Conway AR 72032

JOHNSON, JAMES GANN, JR., lawyer; b. Jackson, Miss., Oct. 15, 1915; s. James Gann and Marguerite (Willing) J.; m. Mary Anne Scott, July 12, 1940; children: Robert W., Carol Johnson Ornitz, James Gann, William F. B.A., Yale U., 1936, LL.B., 1939. Bar: N.Y. 1939, D.C. 1947. Pvt. practice, N.Y.C., 1939-42; atty. Lend Lease Adminstrn., also Dept. State, 1942-43; asst. gen. counsel UNRRA, 1944; legal adv. China mission, 1945-46; with legal dept. UN, 1946; with firm Cleary, Gottlieb, Steen & Hamilton, Washington, Paris, France and N.Y.C., 1946—, partner, 1951-83, of counsel, 1983—; pres., dir. Allied-Lyons N.Am. Corp., 1973—; dir. LTCB Trust Co., Tetley Inc., BNP Internat. Fin. Services Corp.; Trustee Internat. Inst. Rural Reconstrn., 1965—, vice chmn., 1979—. Pres. trustees Friends of Reservoir, Larchmont, N.Y., 1980—; mem. Mamaroneck (N.Y.) Bd. Edn., 1958-61. Decorated chevalier Ordre de la Couronne, Belgium; chevalier Légion de Honneur, France). Mem. Am. Bar Assn., Am. Bar Found., Am. Soc. Internat. Law, Assn. Bar City N.Y., N.Y. County Lawyers Assn., N.Y. State Bar Assn. Democrat. Clubs: Broad St., Yale (N.Y.C.). Home: 17 Pryer Ln Larchmont NY 10538 Office: 1 State St Plaza New York NY 10004

JOHNSON, JAMES GIBB, physician; b. Knoxville, Tenn., Nov. 2, 1937; s. James William Kelly and Katherine Elizabeth (Goodlett) J.; m. Mackie Lou Stooksbury, June 20, 1961; children—Lee Anne and Leslie Lou (twins). A.B., U. Tenn., 1959, M.D., 1963. Diplomate: Am. Bd. Internal Medicine. Intern City of Memphis Hosp., 1963, resident in internal medicine, 1964-66, chief resident in internal medicine, 1966-67, med. dir., 1975-77, profl. dir., 1978-79; intern Columbia div. Bellevue Hosp., N.Y.C., 1963-64; NIH fellow in nephrology U. Tenn., Memphis, 1967-68, NIH spl. fellow in nephrology, 1968-69, instr. medicine, 1966-69, asst. prof., 1969-72, asso. prof., 1972-74, prof., 1975—, asso. dean for hosp. affairs, 1975-78, asso. dean grad. med. edn., 1979—; Bd. dirs. Kidney Found. Western Tenn., 1975-77; chmn. med. adv. com. Tenn./Venezuela Partners of Americas, 1974-77, mem. state bd. dirs., 1974-77. Contbr. articles to med. jours. Fellow A.C.P.; mem. Am. Fedn. Clin. Research, Am. Heart Assn., AMA, Am., Internat. socs. nephrology, Memphis Acad. Internal Medicine, So., Tenn. med. assns., Memphis and Shelby County Med. Soc., Am. Soc. Internal Medicine, Tenn. Soc. Internal Medicine, Tenn., Memphis heart assns., S.E. Dialysis and Transplantation Assn., Alpha Omega Alpha (counsellor 1978-80, sec.-treas. 1975-78). Home: 59 East Pkwy N Memphis TN 38104 Office: 800 Madison Ave Memphis TN 38163

JOHNSON, JAMES HARRY, army officer; b. Washington, May 24, 1929; m. Katherine June Collins, Aug. 5, 1950; 1 son, Richard Allen. B.S., U. Md., 1950. Commd. 2d lt. U.S. Army, 1950; advanced through grades to maj. gen.; comdg. officer 4th Bn. 5030 Airborne, Vietnam, 1967-68, 3rd Brigade 82nd Airborne Div., 1970-71, 2d Inf. Div., Korea, 1981-83; asst. dep. chief of staff for ops. and plans Dept. Army/Pentagon, Washington, 1983—. Decorated D.S.C., Silver Star, Air medal, Legion of Merit. Home: 3384 Ardley Ct Falls Church VA 20041 Office: Dept Army/Pentagon Washington DC 26301

JOHNSON, JAMES HOWARD, government official; b. Laurel, Miss., Nov. 9, 1943; s. Ernest Howard and Juanita (Sumrall) J.; m. Vicki Lynn Sullivan, Aug. 28, 1965; children: Christian, Ashley, Myra, Anne Elisabeth. B.A, U. Miss., 1965. Pres. Johnson Devel. Corp., Laurel, 1973-81; spl. asst. to sec. Dept. Agr., Washington, 1981-82, dep. under sec. small community and rural devel., 1982—. Chmn. Planning Commn., Laurel, 1979-81. Recipient Faith in God Laurel Jaycees, 1978. Mem. Phi Kappa Alpha. Republican. Baptist. Lodge: Laurel Rotary. Office: US Dept Agr 14 and Independence Ave SW Washington DC 20250 *

JOHNSON, JAMES JOSEPH, corporate executive; b. Balt., Mar. 10, 1929; s. Joseph G. and Genevieve (Campagna) J.; m. Eloise Ray, Apr. 19, 1974; 1 dau., Erica; children by previous marriage: James, Jeffrey, Janet. B.S., Northwestern U., 1951. Dir. mktg. IBM, 1955-70; v.p. mktg. RCA, 1970-74; exec. v.p. Western Union Telegraph Co., 1974-77, Singer Co., Stamford, Conn., 1977-82; chief exec. officer Group L Corp., Herndon, Va., 1982—. Served to lt., j.g. USN, 1951-55. Home: Box 13 Niamogue Ln Quogue NY 11959 Office: Group L Corp Herndon VA

JOHNSON, JAMES LAWRENCE, telephone co. exec.; b. Vernon, Tex., Apr. 12, 1927; s. Samuel Lonzo and Adeline Mary (Donges) J.; m. Ruth Helen Zweig, Aug. 5, 1949; children—James Lawrence, Helayne, Barry, Todd. B.B.A. in Accounting, Tex. Tech. Coll., Lubbock, 1949. Accountant Whiteside Laundry, Lubbock, 1949; with Gen. Telephone Co. S.W., San Angelo, Tex., 1949-59, asst. controller, 1953-59; controller Gen. Telephone Co. Mich., Muskegon, 1959-63; asst. controller telephone ops., then chief accountant consol. ops. GTE Service Corp., N.Y.C., 1963-66; v.p., controller, treas. Gen. Telephone Co. S.W., 1966-69; v.p., controller telephone ops. GTE Service Corp., 1969-74; v.p. revenue requirements Gen. Telephone & Electronics Corp., Stamford, Conn., 1974-76; pres. Gen. Telephone Co. Ill., Bloomington, 1976-81, also dir., also group v.p.; pres. GTE telephone operating group Gen. Telephone & Electronics Corp., 1981—; dir. First Fed. Savs. & Loan Assn., Bloomington.; Mem. adv. council Coll. Bus., Ill. State U., Normal. Trustee, adv. council Mennonite Hosp., Bloomington; bd. dirs. Bloomington Unlimited; mem. Wesleyan Assos., Ill. Wesleyan U., Bloomington. Served with USNR, 1945-47. Mem. Nat. Accountants Assn., Fin. Execs. Inst., Ill. Telephone Assn. (dir.), McLean County Assn. Commerce and Industry (dir.). Republican. Methodist. Clubs: Bloomington Country, Crestwicke Country, Rotary (Bloomington); Woodway Country (Darien, Conn.)

JOHNSON, JAMES MYRON, educator, psychologist; b. Sauk Centre, Minn., Aug. 4, 1927; s. Walfred and Sophie (Koelzer) J.; m. Constance Mary Blodgett, Apr. 15, 1950; children—Kathryn, Peter, Donna, Daniel, Amy, Linda, Eric, Christian. B.A., U. Minn., 1948; M.A., Clark U., 1950; Ph.D., Columbia, 1958. Adj. prof. Grad. Sch. Indsl. Engring., N.Y.U., 1963-66; dep. dir. lab. psychol. studies Stevens Inst. Tech., 1964-67, dir., 1967-73, prof. mgmt. sci. and psychology, 1966—, asso. dean acad. affairs, 1972-76, dir. tech. and soc. curriculum, 1972-75; dir. Center for Mgmt. of Organizational Resources, 1976-81; sr. partner Organizational Scis. Assos., 1980—; Sr. assoc. G. W. Fotis Assocs., Inc., 1982—; cons. to industry. Pres. Darien (Conn.) Mental Health Assn., 1961-64, 68-70; Mem. Darien Democratic Town Com.; Bd. dirs. Stamford (Conn.) Psychiat. Clinic Children, Gateway, Inc., 1979—. Served with USNR, 1945-46. Mem. Am., N.J. psychol. assns., Met. N.Y. Assn. Applied Psychology (pres. 1966-67), AAAS, Inst. Mgmt. Sci., AAUP, Sigma Xi. Home: 62 Brookside Rd Darien CT 06820 Office: Stevens Inst Tech Castle Point Sta Hoboken NJ 07030

JOHNSON, JAMES ROBERT, ceramic engineer, educator; b. Cin., Jan. 2, 1923; s. Charles William and Della Ramona (Schubert) J.; m. Virginia M. Bowen, Apr. 3, 1945; children—Cathy (Mrs. John Whitman), Barbara (Mrs. Charles Kallusky), Randy, John, Jamie (Mrs. J.R. Myers), Brian. B.S., Ohio State U., 1947, M.S., 1948, Ph.D., 1950. Asst. prof. U. Tex., 1950-51; tech. adviser ceramics Oak Ridge Nat. Lab., 1951-56; lab. mgr., dir., exec. scientist Minn. Mining & Mfg. Co., St. Paul, 1956-79, cons., 1979—; adj. prof. U. Wis.-Stout; U. Minn., 1979—. Contbr. articles to profl. jours. Served with C.E. AUS, 1943-46. Recipient Distinguished Alumnus award Ohio State U., 1970, 3M Carlton award, 1970. Fellow Am. Ceramic Soc. (pres. 1973-74, disting. life mem.); mem. Nat. Acad. Engring., Nat. Inst. Ceramics Engrs. (Pace award 1959), Research Engring. Soc. Am. Patentee in field. Home: Route 1 Box 231B River Falls WI 54022

JOHNSON, JAMES ROSSER, educator; b. Scranton, Pa., Sept. 2, 1916; s. John Solomon and Rose Anne (Rosser) J.; m. Ida McCabe, Nov. 19, 1949; children—David, Eric, Ethan. B.S., Harvard U., 1941; postgrad., U. Paris, 1947; Ph.D., Columbia U., 1960. Instr. humanities Columbia U., N.Y.C., 1952-53; asst. prof. art history Western Res. U., Cleve., 1954-59, chmn. humanities, 1958-59; asso. curator edn. Cleve. Mus. Art, 1959-67; curator art history and edn., also adj. prof. Case Western Res. U., Cleve., 1967-72; prof. art U. Conn., Storrs, 1972—, dean, 1972-78. Author: The Radiance of Chartres, 1964; contbr. articles to profl. jours. Served with USAAF, 1943-45; 2d lt. Transp. Corps AUS, 1945-46. Fellow Royal Soc. Arts (London); mem. Mediaeval Acad. Am. (councillor 1968-70), Am. Council Learned Socs., Coll. Art Assn. Am., Am. Soc. Aesthetics (nat. sec.-treas. 1959-78, hon. trustee), 1978, Phi Kappa Phi. Home: 154 Hanks Hill Rd Storrs CT 06268

JOHNSON, JAMES TERENCE, college president, lawyer; b. Springfield, Mo., Oct. 25, 1942; s. Clifford Lester and Margaret Jeanne (Wallace) J.; m. Martha Susan Mitchell, May 2, 1964; children: Jennifer Jeanne, Emily Jill, Tiffanie Michelle. B.A., Okla. Christian Coll., 1964; J.D., So. Meth. U., 1967; LL.D., Pepperdine U., 1980. Staff counsel, asst. prof. Okla. Christian Coll., Oklahoma City, 1968-72, v.p., 1972-73, exec. v.p., 1973-74, pres., 1974—; minister, Okla., Tex., 1961—, pvt. practice law, Oklahoma City, 1969—; co-founder Enterprise Sq., U.S.A., 1982; dir. Alliance Bank N.A. Pres. Okla. Christian Coll. Investment Corp.; trustee Freedom Found.; bd. dirs. Okla. Ind. Coll. Found.; mem. adv. council Found. Am. Agr., 1977. Mem. Okla. Bar Assn., Newcomen Soc., Phi Delta Theta. Mem. Ch. of Christ. Club: Rotary. Office: Okla Christian Coll Oklahoma City OK 73111

JOHNSON, JAMES WILLIAM, educator, author; b. Birmingham, Ala., Mar. 1, 1927; s. James Terry and Maude Belle (Brown) J.; m. Nan Heffelfinger, Oct. 5, 1957; children—Miranda, Reed. B.A. cum laude, Birmingham-So. Coll., 1950; M.A. (Am. Council Learned Socs. fellow), Harvard U., 1950; Ph.D., Vanderbilt U., 1954; Fulbright scholar, Univ. Coll., U. London, 1954-55. Instr. English Vanderbilt U., 1953-54; instr. English U. Rochester, N.Y., 1955-58, asst. prof., 1958-61, asso. prof., 1961-65, prof. English, 1965—; cons. various pubs. Author: Logic and Rhetoric, 1962, The Formation of English Neo-Classical Thought, 1967, Utopian Literature, 1968, The Plays of John

Dennis, 1980; Contbr. articles to scholarly jours. Served with USN, 1945-46. Folger Library fellow, 1963; Am. Council Learned Socs. fellow, 1966-67; Guggenheim fellow, 1970-71. Mem. MLA, English Inst., Am. Soc. for 18th Century Studies, North Eastern Am. Assn. for 18th Century Studies (v.p. 1979, pres. 1980—), Alpha Tau Omega. Democrat. Home: 64 Oliver St Rochester NY 14607 Office: English Dept U Rochester Rochester NY 14627 *I subscribe to two maxims: The end of all public ambition is to be happy at home (Samuel Johnson), and Happiness is nobody sick and no bill collectors at the door (Chinese proverb).*

JOHNSON, JAMES WINSTON, educator; b. Quinton, Okla., May 25, 1930; s. Fred M. and Lois Amelia (Sands) J.; m. Vera Mae Hamman, Oct. 17, 1953; children—Christopher James, Victor Andrew. B.S. in Chemistry-Math, Southeastern Okla. U., 1953, Mo. Sch. Mines and Metallurgy, 1957; M.S. in Chem. Engring. (AEC fellow), Mo. Sch. Mines and Metallurgy, 1958; Ph.D. (NSF fellow), U. Mo., 1961. Instr. Mo. Sch. Mines and Metallurgy, 1958-60, asst. prof., 1961-62; research asso. U. Pa., 1962-63; asso. prof. U. Mo. at, Rolla, 1963-66, prof. chem. engring., 1966—, chmn. chem. engring. dept., 1979—; research asso. Grad. Center Materials Research, 1965—. Contbr. articles tech. jours. Served with AUS, 1953-55. Mem. Am. Inst. Chem. Engrs., Nat. Assn. Corrosion Engrs., Electrochem. Soc., Am. Soc. Engring. Edn., Blue Key, Sigma Xi, Tau Beta Pi, Alpha Chi Sigma, Sigma Pi Sigma, Phi Kappa Phi, Kappa Delta Pi, Sigma Tau Gamma. Republican. Club: Rotary. Home: PO Box 486 Rolla MO 65401

JOHNSON, JANET HELEN, Egytology educator; b. Everett, Wash., Dec. 24, 1944; d. Robert A. and Jane N. (Osborn) J.; m. Donald S. Whitcomb, Sept. 2, 1978. B.A., U. Chgo., 1967, Ph.D., 1972. Instr. Egyptology U. Chgo., 1971-72, asst. prof., 1972-79, assoc. prof., 1979-81, prof., 1981—; dir. Oriental Inst., 1983—; research assoc. dept. anthropology Field Mus. of Natural History, 1980—. Author: Deomotic Verbal System, 1977, (with Donald S. Whitcomb) Quseir al-Qadim, 1978; editor: (with E.F. Wente) Studies in Honor of G.R. Hughes, 1977. Smithsonian Instn. grantee, 1977-83; NEH grantee, 1978-81, 81-84; Nat. Geog. Soc. grantee, 1978-80, 80-82. Mem. Am. Research Ctr. in Egypt (bd. govs. 1979—). Office: Oriental Inst Chicago 1155 E 58th St Chicago IL 60637

JOHNSON, JEAN ELAINE, nurse, psychologist; b. Wilsey, Kans., Mar. 11, 1925; d. William H. and Rosa L. (Welty) Irwin. B.S., Kans. State U., 1948; M.S. in Nursing, Yale, 1965, U. Wis., 1969, Ph.D., 1971. Instr. nursing, Iowa, Kans. and Colo., 1948-58; staff nurse Swedish Hosp., Englewood, Colo., 1958-60; in-service edn. coordinator Gen. Rose Hosp., Denver, 1960-63; research asst. Yale, New Haven, 1965-67; asso. prof. nursing Wayne State U., Detroit, 1971-74, prof., 1974-79; dir. Center for Health Research, 1974-79; prof. nursing, asso. dir. oncology nursing Cancer Center, U. Rochester, 1979—. Contbg. author: Stress and Anxiety, vol. 2, 1975; contbr. articles to profl. jours. Recipient Bd. Govs. Faculty Recognition award Wayne State U., 1975; grantee NIH, 1972—. Mem. Inst. Medicine, Nat. Acad. Sci. (com. on patient injury compensation 1976-77, membership com. 1981—), Am. Nurses Assn. (chmn. council for nurse researchers 1976-78, mem. commn. for research 1978-82), AAAS, Acad. for Behavioral Medicine Research, Sigma Xi, Am. Psychol. Assn., Omicron Nu, Phi Kappa Phi. Home: 1412 East Ave Rochester NY 14610 Office: Cancer Center U Rochester Rochester NY 14642

JOHNSON, JEH VINCENT, architect; b. Nashville, July 8, 1931; s. Charles Spurgeon and Marie Antoinette (Burguette) J.; m. Norma Edelin, Dec. 28, 1956; children—Jeh Charles, Marguerite Marie. A.B., Columbia U., 1953, M.Arch., 1958. Architect/designer Paul R. Williams, Los Angeles, 1956; designer Adams & Woodbridge, N.Y.C., 1957-62; asso. Gindele & Johnson (P.C. Architects and predecessors), Poughkeepsie, N.Y., 1967-69, partner, 1969-71, pres., 1971-80; partner LeGendre Johnson McNeil Assos., 1980—; lectr. Vassar Coll., 1964—; vice chmn. N.Y. State Bd. for Architecture, 1974—; mem. Nat. Commn. Urban Problems, 1967-69. Designer: Dutchess County (N.Y.) Mental Health Center, 1969, Lagrange (N.Y.) Town Hall, 1969, Newburgh (N.Y.) Houses on the Lake, 1970, Whitney Young Health Center, Albany, N.Y., 1973, St. Simeon Apts. for Elderly, Poughkeepsie, N.Y., 1973, Bedford-Stuyvesant Comml. Center, N.Y.C., 1978. Trustee Poughkeepsie Savs. Bank. Served with CIC U.S. Army, 1953-55. William Kinne Fellows traveling fellow, 1958. Fellow AIA (Students medal 1958); mem. Nat. Orgn. Minority Architects, AAUP, NAACP, Nat. Council Archtl. Registration Bds., Sigma Pi Phi. Club: Masons. Home and Office: 14 Edgehill Rd Wappingers Falls NY 12590

JOHNSON, JERRY A., occupational therapy educator; b. Lubbock, Tex., Sept. 21, 1931; d. Weldon F. Johnson and Geraldine (Buckner) Mallory. B.S., Tex. Womans U., 1953; postgrad., Washington U., St. Louis, Radcliffe Coll., 1959-60; M.B.A., Harvard U., 1961; Ed.D., Boston U., 1970. Staff occupational therapist U.S. Naval Hosp, Oakland, Calif., 1954-56; dir. occupational therapy Easter Seal Soc., Alton, Ill., 1956, exec. dir., 1957-59; asst. hosp. adminstr. U.S. Naval Hosp., Newport, R.I., 1961-62; legal counsel for party Phys. Evaluation Bd., USN, Chelsea, Mass., 1962-63; assoc. prof., chmn. div. occupational therapy Sargent Coll. Allied Health Professions, Boston, 1963-69; acting exec. dir. rehab. council Boston U., 1969-70; prof., chmn. Center for Allied Health Instructional Personnel, U. Fla., 1971-72; prof., chmn. div. grad. studies Sargent Coll. Allied Health Professions, Boston, 1972-73, asso. dean, 1973-74; prof. dir. occupational therapy grad. studies and research Colo. State U., Fort Collins, 1974-76; prof., dir. Sch. Occupational Therapy Washington U., St. Louis, 1976—; vis. scholar speech communication dept. U. Denver, 1982-83; pres., dir. Context, Inc., Denver, 1982—; Project dir., ednl. cons. Am. Occupational Therapy Assn., Detroit and Chgo., 1966-67, 69-70, mem. exec. bd., 1967-72, pres., 1973-79; ednl. cons. U. Ala., 1968; mem. panel cons. to adv. com. on edn. Allied Health Professions, Council on Med. Edn. AMA, 1969-73; cons. Hebrew U., Jerusalem, 1971—; mem. med. adv. com. Bay State Soc. for Crippled, 1969-70; mem. Govs. Task Force on Tng. and Manpower in Mental Health, Boston, 1964-66; mem. adv. bd. Grace Hill Community Health Center, 1977—, Ctr. for Creative Arts, Denver, 1982—; mem. exec. bd. Nat. Easter Seal Soc., 1981—. Contbr. articles to profl. jours. Mem. Mass. Assn. Occupational Therapy (pres. 1964-66), Internat. Soc. Rehab. Disabled, World Fedn. Occupational Therapists, Harvard Bus. Sch. Assn., Am. Occupational Therapy Assn. (pres. 1973-78, chmn. polit. action com. 1977-79), Mo. Occupational Therapy Assn., Am. Mgmt. Assn., Am. Pub. Health Assn., Common Cause, Mo. Bot. Gardens, Wildlife Fedn., League Women Voters. Democrat. Episcopalian. Clubs: Radcliffe Coll., Harvard Bus. Coll., Zonta Internat. Home: 400 Fairfax St Denver CO 80206

JOHNSON, JERRY RAY, textile company executive; b. Savannah, Ga., Sept. 7, 1926; m. Billie Wannamaker, Dec. 31, 1948; children: Rupert Ray, Wanna Bee Johnson Towler, William Elliott. B.S.M.E., U. S.C., 1950. Registered profl. engr., S.C. With Graniteville Co., S.C., 1942—, beginning as machinist, successively maintenance engr., asst. maintenance supt., asst. gen. supt., gen. supt. maintenance, power and constrn., asst. v.p. ops., v.p. ops., 1942-79, exec. v.p., 1979—; dir. Community Services, Inc., C.H. Patrick & Co., Inc., Graniteville Internat., Inc. Trustee Columbia Coll., S.C., 1980—. Served with USNR, 1944-46. Mem. ASME (sect. chmn.), S.C. Textile Mfrs. Assn. (bd. dirs.). Methodist. Clubs: Houndslake Country (Aiken, S.C.); Pinnacle (Augusta, Ga.); Graniteville Exchange (past pres.). Lodge: Rotary (past pres.). Home: 904 Wildwood Rd Aiken SC 29801 Office: Graniteville Co Marshall St Graniteville SC 29829

JOHNSON, J.M. HAMLIN, manufacturing company executive; b. Ridgway, Pa., Oct. 10, 1925; s. Manferd H. and Esther (Hallstrom) J.; m. Sara N. Richardson, Sept. 11, 1948; children: Stephanie (Mrs. William G. Cox), Robert H., Elizabeth E., Lara, David L., Christine M. B.S., Grove City Coll., 1949; student, Pa. State U., 1969. With Stackpole Corp., St. Mary's, Pa., 1950—, supr. accounting, to 1960, operational auditor, 1960-64, mgr. accounting, 1964-68, asst. treas., 1968-71, treas., asst. sec., 1971-79, v.p., treas., asst. sec., dir., 1979—; treas., asst. sec. Stackpole Components Co.; treas. Stackpole Fibers Co.; treas., sec., dir. Stackpole Machinery Co.; partner J. & B. Co., Ridgway, Pa.; dir. Hamlin Bank & Trust Co. Past mem. Ridgway Area Sch. Bd.; trustee Ridgway YMCA, A. Kaul Meml. Hosp.; bd. dirs., pres. ELCAM Vocat. Rehab. Center. Served with USAAF. Mem. Nat. Assn. Accountants (pres. 1958-59). Clubs: Kiwanian (pres. 1973-74), St. Marys Country.). Home: 517 Center St Saint Marys PA 15857 Office: 201 Stackpole St Saint Mary's PA 15857

JOHNSON, JOAN D., physical education educator; b. Wyandotte, Mich., Oct. 10, 1929; d. Joel C. and Emily Carla (Timm) J. Student, Western Mich. Coll., 1947-49; B.S., U. Wis., 1951; M.S., U. So. Calif., 1955, Ph.D., 1965; postgrad., U. Mich., 1958. Tchr. phys. edn. Bloom Twp. High Sch., Chicago Heights, Ill., 1951-53; teaching asst. U. So. Calif., Los Angeles, 1953-55, vis. prof., 1960; asst. prof. phys. edn. Calif. State U., Los Angeles, 1955-65, asso. prof., 1965-70, prof., 1970—, asso. chmn. dept. phys. edn. and athletics, 1969-77, chmn. dept., 1977-80; vis. prof. Tex. Woman's U., 1973; coach U.S. Women's Tennis Team, World U. Games, Sofia, Bulgaria, 1977; chmn. tennis com. Assn. Intercollegiate Athletics for Women, 1976-80. Author: (with P. J. Xanthos) Tennis, 4th edit, 1981, (with D.F. Kelley) A Workbook for Tests and Measurements in Physical Education, 1967. Recipient Women's Tennis Leadership award U.S. Lawn Tennis Assn., 1970; Outstanding Prof. award Calif. State U., Los Angeles, 1978. Mem. Calif. Assn. Health, Phys. Edn., Recreation and Dance, AAHPERD, Western Soc. Phys. Edn. Coll. Women (sec. 1967-68, treas. 1972-73, pres. 1977-78, exec. bd. 1980—), Nat. Assn. Phys. Edn. in Higher Edn., So. Calif. Tennis Umpires Assn., Phi Kappa Phi. Club: Soroptimist Internat. (Los Angeles) (pres. bd. Found. 1982—). Office: Dept Phys Edn and Recreation/Leisure Studies Calif State U Los Angeles 5151 State University Dr Los Angeles CA 90032

JOHNSON, JOHN A., communications company executive; b. Milw., 1915; s. John W. and Amy (Nelson) J.; m. Harriet Nelson, Sept. 11, 1938; children: Barbara (Mrs. James A. Groff), John Vance, Susan (Mrs. Don H. Boatwright), Richard Bailey. A.B., DePauw U., 1937; J.D., U. Chgo., 1940; LL.M., Harvard U., 1946. Bar: Ill. 1946, D.C. 1979. Atty. Office Gen. Counsel, Burlington & Quincy R.R., 1940-41; with firm Wilson & McIlvaine, 1941-43; asst. Office UN Affairs, Dept. State, Washington, 1946-48; atty., asst. gen. counsel, assoc. gen. counsel Dept. of Air Force, 1948-52, gen. counsel, 1952-58, NASA, 1958-63; staff Communications Satellite Corp. (COMSAT), Washington, 1963-64, v.p. internat., 1964-73, sr. v.p., 1973-74; pres. COMSAT Gen. Corp., 1973-77, chmn. bd., chief exec. officer, 1977-80; chmn. Satellite TV Corp., 1980-81; dir. Intercontinental de Communicaciones por Satelite, S.A. (INTERCOMSA), Panama; U.S. rep. Interim Communications Satellite Com. of INTELSAT, 1964-67, 68-69, INTELSAT bd. govs., 1973-74, INMARSAT Council, 1979; dir. World Christian Broadcasting Corp. Contbr.: articles to profl. jours., also to Ency. Brit. Mem. Falls Church (Va.) Sch. Bd., 1949-56, chmn., 1951-56; mem. exec. bd. Va. Sch. Bds. Assn., 1953-56; trustee Northeastern Christian Jr. Coll., 1955—, chmn. bd. trustees, 1958-73; bd. visitors Coll. of U. Chgo., 1966-71, Western Res. Law Sch., 1964-67; bd. dirs. Pan Am. Devel. Found. Served to lt. (j.g.) USNR, 1943-46. Recipient Exceptional Civilian Service award Dept. Air Force; medal for outstanding leadership NASA; Alumni citation for pub. service U. Chgo., DePauw U. Mem. Am. Soc. Internat. Law, Inter-am Bar Assn., Internat. Acad. Astronautics. Mem. Ch. of Christ. Club: Federal City. Home: 3643 N Nelson St Arlington VA 22207 Office: 950 L'Enfant Plaza SW Washington DC 20004

JOHNSON, JOHN BRAYTON, editor, publisher; b. Watertown, N.Y., Dec. 14, 1916; s. Harold Bowtell and Jessie R. (Parsons) J.; m. Catherine Amelia Common, June 21, 1941; children: John Brayton, Ann, Deborah (Mrs. Fitzhugh Elder III), Harold Bowtell II. A.B., Princeton, 1939; L.H.D., St. Lawrence U., 1978. Reporter Watertown (N.Y.) Daily Times, 1939-41, 46-49, editor and pub., 1949—; dir. Key Bank No. Watertown, Key Bank, Inc., Albany, N.Y.; Chmn. Council to Upstate Med. Center, Syracuse, 1964—. Bd. dirs. N.Y. State Dormitory Authority, Elsmere, 1962—; Trustee St. Lawrence U., Canton, N.Y. Served with M.I. AUS, 1941-46. Mem. A.I.A. (hon.). Republican. Presbyterian. Clubs: Princeton N.Y.; Black River Valley (Watertown). Home: 221 Flower Ave W Watertown NY 13601 Office: Watertown Daily Times 260 Washington St Watertown NY 13601

JOHNSON, JOHN CLARK, emeritus physics educator; b. Waterbury, Conn., Aug. 17, 1919; s. John Mauritz Eugene and Aletha (Clark) J.; m. Frances Elizabeth Barrett, July 1, 1941 (div. June 1961); children: Eric Arthur, Signe Lee. A.B., Middlebury Coll., 1941; S.M., Mass. Inst. Tech., 1946; Sc.D., 1948. Asst. prof. Mass. Inst. Tech., 1950-53; lectr., research asso. Tufts U., 1953-54; faculty Worcester (Mass.) Poly. Inst., 1954—, prof. physics, 1965-81, prof. emeritus, 1981—. Author: Physical Meteorology, 1954. Served to 1st lt. USAAF, 1941-45; ETO. Decorated Air medal. Mem. Am. Phys. Soc., Am. Meteorol. Soc., Optical Soc. Am., Am. Assn. Physics Tchrs., Sigma Xi, Alpha Sigma Phi. Office: Physics Dept Worcester Poly Inst Worcester MA 01609

JOHNSON, JOHN DAVID, banker; b. Ft. Dodge, Iowa, Apr. 22, 1939; s. Morris Obed Filmore and Florence Marie (Carlson) J.; m. Sandra Kay Kallestad, Jan. 19, 1963; children: Catherine Jane, James Mark, Karen Louise. B.S. in Bus., U. Minn., 1970; grad., Stonier Grad. Sch. Banking, Rutgers U., 1973. Auditor Fed. Res. Bank, Mpls., 1960-65, anaylst,programmer, 1965-70, asst. v.p., 1970-75, v.p., Helena, Mont., 1975-79, sr. v.p., Phila., 1975-82, exec. v.p., 1982—. Treas., dir. Afro-Am. Hist. and Cultural Mus., Phila., 1981—; dir. Mont. Council Econ. Edn., 1976-78; pres. Marple Newton Band Assn., 1983; adv. com. Phila. Assn. Retarded Citizens, 1982; chmn. Lewis and Clark County United Fund, 1979; bd. dirs. Helena YMCA, 1976-79. Fellow Am. Mgmt. Assn. Republican. Club: Kiwanis. Office: Federal Reserve Bank 100 N 6th St Philadelphia PA 19106

JOHNSON, JOHN F., mfg. co. exec. B.S. in Elec. Engring, U.S. Mil. Acad., M.S., U. Pa. Mgr. electronics research and devel. Am. Machine and Foundry Corp.; v.p. Aiken Industries, pres., gen. mgr.; tech. advisor to v.p. engring. Avonics div. ITT, N.Y.C., 1968—; pres., gen. mgr. Electro-Optical products div.; group gen. mgr. North Group of Telephone Equipment Mfg. Cos., Nutley, N.J., 1979—, v.p., 1981— *

JOHNSON, JOHN GRAY, university president; b. Irwin, Pa., Aug. 8, 1924; s. John Arthur and Elizabeth (Gray) J.; m. Jane Wyncoop, Aug. 28, 1948; children: Scott Raymond, Lynn. B.S., Carnegie-Mellon U., 1949; LL.D. (hon.), Ind. Central U., 1980. Alumni dir. Carnegie-Mellon U., 1955-60; exec. dir. Am. Alumni Council, Washington, 1960-64; v.p. devel. Butler U., Indpls., 1964-66, pres., 1978—; v.p. for devel. Carnegie-Mellon U., 1966-78; dir. Ind. Nat. Bank, Indpls. Water Co., Meridian Ins. Co. Bd. dirs. Greater Indpls. Progress Com.; vice chmn. United Way. Served with U.S. Army, 1943-46. Decorated Air medal. Mem. Council Advancement and Support of Edn., Ind. C. of C. (dir.), Indpls. C. of C. (dir.), Phi Kappa Phi. Clubs: University (N.Y.C.); Meridian Hills, Sagamore of Wabash, Economic (pres.), Skyline (Indpls.) (dir.); The Pointe). Home: 8485 Olde Mill Circle West Dr Indianapolis IN 46260 Office: 4600 Sunset Ave Indianapolis IN 46208

JOHNSON, JOHN H., editor, publisher; b. Arkansas City, Ark., Jan. 19, 1918; m. Eunice Johnson; children: John Harold (dec.), Linda. Student, U. Chgo., Northwestern U.; LL.D., Central State Coll., Shaw U., N.C. Coll., Benedict Coll., Carnegie-Mellon Inst., Morehouse Coll., N.C. A. and T. State U., Syracuse U., Eastern Mich. U., Hamilton Coll., Lincoln U., Malcolm X Coll., Upper Iowa Coll., Wayne State U., Pratt Inst., Chgo. State U., Northeastern U. Pres., pub. Johnson Pub. Co., Inc., Chgo. N.Y.C., Los Angeles, Washington, 1942—; pub., editor Ebony, Jet, Ebony Jr. (mags.); pres. Sta. WJPC, Chgo., Sta. WLOU, Louisville, Fashion Fair Cosmetics, Chgo.; chmn., chief exec. officer Supreme Life Ins. Co., Chgo.; dir. Marina Bank, Chgo., Greyhound Corp., 20th Century-Fox Film Corp., Zenith Radio Corp. Trustee Art Inst., Chgo. Named Outstanding Young Man U.S. Jaycees, 1951; recipient Horatio Alger award, 1966; John Russwurm award Nat. Newspaper Pubs. Assn., 1966; Spingarn medal NAACP, 1966; Henry Johnson Fisher award Mag. Pubs. Assn., 1971; Communicator of Year award U. Chgo. Alumni Assn., 1974; Columbia Journalism award, 1974; named to Acad. Disting. Entrepreneurs Babson Coll., 1979. Fellow Sigma Delta Chi; mem. U.S. C. of C. (dir.), Mag. Pubs. Assn. Office: 820 S Michigan Ave Chicago IL 60605 also 1270 Avenue of Americas New York NY 10020 also 1750 Pennsylvania Ave NW Washington DC 20006 also 3600 Wilshire Blvd Los Angeles CA 90005

JOHNSON, JOHN HAROLD, sports assn. exec.; b. S.I., Sept. 26, 1921; s. John Walter and Alexandra (Niiles) J.; m. Lillian Alice Bauer, Nov. 1, 1947; children—Barbara Ann, Thomas Walter. Student public schs., S.I. Gen. mgr. Binghamton (N.Y.) Baseball Club, 1951-54; farm dir. N.Y. Yankees, 1956-64, v.p., 1965-69; adminstr. Office of Baseball Commr., N.Y.C., 1970-78; pres. Nat. Assn. Profl. Baseball Leagues, St. Petersburg, Fla., 1979—; chmn. Ofcl. Baseball Rules Com. Served with USCG, 1942-46; MTO; ETO. Mem. Am. Legion. Lutheran. Office: PO Box A Saint Petersburg FL 33731

JOHNSON, JOHN IRWIN, JR., neuroscientist; b. Salt Lake City, Aug. 18, 1931; s. John Irwin and Ann Josephine (Freeman) J. A.B., U. Notre Dame, 1952; M.S., Purdue U., 1955, Ph.D., 1957. Instr., then asst. prof. Marquette U., Milw., 1958-60; USPHS spl. research fellow U. Wis., Madison, 1960-63; Fulbright-Hays research scholar U. Sydney, Australia, 1964-65; asso. prof. biophysics, psychology and zoology Mich. State U., E. Lansing, 1965-69, prof., 1969-81, prof. anatomy, 1981—, chmn. dept. biophysics, 1973-78; vis. fellow psychology dept. Yale U., New Haven, 1975-76. Recipient Career Devel. award NIH, 1965-72, research grantee, 1966-79; research grantee NSF, 1969-71, 71-73, 73-76, 78—; 3d hon. life mem. Anat. Assn. Australia and N.Z., 1973. Mem. Soc. Neurosci., Am. Assn. Anatomists, Am. Soc. Zoologists, Am. Psychol. Assn., Assn. Gay Psychologists, Am. Soc. Mammalogists, Animal Behavior Soc., AAUP, Nat. Gay Task Force, Gay Rights Alumni Notre Dame U., ACLU, Sigma Xi. Home: 2494 W Grand River Ave Okemos MI 48864 Office: Dept Anatomy A514 E Fee Hall Mich State U East Lansing MI 48824

JOHNSON, JOHN J., educator, historian; b. White Swan, Wash., Mar. 26, 1912; s. George E. and Mary (Whitford) J.; m. Maurine Amstutz, June 8, 1942; 1 son, Michael G. B.A., Central Wash. Coll., 1940; M.A., U. Calif.-Berkeley, 1943, Ph.D., 1947; postgrad., U. Chgo., 1943-44, U. Chile, 1946. Tchr. pub. schs., Wash., 1935-41; mem. faculty Stanford U., 1946-78, prof. history, 1958-78, emeritus prof., 1977—; chmn. com. Latin Am. studies, 1966-72; prof. U. N.Mex., Albuquerque, 1980—; acting chief S. Am. br., div. research Am. Republic, State Dept., 1952-53; lectr. U. Ariz. Summer Sch., Guadalajara, Mex., 1955, 58, 61; cons. to industry and govt., 1959—; Fulbright lectr. U. Auckland, New Zealand, 1974; vis. prof. U. N.Mex., 1977, 79, Ariz. State U., 1980. Author: Pioneer Telegraphy in Chile, 1948, Political Change in Latin America; The Emergence of the Middle Sectors, 1958, The Military and Society in Latin America, 1964, Simon Bolivar and Spanish American Independence: 1783-1830, 1967, Latin America in Caricature, 1980; Mng. editor: Hispanic Am. Hist. Rev, 1980—; Editor, contbr.: Role of the Military in Underdeveloped Countries, 1962, Continuity and Change in Latin America, 1964, The Mexican American: A Selected and Annotated Bibliography, 1969. Recipient Bolton prize Conf. Latin Am. History, 1959, Distinguished Alumnus award Central Wash. U., 1977. Mem. Am. Hist. Assn. (chmn. conf. Latin Am. history 1961, mem. council 1976-79), Latin Am. Studies Assn. (pres. 1970, 1st Kalman Silvert Pres.'s prize 1983). Home: 2912 Cutler NE Albuquerque NM 87106 Office: History Dept U NMex Albuquerque NM 87131

JOHNSON, JOHN PRESCOTT, philosophy educator; b. Tumalo, Oreg., Apr. 24, 1921; s. John Edward and Caroline Prescott (Eaton) J.; m. Mable Alice Dougherty, June 9, 1943; children: Grace Beth (Mrs. Thomas Collins Booth), John Paul, Carol Ruth. A.B., Kans. State Coll., 1947; M.S., Pittsburg State U., 1948; Ph.D., Northwestern U., 1959. Asst. prof. philosophy Bethany (Okla.) Nazarene Coll., 1949-57; asst. prof. U. Okla., Norman, 1957-62; asso. prof. philosophy Monmouth (Ill.) Coll., 1962-69; prof. Monmouth (Ill.) Coll., 1969—; chmn. dept. Monmouth (Ill.) Coll., 1967—; Vis. asst. prof. Northwestern U., summer 1961; Cons. research project student values U.S. Office Edn., 1967. Contbr. articles to philos. jours. Mem. Am. Philos. Assn., Ill. Philos. Assn. (sec.-treas. 1967-69, pres. 1971-73), Metaphys. Soc. Am. Home: 1040 E 3d Ave Monmouth IL 61462

JOHNSON, JOHN WARREN, assn. exec.; b. Mpls., Jan. 29, 1929; s. Walter E. and Eileen L. J.; m. Marion Louise Myrland; children—Daniel Warren, Karen Louise, Nancy Marie. B.A., U. Minn., 1951. Exec. v.p. Am. Collectors Assn., Inc., Mpls., 1955—. Author: Political Christians, 1979, You Can Manage Your Money, 1981, 38 Days to Cape Town, 1981. Mem. Mpls. City Council, 1963-67; mem. Minn. State Ho. of Reps., 1967-75, asst. majority leader, 1972-74; Republican candidate for Gov. of Minn., 1974. Served with USNR, 1947-53. Mem. Am. Soc. Assn. Execs. (past dir., mem. exec. com.), U.S. C. of C. (past chmn. bd. regents), Minn. Soc. Assn. Execs. (past pres.). Lutheran. Office: 4040 W 70th St Minneapolis MN 55435

JOHNSON, JOHN WILBUR, communications executive; b. Aitkin, Minn., Apr. 11, 1921; s. John Edward and Adele Marie (Raboin) J.; m. Barbara Jean Gottlich, Oct. 16, 1943; children: Stephen, Timothy, Revecca, Mary, Peter. B.A., U. Minn.-Mpls., 1948; student, St. John's U., 1939-41. Ordained priest, Episcopal Ch., 1970. Reporter LaCrosse Tribune, Wis., 1948; reporter, asst. city editor Corpus Christi Caller, Tex., 1949-53; pub. relations exec. United Aircraft Corp., East Hartford, Conn., 1953-54; pub. relations and advt. The LTV Corp., Dallas, 1961—; dir. Wilson Sporting Goods Co., 1967-70, Okonite Co., 1966-70, Wilson Foods, 1967-70, Wilson Pharm., 1967-70. Contbr. articles to profl. jours. Bd. dirs. Irving Community Hosp., Tex., 1977-80; mem. Commn. on Ministry, Diocese of Dallas, 1977-81. Served to lt. USN, 1942-46; PTO. Mem. Pub. Relations Soc. Am., Am. Film Inst., Dallas Advt. League, Dallas Press Club, Sigma Delta Chi. Clubs: Las Colinas, Admirals. Office: The LTV Corp LTV Cower Dallas TX 75265

JOHNSON, JOHN WILLIAM, JR., executive recruiter; b. St. Petersburg, Fla., Dec. 10, 1932; s. John William and Elizabeth (Lowitz) J.; m. Cecelia Lynn Wescott, Feb. 6, 1960; children: William Wescott, James Robert, Gayle McCrimmon. A.B., Wesleyan U., Middletown, Conn., 1954; postgrad., NYU, 1958-59. With Benton and Bowles, Inc., N.Y.C., 1958-82, v.p., account supr., 1963-70, sr. v.p., mgmt. supr., 1970-82, adminstr. profit sharing plan, 1969-82, also dir.; ptnr., dir. George Webb Assocs., Inc., 1982—; founder, former pres. Scarsdale Hardware Co., Inc.; dir. Scarsdale Nat. Bank. Mem. Scarsdale Planning Bd.; mem. Scarsdale Citizens Nominating Com.; pres. Rainsford House Assn., N.Y.C., 1964-66, now bd. dirs.; bd. dirs. Jacob A. Riis Settlement, Long Island City, St. Christopher's-Jennie Clarkson Child Care; vestry Ch. St. James the Less, Scarsdale. Served as pilot USNR, 1954-58. Decorated Air medal.; S.C. Davis fellow in bus. ethics Wesleyan U., 1979—. Clubs: Winged Foot, Town. Home: 43 Axtell Dr Scarsdale NY 10583 Office: 280 Park Ave New York NY 10017

JOHNSON, JOHNNY RAY, educator; b. Chatham, La., Dec. 19, 1929; s. Dave Ernest and Bessie (Morris) J.; m. Betty Ann Moore, Oct. 21, 1960; children—Todd Michael, John Fitzgerald, Shauna Renee. B.S., La. Tech. U., 1951; M.S., Auburn U., 1953, Ph.D., 1959. Registered profl. engr., La. Asst. prof. math. La. Tech. U., 1958-62; asso. prof. math. Appalachian State U., 1962-63; prof. elec. engring. La. State U., Baton Rouge, 1963—; adj. prof. elec. engring. U. Fla., Gainesville, 1976-77; mem. staff Combat Ops. Research Group, Ft. Monroe, Va., summer 1957; mathematician Boeing Co., New Orleans, summer 1965. Author: (with David E. Johnson) Mathematical Methods in Engrineering and Physics, 1965, Graph Theory with Engineering Applications, 1972, Introductory Electric Circuit Analysis, 1981, Linear Systems Analysis, 1975, (with David E. Johnson and John L. Hilburn) Basic Electric Circuit Analysis, 1978, (with David E. Johnson and Harry P. Moore) A Handbook of Active Filters, 1980. Pres. Wildwood PTA, 1973-74. Served with AUS, 1954-56. Mem. La. Engring. Soc., IEEE (sr. mem.), AAUP, Sigma Xi, Tau Beta Pi, Phi Kappa Phi, Eta Kappa Nu, Pi Mu Epsilon. Home: 953 W Lakeview Dr Baton Rouge LA 70810

JOHNSON, JONATHAN EDWIN, II, lawyer; b. Whittier, Calif., May 1, 1936; s. Roger Edwin and Louise (Thompson) J.; m. Clare Hardy, June 23, 1964; children—Jonathan III, Hardy, Benjamin, Adam, Rufus, Bradford. B.Chem.Engring., Cornell U., 1959, M.B.A., 1960; J.D. with honors, George Washington U., 1963. Bar: Calif. bar 1964. Asso. Tuttle & Taylor, Los Angeles, 1963-65; individual practice law, Los Angeles, 1965-67; partner Johnson & Jarvis, Los Angeles, 1967-68, Carmack, Johnson & Poulson, 1968—; instr. paralegal probate U. West Los Angeles Sch. Law, 1974; clergy adv. com. to supt. edn., City of Los Angeles, 1978—. Mem. State Bar Calif. (legis. com. family law sect. 1978—, chmn. 1980), Beverly Hills Bar Assn. (exec. com. family law sect. 1977—), Inter-stake Bus. and Profl. Assn. Los Angeles (pres. 1974), Sigma Chi, Phi Delta Phi, Order Coif. Mem. Ch. of Jesus Christ of Latter-Day Saints. Club: Cornell of So. Calif. (pres. 1966-68). Home: 1094 Acanto Pl Los Angeles CA 90049 Office: 10880 Wilshire Blvd Suite 1800 Los Angeles CA 90024

JOHNSON, JOSEPH BENJAMIN, univ. pres.; b. New Orleans, Sept. 16, 1934; s. Sidney Thomas and Lillie Mickens J.; m. Lula Young; children—Yolanda, Joseph, Juliet, Julie. B.S., Grambling State U., 1957; M.S., U. Colo., 1967, Ed.D., 1973; postgrad., Harvard U., 1975-76. Tchr. George Washington Carver High Sch., Shreveport, La., 1960-61, Booker T. Washington High Sch., Shreveport, 1962-63; with U. Colo., Boulder, 1969-77, exec. asst. to pres., 1975-77; pres. Grambling (La.) State U., 1977—. Mem. Task Force on Econ. Devel., State of La.; trustee Gulf South Research Inst.; mem. nat. adv. com. United Negro Coll. Fund's Dept. of Employment and Tng. Devel.; mem. adv. com. Office for Advancement of Public Negro Colls.; mem. acad. adv. com. Black Entertainment TV; mem. La. State Fair. Served with U.S. Army, 1958-60, 61-62. Mem. Am. Assn. Adminstrs. Higher Edn., Am. Assn. Univ. Adminstrs., Nat. Assn. Black Sch. Educators, La. Assn. Educators, AAHPER, Am. Council Edn., Am. Assn. State Colls. and Univs. (mem. humanities com., com. on acad. and student personnel), Nat. Assn. State Univs. and Land-Grant Colls., Nat. Black Alliance Grad. Level Educators, La. Edn. Research Assn., Phi Delta Kappa, Kappa Alpha Psi, Kappa Delta Pi. Office: PO Box 607 Grambling LA 71245

JOHNSON, JOSEPH EGGLESTON, III, medical educator; b. Elberton, Ga., Sept. 17, 1930; s. Joseph Eggleston and Marie (Williams) J.; m. Judith H. Kemp, Jan. 21, 1956; children: Joseph Eggleston IV, Judith Ann, Julie Marie. B.A. cum laude, Vanderbilt U., 1951, M.D., 1954. Diplomate: Am. Bd. Internal Medicine (bd. govs. 1977—, exec. com. 1981), Am. Bd. Allergy and Immunology. Intern Johns Hopkins Hosp., 1954-55, resident, 1957-61, physician, 1961-66; mem. faculty Johns Hopkins Med. Sch., 1961-66, asst. dean, 1963-66; mem. staff U. Fla. Teaching Hosp. (J. Hillis Miller Health Center); mem. faculty U. Fla. Med. Sch., 1966-72, prof. medicine, head div. infectious disease and clin. immunology, 1968-72, assoc. dean, 1970-72; prof. chmn. dept. medicine Bowman Gray Sch. Medicine, Winston-Salem, N.C., 1972—; chief med. service N.C. Baptist Hosp.; vice-chmn. residency rev. com. internal medicine, 1978-83, chmn. residency rev. com. internal medicine, 1983—. Contbr. articles to profl. jours. Served to lt. USNR, 1956-57. John and Mary R. Markle scholar, 1962-67; Mead-Johnson postgrad. scholar, 1960-61. Fellow ACP (sci. program com. 1979—, chmn. sci. program com. 1982—, gov.-elect N.C. 1981-82, gov. N.C. 1982), Am. Acad. Allergy, Royal Soc. Medicine (travelling fellow 1970-71); mem. Am. Fedn. Clin. Research, Assn. Am. Physicians, Infectious Diseases Soc. Am., Soc. Exptl. Biology and Medicine, N.Y. Acad. Scis., Am. Assn. Immunologists, So. Soc. Clin. Investigation, Am. Soc. for Microbiology, Assn. Profs. Medicine (sec.-treas. 1978-81, pres.-elect 1981-82, pres. 1982-83), Am. Clin. and Climatol. Assn., Société Francaise de la Tuberculose et des Maladies Respiratoires, Assn. Program Dirs. in Internal Medicine (exec. council 1980—), Assn. Am. Med. Colls. (exec. council 1983—), Council of Acad. Socs. (adminstrv. bd. 1978—), Federated Council for Internal Medicine (vice chmn. 1981-82, chmn. 1982-83), Phi Beta Kappa, Sigma Alpha Epsilon, Phi Chi, Omicron Delta Kappa, Alpha Omega Alpha. Home: 3500 Quarterstaff Pl Winston-Salem NC 27104

JOHNSON, JOSEPH HARRY, communication company executive; b. Willcox, Ariz., Mar. 14, 1919; s. John Harry and Ona Hettie (Butler) J.; m. Esther J. Chappuis, Nov. 14, 1942; children—Joseph C., Craig M., Evan R. Student, George Washington U., Ill. Bus. Coll., Washington U., St. Louis. Bookkeeper Springfield (Ill.) Marine Bank, 1937-40; personnel clk. SEC, Washington, 1940-41; with Ill. Bell Telephone Co., 1946-82; v.p. Chgo. ops., 1965-74, v.p. mktg., 1974-78, exec. v.p. bus., 1978-81, exec. v.p. mktg., 1982, Am. Info. Techs. Corp. Ameritech, 1982—. Vice chmn. bd. trustees Nat. Coll. Edn. Served to capt. USAF, 1941-46. Mem. Ill. State C. of C. Clubs: Met. (Chgo.); Skokie Country. Home: 710 Cummings Ave Kenilworth IL 60043 Office: Am Info Techs Corp (Ameritech) 225 W Randolph St Chicago IL 60606

JOHNSON, JOSEPHINE WINSLOW (MRS. GRANT G. CANNON), author; b. Kirkwood, Mo., June 20, 1910; d. Benjamin H. and Ethel (Franklin) J.; m. Grant G. Cannon, Apr. 5, 1942; children—Terence, Jane Ann, Carol Lynn. Student, Washington U., 1933, L.H.D. (hon.), 1970. Author: Now in November, 1934 (Pulitzer prize 1935), Jordanstown, 1937, Wildwood, 1947; short stories Winter Orchard, 1936; poetry Years End, 1939; novel The Dark Traveler, 1963, The Sorcerer's Son; short stories, 1965, The Inland Island, 1969; autobiog. memoir Seven Houses, 1973, Circle of Seasons, (pictures by Dennis Stock), 1974; also; writer: numerous stories in Best Short Stories; other anthologies, 1944-46 (O. Henry Meml. award 1934, 35, 42-45). Recipient Alumnae citation Washington U., 1955; Cin. Inst. Fine Arts award, 1964; Ohioana Library citation, 1964; Sarah Chapman Francis medal Ganden Club Am., 1970; Am. Acad. Arts and Letters award, 1974. Mem. Authors Guild. Home: 4907 Klatte Rd Cincinnati OH 45244

JOHNSON, JOYCE, writer, editor; b. N.Y.C., Sept. 27, 1935; d. Daniel and Rosalind (Ross) Glassman; m. James Johnson, Dec. 12, 1962 (div. 1963); m. 2d Peter Pinchbeck, Nov. 21, 1965 (div. 1971); 1 son, Daniel. Student, Barnard Coll., 1951-55. Assoc. editor William Morrow & Co, N.Y.C., 1965-67; sr. editor Dial Press, N.Y.C., 1967-70, exec. editor, 1977—; sr. editor McGraw Hill Book Co., N.Y.C., 1970-77. Author: Come and Join the Dance, 1962, Bad Connections, 1978, Minor Characters, 1983 (Nat. Book Critics 1983). John Gardner fellow Breadloaf Writers Conf., 1983. Mem. PEN. Jewish. Office: Dial Press 245 Park Ave New York NY 10167

JOHNSON, JUDITH ANNE, English language educator; b. Fargo, N.D., Aug. 31, 1934; d. Raymond Orlando and Floy Blanche (Beatty) Gregerson; m. Neil Burnett Johnson, Aug. 14, 1956 (div. May 1974); children: Catherine Elisabeth, Wendy Gillian Johnson Lange. B.A., Carleton Coll., 1956; M.A., N.D. State U., 1965; Ph.D., U. Mich., 1969. Lectr. Moorhead State Coll., (Minn.), 1965-66; teaching fellow U. Mich., Ann Arbor, 1966-70; from instr. to prof. Eastern Mich. U., Ypsilanti, 1970-81, head English dept., 1981—. Author: A Transformational Analysis of the Syntax of AElfric's Lives of Saints, 1975, Writing Strategies for ESL Students, 1983. Mem. Linguistic Soc. Am., Medieval Acad. Am., Coll. English Assn., MLA, tchrs. English to Speakers Other Langs. Democrat. Episcopalian. Office: English Dept Eastern Mich U Ypsilanti MI 48197

JOHNSON, JUDITH SALTER, international public relations consultant; b. Modesto, Calif., Aug. 17, 1937; d. John West and Agnes Mayes (Zimmerman) Salter. Student, U. Calif., Berkeley, 1955-58, Smaller Co. Mgmt. Program, Harvard Bus. Sch., 1975-77. With Calif. Farm Bur. Fedn., Berkeley, 1959-63; with Buttes Gas & Oil Co., Oakland, Calif., 1963-83, v.p. adminstrn., 1976-83; cons., v.p. Susan Davis & Assocs., Oakland, 1983—; dir. Oakland City Center Hotel Corp. Bd. dirs. Oakland Mus. Assn., Oakland Symphony, Oakland Council Econ. Devel., Coro Found.; bd. dirs. Women's Forum-West, 1978—, U. Calif. Bear Boosters; pres. Women's Forum-West, 1978-80; trustee East Oakland Youth Devel. Center Found. Mem. Com. of 200, Am. Women for Internat. Understanding, San Francisco Bay Area Internat. Hospitality Center. Republican. Club: Commonwealth. (bd. govs.). Office: Susan Davis & Assocs 1440 Broadway Suite 601 Oakland CA 94612

JOHNSON, JULIAN FRANK, chemist; b. Baxter Springs, Kans., Aug. 20, 1923; s. Julian Frank and Blanche Elizabeth (Williams) J.; m. Jean Ellen Stelzner, Dec. 21, 1943. B.A., Coll. of Wooster (Ohio), 1943; Ph.D., Brown U., 1950. Chemist Chevron Research Co., Richmond, Calif., 1950-68, supervising research asso., sr. research asso., until 1968; lectr. U. Calif. Extension, Berkeley, 1960-67; asso. prof. U. Conn., Storrs, 1968-70, prof. dept. chemistry, 1970—; asso. dir. Inst. Materials Sci., 1971—; vis. scientist IBM Labs, San Jose, Calif., 1974-75; indsl., govt. cons.; mem. adv. panel, polymer div. Nat. Bur. Standards, 1973-76; mem. council Gordon Research Confs., 1974-76. Co-editor: Ordered Fluids and Liquid Crystals, 1967, Analytical Gel Permeation Chromatography, 1968, Analytical Calorimetry, 1968, Liquid Crystals and Ordered Fluids, 1970, vol. 2, 1974, Analytical Calorimetry, vol. 2, 1970, vol. 3, 1974; Adv. bd.: Polymer Sci. and Engring, 1975—, Revs. of Macromolecular Chemistry, 1970-72; Contbr. numerous articles to profl. jours. Served to lt. USNR, 1943-46. Recipient U. Conn. Alumni Assn. award, 1976. Fellow Am. Physics Soc.; mem. Am. Chem. Soc. (Nat. award in chromatography and electrophoresis 1970), Am. Phys. Soc. (program chmn. div. high polymer physics 1976-77), N. Am. Thermal Analysis Soc. (exec. com. 1973-75, treas. 1975-76, editor Jour. 1970-77), Brit. Soc. Rheology, Soc. Rheology, Conn. Acad. Sci. and Engring., Phi Beta Kappa, Sigma Xi, Kappa Mu Epsilon. Home: 4 Hillyndale Rd Storrs CT 06268 Office: Inst Materials Sci U Conn U-136 Storrs CT 06268

JOHNSON, KEITH HUBER, educator; b. Reading, Pa., Sept. 1, 1936; s. Clyde Huber and Rachel Naomi J.; 1 dau., Natalie. A.B. in Physics, Princeton U., 1958, Ph.D., Temple U., 1965. Fellow, Quantum Theory Project U. Fla., 1965-67; asst. prof. materials sci. M.I.T., 1967-72, asso. prof., 1972-74, prof., 1974—; cons. Contbr. numerous articles to profl. jours. Recipient Internat. Acad. Quantum Molecular Sci. medal, 1973. Mem. Am. Phys. Soc. Office: Mass Inst Tech Cambridge MA 02139

JOHNSON, KEITH W., labor union official. Pres. Internat. Woodworkers Am. Office: 1622 N Lombard St Portland OR 97217§

JOHNSON, KENNETH HARVEY, veterinary pathologist; b. Hallock, Minn., Feb. 17, 1936; s. Clifford H. and Alma (Anderson) J.; Sept. 17, 1960; children—Jeffrey, Gregory, Sandra. B.S., U. Minn., 1958, D.V.M., 1960, Ph.D., 1965. Jr. asst. health officer NIH, Bethesda, Md., 1958; practice vet. medicine, Edina, Minn., 1960; USPHS-NIH non-service fellow U. Minn., St. Paul, 1960-65, asst. prof. dept. vet. pathology and parasitology, 1965-69, asso. prof., 1969-73, prof. dept. vet. biology, 1973-76, head, sect. pathology, dept. vet. biology, 1974-76; chmn. dept. vet. pathobiology Coll. Vet. Medicine, 1976-83; cons. Minn. Mining & Mfg. Co., Medtronic Inc.; Co-investigator several NIH grants, 1965—. Contbr.: chpts. to Veterinary Clinics of North America, 1971, Spontaneous Animal Models of Human Disease, 1979; articles to sci. jours. Councilman Nativity Lutheran Ch., St. Anthony Village, Minn., 1972-75. Recipient Tchr.-of-Year award, 1968-69, Norden award for disting. tchr. in vet. medicine, 1970. Mem. AAUP, Electron Microscopy Soc. Am., Am. Assn. Feline Practitioners, Minn. Vet. Med. Assn., Minn. Electron Microscopy Soc., Sigma Xi, Phi Zeta, Gamma Sigma Delta. Home: 3510 Skycroft Dr Minneapolis MN 55418 Office: Dept Vet Pathobiology Coll Vet Medicine U Minn Saint Paul MN 55108

JOHNSON, KENNETH JAMES, business executive; b. Chgo., Mar. 1, 1935; s. Herbert Gordon and Edna (Kirst) J.; m. Sally Logan, Apr. 21, 1960; children: Brian, Douglas, Laura. B.A., U. Ill., 1958; M.B.A., U. Chgo., 1970. C.P.A. Pub. acct. Touche Rose, Chgo., 1958-63; controller Kinkead Industries, Chgo., 1963-69, Nuclear Chgo., Des Plaines, Ill., 1969-71; dir. fin. reporting Motorola Inc., Schaumburg, Ill., 1971-80, v.p., corp. controller, 1980—. Mem. Fin. Exec. Inst. Home: 520 Grand Bldv Park Ridge IL 60068 Office: Motorola Inc 1303 Algonquin Rd Schaumburg IL 60196

JOHNSON, KENNETH OSCAR, oil company executive; b. Center City, Minn., Apr. 11, 1920; s. Oscar W. and Sigrid (Hollsten) J.; m. Margery Wheeler, Apr. 18, 1945; 1 son, Eric W. B.S. in Chem. Engring., U. Minn., 1942. With Exxon Corp., Houston, 1942-74, heavy fuels mgr. supply dept., 1968-72, wholesale fuels sales mgr., mktg. dept., 1972-74; pres., chief exec. officer Belcher Oil Co., Miami, Fla., 1974—; sr. v.p. Coastal Corp.; dir. S.E. 1st Nat. Bank, Petroleum Industry Found. Mem. Fla. C. of C. (bd. dirs.), Greater Miami C. of C., Bus. Devel. Action Com., S. Fla. Coordinating Council. Clubs: Bankers (Miami); Port Royal (Naples). Patentee in field. Home: 845 Admiralty Parade Naples FL 33940 Office: PO Box 525500 Miami FL 33152

JOHNSON, KENNETH OWEN, audiologist, assn. exec.; b. St. Paul, Jan. 26, 1920; s. Ernest Wilbert and Anna Mae (Little) J.; m. Dorothy Schlesselman, Sept. 5, 1949. B.A., Macalester Coll., St. Paul, 1946; M.A., U. Minn., 1948; Ph.D., Stanford, 1952. Chief, audiology and speech correction program VA, Washington, 1954-56; past. cons. acoustical audiology; dir. San Francisco Hearing and Speech Center, 1956-57; asst. clin. prof. dept. surgery Stanford Med. Sch., 1957; exec. sec. Am. Speech and Hearing Assn., 1957-80; dir. Deafness, Speech and Hearing Publs., 1959-78; sec.-treas., past pres.; chmn. Coalition Ind. Health Professions, 1970-71; cons. for speech, hearing and lang. to Head Start program, 1968-72; mem. research fellowship bd. U.S. Vocational Rehab. Adminstrn., 1964-71. Bd. dirs. Com. Handicapped People to People Program; trustee Am. Speech and Hearing Found. Fellow Am. Speech and Hearing Assn. (certified in speech pathology and audiology, editor jour.); mem. AAAS, Am. Psychol. Assn., Speech Assn. Am., Internat. Assn. Logopedics and Phoniatrics (v.p. 1977-80). Home: 18630 Polvera Dr San Diego CA 92128

JOHNSON, KENNETH PARKER, newspaper editor; b. Huntington, W.Va., Aug. 24, 1934; s. Fred Leonard and Faye Pauline (Dotson) J.; m. Margaret Louise Vandervalk, Jan. 20, 1979; children: Kenneth Parker, Elizabeth Faye, Jarrett William. E., Tenn. State U., 1952-55. Reporter, city editor Bristol (Va.) Herald-Courier, 1953-60; mng. and city editor Savannah (Ga.) Morning News, 1960-65; asst. mng. editor Washington Post, 1966-72, v.p. ops., 1972-75; exec. v.p., editor, dir. Dallas Times Herald, 1975—. Pres. Tex. Election Bur., 1979-80; adv. bd. U. Tex., Dallas, 1979-80. Mem. Tex. UPI (pres. 1980-81), Am. Soc. Newspaper Editors (freedom of info. com. 1979-80), Dallas Press Club (dir. 1980-81). Clubs: Los Colinas Country, The Lancers, City, Tower. Home: 4526 Kelsey Rd Dallas TX 75229 Office: 1101 Pacific Ave Dallas TX 75202

JOHNSON, KENNETH WILLIAM, publishing company executive; b. Seattle, Oct. 31, 1932; s. Everett Frank and Eleanor Elizabeth (Johnson) J.; m. Marie Martha Herning, Aug. 17, 1954; 1 son, Jeffrie Scott. B.A. in Bus. Adminstrn, U. Wash., 1954. Mgr. mktg. Hunt Foods, Fullerton, Calif., 1956-61; mgr. advt. Campbell Soup, Camden, N.J., 1961-66; asst. dir. civil systems TRW, Inc., Redondo Beach, Calif., 1966-67; account rep. J.W. Thompson Co., Chgo., 1967-68; brand dir. RJR Foods, N.Y.C., 1968-71; dir. mktg. Pillsbury Co., Mpls., 1971-72; exec. v.p. The Walpert Co., Cherry Hill, N.J., 1972-76; v.p. Lewis & Gilman, Inc., Phila., 1976-79; dir. devel. Pocket Testament League, Inc., Lincoln Park, N.J., 1980-83; advt. mgr. Christianity Today Inc., Carol Stream, Ill., 1983—. Served to lt. (j.g.) USNR, 1954-56. Mem. Common Cause, World Future Soc., Big Bros. Assn. Home: 28 W 032 Roosevelt Rd Winfield IL 60190 Office: Christianity Today 465 Gundersen Dr Carol Stream IL 60187

JOHNSON, KENNETT CONRAD, advertising agency executive; b. Crystal City, Mo., Feb. 5, 1927; s. Robert Winthrop and Gladys Agnes (Butler) J.; m. Norren Ellen Driscoll, July 25, 1953; children: Lydia, Burke. B.A. in Journalism, U. Mo., 1950. State editor Binghamton Press, N.Y., 1950-55; advt. supr. Southwestern Bell, St. Louis, 1955-59; v.p. Butler & Gardner Ltd., London, 1964-65; sr. v.p. Gardner Advt., N.Y.C., 1959-63, St. Louis, 1966-75; exec. v.p. Kenrick Advt., St. Louis, 1975-77; pres., chief exec. officerr Batz Hodgson Neuwoehner, St. Louis, 1977—. Campaign communications chmn. United Way, St. Louis, 1981-83, bd. dirs., St. Louis, 1982. Served as officer CIC, 1946-47; Japan. Recipient Clio award Am. TV and Radio Commls. Festival N.Y., 1971. Mem. Am. Assn. Advt. Agys. (chmn. Mo. council 1973-74), Advt. Club Greater St. Louis (gov. 1976—). Club: Bellerive Country (St. Louis). Home: 13330 Thornhill Dr Saint Louis MO 63131 Office: Batz Hodgson Neuwoehner Inc 910 N 11th St Saint Louis MO 63101

JOHNSON, LADY BIRD (CLAUDIA ALTA TAYLOR, MRS. LYNDON BAINES JOHNSON), former first lady; b. Karnack, Tex., Dec. 22, 1912; d. Thomas Jefferson and Taylor; m. Lyndon Baines Johnson (36th Pres. U.S.), Nov. 17, 1934 (dec. 1973); children: Lynda Bird Johnson Robb, Luci Baines Johnson Nugent. B.A., U. Tex., 1933, B.J., 1934; LL.D., Tex. Woman's U., 1964; Litt.D., U. Tex., 1964, Middlebury (Vt.) Coll., 1967; L.H.D., Williams Coll., 1967, U. Ala., 1975; H.H.D., Southwestern U., 1967. Mgr. husband's congressional office, Washington, 1941-42; owner Tex. Broadcasting Corp., Austin, cattle rancher, Tex., 1943-73, also cotton and timberlands, Ala. Author: A White House Diary, 1970.; Narrator: TV prodn. A Visit to Washington with Mrs. Lyndon B. Johnson, 1965. Hon. chmn. numerous civic and charitable orgns., drives; founder Com. for More Beautiful Capital, 1965; mem. Adv. Council Nat. Parks, Historic Sites, Bldgs. and Monuments; mem. nat. com. Helen Keller World Crusade for Blind; hon. chmn. Town Lake Beautification Com., Austin, LBJ Meml. Grove, Washington; active environ., nat. beautification projects; hon. trustee Washington Gallery Modern Art; regent U. Tex. System, 1971-77; trustee Nat. Geog. Soc. Recipient Togetherness award McCall's Mag., 1958, Crystal citation Fashion Group Phila., 1961, Distinguished Achievement award Washington Heart Assn., 1962, citation Nat. Assn. Colored Women's Clubs, 1962, Humanitarian award Ararat chpt. B'nai B'rith, Industry citation Am. Women in Radio and TV, 1963, Humanitarian citation Vols. Am., 1963; Conservation Service award Dept. Interior, 1974; named Woman of Year for quality of life Ladies Home Jour., 1975; Medal of Freedom Pres. Ford, 1977; numerous others. Mem. Federated Bus. and Profl. Women's Club (Bus. Woman's award 1961), AAUW (life mem. Tex. div.), Internat. Club II, Theta Sigma Phi (citation 1961), others. Episcopalian. Address: LBJ Library 2313 Red River Austin TX 78705 *

JOHNSON, LAEL FREDERIC, pharm. co. exec.; b. Yakima, Wash., Jan. 22, 1938; s. Andrew Cabot and Gudney M. (Fredrickson) J.; m. Eugenie Rae Call, June 9, 1960; children—Eva Marie, Inga Margaret. A.B., Wheaton Coll., 1960; J.D., Northwestern U., 1963. Vice pres., gen. counsel Abbott Labs. Office: Abbott Labs Abbott Park North Chicago IL 60064

JOHNSON, LARRY WILSON, association executive; b. Raleigh, N.C., Jan. 24, 1938; s. Lewis Marvin and Della (Wilson) J.; m. Sondra Elizabeth Baker, Nov. 29, 1974; children: Elizabeth, Anne, John, Robert, Patricia, Larry, Jr. A.A., Campbell Coll., 1958; A.B., U. N.C., 1960, M.Ed., 1965. Tchr. indsl. edn. pub. schs., Cary, N.C., 1960-63; asst. state supr. State Bd. Edn., Raleigh, 1963-65; founder, hon. life mem., chief exec. officer Vocat. Indsl. Clubs of Am., Falls Church, Va., 1965—; Founder, chmn. Loudoun County Pub. Nominating Fedn., 1970-71; mem. Loudoun County Adv. Com. on Vocational Edn., Leesburg, Va., 1974—. U.S.A. del. Internat. Skill Olympics Organizing

Council, Madrid, Spain, 1973—; chmn. Nat. Coordinating Council for Vocat. Student Orgn., Washington, 1972, 77; chmn. bus. edn. adv. com. Fairfax County Bd. Edn., 1972, mem. adult edn. adv. com., 1972-73; deacon Anglican Catholic Ch., 1983—. Mem. Nat. Assn. for Trade and Indsl. Edn. (founder, dir. 1973—), Am. Vocat. Assn. (mem. policy and planning com., mem. nat. adv. council trade and indsl. edn. 1974—), Am. Soc. Assn. Execs. (certified). Home: Scarlet Oak Farm Route 1 Purcellville VA 22132 Office: Box 3000 Leesburg VA 22075

JOHNSON, LAURENCE MICHAEL, lawyer; b. N.Y.C., Feb. 8, 1940; s. Edgar and Eleanor (Kraus) J.; m. Benita Kalnins, Feb. 15, 1975; children: Mark Steven, Lisa Arienne, Laura Elizabeth, Daniel Milton. A.B. cum laude, Harvard U., 1961, LL.B., Columbia U., 1964. Bar: Mass. 1964. Research asst. Columbia U., 1962-64; law clk. Supreme Jud. Ct. Mass., 1964-65; asso. to partner firm Nutter, McClennen & Fish, Boston, 1965-77; partner firm Newman & Meserve, Boston, 1977-78, Palmer & Dodge, 1978-83; sole practice law, Boston, 1983—; teaching team Harvard Trial Adv. Workshop, 1976—; mem. trial adv. faculty Mass. Continuing Legal Edn. of New Eng. Law Inst., 1979—; arbitrator Am. Arbitration Assn., 1976—. Group chmn. larger law firms United Way of Mass. Bay, 1976; mem. Sudbury Human Rights Council, 1964-68, pres., 1965-66; mem. steering com. Lawyers Com. for Civil Rights under Law, Boston Bar Assn., 1976—. Patriot award, 1976. Fellow Am. Coll. Trial Lawyers; mem. Boston Bar Assn., Am. Bar Assn., Am. Law Inst. Democrat. Club: Union (Boston). Home: 55 Lee St Brookline MA 02146 Office: 77 N Washington St Boston MA 02114 *The trial lawyer's art requires a combination of knowledge, both specialized and general, experience (and the judgment that comes with it), energy, determination, uncompromising self-appraisal and receptivity to the ideas of others. Its object is effective communication and to achieve it, it draws upon not only the law, but every area of human interest. It provides boundless opportunities for creative achievement, but they are realized only in proportion to the effort actually expended.*

JOHNSON, LAURENCE ROBERT, biotechnology company executive, venture capitalist; b. Colon, Panama, Dec. 6, 1941; s. Bernard Carl and Roberta (Sollisch) J.; m. Julia Wheaton Keyes, Apr. 6, 1966; children: Alexander Keyes, Matthew Taylor. S.B. in Physics, MIT, 1963; M.B.A. with distinction, Harvard U., 1965. Asso. buyer Burdines div. Federated Dept. Stores, Miami, Fla., 1965-66; asst. v.p. Kidder & Peabody & Co., N.Y.C., 1966-69; with DLJ Capital Corp., N.Y.C., 1969-81, exec. v.p., 1975-78, pres., chief exec. officer, 1978-81; sr. partner Sprout Capital Group, N.Y.C., 1969-82; founder, chmn. bd., chief exec. officer Angenics, Inc., 1981—; founding dir. Geosource, Inc.; dir. Index Systems Inc., Baldt Inc. Mem. Nat. Venture Capital Assn. (past dir.), Nat. Assn. Small Bus. Investment Cos. (past bd. govs.). Republican. Club: Country (Brookline, Mass.). Home: 188 Heath St Chestnut Hill MA 02167 Office: 100 Inman St Cambridge MA 02139

JOHNSON, LEANDER FLOYD, plant pathologist; b. Lecompte, La., Aug. 3, 1926; s. Francis Menard and Margarete Mae (Hearn) J.; m. Jean Perry Cawood, May 24, 1978; children: Darryl Leander, James Menard. B.S., U. Southwestern La., 1948; M.S., La. State U., 1951, Ph.D., 1953. Tchr. sci. Urania (La.) High Sch., 1948-49; research asst. dept. botany La. State U., Baton Rouge, 1949-53; mem. faculty U. Tenn., Knoxville, 1953—, prof. plant pathology, 1970—. Author numerous works in field.; Editor: Phytopathology, 1961-64. Served with USNR, 1944-45. Mem. Am. Phytopath. Soc., Tenn. Rose Soc. (pres. 1971), Am. Rose Soc., Sigma Xi, Gamma Sigma Delta. Roman Catholic. Club: Knoxville Sci. (pres. 1983-84). Home: 8617 Fox-Lonas Rd Knoxville TN 37923 Office: Dept Entomology and Plant Pathology U of Tenn Knoxville TN 37916

JOHNSON, LEE HARNIE, emeritus dean, educator; b. Houston, Jan. 4, 1909; s. Lee Harnie and Isabelle (Smart) J.; m. Eulalie Woolverton McKay, Oct. 19, 1940 (dec.); children: Lee McKay, William Irving; m. Kate Chamness O'Meallie, Aug. 21, 1976. B.A., Rice Inst., 1930, M.A., 1931; M.S., Harvard, 1932, Sc.D., 1935. Fellow in math. Rice Inst., 1930-31; asst. in civil engring. Harvard, 1932-35; asst. engring. aide U.S. Waterways Expt. Sta., Vicksburg, Miss., 1935-36; asst. to engr. in charge design U.S. Engr. Office, Mobile, Ala., 1936-37; dean engring. and prof. civil engring. U. Miss., 1937-50, dir. def., war tng. program, 1941-45; dean engring., prof. civil engring. Tulane U., 1950-72, emeritus dean, 1972—, W.R. Irby prof. engring., 1972-79; tchr. math Newman High Sch., 1979—. Author: The Slide Rule, 1947, Nomography and Empirical Equations, 1952, Engineering: Principles and Problems, 1960; Contbr. to engring. jours. Graham Baker and Hohenthal scholar Rice Inst.; Hilton scholar Harvard U.; Lee H. Johnson award for excellence in teaching established in his honor Tulane U. Mem. ASCE, Am. Soc. Engring. Edn., La. Engring. Soc., Phi Beta Kappa, Kappa Delta Phi, Tau Beta Pi, Chi Epsilon, Gamma Alpha, Omicron Delta Kappa. Democrat. Presbyn. Clubs: New Orleans Country, Boston (New Orleans); City. Home: 211 Fairway Dr New Orleans LA 70124

JOHNSON, LELAND PARRISH, biologist, emeritus educator; b. Ponemah, Ill., Nov. 14, 1910; s. Carl W. and Dora M. (Parrish) J.; m. Marion E. Schiess, Aug. 25, 1940 (dec. 1976); children: Christine Ann, Don Alan; m. Carolyn Jones Eades, July 29, 1979. B.S., Monmouth Coll., 1932; M.S., State U. Iowa, 1937, Ph.D., 1942; Ford faculty fellow, Harvard U., 1955-56. Sci. tchr. Reynolds (Ill.) High Sch., 1933-36; mem. faculty Drake U., 1937—, prof. biology, 1947-81, prof. emeritus, 1981—, chmn. dept., 1956, coordinator sci. div., 1958, dean, 1971-76, dir. cancer research, 1958—; dir. insts. tchr. research participation programs NSF, 1959—; cons. gen. edn. Iowa League Nursing, 1958—; ednl. adv. bd. Iowa Meth. Hosp., 1952—; chmn. Iowa Bd. Basic Sci. Examiners, 1957—. Contbr. to lab. manuals, monographs, articles. Recipient Distinguished Alumni award Monmouth Coll., 1957. Mem. NEA, AAAS, Am. Micros. Soc., N. Y. Acad. Sci., Iowa Acad. Sci. (pres. 1965-66), Soc. Protozoologists, Am. Inst. Biol. Scis., Nat. Assn. Research Sci. Teaching, Nat. Assn. Biology Tchrs., Assn. Midwest Biology Tchrs. (pres. 1958), Soc. History Sci., Phi Beta Kappa, Sigma Xi. Home: 6340 Harwood Ct Des Moines IA 50312

JOHNSON, LENHARD H., food distribution company executive. Chmn. Associated Grocers Colo., Inc. Office: 5151 Bannock St Denver CO 80217§

JOHNSON, LESTER ELWIN, hospital administrator; b. Winthrop, Minn., Apr. 2, 1923; s. Louis Magnus and Blenda (Nelson) J.; m. Margaret Lenore Foley, Oct. 7, 1945; children: Stephen Willard, Blenda Alice J. Ingalls, Katherine Sue J. Landers, Peter Eric. A.B. in Econs., Ill. Coll., 1948; M.Hosp. Adminstrn., Washington U., St. Louis, 1954. Br. office cashier Swift and Co., Jacksonville, Ill., 1948-49; prodn. cost accountant Eli Bridge Co., Jacksonville, 1949-51; asst. adminstrn. Bapt. Hosp., Alexandria, La., 1954-56; asst. supt. Willmar (Minn.) State Hosp., 1956-61, adminstr., 1961—; Pres. Dist. E Minn. Hosp. Council, 1972-73; mem. Minn. Dept. Health Hosp. Adminstr. Registration Adv. Bd., 1971-79; chmn. hosp. adminstr. registration council Dept. Health, 1975-79. Treas. Kandiyohi County Hist. Soc., 1966-68, bd. dirs., 1971—. Served with AUS, World War II. Decorated Purple Heart, Bronze Star medal. Fellow Am. Coll. Hosp. Adminstrs.; mem. Am. Hosp. Assn., Internat. Hosp. Fedn., Wilmar C. of C. (dir. 1975—, sec. 1977). Presbyterian (deacon, elder). Clubs: Kiwanian (dir. 1962-63, pres. Willmar 1968. Home: Rt 4 Box 736 Pleasant Acres Willmar MN 56201 Office:: Box 1128 Willmar MN 56201 *Being a handicapped person, I have been most grateful for the quality of rehabilitation provided by our military. Following that I have looked positively at things, respected others in their momentary adversity, and have worked with the idea of changing things by "reasonable adjustment" rather than by dramatic upheaval.*

JOHNSON, LESTER FREDRICK, painter; b. Mpls., Jan. 27, 1919; s. Edwin August and Helma Marie (Holmes) J.; m. Josephine Valenti, Feb. 12, 1949; children: Leslie Maria, Anthony Edwin. Student, Mpls. Art Inst., 1939-41, St. Paul Art Sch., 1939-41, Art Inst. Chgo., 1943. Prof. painting Yale U., 1964—, dir. studies, 1968—; Mem. Milford (Conn.) Fine Arts Council, 1972-73; mem. art adv. com. Housatonic Community Coll., Stratford, Conn., 1969—. One-man shows, Zabriskei Gallery, N.Y.C., Martha Jackson Gallery, N.Y.C., Donald Morris, Detroit, Mpls. Art Inst., Dayton Art Inst., Fort Worth Art Inst., Yale Univ. Mus., Gimpel Fils Gallery, London, Gimpel Hanover Gallery, Zurich, Switzerland; exhibited in numerous group shows; represented in permanent collections, Albright Knox Mus., Dayton Art Inst., Met. Mus. Art, N.Y.C., Mus. Modern Art, New Sch. for Social Research, Phoenix Art Mus., U. Nebr., Walker Art Mus. Recipient fellowship Trumbull Coll., 1966—; Creative Arts award Brandeis U., 1978; Guggenheim fellow, 1973. Home: 191 Milbank Ave Greenwich CT 06830 Office: Yale U Sch Art York and Chapel Sts New Haven CT 06520

JOHNSON, LINCOLN F., JR., educator, art and film historian, critic; b. Lynn, Mass., May 21, 1920; s. Lincoln F. and Theresa (McGowan) J.; m. Rodica H. Isaila, Aug. 10, 1974. A.B., Bowdoin Coll., 1942; M.A., Harvard U., 1947, Ph.D., 1956. Vis. lectr. Wellesley Coll., 1949-50; mem. faculty Goucher Coll., 1950—, chmn. dept. fine arts, 1959-69, 78—, prof. art, 1963—; art critic Balt. Sun, 1971-78; mem. accessions com. Balt. Mus. Art, 1963-69; mem. Balt. Mcpl. Arts. Commn., 1960-72, 78—; mem. visual arts panel Md. Arts Council, 1969-80, 82—; adv. panel for sculpture Balt. Office Housing and Community Devel., 1976—. Author: Film Space, Time, Light and Sound, 1974. Trustee Md. Inst. Coll. Art, 1957-78, Balt. Film Forum, 1976—; mem. adv. com. Mass Transit Adminstrn., 1978—. Served with USAAF, 1942-46. Recipient Merit award Artists Equity Assn., 1976; Longfellow fellow, 1942; Bacon fellow, 1948-49; Fulbright fellow, 1962; Ford Found. fellow, 1970-71; Nietsche grantee, 1976. Mem. Coll. Art Assn., AAUP, Univ. Film Assn., Internat. Assn. Art Critics, Phi Beta Kappa. Home: 1611 Templeton Rd Towson MD 21204 Office: Goucher Coll Towson MD 21204

JOHNSON, LLOYD PETER, banker; b. Mpls., May 1, 1930; s. Lloyd Percy and Edna (Schlampp) J.; m. Rosalind Gesner, July 3, 1954; children—Marcia, Russell, Paul. B.A., Carleton Coll., Northfield, Minn., 1952; M.B.A., Stanford U., 1954. With Security Trust & Savs. Bank, San Diego, 1954-57; with Security Pacific Nat. Bank, Los Angeles, 1957—, now vice chmn. charge corp. banking, fiduciary services, internat. banking group; mem. faculty Pacific Coast Banking Sch., 1969-72, chmn., 1979-80. Trustee Harvey Mudd Coll., Carleton Coll.; regent emeritus U. San Francisco; adv. bd. U. Wash. Grad. Sch. Bus. Mem. Assn. Res. City Bankers, Calif. Bankers Assn. (pres. 1977—). Home: 206 Inverness Dr Flintridge CA 91011 Office: 333 S Hope St Los Angeles CA 90071

JOHNSON, LOWELL FERRIS, drug and food manufacturer; b. Butler, N.J., Sept. 21, 1912; s. George F. and Eliza (James) J.; m. Josephine Herche, July 7, 1939 (dec. Jan. 1964); children: Don W., Joy C. Johnson; m. Beverly Herman, Sept. 25, 1965 (dec. June 1979). B.S., N.J. State U., 1934; Ed.M., Rutgers U., 1938; postgrad., N.Y. U; LL.D., Sch. of Ozarks, 1977. Mem. faculty Rutgers U., 1941-45; with Am. Home Products Corp., N.Y.C., 1945—, mem. ops. com., 1957—, v.p. indsl. relations, 1959-61, v.p., 1961-77, cons., 1977—; chmn. bd. AHPC Coordinated Bargaining Trust; v.p., dir. Citizen's Realty Co.; exec. com., trust com., dir. United Nat. Bank Central Jersey; dir. Mid Jersey Savs. & Loan Assn., Bankers Nat. Life Ins. Co.; pres., dir. LOR, Inc.; former spl. lectr. Rutgers U., Columbia, N.Y. U., George Washington U., U. Balt. Mem. mgmt. team U.S. Dept. State Mission to Guatemala, 1961; mem. Mayor's Labor-Mgmt. Adv. Com., N.Y.C.; mem. adv. com. Social Welfare Center, Columbia U.; also affiliated bus. fellow Grad. Sch. Bus.; chmn. bd. govs. Mulhlenberg Hosp.; bd. dirs. Internat. Council for Operation Enterprise; chmn. bd., chmn. exec. com., mem. internat. com., nat. fund raising chmn. Am. Heart Assn.; trustee, vice chmn. bd. N.J. State Coll.; bd. dirs. Nat. Health Council; v.p., mem. exec. com. U.S.O.; councilman North Plainfield (N.J.) City Council; vice chmn. Gantt Gold Medal Award Bd. Recipient Boss-of-the-Year award N.Y. chpt. Nat. Secs. Assn., 1959; Distinguished Alumnus award N.J. State Coll.; Gold Heart award Am. Heart Assn.; Distinguished Service award N.J. Heart Assn.; certificate appreciation Council for Internat. Progress in Mgmt., U.S.A.).; Lowell F. Johnson award Muhlenberg Hosp. Mem. N.J. C. of C. (chmn. mgmt.-employee relations com.), Commerce and Industry Assn. (chmn. state and local affairs com, mem. council), U.S. C. of C., Council State Chambers Commerce U.S., Soc. Advancement Mgmt., Am. Arbitration Assn. (nat. labor panel), Am. Mgmt. Assn. (life; v.p., trustee, exec. com., chmn. human resources council, Disting. Service award 1979, Man of Yr. award 1980, pres.'s council 1979—), NAM (mem. labor relations policy com.), Nat Indsl. Conf. Bd., N.Y. Indsl. Relations Assn. (past pres.), Internat. Platform Assn., Phi Delta Kappa. Clubs: Plainfield Country, Vanderbilt Athletic, T.D. of N.Y. Home and Office: 40 Mali Dr North Plainfield NJ 07062

JOHNSON, M. ALANSON, paper company executive; b. Williamsport, Pa., June 1, 1933; s. Miller A. and Naomi (Plitt) J.; m. Delores Secrist, June 18, 1955; children: M. Alanson III, Christopher R., Keith F. B.A., Haverford Coll., 1955. With Hamilton Watch Co., Lancaster, Pa., 1958-67, asst. controller budgets, Lancaster, 1965-67; comptoller P.H. Glatfelter Co., Spring Grove, Pa., 1967-68, v.p. fin., Spring Grove, 1968-80, exec. v.p., treas. chief fin. officer, 1980—. Pres. East Lampeter P.T.O., Lancaster, Pa., 1965, Eastern York County Boys Club Football, York, Pa., 1978; mem. bd. Jr. Achievement, York, Pa., 1975-79; chmn. bd. York Hosp., 1982—. Served to lt. (j.g.) USNR, 1955-58; PTO. Republican. Presbyterian. Office: P H Glatfelter Co 228 S Main St Spring Grove PA 17403

JOHNSON, MALCOLM CLINTON, JR., publishing consultant; b. Jersey City, Sept. 4, 1925; s. Malcolm Clinton and Edna Menard (Freeman) J.; m. Jean Anne Guinane, Dec. 28, 1963 (div. 1974); children: Clinton, Brian. Student, Harvard U., 1943-44; A.B., Dartmouth Coll., 1946; M.S., U. Ill., 1947. Editor, McGraw Hill Book Co., N.Y.C., 1949-60, sr. editor, 1960-62, editor in chief engring. and sci., 1962-65; editor, pub. coll. dept. Time Life Books, N.Y.C., 1965-67; v.p. publ. W.A. Benjamin Inc., N.Y.C., 1967-70; v.p., editorial dir. book div. R.R. Bowker, N.Y.C., 1970-73; dir. NYU Press, N.Y.C., 1973-80; pres. Malcolm Johnson Assos. (Publ. Cons.), N.Y.C., 1980—. Served to lt. (j.g.) USNR, 1943-45. Mem. Coll. Publs. Group (chmn. 1968-69), N.Y. Acad. Scis., Motovun Group European Publs., Chi Phi. Clubs: Harvard, Yale, Saltaire Yacht, N.Y. U. (N.Y.C.); Potlach (Eluthera, B.W.I.); Publishers Lunch (sec.-treas. 1978-79).

JOHNSON, MARGARET KATHLEEN, educator; b. Baylor County, Tex., Oct. 30, 1920; d. George W. and Julie Rivers (Turner) Higgins; m. Herman Clyde Johnson, Jr., July 27, 1949 (dec.); 1 dau., Carolyn Kay. B.S., Hardin-Simmons U., 1940; M.Bus. Edn., North Tex. State U., 1957, Ed.D., 1962. Clk. Farmers Nat. Bank, Seymour, Tex., 1940-41; adminstrv. sec. U.S. Navy, Corpus Christi, Tex., 1941-46; adminstrv. asst. Hdqrs. 8th Army, Yokohama, Japan, 1946-49; instr. Coll. Bus. Adminstrn., U. Ark., 1957-60; teaching fellow Sch. Bus. Adminstrn., North Tex. State U., 1960-62, instr., 1962-63; asst. prof. bus., tchr. edn. and secondary edn. Tchrs. Coll., U. Nebr., Lincoln, 1963-65, asso. prof., 1966-70, prof., 1970—; guest lectr. U. N.Mex., 1967, Curriculum Devel. in Bus. Edn., N.S. Dept. Edn., 1969, North Tex. State U., 1970, East Tex. State U., 1972; in Policies Commn. for Bus. and Econ. Edn., 1979—. Author: Standardized Production Typewriting Tests series, 1964-65, National Structure for Research in Vocational Education, 1966; co-author: Introduction to Word Processing, 1980, Introduction to Business Communication, 1981; editor: Nat. Bus. Edn. Assn. Yearbook, 1980. Recipient United Bus. Edn. Assn. award as outstanding grad. student in bus. edn. North Tex. State U., 1957, award for outstanding service Nebr. Future Bus. Leaders Am., 1968; Mountain-Plains Bus. Edn. Leadership award, 1977; merit award Nebr. Bus. Assn., 1979. Mem. Nat. Bus. Edn. Assn. (exec. bd. 1975, 76-78), Mountain-Plains Bus. Edn. Assn. (exec. sec. 1970-73, pres. 1975), Nebr. Bus. Edn. Assn. (pres. 1966-67), Nebr. Council on Occupational Tchr. Edn., Delta Pi Epsilon. Office: 303 Tchrs Coll U Nebr Lincoln NE 68588

JOHNSON, MARIE-LOUISE TULLY, physician; b. N.Y.C., July 26, 1927; d. James Henry and Mary Frances (Dobbins) Tully; m. Kenneth Gerald Johnson, June 10, 1950. A.B., Manhattanville Coll., 1948; Ph.D., Yale U., 1954; M.D., 1956. Diplomate: Am. Bd. Dermatology. Intern Yale-New Haven Med. Center, 1956-57, resident, 1957-60; chief dermatology Atomic Bomb Casualty Commn., Hiroshima, Japan, 1964-67; asso. prof. dermatology N.Y. U. Sch. Medicine, 1967-70, prof., 1974-80; chief dermatology Bellevue Med. Center, N.Y.C., 1974-80; asso. prof. medicine (dermatology) Dartmouth Med. Sch., 1970-74; asst. prof. medicine (dermatology) Yale U. Sch. Medicine, 1961-64, clin. prof. dermatology, 1980—; dir. med. edn., v.p. med. affairs Benedictine Hosp., Kingston, N.Y., 1980—; cons. HHS Nat. Center for Health Stats., 1969—. Contbg. author: Textbook of Medicine, 15th edit, 1979, Dermatology in General Medicine, 1979; composer: Mass for Organ and Choir, 1962. Recipient Dasey award Yale U. Sch. Medicine, 1956; Disting. Alumni award Manhattanville Coll., 1977. Mem. Inst. of Medicine of Nat. Acad. Scis., Am. Acad. Dermatology (dir. 1976-80), Am. Dermatol. Assn., N.Y. Acad. Medicine, New Eng. Dermatology Assn., Soc. Investigative Dermatology, Soc. for Tropical Dermatology, Can. Dermatol. Assn., Med. Soc. N.Y. State, AMA, Alpha Omega Alpha. Roman Catholic. Club: Yale (N.Y.C.). Home: Strawberry Bank High Falls NY 12440 Office: Benedictine Hosp Kingston NY 12401

JOHNSON, MARION PHILLIP, hospital administrator; b. Ft. Valley, Ga., Oct. 12, 1931; s. Robert Wesley and Hazel (Causey) J.; m. Rebecca Clement, Oct. 3, 1952; children: Donald, Steven, Marian. B.S. in Edn., U. Ga., 1953; M.H.A., Baylor U., 1965. Commd. 2d lt. U.S. Army, 1953, advanced through grades to col., 1974; exec. officer 45th Surg. Hosp., Vietnam, 1966-67, Dunham Army Hosp., Carlisle Barracks, Pa., 1967-71; insp. gen. Hdqrs. Dept. Army, Washington, 1971-73, Army Health Services Command, Ft. Sam Houston, Tex., 1973-77; exec. officer Eisenhower Army Med. Ctr., Ft. Gordon, Ga., 1977-79, Brooke Army Med. Ctr., Ft. Sam Houston, 1979-83; ret., 1983; chmn. acad. adv. com. Army-Baylor Program in Health Care Adminstrn., San Antonio, 1979-83; mem. adv. com. Trinity U., San Antonio, 1979-83; adminstr. McKenna Meml. Hosp., New Braunfels, Tex., 1983—. Pres. adv. com. Ft. Sam Houston Golf Course, 1981. Decorated Bronze Star, Meritorious Service medal, Legion of Merit. Fellow Am. Coll. Hosp. Adminsts. (adviser to regent); mem. Army Med. Dept. Museum Found. Home: 19 Mission Dr New Braunfels TX 78130 Office: McKenna Meml Hosp New Braunfels TX 78130

JOHNSON, MARLENE, lieutenant governor state of Minnesota; b. Braham, Minn., Jan. 11, 1946; d. Beauford and Helen (Nelson) J. B.A., Macalester U., 1968. Lt. gov. State of Minn., St. Paul, 1983—; bd. dirs. Minn. Outward Bound Sch., Mpls., Spring Hill Conf. Ctr. Chmn. minn. Women's Polit. Caucus, 1973-76; recipient Outstanding Achievement award, St. Paul YWCA, 1980, Disting. Citizen citation, Macalester Coll., 1982; named World Press Inst., dir. Home: 24 S St Albans Pl Saint Paul MN 55105 Office: Office of Lt Gov Room 122 State Capitol Saint Paul MN 55155

JOHNSON, MARQUES KEVIN, professional basketball player; b. Nachitoches, La., Feb. 8, 1956; s. Jeff David and Baasha Violet (Kessee) J.; 1 son, Kristaan Iman. B.A., UCLA, 1977. Mem. UCLA Varsity Basketball Team, 1973-77, Milw. Bucks, Nat. Basketball Assn., 1977—. Producer, dir., editor: film Livin' for the Weekend, 1979; producer: TV film On the Road with the Milwaukee Bucks, 1984. Recipient Bob Hope Youth award, 1979, John W. Wooden sports award, 1977, Inspiration to Youth award, 1983; named Coll. Player of Yr., 1977; named to Nat. Basketball Assn. All-Star Team, 1979, 80, 81, 83, Nat. Basketball Assn. All-Pro 1st Team, 1979. Democrat. Baptist. Office: Milw Bucks 901 N Fourth St Milwaukee WI 53203

JOHNSON, MARTIN ALLEN, publisher; b. Bklyn., Aug. 20, 1931; s. Ellis A. and Estelle (Rudnick) J.; m. Suzanne Cornbleet, Dec. 12, 1964 (div. Feb. 1979); 1 dau., Sarah.; m. Diane Krull, Aug. 19, 1981. A.B., Bard Coll., 1954. Asso. editor Am. Printer and Lithographer mag., N.Y.C., 1956-57, mng. editor, 1957-58, editor, 1958; mng. editor Printing Impressions mag., Phila., also; Delaware Valley Printing Impressions, 1958-61; pub. PTM mag., Chgo., 1961-68; v.p. Ednl. Screen and Audio Visual Guide, Chgo., 1962-68; pres. Trade Periodical Co., Chgo., 1968—, Pub. Dynamics, Inc., Stamford, Conn., 1968—, U.S. Indsl. Publs., Inc., Stamford, 1971—, U.S. Graphics Corp., 1974—, Landmark Communications Corp., Landmark Type, Inc., Stamford. Contbr. articles to profl. jours. Served with AUS, 1954-56. Mem. Typophiles (N.Y.C.), Ams. for Music Library in Israel, Am. Soc. Interior Designers. Clubs: Chgo. Press, Execs. (Chgo.); Landmark (Stamford). Home: 1 Strawberry Hill Ct Stamford CT 06902 Office: 2 Selleck St Stamford CT 06902

JOHNSON, MARTIN EARL, publishing corporation financial executive; b. Argonia, Kans., Mar. 12, 1929; s. Alfred W. and Maggie (Martin) J.; m. Rozella Marie Stephens, Sept. 4, 1949; children: Stephen, Kay L. Johnson Hossner, Jan M. Johnson Karr. B.S. in Bus. Adminstrn., Wichita State U., 1951. C.P.A., Kans. Acct. Excel Packing Co., Wichita, Kans., 1951; staff acct. Arthur Young & Co., Wichita, 1951-54; auditor Wichita Eagle & Beacon Pub. Co., Inc., 1954-61, controller, 1961-83, dir. fin., 1983—. Mem. Nat. Assn. Accts. (pres. Wichita 1969-70), Inst. Newspaper Controllers and Fin. Officers. Republican. Presbyterian. Home: 1730 N Clarence Wichita KS 67203 Office: Wichita Eagle & Beacon Pub Co Inc 825 E Douglas Wichita KS 67201

JOHNSON, MARVIN DONALD, university official; b. Willcox, Ariz., Nov. 2, 1928; s. Wellington Lott and Hazel Valentine (Bendure) J.; m. Stella C. Pacheco, Feb. 14, 1953; children: Lynn Anne, Marshall Donald, Karen Marie. B.S., U. Ariz., 1950, M.S., 1957; Ed.D. (hon.), Lincoln Coll., 1970. Asst. grad. mgr. U. Ariz., 1950-52, dir. student union, 1952-58, dir. alumni assn., 1958-63, v.p. univ relations, 1963-77; adminstrv. v.p. student affairs alumni relations and devel. U. N.Mex., Albuquerque, 1977—; dir. Radio Fiesta, Ariz. Pres., Palo Verde

Mental Health Assn., Ariz., 1967-69. Editor: Successful Governmental Relations, 1981. Chmn. Tucson Crime Commn., Ariz., 1969-71; pres. Catalina council Boy Scouts Am., 1966, bd. dirs. Gt. S.W. council, 1983—; bd. dirs. Fund for Tucson, 1960-65, Maxwell Mus., 1977—, Sta. KNME-TV, 1977—, N.Mex. div. Am. Cancer Soc., 1978—, United Way Albuquerque, 1978-79, 83—; mem. White House Conf. on Youth, 1971, Gov's. Film Commn., Ariz., 1972-77. Recipient Outstanding Alumni award Future Farmers Am., Ariz., 1964, Ariz. 4-H, 1970; Silver Antelope award Boy Scouts Am., 1975; Super P.R. award Am. Cancer Soc. N.Mex., 1979; N.Mex. Disting. Pub. Service award, 1982. Mem. Inst. Ednl. Mgmt. (trustee 1972-76), Nat. Assn. State Univs. and Land Grant Colls. (mem. exec. com. 1973-77), Council Advancement and Support Edn. (trustee 1976—, nat. chmn. 1980-81), Newcomen Soc. N. Am., Western Athletic Conf. (chmn. council 1978-79), Ariz. Cattle Growers Assn., Lamplighters Ednl. Round Table, Alpha Zeta, Kappa Kappa Psi, Gamma Sigma Delta, Alpha Kappa Psi, Phi Eta Sigma, Sigma Chi (grand trustee 1973—). Democrat. Methodist. Club: Albuquerque Petroleum. Home: 1616 Sigma Chi Rd NE Albuquerque NM 87106 Office: Room 152 Scholes Hall U NM Albuquerque NM 87131

JOHNSON, MARVIN MELROSE, industrial engineer; b. Neligh, Nebr., Apr. 21, 1925; s. Harold Nighram and Melissa (Bare) J.; m. Anne Stuart Campbell, Nov. 10, 1951; children: Douglas Blake, Harold James, Phyllis Anne, Nighram Marvin, Melissa Joan. B.S., Purdue U., 1949; postgrad., Ill. Inst. Tech., 1953; M.S. in Indsl. Engring, U. Iowa, 1966, Ph.D., 1968. Registered profl. engr., Iowa, Mo., Nebr. Quality control supr., indsl. engr. Houdaille Hershey, Chgo., 1949-52; indsl. engr. Bell & Howell, Chgo., 1952-54; with Bendix Aviation Corp., Davenport, Iowa, 1954-64, successively chief indsl. engr., staff asst., supr. procedures and systems, 1954-63, reliability engr., 1963-64, cons., 1964—; lectr. indsl. engring. State U. Iowa, 1963-64; instr. indsl. engring. U. Iowa, 1965-66; asso. prof. U. Nebr., 1968-73, prof., 1973—; AID adv., mgmt. engring. and food processing Kabul (Afghanistan) U., 1975-76; vis. prof. indsl. engring. U. P.R., Mayaguez, 1982-83; NSF trainee U. Iowa, 1964-67. Served with AUS, 1943-46; ETO. Fellow Am. Inst. Indsl. Engrs.; Mem. Am. Soc. Engring. Educators, Am. Statis. Assn., ASME, Ops. Research Soc. Am., Inst. Mgmt. Sci., Sigma Xi, Tau Beta Pi, Pi Tau Sigma, Alpha Pi Mu. Presbyterian. Home: 2507 Ammon Ave Lincoln NE 68507 Office: 175 Nebraska Hall U Nebr Lincoln NE 68588 *Education is the foundation of democracy.*

JOHNSON, MARVIN RICHARD ALOIS, architect; b. Humphrey, Nebr., Aug. 13, 1916; s. Otto Henry and Reenste (Berends) J. A.B., U. Nebr., 1943, B.A. in Architecture, 1943; M.Architecture, Harvard U., 1948. Designer, draftsman firm Clark & Enersen, Lincoln, Nebr., 1946-47, 48-50; cons. architect div. sch. planning N.C. Dept. Public Instrn., Raleigh, 1950-80; architect, cons. ednl. facilities, 1981—; cons. HEW, Washington, 1960. Contbr. articles to profl. jours. Served with USNR, 1943-46. Fellow AIA (recipient Distinguished Service citation N.C. chpt. 1960, v.p. N.C. chpt. 1977-78, pres.-elect 1979, pres. 1980); mem. Council Ednl. Facility Planners, Am. Assn. School Adminstrs., N.C. Arts Soc., Phi Beta Kappa. Democrat. Lutheran. Home: L5 Raleigh Apts 1020 W Peace St Raleigh NC 27605

JOHNSON, MILTON AXEL, lawyer; b. Marinette, Wis., July 10, 1906; s. Charles Alfred and Hilma (Lindlof) J.; m. Clara Bauer, Sept. 6, 1934; 1 dau., Linda C. (Mrs. James F. Hayden). LL.B., Ind. U., 1930. Bar: Ind. bar 1930. Since practiced in, South Bend; mem. firms Hammerschmidt & Johnson, South Bend, 1935-56, Jones, Obenchain, Johnson, Ford, Pankow & Lewis, 1957—; Dir. H.G. Christman Constrn. Co., Inc. City chmn. Republican party, 1942. Mem. ABA, Ind. Bar Assn. (bd. govs. 1949-51), St. Joseph County Bar Assn. (pres. 1944), Lambda Chi Alpha, Phi Delta Phi. Clubs: Kiwanian, Elk., Summit. Home: 605 W North Shore Dr South Bend IN 46617 Office: 1800 Am Nat Bank Bldg South Bend IN 44601

JOHNSON, NED (EDWARD CHRISTOPHER JOHNSON), pub. co. exec.; b. Lexington, Mass., Dec. 6, 1926; s. Edward J. and Mary A. (MacInnes) J.; m. Irma Di Lonardo, Mar. 13, 1946; children—Dana Elizabeth, Blair Christopher. B.S., Boston U., 1948. Vice pres. Moore Pub. Co., N.Y.C., 1948-57; sr. v.p. Cahners Pub. Co., Boston, 1957—; pub. Design News mag., 1977—; founder, chmn. Cahners Advt. Research Reports, 1976—. Served with USNR, 1944-46. Mem. Am. Bus. Publs., Bus. and Profl. Advt. Assn. Democrat. Clubs: Boston Yacht (Marblehead, Mass.); Univ. (Boston); Jackson (N.H.); Ski and Tennis. Home: 15 Waldron Ct Marblehead MA 01945 also Valley Cross Rd Jackson NH 03846 Office: Cahners Pub Co 221 Columbus Ave Boston MA 02116 *I thoroughly believe in the principle that each of us can accomplish anything we wish to accomplish, once the desire for accomplishment is firmly established and recognized within. I also believe that each of us has a responsibility to create an atmosphere among our fellow workers which will make it possible for each individual to accomplish the level of excellence within himself.*

JOHNSON, NICHOLAS, lecturer, writer; b. Iowa City, Sept. 23, 1934; s. Wendell A.L. and Edna (Bockwoldt) J.; m. Karen Mary Chapman, 1952 (div. 1972); children: Julie, Sherman, Gregory. B.A., U. Tex., 1956, LL.B., 1958; L.H.D., Windham Coll., 1971. Bar: Tex. 1958, D.C. 1963, U.S. Supreme Ct. 1963, Iowa 1974. Law clk. to judge John R. Brown, U.S. 5th Circuit Ct. Appeals, 1958-59; law clk. to U.S. Supreme Ct. Justice Hugo L. Black, 1959-60; acting asso. prof. law U. Calif. at Berkeley, 1960-63; asso. firm Covington & Burling, Washington, 1963-64; adminstr. Maritime Adminstrn., U.S. Dept. Commerce, 1964-66; commr. FCC, 1966-73; adj. prof. law Georgetown U., 1971-73; Poynter fellow Yale U., 1971; vis. prof. U. Ill., Champaign-Urbana, 1976, U. Okla., Norman, 1978, Ill. State U., Normal, 1979, U. Wis., Madison, 1980, Newhouse Sch., Syracuse U., 1980, dept. communications and Coll. Law, U. Iowa, 1981—; chairperson, dir. Nat. Citizens Communications Lobby, 1975—, Nat. Citizens Com. for Broadcasting, 1974-78; pub. access, 1975-77; commentator Nat. Pub. Radio, 1975-77, 83—, Sta. WRC-AM, Washington, 1977, Sta. WSUI, Iowa City, 1982—; presdl. advisor White House Conf. on Libraries and Info. Services, 1979. Author: Cases and Materials on Oil and Gas Law, 1962, How to Talk Back to Your Television Set, 1970, Japanese transl., 1971, Life Before Death in the Corporate State, 1971, Test Pattern for Living, 1972, Broadcasting in America, 1973, Cases and Materials on Communications Law and Policy, 1981, 82, 83; syndicated columnist: Gannett News Service, 1982-84, Register and Tribune Syndicate, 1984—; contbr. to legal, gen., internat. publs.; contbg. editor, host: PBS The New Tech Times, 1983-84. Bd. dirs. Churches Center for Theology and Public Policy; bd. dirs. Iowa Freedom Found.; mem. adv. bd. In the Public Interest, Project Censored; commr. Broadbend and Telecommunications Commn., Iowa City, 1981—. Named 1 of 10 Outstanding Young Men in U.S. U.S. Jaycees, 1967; recipient New Republic Pub. Defender award, 1970; Civil Liberties award Ga. ACLU, 1972; DeWitt Carter Reddick award U. Tex., 1977. Mem. D.C., Iowa bar assns., State Bar Tex., Internat. Soc. Gen. Semantics (dir.), Order of Coif, Phi Beta Kappa, Phi Delta Phi, Phi Eta Sigma, Pi Sigma Alpha. Democrat. Unitarian. Home and Office: PO Box 1876 Iowa City IA 52244 Office: care Leigh Lecture Bureau 49 State Rd Princeton NJ 08540

JOHNSON, NORMA HOLLOWAY, fed. judge; b. Lake Charles, La. B.S., D.C. Tchrs. Coll., 1955; J.D., Georgetown U., 1962. Bar: D.C. bar 1962, U.S. Supreme Ct. bar 1967. Practiced in, Washington, 1963; atty. Dept. Justice, Washington, 1963-67; asst. corp. counsel D.C., 1967-70; judge D.C. Superior Ct., 1970-80, U.S. Dist. Ct. for D.C., 1980—; Bd. dirs. Nat. Children's Center, Washington, National Street Law Inst. Mem. Am. Bar Assn., Nat. Bar Assn., D.C. Bar, Nat. Council Juvenile Ct. Judges, Am. Judicature Soc. (dir.), Nat. Assn. Women Judges (dir.). Office: US Courthouse 3d and Constitution Ave NW Washington DC 20001

JOHNSON, NORMAN, music director; b. Oneida, N.Y., Nov. 12, 1928; s. James Kenneth and Mildred (Sevy) J.; m. Matilda Nickel, Dec. 31, 1962. B.S., Juilliard Sch. Music, 1950, M.S., 1951. Recorded for Riverside and SMC; Coach, accompanist leading opera singers, concert artists, 1951-64; guest lectr. U. Colo., 1970; dir. opera N.C. Sch. of Arts, Winston-Salem, N.C., 1968—. Asso. condr., Oratorio Soc. N.Y., 1955-64; mem. conducting staff, Central City Opera Festival, Colo., 1962-70; coach, Met. Opera Nat. Co., 1965; guest music dir., Center Stage, Balt., 1968; artistic dir., condr., Denver Lyric Opera, 1967-72; music dir., N.C. Summer Festival, 1973; condr., Winston-Salem Symphony Chorale, 1975-80; music dir., Manhattanville Summer Opera Workshop, 1979-80; mem. conducting faculty, Peabody Conservatory, Balt., 1964-68; condr.: world premiere Argento's Colonel Jonathan The Saint, Denver, 1971, Agnes DeMille's Heritage Dance Theatre, 1973; guest condr., Cin. Opera, 1974, Charlotte Symphony, 1976, Augusta Opera, 1977-79, Artists Internationale, Providence, 1979; founder, artistic dir., Piedmont Opera Theatre, 1976-82; gen. dir., Piedmont Opera Theatre, 1982—, Donizetti's The Daughter of the Regiment; performing: translations in use Humperdinck's Hansel and Gretel. Mem. Am. Fedn. Musicians. Office: NC Sch of the Arts PO Box 12189 Winston-Salem NC 27107

JOHNSON, OGDEN CARL, food products company executive; b. Rockford, Ill., Aug. 15, 1929; s. Martin and Hildur Marie J.; m. Lucille Bruner, June 15, 1955; children: Timothy, Debra, Jonathan, Suzanne. B.S., U. Ill., 1951, M.S., 1952, Ph.D., 1956. Research chemist A.E. Staley Mfg. Co., 1957-60; asst. dir. dept. food and nutrition AMA, 1960-66; asst. dir. nutrition sect. USPHS, 1966-70; dir. Office Nutrition-FDA, 1970-74; v.p. sci. and tech. Hershey Foods Corp. (Pa.), 1974—, now sr. v.p., dir. Served with AUS; 1952-54. Mem. Inst. Food Technologists, Am. Chem. Soc., Am. Pub. Health Assn., Am. Inst. Nutrition. Home: RD 1 Box 400 Palmyra PA 17078 Office: Hershey Foods Corp 100 E Mansion Rd Hershey PA 17033

JOHNSON, PAUL CHRISTIAN, physiologist, educator; b. Ironwood, Mich., Feb. 3, 1928; s. George Herman and Sophia (Kliemola) J.; m. Genevieve Ruth Shanklin, Sept. 3, 1955; children: Ciri, Philip, Christopher. A.A., Gogebic Jr. Coll., 1948; B.S. in Physics, U. Mich., 1951; M.A. in Physiology, U. Mich., 1953, Ph.D., 1955. Instr. dept. physiology U. Mich., 1955-56; instr. Western Res. U., 1956-58; asst. prof. Ind. U., Bloomington, 1958-61, asso. prof., 1961-67; prof., head dept. physiology U. Ariz., Tucson, 1967—; mem. study sect. on physiology NIH, 1968-72. Contbr. research articles on regulation of blood flow to tech. jours.; editorial bd.: Am. Jour. Physiology, 1964-70; co-editor, 1975-78; editorial bd.: Jour. Applied Physiology, 1964-70, Circulation Research, 1971-76, 81—. NIH Spl. Postdoctoral fellow, 1965-66; research grantee NIH, 1960—; Am. Heart Assn., 1960-72. Mem. Am. Physiol. Soc. (chmn. circulation group 1973-74, mem. council 1978-82, Wiggers award lecture 1981), Microcirculatory Soc. (pres. 1967-68, Landis award lecture 1976), Basic Sci. Council, Am. Heart Assn. (exec. com. 1973-75, 82—), Assn. Chmn. Depts. Physiology (pres. 1980-81). Democrat. Club: Tucson Sailing. Home: 5345 Calle La Cima Tucson AZ 85718

JOHNSON, PAUL H., banker, lawyer; b. New Haven, Oct. 26, 1936; s. Harold Ragnar and Esther (Lindskog) J.; m. Gwendolyn Davies, Aug. 4, 1962; children: Kirsten, Philip, Peter. A.B., Brown U., 1958; J.D., U. Conn., Hartford, 1966; P.M.D., Harvard Grad. Sch. Bus., 1971; LL.D. hon., U. New Haven, 1981. Bar: Conn. 1966. V.p. 1st Bank, New Haven, 1961-71; pres., chief exec. officer Conn. Savs. Bank, New Haven, 1971—; dir. Cooper Thermometer Co., Middlefield, Conn., Conn. Energy Corp., Bridgeport, So. Conn. Gas., Gordon Techs. Served to lt. comdr. USNR, 1958-61. Named Man of Yr. New Haven C. of C., 1980. Clubs: New Haven Lawn (v.p.), New Haven Country; Mory's (New Haven). Home: Andrews Rd Leetes Island Guilford CT 06437 Office: Connecticut Savings Bank 55 Church St New Haven CT 06437

JOHNSON, PAUL HOWARD, librarian; b. N.Y.C., Jan. 30, 1924; s. Frederick George and Adelaide (Wilson) J. B.A., Yale U., 1949; M.A., Columbia U., 1954; M.A.L.S., U. Mich., 1956. Historian First Air Force, US Air Force Res., 1960-67; dir. undergrad. library system Yale U., New Haven, 1956-62; dir. U.S. Coast Guart Acad. Library, New London, Conn., 1962—; dir., curator, founder U.S. Coast Guard Mus., 1967—. Co-author: Eagle Seamanship, 1979, U.S. Coast Guard Academy: First 100 Years, 1976. Bd. mgrs. Old Lyme Publ. Lib., Old Lyme, Conn., 1969-71. Served to maj. USAAF, 1942-45; ETO; served USAF, 1951-52. Recipient Air medal with 2 oak leaf clusters, Purple Heart. Mem. ALA, Council Am. Maritime Museums (dir. 1977-81), Internat. Congress Maritime Museums. Office: US Coast Guard Acad New London CT 06320

JOHNSON, PAUL OREN, chem. co. exec., lawyer; b. Mpls., Feb. 2, 1937; s. Andrew Richard and LaVerne Delores (Slater) J.; m. Georgene Howalt, July 1, 1961; children—Scott, Paula, Amy. B.A., Carlton Coll., 1958; J.D., U. Minn., 1961. Bar: Minn. bar 1961. Atty. law firm Briggs & Morgan, St. Paul, 1961-62; atty. Green Giant Co., Le Sueur, Minn., 1961—, asst. sec., 1967-74, sec., 1975-79, gen. counsel, 1971-79, v.p. corporate relations, 1973-79, mem. mgmt. com., 1976-79; v.p., gen. counsel, sec. H.B. Fuller Co., 1979—, v.p., 1980—, mem. mgmt. com., 1981—. Active Boy Scouts Am. Chmn., Republican County Com., 1965; bd. dirs. Minn. State U., 1979—, v.p., 1980—. Served with U.S. Air N.G., 1961. Mem. Ramsey County, Minn. State, Am. bar assns., Minn. Corporate Counsel Assn., Nat. Canners Assn. (mem. claims com. 1969-79, mem. lawyers com. 1969-79). Home: 115 Outer Dr Le Sueur MN 56068 Office: 2400 Kasota Ave Saint Paul MN 55108

JOHNSON, PAUL ROBERT, banker; b. Cleve., July 22, 1932; s. Theodore H. and Ann Marie (Kollie) J.; m. Lois Little, Dec. 14, 1978; children: Scott, Cheryl, Debbie. B.S.I.E., U. Dayton, 1957, B.S.E.E., 1960; M.B.A., Xavier U., 1959; postgrad., U. Mich., 1960, Ohio State U., 1962; Ph.D. in Bus.-Ops. Research, Stanford U., 1968. Devel. and research engr. Standard Register Co., 1955-58; with IBM, 1958-68; v.p., dir. info. systems Irving Trust, 1968-70; exec. v.p., div. mgr. ops./automation European Am. Bancorp., N.Y.C., 1970-82; pres. Sincere Press Inc., 1982-83; pres., chief exec. officer First Central Bank, Phoenix, 1983—; mem. faculty, thesis review panel chmn., library rev. com. Stonier Grad. Sch. Banking, Rutgers U.; adj. prof. world bus. dept. Am. Grad Sch. Internat. Mgmt., Glendale, Ariz., 1982—. Author IBM manuals application guides; contbr. articles to profl. Jours. Div. chmn. United Fund; bd. rep. Edgemont Sch. Dist.; also bd. dirs. PTA and PTSA; bd. dirs. Greenville Community Council, Greenburgh Council Civic Assns.; formerly pres. Greenridge Civic Assn.; sch. dist. election supr. IBM resident grad. study fellow, 3 yrs. Mem. Am. Mgmt. Assn., Inst. Mgmt. Scis., Ops. Research Soc. Am. (charter), Assn. Computing Machinery, Am. Inst. Elec. Engrs., Am. Inst. Indsl. Engrs., Am. Bankers Assn. (chmn. ops. conf. Boston), Bank Adminstrn. Inst., Ancient Astronaut Soc., Phi Beta Kappa, Tau Beta Pi. Office: First Central Bank 3443 N Central Ave Phoenix AZ 85012

JOHNSON, PHILIP CORTELYOU, architect; b. Cleve., July 8, 1906; s. Homer M. and Louise (Pope) J. A.B., Harvard, 1930, B.Arch., 1943. Dir. dept. architecture and design Mus. Modern Art, 1930-36, 46-54, trustee, 1958—. Architect: Lincoln Center, N.Y.C., Glass House, New Canaan, Conn.; co-architect: Seagram Bldg, N.Y.C.; Works include Pennzoil Pl, Houston, IDS Center, Mpls., Niagara Falls (N.Y.) Conv. Center, addition to Boston Pub. Library, Bobst N.Y. U. Library; Author: (with Henry-Russel Hitchcock) Architecture Since 1922, 1932, Mies van der Rohe, 1947, rev., 1953. Recipient Bronze Medallion City of N.Y., 1978; Pritzker prize, 1979; AIA Gold medal, 1978; fellows award R.I. Sch. Design, 1983. Mem. Acad. Arts and Letters. Office: 375 Park Ave New York NY 10022 *

JOHNSON, PHILIP LEWIS, research and educational association executive; b. Oneonta, N.Y., May 26, 1931; s. Robert A. and Hazel S. (Shaffer) J.; m. Judy Rodgers, Nov. 17, 1973. B.S. in Agr, Purdue U., 1953, M.S. in Natural Resources, 1955; Ph.D. in Ecology, Duke U., 1961. Agrl. economist fruit and vegetable div., sect. program analysis Dept. Agr., 1955; instr. botany U. Wyo., Laramie, 1959-61; botanist U.S. Forest Service, Laramie, 1961-62; ecologist U.S. Cold Regions Research and Engring. Lab., Hanover, N.H., 1962-67; asst. prof. biology Dartmouth Coll., 1963-67; asso. prof. botany and forestry U. Ga., 1967-70; program dir. ecosystem analysis program NSF, 1968-69; dep. head Office Interdisciplinary Research, 1970-71, dir. div. environ. systems and resources, 1971-74; exec. dir. Oak Ridge Asso. Univs., 1974-81, John E. Gray Inst., Lamar U., Beaumont, Tex., 1981—; also pres. John E. Gray Found.; research collaborator Brookhaven Nat. Lab., 1963-65; mem. N.H. Pesticide Control Bd., 1965-67; mem. primary productivity com. Internat. Biol. Program, 1967-68, adv. com. tundra biome, 1968-70, deciduous forest biome coordinating com., 1968, 70; mem. environ. panel fgn. currency program Smithsonian Instn., 1969-70; adv. council Public Broadcast Environ. Center, Washington, 1970; vice chmn. interagy. com. ecol. research Fed. Council Sci. and Tech./Council Environ. Quality, 1972; mem. U.S. com. Man and Biosphere Program, 1973-74; exec. com. E. Tenn. Cancer Research Center, Knoxville, 1975-77; regional com. Southeastern Plant Environ. Lab., 1975-80; fellowship adv. panel environ. affairs Rockefeller Found., 1974-78; chmn. com. on environ. research and devel. Nat. Acad. Scis., 1978-79, mem. polar research bd., 1981—. Editorial bd.: Ecol. Monographs, 1968-70, Jour. Remote Sensing of Environ, 1971-75. Trustee Inst. of Ecology, 1976-79, chmn. bd., 1980-81; bd. dirs. Center for Natural Areas, 1979-81; mem. U.S. Commn. for UNESCO, 1978-80. Served with AUS, 1955-57. Recipient Commendation award Cold Regions Research and Engring. Lab., 1964, 66, Meritorious Sch. Achievement award, 1966; Meritorious Service award NSF, 1973; James B. Duke fellow 1957-59. Fellow Arctic Inst. N. Am.; mem. Ecol. Soc. Am., Brit. Ecol. Soc., N.Y. Acad. Scis., AAAS, Sigma Xi, Phi Eta Sigma, Alpha Zeta, Kappa Delta Pi, Xi Sigma Pi. Club: Cosmos (Washington). Home: 5815 Honeysuckle St Beaumont TX 77706 Office: John E Gray Inst Lamar U Beaumont TX 77710

JOHNSON, PHILIP MCBRIDE, lawyer; b. Springfield, Ohio, June 18, 1938. A.B. with honors, Ind. U., 1959; LL.B., Yale U., 1962. Bar: Ill. 1962, D.C. 1983. Partner firm Kirkland & Ellis, Chgo., 1962-81; chmn. Commodity Futures Trading Commn., Washington, 1981-83; ptnr. Wiley, Johnson & Rein, Washington, 1983—; speaker, panelist on Commodity Exchange Act Fed. Bar Assn., others; past mem. adv. com. definition and regulation Commodity Futures Trading Commn., adv. com. state jurisdiction and responsibility. Author: Commodities Regulation, 2 vols., 1982; Mng. editor: Yale U. Law Jour, 1962, Agrl. Law Jour; contbr. articles to legal jours. Mem. ABA (chmn. com. on commodities regulation, governing council sect. corp. banking and bus. law). Office: 1776 K St Washington DC 20006

JOHNSON, PHILLIP EUGENE, educator; b. Bostic, N.C., Feb. 25, 1937; s. Lin Joe and Gertrude (Pitman) J.; m. Carolyn Roberta Long, Dec. 23, 1959; 1 son, Philip Marc. B.S., Appalachian State U., 1959; M.A., Am. U., 1966, George Peabody Coll., 1963, Ph.D., 1968; postgrad., N.C. State U., 1971, Cambridge U., 1973. Tchr. math., Fredericksburg, Va., 1960-61, Fairfax County, Va., 1961-63; faculty U. Richmond, 1963-65, Vanderbilt U., 1966-71; prof. math. U. N.C., Charlotte, 1971—. Author: A History of Set Theory, 1972; Contbr. articles to profl. jours. Served with USMCR, 1960. Grantee NSF, 1960-63, summers 1961-63, Ga. U. summer, 1965. Mem. Math. Assn. Am., Nat., N.C. councils tchrs. math., AAUP, Pi Mu Epsilon. Home: 6717 Pencade Ln Charlotte NC 28215 Office: Math Dept U NC Charlotte NC 28223

JOHNSON, RAFER LEWIS, actor, athlete, telephone co. exec.; b. Hillsboro, Tex., Aug. 18, 1935; s. Lewis and Elma (Gibson) J. A.B., U. Calif. at, Los Angeles, 1959. V.p. community relations Continental Telephone Corp., Atlanta, 1979—. Formerly sports commentator, NBC-TV; film appearances include Sergeant Rutledge, Sins of Rachel Cade, Pirates of Tortuga, Wild in the Country, A Global Affair, None But the Brave, Games, The Last Grenade, The Red White and Black; appeared: in TV movie The Loneliest Runner. Active presdl. campaign Robert F. Kennedy, 1968; active Pres.'s Council Phys. Fitness, Spl. Olympics for Retarded. Recipient Gold medal Pan Am. Games, 1955, Silver medal Olympics, 1956, Gold medal as Decathlon Champion Olympics, 1960, Sullivan trophy AAU, 1960. Office: care Mishkin Agy Inc 9255 Sunset Blvd Los Angeles CA 90069 *

JOHNSON, RALPH M., university dean; b. Ririe, Idaho, Apr. 9, 1918; s. Ralph Melvin and Millie (Marler) J.; m. Genevieve Porter, Aug. 8, 1940; children: Karen (Mrs. Warren Eugene Babcock), Robert Christian, Wilford Preece. B.S., Utah State U., 1940; M.S., U. Wis., 1947, Ph.D., 1948. Fellow Wis. Alumni Research Found., U. Wis., 1940-41, 46-47; fellow NIH, 1947-48; research asso., asst. to sci. dir. Detroit Inst. Cancer Research, 1948-59; asst. prof. physiol. chemistry Coll. Medicine, Wayne State U., 1951-59; research prof., dir. research labs. Inst. Nutrition and Food Tech. Ohio State U., Columbus, 1959-63; dir. Inst. Nutrition, 1963-66, dean Inst. Nutrition, Coll. Biol. Scis., 1966-68; prof. chemistry, dean Coll. Sci. Utah State U., 1968—, also pres. found. Contbr. articles to profl. jours. Pres. United Way of Cache Valley, 1977—. Served to maj. U.S. Army, 1941-46. Mem. Am. Soc. Biol. Chemists, Am. Inst. Nutrition, Cache C. of C. (dir. 1975—), Sigma Xi, Phi Kappa Phi, Gamma Sigma Delta. Republican. Mem. Ch. of Jesus Christ of Latter-day Saints (pres. stake). Home: 2044 N 13th E Logan UT 84321 *If there is a single characteristic that might contribute to any personal success, it is the almost subconscious urge to utilize time fully and well. . . .Somewhere I seemed to have acquired the habit of thoroughness in almost any task undertaken. This has on important occasions served me well. No one seems to appreciate slip-shod or partially completed efforts.*

JOHNSON, RAY, painter; b. Detroit, Oct. 16, 1927. Student, Art Students' League, N.Y.C., Black Mountain Coll. Asso. with Am. Abstract Artists, 1949-52; founded N.Y. Corr. Sch. Art, 1962. Exhibited one-man shows, Willard Gallery, N.Y.C., 1965, 66, 67, Feigen Gallery, Chgo., 1966, 67, Whitney Mus. Am. Art, N.Y.C., 1970, Art Inst. Chgo., 1972, N.C. Mus. Art, Raleigh, 1976, in group shows including, Boylston St. Print Gallery, Cambridge, Mass., 1955, contemporary Arts Assn. Houston, 1959, Batman Gallery, San

Francisco, 1961, Pitts. Internat., Carnegie Inst., AG Gallery, N.Y.C., Oakland Art Mus., 1963, Mus. Modern Art, N.Y.C., 1966, Finch Coll. Mus. Art, N.Y.C., 1967, Chgo. Mus. Contemporary Art, Hayward Gallery, London, 1969, U. B.C.; represented in permanent collections, Art Inst. Chgo., Dulin Gallery, Houston Mus. Fine Arts, DeCordova Mus., Lincoln, Mass., Mus. Modern Art, N.Y.C.; Pub.: The Paper Snake, 1965. Recipient award Nat. Inst. Arts and Letters, 1966 *

JOHNSON, RAY ARVIN, construction company executive; b. Long Prairie, Minn., May 2, 1920; s. Walter David and Rosalind (Hesser) J.; m. Kay Meredith Durbahn, May 14, 1960; children: Sherry Kay, Diane Rosalind, Laura Faye. Student, Iowa State U., 1942, U. Minn., 1948-51, Coll. William and Mary, 1969. Operating engr. for U.S. mil. airfields, ship repair drydocks and roads, Minn., W.I., Jamaica, P.R., 1938-42; partner Johnson Constrn. Co., Litchfield, Minn., 1941—; co-founder, dir. Johnson Bros. Hwy. & Heavy Constructors, Inc. (name changed to Johnson Bros. Corp. 1974), Litchfield, 1959—, v.p., 1959-67, sr. v.p., 1968-72, chmn. bd., 1973-80; instr. equipment mgmt. Mankato (Minn.) State Coll., 1975-76; mem. joint task force Assn. Gen. Contractors Am. and Bur. Reclamation, U.S. Dept. Interior, 1969-77; mgmt. trustee joint trusteed Teamster funds for mgmt. health, welfare and pension funds Asso. Gen. Contractors Minn. and Minn. Teamsters Constrn. Unions, 1970—; bd. dirs. Regional Congress Constrn. Employers Minn., 1973-75; mem. adv. com. for heavy equipment Vocat. Tech. Inst., Staples, Minn., 1974. Author: Construction Equipment Cost Manual for Value Recovery Rates. Commr. Minnetonka (Minn.) Park Bd., 1973-75. Served with USNR, 1942-45. Mem. Asso. Gen. Contractors Am. (nat. heavy dir. 1973-74, nat. mcpl.-utilities dir. 1974—, equipment expense com. 1974-83, internat. constrn. com. 1979-83, energy and materials com. 1979-82, constrn. mgmt. com. 1983—), Asso. Gen. Contractors Minn. (hwy. dir. 1973-74, v.p. hwy. div. 1974, mem. statewide labor negotiations for hwy. and heavy constrn. industry 1970-78, chmn. hwy. force account com. 1970-83, equipment cost manual for value recovery rates com. 1971-83, mem. joint task force com. with Minn. Hwy. Dept. 1971-83, mem. legis. com. 1978—), Soc. for Preservation and Encouragement Barbershop Quartet Singing in Am., East Africa Wild Life Soc. Lutheran. Clubs: Masons., Shriners, Scottish Rite. Office: PO Box 1002 Litchfield MN 55355

JOHNSON, RAY CLIFFORD, mechanical engineering educator; b. Canton, Ohio, Aug. 26, 1927; s. Olaf Andreas and Hilma D. (Blomberg) J.; m. Helen Frances Lindgren, July 2, 1949; children: Glen Eric, Barbara Ann, Carol Marie. B.S. with high distinction, U. Rochester, 1950, M.S., 1954, Ph.D., 1983. Registered profl. engr., N.Y., Conn., Mass., Mich., N.J., Ohio. Mech. design engr. Gleason Works, Rochester, N.Y., 1950-51; instr. U. Rochester, 1951-54; sr. design engr. Eastman Kodak Co., 1954-58; asst. prof. mech. engring. Yale, 1958-61; staff engr. IBM Corp., 1961-62; John Woodman Higgins prof. mech. engring. Worcester (Mass.) Poly. Inst., 1962-80; Gleason prof. mech. engring. Rochester (N.Y.) Inst. Tech., 1980—; lectr. and cons. to major univs. and industries, 1957—; keynote speaker Symposium on Mech. Design, U. Mex., 1975; vis. fellow mech. engring. U. Salford (Eng.), 1976-77, Nat. Acad. Engring., Mex., 1978—. Author: Optimum Design of Mechanical Elements, 1961, 80, Mechanical Design Synthesis with Optimization Applications, 1971, 78, also tech. papers. Served with USNR, 1945-46. Recipient Emil Kuichling prize U. Rochester, 1948. Fellow ASME; Mem. Soc. Exptl. Stress Analysis, Am. Soc. Engring. Edn., Nat. Soc. Profl. Engrs., AAUP, Phi Beta Kappa, Sigma Xi, Tau Beta Pi, Pi Tau Sigma. Patentee in field. Home: 698 Ashdon Circle Webster NY 14580 Office: Rochester Inst Tech Rochester NY 14623

JOHNSON, RAYMOND COLES, insurance executive; b. Bisbee, Ariz., June 19, 1907; s. Ira J. and Carolyn (Coles) J.; m. Alice Elizabeth Abbott, June 21, 1930 (dec. July 21, 1949); children: Carolyn C. Johnson Smith, Eleanor Johnson Palmer; m. Alice Hall Willard, July 16, 1954. B.S. magna cum laude, U. Ariz., 1928, LL.D., 1976. With N.Y. Life Ins. Co., 1927—, agt., Phoenix, 1927-29, asst. mgr., 1929-33, mgr., 1933-38, mgr. Los Angeles br., 1938-42, supt. agys. home office, N.Y.C., 1942- 43, asst. v.p., 1942-49, agy. v.p. and exec. officer, 1949-51, v.p. charge agy. admistrn., 1951-56, v.p. charge agy. affairs, 1956-59, v.p. charge mktg., 1959-62, exec. v.p., 1962-69, dir., 1968—, vice chmn., 1969-73; pres. Council Fin. Aid to Edn., 1973-78, chmn. exec. com., 1979—; dir. Western World Ins. Co., Am. Life Ins. Co. Contbr. articles mags. and trade jours. Bd. govs. Internat. Ins. Seminars, 1968—; agy. chmn. Am. Life Conv., 1962; mem. Republican Nat. Fin. Com.; mem., trustee NYU Med. Center, 1965; chmn. N.Y. chpt. ARC, 1968—, United Negro Coll. Fund, Ind. Coll. Funds Am. Recipient U. Ariz. Alumni Achievement award, 1956. Mem. Am. Coll. Life Underwriters (Huebner Gold medal 1979, life trustee), Am. Soc. C.L.U.S., Life Ins. Agy. Mgmt. Assn. (dir., past pres.), Better Bus. Bur. Met. N.Y. (dir. 1968, council 1969), Pilgrims U.S., Newcomen Soc., Phi Beta Kappa, Phi Delta Theta, Pi Delta Epsilon, Alpha Kappa Psi. Clubs: Knights of Malta, University (N.Y.C.); Southampton (L.I., N.Y.); Bath and Tennis, Soc. Four Arts (Palm Beach, Fla.); Sales Execs. (dir.), Economic; Metropolitan (N.Y.C.); Confrerie des Chevaliers, Tastevin. Home: 265 E 66th St New York NY 10021 Office: 680 Fifth Ave New York NY 10019

JOHNSON, RAYMOND EDWARD, former newspaper editor; b. McEwen, Tenn., Feb. 27, 1904; s. Edward and Lina (Adams) J.; m. Mae Louthan; children: Robert Edward, Raymond Eugene. Grad. high sch. Office boy Nashville Tennessean, 1918-20, sports writer, 1920-25, asst. sports editor, 1926-37, sports editor, 1937-70, Evening Tennessean, 1925-26; publicity dir. Churchill Downs, 1971-73, dir. press relations, 1973-81; commr. So. Basketball League, 1947-49. Recipient George Barton award, 1959, Southeastern Conf. Sportsman award, 1966, Jake Wade award, 1969, Tenn. Press Assn. award, 1969; named Man of Year Capital City Golf Assn., 1971, to Tenn. Sports Hall of Fame, 1972, Nat. Softball Hall of Fame, 1976, So. Amateur Boxing Hall of Fame, 1980. Mem. Football Writers Assn. Am. (past pres., life), Amateur Softball Assn. Am. (past pres.), Golden Gloves Nat. (past pres.), So. Assn. Baseball Writers (past pres.), Nat. Turf Writers Assn. (past pres.), Golf Writers Am. (life), Nat. Assn. Softball Writers, Southeastern Amateur Athletic Union (past pres.), Nat. Football Hall Fame (charter), Sigma Delta Chi. Democrat. Lutheran. Club: Elk (life). Home: 1604 17th Ave Nashville TN 37212 *Treat everyone the way you want to be treated.*

JOHNSON, REVERDY, lawyer; b. N.Y.C., Aug. 24, 1937; s. Reverdy and Reva (Payne) J.; m. Marta Schneebeli, Apr. 4, 1970; children: Deborah Ghiselin, Reverdy Payne. A.B. cum laude, Harvard U., 1960, LL.B., 1963. Bar: Fla. 1963, Calif. 1964. Assoc. mem. firm Brobeck, Phleger & Harrison, San Francisco, 1963-66, Pettit & Martin, 1966-69, partner, 1970—; co-owner Johnson Turnbull Vineyards, Napa Valley, Calif., 1977—; mem. tech. adv. com., com. open space lands Calif. Joint Legislature, 1968-69, chmn., 1969-70. Bd. dirs. Planning and Conservation League, 1966-72, League to Save Lake Tahoe, 1972-77, Found. for San Francisco's Archtl. Heritage, 1975—. Mem. Urban Land Inst. (vice chmn. recreational devel. council 1975-78, comml. and retail devel. council 1980—), Am. Coll. Real Estate Lawyers, Lambda Alpha. Home: 2503 Broadway San Francisco CA 94115 Office: 101 California St San Francisco CA 94111

JOHNSON, REX D., investor, financial adviser; b. Ardmore, Okla., Sept. 19, 1926; s. Robert Bruce and Opal (Williams) J.; m. Helen Anne Duboc, Dec. 28, 1957; children: Dianne Elizabeth, Bradley Duboc. B.B.A., U. Okla., 1949; M.B.A., Stanford U., 1951; grad., Advanced Mgmt. Program, Harvard U., 1967. With Republic Nat. Bank, Dallas, 1951-72, staff credit analyst, 1951-53, asst. cashier comml. loans, 1953-57, asst. v.p. comml. loans, 1957-60, v.p. comml. loans, 1960-66, sr. v.p. comml. loans, 1966-67, exec. v.p. finance, adminstrn., chmn. investment com., 1967-72; pres. Security Nat. Bank, N.Y.C., 1972-73; prin. Johnson & Bingham, N.Y.C. and Dallas, 1973—; Mem. adv. com. Children's Med. Center, Dallas, 1970-71; com. chmn. corps. and founds. Greenwich Acad. anniversary campaign, 1972-74. Bd. dirs. Tejas council Girl Scouts U.S.A., 1968-72; chmn. Tex. Girl Scout Endowment Found., 1976—. Served with USMCR, 1944-46. Fellow Acad. U.; Fellows U. Okla. Mem. L.I. Assn. (dir., exec. com. 1972-73), Stanford Bus. Sch. Assn. (dir.), N.Y.C. Chamber Commerce and Industry (com. on fin. and currency), Am. Bankers Assn. (internat. lending com. 1972-74), L.I. World Trade Club (bd. govs. 1972-74), Phi Kappa Sigma, Delta Sigma Pi. Presbyterian. Clubs: Dallas, Rush Creek Yacht, Masons, Shriners, Dallas. Home: 8 Royal Way Dallas TX 75229 Office: Mathiesson Park Irvington-on-Hudson NY 10533

JOHNSON, RICHARD ABRAHAM, historian, educator; b. Moline, Ill., Apr. 17, 1910; s. Andrew and Harriet May (Abrahamson) J.; m. Irene E. Beam, June 15, 1946; children: Cristina Anne, Richard Alexander, Daniel Anders Lowell. A.B., Augustana Coll., 1932; M.A., U. Tex., 1933, Ph.D., 1938. Instr. Montezuma Coll., 1933-34, U. Tex., 1935-38; prof. Augustana Coll., Rock Island, Ill., 1938-40; apptd. fgn. service officer, 1940, vice consul, Naples, Italy, 1940-41, vice consul, 3d sec., London, 1941-46; U.S. observer Conf. Allied Ministers Edn., 1943-45; tech. sec. U.S. del. UN Conf. Orgn. of UNESCO, 1945, acting rep. preparatory com., 1945-46; adviser U.S. del. 1st Gen. Conf. UNESCO, 1946; staff Dept. State, 1946-48; consul, 1st sec., La Paz, Bolivia, 1948-50, consul, prin. officer, Guadalajara, Mex., 1950-52, consul, 1st sec., dep. chief mission, Ciudad, Trujillo, 1952-54; assigned to Nat. War Coll., 1954-55; counselor of embassy, Madrid, Spain, 1955-57; dep. dir. Office of Intelligence and Research, Dept. of State, Washington, 1957-59; dir. Office Functional and Biographic Intelligence, 1959-61; exec. dir. Bd. Examiners for Fgn. Service, 1961-62; consul gen., Monterrey, Mex., 1962-65; prof., coordinator Inter-Am. studies Trinity U., San Antonio, 1965-70; dir. Interdisciplinary Area Tng. Program, 1966-70; adj. prof. U. West Fla., 1974; lectr. George Washington U., 1959-60. Author: The Mexican Revolution of Ayutla, 1939, The Administration of U.S. Fgn. Affairs, 1971; Contbr. articles to profl. publs. Chmn. ednl. exhibits com. Hemis Fair, 1966-68; pres. Scolas, 1967-68. Mem. Am. Hist. Soc., Am. Fgn. Service Assn., Mexican Acad. Internat. Law (academician). Home: 5822 Rue Burgundy San Antonio TX 78240

JOHNSON, RICHARD CLAYTON, engineer, physicist; b. Eveleth, Minn., May 9, 1930; s. Elvin and Sadie (Abramson) J.; m. Sallie Staples Hairston, Aug. 2, 1958 (div. 1971); children: Karen Louise, Diana Elizabeth.; m. Margaret R. Campbell, Jan. 1, 1984. B.S. in Physics, Ga. Inst. Tech., 1953, M.S., 1958, Ph.D., 1961. Registered profl. engr., Ga. Co-op student Ga. Power Co., 1949-51; with Ga. Inst. Tech., 1952—, prin. research engr., 1967—; asso. dir. Engring. Expt. Sta., 1975-79; cons. to govt. and industry, 1966—; mem. sci. adv. group for U.S. Army Missile Command, 1975-78. Editor: Antenna Engineering Handbook, 1984; Contbr. research papers, chpt. in book. Served to lt. (j.g.) USNR, 1953-55. Fellow IEEE (editor newsletter Antennas and Propagation Soc. 1975-77, v.p. Antennas and Propagation Soc. 1979, pres. 1980, Disting. lectr. 1978-79, mem. adminstrv. com. 1978—, leader study group to China 1980); mem. Am. Phys. Soc., Sigma Xi, Phi Kappa Phi, Tau Beta Pi, Phi Eta Sigma, Sigma Pi Sigma, Phi Kappa Sigma. Patentee in field. Home: 467 Tenth St NW Atlanta GA 30318

JOHNSON, RICHARD DAMERAU, aeronautic scientist; b. Zanesville, Ohio, Oct. 28, 1934; s. Earl G. and Merlie D. J.; m. Catherine Collins, Dec. 30, 1969; children: Laurana, Karen, Eric, Gregory. B.A., Oberlin Coll., 1956; M.S., Carnegie-Mellon U., 1960, Ph.D., 1961; postdoctoral fellow, UCLA, 1961-62. Sr. scientist Jet Propulsion Lab., Pasadena, Calif., 1962-63; with NASA, 1963—, chief life scis. flight expts. office, 1973-76, chief bio-systems div. Ames Research Center, Moffett Field, Calif., 1976—; vis. lectr. Stanford U. Contbr. papers in field. Recipient Exceptional Service medal NASA, 1976; Alfred P. Sloan fellow M.I.T., 1981-82. Mem. Am. Chem. Soc., AAAS, AIAA, N.Y. Acad. Scis., Peninsula Home Enologists Workshop. Club: Stanford (Palo Alto, Calif.). Office: Mail Stop 236-5 Code LB NASA-Ames Research Center Moffett Field CA 94035

JOHNSON, RICHARD DAVID, librarian; b. Cleve., June 10, 1927; s. Robert Emanuel and Emma (Lindhorst) J.; m. Harriett Herzog, Sept. 8, 1956; children: Ruth Ellen, Royce Emanuel. B.A., Yale U., 1949; M.A. in Internat. Relations, U. Chgo., 1950, U. Chgo., 1957. Librarian Nat. Opinion Research Center, U. Chgo., 1956-57; reference librarian Stanford, 1957-59; cataloger Stanford U., 1959-60, 61-62, adminstrv. asst. to dir., 1960-61, head acquisitions, 1962-64, chief undergrad. library project, 1964-67, chief librarian tech. services, 1967-68; dir. libraries Claremont (Calif.) Colls., 1968-73, SUNY, Oneonta, 1973—. Editor: California Librarian, 1966-68, Coll. and Research Libraries, 1974-80, Choice, 1982, Lexington Books series on libraries, 1981—; mng. editor: Jour. Library Automation, 1980. Trustee Four County Library System, Binghamton, N.Y., 1978—. Served with inf. AUS, 1952-54. Decorated Bronze Star. Mem. ALA, Calif. Library Assn. (pres. 1972), N.Y. Library Assn. (pres. acad. and spl. libraries sect. 1981—, 2d v.p. 1982), Soc. Scholarly Publishing, Beta Phi Mu. Presbyterian. Home: 2 Walling Blvd Oneonta NY 13820 Office: Milne Library State U Coll Oneonta NY 13820

JOHNSON, RICHARD JAMES VAUGHN, newspaper executive; b. San Luis, Potosi, Mexico, Sept. 22, 1930; s. Clifton Whatford and Myrtle Louise (Hinman) J.; m. Belle Beraud Griggs, Aug. 6, 1955; children: Shelley Beraud, Mark Hinman. B.B.A., U. Tex., Austin, 1954. Asst. dir., exec. dir. Tex. Daily Newspaper Assn., 1955-56; with Houston Chronicle Pub. Co., 1956—, v.p. sales and mktg., 1970, exec. v.p., 1971, pres., 1972—, also dir.; dir. Lakeside Commerce Bank, Anderson Clayton Co., Newspaper Advt. Bur. Inc. Bd. dirs. Soc. for Performing Arts; chmn. bd. Tex. Med. Center; trustee Robert A. Welch Found.; bd. visitors Anderson Cancer and Tumor Inst., Meth. Hosp. Served with U.S. Army, 1952-54. Recipient Silver medal Houston Advt. Club, 1974. Mem. Tex. Daily Newspaper Assn. (pres. 1978, dir.), Am. Newspaper Pubs. Assn. (pres., chmn.), Houston C. of C. Unitarian. Clubs: River Oaks, Houston, Petroleum, Coronado. Office: 801 Texas Ave Houston TX 77002

JOHNSON, RICHARD J.V., newspaper publisher. Pres. Houston Chronicle Pub. Co. Address: Houston Chronicle Pub Co 801 Texas St Houston TX 77002 *

JOHNSON, RICHARD LOUIS, paper company executive; b. Madison, Wis., May 16, 1916; s. Harry J. and Louise (Nisalk) J.; m. Virginia Eckman, Jan. 1, 1943; children: Gregg E., Timothy D. B.A., U. Wis., 1939, J.D., 1942. Bar: Wis. 1942. Atty. Chief Counsel Office, IRS, Washington, 1943-44; gen. atty, tax mgr., asst. controller Marathon Corp., Menasha, Wis., 1944-55; controller Menasha Corp., 1955-60, pres., 1960-80, chmn. bd., 1980—, also dir.; dir. N.E. Wooden Ware Co., Radford Co., 1st Nat. Bank Menasha, Wis. Electric Power Co., Neenah-Menasha Water Power Co. Trustee Theda Clara Meml. Hosp.; bd. dirs. Bergstrom Art Mus. Mem. Phi Delta Phi. Republican. Presbyterian. Club: North Shore Golf. Home: 856 Bayview Rd Neenah WI 54956 Office: Menasha Corp Hwy 41 Neenah WI 54956

JOHNSON, RICHARD MERRILL, educator; b. Ft. Wayne, Ind., Oct. 31, 1934; s. Merrill C. and Blanche A. (Haberkorn) J.; m. Nancy K. Burris, Apr. 20, 1957; children—Kathleen A., Deborah L. B.A., Miami U., Oxford, Ohio, 1956; M.A., Am. U., 1961; Ph.D., U. Ill., 1965. Instr. U.S. Naval Acad., Annapolis, Md., 1959-61; staff asst. Gov. Ill., 1963; instr. U. Ill. at Urbana, 1963-64; asst. prof. polit. sci. State U. N.Y. at Buffalo, 1964-68, asso. prof., 1968-69, vice-chmn. dept., 1966-68; prof., head dept. polit. sci. U. Ill. at Chgo. Circle, 1969-72, asso. dean, 1972-74, acting dean, 1973-74, asso. vice chancellor for acad. affairs, 1976-78, vice chancellor acad. affairs, 1978—. Author: Supreme Court Decision-Making From a New Prespective, 1967. Served to lt. USNR, 1956-61. Mem. Am., Midwest polit sci. assns. Democrat. Unitarian. Home: 2753 Girard Evanston IL 60201

JOHNSON, RICHARD TENNEY, lawyer; b. Evanston, Ill., Mar. 24, 1930; s. Ernest Levin and Margaret Abbott (Higgins) J.; m. Marilyn Bliss Meuth, May 1, 1954; children: Ross Tenney, Lenore, Jocelyn. A.B. with high honors, U. Rochester, 1951; postgrad., Trinity Coll., Dublin, Ireland, 1954-55; LL.B., Harvard, 1958. Bar: D.C. 1959. Trainee Office Sec. Def., 1957-59; atty. Office Gen. Counsel. Dept. Def., 1959-63; dep. gen. counsel Dept. Army, 1963-67, Dept. Transp., 1967-70; gen. counsel CAB, 1970-73, NASA, 1973-75, ERDA, 1975-76; mem. CAB, 1976-77; chmn. organizational integration Dept. Energy Activation, Exec. Office of Pres., 1977; ptnr. firm Sullivan & Beauregard, 1978-81; gen. counsel Dept. Energy, 1981-83; ptnr. firm Zuckert, Scoutt, Rasenberger & Johnson, 1983—. Served to lt. USNR, 1951-54. Mem. ABA, Fed. Bar Assn., Phi Beta Kappa, Theta Delta Chi. Office: 888 17th St NW Washington DC 20006

JOHNSON, RICHARD WALTER, investment executive; b. Mpls., Oct. 2, 1928; s. Walter Benjamin and Evelyn (Peterson) J.; children: Richard Walter, William Charles, Nancy Ann, Thomas Gregory, Michael Richard, Jeffrey Wayne. B.B.A. with distinction, U. Minn., 1949. C.P.A., Nebr., Ill. With Arthur Andersen & Co. (C.P.A.'s), 1949-74, mng. partner, Omaha, 1960-74; chmn. bd., chief exec. officer Western Securities Co. of Del., Omaha, 1975—; pres. Modern Equipment Co., Omaha, 1975—. Bd. dirs., exec. com. Jr. Achievement Omaha, 1962—, pres., 1966-67; gen. campaign chmn. Heart of the Midlands United Way, 1972, chmn. pacemaker sect. fund raising campaign, 1964, chmn. corporate standards com., 1966, asso. gen. chmn., 1968, treas., mem. exec. com., 1969; bd. dirs. Mid-Am. council Boy Scouts of Am., Omaha Symphony Assn., Omaha Big Bros. Assn., Omaha Playhouse Assn.; Trustee Fontenelle Forest Assn., Creighton U. Pres.'s Council. Recipient One of Outstanding Young Men in Am. award, 1965. Mem. Am. Inst. C.P.A.'s, Nebr. Soc. C.P.A.'s, Omaha-Lincoln Soc. Financial Analysts, Newcomen Soc. N.Am., Omaha C. of C. (chmn. membership relations com. 1962—, bd. dirs. 1965—, mem. exec. com., v.p. 1968), Beta Gamma Sigma, Beta Alpha Psi. Clubs: Masons, Shriners; Garden of the Gods (Colorado Springs); Omaha, Omaha Country; Palm Bay (Miami). Home: 3008 Paddock Rd Omaha NE 68124 Office: 2011 Cuming St Omaha NE 68102

JOHNSON, RICHARD WARREN, civil engineer; b. Litchfield, Minn., Aug. 24, 1939; s. Paul Revere and Hazel Edna (West) Johnson-W.; m. Bonita Louise Stevenson, June 22, 1963; children: Wendy, Jenny, Christopher, Katy. B.C.E., U. Minn., 1962. Registered profl. engr., Minn., Iowa., Wis., N.D., S.D., La., Wash. Div. engr. Johnson Bros. Corp., Litchfield, Minn., 1962-68, v.p., 1968-76, exec. v.p., 1976-82, pres., 1983—. Mem. ASCE, Constrn. Mgmt. Assn. Am., Chi Epsilon. Republican. Home: 410 E 6th St Litchfield MN 55355 Office: Johnson Bros Corp S Hwy 22 Litchfield MN 55355 *The effective accumulation of initiative, intelligence, judgement, patience, courage and follow-thorough will develop success in the individual. However, it is the recognition of the value of others that develops success in an organization*

JOHNSON, RICHARD WILLIAM, newspaper executive; b. Pawnee, Okla., Nov. 25, 1916; s. Ralph Waldo and Ollie May (Colvin) J.; m. Gloria Scott, Dec. 28, 1945; children—Richard, Daniel, Ellen. B.A. in Journalism, U. Okla., 1940. Sales rep. Newspaper Enterprise Assn., Cleve., 1940-41, Eastern sales mgr., N.Y.C., 1945-63, dir. spl. services, Cleve., 1963-68, v.p. publs., N.Y.C., 1968-72, sr. v.p., 1978—, Cleve., 1972-78, also dir., N.Y.C.; exec. cons. United Media Enterprises, Newspaper Enterprise Assn., United Features Syndicate, 1978-81; dir. Berkley-Small, Inc., Mobile, Ala. Served with USNR, 1941-45; PTO. Mem. Inland Daily Press Assn. (asso.), So. Newspaper Pubs. Assn. (asso.). Clubs: Cleve. Athletic., Rotary. Office: 200 Park Ave New York NY 10166 also Water St Morristown NY 13664

JOHNSON, ROBERT ALLAN, foundation executive; b. Mishawaka, Ind., Jan. 28, 1919; s. Ralph Wallace and Inez D. (Jones) J.; m. Elizabeth Jane Flinn, July 24, 1941; children: Susan, David, Roger. B.A., Franklin (Ind.) Coll., 1940. Mgr. accounting Eli Lilly Internat. Corp., 1947-48; controller Eli Lilly y Cia. de Mexico, Mexico City, 1958-59; pres., gen. mgr. Eli Lilly (S.A.), Geneva, Switzerland, 1960-63, dir., chmn. bd., 1960-64; asst. treas. Eli Lilly Internat. Corp., London, 1963-66, Indpls., 1966-69; asst. treas., then gen. auditor Eli Lilly and Co., Indpls., 1970-72; treas. Lilly Endowment, Inc., Indpls., 1972—, exec. v.p., 1975—; sec. Eli Lilly and Co. Ltd., U.K., 1963-66. Mem. Franklin City Council, 1955-58; trustee Franklin Coll., 1969—, sec. bd., 1970-76, chmn., 1976-79, mem. pres.'s adv. council, 1966—. Served with USNR, 1944-46. Recipient Alumni citation Franklin Coll., 1965. Mem. Alpha Phi Gamma, Pi Kappa Delta, Sigma Alpha Epsilon. Republican. Presbyterian. Club: Skyline. Home: 7973 N Pennsylvania St Indianapolis IN 46240 Office: 2801 N Meridian St Indianapolis IN 46208

JOHNSON, ROBERT ALLISON, life ins. co. exec.; b. Canandaigua, N.Y., Sept. 8, 1928; s. Allison Fisher and Thelma Marie (Beers) J.; m. Suzanne Amundsen Stone, Dec. 18, 1951; children—Pamela Suzanne, Carol Alison, Elizabeth Stone, Cynthia Marie. B.A. in History, Harvard U., 1950; M.B.A., Western New Eng. Coll., 1963. With Mass. Mut. Life Ins. Co., Springfield, 1951—, employment mgr., 1958-72, dir. personnel, 1972-76, sr. v.p., 1976—. Active ARC. Served with U.S. Army, 1951-53. Mem. Life Office Mgmt. Assn., Am. Soc. C.L.U.'s. Home: 33 Woodland Rd Longmeadow MA 01106 Office: 1295 State St Springfield MA 01111

JOHNSON, ROBERT BRITTEN, educator; b. Cortland, N.Y., Sept. 24, 1924; s. William and Christine (Hofer) J.; m. Garnet Marion Brown, Aug. 30, 1947; children—Robert Britten, Richard Karl, Elizabeth Anne. Student, Wheaton (Ill.) Coll., 1942-43, 46-47; A.B. summa cum laude, Syracuse U., 1949, M.S., 1950; Ph.D., U. Ill., 1954. Asst. geologist Ill. Geol. Survey, 1951-54; asst. prof. geology Syracuse U., 1954-55; sr. geologist and geophysicist C.A. Bays & Asso., Urbana, Ill., 1955-56; from asst. prof. to prof. engring. geology Purdue U., 1956-66, head, engring. geology dept., 1964-66; prof. geology DePauw U., 1966-67, head, dept. geology, 1966-67; prof. geology Colo. State U., 1967—, acting chmn. dept. geology, 1968, chmn. dept., 1969-73, prof. in charge geology programs, dept. earth resources, 1973-77, acting head dept. earth resources, 1979-81; geologist U.S. Geol. Survey, 1976—; cons. in field, 1957—. Active local Boy Scouts Am., 4-H Club, Sci. Fair. Served with USAAF, 1943-46. Fellow Geol. Soc. Am.; mem. Assn. Engring. Geologists, Transp. Research Bd., Internat.

Assn. Engring. Geology, Phi Beta Kappa. Republican. Home: 2309 Moffett Dr Fort Collins CO 80526

JOHNSON, ROBERT BRUCE, pub. relations exec.; b. Mpls., Sept. 10, 1912; s. Edward and Kristine (Anderson) J.; m. Grace Burns, Dec. 8, 1943; children—Randi Elizabeth, Kristin Anne. A.B., Colo. Coll., 1934. Advt. supr. Proctor & Gamble, 1939-42; dir. pub. relations Marshall Field & Co., Chgo., 1945-49; sales promotion mgr. Mdse. Mart, Chgo., 1949-56; v.p., dir. merchandising Harshe-Rotman, Inc., Chgo., 1956-57; mng. dir. State St. Council, Chgo., 1957-64; pres. Robert Bruce Johnson & Assos., Inc., 1964—. Trustee Chgo. YWCA, Mus. Contemporary Art; bd. dirs. Inst. Internat. Edn. Adult Edn. Council Chgo., Chgo. Maternity Center; mem. Bright New City Com. Served to lt. comdr. USNR, 1942-45. Mem. Pub. Relations Soc. Am., Chgo. Federated Advt. Clubs, Soc. Typographic Arts, Soc. Contemporary Am. Art, Am. Marketing Assn., Internat. Downtown Execs. Assn., Phi Delta Theta. Clubs: Chicago Press, Arts, Publicity (past pres.), University, Economic (Chgo.). Home: 489 Willow Rd Winnetka IL 60093 Office: 333 N Michigan Ave Chicago IL 60601

JOHNSON, ROBERT CALVIN, JR., lawyer; b. Dallas, May 7, 1944; s. Robert Calvin and Nancy Elizabeth (Kerr) J.; m. Kathleen Luebert; children—Courtney Ann, Robert Calvin III, Marissa Elizabeth, Hilary Laine, Allison Anne, Zachary Everett. B.A., U. Tex., Austin, 1965, J.D., 1968. Bar: Tex. bar 1968, D.C. bar 1969. Partner firm Grady, Johnson, Blakeley, Johnson & Smith, Dallas, 1970—; mng. dir. Robinson Media, Ltd.; dir. Dynasty Oil Co. Chmn. finance com. Dallas chpt. A.R.C., 1975. Mem. Am., D.C., Dallas bar assns., State Bar Tex., Phi Delta Theta (v.p. 1962), Phi Delta Phi. Clubs: Dervish, Dallas Country. Home: 4237 Armstrong Pkwy Dallas TX 75205 Office: 2130 Republic Nat Bank Bldg Dallas TX 75201

JOHNSON, ROBERT CLYDE, educator; b. Knoxville, Tenn., Aug. 17, 1919; s. Robert Clyde and Lucille (Davis) J.; m. Elizabeth Childs, June 26, 1942; children—Robert Clyde III, Richard Albert, Catherine Barton, Anne Elizabeth. B.S., Davidson Coll., 1941, D.D., 1963; postgrad., Princeton Theol. Sem., 1941-43; B.D., Union Theol. Sem., N.Y.C., 1944, S.T.M., 1953; M.A., Columbia, 1947, Yale, 1963; D.D., Tusculum Coll., 1953; Ph.D., Vanderbilt U., 1957. Ordained to ministry Presbyterian Ch., 1943; minister in, Shrewsbury, N.J., 1943-47, Greeneville, Tenn., 1947-55; asst. prof. theology Pitts. Theol. Sem., 1955-57, prof., 1957- 63; prof. thelogy Yale Div. Sch., 1963—, dean, 1963-69; fellow Ezra Stiles Coll., Yale, 1963—. Author: The Meaning of Christ, 1958, Authority in Protestant Theology, 1959, The Church and Its Changing Ministry, 1962. Served as chaplain USNR, 1944-46. Mem. Am. Theol. Soc. Home: 141 Garfield Ave North Haven CT 06518 Office: Yale Div Sch 409 Prospect St New Haven CT 06510

JOHNSON, ROBERT CURTIS, chemical engineer, educator; b. Danville, Ill., Oct. 8, 1922; s. George Ernest and Jessie Rae (Tuttle) J.; m. Claranne Von Fossen, Aug. 26, 1944; 1 dau., Julie Anne. B.S., U. Ill., 1944, M.S., 1946; Ph.D., Pa. State U., 1951. Instr. Pa. State U., 1946-51; asst. prof., asso. prof. Washington U., 1951-57; dir. sci. computation Compumatix, St. Louis, 1957-58; asso. mgr. process analysis dept. computer div. TRW, Los Angeles, 1958-64; prof. chem. engring. dept. U. Colo., Boulder, 1964—, dir. internat. edn., 1973-74, dean internat. edn., 1974-82; cons. Mitsubishi-TRW, Tokyo, 1962-63. Author: (with Edwin T. Williams) Stoichiometry for Chemical Engineers, 1958. Mem. Am. Inst. Chem. Engrs., Japan Soc., Nat. Assn. Fgn. Student Affairs, AAAS, Sigma Xi, Beta Theta Pi, Tau Beta Pi, Sigma Tau. Home: 1400 Mariposa St Boulder CO 80302

JOHNSON, ROBERT EDWARD, editor; b. Montgomery, Ala., Aug. 13, 1922; s. Robert and Delia (Davis) J.; m. Naomi Cole, Dec. 16, 1948; children: Bobbye LaVerne, Janet Bernice, Robert Edward III. B.A., Morehouse Coll., 1948; M.A., Syracuse U., 1952; Litt.D., Miles Coll., 1973. Reporter Atlanta Daily World, 1948-49, city editor, 1949-50; asso. editor Jet News mag., Chgo., 1953-54, asst. mng. editor, 1954-56, mng. editor, 1956-63, exec. editor, 1963—; Dir. Project Upward Bound, 1966-68. Bd. dirs. Martin Luther King Jr. Center Social Change, DuSable Mus. Afro-Am. History. Served with USNR, 1943-46. Mem. World Fedn. Scottish Socs., Sigma Delta Chi, Alpha Phi Alpha, Alpha Kappa Delta. Clubs: Mason., Helms Athletic Found., Chgo. Headline (dir. 1968-70). Office: 820 S Michigan Ave Chicago IL 60605 *

JOHNSON, ROBERT EUGENE, physiologist; b. Conrad, Mont., Apr. 8, 1911; s. Arthur and Florence May (Disbrow) J.; m. Margaret Hunter, Jan. 11, 1935; children: Thomas Arthur, Charles William, Katherine Helen (dec.). B.S. in Chemistry, U. Wash., 1931; B.A. in Physiology (Rhodes scholar), U. Oxford, Eng., 1934; D.Phil. in Biochemistry, U. Oxford, Eng., 1935; M.D., Harvard U., 1941. Research asst. advancing to asst. prof. indsl. physiology Harvard Fatigue Lab., 1935-46; expert cons. QMC 3, AUS, 1941-46; dir. U.S. Army Med. Nutrition Lab., Chgo., 1946-49; prof. physiology U. Ill. at Urbana, 1949-73, head dept., 1949-60, dir. univ. honors program, 1959-67, acting dean Grad. Coll., 1952-53; prof. biology Knox Coll., Galesburg, Ill., 1973-79; coordinator Knox Coll.-Rush U. Med. Program, 1973-79; sci. cons. Presbyn.-St. Luke's Hosp., Chgo., 1973-83; pres. Horn of the Moon Enterprises, Montpelier, Vt., 1980—. Co-author: Metabolic Methods, 1951, Physiological Measurements of Metabolic Functions in Man, 1963; author: Sir John Richardson, 1976; also articles in profl. jours. NSF Sr. Postdoctoral Research fellow, 1957-58; Guggenheim Meml. Found. fellow, 1964-65. Mem. Am. Soc. Clin. Investigation, Am. Physiol. Soc., Nutrition Today. Home: Horn of the Moon RFD 1 Box 5100 Montpelier VT 05602 *These I believe: Work hard. Deal honestly and straightforwardly with everyone. Be temperate in all aspects of life. Respect the rights and privileges of all living creatures.*

JOHNSON, ROBERT GERALD, consultant; b. Omaha, Mar. 13, 1928; s. Enoch and Helen Christine (Peterson) J.; m. Patsy Ruth Green, Feb. 24, 1950; children: Cynthia Marie, Cheryl Leigh, Christina Ruth. A.B., U. Colo., 1951; M.Sc., U. Omaha, 1953; Ed.D., Fla. State U., 1959. Pub. sch. tchr., Omaha, 1951-53; instr. Fla. State U., 1953-55; supr. elem. and jr. high sch., Guam, 1955-57; edn. adviser AID, Bangkok, Thailand, 1959-63, dep. chief East South Africa edn. div., Washington, 1963-65, chief East South Africa edn. br., 1965-66, dep. chief edn. div., 1966-67, chief Africa edn. div., 1967-69, asst. dir. edn., Thailand, 1969-72, assigned, Washington, 1972-75, chief human resources devel., La Paz, Bolivia, 1975-77, Kingston, Jamaica, 1977-80, cons., 1980—, U.S. Dept. State, 1980. Mem. bd. Internat. Sch., Bangkok, 1961-63. Served with AUS, 1946-48. Mem. Am. Fgn. Service Assn., Phi Delta Kappa. Club: Royal Bangkok Sports. Home: 7419 Park Terrace Dr Alexandria VA 22307

JOHNSON, ROBERT HENRY, political science educator; b. Hannaford, N.D., Jan. 23, 1921; s. Albert Idan and Alma (Peterson) J.; (div.)children: Mark Olin, Eric Lowell, Hilary Jean. B.A., Concordia Coll., Moorhead, Minn., 1942; M.S., Syracuse U., 1943; Ph.D., Harvard U., 1949. Teaching fellow Harvard U., 1948-49, instr. govt., 1949-51; asst. to exec. sec. NSC, 1951-54, mem., sec. spl. staff, 1954-59, dir. planning bd. secretariat, 1959-61; mem. policy planning council State Dept., 1962-67; sr. fellow Brookings Instn., 1966-68, guest scholar, 1970, 71, 73, 80; Harvey Picker prof. internat. relations Colgate U., 1968-71, 80—, Charles Evans Hughes prof. govt., 1971-80, chmn. dept. polit. sci., 1979-82, 83-84; vis. sr. fellow Overseas Devel. Council, 1974-75, 76-77; cons. to dir. internat. div. GAO, 1978-82; resident assoc. Carnegie Endowment for Internat. Peace, 1982-83. Contbr. articles to profl. jours. Served with USNR, 1943-46. Recipient Rockefeller Pub. Service award, 1958; Alumni Achievement award Concordia Coll., 1975; fellow Social Sci. Research Council, 1948-49; Ford Found. grantee, 1966. Mem. Am. Polit. Sci. Assn., Assn. Asian Studies. Congregationalist. Home: RD 1 Hamilton NY 13346 Office: Polit Sci Dept Colgate U Hamilton NY 13346

JOHNSON, ROBERT HERSEL, journalist; b. Colorado City, Tex., May 28, 1923; s. Robert Hersel and Leah (Sikes) J.; m. Luise Putcamp, Jr., Feb. 24, 1945; children: Robert Hersel, III, Luise Robin, Jan Leah, Stephanie Neale, Jennifer Anne. B.S. in Journalism, So. Methodist U., 1947. Reporter Phoenix Gazette, 1940-42; asst. sports editor Ariz. Republic, Phoenix, 1942-43; newscast writer Sta. KOY, Phoenix, 1943; reporter Dallas Times-Herald, 1946; with AP, 1946—, Utah-Idaho bur. chief, 1954-59, Ind. bur. chief, 1959-62, Tex. bur. chief, 1962-69, gen. sports editor, 1969-73, mng. editor, 1973-77, asst. gen. mgr., spl. asst. to pres., 1977—; Mem. Newspaper Readership Council, 1977-82. Served to capt. USMCR, 1943-46, 51-52. Home: 15 Cobblers Green New Canaan CT 06840 Office: 50 Rockefeller Plaza New York NY 10020 *The kind of journalism that is likely to bring about change for the better is journalism that is painfully honest, painfully clear, that illuminates large issues with small details, and in which the reporter is not a participant or an advocate but a dispassionate observer who keeps his own emotions at bay until the story is told.*

JOHNSON, ROBERT IVAR, business executive; b. Chgo., Aug. 18, 1933; s. Ivar Carl and Anna Elina (Wirkula) J.; m. Patricia A. Horgan, June 30, 1962; children: Christine Anne, Selenie Anne. Diploma, Wright Jr. Coll., 1953; A.B., Northwestern U., 1957; postgrad., U. Mich., 1958-59. Research asst. Dearborn Obs., Northwestern U., 1953-54, 57; planetarium tech. Adler Planetarium and Astron. Mus., 1953-55, asst. dir., acting dir., 1959, dir., 1960-66; staff Mus. Expdn. Observation Total Solar Eclipse, 1954, 63; dir. Kansas City Mus. History and Sci., 1966-70; exec. v.p., asst. sec., asst. treas., dir. Envirco, Inc., Northbrook, Ill., 1970-72; partner, exec. v.p. Tomorrow's Products Co., 1972-73; spectrographic observer U. Mich., 1958-59; adult edn. faculty Central YMCA, Chgo., 1959-61; lectr. astronomy Chgo. Acad. Scis., 1959-66, Chgo. Tchrs. Coll., 1960-66; spl. lectr. astronomy Ind. U., 1960-65; cons. Field Enterprises Ednl. Corp., 1960-66, Hubbard Sci. Co., 1961, Replogle Globe Co., 1962-63, 68, Compton's Ency., 1961-73, No. Ill. U., 1961-65, Ency. Brit. Films, Inc., 1962-64, McGraw-Hill, Inc., 1963, Mus. Sci. and Tech., Tel Aviv, 1965-70, Rand McNally & Co., 1966, NSF Earth Sci. Curriculum Project, 1966, Coll. Am. Pathologists, 1970, 73-76, 79—, MCR, Inc., 1972-76, McCrone Research Inst., 1972-83, Frank J. Corbett, Inc., 1972-75, Johnson & Johnson Advt., 1972-83, Dynamic Mktg. Programs, Inc., 1972-73, McCrone Assos., Inc., 1972-77, Yunker Industries, Inc., 1977—, Clay Engring. & Mfg. Co., 1977—, Sci. Teaching Aids Co., Inc., 1977—, Sonoscan Inc., 1977-83, F.E. Fryer Co., Inc., 1978-83, Andreas Assos., Inc., 1979-80; Scott Abbott Mfg. Co., 1978—, Tech. Mktg. Group Ltd., 1979—, Intermatic, Inc., 1979-83, others; dir. NSF Summer Inst. in Astronomy, 1963, 64, 66; partner TBM Investments Co., 1964-65; tech. cons. Follett Pub. Co., 1966-68; mem. citizens adv. com. for natural scis. Lake Forest Coll., 1961-66; bd. advisers World Book Ency. Sci. Service, 1964-66; program adv. bd. Inter-Univ. Center, 1966-73; mem. Am. Nat. ICOM Com. Edn. and Cultural Action; cons. astronomy and allied scis., planetarium design and ednl. films prodn. various orgns. Author: Teachers Guide for the Celestial Globe, 1961, Astronomy-Our Solar System and Beyond, 1963, Galaxy Model Study Guide, 1963, The Story of the Moon, 1963, rev. edit., 1968, 2d revision, 1971, Celestial Planetarium Guide Book, 1964, Meteorite Kit Study Guide, 1968, Sundials, 1968; editor: Insight, 1972-77, Techniques, Instruments and Accessories for Microanalysts—A User's Manual, 1972-83; editorial bd.: Space Frontiers, 1962-66; contbr. articles to profl. jours., other publs. Sci. fair judge high sch. div. Chgo. Bd. Edn., Parochial Schs., 1959-66; mem. U.S. com. for ednl. and cultural affairs Internat. Council Museums, 1966-70; mem. fine arts com. Ill. Sesquicentennial Commn., 1967-68; mem. Model Cities Com., Liberty Meml. Exhbn. Com., 1967-70 mem. Model Cities Com., Liberty Meml. Exhbn. Com., both Kansas City, Regional Health and Welfare Council, 1967-70, Kansas City Assembly on U.S. and Eastern Europe, 1968, NSF panel Summer Inst. for Secondary Schs., 1968-76, Midwest Mus. Conf., 1964-70; fin. com. Midwest Mus. Conf., 1967-70; mem. spl. events com. Kansas City Jewish Community Center, 1968-70; mem. Twin Lakes Bicentennial Com., 1976; v.p. Lakewood Sch. Parent Tchr. Orgn., 1976-77, pres., 1977-78, 80; bd. govs. Bacchus Cultural and Ednl. Found., 1968-70. Served with AUS, 1955-56; intelligence analyst; Chgo.-Gary Nike Def. Hdqrs. Recipient certificate for service Gary (Ind.) Pub. Schs., 1959; Indsl. Research 100 award, 1973; named One of 10 Outstanding Young Men Chgo. Jr. C. of C. and Industry, 1961. Fellow AAAS; mem. Am. Astron. Soc. (co-chmn. com. spl. events 1964), Chgo. Astron. Soc., Internat. Platform Assn., Chgo. Planetarium Soc., Chgo. Physics Club (dir., pres. 1960-66), Royal Astron. Soc. Can., Assn. Sci. Mus. Dirs., Chgo. Geog. Soc., Adult Edn. Council Greater Chgo. (speakers bur., dir.), Am. Assn. Museums (chmn. planetarium sect. 1962-66, program chmn. 1966), Northwestern U. Alumni Assn., Nat. Adult Edn. Assn. (tours com. 1966), Golf (Ill.) Civic Assn., Mu Beta Phi (hon.). Clubs: Execs. (Chgo.); Carriage. Home: 21 Spring Lake Dr New Port Richey FL 33552 Office: HLA Advt and Pub Relations 3502 Henderson Blvd Tampa FL 33609

JOHNSON, ROBERT KELLOGG, librarian, educator; b. Grand Rapids, Mich., July 27, 1913; s. Maurice Flower and Hazel Jeannette (Kellogg) J.; m. Mary Loretta Franks, Aug. 22, 1950; children: Phillip, Emily (dec.), Peter, Sarah, Robert Kellogg. A.B., U. Mont., 1937; B.A. in Librarianship, U. Wash., 1938; M.S., U. Ill., 1946, Ph.D., 1957. Reference asst. Library Assn. Portland, Oreg., summer 1938; circulation and reference librarian, instr. French Pacific U., 1938-39, acting librarian, instr. library sci., 1939-40, head librarian, asso. prof. library sci., acting head audio-visual dept., 1946-48; head librarian, instr. library sci. Central Coll., Fayette, Mo., 1940-42; payroll auditor, spl. asst. to plant exec. central devel, and expt. unit Gen. Motors Corp., 1942-43; bibliographer U. Ill. Library, 1948-50, cataloger, 1950-52; mem. staff Air U. Library, Maxwell AFB, Ala., 1952-59; asst. dir. libraries Drexel U., 1959-62; prof. library sci. Grad. Sch. Library Sci., 1959-64, dir. libraries, 1962-64; prof. library sci. U. Ariz., 1964—, univ. librarian, 1964-72, prof., 1972—, individual studies dir., 1979—; cons. Westerners Internat., 1968—; Chmn. Library Council Met. Phila., 1963-64; mem. Ariz. Library Survey Adv. Com., 1966-68, Com. Jr. Colls. in Phila. Area, 1962-63, Media (Pa.) Free Library Bd., 1959-60; mem. exec. and editorial bds. Seminar Acquisition Latin Am. Library Materials, 1969-72; Cons. in field. Contbr. numerous articles to profl. jours. Trustee Bibliog. Center for Research, Rocky Mountain Region, Inc., 1968-72, pres., 1970-71. Served with USNR, 1943-46. Recipient Distinguished Alumnus award U. Wash. Sch. Librarianship Alumni Assn., 1973. Mem A.L.A. (mem. council 1969-72), Ariz. State Library Assn. (exec. bd. 1965-69, v.p. 1967-68, pres. 1968-69), Assn. Coll. and Research Libraries (bd. dirs. 1969-72), Seminar on Acquisition of Latin Am. Library Materials-Assn. Research Libraries (chmn. joint Latin Am. Farmington Plan subcom. 1970-73), Western Writers Am. (bd. of judges for non-fiction awards 1971-82), Southwestern Library Assn. (chmn. awards com. 1976-77). Home: 3020 E 3d St Tucson AZ 85716

JOHNSON, ROBERT LAWRENCE, mechanical engineering educator; b. Glasgow, Mont., June 18, 1919; s. Elmer and Hilma Otilia (Lindstrom) J.; m. Josephine Marie Saetre, Feb. 3, 1945; children: Robert Lawrence, Elizabeth Marie, Richard Paul. B.S. in Mech. Engring, Mont. State U., 1942. Research mech. engr. NACA (now NASA), Langley Field, Va., 1942-43, research engr., 1943-58; project engr., head lubrication, then chief lubrication br. NASA, Cleve., 1958-75; ret., 1975; adj. prof. mech. engring. Rensselaer Poly. Inst., Troy, N.Y., 1975—; cons. in field; chmn. ASME-RCL adv. bd. on energy conservation through tribology U.S. Dept. Energy, 1976-82; lectr. lubrication Gordon Research Confs., 1960—, chmn., 1974; U.S. del., chmn. Internat. Research Group on Wear of Engring. Materials OECD, 1964-73. Contbr. articles to profl. jours. Recipient medal for exceptional sci. achievement NASA, 1973; IR100 award, 1966, 73. Fellow Am. Soc. Lubrication Engrs. (Alfred E. Hunt award 1961, 65, nat. award 1971, nat. pres. 1968-69), Instn. Mech. Engrs. Gt. Britain (gold medal for tribology 1976); mem. ASTM, AAAS, ASME (research com. on tribology, Mayo D. Hersey award 1977), Soc. Automotive Engrs., Lambda Chi Alpha. Lutheran. Clubs: Masons, Shriners. Patentee in field. Home: 5304 W 62d St Edina MN 55436 Office: Dept Mech Engring Rensselaer Poly Inst Troy NY 12181

JOHNSON, ROBERT LOUIS, astronautics company executive; b. Winslow, Ariz., May 16, 1920; s. Ernest Conrad and Carrie Arora (Saunders) J.; m. Betty Tuft, Oct. 24, 1942; children: Jeanne Johnson Dillon, Robert C., Louise Buck, Bruce T., Kirk T. B.S. in Mech. Engring., U. Calif., Berkeley, 1941, M.S., 1942. Vice pres. research and engring., then v.p. manned orbit lab. Douglas Aircraft Co., 1946-69; asst. sec. army for research and devel., 1969-73; v.p. engring. and research McDonnell Douglas Corp., 1973-75; pres. McDonnell Douglas Astronautics Co., Huntington Beach, Calif., 1975—; corp. v.p., aerospace group exec. McDonnell Douglas Corp., 1980—; mem. engring. adv. council U. Calif., Berkeley. Served to lt. USNR, 1942-46. Recipient James H. Wyld Meml. award Am. Rocket Soc., 1960. Fellow Am. Inst. Aeros. and Astronautics; mem. Nat. Acad. Engring., Nat. Space Club, Assn. U.S. Army (dir.). Episcopalian. Club: El Niguel Country. Address: McDonnell Douglas Corp 3855 Lakewood Blvd Long Beach CA 90846

JOHNSON, ROBERT MAURICE, newspaper executive; b. Lockport, Ill., July 14, 1945; s. Norman Herman and Virginia (Keith) J.; m. Susan Elaine Chadwick, Jan. 19, 1971; children—Stephanie Chadwick, Chadwick Robert. B.S. in Bus. and Fin, La. State U., 1968; J.D., U. Mich., 1971. Bar: D.C. bar 1972, Ill. bar 1971. Asso., then partner firm Seyfarth, Shaw, Fairweather & Geraldson, Washington, 1971-75, Chgo., 1975-79; v.p., gen. mgr. Dispatch Printing Co.; pubs. Columbus (Ohio) Dispatch, 1979-82; pres., chief operating officer Newsday, Inc., 1982—. Mem. Ill. Bar Assn., D.C. Bar Assn., Am. Newspaper Publishers Assn.

JOHNSON, ROBERT MERRILL, coll. adminstr.; b. Detroit, Sept. 17, 1926; s. Austin George and Jeanne Maude (Parkin) J.; m. Eleonore Maria Wegele, June 14, 1947; children—Barbara Jeanne (Mrs. Patrick Burns), Eric Merrill, Kristopher James, Kim Marie. B.S., U. Detroit, 1951, M.S., 1953; Ph.D., Mich. State U., 1957. Grad. teaching fellow U. Detroit, 1951-52; mfr. agt. Baker & Collinson, Detroit, 1953-54; grad. asst. Mich. State U., 1954-57; instr. Colo. State U., 1957-58, asst. prof., 1958-61, asso. prof., 1961-64, prof., 1964, asst. dir.research found., 1958-62, dir. facilities devel., 1964-66; program dir. NSF, Washington, 1962-64, staff asso., 1966-68; grad. dean, dir. research Fla. State U., 1968-73, provost grad. studies and research, 1973—. Contbr. articles to profl. jours. Served with USAAF, 1944-46. Mem. Am. Physiol. Soc., AAAS, Electron Microscope Soc. Am., Sigma Xi. Home: 306 Saratoga Dr Tallahassee FL 32312

JOHNSON, ROBERT RAYMOND, mgmt. cons., educator; b. Anthony, Kans., Feb. 22, 1917; s. Wallace Blaine and Marie Frances (Mulholl) J.; m. Elizabeth Forsythe Griffin, Feb. 5, 1941; children—Elizabeth Ann, Alan, Brian, Eleanor. B.S., Northwestern U., 1939; postgrad., U. Oreg., 1951-55, U. Pitts., 1964. Personnel examiner, City of Kansas City, Mo., 1940-41; cons. Pub. Adminstrn. Service Chgo., 1941-46; dir. Oreg. Civil Service Commn., 1946-51; exec. dir. Oreg. Legis. Commn. State Govt. Reorgn., 1949-50; civil govt. adviser to Greece ECA, 1951-55; exec. dir. Oreg. Legis. Commn. Local Govt. Orgn., 1955-56; dir. Oreg. Dept. Fin. and Adminstrn., 1956-57; cons. League Oreg. Cities, 1957-58; orgn. and mgmt. adviser to India ICA, 1958-61; chief public adminstrn. adviser to Iran AID, 1961-64, asst. dir. for East Pakistan, Dacca, 1965-67; asst. dir. pub. adminstrn. AID mission to Vietnam, 1967-68; asso. dir. for local devel., Vietnam, 1968-69; dir. tech. assistance AID (East Asia Bur.), Washington, 1969-73; exec. dir. adv. com. Vol. for Assistance, 1973; asst. dean Grad. Sch. Adminstrn., Willamette U., 1975-78; mgmt. cons., 1975—. Mem. Oreg. Interstate Coop. Commn., 1957-58; U.S. observer pub. sect. mgmt. UN-ECAFE, 1959. Mem. Am. Soc. Pub. Adminstrn. (pres. Oreg. 1957-58), Asia Soc., Middle East Inst., Eastern Region Orgn. Pub. Adminstrn., Indian Inst. Pub. Adminstrn., Sigma Alpha Epsilon. Clubs: Rotarian, Mason., Internat. (Washington). Home: 830 Clarmount NW Salem OR 97304 Office: PO Box 2312 Salem OR 97308

JOHNSON, ROBERT REED, paper company executive, lawyer; b. Plainfield, Wis., June 1, 1919; s. Buchanan and Grace (Walker) J.; m. Anna M. Buschor, June 1, 1946; 1 son, Reed Buchanan. Ph.B., U Wis., 1941; LL.B., U. Wis. Law Sch., 1948. Bar: Wis. 1948. Practice law, Plainfield, Wis., 1948-49; with Nekoosa Papers, Inc., Port Edwards, Wis., 1949—; sec. Nekoosa Papers Inc., 1962; gen. counsel Nekoosa Papers, Inc., 1962; sec., gen. counsel Butler Paper Co., 1963—; pres. Nekoosa Port Edwards Savs. & Loan Assn., 1959-70, chmn. bd. dirs., 1970—; v.p., dir. Nekoosa Found., Inc., 1956—. Justice of Peace Village of Port Edwards; supr. Wood County Bd. Suprs., 1963-70; bd. visitors U. Wis. Law Sch., 1966-69, chmn., 1968-69. Served with AUS, 1941-45. Mem. Wis. Bar Assn., Wood County Bar Assn., Wis. Law Alumni Assn., U. Wis. Law Sch. Benchers Soc., Chi Psi. Republican. Methodist. Home: 50 Ver Bunker Ave Port Edwards WI 54469 Office: 100 Wisconsin River Dr Port Edwards WI 54469

JOHNSON, ROBERT ROYCE, computer co. exec.; b. Madison, Wis., June 20, 1928; s. Royce E. and Olga S. (Wellberg) J.; m. Mary Perrine, Dec. 30, 1953; children—Perrine, Royce, Allegra. B.S. in Engring, U. Wis., 1950; M.Engring., Yale U., 1951; Ph.D., Calif. Inst. Tech., 1956. Sr. scientist Hughes Aircraft Co., Culver City, Calif., 1951-55; mgr. engring., computer dept. Gen. Electric Co., Phoenix, 1956-64; with Burroughs Corp., Detroit, 1964-81, v.p. engring., 1968-81, v.p. tech., 1979-81; sr. v.p. engring. and info. systems, dir. energy Energy Conversion Devices Inc., Troy, Mich., 1981—. Village trustee Village of Franklin, Mich., 1972-76. Recipient Outstanding Alumnus award U. Wis., 1970. Fellow IEEE; mem. Assn. Computing Machinery, Engring. Soc. Detroit (pres. 1975-76), Sigma Xi. Clubs: Catawba Island, Detroit Athletic. Office: Energy Conversion Devices Inc 1675 W Maple St Troy MI 48084

JOHNSON, ROBERT WILLARD, management educator; b. Denver, Dec. 23, 1921; s. Ernest A. and Edith (Glassford) J.; m. Mary McCormack, Jan. 7, 1945 (div. Oct. 1983); children: Judith L., Cynthia L.; m. Dixie P. Jackson, Oct. 22, 1983. Student, Oberlin Coll., 1939-42; M.B.A., Harvard U., 1946; Ph.D., Northwestern U., 1952. Asst. prof. Southwestern at Memphis, 1948-50; chmn. Mfrs. and Traders Trust

Co.; prof. fin., dir. exec. devel. program, dir. mgmt. tng. program, chmn. dept. U. Buffalo, until 1959; economist Fed. Res. Bd., 1956-57; prof. fin. adminstrn. Mich. State U., 1959-64; prof. mgmt., dir. Credit Research Center, Purdue U., Lafayette, Ind., 1964—; Reporter-economist Nat. Conf. Commrs. on Uniform State Laws, 1964-76; Fellow Inst. Basic Math. for Application to Bus., Harvard, 1959-60; mem. Nat. Commn. Consumer Fin., 1969-72. Author: (with others) Financial Management, 5th edit., 1982, Self-Correcting Problems in Finance, 3d edit., 1976, Capital Budgeting, 1977. Served with Supply Corps, USNR, 1943-46. Mem. Am. Fin. Assn., Am. Econs. Assn., Fin. Mgmt. Assn. (pres. 1971). Home: 1001 Digby Dr Lafayette IN 47905

JOHNSON, ROGERS BRUCE, chemical company executive; b. Boston, Apr. 8, 1928; s. Rogers Bruce and Dorothy Squires (Aiken) J.; m. Margery Ruth Howe, June 25, 1951; children: Wynn, Carol, Stephen, Herrick. B.A., Harvard U., 1949, M.B.A., 1955. Field salesman Dow U.S.A., Pitts., 1956-61; mgr. molding materials Dow Europe, Zurich, Switzerland, 1961-65; bus. mgr. styrene polymers Dow U.S.A., Midland, Mich., 1965-70; corp. products dir. Dow Chem. Co., Midland, Mich., 1970-76; v.p. supply, distbn. and planning Dow Chem. U.S.A., Midland, Mich., 1976-81, group v.p. adminstrv. services, 1981—; dir. Dow Can., Sarnia, Ont., Can., 1973-76. Bd. dirs. Midland Community Tennis Ctr., (Mich.), 1974—; pres. Midland Community Tennis Ctr. (Mich.), 1975-78, treas., 1979-80. Served to 1st lt. USAF, 1951-53. Decorated Bronze Star. Republican. Office: Dow Chem Co 2020 Dow Center Midland MI 48640 *My success in business has been based on: (1) selecting good people; (2) establishing sound strategy with assistance of involved people consistant with overall objectives; (3) providing people freedom to implement strategy while at the same time monitoring that important process and suggesting modifications as necessary. It goes without saying that people are a company's most important asset.*

JOHNSON, RONALD, poet; b. Ashland, Kans., Nov. 25, 1935; s. Albert Theodore and Helen (Mayse) J. B.A., Columbia, 1960. Writer-in-residence U. Ky., 1970-71; Theodore Roethke chair for poetry U. Wash., 1973. Author: A Line of Poetry, A Row of Trees, 1964, Sports & Divertissments, 1965, The Book of the Green Man, 1967, Valley of the Many-Colored Grasses, 1969, Balloons for Moonless Nights, 1969, The Spirit Walks, The Rocks Will Talk, 1969, Songs of the Earth, 1970, Eyes & Objects, 1975, RADI OS, 1977, Ark: The Foundations, 1980. Recipient Boar's Head prize Columbia, 1960, Inez Boulton award Poetry, Chgo., 1965, Nat. Endowment for Arts award, 1970, 74. Address: 73 Elgin Park San Francisco CA 94103

JOHNSON, ROY E., Pres. United Union of Roofers, Waterproofers and Allied Workers. Office: 1125 17th St NW Washington DC 20036§

JOHNSON, ROY RAGNAR, electrical engineer; b. Chgo., Jan. 23, 1932; s. Ragnar Anders and Ann Viktoria (Lundquist) J.; m. Martha Ann Mattson, June 21, 1963; children: Linnea Marit, Kaisa Ann. B.S. in Elec. Engring, U. Minn., 1954, M.S., 1956, Ph.D., 1959. Research fellow U. Minn., 1957-59; research scientist Boeing Sci. Research Labs., Seattle, 1959-72; prin. scientist KMS Fusion, Inc., Ann Arbor, Mich., 1972-74, dir. fusion expts., 1974-78, tech. dir., 1978—; vis. lectr. U. Wash., Seattle, 1959-60; vis. scientist Royal Inst. Tech., Stockholm, 1963-64. Author: Nonlinear Effects in Plasmas, 1969, Plasma Physics, 1977; contbr. to profl. publs. Bd. advisors Rose-Hulman Inst. Tech., 1982—. Fellow Am. Phys. Soc.; Mem. N.Y. Acad. Scis., IEEE, AAAS, Vasa Order Am., Am. Swedish Inst., Torpar Riddar Orden, Swedish Pioneer Hist. Soc., Swedish Council Am., Eta Kappa Nu, Gamma Alpha. Lutheran. Patentee in field. Home: 671 Adrienne Ln Ann Arbor MI 48103 Office: 3621 S State Rd Ann Arbor MI 48104

JOHNSON, RUSSELL SIMMS, lawyer; b. Dallas, Mar. 29, 1947; s. William E., Jr. and Jane (Warner) J.; m. Lisa Andrews, Sept. 25, 1976. B.A., Princeton U., 1969; J.D., U. Tex., 1972. Bar: Tex. 1972. Since practiced in, Dallas; partner firm Johnson, Johnson & Johnson; v.p. Johnson Energy Corp.; pres. Agro-Pacific Devel., Inc. Bd. dirs. Dallas Summer Musicals. Mem. Am., Tex., Dallas bar assns. Presbyterian. Address: 1725 One Dallas Centre Dallas TX 75201

JOHNSON, SAM, judge; b. Hubbard, Tex., Nov. 17, 1920; s. Sam D. and Flora (Brown) J.; m. June Page, June 1, 1946; children: Page Johnson Harris, Janet Johnson Clements, Sam. J. B.B.A., Baylor U., 1946; LL.B., U. Tex., 1949. Bar: Tex. bar 1949. Former county atty. Hill County, Tex.; dist. atty. and dist. judge 66th Jud. Dist. of Hill County, Tex.; judge 14th Ct. Civil Appeals, Houston; assoc. justice Supreme Ct. Tex., Austin; now judge U.S. Ct. of Appeals for 5th Circuit.; Bd. dirs. Nat. Legal Aid and Defender Assn.; past bd. dirs. Houston Legal Found. Served with AUS, 1942-45. Recipient Disting. Alumnus award Baylor U., 1978-79. Mem. ABA (chmn. appellate judges conf., bd. govs., bd. govs. 1979-82), Baylor Ex-Students Assn. (pres. 1972-73). Democrat. Home: 1811 Exposition Blvd Austin TX 78703 Office: 999 American Bank Tower Austin TX 78701

JOHNSON, SAMUEL CURTIS, wax company executive; b. Racine, Wis., Mar. 2, 1928; s. Herbert Fisk and Gertrude (Brauner) J.; m. Imogene Powers, May 8, 1954; children: Samuel Curtis III, Helen Powers, Herbert Fisk III, Winifred Johnson Marquart. B.A., Cornell U., 1950; M.B.A., Harvard U., 1952; LL.D., Carthage Coll., 1974, Northland Coll., 1974, Ripon Coll., 1980. With S.C. Johnson & Son, Inc., Racine, 1954—, internat. v.p., 1962-63, exec. v.p., 1963-66, pres., 1966-67, chmn., pres., chief exec. officer, 1967-72, chmn., chief exec. officer, 1972-79, chmn., 1979-80, chmn., chief exec. officer, 1980—; dir. Johnson Wax cos., Eng., Japan, Germany, Switzerland, Can., Australia, France; chmn. Heritage Bank & Trust of Racine; dir., chmn. exec. com. Heritage Wis. Corp., Milw.; dir. Deere & Co., Moline, Ill., Mobil Corp., N.Y.C. Chmn. The Mayo Found.; trustee, mem. exec. com. Cornell U.; chmn. Johnson's Wax Fund, Inc.; founding chmn. emeritus Prairie Sch., Racine; chmn. Johnson Found., Inc.; chmn., dir. Heritage Racine Corp.; mem. adv. council Cornell U. Grad. Sch. Mgmt.; bd. regents Smithsonian Assn.; mem. Bus. Council. Mem. Chgo. Council on Fgn. Relations (dir.), Chi Psi. Clubs: Cornell (N.Y.C., Milw.); Univ. (Milw.); Racine Country; American (London). Home: 4815 Lighthouse Dr Racine WI 53402 Office: 1525 Howe St Racine WI 53403

JOHNSON, SANKEY ANTON, manufacturing company executive; b. Bremerton, Wash., May 14, 1940; s. Sankey Broyd and Alice Mildred (Norum) J.; m. Carolyn Lee Rogers, Nov. 30, 1969; children: Marni Lee, Ronald Anton. B.S. in M.E, U. Wash.; M.B.A., Stanford U. Vice pres. gen. mgr. Cummins Asia Pacific, Manila, Philippines, 1974-78; v.p. automotive Cummins Engine Co., Columbus, Ind., 1978-79; v.p. N. Am. bus., 1979-81; pres., chief exec. officer Onan Corp., Mpls., 1981—; dir. Roger's Electromatics Inc., Donaldson Co. Mem. Am. Mgmt. Assn., Western Hwy. Inst., Am. Electronics Assn. Clubs: Minneapolis, Wayzata Country. Home: 2709 Hidden Creek Ln Wayzata MN 55391 Office: 1400 73d Ave NE Minneapolis MN 55432

JOHNSON, SEARCY LEE, lawyer; b. Dallas, Aug. 30, 1908; s. Jesse Lee and Annie Clyde (Searcy) J.; m. Lillian Cox; 1 dau., Susan Lee (Mrs. Keyes). A.B., Williams Coll., 1929; LL.B., U. Tex., 1933. Bar: Tex. 1933. Since practiced in, Dallas; partner Lawther, Cramer, Perry & Johnson, 1941, then Johnson, Guthrie, White & Stanfield; now Johnson, Shanklin, Billings & Porter.; Legal adv. Gen. Hershey (on vets. reemployment), 1944-45; spl. asst. to U.S. Atty. Gen., organizer, chief Veterans Affairs sect. Dept. Justice, 1945-47. Author: Feast of Tabernacles; Contbr. to: Hildebrand's Texas Corporations, 1942, also articles to legal jours.; Composer: others. The Ballad of the Thresher. Served as lt. comdr. USNR, 1941-45. Decorated Army Commendation award. Mem. Washington Bar Assn., Tex. Bar Assn., Dallas Bar Assn. (spl. prosecutor 1938), Am. Legion, Amvets (charter mem.), ASCAP, Am. Authors and Composers, S.A.R., Am. Judicature Soc., Fellows Tex. Bar, Psi Upsilon. Clubs: Masons (33 deg.), Chaparral, Dallas; City, Insurance (N.Y.C.); Dallas Country. Home: 3901 Gillon Ave Dallas TX 75205 Office: 1410 Republic Nat Bank Bldg Dallas TX 75201

JOHNSON, SIDNEY MALCOLM, educator; b. New Haven, Aug. 17, 1924; s. Everett Caswell and Eleanor (Eckman) J.; m. Lora Louise Dunbar, Sept. 29, 1945; children: Thomas Malcolm, Frederick William, Karl Everett. B.A., Yale U., 1944, M.A., 1948, Ph.D., 1953. Asst. instr. Yale U., 1946-51; instr. U. Kans., 1951-53, asst. prof., 1953-58, asso. prof., 1958-62, prof., 1962-65; prof. German, chmn. dept. Emory U., Atlanta, 1965-72; prof. German, Ind. U., Bloomington, 1972—, chmn. dept., 1972-78; dir. Ind.-Purdue U. Study Program, U. Hamburg, W.Ger., 1978-79. Contbr. articles on medieval German lit. to profl. jours. Served to lt. (j.g.) USNR, 1943-46. Research grantee Am. Philos. Soc., 1963. Mem. MLA, Am. Assn. Tchrs. German, AAUP, Wolfram von Eschenbach Gesellschaft, Internat. Assn. Germanic Studies, Medieval Acad. Home: 2320 Covenanter Dr Bloomington IN 47401

JOHNSON, STANFORD LELAND, marketing educator; b. Mapleton, Utah, July 31, 1924; s. Leland Stanford and Mary Alice (Thompson) J.; m. Lucy E. Watts, Sept. 14, 1945 (div. 1976); children: Janet, Debbie, Stanford Leland, Robert, Gregory, Kent; m. Heidi G. Ivanoff, Jan. 1977. B.S. in Bus. and Social Sci., Utah State U., 1949; M.S. in Mktg. and Retailing, NYU, 1950; Ph.D. in Bus, N.Y. U., 1965. Field research Dept. Commerce, 1949-51; asst. mgr. Wickel's Men's Wear Store, Logan, Utah, 1951-52; asst. office mgr. Raymond Constrn. Co., Logan, 1952-54; asst. prof. Sch. Bus., Utah State U., 1951-54; asst. dean, instr. N.Y. U., 1954-64; mem. faculty San Francisco State U., 1964—, prof. mktg., transp. and world bus., 1968—, chmn. dept., 1972-76; cons. to industry, 1960—. Editorial cons., McGraw-Hill Book Co., Houghton Mifflin Co., Wadsworth Pub. Co., Sci. Research Assos. Bd. dirs., acad. adviser Schiller Internat. U., Heidelberg, Germany, 1969—. Served as pilot USAAF, 1943-45. Ins. fellow Am. Assn. U. Tchrs., 1953; Forum and Finance fellow, 1954; Found. for Econ. Edn. fellow, 1955; recipient Founder's Day award N.Y. U., 1965. Mem. Am. Mktg. Assn. Republican. Mem. Ch. of Jesus Christ of Latter Day Saints. Home: 648 Clarendon Ave San Francisco CA 94131 Office: Sch Business San Francisco State Univ 19th Ave at Holloway St San Francisco CA 94132

JOHNSON, THEODORE MEBANE, investment executive; b. Denver, Jan. 25, 1934; s. Harold Theodore and Flora Luella (Cunningham) J.; m. Sandra Hall, May 23, 1970. B.S., U. Denver, 1956. Partner, Hornblower Weeks-Hemphill, Noyes, 1961-78, sr. v.p., dir., exec. com., until 1978; sr. v.p., dir. Eastern div., mgr. Paine Webber Jackson & Curtis, N.Y.C., 1978—. Co-founder, past dir. N.Am. Housing Corp. Served to lt. (j.g.) USNR, 1956-57. Mem. Bond Club D.C. Presbyterian. Clubs: Congressional Country, Univ., City Tavern (Washington); N.Y. Athletic. Home: 6223 Kennedy Dr Chevy Chase MD 20015 Office: 1120 20th St Washington DC 20036

JOHNSON, THEODORE OLIVER, JR., musician, educator; b. Elkhart, Ind., Oct. 9, 1929; s. Theodore Oliver and Harriet Koehler (Herrold) J.; m. Carol Ann Jolliff, June 22, 1968; children: Karen, Nancy, Steven, David. Mus.B., U. Mich., 1951, Mus.M., 1952, D.Mus. Arts (Rackham fellow), 1959. Mem. music-theory faculty, violinist in faculty string quartet Sch. Fine Arts, U. Kans., 1958-64; mem. music theory and lit. faculty dept. music Coll. Arts and Letters, Mich. State U., East Lansing, 1964—, prof. music, 1977—, chair music theory, 1984—. Violist and violinist, Beaumount String Quartet, 1964-80; concertmaster, Lansing Symphony Orch., 1967-69; prin. violist, Lansing Symphony Orch., 1982—; concertmaster, Grand Rapids Symphony Orch., 1972-73; dir. music, Bethel Baptist Ch., 1969-82; solo recitalist.; Composer motets; author: An Analytical Survey of the Fifteen Two-Part Inventions by J.S. Bach, 1982. Served in U.S. Army, 1952-55; Korea, Japan. Fulbright scholar, 1956-57; recipient Stanley award U. Mich. Sch. Music, 1951. Mem. Phi Mu Alpha Sinfonia, Phi Kappa Phi, Pi Kappa Lambda, Phi Eta Sigma. Home: 651 Hillcrest Ave East Lansing MI 48823 Office: 417 Music Practice Bldg Mich State U East Lansing MI 48824

JOHNSON, THOMAS S., banker; b. Racine, Wis., Nov. 19, 1940; s. H. Norman and Jane Agnes (McAvoy) J.; m. Margaret Ann Werner, Apr. 18, 1970; children: Thomas Philip, Scott Michael, Margaret Ann. A.B. in Econs., Trinity Coll., 1962; M.B.A., Harvard U., 1964. Instr. Ateneo de Manila U. Grad. Bus. Sch., Philippines, 1964-66; spl. asst. to controller U.S. Dept. Def., Washington, 1966-69; with Chem. Bank, N.Y.C., 1969—, pres., dir., 1983—; dir. Pan Atlantic Group Inc. Co-author: Condominium Housing of the Future, 1964. Chmn. bd. dirs. Union Theol. Sem.; bd. dirs. Montclair Art Mus. (N.J.); trustee Trinity Coll. Recipient Trinity Coll. Alumni Medal Excellence, 1976. Mem. Fin. Execs. Inst., Assn. Res. City Bankers. Democrat. Roman Catholic. Clubs: Montclair Golf; Wall St., Bond (N.Y.C.). Office: Chemical Bank 277 Park Ave New York NY 10010

JOHNSON, TORRENCE VAINO, astronomer; b. Rockville, N.Y., Dec. 1, 1944; s. Vaino Oliver and Priscilla Welch (Sneed) J.; m. Mary Eleanor Zachman, Mar. 31, 1967; children: Aaron Torrence, Eleanor Nancy. B.S. with honors, Washington U., St. Louis, 1966; Ph.D., Calif. Inst. Tech., 1970. Research assoc. Planetary Astronomy Lab., MIT, 1969-71; resident research assoc. NRC, Jet Propulsion Lab., Pasadena, 1971-73, sr. scientist, mem. tech. staff, 1973-74; group supr. Optical Astronomy Group, 1974—, project scientist Project Galileo, 1977—, research scientist, 1980-81, sr. research scientist, 1981—; vis. assoc. prof. Calif. Inst. Tech., 1981-83; cons. Jet Propulsion Lab., Pasadena, 1971. NASA trainee Calif. Inst. Tech., 1966-69; recipient Exceptional Sci. Achievement medal NASA, 1980, 81. Fellow Explorers Club; mem. Am. Astron. Soc. (sec.-treas. div. planetary sci. 1977-80), Am. Geophys. Union, AAAS, Internat. Astron. Union, Planetary Soc. (founding mem.), Sigma Xi. Office: 183-301 Jet Propulsion Lab 4800 Oak Grove Dr Pasadena CA 91103 *A major Theme in my life has been curiosity. My parents encouraged this trait, as did a variety of schools around the United States, and I have been fortunate to be allowed to satisfy my curiosity professionally, and occasionally to get paid for it. To date, one of the greatest fullfillments in my life has been the opportunity to participate in the Voyager mission, which has opened our eyes to worlds which I had previously only glimpsed dimly, through earth bound telescopes as a boy and a young astronomer.*

JOHNSON, VAN, actor; b. Newport, R.I., Aug. 25, 1916; s. Charles and Loretta J.; m. Eve Abbott Wynn, Jan. 25, 1947 (div.); 1 dau., Schuyler Van. Grad. high sch. Began as worker in father's plumbing office, 1936. 1st stage appearance in chorus of musical New Faces, 1937; later toured as singer with vaudeville act; joined, Eight Men of Manhattan; appearing (with Mary Martin at), Rainbow Room; appeared: in roles in Too Many Girls, 1940, Pal Joey, 1941; in more than 30 motion pictures, 1941—; appearances include: Murder in the Big House, Remains to Be Seen, Easy to Love, The Caine Mutiny, The End of the Affair, Mating Game; appeared: in more than 30 motion pictures Kidnapping of the President; TV appearances include Rich Man, Poor Man, Kennedy Ctr. Honors, 1982; has appeared in: stage appearances include Tribute; toured in: musicals Damn Yankees, summer 1963. Address: care William Morris Agy 151 El Camino Beverly Hills CA 90212 *

JOHNSON, VERDENAL HOAG, English educator, art editor, writer; b. Newark, Nov. 22, 1924; d. Philip Osborne and Frances (Verdenal) Hoag; m. Edward F. Johnson, June 29, 1945; children: Candida Ann, David Bladen, Frances Verdenal Meffen. B.A., Swarthmore Coll., 1945; postgrad., Temple U., 1945-46, Rutgers U., 1956-57, Newark State Coll., 1961-63; M.A. in Am. Studies, Seton Hall U., 1973. Psychometrician VA, Phila., Bklyn., 1944-46; founder, dir. Argus Gallery, Madison, N.J., 1961-67; psychol. cons. Hooper Holmes Bur., Basking Ridge, N.J., 1965-73; art editor Newark Star Ledger, 1969-74; tchr. English, Morristown (N.J.) High Sch., 1963-82, chmn. dept., 1970-82, coordinator student vol. program, 1982-84; prof. English, Seton Hall U., South Orange, N.J., 1982—; lectr., art judge; curator Acorn Hall, Morristown, N.J., 1980—. Originator: exhbn. Brit. Printmakers Council. Charter pres. Vols. of Newark Mus., 1975-77; Active Girl Scouts Am., ARC, various community activities; mem. Gov.'s Commn. Study Arts N.J., 1965-66; founding mem. Costume and Textiles Group Museums Council of N.J. Mem. NEA, N.J. Edn. Assn., Morris County Hist. Soc. (trustee). Home: 88 Garfield Ave Madison NJ 07940

JOHNSON, VERNON ARTHUR, former aircraft mfr.; b. Heavener, Okla., Dec. 15, 1914; s. Arthur and Lillian Bell (Bradley) J.; m. Dorothy Lee Thompson, June 18, 1939; children—Brian A., Curtis B., Shirley L. (Mrs. Joseph E. Henderson). A.B., U. Calif., 1936; postgrad., Harvard Advanced Mgmt. Program, 1963. Asst. mgr. San Bernardino (Calif.) C. of C., 1937-38, mgr., Redlands, Calif., 1939-40, Bakersfield, 1941-42; staff assembly div. Lockheed Aircraft Corp., 1943, asst. pub. relations mgr., 1944-47, staff Washington office, asst. to pres., 1948-54, Washington mgr., 1954-58, v.p. Eastern region, 1958-72, sr. v.p. Eastern region, 1972-74, sr. adviser, 1974-80. Trustee Palm Beach-Martin County Med. Center, 1979—. Mem. Phi Sigma Kappa. Clubs: Aero (pres. 1953), Congressional Country (v.p. 1957-58), Burning Tree (Washington) (pres. 1970-71); Turtle Creek (Tequesta, Fla.) (pres. 1977-78). Home: 14 Turtle Creek Dr Tequesta FL 33458

JOHNSON, VICTOR LAWRENCE, banker; b. Phila., Feb. 8, 1928; s. Paul J. and Eleanor (Moskowitz) J.; m. Joan Markovitz, Dec. 4, 1955; children: Linda E., Sally A. Grad., Phillips Exeter Acad., 1945; B.A., Haverford Coll., 1949; M.B.A., Wharton Sch. of U. Pa., 1951. Vice pres. Ocean City Mfg. Co., Phila., 1953-58; pres. Johnson Computing Co., Phila., 1958-68, chmn. bd., dir., 1968—; with Provident Nat. Bank, Phila., 1969—, sr. v.p., 1971—; pres., dir. Allen Data Systems, Inc., Phila., 1970; pres. JCI Data Processing Inc., 1976—; dir. Sircom Knitting Co., Spring City, Pa., pres., 1980-81. Bd. dirs., mem. budget com. Phila. United Fund, 1954-67; bd. dirs. Nicetown Club Boys and Girls, Phila., 1954-57, Huntingdon Valley (Pa.) Civic Assn., 1956-64; bd. dirs., exec. com. Ridal/Meadowbrook (Pa.) Civic Assn., 1969—; mem. planning and devel. com. Germantown Friends Sch., 1970—; trustee, exec. com. Albert Einstein Med. Center, 1973—, vice chmn., 1980, chmn. bd. govs. No. div., 1981—; sec., treas. Delaware Valley Hosp. Councils, 1982—; chmn. bd. Delaware Valley Health, Edn. and Research Found., 1982—. Served with U.S. Army, 1951-52. Mem. Pa. Bankers Assn., Bank Automation Assn. Delaware Valley. Clubs: Locust (Phila.); Philmont Country (Huntingdon Valley) (bd. dirs., exec. v.p.). Home: Hidden Glen Meadowbrook PA 19046 Office: 1617 JFK Blvd Suburban Station Bldg Philadelphia PA 19103

JOHNSON, VIRGIL ALLEN, agronomist; b. Newman Grove, Nebr., June 28, 1921; s. Oscar Johannas and Fairy Bell (Johnson) J.; m. Betty Ann Tisthammer, July 27, 1943; children—Karen (Mrs. Ronald Eakes), Leslie (dec.), Reed, Scott. B.S. with distinction, U. Nebr., 1948, Ph.D. (Regents Grad. fellow, Ak-Sar-Ben grad. fellow, Sears, Roebuck Grad. fellow), 1952. Agt. Agrl. Research Service, U.S. Dept. Agr., Lincoln, Nebr., 1951-52, research agronomist, 1954-75, supervisory research agronomist, 1975-78; leader wheat research, asst. agronomist U. Nebr., Lincoln, 1952-54, asso. prof., 1954-63, prof. agronomy dept., 1963—; cons. Gt. Plains Wheat, Inc.; mem. Nat. Wheat Improvement Com.; mem. tech. com. Wheat Quality Council. Contbr. articles to profl. publs. Served in inf. U.S. Army, 1940-43, AC; Served in inf. U.S. Army, 1943-45. Decorated D.F.C., Air medal with 3 oak leaf clusters; recipient Agrl. Achievement award Ak-Sar-Ben, 1970, Disting. Service award Dept. Agr., 1981; AID grantee, 1966-79. Fellow Am. Soc. Agronomy, AAAS; mem. Crop Sci. Soc. Am. (Crop Sci. award 1975, pres. 1978), Am. Genetics Assn., Sigma Xi, Gamma Sigma Delta (Internat. award 1969), Alpha Zeta. Lutheran. Co-developer 22 varieties of hard red winter wheat. Home: 3849 Dudley St Lincoln NE 68503 Office: 324 Keim Hall East Campus U Nebr Lincoln NE 68583

JOHNSON, VIRGINIA ALMA FAIRFAX, ballerina; b. Washington, Jan. 25, 1950; d. James Lee and Madeline (Murray) J. Student, pub. schs.; grad., Academy Wash. Sch. Ballet. Prin. ballerina Dance Theatre Harlem, N.Y.C., 1969—; solo concert Concert Socials, Marymount Coll., N.Y.C., 1978; prin. dancer Star World Ballet, Australia, 1979; performer White House, Washington, 1980, 81. Recipient Monarch award Nat. Council Culture and Art, N.Y.C., 1983. Office: Dance Theatre Harlem 466 W 152d St New York NY 10031

JOHNSON, WAINE CECIL, dermatologist; b. Mt. Vernon, Tex., Sept. 30, 1928; s. Tulley Bell and Lizzie J.; m. Deanna Glutz, Dec. 1973; children: Susan Lynn, Carol Ann, Sandra Kay. B.S., E. Tex. State U., 1949; M.D., U. Tex., 1953. Intern Brooke Army Hosp., 1953-54; resident in dermatology Walter Reed Army Hosp., 1955-58; fellow in dermal pathology Armed Forces Inst. Pathology, 1960-61; mem. staff Skin and Cancer Hosp., Phila., 1962-78, asst. dir. lab., 1962, dir., 1970-78; mem. faculty Temple U. Med. Sch., Phila., 1962-78, prof. dermatology, 1970-78; clin. prof. U. Pa. Med. Sch., 1978—; chmn. dept. dermatology Grad. Hosp. U. Pa., 1978—, dir. immunofluorescent lab. of dermatology assos., 1978; pres. Johnson Dermatology Assns., 1980—. Author numerous papers in field.; Co-editor: Dermal Pathology, 1974. Served to maj. M.C. USAR, 1953-62. Recipient Gold medal sci. exhibit Am. Soc. Clin. Pathologists-Coll. Am. Pathologists, 1962. Mem. Am. Acad. Dermatology (chmn. com. pathology 1976-80), AMA, ACP, Sm. Dermatol. Assn., Internat. Acad. Pathology, Am. Soc. Dermapathology, Soc. Investigative Dermatology, Histochem. Soc., Phila. Dermatol. Soc. (pres. 1979-80), Atlantic Dermatol. Conf. (pres. 1979-80). Home: 611 Chelten Hills Dr Elkins Park PA 19117 Office: 415 S 19th St Philadelphia PA 19146

JOHNSON, WALTER, history educator; b. Nahant, Mass., June 27, 1915; s. Alfred and Annie (Hogan) J.; m. Bette Gifford, Sept. 13, 1955; 1 son, Gifford; children by previous marriage: Deborah, Richard. A.B., Dartmouth Coll., 1937; M.A., U. Chgo., 1938, Ph.D., 1941. Instr. history U. Chgo., 1940-43, asst. prof., 1943-49, assoc. prof., 1949-50, prof., 1950-66, chmn. dept., 1950-61, Preston and Sterling Morton prof. history, 1963-66; prof. history U. Hawaii, 1966-82; Harmsworth prof. Am. history Oxford U., 1957-58; vis. prof. history Grand Valley State Coll., Allendale, Mich., 1980—; mem. U.S. Adv. Commn. Internat. Ednl. and Cultural Affairs, 1962-67. Author: The Battle Against Isolation, 1944, William Allen White's America, 1947, (with

Avery Craven) The United States: Experiment in Democracy, 1947, How We Drafted Adlai Stevenson, 1955, American Studies Abroad, 1963; co-author: The Fulbright Program: A History, 1965; editor: Selected Letters of William Allen White, 1947, Roosevelt and The Russians, The Yalta Conference (Edward R. Stettinius, Jr.), 1949, Turbulent Era: A Diplomatic Record of Forty Years (Ambassador Joseph C. Grew), 1952, 1600 Pennsylvania Avenue: Presidents and the People, 1929-59, 1960, The Papers of Adlai E. Stevenson, 8 vols. Bd. fgn. scholarships Fulbright Program, 1947-54, chmn. bd., 1950-53; co-chmn. Nat. Com. Stevenson for Pres., 1952. Recipient prize for excellence in teaching U. Chgo., 1943; Newberry Library fellow, 1945. Mem. Am., Miss. Valley hist. assns. Accompanied Gov. Stevenson around the world, 1953. Home: Bass Lake Route 1 Pentwater MI 49449

JOHNSON, WALTER CONRAD, banker; b. Mpls., Oct. 4, 1925; s. John Conrad and Edna (Gustafson) J.; m. Janet Patricia Baker, Aug. 27, 1949; children: Karen, Steven, James. B.B.A., U. Minn., 1948. C.P.A., Minn., Ill. Accountant George Rossetter & Co., Chgo., 1949-53, Peat, Marwick, Mitchell & Co., Mpls., 1953-57; controller Norwest Bancorp., Mpls., 1957-71; treas. NW Bancorp., 1962-74, v.p., 1967-72, sr. v.p., 1972-75, exec. v.p., 1975-82; pres. Fin. Services Cos., 1982—; chmn., dir. Norwest Bus. Credit, Inc., Norwest Mortgage, Inc.; dir. Norwest Credit Life Ins., Norwest Leasing, Inc., Norwest Ins. Mgmt., Inc., Norwest Growth Fund. Mem. Mpls. Citizens League. Served to ensign AC USNR, 1943-46. Mem. Fin. Execs. Inst. (nat. dir. 1971-74), Am. Inst. C.P.A.s, Minn. Soc. C.P.A.s, Bank Adminstrn. Inst. (mem. bank holding co. commn. 1973-76, chmn. bank holding co. council 1975), Am. Inst. Banking, U. Minn. Sch. Bus. Adminstrn. Alumni Assn. (dir. 1967-70), Beta Alpha Psi. Lutheran. Clubs: Minneapolis; Wayzata (Minn.); Country. Home: 4743 E Coventry Rd Minnetonka MN 55343 Office: 1200 Peavey Bldg Minneapolis MN 55479

JOHNSON, WALTER CURTIS, electrical engineering educator; b. Weikert, Pa., Jan. 6, 1913; s. David C. and Mary (Ely) J.; m. Carolyn Shirk, Sept. 1, 1934; children: Walter Curtis, William Stanford, David Edward. B.S., Pa. State Coll., 1934, E.E., 1942. Engr. Gen. Electric Co., Schenectady, 1934-37; instr., dept. elec. engring. Princeton, 1937, prof. elec. engring., 1948—, Arthur LeGrand Doty prof. engring., 1963-81, Arthur LeGrand Doty prof. emeritus, 1981—, chmn. dept., 1950-65; engring. cons. various cos.; resident visitor Bell Telephone Labs., 1968. Author: Mathematical and Physical Principles of Engineering Analysis, 1944, Transmission Lines and Networks, 1950, (with P.R. Clement) Electrical Engineering Science, 1960; articles tech. and sci. publs. Recipient Western Elec. award for excellence in engring. edn.; Am. Soc. Engring. Edn., 1967; Nat. award for Best Initial Paper Am. Inst. Elec. Engrs., 1939. Fellow IEEE (profl. groups on edn., electron devices); mem. Am. Soc. Engring. Edn. (chmn. elec. engring. div. 1955-56), Am. Phys. Soc., Sigma Xi. Presbyterian. Home: 20 McCosh Circle Princeton NJ 08540

JOHNSON, WALTER HEINRICK, JR., educator, univ. adminstr.; b. Mpls., Sept. 20, 1928; s. Walter H. and Ruby A. (Tronsgaard) J.; m. Harriet R. Willingham, June 28, 1958; children—Bradford, Lee. B.A., U. Minn., 1950, M.A., 1953, Ph.D., 1956. Research asso. U. Minn., Mpls., 1956-57, asst. prof., 1958-62, asso. prof., 1962-68, prof., 1968—, asso. dean, 1971-76, acting dean, 1977-79; physicist Gen. Electric Co., Schenectady, 1957-58; Commr. Internat. Union Pure and Applied Physics Commn. on Atomic Masses and Fundamental Constants, 1966-78; mem. com. on atomic weights Internat. Union Pure and Applied Chemistry, 1971-83. Fellow Am. Phys. Soc.; mem. Phi Beta Kappa, Sigma Xi. Research in field of measurement of atomic masses with mass spectrometer. Home: 619 8th Ave SE Minneapolis MN 55414

JOHNSON, WALTER J., publisher; b. July 29, 1912; m. Thekla E. Johnson; 3 children. Ed., U. Heidelberg, U. de Paris á la Sorbonne, Paris, U. Coll., London; Sc.D. (hon.), Albany Med. Coll., 1978. Founder, pres. Walter J. Johnson, Inc., N.Y.C. and London, 1942—; founder, pres. Academic Press, N.Y.C. and London, 1942-72, Johnson Reprint Corp.; (became subsidiary of Academic Press 1967), 1946-72; merger Academic Press and Harcourt Brace Jovanovich, N.Y.C., 1969; pres. Ablex Pub. Co., 1977—; dir. Harcourt Brace Jovanovich. Trustee Albany (N.Y.) Med. Coll.; Fellow Pierpont Morgan Library. Served with N.G., 1941-44. Mem. A.L.A., Am. Med. Library Assn., Friends of Columbia U. Club: Grolier (N.Y.C.). Office: 355 Chestnut St Norwood NJ 07648

JOHNSON, WARREN DONALD, former air force officer, pharmaceutical executive; b. Blackwell, Okla., Sept. 2, 1922; s. Charles Leon and Vera Ruth (Tucker) J.; children: Patricia Suzanne Johnson Peak, Lindabeth Johnson Brown. Student, Oklahoma City U., 1940-41. Served to 1st lt. U.S. Army, 1942-45; commd. 1st lt. USAAF, 1945; advanced through grades to lt. gen. USAF, 1973; chief of staff SAC, Offutt AFB, Nebr., 1971-73; dir. Def. Nuclear Agy., Washington, 1973-77; ret., 1977; corp. v.p. Baxter-Travenol Labs., Inc., Deerfield, Ill., 1977—. Decorated D.S.M., Legion of Merit with 2 oak leaf clusters, Joint Commendation medal. Office: Baxter-Travenol Labs Inc One Baxter Pkwy Deerfield IL 60015

JOHNSON, WAYNE D., utility co. exec.; b. Winterset, Iowa, Sept. 20, 1932; s. Leslie E. and Ruth N. J.; m. Lynne Alice Brouwer, June 15, 1963; children—Christopher W., Kevin B. B.A., U. Nebr., 1954; LL.B., Harvard U., 1959. Bar: Ill. bar 1959. Asso. to partner firm Ross, Hardies, O'Keefe, Babcock & Parsons, Chgo., 1959-72; asst. gen. counsel Peoples Gas Co., Chgo., 1972-75; sr. v.p., gen. counsel Entex, Inc., Houston, 1975-78, pres., 1978—; dir. simmons & Co. Served with U.S. Army, 1954-56. Woodrow Wilson fellow, 1954. Mem. Am. Bar Assn., Am., So. gas assns., Tex. Utilities Lawyers Assn. Clubs: Petroleum, Houstonian (Houston); Legal (Chgo.). Home: 710 Marchmont Houston TX 77024 Office: Entex Inc PO Box 2628 Houston TX 77001

JOHNSON, WAYNE EATON, drama critic; b. Phoenix, May 9, 1930; s. Roscoe and Marion (Eaton) J.; children: Katherine, Jeffrey. B.A., U. Colo., 1952; postgrad., Duke U., 1952-53, U. Vienna, Austria, 1955-56; M.A., UCLA, 1957. Reporter Internat. News Service, Des Moines, 1958, Wheat Ridge (Colo.) Advocate, 1957, Pueblo (Colo.) Chieftain, 1959; reporter Denver Post, 1960, editorial writer, music critic, 1961-65; arts and entertainment editor Seattle Times, 1965-80, drama critic, 1980—; instr. journalism Colo. Woman's Coll., 1962. Author: Show: A Concert Program for Actor and Orchestra, 1971, America! A Concert of American Images, Words and Music, 1973, From Where the Sun Now Stands: The Indian Experience, 1973. Served with CIC AUS, 1953-55. Home: 11303 Durland Pl NE Seattle WA 98125 Office: Seattle Times Fairview Ave N and John St Seattle WA 98111

JOHNSON, WAYNE HAROLD, librarian, state ofcl.; b. El Paso, Tex., May 2, 1942; s. Earl Harold and Cathryn Louise (Greeno) J.; m. Patricia Ann Froedge, June 15, 1973; 1 dau., Meredith Jessica. B.S., Utah State U., 1968; M.P.A., U. Colo., 1970; M.L.S., U. Okla., 1972. Circulation librarian Utah State U., Logan, 1968, adminstrv. asst. librarian, 1969; research Okla. Mgmt. and Engring. Cons., Norman, 1972; chief adminstrv. services Wyo. State Library, Cheyenne, 1973-76, chief bus. officer library archives and hist. dept., 1976-78, Wyo. state librarian, 1978—. Trustee Bibliog. Center for Research, Denver.; Chmn. bd. dirs. Cheyenne dist. Longs Peak council Boy Scouts Am., 1982—; v.p. Cheyenne/Laramie County Airport Bd., 1980, pres., 1981. Served with USCG, 1960-64. Mem. ALA, Wyo. Library Assn., Aircraft Owners and Pilots Assn., Cheyenne C. of C. (chmn. transp. com. 1982, 83). Democrat. Presbyterian. Clubs: Masons, Kiwanis. Office: Wyo State Library Cheyenne WY 82002

JOHNSON, WESLEY ROBERT, plastic manufacturing executive; b. Cleve., Dec. 27, 1919; m. Doris Faye Meadows, Feb. 14, 1945; children: Elizabeth N. Johnson Tucker, Wesley Robert, Philip Meadows, Gillian Smith. B.S. summa cum laude, Ohio State U., 1948; M.B.A., Northwestern U., 1949; postgrad., Columbia U., 1950-53. Mgmt. cons. George Fry & Assos., Chgo., 1949-51; v.p. internat. Ill. Tool Works, Inc., Chgo., 1958-61, London, 1956-61; exec. v.p. Woodall Industries, Inc., Detroit, 1962-66, pres., 1966-75; pres., dir. LOF Plastics Inc., Detroit, 1976—. Mem. bus. and industry com. United Negro Coll. Fund, Detroit, 1972; bd. dirs. Jr. Achievement S.E. Mich., 1972, Detroit Swedish Council, 1975, YMCA-Met., Detroit, 1975, Bus./Edn. Alliance, Detroit, 1976; trustee Children's Hosp. of Mich., Detroit, 1976; mem. adv. bd. U. Detroit Coll. Engring., 1971. Clubs: American (London); Economic of Detroit (dir. 1971—), Country of Detroit, Detroit, Detroit Athletic. Office: 1150 Stephenson Hwy PO Box 3230 Troy MI 48099

JOHNSON, WILLARD LYON, orgn. exec.; b. Sterling, Ill., Dec. 1, 1905; s. James William and Anna Laura (Lyon) J.; m. Marjorie Elta Hackenberg, Feb. 9, 1936; children—Willard Lyon, Miriam Ellen. A.B., Drake U., 1930, M.A., 1932; B.D., Colgate-Rochester Div. Sch., 1933. Ordained to ministry Disciples of Christ Ch., 1930; asso. minister Plymouth Congl. Ch., Des Moines, 1939-41; dean men, dir. personnel Drake U., 1934-38; regional dir. NCCJ, 1938-42, 58, dir., Chgo., 1955-58; asst. to pres., 1942-45, v.p., 1945-47, nat. program dir., 1947-51; European dir. World Brotherhood, 1951, sec.-gen., 1951-55; pres. Com. Internat. Econ. Growth, 1958-60; v.p. Am. Edn. Found., Geneva, Switzerland, sec. human rights com., 1947-49; chief mission CARE, Berlin, Germany, 1960-62; exec. dir. Unitarian Universalist Service Com., 1962-65, Am. Freedom from Hunger Found., Inc., FAO, 1965-66, Center for Research and Edn., 1966-67; dir. internat. devel. Calif. Western U., 1967-68; exec. dir. Planned Parenthood, San Diego, 1968-70; 1st v.p. Zero Population Growth, Inc., 1971, chmn., 1972-73; dir. Population Study Center, 1974—; Cons. State Dept., Germany, 1950; gen. sec. U.S. com. UN Genocide Conv., 1948; exec. com. Nat. Assn. Intergroup Relations Ofcls., 1950—; cons. nat. radio network programs Light of the World and Superman; religious news reporter sta. WHO, Des Moines, 1938-41, sta. KWK, St. Louis, 1941-42; asst. commentator Religion in the News, NBC, 1947-49; del. World Council Chs. Consultations, Salonika, Greece, 1959; mem. adv. bd. Integrated Planning Office County of San Diego, 1975—. Author: Population and Quality of Life, 1971, Better Organizations, 1974, Population Primer, 1974; Contbr. chpts., articles to various publs., also profl. jours. Trustee Bur. Intercultural Edn., Inst. Am. Democracy, World Alliance Internat. Friendship Through Religion; chmn. scholarship fund, Pleasantville, N.Y. Recipient Distinguished Service award Drake U., 1956. Mem. Religious Radio Assn. (pres. 1947-49), Soc. Psychol. Study Social Issues, Soc. Internat. Devel. (mem. council, pres. Boston chpt.), UN Assn. (pres. San Diego 1970-75), Phi Beta Kappa, Omicron Delta Kappa, Psi Chi. Unitarian. Home: 4149 6th Ave San Diego CA 92103 Office: 4149 6th Ave: San Diego CA 92103 *Ideals, sound administration, and accountability—these have been my watchwords.*

JOHNSON, WILLARD RAYMOND, political science educator, consultant; b. St. Louis, Nov. 22, 1935; s. Willard and Dorothy (Stovall) J.; m. Vivian Robinson, Dec. 15, 1957; children: Caryn L., Kimberly E. B.A., UCLA, 1957; M.A., Johns Hopkins U., 1961; Ph.D., Harvard U., 1965. Asst. prof. polit. sci. MIT, Cambridge, Mass., 1964-69, assoc. prof., 1969-73, prof. polit. sci., 1973—; vis. assoc. prof. Harvard U. Sch. Bus., Cambridge, 1969; exec. dir. Circle Inc., Roxbury, Mass., 1968-70; adj. prof. Fletcher Sch., Medford, Mass., 1971—; cons. U.S. Nat. Commn. for Minority Enterprise, Washington, 1969; bd. dirs. Interfaith Housing Corp., Boston, 1970; chmn. bd. Circle Inc. subs. Greater Roxbury Devel. Corp., 1970; mem. U.S. Commn. for UNESCO, Washington, 1960-66. Author: The Cameroon Federation, 1970; contbr. articles to Daedalus, 1973-82; New Eng. dir.: Jour. African Civilizations, 1979—. Bd. dirs. TransAfrica and TransAfrica Forum, Washington, 1978—; pres. TransAfrica Boston Support Group, 1980—; chmn. Africa Policy Task Force McGovern for Pres. campaign, Boston, 1972. Recipient M.L. King Jr. award MIT Pres.'s Office, 1982—; fellow and grantee Ford Found.; grantee Social Sci. Research Council, 1975, Rockefeller Found., 1977. Mem. Council Fgn. Relations, Assn. Concerned African Scholars (bd. dirs. 1977—). Democrat. Baptist. Office: Dept Polit Sci MIT 30 Wadsworth St Cambridge MA 02139 *I believe that personal and social health is based on responsible engagememt, creative action, reflective credulity, disciplined energy, and respect for others.*

JOHNSON, WILLIAM ALEXANDER, poultry science educator; b. Ennis, Tex., June 22, 1922; s. William Frederick and Lillian (Wilson) J.; m. Joy Maxine Marchand, Apr. 2, 1946; children: Mary Judith, David William. Student, U. S.W. La., 1939-40; B.S., La. State U., 1943, M.S., 1949; Ph.D., U. Minn., 1952. Faculty dept. animal industry La. State U., Baton Rouge, 1947-49, instr. poultry sci., assoc. prof., 1952-65, prof., 1965—, chmn. dept., 1981—; vis. prof. Iowa State U., Ames, 1959-60. Mem. Istrouma Area council Boy Scouts Am., 1960-70; chmn. bd. Internat. Hospitality Found., 1971-76; chmn. adminstrv. bd. Univ. United Meth. Ch., 1977. Served with USNR, 1943-46. Mem. Poultry Sci. Assn. (asso. editor 1978—), World Poultry Sci. Assn., Poultry Industries La., Nat. Assn. Colls. and Tchrs. Agr., Am. Genetics Assn., La. State U. Sci. Club, Sigma XI, Gamma Sigma Delta, Alpha Zeta. Home: 5757 Chandler Dr Baton Rouge LA 70808 Office: Dept Poultry Sci La State U Baton Rouge LA 70803

JOHNSON, WILLIAM ALEXANDER, clergyman, educator; b. Bklyn., Aug. 20, 1934; s. Charles Raphael and Ruth Augusta (Anderson) J.; m. Carol Genevieve Lundquist, June 11, 1955; children—Karin Ruth, Karl William, Krister Frederick. B.A., Queens Coll., City U. N.Y., 1953; B.D. (Univ. fellow, Morrow Meml. fellow, Daniel Delaplaine fellow), Union Theol. Sem., 1956; Teol. Kand., Lund U., 1957, Teol. Lic., 1958, Teologie Doktor, 1962; M.A., Columbia U., 1958, Ph.D. (Univ. fellow, Rockefeller Bros. fellow), 1959. Profl. baseball player New York Giants, 1949-51; dir. Boys Club, Salvation Army, Jamaica, N.Y., 1952-54; minister Mt. Hope and Teabo Methodist chs., Wharton, N.J., 1954-56; ordained deacon Meth. Ch., 1955, elder, 1958; minister Immanuel and Union Meth. chs., Bklyn., 1957-59; asst. in instrn. Columbia, 1957, Union Theol. Sem., N.Y.C., 1958; instr., asst. prof. religion Trinity Coll., Hartford, Conn., 1959-63; lectr. philosophy and theology Hartford Sem. Found., 1961-62; asso. prof. religion, chmn. dept. Drew U., Madison, N.J., 1963-66; research prof. religion N.Y. U., 1966; vis. lectr. Union Theol. Sem., N.Y.C., 1966; vis. prof. religion Princeton, 1966-68; prof. religion, chmn. dept. Manhattanville Coll., Purchase, N.Y., 1967-71; ordained priest Episcopal Ch., 1968; vis. prof. Christian ethics Gen. Theol. Sem., N.Y.C., 1970; Albert V. Danielsen prof. Christian thought, prof. philosophy and history of ideas Brandeis U., Waltham, Mass., 1971—; canon residentiary Cathedral Ch. of St. John The Divine, N.Y.C., 1973—; vis. prof. Protestant theology N.Am. Coll., Vatican City, 1969-75; vis. scholar MIT, Cambridge, 1974-75; vis. prof., Tokyo, Japan, Stockholm, Sweden, 1979, U. Gothenburg, 1979; examining chaplain Diocese of the Arctic, 1982. Author: The Philosophy of Religion of Anders Nygren, 1958, Christopher Polhem: The Father of Swedish Technology, 1963, Nature and the Supernatural in the Theology of Horace Bushnell, 1963, On Religion: A Study of Theological Method in Schleiermacher and Nygren, 1964, Problems in Christian Ethics, 1965, (with Nels F.S. Ferre) Swedish Contributions to Modern Theology, 1966, The Search for Transcendence, 1974, The Christian Way of Death, 1974, Invitation to Theology, 1979, Philosophy and the Gospel, 1979; contbr. articles to profl. jours.; lectr., Europe, Asia, Africa, South Am., Caribbean., Arctic. Democratic committeeman Hartford, 1960-63; mem. exec. com. Am. Friends Service Com., Coll. Div., 1966-70. Recipient David F. Swenson-Kierkegaard Meml. award, 1964, Harbison award for Tchr. of Yr. Danforth Found., 1965; named Outstanding Young Man in Am. Jr. C. of C., 1964; Disting. Alumnus Queens Coll., 1980; Scandinavian-Am. Found. fellow, 1956; Fulbright scholar U. Copenhagen, 1957-58; Dempster Grad. fellow Meth. Ch., 1958; vis. research fellow Princeton, 1972; Guggenheim fellow for study in, Rome, Italy, 1972; NSF grantee, 1978; Rockefeller fellow Aspen Inst., 1978; Fellow Aspen Inst., Jerusalem, 1982; Nat. Endowment Humanities grantee, 1978; grantee Arthur Viking Davis Found., 1981, Trinity Ch. of N.Y.C., 1982. Mem. Am. Acad. Religion, Asia Soc., Japan Soc., Scandinavian-Am. Heritage Soc., Am. Philos. Assn., Danforth Assos., Soc. for Sci. Study Religion, Soc. for Religion in Higher Edn. (Kent fellow 1959), Soc. Anglican Theologians, Vasa Order Am., Am. Soc. Christian Ethics, Swedish Pioneer Hist. Soc., Soc. for Scandinavian Study, Willa Cather Pioneer Meml. Found., Authors Guild, Episcopal Churchmen for S.Africa, New Haven Theol. Group, Ecumenical Found. for Christian Ministry, English Speaking Union, Ch. Soc. for Coll. Work, Phi Beta Kappa, Pi Gamma Mu, Phi Sigma Tau. Clubs: Columbia U., Univ., Met. Opera. Home: 27 Fox Meadow Rd Scarsdale NY 10583 45 Pascal Ave Rockport ME 04856 Office: Rabb Grad Center Brandeis U Waltham MA 02154 *I have attempted in my life to fulfill the simple prayer of St. Francis: Lord, make me an instrument of your peace/ Where there is hatred... let me sow love/ Where there is injury... pardon/ Where there is doubt... faith/ Where there is despair... hope/ Where there is darkness... light/ Where there is sadness... joy.*

JOHNSON, WILLIAM BENJAMIN, industrial executive; b. Salisbury, Md., Dec. 28, 1918; s. Benjamin A. and Ethel (Holloway) J.; m. Mary Barb, Dec. 19, 1942; children: Benjamin H., Kirk B., John P., Kathleen M. A.B. maxima cum laude, Washington Coll., 1940, LL.B. (hon.), 1975, U. Pa., 1943. Bar: Md. bar 1943, Pa. bar 1947. Editor-in-chief U. Pa. Law Rev.; atty. U.S. Tax Ct., 1945-47; asst. solicitor Pa. R.R., 947-48, asst. gen. solicitor, 1948-51, asst. to gen. counsel, 1951-52, asst. gen. counsel, 1952-59; pres., dir. REA Express (formerly Ry. Express Agy., Inc.), N.Y.C., 1959-66, chmn. bd., 1966; pres., chief exec. officer, dir. Ill. Central Industries and I.C. R.R., 1966-68; chmn., pres., chief exec. officer Ill. Central Industries, 1968-72, chmn., chief exec. officer, 1972—; chmn., chief exec. Officer I.C. R.R., 1969-72, chmn. exec. com., 1972-76; dir. Continental Ill. Corp., Chgo., Continental Ill. Nat. Bank, Abex Corp., N.Y.C., Ill. Central Gulf R.R., Midas-Internat., Chgo., Esmark, Pet Inc., St. Louis, Pepsi-Cola Gen. Bottlers, Inc., Chgo. Bd. dirs. Chgo. Central Area Com.; trustee Com. for Econ. Devel.; mem. citizens bd., life trustee U. Chgo.; governing mem. Shedd Aquarium; mem. Northwestern U. Assocs.; bd. overseers U. Pa. Served as spl. agt., Security Intelligence Corps AUS, 1943-45. Mem. Am., Phila. bar assns., ICC Practitioners Assn., Juristic Soc., Conf. Bd., Newcomen Soc. N.Am., Assn. Am. Railroads (dir.), Nat. Def. Transp. Assn. (life, past chmn. bd.), Am. Productivity Ctr. (dir.), Md. Soc. Pa., S.A.R., Order of Coif, Kappa Alpha, Omicron Delta Kappa. Clubs: Sky, Economic, Links (N.Y.C.); Commercial, Economic, Chicago, Executives, Metropolitan, Mid-America (Chgo.); Onwentsia (Lake Forest); Old Elm (Highland Park). Office: Room 2700 111 E Wacker Dr Chicago IL 60601

JOHNSON, WILLIAM HALL, lawyer, government official; b. Washington, June 14, 1943; s. Helmer R. and Ramona Louise (Gratten) J.; m. Debora Carol Bergmann, May 25, 1974; 1 dau., Lindsey Elizabeth. B.A., Colgate U., 1965; J.D., Northwestern U., 1968. Bar: N.Y. 1968. Staff atty. Cable TV Bur., FCC, Washington, 1968-73, chief policy rev. and devel. div., 1973-81; chief Cable TV Bur., Washington, 1981-82, dep. chief mass media bur., 1982—. Home: 1823 21st St NW Washington DC 20009 Office: FCC 1919 M St NW Washington DC 20554

JOHNSON, WILLIAM HOWARD, educator, agricultural engineer; b. Sidney, Ohio, Sept. 3, 1922; s. Russell Earl and Dollie (Gamble) J.; m. Wyoma Jean Swift, Oct. 2, 1943; children: Lawrence Alan, Cheri Ellen, Dana Sue. B.S., Ohio State U., 1948, M.S., 1953; Ph.D., Mich. State U., 1960. Registered profl. engr. Mem. faculty Ohio Agrl. Expt. Sta., Wooster, 1948-64; mem. faculty Ohio Agrl. Research and Devel. Center, Wooster, 1964-70, prof., asso. chmn. dept. agrl. engring., 1959-70; part-time prof. Ohio State U., 1964-70; prof., head dept. agrl. engring. Kans. State U., Manhattan, 1970-81, dir. Engring. Experiment Sta., 1981—; cons. farm equipment cos. Author: (with B.J. Lamp) Principles, Equipment and Systems for Corn Harvesting, 1966; also articles. Recipient Distinguished Alumnus award Coll. Engring., Ohio State U., 1974. Fellow Am. Soc. Agrl. Engrs.; mem. Sigma Xi, Tau Beta Pi. Research on soil-plant-machine relationships, harvesting, design for soiltillers, planters, harvesters. Home: 2025 Blue Hills Rd Manhattan KS 66502

JOHNSON, WILLIAM HUGH, JR., hospital administrator, consultant; b. N.Y.C., Oct. 29, 1935; s. William H. and Florence P. (Seinsoth) J.; m. Gloria C. Stube., Jan. 23, 1960; children: Karen A., William H. III. B.A., Hofstra U., 1957; M.Ed., U. Hawaii, 1969. Commd. 2d lt. U.S. Army, 1957, advanced through grades to lt. col., 1972, health adminstr., world wide, 1957-77, health adminstr., world wide, ret., 1977; chief exec. officer U. N. Mex. Hosp., Albuquerque, 1977—; asst. prof. U.S. Mil. Acad., West Point, N.Y., 1962-65; mem. clin. faculty U. Minn., Mpls., 1980-83; preceptor Ariz. State U., Tempe, 1982-83; pres. Albuquerque Area Hosp. Council, 1980. Vice pres. Vis Nurse Service, Albuquerque, 1979. Decorated Army Commendation Medal with 2 oak leaf clusters, 1979-80, Meritorious Service Medal, Order of Merit, Legion of Merit. Mem. Am. Hosp. Assn. (governing bd. pub-gen. hosp. sect. 1982-86), Am. Coll. Hosp. Adminstrs., N. Mex. Hosp. Assn. (bd. dirs. 1983, chmn. elect). Roman Catholic. Club: Tanoan Country (Albuquerque). Home: 7920 Sartan Way NE Albuquerque NM 87109 Office: U N Mex Hosp 2211 Lomas Blvd NE Albuquerque NM 87106

JOHNSON, WILLIAM LEE, lawyer; b. N.Y.C., Jan. 11, 1929; s. Reginald Lee and Dorothy (Maloney) J.; m. Marjory Bruce Hughes, Apr. 26, 1952; children: Susan D., Helen W., Marjory S. Grad., Horace Mann Sch., N.Y.C., 1946; A.B., Princeton U., 1950; LL.B., Columbia U., 1955. Bar: N.Y. 1955. Assoc. firm Hughes, Hubbard, Blair & Reed, 1955-61; sec., gen. counsel Otis Elevator Co., N.Y.C., 1968-78; gen. counsel Newmont Mining Corp., 1978-82. Trustee Village of Irvington, N.Y., 1963-67; bd. dirs. Phelps Meml. Hosp. Center. Mem. ABA, Assn. Bar City N.Y. Clubs: Princeton, Riverdale Yacht (N.Y.C.); Ardsley Curling (Ardsley-on-Hudson). Home: 240 Harriman Rd Irvington-on-Hudson NY 10533

JOHNSON, WILLIAM MCALLISTER, fine arts educator, art historian; b. Columbia, Mo., Oct. 24, 1939; s. Durfee McAllister and Fern Dolores (Hammer) J. B.A., U. Mo.-Columbia, 1960, M.A., 1962;

M.F.A., Princeton U., N.J., 1964, Ph.D., 1965. Lectr. dept. fine arts U. Toronto, 1965-67, asst. prof., 1967-69, assoc. prof., 1969-77, prof., 1977—. Author: French Lithography: The Restoration Salons, 1817-1824, 1977; auhtor: The Royal Tour of Charles IX and Catherine de'Medici, 1564-1566, 1979, French Royal Academy of Painting & Sculpture: Engraved Reception Pieces, 1673-1789, 1982; editor: Canadian Art Review, 1977—. Recipient Fulbright award, 1960-61, Prix Bernier award Inst. de France, 1982; Guggenheim fellow, 1978-79. Mem. Am. Numismatic Soc., Renaissance Soc. Am., Societe de l'Histoire de l'Art Francais, Phi Beta Kappa. Office: Dept Fine Art Univ Toronto 100 St George St Toronto ON Canada M5S 1A1

JOHNSON, WILLIAM MCKINLEY, JR., fgn. service officer; b. Columbus, Ohio, June 15, 1920; s. William McKinley and Maria Valentine (Pierce) J.; m. Margaret Hodge Urban, Oct. 23, 1948; children—Mary V., Christopher H., Margaret P. A.B., Princeton U., 1941; M.A., Fletcher Sch. Law and Diplomacy, 1947. Commd. fgn. service officer Dept. State; vice consul, Munich, Regensburg, 1950-52; 2d sec. Am. embassy, Pretoria, South Africa, 1952-55, 1st sec., Rabat, 1959-63; assigned Can. Def. Coll., 1963-64; polit. counselor Am. embassy, Ottawa, Can., 1964-69, minister, 1973-76; consul gen., Johannesburg, South Africa, 1976-80; internat. affairs officer Dept. State, Washington, 1980—. Served with USNR, 1942-46. Episcopalian. Home: 3514 Leland St Chevy Chase MD 20015 Office: 2201 C St NW Washington DC 20520

JOHNSON, WILLIAM R., university administrator; b. Houston, Jan. 12, 1933; s. Ernest H. and Rosabelle (Thompson) J.; m. Freida Marilyn Kennedy, June 26, 1954; children: William Scott, Alison Gaye. B.S., U. Houston, 1958, M.A., 1959; Ph.D., U. Okla., 1963. Assoc. prof. history Tex. Tech. U., Lubbock, 1968-76, assoc. dean arts and scis., 1972-73, interim v.p. acad. affairs, 1973-75, v.p. acad. affairs, 1975-76; pres. Stephen F. Austin State U., Nacogdoches, Tex., 1976—. Author: A Short History of the Sugar Industry in Texas, 1961. Served with USAF, 1951-55. Recipient L.R. Bryan Jr. award Tex. Gulf Coast Hist. Assn., 1961. Mem. Tex. Sr. Colls. and Univs. (chmn. council of pres.'s 1979-81), Am. Hist. Assn., Orgn. Am. Historians, Assn. Tex. Colls. and Univs. (pres. 1981-82). Methodist. Club: Boosters. Lodge: Rotary. Home: 505 E Starr St Nacogdouches TX 75961 Office: Stephen F Austin State U PO Box 6078 SEA Station Nacogdouches TX 75962

JOHNSON, WILLIAM RICHARD, retail chain exec.; b. N.Y.C., July 15, 1928; s. John M. and Olivia B. (Wagner) J.; m. Donna Mae Means, Mar. 12, 1955; children—Bonnie Johnson See, Jill, Wendy, Bobby. B.S., Yale U., 1950. With J.C. Penney Co., Inc., 1950—, dir. mktg. services, 1976-79, v.p., dir. public affairs and co. communication, N.Y.C., 1979—. Bd. dirs. Greeville Bakers Boys Club, Locust Valley, N.Y., Ave. of Americas Assn.; vestryman St. John's Episcopal Ch., Lattingtown, N.Y. Served to capt. USMCR, 1950-52. Mem. Bus. Rountable. Clubs: Beaver Dam Winter Sports, Creek. Office: 1301 Ave of Americas New York NY 10019

JOHNSON, WILLIAM ROBERT, bishop; b. Tonopah, Nev., Nov. 19, 1918. Ed., St. Patrick's Sem., St. John's Sem., Nat. Cath. Sch. Social Service, Cath. U. Am. Registered social worker, clin. social worker, Calif. Ordained priest Roman Cath. Ch., 1944; consecrated bishop, 1971; asst. pastor St. Anthony of Padua Parish, Gardena, Calif., 1944-45, San Antonio de Padua Parish, Los Angeles, 1946; resident various parishes, 1948-62; pastor Holy Name Jesus Ch., Los Angeles, 1962-68, Am. Martyrs Ch., Manhattan Beach, Calif., 1968-70; parochial vicar St. Vibiana's Cathedral, Los Angeles, 1970-76; with Cath. Welfare Bur., 1948—, asst. dir., Los Angeles, 1954-56; dir. Cath. Welfare Bur. Archdiocese Los Angeles, also; archdiocesan dir. charities, 1956—, aux. bishop of, Los Angeles, bishop of, Orange, Calif., 1976—. Named Papal Chamberlain, 1960, Domestic Prelate, 1966. Mem. Nat. Assn. Social Workers, Acad. Cert. Social Workers. Address: 2811 E Villa Real Dr Orange CA 92667

JOHNSON, WILLIAM RUDOLPH, university president; b. Houston, Jan. 12, 1933; s. Ernest Henry and Rosa Belle (Thompson) J.; m. Freida Marilyn Kennedy, June 24, 1954; children: William Scott, Alison Gaye. B.S. in Edn. cum laude, U. Houston, 1958, M.A., 1959; Ph.D., U. Okla., 1963. Grad. asst. U. Houston, 1958-59; teaching asst. U. Okla., 1959-62; asst. prof. history Austin Peay State Coll., 1962-64; asst. prof. Tex. Tech. U., 1964-67, asso. prof., 1967-76, prof., 1976, v.p. acad. affairs, 1973-76; pres. Stephen F. Austin State U., 1976—. Author: A Short History of the Sugar Industry in Texas, 1961. Served with USAF, 1951-55. Recipient L.R. Bryan Jr. award Tex. Gulf Coast Hist. Assn., 1961; Am. Council Edn. fellow, 1971-72. Mem. Am. Hist. Assn., Assn. Tex. Colls. and Univs. (pres. 1982-83), Orgn. Am. Historians, Tex. Hist. Assn., East Tex. Hist. Assn., Forest History Assn., Nacogdoches County C. of C. (dir. 1979). Democrat. Methodist. Clubs: Rotary, Boosters. Office: Box 6078—SFA Sta Nacogdoches TX 75962

JOHNSON, WILLIAM SUMMER, chemistry educator; b. New Rochelle, N.Y., Feb. 24, 1913; s. Roy Wilder and Josephine (Summer) J.; m. Barbara Allen, Dec. 27, 1940. Grad., Gov. Dummer Acad., 1932; B.A., Amherst Coll., 1936, Sc.D., 1956; M.A., Harvard U., 1938, Ph.D., 1940; Sc.D, L.I. U., 1968. Instr. Amherst Coll., 1936-37; research chemist Eastman Kodak Co., summer, 1936-39; instr. U. Wis., 1940-42, asst. prof., 1942-44, assoc. prof., 1944-49; Homer Adkins prof. chemistry U. Wis., 1954-60; prof. dept. chemistry Stanford U., Calif., 1960-78, Jackson-Wood prof., 1974-78, prof. emeritus, 1978—, chmn. dept., 1960-69; vis. prof. Harvard U., 1954-55; mem. exec. bd. Jour. Organic Chemistry, 1954-56; mem. chem. adv. panel NSF, 1952-56; sec. organic sect. Internat. Congress Pure and Applied Chemistry, 1951. Contbr. chpts. to chemistry books, articles to assn. jours.; mem. bd. editors: Organic Syntheses, vol. 34, 1954, Jour. Am. Chem. Soc., 1956-65, Jour. Organic Chemistry, 1954-56, Tetrahedron, 1957—. Recipient award for creative works in synthetic organic chemistry, 1958, medal Synthetic Organic Chem. Mfrs. Assn., 1963, Nichols medal Am. Chem. Soc., 1968, Roussel prize, 1970, Roger Adams award in Organic Chemistry, 1977. Fellow London Chem. Soc.; mem. Am. Acad. Arts and Scis., Swiss Chem. Soc., Am. Chem. Soc. (chmn. organic div 1951-52), Nat. Acad. Scis., Phi Beta Kappa, Sigma Xi. Home: 191 Meadowood Dr Portola Valley CA 94025 Office: Dept Chemistry Stanford Univ Stanford CA 94305

JOHNSON, WYATT THOMAS, JR., newspaper publisher; b. Macon, Ga., Sept. 30, 1941; s. Wyatt Thomas and Josephine Victoria (Brown) J.; m. Edwina Mac Chastain, Dec. 29, 1963; children: Wyatt Thomas III, Christa Farie. A.B. in Journalism, U. Ga., 1963; M.B.A., Harvard, 1965. Reporter, mgmt. trainee Macon Telegraph and News, 1957-65; White House fellow, 1965-66; asst. press sec. to Pres. U.S., 1966, dep. press sec., 1967; spl. asst. to Pres., 1968, exec. asst., 1969-70; exec. v.p., dir. Tex. Broadcasting Corp., Sta. KTBC-AM-FM-TV, Austin, 1970-73; exec. editor, v.p., dir. Dallas Times Herald, 1973-75, publisher, 1975-77; pres. Los Angeles Times, 1977-80, publisher, 1980—; Mem. Pres.'s Commn. on White House Fellows, 1979, Nieman Fellows Selection Com., Harvard U., 1977; Pres. adv. bd. Henry W. Grady Sch. Journalism, 1974-75. Co-author: Automating Newspaper Composition, 1965. Bd. dirs. U. Ga. Sch. Journalism, Peabody Awards, ARC, Rockefeller Found., Trilateral Commn., Reading is Fundamental; chmn. bd. Lyndon B. Johnson Found., John S. Knight/Stanford Profl. Journalism Fellows. Named Nat. Man of Year Sigma Nu, 1962, Outstanding Young Man of Ga. Jr. C. of C., 1967, One of Five Outstanding Young Texans Tex. Jaycees, 1969, One of 10 Outstanding Men of U.S., 1975. Mem. Am. Newspaper Pubs. Assn., Newspaper Advt. Bur. (dir.), Ga. Alumni Soc. (pres. 1979), Council on Fgn. Relations N.Y., Sphinx Soc., Young Pres.'s Orgn., Gridiron Soc. (Ga.), Sigma Delta Chi, Sigma Nu. Presbyterian. Club: Harvard Business School Alumni. Office: Los Angeles Times Times Mirror Sq Los Angeles CA 90053

JOHNSON, ZANE QUENTIN, retired petroleum company executive; b. Bristow, Okla., Mar. 5, 1924; s. Sylvester B. and Meta B. (Biggs) J.; m. Nila Jean Caylor, June 4, 1949; children: Zane Quentin, Mark Caylor, Janis Lyn. B.S. in Chem. Engring, U. Okla., 1947. With Gulf Oil Corp. (and subs. cos.), from 1947; pres., chief operating officer Gen. Atomic, Inc., San Diego, 1969-70; exec. v.p. Gulf Oil Corp., Pitts., 1970-75; pres. Gulf Sci. & Tech. Co., Pitts., from 1975, now ret.; faculty Sch. Chem. Engring., U. Okla. Mayor, Port Arthur, Tex., 1957-58; bd. dirs. United Community Services of San Diego County, 1969-70, Boy Scouts Am., Duquesne U.; trustee Shadyside Hosp. Served to 1st lt. USAAF; PTO. Decorated Air medal with three oak leaf clusters; recipient U. Okla. Coll. Engring. Hall of Fame award. Mem. Am. Inst. Chem. Engrs., Am. Petroleum Inst., Petroleum Club Houston. Republican. Presbyterian. Clubs: Duquesne, Fox Chapel Golf, Port Royal, Laurel Valley Golf, Wyndemere Country, Rolling Rock, Wilderness Country, 25 Year of Petroleum Industry. Home: 3833 Rum Row Naples FL 33940

JOHNSON-MASTERS, VIRGINIA E. (MRS. WILLIAM H. MASTERS), psychologist; b. Springfield, Mo., Feb. 11, 1925; d. Harry Hershel and Edna (Evans) Eshelman; m. George Johnson, June 13, 1950 (div. 1956); children: Scott Forstall, Lisa Evans; m. William H. Masters, Jan. 7, 1971. Student music, Drury Coll., Springfield, 1940-42, U. Mo., 1944-47, Washington U., St. Louis, 1963-64; D.Sc. (hon.), U. Louisville, 1978. With St. Louis Daily Record, 1947-50, Sta. KMOX, St. Louis, 1950-51; with div. reproductive biology, dept. obstetrics and gynecology Washington U. Sch. Medicine, 1957-64, research instr., 1962-64; research asst. Masters & Johnson Inst. (formerly Reproductive Biology Research Found.), St. Louis, 1964-69, asst. dir., 1969-73, co-dir., 1973-80, pres., dir., 1981—; pres. MVM Enterprises, Inc., 1981—; Am. Geriatrics Soc. Edward Henderson lectr. Author: (with Dr. William H. Masters) Human Sexual Response, 1966, Human Sexual Inadequacy, 1970, The Pleasure Bond, 1975, Homosexuality in Perspective, 1979, (with Kolodny and others) Textbook of Human Sexuality for Nurses, 1979, Textbook of Sexual Medicine, 1979, Human Sexuality, 1982; Editor: (with Masters and Kolodny) Ethical Issues in Sex Therapy and Research, Vol. 1, 1977, Vol. 2, 1980. Recipient Paul H. Hoch award Am. Psychopathol. Soc., 1971; SIECUS citation award, 1971; Distinguished Service award Am. Assn. Marriage and Family Counselors, 1976; Modern Medicine award for Disting. Achievement, 1977; Biomed. Research award World Assn. Sexology, 1979; named One of 25 Most Influential Women in Am. World Almanae, 1975, 78, 79, 80; Paul Harris fellow Rotary Internat., 1976. Fellow Soc. Sci. Study of Sex; mem. AAAS, Soc. Study of Reprodn., Internat. Soc. Research in Biology Reprodn., Internat. Acad. Sex Research (treas. 1975-76), Am. Assn. Sex Educators, Counselors and Therapists (Modern Medicine award 1977), Internat. Platform Assn., Authors Guild. Episcopalian. Office: 24 S Kingshighway Saint Louis MO 63108

JOHNSON MORNER, ANTONIA MARGARET, business executive; b. N.Y.C., Sept. 6, 1943; d. Axel and Antonia (de Souza Toledo) Johnson; m. Nils Morner, Apr. 10, 1965 (div.); children: Alexandra, Caroline, Axel, Sophie. Student, Radcliffe Coll., 1963-64; B.A., U. Stockholm, 1971. With Axel Johnson Group-Cos., 1971—; chmn. A. Johnson & Co. HAB, Stockholm, 1982—, A. Johnson & Co., Inc., N.Y.C., 1983—; dep. bd. dirs. Skandinaviska Enskilda Banken, Stockholm, 1982—; tech. and indsl. adv. bd. Swedish Ministry Industry, Stockholm, 1982—; tech. and indsl. adv. bd Swedish Work Environ. Fund, Stockholm, 1982—. Trustee Carnegie Instn., Washington, 1982-85; chmn. Carlsson Sch. Stockholm, 1981. Clubs: Am. Stockholm; Merchants (Stockholm); Port Royal (Naples, Fla.). Office: A Johnson & Co HAB Jakobsbergsgatan 7 Stockholm Sweden S-103 75

JOHNSRUD, RUSSELL LLOYD, surgeon, ins. co. exec.; b. Portland, Oreg., June 4, 1909; s. Joseph Andrus and Mignonette Josephine (Fleischer) J.; m. Barbara Faire Pittock, Apr. 18, 1939; children—Georgiana Johnsrud Rathman, Nancy Johnsrud Dudley, Stephen Russell. B.A., U. Oreg., 1930, IM.D., 1933. Diplomate: Am. Bd. Surgery. Intern U. Oreg. Med. Sch. Hosps., 1933-34; resident St. Luke's Hosp., San Francisco, 1934-35; practice medicine specializing in surgery, Portland, 1935-76; asst. prof. surgery U. Oreg., 1952—; dir. Blue Cross of Oreg., Portland, 1949-79, vice chmn., 1965-79; dir., treas. Gearhart Condominium Mgmt. Co., Oreg., 1973-79, v.p., 1979-80; mem. staff St. Vincent Hosp.; mem. staff, dir. Med. Center Hosp., 1961-76. Served to comdr. USNR, 1939-45; PTO. Mem. ACS, AMA, North Pacific Surg. Assn., Portland Surg. Soc. (pres. 1957-58), Nu Sigma Nu, Alpha Omega Alpha. Clubs: Multnomah Athletic, Arlington, Waverley Country (Portland); Charbonneau Golf and Country (Wilsonville, Oreg.). Home: 8220 Fairway Dr Wilsonville OR 97070 *Intellectual curiosity with a prepared open mind is the best road to learning. Everything that I have ever learned has been worthwhile. I do not recall any knowledge that has not been useful in some way.*

JOHNSTON, ALAN ROGERS, lawyer; b. Chgo., Apr. 21, 1914; s. Edward Raymond and Caroline (Rogers) J.; m. Eleanor Cope Smith, Apr. 7, 1945; children: Alan Cope, Margaret Meade, Edward Raymond. B.S. in Mech. Engring., Princeton U., 1937; J.D., U. Mich., 1941. Bar: Ill. 1941. Assoc. firm Jenner & Block, Chgo., 1941-50, ptnr., 1950—. Bd. dirs. Chgo. Crime Commn., 1972—; rep. Ill. Gen. Assembly, Springfield, 1963-70; pres. New Trier Citizens League, Winnetka, Ill., 1973-83, Lake Mich. Fedn., Chgo., 1979-81; exec. com. Lawson YMCA, Chgo., 1975—; trustee New Trier Twp. Sch., 1975—. Fellow Ill. Bar Assn. Republican. Episcopalian. Clubs: Indian Hill (Winnetka); Chgo Yacht (bd. dirs 1976-81), Legal (pres. 1967-68), Law (dir. 1964-66). Home: 504 Park Dr Kenilworth IL 60043 Office: Jenner & Block One IBM Plaza Chicago IL 60611

JOHNSTON, BRUCE GILBERT, civil engr.; b. Detroit, Oct. 13, 1905; s. Sterling and Ida (Peake) J.; m. Ruth Elizabeth Barker, Aug. 5, 1939; children—Sterling, Carol Anne. Snow, David. B.S. in Civil Engring, U. Ill., 1930; M.S., Lehigh U., Bethlehem, Pa., 1934; Ph.D. in Sci, Columbia U., 1938. Engaged in engring. constrn. Coolidge Dam, Ariz., 1927-29; with design office Roberts & Schaefer Co., Chgo., 1930; instr. civil engring. Columbia U., 1934-38; charge structural research Fritz Engring. Lab., Lehigh U., 1938-50, asst. dir. lab., 1938-47, dir., 1947-50, mem. univ. faculty, 1938-50, prof. civil engring., 1945-50; prof. structural engring. U. Mich., 1950-68, emeritus, 1968—; prof. civil engring. U. Ariz., Tucson, 1968-70; engr. Johns Hopkins Applied Physics Lab., Silver Spring, Md., 1942-45; chmn. Column Research Council, 1956-62. Author: Basic Steel Design, 2d edit, 1980, also tech. papers.; Editor: Column Research Council Design Guide, 3 edits, 1960-76. Recipient Alumni Honor award for disting. service in engring. U. Ill., 1981. Hon. mem. ASCE (chmn. structural div. 1965-66, chmn. engring. mechanics div. 1961-62, J.J.R. Croes medal 1937, 54, Ernest E. Howard medal 1974); mem. Nat. Acad. Engring., Sigma Xi, Phi Kappa Phi, Tau Beta Pi, Chi Epsilon. Methodist. Address: 5025 E Calle Barril Tucson AZ 85718

JOHNSTON, CHARLES BERNIE, JR., business educator, university dean; b. Sudbury, Ont., Can., June 3, 1931; s. Charles Bernie and Beatrice Eileen J.; m. Carol Jean Querney, Aug. 22, 1953; children: Charles David, Jeffrey Philip, Craig Matthew, Laura Isabel Myerling, Nancy Anne Beatrice. B.A., U. Western Ont., 1954; M.B.A., 1957; postgrad., Northwestern U., 1959-61. Promotion coordinator Proctor and Gamble Co. of Can., Ltd., 1954; gen. mgr. C.B. Johnston Ltd., London, Ont., 1955-70, pres., 1970—; mem. faculty Sch. Bus. Adminstrn. U. Western Ont., 1957—, prof., 1971—, chmn. continuing edn., 1972—, dir. mgmt. tng. course, 1972—, asso. dean, 1975-78, dean, 1978—; dir. Quaker Oats Co. of Can. Ltd., Pathex Ltd., Photochemical Research Assos., Inc. Author: (with D.S.R. Leighton and D.H. Thain) How Industry Buys, 1959, (with D.S.R. Leighton et al) Canadian Problems in Marketing, 3d edit, 1972; Contbr. articles in field to profl. jours. Pres. Oak Park Home and Sch. Assn., London, 1967; chmn. bd. London French Sch., London, 1970-71. Wilhelmina and J. Gordon McIntosh scholar, 1956-57; Allstate fellow, 1959-61. Mem. Am. Mktg. Assn., Adminstrv. Scis. Assn. Can. Home: 165 Hunt Club Dr London ON Canada N6H 3Y8 Office: School of Business Adminstrn The University of Western Ontario Richmond St N London ON Canada N6A 3K7

JOHNSTON, DAVID LLOYD, lawyer, univ. adminstr.; b. Sudbury, Ont., Can., June 28, 1941; s. Lloyd Allen and Dorothy Isobelle (Stonehouse) J.; m. Sharon Jean Downey, Aug. 29, 1964; children—Deborah Nicole, Barbara Alexandra, Sharon Elisabeth, Jenifer Joan, Catherine Ives. A.B., Harvard U., 1963; LL.B., Cambridge U., 1965, Queen's U., 1966. Bar: Called to Ont. bar 1969. Asst. prof. law Queen's U., Kingston, Ont., Can., 1966-68; prof. law U. Toronto, Ont., 1968-74; dean, prof. law U. Western Ont., London, 1974-79; prin., vice chancellor, prof. law McGill U., Montreal, Que., Can., 1979—; commr. Ont. Securities Commn., 1972-79. Author: Canadian Securities Regulation, 1977, Business Associations, 1979, Canadian Companies and the Stock Exchanges, 1979. Mem. Law Soc. Upper Can., Can. Bar Assn. Anglican. Office: Office of Prin and Vice Chancellor McGill U 845 Sherbrooke St W Montreal PQ H3A 2T5 Canada

JOHNSTON, DAVID TOWNSEND, commodity broker; b. Richmond Hill, N.Y., Feb. 12, 1921; s. Alexander S. and Ruth J.; 1 son, Peter A. B.S. in Econs, Wharton Sch., U. Pa., 1942. Asst. v.p. commodity dept. Merrill Lynch, Pierce, Fenner & Smith, N.Y.C., 1946-68; sr. v.p. commodities, dir. E.F. Hutton & Co. Inc., N.Y.C., 1968—; dir. E.F. Hutton Group Inc., E.F. Hutton London Ltd.; mem., past chmn. bd. govs. Commodity Exchange, Inc.; mem. Chgo. Bd. Trade, Coffee, Sugar and Cocoa Exchange, Inc.; N.Y. Cotton Exchange, Winnipeg Commodity Exchange, Mpls. Grain Exchange. Trustee Northfield Mt. Hermon Sch., N.Y.C., Mission Soc. Served to lt. USNR, 1942-45. Mem. Futures Industry Assn. (past chmn. bd. dirs.), Nat/Futures Assn. (vice chmn., dir.). Clubs: Ridgewood (N.J.); Country. Office: 1 Battery Park Plaza New York NY 10004

JOHNSTON, DAVID WHITE, JR., textile manufacturing company executive; b. Atlanta, Mar. 31, 1921; s. David White and Annie Kate (Johnston); m. Sally Onie Ingram, July 30, 1949; children—Elizabeth, David. B.S. in Indsl. Mgmt, Ga. Inst. Tech., 1942; postgrad., U. Western Ont., U. N.C. Plant mgr. Dominion Textile Co., Ltd., Drummondville, Que., Can., 1952-60, v.p. mfg., 1963-68; div. v.p. Deering Milliken Co., Spartanburg, S.C., 1960-64; v.p. mfg. Bibb Mfg. Co., Macon, Ga., 1968-70; chmn. bd., chief exec. officer Dan River Inc., Danville, Va., 1970—, also dir.; dir. Dibrrell Bros., Bank Va. Co., Liberty Life Ins. Co. Trustee Averett Coll., Danville; bd. dirs. Roman Eagle Nursing Home, Danville, Meml. Hosp., Danville; adv. bd. Duke U. Hosp., Durham, N.C. Served to lt. USNR, 1942-46. Mem. Danville C. of C. (dir.). Presbyterian. Club: Danville Golf. Home: 134 Acorn Ln Danville VA 24541 Office: 2291 Memorial Dr Danville VA 24541

JOHNSTON, DON, advt. exec.; b. Elmira, N.Y., 1927. B.A., Mich. State U., 1950; M.A., Johns Hopkins U., 1952. With J. Walter Thompson Co., N.Y.C., 1951—, chief exec. officer, dir., 1978—; dir. Continental Group. Home: 33 Woodridge Dr New Canaan CT 06840 Office: 420 Lexington Ave New York NY 10017 *

JOHNSTON, DONALD JAMES, Canadian government official; b. Ottawa, Ont., Can., June 26, 1936; s. Wilbur Austin and Florence Jean (Moffat) Tucker) J.; m. Heather Bell Maclaren, Dec. 11, 1965; children: Kristina, Allison, Rachel, Sara. LL.B., McGill U., 1958; student (World U. scholar, MacDonald Travelling scholar), Grenoble U., 1958-59. Asso., Stikeman & Elliott, 1961-67; partner Johnston, Heenan & Blaikie, 1967-78; lectr. Faculty of Law, McGill U., 1964-77; M.P. from St. Henri-Westmount, 1978-80. Author: How to Survive Canada's Tax Chaos; contbr. articles to profl. jours. Pres. Treasury Bd. Can., 1980-82; minister econ. devel., sci. and tech., 1982—; chmn. public accounts com. Treasury Bd. Can., 1979. Liberal. Clubs: St. James, Montreal Indoor Tennis, Rideau Tennis and Squash. Office: House of Commons Ottawa ON K1A 0A6 Canada *

JOHNSTON, DONALD MACTAVISH, natural gas transmission line executive; b. Moose Jaw, Sask., Can., July 25, 1925; s. Donald Murdoch and Bessie May (Phillips) J.; m. Isabelle MacMillan Murray, Apr. 19, 1952. B.A., U. Sask.-Saskatoon, 1946, LL.B., 1948. Legal counsel Chevron Standard, Calgary, Alta., 1950-57; asst. gen. counsel Transcan. Pipelines, Toronto, 1957—. Mem. Sask. Law Soc., Alta. Law Soc. Progressive Conservative. Anglican. Club: Albany (Toronto). Home: 1631 Pinetree Crescent Mississauga ON Canada L5G 2S9 Office: Transcanada Pipelines 5500 Commerce Ct W Toronto ON Canada M5L 1C2

JOHNSTON, EDWARD ALLAN, lawyer; b. Balt., Sept. 25, 1921; s. William Henry and Hattie Frisby (Sanner) J.; m. Dorothy Janet Swart, June 23, 1951; children: Elizabeth Janet, Jean Taylor. B.B.A., U. Balt., 1942, B.S., 1947, LL.B., 1949, LL.M., 1957. Bar: Md. 1949; C.P.A., Md. With Johnston & Co., C.P.A.s, Balt., 1946-52; partner firm Whiteford, Taylor, Preston, Trimble and Johnston, Balt., 1954—; lectr. taxes U. Balt., 1948-65; Dir. Poole and Kent Co., Balt. Pres. Dickeyville Assn., 1960; Bd. dirs. Contact-Balt., 1974—, chmn. bd., 1976-80; trustee Asbury Found., 1970—. Recipient Alumnus of Yr. award U. Balt., 1980. Mem. U. Balt. Alumni Assn. (pres. 1975-76), Md. Golf Assn. (pres. 1968), Middle Atlantic Golf Assn. (v.p. 1978-82), Methodist (chmn. ofcl. bd. 1965-69, chmn. bd. trustees 1977—). Club: Balt. Country (golf com.). Home: 2449 Pickwick Rd Baltimore MD 21207 Office: 2000 First Md Bldg 25 S Charles St Baltimore MD 21201

JOHNSTON, EDWARD ELLIOTT, insurance and management consultant; b. Jacksonville, Ill., Jan. 3, 1918; s. Leonard Edward and Erma Lytle (Elliott) J.; m. Clara Margaret Stacey, Aug. 26, 1950; children: Janice Linell Johnston Regine, Karen Elleen Johnston Blois. A.B. in Psychology and Econs., Ill. Coll., Jacksonville, 1939, LL.D., 1970. Engaged in ins. industry, Hawaii, 1947-69; pres., gen. mgr. 50th State Ins. Assos., Inc., 1960-66; v.p. Hawaiian Ins. & Guaranty Co. Ltd., 1966-69; sec. (lt. gov.), Hawaii, 1958-59; high commr. Trust Ter. Pacific Islands, Saipan, Mariana Islands, 1969-76; exec. v.p. Pacific Area Travel Assn., San Francisco, 1976-80, Gt. Atlantic Ins. Co., 1980-

82, also dir.; research assoc. Greenwich Research Assocs. (Conn.), 1983—; dir. Longs Drug Stores Inc.; frequent guest lectr. polit. sci. U. Hawaii. Trustee Internationale Tourismus-Börse, Berlin.; Oahu County chmn. Republican party, 1965-69, State of Hawaii chmn., 1965-69; del. Nat. Rep. convs., 1960, 68, alt. del., 1964; chmn. Hawaii State Bd. Econ. Devel., 1960-63; pres., trustee Hawaii chpt. Easter Seal Soc.; mem. adv. bd. Sch. Travel Industry Mgmt., U. Hawaii. Served to capt. USAAF, 1942-48; to maj. USAF, 1951-52. Fellow Inst. Cert. Travel Agts.; mem. Assn. C.P.C.U.s, Phi Beta Kappa. Congregationalist. Clubs: Kiwanis; Whispering Palms Country (Saipan). Home: 15 Lyonridge Ln San Mateo CA 94403 *Many years ago, as a youth in the farming country of Southern Illinois, I saw a sign in a small country store which read "I cried because I had no shoes until I met a man who had no feet." This simple philosophy, which I never forgot, has helped me through many crises in both public and personal life. Regardless of what may happen, it could always be worse*

JOHNSTON, EDWARD JOSEPH, professional hockey team executive; b. Montreal, Que., Can., Nov. 24, 1935; m. Diane Johnston; 3 children. Former profl. hockey goaltender NHL with Boston Bruins, Toronto Maple Leafs, St. Louis Blues, Chgo. Black Hawks; coach N.B. Hawks, Am. Hockey League, 1978-79, Chgo. Black Hawks, NHL, 1979, Pitts. Penguins, NHL, 1980-83, gen. mgr., 1983—. Office: Pitts Penguins Civic Arena Gate 7 Pittsburgh PA 15219 *

JOHNSTON, EDWARD RICHARD, college president; b. Pitts., Sept. 30, 1939; s. Elmer F. and Margaret J.; m. Eugenia L. Mettrick, Apr. 6, 1963; children: Christine Lynn, Megan Louise. B.S., Muskingum Coll., 1961; O.D., Pa. Coll. Optometry, 1968; M.P.A., N.Y. U., 1971. Asso. dir. Optometric Center N.Y., N.Y.C., 1968-76; dean acad. affairs State Coll. Optometry, SUNY, N.Y.C., 1977-80, pres., 1980—; exec. dir. Optometric Center N.Y. Found. Mem. Health Service Agy., N.Y.C., from 1981. Mem. Am. Optometric Assn., Am. Public Health Assn., Am. Acad. Optometry. Presbyterian. Office: SUNY Coll Optometry 100 E 24th St New York NY 10010 *

JOHNSTON, ELTON E., business executive; b. Columbus, Ohio, Feb. 16, 1927; s. Ross Festus and Esta Ozella (Morrow) J.; m. Shirley Kretschmer, Mar. 5, 1949; children: Gary, Gail. B.S. in Bus. Adminstrn, U. Louisville, 1949. With Am. Greetings Corp., Cleve., 1949—, dir. data processing, 1960-62, asst. treas., 1962-64, asst. v.p., 1964-67, v.p. adminstrn., 1967-78, sr. v.p. adminstrn. and research, 1978—. Bd. dirs. Goodwill Industries Greater Cleve., 1981—. Served with USNR, 1945-46. Mem. Assn. Systems Mgmt. (pres. 1957-58). Methodist. Lodges: Kiwanis (past pres.); Masons. Home: 4932 Berkshire Dr North Olmsted OH 44070 Office: 10500 American Rd Cleveland OH 44144

JOHNSTON, ERNEST B., JR., oil company executive; b. Selma, Ala., June 26, 1930; s. Ernest Barnwell and Emma Julia (Thomas) J.; m. Joan Lord, Jan. 25, 1958; children: Johanna, Lucy Peabody Pevey, Julia Caroline Kimball, Rebeckah Eliza. A.B., Harvard U., 1952; postgrad., U. Paris, France, 1953; M.A., U. Calif. at Berkeley, 1966. Joined U.S. Fgn. Service, 1956; with Dept. State, Washington, 1956-58; consular officer, Colombo, Ceylon (now Sri Lanka), 1958; econ.-comml. officer Am. embassy, Madrid, Spain, 1960-65; with Dept. State, Washington, 1966-69, asst. chief trade agreements div., 1968-69; staff Nat. Security Council, 1969-71; Sloan fellow Stanford U., 1971-72; econ. counselor U.S. mission to European Communities, Brussels, Belgium, 1974-77; exec. asst. Under Sec. of State for econ. affairs, Washington, 1977-79; dep. asst. Sec. State for econ. and bus. affairs, 1979-82; prin. internat. affairs rep. Phillips Petroleum, 1982. Served with AUS, 1953-55. Home: 6900 Benjamin St McLean VA 22101 Office: Phillips Petroleum 1825 K St NW Suite 1107 Washington DC 20006

JOHNSTON, EUGENE, Congressman; b. Winston-Salem, N.C., Mar. 3, 1936. Student, Duke U., Wake Forest U. Former acct. A.M. Pullen and Co.; former pres., dir. Fisher-Harrison Corp., Johnston Properties (real estate holding co.); mem. 97th Congress from 6th N.C. dist. Mem. Am. Inst. C.P.A.'s, Young Pres.'s Orgn. *

JOHNSTON, FRANK RANDOLPH, surgeon; b. Aiken, S.C., Oct. 29, 1915; s. Thomas Dabney and Mary Elizabeth (Withers) J.; m. Era Leigh McIntosh, Jan. 6, 1946; children: Elizabeth Ann., Randolph Leigh, Mary Withers. B.S., Presbyn. Coll., S.C., 1938; M.D., Duke U., 1942; D.Humanities (hon.), Presbyn. Coll., S.C., 1965. Intern in gen. and thoracic surgery Bowman Gray Sch. Medicine, Winston-Salem, N.C., 1942-43; resident in gen. and thoracic surgery, 1946-50, practice medicine specializing in gen. and thoracic surgery, Winston-Salem, 1950-77, in thoracic surgery, 1977—; instr. surgery Bowman Gray Sch. Medicine, Winston-Salem, 1950-55, asst. prof., 1955-63, asso. prof., 1963-68, prof., 1968—. Served to capt. M.C. USAAF, 1943-46. Mem. Am. Assn. Thoracic Surgery, ACS, AMA, Internat. Cardiovascular Soc., So. Thoracic Surg. Assn., Soc. Thoracic Surgeons, S.E. Surg. Congress, So. Surg. Assn., N.C., Forsyth County med. socs., N.C. Surg. Assn., Sigma Xi, Alpha Omega Alpha. Home: 735 Arbor Rd Winston-Salem NC 27104 Office: Cardiothoracic Surgery Sect Bowman Gray Sch Medicine Winston-Salem NC 27103

JOHNSTON, FRED WILLIAM, JR., naval officer; b. Chgo., Nov. 16, 1933; s. Fred William and Maybelle (Shuman) J.; m. Sally Hale, May 29, 1958; children: Fred William III, Mary. Student, Emory U., 1951-53; B.A., Navy Postgrad. Sch., 1961; tng., Naval War Coll., 1968. Served as naval aviation cadet U.S. Navy, 1953-55, commd. ensign, 1955, advanced through grades to rear adm., 1980; flew helicopters and fixed wing carrier-based aircraft, 1955-73; exec. officer U.S.S. Tarawa, San Diego, 1974-76; 1st comdg. officer U.S.S. Saipan, Norfolk, Va., 1977-79; served on Joint Chiefs of Staff, Washington, 1980-81; comdr. Sea-based Air Anti-Submarine Warfare Wings, Atlantic, Jacksonville, Fla., 1981—. Mem. exec. bd. Jacksonville United Way, 1981-83. Decorated Def. Meritorious Service medal, Navy Meritorious medal, Navy Commendation medal. Mem. Jacksonville C. of C. (bd. govs. 1981-83), Phi Delta Theta. Lodge: Rotary. Home: OTRS A Naval Air Sta Jacksonville FL 32212 Office: PO Box 102 Naval Air Sta Jacksonville FL 32212

JOHNSTON, GEORGE SIM, investment counsel; b. Memphis, Nov. 30, 1924; s. George Sim and Marguerite (Aden) J.; m. Cynthia M. Cogswell, Feb. 23, 1951; children: George Sim III, William C., Scott Christian, Bart Alexander. B.S., Yale U., 1948; postgrad., N.Y. U., 1949-51. With Scudder, Stevens & Clark, N.Y.C., 1948—, pres., chief exec. officer, 1970—; chmn. bd. Scudder Internat. Fund, Inc.; chmn. bd., dir. Scudder Capital Growth Fund, Inc.; v.p., dir. Scudder Fund Distbrs., Inc.; chmn. bd., dir. Scudder Internat. Fund; pres., trustee Scudder Target Fund; trustee Bowery Savs. Bank, Scudder Managed Municipal Bonds, Scudder N.Y. Tax Free Fund, Scudder Cash Investment Trust, Scudder Tax Free Target Fund, Scudder Govt. Money Fund, Scudder Calif. Tax Free Fund; dir. 580 Park Ave., Inc., Bessemer Securities Corp., N.Y.C., Fiduciary Trust Co., Boston, Scudder Income Fund, Inc., Scudder Common Stock Fund, Inc., Scudder Devel. Fund, Scudder Realty Advisors, Inc.; mem. U.S. adv. bd. Zurich Ins. Co. Bd. dirs. N.Y. Soc. for Prevention Cruelty to Children; mem. Am. Council on Germany, Brit.-N.Am. Com. Served to 1st lt. AUS, 1942-46, 51-52. Decorated Army Commendation medal; mem. Am. Soc. of Most Venerable Order of Hosp. of St. John of Jerusalem. Mem. Investment Counsel Assn. Am., Nat. Golf Links of Am. (dir. 1959—, pres. 1978—). Clubs: Racquet and Tennis (dir. 1962—), Links (N.Y.C.); Sky; Met. (Washington). Home: New York NY Office: 345 Park Ave New York NY 10154

JOHNSTON, HAROLD SLEDGE, chemistry educator; b. Woodstock, Ga., Oct. 11, 1920; s. Smith L. and Florine (Dial) J.; m. Mary Ella Stay, Dec. 29, 1948; children—Shirley Louise, Linda Marie, David Finley, Barbara Dial. A.B., Emory U., 1941, D.Sc., 1965; Ph.D., Calif. Inst. Tech., 1948. From instr. to asso. prof. chemistry Stanford, 1947-56; asso. prof. Calif. Inst. Tech., 1956-57; prof. chemistry U. Calif. at, Berkeley, 1957—, dean, 1966-70. Author: Gas Phase Reaction Rate Theory, 1966, Gas Phase Kinetics of Neutral Oxygen Species, 1968, Reduction of Stratospheric Ozone by Nitrogen Oxide Catalysts from Supersonic Transport Exhaust, 1971; Contbr. articles to profl. publs. Recipient Tyler prize for environ. achievement, 1983. Mem. Am. Chem. Soc. (Gold medal Calif. sect. 1956, Pollution Control award 1974), Am. Phys. Soc., Nat. Acad. Scis., Am. Acad. Arts and Scis., Am. Geophys. Union. Home: 132 Highland Blvd Berkeley CA 94708

JOHNSTON, J. BENNETT, U.S. senator; b. Shreveport, La., June 10, 1932; m. Mary Gunn, 1956; children: Bennett, Hunter, Mary, Sally. Student, Washington and Lee U., U.S. Mil. Acad.; LL.B., La. State U., 1956. Bar: La. 1956. Formerly mem. firm Johnston, Johnston & Thornton; mem. U.S. Senate from La., 1972—, mem. spl. com. on aging; chmn. Democratic senatorial campaign com., 1975-76, La. Ho. of Reps., 1964-68, mem. appropriations com., ranking minority mem. subcom. energy and water devel., mem. com. energy and natural resources, ranking minority mem. com. on energy and natural resources, mem. budget com.; chmn. La. Senate, 1968-72, mem. appropriations com., ranking minority mem. subcom. energy and water devel., mem. com. energy and natural resources, ranking minority mem. subcom. energy regulation, mem. budget com.; mem. Served with U.S. Army, 1956-59. Mem. Am., La., Shreveport bar assns. Democrat. Address: US Senate 136 Hart Senate Office Bldg Washington DC 20510

JOHNSTON, JAMES I., pharmaceutical company executive; m. Marjorie; children: Lana, Robert, Cathryn, Jennifer. B.S. in Indsl. Mgmt., U. Calif.-Berkeley, 1949. With Edgewater Gulf Hotel, Gulfport, Miss., 1949-50, Colonial Banking Co., Gulfport, 1950-51, J.F. Pryun Bldg. Contractor, Berkeley, Calif., 1951-52; personnel analyst San Francisco office Shell Oil & Chem. Co., 1952, personnel sr. clk. Martinez refinery, 1952-55, personnel asst. Shell Point, 1955-57; with Monsanto Co., 1957-72, gen. supt. personnel J.F. Queeny plant, St. Louis, 1961-64, gen. supt. mfg., 1964-66, mgr. mfg. personnel devel., 1966-67, dir. personnel planning and devel., 1967-72; with Foremost-McKesson, Inc. and successor firm McKesson Corp., San Francisco, 1972—, corp. dir. employee and labor relations and compensation, 1972-73, corp. dir. employee relations and compensation, 1973-74, corp. dir. personnel, Sna Francisco, 1974-75, v.p. personnel, San Francisco, 1975—. Author: (with others) Organization Planning. Pres. Knollwood Townhouse, Inc. Served with U.S. Navy, 1945-47. Mem. Nat. Conf. Bd. (orgn. planning council), Am. Soc. Personnel Adminstrn., Federated Employers of San Francisco (chmn. exec. com.), Alpha Delta Phi. Clubs: Olympic, Peacock Gap Country. Home: 187 Knollwood Dr San Rafael CA 94901 Office: McKesson Corp One Post St San Francisco CA 94101

JOHNSTON, JAMES JORDON, advt. exec.; b. Sedalia, Mo., Jan. 17, 1931; s. E.O. and Hildah (Pease) J. Student, U. Calif., 1951-52, U. Mo., 1955-56, U. Wichita, 1956-57. Dir. advt. and promotion WMBD-TV, Peoria, Ill., 1957-59; v.p., creative dir. Kane Advt., Bloomington, Ill., 1959-62; partner, creative dir. Howard Advt., Raleigh, N.C., 1962-64; v.p., creative dir. Griswold-Eshleman Co., Cleve., 1964-69, pres., 1969-74, chmn. bd., chief exec. officer, 1970-74; pres., chief exec. officer Jim Johnston Advt., N.Y.C., 1974—; mng. dir. Strategic Planning Center, Chapel Hill, N.C., 1974—. Promotion chmn. Cleve. Plan, 1968-70. Served with USAF, 1951-55. Named Man of Year Cleve. Soc. Communicating Arts, 1968; named One of Am.'s Top 100 Creative People Ad Day poll of industry leaders, 1973, 75. Mem. Am. Assn. Advt. Agys. Clubs: Metropolitan (N.Y.C.); Chapel Hill (N.C.) Country. Home: Morgan Creek Rd Chapel Hill NC 27514 also 17 W 54th St New York NY 10019 Office: 551 Fifth Ave New York NY 10176 *Reach should exceed grasp; dreams should be larger than reality; or else we settle for too little, too late, restricting ourselves to petty gain and studied mediocrity.*

JOHNSTON, JAMES WESLEY, tobacco company executive; b. Chgo., Apr. 11, 1946; s. Ted and Irma (Hacker) J.; m. Beverly S. Cline, Nov. 10, 1967; children—Amanda E., Emily S., J. Michael. B.S. in Accountancy, U. Ill., 1967; M.B.A., Northwestern U., 1971. C.P.A., Ill. Fin. analyst Ford Motor Co., 1967-69; with N.W. Industries, 1969-79, dir. corp. devel., 1973-75, v.p. mktg., 1975-79; exec. v.p. Asia/Pacific R. J. Reynolds Tobacco Internat. Inc., 1979, pres., chief exec. officer Asia/Pacific, Hong Kong, 1979-81; exec. v.p. R.J. Reynolds Tobacco, U.S., 1981—. Village treas., trustee, acting village pres. Village of Bollingbrook, Ill., 1973-75. Mem. Ill. Soc. C.P.A.s. Clubs: Twin City, American. Office: 10th Floor RJ Reynolds Tobacco Co Winston-Salem NC 27102

JOHNSTON, JOHN ANDREW, air force officer; b. Ont., Can., Jan. 30, 1923; s. Robert Andrew and Rebecca Ellen (McKenzie) J.; m. Dorothy L. Crabb, Aug. 17, 1945; children: Robert H., Susan L., James J., William G. Grad., Air Force Command Staff Coll., 1955, Armed Forces Inst., 1962. Commd. 2d lt. USAAF (named changed to USAF 1947), 1942, advanced through grades to maj. gen., 1974; base comdr. Detroit Met. Airport, 1952-60; asst. adj. gen., Mich., 1960-74, adj. gen.; dir. Mich. Dept. Mil. Affairs, 1974—; Bd. dirs. Dept. Def. Res. Forces Policy Bd., St. Lawrence Hosp., Lansing, Mich., 1972—. Decorated Air medal with 16 oak leaf clusters, Purple Heart., D.S.M. Mem. N.G. Assn. U.S., N.G. Assn. Mich., Am. Legion, Am. Def. Preparedness Assn., Air Force Assn. Clubs: Rotary, Quiet Birdmen. Home: 1708 Briarwood Rd Lansing MI 48917 Office: 2500 S Washington Lansing MI 48913

JOHNSTON, JOHN MARTIN, lawyer; b. Bklyn., July 19, 1923; s. John Brown and Helen Agatha (Connelly) J.; m. Marie Ann Kelly, June 30, 1944 (div. 1966); children: Nancy Elting, John W., David P., Peter K.; m. Suzanne Shepardson, July 30, 1966; children: Philip C., Jacqueline S. Student, Princeton U., 1941-43, A.B., 1947; LL.B., Columbia U., 1949. Bar: N.Y. 1949. Assoc. firm White & Case, N.Y.C., 1949-62, ptnr., 1962—, resident ptnr., Palm Beach, Fla., 1978—; mem. character com. 1st dept. N.Y. Supreme Ct., 1974-78; chmn. supreme ct. com. N.Y. City Lawyers Assn., 1975-78. Trustee Trinity Sch., N.Y.C., 1978, Presentation Found., Palm Beach, 1982, Planned Parenthood, Palm Beach, 1982, Cripple Children Assn., Palm Beach, 1982. Served to 1st lt. U.S. Army, 1943-46. Decorated Silver Star, Purple Heart. Fellow Am. Bar Found., Am. Coll. Trial Lawyers; mem. ABA, Assn. Bar City of N.Y. Clubs: Piping Rock (Locust Valley, N.Y.); Everglades (Palm Beach). Home: 570 Park Ave New York NY 10021 Office: White & Case 14 Wall St New York NY 10005

JOHNSTON, JOHN PHILIP, orgn. exec.; b. Newton, Mass., Dec. 14, 1935; s. William James and Gladys J.; m. Inada Hiltrud Pasewald, Feb. 26, 1969; 1 dau., Dawn. B.S., Northeastern U., Boston, 1963, M.Ed., 1966; Ph.D., Madras (India) U., 1971. With CARE, 1963—; dir. programming Sierra Leone, 1970-75; dir. CARE, Deutschland, 1976-80, worldwide exec. dir., N.Y.C., 1980—. Served with AUS, 1955-58. Episcopalian. Home: Apt 3B Eastbourne Alger Ct Bronxville NY 10708 Office: 660 1st Ave New York NY 10016

JOHNSTON, JOHNNY JONES, army officer; b. Farmersville, Tex., Dec. 23, 1928; s. Herman and Mary McGee J.; m. Beverly Hale, June 11, 1949; children: John G., Katherine R. B.A., U. Omaha, 1967. Joined U.S. Army, 1952; grad. (Officers Candidate Sch.), 1953, commd. 2d lt., advanced through grades to maj. gen.; served as co. comdr., Ft. Ord, Calif., Korea, commd. 2d lt., advanced through grades to brig. gen.; served as co. comdr., Ft. Jackson, S.C., bn. comdr., Ft. Benning, Ga., also Vietnam, brigade comdr., Ft. Riley, Kans., asst. div. comdr., Ger., now armored comdr., Ft. Sheridan, Ill. Decorated Legion of Merit, Bronze Star, others. Mem. Ch. of Christ. Home: 111 Logan Loop Sheridan IL 60037 Office: Comdr USARMR V Sheridan IL 60037

JOHNSTON, KENNETH RICHARD, English literature educator; b. Marquette, Mich., Apr. 20, 1938; s. John Martin McKinley and Eva Alice Amalia (Nelson) J.; m. Elizabeth Louise Adolphson, Aug. 12, 1961 (div. 1976); children: Kate, Lucas, Matthew; m. Ilinca Marina Zarifopol, Dec. 30, 1976; 1 son, Theodore. B.A., Augustana Coll., Rock Island, Ill., 1959; M.A., U. Chgo., 1961, Yale U., 1962, Ph.D., 1966. Asst. prof. to prof. lit. Ind. U., Bloomington, 1966—, assoc. dean Coll. Arts and Sics., 1973-75; prof. U. Bucharest, Romania, 1974-75; exec. sec. English Inst., 1979—. Author: Wordsworth and "The Recluse", 1984. Recipient Disting. Teaching award Amoco Found.-Ind. U., 1973; NEH fellow, 1979-80. Mem. MLA (del. 1973-75, mem. exec. dom. 1978-82). Lutheran. Office: Dept English Ind U Bloomington IN 47405

JOHNSTON, LLOYD DOUGLAS, research psychologist; b. Boston, Apr. 18, 1940; s. Leslie D. and Madeline B. (Irvin) J.; 1 son, Douglas Leslie. B.A. in Econs., Williams Coll., 1962; M.B.A., Harvard U., 1965, postgrad., 1965-66; M.A. in Social Psychology, U. Mich., 1971, Ph.D., 1973. Research asst. Grad. Sch. Bus. Adminstr., Harvard U., Boston, 1965-66; asst. study dir. Inst. Social Research, U. Mich., Ann Arbor, 1966-73, asst. research scientist, 1973-75, assoc. research scientist, 1975-78, research scientist and program dir., 1978—; prin. investigator Monitoring the Future: A Continuing Study of Lifestyles and Values of Am. Youth, 1975—; cons. to WHO, UN White House, fgn. govts., fed. agys. and various univs., 1975—; mem. Nat. Adv. Council on Drug Abuse, 1982—; chmn. drug epidemiology sect. Internat. Council on Alcohol and Addictions, 1982—; mem. Com. on Problems of Drug Dependence, 1982—; mem. adv. com. Drug Abuse Epidemiology Data Ctr., Tex. Christian U., 1974-80; mem. various coms. and adv. groups Nat. Inst. Drug Abuse, 1975—. Author: Drugs and American Youth, 1973, Student Drug Use in America, 1975-81, 82, various monographs on drug use and lifestyles of Am. high sch. students, 1972—; editor: Conducting Follow Up Research on Drug Treatment Programs, 1977; contbr. chpts. to books, articles to profl. jours. Recipient nat. Pacesetter award in research Nat. Inst. on Drug Abuse, 1982. Mem. Am. Psychol. Assn., Soc. for Psychol. Study Social Issues (sec.-treas. 1976-79), AAAS. Home: 4231 Shetland Dr Ann Arbor MI 48104 Office: Inst Social Research U Mich Ann Arbor MI 48109

JOHNSTON, MARGUERITE, journalist, author; b. Birmingham, Ala., Aug. 7, 1917; d. Robert C. and Marguerite (Spaling) J.; m. Charles Wynn Barnes, Aug. 31, 1946; children: Susan, Patricia, Steven, Polly. A.B., Birmingham-So. Coll., 1938. Reporter Birmingham News, 1939-44; Washington corr. Birmingham News, Birmingham Age-Herald, London Daily Mirror, 1945-46; columnist Houston Post, 1947-69, fgn. news editor, mem. editorial bd., 1969—; assoc. editor editorial page Houston Page, 1972-77, asst. editor editorial page, 1977—; lectr. in field, 1947—; instr. creative writing U. Houston, 1946-47, lectr. feature writing, 1965-66; lectr. Baker Coll., Rice U., 1977-78; del. Asian Am. Women Journalists Conf., Honolulu, 1965, 1st World Conf. Women Journalists, Mexico City, 1969. Author: Public Manners, 1957, A Happy Worlding Abode, 1964. Bd. dirs. Tex. Bill of Rights Found., 1962-64, Planned Parenthood, 1953-55, Homes St. Mark, 1962-63, Rice Ctr., 1980—; mem. Mcpl. Art Commn., 1971-76, Houston Com. Fgn. Relations. Recipient Theta Sigma Phi Headliner award, 1954, 1st ann. award of merit Houston Com. Alcoholism, 1956, cert. of merit Gulf Coast chpt. Am. Soc. Safety Engrs., 1960, Agnes Carter Nelms award Planned Parenthood, 1968, Sch. Bell award Tex. State Tchrs. Assn., 1974, 75, Gold Key award Nat. Council Alcoholism, 1975, Population Action Council award, 1981. Mem. Tex. Soc. Architects (hon.), Mortar Bd., Phi Beta Kappa, Pi Beta Phi. Home: 5319 Cherokee Houston TX 77005

JOHNSTON, NORMAN JOHN, architecture educator, architect; b. Seattle, Dec. 3, 1918; s. Jay and Helen May (Shultis) J.; m. Lois Jane Hastings, Nov. 22, 1969. B.A., U. Wash.-Seattle, 1942; B.Arch., U. Oreg., 1949; M., Urban Planning, U. Pa.-Phila., 1959, Ph.D., 1964. Registered architect, Wash. City planner Seattle City Planning Commn., 1951-55; asst. prof. arch. U. Oreg.-Eugene, 1956-58; assoc. prof. architecture and urban planning U. Wash.-Seattle, 1960-64, prof., 1964—, assoc. dean, 1964-76, 79—; mem. nat. examinations com. Nat. Council Archtl. Registration Bds., Washington, 1970-81. Author: Cities in the Round, 1983; editor: NCARB Architectural Registration Handbook, 1980. Commr. King County Policy Devel. Commn., Seattle, 1970-76; chmn. Capitol Area Master Plan Adv. Com. State of Wash., Olympia, 1980—. Served with AUS, 1942-45. Fellow AIA (pres. Seattle chpt. 1981); mem. Soc. Archtl. Historians, Inst. Urban Design, Phi Beta Kappa, Tau Sigma Delta, Lambda Alpha. Presbyterian. Home: 3905 NE Belvoir Pl Seattle WA 98105 Office: Coll Architecture and Urban Planning U Wash JO-26 Seattle WA 98195

JOHNSTON, PAUL ALEXANDER, bus. exec.; b. Smithfield, N.C., May 17, 1916; s. Albert S. and Gayle (Makepeace) J.; m. Margaret McGirt, Aug. 31, 1949; 1 son, Paul A. A.B., U. N.C., 1950, LL.B., 1952. Bar: N.C. bar 1952. Asso. Satterlee, Warfield and Stephens, N.Y.C., 1952; asst. dir. Inst. Govt., U. N.C., 1953; adminstrv. asst. to Gov. Luther H. Hodges, 1954-57; dir. adminstrn., N.C., 1957-60; asst. to controller Burlington Industries, Greensboro, N.C., 1960; exec. asst. to sec. Dept. Commerce, 1961; v.p. contracts Martin Co. div. Martin Marietta Corp., 1961-63, pres. cement and lime div., N.Y.C., 1963-65; v.p. Martin Marietta Corp., 1963-65; pres. Glen Alden Corp., 1965-72; chmn. bd., chief exec. officer Johnston Industries, Inc., 1972—; chmn. bd. Whitehead & Kales, Inc., Detroit, 1977—, Johnston Industries Ltd., London, Eng.; dir. Beaufort Engring., Kirby-in-Ashfield, Eng. Editor-in-chief: N.C. Law Rev, 1952. Served with AUS, 1944-46. Mem. N.C. State Bar, N.C. Bar Assn., Bar Eastern Dist. N.C., Order of Coif, Phi Delta Phi. Democrat. Presbyn. Office: 111 W 40th St New York NY 10018

JOHNSTON, PERCY WALKER, JR., railroad executive, lawyer; b. Shubuta, Miss., Jan. 8, 1921; s. Percy Walker and Lyda (Brashier) J.; m. Mary Gibson, Oct. 19, 1946; children: Stephen Gibson, David Bruce. B.A., U. Miss., 1941; LL.B., U. Va., 1947. Bar: Ala. 1948, Ill. 1974. Assoc. Johnston, McCall & Johnston, Mobile, Ala., 1948-54; with Gulf, Mobile & Ohio R.R., 1954-72, gen. atty., 1956-68, gen. solicitor, 1968-72, Ill. Central Gulf R.R. (merger Ill. Central R.R. and Gulf, Mobile & Ohio R.R. 1972), Chgo., 1972-73, gen. counsel, 1973-76, v.p. law, 1976-80, sr. v.p. law, 1980—, also dir.; dir. G M & O Land

Co., Peoria & Pekin Union Ry. Mem. ofcl. bd. Dauphin Way Methodist Ch., Mobile, Ala., 1971-73. Served to capt. USAAF, 1945. Mem. Ala., Ill. bar assns., ABA, Assn. Am. Railroads (legal affairs com.), Western Conf. Ry. Counsel (chmn. 1977-78), Order of Coif, Pi Kappa Alpha, Phi Delta Phi. Home: 2245 Willow Rd Homewood IL 60430 Office: 233 N Michigan Ave Chicago IL 60601

JOHNSTON, RICHARD FOURNESS, biologist; b. Oakland, Calif., July 27, 1925; s. Arthur Nathaniel and Marie (Johnson) J.; m. Lora Lee Bliler, Feb. 7, 1948; children—Regan (Mrs. David Harsha), Janet, Cassandra (Mrs. Douglas McEnery). B.A., U. Calif.-, Berkeley, 1950, M.A., 1953, Ph.D., 1955. Asst. prof. dept. biology N.Mex. State U., 1956-58; mem. faculty depts. zoology and ecology U. Kans. at Lawrence, 1958—, prof., 1968—, chmn., 1979, editor, 1974-76; program dir. systematic biology NSF, Washington, 1968-69; editor Ann. Rev. Ecology and Systematics, 1968—, Current Ornithology, 1981—; Mem. adv. panel biol. scis. Smithsonian Fgn. Currency Program, 1969-71. Served with AUS, 1943-46. Am. Acad. Arts and Scis. grantee, 1957; Nat. Acad. Sci. grantee, 1959; NSF grantee, 1959—. Fellow Am. Ornithol. Union (Coues award 1975), AAAS; mem. Ecol. Soc. Am., Soc. Systematic Zoology (editor jour. 1967-70, pres. 1977), Soc. Study Evolution, Am. Soc. Naturalists, Animal Behavior Soc. Home: 615 Louisiana St Lawrence KS 66044 Office: Mus Natural History U Kans Lawrence KS 66045 *Variability or heterogeneity or pluralism is present in nearly everything humans do or to which they are exposed.*

JOHNSTON, RICHARD SMITH, medical center executive; b. Keyser, W.Va., Oct. 1, 1926; s. Fred R. and Bernedetta H. J.; m. Jean E. Armbruster, June 14, 1949; children: Susan J., Richard A. B.S., U. Md. Research chemist Naval Research Lab., Washington, 1946-55; engr. U.S. Naval Bur. Aeros., Washington, 1955-59; engr., chief crew systems div. NASA, Space Task Group, Langley Field, Va., 1959-63; chief crew systems div. Manned Spacecraft Center, Houston, 1963-68, spl. asst. to dir., 1968-69; dir. Lunar Receiving Lab Apollo/11, mgr. Apollo Lunar Expt. Program, 1969-70, dep. dir. med. research and ops., 1970-72; dir. life scis. Johnson Space Center, 1972-75, dir. space and life scis., 1977-79; dir. sci. and tech., spl. asst. to pres. U. Tex. Health Sci. Center, Houston, 1979-81; now v.p. Tex. Med. Ctr., Inc., Houston; dir. engring. Bunker Ramo Corp., Oak Brook, Ill., 1976-77; lectr. 125th Royal Soc. Medicine, Amsterdam, The Netherlands and Inst. Medicine, Toronto, Ont., Can., 1974-75; guest lectr. Purdue U., Trinity U., Tex. A & M U., Tex. Tech., Rice U. Contbr. sci. articles to profl. jours. Served with USN. Recipient Exceptional Service medals NASA, 1968, 69, Distinguished Service medal NASA, 1973, Distinguished Citizen award U. Md. Fellow Am. Astron. Soc. (Victor A. Prather award 1966); mem. Am. Inst. Aeros. and Astronautics (John Jefferies award 1971, contbn. to Soc. award 1979), Aerospace Med. Assn., Internat. Acad. Astronautics. Methodist. Club: Masons. Home: 2311 Green Tee Dr Pearland TX 77581 Office: Texas Medical Center Inc Houston TX 77030

JOHNSTON, ROBERT ATKINSON, educator, psychologist; b. Allentown, Pa., July 8, 1931; s. Robert and Marion (McBride) J.; children: Robert Paul, Kenneth Moffett, Scott Andrew. A.B., Haverford Coll., 1952; M.A., State U. Iowa, 1954, Ph.D., 1955. Intern VA Hosp., Knoxville, Iowa, 1955-56, staff psychologist, Coatesville, Pa., 1956; asso. prof. psychology, dir. Univ. Center for Psychol. Services, U. Richmond, 1957-63; prof. psychology, asso. dean faculty Coll. William and Mary, 1963-74, dept. psychology, 1974—. Pres. Williamsburg PTA Council, 1967-69; chmn. bd. dirs. Williamsburg Pre-sch. for Spl. Children, 1968-69. Mem. Am., Eastern psychol. assns., Va. Acad. Sci., AAUP. Home: PO Box 455 Williamsburg VA 23187

JOHNSTON, ROBERT COSSIN, consulting engineer; b. N.Y.C., Jan. 10, 1913; s. James Weeks and Caroline Agatha (Cossin) J.; m. Charlotte E. Shiels, June 17, 1939; 1 dau., Barbara Shiels Johnston Adams. B.S. magna cum laude in Engring, Princeton U., 1935. With Mueser, Rutledge, Johnston & DeSimone (and predecessor firms), N.Y.C., 1935—, asso., 1947-51, partner, 1951—. Contbr.: articles to Engring. News Record; others. Served to lt. C.E. USN, 1944-46. Fellow ASCE (lectr.), Am. Cons. Engrs. Council; mem. N.Y. Bldg. Congress, Soc. Am. Mil. Engrs., Concrete Industry Bd., The Moles, Am. Shore and Beach Assn. Episcopalian. Club: Princeton of N.Y. Home: 95 Bronxville Rd Bronxville NY 10708

JOHNSTON, ROBERT ELLIOTT, former steel company executive; b. Johnstown, Pa., June 29, 1921; s. David Blair and Anna (Stephenson) J.; m. Nancy Jane Pyle, June 19, 1943; children: Michael, Lawrence, Susan (Mrs. Ronald Lindbeck), Martha. B.S., U. Pitts., 1942; postgrad., Harvard Sch. Bus. Adminstrn., 1973. Research engr. Bethlehem Steel Corp., Lackawanna, N.Y., 1942-51, plant indsl. engr., Steelton, Pa., 1951-56, asst. gen. mgr., Sparrows Point, Md., 1956-72, v.p. manufactured products, steel ops., Bethlehem, Pa., 1972-74, v.p. prodn., 1974-77, v.p. steel ops., 1977-82. Served with AUS, 1943-44. Mem. Am. Iron and Steel Inst., Assn. Iron and Steel Engrs., U.S. Power Squardron, Sigma Chi. Republican. Presbyterian. Clubs: Saucon Valley Country (Bethlehem); Talbot Country, Sparrow Point Country, Miles River Yacht. Home: PO Box 826 Saint Michael's MD 21663

JOHNSTON, SAMUEL THOMAS, entertainment co. exec.; b. Cin., July 25, 1924; s. Alexander Robert and Betty Adeline (Hanna) J.; children from previous marriage—Jill, Susan, Melissa, Samuel Thomas. Grad., U. Cin., 1946; J.D., Chase Coll., 1953. Bar: Ohio bar 1953. Exec. v.p., dir. Hanna Barbera Prodns., Los Angeles, 1972-80; sr. v.p. Taft Broadcasting Co., Los Angeles, 1980—; vice chmn. Solo Prodn. Co., Los Angeles, 1977-80; pres., dir. Cine Guarantors II, Los Angeles, 1979. Served to lt. (j.g.) USN, 1942-45. Mem. Sigma Chi. Republican. Clubs: Coldstream Country, Lakeside Country (Hollywood, Calif.). Home: 2401 Ingleside St Cincinnati OH 45206 Office: 1718 Young St Cincinnati OH 45210

JOHNSTON, SCOTT DORAN, educator; b. Evanston, Ill., Oct. 8, 1922; s. Ralph Estes and Helen Annette (Doran) J.; m. Laura Lydia Wallace, Aug. 5, 1943; children—Linda, Laurance. B.A. magna cum laude, U. Minn., 1944, B.S. in Edn, 1945, M.A. in Polit. Sci, 1947, Ph.D., 1952. Tchr. high sch. social studies and history, Cloquet, Minn., 1945-46; mem. faculty Hamline U., St. Paul, 1947—, prof. polit. sci., chmn. dept., 1957—; dir. summer coll. faculty insts. in East Asian and Middle Eastern Studies, 1964—; cons. Islamic civilization teaching materials project Am. Council Learned Socs., 1978-80. Author articles, chpts. in field; cons. editor: World Affairs, 1976—. Mem. commn. social concerns Minn. Council Chs., 1960-65; del. county and state convs. Democratic-Farmer-Labor Party Minn. Served with USAAF, 1943-44. Social Sci. Research Council grantee, 1960; also 13 grants Hill Family Found. Mem. Associated Colls. Twin Cities (dir. 1975-79), Middle East Studies Assn. N.Am. (research and tng. com. 1976-80), Midwest Polit. Sci. Assn. (exec. council 1969-72), Assn. N.Am., Phi Beta Kappa, Pi Gamma Mu (nat. pres. 1978—, trustee). Methodist. Home: 2837 Lakeview Ave Saint Paul MN 55113

JOHNSTON, THOMAS ALEXANDER, III, lawyer; b. Mobile, Ala., Sept. 7, 1916; s. Thomas Alexander, Jr. and Pauline (Sheldon) J.; m. Helen Torrey DuBois, July 16, 1941; children: Helen DuBois Johnston Sargent, Leslie Sheldon Johnston Krempa, Thomas Alexander. J.D., U. Ala., 1938. Bar: Ala. 1938. Since practiced in, Mobile; partner firm Howell, Johnston & Langford and predecessors, 1938—; mem. Ala. Ho. of Reps., 1941-49, Ala. Senate, 1949-53, Ala. Constl. Revision Com., 1970-76, Ala. Jud. Compensation Commn., 1976-78. Holder Scottish title 13th Baronet of Caskieben. Mem. ABA, Ala. Bar Assn., Mobile County Bar Assn. (past pres.), Mobile Wildlife Conservation Assn. (pres. 1978), English Speaking Union (past pres. Mobile chpt.), St. Andrews Soc. Middle South, Pi Kappa Phi. Clubs: Mobile Country, Athelstan (Mobile). Home: 350 W Delwood Dr Mobile AL 36606 Office: South Trust Bank Bldg Mobile AL 36601

JOHNSTON, WALDO CORY MELROSE, museum executive; b. Cooperstown, N.Y., Sept. 21, 1913; s. Waldo Cory and Marie (Jones) J.; m. Elinor Doolittle, July 1, 1939; children: Waldo Cory Melrose, Elinor (Mrs. Jonathan Smith), Carol (Mrs. Amos Galpin), James Andrews Melrose. Grad., Hill Sch., Pottstown, Pa., 1933; A.B., Yale U., 1937; postgrad., Harvard U., 1938. Tchr. Pomfret (Conn.) Sch., 1939-41, asst. headmaster, 1946-51; exec. sec. Yale Alumni Bd., New Haven, 1951-59, dir. com. on enrollment and scholarships, 1960-65, asso. dir. alumni relations, 1960-65; dir. Marine Hist. Assn., Inc., Mystic Seaport, Conn., 1965-78, dir. emeritus, 1978—; headmaster Berkshire Sch., 1978-79, headmaster emeritus, 1979—. Contbr. articles profl. jours. Mem. adv. com. South St. Seaport Mus., N.Y.C., 1969—; trustee Sail Edn. Assn., Boston, 1971—, Mystic Seaport Mus., 1978—, Connecticut River Found., 1982—; bd. govs. Chesapeake Bay Maritime Mus., St. Michaels, Md., 1971-82; mem. adv. com. Eleutherian Mills-Hagley Found., Wilmington, Del., 1974-77; adv. council Soc. for Preservation of New Eng. Antiquities, Boston, 1976—; Bd. dirs. Am. Alumni Council, 1953-60, sec., treas., 1953-58, pres., 1960-61; bd. admissions Yale, 1955-65; dir. Dwight Hall, 1952-65; bd. dirs. New Haven Council Social Agys., 1952-65, Cooperstown Art Assn.; pres. Cooperstown Art Assn., 1955-56, hon., 1961—; trustee Berkshire Sch., Sheffield, Mass., 1956-78, 79—, exec. com., 1963-78; bd. incorporators Lawrence and Meml. Hosps., New London, Conn., 1965-79, Conn. Blue Cross, 1973-74; bd. dirs. Conn. Blue Cross, 1974-79; trustee Nat. Trust for Hist. Preservation, Washington, 1974-80, mem. exec. com., 1975-80, chmn. maritime preservation com., 1976—, mem. Maritime Task Force, 1982—; mem. adv. bd. Hartford Nat. Bank, 1965-78. Served from 2d lt. to lt. col. USAAF, 1941-45. Fellow Davenport Coll., Yale U., 1955—. Mem. Am. Assn. Museums, Council Am. Maritime Museums (pres. 1973-78, hon. fellow 1978—), Am. Assn. State and Local History, Newcomen Soc. (hon. mem.), Internat. Congress Maritime Museums (exec. com. 1974-81, hon. founding fellow 1981—), N.Y. State Hist. Assn., Conn. Antiquarian Soc., Am. Sail Tng. Assn., Am. Catboat Assn. (hon. mem.), Century Assn. N.Y.C., Scroll and Key. Republican. Episcopalian. Clubs: Yale, N.Am. Sta. Royal Scandinavian Yacht (gov. 1973-78), N.Y. Yacht, Explorers (N.Y.C.); New Haven Lawn, Mory's Assn. (New Haven); Essex (Conn.); Yacht; Off Soundings (Conn.); Cruising of Am. Home: Smith Neck Rd Old Lyme CT 06371 Office: Mystic Seaport Mystic CT 06355

JOHNSTON, WILLIAM NOEL, educational consultant; b. Balt., Mar. 21, 1919; s. Howard Thomas and Irene Louise (Noellert) J.; m. Virginia Miles Vogts, Sept. 26, 1943; children: Virginia Gail, William Noel, Jeffrey. A.B., Johns Hopkins, 1949, M.Ed., 1951; LL.D., Heidelberg Coll., 1965. Asst. dir. pub. relations Johns Hopkins, 1947-49; supr. personnel Locke dept. Gen. Electric Co., 1949-51; dir. pub. relations Goucher Coll., 1951-53; asst. to pres. Evansville (Ind.) Coll., 1953-54, Pratt Inst., Bklyn., 1954-56; exec. dir. Am. Coll. Pub. Relations Assn., 1956-59; v.p. Ohio Wesleyan U., 1959-64; pres. Defiance (O.) Coll., 1964-74, Assn. Ind. Colls. and Univs. of N.J., 1974-79; sr. v.p. Kersting, Holding & Street, 1979-80, Ross, Johnston & Kersting, 1980—; Dir. summer insts. coll. devel. officers, 1959, 60, 61, 63, 64; faculty Case Snowmass Seminar, 1981, 83. Chmn. United Ch. Christ Council Higher Edn., 1966, 67; trustee Peace Coll., 1984—. Served with F.A. U.S. Army, 1941-45; ETO. Mem. Ohio Coll. Assn. (pres. 1971—). Presbyterian. Club: Rotarian (pres. Delaware, O. 1962-63). Home: 2911 Quincemoor Rd Durham NC 27712

JOHNSTON, WILLIAM NORVILLE, shipping bureau executive; b. Mobile, Ala., July 11, 1922; s. William Norville and Catherine Mary (Murray) J.; m. Kathryn Pauline Solberg, June 14, 1952; children: Kathryn Mary Johnston, William Norville, Stephen Gregory, Paul Brady. B.S. in Mech. Engring., Auburn U., 1947, MIT, 1950. Engr. Gulf Shipbuilding Corp., Mobile, Ala., 1957, Ala. Drydock and Shipbuilding Co., Mobile, 1947-48; hull surveyor United Fruit Co., New Orleans, 1950-51; from surveyor to area prin. surveyor Am. Bur. Shipping, N.Y.C., 1951-72, asst. to chmn., 1974-76, v.p., 1976-77, sr. v.p., 1977-79, pres., chmn., 1979—; chmn. ABS Worldwide Tech. Services, ABS Computers Inc., ABS Group of Cos. Inc., ABS Properties Inc., Exam Co., Abstech Assocs. Inc.; trustee Webb Inst. Naval Architecture. Served with C.E. U.S. Army, 1943-46. Fellow Royal Instn. Naval Architects and Marine Engrs.; mem. Soc. Naval Architects and Marine Engrs., Am. Welding Soc., Am. Mcht. Marine Library Assn. Roman Catholic. Clubs: Union League, India House, N.Y. Yacht, Whitehall Lunch (N.Y.C.); Army and Navy (Washington). Home: 107 Wellington Ave Short Hills NJ 07078 Office: Am Bur of Shipping 65 Broadway New York NY 10006

JOHNSTON, WILLIAM WEBB, pathologist; b. Statesville, N.C., Aug. 26, 1933; s. Jesse Clyde and Pauline Elizabeth (Massey) J. B.S., Davidson Coll., 1954; M.D., Duke U., 1959. Diplomate: Am. Bd. Pathology, Internat. Bd. Cytopathology. Intern Duke U., 1959-60, resident in pathology, 1960-63, mem. faculty, 1963—, prof. pathology, 1972—, dir. div. cytopathology and cytotechnology tng. program, 1966—; cons. pathologist Durham VA Hosp., Durham County Hosp. Author: (with W.J. Frable) Respiratory Cytopathology, 1974, Diagnostic Respiratory Cytopathology, 1979, (with S.H. Bigner) The Cytopathology of Cerebral Spinal Fluid, 1981; Asso. editor: Acta Cytologica, 1978—; editor: Masson Monographs in Cytopathology; editorial cons., Masson Publs., N.Y.C. Fellow Internat. Acad. Cytology, Am. Soc. Clin. Pathology, Coll. Am. Pathologists; mem. Am. Soc. Cytology (rev. bd.), pres. 1981-82), Am. Assn. Pathologists, Arthur Purdy Stout Soc. Surg. Pathology, Internat. Acad. Pathology. Republican. Presbyterian (organist). Home: 1608 University Dr Durham NC 27707 Office: Box 3712 Duke U Med Center Durham NC 27710

JOHNSTON, YNEZ, artist; b. Berkeley, Calif., May 12, 1920. B.F.A., U. Calif., Berkeley, 1941, M.F.A., 1946. Lectr. art U. Calif., Berkeley, 1950-51, Colorado Springs Fine Arts Center, 1954, 55, Chouinard Art Inst., 1956, Calif. State U.-Los Angeles, 1966, 67, U. Judaism Sch. Fine Arts, Los Angeles, 1967, Otis Art Inst., 1978-81; artist-in-residence Fullerton Coll. (Calif.), 1982. One-man exhbns. include, San Francisco Mus. Art, 1943, Redlands U., 1947, Santa Barbara (Calif.) Mus. Art, 1952, 57, Pasadena (Calif.) Mus. Art, 1955, 62, Colorado Springs (Colo.) Fine Arts Center, 1955, Calif. Palace Legion of Honor, 1956, The O'Hana Gallery, London, 1958, Paul Kantor Gallery, Los Angeles, 1952, 53, 55, 57, 58, 61-62, 63, Beloit (Wis.) Coll., 1961, Barbara Cecil Gallery, New Orleans, 1963, Barbara Cecil Gallery, Mex., 1959, Occidental Coll., Los Angeles, 1955, Esther Bear Gallery, 1967, Ball State U., Stewart-Verde Galleries, San Francisco, 1966, San Francisco Mus. Art, 1967, Mekler Gallery, Los Angeles, 1970-82, Tokyo Shoten Gallery, N.Y.C., 1976, Mitsukoshi Gallery, Tokyo, 1977, Wiener Gallery, N.Y.C., Worthington Gallery, Chgo., also exhibited numerous small group shows including, Whitney Mus. Am. Art, 1953-56, Mus. Modern Art, 1952, 54, Carnegie Inst., 1951, 55, I.F.A. Gallery, Washington, 1963, 100 Prints of the Year, N.Y.C., Bklyn. Mus., 1966, Vancouver (B.C., Can.) Print Internat., World Print Competition, San Francisco, 1977, Met. Mus., 1978, Ericson Gallery, N.Y.C., Los Angeles County Mus., 1980-81, others; represented in permanent collections numerous museums including, Santa Barbara Mus. Art, Mus. Modern Art, Philbrook Art Center, Los Angeles County Mus., City Art Mus. St. Louis, Whitney Mus. Am. Art, Phila. Mus. Art, San Diego Mus. Art, U. Ill., Met. Mus. Art, Hirshhorn Collection, Herbert F. Johnson Collection (Cornell U.), San Francisco Mus. Art, Otis Art Inst., Milw. Art Center, numerous schs. and colls., other museums, also pvt. collections. Recipient San Francisco Mus. Art award oil painting, 1946; awards Calif. State Fair, 1951, 61, 62; award etching Los Angeles County Mus., 1950; exhbn. first award Met. Mus. Art, 1952; purchase award Exhbn. Fgn. Artists, Rome, Italy, 1952, Otis Art Inst., 1963, Los Angeles Municipal Art Dept., 1967; also commns.; John Simon Guggenheim Found. grantee, 1952; Louis Comfort Tiffany grantee, 1955, 56; Huntington Hartford grantee, 1957; James Phelan grantee, 1958; MacDowell Colony grantee, 1959; Tamarind workshop fellow, 1966; Nat. Endowment Arts painting grantee, 1976. Address: 579 Crane Blvd Los Angeles CA 90065

JOHNSTONE, DONALD BRUCE, college president; b. Mpls., Jan. 13, 1941; s. Donald Bruce and Florence Morton (Elliott) J.; m. Gail Eberhardt, July 30, 1965; children—Duncan Bruce, Cameron. B.A., Harvard U., 1963, M.A.T., 1964; Ph.D., U. Minn., 1969. Tchr. econs. and history, Westport, Conn., 1964-65; asst. dir. U. Minn. Center for Econ. Edn., 1966-69; adminstrv. asst. to Sen. Walter F. Mondale, 1969-71; project specialist Ford Found., 1971-72; exec. asst. to pres. U. Pa., 1972-77, asso. prof. edn., 1976-79, v.p. for adminstrn., 1977-79; pres. State U. Coll. at Buffalo, 1979—; dir. Western region Bank of N.Y.; Mem. adv. com. Coop. Institutional Research Program of the Am. Council on Edn. and UCLA. Author: New Patterns for College Lending, 1973; Contbr. articles to profl. jours. Vice pres. Studio Arena theatre, Niagara Frontier Vocat. Rehab. Ctr.; chmn. Buffalo and Erie County Enterprise Zone Task Force; bd. dirs. Greater Buffalo Devel. Found., Buffalo Urban League, Geneva B. Scruggs Community Health Ctr., Western N.Y. Inst. for Arts in Edn. Mem. Am. Assn. Higher Edn. Democrat. Episcopalian. Club: Harvard-Radcliffe of Western N.Y. (treas.). Home: 152 Lincoln Pkwy Buffalo NY 14222 Office: SUNY Buffalo 1300 Elmwood Ave Buffalo NY 14222

JOHNSTONE, EDMUND FRANK, advt. exec.; b. Rochester, N.Y., Apr. 28, 1909; s. Charles T. and Ida M. (Hilgenreiner) J.; m. Margaret Horan, Apr. 1, 1940; children—Heather, Dawn; m. Janet Olcott, June 2, 1951; children—Charles, Jill, Edmund, Chauncey, Rita. Student, Ohio State U., 1928. With E. F. Johnstone Advt. Co., N.Y.C., 1939-51; exec. v.p. Dowd, Redfield & Johnstone, Inc., N.Y.C., 1951—; vice chmn. bd. Calkins Holden. Inc., 1959; sr. v.p. Fletcher Richards, Calkins & Holden, N.Y.C., 1959-60; exec. v.p. Kastor Hilton Advt. Agy., from 1960; vice chmn. exec. com., dir. Kastor, Hilton, Chesley, Clifford and Atherton, Inc., 1960; advt. dir. Fox Pharmacal, Fort Lauderdale, Fla. Contbr. articles to trade jours. Served as lt. col. USAAF, WW II. Mem. Mil. Order Fgn. Wars. Episcopalian. Clubs: New York Athletic, St. Bartholomew's (N.Y.C.); St. Andrews (Delray Beach, Fla.); New Canaan Field, Manalapan. Home: 95 Spoonbill Rd Point Manalapan FL 33462 also Trinity Pass Rd Pound Ridge NY 10576

JOHNSTONE, HARRY INGE, architect; b. Mobile, Ala., Nov. 27, 1903; s. Charles Albert Lesesne and Virginia (Inge) J.; m. Kathleen Cawthorn Yerger, June 24, 1930; children—Montgomery Inge, Yerger, Douglas. Student, Univ. Mil. Sch., Mobile, 1912-21; B.Arch., Cornell, 1927. Archeol. research restoration, Mex., 1926; draftsman, designer Shreve & Lamb, N.Y.C., 1927-28; archtl. study, England, Italy, 1928-29; designer T.O. Foster, London, 1928-29; instr. archtl. design, theory architecture Cornell, 1929-30; chief designer Marston-Maybury, Pasadena, Calif., 1930-31; asso. Douglas Honnold, Los Angeles, 1931; instr. architecture John Herron Art Sch. Indpls., 1933-36; pvt. practice architecture, Indpls., 1933-36, Mobile, 1937—; propr. Harry Inge Johnstone, 1937—; co-venturer J.B. Converse & Co., Inc. & Harry Inge Johnstone, 1950—. Illustrator: Collecting Seashells, 1970, The Lore of Seashells, 1974. Trustee Mobile Pub. Library, 1953-57, chmn., 1956-57. Served as maj. AUS, 1943-45. Fellow AIA (v.p. Ala. chpt. 1940); mem. Ala. Assn. Architects (pres. 1941, 47), Mobile Assn. Architects (pres. 1959), Am. Malacological Union, Phi Delta Theta. Episcopalian. Home: 2209 River Forest Dr Mobile AL 36605

JOHNSTONE, HENRY WEBB, JR., philosophy educator; b. Montclair, N.J., Feb. 22, 1920; s. Henry Webb and Beatrice (Grieb) J.; m. Margery Vaughan Coffin, July 17, 1948; children: Barbara C., Anne C., Henry Webb III. B.S., Haverford Coll., 1942; M.A., Harvard U., 1947, Ph.D., 1950. Instr. philosophy Williams Coll., 1948-52; mem. faculty Pa. State U., 1952—, prof. philosophy, 1961—, asst. to v.p. for research, 1966-70, dir., 1968-70; Spl. Am. fellow Belgian Am. Ednl. Found., 1957; Fulbright sr. lectr. Trinity Coll., Dublin, 1960-61; guest prof. U. Bonn, Germany, 1969; Fulbright-Hays sr. lectr. Am. U. Beirut, 1971-72. Author: Elementary Deductive Logic, 1954, Philosophy and Argument, 1959, (with J.M. Anderson) Natural Deduction, 1962, What is Philosophy?, 1965, (with M. Natanson) Philosophy, Rhetoric and Argumentation, 1965, The Problem of Self, 1970, Validity and Rhetoric in Philosophical Argument, 1978; also articles in profl. jours.; editor: Philosophy and Rhetoric, 1968-76. Served to capt. AUS, 1942-46. Home: 262 Woodland Dr State College PA 16801

JOHNSTONE, JAMES GEORGE, educator; b. LaPorte, Ind., July 29, 1920; s. Arthur Paul and Lydia Henrietta (Werremeyer) J.; m. Louise Moffit, Aug. 24, 1946; 1 dau., Nancy Louise Johnstone Ratay. Student, Western Ky. State U., 1939-41; Geol. Engr., Colo. Sch. Mines, 1948; M.S. in Engring, Purdue U., 1952. Registered profl. engr., Ind., Colo. Plant engr. Ford Motor Co., Detroit, 1942-45; asst. prof. geology Purdue U., Lafayette, Ind., 1948-55; project engr. Geophoto Services, Denver, 1955-57; prof. engring. Colo. Sch. Mines, Golden, 1957—; partner Colo. Central Narrow Gauge R.R., Central City, 1970—; cons. engr. Ind. Toll Rd., Dewline Mass. Turnpike, Colo. Dept. Hwys.; mem. Colo. Bd. Registration Profl. Engrs. and Land Surveyors, 1971-79, chmn., 1978-79. Mem. Wheatridge (Colo.) Incorporation Commn., 1968-69, Wheatridge St. Commn., 1969-71. Named Colo. Profl. Engr. of Year, 1967, 79. Mem. Nat. Soc. Profl. Engrs. (dir. 1967-74, 77—, nat. v.p. 1974-76), ASCE, Am. Soc. Engring. Edn., Nat. Council Engring. Examiners, Profl. Engrs. Colo. (pres. 1965-66, dir. 1967-74, 76-79), Engrs. Council for Profl. Devel. (council 1975-79), Sigma Xi, Tau Beta Pi, Sigma Gamma Epsilon. Republican. Methodist. Home: 13079 W Ohio Ave Lakewood CO 80228 Office: Colo Sch Mines Golden CO 80401 *If I had stopped to ask, "What's in it for me?" I would have missed most of the rewards of my life.*

JOHNSTONE, JOHN WILLIAM, JR., chem. co. exec.; b. Bklyn., Nov. 19, 1932; s. John William and Sarah J. (Singleton) J.; m. Claire Lundberg, Apr. 14, 1956; children—Thomas Edward, James Robert, Robert Andrew. B.A., Hartwick Coll., Oneonta, N.Y., 1954; grad., Advanced Mgmt. Program, Harvard U., 1970. With Hooker Chem. Corp., 1954-75, group v.p., 1973-75; pres. Airco Alloys div. Airco, Inc., 1976-79; v.p., gen. mgr. indsl. products, then sr. v.p. chems. group Olin

Corp., 1979-80, corp. v.p., pres. chems. group, Stamford, Conn., 1980—. Bd. dirs. SPUR, Niagara Falls, N.Y., 1974-79, United Way Niagara Falls, 1974-77. Mem. Am. Mgmt. Assn., Soc. Chem. Industry. Episcopalian. Clubs: Landmark; Duquesne (Pitts.). Office: 120 Long Ridge Rd Stamford CT 06904

JOHNSTONE, PAUL MEREDITH, retired airline executive, consultant; b. Oak Park, Ill., Aug. 29, 1925; s. Paul M. and Marjorie (Scott) J.; m. Joan Cory Chandler, June 25, 1949; children: Paul Scott, Joel Chandler, Cory Anne. B.S. Aero. Engring., U. Notre Dame, 1946. Engring. officer Naval Air Transport Service, 1946; design aerodynamicist Douglas Aircraft Co., Santa Monica, Calif., 1946-59; chief engr. Hawaiian Airlines, Honolulu, 1959-64; ops. engr. Eastern Airlines, Miami, Fla., 1964-68, v.p. engring., 1968-77, sr. v.p. ops. services, 1977-83; cons., 1983—. Served with USNR, 1943-46. Fellow AIAA. Club: Coral Reef Yacht. Office: Miami FL 33172

JOHNSTONE, QUINTIN, legal educator; b. Chgo., Mar. 29, 1915; s. Quintin and Wegia (Metsker) J.; m. Nancy McMullen; children: Robert Dale, Katherine Mary. A.B., U. Chgo., 1936, J.D., 1938; LL.M., Cornell U., 1941; J.S.D., Yale U., 1951. Bar: Ill. 1939, Oreg. 1948. Sole practice, Chgo., 1939-41; atty. OPA, 1941-47; mem. law faculty U. Willamette, 1947-50, U. Kans., 1950-55, Yale U., 1955—, Justus S. Hotchkiss prof., 1969—; dean law, prof. Haile Sellassie I U., Ethiopia, 1967-69. Author: (with D. Hopson) Lawyers and Their Work, 1967, (with A. Axelrod and C. Berger) Land Transfer and Finance, 2d edit, 1978; Contbr. articles profl. jours. Mem. ABA, Conn. Bar Assn., Oreg. Bar Assn. Home: 22 Morris St Hamden CT 06517 Office: Yale Law Sch New Haven CT 06520

JOHNSTONE, ROBERT LAWRENCE, agricultural economist, educator; b. Paducah, Ky., Sept. 14, 1926; s. William Clarkson and Katherine (Huggins) J.; m. Mary Ann Moser, June 18, 1948; children: John Moser, Frank Andrew, William Henry, Sarah Beaumont. B.S., U. Ky., 1948, M.S., 1957; Ph.D., U. Ill., 1961. Tchr. Logan County (Ky.) schs., 1948-53, Todd County (Ky.) schs., 1953-54; farm mgr., Todd County, 1949-54; asst., agrl. econs. U. Ky., 1955-56; research asst. U. Ill., 1956-59; extension specialist agrl. econs. N.C. State U., 1959-64; chmn. dept. agr. Berea Coll., prof. econs. and agr., 1964—, C.M. Clark prof. mountain agr., 1965—; Chmn. Ky. Agrl. Council, 1972-73. Mem. Berea Bd. Edn., 1970-74; Bd. dirs. Scientists and Engrs. for Appalachia, 1968-70, Berea Hosp., 1970-82. Served with AUS, 1944-46. Mem. Am. Agrl. Econs. Assn., Gamma Sigma Delta, Kappa Delta Phi, Delta Tau Alpha, Phi Kappa Phi. Episcopalian. Home: 319 Forest St Berea KY 40403

JOHNSTONE, ROBERT M., JR., insurance company executive; b. Richmond Hill, N.Y., May 6, 1925; s. Robert M. and Freda (Ammarell) A.; m. Margaret Ann Schmitt, Nov. 11, 1950; children: Douglas S., Richard B. B.S., U. Mich., 1951. With Equitable Life Assurance Soc. U.S., N.Y.C., 1951—, assoc. actuary, 1954—, v.p., 1972-77, sr. v.p., 1977-82; pres., chief exec. officer, dir. Equitable Casualty Ins. Co., Equitable Gen. of Okla., 1983—; dir. Equico Capital. Served with AUS, 1943-45. Fellow Soc. Actuaries; mem. Am. Acad. Actuaries, Fin. Execs. Inst. Office: 1285 Ave of Americas Equitable Life Assurance Soc US New York NY 10019

JOHNSTONE, ROSE MAMELAK (MRS. DOUGLAS JOHNSTONE), educator; b. Lodz, Poland, May 14, 1928; d. Jacob Shea and Esther (Rotholz) Mamelak; m. Douglas Johnstone, Aug. 9, 1953; children—Michael, Eric. B.Sc., McGill U., 1950, Ph.D., 1953. Nat. Cancer Inst. of Can. fellow Nat. Inst. for Med. Research and Strangeway Research Lab., Cambridge, England, 1954-56; research asso. McGill-Montreal Gen. Hosp. Research Inst., 1956-60; faculty McGill U., Montreal, Que., Can., 1961—, asso. prof. biochemistry, 1967-76, prof., 1977—, chmn. dept., 1980—. Contbr. articles to profl. jours. Nat. Cancer Inst. of Can. grantee, 1965-68; Med. Research Council of Can. grantee, 1965—. Mem. McGill Assn. U. Tchrs. (treas., membership sec. 1967-70), Biol. Chemists Am., Canadian Soc. Biochemistry, Biochem. Soc. London. Home: 4064 Oxford Montreal PQ Canada Office: McGill University Dept Biochemistry McIntyre Med Sci Center 3655 Drummond Montreal PQ H3G 1Y6 Canada

JOHSON, KENNETH PETER, neurologist, medical researcher; b. Jamestown, N.Y., Mar. 12, 1932; s. Kenneth Peter and Nina (Bengtson) Johnson; m. Jacquelyn Johnson, June 23, 1956; children: Peter, Thomas, Diane, Douglas. B.A., Upsala Coll., East Orange, N.J., 1955; M.D., Jefferson Med. Coll., Phila., 1959. Diplomate: Am. Bd. Psychiatry and Neurology. Intern Buffalo Gen. Hosp., 1959-60; resident Hosp. of Cleve., 1963-65; asst. prof. neurology Case Western Res. U., Cleve., 1968-71, assoc. prof., 1971-74; prof. U. Calif., San Francisco, 1974-81; prof., chmn. U. Md., Balt., 1981—; chief neurology VA Hosp., Balt., 1981-83. Editor: Neurovirology, 1984; contbr. numerous articles in field to profl. jours. Served to lt. U.S. Navy, 1961-63. Recipient Weil award Am. Assn. Neuropathology, 1967, Research Ctr. Devel. award NIH, 1968-73; Zimmerman lectr. Stanford U., 1981. Fellow Am. Neurol Assn.; mem. Am. Acad. Neurology, Teratology Soc., Am. Soc. Virology. Democrat. Lutheran. Home: 6114 Maywood Ave Baltimore MD 21209 Office: Univ Md Hosp 22 S Greene St Baltimore MD 21201

JOINER, CHARLES WYCLIFFE, judge; b. Maquoketa, Iowa, Feb. 14, 1916; s. Melvin William and Mary (von Schrader) J.; m. Ann Martin, Sept. 29, 1939; children: Charles Wycliffe, Nancy Caroline, Richard Martin. B.A., U. Iowa, 1937, J.D., 1939. Bar: Iowa 1939, Mich. 1947. With firm Miller, Huebner & Miller, Des Moines, 1939-47; part-time lectr. Des Moines Coll. Law, 1940-41; faculty U. Mich. Law, 1947-68, assoc. dean, 1960-65, acting dean, 1964-65; dean Wayne State U. Law Sch., Detroit, 1968-72; U.S. dist. judge, 1972—; assoc. dir. Preparatory Commn. Mich. Constl. Conv., 1961, co-dir. research and drafting com., 1961-62; civil rules adv. com. U.S. Jud. Conf. Com. Rules Practice and Procedure, 1959-70, evidence rules adv. com., 1965-70; rep. Mich. Atty. Gens. Com. Ct. Congestion, 1959-60. Author: Civil Justice and the Jury, 1962, Trials and Appeals, 1957, Trial and Appellate Practice, 1968; Co-author: Introduction to Civil Procedures, 1949, Jurisdiction and Judgments, 1953, (with Delmar Karten) Trials and Appeals, 1971. Mem. charter rev. com. Ann Arbor Citizens Council, 1959-61; mem. Mich. Commn. on Uniform State Laws, 1963—; Mem. Ann Arbor City Council, 1955-59. Served to 1st lt. USAAF, 1942-45. Fellow Am. Bar Found. (chmn. 1977-78); mem. ABA (chmn. com. specialization 1952-56, spl. com. uniform evidence rules fed. cts. 1959-64, adv. bd. jour. 1961-67, spl. com. on specialization 1966-69, ethics com. 1961-70, council mem. sect. individual rights and responsibilities 1967-77, chairperson 1976-77), State Bar Mich. (pres. 1970-71, chmn. joint com. Mich. procedural revision 1956-62, commr. 1964—), Am. Judicature Soc. (chmn. publs. com. 1959-62), Am. Law Student Assn. (bd. govs.), Am. Law Inst., Am. Bar Found., Scribes (pres. 1963-64). Office: 200 E Liberty Suite 400 PO Box 7880 Ann Arbor MI 48107

JOINER, WEBB FRANCIS, helicopter manufacturing company executive; b. Arlington, Tex., Aug. 29, 1933; s. Webb Monroe and Virginia Francis (Kidwill) J.; m. Rosemary Lee, Apr. 15, 1954; children: Cherilyn Jenee, Rosemary Melisa, Webb Francis. B.S. in Commerce, Tex. Christian U., 1955; postgrad., Stanford U., 1971. C.P.A., Tex. Sr. audit staff Arthur Andersen & Co., Dallas, 1955-60; asst. to treas., mgr. indsl. acctg., mgr. program controls and controller Bell Helicopter Textron, Ft. Worth, 1960-75; treas., controller Bell Ops. Corp., 1976-78; v.p. fin. Bell Helicopter Textron, 1978-84, sr. v.p. fin., 1984—; dir. Tex. Commerce Bank, Hurst, 1978-80. Ruling elder St. James Presbyn. Ch., 1980—. Served to 1st lt. U.S. Army, 1958. Mem. Am. Inst. C.P.A.'s, Tex. Soc. C.P.A.'s, Assn. U.S. Army, Am. Helicopter Soc., Fin. Execs. Inst. Office: PO Box 482 Fort Worth TX 76101 *

JOKLIK, WOLFGANG KARL, biochemist, virologist, educator; b. Vienna, Austria, Nov. 16, 1926; s. Karl F. and Helene (Giessl) J.; m. Judith Vivien Nicholas, Apr. 9, 1955 (dec. Apr. 1975); children: Richard G., Vivien H.; m. Patricia Hunter Downey, Apr. 23, 1977. B.Sc. with 1st class honors, U. Sydney, Australia, 1948, M.Sc., 1949; D.Phil. (Australian Nat. U. scholar), U. Oxford, Eng., 1952. Australian Nat. U. research fellow, Copenhagen, Denmark, 1953, Canberra, Australia, 1954-56, fellow, 1957-62; assoc. prof. cell biology Albert Einstein Coll. Medicine, Bronx, N.Y., 1962-65, prof. cell biology, 1965-68, Siegfried Ullmann prof. biochem. virology, 1966-68; prof., chmn. dept. microbiology and immunology Duke U. Med. Center, Durham, N.C., 1968—, James B. Duke Distinguished prof. microbiology and immunology, 1972—. Sr. author: Zinsser Microbiology, 15th, 16th, 17th and 18th edits; Contbr. articles profl. jours. Mem. Am. Soc. Cell Biology, Am. Soc. Microbiology, Am. Soc. Biol. Chemists, Am. Soc. Immunology, Nat. Acad. Scis., Inst. Medicine of Nat. Acad. Scis. Address: Dept Microbiology and Immunology Duke U Med Center Durham NC 27710

JOLLEY, HOMER RICHARD, ednl. adminstr.; b. Morgan City, La., May 28, 1916; s. Homer Levi and Frances (Shannon) J.; m. Mary P. Allen, Oct. 7, 1972. A.B., Gonzaga U., 1938, M.A., 1939; M.S., Fordham U., 1941; S.T.L., St. Louis U., 1946; Ph.D. (Allied Chem. & Dye fellow), Princeton U., 1951. Fulbright fellow U. Nottingham, Eng., 1950-51; Entered S.J., 1932; ordained priest Roman Catholic Ch., 1945; asst. prof. chemistry Loyola U., New Orleans, 1951-54, asso. prof., 1954-58, prof., 1958-70, chmn. chemistry dept., 1956-64, v.p. devel., 1964-66, pres., 1966-70; dir. Office Program Innovation, Med. Services Adminstrn., HEW, Washington, 1970-75, dir. health delivery systems, 1975-77; dir. instl. research, asst. v.p. for acad. affairs, asso. prof. adminstrv. medicine Med. U. S.C., 1977—; summer research participant Oak Ridge Nat. Lab., 1957-64, cons., 1964—. Bd. dirs. Gulf South Research Inst., Total Community Action, Internat. House, Internat. Trade Mart, Met Area com. La. Council for Music and Performing Arts, Fgn. Relations Assn., New Orleans, Nat. Found., New Orleans chpt.; trustee Greater New Orleans Ednl. TV Found.; mem. adv. bd. La. Council Human Relations; mem. Adv. Council Naval Affairs New Orleans; mem. adv. bd. Delta Regional Primate Research Center. Fellow Am. Inst. Chemists (past chmn. La. chpt.); mem. Chem. Soc. London, Faraday Soc., N.Y. Acad. Sci., Am. Chem. Soc. (past chmn. La. sect.), New Orleans Jr. Acad. Sci. (past pres.), Sigma Xi. Home: 33 Devereaux Ave Charleston SC 29403

JOLLEY, JACK J., transporation equipment executive; b. Bellingham, Wash., Oct. 4, 1925; s. John Jay and Cicily Ann (McDougall) J.; m. Joyce Werttemberger, Aug. 3, 1957; children: Jack, Elizabeth, Monica, Bill, Sheila. B.A., U. Portland, 1950. With PACCAR Inc, Bellevue, Wash., 1952-; asst. treas. PACCAR Inc., 1971-73, v.p., treas., 1973-78, v.p., 1978-83, v.p., treas., 1983—. Served with AUS, 1943-46. Home: 9820 NE 20th St Bellevue WA 98004 Office: Business Center Bldg 777 106th Ave NE Bellevue WA 98004

JOLLY, ALDWIN E., department store executive; b. Jonesboro, Ark., Nov. 13, 1939; s. Evans Estes and Ethelene Jewel (Wimberley) J.; m. Bonnie Lee Oscarson, Nov. 26, 1958; children: Andrew, Todd, Kristie, Katy, Jacob. Student, Brigham Young U., 1957-60. Dir. personnel Edison Bros. Stores, St. Louis, 1961-70; sr. v.p. orgnl. planning and devel. May Dept. Stores, St. Louis, 1970-80; sr. v.p. human resources J.L. Hudson Co., Detroit, 1980—. Pres. Minority Tng. and Devel., St. Louis, 1975-76; bd. dirs. Employs Assn., Detroit, 1980—, Urban Housing Devel., St. Louis, 1976-80, Mich. Jr. Achievement, 1979-80, St. Louis Opportunities Indsl. Corp., 1976-80. Mem. Nat. Retail Mchts. Assn. (bd. dirs. 1980—), Am. Soc. Tng. and Devel., Am. Soc. Personnel Adminstrn., Am. Mgmt. Assn. Mormon. Club: Detroit Athletic. Lodge: Kiwanis. Home: 4063 Fox Lake Dr Bloomfield Hills MI 48013 Office: JL Hudson Co 1206 Woodward Ave Detroit MI 48226

JOLLY, BRUCE DWIGHT, agrl. equipment mfg. co. exec.; b. Wheeling, W.Va., Aug. 27, 1943; s. Edward and Martha Elizabeth (Glass) J.; m. Alice Marie O'Beirne, May 25, 1974; children—Mara O'Beirne, Brock Thomas. A.B., Dartmouth Coll., 1965; M.B.A., U. Va., 1967. Systems engr. IBM Corp., Richmond, Va., 1967-68; financial analyst Keystone Consol. Industries, Peoria, Ill., 1970-73; controller HON Industries, Inc., Muscatine, Iowa, 1973-76, sec., treas., 1976-79; v.p. fin. Hawkeye Steel Products, Inc., Waterloo, Iowa, 1979—. Served with AUS, 1968-70; Vietnam. Decorated Bronze Star. Mem. Phi Kappa Psi. Republican. Presbyn. Home: Rural Route 1 Box 86B Denver IA 50622 Office: 324 Duryea St Waterloo IA

JOLLY, WAYNE TRAVIS, geologist, educator; b. Jacksonville, Tex., Aug. 15, 1940; s. Edward B. and Alfreda J. (Sharp) J. B.F.A., U. Tex., 1963; M.A., SUNY, Binghamton, 1967, Ph.D. (univ. fellow), 1970. Postdoctoral fellow U. Sask., Saskatoon, 1970-71; chmn., prof. Brock U., St. Catherines, Ont., Can., 1971—. NRC Can. grantee, 1971—. Mem. Geol. Soc. Am., Am. Geophys. Union, Geol. Assn. Can. Office: Dept Geol Science Brock U Saint Catharines ON Canada

JOLLY, WILLIAM LEE, chemistry educator; b. Chgo., Dec. 27, 1927; s. John McGown and Marjorie (Farmer) J.; m. Frances Ann Adams Bartholomew, Nov. 18, 1950; children: Jeffrey Lee, Steven William, Jennifer Frances. B.S., U. Ill., 1948, M.S., 1949; Ph.D., U. Calif. at Berkeley, 1952. Instr. chemistry dept. U. Calif. at Berkeley, 1952-53; group leader Radiation Lab., Livermore, 1953-55, asst. prof., asso. prof., prof. chemistry, Berkeley, 1955—; prin. investigator materials and molecular research div. Lawrence Berkeley Lab., Berkeley, 1955—. Author: The Synthesis and Characterization of Inorganic Compounds, 1970, The Principles of Inorganic Chemistry, 1976; Editor: Preparative Inorganic Reactions, Vols. 1-7, 1964—; Mem. editorial bd.: Inorganic Syntheses, 1959—. Guggenheim fellow, 1960. Mem. Am. Chem. Soc., AAAS (sec. sect. C 1978—), Royal Soc. Chemistry (London), Sigma Xi, Alpha Chi Sigma. Home: 2621 La Honda St El Cerrito CA 94530 Office: Chemistry Dept U Calif Berkeley CA 94720

JOLSON, MARVIN ARNOLD, marketing educator, consultant; b. Chgo., June 7, 1922; s. George and Bess (Sweetow) J.; m. Betty Harris, July 8, 1944; children: Robert, Nancy. B.E.E., George Washington U., 1949; M.B.A., U. Chgo., 6965; D.B.A., U. Md., 1969. With Ency. Brit., Inc., Chgo., 1949-68, mgr. Eastern nat. sales, 1960-62, sr. v.p., 1962-68; asst. prof. mktg. U. Md., College Park, 1968-77, asso. prof., 1977-79, prof., 1979—; dir. Mktg. Systems, Inc., Crime Prevention Co. Am., Inc., Public Telephone Answering Service Inc. Author: Consumer Attitudes Toward Direct-To-Home Marketing Systems, 1970, Sales Management-A Tactical Approach, 1977, Contemporary Readings in Sales Management, 1977, Marketing Management, 1978; co-author Quantitative Techniques for Marketing Decisions, 1973; contbr. articles to profl. jours. Served with Signal Corps AUS, 1944-46. Mem. Sales Exec. Club, Am. Mktg. Assn., So. Mktg. Assn., Assn. Consumer Research, Beta Gamma Sigma. Club: Masons. Office: Coll Bus and Mgmt U Md College Park MD 20742 *A person is not judged by his talk, looks, abilities, or past accomplishments. He is judged by his current results.*

JOMARRON, WILL C., publishing executive; b. Puerto Padre, Oriente, Cuba, Nov. 1, 1944; came to U.S., Mar. 22, 1958; s. Wilfredo Vicente and Racquel (Morell) J. B.A. in Acctg., U. Munich, Germany, 1963, 1968. Prodn. mgr. Academic Press, N.Y.C., 1968-74, mgr. book prodn., 1974-77, assoc. dir., 1977-79, dir. book prodn., San Diego, 1979-81, v.p., 1981-82, sr. v.p., Orlando, Fla., 1982—. Served to sgt. AUS, 1963-65; West Germany. Republican. Roman Catholic. Home: 722 N Lake Formosa Dr Orlando FL 32803 Office: Academic Press Inc Orlando FL 32887

JONAS, FEDERICO ROQUE, physician; b. San Carlos Centra, Santa Fe, Argentina, Jan. 3, 1943; came to U.S., 1968, naturalized, 1974. M.D., Cath. U. Cordoba, Argentina, 1967, Nat. U. Cordoba, 1968; M.S. in Preventive Medicine, Ohio State U., 1971. Diplomate: Am. Bd. Preventive Medicine. Rotating intern Providence Hosp., Washington, 1968-69; resident preventive medicine Ohio State U., 1969-71, Lovelace Found. Med. Edn. and Research, Albuquerque, 1971, NASA Flight Research Center, Edwards, Calif., 1972; staff physician Kelsey-Seybold Clinic, Houston, 1972-77, head med. ops. testing, 1972-76; med. officer Skylab Med. Experiments Altitude Test, NASA, 1972; surgeon Skylab Mission Control Center, 1973-74, Apollo/Soyuz Test Project, Mission Control Center, 1975—; med. dir. So. region corp. med. dept. Shell Oil Co., Houston, 1977-79. Contbr. articles to med. jours. Recipient Skylab Med. Expts. Altitude Test Team Group Achievement award NASA Manned Spacecraft Center, 1972, Lunar Landing Tng. Vehicle Support Team Group Achievement award NASA, Washington, 1973, Skylab Med. Team Group Achievement award, 1974. Fellow A.C.P., Am. Coll. Preventive Medicine, Am. Occupational Med. Assn., Aerospace Med. Assn. (asso.), Am. Acad. Occupational Medicine; mem. AMA. Office: EG&G Idaho Inc Idaho Falls ID

JONAS, HARRY S., univ. adminstr., physician; b. Kirksville, Mo., Dec. 3, 1926; s. Harry S. and Sarah (Laird) J.; m. Connie Kirby, Aug. 6, 1949; children—Harry S., III, William Reed, Sarah Elizabeth. B.A., Washington U., St. Louis, 1949, M.D., 1952. Intern St. Luke's Hosp., St. Louis, 1952-53; resident Barnes Hosp., St. Louis, St. Louis Maternity Hosp., St. Luke's Hosp., 1952-56; practiced medicine specializing in ob-gyn, Independence, Mo., 1956-74; prof. ob-gyn, chmn. dept. ob-gyn Truman Med. Center; asst. dean U. Mo-Kansas City Sch. Medicine, 1975-78, dean, 1978—. Mem. Independence City Council, 1964-68; mem. Jackson County (Mo.) Legislature, 1973-74, Pres.'s Commn. of White House Fellowships, 1975-76. Recipient Disting. Service award Independence Jaycees, 1960. Mem. Am. Coll. Obstetricians and Gynecologists, Central Assn. Obstetricians and Gynecologists, Assn. Profs. Gynecology and Obstetrics, Assn. Am. Med. Colls., A.C.S., AMA, Mo. State Med. Assn., Jackson County Med. Soc., Kansas City (Mo.) Gynecol. Soc. Home: 207 Spruce Lee's Summit MO 64063 Office: 2411 Holmes Kansas City MO 64108

JONAS, MANFRED, historian, educator; b. Mannheim, Germany, Apr. 9, 1927; came to U.S., 1937, naturalized, 1944; s. Walter and Antonie (Dannheisser) J.; m. Nancy Jane Greene, July 19, 1952; children: Andrew Miles, Kathryn Leslie, Emily Susan, Matthew Greene. B.S., CCNY, 1949; A.M., Harvard U., 1950, Ph.D. (Teaching fellow), 1959. Mil. intelligence analyst U.S. Dept. Def., 1951-54; teaching fellow Harvard, 1954-59; vis. prof. Am. history Free U., Berlin, 1959-62; asso. prof. PMC Colls., 1962-63; faculty Union Coll., Schenectady, 1963—, dir. grad. program Am. studies, 1964-74, prof. history, 1967—, Washington Irving prof. modern lit. and hist. studies, 1981—, chmn. dept. history, 1970-81, chmn. div. social sci., 1971-74; lectr. City Coll. N.Y., 1950, U. Md. Extension, 1954, Northeastern U., 1958; dir. NDEA Insts. for Advanced Study in History, 1966-68; cons. U.S. Office Edn., 1966; sr. Fulbright-Hays lectr. U. Saarland, Germany, 1973; Charles Warren fellow Harvard U., 1977-78. Author: Die Unabhängigkeitserklärung der Vereinigten Staaten, 1964, Isolationism in America, 1935-41, 1966, American Foreign Relations in the Twentieth Century, 1967, The United States and Germany, 1984; Co-editor: Roosevelt and Churchill: Their Secret Wartime Correspondence, 1975, New Opportunities in a New Nation, 1982; Contbr. articles profl. jours. Mem. N.Y. State Coll. Proficiency Exam. Com. in Am. History, 1970—; Moderator Forum 17 WMHT-TV, 1965; Bd. dirs. Freedom Forum, Inc., 1965-76, chmn., 1969-70, 75-76. Served with USNR, 1945-46. Mem. Am. Hist. Assn., Orgn. Am. Historians, Soc. for Historians Am. Fgn. Relations, AAUP (chpt. pres. 1969-71), German Assn. Am. Studies, Phi Beta Kappa, Phi Alpha Theta. Home: 2471 Hilltop Rd Schenectady NY 12309

JONAS, SARAN, neurologist, educator; b. N.Y.C., June 24, 1931; s. Myron and Margaret (Wurmfeld) J.; m. Ruth Haber, Sept. 16, 1956; children: Elizabeth Ann, Frederick Jonathan. B.S., Yale U., 1952; M.D., Columbia U., 1956. Diplomate: Am. Bd. Psychiatry and Neurology, Am. Bd. Internal Medicine. Intern Bellevue Hosp., N.Y.C., 1956-57, resident and fellow in medicine and neurology, 1957-62; practice medicine specializing in neurology, N.Y.C., 1964—; from clin. instr. to assoc. prof. clin. neurology N.Y. U. Sch. Medicine, 1964-77, prof. clin. neurology, 1977—; assoc. dir. neurology N.Y. U. Hosp., 1970—, dir. electroencephalography, 1969—. Served with USN, 1962-64. N.Y. State fellow in rheumatic diseases, 1962-64. Mem. Am. Acad. Neurology, Am. Med. Electroencephalographic Assn., Assn. for Research in Nervous and Mental Diseases, Am. Heart Assn. (Stroke Council). Office: 530 1st Ave New York NY 10016

JONASSEN, HANS BOEGH, educator, chemist; b. Seelze, Hannover, Germany, Aug. 18, 1912; came to U.S., 1940, naturalized, 1943; s. Hans Adolph Leire Boegh and Ida (von Droege) J.; m. Fannie Taylor Baumgartner, Aug. 30, 1939; children—Hans Boegh, Ida Frances, Ellen Taylor. B.S., Tulane U., 1942, M.S., 1944; Ph.D., U. Ill., 1946; Abitur, Leibniz Realgymnasium, Germany, 1931. Instr. Tulane U., 1942-44, asst. prof., 1946-48, asso. prof., 1948-52, prof., 1952—, chmn. dept. chemistry, 1962-68, W.R. Irby prof. chemistry, 1972-78, W.R. Irby prof. chemistry emeritus, 1978—, prof. engring., 1978—; Sci. liaison officer London br. Office Naval Research, 1958-59; mem. Nat. Adv. Council Coll. Chemistry, 1962-66; mem. divisional coms. for postdoctoral fellowship Nat. Acad. Scis.-NRC, 1960-63; Reilly lectr. U. Notre Dame, 1964; 5th F.P. Dwyer Meml. lectr., Sydney, Australia, 1967. Asso. editor: Chem. Rev, 1959-62; bd. editors: Jour. Am. Chem. Soc, 1960-69, Jour. Inorganic and Nuclear Chemistry, 1961—, Inorganic and Nuclear Letters, 1966—; bd. advisers: Chem. and Engring. News, 1962-65; co-editor: Techniques of Inorganic Chemistry, 1962-69; bd. cons. editors: Inorganic and Nuclear Chemistry Letters, 1965—. Bd. dirs. New Orleans YMCA, 1950, trustee, 1963—; pres. Met. YMCA, New Orleans, 1972-74; mem. internat. com. YMCA, 1965-70, So. area chmn. for, La., 1968-70. Recipient So. Chem. award, 1954, Coll. Chem. Tchrs. award Mfg. Chemist's Assn., 1959; Fulbright-Hayes sr. scholar fellow U. Sydney, Australia, 1971. Fellow AAAS; mem. Am. Chem. Soc., AAUP, Chem. Soc. London. Presbyterian (elder). Home: 7729 Belfast St New Orleans LA 70125

JONASSOHN, KURT, sociologist, educator; b. Cologne, Germany, Aug. 31, 1920; emigrated to Can., 1940, naturalized, 1946; s. Richard and Frieda; m. Pearl Pepper, Jan. 26, 1956; children—Frieda, Joseph David. B.A., Sir George Williams Coll., 1953; M.A. (Samuel Lapitsky fellow), McGill U., 1955; postgrad. (Univ. scholar), U. Chgo., 1955-56. Asst. study dir. U. Chgo., 1957-59; research sociologist Directorate of Personnel Planning, RCAF Hdqrs., Ottawa, Ont., Can., 1959-61; asst. prof., then prof. sociology Sir George Williams U. (now Concordia U., Sir George Williams campus), Montreal, Que., Can., 1961—. Contbr. articles and revs. to profl. jours.; co-editor: ISA Bull. Bd. dirs. Can. Youth Hostels Assn., 1975-77; bd. dirs. Hostelling Tours Agy. Inc., pres., 1976-77. Imperial Oil grad. research fellow, 1955-58. Mem. Internat. Sociol. Assn. (dep. exec. sec. 1974-78, exec. sec. 1978-82), Can. Sociology and Anthropology Assn. (sec.-treas. 1971-74), Am. Sociology Assn. Jewish. Office: Dept Sociology Concordia Univ SGW Campus 1455 de Maisonneuve Blvd W Montreal PQ H3G 1M8 Canada

JONASSON, OLGA, physician; b. Peoria, Ill., Aug. 12, 1934; d. Olav R. and Swea C. J. M.D. with honors, U. Ill., 1958. Intern U. Ill. Research and Ednl. Hosps., Chgo., 1958-59, resident in surgery, 1960-64, chief resident, 1963-64; postdoctoral research fellow Walter Reed Army Inst. Research, 1964-65, Mass. Gen. Hosp., 1965-66; mem. faculty dept. surgery U. Ill., Chgo., 1967—, prof., 1975—; chief surgery Cook County Hosp., Chgo., 1977—; cons. NIH, FDA. Fellow A.C.S.; mem. Soc. Univ. Surgeons, Am. Surg. Assn., Soc. Clin. Surgery, Transplantation Soc. Lutheran. Office: 1825 W Harrison Chicago IL 60612

JONCKHEERS, ALAN MATHEW, physicist; b. Howell, Mich., Feb. 12, 1947; s. August Peter and Elizabeth Gertrude (Nash) Jonckheere; m. Barbara Jean Minter, Aug. 16; children: Jessica, Susan, Laura Jean and Amanda Jean (twins). B.S., Mich. State U., 1969; M.S., U. Wash., 1970, Ph.D., 1976. Instr. physics dept. Fermi Nat. Accelerator Lab., Batavia, Ill., 1976-78; staff physics Fermilab, 1978—, assoc. dept. head meson dept., 1981—; researcher elem. particle physics Stanford Linear Accelerator Ctr., Lawrence Berkeley Lab., Calif. Contbr. papers to physics publs. Home: 637 Church St Batavia IL 60510

JONES, ABBOTT C., advertising agency executive; b. Lexington, Ky., Aug. 14, 1934; s. John Catron and Lois (Sauters) J.; m. Carol Donahue, June 29, 1957; children: Cynthia, Alison, Hilary. B.A., Principia Coll., 1956; M.B.A., Harvard U., 1958. Salesman Carnation Co., 1959-60; account exec. Benton & Bowles, N.Y.C., 1960-63; with Ogilvy & Mather, N.Y.C., 1963-77, sr. v.p., dir., 1973-77; exec. v.p., gen. mgr. Foote, Cone & Belding, N.Y.C., 1977-81, pres., 1981-82, Assoc. Communications Cos., 1982—. Served with U.S. Army, 1958-59. Clubs: University, Sky, Harvard Bus. Sch. of Greater N.Y. (dir.); Belle Haven (Greenwich, Conn.)). Home: 18 Echo Ln Greenwich CT 06830 Office: 101 Park Ave New York NY 10178

JONES, ALEXANDER ELVIN, foundation executive; b. Independence, Mo., Oct. 11, 1920; s. Joseph Elvin and Tessie (Watson) J; m. Sara Elisabeth Mullins, Jan. 16, 1946; children: Jo Ellen, Sara Elisabeth. B.A. with high distinction, DePauw U., 1942, LL.D., 1964; M.A., U. Minn., 1949, Ph.D., 1950; LL.D., U. Ark., 1967, Wabash Coll., 1975; D.H.L., Ind. Central Coll., 1970. Mem. faculty U. Minn., 1949-50, U. Ark., 1950-56, MacMurray Coll., 1956-59; dean Coll. Liberal Arts and Scis.; prof. English Butler U., 1959-63, pres., 1963-77; exec. v.p. Winona Meml. Found., 1977—; dir. Am. United Life Ins. Co. Author: Creative Exposition, 1957; co-author: Writing Good Prose, 1961, 4th edit., 1977; contbr. articles on Mark Twain, other Am. writers. Served with USNR, 1942-45. Mem. Phi Beta Kappa, Phi Eta Sigma, Phi Kappa Phi, Kappa Delta Pi. Club: Kiwanian (pres. 1971). Home: 17 Hilltop Dr Danville IN 46122

JONES, ALICE HANSON, economist; b. Seattle, Nov. 7, 1904; d. Olof and Agatha Marie (Tiegel) Hanson; m. Homer Jones, Apr. 21, 1930; children: Robert Hanson, Richard John, Douglas Coulthurst. A.B., U. Wash., 1925, M.A., 1928; Ph.D., U. Chgo., 1968. Teaching fellow U. Wash., 1927-28; fellow, research asst. econs. U. Chgo., 1928-29, 32-34; asst. editor Ency. Social Scis., N.Y.C., 1930; researcher, writer Pres.'s Com. Social Trends, N.Y.C., 1931; economist, asst. chief Cost of Living div. Bur. Labor Stats., Washington, 1934-44; economist div. statis. standards Bur. Budget, Washington, 1945-48; sec. com. nat. accounts Nat. Bur. Econ. Research, Washington, 1957; supervising economist, cons. Dept. Agr. Econ. Research, Washington, 1958-61; lectr. econs. Washington U., St. Louis, 1963-68, asst. prof., 1968-71, assoc. prof., 1971-73, adj. prof., 1973-77, prof. emeritus, 1977—; prin. investigator Social Sci. Inst., 1969—; adj. prof. econs. Claremont Men's Coll., 1973-74; econ. adviser Bank of Korea, 1967-68, AID, 1967-68. Author: American Colonial Wealth: Documents and Methods, 3 vols., rev. edit., 1978, Wealth of a Nation to Be: The American Colonies on the Eve of the Revolution, 1980. Named Woman of Achievement St. Louis Globe Democrat, 1980; research grantee NSF, 1969-75, NEH, 1970-76. Mem. Am. Econ. Assn., Econ. History Assn. (v.p. 1976-77, pres. 1982-83, trustee 1983—), Orgn. Am. Historians, Internat. Assn. Reearch in Income and Wealth, Social Sci. History Assn., Mortar Board, Phi Beta Kappa, Delta Zeta (Nat. Woman of Yr. 1981), Beta Phi Alpha (nat. pres. 1932-32), Omicron Delta Epsilon. Congregationalist. Home: 404 Yorkshire Pl Webster MO 63119 Office: Dept Econs Washington U St Louis MO 63130

JONES, ALLAN BARRY, clergyman, religious assn. exec.; b. Liverpool, Eng., June 25, 1936; came to U.S., 1968; s. Alfred William and Ethel May (Sumner) J.; m. Christine A. Lidster, Oct. 17, 1959; children—Glyn, Owen. Diploma, Skerry's Coll., Liverpool, 1953, Cliff Coll., Calver, Eng., 1957; B.Th., Toronto (Ont., Can.) Bible Coll., 1964; M.A., Calif. Grad. Sch. Theology, 1980. Ordained to ministry Congl. Christian Conf., 1962; pastor Murray Hall Ch., Liverpool, 1958-60, Ringwood (Ont.) Congl. Christian Ch., 1960-65, Univ. Ave. Congl. Ch., St. Paul, 1968-73, Carlsbad (Calif.) Union Ch., 1973—; pres. Conservative Congl. Christian Conf., Carlsbad, 1972-75; Tchr. Northwestern Coll., St. Paul, 1971-73. Mem. St. David's Soc. of San Diego. Home: 3760 Catalina St Carlsbad CA 92008 Office: 3175 Harding St Carlsbad CA 92008

JONES, ARCHER, educator, historian; b. Richmond, Va., Oct. 14, 1926; s. Montgomery Osborne and Helen Rutherfoord (Johnston) J.; m. Louise Fairfax Coleman, June 16, 1956 (div. 1977); 1 son, Caruthers Coleman; m. Joanne Leach Gatewood, Feb. 11, 1978. Student, St. John's Coll., 1943-46; B.A., Hampden-Sydney Coll., 1949; M.A., U. Va., 1953, Ph.D., 1958. Part-time instr. Randolph-Macon Woman's Coll., 1953-54, U. Va., 1954-55; instr. Hampden-Sydney Coll., 1957-58; dean, assoc. prof. history Clinch Valley Coll., U. Va., 1958-61; prof. history, chmn. dept. history and polit. sci. Va. Poly. Inst., 1961-66; assoc. dean arts and scis., prof. history U. S.C., 1966-68; Morrison vis. prof. history Command and Gen. Staff Coll., 1976-77; prof. history, dean Coll. Humanities and Social Sci. N.D. State U., 1968—. Author: Confederate Strategy from Shiloh to Vicksburg, 1961, (with T.L. Connelly) Politics of Command, 1973, (with H.M. Hattaway) How the North Won, 1983; contbr. Civil War books. Served to 1st lt. AUS, 1946-47, 55-57. Mem. Am. Mil. Inst. (trustee, prize com., army history adv. com.), Phi Beta Kappa, Omicron Delta Kappa. Home: 1616 15th Ave S Fargo ND 58103

JONES, BENJAMIN FRANKLIN, financial services company executive; b. Orange, N.J., Sept. 21, 1922; s. Benjamin Franklin and Mabel Louise (Stevens) J.; m. Betty Jane Thompson, Oct. 14, 1944; children: Douglas Thompson, Susan Leigh, Nancy Lynn. A.B., Dartmouth Coll., 1944. With Monarch Life Ins. Co., Springfield, Mass., 1947—, v.p., dir., 1962-66, exec. v.p., 1966-68, pres., 1968—; v.p., dir. Springfield Life Ins. Co., 1962-66, exec. v.p., 1966-68, pres., 1968—, Monarch Capital Corp., 1968-83, chmn. bd., 1983—; dir. Multibank, Springfield, Multibank Fin. Corp., Fidelity Bankers Life Ins. Co., Richmond, Va., 1st Variable Life Ins. Co., Little Rock, Great Oak Ins. Co., Springfield, Monarch Resources, Inc., N.Y.C. Trustee Western New Eng. Coll.; bd. dirs. Bus. Fund for Arts, Springfield, Mass. Served with inf. AUS, 1942-46; ETO. Mem. Am. Soc. Chartered Life Underwriters. Methodist. Clubs: Colony (Springfield); Longmeadow (Mass.); Country. Home: 565 Hall Hill Rd Somers CT 06071 Office: 1250 State St Springfield MA 01133

JONES, BOB GORDON, bishop; b. Paragould, Ark., Aug. 22, 1932; s. F.H. and Helen Truman (Ellis) J.; m. Judith Munroe, Feb. 22, 1963; children: Robert Gordon, Timothy Andrew. B.B.A., U. Miss., 1956; M.Div., Episcopal Sem. S.W., 1959, D.D. hon., 1978. Asst. to dean Trinity Cathedral, Little Rock, 1959-62; vicar St. George-in-Arctic, Kotzebue, Alaska, 1962-67; rector St. Christopher's Ch., Anchorage, 1967-77; bishop Episcopal Diocese Wyo., Laramie, 1977—; chmn. bd. Cathedral Home Children, Laramie, 1977—; mem. exec. com. Provence N.W., Helena, Mont., 1980-83, Coalition 14, Phoenix, 1982-84. Pres. Arctic Circle C. of C., Kotzebue, 1966; mem. exec. com. Alaska C. of C., Juneau, 1967; chmn. allocations com. United Way, Anchorage, 1973-75; pres. United Way Anchorage, 1975-76. Served with USN, 1950-55; Korea. Republican. Lodges: Lions; Elks. Home: 3207 Alta Vista Dr Laramie WY 82070 Office: Episcopal Dioces Wyo 104 S 4th Laramie WY 82070

JONES, BOB, JR., educator, lecturer, minister; b. Montgomery, Ala., Oct. 19, 1911; s. Bob and Mary Gaston (Stollenwerck) J.; m. Fannie May Holmes, 1938; children: Bob III, Jon Edward, Joy Estelle. Grad., Bob Jones Coll., 1930; M.A., U. Pitts., 1932; student, U. Chgo., U. Ala., Northwestern U.; Litt.D. (hon.), Asbury Coll., Wilmore, Ky., 1935, Chung-ang U., Seoul, Korea, 1972; L.H.D., John Brown U., Siloam Springs, Ark., 1941; LL.D., Houghton Coll., 1943; D.D., Northwestern Schs., Mpls., 1950; S.T.D., Midwestern Bible Coll., Pontiac, Mich., 1974. Acting pres. Bob Jones Coll., 1932-47; pres. Bob Jones U., 1947-71, chmn. bd. trustees, 1964—, chancellor, 1971—; Shakespearean authority and interpreter. Minister; lectr.; radio speaker.; Author: All Fullness Dwells, How to Improve Your Preaching, As the Small Rain, Inspirational and Devotional Verse, Wine of Morning, Ancient Truths for Modern Days, Revealed Religion: Paintings by Benjamin West, Prologue: A Drama of Jon Hus; Contbr. writings to various religious and profl. periodicals.; Author: weekly syndicated article A Look at the Book; Editor: Faith for the Family. Col. Gov's. Staff, S.C., Gov's. Staff, Tenn.; recipient Order of Palmetto State of S.C. Mem. Gospel Fellowship Assn. (pres. bd.), Internat. Cultural Soc. Korea (hon.). Home: Bob Jones U Greenville SC 29614 *As a Christian, I have always sought in all things to honor the Lord Jesus Christ; to be obedient to the Bible; to be frank, open and honest in my dealings; and never to compromise principle but be always ready to bend where no principle was involved.*

JONES, BOBETTE LAVELLE, lawyer, business executive; b. Los Angeles, Sept. 21, 1928; d. Ernest Lavelle and Alexandria Q. (Tufts) Camp; m. Paul LeRoi Jones, May 6, 1951; children—M'Liss LaVelle Jones Kane, Buff Laurie. B.S., UCLA, 1950; J.D., Loyola U., 1978. Editorial asst. Los Angeles Daily Jour., 1951-52; legal sec., 1953; with System Devel. Corp., Santa Monica, Calif., 1954-83, dir. bus. ops., 1967-71, corp. sec., 1971—; asst. corporate sec. Burroughs Corp., 1983—. Mem. ABA, Calif. State Bar, Am. Soc. Corp. Secs., U. Calif. at Los Angeles Gold Shield. Office: 2500 Colorado Ave Santa Monica CA 90406

JONES, BOISFEUILLET, JR., lawyer, newspaper executive; b. Atlanta, Nov. 14, 1946; s. Boisfeuillet and Laura (Coit) J.; m. Barbara Frost Pendleton, Sept. 13, 1969; children: Lindsay Pendleton, Theodore Boisfeuillet. A.B., Harvard U., 1968, J.D., 1974; D.Phil., Oxford U., 1981. Bar: Mass. 1974, D.C. 1979. Law clk. Judge Levin H. Campbell, U.S. Ct. Appeals (1st cir.), Boston, 1974-75; atty. Hill and Barlow, Boston, 1975-80; v.p., counsel Washington Post, 1980—; dir. Bowater Mersey Paper Co. Ltd., N.S., Newsprint, Inc., Richmond, Va., Robinson Terminal Warehouse Corp., Alexandria, Va. Rhodes scholar Rhodes Trust, 1968. Episcopalian. Home: 4331 Forest Ln NW Washington DC 20007 Office: Washington Post 1150 15th St NW Washington DC 20071

JONES, CARROLL FRANCIS, government official; b. Boston, Sept. 7, 1938; s. John P. and Jessie (Gillis) J.; m. Colleen Haney, Nov. 16, 1963 (div. 1968); children: Jessica M., Sarah M.; m. Louise Bennett, June 27, 1970; children: Emily C., Bennett P. B.S., Boston U., 1960, J.D., 1970. Bar: N.H. Ptnr. McSwiney, Jones & Semple, 1973-82; commr. Fed Property Resources, Gen. Services Adminstrn., Washington, 1982. Home: 4005 Thornapple St Chevy Chase MD 20815 Office: 18th and F Sts NW Washington DC 20405

JONES, CATESBY BROOKE, banker; b. Lexington, Va., Mar. 7, 1925; s. Catesby and Elizabeth (Cox) J.; m. Margaret Gordon Gaffney, June 13, 1953; children: Catesby II, Margaret Brooke, Elizabeth Gordon. Grad., St. Paul's Sch., 1943; B.A. in Econs, Yale, 1949, Stonier Grad. Sch. Banking, Rutgers U., 1956, U. Va. Grad. Sch. Bus., 1961. With United Va. Bank, Richmond, 1949—, sr. v.p., head nat. div., 1965—; pres., dir. Buffalo Creek & Gauley R.R. Co.; dir. Spindale Mills, Inc. Chmn. finance com., dir. Richmond Area Community Council, 1959-63; div. chmn. United Givers Fund, 1965, 72. Served to 1st lt. AUS, 1944-46. Mem. Am. Inst. Banking, Robert Morris Assos., Va. C. of C. (treas., dir. 1964-67), Richmond C. of C. (chmn. membership relations com. 1957-59), Soc. Colonial Wars in Va. (gov. 1976), Soc. Cincinnati (pres. 1979-82), Soc. Cincinnati in Va. (pres. gen. 1983), Jamestown Soc., Newcomen Soc., Beta Theta Pi. Episcopalian. Clubs: Yale of Va. (past pres.); Yale (N.Y.C.); Country of Va. (Richmond). Home: 19 Glenbrooke Circle W Richmond VA 23229 Office: 919 E Main St Richmond VA 23219

JONES, CHARLES EDWARD, mech. engr.; b. Bklyn., Apr. 20, 1929; s. Charles Edward and Mary Margaret (Decker) J.; m. Noel Catherine McDonald, Feb. 12, 1944; children—Claudia, Geoffrey, Kathryn, Jonathan. B.M.E., CCNY, 1947; M.S., Tex. A&M U., 1951; Ph.D., Cornell U., 1957. Lectr. mech. engring. CCNY, 1947-49; asst. prof. Tex. A&M U., 1949-52; instr. Cornell U., 1952-54; research engr. B & W Research Center, Alliance, Ohio, 1954-59, mgr. research and devel. lab., 1959-67, asst. dir., 1967-68, dir., 1968-71; v.p. ops. Bailey Meter Co., Wickliffe, Ohio, 1970-71, pres., 1971-75; asst. to group v.p. Babcock & Wilcox Indsl. Products Group, N.Y.C., 1975-80; pvt. practice mech. engring. cons., Mentor, Ohio, 1980—. Contbr. articles in field to profl. jours. Trustee Euclid Gen. Hosp., 1972-75. Served to capt. USAR, 1943-46. Fellow ASME (pres. 1980-81), Sigma Xi., Tau Beta Pi, Phi Kappa Phi, Pi Tau Sigma. Home and Office: 9200 Idlewood Dr Mentor OH 44060

JONES, CHARLES EDWARD, advt. exec.; b. Mound City, Ill., Oct. 1, 1918; s. William M. and Daisy D. (Rivers) J.; m. Doris E. Hogendobler, June 26, 1938; children—Eleanor Ann, Philip Alan; m. Greta Jane Houston., Dec. 3O, 1955; 1 dau., Emily Susan. Student, McKendree Coll., Lebanon, Ill., 1936-38; B.J., U. Mo., 1940. Account supr. Schwimmer & Scott (Ins.), Chgo., 1950-52; adminstrv. v.p., dir. Potts-Woodbury, Inc., 1952-60, pres., chmn. bd., chief exec. officer, 1962-67; sr. v.p. Biddle Advt., 1967—; chmn. Blue Anchor Marina, Inc., Gravois Mills, Mo., 1969—; owner Anchor Advt., Anchor Bus. Communications, Gravois Mills, 1972—; gen. sales mgr. WHB Radio, Kansas City, Mo., 1960-62. Former dir. Greater Kansas City Sports Commn.; ambassador Am. Royal. Served as 1st lt. USMC, 1943-46. Mem. Kansas City C. of C. (past dir.). Clubs: Kansas City, Masons. Home: Blue Anchor Marina Gravois Mills MO 65037 Office: Suite 309 6400 Glenwood St Overland Park KS 66202 also Box 594 Gravois Mills MO 65037

JONES, CHARLES FRANKLIN, petroleum company executive; b. Bartlett, Tex., Nov. 23, 1911; s. Charles Edward and Pearl Lee (Keeton) J.; m. Edith Temple Houston, Apr. 1, 1938; children: Dianne (Mrs. Orson C. Clay), Kenneth Franklin. B.S. in Chem. Engring, U. Tex., 1933, M.S., 1934, Ph.D. in Phys. Chemistry, 1937; LL.D., Austin Coll., 1965. Registered profl. engr., Tex. With Humble Oil and Refining Co., 1937-47, 49-63, mgr. econs. and planning dept., Houston, 1960-62, gen. mgr. central region, Tulsa, 1962-63; asst. to mgr. coordination and econs. dept. Standard Oil Co., N.J., 1947-49; pres., dir. Esso Research and Engring. Co., Linden, N.J., 1963-64; exec. v.p. Humble Oil & Refining Co., Houston, 1964, pres., 1964-70, vice chmn., 1970-72; also dir.; dean Coll. Bus. Adminstrn., U. Houston, 1972-74; mgmt. cons., 1974—; dir. Howell Corp., Coastal Corp., Western Co. of N.Am., Mosher, Inc., AIM Mgmt. Investment Funds; chmn. bd. Fed. Res. Bank of Dallas, 1969-73. Mem. Nat. sci. bd. NSF, 1966-72; former mem. Nat. Indsl. Conf. Bd.; former vice chmn. Tex. Research League; pres. Houston Symphony Soc., 1970-75, chmn., 1975-80; chmn. bd. trustees Houston Pub. Library, 1975—. Recipient Distinguished Engring. Grad. award U. Tex., 1964. Mem. AAAS, Am. Chem. Soc., Am. Inst. Chem. Engrs., Sigma Xi, Tau Beta Pi, Phi Lambda Upsilon, Beta Gamma Sigma, Omicron Delta Epsilon. Presbyterian (elder). Home: 3706 Del Monte Houston TX 77019 Office: 2315 Houston Natural Gas Bldg Houston TX 77002

JONES, CHARLES MARTIN (CHUCK JONES), author, producer, dir.; b. Spokane, Sept. 21, 1912; s. Charles Adams and Mabel (Martin) J.; m. Dorothy Webster, Jan. 31, 1935 (dec. 1978); 1 dau., Linda Jones Clough. Grad., Chouinard Art Inst., Los Angeles, 1931. Animator Warner Bros., 1933-38, dir., 1938-63; tchr., lectr. schs. and colls. throughout U.S. Creator: Pepe le Pew, Road Runner, Coyote, other animated characters; writer, producer, dir. TV spls. for, ABS and, CBS, including, The Cricket in Times Square, How the Grinch Stole Christmas, Rikki-Tikki-Tavi, Bugs Bunny in King Arthur's Court, Raggedy Ann and Andy in the Great Santa Claus Caper; numerous others, 1963—; Author articles. Recipient Acad. award for best animated cartoons for Scenti-Mental Reasons, 1950, The Dot and the Line, 1965, best documentary short subject for So Much for So Little, 1950; Peabody award for TV program excellence, 1971; Best Ednl. Films for 24th Ann. Columbus Film Festival, 1976; 1st prize Tehran Festival Films for Children, 1977; Brit. Film Inst. tribute, 1979; Am. Film Inst. tributes, 1975, 80; N.Y. Film Festival tribute, 1979; Cine award for The Dot and the Line, The Cricket in Times Square, Rikki-Tikki-Tavi, The White Seal and Mowgli's Brothers. Mem. Nat. Council Children and TV, Acad. Motion Picture Arts and Scis., Screen Actors Guild. Democrat. Unitarian.

JONES, CHARLES OSCAR, political science educator; b. Worthing, S.D., Oct. 28, 1931; s. Llewellyn F. and Marjorie (Tye) J.; m. Vera B. Mire, June 6, 1959; children—Joseph B., Daniel C. B.A. magna cum laude, U. S.D., 1953; M.S., U. Wis., 1956, Ph.D., 1960; student, London Sch. Econs. and Polit. Sci., 1956-57. Instr. Wellesley Coll., 1959-61, asst. prof., 1961-62; vis. lectr. U. Wis., summer 1961; asso. prof. U. Ariz., 1963-65, prof., 1965-69; Maurice Falk prof. politics U. Pitts., 1969-81; Robert Kent Gooch prof. U. Va., 1981—; asso. dir. Nat. Center for Edn. in Politics, N.Y., 1962-63; cons. for elections analysis NBC News, N.Y.C., 1964, 66; fellow Center for Advanced Study in Behavioral Scis., 1971-72; guest scholar Am. Enterprise Inst., 1983. Author: The Republican Party in American Politics, 1965, Every Second Year: Congressional Behavior and the Two-Year Term, 1967, The Minority Party in Congress, 1970, Clean Air: The Policies and Politics of Pollution Control, 1975, An Introduction to the Study of Public Policy, 1977, The United States Congress: People, Place and Policy, 1982, The Politics of the Policy Process, 1984; co-author: American Democracy, 1983; Mng. editor: Am. Polit. Sci. Rev, 1977-81. Mem. Commn. on Polit. Activity of Govt. Personnel U.S. Congress, 1966-67; chmn. council Inter-Univ. Consortium for Polit. Research, 1971-73, Social Sci. Research Council, 1980—. Served with AUS, 1953-55. Mem. Am. Polit. Sci. Assn. (mem. council 1967-69, treas. 1972-74), Policy Studies Orgn. (pres. 1980-81), Phi Beta Kappa, Pi Sigma Alpha (nat. pres.-elect 1982-84), Omicron Delta Kappa. Home: Route 5 Box 204 Charlottesville VA 22901

JONES, CHARLES WILLIAMS, educator; b. Lincoln, Nebr., Sept. 23, 1905; s. Charles Williams and Grace Elizabeth (Cook) J.; m. Sarah Frances Bosworth, June 30, 1928; children—Frances Elizabeth, Charles Bosworth (dec.), Lawrence Wager, Gregory Hunt. A.B., Oberlin Coll., 1926; Litt.D. (hon.), 1951; A.M., Cornell U., 1930, Ph.D., 1932. Rep. Allyn and Bacon (ednl. pubs.), 1926-29; instr. English Oberlin Coll., 1932-35, Cornell U., 1936-38, asst. prof., 1938-41, asso. prof., 1941-48, prof., 1948-54, dir. summer sessions, 1946-48, dean Grad. Sch., 1948-53; prof. English U. Calif., Berkeley, 1954-73, prof. emeritus, 1973—; dir. U.S. Mil. Acad. Preparatory, 1943-45. Author: Bedae Pseudepigrapha, 1939, Writing and Speaking, Bedae Opera de Temporibus, 1943, Saints' Lives and Chronicles in Early England, 1947, Medieval Literature in Translation, 1950, The St. Nicholas Liturgy, 1963, Bedae Opera Exegetica: in Genesim, 1967, Opera Didascalica, 1977, 79, 80, (with Horn and Crocker) Carolingian Aesthetics, 1976, St. Nicholas of Myra, Bari and Manhattan, 1978; Editor or contbr.: others. Dictionary Sci. Biography; Dictionary Middle Ages. Research fellow Am. Council Learned Socs., 1935-36; Guggenheim Meml. Found., 1939-40, 45-46; recipient Berkeley citation, 1973; Shea prize Am. Cath. Hist. Assn., 1978; nonfiction medal Commonwealth Club, 1979. Home: 670 Vernon St Oakland CA 94610

JONES, CHRISTINE MASSEY, furniture co. exec.; b. Columbus, Ga., Nov. 7, 1929; d. Lewis Everett and Donia (Spivey) Massey; (m), Dec. 24, 1948 (div. 1970); children—James Raymond, Jr., James David. Student, Ga. Southwestern Coll., 1947-48. With Muscogee Mfg. Co., Columbus, Ga., 1948-56, sec. to pres., 1956; sec. to pres., corp. sec. Haverty Furniture Cos., Inc., Atlanta, 1956-59, sec., asst. to pres., 1959-72, adminstrv. asst. to pres., 1972-78, asst. corp. sec., 1974-78, corp. sec., 1978—. Mem. Am. Soc. Corp. Secs. Home: 5245 Chemin de Vie NW Atlanta GA 30342 Office: 866 W Peachtree St NW Atlanta GA 30308

JONES, CHUCK *See* **JONES, CHARLES MARTIN**

JONES, CLAIBORNE STRIBLING, univ. adminstr.; b. Petersburg, Va., Dec. 20, 1914; s. Claiborne Turner and Elizabeth (Stribling) J.; m. Annie Goodwyn Boisseau, June 12, 1940; children—Anne Goodwyn, Maria de Saussure, Elizabeth Claiborne. A.B., Hampden-Sydney Coll., 1935; M.A., U. Va., 1940, Ph.D., 1944. Faculty U. N.C., 1944—, prof. zoology, 1956—; asso. dean Gen. Coll., 1958-65, asst. vice chancellor, 1965-66, asst. to chancellor, 1966-73, vice chancellor for bus. and finance, 1973-77, exec. asst. to chancellor, 1977-80, spl. asst. to chancellor, 1980—. Mem. Am. Soc. Zoologists, Phi Beta Kappa, Sigma Xi, Omicron Delta Kappa, Pi Kappa Alpha. Democrat. Episcopalian. Home: 419 Westwood Dr Chapel Hill NC 27514

JONES, CLARA PADILLA, state official; b. Albuquerque, N.Mex., Oct. 2, 1940; d. Julian and Suzanna Padilla; m. Ronald A. Jones, Apr. 28, 1960; children: Mary Padilla Davis, Suzanna. Student, El Camino Jr. Coll., Albuquerque Career Inst. V.p. Southwest Bankers Investment Co., Albuquerque; realtor Julian Padilla & Assocs., Albuquerque; sec. state State of N.Mex., Santa Fe, 1983-86. Bd. dirs. Albuquerque Career Inst.; vice-chmn. Bernalillo County Democratic Party Com.; pres. Bernalillo County Valley Dem. Women; mem. rules com. La Compania del Teatro; active Kidney Found.; pres., founder Las Amigas de Nuevo Mejico. Mem. Orgn. Bus. and Profl. Women, Nat. Assn. Secs. State, Am. G.I. Forum. Roman Catholic. Club: Zonta Internat. Home: 228 Crestview Dr SW Albuquerque NM 87105 Office: Sec State Executive Legislative Bldg Santa Fe NM 87503

JONES, CLARIS EUGENE, JR., botanist, educator; b. Columbus, Ohio, Dec. 15, 1942; s. Claris Eugene and Clara Elizabeth (Elliott) J.; m. Teresa Diane Wagner, June 26, 1966; children: Douglas Eugene, Philip Charles, Elizabeth Lynne. B.S., Ohio U., 1964; Ph.D., Ind. U., 1969. Asst. prof. Calif. State U.-Fullerton, 1969-73, assoc. prof., 1973-77, prof. botany, 1977—, dir. Fullerton Arboretum, 1970-80, dir. Faye MacFadden Herbarium, 1969—. Author: A Dictionary of Botany, 1980; editor: Handbook of Experimental Pollination Biology, 1983; contbr. articles to profl. jours. Mem. Am. Inst. Biol. Sci., AAAS, Bot. Soc. Am., Internat. Assn. Plant Taxonomy, Am. Soc. Plant Taxonomists, Soc. Study Evolution, Systematics Assn., Ecol. Soc. Am., Calif. Bot. Soc., Sigma Xi. Methodist. Office: 800 N State College Blvd Fullerton CA 92634

JONES, CLIFFORD AARON, lawyer, international businessman; b. Long Lane, Mo., Feb. 19, 1912; s. Burley Monroe and Arlie (Benton) J.; (m. 1st), 1942 (dec. 1975); m. Christina Wagner, Dec. 24, 1978. LL.B., U. Mo., 1938, J.D., 1969. Bar: Nev. bar 1938. Founder, sr. partner firm Jones, Jones, Bell, Close & Brown, Las Vegas, Nev., 1938—; majority leader Nev. Legislature, 1941-42; judge 8th Jud. Dist., Nev., 1945-46; lt. gov., State of Nev., 1947-54; owner, builder, chmn. bd. Thunderbird Hotel, Inc., Las Vegas, 1948-64; founder Valley Bank of Nev., 1953; founder, sec., dir. First Western Savs. and Loan Assn., 1954-66; pres., chmn. bd. Caribbean-Am. Investment Co., Inc., 1960-78; pres., dir. Income Investments, Inc., 1963-65; sr. v.p., dir. First Western Fin. Corp., 1963-66; dir., past pres. Baker & Hazard, 1966—; dir. Barrington Industries, Inc., 1966-70, Internat. Commodities Exchange, 1973—; chmn. bd., pres. Central African Land and Cattle Co., 1974-76. Mem. Clark County (Nev.) Democratic Central Com., 1940—, chmn., 1948; nat. committeeman from Nev. Dem. Party, 1954; mem. Nev. Dem. State Central Com., 1945-60; 4 time del. Dem. Nat. Conv. Served as lt. col. F.A. U.S. Army, 1942-46; ETO. Mem. ABA (past mem. tax sect.), Am. Coll. Probate Counsel, Nev. Bar Assn., D.C. Bar Assn., Am. Legion, V.F.W., Phi Delta Phi, Kappa Sigma. Clubs: United Nations Lions, Elks, Lions (Las Vegas) (past pres.). Office: Suite 700 Valley Bank Plaza 300 S 4th St Las Vegas NV 89101 and Suite 1060 1110 Vermont Ave NW Washington DC 20005

JONES, CLIFTON CLYDE, business educator; b. Huntington, W.Va., Dec. 21, 1922; s. Clifton Clark and Goldie (Williams) J.; m. Margaret Esther Scheldrup, 1948; children—Karen Eileen, Kristin Ann, Clifton Carl. A.B., Marshall Coll., 1944; student, Bethany Coll., 1943; M.A., Northwestern U., 1950, Ph.D., 1954. Instr. dept. bus. history Northwestern U., 1951-53; asst. prof. econs. Atlanta div. U. Ga., 1953-55, U. Ill., 1955-58, asso. prof., 1958-60; prof., head dept. bus. adminstrn. Kans. State U., 1960-62; dean Coll. Commerce, 1962-67, v.p. univ. devel., 1966-70, prof. bus. adminstrn., 1970—; dir. Overland Enterprises, Overland Park, Kans., Manhattan Fed. Savs. and Loan Assn. Author: (with D.L. Kemmerer) American Economic History, 1959, Caring for the Aged: An Appraisal of Nursing Homes and their Alternatives, 1982; Editor: Agricultural History, 1958-60. Mem. Kans. Council for Econ. Analysis, 1963-67; pres. Kans. Council Econ. Edn., 1965-66. Served from ensign to lt. (j.g.) USNR, 1944-46. Mem. Bus. History Conf., Agrl. History Soc. (pres. 1967-68), Manhattan C. of C. (pres. 1965), Delta Sigma Pi, Beta Gamma Sigma. Presbyterian. Club: Rotary. Home: 2015 Rockhill Circle Manhattan KS 66502

JONES, COURTNEY FREDERICK, automotive corporation executive; b. Detroit, Mar. 6, 1940; s. Hugh Frederick and Evelyn Matilda Corinne (Herzog) J.; m. Judette Natalie Banket, Sept. 14, 1975; children: Dawn M. Banket, Jessica D. Jones. B.S., Wayne State U., 1963, postgrad., 1963-64; postgrad., U. Chgo., 1965-68, M.B.A., 1968. With Gen. Motors Corp., 1963—; analyst Gen. Motors Assembly Div., Detroit, 1963-67, Fisher Body Div., Warren, Mich., 1968-71; analyst-dir. Gen. Motors Corp. Fin. Staff, N.Y.C., 1971-74; mgr. Gen. Motors Overseas Div., N.Y.C., 1974-77; asst. div. comptroller, chief product planner Pontiac Motor Div., Pontiac, Mich., 1977-78; asst. treas. Gen. Motors Corp. Fin. Staff, N.Y.C., 1978-82; treas., sec. fin. com. Gen. Motors Corp., N.Y.C., 1982—; bd. dirs. Gen. Motors Acceptance Corp., Detroit, 1981—, Motors Ins. Corp., 1981—, Tax Found., Inc., Washington, 1982—. Mem. Fin. Execs. Inst., Nat. Assn. Corp. Treas. Office: General Motors Corp 767 Fifth Ave New York NY 10153

JONES, CRANSTON EDWARD, magazine editor, writer; b. Albany, N.Y., Mar. 12, 1918; s. Edward Thomas and Katharine Phoebe (Lamson) J.; m. Jean Campbell, Dec. 24, 1949; children: Abigail Ainsworth, Baird Campbell. Grad., Phillips Acad., Andover, Mass., 1936; B.S., Harvard, 1940. Corr. for Time-Life mag., San Francisco, London and Paris, 1946-52, bur. chief, Rio de Janeiro, 1952-55; mem. staff Time mag., 1955-69, sr. editor, 1961-69; editor-in-chief Travel & Camera, 1969-70, Travel & Leisure, 1970-71; exec. v.p. U.S. Camera Pub. Corp., 1969-71; exec. dir. Atlas Mag., 1971-73, editor, 1973; sr. editor People mag., 1974—. Author: America Liberty and Natural Law, America's Advocate: Robert H. Jackson, Robert H. Jackson: Lawyer's Judge, Quote It: Memorable Legal Quotations, Architecture Today and Tomorrow, 1961, Homes of American Presidents, 1962, Marcel Breuer: Works and Projects, 1921-1961, 1963; editor: The Best of People: The First Decade; Author also articles. Served to lt. USNR, 1941-45. Recipient award for excellence in archtl. journalism A.I.A., 1956, 58, 59, 60. Mem. Municipal Art Soc., Soc. Mayflower Descs., Soc. Archtl. Historians. Clubs: Century, Edgartown Yacht. Home: 8 E 96th St New York NY 10128 Office: Time-Life Bldg New York NY 10020

JONES, D. PAUL, JR., banker, lawyer; b. Birmingham, Ala., Sept. 26, 1942; s. D. Paul and Virginia Lee (Mount) J.; m. Charlene Dale Angelich, Aug. 1964; children—Elizabeth Holly, Allison Leigh, D. Paul, III. B.S., U. Ala., 1964, J.D., 1967; LL.M., N.Y. U., 1968. Bar: Ala. Mem. firm Balch, Bingham, Baker, Hawthorne, Williams & Ward, Birmingham, 1970-78, of counsel, 1978—; exec. v.p., gen. counsel, dir. Central Bancshares South, Inc., Birmingham, 1978—; dir. Central Bank of South, Marathon Corp. Bd. editors: U. Ala. Law Rev, 1965-67. Trustee Advent Episcopal Day Sch., Birmingham, 1969-71. Mem. Am. Bar Assn., Ala. Bar Assn. (chmn. sect. corp., banking and bus. law 1973-75, bd. bar examiners 1975-78), Birmingham Bar Assn. Clubs: Downtown (Birmingham); Country of Birmingham. Home: 2880 Balmoral Rd Birmingham AL 35223 Office: 701 S 20th St Birmingham AL 35205

JONES, DALLIS CLIFFORD, electric utility executive; b. Augusta, Ga., Apr. 5, 1929; s. Dallis Clifford and Rose Vernon (Owens) J.; m. Virginia P. Prothro, Nov. 22, 1951; children: Virginia, Nancy, Michael, Anthony. B.S. in Civil Engring., Clemson U., 1950. Registered profl. engr. Engr. Dawson Engring. Co., Charleston, S.C., 1950-52; contracts engr. E.I. du Pont Nuclear Project, Augusta, Ga., 1952-54; sales and mgmt. Pacific Power & Light Co., Ga., 1956-77, v.p. and div. mgr., Yakima, Wash., 1977-82, sr. v.p., Portland, Oreg., 1982—. Served to 1st lt. USAF, 1954-56. Disting. mil. student Clemson U., 1950. Mem. Associated Oreg. Industries. Republican. Presbyterian. Clubs: International; Aero (Portland). Office: Pacific Power & Light Co 920 SW 6th Ave Portland OR 97204

JONES, DAVID CARLTON, oil consultant; b. Calgary, Alta., Can., Dec. 14, 1914; s. D. Charles and Norah (Browne) J.; m. Marian Lilian Glover, Nov. 30, 1940; children: Donna Marian (Mrs. Jeffrey King Motherwell), Linda Noreen (Mrs. Melvin Ernest Feddersen). Student, U. Alta., 1933-35; B.Eng., McGill U., 1937; postgrad., Harvard U., 1963. Engr. Dominion Bridge Co., Calgary, 1944; engr. Can. Western Natural Gas Co., 1945-51; Cons. engr. Denton Spencer Co., Calgary, 1951-54; engr. Hudson's Bay Oil & Gas Co., Ltd., Calgary, 1955-59, v.p. prodn., 1960-66, exec. v.p., 1966-69, pres., 1970-77, Carlton Resource Mgmt., 1977—; v.p., dir. Alta. Gas Trunk Line, 1955-70; dir. DuPont of Can. Ltd., Polysar Ltd., Onyx Petroleum Co. Ltd., Canterra Energy. Vice pres., bd. dirs. Calgary Philharmonic Soc., 1967-73, Calgary YMCA, 1964-69; mem. bd. mgmt. Foothills Gen. Hosp., 1969-76. Mem. Assn. Profl. Engrs. Alta. (pres. 1960), Petroleum Recovery Research Inst. (pres. 1966-71). Clubs: Calgary Golf and Country, Calgary Petroleum (pres. 1973). Home: 1411 Beverley Pl Calgary AB Canada T2V 2C7 Office: 200 Iveagh House 707 7th Ave W Calgary AB Canada T2P 0Z2

JONES, DAVID CHARLES, retired air force officer, former chairman Joint Chiefs of Staff; b. Aberdeen, S.D., July 9, 1921; s. Maurice and Helen Alice (Meade) J.; m. Lois M. Tarbell, Jan. 23, 1942; children: Susan Jones Coffin, Kathy Jones Franklin, David Curtis. Student, U. N.D., Minot State Coll.; grad., Flying Sch., Roswell, N.Mex., 1943, Nat. War Coll., Washington, 1960; H.L.D., U. Nebr., 1974, La. Tech. U., 1975, Minot State Coll., 1979, Boston U., 1980, Troy State U. Commd. 2d lt. U.S. Air Force, 1943, advanced through grades to gen., 1971; dep. comdr. ops., Vietnam, vice comdr., comdr.-in-chief; comdr. 4th Allied Tactical Air Force; chief of staff (U.S. Air Force), Washington, 1974-78; chmn. Joint Chiefs of Staff, Dept. Def., Washington, 1978-82, ret., 1982. Decorated Def. D.S.M., Air Force D.S.M., Legion of Merit, D.F.C., Bronze star, Air medal, numerous others. Mem. Air Force Assn. Clubs: Alfalfa, Army-Navy Country, International.

JONES, DAVID CHARLES, interior designer, syndicated columnist; b. Marion, Ind., Feb. 23, 1929; s. Herschel Edward and Georgia Madeline (Hendey) Conner; m. Susanna Stephenson Hughes, June 16, 1951; children: Beth Jones Newman, Laura Jones Thayer, Margaret Jones Baker, Amy Jones Powell. B.A., DePauw U., 1951. Vice pres. Jones Inc., Columbus, Ind., 1951-59, Gallery Shop, 1959-70; pres. Franklin Square Interiors, Columbus, 1970—. Creator: Breakfast in the Courtyard, Indpls. Mus. Art, 1972; designer decorations, Cooper-Hewitt Mus., N.Y.C., 1976; work appeared in: Interior Design, 1970. Mem. Columbus Redevel. Design Rev. Commn., 1969-74; pres. Bartholomew County Hist. Soc., 1977. Recipient award Nat. Soc. Interior Designers, 1975; named Sagamore of Wabash State of Ind., 1975. Fellow Am. Soc. Interior Designers (Ind. pres. 1968-70, v.p. nat. bd. 1976); mem. Decorator's Group (pres. 1972—), Sigma Delta Chi, Sigma Chi. Republican. Presbyterian. Clubs: Mchts. and Mfrs. (Chgo.); Columbia (Indpls.); Harrison Lake Country (Columbus). Home: 2830 S Crossing Ln Columbus IN 47201 Office: 538 Franklin St Columbus IN 47201

JONES, DAVID HUGH, theatre, film and TV director; b. Poole, Dorset, Eng., Feb. 19, 1934; came to U.S., 1979; s. John David and Gwendolen Agnes (Ricketts) J.; m. Sheila Marion Essex Allen, Oct. 20, 1964; children: Joseph Luke Allen, Jesse Gawain Allen. B.A. in English with 1st class honours, Christ's Coll., Cambridge U., 1954, M.A., 1957. Producer BBC TV program "Monitor" Arts Mag., 1958-64; artistic controller, then asso. dir. Royal Shakespeare Co., 1964-75; artistic dir. Royal Shakespeare Co., Aldwych, 1975-78; artistic dir. BAM Theatre Co., Bklyn., 1979-81; prof. Yale Sch. Drama, New Haven, 1981. Producer: BBC TV program Play of the Month, 1978-79; dir.: (film) Betrayal, 1982; BBC TV Shakespeare Series, 1982-83. Served to 1st lt. Brit. Army, 1954-56. Recipient Obie award for direction of Summerfolk, 1976, for innovative programming at B.A.M., 1980. Office: Care Lantz Inc 888 7th Ave New York NY 10106

JONES, DAVID MILTON, economist, educator; b. Newton, Iowa, June 22, 1938; s. Charles Raymond and Mary Evelyn (Corrough) J.; m. Becky Ann Jones Strait, Aug. 4, 1962; children: David, Jennifer, Stephen. B.A. with honors, Coe Coll., 1960; M.A., U. Pa., 1961, Ph.D., 1969. Economist Fed. Res. Bank N.Y., N.Y.C., 1963-68; v.p., fin. economist Irving Trust Co., N.Y.C., 1968-72; sr. v.p., economist Aubrey G. Lanston & Co., Inc., N.Y.C., 1972—; advisor Fed. Res. Bank N.Y., 1982—; mem. econ. adv. bd. Columbia U., 1982—; dir. Suffolk County Savs. & Loan, Centerreach, N.Y. Chmn. fin. and investment com. United Ch. Bd. for World Ministries, N.Y.C., 1975—; mem. bonding com. City of Montclair, 1982-83. Woodrow Wilson Found. fellow, 1960; NDEA fellow, 1960. Mem. Nat. Assn. Bus. Economists. Home: 168 Gates Ave Montclair NJ 07042 Office: 20 Broad St New York NY 10005

JONES, DAVID RHODES, newspaper editor; b. Connellsville, Pa., Sept. 13, 1932; s. David Rhodes and Ruth Elizabeth (Dillon) J.; m. Mary Lee Lauffer, Oct. 8, 1955; 1 dau., Elizabeth Lee. B.A., Pa. State U., 1954; M.A., N.Y. U., 1961. Reporter Wall Street Jour., N.Y.C., 1957-61, bur. chief, Pitts., 1961-63; corr. N.Y. Times, Detroit, 1963-65, nat. labor reporter, Washington, 1965-68, asst. nat. editor, N.Y.C., 1969-72, nat. editor, 1972—. Served to 1st lt. USAF, 1955-57. Mem. Sigma Delta Chi, Tau Kappa Epsilon. Office: 229 W 43d St New York NY 10036

JONES, DEAN CARROLL, actor; b. Morgan City, Ala., Jan. 25; s. Andrew Guy and Nolia Elizabeth (Wilhite) J.; m. Mae Inez Entwisle, Jan. 1, 1954 (div.); children: Carol Elizabeth, Deanna Mae. Student, Asbury Coll., UCLA, 1957. Blues singer, New Orleans; actor: films including Handle With Care, 1958, Never So Few, 1959, Under the Yum-Yum Tree, 1963, New Interns, 1964, That Darn Cat, 1965, Two On a Guillotine, 1965, Ugly Dachshund, 1966, Monkeys, Go Home, 1967, Blackbeard's Ghost, 1968, Love Bug, 1969, The $1,000,000 Duck, 1971, Snowball Express, 1972, Mr. Superinvisible, 1976, Shaggy D.A, 1976, Herbie Goes to Monte Carlo, 1977, Born Again, 1978; TV series What's It All About, World?; TV films When Every Day Was the 4th of July, NBC-TV, 1978, The Long Day of Summer, ABC-TV, 1980; appeared: Broadway plays Company; recording artist. Mem. Acad. Motion Picture Arts and Scis., Acad. TV Arts and Scis., Acad. Rec. Arts and Scis. Address: care Contemporary-Korman Artists Ltd Contemporary Artists Bldg 132 Lasky Dr Beverly Hills CA 90212 *

JONES, DONALD EDWARD, advt. exec.; b. Jamestown, N.Y., June 2, 1922; s. Albin Ernest and Anna (Anderson) J.; m. Marilyn Ahlstrom, June 26, 1948; children—Jeffrey, Barbara, Cynthia, Kathleen. Student, Mass. Inst. Tech., 1943-44; B.S., U. Mich., 1948. Bus. mgr. Rogers Pub. Co., Detroit, 1948-54; with MacManus, John & Adams, Inc., Bloomfield Hills, Mich., 1954—, v.p., mgr., Los Angeles, 1958-64, exec. v.p., mgr. N.Y. office, 1964-69, exec. v.p. central ops., 1969—, dir., 1964—; corp. exec. v.p., dir. D'Arcy-MacManus-Masius, Inc. Served with Signal Corps AUS, 1943-46. Home: 2338 Claymoor Dr Chesterfield MO 63017 Office: 1 Memorial Dr St Louis MO 63102

JONES, DONALD RICHARD, electronics company executive; b. Oak Park, Ill., Jan. 17, 1930; s. Harold and Esther (Christiansen) J.; m. Susan Jane Elworthy, July 27, 1957; children: Linda C., David R., Donna S., Bradley R. B.S.E.E., U. Ill., 1951; postgrad., Northwestern U., Chg., 1956-58. With Motorola, Inc., 1951—; sr. v.p., treas. Motorola, Inc., Schaumburg, Ill., 1971—. Served to 1st lt. Signal Corps U.S. Army, 1951-53; Korea. Mem. Fin. Execs. Inst. Republican. Club: Inverness Golf (Ill.) (pres. 1981). Office: Motorola Inc 1303 E Algonquin St Schaumburg IL 60196

JONES, DONALD WAYNE, publisher; b. LaCrosse, Wis., Sept. 25, 1922; s. Lester Martin and Nelle (Roach) J.; m. Barbara Causey, Sept. 2, 1950; children: Donald Wayne, Nona Lane, Clayton. A.B., DePauw U., 1943. Sci. editor Prentice-Hall, Inc., 1946-56; editor-in-chief Allyn & Bacon, Inc., 1956-58; pres. Addison-Wesley Pub. Co., Reading, Mass., 1958-76; with Jones and Bartlett Pubs., Inc., Boston; dir. Wadsworth Pub. Co., Stephen Greene Press. Vice pres. Am. Ednl. Pubs. Inst., 1967-69. Served with USAF, 1943-46. Mem. Woods Hole Oceanographic Inst. (asso.), Assn. Am. Pubs., Sierra Club, Sigma Chi. Club: Woods Hole (Mass.) Golf. Home: Amrita Island Cataumet MA Office: Jones and Bartlett Pubs Inc 20 Park Plaza Boston MA

JONES, DOROTHY CAMERON, educator; b. Detroit, Feb. 5, 1922; d. Vinton Ernest and Beatrice Olive (Cameron) J. B.A., Wayne State U., 1943, M.A., 1944; Ph.D., U. Colo., 1965. Attendance officer Detroit Bd. Edn., 1943-44; tchr. English Denby High Sch., Detroit, 1946-56, 57-58; exchange tchr., Honolulu, 1956-57; instr., asst. prof. English Colo. Women's Coll., Denver, 1962-66; mem. faculty U. No. Colo., Greeley, 1966—, prof. English, 1974—. Contbr. articles to profl. lit. Served with WAVES USNR, 1944-46. Faculty research grantee, 1970, 76. Mem. Internat. Shakespeare Assn., Central States Renaissance Soc., Patristic, Medieval and Renaissance Conf., Rocky Mountain Medieval and Renaissance Soc., Rocky Mountain MLA, Delta Kappa Gamma, Pi Lambda Theta. Home: Apt 312 1009 13th Ave Greeley CO 80631 Office: Dept English 40 Michener Library U No Colo Greeley CO 80639

JONES, DOUGLAS A., bldg. products mfg. co. exec.; b. 1917. With Steel Co. Can., prior to 1950; with steel constrn. div. Can. Govt. Dept. Reconstrn. and Supply, World War II; with H.H. Robertson Co., 1950—, pres., 1950-60, corp. exec. v.p., then pres., chief exec. officer, 1960-79, chmn. bd., chief exec. officer, 1979—, pres., 1981, also dir. and dir. Office: HH Robertson Co 2 Gateway Center Pittsburgh PA 15222 *

JONES, DOUGLAS CLYDE, author; b. Winslow, Ark., Dec. 6, 1924; s. Marvin Clyde and Bethel Mae (Stockburger) J.; m. Mary Arnold, Jan. 1, 1949; children: Mary Glenn, Martha Claire, Kathryn Greer, Douglas Eben. B.A. in Journalism, U. Ark., 1949; M.S. in Mass Communications, U. Wis., Madison, 1962. Commd. U.S. Army, 1949, advanced through grades to lt. col., 1968; service in, W. Ger. and Korea; chief armed forces news br. Dept. Def., 1966-68, ret., 1968; prof. U. Wis. Sch. Journalism, Madison, 1968-74. Painter of plains Indians, 1974-75; novelist, 1976—; author: Treaty of Medicine Lodge, 1966, Court Martial of G.A. Custer, 1976 (Spur award Western Writers Am. 1976), Arrest Sitting Bull, 1977, Creek Called Wounded Knee, 1978, Winding Stair, 1979, Elkhorn Tavern, 1980 (Friends of Am. Writers award 1980), Weedy Rough, 1981, The Barefoot Brigade, 1982, Season of Yellow Leaf, 1983. Served with U.S. Army, World War II; PTO. Decorated Commendation medal (3) Legion of Merit. Address: 1987 Greenview Dr Fayetteville AR 72701

JONES, DOUGLAS EPPS, educator, geologist; b. Tuscaloosa, Ala., May 28, 1930; s. Walter Bryan and Hazel (Phelps) J.; m. Bonnie Ann Cook, June 4, 1955; children—Susan Lucile, Elizabeth Tannahill, Walter Bryan II. B.S., U. Ala., 1952; Ph.D., La. State U., 1959. Research geologist La. Geol. Survey, 1955-58; mem. faculty U. Ala., 1958—, prof. geology, head dept. geology and geography, 1966-68; asst. dean Coll. Arts and Scis., 1967-68, interim dean, 1968-69, dean, 1969—. Contbr. articles on gulf coastal plain paleontology and stratigraphy. Served with U.S. Army, 1952-54. Mem. Am. Assn. Petroleum Geologists, Geol. Soc. Am., Assn. Profl. Geol. Scientists, Sigma Xi. Home: 23 High Forest Tuscaloosa AL 35406 Office: PO Box 2906 University AL 35486

JONES, EARL, former college president, research specialist; b. Canton, Okla, Aug. 4, 1925; s. Hercel C. and Florence (Hill) J.; m. Eleanor Harriett Vance, July 15, 1952; children: Beverly Anne, Mark Earl, James Richard, Cindy Kay. B.S., 1949; M.S., Inter-Am. Inst. of OAS, Turrialba, Costa Rica, 1958; Ed.D., Mont. State U., 1962. Tchr. pub. schs., Ontario, Oreg., 1949-55; dir. rural programs Sta. KSRV, Ontario, 1955-56; dir. Sta. KSLM, Salem, Oreg., 1956; vocat. dir. Arcata Pub. Schs., Calif., 1956-57; instr. Inter-Am. Inst., 1957-58, asst. prof., 1960-62; assoc. prof. sociology UCLA, 1963-66; prof. sociology and edn., assoc. dean Tex. A&M U. Coll. Edn., 1967-71; pres. Incarnate Word Coll., San Antonio, 1971-73; sr. research specialist Devel. Assocs., San Antonio, 1974—, dir. research office, 1977—; prof. Antioch U., West San Antonio, 1977—; dir. research Caribbean Inst. Sociology and Anthropology, Caracas, Venezuela, 1963-65; chair prof. U. Chile Sch. Law, Santiago, Valparaiso, 1965-66; vis. prof. Royal Danish Acad., Copenhagen, 1955, U. P.R., Mayaguez, 1960, Cath. U., Caracas, 1963-65, U. Pacific, 1966, Calif. State Coll.-Los Angeles, Calif. State Coll.-San Francisco, 1968; prof. Antioch Coll., 1973—; cons. Mexican-Am. Cultural Ctr., San Antonio, 1973-75; mem. Gov.'s Com. on Confluence of Tex. Cultures, 1969-76, Gov's Com. to Reconstruct Tchr. Edn., 1969-72; cons. Cabinet Com. on Spanish Speaking Peoples, 1972-75. Author: Rural Youth in the Americas, 1960, Lideracao, 1961, A Study of the Costa Rican Extension Service, 1962, The Cooperative Extension Services of Jamaica, 1962, Supervision en Extension Agricola, 1963, Latin American Literature for Youth, 1968, Some Perspectives on the Americas, 1968, Self-Identification and the Americas, 1970, Social Atitudes of South Texas Primary Children, 1976, (with others) Teacher Classroom Behaviors, 1977, Case Studies in Educational Change, 1978, Client Satisfaction with Services to Limited and Non-English-Speaking Students In California, 1980. Served with USMCR, 1943-46. Recipient Presdl. citation, Republic of Guatemala, 1969, Standard Oil Disting. Teaching Award, 1970. Mem. Am. Sociol Assn., Rural Sociol. Soc., Alpha Zeta, Phi Kappa Delta. Democrat. Roman Catholic. Lodge: Lions. Home: 2695 37th Ave San Francisco CA 94116 office: 693 Sutter St 3d Floor San Francisco CA 94102 *This:The support of family, friends and colleagues has made it possible to serve in many fields. Dedication to these three, to my affiliated institutions, and to the people who were to benefit from my efforts, brought about continued and new opportunities. Those expressions of confidence caused me to work longer and harder than* *almost anyone else, and together, these factors engendered a considerably successful career in helping others.*

JONES, E(BEN) BRADLEY, steel company executive; b. Cleve., Nov. 8, 1927; s. Eben Hoyt and Alfreda Sarah (Bradley) J.; m. Ann Louise Jones, July 24, 1954; children: Susan Robb, Elizabeth Hoyt, Bradley Hoyt, Ann Campbell. B.A., Yale U., 1950. With Republic Steel Corp., Cleve., 1954—, v.p. mktg., 1971-74, v.p. comml., 1974-76, exec. v.p., 1976-79, pres., 1979-82, chief operating officer, 1980-82, also dir., chmn., chief exec. officer, 1982—; officer and/or dir. Republic Steel Corp. subs. and affiliated cos.; dir. TRW Inc., Nat. City Bank Cleve., Nat. City Corp. Trustee, v.p., mem. exec. com. Cleve. Clinic Found.; trustee, exec. com. Univ. Sch., Cleve.; trustee Cleve. Mus. Art, Greater Cleve. Roundtable; bd. dirs. Greater Cleve. Growth Assn., INROADS/Cleve., Inc.; mem. Cleve. Com. for Corp. Support of Edn., Council for Fin. Aid to Edn.; trustee United Way Services, Cleve., chmn. 1981 Cleve. Campaign. Served with U.S. Army, 1950-53. Mem. Am. Iron and Steel Inst (dir.), Delta Kappa Epsilon. Office: PO Box 6778 Cleveland OH 44101

JONES, EBON RICHARD, retailing executive; b. Oak Park, Ill., Aug. 23, 1944; s. Ebon Clark and Marilyn B. (Dow) J.; m. Sally Samuelson, Jan. 27, 1968; children: Stephanie Blythe, Heather Denise. B.A., Priceton U., 1966; M.B.A., Stanford U., 1968. Adminstrv. asst. Nat. Air Pollution Control Adminstrn., Washington, 1968-70; cons. McKinsey & Co., San Francisco and Paris, 1970-83; exec. v.p. Safeway Stores Inc., Oakland, Calif., 1983—. Chmn. bd. San Francisco Zool. Soc., 1979-83; trustee San Francisco Trust. Served to lt. USPHS, 1968-70. Mem. Phi Beta Kappa. Home: 58 Chester Way San Mateo CA 94402 Office: Safeway Stores Inc 201 4th St Oakland CA 94660

JONES, ED, congressman; b. Yorkville, Tenn., Apr. 20, 1912; s. William Frank and Hortense (Pipkin) J.; m. Mary Llewellyn Wyatt, June 9, 1938; children: Mary Llew Jones McGuire (dec.), Jennifer Wilson Kinnard. B.S., U. Tenn., 1934; student, U. Wis., 1944, U. Mo., 1945. With Tenn. Dept. Agr., 1934-41, Tenn. Dairy Products Assn., 1941-43; agrl. agt. I.C. R.R., 1943-49, 52-69; Tenn. commr. agr., 1949-52; mem. 91st-98th congresses from 8th dist. Tenn.; mem. com. on adminstrn., mem. com. on agr. Chmn. Tenn. Agrl. Stablzn. Conservation Commn., 1962-69. Trustee Bethel Coll., McKenzie, Tenn. Named Man of Year Progressive Farmer mag., 1951, Memphis Agrl. Club, 1957, Nat. Limestone Inst., 1979; recipient Distinguished Dairy Service award U. Tenn. Dairy Club, 1966; Distinguished Pub. Service award Am. R.R. Assn., 1970; Distinguished Nat. Leadership award Future Farmers Am., 1970; award U. Tenn. Block and Bridle Club, 1972; Disting. Service to Agr. award Gamma Sigma Delta, 1980; award for disting. service to so. agr. Progressive Farmer mag., 1980; disting. service award Nat. Assn. Conservation Dists., 1984. Mem. Alpha Gamma Rho. Democrat. Presbyn. Clubs: Mason (Shriner), Elk. Home: Yorkville TN 38389 Office: House Office Bldg Washington DC 20515

JONES, EDDIE, professional sports team executive; b. Houston; m. Marilyn Jones; children: Wendy, Todd, Jeffrey. B.S. in Acctg., La. State U. Bus. mgr. New Orleans Saints, 1968-73, treas., 1973-77, v.p., 1977-78, exec. v.p., 1978-80, pres., 1982—; v.p. John Mecom Co., Houston, 1980-82. Served with USAF. Office: New Orleans Saints 1500 Poydras St New Orleans LA 70112 *

JONES, EDGAR ALLAN, JR., educator, arbitrator, lawyer; b. Bklyn., Jan. 8, 1921; s. Edgar Allan and Isabel (Morris) J.; m. Helen Callaghan, Sept. 15, 1945; children: Linda Marie, Anne Marie, Carol Marie, Edgar Allan III, Denis James, Robert Morris, David Llewellyn, Therese Marie, Catherine Marie, Nancy Marie, Daniel Anthony. B.A., Wesleyan U., 1942; LL.B., U. Va., 1950. Bar: Va. bar 1948. Faculty U. Calif. at Los Angeles Law Sch., 1951—, prof. law, 1958—, asst. dean, 1957-58; dir. Law-Sci. Research Center, 1963-66; labor dispute arbitrator, mediator, fact finder for pvt. and pub. employers and unions, 1953—. Appeared as judge: network TV programs Accused, 1958-59, Traffic Ct, 1958-61, Day in Court, 1958-64; moderator: ednl. TV program Forum West, 1966; Contbr. numerous law rev. articles.; Editor: Law and Electronics: The Challenge of a New Era, 1960; founding editor: Va. Law Weekly, 1948-50, NAA Chronicle, 1977-78. Pres. Creddalt Research, Inc., 1959—; dir. Deauville Restaurant, Inc. (Jimmy's); Pub. mem. Calif. Commn. Manpower Automation and Tech., 1963-67, Calif. Manpower Adv. Com., 1964-67; nat. enforcement commr. WSB, 1951; Sec. Californians for Kennedy, 1960. Served to 1st lt. USMCR, 1942-45. Mem. Nat. Acad. Arbitrators (pres. 1980-81), ABA, Va. State Bar, AFTRA. Office: U Calif at Los Angeles Law Sch 405 Hilgard Ave Los Angeles CA 90024

JONES, EDITH AUGUSTA, dietitian; b. Muscle Shoals, Ala.; d. Leonidas and Ora (Phillips) J. B.S., U. Ala., 1941; M.S., U. Tenn., 1949. Dietetic intern Johns Hopkins Hosp., 1941-42, staff dietitian, 1942-43; dir. student curriculum Sch. Dietetics, 1946-49; dietitian AUS, 1943-46; nutritionist Bur. State Services, USPHS, 1950-51; dietitian cons. hosp. facilities div. Bur. Med. Service, 1951-52; chief, nutrition dept. Clin. Center, NIH, Bethesda, Md., 1952-83; Chnm. Internat. Com. Dietetic Assns., 1965-69; gen. chmn. 5th Internat. Congress Dietetics, 1969. Contbr. articles in field. Recipient Distinguished Service award U. Ala, 1956; McLester award Assn. Mil. Surgeons U.S., 1957; Meritorious Achievement award USPHS, 1971; Majorie Hulsizer Copher Meml. award, 1971; hon. sesquicentennial professorship U. Ala., 1981. Fellow Am. Pub. Heath Assn.; mem. Am. Dietetic Assn. (pres 1962-63), D.C. Dietetic Assn. (rep. ho. dels. Am. assn.), Am. Home Econs. Assn. (named one of 50 outstanding grads. of U. Ala. 50th anniversary of home. econs. 1981), Mortar Bd., Alpha Chi Omega (award achievement 1962), Phi Kappa Phi, Phi Upsilon Omicron, Alpha Lambda Delta, Omicron Nu. Address: 4977 Battery Ln Bethesda MD 20014

JONES, EDWARD ELLSWORTH, psychology educator; b. Buffalo, Aug. 11, 1926; s. Edward Safford and Frances Christine (Jeffery) J.; m. Virginia Sweetnam, Apr. 5, 1947; children: Sarah E., Caroline A., Todd E., Amelia G., Jason L., Janet P. A.B., Harvard U., 1949, Ph.D., 1953. Mem. faculty Duke U., 1953-77, prof. psychology, 1961-77, chmn. dept., 1970-73; Stuart prof. psychology Princeton U., 1977—. Author: Ingratiation, 1964, (with H.B. Gerard) Foundations of Social Psychology, 1967, (with others) Attribution, 1972, Social Stigma, 1984; editor: Jour. Personality, 1954-62; contbr. articles to profl. jours. Served with AUS, 1944-47. NSF research grantee, 1956—; NIMH spl. fellow, 1963-64; recipient Distinguished Sci. Contbn. award Am. Psychol. Assn., 1977; Fellow Center for Advanced Study in Behavioral Scis., Stanford, Calif., 1963-64, 80-81. Fellow Am. Psychol. Assn., Am. Acad. Arts and Scis. Home: 32 Mason Dr Princeton NJ 08540 Office: Princeton U Princeton NJ 08544

JONES, EDWARD MAGRUDER, TV producer-writer, correspondent; b. Orlando, Fla., Feb. 25, 1928; m. Lilian Marie Jones. Reporter, Tokyo edit. Pacific Stars and Stripes, 1946; copy-boy N.Y. Times, 1947-48; freelance writer, 1949-50; from mail boy to producer CBS, 1952-62. Prodns. including CBS Reports; producer news and pub. affairs, WABC-TV, 1963-66; prodns. including New York, New York; also specials; producer-writer-dir., ABC News, 1966-67, ABC News, Africa, Nurses: Crisis in Medicine, Westinghouse Broadcasting Co.; co-producer, dir.: One Nation, Indivisible, 1968; producer, writer, director: Night Call for Television Radio Film Commn, United Meth. Ch., 1968; producer, writer, editor news and pub. affairs spls., Nat. Ednl. TV, 1969-70; producer, writer, corr. news and pub. affairs spls. and series, WHYY-TV, 1971; exec. producer, UNTV, N.Y.C., 1972-80; media cons., freelance prodn. and writing, Hollywood, Fla., 1981—. Served with the AUS, 1945-47; Served with the AFUS, 1951. Recipient Brotherhood award NCCJ, 196l, 1969; award Overseas Press Club, 1962; Freedoms Found. award, 1968, 69; Emmy award, 1964, 66, 1968; Peabody award, 1968, 1969; Albert J. Lasker Med. Journalism award, 1966; TV Pub. Service award Sigma Delta Chi, 1966. Mem. Am. Writers Guild East, Nat. Radio and TV News Dirs. Assn. Address: PO Box 6855 Hollywood FL 33081

JONES, EDWARD MARSHALL, automotive parts distbg. co. exec.; b. Decatur, Ga., Feb. 3, 1926; S. Henry L. and Stella (Moessner) J.; m. Shirlie McCleary, June 13, 1947; children—Glenn Steven, Gary Lynn, Michael Alan. Student, Ga. Inst. Tech., 1946-48, Ga. State Coll., 1948-49. With Genuine Parts Co., Atlanta and Jacksonville, Fla., 1947—, asst. to pres., 1961-65, treas., 1965—, v.p. ops., 1967-79, sr. v.p. ops., 1979-81, group v.p., 1981—. Active United Way. Served with USAAF, 1944-45. Lutheran. Home: 4170 Thunderbird Dr Marietta GA 30067 Office: 2999 Circle 75 Pkwy Atlanta GA 30339

JONES, EDWARD POWIS, artist; b. N.Y.C., Jan. 8, 1919; s. Edward Powis and Julia (Zabriskie) J.; m. Anne Keating, May 25, 1945; children: Elizabeth Jones White, Edward Powis, Peter C. Student, Harvard U., 1936-37. Author: Images of Torment, 1980; One-man exhbns. include, Bard Coll., 1948, Kraushaar Galleries, 1949, 53, New Gallery, N.Y.C., 1955, 57, 58, Pomfret Sch., 1957, Interfaith Center, N.Y.C., 1962, Norfolk Mus. Arts and Scis., 1966, 1st Nat. City Bank, Paris, 1972, World Trade Center, 1975, Vassar Coll. Art Gallery, Poughkeepsie, N.Y., 1978, Ringwood Manor, N.J., 1980, Inst. Art and Urban Resources, Long Island City, one-man exhbns. include, Books & Co., N.Y.C., 1983, Meads Art Gallery, Amherst Coll.; represented in permanent collections, Met. Mus. Art, N.Y.C., Mus. Modern Art, N.Y.C., Library Congress, Washington, Brandeis U., Phila. Mus. Art, Bklyn. Mus., others. Fellow Pierpont Morgan Library, chmn. council of fellows, 1972-73. Served with C.E. U.S. Army, 1941-45. Mem. Artists Equity Assn. Roman Catholic. Clubs: Union, Grolier. Home: 925 Park Ave New York NY 10028

JONES, EDWARD WITKER, bishop; b. Toledo, Mar. 25, 1929; s. Mason Beach and Gertrude (Witker) J.; m. Anne Shelburne, July 13, 1963; children: Martha, Caroline, David. B.A., William Coll., 1951; B.D., Va. Theol. Sem., 1954, D.D., 1978. Ordained to ministry Episcopal Ch., 1954; rector Christ Ch., Oberlin, Ohio, 1957-68; exec. asst. to bishop and planning officer Diocese of Ohio, Cleve., 1968-71; rector St. James' Ch., Lancaster, Pa., 1971-77; bishop Episc. Diocese of Indpls., 1977—; lectr. homiletics, 1963-67. Bd. dirs. Ohio Chpt. ACLU, 1964-67, Loraine County Child Welfare Dept., Ohio, 1964-68, Lancaster Tomorrow, 1975-77, Indpls. United Way, 1978—, Indpls. Urban League, 1982—; bd. visitors DePauw U., 1982—. Mem. Urban Bishops Coalition. Democrat. Home: 5008 Derby Ln Indianapolis IN 46226 Office: The Episcopal Ch 1100 W 42d St Indianapolis IN 46208

JONES, EDWIN HOWARD, JR., retired paper executive; b. Waterbury, Conn., July 21, 1917; s. Edwin Howard and Ruth (Angrave) J.; m. Evelyn Mae Rowe, Aug. 28, 1948; children: Edwin Howard, Stephen Rowe, Bruce Angrave, Sherrill Chapman. A.B., Yale U., 1939; M.B.A., Harvard U., 1941. With St. Regis Paper Co., N.Y.C., 1946-82, adminstrv. asst. to v.p., 1955-59, gen. sales mgr. Kraft div., 1960-61, exec. asst. to v.p., chief adminstrv. officer, 1962-68, v.p., gen. mgr. printing paper div., 1968-72, v.p. internat. div., 1972-74, exec. v.p. fin. and adminstrn., 1974-79, vice chmn., chief fin. officer, dir. internat. ops., 1979-82, chmn. exec. com., 1981-82; chmn. bd. Flakt, Inc., Gotaverken Energy Systems, Inc. Mem. Rep. Town Meeting, Darien, Conn., 1957-64, chmn. fin. com., 1962-64; mem. Bd. Edn., Darien, 1964-70, chmn., 1968-70. Served with USNR, 1941-46; Atlantic, European, Far Eastern theatres; comdr. Res. ret. Methodist. Clubs: Masons, Wee Burn Country. Home: 12 Harbor Rd Darien CT 06820 Office: 301 Perimeter Center North Suite 170 Atlanta GA 30346

JONES, EDWIN LEE, JR., construction company executive; b. Charlotte, N.C., May 6, 1921; s. Edwin Lee and Annabel (Lambeth) J.; m. Lucille Finch, Oct. 16, 1943; children: Edwin Lee, Annabel Lambeth Jones Link, Sam Finch, John Wesley, David Gilchrist. Student, U.S. Mil. Acad., 1940-41; B.C.E., Duke U., 1948. With J.A. Jones Constrn. Co., Charlotte, 1948—, pres., 1960-78, pres., chmn., 1978—; dir. First Union Nat. Bank, William L. Crow Constrn. Co., Charles H. Tompkins Co., First Union Corp. Bd. dirs. N.C. Citizens for Bus. and Industry, Univ. Research Park, Charlotte YMCA; trustee emeritus Duke U., 1970-81; trustee Western N.C. Super Annuate Endowment Fund, Queens Coll.; mem. N.C. Gov.'s Council on Arts and Humanities. Served to 1st lt. USMC, 1942-46. Mem. Charlotte C. of C. (dir.), Beavers, Moles, Chi Epsilon, Omicron Delta Kappa, Pi Mu Epsilon, Pi Kappa Phi. Home: 2633/3D Richardson Dr Charlotte NC 28211 Office: 6060 St Albans St Charlotte NC 28287

JONES, EDWIN MICHAEL, lawyer, insurance company executive; b. Bridgeport, Conn., May 15, 1916; s. Edward Henry and Mary Ellen (Carroll) J.; m. Alberta Irene Conway, Aug. 21, 1948; children: Michelle, Karen, Alberta, Edwin, Marianne. B.A., Yale U., 1937; LL.B., NYU, 1942, LL.M. in Taxation, 1951. Bar: N.Y. 1943, Conn. 1947, U.S. Supreme Ct. 1959. Security analyst Goodbody & Co., N.Y.C., 1937-42; economist War Prodn. Bd., Washington, 1942-43; assoc. firm Root, Ballantine, Harlan, Bushby & Palmer, N.Y.C., 1946-48; sole practice, N.Y.C., 1948-52; atty., officer N.Y. Life Ins. Co., N.Y.C., 1952-72; ptnr. firm Shea & Gould, N.Y.C., 1972-81, Lane & Mittendorf, 1981-82; exec. dir. Pension Benefit Guaranty Corp., Washington, 1982—; pres. Talisman Corp., N.Y.C., 1952—, dir.; pres., trustee Nat. Ctr. for Automated Info. Retrieval, N.Y.C., 1972-83. Contbr. articles to profl. jours. Mem. Adv. Council of Non-Pub. Sch. Secular Edn., Conn., 1971-72; pres. Fairfield (Conn.) Found. of Diocese of Bridgeport, 1973—. Served to maj. USAAF, 1943-46. Decorated Army Commendation medal. Mem. ABA (chmn. ins. com. 1960-82, chmn. employee benefits com. of tax sect. 1976-82), N.Y. State Bar Assn. (chmn. tax sect. 1966-6 7), Assn. Bar City N.Y., Assn. Life Ins. Counsel. Roman Catholic. Clubs: Yale (N.Y.C.); Belle Haven Yacht (Greewich, Conn.) (vice commodore, dir. 1970-75). Home: 197 Otter Rock Dr Greenwich CT 06830 Office: Pension Benefit Guaranty Corp 2020 K St NW Washington DC 20006

JONES, EDWIN S., retired banker; b. St. Louis, Dec. 16, 1915; s. C. Norman and Josephine (Calhoun) J.; m. Hope DePew, Nov. 3O, 1946; children: Stephen C., Douglas D., Hope F. Student, Yale, 1934-36, U. Wis., 1948. With Ely & Walker, Inc., St. Louis, 1936-41; with 1st Nat. Bank St. Louis, 1946—, exec. v.p., 1960-68, pres., 1968-70, chmn. bd., 1970-76, chmn. exec. com., 1976—, also dir.; pres. First Union Bancorp., 1971-73, chmn., pres., 1973-78, chmn. exec. com., 1978—; dir. Angelica Corp., Anheuser-Busch, Inc., Gen. Am. Life Ins. Co., Jefferson-Smurfit Corp., INTERCO, Inc., McDonnell-Douglas Corp., Union Electric Co., Automobile Club Mo. Trustee Washington U., St. Louis, St. Louis council Boy Scouts Am., St. Louis YMCA; bd. dirs. Mcpl. Theatre Assn. Served to capt. USAAF, 1941-46. Decorated D.F.C., Air medal. Clubs: Noonday, St. Louis Country, Log Cabin (St. Louis); Dardenne Shooting, Round Table. Home and Office: 765 Cella Rd Saint Louis MO 63124

JONES, EIDDON LLOYD, real estate co. exec.; b. Utica, N.Y., Oct. 25, 1904; s. David and Jane (Lloyd) J.; m. Ruth A Davies, Apr. 23, 1932 (dec. Apr. 1964); 1 son, Robert E; m. Alice Liddy, Aug. 30, 1965. Student pub. schs., Utica. With Marine Midland Trust Co. of Mohawk Valley (formerly 1st Bank and Trust Co.), Utica, 1923—, v.p., 1950-62, exec. v.p., 1962-64, pres., chmn. bd., 1964-68, chmn. bd., chief exec. officer, 1968-69, also dir., until 1971; now mem. adv. com.; exec. council Marine Midland Bank, 1964-69; v.p., adminstr. shopping centers Cale Devel. Corp., 1971-81; owner real estate co., Utica, 1981—. Asst. treas. Greater Utica Community Chest, 1955, treas., 1956, campaign mgr., 1957—, pres., 1959—; chmn. Utica Cerebral Palsy and Handicappped Children's Assn., 1950—; campaign chmn. United Fund Campaign, 1957; mem. planning bd. City of Utica, 1950-74; trustee St. Luke's Meml. Hosp., Utica Coll. Found., 1964-74; trustee emeritus Utica Coll. Found., 1974—; bd. dirs. Faxton, Sunset, St. Luke's Nursing Home & Health Related Facility, 1974—, Boys Club Utica, 1965—. Mem. N.Y. State Bankers Assn. (chmn group IV 1955-56), Greater Utica C. of C. (pres. 1967-69). Home and office: 143 Eastwood Ave Utica NY 13501

JONES, ELMER RUTLEDGE, journal executive; b. Balt., Aug. 18, 1921; s. Elmer O. and Elizabeth Virginia (Meyers) J.; m. Edith M. Averell, Feb. 8, 1948; 1 son, Christopher Warren. B.A. in Journalism, U. So. Cal., 1951. Circulation mgr. Annals of Internal Medicine; publ. Am. Coll. Physicians, Phila., 1957-63, conv. mgr. for assn., 1963-73, publs. mgr. for assn., 1973-82; dir. bus. dept. Annals Internal Medicine, 1983—; partner Sugarbush Antiques, Strasburg, Pa., 1972—. Served with USAAF, 1942-45. Home: 4205 Pine St Philadelphia PA 19104 also RD 1 May Post Office Rd Strasburg PA 17579 Office: 4200 Pine St Philadelphia PA 19104

JONES, ELVIN RAY, drummer; b. Pontiac, Mich., Sept. 9, 1927. Drummer with, John Coltrane; now leader own jazz group, 1966—; film appearance Zachariah, 1971; composer: songs Elvin's Guitar Blues, Three Card Molly, Keiko's Birthday March; also several rec. albums. Winner Downbeat Critics Poll, 1966-77, Downbeat Readers Poll, 1966, 68, 69, 77, 78. Office: care PAUSA Rees PO Box 10069 Glendale CA 91202 *

JONES, EMILY STRANGE, educational film consultant; b. Rochester, N.Y., June 24, 1919; d. Leonard Warburton and Helen (Stone) J. A.B., Vassar Coll., 1940. Asst. in children's room N.Y. Pub. Library, 1941-43; editorial asst. Trained Nurse mag., 1943-44; film prodn. asst. Emerson Yorke Studio, 1944-46; adminstrv. dir. Ednl. Film Library Assn., Inc., N.Y.C., 1946-69; ednl. film cons., 1969—; pres. Acorn Films, Inc., N.Y.C.; exec. dir. Am. Film Festival, 1959-69; treas., bd. dirs. Ednl. Media Council, 1965-68; chmn. bd. dirs. Dance Films, Inc., 1966-69, 80—; sec. bd. dirs. Internat. Film Found., 1970—; mem. internat. jury Teheran Festival Films for Children, 1970; mem. adv. com. N.Y. Council on Arts, 1969-72; bd. dirs. N.Y. Film Council, 1978—; adj. prof. film dept. C.W. Post Ctr., L.I. U., 1983—. Author: (with Jessie Kitching) Index to Selected Film Lists, 1950, Films and People, 1951, Manual on Film Evaluation, 1968, rev. edit., 1975; editor: Sightlines Mag., 1966-69, College Film Library Collection; supervising editor: Film Evaluation Guide; contbr. articles to mags. Girl Scout leader, N.Y.C., 1944-49; corr. sec. N.Y. chpt. Am. Gloxinia and Gesneriad Soc., 1983—. Mem. Council Internat. Non-Theatrical Events (dir. 1959-75, hon. life dir. 1975—), N.Y.C. Audubon Soc. (pres. 1979-81, dir. 1981-83). Address: 72-61 113th St Forest Hills New York NY 11375

JONES, ERNEST CARL, finance educator; b. Atlanta, La., Feb. 17, 1921; s. Rufus T. and Nena (Franks) J.; m. Helen L. Worsham, Dec. 25, 1944; children: Kenneth Carl, Carol Annette. B.S., Southwestern La. Inst., 1941; M.S., La. State U., 1947, Ph.D., 1962. Grad. research asst. agrl. econs. La. State U., 1945-47; mem. faculty dept. econs. La. Tech. U., Ruston, 1947-74, prof. econs., 1962-74, head dept. econs. and fin., 1964-74; head dept. fin. Miss. State U., 1974—; cons. Gulf South Research Inst., 1966, La. Revenue Dept., 1970-71. Author: Lincoln Parish, Louisiana, 1939-57, 1957, An Economic Appraisal of Public Revenues and Expenditures in Lincoln Parish, Louisiana, 1962, A Severance Damage Study on Interstate System, Louisiana, 1967, Louisiana's Agriculture: Some Observations, 1973, Contribution and Benefits from Louisiana's Fiscal Process, By Parish, Fiscal Year, 1969, Financing Agricultural Firms in Mississippi, 1976, Agricultural Credit Agencies in Mississippi, 1976. Served with U.S. Army, 1942-45. Mem. So. Econs. Assn., Southwestern Fedn. Adminstrv. Disciplines, Fin. Mgmt. Assn., La. Tchrs. Assn. (unit pres. 1963-64), Beta Gamma Sigma, Delta Sigma Pi, Omicron Delta Epsilon, Omicron Delta Kappa. Clubs: Lions (chmn. edn. com. 1967-68, 1st v.p. 1968), Lions (pres. 1969); Kiwanis (Starkville, Miss.); Nat. Block and Bridle (hon.). Home: 36 Colonial Circle Starkville MS 39759 Office: Drawer DF Mississippi State MS 39762

JONES, ERNEST OLIN, educator, radiation physicist; b. Atlanta, Feb. 1, 1923; s. Ernest and Annie Jane (Bryan) J.; m. Dorothy Irene Berg, May 20, 1946; children: Michael Bruce, Jacquelyn Ann (Mrs. Robert H. Hanks). B.A., Emory U., 1948, M.A. (Research Corp. fellow), 1949; M.S., U.S. Naval Postgrad. Sch., 1959; Ph.D., N.C. State U., 1964. Diplomate: radiol. physics Am. Bd. Radiology, 1975. Commd. 2d lt. U.S. Army, 1950, advanced through grades to lt. col., 1965; dep. dir. div. nuclear medicine WRAIR, 1964-67, dir. div. biometrics, 1967-68; ret., 1968; asso. prof. radiology U. Nebr., Omaha, 1968-72, prof., 1972—; Cons. in field. Decorated Legion of Merit. Mem. Am. Assn. Phys. Medicine (pres. Mo. River Valley chpt. 1972-73), Midlands Soc. Therapeutic Radiologists (pres. 1983-84), Nebr. Radiol. Soc., Assn. Mil. Surgeons, Am. Coll. Nuclear Physicians, Am. Coll. Radiology. Research minority carrier lifetimes in silicon radiation detectors, 1961-64, dosimetry of neutrons in modified research reactor, 1964-67. Home: 12823 Jones St Omaha NE 68154

JONES, EUINE FAY, architect, educator; b. Pine Bluff, Ark., Jan. 31, 1921; s. Euine Fay and Candie Louise (Alston) J.; m. Mary Elizabeth Knox, Jan. 6, 1943; children: Janis Fay, Jean Cameron. B.Arch., U. Ark., 1950; M.Arch., Rice U., 1951. Asst. prof. architecture U. Okla., 1951-53; Frank Lloyd Wright Taliesin fellow, 1953; prof. architecture U. Ark., 1953—, chmn. dept., 1966-74, dean, 1974-76; pvt. practice architecture, 1953—; Rome Prize fellow in architecture and design, 1981; Mem. Nat. Council Archtl. Registration Bds., Ark. Bd. Architects. Served as lt., naval aviator USNR, 1942-45. Recipient nat. awards for archtl. design. Fellow AIA; mem. Assn. Collegiate Schs. Architecture, Soc. Archtl. Historians. Home: 1330 N Hillcrest St Fayetteville AR 72701

JONES, FERDINAND TAYLOR, JR., psychologist, educator; b. N.Y.C., May 15, 1932; s. Ferdinand Taylor and Esther (Haggie) J.; m. Antonina Laub, Sept. 26, 1953 (div. Mar. 1967); children: Joanne Esther, Terrie Lynn; m. Myra Jean Rogers, Nov. 25, 1967. A.B., Drew U., 1953; Ph.D., U. Vienna, Austria, 1959. Staff psychologist Riverside Hosp., Bronx, N.Y., 1959-62; chief psychologist Westchester County Community Mental Hosp. Bd., White Plains, N.Y., 1962-67; tng. cons. Lincoln Hosp. Mental Health Services, Bronx, 1967-69; tchr. psychology, black social change Sarah Lawrence Coll., Bronxville, N.Y., 1968-72; prof. psychology, dir. psychol. services Brown U., Providence, 1972—; Cons. St. Peter's Head Start, Yonkers, N.Y., 1967-71, Bronx State Hosp., 1969-72. Served with AUS, 1953-56. Mem. Am. Psychol. Assn., Eastern Psychol. Assn., Westchester

County Psychol. Assn. (past pres.), Assn. Black Psychologists, Soc. Psychol. Study Social Issues. Developed (with Myron W. Harris) small group method for reduction of distance and dissonance in interracial communication. Home: 30 Langham Rd Providence RI 02906 *Dedicated to channeling a lifelong fascination with people into skilled understanding of human behavior and the alleviation of problems in human functioning.*

JONES, FRANCES FOLLIN, mus. curator; b. N.Y.C., Sept. 8, 1913; d. T. Carlyle and Rosalie (Warner) J. A.B., Bryn Mawr Coll., 1934, M.A., 1936, Ph.D., 1952; postgrad., Am. Sch. Classical Studies, Athens, Greece, 1937-38. Research asst. Inst. for Advanced Study, Princeton, 1939-46; sec., asst. curator classical art Art Mus., Princeton, N.J., 1943-46, asst. to dir., curator classical art, 1946-65, chief curator, curator classical art, 1965-71, curator of collections, 1971—. Contbr. articles to profl. jours.; Author: Ancient Art in the Art Museum, 1960. Mem. Museums Council N.J. (past chmn.), Archaeol. Inst. Am., Am. Assn. Museums, Rei Cretariae Romanae Fautores. Home: 1041 Kingston Rd Princton NJ 08540 Office: Art Museum Princeton U Princeton NJ 08544

JONES, FRANK CATER, lawyer; b. Macon, Ga., June 19, 1925; s. Charles Baxter and Carolyn (Cater) J.; m. Annie Gantt Anderson, Mar. 31, 1951; children: Eugenia Anderson Henderson, Annie Gantt Rossetti, Carolyn Cater, Frank Cater. B.B.A., Emory U., 1947; LL.B., Mercer U., 1950. Bar: Ga. bar 1950. Practiced in, Macon, 1952-77; mem. firm Jones, Cork, Miller & Benton (and predecessor), 1952-77, King & Spalding, Atlanta, 1977—; dir. Bibb Co., So. Trust Corp. Pres. United Givers Fund Macon-Bibb County, 1965; chmn. bd. trustees Wesleyan Coll., Macon; vice chmn. bd. sponsors Atlanta Symphony Orch. League; chmn. Great Park Authority, State of Ga., Ga. Pub. Telecommunications Commn. Served to lt. USNR, 1943-46. Fellow Am. Bar Found., Am. Coll. Trial Lawyers (chmn. Ga. state com.); mem. ABA (ho. of dels. 1972—), Macon Bar Assn. (pres. 1954), Ga. Bar Assn. (pres. young lawyers assn. 1956-57), State Bar Ga. (pres. 1968-69), Greater Macon C. of C. (pres. 1965). Home: 105 W Paces Ferry Rd NW Atlanta GA 30305 Office: 2500 Trust Co Tower Atlanta GA 30303

JONES, FRANK CHARLES, insurance company executive; b. Binghamton, N.Y., Mar. 11, 1941; s. George Hiles and Florence (Harris) J.; m. Laura Anne Benedict, July 29, 1967; children: Laura, Caldwell. B.A., U. of South, Sewanee, Tenn., 1962; postgrad., MIT, 1962-63; M.A., U. Mich., 1964. Various positions Liberty Nat. Life Ins. Co., Birmingham, Ala., 1963-74, v.p., 1974-82; exec. v.p. Globe Life & Accident Ins. Co., Oklahoma City, 1982, pres., chief exec. officer, 1982—. Fellow Soc. Actuaries; mem. Am. Acad. Actuaries. Republican. Episcopalian. Office: Globe Life & Accident Ins Co 120 Robert S Kerr Ave Oklahoma City OK 73184

JONES, FRANK EDWARD, educator; b. Montreal, Que., Can., Oct. 28, 1917; s. Richard Thomas and Victoria Lemire (Hughes) J.; m. Jean E. McEachran, Sept. 14, 1946; children: David, Dilys. Ph.D. in Sociology, Harvard U., 1954. Chief research div. Can. Citizenship Br., Dept. Citizenship and Immigration, Ont., 1953-55; asst. prof. sociology McMaster U., 1955-59, chmn. dept., 1959-64, 82—, asso. prof., 1959-64, prof., 1964—, chmn. degree program in labor studies, 1981—; vis. prof. U. B.C., summers 1957-67, Australian Nat. U., 1961, 71, McGill U., 1966-67. Author: An Introduction to Sociology, 1961, (with others) Canadian Society Sociological Persectives, 1961, 64, 68, 70, 71, 72; editor: Canadian Rev. Sociology and Anthropology, 1968-73; contbr. articles to profl. jours. Served with Royal Can. Navy, 1940-45. Home: 19 Brentwood Dr Dundas ON Canada L9H 3N2

JONES, FRANK HENRY, railroad executive; b. Detroit, Nov. 13, 1927; s. Frank and Hanna (Cameron) J.; m. Norma Routon, Oct. 8, 1947; children: Janice, Robert, Laura, Jeffrey,James. A.A., Walsh Inst., 1949. Various mgmt. positions N.Y. Central, Detroit, Chgo., Cleve., 1951-71, terminal supt., Cleve., 1970-71; div. supt. Pitts. Penn Central R.R., 1971-73; div. supt. N.J. div. Penn. Central R.R., N.Y.C., 1973-76; asst. gen. mgr. CONRAIL-Atlantic Region, Newark, 1976; pres., chief exec. officer Colo. & Wyoming R.R. Co., Pueblo, Colo., 1976-79; v.p. ops. Isringhausen,Inc., Jerseyville, Ill., 1979; gen. mgr., chief exec. officer Alaska R.R., Anchorage, 1980—; mem. dist. export council Dept. Commerce, Anchorage, 1981—; staff cons. Resource Devel. Council, Anchorage; bd. dirs. Alaska-Korea Bus. Council, Anchorage, 1983—. Bd. dirs. ARC, Anchorage, 1982-83. Recipient Silver medal Sec. Transp., 1981. Mem. Commonwealth North, Anchorage C. of C. Lodge: Masons. Office: Alaska RR Pouch 7-2111 419 W 1st Ave Anchorage AK 99510

JONES, FRANK WILLIAM, emeritus English language educator; b. Liverpool, Eng., Jan. 5, 1915; came to U.S., 1939, naturalized, 1943; s. Reginald Foy and Anna Carolina (Zartmann) J.; m. Margaret Rose Puchner, 1943 (div. 1957); children: Liza Carolyn, Ann Rosalind; m. Dorothy Stearns, 1958 (div. 1965); m. Sumie Amikura, May 27, 1966 (div. 1979); 1 dau., Laura Frances; m. Gloria Bien, 1979. B.A., U. Man., Can., 1934, Oxford (Eng.) U., 1937, M.A., 1955; Ph.D., U. Wis., 1941. Instr. classics Yale, 1942-43, 46; instr. humanities Coll. of U. Chgo., 1946-48; mem. faculty lit. and humanities Reed Coll., 1948-54, prof., 1952-54; asso. prof. U. Wash., Seattle, 1955-70, prof. English and comparative lit., 1970-78, prof. emeritus, 1978—; Chmn. region XIV Woodrow Wilson Nat. Fellowship Found., 1966. Translator: Saint Joan of the Stockyards, 1956, 70, Drums in the Night, 1966, The Trial of Lucullus, 1972, (Bertolt Brecht), The Suppliant Women (Euripides), 1957, (with S. Mpondo) Hammer Blows and other Writings (David Diop), 1973; Acting asst. editor: Liverpool (Eng.) Daily Post, 1937-38; co-editor: (with Arthur Blair) Diogenes, Madison, Wis., 1939-41; assoc. editor: Poetry Northwest, Seattle, 1963-66. Served with AUS, 1943-45. Rhodes scholar, 1934; Ford Found. Faculty fellow, 1955; recipient Nat. Book award, 1971. Mem. Modern Lang. Assn., Philol. Assn. Pacific Coast, Nat. Audubon Soc., Am. Comparative Lit. Assn., Am. Assns. Rhodes Scholars, Can. Assn. Rhodes Scholars, P.E.N. Am. Center. Home: 418 E Loretta Pl Apt 701 Seattle WA 98102

JONES, FRANK WYMAN, company executive, mechanical engineer; b. Ironton, Ohio, Jan. 20, 1940; s. Kylius and Kathleen (McDonald) J.; m. Margaret Kwitek, Sept. 2, 1962; children: Kelly, Connie, Katie, Colleen, Carolyn. B.S.M.E., U. Cin., 1963; M.B.A., Ind. U., 1965. V.p., gen. mgr. G & L Machine Tool Div., Fond du Lac, Wis., 1976-80; exec. v.p. Giddings & Lewis Inc., Fond du Lac, Wis., 1980-82, pres., chief exec. officer, 1982—; dir. 1st Wis. Bank, Fond du Lac, Modine, Racine, Wis. Mem. Am. Mgmt. Assn., Nat. Mgmt. Assn. Republican. Roman Catholic. Club: South Hills (Fond du Lac). Home: Brookhaven Beach Fond du Lac WI 54935 Office: Giddings & Lewis Inc Doty St Fond du Lac WI 54935

JONES, FRANKLIN ROSS, educator; b. Charlotte, N.C., Jan. 3, 1921; s. William Morton and Olive Ruth (Moser) J.; (div.)children: Franklin Ross, C. Morton, Susan Noel. A.B., Lenoir Rhyne Coll., 1941; M.A., U. N.C., 1951; D.Ed., Duke, 1960. Tchr. schs., N.C., 1944-48; prin. Jr. High Sch., Henderson, N.C., 1948-54; dist. sch. prin., Wake County, N.C., 1954-56; dist. supt. Roxboro (N.C.) schs., 1956-58; chmn. dept. edn. Randolph-Macon Coll., Ashland, Va., 1959-64; dean Sch. Edn. Old Dominion U., 1964-69; founder Child Study Center, 1965, distinguished prof., 1969—, social founds. program leader, 1973-77, doctoral program liaison rep., 1974-77, faculty chmn., 1981—; vis. research scholar Duke, 1967; cons. HEW, State Sch. Systems and Colls.; lectr. in field. Mem. com. White House Conf. Children and Youth, 1968-71, Eastern regional chmn., 1968-71; mem. Va. Gov.'s Com. Implementation, 1971-73. Author: Psychology of Human Development, 1969, 2d edit., 1984, Handbook on Testing, 1972, Understanding the Middlescent Years, 1978, Theory of Adult Development, 1980, Radio series, WTAR, Norfolk, 1973-75. Mem. Norfolk Urban Coalition, 1969-73; chmn. March of Dimes, Person County, N.C., 1956-57; Adv. bd. Tidewater Rehab. Center, 1967-69; chmn. Hull Scholarship Fund, 1983—; univ. chmn. United Fund, 1982, 84. Named Eminent Prof. Old Domion U., 1973. Mem. Va. Assn. U. Profs. (dir. 1962-64), South Atlantic Philosophy Edn. Soc. (pres. 1966-69, dir. 1969—), Va. Assn. Research in Edn. (distinguished research awards 1972, 73, 78), Southeast Psychol. Assn., N.C. Edn. Assn. (pres. North Central chpt. 1951, pres. North Central Prins. 1956), Eastern Ednl. Research Assn., Nat. Urban Edn. Assn., Alpha Tau Kappa, Kappa Delta Pi, Phi Delta Kappa, Phi Kappa Phi, Pi Gamma Mu (sec. 1962-64). Clubs: Rotarian, Lion.; Harbor (Norfolk). Home: 1026 Manchester Ave Norfolk VA 23508

JONES, FRED EUGENE, state judge; b. Detroit, Aug. 22, 1926; s. Fred McKinley and Thelma (Riddell) J.; m. Colleen F. Cranmer, July 19, 1948; children: Jennifer Lynn, Daniel Frederick, Matthew Charles, Barbara Ellen. Student, Miami U., Oxford, Ohio, 1944-45, Ohio State U., 1946-48; LL.B., Salmon P. Chase Coll. Law, 1951. Bar: Ohio 1951. Practiced law, Lebanon, pros. atty., Warren County, 1957-61; mem. Young & Jones, 1954-79, Jones, Kaufman & Jones, 1979-82; judge 12th Dist. Ohio Ct. Appeals, 1982—. Chmn. Warren County Republicans, 1962-68; mem. Warren County Bd. Elections, 1962-70; state committeeman Ohio 24th Dist., 1966-70; del. Rep. Nat. Conv., 1964-68; Rep. candidate for Congress, 1970. Served with AUS, 1944-45. Fellow Am. Coll. Trial Lawyers. Home: 2206 Drake Rd Lebanon OH 45036 Office: One City Centre Middletown OH 45042

JONES, GALEN EVERTS, microbiologist, educator; b. Milw., Sept. 9, 1928; s. Galen and Grace (Everts) J.; m. Edith Agnes Boehme, July 17, 1954; children: Galen Randolph, Gwenith Grace, Christopher Thomas. A.B., Dartmouth Coll., 1950; M.A., Williams Coll., 1952; Ph.D., Rutgers U., 1956. With Scripps Inst. Oceanography, U. Calif., La Jolla, 1955-63, asst. research microbiologist, 1957-63; asso. prof. biology Boston U., 1963-66; prof. microbiology U. N.H., Durham, 1966—, chmn. dept., 1975-80; dir. Jackson Estuarine Lab., 1966-72, 83—; vis. prof. U. Liverpool, Eng., 1972-73, Scripps Inst. Oceanographic, U. Calif., La Jolla, 1981; Mem. Pres.'s Santa Barbara Oil Spill Panel, 1969; mem. adv. com. to biol. oceanography NSF, 1971-72, 74-75; mem. water ecosystems adv. com. Inst. of Ecology to Nat. Commn. on Water Quality, 1974-77; mem. adv. com. for ocean scis. NSF, 1979-80. Contbr. articles to profl. jours. Fellow Am. Acad. Microbiology, AAAS; mem. Am. Inst. Biol. Sci., Soc. Gen. Microbiology, Estuarine Research Found., Western Soc. Naturalists, Geochem. Soc., Am. Soc. Microbiology, Am. Soc. Limnology and Oceanography, Sigma Xi. Home: 22 Faculty Rd Durham NH 03824 *In our brief life on this planet, our striving for understanding and the success it brings leads to the conviction that we are part of a masterful continuity and evolution.*

JONES, GARDNER MONORE, accounting and finance educator; b. Hesperia, Mich., Dec. 4, 1918. B.B.A., U. Mich., 1949, M.B.A., 1950; Ph.D., La. State U., 1956. C.P.A., La. Instr. La. State U., 1950-56; asst. prof. acctg. Mich. State U., 1956-59, assoc. prof., 1959-62, prof., 1962—, chmn. dept. accountcy and fin., 1971-75, assoc. dean, 1976-83; vis. prof. U. Colo., 1966, Instituto Post-Universitario por lo Studio Del Organizazione Aziendale, Torino, Italy, 1963. Author: Electronics in Business, 1959. Served with U.S. Army, 1942-45. Mem. Am. Inst. C.P.A.s, Mich. Assn. C.P.A.s, Am. Acctg. Assn., Nat. Assn. Accts. Office: Grad Sch Bus Adminstrn Mich State U East Lansing MI 48824

JONES, GARTH NELSON, educator; b. Salt Lake City, Feb. 25, 1925; s. Harry H. and Sophronia Dubois (Nelson) J.; m. Verda Marie Clegg, Sept. 29, 1950; children: Edward Hood, Garth Kevin, Drew Luke. B.S., Utah State U., 1947; M.S., U. Utah, 1948, Ph.D., 1954. Mem. faculty Brigham Young U., Provo, Utah, 1953-56; with AID, Indonesia, 1957-61, Pakistan, 1967-69; mem. faculty U. So. Calif., 1961-67; sr. scholar East-West Center, U. Hawaii, 1969-70; mem. faculty Colo. State U., 1970-72; with UN, 1972-73; mem. faculty U. Alaska, Anchorage, 1973—, former dean Sch. Bus. and Public Adminstrn.; vice chmn. Alaska Council Edn.; cons. to govt. and industry. Contbr. articles to profl. jours. Chmn. Anchorage Mayor's Ad Hoc Govtl. Rev. Bd., Anchorage Urban Obs. Fulbright-Hayes scholar, Taiwan, 1982. Mormon. Office: 3221 Providence Dr Anchorage AK 99504

JONES, GARY LELAND, government official; b. Jackson, Mich., May 6, 1944; s. Jack B. and Charlotte T. J.; m. Barbara Crippen, Dec. 30, 1967; children: Julie Kay, Gary Leland. A.B., Albion Coll., 1966; M.A., Mich. State U., 1968, Ph.D., 1975. Admissions officer Albion (Mich.) Coll., 1967-70; exec. asst. to U.S. Senator Robert P. Griffin, Washington, 1970-73; v.p. Am. Enterprise Inst., Washington, 1973-79; dir. research and policy coordination Regan for Pres. Campaign, Washington, 1979-80; v.p. MacArthur Found., Chgo., 1980-81; dep. under-sec. U.S. Dept. Edn., Washington, 1981-82, under-sec., 1982—. Mem. vis. com. Gerald R. Ford Inst. Pub. Service, Albion Coll.; mem. vis. com. student affairs Case Western Res. U., Cleve.; mem. Fairfax (Va.) County Sch. Bd., 1977-81. Recipient Albion Coll. Disting. Alumni award, 1979. Methodist. Home: 5265 O'Faly Rd Fairfax VA 22030 Office: US Dept Education 400 Maryland Ave SW Washington DC 20202

JONES, GEORGE, country music singer, songwriter; b. Saratoga, Tex., Sept. 12, 1931; s. George Washington and Clara J.; m. Tammy Wynette, 1968 (div. 1975); m. Nancy Sepucao, Mar. 4, 1983. Played guitar and sang professionally from age 16: first rec. Why Baby, Why, 1955; first No. 1 record White Lightning, 1959; propr.: Jones Country Music Park, 1983; sang (with Tammy Wynette) duets; composer: songs The Race Is On. Served with USMC, 1950-53. Named Male Vocalist of Yr. by country music trade assn., 1962, 63; named Country Singer of Yr. Rolling Stone, 1976, Best Male Vocalist Country Music Assn., 1980, 81. Office: care CBS Records 51 W 52d St New York NY 10019 *

JONES, GEORGE EDWARD, magazine editor; b. Eugene, Oreg., Jan. 10, 1916; s. Walter Bancroft and Susie Belle (Seaver) J.; m. Antonia Greene, Aug. 17, 1946; 1 son, Brett Michael. B.S., U. Oreg., 1937. Reporter-writer Eugene Register Guard, 1934-37, Salem (Oreg.) Capitol Jour., 1937-39; corr. UP, 1939-44, N.Y. Times, 1944-47, Time-Life, 1948-52; public relations work with UN Korean Reconstrn. Agy., 1952-53; with U.S. News & World Report, 1953—, gen. editor, then asso. exec. editor, 1966-76, dep. editor, Washington, 1976-82; editorial cons., 1982—. Author: Tumult in India, 1948. Recipient award for valor Headliners Club, 1944; co-recipient Penney-U. Mo. award, 1980. Mem. Am. Acad. Polit. and Social Sci., Authors Guild, Sigma Delta Chi. Club: Cosmos (Washington). Home: 2 Concord Dr Saratoga Springs NY 12866

JONES, GOMER EDWARD, JR., wildlife institute executive; b. Kingston, Pa., Mar. 8, 1927; s. Gomer E. and Margaret (Bender) J.; m. Dorothy Ann Pugh, Dec. 26, 1947; children: Robert Gomer, Cathy Lee, Margaret Bender. B.S. in Chem. Engring., Wilkes Coll., 1948. Photographer, Bert Husband Studios, 1946-48; scout exec. Boy Scouts Am., Washington, Norfolk, Va., 1948-76; v.p. Nat. Wildlife Fedn., Washington, 1976-80; sr. v.p. Nat. Audubon Soc., N.Y.C., 1980-81, Nat. Wildlife Fedn., 1981-83; pres. Nat. Inst. Urban Wildlife, 1983—. Vice chmn. Presidential Inaugural Com., 1961, exec. vice chmn., 1965. Served as sgt. maj. C.E., U.S. Army, 1943-46. Recipient Profl. Fund Raiser of Year award Nat. Soc. Fund Raising Execs., 1978, disting. citizens award Citizens Adv. Com. of Norfolk, Va., 1973. Mem. Nat. Soc. Fund Raising Execs., No. Va. Estate Planning Council., Am. Mgmt. Assn., Wildlife Soc., Am. Rifle Assn., Nat. Wildlife Fedn. Presbyterian. Clubs: Republican., Lions (Lion of Yr. award 1969), Rotary.). Home: 12317 Ox Hill Rd Fairfax VA 22033 Office: 10921 Trotting Ridge Way Columbia MD 21044

JONES, GORDON, banker; b. Atlanta, Jan. 14, 1918; s. Harrison and Kathryn (Gordon) J.; m. Ann Creekmore, Oct. 8, 1940; children: Harrison II, Caroline C., Ann Gordon, Kathryn Helene. B.S., U. Ga., 1940. With Bank of the South, N.A. (formerly Fulton Nat. Bank of Atlanta), 1941—, successively asst. cashier, asst v.p., v.p., exec. v.p., 1941-58, pres. and chief exec. officer, 1958-80, also dir.; pres. and chief exec. officer Bank South Corp., 1969-81, chmn. exec. com., 1981—; also dir.; dir. Atlanta Stove Works, Inc., Haverty Furniture Cos., Inc., Atlanta Gas Light Co., Asso. Distbrs., Inc., Atlanta. Trustee U. Ga. Found., Met. Found. Atlanta; bd. dirs., mem. exec. com. Central Atlanta Progress, Inc. Mem. Assn. Res. City Bankers, Am. Bankers Assn. (former mem. exec. council), Ga. Bankers Assn. Office: 55 Marietta St NW Atlanta GA 30303

JONES, GORMAN ROBINSON, JR., lawyer; b. Sheffield, Ala., Oct. 24, 1919; s. Gorman Robinson and Aline (Drake) J.; m. Llewellyn Childress, Oct. 25, 1941; children—Aline Llewellyn (Mrs. Don R. Parks), Elizabeth Cecelia (Mrs. David Talley), Martha Shaler (Mrs. Charles Gentry), Gorman Robinson III. Student, Marion Mil. Inst., 1937-38; A.B., U. Ala., 1940, LL.B., 1943. Bar: Ala. bar 1943. Law clk. U.S. dist. judge, 1943-45; asst. U.S. atty., 1945-47, practice law, Sheffield, 1947—; partner McDonnell & Jones, 1947—; Sec., dir. So. Tire Co., Inc., Asso. Developers, Inc.; Mem. Commn. on Minister and His Work N. Ala. Presbytery, Presbyn. Ch. in U.S., 1969-72, commr., 1969. Author: (with others) Alabama Appellate Practice, 1963. Past pres. Colbert County United Fund.; Past mem. Sheffield City Bd. Edn. Mem. Colbert C. of C. (past pres.). Home: 120 Rivermont Ct Sheffield AL 35660 Office: Valley Fed Savs & Loan Bldg Sheffield AL 35660

JONES, GRANT RICHARD, landscape architect, environ mental planner; b. Seattle, Aug. 29, 1938; s. Victor Noble and Ione Bell (Thomas) J.; m. Ilze Grinbergs, July 12, 1965 (div. July 1983); children: Victor, Kaija.; m. Lucy Cantril, July 30, 1983; children: Laura, Christopher, Sara. Student, Colo. Coll., 1956-58; B.Arch., U. Wash., 1962; M.Landscape Architecture, Harvard U., 1966, postgrad. (Frederick Sheldon fellow), 1967-68. Draftsman, Jones Lovegren Helms & Jones, Seattle, 1958-59; asso. Richard Haag Assos., Seattle, 1961-65; research asso. landscape architecture research office Harvard U., 1966-67; land planner Eckbo Dean Austin & Williams, Honolulu, 1968-69; prin. Grant Jones & Assos., Seattle, 1969-71; partner Jones & Jones, Seattle, 1972—, chmn. bd., 1983—; lectr. in field. Mem. vis. com. Coll. Architecture and Urban Planning, U. Wash.; chmn. landscape archtl. registration bd., State of Wash., 1974-79; mem. council Harvard Grad. Sch. Design, 1978—. Author: The Nooksack Plan: An Approach to the Investigation and Evaluation of a River System, 1973, (with B. Gray and J. Burnham) A Method for the Quantification of Aesthetic Values for Environmental Decision Making, 1975, Design as Ecogram, 1975, (with J. Coe and D. Paulson) Woodland Park Zoo: Long Range Plan, Development Guidelines and Exhibit Scenarios, 1976, Landscape Assessment. .Where Logic and Feelings Meet, 1978; Major landscape archtl. and planning works include Nooksack River Plan, Bellingham, Wash.; Yakima River Regional Greenway, Yakima, Wash., Union Bay Teaching and Research Arboretum, U. Wash., Seattle, Newhalem Campground, N. Cascades Nat. Park, Woodland Park Zool. Gardens, Seattle, Washington Park Arboretum, U. Wash., Seattle, Galapagos Archipelago exhibit, San Diego Zoo. Fellow Am. Soc. Landscape Architects (chmn. Wash. chpt. 1972-73, trustee 1979—, Merit award in community design 1972, Honor award in regional planning 1974, Merit award in regional planning 1977, Merit award in park planning 1977, Merit award in instnl. planning 1977, Pres.'s award of excellence 1980), others; mem. Am. Planning Assn., Nat. Recreation and Park Assn., Audubon Soc., Sierra Club, Nat. Trust Hist. Preservation, Nature Conservancy, Am. Hort. Soc., N.W. Ornamental Hort. Soc., Am. Assn. Bot. Gardens and Arboreta, Wash. Environ. Council, Pioneer Sq. Assn., Rainier Club, AIA (affiliate), Phi Gamma Delta. Home: 2244 39th Pl E Seattle WA 98112 Office: 105 S Main St Seattle WA 98104

JONES, GREYDON G., real estate development executive; b. Warsaw, N.Y., Feb. 16, 1926; s. Onias S. and Dorothy M. (Goetz) J.; m. Janis R. Anderson, June 21, 1946; children: Carrell Jones Tysver, Melodee K. Jones Hyslop. Student, Syracuse U., 1943-44, Ohio State U., 1944-45, Tex. A&M U., 1945; B.C.S., Auerswald Bus. U., 1949. C.P.A., Wash. Partner V.L. Maxfield & Co., Seattle, 1949-57; prin. Haskins & Sells, Seattle, 1958-68; v.p., treas. Weisfield's, Inc., Seattle, 1968-75; chief financial officer Roland and Roland, Inc., Gig Harbor, Wash., 1975—. Served with AUS, 1943-46. Mem. Wash. Soc. C.P.A.s, Am. Inst. C.P.A.s, Fin. Execs. Inst. Home: 209 240th St SE Bothell WA 98011 Office: PO Box 235 Gig Harbor WA 98335

JONES, GWYNETH, soprano; b. Pontnewynydd, Wales, Nov. 7, 1936; d. Edward George and Violet (Webster) J.; m. Till Haberfeld, Mar. 7, 1969. Ed., Royal Coll. Music, London, Accademia Chigiana, Siena, Italy, Internat. Opera Center, Zurich, Switzerland; Dr. h.c. musica, U. Wales. Mem. Royal Opera, Covent Garden, Eng., 1963—, Vienna (Austria) State Opera, 1966—; also mem. Munich Bavarian State Opera. Guest performances in numerous opera houses including, Hamburg, Bayreuth, Berlin, Paris, Zurich, Rome, Chgo., San Francisco, Los Angeles, Tokyo, Buenos Aires, Munich, La Scala, Milan, Met. Opera, N.Y.C., Salzburg Festival, Verona; appeared in 30 leading roles including; Tosca; Leonora in: Il Trovatore; Desdemona in: Otello; Lady MacBeth; Fidelio; Aida; Senta; Sieglinde; Marschallin; Salome; Brunnhilde; Medea; Kundry; Madame Butterfly; Elizabeth/Venus in: Tannhauser; Ariadne; Chrysothemis; Elektra; Turaudot; Helena in: Aegyptische Helena; Poppea in: Färberin in Frau ohne Schatten; court singer, Bavaria, Austria; rec. artist for, Decca, Deutsche Grammophon, EMI, CBS, films, TV and concert appearances. Decorated comdr. Order Brit. Empire. Home: Box 380 8040 Zurich Switzerland *

JONES, HAROLD ANTONY, banker; b. Bklyn., Nov. 5, 1943; s. Harold Edward and Marie Albertine (Schwietering) J.; m. Jo Ann T. Titone, Oct. 8, 1966; children: Christopher, Gregory. Student, Pace Coll., 1968; A.A.S., Am. Inst. Banking, 1970, Grad. Sch. Savs. Banking, Brown U., 1975; grad., Exec. Mgmt. Program, U. Mass., 1977. Trainee Mfrs. Trust Co., N.Y.C., 1961-62, ops. supr. div. internat. banking, 1962-64; with Lincoln Savs. Bank, N.Y.C., 1964—, dir. mktg., 1978-79, sr. v.p., corp. sec., 1979—, dir. retail banking div., 1980; guest lectr. money and banking NYU; guest lectr. corp. social responsibility Columbia U.; exec. com. Savs. Bank Life Ins. Fund.

Named Outstanding Banker in Community Revitalization Brighton Beach Neighborhood Assn., 1978. Mem. Fin. Advt. and Mktg. Assn. N.Y. (dir.), Savs. Instn. Mktg. Soc. Am., Bank Mktg. Assn., Savs. Banks Assn. N.Y. State (commn. on electronic funds transfer systems), Thrift Transfer Services (dir.), Nat. Assn. Corp. Secs. Office: Lincoln Savs Bank 200 Park Ave New York NY 10166

JONES, H(AROLD) GILBERT, JR., lawyer; b. Fargo, N.D., Nov. 2, 1927; s. Harold Gilbert and Charlotte Viola (Chambers) J.; m. Julie Squier, Feb. 15, 1964; children: Lenna Lettice Mills Jones Carroll, Thomas Squier, Christopher Lee. B.Eng., Yale U., 1947; postgrad., Mich. U., 1948-49; J.D., UCLA, 1956. Bar: Calif. bar 1957. Mem. firm Overton, Lyman & Prince, Los Angeles, 1956-61; founding partner Bonne, Jones Bridges, Muellers' O'Keefe, Los Angeles, 1961—. Bd. dirs. Wilshire YMCA, 1969—. Served with U.S. Army, 1950-52. Fellow Am. Coll. Trial Lawyers, Internat. Acad. Trial Lawyers; mem. State Bar Calif., ABA, Los Angeles County Bar Assn. (past chmn. legal-med. relations com.), Orange County Bar Assn., Wilshire Bar Assn., Am. Bd. Trial Advs. (nat. exec. com., past pres. Los Angeles chpt.), Am. Acad. Forensic Scis., So. Calif. Assn. Def. Counsel. Clubs: Jonathan, Calif. Yacht, Los Angeles Yacht, Jonathan Yacht. (Los Angeles). Home: 7 Morning Glory Irvine CA 92715 Office: 1700 CNA Park Pl 600 S Commonwealth Ave Los Angeles CA 90005 Office: #302 1200 N Main St Santa Ana CA 92701

JONES, HAROLD HENRY, photographer; b. Morristown, N.J., Sept. 29, 1940; m. Frances Ellen Murray, May 16, 1970; 2 daus. Diploma, Newark Sch. Fine and Indsl. Art, 1963; B.F.A., Md. Inst. Art, 1965; M.F.A., U. N.Mex., 1972. Advt. chmn. Gallery 61, Newark, 1962-63; wedding photographer Udel Studios, Balt., 1964; ofcl. sch. photographer Md. Art Inst., Balt., 1964; portrait photographer Jordan Studios, Balt., 1965-66; mus. asst. U. N.Mex., Albuquerque, 1966-68; instr. painting and drawing Barelas Community Center, Albuquerque, 1966-67; tech. adv. Quivera Bookshop and Gallery, Corrales, N.Mex., 1966-67; asst. curator exhbns. George Eastman House, Rochester, N.Y., 1968-69, asso. curator, 1970-71; vis. lectr. photography U. Rochester, 1970-71, Cooper Union, N.Y.C., 1971-72; dir. Light Gallery, N.Y.C., 1971-75; adj. asso. prof. art history Queens Coll., N.Y.C., 1974-75; dir. Center for Creative Photography, U. Ariz., Tucson, 1975-77, asso. prof. dept. art, 1977—, coordinator photography program, 1977—; instr. Colo. Mountain Coll. Summervail workshop, Vail, 1976; vis. artist U. Colo., 1976. One-man shows photography and/or prints, 1969—, latest being, Harris 125 Gallery, U. So. Calif., Los Angeles, 1978, Northlight Gallery, Ariz. State U., Tempe, 1979, Slocumb Gallery, E. Tenn. State U., Johnson City, Light Factory Gallery, Charlotte, N.C., 1980, Light Gallery, N.Y.C., Etherton Gallery, Tucson, 1982, Ctr. Creative Photography, Tucson, B.C. Space, Laguna Beach, Calif., 1983, numerous group shows, including, San Francisco Mus. Modern Art, 1980, Lynn Mayhew Gallery, Delaware, Ohio, Freedman Gallery, Reading, Pa., DeCordova Mus., Lincoln, Mass., Joseph Gross Gallery, U. Ariz., Tucson, Addison Gallery Am. Art, Andover, Mass., 1981, de Saisset Art Gallery, U. Santa Clara, Calif., Gallery Atelier 696, Rochester, George Eastman House, Rochester, N.Y., U. Colo.-Denver, 1982, Calif. State U.-Fullerton, San Francisco Mus. Modern Art, Dinnerware Gallery, Tucson, 1983, Meridian Gallery, Albuquerque; represented in permanent collections, Mus. Modern Art, N.Y.C., DeCordova Mus., Lincoln, Mass., Norton Simon Mus. Art, Pasadena, Calif., Internat. Mus. Photography, George Eastman House, Nat. Gallery Can., Ottawa, Ont., UCLA Art Mus., U. Colo., Boulder, U. Louisville Photog. Archive, Santa Fe Mus., U. Ariz., Tucson, also pvt. collections. Recipient Gold award Univ. and Coll. Designers Assn., 1977; Nat. Endowment Arts Photographers fellow, 1977. Mem. Soc. Photog. Edn. Home: 420 E 4th St Tucson AZ 85705 Office: Art Dept Univ Arizona Tucson AZ 85721

JONES, HARRY WILLMER, lawyer, educator; b. N.Y.C., Mar. 4, 1911; s. Harry and Leona May (Coffin) J.; m. Shirley O'Neal Coggeshall, Nov. 21, 1935 (dec. 1955); m. Alice Neuburger Katz, July 11, 1956. Student, Westminster Coll., Fulton, Mo., 1929-31; LL.B., Washington U., St., Louis, 1934, A.B., 1937; postgrad., Oxford U., Eng., 1934-35; LL.M., Columbia, 1939; LL.D., Jewish Theol. Sem. Am., 1967; L.H.D., Villanova U., 1972. Bar: Mo. bar 1934, Calif. bar 1946. Part-time law practice, lecture series on public and internat. affairs, 1935-38; instr., asst. prof. law Washington U., 1935-39; vis. lectr. in law Columbia, 1939-40, Stanford, summer 1940; asso. prof. law U. Calif., 1940-41, prof., 1946; prof. law Columbia, 1947-57, Cardozo prof. jurisprudence, 1957-79, Cardozo prof. emeritus, 1979—; prof. law U. Chgo., 1963-64; dir. research Am. Bar Found., 1963-64; with O.P.A., Washington, 1941-43; successively as head, research and opinion unit, chief appellate litigation branch, asst. gen. counsel, dir. food enforcement div.; vis. prof. Columbia, summer 1947; vis. prof. law U. Delhi, Inda, 1968; Phi Beta Kappa vis. scholar, 1981-82; Chmn. O.D.M. shipbldg. industry panel, summer 1952; research dir. Am. Assembly, 1953; faculty Salzburg Seminar in Am. Studies, summers 1955-59. Author: (with N.T. Dowling, E.W. Patterson and R.R. Powell) Materials for Legal Method, 1952, Economic Security for Americans, 1954, Legal Realism and Natural Law (Riverside lectures), 1956, Cases on Contract, (with E.W. Patterson and G.W. Goble), 1957, The Courts, The Public and The Law Explosion, 1965, (with E.A. Farnsworth, William F. Young) Cases and Materials on Contracts, 1965, Law and the Social Role of Science, 1966, The Efficacy of Law, 1969, Political Separation and Legal Continuity, 1976, Legal Institutions Today, 1976, (with J.M. Kernochen and A.W. Murphy) Legal Method: Cases and Text Materials, 1980; Editor in charge of dept. legislation: Am. Bar Assn. Jour, 1948-51; directing editor: Univ. Textbook Series. Trustee W.E. Meyer Research Inst. Law, 1957-73. Served as asst. counsel Bur. Aercs. and counsel for Bur. Aeronautics gen. rep., Western Dist., with rank of lt. (j.g.) and lt. comdr. USNR, 1943-46; cons. on legis. research and drafting problems for conl. and state legis. coms. Recipient Alumni citation Washington U., 1958, Westminster Coll., 1960; Henry M. Phillips award for jurisprudence, 1976. Mem. Am. Law Inst., Am. Philos. Soc., Am. Acad. Arts and Scis., Am. Bar Assn., Am. Bar Found., Order of Coif, Phi Delta Theta, Phi Delta Phi. Democrat. Presbyterian. Home: RFD 1 Box 385 Kent CT 06757

JONES, HARVIE PAUL, architect; b. Huntsville, Ala., June 9, 1930; s. Howard Criner and Kathleen (Paul) J.; m. Hattie Marie Webb, July 1960 (div. 1972); children: Anne Marie, Steven Criner, Martha, Evelyn; m. 2d Marilyn Jean Miller, June 25, 1977. B.S., Ga. Inst. Tech., 1952, B. Arch., 1953. Registered architect, Ala., Tenn. Archtl. designer G. W. Jones & Sons, Engrs., Huntsville, Ala., 1955-57, W. R. Dickson, Architect, 1957-64; ptnr. Dickson, Jones & Davis, Architects, Huntsville, 1964-67, Jones & Harrin, Architects, 1967—. Chmn. Huntsville Historic Commn., 1982-84, City of Huntsville Beautification Bd., 1973, Local Govt. Study Commn. Culture and Recreation Subcom., Huntsville, 1973; pres. Central City Assn., Huntsville, 1975; preservation architect numerous bldgs., 1970-83. Recipient Dist. Service Honor award Ala. Hist. Commn., 1980, Honor award AIA, 1975, 78, 79, 82, 83. Fellow AIA (com. on hist. resources chmn. 1980); mem. Ala. Hist. Commn. (chmn. Ala. council of AIA com. on hist resources 1973-84), Assn. Preservation Tech., Nat. Trust Hist. Preservation. Presbyterian. Office: Jones & Herrin Architects 104 Jefferson St Huntsville AL 35801

JONES, HAZEL LUCILE JAMES, univ. ofcl.; b. Eckert, Colo., Feb. 3, 1915; d. Robert Phelps and Ethel (Hart) James; 1 dau., Annette. B.A., Western State Coll., 1937; M.A., U. So. Calif., 1958, Ed.D., 1963. Tchr. English, high schs., Colo., 1938-50, Calif. high schs., 1950-59; prof. edn. Los Angeles State Coll., 1959-60; prof. English Calif. State U., Fullerton, 1960-74, asso. dean, 1967-70, dean, 1970-72, 1972-74; v.p. acad. affairs Calif. Poly. State U., San Luis Obispo, 1974—; Chmn. Calif. Com. Tchr. Preparation in English, 1969-70; Mem. exec. bd. Whittier (Calif.) Library, 1956-59. Delta Kappa Gamma fellow, 1961-62. Mem. Calif. Assn. Tchrs. English (pres. 1965-66), Cal. Assn. Econ. Edn. (exec. bd. 1965-74), Nat. Council Tchrs. English, Coll. English Edn. Home: 1451 Sierra Dr Arroyo Grande CA 93420

JONES, HELEN HART, lawyer; b. Lakewood, Ohio, July 30, 1921; d. Bert C. and Ellen M. (Moran) H.; m. Richard J. Jones, Oct. 5, 1946; children: Christopher, Ruth, Jeffrey, Catherine. A.B., Miami (Ohio) U., 1943; LL.B., Case Western Res. U., 1945; LL.M., Northwestern U., 1950. Bar: Ohio 1945, Ill. 1952. Atty. NLRB, Washington, 1945-46; individual practice law, Buffalo, 1946-47; asst. gen. counsel Chgo. Housing Authority, 1947-48; practice law, Chgo., 1952—; mem. firm Cotton, Watt, Jones, King & Bowlus, 1954—, partner, 1959—; lectr. Northwestern U., 1974—. Mem. Ill., Chgo. bar assns., Chgo. Council Lawyers (bd. 1974-76), Women's Bar Assn. Ill. (pres. 1967-68), A.C.L.U. (bd. 1976-82), Phi Beta Kappa. Home: 4820 S Kenwood Ave Chicago IL 60615 Office: One IBM Plaza Suite 4750 330 N Wabash Ave Chicago IL 60611

JONES, HENRY, actor; b. Phila., Aug. 21, 1912; s. John F.X. and Helen (Burk) J.; m. Yvonne Bergere, Jan. 1942 (dec. Oct. 1942); m. Judy Briggs, June 1946 (div. 1961); children—David, Jocelyn. A.B., St. Joseph's Coll., Phila., 1935. Actor starring in Broadway shows, motion pictures and television; theatrical credits include Hamlet, Henry IV, Part 2, The Time of Your Life, Village Green, My Sister Eileen, This is the Army, January Thaw, Alice in Wonderland, How I Wonder, Advise and Consent, Kathleen, Town House, They Knew What They Wanted, Metropole, A Story for a Sunday Evening, The Solid Gold Cadillac, The Bad Seed, Sunrise at Campobello, Advise and Consent; films include The Girl Can't Help It, Will Success Spoil Rock Hunter?, Vertigo, Never too Late, The Champagne Murders, Stay Away Joe, Support Your Local Sheriff, Butch Cassidy and the Sundance Kid, Rabbit Run, Dirty Dingus Magee, Tom Sawyer, Pete n' Tillie, Nine to Five, 1980; numerous TV appearances, including role of; Judge Dexter in: series Phyllis; (Recipient Tony award for Sunrise at Campobello 1958, also, winner Variety N.Y. Drama Critics Poll.). Served with AUS, 1942-45. Mem. Acad. Motion Picture Arts and Scis., Acad. TV Arts and Scis., Screen Actors Guild, Actors Equity Assn., A.F.T.R.A. Club: Players (N.Y.C.) *

JONES, HENRY EARL, dermatologist, educator; b. Detroit, Jan. 24, 1940; s. Henry Clay and Treva Jewel (Jones) J.; m. Hilda Ann Skagfield; children: Gregory, Laronda, Tamara, Hanna. B.S., Murray State U., 1961; M.D., Tulane U., 1965. Diplomate Am. Bd. Dermatology. Intern, Tripler Gen. Hosp., Honolulu, 1965-66; resident in dermatology Letterman Gen. Hosp. and U. Calif.-San Francisco, 1966-69; asst. chief div. dermatology Letterman Army Inst. Research, San Francisco, 1970-73; asst. prof. dermatology and head immunodermatology U. Mich., 1973-76; prof. dermatology, chmn. dept. Emory U., 1976-84, clin. prof., 1984—, dir. Emory affiliated dermatology tng. program, 1976-84. Served to lt. col. U.S. Army, 1965-73. Decorated Bronze star; recipient John Herr Musser Meml. award Tulane U., 1965. Mem. Soc. Investigative Dermatology, Am. Acad. Dermatology, Am. Dermatol. Assn., Am. Dermatologic Soc., Allergy, Immunology, Dermatology Found., Am. Soc. Microbiology, Ga. Dermatology Soc., Atlanta Dermatol. Assn., Am. Assn. Immunology, Alpha Omega Alpha. Home: 865 Sea Cliff Dr Fairhope AL 36532 Office: Bldg E Montrose Park Hwy 98 PO Box 1106 Fairhope AL 36533

JONES, HORACE CHARLES, former sales company executive; b. Benton, Ky., Nov. 12, 1910; s. Horace Cleveland and Evalena (Darnall) J.; m. Loretta Louise Schille, June 12, 1937 (dec. Dec. 1979); children: Charles D., Margaret L.; m. Ruth Moss, May 3, 1980. Diploma commerce, Northwestern U., 1929-35. C.P.A., Ohio. Investment analyst City Nat. Bank & Trust Co., Chgo., 1930-38; treas. Fed. Home Loan Bank of, Chgo., 1938-43; with Hickman, Williams & Co., Cin., 1947—, sec., dir., 1955-59, v.p., 1959-64, pres., 1964-76, chmn., 1976-77, ret., 1977; dir. Covington Trust & Banking Co., 1974-84. Bd. dirs. YMCA of No. Ky., 1965-75; exec. allocation bd. Community Chest of Cin., 1969; mem. adv. council William Booth Meml. Hosp., Florence, Ky., 1967-80, chmn., 1976. Served to lt. USNR, 1943-46. Mem. Am. Inst. C.P.A.'s. Baptist. Clubs: Bradenton (Fla.) Country, Cin. Home: 1403 Water Oak Way N Bradenton FL 33529

JONES, HORACE HERBERT(BUD), JR., coal company executive; b. N. Reading, Mass., Feb. 21, 1923; s. Horace Herbert and Ruby (Power) J.; m. Patricia Maddox, June 17, 1945; children: Stephen Kenneth, Randall Power, Richard Dwight. B.S., U. Pa., 1948. Vice pres. fin. and ops. RCA Corp., Hertz Corp., N.Y.C., 1948-73; v.p., chief fin. officer Magnavox Consumer Electronics Co., Fort Wayne, Ind., 1973-75; v.p. fin. and planning Midland Enterprises, Inc., Cin., 1975-80; sr. v.p. fin. Eastern Assoc. Coal Corp., Pitts., 1980—, dir.; dir. Affinity Mining Co., Pitts., Assoc. Coal Sales Corp., Charles Coal Co., Boston, Sterling Smokeless Coal Co., Beckley, W.Va.; adv. Burlington County Coll., 1971. Bd. dirs. council boy Scouts Am., 1960-66. Mem. Fin. Exec. Inst. (dir. 1977-80). Republican. Methodist. Lodge: Rotary. Home: 108 Saybrook Harbor Dr Bradford Woods PA 15015 Office: Eastern Assoc Coal Corp 1750 Koppers Bldg Pittsburgh PA 15219

JONES, HOWARD ALDRED, advertising executive; b. Jamestown, N.Y., Dec. 6, 1900; s. Aldred James and Edith (Walker) J.; m. Eleanor Talcott, July 25, 1926; children: Challis Jones Snyder, Talcott Aldred. Ph.B., U. Chgo., 1922. Tchr. Shadyside Acad., Pitts., 1922-23; writer, editor mail order catalogue Butler Bros., Chgo., 1923; sales corr. U.S. Gypsum Co., 1924; with advt. dept. B. Kuppenheimer & Co., 1924-27; propr. own advt. agy., 1927-30; with Insul Securities Co., 1929-30; advt. exec. Albert Frank & Co., N.Y.C. and Chgo., 1930-31, Ruthrauff & Ryan, Chgo., 1931-34; v.p. Blackett Sample Hummert, Chgo., 1934-38; with Lord & Thomas, N.Y.C., 1939-40, v.p., Chgo., 1940-42; exec. v.p. Grant Advt., Chgo., 1943-57; pres. Keyes Madden & Jones, Chgo., 1957-65; cons. J. Walter Thompson Co., Chgo., 1965-69, N.Y.C., 1971-76, Ted Bates Advt., 1977, Kenyon & Eckhardt, 1978-80, 82-83; engaged in breeding, raising and racing thoroughbred horses, 1944-65. Author: 50 Years Behind the Scenes in Advertising, 1975, Hooked on Horses, 1982. Mem. Beta Theta Pi. Republican. Episcopalian. Office: 919 N Michigan Ave Suite 1920 Chicago IL 60611

JONES, HOWARD LANGWORTHY, educational administrator; b. Pelham, N.Y., Nov. 16, 1917; s. Dyer Tillinghast and Margaret (Longworthy) J.; m. Margaret Irene Lloyd, Apr. 27, 1940; 1 son, D. Lloyd. A.B., Colgate U., 1939; M.A., Syracuse U., 1948, Ed.D., 1951; LL.D., Colgate, 1969. Tchr., coach secondary sch., East Hampton, N.Y., 1939-42; mem. faculty Colgate U., 1947-61, prof., 1947-55, v.p., 1956-61; pres. Northfield (Mass.) Mt. Hermon Sch., 1961-79; spl. asst. to pres. Colgate U., Hamilton, N.Y., 1979—; dir. Imagetics Corp., Greenfield.; Bd. dirs. A Better Chance, Inc., Boston, 1962—, Elderhostel Inc.; trustee Good Hope Sch., St. Croix, V.I., 1966-73, Cushing Acad., Asburnham, Mass., 1967-73, Colgate U., 1969—, Coll. V.I., 1962—. Served as pilot USAAF, 1943-47. Mem. Am. Mgmt. Assn. (dir. 1965-71), Nat. Assn. Ind. Schs. (dir. 1971—), Phi Delta Kappa, Phi Kappa Tau. Clubs: Anglers, Univ. (N.Y.C.). Home: 22 E Pleasant St Hamilton NY 13346

JONES, HOWARD LEON, educator; b. Phoenixville, Pa., Oct. 20, 1940; s. Walter R. and Marie (McCann) J.; m. Renda M. Nowell, Dec. 28, 1963. B.S., Millersville (Pa.) State Coll., 1962; M.A., U. Tex., 1964, Ph.D., 1966. Project asso., research asso., instr. U. Tex., 1964-66; vis. prof. Okla. State U., summer 1965; asst. prof. sci. edn. Syracuse U., 1966-68; asso. prof. edn. U. Houston, 1968-73, prof. edn., 1973—, asso. dir. competency-based tchr. edn. program, 1971-73, dir., 1973-74, coordinator elem. edn., 1974-75, chmn. tchr. edn., 1976-78, chmn. dept. curriculum instrn., 1978-80, dir. Center for Study of Teaching, 1980—, dir. in formal sci. study, 1981—; program mgr. div. pre-coll. edn. in sci. NSF, 1975-76; sci. cons. Eastern Regional Inst. for Edn., 1967-69; cons. Exploratory Com. for Assessment of Edn. Progress, Ednl. Testing Service; mem. Tex. Bd. Examiners for Tchrs. Edn., 1974-76. Author: (with G.E. Hall) Competency-Based Education: A Process for the Improvement of Education, 1976; contbr. articles to profl. jours. Fellow AAAS. Home: 1503 Ashford Pkwy Houston TX 77077

JONES, HOWARD ST. CLAIRE, JR., electronic engineering executive; b. Richmond, Va., Aug. 18, 1921; s. Howard St. Claire and Martha Lillian (Mason) J.; m. Evelyn Mercer Saunders, Nov. 27, 1946. B.S., Va. Union U., 1943, D.Sc., 1971; certificate engring., Howard U., 1944; M.S.E.E., Bucknell U., 1973. Registered profl. engr., D.C. Indsl. engring. aid Bur. Ships USN, Washington, 1943; electro mech. engring. aide U.S. Bur. Standards, Washington, 1944, electronic physicist, 1946-53; electronic scientist, engr., supervisory phys. scientist Harry Diamond Labs., AUS, Washington, 1953-80; tech. cons. microwave electronics, 1980—; Tchr. radio physics Hilltop Radio-Electronics Inst., Washington, 1946-52; asso. prof. elec. engring. Howard U., 1958-63, adj. prof., 1982; cons. microwave engring., 1965-69. Contbr. tech. reports and publs. Served as instr. mech. engring. AUS, 1944-46. Recipient four Sustained Superior Performance or Spl. Act awards Harry Diamond Labs AUS, 1956, 68, 70, 75, Inventor of Year award, 1972; Sec. Army Fellowship award, 1972; Army Research and Devel. award, 1975; Meritorious Civilian Service award, 1976, 80. Fellow IEEE, AAAS, Washington Acad. Sci. Inventor, holder 31 U.S. patents microwave field. Home: 6200 Sligo Mill Rd NE Washington DC 20011 Office: 6200 Sligo Mill Rd NE Washington DC

JONES, HOWARD WESLEY, mag. pub.; b. Verdon, S.D., Nov. 10, 1924; s. Franklin Evan and Lydia Anna (Krueger) J.; m. Greta Ann Nelson, Oct. 20, 1950; children—Kirby William, Dana Ann, Nancy Kathryn. B.A., U. Minn., 1947. Field research and advt. rep. The Webb Co., 1947-51; advt. mgr. Bride and Homemaker, 1951; pub. Equipment Blueprint mag., 1952-67; account exec., v.p. Knox Reeves Advt., 1967-68; partner Sielaff, Herder, Grawert and Jones Advt., 1968-69; pres. HPC Corp., Bethel, Minn., 1969-72; gen. mgr. Webb Travel mags., St. Paul, 1976-81; pub. Webb Family Mags., St. Paul. State del. Republican Party. Served with USAAF, 1943-45. Lutheran. Club: St. Paul Athletic. Office: 1999 Shepard Rd St Paul MN 55116

JONES, HOWARD WILBUR, JR., gynecologist; b. Balt., Dec. 30, 1910; s. Howard Wilbur and Ethel Ruth (Marling) J.; m. Georgeanna Emory Seegar, June 22, 1940; children—Howard Wilbur III, Georgeanna S., Lawrence M. A.B., Amherst Coll., 1931; M.D., Johns Hopkins, 1935; Dr. Honoris Causa, Cordoba, 1968. Intern, asst. resident, resident gynecology Johns Hopkins Hosp., 1935-37, 46-48; asst. resident, resident surgery Ch. Home and Hosp., Balt., 1937-40; practice medicine, specializing in obstetrics and gynecology, Balt., 1948—; instr., asst. prof., asso. prof., prof. gynecology and obstetrics Sch. Medicine Johns Hopkins, 1948-79, prof. emeritus, 1979—; prof. obstetrics and gynecology Eastern Va. U. Med. Sch., 1978—; nat. cons. USAF, 1968-78; Dir. William & Wilkins Co. Author: (with W.W. Scott) Genital Anomalies and Related Endocrine Disorders, 1958, rev. edit., 1971, (with G.S. Jones) Textbook of Gynecology, 1965, 10th edit., 1981, (with R. Heller) Pediatric and Adolescent Gynecology, 1968, (with J.A. Rock) Reparative and Constructive Surgery of the Female Generative Tract, 1983; Editor in chief: (with G.E.S. Jones) Obstetrical and Gynecological Survey, 1957—; Contbr. articles to profl. jours. Served to maj. M.C. AUS, 1943-46. Decorated Bronze Star medal. Mem. AMA, Am. Assn. Cancer Research, Am. Cancer Soc. (dir. Md. div.), Am. Coll. Obstetrics and Gynecology, Soc. Pelvic Surgeons, Sociedad de Obstetricia Y Gynecologia die Buenos Aires, Sociedad Peruana de Obstetricia Y Ginecologia. Home: 7506 Shirland Norfolk VA 23505 Office: 603 Med Tower Norfolk VA 23507

JONES, HOWARD WILLIAM, artist, educator; b. Ilion, N.Y., June 20, 1922; s. Harry and Kezia (White) J.; m. Helen M. Frick, Jan. 31, 1948; 1 dau., Brandyn Marion. Student, U. Toledo, 1942, Columbia U., 1947; B.F.A. cum laude, Syracuse U., 1948; postgrad., Cranbrook Acad. Art, 1953. Instr. Tulane U., New Orleans, 1951-54; asst. prof. dept. art Fla. State U., Tallahassee, 1954-57; prof. fine arts Washington U., St. Louis, 1957—; vis. artist U. So. Ill., Carbondale, 1969, Edwardsville, 1970, U. Ind., Evansville, 1971; lectr., panelist Internat. Sculpture Conf., U. Kans., Lawrence, 1974. One-man shows of paintings, sound and light shows and environments include, Nelson Atkins Mus., Kansas City, Mo., 1965, 73, Royal Marks Gallery, N.Y.C., 1966, Howard Wise Gallery, N.Y.C., 1968, 70, Fla. State U., Tallahassee, 1969, Electric Gallery, Toronto, Ont., Can., 1971, St. Louis Art Mus., 1973, Wadsworth Atheneum, Hartford, Conn., 1974, Forbes Found., N.Y.C., 1976, numerous group shows, 1966—, latest being, Whitney Mus., 1968, Hayward Gallery, London, Eng., 1970, N.J. State Mus., Trenton, 1972, Brooks Meml. Art Gallery, Memphis, Tenn., 1977, Huntsville Mus. Art, Ala., 1978, U. Rochester, N.Y., Ind. Curators, Inc., Kltouring, U.S., 1981-83, Newberger Mus., SUNY, 1981; represented in permanent collections, Milw. Art Center, Rockefeller U., N.Y.C., Smithsonian Inst., Washington, Jewish Mus., N.Y.C., Albright-Knox Mus., Buffalo, Mpls. Inst. Art, Mus. Contemporary Art, Ridgefield, Conn., St. Louis Art Mus., Princeton U. Art Mus., Princeton, N.J., U. Mo., St. Louis, Lannon Found., N.Y.C., Lannon Found., Palm Beach, Fla. Served with USAAF, 1942-45. Nat. Endowment for the Arts grantee, 1977; Graham Found. fellow, 1966-67; Nat. Endowment Arts-Corp. Public Broadcasting grantee, 1971. Home: 12 N Newstead St Louis MO 63108 Office: School of Fine Arts Washington Univ St Louis MO 63130

JONES, HUGH HENRY, JR., banker; b. Pitts., Apr. 22, 1930; s. Hugh Henry and Merriem R. J.; m. Mary Joyce Mackie, Feb. 5, 1955; children: Cynthia A., Merriem R., Laura E. A.B. in Econs., Lafayette Coll., Easton, Pa., 1952; M.B.A. in Banking, NYU, 1956. With Chem. Bank N.Y. Trust Co., N.Y.C., 1954-70, v.p., 1970; 1st v.p. Barnett Banks, Fla., 1970-80; vice chmn., dir. Barnett Bank, Jacksonville, Fla., 1980-82, chmn., chief exec. officer, 1982—. Bd. dirs. N.C. Outward Bound Sch., Morganton; chmn. Jacksonville Sports and Entertainment Commn.; tournament dir. Jacksonville Internat. Invitational Tennis Tournament, 1971; chmn. N. Fla. chpt. Nat. Multiple Sclerosis Soc., 1976, pres., dir., 1978-80; mem. Duval County Hosp. Authority, 1978-79. Served with AUS, 1952-54. Named Boss of Year Jacksonville chpt. Nat. Secs. Assn., 1975. Mem. U.S. C. of C., Assn. Tournament Dirs. (founder, 1st pres.), Jacksonville Area C. of C., Com. 100 Jacksonville. Presbyterian. Clubs: University (N.Y.C.); River (Jacksonville). Home:

4933 Long Bow Rd Jacksonville FL 32210 Office: 100 Laura St Jacksonville FL 32202

JONES, HUGH MCKITTRICK, architect; b. St. Louis, Oct. 6, 1919; s. Hugh McKittrick and Carroll (West) J.; m. Elizabeth Siddons Mowbray, Sept. 9, 1940 (dec. July 1978); children: Cynthia Siddons Jones Benjamin, Terry West (Mrs. James Henry Eddy, Jr.), Hugh McKittrick III, Timothy Millard.; m. Margaret Twichell Mowbray, Mar. 17, 1984; stepchildren: Burton Twichell Mowbray, Katharine Siddons Mowbray Michie. B.S., Harvard, 1940, B.Arch., 1942, M.Arch., 1947. Registered profl. architect, Conn. Trainee Office Walter Bogner, Cambridge, Mass., 1945-47, Office Douglas Orr, New Haven, 1947-49; architect Jones & Mowbray, New Haven and Guilford, Conn., 1949-54, Office Hugh Jones, Guilford, 1954—, now cons.; corporator, trustee Guilford Savs. Bank, 1954—, v.p., 1975-77, vice chmn., 1977—; v.p. Envirland Co., 1976—. Mem. Guilford Republican Party Town Com., 1952—; mem. Guilford Town Planning Commn., 1953-58, chmn., 1956; mem. Regional Planning Agy., 1961-69; rep. Conn. Ho. Reps., 1963-67; mem. Conn. Commn. to Study Metro Govt., 1965-67, Conn. Gov.'s Task Force on Housing, 1971-73; chmn. Regional Housing Council for S. Central Planning Region, 1974-80; mem. Guilford Land Conservation Trust, 1965—; pres. Guilford Found., 1976-80, 83—, dir., 1977-82; treas. Guilford Preservation Alliance, 1981—; mem. Guilford Keeping Soc., 1979—. Served to lt. USNR, 1942-46; PTO. Fellow AIA (pres. Conn. chpt. 1962, 63, Nat. dir. 1970-73), Guilford C. of C., Sierra Club, Am. Arbitration Assn. (nat. panel arbitrators 1956—). Home and Office: 265 Dromara Rd PO Box 361 Guilford CT 06437

JONES, HUGH RICHARD, judge; b. New Hartford, N.Y., Mar. 19, 1914; s. Hugh Richard and Anna (Jones) J.; m. Jean McMillen, July 3, 1937; children: Hugh Richard, Anne E., Thomas McM., Jean C., David B. A.B., Hamilton Coll., Clinton, N.Y., 1935, LL.D., 1974; J.D., Harvard U., 1939; LL.D., Albany Law Sch., 1981. Bar: N.Y. 1940, U.S. Supreme Ct. 1963. Instr. Am. U. at, Cairo, 1935-36; asso. firm Burke & Burke, N.Y.C., 1939-42, Miller, Hubbell & Evans, Utica, N.Y., 1945, partner, to 1953; partner firm Evans, Pirnie & Burdick, Utica, 1953-69, Evans, Burdick, Severn & Jones, 1970-72; assoc. judge N.Y. Ct. Appeals, Albany, 1973—; adviser Restatement 2d Restitution, 1981—. Mem. N.Y. State Bd. Social Welfare, 1959-69, chmn., 1964-69; dir. local health and welfare agys., Utica; trustee Hamilton Coll., 1967—, State U. N.Y., 1969-72; chancellor Episcopalian Diocese of, Central N.Y. Served to lt. comdr. USNR, 1942-45. Decorated Bronze Star with combat V.; recipient Humanitarian award for services to Spanish Speaking Community of N.Y. State, 1969; Civic award Colgate U., 1970; William R. Hopkins Bronze medal St. David's Soc. State of N.Y., 1974. Fellow Am. Coll. Probate Counsel, Am. Bar Found.; mem. Am. Law Inst., ABA, N.Y. State Bar Assn. (pres. 1971-72, Root-Stimson award 1978), Oneida County Bar Assn. (pres. 1962), Am. Judicature Soc., Assn. Bar City N.Y. Home: 111 Paris Rd New Hartford NY 13413 Office: Oneida County Courthouse Utica NY 13501

JONES, HYWEL JAMES, bishop; b. Porthcawl, Glamoargan, Wales, Mar. 4, 1918; s. Ifor James and Ann (Twiss) J.; m. Dorothy Margaret Wilcox; children: Margaret Lindsay, Peter Hywel. L.Th., Coll. Emmanuel and St. Chad, Saskatoon, Sask., Can.; D.D. hon. Ordained to ministry Anglican Ch. Can. Bishop Anglican Synod of Diocese of B.C., Victoria. Home: 2028 Frderick Norris Rd Victoria BC Canada V8P 2B2 Office: Anglican Synod of Diocese of BC 912 Vancouver St Victoria BC Canada V8V 3V7

JONES, J. BENTON, JR., agronomist, educator; b. Tyrone, Pa., Apr. 4, 1930; m. J. Benton and Ethel May (Reynolds) J.; children—J. Benton III, Karin, Kristin. B.S. in Agrl. Sci, U. Ill., 1952; M.S. in Agronomy, Pa. State U., 1956, Ph.D., 1959. Asst. prof. Ohio Agrl. Research and Devel. Center, Wooster, 1959-63, asso. prof., 1963-66, prof., 1966-68; extension agronomist, prof. agronomy U. Ga., Athens, 1968-74, div. chmn. dept. horticulture, prof. plant sci., 1974-80, prof. horticulture, 1980—; pres. Benton Labs., Inc., 1978—; Bd. dirs. Council Agrl. Sci. and Tech., 1974-79. Editor: Com. Soil Sci. and Plant Analysis, 1970—, Jour. Plant Nutrition, 1979—. Served with USNR, 1952-54. Fellow AAAS; mem. Am. Soc. Agronomy, Soil Sci. Soc. Am., Soc. Hort. Sci., Internat. Soc. Soil Sci., Council Soil Testing and Plant Analysis (chmn. 1970-72, sec.-treas 1972—), Applied Spectroscopy Soc., Am. Chem. Soc., Sigma Xi. Christian Scientist (chmn. bd. Athens 1969-70, 79—, treas. 1970-72). Home: 345 Brookwood Dr Athens GA 30605 Office: Plant Sci Bldg U Ga Athens GA 30602

JONES, J. KENLEY, journalist; b. Greenville, S.C., Feb. 24, 1935; s. J. Clyde and Mildred Idel (Smith) J.; m. Margaret Jean McPherson, Dec. 11, 1965; children—Stephanie, Jason, Eleanor. Student, Furman U., 1953-55; B.S. in Speech, Northwestern U., 1957; M.S. in Journalism, Northwestern U., 1963; postgrad., Columbia U., 1964-65. Reporter City News Bur. of Chgo., 1962; reporter, cameraman KRNT-TV, Des Moines, 1963-64, WSB-TV, Atlanta, 1965-69; fgn. corr. NBC News, Asia, 1969-72, corr., Atlanta, 1972—. Served with USNR, 1958-61. Recipient Overseas Press Club award for best television reporting from abroad, 1970. Mem. AFTRA, Nat. Acad. Television Arts and Scis. Presbyterian. Office: 100 Colony Sq Suite 300 1175 Peachtree St Atlanta GA 30361

JONES, J. KENNETH, curator; b. Syracuse, N.Y., Jan. 1, 1945; s. John Paul and Esther Elizabeth (Auborn) J. B.F.A., Ringling Sch. Art, Sarasota, Fla., 1969. Designer Southeastern Galleries, Charleston, S.C., 1969, designer, warehouse mgr., display coordinator, 1973; designer Engel Bros. Furnitue, Charleston, 1969-70; designer, buyer Maxwell Bros. Furniture, Charleston, 1970-73; curator decorative arts and cultural history Charleston Mus., 1973—. Mem. Mayor's Com. for Econs. of Amenity, Charleston, 1982-83, Save the Ft. Sumter Flag Com., Ft. Moultrie, Sullivans Island, S.C., 1983. Mem. Victirian Soc. Am., Nat. Trust Hist. Preservation. Episcopalian. Home: 79 Alexander St Charleston SC 29403 Office: Charleston Mus 360 Meeting St Charleston SC 29403

JONES, J. KNOX, JR., biologist; b. Lincoln, Nebr., Mar. 16, 1929; s. James Knox and Virginia E. (Bowen) J.; m. Janet Helen Glock, Sept. 12, 1953; children—Amy Sue, Sarah Ann, Laura Lee. B.S., U. Nebr., 1951; M.A., U. Kans., 1953, Ph.D., 1962. Mem. faculty U. Kans., 1959-71; prof. zoology, curator Mus. Natural History, 1968-71, asso. dir. mus., 1967-71; dean Grad. Sch., prof. biol. scis. Tex. Tech. U., Lubbock, 1971—, asso. v.p. research, 1972-74, v.p. research and grad. studies, 1974—, adj. prof. pathology, 1973—; cons. in field. Author monographs, sects. books, articles. Served with U.S. Army, 1953-55. Mem. Am. Soc. Mammalogists (pres. 1972-74), Orgn. Tropical Studies (treas. 1974-76), Gulf Univs. Research Consortium (sec. 1979-80), Soc. Study Evolution, Soc. Systematic Zoology, Biol. Soc. Washington, AAAS, Southwestern Assn. Naturalists, Lubbock C. of C., Sigma Xi, Alpha Tau Omega. Clubs: Southwest Rotary, Lubbock Swim (dir.). Home: 6807 Nashville Ave Lubbock TX 79413 Office: Grad Sch Tex Tech U Lubbock TX 79409

JONES, JACK DELLIS, oil co. exec.; b. Carnegie, Okla., Mar. 3, 1925; s. Henry Clifford and Dora Dean (Dellis) J.; m. Sally Kramer, Dec. 19, 1953; children—Margaret K., Elizabeth D., Susan L. B.S., U.S. Naval Acad., 1947; J.D., U. Tulsa, 1955. Bar: Okla. bar 1955, Tex. bar 1960, Calif. bar 1962. Engr. Sunray Oil Co., 1953-55; asst. county atty., Tulsa County, 1955-56; with Getty Oil Co., 1956—, v.p., 1966-80, group v.p., 1980—; pres. Getty Refining and Mktg. Co., Tulsa, 1973—; also dir.; dir. Nuclear Fuel Services Co., First Nat. Bank & Trust Co., Tulsa. Trustee Hillcrest Med. Center, Tulsa, 1977—; bd. dirs. Tulsa Salvation Army, 1977—, Tulsa Opera, 1977—, Ark. Basin Devel. Assn., 1978—. With U.S. Navy, 1943-50, 51-53. Mem. Calif. Bar Assn., Tex. Bar Assn., Okla. Bar Assn., Am. Petroleum Inst. (dir. 1980—), Met. Tulsa C. of C. (dir. 1977—). Episcopalian. Clubs: Tulsa (So. Hills Country); (Tulsa); Shriners. Office: PO Box 1650 Tulsa OK 74102

JONES, JAMES ARTHUR, utility co. exec.; b. Anderson, S.C., Sept. 18, 1917; s. James Rol and Maude Magdalene (Pendleton) J.; m. Clara Melba Sharpe, May 7, 1942; children—Elva Jones Summerlin, James Roland, Michael Arthur, Robert Franklin, William Lawrence. B.S., N.C. State U., 1951. With Carolina Power & Light Co., Wilmington and Raleigh, N.C., 1951—, v.p., Raleigh, 1969-70, sr. v.p., 1970-73, exec. v.p., 1973—, chief operating officer, 1976, vice chmn., 1981—, also dir.; Past pres. N.C. State U. Engring. Found. Named Distinguished Engring. Alumnus N.C. State U., 1974, Outstanding Engr. N.C. Soc. Engrs., 1974, Raleigh Engrs., 1976. Fellow ASME; mem. Am. Soc. Nuclear Engrs., Am. Inst. Indsl. Engrs., Nat. Soc. Profl. Engrs., N.C. Soc. Engrs., N.C. Health Physics Soc., Pi Tau Sigma, Phi Kappa Phi. Club: Masons. Home: 3004 Sandia Dr Raleigh NC 27607 Office: 411 Fayetteville St Raleigh NC 27602 *What a man can accomplish is unlimited, provided he is not concerned with receiving the credit.*

JONES, JAMES BEVERLY, engineer, educator; b. Kansas City, Mo., Aug. 21, 1923; s. Alonzo Lewis and Bertha (Crockett) J.; m. Jane Hardcastle, Oct. 20, 1945; children: Ellen Elizabeth, Warren Howard. B.S., Va. Poly. Inst., 1944; M.S.M.E., Purdue U., 1947, Ph.D., 1951. Asst. mech. engr. Engr. Bd., U.S. War Dept., Ft. Belvoir, Va., 1944-45; devel. engr. Gen. Electric Co., Schenectady, 1951-52; asst. instr. Purdue U., Lafayette, Ind., 1945-47, instr., 1947-51, asst. prof., 1951-54, assoc. prof., 1954-57, prof., 1957-64; head dept. mech. engring. Va. Poly. Inst. and State U., Blacksburg, 1964-83, prof., 1964—, head dept., Blacksburg, 1964-83; faculty fellow Swiss Fed. Inst. Tech., Zurich, 1961-62; bd. dirs. Accreditation Bd. for Engring. and Tech., 1981—; cons. mech. engring. Author: (with G.A. Hawkins) Engineering Thermodynamics, 1960. Assoc. fellow AIAA; fellow ASME (v.p. edn. 1984—); mem. Am. Soc. Engring. Edn., Nat. Soc. Profl. Engrs. Presbyterian. Clubs: Rotary, Torch (Blacksburg). Home: 1503 Palmer Dr SE Blacksburg VA 24060

JONES, JAMES EARL, actor; b. Tate County, Miss., Jan. 17, 1931; s. Robert Earl and Ruth (Williams) J.; m. Cecilia Hart, Mar. 15, 1982. B.A., U. Mich., 1953; diploma, Am. Theatre Wing, 1957. Appeared in: plays Romeo and Juliet, 1955, Wedding in Japan, 1957, Sunrise at Campobello, 1958, The Pretender, 1959, The Cool World, 1960, King Henry V, 1960, Measure for Measure, 1960, The Blacks, 1961, A Midsummer Night's Dream, 1961, The Apple, 1961, Moon on a Rainbow Shawl, 1962, Infidel Caesar, 1962, The Merchant of Venice, 1962, The Tempest, 1962, Toys in the Attic, 1962, P.S. 193, 1962, Macbeth, 1962, The Love Nest, 1963, The Last Minstrel, 1963, Othello, numerous appearances, The Winter's Tale, 1963, Mr. Johnson, 1963, Next Time I'll Sing to You, 1963, Bloodknot, 1964, King Lear, 1973, Of Mice and Men, 1974, Paul Robeson, 1977, Master Harold and The Boys, 1982-83; appeared in: movies Dr. Strangelove, 1963, The Man, 1972, Claudine, 1973, The River Niger, 1975, Swashbuckler, 1976, Bingo Long Traveling All-Stars and Motor Kings, 1976, Exorcist II: The Heretic, 1977, The Greatest, 1977, The Last Remake of Beau Geste, 1977, A Piece of the Action, 1978, The Bushido Blade, 1981, Conan the Barbarian, 1982, Blood Tide, 1982; TV appearances include The Defenders, 1962, East Side/West Side, 1963, Camera 3, 1963, Look Up and Live, 1963, The Cay, 1974, King Lear, 1974, Big Joe and Kansas, 1975, UFO Incident, 1975; TV appearances Jesus of Nazareth, 1977, The Greatest Thinks That Almost Happened, 1977, Guyana Tragedy: The Story of Jim Jones, 1980; TV appearances include The Golden Movement: An Olympic Love Story, 1980; narrated: Malcolm X, 1972, Sojourner, 1975, A Day Without Sunshine, 1976; star: TV series Paris, 1979-80; (Recipient The Village Voice Off-Broadway awards 1962, Theatre World award 1962, Tony award for best actor in Great White Hope 1969, Grammy award 1976, medal for spoken lang. Am. Acad. Arts and Letters 1981). Mem. Nat. Council of Arts. Address: care Jack Fields & Assoc Inc 9255 Sunset Blvd Suite 1105 Los Angeles CA 90069 *

JONES, JAMES PICKETT, historian, educator, academic administrator; b. Jacksonville, Fla., June 17, 1931; s. James Pickett and Clare (Brobston) J.; m. Berlin Louise Gabbert, Aug. 27, 1955 (div. 1963); 1 dau., Nancy Berin; m. Clare Elsine Langley, Mar. 21, 1981. B.A., U. Fla., 1953, M.A., 1954, Ph.D., 1960. Instr. history Fla. State U., 1957-61, asst. prof., 1961-66, assoc. prof., 1966-69, prof., 1969—, chmn. dept. history, 1980—, chmn. athletic bd., 1981—; faculty rep. Nat. Collegiate Athletic Assn., 1981—. Author: Black Jack: John A. Logan and Southern Illinois in the Civil War Era, 1967, Frank Church, Civil War Marine, 1974, Yankee Blitzkrieg: Wilson's Raid through Alabama and Georgia, 1976, John A. Logan, Stalwart Republican from Illinois, 1982; editor: Fla. State, 1977—. Recipient Pres.'s Teaching award Fla. State U., 1978. Mem. Orgn. Am. Historians, So. Hist. Assn., Ill. State Hist. Soc., Fla. Hist. Soc. Democrat. Office: Dept History Fla State U Tallahassee FL 32306

JONES, JAMES R., congressman; b. Muskogee, Okla., May 5, 1939; m. Olivia Barclay, 1968; children—Geoffrey Gardner, Adam Winston. A.B. in Journalism and Govt, U. Okla., 1961; LL.B., Georgetown U., 1964. Bar: Okla. bar 1964. Legis. asst. to Congressman Ed Edmondson, 1961-64; spl. asst. to Pres. Lyndon Johnson, 1965-69; mem. 93d-97th congresses from 1st Dist. Okla., chmn. budget com. Served as capt. CIC AUS, 1964-65. Mem. Am., Okla., Tulsa bar assns., Am. Legion, Tulsa C. of C. Democrat. Club: Rotarian. Home: Tulsa OK Office: 203 Cannon House Office Bldg Washington DC 20515 *In essence, I try to follow the admonition of Thomas Aquinas, "To work as if everything depends upon you, and pray as if everything depends on God." By attempting to pursue a daily course of excellence in all responsibilities, I hope that when my earthly work is completed, they will say of me, "that I gave it my all."*

JONES, JAMES REES, ret. oil co. exec.; b. Britton, S.D., Nov. 26, 1916; s. Buell Fay and Florence (Bockler) J.; m. Betty Jane Preston, May 28, 1943; children—Quentin Buell, Newton James, Preston Lee. B.S. in Accountancy, U. Ill., 1938. From accountant to sr. accountant Ernst & Ernst (C.P.A.'s), Detroit and Kalamazoo, 1938-41, 46-48; auditor, then div. auditor, chem. plant office mgr. Pan Am. Petroleum Corp., 1948-56; comptroller Amoco Chems. Corp., Chgo., 1956-62; mgr. auditing Standard Oil Co., Ind., 1962-63; controller Murphy Oil Corp., El Dorado, Ark., 1963-74, v.p., 1974-75; also dir.; chmn., mng. dir. Canam Offshore Ltd., Hamilton, Bermuda, 1975—; pres., dir. Mentor Ins. Ltd., Hamilton, 1975—; controller Ocean Drilling & Exploration Co., El Dorado, 1963-66, also dir.; controller, dir. Deltic Farm & Timber Co., Inc., El Dorado, 1963-72, v.p., 1963-75. Past mem. El Dorado Water Utilities Commn.; past pres., bd. dirs. United Campaign El Dorado. Served to capt. AUS, 1941-46. Mem. Fin. Execs. Inst., Am. Petroleum Inst., Mid-Continent Oil and Gas Assn., Phi Kappa Psi. Home: 15 Cedarwood Ln Russelville AR 72801

JONES, JAMES RICHARD, educator; b. Saginaw, Mich., May 25, 1940; s. George B. and F. Rena (Jerome) J.; m. children—Kimme Ann, Kriste Gay, Kelle Lyn, Karme Jill. B.A., Mich. State U., 1962, M.B.A., 1964; D.B.A., Ariz. State U., 1969. Research analyst Mich. Public Service Commn., Lansing, 1962; systems analyst Allis-Chalmers Mfg. Co., West Allis, Wis., 1964-65; asst. prof. transp. U. Houston, 1967-70; asso. prof. mktg. U. Ga., Athens, 197—72; spl. asst. Dept. Transp., Washington, 1972-74, transp. economist, 1974-76; Disting. prof. transp. Memphis State U., 1976-81; George R. Brown Disting. prof. bus. Trinity U., San Antonio, 1981—; cons. in field. Author books in field; contbr. articles to profl. jours.; bd. editors: Jour. Bus. Logistics, 1978—. Keeshin fellow, 1963. Mem. Am. Soc. Traffic and Transp. (exam. bd.), Am. Mktg. Assn., Nat. Council Phys. Distbn. Mgmt., Transp. Research Forum, Transp. Research Bd., So. Mktg. Assn., Acad. Mktg. Sci., Am. Inst. Decision Scis. Home: 2811 Woodbury Dr San Antonio TX 78217 Office: Trinity U 715 Stadium Dr San Antonio TX 78284

JONES, JAMES ROBERT, obstetrician, gynecologist, educator; b. Bklyn., Dec. 16, 1934; s. Harold Edward and Elenor Jean (O'Connor) J.; m. Carolann Patricia Contiguglia, Aug. 1, 1972; children—Michael, Francis, Leslie, Laurie, Christopher. B.S., Manhattan Coll., 1956; M.D., SUNY, Bklyn., 1960. Diplomate Am. Bd. Obstetrics and Gynecology. Intern L.I. Coll. Hosp., Bklyn., 1960-61, resident in obstetrics and gynecology, 1961-64, cons. reproductive endocrinology, 1964-66; NIH fellow reproductive endocrinology U. Calif., San Francisco, 1964-66; practice medicine specializing in obstetrics and gynecology, San Francisco, 1964-66; asst. prof. obstetrics gynecology SUNY, Bklyn., 1969-72, dir. reproductive endocrinology, 1969-77, dir. residency obstetrics and gynecology, 1970-75, asso. prof. obstetrics and gynecology, dir. gender identification service, 1972-77; prof., chmn. dept. obstetrics and gynecology Rutgers Med. Sch., Piscataway, N.J., 1977—; cons. reproductive endocrinology Wycoff Heights Hosp., Bklyn.-Cumberland Hosp., L.I. Coll. Hosp., Glen Cove Hosp. Editor: Am. Cancer Soc. teaching tapes Advances in Cancer Management, 1971, Gynecologic Oncology, 1975; asso. editor: N.Y. Jour. Medicine, 1970—; contbr. articles in field to profl. jours. and books. Served to maj. USMCR, 1966-68; Vietnam. Decorated Bronze Star medal. Mem. Am. Coll. Obstetrics and Gynecology, AMA, AAAS, Assn. Prof. Gynecology and Obstetrics, Endocrine Soc., Am. Fertility Soc., Bklyn. Gynecol. Soc. (sec. 1976—), N.Y. Obstet. Soc., N. Shore Sci. Mus., Am. Mus. Natural History. Democrat. Home: Private Rd Mendham NJ 07945 Office: Dept Obstetrics Gynecology Rutgers Med Sch new brunswick NJ 08903

JONES, JAMES ROBERT, coal mining and sales company executive; b. Chgo., Jan. 19, 1921; s. Charles Henry and Ragna (Rasmussen) J.; m. Anita M. Hertz, June 16, 1956; 1 son, Gregory A. B.S. in M.E., Purdue U., 1942. Group leader engring. goodyear Aircraft Corp., Akron, Ohio, 1942-46; mgr. coal utilization services Peabody Coal and Predecessors, Chgo., 1946-69, dir. tech. services, St. Louis, 1970, dir. environ. quality, 1970-79, v.p. environ. affairs, 1979—. Mem. Ky. Air Pollution Control Commn., 1966-72; mem. tech. adv. com. Ill. Air Pollution Control Bd., 1967-69. Served 2d lt. U.S. Army, 1946. Recipient Percy Nicholls award ASME, 1982. Mem. Am. Soc. Mech. Engrs. (mem. bd. govs. 1983—), Am. Mining Congress (chmn. com. 1980—). Republican. Episcopalian. Home: 21 Meadowbrook Country Club Ballwin MO 63011 Office: Peabody Coal Co 301 N Memorial Dr Saint Louis MO 63102

JONES, JAMES THOMAS, state official, lawyer; b. Twin Falls, Idaho, May 13, 1942; s. Henry C. and Eunice Irene (Martens) J.; m. Nancy June Babson, Nov. 25, 1972; 1 dau., Katherine A. Student, Idaho State U., 1960-61; B.A., U. Oreg., 1964; J.D., Northwestern U., 1967. Bar: Idaho 1967. Legis. asst. to U.S. Senator, Washington, 1970-72; law practice, Jerome, Idaho, 1973-82; atty. gen. State of Idaho, Boise, 1973—. Bd. dirs. Idaho Vietnam Vets Leadership Program, Boise, Idaho Cancer Soc., Boise. Served to capt. U.S. Army, 1967-79; Vietnam. Decorated Bronze Star, Air medal with 4 oak leaf clusters, Cross of Gallantry (Vietnam), Army Commendation medal. Mem. Idaho State Bar Assn., Idaho Trial Lawyers Assn., ABA, Am. Legion, Idaho Farm Bur., VFW. Republican. Lutheran. Lodge: Rotary. Office: Atty Gen Idaho Statehouse Boise ID 83720

JONES, JENKIN LLOYD, newspaper publisher; b. Madison, Wis., Nov. 1, 1911; s. Richard Lloyd and Georgia (Hayden) J.; m. Ana Maria de Andrada Rocha, July 30, 1976; children: Jenkin Lloyd, David, Georgia; step-children: Maria Alice Rocha, Paulo Rocha. Ph.B., U. Wis., 1933; various hon. degrees. Reporter, Tulsa Tribune, 1933, mng. editor, 1938, editor, 1941—, pub., 1963—; dir. Newspaper Printing Corp., Tulsa. Author: The Changing World, 1966; writer syndicated weekly column. Served to lt. comdr. USNR, 1944-46; PTO. Recipient William Allen White award Okla. Hall of Fame, 1957; Fourth Estate award Am. Legion, 1970; Freedom Leadership award Freedoms Found., 1969; Disting. Service award U. Wis., 1970, U. Okla., 1971, Okla. State U., 1972. Mem. Am. Soc. Newspaper Editors (pres. 1957), Inter Am. Press Assn. (dir.), U.S. C. of C. (pres. 1969), Internat. Press Inst. Republican. Unitarian. Clubs: So. Hills Country, Summit (Tulsa). Home: 6683 S Jamestown Pl Tulsa OK 74136 Office: Tulsa Tribune Box 1770 Tulsa OK 74102 *My theory that human history is like a point on the rim of a wheel — an endless series of downs and ups, accompanied by forward progress, has saved me from the cynicism, if not despair, characteristic of many journalists. The lesson of fallen civilizations is that all good things decay, and the lesson of nature is that out of decay new life springs.*

JONES, JENNIFER, actress; b. Tulsa; d. Philip R. and Flora Mae (Suber) Isley; m. Robert Walker, Jan. 2, 1939 (div. June 1945); children: Robert Hudson, Michael Ross; m. David O. Selznick, July 13, 1949 (dec. 1965); 1 dau., Mary Jennifer; m. Norton Simon, May 30, 1971. Ed., pub. schs., Dallas; student, Monte Cassino Jr. Coll., Northwestern U., Am. Acad. Dramatic Arts. Appeared stock cos.; actress in motion pictures, 1943—, The Song of Bernadette, Since You Went Away, Cluny Brown, Love Letters, Duel in the Sun, We Were Strangers, Madame Bovary, Portrait of Jennie, Carrie, Wild Heart, Ruby Gentry, Indiscretion of an American Wife, Beat the Devil, Love is a Many-Splendored Thing, Good Morning, Miss Dove, The Man in the Gray Flannel Suit, The Barretts of Wimpole Street, A Farewell to Arms, Tender Is The Night, The Idol, The Towering Inferno, Eagles over London. Recipient Acad. Motion Pictures Arts and Scis. award for best performance by an actress (for work in Song of Bernadette), 1943; Winged Victory award, France, 1948; Triunfo award, Spain, 1953; Film Critics Award, Japan, 1953; First Ann. Audience award, 1955; winner Nat. Critics Poll, 1955; award Stars and Stripes citation for war work ARC; medal and citation for work at front during Korean War. Office: PO Box 367 Malibu CA 90265 *

JONES, JENNINGS HINCH, educator; b. Petrolia, Pa., Aug. 19, 1913; s. George Findred and Florence Jennings (Hinch) J.; m. Katherine E. Campbell, Nov. 16, 1940; children—Ellen F. (Mrs. Frank La Belle), Trudy K. (Mrs. Michael Schobinger). B.S., Pa. State U., 1934, M.S., 1937, Ph.D., 1941. Chemist Pa. Coal Products Co., Petrolia, 1934-36; faculty Pa. State U., University Park, 1941—, prof. chem. engring., 1964-79, prof. emeritus, 1979—; cons. in field. Mem. Am. Chem. Soc., Am. Inst. Chem. Engrs., Combustion Inst., Sigma Xi, Phi Lambda Upsilon. Patentee in field. Home: 229 S Gill St State College PA 16801 Office: Fenske Lab University Park PA 16802

JONES, JERRY LYNN, educator; b. Grandfield, Okla., Mar. 28, 1933; s. Euel Taylor and Margie Leona (DeVaughan) J.; m. Gail Kathleen Jones, Aug. 8, 1954; children—Kathleen DeVaughan, Jerry Clifton, Gregory Taylor. B.A., Okla. State U., 1957; M.S. (NSF fellow 1959-60), 1960; postgrad., U. Oreg., 1957-58; Ph.D. (Am. Oil Co. fellow 1961-62), U. Ark., 1963. Asst. prof. chemistry Tex. A&M U. (College Station), 1962-68; asso. prof. chemistry Central Wash U., Ellensburg, 1968-73, prof., 1973—, interim dean grad. sch. and research, 1976-77, spl. asst. to pres., 1979—. Asso. editor: sci. and tech. USA Today; contbr. articles to profl. jours. Served with AUS, 1954-56. Fellow Am. Inst. Chemists; mem. N.Y. Acad. Scis., Am. Chem. Soc., Sigma Xi, Phi Lambda Upsilon. Club: Masons. Home: 405 N Anderson St Ellensburg WA 98926

JONES, JOHN BARCLAY, JR., lawyer; b. Hinsdale, Ill., Jan. 4, 1928; s. John Barclay and Anna Bishop (Harvey) J.; m. Anita Evelyn Bills, Dec. 30, 1950; children: Katherine Anita, Phoebe Bishop, Jonathan Barclay. A.B., Harvard U., 1950, LL.B. magna cum laude, 1953. Bar: D.C. 1953, U.S. Supreme Ct. 1957. Assoc. firm Covington & Burling, Washington, 1953-61, partner, 1965—; first asst. tax div. Dept. Justice, Washington, 1961-65; Chmn. bd. trustees Sidwell Friends Sch., Washington, 1975-77; bd. mgrs. Haverford Coll., 1976—, chmn. bd. mgrs., 1982—; co-chmn. Lawyers Com. Civil Rights Under Law, 1979-81. Mem. Am. Bar Assn. (council sect. taxation 1978-81, vice chmn. 1981—). Quaker. Club: Met. (Washington). Office: 1201 Pennsylvania Ave NW Washington DC 20004

JONES, J(OHN) CHARLES, educator; b. Library, Pa., Mar. 18, 1921; s. Clarence Gibson and Frances Mary (Bradshaw) J.; m. Marguerite Alice Strouse, June 29, 1944; children—Marilyn, Steven Ralph, Eric Donald, Lawrence Walter (dec.). A.B., Bucknell U., 1942; M.S., Cornell U., 1950, Ph.D., 1953. Asst. prof. child devel. U. Ill., 1953-54; asst. prof. edn. Bucknell U., 1954-56, asso. prof., 1956-58, prof., 1958—, chmn. dept., 1958-63, acting chmn. dept., 1971-72; dir. Instructional Media Center, 1970-71; vis. prof. Inst. Child Study, U. Md., summer 1956—, Western Wash. State Coll., 1962-63; sr. lectr. Victoria U., New Zealand, 1968. Author: Learning, 1968, Growing Children, 1974, also monograph. Served with AUS, 1942-46. Recipient research grants Ford Found., 1958, AAAS, 1960, U.S. Office Edn., 1961, 72, postdoctoral fellowship NSF, 1963. Home: River Rd RD 1 Lewisburg PA 17837

JONES, JOHN DAVID, electrical engineering executive; b. Natural Bridge, Ala., Oct. 1, 1922; s. Will H. and Minnie (Shank) J.; m. Barbara Lobb, July 18, 1946 (div. Apr. 1970); children: Judith Ann, Mark Lobb; m. Dolphine Disheroon, June 5, 1971. B.E.E., Auburn U., 1947. Utility engr. Ala. Power Co., Birmingham, 1947-62, asst. mgr. trans. and dist., 1962-63, asst. to sr. exec. v.p., 1963-65, div. mgr., 1965-68, v.p. power delivery, 1968-77, sr. v.p., 1977—. Served to maj. gen. AUSR, 1942-79. Mem. Edison Electric Inst., Southeastern Electric Exchange. Clubs: Downtown, Relay House (Birmingham). Home: 2651 Swiss Ln Birmingham AL 35226 Office: Alabama Power Co 600N 18th St Birmingham Al 3529

JONES, JOHN EARL, construction company executive. B.A., Carleton Coll., 1956; postgrad., U. Chgo., 1958-60, Northwestern U., 1960-61. Sr. v.p. Continental Ill. Nat. Bank and Trust Co., Chgo., 1957-80; with CBI Industries, Inc., Oak Brook, Ill., 1980—, exec. v.p., treas., 1982—, also dir.; dir. Allied Products Corp., Imperial Clevite, Inc. Bd. dirs. ann. meeting chmn. Am. Cancer Soc., Ill.; trustee Glenwood Sch., Ill.; mem. bus. adv. council U. Ill. Office: CBI Industries Inc 800 Jorie Blvd Oak Brook IL 60521

JONES, JOHN EVAN, medical educator; b. Mt. Pleasant, Utah, Oct. 29, 1930; s. Aaron Eugene and Malinda May (Flowers) J.; m. Judith Carolyn Watson, Dec. 22, 1954; children: Malinda Anne, Evan Alan, Nathan Keith. A.A., Coll. Eastern Utah, 1950; B.S., U. Utah, 1952, M.D., 1955. Diplomate Am. Bd. Internal Medicine. Intern U. Minn. Hosps., Mpls., 1955-56, resident, 1956-59; dir. tng. endocrinology USPHS, Mpls. and Morgantown, W.Va., 1959-61; mem. faculty W.Va. U., Morgantown, 1961—, assoc. prof. medicine, 1967-70, prof. medicine, 1970—, chmn. div. metabolism and endocrinology, 1970-74, dean, 1974-82, v.p. for health scis., 1982—. Served with USNR, 1957-59. Fellow A.C.P. (gov. for W.Va. 1975-79); mem. Am. Soc. Clin. Nutrition, Endocrine Soc., Central Soc. Clin. Research, Alpha Omega Alpha. Home: 1286 Woodhaven Dr Morgantown WV 26505

JONES, JOHN GRANDEL, finance management executive; b. Mpls., 1920; m. Eleanor E'we, 1944; children: Jeryl Gulin, Grandel. Ed., U. Minn., 1941; postgrad., Harvard Bus. Sch., NYU. Former chief fin. officer, treas., dir. Chesebrough-Pond's, Inc., N.Y.C.; controller, gen. mgr. container Machinery Bostitch div. Textron, East Greenwich, R.I., 1948-62; mgmt. positions Gen. Electric Co., Bridgeport, Conn., 1941-42, 45-46; sr. v.p. finance, dir., chmn. fin. com., chmn. sr. mgmt. com. Econ. Lab. Inc., St. Paul, 1970-73; v.p., mem. mgmt. com., corp. planning com. CBS, Inc., N.Y.C., 1973-77; v.p., dir. Ross Stebbins, Inc., N.Y.C., 1978-82; fin. cons. Frank Henjes Co., Inc., 1982—; cons. Spencer Group, New Canaan, Conn.; dir. Chartwell Ltd.; past dir. Associated Engrs., First Trust Co., Clinton Oil Co., Real Petroleum. Served to lt. USNR, 1942-45. Mem. Fin. Execs. Inst. Nat. Metal Trades Assn. (pres. New Eng. 1961-62); Mem. Financial Execs. Inst. Beta Theta Pi. Presbyn. Clubs: Watch Hill (R.I.) Yacht; Landmark (Stamford, Conn.); Wee Burn Country (Darien, Conn.). Home: 30 Sunswyck Rd Darien CT 06820 Office: 111 Broadway #1400 New York NY 10006

JONES, JOHN HARRIS, lawyer, banker; b. New Blaine, Ark., Apr. 9, 1922; s. Ira Burton and Byrd (Harris); m. Marjorie Crosby Hart, 1983. A.B., State Coll. Ark., 1941; postgrad., George Washington U. Law Sch., 1941-42; LL.B., Yale, 1947. Bar: Ark. 1946, U.S. Supreme Ct 1946. Communications clk. FBI, 1941-42; practice in, Pine Bluff, 1947—; spl. judge Circuit Ct., 1950; chmn. bd. Pine Bluff Nat. Bank, 1964-77, pres., 1966-76; Mem. Ark. Bd. Law Examiners, 1953-59; Republican nominee for U.S. Senate, 1974; Rep. presdl. elector, 1980; v.p., dir. John Rust Found., 1953-60. Served to 1st lt. USAAF, 1943-45. Decorated Purple Heart, Air medal. Mem. ABA, Ark. Bar Assn., Jefferson County Bar Assn. (pres. 1959-60), Am. Judicature Soc., Res. Officers Assn. Mem. Christian Ch. (elder 1963-65, trustee 1965-71, 78—). Club: Pine Bluff Country. Home: 4001 Cherry St Pine Bluff AR 71603 Office: National Bldg Pine Bluff AR 71611

JONES, JOHN MARTIN, JR., lawyer; b. Balt., Dec. 31, 1928; s. John Martin and Nannalee (Rogers) J.; m. Dayle Joan Fort, July 27, 1969; children—David Mallory, Kelly Anne, Jeffrey Wallace Arthur, Kathleen Celeste; stepchildren—Martha Dayle Nesbitt, William Fort Nesbitt, Howard Scott Nesbitt. A.B., U. Md., 1951, LL.B., 1953. Bar: Md. Ct. Appeals bar 1953, U.S. Dist. Ct. bar for Dist. Md 1953, U.S. Ct. Appeals bar for 4th Circuit 1954, ICC 1956, U.S. Supreme Ct. bar 1959. Assoc. firm Piper & Marbury, Balt., 1954-59, ptnr., 1960—; asst. atty. gen. State of Md., 1959-60; mem. Md. Gov.'s Commn. to Study Tax Laws. Mem. Balt. Area council Boy Scouts Am.; publ. adv. Regional Planning Council, Greater Balt., 1977. Mem. Am. Bar Assn., Md. State Bar Assn., Bar Assn. Balt. City, Am. Judicature Soc., Am. Law Inst., Order of Coif, Delta Theta Phi, Delta Kappa Epsilon. Clubs: Center, Yale of N.Y.C., DKE of N.Y.C., Rule Day.; Univ. (Washington). Mem. adv. com. in drafting and preparation of Am. Law Inst.'s Model Land Development Code, 1970-77. Home: 8025 Strauff Rd Baltimore MD 21204 Office: 36 S Charles St Baltimore MD 21201 Office: 888 16th St NW Washington DC 20006 *Palma Non Sine Pulvere.*

JONES, JOHN PAUL *See* **BALDWIN, JOHN**

JONES, JOHN TILFORD, JR., broadcasting executive; b. Dallas, Dec. 2, 1917; s. John Tilford and Margaret (Wilson) J.; m. Winifred Ann Small, Oct. 20, 1945; children: Melissa Ann, Jesse Holman II, John Clinton. Student, N. Mex. Mil. Inst., 1935-38, U. Tex., 1938-40. Pres. Houston Chronicle Pub. Co., 1949-66, Houston Consol. TV Co., 1954-67, Rusk Corp., 1965—; broadcast exec. KTRH-AM, KLOL-FM; pres. Battleground Corp.; dir. Fischback Corp., Am. Gen. Ins. Co., CRS Group, Inc. Vice pres., dir. Tex. Med. Center, Inc. Served from lt. to capt. AUS, 1940-45; ETO. Presbyterian. Office: 811 Rusk Ave Suite 1313 Houston TX 77002

JONES, JOHN WILEY, chem. co. exec.; b. Emporium, Pa., Apr. 10, 1901; s. George Poole and Sarah (Wiley) J.; m. Helen Lucille Kline, Sept. 5, 1924; children—Jack, Robert, David, Nancy. Grad., U. Pa., 1924; LL.D., Lycoming Coll., Williamsport, Pa. With Butterick Pub. Co., 1924-28, Erwin Wasey Co., 1928-30; owner, chmn. bd. Jones Chems. Inc., Caledonia, N.Y. Author books on bus., self-devel. Pres., exec. com. Genesee council Boy Scouts Am.; trustee Rochester (N.Y.) Inst. Tech.; trustee, mem. exec. com. Eisenhower Coll., Seneca Falls, N.Y. Recipient Silver Beaver award Boy Scouts Am.; named Man of Yr. Nathaniel Rochester Soc., Rochester Inst. Tech., 1977. Mem. N.A.M., U.S. C. of C., Rochester C. of C., Livingston C. of C., Beta Theta Pi. Lay reader Presbyterian Ch. Clubs: Masons, Lions (N.Y.C.); Rochester; Ponte Vedra (Jacksonville, Fla.); Batavia (N.Y.); Stafford Country; Capitol Hill (Washington); Indpls. Athletic; Lake Shore Country (Geneva, N.Y.). Home: 3225 East Ave Caldeonia NY 14423 Office: 10 Iroquis Rd Caldeonia NY 14423

JONES, JOIE PIERCE, scientist, educator, writer; b. Brownwood, Tex., Mar. 4, 1941; s. Aubrey M. and Mildred K. (Pierce) J.; m. Kay Becknell, June 12, 1965. B.A. (Jr. fellow 1961-63), U. Tex., Austin, 1963, M.A., 1965; Ph.D., Brown U., 1970. Sr. scientist Bolt Beranek & Newman, Inc., Cambridge, Mass., 1970-75; asso. prof., dir. ultrasonics research lab. Case Western Res. U. Sch. Medicine, Cleve., 1975-77; prof., chief med. imaging, dir. grad. studies, dept. radiol. scis. U. Calif., Irvine, 1977—; cons. acoustics; pres. Computer Sci. Systems, 1978—; founding gen. ptnr. Of Food and Wine, 1982—, Meditherm Assocs., Ltd., 1983—; proposal reviewer NSF and NIH, 1974—; Appointee sci. and tech. adv. com. Pres. Carter, 1977-81. Author 2 books; editor: Ultrasound in Medicine and Biology, 1976, IEEE Procs, 1976; mem.: editorial bd. Jour. Clin. Ultrasound, 1977—; contbr. 100 articles to profl. jours. Active vol. local govt. Mem. Am. Inst. Ultrasound in Medicine, Acoustical Soc. Am., Am. Phys. Soc., IEEE, AAAS, Am. Assn. Physicists in Medicine, Fedn. Am. Scientists, Phi Beta Kappa. Democrat. Patentee in field (5). Home: 2094 San Remo Dr Laguna Beach CA 92651 Office: Dept Radiol Sci U Calif Irvine CA 92717

JONES, JOSEPH FRECH, food co. exec.; b. DeSoto, Mo., Nov. 5, 1914; s. Roscoe B. and Eva (Frech) J.; m. Frances K. McLaughlin, June 27, 1945; children—Michael F., Christopher J., Mark J., Nancy K., Sarah M. B.S. in Mech. Engring, U. Mo., 1936. Registered profl. engr., Ind., Mo. Mem. NAM (dir. 1974-80). With prodn. dept. Ralston Purina Co., St. Louis, 1936-42, mgr. prodn. div., 1945-60; v.p. Central Soya Co., Inc., Ft. Wayne, Ind., 1960-65, exec. v.p., 1965-70, pres., 1970-79, chief exec. officer, 1975-79, chmn. bd., 1976-79, ret., 1979, dir., 1965—; dir. Lincoln Fin. Corp., Ft. Wayne.; Bd. dirs. Mo. U. Devel. Fund, 1974—. Served to lt. comdr. USNR, 1942-45

JONES, JOSEPH LOUIS, manufacturing company executive; b. Sheppards, Va., Feb. 27, 1923; s. Joseph Louis and Edna (Elcan) J.; m. Dorothy Jeanne Jennings, June 21, 1949; children: Joseph, Catherine, Carolyn. B.A., Va. Poly Inst., 1947. With Armstrong World Industries, Lancaster, Pa., 1947—, prodn. mgr., 1961-66, v.p. carpet ops., 1966-74, exec. v.p., dir., 1974-83, chmn., pres., chief exec. officer, 1983—; dir. Carpenter Technology, Reading, Pa. Trustee Lancaster Gen. Hosp. Served to capt., inf. AUS, 1943-46. Decorated Bronze Star. Mem. Lancaster C. of C., NAM (dir.). Republican. Presbyterian (trustee). Club: Lancaster Country. Home: 121 Eshelman Rd Lancaster PA 17601 Office: Liberty and Charlotte Sts Lancaster PA 17604

JONES, JULIAN WARD, classical studies educator. Chancellor, prof. classical studies Coll. William and Mary, Williamsburg, Va. Office: Coll William and Mary Dept Classical Studies Williamsburg VA 23185§

JONES, K.C., professional basketball coach; b. San Francisco, May 25, 1932. Ed., U. San Francisco. Player Boston Celtics, NBA, 1958-67; coach Brandeis U., Waltham, Mass., 1967-71; asst. coach Los Angeles Lakers, NBA, 1971-72; coach San Diego Conquistadores, ABA, 1972-73, Capital Bullets (later Washington), 1973-76; asst. coach Boston Celtics, NBA, 1977-83, coach, 1983—; mem. U.S. Olympic Basketball Team, 1956, NCAA Championship Team, 1955, NBA Championship Team, 1959-66; coach NBA All-Star Game, 1975, 84. Served with U.S. Army, 1956-58. Office: Boston Celtics Boston Garden North Sta Boston MA 02114 *

JONES, KENSINGER, advertising executive; b. St. Louis, Oct. 18, 1919; s. Walter C. and Anna (Kensinger) J.; m. Alice May Guseman, Oct. 7, 1944; children: Jeffrey, Janice A. Jones Geary. Student, Washington U., St. Louis, 1938-39. TV writer, advt. agy. supr., 1952-57; exec. v.p., creative dir. Campbell-Ewald Co., Detroit, 1957-68; sr. v.p., creative dir. D.P. Brother & Co., Detroit, 1968-70; sr. v.p., exec. creative dir. Leo Burnett Co., Inc., Chgo., 1970-73; regional creative dir. Leo Burnett Pty. Ltd., Sydney, Australia, 1973-75, Leo Burnett, S.E. Asia, 1975-77, advt. cons., 1977—; creative supr. Biggs/Gilmore, 1981-83; lectr. Mich. State U., 1982—. Writer: radio series Land We Live In, 1945-52; Author: Enter Singapore, 1974. Chmn. Barry County Planning and Zoning Commn., Parks and Recreation Commn.; county grants coordinator, Barry County, 1977-78; mem. communications and exploring com. Nat. council Boy Scouts Am.; bd. dirs. World Med. Relief, Inc. Served with inf. U.S. Army, 1940-45. Recipient Silver Beaver award, Silver Salute Mich. State U., 1982. Mem. Nat. Def. Exec. Res., Am. Angus Assn., Vet. Car Club Am. Clubs: The Players, Recess, Circumnavigators, Adcraft of Detroit. Home: 425 Pritchardville Rd Hastings MI 49058 Office: 312 Com Arts Bldg Mich State U East Lansing MI 48824 *The opportunity to absorb, examine, synthesize and then utilize facts and experience is what makes creative endeavor fascinating. Somehow the individual mind finds new and meaningful relationships between previously unrelated data. An idea is born. It becomes an advertising campaign, a book or movie, a new product. Trying to find those new relationships makes life rewarding in so many ways. Dissatisfaction with the status quo is the prod toward all progress.*

JONES, LAURIE LYNN, editor; b. Kerrville, Tex., Sept. 2, 1947; d. Charles Clinton and Jean Laurie (Davidson) J.; m. C. Frederick Childs, June 26, 1976; children: Charles Newell, Cyrus Trevor. B.A., U. Tex., 1969. Asst. to dir. coll. admissions Columbia U., N.Y.C., 1969-70; asst. to dir. Office Alumni-Columbia U., N.Y.C., 1970-71; asst. advt. mgr. Book World, 1971-72, Washington Post-Chgo. Tribune, 1971-72; editorial asst. N.Y. Mag., N.Y.C., 1972-74, asst. editor, 1974, sr. editor, 1974-76, mng. editor, 1976—. Mem. Am. Soc. Mag. Editors, Women in Coummunication, Advt. Women N.Y. Republican. Methodist. Home: 40 Great Jones St New York NY 10012 Office: NY Mag 755 2d Ave New York NY 10017

JONES, LAURIE PITTS, energy co. exec.; b. New Canton, Va., Mar. 12, 1921; s. Plummer Flippen and Lottie (Pitts) J.; m. Naomi Jones, Oct. 19, 1946; children—Judith Jones Snyder, Laurie Pitts, Louis Dibrell. B.A., U. Richmond, Va., M.A., 1948. With Entex Inc. (and predecessors), 1948—, Fla. div. mgr., 1965-66, v.p., dir. mktg., 1967-75, sr. v.p. mktg. and personnel, Houston, 1975—. Past mem. budget com. Houston United Fund; exec. bd. mem.-at-large local Boy Scouts Am; past sec. Mental Health Assn., Houston. Served to lt. (j.g.) USNR, 1942-46. Mem. Am. Gas Assn., So. Gas Assn. (dir. 1975-78), Natural Gas Men Houston, Houston C. of C., Tex. C. of C. (dir.), East Tex. C. of C. (dir.), South Tex. C. of C. (dir.). Presbyterian. Clubs: Rotary, Petroleum (Houston). Home: 13418 Myrtlea St Houston TX 77079 Office: 1200 Milam St Houston TX 77002

JONES, LAWRENCE CAMPBELL, manufacturing company executive; b. Cleve., Aug. 30, 1913; s. Norton Taylor and Anna (Campbell) J.; m. Nancy Ellen Jackman, Oct. 7, 1939; children: Judy Jackman Jones Gordon, Robert Norton. B.A., Colgate U., 1935. With sales dept. Una Welding Co., Cleve., 1935-36; salesman N.Am. Coal Corp., Clevel., 1937-38, Davies Can Co. div. Van Dorn Co., 1939-45, gen. mgr., 1945-52; pres. Van Dorn Co., Clevel., 1952—, chmn. bd., 1974—; dir. Scott Fetzer Co., Cleve., RPM, Inc., Nat. Solvent Corp. Trustee Dyke Coll., Cleve.; chmn. bd. dirs. Cleanland Ohio, Cleve., 1978; assoc. trustee Woodland East Community Orgn., Cleve.; bd. dirs., mem. exec. com. Greater Cleve. Growth Assn.; mem. adv. bd. Bond Ct. Hotel, Cleve. Republican. Presbyterian. Clubs: Union, Peeper Pike, Canterbury Golf (Cleve.); Cleve. Skating; University (Cleve.); Cleve. Playhouse; La Quinta Hotel and Golf (Calif.). Home: 20925 Colby Rd Shaker Heights OH 44122 Office: Van Dorn Co 2700 E 79th St Cleveland OH 44104

JONES, LAWRENCE MARION, recreational equipment manufacturing company executive; b. Southard, Okla., 1931. M.S., Wichita State U.; Ph.D., Harvard U. With Coleman Co. Inc., Wichita, Kans., 1950-52, market analyst, asst. to pres., 1956-64, treas., 1964-66, sr. v.p., gen. mgr. outing products group, 1966-71, pres., chief exec. officer, 1971—; dir. Fourth Nat. Bank & Trust Co. Wichita, Fleming Cos. Inc., Cessna Aircraft Co. Bd. dirs. Wichita State U. Endowment Assn. Office: Coleman Co Inc 250 N St Francis Ave Wichita KS 67201 *

JONES, LAWRENCE MCCENEY, JR., army officer, legal adminstr.; b. West Point, N.Y., Aug. 30, 1924; s. Lawrence McCeney and Elizabeth Trueman (King) J.; m. Janis Irene Owens, May 22, 1948; children—Douglas Owen, Stephen Anderson. B.S., U.S. Mil. Acad., 1945; M.S., U. So. Calif., 1950. Commd. 2d lt. U.S. Army, 1945, advanced through grades to maj. gen., 1974; service in, Japan, Korea, Ger. and Vietnam; asst. dep. chief staff ops. U.S. Army (Continental Army Command), 1970-73, dep. chief staff logistics, Ft. McPherson, Ga., 1974-76; comdr. (21st Support Command), Kaiserslautern, Ger., 1976-79, U.S. Army (Readiness Region III), Ft. George G. Meade, Md., 1979-80, ret., 1980; chief of staff firm Patton, Boggs & Blow, Washington, 1980—. Contbr. articles to mil. jours. Decorated Disting. Service medal, Legion of Merit with 3 oak leaf clusters, Air medal with 11 oak leaf clusters, Army Commendation medal with 2 oak leaf clusters. Mem. Assn. U.S. Army, Assn. Grads. U.S. Mil. Acad., Assn. Legal Adminstrs. Republican. Episcopalian. Clubs: Army-Navy (Washington); (Army-Navy Country); Army-Navy (Alexandria, Va.). Home: 4336 Westover Pl NW Washington DC 20016 Office: Patton Boggs & Blow 2550 M St NW Washington DC 20037

JONES, LAWRENCE NEALE, university dean, clergyman; b. Moundsville, W.Va., Apr. 24, 1921; s. Eugene Wayman and Rosa (Bruce) J.; m. Mary Ellen Cooley, Mar. 29, 1945; children: Mary Lynn (Mrs. Gary C. Walker), Rodney Bruce. B.Ed., W. Va. State Coll., 1942, LL.D., 1965; M.A., U. Chgo., 1948; B.D., Oberlin Grad. Sch., 1956; Ph.D., Yale U., 1961; LL.D., Jewish Theol. Sem., 1971. Ordained to ministry United Ch. Christ, 1956; student Christian Movement Middle Atlantic Region, 1957-60; dean chapel Fisk U., 1960-65; dean students Union Theol. Sem., N.Y.C., 1965-71, prof., 1970, dean, 1971-74, acting pres., 1970; dean Sch. Religion, Howard U., Washington, 1975—; Pres. Civil Rights Coordinating Council, Nashville, 1963-64. Bd. dirs. Sheltering Arms and Children's Service, 1970-75, Inst. Social and Religious Studies Jewish Sem., United Ch. Bd. for World Ministries, 1969-75; bd. dirs., sec. exec. com. Assn. Theol. Schs., U.S. and Can.; chmn. exec. com. Fund for Theol. Edn., 1978—. Served with AUS, 1943-46, 47-51. Rockefeller Doctoral grantee; Lucy Monroe scholar; Rosenwald scholar; Am. Assn. Theol. Schs. Study grantee. Mem. Am. Ch. History Soc., Am. Acad. Religion, Soc. Study Black Religion (pres. 1973-75), Nat. Com. Black Churchmen. Office: Office of Dean Sch Divinity Howard U Washington DC 20017

JONES, LAWRENCE WILLIAM, educator, physicist; b. Evanston, Ill., Nov. 16, 1925; s. Charles Herbert and Fern (Storm) J.; m. Ruth Reavley Drummond, June 24, 1950; children: Douglas Warren, Carol Anne, Ellen Louise. B.S., Northwestern U., 1948, M.S., 1949; Ph.D., U. Calif. at Berkeley, 1952. Research asst. U. Calif. Radiation Lab., Berkeley, 1950-52; mem. faculty U. Mich., Ann Arbor, 1952—, prof. physics, 1963—, chmn. dept. physics, 1982—; vis. physicist Lawrence Radiation Lab., Berkeley, 1959, cons., 1964—; vis. scientist CERN, Geneva, Switzerland, 1961-62, 65; vis. physicist Brookhaven Nat. Lab., Upton, N.Y., 1963—; cons. Argonne (Ill.) Nat. Lab., 1963—; vis. physicist Nat. Accelerator Lab., Batavia, Ill., 1971—; vis. prof. Tata Inst. Fundamental Research, Bombay, India, 1979; mem. elem. particle physics panel of physics survey com. NRC; trustee Univs. Research Assn., 1982—. Guggenheim fellow, 1965; Sci. Research Council fellow, 1977. Fellow Am. Phys. Soc. Home: 2666 Park Ridge Dr Ann Arbor MI 48103

JONES, LEE BENNETT, chemist; b. Memphis, Mar. 14, 1938; s. Harold S. and Martha B. J.; m. Vera Kramar, Feb. 8, 1964; children: David B., Michael B. B.A. magna cum laude, Wabash Coll, 1960; Ph.D., M.I.T., 1964. Faculty U. Ariz., Tucson, 1964—, prof. chemistry, 1972—, asst. head dept. chemistry, 1971-73, head dept., 1973-77, dean Grad. Coll., 1977-79, 82—, provost Grad. Studies and Health Scis., 1979-82, v.p. research, 1982—. Contbr. numerous articles to profl. jours.; Editorial bd.: Jour. Chem. Edn, 1975-79. NSF fellow, 1961-63, 64—. Mem. Am. Chem. Soc., Chem. Soc. (London), AAAS, AAUP, Phi Beta Kappa. Home: 5645 E Towner St Tucson AZ 85712 Office: Adminstrn Bldg Univ Arizona Tucson AZ 85721

JONES, LEROI *See* **BARAKA, IMAMU AMIRI**

JONES, LESLIE ALAN, dental supply executive; b. Liverpool, England, Sept. 30, 1939; came to Can. citizen; s. Richard and Florence (Davies) J.; m. Jill Robinson, Oct. 16, 1965; children: Mathew Charles, Katherine Luisa. With Amalgamated Denta., 1962-73, Eng., 1962-68, pres., Can., 1968-73; gen. mgr. L.D. Caulk Co., Milford, Del., 1978-81; sr. v.p. Dentsply Internat. Inc., York, Pa., 1981—. Home: 3550 Springettes Dr York PA 17402 Office: Dentsply Internat Inc 570 W College Ave York PA 17405

JONES, LINCOLN, III, army officer; b. Ft. Benning, Ga., Jan. 23, 1933; s. Lincoln and Doris G. (Baltz) J.; m. Alexandra Ann Archbald, June 21, 1958; children: Peter L., Patricia A. B.S., U.S. Mil. Acad., 1958; M.S., Auburn U., 1969. Commd. 2d lt. U.S. Army, 1958, advanced through grades to brig. gen.; dep. bridgade comdr., C.Z., 1976-78; brigade comdr. 9th Inf. Div., 1978-79, chief staff div. and, Ft. Lewis, 1980, asst. div. comdr., 1980—; also dep. chief of staff Landsouth, Verona, Italy. Decorated Legion of Merit with oak leaf cluster, D.F.C., Bronze Star, others. Mem. Assn. U.S. Army. Episcopalian. Home: DCS HQS Landsouth APO New York NY 09453 Office: Hdrs 9th Inf Div WA 98433

JONES, LOIS MAILOU (MRS. V. PIERRE-NOEL), designer, artist, educator; b. Boston, Nov. 3, 1905; d. Thomas Vreel and Carolyn Dorinda (Adams) J.; m. Vergniaud Pierre-Noel, Aug. 18, 1953. Diploma, Mus. Sch. Fine Arts, Boston, 1927, Designers Art Sch., Boston, 1928; A.B. magna cum laude, Howard U., 1945; student, Harvard, summer 1928, Columbia U., summers 1934, 35, 36; Certificate, Academie Julian, Paris, France, 1937-38, Academie de la Grande Chaumiere, Paris, 1962; Ph.D. (hon.), Colo. State Christian Coll., 1973, Suffolk U., Boston, 1981. Head dept. art Palmer Meml. Inst., Sedalia, N.C., 1928-30; prof. design and watercolor painting Howard U., 1930-77; guest prof. Centre d'Art, Port-au Prince, Haiti, summer 1954; pres. Leopold Sedar Sanghor collection, Dakar Senegal. Costume designer, Grace Ripley Studios, Boston, 1920-25; free-lance textile designer, F.A. Foster Co., Boston, Schumacher Co., N.Y.C., 1927-31; illustrator, Assn. Study of Negro Life and History, Washington, 1930-53; exhibited, Salon des Artistes Français, France, Rhodes Nat. Gallery, S. Rhodesia, NAD, N.Y.C., Galerie Soulanges, Paris, A.C.A. Gallery, N.Y.C., Mus. Modern Art, N.Y.C., Pan Am. Union, Boston Mus. Fine Arts, San Jose (Calif.) Mus., Los Angeles County Mus. Art, Festac, Nigeria; paintings represented in permanent collections, Boston Mus. Fine Arts, Bklyn. Mus., IBM, Phillips Collection, Corcoran Gallery of Art, U. Panjab, Pakistan, Internat. Fair Gallery, Walker Art Mus., Bowdoin Coll., Atlanta U., Palais Nationale, Haiti, Walker Art Mus., Hirshhorn Mus. and Sculpture Garden, Washington, Howard U., Rosenwald Found., Chgo., Johnson Pub. Co., Chgo., 135th St. Pub. Library, Atlanta U., Fisk U., Met. Mus. Art, N.Y.C., Nat. Portrait Gallery, Washington; Author: Peintures, Lois Mailou Jones, 1937-51, 1952. Recipient Nathaniel Thayer prize for Excellence in Design, 1925; Luban Watercolor award, 1958; 1st award Painting Nat. Mus. Art, Washington, 1940, 47, 60, 64, 1st; Honorable Mention Salon des Artistes Française, Paris, 1966; Alumni Achievement award Howard U., 1978; decorated the Diplome and Decoration de l'Ordre Honneur et Merit au Grade de Chevalier Govt. of Haiti, 1955; Gen. Edn. Bd. fellow, 1937-38; Howard U. Research grantee, 1969, 71, 73. Fellow Royal Soc. Arts (London, Eng.); mem. Washington Water Colour Assn., Art Dirs. Club of Washington, Washington Soc. Artists, Artists' Equity, Alpha Kappa Alpha. Home: 4706 17th St NW Washington DC 20011 Office: Box 893 Howard U Washington DC 20059

JONES, L.Q. *See* **MCQUEEN, JUSTICE ELLIS**

JONES, LYLE VINCENT, psychology educator; b. Grandview, Wash., Mar. 11, 1924; s. Vincent F. and Matilda M. (Abraham) J.; m. Patricia Edison Powers, Dec. 17, 1949 (div. 1979); children: Christopher V., Susan E., Tad W. Student, Reed Coll., 1942-43; B.S., U. Wash., 1947, M.S., 1948; Ph.D., Stanford, 1950. Nat. Research fellow, 1950-51; asst. prof. psychology U. Chgo., 1951-57; vis. asso. prof. U. Tex., 1956-57; asso. prof. U. N.C., 1957-60, prof., 1960-69, Alumni disting. prof., 1969—, dir., 1957-74, 79—, vice chancellor, dean, 1969-79; pres. Assn. Grad. Schs., 1976-77; cons. in field. Author: (with others) Studies in Aphasia: An Approach to Testing, 1961, The Measurement and Prediction of Judgment and Choice, 1968, (with others) An Assessment of Research-Doctorate Programs in the United States, 5 vols.; Mng. editor: Psychometrika, 1956-61; Editorial com. for psychology, Mc-Graw-Hill, 1965-77; Contbr. articles to profl. jours. Served with USAF, 1943-46. Recipient Thomas Jefferson award U. N.C., 1979; Fellow Center Advanced Study in Behavioral Scis., 1964-65, 81-82; grantee NIH, 1957-63, NSF, 1960-63, 71-74, NIMH, 1963-74, 79—. Fellow AAAS, Am. Psychol. Assn. (pres. div. 1963-64); mem. Psychometric Soc. (pres. 1962-63), Am. Statis. Assn., Am. Ednl. Research Assn. Home: Rt 1 Pittsboro NC 27312 Office: Davie Hall U NC Chapel Hill NC 27514

JONES, LYNN EDWIN, television journalist; b. Muncie, Ind., Sept. 17, 1939; s. John H. and Louise Katherine (Ripley) J.; m. Joanna Hill, May 26, 1962; children—Michele Louise, Nicole Ellen. B.A. summa cum laude, U. Cin., 1962; M.A. in History, Ind. U., 1964, Ind. U., 1966. Midwest corr., producer TV News, Inc., Chgo., 1973-75; info. dir. Calif. Farm Bur., Berkeley, Calif., 1975; Moscow corr. ABC News, 1976-78, West Coast producer, 1978—; lectr. various univs. Editor: NBC Today Show, N.Y.C., 1968-70; producer, radio news dir., KING-TV and AM, Seattle, 1970-73; Asso. editor, contbg. author: NBC News Year of 1969. Ford Found. fellow, 1962-63. Mem. Phi Beta Kappa, Sigma Delta Chi, Pi Delta Epsilon, Phi Alpha Theta, Omicron Delta Kappa. Club: Overseas Press. Office: 277 Golden Gate Ave San Francisco CA 94102

JONES, MALCOLM DAVID, physician, educator; b. Orange, Calif., Feb. 16, 1923; s. LeRoy and Wilhelmina (Barth) J.; m. Margaret Fisher, June 25, 1945; children: Malcolm David, Sheryl Jones Parker, Roger, Margaret Jones Aycinene, Linda Jones Rohan. A.B., U. Calif., 1943, M.D., 1946. Instr. radiology U. Calif. at San Francisco, 1953-54, asst. prof., 1954-61, assoc. prof., 1961-65, prof., vice chmn. dept., 1965-74; prof., chmn. dept. radiology U. Tex. Health Sci. Center, San Antonio, 1974-79; prof., vice chmn. dept. radiology U. Calif., San Francisco, 1979-83, prof. dept. radiology, Irvine, 1983—; chief radiology service VA Center, Fresno, Calif., 1979-83; chief diagnostic radiology U. Calif. Hosps., Irvine, 1983—; dir. radiology ednl. program Fresno Med. Program, 1979-83. Author: Basic Diagnostic Radiology, 1969. Served with USNR, 1943-50. Mem. Am. Coll. Radiology, Tex. Med. Assn., AMA, Radiol. Soc. N.A., Assn. Univ. Radiologists, Am. Roentgen Ray Soc., AAAS, Alpha Omega Alpha. Home: 2105 N Louise Ave Santa Ana CA Office: 101 City Dr S Orange CA 92668

JONES, MARGARET EILEEN ZEE, physician, educator; b. Swedesboro, N.J., June 24, 1936; d. Wilmer and Elsie (Schober) Zee; m. John Walker Jones, Aug. 29, 1959; children—John Stewart, Mary Cassaday, Amanda Worthington. B.A., U. Pa., 1957; M.D., Med. Coll. Va., 1961. Intern U. Wash., Seattle, 1962-63, resident in pathology and neuropathology, 1963-65; resident in pathology Med. Coll. Va., Richmond, 1966-67, instr. pathology, 1967-68, acting dir. neuropathology, 1967, 68-69, asst. prof., 1968-69; asst. prof. pathology Mich. State U., East Lansing, 1969-73, asso. prof., 1973-78, prof., 1978—, dir., 1972—; lectr. neurosurgery Med. Sch. Yale, 1969—. Contbr. articles to tech. jours. Recipient Disting. Faculty award Mich. State U., 1978; A.D. Williams summer fellow, 1959, 60; cert. of excellence in teaching Coll. Human Medicine, 1981; cert. of recognition Lansing (Mich.) YWCA, 1980; Nat. Inst. Neurol. Diseases and Blindness NIH fellow, 1970-71; Nat. Endowment Humanities summer fellow, 1979. Fellow Am. Soc. Clin. Pathologists; mem. Am. Assn. Neuropathologists (Weil award 1980), Am. Assn. Pathologists, Am. Fedn. Clin. Research, Soc. Neuroscience (pres. chpt. 1974—), Mich. State Med. Soc. Office: Dept Pathology Mich State U East Lansing MI 48824

JONES, MARK ELMER, JR., lawyer, artist; b. Indpls., Oct. 15, 1920; s. Mark Elmer and Pearl (Campbell) J.; m. Jeanne L. Roger, Apr. 17, 1944; children: Marquita, Marcus, Marvin, Julie. A.B., Roosevelt U., 1948; J.D., Loyola U., 1950. Bar: Ill. 1950. Practiced in, Chgo., 1950-63; partner firm McCoy, Ming & Leighton, Chgo., 1957-62; asst. state's atty., Chgo., 1951-57; judge Circuit Ct. of Cook County, Ill., from 1963; now ptnr. firm Jones, Ware & Grenard, Chgo.; Mem. exec. com. Chgo. br. NAACP, 1959—. Bd. dirs. Better Boys Found., Inst. Cultural Devel., Urban Gateways, South Side Community Art Center; trustee Roosevelt U., 1962-66; mem. Chgo. Cable TV Commn. Mem. ABA, Ill. Bar Assn., Chgo. Bar Assn., Cook County Bar Assn., Nat. Bar Assn. (founding mem., exec. com. jud. council), John Howard Assn. (dir.). Democrat. Unitarian. Club: Druids. Home: 1310 N Ritchie Ct Chicago IL 60610 Office: Chicago Civic Center Chicago IL 60602

JONES, MARK MANDERVILLE, management consultant; b. Cedar Falls, Iowa, 1890; s. Fred Soule and Ada (Thompson) J.; m. May Irene Rinehart; 1 dau., Helen May Evatt Jones. Student, East Waterloo (Iowa) High Sch.; LL.D., Bethany Coll., 1940. Successively chief clk. to gen. mgr. and traffic mgr., Waterloo, Cedar Falls and No. Ry.; traffic mgr. William Galloway Co., Waterloo, Iowa; indsl. sec. C. of C., Oakland, Calif.; dir. personnel Thomas A. Edison Industries, Orange, N.J., 1916-21; civilian rep. Sec. of War on devel. Army personnel system, 1917; dir. Div. Trade Tests of Army, 1917-18; dir. econ. staff Curtis, Fosdick and Belknap, N.Y.C.; on affairs of John D. Rockefeller, Jr., 1921-26; mgmt. cons. and econ. economist, N.Y.C. and Princeton, N.J., 1926—; cons. to pres. U.S. Steel Corp., 1953-59; pres. Akron Belting Co., 1934-54, Leadership Publs., Inc., 1948-54; editor Execs. Policy Letter, 1948-53; pres. Nat. Econ. Council, 1963-69; 1st sec. Nat. Assn. Employment Mgrs., 1916-21. Editor: Economic Council Letter, 1963-69. Republican. Presbyterian. Club: Union League (N.Y.C.). Donated archives to Edison Nat. Hist. Site, U.S. Nat. Park Service, Orange, N.J., 1980. Address: 159 Library Pl Princeton NJ 08540 *We are born into a universe of natural law without being consulted and have but three choices. The first is to identify and define these laws. The second is to capitalize upon them. The third is to ignore them and suffer.*

JONES, MARNIE, designer; b. Orange, N.J., Mar. 19, 1948; d. Howland Barton and Elizabeth (Lyon) J. A.A., Pine Manor Jr. Coll., 1968; B.F.A. in Indsl. Design, R.I. Sch. Design, 1971; postgrad., MIT, 1974, Stanford U., 1976-78. Indsl. designer, product mgr. Voltek, Inc., Lawrence, Mass., 1971-73; assoc. designer Lonberger & Assocs., Campbell, Calif., 1979; coordinator, editor, store mgr. Center for Design, Palo Alto, Calif., 1979-80; toy designer Tonka Corp., Spring Park, Minn., 1982-83; cons. Marnie-Jones, Designer, Mpls., 1983—; instr. product design N.C. State U., Raleigh, 1974-76; lectr. in indsl. design San Jose State U., Calif., 1977, 81. Editor: Cenerline (monthly tabloid), 1979-80. Fellow Indsl. Designers Soc. Am. (editor newsletter 1976-80, bd. dirs. 1978-81, sec. San Francisco chpt. 1976-78, program chmn. ann conf. 1978). Home and Office: 4608 Chowen Ave S Minneapolis MN 55410

JONES, MARY ELLEN, biochemist; b. La Grange, Ill., Dec. 25, 1922; d. Elmer E. and Laura A. (Klein) J.; children: Ethan Vincent Munson, Catherine Laura Munson. B.S., U. Chgo., 1944; Ph.D., Yale U., 1951. AEC fellow Am. Cancer Soc.; fellow, asso. biochemist Mass. Gen. Hosp., Boston, 1951-57; asst. prof. grad. dept. biochemistry Brandeis U., Watham, Mass., 1957-60, asso. prof., 1960-66; asso. prof. dept. biochemistry Sch. Medicine, U. N.C., Chapel Hill, 1966-68, prof. depts. biochemistry and zoology, 1968-71; prof. dept. biochemistry Sch. Medicine, U. So. Calif., 1971-78; prof., chmn. dept. biochemistry Sch. Medicine, U. N.C., Chapel Hill, 1978—, Kenan prof. biochemistry, 1980—; mem. study sect. Am. Cancer Soc., 1971-73, NIH, 1971-75; mem. sci. adv. bd. Nat. Heart, Lung and Blood Inst., 1980-84; mem. metabolic biology study sect. NSF, 1978-81; mem. Merit rev. bd., VA, 1975-78; mem. life sci. com. NASA, 1976-78. Contbr. numerous articles on biochem.; editorial bd.: Jour. Biol. Chemistry, 1975-80, Cancer Research, 1982—; assoc. editor: Can. Jour. Biochemistry, 1969-74. Recipient Wilbur Lucius Cross award Yale U., 1982; Am. Cancer Soc. scholar, 1957-62; NIH grantee, 1957—; NSF grantee, 1957—. Fellow AAAS; Mem. Am. Chem. Soc. (councilor 1975-79, mem. nominating com. 1971-72, chair 1973-74, Am. Soc. Biol. Chemists, councilor 1975-78, 81-84), Inst. Medicine of Nat. Acad. Scis., Assn. Women in Sci., N.Y. Acad. Sci., Sierra Club, Sigma Xi. Democrat. Unitarian. Club: Appalachian Mountain. Research to sci. publs. Office: Dept Biochemistry Sch Medicine U NC Chapel Hill NC 27514

JONES, MASON, musician, educator; b. Hamilton, N.Y., June 16, 1919; s. Frederick Mason and Elizabeth (Piotrow) J.; m. Eve Furlong, July 20, 1941; children—Frederick Mason III, Saralinda Mason. Student, Curtis Inst. Music, 1936-38; Mus.D. (hon.), Colgate U., 1970. Tchr. horn and brass ensemble Curtis Inst. Music, 1946—; faculty Temple U. Coll. Music, 1976—; condr. Episcopal Acad. Orch., 1958-60; condr. sch. concerts Phila. Orch., 1972—; founder-mem. Phila. Woodwind Quintet, 1950—; co-founder Phila. Brass Ensemble, 1957—; asst. condr. Phila. Chamber Orch., 1961-64. Mem., Phila. Orch., 1938-78; first hornist, 1940-78; personnel mgr., 1963—; Editor: Solos for the Horn Player, 1962, 20th Century Orch. Studies, 1971. Served with USMC, 1942-46. Recipient C. Hartman Kuhn award for service to Phila. Orch., 1953, 56, 68. Mem. Phila. Art Alliance. Episcopalian. Clubs: Union League (Phila.); Merion (Pa.) Golf. Home: Box 37 Gladwyne PA 19035 Office: 1420 Locust St Philadelphia PA 19102

JONES, MAX LAMAR, JR., utility company executive; b. Ogden, Utah, June 13, 1937; s. Max LaMar and Lura Ida (Miller) J.; m. Honor Katrina Settelmeyer, Dec. 16, 1956; children: Max LaMar, Lynne K. B.S.E.E., U. Nev., Reno, 1960. Asst. engr. Pacific Gas & Electric Co., San Jose, Calif., 1960-61; with Sierra Pacific Power Co., 1963—, asst. engr., 1963-65, electric transmission engr., 1965-67, electric system planning, design engr., 1967-72, engring. mgr., 1972-73, v.p. planning, engring., 1977-80, sr. v.p. planning, engring., 1980-83, sr. v.p. planning, engring. and constrn., 1983—; v.p. Sierra Energy Co., 1980—. Dir. Washoe County unit Am. Cancer Soc., 1978-81; mem. adv. council Water Resources Research; mem. adv. com. multiple use State of Wash.; active Boy Scouts Am., Campfire Girls. Served with C.E. U.S. Army, 1961-63. Mem. Nat., Nev. socs. profl. engr., IEEE, Am. Mgmt. Assn., Pacific Coast Gas Assn. (dir.), Edison Electric Inst., Am. Gas Assn. Republican. Club: Reno Men's Golf. Lodge: Elks. Home: 1160 Harvey Ln Reno NV 89509 Office: 100 E Moana Ln Reno NV 89520 *The ability to focus on planning and results while allowing subordinates to develop by working out the "How To" element of management has been the cornerstone of my success and satisfaction at work and in community activities.*

JONES, MILTON WAKEFIELD, publisher; b. Burbank, Calif., Apr. 18, 1930; s. Franklin M. and Lydia (Sinclair) J.; m. Rita Strong, May 4, 1959; 1 son, Franklin Wayne. Student, Santa Monica City Coll., 1948-50; A.A., U. So. Calif., 1950-52; B.S. Vice pres. mktg. Sav-Ink Co., Newport Beach, Calif., 1956-58; account exec. KDES-Radio, Palm Springs, 1958-60; pres. Milton W. Jones Advt. & Pub. Relations Agy., 1960—, Desert Publs., Inc., Palm Springs, 1965—, Riverside Color Press, Inc., Olman Travel Service, Palm Springs, 1979—. Pub.: Palm Spring (Calif.) Life Mag, 1965—, Wheeler Bus. Letter, Palm Springs, 1969-77, San Francisco mag, 1973-79, Vail, 1978—. Club: Desert Press (pres. 1965). Home: 422 Farrell Dr Palm Springs CA 92262 also 206 Abalone Ave Balboa Island CA Office: 303 N Indian Ave Palm Springs CA 92262

JONES, MORTON EDWARD, company executive; b. Alhambra, Calif., Apr. 12, 1928; s. Edward P. and Bonnibel (Sanford) J.; m. Patricia Walker, Mar. 18, 1951; children: Shelley, Steven Kent, Kay. B.S. in Chemistry, U. Calif., Berkeley, 1949; Ph.D. in Chemistry and Physicis, Calif. Inst. Tech., 1953. Mem. tech. staff Tex. Instruments, Dallas, 1953-61, sr. scientist, 1961-65, lab. dir., Dallas, TX, 1965-79, dir. dept., Dallas, 1979—. Contbr. articles to various publs. Chmn. judging Internat. Sci. Fair, Dallas, 1966; chmn. Regional Sci. Fair, Dallas, 1972-74. Fellow IEEE; mem. Electrochem. Soc. (mem. exec. com. 1976—). Republican. Episcopalian. Home: 619 Northhill Richardson TX 75080 Office: Texas Instruments Inc PO Box 225936 MS 145 Dallas TX 75265

JONES, MURIEL KATHLEEN, university dean; b. Charleroi, Pa., Apr. 2, 1934; d. David Alexander and Muriel Mae (Baker) J. B.S., Indiana U. of Pa., 1956; M.Ed., Pa. State U., 1960; Ph.D. (Gen. Foods fellow), Ohio State U., 1968. Tchr. Penn Hills Sch. Dist., 1956-63; prof. Indiana U. of Pa., 1963-71; dean Coll. Home Econs., 1971—; cons. Pitts. Public Schs. Mem. Am. Home Econs. Assn., Pa. Home Econs. Assn. (pres. 1978-79), Assn. Adminstrs. in Home Econs. (exec. bd.), AAUW (pres. Indiana br. 1970-72), Nat. Council Adminstrs. of Home Econs., Assn. Adminstrs. in Higher Edn., Elec. Women's Roundtable, Delta Kappa Gamma, Kappa Omicron Phi, Phi Mu, Omicron Nu, Phi Upsilon Omicron. Methodist. Club: College (Indiana, Pa.). Office: Ackerman Hall Indiana U of Pa Indiana PA 15705

JONES, NATHANIEL RAPHAEL, federal judge; b. Youngstown, Ohio, May 13, 1926; s. Nathaniel B. and Lillian J. (Rafe) J.; m. Lillian Graham, Mar. 22, 1974; 1 dau., Stephanie Joyce; stepchildren: William Hawthorne, Rickey Hawthorne, Marc Hawthorne, Pamela Haley. A.B., Youngstown State U., 1951, LL.B., 1955, LL.D. (hon.), 1969, Syracuse U., 1972. Editor Buckeye Rev. newspaper, up to 1956; exec. dir. FEPC, Youngstown, 1956-59; practiced law, 1959-61, 68-69, asst. U.S. atty., 1961-67; asst. gen. counsel Nat. Adv. Commn. on Civil Disorders, 1967-68; gen. counsel NAACP, 1969-79; judge U.S. Ct. of Appeals, 6th Circuit, 1979—; dir. Buckeye Rev. Pub. Co.; chmn. Con. on Adequate Def. and Incentives in Mil.; mem. Task Force-Vets. Benefits. Served with USAAF, 1945-47. Mem. Ohio State Bar Assn., Mahoning County Bar Assn., Fed. Bar Assn., Nat. Bar Assn., Am. Arbitration Assn., Youngstown Area Devel. Corp., Urban League, Nat. Conf. Black Lawyers, Am. Bar Assn. (co-chmn. com. constl. rights criminal sect.), Kappa Alpha Psi. Baptist. Clubs: Houston Law (Youngstown); Elks. Office: 541 US Courthouse Cincinnati OH 45202

JONES, NORMA LOUISE, educator; b. Poplar, Wis.; d. George Elmer and Hilma June (Wiberg) J. B.E., U. Wis.; M.A., U. Minn., 1952; postgrad, U. Ill., 1957; Ph.D., U. Mich., 1965; postgrad. archivestng., NARS, 1978, 79, 80. Librarian Grand Rapids (Mich.) Public Schs., 1947-62; with Grand Rapids Public Library, 1948-49; instr. Central Mich. U., Mt. Pleasant, 1954, 55; librarian Benton Harbor (Mich.) Public Schs., 1962-63; asst. prof. library sci. U. Wis., Oshkosh, 1968-70, assoc. prof., 1970-75, prof., 1975—, chmn. dept. library sci., 1980—; lectr. U. Mich., Ann Arbor, 1954, 55, 61, 63-65, asst. prof., 1966-68. Recipient Disting. Teaching award U. Wis.-Oshkosh, 1977. Mem. ALA (chmn. reference conf. 1975—), Assn. Library and Info. Sci. Educators, Spl. Library Assn., Soc. Am. Archivists, Phi Beta Kappa, Phi Kappa Phi, Pi Lambda Theta, Beta Phi Mu, Sigma Pi Epsilon. Home: 1220 Maricopa Dr Oshkosh WI 54901

JONES, OLEN E., educational administrator; b. Charleston, W.Va., May 7, 1937; s. Olen E. and Anna F. (Crislip) J.; m. Patty Gaye Barber, Nov. 9, 1936; children: Jeffrey, Kimberly, Jay. A.B., Marshall U., 1959, M.A., 1960; Ph.D., Northwestern U., 1972. Asst. dir. admissions Marshall U., Huntington, W.Va., 1963-65; dir. records Am. Coll. Testing Program, Iowa City, 1966-67; asst. to dean Sch. Edn., Northwestern U., Evanston, Ill., 1970-71, admissions asst., 1972; dir. test adminstrn. and security Am. Coll. Testing Program, 1972-73, asst. v.p., 1973-74; exec. v.p. Marshall U., 1975-79, provost, 1980—; instl. rep. North Central Accrediting Agy., 1977—; state rep. for Resource Ctr. Planner Change Am. Assn. State Colls. and Univs., 1982—; acting pres. W.Va. Bd. Regents, 1980-81; chmn. search and screening com. for vice chancellor, 1981. Bd. dirs. Huntington YMCA, 1981—; pres. Tri-State Chpt. ARC, 1980-82; trustee Huntington Galleries, 1979-82. Mem. Am. Assn. State Colls. and Univs., NEA, Nat. Assn. Guidance and Counseling Personnel. Home: 52 Roland Park Dr Huntington WV 25705 Office: Marshall U Huntington WV

JONES, OLIVER HASTINGS, consulting economist; b. Altoona, Pa., Dec. 9, 1922; s. Oliver Hastings and Mary (Herman) J.; m. Margaret Ann Vogel, July 4, 1942; children: Thomas, William, David, Robert, Richard. B.A., St. Francis Coll., Loretto, Pa., 1948; M.A., Pa. State U., 1949, Ph.D., 1961. Analyst, div. bank ops., bd. govs. Fed. Res. System, 1951-55; sr. economist, research dept. Fed. Res. Bank, Cleve., 1955-59; assoc. research economist, real estate research program Grad. Sch. Bus. Adminstrn., U. Calif. at Los Angeles, 1959-61; economist Stanford Research Inst., 1961-62; dir. research Mortgage Bankers Assn. Am., 1962-67; cons. economist Oliver Jones & Assos., Washington, 1967-68; exec. v.p. Mortgage Bankers Assn. Am., 1968-77; cons. economist Oliver Jones & Assos., Washington, 1977—; professorial lectr. Am. U., 1967—. Author: (with Leo Grebler) The Secondary Mortgage Market, 1961, Financial Futures Market, 1983. Served with AUS, 1942-45. Mem. Am. Statis. Assn., Am. Econ. Assn., Am. Finance Assn., Nat. Assn. Bus. Economists, Conf. Bus. Economists, Lambda Alpha. (internat. pres. 1976-77). Clubs: Cosmos, Metropolitan (Washington). Home: Box 42 Manns Choice PA 15550 Office: 1629 K St NW Washington DC 20006 also Manns Choice PA

JONES, ORLO DOW, lawyer, drug store exec.; b. Logan, Utah, June 10, 1938; s. Orlo Elijah and Joyce (Lewis) J.; m. Ilarene Balls, July 9, 1958; children—Monica, Orlo Courtney. B.S., Utah State U., 1960; LL.B., U. Calif., Berkeley, 1963. Bar: Calif. bar 1964. Atty. Carlson, Collins & Bold, Richmond, Calif., 1968-69, A.T. and T., San Francisco, 1969-71, Longs Drug Stores, Inc., Walnut Creek, Calif., 1971-76, sec., gen. counsel, 1976—, v.p., 1979—; lectr. comml. leases Continuing Edn. of Bar Univ. Extension U. Calif., Berkeley. Served to capt. JAGC AUS, 1964-68. Republican. Mormon. Home: 156 Santiago Dr Danville CA 94526 Office: 141 N Civic Dr Walnut Creek CA 94596

JONES, OWEN CRAVEN, JR., mechanical and nuclear engineer, educator; b. N.Y.C., Oct. 18, 1936; s. Owen C. and Lois B. (Wright) J.; children: Jennifer, Douglas, Kevin. B.S. in Mech. Engring. magna cum laude, U. Mass., 1962; M.S., Rensselaer Poly. Inst., 1966, Ph.D., 1974. Mech. engr. Gen. Electric Co. Knolls Atomic Power Lab., Schenectady, 1962-74; mech. engr. reactor analysis and safety div. Argonne Nat. Lab., Ill., 1974-76; group leader dept. applied sci. Brookhaven Nat. Lab., Upton, N.Y., 1976-77, prin. investigator reactor safety program, 1976-80, head thermal hydraulic devel. div.,

1977-80, staff research mech. engr., Upton, NY, 1980-81; prof. nuclear engring. Rensselaer Poly. Inst., Troy, NY, 1981—; adj. prof. Union Coll., Schenectady, 1968-74; guest lectr. (various univs.), Japan, U.S. Europe. Author: (with S.G. Bankoff) Thermal Hydraulic Aspects of Nuclear Reactor Safety, 2 vols., 1977, Nuclear Reactor Safety Heat Transfer, 1981; contbr. articles to profl. jours. Served with USN, 1955-59. Fellow ASME (mem. standing com. theory and fundamental research heat transfer div.); mem. Am. Nuclear Soc. (exec. bd. thermal hydraulic div.), Sigma Xi, Tau Beta Pi, Phi Kappa Phi, Phi Eta Sigma. Home: L-B Candlelight Ct Twin Lakes Clifton Park NY 12065 Office: Rensselear Poly Inst NES Bldg Troy NY 12181

JONES, PETER D'ALROY, educator, author; b. Hull, Eng., June 9, 1931; came to U.S., 1959, naturalized, 1968; s. Alfred and Margery (Rutter) J.; m. Beau Fly, June 10, 1961 (div. Dec. 22, 1980); children: Kathryn Beauchamp, Barbara Collier. B.A., Manchester (Eng.), U., 1952, M.A., 1953; Ph.D., London U., 1963; postgrad., U. Brussels, 1954. Freelance editor, London, 1953-56; lectr. U.S. history dept. Am. studies Manchester U., 1957-58; vis. asst. prof. econs. Tulane U., 1959-60; from asst. to full prof. Smith Coll., 1960-68; prof. history U. Ill.-Chgo., 1968—; Kennan prof. Am. instns. and values Trinity Coll., Hartford, 1980-81; vis. prof. Columbia U.; U. Mass., U. Hawaii, U. Warsaw, Poland, U. Düsseldorf, Germany; Mem. com. examiners Grad. Record Exams Ednl. Testing Service, Princeton, N.J., 1966-70; mem. Am. Studies com. Am. Council Learned Socs., 1973-75; Am. specialist U.S. Dept. State, Internat. Communications Agy., 1976—; adviser pubs. Author: Economic History of U.S.A since 1783, 2d edit., 1965, The Story of the Saw, 1961, America's Wealth, 1963, The Consumer Society, 2d edit., 1967, The Christian Socialist Revival, 1968, The Robber Barons Revisited, 1968, Robert Hunter's Poverty; Social Conscience in the Progressive Era, 1965, La Sociedad Consumidora, 1968, Since Columbus: Poverty and Pluralism in the History of the Americas, 1975, The U.S.A.: A History of Its People and Society, 2 vols., 1976; editor: Pegasus, 1966-68; Editor: (with M.G. Holli) The Ethnic Frontier: Group Survival in Chicago and the Midwest, 1977, Ethnic Chicago, 1981, rev. and enlarged edit., 1984, Biographical Dictionary of American Mayors, 1820-1980, 1981. Served with RAF, 1956-57. Mem. Am. Hist. Assn., Orgn. Am. Historians, Econ. History Assn., Am. Sociol. Assn., London Sch. Econs. Soc. (life). Office: Dept History U Ill at Chgo Chicago IL 60680

JONES, PHILIP ALAN, broadcasting executive; b. Cairo, Ill., June 27, 1944; s. Charles E. and Doris E. (Hogendobler) J.; m. Lynnsay Williams, Sept. 6, 1967; children: Whitney, Spencer. B.J., U. Mo., Columbia, 1966; postgrad., Harvard U., 1976. Salesman KCMO-FM, Kansas City, Mo., 1966-67, KMBR Radio, Kansas City, 1967-68; local salesman WDAF-TV, Kansas City, Mo., 1968-70, local sales mgr., 1970-74; gen. sales mgr. WTAF-TV, Phila., 1974-76; gen. mgr. WGR-TV, Buffalo, 1976-79; v.p., gen. mgr. KCTV, Kansas City, Mo., 1979—; dir. CBS-TV affiliates. Bd. dirs. March of Dimes, 1980-81, Conv. Bur. Greater Kansas City, 1980—, Greater Kansas City YMCA, Learning Exchange; bd. dirs., exec. com. Starlight Theatre, 1980—; mem. communications com. United Way, 1979—; mem. Nelson Gallery Soc. Fellows, 1980—; bd. govs. Mayor's Task Force on Neighborhood Crime, 1981. Mem. Nat. Assn. Broadcasters, TV Bur. Advt., Assn. Maximum Service Telecasters, United Minority Media Assn. (dir. 1979—, mem. adv. bd.), Am. Women in Radio and TV, Kans. Broadcasters Assn., Mo. Broadcasters Assn. (program com.), C. of C. Greater Kansas City, Alpha Delta Sigma, Phi Delta Theta. Methodist. Clubs: Carriage (Kansas City, Mo.); Ducks Unlimited, Woodside Racquet, Overland Park Racquet, Confrerie de la Chaine des Rotisseurs. Home: 2730 Verons Terr Mission Hills KS 66208 Office: 4500 Johnson Dr Fairway KS 66205

JONES, PHILIP DAVIS, book pub. cons.; b. Kingston, Pa., Mar. 24, 1932; s. Scott and Catherine (Davis) J.; m. Kay Wharen, July 7, 1957 (div. Nov. 1965); children—Philip B., Bradford D., Duncan S.; m. Jean Elizabeth LeGwin, Aug. 26, 1967 (div. Aug. 1975); m. Sheryl Diane Stephens, Mar. 20, 1977. B.S., Wilkes Coll., 1954. Licensed pvt. pilot. Sales rep. Ronald Press Co., 1956-59; editor Macmillan Co., 1959-62, Random House-Alfred A. Knopf, 1964-67; registered rep. Auchincloss Parker & Redpath, N.Y.C., 1962-64; asst. dir., editor-in-chief U. Chgo. Press, 1967-74; dir. U. Tex. Press, Austin, 1974-77, Am. Univ. Press Group, London, 1974-77, Kluwer-Nijhoff Pub., Boston, 1978-83; v.p. Kluwer-Boston Inc.; book pub. cons., 1977—; cons. Nat. Endowment for Humanities, 1975—. Served with USAF, 1954-56. Mem. Ops. Research Soc. Am. Home: 3919 Beverly Dr Dallas TX 75205

JONES, PHILIP HOWARD, broadcast journalist; b. Marion, Ind., Apr. 27, 1937; s. Thomas Howard and Charline (Shugart) J.; m. Patricia Ann Powell, June 4, 1961; children: Pamela Lynn, Paul Howard. B.S. in Arts and Scis, Ind. U., 1959. Dir. news Sta. WTHI-TV, Terre Haute, Ind., 1960-61; polit. corr. Sta. WCCO-TV, Mpls., 1961-69; White House corr. CBS News, Washington, 1974-76, Capitol Hill. corr., 1977—. Served with USAF, 1961-62. Recipient Internat. News award Radio-TV News Dirs. Assn., 1965, award for Vietnam war reporting, 1966; Emmy award for CBS Indochina air war coverage Nat. Acad. TV Arts and Scis., 1971. Club: Masons. Home: 5105 Westport Rd Chevy Chase MD 20815 Office: 2020 M St NW Washington DC 20036

JONES, PHILIP NEWTON, physician, medical educator; b. Billings, Mont., May 27, 1924; s. Robert Newton and Edith (Woodbury) J.; m. Rebecca Ann Means, June 13, 1948; children: Robert Newton II, Rebecca Ann, Margaret Jane. Student, Stanford, 1942-43, U. Wis., 1944; M.D., Washington U., St. Louis, 1948. Diplomate: Am. Bd. Internal Medicine. Intern St. Luke's Hosp., Chgo., 1948-49, resident internal medicine, 1949-51; research fellow internal medicine Northwestern U., Chgo., 1953, clin. asst. medicine, 1954-57; practice medicine, specializing in internal medicine and hepatology, Chgo., 1954—; clin. asst. medicine U. Ill., Chgo., 1957-58, clin. instr. medicine, 1958-61, clin. asst. prof. medicine, 1961-68, clin. asso. prof. medicine, 1968-71; asso. prof. medicine Rush Coll. Medicine Chgo., 1971-75, prof. medicine, 1975—; sr. attending physician Presbyn.-St. Luke's Hosp., Chgo., 1954—, treas. med. staff, 1960-62, mem. exec. com., med. staff, 1960-62, 72-77, sec. med. staff, 1972-73, pres. med. staff, 1973-75; mem. exec. bd. Rush Presbyn.-St. Luke's Med. Center, Chgo., 1973-75, trustee, 1973-77. Contbr. articles to books and profl. jours. Mem. bd. edn., Kenilworth, Ill., 1962-68, pres., 1965; mem. Welfare Council Met., Chgo., 1965-66; bd. dirs. Presbyn. Home, Evanston, Ill., 1978—. Served with AUS, 1943-46, to; capt. USAF, 1951-53. Fellow Am. Coll. Physicians, Inst. Medicine Chgo.; mem. Am. Assn. Study Liver Disease, Chgo. Soc. Internal Medicine, Am. Fedn. Clin. Research, AMA, Ill. Med. Assn., Chgo. Med. Soc., Nu Sigma Nu. Republican. Congregationalist (pres. bd. trustees). Clubs: Comml. (Chgo.); Indian Hill. Home: 328 Warwick Rd Kenilworth IL 60043 Office: 1725 W Harrison Chicago IL 60612

JONES, PHILLIP SANFORD, mathematics educator emeritus; b. Elyria, Ohio, Feb. 26, 1912; s. Albert Thomas and Pearl (Fitch) J.; m. Helen Louise Campbell, Nov. 28, 1935; children—Anne Louise (Mrs. Steven V. Hansen), Phillip S. Jr., Kristin G. (Mrs. Nicholas W. Jones), Roger Thomas. A.A., Jackson Jr. Coll., 1931; A.B., U. Mich., 1933, M.A. in Math, 1935, Ph.D., 1948; L.H.D., No. Mich. U., 1972. Instr. Edison Inst. Tech., Dearborn, Mich., 1937-42; mem. faculty dept. math. U. Mich., Ann Arbor, 1942-44, 47—, asso. prof., 1953-58, prof., 1958-82, prof. emeritus, 1982—; instr. Univ. Sch., Ohio State U., Columbus, 1944-45; vis. asso. prof. U. Calif. at Los Angeles, summer 1958. Univ. Mich. faculty summer research fellow, 1953, 65; NSF research grantee, 1962-63. Mem. Nat. Council Tchrs. Math. (past pres.; editor 24th, 32d yearbooks 1959, 70, chmn. edit. panel Math. Tchr. Jour. 1970-72), Math. Assn. Am. (gov. 1953-56, 65-68), AAAS, Am. Math. Soc., History Sci. Soc., Sigma Xi, Phi Kappa Phi, Delta Sigma Pi. Baptist. Home: 1701 Shadford Rd Ann Arbor MI 48104

JONES, PHYLLIS EDITH, coll. dean; b. Barrie, Ont., Can., Sept. 16, 1924; d. Colston Graham and Edith Luella (Sh) J. B.Sc.N., U. Toronto, 1950, M.Sc., 1969. With Victorian Order Nurses, Toronto, 1950-53; supr. Vancouver Dept. Health, 1953-58; asst. dir. Victorian Order Nurses, Toronto, 1959-63; prof. nursing U. Toronto, 1963—, dean, 1979—. Contbr. articles to profl. jours. Can. Nurses Found. fellow, 1967-69; recipient grants Nat. Health Research and Devel., Ont. Ministry Health. Fellow Am. Public Health Assn.; mem. Coll. Nurses Ont., Registered Nurses Assn. Ont., Can. Public Health Assn., Can. Soc. Study Higher Edn. Home: 81 Sutherland Dr Toronto ON M4G 1H6 Canada Office: 50 George St Toronto ON M5S 1A1 Canada

JONES, PIRKLE, photographer, educator; b. Shreveport, La., Jan. 2, 1914; s. Alfred Charles and Wilie (Tilton) J.; m. Ruth-Marion Baruch, Jan. 15, 1949. Grad., Calif. Sch. Fine Arts, 1949. Profl. free-lance photographer, 1949—; asst. to Ansel Adams, 1949-52; faculty Calif. Sch. Fine Arts, 1953-58, San Francisco Art Inst., 1971—; tchr. Ansel Adams Workshops, Yosemite.; Mem. Archtl. Adv. Com., Mill Valley, Calif., 1963-67. Exhibited in leading art museums; Author: Portfolio One, 1955, (with Dorothea Lange) Death of a Valley, 1960, Portfolio Two, 1968, (with Ruth-Marion Baruch) The Vanguard, A Photographic Essay on the Black Panthers, 1970. Nat. Endowment for Arts photography fellow, 1977; recipient award of honor for exceptional achievement in field of photography Arts Commn. of City and County of San Francisco, 1983. Home: 663 Lovell Ave Mill Valley CA 94941 Office: 800 Chestnut St San Francisco CA 94133

JONES, QUENTIN, government official; b. Montesano, Wash., Dec. 15, 1920; s. LeRoy Ansel and Janet Content (Crawford) J.; m. June M. Moore, Oct. 3, 1959; children by previous marriage: Richard Q., Barbara L., J. Patrice, Garth S. B.S., Wash. State U., 1948, M.S., 1950; Ph.D., Harvard U., 1954. Field cons. Boston U.; with U.S. Dept. Agr., 1956—, now nat. coordinator Nat. Plant Germplasm System,; Mem., exec. committeeman Internat. Bd. Plant Genetic Resources; mem., exec. sec. Nat. Plant Germplasm Commn. Contbr. 65 articles to various sci. publs. Served with USMC; Served with USN. Recipient Superior Service award U.S. Dept. Agr., also; Disting. Service award; NSF Grad. Program fellow; Anna C. Ames Meml. scholar Harvard U.; recipient Frank Meyer Meml. medal Am. Genetics Soc. Mem. AAAS, Soc. Econ. Botany, Smithsonian Assos., Applied Botany Abstracts (mem. adv. bd.), Am. Legion. Clubs: Elks., Moose. Home: 7997 Brown Bridge Rd Fulton MD 20759 Office: Agr Research Center U S Dept Agr Beltsville MD 20705

JONES, QUINCY, composer, arranger, conductor, trumpeter; b. Chgo., Mar. 14, 1933; s. Quincy Delight and Sarah J.; m. Peggy Lipton; children: Kidada, Rashida; children by previous marriage: Jolie, Martina-Lisa, Quincy III. Ed., Seattle U., Berklee Sch. Music, Boston Conservatory; hon. degree, Berklee Coll. Music, 1983. Trumpeter, arranger, Lionel Hampton Orch., 1950-53; arranger for orchs., singers including, Frank Sinatra, Dinah Washington, Count Basie, Sarah Vaughan, Peggy Lee; organizer, trumpeter, Dizzy Gillespie Orch. for Dept. of State tour of Near East, Middle East, S.Am., 1956; music dir., Barchlay Disques, Paris, France; leader own orch. European tour, concerts, TV, radio, 1960; music dir., Mercury Records, 1961; v.p., 1964; composer: fill background scores The Boy in the Tree; conductor: film music The Pawnbroker, 1965, Mirage, 1965, The Slender Thread, 1968, MacKenna's Gold, 1968, For Love of Ivy, 1968, In Cold Blood, 1967, In the Heat of the Night, 1967; conductor other movie scores include: Banning, 1967, The Split, 1968, Bob and Carol and Ted and Alice, 1969, The Out-of Towners, 1970, Cactus Flower, 1969, John and Mary, 1969, They Call Me Mr. Tibbs, 1970, The Anderson Tapes, 1971, The Hot Rock, 1972, The New Centurions, 1972, The Getaway, 1972, The Wiz, 1978; composer, actor: film Blues for Trumpet and Koto; Recs. include Body Heat, 1974 (Gold record); numerous others. Recipient Grammy award, 1963, 69, 71, 73, 81; award German Jazz Fedn., Edison Internat. award of Sweden; awards Downbeat Critics Poll, Downbeat Readers Poll; Billboard Trendsetters award, 1983; ASCAP Golden Note award, 1982; Antonio Carlos Jobim award. Address: care Quincy Jones Prodns 7250 Beverly Blvd Los Angeles CA 90036 *

JONES, RALPH WOOD, educator; b. Streator, Ill., July 9, 1918; s. Ralph A. and Jane (Wood) J.; m. Ruthelle Lorraine Schroeder, June 20, 1942; children—Kyra Lee (Mrs. Richard Osmus), Amelia Kay (Mrs. Milton Ward). B.Mus., Ill. Wesleyan U., 1940; M. Mus. Edn., Okla. U., 1941; postgrad., U. Mich., 1946; Ph.D., U. Tex., 1959. Asso. prof., head wind instrument dept. Southwestern U., Georgetown, Tex., 1946-57, asso. prof., then prof. history, 1957-61; prof., chmn. dept. history and philosophy edn. U. Ala., 1961-68; prof., dir. grad. studies Coll. Edn. U. South Ala., 1968-77, asst. to pres., 1977—. Author: A History of Southwestern University, 1960, (with others) Problem Solving Processes in Social Studies, 1968, Southwestern University, 1840-1961, 1973. Served to lt. (j.g.) USNR, 1942-46. Fellow Philosophy Edn. Soc.; mem. Am. Edn. Research Assn., Phi Delta Kappa, Phi Mu Alpha, Phi Kappa Phi. Home: 1242 Anchor Dr Mobile AL 36609

JONES, RAYMOND ALLEN, JR., constrn. co. exec.; b. Charlotte, N.C., Jan. 19, 1925; s. Raymond Allen and Lucille (Hubbard) J.; m. Donna Louise Bridges, Dec. 28, 1946; children—Sharon Lucille (Mrs. Madison F. Cole, Jr.), Donna Lee (Mrs. Richard C. Handford, Jr.), Raymond Allen III. B.C.E., Ga. Inst. Tech., 1949; exec. program, U. N.C., 1961-62. Exec. v.p., dir. J.A. Jones Constrn. Co., Charlotte; pres., dir. Highlands Hotels Co., Charlotte, Peachtree Hills Apts. Corp., Atlanta; chmn. bd. J.A. Jones Internat., Charlotte; dir. Technology Park/Atlanta, William L. Crow Constrn. Co., N.Y.C., Chas. H. Tompkins Co., Washington, Branch Corp., Wilson, N.C., Branch Banking & Trust Co., Wilson; adv. dir. Ga. Internat. Life Ins. Co., Atlanta. Trustee Pfeiffer Coll., Misenheimer, N.C., N.C. Assn. Ind. Colls. and Univs., Ga. Tech. Found., Atlanta, Southeastern Legal Found., Atlanta; exec. bd. Mecklenburg County council Boy Scouts Am.; hon. bd. dirs. Ga. Engring. Found., Atlanta. Served with AUS, World War II; CBI. Mem. ASCE, Assn. Gen. Contractors Am. (nat. dir., pres. Carolinas br.), Newcomen Soc.), N.Am., Moles, Sigma Chi. Clubs: Charlotte Country, Charlotte City; Capital City (Atlanta). Home: 335 Eastover Rd Charlotte NC 28207 Office: One S Executive Park 6060 St Albans St Charlotte NC 28287

JONES, RAYMOND EDWARD, JR., brewing exec.; b. New Bern, N.C., Jan. 27, 1927; s. Raymond Edward and Ellen LaVerne (Mallard) J.; m. Sarra Gordon O'Bryan, Aug.29, 1958; children—Leslie Anne, Raymond Edward III. B.S., U. Md., 1953; LL.B., U. Balt., 1962. Bar: Md. bar 1962. Office mgr. Hopkins Furniture Co., Annapolis, Md., 1953-55; sr. v.p. legal, sec. Nat. Brewing Co., Balt., 1956-75; (merged with Carling Brewing Co. 1975); sr. v.p. legal and indsl. relations, dir. Carling Nat. Breweries, Inc., 1975-78; sec., asso. gen. counsel Miller Brewing Co., 1978—; house counsel and/or officer Divex, Inc., Laco Products, Inc., Laco Corp., C.W. Abbott, Inc., Pompeian, Inc., Interhost Corp., Solarine Co., Balt. Baseball Club, Inc., 1967-75. Bd. dirs. Soc. Preservation Md. Antiquities, 1969—. Served with USNR, 1942-45. Mem. U.S. Brewers Assn., Am., Md., Balt. City bar assns., Sigma Chi, Sigma Delta Chi. Democrat. Presbyterian. Home: 7749 Hawthorne Rd Mequon WI 53092 Office: 3939 W Highland Blvd Milwaukee WI 53208

JONES, REGINA NICKERSON, public relations executive; b. Los Angeles, Sept. 23, 1942; d. Leslie Augustus and Luedelia (Triggs) Nickerson; m. Kenneth Leon Jones, Apr. 5, 1958; children: Kenneth Leon, Kevin Christopher, Keith Fitzgerald, Kory Reginald, Karen Regina. Bookkeeper, sec. Carson Realty, Los Angeles, 1958; radio telephone operator Los Angeles Police Dept., 1962-66; owner, publisher Soul Publs., Los Angeles, 1966-83; v.p. pub. relations Solar Records-Dick Griffey Prodns., Los Angeles, 1983—. Mem. Nat. Assn. Media Women, Black Music Assn. (exec. council), NAACP, Urban League. Office: 1635 N Cahuenga Blvd Los Angeles CA 90028

JONES, REGINALD LANIER, educator; b. Clearwater, Fla., Jan. 21, 1931; s. Moses and Naomi Modestine (Henry) J.; m. Johnette Turner, Sept. 6, 1958; children: Juliette Melinda, Angela Michele, Cynthia Ann. B.A. in Psychology, Morehouse Coll., 1952; M.A. in Clin. Psychology, Wayne State U., 1954; Ph.D. in Psychology, Ohio State U., 1959. Clin. psychologist Logansport State Hosp., 1956; research asst. prof. instructional research service Miami U., Oxford, Ohio, 1959-63; assoc. prof. psychology Fisk U., 1963-64; asst. prof. edn. UCLA, 1964-66; prof., vice chmn. dept. psychology Ohio State U., 1966-69; chmn., prof. dept. edn. U. Calif.-Riverside, 1969—; dir. Univ. Testing Center Haile Selaisse U., Ethiopia, 1972-74; prof. edn. and Afro-Am. studies U. Calif.-Berkeley, 1973. Editor: New Directions in Special Education, 1970, Problems and Issues in the Education of Exceptional Children, (with (I.G. Hendrick) Student Dissent in the Schools, 1971, Black Psychology, 1972, (with D.L. MacMillan) Special Education in Transition, 1974, Mainstreaming and the Minority Child, 1976, Sourcebook on the Teaching of Black Psychology, 1980, Reflections on Growing Up Disabled, 1983. Served with M.C. AUS, 1954-56. Fellow Am. Psychol. Assn.; mem. Assn. Black Psychologists (nat. chmn. 1971-72), Am. Assn. on Mental Deficiency, Council on Exceptional Children, Am. Ednl. Research Assn. Office: Dept Afro Am Studies U Calif at Berkeley Berkeley CA 94720

JONES, RICHARD HUTTON, history educator; b. Rye, Colo., Aug. 11, 1914; s. John Wiley and Jessie (Hutton) J.; m. Alyce Decker, Aug. 15, 1935; 1 son, Robert Charles. B.A., U. No. Colo., 1934, M.A., 1937; Ph.D., Stanford U., 1947; LL.D., Reed Coll., 1982. High sch. tchr., Ft. Lupton, Colo., 1934-38; instr. Stanford, 1940-41; mem. faculty Reed Coll., Portland, Oreg., 1941—, Richard F. Scholz prof. history, 1962—; dir. Nat. Endowment Humanities Inst., 1978; profector Oreg. Shakespearean Festival, 1964; Chmn. com. European history Coll. Entrance Exam. Bd., 1961-69, mem. com. exams., 1965-68; spl. cons. Ednl. Assos., Inc., 1968-70; vis. scholar Wolfson Coll., Cambridge, Eng., 1983. Author: The Royal Policy of Richard II, 1966; Contbg. editor: medieval sect. London Times Atlas of World History, 1978. Pub. mem. Oreg. Legis. Interim Com. Labor, 1958-60; mem. Oreg. Commn. Constl. Revision, 1961, 62; exec. sec. Citizens Com. Constl. Revision, 1963-65; Oreg. chmn. Rep. Com. Arts and Scis., 1965-66; chmn. Oreg. Reps. for McCarthy; mem. Oreg. Gov.'s Com. on Humanities, 1965-66; mem. adv. council Oreg. Commn. for Humanities, 1973—; mem. State Panel of Fact Finders, 1976—. Social Sci. Research Council faculty fellow, 1951-53; Ford Found. fellow, 1953-54; sr. fellow law and behavioral sci. U. Chgo., 1956-57. Mem. Am. Arbitration Assn. (panel on arbitrators). Home: 3908 SE Reedway Portland OR 97202

JONES, RICHARD L., justice Ala. Supreme Ct.; b. Carrollton, Ala., Mar. 3, 1923; m. Jean Leslie; children—Rick, Marilyn, Leslie. LL.B., U. Ala. Bar: Ala. bar. Practiced law, Aliceville, Ala., Bessemer, Ala., Birmingham, Ala.; asso. justice Ala. Supreme Ct., Montgomery; mem. Uniform State Law Commn., Ala. Jud. Conf. and Code Revision Com. Elder, tchr. Shades Valley Presbyterian Ch. Served to col. USAR. Mem. Ala. Trial Lawyers Assn. (pres.). Office: PO Box 218 Montgomery AL 36101 *

JONES, RICHARD M., business executive; b. Eldon, Mo., Nov. 26, 1926; m. Sylvia A. Richardson, 1950; 3 children. B.S. in Bus. Adminstrn., Olivet Nazarene Coll., 1950, LL.D. (hon.), 1983; grad. Advanced Mgmt. Program, Harvard U., 1973. With Sears, Roebuck & Co., 1950—, store mgr., 1963-68, gen. mgr., Washington and Balt., 1974, exec. v.p.-East, 1974-80, corp. v.p., 1980, vice chmn. bd., chief fin. officer, 1980—, also dir., chmn. fin. and investment coms.; chmn., chief exec. officer Sears World Trade; dir. Sears Roebuck Acceptance Corp. Trustee Field Mus. Natural History, Chgo., Sears-Roebuck Found. Office: Sears Roebuck & Co Sears Tower Chicago IL 60684

JONES, RICHARD NORMAN, scientist; b. Manchester, Eng., Mar. 20, 1913; s. Richard Leonard and Blanche (Mason) J.; m. Magda Kemeny, July 12, 1939; children: Richard Kemeny, David Leonard. B.Sc., Manchester U., 1933, M.Sc., 1934, Ph.D., 1936, D.Sc., 1954; D.Sc. (hon.), U. Poznan, 1972, Tokyo Inst. Tech., 1982. Commonwealth Fund fellow, tutor in biochemistry Harvard U., Cambridge, Mass., 1937-42; asst. prof. Queens U., Kingston, Ont., Can., 1942-46; assoc. research officer in analytical spectroscopy Nat. Research Council Can., Ottawa, 1949-65, prin. research officer, 1965-78; guest prof. Tokyo Inst. Tech., 1979-82; Disting. visitor U. Alta., 1982-83. Contbr. articles to profl. jours. Recipient Fisher award Chem. Inst. Can., 1971; Herzberg award Spectroscopy Soc. Can., 1979. Fellow Royal Soc. Can., Chem. Soc. (London), Chem. Inst. Can., Spectroscopy Soc. Can. (hon., v.p. 1983); mem. Am. Chem. Soc., Internat. Union Pure and Applied Chemists (pres. phys. chemistry div. 1973-77), Internat. Council of Sci. Unions (v.p. com. on data for sci. and tech. 1970-74). Home: Apt 601 71 Somerset St W Ottawa ON K2P 2G2 Canada

JONES, RICHARD THEODORE, biochemistry educator; b. Portland, Oreg., Nov. 9, 1929; s. Lester Tallman and Olene (Johnson) J.; m. Marilyn Virginia Beam, June 20, 1953; children: Gary Richard, Alan Donald, Neil William. Student, Calif. Inst. Tech., 1948-51, Ph.D., 1961; B.S., U. Oreg., 1953, M.S., M.D., 1956. Student asst. dept. physiology U. Oreg. Med. Sch., Portland, 1953-56, asst. prof., 1961-64, assoc. prof. exptl. medicine and biochemistry, 1964-67, prof., chmn. dept. biochemistry, 1967—; acting pres. U. Oreg. Health Scis. Center, 1977-78; intern Hosp. U. Pa., 1956-57; research asst. dept. chemistry Calif. Inst. Tech., 1959-60; Mem. biochemistry tng. com. Nat. Inst. Gen. Med. Scis., NIH, 1968-73, med. sci. tng. com., 1971-74; comprehensive sickle cell centers ad hoc rev. com. Nat. Heart, Lung and Blood Inst., 1974-77; biochemistry test com. Nat. Bd. Med. Examiners, 1968-74. Contbr. articles to profl. jours. Mem. Am. Soc. Biol. Chemists, Am. Chem. Soc., AAAS, Sigma Xi, Alpha Omega Alpha, Tau Beta Pi. Home: 2634 SW Fairmount Blvd Portland OR 97201 Office: 3181 SW Sam Jackson Park Rd Portland OR 97201

JONES, RICHARD VICTOR, physics educator; b. Oakland, Calif., June 8, 1929; 3 children. A.B., U. Calif., 1951, Ph.D. in Physics, 1956; M.A. hon., Harvard U., 1961. Sr. engr. Shockley Semiconductor Lab., Beckman Instruments, Inc., 1955-57; from asst. prof. to assoc. prof. applied physics Harvard U., 1957-71, assoc. dean div. engring. and applied physics, 1969-71, dean Grad. Sch. Arts and Sci., 1971-72, prof. applied physics, now Robert L. Wallace prof. applied physics; vis. MacKay prof. U. Calif.-Berkeley, 1967-68. Guggenheim fellow, 1960-61. Office: Div Applied Scis Harvard U 201 Gordon McKay Cambridge MA 02138 *

JONES, ROBERT C., symphony orchestra administrator; b. Needham, Mass., July 21, 1943; s. William Arthur and Roberta (Cushman) J.; m. Susan Christine Anderson, Mar. 19, 1966; children: Jeffrey Howard, William Oscar. B.S. in Econs., Portland State U., 1966. Sec.-treas. Musicians Mut. Assn., Local 99, Portland, Oreg., 1969-80; exec. officer Am. Fedn. Musician of U.S. and Can., N.Y.C., 1978-80; v.p., gen. mgr. Minn. Orchestral Assn., Mpls., 1980-83; exec. dir. Indpls. Symphony Orch., 1983—; pres. Northwest Conf. of Musicians, 1976; founding dir. Pacific Northwest Labor Coll., 1977-80; panelist NEA, Washington, 1977-80; dir. Greater Twin Cities Youth Symphonies, Mpls., 1980-83, West Coast Chamber Orch., Portland, 1978-80. Chmn. Met. Arts Commn., Portland, 1977-80; mem. Performing Arts Theatre Task Force, Portland, 1979-80; producer Artquake, Portland, 1977-80; dir. Arts Celebration, Inc., Portland, 1977-80. Mem. Am. Symphony Orch. League, Am. Fedn. Musicians (Oreg. state rep. and legis. dir. 1971-80), Minn. Orchestral Assn. N.Am. Saxaphone Alliance (northwest regional coordinator 1970-80). Democrat. Office: Indianapolis Symphony Orchestra PO Box 88207 Indianapolis IN 46208

JONES, ROBERT DOYNE, retail grocery executive; b. Huntington, Ind., May 26, 1933; s. Cecil Earl and Doris Eden (Kindig) J.; m. Suzanne English, May 18, 1963; children: Anthony, Christopher. B.S., Ind. U., 1955. Supr. Travelers Ins. Co., Hartford, Conn., 1958-62; adminstrv. asst. to Congressman Donald Rumsfeld of Ill., Washington, 1963-65; v.p pub. affairs Jewel Co. Inc., Chgo., 1965—. Bd. dirs. Donors Forum, Chgo., Police and Fire Com., Winnetka, 1983. Served to 1st lt. U.S. Army, 1956-58. Mem. Ill. Retail Mchts. Assn. (vice chmn.). Republican. Episcopalian. Clubs: University (Chgo.); Indian Hill (Winnetka). Home: 326Woodland Winnetka IL 60093 Office: Jewel Co Inc 5725 N East River Rd Chicago IL 60631

JONES, ROBERT EMMET, educator; b. N.Y.C., Sept. 16, 1928; s. Robert Emmet and Lois Kathryn (UpdeGrove) J. A.B., Columbia U., 1948, Ph.D., 1954; certificat de phonetique Sorbonne, Paris, 1949. Vis. instr. French Columbia U., 1953-54; asst. prof. French U. Ga., Athens, 1954-61, U. Pa., 1961-67; asso. prof. French and humanities M.I.T., 1967-71, prof. French and humanities, 1971—; tchr. French cooking, 1976—. Author: The Alienated Hero in Modern French Drama, 1961, Panorama de la nouvelle critique en France, 1968, Gerard de Nerval, 1974; contbr. articles to profl. jours. Mem. MLA, Am. Assn. Tchrs. French, French Library Boston. Episcopalian. Clubs: St. Anthony, St. Botolph. Home: 452 Beacon St Boston MA 02115 Office: 14N 212 MIT Cambridge MA 02139

JONES, ROBERT EUGENE, architect, architectural critic; b. Lawton, Okla., Nov. 13, 1930; s. James Cecil and Ernestine Alberta (Huber) J.; m. Sara Carol Price, Dec. 31, 1955 (div.); children: Brent, Brigette; m. Elizabeth S. Dorland, May 28, 1977. B.Arch., U. So. Calif., 1955. Partner Hester-Jones & Assocs., La Jolla, Calif., 1962-64; prin. Robert E. Jones (Architect), La Jolla, 1964-66; partner Robert E. Jones & Edwin K. Hom (architects), La Jolla, 1966-69, pres., 1969-76; v.p. Koizumi & Jones Internat. Design Corp., Newport Beach, Calif., 1971-76; pres. Robert E. Jones (Architect), 1976—; v.p., dir. design Frank L. Hope & Assocs., 1977-78; partner Colonial Inn Properties, 1975—, Jones & Greene, 1980-82; archtl. critic San Diego Union. Important works include Bruck Residence, La Jolla; 1st patio home community Casas Capistrano; 2d patio home community Jones Residence, Del Mar, Busch Residence, Del Mar. Planning commr. City of Del Mar, Calif., 1970-72; mem. Del Mar Design Rev. Bd., 1970-72, Urban Design Center, S.E. San Diego Model Cities Area, 1970. Served to 1st lt. USAF, 1955-57. Recipient 13 nat. and local AIA design awards; named One of 12 Top Performers of 1969 by House & Home Mag. for contbn. of patio-home concept to housing industry. Mem. AIA, San Diego C. of C., Urban Land Inst., Nat. Council Archtl. Registration Bds., Blue Key, Skull and Dagger, Tau Sigma Delta, Scarab. Office: 7713 Fay Ave La Jolla CA 92037

JONES, ROBERT GEAN, educator; b. Magnolia, Ark., Feb. 17, 1925; s. Emless Bunyan and Eunice (Gean) J.; m. Marian Laverne Alexander, July 23, 1946; 1 dau., Carolyn Ann. B.A. cum laude, Baylor U., 1947, B.D., Yale, 1950, M.A., 1957, Ph.D., 1959. Ordained to ministry Bapt. Ch., 1946; minister Deep River (Conn.) Bapt. Ch. and; First Bapt. Ch. of, Saybrook, 1950-59; asst. prof. religion George Washington U., Washington, 1959-61, asso. prof., 1961-64, prof., 1964—, chmn. dept. religion, 1963-79, univ. marshal, 1969—. Author: The Rules for the War of the Sons of Light With the Sons of Darkness, 1957, The Manual of Discipline (1QS), The Old Testament and Persian Religion, 1964. Mem. Soc. Bibl. Lit. and Exegesis, Am. Acad. Religion, Alpha Chi, Omicron Delta Kappa. Home: 11835 Goya Dr Potomac MD 20854 Office: George Washington U Washington DC 20052

JONES, ROBERT HUHN, history educator; b. Chgo., July 30, 1927; s. Merton Oakes and Ethel (Huhn) J.; m. Estelle Marie Long, June 12, 1948 (dec.); children: Judith Caroline, Robert Paul.; m. Hedy J. Kish, July 17, 1982. A.B., U. Ill. at Champaign, 1950, M.A., 1951, Ph.D., 1957. Mem. faculty Kent (Ohio) State U., 1957-65, Case Western Res. U., Cleve., 1965-71; prof. history, chmn. dept. U. Akron, 1971—; vis. research prof. U. Ill. at Champaign, 1962-63. Author: The Civil War in the Northwest, 1960, (with Fred A. Shannon) The Centennial Years, 1967, The Roads to Russia: United States Lend-Lease to the Soviet Union, 1969, Disrupted Decades: The Civil War and Reconstruction Years, 1973, 79. Mem. Stow (Ohio) City Sch. Dist. Bd. Edn., 1968-80; pres. Stow Bd. Edn., 1971-76. Served with Signal Corps U.S. Army, 1945-47. Lilly Endowment postdoctoral fellow, 1964. Mem. Ohio Acad. History (chmn. standards com. 1970-73, exec. com. 1981—), Am. Hist. Assn., Western History Assn., Orgn. Am. Historians, Author's Guild. Home: 1870 Oakridge Dr Akron OH 44313

JONES, ROBERT LAWTON, architect, planner; b. McAlester, Okla., May 12, 1925; s. Lawton Henry and Josephine (Troy) J.; m. Lynn Scott, Dec. 2, 1950; children: Jayme, Mark, Paul, Gregory, Laure, Christi, Matthew. B.Arch. cum laude, U. Notre Dame, 1949; M.S., Ill. Inst. Tech., 1953; postgrad., Tech. U., Karlsruhe, Germany, 1954. With Perkins & Will, Chgo., 1949-52; mgr. Civic Center Project, Tulsa, 1954-55; architect David G. Murray & Assos., Tulsa, 1955-56; dir. planning and design Murray Jones Murray Inc., Tulsa, 1957—; Chmn. Community Relations Commn., Tulsa, 1968; chmn. Art Commn., Tulsa, 1970-71; v.p. NCCJ, Tulsa, 1970-73. Important works include Chapman Hall, Tulsa U., Tulsa Internat. Airport, Okla. U. Coll. Nursing, St. Patrick's Ch., Hissom Meml. Center, First Nat. Bank, Hillcrest Med. Center, Okla. Coll. Osteo. Medicine and Surgery, Hilti Western Hemisphere Hdqrs, Cities Service Tech. Center. Chmn. Tulsa Pollution Control Task Force, 1970; v.p. Arts and Humanities Council, Tulsa, 1971-74, pres., 1975-76; chmn. Community of the Living Christ, 1973; Bd. dirs. Tulsa Area Health and Hosp. Planning Council, 1972-78, Nat. Research Found. and Aging, 1974-78, Tulsa Met. Ministry, 1977-82. Served with USNR, 1943-46. Fellow AIA; mem. Am. Planning Assn., Am. Inst. Cert. Planners, Met. Tulsa C. of C. (dir. 1974-76). Democrat. Roman Catholic. Home: 1916 E 47th St Tulsa OK 74105 Office: 201 W 5th St Tulsa OK 74103

JONES, ROBERT LEE, educator; b. Sapulpa, Okla., June 17, 1920; s. Clyde William and Arminia (Harris) J.; m. Mary Claire Collingsworth, June 12, 1948; 1 dau., Mary Lee. B.A, Oklahoma City U., 1948; B.D., So. Methodist U., 1951; M.A., 1952; Ph.D., St. Mary's Coll., U. St. Andrews, Scotland, 1961. Ordained to ministry Meth. Ch., 1952; asso. pastor Wesley Meth. Ch., Oklahoma City, 1947-48, Dallas, 1948-52; pastor Grove (Okla.) Meth. Ch., 1952-54, Ch. of Scotland, 1954-56; pastor, dir. Wesley Found. Meth. Ch., Goodwell, Okla., 1956-57; asst. prof. religion Oklahoma City U., 1957-61, asso. prof., 1961-65, prof., 1965—, dean of men, 1960-62, asso. dean, 1962-63, dean, 1963-70, v.p. acad. affairs, 1970-79, dir.; del. 3d Oxford Inst. Meth. Theol. Studies, 1965; Internat. Conf. on Higher Edn., Oxford, Eng., 1965; Chmn. com. on edn. Community Relations Commn., Oklahoma City, 1966-70, vice chmn. Commn., 1970; mem. editorial bd. Intercollegiate Press, Am. Soc. Ch. History. Serve with F.A. U.S. Army, 1941-45. Decorated Bronze Star. Mem. Am. Acad. Religion, Am. Assn. Higher Edn. Home: 3240 N W 18th St Oklahoma City OK 73107 Office: N W 23d at Blackwelder Oklahoma City OK 73106

JONES, ROBERT LEWIS, soil mineralogy and ecology educator; b. Wellston, Ohio, Jan. 26, 1936; s. Robert Davis and Laura (Lewis) J.; m. Katharine Anne King, July 8, 1958; children: Kevin, Laura, Dylan. B.Sc., Ohio State U., 1958, M.Sc., 1959; Ph.D., U. Ill., 1962. Research assoc. U. Ill., Champaign-Urbana, 1962-64, asst. prof., 1964-67, assoc. prof., 1967-72, prof. soil mineralogy and ecology, 1972—; Fulbright lectr., 1968. Co-author: (with H.C. Hanson) Biogeochemistry of Blue, Snow and Ross Geese, 1978, Mineral licks, geophagy and biogeochemistry of North American ungulates, 1984. Mem. Soil Sci. Soc. Am., Mineral So. Am., Wildlife Soc., Am. Soc. Agronomy. Home: 16 Ashley Ln Champaign IL 61820 Office: N 415 Turner Hall 1102 S Goodwin St Urbana IL 61801

JONES, ROBERT MARION, book and magazine consultant; b. Fulda, Minn., May 31, 1919; s. John Webster and Emma Louella (Price) J.; m. Mary Catherine Burd, Nov. 16, 1940; children—Sheila Jones Reagan, Robert Michael, Jeffrey Paul, Molly Jones Marshall, Christopher Francis. B.A., U. Minn., 1940. Newspaper reporter Hennepin County (Minn.) Rev., 1938-40, Madison (S.D.) Daily Leader, 1940-42, Sioux Falls (S.D.) Daily Argus-Leader, 1942-45; editorial asst., asso. editor, mng. editor Better Homes & Gardens, Meredith Pub. Co., Des Moines, 1945-54; editor Family Circle, N.Y.C.; v.p. Family Circle, Inc., 1955-67; series editor Time-Life Books, Inc., 1967-81, corp. planning cons., 1982—. Editor: Better Homes and Gardens Handyman's Book, 1951, Can Elephants Swim? Unlikely Answers to Improbable Questions, 1969, The Time-Life Book of Family Finance, 1969, The Time-Life Ency. of Gardening, 1971-72, extension, 1976-79, Time-Life Home Repair and Improvement series, 1979-81; supervising editor: The Family Creative Workshop, 1974-75. Mem. Mag. Publishers Assn., U. Minn. Alumni Assn., Am. Soc. Mag. Editors (exec. com.), Sigma Delta Chi. Home: 1507 Wake Forest Dr Alexandria VA 22307

JONES, ROBERT RUSSELL, mag. editor; b. Topeka, Oct. 19, 1927; s. Russell Alonzo and and Marie (Carter) J.; m. Dorothy Jean Vincent, Sept. 3, 1947; children—Daniel Robert, Mark Alan. A.B. in Polit. Sci. and History, Washburn U., Topeka, 1949; M.S. in Tech. Journalism, Kans. State U., Manhattan, 1959. Expt. sta. editor, asst. prof. agrl. econs. Kans. State U., 1957-60; asst. editor Agrl. Pubs. Inc., Milw., 1960-67; sci. editor, asst. prof. expt. sta. U. Mo., Columbia, 1967-72; asso. editor Indsl. Research mag., Chgo., 1972-74, editor, 1974-78; editor, editorial dir. Indsl. Research & Devel. mag., Barrington, Ill., 1978—; chmn. I-R 100 new products awards ann. program, 1974—. Editor: The Unsettled Earth, 1975. Served with USNR, 1945-46. Mem. Am. Bus. Press (Jesse H. Neal Editorial Achievement award 1976), Am. Soc. Bus. Press Editors, Nat. Assn. Sci. Writers. Democrat. Baptist. Home: 1213 Main St Evanston IL 60202 Office: 1301 S Grove Ave Barrington IL 60010

JONES, ROBERT THOMAS, aero. scientist; b. Macon, Mo., May 28, 1910; s. Edward Seward and Harriet Ellen (Johnson) J.; m. Barbara Jeanne Spagnoli, Nov. 23, 1964; children—Edward, Patricia, Harriet, David, Gregory, John. Student, U. Mo., 1928; Sc.D. (hon.), U. Colo., 1971. Aero. research scientist NACA, Langley Field, Va., 1934-46; research scientist Ames Research Center NACA-NASA, Moffet Field, Calif., 1946-62; sr. staff scientist Ames Research Center, NASA, 1970-81, research asso., 1981—; scientist Avco-Everett Research Lab., Everett, Mass., 1962-70; cons. prof. Stanford U., 1981. Author: (with Doris Cohen) High Speed Wing Theory, 1960, Collected Works of Robert T. Jones, 1976; contbr.: articles to profl. jours. Collected Works of Robert T. Jones. Recipient Reed award Inst. Aero. Scis., 1946; Inventions and Contbns. award NASA, 1975; Prandtl Ring award Deutsche Gesellschaft für Luft and Raumfahrt, 1978; Pres.'s medal for disting. fed. service, 1980; Langley medal Smithsonian Instn., 1981. Fellow Am. Inst. Aeros. and Astronautics (hon.); mem. Am. Acad. Arts and Scis., Nat. Acad. Scis., Nat. Acad. Engring. Home: 25005 La Loma Dr Los Altos Hills CA 94022 Office: NASA Ames Research Center Moffett Field CA 94035

JONES, ROBERT TRENT, golf course architect; b. nr. Ince, Eng., June 20, 1906; came to U.S., 1911; s. William Rees and Jane (Sothern) J.; m. Ione Tefft Davis, May 11, 1934; children: Robert Trent, Jr., Rees Lee. Spl. student, Cornell, 1927-30. Partner Stanley Thompson (Canadian golf course architect), N.Y.C., 1930-40; pvt. practice as golf course architect, 1940—. Co-author: The Complete Golfer, 1954, Golf-Its History, People and Events, 1966; author: Great Golf Stories; Contbr. articles golf publs. Recipient Golden Plate award, 1972; Disting. Service award Met. Golf Writer's Assn., 1976; Outstanding Achievement award Am. Soc. Golf Course Architects, 1976; William D. Richardson award Golf Writers Assn. Am., 1981; Disting. Alumni award Cornell U., 1982. Mem. Delta Kappa Epsilon. Episcopalian. Clubs: Montclair (N.J.) Golf; Pine Valley Golf (Clementon, N. J.); Yale (N.Y.C.); Coral Ridge Country (Fort Lauderdale, Fla.) (pres.); Royal and Ancient Golf (St. Andrews, Scotland); Cotton Bay (dir.); Eleuthera (Bahamas); Burning Tree (Washington); Oakmont Country (Pitts.); Sleepy Hollow Country (Scarborough, N.Y.); Metropolitan (N.Y.C.); Spyglass Hill (Pebble Beach, Calif.); Birnam Woods Golf (Santa Barbara, Calif.); Point o' Woods (Benton Harbor, Mich.). Designed more than 350 world's most outstanding courses. Home: 173 Gates Ave Montclair NJ 07042 also Breakwater Towers Fort Lauderdale FL 32016 Office: 31 Park St Montclair NJ 07042

JONES, ROBERT TRENT, JR., golf course architect; b. Montclair, N.J., July 24, 1939; s. Robert Trent J. and Ione J. (Jones). B.A., Yale U., 1961; postgrad. in law, Stanford U. Pres., prin. designer Robert Trent Jones II, Palo Alto, Calif., Robert Trent Jones II Internat., Internat. assoc. SRI Internat., 1983; amateur golfer numerous tournaments, speaker in field. Contbr. articles to prof., jours. Chmn. Calif. Parks and Recreation Commn., 1983; mem. San Francisco Com. on Fgn. Relations, 1983. Recipient Family of the Yr. award Met. Golf Writers and Golf Owners Assn. Mem. Am. Soc. Golf Course Architects (exec. com.), Urban Land Inst. (exec. com.). Democrat. Clubs: Bohamian Golf, San Francisco Golf; Royal and Ancient Golf (St. Andrews, Scotland); Spyglass Hill Golf, Pine Valley Golf. Office: 705 Forest Ave Palo Alto CA 94301

JONES, ROGER CLYDE, electrical engineer, educator; b. Lake Andes, S.D., Aug. 17, 1919; s. Robert Clyde and Martha (Albertson) J.; m. Katherine M. Tucker, June 7, 1952; children: Linda Lee, Vonnie Lynette. B.S., U. Nebr., 1949; M.S., U. Md., 1953; Ph.D., 1963. With U.S. Naval Research Lab., Washington, 1949-57; staff sr. engr. to chief engr. Melpar, Inc., Falls Church, Va., 1957-58, cons. project engr., 1958-59, sect. head physics, 1959-64, chief scientist for physics, 1964; prof. dept. elec. engring. U. Ariz., Tucson, 1964—, dir. quantum electronics lab., 1968—, adj. prof. radiology, 1978—; guest prof. in exptl. oncology Inst. Cancer Research, Aarhus, Denmark, 1982-83. Served with AUS, 1942-45. Mem. Am. Phys. Soc., Optical Soc. Am., Bioelectromagnetics Soc., IEEE, AAAS, Eta Kappa Nu, Pi Mu Epsilon. Patentee in field. Home: 5809 E 3d St Tucson AZ 85711 Office: Dept Elec Engring U Ariz Tucson AZ

JONES, RUSSEL CAMERON, educator; b. Tarentum, Pa., Oct. 18, 1935; s. Frederick Russel and Helena Doris (Elliot) J.; m. Sharon Ann Keillor; children—Amy Sue, Kimberly Nicole, Tamara Melissa. B.S., Carnegie Inst. Tech., 1957, M.S., 1960, Ph.D., 1963. Structural engr. Hunting, Larsen & Dunnels, Pitts., 1957-59; asst. prof. civil engring. M.I.T., 1963-66, asso. prof., 1966-71; prof., chmn. dept. civil engring. Ohio State U., Columbus, 1971-76; dean Sch. Engring., U. Mass., Amherst, 1977-81; v.p. acad. affairs Boston U., 1981—. Recipient fellowship NDEA, 1959-62, ASCE, 1962-63, Collingwood prize, 1966, Edmund Friedman profl. recognition award, 1981. Mem. ASCE (dir. 1969-71, 72-75, v.p. 1976-77), ASTM, Am. Soc. Engring. Edn., Nat. Soc. Profl. Engrs., Am. Concrete Inst., Am. Soc. Metals, AIME Engrs., Sigma Xi, Tau Beta Pi, Phi Kappa Phi, Chi Epsilon, Sigma Nu. Home: 405 Commonwealth Ave Newton Centre MA 02159 Office: Vice Pres Acad Affairs Boston U 145 Bay State Rd Boston MA 02215

JONES, SAMUEL, conductor; b. Inverness, Miss., June 2, 1935; s. Samuel Leander and Ella Mae (Spencer) J.; m. Kristin Barbara Schutte, Dec. 22, 1975; children by previous marriage: Rachel Ann, Alison Frances. B.A., Millsaps Coll., 1957; M.A. (Woodrow Wilson fellow), Eastman Sch. Music, U. Rochester, 1958, Ph.D., 1960. Dir. instrumental music Alma (Mich.) Coll., 1960-62, instr., 1960-61, asst. prof., 1961-62; prof. conducting and composition Shepherd Sch. Music, Rice U., Houston, 1973—; dean, 1973-79. Founder: Alma Symphony, 1961; condr., Saginaw (Mich.) Symphony, 1962-65, also; dir., Saginaw Choral Soc.; composer-in-residence, Delta Coll., University Center, Mich., 1964-65; founder, conductor: Festival Orch, University Center, 1964-65; with, Rochester Philharmonic Orch., 1965-73; condr., 1971-73; guest condr., Pitts. Symphony, Buffalo Philharmonic, Shenandoah Valley Music Festival, Naumberg, Detroit, Prague, Houston, Iceland symphonies, others.; Composer: Symphony 1, 1960, In Retrospect, 1959, Overture for a City, 1964, Festival Fanfare (commd. Am. Symphony Orch. League), 1964, Elegy in Memory of John Fitzgerald Kennedy, 1917-63, 1963, Let Us Now Praise Famous Men (commd. Shenandoah County Bicentennial Commn.), 1972, Spaces, 1974, Contours of Time, 1975, Fanfare and Celebration (commd. Houston Symphony), 1980, A Symphonic Requiem (commd. Sioux City Symphony), 1983; Writer/narrator: ednl. TV series for N.Y. State Dept. Edn. The World of Music. Recipient Founders medal Millsaps Coll., 1957. Mem. Houston Profl. Musicians Assn., Am. Music Center, Nat. Assn. Am. Composers and Condrs., Nat. Assn. Humanities Edn., Omicron Delta Kappa, Lambda Chi Alpha. Methodist. Home: 2235 Southgate Blvd Houston TX 77030 Office: Shepherd School of Music Rice U Houston TX 77251

JONES, SHIRLEY, actress, singer; b. Smithton, Pa., Mar. 31; d. Paul and Marjorie (Williams) J.; m. Jack Cassidy, Aug. 5, 1956 (div. 1975); children—Shaun, Patrick, Ryan; m. Marty Ingels, 1977. Grad. high sch., 1952; student, Pitts. Playhouse. Appeared: with chorus South Pacific, 1953, also; also: Broadway prodn. Me and Juliet; leading role in road tour; role of Laurey: motion picture Oklahoma, 1954; later stage tour of Paris and Rome, sponsorship U.S. Dept. State, Am. stage in summer stock, 1960; appeared in role of Julie: motion picture Carousel, 1956; other films include April Love, 1957, Never Steal Anything Small, 1959, Elmer Gantry, 1960, Pepe, 1960, The Music Man, 1962, A Ticklish Affair, 1963, Bedtime Story, 1964, The Secret of My Success, 1965, Fluffy, 1965; appeared in a night club tour with husband, 1958, later; later TV and summer stock; appeared in, CBS-TV prodn. Victor Herbert operetta; The Red Mill, 1958; appeared in: Broadway play Maggie Flynn, 1968; star: TV series The Partridge Family, 1970-74, Shirley, 1979; TV role: The Big Slide; toured in: On A Clear Day, 1975, Show Boat, 1976; guest star: TV series McMillan, 1976; one-woman concert: Shirley Jones' Am, 1981—; (Recipient Acad. award for best supporting actress in Elmer Gantry 1961, named Mother of Year, Women's Found. 1978). Nat. chairwoman Leukemia Found. Address: care Ingels Inc 7560 Hollywood Blvd Hollywood CA 90046

JONES, SIDNEY LEWIS, economist, former govt. ofcl.; b. Ogden, Utah, Sept. 23, 1933; s. Lewis W. and Anna Vernal (Evans) J.; m. Marlene Stewart, Nov. 24, 1953; children—Randall Sidney, Stanna, Bryan Lewis, Blake Stewart, Allyson. B.S. with honors in Econs, Utah State U., 1954; M.B.A., Stanford, 1958, Ph.D., 1960. Asst. prof. finance Northwestern U., Evanston, Ill., 1960-64, asso. prof., 1964-65; prof. finance U. Mich., Ann Arbor, 1965-69, 71-72; sr. staff economist Pres.'s Council Econ Advisers, 1969-71, spl. asst. to chmn., 1970-71; minister-counselor for econ. affairs to NATO, Brussels, Belgium, 1972-73; asst. sec. for econ. affairs Dept. Commerce, Washington, 1973-74; dep. asst. to Pres., also; dep. counsellor for econ. policy White House, 1974-75; counselor to sec. Treasury, Washington, 1975; asst. sec. for econ. policy Dept. Treasury, 1975-77; fellow Woodrow Wilson Internat. Center for Scholars, Washington, 1977-78; asst. to bd. govs. FRS, 1978; research scholar Am. Enterprise Inst.; Public Policy Research and lectr. Georgetown U., 1979-84; under secretary for economic affairs Commerce Dept., Washington, D.C., 1984—; Conf. program dir. NASA 3d Nat. Conf. on Peaceful Uses of Space, 1962. Co-author: The Generalist-Specialist Dichotomy in the Management of Creative Personnel, 1960, Managerial Problems in Finance, 1964, Financial Institutions, 4th edit, 1966, The Development of Economic Policy, 1980. Served to 1st lt. Q.M.C. AUS, 1954-56. Recipient Distinguished Alumni award Utah State U., 1971; Newell scholar; McKinsey fellow; Ford Found. fellow, 1957-60. Home: 8505 Parliament Dr Potomac MD 20854 Office: Commerce Dept Main Bldg Washington DC 20230

JONES, STANLEY BOYD, health policy analyst; b. Balt., July 27, 1938; s. Arthur Boyd and Lillian Ailene (Powell) J.; m. Judith K. Miller, Mar. 9, 1981; children—Andrew, Jeffrey, Lisa, Julia. B.A., Dartmouth Coll., 1960; postgrad., Yale U., 1960-63. Mem. profl. staff, staff dir. Subcom. on Health, U.S. Senate, Washington, 1970-76; program devel. officer Inst. of Medicine, Nat. Acad. Scis., Washington, 1976-78; v.p. Fullerton, Jones & Wollkstein (Health Policy Alternatives), Washington, 1978-80; v.p. for Washington representation Nat. Assns. Blue Cross and Blue Shield Plans, 1980—; Mem. adv. bd. Health Policy Center, U. Calif., San Francisco. Sr. warden, vestryman Episcopal Ch. Fellow Inst. of Soc., Ethics and the Life Scis.; mem. Inst. of Medicine of Nat. Acad. Scis., Am. Public Health Assn. Home: 9005 Fairview Rd Silver Spring MD 20910 Office: 1700 Pennsylvania Ave NW Washington DC 20006

JONES, TERRY, film director, author; b. Colwyn Bay, North Wales, U.K., Feb. 1, 1942; s. Alick George Parry and Dilys Louisa (Newnes)

J.; m. Alison Telfer; children—Sally, Bill. Student, St Edmund Hall, Oxford U. Writer, performer on TV in: Monty Python's Flying Circus; co-author: TV play Secrets; co-dir.: film Monty Python and the Holy Grail; dir.: Monty Python's Life of Brian, Monty Python's The Meaning of Life; author: Chaucer's Knight, 1980, Fairy Tales, 1981, The Saga of Erik the Viking, 1983; co-author: Dr. Fegg's Nasty Book of Knowledge. Address: Python Prodns 6 Cambridge Gate London NW1 England

JONES, THEODORE LAWRENCE, association executive, lawyer; b. Dallas, Nov. 29, 1920; s. Theodore Evan and Ernestine Lucy (Douthit) J.; m. Marion Elizabeth Thomas, Feb. 29, 1944; children: Suzanne Lynn, Scott Evan, Stephen Lawrence, Shannon Elizabeth. B.B.A., U. Tex., 1944, J.D., 1948; postgrad., So. Meth. U., 1950-52, Am. U., 1965-66. Bar: Tex. 1948, U.S. Supreme Ct. 1962. Asso. Carrington, Gowan, Johnson & Walker, Dallas, 1948-51; gen. counsel W. H. Cothrum & Co., Dallas, 1951-54; practice law, Dallas, 1955-56, asst. atty. gen., Tex., chief div. ins., banking and corp., 1957-60; partner Herring & Jones, Austin, Tex., 1960-61; gen. counsel Maritime Adminstrn., U.S. Dept. Commerce, 1961-63; dep. gen. counsel Dept. Commerce, 1963-64, dep. fed. hwy. adminstr., 1964-66; pres. Am. Ins. Assn., N.Y.C., 1967—; chmn. interdeptl. com. for bilateral agreements for acceptance of nuclear ship, Savannah, 1962-63; lectr. Fgn. Service Inst., 1962-64; alt. U.S. rep. 11th session Diplomatic Conf. on Maritime Law, Brussels, 1962; advisor U.S. del. 6th session Council, Intergovtl. Maritime Consultative Orgn., London, 1962; mem. maritime subsidy bd. U.S. Dept. Commerce, 1962-63; acting hwy. beautification coordinator, 1965-66; del. White House Conf. on Internat. Cooperation; mem. Property-Casualty Ins. Council, 1976—, Internat. Ins. Adv. Council, 1980—; mem. adv. com. Pension Benefit Guaranty Corp., 1977; mem. Time Newstour, Eastern Europe and Persian Gulf, 1981, Mexico and Panama, 1983; bd. dirs. Nat. Safety Council, 1967, Ins. Inst. for Hwy. Safety, 1967. Contbr. articles to legal, ins. and fin. jours. Served to lt. (j.g.) USNR, 1944-46. Mem. ABA, Fed. Bar Assn. (chmn. nat. speakers bur. 1964), Tex. Bar Assn., Friars, Phi Delta Phi, Beta Gamma Sigma, Phi Eta Sigma. Democrat. Presbyterian. Clubs: Met. (Washington); Great Oaks Country (Floyd, Va.); Drug and Chem. World Trade Center (N.Y.C.). Home: 160 E 48th St New York NY 10017 Home: Route 3 Box 182-B Floyd VA 24091 Office: 85 John St New York NY 10038

JONES, THOMAS BAKER, retired social work educator; b. Phila., Nov. 7, 1918; s. Wilberforce Thomas and Nannie Virginia (Burnett); married; 1 dau., Yvonne. A.B., Va. Union U., 1941; M.S.W., Atlanta U., 1943; Ph.D., Ohio State U., 1947; vis. scholar, Columbia U., spring 1956, Harvard Sch. Public Health, 1962-63, U. London, summer 1963. Prof. Sch. Social Work Atlanta U., 1947-48, U. P.R., 1948-68; prof. Howard U. Sch. Social Work, 1968-71; prof., dir. Coll. Counseling Center, Bowie State Coll., 1971-73; prof. Ind. U. Sch. Social Work, Indpls., 1973-84; sr. Fulbright prof. Higher Inst. Social Service, Alexandria, Egypt, 1951-52; research assoc. Am. U., Cairo, fall, 1955; mem. faculty Internat. Coll., Copenhagen, summer 1966; dir. 1st nat. community devel. seminar, vis. prof. U. Ibadan (Nigeria), spring 1980; Bd. dirs. Indpls. Pre-sch. Centers, 1974-77. Author publs. in field of social work and community devel. Mem. Nat. Assn. Social Workers (dir. 1977—), Acad. Cert. Social Workers, Internat. Assn. Schs. Social Work, NEA, Asociación de Maestros de P.R., Kappa Alpha Psi. Democrat. Unitarian. Home: 3843 Kessler Blvd N Dr 3019 Indianapolis IN 46208

JONES, THOMAS CARLYLE, veterinary science educator; b. Boise, Idaho, Sept. 29, 1912; s. Thomas Daniel and Lillie Marion (Jones) J.; m. Dorotha Anne Bratt, Sept. 13, 1935; children: Sylvia M., Don Carl, Anne Louise. B.S., D.V.M., Wash. State U., 1935; D.Sc. (hon.), Ohio State U., 1970. Commd. 1st lt. Vet. Corps U.S. Army, 1935, advanced through grades to lt. col., 1950; ret., 1957; officer-in-charge U.S. Army Vet. Research Lab., 1939-45; chief vet. pathology sect. Armed Forces Inst. Pathology, 1946-50, 53-57; clin. assoc. in pathology Harvard U. Med. Sch., 1957-63, assoc. clin. prof., 1963-71, prof. comparative pathology, 1971-82, prof. emeritus, 1982—; dir. pathology Angell Meml. Animal Hosp.; cons. NIH, Armed Forces Inst. Pathology.; Mem. bd. of health, Dover, Mass., 1966-75. Author: (with R.D. Hunt) Veterinary Pathology, 5th edit, 1983; editor monographs, Internat. Life Scis. Inst., 1980—; contbr. articles to profl. jours. Fogarty internat. fellow, 1979-80. Mem. Am. Coll. Vet. Pathologists, Am. Coll. Lab. Animal Medicine, AVMA, Internat. Acad. Pathology, Am. Soc. Pathologists, New Eng. Soc. Pathologists, Comparative Pathology Colloquy. Home: 8 Crest Dr Dover MA 02030 Office: New Eng Regional Primate Research Center Southborough MA 01772

JONES, THOMAS K., government administrator; b. Tacoma, Wash. B.S. in Mech. Engring., U. Wash., 1954. Various design and systems engring. assignments Boeing Co., 1954-71; mgr. requirements and strategic planning Boeing Aerospace, 1974-81; sr. advisor US SALT Del., 1971-74; dep. undersec. for research and engring. Dept. Def., Washington, 1981—. Office: Strategic and Theater Nuclear Forces Dept Defense The Pentagon Washington DC 20301

JONES, THOMAS L., lawyer, coll. dean; b. Breckinridge County, Ky., Apr. 10, 1931; s. V.A. and Elizabeth (Lambirth) J.; m. Shelley Edwards, July 15, 1961. B.S., U. Ky., 1959, LL.B., 1961; LL.M., U. Mich., 1965. Asst. prof. law U. Ala., Tuscaloosa, 1962-65, asso. prof., 1965-68, prof., 1968—; acting dean Sch. Law, 1970-71, asso. dean, 1971-76; acting dir. Ala. Law Inst., 1972-75; vis. prof. U. Ky., Lexington, 1965, U. Ill. Coll. Law, 1971-72; Ala. commr. to Nat. Conf. Commrs. on Uniform State Laws, 1967—, mem. exec. com., 1975-77. Editor: Ala. Will Manual Service, 1965—. Served with USAF, 1951-55. Mem. Am. Law Inst., Assn. Am. Law Schs. (exec. com. 1975-77). Home: 907 Indian Hills Dr Tuscaloosa AL 35406 Office: Sch Law Univ Ala Box 5557 University AL 35486

JONES, THOMAS VICTOR, aerospace company executive; b. Pomona, Calif., July 21, 1920; s. Victor March and Elizabeth (Brettelle) J.; m. Ruth Nagel, Aug. 10, 1946; children: Ruth Marilyn, Peter Thomas. Student, Pomona Jr. Coll., 1938-40; B.A. with gt. distinction, Stanford U., 1942; LL.D., George Washington U., 1967. Engr. El Segundo div. Douglas Aircraft Co., 1941-47; tech. adviser Brazilian Air Ministry, 1947-51; prof., head dept. Brazilian Inst. Tech., 1947-51; staff cons. Air Staff of USAF, Rand Corp., 1951-53; asst. to chief engr. Northrop Corp., 1953, dep. chief engr., 1954-56, dir. devel. planning, 1956-57, corporate v.p., 1957, sr. v.p., 1958-59, pres., 1959-76, chief exec. officer, 1960—, chmn. bd., 1963—; dir. MCA Inc. Author: Capabilities and Operating Costs of Possible Future Transport Airplanes, 1953. Bd. dirs. Los Angeles World Affairs Council; trustee Inst. for Strategic Studies, London. Fellow AIAA; mem. Los Angeles C. of C., Navy League U.S. (life), Aerospace Industries Assn., U. So. Calif. Assos., Town Hall. Clubs: California; The Beach (Santa Monica); Georgetown, California Yacht, Bohemian. Home: 1050 Moraga Dr Los Angeles CA 90049 Office: 1800 Century Park E Century City Los Angeles CA 90067

JONES, TOM, singer; b. Pontypridd, Wales, June 7, 1940; s. Thomas and Freda (Jones) Woodward; m. Malinda Trenchard, 1956; 1 son, Mark. Attended, Treforrest Secondary Modern Sch. Bricklayer, factory and constrn. laborer. Sang in local pubs.; changed name to Tom Jones, 1963; organized backup group the Playboys to sing in London clubs; first hit record was It's Not Unusual, 1964; appeared on Brit. radio and TV; toured, U.S. in, 1965, 68; appearing on: Ed Sullivan Show; star of: TV show This is Tom Jones, 1969-71; regular appearances in nightclubs and on TV; songs recorded include What's New Pussycat, 1965, Thunderball, 1965, Green Green Grass of Home, 1966, Delilah, 1968, Love Me Tonight, 1969, Can't Stop Loving You, 1970, She's A Lady, 1971, Letter to Lucille, 1973, Say You'll Stay Until Tomorrow, 1976; album Darlin, 1981. Public singing debut at age 3 in village stores in Wales. Office: care Internat Creative Mgmt 8899 Beverly Blvd Los Angeles CA 90048 *

JONES, TOMMY LEE, actor; b. San Saba, Tex., Sept. 15, 1946; s. Clyde L. and Lucille Marie (Scott) J.; m. Kimberlea Gayle Cloughley, May 30, 1981. B.A. cum laude in English, Harvard U., 1969. Broadway debut in A Patriot for Me; other stage appearances include Fortune and Men's Eyes; film debut in Love Story; film appearances include Coal Miner's Daughter, Back Roads, 1981; television movie The Amazing Howard Hughes, The Executioner's Song, 1982.

JONES, TONY EVERETT, educator; b. Leonard, Tex., Sept. 5, 1920; s. Pink and Nancy Lee (Duvall) J.; m. Imogene Brown, May 28, 1947; children—Everett Eugene, Susan Renee. B.S., U. Tex., 1948, M.S., 1950; Ph.D., U. Colo., 1957. With Inst. Pharm. Chemistry, U. Tex., Austin, 1949-53; registered pharmacist M.D.'s Pharmacy, Austin, 1949-51, Seton Hosp., 1951-54; asst. prof. pharm. chemistry U. Tex., 1953-54; asst. prof. U. Colo., Boulder, 1956-59, asso. prof., 1959-63, prof. pharm. chemistry, 1964—; dir. pharm. research, also cons. Carbisulphoil Co. (div. Blistex Inc.), Oak Brook, Ill., 1954—. Co-author: American Drug Index, 1956-76. Served with USNR, World War II. Mem. Am. Pharm. Assn., Am. Chem. Soc., Sigma Xi, Phi Delta Chi, Rho Chi, Phi Lambda Upsilon. Baptist (exec. bd. Colo. Baptist Conv. 1968-72). Research and publ. in local anesthetics, toxicology, drug assay. Home: 7631 Watonga Way Boulder CO 80303

JONES, TRACEY KIRK, JR., clergyman, educator; b. Boston, Mar. 16, 1917; s. Tracey Kirk and Marion (Flowers) J.; m. Martha Clayton, Sept. 12, 1942 (dec. June 1975); children: Judith Grace (Mrs. Larry Watson), Tracey Kirk Jones, III, Deborah Anita Jones; m. Junia K. Moss, July 1, 1978. B.A., B.D., D.D., Ohio Wesleyan U.; B.D., Yale Div. Sch., 1942. Ordained to ministry Meth. Church, 1945; liaison officer Chinese Govt., 1945; missionary Meth. Ch., China, 1946-50, Malaya, 1952-55, exec. bd. mission, 1955; exec. sec., S.E. Asia, 1955-62, asso. gen. sec. div. world missions, 1962-64, asso. gen. sec. world div., 1964-68, gen. sec. bd. missions, 1968-72, gen. sec. bd. global ministries, 1972-80; vis. prof. Drew Theol. Sch., Madison, N.J.; Mem. governing bd. Nat. Council Chs., 1st v.p., 1978—. Author: Our Mission Today, 1963. Home: 87 Alexander Ave Upper Montclair NJ 07043 Office: Drew U Madison NJ 07940

JONES, TREVOR OWEN, automobile supply company executive; b. Maidstone, Kent, Eng., Nov. 3, 1930; came to U.S., 1957, naturalized, 1971; s. Richard Owen and Ruby Edith (Martin) J.; m. Jennie Lou Singleton, Sept. 12, 1959; children: Pembroke Robinson, Bronwyn Elizabeth. Higher Nat. Cert. in Elec. Engring., Aston Tech. Coll., Birmingham, Eng., 1952; Ordinary Nat. Cert. in Mech. Engring., Liverpool (Eng.) Tech. Coll., 1957. Registered profl. engr., Wis.; chartered engr., U.K. Student engr., elec. machine design engr. Brit. Gen. Electric Co., 1950-57; project engr., project mgr. Nuclear Ship Savannah, Allis-Chalmers Mfg. Co., 1957-59; with (Gen. Motors Corp.), 1959-78, staff engr. in charge Apollo computers, 1967, dir. electronic control systems, 1970-72, dir. advanced product engring., 1972-74; dir. Gen. Motors Proving Grounds, 1974-78; v.p. engring., automotive worldwide TRW Inc., 1978-80, pres., gen. mgr. transp. electronics group, 1980—; vice chmn. Motor Vehicle Safety Adv. Council, 1971; chmn. Nat. Hwy. Safety Adv. Com., 1976. Author. Trustee Lawrence Inst. Tech., 1973-76; mem. exec. bd. Clinton Valley council Boy Scouts Am., 1975; bd. govs. Cranbrook Inst. Sci., 1977. Served as officer Brit. Army, 1955-57. Recipient Safety award for engring. excellence U.S. Dept. Transp., 1978. Fellow Brit. Instn. Elec. Engrs. (Hooper Meml. prize 1950), IEEE (exec. com. vehicle tech. soc. 1977—), Soc. Automotive Engrs. (Arch T. Colwell paper award 1974, 75, Vincent Bendix Automotive Electronics award 1976); mem. Nat. Acad. Engring., Engring. Soc. Detroit and Cleve. Republican. Episcopalian. Clubs: Birmingham (Mich.) Athletic; Capitol Hill (Washington); Kirtland Country. Patentee automotive safety and electronics. Home: 18400 Shelburne Rd Shaker Heights OH 44118 Office: TRW Inc 30000 Aurora Rd Solon OH 44139 *Innovation and the acceptance of change are fundamental seeds of progress, and only hard work and an open mind will permit you to harvest its fruits.*

JONES, VICTOR EMORY, police chief; b. Long Beach, Calif., July 10, 1935; s. Walter Jacob and Lillian Merble (Roberts) J.; m. Sharon Kaye Burns, Dec. 24, 1961; children: Victoria Suzanne, Robert Eugene. A.A., Riverside City Coll., 1971; B.S., Calif. State U., Los Angeles, 1973; M.P.A., U. So. Calif., 1975; grad., FBI Nat. Acad., Quantico, Va., 1976. With Rohr Corp., Riverside, Calif., 1958-61; with Riverside (Calif.) Police Dept., 1961—, chief of police, 1977—; Exec. v.p. Nick Tavaglione Constrn. Co.; pres. Nat. Utility Vehicle Corp. Mem. Internat. Assn. Chiefs of Police, U. So. Calif. Scapa Practor, FBI Nat. Acad. Assos., Calif. Police Chiefs Assn. Republican. Clubs: U. So. Calif. Lifetime Alumnae, Masons, Shriners, Jesters, Elks, Moose, Riverside, Kiwanis (dir.). Home: 4020 Rosewood Pl Riverside CA 92506 Office: 9000 Arlington Ave Riverside CA 92503

JONES, VINCENT STARBUCK, retired newspaper editor; b. Utica, N.Y., Dec. 4, 1906; s. William Vincent and Susan B. (Starbuck) J.; m. Nancy van Dyke Parsons, May 25, 1940; children: Suzanne Cansler, Margot Mabie. A.B., Hamilton Coll., 1928; postgrad., Harvard U., 1929-30; LL.D., Hamilton Coll., 1971. Reporter Utica Daily Press, 1928-29, night city editor, 1930-37, city editor, 1937-38, mng. editor, 1938, Utica Observer-Dispatch, 1938-42; exec. editor Utica Observer-Dispatch and Utica Daily Press, 1942-50; dir. news and editorial office Gannett Newspapers, 1950-55, exec. editor, 1955-70, v.p., 1965-70; trustee Gannett Found., exec. v.p., sec., 1970-75; Lectr. Am. Press Inst., 1946-68; lectr., writer newspaper readership, readability, photography; dir. Kent State U. photo short course, 1952. Directed, edited: The Road to Integration (Pulitzer prize citation 1964). Mem. Utica City Planning Bd., 1946-50; v.p. St. Luke's Meml. Hosp., Utica, N.Y., 1950; bd. govs. Genesee Hosp., Rochester, 1957—; treas. Gannett Newspaper Carrier Scholarships, Inc., 1967-75; bd. dirs. Rochester Civic Music Assn., 1954-62; trustee Monroe Community Coll., Rochester, 1961-78, chmn., 1969-74; trustee Internat. Mus. Photography at George Eastman House, Rochester, chmn., 1974-77; bd. overseers Sweet Briar Coll., 1968-75; past trustee Hamilton Coll. Recipient distinguished service medal Syracuse Journalism Sch., 1969. Mem. N.Y. State AP Assn. (pres. 1947), Am. Soc. Newspaper Editors (dir. 1962-70, pres. 1968-69), Asso. Press Mng. Editors Assn. (dir. 1949-56, pres. 1955), N.Y. State Soc. Editors (pres. 1962-63), Internat. Press. Inst. (chmn. Am. com. 1965-68), Nat. Press Photographers Assn. (Sprague award 1954), Rochester Inst. Tech. Inst. of Fellows, Sigma Delta Chi, Psi Upsilon. Episcopalian. Clubs: Genesee Valley, Country, Torch (Rochester.). Home: 5 Highland Heights Rochester NY 14618

JONES, VIRGINIA LACY (MRS. E.A. JONES), library director; b. Cin., June 25, 1912; d. Edward and Ellen Louise (Parker) Lacy; m. Edward Allen Jones, Nov. 27, 1941. B.S., Sch. Edn., Hampton Inst., 1936, 1933, M.S., U. Ill., 1938; Ph.D., Chgo.; Ph.D. (Gen. Edn. Bd. fellow 1943-45), 1945. Asst. Librarian Louisville Municipal Coll., 1934-35, librarian, 1936-37; asst. circulation dept. Hampton Inst. Library, 1935-36; dir. dept. library sci. Prairie View (Tex.) State Coll., summers 1936-39; catalog librarian Atlanta U., 1939-41; instr. Sch. Library Service, 1941-43, dean, 1945-82; dir. Atlanta U. Center Library, 1982—. Recipient Joseph W. Lippincott award, 1977. Mem. ALA (exec. bd. 1971—, Melvil Dewey award 1973, now hon.), Assn. Am. Library Schs. (pres. 1967-68), NAACP, Delta Sigma Theta, Beta Phi Mu. Democrat. Conglist. Home: 1341 Thurgood St SW Atlanta GA 30314

JONES, WALLACE SYLVESTER, lawyer, former mayor; b. N.Y.C., May 23, 1917; s. Adam Leroy and Lily Sylvester (Murray) J.; m. Barbara Hardenbergh Ostgren, June 7, 1941 (dec. Dec. 1964); children—Karen Ostgren (Mrs. John Gordon Fraser, Jr.), Ellen Wallace (Mrs. Robert Q. Barr), Mark Lawrence, Sara Sylvester (Mrs. Tim Kaylor), Caroline Murray (Mrs. Gary Gooden); m. Helen Marion Nelson Anderson, Jan. 7, 1967. A.B., Columbia U., 1938, J.D. (Kent Scholar 1941, editor Law Rev. 1939-41), 1941. Bar: N.Y. 1941, U.S. Supreme Ct. 1948. Assoc. firm Davis Polk & Wardwell, and (predecessors), N.Y.C., 1941—, mem., 1957-82, sr. counsel, 1982—; mayor of, Essex Fells, N.J., 1974-81; Mem. Essex Fells Bd. Edn., 1955-58; commr. Essex County Ednl. Audio-Visual Aid Commn., 1955-58; pres. W. Essex Regional Sch. Dist., Essex County, 1957-60; moderator No. N.J. Assn., United Ch. Christ, 1966-67, Central Atlantic Conf., 1969-70. Trustee Barnard Coll., 1958-76, trustee emeritus, 1976—, chmn. bd., 1967-73; trustee Seeing Eye, Inc., 1971—, sec., 1973-81, pres. and chmn., 1981—; trustee Internat. Found., 1972—, v.p., 1977—; bd. dirs. Kimberly Sch., Montclair, N.J., 1968-70, United Ch. Homes N.J., 1967-75; sec. Scottish Heritage USA, Inc., 1969-74, v.p., 1974-77, pres., 1977-82, chmn., 1982—; Lay reader Episcopal Ch., 1980—. Served to lt. comdr. USNR, 1942-46; PTO. Mem. Am., N.Y. State bar assns., Assn. Bar City N.Y., N.Y. County Lawyers Assn., Psi Upsilon, Phi Delta Phi. Clubs: Ausable (St. Huberts, N.Y.); Essex Fells Country, Fells Brook (Essex Fells); Adirondack Mountain (chmn. Hurricane Mountain chpt. 1952-53); Down Town, Wall Street (N.Y.C.); Montclair (N.J.); Golf. Home: 21 Inwood Rd Essex Fells NJ 07021 Office: 1 Chase Manhattan Plaza New York City NY 10005 *He who does not seek to serve others, serves himself poorly.*

JONES, WALTER BEAMAN, congressman; b. Fayetteville, N.C., Aug. 19, 1913; s. Walter George and Fannie (Anderson) J.; m. Doris Long, Apr. 26, 1934; children: Mrs. Dotdee Moye, Walter Beaman II. B.S., N.C. State U., 1934. Mem. N.C. Gen. Assembly, 1955-59; mem. N.C. Senate, 1965, 90th-98th Congresses from 1st Dist. N.C.; Dir. Security Savs. & Loan Assn., Farmville, N.C.; Mayor Farmville, 1949-53. Recipient Watchdog of Treasury award Nat. Assn. Businessmen, 1966; named Farmville Man of Year, 1955. Democrat. Baptist (deacon). Clubs: Mason (32 deg., Shriner), Elk, Rotarian, Moose. Office: Cannon Bldg Washington DC 20515 *

JONES, WALTER HEATH, bishop; b. St. Boniface, Man., Can., Dec. 25, 1928; s. Harry Heath and Anne Grace (Stoddart) J.; m. L. Marilyn Lunney, Aug. 25, 1951; children: Irene Lenore Jones Mihara, Leah Anne, Barry Malcolm Heath, Kristin Maureen. B.A., U. Man., 1951; B.Th., St. Johns Coll., 1951, S.T.D., 1970. Received in Episcopal Ch., 1958; founding rector St. Peters Ch., Flin Flon, 1951-56; rector St. John The Baptist Ch., Winnipeg, Man., 1956-58, St. Mary Ch., Mitchell, S.D., 1958-62; dean Calvary Cathedral, Sioux Falls, S.D., 1968-70, v.p. chpt., 1962-67; bishop Diocese of S.D., Sioux Falls, 1970—. Editor: S.D. Churchman, 1962-67. Mem. exec. bd. Sioux council Boy Scouts Am., from 1958. Hon. citizen, St. Boniface, 1964. Clubs: Masons, Kiwanis. Office: 200 W 18th St Sioux Falls SD 57102 *

JONES, WARREN LEROY, judge; b. Gordon, Nebr., July 2, 1895; S. Lauren and Katherine (Ballengee) J.; m. Edith Ann Le Prouse, Dec. 23, 1921; 1 dau., Dorothy Lauren Jones Shakely (dec.). LL.B. cum laude, U. Denver, 1924; LL.D., Stetson U., 1955; D.H.L. (hon.), La. State U., 1977; D.C.L., Jacksonville U., 1978. Bar: Colo. 1924, Fla. 1926. Dep. dist. atty., City and County Denver, 1924; mem. Jones, Gandy & Wilson, Denver, 1925; asso. Fleming, Hamilton, Diver & Lichliter, Jacksonville, 1926-37; mem. Fleming, Hamilton, Diver & Jones, 1938-41, Fleming, Jones, Scott & Botts, 1942-55, sr. mem., 1948-55; judge U.S. Ct. Appeals 5th Circuit, 1955-65, sr. judge, 1965—. Sec., dir. Jacksonville Blood Bank, 1942-55. Recipient Lincoln diploma of honor Lincoln Meml. U., 1971. Fellow Am. Coll. Probate Counsel; mem. Fla. C. of C., Jacksonville C. of C. (pres. 1955), SAR, Am. Judicature Soc., Am. Law Inst., ABA, Fla. Bar Assn. (pres. 1944), Jacksonville Bar Assn. (pres. 1939), Nat. Lawyers Club (Washington), Newcomen Soc., Phi Alpha Delta. Episcopalian. Clubs: Timuquana Country, Fla. Yacht, Seminole, River, Ponte Vedra, Civitan (past pres.); Univ. (Jacksonville); Masons (33 deg.), Shriners.). Collector Lincolniana. Home: 1560 Lancaster Terr Jacksonville FL 32204 Office: US PO and Ct House Bldg Jacksonville FL 32201

JONES, WARREN THOMAS, computer science educator; b. Gainesville, Ga., Nov. 5, 1942; s. Hammond C. and Thelma (Brewer) J.; m. Bobbie Jean Collins, June 12, 1964; children: Warren Thomas. B.E.E., Ga. Inst. Tech., 1965, M.S., 1971, Ph.D., 1973. Registered profl. engr., Ky. Asst. prof. engring. U. Louisville, 1973-77, assoc. prof., 1977-79; prof., chmn. computer sci. U. Ala., Brimingham, 1979—. Author: Computer Literacy, 1983. Mem. Assn. Computing Machiners (pres. 1977-79). Home: 3926 S River Cir Birmingham AL 35243 Office: Dept Computer and Info Sci Univ Ala Birmingham AL 35294

JONES, WAYNE VAN LEER, private investor, retired petroleum industry executive; b. Chgo., June 18, 1902; s. Frank Edgar and Josephine Louella (Van Leer) J.; m. Elizabeth Rieke, Jan. 14, 1926; 1 son, Wayne Van Leer II. A.B., Northwestern U., 1923. Accountant, then chief auditor Mission Oil Co., Kansas City, Mo., 1923-28; mem. firm F. E. Jones & Son, oil operators, Wichita, Kans., 1928-29; asst. mgr. Exchange Petroleum Co., Shreveport, La., 1930- 34; geologist Midcontinent div., Tidewater Asso. Oil Co., Houston, 1934- 41, chief geologist, 1941-53; v.p., charge exploration Union Tex. Natural Gas Corp. (formerly Union Sulphur & Oil Corp., Union Oil & Gas Corp. of La.), Houston, 1953-59, sr. v.p., 1959-62, Union Tex. Petroleum div. Allied Chem. Corp., 1962-63; pvt. investor, 1963—; Mem. Am. Commn. on Stratigraphic Nomenclature, 1947-53; Alumni regent for Tex. Northwestern U., 1965-75, life regent, 1975—, donor Wayne V. and Elizabeth R. Jones Film and Performing Arts Residential Coll., 1980. Author: Jacob Woodward Colladay and his Descendants, 1976, The Rieke Family of Bavenhausen and America, 1979. Mem. Am. Assn. Petroleum Geologists, geneal. socs. Pa., N.J., Md., Houston Geol. Soc., N.Y. Geneal. and Biog. Soc., Soc. Genealogists (London), Phi Beta Kappa, Sigma Xi, Sigma Alpha Epsilon. Clubs: Houston, Memorial Drive Country (Houston). Address: 5672 Longmont Dr Houston TX 77056

JONES, WILLIAM ARNOLD, newspaper columnist; b. Dover, Ohio, Jan. 29, 1924; s. Vinton W. and Eva M. (Ringheimer) J.; m. Ruth Hines Johnson, May 4, 1968; children by previous marriage—Judson D., Jeffrey B., Brinley W., Megan A., Jenny C. Student, Ohio State U., 1942-45, U. Minn. Law Sch., 1945-46. Movie reviewer Tuscarawas County (Ohio) Republican News, 1938-39; reporter Dover Daily Reporter, 1939-42, Columbus (Ohio) Citizen, 1942-45, Mpls. Tribune, 1945-47, entertainment and food columnist, 1947—; creative cons., freelance writer advt. agencies 1962. Author: cook book Wild in the

Kitchen, 1961; also numerous articles. Founder S.H.A.M.E. Smokers, anti-smoking group, 1964. Served with USAAF, 1943. Home: 2102 Cedar Lake Parkway Minneapolis MN 55416 Office: 425 Portland Ave Minneapolis MN 55488

JONES, WILLIAM AUGUSTUS, JR., bishop; b. Memphis, Jan. 24, 1927; s. William Augustus and Martha (Wharton) J.; m. Margaret Loaring-Clark, Aug. 26, 1949; 4 children. B.A., Southwestern at Memphis, 1948; B.D., Yale U., 1951. Ordained priest Episcopal Ch., 1952; priest in charge Messiah Ch., Pulaski, Tenn., 1952-57; curate Christ Ch., Nashville, 1957-58; rector St. Mark Ch., LaGrange, Ga., 1958-65; asso. rector St. Luke Ch., Mountainbrook, Ala., 1965-66; dir. research So. region Assn. Christian Tng. and Service, Memphis, 1966-67, exec. dir., 1968; rector St. John's, Johnson City, Tenn., 1972-75; bishop of Mo., St. Louis, 1975—. Office: 1210 Locust St Saint Louis MO 63103

JONES, WILLIAM BENJAMIN, JR., electrical engineering educator; b. Fairburn, Ga., Sept. 17, 1924; s. William Benjamin and Katherine (Davenport) J.; m. Mary Pierce Hammond, Sept. 8, 1948; children: William Benjamin III, Katherine P., Joseph L. B.S., Ga. Inst. Tech., 1945, M.S., 1948, Ph.D., 1953. Mem. tech. staff Hughes Aircraft Co., Culver City, Calif., 1954-58; prof. elec. engring. Ga. Inst. Tech., 1958-67; prof., head dept. elec. engring. Tex. A. and M. U., 1967—. Served with USNR, 1943-46. Mem. IEEE (editor transactions on communication systems 1960-61, chmn. communication tech. group 1966-67, mem. tech. activities bd. 1966-69, v.p. communications soc. 1972-73, chmn. elec. engring. dept. heads assn. 1983-84), Am. Soc. Engring. Edn., Nat. Soc. Profl. Engrs., Optical Soc. Am., Sigma Xi, Tau Beta Pi, Eta Kappa Nu. Home: 2612 Melba Circle Bryan TX 77802 Office: Tex A and M U College Station TX 77843

JONES, WILLIAM BOWDOIN, diplomat; b. Los Angeles, May 2, 1928; s. William T. and LaValle (Bowdoin) J.; m. Joanne Fairchild Garland, June 27, 1953; children: Lisa, Stephanie, Walter. A.B. in Polit. Sci, UCLA, 1949; J.D., U. So. Calif., 1952; postgrad., U. Southhampton, Eng., 1949, U. So. Calif. Sch. Internat. Relations, 1955-60. Bar: Calif. 1953, U.S. Supreme Ct. 1964, D.C. 1968. Sole practice, Los Angeles, 1953-62; with Fgn. Service Res., 1962-68, Fgn. Service, 1968—; dep. dir. Office African Programs, 1964-67, dir. program analysis staff, 1967-68; dir. Office Program Devel. and Evaluation, 1968, dep. asst. sec. state for edn. and cultural affairs, 1969-73; chmn. U.S. del. to 17th gen. conf. UNESCO, Paris, 1972, permanent rep., minister, 1973-77; ambassador to, Haiti, 1977-80; diplomat-in-residence Hampton (Va.) Inst., 1980-81; with law of sea mgmt. ops. Dept. State, 1981-84, ret., 1984; ambassador in residence prof. U. Va., 1984-85; mem. U.S. del. European Ministers Edn. Conf., Bucharest, Romania, 1973, Internat. Oceanographic Commn. Gen. Conf., Paris, 1973, 18th gen. conf. UNESCO, 1974; head U.S. del. Conf. on Cultural Policies, Africa, Accra, Ghana, 1975; mem. U.S. del., chmn. legal com. 19th gen. conf. UNESCO, Nairobi, Kenya, 1976; chmn. performance standards bds. U.S. Fgn. Service, 1976; Chmn. exec. com. Am. Soc. African Culture, 1961-62; mem. Los Angeles World Affairs Council, 1954-62. Recipient Alumni Profl. Achievement award UCLA, 1978; Alumni Merit award U. So. Calif., 1980. Mem. ABA, Am. Acad. Polit. and Social Sci., Academia de Derecho Internacional, Am. Fgn. Service Assn., Kappa Alpha Psi, Pi Sigma Alpha, Sigma Pi Phi Boule. Clubs: Internat. (Washington); American (Paris); Petionville (Port-au-Prince, Haiti). Address: 4807 17th St NW Washington DC 20011 *As a Black American, I have always strongly resisted being stereotyped. My family, for generations were well educated, with a tradition of excellence, pride and achievement. I have always felt I could compete with anyone and that I had a right to expect to achieve positions of highest authority. My advice is to stand on your own two feet. Work with determination to achieve.*

JONES, WILLIAM ERNEST, educator; b. Sackville, N.B., Can., Aug. 7, 1936; s. Frederick W. and Jennie E. (Tuttle) J.; m. Norma Florence McKinney Reig, Aug. 9, 1958; children: Mary Ellen, Jennifer A.J., Sarah A.L., Martha M. B.Sc., Mt. Allison U., 1958, M.Sc., 1959; Ph.D., McGill U., 1963. Asst. prof. Dalhousie U., Halifax, N.S., 1962-68, assoc. prof., 1968-73, prof. chemistry, Halifax, 1973—, chmn. dept. chemistry, 1974-83. Contbr. articles to profl. jours. Fellow Chem. Inst. Can.; mem. Canadian Assn. Physicists, Spectroscopy Soc. Can., Inter-Am. Photochem. Soc. Home: 17 Shaw Crescent Halifax NS Canada B3P 1V2 Office: Dept Chemistry Dalhousie Univ Halifax NS Canada B3H 4J3

JONES, WILLIAM KENEFICK, marine corps officer; b. Joplin, Mo., Oct. 23, 1916; s. Charles Vernon and Irene (Kenefick) J.; m. Charlotte McIndoe, Nov. 15, 1945; children—Carol (Mrs. Donald W. Hatton), William Kenefick, Hugh M., Charles V. B.A., U. Kan., 1937; postgrad., Naval War Coll., 1960-61. Commd. 2d lt. USMC, 1938, advanced through grades to lt. gen., 1970; comdg. officer (1st Bn., 6th Marines), Tarawa, Saipan, Tinian, Okinawa, 1943-45, head tactics and tech. sect. and inf. sect., Quantico, Va., 1945-48, asst. Naval attache, Stockholm, Sweden, 1948-50, asst. chief staff, 1953, comdr., 1954, asst. chief staff, Quantico, 1954-56, comdr., 1956-58, Parris Island, S.C., 1958-60, chief gen. operations div., 1961-62; legislative asst. to comdt. Marine Corps, 1962-64; comdr. (Force Troops, FMF), Pacific and Marine Corps Base, Twentynine Palms, 1964-65, dir., Vietnam, 1966-67; dep. dir. personnel Hdqrs. Marine Corps, Washington, 1967-69; comdr. (3d Marine Div.), Vietnam, 1969, Okinawa, 1969-70; spl. asst. to chief of staff Hdqrs. Marine Corps, 1970; comdg. gen. (Fleet Marine Force Pacific), Camp H.M. Smith, Oahu, Hawaii, 1970—. Decorated Silver Star medal, Navy Cross, Legion of Merit, Bronze Star medal, D.S.M. (3), Purple Heart. Mem. Sigma Alpha Epsilon. Home: 1211 Huntly Pl Alexandria VA 22307

JONES, WILLIAM KENNETH, educator; b. N.Y.C., Sept 1, 1930; s. William Arthur and and Mary (Cody) J.; m. Cecile Patricia Flower, June 7, 1952; children—Deborah Ann, Patricia Lynn, John William. A.B., Columbia, 1952, LL.B., 1954. Bar: N.Y. bar 1955, Ohio bar 1957. Law clk. to U.S. Supreme Ct. Justice Tom C. Clark, 1954-55; atty. Dept. Air Force, 1955-56; asso. firm Jones, Day, Cockley & Reavis, Cleve., 1956-59; mem. faculty, Columbia, 1959—, prof. law, 1962-72, James Dohr prof., 1972-75, Milton Handler prof., 1975—; pub. service commr., N.Y. State, 1970-74; Cons. Am. Law Inst., 1959; research dir. com. licenses and authorizations Administrv. Conf. U.S., 1961-62. Author: Regulated Industries, 1967, 2d edit., 1976, Electronic Mass Media, 1976, 2d edit., 1979. Served to 1st lt. USAF, 1955-56. Home: 20 Creston Ave Tenafly NJ 07670 Office: 435 W 116th St New York NY 10027

JONES, WILLIAM MARCELLUS, university official; b. Sioux Falls, S.D., May 1, 1922; s. James Ernest and Mary L. (Crocker) J.; m. Audrey Zube, Aug. 20, 1944; children: James Paul, Christopher Mark, Jeffrey Lyle, Karen Louise. B.A., Concordia Coll., 1944; M.A., U. Rochester, 1946; Ph.D., Ind. U., 1963. Tchr. Lincoln High Sch., Thief River Falls, Minn., 1944-45; asso. prof. music Linfield Coll., McMinnville, Oreg., 1946-58; prof. music, dept. chmn. Beloit (Wis.) Coll., 1958-69; acad. v.p., dean Berea (Ky.) Coll., 1969-72; dean arts, humanities and social scis. Moorhead (Minn.) State U., 1972-77, acad. v.p., 1977—; Curriculum cons. Northland, Carthage, W.Va. Wesleyan colls. Contbr. articles to music jours.; Choral condr., dir. many maj. works. Founder, dir. Beloit Symphonic Choir; pres. Beloit Community Concerts Assn., 1960-63; mem. Beloit Human Relations Commn., 1967-69; Bd. dirs. Affiliate Artists, Inc., 1966-70, Univ. Press of Ky., 1969-72; pres. Fargo-Moorhead Symphony Bd., 1980-81. Served with USAAF, 1943. Mem. Danforth Assos. (Pacific N.W. chmn. 1956-57). Home: 1303 18th Ave S Moorhead MN 56560

JONES, WILLIAM MAURICE, chemistry educator; b. Campbellsville, Ky., Jan. 12, 1930; s. Warren Francis and Margaret (Scott) J.; m. Elizabeth Rose Nordwall, Jan. 28, 1956; children: Kevin Scott, Sigrid Elizabeth, Kimberly Anne. B.S., Union U., 1951; M.S., U. Ga., 1953; Ph.D., U. So. Calif., 1955. Instr. U. So. Calif., 1955-56; asst. prof. U. Fla., 1956-61, asso. prof., 1961-65, prof., 1965—, chmn. dept. chemistry, 1968-73. Editorial bd.: Chem. Rev., 1972-75, Jour. Organic Chemistry, 1974-78; contbr. articles profl. jours. Recipient Tour Speaker of Yr. award Am. Chem. Soc., 1970, Fla. award Am. Chem. Soc., 1976; Alfred P. Sloan fellow, 1963-67; NATO fellow, 1971. Mem. Am. Chem. Soc. (nat. symposium exec. officer organic div., chmn. nat. advanced organic exams. com. 1974-82, exec. com. organic div. 1984—), Phi Beta Kappa, Sigma Xi. Home: 5915 NW 27th Ave Gainesville FL 32601

JONES, WILLIAM MCKENDREY, educator; b. Dothan, Ala., Sept. 19, 1927; s. William McKendrey and Margaret (Farmer) J.; m. Ruth Ann Roberts, Aug. 14, 1952; children: Margaret, Elizabeth, Bronwen. B.A., U. Ala., 1949, M.A., 1950; Ph.D., Northwestern U., 1953. Asst. prof. English Wis. State U., Eau Claire, 1953-55; asst. prof. U. Mich., Ann Arbor, 1955-59; mem. faculty U. Mo., Columbia, 1959—, prof. English, 1964—, assoc. dean, 1966-68. Author: Stages of Composition, 1964, Form and Experience, 1969, Guide to Living Power, 1975, (with Ruth Ann Jones) Living in Love, 1976, Two Careers—One Marriage, 1980, Speaking Up in Church, 1977, The Present State of Scholarship in 16th Century Literature, 1978, Survival: A Manual on Manipulating, 1979, Protestant Romance, 1980, John Steinbeck, 1982. Served with U.S. Army, 1946-47. Folger Library summer fellow, 1955; U. Mo. distinguished prof., 1972. Home: 209 Russell Blvd Columbia MO 65201 Office: Dept English U Mo Columbia MO 65201

JONES, WILLIAM ORVILLE, economist, educator; b. Lincoln, Nebr., July 6, 1910; s. Ralph Wilson and Nelle (McFall) J.; m. Kay Kelly, Oct. 4, 1943; children: Peter Richard, Stephen Robert, Brian Kelly. A.B., U. Nebr., 1932, Sc.D. (hon.), 1965; Ph.D., Stanford, 1947. With Standard Oil Co., Nebr., 1933-34, Graybar Elec. Co., Inc., 1935-38; acting instr. econs. Stanford, 1940-41, U. Santa Clara, Calif., 1942; assoc. instr. ground sch. tng. Pre-Flight Sch., Santa Ana Army Air Base, 1942-44; mem. faculty Stanford, 1944-75, economist, prof., 1953-75; exec. sec. Food Research Inst., 1955-62, dir. inst., 1964-72; editor Food Research Inst. Studies, 1970-75, asso. editor, 1980—; cons. World Bank, 1974-75, 78, Caribbean Food and Nutrition Inst., 1975, Internat. Inst. Tropical Agr., 1976, U.S. AID, 1976-77, Ford Found., 1978, Food Research Inst., 1978—; dir. Avondale Corp.; pres. Consumers Coop. Soc. Palo Alto, 1952-53; Mem. adv. council on Africa Bur. African Affairs, State Dept., 1962-68; mem. Africa sci. bd. Nat. Acad. Scis.-NRC, 1961-68; mem. joint com. African studies Social Sci. Research Council-Am. Council Learned Socs., 1960-71, chmn., 1965-68. Author: Manioc in Africa, 1959, Marketing Staple Food Crops in Tropical Africa, 1972; co-author, editor: Agricultural Change in Tropical Africa, 1978; co-editor: Cassava Economy of Java, 1984; also articles and chpts. in books. Bd. dirs. Consumers Coop. Soc. Palo Alto, 1951-53. Guggenheim fellow, 1953. Mem. Am. Econ. Assn., Western Econ. Assn. (pres. 1961-62), African Studies Assn. (pres. 1960-61), Am., Western farm econ. assns., Internat. Assn. Agrl. Economists, Internat. Soc. Tropical Root Crops. Home: 590 San Juan Stanford CA 94305

JONES, WILLIAM THOMAS, philosophy educator; b. Natchez, Miss., Apr. 29, 1910; s. William Thomas and Mary Fleming (Chamberlain) J.; m. Molly Mason, Mar. 29, 1941; children: Jeffery, Gregory. A.B., Swarthmore Coll., 1931; B.Litt. (Rhodes scholar 1931-34), Oxford (Eng.) U., 1933; A.M., Princeton, 1936; Ph.D. (Lippincott fellow 1935-36, Proctor fellow 1936-38), Princeton, 1937. Instr. philosophy Pomona Coll., 1938-40, asst. prof., 1940-42, asso. prof., 1945-50, prof., 1950-72, dean men, 1947-49; Nimitz prof. social and polit. philosophy U.S. Naval War Coll., 1953-54; vis. prof. Calif. Inst. Tech., 1970-72, prof., 1972—; Cons. and/or panelist Nat. Endowment for Humanities, Nat. Humanities Faculty, World Book Ency., others.; Bd. dirs. Wenner-Gren Found. Anthrop. Research, 1966—; trustee Pomona Coll., 1972—. Author: Morality and Freedom in Kant, 1941, Masters of Political Thought, 1947, A History of Western Philosophy, 1952, Facts and Values, 1961, Approaches to Ethics, 1962, The Romantic Syndrome, 1962, The Sciences and the Humanities, 1965, The Classical Mind, 1969, The Medieval Mind, 1969, Hobbes to Hume, 1969, Kant and the Nineteenth Century, 1975, The Twentieth Century to Wittgenstein and Sartre, 1976; also articles. Served to lt. comdr. USNR, 1942-46. Guggenheim fellow, 1958-59; Ford Faculty fellow, 1955-56; Phi Beta Kappa vis. scholar, 1963-64. Mem. Am. Philos. Assn. (pres. Pacific div. 1969-70), Phi Beta Kappa. Home: 4201 Via Padova Claremont CA 91711

JONES, WOODROW WILSON, judge; b. Rutherfordton, N.C., Jan. 26, 1914; s. Bernard Bartlett and Karl Jane (Nanney) J.; m. Rachel Elizabeth Phelps, Nov. 22, 1936; children—Woodrow Wilson, Michael Anthony. Student, Mars Hill Coll., 1932-34; LL.B., Wake Forest U., 1937. Bar: N.C. bar 1937. Practiced law, Rutherfordton, 1937-67; solicitor Rutherford County Recorders Ct., 1941-43; mem. N.C. Gen. Assembly, 1947-49, U.S. Ho. of Reps., 1950-56; judge U.S. Dist. Ct. for Western N.C., Rutherfordton, 1967—, chief judge, 1968—; Dir. Union Trust Co., Shelby, N.C., Citizens Fed. Savs. & Loan Assn., Rutherfordton.; Chmn. N.C. Democratic Exec. Com., 1958-60; Trustee Gardner-Webb Coll., Boiling Springs, N.C. Served to lt. (j.g.) USNR, 1943-45. Recipient spl. citation for outstanding service Gardner-Webb Coll., 1968. Mem. Am., N.C., Rutherford County bar assns., Am. Judicature Soc. Baptist (deacon). Club: Kiwanian. Office: Box 741 Rutherfordton NC 28139 *

JONES, WYMAN H., librarian; b. St. Louis, Dec. 17, 1929; s. Jay Hugh and Marie (Dallas) J.; m. Janet Grigsby, Jan. 17, 1953; children—Gregory Foster, Mark Jay, Manson Matthew, Ross Christopher. Student, So. Ill. U., 1945-47, Washington U., St. Louis, 1948-50; B.A., Adams State Coll., Alamosa, Colo., 1956; postgrad., U. Iowa, 1956-57; M.S. in L.S, U. Tex., 1958. Head sci. and industry div. Dallas Pub. Library, 1958-60, chief br. services, 1960-64; dir. Ft. Worth Pub. Library, 1964-70; city librarian Los Angeles Pub. Library, 1970—; cons. library bldg. and site selections, 1962—; Mem. Gov. Tex. Adv. Bd., 1969-70, Calif. Bd. Library Examiners, 1970—. Author: (with E. Castagna) The Library Reaches Out, 1964; also articles. Bd. dirs. Young Symphony Orch., Ft. Worth, 1967-69. Served with USAF, 1951-55. Mem. ALA (legis. com. 1974-78), S.W. Library Assn. (pres.-elect 1967), Tex. Library Assn. (pres. pub. library div. 1966), Calif. Library Assn. (council 1972—). Home: 1433 Via Cataluna Palos Verdes Estates CA 90274 Office: Pub Library 630 W 5th St Los Angeles CA 90017

JONES-WILSON, FAUSTINE CLARISSE, education educator; b. Little Rock, Ark., Dec. 3, 1927; d. James Edward and Perrine Marie (Childress) Thomas; m. James T. Jones, June 20, 1948 (div. 1977); children: Yvonne Dianne, Brian Vincent; m. Edwin L. Wilson, July 10, 1981. A.B., Ark. A.M.&N. Coll., 1948; A.M., U. Ill., 1951, Ed.D., 1967. Tchr., sch. librarian Gary pub. schs. (Ind.), 1955-62, 1964-67; asst. prof. Coll. Edn., U. Ill., Chgo., 1967-69; asst. prof. adult edn. Fed. City Coll., Washington, 1970-71; prof. edn., grad. prof. Howard U., Washington, 1969-70, 71. Editor: Jour. Negro Edn., 1978—; author: The Changing Mood in America; Eroding Commitment, 1977, A Traditional Model of Educational Excellence: Dunbar High School of Little Rock, Arkansas, 1981. Recipient Frederick Douglass award Nat. Assn. Black Journalists, 1979. Mem. Am. Ednl. Studies Assn., John Dewey Soc., Soc. Profs. of Edn., Adult Edn. Assn. Met. Washington, Washington Women's Forum, NAACP. Democrat. Methodist. Home: 908 Dryden Ct Silver Spring MD 20901 Office: Sch Edn Howard U. 2400 6th St NW Washington DC 20059

JONG, ANTHONY, public health dentist, educator; b. Hong Kong, Aug. 1, 1938; s. Goddard S. and Lily (Fung) J. (mother Am. citizen). B.S., CCNY, 1960; D.D.S., NYU, 1964; M.P.H., Harvard U., 1966; certificate, Sch. Dental Medicine, 1968; D.Sc. in Dentistry, Boston U., 1976. Diplomate: Am. Bd. Dental Public Health. Intern Jewish Meml. Hosp., N.Y.C., 1964-65; resident Mass. Dept. Public Health, 1966-67; dental supr. Project Head Start, Boston, 1966; dir. dental services Boston Maternity and Infant Care Project, 1968-69; dir. Boston Maternity, Infant Care and Children and Youth Projects, 1969-70; asst. dean student affairs Harvard Sch. Dental Medicine, 1971-73; prof., chmn. dept. dental care mgmt. Boston U. Sch. Grad. Dentistry, 1973—, asst. dean postdoctoral studies, 1978-80, assoc. dean for acad. affairs, 1980—; Research fellow Harvard Sch. Dental Medicine, 1966-68, research assoc., 1968-69, asst. prof. dental ecology, 1969-73; cons. Boston Head Start Health Services, 1966-70; mem. dental health research and edn. adv. com. U.S. Dept. HEW, 1971-73. Editor: Dental Pub. Health and Community Dentistry; Contbr. articles to profl. jours. Recipient USPHS Research Career Devel. award, 1969. Mem. Am. Public Health Assn. (mem. dental sect. council 1974-77, chmn. dental sect. 1978-79, governing council 1979-83), Mass. Public Health Assn. (chmn. dental sect. 1971-72), Am. Dental Assn., Internat. Assn. for Dental Research, Am. Assn. Public Health Dentists, Omicron Kappa Upsilon (treas.-sec. 1972-74). Home: 120 Goddard Ave Brookline MA 02146 Office: 100 E Newton St Boston MA 02118

JONG, ERICA MANN, author, poet; b. N.Y.C., Mar. 26, 1942; d. Seymour and Eda (Mirsky) Mann; m. Allan Jong (div. Sept. 1975); m. Jonathan Fast, Dec. 1977 (div. Jan. 1983); 1 dau., Molly. B.A., Barnard Coll., 1963; M.A., Columbia U., 1965. Faculty, English dept. CUNY, 1964-65, 69-70, overseas div. U. Md., 1967-69; mem. lit. panel N.Y. State Council on Arts, 1972-74. Author: poems Fruits & Vegetables, 1971; (poems) Half-Lives, 1973; (novel) Fear of Flying, 1973; Loveroot, 1975; (novel) How to Save Your Own Life, 1977; (poems) At the Edge of the Body, 1979; (novel) Fanny, 1980; (poetry and non-fiction) Witches, 1981; (poems) Ordinary Miracles, 1983; (juvenile) Megan's Book of Divorce, 1984. Recipient Bess Hokin prize Poetry mag., 1971, Alice Faye di Castagnola award Poetry Soc. Am., 1972; Nat. Endowment Arts grantee, 1973. Mem. Authors Guild (dir. 1975), Poets and Writers Bd., Writers Guild Am.-West, P.E.N., Phi Beta Kappa. Office: care Sterling Lord Agy 660 Madison Ave New York NY 10021

JONISH, JAMES EDWARD, economist; b. Chgo., Apr. 16, 1941; s. Edward and Irene (Smith) J.; m. Geri Kazlauskas, Sept. 5, 1964; children—Lisa, Debra. B.A., U. Ill., 1963, M.A., 1964; Ph.D., U. Mich., 1969. Asst. prof., asso. prof. U. Hawaii, 1969-73; prof., chmn. Tex. Tech U., Lubbock, 1973-80, prof. econs., 1976—; vis. prof. Dartmouth Coll., 1975-76, U. Minn., 1977; cons. energy and labor. Mem. Am. Econ. Assn., Internat. Assn. Energy Economists, Indsl. and Labor Relations Assn. Office: Dept of Economics Texas Tech University Lubbock TX 79409

JONSEN, ALBERT R., philosophy educator; b. San Francisco, Apr. 4, 1931; s. Albert R. and Helen (Sweigert) J. B.A., Gonzaga U., 1955, M.A., 1956; S.T.M., U. Santa Clara, 1963; Ph.D., Yale U., 1967. Mem. S.J.; ordained priest Roman Catholic Ch.; instr. philosophy Loyola U., Los Angeles, 1956-59; asst. in instrn. Yale Div. Sch., 1966-67; asst. prof. theology and philosophy U. San Francisco, 1967-72, pres., 1969-72; prof. med. ethics Sch. Medicine, U. Calif.-San Francisco, 1972—; adj. asso. prof. dept. community medicine and internat. health Sch. Medicine, Georgetown U., 1977; mem. artificial heart assessment panel Nat. Heart and Lung Inst., 1972-73; mem. Am. Bd. Med. Spltys., 1978-81; cons. Am. Bd. Internal Medicine, 1978—; mem. Pres.'s Commn. for Study of Ethical Problems in Medicine, 1979-82, Nat. Commn. for Protection Human Subjects of Biomed. and Behavioral Research, HEW, 1974-78; mem. adv. com. Center for Ulcer Research and Edn. Author: Responsibility in Modern Religious Ethics, 1968, Patterns of Moral Responsibility, 1969, Christian Decision and Action, 1970, Ethics of Newborn Intensive Care, 1976, Clinical Ethics, 1982; Mem. editorial bd.: Jour. Religious Ethics. Trustee Inst. Ednl. Mgmt., Harvard U., 1971-74; mem. San Francisco Crime Com., 1969-71; bd. dirs. Found. Critical Care Medicine, 1983—. Fellow Inst. for Soc., Ethics and Life Scis.; mem. Soc. Health and Human Values, Am. Soc. Law and Medicine (dir. 1981—), Soc. Christian Ethics, Inst. Medicine of Nat. Acad. Scis. (com. human values 1973, council 1983). Address: Sch Medicine U Calif 1326 3d Ave San Francisco CA 94143

JONSSON, BJARNI, educator, mathematician; b. Draghals, Iceland, Feb. 15, 1920; came to U.S., 1941, naturalized, 1963; s. Jon and Steinunn (Bjarnadottir) Petursson; m. Amy Sprague, Dec. 16, 1950 (div. 1967); children: Eric M., Meryl S.; m. Harriet Parkes, Jan. 17, 1970; child, M. Kristin. B.A., U. Calif. at Berkeley, 1943, Ph.D., 1946. Faculty Brown U., 1946-56, asst. prof., 1948-56; vis. prof. U. Iceland, 1954-55; vis. asso. prof. U. Calif. at, Berkeley, 1955-56, vis. prof., research mathematician, 1962-63; faculty U. Minn., 1956-66, asso. prof., 1956-59, prof., 1959-66; distinguished prof. Vanderbilt U., Nashville, 1966—. Mem. Am. Math. Soc., Assn. for Symbolic Logic, AAUP, Icelandic Math. Soc., Societas Scientiarum Islandica. Research, publs. in lattice theory, universal algebra, founds. of algebra, group theory. Home: 5810 Vineridge Dr Nashville TN 37205

JONSSON, JENS JOHANNES, engineering educator; b. Mildstedt, Germany, Apr. 4, 1922; came to U.S., 1927, naturalized, 1933; s. John Fredrich and Catharina Maria (Latre) J.; m. Helen Broadbent, Sept. 5, 1945; children: Craig, Diane, Karen, Catherine, Eric. B.S., U. Utah, 1944, 1947; M.S., Purdue U., 1948, Ph.D., 1951; postgrad., Poly. Inst. Bklyn., 1960-61. Registered profl. engr., Utah. Supr., N.Am. Aviation, 1951-53; prof. elec. engring. Brigham Young U., Provo, Utah, 1953—, dir. Engring. Analysis Center, 1964-72, chmn. engring. dept., 1954-55, chmn. elec. engring. sci. dept., 1955-60, 77-83; vis. prof. Gen. Electric Co., 1957; mem. sr. staff Convair Astronautics, San Diego, 1958; mem. sr. research staff Bell Telephone Labs., Whippany, N.J., 1959; field expert UNESCO, Ankara, Turkey, 1967; chief tech. adviser UNESCO-Poly. Inst. Bucharest project, Romania, 1974-76. Contbr. to profl. lit. Served with USNR, 1944-46. Recipient award for teaching excellence Western Electric Fund, 1969; certificate of recognition for contbn. to engring. edn. Utah Engring. Council, 1965. Mem. Utah Acad. Scis., Arts and Letters, Am. Soc. Engring. Edn. (chmn. Utah relations with industry com. 1963-66), IEEE (pres. Utah sect. 1963, Community Service award 1973), Sigma Xi (pres. Brigham Young U. chpt. 1970-71). Home: 1710 N Lambert Ln Provo UT 84601

JONTE, JOHN HAWORTH, chemistry educator; b. Moscow, Idaho, Oct. 21, 1918; s. John Herbert and Bada Sophia (Johnson) J.; m. Eloise

Nyra Bailiss, June 15, 1942; children: Barbara (Mrs. Garry Wayne Boswell), Sharon (Mrs. Rex Lee Page), J. Michael, Dorothy. Student, Stockton Jr. Coll., 1936-38; A.B., U. of Pacific, 1940; M.S., Wash. State U., 1942; postgrad., Ia. State U., 1946-51; Ph.D., U. Ark., 1956. Jr. chemist U.S. Bur. Mines Expt. Sta., Reno, Nev., 1942-44; chemist Shell Devel. Co., Emeryville, Calif., 1944-46; instr. Iowa State U., 1946-51; grad. asst. U. Ark., 1951-55, instr., 1954-55; research chemist, group leader Texaco, Inc., Bellaire, Tex., 1955-66; asso. prof. S.D. Sch. Mines and Tech., Rapid City, 1966-69, prof., head chemistry dept., 1969—. Mem. Am. Chem. Soc., AAAS, Am. Inst. Chemists, Geochem. Soc., N.Y. Acad. Sci., Alpha Chi Sigma (dist. counselor 1959-66, 72—, pres. 1970-72), Phi Lambda Upsilon. Home: 2126 Cedar Dr Rapid City SD 57701

JONTRY, JERRY, magazine executive; b. Chenoa, Ill., May 19, 1911; s. Charles F. and Minnie B. (Reid) J.; m. Mary McLaughlin, Nov. 17, 1962; 1 son, Jonathan Charles. Ph.B., U. Chgo., (1933). Vice pres. Howland & Howland (newspaper reps.), 1933-36, Nixon Newspapers, Wabash, Ind., 1936-42; west coast mgr. Esquire, Inc., 1945-54; v.p., advt. dir. Esquire mag., 1954-64, sr. v.p., advt. dir., 1964-70; pres. Jonson Pub. Group, 1970-75; also dir.; pres. Jontry Communications, Inc., N.Y.C., 1975—. Served with USNR, 1942-45. Clubs: Town Tennis, Univ. (N.Y.C.). Home: 440 E 57th St New York NY 10022 Office: 350 Fifth Ave #4210 New York NY 10118

JOPLING, ALAN VICTOR, geography, geology educator, researcher, consultant; b. Sydney, New South Wales, Australia, Oct. 3, 1924; emigrated to Can., 1953; s. Victor and Gwendoline Ellen (Best) J.; m. Rhoda Marie Robson, Feb. 10, 1950; children: David Alan, Jennifer Marie. B.S., U. Sydney, 1946, B.Engring., 1947; M.A., Harvard U., 1958, Ph.D., 1961. Registered profl. engr., Ont. Lectr. in charge geology New South Wales U. Tech., Sydney, 1949-53; geologist Socony Vacuum Oil Co. Can., Alta., 1954-56; engr., research geologist U.S. Geol. Survey, Boston, Washington, 1958-61; asst. prof. geology Harvard U., Cambridge, Mass., 1961-66; prof. geography U. Toronto, 1968—, prof. geology, 1980—; cons. in field. Contbr. articles in field to profl. jours. Grantee Nat. Sci. Found., 1963, Nat. Sci. and Engring. Research Council Can., 1968-80, Donner Canadian Found., 1980-83. Fellow Geol. Soc. Am.; mem. Can. Assn. Geographers, Engring. Inst. Can., Am. Soc. Civil Engrs., Soc. Econ. Paleontologists & Mineralogists (Best paper award 1965). Home: 69 Jackson Ave Toronto ON Canada M8X 2J7 Office: Dept Geography 100 St George St Toronto ON Canada M5S 1A1

JOPPA, ROBERT GLENN, educator; b. Orchard, Colo., Aug. 25, 1922; s. Martin and Beatrice Virginia (Winkelseth) J.; m. Dorris Eileen Campbell, Mar. 3, 1944; children—Paul Douglas, Susan Elise. B.S., U. Wash., 1945, M.S., 1951; M.A., Princeton, 1962, Ph.D., 1972. Wind tunnel operator U. Wash., Seattle, 1942-49, instr., 1949-53, asst. prof., 1953, asso. prof., 1956, prof. aeronautics, 1970—; faculty fellow NSF, Princeton (N.J.) U., 1960-62; with Boeing Co., Seattle, summers; 1955-61; aircraft accident analyst cons. and expert witness in field. Contbr. articles in field to profl. jours. Mem. Am. Inst. Aeronautics and Astronautics, Am. Helicopter Soc., Soc. Flight Test Engrs., AAUP, Sigma Xi. Unitarian. Patentee in field of gliding anchor. Office: Dept of Aeronautics and Astronautics FS10 U Wash Seattle WA 98195

JORAVSKY, DAVID, history educator; b. Chgo., Sept. 9, 1925; s. Joseph and Bertha (Segal) J.; m. Doris Rubin, June 19, 1949; children: Deborah, Benjamin. B.A., U. Pa., 1947; M.A., Columbia, 1949; Ph.D., certificate, Russian Inst., 1958. Instr. history Marietta (Ohio) Coll., 1953-54, U. Conn., Storrs, 1954-58; mem. faculty Brown U., Providence, 1958-65, asso. prof., 1961-65; prof. Northwestern U., Evanston, Ill., 1965—, chmn. dept. history, 1980-83; fellow Woodrow Wilson Center, Smithsonian Instn., 1977-78; trustee Nat. Council Soviet and East European Research, 1982—. Author: Soviet Marxism and Natural Science, 1917-32, 1961, The Lysenko Affair, 1970 (Pfizer prize History Sci. Soc.); Editor and introduction: Let History Judge: The Origins and Consequences of Stalinism (Roy Medvedev), 1972; contbr.: articles to N.Y. Rev. Books, Sci; other jours. Served with AUS, 1944-46. Guggenheim fellow, 1961-62; grantee Am. Philos. Soc., Am. Acad. Arts and Sci., NSF, Social Sci. Research Council, Am. Council Learned Socs., Nat. Endowment for Humanities. Mem. Am. Assn. Advancement Slavic Studies (dir. 1966-69). Home: 1050 Hinman Ave Evanston IL 60202

JORDAN, AMOS AZARIAH, JR., educator, retired army officer; b. Twin Falls, Idaho, Feb. 11, 1922; s. Amos Azariah and Olive (Fisher) J.; m. MarDeane Carver, June 5, 1946; children: Peggy Jordan Chu, Diana Jordan Paxton, Keith, David, Linda, Kent. B.S., U.S. Mil. Acad., 1946; B.A., Oxford U., Eng., 1950, M.A., 1955; Ph.D., Columbia U., 1961. Commd. 2d lt. U.S. Army, 1946, advanced through grades to brig. gen., 1972; instr. U.S. Mil. Acad., 1950-53; arty. battery comdr. U.S. Army, Korea, 1954-55; asst. S-3 7th Div. Arty, Korea, 1955; econ., fiscal policy adviser U.S. Econ. Mission to Korea, 1955; prof. social scis. U.S. Mil. Acad., 1955-72, head dept., 1969-72; ret., 1972; dir. Aspen Inst., 1972-74; prin. dep. asst. sec. for internat. security affairs Dept. Def., Washington, 1974-76; dep. undersec. and acting undersec. for security assistance Dept. State, Washington, 1976-77; with Ctr. for Strategic and Internat. Studies, Georgetown U., Washington, 1977—, pres, chief exec. officer, 1983—; mem. staff Pres.'s Com. to Study Fgn. Assistance Program, 1959; staff dir. Adv. Com. Sec. Def. on Non-Mil. Instrn., 1972; spl. polit. adviser U.S. ambassador to India, 1963-64; dir. Near East and So Asia Region Office Sec. Def., 1966-67; cons. Nat. Security Council, 1969. Author: Foreign Aid and the Defense of Southwest Asia, 1962, Issues of National Security in the 1970's, 1967; contbr. articles to profl. jours., chpts. to books. Decorated D.S.M., Legion of Merit with oak leaf cluster. Mem. Council Fgn. Relations, Inst. Strategic Studiess (London), Asia Soc., Assn. Am. Rhodes Scholars, Middle East Inst. Home: 4000 Oakhill Dr Annandale VA 22003 Office: Ctr for Strategic and Internat Studies 1800 K St NW Suite 400 Washington DC 20006

JORDAN, ANGEL GONI, engineering educator; b. Pamplona, Spain, Sept. 19, 1930; came to U.S., 1956, naturalized, 1966; s. Hilario and Perpetua (Goni) J.; m. Nieves Alfonso Cuartero, July 8, 1956; children: Xavier, Edward, Arthur. M.S., U. Zaragoza, Spain, 1952, Carnegie Inst. Tech., 1959, Ph.D., 1959. With NavalOrdnance Lab., Madrid, 1952-56; instr. elec. engring. Carnegie-Mellon U., 1956-58, asst. prof. elec. engring., 1959-62, asso. prof., 1962-65, prof., 1965—, U.A. and Helen Whitaker prof., 1972-80, head dept., 1969-79, dean engineering, 1979-82, provost, 1983—; research fellow Mellon Inst. Indsl. Research, 1958-59; cons. to industry.; chmn. bd. MPC Corp., 1983—. Contbr. articles to profl. jours. Chmn. Pitts. High Tech. Council, 1983—; bd. dirs. Pa. Sci. and Engring. Found, 1981-83, Keithley Inst., Inc., 1983—. NATO sr. scientist fellow, 1976. Fellow IEEE (past chmn. profl. tech. group electron devices Pitts. chpts.); mem. Am. Phys. Soc., Am. Inst. Physics, Am. Soc. Engring. Edn., Sigma Xi, Eta Kappa Nu, Phi Kappa Phi, Tau Beta Pi. Home: 5874 Aylesboro Ave Pittsburgh PA 15217 Office: Office of Provost Carnegie Inst Tech Carnegie-Mellon U Pittsburgh PA 15213

JORDAN, BARBARA C., lawyer, educator, former congresswoman; b. Houston, Feb. 21, 1936; d. and Arlyne J. B.A. in Polit. Sci. and History magna cum laude, Tex. So. U.; J.D., Boston U., 1959. Bar: Mass. bar 1959, Tex. bar 1959. Adminstrv. asst. to county judge, Harris County, Tex.; mem. Tex. Senate, 1966-72; pres. pro tem, chmn. Labor and Mgmt. Relations Com. and Urban Affairs Study Com.; mem. 93d-95th congresses from 18th Dist. Tex.; mem. com. judiciary, com. govt. ops.; mem. spl. task force 94th Congress; mem. steering and policy com. (House Democratic Caucus); Lyndon B. Johnson public service prof. U. Tex., Austin, 1979—; dir. numerous cos. Author: Barbara Jordan—Self Portrait, 1979. Named One of 10 Most Influential Women in Tex., One of 100 Women in Touch With Our Time, Harpers Bazaar mag.; Dem. Woman of Year Women's Nat. Dem. Club; Woman of Year in Politics Ladies Home Jour. Mem. Am., Tex., Mass., Houston bar assns., NAACP, Delta Sigma Theta. Baptist. Headed poll Redbook mag. Women Who Could Be Pres. Office: Lyndon B Johnson Sch Public Affairs U Tex Austin TX 78712 *

JORDAN, BONITA ADELE, television producer; b. Dayton, Ohio, Mar. 9, 1948; d. Theodore and Faye Annette (Fields) Sampson; (div.) 1 son, Brett Anthony. Student, Habor Jr. Coll., Wilmington, Calif., 1966-68. Assoc. producer Dick Clark Prodns., Hollywood, Calif., 1972-73, Sta. KNBC-TV, Los Angeles, Calif., 1973-75; account exec. Ameron co., Monterey Park, Calif., 1976; prodn. coordinator Movie of the Week for CBS, Paramount Studios, Hollywood, 1977-78; asst. to producer Glen Larson Prodns., Film TV Devel. and Casting, 20th Century Fox, Beverly Hills, Calif., 1978—. Co-chmn., asst. to producer telethon United High Blood Pressure Found., 1977, mem. exec. bd., 1975-78, treas., 1977. Recipient cert. achievement City of Los Angeles and UCLA Mardi Gras, 1974. Mem. Nat. Assn. Media Women (corr. rec. sec. 1974-75). Home: 15050 Sherman Way Apt 207 Van Nuys CA 91405 Office: PO Box 900 Beverly Hills CA 90213

JORDAN, BRYCE, university president; b. Clovis, N.Mex., Sept. 22, 1924; s. W. Joseph and Kittie (Cole) J.; m. Patricia Jonelle Thornberry, June 10, 1948; children: Julia Cole, Christopher Joseph. Student, Hardin-Simmons U., 1941-42; B.Mus., U. Tex., 1948, M.Mus., 1949; Ph.D., U. N.C., 1956. Asst. prof. music Hardin-Simmons U., 1949-51; from asst. prof. to prof. music U. Md., 1954-63; prof. music, chmn. dept. U. Ky., 1963-65, U. Tex., 1965-68; v.p. student affairs U. Tex. at Austin, 1968-70, pres. ad interim, 1970-71; pres. U. Tex. at Dallas, 1971-81; exec. vice chancellor for acad. affairs U. Tex. System, 1981-83; pres. Pa. State U., 1983—; mem. faculty Salzburg (Austria) Seminar Am. Studies, 1960, 62; occasional lectr. Fgn. Service Inst., State Dept., 1962-63; Mem. Yale Council on Music, 1971-73, Nat. Commn. on Higher Edn. Issues, 1982-83; dir. Harleysville Mut. Ins. Co., Harleysville Life Ins. Co., Mellon Bank Central. Author: (with Homer Ulrich) Student Manual for Music: A Design for Listening, 1957, Designed for Listening, 1962, also articles, revs.; Assoc. editor: Coll. Music Symposium, 1961-66. Bd. dirs. Dallas Grand Opera Assn., 1973-75; trustee St. Marks Sch. Tex., 1973-81, Dallas Symphony Assn., 1972-81, Presbyterian Hosp., Dallas, 1976-83; v.p. Dallas Civic Music Assn., 1978-79, pres., 1979-80, exec. com., 1980—; bd. dirs. Dallas County chpt. ARC, 1976-79; div. chmn. United Way of Met. Dallas, 1979; Pa. state chmn. Am. Heart Assn., 1983-84. Served with USAAF, 1942-46. Mem. Coll. Music Soc. (v.p. 1963-65, council 1968—), Am. Musicol. Soc. (chmn. greater Washington chpt. 1958-60), Music Educators Nat. Conf. (pres. Md. br. 1963), Music Tchrs. Nat. Assn., Philos. Soc. Tex., Dallas C. of C. (dir. 1979—), So. Assn. Colls. and Schs. (commn. on colls. 1981-83), Phi Kappa Phi, Pi Kappa Lambda, Phi Mu Alpha. Presbyn. (presiding elder). Home: 639 Kennard Rd State College PA 16801

JORDAN, CARL FREDERICK, ecologist; b. New Brunswick, N.J., Dec. 10, 1935; s. Emil Leopold and Ethel Anabel (Augustine) J.; m. Carmen S. Vega Rivera, Jan. 14, 1967; children—Anabel, Christopher. B.S., U. Mich., 1958; M.S., Rutgers U., 1964, Ph.D., 1966. Asst. scientist, asso. scientist P.R. Nuclear Center, San Juan, 1966-69; ecologist Argonne (Ill.) Nat. Lab., 1969-74; adj. prof. Inst. Ecology U. Ga., Athens, 1974—, sr. ecologist, 1979—; vis. scientist Centro de Ecologia Insituto Venezelano de Investigaciones Cientificas, Caracas, 1974—; coordinator Internat. Study of Ecosystems., Amazon Basin, 1974—. Contbr. articles to profl. jours. Served with USNR, 1958-62. NSF grantee, 1974—; Man and Biosphere grantee, 1979—. Mem. AAAS, Ecol. Soc. Am., Sigma Xi. Address: Inst of Ecology U Ga Athens GA 30602

JORDAN, CASTLE WILLIAM, diversified management company executive; b. Oak Park, Ill., Nov. 20, 1924; s. William R. and Ina (Castle) J.; m. Jean Pringle, Jan. 10, 1945; children: Gail Jordan Bradbury, Deborah Jordan Gordon, Timothy, Peter. Student, Ill. Inst. Tech., 1943-44; J.D., John Marshall Law Sch., Chgo., 1951. Bar: Ill. 1951, Fla. 1960. Sole practice law, Chgo., 1951-58; with Ryder System Inc., Miami, Fla., 1958-67; pres., chief exec. officer, dir. Aegis Corp., Coral Gables, Fla., 1967—. Served with USNR, WW II. Mem. ABA, Fla. Bar Assn. Episcopalian. Home: 6020 Riviera Dr Coral Gables FL 33146 Office: Suite 705 250 Catalonia Ave Coral Gables FL 33134

JORDAN, CLIFFORD HENRY, association executive; b. New Orleans, Dec. 27, 1921; s. Clifford Henry and May Rosalie (Duke) J.; m. Clara H. Nordberg, June 1, 1955. R.N., Pa. Hosp. Sch. Nursing, 1949; B.S. in Nursing Edn., Temple U., 1954, Ed.D., 1975; M.Sc. in Edn., U. Pa., 1957. R.N., Pa. Staff nurse, then head nurse Pa. Hosp., Phila., 1949-53; instr. Episcopal Hosp., Phila., 1954-58, dir. nursing, 1958-66; asst., then assoc. prof. U. Pa., Phila., 1966-75, prof., 1975-82; exec. dir. Assn. Operating Room Nurses, Denver, 1981—; cons. in nursing adminstrn. Pa., N.J., Calif. hosps.; edn. cons. in organizational devel. Pa., Kans., N.J. univs. Mem. Pa. Gov.'s Commn. on Health, 1975-77; bd. govs. Health Systems Agy. So. Pa., 1975-79. Recipient U. Pa. Lindbach award, 1980; named Outstanding alumni U. Pa., 1982. Fellow Am. Acad. Nursing; mem. Am. Nurses Assn. (bd. dirs.), Pa. Nurses Assn. (pres. 1962-66, 72-76), Am. Nurses Found. (v.p. 1980-82). Republican. Roman Catholic. Home: 7787 Gunnison Pl Denver CO 80231 Office: Association of Operating Room Nurses 10170 Mississippi Denver CO 80231

JORDAN, D.D., electric utility company executive; b. Corpus Christi, 1932; married. B.B.A., U. Tex., 1954; J.D., So. Tex. Coll. of Law, 1969. With Houston Lighting & Power Co., 1956—, mgr. comml. sales, 1967-69, mgr. personnel relations, 1969-71, v.p., asst. to pres., 1971-73, group v.p., 1973-74, pres., 1974—, chief exec. officer, dir., 1977—; also pres., chief exec. officer Houston Industries, Inc.; dir. Great So. Corp., Hughes Tool Corp. Office: Houston Lighting & Power Co Inc 611 Walker Ave Electric Tower PO Box 1700 Houston TX 77001 *

JORDAN, EDWARD DANIEL, educator, engineer; b. Bridgeport, Conn., Mar. 14, 1931; s. Edward James and Jessie (Palsak) J.; m. Margaret Ann Moran, July 20, 1957; children: Christopher, Kathleen, Daniel, David, Margaret. B.S. in Physics, Fairfield U., 1953, M.S., N.Y.U., 1955; Ph.D. in Nuclear Engring, U. Md., 1965. Registered profl. engr., D.C. Teaching fellow N.Y.U., 1953-55, instr., 1955; guest scientist Brookhaven Nat. Lab., Upton, N.Y., 1955; reactor physicist Foster Wheeler Corp., N.Y.C., 1955-57, U.S. AEC, Washington, 1957-59; chmn. dept. nuclear sci. and engring., prof. Catholic U. Am., Washington, 1959-68; dir. Info. Systems and Planning Office, 1968-83; prof. engring. Cath. U. Am., 1983—. Named Inventor of Month Sci. Digest mag., 1964; recipient Fairfield U. Alumni citation for outstanding achievement, 1962. Mem. Am. Nuclear Soc., Am. Soc. Elec. Engring., AAAS, Assn. Instl. Research, Soc. Coll. and Univ. Planners, Sigma Xi. Research and publs. on sci. and engring., ednl. planning and mgmt., engring. edn. planning. Home: 5925 Searl Terr Bethesda MD 20816

JORDAN, EDWARD GEORGE, college president, former r.r. exec.; b. Oakland, Cal., Nov. 13, 1929; s. Edward A. and Alice (Smith) J.; m. Nancy Phyllis Schmidt, June 20, 1954; children: Susan Gail, Kathryn Claire, Jonathan Edward, Christopher Austin. B.A. in Econs. with honors, U. Calif. at Berkeley, 1951; M.B.A., Stanford U., 1953. Pres. Pinehurst Corp. (ins. and pension plans), Los Angeles, 1973-74, U.S. Ry. Assn., Washington, 1974-75; chmn., chief exec. officer Consol. Rail Corp., 1975-80; dean Cornell U. Grad. Sch. Bus. and Public Adminstrn., Ithaca, N.Y., 1980-82; pres. Am. Coll., Bryn Mawr, Pa., 1982—; dir. ARA Services. Bd. dirs. Franklin Inst. Clubs: University (Washington); Merion Golf, Philadelphia (Phila.). Home: 414 Mill Creek Rd Gladwyne PA 19035 Office: Am Coll 270 Bryn Mawr Ave Bryn Mawr PA 19010

JORDAN, ELKE, molecular biologist, government medical research institute executive; b. Gottingen, Germany, Apr. 8, 1937; came to U.S., 1953, naturalized, 1961; d. Peter Friederich and Elisabeth A.K. (Lehmann) J.; m. Thomas H. Edelson, Aug. 21, 1972. B.A., Goucher Coll., 1957; Ph.D, Johns Hopkins U., 1962. In various research positions Harvard U., 1962-64, U. Cologne, W. Ger., 1964-68, U. Wis., Madison, 1968-69, U. Calif.-Berkeley, 1969-72; grants assoc. NIH, Bethesda, Md., 1972-73; coordinator for collaborative research Nat. Cancer Inst., NIH, Bethesda, Md., 1973-76; health scientist adminstr. Nat. Inst. Gen. Med. Scis., Bethesda, 1976-82, assoc. dir., 1982—. Contbr. articles on molecular biology of e. coli and bacteriophage lambda to profl. jours. NIH fellow, 1959-65; Helen Hay Whitney Found. fellow, 1965-68. Mem. Genetics Soc. Am., AAAS. Office: Nat Inst Gen Med Scis NIH 9000 Rockville Pike Bethesda MD 20205

JORDAN, GEORGE LYMAN, JR., surgeon; b. Kinston, N.C., July 10, 1921; s. George L. and Sally (Herndon) J.; m. Florence Fisher Henszey, June 23, 1945; children: George Lyman III, Florence Elizabeth, Amy Henszey, Jacob Henszey. B.S., U. N.C., 1942; M.D., U. Pa., 1944; M.S. in Surgery, Tulane U., 1949. Diplomate: Am. Bd. Surgery (dir. 1971-77, vice chmn. 1975-77), Am. Bd. Thoracic Surgery. Intern Grady Meml. Hosp., Atlanta, 1944-45; fellow in surgery Tulane U., New Orleans, 1947-49, Mayo Found., Rochester, Minn., 1949-52; practice medicine specializing in surgery, Houston, 1952—; instr. surgery Baylor U. Coll. Medicine, Houston, 1952-54, asst. prof. surgery, 1954-57, asso. prof., 1958-64, prof., 1964—, disting. prof. surgery, 1978—; dep. chief surgery Ben Taub Gen. Hosp., Houston, 1961-68; chief med. staff Harris County (Tex.) Hosp. Dist., Houston, 1968—; med. adv. HEW, Social Security Adminstrn., Region IV, 1965—; sr. cons. surgery Nat. Inst. Gen. Med. Scis., 1966; mem. surg. research tng. grants com. NIH, 1968-70; adv. Houston chpt. Nat. Found. for Ileitis and Colitis, 1974—; Chmn. commn. on edn. St. Paul's Meth. Ch., 1967-69, mem. adminstrv. bd., 1963—, chmn., 1978, chmn. council on ministries, 1973-75, chmn. pastor-parish relations com., 1977, charge lay leader, 1980-81. Author: (with John M. Howard) Surgical Diseases of the Pancreas, 1960; contbr. numerous articles to profl. jours.; editorial bd.: Am. Jour. Surgery, 1968—, Advances in Surgery, 1971—. Served to capt., M.C. U.S. Army, 1945-47. Fellow A.C.S. (pres. Southeastern Tex. chpt. 1966-67, gov. 1976-82, chmn. bd. govs. 1980-82, exec. com. 1977-82, regent 1982—); mem. Western Surg. Assn. (dist. rep. on exec. com. 1976-80, pres. 1984), Pan-Pacific Surg. Assn., So. Surg. Assn. (pres. 1984), Am. Surg. Assn. (2d v.p. 1980), Tex. Surg. Soc. (council mem. 1975-78, chmn. council 1978, pres.-elect 1982, pres. 1983), Houston Surg. Soc. (pres. 1980), Am. Assn. Surgery Trauma, Soc. Surgery Alimentary Tract (pres. 1978, chmn. bd. trustees 1979), Univ. Assn. Emergency Med. Services, Am. Assn. Cancer Research (sec. Southwestern sect. 1959-60), Pan Am. med. assns., AMA (residency rev. com. for surgery 1974—), Harris County Med. Soc., Am. Trauma Soc. (dir. Harris County unit 1974—), Am. Cancer Soc. (dir. Tex. div. 1966-68), Southwestern Surg. Congress, Transplantation Soc., Internat. Cardiovascular Soc., Soc. Univ. Surgeons, Houston Gastroenterol. Soc., Soc. Exptl. Biology and Medicine, N.Y. Acad. Scis., Collegium Internat. Chirurgiae Digestivae, So. Soc. Clin. Investigation, Pancreas Club, Am. Soc. Exptl. Pathology, Assn. Advancement Med. Instrumentation, Phi Beta Kappa, Alpha Omega Alpha. Methodist. Home: 1748 North Blvd Houston TX 77098 Office: 1200 Moursund Ave Houston TX 77030

JORDAN, GEORGE ROYAL, JR., life insurance company executive; b. Forney, Tex., June 9, 1920; s. George R. and Lucile (Hailey) J.; m. Mary Julia von Blucher, Feb. 6, 1944; children: Carol Julia, Claudia Louise, Mary Lucile. B.S., Tex. A. and M. Coll., 1946; M.S., U. Iowa, 1948. With life actuarial dept. Travelers Ins. Co., 1948-50; with Southland Life Ins. Co., Dallas, 1950-70, 1st v.p., actuary, 1959-61, exec. v.p., 1961-70; also dir., mem. exec. and investment coms.; now chmn., chief operating officer Gt. So. Life Ins. Co., Houston. Chmn. of ins. unit Dallas County United Fund, 1963-65, chmn. bus. div., 1967; chmn. Dallas Heart Assn. drive, 1962; div. chmn. United Fund Houston and Harris County, 1972; gen. chmn. excellence campaign U. Houston, 1976-77; bd. dirs. YMCA Camp Grady Spruce, 1962-70; trustee So. Meth. U., Tex. Children's Hosp. Found., Austin Coll. Served to maj. AUS; World War II. Mem. Actuaries Club Southwest (past pres.), Soc. Actuaries (asso.), Salesmanship Club, Tex. Life Conv. (past pres.), Dallas Assembly. Clubs: Mason (32 deg.), Las Colinas Country (Dallas); River Oaks Country, Houston Met. Racquet, Ramada, Riverhill, Warwick. Home: PO Box 1972 Houston TX 77251 Office: Gt So Life Ins Co 3121 Buffalo Speedway Houston TX 77098

JORDAN, GLENN, director; b. San Antonio, Apr. 5, 1936. B.A., Harvard U., 1957; postgrad., Yale U. Drama Sch., 1957-58. Dir.: regional and stock theatre, including Cafe La Mama, late 1950s; N.Y. directorial debut with Another Evening With Harry Stoones, 1961; other plays include A Taste of Honey, 1968; Rosencrantz and Guildenstern Are Dead, 1969, A Streetcar Named Desire at, Cin. Playhouse in the Park, 1973, All My Sons at, Huntington Hartford Theatre, 1975; founder, N.Y. TV Theater, 1965, dir. various plays, including Paradise Lost and Hogan's Goat; dir.: mini-series Benjamin Franklin, CBS, 1974 (Emmy award 1975); Family, ABC-TV series, 1976-77, including segment Rights of Friendship; numerous TV plays for public TV, including Eccentricities of a Nightingale, 1976; The Displaced Person, 1976; TV movies, including Shell Game, 1975; One Of My Wives Is Missing, 1975, Delta County U.S.A, 1977, In The Matter of Karen Ann Quinlan, 1977, Sunshine Christmas, 1977, Les Miserables, 1978, Son-Rise, A Miracle of Love, 1979, The Family Man, 1979, The Women's Room, 1980, Lois Gibbs and the Love Canal, 1982, The Buddy System, 1983; dir: feature film Only When I Laugh (Neil Simon), 1981. Recipient Emmy awards for N.Y. TV Theater Plays, 1970. Office: care Bill Haber Creative Artists Agy 1888 Century Park E Suite 1400 Los Angeles CA 10067

JORDAN, HAMILTON (WILLIAM HAMILTON MCWHORTER JORDAN), former govt. ofcl., news corr.; b. Charlotte, N.C., Sept. 21, 1944; s. Richard and Adelaide J.; m. Nancy Konigsmark, 1970 (div. Nov. 1978). B.A. in Polit. Sci, U. Ga. With Internat. Voluntary Services (social worker), Vietnam, 1967-68; campaign mgr. Jimmy Carter for Gov. Ga., 1970; exec. sec., adviser to Gov. Carter; campaign mgr. Jimmy Carter for Pres., 1976; asst. to Pres., chief polit. adviser, 1977-79, chief staff to, 1979-1981; polit. commentator Cable News Network, Atlanta, 1981—; disting. vis. fellow in polit. sci. Emory U., Atlanta, 1981-82. Democrat. Office: Cable News Network Inc 1050 Techwood Dr NW Atlanta GA 30318 *

JORDAN, HOWARD, JR., university chancellor; b. Beaufort, S.C., Dec. 28, 1916; s. Howard and Julia (Glover) J.; m. Ruth Menafee, Feb 14, 1943; 1 dau., Judith Louise. A.B., S.C. State Coll., 1938; spl. student, Howard U., 1938-39; Ed.D., N.Y. U., 1956. Faculty S.C. State Coll., Orangeburg, 1941—, prof. edn. and psychology, chmn. dept. edn., dean, 1950-60, dean faculty, 1960-63; pres. Savannah (Ga.) State Coll., 1963-71; vice chancellor for Services U. System Ga., 1971—. Mem. Savannah-Chatham County Area Econ. Opportunity Authority; chmn. Orangeburg County Cancer dr., 1948-49, Orangeburg County Crippled Childrens Soc. dr., 1950; mem. State Adv. Com. for Adult Edn., State Adv. Council on Vocat. Edn.; bd. dirs. Greater Savannah Council, Interfaith Atlanta; bd. dels. United Way, Atlanta; bd. mgrs. SW YMCA, Atlanta; new bd. mentor Assn. Governing Bds.; mem. SE regional bd., Atlanta council exec. bd. Boy Scouts Am.; trustee Mather Sch. and Jr. Coll. Served with AUS, 1942-46; ETO. Mem. Am., S.C. psychol. assns., Nat. Soc. Study Edn., Nat. (dept. higher edn.), Palmetto edn. assns., Ga. Planning Assn., Assn. U.S. Army, Phi Delta Kappa, Kappa Delta Pi, Alpha Kappa Mu, Alpha Phi Alpha, Sigma Pi Phi. Episcopalian (vestryman, sec.). Clubs: West End Rotary (pres.), Masons.). Address: 244 Washington St SW Atlanta GA 30334

JORDAN, JAMES DEMPSEY, lawyer; b. Hennessey, Okla., July 18, 1934; s. Truman James and Nora LaVauna (Brown) J.; m. Marian Gayle Pickett, June 2, 1962; 1 dau., Alies LaVauna. B.B.A., U. Okla., 1956; J.D., Oklahoma City U., 1969; certificate, Nat. Coll. State Judiciary, 1972. Bar: Okla. 1969. Financial reporter Dunn & Bradstreet, Inc., Oklahoma City, 1958-61; asst. v.p. claims Am. Fidelity Assurance Co., Oklahoma City, 1961-7O; asst. dist. atty. State of Okla., Okmulgee, 1970-71; judge Dist. Ct. State of Okla., Okmulgee, 1971-74; practice in, Okmulgee, 1974-78, 83—, dist. atty., Okmulgee and McIntosh Counties, 1979-83. Served with AUS, 1956-58. Mem. Okla. Bar Assn. Baptist. Clubs: Masons, Rotarian. Office: PO Box 123 Okmulgee OK 74447 *One man can not change the world, but one man can stand for right, and he can make a difference.*

JORDAN, JAMES JOSEPH, JR., advertising executive; b. Phila., Aug. 3, 1930; s. James Joseph and Dorothy (Morgan) J.; m. Mary Helen Cronin, Sept. 13, 1958; children: James, Michael, Mary Elizabeth, Thomas. Jennifer, Anne, Laura. B.A., Amherst Coll., 1952. Copywriter Batten Barton Durstine & Osborn, N.Y.C., 1953-59, v.p., copy supr., 1960-64, sr. v.p. assoc. creative dir., 1964-66, exec. v.p., creative dir., 1966-74, pres., 1975-78; chmn. bd. James Jordan, Inc., N.Y.C., 1978-80, Jordan, Case & McGrath, 1981—. Trustee Amherst Coll., 1977—. Recipient Clio award, 1973, Effie award, 1981. Republican. Roman Catholic. Club: Larchmont Yacht. Home: 19 Robinhood Rd White Plains NY 10605 Office: 445 Park Ave New York NY 10022

JORDAN, JAMES PHILLIP, lawyer; b. Dothan, Ala., Dec. 19, 1948; s. James Monroe and Agnes Lorraine (Fowler) J.; m. Christine Loftin Rinehart, Sept. 4, 1976; 1 dau., Elizabeth Young. A.B. magna cum laude (Nat. Merit scholar 1967, Presdl. scholar 1967), Princeton U., 1971; J.D., U. Va., 1974. Bar: Ga. 1974, D.C. 1979. Law clk. to judge U.S. Ct. Appeals, 4th Circuit, 1974-75, to Hon. Lewis F. Powell, Jr., U.S. Supreme Ct., 1975-76; asso. firm King & Spalding, Atlanta, 1976-77; spl. asst. to Atty. Gen. U.S., Washington, 1977-79; asso. firm Leva, Hawes, Symington, Martin & Oppenheimer, Washington, 1979-81, ptnr., 1982-83, Venable, Baetjer, Howard & Civiletti, Washington, 1983—. Editor-in-chief: Va. Law Rev, 1973-74. Mem. ABA; Mem. Ga. Bar Assn., D.C. Bar Assn., Order of Coif, Phi Beta Kappa. Home: 4616 Bayard Blvd Bethesda MD 20816 Office: 1301 Pennsylvania Ave NW Washington DC 20004

JORDAN, JERRY NEVILLE, advt. exec.; b. Phila., June 15, 1928; s. Clarence L. and Helen (Wagner) J.; m. Barbara Claire Moore, Sept. 12, 1953; children—Mark, Elizabeth, Douglas. A.B., Princeton, 1949; M.A., U. Pa., 1951. With N.W. Ayer & Son, Inc., Phila., 1953-66, v.p., 1960-66, asst. to pres., 1963-66; v.p., market research Am. Airlines, N.Y.C., 1966-67, v.p. advt., 1967-68, v.p. passenger sales, 1968-69, v.p. marketing planning, 1969-70, v.p. market and schedule devel., 1970; pres. subsidiary Reservations World, 1970-71, v.p. corporate planning, 1971-73; pres. Thomas Cook & Son, Inc., 1973-76; exec. v.p. N.W. Ayer ABH Internat., N.Y.C., 1976-81; pres. Ayer Internat., 1981—. Served to 1st lt. AUS, 1951. Mem. Royal Soc. Arts, Phi Beta Kappa. Clubs: Union League, Sky (N.Y.C.); Greenwich (Conn.) Country, Old Greenwich Yacht; Skytop (Cresco, Pa.). Home: Saw Mill Ln Greenwich CT 06830 Office: 1345 Ave of Americas New York NY 10019

JORDAN, JOHN ALLEN, JR., steel company executive; b. St. Louis, Nov. 5, 1935; s. John Allen and Nelle Gail (Koehne) J.; m. Betsy Lockhart Belsterling, June 11, 1960; children: Constance Mary, Julia Gibson, John Innes. B.S. in Indsl. Engring., 1957; M.B.A. with distinction, Harvard U., 1969. Salesman Bethlehem Steel Corp., Pa., 1961-67, bus. analyst, 1969-71; asst. mgr. planning Bethlehem Steel Corp, Pa., 1971-76; mgr. fin. planning Bethlehem Steel Corp., Pa., 1976-82, v.p. planning, 1982-83, v.p. human resources, 1983—; mem. vis. com. Sch. Internat. Relations Lehigh U., Bethlehem, 1979—; mem. Moravian council Moravian Coll., Bethlehem, 1983—. Bd. dirs. Sr. Citizens' Council, Bethlehem, 1979—; pres. Girls Club of Bethlehem, 1979-80. Served to lt. (j.g.) USN, 1957-60; PTO. Baker scholar, 1969. Mem. Am. Iron and Steel Inst. Republican. Presbyterian. Clubs: Harvard (N.Y.C.); Saucon Valley Country (Bethlehem) (bd. govs.). Home: 2354 Overlook Dr Bethlehem PA 18017 Office: Bethlehem Steel Corp Martin Tower Bethlehem PA 18016

JORDAN, JOHN EMORY, educator; b. Richmond, Va., Apr. 8, 1919; s. Emory DeShazo and Magdalene (Yarbrough) J.; m. Marie Estelle Keyser, June 14, 1943; children—John Craig, Leigh Keyser, Hugh DeShazo. B.A., U. Richmond, 1940; M.A., Johns Hopkins, 1942, Ph.D., 1947. Jr. instr. English Johns Hopkins, 1946-47; mem. faculty U. Calif. at Berkeley, 1947—, prof. English, 1959—, vice chmn. dept., 1960-69, chmn. dept., 1969-73, acad. asst. to chancellor, 1962-65, acad. asst. v.p. acad. affairs and personnel, 1974-75; Mem. Calif. Adv. Com. English Framework, 1964-67. Author: Thomas de Quincey, Literary Critic, 1952, reprinted 1972, Stevenson's Silverado Journal, 1954, De Quincey to Wordsworth, 1962, Using Rhetoric, 1965, Why The Lyrical Ballads?, 1976; co-author: English Romantic Poets and Essayists, 2d edit, 1966, English Language Framework, 1968; Editor: (Thomas de Quincey) Confessions of an English Opium Eater, 1960, English Mail Coach, 1960, Reminiscences of the English Lake Poets, 1961, (Shelley and Peacock) Defence of Poetry and the Four Ages of Poetry, 1965, Questions of Rhetoric, 1971, Sackville West, A Flame in Sunlight, 1974; co-editor: Some British Romantics, 1966. Served with USNR, 1942-46. Ford fellow, 1954-55; Guggenheim fellow, 1958-59; Humanities research fellow, 1967-68, 73-74; Gayley lectr., 1964. Mem. Modern Lang. Assn. (chmn. sect. 9 1963-64, contbr. Romantic Bibliography 1965—), Nat. Council Tchrs. English (dir. 1965-68), Phi Beta Kappa. Home: 834 Santa Barbara Rd Berkeley CA 94707

JORDAN, JOHN PATRICK, government agency executive, research scientist; b. Salt Lake City, Apr. 23, 1934; s. Herbert Spencer and Madalene (Driscoll) J.; m. Thelma Marie Marsh, Sept. 4, 1954; children: Sharon Ann, Dennis Patrick, Jeffrey Terrance, Kevin Brian, Maureen Kathleen, Shaun Timothy, Kelly Christopher, John Clancy. B.S. in Animal Sci, U. Calif. at, Davis, 1955, Ph.D. in Comparative Biochemistry, 1963; postdoctoral tng. Inst. Ednl. Mgmt., Harvard U., 1974. NIH predoctoral fellow U. Calif., Davis, 1959-62; asst. prof. chemistry Oklahoma City U., 1962-65, assoc. prof., 1965-68; assoc. prof. biochemistry Colo. State U., 1968-71, prof., 1971-83; assoc. dean Coll. Natural Scis., 1968-72; dir. core curriculum in biology Univ. Expt. Sta., 1968-73, dir., 1972-83; exec. dir. Inst. Agr., 1982-83; dir. Coop. Extension Service, 1983; adminstr. Coop. State Research Service U.S. Dept. Agr., 1983—; cons. NASA (Manned Orbiting Research Lab., Lunar Receiving Lab.), NIH, NSF, Dept. Def.; Ency. Brit., several univs.; rep. Joint Council for Food and Agrl. Scis., 1980—; co-chmn. Western Regional Agrl. Research Planning Com., 1975-78; mem. Nat. Expt. Sta. Com. on Agrl. Research Policy and Orgn., 1977-78, chmn., 1979; Pres. St. Patrick's Sch. Bd., Oklahoma City, 1966-68, St. Joseph's Sch. Bd., Ft. Collins, 1970-76; Dep. chief of staff 95th div. (tng.) USAR, 1963-65; mobilization designee Office of Chief of Research and Devel., U.S. Army, 1965-77; ret. Res., 1977. Served to 1st lt. 101st Airborne Div. RA, 1955-58. Recipient 1967 Bond award Am. Oil Chemists Soc.; Gustav Ohaus award Nat. Sci. Tchrs. Assn., 1972. Fellow Am. Inst. Chemists, AAAS; mem. Biochem. Soc., Am. Physiol. Soc., Aerospace Med. Assn., Soc. Exptl. Biology and Medicine, Am. Inst. Biol. Sci. (chmn. nat. com. public policy 1979—), Sigma Xi, Phi Beta Kappa. Agrl. research adminstrn., ednl. innovation and effects of proposed space capsule environs. and metabolism of animals. Home: 917 Edwards St Fort Collins CO 80524 Office: Coop State Research Service US Dept Agr Washington DC 20250 *The role of higher education is to help people become maximally effective during that period of life when they will have maximum impact on their professions and society. Thus, although curricula, courses and programs are important vehicles, people are the major product of higher education. The day that faculty and administrators lose sight of this is the day they begin to fail in their responsibilities. Next in importance is the genesis of newer knowledge, we call it research. For it is today's research that significantly defines tomorrow's America.*

JORDAN, JOHN RICHARD, JR., lawyer; b. Winton, N.C., Jan. 16, 1921; s. John Richard Jordan and Ina Love (Mitchell) J.; m. Patricia Exum Weaver, June 19, 1949 (div.); children: Ellen Meares Jordan McCarren, John Richard, III.; m. Brenda Moore Harlow, June 27, 1982. B.A., U. N.C., 1942, J.D., 1948. Now sr. partner firm Jordan, Brown, Price & Wall, Raleigh and Chapel Hill, N.C.; mem. staff Atty. Gen. N.C., 1948-51; mem. N.C. Senate (3 regular sessions, 1 spl. session), 1959, 61, 63. Contbr. articles and revs. to newspapers and mags.; editor: Why the Democratic Party, 1955. Mem. N.C. Bd. Higher Edn., 1964; mem. N.C. Commn. Higher Edn. Facilities, 1964—; chmn. N.C. Bd. Social Services, 1969-73; trustee Ravenscroft Found., 1971—; bd. govs. U. N.C., 1973—, chmn. bd. govs., 1980—; trustee Chowan Coll., 1981—; permanent chmn. N.C. Dem. Conv., 1974; chmn. bd. dirs. N.C. div. Am. Cancer soc., 1959, pres., 1960; mem. Gov.'s Cancer Commn., 1962-64; N.C. chmn. ARC, 1966, Nat. Soc. Crippled Children and Adults, 1963; pres. N.C. Arthritis Found., 1966-70; bd. dirs. N.C. Med. Found., State Capitol Found., N.C. Mus. History Assocs., 1983—, N.C. Archives. Recipient award for scholarship and leadership Phi Delta Phi, 1948; Disting. Service award as Raleigh's Young Man of Yr., 1955, N.C. Public Health Assn., 1964; Gold Medal award Am. Cancer Soc.; Disting. Alumni award Chowan Coll., 1983. Mem. Wake County Bar Assn. (chmn. exec. com. 1955), N.C. Bar Assn., Am. Bar Assn., Am. Judicature Soc., N.C. Acad. Trial Lawyers, Internat. Bar Assn., English Speaking Union (dir.), Pi Kappa Alpha, Phi Delta Phi. Baptist. Clubs: Carolina Country, Sphinx, City of Raleigh, Exec. of Raleigh, Torch, Lions, Assembly of Raleigh. Home: 809 Westwood Dr Raleigh NC 27607 Office: Branch Banking & Trust Bldg Suite 1414 Raleigh NC 27602

JORDAN, JOSEPH, chemist, educator; b. Timisoara, Rumania, June 29, 1919; came to U.S., 1950, naturalized, 1959; s. Victor and Maria (Purjusz) J.; m. Colina L. Fischer, Nov. 26, 1952; children—Saskia Audrey, Sharon Leah, Naomi Esther, Adlai David. M.Sc., Hebrew U., Jerusalem, 1942, Ph.D., 1945. Faculty asst., instr. Hebrew U., 1945-49; research fellow Harvard, 1950; research fellow, instr. U. Minn., Mpls., 1951-54; asst. prof. Pa. State U., University Park, 1954-57, asso. prof., 1957-60, prof. chemistry, 1960—; research collaborator Brookhaven Nat. Lab., 1960-63; vis. prof. U. Calif. at Berkeley, 1959, Swiss Fed. Inst. Tech., 1961-62, Cornell U., 1965, Hebrew U., Jerusalem, 1972, Centre National de Recherches Scientifiques, Paris, 1975-76, Ecole Supérieure de Physique et Chimie, 1975-76, Pierre and Marie Curie U., 1976; Fulbright exchange lectr. U. Paris, 1968-69; Mem. com. on symbols, units and terminology, numerical data adv. bd. NRC-Nat. Acad. Scis., 1973—; mem. evaluation panel for phys. chemistry div. Nat. Bur. Standards, 1975-78. Editor-in-chief: Treatise on Titrimetry, 1971—; editor: New Developments in Titrimetry, 1974; mem. editorial bd.: Analytical Letters, 1967—, Talanta, 1972-74; editorial adv. bd.: Jour. Analytical Chemistry, 1968-70; Contbr. articles to profl. jours. and chpts. to books. Recipient Benedetti-Pichler award Am. Microchem. Soc., 1978; hon. fellow U. Minn., 1950; Frontier of Chemistry lectr. Wayne State U., 1958; Robert Guehm lectr. Swiss Fed. Inst. Tech., 1969; I.M. Kolthoff sr. fellow in analytic chemistry Hebrew U., Jerusalem, 1972. Fellow AAAS, Am. Inst. Chemists; mem. Am. Chem. Soc., Royal Soc. Chemistry, Bioelectrochem. Soc., Internat. Union Pure and Applied Chemistry (chmn. electrochemistry commn. 1967-71, titular mem. phys. chemistry div. com. 1969-73, commn. on electroanalytical chemistry 1971—, sec. 1979-81, chmn. 1981—), Assn. Harvard Chemists, AAUP, Internat. Soc. Electrochemistry, Sigma Xi, Phi Lambda Upsilon. Home: 1007 Glenn Circle N State College PA 16801 Office: Dept Chemistry Pa State U 152 Davey Lab University Park PA 16802

JORDAN, JOSEPH MICHAEL, commr. police, Boston; b. Boston, Nov. 9, 1922; s. John Francis and Mary Agnes (Shea) J.; m. Jacqueline Therese Hoar, June 26, 1949; children—Jacquelyn, Janine, Jolienne, Joseph Michael, Johnna. A.S., Northeastern U., 1969, B.S., 1970, M.P.A., 1974; postgrad., FBI Nat. Acad., 1970. With Boston Police Dept., 1946—, supt., 1974-75, supt.-in-chief, 1975-76, police commr., 1976—; lectr., cons. Northeastern U., 1976-81. Served with USN, 1943-46; PTO. Recipient eight awards for outstanding police work. Mem. Internat. Assn. Chiefs of Police, Mass. Assn. Chiefs of Police, Nat. Exec. Inst. FBI, M.P.A. Alumni Northeastern U. Roman Catholic. Home: 16 Auriga St Boston MA 02122 Office: 154 Berkeley St Boston MA 02116

JORDAN, JUNE M., poet, English language educator; b. N.Y.C., July 9, 1936; d. Granville I. and Mildred (Fisher) J.; m. Michael Mayer, Apr. 5, 1955 (div. 1966); 1 son, Christopher David. Student, Barnard Coll., 1953-55, 56-57, U. Chgo., 1955-56. Mem. English faculty Sarah Lawrence Coll., CCNY, Yale U., New Haven; research assoc. Tech. Housing Dept. Mobilization for Youth; asst. to producer The Cool World, 1964-65; prof. English SUNY, Stony Brook, 1982—; vis. poet-in-residence MacAlester Coll., 1980, Tchrs. and Writers Collaborative, 1966-68. Author: Civil Wars, Selected Essays 1963-1980, 1981, Things That I Do in the Dark, Selected Poems 1954-77, 1981, Kimako's Story, 1981, Passion, New Poems, 1977-80, 1980, Things That I Do in The Dark, 1977, New Life: New Room, 1975, New Days, Poems of Exile and Return, 1974, Fannie Lou Hamer, 1971, Dry Victories, 1972, His Own Where, 1971, The Voice of the Children, 1970, Who Look at Me, 1969; editor soulsript, 1970; contbr. articles, poems to profl. jours. Rockfeller grantee, 1969; recipient Prix de Rome, 1970; CAPS grantee in poetry, 1978; Yaddo fellow, 1979, 80; NEA fellow in creative writing, 1982. Mem. Poets and Writers Inc. (dir.), PEN Am. Center (exec. bd.), Am. Writers Congress (exec. bd.). Address: Dept English SUNY Stony Brook NY 11794

JORDAN, KENNETH ALLAN, agricultural engineering educator; b. Plainfield, N.J., June 30, 1930; s. Homer Glenn and Lucy Marie (Rutledge) J.; m. Phyllis A. Deck, June 1, 1952; children: Jeanette Arlene, Genevieve Jean, Kenneth Allan, David Mark. B.S., Purdue U., 1952, M.S., 1956, Ph.D., 1959. Instr. Purdue U., 1957-58; asst. prof. agrl. engring. N.C. State U., 1958-63, asso. prof., 1963-67; prof. agrl. engring. U. Minn., St. Paul, 1967—; with Bioengring. Assos., Raleigh, 1965-66; ordained to ministry Christian Ch., 1974. Instrumentation news editor: Agrl. Engr, 1962-65, ASHRAE Guide & Data Book, 1964-66. Served with USNR, 1952-54. Mem. Am. Soc. Agrl. Engrs., Japan Soc. for Promotion Sci., Sigma Xi, Alpha Epsilon, Gamma Sigma Delta. Home: 2613 Winbledon Dr Woodbury MN 55125 Office: 309 Agrl Engring Bldg U Minn Saint Paul MN 55108

JORDAN, LEMUEL RUSSELL, hospital administrator; b. Smithfield, N.C., Oct. 21, 1924; s. Thomas and Sophronia Lee (Creech) J.; m. Jean Marrow, Dec. 15, 1951; children: Jean H., Rebecca, Judy. B.A., Amherst Coll., 1947; M.A., Columbia U., 1949; postgrad. mgmt, U. N.C., 1949-50, 51-54, Ernest H. Abernathy fellow, 1952-53. Instr. personnel relations Sch. Bus. Adminstrn., U. N.C., 1953-55; asst. dir., asst. prof. hosp. mgmt. Duke U. Med. Center, 1955-59; dir. teaching hosps. and clinics, asso. prof. mgmt. Coll. Bus. Adminstrn., J. Hillis Miller Health Center, U. Fla., Gainesville, 1959-65; asso. prof. health and hosp. adminstrn. Coll. Health Related Professions, chmn. grad. program health and hosp. adminstrn., 1963-65; exec. dir., chief exec. officer Baptist Med. Center, Birmingham, Ala., 1965-71, pres., chief exec. officer, 1971-74, Alton Ochsner Med. Found., New Orleans, 1974-78; chmn. bd., chief exec. officer Eye, Ear, Nose and Throat Hosp. and Clinics, New Orleans, 1976-78; pres., chief exec. officer, dir. Miami Valley Hosp., Dayton, Ohio, 1978—; pres., chief exec. officer MedAm. Health Systems Corp.; adj. prof. U. Ala., Birmingham, 1969—, Sch. Public Health and Tropical Medicine, Tulane U., 1975—, Washington U., St. Louis, 1971—; Kellogg Found. vis. prof., San Salvador, 1964; chmn. Accrediting Commn. Edn. Health Services Adminstrn., 1975-77; adv. com. Robert Wood Johnson Community Hosp.-Med. Staff, Washington, 1974—; guest lectr. Xavier U., Cin., 1978—; adj. asso. prof. Wright State U. Coll. Medicine, Dayton, 1978—. Author papers in field. Bd. dirs. Dayton Philharm. Orch., VHA Health Ventures, Voluntary Hosps. Am.; mem. adv. bd. Salvation Army. Served as officer USAAF, World War II; Korea. Named hon. alumnus Duke U., U. Ala., George Washington U. Fellow Am. Coll. Hosp. Adminstrs. (chmn. com. article-of-year awards 1969-70); mem. Am. Heart Assn., Am. Hosp. Assn., Am. Mgmt. Assn., Am. Public Health Assn., Nat. League Nursing, Alpha Kappa Psi (nat. pres. 1959-65, dir. found. 1965-72, 76—, Disting. Service award 1952, 62, 63). Republican. Presbyterian. Clubs: Racquet, Dayton Country, Rotary (Dayton). L. R. Jordan Library dedicated at Ida V. Moffett Sch. Nursing, Birmingham, 1975; L. R. Jordan Health Care Mgmt. Soc. founded as nat. ednl. soc., New Orleans, 1978. Office: 1 Wyoming St Dayton OH 45409

JORDAN, LEONARD EDWARD, gas and oil company executive; b. Jonesboro, La., Aug. 10, 1930; s. Hilton Edward and Audye (Martin) J.; m. Patricia Joy Jolley, May 31, 1952; children: Kathryn Lynn, Jordan Ware, Linda Lee Jordan Turner, Keith Edward. B.S. in Geology, La. Statae U., 1953. With Ark. La. Gas Co. (now Arkla Inc.), 1953—, v.p., Shreveport, La., 1970-82, sr. v.p. exploration and prodn., 1982—, Arkla Exploration Co. subs. Arkla Inc., Shreveport, 1982—, dir.; dir. N.Am. Drilling Co. P.L.C., Edinburgh, Scotland. Bd. dirs. South Broadmoor YMCA, Shreveport, 1963-67; div. chmn. United Fund, Shreveport, 1968; asst. scoutmaster Norwela council Boy Scouts Am., 1967-72; mem. adv. council La. State U.Geology Endowment, Baton Rouge. Mem. Am. Assn. Petroleum Geologists (cert.), Am. Assn. Petroleum Landmen (cert.), Soc. Petroleum Engrs., Mid-Continent Oil and Gas Assn., Gulf Coast Assn. Geol. Socs., Shreveport Geol. Socs., Ark.-La.-Tex. Landman Soc., Shreveport C. of C., Shreveport Desk and Derrick Club (industry adviser), Alpha Phi Omega. Republican. Baptist. Clubs: Sherveport Petroleum, Riverside Swim and Tennis. Home: 1901 Audubon Pl Shareveport LA 71105 Office: PO Box 21734 Shareveport LA 71151

JORDAN, LOUIS HAMPTON, educator; b. Owassa, Ala., Jan. 1, 1922; s. Issac Newton and Bertha (Edeker) J.; m. Carolyn Maureen Carter, June 2, 1956; children—Louis Hampton, Mark Stephen. B.S., Auburn U., 1947; M.B.A., Northwestern U., 1951; Ph.D., Columbia U., 1954. Asso. prof. Tulane U., New Orleans, 1955-60; prof. acctg. Columbia U., 1960-75; prof. acctg., asso. dean Grad. Sch. Bus. Adminstrn., Fordham U., N.Y.C., 1975—; cons. Westinghouse Electric Corp., Touche Ross & Price Waterhouse; vis. prof. Robert Coll., Instanbul, Turkey, 1966-67, 70-71. Author: (with M. Moonitz) Accounting: An Analysis of Its Problems, 2 vols, 1963, 64. Served to capt., arty. U.S. Army, 1942-46. Mem. Am. Inst. C.P.A.'s, Am. Acctg. Assn. Democrat. Roman Catholic. Home: 20 Kingston Ave Yonkers NY 10701 Office: Fordham U 624 Lincoln Center New York NY 10023

JORDAN, MARK HENRY, consulting engineer; b. Lawrence, Mass., Apr. 10, 1915; s. Joseph Augustine and Gertrude (O'Connell) J.; m. Louise Sullivan, June 23, 1939; children: Mary Elizabeth (Mrs. Delio Gianturco), Margaret Michaela. B.S., U.S. Naval Acad., 1937; M. Civil Engring., Rensselaer Poly. Inst., 1942, M.S., 1965, Ph.D., 1968. Registered profl. engr., N.J., N.Y. Commd. ensign U.S. Navy, 1937, advanced through grades to capt., 1955; comdr. 6th Seabee Battalion, South Pacific, 1943-44, comdr. 103d Seabee Battalion, Central Pacific, 1951-52, comdr. Civil Engr. Corps. Sch., Port Hueneme, Calif., 1960-63, ret., 1963; assoc. prof. civil engring. U. Mo., Columbia, 1966-67; prof. civil engring. Rensselaer Poly. Inst., 1968-77, prof. emeritus, 1977—, dean continuing studies, 1967-72, chmn. civil engring., 1972-73; cons. engr. Smith & Mahoney, Albany, N.Y., 1975-78; individual practice as cons. engr., 1978—. Author: (with others) Saga of the Sixth, 1950. Mem. Rensselaer County Charter Commn., 1969-71; Bd. dirs. United Community Services, Troy, N.Y., 1969-75. Decorated Bronze Star with V, Presdl. Unit citation. Fellow ASCE (life); mem. Am. Soc. Engring. Edn., Soc. Am. Mil. Engrs. (local post pres.), Am. Pub. Works Assn., Nat. Soc. Profl. Engrs., Sigma Xi, Chi Epsilon. Roman Catholic. Club: Fort Orange (Albany, N.Y.). Home: East Rd Brunswick Hills NY 12180 Office: 40 Steuben St Albany NY 12207

JORDAN, MICHELLE H., pub. relations co. exec.; b. Sussex, Eng., Sept. 19, 1948; came to U.S., 1975; d. Raymond Cameron and Liliane (Ambar) J. Student, Sorbonne, 1966-67. With Coordinated Mktg. Services Ltd., London, 1967-71; dir. Spectrum Public Relations, London, 1971-74; with Rowland Co., N.Y.C., 1975—, exec. v.p., 1980—. Mem. Mayor N.Y.C. Commn. Status Women, 1980—. Office: 415 Madison Ave New York NY 10017

JORDAN, PAUL HOWARD, JR., surgeon; b. Bigelow, Ark., Nov. 22, 1919; s. Paul Howard and Marie Theresa (Lewis) J.; m. Lois Regnell, Apr. 6, 1944; children: Kristine Jordan Henyey, Craig T., Patricia Jordan Johnson. B.S., U. Chgo., 1941, M.D., 1944; M.S., U. Ill., 1950. Intern St. Luke's Hosp., Chgo., 1944-46; resident in surgery U. Ill., Chgo., 1948-50, Hines VA Hosp., 1950-53; from instr. to clin. prof. surgery UCLA Med. Sch., 1953-58; asso. prof. U. Fla. Med. Sch., Gainesville, 1959-64; prof. surgery Baylor Coll. Medicine, Houston,

1964—; chief surgery VA Hosp., Houston, 1964—, chief staff, 1969; mem. sr. attending staff Methodist Hosp., Houston; cons. staff St. Luke's Episcopal Hosp., Houston. Author articles in field, chpts. in books. Served to capt. M.C. AUS, 1946-48. Spl. NIH fellow Karolinska Inst., Stockholm, 1958-59; recipient Acrel medal Swedish Surg. Soc., 1974; corr. fellow Brazilian Surg. Soc., 1976. Mem. ACS (chpt. councilor 1978—), Soc. Surgery Alimentary tract (past recorder, pres. 1983-84), Assn. VA Surgeons (past pres., Disting. Service award 1979), Am. Surg. Assn., Soc. Internat. Chururgie, Soc. Univ. Surgeons, Am. Physiol. Soc., Am. Gastroenterol. Assn., Am. Soc. Gastrointestinal Endoscopy, Soc., Exptl. Biology and Medicine, Western Surg. Assn., So. Surg. Assn., Tex. Surg. Soc., Harris County Med. Soc., Houston Surg. Soc. (past pres.), Houston Gastroenterol. Soc. (past pres.). Methodist. Club: Doctors (Houston). Office: 1200 Moursund Houston TX 77030

JORDAN, PHILIP HARDING, JR., coll. exec.; b. N.Y.C., June 2, 1931; m. Sheila Anne Gray; children: Philip Harding, III, John, II. B.A. in Philosophy summa cum laude, Princeton U., 1954; M.A. in History (Univ. fellow), Yale U., 1956; Ph.D. in History (Conn. Soc. Colonial Dames fellow), Yale U., 1962. Asst. in instrn. Yale U., 1956-57, 58-59; instr. in history Conn. Coll., 1959-63, asst. prof. history, 1963-67, asso. prof., 1967-73, prof., 1973-75, asso. dean acad. affairs, 1968-69, dean of faculty, 1969-74; pres. Kenyon Coll., 1975—; mem. governing bd. Conn. Faculty Talent Search for recruitment of black faculty into Conn. colls. and univs., 1970-75; mem. regional adv. council Mohegan Community Coll., 1974-75; mem. faculty cons. examiners, com. on asso. degree Conn. Bd. State Acad. Awards, 1974-75; mem. Ohio Com. Public Programs in Humanities, 1977-79; mem. Ohio state panel Nat. Indentification Program Advancement Women in Higher Edn., 1979—. Author: Student Guide to Accompany John A. Garraty's The American Nation, 1966, (with Patrick J. Abbazia) Instructor's Manual to Accompany John A. Garraty's The American Nation, 1966. Trustee Williams Sch., New London, Conn., 1971-75, Pine Point Sch., Stonington, Conn., 1973-75, Rutherford B. Hayes and Lucy Webb Hayes Found., 1977—, Lawrenceville Sch., 1979—. Recipient Class of 1869 prize in ethics Princeton U., 1954, Salgo-Noren prize Conn. Coll., 1965. Mem. AAUP (ad hoc com. to investigate acad. freedom and tenure at Tufts U. 1964-65), Am. Council Edn. (dir. 1981—), Assn. Ind. Colls. and Univs. Ohio (vice chmn. 1977-79, dir. 1975—, chmn. 1980—), Ohio Coll. Assn. (exec. com.), Phi Beta Kappa. Office: Office of Pres Kenyon Coll Gambier OH 43022

JORDAN, RALPH WILBUR, insurance company executive; b. Columbus, Ohio, June 30, 1920; s. Ralph W. and Helen (Mougey) J.; m. Violet Elizabeth Hartinger, June 20, 1947; children: Judy, Deborah, Nancy, Thomas, Ralph. B.Sc., Ohio State U., 1946; LL.B., Franklin U., 1951; J.D. (hon.), Capital U., 1965. Bar: Ohio 1951; C.L.U.; registered health underwriter, Ohio. Regional adminstrv. mgr. Nationwide Ins. Co., Canton, Ohio, 1952-59, dir. systems, Columbus, 1959-69, v.p., regional mgr., Syracuse, N.Y., 1969-73, v.p. health care devel., Columbus, 1973—; v.p., gen. mgr. Nat. Profl. Services, Columbus, 1974-82; developer Primary Care Network Health Maintenance Orgn., Akron and Columbus, 1981-82. Trustee First Community Retirement Village, Columbus, 1978—, vice chmn. bd., Columbus, 1978—; trustee Marion Health Maintenance Orgn., Ohio, 1974-83; chmn. State Cert. of Need Rev. Bd., Columbus, 1979—; mem. Bd. Regents Adv. Com., Columbus, 1979-82; mem. med. adv. com. Ohio Welfare Dept., Columbus, 1980—; sponser health edn. program Columbus Pub. Schs., 1981—; mem. Affordable Health Council, Columbus, 1983, Gov.'s Commn. on Health Care, Columbus, 1983, Pres.'s Pvt. Sector Survey on Cost Control Com., 1982-83. Served with AUS, 1942-45; ETO. Mem. Health Ins. Assn. Am. (state chmn. 1974—), Am. Soc. C.L.U.s, Ohio Health Underwriters Assn. Republican. Home: 4270 Shelbourne Ln Columbus OH 43220 Office: Nationwide Ins Cos 1 Nationwide Plaza Columbus OH 43215

JORDAN, RICHARD CHARLES, engineering educator; b. Mpls., Apr. 16, 1909; s. C. and Estelle R. (Martin) J.; m. Freda M. Laudon, Aug. 10, 1935; children: Mary Ann, Carol Lynn, Linda Lee. B. Aero. Engring., U. Minn., 1931, M.S., 1933, Ph.D., 1940. In charge air conditioning div. Mpls. br. Am. Radiator & Standard San. Corp., 1933-36; instr. petroleum engring. U. Tulsa, 1936-37; instr. engring. expt. sta. U. Minn., 1937-41, asst. dir., 1941-44, asso. prof., 1944-45, prof., asst. head mech. engring. dept., 1946-49, prof., head dept. mech. engring., 1950-77, prof., head, 1966-77, acting asso. dean, 1977-78, asso. dean, 1978—; dir. Onan Corp. of McGraw-Edison; cons. various refrigeration and air conditioning cos., 1937—; cons. NSF, U.S. Dept. State, Control Data Corp., others.; Mem. engring. sci. adv. panel NSF, 1954-57, chmn., 1957; mem. div. engring. and indsl. research NRC, mem. exec. com., 1957-69, chmn., 1962-65; del. OAS Conf. on Strategy for Tech. Devel. Latin Am., Chile, 1969; chmn. U.S.-Brazil Sci. Coop. Program Com. on Indsl. Research, Rio de Janeiro, 1967, Washington, 1967, Belo Horizonte, 1968, Houston, 1968; del. World Power Conf., Melbourne, 1962; v.p. sci. council Internat. Institut de du Froid, 1967-71; cons. to World Bank on alternative energy for Northeastern Brazil, 1976. Author: (with Priester) Refrigeration and Air Conditioning, 1948, rev. edit., 1956, also numerous publs. on mech. engring., environ. control, solar energy, energy resources, engring. edn., tech. transfer.; Contbr. Mech. Engring. Recipient F. Paul Anderson medal ASHRAE, 1966, E.K. Campbell award, 1966, Outstanding Publs. Golden Key award, 1949; Outstanding Achievement award U. Minn., 1979; elected to Solar Energy Hall of Fame, 1980. Fellow ASME, AAAS, ASHRAE (presdl. mem.); mem. Nat. Acad. Engring., Assn. Applied Solar Energy (adv. council 1958-61), Am. Soc. Refrigerating Engrs. (1st v.p. 1952, pres. 1953, dir., council mem. 1946-53), Am. Soc. Engring. Edn., AAAS, Nat., Minn. (Engr. of Yr. award 1972), socs. profl. engrs., Internat. Inst. Refrigeration (hon. mem., del. NRC to exec. com. 1957-76, v.p. exec. com. 1959-63, v.p. sci. council 1963-71), Engr. Council Profl. Devel. (chmn. regional edn. and accreditation com.), Sigma Xi, Tau Beta Pi, Pi Tau Sigma, Sigma Chi. Club: Campus. Office: Dept Mech Engring U Minn Minneapolis MN 55455

JORDAN, ROBERT, pianist, educator; b. Chattanooga, May 2, 1940; s. Ira and Mamie (McCamey) J. Mus.B., Eastman Sch. Music, 1962; M.S., Juilliard Sch. Music, 1965; diploma, Goethe Inst. for German Lang., 1965, Hochschule fur Musik, Germany, 1967, Sorbonne, Paris, 1969. Assoc. prof. SUNY—Fredonia, 1980—; bd. dirs., mem. adv. council Triad Presentations, Inc.; pres. Paris Inst. Music, N.Y.C.; artist-in-residence U. Del., 1979. Represented Afro-Am. classical performer: 2d World Black and African Festival, Lagos, Nigeria, 1977; Extensive concertizing in, Europe, 1966-70; appeared at, Avery Fischer Hall and Alice Tully Hall, Lincoln Center, N.Y.C., 1971, 72, recital debut, Kennedy Center, Washington, 1975; soloist with, Buffalo, Balt., Chattanooga and Symphony of New World orchs., Prague Symphony, Bavarian Radio Orch. Tchr., Bronx Community Coll., 1972—, U. Mich. div. Nat. Music Camp, summer 1974; artist in residence, Morgan State U., Balt.; recital, tour, Brazil, summer 1978, Surinam, S. Am., 1982, Lagos, Nigeria; recs. on Orion Records. Established Minority Scholarship Fund, U. Del., 1979, Jessie Hillman Scholarship Fund for Pianists, SUNY, Fredonia, 1981. Recipient Chancellors award for excellence in teaching SUNY-Fredonia; Fulbright scholar, 1965-67. Invited by USIS to tour France and Germany, 1969; chosen as one of 13 pianists nationally to commn. composition from an Am. composer and to give world premiere at Kennedy Center. Home: 52 E Main St Fredonia NY 14063 Office: SUNY Fredonia NY 14063 *In retrospect, I see that my entire growth as an artist has been inextricably linked with my growth as a human being, and that they are indeed, inseparable. To totally realize my potential, on every level, as both artist and man, has been the strongest single motivating force in my life. I acknowledge with gratitude the support I have received throughout my career, and trust that whatever I do, I will always bring honor to those who have done so much for me.*

JORDAN, ROBERT CHARLES, insurance company executive; b. Ft. Worth; s. James B. and Viola (Wood) J.; m. Alison Smith Jordan; children: Julia W., Robert Charles, Lindsay F. B.B.A., Tex. Tech U., 1941; grad., Advanced Mgmt. Program Harvard U., 1958. With John Hancock Mut. Life Ins. Co., Boston, 1946-68; exec. v.p. fin. New Eng. Mut. Life Ins. Co., Boston, 1968—, vice chmn., 1982—, dir., until 1983; pres., dir. subs. mut. and annuity funds NEL Equity Service Corp.; Trustee, mem. fin. com. Mt. Holyoke Coll., Derby Acad., Hingham, Mass.; trustee Mus. Sci., Boston; pres. Mass. Eye and Ear Infirmary, Boston. Mem. exec. com. Mass. Bus. Devel. Corp.; trustee Eastern Gas and Fuel Assos. Served with USAAF, 1942-46. Mem. Greater Boston C. of C. (past dir.). Clubs: Algonquin, Boston Econ., Commercial, Executives. Office: 501 Boylston St Boston MA 02117 *

JORDAN, ROBERT ELIJAH, III, lawyer; b. South Boston, Va., June 20, 1936; s. Robert Elijah and Lucy (Webb) J.; m. Karen Wise Rosenberg, Sept. 14, 1968; children—Janet Elizabeth, Jennifer Anne, Robert Elijah IV. S.B. (Sloan Found. scholar), Mass. Inst. Tech., 1958; J.D. magna cum laude (Edward J. Noble Found. fellow), Harvard U., 1961. Bar: D.C. bar 1962, Va. bar 1964. Spl. asst. civil rights Office Sec. Def., Washington, 1963-64; asst. U.S. atty. for D.C., 1964-65; exec. asst. for enforcement Office Sec. Treasury, 1965-67; dep. gen. counsel Dept. Army, 1967, acting gen. counsel, 1967-68; gen. counsel of Army, spl. asst. for civil functions to Sec. Army, 1968-71; partner firm Steptoe & Johnson, Washington, 1971—; mem. Jud. Conf., D.C. Circuit, 1973; Pres. Langley Sch., 1981-82. Contbr. articles to profl. jours. Served to 1st lt. AUS, 1961-63. Recipient Karl Taylor Compton award, 1958, Arthur S. Flemming award, 1970, award for exceptional civilian service Dept. Army, 1971. Mem. Am. (chmn. oil pipeline com. of public utility sect. 1978-82), Va. bar assns., D.C. Bar (chmn. ethics com. 1978-82), Tau Beta Pi, Tau Kappa Alpha. Democrat. Club: Met. (Washington). Home: 6963 Duncraig Ct McLean VA 22101 Office: 1250 Connecticut Ave NW Washington DC 20036

JORDAN, ROBERT HENRY, chief justice Supreme Ct. Ga.; b. Talbotton, Ga., Feb. 6, 1916; s. James Weaver and Maude Marie (Jossey) J.; m. Jean Ingram, Jan. 9, 1944; children—Barbara Jordan Holder, David, William. LL.B., J.D., U. Ga., 1941. Bar: Ga. bar 1941. Practiced in, Talbotton, 1946-60; judge Ga. Ct. Appeals, 1960-72; justice Ga. Supreme Ct., 1972-80, chief justice, 1980—; mem. Jud. Council Ga.; Mem. Ga. Warm Springs Meml. Commn., 1959—; mem. Ga. Senate, 1953-54, 59, Ga. Hwy. Bd., 1959-60. Author: There Was a Land, 1970. Served to maj. AUS, 1941-45. Democrat. Office: 539 State Jud Bldg Atlanta GA 30303

JORDAN, ROBERT MAYNARD, educator; b. Chgo., June 16, 1924; s. David O. and Annette G. (Cohen) J.; m. C. Jean Schneider, Aug. 16, 1955; children—Jennifer, John, David. Student, Antioch Coll., 1941-42; B.A., Colo. Coll., 1949; Ph.D., U. Calif.-Berkeley, 1955. Instr. English Amherst (Mass.) Coll., 1955-58; asst. prof. U. B.C., Vancouver, Can., 1958-63; asso. prof. to prof., dean grad. sch. State U. N.Y. at Stony Brook, 1963-68; prof. U. Wis., Madison, 1968-69; prof. English U. B.C., 1969—, head dept. English, 1969-81; Bd. councillors Medieval Acad. Am., 1970-73. Author: Chaucer and the Shape of Creation, 1967. Served with USAAF, 1942-45. Can. Council Research fellow, 1960-61, 72-73, 79-80. Home: 5750 Larch Vancouver BC V6M 4E2 Canada Office: Dept English U BC Vancouver BC V6T 1W5 Canada

JORDAN, ROBERT SMITH, educator; b. Los Angeles, June 11, 1929; s. Ralph Burdette and Mary Wright (Smith) J.; m. Sara Jane Hatch, Sept. 19, 1961; children: Sara Jane, Mary Rebecca, Robert Hatch, David Thomas. A.B., UCLA, 1951; M.S., U. Utah, 1955; M.A. (E.I. DuBois fellow), Princeton U., 1957, Ph.D., 1960; D.Phil. (Fulbright scholar), Oxford U., Eng., 1960. Asst. to v.p. academic affairs U. Utah, 1954-55; budget examiner internat. div. U.S. Bur. Budget, 1956; instr. dept. politics Princeton U., 1956-57; mem. St. Antony's Coll., Oxford, 1957-59; asst. prof. pub. and internat. affairs, exec. asst. to dean Grad. Sch. Pub. and Internat. Affairs, U. Pitts., 1959-60; asso. professorial lectr. George Washington U., 1960-62; asst. dir. Army War Coll. Center, 1960-61; dir. Air U. Center, 1961-62, asso. prof. polit. sci. and internat. affairs, 1962-70, asst. to pres., 1962-64; asso. dir. internat. orgn. and internat. security studies Program of Policy Studies, 1964-65; dir. Fgn. Affairs Intern Program, Sch. Pub. and Internat. Affairs, 1968-70; dean faculty econ. and social studies, head dept. polit. sci. U. Sierra Leone, 1965-67; prof. polit. sci. State U. N.Y. at Binghamton, 1970-76, chmn. dept., 1970-74; dir. research UN Inst. for Tng. and Research, N.Y.C., 1975-79; Dag Hammarskold vis. prof. internat. relations U.S.C., Columbia, 1979-80; prof. polit. sci., dean Grad. Sch., U. New Orleans, 1980-82; adj. prof. polit. sci. Columbia U., 1978-79. Author/editor: The NATO International Staff/Secretariat, 1967, Problems in International Relations, 1970, Government and Power in West Africa, 1970, rev. edit., 1977, Europe and the Superpowers, 1971, International Administration, 1971, Multinational Cooperation, 1972, Basic Issues in International Relations, 1974, Political Handbook of the World, 1975, The World Food Conference and Global Problem Solving, 1976, Political Leadership in NATO, 1979, Changing Role and Concepts in the International Civil Service, 1980, Dag Hammarskjold Revisited: The UN Secretary-General as a Force in World Politics, 1983, International Organizations: A Comparative Approach, 1983. Mem. Commn. to Study Orgn. of Peace.; Bd. dirs. Scarsdale-Hartsdale chpt. UN Assn., 1976-79. Served with USAF, 1951-53. Decorated Bronze Star; named Distinguished Alumnus Hinckley Inst., U. Utah, 1964; NATO research fellow, 1969-70; Fellow African Studies Assn. Mem. Assn. Princeton Grad. Alumni (pres.), Am. Polit. Sci. Assn., Internat. Studies Assn. (v.p.), Am. Soc. Pub. Adminstrn. (exec. com. sect. on internat. adminstrn.), Am. Soc. Internat. Law, Internat. Inst. Strategic Studies, Sigma Chi, Pi Sigma Alpha. Mem. Ch. Jesus Christ of Latter-day Saints. Clubs: Plimsoll (New Orleans); Cosmos (Washington). Home: 140 Belle Terre Blvd Covington LA 70433 Office: Dept Polit Sci U New Orleans Lake Front New Orleans LA 70122

JORDAN, ROY WILCOX, investment company executive; b. St. Louis, May 19, 1911; s. William Edgar and Martha (Hazzard) J.; m. Helen Fusz, June 24, 1936 (dec. Nov. 1974); children: Eugene Fusz, Martha Jordan Weiss, David Allen, Cicely Ann Jordon Drennan.; m. Georgia Willmore Hatton, Nov. 26, 1981. Student, Washington U., 1928. Trader, prin. Gatch Bros., Jordan & McKinney, St. Louis, 1932-41; partner G.H. Walker & Co., St. Louis, 1941-71, sr. v.p., 1971-73; sr. v.p., dir. G.H. Walker, Laird Inc., 1973-74; 1st v.p. White Weld & Co. Inc., 1974-78; v.p. Merrill Lynch Pierce Fenner & Smith, 1978—; staff asst. to pres. McDonnell Aircraft Co., St. Louis, 1941-44; chmn. Clayton (Mo.) Fed. Savs. and Loan Assn.; dir. Whitaker Cable Corp., Kansas City, Mo., Boatmen's Bank St. Louis County, G.H. Walker & Co. Active Boy Scouts Am., 1940—, chmn., mem. exec. bd. Region VIII, 1966-68, mem. nat. adv. bd., 1940—, pres. St. Louis Area council, 1973-75; chmn. Park and Recreation Commn., Clayton, 1954-58, Clayton Planning Commn., 1960-68, 71—; vice chmn. Clayton Planning Commn., 1968-71; chmn. St. Louis County Plan Commn., 1963-67; chmn. adv. com. Hanley House, Clayton, 1966—; mem. investment adv. com. St. Louis County Funds, 1967-74; pres. Arts and Edn. Found. Greater St. Louis, 1971-73; mem. Arts and Edn. Council Greater St. Louis, 1965—, pres., 1971-73; chmn. Met. Zool. Park and Mus. Dist.; mem. Mo. Hwy. Commn., 1975-81, vice chmn., 1979-81; chmn. bd. trustees YWCA, St. Louis, 1960-78; trustee Sch. of the Ozarks, 1974—. Recipient Silver Beaver award Boy Scouts Am., 1949, Silver Antelope award, 1966, Silver Buffalo award, 1978; named Clayton Man of Yr., 1972, St. Louis County Bus. Person of Yr., 1982. Mem. Investment Bankers Assn. (dir.), Securities Industry Assn. (governing council 1974-78, chmn. dist. 1974-75), SAR (past pres. St. Louis, past pres. Mo.), Am. Badminton Assn. (past pres.). Clubs: Rotary, Clayton; Noonday, Racquet, St. Louis (St. Louis). Home: 140 N Bemiston Clayton MO 63105 Office: 120 S Central Clayton MO 63105 *My life has been an affirmation of the motto that is shown on the Jordan Coat of Arms on the Old Brick Church at Smithfield, Virginia, the first brick church in America. The motto is "Percusa Resurgo" (Stricken Down I Will Rise Again). This has meant much to me and my family.*

JORDAN, THOMAS RICHARD, pub. relations exec.; b. Ridgewood, N.Y., Jan. 28, 1928; s. Henry C. and Marie (Mills) J.; m. Joann Harriet Schneider, Nov. 2, 1957; children—Craig Mills, Eve Suzanne. B.S., USCG Acad., 1950. Commd. officer USCG, 1950-53; resigned, 1953; newspaperman News Rev., Riverhead, N.Y., 1954-56; with McGraw-Hill Pub. Co., 1956-60; acting mng. editor Elec. World, 1958-60; with Bozell & Jacobs, 1960-67; organizer, pres. Underwood, Jordan, Yulish Assos. Inc. (sold to Ogilvy & Mather 1981), N.Y.C., 1967—; exec. v.p. Ogilvy & Mather Public Relations, 1981—. Mem. Pub. Relations Soc. Am., Pub. Relations Seminar. Club: Nat. Press (Washington). Home: 60 East End Ave New York NY 10028 Office: 230 Park Ave New York NY 10169

JORDAN, VERNON EULION, JR., urban league ofcl.; b. Atlanta, Aug. 15, 1935; s. Vernon Eulion and Mary (Griggs) J.; m. Shirley M. Yarbrough, Dec. 13, 1958; 1 dau., Vickee. B.A., DePauw U., 1957; J.D., Howard U., 1960, Baldwin-Wallace Coll., Bloomfield Coll., Brandeis U., Bklyn., Center of L.I. U., Brown U., City U. N.Y., Dartmouth Coll., Davidson Coll., Dillard U., U. Evansville, Fordham U., Mich. State U., Morris Brown Coll., Harvard U., Coll. of Holy Cross, Lafayette Coll., N.Y. U., Benedict Coll., Boston Coll., Duke U., Hamilton Coll., N.C. A&T U., Notre Dame U., U. Pa., Princeton U., Tougaloo Coll., Tuskegee Inst., Rutgers U., Suffolk U. Law Sch., Wilberforce U., Williams Coll., Yale U., Morehouse U., Winston-Salem State U. Bar: Ga. bar 1960, Ark. bar 1964. Practice law, Atlanta, 1960-61, Pine Bluff, Ark., 1964-65; Ga. field sec. N.A.A.C.P., 1961-63; dir. Voter Edn. Project So. Regional Council, 1964-68; atty. Office Econ. Opportunity, Atlanta, 1969; exec. dir. United Negro Coll. Fund, N.Y.C., 1970-71; pres. Nat. Urban League, 1972-81; dir. Am. Express Co., Bankers Trust Co., Bankers Trust N.Y. Corp., Celanese Corp., J.C. Penney Co., Inc., R.J. Reynolds Industries, Inc., Xerox Corp. Contbr.: column To Be Equal to newspapers throughout U.S. Mem. Am. Revolution Bi-Centennial Commn., 1972—, Presdl. Clemency Bd., 1974; adv. bd. Social Security.; Bd. dirs. Am. Mus. Natural History, Atlanta U. Center, Clark Coll., John Hay Whitney Found., Nat. Council Crime and Delinquency, Nat. Multiple Sclerosis Soc., Nat. Urban Coalition, New World Found., Taconic Found., Rockefeller Found.; mem. corp. Mass. Inst. Tech. Fellow 2Met. Applied Research Center, 1968, Harvard Inst. Politics, 1969. Mem. Am., Nat. bar assns., Nat. Conf. Black Lawyers, Council on Fgn. Relations. Mem. A.M.E. Ch. Office: 500 E 62d St New York NY 10021

JORDAN, WILLIAM BRYAN, JR., art historian; b. Nashville, May 8, 1940; s. William Bryan and Dixie (Owen) J. B.A. cum laude, Washington and Lee U., Lexington, Va., 1962; M.A., N.Y. U., 1964, Ph.D., 1967. Mem. faculty So. Meth. U., 1967-81, chmn. div. fine arts, 1967-73, prof. art history, 1975-81; dir. Meadows Mus., 1967-81; curator European art Dallas Mus. Fine Arts, 1976-81; dep. dir. Kimbell Art Mus., Ft. Worth, 1981—. Author papers in field, also mus. catalogues. Trustee Dallas Symphony Orch., 1969-71. Mem. Am. Soc. Hispanic Art Hist. Studies (gen. sec. 1976-78), Coll. Art Assn. Am., Hispanic Soc. Am. (corr.). Office: Kimbell Art Museum PO Box 9440 Fort Worth TX 76107

JORDAN, WILLIAM BURNAP, III, financial executive; b. Pine Plains, N.Y., May 13, 1920; s. William Burnap and Julia Duxbury (Slingerland) J.; m. Jean Doris Costello, July 22, 1944; children: Laura Jordan Sawyer, W. Cyrus, James C. Grad., Hotchkiss Sch., 1939; B.S., Yale, 1942; night student, Walsh Inst. Accountancy, Detroit, 1947-50. With Am. Brake Shoe Co., 1945-58, comptroller Am. Brakeblok div., 1950-51, treas., 1952-58; v.p. finance and adminstrn. S.H. Kress & Co., 1958-61; treas. Chesebrough-Pond's, Inc., 1961-63, Kraft, Inc., 1963-71, v.p., treas., 1971-80, Dart & Kraft, Inc., 1980—; dir. Optimum Holdings Corp., Benchmark Fund; adv. bd. Mfrs. Hanover Trust Co., N.Y.C. Bd. dirs. Dr. Scholl Found. Served as aviator Pacific Fleet USNR, 1942-45. Clubs: Union League (N.Y.C.); Univ. (Chgo.); Barrington Hills (Ill.) Country. Office: Dart & Kraft Inc 2211 Sanders Rd Northbrook IL 60062

JORDAN, WILLIAM DITMER, educator; b. Selma, Ala., Feb. 5, 1922; s. John Bryant and Leona (Sanders) J.; m. Carolyn Carter, Aug. 30, 1947; children—William Ditmer, Lucy Carolyn (Mrs. Jack R. Altherr, Jr.), Rebecca Newton (Mrs. William A. Pow). B.S. in Mech. Engring, U. Ala., 1942, M.S. in Civil Engring, 1949; Ph.D., U. Ill., 1952. Mem. faculty U. Ala., 1946—, prof. engring. mechanics, 1957—; head engring. mechanics dept., 1961-68, head aerospace engring., mech. engring. and engring mechanics dept., 1968; cons. to govt. and industry, 1953—. Bd. dirs. Tuscaloosa County YMCA, 1963—, chmn., 1977. Served to capt. C.E. U.S. Army, 1942-46. Mem. Am. Soc. Engring. Edn. (chmn. mechanics div. 1965), ASME, Sigma Xi, Tau Beta Pi, Phi Eta Sigma, Pi Mu Epsilon, Pi Tau Sigma, Omicron Delta Kappa, Kappa Alpha. Presbyn. Clubs: Exchange (pres. 1962), Indian Hills Country (bd. dirs. Tuscaloosa). Home: 1501 High Forest Drive North Tuscaloosa AL 35406 Office: Box 2908 University AL 35486

JORDAN, WILLIAM JOHN, banker; b. Jersey City, Aug. 21, 1919; s. John Thomas and Ethel (Rule) J.; m. Mary Evelyn Kelly, Nov. 14, 1942; children—Janet Mary, William John. Grad., Am. Inst. Banking, 1948, Stonier Grad. Sch. Banking, 1960. Teller Trust Co., N.J., 1937-41; teller Provident Savs. Bank, Jersey City, 1946-50, auditor, 1950, comptroller, 1960-71, v.p., comptroller, 1971-79, sr. v.p., comptroller, 1979—. Served with AUS, 1941-45. Mem. Am. Inst. Banking (past pres. chpt.), Nat. Assn. Bank Auditors and Comptrollers (past pres. N.J. chpt.). Club: Rotarian (treas.). Home: 14 Britton St Jersey City NJ 07306 Office: 239 Washington St Jersey City NJ 07302

JORDAN, WILLIAM STONE, JR., physician, educator; b. Fayetteville, N.C., Sept. 28, 1917; s. William Stone and Louise Manning (Huske) J.; m. Marion Elizabeth Anderson, May 17, 1947; children—William Stone, Marion Anderson. A.B., U. N.C., 1938; M.D., Harvard, 1942. Diplomate: Am. Bd. Preventive Medicine, Am. Bd. Microbiology. Intern, resident Boston City Hosp., 1942-43, 46-47; teaching fellow Univ. Hosps., Cleve., 1947-48; mem. faculty Sch. Medicine, Western Res. U., 1948-58, asso. prof. preventive medicine, asst. prof. medicine, 1954-58; prof. preventive medicine, chmn. dept.

U. Va. Sch. Medicine, also prof. medicine, 1958-67; dean Coll. Medicine, U. Ky., 1967-74, prof. community medicine, prof. medicine, 1967-80; on leave as dir. microbiology and infectious diseases program Nat. Inst. Allergy and Infectious Diseases, NIH, Bethesda, Md., 1976-80; mem. Sr. Exec. Service, 1980—; cons. to surgeon gen. U.S., 1956—; dir. commn. acute respiratory diseases Armed Forces Epidemiol. Bd., 1959-67, mem. bd., 1967-75, 77-81; chmn. panel on respiratory and related viruses NIH, 1960-64, mem. bd. for virus reference reagents, 1962-64, mem. vaccine devel. com., 1967-70; chmn. pub. health and preventive medicine test com. Nat. Bd. Med. Examiners, 1962-65; mem. com. epidemiology and vet. followup studies Nat. Acad. Scis.-NRC, 1965-72; health adv. com. Region III HEW, 1967-71; mem. infectious diseases adv. com. Nat. Inst. Allergy and Infectious Diseases, 1970-71, chmn., 1970-71; sci. adv. com. Nat. Found., 1959-72; mem. panel on rev. viral vaccines and Rickettsial vaccines FDA, Adminstrn., 1973-79. Contbr. sci. papers.; Author: Community Medicine in the United Kingdom, 1978; Editorial bd.: Am. Rev. Respiratory Diseases, 1962-65. Served to lt. USNR, 1943-46. Markle scholar med. sci., 1953-58. Mem. Assn. Am. Physicians, AMA, Am. Acad. Microbiology, Am. Epidemiol. Soc. (pres. 1972-73), AAAS, Am. Thoracic Soc., Infectious Diseases Soc. Am., Am. Assn. Immunologists, Am. Soc. Clin. Investigation, Am. Fedn. Clin. Research, Am. Pub. Health Assn., Am. Soc. Tropical Medicine and Hygiene, Soc. Med. Cons. Armed Forces (pres. 1982-83), Central Soc. Clin. Research (sec.-treas. 1957), So. Soc. Clin. Research, Soc. Exptl. Biology and Medicine, Assn. Tchrs. Preventive Medicine (sec. 1965-67), Internat. Epidemiol. Assn., Royal Soc. Medicine, Assn. Study Med. Edn., Phi Beta Kappa, Sigma Xi, Alpha Omega Alpha, Alpha Tau Omega. Episcopalian.

JORDEN, ELEANOR HARZ, linguist, educator; b. N.Y.C.; d. William George and Eleanor (Funk) Harz; m. William J. Jorden, Mar. 3, 1944 (div.); children: William Temple, Eleanor Harz, Marion Telva. A.B., Bryn Mawr Coll., 1942; M.A., Yale U., 1943, Ph.D., 1950; D.Litt. (hon.), Williams Coll., 1982. Instr. Japanese Yale U., 1943-46, 47-48; dir. Japanese lang. program and Fgn. Service Inst. Lang. Sch., Am. Embassy, Tokyo, 1950-55; sci. linguist Fgn. Service Inst., Dept. State, Washington, 1959-69; acting head Far Eastern langs, 1961-64, chmn., 1964-67, 69, chmn. Vietnamese lang. div., 1967-69; vis. prof. linguistics Cornell U., 1969-70, prof., 1970—, Mary Donlon Alger prof. linguistics, 1974—; dir. Japanese FALCON program, 1972—; guest scholar Wilson Center Smithsonian Instn., 1982; cons., mem. exec. com. Nat. Assn. Self-Instructional Lang. Programs, pres., 1977-78; mem. Fulbright-Hays Com. on Internat. Exchange Scholars, 1972-75; mem. area adv. com. for, East Asia, 1972-76; chmn. Social Sci. Research Council Task Force on Japanese Lang. Tng., 1976-78; mem. adv. com. Japan Found., 1979-81; mem. Lang. Attrition Project, 1981—. Author: (with Bernard Bloch) Spoken Japanese, 1945, Syntax of Modern Colloquial Japanese, 1955, Gateway to Russian, 1961, Beginning Japanese, Part 1, 1962, Part 2, 1963, (with Sheehan, Quang and others) Basic Vietnamese, vols. I, II, 1965, (with Quang) Vietnamese Familiarization Course, 1969, (with Hamako Chaplin) Reading Japanese, 1976. Recipient Superior Service award Dept. State, 1965, Japan Found. and Social Sci. Research Council sr. fellow, 1976; Toyota Twentieth Anniversary Fund grantee, 1978. Mem. Assn. Asian Studies (v.p. 1979-80), Linguistic Soc. Am., Assn. Asian Studies (pres. 1980-81), Am. Council Tchrs. Fgn. Langs., Assn. Tchrs. Japanese (exec. com., pres. 1978-84), Japan Soc. N.Y. (dir. 1982—). Home: 333 N Sunset Dr Ithaca NY 14850 Office: 321 Morrill Hall Cornell U Ithaca NY 14853

JORDEN, WILLIAM JOHN, writer, retired diplomat; b. Bridger, Mont., May 3, 1923; s. Hugh G. and Jane Ann (Temple) J.; m. Eleanor Harz, 1944 (div.); children: William Temple, Eleanor Harz, Marion Telva; m. V. Mildred Xiarhos, 1972. B.A. with honors, Yale, 1947; M.S., Columbia, 1948. Instr. Japanese Yale, 1945-46; reporter Vineyard Gazette, Edgartown, Mass., 1947; radio news writer N.Y. Herald Tribune, 1948; fgn. corr. A.P., Japan and Korea, 1948-52, N.Y. Times, 1952-55, USSR, 1956-58, 1958-61; mem. Policy Planning Council, State Dept., 1961-62, spl. asst. to under sec. polit. affairs, 1962-65, dep. asst. sec. state pub. affairs, 1965-66; sr. mem. staff NSC, 1966-68, 72-74; mem., spokesman Am. del. Vietnam Peace Talks, Paris, France, 1968-69; asst. to former Pres. Lyndon B. Johnson, 1969-72; U.S. ambassador to, Panama, 1974-78; scholar in residence LBJ Library; adj. prof. LBJ Sch. Public Affairs, U. Tex., 1978-80. Author: Panama Odyssey; co-author: Japan Between East and West. Served with AUS, 1943-45. Shared Pulitzer prize for internat. corr., 1958; Recipient Disting. Honor award Dept. State, 1978; Pulitzer traveling fellow, 1948-49; Council Fgn. Relations fellow, 1955-56; Decorated order of Vasco, Nunez de Balboa (Republic of Panama). Mem. Council Fgn. Relations, Council World Affairs. Clubs: Washington Golf and Country, Fgn. Corrs. Japan (pres. 1952-53).

JORDIN, MARCUS WAYNE, educator; b. Idaho Falls, Idaho, May 23, 1927; s. Clair and Mary Ellen (Kyler) J.; m. Ruth Joan Christensen, July 28, 1956; children—Robert, John. B.S. in Pharmacy, Idaho State U., 1949; M.S. (Am. Found. Pharm. Edn. fellow), Purdue U., 1952, Ph.D., 1954. Faculty dept. pharmacology U. Ark., Little Rock, 1954—, prof., 1964—, chmn. dept., 1954—, dir. outpatient pharmacy, 1967—. Served with USNR, 1945-46. Mem. Am. Pharm. Assn., Sigma Xi, Rho Chi, Phi Lambda Upsilon. Presbyn. Home: 309 Brookside Dr Little Rock AR 72205 Office: 4301 W Markham St Little Rock AR 72001

JORDON, ROBERT EARL, physician; b. Buffalo, May 7, 1938; s. James Wallace and Helen Viola (Sampson) J.; m. Mary Ann Michaels, July 12, 1969; children: James H., Kathryn L., Marie H. B.A., Hamilton Coll., 1960; M.D., SUNY-Buffalo, 1965; M.S., U. Minn., 1970. Diplomate: Am. Bd. Dermatology. Intern straight medicine Buffalo Gen. Hosp., 1965-66; resident, fellow in dermatology Mayo Clinic and Mayo Found., Rochester, Minn., 1966-69, asso. cons., 1971-73, cons. dermatology, 1973-77; instr. pathology U. Minn. Hosps., Mpls., 1971-73; Nat. Inst. Arthritis and Metabolic Diseases spl. research fellow U. Minn., 1972-73; asst. prof. dermatology Mayo Grad. Sch. Medicine, Rochester, Minn., 1971-73, Mayo Sch. Medicine, Rochester, 1973-76, asst. prof. immunology, 1974-77, asso. prof. dermatology, 1976-77; prof. medicine, chmn. dermatology Med. Coll. Wis., Milw., 1977-82; med. career investigator VA, 1978-82; chief dermatology Froedtert Meml. Luth. Hosp., Milw., 1980-82; prof., chmn. dept. dermatology U. Tex. Health Sci. Center, Houston; chief dermatology Hermann Hosp., Houston, 1983—; mem. study sect. NIH, 1983—. Mem. editorial bd.: Jour. Investigative Dermatology, 1977-82, Jour. Clin. and Lab. Immunology, 1977—, Archives of Dermatology, 1978—; sect. editor: Am. Jour. Dermatopathology, 1981—. Served to lt. comdr. M.C., USN, 1965-71. Recipient Bacelli Research award SUNY, Buffalo, 1965, Med. Spltys. Outstanding Achievement award Mayo Found., 1969, Marion B. Sulzberger award Am. Soc. Dermatology, Allergy and Immunology, 1983. Mem. Soc. Investigative Dermatology (dir. 1977—), Am. Acad. Dermatology (co-chmn. com. lab. proficiency and quality control in immunodermatology 1980—), AAAS, Am. Assn. Immunologists, Am. Dermatol. Assn., Am. Fedn. Clin. Research, AMA, Am. Soc. Clin. Investigation, Assn. Profs. Dermatology, Central Soc. Clin. Research, Dermatology Found. (chmn. med. and sci. com. 1980-81), Soc. Exptl. Biology and Medicine, Lupus Erythematosus Soc. Wis. (mem. med. adv. bd. 1977—), Wis. Dermatol. Soc. (pres. 1979-80), Wis. State Med. Soc., Chgo. Dermatol. Soc., Sigma Xi. Home: 12319 Huntinguick Houston TX 77024 Office: U Tex Health Sci Center Houston TX

JORDY, WILLIAM HENRY, art history educator; b. Poughkeepsie, N.Y., Aug. 31, 1917; s. Elwood Benjamin and Caroline May (Hill) J.; m. Sarah Stoughton Spock, July 25, 1942. B.A., Bard Coll., 1939, L.H.D., 1968; postgrad., Inst. Fine Arts, NYU, 1939-42; Ph.D., Yale U., 1948. Instr., then asst. prof. art and Am. civilization Yale U., 1948-55; faculty Brown U., Providence, 1955—, prof. art, 1960—, chmn. dept., 1963-66, 76-77. Author: Henry Adams, Scientific Historian, 1952, American Buildings and Their Architects, 2 vols., 1972; editor: (with Ralph Coe) Montgomery Schuyler, American Architecture and Other Writings, 1961; cons.: Arts of the United States, 1960; contbr. articles to profl. jours. Mem. Coll. Art Assn., Soc. Archtl. Historians, Victorian Soc. Home: 55 Bond Rd Riverside RI 02915 Office: Brown U Providence RI 02912

JORGENSEN, CHESTER NEIL, manufacturing company executive; b. Hamilton, Ont., Can., Nov. 30, 1925; s. Chester Daniel and Esther (Purrington) J.; m. Ruth Ann Stamper, July 18, 1970; children: Nancy, Richard, Sue; Kevin Brooks; stepchildren: Pamela Baker, Jeff Hawk. A.B., Dartmouth Coll., 1949; M.S. in Elec. Engring, 1950. With NCR Corp., Dayton, Ohio, 1950—, v.p. terminal systems div., 1975-80, v.p. devel. and prodn. group staff, 1980—. Served with USMC, 1944-46. Mem. Dayton Soc. Profl. Engrs. (Outstanding Achievement award 1970), Engrs. Club Dayton (gov.). Home: 732 Stonybrook Dr Kettering OH 45429 Office: 1700 S Patterson Blvd Dayton OH 45479

JORGENSEN, ERICK, forest pathologist, educator; b. Haderslev, Denmark, Oct. 28, 1921; emigrated to Can., 1955, naturalized, 1960; s. Johannes and Eva Bromberg (Hansen) J.; m. Grete Moller, June 13, 1946; children: Marianne, Brithe. M. Forestry, Royal Vet. and Agrl. Coll., Copenhagen, 1946. Forest pathologist Royal Vet. and Agrl. Coll., Copenhagen, 1948-55; forest pathologist sci. service Agr. Can., 1955-59; asst. prof. U. Toronto, 1959-63, assoc. prof., 1963-67, prof. forest pathology and urban forestry, 1967-73; chief urban forestry program Can Forestry Service, Environ. Can., 1973-78; arboretum dir., prof. environ. biology U. Guelph, Ont., 1978—; cons. in field. Author: The Development of an Urban Forestry Concept, 1967; contbr. articles to sci. jours. Served to 2d lt. Danish Army, 1946-48. Recipient Autors citation Internat. Shade Tree Conf., 1970, Maple Leaf award Internat. Shade Tree conf., 1975, Can. Parents and Devel. Ltd. Inventors cert., 1975. Mem. Ont. Profl. Foresters Assn., Can. Inst. Forestry, Internat. Soc. Arboriculture, Ont. Shade Tree Council (Jaap Salm Meml. award 1975), N.Y. Acad. Scis., AAAS, Sigma Xi. Luteran. Home: 47 Sherwood Dr Guelph ON Canada N1E 6E6 Office: University of Guelph Arboretum Guelph ON Canada N1G 2W1 *A dedication to the application of forest science to the service of mankind.*

JORGENSEN, JOHN W., steel and aluminum manufacturing company executive; b. 1925; married. B.A., Pomona Coll., 1947. With Earle W. Jorgensen Co. Inc., Los Angeles, 1948—; v.p. Earle M. Jorgensen Co. Inc., Los Angeles, 1962-67, pres., chief adminstrv. officer, mem. exec. com., dir., 1967—. Served with USN, World War II. Office: Earle W Jorgensen Co Inc Box 54633 Terminal Annex Los Angeles CA 90054 *

JORGENSEN, JOSEPH GILBERT, anthropology educator; b. Salt Lake City, Apr. 15, 1934; s. Joseph Norman and Clela (Bailey) J.; m. Katherine Will, Aug. 31, 1964; children: Brigham Will, Sarah Katherine. B.S., U. Utah, 1956; Ph.D., Ind. U., 1964. Work camp dir. No. Ute Indian Tribe, 1960-62; asst. prof. anthropology Antioch Coll., Yellow Springs, Ohio, 1964-65; asst. prof. U. Oreg., 1965-68; assoc. prof. U. Mich., Ann Arbor, 1968-71, prof., 1971-74; prof., dir. Program in Comparative Culture, U. Calif., Irvine, 1974—; mem. socioecon. subcom., com. on surface mining and reclamation Nat. Acad. Scis., 1978—; Rufus Wood Leigh lectr. U. Utah, 1982; cons. Lake Powell Research Project, No. Cheyenne Research Project, Calif. Energy Commn. Chmn., Faculty-Student Com. to Stop the War in Vietnam, 1965-67; Bd. dirs. Native Struggles Support Group, Toronto, Human Relations Area Files Internat., New Haven, Anthropology Resource Center, Cambridge. Author: Salish Language and Culture, 1969, The Sun Dance Religion, 1972, Native Americans and Energy Development, 1978, 83, Western Indians, 1980; mem. editorial bd.: Behavior Sci. Research, 1973—, The Indian Historian, 1974—, Southwest Economy and Society, 1976—, Xetetic Scholar, 1976—, Social Sci. Jour, 1978—, Environ. Ethics, 1978—, Social Policy Rev, 1981—; Contbr. articles to N.Y. Rev. of Books, also to profl. jours. Recipient NIH grant, 1966-67, Am. Philos. Soc. grant, 1967, 69, NSF grant, 1970-74, 78-80, C. Wright Mills book award, 1973; Horace H. Rackham fellow, 1972; John Simon Guggenheim fellow, 1974-75; F.O. Butler lectr. S.D. State U., 1976. Mem. AAAS, Am. Indian Hist. Soc., Sigma Xi. Home: 1517 Highland Dr Newport Beach CA 92660 Office: Program in Comparative Culture U Calif Irvine CA 92664

JORGENSEN, NEAL ALBERT, educator, administrator; b. Luck, Wis., Feb. 3, 1935; s. Carl and Frances J.; m. Darlyne Rae Olson, July 3, 1955; 1 dau., Pamela Kay. B.S., U. Wis., River Falls, 1960, M.S., 1962, Ph.D., 1964. Asst. prof. dairy sci. U. Wis., Madison, 1964-66, asso. prof., 1968-73, prof. nutrition, 1973—, assoc. dean, dir. CALS, 1984—; asst. prof. dairy sci. S.D. State U., Brookings, 1966-68; mem. com. on animal nutrition NRC. Served with U.S. Army, 1955-56. Recipient Teaching award of Merit U. Wis., Madison, 1972; award for nutrition research Am. Feed Mfrs. Assn., 1978; Teaching award Ralston Purina Co., 1979. Mem. Am. Dairy Sci. Assn., Am. Soc. Animal Sci., Nutrition Soc., Sigma Xi, Gamma Sigma Delta, Alpha Zeta. Mem. United Ch. of Christ. Club: Kiwanis (Middleton, Wis.) (pres. 1974). Office: Ag Hall U Wis Madison WI 53706

JORGENSEN, PAUL ALFRED, emeritus English language educator; b. Lansing, Mich., Feb. 17, 1916; s. Karl and Rose Josephine (Simmons) J.; m. Virginia Frances Elfrink, Jan. 3, 1942; children: Mary Catherine, Elizabeth Ross (Mrs. Gregory S.E. Howard). A.B., Santa Barbara State Coll., 1938; M.A., U. Calif. at Berkeley, 1940, Ph.D., 1945. Instr. English Bakersfield (Calif.) Jr. Coll., 1945-46, U. Calif., Berkeley, summer 1946, U. Calif., Davis, 1946-47; mem. faculty UCLA, 1947—, prof. English, 1960-81, prof. emeritus, 1981—; vis. prof. U. Wash., summer 1966; mem. editorial com. U. Calif. Press, 1957-60; mem. Humanities Inst. U. Calif., 1967-69; mem. acad. adv. council Shakespeare Globe Ctr. N.Am. Author: Shakespeare's Military World, 1956, (with Frederick B. Shroyer) A College Treasury, rev. edit, 1967, (with Shroyer) The Informal Essay, 1961, Redeeming Shakespeare's Words, 1962; Editor: The Comedy of Errors, 1964, Othello: An Outline- Guide to the Play, 1964, (with Shroyer) The Art of Prose, 1965, Lear's Self-Discovery, 1967, Our Naked Frailties; Sensational Art and Meaning in Macbeth, 1971; Mem. bd. editors: Film Quar, 1958-65, Huntington Library Quar, 1965-83, Coll. English, 1966-70; mem. adv. com.: Publs. of MLA of Am, 1978-82. Guggenheim fellow, 1956-57; Regents' Faculty fellow in humanities, 1973-74. Mem. Modern Lang. Assn., Shakespeare Assn. Am. (bibliographer 1954-59), Renaissance Soc. Am., Philol. Assn., Pacific Coast (exec. com. 1962-63). Episcopalian. Home: 234 Tavistock Ave Los Angeles CA 90049

JORGENSEN, WILLIAM ERNEST, ret. librarian; b. Heber, Utah, Oct. 13, 1913; s. George Michael and Mary Annette (Jackman) J.; m. Margaret Louise Boyle, May 25, 1940; children—Robert Ernest, Barry Steven, Mollie Ann. B.A. summa cum laude, U. Idaho, 1938; certificate librarianship, U. Calif. at Berkeley, 1940; M.A., Oreg. State U., 1942. Engring. librarian Oreg. State U., 1940-42; supr. tech. data sect., frequency change dept. So. Calif. Edison Co., 1945-46; chief librarian research library Naval Electronics Lab. Center, San Diego, 1946-74; dir. Research Info. Services, 1974—; John Cotton Dana lectr. U. Calif. at Los Angeles, 1964; Mem. investment bd. Coronado Mgmt. Corp., 1970-72; Mem. inter-library task group San Diego Ednl. Resources Project, 1960-74; library com. Fine Arts Soc., San Diego, 1965-67; chmn. 10th Mil. Librarians Workshop, 1966; mem. Navy Research Library Council W. Coast, 1955-74; expert examiner U.S. Civil Service Examiners for So. Calif. Navy Labs., 1951-68; mem. Com. for Asso. Sci. Libraries San Diego, 1963-74; adv. council edn. for Librarianship U. Calif., Berkeley, Los Angeles, 1965-68; mem. San Diego Met. Area Library Council, 1973-74; vice chmn. library com. U. Calif. at San Diego Sch. Medicine Assos., 1974-77, treas., 1977-78. Author: The Use of a Technical Library, 1942, Naval Electronics Laboratory Reliability Bibliography, 1956-58, Navy Electronics Laboratory and the Point Loma Military Reservation, A Collection of Historical Photographs, 1966; Editor: procs.: Tenth Military Librarians Workshop, 1966; Contbr. articles to profl. jours. Bd. dirs. San Diego chpt. ACLU, 1971-73. Served to lt. comdr. USNR, 1942-45; comdr. Res.; ret. Mem. Calif. Library Assn. (pres. Palomar dist. 1963, councilor 1967-70), Spl. Libraries Assn. (chmn. engring. sect. 1950), U. Calif. Schs. Librarianship Alumni Assn. (pres. 1963), San Diego Writers Assn., Phi Beta Kappa, Phi Kappa Phi. Home: 575 Twin View Ln Soquel CA 95073

JORGENSON, DALE WELDEAU, economist, educator; b. Bozeman, Mont., May 7, 1933; s. Emmett B. and Jewell (Torkelson) J.; m. Linda Ann Mabus, July 27, 1971; children: Eric Mabus, Kari Ann. B.A., Reed Coll., 1955; A.M., Harvard U., 1957, Ph.D., 1959. Mem. faculty U. Calif., Berkeley, 1959-69, prof. econs., 1963-69, Harvard U., 1969-80, Frederic Eaton Abbe prof. econs., 1980—; Ford research prof. econs. U. Chgo., 1962-63. Author: (with J.J. McCall, R. Radner) Optimal Replacement Policy, 1967, Econometric Studies of U.S. Energy Policy, 1975; Contbr. articles profl. jours. Fellow Econometric Soc., Am. Statis. Assn., Am. Acad. Arts and Scis.; mem. Am. Econ. Assn. (John Bates Clark medal 1971), Nat. Acad. Scis., Royal Econ. Soc. Home: 1010 Memorial Dr Cambridge MA 02138

JORGENSON, WALLACE JAMES, broadcasting executive; b. Mpls., Oct. 31, 1923; s. Peter and Adelia Henrietta (Bong) J.; m. Solveig Elizabeth Tvedt, Feb. 24, 1945; children: Kristin, Peter, Mark, Philip, Lisa. Student, St. Olaf Coll., 1941-43, Gustavus Adolphus Coll., 1943; B.A., Bowling Green State U., 1944; L.H.D., Lenoir-Rhyne Coll., 1971. Staff announcer Sta. WCAL, Northfield, Minn., 1941-43; sta. mgr. Sta. KTRF, Thief River Falls, Minn., 1946-48; with Sta. WBT, Charlotte, 1952-67, v.p., asst. gen. mgr., 1966-67; exec. v.p. Jefferson-Pilot Broadcasting Co., Charlotte, 1966-78, pres., 1978—, also dir.; dir. Charlotte br. Fed. Res. Bank; Chmn. mgmt. com. Office for Communications, Lutheran Ch. in Am., 1978—. Pres.-elect United Way campaign, 1978; bd. govs. ARC, 1977-83; chmn. Red Cross Centennial, 1981; trustee Lenoir-Rhyne Coll., 1963-81, chmn., 1971-77; bd. dirs. Central Piedmont Community Coll. Found., 1980—; bd. visitors Davidson Coll., 1979—. Served with USMC, 1943-46. Recipient silver medal award Charlotte Advt. Club, 1975; Abe Lincoln award So. Baptist Conv., 1975; Communications award N.C. Council Chs., 1976; Harriman award ARC, 1982. Mem. Broadcast Pioneers, Nat. Assn. Broadcasters, Am. Mgmt. Assn., N.C. Assn. Broadcasters, Assn. Maximum Service Telecasters (chmn.), U.S. C. of C. (public affairs com.), Greater Charlotte C. of C. (chmn.). Republican. Clubs: Quail Hollow Country, Charlotte City, Broadcasters (Washington). Home: 2742 Meade Ct Charlotte NC 28211 Office: 1 Julian Price Pl Charlotte NC 28208

JORGENSON, WILLIAM LLOYD, manufacturing company executive; b. Phila., Dec. 12, 1942; s. James K. and Mary Jane (Stewart) J.; children by previous marriage: Susan, Todd. B.A., Colgate U., 1965; postgrad., Oslo U., 1966. Mem. mktg. staff Colgate Palmolive Co., 1965-69; with Quaker Oats Co., Chgo., 1969-81, v.p., dir., S. Am. and Central Am., 1974-81; pres., chief operating officer The Terson Co., Inc., Chgo., 1981—; Bd. dirs. Corp. Fund for Dance, Partners of the Americas. Author: Executive Corporate Handbook, 1974, Corporate Profiles, 1975. Office: 310 S Michigan St Chicago IL 60604

JORTBERG, ROBERT FRANCIS, retired naval officer; b. Portland, Maine, Feb. 2, 1926; s. Charles Augustus and Adelaide Cecelia (Mahoney) J.; m. Kathleen Ann Farrell, May 8, 1948; children—Robert Francis, Anna Mary, Christina Francesca. B.S., U.S. Naval Acad., 1947; B.C.E., Rensselaer Poly. Inst., Troy, N.Y., 1951, M.S. in Mgmt, 1958. Commd. ensign U.S. Navy, 1947, advanced through grades to rear adm., 1974; chief staff officer (30th Naval Constrn. Regt.), Vietnam, 1966-67, S.E. Asia program mgr., 1967-69, pub. works officer, dep. supt. mgmt., 1969-72; officer charge constrn. Dept. Def. contracts, Vietnam, 1972; comdr. officer Western div. Naval Facilities Engring. Command, San Bruno, Calif., 1973-74; dir. shore facilities div. Office Chief Naval Ops., Washington, 1974-79, ret., 1979; with Lummus Co. (engrs. and constructors), Bloomfield, N.J., 1979—, v.p. constrn., 1983—. Decorated Legion of Merit (2), D.S.M., Meritorious Service medal, Bronze Star. Mem. Soc. Am. Mil. Engrs., U.S. Naval Inst., Tau Beta Pi, Chi Epsilon. Roman Catholic. Home: 34 Hideaway Ln Sparta NJ 07871

JOSE, JAMES ROBERT, food services company executive; b. Pitts., Jan. 7, 1939; s. John Frederick and Helen Louise (Hunter) J.; m. Joyce Ann Mosser, June 10, 1961; children: Anna Mansfield, Andrew Douglass. B.A., Mt. Union Coll., 1960; M. Internat. Relations, Am. U., 1962, Ph.D., 1968. Registrar, adminstrv. asst. to academic dean, instr. polit. sci. Mt. Union Coll., 1963-65; asst. dean, asst. prof. internat. relations Am. U., 1965-70; dean of coll., prof. polit. sci. Lycoming Coll., 1970-79; v.p., dir. adminstrn. Food Services, Inc., 1979—; vis. lectr. U.S. Mil. Acad., Fgn. Service Inst., U.S. Dept. State. Author: An Inter-American Peacekeeping Force Within the Framework of the Organization of American States, 1970; contbr. to: America's World Role in the 70's (A.A. Said, editor), 1970, Reducing the Dropout Rate (L. Noel, editor), 1978; contbr. articles to profl. jours. Named Outstanding Young Man Am. U.S. Jaycees, 1967. Mem. Phi Kappa Phi, Pi Gamma Mu, Phi Sigma Alpha, Delta Phi Epsilon, Alpha Phi Omega, Blue Key. Home: 7025 Madelynne Way Anchorage AK 99504

JOSEL, NATHAN ABRAM, librarian; b. New Orleans, Sept. 28, 1941; s. Nathan A. and Elise (Goldberger) J.; m. Jacqualine M. Nielsen, Dec. 15, 1979; children: Laura P., Nathan Abram, III. B.A., Tulane U., 1963; M.S., La. State U., 1965. Mem. staff Enoch Pratt Free Library, Balt., 1965-69; head history and travel dept. Memphis-Shelby County Pub. Library, 1969-74; asst. dir. Madison (Wis.) Pub. Library, 1974-80; dir. El Paso (Tex.) Pub. Library, 1980—; lectr. U. Wis. Library Sch., 1975-79. Author articles in field, chpts. on reference books. Commnr. Shelby Country Hist. Records Commn., 1972-74, Shelby County Hist. Commn., 1973-74. Mem. ALA, Tex. Library Assn., S.W. Library Assn., Border Regional Library Assn. Office: 501 N Oregon St El Paso TX 79901

JOSELYN, JO ANN, space scientist; b. St. Francis, Kans., Oct. 5, 1943; d. James Jacob and JosephineFelzien (Firjins) Cram. B.S. in Applied Math., U. Colo., 1965; research asst., NASA-Manned Space Ctr., Houston, 1966; physicist, NOAA-Space Environ. Lab., Boulder, Colo., 1967-78, space scientist, 1978—. Recipient NOAA unit citation, 1971, 80. Mem. Am. Geophys. Union, Union Radio Sci. Internat., Internat. Union Geodesy and Geophysics, Assn. Geomagnetism and Aeronomy, AAAS, AAUW, Assn. Fed. Profl. and Adminstrv. Women, PEO, Sigma Xi, Tau Beta Pi, Sigma Tau. Republican. Methodist. Office: NOAA-Space Environ Lab 325 Broadway St Boulder CO 80303

JOSEPH, ALLAN JAY, lawyer; b. Chgo., Feb. 4, 1938; s. George S. and Emily (Miller) Cohen; m. Phyllis L. Freedman, Sept. 1, 1958; children—Elizabeth, Susan, Katherine. B.B.A., U. Wis., Madison, 1959; J.D. cum laude, 1962. Bar: Wis. bar 1962, Calif. bar 1964. Partner firm Pettit & Martin, San Francisco, 1965-80, Rogers, Joseph, O'Donnell & Quinn, 1981—. Served to capt. JACG AUS, 1962-65. Am. Bar Found. fellow, 1978—. Mem. Am. Bar Assn. (nat. chmn. public contract law sect. 1977-78, ho. of dels. 1980—), State Bar of Calif., Nat. Contract Mgmt. Assn., Fed. Bar Assn., Order of Coif. Home: 2461 Washington San Francisco CA Office: 505 Sansome St San Francisco CA 94111

JOSEPH, BURTON M., grain merchant; b. Mpls., Apr. 2, 1921; s. I.S. and Anna J.; m. Geraldine, Apr. 2, 1953; children—Shelley, Scott, Jonathan. B.A., U. Minn., 1942. Vice pres. I.S. Joseph Co., Inc., Mpls., 1945-53, pres., 1953-80, chmn. bd., 1980—; mem. agrl. policy adv. com. for trade U.S. Dept. Agr., 1980—. Commr. Duluth Port Authority, Mpls. Human Relations Commn.; treas. Nat. Commn. Anti-Defamation League, 1969-76; nat. chmn. Anti-Defamation League of B'nai B'rith, 1976-78, hon. nat. chmn., 1978; trustee Am. Freedom from Hunger Found.; trustee, bd. govs. Hebrew Union Coll.-Jewish Inst. Religion, 1970-75, vice chmn., 1976. Home: 5 Red Cedar Ln Minneapolis MN 55410 Office: Grain Exchange Bldg Minneapolis MN 55415

JOSEPH, DANIEL DONALD, educator, aero. engr.; b. Chgo., Mar. 26, 1929; s. Samuel and Mary (Simon) J.; m. Ellen Broida, Dec. 18, 1949; children—Karen, Michael, Charles. M.A. in Sociology, U. Chgo., 1950; B.S. in Mech. Engring, Ill. Inst. Tech., 1959, M.S., 1960, Ph.D., 1963. Asst. prof. mech. engring. Ill. Inst. Tech., 1962-63; mem. faculty U. Minn., 1963—, asso. prof. fluid mechanics, 1965-69, prof. aerospace engring. and mechanics, 1969—. Editor: SIAM Jour. Applied Math; Contbr. articles to sci. jours. Guggenheim fellow, 1969-70. Mem. Am. Phys. Soc., ASME, Soc. Nat. Philol. Asso. Contbns. to math. theory of hydrodynamic stability; rheology of viscoelastic fluids. Home: 19 S 1st St B1606 Minneapolis MN 55401 Office: Dept Aerospace Engring U Minn Minneapolis MN 55455

JOSEPH, DAVID J., JR., trading company executive; b. Cin., June 5, 1916; s. David J. and Emilie A. (Aram) J.; m. Josephine Iglauer, June 22, 1940; children: David I., Helen E. Joseph Richfield. B.A., Yale U., 1938. With David J. Joseph Co., Cin., 1938—, pres., 1945-78, chmn. bd., 1978—, also dir.; dir. SHV N.Am. Corp.; gen. mgr., group dir. SHV Holdings, NV, The Netherlands. Home: 1763 E McMillan St Cincinnati OH 45206 Office: SHV NAm Corp 300 Pike St PO Box 85331 Cincinnati OH 45202

JOSEPH, EDWARD DAVID, psychiatrist; b. Pitts., Aug. 26, 1919; s. A. Pinto and Hortense (Ury) J.; m. Harriet Bloomfield, Aug. 16, 1942; children: Leila, Alan, Brian. B.Sc., McGill U., 1941, M.D., C.M., 1943; postgrad., N.Y. Psychoanalytic Inst., 1949-55. Intern Montreal (Que., Can.) Gen. Hosp., 1943-44; resident, fellow in psychiatry Mt. Sinai Hosp., N.Y.C., 1947-49, coordinator in-patient psychiat. service, 1965-71, clin. dir. psychiatry, 1971-76, vice chmn., 1976-78; attending psychiatrist, 1949—, practice medicine, specializing in psychiatry and psychoanalysis, N.Y.C., 1949—; tng. analyst N.Y. Psychoanalytic Inst., 1964—, lectr., 1962—; prof. psychiatry Mt. Sinai Med. Sch., N.Y.C., 1968—. Editor: Kris Monograph Series, 1965—; asso. editor: Psychoanalytic Quar, 1965-77, Jour. Am. Psychoanalytic Assn, 1977—; Contbr. articles profl. jours. Served to capt., M.C. AUS, 1944-46. Mem. Am. Psychoanalytic Assn. (exec. councilor 1962-67, treas. 1967-72, pres. 1972-73, 83—), Internat. Psychoanalytic Assn. (treas. 1973-77, pres. 1977-81), N.Y. Psychoanalytic Soc. (sec. 1965-67, v.p. 1975-77), Am. Psychiat. Assn., A.A.A.S., Westchester Mental Health Assn. Club: Town (Scarsdale). Home: 9 Putnam Rd Scarsdale NY 10583 Office: 1 E 100th St New York City NY 10029

JOSEPH, FREDERICK HAROLD, investment banker; b. Boston, Apr. 22, 1937; s. Edward M. and Sarah (Mostowitz) J.; m. Susan Ferran, Aug. 27, 1960; children—Melissa, Melinda, Amy, Tommi Beth, Mark. B.A., Harvard, 1959, M.B.A., 1963. With E.F. Hutton Co., N.Y.C., 1963-70, Shearson Hamill Co., 1970-74; with Drexel Burnham Lambert Inc., N.Y.C., 1974—, sr. exec. v.p., 1981—. Served with USNR, 1959-61. Home: 19 Euclid Ave Maplewood NJ 07040 Office: 60 Broad St New York City NY 10004

JOSEPH, GERI M., former ambassador; b. St. Paul, June 19, 1923. B.S., U. Minn., 1946; LL.D. (hon.), Bates Coll., 1982. Staff writer Mpls. Tribune, 1946-53, contbg. editor, 1972-78; ambassador to The Netherlands, The Hague, 1978-81; dir. internat. program devel. Hubert H. Humphrey Inst. Pub. Affairs, U. Minn.; dir. Norwest Bank, George A. Hormel Co., Honeywell, Twin City Barge Inc.; Mem. U.S. Pres.'s Commn. on Mental Health; mem. Minn. Supreme Ct. Commn. on Mentally Disabled and the Cts. Mem. Gov.'s Commn. on Taxation, 1983—; trustee Carleton Coll., 1975—; mem. Democratic Nat. Com., 1960-72, vice chmn., 1968-72; co-chairperson Minn. Women's Campaign Fund, 1982—.

JOSEPH, JAMES ALFRED, foundation executive; b. Opelousas, La., Mar. 12, 1935; s. Adam and Julia Lee (Jones) J.; m. Doris Taylor, June 27, 1959; children: Jeffrey, Denise. B.A., So. U., 1956; M.Div., Yale U., 1963; L.H.D. (hon.), Shaw U., 1972, LL.D., Fla. Meml. U., 1979. Ordained to ministry United Ch. Christ, 1963; asso. dir. Assn. of Founds., Columbus, Ind., 1967-69; chaplain Claremont (Calif.) Colls., 1969-70; exec. dir. Irwin-Sweeney-Miller Found., Columbus, 1970-72; v.p. Cummins Engine Co., 1972-77, 81—; also pres. Cummins Found., Columbus, 1972-77; under sec. U.S. Dept. Interior, Washington, 1977-81; chmn. Commn. on No. Mariana Islands, 1980—; pres., chief exec. officer Council on Founds.; mem. faculty Stillman Coll., Tuscaloosa, Ala., 1963-64, Pitzer Coll., Claremont, 1966, Claremont Sch. Theology, 1970, Yale U., 1981—; mem. adv. com. Nat. Sci. Acad., AID. Contbr. to profl. publs.; co-editor: Three Perspectives on Ethnicity, 1976. Chmn. Spl. Commn. on Racism and Devel., World Council Chs., Geneva, U.S. del. to UN Conf. in Kenya, Bilateral Consultation with Mex. Pres. Claremont Intercultural Council, 1965-67; mem. City Park and Recreation Commn., Claremont, 1965-67; pres. Nat. Black United Fund; bd. dirs. Pitzer Coll., Opportunity Funding Corp., Union Theol. Sem., N.Y.C., African-Am. Inst. N.Y., Children's Def. Fund, New Transcentury Found.; bd. visitors Inst. Policy Scis., Duke U. Served to 1st lt., Med. Service Corps U.S. Army, 1956-58. Fellow Met. Applied Research Center, N.Y.C., 1958. Mem. Assn. Black Found. Execs. (chmn. 1970-76), Council Fgn. Relations, Alpha Phi Alpha. Home: 8013 Snowpine Way McLean VA 22102 Office: 2550 M St NW Suite 500 Washington DC 20037

JOSEPH, JOHN, history educator; b. Baghdad, Iraq, Sept. 1, 1923; came to U.S., 1946, naturalized, 1961; s. Joseph Shukur and Rebecca (Alkhas) J.; m. Beatrice Paul Malick, July 20, 1956; children: Paul Faris, Lawrence John, Deena Rebecca. B.A., Franklin and Marshall Coll., 1950; M.A., Princeton U., 1953, Ph.D., 1957. Instr. Princeton U., 1956-58, lectr., 1958-59; assoc. prof. history Thiel Coll., Greenville, Pa., 1960-61; assoc. prof. Franklin and Marshall Coll., Lancaster, Pa., 1964-69, prof. history, 1969—, Lewis Audenried prof. history and archaeology, 1972. Author: The Nestorians and Their Muslim Neighbors, 1961, Muslim-Christian Relations and Inter-Christian Rivalries in the Middle East, 1983. Recipient award Christian R. and Mary F. Lindback Found., 1978; fellow Ford Found., 1954-56, NEH, 1979; grantee Am. Council Learned Socs.-Social Sci. Research Council Joint Com., 1966-67. Fellow Middle East Studies Assn.; mem. Am. Hist. Assn., Am. Oriental Soc., Middle East Inst., Phi Beta Kappa. Democrat. Home: 952 Virginia Ave Lancaster PA 17603 Office: Franklin and Marshall Coll College Ave Lancaster PA 17604

JOSEPH, JULES K., public relations exec.; b. Cin., Jan. 18, 1926; s. Leslie Bloch and Ellen (Kaufman) J.; m. Elizabeth Levy, Sept. 9, 1948; children—Ellen Beth, Barbara Ann, John Charles. B.A., U. Wis., 1947. Reporter Cin. Enquirer, 1946; asst. editor Hosp. Mgmt., Chgo., 1947-48; mem. press relations staff Gimbels, Milw., 1948-52; bur. chief Fairchild Publs., Milw., 1952-60; co-founder, co-owner, pres. Zigman-Joseph-Skeen Assos. in Pub. Relations, Milw., 1960—; opened Zigman-Joseph, N.Y., 1968. Pres. Friends of Art of Milw. Art Center, 1961-62; v.p. Milwaukee County Mental Health, 1967; bd. dirs. Milw. Repertory Theatre, Camp Webb, Whitefish Bay Civic Improvement Found., St. John's Home for the Aged, Milw., DePaul Hosp.; trustee Layton Sch. Art and Design, Milw.; bd. dirs. Wis. Olympics Com. Mem. Pub. Relation Soc. Am. (accredited; treas. Wis. 1970-71, del. 1976-77, task force on consumerism), Sigma Delta Chi, Phi Kappa Phi. Episcopalian. Home: 5028 N Lake Dr Milwaukee WI 53217 Office: 700 N Water St Milwaukee WI 53202 *During my first job (summer '47) as a reporter on the Cincinnati Enquirer I was told off for not getting the story. I have translated this to mean there's no excuse for not getting the job done—or reaching your goal.*

JOSEPH, LEONARD, lawyer; b. Phila., June 8, 1919; s. Harry L. and Mary (Pollock) J.; m. Norma Hamberg, 1942; children—Gilbert M., Stuart A., Janet H. B.A., U. Pa., 1941; LL.B., Harvard U., 1947. Bar: N.Y. bar 1949. Since practiced in, N.Y.C.; partner firm Dewey, Ballantine, Bushby, Palmer & Wood, 1957—. Served with AUS, 1943-46. Fellow Am. Bar Found., Am. Coll. Trial Lawyers; mem. Am. Bar Assn., N.Y. State Bar Assn., Bar Assn. City of N.Y. Clubs: Harvard, Wall St. (N.Y.C.). Office: 140 Broadway New York NY 10005

JOSEPH, MARJORY L., home economics educator; b. Milan, Ohio, Oct. 10, 1917; d. Ernest J. and Bertha (Allyn) Lockwood; m. William D. Joseph, Aug. 11, 1941; 1 dau., Nancy-Joyce. B.S., Ohio State U., 1939; M.S., 1952; Ph.D., Pa. State U., 1962. Supr. alteration dept. Collegienne Shop, Lazarus Dept. Store, Columbus, Ohio, 1939-41; ind. designing and constrn. original design clothing, 1941-44; supr. workrooms custom designing shop Ruth Harris, Inc., N.Y.C., 1944-46; mgr., co-owner MarJay Co., Milan, 1946-48; tchr. secondary schs., Ohio, 1948-51; teaching asso. textile div. Ohio State U. Sch. Home Econs., 1951-52; instr. to asso. prof. Juniata Coll., Huntingdon, Pa., 1952-62; part-time instr. in clothing and textiles research Pa. State U., 1957-62; asso. prof. home econs. Calif. State U., Northridge, 1962-66, prof., 1966—, chmn. home econs. dept., 1969-82; cons. textile fiber and fabric care So. Calif. Gas Co., Los Angeles, Springs Mills, Inc., Ft. Mill, S.C., U.S. Borax Co., Los Angeles. Author: Introductory Textile Science, 1966, 4th edit., 1981, Illustrated Guide to Textiles, 1973, 3d edit., 1981, Essentials of Textiles, 2d edit., 1980, 3d edit., 1984, (with W.D. Joseph) Essentials of Research Methodology and Evaluation in Home Economics, 1975, Research Fundamentals in Home Economics, 1979, 2d edit., 1984; contr. articles to profl. jours. Recipient Disting. Alumni award Ohio State U., 1972. Mem. Am. Assn. Textile Chemists and Colorists, ASTM, Am. Home Econs. Assn., Elec. Women's Round Table, Omicron Nu, Sigma Delta Epsilon. Home: 10612 Collett Ave Granada Hills CA 91344 Office: 18111 Nordhoff St Northridge CA 91330

JOSEPH, RAMON RAFAEL, physician, educator; b. N.Y.C., May 17, 1930; s. Felix R. and Helen (Espinet) J.; m. Mary Ann Kowalchik, June 16, 1956; children: Ricardo George, Maria Ann, Lisa Marie. B.S., Manhattan Coll., 1952; M.D., Cornell U., 1956. Diplomate: Nat. Bd. Med. Examiners, Am. Bd. Internal Medicine. Intern Meadowbrook Hosp., Hempstead, N.Y., 1956-57, resident, 1957, Wayne County Gen. Hosp., Westland, Mich., 1959-62, dir. gastroenterology, 1962—, asst. dir. internal medicine, 1964-73, dir., 1973—, pres. med. staff, 1971-72; practice medicine specializing in internal medicine and gastroenterology, 1962—; cons. Annapolis Hosp., 1962—; instr. internal medicine U. Mich., 1962-65, asst. prof., 1965-69, asso. prof., 1969-74, prof., 1975—, asst. dean, 1973—; 1st v.p.-dir. Univ. Med. Affiliates (P.C.), 1981—; cons. gastroenterology St. Mary Hosp., Livonia, Mich., 1966—. Contbr. articles to profl. jours. Mem. Community Commn. on Drug Abuse, Livonia and Westland, Mich., 1970-73; mem. Mich. Dept. Edn. Council on Drug Abuse; cons. on drug abuse public schs., Livonia cons. on drug abuse public schs., 1968-74; pres. Livonia Sch. Bd. Adv. Council, 1970-71. Served as capt. U.S. Army, 1957-59. Fell. ACP; mem. Am. Fedn. Clin. Research, Am. Gastroent., Assn., AAAS, Assn. Am. Med. Colls., AMA, N.Y. Acad. Sci., Detroit Gastroent. Soc. (pres. 1969-70), Mich., Wayne County med. socs., Am. Assn. Lab. Animal Sci., Am. Soc. Gastrointestinal Endoscopy, Am. Soc. Internal Medicine, Mich. Soc. Gastrointestinal Endocsopy (pres. 1982—), Mich. Soc. Internal Medicine, Assn. Program Dirs. in Internal Medicine. Roman Catholic. Home: 5593 Stratford Dr West Bloomfield MI 48033 Office: Wayne County Gen Hosp Westland MI 48185 U Mich Med Sch Ann Arbor MI 48104 PO Box 2625 Livonia MI 48151

JOSEPHS, JESS J., educator, physicist; b. N.Y.C., Jan. 4, 1917; s. Jacob I. and Mollie (Barouch) J.; m. Margaret Milroy Lewis, June 22, 1962; children—John Lewis III (stepson), Kenneth, Nancy Lewis (stepdau.), David. A.B., N.Y. U., 1938, M.Sc., 1940, Ph.D., 1943. Instr. phys. chemistry Northwestern U., 1946-47; asst. prof. phys. scis. U. Chgo., 1947-50; asst. prof. physics Boston U., 1950-56; asst. dir. upper Atmosphere Physics Lab., Boston U., 1951-54; prof. physics Smith Coll., 1956—, chmn. physics dept., 1977—; staff cons. Lincoln Labs., Mass. Inst. Tech., 1956-59, Mitre Corp., 1960-62. Author: The Physics of Musical Sound, 1967; Contbr. to Ency. Physics, 1967, 73. Bd. overseers Williston Northampton Sch., 1970-73. Served with USNR, 1943-46. Mem. Am. Phys. Soc., Am. Assn. Physics Tchrs., Acoustical Soc. Am., Audio Engring. Soc., Sigma Xi, Phi Lambda Upsilon. Home: 56 Ward Ave Northampton MA 01060

JOSEPHS, RAY, public relations consultant, writer; b. Phila., Jan. 1, 1912; s. Isaac and Eva (Borsky) J.; m. Juanita Wegner, Feb. 22, 1941. Student, U. Pa., 1927-29. Staff writer Phila. Evening Bull., 1929-40; columnist Buenos Aires Herald, 1940-44; Latin-Am. corr., 1940—; representing at various times Wash. Post, Christian Sci. Monitor, Pitts. Post-Gazette, Newark Star Ledger, Chgo. Sun, P.M., Variety, Nat. Monthly, others; chmn. Internat. Pub. Relations Co., Ltd., N.Y.; chmn. bd. Ray Josephs-David E Levy, Inc.; pub. relations counsel maj. industries, comml. concerns; regional v.p. Internat. Public Relations Group; dir. Concorde News Bur., N.Y.C.; Lectr. Columbia Inst. Arts and Scis., Ind. U., Cornell Coll., Sweet Briar, Union Coll., Town Hall of West, San Francisco, Detroit, Indpls., Atlanta, Louisville, Spokane, Los Angeles Town Halls, numerous forums, town meetings from coast to coast; broadcaster NBC, CBS, MBS; cons. on Latin Am. affairs to coordinator Inter-Am. Affairs Brit. Ministry Information, RKO Radio Pictures, Asso. Export Adv. Agys. Author: Argentine Diary, 1944, Spies and Saboteurs in Argentina, 1943, Latin America: Continent in Crisis, 1948, Those Perplexing Argentines, 1952, How to Make Money from Your Ideas, 1954, How to Gain an Extra Hour Every Day, 1955, (with David Kemp) Memoirs of a Live Wire, 1956, Streamlining Your Executive Workload, 1958, (with Oscar Steiner) Our Housing Jungle and Your Pocketbook, 1960, (with Stanley Arnold) The Magic Power of Putting Yourself Over with People, 1962 (books pub. in Brit., French, Japanese, Spanish, Italian, German edits). Mem. Brandeis U. Devel. Council. Mem. Writers Guild Am., Public Relations Soc. Am. (charter, accredited), Soc. Mag. Writers. Clubs: American (Buenos Aires); Overseas Press (N.Y.C.). Home: 860 United Nations Plaza New York NY 10017 Office: 230 Park Ave New York NY 10169

JOSEPHSON, BRIAN DAVID, physicist, educator; b. 1940. Attended, U. Cambridge, Eng. Research prof. U. Ill., 1965-66; prof. physics U. Cambridge, 1974—. Recipient Nobel prize for Physics, 1973. Fellow Royal Soc. London (Eng.), Inst. Physics; fgn. mem. Am. Acad. Arts and Scis. Office: Cavendish Lab Madingley Rd Cambridge CB3 0HE England

JOSEPHSON, JOSEPH PAUL, lawyer; b. Trenton, N.J., June 3, 1933; s. David S. and Jenny (Randelman) J.; children: Peter, Andrew, Sarah. B.A., U. Chgo., 1953; J.D., Cath. U. Am., 1960. Bar: Alaska 1961. Since practiced in, Anchorage, Legis. asst. to territorial del. and U.S. Senator from Alaska, Washington, 1957-60; mem. Alaska Ho. of Reps., Juneau, 1963-67; acting mayor, Anchorage, 1968; mem. Alaska Senate, 1969-72, 83, chmn. senate majority caucus, chmn. com. on health, edn. and social services, 1983; co-chmn. Joint Fed.-State Land Use Planning Commn. for Alaska, 1972-74; assemblyman Municipality of Anchorage, 1980-82; lectr. Alaska Pacific U., 1983. Editorial bd.: Cath. U. Am. Law Rev, 1959-60; columnist: Anchorage Daily News, 1976-79; contbg. editor: Alaska Bar Assn. Newspaper. Chmn. South Central Alaska ARC, 1964-65; Candidate U.S. Senate, 1970; mem., dep. chmn. Greater Anchorage Charter Commn., 1975-76. Served with AUS, 1955-57. Mem. Am., Alaska, Anchorage bar assns., Am. Arbitration Assn. (arbitrator 1977—). Democrat. Home: 1526 F St Anchorage AK 99501 Office: 425 G St Anchorage AK 99501

JOSEPHSON, KENNETH BRADLEY, educator, artist; b. Detroit, July 1, 1932; s. Ernest Gustav and Hilda Christine (Wick) J.; m. Carol A. Comdeau, Feb., 1954 (div. Apr. 1958); m. Sherill A. Petro, Oct. 28, 1960 (div. 1960); children: Matthew W. (dec.), Bradley J., Anissa C.; m. Sally D. Garen, Jan. 30, 1973 (div. 1978). B.F.A. Inst. Design, Ill. Inst. Tech., 1957, M.S., 1960. Photographer Chrysler Corp., Detroit, 1957-58; exchange tchr. Konstfackskolan, Stockholm, 1966-67; assoc. prof. U. Hawaii, Honolulu, 1967-68; vis. prof. Tyler Sch. Art, Temple U., Phila., 1975, UCLA, 1981-82; prof. art Sch. Art Inst., Chgo., 1960—; fellowship panelist Nat. Endowment Arts, Washington, 1975. Artist one-man shows, Art Inst., Chgo, 1971, Visual Studies Workshop, Rochester, N.Y., U. Iowa Mus. Art, Iowa City, 1974, 291 Galery, Milan, Cameraworks Gallery, Los Angeles, 1976, Reicher Gallery, Barat Coll., Lake Forest, Ill., 1977, Fotoforum, Kassel, Germany, 1978, Photographer's Gallery, London, 1979, Delpire Galerie, Paris, 1981, Young Hoffman Gallery, Chgo., Swen Parson Gallery, No. Ill. U., 1983, Retrospective Exhbn. Mus. Contemporary Art, Chgo., group shows, Fla. State Mus., Gainesville, 1965, Sheldon Meml. Art Gallery, Lincoln, 1968, Fogg Art Mus., Harvard U., 1967, Eastman House, Rochester and Nat. Gallery of Can., Ottawa, Mus. Contemporary Crafts, N.Y.C., 1971, Corcoran Gallery, 1972, Art Inst., Chgo., 1973, Walker Art Ctr., Mpls., Madison Art Ctr., Mus. Art, Indpls., Incontri Internazionali d'Arte, Prcheggio di Villa Borghese, Rome, 1973-74, Atkins Art Gallery, 1974, Kunsthaus, Zurich, 1977, Mus. Contemporary Art, Chgo., Mus. Art, R.I. Sch. Design, 1978, Mus. Modern Art, N.Y.C., Light Gallery, N.Y.C., 1980, Photokina, Koln, Germany, permanent collections, Mus. Modern Art, N.Y.C., Contemprary Arts Mus., Houston, Addison Gallery Am. Art, Art Inst., Cgho., Bibliotheque Natinale, Paris, Ctr. for Creative Photography, U. Ariz., Fotografiska Museet, Stockholm, Hallmark Collections, Kansas City, Mo., Mus. Art, N.Y.C., Mpls. Inst. Arts, Mus. Fine Arts, Boston, Mus. Modern Art, N.Y.C., Grunwald Ctr. Graphic Arts, UCLA. Served with U.S. Army, 1953-55. Guggenheim fellow, 1972; Nat. Endowment for Arts fellow, 1975, 79; Ruttenberg Arts Found. grantee, 1983. Mem. Soc. for Photog. Edn. (founding mem.). Home: 1914 W Wabansia St Chicago IL 60622

JOSEPHSON, MARVIN, corporation executive; b. Atlantic City, Mar. 6, 1927; s. Joseph and Eva (Rounick) J.; m. Tina Tann Chen, Apr. 12, 1973; children: Celia M., Claire A., Nancy A., Joseph T. Josephson; YiLing L.T. and YiPei R.T. Chen-Josephson. B.A., Cornell U., 1949; LL.B., N.Y. U., 1952. Atty. CBS, N.Y.C., 1952-55; pres., then chmn. Josephson Internat. Inc. (and predecessors), N.Y.C., 1955—; pres., then chmn. exec. com. Internat. Creative Mgmt., Inc. subs. Josephson Internat. Inc., N.Y.C., 1975—. Served with USN, 1945-46. Office: 40 W 57th St New York NY 10019

JOSEPHSON, WILLIAM HOWARD, lawyer; b. Newark, Mar. 22, 1934; s. Maurice and Gertrude (Brooks) J. A.B., U. Chgo., 1952; J.D., Columbia, 1955; commoner, St. Antony's Coll., Oxford (Eng.) U., 1958-59. Bar: N.Y. bar 1956, D.C. bar 1966, U.S. Supreme Ct. bar 1959. Asso. Paul, Weiss, Rifkind, Wharton & Garrison, N.Y.C., 1955-58, Joseph L. Rauh, Jr., Washington, 1959; Far East regional counsel ICA, 1959-61; spl. asst. to dir. Peace Corps, 1961-62, dep. gen. counsel, 1961-63, gen. counsel, 1963-66; asso. Fried, Frank, Harris, Shriver & Jacobson, N.Y.C., 1966-67, ptnr., 1968—; Spl. counsel N.Y.C. Human Resources Adminstrn., 1966-67, N.Y.C. Bd. Edn., 1968-71; Nat. Democratic vice presdl. campaign coordinator, 1972; pres. Peace Corps Inst., 1980—; adv. bd. Nat. Sci. Study, 1982—. Bd. editors: Columbia Law Rev, 1953-55. Recipient William A. Jump award exemplary achievement pub. adminstrn., 1965; Disting. Service award and Valerie Kantor awards Mex. Am. Legal Def. and Edn. Fund, 1980, 81. Mem. Assn. Bar City N.Y. (spl. com. on Congl. ethics 1968-70), Council on Fgn. Relations. Jewish. Home: 58 S Oxford St Brooklyn NY 11217 Office: 1 New York Plaza New York NY 10004

JOSEPHY, ALVIN M., JR., author, editor; b. Woodmere, N.Y., May 18, 1915; s. Alvin M. and Sophia (Knopf) J.; m. Elizabeth Carlisle Peet, Mar. 13, 1948; children: Diane, Alvin M. III, Allison Elizabeth (Mrs. Steven Wolowitz), Katherine Anne (Mrs. John B. Hobbs). Student, Harvard U., 1932-34. Screen writer M.G.M., 1934-35; ednl. editor, reporter, corr. N.Y. Herald Tribune, Mexico, 1937; news and spl. features dir. radio sta. WOR, 1938-42; screen writer M.G.M., Warner Bros., United Artists, 1944-51; mng. editor Santa Monica (Calif.) Ind., 1949-51; asso. editor Time mag., 1951-60; v.p., sr. editor Am. Heritage Pub. Co., 1960-76, v.p., editor-in-chief, dir., 1976-79, sr. editor, dir., 1980—; mem. editorial adv. bd. Am. Heritage mag., 1961-76, editor, 1976-78; Chief spl. events, domestic radio bur. Office Facts and Figures, OWI, 1942-43; cons. sec. Dept. interior, 1963; commr. Indian Arts and Crafts Bd., 1966-70, vice chmn., 1967-70; contbg. editor Indian Historian, 1966-69; mem. editorial bd. Am. West Mag., 1981—; pres., nat. council Inst. of Am. West, Sun Valley, Idaho, 1981—; mem. Author: (with others) The U.S. Marines on Iwo Jima,

1945, The Long and The Short and The Tall, 1946, Uncommon Valor, 1946, American Heritage Book of the Pioneer Spirit, 1959, The Patriot Chiefs, 1961, The Nez Perce Indians and the Opening of the Northwest, 1965, American Heritage Pictorial Atlas of U.S. History, 1966, The Indian Heritage of America, 1968, The Artist Was A Young Man, 1970, Red Power, 1971, American Heritage History of the Congress of the United States, 1975, Black Hills, White Sky, 1979, On the Hill, 1979, Now That the Buffalo's Gone, 1982; Editor: (with others) American Heritage Book of Indians, 1961, Horizon History of Africa, 1971, The Law in America, 1974; Contbr. articles to various jours. Conn. adv. bd. Small Bus. Adminstrn., 1961-63; adv. bd. Atlantic chpt. Sierra Club, 1966-72; cons. Nat. Congress Am. Indians, 1958-65; exec. com. Assn. Am. Indian Affairs, 1967—; nat adv. bd. Indian work Episcopal Ch., 1962-69; mem. council Indian Affairs, 1961-69; writer spl. report on Am. Indian for Pres. Nixon, 1969; trustee Mus. of Am. Indian, N.Y.C., 1976—, pres. nat. council, 1979—; trustee Nat. Resources Def. Council, 1977-82, Environ. Policy Center, 1978—, Sun Valley Center for Arts and Humanities, 1978—; cons. Pub. Land Law Rev. Commn., 1970; Vice chmn. Am. Vets. Com., Calif., 1947-48; pres. Young Democratic Club, Greenwich, Conn., 1952-55; v.p. Conn. Young Dem. Clubs, 1953-55; mem. Conn. Dem. Central Com., 1956-60; Dem. candidate for Conn. Legislature, 1958, 60. Served with USMCR, 1943-45; PTO. Decorated Bronze Star.; Recipient Western Heritage award Cowboy Hall of Fame, 1962, 65; Eagle Feather award Nat. Congress Am. Indians, 1964; award of merit Am. Assn. State and Local History, 1965; Golden Saddleman; Golden Spur and Buffalo awards for history, 1965; Guggenheim fellow, 1966-67. Mem. Soc. Am. Historians, Western History Assn., Am. Indian Ethnohistoric Conf., Am. Assn. State and Local History (exec. council 1977-78), U.S. Capitol Hist. Soc. (council 1977—), 3d Marine Div. Assn., N.Y. Westerners. Club: Harvard (N.Y.C.). Home: 4 Kinsman Ln Greenwich CT 06830 also Joseph OR Office: 10 Rockefeller Plaza New York NY 10020

JOSEY, E(LONNIE) J(UNIUS), librarian, state administrator; b. Norfolk, Va., Jan. 20, 1924; s. Willie and Frances (Bailey) J.; m. Dorothy Johnson, Sept. 11, 1954 (div. Dec. 1961); 1 dau., Elaine Jacqueline. A.B., Howard U., 1949; M.A., Columbia U., 1950; M.L.S., SUNY- Albany, 1953; L.H.D., Shaw U., 1973. Desk asst. Columbia U. Libraries, 1950-52; library tech. asst. central br. N.Y. Pub. Library, N.Y.C., 1952; librarian I Free Library, Phila., 1953-54; instr. social scis. Savannah State Coll., 1954-55, librarian, asso. prof., 1959-66; librarian, asst. prof. Del. State Coll., 1955-59; assoc. div. library devel. N.Y. State Edn. Dept., Albany, 1966-68; chief Bur. Acad. and Research Libraries, 1968-76, Bur. Specialist Library Services, 1976—; mem. bd. advisors Children's Book Rev. Service, Bklyn., 1972—. Contbg. author: The Black Librarian in America, 1970, What Black Librarians Are Saying, 1972, New Dimensions for Academic Library Service, 1975; co-compiler, co-editor: Handbook of Black Librarianship, 1977; co-editor: A Century of Service: Librarianship in the United States and Canada, 1976, Opportunities for Minorities in Librarianship, 1977, The Information Society: Issues and Answers, 1978, Libraries in the Political Process, 1980, Ethnic Collections in Libraries, 1983; editorial bd.: Dictionary of Am. Library History, 1974—; mem. editorial adv. bd.: ALA Yearbook, 1975—; spl. advisor: World Ency. Black People, 1974—; contbr. numerous articles to profl. jours. Mem. Albany Interracial Council, 1972—; mem. exec. bd. Savannah (Ga.) br. NAACP, 1960-66; state youth advisor Ga. Conf., 1962-66; mem. exec. bd. Albany br., 1968—, treas., 1970-72, 1st v.p., 1981-82, pres., 1982—, life mem., 1971—, chmn. program com., 1972-76, also trustee; mem. tech. task force Econ. Opportunity Authority of Savannah, 1964-66; bd. dirs. Corretta Scott King Award; trustee Minority Edn. and Devel. Agy., Central Islip, N.Y., 1973; bd. mgrs. Savannah Pub. Library, 1962-66; mem. adv. council Sch. Library Sci., N.C. Central U., Sch. Library and Info. Sci., SUNY-Albany, Sch. Library and Info. Sci., Queen's Coll., CUNY; mem. exec. bd. Albany County Opportunity Authority. Served with AUS, 1943-46. Recipient cert. of Appreciation Savannah br. NAACP, 1963, NAACP award Savannah State Coll. chpt., 1964, award for work as faculty coach and advisor Savannah State Coll. Debating Soc., 1965, Nat. Office award for leadership in youth work NAACP, 1965, award for youth work Ga. State Conf. NAACP, 1966, Merit award for work on econ. opportunity task force Savannah Chatham County, 1966, award for distinguished service to librarianship Savannah State Coll. Library, 1967, Jour. Library History award, 1970; award of excellence; N.Y. Black Librarians Inc. award, 1979; N.J. Black Librarians Network award, 1984; Joseph W. Lippincott award, 1980; Disting. Alumnus of Yr. award SUNY Albany Sch. Library and Info. Sci., 1981; Disting. Service award Library Assn. of CUNY, 1982; Martin Luther King Jr. award for disting. community leadership SUNY, Albany, 1984; award for contbns. to librarianship D.C. Assn. Sch. Librarians, 1984. Mem. ALA (John Cotton Dana award 1962, 64, founder, chmn. Black Caucus 1970-71, mem. council 1970—, exec. bd. 1979—, v.p./pres.-elect 1983-84, pres. 1984-85, Black Caucus award 1979), Assn. Study Afro-Am. Life and History, AAUP, Am. Acad. Polit. and Social Sci., N.Y. Library Assn., Freedom to Read Found., N.Y. Library Club, ACLU, Internat. Platform Assn., Am. Soc. Info. Scis., Alpha Phi Omega, Kappa Phi Kappa., Sigma Pi Phi. Democrat. Home: 12C Old Hickory Dr Apt 1A Albany NY 12204 Office: Cultural Edn Center Room 10C47 Empire State Plaza Albany NY 12230

JOSLIN, ALFRED HAHN, lawyer, former state justice; b. Providence, Jan. 29, 1914; s. Philip C. and Dorothy (Aisenberg) J.; m. Roberta Grant, Mar. 9, 1941 (dec.); children: Andrew J. (dec.), Susan A. A.B. magna cum laude, Brown U., 1935, LL.D. (hon.), 1980; LL.B. cum laude, Harvard U., 1938; L.H.D. (hon.), Bryant Coll.; D.J.S. (hon.), Roger Williams Coll. Bar: R.I. 1938. Practiced in, Providence, 1938-63; asso. justice Supreme Ct. R.I., 1963-79; of counsel firm Edwards & Angell, Providence, 1979—; Vice pres. R.I. Health Facilities Planning Council, 1965-72; v.p., budget chmn. United Fund R.I., 1955-57; mem. com. to revise corp. laws R.I., 1949-50, com. to revise election laws R.I., 1959-60; del. R.I. Constl. Conv., 1957; pres. Butler Hosp., 1957-65, emeritus, 1965—; pres. Providence Community Fund, 1960-63; trustee Brown U., 1963-69, vice chancellor, 1968-69, fellow, 1969—, Sec. Corp., 1972—. Bd. dirs. R.I. Legal Aid Soc., 1940-65, Greater Providence YMCA, 1955-60, Jewish Children's Home R.I.; bd. dirs. R.I. region NCCJ; bd. dirs. United Fund; hon. trustee Miriam Hosp.; chmn. Capital Ctr. Commn., 1980—. Served from lt. (j.g.) to lt. comdr. USNR, 1942-45. Recipient Big Bro. of Yr. award in R.I., 1957; Outstanding Accomplishment citation Brown U., 1959; named to R.I. Heritage Hall of Fame, 1980, Jewish Man of Yr., 1969, Univ. Club Man of Yr., 1974. Mem. ABA (chmn. jr. bar conf. R.I. 1940-41), R.I. Bar Assn. (chmn. exec. com. 1962-63), Alumni Assn. Brown U. (dir.), Phi Beta Kappa, Phi Alpha Delta (hon.), Pi Lambda Phi. Jewish (hon. trustee temple). Clubs: University, Hope, Ledgemont Country. Office: 2200 Hospital Trust Towers Providence RI 02903

JOSLYN, JAY THOMAS, arts critic; b. Mpls., June 13, 1923; s. William Jay and Hazel Mae (Howlett) J.; m. Ana Julia Blodgett, June 19, 1948; children—William, Thomas, Lyn Joslyn Blackston, Julia Joslyn Carlson, Jennie, Sarah. Student journalism, Marquette U., 1941-47. Reporter North Shore Publs., Shorewood, Wis., 1945-47; reporter, editor Superior (Wis.) Telegram newspaper, 1947-50; asso. editor Torch mag., Milw., 1950-51; reporter, state and farm editor, Sunday editor and arts reviewer Twin City News-Record, Menasha and Appleton (Wis.) Post-Crescent, 1953-65; arts reviewer, reporter Milw. Sentinel, 1965—. Served with USAAF, 1943-45. Recipient Certificate of Merit Wis. Hist. Soc., 1963. Mem. Menasha Hist. Soc. (pres. 1965, founding mem.), Fox Valley Glass Club (pres. 1964). Mem. United Ch. of Christ. Club: Kiwanian (pres. Menasha Club 1963). Home: 8709 W Spokane St Milwaukee WI 53224

JOSLYN, ROBERT BRUCE, lawyer; b. Detroit, Jan. 9, 1945; s. Lee Everett, Jr. and Juanita Constance (McGonegal) J.; m. Karen Sue Glenny, July 8, 1967; children: Gwendolyn Constance, Robert Bruce. B.A., Fla. State U., 1967; J.D., Emory U., 1970. Bar: Mich. 1970. Law clk. Gurney, Gurney & Handley, Orlando, Fla., summer 1969; asso. Joslyn & Keydel, Detroit, 1970-74; partner Joslyn, Keydel, Wallace & Joslyn, 1975—; Vis. instr. Oakland U., Rochester, Mich., 1974; faculty Inst. Continuing Legal Edn., Ann Arbor, Mich., 1975—. Co-author: Manual for Lawyers and Legal Assistants: Probate and Trust Administration, 1977, Manual for Lawyers and Legal Assistants: Taxation of Trusts and Estates, 1977, 3d edit., 1980. Mem. U.S. All Am. Prep. Sch. Swim Team, 1963. Mem. Am., Detroit bar assns., State Bar Mich., Am. Coll. Probate Counsel, Fin. and Estate Planning Council Detroit, Founders Soc. Detroit Inst. Arts, Phi Delta Phi, Phi Kappa Psi. Republican. Methodist. Clubs: Detroit Athletic, Grosse Pointe. Home: 286 Hillcrest Ave Grosse Pointe Farms MI 48236 Office: 2211 Comerica Bldg Detroit MI 48226

JOSSELSON, JACK BERNARD, lawyer; b. Ashland, Ky., June 25, 1905; s. Frank R. and Bella (Goodman) J.; m. Beatrice Elaine Lichtenstein, Dec. 26, 1933 (dec. Feb. 1977); children—Jill (Mrs. Stanley Kamin), John and Frank (twins). A.B., U. Cin., 1926; J.D., Harvard U., 1929. Bar: Ohio bar 1930. Asst. pros. atty., Hamilton County, Ohio, 1931-32, spl. asst. solicitor, City of Cin., 1933, practice in, Cin., 1933—; mem. firm Schmidt, Effron, Josselson & Weber, 1944—; Instr. transp. law U. Cin., 1948-50. Pres. Children's Heart Assn., 1967-69, trustee; trustee Heart Assn. Southwestern Ohio, Cin. Legal Aid Soc., 1965-78. Fellow Ohio State Bar Assn. Found. (trustee 1969-72), Am. Bar Found.; mem. ABA, Ohio Bar Assn. (exec. com. 1969-72, pub. utilities com.), Cin. Bar Assn. (pres. 1965-66), Motor Carrier Lawyers Assn. (pres. 1960-61), Harvard Law Sch. Assn. Clubs: Civic (pres. 1946), Harvard, Losantville Country (Cin.). Home: Regency Apts 2444 Madison Rd Cincinnati OH 45208 Office: Atlas Bank Bldg Cincinnati OH 45202

JOSSEY-BASS, ALLEN QUITMAN, publishing co. exec.; b. Atlanta, Jan. 22, 1928; s. Phillip Quitman Bass and Sarah Elizabeth Jossey. B.A., Emory U., 1950; postgrad., U. Calif., Berkeley, 1953-56. Editor Wadsworth Pub. Co., San Francisco, 1957-60; founder, dir. Atherton Press div. Prentice-Hall, Inc., N.Y.C., 1961-65; founder, pres. Jossey-Bass, Inc., Publisher, San Francisco, 1965—; chmn. Jossey-Bass Ltd., London. Served with USNR, 1945-49, 50-52. Home: 290 Union St San Francisco CA 94133 Office: 433 California St San Francisco CA 94104

JOUDRY, PATRICIA, playwright, author; b. Spirit River, Alta., Can., Oct. 18, 1921; d. Clifford George and Kennatha Beth (Gilbart) J.; m. Delmar Dinsdale (div.); children: Gay, Sharon (Mrs. Michael Martin); m. John Steele (div.); children—Stephanie, Melanie, Felicity. Grad. high sch. Radio and TV dramas include The Aldrich Family, 1945-49, Penny's Diary, 1940-45, Affectionately, Jenny, 1951; plays include Teach Me How To Cry, 1955, Walk Alone Together, 1960, Semi-Detached, 1960, Sand Castle, 1956, Valerie, 1958, The Song of Louise in the Morning, 1957, Three Rings for Michelle, 1956, God Goes Heathen, 1965, Now, 1970, I, Ching, 1971, Think Again, 1969, O Listen!, 1976; author: novel The Dweller on the Threshold, 1973; non-fiction And the Children Played, 1975; novel Spirit River to Angels' Roost, 1976; non-fiction The Selena Tree, 1980. Address: Box 78 Saint Denis SK S0K 3W0 Canada *I was born knowing there was something I had to do. As a child I knew I could think of it if they would only leave me alone long enough. Whatever it was it lay in the opposite direction from the way everybody wanted me to go. So it was a fight from the beginning. I fought my way through school and through two marriages before discovering that what I was meant to do was to become myself and to this give expression. Feeling that the process should not be a perpetual bloodbath I became a champion of children's rights, keeping my own three children out of school so they could educate themselves in their own way, which they did. My search for selfhood led to a deep investigation of the meaning of existence. I became a mystic. It was fated from the beginning. When I was two years old and saw a large body of water for the first time I yelled "Argo! Argo!" and rushed into the lake before my parents could stop me. In the mythical Greek ship Argo sailed Jason in search of the Golden Fleece, the elixir of life. That is my search, in my life and in my writing. To become myself I must become everybody, and eventually with everybody touch the Source. From that Source has come the drive, the energy, the sense of purpose and the will which has propelled me in my unrelenting endeavours to achieve.*

JOULLIE, MADELEINE M., chemist; b. Paris, Mar. 29, 1927; U.S., 1946, naturalized, 1958; d. Leon and Laure J.; m. Richard Prange, June 6, 1958. B.S., Simmons Coll., 1949; M.S., U. Pa., 1950, Ph.D., 1953. Instr. dept. chemistry U. Pa., Phila., 1953-57, asso., 1957-59, asst. prof., 1959-68, asso. prof., 1968-74, prof. chemistry, 1974—, chmn. com. on safety and security, 1974-75, univ. affirmative action officer, 1975—; chmn. Equal Opportunity Council, 1976, asst. chmn. undergrad. curriculum com., 1977—; Fulbright lectr. U. Brazil, 1965; vis. prof. Columbia U., 1968. Contbr. articles to profl. jours. Fellow N.Y. Acad. Scis.; mem. Am. Chem. Soc. (Phila. sect. award 1972, Garvan medal 1978, dir. and councilor Phila. sect., chmn. com. on econ. status), AAAS, English Chem. Soc., Japanese Chem. Soc., Phila. Organic Chemists Club (chmn. 1970), Sigma Xi, Sigma Delta Epsilon. Home: 288 Saint James Pl Philadelphia PA 19106 Office: U Pa Dept Chemistry Philadelphia PA 19104

JOUNO, RANDOLPH JAMES, management consultant, educator; b. Minocqua, Wis.; s. Edwin J. and Rose Ethel (Krzmarcik) J.; m. Dorothy Marion Carlson, Dec. 26, 1936 (dec. 1973); 1 dau., Paulette. B.A. magna cum laude, St. Thomas Coll., 1929; postgrad., U. Minn., 1933-50, U. Iowa, 1944, Am. U., 1958-65; M.A., U. S.D., 1937, U. S.D., 1957; Ph.D., Miss. State U., 1974. Tchr., Cretin High Sch., St. Paul, Minn., 1929-39; instr. history U. Detroit, 1938; claims examiner R.R. Retirement Bd., Cleve., 1939-40; personnel officer CSC, Dayton, Ohio, 1940-41, Omaha, Nebr., 1944, St. Paul, Minn., 1942, 44, 45-57, Air Force Mobile, Ala., 1941-42, IRS, Washington, 1957-58, Office of Edn., 1958-71; personnel mgmt. cons. St. Thomas Coll., St. Paul, 1976-81, prof. public personnel adminstrn., 1979-80; free lance writer, 1976—, also guest lectr. univs. Contbr. numerous articles on polit. sci., history and personnel mgmt. to profl. and popular publs. Mem. Am. Hist. Assn., Orgn. Am. Historians, Fed. Bus. Assn. (v.p. 1953-55), Am. Public Adminstrn. Soc. (bd. dirs. 1948-50), St. Thomas Coll. President's Council, Twin Cities Fed. Personnel Council (v.p. 1948-50), Nat. Assn. Ret. Fed. Employees, Am. Assn. Ret. Persons, Cath. League, Am. Fedn. Govt. Employees (chmn. nat. conv. 1946), Am. Automobile Assn., Phi Theta Alpha, Pi Sigma Alpha. Democrat. Roman Catholic. Clubs: Serra Internat., Midwest, Amhert H. Wilder. Address: 1530 Bellows St West Saint Paul MN 55118

JOURDAIN, ALICE MARIE, philosopher, educator; b. Brussels, Mar. 11, 1923; U.S., 1940, naturalized, 1948; d. Henri and Marthe (Van de Vorst) J.; m. Dietrich von Hildebrand, July 16, 1959. Student, Manhattanville Coll., 1942-44; Ph.D., Fordham U., 1949. Mem. faculty dept. philosophy Hunter Coll., City U. N.Y., 1947—, prof., 1971—; vis. prof. U. de los Andes, Bogotá, Colombia, summer 1955. Author: Greek Culture: The Adventure of the Human Spirit, 1966, Introduction to a Philosophy of Religion, 1971, (with D. von Hildebrand) Situation Ethics, 1966, Art of Living, 1965, Grave Images, 1957. Roman Catholic.

JOURDAN, LOUIS, actor; b. Marseille, France, June 19, 1921; came to U.S., 1946; s. Henry Gendre and Yvonne J.; m. Berthe Frederique, Mar. 11, 1946; 1 son, Louis Henry. Ed. pvt. schs. Profl. actor, 1940—. Appeared in French motion pictures, 1940-46; Am. motion picture appearances include The Paradine Case, 1946, No Minor Vices, 1947, Letter from an Unknown Woman, 1948, Madame Bovary, 1949, Bird of Paradise, 1950, Anne of the Indies, 1950, Three Coins in the Fountain, 1953, The Swan, 1955, Julie, 1956, Gigi, 1957, Best of Everything, 1959, Can-Can, 1960, The V.I.P.'s, 1963, Made in Paris, 1966, A Flea In Her Ear, 1968, To Commit a Murder, 1970; TV movies include The Great American Beauty Contest, 1973; Am. motion picture appearances include Silver Bears, 1978, Octopussy, 1983; TV movies include The Man in the Iron Mask, 1977, The French Atlantic Affair, 1979, Dracula, PBS; various Broadway appearances include Tonight at Sammarkand; numerous appearances in, U.S., Eng. Office: care Internat Creative Mgmt 8899 Beverly Blvd Los Angeles CA 90048

JOURDIAN, GEORGE WILLIAM, biochemist, educator; b. Northampton, Mass., Apr. 21, 1929; s. Charles Loomis and Florence (Brooks) J.; m. Joan Kettell, June 12, 1954; children: Susan, Robert. B.A., Amherst Coll., 1949; M.S., U. Mass., 1953; Ph.D., Purdue U., 1958. Instr. biol. chemistry Med. Sch. U. Mich., Ann Arbor, 1961-63, asst. prof., 1963-65, research asso., 1965-74, asso. prof., 1965-74, prof. depts. internal medicine and biol. chemistry, 1974—. Contbr. articles to profl. jours. Fellow Arthritis Found., 1958-61; grantee, 1965—, NIH, 1965—, Nat. Found. March of Dimes, 1976—; sr. internat. fellow Fogarty Internat. Center, 1978-79. Mem. Am. Soc. Biol. Chemists, Am. Chem. Soc., Soc. Complex Carbohydrates. Home: 4455 Kuebler Ct Ann Arbor MI 48103 Office: Room 4633 Kresge Bldg I Univ Mich Med Sch Ann Arbor MI 48109

JOURDONAIS, LEONARD FRANCIS, educator, physician; b. Havre, Mont., July 27, 1904; s. Lucien A. and Camille (Wyrn) J.; m. Marjorie M. Smith, Oct. 26, 1974. B.A., U. Mont., 1926; M.A., Northwestern U., 1932, M.D., 1933. Diplomate: Am. Bd. Preventive Medicine. Intern Evanston Hosp., 1933-34; fellow N.Y. Postgrad. Med. Sch. and Hosp., 1936-37; prof. medicine Northwestern U. Med. Sch., 1964-74, prof. emeritus, 1974—; chmn. dept. medicine Evanston Hosp., 1956-74, chmn. emeritus, 1974—, Louise W. Coon chair dept. medicine, 1968-74. Fellow ACP (life); mem. Am. Diabetes Assn., AMA, Endocrine Soc., Chgo. Soc. Internal Medicine, Assn. Tchrs. Preventive Medicine, Alpha Omega Alpha. Home: 10702 Roundelay Circle Sun City AZ 85351

JOURNEY, DREXEL DAHLKE, lawyer; b. Westfield, Wis., Feb. 23, 1926; s. Clarence Earl and Verna L. Gilmore (Dahlke) J.; m. Vergene Harriet Sandsmark, Oct. 24, 1952; 1 dau., Ann Marie. Student, U.S. Mcht. Marine Acad., 1944-45; B.B.A., U. Wis., 1950; LL.B., 1952; LL.M., George Washington U., 1957. Bar: Wis. 1952, U.S. Supreme Ct. 1955, D.C. 1970, also other fed. cts. 1970. Practice utility law; with FPC, Washington, 1952-77, dep. gen. counsel, 1970-74, gen. counsel, 1974-77; partner firm Schiff Hardin & Waite, Washington, 1977—. Contbr. articles to profl. jours. Served with Mcht. Marine Res. USNR, 1944-46; with U.S.N.G., 1948-50. Knapp scholar U. Wis., 1952. Mem. Am., Fed. bar assns., Phi Kappa Phi, Phi Eta Sigma, Theta Delta Chi. Club: Mason. Home: 4540 Windom Pl NW Washington DC 20016 Office: 1101 Connecticut Ave NW Washington DC 20036

JOVA, HENRI VATABLE, architect; b. Newburgh, N.Y., May 11, 1919; s. Joseph Luis and Maria Gonzalez (Cavada) J. B.Arch., Cornell U., 1949. Fellow Am. Acad. Rome, 1949-50; Designer Harrison & Abramowitz, N.Y.C., 1952-54; chief of design Abreu & Robeson, Atlanta, 1954-66; chmn. bd., ptnr. Jova/Daniels/Busby, Atlanta, 1966—. Works include Progressive Farmer Hdqrs, Birmingham, Ala., 1974, Colony Sq, Atlanta, 1973, Atlanta Newspapers Bldg, 1971, Multi-Use Bldg., Ga. State U, 1979, McWane Hdqrs, Monarch Condominiums, Hilton Head, N.C., Birmingham, 1979, Jimmy Carter Presdl. Library, Atlanta, VA Med. Center, Augusta, Ga. Served with U.S. Army, 1942-45. Fulbright fellow, 1951. Fellow AIA; mem. L'Ogive, Tau Sigma Delta. Club: Piedmont Driving. Home: 861 Mentelle Dr NE Atlanta GA 30308 Office: 909 W Peachtree St Atlanta GA 30309

JOVA, JOSEPH JOHN, foundation executive, former ambassador; b. Newburgh, N.Y., Nov. 7, 1916; s. Joseph Luis and Maria Josefa (Gonzalez-Cavada) J.; m. Pamela Johnson, Feb. 9, 1949; children: Henry Christopher, John Thomas, Margaret Ynes. A.B., Dartmouth, 1938; grad. sr. seminar on fgn. policy, Fgn. Service Inst., 1959; L.H.D., Mt. St. Mary Coll., 1973; LL.D., Dowling Coll., 1973. With Guatemala div. United Fruit Co., 1938-41; fgn. service officer Dept. State, 1947—, vice consul, Basra, 1947-49, 2d sec., vice consul, Tangier, 1949-52; consul, Oporto, 1952-54, 1st sec., Lisbon, 1954-57; officer-in-charge French-Iberian affairs, 1957-58, asst. chief personnel ops. div., 1959-60, chief personnel operations div., 1960-61; dep. chief of mission, Santiago, Chile, 1961-65, ambassador to Honduras, Tegucigalpa, 1965-69, ambassador to OAS, Washington, 1969-74, ambassador to Mexico, Mexico City, 1974-77; pres. Meridian House Internat., 1977—; chmn. Dept. State Mgmt. Reform Task Force, U.S. dels. to Inter-Am. Council on Edn., Sci. and Culture at Panama, 1972, Mar del Plata, 1973, UN Econ. Commn. for Latin Am., Santiago, 1971, UNEcon. Commn. Latin Am. Population Conf., Mexico, 1974; vice chmn. U.S. del. to gen. assembly OAS, 1970, 71, 72, 73; dir. First Am. Bank of Washington. Contbr. articles to profl. jours. Trustee Mt. St. Mary's Coll., Ariz., Desert Mus., Pan-Am. Devel. Found. Served to lt. USNR, 1942-47. Named knight Malta-Am. Assn.; decorated Grand Cross Order Morazan, Honduras, Constantinian Order St. George; Order of Aztec Eagle, Mexico; Order of Orange-Nassau (Netherlands); recipient Presdl. Mgmt. Improvement award, 1970, Conquistador award, El Paso, Tex., 1975; T.A. Cunningham award New Orleans Internat. House, 1975; Wilbur J. Carr award U.S. Dept. State, 1977. Mem. Mexican Acad. Internat. Law, Mexican Acad. History, Mex. Inst. Hist. and Geneal. Studies, U.S. Fgn. Service Assn., Center Interam. Relations, Inst. Hispanic Culture (Spain), Asociacion de Hidalgos a Fuero de España, Sigma Phi Epsilon. Roman Catholic. Clubs: Rotarian., Sulgrave, Internat. of Washington, Chapultepec Golf, Dacor House. Address: Meridian House Internat 1630 Crescent Pl NW Washington DC 20009

JOVANOVIC, DRASKO, physicist; b. Belgrade, Yugoslavia, May 24, 1930; came to U.S., 1954; s. Dragoljub and Mira (Trbojevic) J.; m. Stanka Dimitrijevic, Aug. 8, 1954; children: Jasna, Vesna. B.S., Belgrade U., 1953; M.S., U. Chgo., 1956, Ph.D., 1959. Research assoc. U. Chgo., 1959-60; research asst. U. Calif., San Diego, 1960-62; physicist Argonne Nat. Lab., Ill., 1962-72; chmn. physics dept., head physics sect. Fermilab, Batavia, Ill., 1972—, assoc. head research div., 1974-79. Fellow Am. Phys. Soc. Home: 4808 Wallbank Downers Grove IL 60515 Office: Fermilab PO Box 500 Batavia IL 60510

JOVANOVIC, MIODRAG, surgeon, educator; b. Tabonovic, Yugoslavia, May 3, 1936; s. Stevan and Zivina Jelena (Antonic) J.; 3

children. B.A., Coll. Sabac, 1954; M.D., Faculty of Medicine, Belgarde, Yugoslavia, 1963. Intern in, France and Can., resident in surgery in, Can., 1965-72, practice surgery, Quebec, Que., Can., 1972—; mem. staff Jeffery Halle Hosp., Notre Dame Hosp.; prof. Faculty Medicine, Laval U., Quebec, 1972—. Fellow Royal Coll. Surgeons Can., Am. Coll. Chest Physicians, Med. Council Can., A.C.S., Internat. Coll. Surgeons; mem. Can. Med. Assn., Assn. des Medecins de Langue Francaise du Canada, Royal Coll. Surgeons and Physicians Can. Home: 2219 Bourbonniere Quebec PQ Canada Office: Dept Anatomy Faculty Medicine Laval U Quebec PQ Canada

JOVANOVICH, PETER, publisher; b. Mineola, N.Y., Feb. 4, 1949; s. William and Marshall (David) J.; m. Robin Jovanovich, June 14, 1976; children: Nicholas, William. A.B., Princeton U., 1972. Pub. Harcourt Brace Jovanovich Inc., N.Y.C. Home: 24-28 Oval Rd London England NW1 7DX Office: Harcourt Brace Jovanovich Inc 111 Fifth Ave New York NY 10003

JOVANOVICH, WILLIAM, publisher; b. Louisville, Colo., Feb. 6, 1920; s. Iliya M. and Hedviga (Garbatz) J.; m. Martha Evelyn Davis, Aug. 21, 1943. A.B., U. Colo., 1941; grad. study, Harvard, 1941-42, Columbia, 1946-47; Litt.D., Colo. Coll., 1966, U. Colo., 1971, Adelphi Coll., 1971, Middlebury Coll., 1971, Ohio State U., 1971; LL.D., U. Alaska, 1971. With Harcourt Brace Jovanovich, Inc. (formerly Harcourt, Brace & Co.), N.Y.C., 1947—, asso. editor, 1947-53, v.p., dir., 1953-54, pres., dir., 1955-70, chmn., dir., 1970—; Regent prof. U. Calif.-Berkeley, 1967; lectr. Adelphi U., 1973. Author: Now Barabbas, 1964, Madmen Must, 1978; also essays. Regent State of N.Y., from 1974. Recipient Norlin award distinguished achievement U. Colo., 1963; Fellow Morgan Library, N.Y.C. Mem. Phi Beta Kappa. William Jovanovich lectrs. in pub. affairs named in honor, Colo. Coll., 1976-79. Office: orlando fl 32887 *

JOY, JAMES, JR., labor union official. Pres. Utility Workers Union Am. Office: 815 16th St NW Washington DC 20006§

JOY, WILLIAM FRANCIS, lawyer; b. Somerville, Mass., Feb. 2, 1918; s. Thomas J. and Margaret M. (Ryan) J.; m. Mary E. O'Brien, July 27, 1946; children: William F., John P., Robert P., Mary M., David M., Anne E., Thomas M., Ellen L., Richard J. A.B., Boston Coll., 1940, J.D., 1943; M.B.A., Boston U., 1950. Bar: Mass. Asso. firm Ropes Gray Best Coolidge & Rugg, Boston, 1943-44; lawyer Swift & Co., Chgo., Boston, 1944-61; partner firm Morgan, Brown & Joy, Boston, 1961—; lectr. Boston U., 1949-66, Boston Coll., 1950. Contbr. articles to legal jours. Mem. Greater Boston C. of C. (v.p. 1974-77, dir. 1971-74), ABA (del. 1975-76), Mass. Bar Assn., Boston Bar Assn., Am., Mass. bar founds. Clubs: Algonquin, Bay (Boston); Winchester (Mass.) Country. Home: 39 Everett Ave Winchester MA 01890 Office: One Boston Pl Boston MA 02108

JOYAL, SERGE, Canadian government official, lawyer; b. Montreal, Que., Can., Feb. 1, 1945. Student, U. Montreal, Faculty Internat. Law, Strasbourg, France, London Sch. Econs. and Polit. Sci. Bar: Que. 1969. Mem. Can. Parliament, 1974, co-chmn. spl. joint com. on constitution of Can., 1980, parliamentary sec., founding mem. spl. joint com. ofcl. langs., 1980; minister of state Can., 1981-82, Sec. of State, Ottawa, 1982—. Home: 4234 Ste Catherine E Montreal PQ Canada H1V 1X3 Office: House of Commons Room 435 Confederation Bldg Ottawa ON Canada K1A OA6

JOYCE, CHARLES RAYMOND, JR., librarian; b. West Tremont, Maine, Jan. 3, 1929; s. Charles Raymond and Lessie Emeline (Bridges) J.; m. Ingrid Maria Thale, June 1, 1963; children—Lillian, Gareth. B.A., Tufts Coll., 1951; M.S., Simmons Coll. Library Sci., 1955. Librarian Detroit Pub. Library, 1955-57, Branford (Conn.) Pub. Library, 1957-59; asst. librarian Wellesley (Mass.) Pub. Library, 1959-61, Winchester (Mass.) Pub. Library, 1961-62; dir. Norwood (Mass.) Pub. Library, 1962-68; asso. state librarian State of Conn., 1968-73; dir. Bur. Library Extension Mass., Boston, 1973-78, Kansas City (Kans.) Public Library, 1978—; Mass. adminstr. Interstate Library Compact, 1974-78; chmn. New Eng. Library Bd., 1975-77, New Eng. Document Conservation Center, North Andover, Mass., 1975-77. Served to 2d lt. AUS, 1951-53. Mem. ALA, Kans., Mountain Plains library assns. Home: 7708 Corona Kansas City KS 66112 Office: 625 Minnesota Kansas City KS 66101

JOYCE, CLAUDE CLINTON, retail food and drug chain executive; b. Lordsburg, N.Mex., May 10, 1931; s. William Claude and Minnie Merlina (Gibson) J.; m. Wanda Clifitine Land, Dec. 7, 1951; children: Clifton Claude, Lani Caprice. B.S. in Acctg., San Diego State U., 1956. Supr. machine reports U.S. Navy, San Diego, 1952-55; sales rep. Service Bur. Corp., San Francisco, 1955-59; dir. mgmt. service Price Waterhouse, San Francisco, 1959-68; sr. v.p. Mgmt. Info. System, Boise, Idaho, 1968—. Served with USN, 1948-52; PTO. Mem. Assn. Systems Mgmt. (pres. chpt. 1972-73). Republican. Methodist. Lodges: Masons; Shriners. Home: 1400 Shoshone Boise ID 83705 Office: Albertsons Inc 250 Parkcenter Blvd Boise ID 83726

JOYCE, EDMUND PATRICK, clergyman, univ. exec.; b. Tela, Honduras, Jan. 26, 1917; s. Edmund Patrick and Genevieve (Block) J. (parents U.S. citizens). B.S.C., U. Notre Dame, 1937; postgrad., Holy Cross Coll., 1945-49, Oxford U., 1950-51; LL.D., St. Thomas Coll., St. Paul, 1958; L.H.D., Belmont Abbey Coll., 1967, U. S.C., 1984. C.P.A., Spartanburg, S.C., 1939. Entered Congregation of Holy Cross, 1943; ordained priest Roman Cath. Ch., 1949; tchr. religion U. Notre Dame, 1949-51, v.p. bus. affairs, 1951 -52, exec. v.p., 1952—; U.S. del. Atlantic Congress, London, 1959. Trustee Jr. Achievement; bd. visitors U.S. Naval Acad. Recipient Disting. Am. award Nat. Football Found. and Hall of Fame, 1977. Mem. S.C. Assn. C.P.A.s, Oxford Soc. K.C. Home: Corby Hall Notre Dame IN 46556

JOYCE, EDWARD M., broadcasting executive; b. Phoenix, Dec. 13, 1932; m. Maureen Jarry; children: Brenda, Randall. Student, U. Wyo. With Sta. WBBM, CBS, Chgo., 1954-59, Sta. WCBS, CBS, N.Y.C., 1959-69, dir. news and pub. affairs, 1966-69; exec. producer spl. events for radio CBS News, N.Y.C., 1969-71; dir. news Sta. WCBS-TV, 1970-77, v.p. news CBS TV Stas. div., 1977-78; v.p., gen. mgr. Sta.-WBBM-TV, 1978-80, Sta. KNXT-TV, Los Angeles, 1980, WCBS-TV, 1981; exec. v.p. CBS News, 1981-83, pres., 1983—. Recipient award for reporting of Chappaquiddick Soc. Silurians, 1969, award for reportin of Chappaquiddick N.Y. State AP Broadcasters Assn., 1969. Mem. Radio-TV News Dirs. Assn., Internat. Radio and TV Soc., Acad. TV Arts and Scis. Investigative Reporters and Editors, Sigma Delta Chi (Disting. Serviceaward 1969). Office: 524 W 57th St New York NY 10019

JOYCE, JAMES AVERY, international law educator, economist, author; b. London, May 24, 1902; s. George Thomas Simeon and Mary Elizabeth (Leng) J. Student, Geneva Sch. Internat. Studies; Ph.D.; B.Sc. in Econs, London U.; grad., Inns. of Ct. law Sch.; LL.D., Morningside Coll., 1970. Bar: called to bar to practice common and criminal law on S.E. Circuit, also before High Ct. in London 1943. Lectr. London U.; popular law broadcasts BBC; faculty U. Denver Inst. Internat. Adminstrn., also Inst. Internal Affairs, Grinnell Coll., San Diego State Coll., NYU, Amherst Coll.; prof. Webster U. Coll. (Geneva (Switzerland) campus), 1980—; vis. lectr. other U.S. univs., colls., also New Delhi U.; speaker auspices Am. Friends Service Com., Midwest and N.E. communities, 1948—; Disting. prof. Lambuth Coll., 1969-70; sr. research asso. Fletcher Sch. Law and Diplomacy, 1970. Author: World Organization, 1944, Justice at Work, 1950, World in the Making, 1953, Revolution on East River, 1956, Red Cross International, 1959, Capital Punishment, A World View, 1960, Target for Tomorrow, 1962, Going One Way, 1963, Worker's Education Handbook, 1963, Education and Training, 1963, The Story of International Cooperation, 1964, World of Promise, 1965, Decade of Development, 1966, End of An Illusion, 1969, Story of the League of Nations, 1971, Which Way Europe, 1971, Jobs Versus People, 1974, New Politics of Human Rights, 1979, World Labour Rights and New Protection, 1980, The War Machine, 1980, One Increasing Purpose, 1981, Animals Too Have Rights, 1982, Planning Disarmament, 1982; Contbr. articles to profl. jours., nat. mags. Founder World Unity Movement (later became World Citizenship Movement), 1939, founder, 1929; nat. chmn. League of Nations Youth Movement; staff League of Nations Union; sec. Internat. Conf. Minorities of Lang., Race and Religion; Brit. sec. Internat. Assn. Labour Legislation; staff Internat. Labour Office, Geneva; cons. UNESCO and ECOSOC of UN.; Candidate for Parliament from, Oldham, 1951 Candidate for Parliament from, Lambeth, 1955, UN, 1971. Fellow Royal Geog. Soc., Royal Statis. Soc., Royal Econ. Soc.; mem. Royal Inst. Public Adminstrn., Internat. Law Assn., Howard League, World Calendar Assn. (UN rep.), Parliamentary Labour Assn., Brit. Inst. Internat. and Comparative Law, Internat. Lawyers Club, Internat. Center Criminological Studies (v.p.), Soc. Labour Lawyers, Internat. P.E.N., Translators Assn., AAUP, Am. Polit. Sci. Assn., UN Assn., World Federalists. Mem. Labour Party. Methodist. Address: 7 rue de Courvoisier Versoix 1290 Geneva Switzerland also 3 King's Bench Walk Temple London EC4 England also care Am Friends Service Com 1515 Cherry St Philadelphia PA 19102 *World peace is the first human right and must be pursued today as a priority of foreign policy through the UN system of security, disarmament, and development.*

JOYCE, JAMES NEAL, educator, psychologist; b. Buhl, Idaho, July 8, 1925; s. Patrick William and Margaret (McFerran) J.; m. Maxine Petterborg, Aug. 29, 1948; children: Jeffrey Neal, Timothy Kevin, Patricia Alice, Michael David. Student, Idaho State Coll., 1946-48; B.A., Ind. U., 1950; M.A., Ohio State U., 1952, Ph.D., 1955. Psychologist Columbus (Ohio) Sch. Retarded, 1955; from asst. prof. to asso. prof. Coe Coll., Cedar Rapids, Iowa, 1955-60; faculty Western Ill. U., Macomb, 1960—, prof. psychology, 1966—, chmn. dept., 1962-70, acting dean, 1969-70; Exec. dir. Illowa Higher Edn. Consortium, 1973-76. Served with USNR, 1943-46. Mem. Am. Psychol. Assn., Midwestern Psychol. Assn., Ill. Psychol. Assn., AAUP, AAAS. Home: 514 N McArthur St Macomb IL 61455

JOYCE, JAMES VINCENT, pubic relations executive, writer; b. Port Chester, N.Y., Jan. 14, 1925; s. James R. and Frances M. (Joyce) J.; m. Veronica L. Tookey; children: Cecilia M., Rosemary, Francesca, Anthony. B.A. cum laude, U. Pitts. Formerly with pub. relations dept. Batton, Barton, Durstine & Osborne; joined U.S. Fgn. Service, 1951; assigned, Turkey, 1951-52, Iran, 1953-54, India, 1954-55, pub. affairs officer, Jordan, 1960-63, counsellor of embassy for pub. affairs, Athens, Greece, 1963-64; counselor for public affairs U.S. delegation to NATO, 1964-67; public affairs dir. Asia/Pacific, Europe, Middle East and N. Africa, Citibank (N.A.). Author stage and TV plays, novels, articles, studies. Served with parachute troops AUS; ETO.

JOYCE, JOHN MICHAEL, beverage company executive; b. Grand Rapids, Mich., Sept. 18, 1908; s. John Michael and Mary Agnes (McCann) J.; m. Catherine Bernice Peet, Oct. 16, 1934; children: John Michael III, Thomas Patrick, Patricia Anne (Mrs. John K. Figge), Mary Catherine (Mrs. Robert H. McCooey), Anne Elizabeth (Mrs. Thomas G. Grace), Timothy Joseph, Cathleen (Mrs. Thomas F. Egan). B.C.S., St. Louis U., 1930; LL.D. (hon.), Iona Coll., 1962, Coll. of Holy Cross, 1979. With Travelers Ins. Co., 1930-37; with Joyce 7-Up, Chgo., 1937-39; pres. N.Y. Seven-Up Bottling Co., New Rochelle, 1939-65, chmn. bd., 1965-73; chmn. bd., dir. Joyce Beverages, Inc., New Rochelle, 1973—; dir. Joyce Beverages (subsidiaries in), N.Y., Ill., Wis., N.J., Washington, Conn.; past dir. Bookmatches, Inc., D.D. Bean & Sons Co., Jaffrey, N.H.; trustee Emigrant Savs. Bank, N.Y.C.; dir., chmn. exec. com. Nat. Bank of Westchester, White Plains, N.Y., 1960—; dir., mem. exec. com. Lincoln First Banks, Inc., Rochester, N.Y. Chmn. bd. govs. New Rochelle Hosp. Med. Center; past trustee, past chmn. bd. lay trustees Iona Coll., New Rochelle; past pres. New Rochelle C. of C.; mem. pres.'s com. Notre Dame U.; trustee Alfred E. Smith Meml. Found., Inc., Cath. Charities of Archdiocese of N.Y., 1978—; pres. John M. and Mary A. Joyce Found.; bd. dirs. N.Y. Med. Coll., Valhalla, N.Y. Decorated Knight of Malta, Knight of Holy Sepulchre.; Recipient Merit award St. Louis U., Brother William B. Cornelia Founders award, 1965; charter mem. St. Louis U. Sports Hall of Fame, 1976. Clubs: Westchester Country, Minocqua (Wis.) Country; Metropolitan (N.Y.C. and Washington); Winged Foot Country (Mamaroneck, N.Y); St. Louis. Home: 7 Forest Circle New Rochelle NY 10804 Office: Joyce Rd New Rochelle NY 10802

JOYCE, JOHN T., labor union ofcl.; b. Chgo., 1935. Ed., U. Notre Dame. Staff Masonry Inst., Cook County, 1960; adminstr. local pension fund. Internat. Bricklayers Union, adminstr. apprenticeship and tng. fund, treas. internat. union, 1971, sec., 1971; now pres. Internat. Union Bricklayers and Allied Craftsmen; v.p. bldg. and constrn. trades dept. AFL-CIO; founding pres. Masonry Research Found.; founding sec. Masonry Industry Com., Trowel Trades Internat. Pension Fund; dir. Internat. Masonry Inst., Internat. Masonry Apprentice Trust.; Bd. dirs. Mus. Bldg. Arts; mem. bldg. research adv. bd. Nat. Acad. Scis. Mem. Human Resources Devel. Inst., League Indsl. Democracy.

JOYCE, LEO HAROLD, III, retail exec.; b. N.J., Feb. 24, 1942; s. Leo Harold and Theresa (Alvino) J.; Apr. 18, 1981; 1 dau., Cheryl. Ed., Fairleigh Dickenson U. With Bambergers Dept. Store, Newark, now sr. v.p., dir. mdse. sportswear. Club: Braidburn Country. Office: Bambergers Dept Store 131 Market St Newark NJ 07102 *

JOYCE, PATRICK VINCENT, newspaper editor; b. Chgo., July 19, 1940; s. John and Catherine Agnes (Callaghan) J.; m. Catherine Ann Somers, May 3, 1969; children: Sara, John, Matthew, Thomas, Michael. B.S., Loyola U., Chgo., 1962; postgrad., McCormick Theol. Sem., 1967-68. Reporter City News Bur. Chgo., 1963-65, Chgo's. American, 1965-67; reporter, news editor Catholic Rev., Balt., 1968-70, editor, 1974-77; city editor Wheeling (Ill.) Herald, 1970-72; news editor N.C. News Service, Washington, 1972-74; editor, gen. mgr. Joliet (Ill.) Cath. Explorer, 1977-79; copy editor Balt. Evening Sun, 1979-82, asst. met. editor, 1982—. Mem. Cath. Press Assn. Roman Catholic. Office: Balt Evening Sun Calvert and Centre Sts Baltimore MD 21203

JOYCE, PHILIP HALTON, journalist; b. Albany, N.Y., Dec. 15, 1928; s. Raymond F. and Edna (Crist) J.; m. Mary Frances Tessier, Feb. 11, 1961; children—Marie Elizabeth, Thomas Patrick. B.A. in Sociology, Siena Coll., 1952. Sports writer Glens Falls (N.Y.) Post-Star, 1954-55; reporter The Saratogian, Saratoga, N.Y., 1955-56, Times-Union, Albany, N.Y., 1956-62, Buffalo Courier-Express, 1962-64, legislative corr., 1965, copy editor, 1966-68; editorial writer Phila. Inquirer, 1968—. Served with AUS, 1952-54. Roman Catholic. Home: 22 Erindale Dr Marlton NJ 08053 Office: Phila Inquirer 400 N Broad St Philadelphia PA 19101

JOYCE, ROBERT HYLAND, lawyer; b. Chgo., July 16, 1928; s. James Michael and Mary (Dunne) J.; m. Barbara Lee Novak, Nov. 15, 1958; children: James Michael, Jonathan David, Matthew Paul. B.A., Loras Coll.; J.D., DePaul U. Bar: Ill. Trial atty. Liberty Mut. Ins. Co., Chgo., 1956-58; assoc. Seyfarth, Shaw, Fairweather & Geraldson, Chgo., 1958-64, ptnr., 1964—. Served with U.S. Army, 1951-53. Mem. ABA, Ill. Bar Assn. Roman Catholic. Club: Chgo. Athletic Assn. Home: 5005 Lawn Ave Western Springs IL 60558 Office: Seyfarth Shaw Fairweather & Geraldson 55 E Monroe St Suite 4200 Chicago IL 60603

JOYCE, WILLIAM LEONARD, research librarian; b. Rockville Centre, N.Y., Mar. 29, 1942; s. John Francis and Mabel Clare (Leonard) J.; m. Carol Gail Bertani, Aug. 13, 1967; children: Susan, Michael. B.A., Providence Coll., 1964; M.A., St. John's U., 1966; Ph.D., U. Mich., 1974. Manuscripts librarian William L. Clements Library, U. Mich., Ann Arbor, 1968-72; curator manuscripts Am. Antiquarian Soc., Worcester, Mass., 1972-81, edn. officer, 1977-81; asst. dir. for rare books and manuscripts N.Y. Pub. Library, N.Y.C., 1981—; cons. Dukes County (Mass.) Hist. Soc., 1979, R.I. Hist. Soc., 1979-81, U. Wyo., 1980, Essex Inst., 1980-81, New Bedford (Mass.) Whaling Mus., 1980-82, U. Minn.-Orthodox Ch. Am., 1981; chmn. Worcester Pub. Library Adv. Com., 1980-81; lectr. Clark U., 1975-77, Case Western Res. U., 1979, Modern Archives Inst., Nat. Archives and Records Service, 1980; cons. assessment-reporting project Nat. Hist. Publs. and Rocords. Commn., Washington, 1982. Author: booklet Evaluation of Archival Institutions, 1982; contbr. articles, revs. to profl. jours.; editor: Printing and Society in Early America, 1983; compiler, editor: Catalog of Manuscripts, 4 vols., 1979; compiler: Collections of the American Antiquarian Society, 4 vols., 1979. Team leader Mechanics Hall Restoration Fund, Worcester, 1976; mem. Worcester Social Service Corp., 1977-79; v.p. Elm Park Ctr. for Early Childhood Edn., Worcester, 1977-81. Nat. Endowment for Humanities grantee, 1974, 76, 81. Fellow Soc. Am. Archivists (chmn. task force on instl. evaluation 1977-82, council mem. 1981—, com. mem. archival info. exchange 1982—); mem. Am. Hist. Assn. (mem. profl. div. com. 1979-81, chmn. task Force on employment opportunities for historians 1980), New Eng. Archivists (pres. 1977-78, mem. exec. bd. 1976-79), Bibliog. Soc. Am. (chmn. fellowship com. 1981—), Orgn. Am. Historians. Club: Grolier (N.Y.C.). Home: q 433 Wolf's Ln Pelham Manor NY 10803 Office: Rare Books and Manuscripts Div NY Pub Library 476 Fifth Ave New York NY 10018

JOYNER, CLAUDE REUBEN, JR., physician; b. Winston-Salem, N.C., Dec. 4, 1925; s. Claude R. and Lytle (Mackie) J.; m. Nina Glenn Michael, Sept. 21, 1950; children: Emily Glenn, Claude Courtney. B.S., U. N.C., 1947; M.D., U. Pa., 1949. Intern Hosp. U. Pa., 1949-50; resident Bowman grey Med. Sch., 1950, U. Pa., 1954-55, fellow in cardiology; Nat. Heart Inst. trainee, 1952-53; asst. instr. medicine Hosp. U. Pa., Phila., 1951-53, instr., 1953-56, asso. medicine, 1956-59, asst. prof., 1959-64, asso. prof., 1964-72; prof. medicine U. Pitts., 1972—; chief medicine Allegheny Gen. Hosp., Pitts., 1972—. Contbr. articles to profl. jours. Served to lt. M.C. USNR, 1950-52. Fellow Am. Coll. Cardiology, ACP, Councils on Circulation, Arteriosclerosis and Cardiovascular Radiology of Am. Heart Assn.; mem. AAAS, Am. Heart Assn., Am. Clin. and Climatol. Soc. Home: Pulpit Rock Little Sewickley Creek Rd Sewickley PA 15143 Office: Allegheny Gen Hosp Pittsburgh PA 15212

JOYNER, CONRAD FRANCIS, political educator; b. Connersville, Ind., Oct. 21, 1931; s. Hubert Williams and Louise Agatha (Ariens) J.; m. Arabella Ann Maxey, July 9, 1955; children: Conrad, Jr. Michael, Mark. B.A., Earlham Coll., 1953; M.A., U. Fla., 1954, Ph.D., 1957; student (Fulbright scholar), Sydney U., Australia, 1956. Instr. W.Va. U., Morgantown, 1956-57; asst. prof. U. Southwestern La., Lafayette, 1957-61; prof. polit. sci. U. Ariz., Tucson, 1961—; spl. cons. program evaluation HEW, 1969-70; del. Internat. Energy Conf., Paris, 1975; expert cons. EPA, 1981. Author: The Commonwealth and Monopolies, 1963, The Republican Dilemma, 1963, The American Politician, 1971; contbr. articles to profl. jours. 1st v.p. Ariz. Acad., 1972-75; sec.-treas. So. Ariz. Environ. Council, Tucson, 1971; mem. U.S. Commn. for UNESCO, 1975-79, Tucson City Council, 1967-71; vice mayor Tucson City Council, 1969-70; vice chmn. Council Orgn. Ariz. State Govt., 1967-70; mem. Pima County Bd. Suprs., Tucson, 1972—, U.S. Census Adv. Commn., 1972-75, Ariz. Manpower Services Council, 1975—; bd. dirs. Ariz. Center Edn. in Politics, Palo Verde Found. Mental Health, 1969-72, Lighthouse YMCA, 1967-72; mem. alumni council Earlham Coll., 1974—. Recipient Outstanding Faculty Mem. award U. Ariz., 1965-66; E. Harris Harbison award Danford Found., 1967. Mem. John Henry Newman Honor Soc., AAUP (pres. 1960, 66), Am. Polit. Sci. Assn., Phi Beta Kappa. Republican. Roman Catholic (council). Home: 630 N Hayden St Tucson AZ 85710

JOYNER, LEON FELIX, university administrator; b. Savannah, Ga., Nov. 20, 1924; s. Leon Felix and Sarah (Thompson) J.; m. Margaret Ruth Barrett, June 28, 1944; children-Leon Stephens, Barrett Ray. Student, Harvard, 1944-45; A.B., Berea Coll., 1947; postgrad., Univs. Ala., Tenn., Ky., 1947-48. Mem. budget staff Ky. State Govt., 1948-55; mem. field staff Pub. Adminstrn. Service, Chgo., 1956-60; commr. personnel Ky. State Govt., 1960-62, health welfare adminstr., 1962-63, commr. fin., 1963-67; v.p. fin. U. N.C., 1968—; cons. Govts. of Burma, Thailand, 1956-59, Auditor-Gen., Pakistan, 1968. Chmn. Commn. on Reorganization of Exec. Br. State Govt. Ky., 1962; Bd. dirs. Research Triangle Found., N.C. Served to lt. (j.g.), Supply Corps USNR, 1943-46. Named Pub. Adminstr. of Year Ky. chpt. Am. Soc. Pub. Adminstrn., 1961. Mem. Am. Soc. Pub. Adminstrn. (past pres. Ky. chpt.), Nat. Assn. State Budget Officers (past mem. exec. com.), Internat. Bridge, Tunnel and Turnpike Assn. (past dir.), Am. Acad. Polit. and Social Sci., Phi Kappa Phi. Democrat. Presbyn. Home: 616 Churchill Dr Chapel Hill NC 27514

JOYNER, POWELL AUSTIN, manufacturing company executive; b. Dallas, July 20, 1925; s. Calvin N. and Isabel F. (Powell) J.; m. Wallene L. Schaper, July 12, 1952. B.S. in Physics, Centenary Coll., 1946; Ph.D. in Phys. Chemistry, U. Iowa, 1951. Asst. U. Iowa, 1946-50; research chemist Mpls.-Honeywell Regulator Co., 1950-52; head analysis sect. Callery Chem. Co., 1952-53, head measurements div., 1953-54; sr. research scientist Research Center, Mpls.-Honeywell Regulator Co., 1954-56, research supr., 1956-58, head chem. sect., 1958-60, project mgr. fuel cell controls, 1960-62, staff scientist, 1962-63; asst. dir. research div. Allis Chalmers Mfg. Co., 1963-64, gen. mgr. space and def. sci., 1964-67, dir. planning and evaluation, 1967-68; dir. research Trane Co., La Crosse, Wis., 1968-79, v.p. research, 1979—. Mem. Am. Chem. Soc., AAAS, Combustion Inst., Am. Flame Research Com. Club: Rotary. Home: W5369 Norseman Dr La Crosse WI 54601 Office: Trane Co 3600 Pammel Creek Rd La Crosse WI 65401

JOYNER, ROY ELTON, physician; b. Macon, Ga., Nov. 24, 1922; s. Van Buren and Lila Adelle (Phlieger) J.; children—David, Kathie Shayne, Julia, Joseph, Gregory, Elizabeth. Student, North Ga. Coll., Dahlonega, 1940-42; M.D., Med. Coll. Ga., Augusta, 1950. Diplomate: Am. Bd. Preventive Medicine. Intern USPHS Hosp., Galveston, Tex., 1950-51; staff physician Union Carbide Corp., South

Charleston, W.Va., 1951-55, med. dir., Texas City, Tex., 1955-72; corp. med. dir. Shell Oil Co., Houston, 1972—; Asso. adj. prof. U. Tex. Sch. Pub. Health at Houston, 1973—; mem. cons. faculty Inst. Clin. Toxicology, Houston, 1974-75. Contbr. articles to profl. jours. Mem. adv. bd. Houston Regional Council on Alcoholism, 1973—. Served with USAAF, 1942-45; asst. surgeon USPHS, 1950-51. Decorated Air medal with five clusters. Fellow Am. Acad. Occupational Medicine, Am. Occupational Med. Assn., Am. Coll. Preventive Medicine; mem. Tex. Occupational Med. Assn. (pres. 1964-65, dir. 1966-69), Texas City Optimists Club (pres. 1959). Home: 499 N Post Oak Ln Houston TX 77024 Office: PO Box 2463 Houston TX 77001

JOYNER, WEYLAND THOMAS, educator, physicist; b. Suffolk, Va., Aug. 9, 1929; s. Weyland T. and Thelma (Neal) J.; m. Marianne Steele, Dec. 3, 1955; children: Anne, Weyland, Leigh. B.S., Hampden-Sydney Coll., 1951; M.A., Duke, 1952, Ph.D., 1955. Teaching fellow Duke, 1954, research asso., 1958; physicist Dept. Def., Washington, 1954-57; research physicist U. Md., 1955-57; asst. prof. physics Hampden-Sydney Coll., 1957-59, asso. prof., 1959-63, prof., 1963—, physics chmn., 1968-82; research asso. Ames Lab. AEC, 1964-65; vis. prof. Pomona Coll., 1965; staff Commn. on Coll. Physics, Ann Arbor, Mich., 1966-67; vis. fellow Dartmouth Coll., 1981; mem. Panel on Preparation Physics Tchrs., 1967-68; nuclear phys. cons. Oak Ridge Inst. Nuclear Studies, 1960-67; NASA-Lewis faculty fellow, 1982-84; Pres. Piedmont Farms, Inc., 1958-75; ednl. cons. numerous colls. and univs., 1965-75; pres. Windsor Supply Corp., 1966-82, Three Rivers Farms, Inc., 1971—; mgmt. cons., 1966—; pres. Windsor Seed & Livestock Co., 1969—. Contbr. articles profl. jours. Bd. dirs. Prince Edward Acad., 1971—, exec. com., 1975—; trustee Prince Edward Sch. Electoral Bd., 1979—. Fellow AAAS; mem. Am. Phys. Soc., Am. Assn. Physics Tchrs., IEEE, Va. Acad. Sci. (past mem. council, sect. pres.), Am. Inst. Physics (regional counselor, past dir. Coll. Program), Phi Beta Kappa, Sigma Xi, Lambda Chi Alpha. Presbyn. (elder). Home: Venable Pl Hampden-Sydney VA 23943

JOYNES, RALPH CARLISLE, construction material company executive; b. Cheriton, Va., May 15, 1928; s. Ralph Havord and Irma Blanche (Sexton) J.; m. Roxanna Edge, June 7, 1952; children: Linda Carter, Ralph Carlisle, Jr., Karen Edge. B.A. in Econs., U. Va. Sales rep. U.S. Gypsum Co., 1952-60, dist. sales mgr., 1960-63, div. sales mgr., Charlotte, N.C., 1964-69, mgr. sales, Atlanta, 1970-74, mgr. mktg., 1975-77, gen. mgr., Chgo., 1977-80, group v.p., 1980—. Served with USMC, 1950-52.

JOYNT, CAREY BONTHRON, educator; b. Hensall, Ont., Can., 1924; came to U.S., 1948, naturalized, 1958; s. Thomas Clevel and Florence (Bonthron) J.; m. Anne Wilson Morgan, Aug. 21, 1948; 1 son, David Morgan. B.A., U. Western Ont., 1945, M.A., 1948; Ph.D., Clark U., 1951. Asst. prof. Lehigh U., Bethlehem, Pa., 1951-56, prof., chmn. dept. internat. relations, 1956-74, Monro J. Rathbone prof., 1975—. Co-author: Theory and Reality in World Politics, 1978, Ethics and International Affairs, 1982; Contbr. articles to profl. jours. Mem. Council on Ch. and Soc., United Presbyn. Ch. U.S.A., 1969-73. Ford Found. fellow, 1957-58; Am. Council Learned Socs. fellow, 1960; John S. Guggenheim fellow, 1963. Home: 1415 Oakwood Dr Bethlehem PA 18017

JOYS, DAVID SANDERSON, exec. recruiting cons.; b. Milw., July 17, 1943; s. J. Hartley and Anne (Welser) J.; m. Sandra Schuette, May 6. 1967; children—William Sanderson, Jonathan Hartley. B.A., Amherst Coll., 1965; M.B.A., Columbia U., 1967. With Am. Airlines, N.Y.C., Dallas and Los Angeles, 1967-72, zone sales mgr., 1968-70, mgr. reservations services, 1970-71, v.p. gen. sales, 1971-72; v.p. mktg. Hertz Corp., N.Y.C., 1972-73, v.p. mktg. ops. and services, 1973-74; v.p. Russell Reynolds Assos., N.Y.C., 1974-78, sr. v.p., 1978-80, exec. v.p., 1980—. Trustee Hurricane Island Outward Bound Sch., Rockland, Maine. Clubs: Stanwich, Field, Verbank, Racquet, Recess, Greenwich skating. Home: 57 Clapboard Ridge Rd Greenwich CT 06830 Office: 245 Park Ave New York NY 10167

JOZOFF, MALCOLM, consumer products company marketing executive; b. Allentown, Pa., May 2, 1939; s. Martin and Frieda (Wiener) J.; m. JoAnne Flynn, May 7, 1963; 1 son, Matthew James. B.A., Columbia U., 1961. With Procter & Gamble, 1967—; v.p. packaged soap and detergent div., 1981, v.p. So. Europe, 1982—. Bd. dirs. Arthristis Found. Southwestern Ohio, Cin., 1980; trustee Cin. Symphony Orch., 1981. Served to capt. USAF, 1962-67. Clubs: Queen City (Cin.); Briarwood (Bellefontaine, Ohio). Home: 223 Chaussee de Vleurgat 1050 Brussels Belgium Office: Procter and Gamble European Tech Ctr Temselaan 100 1820 Strombeek-Bever Belgium

JUBINVILLE, ALAIN MAURICE JOSEPH, economist, banker; b. Somerset, Man., Can., Aug. 23, 1928; s. Laurent and Eliane (Landry) J.; m. Marguerite Taillefer, Jan. 23, 1960; children: Yves, Louise, Denis, Francois. M.Soc.Sc., Universite Laval, Que., 1953. Research economist Bank of Can., Ottawa, 1953-63, research officer, 1963, chief fgn. exchange, 1963-71, chief internat., 1971-74, dep. gov., 1974—; on assignment with IMF as prin. dir. Bank of Zaire, 1981-83. Mem. Societe Canadienne de Scis. Economiques, Can. Econs. Assn. Club: Le Club de Golf Outaouais (Rockland, Ont.). Office: Bank of Can 234 Wellington St Ottawa ONCanada K1A OG9

JUCKEM, WILFRED PHILIP, mfg. co. exec.; b. Sheboygan, Wis., Apr. 27, 1915; s. Arvin M. and Martha (Henning) J.; m. Dorothy Iris Dean, Dec. 8, 1941; children—Jean Audrey, Philip Dean. Grad., Sheboygan Bus. Coll., 1934. With Jenkins Machine Co., Sheboygan Falls, Wis., 1933-34, Kohler of Kohler, Wis., 1934-42, Rock Island (Ill.) Arsenal, 1942-45; with Eagle Signal Corp., Moline, Ill., 1947-63, v.p. mfg., 1958-63; asst. to pres. E.W. Bliss Co., Canton, Ohio, 1963-64, adminstrv. v.p., 1964-66, v.p. press div., 1966-67, v.p. corporate devel., 1967-68, v.p., div. mgr., 1968-77; chmn. bd. Sears Mfg. Co., Davenport, Iowa, 1977—. Chmn. bd. dirs. Davenport Osteo. Hosp., 1979-80, vice chmn., 1980-82; bd. dirs. Ridgecrest Retirement Village. Mem. Nat. Elec. Mfrs. Assn. (chmn. emeritus traffic control systems sect. 1972-77), Am. Ordnance Assn. (pres. Iowa-Ill. chpt. 1975-76), Asso. Employers Quad Cities (dir., past pres.). Lutheran. Clubs: Town, Davenport, Iowa, Rock Island Arsenal Golf. Home: 2428 Salem Ct Bettendorf IA 52722 Office: 1718 S Concord St Davenport IA 52808

JUCKETT, J(ACOB) WALTER, manufacturing executive, religious association official; b. West Springfield, Mass., May 26, 1908; s. Frank A. and Laura P. (Fassett) J.; m. Elizabeth Brown, Aug. 24, 1940; children: David Warren, Nancy Elizabeth. B.S. in Elec. Engring., Norwich U., 1930, D.Sc. (hon.), 1962. With Hurlbut Paper Co., 1930-36, asst. treas., 1935-36; office mgr. Sandy Hill Corp. (formerly The Sandy Hill Iron & Brass Works), Hudson Falls, N.Y., 1936-42, asst. treas., 1937-42, sec., asst. treas., 1942-49, sec.-treas., gen. mgr., 1952-57, pres., 1957—, also dir.; Pres. bd. edn. Hudson Falls Central Sch. Dist., 1957-74; mem. exec. com. Nat. Bd. Missions Commn. on Evangelism, United Presbyn. Ch. U.S.A., 1954-59; mem. gen. council Presbytery of Albany, United Presbyn. Ch. U.S., 1958-61, Presbyn. Ch. U.S.A., 1959-60, exec. com. cons. conf. missions under gen. council, also elder local ch.; pres. Richmor Aviation, Inc.; dir. Kamyr, Inc.; mem. area adv. com. N.Y. Bus. Devel. Corp. Author: (autobiography) In Retrospect. Mem. at large nat. council Boy Scouts Am.; trustee Sandy Hill Found., 1951—; vice chmn. bd. trustees Norwich U.; trustee Citizens Pub. Expenditure Survey Inc. in, N.Y. State, Adirondack Community Coll., 1971-81; past chmn. N.Y. State Adv. Council Vocat. Edn.; mem. adv. council Bd. Coop. Ednl. Services, Washington-Warren-Hamilton Counties; chmn. bd. Lake Champlain Cancer Research Orgn.; pres. Sandy Hill Ednl. Fund Inc.; advisor Salvation Army. Served to capt. AUS, 1942-45. Recipient Silver Beaver award Boy Scouts Am. Mem. Nat. Council United Presbyn. Men (pres. 1959-60), Nat. Council Chs. (mem. dept. evangelism 1958-60), TAPPI, Newcomen Soc. N.Am., Tau Beta Pi, Sigma Alpha Epsilon, Eta Kappa Nu. Home: 31 Pearl St Hudson Falls NY 12839 Office: 27 Allen S Hudson Falls NY 12839

JUDAH, JAY STILLSON, historian, educator; b. Leavenworth, Wash., July 7, 1911; s. Stillson and Maude Alice (Cannon) J.; m. Lucile Elaine Baker, Dec. 2, 1935; children—Jay Stillson Jr., Elaine Judah Keller, Diane Judah Moore. A.B., U. Wash., 1934; Library cert., U. Calif., Berkeley, 1941; Litt.D., Chapman Coll., 1955. Mem. Christian Church (Disciples of Christ); with Pacific Sch. Religion, Berkeley, 1941-69, head librarian, 1941-69, prof. history of religion, 1955-69; librarian, dir. Bibliog. Center, Grad. Theol. Union, Berkeley, 1966-69, dir., prof. history of religion, 1969-76; adj. prof. Pacific Sch. Religion, 1974-79; Nat. v.p. Alliance for Preservation of Religious Liberty, 1978-79. Author: Jehovah's Witnesses, 1964, History and Philosophy of the Metaphysical Movements in America, 1967, Hare Krishna and the Counterculture, 1974; compiler, editor: Index to Religious Periodical Literature, 1949-52, 1952. Guggenheim fellow, 1934; Sealantic Fund fellow, 1957-58. Fellow Internat. Inst. Arts and Letters; mem. Am. Theol. Library Assn. (v.p. 1962-63, pres. 1963-64), Western Theol. Library Assn. (pres. 1954-55), Internat. Assn. Theol. Libraries (sec.-treas. 1955-60). Clubs: El Cerrito (Calif.); Tennis (pres. 1958-65). Home: 2705 Saklan Indian Dr 8 Walnut Creek CA 94595 *My goal and motivation as a Christian have been to practice to the best of my ability my belief in a sacrificial love for God and humanity without any reservations, and to contribute whatever possible toward the furtherance of justice and truth.*

JUDD, BRIAN RAYMOND, educator, physicist; b. Chelmsford, Eng., Feb. 13, 1931; s. Harry and Edith (Saltmarsh) J. B.A., Brasenose Coll., Oxford U., 1952, M.A., 1955, D.Phil., 1955. Fellow Magdalen Coll., Oxford U., 1955-62; instr. U. Chgo., 1957-58; asso. prof. U. Paris, 1962-64; staff mem. Lawrence Radiation Lab., Berkeley, Cal., 1964-66; prof. physics Johns Hopkins, Balt., 1966—, chmn. dept., 1979—; Vis. Erskine fellow U. Canterbury, Christchurch, New Zealand, 1968; vis. fellow Australian Nat. U., Canberra, 1975. Author: Operator Techniques in Atomic Spectroscopy, 1963, Second Quantization and Atomic Spectroscopy, 1967, (with J.P. Elliott) Topics in Atomic and Nuclear Theory, 1970, Angular Momentum Theory For Diatomic Molecules, 1975. Office: Physics Dept Johns Hopkins Baltimore MD 21218

JUDD, DONALD CLARENCE, sculptor; b. Excelsior Springs, Mo., June 3, 1928; s. Roy Clarence and Effie (Cowsert) J.; children: Flavin Starbuck, Rainer Yingling. Student, Coll. William and Mary, 1948-49, Art Students League, 1949-53; B.S. in Philosophy, Columbia U., 1953, postgrad., 1957-62. Tchr., Bklyn. Inst. Arts and Sci., 1962-64; vis. artist Darmouth Coll., 1966. Author: Complete Writings 1959-75, 1975; one-man shows include, Green Gallery, N.Y.C., 1963, Leo Castelli Gallery, N.Y.C., 1966, 69, 70, 73, 75, Whitney Mus. Am. Art, 1968, Locksley-Shea Gallery, Mpls., 1970, 71, 73, 75, 81, Greenberg Gallery, St. Louis, 1970, Pasadena Art Mus., 1971, Ace Gallery, Venice, Calif., 1974-77, Nat. Gallery Can., 1975, Art Mus. S. Tex., 1977, also numerous European galleries, numerous commns. Swedish Inst. fellow, 1965; Guggenheim fellow, 1968; Nat. Endowment Arts grantee, 1967, 76. Address: care Leo Castelli Gallery 420 W Broadway New York NY 10013 *

JUDD, GARY, university administrator; b. Czechoslovakia, Sept. 24, 1942; came to U.S., 1946, naturalized, 1951; s. Joe and Arlene (Zipser) J.; m. Rosalind Sandra Dixter, July 26, 1964; children: Robin, Jennifer, Jason. B.Mat.E., Rensselaer Poly. Inst., 1963, Ph.D. in Phys. Metallurgy, 1967. Mem. faculty dept. materials engring. Rensselaer Poly. Inst., Troy, N.Y., 1967—, assoc. prof., 1972-76, prof., 1976—, acting dept. chmn., 1974-75, vice provost plans and resources, 1975-78, dean Grad. Sch. and vice provost for acad. affairs, 1979—, acting provost, 1982-83; cons. Oak Ridge Nat. Labs., Watervliet Arsenal. Contbr. articles to profl. jours. Mem. bd. of edn. Hebrew Acad. of Capital Dist., 1974-79, 81-83. NSF fellow, 1963-66; Recipient Alfred Geisler award Eastern N.Y. chpt. Am. Soc. Metals, 1974. Mem. Am. Soc. Metals, AIME, Microbeam Analysis Soc., AAAS, Sigma Xi, Tau Beta Pi, Alpha Sigma Mu, Phi Lambda Upsilon. Jewish. Home: 3 Harding Albany NY 12208 Office: 110 8th Troy NY 12181

JUDD, ROBERT CARPENTER, business administration educator; b. Maui, Hawaii, July 6, 1921; s. Robert Augustine and Marguerite (Schoonmaker) J.; m. Dorothy May Heiple, Sept. 19, 1964; children: Dianna Kay (Mrs. Joseph R. Carlisi), Nancy Carol (Mrs. David E. Wilber), Linda Sue (Mrs. Bernard Pucci); stepchildren: Patricia Ann (Mrs. Michael J. Konkoly), Catherine Rafferty, Deborah Rafferty-Brown (Mrs. Herb Brown), Nancy Rafferty (Mrs. Steve Arrington). A.B., U. Chgo., 1942; Ph.D., U. Wis., 1963. Statis. analyst Montgomery Ward & Co., 1943; statis. mgr. Manning, Maxwell & Moore, Inc., 1943-46; market research mgr. R.G. LeTourneau, Inc., 1946-47; instr. statistics Bradley U., 1947-50; spl. risks supr. Continental Casualty Co., 1950-52; asst. to v.p. Mut. of Omaha, 1952-55; Eastern regional mgr. Fed. Life & Casualty Co., 1955-57; asst. prof. econs. and bus., dir. continuing edn. Beloit Coll., 1957-62; asst. prof. bus. orgn. and mgmt. U. Nebr., 1962-63; asso. prof. mktg. DePaul U., 1963-66, No. Ill. U., 1966-68; prof. ops. analysis U. Toledo, 1968-73, chmn. dept. ops. analysis, 1968-71; v.p. acad. affairs Dyke Coll., 1973-74; prof. Troy (Ala.) State U., 1974-76; Univ. prof. bus. adminstrn. Gov.'s State U., 1976—. Contbr. articles to profl. jours. Fellow AAAS; mem. Am. Mktg. Assn., Am. Inst. Decision Scis., Ops. Research Soc. Am., Am. Statis. Assn., Delta Sigma Pi, Beta Gamma Sigma. Club: Rotary. Home: 1990 Flagstaff Ct Glendale Heights IL 60139

JUDD, WILLIAM ROBERT, engineering geologist, educator; b. Denver, Aug. 16, 1917; s. Samuel and Lillian (Israelske) J.; m. Rachel Elizabeth Douglas, Apr. 18, 1942; children: Stephanie (Mrs. Chris Wadley), Judith (Mrs. John Soden), Dayna (Mrs. Erick Grandmason), Pamela, Connie. A.B., U. Colo., 1941, postgrad., 1941-50. Registered profl. engr., Colo., engring. geologist, Calif., Oreg., Ind. Engring. geologist Colo. Water Conservation Bd., 1941-42; supervisory engring. geologist Denver, Rio Grande Western R.R., Colo. and Utah, 1942-44; head geology sect. No. 1, acting dist. geologist-Alaska U.S. Bur. Reclamation, Office of Chief Engr., Denver, 1945-60; head basing tech. group RAND Corp., Santa Monica, Calif., 1960-65; prof. rock mechanics Purdue U., Lafayette, Ind., 1966—, head geotech. engring., 1976—, tech. dir., 1972-79; Geotech. cons., U.S., Mexico, Cuba, Honduras, Greece, 1950—; geoscience editor Am. Elsevier Pub. Co., 1967-71; chmn. panel on ocean scis. Com. on Instl. Cooperation, 1971—; chmn. Nat. Acad. Sci. U.S. Nat. Com. on Rock Mechanics, 1963-69, co-chmn. panel on research requirements, 1977-81, chmn. panel on awards, 1972-82; mem. U.S. Army Adv. Bd. on Mountain and Arctic Warfare, 1956-62, USAF Sci. Adv. Bd. Geophysics Panel Study Group, 1964-67; mem. com. on safety dams NRC, 1977-78, 82-83; Nat. dir. Nat. Ski Patrol System, Inc., 1956-62; Alex du Toit Meml. lectr., S.Africa, 1967. Author: (with E.F. Taylor) Ski Patrol Manual, 1956, (with D. Krynine) Principles of Engineering Geology and Geotechnics, 1957, Sitzmarks or Safety, 1960; Editor: Rock Mechanics Research, 1966, State of Stress In The Earth's Crust, 1964; co-editor: Physical Properties of Rocks and Minerals, 1981; editor-in-chief: Engring. Geology, 1972—. Recipient Spl. Research award NRC, 1982; named to Colo. Ski Hall of Fame, 1983. Fellow ASCE (com. on rock mechanics), Geol. Soc. Am., S.African Inst. Mining and Metallurgy; mem. Internat. Soc. Rock Mechanics (1st v.p. 1967-70), Am. Arbitration Assn. (panel arbitrators), Assn. Engring. Geologists, Internat. Assn. Engring. Geologists, Ind. Soc. Engring. Geology (life), U.S. Com. on Large Dams (mem. exec. council 1977—), Sigma Xi. Club: Explorers. Home: 200 Quincy St West Lafayette IN 47906 Office: Sch Civil Engring Purdue U West Lafayette IN 47907 *Any new idea may have merit, so don't hesitate to introduce it; you occasionally may be ridiculed but the ideas that are accepted make such ridicule unimportant.*

JUDE, JAMES RODERICK, cardiac surgeon; b. Maple Lake, Minn., June 2, 1928; s. Bernard Benedict and Cecilia Mary (Leick) J.; m. Sallye Garrigan, Aug. 4, 1951; children—Roderick, John, Cecilia, Victoria, Peter, Robert, Chris. B.S., Coll. St. Thomas, 1949; M.D., U. Minn., 1953. Intern Johns Hopkins Hosp., 1953-54, resident in surgery, 1954-55, 58-61, fellow in cardiovascular research, 1955-56; instr. surgery Johns Hopkins U. and Med. Sch., 1961-62, asst. prof., 1962-64; prof. surgery, chief thoracic and cardiovascular surgery U. Miami Sch. Medicine, 1964-71, clin. prof., 1971—; practice medicine specializing in cardiovascular surgery, Miami and Ft. Lauderdale, 1971—. Contbr. articles to med. jours. Trustee Sir Victor Sasson Heart Found., Bahamas, 1973—; mem. Coral Gables (Fla.) Planning Bd., 1973-77. Served with USPHS, 1956-58. Fellow Am. Coll. Chest Physicians, Am. Coll. Cardiology, A.C.S.; mem. Am. Assn. Thoracic Surgery, Am. Surg. Assn., So. Surg. Assn., Soc. Vascular Surgery, Soc. Thoracic Surgeons, Am. Heart Assn., Soc. Univ. Surgeons. Democrat. Roman Catholic. Co-developer cardiopulmonary resuscitation. Home: 200 Edgewater Dr Coral Gables FL 33133 Office: 3661 S Miami Ave Miami FL 33133 also 5601 N Dixie Hwy Fort Lauderdale FL 33334

JUDELSON, ALAN I., advertising agency executive; b. N.Y.C., May 24, 1931; s. Herman W. and Anne (Retman) J.; m. Tommi Wilson, Dec. 19, 1966 (div. 1980); children: Marcie, Howard; m. Jean Anne Johnson, Jan. 1, 1982. B.F.A., Cooper Union. Art dir. Galbraith, Hoffman & Rogers, N.Y.C., 1957-61; art dir., ptnr. Judelson-Trooper Assoc., N.Y.C., 1961-64; art dir. Tathum Laird 7 Kudner, N.Y.C., 1964-68; creative dir., v.p. Interpub. Corp., N.Y.C., 1968-69; creative dir., sr. v.p. Ted Bates Worldwide, N.Y.C., 1969—; cons. Black Enterprise Mag., 1971—, J.P. Stevens Co. Served with U.S. Army, 1953-55. Jewish. Office: 1515 Broadway New York NY 10036

JUDELSON, DAVID N., business executive; b. 1928. B.S. in Mech. Engring, N.Y.U., 1949. Chmn. bd. Oscar I. Judelson, Inc. (mfrs. indsl. equipment), Jersey City, 1949-58; with Gulf & Western Industries, Inc., 1958-83, v.p., dir., 1959-61, mem. exec. com., 1961-65, chmn. exec. com., 1965-66, exec. v.p., 1966-67, pres., 1967-83, also dir.; dir. Madison Sq. Garden Corp., A.P.S., Inc., Brown Co. Address: 375 Park Ave Suite 2507 New York NY 10152 *

JUDGE, BERNARD MARTIN, newswire editor; b. Chgo., Jan. 6, 1940; s. Bernard A. and Catherine Elizabeth (Halloran) J.; m. Kimbeth A. Wehrli, July 9, 1966; children—Kelly, Bernard R., Jessica. Student, John Carroll U., 1957-61. Reporter City News Bur., Chgo., 1965-66, pres., 1978-80, dir., 1980-83; reporter Chgo. Tribune, 1966-72, asst. city editor, 1972-73, night city editor, Sunday city editor, 1973-74, city editor, 1974-79, asst. mng. editor met. news, 1979-83; editor, gen. mgr. City News Bur. Chgo., 1983—. Served with U.S. Army, 1962-64. Mem. Chgo. Headline Club, Chgo. Press Club, Sigma Delta Chi. Club: Skyline. Home: 216 W Lake St Barrington IL 60010 Office: Chgo Tribune 435 N Michigan Ave Chicago IL 60611

JUDGE, CURTIS HERBERT, tobacco co. exec.; b. Valdosta, Ga., July 13, 1924; s. Curtis Herbert and Iris (Herbert) J.; m. Rosemary Tom, Sept. 5, 1947; children—Curtis Herbert, III, Kate. J.D., U. Tex., 1947; postgrad., Harvard U., 1962. Bar: Tex. bar 1947. Individual practice law, Texas City, 1947-48; with Colgate-Palmolive Co., Houston, Omaha and St. Louis, 1948-65; salesman to gen. sales mgr. R.J. Reynolds Co., Winston-Salem, N.C., 1965-70; sales mgr. to v.p. mktg. Lorillard div. Loews Corp., N.Y.C., 1970—; pres., dir. Loews Corp. Served with USAAF, 1943-45. Mem. Sigma Nu. Republican. Episcopalian. Clubs: Winged Foot Golf, Sky, Pinnacle, Harvard, Tex. Ex, Tex. Cowboys. Home: 518 W Lyon Farm Dr Greenwich CT 06830 Office: 666 Fifth Ave New York NY 10103

JUDGE, JOHN EMMET, manufacturing company marketing executive; b. Grafton, N.D., May 5, 1912; s. Charles and Lillian (Johnson) J.; m. Clarita Garcia, Apr. 18, 1940; children: Carolyn (Mrs. Samuel Stanley), John Emmet, Maureen, Eileen, Susan. B.S. in Elec. Engring., U. N.D., 1935. Asst. to adminstr. Fed. Works Agy., Washington, 1939-42; staff Wallace Clark & Co. (mgmt. cons.), N.Y.C., 1942-46; v.p. Morgan Furniture Co., Asheville, N.C., 1946-48; mgr. financial analysis Lincoln-Mercury div. Ford Motor Co., 1949-53, asst. gen. purchasing agt., 1953-55, mgr. mdsg. and product planning, 1955-58, marketing mgr., 1958-60, product planning mgr., Dearborn, Mich., 1960-62; v.p. mktg. services Westinghouse Elec. Corp., Pitts., 1963-67; v.p. mktg. Indian Head, Inc., 1967-68; mktg. cons., 1969—; dir. Capital Corp. of Am. (investments), Intertek Industries, Kratos, Inc., Cashiers Plastics Corp., Cambridge Instruments, Inc.; Mem. adv. com. to U.S. sec. of commerce. Chmn. Birmingham Library Com., 1957; mem. bd. Boysville of Mich., 1957—. Mem. Am. Ordnance Assn., Soc. Advancement Mgmt., N.A.M. (chmn. marketing com.), Am. Soc. M.E., Engring. Soc. Detroit, Nat. Assn. Accountants, Soc. Automotive Engrs., U. N.D. Alumni Assn. (pres.), Sigma Tau, Alpha Tau Omega. Roman Catholic. Clubs: Detroit Athletic, Economic (Detroit); Orchard Lake (Mich.). Address: S Lake Shore Dr Harbor Springs MI 49740

JUDGE, ROSEMARY ANN, oil company executive; b. Jersey City; d. Frank T. and Frances M. (O'Brien) J. A.B., Seton Hall U. Exec. sec. Socony Vacuum, N.Y.C., 1944-56; sec., confidential asst. to v.p. and dir. Socony Mobil, N.Y.C., 1956-59; sec., confidential asst. to pres. Mobil Oil Co. Div., N.Y.C., 1959-61; sec., adminstrv. asst. to pres. Mobil Oil Corp., N.Y.C., 1961-69, adminstrv. asst. to chmn., 1969-71, asst. to chmn., sec. exec com., 1971-84, corp. sec., 1975-76; asst. to chmn., sec. bd. and exec. com. Mobil Corp., 1976-84; pres. Mobil Found., N.Y.C., 1973—. Bd. regents Seton Hall U. Club: Women's Econ. Round Table. Office: 150 E 42nd St New York NY 10017

JUDGE, THOMAS LEE, management company executive, former state official; b. Helena, Mont., Oct. 12, 1934; s. Thomas Patrick and Blanch (Guillot) J.; m. Suzie Koch, June 27, 1981; children: Tommy, Patrick. B.A., U. Notre Dame, 1957; student, U. Louisville, 1958-60. Sales exec. Nat. Starch Products & Chem. Co., Louisville, 1957-58; merchandising dir. Louisville Courier-Jour., 1958-60; owner, pres. Judge Advt.-Pub. Relations, Helena, 1960-72; lt. gov. Mont., 1969-73, gov. Mont., 1973-81; mng. partner Mountain States Mgmt. Co., 1981—; chmn. Nat. Conf. Lt. Govs., 1972; mem. exec. com. Nat. Govs. Conf., 1979-80; chmn. Western Govs. Policy Office, 1978. Chmn. Old West Region Commn., 1973, Fedn. Rocky Mountain States, 1974; Mem. Mont. Ho. of Reps., 1960-65, asst. minority leader,

1962; mem. Mont. Senate, 1967-69; Bd. dirs. YMCA, 1962-64. Served with AUS, 1958-59. Eisenhower fellow, Taiwan, 1981; Named Notre Dame Man of Year for Mont., 1966, 1 of 100 Outstanding Young Men Am. Time mag., 1974. Democrat. Clubs: KC, Elks, Eagles. Home: 493 S Park Helena MT 59601 Office: Box 503 Helena MT 59624

JUDIS, JOSEPH, educator; b. Toledo, Sept. 23, 1929; s. Max and Thelma (Rabinovitz) J.; m. Hana Kiryati, Mar. 20, 1955; children-Linda Susan, Allen Sydney. B.S. in Pharmacy, U. Toledo, 1949; M.S., Purdue U., 1951, Ph.D., 1954. Postdoctoral research fellow microbiology Western Res. U. Med. Sch., 1954-55; research microbiologist Toledo Hosp. Inst. Med. Research, 1955-56; mem. faculty U. Toledo, 1956—, prof. pharmacy, 1962—, chmn. dept. biology, 1964-66, dean, 1966-76. Author articles in field. Mem. Am. Pharm. Assn., Am. Chem. Soc., Am. Soc. Microbiology, Soc. Gen. Microbiology (London), A.A.A.S., Sigma Xi, Phi Lambda Upsilon, Rho Chi, Phi Kappa Phi. Home: 2806 Meadowwood Dr Toledo OH 43606

JUDKINS, DONALD WARD, retired banker, art historian; b. Seattle, Apr. 2, 1912; s. Earl Henry and Laura (Lundberg) J.; m. Elizabeth Waltz Dickey, Jan. 23, 1954. Student, U. Minn., 1929-32, 75—, B.A., 1976; grad., Am. Inst. Banking, 1939. With First Nat. Bank, Mpls., 1933-41, asst. cashier, 1946-49; cashier First Hennepin Nat. Bank, Mpls., 1949-56; pres. First Southdale Nat. Bank, Mpls., 1955-74, chmn. bd., 1974-75, also dir., 1955-78; dir. Contech, Inc., Mpls., 1972-83. Bd. dirs. Walker Art Center, Mpls., 1953-74, pres. bd. dirs., 1955-58; bd. dirs. Minn. Opera Co., 1968—, v.p., 1969-71, pres., 1971-72; bd. dirs. Ft. Snelling State Park Assn., 1962—, Boys Clubs Mpls., 1972-80, Family and Welfare Soc., Mpls., 1970-72, Mpls. Coll. Art and Design, 1977—; 1st v.p. Mpls. Coll. Art and Design, 1978, pres., 1979-81; bd. dirs., treas. Southdale Center Mchts. Assn., 1956-68. Served to capt. AUS, 1942-46. Mem. Greater Southdale Area C. of C. (pres. 1967-68), Walker Art Center, Mpls. Soc. Fine Arts, Minn. Orch. Assn., Coll. Art Assn. Am., Smithsonian Instn., English Speaking Union, Minn. Hist. Soc., Minn. Mus. Art, Minn. Alumni Assn., Phi Sigma Kappa. Clubs: Rotary (recipient Paul Harris award 1974, dir. 1957-62), Rotary (pres. 1959-60), Rotary (dist. treas. 1960-66); Minneapolis, North Star Tennis (Mpls.); Mill Reef (Antigua, W.I.). Home: 2310 Huntington Point Rd W Wayzata MN 55391

JUDSON, FRANKLYN SYLVANUS, lawyer, consultant; b. Cleve., May 13, 1915; s. Calvin Albert and Beatrice (Harding) J.; m. Nancy E. Nevin, July 29, 1939; children: Franklyn N., William W., Ann Louise, Kenneth G., Carolyn. A.B., Case Western Res. U., 1938, J.D., 1940. Bar: Ohio 1940, Pa. 1954. Law librarian Western Res. U., Cleve., 1940-41; jr. atty., prin. trial atty., asst. regional adminstr. SEC, Cleve., 1942-53; atty., asst. sec. I-T-E Circuit Breaker Co., Phila., 1953-55, sec., 1955-67; sec., gen. counsel I-T-E Imperial Corp., 1967—, v.p., sec., gen. counsel, 1969-72, v.p., gen. counsel, 1972-75, sr. v.p., gen. counsel, 1975-77, cons. corp. law depts., 1978—. Chmn. div. C maj. firms dept. United Fund, Phila., 1957-59; Bd. dirs. Health and Welfare Council, 1963, United Cerebral Palsy Assn. Phila., 1959-68; past pres. bd. trustees Friends' Central Sch. Mem. Internat., Am., Cleve., Phila. bar assns., World Assn. Lawyers, Am. Soc. Corp. Secs. (past pres. Middle Atlantic regional group, bd. dirs. 1968), Am. Arbitration Assn. (panel mem.), Com. for Edn. in Bus. Ethics. Quaker (clk. Old Haverford monthly meeting). Club: Union League (Phila.). Home: 820 Colony Rd Bryn Mawr PA 19010

JUDSON, JEANNETTE ALEXANDER, artist; b. N.Y.C., Feb. 23, 1912; d. Philip George and Gertrude (Leichter) Alexander; m. Henry Judson, Sept. 23, 1945; children: S. Robert Weltz, Jr., Pauline Raiff; 1 stepson, E. William Judson. Student, N.A.D., 1956-59, Art Student League, N.Y.C., 1959-61. One-man shows, Fairleigh Dickinson U., 1965, Bodley Gallery, N.Y.C., 1967, 69, 71, 73, N.Y. U., 1969, Pa. State U., Laura Musser Mus. Art, Muscatine, Iowa, Syracuse U. House, N.Y.C., 1975, Ludlow-Hyland Gallery, 1980, Key Gallery, N.Y.C., 1982, 2 person show, Am. Standard Gallery, 1980; exhibited in group shows, including: anns., Nat. Assn. Women Artists, N.Y.C., France, Italy, 1965—, Audubon Artists, N.Y.C., 1962, 64, 65-67, Allied Artists, N.Y.C., 1966-67, group show, Key Gallery, N.Y.C., 1981, Key Gallery small works exhibit, 1983, N.Y.U. small works, N.Y.C., 1982; represented in permanent collections, Joseph H. Hirshhorn, N.Y. U., Norfolk (Va.) Mus. Arts and Scis., Brandeis U., Peabody Art Mus., Mus. N.Mex., Sheldon Swope Art Mus., Syracuse U., Evansville Mus. Arts and Scis., Rutgers U., Colby Coll., Butler Inst. Am. Art, Laura Musser Mus., Fordham U., Lehigh U., Ga. Mus. Art, U. Ga., Fairleigh Dickinson U., Lowe Mus., U. Miami, Washington County (Md.) Mus. Fine Arts, Miami Mus. Modern Art, Bruce Mus., Greenwich, Conn., Bklyn. Mus., Hudson River Mus., Dartmouth Coll., Mus., Mus. Modern Art, Lending Service, Columbia U., Art In Embassies program Dept. State, Am. embassy., Stockholm, also numerous pvt. collections. Mem. Nat. Assn. Women Artists (Grumbacher award 1967, Lillian Cottan award 1979, oil nominating com. 1977-79), Artists Equity, N.Y., Art Students League (life), Am. Soc. Contemporary Artists (Dorothy Feigin award 1976, House of Heydenriek award 1977). Home and Studio: 1130 Park Ave New York NY 10028

JUDSON, LOWELL HOLLANDER, fashion designer; b. N.Y.C.,; s. Chester Donald and Anita Weiser (Hollander) J. B.A., Lehigh U., 1944. Fashion designer Roytex Robes, Dorian Loungewear, Jasper House; also free-lance fashion designer; designer Kay Windsor Dresses., R&K Dresses, Patty O'Neil Dresses, Pierre Cardin Sportswear. Recipient Spl. Coty award in Men's Fashion, 1976, Tommy award in fashion, 1975, 76, 77, 78, 79. Mem. Inner Circle, Fashion News Workshop. Home: 15 W 75th St New York NY 10023

JUDSON, LYMAN SPICER VINCENT, author, artist; b. Plymouth, Mich., Mar. 27, 1903; s. Ernest W. and Fannie Louise (Spicer) J.; m. E. Ellen MacKechnie, 1933 (dec. 1964); m. S. Adele H. Christensen, 1968. A.B., Albion Coll., 1925; postgrad., S.E. Mich. U., 1926, U. Iowa, 1929-30, U. So. Calif., 1927, Harvard, 1942, U. San Francisco, Palma, Mallorca, Spain, 1967; M.S., U. Mich., 1929; Ph.D., U. Wis., 1933. Chief motion picture and visual edn. divs. OAS, 1946-51; served to comdr. USNR, 1942-65; mem. joint bd. control USN tng. films, 1944-46; vis. prof. Latin Am. affairs Assn. Am. Colls., 1952; speech writer for Hon. Christian A. Herter, 1954-57; staff Supreme Allied Comdr. Atlantic; liaison officer staff Supreme Allied Comdr. Europe and European Hdqrs.; dir. gen. NATO, 1953-54; spl. mission, Vietnam and 7th Fleet, 1966; TV cons. Johnson Found., 1963-64; devel. and long-range planning cons., 1965—; chmn. bd., treas. Am. Fine Arts Found., Rochester, Minn., 1964—. Author: Electrodynamic Recorder, 1930, Objective Studies on the Influence of the Speaker and the Listener, 1930, Combining the Breathing Undae of Speaker and the Listener, 1932, Preliminary Study of the Offerings of Speech-Content Courses in the Technical Colleges of the United States, 1932, The Vegetative Versus the Speech Use of Biological Systems, 1932, Basic Speech and Voice Science, 1933, The Fundamentals of the Speaker-Audience Relationship, 1934, Modern Group Discussion, 1935, Manual of Group Discussion, 1936, Public Speaking for Future Farmers, 1936, After-Dinner Speaking, 1937, Winning Future Farmers Speeches, 1939, The Student Congress Movement, 1940, The Monroe Doctrine and the Growth of Western Hemisphere Solidarity, 1941, Voice Science, 1942, rev. edit., 1965, The Judson Guides to Latin America, including: Let's Go to Colombia, 1949, Let's Go to Guatemala, 1950, Let's Go to Peru, 1951, Your Holiday in Cuba, 1952, Report of Command Information Bureau 47 on Operation Inland Seas, 1959, The Interview, 1966, The Business Conference, 1969, Vincent Judson: The Island Series, 1973, Solution: PNC and PNCLAND, 1973, The AQUA Declaration, 1976, Happy 60th Birthday, 1982, The Shadow(s), 1983. Propr. Boston Athenaeum.; Mem. Explorers Scout bd.; cabinet mem., bd. mem., exec. com. mem., treas. Twin Lakes council Boy Scouts Am., 1972-73; sustaining mem. Rochester Civic Theater. Fellow Am. Geog. Soc.; mem. Inter-Am. Soc. Anthropology and Geography, Soc. Am. Archeology, Am. Soc. Agrl. Scis., Am. Acad. Polit. and Social Scis., Pub. Relations Soc. Am., Rochester Art Center, Judson Latin Am. Collection, Smithsonian Instn., Walker Art Center, Archeol. Inst. Am. (pres. Winona-Hiawatha Valley chpt.), AAAS, Am. Micros. Soc., Navy League, Service Corps Ret. Execs., Sigma Xi (Mayo Found. chpt.), Alpha Phi Omega, Delta Sigma Rho (nat. sec., nat. editor), Tau Kappa Alpha, Pi Kappa Delta, Sigma Delta Chi, Sigma Chi. Episcopalian. Clubs: Rotary; Explorers (N.Y.C.); Cosmos (Washington). Home: Rochester Towers 207 SW 5th Ave Rochester MN 55902 Office: APEX U Press PO Box 277 Rochester MN 55903 *New ideas may be judged successful (even though they, themselves, are not adopted) if they open up new areas of thought and, thus, stimulate other new ideas which are acceptable and successful.*

JUDSON, SHELDON, geology educator; b. Utica, N.Y., Oct. 18, 1918; s. Salmon Sheldon and Dorothy (Eurich) J.; m. Anne Perrin Galpin, Feb. 13, 1943; children: Stephanie Dean, Anne Perrin, Lucy Sheldon. A.B., Princeton U., 1940; M.A., Harvard U., 1946, Ph.D., 1948. Faculty U. Wis., 1948-55, asso. prof. geology, 1955-64; Knox Taylor prof. geology, Princeton, 1964—, chmn. dept., 1970-82; dir. Princeton Coop. Sch. Program, 1964-66; pres. Princeton Jr. Mus., 1964-67; trustee Daily Princetonian; chmn. Univ. Research Bd., Princeton U., 1972-77. Author articles in field; asso. editor: Am. Scientist, 1956-69. Served to lt. USNR, 1942-46. Faculty fellow Fund Advancement Edn., 1954-55; Guggenheim fellow, 1960-61, 66-67; Fulbright fellow, 1960-61. Fellow AAAS, Geol. Soc. Am.; mem. Arctic Inst., Sigma Xi. Clubs: Nassau (Princeton); Princeton of N.Y., Century Assn. N.Y. Home: 18 Aiken Ave Princeton NJ 08540

JUDSON, THOMAS FEAREY, JR., construction company executive; b. Rochester, N.Y., Apr. 2, 1945; s. Thomas F. and Virginia (Pike) J.; m. Elisabeth Wesson, June 22, 1968; children: Rufus Morgan, Elisabeth. B.S., Yale U., 1967; M.B.A., Cornell U., 1970. With John B. Pike & Son, Rochester, 1963—, field engr., 1968-69, asst. to treas., 1969-71, asst. treas., 1971-73, v.p., sec.-treas., 1973-75, pres., chief exec. officer, 1975—. Bd. dirs. Genesee Hosp., Rochester, 1982-83, Hochstein Sch. Music, Rochester, 1983, George Eastman House, 1983; treas. Convalescent Children's Hosp., Rochester, 1978-81. Mem. Gen. Bldg. Contractors, N.Y. Assn. Gen. Contractors (pres. 1983-84), Young Pres.'s Orgn. Clubs: Genesee Valley (pres. 1981-82), Country of Rochester). Home: 1752 Murray Rd Victor NY 14564 Office: 1 Circle St Rochester NY 14607

JUDY, BERNARD FRANCIS, newspaper editor; b. Grove City, Pa., Mar. 20, 1920; s. Francis Xavier and Catherine Veronica (Toomey) J.; m. Jane Elizabeth Urey, Apr. 3, 1945; children—Kathleen, Cynthia, Jill, Mark. B.S. in Commerce, Grove City Coll., 1941; A.B. in Econs, Washington and Lee U., Lexington, Va., 1947; M.S. in Journalism, Columbia, 1948. Mem. staff Toledo Blade, 1948—, asso. editor, 1969-73, editor, 1973—; dir. Toledo Blade Co. Served with USAAF, 1942-44; CIC AUS, 1945. Mem. Am. Soc. Newspaper Editors, Phi Beta Kappa, Sigma Delta Chi. Roman Catholic. Home: 3405 Kenwood Blvd Toledo OH 43606 Office: 241 Superior St Toledo OH 43660

JUDY, HUBERT STONEWALL, ret. def. industry cons.; b. Woodward, Okla., June 20, 1915; s. Hubert Stonewall and May (Pierson) J.; m. Mae Summers, Oct. 10, 1942. B.S. in Bus. Adminstrn, Okla. U., 1940; grad., Advanced Flying Sch., Kelly Field, Tex., 1941, Air War Coll., 1952, Nat. War Coll., 1959, Advanced Mgmt. Program Harvard, 1956. Commd. 2d lt. USAAF, 1941; advanced through grades to brig. gen. USAF, 1962; various assignments in, U.S., 1941-43; dep. comdr. 448th Heavy Bomb Group, Eng., 1943-45; plans and operations staff officer SHAPE; air dep. to air comdr. Office Allied Mil. Govt., Berlin, Germany, 1945-46; staff plans and operations officer, directorate plans and operations Hdqrs. USAF, 1946- 48; USAF liasion officer to State Dept., 1948-49; asst. exec., exec. directorate plans and operations Hdqrs. USAF, 1949-51; asst. chief staff, plans and operations NATO, 1952-55; dep. comdr. Air Force Missile Devel. Center, Holloman AFB, N.M., 1955-58; asst. chief staff, plans and operations J-3, Hdqrs. Alaskan Command, 1959-62; comdr. Montgomery Air Def. Sector, Gunter AFB, Ala., 1962-64, 32 NORAD/CONAD Region, 1963-64; dep. dir. plans for advanced planning, directorate plans DCS/P&O, Hdqrs. USAF, 1964-65; dep. dir. plans NATO Mil. Com. and Standing Group, Washington, 1965-67, ret., 1967; partner in ins. and real estate firm, Hot Springs, Va., also cons. to def. industry, until 1977, now engaged in farming and oil leasing, Woodward, Okla. Decorated Legion Merit with 2 oak leaf clusters, D.F.C. with 2 oak leaf clusters, Bronze Star with oak leaf cluster, Air medal with 3 oak leaf cluster; Croix de Guerre with palm, France). Home: 2404 Wildwood Dr Woodward OK 73801

JUDY, JOHN WAYNE, JR., veterinary educator; b. Indpls., Oct. 11, 1931; s. John Wayne and Doris Lucille (Lane) J.; m. Nan Bond, Aug. 20, 1983; children: Charles W., Martha L., Douglas B. Student, Wabash Coll., 1949-52; B.S., Purdue U., 1954; Ph.D., D.V.M., Kans. State U., 1958. Individual practice vet. medicine, Greencastle, Ind., 1958-61; research fellow Coll. Vet. Medicine, Iowa State U., 1961-62; instr. Purdue U., 1962-68, asst. to dean, 1964-66, asst. prof., 1968-69; prof., head dept. med. and surgery Coll. Vet. Medicine, U. Ga., 1969-71; prof. comparative medicine and clin. medicine Coll. Vet. Medicine, U. Ill., 1971-76; asso. dean Coll. Vet. Medicine, Mich. State U., 1976—; vet. cons. Contbr. articles to profl. jours. Named Tchr. of Year, 1969. Mem. AVMA, Ill., Mich., Ind. vet. med. assns., Am. Assn. Vet. Clinicians (pres. 1981—), Am. Farm Econ. Assn., Assn. Am. Vet. Med. Colls. (sec.-treas., pres.), Sigma Xi, Sigma Chi, Phi Zeta. Republican. Methodist. Club: Mason. Home: 1854 Penobscot St Okemos MI 48864 Office: Coll Veterinary Medicine Mich State U East Lansing MI 48824

JUDY, JOHN WILLIAM, JR., wholesale forest products executive; b. San Francisco, July 8, 1938; s. John William and Sara Christine (Brown) J.; m. Patricia Ann Snead, May 24, 1968; children: Christopher Allan, Jennifer Ann. A.B., Stanford U., 1960. Personnel mgr. St. Regis Paper Co., Tacoma, Wash., 1962-66; trader Brazier Forest Products, Tacoma, 1966-68; salesman Pack River Tree Farm, Spokane, Wash., 1968-72; v.p. Am. Internat. Forest Products, Beaverton, Oreg., 1972-76, pres., 1976—. Republican. Presbyterian. Office: Am Internat Forest Products 5560 SW 107th Beaverton OR 97005

JUDY, LEONARD P., food company executive; b. Chgo., May 16, 1939; s. Leonard A. and Lillian M. (Dedera) J.; m. Nicolette H. deMattencloit, Dec. 28, 1963; children: Karen, Stephen, Michael. B.S. in Bus. Adminstrn., John Carroll U.; M.B.A., Northwestern U. Mktg. dir. canned foods Libby, McNeill & Libby Inc., Chgo., 1971-76, v.p., gen. mgr., 1976-78, v.p. planning and fin., 1978-82, exec. v.p., 1982-83, pres., 1983—; dir. Dunkley Co., Kalamazoo, Latas Dos Inc., P.R., Condmix Corp. Served to lt. U.S. Army, 1961-63. Mem. Am. Mktg. Assn., Nat. Food Processors Assn. (bd. dirs. 1982-83), Midwest Planning Assn. Roman Catholic. Clubs: Chgo. Athletic Assn.; Oak Park Tennis (River Forest) (pres. 1981-83). Office: Libby McNeill & Libby Inc 200 S Michigan Ave Chicago IL 60604

JUENGER, FRIEDRICH KLAUS, lawyer, educator; b. FrankfurtMain, Ger., Feb. 18, 1930; came to U.S., 1955, naturalized, 1961; s. Wilhelm and Margarete J.; m. Baerbel Thierfelder, Sept. 15, 1967; children: J. Thomas, John F. Referendarexamen (Studienstiftung des deutschen Volkes scholar), J.W. Goethe-Universität, 1955; M.C.L. U. Mich, 1957; J.D. (Harlan-Fiske-Stone scholar), Columbia U., 1960. Bar: N.Y. State 1962, Mich. 1970, U.S. Supreme Ct. 1970. Asso. firm Cahill, Gordon, Reindel & Ohl, N.Y.C., 1960-61, Baker & McKenzie, N.Y.C., Chgo., Madrid, 1961-66; asso. prof. law Wayne State U., Detroit, 1966-68, prof., 1968-75; vis. prof. Albert-Ludwigs U., Freiburg, Ger., 1972-73, 74, U. Calif., Davis, 1975—; vis. prof. Max-Planck-Institut für ausländisches und in ternationales Privatrecht, Hamburg, W. Ger., 1981-82. Author: (with L. Schmidt) German Stock Corporation Act, 1967, Zum Wandel des Internationalen Privatrechts, 1974; Editor: Columbia Law Rev, 1959-60; Bd. editors: Am. Jour. Comparative Law, 1977—; Contbr. articles on the conflict of laws, fgn. and comparative law to legal jours. Recipient Faculty Research award Wayne State U., 1971; Fulbright scholar, 1953-55; Volkswagen Found. research grantee, 1972-73; Fulbright sr. research fellow, 1981-82. Mem. Am. Bar Assn., Am. Fgn. Law Assn., Am. Law Inst., Am. Soc. Internat. Law, Assn. Bar City N.Y., Assn. Can. Law Tchrs., Gesellschaft für Rechtsvergleichung, Internat. Acad. Comparative Law (assoc. mem.). Office: King Hall U Calif Davis CA 95616

JUERGENS, GEORGE IVAR, history educator; b. Bklyn., Mar. 20, 1932; s. George deGaard and Magnhild (Julin) J.; m. Jenifer Jane Beattie, Mar. 21, 1959; children: Steven Erik, Paul Andreas. B.A., Columbia Coll., 1953, Oxford U., 1956, M.A., 1956; Ph.D., Columbia U., 1965. Instr. Dartmouth Coll., Hanover, N.H., 1962-65; asst. prof. Amherst (Mass.) Coll., 1965-67; assoc. prof. Ind. U., Bloomington, 1967-80, prof. history, 1980—; cons. Nat. Endowment Humanities, Washington, 1971—. Author: Joseph Pulitzer and the New York World, 1966, News From The White House, 1981; assoc. editor: Jour. Am. History, 1968-69. Served with U.S. Army, 1956-58. Recipient Disting. Teaching award Amoco Found., 1982; Kellett fellow Columbia U., 1954-56; sr. faculty fellow Nat. Endowment Humanities, 1971-72; fellow Rockefeller Found., 1981-82. Mem. AAUP, Orgn. Am. Historians, Phi Beta Kappa. Home: 2111 Meadowbluff Ct Bloomington IN 47401 Office: Dept History Ind U Bloomington IN 47405

JUERGENS, WILLIAM GEORGE, judge; b. Steeleville, Ill., Sept. 7, 1904; s. H.F. William and Mathilda (Nolte) J.; m. Helen A. Young, Dec. 14, 1929 (dec. Feb. 1966); children: Jane Juergens Hays, William G.; m. Charlotte Louise Mann, Mar. 18, 1967. A.B., Carthage Coll., 1925, LL.D., 1970; J.D., U. Mich., 1928; S.J.D. (hon.), William Woods Coll., 1977. Bar: Ill. bar 1928. County judge, Randolph County, 1938-50; judge 3d Jud. Circuit Ct. Ill., 1951-56, U.S. Dist. Ct. So. Dist. Ill. (formerly Eastern Dist. Ill.), 1956—, chief judge, 1965-72, U.S. sr. dist. judge, 1972—; Adv. bd. Inst. Juvenile Research, Ill., 1945-56. Recipient 1st Ann. Honor Alumnus award Carthage Coll., 1961; George Washington Honor Medal award Freedoms Found. at Valley Forge, 1978. Mem. Fed., Ill., Randolph County bar assns., Bar Assn. 7th Fed. Circuit, Nat. Lawyers Club. Republican. Presbyn. Clubs: Masons (32 deg.), Shriners.). Home: 1836 Swanwick St Chester IL 62233 Office: First Nat Bank Bldg: Chester IL 62233 *The foundation of this nation is spiritual. It was founded on the belief that God was the sovereign and that He, rather than the government, granted men their rights.*

JUETTNER, THOMAS RICHARD, patent lawyer; b. Mpls., Aug. 9, 1924; s. Paul Albert and Alice Helen (Stevens) J.; m. Vivian Dorothy Bajork, May 4, 1946; children: Timothy, Paul, Ann Juettner Shadyac, Carol. Student, St. John's U., 1942-43; B. Mech. Engring., Marquette U., 1945; J.D., Loyola U., 1950. Bar: Ill. bar 1950, Calif. bar 1978, U.S. Supreme Ct. bar 1978, U.S. Patent Office bar 1948. Patent engr. Stewart Warner Corp., Chgo., 1946-49; patent agt. Singer, Stern & Carlberg, 1949-50; patent lawyer Brown, Jackson, Boettcher & Dienner, 1951-60, Gary, Juettner & Pyle, 1960—; Dir. Binks Research & Devel. Corp. Trustee St. Joseph's Coll., Rensselear, Ind. Served to lt. (j.g.) USN, 1943-46. Mem. Am., Ill., San Diego, Chgo. bar assns., State Bar Calif., Bar Assn. 7th Fed. Circuit, Am. Intellectual Property Law Assn., San Diego Patent Law Assn., Patent Law Assn. Chgo. (sec. 1968-70, pres. 1975), Loyola Law Alumni Assn. (pres. 1959-60). Clubs: Serra (Chgo.) (v.p. 1968-69, pres. 1972-74. Office: Suite 2301 33 N Dearborn St Chicago IL 60602 also Suite 1200 1200 3d Ave San Diego CA 92101

JUHL, JOHN HAROLD, physician, educator; b. Thompson, Iowa, Nov. 21, 1913; s. Hans Peter and Helen (Halverson) J.; m. Helen B. Harris, Sept. 12, 1938 (dec. Mar. 1977); children: John Harold, Susan; m. Barbara P. Johnson, Nov. 24, 1978. A.B., U. Mich., 1936, M.D., 1940. Diplomate: Am. Bd. Radiology. Intern U. Hosp., Madison, Wis., 1941, resident radiology, 1946-49; faculty U. Wis. Med. Sch., 1949-52, 54-80, prof. radiology, 1960-80, chmn. dept., 1963-76; radiologist St. Barnabas Hosp., Mpls.; prof. radiology U. N.Mex., 1980—; acting chief radiology VA Med. Center, Albuquerque, 1980—; engaged in private practice, 1952-54. Author: Essentials of Roentgen Interpretation, 4th edit, 1981. Served with USNR, 1943-46. Fellow Am. Coll. Radiology; mem. Assn. U. Radiologists, Radiol. Soc. N.Am., N.Y. Acad. Scis., Am. Roentgen Ray Soc., AAAS, N.Mex. Med. Soc., Wis. Radiol. Soc., N.Mex. Radiol. Soc., A.M.A., Wis., Dane County med. socs. Home: 2617 Cutler Ave NE Albuquerque NM 87106

JUHL, LOREN EARL, lawyer; b. New Holland, Ill., Nov. 19, 1918; s. Albert H. and Margaret (Krusemark) J.; m. Harriet Hanson, Mar. 8, 1941 (dec.); children: Cynthia Juhl Carpenter, Gloria Juhl Raney, Roger C.; m. Elaine M. Morey, Oct. 8, 1970. B.S., U. Ill.-Urbana, 1940; LL.B., Harvard U., 1948. Bar: Ill. 1949. Assoc. Sidley & Austin, Chgo., 1948-56, ptnr., 1957—. Co-author: Drafting Wills and Trust Agreements in Illinois, 1983. Bd. dirs. Northwestern Meml. Found., Chgo., The Thresholds, Chgo., Chgo. Maternity Ctr. Served to maj. U.S. Army, 1941-45. Fellow Am. Coll. Probate Counsel; mem. Illini Club Chgo., ABA, Ill. State Bar Assn. (sec. 1971-72), Chgo. Bar Assn. Republican. Lutheran. Clubs: Westmoreland Country (Wilmette); Univ. Chgo.; Mid-Day (Chgo.). Home: 2245 Sanders Rd Northbrook IL 60062 Office: Sidley & Austin 1 First Nat Plaza Chicago IL 60603

JUKES, THOMAS HUGHES, biological chemist; b. Hastings, Eng., Aug. 25, 1906; came to U.S., 1925, naturalized, 1939; s. Edward Hughes and Ann Mary (Barton) J.; m. Marguerite Esposito, July 2, 1942; children—Kenneth Hughes, Caroline Elizabeth (Mrs. Nicholas Knueppel), Dorothy Mavis (Mrs. Robert Hudson). B.S.A., U. Toronto, 1930, Ph.D., 1933; NRC fellow med. scis., U. Calif. at Berkeley, 1933-34; D.Sc. (honoris causa), U. Guelph, 1972. Instr., asst. prof. U. Calif. at Davis, 1934-42; with pharm. div. Lederle Labs., 1942-45; dir. nutrition and physiology research sect. research div. Am. Cyanamid Co., Pearl River, N.Y., 1945-58, dir. research agrl. div., 1958-59, dir. biochemistry, 1960-62; vis. sr. research fellow in biochemistry Princeton, 1962-63; prof. in residence dept. biophysics and med. physics, lectr. dept. nutritional scis., research biochemist Space Scis. Lab., U. Calif. at Berkeley, 1963—, asso. dir., 1968-70; cons. C.W.S., AUS, 1944-45, NASA, 1969-70; guest lectr. various univs.; Storer lectr. U. Calif. at Davis, 1973; Fred W. Tanner lectr. Inst. Food Technologists, 1979. Author: B Vitamins for Blood Formation, 1952, Antibiotics in Nutrition, 1955, Molecules and Evolution, 1965; Editorial bds.: Biochem. Genetics; biog. editor: Jour. Nutrition; assoc. editor: Jour. Molecular Evolution; Contbr. articles to profl. jours. Mem. Nat. Adv. Bd. Accuracy in Media, Washington, 1976—; mem. acad. adv. council Nat. Legal Center for Pub. Interest, Washington, 1976—; adv. bd. Consumer Alert, 1978—, Media Inst., 1979—; bd. dirs. Council Environ. Balance, 1976—. Recipient Borden award Poultry Sci. Assn., 1947; Spencer award Am. Chem. Soc., 1976; Agrl. and Food Chemistry award, 1979; Disting. Service award Am. Agrl. Editors Assn., 1978. Fellow Am. Soc. Animal Sci., Poultry Sci. Assn., Am. Inst. Nutrition (council 1941-45, pub. affairs officer 1978-81, chmn. com. on history 1979-83); mem. Internat. Council Sci. Unions (chmn. biology working group COSPAR 1978-80, chmn. interdisciplinary sci. commn. F 1980—), Am. Soc. Biol. Chemists, Biophys. Soc., Soc. for Exptl. Biology and Medicine, Am. Chem. Soc., Trustees for Conservation (San Francisco) (pres. 1970-71), Sigma Xi, Delta Tau Delta. Clubs: Am. Alpine, Explorers (N.Y.C.); Chit Chat, Sierra (San Francisco); Faculty (Berkeley). Home: 170 Arlington Ave Berkeley CA 94707

JULES, MERVIN, artist, educator; b. Balt., Mar. 21, 1912; s. Sidney and Anna (Goldenberg) J.; m. Rita Albers, Apr. 20, 1940; children: Gabriel, Fredrick. Student, Balt. City Coll., 1930, Md. Inst. Fine Arts, 1930-33, Art Students League, 1933-34. Instr. art Fieldston Sch., N.Y.C., 1942-44, Mus. Modern Art, 1943-44, 1946-48, War Vets. Art Center, 1944; vis. artist Smith Coll., 1945-45, asso. prof. art, 1946-63, prof., 1963—, chmn. art dept., 1963-67; prof., chmn. art dept. CCNY, 1969—; mem. staff, univ. extension div., dept. edn. Commonwealth Mass., 1950-52; Lectr. U. Wis., summer 1951; staff George Vincent Smith Mus., Springfield, 1952-53; Lectr. Hillyer Coll., Hartford, Conn., 1953; fellow McDowell Colony, 1938, 61, Yaddo, 1941. Held many one man shows including, A.A.A. Gallery, N.Y.C., 1961; represented in collections including, Met. Mus. Art, Mus. Modern Art, Art Inst. Chgo., Mus. Fine Arts Boston, Portland (Oreg.) Mus., Library Congress, Balt. Mus. Art, Duncan Phillips Gallery, Walker Art Center, Tel Aviv Mus., N.Y. Library, La. Art Commn., Fogg Mus., Carnegie Inst., colls., univs. Bd. dirs. Fine Arts Work Center, Provincetown, Mass.; mem. governing bd. Inst. for Study Art in Edn. Recipient Wilson Levering Smith medal, 1939, 41; Purchase prize Balt. Mus. Art, 1941, Mus. Modern Art, 1941, Library Congress, 1945, Bklyn. Mus., 1946; Springfield Art League prize, 1952; 1st prize, 1955, Cape Cod Art Assn., 1957; Hollis M. Carlyle purchase prize Eastern States Art Exhbn., 1957; medal CCNY, 1973; McDowell Colony fellow, 1978; grant to study in Japan Asian African Study Program, 1967. Fellow Royal Soc. Arts; mem. Provincetown Art Assn. (trustee, pres. 1982), Audubon Artists, Nat. Acad., Artists League Am., Com. Art Edn., Soc. Am. Graphic Artists, Artist Equity Assn., Springfield Art League, Boston Printmakers (hon. mention 19th Ann. Exhbn. 1967), AAUP, Century Assn. Home: 720 Burns St Forest Hills Gardens NY 11375

JULIA, RAUL RAFAEL CARLOS, actor; b. San Juan, P.R., Mar. 9, 1944; s. Paul and Olga (Arcelay) J.; m. 2d Merel Poloway, June 28, 1976; 1 son, Raul Sigmund. B.A. in Humanities, U. P.R.; student in drama, Wynn Handman, 1964. Mem. Phoebe Brand's Theatre in St., N.Y.C., 1964—. (Spanish-lang. prodn.) Life Is A Dream, Astor Playhouse, 1964; N.Y. Shakespeare Festival prodns. Macbeth, 1966, Titus Andronicus, summer 1967, Hamlet, 1972, As You Like It, 1973, King Lear, 1973, The Threepenny Opera, 1976, The Cherry Orchard, 1977, The Taming of the Shrew, 1978, Othello, 1979; off-Broadway plays The Ox Cart, 1966, The Memorandum, 1968, No Exit, 1967, Your Own Thing, 1968, The Persians, 1970, The Emperor of Late Night Radio, 1974, The Robber Bridegroom, 1974; Broadway debut, The Cuban Thing, 1968; Broadway plays Frank Gagliano's City Scene, 1969, Indians, 1969; Broadways plays The Castro Complex, 1970; Broadway plays The Two gentlemen of Verona, 1971, Where's Charley, 1974, Betrayal, 1980, Nine, 1982; rd.-co. prodn. Dracula, 1978, Broadway prodn., 1979; films The Organization Man, 1971, Been Down So Long It Looks Like Up To Me, 1971, The Panic in Needle Park, 1971, The Gumball Rally, 1976, The Eyes of Laura Mars, 1978, The Escape Artist, 1982, One From The Heart, 1982, The Tempest, 1982, TV appearances, Death Scream, Love of Life; TV pilot appearances Aces UP, CBS, 1974; Rafael the Fixit Man: series Sesame Street, Pub. Broadcasting System. Active Internat. Hunger Project. Mem. Hispanic Orgn. Latin Actors. Office: care Susan Wright 449 E 84th St 4A New York NY 10028

JULIAN, ALEXANDER, II, menswear designer; b. Chapel Hill, N.C., Feb. 8, 1948; s. Maurice S. and Mary L. (Brady) J.; m. Lynn A. Forberg, Dec. 30, 1973; 1 dau., Alystyre. Student, U. N.C. Operator Alexander's Ambition (splty. store), Chapel Hill, 1969-73; designer men's clothing for Baker Clothes, Phila., 1973-76; dir. market research and devel. Trimingham Bros., Bermuda, 1974—; designer sweater collections for Pringle of Scotland, 1975—; pres. Alexander Julian, Inc., N.Y.C., 1975—; guest lectr. Fashion Inst. Tech. Mem. Chapel Hill Appearance Commn. Recipient Coty award, 1977, 79, 80; named to Coty Hall of Fame, 1980; Cutty Sark award as Outstanding U.S. Designer, 1980. Mem. Council Fashion Designers Am. (dir., award for outstanding U.S. men's wear), Men's Fashion Assn. Clubs: Burke's, Alibi (London). Address: Alexander Julian Inc 8 W 40th St New York NY 10018 *To be successful you must liken your endeavours to "defensive driving." You have to be more concerned with what others are doing wrong around you than what you're doing right to really get where you're going.* *

JULIAN, BROOKS PATTON, former banker; b. Mt. Sterling, Ohio, Oct. 7, 1917; s. Earl R. and Stella L. (Brooks) J.; m. Helen McCoy, Feb. 7, 1942; children: Kathryn Julian Goldberg, Constance Julian Glierman, Jeanne. B.S., Ohio State U., 1940; grad., U. Wis. Sch. Banking, 1954. Asst. cashier Ohio Nat. Bank, Columbus, 1951-53, asst. v.p., 1953-56, v.p., 1956-68, exec. v.p., 1970-76; v.p. BancOhio Corp., 1968-70; pres. BancOhio/Ohio Nat. Bank, 1976-79, chief exec. officer, 1979; sr. v.p. BancOhio Corp., 1977-82; pres. BancOhio Nat. Bank, 1979-82, also dir.; dir. Scioto Investment Co. Trustee Grant Hosp., 1972—; bd. dirs. Franklin County unit Am. Cancer Soc.; adv. bd. Whetstone Convalescent Center. Served to capt. Mil. Intelligence AUS, 1941-45; lt. col. Res. ret. Mem. Assn. Res. City Bankers. Republican. Episcopalian. Clubs: University, Columbus Country, Columbus Athletic, Ohio Automobile (trustee 1964—). Office: BancOhio Corp/BancOhio Nat Bank 155 E Broad St Columbus OH 43265

JULIAN, ORMAND CLINKINBEARD, surgeon; b. Omaha, May 6, 1913; s. William Harold and Ella (Clinkinbeard) J.; m. Rosemary Stirling Becker, Sept. 14, 1935; children—William H., Gail Elizabeth. B.S., U. Chgo., 1934, M.D., 1937, Ph.D., 1941. Intern St. Luke's Hosp., Chgo., 1937-38; resident U. Chgo. Clinics, 1938-42; practice medicine, specializing in cardiovascular surgery, Chgo., 1945—; prof. surgery U. Ill. Coll. Medicine, 1947-71; chmn. div. surgery Presbyn.-St. Luke's Hosp., Chgo., 1965-72, chmn. dept. cardiovascular-thoracic surgery, 1970-72; prof. Rush Med. Coll. Rush-Presbyn.-St. Luke's Med. Center, Chgo., 1971—; emeritus staff surgeon Eisenhower Med. Center, Rancho Mirage, Calif. Served to maj. M.C. AUS, 1942-45. Fellow A.C.S.; mem. Am. Surg. Assn., Soc. Clin. Surgery, Internat. Cardiovascular Soc., Soc. Vascular Surgery. Home: 47-190 El Agadir Palm Desert CA 92260 Office: 1725 W Harrison St Chicago IL 60612

JULIANA, JAMES NICHOLAS, govt. ofcl.; b. Camden, N.J., Apr. 1, 1922; s. Nicholas and Rosa (de Noti) J.; m. Elizabeth D. Sutton, Nov. 8, 1947; children—James S., Patrick C., Mary E., Thomas E., David J., Richard S., Robert Francis, Ronald Joseph (dec.). B.S., Washington Coll., Md., 1944. Spl. agt. FBI, Washington, 1947-53; asst. exec. dir., exec. dir., chief counsel to minority Senate Permanent Sub-com. on Investigations, 1953-58; exec. dir. CAB, 1958-61; pres., dir. Internat. Fact Finding Inst., 1961-62; pres. James N. Juliana Assos., Washington, 1962-81; sec., dir. Alaska N.Am. Corp., Washington, 1970-77; v.p. fed. affairs Braniff Internat., 1977-81; prin. dep. asst. sec. for manpower, res. affairs and logistics Dept. Def., Washington, 1981—. Mem. Pres.'s Com. on Mental Retardation, 1971-77; exec. v.p. Armed Forces Mktg. Council, Washington, 1974-81; bd. visitors, bd. govs. Washington Coll., Chestertown, Md., 1978—. Served with USNR, 1944-46. Mem. Soc. Former Spl. Agts. FBI, Assn. Former Senate Aides, Kappa Alpha, Omicron Delta Kappa. Clubs: Internat., Capitol Hill, Atlantic City Country. Home: 11013 Rosemont Dr Rockville MD 20852 also 66 W 17 St Ocean City NJ 08226 Office: Pentagon Room 3E808 Washington DC 20301

JULIBER, IRVING GERARD, management consultant; b. Bklyn., May 22, 1913; s. Irving and Lillian (Feltman) J.; m. Roslyn E. Wolff, June 30, 1940; children: Ilene H., Lois D. B.S., N.Y. U., 1934, postgrad., 1940; M.A., Columbia, 1936. Dep. mgr. N.Y. State Employment Service, 1938-41; dir. personnel OWI, 1941-43, Philharmonic Radio Corp., N.Y.C., 1943-46; dir. personnel, labor relations Waldes Kohinoor, Inc., N.Y.C., 1946-50; with Revlon, Inc., N.Y.C., 1950-71, v.p. indsl. relations, 1950-56, v.p. ops., 1956-60, sr. v.p. adminstrn., 1960-71; pres. Millrose Consultants to Mgmt. Ltd., N.Y.C., 1971—; dir. Master Contact Lens Lab. Inc.; Comml., labor arbitrator Am. Arbitration Assn. Mem. Am. Soc. Personnel Adminstrn. Clubs: N.Y. Univ., Varsity Letter; Pine Hollow Country (East Norwich, L.I.); East Pointe Country (Palm Beach Gardens, Fla.). Home: 635 Bryant Ave Roslyn Harbor NY 11576 Home: 6528 E Pointe Pines St Palm Beach Gardens FL 33410

JULIEN, RICHARD EDWARD HALE, lawyer; b. Detroit, Mar. 20, 1900; s. Edward H. and Katherine (Heard) J.; m. Sophie Hill, Aug. 30, 1926; children—Joan Mary, Richard Edward Hale. A.B., U. Calif. at Berkeley, 1923; LL.B., Harvard, 1926. Bar: Calif. bar 1935. Corporate fiduciary banking, N.Y.C., San Francisco, 1927-35, since practiced in, San Francisco.; Dir. Travelers Aid Soc. San Francisco, 1963-69. Contbr. articles to banking, legal jours. Life mem. Am. Bar Assn. (mem. ho. dels. 1952-62, chmn. com. on hearing 1960-62, rep. Conf. Lawyers and C.P.A.'s 1963-65, mem. bd. govs. 1964-67, assembly del. Ho. of Dels. 1963-66, 71-73); mem. Bar Assn. San Francisco (bd. dirs., chmn. com. judiciary 1958-59), State Bar Calif. (chmn. com. on taxation, com. on Jour. 1958-60), Am. Law Inst., Practicing Law Inst., Am. Bar Found. (charter life fellow), Am. Judicature Soc., Soc. Calif. Pioneers San Francisco County (v.p.), Am. Legion (past post comdr.), Phi Delta Theta, Phi Alpha Delta (hon.). Republican. Clubs: Commonwealth of Calif. (past chmn. sect. on adminstrn. of justice), Harvard, Olympic. Home: 2640 Steiner St San Francisco CA 94115 Office: Mills Tower 220 Bush St San Francisco CA 94104 *Trying to be a good and whole man by playing it straight with clients, wife, children, and grandchildren. A sense of humor and of the earth has helped a lot in the rough spots.*

JULIN, JOSEPH RICHARD, lawyer, educator; b. Chgo., July 5, 1926; s. George Allan and Jennie Elizabeth (Carlsten) J.; m. Dorothy Marie Julian, Oct. 18, 1952; children: Pamela, Thomas, Diane, Linda. Student, Deep Springs Coll., 1944, George Washington U., 1946-49; B.S.L., Northwestern U., 1950, J.D., 1952. Bar: Ill. 1952, Mich. 1960. Asso. firm Schuylur, Stough & Morris, Chgo., 1952-57, partner, 1957-59; asso. prof. law U. Mich., Ann Arbor, 1959-62, prof. law, 1962-70, asso. dean, 1968-70; dean, prof. law U. Fla. Coll. Law, Gainesville, 1971-80, dean emeritus and prof. law, 1980—. Author: (with others) Basic Property Law, 1966, 72, 79. Trustee Ann Arbor Bd. Edn., 1966-69, pres., 1968-69. Served with U.S. Army, 1944-46. Fellow Am. Bar Found.; mem. Legal Club of Chgo., Mich. Bar Assn., Ill. Bar Assn., Chgo. Bar Assn., Am. Bar Assn. (chmn. sect. on legal edn. and admissions to the bar 1977-78), Assn. Am. Law Schs. (pres. 1984), Order of Coif., Phi Beta Kappa. Republican. Home: 1657 NW 19th Circle Gainesville FL 32605 Office: U Fla Coll Law Gainesville FL 32611

JULIUS, STEVO, physician; b. Kovin, Yugoslavia, Apr. 15, 1929; came to U.S., 1965, naturalized, 1971; s. Dezider and Jelena (Engel) J.; m. Susan P. Durrant, Sept. 17, 1971; children: Nicholas, Natasha. M.D., U. Zagreb, 1953, Sc.D., 1964; M.D. (hon.), U. Goteborg, Sweden, 1979. Intern, then resident in internal medicine Univ. Hosp., Zagreb, 1953-60, sr. instr. internal medicine, 1962-64; research asst. U. Mich. Med. Sch., 1961-62, mem. faculty, 1965—, prof. internal medicine, 1974—, assoc. prof. physiology, 1980-83, prof. physiology, 1983—, dir. div. hypertension, 1974—. Co-editor: The Nervous System in Arterial Hypertension, 1976; contbr. articles med. jours. Fellow Am. Coll. Cardiology; mem. Internat. Soc. Hypertension, Interam. Soc. Hypertension (treas. 1978-83), Am. Heart Assn. (councils high blood pressure research and epidemiology); med. adv. bd. Am. Physiol. Soc., Am. Fedn. Clin. Research, Am. Soc. Clin. Pharmacology and Therapeutics, Soc. Exptl. Biology and Medicine. Office: Div Hypertension Univ Mich Med Sch Box 48 R6669 Kresge Bldg Ann Arbor MI 48109 *Research has a way of turning some people into deadly serious dry bores. Luckily many resist the danger. The biggest reward of my career is the chance to meet brilliant, witty and knowledgeable scientists.*

JUMONVILLE, FELIX JOSEPH, JR., physical education educator; b. Crowley, La., Nov. 20, 1920; s. Felix Joseph and Mabel (Rogers) J.; m. Mary Louise Hoke, Jan. 11, 1952; children: Carol, Susan. B.S., La. State U., 1942; M.S., U. So. Calif., 1948, Ed.D., 1952. Asso. prof. phys. edn. Los Angeles State Coll., 1948-60; prof. phys. edn. Calif. State U., Northridge, 1960—; Owner Felix Jumonville Realty, Northridge, 1974-82, Big Valley Realty, Inc., 1982-83, Century 21 Lamb Realtors, 1983—. Served with USCGR, 1942-46. Mem. Assn. Calif. State Univ. Profs., AAHPER, San Fernando Valley Bd. Realtors, Calif. Assn. Realtors, Nat. Assn. Realtors, Pi Tau Pi, Phi Epsilon Kappa. Home: 8816 Whitaker Ave Sepulveda CA 91343 Office: 18111 Nordhoff St Northridge CA 91330

JUMP, CHESTER JACKSON, JR., clergyman, church official; b. Covington, Ky., Mar. 31, 1918; s. Chester Jackson and Inez (Moore) J.; m. Margaret Elizabeth Savidge, Sept. 5, 1942; children—Karen Jane, Richard Alan, Catherine Louise, Robert Jon. A.B., Albright Coll., 1938; M.A., Columbia, 1940; B.D., Union Theol. Sem. N.Y.C., 1943; postgrad., Ecole Coloniale, Brussels, Belgium, 1950-51; D.D., Eastern Bapt. Theol. Sem., 1965. Ordained to ministry Bapt. Ch., 1943; pastor N.E. Larger Parish, Lyndon Center, Vt., 1943-44; missionary, Belgian Congo, Republic of Congo, 1945-62; regional rep. Am. Bapt. Fgn. Mission Socs., Valley Forge, Pa., 1961-64, exec. dir., 1965—; Assoc. gen. sec. Am. Bapt. Chs., 1965—, dir. world relief, 1983—; mem. gen. bd. Nat. Council Chs., 1965-75, mem. program bd., exec. com. div. overseas ministries, 1965-83; mem. exec. com. Bapt. World Alliance, 1965-83, v.p., 1980—; Trustee Eastern Bapt. Theol. Sem. Author: (with wife) Congo Diary, 1950, Coming, Ready or Not, 1959. Mem. Pi Gamma Mu. Home: 2548 DuPont St Coatesville PA 19320 Office: Am Bapt Fgn Mission Socs Valley Forge PA 19481

JUMP, GORDON, actor; b. Dayton, Ohio, Apr. 1; m. Anna; children—Cindy, Kiva, Maggi-Jo. Grad., Kans. State U. Prodn. dir. Sta. WIBW-TV, Topeka; later managed spl. broadcast services dept. Sta. WLWD, Dayton and also. Wrote and produced: several shows, including High Times; worked as actor in little theaters and showcases, Calif., beginning 1963; regular on: TV series McDuff, the Talking Dog, 1976, Soap, 1977, WKRP In Cincinnati, 1978—; other TV appearances include Get Smart, Daniel Boone, Mannix, The Mary Tyler Moore Show, Bewitched, Ruby and Oswald, The Phantom Rebel, Fawn Story, Alice, Starsky and Hutch; films include Adam at Six A.M, Conquest of the Planet of the Apes, Trouble Man; TV films Big Stuffed Dog, Goldie and the Boxer. Office: care The Artists Agy 190 N Canon Dr Beverly Hills CA 90210

JUNEAU, PIERRE, broadcasting company executive; b. Verdun, Que., Can., Oct. 17, 1922; s. Laurent Edmond and Marguerite (Angrignon) J.; m. Fernande Martin, Mar. 17, 1947; children: Andre, Martin, Isabelle. B.A., College Sainte-Marie, Montreal, 1944; postgrad. in philosophy, Sorbonne, Paris, 1949; licentiate in Philosophy, Institut Catholique, Paris, 1949; LL.D. (hon.), York U., Toronto, 1973. With Nat. Film Bd. Can., 1949-66, dist. rep., asst. regional supr. of Que., chief internat. distbn., Montreal, 1951, asst. head European office, London, 1952-54, sec., Montreal, 1954-64, sr. asst. to commr. and dir. French Lang. prodn., 1964-66, bd. dirs., vice chmn. bd. Broadcast Govs., Ottawa, 1966-68; chmn. Can. Radio-TV Commn., Ottawa, 1968-75; minister communications Govt. Can., Ottawa, 1975, adviser to Prime Minister, 1975—; chmn. Nat. Capital Commn., 1976-78; under sec. state Govt. Can., 1978-80, dep. minister communications, 1980-82; pres. Can. Broadcasting Corp., Ottawa, 1982—; co-founder, 1st pres. La Federation des Mouvements de jeunesse au Que. Co-founder Montreal Internat. Film Festival, 1950's, pres., 1959-68; sec., bd. dirs. Albert-Prevost Psychiat. Inst., Montreal, 1960's; chmn. bd. Ecole nouvelle St.-Germain, Montreal; founder, bd. dirs. Institut Canadien d'Education des Adultes. Decorated officer Order Can. Mem. Royal Soc. Can., Nat. Arts Centre (bd. dirs.). Office: Can Broadcasting Corp 1500 Bronson Ave Ottawa ON Canada K1G 3J5

JUNG, DORIS, dramatic soprano; b. Centralia, Ill., Jan. 5, 1924; d. John Jay and May (Middleton) Crittenden; m. Felix Popper, Nov. 3, 1951; 1 son, Richard Dorian. Ed., U. Ill., Mannes Coll. Music, Vienna Acad. Performing Arts; student of, Julius Cohen, Emma Zador, Luise Helletsgruber, Winifred Cecil. Debut as Vitellia in: Clemenza di Tito, Zurich (Switzerland) Opera, 1955, other appearances with, Hamburg State Opera, Munich State Opera, Vienna State Opera, Royal Opera Copenhagen, Royal Opera Stockholm, Marseille and Strasbourg, France, Naples (Italy) Opera Co., Catania (Italy) Opera Co., N.Y.C. Opera, Met. Opera, also in Mpls., Portland, Oreg., Washington and Aspen, Colo.; soloist: Wagner concert conducted by Leopold Stokowski, 1971; with, Syracuse (N.Y.) Symphony, 1981; voice tchr., N.Y.C., 1970—. Home: 40 W 84 St New York NY 10024

JUNG, JAMES DONALD, financial executive; b. Cin., Oct. 9, 1942; s. Herman and Edna Marian (Christen) J.; m. Kathryn Joy Bingham, Mar. 31, 1973; 1 son, Matthew Austin. B.S., U. Cin., 1969; M.B.A., Ind. U., 1970. Sr. acct. Coopers & Lybrand, Detroit, 1970-73; project controller Joseph Schlitz Brewing Co., Milw., 1973-74; v.p., treas. Midland-Ross Corp., Cleve., 1974—. Panel mem. United Way Services, Cleve. Served with USN, 1960-63. Mem. Fin. Exec. Inst. Club: Chagrin Valley Country. Office: Midland-Ross Corp 20600 Chagrin Blvd Cleveland OH 44122

JUNG, RODNEY C., physician; b. New Orleans, Oct. 9, 1920; s. Frederick Charles and Clara (Cuevas) J. B.S. in Zoology with honors, Tulane U., 1941, M.D., 1945, M.S. in Parasitology, 1950, Ph.D., 1953. Diplomate: Am. Bd. Internal Medicine. Intern Charity Hosp. La., New Orleans, 1945-46; dir. Hutchinson Meml. Clinic, 1948; asst. parasitology Tulane U., 1948-50, instr. tropical medicine, 1950-53, asst. prof., 1953-57, asso. prof. tropical medicine, 1951-63, prof. tropical medicine, 1963-73, clin. prof. internal medicine, 1955-63, 73—, clin. prof. tropical medicine, 1983—, head div. tropical medicine, 1960-63; health dir., City of New Orleans, 1963-70, 79-82; internist in charge Ill. Central Hosp., New Orleans, 1956-70; sr. vis. physician Charity Hosp., 1959—; mem. study sect. on tropical medicine and parasitology Nat. Inst. Allergy and Infectious Disease, 1963-67; mem. Commn. on Parasitic Diseases Armed Forces Epidemiol. Bd., 1967-73; chief communicable disease control, City of New Orleans, 1978; sr. in internal medicine Touro Infirmary. Co-author chpt. in: Clinical Parasitology; editorial bd.: Am. Jour. Tropical Medicine and Hygiene, 1972—; Contbr. articles to profl. jours. Chmn. New Orleans chpt. Irish Lang. League, 1977-79; pres. Irish Cultural Soc. New Orleans, 1980—; officer res. div. New Orleans Police Dept. Served as lt. (j.g.) M.C. USNR, 1946-48. John and Mary Markle Scholar in med. sci. Fellow ACP; hon. fellow Brazilian Soc. Tropical Medicine; mem. Am., Royal socs. tropical medicine and hygiene, Am. Soc. Parasitologists, La. State Med. Soc. (chmn. com. on disaster medicine), Orleans Parish Med. Soc. (chmn. com. on disaster medicine and emergency med. services), Nat. Rifle Assn., Irish Georgian Soc., La. Mosquito Control Assn., La. Soc. Internal Medicine, Am. Soc. Internal Medicine, New Orleans Acad. Internal Medicine, Am. Def. Preparedness Assn., Irish-Am. Cultural Inst., Nat. Trust. Historic Preservation, La. Landmarks Soc., Naval Inst., New Orleans Mus. Art, New Orleans Opera Assn., La. Wildlife Fedn., Irish Lang. League, Phi Beta Kappa, Sigma Xi, Delta Omega, Alpha Omega Alpha. Presbyn. Office: 3600 Chestnut New Orleans LA 70115

JUNGE, JAMES F., corp. exec.; b. Chgo., June 18, 1921; s. William F. and Eleanore (Rauch) J.; m. Bethel Pitcairn, Sept. 4, 1943; children—Danna J. Kistner, Dirk, Wenda J. Critchlow, Kim, Nita J. Holmes, Kaye J. Lermitte. B.A. in Chem. Engring, U. Ill., 1943. Engr. Gulf Oil Corp., 1943-49; partner Custom Refining Co., 1949-54; cons. engr. Welling & Woodward, Inc., 1954-58; exec. v.p. Pitcairn Co., Jenkintown, Pa., 1958-63, pres., 1963-70, Pitcairn Inc., 1971-78, chmn. bd., 1979—, also dir.; dir. PPG Industries, Inc., Ins. Services Corp., 77 Capital Corp., Indsl. Chem. Corp., Paramount Resources Ltd.; Evans-Pitcairn Corp., Cairntrust Co.; Bd. dirs. PPG Industries Found. Mem. Am. Chem. Soc., Am. Inst. Chem. Engrs. Office: Jenkintown Plaza Jenkintown PA 19046 *

JUNGER, MIGUEL CHAPERO, acoustics researcher; b. Dresden, Germany, Jan. 29, 1923; came to U.S., 1941, naturalized, 1946; s. José and Adrienne (Junger) Chapiro; m. Ellen Sinclair, 1960; children: M. Sebastian, A. Carlotta. B.S., MIT, 1944, S.M., 1946; Sc.D. (Gordon McKay scholar), Harvard U., 1951. Engr., research fellow in acoustics Harvard U., 1951-55; partner Cambridge Acoustical Assos., Inc., 1955-59, pres., 1959—; sr. vis. lectr. ocean engring. dept. MIT, Cambridge, 1968-78; vis. prof. U. Technologie de Compiègne, 1975, 77-82. Author: Sound, Structures and Their Interaction, 1972, Eléments d'Acoustique Physique, 1978; contbr. articles to profl. jours. Fellow Acoustical Soc. Am., ASME. Patentee in field. Home: 90

Fletcher Rd Belmont MA 02178 Office: 54 Rindge Ave Extension Cambridge MA 02140

JUNGERS, FRANCIS, consultant; b. July 12, 1926; s. Frank Nicholas and Elizabeth (Becker) J.; m. Allison Frances Morris, Oct. 16, 1947; children—Gary M., Randall O. B.S. in Mech. Engring, U. Wash., 1947; student, Advanced Mgmt. Program, Harvard U., 1967. With Arabian Am. Oil Co., 1947-78, chmn. bd., chief exec. officer, 1973-78; cons. Bechtel Group; dir. Ga. Pacific Co., Hyster Co., Donaldson Lufkin & Jenrette, Orbanco Fin., Thermo Electron., Welltech, Dual Drilling Co. Trustee Am. U. in Cairo. Served with U.S. Navy, 1944-46. Mem. Council on Fgn. Relations. Republican. Roman Catholic. Clubs: N.Y. Athletic, San Francisco Golf; Arlington, Waverly Golf (Portland, Oreg.). Home: PO Box 3242 Sunriver OR 97701 Office: care Bechtel 50 Beale St San Francisco CA 94108

JUNGKUNTZ, RICHARD PAUL, univ. provost; b. Cleve., Oct. 1, 1918; s. Otto William and Clara Magdalen (Lange) J.; m. Grace Elizabeth Kowalke, Aug. 16, 1943; children—Gay (Mrs. Jeffrey Osborn), Paula (Mrs. Thomas Warren III), Richard, Lisa (Mrs. Richard Campbell), Andrea, William, Laura. B.A., Northwestern Coll., 1939; student, Concordia Sem., 1939-40, Wis. Luth. Sem., 1940-42, Ind. U., 1951; M.A., U. Wis., 1955, Ph.D., 1961. Ordained to ministry Luth. Ch., 1942; pastor St. Matthews Ch., Janesville, Wis., 1942-46, Bethany Ch., Ft. Atkinson, Wis., 1946-49; prof. Northwestern Coll., Watertown, Wis., 1949-61; asst. prof. Concordia Theol. Sem., Springfield, Ill., 1961-65; exec. sec. Commn. Theology and Church Relations of Luth. Ch. Mo. Synod, St. Louis, 1965-70; provost Pacific Luth U., Tacoma, 1970—, acting pres., 1974-75; vis. prof. Concordia Sem., 1970; lectr. Eden Sem., Webster Groves, Mo., 1970; Mem. Commn. Faith and Order of World Council Chs., 1968-77; pres. Lutheran Acad. for Scholarship; chmn. bd. dirs. Christ Sem.-Seminex, St. Louis. Author: Luther's (1519) Lectures on Galatians, 1964, The Gospel of Baptism, 1968, Kasteen Evankeliumi, 1976; Editor: A Project in Biblical Hermeneutics, 1969. Mem. Soc. Bibl. Lit., Luth. Acad. Scholarship, Am. Assn. Higher Edn., Am. Conf. Acad. Deans, Am. Assn. Univ. Adminstrs. Home: 6310 Hillcrest Dr SW Tacoma WA 98499

JUNIOR, LEWIS DONALD, foreign service officer; b. Hutchinson, Kans., Aug. 23, 1925; s. Frederick Emerson and Florence (Wilcott) J.; m. Jean Marie Mazet; children: Christina Marie, Melissa Anne. Student, U. Ky., 1942-43, Tex. Christian U., 1946-47, U. Mex., 1947; B.S. in Fgn. Service, Georgetown U., 1950. Commd. U.S. Fgn. Service, 1951; consular officer Am. Consulates Gen., Nigeria, Sicily, W.Ger., 1951-59; spl. asst. multilaterial forces negotiation team Dept. State, Washington, 1963; polit. officer Am. Embassy, Addis Ababa, Ethiopia, 1963-66; Am. consul gen. Consulate Gen., Lubumbashi, Zaire, 1972-74; country dir. Dept. State, 1977-80; consul. gen. Consulate Gen., Rotterdam, Netherlands, 1982—; mem. Sr. Seminar in Fgn. Policy, Washington, 1971. Bd. dirs. Am. Internat. Sch., Rotterdam, 1982-83. Served with USAAF, 1943-45. Decorated Air medal with 3 oak leaf clusters; recipient Superior Honor award Dept. State, 1971, Meritorious Honor award Dept. State, 1982. Democrat. Roman Catholic. Address: Am Consulate Gen Vlasmarkt 1 Rotterdam The Netherlands 3011 PW

JUNIPER, KERRISON, JR., physician, educator; b. St. Petersburg, Fla., Aug. 3, 1924; s. Kerrison and Dorothy (Drew) J.; m. Catherine Durant, July 10, 1943; children: Kevin Alan, Karen Ann. Student, Duke, 1941-43, U. Miss., 1943-45; M.D., Emory U., 1949. Diplomate: Am. Bd. Internal Medicine, Am. Bd. Gastroenterology, Am. Bd. Microbiology in Pub. Health and Med. Lab. Parasitology. Intern Roper Hosp., Charleston, S.C., 1949-50; resident VA Hosp., Atlanta, 1950-51, 52-54; asst. in medicine Boston U., 1954-56; asst. prof. medicine U. Ark. Med. Center, Little Rock, 1956-62, asso. prof., 1962-67, prof., 1967-73, chief gastroenterology sect., 1956-70, dir. Postgrad. Tng. Program in Gastroenterology, 1960-70, dir. Office Biomedical Communications, 1969-70, coordinator tech. research med. edn., 1970-73; prof. medicine, chief gastroenterology div. So. Ill. U. Sch. Medicine, Springfield, 1973—; vis. prof. Nat. Def. Med. Center, Taipei, Taiwan, 1971-72; cons. Naval Med. Research Unit 2, Taipei, 1971-72; attending physician in medicine VA Hosp., Little Rock, 1956-62, cons. in medicine, 1962-73; vis. lectr. tropical medicine Walter Reed Army Inst. Research, 1967—. Mem. editorial bd.: Am. Jour. Digestive Diseases, 1966-68. Mem. health occupations adv. council Met. Vocational-Indsl. High Sch., Little Rock; cons. in continuing edn. Ark. Regional Med. Programs, 1970-73; cons. HEW Bur. Hearings and Appeals, Social Security Adminstrn., 1976—, McFarland Mental Health Center, Ill. Dept. Mental Health and Development Disabilities, 1976—; mem. med. adv. com. Refugee Health Services Program, Ill. Dept. Public Health, 1980—; mem. utilization rev. com. CIPRO, 1980—; Hon. mem. faculty com. Nat. Def. Med. Center, Taipei, Taiwan, Republic China, 1972—. Served with AUS, 1943-46; to capt., 1951-52; maj. Res., 1952-62. Decorated Bronze Star medal.; USPHS postdoctoral research fellow in gastroenterology Boston U., 1954-56. Mem. A.A.A.S., Am. Fedn. Clin. Research, A.C.P., Am. Soc. Gastrointestinal Endoscopy, Central Soc. Clin. Research, Ill. Med. Soc. (cons. com. on drugs and therapeutics), Am. Gastroenterol. Assn. (com. on exhibits 1970-76), Am. Soc. Tropical Medicine and Hygiene, A.M.A., Am. Med. Writers Assn. (chmn. audiovisual sect. 1973-75), Am. Assn. for Study of Liver Diseases, Sigma Xi. Home: Rural Route 2 Box 12C Edinburg IL 62531 Office: SIU Sch Medicine PO Box 3926 Springfield IL 62708

JUNZ, HELEN B., economist; d. Samson and Dobra Bachner. B.A., U. Amsterdam; M.A., New Sch. Social Research, 1956. Acting chief consumer price sect. Nat. Indsl. Conf. Bd., N.Y.C., 1953-58; research officer Nat. Inst. Econ. and Social Research, London, 1958-60; economist Bur. Econ. Analysis, Dept. Commerce, Washington, 1960-62; adviser div. internat. fin. bd. govs. Fed. Res. System, Washington, 1962-77; adviser OECD, Paris, 1967-69; sr. internat. economist Council of Econ. Advisers, The White House, Washington, 1975-77; dep. asst. sec. Office of Asst. Sec. for Internat. Affairs, Dept. Treasury, Washington, 1977-79; v.p., sr. adviser First Nat. Bank Chgo., 1979-80; v.p. Townsend Greenspan & Co., Inc., N.Y.C., 1980-82; sr. adviser IMF, Washington, 1982—. Contbr. articles to profl. jours. Mem. Am. Econ. Assn., Nat. Assn. Bus. Economists, Council Fgn. Relations, Nat. Women's Polit. Caucus., Women's Econ. Round Table. Office: Internat Monetary Fund Washington DC 20431

JURAN, JOSEPH MOSES, engineer; b. Braila, Rumania, Dec. 24, 1904; came to U.S., 1912, naturalized, 1917; s. Jakob and Gitel (Goldenberg) J.; m. Sadie Shapiro, June 5, 1926; children: Robert, Sylvia, Charles, Donald. B.S. in Elec. Engring, U. Minn., 1924; J.D., Loyola U., 1935. Bar: Ill.; Registered profl. engr., N.Y. State, N.J. With Western Electric Co., Inc., 1924-41; asst. adminstr. Office Lend-Lease Adminstrn., 1941-43, Fgn. Econ. Adminstrn., 1943-45; prof., chmn. dept. adminstrv. engring. N.Y.U., 1945-51; cons. numerous indsl. cos. and govt. agys., 1951—, vis. lectr. numerous Am. and Fgn. univs.; founder, chmn. Juran Inst., Inc., 1979—. Editor: Quality Control Handbook, 3d edit, 1974 (translated into Japanese, Spanish, Russian, Hungarian, Chinese); Author numerous books in field quality control, including: (with N.N. Barish) Case Studies in Industrial Management, 1955; Author: Managerial Breakthrough, 1964, (with J.K. Louden) the Corporate Director, 1966, (with F.M. Gryna, Jr.) Quality Planning and Analysis, 1970, 2d edit., 1980, (video cassette series) Juran on Quality Improvement, 1981; Lectr., author numerous papers on mgmt. Decorated Order of Sacred Treasure (Japan); recipient alumni medal U. Minn., 1954; Recipient Scroll of Appreciation Japanese Union Scientists and Engrs., 1961, 250th Anniversary medal Czech Higher Inst. Tech., 1965, Wallace Clark medal, 1967, ann. medal Technikhaza Esztergom, Hungary, 1968, medal Fedn. Tech. and Sci. Industries, Hungary, 1968; medal of honor camera Official de la Industria, Madrid, 1970. Fellow Internat. Acad. Mgmt., A.A.A.S., Am. Soc. for Quality Control (hon., Brumbaugh award 1958, Edwards medal 1962, Eugene L. Grant medal 1967), Am. Inst. Indsl. Engrs. (Gilbreth medal 1981), Am. Mgmt. Assn., ASME (Warner medal 1945); mem. Sigma Xi, Tau Beta Pi, Alpha Pi Mu; hon. mem. European Orgn. for Quality Control, Australian Orgn. for Quality Control (established Juran medal 1975), Argentine Orgn. for Quality Control, Philippine Soc. for Quality Control, Brit. Inst. Quality Assurance.; mem., sometime officer many profl. assns. Address: 866 UN Plaza New York NY 10017

JURASAS, JONAS RIMGAUDAS, theatre director; b. Lithuania, June 19, 1936; came to U.S., 1976, naturalized, 1981; s. Jonas and Sofia (Jurksaite) J.; m. Ausra-Maria Sluckaite, 1968; 1 son, Chris-Joris. G.I.T.I.S., Moscow Acad. Theater Arts, 1964. Artistic dir. State Drama Theater, Kaunas, Lithuania, 1967-71. Guest dir. various theaters, 1976-81, the most recent being; The Suicide, Anta theater on Broadway, 1980, The Magnificent Cuckold, Yale Repertory Theatre, 1981, The Three Sisters, Japan Waseda Shosekijo Co.; guest tchr.-dir., Yale Drama Sch., drama sch. at, Trinity Repertory Theatre, Providence, drama sch. of, Hartman Conservatory, Stamford, Conn. Recipient various Soviet theater awards, 1967-71. Mem. Soc. Stage Dirs. and Choreographers.

JUREIT, WILLIAM FREDERICK, structural and computer design co. exec.; b. Balt., Oct. 10, 1921; s. William F. and Lillian E. (Rau) J.; m. Carolyn J. Hiserodt, Oct. 21, 1976; children—April J. Major, Leslie J. Taylor, William F., Ross C. B.S., Columbia U., 1947; J.D., U. Miami, 1950. Bar: Fla. bar 1950. Partner Ayers, Jureit & Bond (C.P.A.'s), Miami, Fla., 1950-62; mem. firm McHenry & Jureit, Miami, 1951-62; exec. v.p., gen. counsel Automated Bldg. Components, Inc., Miami, 1963-77, pres., 1978—; dir. Gang Nail Systems, Inc., Multivisions, Inc. Served with U.S. Army, 1942-45. Mem. Am. Bar Assn., Fla. Bar Assn., Am. Inst. C.P.A.'s, Fla. Inst. C.P.A.'s, Am. Soc. Atty- C.P.A.'s. Republican. Christian Scientist. Home: 10850 SW 53d Ave Miami FL 33156 Office: 7525 NW 37th Ave Miami FL 33147

JURGENSEN, CHRISTIAN ADOLPH, III, sports commentator; b. Wilmington, N.C., Aug. 23, 1934; s. Christian Adolph II and Lola (Johnson) J.; m. Margo Hurt, June 8, 1967; children: Gregory, Scott, Erik, Gunnar. B.A. in Edn., Duke U., 1957. Quarterback Phila. Eagles, 1957-64, Washington Redskins, 1964-74; sports commentator, TV analyst WTOP-TV, CBS Sports, Washington, 1974-81. Hon. chmn. Cerebral Palsy Assn. Va., 1972, No. Va. Mental Health Assn., 1972, Children's Hosp. Fund Raising Com., 1973. Recipient NFL passing title, 1967, 69, 74; named All Pro, 1961, 64, 66, 67, 69; named to N.C. Hall of Fame, 1972, S.C. Hall of Fame, 1975, Pro Football Hall of Fame, 1983. Home: PO Box 53 Mount Vernon VA 22121

JURGENSEN, WARREN PETER, educator, psychiatrist; b. Sioux City, Ia., June 30, 1921; s. Matthias Peter and Dagmar (Jensen) J.; m. Gwenda Doris Downey, Mar. 30, 1946; children—Gail Ruth, Karen Sue, Timothy Allan. B.S., Northwestern U., 1945; M.D., Creighton U., 1950. Diplomate: Am. Bd. Psychiatry and Neurology. Intern Edward W. Sparrow Hosp., Lansing, Mich., 1950-51; regional health dir., then asst. chief U.S. Health Mission to Iran, 1951-54; psychiat. resident USPHS Hosp., Lexington, Ky., 1955-57, Cin. Gen. Hosp., 1957-58; with USPHS, 1951-70; chief Clin. Research Center, Nat. Inst. Mental Health, Ft. Worth, 1969-70; dir. student health services U. Tex. at Arlington, 1970-77; also adj. prof. biology; psychiatrist Tarrant County Mental Health Mental Retardation Services, Ft. Worth, 1977—; clin. asst. prof. psychiatry U. Tex. Southwestern Med. Sch., 1966-72; vis. research scientist Inst. Behavorial Research, Tex. Christian U., 1967-72; vis. lectr. Regional Tng. Center, North Central Tex. Council Govts., 1967-77; cons. Alive and Well Program, U. Tex. Southwestern Med. Sch., 1974-79. Mem. Gov.'s Adv. Council on Drug Abuse, 1973-79. Served with USNR, 1942-45. Fellow Am. Psychiat. Assn., Am. Pub. Health Assn., Royal Soc. Health. Episcopalian. Club: Woodhaven Country (Fort Worth). Home: 5000 Marble Falls Rd Fort Worth TX 76103 Office: PO Box 2603 Fort Worth TX 76101

JURIS, HERVEY ASHER, management educator; b. Lawrenceville, N.J., Sept. 5, 1938; s. Edward and Justa (Novik) J.; m. Leslie Nathanson; children: Steven Jerome, Robin Lynn. A.B., Princeton U., 1960; M.B.A., U. Chgo., 1962, Ph.D., 1967. Asst. dean students Grad. Sch. Bus., U. Chgo., 1962-64; asst. prof. Sch. for Workers, U. Wis., Madison, 1965-70, assoc. prof., 1970, Grad Sch. Mgmt., Northwestern U., Evanston, Ill., 1970-75, prof. indsl. relations and urban affairs, 1975—, chmn. dept. indsl. relations and urban affairs, 1982—, assoc. dean acad. affairs, 1978-80. Author: (with Peter Feuille) Police Unionism, 1973; editor, contbg. author: (with Myron Roomkin) The Shrinking Perimeter: Manufacturing Unionism in the 1980s, 1980; contbr. articles to profl. jours. Nat. Center for Health Services Research grantee, 1975-78; Law Enforcement Asst. Adminstrn. grantee, 1970-72; Spencer Found grantee, 1976-77; Ford Found. grantee, 1977-78. Mem. Am. Econ. Assn., Indsl. Relations Research Assn. (exec. bd. 1980-83), Human Resources Mgmt. Assn. Chgo. Address: 2001 Sheridan Rd Evanston IL 60201

JURIST, JAMES ALFRED, broadcasting and marketing company executive; s. Alfred Edward and Rachel (Graff) J.; m. Janet Calodny, June 28, 1953; children: Louis, Carolyn. B.A., Columbia U., 1947, M.B.A., 1949. C.P.A., N.Y. Sr. acct. Arthur Young & Co., N.Y.C., 1949-51, 53-56; in various fin. positions NBC, 1956-65; dir. bus. affairs NBC Films, NBC, N.Y.C., 1960-61, NBC News, NBC, 1961-65; controller Columbia Pictures Corp., N.Y.C., 1965-67; v.p., treas., chief fin. officer John Blair & Co., N.Y.C., 1967—. Served to 1st lt. USAAF, 1943-46; then USAF, 1951-52; CBI, Korea. Mem. Am. Inst. C.P.A.s, N.Y. State Soc. C.P.A.s, Broadcasting Fin. Mgmt. Assn., Phi Beta Kappa, Beta Gamma Sigma. Home: 510 E 86 St New York NY 10028 Office: John Blair & Co 1290 Ave of Americas New York NY 10104 *If one must ask if a specific action, or proposed action, is ethical, the question has already been answered.*

JURJI, EDWARD J., educator, writer, lecturer; b. Latakia, Syria, Mar. 27, 1907; came to the U.S., 1933, naturalized, 1947; s. Jabra and Mary (Jureidini) J.; m. Nahia K. Khuri, Aug. 20, 1932 (dec. April 1957); children: Layla (dec.), Edward David; m. Ruth Guinter, Nov. 27, 1958. B.A., Am. U., Beirut, Lebanon, 1928, M.A., 1934; Ph.D., Princeton, 1936, B.D., 1942. Tchr. dept. edn., Iraq, 1928-30, Am. Sch. for Boys, Baghdad, 1930-33; ordained to ministry Presbyterian Ch., 1942; mem. Inst. Advanced Study, Princeton, N.J., 1936-38; faculty Princeton Theol. Sem., 1939—; lectr. univ. Theol. Sem., Princeton U., 1942-52, book rev. editor, 1945-77, asso. prof. Islamics, comparative religion, 1946-54, prof., 1954-63, prof. history religions, 1963-77, prof. emeritus, 1977—; interim minister Christ Presbyn. Ch., Trenton, N.J., 1939-41, Hopewell, N.J., 1943-45, 4th Ave. Presbyn. Ch., Bay Ridge, N.Y., 1977-81; vis. prof. numerous colls., univs., sems.; lectr. Middle East internat. and intercultural affairs; lectr. advanced program world religions Union Theol. Sem., N.Y.C., 1958, 60; Haskell lectr. Oberlin, 1959; Fulbright research prof. U. Madras, India, 1960; Mem. Presbytery of N.Y.C.; chmn. Sesquicentennial Comparative Religion Conf., 1963; dir. World Religious Conf., 1964, 66. Author: Illumination in Islamic Mysticism, 1938, Christian Interpretation of Religion, 1952, The Middle East, Its Religion and Culture, 1957, 2d edit., 1973, The Phenomenology of Religion, 1963; Editor: Great Religions of the Modern World, 1947, most recent edit., 1981, Portuguese transl., 1956, The Ecumenical Era in Church and Society: Symposium in Honor of John A. Mackay, 1959, Religious Pluralism and World Community, 1969; Co-editor: Proc. of First Gallahue Conf. on World Religions, 1966; editorial bd.: Muslim World Jour. Collaborator: Tarikh el Arab (3 vols.); Saudi Arabia; Contbr.: articles on religion, Eastern religions to Colliers Ency., 1957; book revs. to Jour. Ch. and State; also articles and essays on Arabic philosophy, Islamic law, religious pluralism fgn. affairs, intercultural dialogue, world religions to profl. publs.; Cons. staff: Random House Dictionary of the English Language, 1966, coll. edit., 1968, Great Religions of World, Nat. Geog. Soc., 1971, rev. edit., 1978, Funk and Wagnalls New Ency, 1972; editorial cons.: Berlitz Sch. Langs. of Am., Inc., 1981. Bd. dirs. St. Nicholas Cathedral Home, 1980-82; mem. acad. and mus. adv. com. Islam Centennial, 1980—. Recipient Author award N.J. Assn. Tchrs. English, 1964; Edward F. Gallahue grantee. Mem. Soc. Sci. Study Religion, Internat. Assn. History Religions, AAUP. Home: 89 Castle Howard Ct Princeton NJ 08540

JURKAT, MARTIN PETER, management educator; b. Berlin, July 23, 1935; U.S., 1946, naturalized, 1951; s. Ernest Herman and Dorothy (Bergas) J.; m. Mayme Porter, May 31, 1958; children: Martin Alexander, Susanna, Maria. B.A. in Math. and Stats. with honors, Swarthmore (Pa.) Coll., 1957; M.A., U. N.C., 1961; Ph.D., Stevens Inst. Tech., Hoboken, N.J., 1972. Programmer Burroughs Corp. Research Lab., Paoli, Pa., 1960-61; sr. program analyst ITT Corp., Paramus, N.J., 1961-64; chief transp. analysis div. Davidson Lab., Stevens Inst. Tech., 1964-77, dir., 1977-79, Alexander Crombie Humphreys prof. mgmt. sci., 1979—; cons. Tank-Automotive Devel. Command, U.S. Army, 1980—; dir. Cause project NSF, 1978—. Co-author: The NATO Reference Mobility Model, 1980; author studies, reports on mobility, transp., human factors. Mem. Assn. Computing Machinery, Am. Statis. Assn., Soc. Indsl. and Applied Math., IEEE Computer Soc., Sigma Xi. Democrat. Quaker. Home: 706 Hudson St Hoboken NJ 07030 Office: Dept Mgmt Stevens Inst Tech Castle Point Sta Hoboken NJ 07030

JURKIEWICZ, MAURICE JOHN, educator, surgeon; b. Claremont, N.H., Sept. 24, 1923; s. Charles B. and Mary (Ostrowska) J.; m. Mary de Forest Freeman, July 7, 1951; children—Elizabeth de Forest, John Christopher. D.D.S. magna cum laude, U. Md., 1946; M.D., Harvard, 1952. Diplomate: Am. Bd. Surgery, Am. Bd. Plastic Surgery (mem. bd. 1971-77, chmn. 1977—). Intern Barnes Hosp., Washington U., St. Louis, 1952-53, resident, 1953-58, clin. fellow, 1958-59, instr. surgery, 1957-59; mem. staff U. Fla. Hosp., Gainesville; asst. prof. surgery U. Fla., 1959-64, asso. prof., 1964-67, prof., 1967-71, chief div. plastic and reconstructive surgery, 1959-71; chief of surgery VA Hosp., Gainesville, 1968-71; prof. surgery, chief of plastic and reconstructive surgery Emory Affiliated Hosps., Atlanta, 1971—; chief surg. services Grady Meml. Hosp., Atlanta, 1972-77; cons. in plastic surgery Walter Reed Gen. Hosp., Washington, 1971—; sci. counselor Nat. Inst. Dental Research, 1966-71; chmn. com. on study of evaluation procedures Am. Bd. Med. Spltys., 1979-81. Assoc. editor: Plastic and Reconstructive Surgery, 1972-78, 79—, Am. Surgeon, 1977—. Served to lt. (j.g.) USNR, 1946-48. Mem. AAAS, Am. Cancer Soc., Am. Cleft Palate Assn., A.C.S. (bd. regents 1979—), AMA, Am., Southeastern, Ga. socs. plastic and reconstructive surgeons, Southeastern Surg. Congress, Am. Soc. Human Genetics, Soc. Head and Neck Surgeons, Ednl. Founds. Plastic Surgery Research Council, Am. Assn. Plastic Surgeons (pres. 1980-81), Am., So. surg. assns., Med. Assn. Ga. Home: 715 Old Post Rd Atlanta GA 30328 Office: Emory U Clinic 25 Prescott St NE Atlanta GA 30308

JURNEY, DOROTHY MISENER, journalist; b. Michigan City, Ind., May 8, 1909; d. Herbert Roy and Mary Zeola (Hershey) Misener; m. Frank J. Jurney, Sept. 1940 (dec.). Student, Western Coll. Women, 1926-28; B.S. in Journalism, Northwestern U., 1930. Reporter Michigan City News and News Dispatch, 1930-39; women's editor Gary (Ind.) Post-Tribune, 1939-41; asst. to press rep., Panama Canal, 1941-42; editor in women's dept. Miami (Fla.) News, 1943-44, 46-49; asst. city editor Washington News, 1944-46; women's editor Miami Herald, 1949-59, Detroit Free Press, 1959-73, asst. mng. editor, 1973, Phila. Inquirer, 1973-75; cons. Nat. Commn. Internat. Women's Year, 1975—; owner, dir. The Woman's Network, Wayne, Pa., 1975—; Lectr., cons. in field. Mem. Women in Communications, Am. Soc. Newspaper Editors. Clubs: Florida Women's Press (life), Michigan Women's Press (life). Home: 325 West Ave Wayne PA 19087

JURTSHUK, PETER, JR., microbiologist; b. N.Y.C., July 28, 1929; s. Peter and Mary (Ferens) J.; m. Rebecca Jones, Jan. 2, 1971; children: Peter, Larissa. A.B., NYU, 1951; M.S., Creighton U., 1953; Ph.D., U. Md., 1957. Asst. prof. pharmacology Bklyn. Coll. Pharmacy, L.I. U., 1957-59; asst. prof. enzyme chemistry U. Wis.-Madison, 1962-63; asst. prof. microbiology U. Tex., Austin, 1963-69; asso. prof. biology U. Houston, 1970-76, prof., 1976—; mem. vis. biol. program Am. Inst. Biol. Scis., 1969-72. Contbr. chpts. to books. Recipient Disting. Service award Am. Soc. Microbiology, 1982; NIH grantee, 1964-75. Fellow Am. Acad. Microbiology, Am. Inst. Chemists; mem. Am. Soc. Microbiology (pres. Tex. br. 1972-74), N.Y. Acad. Scis., Am. Soc. Biol. Chemists, Am. Chem. Soc., Sigma Xi. (pres. U. Houston chpt. 1979-80). Russian Orthodox. Office: Biology Dept U Houston Houston TX 77004

JUST, CAROLYN ROYALL, lawyer; b. Shanghai, China, Sept. 15, 1907; d. Francis Martin and Mary Dunklin (Sullivan) Royall; m. Robert Just, Dec. 17, 1925 (dec. Nov. 1943). Ph.B., U. Chgo., 1934; J.D., DePaul U., 1938; LL.M., George Washington U., 1940; grad., Inter-Am. Acad. Comparative Internat. Law, Havana, Cuba, 4th, 5th, 7th sessions, 1949, 50, 55, 9th Session; cert., Hague Acad. Internat. Law, 31st Session, 1960, Escuela de Verano, San Carlos U., Guatemala City, 1965. Bar: D.C. 1938, Ill. 1940, U.S. Supreme Ct. 1941. Violin tchr., 1925-30; chief of staff concessions dept. Century of Progress Chgo. Expn., 1933; editorial asst., sec. to Dr. Forest Ray Moulton AAAS, 1930-38; practiced law, Washington, 1938, 77—; atty. Lands Div. U.S. Dept. Justice, 1938-43, atty. antitust div., 1943-50, atty. Tax Div., 1950-77; Mem. D.C. Citizenship (formerly I Am An American) Day Com., chmn. com. citizenship recognition, 1946, gen. sec., 1947-50; mem. Atty. Gen's. Adv. Com. on Citizenship and; del. representing Dept. Justice to nat. confs. on citizenship at, Phila., 1946, Washington, 1947, 48, 50-55, N.Y.C., 1949. Mem. Am. Bar Assn. (sects. of taxation, internat. law, chmn. com. on relations with internat. bar orgns. 1950-71, adv. com. on pub. relations 1962-65, mem. com. facilities Law Library Congress 1952-59), Fed. Bar Assn. (formerly asst. editor Fed. Bar Jour.), Nat. Assn. Women Lawyers, Bar Assn. D.C., Women's Bar Assn. D.C., Internat. Bar Assn. (charter patron, del. to confs. N.Y.C. 1947, London 1951, Madrid, 1952, Salzburg, 1960, Mexico City, 1964, Sydney, Australia, 1978, chmn. credentials com. Madrid 1952), Inter-Am. Bar Assn. (del. confs. Havana, Cuba 1941, Mexico City, 1944, Santiago, Chile, 1945, Lima, Peru, 1947, Detroit, 1949, Sao Paulo, Brazil, 1954, Dallas, 1956, Buenos Aires, 1957, Miami, 1959, Bogota, Colombia, 1961, San Jose, Costa Rica, 1967, 77, Caracas, Venezuela,

1969, Quito, Ecuador, 1972, Rio de Janeiro, 1973, Cartagena, Colombia, 1975, reporter gen. 1951-72, council 1951-72, Gold medal 1972, Vallance award found. 1979), Am. Law Inst., Am. Soc. Internat. Law, George Washington U. Alumni Assn., U. Chgo. Alumni Assn., Am. Judicature Soc., AAUW, Club de las Americas (pres. 1964-65), D.A.R., Internat. Law Assn. (Am. br.), Internat. Fiscal Assn., Am. Assn. for Internat. Commn. Jurists, English Speaking Union, Columbian Women of George Washington U., Georgetown Symphony Orch., Amateur Chamber Music Players, Friday Morning Music Club, Norwegian Chamber Music Soc. (Trondheim, Norway), Pi Gamma Mu, Kappa Beta Pi, Phi Delta Gamma. Home: Harbour Sq 520 N St SW Washington DC 20024 Office: 927 15th St NW Washington DC 20005

JUST, WARD SWIFT, author; b. Michigan City, Ind., Sept. 5, 1935; s. F. Ward and Elizabeth (Swift) J. Student, Lake Forest (Ill.) Acad., 1949-51, Cranbrook (Mich.) Sch., 1951-53, Trinity Coll., Hartford, Conn., 1953-57. Reporter Waukegan (Ill.) News-Sun, 1957-59, Newsweek, 1959-61, Reporter mag., 1962-63; corr. Newsweek, 1963-65, Washington Post, 1965-70; contbg. editor Atlantic Monthly, 1972—. Author: To What End, 1968, A Soldier of the Revolution, 1970, Military Men, 1970, The Congressman Who Loved Flaubert and Other Washington Stories, 1973, Stringer, 1974, Nicholson at Large, 1975, A Family Trust, 1978, Honor, Power, Riches, Fame, and the Love of Women, 1979, In the City of Fear, 1982, The American Blues, 1984; Contbr. to: Best Am. Short Stories, 1972, 73, 76.

JUSTESEN, DON ROBERT, psychologist; b. Salt Lake City, Mar. 8, 1930; s. Richard Carvel and Elizabeth Agnes (Gustafson) J.; m. Patricia Ann Larson, Feb. 14, 1957; children: Lyle Richard, Jonille Jacelyn, Tracy Ann, Anthony Ray. B.A. in Psychology, U. Utah, 1955, M.A., 1957, Ph.D., 1960. Asst. prof., chmn. dept. psychology Westminster Coll., Salt Lake City, 1959-62; lectr. to prof. dept. psychology U. Mo.-Kansas City, 1963-75; vis. prof. U. Colo., Boulder, 1965; asst. prof. to prof. dept. psychiatry U. Kans. Sch. Medicine, Kansas City, 1963—; dir. behavioral radiology labs. VA Med. Ctr., Kansas City, 1962—; cons. Nat. Council on Radiation Protection and Measurements, Washington, 1977—, EPA, NAS, NIH, NSF, USN, 1972—. Contbr. articles to profl. jours.; assoc. editor: Jour. Microwave Power, 1975-83; editor: Spl. Supplements to Radio Sci., Washington, 1977—; editorial bd.: Bioelectromagnetics Soc., 1979-83. Pres. Fountains Homes Assn., Grandview, Mo., 1974-75. Served to lt. USNR, 1962-65; served to lt. USN, 1948-52; ATO. Recipient First Cash prize in psychopharmacology Am. Psychol. Assn., 1968; VA Research Career Scientist, 1980; USPHS grantee, 1971—. Fellow AAAS, Am. Psychol. Assn.; mem. IEEE (sr.), Soc. for Neurosci., Bioelectromagnetics Soc. (pres. 1984—), Brit. Soc. Philosophy of Sci., Nat. Acad. Sci. (U.S. nat. com.), Internat. Radio Sci. (mem. commn. on meteorology). Home: 12416 Ewing Cir Grandview MO 64030 Office: VA Med Center 4801 Linwood Blvd Kansas City MO 64128

JUSTICE, (DAVID) BLAIR, psychologist, author; b. Dallas, July 2, 1927; s. Sam Hugh and Lou-Reine (Hunter) J.; m. Rita Norwood, July 26, 1972; children by previous marriage: Cynthia, David, Elizabeth. B.A., U. Tex. at Austin, 1948; M.S., Columbia U., 1949; M.A., Tex. Christian U., 1963; Ph.D., Rice U., 1966. Reporter Ft. Worth Star-Telegram, 1952-55; sci. writer N.Y. Daily News, 1955-56, Ft. Worth Star-Telegram, 1956-64; sci. editor, columnist Houston Post, 1964-73; exec. asst. to Mayor Houston, 1966-72; prof. psychology Sch. Public Health, U. Tex., Houston, 1968—; sr. psychologist, group therapist, psychiat. residency faculty Tex. Research Inst. Mental Scis.; community assoc. Rice U., Lovett Coll.; cons. child abuse Tex. Dept. Human Resources. Author: Violence in the City, 1969, Detection of Potential Community Violence, 1967, (with Rita Justice) The Abusing Family, 1976, The Broken Taboo: Sex in the Family, 1979, Perspectives in Public Mental Health, 1982; editor: Your Child's Behavior, 1972; editorial bd.: Internat. Jour Mental Health, 1980—. Gen. chmn. Houston Job Fair, 1967-73; chmn. Houston Manpower Area Planning Council, 1972-74; mem. Tex. Urban Devel. Commn., 1970-72; Bd. dirs. Houston Housing Devel. Corp., Tex. Citizens Human Devel., 1979—, Greater Houston Com. Prevention of Child Abuse, 1982—; sec. bd. mgrs. Tarrant County Hosp., Dist., 1961-64; pres. Greater Houston Youth Council, 1978-79, Houston Area Council on Sudden Infant Death Syndrome, 1977-78; mem. nat. adv. com. Marine Biomed. Inst., U. Tex. Med. Br., 1971—; mem. community bd. Tex. Youth Council. Served with USNR, 1945-46. Recipient most outstanding book award Tex. Writers Roundup, 1970, award of recognition City of Houston, 1973; named One of Five Outstanding Young Men of Tex., 1962; recipient numerous awards for sci. writing. Fellow Am. Coll. Psychology, Menninger Found.; Mem. Nat. Assn. Sci. Writers (life; exec. com. 1965-67), Houston Psychol. Assn. (pres. 1975), Am. Public Health Assn. (chmn. mental health sect. 1980-81), Phi Beta Kappa (dir. Houston chpt. 1979—), Phi Beta Kappa Assocs. Clubs: Houston Racquet, N.Y. Road Runners. Finished 1981 Boston Marathon, 1981 and 1982 Houston Marathon, 1980 N.Y.C. Marathon. Home: 6331 Brompton Rd Houston TX 77005 Office: 6901 Bertner St Houston TX 77030

JUSTICE, DONALD RODNEY, poet, educator; b. Miami, Fla., Aug. 12, 1925; s. Vascoe J. and Mary Ethel (Cook) J.; m. Jean Catherine Ross, Aug. 22, 1947; 1 son, Nathaniel Ross. B.A., U. Miami, 1945; M.A., U. N.C., 1947; postgrad., Stanford U., 1948-49; Ph.D., U. Iowa, 1954. Instr. English U. Miami, 1947-51; asst. prof. Hamline U., St. Paul, Minn., 1956-57; lectr. U. Iowa, 1957-60, asst. prof., 1960-63, asso. prof., 1963-66, prof., 1971—, Syracuse U., 1966-70. Author: The Summer Anniversaries, 1960, Night Light, 1967, Departures, 1973, Selected Poems, 1979; Editor: The Collected Poems of Weldon Kees, 1962. Rockefeller Found. fellow in poetry, 1954; Ford Found. fellow, 1964; Nat. Endowment for the Humanities grantee, 1967, 73, 80; Guggenheim Found. fellow in poetry, 1976; recipient Pulitzer Prize in poetry for Selected Poems, 1980. Home: English Dept Univ of Florida Gainesville FL 32611

JUSTICE, FRANKLIN PIERCE, JR., oil company executive; b. Wanego, W.Va., May 5, 1938; s. Franklin Pierce and Jeneta Ruth (Cooley) J.; m. Eva Mae Hartley, June 8, 1960; children: Kerry, Kelly, Kevin. B.S. in Bus. Adminstrn., W.Va. State Coll., 1967; M.B.A., Marshall U., 1977; postgrad., U. Louisville, 1971-72. Reporter Dun & Bradstreet, Inc., Charleston, W.Va., 1960-63, reporting mgr., 1963-65, office mgr., Huntington, W.Va., 1966-68; domestic trade specialist U.S. Dept. Commerce, Charleston, 1968-70; pres., investment mgr. Equal Opportunity Fin., Inc., Ashland, Ky., 1970—, adminstrv. asst. to v.p. personnel, 1973-74, adminstrv. asst. to v.p. external affairs, 1974-75, mgr. spl. projects, 1975-76, dir. pub. affairs, 1976—; v.p. pub. relations Ashland Oil, Inc., 1979-81; v.p. ops. support Ashland Services Co., 1981—. Cons. Ashland Tennis Commn., 1975-79; mem. Ashland Human Rights Commn., 1977-79; bd. dirs. Tri-State Fair & Regatta, 1978-79, Ky. Ctr. for Arts, Lousiville, 1982—, Pub. Affairs Council, Washington, 1978—, Ky. Council Econ. Edn., 1978—; chmn. bd. Ky. Council Econ. Edn., 1983; pres. bd. dirs. Greater Ashland Found., 1979—. Mem. Ashland Area C. of C. (1st v.p. 1978-79, pres. 1980), Ashland Area. C. of C. (dir. 1978-80), Ky. C. of C. (dir. 1978—, chmn. 1983). Republican. Home: 128 Stonybrooke Dr Ashland KY 41101 Office: PO Box 391 Ashland KY 41114

JUSTICE, JACK BURTON, lawyer; b. Hardy, Ky., Aug. 2, 1931; s. George Edward and Goldia (Alley) J.; m. Martha Monser, Dec. 28, 1957 (dec. Feb. 1974); m. Judith Farquhar Lang, Apr. 26, 1975; children—Jonathan Burton, George Lewis, Paul Williamson. A.B. in Polit. Sci, W.Va. U., 1952, postgrad. in law, 1954-55; B.A. in Jurisprudence, Oxford (Eng.) U., 1954, M.A., 1960. Bar: Pa. bar 1956. Assoc. firm Drinker Biddle & Reath, Phila., 1956-62, ptnr., 1962-82, White & Williams, Phila., 1982—; bus. mgr. Am. Oxonian, 1967—. Pres. Youth Service, Phila., 1962-65; chmn. Phila. Com. on City Policy, 1966-67, Southeastern Pa. chpt. Ams. for Democratic Action, 1968-70; bd. dirs. Greater Phila. br. ACLU; bd. overseers William Penn Charter Sch., Phila. Rhodes scholar, 1952-54. Mem. Am. Law Inst., Am. Bar Assn., Pa. Bar Assn., Phila. Bar Assn., City N.Y. Bar Assn., Assn. Am. Rhodes Scholars (sec. 1967—). Democrat. Unitarian. Clubs: Racquet, Germantown Cricket. Home: 3805 The Oak Rd Philadelphia PA 19129 Office: 1234 Market St Philadelphia PA 19107

JUSTICE, JOHN ELLIS, III, investment banker; b. North Wilkesboro, N.C., Nov. 25, 1928; s. John Ellis and Gozeal (Call) J.; m. Sandra Dunnam, Dec. 29, 1958; children: Jennifer Ann, Amanda Dunnan. B.S., Yale U., 1950. Dir. fin. div. Continental Oil Ltd., London, 1965-66; vice-chmn. Rotan Mosle Inc., Houston, 1978—; dir. Petroleum Analysts Investment Assn., Am. Exploration Co., Houtech Energy, Inc., Leam Transp., Inc. Served with USAF, 1953-55. Mem. Fin. Execs. Inst. Club: River Oaks Country. Home: 5432 Tilbury St Houston TX 77056 Office: Rotan Mosle Inc 1500 S Tower Pennzoil Pl Houston TX 77002

JUSTICE, WILLIAM WAYNE, judge; b. Athens, Tex., Feb. 25, 1920; s. William Davis and Jackie May (Hanson) J.; m. Sue Tom Ellen Rowan, Mar. 16, 1947; 1 dau., Ellen Rowan. LL.B., U. Tex., 1942. Bar: Tex. bar. Ptnr. firm Justice & Justice, Athens, 1946-61; city atty., Athens, 1948-50, 52-58; U.S. atty. Eastern Dist. Tex., 1961-68, U.S. dist. judge, Tyler, 1968-80, chief judge, 1980—. Vice pres. Young Democrats Tex., 1948; adv. council Dem. Nat. Com., 1954; alternate del. Dem. Nat. Conv., 1956; presdl. elector., 1960. Served to 1st lt. F.A. AUS, 1942-46; CBI. Recipient award Outstanding Fed. Judge Assn. Trial Lawyers Am., 1982. Mem. Am. Judicature Soc., VFW (past post comdr.). Baptist. Clubs: Rotarian (pres. Athens 1961), Mason (K.T.). Office: Fed Bldg Tyler TX 75701 *

JUTEN, JOHN RUSSELL, lawyer, arbitrator, cons., educator, former manufacturing company executive; b. Sparta, Minn., June 20, 1907; s. John Amandus and Edith (Nelson) J.; m. Beulah Greenstreet, June 16, 1930; 1 dau., Joan Alice (Mrs. Richard Dube Casper). B.S. in Chem. Engring, Cath. U. Am., 1929; J.D., Georgetown U., 1933. Bar: D.C. bar 1932, also Supreme Ct 1932. Examiner U.S. Patent Office, 1929-31; practice patent law, Washington and N.Y.C., 1931-40; legal counsel, dir. indsl. relations Keuffel & Esser Co., Morristown, N.J., 1940—, v.p., sec., gen. counsel, 1960—; Mgmt. mem. labor-mgmt. com. def. manpower region II Dept. Labor, 1951—; prof. Fairleigh Dickinson U., Teaneck, N.J., 1979—; cons. Edn. Law Center, Newark and; Phila. Mem. bd. edn., West Orange, N.J., 1967-74, pres., 1971. Mem. Am., Fed. bar assns., N.Y., N.J. patent law assns., Am. Soc. Corporate Secs., Am. Arbitration Assn. (nat. arbitration panel). Home: 7 Undercliff Terr West Orange NJ 07052

JUVET, RICHARD SPALDING, JR., scientist, chemistry educator; b. Los Angeles, Aug. 8, 1930; s. Richard Spalding and Marion Elizabeth (Dalton) J.; m. Martha Joy Myers, Jan. 29, 1955 (div. Nov. 1978); children: Victoria, David, Stephen, Richard P. B.S., UCLA, 1952, Ph.D., 1955. Research chemist Dupont, 1955; instr. U. Ill., 1955-57, asst. prof., 1957-61, asso. prof., 1961-70; prof. analytical chemistry Ariz. State U., Tempe, 1970—; vis. prof. U. Calif. at Los Angeles, 1960, U. Cambridge, Eng., 1964-65, Nat. Taiwan U., 1968, Ecole Polytechnique, France, 1976-77; Mem. air pollution chemistry and physics adv. com. EPA, HEW, 1969-72; cons. R.J. Reynolds Industries, 1966-72; mem. adv. panel on advanced chem. alarm tech., devel. and engring. directorate Def. Systems div. Edgewood Arsenal, 1975. Author: Gas-Liquid Chromatography, Theory and Practice, 1962; Editorial advisor to: Jour. Chromatographic Sci, 1969—, Jour. Gas Chromatography, 1963-68, Analytica Chimica Acta, 1972-74, Analytical Chemistry, 1974-77; biennial reviewer in, 1962-76. NSF sr. postdoctoral fellow, 1964-65; Sci. Exchange Agreement awardee, Czechoslovakia, Hungary, Romania and Yugoslavia, 1977. Fellow Am. Inst. Chemists; mem. Am. Chem. Soc. (nat. chmn. div. analytical chemistry 1972-73, nat. sec.-treas. div. analytical chemistry 1969-71, councilor 1978—, chmn. U. Ill. sect. 1968-69, sec. 1962-63), AAAS, Internat. Platform Assn., Am. Radio Relay League, Sigma Xi, Phi Lambda Upsilon, Alpha Chi Sigma. Presbyn. (deacon 1960—, ruling elder 1972—, commr. Grand Canyon Presbytery 1974-76). Research on gas and liquid chromatography, instrumental analysis, computer interfacing. Patentee in field. Home: 4821 E Calle Tuberia Phoenix AZ 85018 Office: Dept Chemistry Arizona State Univ Tempe AZ 85287

JUVILER, PETER HENRY, political scientist; b. London, Mar. 26, 1926; U.S., 1939, naturalized, 1945; s. Adolphe Adam and Katie (Henry) J.; m. Anne C. Stephens, June 20, 1982; children: Gregory, Geoffry. B.E., Yale U., 1948, M.E., 1949; M.A., Columbia U., 1954, Ph.D., 1960. Project engr. Sperry Gyroscope Co., 1949-52; instr. in politics Princeton U., 1957-58; researcher Law Faculty, Moscow U., 1958-59, 64; instr. Columbia U., 1959-60; asso. prof. polit. sci. Barnard Coll., 1964-74, prof., 1974—; asso. Russian Inst. Columbia U., 1964—; instr. Hunter Coll., 1960-61, asst. prof., 1961-64; mem. acad. council Citizen Exchange Corps, 1967-77, trustee, 1971-77, mem. advisory bd., 1977—; mem. com. on Soviet studies Am. Council Learned Socs., 1971-75; mem. advisory bd. Columbia U. Center for Study Human Rights, 1978—. Author: Revolutionary Law and Order: Politics and Social Change in the USSR, 1976; editor: (with Henry W. Morton) Soviet Policy Making: Studies of Communism on Transition, 1967; co-editor, contbg. author: Foreign Affairs 50-Year Bibliography, 1972; contbr. numerous articles to profl. publs., newspapers, encys. Founding mem., bd. dirs. West Kortright Community Centre, Delaware County, N.Y. Served with USN, 1944-66. Mem. AAUP (investigating com. 1970, 74, 77), Am. Polit. Sci. Assn., Am. Assn. Advancement Slavic Studies (publs. com. 1975-78, program com. 1984). Office: 408 Lehman Hall Barnard Coll Columbia U New York NY 10027

KAAPCKE, BERNARD EMERSON, editor; b. Chgo., Nov. 16, 1920; s. Ernest Herman and Ophelia Bohannon (Jones) K.; m. Naomi Schiller, July 29, 1960; children: David Michael, Karen Maya. Student, Columbia, 1949-50, U. Calif., Berkeley, 1953; B.A., U. Wash., 1952. Newsman U.P., Seattle, San Francisco, 1951-53; info. specialist Navy Dept., Port Hueneme, Calif., 1954-55; writer-editor Kaiser Cos., Oakland, Calif., 1955-56, Am. Gas Assn., N.Y.C., 1956-63; copywriter David Altman Advt., N.Y.C., 1964-65; editor, writer Ins. Info. Inst., N.Y.C., 1965—, dir. publs., 1972—; Free lance fiction writer and editor, N.Y.C., 1946-50; tchr. short story writing Scott Meredith Sch. for Writers, 1949. Author: Report on Tomorrow, 1970; Editor: Jour. of Ins, 1967—; Contbr. fiction stories and articles to nat. publs. Served with AUS, 1942-45. Recipient Silver Anvil award Pub. Relations Soc. Am., 1971, Writing award Am. Assn. Indsl. Editors, 1970, Graphic Arts award Printing Industries Am., 1970. Mem. Internat. Assn. Bus. Communicators (Traffic Safety award, Gold Quill award for writing). Unitarian-Universalist. Club: Seaford Tennis. Home: 1453 Gaston St Wantagh NY 11793 Office: 110 William St New York NY 10038 *I have always believed that the greatest power for good is that which God has given to writers. My greatest satisfaction is the feeling that through the power of words I may have been able to inform some people, entertain a few, and just possibly help to save the lives of many, in ways they may never know.*

KAAPCKE, WALLACE LETCHER, lawyer; b. Chgo., Oct. 3, 1916; s. Ernest Herman and Ophelia Bohannon (Jones) K.; m. Ellen Adams, Apr. 4, 1942; children: Peter L., Brian E., Gretchen. B.S., U. Oreg., 1937, J.D., 1939; postgrad. (Sterling fellow), Yale U. Law Sch., 1939-40. Bar: Oreg. bar 1939, Calif. bar 1941. Atty. Bonneville Power Adminstrn., Portland, Oreg., 1940; asso. firm Hughes, Hubbard & Ewing, N.Y.C., 1940-41, Pillsbury, Madison & Sutro, San Francisco, 1941-51, mem. firm, 1951—, chmn., 1977-80; gen. counsel San Francisco Bay Area Rapid Transit, 1958-69; lectr. U. Calif., 1961, 73. Contbr. articles to legal jours. Bd. dirs. U. Oreg. Found.; bd. dirs., mem. exec. com., sec. San Francisco Opera Assn.; bd. visitors U. Oreg. Law Sch. Fellow Am. Bar Found.; mem. Am., Calif., Oreg. bar assns. Clubs: Stock Exchange (dir., past pres.), Bohemian (San Francisco); Claremont (Berkeley). Home: 18 Roble Ct Berkeley CA 94705 Office: 225 Bush St 19th Floor San Francisco CA 94104

KAATZ, RONALD B., advertising agency executive; b. Kansas City, Mo., Apr. 27, 1934; s. Lester M. and Jeannette (Rice) K.; m. Suzanne K. Klemperer, June 22, 1958; children: Kathy, Roberta. B.S.J., Northwestern U., 1956, M.S.J., 1957. Media research dir. Leo Burnett Co., Chgo., 1957-64; dir. sales adminstrn. CBS TV Network, Chgo., 1964-67; v.p., network broadcast supr. J. Walter Thompson Co., Chgo., 1967—, v.p., dir. network relations, 1978—; sr. v.p., dir. media resources and research J. Walter Thomspson Co., Chgo., 1980—; instr. advt. Northwestern U., Evanston, 1963-77. Author: Cable: An Advertiser's Guide to the New Electronic Media, 1982; contbr. articles to profl. jours. Served with U.S. Army, 1957-58. Recipient Leadership award Traffic Audit Bur., 1982. Mem. Nat. Acad. TV Arts and Scis., Country Music Assn., Broadcast Ad Club of Chgo., Traffic Audit Bur. (dir.).

KABAK, ROBERT, artist, educator; b. Bronx, N.Y., Feb. 15, 1930; s. William and Dorothy (Branin) K. B.A. cum laude, Bklyn. Coll., 1952; M.F.A. in Painting, Yale U., 1954. Tchr. Greenport (N.Y.) Public Schs., 1953-54, N.Y.C. Bd. Edn., 1954-56, High Sch. Mus. and Art, N.Y.C., 1956-60; mem. faculty Bklyn. Coll. N.Y., 1960-62, U. Calif., Berkeley, 1962-68, No. Ill. U., DeKalb, 1968-74; prof. housing and interior design U. Mo., Columbia, 1974—. One-man shows, Mus. Modern Art, N.Y.C., 1956, San Francisco Mus. Art, 1964, Santa Barbara Mus. Art, 1965, Oakland Art Mus., 1966, U. Mo., 1980, William Woods Coll., Fulton, Mo., 1982, Western Assn. Art Mus. traveling one-man show, 1971, 80. Huntington Hartford Found grantee; Helene Wurlitzer Found fellow; MacDowell Colony painting grantee, Peterborough, N.H. Office: Stanley Hall U Mo Columbia MO 65211 *

KABARA, JON JOSEPH, biochemical pharmacology educator; b. Chgo., Nov. 26, 1926; s. John Stanley and Mary Elizabeth (Wielgus) K.; m. Annette Elser Sproull, Aug. 18, 1971; children: Christie Anne, Mary K., Sheila Jon, Pat Lee, Tim S., Steve S. B.S., St. Mary's Coll., Minn., 1948; M.S., U. Miami, 1950; Ph.D. (Univ. scholar), U. Chgo., 1959. Prof. chemistry U. Detroit, 1965-68; prof., assoc. dean Mich. Coll. Osteo. Medicine, Pontiac, 1967-70; prof. assoc. dean pharmacology Mich. State U., E. Lansing, 1970-71, prof. biomechanics, 1971—; dir. research and devel. Med.-Chem. Labs., Okemos, Mich., 1975—; cons. in neurochemistry and microbiology. Contbr. over 150 articles to profl. jours.; patentee in field. Pres. Mich. NE PTA, 1959; active Little League, 1973-75. Damon Runyon Cancer fellow, 1949-50; Mt. Sinai fellow, 1949-51; Bishop Heffron awardee St. Mary's Coll., 1970; named Man of Year St. George High Sch. Alumni Club, 1970. Fellow Am. Inst. Chemists; mem. Am. Oil Chem. Soc., N.Y. Acad. Sci., Detroit Physiology Soc., Assn. Analytical Chemists, AAAS, Am. Soc. Clin. Pathologists, Sigma Xi, other orgns. Home: 2088 Riverwood Dr Okemos MI 48864 Office: A407 E Fee Hall Michigan State University East Lansing MI 48824 *One of the more important rules in life is good communication. Communication (speaking and listening) is the keystone to understanding.*

KABAT, ELVIN ABRAHAM, immunochemist, biochemist, educator; b. N.Y.C., Sept. 1, 1914; s. Harris and Doreen (Otis) K.; m. Sally Lennick, Nov. 28, 1942; children: Jonathan, Geoffrey, David. B.S., CCNY, 1932; M.A., Columbia U., 1934, Ph.D., 1937; LL.D. (hon.), U. Glasgow, 1976, Doctoral degree, U. Orleans (France), Ph.D., Weizmann Inst. Sci., Rehovot, Israel. Lab. asst. immunochemistry Presbyn. Hosp., 1933-37; Rockefeller Found. fellow Inst. Phys. Chem., Upsala, Sweden, 1937-38; instr. pathology Cornell U., 1938-41; mem. faculty Columbia U., N.Y.C., 1941—, asst. prof. bacteriology, 1946-48, assoc. prof., 1948-52, prof. microbiology, 1952—, prof. human genetics and devel., 1969—, Higgins prof. Microbiology, 1984—; mem. adv. panel on immunology WHO, 1965—; expert cons. Nat. Cancer Inst., 1975-82, Nat. Inst. Allergy and Infectious Disease, 1983—; Alexander S. Wiener lectr. N.Y. Blood Center, 1979. Author: (with M.M. Mayer) Experimental Immunochemistry, 1948, 2d edition, 1961, Blood Group Substances, Their Chemistry and Immunochemistry, 1956, Structural Concepts in Immunology and Immunochemistry, 1968, 2d edit., 1976, (with T.T. Wu and H. Bilofsky) Variable Regions of Immunoglobulin Chains, 1976, Sequences of Immunoglobulin Chains, (with others) Sequences of Proteins of Immunological Interest, 1983; Mem. editorial bd.: Jour. Immunology, 1961-76, Transplantation Bull, 1957-60. Recipient numerous awards including; Ann. Research award City of Hope, 1974; award Center for Immunology, State U. N.Y., Buffalo, 1976; Louisa Gross Horwitz award Columbia U., 1977; R.E. Dyer lectr. award NIH, 1979; Townsend Harris medal CCNY, 1980, Philip Levine award Am. Soc. Clin. Pathology, 1982, award for excellence Grad. Faculties Alumni Columbia U., 1982; Fogarty scholar NIH, 1974-75. Fellow AAAS, Am. Acad. Allergy (hon.); mem. Nat. Acad. Scis., Am. Acad. Arts and Scis., Am. Assn. Immunologists (past pres.), Am. Soc. Biol. Chemists, Am. Chem. Soc., Harvey Soc. (pres. 1976-77), Am. Soc. Microbiology, Internat. Assn. Allergists, Societe Franciaise d'Allergie (hon.), Biochem. Soc. (Eng.), Assn. for Research in Nervous and Mental Diseases, AAUP, Assn. de Microbiologists de Langue Francaise, Société de Biologie, Société de Immunologie (hon.), Phi Beta Kappa, Sigma Xi. Home: 70 Haven Ave New York NY 10032 Office: Dept Microbiology Coll Physicians and Surgeons Columbia U 701 W 168th St New York NY 10032

KABLE, EDWARD EVERETT, textile co. exec.; b. Bklyn., Feb. 17, 1939; s. Charles W. and Ruth E. (Combs) K.; m. Lynn Waterson Middleton, June 1, 1968; children—Lisa Middleton, Amelia Hammond. B.A., Williams Coll., 1961; LL.B., Harvard, 1964; LL.M., N.Y. U., 1967. Bar: N.Y. bar 1965. Asso. firm Curtis, Mallet-Prevost, Colt & Mosle, N.Y.C., 1965-67; asso. counsel Greenwood Mills, Inc., N.Y.C., 1967—, sec., asst. treas., 1969-72, sec., treas., gen. counsel, 1972—, 1975—. Mem. N.Y. State Bar Assn., Bar Assn. City N.Y., Am. Textile Mfrs. Inst. Home: 161 W 75th St New York City NY 10023 Office: 111 W 40th St New York City NY 10018

KABOT, RONALD H., financial executive; b. Newark, Dec. 1, 1937; s. Martin and Betty (Weber) K.; m. Barbara S. Sherwin, Dec. 4, 1960; children: Lisa, M., Jeffrey D. A.B., Dartmouth Coll., 1959, M.B.A., 1960. Sr. v.p. Kaufman & Broad Inc., Los Angeles, 1969—; pres. Internat. Mortgage Co., Santa Monica, Calif., 1974—. Pres. Nat. Little League, Los Angeles, 1976-78. Served to lt. (j.g.) USN, 1960-62. Mem.

Am. Inst. C.P.A.s, Calif. Soc. C.P.A.s. Club: Dartmouth of So. Calif. Office: 3000 Ocean Park Blvd Santa Monica CA 90405

KAC, MARK, educator, mathematician; b. Krzemieniec, Poland, Aug. 3, 1914; came to U.S., 1938, naturalized, 1943; s. Bencion and Chana (Rojchel) K.; m. Katherine Elizabeth Mayberry, Apr. 4, 1942; children—Michael Benedict, Deborah Katherine. Magister of Philosophy, U. Lwow, Poland, 1935, Ph.D., 1937; D.Sc. (hon.), Case Inst. Tech., 1966. Teaching asst. U. Lwow, 1935-37; jr. actuary Phoenix Co., Lwow, 1937-38; fellow Parnas Found., Johns Hopkins, 1938-39; instr. Cornell U., 1939-43, asst. prof., 1943-46, prof. math., 1947-61, Andrew D. White prof.-at-large, 1965-71; mem. Inst. Advanced Study, Princeton, 1951-52; prof. Rockefeller U., N.Y.C., 1961-81, U. So. Calif., Los Angeles, 1981—; H.A. Lorentz vis prof. U. Leiden, Netherlands, 1963; vis. fellow Brasenose Coll.; sr. vis. fellow Oxford (Eng.) U., spring, 1969; Solvay lectr. U. Brussels, Belgium, 1971. Contbr. articles to profl. jours. Guggenheim fellow, 1946-47; recipient Chauvenet prize for paper Random Walk and the Theory of Brownian Motion Math. Assn. Am., 1950, Chauvenet prize for paper Can One Hear the Shape of A Drum, 1968; Alfred Jurzykowski Found. award in sci., 1976; Birkhoff prize Am. Math. Soc.-Soc. Indsl. and Applied Math., 1978. Mem. Am. Acad. Arts and Scis., Am. Philos. Soc., Am. Math. Soc., Math. Assn. Am., Nat. Acad. Scis., Inst. Math. Stats., Royal Netherlands Acad. Arts and Sci. (fgn.), Royal Norwegian Acad. (fgn.), Sigma Xi. Home: 3980 Astaire Ave Culver City CA 90230 Office: Dept Math U So Calif Los Angeles CA 90007

KACEK, DON J., manufacturing company executive; b. Berwyn, Ill., May 4, 1936; s. George J. and Rose K.; m. Carolyn Hiner, July 22, 1961; children: Scott M., Stacey M. B.S. in Mech. Engring, Ill. Inst. Tech., 1958. With Sunstrand Corp., 1958-72; with Kysor Indsl. Corp., 1972-76, group v.p., 1975-76; dir. product devel. Ransburg Corp., Indpls., 1976-77, pres., 1977—, chmn. bd., chief exec. officer, 1978—; dir. CTS Corp., Arvin Industries, Inc., Ind. Nat. Corp., Ind. Corp. for Sci. & Tech. Served with AUS, 1960. Office: 3939 W 56th St Indianapolis IN 46254

KACERE, JOHN C., artist, educator; b. Walker, Iowa, 1920. B.F.A., U. Iowa, M.F.A. Tchr. U. Man., Can., 1950-53, U. Fla., Gainesville, 1953-58, Cooper Union, N.Y.C., 1958-64, 81, Parson's Sch. Design, 1959-64, U. N.Mex., Albuquerque, 1964-73, NYU, 1974-77, Sch. Visual Arts, N.Y.C., 1971, R.I. Sch. Design, 1981; vis. artist U. Ariz., Tucson, 1978, Ariz. State U., Tempe, 1979. Artist one-man shows, Zabriskie Gallery, N.Y.C., 1954-56, Allan Stone Gallery, N.Y.C., 1961, 63, O.K. Harris Works of Art, N.Y.C., 1971, 73, 75, 78, 80, 82, Galerie de Gestlo, Hamburg, Germany, 1972, 73, Galerie Jean-Pierre Lavignes, Paris, 1981, group shows, Mus. Modern Art, N.Y.C., 1961-62, 63, Corcoran Gallery Art, Washington, 1963, Bryon Gallery, N.Y.C., 1964, Mus. Fine Arts, Boston, 1966, Galerie des 4 Mouvements, Paris, 1972, Cleve. Inst. Art, DeCordova Mus., Lincoln, Mass., 1973, Galerie Arditti, Paris, Galerie Isy Brachot, Brussels, Belgium, Freedom Art Gallery, Buffalo, 1976, Whitney Mus. Am. Art, N.Y.C., 1977, Wesleyan U. Sch. Art, Bloomington, Ill., 1971, Fine Arts Festival, 1977, Butler Inst. Am. Art, Youngstown, Ohio, 1981, Brainerd Art Gallery, Potsdam, N.Y., 1982. Office: OK Harris Works of Art 383 Broadway St New York NY 10012

KACHADOORIAN, ZUBEL, painter, educator; b. Detroit, Feb. 7, 1924; s. Simpat and Queen (Kegulian) K.; m. Deena Morguloff, Aug. 17, 1974; children: Karina, Nika. Student, Meinzinger Art Sch., Detroit, 1953-44, Ox-Bow Summer Sch. Painting, Saugatuck, Mich., 1944-45, Skowhegan (Maine) Sch. Painting-Sculpture, 1946, Colo. Fine Arts Center, Colorado Springs, 1947. Artist-in-residence Art Inst. Chgo. Sch., 1960-61, Norton Gallery Sch., West Palm Beach, Fla., 1961, Mich. Council of Arts, 1981—; instr. Ox-Bow Summer Sch. Painting, 1960-61, 68-69, Skowhegan Sch. Painting-Sculpture, 1964; asst. prof. art Wayne State U., 1967-73; art dir. Detroit Repertory Theatre, 1970-75; mem. adv. panel Detroit Council of Arts, 1979-81. Exhibited in one-man shows, Art Inst. Chgo., 1961, Nordness Gallery, N.Y.C., 1960, 62, 64, Main St. Gallery, Chgo., 1957-61, Detroit Artists Market, 1949, 50, 53, 66, 76, Forsythe Gallery, Ann Arbor, Mich., 1953-57, 61, 65, 76, Battle Creek Art Ctr. (Mich.), 1983; exhibited in group shows, Johnson Wax Collection, 1962, 66, N.Y. World's Fair, 1963, 64, Ball State Ann., Muncie, Ind., 1973, 74, 77, 78, 79, 80, 81, Am. Drawing III Touring Exhibit, 1980-83; represented in permanent collections, Detroit Inst. Art, Art Inst. Chgo., Smithsonian Instn., Worcester (Mass.) Art Mus., Tate Gallery, London; works include gold leaf and oil Altar painting, St. John's Armenian Ch. Greater Detroit, 1966-67; sculptured silver medallion, Henry Ford Community Coll., 1978 (Eleanor Heth Art award 1976). Recipient Richard-Linda Rosenthal award Nat. Inst. Arts and Letters, 1961; Midwest Pepsi-Cola fellow, 1946; Prix de Rome fellow, 1956-59; Mich. Arts Council grantee, 1983-84. Home and Office: 1214 Beaubien Detroit MI 48226

KACHLEIN, GEORGE FREDERICK, JR., lawyer, association executive; b. Tacoma, May 9, 1907; s. George Frederick and Edna June (Burt) K.; m. Retha Hicks, Aug. 30, 1930; 1 son, George Frederick. A.B., Stanford U., 1929; LL.B., Harvard U., 1932. Bar: Wash. 1933. Asso. firm Bogle, Bogle & Gates, Seattle, 1933-37, partner, 1937-42, 46-65; asst. gen. mgr., asst. sec. Seattle-Tacoma Shipbldg. Corp., 1942-46; sec. Greater Seattle, Inc., 1952-57, pres., 1958-59, Am. Automobile Assn., 1962-64, exec. v.p., 1965-70, cons. internat. affairs, 1971—, also trustee; mcpl. ct. judge, City of Langley, Wash., 1974-78, dist. justice ct. commr., Island County, Wash., 1974-78. Sec. King Neptune VI, 1955-56. Named Seattle's Man of Year, 1963. Mem. Inter-Am. Fedn. Touring and Automobile Clubs, Am., Wash., Island County bar assns., C. of C. Clubs: O'Donnel Golf, Seattle Golf, Wash. Athletic (sec. 1950-51), Broadmoor Golf (pres. 1950-51). Lodge: Rotary. Home and office: 620 W Mercer Pl Seattle WA 98119

KACHRU, BRAJ BEHARI, linguist; b. Srinager, Kashmir, India, May 15, 1932; came to U.S., 1963; s. Shyam Lal and Shobhavati (Tulsidevi) K.; m. Yamuna Keskar, Jan. 22, 1965; children: Amita, Shamit. B.A. with honours, U. Kashmir, 1952; M.A., U. Allahabad, India, 1955; diploma applied linguistics, U. Edinburgh, Scotland, 1959, Ph.D., 1961. Research fellow Research Inst., Deccan Coll., Poona, India, 1957-58; asst. prof. Lucknow (India) U., 1962-63; research asso. U. Ill., Urbana, 1963-64, mem. faculty, 1964—, prof. linguistics, 1970—, head dept., 1969-79, coordinator div. applied linguistics, 1976—; vis. prof. Nat. U. Singapore, 1984; dir. summer program S. Asian studies Com. for Instl. Cooperation, 1967; chmn. com. regional varieties English, Assn. Commonwealth Lit. and Lang., Brisbane, Australia, 1968; mem. internat. adv. com. English, East-West Center, Hawaii, 1978—; mem. lang. com. Am. Inst. Indian Studies, 1971-77; lang. and lit. com. S. Asian Regional Council, 1977-79; cons. in field. Author: A Reference Grammar of Kashmiri, 1966, An Introduction to Spoken Kashmiri, 1973, Kashmiri Literature, 1981, The Indianization of English: The English Language in India, 1983, The Alchemy of English: The Spread, Functions and Models of Non-Native Englishes, 1985; editor: Dimensions of Bilingualism: Theory and Case Studies, 1976, Studies in the Linguistic Sciences, 1971—, Studies in Language Learning, 1976-77, (with S.N. Sridhar) Aspects of Sociolinguistics in South Asia, 1978, The Other Tongue: English Across Cultures, 1982; co-editor: Current Trends in Stylistics, 1971, Issues in Linguistics: Papers in Honor of Henry and Renée Kahane, 1973; editorial adv. bd.: Papers in Linguistics, 1972-83, Internat. Jour. Sociology of Lang., 1974—, TESOL Quar., 1978-84, Jour. South Asian Lit., 1980—, English World-Wide: A Jour. of Varieties of English, 1981-83; co-editor, 1983—; permanent editorial bd.: Ann. Rev. Applied Linguistics, 1980—. Fellow Brit. Council, 1958-60; Faculty Research fellow Am. Inst. Indian Studies, 1967-68; asso. Center Advanced Study, U. Ill., 1971-72, 79-80; fellow Culture Learning Inst., East-West Ctr., Honolulu, summer 1983. Mem. Linguistic Soc. Am. (dir. linguistic inst. 1978—), India Linguistic Soc., TESOL, Am. Assn. Applied Linguistics (v.p. 1983, pres. 1984), Linguistic Assn. Can. and U.S. Home: 2016 Cureton Dr Urbana IL 61801 Office: Dept Linguistics Univ Ill Urbana IL 61801 *I believe that the world will be a better place if we follow what the Indian pragmatist and thinker Mohandas K. Gandhi (1869-1948) has said so well: "I do not want my house to be walled in on all sides and my windows to be stuffed. I want cultures of all lands to be blown about my house as freely as possible. But I refuse to be blown off my feet anyway."*

KACHRU, YAMUNA, linguist; b. Purulia, India, Mar. 5, 1933; d. Raghunath G. and Sita Keskar; m. Braj B. Kachru, Jan. 22, 1965; children: Amita, Shamit. B.A., Bihar U., 1953; M.A., Patna U., 1955; Ph.D., London U., 1965. Lectr. Ranchi Women's Coll., India, 1956-58; lectr. Sch. Oriental and African Studies, London U., 1959-65; mem. faculty U. Ill., Urbana, 1965—, prof. linguistics and English, 1971—; Rockefeller fellow Deccan Coll., Poona, India, 1958-59; Am. Inst. Indian Studies faculty fellow, India, 1967-68, 71-72, 78-79, 81-82; assoc. Center for Advanced Study, U. Ill., 1975. Author: An Introduction to Hindi Syntax, 1966, Topics in a Transformational Grammar of Hindi, 1972, Aspects of Hindi Grammar, 1980, A Contemporary Grammar of Hindi, 1980; contbr. articles profl. jours. Mem. Linguistic Soc. India, Linguistic Soc. Am., Modern Lang. Assn. Tchrs. English to Speakers of Other Langs., Am. Assn. Applied Linguistics. Home: 2016 Cureton Dr Urbana IL 61801 Office: Dept of Linguistics University of Illinois Urbana IL 61801

KADANE, DAVID KURZMAN, educator, lawyer; b. N.Y.C., Apr. 9, 1914; s. Joseph Carlisle and Fannie (Kurzman) K.; m. Helene Born, Oct. 5, 1936; children—Joseph B., Kathryn Ann (Mrs. Garry Crane). B.S.S., Coll. City N.Y., 1933; LL.B., Harvard, 1936. Asst. counsel U.S. Senate com. on interstate commerce investigation r.r. finance, N.Y.C., 1936-38; atty. SEC, Washington and Phila., 1938-41, spl. counsel and asst. dir., 1942-46; asst. to fed. housing expediter and nat. housing adminstr., Washington, 1946; gen. counsel L.I. Lighting Co., 1949-70; on leave as vol. Peace Corps, 1964-66; prof. law Hofstra Law Sch., 1970—. Chmn. Nassau County Youth Bd. Jewish. Home: 190 Voorhis Ave Rockville Centre NY 11570 Office: 73 Main St Hempstead NY 11550

KADANE, JOSEPH B., statistics educator; b. Washington, Jan. 10, 1941; s. David Kurzman and Helen Margret (Born) K.; m. Kathleen Coleman, 1969 (div. 1975). B.A. cum laude in Math., Harvard Coll., 1962; Ph.D. in Stats., Stanford U., 1966. Asst. prof. Yale U., New Haven, 1966-68; staff analyst Ctr. for Naval Analysts, Arlington, VA., 1968-71; prof. stats. Carnegie-Mellon U., Pitts., 1971—. Assoc. editor: Jour. Am. Statis. Assn., 1968-73; dep. editor, 1976-78; editor, 1983—; assoc. editor: Annals of Stats., 1974-76; contbr. articles to profl. jours. NSF grantee; Office Naval Research grantee; Japan Soc. for Promotion of Sci. fellow, 1978. Fellow Am. Statis. Assn. (Pitts. statistician of yr. 1980), Inst. Math. Stats., AAAS; mem. Internat. Statis. Inst. Democrat. Jewish. Home: 5289 Forbes Ave Pittsburgh PA 15217 Office: Dept Stats and Social Scis Carnegie-Mellon U Schenley Park Pittsburgh PA 15213

KADANOFF, LEO PHILIP, physicist; b. N.Y.C., Jan. 14, 1937; s. Abraham and Celia (Kibrick) K.; children: Marcia, Felice, Betsy. A.B., Harvard U., 1957, M.A., 1958, Ph.D., 1960. Fellow Neils Bohr Inst., Copenhagen, 1960-61; from asst. prof. to prof. physics U. Ill., Urbana, 1961-69; prof. physics and engring., univ. prof. Brown U., Providence, 1969-78; prof. physics U. Chgo., 1978-82, John D. MacArthur Disting. Service prof., 1982—; Mem. tech. com. R.I. Planning Program, 1972-78, mem. human services rev. com., 1977-78; pres. Urban Obs. R.I., 1972-78. Author: Electricity Magnetism and Heat, 1967; co-author: Quantum Statistical Mechanics, 1963; Adv. bd.: Sci. Year, 1975-79; editorial bd.: Statis. Physics, 1972-79, Nuclear Physics, 1980—, Annals of Physics, 1982—; contbr. articles to profl. jours. NSF fellow, 1957-61; Sloan Found. fellow, 1963-67; recipient Wolf Found. prize, 1980. Fellow Am. Phys. Soc. (Buckley prize 1977), Am. Acad. Arts and Scis.; mem. Nat. Acad. Scis. Home: 5424 S Eastview Park Chicago IL 60615 Office: James Franck Inst U Chgo Chicago IL 60637

KADES, CHARLES LOUIS, retired lawyer; b. Newburgh, N.Y., Mar. 12, 1906; s. Louis and Carrie (Kahn) K.; m. Dorothy Lawrence (dec.); m. Phyllis Taber; 1 dau., Caroline Jeanne. A.B., Cornell U., 1927; LL.B., Harvard, 1930; grad., Inf. Sch., 1942, Command and Gen. Staff Sch., 1943. Bar: N.Y. 1931, D.C. 1931. Atty. Hawkins, Delafield & Longfellow, N.Y.C.; asst. gen. counsel Fed. Emergency Adminstrn. Public Works, 1933-37, Treasury Dept., 1938-42; commd. 2d lt. inf. U.S. Army Res., 1928, advanced through grades to col.; assigned to duty with gen. staff War Dept., 1943-45; served with Army and 1st Airborne Task Force in So. France operation, 1944-45, regional liaison officer D-Day, Alpes-Maritimes, landed, Atsugi, Japan, 1945, dep. chief govt. sect. G.H.Q., SCAP, 1945-49; partner firm Hawkins, Delafield & Wood (attys. and counselors), N.Y.C., 1949-79. Decorated Legion of Merit with oak leaf cluster. Mem. N.Y. State Bar Assn. (past chmn. sect. on taxation), Japan Soc., Sphinx Head (Cornell U.), Phi Beta Kappa, Phi Kappa Phi. Democrat. Clubs: City Mid-Day, Nat. Lawyers. Home: Green Bough Heath MA 01346

KADIN, FRED MARTIN, banker; b. N.Y.C., July 4, 1942; s. Sidney Stanley and Adelaide (Harris) K.; m. Christine Kadin-Stadler, June 29, 1972; children: Katherine-Anne, Karen Lee. Student, U. Geneva, 1962-63; B.S. (N.Y. State Regents scholar 1966-71), Columbia U., 1971. Retail bank tng.-ops. officer Bankers Trust Co., N.Y.C., 1967-69; asst. mgr. met. banking div. Irving Trust Co., N.Y.C., 1969-72; asst. v.p. Bank of Am. Internat., Paris, 1972-74, mgr., London, 1974-75; asst. v.p. corp. fin. Crocker Nat. Bank, London, 1975-76, regional rep., Amsterdam, 1976-77, v.p., 1977-79, v.p. Europe, Middle East, Africa, N.Y.C., 1979-81; prin. Kadin Bros., Inc. (mfr. leather goods), N.Y.C., 1981—; v.p., chief fin. officer Zunkel & Co., Inc.; Notary public, N.Y., 1967-72. Contbr. articles to publs. Served with Center for Naval Analysis, 1963-64. Mem. N.Y. Inst. Credit, N.Y. Credit and Fin. Mgmt. Assn. Roman Catholic. Clubs: Hilversumse Golf Netherlands, Hilsversumse Lawn Tennis (Melkhulsje, Netherlands). Home: 21 Northridge Rd Old Greenwich CT 06870 Office: Kadin Bros Inc 10 W 33d St New York NY 10001 Zunkel & Co 100 Wall St New York NY 10005 also

KADISH, SANFORD HAROLD, law educator; b. N.Y.C., Sept. 7, 1921; s. Samuel J. and Frances R. (Klein) K.; m. June Kurtin, Sept. 29, 1942; children: Joshua, Peter. B.S.S., CCNY, 1942; LL.B., Columbia U., 1948; Dr. Jur. (hon.), U. Cologne, 1983. Bar: N.Y. 1948, Utah 1954. Practice law, N.Y.C., 1948-51; prof. law U. Utah, 1951-60, U. Mich., 1961-64, U. Calif.-Berkeley, 1964—; dean Law Sch. U. Calif. at Berkeley, 1975-82, Morrison prof., 1976—; Fulbright lectr. Melbourne (Australia) U., 1956; vis. prof. Harvard U., 1960-61, Freiburg U., 1967, Stanford U., 1970; lectr. Salzburg Seminar Am. Studies, 1965; Fulbright disting. lectr. Kyoto (Japan) U., 1975; vis. fellow Inst. Criminology, Cambridge (Eng.) U., winter 1968. Author: (with Schulhofer and Paulsen) Criminal Law and Its Processes, 4th edit., 1983, (with M.R. Kadish) Discretion to Disobey—A Study of Lawful Departures from Legal Rules, 1973; also articles; editor-in-chief Ency. Crime and Justice, 1983. Reporter Calif. Legis. Penal Code Project, 1964-68; public mem. Wage Stblzn. Bd., region XII, 1951-53; cons. Pres.'s Commn. Adminstrn. of Justice, 1966; mem. Calif. Council Criminal Justice, 1968-69. Served to lt. USNR, 1943-46. Fellow Center Advanced Study Behavioral Scis., 1967-68; Guggenheim fellow, Oxford U., 1974-75; vis. fellow All Souls Coll., Oxford U. Fellow Am. Acad. Arts and Sci. (v.p. 1984-85); mem. AAUP (nat. pres. 1970-72), Nat. Acad. Arbitrators, Am. Soc. Legal and Polit. Philosophy, Am. Assn. Law Schs. (exec. com. 1960, pres. 1982), Phi Beta Kappa, Order of Coif (exec. com. 1966-67, 74-75). Home: 774 Hilldale Ave Berkeley CA 94708

KADISON, STUART, lawyer; b. Richmond, Va., Nov. 17, 1923; s. Elliot Theodore and Rebecca (Lesser) K.; m. Carita Silverman, June 23, 1946; children: Dana, Brian, Warne. Student, NYU, 1938-40; A.B., U. Md., 1942; LL.B., Stanford U., 1948. Bar: Calif. 1948. Practiced law, Los Angeles; partner Kadison, Pfaelzer, Woodard, Quinn & Rossi, Los Angeles, 1967—; lectr. Southwestern U. Sch. Law, Los Angeles, 1948-52, Stanford U. Sch. Law, 1977—; co-chmn. Am. Bar Assn.-Am. Newspaper Pubs. Assn. Task Force, 1977-83. Bd. visitors Stanford Law Sch., 1964-72, chmn., 1969-70; exec. com. Friends of Stanford Law Library, 1965—; bd. dirs. Friends of Huntington Library, v.p. and treas., 1977-82, pres., 1983—, bd. overseers, 1978—; chmn. lawyers adv. com. Constl. Rights Found., 1978-81; bd. dirs. Lawyers Com. for Civil Rights, Los Angeles County Bar Found., Council for Advancement of Legal Edn. Served to lt. USNR, 1942-46. Fellow Am. Coll. Trial Lawyers, Am. Bar Found.; mem. ABA (chmn. spl. com. on delivery of legal services 1973-75, chmn. resource devel. council 1983—), Los Angeles County Bar Assn. (pres. 1971-72, chmn. com. on judiciary 1976-77), State Bar Calif. (gov. 1973-76). Clubs: Univ., Chancery; Century Assn. (N.Y.C.). Office: 707 Wilshire Blvd Los Angeles CA 90017

KADO, CLARENCE ISAO, molecular biologist; b. Santa Rosa, Calif., June 10, 1936; s. James Y. and Chiyoko K.; m. Barbara M. Kawahara, June 30, 1963; children—Deborah, Diana M. B.Sc., U. Calif., Berkeley, 1959, Ph.D., 1964. Research asst. Virus Lab., U. Calif., Berkeley, 1960-64, NIH postdoctoral fellow, 1964-67, asst. research biochemist, 1967-68; asst. prof. plant pathology U. Calif., Davis, 1968-72, asso. prof., 1972-76, prof., 1976—. Author: Principles and Techniques in Plant Virology, 1972; contbr. articles to profl. jours. Recipient Bronze medal for virus research WHO, 1968; NATO sr. fellow, 1974-75; NIH grantee, 1968-82; Am. Cancer Soc. grantee, 1969-73, 1980-82; SEA grantee, 1979-82. Mem. AAAS, N.Y. Acad. Scis., Am. Phytopath. Soc., Genetic Soc. Am., Am. Soc. Microbiology, Am. Soc. Biol. Chemists, Sigma Xi. Clubs: Fedn. Fly Fishers, Fly Fishers Davis (dir., (pres.). Home: 1106 Villanova Dr Davis CA 95616 Office: Dept Plant Pathology Univ Calif Davis CA 95616

KAEFER, GENE JOHN, oil company executive; b. Hamilton, Ohio, Oct. 9, 1928; s. Walter Martin and Sadie (Williams) K.; m. Beatrice Chase, Oct. 10, 1953; children: John Wesley, Susan Chase. B. Petroleum Engring., Colo. Sch. Mines, 1953. Registered prof. engr., Kans., Okla., Tex. Sr. engr. Trunkline Gas, Houston, 1955-59; v.p. ops. Parkersburg, Coffeyville, Kans., 1959-67; pres. FWI, Tulsa, 1967-73; overseas ops. mgr. John Zink Co., Tulsa, 1974-78; pres., gen. mgr. Wheatley-Geosource, Tulsa, 1978—. Mem. AIME, ASME, IEEE. Republican. Office: Wheatley-Geosource 3303 Charles Page Blvd Tulsa OK 74127

KAEGEL, RICHARD JAMES, journalist; b. Belleville, Ill., Oct. 27, 1939; s. Raymond C. and Margaret E. (Welch) K.; m. Pamela Lambert, Apr. 11, 1963; children: James, Daniel. B. in Journalism, U. Mo., 1961. Sports writer Daily Tribune, Columbia, Mo., 1962-63; sports editor Press-Record, Granite City, Ill., 1963-65; assoc. editor The Sporting News, St. Louis, 1965-68, editor, 1979—; exec. sports editor Post-Dispatch, St. Louis, 1968-79. Mem. Baseball Writers Assn. Am. Mem. United Ch. Christ. Home: 70 Cliff Forest Dr Pacific MO 63069 Office: 1212 N Lindbergh Blvd St Louis MO 63132

KAEL, PAULINE, author, film critic; b. Petaluma, Calif., June 19, 1919; d. Isaac Paul and Judith (Friedman) K.; 1 dau., Gina James. Student, U. Calif. at Berkeley, 1936-40; LL.D., Georgetown U., 1972; D.Arts and Letters, Columbia Coll., Chgo., 1972; Litt.D., Smith Coll., 1973, Allegheny Coll., 1979; L.H.D., Kalamazoo Coll., 1973, Reed Coll., 1975, Haverford Coll., 1975; D.F.A., Sch. Visual Arts, N.Y.C., 1980. Movie critic New Republic mag., 1966-67, New Yorker mag., 1968—. Author: I Lost it at the Movies, 1965, Kiss Kiss Bang Bang, 1968, Going Steady, 1970, Deeper into Movies, 1973, Reeling, 1976, When the Lights Go Down, 1980, 5001 Nights at the Movies, 1982, Taking It All In, 1984; contbg. author: The Citizen Kane Book, 1971; contbr. to: other mags. Recipient Polk award in criticism, 1970, Nat. Book award for Deeper into Movies, 1974, Front Page award Newswomen's Club N.Y., 1974, 83; Guggenheim fellow, 1964. Address: New Yorker 25 W 43d St New York NY 10036

KAELIN, EUGENE FRANCIS, philosophy educator; b. St. Louis, Oct. 14, 1926; s. Albert Aloysius and Bertha (Earni) K.; m. Pierrette Nicole Demartini, Dec. 30, 1952; children: Valerie Chantal, Carolyne Pascale, Martine Laurence. B.A. with distinction, U. Mo., 1949, M.A., 1950; D.E.S., U. Bordeaux, France, 1951; Ph.D., U. Ill., 1954. Instr. philosophy U. Mo., 1952-53; fellow philosophy U. Ill., 1953-54, post-doctoral fellow, 1954-55; instr. philosophy U. Wis., 1955-57, asst. prof., 1957-61, asso. prof., 1961-65, Fla. State U., 1965-67, prof., 1967—, chmn. dept., 1969-72; mem. nat. adv. bd. aesthetic edn. program Central Midwestern Regional Ednl. Lab., 1968-76. Author: An Existentialist Aesthetic, 1962, Art and Existence, 1970, The Unhappy Consciousness, 1981. Served with USMC, 1945-46. Recipient William Henry Kiekhofer Meml. Teaching award U. Wis., 1959. Mem. Am. Philos. Assn., Am. Soc. Aesthetics, Am. Soc. Phenomenology and Existential Philosophy, Fla. Philos. Assn. (pres. 1977-78). Home: 604 Hillcrest St Tallahassee FL 32308

KAEMPFER, WALBERT WALDEMAR, political scientist; b. Anderson, Mo., May 3, 1923; s. Walbert Waldemar and Hazel Hughla (McDonald) K.; m. Nancy Pearl Sprinkle, Jan. 2, 1948; children: Pamela, Geoffrey, Eric. B.Public Adminstrn. with spl. distinction, U. Miss., 1953; M.A. (grad. scholar), U. Ala., 1954; Ph.D. (grad. fellow), U. Ala., 1957. Research asst. Bur. Govt. Research, W.Va. U., 1955-57; asst. prof. govt. So. Meth. U., 1957-59; dir. U. Ala. Montgomery Center; dean's rep. Selma Extension Class Program, 1959-63; dean faculty, prof. govt. U. N.C., Asheville, 1963-67; dean Coll. Arts and Scis., prof. polit. sci. U. South Ala., Mobile, 1967-81, prof. polit. sci., 1967—. Served with USAAF, 1942-45. Fulbright scholar, Pakistan, 1954. Mem. Omicron Delta Kappa, Beta Gamma Sigma, Beta Sigma Pi, Pi Sigma Alpha. Republican. Baptist. Office: Dept Polit Sci Coll Arts and Scis Univ South Ala Mobile AL 36688

KAENEL, REG ALFRED, electrical engineer; b. Berne, Switzerland, Oct. 22, 1929; came to U.S., 1958, naturalized, 1966; s. Alfred and Nellie M. (Walker) K.; children: Alfa R., Marina A. M.S.E.E., Swiss Fed. Inst. Tech., 1955, Sc.D., 1958. Supr. Bell Telephone Labs., Inc., Murray Hill, N.J., 1958-71; dir. AMF, Inc., Stamford, Conn., 1971-78; mgr. NL Petroleum Services, Houston, 1978-80; pres. Big Systems,

Inc., Houston, 1980—. Contbr. articles to profl. jours. Recipient Morehead Patterson Highest Merit award AMF, Inc., 1977. Fellow IEEE; mem. Soc. Audio and Electroacoustics of IEEE (pres. 1971-72), Internat. Council on Computer Communications (v.p. 1971—, co-founder), Assn. for Computing Machinery. Patentee in field of devieces/systems of computers/communication. Office: PO Box 2495 Humble TX 77338

KAESBERG, PAUL JOSEPH, educator; b. Engers, Germany, Sept. 26, 1923; came to U.S., 1926, naturalized, 1933; s. Peter Ernst and Gertrude (Mueller) K.; m. Marian Lavon Hanneman, June 13, 1953; children—Paul Richard, James Kevin, Peter Roy. B.S. in Engring, U. Wis., Madison, 1945, Ph.D. in Physics, 1949; D. Natural Scis. (hon.), U. Leiden, The Netherlands, 1975. Instr. biometry and physics U. Wis., 1949-51, asst. prof. biochemistry, 1956-58, asso. prof., 1958-60, prof., 1960-63, prof. biophysics and biochemistry, 1963—; chmn. Biophysics Lab., 1970—, Wis. Alumni Research Found. prof., 1981—; cons. in field. Contbr. chapts. to books and articles to profl. jours. Home: 5002 Bayfield Terr Madison WI 53705 Office: 1525 Linden Dr Madison WI 53706

KAFARSKI, MITCHELL I., chemical processing company executive; b. Detroit, Dec. 15, 1917; s. Ignacy A. and Anastasia (Drzazgowski) K.; m. Zofia Drozdowska, July 11, 1967; children: Erik Michael, Konrad Christian. Student, U. Detroit, 1939-41, Shrivenham (Eng.) Am. U., 1946. Process engr. Packard Motor Car Co., Detroit, 1941-44; organizer, dir. Artist and Craftsman Sch., Esslingen, Germany, 1945-46; with Nat. Bank of Detroit, 1946-50; founder, pres. Chem. Processing Inc., Detroit, 1950-65; also dir.; chmn. bd., pres., treas. Aactron Inc., Madison Heights, Mich., 1965—; treas. Detroit Magnetic Insp. Co., 1960-65; also dir.; v.p. KMH Inc., Detroit, 1960-64; also dir.; treas. Packard Plating Inc., Detroit, 1962-67, also dir. Commr. Mich. State Fair, 1965-72; mem. com. devel. and planning to build Municipal Stadium State of Mich., 1965-69; fellow, mem. Founders Soc., Detroit Inst. Arts, 1965—; trustee Founders' Soc., Detroit Inst. Arts, 1982—; sponsor, host world celebrity for World Preview Mich., 1965-66; mem. dist. adv. council SBA, 1971-73; del. White House Conf. on Aging, 1971; organizer, treas. Mich. Reagan for Pres. Com., 1980; treas. Straith Meml. Hosp., Southfield, Mich., 1972—, chmn. bd., 1976; trustee Mich. Opera Theater, 1982—; White House rep. to opening of first U.S. Trade Center, Warsaw, Poland, 1972; chmn. fund raising Bloomfield Arts Assn., Birmingham, Mich., 1973-74; mem. Space Theatre Consortium, Inc., Seattle, 1981—; bd. regents Orchard Lake (Mich.) Schs., 1981—; Vice chmn. Republican State Nationalities Council Mich., 1969-73; bd. dirs. Bloomfield Arts Assn., 1973—, Friends of Kresge Library, Oakland U., 1973—; Bd. dirs. U.S.A. Pennsylvania Ave. Devel. Corp., Washington, 1973—; trustee Straith Meml. Hosp., Detroit, 1971—, Detroit Sci. Center, 1972—. Served with AUS, 1944-46; ETO. Recipient Nat. award for war prodn. invention War Prodn. Bd., 1943; decorated knight's Cross Order of Poland's Rebirth Restituta, 1975, chevalier Chaine des Rotisseurs, 1982. Mem. Nat. Assn. Metal Finishers, Mich. Assn. Metal Finishers (dir., chmn. bd. 1976), N.A.M., Am. Electroplaters Soc., Cranbrook Acad. Arts, Am.-Polish Action Council (chmn. 1971-76), Am. Assn. Museums (treas. Detroit). Clubs: Capitol Hill (Washington); Detroit Athletic; La Coquille (Palm Beach, Fla.). Home: 240 Chesterfield Rd Bloomfield Hills MI 48013 Office: Aactron Inc 29306 Stephenson Hwy Madison Heights MI 48071 *A basic ingredient to success usually is determined by special events in one's life. In the course of my experiences, a sprinkling of tribulations were a must. From these were gleaned the principles, goals and conduct in attaining success. During the course of my life's pursuit, the ability to help others ensured a complete fulfillment of my goals.*

KAFER, HOWARD GILMOUR, lawyer; b. Plainfield, N.J., Apr. 5, 1923; s. Lester Scott and Marie Paullin (Gilmour) K.; m. Nancy Kinnear, May 26, 1951; children: Karen, Peter Kinnear, Lynn. A.B., Princeton U., 1947; J.D., N.Y. U., 1951. Bar: N.Y. bar 1953. Since practiced in, N.Y.C.; partner Chamberlin, Jube, Byrne & Kafer, 1963-70; partner firm Burns, Van Kirk, Greene & Kafer, 1970-79, Abberley, Kooiman, Marcellino & Clay, 1979-81, Byrne & Kafer, 1982—; pres., dir. Alamo Corp. Trustee Sexauer Found., Short Hills (N.J.) Country Day Sch., 1964-73. Served with AUS, 1943-46. Mem. Am., N.Y. State bar assns. Congregationalist. Clubs: Short Hills; Princeton (N.Y.C.); Nantucket (Mass.) Yacht, Sankaty Head (Mass.) Golf. Home: 33 Crescent Pl Short Hills NJ 07078 Office: 25 W 43d St New York NY 10036

KAFF, ALBERT ERNEST, journalist, news agency executive; b. Atchison, Kans., June 14, 1920; s. John and Ethel Mae (Worley) K.; m. Lee Chuan Diana Fong, Oct. 15, 1960; children: Arthur Fong, Alban Fong. B.A. in Econs., U. Colo., 1942. Reporter, Atchison Globe, summers 1939-41, Ponca City (Okla.) News, 1946-48, Daily Oklahoman, Oklahoma City, 1948-50; fgn. corr. U.P.I., Korea and Japan, 1952-56, bur. mgr., Vietnam, 1956-58, Taiwan, 1958-61, Philippines, 1961-63, news editor, Japan, 1963-72, dir. Asian services, Hong Kong, 1972-75, asst. dir., dir. personnel relations, N.Y.C., 1975-78, v.p., gen. mgr. Asia-Pacific, Hong Kong, 1978-84, vp., mgr. N.Y., 1984—. Contbr.: chpt. to How I Got That Story, 1967. Served with AUS, 1943-46; Served with U.S. Army, 1950-52. Decorated Bronze Star. Mem. Internat. Press Inst., Fgn. Corrs. Club of Japan (pres. 1967-68), Fgn. Corrs. Club of Hong Kong (pres. 1974-75), Overseas Press Club Am., Sigma Chi. Episcopalian. Home: 90 Brooklawn Terr Fairfield CT 06430 Office: 220 E 42d St New York NY 10017

KAFOED, E. J., banker; b. New Orleans, July 31, 1914; s. Harold James and Marie (Bouchon) K.; m. Ruth Gertrude Hingle, Aug. 3, 1940; 1 son, LeRoy John (dec. 1960). Student, Spencer Bus. Coll. With Hibernia Nat. Bank, New Orleans, 1935—, sr. v.p., 1968-73, exec. v.p., 1973—, also dir.; cons. M&L Mortgage Co., New Orleans; adviser LaMor Land Co. Active local Boy Scouts Am. Served with USNR, 1942-46. Mem. New Orleans C. of C. Clubs: Internat. House, Vista Shores Country (New Orleans). Home: 6208 Bertha Dr New Orleans LA 70122 Office: PO Box 61540 New Orleans LA 70160

KAFOGLIS, MILTON ZACHARY, economics educator; b. Lexington, Ky., May 2, 1925; s. Zachary and Kay (Sophos) K.; m. Virginia Elizabeth Rogers, Aug. 26, 1978; children by previous marriage: Mary, Charles. B.S., U. Ky., 1949, M.A., 1951; Ph.D., Ohio State U., 1958. Prof. econs. U. Fla., Gainesville, 1958-76; sr. economist Council on Wage and Price Stability, Washington, 1976-78; prof., chmn. Dept. Econs., U. S.Fla., Tampa, 1978-79; chmn., John H. Harland prof. econs. Emory U., Atlanta, 1979—; cons. in field. Author: Economic Status of the Legal Profession, 1958, Welfare Economics and Subsidy Programs, 1963; contbr. articles to profl. jours. Served with U.S. Army, 1943-46; ETO. Ford Found. fellow; research grantee Ford Found., 1957-58; Social Studies Research Council, 1973-74, FTC, 1978. Mem. Am. Econ. Assn., So. Econ. Assn., Nat. Acad. Sci. Democrat. Home: 209 E Parkwood St Decatur GA 30030 Office: Dept Econs Emory Univ Atlanta GA 30322

KAGAN, DONALD, historian, educator; b. Kurshan, Lithuania, May 1, 1932; came to U.S., 1934, naturalized, 1940; s. Max and Leah (Benjamin) K.; m. Myrna Dabrusky, Jan. 13, 1955; children: Robert William, Frederick Walter. A.B., Bklyn. Coll., 1954; M.A., Brown U., 1955; Ph.D., Ohio State U., 1958. Instr. history Pa. State U., University Park, 1959-60; asst. prof. ancient history Cornell, 1960-64, asso. prof., 1964-67, prof., 1967; prof. history and classics Yale, 1969—; master Timothy Dwight Coll., 1976-78. Author: The Great Dialogue, 1965, The Outbreak of the Peloponnesian War, 1969, The Archidamian War, 1974, The Western Heritage, 1979, (with Frank Turner and Steven Ozment) The Peace of Nicias and the Sicilian Expedition, 1981. Mem. Am. Hist. Assn., Am. Assn. Ancient Historians, Am. Philol. Assn. Home: 37 Woodstock Rd Hamden CT 06517 Office: 215 Hall of Grad Studies Yale Univ New Haven CT 06502

KAGAN, IRVING, vehicle renting and leasing company executive; b. N.Y.C., Mar. 14, 1936; s. Abraham and Yetta (Hochberg) K.; m. Shirley Anne Wolfe, May 29, 1956; children: Michael A., David M., Joshua A. B.S., N.Y. U., 1956, LL.B., 1958. Bar: N.Y. 1958, U.S. Supreme Ct. 1964. Practice law, N.Y.C., 1958-60; with antitrust div. Dept. Justice, 1960-68, acting chief evaluation sect., 1965, acting asst. chief N.Y. Field Office, 1968; trade regulation counsel, then asst. gen. counsel Hertz Corp., N.Y.C., 1968-74, v.p., gen. counsel, 1974-83, sr. v.p., gen. counsel, 1983—. Asso. editor: N.Y. U. Law Rev, 1957-58. Mem. Am., N.Y. State, N.Y. County bar assns., N.Y.U. Law Rev. Alumni Assn. (gov.), Am.-Israel Chamber of Commerce and Industry (dir.), Internat. League Human Rights. Office: 660 Madison Ave New York NY 10021

KAGAN, JEREMY PAUL, filmmaker; b. Mt. Vernon, N.Y., Dec. 14, 1945; s. Henry Enoch and Esther (Miller) K.; m. Elaine Goren, Mar. 17, 1974; 1 dau., Eve Laura. B.A. magna cum laude, Harvard U., 1967; M.F.A., N.Y. U., 1969; student, Am. Film Inst., 1971. Film animator, 1968; multimedia show designer White House Conf. on Youth and Edn., 1970; trustee Filmex; Phi Beta Kappa vis. scholar univs. Dir.: TV series, including Columbo, 1971-72; Movies of the Week: Unwed Father, 1974; TV series, including Judge Dee, 1974; dir., writer: Movies of the Week: Katherine, 1975; dir.: children's TV spl. My Dad Lives in a Downtown Hotel, 1973 (Emmy nominee); feature motion pictures Scott Joplin, 1976, Heroes, 1977, The Big Fix, 1978, The Chosen, 1981 (Grand prize Montreal Film Festival), The Sting II, 1983. Recipient numerous film festival awards, including Chgo. Film Festival, 1968, 69, 75, N.Y. Film Festival, 1969, 70, San Francisco Film Festival, 1975; Silver Knight award Malta Film Festival, 1973; awards Edinborough Festival, 1973, London Film Festival, 1977; Royan Grand prize, 1979. Mem. Writers Guild Am., Dirs. Guild Am., Phi Beta Kappa. Office: care Rosenberg Ray & Rosenberg 9200 Sunset Blvd Penthouse 25 Los Angeles CA 90069 *

KAGAN, JEROME, psychologist, educator; b. Newark, Feb. 25, 1929; s. Joseph and Myrtle (Liebermann) K.; m. Cele Katzman, June 20, 1951; 1 dau., Janet Ina. B.S., Rutgers U., 1950; Ph.D., Yale, 1954. Instr. psychology Ohio State U., 1954-55; research asso. Fels Research Inst., Yellow Springs, Ohio, 1957-59, chmn. dept. psychology, 1959-64; asso. prof. psychology Antioch Coll., 1959-64; prof. social relations Harvard, 1964—; Adv. com. Nat. Inst. Child Health and Devel. Author: (with G.S. Lesser) Contemporary Issues in Thematic Apperceptive Methods, 1961, (with Moss) Birth to Maturity, 1962, (with Mussen and Conger) Child Development and Personality, 5th edit, 1979, (with Havemann) Psychology, 4th edit, 1980, (with Janis, Mahl and Holt) Personality, 1969, Understanding Children, 1971, Change and Continuity in Infancy, 1971, (with Kearsley and Zelazo) Infancy, 1978, (with Brim) Constancy and Change, 1980, The Second Year, 1981. Served with AUS, 1955-57. Recipient Lucius Cross medal Yale U., 1981. Fellow Am. Psychol. Assn., Am. Acad. Arts and Scis., Soc. Research Child Devel.; mem. Eastern Psychol. Assn. Home: 210 Clifton St Belmont MA 02178 Office: William James Hall Harvard U Cambridge MA 02138 *My success has been aided by a combination of hard work, openess to new ideas, a readiness to discard beliefs that are proven invalid; a desire to nurture the growth of others; and belief in the beauty of ideas and the perfectibility of man.*

KAGAN, RICHARD LAUREN, history educator; b. Newark, Sept. 8, 1943; s. George M. and Sylvia (Gurkin) K. B.A., Columbia U., 1965; Ph.D., Cambridge (Eng.) U., 1968. Asst. prof. Ind. U., 1968-72; asst. prof. Johns Hopkins, 1973-74, asso. prof., 1974-79, prof., 1979—. Author: Students and Society in Early Modern Spain, 1974, Lawsuits and Litigants in Castile, 1500-1700, 1981. Mem. Am. Hist. Assn. Home: 333 Tuscany Rd Baltimore MD 21210 Office: Dept History Johns Hopkins U Baltimore MD 21218

KAGAN, SIOMA, educator; b. Riga, Russia, Sept. 29, 1907; came to U.S., 1941, naturalized, 1950; s. Jacques and Berta (Kaplan) K.; m. Jean Batt, Apr. 5, 1947 (div. 1969). Diplom Ingenieur, Technische Hochschule, Berlin, 1931; M.A., Am. U., 1949; Ph.D. in Econs, Columbia U., 1954. Sci. asst. Heinrich Hertz Inst., Berlin, 1931-33; partner Laboratoire Electro-Acoustique, Neuilly-sur-Seine, France, 1933-48; chief French Mission Telecommunications, French Supply Council in N.Am., Washington, 1943-45; mem. telecommunications bd. UN, 1946-47, econ. affairs officer, 1947-48; econs. cons. to govt. and industry; asso. prof. econs. Washington U., St. Louis, 1956-59; staff economist Joint Council Econ. Edn., N.Y.C., 1959-60; prof. internat. bus. U. Oreg., Eugene, 1960- 67, U. Mo., St. Louis, 1967—; faculty leader exec. devel. programs Columbia, Northwestern U., NATO Def. Coll., Rome, others. Contbr. numerous articles profl. publs. Served with Free French Army, 1941-43. Decorated Legion of Honor, France).; recipient Thomas Jefferson award U. Mo., 1984. Fellow Latin Am. Studies Assn.; mem. Am. Econ. Assn., Acad. Polit. Sci., Assn. Asian Studies. Clubs: University (St. Louis); Conanicut Yacht (Jamestown, R.I.). Home: 8132 Roxburgh Dr Saint Louis MO 63105 Office: U Mo Saint Louis MO 63121

KAGLE, JOSEPH LOUIS, JR., arts adminstr., artist; b. Pitts., May 2, 1932; s. Joseph Louis and Edith (Marcellus) K.; m. Anne Cornelia Schiller, Jan. 19, 1957; children—Samantha Anne, Christopher Yung Wook. Student, Carnegie Mus. Sch. Art, 1938-51; A.B., Dartmouth Coll., 1955; M.F.A., U. Colo., 1958. Instr. Wis. State U., Whitewater, 1958-60; head dept. art, asst. prof. Washington and Jefferson Coll., 1960-63; had dept. art, asso. prof. Keuka Coll., 1964-68, Wash. State U., 1965-66; artist in residence Chapman Coll., World Campus Afloat, 1968-69; asso. prof. art Eastern Wash. State Coll., 1968-69; prof. fine arts U. Guam, 1970-76; prof. art Community Coll. Finger Lakes, 1976-78; exec. dir. S.E. Ark. Arts and Sci. Center, Pine Bluff, 1978—; artist in residence Naples Mill Sch., 1976-78; lectr. USIS, Taiwan, 1970-76; critic Pine Bluff (Ark.) News. Work exhibited more than 300 nat. and internat. exhbns.; dir. 50 TV shows on art; muralist, Hafa Adai Theatre, Bank of Guam, Fine Arts Bldg. U. Guam; Author: Death Is All the Time, 1976. Mem. planning bd. Pine Bluff Com. Gifted and Talented, 1979-80. Named artist of year Pacific chpt. A.I.A., 1976-77. Mem. Am. Mus. Assn., Coll. Art Assn., S.E. Mus. Assn. (planning bd.), Ark. Mus. Assn., Ward Nasse Gallery of N.Y.C., Cedars Gallery of Binghamton, N.Y., Mid Am. Coll. Art Assn., S.E. Coll. Art Assn. Home: Rt 11 Box 2300 Pine Bluff AR 71603 Office: Civic Center Pine Bluff AR 91601

KAGLER, WILLIAM GEORGE, retail food chain executive; b. Scranton, Pa., June 4, 1932; s. George M. and Marion B. (Lewis) K.; m. Gail A. Whitehead, Sept. 12, 1959; children: Kim Noel, Kristen Amy, Kerri Lu. B.S. in Journalism, Syracuse U., 1954; postgrad., Columbia U., 1958, U. Pa., 1959-60, U. Cin., 1963. Pub. relations counsel The Kroger Co., Cin., 1964-66, dir. pub. relations, 1966-71, v.p. corp. affairs, personnel and human resources, 1971-74, corp. v.p., 1974-77, group v.p., 1977, sr. v.p., 1977-83, pres., 1983—, dir., 1982—; dir. The 5th 3d Bank, Cin., 1983. Group chmn. pub. service div. United Appeal, Cin., 1979; trustee Good Samaritan Hosp., Cin., 1980—; mem. nat. corps. com. United Negro Coll. Fund, N.Y.C., 1980—; fin. chmn. Hamilton county Clarence J. Brown for Gov. com., Cin., 1982. Served with CIC U.S. Army, 1955-57. Am. Polit. Assn. Congl. fellow, 1963-64. Clubs: Queen City (bd. dirs.) (1982—); Commonwealth (sec.) (1983—). Office: The Kroger Co 1014 Vine St Cincinnati OH 45202

KAHAN, BARRY DONALD, surgeon; b. Cleve., July 25, 1939; s. Jacob Marvin and Pearl (Schultz) K.; m. Rochelle Liebling, Sept. 5, 1962; 1 dau., Kara. B.S., U. Chgo., 1960, Ph.D., 1964, M.D., 1965. Intern Mass. Gen. Hosp., Boston, 1965-66, resident in surgery, 1968-72; staff asso. in immunology NIH, 1966-68; asst. prof. surgery and physiology Northwestern U. Sch. Medicine, Chgo., 1972-74, asso. prof., 1975-76; prof. surgery U. Tex. Med. Sch., Houston, 1977—, also dir. divs. organ transplantation dept. surgery, dir. program immunology, grad. sch. Bd. dirs. Ill. Kidney Found., 1974-76. Mem. A.C.S., AAAS, Soc. Univ. Surgeons, Am. Soc. Clin. Investigation, Am. Soc. Transplant Surgeons, Internat. Transplantation Soc. (charter), Am. Assn. Immunologists, Am. Assn. Cancer Research, Am. Physiol. Soc. Home: 4 Rain Hollow St Houston TX 77024 Office: 6431 Fannin Ave Houston TX 77030

KAHAN, IRVING, ret. editor; b. Passaic, N.J., Feb. 12, 1912; s. Harry R. and Sonia (Abbot) K.; m. Minna Richman, Sept. 11, 1941; children—Harriet R., Justine S. B.A., State U. Iowa, 1935, certificate in journalism, 1935. Editor Passaic Citizen, 1936-38, Paterson (N.J.) Sunday Chronicle, 1939-40, Textile Dyer, Paterson, 1940-48; mng. editor Textile Labor mag., N.Y.C., 1949-56, editor, 1957-69; pub. relations dir. Textile Workers Union Am., AFL-CIO, 1957-76, publs. dir., 1969-76. Author: Behind Taft-Hartley's Mumbo-Jumbo, 1949, The TWUA Story: They Said it Couldn't Be Done, 1964. Publicity dir. United Italian Appeal, Paterson, 1946. Served with inf. AUS, 1943-45. Sigma Delta Chi Scholar, 1935. Home: 463-C Portsmouth Dr Lakewood NJ 08701 *I try, day by day, not to do unto others what I would not have them do unto me. This is an exercise in human relations based, I believe, on Confucian teaching. I pursue it because it is far more achievable than complying with the admonition of Jesus Christ to "do unto others as you would have them do unto you." The latter demands saintliness and dedication that I do not possess. So I do my best not to injure my fellowman whenever I cannot measure up to the greater challenge of actively helping him.*

KAHAN, NANCY WHITE, publishing executive; b. Paterson, N.J., Aug. 5, 1944; d. Thomas James and Kathryn (Breslin) White; m. Stuart Marvin Kahan, Mar. 12, 1972 (div. 1982); 1 son, William White. B.A., Dunbarton Coll., 1969. Publicist Charles Scribners Sons, N.Y.C., 1969-73; publicity dir. MacMillan Pub., N.Y.C., 1973-76; v.p., dir. publicity and pub. relations Crown Publishers, N.Y.C., 1976—. Mem. Pub. Relations Soc. Am., Pubs. Publicity Assn. (dir.). Democrat. Roman Catholic. Office: Crown Publishers 1 Park Ave New York NY 10028

KAHANE, HENRY, educator, linguist, medievalist; b. Berlin, Germany, Nov. 2, 1902; came to U.S., 1939, naturalized, 1945; s. Arthur and Paula (Ornstein) K.; m. Renée Toole, Dec. 5, 1931; children: Roberta, Charles. Student univs., Berlin, Rome and Greifswald, 1922-30; Ph.D., U. Berlin, 1930; D.Litt. (hon.), U. Ill., 1977; alumnus, Am. Sch. Classical Studies, Athens. Departmental asst. Romance linguistics U. Berlin, 1932; lectr. U. Florence, Italy, 1934-38; research asst. U. So. Calif., 1939-41; mem. faculty U. Ill., Urbana, 1941—; now prof. linguistics, also prof. Center Advanced Study, acting dir., 1971-72; Bd. dirs. Mediterranean Linguistic Atlas, Venice, Italy; mem. U.S. Nat. Com. for Byzantine Studies, 1981. Author: (mostly in coop. with wife) Italian Placenames in Greece, 1940, Spoken Greek, 1945-46, Descriptive Studies in Spanish Grammar, 1954, Development of Verbal Categories in Child Language, 1958, Lingua Franca in the Levant, 1958, Structural Studies on Spanish Themes, 1959, The Krater and the Grail, 1965, Glossary of Old Italian Portolani, 1967, Linguistic Relations between Byzantium and the West, 1976, Graeca et Romanica: Scripta Selecta, 1979-81; also articles.; Assoc. editor: Romance Philology, 1947—. Guggenheim fellow, 1955, 62; recipient Silver award Acad. of Athens, 1977. Mem. Linguistic Soc. Am. (v.p., pres. elect 1983, pres. 1984), MLA, Arthurian Soc., Wolfram von Eschenbach Gesellchaft, Linguistic Soc. Paris, Soc. Romance Linguistics. Home: 808 W Oregon St Urbana IL 61801

KAHANE, MELANIE, interior and industrial designer; b. N.Y.C., Nov. 26, 1910; d. Morris and Rose (Roth) K.; m. Theodore Earl Ebenstein, Dec. 22, 1934 (div. 1945); 1 dau., Joan Lynn (Mrs. Porter); m. Ben Grauer, Sept. 25, 1954 (dec. June 1977). Grad., Parsons Sch. Design, Paris, France, 1932. Illustrator Tobias Green Advt. Co., 1931-32; designer Lord & Taylor, 1933-34; founder, pres. Melanie Kahane, Inc., 1935-52; founder, 1952; since pres. Melanie Kahane Assos. (indsl. design); designer for SBF Dept. and suburban stores, St. Louis, 1958—, Charles of Ritz (beauty salons), throughout U.S., 1957—, Playbill Restaurant, N.Y.C., 1958, Children's Mus., Ft. Worth, 1955, Ziegfield Theatre, N.Y.C., 1963, Gov. Shivers mansion, Austin, Tex., 1957, Pres. Goheen of Princeton ofcl. residence, 1958, Reid Hall, Paris, France, 1948, First Nat. Bank, Ft. Worth, 1962, Shubert Theaters, N.Y.C., Chgo., Phila., Boston, 1977—, others; dir. styling and design Sprague & Carleton Furniture Co., Inc., 1962—; lectr. Parsons Sch. Design, 1950—; design, color and fabric cons., 1952—. Author: There's a Decorator in Your Doll House, 1968; Prod.: documentary film Decorating, A Way of Life, 1949; Contbr. to books, encys. Mem. commn. to S.E. Asia for N.Y. World's Fair, 1964-65; mem. Nat. Panel Arbitrators, 1963—, NBC Monitor program mission to, Russia, 1959, A.I.D. Design Team for NASA, 1972-73; Chmn. Greater N.Y. Fund, 1961. Named hon. citizen Knoxville, Tenn., Wichita, Kan. and Houston; recipient Decorator of Year award Carpet Assn. Am., 1953; Designer citation U.S. Commr. Gen. Cullman, 1958; award Brussels World Fair, 1958; Career Key award Girl's Club Am., 1961; chosen as one of 100 Am. Women of Accomplishment Harper's Bazaar mag., 1967; Eleanor Roosevelt humanities award, 1981. Fellow Am. Inst. Interior Designers (past nat. sec., dir., past pres. N.Y. chpt., nat. treas. 1971-75), Municipal Art Soc., Decorator's Club N.Y.C. (pres. 1982-84), Archtl. League N.Y., Nat. Soc. Lit. and the Arts, Illuminating Engring. Soc., Inter-Soc. Color Council, Nat. Home Fashions League, Inst. Practising Designers (Eng.), Women's Forum, Am. Theatre Wing. Home: 29 E 63d St New York NY 10021 Office: 251 E 61st St New York NY 10021

KAHEN, HAROLD I., lawyer; b. Chgo., Aug. 14, 1918; s. Gabriel and Jennie (Weisberg) K.; m. Florence Gold, Dec. 21, 1946; children—Deborah Judith Kayman, Daniel Seth, David Ezra. A.B., U. Chgo., 1938, J.D., 1940. Bar: Ill. bar 1940, N.Y. bar 1947. Spl. asst. to fed. circuit judge Evan A. Evans, 1940; mem. legal staff SEC, 1941-46; asso. firm Poletti, Diamond, Rabin, Freidin & Mackay, 1946-50; gen. atty. Hudson & Manhattan R.R. Co., 1950-55; assoc. counsel N.Y. Supt. of Ins., 1955 Welfare Fund Inquiry; mem. firm Delson & Gordon, 1956-72, Burns Summit Rovins & Feldesman, N.Y.C., 1973—; spl. prof. Hofstra U. Law Sch., 1971—. Mem. N.Y. State Bar Assn. (com. corp. law), Assn. Bar City N.Y. (past spl. com. securities regulation), Order of Coif, Phi Beta Kappa. Home: 85-26 Kendrick Pl Jamaica NY 11432 Office: 445 Park Ave New York NY 10022

KAHIN, GEORGE MCTURNAN, political science and history educator; b. Balt., Jan. 25, 1918; s. George Stanley and Helen Agnew (Andrews) K.; m. Margaret Baker, July 4, 1942 (div.); children: Brian, Sharon; m. 2d Audrey Richey, Mar. 8, 1967. B.A., Harvard U., 1940; M.A., Stanford U., 1946; Ph.D., Johns Hopkins U., 1951. Instr. Johns Hopkins U., Balt., 1949-51; asst. prof. Cornell U., Ithaca, N.Y., 1951-54, assoc. prof., 1954-59, prof., 1959-68, Aaron L. Binenkorb prof. internal studies, 1968—; exec. dir. Cornell South East Asia Program, Ithaca, 1951-60, dir., 1961-70, Cornell Modern Indonesia Project, 1954—; vis. prof. U. London, 1962-63; cons. Rockefeller Found., N.Y.C., 1964-65. Author: Nationalism and Revolution in Indonesia, 1952, (with John Lewis) The United States in Vietnam, 1967; editor: Major Governments of Asia, 1958, Governments and Politics of Southeast Asia, 1959. Served to sgt. U.S. Army, 1942-45; ETO. Fellow Social Sci. Research Council, Indonesia, 1948-49; John Simon Guggenheim fellow, 1975; Henry Luce Found. fellow, 1977; NEH fellow, 1981-82. Fellow Am. Acad. of Arts and Scis., Center Study Democratic Instns.; mem. Council Fgn. Relations, Asia Soc. (chmn. Indonesia council 1962-66), Assn. Asian Studies (pres. 1973-74). Club: Cosmos (Washington). Home: 988 Cayuga Heights Rd Ithaca NY 14850 Office: Dept of Govt McGraw Hall Cornell U Ithaca NY 14853

KAHL, VIRGINIA CAROLINE, librarian, author, illustrator; b. Milw., Feb. 18, 1919; d. Arthur Henry and Frieda Emily (Krause) K. B.A., Milw-Downer Coll., 1940; M.L.S., U. Wis., 1956. Librarian Milw. Public Library, 1942-48, U.S. Army, Berlin, W. Ger., 1948-49, Salzburg, Austria, 1949-52; command librarian U.S. Forces, Austria, 1952-55; sch. librarian, Madison, Wis., 1958-61; dir. Menomonee Falls (Wis.) Library, 1961-68; coordinator public services Alexandria (Va.) Library, 1970—; mem. faculty George Washington U. Continuing Edn. for Women Center, 1970-80. Author, illustrator: children's books Away Went Wolfgang, 1954, The Duchess Bakes a Cake, 1955, The Plum Pudding for Christman, 1955, Maxie, 1956, The Habits of Rabbits, 1957, Droopsi, 1958, Voice Henri, 1959, The Perfect Pancake, 1960, Encore Henri, 1961, The Baron's Booty, 1963, How do you Ride a Monster?, 1971, Gunhilde's Christmas Booke, 1972, Giants, Indeed!, 1974, Gunhilde and the Hallowe'en Spell, 1975, How Many Dragons are Behind the Door?, 1977, Whose Cat is That?, 1979. Office: 717 Queen St Alexandria VA 22314 Address: care Charles Scribner's Sons 597 Fifth Ave New York NY 10017

KAHL, WILLIAM FREDERICK, college president; b. May 23, 1922; s. William Frederick and Bessie (Gladding) K.; m. Mary Carson, Jan. 25, 1964; children: Frederick Gladding, Sarah Hartwell. B.A., Brown U., 1945; M.A., Harvard U., 1947, Ph.D., 1955. Lectr. history Boston U., 1947-48, 50; instr. Simmons Coll., Boston, 1948-52, asst. prof., 1952-59, asso. prof., 1959-62, prof., 1962-76, provost, 1965-76; pres. Russell Sage Coll., Troy, N.Y., 1976—; dir. State Bank of Albany. Author: The London Livery Companies: An essay and bibliography, 1960; contbr. articles to profl. jours. Trustee Samaritan Hosp.; bd. dirs. Albany Symphony Orch. Social Sci. Council research grantee, 1957-58. Mem. Am. Hist. Assn., Commn. on Ind. Colls. and Univs. (dir.), Anglo-Am. Hist. Conf. Episcopalian. Club: Harvard (Boston and N.Y.C.). Home: 29 Old Niskayuna Rd Loudonville NY 12211 Office: Russell Sage Coll Troy NY 12180

KAHLER, ELIZABETH SARTOR (MRS. ERVIN NEWTON CHAPMAN), physician; b. Washington, Oct. 20, 1911; d. Armin Adolphus and Lenore Elome (Sartor) K.; m. Dr. Ervin Newton Chapman, Feb. 24, 1942. B.S., George Washington U., 1933, M.A., 1935, M.D. with distinction, 1940. Intern Gallinger Municipal Hosp. (now D.C. Gen. Hosp.), Washington, 1940-41; resident Children's Hosp., Washington, 1941-42; practice medicine, Washington, 1942-78; assoc. univ. physician George Washington U., 1942-50; examining physician YWCA, 1942-45; courtesy staff Washington Hosp. Center, until 1978, George Washington U. Hosp., until 1978; physician for health services br. resources div. Bur. Social Services and Resources Social Services Adminstrn. D.C. Dept. Human Services, 1953-75; sch. physician D.C. public schs., 1959—; Mem. cons. com. D.C. Pub. Schs. (for practical nursing program), 1962-70. Trustee Wilson Coll. Mem. Women's Med. Soc. D.C. (pres. 1950-51), Am. Med. Women's Assn. (pres. 1957-58, treas. Past Presidents Club 1976-78, liaison to NVOILA 1975-82), Nat. Voluntary Orgns. for Ind. Living for the Aging (exec. com. 1978-82), AMA, Med. Soc. D.C. (chmn. com. on medicine and religion 1967-72), D.C. Assn. Mental Health, Am. Heart Assn., Camp Fire Girls Inc. (nat. program com.), Columbian Women of George Washington U. (life), Women's Assn. of Nat. Presbyn. Ch. (treas. 1981-83, fin. chmn. 1983-85). Republican. Presbyterian. Home: 2600 36th St NW Washington DC 20007 Office: 3601 Davis St NW: Washington DC 20007

KAHLER, HERBERT FREDERICK, business executive; b. St. Augustine, Fla., Sept. 20, 1936; s. Herbert E. and Marie (Strieter) K.; m. Erika Rozsypal, May 16, 1964; children: Erik, Stephen, Christopher, Michael, Craig. A.B., Johns Hopkins, 1958; LL.B., Harvard, 1961. Bar: N.Y. bar 1962. With firm Simpson, Thacher & Bartlett, N.Y.C., 1961-65; sec., gen. counsel Insilco Corp., Meriden, Conn., 1965-70; pres., chief exec. officer W.H. Hutchinson & Son, Inc., Chgo., 1970-73, Miles Homes Co., Mpls., 1973—; v.p., dir. Insilco Corp., 1979—. Bd. corporators Meriden Hosp., 1965-70, Harvard, 1970; bd. dirs. St. Paul Chamber Orch., 1974—, St. Paul Opera Assn., 1975-77, Minn. Opera Co., 1977—. Served to lt., arty. AUS, 1962-64. Mem. Am. Bar Assn., Newcomen Soc., Phi Beta Kappa. Clubs: Mpls., Mpls. Athletic. Office: 4700 Nathan Ln Minneapolis MN 55442

KAHLER, STEVE, advertising executive; b. New Rochelle, N.Y., Sept. 11, 1939; s. Carl Christian and Helen Maude (Hancock) K.; m. Carollyn Ann Coghill, Aug. 24, 1963; children: Brett Hancock, Christopher William. B.S.M.E., Purdue U., 1962; M.B.A., U. Mich., 1964. Fin. analyst. Exxon Corp., N.Y.C., 1965-68; adv. Esso Europe, London, 1968-70; asst. Treas. Esso U.K., London, 1970-71; treas. Esso Germany, Hamburg, 1971-73; fin. planning mgr. Exxon Corp., N.Y.C., 1973-75, strategic planning mgr., 1975-77; exec. v.p. fin. & adminstrn. BBDO Internat., Inc., N.Y.C., 1977—, also dir. Republican. Club: Racquet and Tennis (N.Y.C.). Home: 6 Woodley Rd Darien CT 06820 Office: 383 Madison Ave New York NY 10017

KAHLOR, ROBERT A., newspaper executive; b. Akron, Ohio, Nov. 20, 1933; s. Ernest M. and Mabel U. (Marhofer) K.; m. Jane Ann Mace, Dec. 13, 1952; children: Vickie Kahlor Jakubowski, Linda Kahlor Wright, Brian, Todd, Lee Ann. Student, Kent State U., 1951-52, U. Akron, 1960-66. Asst. mech. supt. Akron Beacon Jour., 1952-67; v.p., gen. mgr. Morristown Daily Record, N.J., 1967-70; asst. prodn. mgr. N.Y. Times, N.Y.C., 1970-71; sr. v.p. The Jour. Co. and Newpapers, Inc., Milw., after 1971, now pres. Mem. Zool. Soc. Milw. County. Club: Wis. (Milw.). Lodge: Masons. Home: 19195 Killarney Way Brookfield WI 53005 Office: The Journal Co Newpapers Inc 3333 W State St Milwaukee WI 53201

KAHN, ALFRED EDWARD, economist, educator, government official; b. Paterson, N.J., Oct. 17, 1917; s. Jacob and Bertha (Orlean) K.; m. Mary Simmons, Oct. 10, 1943; children: Joel, Rachel, Hannah. A.B., NYU, 1936, M.A., 1937; postgrad., U. Mo., 1937-38; Ph.D., Yale U., 1942; LL.D. (hon.), Colby Coll., 1978, U. Mass., 1979, Ripon Coll., 1980, Northwestern U., 1982, Colgate U., 1983. Mem. staff Brookings Inst., 1940, 51-52; with anti-trust div. Dept. Justice, 1941-42, Dept. Commerce, 1942, WPB, 1943; economist on Palestine surveys, 1943-44, Twentieth Century Fund, 1944-45; asst. prof., chmn. dept. econs. Ripon Coll., 1945-47; asst. prof. Cornell U., 1947-50, asso. prof., 1950-55, prof., 1955—, chmn. dept. econs., 1958-63, Robert Julius Thorne prof. econs., 1967—, dean Coll. Arts and Scis., 1969-74; chmn. N.Y. State Pub. Service Commn., 1974-77, CAB, 1977-78, Council on Wage and Price Stability (adviser to Pres. on inflation), 1978-80; dir. Tompkins Co. Econ. Opportunity Corp., 1968-69, N.Y. Airlines, 1980—; mem. atty. gen.'s nat. com. to study anti-trust laws, 1953-55; sr. staff U.S. Council Econ. Advisers, 1955-57; spl. cons. Boni, Watkins, Jason & Co., N.Y.C., 1957-61, Nat. Econ. Research Assos., 1961-74, 80—, U.S. Fgn. Agrl. Service, Israel, 1960-61, Dept. Justice, 1963-64, FTC, 1965, Ford Found., 1967; econ. adv. council AT&T, 1968-74; econ. adv. com. U.S. C. of C., 1964-66; mem. environ. adv. com. Fed. Energy Adminstrn., 1974-77; mem. rev. com. sulfur emissions from power plants Nat. Acad. Scis., 1974-75; adv. bd. Electric Power Research Inst., 1974-77; mem. Nat. Antitrust Law Rev. Com., 1978-79; adv. to N.Y. gov. on communications regulation, 1980-82; mem. N.Y. Gov.'s Fact-Finding Panel on Shoreham Nuclear Plant, 1983, N.Y. State Council on Fiscal and Econ. Priorities, 1983—; biweekly econ. commentator Nightly Bus. Report (pub. TV), 1981—. Author: Great Britain in the World Economy, 1946, (with J.B. Dirlam) Fair Competition, The Law and Economics of Anti-trust Policy, 1954, (with M.G. de Chazeau) Integration and Competition in the Petroleum Industry, 1959, The Economics of Regulation, 2 vols., 1970, 71; bd. editors: Am. Econ. Rev., 1961-64. Trustee Cornell U., 1964-69; mem. nat. governing bd. Common Cause, 1982—. Fulbright research fellow, Italy, 1954-55. Mem. Am. Econ. Assn. (v.p. 1981-82), Nat. Assn. Regulatory Utility Commrs. (exec. com., chmn. com. on electricity 1975-77), Am. Acad. Arts and Scis., Phi Beta Kappa. Home: RD 3 Trumansburg NY 14886 Office: Dept Econs Cornell U Ithaca NY 14853

KAHN, ALFRED JOSEPH, educator, social worker and planner; b. N.Y.C., Feb. 8, 1919; s. Meyer and Sophie (Levine) K.; m. Miriam Kadin, Sept. 3, 1949 (div. 1980); 1 dau., Nancy Valerie. B.S.S., CCNY, 1939; B.Hebrew Lit., Sem. Coll. Jewish Studies, N.Y.C., 1940; M.S., Columbia U., 1946, D.Social Welfare, 1952. Psychiat. social worker Jewish Bd. Guardians, N.Y.C., 1946-47; mem. faculty Columbia Sch. Social Work, 1947—, prof., 1954—; co-dir. Cross Nat. Studies of Social Service Systems and Family Policy, 1973—; staff cons. Citizens Com. for Children, N.Y.C., 1948-72; mem. summer faculty Smith Coll. Sch. Social Work, 1949-54; cons. govts., founds., vol. agys., 1949—; mem. adv. com. Urban Inst.; mem. adv. com. child devel. NRC-Nat. Acad. Scis., 1971-76, mem. com. child devel. research and pub. policy, Acad. Scis., 1977—, chmn., 1980-83; mem. adv. bd. Inst. Research Poverty, U. Wis. Author: A Court for Children, 1953, Planning Community Services for Children in Trouble, 1963, Neighborhood Information Centers, 1966, (with Anna Mayer) Day Care as a Social Instrument, 1966, Theory and Practice of Social Planning, 1969, Studies in Social Policy and Planning, 1969, Social Policy and Social Services, 1973; co-author: Not for the Poor Alone, 1975, Social Service in the U.S, 1976, Social Services in International Perspective, 1977, Child Care, Family Benefits and Working Parents, 1980, Helping America's Families, 1982, Maternity Policies and Working Women, 1983, Income Transfers for Families with Children, 1983; contbr. monographs, articles to profl. jours., chpts. to books.; Editor: Issues in American Social Work, 1959, Shaping The New Social Work, 1973; co-editor: Family Policy: Government and Families in Fourteen Countries, 1978. Served with USAAF, 1942-46. Mem. Nat. Assn. Social Workers (chmn. div. practice and knowledge 1963-66, bd. dirs. 1967-70), Council Social Work Edn., AAUP, Am. Planning Assn. Home: 250 Gorge Rd Cliffside Park NJ 07010 Office: Columbia Univ New York NY 10025

KAHN, CHARLES HOWARD, university dean; b. Birmingham, Ala., Feb. 10, 1926; s. Benjamin Arthur and Dorothy (Goldman) K.; m. Annette Lee, May 12, 1956; children: Kathryn Lauren, Sarah Elizabeth, Benjamin Arthur. A.B., U. N.C., 1946; B.C.E., N.C. State U., 1948; B. Arch., 1956; M.S., M.I.T., 1949; Fulbright grantee, Inst. di Urbanistico, Rome, 1957-58. With Robert & Co. (architects and engr.), Atlanta, 1949-51, Frederick Snare Corp., N.Y.C., 1951-52, F. Carter Williams (AIA), Raleigh, N.C., 1952-54; propr. Charles Howard Kahn & Assos., Architects and Engrs., Lawrence, Kans., 1959—; dean Sch. Architecture and Urban Design, U. Kans., Lawrence, 1968-81, prof., 1968—. Works include Carter Stadium, N.C. State U., 1966, Minges Auditorium, E. Carolina Coll., 1967, Poliedró, Caracus, Venezuela, 1973; mem. editorial bd.: Jour. Archtl. and Planning Research. Bd. Dirs. Community Devel. Center, 1968—, Environ. Research and Devel. Found., 1968; mem. Kans. Bldg. Commn., 1978. Fulbright vis. research scholar, Gt. Brit., 1977-78. Fellow AIA; Mem. Assn. Collegiate Schs. of Architecture, Phi Beta Kappa, Phi Kappa Phi, Sigma Xi, Tau Beta Pi. Democrat. Jewish. Office: Sch Architecture and Urban Design Lawrence KS 66045

KAHN, DONALD ROY, surgeon, educator; b. Birmingham, Ala., May 21, 1929; s. Nathan Aaron and Bertha (Goldner) K.; m. Ellen Rhee Levy, Aug. 9, 1953; children: Elizabeth, Gayle, Donald Roy, Tamara. B.S., Birmingham So. Coll., 1950; M.D., Ala. Med. Sch., 1954. Diplomate: Am. Bd. Surgery, Bd. Thoracic Surgery. Intern St. Louis City Hosp., 1954-55; resident in surgery U. Mich. Hosp., 1955-61, in thoracic surgery, 1961-63, instr. thoracic surgery, 1963-64, asst. prof. thoracic surgery, 1964-67, asso. prof., 1967-71; prof. surgery, chmn. dept. thoracic surgery U. Wis., Madison, 1971-80; chmn. dept. cardiac surgery Bapt.-Princeton Med. Center, Birmingham, Ala., 1980—; dir. Princeton Heart Inst., 1983—. Author: (with W. Wilson and R. Strang) Clinical Aspects of Operable Heart Disease, 1967; contbr. articles on various aspects cardiac surgery and organ transplantation to med. jours. Served to capt. USMCR, 1956-58. Fellow ACS, Am. Coll. Cardiology; mem. Assn. Acad. Surgeons, Soc. Vascular Surgeons, Internat. Soc. Transplantation, Mich. Soc. Thoracic Surgeons, Am. Thoracic Soc., John Alexander Soc., Am. Heart Assn., Am. Soc. Transplantation, Soc. Univ. Surgeons, Soc. Thoracic Surgeons, Am. Assn. Thoracic Surgeons, Transplant Soc. Home: 3829 White Oak Dr Birmingham AL 35243 Office: Baptist-Princeton Med Center Birmingham AL 35211 *Don't try for success in itself, as it can be judged only through your own eyes; just enjoy what you do.*

KAHN, DORIS J., advertising writer; b. N.Y.C., Apr. 2, 1948; d. Hans and Grete (Silberberg) K. B.A., Am. U., 1969. Producer Compton Advt., N.Y.C., 1969-72, writer-producer, 1972-75, creative supr., 1975-80, assoc. creative dir., 1980-83, dep. creative dir., 1983—. Recipient Clio Award, 1970, Advt. Age Award, 1982. Office: 625 Madison Ave New York NY 10022

KAHN, EDWIN LEONARD, lawyer; b. N.Y.C., Aug. 1, 1918; s. Max L. and Julia (Rich) K.; m. Myra J. Green, Oct. 20, 1946; children: Martha Lynn, Deborah Jane. A.B., U. N.C., 1937; LL.B. cum laude, Harvard U., 1940. Bar: N.C. 1940, D.C. 1949. Atty., asst. head legislation and regulations div. Office Chief Counsel, IRS, 1940-52, dir. tech. planning div., 1952-55; ptnr. Arent, Fox, Kintner, Plotkin & Kahn, Washington, 1955—; Lectr. tax insts. N.Y. U., Coll. William and Mary, U. Chgo., U. Tex.; Mem. adv. bd. N.Y. U. Tax Inst., 1959-70. Editor: Harvard Law Rev., 1939-40; editorial adv. bd.: Tax Advisor of Am. Inst. C.P.A.'s, 1974—. Bd. dirs. Jewish Community Center Greater Washington, 1972-78. Served with AUS, 1943-46; ETO. Decorated Bronze Star. Fellow Am. Bar Found.; mem. ABA (council 1963-66, vice chmn. sect. taxation 1965-66), Fed. Bar Assn. (chmn. taxation com. 1967-68), D.C. Bar Assn., Nat. Tax Assn.-Tax Inst. Am. (adv. council 1967-69, dir. 1969-73), Am. Law Inst., Phi Beta Kappa Assos. Jewish. Home: 4104 N 40th St Arlington VA 22207 Office: 1050 Connecticut Ave NW Washington DC 20036

KAHN, ELY JACQUES, JR., writer; b. N.Y.C., Dec. 4, 1916; s. Ely Jacques and Elsie Plaut Mayer; m. Virginia Rice, 1945 (div. 1969); children: Ely Jacques III, Joseph Plaut, Hamilton Rice; m. Eleanor Munro, 1969. Grad., Horace Mann Sch., 1933; A.B., Harvard U., 1937. Writer, reporter, N.Y.C., 1937—; adj. prof. writing Columbia, 1974-75, 81-82. Author: The Army Life, 1942, G. I. Jungle, 1943, McNair: Educator of an Army, 1945, The Voice, 1947, Who, Me?, 1949, The Peculiar War, 1952, The Merry Partners, 1955, The Big Drink, 1960, A Reporter Here and There, 1961, The Stragglers, 1962, The World of Swope, 1965, A Reporter in Micronesia, 1966, The Separated People, 1968, Harvard: Through Change and Through Storm, 1969, The First Decade, 1972, (with Joseph P. Kahn) The Boston Underground Gourmet, 1972, Fraud, 1973, The American People, 1974, The China Hands, 1975 (Sidney Hillman prize), Georgia: From Rabun Gap to Tybee Light, 1978, About The New Yorker and Me, 1979, Far-flung and Footloose, 1980, Jock: The Life and Times of John Hay Whitney, 1981; contbr.: New Yorker, other nat. mags. Bd. dirs. Asso. Harvard Alumni, 1969-72. Served with AUS, 1941-45. Mem. Authors Guild Am., Authors League Am., PEN (exec. com. 1976-79), Phi Beta Kappa, Kappa Alpha Tau. Clubs: Harvard (N.Y.); Century Assn. Home: 1095 Park Ave New York NY 10128 Office: The New Yorker 25 W 43d St New York NY 10036

KAHN, EVERETT FISHER, lawyer, mfg. corp. exec.; b. N.Y.C., Sept. 12, 1924; s. Samuel and Lillian K.; m. Edith S. Adler, Sept. 2, 1951; children—Alison, Lisa, Claudia. A.B., Columbia U., 1947, J.D., 1949. Bar: N.Y. State bar 1950, D.C. bar 1973. Practice law, N.Y.C., 1950-53, 67-69; with Bendix Corp., Southfield, Mich., 1969—, govt. relations counsel, 1972—; sec., dir. Bendix Comml. Service Corp., 1972—, Bendix Field Engring. Corp., 1972—. Served with AUS, 1943-46. Mem. Am. Bar Assn., D.C. Bar Assn., Nat. Security Indsl. Assn. (life). Home: 9601 Kentsdale Dr Potomac MD 20854 Office: Bendix Corp 1000 Wilson Blvd Arlington VA 22209

KAHN, GORDON BARRY, judge; b. Mobile, Ala., Dec. 3, 1931; s. Al and Molly (Prince) K.; 1 son, Andrew Fortier. B.S., U. Ala., 1953, LL.B., 1958; LL.M., N.Y. U., 1959; postgrad., U. London, 1957—. Bar: Ala. bar 1958. Practice in, Mobile, 1959; mem. firm Lyons, Pipes & Cook, 1959-74; bankruptcy judge U.S. Dist. Ct. for So. Ala., 1974—. Chmn. Mobile United Jewish Appeal, 1963-64; pres. Friends of Mobile Pub. Library, Jewish Community Center of Mobile, 1974; Trustee Mobile Pub. Library, 1973-74; bd. dirs. Salvation Army Mobile, 1973-74, B'nai B'rith Home for Aged, Memphis, 1973-74. Served to 1st lt. U.S. Army, 1953-55. Mem. Ala., Mobile County bar assns. Democrat. Jewish. Clubs: Mason, Shriner, Internat. Trade, Athelstan. Home: 230 S McGregor Ave Mobile AL 36608 Office: 317 US Courthouse Mobile AL 36602

KAHN, HERMAN BERNARD, construction company executive; b. Cleve., Feb. 12, 1923; s. Myron Bernard and Bessie (Shur) K.; m. Revera C. Tolochko, Aug. 1, 1948 (div. Feb. 1970); children: Meryl Denise, David Geoffrey.; m. Gerda Moore, June 10, 1983. B.S. in Gen. Engring, N.C. State U., 1949. Partner M.B. Kahn Constrn. Co., Columbia U., S.C., 1949-74; pres. M.B. Kahn Constrn. Co., Inc., 1965-76, Kahn Southern, 1976-77, Kahn-Lockwood, Inc. (gen. contractors), 1977—; dir. Habak, Inc., Nix Volkswagens, Eikay Corp., Stadium Realty Co., S.R. Charleston, Inc., all Columbia. Mem. adv. bd. S.C. Fire Marshall, 1969-79, UN Day com., 1969-74; Bd. dirs. M.B. Kahn Found. Served with AUS, 1943-46. Mem. Associated Gen. Contractors Am., Columbia Contractors Assn. Jewish. Home: 2307 Lincoln St Columbia SC 29201 Office: 731 Elmwood Ave Columbia SC 29201

KAHN, HERTA HESS (MRS. HOWARD KAHN), stockbroker; b. Wuerzburg, Germany, Apr. 1, 1919; came to U.S., 1939, naturalized, 1944; d. Ferdinand and Lilly (Suesser) Hess; m. Herbert Levy, Jan. 4, 1947 (dec. 1966); 1 dau., Linda; m. Howard Kahn, 1970. Student, Northwestern U. Sch. Commerce, 1947-49, 51-56. Joined Paine, Webber, Jackson & Curtis, Inc., Chgo., 1941, registered rep., 1955—, account v.p.; Nat. commn., mem. Chgo. exec. com. Anti-Defamation League B'nai B'rith. Author: What Every Woman Should Know About Investing Her Money, 1968. Hon. bd. dirs. Found. Hearing and Speech Rehab., Michael Reese Hosp. Mem. N.Y. Soc. Security Analysts, Investment Analysts Soc. Chgo. Clubs: Northmoor Country (Highland Park, Ill.); Standard, Economic, Execs. (Chgo.); Tamarisk Country (Palm Springs, Calif.). Home: 1000 Lake Shore Plaza Apt 29-A Chicago IL 60611 Office: 4000 Xerox Center 55 W Monroe St Chicago IL 60603

KAHN, IRVING B., communications exec.; b. N.Y.C., Sept. 30, 1917; s. Abraham and Ruth (Baline) K.; m. Elizabeth Heslin, Sept. 17, 1949; children—Ruth, Jean. B.S., U. Ala., 1939. Advt., publicity mgr. Wilby-Kincey theatres, Tuscaloosa, Ala., 1935-38; publicity mgr. orchs., 1938-39; radio contact, advt. and publicity dept. 20th Century Fox, 1939-42, radio mgr., 1945-46; TV program mgr., spl. asst. to Spyros P. Skouras, 1946-51; pres., chmn. TelePrompTer Corp., 1951-71, Irving B. Kahn & Co., 1972-75; pres., chmn. bd. BroadBand Communications, Inc., 1975—; chmn. exec. com., dir. Times Fiber Communications, Inc., 1977-80; chmn. bd. Gen. Optronics Corp., 1977—, Electro-Optic Devices Corp., 1977-81; dir. Nat. Cable TV Assn., 1965-68. Served as 1st lt. USAAF, 1942-45. NCTA Larry Boggs Man of Year award, 1970. Mem. Soc. Motion Picture and TV Engrs., Internat. Radio and TV Soc. N.Y., Am. Rocket Soc., Young Pres. Orgn., Internat. Inst. Communications (trustee 1980—), Phi Sigma Delta. Clubs: Nat. Press (Washington); Variety of Am. Pioneered closed-circuit TV for teaching missile men Redstone Arsenal, Huntsville, Ala.; co-designer automated electronic audio-visual systems; staging cons. Dem. and Rep. nat. convs., 1952, 56, 60; pioneered large-screen closed-circuit telecasts. Home: 1260 Flagler Dr Edgewater Point Mamaroneck NY 10543 Office: 375 Park Ave New York NY 10022

KAHN, JACOB PHILIP, psychiatrist; b. Melitopol, Russia, May 16, 1914; s. Philip and Elizabeth (Kahn) K.; m. Doris Woodhouse, May 9, 1947; children—Philip, Victoria, Elizabeth (Mrs. Steven Davenport), Madeleine. M.D., U. Calif. at San Francisco, 1941. Diplomate: in psychiatry and child psychiatry Am. Bd. Psychiatry and Neurology. Rotating intern Franklin Hosp., San Francisco, 1940-41, asst. resident medicine, 1941-42; resident psychiatry Langley-Porter Clinic, San Francisco, 1946-49; research fellow child psychiatry James Jackson Putnam Children's Center, Boston, 1949-50, fellow child psychiatry, 1950-51, Judge Baker Guidance Center, Boston, 1950-51; faculty Stanford Sch. Medicine, 1952—, asso. clin. prof. psychiatry, 1959—; chief psychiatry Presbyn. Hosp., Pacific Med. Center, San Francisco, 1959-71, cons., 1971—. Contbr. articles to profl. jours. and textbooks. Served to capt., M.C. AUS, 1942-46. Fellow Am. Psychiat. Assn. (life), Am. Acad. Child Psychiatry, Royal Soc. Medicine, Calif. Acad. Medicine; mem. Royal Coll. Psychiatrists (founding mem.), N.Y.

Acad. Scis. Home: 3259 Clay St San Francisco CA 94115 Office: 3261 Clay St San Francisco CA 94115

KAHN, JENETTE SARAH, publishing company executive; b. Altoona, Pa., May 16, 1947; d. Benjamin and Rosalind (Aronson) K. B.A. cum laude, Radcliffe Coll., 1968. Co-founder, editor Kids mag., Cambridge, Mass., 1970-73; creator, editor Dynamite mag., 1973-74; pub., editor Smash mag., 1974-76; pub. DC Comics Inc., N.Y.C., 1976-81, pres., pub., 1981—. Jr. council Mus. Modern Art, 1975-81; active Big Sisters and Big Bros., 1978—; mem. nat. adv. council Nat. Network of Runaways and Youth Services; pres. Wonder Woman Found. Kress Found. grantee, 1969. Home: 25 Central Park W New York NY 10023 Office: 666 Fifth Ave New York NY 10103

KAHN, JOAN, editor; b. N.Y.C., Apr. 13, 1914; d. Ely Jacques and Elsie (Plaut) K. Student, Barnard Coll., Art Students League. Editor Harper & Row, N.Y.C., 1945-80, Ticknor & Fields, 1980-82, E.P. Dutton, 1982-83, St. Martins Press, 1983—. Mem. Authors Guild, PEN, Mystery Writers Am. Club: National Arts (N.Y.C.). Home: 201 E 36th St New York NY Office: St Martins Press 175 Fifth Ave New York

KAHN, JOSEPH GABRIEL, newspaperman; b. N.Y.C., May 11, 1913; s. Max and Helen (Tigner) K.; m. Lenore Ferber, June 12, 1947; children: Richard, Robert, William. Student, Nat. Acad. Design. With N.Y. Post, 1942-79, reporter, 1943-80; adj. instr. journalism New Sch Center for N.Y.C. Affairs; free-lance writer nat. mags.; water colorist. Recipient Nat. Journalism award Assn. Improvement Mental Hosps., 1953, Albert Lasker award, 1959, Page One award Newspaper Guild, 1959, 60, Service award N.Y. City Protestant Council, 1959, award Planned Parenthood Fedn. Am., 1959, Heywood Broun meml. award, 1960, George Polk meml. award, 1960, Reporters Assn. N.Y.C. award, 1960; award for dedicated service Rotary Club N.Y., 1968; Silurians award, 1971. *Often people ask me how I managed to achieve success as a news reporter. My answer is simple—by treating others decently, honestly and equally. I have followed a road to individual contentment by ignoring such obvious pitfalls as greed and envy.*

KAHN, LAWRENCE R., investment company executive, financial consultant; b. N.Y.C., May 15, 1912; s. Sigmund and Emma (Isenberg) K.; m. Helen Beling, Sept. 30, 1937; children—Kathe (Mrs. James H. Mayer), Victoria (Mrs. Mark Tierney). B.S.S., Coll. City N.Y., 1937; M.A., Columbia, 1939. Economist, asst. gen. mdse. mgr. Bloomingdale Bros. Inc., N.Y.C., 1942-47; mdse. mgr. Oppenheim Collins & Co., N.Y.C., 1947-49; propr. L.R. Kahn Co., N.Y.C., 1949-51; dir. research E.F. Hutton & Co., N.Y.C., 1951-55; v.p. research A.G. Becker & Co. Inc., N.Y.C., 1955-62; sr. v.p. investments Nat. Securities & Research Corp., N.Y.C., 1962—; pres. NSR Adv. Corp., 1969-72; asso. prof. mktg. Pace Coll., 1952-62; cons. Amanah Internat. Fin., Kuala Lampur, Malaysia, 1978. Bd. dirs., mem. exec. com., chmn. fin. com. George Jr. Republic, 1964—; bd. dirs. Westchester Ethical Soc., 1960-65. Mem. N.Y. Soc. Security Analysts (pres. 1959-60, dir. 1954-66), Nat. Assn. Bus. Economists, Phi Beta Kappa (dir. N.Y. assn. 1965—, pres. 1976—), Phi Beta Kappa Assocs. (v.p. 1979—). Club: Sheldrake Yacht. Home and Office: 287 Weyman Ave New Rochelle NY 10805

KAHN, LUDWIG WERNER, educator; b. Berlin, Germany, Oct. 18, 1910; came to U.S., 1936. naturalized, 1943; s. Bernhard and Dora (Frishberg) K.; m. Tatyana Uffner, July 12, 1941; children—Andrée S., Miriam. Student, U. Berlin, 1928-30, 31-33, U. Paris, 1931; M.A., U. London, 1936; Ph.D., U. Berne, 1934. Staff mem. Warburg Inst., London, 1934-36; asst. lectr. Univ. Coll., U. London, 1935-36; instr. U. Rochester, 1936-40, Bryn Mawr Coll., 1940-42; editor Strategic Index of Latin Am., 1942-43; instr. Vassar Coll., 1942-45, asst. prof., 1945-47, Coll. City N.Y., 1947-53, asso. prof., 1953-62, prof., 1963-67, chmn. dept. Germanic and Slavic langs., 1961-67; prof. Columbia, 1967—, Gebhard prof. Germanic langs. and lits., 1973-79, Gebhard prof. emeritus, 1979—; dir. Deutsches Haus, 1973—; vis. prof. Yale Grad. Sch., 1968, 79, Tech. U., Stuttgart, Germany, 1959-60, Grad. Center, City U. N.Y., 1971. Author: Shakespeares Sonette in Deutschland, 1935, Social Ideals in German Literature, 1939, Literatur und Glaubenskrise, 1964; contbr. numerous articles to profl. jours.; Asso. editor: Germanic Rev, 1967—. Mem. regional selection com. Woodrow Wilson Found., 1962-66; mem. Fulbright Screening Com., 1971-73. Decorated grand cross 1st class, Fed. Republic of Germany).; Sr. Fulbright lectr.; Faculty fellow Fund Advancement Edn., 1951-52; Guggenheim fellow, 1969-70; Fulbright research fellow, 1959-60, 69-70. Mem. Modern Lang. Assn. (sect. chmn. 1955), AAUP, Am. Assn. Tchrs. German, Germanistic Soc. Am. (dir. 1968—). Home: 9 Atherstone Rd Scarsdale NY 10583

KAHN, MADELINE GAIL, actress; b. Boston, Sept. 29; d. Bernard B. Wolfson and Paula K. B.A., Hofstra U., 1964; trained as opera singer. Appeared in: satirical revue Upstairs at the Downstairs, N.Y.C., 1966-67, New Faces of 1968, Candide, Booth Theatre, N.Y.C.; Philharmonic Hall, 1968, Two By Two; satirical revue, Imperial Theatre, N.Y.C., 1970-71; appeared in: motion pictures What's Up Doc?, 1972, Paper Moon, 1973 (Oscar nominee, Golden Globe nominee), Blazing Saddles (Oscar nominee 1974), 1974 (First Ann. Acad. of Humor award 1975), Young Frankenstein, 1975 (Golden Globe nominee), At Long Last Love, 1975, The Adventure of Sherlock Holmes, 1975, Smarter Brother, 1975, Won-Ton-Ton, 1976, High Anxiety, 1977, The Cheap Detective, 1978, Simon, 1980, Happy Birthday Gemini, 1980, First Family, 1980, History of the World, Part I, 1981, Yellowbeard, 1983; Boom Boom Room at, Vivian Beaumont Theater, 1973 (Tony nominee, Drama Desk award); Broadway prodn. On the 20th Century, 1978 (Tony nominee); TV series Oh, Madeline, ABC, from 1983; appeared as Madame Arcati in: Blithe Spirit, Santa Fe Festival Theater, 1983. Recipient Distinguished Service award Hofstra Alumni Assn., 1975 *

KAHN, MICHAEL, stage director; b. N.Y.C.; s. Frederick J. and Adele (Gaberman) K. B.A., Columbia U. Artistic dir. Am. Shakespeare Theatre, Stratford, Conn., 1969-77; head dept. interpretation Drama div. Juilliard Sch., N.Y.C.; mem. faculty Circle in the Square, Princeton U.; mem. faculty grad. program NYU Sch. Arts.; Mem. panel League of Profl. Theatre Tng. Programs; bd. dirs. Theatre Communications Group, Theatre Panel, N.Y. State Council of Arts. Dir.: Merchant of Venice; producing dir., McCarter Theater, Princeton, N.J.; plays including Beyond The Horizon, Mother Courage, Grave Undertaking, The Heiress, Angel City, The Torchbearers, A Month in the Country, Put Them All Together, 1974—; dir.: Broadway prodns. The Death of Bessie Smith, 1967, Here's Where I Belong, 1968, Cat On A Hot Tin Roof, 1974, Night of the Tribades, 1977, Whodunnit, 1983, Showboat, 1983; off-Broadway prodns. Funnyhouse of A Negro, 1966, Rimers of Eldritch, 1967, Thorton Wilder plays, 1967, N.Y. Shakespeare Festival's Measure for Measure, 1966, Grand Magic, Manhattan Theatre Club, 1978, A Month in the Country, Roundabout, 1980, Hedda Gabler, Roundabout, 1981, Flux, 1982, Something Different, 1983, Goodman Theatre, Chgo., Old Times, 1972, Tooth of Crime, 1973, Tis Pity She's a Whore, 1974; TV prodn. Beyond the Horizon, WNET, 1975; San Francisco Opera Guild prodn. Cesare, 1978; co-dir., The Acting Co., 1978—, The White Devil, 1979, Carmen, Houston Grand Opera, 1981; Merry Wives of Windsor, Houston Grand Opera, 1983, Washington Opera, Carmen, 1982. Recipient best dir. revival award Saturday Rev., 1966; Charles MacArthur award for best dir. Old Times, 1973; Best dir. award N.J. Drama Critics, 1974, 76; nominated for 4 Vernon Rice awards, 1967; Joseph Jefferson award, 1974; Tony nomination for best director for Showboat, 1983. Home: 1 W 72d St New York NY 10023 Office: The Acting Co 420 W 42d St New York NY 10036

KAHN, PAUL FREDERICK, diversified food company executive; b. Indpls., Oct. 10, 1935; s. Paul L. and Florence (Copeland) K.; m. Helen Gail Bass, Dec. 27, 1961; children—Hartley, Meredith. B.S., Purdue U., 1957; M.B.A., Harvard U., 1963. Brand mgr. Procter and Gamble, Cin., 1963-69; v.p. Foote, Cone & Belding, N.Y.C., 1969-70; sr. v.p. Wilson Sporting Goods, Chgo., 1970-78, Consol. Foods Corp., 1978—. Served with USMC, 1957-60. Presbyterian. Clubs: Indian Hill Country, University. Home: 177 Scott Ave Winnetka IL 60093

KAHN, RAYMOND LEE, lawyer; b. Chgo., Apr. 2, 1917; s. William and Gertrude (Weinberg) K.; m. Gloria Kornberg, Feb. 20, 1949; children—Patricia Ellen, Carole Eileen. A.B., U. So. Calif., 1938, LL.B., 1940. Bar: Cal. bar 1940. Law clk. to justice U.S. Ct. of Appeals, Washington, 1940-41; practice in, Beverly Hills, 1945—; v.p. bus. affairs Aaron Spelling Prodns., Inc., Hollywood, Calif., 1970. Served to capt. USAAF, 1941-45. Mem. Am., Calif., Los Angeles County, Beverly Hills bar assns., Los Angeles Copyright Soc. Home: 5241 Purdue Ave Culver City CA 90230 Office: 132 S Rodeo Dr Beverly Hills CA 90212

KAHN, RICHARD, film co. exec.; b. New Rochelle, N.Y., Aug. 19, 1929; s. Max and Fanny K.; m. Marianne Fletcher, Nov. 22, 1953; children—Lisa, Sharon. B.S. in Econs, U. Pa., 1951. With Buchanan & Co., 1954; with Columbia Pictures, 1955-75, nat. coordinator advt. and publicity, 1963-67, nat. dir. advt. and publicity, 1967-69, v.p., 1969-75; with Metro-Goldwyn-Mayer, Inc., Culver City, Calif., 1975—; now sr. v.p. worldwide mktg., also pres. Metro-Goldwyn-Mayer Internat. Served with U.S. Navy, 1951-54. Mem. Acad. Motion Picture Arts and Scis. (gov.), Film Info. Council. Office: 10202 W Washington Blvd Culver City CA 90230

KAHN, ROBERT IRVING, management consultant; b. Oakland, Calif., May 17, 1918; s. Irving Herman and Francesca (Lowenthal) K.; m. Patricia E. Glenn, Feb. 14, 1946; children: Christopher, Roberta Anne. B.A. cum laude, Stanford U., 1938; M.B.A. (Baker scholar), Harvard U., 1940; LL.D. (hon.), Franklin Pierce Coll., 1977. Exec. researcher R.H. Macy's, Inc., N.Y.C., 1940-41; controller Smith's, Oakland, 1946-51; v.p., treas. Sherwood Swan & Co., Oakland, 1952-56; prin. Robert Kahn & Assocs. (mgmt. cons.), Lafayette, Calif., 1956—; pres. Kahn Harris & Dakin Inc. (fin. cons.), San Francisco, 1971—; v.p. Hambrecht & Quist (investment bankers), San Francisco, 1977-80; dir. Wal-Mart Stores, Inc., Marc Paul, Inc., Piedmont Grocery Co., Components Corp. Am., Lipps, Inc., Vita Plus Industries Inc., Menlo Trading Co., Berkeley Enterprises Inc., Coast Med. Corp., Ear Peace Inc. Publisher: newsletter Retailing Today, 1965—; author: weekly newspaper column Pro and Kahn, 1963-77. Past bd. dirs. Oakland council Boy Scouts Am.; past bd. dirs. Oakland Area ARC; trustee Kahn Found.; past sec. League to Save Lake Tahoe. Served with USAAF, 1941-46; Served with USAF, 1951-52; lt. col. Res. ret. Recipient Mortimer Fleishhacker award as outstanding vol. United Way Bay Area, 1980. Mem. Assn. Mgmt. Consultants (pres. 1977), Inst. Mgmt. Consultants (a founder), Nat. Retail Mchts. Assn. (asso. cons. mem.), Mensa, Phi Beta Kappa. Home: 3684 Happy Valley Rd Lafayette CA 94549 Office: PO Box 249 Lafayette CA 94549 *Only I know how I spend each day. Each night as I put my head on my pillow I think back over how I spent that day. I try to spend it so that I can say, "I spent this day the way I know I should have spent it."*

KAHN, ROBERT THEODORE, photojournalist; b. N.Y.C., Oct. 15, 1933; s. Edward Harold and Helen Dorothy (Dworsky) K.; m. Bettina Kaufman, Mar. 26, 1964; 1 dau., Elizabeth Joan. Student, Bklyn. Coll., 1951-55, CCNY, 1957-59, Columbia U., 1960-63, Domaine Sch. Music, 1963. Writer, photographer Life mag., 1964-66; exec. Young & Rubicam, 1967-70; photojournalist R.T. Kahn Assocs., N.Y.C., 1970—; Tchr. Famous Photographers Sch., Westport, Conn.; vis. lectr. photojournalism N.Y. Inst. Tech., 1975. One-man show Famous Faces, Caldwell Coll., N.J., 1975; represented in permanent collections at, Met. and Stockholm Opera houses. Served with U.S. Army, 1953-55. Mem. Am. Soc. Mag. Photographers, Royal Photog. Soc. Gt. Britain. Clubs: Union League, Royal Thames Yacht. Photographed and interviewed numerous statesmen, celebrities and notables, including Royal Families of Gt. Britain, Denmark and Sweden, Pope Paul VI, Pres. Urho Kekkonen, Earl Mountbatten of Burma, Duchess of Windsor, Duke and Duchess of Marlborough, Prince and Princess Alfonse de Borbon, Countess Estelle Bernadotte, Pablo Casals, Joseph Szigeti, Vladimir Nabokov, David Niven, Douglas Fairbanks, Jr., Cary Grant, Bob Hope, Lord Laurence Olivier, Michael Caine, Jackie Gleason, Oskar Kokoschka, Gov. and Mrs. William H. Vanderbilt, Gov. Raphael Hernandez-Colon, The Hon. John V. Lindsay, The Hon. Tom Bradley, The Hon. Moon Landrieu, Rep. Lindy Boggs, Hernando Courtright, Jack Dempsey, Gunnar Myrdal, Goeran Gentele, Peter F. Heering, many others. Address: 156 E 79th St New York NY 10021

KAHN, ROGER, author, educator; b. Bklyn., Oct. 31, 1927; s. Gordon Jacques and Olga K. K.; m. Joan Rappapert, July 14, 1950 (div. Oct. 1963); 1 son, Gordon Jacques II; m. Alice Lippincott Russell, Sept. 22, 1963 (div. Apr. 1974); children: Roger Lawrence, Alissa Avril; m. Wendy Meeker, Sept. 27, 1974. Student, Univ. Coll., NYU, 1944-47. Sports reporter N.Y. Herald Tribune, N.Y.C., 1948-55; sports editor Newsweek Mag., N.Y.C., 1956-60; editor-at-large Saturday Evening Post, N.Y.C., 1963-69; asst. prof. journalism L.I.U., 1967; adj. prof. creative writing Colo. Coll., 1972; dir. non-fiction writers workshop U. Rochester, 1974, 75, 77; pres. Columbia Mets Baseball Team, S.C., 1983—. Author: The Passionate People, 1968, The Battle for Morningside Height, 1970, The Boys of Summer, 1972, But Not to Keep, 1978, The Seventh Game, 1982. Recipient Best Mag. Sports Article of Yr. award E. P. Dutton Pubs., 1960, 69, 70, 80, 82, Disting. Alumni Sesquicentennial award NYU, 1981. Mem. Author Guild U.S., Soc. Authors and Journalists. Home and Office: 234 Pine Rd Briarcliff Manor New York NY 10510

KAHN, SANDERS ARTHUR, realty consultant; b. N.Y.C., Jan. 20, 1919; s. Robert and Hattie (Grossman) K.; m. Miriam Lefkowitz, Mar. 19, 1948; children: Leslie Arlene, Susan Betty, Richard Steven. With Adams & Co., Real Estate, Inc., 1939-42; v.p. Walter Oertly Assos., Inc., 1946-48; with Dwight-Helmsley, 1948-49; asst. prof. real estate U. Fla., 1949-50; mgr. real estate planning div. Port N.Y. Authority, 1951-53; pres., dir. Sanders A. Kahn Assos., Inc., N.Y.C., 1953—; pres. Transp. Realty Devel. Corp., Clifton, N.J., 1965—; adj. prof., supr. real estate edn. CCNY, 1953-76. Co-author: Principles of Right of Way Negotiation, Real Estate Appraisal and Investment; contbr. articles to profl. jours. Bd. dirs. Citizens Housing and Planning Council N.Y.; past pres. adv. bd. Mercy Coll., Dobbs Ferry, N.Y. Served with USAAF, 1942-45. Recipient George L. Schmutz award Am. Inst. Real Estate Appraisers, 1979; scholarship fund established in his honor Bernard M. Baruch Coll. Fellow Valuers and Auctioneers Instn. (Gt. Britain), Am. Soc. Appraisers (past chmn. internat. edn. com., past internat. gov., Man of Yr. award N.Y. chpt. 1980); mem. Am. Soc. Planning Ofcls., Am. Soc. Real Estate Counselors, Soc. Bus. Adv. Professions, Planning Assn. N. Jersey (dir.), So. Econ. Assn., Am. Right of Way Assn. (past state pres., nat. dir., chmn. valuation com.), Urban Land Inst., Am. Arbitration Assn., Lambda Alpha, Alpha Epsilon Pi. Club: N.Y. U. Alumni (N.Y.C.). Home: 428 Green Hill Rd Smoke Rise Kinnelon NJ 07405 Office: 341 Madison Ave New York NY 10017 also Styertowne Shopping Center 1051 Bloomfield Ave Clifton NJ 07012 also 23 Lawrence Ln London EC 2 England *To rise above the status of the beast in the field, one must dedicate himself to the improvement of society and advancement in his field of endeavor. To consume scarce resources is a privilege, the payment for which is full personal performance.*

KAHN, SIDNEY S(AMUEL), securities firm executive; b. Englewood, N.J., Mar. 27, 1937; s. Herman Wayward and Ruth (Schulman) K.; m. Maxine Rabin, Sept. 17, 1957; children: Jeffrey, Robin, Stephen, Anne. B.A., Yale Coll., 1959; postgrad., Harvard U. Law Sch., 1959-60. Ptnr. Lehman Bros., N.Y.C., 1966-76; sr. v.p. E.F. Hutton, N.Y.C., 1976—; dir. M/A COM, Inc., Boston, 1973—, Belding Heminway, N.Y.C., 1973—, Elder Beerman Stores, Dayton, Ohio, 1975—, Microtel, Inc., Boca Raton, Fla., 1982—. Trustee Yale U. Art Museum, 1972—; mem. chmn.'s council Met. Mus. Art, N.Y.C., 1982—. Republican. Clubs: L.I. Creek; Deepdale (L.I., N.Y.); Knickerbocker (N.Y.C.). Office: EF Hutton 1 Battery Park Pl New York NY 10004

KAHN, SUSAN BETH, artist; b. N.Y.C., Aug. 26, 1924; d. Jesse B. and Jenny Carol (Peshkin) Cohen; m. Joseph Kahn, Sept. 15, 1946 (dec.); m. Richard Rosenkranz, Feb. 1, 1981. Grad., Parsons Sch. Design, 1945; pupil, Moses Soyer, 1950-57. Subject of: book Susan Kahn, with an essay by Lincoln Rothschild, 1980; One-man shows, Sagittarius Gallery, 1960, A.C.A., Galleries, 1964, 68, 71, 76, 80, Charles B. Goddard Art Center, Ardmore, Okla., 1973, Albrecht Gallery Mus. Art, St. Joseph, Mo., 1974, N.Y. Cultural Center, N.Y.C., St. Peter's Coll., Jersey City, 1978; exhibited in group shows, Audubon Artists, N.Y.C., Nat. Acad., N.Y.C., Springfield (Mass.) Mus., City Center, N.Y.C., A.C.A., Galleries, N.Y.C., Nat. Arts Club, N.Y.C., Butler Inst., Youngstown, Ohio; represented in permanent collections, Tyler (Tex.) Mus., St. Lawrence U. Mus., Canton, N.Y., Fairleigh Dickinson U. Mus., Rutherford, N.J., Syracuse U. Mus., Sheldon Swope Gallery, Terre Haute, Ind., Montclair (N.J.) Mus. Fine Arts, Butler Inst. Am. Art, Youngstown, Ohio, Reading (Pa.) Mus., Albrecht Gallery Mus. Art, St. Joseph(Mo.), Cedar Rapids (Iowa) Art Center, N.Y. Cultural Center, N.Y.C., Edwin A. Ulrich Mus., Wichita, Kans., Wichita State U., Johns Hopkins Sch. Advanced Internat. Studies, Washington, Joslyn Mus., Omaha, U. Wyo., Laramie. Recipient Knickerbocker prize for best religious painting, 1956; Edith Lehman award Nat. Assn. Women Artists, 1958; Simmons award, 1961; Knickerbocker Artists award, 1961; Nat. Arts Club award, 1967; Knickerbocker Medal of Honor, 1964; Famous Artists Sch. award, 1967. Mem. Nat. Assn. Women Artists (Anne Barnett Meml. prize 1981), Artists Equity, Knickerbocker Artists, Met. Mus., Mus. Modern Art. *I choose to be a realist and humanist in my work. The most important objects of my concern are people, their lives and times. I believe that art is a way of communicating, subject matter translated into color, form and line, so that the work will express the idea convincingly.*

KAHN, THEODORE CHARLES, educator, behavioral scientist; b. Germany, Oct. 13, 1912; came to U.S., 1922, naturalized, 1927; s. Samuel and Julia (Mayer) K.; m. Shirley Rich, June 7, 1948; children—Donald Alan, Susan, Steven James. B.A., Yale, 1935; M.A., Columbia, 1940; Ph.D., U. So. Calif., 1950; M.A., Mills Coll., 1952; Doktor Rerum Naturalium, Johannes Gutenberg U., Mainz, Germany, 1960. Diplomate: in clin. psychology Am. Bd. Examiners in Profl. Psychology. Sr. counselor Vocational Guidance Center, U. Calif. at Los Angeles, 1947-49; psychologist Los Angeles City Schs., 1949-51; prof. behavioral sci. So. Colo. State Coll., 1965—, chmn. dept., 1965-75; prof. Sch. Social and Behavioral Scis., U. So. Colo., 1975-78; staff psychologist Yuma County Assn. for Behavioral Health Services, 1979—; lectr. U. Colo., 1972; mem. tech. rev. bd., aeromed. div. USAF, 1963-65, task scientist biomed. service corps., 1963-65; cons. psychiatry Wilford Hall USAF Hosp., 1966-69; liaison fellow Am. Anthrop. Assn., 1958-60. Author: Kahn Test of Symbol Arrangement, 1947, Audio-visual-tactile Rhythm Therapy Experiments, 1950-53, Kahn Intelligence Test, 1958, (with M.B. Giffen) Psychological Techniques in Diagnosis and Evaluation, 1960, Four Methods Having Medical and Diagnostic Potential, 1964, Introduction to Hominology, 1965, Introduction to Hominology—The Study of the Whole Man, 1969, 3d edit., 1976, Hominology-A New Therapeutic Dimension, 1972; sr. author: Methods and Evaluation in Clinical Psychology and Counseling, 1974; contbg. author: What Is Hominology and Why Is It?, 1969; founder: Hominology, 1965. Served to maj. AUS, 1940-46; to col. USAF, 1951-65. Decorated N.Y. State Distinguished Service Cross. Fellow Am. Psychol. Assn., AAAS (chmn. social sci. sect. Southwestern and Rocky Mountain div. 1973); mem. Internat. Soc. Study Symbols (founder, pres. 1958-61), Deutsche Gesellschaft fuer Anthropologie, USAF Soc. Psychologists (hon. past pres.), Japanese Soc. (hon. pres.). Home: 1412 Cypress Point Yuma AZ 85365 *For me there is only one meaningful measure of success: How much has my work been able to contribute to the enlightenment and welfare of others*

KAHN, TOM, labor union official; b. N.Y.C., Sept. 15, 1938; s. David and Adele (Klaus) K. Student, Bklyn. Coll., 1955-57; B.A., Howard U., 1963. Asst. organizer Youth Marches for Integrated Schs., 1958-59; mem. staff Am. Com. Africa, 1959-60; mem. Com. to Defend Martin Luther King, 1960-61; asst. dep. dir. March on Washington for Jobs and Freedom, 1963; exec. dir. League Indsl. Democracy, N.Y.C., 1964-72; chief speechwriter for Senator Henry M. Jackson, 1971-72; asst. to pres. AFL-CIO, Washington, 1972—; mem. faculty Urban Affairs Center, New Sch. Social Research, 1969-70; Co-chmn. ad hoc com. to defend right to teach, 1968, chmn. ad hoc com for justice in schs., 1968; mem. guiding com. Nat. Com. for A Polit. Settlement in Vietnam, 1968—; dir. AFL-CIO Polish Workers Aid Fund, 1980—; mem. Com. in Suppport of Solidarity, 1981—, Vol. Service Adv. Council, 1982—; mem. radio programming adv. com. Voice of Am., 1983. Editor: AFL-CIO Free Trade Union News, 1974—; Contbr. articles to various jours. Mem. nat. action com. Socialist Party U.S., 1965—; bd. dirs. A. Philip Randolph Inst., Nat. Com. Against Discrimination in Housing, Workers Def. League, Internat. Rescue Com., 1978, Leadership Conf. on Civil Rights, N.Y. Friends; co-dir. Norman Thomas Fund. Mem. Center War/Peace Studies. Office: 815 16th St NW Washington DC 20006

KAHN, WOLF, artist; b. Stuttgart, Germany, Oct. 4, 1927; came to U.S., 1940, naturalized, 1946; s. Emil and Nellie (Budge) K.; m. Emily Mason, Mar. 2, 1957; children: Cecily, Melany. Student, Hans Hofmann Sch., 1948-50; B.A., U. Chgo., 1951. Vis. prof. painting U. Calif., Berkeley, 1960; adj. asso. prof. Cooper Union Art Sch., 1961-77; jury mem. numerous regional art shows. One-man shows, Borgenicht Gallery, N.Y.C., 1957—, Waddington Gallery, London, 1968—, Meredith Long Gallery, Houston, 1970—, Chgo. Arts Club, 1981, group shows include, Whitney Mus., N.Y.C., 1960, 77, "Sense of Place," (Midwest tour), 1975-76; represented in permanent collections, Mus. Modern Art, N.Y.C., Whitney Mus., Houston Mus. Fine Arts, Chase Manhattan Coll., Va. Mus., Met. Mus., N.Y.C., Los Angeles County Mus., Sheldon Galleries of U. Nebr.; author: Pastel Light, 1983. Served with USNR, 1945-46. Recipient award for art Am. Acad. Arts and Letters, 1979; Fulbright fellow, Italy, 1964-65; Guggenheim fellow, 1967-68; Ford Found. grantee, 1969. Mem. NAD (council), Am. Acad. and Inst. of Arts and Letters. Independent Democrat.

Jewish. Office: care Borgenicht Gallery 724 Fifth Ave New York NY 10019

KAHNE, STEPHEN JAMES, systems engineer, educator; b. N.Y.C., Apr. 5, 1937; s. Arnold W. and Janet (Weatherlow) K.; m. Irena Nowacka, Dec. 11, 1970; children: Christopher, Katarzyna. B.E.E., Cornell U., 1960; M.S., U. Ill., 1961, Ph.D., 1963. Asst. prof. elec. engring. U. Minn., Mpls., 1966-69, asso. prof., 1969-76; dir. Hybrid Computer Lab., 1968-76; founder, dir., cons. InterDesign Inc., Mpls., 1968-76; prof. dept. systems engring. Case Western Res. U., Cleve., 1976-83, chmn. dept., 1976-80; dir. div. elec., computer and systems engring. NSF, Washington, 1980-81; cons. in field; exchange scientist Nat. Acad. Scis., 1968, 75. Editor: IEEE Transactions on Automatic Control, 1975-79; hon. editor: Internat. Fedn. of Automatic Control, 1975-81; editorial bd.: IEEE Spectrum, 1979-82; dep. chmn. editorial bd.: Automatica, 1976-82; dep. chmn. mng. bd.: Internat. Fedn. Automatic Control Publs, 1976—; contbr. articles to sci. jours. Active Mpls. Citizens League, 1968-75. Served with USAF, 1963-66. Recipient Amicus Poloniae award POLAND Mag., 1975; John A. Curtis award Am. Soc. Engring. Edn.; Case Centennial scholar, 1980. Fellow IEEE (pres. Control Systems Soc. 1981, bd. dirs. 1982-83), AAAS. Office: Office of Dean of Engring Poly Inst NY 333 Jay St Brooklyn NY 11201

KAHNG, DAWON, physicist; b. Seoul, Korea, May 4, 1931; came to U.S., 1954, naturalized, 1964; s. Chung-Ryong and Kyong-Hee (Lee) K.; m. Young-Hee Kim, Jan. 21, 1956; children—Kim, Vivienne, Lillian, Dwight, Eileen. B.Sc., Seoul U., 1955; M.Sc., Ohio State U., 1956, Ph.D., 1959. Research asso., then instr. elec. engring. Ohio State U., 1957-59; mem. tech. staff Bell Labs., Murray Hill, N.J., 1959-64, supr., 1964—. Author, editor. Recipient Stuart Ballantine medal Franklin Inst., 1975. Fellow IEEE; mem. Sigma Xi, Pi Mu Epsilon. Patentee in field. Home: 956 Severin Dr Bridgewater NJ 08807 Office: 600 Mountain Ave Murray Hill NJ 07974

KAHRL, STANLEY J., educator; b. Mount Vernon, Ohio, June 30, 1931; s. George Morrow and Faith Jadwin (Jessup) K.; m. Julia Gamble, June 20, 1954; children—Jennifer, George, Sarah, Benjamin. A.B. magna cum laude, Harvard U., 1953, Ph.D., 1962; B.A. with first class honors, Cambridge U., Eng., 1958, M.A., 1962. Teaching fellow Harvard U., 1960-62; instr. U. Rochester, N.Y., 1962-65, asst. prof., 1965-69; dir. Center for Medieval and Renaissance Studies, Ohio State U., Columbus, 1969-78, prof. English, 1969—, asso. dean coll. humanities, 1970-72. Author: Traditions of Medieval English Drama, 1974; Editor: Merry Tales of the Mad Men of Gotham, 1965, Essential Articles for the Study of Old English Poetry, 1968, Collections VIII: Records of Plays and Players in Lincolnshire, 1300-1585, 1974; producer: TV series Early English Drama, WOSU-TV. Bd. dirs. Pathfinder Fund. Served to lt. j.g. USNR, 1953-56. Mem. Mediaeval Acad. (chmn. centers and regional assns. standing com. 1972-75), Modern Lang. Assn., Bibliog. Soc., Modern Humanities Research Assn. Episcopalian. Clubs: Athletic of Columbus; Grolier (N.Y.C.). Home: 209 S Columbia Ave Columbus OH 43209

KAHT, JOSEPH EDWARD, banker, lawyer; b. Bklyn., Feb. 4, 1928; s. Joseph Martin and Isabelle (Stewart) K.; m. Rose Perazzo, Apr. 24, 1954; 1 dau., Jo Ann. Student, St. Francis Coll., 1946-48; LL.B., N.Y. Law Sch., 1952. Bar: N.Y. 1953, U.S. Supreme Ct. 1961, D.C. 1978. Assoc. atty. Dewey, Ballantine, Bushby, Palmer & Wood, N.Y.C., 1952-61; house counsel Irwin, Wolfson, N.Y.C., 1961-63; asst. v.p., atty. Dry Dock Savs. Bank, 1963-67, v.p., atty., 1967-69, sr. v.p., gen. counsel, 1970-82; assoc. gen. counsel Anchor Savs. Bank, 1983—; lectr. real estate Practising Law Inst., 1965—; assoc. Finley, Kumble, Wagner, Heine, Underberg & Casey, 1982-83; mem. adv. bd. Security Title & Guaranty Co., N.Y.C., 1961—. Mem. adv. bd. Little Village Sch. Mem. ABA (com. on econs. and real estate, real property and probate sect., com. mut. savs. banks), N.Y. State Bar Assn., N.Y. County Bar Assn., Catholic Lawyers Guild, Mortgage Bankers Assn. Am. (com. on income producing property), Nat. Assn. Mut. Savs. Banks (mortgage investments). Club: Hempstead (N.Y.) Golf. Home: 3309 Milburn Ave Baldwin Harbor NY 11510 Office: 742 Lexington Ave New York NY 10022

KAILATH, THOMAS, electrical engineer; b. Poona, India, June 7, 1935; came to U.S., 1957, naturalized, 1976; s. Mamman and Kunjamma (George) K.; m. Sarah Jacob, June 11, 1962; children—Ann, Paul, Priya, Ryan. B.E., U. Poona, 1956; S.M., M.I.T., 1959, Sc.D., 1961. Communications researcher Jet Propulsion Labs., Pasadena, Calif., 1961-62; mem. faculty Stanford (Calif.) U., 1963—, prof. elec. engring., 1968—; dir. Info. Systems Lab., 1971-81, asso. chmn. dept., 1981—; vis. prof., cons. univs., industry, govt. Author: Linear Systems, 1980, Least-Squares Estimation, 2d edit, 1981; edit. bd. various jours.; contbr. articles to profl. jours. Guggenheim fellow, 1970; Churchill fellow, 1977. Fellow IEEE, Inst. Math Stats.; mem. Am. Math Soc., Soc. Indsl. and Applied Math, Soc. Exploration Geophysics, Sigma Xi. Home: 1024 Cathcart Way Stanford CA 94305 Office: Dept Elec Engring Stanford U Stanford CA 94305

KAIN, JOHN FORREST, educator; b. Ft. Wayne, Ind., Nov. 9, 1935; s. Forrest and Bessie (Wilder) K.; m. Mary Fan Kiracofe, Aug. 17, 1957; children-Mary Jo, Joanna. B.A. with honors in Econs. and Polit. Sci, Bowling Green State U., 1957; M.A., U. Calif. at Berkeley, 1961, Ph.D., 1961; A.M. (hon.), Harvard U., 1969. Grad. research asst. U. Calif. at Berkeley, 1957-59, lectr. bus. adminstrn. and econs., extension div., 1959-61; research economist RAND Corps., 1961-62; mem. faculty Harvard, 1966—, prof. econs., 1969—, prof., chmn. program in city and regional planning, 1975-81; sr. staff mem. Nat. Bur. Econ. Research, 1967-76; cons. to govt. Author: (with John R. Meyer and Martin Wohl) The Urban Transportation Problem, 1965, (with Gregory K. Ingram and J. Royce Ginn) The Detroit Prototype of the NBER Urban Simulation Model, 1972, Essays on Urban Spatial Structure, 1975, (with John M. Quigley) Housing Markets and Racial Discrimination, 1975; also articles; editor: Race and Poverty: The Economics of Discrimination, 1969. Mem. task force housing Urban Coalition. Served to 1st lt. USAF, 1962-65. Mem. Am. Econ. Assn., Am. Statis. Assn., Econometric Soc., Regional Sci. Assn., Am. Planning Assn., Urban Land Inst., Am. Inst. Cert. Planners. Home: 335 1/2 Harvard St Cambridge MA 02139 Office: Littauer Center Harvard Univ Cambridge MA 02138

KAIN, KAREN ALEXANDRIA, ballet dancer; b. Hamilton, Ont., Can., Mar. 28; d. Charles Alexander and Winifred (Kelly) K. Student, Nat. Ballet Sch., Toronto; Litt.D. (hon.), York U., Toronto, 1977. Mem. corps de ballet Nat. Ballet Can., 1969-70, prin. dancer, 1970—. Roles include: chosen maiden in Rite of Spring, bride in The Seven Daggers; also danced in: Inventions, Whispers of Darkness, Tales of Hoffmann; guest artist: Bolshoi Ballet, London Festival Ballet, others. Decorated Order Can., 1977; recipient Silver medal Internat. Competition, Moscow, 1973. Mem. Canadian Actors Equity Assn., Assn. Radio and TV Artists. Address: Nat Ballet Can 157 King St E Toronto ON Canada M5C 1G9 *

KAIN, RONALD STUART, editor, writer; b. nr. Helena, Mont., Mar. 5, 1899; s. Henry and Fanny (Clift) K.; m. Olive McKay, June 29, 1929. B.A., Mont. State U., 1922; postgrad., Harvard, 1925-26; M.A., Columbia, 1936. Asso. editor Mont. Banker, Great Falls, 1922; reporter Yakima (Wash.) Herald, 1923, Butte (Mont.) Miner, 1923-25, N.Y. Herald Tribune, 1926-29; editor for Am. Biography (supplement New Internat. Ency.), 1929; asso. editor New Internat. Year Book, 1929-44; fgn. news editor, N.Y. office, news and features div. Outpost Service Bur., OWI, 1944; with Psychol. Warfare Dept., SHAEF, London, 1944-45; chief press sect. Netherlands Unit of OWI in, London, 1945, Brussels, 1945, The Hague, 1945; (attached as press officer to psychol. warfare consolidation team 11, Allied mil. mission to Netherlands); chief press and photo sects. USIS, Am. embassy, The Hague, 1945-46; with State Dept., 1946; free-lance writer and editorial cons., 1946-49; chief rev. officer Dept. State, 1949-61; dir. Internat. Surveys Staff, Office Sec. HEW, 1961-66; free-lance writer, 1967—. Author: Europe: Versailles to Warsaw, 1939; Contbr. articles to mags. Mem. English-Speaking Union, Am. Security Council. Club: Cosmos (Washington). Visited Netherlands and Indonesia to study Indonesian revolution during 1947. Home: 3611 N St NW Washington DC 20007

KAINEN, JACOB, former museum curator, artist; b. Waterbury, Conn., Dec. 7, 1909; s. Joseph and Fannie (Levin) K.; m. Bertha Friedman, Aug. 28, 1938; children: Paul Chester, Daniel Bernard; m. Ruth Priscilla Cole, Feb. 19, 1969. Grad., Pratt Inst., 1930; postgrad., N.Y.U., 1936-38, George Washington U., 1944-46. Aide div. graphic arts U.S. Nat. Mus., Smithsonian Instn., Washington, 1942-44, asst. curator, 1944-46, curator, 1946-66, Nat. Collection Fine Arts, 1966-70, spl. cons., 1970—; lectr. painting and history graphic arts U. Md., 1970-71. Work represented in permanent collections, Met. Mus. Art, Bklyn. Mus., Corcoran Gallery of Art, Phillips Collection, Carnegie Inst., Balt. Mus. Art, Art Inst. Chgo., Bklyn. Pub. Library, Kunsthalle, Hamburg, Germany, Brit. Mus., London, Hirshhorn Mus. and Sculpture Garden, Yale U. Mus. Art, Phila. Mus. Art, Queens Coll., Howard U., Bard Coll., N.Y. U., Newark Mus., U. Neb., Bezalel Nat. Mus., Jerusalem, Nat. Gallery of Art, Mus. Modern Art, Whitney Mus. Am. Art, Bklyn. Mus. Art, Portland (Ore.) Mus. Art, Achenbach Found. Graphic Arts, Grunwald Center Graphic Arts, San Francisco Mus. Art, Cleve. Mus. Art, others.; Author: George Clymer and the Columbian Press, 1950, The Half Tone Screen, 1951, Why Bewick Succeeded, 1959, John Baptist Jackson: 18th Century Master of the Color Woodcut, 1962, The Etchings of Canaletto, 1967; also articles. Research grantee Am. Philos. Soc., 1956. Mem. Print Council Am. (dir.). Home: 27 W Irving St Chevy Chase MD 20815

KAINLAURI, EINO OLAVI, architect; b. Lahti, Finland, June 13, 1922; came to U.S., 1947, naturalized, 1954; s. William and Eva K.; m. Genevieve Marjorie Mobley, Aug. 20, 1949; children: John Stanford, William Eino, Mary Ann. Student, Finland Inst. Tech., 1945-47; B.Arch., U. Mich., 1950, M.Arch., 1959, Ph.D., 1975. Draftsman U. Mich. Architect's Office, Ann Arbor, 1951-55; dealer systems planner Ford div. Ford Motor Co., Livonia, Mich., 1955-56; ptnr., gen. mgr. Davis, Kainlauri & MacMullan (architects, engrs., planners), Ann Arbor, 1956-59; pres. KMM Assocs. (architects, engrs., planners), Ann Arbor, 1959-75; prof. architecture Iowa State U., Ames, 1975—; mem. consultative council Nat. Inst. Bldg. Sci.; mem. profl. devel. group. Union Internationale des Architectes. Works include Finnish Cultural Ctr., Farmington, Mich., also schs. and chs.; Author: Multinational Cooperation in Regional Planning for Lapland, 1976. Bd. dirs. Des Moines chpt. Am. Scandinavian Found.; mem. bldg. energy utilization adv. com. Iowa State Energy Policy Council. Served to 1st lt. Finnish Army, World War II. Decorated cross and medal of Liberty; Fulbright Hayes sr. scholar, 1973-74, 83-84; Fulbright research scholar, 1983-84. Mem. AIA (edn. chmn. energy com.), Am. Planning Assn., ASTM, ASHRAE (edn. chmn. of internat. activities com.), Am. Nat. Metric Council, ASHRAE (internat. activities com.), Internat. Soc. Housing Sci., Nat. Trust Hist. Preservation, Am. Solar Energy Assn. Lutheran. Clubs: Optimist (life), Lions.). Home: 1305 Wisconsin Circle Ames IA 50010 Office: 290 Coll Design Iowa State U Ames IA 50011 *As an advocate of life-long learning, Ifeel that what really counts is what you learn after you "know it all." Too often, we limit our opportunities by what we learn at a university or during the first years in a profession. We need to continue and expand our knowledge for wider opportunites in the world.*

KAISEL, STANLEY FRANCIS, engineering management consultant; b. St. Louis, Aug. 2, 1922; s. Samuel and Dora (Sincoff) K.; m. Mary Ann Jones, Mar. 2, 1958; children: David Allen, Ann Penland. B.S.E.E., Washington U., St. Louis, 1943; M.S.E.E., Stanford U., 1946, Ph.D. in Elec. Engring, 1949. Research assoc. Radio Research Lab., Harvard U., 1943-45, Stanford U., 1946-55, lectr., mem. sr. staff electronics research lab., 1951-55; research engr. RCA Labs., 1949-51; engring. mgr. electron tube div. Litton Industries, San Carlos, Calif., 1955-58; founder, pres., chief exec. officer Microwave Electronics Corp. (became div. Teledyne Inc.), Palo Alto, Calif., 1959-65, pres., gen. mgr., 1965-69; pvt. practice engring. mgmt. cons., Woodside, Calif., 1969—; dir. Impell Corp.; vis. com. Washington U. Sch. Engring.; adv. council Sch. Engring. Stanford U. Contbr. papers to profl. publs. Trustee Woodside Elementary Sch. Dist., 1976-82. Recipient engring. achievement award Washington U., 1977; Gold Spike award Stanford U. Annual Fund, 1980. Fellow IEEE (dir. Region 6 1966-68); mem. Assn. Old Crows, Sigma Xi, Tau Beta Pi, Pi Mu Epsilon. Patentee. Home: 595 Albion Way Woodside CA 94062 Office: PO Box 4153 Woodside CA 94062

KAISER, ALBERT FARR, diversified corporation executive; b. N.Y.C., May 14, 1933; s. Albert Louis and Lucille (Daggett) K.; m. Joy E. White, Sept. 16, 1961; children—Elizabeth Ann, Albert Farr. B.A., Hamilton Coll., Clinton, N.Y., 1955; M.B.A., Harvard U., 1960. With acquisitons dept. AMF Inc., 1960-61; with data processing div. IBM Corp., 1961-64; with Sperry and Hutchinson Co., 1964—; pres. The Gunlocke Co., Inc., 1974-77, pres. promotional services div., also chmn. motivation and travel div., 1977-80, corp. exec. v.p., N.Y.C., 1980-82; investment banker J.J. Lowrey & Co., N.Y.C., 1983—. Served to lt. (j.g.) USNR, 1955-58. Mem. So. Furniture Mfrs. Assn. (past dir.), Bus. and Instl. Furniture Mfrs. Assn. (past dir.), Newcomen Soc., Hamilton Coll. Alumni Assn. (pres. Westchester County chpt.). Republican. Mem. Reformed Ch. Am. Clubs: Harvard, Harvard Bus. Sch. (N.Y.C.); Fox Meadow Tennis (Scarsdale); Shenorock Shore (Rye, N.Y.C.). Home: 13 Forest Ln Scarsdale NY 10583 Office: 110 Wall St New York NY 10005

KAISER, ARMIN DALE, biochemist; b. Piqua, Ohio, Nov. 10, 1927; s. Armin Jacob and Elsa Catherine (Brunner) K.; m. Mary Eleanor Durrell, Aug. 9, 1953; children: Jennifer Lee, Christopher Alan. B.S., Purdue U., 1950; Ph.D., Calif. Inst. Tech., 1955. Postdoctoral research fellow Inst. Pasteur, Paris, 1954-56; asst. prof. microbiology Washington U., St. Louis, 1956-59; mem. faculty Stanford U., 1959—, prof. biochemistry. Served with AUS, 1945-47. Recipient molecular biology award U.S. Steel Corp., 1971; Lasker award in basic med. sci., 1980. Mem. Nat. Acad. Scis., Am. Acad. Arts and Scis., Am. Soc. Biochemists, Genetic Soc. Am. Research on virus multiplication, microbial devel. Office: Biochemistry Dept Stanford Univ Stanford CA 94305

KAISER, EDGAR FOSBURGH, JR., coal, oil, gas co. exec.; b. Portland, Oreg., July 5, 1942; s. Edgar Fosburgh and Sue (Mead) K. B.A., Stanford U., 1965; M.B.A., Harvard U., 1967. With AID, Vietnam, 1967-68; White House fellow, 1968, spl. asst. to sec. interior, 1969; mgr. corp. planning and devel. Kaiser Resources, Ltd., Vancouver, B.C., Can., 1970, v.p., treas., 1971-72, exec. v.p. ops., 1972-73, pres., chief exec. officer, 1973-78, chmn. bd., chief exec. officer, 1978-80, chmn. exec. com., 1974-80; mgr. resources devel. Kaiser Steel Corp., 1970-71, chmn. exec. com., 1979—, chmn. bd., 1980—; dir. Toronto-Dominion Bank, Daon Devel. Corp., B.C. Coal Ltd., B.C. Resources Investment Corp., B.C. Place Ltd.; adv.-dir. Pvt. Investment Co. Asia.; Mem. Can. Japan Bus. Cooperation Com., Can.-Korea Bus. Council; mem. Can. com. Pacific Basin Econ. Council, Bus. Council on Nat. Issues, SRI Internat. Council. Hon. bd. dirs. Vancouver Boys' and Girls' Clubs; bd. govs. Jr. Achievement of B.C., Arts and Scis. Centre Soc.; trustee Gov. Dummer Acad., Acad., Byfield, Mass., Calif. Inst. Tech., Henry J. Kaiser Family Found.; bd. dirs. Am. Iron and Steel Inst., Internat. Iron and Steel Inst. Mem. Coal Assn. Can. (past pres.), Mining Assn. B.C. (v.p. 1973-76), Young President's Orgn., Trilateral Commn., White House Fellows Assn. Home: Vancouver BC Canada Office: 1500 W Georgia St Vancouver BC V6G 2Z8 Canada

KAISER, EMIL THOMAS, chemistry educator; b. Budapest, Hungary, Feb. 15, 1938; s. Emil and Elizabeth (Timar) K.; m. Bonnie Lu Togias, Mar. 30, 1968; children: Elizabeth Ann, Charlotte Emily. B.S., U. Chgo., 1956; M.A., Harvard, 1957, Ph.D., 1959. Asst. prof. chemistry Washington U., St. Louis, 1961-63; mem. faculty dept. chemistry U. Chgo., 1963—, asso. prof., 1967-70, prof., 1970-81, Louis Block prof., 1981-82; dir. Center Bioorganic and Bioinorganic Chemistry, 1981-82; prof. Rockefeller U., N.Y.C., 1982—; vis. prof. U. Nice, France, 1976; Japan Soc. for Promotion Sci. prof., 1976; cons. Wiley-Intersci. Co., Kureha Chem. Industry Ltd., Japan, Merck, Sharp and Dohme Labs.; mem. medicinal chem. study sect. A NIH, 1973-77; vis. com. dept. chemistry Brookhaven Nat. Lab., 1978-81, chmn., 1981; vis. com. dept. chemistry Purdue U., 1979; mem. sci. adv. bd. Robert A. Welch Found., 1982—. Editor: Radical Ions, 1969, Progress in Bioorganic Chemistry, 1971, 73, 74, 76; editorial bd.: Jour. Am. Chem. Soc, 1973-82. NSF predoctoral fellow, 1956-58; NIH predoctoral fellow, 1958-59; NIH postdoctoral fellow, 1959-61; Alfred P. Sloan Found. fellow, 1968-70; Guggenheim Meml. Found. fellow, 1975-76. Mem. Phi Beta Kappa, Sigma Xi. Office: Rockefeller Univ Dept of Chemistry York Ave and 66th Street New York NY 10021

KAISER, ERNEST DANIEL, writer, editor; b. Petersburg, Va., Dec. 5, 1915; s. Ernest Bascom and Elnora Blanche (Ellis) K.; m. Mary Gertrude Orford, 1949; children—Eric, Joan. Student, CCNY, 1935-38. Adminstrv. asso. Schomburg Center for Research in Black Culture, N.Y. Pub. Library, N.Y.C., 1945—; cons., reviewer, editor manuscripts about Blacks for McGraw-Hill Pub. Co., R.R. Bowker Co., W.E.B. Du Bois papers U. Mass. Press, Chelsea House Pubs. Adviser: Arno Press series The American Negro: His History and Literature, 145 vols; Author: In Defense of the People's Black and White History and Culture, 1970; co-author: Harlem: A History of Broken Dreams, 1974; editor: A Freedomways Reader, 1978; co-founder, asso. editor: Freedomways mag, 1961—; contbg. editor: Science and Society; co-editor: The Negro Almanac, 1971, Black Titan: W.E.B. Du Bois, 1970, Paul Robeson: The Great Forerunner, 1978; contbr. essays, book reviews, introductions, bibliographies to numerous books, mags., newspapers. Mem. Martin Luther King, Jr. Ind. Democratic Assn., Corona, N.Y.; Bd. dirs. Am. Inst. for Marxist Studies, N.Y.C. Home: 31-37 95th St East Elmhurst NY 11369 Office: 515 Lenox Ave New York NY 10037

KAISER, FRED, computer leasing co. exec.; b. Bklyn., Nov. 22, 1906; s. Fred and Elizabeth (Kleber) K.; m. Jeannette Nelson, June 17, 1930; children: Carol Kaiser Oliver, Janice Kaiser Smith. Student indsl. electricity, Pratt Inst., 1922; grad., Marconi Inst., 1924. Comml. radio operator on shipboard Tropical Radio Co., 1925-26; with Mpls.-Honeywell Regulator Co., 1926-71, regional Midwest mgr., Chgo., 1942-50, field sales mgr., 1950-53, regional mgr. Eastern states, N.Y.C., 1953-60, v.p., 1960-64, v.p. So. area, 1964-71; owner, pres. Nelson Cons. and Mgmt. Corp., Atlanta, 1971—. Office: 3747 Peachtree Rd NE Suite 1613 Atlanta GA 30319

KAISER, GEORGE CHARLES, surgeon; b. Bronx, N.Y., July 30, 1928; s. George P. and Bertha B. (Schwehla) K.; m. Jane Haggart, Nov. 21, 1953; children—Barbara, G. Charles, James H. A.B. in Biology, Lehigh U., 1949; M.D., Johns Hopkins U., 1953. Diplomate: Am. Bd. Surgery, Am. Bd. Thoracic Surgery. Intern in surgery Johns Hopkins Hosp., Balt., 1953-54; resident in gen. and thoracic surgery Ind. U. Med. Center, Indpls., 1956-61, instr. surgery, 1961-63, asst. prof. surgery, 1963; practice medicine specializing in cardiovascular and thoracic surgery, St. Louis, 1963—; staff surgeon VA Hosp., Indpls., 1961-63, St. Louis U. Hosps., chief thoracic and cardiovascular surgery, 1975—; mem. staff St. Mary's Health Center, St. Louis City Hosp., chief surgery, 1967-68, cons. surgery, 1968—, John Cochran Va Hosp., 1965—; asst. prof. surgery St. Louis U. Sch. Medicine, 1963-65, asso. prof., 1965-70, prof. surgery, 1970—. Contbr. numerous articles on cardiology and cardiovascular surgery to profl. jours. Served with USPHS, 1954-56. Fellow A.C.S., Am. Heart Assn. Council Cardiovascular Surgery; mem. Am. Assn. Thoracic Surgery, Internat. Cardiovascular Soc., Midwestern Vascular Surg. Soc., Soc. Vascular Surgery, Soc. Thoracic Surgeons, Am. Coll. Cardiology, Am. Coll. Angiology, Am. Surg. Assn., Central Surg. Assn., So. Surg. Assn., St. Louis Thoracic Surg. Soc., Am. Fedn. Clin. Research, So. Thoracic Surg. Soc., St. Louis Cardiac Club, Am. Soc. Artificial Internal Organs, St. Louis Heart Assn. (Arthur E. Strauss award 1981), AMA, Mo. Med. Assn., Mo. Heart Assn., Sigma Xi, Alpha Omega Alpha. Episcopalian. Home: 30 Joy Ave Webster Groves MO 63119 Office: 1325 S Grand Blvd St Louis MO 63104

KAISER, IRWIN HERBERT, educator, physician; b. N.Y.C., Jan. 27, 1918; s. Leon S. and Helen (Kessler) K.; m. Barbara J. Lieberman, June 12, 1938; children—Susan, Peter, Richard, Margaret, Steven, James. B.A., Columbia, 1938; M.D., Johns Hopkins, 1942; Ph.D., U. Minn., 1953. Intern Johns Hopkins Hosp., 1942-43; research fellow embryology Carnegie Instn., Washington, 1946-47; resident physician Sinai Hosp., Balt., 1947-50; from instr. to asso. prof. U. Minn., 1950-59; prof. obstetrics and gynecology, chmn. dept. U. Utah Med. Sch., 1959-68; prof. gynecology and obstetrics Albert Einstein Coll. Medicine, 1968—. Served to capt. M.C. AUS, 1943-46. Home: 20 Dimitri Pl Larchmont NY 10538

KAISER, LEO MAX, classics educator; b. St. Louis, Dec. 5, 1918; s. Max J. and Rose C. (Speh) K.; m. Aurelia T. Mueth, May 26, 1945; children: Gerold, Joan (Mrs. Neil M. Tomiuk), Leo, James, Andrea, Jeffrey. A.B., St. Louis U., 1940; A.M., U. Ill., 1941, Ph.D., 1943. Instr. classics U. Ill., 1943-46; asst. prof. classics St. Louis U., 1946-51; asst. prof. German and classics, chmn. dept. St. Joseph Coll., Phila., 1952-54; asst. prof. classics Loyola U., Chgo., 1954-63, prof., 1963—; vis. prof. Ohio State U., 1948. Author: The Captivi of Plautus, 1951, 500 German Proverbs, 1955, Thoreau's Translation of the Seven Against Thebes, 1960, Index Verborum to Cicero's Rhetorica, 1964, Anthology of American Latin Verse, 1984; Contbr. articles to profl. jours. Mem. Am. Philol. Assn., Am. Classical League, Classical Assn. Middle West and South. Roman Catholic. Home: 7147 N McAlpin Ave Chicago IL 60646 *Successful or not, one must abide by a personal philosophy honestly—and hopefully intelligently and honorably—developed.*

KAISER, LLOYD EUGENE, broadcasting exec.; b. Alpena, Mich., Aug. 1, 1927; s. Albert W. and Adele V. (Diemond) K.; m. Barbara Jane Wieand, June 17, 1957; children—Kristina, Timothy. B.A., U. Mich., 1950, M.A., 1951. Communications instr. Fla. secondary schs.,

Hollywood, 1951-52; instr. radio and TV Lehigh U., Bethlehem, Pa., 1952-54; asst. prof. communications SUNY, Fredonia, 1954-58; ednl. TV programming exec. Rochester (N.Y.) Ednl. TV Assn., 1958-63; founder, gen. mgr. Sta. WITF-TV, Hershey, Pa., 1963-70; pres., gen. mgr. WQED/WQEX-TV, WQED-FM and Pitts. Mag. (pub. broadcasting), Pitts., 1970—; Vice chmn. bd. Pub. Broadcasting Service, 1969-71; v.p. Eastern Ednl. Network, 1970-72; chmn. operating com. Pa. Pub. TV Network, 1973-75; mem. Pa. Pub. TV Network Commn., Pres.'s Com. on Health Edn. Adminstr.: network prodns. Nat. Geog. Spls (4 Emmy awards, Peabody award 1979-80), Previn and the Pittsburgh, Once Upon a Classic, Kennedy Center Tonight, Newsweek's Cover Story. Bd. dirs. Pitts. March of Dimes, 1970-74; media adv. bd. Point Park Coll., Pitts., 1970-74; bd. dirs. Am. Wind Symphony, 1975—, United Way Allegheny County; mem. Health Edn. Center. Mem. Nat. Ednl. TV Affiliates Council (sec. 1967-68), Nat. Assn. Ednl. Broadcasters (bd. dirs. 1969-71, chmn. 1972, sec. Ednl. TV Stas. 1968—), Pitts. C. of C. (edn. com. 1970-71), Pitts. Health Conf. (chmn. 1980-81). Home: 1204 Hulton Rd Oakmont PA 15139 Office: 4802 5th Ave Pittsburgh PA 15213

KAISER, PHILIP M., diplomat; b. Bklyn., July 12, 1913; s. Morris and Temma (Sloven) K.; m. Hannah Greeley, June 16, 1939; children: Robert Greeley, David Elmore, Charles Roger. A.B., U. Wis., 1935; B.A., M.A. (Rhodes scholar), Balliol Coll., Oxford (Eng.) U., 1939. Economist, mem. bd. govs. Fed. Res. System, 1939-42; chief project ops. staff, also chief planning staff enemy br. Bd. Econ. Warfare and Fgn. Econ. Adminstrn., 1942-46; expert on internat. orgn. affairs State Dept., 1946; exec. asst. to asst. sec. labor in charge internat. labor affairs, 1946-47; dir. Office Internat. Labor Affairs, Dept. Labor, 1947-49, asst. sec. labor for internat. labor affairs, 1949-53; labor adviser to Com. for Free Europe, 1954; spl. asst. to Gov. W. Averell Harriman of N.Y., 1955-58; prof. internat. labor relations Sch. Internat. Service, Am. U., 1958-61; U.S. ambassador to Republic Senegal, Islamic Republic Mauritania, 1961-64; minister Am. embassy, London, Eng., 1964-69; chmn. Ency. Brit. Internat. Ltd., London, 1969-75; dir. Guinness Mahon Holdings, Ltd., 1975-77; ambassador to, People's Republic of Hungary, 1977-80, Austria, 1980-81; professorial lectr. Johns Hopkins Sch. Advanced Internat. Studies, 1981—; Woodrow Wilson vis. fellow; Mem. interdept. com. to develop programs under Marshall Plan, 1947-48, interdept. com. to develop programs for Greek-Turkish aid and Point 4 Tech. Assistance, 1947-49. Bd. govs. Ditchley Found. Mem. Am. Assn. Rhodes Scholars, Council Fgn. Relations, Phi Beta Kappa.

KAISER, ROBERT GREELEY, journalist, columnist; b. Washington, Apr. 7, 1943; s. Philip Mayer and Hannah (Greeley) K.; m. Hannah Jopling, July 14, 1965; children: Charlotte Jerome, Emily Eli. B.A., Yale, 1964; M.Sc., London Sch. Econs., 1967; postgrad., Columbia U., 1970-71. Reporter met. staff Washington Post, 1967-69, corr. Saigon Bur.,, 1969-70, bur. chief Moscow Bur.,, 1971-74, nat. corr., 1975-82, assoc. editor, columnist, 1982—; Vis. prof. Duke U., 1974-75, adj. prof., 1980—. Author: Cold Winter, Cold War, 1974, Russia, The People and The Power, 1976, (with Jon Lowell) Great American Dreams, 1979, (with Hannah Jopling Kaiser) Russia From the Inside, 1980. Recipient Front Page award Balt.-Washington Newspaper Guild, 1973, Overseas Press Club award for best reporting from abroad, 1975. Mem. Council Fgn. Relations, Lehrman Inst. (asso.). Club: Elihu. Home: 1711 S St NW Washington DC 20009 Office: 1150 15th St NW Washington DC 20071

KAISER, WALTER JACOB, English literature educator; b. Bellevue, Ohio, May 31, 1931; s. Walter O. and Joyce (Drexel) K.; children: David Walter, Miranda Margaret. A.B., Harvard U., 1954, Ph.D., 1960; postgrad., U. Paris, 1954-55, Ecole Normale Superieure, Paris, 1955-56. Instr. Harvard, 1960-62, asst. prof., 1962-65, asso. prof. English and comparative lit., 1965-69, prof., 1969—, chmn. dept. comparative lit., 1969-75, Walter Cabot Channing fellow, 1977-78; vice-dir. Villa I Tatti, Florence, Italy. Author: Praisers of Folly: Erasmus, Rabelais, Shakespeare, 1963; Editor: Selected Essays of Montaigne, 1964; Translator: (George Seferis) Three Secret Poems, 1969; contbr.: Dictionary of the History of Ideas, 1973, Atlantic Brief Lives, 1971. Mem. vis. com. Boston Mus. Fine Arts, 1970-72, trustee, 1978—; bd. dirs. Philip H. and A.S.W. Rosenbach Found., 1974-78; chmn. vis. com. Addison Gallery Am. Art, Andover, 1978. Fulbright fellow, 1954-55; Tower fellow, 1955-56; Am. Council Learned Socs. fellow to, Rome, 1964-65; recipient faculty prize Harvard Univ. Press, 1963. Mem. Renaissance Soc. Am., Am. Comparative Lit. Assn., Modern Greek Studies Assn., Council Fgn. Relations, Signet Soc., P.E.N., Phi Beta Kappa. Clubs: Somerset, Belmont Hill. Office: 401 Boylston Hall Harvard U Cambridge MA 02138

KAISERMAN, WILLIAM, fashion designer; b. N.Y.C., Sept. 8, 1942; s. Bert and Sarah (LaVerne) K.; m. Mildred Lyons, Dec. 11, 1971. Student, U. Fla. Pres., owner Rafael Fashions (hat design and mfg.), N.Y.C., 1966-68; designer leather collections in, Paris, 1968-70; pres., owner Rafael Fashions, Ltd., N.Y.C., from 1970; also owner Bill Kaiserman Ltd., N.Y.C. Recipient Coty award, 1974, 75; named to Coty Hall of Fame, 1976. Mem. Council Fashion Designers Am. *

KAISH, LUISE, sculptor; b. Atlanta; d. Harry and Elsa (Brown) Meyers; m. Morton Kaish, Aug. 15, 1948; 1 dau., Melissa. B.F.A., Syracuse U., 1946, M.F.A., 1951; student, Escuela de Pintura y Escultura, Escuela de las Artes del Libro, Taller Grafico, Mexico, 1946-47. Artist-in-residence Dartmouth Coll., 1974; lectr. sculpture Columbia U., 1974, 75, prof. sculpture and chmn. div. painting and sculpture, 1980—; vis. artist U. Wash., Seattle, Battelle seminars and study program, 1979. One artist shows, Rochester (N.Y.) Meml. Art Gallery, 1954, Sculpture Center, N.Y.C., 1955, 58, Staempfli Gallery, N.Y.C., 1968, 81, 84, Minn. Mus. Art, St. Paul, 1969, Jewish Mus., N.Y.C., 1973; exhibited (with Morton Kaish), Manhattanville Coll., Purchase, N.Y., 1955, Rochester Meml. Art Gallery, 1958, USIS, Rome, 1973, Dartmouth Coll., 1974; represented in permanent collections, Whitney Mus. Am. Art, N.Y.C., Met. Mus. Art, N.Y.C., Jewish Mus., N.Y.C., Export Khleb, Moscow, Minn. Mus. Art, Gen. Mills Corp., Minn., High Mus. Art, Atlanta, Rochester Meml. Art Gallery, Lowe Mus., Coral Gables, Fla., also numerous pvt. collections, commns., Syracuse U., Temple B'rith Kodesh, Rochester, Temple Israel, Westport, Conn., Holy Trinity Mission Sem., Silver Springs, Md., Temple Beth Shalom, Wilmington, Del., Beth-El Synagogue Center, New Rochelle, N.Y., Temple B'nai Abraham, Essex City, N.J., Continental Grain Co., N.Y. Trustee Am. Acad. in Rome, 1973-81, mem. exec. com., 1975-81; trustee St. Gaudens Found., 1978—. Recipient awards Everson Mus., Syracuse, 1947, Rochester Meml. Art Gallery, 1951, Ball State U., 1963, Ch. World Service, 1960, Council for Arts in Westchester, 1974; Emily Lowe award, 1956; Audubon Artists medal, 1963; Honor award AIA, 1975; Louis Comfort Tiffany grantee, 1951; Guggenheim fellow, 1959; Rome prize fellow Am. Acad. in Rome, 1970-72. Mem. Sculptors Guild (v.p.), Eta Pi Upsilon, Pi Lambda Theta. Address: 610 West End Ave New York NY 10024

KAISH, MORTON, painter, educator; b. Newark, Jan. 8, 1927; s. Morris and Sophie (Furman) K.; m. Luise H. Meyers, Aug. 15, 1948; 1 dau., Melissa. B.F.A., Syracuse U., 1949; postgrad., Academie de la Grande Chaumiere, Paris, 1951, Istituto d' Arte, Florence, Italy, 1952, Accademia dell Belle Arti, Rome, 1957. Vis. critic Parsons Sch. Design, N.Y.C., 1966-70, Phila. Coll. Art, 1983; mem. faculty Art Students League, N.Y.C., 1974—; guest critic Sch. Visual Arts, N.Y.C., 1967; vis. prof. Queens Coll., Flushing, N.Y., 1979; vis. artist U. Wash., Seattle, 1979; fellow MacDowell Colony, 1976; artist-in-residence Dartmouth Coll., 1974; mem. faculty Fashion Inst. Tech., SUNY, N.Y.C., 1973—; dir. Carl Fischer Mus. Instrument Co., N.Y.C., 1964-70. Exhibited one-man shows, Manhattanville Coll., Purchase, N.Y., 1955, Rochester (N.Y.) Meml. Art Gallery, Guild Hall, Easthompton, L.I., 1969, U.S. Info. Service, Rome, 1973, Dartmouth Coll., Hanover, N.H., 1974, Staempfli Gallery, N.Y.C., 1964, 67, 71, 73, 79, 83, group shows, Mus. Galleria 11 Torcoliere, Rome, 1957, Barone Gallery, N.Y.C., 1959, Art Inst. Chgo., 1964, Sheldon Meml. Art Gallery, Lincoln, Nebr., U. Nebr., Lincoln, Krannert Art Mus., U. Ill., Urbana, 1965, 68, Herron Mus. Art, Indpls., 1965, Mary Washington Coll., Fredericksburg, Va., Am. Acad. Arts and Letters, N.Y.C., 1966, Pa. Acad. Fine Arts, Phila., Ark. Art Ctr., Little Rock, Whitney Mus. Am. Art, N.Y.C., Finch Coll. Mus. Art, N.Y.C., N.J. State Mus., Trenton, Krannert Art Mus., 1968, Kent (Ohio) State U., 1970, U.S. Info. Service, Rome, 1972, New Sch. Social Research, N.Y.C., 1973, Child Hassam Purchase Fund Exhbn., N.Y.C., invitational exhbns., Child Hassam Purchase Fund, 1975, Am. Acad. Arts and Letters, Drawings U.S.A., Minn. Mus. Art, St. Paul, Springfield Art Mus., Springfield Mus. Art, Mo., Galerie Brusberg, Berlin, W.Ger., 1980, Taft Mus., Cin., 1981; represented in permanent collections, Whitney Mus. Am. Art, N.Y.C., Bklyn. Mus., Nat. Mus. Art, Smithsonian Instn., Washington, Guild Hall, Easthampton, N.Y., Williams Coll., Williamstown. Mass., Syracuse U., N.Y.; exhibited group shows, N.J. State Mus. Art, Trenton, 1966. Recipient Harriet T. Leavenworth award Syracuse U., 1949, award Everson Mus. Art, 1950, Meml. Art Gallery, 1952, SUNY Research Found., 1983. Mem. Century Assn., Nat. Acad. Design (assoc., William A. Paton prize 1983). Address: 610 West End Ave New York NY 10024

KALABA, ROBERT EDWIN, engineering educator; b. Mt. Vernon, N.Y., Sept. 21, 1926; s. Edwin Albert and Leona Margaret (Winkler) K.; m. Wilma Joy Becker, Dec. 23, 1950; children: Robert John, Darlene Day, Kathy Lynn, Richard William. B.A., NYU, 1948, Ph.D., 1958. Mathematician Rand Corp., Santa Monica, Calif., 1951-70; prof. econs., elec. and biomed. engring U. So. Calif., Los Angeles, Calif., 1969—; sr. scientist Hughes Aircraft Co., El Segundo, Calif., 1982—. Founding editor: Jour. Applied Math. and Computation, 1975; contbr. articles to profl. jours.; author: Integral Equations via Imbedding Methods, 1974, Control, Identification and Input Organization, 1982. Served with USN, 1945-46. Mem. IEEE, Assn. Computing Machinery, Math. Assn. Am., Phi Beta Kappa. Home: 370 Aderno Way Pacific Palisades CA 90272 Office: U So Calif Los Angeles CA 90089

KALAINOV, SAM CHARLES, insurance company executive; b. Steele, N.D., May 11, 1930; s. George and Celia Mae (Makedonsky) K.; m. Delores L. Holm., Aug. 10, 1957; children: John Charles, David Mark. B.S., N.D. State U., 1956. C.L.U. Life ins. agt. Am. Mut. Life Ins. Co., Fargo, N.D., 1956-60, supt. agys., Des Moines, 1960-70, sr. v.p. mktg., 1972-80, pres., chmn., chief exec. officer, 1980—; v.p. agy. Western States Life Ins. Co., Fargo, 1970-72. Bd. dirs. Luth. Hosp. and Homes, Fargo, 1974—, City Corp., Des Moines, 1981—, Civic Ctr. Ct., Des Moines, 1981—, Iowa Luth. Hosp, Des Moines, 1982—; mem. Republican Central Com., Des Moines, 1980, Presdl. Task Force, Washington, 1981. Served with inf. AUS, 1947-49; served to lt. AUS, 1952-55. Decorated Bronze Star. Mem. Nat. Assn. Life Underwriters, Am. Coll. Life Underwriters, Greater Des Moines C. of C. (Nat. Leadership award 1978), Am. Legion. Lodge: Rotary. Home: 681 50th St Des Moines IA 50312 Office: Am Mut Life Ins Co 418 6th Ave Des Moines IA 50307

KALAMAROS, EDWARD NICHOLAS, lawyer; b. Williamsport, Ind., July 5, 1934; s. Nicholas John and Margaret Louise (Riley) K.; m. Marilyn Jane Foster, June 14, 1958; children: Alexander, Philip, Anastasia, Timothy. B.S. in Commerce, U. Notre Dame, 1956, LL.B., J.D., 1959. Bar: Ind. 1959. Chief dep. prosecutor 60th Jud. Circuit of Ind., 1963-67; practiced in, South Bend, 1960—; pres. Edward N. Kalamaros & Assos., 1971—; U.S. govt. appeal agt. SSS, 1967-71, adviser to registrants, 1971-75; mem. St. Joseph County Tax Adjustment Bd., 1970-73, pres., 1972-73. Past deacon, elder, trustee Presbyn. Ch.; v.p. bd. dirs. Council for Retarded of St. Joseph County, 1972-78, sec., 1966-72; bd. dirs., sec. Alcoholism Council; bd. edn. St. Joseph High Sch., 1975-82. Served with USNG and U.S. Army Res., 1960-66. Mem. Am. Arbitration Assn. (panel of arbitrators), Lawyers and Pilots Bar Assn., Am., Ind., St. Joseph County, 7th Fed. Circuit bar assns., Am. Judicature Soc., Def. Research Inst., Internat. Assn. Indsl. Accident Bds. and Commns., Am., Ind. trial lawyers assns., Ind. Def. Lawyers Assn., Comml. Law League. Clubs: Masons (32 deg.), Shriners, Macatawa Bay Yacht, South Bend Press (hon.). Home: 1829 Portage Ave South Bend IN 46616 also 5209 Lakeshore Dr Holland MI 49423 Office: 129 N Michigan Ave PO Box 4156 South Bend IN 46601

KALAMOTOUSAKIS, GEORGE JOHN, economist; b. Chios, Greece, July 26, 1936; came to U.S., 1953; s. John S. and Marika (Nikolaides) K.; m. Elena Manta; 1 son, Yannis. B.A., City U. N.Y., 1956, M.A., 1958; Ph.D., N.Y. U., 1966. Instr. Fairleigh Dickinson, U., Teaneck, N.J., 1958-59; asst. prof. Ithaca (N.Y.) Coll., 1959-62; chief economist Brown Engr., N.Y.C., 1963-64; instr. Washington Sq. Coll., City U. N.Y., 1963-65; econ. cons. N.Y. State Office Regional Devel., Albany, 1964-66; adv. economist IBM, Armonk, N.Y., 1969-73; internat. economist Am. Standard, Inc., N.Y.C., 1973-76; prof. finance Grad. Sch. Bus., N.Y. U., 1971—; external dir. Rank-Xerox, Greece; vis. prof. U. Md. European div. USAF, 1960, 67-68; head dept. pub. finance Center of Planning and Econ. Research, Athens, Greece, 1966-69; dir. econ. research Bank of Greece, 1977-79; chief exec. officer, vice-chmn. bd. Bank of Crete, Athens, 1979—. Contbr. articles to profl. jours.; Author books on internat. fin., Cyprus and self determination, common market and econ. devel. Greece. Bd. dirs., trustee Hellenic Theatre Found. Am. Ford Found. Faculty Research fellow, 1962. Mem. Am. Econ. Assn., AAUP (v.p. chpt. 1961), Omicron Delta Epsilon. Home: 124 Lakeview Ave Lynbrook NY 11563 Office: 22 Voukourestiou St Athens 134 Greece

KALANT, HAROLD, physician, educator; b. Toronto, Ont., Can., Nov. 15, 1923; s. Max Isaac and Sophia (Shankman) K.; m. Oriana Josseau, July 22, 1948. M.D., U. Toronto, 1945, B.S. in Medicine, 1948, Ph.D., 1955. Intern. Toronto Gen. Hosp., 1945-46; resident in medicine Saskatoon Dept. Vets. Affairs Hosp., 1947, Toronto Gen. Hosp., 1948-49, Hospital del Salvador, Santiago, Chile, 1949-50; attending physician Bell Clinic, Toronto, 1952-55; Med. Research Council postdoctoral fellow in biochemistry, Cambridge, Eng., 1955-56; biochemistry sect. head Def. Research Med. Labs., Toronto, 1956-59; asso. prof., prof. pharmacology U. Toronto, 1959—; asso. research dir. Addiction Research Found., Toronto, 1959—. Author: Experimental Approaches to the Study of Drug Dependence, 1969, Drugs, Society and Personal Choice, 1971, Alcoholic Liver Pathology, 1975. Served with M.C. Royal Can. Army, 1943-47. Silver medallist in medicine U. Toronto, 1945; recipient Starr medal for research, 1955; Jellinek Meml. award, Amsterdam, 1972; Raleigh Hills Found. gold medal, Irvine, Calif., 1981; Royal Soc. Can. fellow, 1981, ann. research award Am. Research Soc. on Alcoholism, 1983. Mem. Pharmacol. Soc. Can., Biochem. Soc. (U.K.), AAAS, Internat. Soc. Biomed. Research on Alcoholism, Acad. Scis. Can. Office: Dept Pharmacology Univ Toronto Toronto M5S 1A8 Canada

KALB, MARVIN LEONARD, radio and TV corr.; b. U.S., June 9, 1930; s. Max and Bella (Portnoy) K.; m. Madeleine J. Green, June 1, 1958; children—Deborah, Judith. B.S.S., Coll. City N.Y., 1951; M.A., Harvard, 1953, Ph.D. candidate, 1955. Press attache Am. embassy, Moscow, 1956-57; corr. CBS News, Moscow, 1960-63, diplomatic corr., Washington, 1963-1980; Chief Diplomatic Correspondent NBC News, 1980-. Panel member: Meet The Press; Author: Eastern Exposure, 1958, Dragon in the Kremlin, 1961, The Volga, A Political Journey Through Russia, 1967; introduction to One Day in Life of Ivan Denisovich, 1964, (with Elie Abel) Roots of Involvement: The U.S. in Asia 1784-1971, 1971, (with Bernard Kalb) Kissinger, 1974. Served with U.S. Army, 1953-55. Recipient award for best radio analysis Overseas Press Club, 1962, award for best TV analysis, 1965; award for best interpretation fgn. news on TV Internat. Cinema Soc., 1967. Mem. Overseas Writers (pres.), State Dept. Corrs. Assn. Clubs: Nat. Press (Washington); Harvard (N.Y.C.). Office: NBC News 30 Rockefeller Plaza New York NY 10020

KALBER, FLOYD, TV journalist; b. Omaha, Dec. 23, 1924. Student, Creighton U. Announcer Sta. KGF, Kearney, Nebr., 1946-48; sports dir. Sta. WIRL, Peoria, Ill., 1948-49; news dir. Sta. KMTV, Omaha, 1949-60; anchorman evening news WMAQ-TV, Chgo., 1960-76; Reporter nat. polit. convs., 1960, 64, 68, 72. Newscaster: The Today Show, NBC-TV, N.Y.C., 1976-79; reporter: NBC News, 1979—; anchorman: covering Apollo 11 and 12 space flights. NBC Sunday News. Served in U.S. Army, World War II. Office: WLS-TV 190 N State Street Chicago IL 60611 *

KALBFLEISCH, GIRARD EDWARD, U.S. judge; b. Piqua, Ohio, Aug. 3, 1899; s. Oscar Conrad and Magdalena Margaret (Gerstmeyer) K.; m. Chattie Lenora Spohn, May 1, 1929. LL.B., Ohio No. U., Ada, 1923, LL.D., 1960. Bar: Ohio bar 1924. Pvt. practice, Mansfield, Ohio, 1929, pros. atty., Richland County, 1929-33, mcpl. judge, Mansfield, 1936-42; judge Ct. Common Pleas, Richland County, 1943-58; sr. U.S. dist. judge for, No. Ohio, 1959—; pres. Common Pleas Judges Assn. Ohio, 1952. Served with S.A.T.C., 1918. Fellow Ohio State Bar Found.; mem. Am. Bar Assn., Fed. Bar Assn., Ohio Bar Assn., Richland County Bar Assn., Soc. Benchers Case Western Res. U. Law Sch. Home: 545 Stewart Ln Mansfield OH 44907

KALBFLEISCH, JOHN MCDOWELL, cardiologist; b. Lawton, Okla., Nov. 15, 1930; s. George and Etta Lillian (McDowell) K.; m. Jolie Harper, Dec. 30, 1961. A.S., Cameron A&M U., Lawton, 1950; B.S., U. Okla., 1953, M.D., 1957. Diplomate: Am. Bd. Internal Medicine. Intern U. Va. Hosp., 1957-58; resident and fellow U. Okla. Med. Center, 1958-61, instr. medicine, 1964-66, asst. prof., 1966-69, asso. clin. prof., 1970-78, clin. prof., 1978—; practice medicine specializing in cardiology, Tulsa, 1969—; dir. cardiovascular services St. Francis Hosp., Tulsa, 1975—; mem. physician adv. bd., City of Tulsa. Contbr. articles in field to profl. jours. Served with USPHS, 1962-64. Fellow A.C.P., Am. Coll. Cardiology (gov. Okla. 1978-81); mem. Tulsa County Med. Soc., Okla. State Med. Assn., AMA, Am. Heart Assn. (teaching scholar 1967-69), Okla. Soc. Internal Medicine (v.p., pres.-elect 1983—), Am. Soc. Internal Medicine, AAAS, Am. Fedn. Clin. Research, Am. Inst. Nutrition, Delta Upsilon. Republican. Presbyterian. Office: 6565 S Yale St Suite 310 Tulsa OK 74136

KALCKAR, HERMAN M., educator, scientist; b. Copenhagen, Denmark, Mar. 26, 1908; came to U.S., 1953, naturalized, 1956; s. Ludvig and Bertha (Melchior) K.; children—Sonja, Nina, Niels. M.D., U. Copenhagen, 1933, Ph.D., 1938; M.A. (hon.), Harvard U., D.Sc., Washington U., St. Louis, U. Chgo., U. Copenhagen. Sci. asst., also instr. Inst. Med. Physiology, U. Copenhagen, 1934-37, asst. prof., 1937; Rockefeller research fellow biology Calif. Inst. Tech., Washington U. Sch. Medicine, 1939-42; research asso. Pub. Health Research Inst., N.Y.C., 1943-46; asso. prof. physiology U. Copenhagen, 1946-49; research prof., dir. Inst. for Cytophysiology, 1949-54; vis. scientist NIH, Bethesda, Md., 1953-56, chief sect. metabolic enzymes, 1956-58; prof. biology and biochemistry, dept. biology Johns Hopkins, 1958-61; prof. biol. chemistry Harvard Med. Sch., 1961—; now emeritus; chief biochemistry, biochem. research lab. Mass. Gen. Hosp., Boston, 1961-74, vis. biochemist, 1974—; Disting. research prof. biochemistry Sch. Arts and Scis., Boston U., 1979—. Author numerous articles, monographs on phosphorylation and galactose metabolism.; Asso. editor: Cellular Physiology, 1976—. Recipient Saunders award, Phila., 1964. Fellow Am. Acad. Arts and Scis.; mem. Soc. Biol. Chemists, Harvey Soc. (hon.), Royal Danish Acad. (fgn.), Nat. Acad. Scis. Office: Boston U Boston MA 02114

KALDAHL, WESLEY GLEN, airline executive; b. Sauk Centre, Minn., Aug. 26, 1924; s. Axel M. and Alena (DeMeyer) K.; m. Rosemary Stevens, Jan. 9, 1949; children: Steven, Susan, Scott, Mary Beth, Gregory, Jerry, Patricia Elizabeth. Student, U. Detroit, 1945-46; cert. advanced mgmt., Harvard U., 1971. Dir. schedules Capital Airlines Co., Washington, 1945-61; dir. schedule planning Am. Airlines Inc., N.Y.C., 1961-64, v.p. mktg. resources, N.Y.C., Dallas, 1974-82; sr. v.p. airline planning Am. Airlines Co., Dallas, 1982—; v.p. schedules Eastern Airlines Inc., Miami, Fla., N.Y., 1964-72; sr. v.p. airline planning Pan Am. Co., N.Y.C., 1972-74. Mem. Dallas-Fort Worth C. of C. Republican. Roman Catholic. Club: Dallas Economists. Home: 15818 Ranchita Dr Dallas TX 75248 Office: Am Airlines Inc PO Box 61616 Dallas Fort Worth Airport TX 75261

KALED, DAVID ALEC, apparel manufacturer; b. Sioux City, Iowa, Feb. 3, 1943; s. Abraham and Bertha Watfe (Ferris) K.; m. Linda Cecilia Caluya, May 12, 1973; children: Eric Abraham, Gregory Michael. B.S., Iowa State U., 1965; M.B.A., U. Pa., 1967. Market analyst Vertol div., Boeing Co., 1967-68; with Levi Strauss & Co., San Francisco, 1970—, successively asst. to gen. mgr. Sportswear, planning mgr. sportswear dir., gen. mdse. mgr. sportwear, dir. corp. planning and policy, v.p. corp. planning and policy, 1970-81, sr. v.p. corp. devel. and poly, 1981—. Bd. dirs. Ind. Colls. No. Calif., 1983—. Mem. Lambda Chi Alpha. Home: 368 Mountain View Ave San Rafael CA 94901 Office: Levi Strauss & Co 1155 Battery St San Francisco CA 94120

KALER, JAMES BAILEY, astronomer, educator; b. Albany, N.Y., Dec. 29, 1938; s. Earl Bailey and Hazel Alfrieda (Holmgren) K.; m. Maxine Ellen Grossman, June 15, 1960; children: Lauren Lynn Johnson, Bruce Jeffrey, Lisa Suzanne, Jill Lenore. A.B., U. Mich., 1960, postgrad., 1960-61; postgrad., Christian Albrechts U., Kiel, Germany, 1961-62; Ph.D, UCLA, 1964. Asst. prof. astronomy U. Ill., Urbana, 1964-68, assoc. prof., 1968-76, prof., 1976—. Co-author: (with S.P. Wyatt) Principles of Astronomy: A Short Version, 1974, 2d edit., 1981; contbr. articles to profl. jours. Grantee in field; grants coordinator Nat. Acad. Arts; Fulbright fellow, 1961-62; Guggenheim fellow, 1972-73. Mem. Am. Astron. Soc., Internat. Astron. Union, Astron. Soc. Pacific, Ill. Track Club. Home: 907 Sunnycrest Dr Urbana IL 61801 Office: Astronomy Bldg 1011 W Springfield Ave Urbana IL 61801

KALES, ROBERT GRAY, mgmt., finance, mfg., real estate exec.; b. Detroit, Mar. 14, 1904; s. William R. and Alice (Gray) K.; m. Jane Webster, Nov. 27, 1932; children—Jane (Mrs. William H. Ryan),

Robert Gray, William R., Anne W. (Mrs. Jeffrey Howson); m. Miriam Wallin, Jan. 6, 1945; 1 son, David Wallin; m. Herma Lou Boyd, Mar. 6, 1951; m. Shirley L. McBride, Feb. 14, 1961; children—John Gray, Nancy Davis. B.S., Mass. Inst. Tech., 1928; M.B.A., Harvard U., 1933. With Whitehead & Kales Co., Detroit, 1928-31, 43—, v.p., 1943—, now chmn. bd., River Rouge, Mich.; also dir.; with Union Guardian Trust Co., Detroit, 1933-34; analyst, sec.-treas. Investment Counsel, Inc., Detroit, 1934-35; organizer Kales Kramer Investment Co., Detroit, 1935, pres., dir., 1935—, Indsl. Resources, Inc., 1955-74, Automotive Bin Service Co., Inc., 1955—, Jefferson Terminal Warehouse, 1934—, Kales Bldg. Co., 1944-73, Kales Realty Co., 1935-73, Midwest Underwriters, Inc., 1938—, Modern Constrn., Inc., 1938; all Detroit; v.p., dir. Basin Oil Co., Metamora, Mich., 1947-75; dir. Independent Liberty Life Ins. Co., Grand Rapids, Mich., Atlas Energy Corp., Detroit. Chmn. vets. com. Detroit Armed Forces Week.; Adv. bd. Patriotic Edn., Deland, Fla.; chmn. trustees, pres. Kales Found. Served to lt. comdr. USNR, 1942-45; capt. Res. Mem. Am. Legion, Navy League U.S. (pres. Southeastern Mich. council), Mil. Order World Wars (past nat. comdr.-in-chief), Nat. Sojourners, Naval Order U.S., S.A.R., U.S. Naval Inst., Sigma Chi. Episcopalian. Clubs: Army and Navy, Univ., Capitol Hill (Washington); Bayview Yacht, Detroit Country, Detroit Athletic, Detroit, Curling, Detroit Power Squadron, The Players, St. Clair Yacht, Scarab, Univ. (Detroit); Black River Ranch (Onaway, Mich.); Longwood Cricket, Union Boat (Boston); Stone Horse Yacht (Harwich, Mass.); Triton Fish and Game (Quebec, Can.); Grosse Pointe (Mich.) Hunt, Grosse Pointe Yacht, Otsego Ski, Pelee, Masons, Shriners, K.T. Home: 87 Cloverly Rd Grosse Pointe Farms MI 48236 Office: 58 Haltiner St River Rouge MI 48218 also 1900 E Jefferson St Detroit MI 48207 *1) Be considerate of others. (2) Be fair and straightforward in all business and private relationships. (3) Be loyal to your friends and family. (4) Be ready to help where possible in community services and enterprises. (5) Be ever ready to serve your country. (6) Be mindful of your church and religious belief.*

KALEY, ARTHUR WARREN, fin. cons. co. exec.; b. St. Louis, Nov. 14, 1921; s. Clarence Francis and Alma Pauline (Otto) K.; m. Jean Maxine Schwartz, Nov. 23, 1949; children—Susan, Scott, Brian, Matt. Student, Washington U., St. Louis, 1947-49, Grad. Sch. Fin. Mgmt., Dartmouth Coll., 1965-67; grad. Advanced Mgmt. Program, Harvard, 1973. Salesman Swift & Co. (various locations), 1946-48, credit mgr., St. Louis, 1948-54, Memphis, 1954-55, Chgo., 1955-63, asst. treas., 1963-73, treas., 1973-79; pres., treas. Fin. Futures, Inc., Hilton Head, S.C., 1979—; former treas., dir. Trans Pacific Resources, Inc., Swift and Co., N.J., Ky., Derby Foods Inc.; former treas. Nat. Packing Co., Inc., Strongheart Products, Inc., Nutri Products Ltd.; former dir. Swift S.p.A., Genoa, Italy, Swift & Co. (Belgium) N.V., ProTen, Inc., Swift & Co. Ltd., Swift Canadian Co. Ltd.; lectr. cash mgmt. Advanced Mgmt. Research, also Am. Mgmt. Assn. Contbr. articles to various fin. publs. Served to capt. USAAF, 1943-46. Decorated Air medal with five oak leaf clusters. Mem. Fin. Mgrs. Assn. Chgo. (pres. 1970-71), Art Inst. Chgo. Clubs: Execs., Union League, Harvard Bus. (dir.), Internat. Monetary Market (Chgo.); Port Royal Golf, Hilton Head Art League (Hilton Head). Home and Office: 8 Robbers Row Hilton Head Island SC 29928

KALEY, GABOR, educator, scientist; b. Budapest, Hungary, Nov. 16, 1926; came to U.S., 1947, naturalized, 1953; s. Geza and Ilona (Steiner) Kalocsay; m. Harriette Weintraub, July 20, 1969; children—Sharon, David Jason. B.S., Columbia U, 1950; M.S., N.Y. U., 1957, Ph.D., 1960. Research asso. dept. pathology N.Y. U. Med. Center, 1956-60, USPHS postdoctoral fellow, 1960-62, instr., 1961-62, asst. prof., 1962-64; asso. prof. physiology N.Y. Med. Coll., 1964-70, prof., 1970—, acting chmn., 1970-72, chmn., 1972—. Served with AUS, 1952-54. Recipient NIH research grants, 1962—, tng. grants, 1971—. Home: 142 E 71st St New York City NY 10021 Office: Dept Physiology NY Med Coll Valhalla NY 10595

KALIFF, JOSEPH ALFRED, artist, writer, publishing syndicate executive; b. Fall River, Mass., Apr. 3, 1922; s. George and Marie (Fata) K. Student, Pratt Inst., 1940-41, Brown U., 1942, N.Y. Sch. Indsl. Arts, 1950-51. Free-lance artist, writer, 1940-43, and free-lance caricaturist for newspapers and mags., 1945-50; pres. Republic Features Syndicate, N.Y.C., 1950-55, Amusement Features Syndicate, 1979—; entertainment editor Broadway columnist Bklyn. Daily, 1951-71; mem. bd. judges Miss Universe Contest, 1955, Mrs. Am. Contest, 1951-52, Coll. Queen Contest, 1951-55. Starred in 2 TV programs, Sta.-WPIX; author: nationally syndicated columns Did You Know That?, 1950-52, Magic Carpet Over Broadway, 1950—, It's A Cockeyed World, 1953-79, Karikature Karnival, 1979—. Served with U.S. Army, 1943-45; ETO. Mem. Caricaturists Soc. Am. (founder, dir. 1950—, pres. 1979—), Am. Legion. Clubs: Odd Fellows, Circus Saints and Sinners. Sketched Presidents Roosevelt, Truman, Eisenhower, Kennedy and Johnson, also caricatures of numerous entertainers. Home: 224 Highland Blvd Brooklyn NY 11207 Office: 218 W 47th St New York NY 10036 *It was the late President Franklin Delano Roosevelt who most contributed to my success in life. After finishing a caricature of him, many years ago, I showed him the sketch for his approval and expecting a turndown, he surprised me with a loud guffaw. "You know something," he opined, "a man can never become successful in life if he can't laugh at himself, and what better way than at his own caricature."*

KALIN, ROBERT, mathematics education educator; b. Everett, Mass., Dec. 11, 1921; s. Benjamin and Celia (Kraff) K.; m. Madelyn Pildish, Aug. 17, 1962; children: Susan Leslie, John Benjamin, Sandra Kim, Richard Dean. Student, Northeastern U., 1940-43; B.S., U. Chgo., 1947; M.A.T., Harvard U., 1948; Ph.D., Fla. State U., 1961. Tchr. math. Holten High Sch., Danvers, Mass., 1948-49, Beaumont High Sch., Hadley Tech. Sch., Soldan-Blewitt High Sch., St. Louis, 1949-52; ednl. statistician Naval Air Tech. Tng. Center, Norman, Okla., 1952-53; test specialist, asso. in research Ednl. Testing Service, Princeton, N.J., 1953-55; exec. asst. Commn. on Math. of Coll. Entrance Exam. Bd., 1955-56; instr. dept. math. edn. Fla. State U., Tallahassee, 1956-61, asst. prof., 1961-63, asso. prof., 1963-65, prof., 1965—, asso. dept. head, 1968-73, program leader, 1975-78. Co-author: Elementary Mathematics, Patterns and Structure, 11 vols, 1966, (with E.D. Nichols) Analytic Geometry, 1973; co-author: Holt School Mathematics, 9 vols, 1974, Holt Mathematics, 9 vols, 1981. Served with U.S. Army, 1943-46. Mem. Nat. Council Tchrs. Math (chmn. external affairs com. 1972-73), Fla. Council Tchrs. Math. (pres. 1960-61), Nat. High Sch. and Jr. Coll. Math. Clubs (gov. 1972-75, pres. 1978-80), Math. Assn. Am., Assn. Tchrs. Math., Spl. Interest Group for Research in Math. Edn., Internat. Group for Psychology of Math. Edn., Sch. Sci. and Math Assn. Home: 1120 Cherokee Dr Tallahassee FL 32301 Office: Coll Education Fla State U Tallahassee FL 32306

KALINA, RICHARD, artist; b. N.Y.C., May 21, 1946; s. Jacob Wilbert and Helen Ruth (Weinberg) K.; m. Valerie Jaudon, Oct. 23, 1979. B.A., U. Pa., 1966. One man shows, Jack Glenn Gallery, Los Angeles, 1970, OK Harris Gallery, Tibor de Nagy Gallery, 1979, 80, 82, group shows include, Morris Gallery, Toronto, 1970, Lunn Gallery, Washington, Inst. Contemporary Arts, Boston, U. Ala., 1971, Jack Glenn Gallery, 1970, 71, NYU, 1972, Indpls. Mus. Art, 1971, 74, Walker Art Center, Mpls., 1974, Cas Thomas Jefferson, Brasilia, Brazil, 1975, Lehigh U., Norton Gallery, Palm Beach, Fla., Mus. Am. Found. for Arts, Miami, 1977, Sewall Gallery, 1978, 80, Nobe Gallery, 1978, Rutgers U., Weatherspoon Art Gallery, Greensboro, N.C., Ill. Wesleyan U., 1980, Aldrich Mus., Ridgefield, Conn., 1970, 80, Sidney Janis Gallery, N.Y.C., 1981, Drysdale-McIntosh Gallery, Washington, Ericson Gallery, N.Y.C., 1982, Mus. Art, Ft. Lauderdale, Fla., Okla. Mus. Art, Oklahoma City, Santa Barbara Mus. Art, (Calif.), Grand Rapids Art Mus., (Mich.), Hudson River Mus., Yonkers, N.Y., 1983, U. Tex., Austin, Kalamazoo Inst. Art, Madison Art Ctr., (Wis.), U. Chgo., 1983, Loch Haven Art Ctr., (Fla.), Jacksonville Art Mus., (Fla.), Haber-Theodore Gallery, N.Y.C., others; represented in permanent collections, Indpls. Mus. Art, Norton Gallery Art, Palm Beach, N.Y. U., Aldrich Mus., also numerous pvt. collections. Home: 139 Bowery New York NY 10002

KALINA, ROBERT EDWARD, physician, educator; b. New Prague, Minn., Nov. 13, 1936; s. Edward Robert and Grace Susan (Hess) K.; m. Janet Jessie Larsen, July 18, 1959; children: Paul Edward, Lynne Janet. B.A. magna cum laude, U. Minn., 1957, B.S., 1960, M.D., 1960. Diplomate: Am. Bd. Ophthalmology (dir. 1982—). Intern U. Oreg. Med. Sch. Hosp., Portland, 1961-62, resident in ophthalmology, 1961-62, 63-66; asst. in retina surgery Children's Hosp., San Francisco, 1966-67; Nat. Inst. Neurol. Diseases and Blindness Spl. fellow Mass. Eye and Ear Infirmary, Boston, 1967; instr. ophthalmology U. Wash., 1967-69, asst. prof., 1969-71, acting chmn. dept. ophthalmology, 1970-71, asso. prof., 1971-72, chmn. dept. ophthalmology, 1971—, prof., 1972—; mem. staffs Univ. Hosp., Harborview Hosp., Children's Hosp., Seattle.; Cons. VA Hosp., Seattle, USPHS Hosp., Madigan Hosp., Tacoma; asso. head div. ophthalmology dept. surgery Children's Orthopedic Hosp., Seattle, 1975—. Contbr. author: Introduction to Clinical Pediatrics, 1972, Ophthalmology Study Guide for Medical Students, 1975; Contbr. numerous articles to profl. publs. Served to capt., M.C. USAF, 1962-63. Mem. Am. Acad. Ophthalmology (instr. 1970—), AMA, Assn. Research in Vision and Ophthalmology, AAAS, Pacific Coast Oto-Ophthalmol. Soc. (councilor 1972-74), Assn. U. Profs. Opthalmology (pres. 1982-83), King County (Wash.) Med. Soc., Wash. State Acad. Ophthalmology, Phi Beta Kappa. Home: 2627 96th St NE Bellevue WA 98004 Office: Dept of Ophthalmology RJ10 U Wash Seattle WA 98195

KALINOWSKY, LOTHAR B., neuropsychiatrist; b. Berlin, Dec. 28, 1899; s. Alfred and Anna (Schott) K.; m. Hilda Pohl, Mar. 7, 1925; children—Marion, Ellen. Student univs., Berlin, Heidelberg, Munich, 1917-22; M.D., U. Berlin, 1922, U. Rome, 1934. Diplomate: Am. Bd. Neurology and Psychiatry. Asst. neuro-psychiatry univ. hosps., Berlin, Hamburg, Breslau, Vienna, 1922-32; asst. Univ. Hosp. for Nervous and Mental Diseases, Rome, 1933-39; guest physician various European hosps., 1939-40, Pilgrim State Hosp., 1940-43; attending psychiatrist N.Y. Psychiat. Inst. and Hosp., N.Y.C., 1940-58; asso. neurologist Neurol. Inst., N.Y.C., 1940-57; attending psychiatrist St. Vincent's Hosp., N.Y.C., 1957—; specializing chiefly in somatic treatment in psychiatry, 1938—; teaching, research asso. psychiatry Coll. Physicians and Surgeons, Columbia U., 1942-58; asso. prof. neuropsychiatry N.Y. Sch. Psychiatry, 1958—; clin. prof. psychiatry N.Y. Med. Coll., 1961—; Hon. prof. psychiatry Free U. Berlin, 1970—. Author: (with Paul H. Hoch) Somatic Treatments in Psychiatry, 1961, (with H. Hippius) Pharmacological, Convulsive and Other Somatic Treatments in Psychiatry, 1969; Contbr. numerous articles sci. jours. Mem. Brit. Med. Assn., AMA, Am. Psychiat. Assn., Am. Neurol. Assn., N.Y. Acad. Medicine, Internat. League Against Epilepsy, Royal Medico-Psychol. Assn. (corr.), German Neuropsychiat. Soc. (hon.). Home: 155 E 76th St New York NY 10021 Office: 30 E 76 St New York NY 10021

KALINS, DOROTHY, magazine editor; b. Westport, Conn., Oct. 9, 1942; d. Joseph M. and Gil G. K.; m. J. Carlos Davis, Nov. 23, 1983. Student, Skidmore Coll., 1960-62, Sorbonne U., Paris, 1962-63; B.A., Columbia U., 1965. Design writer Home Furnishings Daily, N.Y.C., 1965-68; freelance writer, 1969-74; exec. editor Apartment Life Mag., N.Y.C., 1974-78, editor-in-chief, 1978-81, Metropolitan Home mag., 1981—. Author: Researching Design in New York, 1968, Cutting Loose, 1972, The Apartment Book, 1979, The New American Cuisine, 1981; contbr.: articles to various mags. including N.Y. Mag. Mem. Am. Soc. Mag. Editors (exec. bd.). Office: Metropolitan Home Magazine 750 3d Ave New York NY 10017

KALISCH, BEATRICE JEAN, nurse; b. Tellahoma, Tenn., Oct. 15, 1943; d. Peter and Margaret Ruth Petersen; m. Philip A. Kalisch, Apr. 17, 1965. B.S., U. Nebr., 1965; M.S. (USPHS fellow), U. Md., 1967, Ph.D., 1970. Pediatric staff nurse Centre County Hosp., Bellefonte, Pa., 1965-66; instr. nursing Philipsburg (Pa.) Gen. Hosp. Sch. Nursing, 1966; pediatric staff nurse Greater Balt. Med. Center, Towson, Md., 1967; asst. prof. maternal-child nursing Am. U., 1967-68; clin. nurse specialist N.W. Tex. Hosp., Amarillo, 1970; asso. prof. maternal-child nursing, curriculum coordinator nursing Amarillo Coll., 1970-71; chmn. baccalaureate nursing program, asso. prof. nursing, prin. investigator USPHS research grant to investigate impact of Cadet Nurse Corps on Am. nursing profession in U.S. U. So. Miss., 1971-74; prof. nursing, chmn. dept. parent-child nursing, prin. investigator USPHS grant to investigate image of nurse in mass media U. Mich. Sch. Nursing, Ann Arbor, 1974—, Shirley C. Titus Disting. prof., 1977—; vis. Disting. prof. U. Ala., 1979, U. Tex., 1981, Tex. Christian U., 1983. Author: Child Abuse and Neglect: An Annotated Bibliography, 1978; Co-author: Nursing Involvement in Health Planning, 1978, The Advance of American Nursing, 1978, Politics of Nursing, 1982, Images of Nurses on Television, 1983; co-editor: Studies in Nursing Mgmt.; Contbr. articles to profl. jours. Recipient Joseph L. Andrews Bibliog. award Am. Assn. Law Libraries, 1979; Book of Yr. award Am. Jour. Nursing, 1978, 83. Fellow Am. Acad. Nursing; mem. Am. Nurses Assn., Nat. League Nursing, Am. Public Health Assn., Soc. Research Child Devel., Assn. Care Children in Hosps., AAAS, Internat. Child Abuse Assn., Internat. Soc. History of Nursing, Am. Heart Assn., Sigma Theta Tau, Phi Kappa Phi. Presbyterian. Home: 5663 Glen Oak Ct Saline MI 48176 Office: 1355 Catherine St Ann Arbor MI 48109

KALISH, ARTHUR, lawyer; b. Bklyn., Mar. 6, 1930; s. Jack and Rebecca (Binianoniotsky) K.; m. Janet J. Wiener, Mar. 7, 1953; children: Philip, Pamela. B.A., Cornell U., 1951; J.D., Columbia U., 1956. Bar: N.Y. 1956, D.C. 1970. Assoc. Paul, Weiss, Rifkind, Wharton & Garrison, N.Y.C., 1956-64, ptnr., 1965—; lectr. NYU Inst. Fedn. Taxation, Hawaii Tax Inst., Law Jour. Seminars. Contbr. articles to legal jours. Assoc. trustee L.I. Jewish-Hillside Med. Ctr., New Hyde Park, N.Y., 1978-82, trustee, New Hyde Park, N.Y., 1982—; bd. dirs. Community Health Progra of Queens Nassau Inc., New Hyde Park, 1978—; pres. Community Health Program of Queens Nassau Inc., New Hyde Park, 1981—. Mem. ABA, N.Y. State Bar Assn., Assn. Bar City N.Y. Home: 2 Bass Pond Dr Old Westbury NY 11568 Office: Paul Weiss Rifkind Wharton & Garrison 345 Park Ave New York NY 10154

KALISH, DONALD, educator; b. Chgo., Dec. 4, 1919; s. Lionel and Mildred K. A.B., U. Calif. at Berkeley, 1943, M.A. in Psychology, 1945, Ph.D. in Philosophy, 1949. Instr. Swarthmore Coll., 1946-47, U. Calif. at Berkeley, 1947-48; mem. faculty U. Calif. at Los Angeles, 1949—, prof. philosophy, 1964—, chmn. dept., 1964-70. Author: (with Richard Montague and Gary Mar) Logic Techniques of Formal Reasoning, 2d edit, 1980; also articles. Co-chmn. Nat. Mblzn. Com. to End War in Vietnam, 1967-68; mem. steering com. Resist, 1967—. Mem. AAUP, Am. Philos. Assn., Assn. Symbolic Logic. Address: Univ Calif Los Angeles CA 90024

KALISH, HARRY ISIDORE, psychologist, educator; b. N.Y.C., Apr. 4, 1921; s. Max and Pearl (Pollack) K.; m. Mildred Armstrong, Apr. 27, 1944; children—Douglas, Gregory. B.A., U. Iowa, 1949, M.A., 1951, Ph.D., 1952. Diplomate: Am. Bd. Profl. Psychology. Postdoctoral trainee VA Hosp., Iowa City, 1952-53; vis. prof. Duke, 1953-55; asst. prof. U. Mo., 1955-56; asso. prof. Adelphi U., Garden City, N.Y., 1956-61; prof., chmn. dept. psychology State U. N.Y. at, Stony Brook, 1961-71, dean profl. and para-profl. programs, 1971—, v.p. for liberal studies, 1973-76, prof. psychology, 1976—, chmn. dept., 1981; cons. VA.; Mem. N.Y. Bd. for Psychology, 1971; mem. Psychology adv. bd. N.Y. State Edn. Dept. Contbr. articles profl. jours. Fellow Am. Psychol. Assn., AAAS; mem. Psychonomic Soc., Sigma Xi. Home: 14 Childs Ln Setauket NY 11733

KALISH, MYRON, lawyer, rubber co. exec.; b. N.Y.C., Dec. 3, 1919; s. Louis and Bertha (Nacht) K.; m. Evelyn J. Zobler, Apr. 1, 1944; children—Nita Jane, Pamela Sue. B.S. in Social Sci, Coll. City N.Y., 1940; LL.B. cum laude, Harvard, 1943. Bar: N.Y. bar 1944. Since practiced in, N.Y.C.; sr. partner firm Arthur, Dry & Kalish P.C. (and predecessors), 1961—; gen. counsel UNIROYAL, Inc., 1961—. Editor: Harvard Law Rev, 1942-43. Adv. bd. Southwestern Legal Found. Served to lt. (s.g.) USNR, 1943-46. Mem. Am., N.Y. State bar assns., Assn. Bar City N.Y., N.A.M. (mem. lawyers adv. com. to gen. counsel). Clubs: Mason., Harvard. Home: Halsey Ln Remsenburg NY 11960 Office: 1230 Ave of Americas New York NY 10020

KALISKI, STEPHAN FELIX, economics educator; b. Warsaw, Poland, Nov. 4, 1928; emigrated to Can., 1941, naturalized, 1947; s. Jacob and Ludwika (Romanus) K.; m. Marian Ieleen Nelson, Oct. 6, 1960; 1 dau., Susan Maria. B.A., U. B.C., 1951; M.A., U. Toronto, 1953, postgrad., 1953-54; Ph.D., U. Cambridge, Eng., 1959. Statistician I Dominion Bur. Statistics, 1951-52; Alexander Mackenzie Research fellow U. Toronto, 1953-54; lectr. Queen's U., Kingston, Ont., 1954-56, prof. econs., 1969—, chmn. div II, 1971-73; research fellow in econ. statistics Manchester (Eng.) U., 1958-59; asst. prof. Carleton U., Ottawa, Ont., 1959-62, asso. prof., 1962-65, prof., 1965-69, cmn. dept. econs., 1962-63, 64-66; research supr. Royal Commn. Taxation, 1963-64; Can. Council Sr. fellow, Dept. Labour-Univs. Research Com. research grantee, research asso. U. Calif., Berkeley, 1966-67; Can. Council leave fellow, 1973-74; hon. research asso. in econs. Harvard U., 1973-74; Social Sci. and Humanities Research Council Can. leave fellow, 1980-81, research grantee, 1978, 81; Bd. dirs. Nat. Bur. Econ. Research. Author: Adjustment Assistance under the U.S. Trade Expansion Act, 1963, The Tradeoff Between Inflation and Unemployment, Some Explorations of Recent Evidence for Canada, 1972; editor, author: introduction Canadian Economic Policy since the War, a Series of Six Public Lectures in Commemoration of the Twentieth Anniversary of the White Paper on Employment and Income of 1945, 1966; mng. editor: Can. Jour. Econs, 1976-79; contbr. articles to profl. publs. Can. Council research grantee, 1969, 77-81; Social Sci. Research Council research fellow, 1956-57. Fellow Royal Soc. Can.; mem. Queen's Faculty Assn., Am. Econ. Assn., Can. Econs. Assn. Club: Queen's Faculty. Home: 72 Fairway Hill Crescent Kingston ON K7M 2B4 Canada Office: Dept Econs Queen's U Kingston ON K7L 3N6 Canada

KALKHOFF, RONALD KENNETH, internist, medical educator; b. Milw., Dec. 6, 1933; s. Glenn Charles and Theodora Mathilde (Peterson) K.; m. Rhea Lynn Widerborg, June 12, 1956; children: Stephanie Lynn, Cynthia Lee, Richard Graham, William Webster. B.A., Yale U., 1956; M.D., Washington U., St. Louis, 1960. Diplomate: Am. Bd. Internal Medicine. Intern St. Louis City Hosp., 1960-61; resident in internal medicine Barnes Hosp., St. Louis, 1961-62, 64-65; fellow in endocrinology and metabolism Washington U., 1962-64; asst. prof. medicine Med. Coll. Wis., Milw., 1965-71, assoc. prof., 1971-74, prof., chief endocrine-metabolic sect., 1974—; sr. staff Milw. County Med. Complex and Froedert Hosp. Editorial bd.: Diabetes: Jour. Am. Diabetes Assn, 1971-78; conbr. articles and revs. on diabetes mellitus, obesity and pancreatic islet physiology to sci. jours., chpts. to books. Fellow A.C.P.; mem. Am. Soc. Clin. Investigation, Am. Soc. Pharmacology and Exptl. Therapeutics, Am. Soc. Clin. Research, Central Soc. Clin. Research, Endocrine Soc., Am. Diabetes Assn. (Wis. dir.), AAAS. Office: Med Coll Wis 9200 W Wisconsin Ave Milwaukee WI 53226

KALLAND, LLOYD AUSTIN, clergyman; b. Superior, Wis., Aug. 8, 1914; m. Jean Williams, July 20, 1945; children—Doris Jean Kalland McDowell. A.B., Gordon Coll., 1942; B.D., Theol. Sem. Ref. Episcopal Ch., 1945; M.A., U. Pa., 1946; M.Th., Westminster Theol. Sem., 1946; Th.D., No. Bapt. Theol. Sem., 1955. Ordained to ministry Am. Bapt. Chs. in U.S.A., 1947; pastor ch., Slatington, Pa., 1946-49, Calvary Bapt. Ch., Chgo., 1949-55; lectr. N.T., No. Bapt. Theol. Sem., Chgo., 1949-51; exec. v.p. Gordon-Conwell Theol. Sem., South Hamilton, Mass., 1973—; prof. Christian ethics, 1955—. Cons. editor: The Bible Newsletter; contbr. articles to religious jours. Mem. Evang. Theol. Soc. Home: 102 Chebacco Rd South Hamilton MA 01982

KALLENBERG, JOHN KENNETH, librarian; b. Anderson, Ind., June 10, 1942; s. Herbert A. and Helen S. K.; m. Ruth Barrett, Aug. 19, 1965; children—Jennifer Anne, Gregory John. A.B., Ind. U., 1964, M.L.S., 1969. With Fresno County Library, 1965—; librarian Fig Garden Br., 1968-70, asst. library dir., Santa Barbara, Calif., 1970-76, Fresno County librarian, 1976—. Mem. Calif. Library Assn. (councilor 1975-77), Calif. County Librarians Assn. (pres. 1977), Calif. Library Authority for Systems and Services (chmn. authority adv. council 1978-80). Presbyterian. Club: Kiwanis (pres. Fresno 1981-82). Office: Fresno County Library 2420 Mariposa St Fresno CA 93721

KALLMANN, HELMUT MAX, music historian; b. Berlin, Aug. 7, 1922; emigrated to Can., 1940, naturalized, 1946; s. Arthur and Fanny (Paradies) K.; m. Ruth Singer, Dec. 31, 1955; 1 stepdau., Lynn Salter. B.Mus., U. Toronto, Ont., Can., 1949, LL.D., 1971. With CBC Music Library, Toronto, 1950-70, supr., 1962-70; chief music div. Nat. Library Can., Ottawa, Ont., 1970—; Can. del. Internat. Assn. Music Libraries, 1959-71. Author: A History of Music in Canada, 1534-1914, 1960; also articles.; editor: Catalogue of Canadian Composers, 1952; Editor: (with Gilles Potvin and Kenneth Winters) Encyclopedia of Music in Canada, 1981, French edit., 1983. Mem. Can. Music Council (v.p. 1971-76, medal 1977), Can. Assn. Music Libraries (co-founder 1956, past chmn.), Bibliog. Soc. Can., Can. Folk Music Soc., Faculty Music Alumni Assn. U. Toronto (pres. 1963-64). Home: 38 Foothills Dr Nepean ON K2H 6K3 Canada Office: 395 Wellington St Ottawa ON K1A 0N4 Canada

KALLSEN, THEODORE JOHN, retired educator; b. Jasper, Minn., Mar. 27, 1915; s. Bernhart H. and Irene (Wehrman) K.; m. Marvel J. Stordahl, Aug. 27, 1939; children: Carolyn Irene (Mrs. Harold Pate), Tonya Jo. B.S., Mankato State Coll., 1936; M.A., U. Iowa, 1940, Ph.D., 1949. Various teaching positions, Minn., Mo., Iowa, 1936-49; asst. prof. integrated studies W.Va. U., Morgantown, 1949-55; prof. English, head dept. Stephen F. Austin State U., Nacogdoches, Tex., 1955-65; prof., dean Sch. Liberal Arts, 1965-76, Disting. prof. English, 1976-80, Disting. prof. emeritus, 1980—; Cons. English curriculum pub. schs. Author: Modern Rhetoric and Usage, 1955, (with D.E.

McCoy) Reading and Rhetoric: Order and Idea, 1963, Teachers' Use of Dictating Machines, 1965, Making: Selected Poems, 1981; also traditional and concrete poetry, profl. articles. Served to lt. (j.g.) USNR, 1944-46. Mem. Nat. Council Tchrs. English, Conf. Coll. Composition and Communication (past mem. exec. com.), AAUP, Tex. Conf. Coll. Tchrs. English, Tex. Coll. English Assn. (past pres.), Modern Lang. Assn., So. Humanities Conf. Clubs: Piney Woods Country (Nacogdoches) (past dir.); East Tex. German-Am. Social (pres. 1974-76). Home: 600 Bostwick Nacogdoches TX 75961

KALMAN, ANDREW, manufacturing company executive; b. Hungary, Aug. 14, 1919; came to U.S., 1922, naturalized, 1935; s. Louis and Julia (Bognar) K.; m. Violet Margaret Kish, June 11, 1949; children: Andrew Joseph, Richard Louis, Laurie Ann. With Detroit Engring. & Machine Co., 1947-66, exec. v.p., gen. mgr., 1952-66; exec. v.p. Indian Head, Inc., 1966-75, also dir.; dir. Acme Precision Products, 1959-80, Reef Energy Corp., 1980—. Trustee Alma (Mich.) Coll.; bd. dirs. Am. Hungarian Found., New Brunswick, N.J. Home: 708 S Military Dearborn MI 48124 Office: 2616 Comerica Bldg Detroit MI 48226

KALMAN, RUDOLF EMIL, research mathematician, system scientist; b. Budapest, Hungary, May 19, 1930; s. Otto and Ursula (Grundmann) K.; m. Constantina Stavrou, Sept. 12, 1959; children: Andrew E.F.C., Elisabeth K. S.B., MIT, 1953, S.M., 1954; D.Sc., Columbia U., 1957. Staff engr. IBM Research Lab., Poughkeepsie, N.Y., 1957-58; research mathematician Research Inst. Advanced Studies, Balt., 1958-64; prof. engring. mech. and elec. engring. Stanford U., 1964-67, prof. math. system theory, 1967-71; grad. research prof., dir. Center for Math. System Theory, U. Fla., 1971—; prof. math. system theory Swiss Fed. Inst. Tech., Zurich, 1973—; sci. adviser Ecole Nationale Superieure des Mines de Paris, 1968—; mem. sci. adv. bd. Laboratorio di Cibernetica, Naples, 1970-73. Author: Topics in Mathematical System Theory, 1969; over 120 sci. and tech. papers.; editorial bd.: Jour. Math. Modelling, Math. Systems Theory, Jour. Computer and Systems Scis.; Jour. Nonlinear Analysis, Advances in Applied Math., Jour. Optimization Theory and Applications. Named outstanding young scientist Md. Acad. Sci., 1962; recipient IEEE medal of honor, 1974; Guggenheim fellow IHES Bures-sur-Yvette, 1971; Rufus Oldenburger medal ASME, 1976; Centennial medal IEEE, 1984. Fgn. hon. mem. Hungarian Acad. Scis. Office: Dept Math U Fla Gainesville FL 32611 *It is good to do everything as it was done yesterday, but it is better to examine all accepted assumptions. This is the key to scientific progress as well as to happier interpersonal relations.*

KALMANOFF, MARTIN, composer; b. Bklyn., May 24, 1920; s. Joseph and Anna (Mirin) K.; m. Margaret E. Tharaldsen, Sept. 21, 1974. B.A. cum laude, Harvard U., 1941, M.A., 1942. Composer numerous works for mus. theatre, 17 operas, including collaborations with, Saroyan, Ionesco, Eric Bentley and, Gertrude Stein; Composer works performed on, NBC, CBS and ABC Radio and TV networks; Composer works, also Carnegie Hall; composer works, Town Hall, Philharmonic Hall, Toronto Arts Centre; wrote: words and music for original mus. version of Fourposter, 1963; composer-lyricist: Young Tom Edison, 1962-78; revived, 1976; composer: children's musical Give Me Liberty, Edison Theatre, N.Y.C., 1975; on tour, 1975-76, 84-85; provided music for: movie Puccini: Portrait of a Bohemian; composer: The Joy of Prayer (Sacred Service), 1981 (Winner, Robert Merrill Contest for best one-act opera 1950, recorded by Sherrill Milnes and Am. Symphony Orch. and Chorus); Contbr. articles to profl. jours. Mem. ASCAP, Nat. Opera Assn., Central Opera Service. Home: 392 Central Park W New York NY 10025

KALMUS, ALLAN HENRY, public relations executive; b. N.Y.C., Nov. 7, 1917; s. Nathaniel I. and Louise (Simson) K.; m. Jane Waring, Sept. 9, 1944 (div. Apr. 1968); children—Susan Jane Partier, John Allan; m. Ellin Silberstein, May 16, 1969. B.A. magna cum laude, Harvard U., 1939; M.S., Columbia Grad. Sch. Journalism, 1940. News editor, pub. relations dir. Radio Sta. WQXR, N.Y.C., 1942-43; publicity dir. NBC-TV, N.Y.C., 1944-52, Lever Bros. Co., 1952-54; owner, pres. Kalmus Corp., N.Y.C., 1954—; Lectr. Columbia U. Grad. Sch., N.Y.C., 1948-53. Trustee Harry S. Truman Library Found. Mem. Tri-State Pollution Found., Pub. Relations Soc. Am., Internat. Radio and TV Soc., Overseas Press Club Am., Broadcast Pioneers, Acad. TV Arts and Scis., Phi Beta Kappa. Clubs: Sunningdale Country (Scarsdale, N.Y.); Yale of N.Y., Friars. Home: 125 E 72d St New York NY 10021 Office: Waldorf Astoria New York NY 10022

KALMUS, GEOFFREY MARTIN, lawyer; b. Long Branch, N.J., May 27, 1934; s. Arnold Jay and Muriel (Berg) K.; m. Julia H. Weinstein, Sept. 13, 1977; children—Cynthia, Theodore, Rebecca, Johanna. A.B., Harvard U., 1956, LL.B., 1959. Bar: D.C. bar 1959, N.Y. bar 1961. Law clk. to Hon. J. Edward Lumbard, U.S. Ct. Appeals for 2d Circuit, 1959-60; mem. firm Skadden, Arps, Slate, Meaghen & Flam, N.Y.C., 1960-66; partner firm Kramer, Levin, Nessen, Kamin & Soll, N.Y.C., 1968—; adj. prof. law St. John's U. Law Sch., 1961-71, Fordham U. Law Sch., 1971—. Mem. Bar Assn. of the City of N.Y., Am. Bar Assn. Home: 14 Alta Ln Chappaqua NY 10514 Office: 919 3d Ave New York NY 10022

KALOW, WERNER, pharmacologist, toxicologist; b. Cottbus, Germany, Feb. 15, 1917; emigrated to Can., 1951, naturalized, 1957; s. Johannes Bernhard and Maria Elisabeth (Heyde) K.; m. Brigitte D. von Gaza, Dec. 21, 1946; children—Peter Bernard, Barbara Irene. Student in medicine, U. Greifswald, Ger., 1935-36, U. Graz, Austria, 1936-37, U. Gottingen, Ger., 1939-40; M.D., U. Konigsberg, Ger., 1941. Research asst. Berlin U., 1947-49; research fellow, instr. U. Pa., 1949-51; lectr. U. Toronto, Ont., Can., 1951-53, asst. prof. pharmacology, 1953-55, asso. prof., 1955-62, prof., 1962—, chmn. dept. pharmacology, 1966-77; dir. biol. research C.H. Boehringer Sohn, Ingelheim, Ger., 1965-66. Author: Pharmacogenetics, Heredity and the Response to Drugs, 1962; editor: (with B.N. La Du) Pharmacogenetics, 1968. Fellow Royal Soc. Can.; Mem. Pharm. Soc. Can. (pres. 1963-64), Can. Physiol. Soc., Am. Soc. Human Genetics, Am. Soc. Pharmacology and Exptl. Therapeutics, N.Y. Acad. Scis., Deutsche Pharmakologische Gesellschaft. Discovered pharmacogenetic variants of cholinesterase, 1956; devel. pharmacodiagnosis of skeletal muscle disorders, 1970. Home: 361 Blythwood Rd Toronto ON M4N 1A7 Canada Office: Med Scis Bldg U Toronto Toronto ON M5S 1A8 Canada

KALSNER, STANLEY, educator, pharmacologist; b. N.Y.C., Aug. 21, 1936; s. William Louise and Sadie (Feldman) K.; m. Jenny Book, Aug. 4, 1963; children—Lydia, Pamela, Louisa. A.B., N.Y. U., 1958; postgrad., SUNY Downstate Med. Center, 1959-62; Ph.D., U. Man., Can., 1966, Cambridge (Eng.) U., 1966-67. Asst. prof. pharmacology U. Ottawa, Ont., Can., 1967-72, asso. prof., 1972-77, prof., 1977—; also med. research scientist; sci. referee Med. Research Council Can., Can. Heart Found. Editor, contbr. chpts. to books, articles to jours.; assoc. editor: Can. Jour. Physiology and Pharmacology; mem. editorial bd.: Jour. Autonomic Pharmacology, Blood Vessels. USPHS fellow, 1960-67; Med. Research Council-NRC and Ont. Heart Found. grantee, 1970—. Mem. AAAS, Can. Pharmacology Soc., Am. Soc. Pharmacology and Therapeutics, AAUP. Home: 994 Bronson Ave Ottawa ON Canada Office: 275 Nicholas St Ottawa ON K1N 9A9 Canada *I believe that the greatest mystery of all is life and that it is worth devoting oneself to its solution.*

KALTER, SEYMOUR SANFORD, educator, virologist; b. N.Y.C., Mar. 19, 1918; s. Aaron H. and Jessie (Schulman) K.; m. Gloria V. Verstein, Mar. 3, 1946 (dec.); children: Susan P., Steven P., Debra I.; m. Yvette L. Levine, Apr. 15, 1982. B.S., St. Joseph's Coll., Phila., 1940; M.A., U. Kans., 1943; postgrad., U. Pa., 1943-45; Ph.D., Syracuse U., 1947. Diplomate: Am. Bd. Microbiology. Asst. instr. microbiology U. Kans., 1941-43; research asst. dept. med. bacteriology U. Pa., 1943-45; asst. and asso. prof. med. microbiology Upstate Med. Center, N.Y. State U., Syracuse, 1945-56; cons. virology Pan Am. San. Bur., 1959-62, Cologne (Germany) U.; adj. prof. dept. biology Trinity U., San Antonio, 1967—; dept. pediatrics U. Tex. Health Sci. Center, San Antonio, 1971—; dept. life scis. (microbiology) U. Tex., San Antonio, 1976—; dental br. Dental Sci. Inst., U. Tex. Health Sci. Center, Houston, 1976—; adj. prof. dept. microbiology U. Tex. Health Sci. Center, San Antonio, 1973-75; chief virus diagnostic methodology unit Communicable Disease Center, USPHS, Atlanta, 1956-61; chief virology sect. Sch. Aerospace Medicine, Brooks AFB, Tex., 1961-63; chmn. dept. microbiology Southwest Found. Research and Edn., 1963-66, dir. dept. microbiology and infectious diseases, 1966—; cons. M.D. Anderson Hosp. and Tumor Inst., Houston, 1974—; cons. study zoonoses of primates WHO, also WHO Smallpox Eradication Unit, 1976—; cons. biohazards control and containment sect. Nat. Cancer Inst., 1968-74; chmn. com. simian viruses WHO/FAO; cons. Office Pesticide Programs, EPA, 1973-75, Diagnostic Products Adv. Com., FDA, 1975-83; research adv. Alamo chpt. Nat. Multiple Sclerosis Soc., San Antonio, 1970—. Fellow AAAS, Am. Pub. Health Assn., Tex. Pub. Health Assn.; mem. Am. Assn. Lab. Animal Sci., Am. Inst. Biol. Scis., Am. Soc. Primatologists, Assn. Gnotobiotics, Internat. Assn. Biol. Standardization, Internat. Assn. Comparative Research on Leukemia and Related Diseases, Tissue Culture Assn., U.S. Fedn. Culture Collection, Internat. Primatol. Soc., Am. Acad. Microbiology, Am. Soc. Virology, Am. Assn. Immunologists, Am. Assn. Lab. Animal Sci., Soc. Exptl. Biology and Medicine, N.Y., Tex. acads. scis., Am., Tex. socs. microbiologists, Am. Soc. Tropical Medicine and Hygiene, Royal Soc. Health (Eng.), Tex. Soc. Electron Microscopy, Am. Soc. Cryobiology, Wildlife Diseases Assn., Sigma Xi. Office: PO Box 28147 San Antonio TX 78284

KALTHOFF, KLAUS OTTO, zoology educator; b. Iserlohn, Nordrhein-Westfalen, Germany, Feb. 5, 1941; came to U.S., 1978; s. Hugo and Herta (Brenken) K.; m. Karin Dora Losskarn, Dec. 23, 1965; children: Christian, Ulrich, Philipp. B.A., U. Hamburg, 1964; M.A., U. Freiburg, 1967, Ph.D, 1971. Instr. U. Frieburg, W. Germany, 1969-71; asst. prof. U. Freiburg, W. Germany, 1971-76; assoc. prof. U. Frieburg, W. Germany, 1976-78, U. Tex.-Austin, 1978-80, prof. zoology, 1980—; dir. Ctr. for Devel. Biology, 1983—. Recipient prize for outstanding research work Sci. Soc. Freiburg, 1975; hon. guest mem. Arthropodan Embryology Soc. Japan. Mem. AAAS, Am. Soc. Photobiology, Soc. for Devel. Biology, European Devel. Biologist Orgn., Gesellschaft fuer Entwicklungsbiologie. Office: Dept Zoology U Tex Austin TX 78712

KALTINICK, PAUL R., trust co. exec.; b. N.Y.C., Dec. 1, 1932; s. Morris and Vera (Halpern) K.; m. Alice Levy, Dec. 26, 1954; children—Vera, Marjorie, Pamela. B.B.A. in Acctg, Pace U., 1954. Accountant Peat, Marwick, Mitchell, N.Y.C., 1959-61, mgmt. cons., 1961-63; exec. v.p. Flowerized Presentations, N.Y.C., 1963-64; with J.C. Penney Co., Inc., N.Y.C., 1964-80, v.p., 1974-80, dir. fin. mgmt., 1976-78, dir. tech. support ops., 1978-80; pres., chief exec. officer Frank Russell Trust Co., Tacoma, 1980—. Served with USMC, 1954-56. Mem. Am. Inst. C.P.A.'s, N.Y. State Soc. C.P.A.'s, Fin. Execs. Inst., Treasurers Club. Home: 30 Silver Beach Dr Steilacoom WA 98388 Office: First Interstate Plaza Tacoma WA 98402

KAMAL, MUSA RASIM, chemical engineer; b. Tulkarm, Jordan, Dec. 8, 1934; s. Rasim Kamal and Aminah Masoud (Abu-Hadbah) Ismail; m. Nancy Joan Edgar, Dec. 23, 1961; children: Rammie, Basim. B.S., U. Ill., 1958; M.Eng., Carnegie-Mellon U., 1959, Ph.D., 1961; postgrad., Columbia U., 1964. Research chem. engr. Am. Cyanamid Co., Stamford, Conn., 1961-65, research group leader, project mgr., Wallingford, 1965-67; assoc. prof. chem. engring. dept. McGill U., Montreal, Que., Can., 1967-73, prof., 1973—, chmn. dept. chem. engring., 1983—; head indsl. and engring. sect., 5-year Morocco indsl. investment plan project Dar Al-Handasah Consultants, Rabat, 1977—; pres. Tulkarm Enterprises Ltd., Montreal, 1976—; Co-founder, v.p. South-Western Fairfield County UN Assn., 1965; Bd. dirs. Plastics Edn. Found.; adv. bd. engring. and sci.; program chmn. 2d World Congress Chem. Engring., Montreal, 1981. Editor: Weatherability of Plastic Materials, 1967; Contbr. articles to profl. jours. Trustee Student Aid Internat., 1978—. Research grantee NRC of Can., 1967—, Que. Govt., 1971—. Fellow Chem. Inst. Can. (bd. dirs., dir. macromolecular sci. div.); mem. Canadian Soc. Chem. Engring. (treas. 1969-72), Am. Inst. Physics, Soc. Rheology, Am. Inst. Chem. Engrs., Am. Chem. Soc., AAAS, Soc. Plastics Engrs. (dir. plastics analysis div., engring. properties and structure div.), N.Y. Acad. Scis., UN Assn. Can., Sigma Xi, Phi Lambda Upsilon, Pi Mu Epsilon, Tau Beta Pi. Clubs: Montreal Amateur Athletic Assn., Canadian (Montreal). Patentee in field. Home: 338 Roslyn Ave Westmount PQ Canada H3Z 2L6 Office: Chem Engring Dept McGill U Montreal PQ Canada

KAMALI, NORMA, designer; b. N.Y.C., June 27, 1945; d. Sam and Estelle (Grub) Mariategui. Grad., Fashion Inst., 1967-78. With, Kamali Ltd., N.Y.C., 1967-78; owner, designer, O.M.O. Norma Kamali, N.Y.C., 1978—. Office: 11 W 56th St New York NY 10019 *

KAMAN, CHARLES HURON, corporation executive; b. Washington, June 15, 1919; s. Charles W. and Mabel (Davis) K.; m. Helen Sylvander, Oct. 20, 1945 (div.); children: Charles William II, Cathleen, Steven Wardner; m. Roberta C. Hallock, Sept. 1, 1971. B.S. in Aero. Engring. magna cum laude, Cath. U. Am., 1940. With Hamilton Standard Propellers div. United Aircraft Corp., East Hartford, Conn., 1940-45; chmn. bd., pres. Kaman Corp., Bloomfield, Conn., 1945—; dir. Hartford Nat. Corp., Security-Conn. Life Ins. Co., Emhart Corp., Conn. Nat. Bank; chmn. Vertical Lift Aircraft Council, 1954, 64. Bd. govs. Cath. U. Am.; bd. dirs. Inst. of Living; founder, bd. dirs. Fidelco Guide Dog Found., Inc. Recipient Disting. Service award Conn. Jr. C. of C., 1953, Engr. of Year award, 1961; Alumni Achievement award Cath. U. Am., 1961. Fellow Am. Helicopter Soc. (pres. 1958, dir. 1959-61, Dr. Alexander Klemin award 1981), AIAA; mem. Conn. Bus. and Industry Assn. (dir., exec. com.), Nat. Acad. Engring., Conn. Soc. Profl. Engrs., Aviation Hall of Fame (charter), Navy Helicopter Assn. (hon.),, ward 1975), Pi Tau Sigma (hon.), Beta Gamma Sigma. Office: Kaman Corp Old Windsor Rd Bloomfield CT 06002 *

KAMARCK, ANDREW MARTIN, economist; b. Newton Falls, N.Y., Nov. 10, 1914; s. Martin and Frances (Earl) K.; m. Margaret Ellen Goldenweiser, Oct. 25, 1941; children: Ellen Mary, Elizabeth Anne, Martin Alexander. B.S. summa cum laude, Harvard, 1936, M.A., 1939, Ph.D. in Polit. Econs. and Govt, 1951. Economist Fed. Res. Bd., 1939-40; confidential adv. to sec. treasury, 1940-42; dep. dir. finance div. U.S. group Allied Control Council, Germany, 1945; with Treasury Dept., 1946-48; U.S. Treasury rep., Rome, 1948-50; econ. adviser World Bank, 1950-64, dir. econs. dept., 1965-71; dir. and sr. fellow Econ. Devel. Inst., 1971-78; assoc. fellow Harvard Inst. Internat. Devel., 1978—; pres. Housing Assistance Corp. of Cape Cod, 1980—; lectr. Sch. Advanced Internat. Studies, Johns Hopkins U., 1958-76; Regents prof. U. Calif. at Los Angeles, 1964. Author: The Economics of African Development, 1971, The Tropics and Economic Development, 1976, La Politica Finanziara degli Alleati in Italia, 1977, Economics and the Real World, 1983. Served to maj. F.A. AUS, 1942-44; Italy. Recipient Certificate of Merit War Dept., 1945. Fellow African Studies Assn.; mem. Am. Econ. Assn., Council Fgn. Relations, Phi Beta Kappa. Democrat. Unitarian. Home: 118 Pine Ridge Rd Rural Route 1 Brewster MA 02631

KAMATS, GEORGE MICHAEL, airline executive; b. Emporium, Pa., May 7, 1935; s. George and Clara (Zoschg) K.; m. Kathleen D. Sinnes, Feb. 14, 1959; children—Cynthia Louise, Richard Joseph, George Michael, Susan Kathleen. B.B.A., U. Miami, 1964. C.P.A., Calif. Jr. accountant John J. Barry (C.P.A.), Coral Gables, Fla., 1959-61; chief accountant Saturn Airways, Inc., Oakland, Calif., 1961-65, comptroller, 1965-67, asst. sec., asst. treas., 1967-69, treas., 1969-71, sr. v.p. adminstrn., 1972-74; also dir.; exec. v.p., chief operating officer Alaska Internat. Air, Inc., Fairbanks, 1974-75, pres., chief exec. officer, 1975-76; asst. to pres. Capitol Internat. Airways, Inc., Smyrna, Tenn., 1976-77; v.p. adminstrn. and fin. Gt. No. Airlines Inc., Anchorage, 1977-79; v.p. fin. and planning Internat. Air Leases Inc., Miami, Fla., 1979-80; chmn., chief exec. officer chief operating officer Capitol Air,, Smyrna, Tenn., 1980—. Served with USAF, 1955-59. Home: Route 11 Box 386A Murfreesboro TN 37130 Office: Smyrna Airport Smyrna TN 37167

KAMB, WALTER BARCLAY, educator, geologist; b. San Jose, Calif., Dec. 17, 1931; s. Karl Walter and Eleanor (Williams) K.; m. Linda Helen Pauling, Sept. 8, 1957; children: Barclay James, Carl Alexander, Anthony Pauling, Linus Peter. B.S. in Physics, Calif. Inst. Tech., 1952, Ph.D. in Geology, 1956. Mem. faculty Calif. Inst. Tech., 1956—, prof. geology and geophysics, 1961—; chmn. div. geol. and planetary scis., 1972-83. Guggenheim fellow, 1960; Sloan fellow, 1964. Fellow Geol. Soc. Am., Mineral. Soc. Am. (award 1968); mem. Am. Geophys. Union, Am. Assn. Petroleum Geologists. Home: 3500 Fairpoint St Pasadena CA 91107

KAMBARA, GEORGE KIYOSHI, ophthalmologist; b. Sacramento, Feb. 23, 1916; s. Motomu and Kusui K.; m. May Fumiko Tanaka, Sept. 28, 1941; children: Kay Janet Kambara Furuyama, Ken Gene, Kary Ann Kambara, Kim Rae Kambara Dorman. B.A., Stanford U., 1937, M.D., 1941. Intern in surgery Stanford U. Hosps., San Francisco, 1940-41; resident Stanford Ln. Hosp., 1941-42, Memphis Eye, Ear, Nose and Throat Hosp., 1943-44, State of Wis. Hosp., Madison, 1945-46; instr. ophthalmology U. Wis. Med. Sch., Madison, 1946-48, Loma Linda (Calif.) Sch. Medicine, 1948-52, asst. prof., 1952-57, asso. prof., 1957-62, clin. prof., 1962—; clin. prof. ophthalomogy U. Calif.-Calif. Coll Medicine, Irvine, 1969-72, U. So. Calif. Sch. Medicine, Los Angeles, 1972—; mem. staff Los Angeles County Hosp., 1949-66, Olive View Hosp., 1969—; chmn. dept. ophthalmology White Meml. Hosp. Med. Center, 1965—, pres. med. staff, 1968; pres. attending mem.'s assns. Rancho Los Amigos Hosp., 1970; dir. Merit Savs. and Loan, Los Angeles. Mem. Los Angeles Soc. Ophthalmology (pres. 1968), Calif. Med. Assn. (chmn. eye sect. 1970, chmn. adv. panel to eye sect. 1972-74). Office: 321 E 2d St Los Angeles CA 90012

KAMEMOTO, FRED ISAMU, zoologist; b. Honolulu, Mar. 8, 1928; s. Shuichi and Matsu (Murase) K.; m. Alice Takeyo Asayama, July 20, 1963; children: Kenneth, Garett, Janice. Student, U. Hawaii, 1946-48; A.B., George Washington U., 1950, M.S., 1951; Ph.D., Purdue U., 1954. Research asso., acting instr. Wash. State U., 1957-59; asst. prof. zoology U. Mo., 1959-62; asst. prof. U. Hawaii, Honolulu, 1962-64, asso. prof., 1964-69, prof. zoology, 1969—, chmn. dept., 1964-65, 71-80, 81—; vis. research scholar Ocean Research Inst., U. Tokyo, Biol. Lab., Fukuoka U., 1968-69; vis. prof. Coll. Agr. and Vet. Medicine, Nihon U., Tokyo, summer 1973, 1979; vis. scholar dept. biology Conn. Wesleyan U., 1975-76. Contbr. articles to profl. jours. Served with AUS, 1954-57. NSF grantee, 1960-79. Fellow AAAS; mem. Am. Soc. Zoologists, Western Soc. Naturalists, Hawaiian Acad. Sci., Sigma Xi. Buddhist. Home: 3664 Waaloa Way Honolulu HI 96822 Office: Dept Zoology U Hawaii Honolulu HI 96822

KAMEMOTO, HARUYUKI, educator; b. Honolulu, Jan. 19, 1922; s. Shuichi and Matsu (Murase) K.; m. Ethel Hideko Kono, June 7, 1952; children—David Yukio, Mark Toshio, Claire Naomi. B.S., U. Hawaii, 1944, M.S., 1947; Ph.D., Cornell U., 1950. Asst. in horticulture U. Hawaii, Honolulu, 1944-47, asst. prof. horticulture, 1950-54, asso. prof., 1954-58, prof., 1958—, chmn. dept., 1969-75; horticulture adviser Kasetsart U., Bangkok, Thailand, U. Hawaii AID contract, 1962-65; UNFAO hort. cons. to, India, 1971, 80. Author: (with R. Sagarik) Beautiful Thai Orchid Species, 1975; contbr. articles to profl. jours. Fulbright research fellow Kyoto U., Japan, 1956-57; recipient Gold medal Malayan Orchid Soc., 1964; Norman Jay Coleman award Am. Assn. Nurserymen, 1977. Fellow AAAS, Am. Soc. Hort. Sci.; hon. mem. Am. Orchid Soc., Japan Orchid Soc., Orchid Soc. Thailand (award of honor 1978), Orchid Soc. S.E. Asia; mem. Am. Genetic Assn., Am. Hort. Soc., Bot. Soc. Am., Internat. Soc. Hort., Internat. Assn. Plant Taxonomy, Soc. Advancement Breeding Research in Asia and Oceania, Phi Kappa Phi. Home: 3246 Lower Rd Honolulu HI 96822 Office: 3190 Maile Way Honolulu HI 96822

KAMEN, HARRY PAUL, life insurance company executive; b. Montreal, Que., Can., June 17, 1933; came to U.S., 1936, naturalized, 1945; s. Benjamin and Manya (Manishin) K.; m. Susan J. Klein, Feb. 1, 1958; children—Katherine, Abigail. A.B., U. Pa., 1954; LL.B., Harvard U., 1957; Postgrad. Sr. Exec. Program, MIT. Bar: Ohio bar 1957, N.Y. bar 1958. With Met. Life Ins. Co., N.Y.C., 1959—, v.p., sec., asso. gen. counsel, 1979-83, sr. v.p., sec., 1983—. Co-author: Comentaries on Debenture Indentures, 1971. Mem. N.Y.C. Community Bd. 5, 1978—. Served with AUS, 1957. Mem. ABA (sec. com. corp. laws, sect. corp., banking and bus. law 1979—), Assn. Life Ins. Counsel, Am. Soc. Corp. Secs., Phi Beta Kappa. Clubs: Harvard (N.Y.C.); E. Hampton Tennis. Home: 200 E 78th St New York City NY 10021 Office: 1 Madison Ave New York City NY 10010

KAMENETZ, HERMAN LEO, physician; b. Kaunas, Russia, Sept. 1, 1907; came to U.S., 1953, naturalized, 1958; s. Leo I. and Flora (Bernstein) K.; m. Georgette Barbaix, Feb. 13, 1947. M.S., U. Paris, 1945, M.D., 1952. Diplomate: Am. Bd. Phys. Medicine and Rehab. Intern St. Anthony Hosp., Rockford, Ill., 1953-54; resident in phys. medicine State Vets. Hosp., Rocky Hill, Conn., 1954-56, Yale-New Haven Hosp., 1956-57; chief phys. medicine Woodruff Hosp., New Haven, 1957-59, State Vets. Hosp., Rocky Hill, 1959-75, chief profl. services, 1960-66; chief rehab. medicine service VA Med. Center, Washington, 1975—; physician out-patient dept. Yale-New Haven Hosp., 1960-75; cons. phys. medicine St. Francis Hosp., Hartford, Conn., 1964-75, Masonic Hosp., Wallingford, Conn., 1965-74, Waterbury (Conn.) Hosp., 1968-75, Manchester (Conn.) Meml. Hosp., 1969-70, Gaylord Rehab. Hosp., Wallingford, Conn., 1970-75; clin. instr. phys. medicine Yale U., 1958-64, asst. clin. prof. medicine, 1964-70; clin. prof. medicine George Washington U. Sch. Medicine and Health Scis., 1975—; professorial lectr. Dept. Phys. Medicine and Rehab., Georgetown U. Sch. Medicine, 1976—. Author: Physiatric

Dictionary, 1965, The Wheelchair Book, 1969, (with Georgette Kamenetz) Dictionnaire de Medecine Physique, de Reeducation et Readaptation Fonctionnelles, 1972, English-French and French-English Dictionary of Physical Medicine and Rehabilitation, 1972, Dictionary of Rehabilitation Medicine, 1983; asst. editor: Medical Hydrology, 1963, Medical Climatology, 1964, Therapeutic Heat and Cold, 1965, Orthotics Etcetera, 1966, Rehabilitation and Medicine, 1968, Arthritis and Physical Medicine, 1969; editor for U.S.: Editorial Com. of Scandinavian-English Rehab. Terminology; contbr. articles in field to profl. books and jours. Mem. Am. Congress. Rehab. Medicine, AAAS, Conn. Soc. Phys. Medicine (pres.), Am. Med. Writers Assn., Internat. Soc. History Medicine, Conn. Hosp. Assn., Am. Soc. Med. Hydrology, Yale Med. Assn., Internat. Rehab. Medicine Assn., Internat. Soc. Prosthetics and Orthotics. Home: The Chatham Apt 824 4501 Arlington Blvd Arlington VA 22203 Office: VA Med Center 50 Irving St NW Washington DC 20422 *I consider education basic to development, self-reliance basic to achievement, and hardship the best road to both.*

KAMENSKE, BERNARD HAROLD, journalist, communications specialist; b. Nashua, N.H., Oct. 11, 1927; s. Nathan and Golda Baila (Glassman) K.; m. Gloria Lee Cheek, Dec. 19, 1960. Grad. pvt. sch., Boston. Writer, editor AP, Boston, 1944-45; news writer, editor Sta. WCOP, Cowles Communications Corp., Boston, 1946-50; news dir. Sta. WORL, Boston, 1950-51; news writer, editor Voice of Am., USIA, Washington, 1955-81, chief current affairs div., 1972-74, chief news div., 1974-81; sr. news editor Cable News Network, 1981-82; pres. newsviews, Inc., 1982—; lectr. in field. Served with U.S. Army, 1951-52. Recipient Superior Service award USIA, 1966. Mem. Nat. Assn. Radio and TV News Dirs., Nat. Acad. Polit. and Social Sci., Am. Fgn. Service Assn., Photog. Soc. Am., Soc. Profl. Journalists-Sigma Delta Chi. Club: Nat. Press Club. Home and Office: 1 Buttonwood Ln Bethesda MD 20816

KAMENTSKY, LOUIS AARON, biophysicist; b. Newark, July 28, 1930; s. Harry and Etta (Brodsky) K.; m. Marcia Alpern, Aug. 28, 1955; children: Lee, Howard, Ellen. B.S.E.E., N.J. Inst. Tech., 1952; Ph.D., Cornell U., 1956. Mem. staff Colombia U. ERL, N.Y.C., 1954-55, Bell Telephone Labs., Murray Hill, N.J., 1956-60, IBM Research, N.Y.C., 1960-68; pres. Biophysics Systems, Mahopac, N.Y., 1968-76; v.p. research Ortho Diagnostics Systems, Cambridge, Mass., 1976—; mem. staff Colombia U. ERL, N.Y.C., 1954-55; sr. research scientist MIT, Cambridge, 1981—. Patentee in field; contbr. articles to profl. jours. Home: 261 Country Dr Weston MA 02193 Office: Ortho Diagnostic Systems 195 Albany St Cambridge MA 02139

KAMENY, NAT, advertising executive; b. N.Y.C., Nov. 6, 1923; s. Michel and Bessie (Sunshine) K.; m. Ruth Zatal, Mar. 27, 1943; children: Ellen, Leslie, Debra. Student, CCNY, 1941-42, 46-47. Propr. Camenard Studios (profl. photographers), 1945; founder, chmn. KSW & G, Inc. (advt.), N.Y.C., 1946-78; pres. Israel Communications, Inc. (pub. relations), 1969-78, Kameny Communications, Inc., 1978—; dir. Agnekolor Systems Corp. Past pres. Jewish Fedn. Bergen County; vice chmn. pub. relations com. Council Jewish Fedns.; nat. vice-chmn., chmn. nat. communications com., nat. budget com., nat. commr. Anti-Defamation League; sec. N.Am. Jewish Students Appeal; vice-chmn. Nat. Jewish Community Relations Adv. Council; exec. com. Greater N.Y. Conf. on Soviet Jewry; plenum mem. Nat. Conf. Soviet Jewry; mem. exec. com. Jewish Telegraphic Agy.; bd. dirs. Radius Inst., Jewish Hosp. and Rehab. Center, Nat. Yiddish Book Center; asst. to mayor, Bergenfield, N.J., 1960-62, indsl. commr., Bergenfield, 1960-64; vice chmn. Bergenfield Planning Bd., 1960-67; Chmn. Bergen County Democratic Campaign Com., 1960-61. Mem. Am. Assn. Advt. Agys., League Advt. Agys. (pres. 1962-63), Am.-Israel C. of C. (dir), Overseas Press Club. Lodge: B'nai B'rith. Home and Office: 85 Thames Blvd Bergenfield NJ 07621

KAMERICK, JOHN JOSEPH, univ. pres.; b. Ottumwa, Iowa, Dec. 30, 1919; s. Harry Herman and Catherine Cecilia (Doyle) K.; m. Elaine Elizabeth Lenney, Aug. 7, 1948; children—Maureen Margaret, Michael John, Sheila Catherine, Kathleen, Eileen, Megan. B.A., St. Ambrose Coll., 1943, D.Pub. Adminstrn. (hon.), 1973; M.A., State U. Iowa, 1947, Ph.D., 1950; LL.D., Loras Coll., 1971. Reporter, 1940-43; instr. U. Iowa, 1948-50; asst. prof. Marycrest Coll., 1950-51; dean studies Lewis Coll. Sci. and Tech., 1951-56; asst. dean Coll. Arts and Scis., Kent State U., 1956-59, dean, 1959-63, v.p., dean faculties, 1963-66, v.p., provost, 1966-68; pres. N. Tex. State U., Denton, 1968-70, U. No. Iowa Cedar Falls, 1970—; Accreditation examiner, cons. N. Central Assn., 1966—; mem. commn. instns. higher edn.; chmn. Iowa Coordinating Council for Post High Sch. Edn., 1973; pres. Iowa Coll. Assn., 1976-77. Trustee Selwyn Sch., Denton, Tex., Ottumwa (Iowa) Heights Coll., Mercy Coll., Cedar Rapids, Iowa. Served to lt. (s.g.) USNR, 1943-46. Mem. Am. Assn. State Colls. and Univs. (chmn.-elect 1980-81, chmn. 1981-82, dir. 1980—), Am. Council Edn. (dir. 1981-82). Democrat. Roman Catholic. Home: 2501 College St Cedar Falls IA 50613

KAMERMAN, SHEILA BRODY, social worker, educator; b. U.S., Jan. 7, 1928; d. S. Lawrence and Helen (Golding) Brody; m. Morton Kammerman, Sept. 11, 1947; children: Nathan Brody, Elliot Herbert, Laura Kamerman-Barouch. B.A., N.Y.U., 1946; M.S.W., Hunter Coll., 1966; D. Social Welfare, Columbia U., 1973. Social worker N.Y.C. Dept. Social Services, 1966-68; social work supr. Bellevue Psychiat. Hosp., 1968-69; research assoc., sr. research assoc. Columbia U. Sch. Social Work, 1971-77, assoc. prof. social policy and planning, 1979-81, prof., 1981—; co-dir. Cross Nat. Studies, Columbia U. Sch. Social Work; chmn. Nat. Acad. Sci.-NRC panel on work, family and community, 1980-82, com. child devel. researchand pub. policy, 1983—; cons. in field, mem. numerous social welfare program coms. and adv. bds. Author: (with Alfred J. Kahn) Not for the Poor Alone, 1975, Social Services in the United State, 1976, Social Services in International Perspective, 1977, Family Policy: Government and Families in Fourteen Countries, 1978, Child Car, Family Benefits and Working Parents, 1981, Parenting in the Unresponsive Society, 1980, Maternity and Parental Benefits and Leaves, 1980, Helping America's Families, 1982, Maternity Policies and Working Women, 1983, Income Transfers for Families with Children, 1983; contbr. numerous articles to profl. jours. Recipient Hunter Coll. Sch. Social Work Alumna Hexter award, 1977; fellow Ctr. Advanced Study in Behavioral Scis., 1983-84. Mem. Nat. Assn. Social Workers, Am. Pub. Welfare Assn., Am. Soc. Pub. Adminstrn., Assn. Policy Analysis and Mgmt., Gerontol. Soc., Phi Beta Kappa. Home: 1125 Park Ave New York NY 10028

KAMEROW, MARTIN LAURENCE, accountant; b. Washington, Aug. 25, 1931; s. Jacob A. and Anne (Adler) K.; m. Corinne Perlmeter, Mar. 24, 1951; children: Deborah, Jacqueline, Haskell. B.C.S., Benjamin Franklin U., 1951, M.C.S., 1952. C.P.A., Washington. Staff accountant various C.P.A. firms, Washington, 1949-52, individual practice accounting, 1952-59; partner firm Kamerow & Serber, Washington, 1959-63; sr. partner firm Harab, Kamerow & Serber, Washington, 1963-74; pres. Harab, Kamerow & Assos. (P.C.), 1974—; dir. Universal Bindery, Inc., Toledo, Campbell Photo Service, Inc., Washington, other cos.; Lectr. Am. U., 1956-65, tax seminars, insts.; mem. faculty 39th N.Y. U. Inst. on Fed. Taxation, 1980; cons. to editor book div. U.S. News & World Report. Author: (with S.A. Kaufman) Consolidated Financial Statements, 1958, (with S. Green) U.S. News and World Reports Book on Income Taxes, 1971—, 4th edit., 1974, (with Margaret Daly) Teach Your Wife to be a Widow; contbr. articles to profl. jours. Mem. nat. council United Synagogue of Am., 1969-76, regional treas., 1969-76; mem. Zionist Youth Commn., Bd. Jewish Edn.; chmn. advance gifts United Jewish Appeal campaign, 1975; pres. L.D. Brandeis dist. Zionist Orgn. Am., 1971-75; Trustee, mem. exec. com. Jewish Social Service Agys., 1973-76; pres. Shma V'ezer Sch. Spl. Edn.; bd. dirs. World Council Synagogues, Hebrew Acad., Washington; bd. dirs., v.p. Jewish Nat. Fund; bd. dirs., treas., mem. exec. com. United Jewish Appeal D.C.; exec. com. Jewish Community Council; nat. bd. dirs. Zionist Orgn. Am.; bd. dirs. Goldman Endowment Fund, Found. Soviet Studies. Served with inf. AUS, 1951-53. Recipient Nat. Kidney Found. Service award, 1969; Disting. Alumni award Benjamin Franklin U., 1977; award United Jewish Appeal, 1978; Louis D. Brandeis award, 1982. Mem. Am. Inst. C.P.A.s (tax com.), Assn. Practicing C.P.A.s (pres. 1972-74), Inst. C.P.A.s in Israel, Sigma Alpha Rho. Jewish (v.p. temple). Clubs: Nat. Press, Touchdown (Washington). Home: 7420 Westlake Terr Bethesda MD 20034 Office: 805 15th St Suite 327 NW Washington DC 20817 *In all things success depends upon adequate preparation.*

KAMERSCHEN, DAVID ROY, economist, educator; b. Chgo., Dec. 8, 1937; s. Robert R. and Elsie D. K.; m. Patricia Barbara Wait, Dec. 26, 1959; children: Christine, Steven, Laura, Robert. Student, Ind. U., 1959-60; B.S. in Econs., Miami U., Oxford, Ohio, 1959, M.A., 1960; Ph.D. in Econs., Mich. State U., 1964. Instr. dept. econs. Miami U., Oxford, Ohio, 1960-61; asst. instr. Mich. State U., summer 1962, 64; asst. prof. econs. U. Washington, St. Louis, 1964-65 65-66; assoc. prof. econs. U. Mo.-Columbia, 1966-68, prof., 1968-74; prof., head dept. econs. U. Ga., Athens, 1974-80, Disting. prof., Jasper N. Dorsey chair pub. utilities econs., 1980—; cons. antitrust and pub. utilities fields; guest appearance Mac Neil-Lehrer Report; host TV show Kamerschen Report. Author: Readings in Microeconomics, 1969, (with Walter L. Johnson) Macroeconomics: Selected Readings, 1970, Reading in Economic Development, 1972, (with George M. Vredeveld) Economics, 1975, (with Lloyd Valentine) Intermediate Microeconomic Theory, 1977, 2d edit., 1981, Money and Banking, 1976, 8th edit., 1984; editor: Rev. Social Theory, 1973-74; mem. editorial bds.: Bus. and Govt. Rev., 1968-72, Internat. Behavioral Scientist, 1970—, Indsl. Orgn. Rev., 1974-80, Rev. Bus. and Econ. Research, 1974—, So. Econ. Jour., 1978-82. Recipient Outstanding Grad. Tchr. award U. Ga., 1978; Amy Hayden scholar, 1959; Mich. State U. fellow, 1964. Mem. Am. Econ. Assn., So. Econ. Assn., Miss. Valley Econ. Assn., Am. Statis. Assn., Econometric Soc., Phi Kappa Phi, Delta Sigma Pi, Beta Gamma Sigma, Omicron Delta Kappa, Sigma Alpha Epsilon. Roman Catholic. Home: 162 Chalfont ln Apt 4 Athens GA 30606 Office: Dept Econs U Ga Brooks Hall Athens GA 30602

KAMERSCHEN, ROBERT JEROME, consumer products executive; b. Laurium, Mich., Feb. 16, 1936; s. Robert Raymond and Elsie D. (Barsanti) K.; m. Judith A. Campbell, July 26, 1958; children: Kathryn, Carol, Jean. B.S., Miami U., Oxford, Ohio, 1957, M.B.A., 1958. Exec. sales trainee Nat. Cash Register, Gary, Ind., 1958-59; mktg. research analyst Foote Cone & Belding, Chgo., 1959-60; dir. consumer mktg. Scott Paper Co., Phila., 1960-71; v.p. mktg. Revlon Inc., N.Y.C., 1971-73; sr. v.p. mktg. ops. Dunkin Donuts Inc., Randolph, Mass., 1973-77; pres., chief operating officer Chanel Inc. and Christian Dior Parfums Inc., N.Y.C., 1977-79; sr. v.p. Norton Simon Inc., N.Y.C., 1979-80; pres., chief exec. officer Max Factor & Co., Hollywood, Calif., 1979-83; exec. v.p., sector exec. Norton Simon Inc., 1980—; disting. practitioner/lectr. Coll. Bus. Adminstrn., U. Ga., 1978-80; guest lectr. various univs., trade assns. Mem. Bus. Adv. Council, exec.-in-residence Miami U., 1979—. Mem. Cosmetics Fragrance and Toiletries Assn. (dir.), Order Artus, Beta Gamma Sigma, Delta Sigma Pi, Sigma Alpha Epsilon. Clubs: N.Y. Athletic, Met., Can. (N.Y.C.). Home: 204 Parade Hill Rd New Canaan CT 06840 Office: Norton Simon 1114 Ave of Americas 30th Floor New York NY 10036

KAMIN, BENJAMIN ALON, rabbi, writer; b. Kfar-Saba, Israel, Jan. 11, 1953; came to U.S., 1962; s. Jeff Israel K. and Ruth (Flek) Nizar; m. Cathy Jill Rosen, June 8, 1975; children: Sari Judith, Debra Eve. B.A. with honors, U. Cin., 1974; M.A.H.L., Hebrew Union Coll., Cin., 1977, rabbi, 1978. Ordained rabbi, 1978. Asst. rabbi Temple Sinai Congregation, Toronto, Ont., Can., 1978-81; rabbi Sinai Reform Temple, Bay Shore, N.Y., 1981-82; N.Am. dir. World Union for Progressive Judaism, N.Y.C., 1982—; program unit head Union Camp Inst., Zionsville, Ind., 1977; rabbinic dean Can. Fedn. Temple Youth, Toronto, 1979-81; admissions com. Hebrew Union Coll., Cin., 1977-78, instr., N.Y.C., 1983; polit. columnist News Record, Cin., 1970-73. Author: poetry series Everything is Falling Into Place, 1970; Be Glad You Can Feel Enough, 1978 (Kahn oratory prize 1978); contbr. editorials to newspaper and periodicals; author short story. Pres. Cin Council World Affairs, 1969-70. Named Young Citizen of Week City of Cin., 1969. Mem. Central Conf. Am. Rabbis, Assn. Reform Zionists of Am. (bd. dirs.). Democrat. Home: 475 Lenox Ave South Orange NJ 07079 Office: World Union for Progressive Judaism 838 Fifth Ave New York NY 10021

KAMIN, HENRY, biochemist; b. Warsaw, Poland, Oct. 24, 1920; came to U.S., 1926, naturalized, 1932; s. Benjamin and Paula (Mirkowicz) K.; m. Dorothy Lee Lingle, Oct. 30, 1943. B.S., CCNY, 1940; Ph.D., Duke U., 1948. Prin. scientist VA Hosp., Durham, N.C., 1953-68; instr., asso. biochemistry Duke U. Med. Center, 1950-55, asst. prof., 1955-59, asso. prof., 1959-65, prof., 1965—; cons. in field; mem. various profl. coms. including food and nutrition bd. NRC-Nat. Acad. Scis., 1978—, vice chmn., 1979-81, chmn. dietary allowances com., 1980—. Editor: Flavins and Flavoproteins III, 1971; contbr. numerous articles to profl. jours., 1941—; editorial bd.: Jour. Biol. Chemistry, 1974-79, 82—. Served to 1st lt. San Corps, U.S. Army, 1943-46. USPHS postdoctoral fellow, 1948-50; NIH grantee, 1955—; NSF grantee, 1966-69, 80—. Mem. Am. Soc. Biol. Chemists, Am. Inst. Nutrition, AAAS, Am. Chem. Soc. Jewish. Home: 2417 Perkins Rd Durham NC 27706 Office: Duke U Med Center Dept Biochemistry Durham NC 27710

KAMIN, SHERWIN, lawyer; b. N.Y.C., Feb. 5, 1927; s. Theodore and Esther K.; m. June M. Warren, June 28, 1963; children: Lawrence O., Samuel N., Janet C., David W., Julia E. B.B.A., CCNY, 1948; LL.B., Harvard U., 1951. Bar: N.Y. 1953. Asst. to reporter Fed. Income Tax Project, Am. Law Inst., Cambridge, Mass., 1951-52; asso. firm Botein, Hays, Sklar & Herzberg, N.Y.C., 1952-62, partner, 1962-68; partner firm Kramer, Levin, Nessen, Kamin & Frankel, N.Y.C., 1968—. Served with USN, 1945-46. Mem. Assn. Bar City N.Y., N.Y. State Bar Assn., Am. Bar Assn., Am. Law Inst. Home: 8 E 77th St New York NY 10021 Office: 919 3d Ave New York NY 10022

KAMINER, BENJAMIN, educator, physician; b. Slonim, Poland, May 1, 1924; came to U.S., 1959, naturalized, 1973; s. Idel and Bluma (Zayoncik) K.; m. Freda Shnitke, Aug. 22, 1948; children—Brian, Lauren. M.B., B.Ch., U. Witwatersrand, South Africa, 1946; diploma child health, Royal Coll. Physicians and Surgeons, Eng. House physician, surgeon Johannesburg (South Africa) Gen. Hosp., 1947-48; registrar Edgeware Hosp., London, 1949-50; lectr. physiology Med. Sch. Johannesburg, 1951-54, sr. lectr., 1955-59; investigator Marine Biol. Lab., Woods Hole, Mass., 1959-69; lectr. Harvard Med. Sch., Boston, 1968-69; prof., chmn. dept. physiology Boston U. Sch. Medicine, 1970—. Rockefeller fellow, 1959-60. Mem. Marine Biol. Lab., Soc. Gen. Physiology, Am. Physiol. Soc., Soc. Cell Biology, Biophys. Soc. Home: 150 Oliver Rd Waban MA 02168 Office: Sch Medicine Boston Univ Boston MA 12118

KAMINER, PETER H., lawyer; b. Berlin, May 4, 1915; s. S.G. and Lucy K.; m. Marie P. Scott, Dec. 13, 1947; 1 son, Stevenson Scott. Student, U. Berlin, 1932-34, U. Leipzig, 1934-35; Dr.Jur., Basle U., 1936; J.D., Yale U., 1939. Bar: N.Y. bar 1943, D.C. bar 1979. Asso. firm Winthrop, Stimson, Putnam & Roberts, N.Y.C., 1940-42, 43-44, 45-48, partner, 1948—; law clk. Office of Price Adminstrn., Washington, 1942-43; asso. Gen. Counsel's Office, Gen. Motors Corp., N.Y.C., 1944-45; vis. lectr. Yale U. Law Sch., New Haven, 1974—; mem. character and fitness com. Appellate Div., Supreme Ct. State of N.Y., 1st Dept., 1977—; presdl. appointee conciliator Internat. Centre for Settlement of Investment Disputes, 1980—. Editor: Yale Law Jour, 1939. Mem. Am. Law Inst. (adv. Restatement Conflict of Laws 1954-71), Council Fgn. Relations, Am. Coll. Trial Lawyers, Assn. Bar City N.Y. (exec. com. 1958-61, chmn. grievance com. 1961-64, v.p. 1966-68), Am. Bar Assn., Internat. Bar Assn., Internat. Law Assn., Union Internationale des Avocats. Clubs: Century Assn.; Met. (Washington); Down Town Assn., Mory's Assn. Home: 830 Park Ave New York NY 10021 Office: 40 Wall St New York NY 10005

KAMINETZKY, HAROLD ALEXANDER, obstetrician, gynecologist, educator; b. Chgo., Sept. 6, 1923; s. Sam and Kate K.; m. Beverlee Small, Aug. 6, 1957; children: Keith, Eric. Student, Northwestern U., 1941-44; B.S., U. Ill., 1948, M.D., 1950. Intern Cook County Hosp., Chgo., 1950-51; resident Research Ednl. Hosps., U. Ill. Med. Center, Chgo.; instr. Ob-Gyn U. Ill. Coll. Medicine, 1954-56, asst. prof., 1956-58, asso. prof., 1958-62; prof., chmn. dept. Ob-Gyn Coll. Medicine and Dentistry of N.J.ON.J. Med. Sch., 1968—; dean N.J. Med. Sch., 1972-74; mem. exec. bd. Internat. Fedn. Ob-Gyn; mem. com. maternal nutrition NRC; pres. 10th World Congress of Obstetrics and Gynecology, San Francisco, 1982. Author: (with Iffy) Progress in Perinatology, 1977, New Techniques and Concepts in Maternal and Fetal Medicine, 1979, Principles and Practices of Obstetrics and Perinatology, 1981; editor in chief: Internat. Jour. Gynaecology and Obstetrics, 1968—; mem. editorial adv. com.: Excerpta Medica, 1982—. Served with USN, 1944-46. Mem. Am. Coll. Obstetricians and Gynecologists (pres. 1978-79, commr. on edn. 1971-74, rep. to liaison com. for ob-gyn 1979-85), ACS, Am. Gynecol. Soc., Am. Assn. Obstetricians and Gynecologists. Club: Cosmos (Washington). Office: 100 Bergen St Newark NJ 07103

KAMINOW, IVAN PAUL, physicist; b. Union City, N.J., Mar. 3, 1930; s. Benjamin and Belle (Glazer) K.; m. Florence Fischer, Nov. 26, 1952; children: Paula, Leonard, Ellen. B.S. in Elec. Engring., Union Coll., N.Y., 1952; M.S. (Hughes fellow), UCLA, 1954; A.M. (Bell Labs. fellow), Harvard U., 1957, Ph.D., 1960. Physicist Hughes Aircraft Co., Culver City, Calif., 1952-54, Bell Telephone Labs., Holmdel, N.J., 1954—; vis. lectr. Princeton U., 1968, U. Calif., Berkeley, 1977. Author: Introduction to Electrooptic Devices, 1974; Asso. editor: Jour. Quantum Electronics, 1978-83; contbr. articles to profl. jours. Mem. Tinton Falls Bd. Edn., 1966-74. Fellow Am. Phys. Soc., Optical Soc. Am., IEEE. Patentee in field. Office: Bell Labs Box 400 Holmdel NJ 07733

KAMINSKI, DONALD LEON, medical educator, surgeon, gastrointestinal physiologist; b. Elba, Nebr., Nov. 9, 1940; s. Edwin and Irene (Syntek) K.; m. Maureen M. Cudmore, Nov. 28, 1964; children: Christian, Julie, Jane, Kathryn. B.S., Creighton U., 1962, N.D., 1966. Diplomate: Am. Bd. Surgery. Intern. St. Louis U., 1966-67, resident in surgery, 1967-71; attending surgeon St. Louis U. Hosp., 1972—, dir. gen. surgery, 1972—. Mem. Soc. Univ. Surgeons, Am. Physiol. Soc., Am. Gastroent. Assn., Am. Surg. Assn., Central Surg. Soc., Alpha Omega Alpha. Republican. Roman Catholic. Home: 1025 Joanna Ave Glendale MO 63122 Office: St Louis University 1325 S Grand Blvd Saint Louis MO 63104

KAMINSKY, ALICE R., English educator; b. N.Y.C.; d. Morris and Ida (Spivak) Richkin; m. Jack Kaminsky; 1 son, Eric (dec.). B.A., N.Y. U., 1946, M.A., 1947, Ph.D., 1952. Mem. faculty dept. English N.Y. U., 1947-49, Hunter Coll., 1952-53, Cornell U., 1954-57, Broome Community Coll., 1958-59; Cornell U., 1959-63; mem. faculty dept. English SUNY, Cortland, 1963—, prof., 1968—. Author: George Henry Lewes as Critic, 1968, Logic: A Philosophical Introduction, 1974; editor: Literary Criticism of George Henry Lewes, 1964, Chaucer's Troilus and Criseyde and the Critics, 1980; contbr. articles and revs. to numerous jours. Mem. MLA., Chaucer Soc., Am. Soc. for Aesthetics. Office: Dept English SUNY Cortland Cortland NY 13045 *At a very early age I learned that life is fragile, that many loved and lovely things die or disappear. My way of coping with that knowledge was to latch on to the work ethic. This meant working to achieve some end.*

KAMINSKY, HOWARD, publisher; b. Bklyn., Jan. 24, 1940; s. Arthur William and May (Kaminsky) K.; m. Susan Stanwood, Jan. 31, 1970; 1 dau., Jessica May. B.A., Bklyn. Coll., 1961; postgrad., San Francisco State Coll. Various exec. positions Random House Inc., N.Y.C., 1965-71; ind. film producer, N.Y.C.; exec. v.p., editorial dir. Warner Books, Inc., N.Y.C., 1972-73, pres. and pub., 1973—. Script writer: Avco-Embassy release Homebodies, 1971-72; Author: (under pseudonym Brooks Stanwood with Susan Kaminsky) The Glow, 1979, The Seventh Child, 1981. Mem. Assn. Am. Pubs. (chmn. mass market div.). Home: Sharon CT Home: The Apthorp 390 West End Ave New York NY 10024 Office: 666 Fifth Ave New York NY 10103

KAMINSKY, MANFRED STEPHAN, physicist; b. Koenigsberg, Germany, June 4, 1929; came to U.S., 1958; s. Stephan and Kaethe (Gieger) K.; m. Elisabeth Moellering, May 1, 1957; children: Cornelia B., Mark-Peter. Diploma in physics, U. Rostock, Germany, 1951; Ph.D. in Physics magna cum laude, U. Marburg, Germany, 1957. German Research Soc. fellow and grad. asst. in physics U. Rostock, 1950-52; lectr. Rostock Med. Tech. Sch., 1952; German Research Soc. fellow and research asst. Phys. Inst., U. Marburg, 1953-57, sr. asst., 1957-58; research asso. Argonne (Ill.) Nat. Lab., 1958-59, asst. physicist, 1959-62, assoc., 1962-70, sr. physicist, 1970—; dir. Surface Sci. Center-CTR Program, 1974-80; guest prof. Inst. Energy, U. Que., Montreal-Varennes, 1976—; E.W. Mueller lectr. U. Wis., Milw., 1978. Author: Atomic and Ionic Impact Phenomena on Metal Surfaces, 1965; contbr. articles to profl. jours.; editor: Radiation Effects on Solid Surfaces, 1976; co-editor: Surface Effects on Controlled Fusion, 1974, Surface Effects in Controlled Fusion Devices, 1976, Dictionary of Terms for Vacuum Science and Technology, 1980. Bd. dirs. Com. 100, Hinsdale, 1970-75, pres., 1973-74; pres. St. Vincent de Paul Soc., Hinsdale, 1972-73. Named Outstanding New Citizen of Year Citizenship Council Chgo., 1968. Fellow Am. Phys. Soc.; mem. Am. Chem. Soc., Research Soc. Am., AAAS, Union German Phys. Socs., Am. Vacuum Soc. (sr., trustee 1982-84, chmn. Midwest sect. 1967-68, co-founder Gt. Lakes chpt., dir. 1968-70, chmn. fusion tech. div. 1980-81, editorial bd. jour. 1978-83). Patentee in field. Home: 906 S Park Ave Hinsdale IL 60521 Office: Physics Div Argonne Nat Lab 9700 Cass Ave Argonne IL 60439

KAMISAR, YALE, educator; b. N.Y.C., Aug. 29, 1929; s. Samuel and Mollie (Levine) K.; m. Esther Englander, Sept. 7, 1953 (div. Oct. 1973); children: David Graham, Gordon, Jonathan; m. Christine

Keller, May 10, 1974. A.B., NYU, 1950; LL.B., Columbia U., 1954; LL.D., John Jay Coll. Criminal Justice, City U. N.Y., 1978. Bar: D.C. bar 1955. Research asso. Am. Law Inst., N.Y.C., 1953; asso. firm Covington & Burling, Washington, 1955-57; asso. prof. law, then prof. U. Minn. Law Sch., 1957-64; prof. law U. Mich. Law Sch., 1965—; vis. prof. law Harvard, 1964-65; Cons. to Nat. Adv. Commn. Civil Disorders, 1967-68, Nat. Commn. Causes and Prevention Violence, 1968-69. Mem. adv. com. model code pre-arraignment procedure, Am. Law Inst., 1965-75; Reporter-draftsman: Uniform Rules of Criminal Procedure, 1971-73; Author: (with W.B. Lockhart and J.H. Choper) Constitutional Law: Cases, Comments and Questions, 5th edit, 1980, (with W. LaFave and J. Israel) Modern Criminal Procedure: Cases and Commentaries, 5th edit, 1980, (with F. Inbau and T. Arnold) Criminal Justice in Our Time, 1965, (with J. Grano and J. Haddad) Sum and Substance of Criminal Procedure, 1977, Police Interrogation and Confessions: Essays in Law and Policy, 1980; Contbr. articles to profl. jours. Served to 1st lt. AUS, 1951-52. Home: 2910 Daleview Dr Ann Arbor MI 48103

KAMLOT, ROBERT, performing arts exec.; b. Vienna, Austria, Nov. 28, 1926; came to U.S., 1938, naturalized, 1943; s. Paul and Elsa (Wilhelm) K.; m. Jayne Bullard, Sept. 18, 1948. Student, CCNY, Syracuse (N.Y.) U., Hunter Coll., N.Y.C. Freelance mgr. Broadway prodns., 1964-71; prodn. exec. Zev Bufman Prodns., N.Y.C., 1969-71; co.-mgr. Much Ado About Nothing, N.Y.C., 1972, Two Gentle Men From Verona (nat. co.), Los Angeles, 1973; gen. mgr. N.Y. Shakespeare Festival, 1973—. Served with AUS, 1944-47. Mem. League N.Y. Theatres and Producers (gov.), League Off-Broadway Theatres, Assn. Theatrical Press Agts. and Mgrs. Home: 175 W 93d St New York NY 10025 Office: 425 Lafayette St New York NY 10003

KAMM, HENRY, journalist; b. Breslau, Germany, June 3, 1925; came to U.S., 1941, naturalized, 1943; s. Rudolf and Paula (Wischnewski) K.; m. Barbara Lifton, Aug. 30, 1950; children: Alison, Thomas, Nicholas. B.A., N.Y. U., 1949. With N.Y. Times, 1949—, asst. news editor Internat. Edit., Paris, 1960-64, corr., 1964-66, Eastern European corr., Warsaw, Poland, 1966-67, chief corr., Moscow, 1967-69, S.E. Asian corr., 1969-71, roving corr., Paris, 1971-77, chief corr., Tokyo, 1977, Asian diplomatic corr., Bangkok, Thailand, from 1977, later corr., Rome, Italy. Served with U.S. Army, 1943-46. Recipient award for fgn. corr. Sigma Delta Chi, 1969; George Polk Meml. award L.I. U., 1970; Pulitzer prize, 1978. Office: NY Times Fgn Desk 229 W 43d St New York NY 10036 *

KAMM, HERBERT, newspaper editor; b. Long Branch, N.J., Apr. 1, 1917; s. Louis and Rose (Cohen) K.; m. Phyllis I. Silberblatt, Dec. 6, 1936; children: Laurence R., Lewis R., Robert H. Student, Monmouth Jr. Coll., 1935. Reporter, sports editor Asbury Park (N.J.) Press, 1935-42; with AP, 1942-43, N.Y. World-Telegram and Sun, 1943-66, successively rewrite man, picture editor, asst. city editor, feature editor, mag. editor, asst. mng. editor, 1943-63, mng. editor, 1963-66; exec. editor N.Y. World Jour. Tribune, 1966-67; editorial cons. Scripps-Howard Newspapers, 1967-69; asso. editor Cleve. Press, 1969-79, editor, 1980-82; editorial dir. WJKW-TV, Cleve., 1982—; instr. journalism Case Western Res. U., 1972-75. Radio and TV news commentator and panelist, 1950—; TV talk show host, 1974—; Contbr. articles mags.; Editor: Jr. Illus. Ency. Sports, 1960, rev. edit., 1963, 66, 70, 74. Bd. overseers Case Western Res. U., 1974-78. Mem. AFTRA, Sigma Delta Chi. Jewish (bd. dirs. temple 1957-60). Clubs: Nat. Press, City of Cleve. (pres. 1982). Home: 1 Bratenahl Pl Bratenahl OH 44108 Office: 901 Lakeside Ave Cleveland OH 44114

KAMM, JACOB OSWALD, economist; b. Cleve., Nov. 29, 1918; s. Jacob and Minnie K. (Christensen) K.; m. Judith Steinbrenner, Apr. 24, 1965; children: Jacob Oswald II, Christian. A.B. summa cum laude, Baldwin-Wallace Coll., 1940, LL.D., 1963; A.M., Brown U., 1942; Ph.D., Ohio State U., 1948; LL.D., Erskine Coll., 1971. Asst. econs. Brown U., 1942; instr. Ohio State U., 1945, Baldwin-Wallace Coll., 1945-46, asst. prof., 1947-48, assoc. prof., 1948, prof., dir., 1948-53; econ. cons. to U.S. Post Office, 1951; exec. v.p. Cleve. Quarries Co., 1953- 55, pres., 1955-67, chmn. bd., chief exec. officer, dir., 1967—; pres., treas., dir. Am. Shipbldg. Co., 1967-69, pres., 1973-74; vice-chmn. bd., chmn. exec. com. Cardinal Fed. Savs. & Loan Assn.; dir. Nordson Corp., McDonald Money Market Fund, Bibb Co., MTD Products, Inc., United Western Corp.; weekly columnist econ. affairs Cleve. Plain Dealer, 1964-68. Author: Decentralization of Securities Exchanges, 1942, Economics of Investment, 1951, Making Profits in the Stock Market, 3d rev. edit, 1966, Investor's Handbook, 1954; Contbg. author: An Introduction to Modern Economics, 1952, Essays On Business Finance, 1953; Contbr. articles profl. jours. Exec. bd. Lorain County Met. Park Bd., 1961-66; hon. mem. Mental Health Com., 1964-69; mem. St. Luke's Hosp. Assn., 1967—; mem. adv. council Natural Sci. Mus., 1967—; bd. regents State of Ohio, 1969-72; pub. mem. Underground Gas Storage Com. Ohio, 1964-73; Chmn. Lorain County Republican Finance Com., 1968-70, mem. exec. com., 1969-70; mem. Ohio Rep. Finance Com., 1969-70; Charter mem. bd. counselors Erskine Coll., 1962—; life fellow Cleve. Zool. Soc., trustee, 1966-77; trustee Fairview Gen. Hosp., 1966-68, Baldwin-Wallace Coll., 1953-78; mem. exec. and investment coms. Baldwin-Wallace Coll., 1956-78, chmn. investment com., 1974-78, hon. life trustee, 1979—; mem. pres.'s club Ohio State U.; mem. com. grad. edn. and research Brown U., 1977. Recipient Alumni Merit award Baldwin-Wallace Coll., 1956; Wisdom award of honor, 1970; Pro Mundi Beneficio medal Acad. Humanities, Sao Paulo, Brazil, 1975. Mem. Am. Econs. Assn., Royal Econ. Soc., Am. Finance Assn., AAUP, Indsl. Assn. North Central Ohio (pres. 1960), Ohio Mfrs. Assn. (exec. com. 1970—, trustee, chmn. bd. trustees 1975-77), Early Settlers Assn. of Western Res. (life mem.), Newcomen Soc. N.Am., Assn. Ohio Commodores, Nat. Alumni Assn. Baldwin-Wallace Coll. (pres. 1961-63), John Baldwin Soc. (charter), Ohio Soc. N.Y., Phi Beta Kappa, Phi Alpha Kappa, Delta Phi Alpha, Delta Mu Delta, Beta Gamma Sigma. Methodist. Clubs: Masons (Shriner, 33 deg., treas. Cleve.); Brown University (N.Y.C.); Union (Cleve.); Duquesne (Pitts.); Clifton (Lakewood, Ohio). Office: PO Box 261 Amherst OH 44001

KAMM, LAURENCE RICHARD (LARRY), producer, director; b. Long Branch, N.J., Oct. 10, 1939; s. Herbert and Phyllis Irene (Silberblatt) K.; m. Claire Louise Cadieux, Oct. 5, 1977; children: Lauren Michelle, Kristin Marie. B.S. in Speech, Northwestern U., 1961. Prodn. asst. ABC-TV, N.Y.C., 1962-64. Assoc. dir.: ABC Sports, 1964-70; dir./producer, 1970—; dir., producer: ABC Wide World of Sports; dir.: Summer Olympic Games, 1972, 76; Dir.: Winter Olympic Games, 1976 (Emmy award), 1980; producer, dir., 1984; dir.: numerous major sports events, including Great Am. Bike Race (Emmy award 1983); numerous sports events, including Indianapolis 500 (Emmy award 1982). Recipient Emmy award 20th Anniversary of Wide World of Sports Special, 1981. Mem. Dir.'s Guild Am., Nat. Acad. TV Arts and Scis., Acad. TV Arts and Scis. Home: 420 E 51st St New York NY 10022 Office: 1330 Ave of Americas New York NY 10019

KAMM, ROBERT B., educator, author, diplomat; b. West Union, Iowa, Jan. 22, 1919; s. Balthasar and Amelia (Etter) K.; m. Maxine Moen, July 10, 1943; children: Susan, Steven. B.A., U. No. Iowa, 1940; M.A., U. Minn., 1946, Ph.D., 1948; H.H.D., Okla. Christian Coll., 1976. Tchr. Belle Plaine (Iowa) High Sch., 1940-42; research asst., counselor Gen. Coll., U. Minn., 1946-48; dean students Drake U., 1948-55; dean student personnel services Tex. A. and M. U., 1955-56, dean basic div. and student personnel services, 1956-58; dean Coll. Arts and Scis., Okla. State U., 1958-65, v.p. acad. affairs, 1965-66, pres., 1966-77, prof., 1977—; Mem. commn. coll. student Am. Council Edn., 1957-60, mem. commn. acad. affairs, 1976-78; chmn. div. arts and scis. Assn. State Univs. and Land-Grant Colls., 1963-64, co-chmn. home econs. commn., 1968-70, chmn. council pres.'s, 1974-75; chmn. Mid-Am. State Univs. Assn., 1968-69; mem. adv. panel USAF ROTC, 1967-69, U.S. Army ROTC, 1975-78; mem. nat. vocat. rehab. and edn. adv. com. VA, 1970-72; mem. Pres. Nixon's Commn. Observance 25th Anniversary UN, 1970-71; mem. So. regional adv. bd. Inst. Internat. Edn., 1974-78; U.S. mem. exec. bd. UNESCO, 1976-77, mem. and vice-chmn. U.S. del. 19th gen. conf., Nairobi, Kenya, 1976. Author: Leadership for Leadership, They're No One!, It Helps To Laugh; Contbr. articles on student personnel work and higher edn. profl. jours. Pres. Bi-State Mental Health Assn., 1967-69; v.p. Will Rogers council Boy Scouts Am., 1965-66, 72-73, pres., 1977-80; Bd. visitors Air U., 1968-70; v.p. Frontiers Sci. Found. Okla., Inc., 1966-69; chmn. bd. dirs. Wesley Found., 1962-64; chmn. bd. trustees World Neighbors, 1977-79; 2d vice chmn. Okla. State Fair Bd., 1977-78, life mem., 1978—; Republican nominee for U.S. Senate from Okla., 1978; pres. Payne County Heart Assn., 1981-83, Stillwater YMCA, 1982-83; nat. sponsor Yr. of Bible, 1983, mem. Okla. Comm., 1983. Civilian radio instr. USAAF, 1942-44; coordinator on staff, 1944; naval aviation radar technician USNR, 1944-46. Recipient Air Force ROTC Outstanding Service award, 1970; Alumni Achievement award U. No. Iowa, 1970; Outstanding Achievement award U. Minn., 1971; Distinguished Alumnus award Okla. State U., 1977; named to Okla. Hall Fame, 1972; Oklahoman of Year Okla. Broadcasters Assn., 1976; Silver Beaver award Boy Scouts Am., 1980. Fellow Am. Psychol. Assn.; mem. Am. Coll. Personnel Assn. (exec. council 1954-56, pres. 1957), Am. Personnel and Guidance Assn., Assn. Higher Edn. (com. on undergrad. edn. 1961-64), Nat. Vocat. Guidance Assn., NEA (div. higher edn.), Okla. Edn. Assn. (pres. Okla. State U. chpt. 1962-63), Assn. Gen. and Liberal Studies, C. of C. (dir., v.p. 1965, 66), Kappa Kappa Psi, Omicron Delta Kappa (mem.-at-large gen. council 1970-76), Phi Delta Kappa, Psi Chi, Kappa Delta Pi, Theta Alpha Phi, Kappa Mu Epsilon, Alpha Phi Omega, Phi Mu Alpha Sinfonia, Phi Kappa Phi (Distinguished Mem. 1977), Blue Key. Methodist. Clubs: Rotarian (pres. 1962-63, Paul Harris fellow 1977. Home: 1103 Springdale Dr Stillwater OK 74074 *My main concern is people and what happens to people. To assist each individual person "to be" and "to become" the best of which he or she is capable is my task.*

KAMM, ROBERT WILLIAM, univ. ofcl.; b. Mpls., July 10, 1917; s. Gerald Edward and Matilda (Kraus) K.; m. Mary Anne Roper, Apr. 27, 1946; children—Mary Lou, Sallie Anne, Stacey Carolyn; 1 stepson, John Paul Campbell, Jr.; m. Shirley Rogers Male, Aug. 12, 1973; stepchildren—Sherry Male, Peggy Male, Connie Male. B.Aero. Engring., N.Y.U., 1939. Aero. engr. NACA, Langley AFB, Va., 1940-46; sr. aerodynamist Glenn L. Martin Co., Balt., 1946-48; exec. dir. panel facilities com. aero. Research and Devel. Bd., Dept. Def., 1948-50; with USAF Arnold Engring. Devel. Center, 1950-59, chief plans and policy office, 1957-59; dir. Western Support Office, NASA, 1959-68; cons. NASA Hdqrs., 1969-71; asst. to dir. U. Tenn. Space Inst., Tullahoma, 1968-69, exec. asst. to dir., 1970-74, dir. adminstrv. services, 1975-79, asst. dean, 1980—; Chmn. Joint Coll. Fed. Council So. Cal., 1966-67; chmn. Los Angeles Fed. Exec. Bd., 1966-68; mem. Mayor Los Angeles Space Adv. Com., 1964-68, chmn. subcom. utilization space tech., 1964-68. Asso. fellow Am. Inst. Aero. and Astronautics; mem. Psi Upsilon, Perstare et Praestare. Club: Estill Springs (Tenn.) Lions. Home: Route 1 Estill Springs TN 37330 Office: Univ Tenn Space Inst Tullahoma TN 37388

KAMM, THOMAS ALLEN, lawyer, retired naval officer; b. Lynden, Wash., June 10, 1925; s. Charles J. and Teena I. (Kampen) K.; m. Geraldine V. Leek, Sept. 4, 1948; children—Kristine E., Thomas A. B.S., U. Wash., 1947; J.D., U. Detroit, 1957; LL.M., George Washington U., 1973. Bar: Mich. bar 1957, Calif. bar 1980, D.C. bar 1981. Commd. ensign U.S. Navy, 1945, advanced through grades to rear adm., 1975; various assignments antisubmarine warfare, transport squadrons, res. units, 1947-62, assigned, Japan, in support, 1962-65, mgr. antisubmarine program, officer flight tng., Alameda, Calif., 1965-67, mem. staff, Glenview, Ill., 1967-69, asst. naval air reserve coordinator, 1969-71, asst. dir., 1971-72, comdg. officer, Alameda, 1972-75, asst. dep. to dir., Washington, 1975-76, dep. chief, New Orleans, 1976-78, dep. dir., Washington, 1978-80, individual practice law, Calif., 1980—; v.p. Ralph C. Wilson Agy., Detroit, 1952-59; gen. assoc. John M. Grubb Co., Oakland, Calif., 1959-61; lectr. internat. law Golden Gate U. Law Sch., San Francisco. Decorated Legion of Merit, Meritorious Service medal. Mem. Am. Bar Assn., Am. Soc. Internat. Law, Internat. Law Assn., Naval Res. Assn., Res. Officers Assn., Phi Delta Theta, Delta Theta Phi. Clubs: Bohemian, N.Y. Yacht, Berkeley Yacht, Army-Navy Country. Home: 106 Lombardy Ln Orinda CA 94563

KAMMAN, ALAN BERTRAM, communications consulting company executive; b. Phila., Jan. 25, 1931; s. Daniel Lawrence and Sara Belle K.; m. Madeleine Marguerite Pin, Feb. 15, 1960; children: Alan Daniel, Neil Charles. B.C.E., Swarthmore Coll., 1952. With Bell Telephone Co. Pa., Phila., 1952-69; with Arthur D. Little, Inc., Cambridge, Mass., 1969—, v.p. telecommunications scis., 1977—, v.p. corp. staff, 1981—; dir. Modern Gourmet, Inc., Linderhof Assn.; mem. adv. bd. Telecom 75, Telecom #79. Contbr. articles to telecommunications and computer jours. Bd. dirs. U.S. Council World Communications Yr.; mem. North Country bd. Appalachian Mountain Club. Mem. Assn. Computing Machinery (past pres. Del. Valley). Clubs: Engrs. (past pres. Phila.); International (Washington)). Lodge: Lions (past pres. Phila.). Office: Arthur D Little Inc 25 Acorn Park Cambridge MA 02140

KAMMAN, WILLIAM, historian, educator; b. Geneva, Ind., Mar. 23, 1930; s. Harry August and Ruth Lois (Shoemaker) K.; m. Nancy Ellen Prichard, Apr. 19, 1957; children: Frederick William, Elizabeth Ellen, David Paul. A.B., Ind. U., 1952, Ph.D., 1962; M.A., Yale U., 1958. Tchr. pub. schs., Bloomington, Ind., 1955-57, 58-59; asst. prof. history North Tex. State U., Denton, 1962-66, assoc. prof., 1966-69, prof., 1969—, chmn. dept. history, 1977—. Author: A Search for Stability: United States Diplomacy Toward Nicaragua, 1968; contbg. author: Makers of American Diplomacy, 1974, Ency. American Foreign Policy, 1978. Mem. Denton Planning and Zoning Commn., 1976-79. Served with U.S. Army, 1952-54. Mem. Am. Hist. Assn., Orgn. Am. Historians, Soc. Historians Am. Fgn. Relations, Phi Alpha Theta. Methodist. Lodge: Kiwanis. Home: 2225 Scripture St Denton TX 76201 Office: History Dept N Tex State U Denton TX 76203

KAMMEN, MICHAEL GEDALIAH, educator, historian; b. Rochester, N.Y., Oct. 25, 1936; s. Jacob M. and Blanche (Lazerow) K.; m. Carol Koyen, Feb. 26, 1961; children: Daniel Merson, Douglas Anton. A.B., George Washington U., 1958; M.A., Harvard U., 1959, Ph.D. (Bowdoin prize), 1964. Mem. faculty Cornell U., 1965—, prof. Am. history, 1969—, Newton C. Farr prof. Am. history and culture, 1973—, chmn. dept. history, 1974-76, dir. Andrew D. White Center for Humanities, 1977-80; dir. d'etudes associé, also 1st holder chair in Am. history Ecole des Hautes Etudes en Sciences Sociales, Paris, France, 1980-81; USIA Bicentennial lectr., 1975-76; Commonwealth Fund lectr. in Am. history U. London, 1976. Author: A Rope of Sand: The Colonial Agents, British Politics and The American Revolution, 1968, Politics and Society in Colonial America: Democracy or Deference, 1967, Deputyes and Libertyes: The Origins of Representative Government in Colonial America, 1969, Empire and Interest: The American Colonies and the Politics of Mercantilism, 1970, People of Paradox: An Inquiry Concerning the Origins of American Civilization, 1972 (Pulitzer prize for history 1973), What is the Good of History? Selected Letters of Carl L. Becker, 1900-1945, 1973, Colonial New York: A History, 1975, (with others) Society, Freedom, and Conscience: The Coming of the Revolution in Virginia, Massachusetts, and New York, 1976, A Season of Youth: The American Revolution and the Historical Imagination, 1978; editor: The Contrapuntal Civilization: Essays Toward a New Understanding of the American Experience, 1971; co-editor: The Glorious Revolution in America, Documents on Colonial Crisis of 1689, 1964; editorial bd.: N.Y. History, 1973-77, Essex Inst. Hist. Colls, 1973-77; editor-in-chief: the Past Before Us: Contemporary Historical Writing in the United States, 1980; Host: radio series The States of the Union, Nat. Pub. Radio, 1975-76. Bd. dirs. Social Sci. Research Council, 1980-83. Recipient Alumni Achievement award George Washington U., 1974; Fellow NEH, 1967, 72-73, Humanities Center, Johns Hopkins, 1968-69, Center for Advanced Study in Behavioral Scis., Stanford U., 1976-77. Mem. Am. Hist. Assn. (council 1976-79), Am. Acad. Arts and Scis., Orgn. Am. Historians, Johns Hopkins U. Soc. Scholars, Am. Antiquarian Soc., Am. Soc. Legal History (bd. dirs. 1971-74), Colonial Soc. Mass., Mass. Hist. Soc., Soc. Am. Historians, Phi Beta Kappa. Home: 207 Cayuga Heights Rd Ithaca NY 14850

KAMMERER, CHARLES FRANCIS, JR., banker; b. White Plains, N.Y., Nov. 19, 1921; s. Charles Francis and Angela (Cantwell) K.; m. Pam Tatananni, Oct. 8, 1949; children-Lynn Marie, Wendy Ann. Student, Columbia, 1940-42. With County Trust Co. (merged into Bank of N.Y. 1976), White Plains, 1940—, asst. treas., 1952-59, v.p., 1959-67, sr. v.p., 1967—; asst. treas. The Bank of N.Y. Co., 1976—; tchr. Am. Inst. Banking. Bd. dirs., chmn. fin. planning Westchester chpt. ARC. Served with AUS, 1942-45. Mem. Nat. Assn. Cost Accountants, Financial Execs. Inst. (pres. West chpt. 1973), Municipal Finance Officers Am. (dir.), White Plains C. of C. (past treas.), Westchester County Indsl. Devel. Assn. (vice chmn.), Mount Pleasant Indsl. Devel. Assn. (vice chmn.). Club: Westchester Hills Golf. Home: 136 Rolling Hills Rd Thornwood NY 10594 Office: 235 Main St White Plains NY 10502

KAMMERER, WILLIAM HENRY, physician; b. Logansport, Ind., Mar. 4, 1912; s. Henry and Margaret (Halpin) K.; m. Edith B. Langley, Feb. 12, 1938; children—Dr. William S., Kelly C., Athleen B. (Mrs. William Ellington), Hilary J. Student, U. Notre Dame, 1928-31; M.D., Ind. U., 1935. Diplomate: Am. Bd. Internal Medicine. Intern U.S. Marine Hosp., Staten Island, N.Y., U. Chgo. Clinics; fellow gastro-enterology Lahoy Clinic, Boston; asst. resident N.Y. Hosp., 1935-39; pvt. practice specializing internal medicine and rheumatology, N.Y.C., 1939—; clin. prof. medicine emeritus Cornell Med. Coll.; attending physician N.Y. Hosp., Hosp. Special Surgery. Pres. N.Y. chpt. Arthritis Found., 1976-79. Served from lt. to lt. col., M.C. AUS, 1942-46; PTO. Fellow A.C.P.; mem. Harvey Soc., Am. Rheumatism Assn., Century Assn. Home: 215 149th St Whitestone NY 11357 Office: 515 E 71st St New York NY 10021

KAMMHOLZ, THEOPHIL CARL, lawyer; b. Jefferson County, Wis., Mar. 23, 1909; s. Frederic Carl and Emma (Donner) K.; m. Lura Walker, Apr. 22, 1935; children: Carolyn Kammholz Hudson, Robert. LL.B., U. Wis., 1932. Bar: Wis. 1932, Ill. 1945, D.C. 1964. Asso. Stephens, Sletteland & Sutherland, Madison, Wis., 1932-34, Bogue & Sanderson, Portage, Wis., 1934-35; partner Bogue & Sanderson & Kammholz, Portage, 1935-42; regional counsel War Labor Bd., Chgo., 1943; partner Pope and Ballard, Chgo., 1944-52, Vedder, Price, Kaufman & Kammholz, 1952-55, 57—; exec. dir. Chgo. Foundrymen's Assn., 1952; gen. counsel NLRB, Washington, 1955-57; dir. Fosdick Enterprises, Inc. Co-author: Practice and Procedure Before the NLRB; Contbr. articles profl. jours. Adv. U.S. del. ILO Conf., Geneva, 1954; mem. legal adv. council Mid-Am. Legal Found., 1977—. Mem. ABA, Ill., Wis., Chgo., Fed. bar assns., Internat. Soc. Labor Law (U.S. exec. com.), Am. Arbitration Assn. (adv. council 1982), Wis. Law Alumni Assn. (pres. Chgo. 1953-55), Chgo. Assn. Commerce and Industry (chmn. labor-mgmt. relations com. 1966-68, v.p. govtl. affairs 1968-70, dir., mem. policy com. 1968—), Order of Coif, Delta Sigma Rho, Lambda Chi Alpha. Clubs: North Shore Country (bd. govs. 1971-74), Monroe, Law (exec. com. 1976—), Executives, Metropolitan, University (Chgo.); Kenwood Country (Washington); Portage (Wis.) Country. Home: 1323 Sunview Ln Winnetka IL 60093 Office: 115 S LaSalle St Chicago IL 60603 also 1919 Pennsylvania Ave Washington DC 20006 also 1 Dag Hammarskjold Plaza New York NY 10017

KAMP, THOMAS G., corporate executive. Chmn. Centronix Data Computer Corp. Office: Centronix Data Computer Corp One Wall St Hudson NH 03051§

KAMP, THOMAS GEORGE, computer corporation executive; b. Detroit, July 22, 1925; s. James and Frances (Van Zanten) K.; m. Janette Louise Schermer, Sept. 2, 1949; children: Jennifer, Pamela, Thomas, Nancy. Student, Calvin Coll., 1942-43, Middlebury Coll., 1943-44, Columbia U., 1945; B.S. in Elec. Engring., U. Minn., 1949. Registered profl. engr., Minn. With A.C. Spark Plug div. Gen. Motors Corp., Milw., 1949-52, Lear Siegler, Inc., Grand Rapids, Mich., 1952-56, asst. chief prodn. engr., 1956-57; with Control Data Corp., Mpls., 1957—, gen. mgr. peripheral equipment group, 1961-65, v.p. mfg., 1965-68, group v.p. peripheral products and computer mfg. group, 1968-69, sr. v.p., group exec. peripheral products, 1969-73; pres. Control Data Peripheral Products Co., Control Data Corp., Mpls., 1973—. Served to lt. (j.g.) USNR, 1943-46. Mem. Christian Reformed Ch. Club: Decathlon Athletic (Bloomington, Minn.) (bd. dirs.). Home: 5821 Southwood Dr Bloomington MN 55437 Office: Control Data Corp Peripheral Products Co 8100 34th Ave S Minneapolis MN 55440

KAMPELMAN, MAX M., lawyer; b. N.Y.C., Nov. 7, 1920; s. Joseph and Eva (Gottlieb) Kampelmacher; m. Marjorie Buetow, Aug. 21, 1948; children—Anne, Jeffrey, Julie, David, Sarah. A.B., N.Y.U., 1940, J.D., 1945; M.A., U. Minn., 1946, Ph.D., 1951. Bar: N.Y. bar 1947, D.C. bar 1950, Md. bar 1956. Research staff Internat. Ladies Garment Workers Union, N.Y.C., 1940-41; law clk. Phillips, Nizer, Benjamin & Krim, N.Y.C., 1941- 43; instr. polit. sci. U. Minn., 1946-48; mem. faculty dept. polit. economy Bennington Coll., 1948-50; legislative counsel to Senator Hubert H. Humphrey, Washington, 1949-55; partner firm Fried, Frank, Harris, Shriver & Kampelman, Washington, 1956—; sr. adviser U.S. mission to UN, 1966-67; mem. faculty Sch. for Workers, U. Wis., summers 1947-48; vis. professorial lectr. Howard U., 1954-56; vis. distinguished prof. polit. sci. Claremont Colls., summer 1963; chmn. exec. com., dir. D.C. Nat. Bank, 1962-66; moderator Washington Week in Rev., Eastern Ednl. Network, 1967-70. Author: The Communist Party vs. The C.I.O.: A Study in Power Politics, 1957, (with Kirkpatrick) The Strategy of Deception, 1963; co-author: Congress Against the President, 1975; Contbr. articles profl. publs. Vice chmn. Mayor Mpls. Com. Charter Reform, 1947-48; pres. Friends of Nat. Zoo, 1958-60, now hon. pres.; mem. nat. com. Anti-Defamation League B'nai B'rith, 1973-77, vice chmn., 1977—; bd. dirs. Washington Arena Stage, 1974-78; pres. Am. Friends of Hebrew U.,

1975-77, chmn. bd., 1977—; trustee Inst. for Am. Univs., Aix-en-Provence, France, 1959—, Population Refenence Bur., 1966-67, Am. Histadrut Cultural Exchange Inst., 1968-72, Fed. City Council, 1965-75, Hebrew U., Jerusalem, 1973—, Law Center Found., N.Y. U., 1978—; v.p. Helen Dwight Reid Ednl. Found., 1959—; hon. chmn. bd. trustees Greater Washington Ednl. TV Assn., Inc.; bd. dirs. Georgetown U., 1978—, Mt. Vernon Coll., 1972—, Am. Friends Israel Conservatory of Music, 1977—, Am. Peace Soc., 1973—, Am.-Israel Cultural Found., 1974—, Atlantic Council of U.S., 1965-70; mem. exec. com. Com. on Present Danger, 1976—; vice chmn. Coalition for a Democratic Majority, 1977—; bd. overseers Coll. V.I., 1963—. Mem. Am., Fed. bar assns., Bar Assn. D.C., Am. Polit. Sci. Assn. (counsel, past treas.), D.C. Polit. Sci. Assn. (past pres.), Jewish Publ. Soc. Am. (v.p. 1978—), Am. Judicature Soc. Clubs: Cosmos, Federal City, Nat. Press (Washington). Home: 3154 Highland Pl NW Washington DC 20008 Office: American Embassy CSCE APO New York NY 09285 *The fatherhood of God presupposes the brotherhood of man. However defined, this is a good guide for life's conduct.*

KAMPHOEFNER, HENRY LEVEKE, architect, educator; b. Des Moines, May 5, 1907; s. Charles Herman and Mary Amelia (Leveke) K.; m. Mabel C. Franchere, Jan. 5, 1937. Student, Morningside Coll., 1924-26; B.S. in Architecture, U. Ill., 1930, M.S., Columbia U., 1931; certificate in architecture, Beaux Arts Inst. of Design, 1932; D.F.A. (hon.), Morningside Coll., 1967, LL.D., Ball State U., 1972. Pvt. practice architecture, Sioux City, Iowa, 1932-36; asso. architect Rural Resettlement Adminstrn., Washington, 1936-37; asst. prof. architecture U. Okla., Norman, 1937-39, asso. prof., 1939-40, prof., 1940-48; dean N.C. State U. Sch. Design, Raleigh, 1948-73, dean emeritus, prof. emeritus, 1973—; disting. vis. prof. art Meredith Coll., Raleigh, 1979-81; cons. in field. Humanist-in-residence Nat. Endowment on Humanities, Cumberland County, N.C., 1977; participant Princeton U. Bicentennial Conf. on Planning Man's Phys. Environment, 1947. Author: (with others) Cities are Abnormal, 1946, Churches and Temples, 1954, The South Builds, 1960; Contbr. numerous articles in field to profl. jours. Recipient three medals Beaux Arts Inst. Design, 1929-32; Edward Langley Scholar AIA, 1940; recipient Lasting Achievement in Architecture Edn. joint award AIA/Assn. Collegiate Schs. of Architecture, 1977; Gov.'s Gold medal in the Fine Arts, N.C., 1978. Fellow AIA; mem. Assn. of Collegiate Schs. Architecture (nat. pres. 1963-65, treas. 1959-63, dir. 1959-67), Raleigh Council Architects (pres. 1955-56), Raleigh Chamber Music Guild (pres. 1954-56). Democrat. Club: Carolina Country (Raleigh). Grandview Music Pavilion, Sioux City, Iowa, selected by Royal Inst. Brit. Architects as one of Am.'s Outstanding Bldgs. of Post-War Period, 1937. Home: 3060 Granville Dr Raleigh NC 27609 Office: Sch Design NC State U Raleigh NC 27607 *As an educator in architecture during the past fifty years I have dedicated my energy to encourage the production of a lasting excellence in the physical environment. I believe that excellence in the built environment is one of the primary factors in establishing a serene and spiritual quality to our lives.*

KAMPMEIER, JACK AUGUST, chemist, educator; b. Cedar Rapids, Iowa, June 11, 1935; s. Carlos and Nevalou (Brown) K.; m. Anne Margaret Derk, June 14, 1958; children—Scott, Margaret, Stephen. A.B., Amherst Coll., 1957; Ph.D. (NSF fellow), U. Ill., 1960. From instr. to prof. chemistry U. Rochester, N.Y., 1960-71, prof., 1971—, chmn. dept. chemistry, 1975-79, assoc. dean grad. studies Coll. Arts and Scis., 1982—. Contbr. sci. articles to profl. jours. NSF sci. faculty fellow, 1971-72; Fulbright Hays sr. research scholar U. Freiburg, W. Ger., 1979-80; NATO sr. scientist, 1979-80. Mem. Am. Chem. Soc., Sigma Xi. Home: 36 Larchwood Dr Pittsford NY 14534 Office: Dept Chemistry U Rochester Rochester NY 14627

KAMRATH, KARL, SR., architect; b. Enid, Okla., Apr. 25, 1911; s. G. A. and Martha (Kreplin) K.; m. Eugenie Sampson, June 27, 1934 (div. 1975); children: Karl, Eugenie Martha, John Robert, Thomas Ramser; m. Gardina McCarthy, 1977. B.Arch., U. Tex., 1934. Registered architect, Tex., Ill., Okla., La. Designer Pereira & Pereria, Chgo., 1934-36; chief architect interior studios Marshall Field & Co., Chgo., 1936; partner MacKie & Kamrath, Houston, 1937—; vis. archtl. critic U. Ill., U. Oreg., U. Tex., U. Ark., Tex. A. and M. U., Tex. Tech., La. State U., Cath. U. Am.; Mem. four man U.S. archtl. team inspecting W. Germany planning and reconstrn., 1954; chmn. Tex. Planning Com., 1949-56; dir., founder Contemporary Arts Assn. Mus., Houston, 1948-52. Adv. bd. dirs. U.S. Tennis Hall of Fame. Served to capt. C.E. AUS, 1942-45. Mem. Hall of Honor U. Tex., 1978; inducted into Tex. Tennis Hall of Fame, 1984. Fellow AIA (dir. pres. Houston chpt., chmn. Frank Lloyd Wright Meml. Com. 1959, 60); mem. Tex. Soc. Architects, Am. Planning and Civic Assn. (dir.), Nat. Council Archtl. Registration Bds., Houston Fine Arts Mus., Alpha Rho Chi. Clubs: Houston Racquet (founder), River Oaks Country (Houston); Internat. Lawn Tennis of U.S.A. U.S. nat. tennis champion boys doubles, 1927, intercollegiate doubles, 1931, father and son, 1952. Home: 48 Tiel Way Houston TX 77019 Office: 2713 Ferndale Pl Houston TX 77098 *As an architect, I have endeavored to carry on, in the Texas area, the philosophy and principles of Frank Lloyd Wright's organic architecture, since very few of my colleagues, if any, are so doing. Mr. Wright gave us an American architecture worthy of our democratic way of life and I have attempted to carry on these principles. He was a long time friend and great inspiration to me. As a tennis player and enthusiast, I feel fortunate to have won 3 U.S. Lawn Tennis Association national championships over a 25 year period, 1927-52. Tennis, architecture and my family have been my main concern over the years.*

KAMROWSKI, GEROME LEONARDI, artist, art educator; b. Warren, Minn., Jan. 29, 1914; s. Felix and Mary (Rizke) K.; m. Mary Jane Dodman, Sept. 12, 1965; children: Felix, Kirby Jay. Student, St. Paul Sch. Art, 1933-36, art Students League, N.Y.C., 1933-34, New Bau Haus, Chgo., 1937-38, Hans Hofmann Sch., N.Y.C., 1938—. Disting. prof. art U. Mich., Ann Arbor, 1946—. One-man shows, Knowlton, 1980, group shows, Mus. Modern Art Rutgers U., 1978, London, 1981. Horrace H. Rachkam fellow, 1982; Solomon R. Guggenheim fellow, 1938. Home: 1501 Beechwood Dr Ann Arbor MI 48103 Office: U Mich 2000 Bonisteel Blvd Ann Arbor MI 48109

KAMSKY, LEONARD, manufacturing executive, economist; b. Richmond, Va., Oct. 28, 1918; s. Paul and Lillie (Sidenberg) K.; m. Sonya Levien, Mar. 30, 1947; children: Katherine, Susan, Virginia. B.S. in Bus., U. Richmond, 1939; Ph.D. candidate, Johns Hopkins U., 1940-42; A.M.P., Harvard U., 1943. Bus. analyst IBM, 1946-48; economist Dept. Def. and Dept. State, 1948-52, Sylvania Elec. Products, 1952-55; sr. v.p., chief economist W.R. Grace & Co., N.Y.C., 1955—; dir. Sealectro Corp., Workwear Corp.; speaker on econs. Contbr. articles to profl. jours. Served to maj. AUS, 1942-46. Decorated Bronze Star, U.S., Member Order Brit. Empire, Croix de Guerre, France). Mem. Am. Econs. Assn., Nat. Assn. Bus. Economists, Nat. Planning Assn., Georgetown U. Center Strategic Internat. Studies, Phi Beta Kappa. Jewish. Club: Princeton. Home: 150 E 69th St New York NY 10021 Office: 1114 Ave of Americas New York NY 10036

KAN, DIANA ARTEMIS MANN SHU, artist; b. Hong Kong, Mar. 3, 1926; U.S., 1949, naturalized, 1964; d. Kam Shek and Sing-Ying (Hong) K.; m. Paul Schwartz, May 24, 1952; 1 son, Kan Martin Meyer Sing-Si. Student, Art Students League, 1949-51, Beaux Arts, Paris, 1951-52, Grande Chaumiere, Paris, 1951-52. Fgn. corr., city editor Cosmorama Pictorial Mag., Hong Kong, 1968; art reviewer Villager, N.Y.C., 1960-69; lectr. Birmingham So. U., N.Y. U., Mills Coll., St. Joseph's Coll., Phila. Mus. Author: White Cloud, 1938, The How and Why of Chinese Painting, 1974; One-man shows, London, 1949, 63, 64, Paris, 1949, Hong Kong, 1937, 39, 41, 47, 48, 52, Shanghai, 1935, 37, 39, Nanking, 1936, 38, Macao, 1947, 48, Bankok, 1947, Casablanca, 1951, 52, San Francisco, 1950, 67, N.Y.C., 1950, 54, 59, 67, 71, 72, 74, 78, Naples, 1971, Elliot Mus., Stuart, Fla., 1967, 73, Bruce Mus., Greenwich, Conn., 1969, Nat. Hist. Mus., Taipei, Taiwan, 1971, N.Y. Cultural Center Mus., 1972, Galerie Barbarella, Palm Beach, Fla., Hobe Sound (Fla.) Galleries, 1976, 81, Nat. Arts Club, 1979, others; exhibited in group shows, Royal Acad. Fine Arts, London, 1963-64, Royal Soc. Painters, London, 1964, Am. Water Color Soc., N.Y.C., 1966-77, Nat. Acad., N.Y.C., 1967, 69, 70, 74, 75, 76, Nat. Arts Club, N.Y.C., 1964-77, Charles and Emma Frye Mus., Seattle, 1968, Willamette U., Salem, Oreg., Columbia (S.C.) Mus. Art, 1969, Allied Artists of Am., 1957-77, Audubon Artist, 1974, 76; represented permanent collections, Met. Mus. Art, Phila. Mus. Art, Nelson Gallery, Elliot Mus., Fla., Bruce Mus., Dalhousie U., Atkin Mus., Kansas City, Nat. Hist. Mus., Taipei. Recipient Summer Festival award, N.Y.C., 1959, 1st Prize Nat. Art Club, 1982; named Most Outstanding Profl. Woman of Year Washington Sq. chpt. N.Y. League Bus. and Profl. Women's Club, 1971. Mem. Pen and Brush Club (dir. 1968, Brush Fund award 1968, Alice S. Buell Meml. award 1969), Nat. Acad. Design (assoc.), Am. Watercolor Soc. (traveling award 1968, Marthe T. McKinnon award 1978, dir. 1975-77), Art Students League, Nat. League Pen Women, Audubon Artists (v.p. 1983), Allied Artists Am. (Barbara Vassilieff Meml. award 1969, Ralph Fabri Meml. award 1975, corr. sec. 1975-78), Catharine Lorillard Wolf Art Club (Anna Hyatt Huntington bronze medal 1970, 74, Gold medal of honor 1982). Clubs: Overseas Press Am., Lotos. Home: 26 W 9th St New York NY 10011 *Failure is the mother of success.*

KAN, MICHAEL, museum administrator, anthropologist; b. Shanghi, China, July 17, 1933; came to U.S., 1948, naturalized, 1959; m. Mimi Kan; 1 son, Gregory. B.A. in Art History and Anthropology, Columbia U., 1953, M.A., 1969, M.Phil., 1973; M.F.A. in Ceramics, SUNY, 1957. Lectr. dept. environ. design U. Calif., Berkeley, 1964-66; dept. art history Finch Coll., 1966-67; curator dept. African, oceanic and new world cultures Bklyn. Mus., 1968-75, acting dir. mus., 1974, chief curator, 1975-76; dep. dir., curator African, oceanic and new world cultures Detroit Inst. Arts, 1976—; coordinator, curator Jennie Simpson Ednl. Collection African Art, 1969; lectr. N.Y. U., 1970-72, Bklyn. Coll., 1973; McDermott vis. curator Mus. Fine Arts, Dallas, 1974; adj. prof. art history Wayne State U., 1977—; guest curator Los Angeles County Mus., 1970; asso. Univer. Seminar on Primitive and Pre-Columbian Art, Columbia U., 1977-80. Organizer maj. internat. exhbns.: Between Continents/Between Seas: Precolumbia Art of Costa Rica, Treasures of Ancient Nigeria; Author numerous exhbn. catalogues. Served with U.S. Army, 1957-59. Mem. Am. Assn. Museums, Mus's. Collaborative (dir. 1975), Inst. Andean Studies.

KANAGA, WILLIAM SMITH, accounting firm exec.; b. Wichita, Kans., Aug. 2, 1925; s. Clinton Williamson and Ruth Amos (Smith) K.; m. Sarah Rowe, June 14, 1952; children: Christopher, Sarah Ann, Clinton. B.S. in Metall. Engring, U. Kans., 1947. With Arthur Young & Co., N.Y.C., 1949-54, 1958—, chmn., 1977—; mem. staff Mann Kerdolff Kline & Welsh, N.Y.C., 1954-58. Served to ensign USN, 1943-46. Mem. Am. Inst. C.P.A.s (past chmn. bd. dirs.), N.Y. State Soc. C.P.A.s, Am. Acctg. Assn., Tau Beta Pi, Sigma Tau. Congregationalist. Clubs: Sky (dir.), Links, Blind Brook, Hillsboro.; Metropolitan (Washington). Office: Arthur Young & Co 277 Park Ave New York NY 10172

KANAL, LAVEEN N., computer science educator, business executive; b. Dhond, Bombay, India, Sept. 29, 1931; came to U.S., 1948; s. Nanik and Ganga (Gandhi) K.; m. Agnes Raclare Cordis, Aug. 6, 1960; children: Shobhana, Jaynati, Gyan. B.S. in E.E., U. Wash., 1950, M.S., 1953; Ph.D., U. Pa., 1960. Registered profl. engr., Ont. Mgr. Machine Intelligence Lab. Gen. Dynamics, Rochester, N.Y., 1960-62; mgr. adv. engring. Philco-Ford Corp., Willow Grove, Pa., 1962-68; mng. dir. L.N.K. Corp., Silver Springs, Md., 1968—; prof. computer sci. U. Md., College Park, 1970—, dir. Machine Intelligence & Pattern Analysis Lab., 1974—; adj. prof. Lehigh U., Bethlehem, Pa., 1965-70; vis. prof. Wharton Grad. Sch. Bus. U. Pa., Phila., 1963-73; mem. army robotics and artificial intelligence Nat. Reserch Council Nat. Acad. Scis., Washington, 1982—. Editor: Pattern Recognition, 1968, Pattern Recognition Practice, 1980, Progress in Pattern Recognition, 1981, (Vol. 2) Progress in Pattern Recognition, 1984, Handbook of Statistics, Vol. 2, 1982. Mem. College Park Bd. Trade, 1983. Grantee NSF, 1959—, Nat. Research Council, 1960-82. Fellow IEEE, AAAS; mem. Forum for Interdisciplinary Math. (v.p. 1981-84), Robotics Internat., Soc. Mfg. Engring., Am. Soc. Photogrammetry. Home: 302 Notley Ct Silver Spring MD 20904 Office: Univ Md Dept Computer Sci College Park MD 20742

KANALY, STEVEN FRANCIS, actor; b. Burbank, Calif., Mar. 14, 1946; s. Lowell Francis and Marjorie Bell (Hinds) K.; m. Brent Elizabeth Power, Mar. 27, 1975; children: Quinn Kathryn, Evan Elizabeth. Student, Los Angeles Pierce Coll., 1968-70, Calif. State U., Northridge, 1970-71. Film appearances include Judge Roy Bean, 1970, Dillinger, 1972, Sugarland Express, 1973, My Name Is Nobody, 1973, Terminal Man, 1973, The Wind and the Lion, 1974, Midway, 1976, Fear in a Handful of Dust, 1983; numerous TV appearances Amelia Earhart, 1976, Melvin Purvis G Man, 1974, To Find My Son, 1979; appearing as Ray Krebbs in: series Dallas, 1978—. Served with U.S. Army, 1966-68; Vietnam. Decorated air medal, Army Commendation medal. Mem. Screen Actors Guild, AFTRA, Acad. TV Arts and Scis. Republican. Episcopalian. Office: care Michael B Druxman 8831 Sunset Blvd Los Angeles CA 90069

KANAMORI, HIROO, educator; b. Tokyo, Japan, Oct. 17, 1936; came to U.S., 1972; s. Tokujiro and Saki (Sakurai) K.; m. Keiko Ihara, Apr. 21, 1964; children—Atsushi, Tadashi. B.S., Tokyo U., 1959, M.S., 1961, Ph.D., 1964. Research fellow Calif. Inst. Tech., Pasadena, 1965-66, prof. geophysics, 1972—; asso. prof. geophysics Tokyo U., 1966-69, prof., 1970-72; vis. asso. prof. Mass. Inst. Tech., 1969-70. Author: (with Hitoshi Takeuchi, Seiya Uyeda) Debate About the Earth, 1967. Fellow Am. Geophys. Union; mem. Sigma Xi. Home: 375 S Bonnie Ave Pasadena CA 91106

KANBARA, BERTRAM TERUO, judge; b. Honolulu, Jan. 7, 1926; s. Matsuichi and Hama (Hamamura) K. B.A., U. Hawaii, 1950; J.D., Harvard, 1953. Bar: Hawaii bar 1953, also U.S. Supreme Ct 1953. Dep. corp. counsel City and County of Honolulu, 1954-62; dep. atty. gen. State of Hawaii, 1963-68, asst. atty. gen., 1968-69, atty. gen., 1969-71; pvt. practice, Honolulu, 1971-76; judge Hawaii Dist. Ct., 1976-80, Hawaii Circuit Ct., 1980—. Active Multiple Sclerosis Soc. Served with AUS, 1946-47; PTO. Mem. Nat. Assn. Attys. Gen. (v.p. 1970-71), Nat. Conf. Commrs. on Uniform State Laws, ABA, Hawaii Bar Assn. (dir. 1965, treas. 1973, pres. Jr. Bar sect. 1960), Am. Judicature Soc., Hawaii Jr. C. of C. (legal counsel 1959), Harvard Law Sch. Assn., U. Hawaii Alumni Assn., Honolulu Acad. Arts, Indsl. Relations Research Assn., Met. Mus. Art, Asia Soc. Home: 1332 Alewa Dr Honolulu HI 96817 Office: PO Box 619 Honolulu HI 96809

KANCELBAUM, JOSHUA JACOB, lawyer; b. Cleve., May 9, 1936; s. Charles P. and Bertha (Wigotsky) K.; m. Pamela Scotty, Nov. 21, 1973; 1 dau., Barbara R. B.A., Adelbert Coll., Western Res. U., 1958; LL.B., Western Res. U. Sch. Law, 1960. Bar: Ohio 1960, U.S. Mil. Ct. Appeals 1963, U.S. Supreme Ct. 1966, U.S. Tax Ct. 1976. Asso. firm Ulmer, Berne, Laronge, Glickman & Curtis, Cleve., 1961-63, Berkman & Gordon, 1963-65; partner firm Berkman, Gordon, Kancelbaum Levy & Murray, 1966-79; individual practice law, Cleve., 1979—; adj. prof. law Cleve. State U., 1979-80; spl. ch.-state counsel ACLU of Ohio, 1965—. Pres. Am. Jewish Congress of No. Ohio, 1979-81, mem. nat. governing council., chmn. commn. on law and social action, 1982—. Served with U.S. Army, 1961. Recipient award ACLU, 1977. Mem. Am. Bar Assn., Greater Cleve. Bar Assn., Ohio Bar Assn., ACLU, Jewish Community Fedn. Cleve. Home: 23700 Fairmount Blvd Shaker Heights OH 44122 Office: 75 Public Sq Cleveland OH 44113

KANDEL, ERIC RICHARD, neurobiologist; b. Vienna, Austria, Nov. 7, 1929; came to U.S., 1939, naturalized, 1945; s. Harris Z. and Charlotte (Zimels) K.; m. Denise Bystryn, June 10, 1956; children: Paul Iser, Michelle Deborah. B.A., Harvard U., 1952; M.D., N.Y. U., 1956. Intern Montefiore Hosp., N.Y.C., 1956-57; resident psychiatry Mass. Mental Health Center, 1960-62, 63-64; instr. psychiatry Harvard U. Med. Sch., 1964-65; asso. prof., then prof. physiology and psychiatry N.Y. U. Med. Sch., 1965-74; chief dept. neurobiology and behavior Pub. Health Research Inst. City N.Y., 1969-74; prof. physiology and psychiatry, dir. Ctr. Neurobiology and Behavior Columbia Coll. Physicians and Surgeons, 1974—. Author: Cellular Basis of Behavior, 1976, A Cell Biological Approach to Learning, 1978, Behavioral Biology of Aplysia, 1979, Principles of Neural Science, 1981; also articles. Served to sr. asst. surgeon USPHS, 1957-60. Recipient Career Devel. and Scientist awards NIMH, 1967—, Hofheimer award, 1977, Lucy G. Moses award, 1977, Karl Spencer Lashley award, 1981, Dixon prize in biology and medicine, 1982, N.Y. Acad. Scis. prize in biology and medicine, 1982, Lasker award in basic sci., 1983. Mem. Nat. Acad. Scis., Am. Acad. Arts and Scis., Soc. Neurosci. (pres. 1980-81), Neuroscis. Research Program. Home: 9 Sigma Pl Riverdale NY 10471 Office: Coll Physicians and Surgeons Columbia U New York NY 10032

KANDER, JOHN, composer; b. Kansas City, Mo., Mar. 18, 1927; s. Harold S. and Bernice (Aaron) K. B.A., Oberlin Coll., 1951; M.A., Columbia. Composer: A Family Affair, 1961, Flora, the Red Menace, 1964, Cabaret (Tony award), 1966 (N.Y. Drama Critic's Circle award), The Happy Time, 1967, Zorba, 1968, 70 Girls 70, 1971, Chicago, 1975, The Act, 1977, Woman of the Year, 1981, The Rink, 1984; film Cabaret, 1972, Funny Lady, 1975, Lucky Lady, 1976, New York, New York, 1977, Kramer vs. Kramer, 1980, Still of the Night, 1982; TV show Liza with a Z, 1974 (Emmy award). Mem. Dramatists Guild., Nat. Inst. Music Theatre. Address: care Dramatists Guild 234 W 44th St New York NY 10036

KANE, ART, photographer; b. N.Y.C., Apr. 9, 1925; s. Herman and Pauline (Horowitz) K.; children: Anthony, Jonathan, Nikolas. Grad., Cooper Union, 1950. Designer Esquire Mag., N.Y.C., 1950-53; art dir. Seventeen Mag., N.Y.C., 1953-59; pres. Art Kane Studio, Inc., N.Y.C., 1959—. Contbr. photog. essays in leading news and fashion mags., U.S. and Europe; photog. essays in book The Persuasive Photograph, 1975, Colore Emotionale, 1981, Art Kane, 1979. Served with U.S. Army, 1942-45. Recipient Newhouse citation Syracuse U., 1961, awards Soc. Typographic Arts, Art Dirs. Club of N.Y., Art Dirs. Club of Chgo., Art Dirs. Club of N.J., Am. Inst. Graphic Arts, others. Mem. Am. Soc. Mag. Photographers (Photographer of Yr. 1963), Newspaper guild Am. (Page One 1966). Jewish. Office: 1181 Broadway New York NY 10001

KANE, BERTHOLOMEW ALOYSIUS, state librarian; b. Pitts., Nov. 2, 1945; s. Bartholomew A. and Ruth M. (Loerlein) K.; m. Kathlenn Osborne, Aug. 7, 1967; 1 dau., Leah. B.A. in Journalism, Pa. State U., 1967; M.L.S., U. Pitts., 1971. Dir. Bradford Meml. Library, El Dorado, Kans., 1972-74; researcher Hawaii Dept. Planning and Econ. Devel., Honolulu, 1974-75, state librarian, 1982—; librarian Hawaii State Library System, Lanai City, 1975-79, Honolulu, 1979-82. Founder Lanai Community Services Council, 1976-79, Hawaii Visual Arts Consortium Inc., Honolulu, 1976-81; mem. Hawaii Literacy Inc., Honolulu, 1982—. Hazel McCoy fellow Friends of Library of Hawaii, 1971. Mem. ALA, Hawaii Library Assn., Librarians Assn. Hawaii (v.p. 1982). Democrat. Home: 4644 Aukai Ave Honolulu HI 96816 Office: State Dept Edn 809 8th Ave Honolulu HI 96816

KANE, CAROL, actress, b. Cleve., June 18, 1952. Appeared with: touring co. of play The Prime of Miss Jean Brodie, 1966; with, Joseph Papp's Pub. Theatre, Charles St. Playhouse, Boston; appearing in: film appearances include Carnal Knowledge, 1971, The Last Detail, 1974, Dog Day Afternoon, 1975, Hester Street, 1975 (Acad. award nomination for Best Actress), Harry and Walter Go to New York, 1976, Annie Hall, 1977, Valentino, 1977, The World's Greatest Lover, 1977, The Mafu Cage, 1977, When a Stranger Calls, 1979, The Muppet Movie, 1979, La Sabina, 1979, Les Jeux, 1980; stage appearances include The Effect of Gamma Rays on Man in the Moon Marigolds, 1978, Tales from the Vienna Woods, 1979, Benefit of a Doubt, 1979, The Tempest and Macbeth at Lincoln Center, Sunday Runners in the Rain, 1980, A Midsummer Night's Dream; appeared in: TV films Many Mansions; in: TV series Taxi. Office: care Creative Artists Agy Inc 1888 Century Park E Suite 1400 Los Angeles CA 90067

KANE, CHARLES JOSEPH, banker; b. Louisville, Jan. 2, 1920; s. Henry and Lillian (Berger) K.; m. Rosemary Wilder, Oct. 4, 1941; children: Charles Joseph, Michael. Grad., U. Louisville, 1951, Rutgers U. Grad. Sch. Banking, 1954, Columbia U. Comml. Banks Sr. Mgmt. Sch., 1959, Advanced Mgmt. Program Harvard U., 1966. With Citizens Fidelity Bank & Trust Co., Louisville, 1940—, v.p. charge banking, 1961-62, 1st v.p., 1962-67, exec. v.p., 1967-70, pres., 1970-74, also dir.; pres., dir. Third Nat. Bank, Nashville, 1975—, chmn., chief exec. officer, 1976—, Third Nat. Corp., Western Ky. Gas Co.; dir., mem. exec. com. Am. Gen. Corp.; dir. Hosp. Corp. Am., Nashville; past instr. U. Louisville. Author: Bank Financing of Small Loan Companies, 1954. Chmn. for Ky. Crusade for Freedom, 1957-58; bd. dirs. Children's Hosp., Vanderbilt U., Nashville. Served with AUS, 1942-45. Recipient Crusade for Freedom award, 1957; President's Citation for Outstanding Service U. Louisville, 1959; named Chief Exec. Officer of Yr. Advantage Mag. Mem. Assn. Res. City Bankers, Nashville Area C. of C. (past pres.), Am. Bankers Assn. (chmn. exec. com. comml. lending div.), Robert Morris Assos., Newcomen Soc. Republican. Clubs: Louisville Country, Harvard Bus., Filson, Pendennis; Union League (Chgo.); Belle Meade Country, Nashville City. Office: 201 4th Ave N Nashville TN 37219 *

KANE, DANIEL, food company executive; b. N.Y.C., 1915. With Kane-Miller Corp., Tarrytown, N.Y., 1932—, pres., 1959—, chmn. bd., dir.; dir. Am. Meat Packing Corp., Orval Kent Food Co., Inc., Carolina By-Products Co., Inc., KMC Foods, Inc., Monarch Wine Co. of Ga., K & S Wholesalers, Inc., Delsaco Foods Corp., Sunnyland Refining Co., Northfield Cheese Co., Kanie-Miller Internat. Ltd., Tama Meat Packing Corp. Office: Kanie-Miller Corp. 555 White Plains Rd Tarrytown NY 10591 *

KANE, DANIEL HIPWELL, lawyer; b. Far Rockaway, N.Y., Aug. 18, 1908; s. David and Bertha (Schilling) K.; m. Helen Shirkey, July 30, 1932; children: Ailene (Mrs. Edward Lee Rogers), Daniel Hipwell, Patricia (Mrs. Patrice Hennin), Kevin Kane. B.S., NYU, 1929; J.D., 1931. Bar: N.Y. 1932. Since practiced in, N.Y.C.; specializing in patents; sr. partner Kane, Dalsimer, Kane, Sullivan, & Kurucz, 1946—; mem. faculty N.Y.U. Sch. Law, 1947—, adj. prof., 1964—; lectr. Practising Law Inst., 1951—; Vice pres., dir. Dzus Fastener Co., Inc., West Islip, N.Y., 1941—; dir. Pickering & Co., Inc., Plainview, N.Y., 1965—. Author article. Pres. bd. edn. Union Free Sch. Dist. 6, Huntington, N.Y., 1954-55; Trustee William Dzus Fund; bd. dirs. Ukrainian Inst. Am. Mem. Assn. Bar City N.Y., Am. Bar Assn., Am., N.Y. patent law assns., Am. Judicature Soc., Phi Delta Phi. Clubs: NYU (N.Y.C.); Centerport Yacht; Hibernian United Service (Dublin); Ponte Vedra Beach (Fla.). Home: 22 Spring Hollow Rd Centerport NY 11721 Office: 420 Lexington Ave New York City NY 10017 *Like many others who grew up during the early part of this century, I simply assumed that America offered boundless opportunities. Free from doubts, hang ups, or inhibitions, I simply seized a very small portion of the opportunities which were offered.*

KANE, DAVID SCHILLING, lawyer; b. Far Rockway, N.Y., Jan. 20, 1907; s. David and Bertha Dorothy (Schilling) K.; m. Mildred Irene Thompson, Sept. 23, 1931; children—David H., T. Sheila, Kathleen. Student, N.Y. U., 1924-26; LL.B., NYU, 1930. Bar: N.Y. State 1931. Asso. firm Duell, Dunn & Anderson, N.Y.C., 1931-34; partner firm Duell & Kane, 1934-52; sr. partner Kane Dalsimer, Kane, Sullivan & Kurucz (and predecessors), N.Y.C., 1952—; pres. Camloc Fastener Corp., 1942-44; asst. sec., dir. Sci. Devel. Corp.; lectr. grad. div. N.Y. U. Sch. Law, 1946-59, adj. asso. prof. law, 1960-64, adj. prof., 1964—. Contbg. author: Ann. Survey Am. Law, 1945—. Mem. sch. bd., Port Washington, N.Y., 1948-50, mem. bd. appeals, Village of Sands Point (N.Y.), 1948-63, trustee, 1963-65, mayor, 1965-69; Bd. dirs. Vanderbilt Assocs. of NYU Law Sch., 1968—, Sci. Research Ctr.; trustee N.Y. U. Law Center Found., 1967—, C. F. Mueller Scholarship Found. Recipient Cert. Meritorious Service, 1950. Mem. Nat. Council Patent Law Assn. (chmn. 1963-64), Am. Patent Law Assn. (pres. 1962-63), N.Y. Patent Law Assn. (pres. 1958-59), NYU Law Alumni Assn. (bd. dirs.), Am. Bar Assn., N.Y. State Bar Assn., N.Y.C. Bar Assn., N.Y. County Lawyers Assn., Am. Judicature Soc., Fed. Bar Council, Nat. Lawyers Club, Phi Delta Phi. Clubs: Union League, Pinnacle, NYU (N.Y.C.) (founder mem.); Naples (Fla.) Yacht, Masons. Home: Millertown Rd Bedford NY 10506 also 140 2d Ave N Naples FL 33940 Office: 420 Lexington Ave New York NY 10170

KANE, E(DWARD) LEONARD, electronics company executive; b. Danvers, Mass., Sept. 23, 1929; s. Edward Benedict and Rachael Mary (Lyons) K.; m. Anne Tracy Ronan, Apr. 26, 1958; children: James Ronan, Tracy Anne, Edward Leonard, Rasamond Marie, Thomas Henry, Matthew Noel. B.S. in Bus. Adminstrn., Boston Coll., 1951; J.D., Harvard U., 1954. Bar: Mass. 1954, U.S. Supreme Ct. 1970. With Raytheon Co., Lexington, Mass., 1957—, atty., 1957-63, dir. labor relations, 1963-75, v.p. indsl. relations, 1975—; dir. Seiler Corp., Waltham, Mass., Assoc. Industries Mass. Bd. dirs. Mass. Taxpayers Assn., 1978—, Better Bus. Bur. Mass., 1976—, Greater Boston YMCA, 1976—; vice chmn. Greater Boston YMCA, 1982—; trustee Waltham Hosp., 1977—. Served as agt. CIC U.S. Army, 1955-57. Recipient Cardinal Cushing award for excellence in labor relations, 1971. Mem. ABA, Boston Bar Assn., Aerospace Industries Assn. (indsl. relations com.). Roman Catholic. Clubs: Annisquam Yacht; Harvard (Boston). Office: Raytheon Co 141 Spring St Lexington MA 02173

KANE, ENEAS DILLON, retired oil company executive; b. San Francisco, Jan. 8, 1917; s. Eneas and Catherine (Dillon) K.; m. Mary Helen Wainwright, July 15, 1944; children: Mary Nappi, Judith Otto, Therese Haden, Barbara Van der Pol, Eneas A., Timothy, Nancy, Christopher. B.S., U. Calif., Berkeley, 1938, Ph.D., 1949; M.S., Kans. State U., 1939. Design engr. Westinghouse, 1940; instr. U. Calif., Berkeley, 1940-41, asst. prof. mech. engring., 1945-47, asso. prof., 1950-51; project engr. Lawrence Radiation Lab., 1942-43, 51-52; group engr. Tenn. Eastman Co., 1943-45; supr. Calif. Research & Devel. Co., Livermore, 1952-53; research asso. Calif. Research Corp., Richmond, 1954-56; sr. engring. asso., engring. cons., sr. engring. cons., 1956-62, mgr. producing div., La Habra, 1962-64; asst. sec. Standard Oil Co. Calif., San Francisco, 1964-65, v.p. tech., 1970—; v.p. Chevron Research Co., Richmond, 1964-67, pres., 1967-70; cons. AMAX, Inc.; mem. statewide engring. adv. council U. Calif., Berkeley; engring. adv. bd. Stanford U. Contbr. numerous articles to profl. jours. Recipient Berkeley citation U. Calif., 1976. Fellow Soc. Automotive Engrs.; mem. Nat. Acad. Engring., Am. Inst. Chem. Engrs., ASME, Soc. Petroleum Engrs. Republican. Roman Catholic. Clubs: Stock Exchange, Engrs. (San Francisco); Univ. (N.Y.C.). Patentee in field.

KANE, GEORGE JOSEPH, humanities educator; b. July 4, 1916; s. George Michael and Clara K.; m. Katherine Bridget Montgomery, 1946; 2 children. B.A., U. B.C., Can., 1936; M.A., U. Toronto, 1937; postgrad., Northwestern U., 1937-38; Ph.D., U. London, 1946. Asst. lectr. English Univ. Coll., London, 1946, lectr., 1948, reader in English, 1953, fellow, 1971; prof. English lang. and lit., head dept. Royal Holloway Coll., London U., 1955-65; prof. English lang. and Medieval lit., head dept. English King's Coll., London, 1965-76, prof. emeritus, fellow, 1976—; William Rand Kenan Jr. prof. English U. N.C., Chapel Hill, 1976—, chmn. div. humanities, 1980-83; vis. prof. Medieval Acad. Am., 1970, 82. Author: Middle English Literature, 1951, Piers Plowman, the A Version, 1960, Piers Plowman: The Evidence for Authorship, 1965, Piers Plowman: the B Version, 1975; author articles. Served with Brit. Army, World War II. Recipient numerous awards. Fellow Am. Acad. Arts and Scis., Southeastern Inst. Medieval and Renaissance Studies, Brit. Acad. (council 1974-76, Sir Israel Gollancz Meml prize 1963, Haskins medal 1978). Clubs: Athenaeum, Flyfishers. Address: Greenlaw Hall Chapel Hill NC 27514 *

KANE, HARRY JOSEPH, financial executive; b. Spokane, Jan. 5, 1923; s. Harry Joseph and Ann Elizabeth (Hartmeier) K.; m. Antoinette Marie Van Parys, Oct. 28, 1944; 1 son, Thomas Robert. B.S., U. Wash., Seattle, 1948. C.P.A., Wash., Oreg. Mgr. indsl. audits Arthur Andersen & Co., Seattle, 1948-55; with Ga. Pacific Corp., Portland, Oreg., 1955-83, exec. v.p. finance, dir., 1966-83, mem. exec. com., 1973-83; chmn. Fin. Mgmt. Group, 1983—; dir. Portland Gen. Services, Inc. Chmn. bd. Oreg. Ind. Coll. Found.; trustee Com. Econ. Devel.; bd. dirs. NCCJ, Oreg. Investment Council. Served with USMCR, 1941-44. Mem. Am. Inst. C.P.A.'s, Wash., Oreg. socs. C.P.A.'s, Fin. Execs. Inst. Republican. Roman Catholic. Clubs: Waverley Country, Arlington, Multnomah Athletic. Home: 296 SE Spokane St Portland OR 97202 Office: 4640 SW Macadam #250 Portland OR 97201

KANE, HOWARD EDWARD, lawyer; b. Evanston, Ill., Apr. 12, 1927; s. Albert Charles and Ethel May (Forse) K.; m. Gladys Annette Pollock, June 1, 1950 (div.); children: Emily Gail Kane Wallace, Steven Charles, Matthew David; m. Sharon Bea Glazer, Dec. 7, 1975; 1 dau., Robin. B.B.A., U. Mich., 1949; J.D. with honors, Northwestern U., 1952. Bar: Ill. 1952. Assoc. Jenner & Block, Chgo., 1952-60, ptnr., 1961-77, sr. ptnr., 1978—; lectr. profl. and univ. continuing edn. programs. Contbr. articles to profl. jours. Trustee Deerfield Library Bd., 1968-72; mem. North Suburban Mass Transit Dist., State of Ill., 1970-71. Served with USN, 1945-46. Mem. Am. Coll. Real Estate Lawyers, Anglo-Am. Real Property Inst., ABA, Ill. State Bar Assn., Chgo. Bar Assn., Law Club. Home: 414 Greenleaf St Evanston IL 60202 Office: Jenner & Block 1 IBM Plaza Chicago IL 60611

KANE, JAMES MARTIN, union executive; b. Bellow Falls, Vt., Sept. 28, 1923; s. Michael Edward and Flora Mary (Martin) K.; m. Jenny Helen Glerko, May 28, 1955; 1 dau., Kathleen Helen. Pres. United Elec., Radio and Machine Workers of Am., Local 218, Springfield, Vt., 1961-62, bus. agt., 1962-71; sec. treas. Dist. 2 United Elec., Radio and Machine Workers of Am., Boston, 1965-71, pres. Dist. 2, 1971-81, nat. pres., N.Y.C., 1981—. Former mem. Vt. Vocat. Ednl. Adv. Council, Vt. Apprenticeship Council. Served to sgt. AUS, 1943-46; PTO. Roman Catholic. Club: Am. Legion (Bellow Falls Vt.) (adj. 1948). Lodge: K.C. Office: United Electrical Radio and Machine Workers of America 11 E 51st St New York NY 10022

KANE, JOHN DANDRIDGE HENLEY, JR., naval officer; b. Newport, R.I., July 3, 1921; s. John Dandridge Henley and Cordelia Phythian (Pringle) K.; m. Suzanne Day Pattinson, July 29, 1943; children: John Dandridge Henley, Joel P.P., Suzanne P. B.S. in Elec. Engring., U.S. Naval Acad., 1941; postgrad., Nat. War Coll., Washington, 1964-65. Commd. ensign U.S. Navy, 1941, advanced through grades to rear adm., 1970; comdg. officer Destroyer Div. and 6th Fleet Flagship, 1964-65, dir. officer personnel Navy Dept., 1965-67, dir. legis. affairs Navy Dept., 1968-69, dep. U.S. rep. NATO Mil. Com., Brussels, 1970-73, dir. Naval Hist. Center, Washington, 1976—. Decorated Legion of Merit, Bronze Star. Mem. U.S. Naval Inst. Episcopalian. Clubs: Knickerbocker (N.Y.C.); Met., Chevy Chase, Alibi (Washington). Home: 1615 Forest Ln McLean VA 22101 Office: Bldg 220 Room 203 Washington Navy Yard Washington DC 20374

KANE, JOHN LAWRENCE, JR., judge; b. Tucumcari, N.Mex., Feb. 14, 1937; s. John Lawrence and Dorothy Helen (Bottler) K.; m. George Ann Berger, Oct. 17, 1969; children: Molly Francis, Meghan, Sally, John Pattison. B.A., U. Colo., 1958; J.D., U. Denver, 1961. Bar: Colo. 1961. Dep. dist. atty., Adams County, Colo., 1961-62; assoc. firm Gaunt, Byrne & Dirrim, 1961-63; ptnr. firm Andrews and Kane, Denver, 1964; pub. defender Adams County, 1965-67; dep. dir. eastern region of India Peace Corps, 1967-69; with firm Holme Roberts & Owen, 1970-77, ptnr., 1972-77; U.S. dist. judge, Denver, 1978—; adj. prof. law U. Denver. Contbr. articles to profl. jours. Trustee Fountain Valley Sch. Fellow Internat. Soc. Barristers, Internat. Acad. Trial Lawyers. Democrat. Roman Catholic. Club: Cactus. Office: C-218 US Courthouse Denver CO 80294 *There is a tendency to gild the past with uncritical generosity but an even more pronounced one to forget Santayana's dictum that one who forgets history is bound to repeat it. Law is that indispensable mechanism by which we may survive as a free people if we use it to apply a critical understanding of history to a confusing and dynamic present.*

KANE, JOSH, broadcasting executive; b. N.Y.C.; m. Jane Baum; children: Brian, Robin, Alison. B.A. in Speech and Theatre/Broadcasting, Bklyn. Coll., also postgrad.; postgrad. in motion picture and TV, UCLA. Corr. info. dept. NBC, 1965-66, staff writer press dept., N.Y.C., 1966-69, asst. trade news editor, from 1969, mgr. press and publicity, until 1974, dir. info., 1974-76, gen. program exec., 1976-77, v.p. programs East Coast, 1979-82; v.p. East Coast program devel. CBS, 1982—. Office: CBS 51 W 52d St New York NY 10020 *

KANE, KATHARINE DANIELS, dep. mayor; b. Indpls., Apr. 12, 1935; d. Joseph J. and Katharine (Holliday) Daniels; m. Louis Isaac Kane, Sept. 21, 1957; children—Elizabeth Holliday, Jennifer Johnston, Joseph Daniels. B.A. summa cum laude, Smith Coll., 1956; L.H.D. (hon.), Franklin Pierce Coll., 1975. Research asst. for President Eisenhower's Com. on Fgn. Aid Program, 1956-58; asst. to mem. faculty Mt. Holyoke Coll., 1958-59; pres. LWV of Boston, 1961-64; mem. Mass. Ho. of Reps., 1964-68; vice chmn. com. on Social Welfare, clk. com. on merc. affairs; dir. Mayor's Office of Cultural Affairs, Boston, 1968; pres. The Boston 200 Corp., 1972-76; dir. Office of the Boston Bicentennial, 1972-75; dep. mayor City of Boston, 1975—, also supr. Boston environ. programs; dir. Greater Boston Conv. and Tourist Bur., U.S. Trust Co., 1974-76. Vice pres. Mass. Com. on Children and Youth; chmn. Gov.'s Com. on Accessibility of the Arts, State of Mass., 1972; mem. exec. com. Met. Cultural Alliance; mem. adv. bd. Boston Repertory Co.; overseer Boston Symphony Orch.; mem. vis. com. dept. art history Boston U.; del. to Democratic Nat. Conv., 1972; mem. Boston Ward 5 Dem. Com.; bd. dirs. United Way of Massachusetts Bay, Boston Natural Areas Fund, Ellis Meml. Settlement House, Boston, Arts Boston, Inc., Boston Center for Arts, United Community Services; trustee Boston Ballet Co., Miss Porter's Sch., Farmington, Conn., 1969-74, Commonwealth Sch., Boston, 1973-76. Recipient Spl. citation Simmons Coll., 1976, Myron Glazer award, 1976, Woman '76 award Boston YMCA, Presdl. Bicentennial award Boston Coll., 1976, Outstanding Contbns. award Bicentennial Council of 13 Original States, 1977. Mem. Citizens Housing and Planning Assn. (dir.), Mass. Assn. Mental Health (dir.), Smith Coll. Alumnae Assn. (dir. 1971-74).

KANE, LOUIS ISAAC, merchant; b. Boston, Mar. 25, 1931; s. George Ernest and Sally Charlotte (Smith) K.; m. Katharine Fitzhugh Daniels, Sept. 21, 1957; children—Elizabeth Holliday, Jennifer Johnston, Joseph Daniels. A.B., Harvard, 1953. Pres., chief exec. officer, dir. Kane Financial Corp., Boston, 1958-72; chmn. bd., chief exec. officer, dir. Healthco, Inc., Boston, 1967-71; gen. partner Boston Partners, 1972—; chmn., chief exec. officer, dir. Au Bon Pain Co., Inc., 1978—. Democratic Party chmn. McGovern Finance Com. Mass., 1972; Councilor Harvard Coll. Fund, 1971-73, 75—, vice-chmn., 1978—; mem. com. on univ. resources Harvard U., co-chmn. Class of 1953 25th reunion gift com.; hon. trustee Inst. Contemporary Art, Boston, 1961—, pres., 1967-75; trustee West End House, Inc., 1970—, v.p., 1975—; trustee DU Club, Harvard, Boston Zool. Soc.; bd. dirs. Harvard-Radcliffe Hillel, 1976—, Harvard Alumni Assn., 1981—; mem. corp. Mass. Gen. Hosp., Mus. Art, Ogunquit, Maine; past bd. dirs. or trustee Eaglebrook Sch., Deerfield, Mass., Cambridge Sch., Weston, Mass., Artists Found. Boston, Charles Playhouse, Boston. Served to capt. USMC, 1953-58. Clubs: Union Boat, Somerset, Harvard (Boston) (dir. 1977—); Harvard (N.Y.C.)). Home: 10 Chestnut St Boston MA 02108 Office: 660 Summer St Boston MA 02205

KANE, LUCILE MARIE, historian; b. Maiden Rock, Wis., Mar. 17, 1920; d. Emery John and Ruth (Coty) K. B.S., River Falls State Tchrs. Coll., 1942; M.A., U. Minn., 1946. Tchr. Osceola (Wis.) High Sch., 1942-44; asst. publicity dept. U. Minn. Press, Mpls., 1945-46; research fellow, editor Forest Products History Found., St. Paul, 1946-48; curator manuscripts Minn. Hist. Soc., St. Paul, 1948-75, sr. research fellow, 1979—; state archivist, 1975-79. Author: A Guide to the Care and Administration of Manuscripts, 2d edit, 1966, Manuscripts Collections of the Minnesota Historical Society, Guide No. 2, 1955, The Waterfall That Built a City, 1966, Guide to the Public Affairs Collection Minn. Historical Soc; Editor, transl.: Military Life in Dakota, the Jour. Philippe Regis de Trobriand, 1951; editor: (with others) The Northern Expeditions of Major Stephen H. Long, 1978; Contbr. articles to profl. jours. Recipient Disting. Service award Western History Assn., 1982, Minn. Humanities Commn., 1983. Fellow Soc. Am. Archivists. Home: 1298 Fairmount Ave Saint Paul MN 55105 Office: 690 Cedar St Saint Paul MN 55101

KANE, MARGARET BRASSLER, sculptor; b. East Orange, N.J., May 25, 1909; d. Hans and Mathilde (Trumpler) Brassler; m. Arthur Ferris Kane, June 11, 1930; children—Jay Brassler, Gregory Ferris. Student, Packer Collegiate Inst., 1920-26, Syracuse U., 1927, Art Students League, 1927-29, N.Y. Coll. Music, 1928-29, John Hovannes Studio, 1932-34; Ph.D., Colo. State Christian Coll., 1973. Head craftsman for sculpture, arts and skills unit ARC, Halloran Gen. Hosp., N.Y., 1942-43; 2d v.p. Nat. Assn. Woman Artists, Inc., 1943-45; sec. to exec. bd. Sculptors Guild, Inc., 1942-45, chmn. exhbn. com., 1942, 44; Jury mem. Bklyn. Mus., 1948, Am. Machine & Foundry Co., 1957; com. mem. An American Group, Inc. Work has appeared at, Jacques Seligmann Gallery, N.Y., Whitney Ann. Exhbns., all Sculptors Guild Mus. and Outdoor Shows, Nat. Sculpture Soc. Ann. Bas-Relief Exhbn., 1938, Whitney Mus. Sculpture Festival, 1940, Bklyn. Mus. Sculptors Guild, 1938, Bklyn. Soc. Artists, 1942, Lawrence (Mass.) Art Mus., 1938, N.Y. World's Fair, 1939, Sculptors Guild World's Fair Exhbn., 1940, Robinson Gallery, N.Y., 1939, Traveling Museums and Instns., 1938, Lyman Allyn Mus., 1939, Met. Mus., Internat. Exhbns., 1940, 1949, Roosevelt Field Art Center, N.Y.C., 1957, Phila. Mus., N.Y. Archtl. League, Nat. Acad., Penn. Acad., Chgo. Art Inst., Am. Fedn. Arts, Riverside Mus., Montclair Mus., Grand Central Art Galleries, Lever House, N.Y.C., 1959-81, Rye (N.Y.) Library, 1962, Lever House Sculptors Guild Ann. Exhbn., 1973-81, N.Y. Bot. Garden, 1981, also exhbns. of nat. scope, 1938—, solo sculpture exhbn., Friends Greenwich (Conn.) Library, 1962; executed plaque for, Burro Monument, Fairplay, Colo.; exhibited, N.Y. Bank for Savs., 1968, Mattatuck Mus., Con., 1967, Lamont Gallery, N.H.; executed: 18 carvings in limewood depicting History of Man; Contbr.: articles to mags. Reprodns. in Contemporary Stone Sculpture, 1970; articles to mags Contemporary American Sculptures. Recipient Anna Hyatt Huntington award, 1942; Am. Artists Profl. League and Montclair Art Assn. Awards, 1943; 1st Henry O. Avery Prize, 1944; Sculpture Prize Bklyn. Soc. Artists, Bklyn. Mus., 1946; John Rogers Award, 1951; Lawrence Hyder Prize, 1952, 54; David H. Zell Meml. Award, 1954, 63; hon. mention U.S. Maritime Commn., 1941 and; A.C.A. Gallery Competition, 1944; Nat. Assn. Med. of honor for sculpture, 1951, Nat. Assn. Women Artists, Nat. Acad. Galleries, N.Y.; prize for carved sculpture, 1955; animal sculpture, 1956; 1st award for sculpture Greenwich Art Soc., 1958, 60, Annual New Eng. Exhbns., Silvermine, Conn. Fellow Internat. Inst. Arts and Letters (life); mem. Sculptors Guild (charter), Nat. Assn. Women Artists (2d v.p. 1943-44), Artists Council, U.S.A., Bklyn. Soc. Artists, Greenwich Soc. Artists (council), Pen and Brush, Internat. Sculpture Center, Silvermine Guild Artists, Nat. Trust for Historic Preservation.; Mem. Internat. Soc. Artists (charter). Home and studio: 30 Strickland Rd Cos Cob CT 06807 *It is not possible to overestimate the deep satisfaction experienced in having created countless direct carvings in marble, stone, wood and models for bronze. I strongly believe mankind needs to express itself in some meaningful way. My recent mahogany woodcarvings are dedicated to Peace, Love and an end to Violence. If these goals should inspire the many thousands of viewers of my art form, then I am content that my sculpture is a worthwhile contribution to American culture.*

KANE, MARY KAY, legal educator; b. Detroit, Nov. 14, 1946; d. John Francis and Frances (Roberts) K. B.A., U. Mich., 1968, J.D., 1971. Bar: Mich. 1971. Co-dir. NSF grant studying privacy and social sci. research data Harvard U. Law Sch., 1971-74; asst. prof. SUNY Law Sch., Buffalo, 1974-77; prof. law Hastings Coll. Law, U. Calif., San Francisco, 1977—; cons. U.S. Privacy Study Commn., 1975-76. Co-author: Federal Practice and Procedure, vol. 10, 2d edit, 1983. Mem. Am. Bar Assn., Am. Law Inst. Office: 200 McAllister St San Francisco CA 94102

KANE, PATRICIA LANEGRAN, educator; b. St. Paul, June 23, 1926; d. Walter B. and Lita E. (Wilson) Lanegran; m. Donald Patrick Kane, Apr. 1, 1947; children: Laura Kane Gustafson, Maura L. B.A. cum laude, Macalester Coll., St. Paul, 1947; M.A., U. Minn., 1950, Ph.D., 1961. Mem. faculty Macalester Coll., 1950—, prof. English, 1971—, DeWitt Wallace prof., 1978—, chmn. dept., 1977—, faculty asso., office of v.p. acad. affairs, 1979-83; mem. Minn. planning com. nat. identification project advancement women in acad. adminstrn. Nat. Council Edn., 1979-81. Co-author: A St. Paul Omnibus, 1979; Contbr. articles to profl. jours. Recipient Jefferson prize for teaching excellence, 1980; Danforth grantee, 1957-58. Mem. MIA, Soc. Study So. Lit. Office: Macalester Coll St Paul MN 55105

KANE, RICHARD, advertising agency executive; b. N.Y.C., Sept. 5, 1928; s. David K. and Eva (Eicholz) Kaplan; m. Racquel Sheps, Oct. 7,1950; children: Brandi, Cindi. Student, U. Mo., 1946-47, CCNY, 1947-48. Copywriter Sta. WDHN, New Brunswick, N.J., 1948; corywriter Sta. WHEW, N.Y.C., 1948-50; advt. dir. Rodale Mfg. Co., Emmaus, Pa., 1953-55; pres. Marden-Kane Inc., N.Y.C., 1958—. Served with U.S. Army, 1951-53. Jewish. Club: Friars. *If there is a thraed of theme that weaves its way through my life then perhaps it is "the stuff that dreams are made of". My career in radio, advertising and promotion is underscored by the attempt to deliver dreams in varied forms to the public, to add rainbow to the otherwise dull day.*

KANE, STANLEY BRUCE, food co. exec.; b. N.Y.C., June 5, 1920; s. Jacob and Anna (Epstein) K.; m. Janet Marilyn Haas, May 23, 1948; children—Katherine, Betsy, Priscilla. Student, N.Y. U., 1938-39. With Kane-Miller Corp., N.Y.C., 1938—, chmn. bd., 1959-77, pres., chief exec. officer, 1977—. Served with USAAF, 1942-45. Home: 290 Bedford Center Rd Bedford Hills NY 10507 Office: 555 White Plains Rd Tarrytown NY 10591

KANE, STANLEY PHILLIP, insurance company executive; b. St. Paul, Oct. 3, 1930; s. Bernard J. and Bertha (Pusin) K.; m. Judith Zaikaner, July 1, 1952; children: Brian, Debra, Elizabeth, David. Student, Beck Radio Sch., Mpls., 1948-49. V.p. Arlan Agys., Inc., Mpls., 1950-57; pres. BOMA Inc., Mpls., 1957-68, North Central Life, St. Paul, 1972-76; exec. v.p. North Central Cos., St. Paul, 1968-76; pres., chief exec. officer Early Am. Life Ins. Co., St. Paul, 1976—. Radio announcer, writer, WJMC, Rice Lake, Wis., 1949-50. Scoutmaster Boy Scouts Am., 1967-69, dist. chmn., 1971-74; Bd. dirs., v.p. Jewish Family Service, 1975-81; chmn. bd. Alfred Adler Inst. of Minn., 1980—. Served with M.C. AUS, 1952-54. Mem. Life Underwriters Assn., Presidents Assn. Jewish (dir. temple 1960-64, 75-79, pres. men's club 1960-64). Home: 1678 Lilac Ln Saint Paul MN 55118 Office: 2706 Gannon Rd Saint Paul MN 55116

KANE, THOMAS REIF, engineering educator; b. Vienna, Austria, Mar. 23, 1924; came to U.S., 1938, naturalized, 1943; Ernest Kane Gertrude and Reif (Kane); m. Ann Elizabeth Andrews, June 4, 1951; children: Linda Ann, Jeffrey Thomas. B.S., Columbia U., 1949, 1950, M.S., 1952, Ph.D., 1953. Asst. prof., assoc. prof. U. Pa., Phila., 1953-61; prof. Sch. Engring. Stanford U., Calif., 1961—; cons. NASA, Harley-Davidson Motor Co., AMF, Lockheed Missiles and Space Co., Vertol Aircraft Corp., Martin Marietta Co., Kellet Aircraft Co. Author: (vol. 1) Analytical Elements of Mechanics, 1959, (vol. 2) Analytical Elements of Mechanics, 1961, Dynamics, 1972, Spacecraft Dynamics, 1983. Served to cpl. U.S. Army, 1943-45; PTO. Fellow ASME; mem. Am. Astronautical Soc., Sigma Xi, Tau Beta Pi. Club: Stanford Campus Recreation Assn. (Calif.) (pres.). Office: Stanford U. Stanford CA 94305

KANE, WARREN FRANCIS, oilfield service, supply company executive; b. Ozone Park, N.Y., Oct. 2, 1923; s. Francis X. and Anna F. (Twelbeck) K.; m. Kathryn Ann McKevitt, Mar. 24, 1944; children: Kathleen, Warren, Susan, Sharon, Stephan, Therese. B.S. in Mech. Engring., U. Notre Dame, 1947. Registered profl. engr. Dist. sales mgr. Clark Bros. div. Dresser Industries, various locations, 1948-61; sr. v.p. Fluor Corp., various locations, 1961-76; chmn., pres. Baker Drilling Equipment Co., Orange, Calif., 1976—, dir., 1971—; dir. Fluorocarbon Co., Laguna Niguel, Calif., Jacobs Engring. Group Inc., Pasadena, Calif., Globe Marine Inc., Houston. Co-inventor wedge fill cooling towers. Served with U.S. Army, 1943-45; ETO. Met. Club scholar U. Notre dame, 1941. Mem. Am. Petroleum Inst. Republican. Roman Catholic.

KANE, WILLIAM JAMES, physician, educator; b. Bklyn., Feb. 22, 1933; s. William Aloysius and Margaret Helen (Redmond) K.; m. Elizabeth Knoll, June 25, 1960; children: Kathleen E., William James, Stephen F., Patricia M., Anne E. A.B., Holy Cross Coll., 1954; M.D., Columbia, 1958; Ph.D., U. Minn., 1965. Intern surgery U. Minn. Hosps., 1958-59, resident orthopedic surgery, 1959-64; from instr. to asso. prof. orthopaedic surgery U. Minn. Med. Sch., 1964-71; chmn. dept. orthopaedic surgery Northwestern U. Med. Sch., 1971-78, prof., 1971—; chmn. orthopaedic surgery Northwestern Meml. Hosp., 1971-78, attending orthopaedic surgeon, 1978—; attending orthopaedic surgeon Children's Meml., VA Lakeside, Cook County hosps., all Chgo., Great Lakes (Ill.) Naval Hosp. Mem. Am. Acad. Orthopaedic Surgeons (Kappa Delta award 1966), ACS, AMA, Am. Orthopaedic Assn., Am. Orthopaedic Foot Soc., Orthopaedic Research Soc., Scoliosis Research Soc. (pres. 1979-80), Cook County Med. Soc., Ill. Med. Soc., Chgo. Orthopaedic Soc., Ill. Orthopaedic Soc., Inst. Medicine Chgo., Internat. Soc. Orthopaedic Surgery and Traumatology, Internat. Soc. Study of Lumbar Spine. Home: 850 N DeWitt Pl Chicago IL 60611 Office: 845 N Michigan Ave Chicago IL 60611

KANEKO, THOMAS MOTOMI, research chemist; b. Tokyo, Aug. 15, 1914; U.S., 1915, naturalized, 1957; s. Bert Y. and Miwako (Tokunaga) K.; m. Yoko Moro, Mar. 16. 1957. B.S. in Chem. Engring., U. Utah, 1936, Ph.D. in Metallurgy, 1956. Cert. prof. chemist, Am. Inst. Chemists, 1978. Assayer Kennecott Copper Corp., Ruth, Nev., 1936-39; research engr. Mitsubishi Chem. Industries, Tokyo, 1939-41; liaison engr. Mitshibshi Rayon Co., Tokyo, 1950-52; research metallurgist Union Carbide Nuclear Co., Niagara Falls, N.Y., 1956-57, Nat. Distillers & Chem. Co., Cin., 1957-59; sr. research chemist BASF Wyandotte Corp., Wyandotte, Mich., 1959-78, research assoc., 1978—. Contbr. articles to profl. jours.; patentee metallurgy, chemistry, detergents, surfactants and pesticides. AEC research fellow, 1953-56. Fellow AAAS; mem. ASTM (symposium chmn. and editor 1982—), Sigma Xi, Sigma Pi Sigma. Republican. Home: 1579 Bosford Rd Trenton MI 48183 Office: 1609 Biddle Ave Wyandotte MI 48192

KANELY, JAMES RAY, telecommunications executive; b. Balt., July 7, 1941; s. Arthur James and Mary Ellen (Cunningham) K.; m. Kathy Kiser, Dec. 18, 1976; children: Susan, Lisa, Michael. B.S.M.E., Johns Hopkins U., 1967; M.S.A., George Washington U., 1971. Registered profl. engr., Calif. Dept. chief Western Electric Co., Atlanta and Balt., 1963-73; dir. engring. Superior Continental Corp., Hickory, N.C., 1973-76; v.p., gen. mgr. Superior Cable Corp., Brownwood, Tex., 1976-78, regional v.p., Keller, Tex., 1978-80; pres. Valtec Corp., West Boylston, Mass., 1980-81; pres., chief exec. officer Valtec, West Boylston, 1981—; dir. Laser Diode Labs. Mem. Am. Mgmt. Assn. Democrat. Methodist. Office: 99 Hartwell St West Boylston MA 01583

KANEMITSU, MATSUMI, artist; b. Ogden, Utah, May 28, 1922; s. Kichizaemon and Shizuma (Hiraiwa) K.; children: Shizumi Patia, Harumi Zoe, Bunshi Paul. Student, Leger, Kuniyoshi, Sternberg, Auston, Brown, Metzler. Instr. Calif. State Coll., Los Angeles, 1969, Art Center Col. Design, 1970, U. Calif., Berkeley, 1970-71, Otis Art Inst., 1971, Calif. Inst. Arts, Valencia, 1971-72. 34 one-man shows include, Janus Gallery, Los Angeles; represented in permanent collections, Galleria Civica Arte Modern, Turin, Italy, Honolulu Acad. Arts, Mus. Modern Art, N.Y.C., San Francisco Mus. Art, Corcoran Gallery Art, Washington, D.C.; artist in residence, U. Calif., Berkeley, 1966, Honolulu Acad. Arts, 1967-68; Documentary film Four Stones for Kanemitsu, 1969. Ford Found. grantee, 1961, 64; recipient awards Longview Found., 1962, 64, Japan Cultural Forum, 1967. Home and Office: 854 S Berendo St Los Angeles CA 90005

KANET, ROGER EDWARD, political science educator; b. Cin., Sept. 1, 1936; s. Robert George and Edith Mary (Weaver) K.; m. Joan Alice Edwards, Feb. 16, 1963; children—Suzanne Elise, Laurie Alice. A.B., Xavier U., Cin., 1961; Ph.B., Berchmanskolleg, Pullach-bei-Muenchen, Ger., 1960; M.A., Lehigh U., 1963, Princeton U., 1965, Ph.D., 1966. Asst. prof. polit. sci. U. Kans., Lawrence, 1966-69, assoc. prof., 1969-74; joint sr. fellow Russian Inst. and Research Inst. Communist Affairs, Columbia U., N.Y.C., 1972-73; vis. asso. prof. U. Ill., Urbana, 1973-74, asso. prof., 1974-78, prof. polit. sci., 1978—; cons. Inst. Public Policy Devel., Washington, 1977-79. Editor: The Behavioral Revolution and Communist Studies, 1971, On the Road to Communism, 1972, The Soviet Union and the Developing Countries, 1974, Soviet and East European Foreign Policy, 1974, Soviet Economic and Political Relations with the Developing World, 1975, Background to Crisis: Policy and Politics in Gierek's Poland, 1981, Soviet Foreign Policy and East-West Relations, 1982, Soviet Foreign Policy in the 1980's, 1982; Contbr. numerous articles to scholarly jours. and books. Co-founder, pres. Kans. Parents Assn. Hearing-Handicapped Children, 1968-70. NDEA fellow, 1963-66; Am. Council Learned Socs. grantee, 1972-73, 78; NATO fellow, 1976; recipient Research award U.S. Dept. State, 1976; Excellence in Undergrad. Teaching award U. Ill., 1981; Internat. Research and Exchanges Bd. exchange with Hungary and Poland, 1976; Center Advanced Study, U. Ill. asso., 1981-82. Mem. Am. Assn. Advancement of Slavic Studies, Am. Polit. Sci. Assn., Internat. Polit. Sci. Assn., Internat. Studies Assn., Midwest Slavic Conf. (program chmn. 1980-81), Internat. Com. Soviet and East European Studies (program chmn. 1st World Congress 1974), Central Slavic Conf. (pres., program chmn. 1966-67). Roman Catholic. Home: 1007 S Victor St Champaign IL 61820 Office: 702 S Wright St 361 Lincoln Hall U Ill Urbana IL 61801

KANFER, FREDERICK H., psychologist, educator; (married); 2 children. Student, Cooper Union Sch. Tech., Sch. Engring., 1942-44; B.S. cum laude, L.I. U., 1948; M.A., Ind. U., 1952, Ph.D., 1953. Lic. psychologist, Oreg. Research asst. Ind. U., 1949-52; asst. Psychol. Clinic, 1952-53, teaching fellow in abnormal psychology, 1953; trainee VA Hosp., Indpls., 1951-52; asst. prof. psychology, dir. Psychoednl. Clinic, Washington U., St. Louis, 1953-57; cons. and asso. E.H. Parsons, M.D. and Assos., St. Louis, 1955-57; asso. prof. Purdue U., 1957-62; vis. prof. med. psychology U. Oreg. Med. Sch., summers 1958, 60, prof. psychiatry, 1962-69; vis. prof. psychology U. Oreg., Eugene, summers and winters 1967, 79; prof. psychology U. Cin., 1969-73; prof. U. Ill., Champaign, 1973—; Fulbright lectr. Ruhr U., Bochum, W. Ger., 1968; cons., speaker in field; lectr., vis. prof. various European univs., 1968—, including univs. Oxford, Madrid, Heidelberg, Amsterdam, Berlin, Oslo, Cologne, Munich, Munster, Marburg, Wurzburg, London, Nijmegen, Copenhagen, Stockholm, Trondheim, Salzburg, Berne; organizer, supr. post-doctoral tng. program for European psychologists univs. Cin. and Ill., 1969—; vis. lectr. Inst. Environ. Health, U. Cin. Med. Sch., 1970-73, vis. prof. psychiatry, 1973-79; Morton Vis. prof. Ohio U., 1976; sr. lectr. U. Bern (Switzerland), 1980—. Author: (with J.S. Phillips) Learning Foundations of Behavior Therapy, 1970, (with others) Premier Symposium Sobre Apprendizaje y Modificacion de Conducta en Ambientes Educativos, 1975; contbr. numerous articles to profl. pubs.; editor: (with A.P. Goldstein) Helping People Change: A Textbook of Methods, 1975, 2d rev. edit., 1980, Maximizing Treatment Gains: Transfer Enhancement in Psychotherapy, 1979, (with P. Karoly) The Psychology of Self-Management, 1982; assoc. editor: Psychol. Reports, 1961—, Jour. Addictive Behaviors, 1974—; editorial bd.: Behavior Therapy, 1969-74, Behavior Modification, 1975—, Cognitive Therapy and Research, 1976-80, Behavioral Assessment, 1979—, Clin. Psychology Rev., 1980—, Revista de Psicologia Generaly Aplicada, 1980—; study and editorial reviewer; adv. editor: Research Press, 1978—. Served with inf. U.S. Army, 1944-46. USPHS grantee, 1955—; U. Ill. Research Bd. grantee, 1973-78. Fellow Am. Psychol. Assn. (exec. council div. 12); mem. Midwestern Psychol. Assn., AAAS, Assn. Advancement Behavioral Therapies (dir. 1972-74), Am. Bd. Examiners Profl. Psychology (diplomate), Sigma Xi. Office: Dept Psychology U Ill 6th & Daniel Sts 603 E Daniel St Champaign IL 61820

KANFER, JULIAN NORMAN, biochemist, educator; b. Bklyn., May 23, 1930; s. Benjamin N. and Clara (Lichtenberger) K.; m. Shelly F. Brooks, Dec. 20, 1953; children—Brian, Rachel. B.Sc., Bklyn. Coll., 1954; M.Sc., George Washington U., 1958, Ph.D., 1961. Biochemist Mass. Gen. Hosp., Boston, 1969-75; dir. biochem. research E.K. Shriver Center, Waltham, Mass.; also dir. research W.E. Fernald State Sch., Waltham, 1969-75; adj. asso. prof. biochemistry Brandeis U., Waltham, 1969-75; asso. prof. neuropathology Harvard, 1969-75, prin. research asso., 1974-75; prof. U. Man., Winnipeg, Can., 1975—, head dept. biochemistry, 1975—; cons. Health Scis. Centre, Winnipeg, 1976—; mem. med. adv. bd. Nat. Tay-Sachs Found., N.Y.C., 1970—; mem. study sect. on pathobiol. chemistry Nat. Inst. Health, 1974—. Contbr. articles to profl. jours. Bd. dirs. Winnipeg chpt. Multiple Sclerosis Soc. Can., 1976. Mem. Am. Soc. Biol. Chemistry, Am., Internat. neurochemistry socs., Am. Chem. Soc., AAAS, Soc. for Complex Carbohydrates, Fedn. Am. Socs. for Exptl. Biology, Can. Fedn. Biol. Socs., Canadian Biochem. Soc. Home: 116 Kingsway St Winnipeg MB R3M 0G9 Canada Office: 770 Bannatyne St Winnipeg MB R3E 0W3 Canada

KANIA, ARTHUR JOHN, lawyer; b. Moosic, Pa., Feb. 11, 1932; s. Stanley J. and Constance (Jerry) K.; m. Angela Volpe, Apr. 24, 1954; children: Arthur Sandra, Kenneth, Karen, James, Linda, Steven. B.S., U. Scranton, 1953; LL.B., Villanova U., 1956. Bar: Pa. bar 1956. Acct. Peat, Marwick, Mitchell & Co., Phila., 1954-55; ptnr. Davis, Marshall & Crumlish & Kania (now Kania, Lindner, Lasak & Feeney), Phila., 1961—; pres., dir. Greate Bay Hotel Corp. (and affiliated corps.), 1979-81; sec.-treas., dir. Piasecki Aircraft Corp.; sec., dir. Indsl. Ops. Corp., Jordan Chem. Co., Consol. Mortgage Co., Opt-Scis. Corp.; chmn. bd., dir. Center City Assos. Inc.; dir. Continental Bank; chmn. Capitol Exchange Corp. Mem. chmn.'s adv. com. dept. health adminstrn. Temple U.; mem. Phila. Com. of 70.; Bd. dirs. Piasecki Found.; vice chmn. bd. trustees Villanova U.; former chmn. bd. trustees Hahnemann Med. Coll., 1978. Mem. Fed. Bar Assn., ABA, Pa. Bar Assn., Phila. Bar Assn. Clubs: Pine Valley (N.J.) Golf; Overbrook (Bryn Mawr, Pa.); Squires Golf (Phila.); Boca Raton (Fla.). Home: 1030 Mt Pleasant Rd Bryn Mawr PA 19010 Office: Two Bala Cynwyd Plaza Bala Cynwyd PA 19004 *A book half read is unread; a book opened by imagination and ambition is often closed with success.*

KANIDINC, SALAHATTIN, graphic artist; b. Istanbul, Turkey, Aug. 12, 1927; s. Yahya and Remziye (Mujgan) K.; m. Seniha Ustun, Nov. 24, 1957; children—Sanver, Somer. Student, Defenbaugh Sch. Lettering, St. Paul, 1954, Zanerian Coll. Penmanship, Columbus, 1963, State U. Iowa, 1963, U. Minn., 1964, U. Calif. at Berkeley, 1963-64. Editor, writer, Bagimiz, Zonguldak, 1944, writer, Ticaret Postasi, Istanbul, 1947, Dil, Istanbul, 1948; chief calligrapher Naval Printing Office, Istanbul, 1950-62; lettering specialist Buzza Cardozo Greeting Cards, Anaheim, Calif., 1962-63; asst. art dir. Rust Craft Greeting Card Publs., Dedham, Mass., 1964; expert calligrapher Tiffany & Co., N.Y.C., 1964-72; owner Kanidinc Internat. (graphic design), N.Y.C., 1972—; cons. handwriting to govts. Exhibited: One Thousand Years of Calligraphy and Illumination, Peabody Inst. Library, Balt., 1959, Bertrand Russell Centenary Internat. Art Exhbn., London, 1972-73. Mem. nat. adv. bd. Am. Security Council, 1972—. Served with Turkish Army, 1946-49. Recipient High Moral prize Turkish Govt., 1954; named Community Leader Am. News Pub. Co., 1969. Mem. Internat. Assn. Master Penmen and Tchrs. Handwriting, Internat. Center Typographic Arts, Queens Council on Arts. Home: 62-34 99th St Rego Park NY 11374 *Work, but hard work... And imagination, planning, initiative, enthusiasm, optimism, good will, tolerance, admiration, appreciation, sincerity, courtesy, kindness, observation, consideration, research, confidence and, Love... Love... Love...*

KANIN, EUGENE JOHN, sociologist; b. Phila., June 21, 1928; s. Anthony John and Juliana Marcella K.; m. Severine Jane Brocki, Nov. 19, 1977. B.A., U. Bridgeport, Conn., 1951; M.A., Ind. U., 1954, Ph.D., 1963. Mem. faculty Purdue U., 1957—, prof. sociology, 1970—; vis. prof. U. Alta., Edmonton, Can., 1965, U. Calgary, Alta., Can., 1967, Meml. U. Nfld., Can., 1969. Author research papers on sociology and human sexuality. Mem. Am. Sociol. Assn., Soc. Study Social Problems, Nat. Council Crime and Delinquency, N. Central Sociol. Assn. Home: 110 E Delaware Apt 1001 Chicago IL 60611 Office: Dept Sociology Purdue Univ West Lafayette IN 47907

KANIN, FAY, writer; b. N.Y.C.; d. David and Bessie Mitchell; m. Michael Kanin; children: Joel (dec.), Josh. Student, Elmira Coll., 1933-36, L.H.D. (hon.), 1981; B.A., U. So. Calif., 1937. Mem. western regional exec. bd., judge Am. Coll. Theatre Festival, 1975-76; dir. Filmex. Writer: (with Michael Kanin) screenplays including The Opposite Sex, Teacher's Pet; writer: for Broadway, including His and Hers, Rashomon; writer, co-producer: Friendly Fire, ABC-TV (Emmy award for best TV film), ABC-TV (San Francisco Film Festival award), ABC-TV (Peabody award); writer: TV spls. Hustling (Writers Guild award for best original drama), Tell Me Where It Hurts, (Emmy award, Christopher award). Mem. Writers Guild Am., West (pres. screen br. 1971-73, Val Davies award 1975), Am. Film Inst. (trustee), Acad. Motion Picture Arts and Sci. (pres. 1979—).

KANIN, GARSON, writer, dir.; b. Rochester, N.Y., Nov. 24, 1912; s. David and Sadie (Levine) K.; m. Ruth Gordon, Dec. 4, 1942. Grad., Am. Acad. Dramatic Arts, N.Y.C., 1933. Mem. prodn. staff Samuel Goldwyn, Hollywood, Calif., 1937. Actor appearing on: Broadway stage in Star Spangled, 1933-36; asst. dir. to, George Abbott for, Three Men on a Horse, Boy Meets Girl, Room Service, Brother Rat, 1935-37; dir.: Hitch Your Wagon, 1937, Too Many Heroes, 1937; films for, R.K.O., A Man to Remember, 1938, Next Time I Marry, 1938, The Great Man Votes, 1939, Bachelor Mother, 1939, My Favorite Wife, 1940, They Knew What They Wanted, 1940, Tom, Dick and Harry, 1941; play The Rugged Path, with Spencer Tracy, 1945; writer, dir.: Born Yesterday, 1946; dir.: Years Ago, 1946, How I Wonder, 1947, The Leading Lady, 1948, The Diary of Anne Frank, 1955, Into Thin Air, 1955, Small War on Murray Hill, 1957, A Hole in the Head, 1957; writer, dir.: Smile of the World, 1949, The Rat Race, 1949, The Live Wire, 1950, Do Re Mi, 1961, The Good Soup, 1960, Come on Strong, 1962; dir.: Sunday in New York, 1961, Funny Girl, 1964, I Was Dancing, 1964, A Very Rich Woman, 1965, We Have Always Lived in The Castle, 1966, Idiot's Delight, 1970; adapted, directed, appeared in: Remembering Mr. Maugham, 1967; adapted and directed: The Amazing Adele, 1950, The Good Soup, 1960, A Gift of Time, 1962, Dreyfus in Rehearsal, 1974; dir.: Ho! Ho! Ho!, 1976; co-author (with Ruth Gordon); films A Double Life, 1948 (nominated Acad. award), Adam's Rib, 1949, Pat and Mike, 1952, The Marrying Kind, 1952; screenplays The Right Approach, 1961, It Should Happen to You, 1953, The Girl Can't Help It, 1957, The Rat Race, 1959, High Time, 1960, (in collaboration) Woman of the Year, 1942, The More the Merrier, 1943, From This Day Forward, 1976; writer, dir.: Some Kind of A Nut, 1969, Where It's At, 1969; wrote New English libretto; and directed: Fledermaus, Met. Opera Co., 1950, 66; author: Do Re Mi, 1955, Blow Up a Storm, 1959, The Rat Race, 1960, Remembering Mr. Maugham, 1966, Cast of Characters, 1969, Tracy and Hepburn: An Intimate Memoir, 1971, A Thousand Summers, 1973, Hollywood, 1974, One Hell of an Actor, 1977, It Takes A Long Time to Become Young, 1978, Moviola, 1979, Smash, 1980, Together Again!, 1981; collections Second Science Fiction Anthology; contbr.: others. Gt. Love Stories from the Saturday Evening Post; co-dir. (with Carol Reed); Gen. Eisenhower's film report The True Glory; (named best film of 1945 by Nat. Bd. Review., Recipient Acad. Award, citation N.Y. Film Critic's Circle, award Am. Acad. Dramatic Arts Alumni, following awards for play Born Yesterday, Sidney Howard Memorial award, Donaldson award for best 1st play of season 1945-46, Donaldson award for best dir. of season 1945-46, Gold medal Holland Soc. 1980). Served to capt. AUS, 1941-45. Mem. Soc. Stage Dirs. and Choreographers, ANTA, Writers Guild Am.-East, Dramatists Guild (council), Acad. Motion Picture Arts and Sci., Authors League (treas.), Authors Guild, A.S.C.A.P., Actors Fund, AFTRA, Actors' Equity. Clubs: The Players (dir.), The Friars, The Lambs, Coffee House, N.Y. Athletic, Century Assn. (N.Y.C.). Home: PO Box 585 Edgartown Martha's Vineyard MA 02539 Office: 200 W 57th St Suite 1203 New York NY 10019

KANIN, MICHAEL, author, artist; b. Rochester, N.Y., Feb. 1, 1910; s. David and Sadie K.; m. Fay Mitchell; 1 son, Josh. Student, Art Students League, N.Y.C., N.Y. Sch. Design. Comml. and scenic artist, musician, entertainer; author: screenplays They Made Her a Spy, 1939, Panama Lady, 1939, Anne of Windy Poplars, 1940, Centennial Summer, 1944, Honeymoon, 1945, When I Grow Up, 1951, The Outrage, 1964, (with Ring Lardner, Jr.) Woman of the Year, 1941 (Acad. award for Best Original Screenplay 1942), The Cross of Lorraine, 1942, (with Fay Kanin) Sunday Punch, 1942, My Pal Gus, 1951, Rhapsody, 1953, The Opposite Sex, 1956, Teacher's Pet, 1957 (Acad. award nomination, Writers Guild nomination), The Right Approach, 1961, The Swordsman of Sienna, 1962, Teacher's Pet, 1957 (Writers Guild nomination), (with Ben Starr) How to Commit Marriage, 1968; dir.: film When I Grow Up, 1951; producer: A Double Life, 1947 (2 Acad. awards); author: (with Fay Kanin) Broadway plays His and Hers, 1954, Rashomon, 1958, The Gay Life; musical, 1961; co-producer: Broadway plays Goodbye My Fancy, 1948, Seidman and Son, 1962. Mem. Writers Guild (dir. 1943-44, treas. 1944-45), Dramatists Guild, Acad. Motion Picture Arts and Scis. (documentary com.), Am. Film Inst., Am. Coll. Theatre Festival (organizer playwriting awards program). Address: 653 Ocean Front Santa Monica CA 90402

KANN, PETER ROBERT, journalist; b. N.Y.C., Dec. 13, 1942; s. Robert A. and Marie (Breuer) K.; m. Francesca Mayer, Apr. 12, 1969 (dec. July, 1983); 1 dau., Hillary Francesca. B.A., Harvard U., 1964. Journalist The Wall St. Jour., N.Y.C., 1964-67, Vietnam, 1967-68, Hong Kong, 1968-75, pub., editor Asian edit., 1976-79, asso. pub., 1979—; asst. to chmn. Dow Jones & Co., N.Y.C., 1979, v.p., mem. mgmt. com., 1979—; alt. dir. Far Eastern Econ. Review, 1973, South China Morning Post, Hong Kong, to 1979. Recipient Pulitzer prize for internat. reporting, 1972. Club: Spee (Cambridge, Mass.). Home: 47 Westcott Rd Princeton NJ 08540 Office: care Dow Jones & Co 22 Cortlandt St New York NY 10007

KANN, WALTER, chemical company executive; b. Friedberg, Germany, May 25, 1923; came to U.S., 1938, naturalized, 1943; s. Adolph J. and Frieda (Gruenebaum) K.; m. Lore Humpole Forstenzer, Feb. 15, 1973; children by previous marriage: Jacqueline, Michael Andrew. B.S., CCNY, 1948. With United Am. Metals Corp., Bklyn., 1940-43, 46-47, Balt., 1947-49, plant mgr., 1948-49; with Phibro-Salomon, Inc. (and predecessor cos.), N.Y.C., 1949—; now exec. v.p. corp., also dir., mem. exec. com. Philipp Bros. div. Phibro Corp. (and predecessor cos.). Served with M.I. U.S. Army, 1943-46. Decorated Army Commendation medal. Fellow Am. Inst. Chemists; mem. Am. Chem. Soc., Metall Soc., AAAS, Nat. Def. Exec. Res. Assn. Club: Beach Point. Office: 1221 Ave of Americas New York NY 10020

KANNE, GERALD MERLE, bank holding company executive; b. Waterville, Minn., Oct. 28, 1930; s. Merle L. and C. Leona K.; m. Jacquelyn Lee McKeever, June 22, 1952; children: Cheryl, Susan, Betsy. B.A. in Bus, Mankato (Minn.) State Coll., 1952; postgrad., Stonier Grad. Sch. Banking, Rutgers U., 1968. Vice pres. adminstrn. Norwest Bank, Rochester, Minn., 1957-68, exec. v.p., 1968-76; sr. v.p. Norwest Corp., Mpls., 1976-78, exec. v.p., 1979-83, regional pres., 1983—; chmn. bd. Northwest Computer Services, Inc., Mpls., 1979—. Bd. dirs. YMCA, St. Paul, 1983—. Served in USAF, 1952-56. Mem. Minn. Bankers Assn. (dir.), Minn. Assn. Commerce and Industry (dir. 1983). Methodist. Clubs: St. Paul, Minnesota, Town and Country, Pool and Yacht. Home: 3060 Woodlark Ln Saint Paul MN 55121 Office: 55 E 5th St Saint Paul MN 55101

KANNEL, WILLIAM BERNARD, cardiovascular epidemiologist; b. Bklyn., Dec. 13, 1923; s. Joseph M. and Sarah M. (Golden) K.; m. Rita R. Lefkowitz, May 29, 1943; children: Linda J. Kannel Isaacson, Steven Michael, Patricia M. Kannel Hoffman, Forrest S. M.D., Ga. Med. Coll., 1949; M.P.H., Harvard U., 1959. Intern, resident internal medicine S.I. Pub. Health Hosp., 1949-50, 53-56; asso. dir. Framingham (Mass.) Heart Study, Nat. Heart and Lung Inst., 1950-53, 56-67, dir., 1967-79; cons. Framingham Union Hosp., Cushing Hosp.; asso. medicine Boston U. Med. Sch.; lectr. preventive medicine Harvard U. Med. Sch.; prof. medicine, head sect. epidemiology and preventive medicine Boston U. Med. Center; med. dir. USPHS, 1949—. Contbr. med. jours.; mem. editorial bd.: Am. Heart Jour. Served with AUS, 1943-49. Recipient Gairdner Found. award, 1976; Einthoven award Leiden U., Netherlands, 1974; Francis medal U. Mich. Med. Sch., 1975; Polish Copernicus award, 1977; Dana award, 1972; Soc. Prospective Medicine award, 1979. Fellow Am. Coll. Cardiology, Am. Coll. Epidemiology; mem. Am. Heart Assn. (fellow council epidemiology, former chmn. council epidemiology), Assn. Commd. Officers USPHS, Alpha Omega Alpha. Democrat. Jewish. Home: 30 Eliot St South Natick MA 01760 Office: Boston U Med Center 80 E Concord St Boston MA 02118

KANOVITZ, HOWARD EARL, painter; b. Fall River, Mass., Feb. 9, 1929; s. Meyer Julius and Dora (Rems) K.; m. Mary Huntting Rattray, Dec. 25, 1961; 1 dau., Cleo. B.S., Providence Coll., 1949; postgrad., R.I. Sch. Design, 1949-51, NYU, 1959-61. Instr. Bklyn. Coll., 1962-64, Pratt Inst., 1964-66; prof. Southhampton Coll., 1977-78, Sch. Visual Arts, N.Y.C., 1981—. Artist, painter (exhibited), Tibor de Ngy

Gallery, 1956, Stable Gallery, 1962, Jewish Mus., 1966, Waddell Gallery, 1969, (one-man show (locat. U.S. and Europe), Stefanotty Gallery, N.Y.C., 1975, Gallerie Jollenbeck, Cologne, 1977, Benson Gallery, Bridgehampton, L.I., N.Y., Akademie der Kunste, Berlin, 1979, Kestner Gesellschaft, Honnover, (group exhibits include), Whitney Mus., N.Y.C., 1972, Berlin Nat. Gallery, 1976, Guild Hall, East Hampton, L.I., Dokumenta 6, Kassel, 1977, Spectrum Gallery, N.Y.C., 1978, Alex Rosenberg Gallery, Louise Himmelfarb Gallery, Watermill, L.I., 1979. Office: 237 E 18th St New York NY 10003

KANTER, HAL, writer, producer, director; b. Savannah, Ga., Dec. 18, 1918; s. Albert Lewis and Rose (Ehrenreich) K.; m. Doris Prouder, Sept. 5, 1941; children—Lisa Kanter Shafer, Donna, Abigail Kanter Jaye. Student pub. schs., Savannah, Miami, Fla., Long Beach, N.Y. Lectr. UCLA Extension. Newspaper writer, cartoonist; writer for radio, television and motion pictures; writer, dir., producer for motion pictures and television; writer, creative cons.; writer, dir., producer for TV spls. for, Jack Benny, Bob Hope, Lucille Ball, many others; writer-producer, Walt Disney Prodns., 20th Century Fox, Universal, NBC, CBS, ABC,, others; (Recipient Emmy award for comedy writing (George Gobel Show) 1954); Author: Snake in the Glass, 1971; contbr. articles, cartoons, columns, essays and criticisms to various publs. Served with AUS, 1941-45. Citations City of Hope, Jewish War Vets, Beverly Hills Bar, Nat. Council Aging, Variety Internat., Armed Forces Radio and TV Service. Mem. Writers Guild Am.-West (citation), Acad. Motion Picture Arts and Scis., Acad. Television Arts and Scis., AFTRA, Dirs. Guild Am., Producers Guild Am. (citation), Pacific Pioneer Broadcasters (citation). Democrat. Jewish. Clubs: Friars, Masquers, Guardians. Office: care Marvin Moss Inc 9200 Sunset Blvd Los Angeles CA 90069 *My constant goal is the discovery of laughter that can be shared with others on the principle that people who laugh together can live together.*

KANTER, JOSEPH HYMAN, banker, community developer; b. Tarrant, Ala., Nov. 15, 1923; s. Harry O. and Sylvia (Klein) K.; m. Nancy Reed, July 26, 1953; children: Harry, Hilary, Mary Ellen, John. Student, U. Ala., 1942, Georgetown U., 1943. Chmn. bd., dir. Kanter Corp., Cin., Nat. Banking Corp. of Fla., Inc. (bank holding co. for Nat. Bank of Fla.), Bank of Fla., Miami, Kanter Exploration Co., Cin., Kanter Enterprises, Kanter Corp. of Fla.; dir. Kanter Fin. Corp., Cin., Aero-Jet Indsl. City, Miami, Cin., Miami, Internat. Bancorp. Cin., Kanter Prodns., Inc., N&K Low Power TV, Cable Mktg. Systems, Housing Corp. Am. Finance chmn. for Fla., U.S. Com. for UN, 1958, for Ohio, 1959-60; mem. bus. leadership adv. council Office Econ. Opportunity, 1967; chmn., pres. Nat. Conf. on Citizenship; pres., trustee Joseph H. Kanter Found., Cin.; past gen. chmn. Xmas Seal campaign Anti-Tb League, Cin.; nat. chmn. young leadership cabinet United Jewish Appeal, 1963-65; chmn. State Israel Bonds drive, Cin., 1966; chmn. Cin. com. Ohio Council Econ. Edn., 1966; nat. chmn. Israel Ednl. Fund of United Jewish Appeal, 1967-7O; leading gifts chmn. Jewish Welfare Fund Cin., 1967; nat. chmn., founder internat. young leadership cabinet United Jewish Appeal, 1967; hon. pres. Am. Friends of Tel Aviv U., 1968—; bd. assos. Brandeis Univ.; bd. govs. Jewish Community Relations Com.; bd. dirs. Am. Jewish Com., Jewish Welfare Bd. Cin., Am. Com. for Weizmann Inst. Sci., Ohio Council Econ. Edn., Am. Friends of Hebrew U.; mem. exec. com. United Jewish Appeal, 1964-7O, State Israel Bonds, 1964—; trustee United Israel Appeal, Inc.; chmn. Greater Miami Fedn. and United Jewish Appeal Campaign, 1970-71, Nat. Coordinating Com. Hubert Humphrey, 1968. Served with AUS, World War II. Named one of fifty four outstanding bright young men in sci., politics, arts and bus. Esquire mag., 1958; recipient Leadership award United Jewish Appeal, 1962, 63, Herbert Lehman award, 1965; Humanitarian award B'nai B'rith, 1976. Mem. Am. Legion (past post comdr.), Young Pres. Orgn., Jewish War Vets., World Bus. Council, Ala. Soc., VFW; mem. B'nai B'rith. Clubs: Masons, Shriners. Home: 6010 N Bay Rd Miami Beach FL 33140 Office: 3550 Biscayne Blvd Miami FL 33137

KANTER, RICHARD S., musician; b. Chgo., July 7, 1935; s. Martin J. and Audrey M. (Kabb) K.; m. Janet Shagam, Dec. 15, 1968. Diploma, Curtis Inst. Music. With Lyric Opera of Chgo., Grant Park Symphony Orch. of Chgo.; mem. Chgo. Symphony Orch., 1961—. Served with USN, 4 years. Home: 2743 N Pine Grove Chicago IL 60614 Office: 220 S Michigan Ave Chicago IL 60604

KANTNER, ARTHUR HENRY, banker; b. N.Y.C., Sept. 4, 1918; s. Rudolph Julius and Anna (Westen) K.; m. Shelton Valeria Richardson, Dec. 15, 1944; children: Leslie Anne, Neil Arthur, Alyce Marie. Diploma, N.Y. State A. and M. Inst., Farmingdale, 1938; B.S., Cornell U., 1949, M.S., 1950; Ph.D., Advanced Mgmt. Program, Harvard, 1971. Serviceman Coop. Grange League Fedn., Bridgehampton, L.I., N.Y., 1938-42; research asst. Coll. Agr., Cornell U., 1949-52; jr. economist, economist, sr. economist Fed. Res. Bank of Atlanta, 1952-62, asst. cashier, 1963-66, asst. v.p. New Orleans br., 1966-68, v.p. in charge, 1968-72, sr. v.p. Atlanta office, 1972-82, exec. v.p., 1982-84. Served to 1st lt. USAAF, World War II; PTO; lt. col. Res. ret. Mem. Atlanta C. of C. Presbyterian (elder). Club: Kiwanis. Office: Fed Res Bank of Atlanta PO Box 1731 Atlanta GA 30301

KANTNER, JOHN F., educator; b. Somerset, Pa., July 17, 1920; s. Joseph M. and Ethel (McDonald) K.; m. Jane Boose Kantner, June 6, 1943; children—Andrew, JoAnn, Christopher, Julia. A.B., Franklin & Marshall Coll., 1942; M.A., U. Mich., 1947, Ph.D., 1953. Asst. prof. Coll. William and Mary, 1950-53; statistician U.S. Bur. Census, 1953-60; asso. Population Council N.Y., 1960-65; chmn. dept. sociology U. Western Ont., 1965-68; prof., chmn. dept. population dynamics Johns Hopkins U., 1968—; also dir. Hopkins Population Center. Served with AUS, 1943-45. Mem. Am. Sociol. Assn., Population Assn. Am. (pres. 1982-83), Internat. Union for Scientific Study of Population. Home: 1306 Wine Spring Lane Towson MD 21204 Office: Sch Hygiene and Pub Health Johns Hopkins U Baltimore MD 21205

KANTNER, PAUL, rock and roll musician; b. San Francisco, Mar. 17, 1941; s. Paul S. and Cora Lee (Fortier) K.; children: Gareth, China, Alexander. Student, U. Santa Clara, 1959-61, San Jose State Coll., 1961-63. Mem. group, Jefferson Airplane, 1965-71, Jefferson Starship, 1972-84, Planet Earth Rock & Roll Orch., 1984—. Office: care William C Thompson 2400 Fulton St San Francisco CA 94118 *

KANTOR, EDWIN, investment company executive; b. Bklyn., May 24, 1932; s. William and Ann (Friedlander) K.; m. Madeline Liebstein, Sept. 10, 1955; children: Steven Lloyd, Jay Scott, Stacey Lynn. B.S. in Fin, N.Y. U., 1960. With L.F. Rothschild Co., N.Y.C., 1950-55; with Drexel Burnham Lambert & Co. Inc., N.Y.C., 1955—, now sr. exec. v.p., also dir.; v.p. Drexel Bond Fund; pres. Drexel Burnham Lambert G.S.I. Served to sgt. AUS, 1952-54. Decorated Bronze star. Mem. Corp. Bond Traders of N.Y. Club: Bond of N.Y. Inc. Home: 16 Palatine Ct Oyster Bay Cove Syosset NY 11791 Office: 60 Broad St New York NY 10004

KANTOR, SETH, writer, reporter; b. N.Y.C., Jan. 9, 1926; s. Arvid and Ella Kathryn (Reisman) K.; m. Anne Blackman, June 7, 1952; children: Susan E., Amy J. Student, Wayne U., 1946-47. Copy boy Detroit AP Bur., 1947; sports editor Lamar (Colo.) Daily News, 1948; feature writer Pueblo (Colo.) Chieftain, 1949; sports desk Denver Rocky Mountain News, 1949; editor, free-lance writer, numerous mags., N.Y.C. and Ft. Worth, 1950-57; reporter Fort Worth Press, 1957-60, Dallas Times Herald, 1960-62; corr. Scripps-Howard Newspaper Alliance, Washington, 1962-72; corr. Washington Bur., Detroit News, 1972-78; nat. investigative reporter Atlanta Constn., Cox Newspapers, Washington, 1978-81; sr. editor Nation's Bus. Mag., Washington, 1982-83; Washington corr. Austin Am.-Statesman, Cox Newspapers, 1984—; syndicated reporter N. Am. Newspaper Alliance, 1972-79, N.Y. Times News Service, 1980-81, 84—. Author: Who Was Jack Ruby?, 1978, The Ruby Coverup, 1980. Served with USMCR, 1943-46. Recipient numerous profl. awards, including nat. Sigma Delta Chi award for Washington correspondence, 1974. Club: Nat. Press (bd. govs. 1976-78). Home: 5115 Wessling Ln Bethesda MD 20814 Office: Cox Newspapers Suite 10000 2000 Pennsylvania Ave NW Washington DC 20006 *To be a meaningful journalist in a free society one must be more of an alerter than a reporter. The difference between alerting and reporting is illustrated by Paul Revere's ride. As a reporter he might have shouted out a description of the countryside.*

KANTOR, SIMON WILLIAM, chemistry educator; b. Brussels, Belgium, Mar. 23, 1925; came to U.S., 1939, naturalized, 1946; s. Joseph Uszer and Josephine (Perez) K.; m. Molly Glenna O'Keefe Maynard, July 18, 1970; children from previous marriage: Michael Bruce, Sharon Inez; stepchildren—Sally Maynard Martin, David Maynard, Darren Maynard. B.S., City Coll. N.Y., 1945; Ph.D., Duke U., 1949. Postdoctoral fellow Duke U., 1949-51; research asso. Gen. Electric Co. Research and Devel. Center, Schenectady, 1951-60, sect. mgr., 1960-65, br. mgr., 1965-72; v.p. research and devel. GAF Corp., Wayne, N.J., 1972-82; prof. U. Mass., Amherst, 1982—. Contbr. articles to chem. jours. Mem. Am. Chem. Soc., AAAS, Soc. Chem. Industry, Indsl. Research Inst., Phi Beta Kappa, Phi Lambda Upsilon. Patentee in field. Home: 51 N East St Amherst MA 01002 Office: U Mass Amherst MA 01003

KANTROWITZ, ADRIAN, surgeon, educator; b. N.Y.C., Oct. 4, 1918; s. Bernard Abraham and Rose (Esserman) K.; m. Jean Rosensaft, Nov. 25, 1948; children—Niki, Lisa, Allen. A.B., N.Y.U., 1940; M.D., L.I. Coll. Medicine, 1943; postgrad. physiology, Western Res. U., 1950. Diplomate: Am. Bd. Surgery, Am. Bd. Thoracic Surgery. Gen. rotating intern Jewish Hosp. Bklyn., 1944; asst. resident, then resident surgery Mt. Sinai Hosp., N.Y.C., 1947; asst. resident Montefiore Hosp., N.Y.C., 1948, asst. resident pathology, 1949, fellow cardiovascular research group, 1949, chief resident surgery, 1950, adj. surg. service, 1951-55; USPHS fellow cardiovascular research, dept. physiology Western Res. U., 1951-52, teaching fellow physiology, 1951-52; instr. surgery N.Y. Med. Coll., 1952-55; cons. surgeon Good Samaritan Hosp., Suffern, N.Y., 1954-55; asst. prof. surgery State U. N.Y. Coll. Medicine, 1955-56, asso. prof. surgery, 1957-64, prof., 1964-70; dir. cardiovascular surgery Maimonides Med. Center, Bklyn., 1955-64, dir. surgery, 1964-70; chmn. dept. surgery Sinai Hosp. Detroit, 1970—; prof. surgery Wayne State U. Sch. Medicine, 1970—. Contbr. articles profl. jours. Served from 1st lt. to capt., M.C. AUS, 1944-46. Recipient H.L. Moses prize to Montefiore Alumnus for outstanding research accomplishment, 1949; 1st prize sci. exhibit Conv. N.Y. State Med. Soc., 1952; Gold Plate award Am. Acad. Achievement, 1966; Max Berg award for outstanding achievement in prolonging human life, 1966; Theodore and Susan B. Cummings humanitarian award Am. Coll. Cardiology, 1967. Fellow N.Y. Acad. Sci., A.C.S.; mem. Internat. Soc. Angiology, Am. Soc. Artificial Internal Organs (pres. 1968-69), N.Y. County Med. Soc., Harvey Soc., N.Y. Soc. Thoracic Surgery, N.Y. Soc. Cardiovascular Surgery, Am. Heart Assn., Am. Physiol. Soc., Am. Coll. Cardiology, Am. Coll. Chest Physicians, Bklyn. Thoracic Surgery Soc. (pres. 1967-68), Pan Am. Med. Assn., Soaring Soc. Am., Am. Ski Assn. Pub. pioneer motion pictures taken inside living heart, 1950; contbr. to devel. pump-oxygenators for human heart surgey; pioneer devel. mech., artificial hearts; performed 1st permanent partial mech. heart surgery in humans, 1966; 1st use phase-shift intra-aortic balloon pump in patient in cardiogenic shock; 1st human heart transplant in U.S., Dec. 1967. Home: 70 Gallogly Rd Pontiac MI 48053 Office: 6767 W Outer Dr Detroit MI 48253

KANTROWITZ, ARTHUR, physicist; b. N.Y.C., Oct. 20, 1913; s. Bernard A. and Rose (Esserman) K.; m. Rosalind Joseph, Sept. 12, 1943 (div.); children: Barbara, Lore, Andrea; m. Lee Stuart, Dec. 25, 1980. B.S., Columbia U., 1934, M.A., 1936, Ph.D., 1947; Dr.Engring. (hon.), Mont. Coll. Mineral Sci. and Tech., 1975, D.Sc., N.J. Inst Tech., 1981. Physicist NACA, 1935-46; prof. aero. engring. and engring. physics Cornell U., 1946-56; dir. Avco-Everett Research Lab., Everett, Mass., 1955-72, chmn., chief exec. officer, 1972-78; sr. v.p., dir. Avco Corp., 1956-79; prof. Thayer Sch. Engring., Dartmouth Coll., 1979—; vis. lectr. Harvard, 1952; Fulbright and Guggenheim fellow Cambridge and Manchester univs., 1954; fellow Sch. Advanced Study, Mass. Inst. Tech., 1957, vis. inst. prof., 1957—; Messenger lectr. Cornell U., 1978; hon. prof. Huazhong Inst. Tech., Wuhan, China, 1980; mem. Presdl. Adv. Group on Anticipated Advances in Sci. and Tech. (head task force on sci. ct.), 1975-76; mem. tech. adv. bd. U.S. Dept. Commerce, 1974-77; mem. adv. panel NOVA, Sta. WGBH-TV; mem. bd. overseers Center for Naval Analyses, 1973-83; adv. council Israel-U.S. Binational Indsl. Research and Devel. Found.; Hon. trustee, past mem. mech. engring. adv. com. U. Rochester; mem. adv. council dept. aero. and mech. scis. Princeton U., 1959-77; mem. engring. adv. council Stanford U., 1966-82; mem. adv. bd. engring. Rensselaer Poly. Inst., 1982—. Contbr. articles to profl. jours. Recipient Kayan medal Columbia U., 1973, MHD Faraday Meml. medal, 1983, Theodore Roosevelt medal of honor for Distinguished Service in Sci. Fellow Am. Acad. Arts and Scis., Am. Phys. Soc., AAAS, AIAA, Am. Astronautical Soc.; mem. Internat. Acad. Astronautics, Nat. Acad. Scis., Nat. Acad. Engring., Am. Inst. Physics, Sigma Xi. Home: 24 Pinewood Village West Lebanon NH 03784

KANUK, LESLIE LAZAR, educator, management consultant; b. N.Y.C.; d. Charles and Sylvia (Hoffman) Lazar; m. Jack Lawrence Kanuk; children: Randi Ellen Dauler, Alan Robert. M.B.A., Baruch Coll., 1964; Ph.D. honoris causa, CUNY, 1973, Mass. Maritime Acad., 1981. Pres. Leslie Kanuk Assocs., mgmt. cons., 1965-78, 81—; Lippert disting. prof. mktg. Baruch Coll., N.Y.C., 1981—; mem., vice chmn., chmn. Fed. Maritime Commn., 1978-81; chmn. adv. panel on maritime trade and tech. U.S. Congress Office Tech. Assessment, 1982—; cons. Va. Port Authority, N.Y. State Dept. Edn., Revlon Corp., Glemby Internat., Merc. Dept. Stores Corp., Macmillan Corp., N.Y. U., AT&T, N.Y.C. Human Resources Adminstrn., Curtiss Wright Corp., others, 1966—; panelist NRC-Nat. Acad. Scis., 1975-78; adj. prof. dept. command communications U.S. Army Signal Sch., Ft. Monmouth, N.J., 1967-69; adj. prof. U.S. Mcht. Marine Acad., Kings Point, N.Y., 1970-71. Author: Upgrading the Low Wage Worker: An Ergonomic Approach, 1967, Environmental and Behavioral Study of U.S. Merchant Marine Officers, 1971, Improving the Efficiency of Maritime Personnel, 1972, Mail Questionnaire Response Behavior, 1974, Consumer Behavior, 1978, rev. edit., 1983, Toward an Expanding U.S.M.M, 1976, Toward a National Transportation Policy, 1981, How To Use Export Trading Companies To Penetrate Foreign Markets, 1983; Contbg. editor: Breaking Barriers of Occupational Isolation, 1966, Management of a Seaport, 1972; editor: The American Seafarer monographs, Kings Point, 1974; editorial rev. bd.: Jour. Mktg, 1978; contbr. numerous articles on mgmt., mktg., internat. transp. and export trading. Mem. maritime transp. research bd. Nat. Acad. Scis., 1975-78; bd. dirs. Nat. Maritime Resource Ctr., 1982—, Containerization and Intermodal Inst., 1981—. Recipient Connie award Containerization and Intermodal Inst., 1980; Diamond Superwoman award Harpers Bazaar mag., 1980; Person of Yr. award N.Y. Fgn. Freight Forwarders and Brokers Assn., 1981, Baruch Fgn. Trade Soc., 1981; AMA Doctoral Consortium fellow. Mem. Am. Mktg. Assn., Acad. Mgmt., Am. Inst. Decision Scis., Am. Assn. Pub. Opinion Research, Navy League, Beta Gamma Sigma. Home: 594 Floyd St Englewood Cliffs NJ 07632 Office: 46 E 26th St New York NY 10010

KAPCSANDY, LOUIS ENDRE, building products manufacturing executive, chemical engineering consultant; b. Budapest, Hungary, June 5, 1936; came to U.S., 1957; s. Lajos Endre and Margit (Toth) K.; m. Roberta Marie Henson, Jan. 25, 1964; 1 son, Louis. B.S. in Chem. Engring., Tech. U. Hungary, 1956; postgrad. in law, U. San Francisco, 1963-64; M.S. in Petroleum Tech., U. Calif.-Berkeley, 1969. Freedom fighter Hungarian Revolution, Budapest, 1956; profl. football player San Diego Chargers, 1963-65; western regional mgr. Norton Co., San Francisco, 1965-72; product mgr. Koch Industries, Wichita, Kans., 1972-74; v.p., gen. mgr. Flow Systems, Inc., Seattle, 1974-78; pres. Fentron Bldg. Products, Inc., Seattle, 1978—; chem. engring. cons. E & K Assocs., Akron, Ohio, 1974—. Contbr. articles to profl. jours.; patentee vacuum fraction of crude oil, purification of hydrogen. Active United for Wash., Seattle, 1982. Served with U.S. Army, 1959-62. Fellow Am. Inst. Chem. Engrs.; mem. Archtl. Aluminum Mfrs. Assn., Constrn. Specifications Inst., Single Insulated Glass Mfrs. Assn., TAPPI. Republican. Roman Catholic. Clubs: Ranier, Glendale Country. Lodge: Rotary.

KAPLAN, ALBERT SYDNEY, microbiologist; b. Phila., Nov. 29, 1917; s. Harry and Rose K.; m. Tamar Ben-Porat, Feb. 14, 1959; children: Nira I., Daniel H. B.S., Phila. Coll. Pharmacy and Sci., 1941; M.S., Pa. State Coll., 1949; Ph.D., Yale U., 1952. Nat. Found. Infantile Paralysis fellow Pasteur Inst., Paris, 1952-53, 53-54; instr. preventive medicine Yale U., 1954-55; research asso. dept. microbiology U. Ill., Urbana, 1955-58; mem., head dept. microbiology Albert Einstein Med. Center, Phila., 1958-71; research prof. Temple U. Sch. Medicine, Phila., 1963-71; prof., chmn. dept. microbiology Vanderbilt U. Sch. Medicine, Nashville, 1972—; chmn. Am. Cancer Soc. Adv. Panel on Virology and Microbiology, 1980-82; mem. microbiology testing com. Nat. Bd. Med. Examiners, 1979-83; mem. cancer spl. program adv. com. Nat. Cancer Inst., 1981-85, mem. sci. rev. com. virus cancer program, 1976-80; mem. virology study sect. NIH, 1970-73, chmn., 1972-73, chmn. exptl. virology study sect., 1983-85. Editor: The Herpesviruses (Albert S. Kaplan), 1973; editorial bd.: Jour. Virology, 1967-73, Intervirology, 1972—; asso. editor: Virology, 1966-69, 72-76, Cancer Research, 1971-81. Served with U.S. Army, 1943-46. Recipient Research Career Devel. award NIH, 1963-68, grantee NIH, 1956—, NSF, 1966, Nat. Found. March of Dimes, 1977-78. Fellow AAAS; mem. Am. Soc. Microbiology (div. chmn. 1979-80), Am. Assn. Immunologists (program com. 1973-75), Am. Assn. Cancer Research, Am. Soc. Virology, Sigma Xi. Home: 5328 General Forrest Ct Nashville TN 37215 Office: Dept Microbiology Vanderbilt U Sch Medicine Nashville TN 37232

KAPLAN, ALVIN IRVING, lawyer, apparel mfg. co. exec.; b. Providence, Apr. 19, 1925; s. David J. and Pauline (Rosenberg) K.; m. Eleanor Ruth Apt, Apr. 7, 1957; 1 son, Laurence J. A.B., Cornell U., 1948; LL.B., N.Y. U., 1963. Bar: N.Y. bar 1964, U.S. Supreme Ct 1970. Internat. rep., staff engr. Internat. Ladies Garment Workers Union, AFL-CIO, St. Louis and N.Y.C., 1950-56; asst. personnel dir. Lightolier, Inc., Jersey City, 1956-69; dir. indsl. relations Climatic, Inc., Yonkers, N.Y., 1959-67; mgr. indsl. relations Koracorp Industries Inc., San Francisco, 1967-70, dir. indsl. relations, asst. sec., 1971-74, sec., 1974—, v.p., 1978-79; v.p. legal affairs, indsl. relations Diversified Apparel Enterprises, Inc., 1979-80; asst. gen. counsel Levi Strauss & Co., 1980—; mem. wage bd. 1 Calif. Indsl. Welfare Commn., 1976, 79. Trustee Homewood Terrace, San Francisco, 1971-73, Internat. Ladies Garment Workers Nat. Retirement Fund, Nat. Retirement Fund United Hatters, Cap and Millinery Workers Union. Served with C.E. AUS, 1943-46. Mem. Am., N.Y. State, Fed. bar assns., Indsl. Relations Research Assn., Internat. Soc. Labor Law and Social Security, Am. Soc. Corp. Secs. Democrat. Jewish. Club: Cornell No. Calif. Office: 1155 Battery St San Francisco CA 94106

KAPLAN, BENJAMIN, judge; b. N.Y.C., Apr. 9, 1911; s. Morris and Mary (Berman) K.; m. Felicia Lamport, Apr. 16, 1942; children: James L., Nancy L. Mansbach. A.B., CCNY, 1929; LL.B., Columbia, 1933; LL.D., Suffolk U., 1974, Harvard U., 1981, Northeastern U., 1981. Bar: N.Y. 1934, Mass. 1950. Assoc., then mem. firm Greenbaum, Wolff & Ernst, N.Y.C., 1933-42, 46; vis. prof. law Harvard, 1947, prof. law, 1948—, Royall prof. law, 1961-72, emeritus, 1972—; assoc. justice Supreme Jud. Ct. Mass., 1972-81; Reporter to adv. com. on civil rules Jud. Conf. U.S., 1960-66, mem., 1966-70; co-reporter restatement (2d) of judgments to Am. Law Inst., 1970-73. Author: An Unhurried View of Copyright, 1967; co-author: Materials for a Basic Course in Civil Procedure, 4th edit, 1978, Cases on Copyright, 3d edit, 1978. Served to lt. col. AUS, 1942-46. Mem. Am. Law Inst., Assn. Bar City of N.Y., Phi Beta Kappa. Mem. Justice Jackson's staff Nuremberg Trial, 1945. Home: 2 Bond St Cambridge MA 02138 Office: Harvard Law Sch Cambridge MA 02138

KAPLAN, BERNICE ANTOVILLE, anthropologist, educator; b. N.Y.C., Apr. 21, 1923; d. Meyer and Marie (Antoville) K.; m. Gabriel Ward Lasker, July 31, 1949; children: Robert Alexander, Edward Meyer, Anne Titania. B.A., Hunter Coll., N.Y.C., 1943; M.A. (Univ. fellow 1944-45, Univ. and Field Mus. fellow 1945-46), U. Chgo., 1947, Ph.D., 1953. Asso. in anthropology Am. Mus. Natural History, 1941-44, Field Mus. Natural History, 1947-48; instr. anthropology and sociology U. Wis., 1946-47, Hobart and William Smith Colls., 1948-49; instr. to asso. prof. anthropology Wayne State U., Detroit, 1949-67, asso. prof., 1967-79, prof., 1979—; lectr. U. Mich., Ann Arbor and Grand Rapids, summers 1955, 59, U. Calif., Berkeley, 1960-61; field work, Michoacán, Mex., 1948, 52, 53, 59, 61, 65, and, Province of Lambayeque, Peru, 1957-58, London, 1977. Contbr. articles to profl. jours. Rep., Birmingham (Mich.) PTA Council to Birmingham Bd. Edn., 1971-76; bd. dirs. Southfield Jr. Symphony, 1972-75. Fulbright scholar, 1957-58; fellow-commonorship Churchill Coll., Cambridge U. (Eng.), 1983-84. Fellow Am. Anthrop. Assn., AAAS (chmn. sect. H 1973-74), Am. Assn. Phys. Anthropologists, Soc. for Applied Anthropology (mem. exec. bd. 1976-79); mem. Am. Ethnological Soc. (sec. 1978-82), Central State Anthrop. Soc. (pres. 1972-73, co-editor Central Issues in Anthropology 1978—), Sigma Xi. Home: 31339 Pierce Rd Birmingham MI 48009 Office: Dept Anthropology Manoogian Hall Wayne State U Detroit MI 48202

KAPLAN, BURTON B., mattress manufacturing company executive; b. Chgo., Aug. 31, 1940; s. Morris A. and Alice B. (Berline) K.; m. Anne Lerner, Apr. 3, 1961; children: Beth Mira, Michael, Charles. B.A., Wesleyan U., Middletown, Conn.; M.B.A., Harvard U. With Sealy Mattress Co. of Ill., 1962—, exec. v.p., Northbook, Ill., 1973-78, pres., 1978—; dir. First Nat. Bank Highland Park, Ill. Trustee Highland Park Hosp., 1973-80; bd. dirs. N. Shore Mental Health Assn., 1965-72. Jewish. Club: Lake Shore Country. Office: Sealy Mattress Co of Ill 191 Waukegan Rd Northfield IL 60093 *

KAPLAN, GABRIEL, comedian; b. Bklyn., Mar. 31, 1945; s. Charles and Dorothy K. Ed. pub. schs. Night club comedian; creator: regular

TV series Welcome Back, Kotter, 1975-79; other TV appearances include: Gabriel Kaplan Presents the Future Stars; others; actor: TV film Love Boat, Lewis and Clark, 1981; film Fast Break, 1979, Nobody's Perfekt, 1981, Tulips, 1981; tours of theater circuit; Comedy album Holes and Mellow Rolls, 1974. Nat. chmn. Cystic Fibrosis Found., 1977. Mem. AFTRA. Office: Creative Artists Agy Inc 1888 Century Park E Suite 1400 Los Angeles CA 90067 *

KAPLAN, GARY, executive recruiter; b. Phila., Aug. 14, 1939; s. Morris and Minnie (Leve) K.; m. Linda Ann Wilson, May 30, 1968; children: Michael Warren, Marc Jonathan, Jeffrey Russell. B.A. in Polit. Sci., Pa. State U., 1961. Tchr. biology N.E. High Sch., Phila., 1962-63; coll. employment rep. Bell Telephone Labs., Murray Hill, N.J., 1966-67; supr. recruitment and placement Univac, Blue Bell, Pa., 1967-69; pres. Electronic Systems Personnel, Phila., 1969-70; staff selection rep. Booz, Allen & Hamilton, N.Y.C., 1970-72; mgr. exec. recruitment M&T Chems., Rahway, N.J., 1972-74; dir. exec. recruitment IU Internat. Mgmt. Corp., Phila., 1974-78; v.p. personnel Crocker Bank, Los Angeles, 1978-79; mng. v.p. ptnr. western region Korn-Ferry Internat., Los Angeles, 1979—. Mgmt. columnist, Radio and Records newspaper. Bd. dirs. Vis. Nurse Assn., Los Angeles. Served to capt. Adj. Gen. Corps., U.S. Army, 1963-66. Mem. Hollywood Radio and TV Soc. Home: 5150 Solliden Ln La Canada CA 91011 Office: Korn-Ferry Internat 1900 Ave of Stars Los Angeles CA 90067

KAPLAN, HAROLD, editor, former fgn. service officer; b. Newark, July 29, 1918; s. Samuel and Celia K.; m. Celia Scop, Nov. 18, 1938; children—Leslie, Roger Francis, Lionel Philip. B.A., U. Ill., 1938, M.A., 1941. Instr. U. Chgo., 1941; Fgn. service officer, various posts, Europe, North Africa, Asia, 1952-67, dep. asst. sec. state, 1967-68, counselor NATO mission, 1968; mem. del. Vietnam Peace Talks, 1968-69; ret., 1969; v.p. Bendix Corp., 1972-78; editor-in-chief GEO mag., N.Y.C., 1978—. Author: novella The Mohammedans, 1943; novel The Plenipotentaries, 1950, The Spirit and The Bride, 1952; translator: Raymond Queneau's Loin De Rueil (pub. as The Skin of Dreams), 1950. Mem. Council Fgn. Relations, Inst. Ednl. Affairs, Century Assn., Centre int. de Formation europeene (France). Jewish. Office: 450 Park Ave New York NY 10022 *

KAPLAN, HAROLD, humanities educator, author; b. Chgo., Jan. 3, 1916; m. Isabelle M. Ollier, July 29, 1962; three children. B.A., U. Chgo., 1937, M.A., 1938; postgrad., 1938-40. Instr. Rutgers U., New Brunswick, N.J., 1946-49; faculty dept. lit. Bennington (Vt.) Coll., 1949-72; prof. dept. English Northwestern U., Evanston, Ill., 1972—, chmn. Program in Am. Culture, 1973-75, acting chmn. dept. English, 1980-81; Fulbright-Hays lectr. U. Bari, Italy, 1956-57, U. Poitiers, France, 1960, U. Clermont-Ferrand, 1961, U. Aix-Marseille, 1967-68; vis. prof. Hebrew U., Jerusalem, 1981-82; editorial cons. U. Chgo. Press, 1973—; acad. cons. Jan Krukowski Assocs., N.Y.C. Author: The Passive Voice: An Approach to Modern Fiction, 1966, Democratic Humanism and American Literature, 1972, Power and Order: American Fiction and the Mythology of Naturalism, 1981; contbr. articles and lit. criticism on Am. lit. to scholarly publs., book revs. to lit. jours. Served to capt. USAAF, 1942-46. Ford Found. research grantee, 1970; Nat. Endowment Humanities grantee, summer, 1977; Rockefeller Found. fellow, 1981-82. Mem. MLA. Home: 514 Oakdale Ave Glencoe IL 60022 Office: Dept English Northwestern U Evanston IL 60201

KAPLAN, HAROLD IRVING, lawyer; b. Boston, Jan. 6, 1921; s. Bernard A. and Florence R. (Stone) K.; m. Eleanor G. Moranz, Jan. 1, 1949; children—Joanne Sue, Bart Alan. B.S. in Mech. Engring, U. Maine, 1942; J.D., Harvard, 1948; LL.M., George Washington U., 1950. Bar: Mass. bar 1948, N.Y. bar 1951, U.S. Supreme Ct. bar 1964. Patent examiner U.S. Patent Office, Washington, 1948-50; patent atty., N.Y.C., 1950—; with firm Blum, Kaplan, Friedman, Silberman & Beran, N.Y.C., 1960—, mng. partner, 1971—; Mem. Nat. Panel Arbitrators, Am. Assn. Arbitrators, 1967—. Served to capt. USAAF, 1942-46; ETO. Mem. Assn. Bar City N.Y., N.Y., N.J., Am. patent law assns., Am. Bar Assn. Home: 44 Kean Rd Short Hills NJ 07078 Office: Blum Kaplan Friedman Silberman & Beran 730 3d Ave New York NY 10017

KAPLAN, HAROLD IRWIN, psychiatrist, psychoanalyst; b. Bklyn., Oct. 1, 1927; s. William and Fannie Rose K.; m. Helen Singer, June 20, 1953 (div. 1971); children: Phillip, Peter, Jennifer; m. Nancy Barrett, 1980. M.D., N.Y. Med. Coll., 1949, cert. psychoanalysis, 1954. Diplomate: Am. Bd. Psychiatry and Neurology, 1957 (examiner 1961—, asso. examiner 1983). Intern Bklyn. Jewish Hosp., 1949-50; resident in psychiatry VA Hosp., Bronx, N.Y., 1950-53; fellow in psychiatry Mt. Sinai Hosp., N.Y.C., 1952; fellow in child psychiatry Jewish Bd. Guardians, N.Y.C., 1953; practice medicine specializing in psychiatry, practice psychoanalysis, N.Y.C., 1953—;; asst. prof. N.Y. Med. Coll., 1957-61, 1961-65; prof. psychiatry, 1965-80, NYU Sch. Medicine, 1980—; attending psychiatrist Bellevue Hosp., 1980—, Univ. Hosp. of NYU Med. Center, 1980—; attending and vis. psychiatrist Met. Hosp. and Flower Hosp., N.Y.C., 1954-80; chief psychiat. edn. and tng. N.Y. Med. Coll.-Met. Hosp. Center., N.Y.C., 1960-80; mem. med. bd. Met. Hosp., 1964-80; specialist in psychiat. tng.; mem. Prep. Commn. on Psychiat. Edn., NIMH-Am. Psychiat. Assn., 1974-75. Co-author: Modern Group Therapy series, 1972; Studies in Human Behavior series, 1972; co-author: Study Guide and Self-examination Review for Modern Synopsis of Comprehensive Textbook of Psychiatry/IV, 2d edit., 1985; co-editor: Comprehensive Group Psychotherapy, 2d edit., 1983, Comprehensive Textbook of Psychiatry, 4th edit., 1984, Modern Synopsis of Comprehensive Textbook of Psychiatry, 4th edit., 1984, The Sexual Experience, 1976; contbr. numerous articles to med. publs. NIMH grantee, 1960-72. Fellow Am. Psychiat. Assn. (chmn. com. med. edn. 1973-75, cert. commendation 1976), Acad. Psychoanalysis, Acad. Psychosomatic Medicine, ACP (life); mem. Am. Psychosomatic Soc., Assn. Research Nervous and Mental Diseases (life), Med. Soc. County and State N.Y., AMA, Am. Geriatric Soc., World Psychiat. Assn., Assn. Advancement Psychotherapy, Am. Med. Writers Assn., Can. Psychiat. Assn., N.Y. Acad. Scis. (life), N.Y. Acad. Medicine (life), AAAS (life), Pan Am. Med. Assn. (diplomate), Royal Soc. Medicine (London), Am. Public Health Assn., Assn. Dirs. Psychiat. Residency Tng. Programs, Assn. Acad. Psychiatry, Am. Group Psychotherapy Assn., Soc. Med. Psychoanalysts, Alumni Assn. Bklyn. Jewish Hosp., Alumni Assn. N.Y. Med. Coll., AAUP, Alpha Omega Alpha. Office: 50 E 78th St New York NY 10021

KAPLAN, HAROLD MORRIS, physiologist, educator; b. Boston, Sept. 4, 1908; s. Max and Mollie (Smith) K.; m. Bernice Stone, June 1935; children: Elaine Beth, Joyce M., Lee Allan. A.B., Dartmouth Coll., 1930; A.M. (Jeffries Wyman scholar), Harvard U., 1931, Ph.D., 1933. Asst. instr. Harvard, 1933-34; prof. Middlesex Med. Sch., 1934-35, Middlesex Vet. Sch., 1945-47; writer Washington Inst. Medicine, 1946-49; asso. prof. U. Mass., 1947-48; prof. So. Ill. U., 1948—, 1974—, adminstr. engring. biophysics program, 1973—; curriculum cons. Okla. Coll. Osteopathic Medicine and Surgery, 1981; Asso. editor Am. Assn. Lab Animal Sci., 1959, pres., 1966-67; chmn. editorial bd. Lab. Animal Scis., 1959-73; cons. Applied Research and Devel. Lab., Mt. Vernon, Ill. Fellow AAAS; mem. Am. Soc. Zoologists Ill. Acad. Sci. (pres. 1968-69, councilor 1969—), Ill. Soc. Med. Research (dir. 1966—), Inst. Lab. Animal Resources (past adv. council), Am. Physiol. Soc., Electron Microscope Soc. Am., Midwest Soc. Electron Microscopists, Am. Assn. Lab. Animal Sci. (pres., exec. bd. 1969-70), Sigma Xi, Phi Kappa Phi (pres. chpt. 1983), Phi Eta Sigma. Home: 106 N Almond St Carbondale IL 62901 *In the 1980s this statement may seem square, but I find no royal road to success other than working hard, consistently, honestly, and at all times for the common good.*

KAPLAN, HELEN SINGER, psychiatrist; b. Vienna, Austria, Feb. 6, 1929; came to U.S., 1940, naturalized, 1947; d. Phillip Sigmund and Sophie (Lanzi) Singer; m. Harold I. Kaplan, June 20, 1953 (div. 1972); children: Phillip, Peter, Jennifer; m. Charles P. Lazarus, Nov. 1979. B.F.A., Syracuse U., 1949; M.A., Columbia U., 1951, Ph.D., 1955; M.D., N.Y. Med. Coll., 1959. Intern Bronx (N.Y.) Hosp., 1960-61; resident N.Y. Med. Coll., 1962-64; practice medicine specializing in psychiatry, N.Y.C., 1964—; resident Bellevue Hosp., 1961-62; assoc. vis. psychiatrist Met. Hosp.; assoc. prof. psychiatry N.Y. Med. Coll.; clin. prof. psychiatry Cornell U. Med. Coll.; founder, head human sexuality program, clin. attending psychiatrist N.Y. Hosp., N.Y.C., 1970-75; career tchr. in psychiatry NIMH, 1964-66. Co-editor: Progress in Group and Family Therapy, 1972, The Evaluation of Sexual Disorders, 1983; asst. to editors: Comprehensive Textbook Psychiatry, 1967, New Sex Therapy, 1974, Illustrated Manual of Sex Therapy, 1975, Making Sense of Sex, 1979, Disorders of Sexual Desire, 1979; co-editor: Jour. Sex and Marital Therapy; contbr. articles to profl. jours. Fellow Am. Psychiat. Assn., Am. Psychol. Assn., Acad. Psychoanalysis; mem. Sigma Xi, Alpha Omega Alpha. Office: 30 E 76th St New York NY 10021

KAPLAN, HELENE LOIS, lawyer; b. N.Y.C., June 19, 1933; d. Jack and Shirley (Jacobs) Finkelstein; m. Mark N. Kaplan, Sept. 7, 1953; children: Marjorie Ellen, Sue Anne. A.B. cum laude, Barnard Coll., 1953; J.D., N.Y. U., 1967. Bar: N.Y. 1967. Individual practice, N.Y.C., 1967-78; mem. firm Webster & Sheffield, N.Y.C., 1978—; dir. Verde Exploration, Ltd. Trustee N.Y. Council for the Humanities, 1976-82, chmn., 1978-82; trustee Barnard Coll., 1973-83, chmn., 1983—; trustee Columbia U. Press, 1977-80, MITRE Corp., 1978—, N.Y. Found., 1976—, Mt. Sinai Hosp. Med. Center and Med. Sch., 1977—, John Simon Guggenheim Found., 1981—, Carnegie Corp. N.Y., 1979—; vice chmn. Carnegie Corp. N.Y., 1981—; trustee N.Y. C. Public Devel. Corp., 1978-83, vice chmn., 1979-82; trustee Olive Free Library; bd. dirs. Am. Arbitration Assn., 1978-82, Catskill Ctr. for Conservation and Devel., 1981—; mem. Women's Forum, Inc., 1982—. Mem. Assn. of the Bar of the City of N.Y. (com. on philanthropic orgn. 1975-81, recruitment of lawyers 1978-82, com. on profl. responsibility 1980-83), Am. Bar Assn., N.Y. State Bar Assn. Club: Cosmopolitan (N.Y.C.). Home: 146 Central Park W New York NY 10023 Office: 1 Rockefeller Plaza New York NY 10020

KAPLAN, IRVING M.J., steel company executive; b. Pitts., Sept. 5, 1919; s. Frank R.S. and Madeline (Roth) K.; m. Joan Marie Meyerhoff, Nov. 10, 1955; children: William A., Thomas R., Fred M. B.A., Princeton U., 1941. Vice pres., sec., dir. Copperweld Corp., Pitts., 1954—. Republican ward committeeman 14th Ward, Pitts., 1964-74; mem. exec. bd. Rep. Fin. Com. Allegheny County, 1966-74; Rep. state committeeman 43d Dist., 1966-74; Pres. Vocat. Rehab. Center, 1961-63, bd. dirs., 1955-74; bd. dirs. Planned Parenthood Center Pitts., 1968-74, Tb League Pitts.; trustee Alumni Council Shady Side Acad., 1960-63; mem. Union Am. Hebrew Congregations, 1975-78, Western Pa. Conservancy, 1979-83. Mem. Am. Iron and Steel Inst., Newcomen Soc., Am. Ordnance Assn., Am. Soc. Corp. Secs., Am. Soc. Metals, Pa. Soc. Commerce, Pitts. C. of C. Jewish (trustee congregation). Clubs: Masons, Duquesne, Concordia, Standard, Harvard-Yale-Princeton. Home: 5469 Northumberland St Pittsburgh PA 15217 Office: Two Oliver Plaza Pittsburgh PA 15222

KAPLAN, J(ACOB) GORDIN, biologist, educator; b. N.Y.C., Nov. 26, 1922; s. Michael and Nadia (Gordin) K.; m. Sylvia Mary Leadbeater, Aug. 31, 1949; children: Elizabeth, Michael Gordin. B.A., CCNY, 1943; M.A., Columbia U., 1948, Ph.D., 1950; D.Sc. (hon.), Concordia U., 1978. Mem. faculty Dalhousie U. Faculty Medicine, Halifax, N.S., Can., 1950-66; prof. biology U. Ottawa, Ont., Can., 1966-81, chmn. dept., 1975-81; prof. biochemistry, v.p. research U. Alta., Edmonton, Can., 1981—; vice chmn. Tri Univs. Meson Facility; pres. XI Internat. Congress Biochemistry, Toronto, 1979; chmn. com. internat. sci. and tech. affairs Nat. Research Council Can., 1980—; dir. Alta. Research Council, Chembiomed Ltd, Majestic Laser Systems Ltd., Alta. Microelectronic Devel. and Application Centre. Editor: Molecular Basis of Immune Cell Function, 1979, Can. Jour. Biochemistry, 1973-81. Served with AUS, 1942-46. Lalor Found. fellow; NSF sr. postdoctoral fellow; Can.-France Exchange fellow, 1973-74. Fellow Royal Soc. Can.; Mem. Can. Soc. Cell Biology (pres. 1969-70), Can. Soc. Biochemistry (pres. 1978-79), Can. Assn. Univ. Tchrs. (pres. 1970-71), Can. Fedn. Biol. Socs. (pres. 1975-76), Am. Soc. Biol. Chemists, Am. Soc. Cell Biology, Soc. Philomathique de Paris. *

KAPLAN, JACOB MERRILL, merchant; b. Lowell, Mass., Dec. 23, 1891; s. David and Fanny K.; m. Alice M. Kaplan, June 30, 1925; 4 children. Organizer, pres., owner Welch Grape Juice Co., 1940-58; pres. Jemkap Inc., N.Y.C., 1930—. Founder, trustee J.M. Kaplan Fund, Inc., 1947—. Home: Sag Harbor Rd East Hampton NY Office: 330 Madison Ave New York NY 10017 *At 92— still believe there is a meaning to human existence— but do not know anyone who can prove the answer— still wonder the purpose and destiny.*

KAPLAN, JEREMIAH, publisher, editor; b. N.Y.C., July 15, 1926; s. Samuel H. and Fannie (Brafman) K.; m. Charlotte R. Larsen, June 16, 1945; children: Ann Frances, Susanna Ruth, Margaret Jane, David Baruch. Vice pres. Free Press Glencoe, Inc., Ill., 1947-60, pres., 1960-64; editorial dir. gen. pub. div. Crowell-Collier Pub. Co., 1960-62, v.p., 1962-67, sr. v.p., 1967—; chmn. bd. Sci. Materials, Inc., 1962-63; v.p. Macmillan Co., 1960-63, exec. v.p., 1963-65, pres., 1965-73, 77—, chmn., 1983—; exec. v.p. Crowell Collier and Macmillan, Inc., 1968—, head product devel. and corporate marketing planning, 1972—; also dir.; chmn. Collier Macmillan Internat., 1973—; exec. v.p. and dir. Macmillan, Inc., 1979—; chmn. bd. Macmillan Pub. Co., Inc., 1980—; dir. Franklin Book Programs, Inc.; professorial lectr. behavioral scis. Grad. Sch. Bus., U. Chgo., 1960-63. Trustee Telladega Coll., Stoneleigh-Burnham Sch., U. Rochester; nat. adv. council Hampshire Coll. Mem. Assn. Am. Pubs. (dir.). Club: Dutch Treat, Century Assn. (N.Y.C.). Office: 866 3d Ave New York NY 10022 *

KAPLAN, JOHN, legal educator; b. N.Y.C., July 9, 1929; s. Edward I. and Dorothy (Saron) K.; m. Elizabeth Brown, Nov. 5, 1960. A.B. in Physics, Harvard U., 1951, LL.B., 1954. Bar: N.Y., Calif., D.C. Law clerk to Supreme Ct. Justice Tom. C. Clark, 1954-55; spl. atty. Dept. Justice, 1957-58; asst. U.S. atty. No. Dist. Calif., 1958-61; assoc. prof. law Northwestern U. Law Sch., 1962-64; vis. assoc. prof. law U. Calif., Berkeley Law Sch., 1964-65; Jackson Eli Reynolds prof. law Stanford Law Sch., Calif., 1965—. Author: Marijuna-The New Prohibition, 1970, Criminal Justice: Introductory Cases and Materials, 1973; co-author: (with Jon R. Waltz) The Trial of Jack Ruby, 1965; author: (with David Louisell and Jon R. Waltz) Cases and Materials on Evidence, 1968, Principles of Evidence and Proof, 1968, (with William Cohen) The Bill of Rights, 1976. Mem. nat. adv. com. on alcoholism and alcohol abuse HEW. Office: Stanford U Sch of Law Crown Quad Stanford GA 94305

KAPLAN, JONATHAN STEWART, film writer and director; b. Paris, Nov. 25, 1947; s. Sol and Mary Frances (Heflin) K. Student, U. Chgo., 1965-67; B.F.A., N.Y. U., 1969; postgrad., New World Pictures Roger Corman Post-Grad. Sch. Film Making, Hollywood, Calif., 1971-73. Mem. tech. staff Bill Graham's Fillmore East, N.Y.C., 1969-71. Actor: Broadway after Broadway The Dark at the Top of the Stairs, 1956-57; Broadway play Happy Anniversary; film, 1959, Rumplestiltskin; play, 1964; dir.: films Night Call Nurses, 1972, Student Teachers, 1973, The Slams, 1973, Truck Turner, 1974, Over the Edge, 1978, 11th Victim, 1979, Muscle Beach, 1980, Gentleman Bandit, 1981; film Heart Like a Wheel, 1983; dir., co-writer: films White Line Fever, 1974, Mr. Billion, 1976; student film Stanley Stanely, 1970 (1st prize Schlitz Nat. Student Film Festival). Address: care ICM 8899 Beverly Blvd Los Angeles CA 90048

KAPLAN, JUSTIN, author; b. N.Y.C., Sept. 5, 1925; s. Tobias D. and Anna (Rudman) K.; m. Anne F. Bernays, July 29, 1954; children: Susanna Bernays, Hester Margaret, Polly Anne. B.S., Harvard U., 1944, postgrad., 1944-46. Free-lance editing, writing, N.Y.C., 1946-54; sr. editor Simon & Schuster, Inc., N.Y.C., 1954-59; lectr. English Harvard U., 1969, 73, 76, 78; prose writer in residence Emerson Coll., Boston, 1977-78. Author: Mr. Clemens and Mark Twain, 1966, Lincoln Steffens, A Biography, 1974, Mark Twain and His World, 1974, Walt Whitman: A Life, 1980; Editor: Dialogues of Plato, 1948, With Malice Toward Women, 1949, The Pocket Aristotle, 1956, The Gilded Age, 1964, Great Short Works of Mark Twain, 1967, Mark Twain, A Profile, 1967, Walt Whitman: Complete Poetry and Collected Prose, 1982; Contbr. to: N.Y. Times, New Republic, Am. Scholar, others. Recipient Pulitzer prize for biography, 1967, Nat. Book award in arts and letters, 1967, Am. Book award for biography, 1981; Guggenheim fellow, 1975-76. Fellow Am. Acad. Arts and Scis., Soc. Am. Historians. Home: 16 Francis Ave Cambridge MA 02138

KAPLAN, LAWRENCE, biology educator; b. Chgo., Apr. 14, 1926; s. Herman and Fannie (Eisen) K.; m. Lucille Nobler, Aug. 24, 1946; children: Martha, Emily, Elisabeth. Student, Wright Jr. Coll., Chgo., 1946-48; B.A., State U. Iowa, 1949, M.S., 1951; Ph.D., U. Chgo., 1956. Assoc. curator museum Mo. Bot. Gardens, 1955; research assoc. dept. anthropology U. Chgo., 1956-58; mem. faculty Wright Jr. Coll., 1956-57; dept. biology Roosevelt U., Chgo., 1957-65; assoc. prof. biology U. Mass., Boston, 1965-68, prof. biology, 1968—, chmn. dept., 1968-71, 75-78, 82—. Assoc. editor: Econ. Botany. Served with USNR, 1943-46. Mem. Am. Inst. Biol. Scis., Soc. for Econ. Botany (mem. council 1966-69, 80—), Bot. Soc. Am., Soc. for Am. Archaeology, N.E. Bot. Club. Home: 26 Parker St Newton Centre MA 02159 Office: Dept Biology U Mass Boston MA 02125

KAPLAN, LAWRENCE IRVING, physiatrist, educator; b. N.Y.C., June 7, 1917; s. Robert and Lora (Tow) K.; m. Esther Weisfofel, Mar. 3, 1951; children: Robin Meade, laura Verne. Student, N.Y.U. Coll. Arts and Scis., 1935-37, St. Mungo's Coll. Medicine, Glasgow Scotland, 1937-39; M.D., U. Geneva (Switzerland), 1948. Diplomate: Am. Bd. Phys. Medicine and Rehab., Am. Bd. Quality Assurance and Utilization Rev. Physicians. Rotating intern Morrisiania City Hosp., Bronx, N.Y., 1949-50, fellow in neurology, 1950, asst. and sr. resident in internal medicine, 1950-52; NIH fellow in phys. medicine and rehab. N.Y.U. Med. Ctr., N.Y.C., 1952-54, asst. attending physician, 1954-56, instr. phys. medicine and rehab., 1954-56, asst. prof. clin. medicine and rehab., 1960-64; asst. vis. physician Bllevue Hosp. Ctr., N.Y.C., 1954-56; assoc. vis. dir. Bellevue Hosp. Ctr., N.Y.C., 1960-64; mem. staff Queens Gen. Hosp., Jewish Hosp., Jamaica, N.Y., 1954-56; dir. Charles S. Wilson Meml. Hosp., Johnson City, N.Y.; med. dir. Binghamton Rhab. Services Inc., 1956-58; assoc. vis. physician Bird S. Coler Hosp., N.Y.C., 1958-60; asst. prof. N.Y. Med. Coll., 1958-60, Met. Hosp. Ctr., 1958-60; chief physiatrist Elmhurst Hosp. Ctr. (N.Y.), 1960-64; dir. dept. rehab. medicine Mt. Sinai Services, 1964—; attending physician Deepdale Hosp., Queens; assoc. prof. rehab. medicine Mt. Sinai Sch. Medicine, N.Y.C., 1966-69, prof., 1969—; adj. prof. Hunter Coll.; lectr. N.Y.U. Med. Ctr.; mem. Hosp. Rev. Com. Queens PSRO, 1977—, bd. dirs., 1978-81, mem. med. care evaluation com. Contbr. articles to profl. jours. Served with USAAF, 1942-45; PTO. Fellow N.Y. Acad. Medicine; mem. Am. Congress Phys. Medicine and Rehab., Am. Acad. Phys. Medicine and Rehab., N.Y. Soc. Phys. Medicine and Rehab., AMA, N.Y. State Med. Soc., Nassau County Med. Soc., Nat. Rehab. Assn., Am. Acad. Physiatrists, N. Am. Acad. Manipulative Medicine, Am. Acad. Sports Medicine. Home: 11 Shrub Hollow Rd Roslyn NY 11576 Office: Mount Sinai Service City Hosp Ctr 79-01 Broadway Elmhurst NY 11373

KAPLAN, LEO SYLVAN, college administrator; b. N.Y.C., Feb. 14, 1924; s. Max and Frieda (Kuritzky) K.; m. Matilda Correa, Dec. 28, 1946; children: Michael, Harry, Hannah. B.A., CCNY, 1946; M.A., Columbia U., 1949. Mem. faculty econs. dept. Queens Coll., N.Y.C., 1952-54; research dir. Lic. Beverage Industries Inc., N.Y.C., 1955-58; mem. faculty Cooper Union, N.Y.C., 1958—, v.p., provost, 1972—. Author book reviews and articles for profl. jours.; editor: Internat. Jour. Sociology, 1972-78. Served with AUS, 1943-45; PTO. Decorated Purple Heart. Office: Cooper Union for Advancement of Science and Art Cooper Square New York NY 10003

KAPLAN, MANUEL E., physician, educator; b. N.Y.C., Nov. 11, 1928; s. Morris Jacob and Sylvia (Schiff) K.; m. Rita Goldman, May 22, 1955; children—Anne J., Eve D., Joshua M. B.Sc. Diplomate: Am. Bd. Internal Medicine. Intern Boston City Hosp., 1954-55, resident, 1955-56, 58-59; fellow in hematology Thorndike Lab., 1959-62; attending hematologist Mt. Sinai Hosp., N.Y.C., 1962-65, asst. chief hematology, 1963-65; asst. prof. medicine Washington U. Sch. Medicine, St. Louis, 1965-69; asso. prof. medicine U. Minn. Sch. Medicine, Mpls., 1969-72, prof. medicine, 1972—; chief hematology and oncology Mpls. VA Med. Center. Contbr. numerous articles to profl. jours. Served with USPHS, 1956-58. Mem. Am. Fedn. Clin. Research, Am. Soc. Clin. Investigation, Am. Soc. Hematology, Am. Assn. Immunology, AAAS, others. Jewish. Home: 2950 Dean Pkwy Apt 1201 Minneapolis MN 55416 Office: Minneapolis VA Med Center Minneapolis MN 55417

KAPLAN, MARILYN FLASHENBERG, painter; b. Bklyn.; s. Sander E. and Eva (Novak) Flashenberg; m. Donald Henry Kaplan, July 11, 1954; children—Daniel Alan, Bruce Howard. B.F.A., Syracuse (N.Y.) U., 1952; M.A. in Art Edn, Columbia U., 1954. Elementary art coordinator Croton (N.Y.) Harmon Schs., 1953-54; art cons. Jericho (N.Y.) adult edn., 1960-75. One-woman exhbns. include, Hofstra U., 1966, Mad Monk Gallery, N.Y.C., 1968, Syosset (N.Y.) Library, 1971, Jericho (N.Y.) Library, 1977, Madison Ave. Gallery, N.Y.C., 1979-83, group exhbns. include, NAD, N.Y.C., 1970, 72, 75, Corcoran Gallery of Art, Washington, 1976, Contemporary Arts Mus., Houston, Mus. of Sci. and Industry, Chgo., Inst. Contemporary Art, London, 1977, Musée des Arts Decoratifs, Paris; created: poster No More War, 1969; rep. in permanent collection, Smithsonian Instn. Recipient B. Altman award NAD, 1975. Mem. Artists Equity Assn. N.Y. Jewish. Address: 26 Birchwood Park Dr Jericho NY 11753 *Success for me as an artist can only be measured in terms of the pleasure my work bestows upon those who desire to live with it.*

KAPLAN, MARK NORMAN, lawyer; b. N.Y.C., Mar. 7, 1930; s. Louis and Ruth (Hertzberg) K.; m. Helene L. Finkelstein, Sept. 7, 1952; children: Marjorie Ellen, Sue Anne. A.B., Columbia, 1951; J.D.,

1953. Bar: N.Y. 1953. Asso. firm Garey & Garey, N.Y.C., 1953; law clk. Judge William Bondy, U.S. Dist. Ct. for So. Dist. N.Y., 1953-54; asso. at law Columbia Law Sch., 1954-55; asso. Wickes, Riddell, Bloomer, Jacobi & McGuire, N.Y.C., 1955-59; asso., partner, sr. partner Marshall, Bratter, Greene, Allison & Tucker, N.Y.C., 1959-70; sr. partner Burnham & Co., N.Y.C., 1970-71; pres. Drexel Burnham Lambert Inc., N.Y.C., 1972-77, also chief exec. officer, 1976-77; pres. Engelhard Minerals & Chem. Corp., N.Y.C., 1977-79; mem. firm Skadden, Arps, Slate, Meager & Flom, N.Y.C., 1979—; dir. Elgin Nat. Industries, Inc., Am. Biltrite, Grey Advt., Inc., Unimax, Utilities and Industries, REFAC Tech. Devel. Corp., U.S. Adminstrs., Marcade Group, Inc., Polo Fashions, Inc., DFS Group Ltd., Hong Kong, Great Pacific Industries Inc., Vancouver, B.C., Can.; vice chmn. Am. Stock Exchange, N.Y.C., 1974, gov., 1975, vice chmn., 1976-77. Bd. dirs. Am. Place Theatre, N.Y.C.; bd. visitors Columbia Coll. and Law Sch.; mem. adv. council Center for Nat. Policy Rev., Washington; trustee Bard Coll., Simons Rock Coll.; mem. audit com. City of N.Y.; bd. dirs. New Alternatives for Children. Mem. Council Fgn. Relations, Econ. Club N.Y., Harmonie. Club: City Athletic (N.Y.C.). Home: 146 Central Park W New York NY 10023 Office: 919 3d Ave New York NY 10022

KAPLAN, MARSHALL L., university dean, former government official, city planner; b. Roxbury, Mass., Feb. 13, 1935; s. Harry and Gertrude K.; m. Barbara Ann Brodkey, June, 1963; children: Stephanie, Scott. B.A., Boston U., 1956, M.A., 1957; M.C.P., MIT, 1960. Report coordinator Gov.'s Housing Commn., Calif., 1960-62; urban economist HHFA, 1962-63; dep. dir. Community Devel. Project, U. Calif., 1963-65; prin. Marshall, Kaplan, Gan & Kahn, San Francisco, 1965-78; vis. prof. urban policy U. Tex., 1977-78; dep. asst. sec. urban policy HUD, Washington, 1978-80; dean Grad. Sch. Public Affairs, U. Colo., Denver, 1980—. Author numerous books in field. Bd. dirs. Calif. Democratic Forum, 1960; Bd. dirs. Urban League, Dallas, 1973-75, Colo. Ballet, Am. Jewish Com., Jud. Inst.; mem. Mayor's Arts Commn., 1981—. Mem. Am. Inst. Planners., Am. Soc. Pub. Adminstrn. Jewish. Home: 9795 E Maplewood Circle Englewood CO Office: U Colo Denver CO

KAPLAN, MELVIN HYMAN, medical educator; b. Malden, Mass., Dec. 23, 1920; s. Harry and Rena (Chernoff) K. A.B., Harvard U., 1942, M.D., 1952. Intern Boston City Hosp., 1952; research fellow medicine House of Good Samaritan, Boston; also asst. bacteriology and immunology Harvard Med. Sch., 1953; research assoc. medicine, instr., also established investigator Am. Heart Assn., 1954-57, assoc. bacteriology and immunology, 1957-58; practice medicine, specializing in rheumatology and clin. immunology, Cleve., 1958—; asst. prof. medicine Sch. Medicine Western Res. U., 1958-60, assoc. prof., 1960-65, prof., 1965—, dir. div. immunology and rheumatology, 1974-82; acting chmn. lab. medicine U. Mass., 1974-79; assoc. physician Cleve. Met. Gen. Hosp., 1958-62, physician, 1962-74; Cons. allergy and immunology study sect. USPHS, 1964-69; asso. mem. com. streptococcal diseases Armed Forces Epidemiological Bd., 1956-70; temp. adviser WHO Study Cardiomyopathies in Africa, 1965; mem. merit review bd. VA, 1972—. Asso. editor: Jour. Lab. and Clin. Medicine, 1963-68, Jour. Clin. and Exptl. Immunology, 1965-71; Contbr. articles to profl. jours. Served with AUS, 1942-46. Recipient Research Career award USPHS, 1964. Mem. Am. Soc. Clin. Investigation, Am. Rheumatism Assn., Am. Assn. Immunologists, Central Soc. Clin. Research, Am. Soc. Microbiology, Soc. Exptl. Biology and Medicine, Am. Heart Assn. Home: 1500 Worcester Rd Apt 605E Framingham MA 01701 Office: 55 Lake Ave N Worcester MA 01605

KAPLAN, MICHAEL IRVING, bedding manufacturing executive; b. Chgo., May 19, 1941; s. Jerome M. and Rose Lena (Simon) K.; m. Francene Peller, Aug. 29, 1965; children: Kelly Susan, Charles David. B.S.B.A., Roosevelt U., 1963. C.P.A. Sr. auditor Seidman & Seidman, Chgo., 1963-66; v.p.-fin. Sealy, Inc., Chgo., 1966-83, group v.p. owned and operated plants, 1983—. Served with USCGR, 1960-66. Mem. Am. Inst. C.P.A.s, Ill. Soc. C.P.A.s. Clubs: B'nai B'rith, Exec., Mchts. and Mfrs., East Bank (Chgo.). Home: 831 Oak Dr Glencoe IL 60022 Office: Merchandise Mart Suite 470 Chicago IL 60654

KAPLAN, MORTON A., political science educator; b. Phila., May 9, 1921; s. Lewis J. and Anthea (Ginsberg) K.; m. Azie Mortimer, 1967. B.S., Temple U., 1943; Ph.D., Columbia, 1951. Instr. Ohio State U., 1951-52; asst. prof. polit. sci. Haverford Coll., 1953-54; mem. staff Brookings Instn., Washington, 1954-55; asst. prof. polit. sci. U. Chgo., 1956-61, asso. prof., 1961-65, chmn. com. internat. relations, 1959—, prof. polit. sci., 1965—; dir. Ford workshop programs in internat. relations, 1961-76, dir. faculty arms control and fgn. policy seminar, 1970-75; dir. Center for Strategic and Fgn. Policy Studies, 1976—; research asso., Center of Internat. Studies, Princeton, 1958-62; vis. asso. prof. polit. sci. Yale, 1961-62; mem. staff Hudson Inst., 1961-78, cons., 1978-80; lectr. Command and Gen. Staff Sch., 1965-67, Fgn. Service Inst., 1967, Air War Coll., 1967-69, Nat. Def. Coll. Can., 1970—; bd. assocs. Fgn. Policy Research Inst., 1967—; Gabrielson Distinguished lectr. Bowdoin Coll., 1968; Nulton Distinguished lectr., Goucher Coll., 1969; cons. Nat. Endowment for Humanities, 1972—. Author: System and Process in International Politics, 1957, Some Problems in the Strategic Analysis of International Politics, 1959, The Communist Coup in Czechoslovakia, 1960, (with Nicholas de B. Kaztenbach) The Political Foundations of International Law, 1961, (with Reitzel and Coblenz) United States Foreign Policy, 1945-55, 1956, Macropolitics: Essays on the Philosophy and Science of Politics, 1969, On Historical and Political Knowing: An Inquiry into Some Problems of Universal Law and Human Freedom, 1971, Dissent and the State in Peace and War: An Essay on the Grounds of Public Morality, 1970, On Freedom and Human Dignity: The Importance of the Sacred in Politics, 1973, The Rationale for NATO; Past and Future, 1973, (with others) Vietnam Settlement: Why 1973, Not 1969?, 1973, Alienation and Identification, 1976, Towards Professionalism in International Theory: Macrosystem Analysis, 1979, Science, Language and the Human Condition, 1984; Editor: (with others) The Revolution in World Politics, 1962, The New Approaches to International Relations, 1968, SALT: Problems and Prospects, 1973, Strategic Thinking and Its Moral Implications, 1973; editor, contbg. author: Great Issues of International Politics, 1970, 74, Isolation or Interdependence? Today's Choices for Tomorrow's World, 1975, NATO and Dissuasion, 1974, Global Policy: Challenge of the 80s, 1983; co-editor, contbg. author: Japan, America, and the Future World Order, 1976, (with others) Justice, Human Nature, and Political Obligation, 1976, The Life and Death of the Cold War: Selected Studies in Post-War Statecraft, 1976; asso. editor: Jour. Conflict Resolution, 1961—; mem. editorial bd.: World Politics, 1961-71, ORBIS, 1967—; editor, contbr.: The Many Faces of Communism, 1978. Pres. Cetra Music Corp., 1962—, Moraz Prodns., Inc., 1963—; Cons. Com. Econ. Devel., 1965, Braddock, Dunn and McDonald, 1969, 72—; cons. USIA, 1972; sect. chmn. Internat. Confs. on Unity Scis., 1975, 76, 78, 79, chmn., 1980-83; bd. dirs. Univ. Centers for Rational Alternatives, 1969—; bd. govs., research com. STRATIS, Israeli Inst. Strategic Studies and Policy Analysis, 1974-79. Served with AUS, 1943-46. Fellow Center Internat. Studies Princeton, 1952-53; Center Advanced Study in Behavioral Scis., 1955-56; Carnegie fellow, 1959-60. Mem. AAAS, Am. Soc. Internat. Law, Am. Polit. Sci. Assn., Internat. Sociol. Assn. (chmn. standing com. on sociology internat. relations 1974-78), Inst. Strategic Studies London, Instituto Mexicano de Cultura (corr.), Internat. Cultural Soc. Korea (hon.). Address: 5828 S University Ave Chicago IL 60637 *Constantly to seek new ideas, not for their newness, but for their ability to illuminate the condition of man.*

KAPLAN, NATHAN ORAM, biochemist, educator; b. N.Y.C., June 25, 1917; s. Philip and Rebecca (Uttef) K.; m. Goldie Levine, Feb. 9, 1947; 1 son, Jerold Laurence. A.B., UCLA, 1939; Ph.D., U. Calif.-Berkeley, 1943; D.Sc. (hon.), Brandeis U., 1982. Research assoc. Mass. Gen. Hosp., Boston, 1945-49; asst. prof. biochemistry U. Ill., 1949-50; asst. prof. biology Johns Hopkins, 1950-52, assoc. prof., 1952-56, prof., 1956-57; prof. biochemistry, chmn. grad. dept. biochemistry Brandeis U., 1957-68; prof. chemistry U. Calif.-San Diego, 1968—, assoc. dir. Cancer Ctr., La Jolla, 1980—; adj. prof. dept. neoplastic diseases Mt. Sinai Sch. Medicine, CUNY, N.Y.C., 1976—; Fogarty scholar-in-residence NIH, 1982. Adv. com. Oak Ridge Nat. Lab., Nat. Cancer Inst.; Bd. dirs. Am. Cancer Soc. Recipient Sugar Research award, 1946, Eli Lilly award in biochemistry, 1952, travel award NSF, 1952, award Am. Assn. Clin. Chemistry, 1976; Guggenheim fellow, 1965, 75. Fellow Harvey Soc. (hon.); mem. Am. Chem. Soc., Am. Soc. Biochemist, Nat. Acad. Scis., Am. Soc. Bacteriologists, AAAS, AAUP, Am. Cancer Soc. Council Research and Clin. Investigation, Am. Acad. Arts and Scis., Internat. Union Biochemistry (U.S. nat. com.), Sigma Xi. Home: 8587 La Jolla Scenic Dr La Jolla CA 92037

KAPLAN, NORMAN MAYER, medical educator; b. Dallas, Jan. 2, 1931; s. Isadore Joseph and Sarah Rebecca (Bernstein) K.; m. Audrey Belle Richman, Nov. 27, 1975; children: Marcia, Cynthia, Carolyn, Diane, Michael, Daniel, Adam. B.S. in Pharmacy, U. Tex., 1950, M.D., 1954. Intern Parkland Hosp., Dallas, 1954-55, resident in internal medicine, 1955-58; instr. U. Tex. Health Sci. Center, Dallas, 1961-62, asst. prof., 1962-68, asso. prof., 1968-70, prof. internal medicine, 1970—; v.p. research programs Am. Heart Assn., 1975-76; cons. VA, Baylor, St. Paul, Presbyn. hosps. Author: Your Blood Pressure: The Most Deadly High, 1974, Clinical Hypertension, 1973, 3d edit., 1982, Prevent Your Heart Attack, 1982; mem. editorial bd. numerous profl. jours. Pres. League Ednl. Advancement, 1963-68; bd. dirs. Jewish Fedn. Dallas, Congregation Shearith Israel; pres. Jewish Vocat. Counseling Service. Served with USAF, 1958-60. Recipient acad. award preventive cardiology NIH, 1979—; USPHS grantee, 1961-75. Mem. Am. Soc. Clin. Investigation, Am. Fedn. Clin. Research, Endocrine Soc., Council High Blood Pressure Research, Am. Heart Assn. (med. adv. bd. 1969). Home: 12624 Breckenridge Dallas TX 75230 Office: 5223 Harry Hines Blvd Dallas TX 75235

KAPLAN, OSCAR JOEL, psychology educator; b. N.Y.C., Oct. 21, 1915; s. Philip and Rebecca (Uttef) K.; m. Rose Zankan, Dec. 28, 1942; children: Stephen Paul, Robert Malcolm, David T.A. A.B., UCLA, 1937, M.A., 1938; Ph.D., U. Calif.-Berkeley, 1940. Instr., then asso. prof. psychology So. br. U. Idaho, 1941-46; asst. prof. psychology San Diego State U., 1946-49, prof., 1952—; chmn. dept. psychology San Diego State U., 1950-52, 63-66; dir. center for survey research; cons. gerontology USPHS, 1946-50; vis. prof. pub. health U. Calif. at Los Angeles, 1965-66; cons. clin. psychology VA, 1962—. Author: Mental Disorders in Later Life, 2d edit, 1956, Psychopathology of Aging, 1979; Editorial bd.: Jour. Gerontology, 1946-60, VOX MEDICA, 1960—, Geriatrics, 1970-80; editor-in-chief: The Gerontolgist, 1961-66; internat. bd. editors: Gerontology and Geriatrics, Amsterdam, 1958—. Mem. planning com. 1st Nat. Conf. Aging, 1950; mem. Nat. Council on Aging, 1954—, Gov.'s Adv. Com. on Aging, 1963-67; chmn. San Diego Mayor's Adv. Com. Aging, 1973—; mem. Quality of Life Bd., City of San Diego, 1978—. Recipient Outstanding Prof. award San Diego State U., 1982, Trustees' Outstanding Prof. award Calif. State U. System, 1983; Fellow Social Sci. Research Council, 1951; travel fellow NSF, 1954. Mem. Am. Assn. Pub. Opinion Research (council Pacific chpt. 1963—), Am. Psychol. Assn. (pres. div. on maturity and old age 1954-55), Western Gerontological Soc. (pres. 1956-57, award for outstanding contbns. 1976), Gerontol. Soc. (editor Newsletter 1954-60), AAAS (council Pacific div. 1958-59). Home: 5409 Hewlett St San Diego CA 92115

KAPLAN, PETER JAMES, lawyer; b. Cambridge, Mass., Jan. 27, 1943; s. George I. and Ethel B. K.; 1 son by previous marriage, Benjamin D. B.S., Wharton Sch. Fin. and Commerce, U. Pa., 1964; J.D., Georgetown U., 1967; postgrad. in labor law, N.Y. U., 1976—. Bar: Mass. 1967, N.Y. 1976. Investment banker Hallgarten & Co., N.Y.C., 1968-72; dir. ops. Wildcat Service Corp—Vera Inst. Justice, N.Y.C., 1972-74, sec., gen. counsel, 1974-77, Seligman & Latz, Inc., N.Y.C., 1977—; exec. v.p., chief operating officer Nat. Media Group Inc., N.Y.C., 1981—; labor and manpower cons. City of Cin., 1975-76. Mem. Bar Assn. City N.Y. Home: 119 W 77th St New York NY 10024 Office:

KAPLAN, PHILIP THOMAS, lawyer, educator; b. Hartford, Conn., Sept. 30, 1928; s. George Gershon and Eva Lee (Levin) K.; m. Sigrid Margot Dede, Sept. 4, 1971; 1 son, Alexander Thomas. A.B., Yale Coll., 1950; LL.B. cum laude, Harvard U., 1953. Bar: N.Y., Mass., conseil juridique. Assoc. Dewey Ballantyne, Bushby, Palmer & Wood, N.Y.C., 1956-63; ptnr. Weil, Gorshal & Manges, N.Y.C., 1963—; adj. assoc. prof. law NYU; dir. Jakob-Suchard, U.S.A.; Food and Wines of France. Contbr. articles on fgn. investment. taxation to publs. N.Am. and France. Served to lt. USCG, 1954-56. Mem. Internat. Discal Assn., ABA (tax mgmt. adv. bd.), Mass. Bar Assn., N.Y. Bar Assn. Home: 114 E 72nd St New York NY 10021 Office: Weil Gitshall & Manges 767 Fifth Ave New York NY

KAPLAN, REUBEN WILLIAM, tool manufacturing executive; b. Owatonna, Minn., Mar. 30, 1924; s. Reuben Alvin and Florence Elizabeth (Wells) K.; m. Dorothy Lavon Frahman, June 16, 1946; children: Kent, Karen, Kimberly. Student, U. Minn., 1946-48. Prodn. control Owatonna Tool Co., 1948-53; gen. mgr. Truth Tool Co., 1956-62, pres., 1956—; exec. v.p. Owatonna Tool Co., 1956-62, pres., chief exec. officer, 1962-83, chmn. bd., chief exec. officer, 1983—; dir. Northwestern Bank, Tennant Co., Wenger Corp.; Mem. Owatonna Bd. Edn., 1972-77. Served with inf. U.S. Army, 1943-46. Mem. Hand Tool Inst., NAM, Nat. Wood Millwork Assn., Equipment and Tool Inst. Republican. Office: Owatonna Tool Co Owatonna MN 55060 *

KAPLAN, ROBERT ARTHUR, association executive; b. N.Y.C., Oct. 15, 1927; s. David and Jeannette (Wyllins) K.; m. Frimette Spilberg, July 26, 1964; children: Nicole A., Arielle E. B.A. cum laude, CCNY, 1949. Spl. sects. editor Fairchild Publns. Daily News Record, N.Y.C., 1953-59, clothing editor, 1960-67; exec. sec. Clothing Mfrs. Assn. U.S.A., N.Y.C., 1967-79, exec. dir., sec., 1979—; mem. adv. com. on textiles and apparel U.S. Spl. Trade, 1975-82; dir. Amalgamated Life Ins. Co., N.Y.C. Served with AUS, 1950-52. Recipient Fairchild Publs. Frontiersman award, 1957,62,64, Assn. Trends Mag. award, 1980. Jewish. Lodge: B'nai B'rith. Office: Clothing Mfrs Assn 1290 Ave of the Americas New York NY 10104

KAPLAN, ROBERT PHILLIP, Canadian govt. ofcl.; b. Toronto, Ont., Can., Dec. 27, 1936; s. Solomon Charles and Pearl (Grafstein) K.; m. Estherelke Kaplan, Oct. 10, 1961; children—Jennifer Mia, John David, Raquel Katherine. B.A., U. Toronto, 1958, LL.B., 1961. Bar: Called to Ont. bar 1963. Practiced in, Toronto; mem. Ho. of Commons for Don Valley, from 1968; mem. standing com. on fin., trade and econ. affairs M.P. for York Centre, 1974; Solicitor Gen. of Can., 1980—; mem. Canadian delegation to UN Gen. Assembly; mem. Canadian-U.S. Parliamentary Group; parliamentary sec. to Minister of Nat. Health and Welfare, to Minister of Fin.; cons. on Canadian affairs Hudson Inst. N.Y. Co-author: Bicycling in Toronto, 1971. Mem. Canadian Bar Assn., Law Soc. Upper Can., Canadian Civil Liberties Assn. Liberal. Jewish. Office: House of Commons Ottawa ON Canada

KAPLAN, SAMUEL, pediatric cardiologist; b. Johannesburg, South Africa, Mar. 28, 1922; came to U.S., 1950, naturalized, 1958; s. Aron Leib and Tema K.; m. Molly Eileen McKenzie, Oct. 17, 1952. M.B., BcH., U. Witwatersrand, Johannesburg, 1944, M.D., 1949. Diplomate: Am. Bd. Pediatrics. Intern, Johannesburg, 1945, registrar in medicine, 1946; lectr. physiology and medicine U. Witwatersrand, 1946-49; registrar in medicine U. London, 1949-50; fellow in cardiology, research assoc. U. Cin., 1950-54, asst. prof. pediatrics, 1954-61, assoc. prof. pediatrics, 1961-66, prof. pediatrics, 1967—, asst. prof. medicine, 1954-67, assoc. prof. medicine, 1967-82, prof. medicine, 1982—; dir. div. cardiology Children's Hosp. Med. Center; cons. NIH; hon. prof. U. Santa Tomas, Manila. Editorial bd.: Circulation, 1974-80, Am. Jour. Cardiology, 1976-81, Am. Heart Jour, 1981—, Jour. Electrocardiology, 1977—, Clin. Cardiology, 1979—, Jour. Am. Coll. Cardiology, 1983—. Cecil John Adams fellow, 1949-50; grantee Heart, Lung and Blood Inst. of NIH, 1960—. Mem. Am. Pediatric Soc., Am. Soc. Pediatric Research, Am. Heart Assn. (med. adv. bd. sect. circulation), Am. Fedn. Clin. Research, Am. Coll. Cardiology, Internat. Cardiovascular Soc., Am. Coll. Chest Physicians, Am. Acad. Pediatrics, Am. Assn. Artificial Internal Organs, Midwest Soc. Pediatric Research (past pres.), Sigma Xi, Alpha Omega Alpha; hon. mem. Peruvian Soc. Cardiology, Peruvian Soc. Angiology, Chilean Soc. Cardiology, Burma Med. Assn. Research and publs. on cardiovascular physiology, diagnostic methods, oxygen supply to tissues and heart disease in infants, children and adolescents. Office: Childrens Hospital Medical Center Cincinnati OH 45229

KAPLAN, SHELDON, lawyer; b. Mpls., Feb. 16, 1915; s. Max Julius and Harriet (Wolfson) K.; m. Helene Bamberger, Dec. 7, 1941; children—Jay Michael, Mary Jo, Jean Burton, Jeffrey Lee. B.A. summa cum laude, U. Minn., 1935; LL.B., Columbia, 1939. Bar: N.Y. bar 1940, Minn. bar 1946. Practice in, N.Y.C., 1940-42, Mpls., 1946—; mem. firm Lauterstein, Spiller, Bergerman & Dannett, N.Y.C., 1939-42; partner firm Maslon, Kaplan, Edelman, Borman, Brand & McNulty, Mpls., 1946-80; firm Kaplan, Strangis and Kaplan, Mpls., 1980—; dir. Lone Star Industries, Inc., N.Am. Life & Casualty Co., Bangor Punta Corp., Piper Aircraft Corp., Minn. Vikings Football Club, Inc., Stewart-McDonald Co., Stewart Holding Co., Creative Ventures, Inc. Served to capt. AUS, 1942-46. Mem. Minn. Bar Assn., Phi Beta Kappa. Home: 2925 Dean Pkwy Minneapolis MN 55416 Office: M Kaplan Strangis and Kaplan 555 Pillsbury Center Minneapolis MN 55402

KAPLAN, SHELDON Z., international lawyer; b. Boston, Nov. 15, 1911; s. Jacob and Lizzie (Strogoff) K.; m. Megan Vondersmith, May 8, 1947; children: Eldon, Deborah, Daniel, Philip, Rebecca, Abigail. A.B. with honors, Yale U., 1933; postgrad., Harvard U. Law Sch., 1933-34; B.A. in Jurisprudence, Brasenose Coll., Oxford (Eng.) U., 1937; M.A., Oxford (Eng.) U., 1945; Licence en Droit, U. Nancy, France, 1944; internat. law student, U. Paris and l'Ecole Libre des Sciences Politiques, 1945; Dr. honoris causa, Inca Garcilaso de la Vega U., Lima, Peru, 1970, U. San Martin de Porres, 1979. Bar: Mass. bar 1940, D.C. bar 1957, also U.S. Supreme Court 1957, also Gray's Inn of London. Research asso. Elder, Whitman and Weyburn, Boston, 1937-40; law practice, Boston, 1940-42; asst. to legal adviser Dept. State, Washington, 1947-49; staff cons. House Fgn. Affairs Com., 1949-57; legal counsel to Govt. Guatemala in U.S., 1960-62, 77-78; gen. counsel Latin Am. and C.Am. Sugar Council, 1963-65; counsel Central Bank Honduras, 1962-64; counsel firm Martin & Burt, 1959-62, Wilkinson, Cragun & Barker, Washington, 1962-67; counsel SAHSA, Honduras Airlines, 1963-77; spl. internat. counsel Morrison-Knudsen Co., 1971-74; partner Bechhoefer, Sharlitt & Lyman, Washington, 1975-79; Mem. U.S. Spl. Mission to Costa Rica, 1949, El Salvador, 1950, Europe, 1951, 53, Pakistan, India, Thailand, Indochina, 1953, Latin Am., 1954, Uruguay, 1955, C. Am., 1955, Guatemala, 1957, Europe, 1957; congl. adviser, mem. U.S. del. 10th Gen. Assembly of UN, 1955; del. Govt. Nicaragua 18th and 19th sessions Internat. Sugar Council, London, 1964, 65; Bd. dirs. Glaydin Sch., Leesburg, Va., 1965-70; adv. bd. Campion Hall, Oxford U., 1974—. Author govt. pub. documents, reports on fgn. affairs.; Contbr. legal and fgn. affairs jours.; Composer popular songs. Served to capt. AUS, 1942-46; E.T.O. Decorated médaille de la Reconnaissance Française (France); Bronze Star medal, U.S.; Orden Del Quetzal (Guatemala); Orden al Merito (Peru). Mem. Nat. Bar Assn. Peru (hon.), Am. Soc. Internat. Law, Brasenose Soc. (Oxford, Eng.), ASCAP, Brit. Sporting Art Trust. Jewish. Clubs: Nat. Steeplechase and Hunt Assn. (N.Y.C.); Mil. Order of Carabao; Oxford and Cambridge (London); Yale (N.Y.C.); Cosmos, Yale, Capitol Hill, Army and Navy (Washington). Home: 7810 Moorland Ln Bethesda MD 20814

KAPLAN, SIDNEY JOSEPH, educator, sociologist; b. Malden, Mass., Feb. 1, 1924; s. Harry and Rena (Chernoff) K.; m. Shirley Taugher, Aug. 22, 1978; children: Carter, Cydney Rena. B.A. magna cum laude, Boston U., 1949, M.A., 1950; Ph.D., Wash. State U., 1953. From instr. to asso. prof. sociology U. Ky., 1953-62; prof. sociology, chmn. dept. sociology and anthropology U. Toledo, 1962-66, 69-82, prof. sociology, 1962—; asso. dean Coll. Arts and Scis., 1962-68. Served with USAAF, 1946-47. Mem. Am. Sociol. Assn., N. Central Sociol. Soc. (v.p. 1964-65), Phi Beta Kappa. Home: 3319 Beverly Dr Toledo OH 43614 Office: Univ Toledo Toledo OH 43606

KAPLAN, STANLEY HENRY, educational center administrator, editor; b. N.Y.C., May 24, 1919; s. Julius and Ericka (Herson) K.; m. Rita Gwirtzman, Jan. 25, 1949; children: Susan Beth, Nancy Paula, Paul Alan. B.S., CCNY, 1939, M.S., 1941. Owner, founder, chief exec. officer Stanley H. Kaplan Ednl. Center, N.Y.C., 1938—; sec. bd. dirs. Council Non-Collegiate Edn., Richmond, Va., 1979—; editor Barron's How to Prepare for College Entrance Examinations, 1953; editor, author Barron's How to Win a Scholarship, 1957, Barron's Regents Exams Series with Answers, 1945-70. Pres. Bklyn. Philharm. Symphony Orch., 1977—; trustee City Coll. Fund, Manhattan, 1978—; bd. dirs. United Jewish Appeal, N.Y.C., 1980—, Rita and Stanley Kaplam Cancer Center, NYU Med. Ctr., N.Y.C., 1982—, Sutton Pl. Synagogue, N.Y.C., 1982—; v.p., bd. dirs. Jewish Fellowship of Hemlock Farms, Hawley, Pa., 1975—. Mem. Gallatin Soc. (life). Club: 100 bd. dirs. (N.Y.C.) (1980—). Lodges: B'nai B'rith; Am. Jewish Congress. Office: Stanley H Kaplan Ednl Center 131 W 56th St New York NY 10019

KAPLAN, STANLEY MEISEL, psychoanalyst; b. Cin., May 10, 1922; s. Abe and Elka (Meisel) K.; m. Myran Jarson, June 18, 1950; children: Steven, Barbara, Richard. B.S., U. Cin., 1943, M.D., 1946; postgrad., Inst. Psychoanalysis, 1962-67. Intern Jewish Hosp., Cin., 1946-47, resident, 1947-48; resident psychiatry Cin. Gen. Hosp., 1949-51; fellow in psychosomatics, 1951-52; faculty dept. psychiatry U. Cin., 1953—, prof., 1969—, acting dir. dept. psychiatry, 1975-77; vice chmn. bd. G & J Pepsi Cola, Inc., Cin.; Bd. dirs. Bonds for Israel, Cin., Jewish Vocat. Service, Cin., 1963-67, 82—, Travelers Aid Internat., 1970-73, Cin. Cancer Control Council, 1961-66, Playhouse in the Park, 1980—. Contbr. articles to profl. jours. Mem. allocations com.

Community Chest Cin., 1975-81; mem. civilian adv. bd. Rollman Receiving Hosp., 1980—. NIMH fellow, 1954-56. Fellow Am. Psychiat. Assn.; mem. Am. Psychosomatic Soc., Am. Psychoanalytic Assn., AAUP, AMA, Sigma Xi. Home: 7216 Willowbrook Ln Cincinnati OH 45237

KAPLAN, STEVEN B., retail apparel company executive; b. 1940. B.A., Yale U., 1962; M.B.A., Harvard U., 1964. Mdse. controller Tall Girl div. Lane Bryant, Inc., N.Y.C., 1964-66, mdse. mgr. retail and mail order Tall div., 1966-71, dir. mktg., 1971-73, v.p. mktg. and promotion, 1973-75, sr. v.p. mkg. and promotion, 1975-77, pres., 1977—, also now chief operating officer, dir. Office: Lane Bryant Inc 469 Fifth Ave New York NY 10017 *

KAPLAN, YALE JOSEPH, ins. co. exec.; b. Omaha, Aug. 10, 1928; s. Samuel Louis and Pauline K.; m. Marilyn T. Gerber, Oct. 16, 1955; children—Beth Janelle, Lisa Ann. Student, U. Wichita, Kans., 1946-48; J.D., Creighton U., Omaha, 1952. Bar: Nebr. bar 1952. With Empire Fire and Maine Ins. Co., Omaha, 1955, pres., chief exec. officer, 1979—, also pres., chief exec. officer subsidiaries. Vice pres., trustee Beth El Synagogue, 1972-76. Served with AUS, 1953-55. Mem. Nebr. Bar Assn., Truck and Heavy Equipment Claims Council (past pres.). Democrat. Clubs: B'nai B'rith, Rotary. Home: 9231 Woolworth Ave Omaha NE 68124 Office: 1624 Douglas St Omaha NE 68102

KAPLAND, MITCHELL ARTHUR, engineering firm executive; b. Riverside, R.I., July 7, 1906; s. Sidney and Elizabeth (Kasanoff) K.; m. Elise Wilson, July 2, 1949; 1 dau., Karen Kapland Woodcock. B.S., Boston U., 1927, Conn. U., 1943. Registered profl. engr., Md. Dir. tool and product design Colt's Fire Arms, Harford, Conn., 1938-43; exec. asst. to pres., v.p. Gray Audograph, Hartford, Conn., 1945-47, 47-49; v.p. Cummins, Chgo., 1949-54; exec. v.p., gen. mgr. Englander Co., Chgo. and Balt., 1954-61; chmn. bd. Trident Engring. Assocs., Inc., Annapolis, Md., 1961—; chmn. Md. Gov.'s Sci. Adv. Council, Nat. Govs.' Council Sci. and Tech., Adv. Council SBA; bd. dirs. Inst. Transp. Studies; trustee Advance Sci. Inst. Mem. Soc. Plastics Engrs., Nat. Soc. Profl. Engrs., Am. Ordance Assn., Zeta Beta Tau. Clubs: N.Y. Athletic (N.Y.C.); Capitol Hill (Washington); Annapolis Yacht; Center (Balt.). Home: 3000 Friends Rd Annapolis MD 21401 Office: Trident Engring Assocs Inc 48 Maryland Ave Annapolis MD 21401

KAPLANSKY, IRVING, educator, mathematician; b. Toronto, Ont., Can., Mar. 22, 1917; came to U.S., 1940, naturalized, 1955; s. Samuel and Anna (Zuckerman) K.; m. Rachelle Brenner, Mar. 16, 1951; children—Steven, Daniel, Lucille. B.A., U. Toronto, 1938, M.A., 1939; Ph.D., Harvard, 1941; LL.D. (hon.), Queen's U., 1969. Instr. math. Harvard, 1941-44; mem. faculty U. Chgo., 1945—, prof. math., 1956—, chmn. dept., 1962-67, George Herbert Mead Distinguished Service prof. math., 1969—; Mem. exec. com. div. math. NRC, 1959-62. Author books, tech. papers. Mem. Nat. Acad. Scis. Home: 5825 S Dorchester Ave Chicago IL 60637

KAPLON, MORTON F., physics educator; b. Phila., Feb. 11, 1921; s. Myer and Ida (Abramson) K.; m. Anita Joanne Harle, June 16, 1946; children: Keith Victor, Bryna Myra, Andrea Joanne. B.Sc., Lehigh U., 1941, M.S., 1947; Ph.D., U. Rochester, 1951. Research asso. physics U. Rochester, 1951-52, mem. faculty, 1953-71, prof. physics, 1960—, assoc. dean, 1963-64, chmn. dept. physics and astronomy, 1964-69; assoc. provost City Coll. N.Y., 1971-76, v.p. adminstrn., 1976-82, prof. physics, 1982—. Contbr. profl. jours.; Editor: Homage to Galileo, 1965. Served to 1st lt. USAAF, 1942-46. NSF Sr. Postdoctoral fellow, 1959-60. Fellow Am. Phys. Soc.; mem. Am. Geophys. Union, Am. Astrophys. Soc., A.A.A.S., Am. Assn. U. Profs., Sigma Xi. Spl. research cosmic ray physics, fundamental particles, origin cosmic radiation, very high energy interactions, gamma ray astronomy, applications of microcomputers. Home: 11 White Birch Dr Pomona NY 10970

KAPLOW, HERBERT ELIAS, journalist; b. N.Y.C., Feb. 2, 1927; s. Solomon and Belle (Bernstein) K.; m. Betty Koplow, Aug. 10, 1952; children—Steven, Robert, Lawrence. B.A., Queens Coll., N.Y.C., 1948; M.S., Northwestern U., 1951. News corr. NBC, Washington, 1951-72, ABC, 1972—. Served with AUS, 1945-46. Recipient Alumni awards Queens Coll., 1963, Northwestern U., 1959. Mem. Sigma Delta Chi. Jewish. Home: 211 Van Buren St Falls Church VA 22046 Office: 1717 De Sales St NW Washington DC 20036 *Curiosity and an open, receptive mind are essential characteristics of good journalism. So too is a certain humility growing from the realization that peoples' lives can be affected by a journalist's work. It is a sobering responsibility.*

KAPLOW, LEONARD SAMUEL, pathologist, educator; b. N.Y.C., Feb. 11, 1920; s. Max and Rose (Augenstreich) K.; m. Sheila Maureen Briscoe, July 10, 1955; children: Roberta Kit Kaplow Dudenhoeffer, David Ross. B.S., Rutgers U., 1941; M.S., U. Vt., 1955, M.D., 1959; M.A. hon., Yale U., 1975. Diplomate: Am. Bd. Pathology. Asst. prof. pathology Med. Coll. Va., Richmond, 1963-64; asst. clin. prof., then assoc. prof. pathology and lab. medicine Yale U., New Haven, 1964-75, prof., 1975—; chief clin. pathology VA Med. Ctr., West Haven, Conn., 1966-74, acting assoc. chief of staff research, 1974-77, chief lab service, 1974—; med. dir. med. lab. technician program Housatonic Community Coll., Bridgeport, Conn., 1977—; mem. assoc. clin. faculty Quinnipiac Coll., Hamden, Conn., 1968—; chmn. med. adv. com. New Haven chpt. ARC, 1967-74; mem. com. lab. regulation Conn. Health Dept., Hartford, 1977—; del. Internat. Com. Standardization in Hematology, 1974-76; program specialist pathology reserach VA Med. Research Service, Washington, 1974-78. Mem. editorial bd. Jour. Histochemistry and Cytochemistry, 1979—; assoc. editor Jour. Soc. Analytical Cytology, 1979—. Served to capt. AUS, 1942-46; PTO. Cited in Citation Classics Inst. Sci. Info., 1982. Mem. Histochem. Soc. (councilor, pres.-elect 1975-80), Assn. VA Chiefs of Lab. Services (pres. 1978-80), Sigma Xi, Alpha Omega Alpha. Home: 275 Hemlock Dr Orange CT 06477 Office: VA Med Ctr W Spring St West Haven CT 06516

KAPNICK, HARVEY E., JR., accounting co. exec.; b. Palmyra, Mich., June 16, 1925; s. Harvey E. and Beatrice (Bancroft) K.; m. Jean Bradshaw, Apr. 5, 1947 (dec. 1962); m. Mary Redus Johnson, Aug. 5, 1963; children—David Johnson, Richard Bradshaw, Scott Bancroft. Student, James Miliken U., 1942-44; B.S., Cleary Coll., 1947, D.Sc. in Bus. Adminstrn. (hon.), 1971; postgrad., U. Mich., 1947-48; D.H.L. (hon.), DePauw U., 1979. C.P.A., Ill. Mem. staff, mgr. Arthur Andersen & Co. (C.P.A.'s), Chgo., 1948-56, partner, 1956-62, partner in charge, Cleve., 1962-70, chmn., chief exec., 1970-79; dep. chmn. 1st Chgo. Corp., 1st Nat. Bank Chgo., 1979—; mem. Adv. Com. on Internat. Investment, Tech. and Devel., Adv. Com. for Trade Negotiations. Pres.'s Commn. on Pension Policy, Ill. Fiscal Commn., 1977; mem. U.S. del. ad hoc working group acctg. standards, com. internat. investment and multinat. enterprises OECD; chmn. Chgo. Mortgage Revenue Bond Adv. Com., Adv. Com. Fed. Consol. Fin. Statements, 1976-78; Chmn. Ill. crusade Am. Cancer Soc., 1972; chmn. campaign Met. Crusade of Mercy, Chgo., 1976; trustee Fin. Acctg. Found., Meninger Found., Mus. Sci. and Industry, Northwestern U.; bd. dirs. Dearborn Park Corp., Orchestral Assn., Mid-Am. chpt. ARC, Internat. Exec. Service Corps, Lyric Opera Chgo., United Way Met. Chgo., Am. Viewpoint, Inc.; council U. Chgo. Grad. Sch. Bus.; adv. council Stanford Grad. Sch. Bus. Served to 2d lt. USAAF, 1943-46. Mem. Ill. Soc. C.P.A.'s, Assn. Ohio Commodores, U.S. C. of C. (govt. ops. and mgmt. com.; dir. 1973-76), Ill. C. of C. (dir. 1970-74), ASEAN-U.S. Bus. Council (exec. com. U.S. sect.), Am. Inst. C.P.A., Nat. Assn. Accountants, Am. Accounting Assn., Chgo. Council Fgn. Relations (dir.), Iran-U.S. Bus. Council. Clubs: Met. (Washington); Mid-America (Chgo.) (gov. 1971-76, treas. 1974-76); Chgo., Carlton, Univ., Execs., Indian Hill, Econ., Comml. (Chgo.). Home: 100 Woodley Rd Winnetka IL 60093 Office: care 1st Chgo Corp One First Nat Plaza Chicago IL 60670

KAPP, CHARLES A., pharmaceutical company executive. Pres. Beecham Pharms. Western Hemisphere div. Beecham, Inc. Office: Beecham Inc 3 Garret Mountain Plaza West Peterson NJ 07424§

KAPP, RONALD ORMOND, educator; b. nr. Ann Arbor, Mich., Mar. 10, 1935; s. Ormond Emanuel and Anna Louise (Heller) K.; m. Phyllis Isabel Moreen, Jan. 30, 1960; children—Lisa, Marda, Sara, Jon. B.A., U. Mich., 1956, M.S., 1957, Ph.D., 1963. Instr. Alma (Mich.) Coll., 1957-60, asst. prof., 1960-64, asso. prof., 1964-69, prof., provost, 1969—. Author: How to Know Pollen and Spores, 1969; Contbr. articles to profl. jours. Mem. Mich. Wilderness and Natural Areas Bd. Fellow A.A.A.S.; mem. Ecol. Soc. Am., Mich. Acad. Sci., Mich. Natural Areas Council, Phi Beta Kappa, Sigma Xi. Home: 6193 Winans Rd Alma MI 48801

KAPPAS, ATTALLAH, physician; b. Union City, N.J., Nov. 4, 1926; s. Attie and Sofia (Kozam) K.; m. Katharine Bingham Hull, Oct. 26, 1963; children: Peter, Michael, Nicholas. A.B., Columbia U., 1947; M.D. with honors, U. Chgo., 1950; Sc.D., N.Y. Med. Coll., 1978. Diplomate: Am. Bd. Internal Medicine. Med. intern Univ. Service, Kings County Hosp., N.Y.C., 1950-51; research fellow div. steroid biochemistry and metabolism Sloan Kettering Inst., N.Y.C., 1951-54; asst. resident physician and sr. asst. resident physician Peter Bent Brigham Hosp., Boston, 1954-56; assic. div. steroid biochemistry and metabolism Sloan Kettering Inst., 1956-57; asst. prof. to Assoc. prof. dept. medicine U. Chgo. Med. Sch., 1957-67; Guggenheim fellow, guest investigator Rockefeller U., N.Y.C., 1966-67, assoc. prof., physician, 1967-71, prof., sr. physician, 1971-74, physician-in-chief, 1974—, Sherman Fairchild prof., 1981—, v.p., 1983—; Vincent Astor chair clin. sci. Meml. Slaon-Kettering Cancer Ctr. and Cornell U. Med. Coll., 1979-81; bd. dirs. Russell Sage Inst. Pathology Cornell U., 1977—, prof. medicine and pharmacology, 1972—; vis. com. div. biol. scis. Pritzker Sch. Medicine, U. Chgo., 1977—; attending physician N.Y. Hosp., 1972—, Meml Hosp. Cancer and Allied Diseases, 1977—; mem. selection com. John A. Hartford Found. Fellowship program in clin. scis., N.Y.C., 1979-83; co-dir. Rockefeller U.-Cornell U. combined M.D.-Ph.D. program, 1980—; mem. com. pyrene and selected analogs NRC-Nat. Acad. Sci., Washington, 1981-83, mem. Bd. Toxicology and Environ. Health Hazards, 1981-83, mem. Commn. on Life Scis., 1981-83; cons. drug devel. Merck Sharp & Dohme Research Labs., 1982—; mem. sci. adv. bd. Environ. Scis. Lab. Mt. Sinai Med. Ctr., 1983—. Contbr. articles to profl. jours. Bd. dirs. Vis. Nurse Service N.Y., 1982—; mem. gov.'s com. on rev. sci. studies and devel. pub. policy on problems resulting from hazardous wastes, 1980. Served with U.S. Army, 1945-46. Commonwealth Fund fellow, 1961-62; Guggenheim fellow, 1966-67; recipient Spl. award in clin. pharmacology Burroughs Wellcome Fund, 1973; named Sr. Henry Hallet Dale Meml. lectr. and vis. prof. Johns Hopkins Hosp., 1975; recipient Disting. Service award in med. scis. U. Chgo. Sch. Medicine, 1975; named Pfizer lectr. clin. pharmacology Peter Bent Brigham Hosp., Harvard Med. Sch., 1977; recipient ASPET award, 1978; named Pfizer lectr. Pa. State U., 1980. Fellow ACP; mem. Practitioners Soc. N.Y., Assn. Am. Physicians, Am. Soc. Clin. Investigation, Am. Clin. and Climatol. Assn., Am. Soc. Pharmacology and Exptl. Therapeutics (pub. affairs com., awards com.), Central Soc. Clin. Research, Harvey Soc., Endocrine Soc., Interurban Clin. Club. Clubs: Cosmos (Washington); University (N.Y.C.); Manursing Island. Home: Griswold Rd Rye NY 10580 Office: Rockefeller Univ 1230 York Ave New York NY 10021

KAPPAUF, ROBERT EDWIN, management consultant; b. N.Y.C., Oct. 17, 1915; s. William Emil and Juliet T. (Bonnlander) K.; m. Laura E. Garrigus, Nov. 23, 1940; children—Robert Laurance, David Garrigus, Donald Wayne. B.S., Columbia, 1936, M.S., 1937. C.P.A., N.Y., N.J. With Price Waterhouse & Co. (C.P.A.'s), N.Y.C., 1937-54, Newark, 1954- 56; asst. comptroller N.Y.C. R.R. Co., 1956-57, comptroller, 1957-68; asst. v.p. Penn Central, 1968-70; v.p., asst. to pres. Lehigh Valley R.R., 1969-70; self-employed, 1970-72; treas. Sci. Mgmt. Corp., Bridgewater, N.J., 1972-79, v.p., treas., 1979-83, v.p., treas., sec., 1983—. Mem. Am. Inst. C.P.A.'s, Nat. Assn. Accts., Assn. Am. R.R.'s. Home: Box 185 J Ridge Rd Lebanon NJ 08833

KAPPAUF, WILLIAM EMIL, JR., educator, psychologist; b. N.Y.C., Oct. 2, 1913; s. William Emil and Juliet Theodora (Bonnlander) K.; m. Catharine Anne Hamilton, June 16, 1945; children—Barbara, Charles, Katharine, William. A.B., Columbia, 1934; M.A., Brown U., 1935; Ph.D., U. Rochester, 1937. Instr. psychology U. Rochester, 1937-41; research projects under NDRC and OSRD, 1941-46; asso. prof. Princeton, 1946-51; prof. U. Ill., Champaign, 1951-80, asso. head dept. psychology, 1976-78; cons. Bell Telephone Labs.; cons., panel mem. Mil. Agys., NSF, NIH. Editor: Am. Jour. Psychology, 1971—; Contbr. articles to profl. jours. Recipient Presdl. certificate of merit, 1948. Mem. Am., Midwestern psychol. assns., Soc. Exptl. Psychologists (sec.-treas. 1967-70), Am. Assn. U. Profs., A.A.A.S., Phi Beta Kappa, Sigma Xi. Home: 1401 Waverly Dr Champaign IL 61820

KAPPE, RAYMOND, architect; b. Mpls., Aug. 4, 1927; s. Phineas and Betty (Gold) K.; m. Rochelle Diamond, June 25, 1950; children: Ron, Karen, Finn. A.B. in Architecture, U. Calif., Berkeley, 1951. Faculty architecture Calif. State Poly. U., 1969-72; chmn. dept. architecture; dir., founder So. Calif. Inst. Architecture, 1972; pvt. practice architecture, Los Angeles, 1953-68; partner Kahn Kappe Lotery Boccato, Santa Monica, 1968-79, Kappe Lotery Boccato, 1979-80, Raymond Kappe FAIA (architect/planner), 1981—; chmn. housing com. Goals Council Los Angeles, 1968; mem. nat. AIA fellowship jury, 1978-80. Works include Sherman Oaks (Calif.) Residence (So. Calif. chpt. AIA Merit award 1957), Nat. Apts. (So. Calif. chpt. AIA Merit award 1957), Hayes Residence (House and Home award of merit 1960), Calif. Gov's. Mansion, Sacramento (State of Calif. award for Merit 1963), Ravenspur Condominium, Los Angeles (So. Calif. chpt. AIA Honor award 1966), Los Angeles (City of Los Angeles Grand Prix award 1969), Brooktree Residence (AIA Sunset Honor award 1969, AIA House and Home and Am. Home award of Merit 1971, AIA Homes for Better Living award of Merit 1972), Gertler Residence (So. Calif. chpt. AIA award of Merit 1972), Katzenstein Residence (So. Calif. chpt. AIA award of Merit 1975), Sultan Residence (So. Calif. chpt. AIA award of Merit 1977), Inglewood Water Treatment Plant (So. Calif. chpt. AIA award of Merit 1978); author: (with others) A Townhouse Study, 1967, Land Development Control in Hillside and Mountain Areas, 1964. Served with U.S. Army, 1946-47. Fellow AIA (chmn. state environ. com. Calif. Council 1969, dir. So. Calif. chpt. 1969-71, award for Excellence in Edn., Calif. chpt. 1976, award of Honor So. Calif. chpt. 1976, participant Los Angeles 12 Exhbn. 1976, nat. Hon. Mention awards 1963, 64, 65, presdl. citation Los Angeles chpt. 1983). Office: 715 Brooktree Rd Pacific Palisades CA 90272

KAPPE, STANLEY EDWARD, environmental engineer; b. Kingston, Pa., Aug. 11, 1908; s. Anthony and Pauline (Danelowicz) K.; m. Flora Syme Clarke, Nov. 10, 1935; 1 son, David S. B.S. in Civil Engring, Pa. State U., 1930. Engring. asst. Pa. Health Dept., Phila., 1930-35; in charge of pollution abatement program on Del. River U.S. Engrs., Phila., 1935-36; eastern mgr. Chicago Pump Co., Phila., 1936-46; chmn. bd. Kappe Assos., Inc., Rockville, Md., 1946—; spl. cons. to Hdqrs. USAF, 1952-70, USPHS, 1967-70. Lectr. in field. Recipient Ted Haseltine award Pa. Water Pollution Control Assn., 1973. Mem. ASCE, Am. Water Works Assn. (internat. dir. 1973-75, Fuller award Chesapeake sect. 1970, hon. mem. 1976—), Am. Acad. Environ. Engrs. (exec. dir. 1971-81, editor Diplomate newsletter 1971-81, Fair award 1978, hon. diplomate award 1981), Water Pollution Control Assn. (Arthur Sidney Bedell award 1980), Nat. Soc. Profl. Engrs., Izaak Walton League Am., Pa. Water Works Operators Assn. (Harry S. Krum award 1972, pres. 1980). Clubs: Congl. Country, Kenwood Country; Engrs. (Phila.). Patentee. Home: 5200 Massachusetts Ave Bethesda MD 20816 Office: PO Box 1036 Rockville MD 20850

KAPPES, CHARLES WILLIAM, insurance company executive, lawyer; b. Union Hill, N.J., July 5, 1912; s. Charles William and Erna (Braunston) K.; m. Nancy Jean Macfarlan, Nov. 29, 1941; children: Prudence (Mrs. Clark Taylor Montgomery), Leslie, Judith, Robert Addison. A.B., Princeton U., 1933; postgrad., Am. Acad., Rome, 1934; LL.B., Yale U., 1937. Bar: N.J. 1937. Since practiced in, Newark; asso., then partner Riker, Emery & Danzig, 1939-50; asst. counsel Mut. Benefit Life Ins. Co., 1950, asso. counsel, 1951-60, counsel, 1960-64, v.p., counsel, 1964-72, sr. v.p., gen. counsel, 1972-74. Pres. Youth Consultation Service, Newark, 1949-56, Newark Council Social Agys., 1954-55; chmn. Planning Bd., Ridgewood, 1955-63; pres. Hosp. and Health Council Newark and Vicinity, 1962; mem. Bd. Edn., Ridgewood, 1963-70, pres., 1967-70; chancellor Diocese Newark; sr. warden Ch. of the Holy Spirit, Orleans, Mass., 1979—; Pres., bd. mgrs. State Home For Boys, Jamesburg, 1958; trustee Health Facilites Planning Council Met. N.J.; mem. Newark Fiscal Adv. Bd. Served to col. F.A. AUS, 1940-45; CBI. Decorated Bronze Star. Mem. Assn. Life Ins. Counsel (past pres.), Nat. Conf. Lawyers and Life Ins. Cos. (past chmn.). Episcopalian. Home: Highview Ln East Orleans MA 02643

KAPPES, PHILIP SPANGLER, lawyer, laboratory equipment company executive; b. Detroit, Dec. 24, 1925; s. Philip Alexander and Wilma Fern (Spangler) K.; m. Glendora Galena Miles, Nov. 27, 1948; children: Susan Lea, Philip Miles, Mark William. B.A. cum laude, Butler U., 1945; J.D., U. Mich., 1948. Bar: Ind. bar 1948, U.S. Supreme Ct. bar 1970. Practice law, Indpls., 1948—; assoc. firm Armstrong and Gause, 1948-49; assoc. law offices C. B. Dutton, 1950-52; ptnr. firm Dutton, Kappes & Overman, 1952—; ptnr. Labeco Properties; Creston Group; chmn. bd., sec., dir. Lab. Equipment Co., Mooresville, Ind.; sec., dir. Labsonics, Inc.; instr. bus. law Butler U., 1948-49, chmn. bd. govs., 1965-66. Bd. dirs., v.p. finance, mem. exec. com. Crossroads Am. council Boy Scouts Am., pres., 1977-79; trustee Children's Mus., Indpls. Mem. Am. Judicature Soc., ABA (ho. of dels. 1970-71), Ind. Bar Assn. (ho. dels. 1959—, mem. chmn. pub. relations exec. com. 1966-69, sec. 1973-74, bd. mgrs. 1975-77), Indpls. Bar Assn. (treas., 1st v.p. 1965, pres. 1970, bd. mgrs. 1975-77), Indpls. Legal Aid Soc., Indpls. Jr. C. of C. (past 1st v.p., dir.), Butler U. (past pres.), Mich. alumni assns., Phi Delta Theta, Tau Kappa Alpha. Republican. Presbyn. (deacon, elder, past pres. bd. trustees). Clubs: Masons (32 deg.; past master lodge; chpt. Scottish Rite), Shriners, Meridian Hills Country, Lawyers, Gyro (pres. 1966). Home: 624 Somerset Dr Indianapolis IN 46260 Office: Century Bldg Indianapolis IN 46204

KAPRAL, FRANK ALBERT, medical microbiology educator; b. Phila., Mar. 12, 1928; s. John and Erna Louise (Melching) K.; m. Marina Garay, Nov. 22, 1951; children: Frederick, Gloria, Robert. B.S., Phila. Coll. Pharmacy and Scis., 1952; Ph.D, U. Pa., 1956. With U. Pa., Phila., 1952-66, assoc. in microbiology, 1958-66; assoc. microbiologist Phila Gen. Hosp., 1962-64, chief microbiology research, 1964-66, chief microbiology, 1965-66; asst. chief microbiol. research VA Hosp., Phila, 1962-66; assoc. prof. med. microbiology Ohio State U., Columbus, 1966-69, prof. med. microbiology and immunology, 1969—. Contbr. articles to profl. jours.; patentee implant chamber. Served with AUS, 1946-47. NIH research grantee, 1959-82. Fellow Am. Acad. Microbiology, Infectious Diseases Soc. Am.; mem. Am. Soc. for Microbiology, Am. Assn. for Immunologists, Soc. for Exptl. Biology and Medicine, Am. Soc. for Cell Biology, N.Y. Acad. Scis., AAAS, Sigma Xi. Democrat. Roman Catholic. Home: 873 Clubview Blvd Worthington OH 43085 Office: Dept Microbiology and Immunology Ohio State U 5065 Graves Hall Columbus OH 43210

KAPRELIAN, EDWARD K., mechanical engineer, physicist; b. Union Hill, N.J., June 20, 1913; s. Karnig and Haiganoosh (Tatarian) K.; m. Lucy Ainilian, Feb. 29, 1936; children: Charles E., Harold R., Helen Kaprelian Ward. M.E., Stevens Inst. Tech., 1934; student law, George Washington U., 1937-38, 1943-44. Registered profl. engr., N.J., Md. Patent examiner for U.S. Patent Office, 1936-42; physicist Bd. Econ. Warfare, 1942-45; patent adviser U.S. Army Signal Corps, 1945-46; chief photo br. Signal Corps Engring. Labs., Ft. Monmouth, 1946-52; dir. research and engring. Kalart Co., Plainville, Conn., 1952-55; pres. Kaprelian Research & Devel. Co., Simsbury, Conn., 1955-57; dep. dir. research U.S. Army Signal Research & Devel. Lab., Ft. Monmouth, 1957-62; tech. dir. U.S. Army Ltd. War Lab., Aberdeen Proving Ground, Md., 1962-67; v.p., tech. dir. Keuffel & Esser Co., 1967-73; pres. Kaprelian Research and Devel., Mendham, N.J., 1973—; Mem. NRC-Nat. Acad. Scis., 1957-66. Author. Lt. col. Signal Corps, U.S. Army Res. (ret.). Recipient Exceptional Civilian award U.S. Army, 1963. Fellow Soc. Photog. Scientists and Engrs. (past pres.), Am. Photog. Hist. Soc. (past pres.); sr. IEEE; mem. ASME, Optical Soc. Am., Phys. Soc. (London), Soc. Motion Picture and TV Engrs., Royal Photog. Soc. (Eng.), Patent Office Soc., N.Y. Patent Law Assn., Am. Def. Preparedness Assn., AAAS, N.Y. Acad. Sci., Sigma Xi, Tau Beta Pi. Patentee in field. Address: 15 Lowery Ln Mendham NJ 07945

KAPRIELIAN, WALTER, advertising executive; b. N.Y.C., June 2, 1934; s. Vartan and Shoushan (DerBargamian) K.; m. Julia Hachigian, July 7, 1957; children: Victoria Susan, Siran Marion, John Vartan. A.A.S., SUNY, 1953. Art dir. BBD&O, N.Y.C., 1953-64; group head, art dir. Grey Advt., N.Y.C., 1964-65; sr. art dir. Ketchum MacLeod & Grove, N.Y.C., 1965-66; v.p., head art dir., 1966-67, v.p., asso. creative dir., 1967-71, sr. v.p., creative dir., 1971-77, exec. v.p., asst. gen. mgr., 1977-80, gen. mgr., 1980-81; pres., chief exec. officer Ketchum New York, 1981-82; ptnr., co-creative dir., vice chmn. Fearon O'Leary Kaprielian, Inc., 1983—; instr. N.Y.C. Tech. Coll., 1971-79, Sch. Visual Arts, 1982—; mem. adv. bd. N.Y.C. Tech. Coll., 1978—; lectr. Graphic Arts Tech. Found., 1970-81. Author/illustrator: The Captain's Cookbook, 1976; designer: Bliss in Chrysalis, 1968; designer/editor: The Consecration of a Cathedral, 1968. Chmn. parish council Holy Cross Ch. of Armenia, 1965-66, Armenian Ch. of Holy Martyrs, 1968-69. Recipient awards Art Dirs. Club N.Y., Art Dirs. Club N.J., Soc. Illustrators, Am. Inst. Graphic Arts, Type Dirs. Club, CLIO, Graphis, Advt. Club N.Y., Am. Advt. Fedn.; Theodore Rossevelt Meml. medal; St. Gauden's medal. Mem. Art Dirs. Club (dir. 1974-76, 78-81, pres. 1981-83, chmn. adv. bd. 1983—), Am. Inst. Graphic Arts, Nat. Acad. TV Arts and Scis., U.S. Power Squadron, Nat. Party Boat Owners Alliance, Internat. Game Fish Assn., Knights of Vartan. Clubs: Union League, Star Island Yacht. Lic. charterboat capt.

KAPROV, SUSAN LEE, artist; b. N.Y.C., Aug. 11, 1946; d. Irving and Sylvia (Sobel) Brooks. B.A., City Coll. N.Y., 1967; postgrad., Dartmouth Coll., 1968. Represented in permanent collections, Finch Coll. Mus. Art, Rutgers U., Mus. Modern Art, N.Y.C., Library Congress, Corcoran Gallery, Met. Mus. Art, N.Y.C., Bklyn. Mus.; One person shows, Terry Dintenfass Gallery, N.Y.C., 1978, Franz Bader Gallery, Washington, 1972, Bklyn. Mus., 1975,81, Vassar Coll., 1976, Hayden Planetarium, N.Y., 1978, group shows include, Smithsonian Instn., 1973, Rutgers U., 1975,77, Bronx Mus. Arts, 1976, San Francisco, Bklyn. Mus., Phila. Print Club, 1977, Jyvasklya, Finland, 1978, Am. Cultural Center, Paris, France, Nat. Collection Fine Arts, Washington, Northlight Gallery, Tucson, 1979, Everson Mus., Syracuse, Los Angeles County Mus. Art traveling show, 1979-81. Ossabaw Island Project fellow, 1972; MacDowell Colony fellow, 1972,74; Creative Artists Pub. Service fellow, 1980. Mem. Nat. Soc. Mural Painter, Am. Soc. Picture Profls. Home and studio: 149 Willow St Brooklyn Heights NY 11201

KAPSALIS, THOMAS, municipal official; b. Chgo., Mar. 9, 1933; s. George and Harriet (Gkikas) K.; m. Patricia Ann Surgalski, Sept. 12, 1964; children: William, Alexandra. B.S., Purdue U., 1956; postgrad., U. Chgo. Grad. Sch. Bus. With Chgo. Dept. Aviation, 1958-62, with dept. city planning, 1962-65, dir., 1965-77; adminstrv. aide to mayor City of Chgo., 1977; exec. dir. Chgo. Urban Transp. Dist., 1977-78; commr. Chgo. Dept. Planning, City and Community Devel., 1978-79; mgr. O'Hare Airport, Chgo. Dept. Aviation, 1979-80, commr. aviation, 1980—. Mem. Am. Hellenic Democratic Council Ill. Served with U.S. Army, 1956-58. Recipient award Am. Jewish Com. Inst. Human Relations, 1980. Mem. Am. Assn. Airline Execs., Airport Operators Council Internat., Ill.-Ind. Bi-State Commn., Northeastern Ill. Planning Commn., Chgo. Econ. Devel. Commn., Chgo. Commn. Hist. and Archtl. Landmarks, Am. Public Transit Assn., Am. Public Works Assn., Constrn. Specifications Inst., Chgo. Constrn. Coordinating Com., Lambda Alpha. Club: Economic. Office: Dept Aviation City Hall 121 N LaSalle St Room 1111 Chicago IL 60602 *

KAPTUR, MARCIA CAROLYN, congressman; b. Toledo, June 17, 1946. B.A., U. Wis., 1968; M. Urban Planning, U. Mich., 1974; postgrad., U. Manchester, (Eng.), 1974. Urban planner; asst. dir. urban affairs domestic policy staff White House, 1977-79; mem. 98th Congress from 9th Dist. Ohio. Bd. dirs. Nat. Ctr. Urban Ethnic Affairs; adv. com. Gund Found.; exec. com. Lucas County Democratic Com.; mem. Dem. Women's Campaign Assn. Mem. Am. Planning Assn., Am. Inst. Cert. Planners, NAACP, Urban League, Polish Mus., U. Mich. Urban Planning Alumni Assn. (bd. dirs.), Polish Am. Hist. Assn. Roman Catholic. Clubs: Lucas County Dem. Bus. and Profl. Women's, Fulton County Dem. Women's. Office: 1630 Longworth House Office Bldg Washington DC 20515 *

KAPUSCINSKI, LUCIAN, advertising executive; b. Cleve., Aug. 9, 1937; s. Lucian and Mary (Majewski) K.; m. Mary Louise Ruschau, June 26, 1965; children: Mary Kyle, Christopher Lucian. B.F.A., U. Dayton, Ohio, 1960. With Tuvell, Hahn & Costello (advt.), Dayton, 1960-62, Bergan & Patterson (advt.), 1962-65; art dir. Henderson Advt., Greenville, S.C., 1965-71; pres., creative dir. Liller Neal Inc., Atlanta, 1971—; also dir. Liller Neal Weltin Inc.; tchr. comml. advt. design Greenville County Mus. Art, 1969. Prin. designer 3 books for, S.C. Tricentennial. Recipient Best Comml. Package Design award Packaging Mag., 1974; also over 20 gold awards from advt. clubs. Mem. Atlanta Advt. Club. Roman Catholic. Club: Dunwoody Country. Office: 2700 Cumberland Pkwy Suite 200 Atlanta GA 30339 *In the forty-five years I have lived, I now know that I still have far too much to learn to be able to make any kind of statement on what makes success. However, one thing seems to be emerging; Work at being the best person you can be.*

KARABA, FRANK ANDREW, lawyer; b. Chgo., Jan. 23, 1927; s. Frank and Katherine (Danihel) K.; m. Alice June Olsen, June 2, 1951; children: Thomas Frank, Stephen Milton, Catherine Alice. B.S. with highest distinction, Northwestern U., 1949, J.D., 1951. Bar: Ill. 1951. Teaching asso. Northwestern U. Law Sch., 1951-52; law sec. Ill. Supreme Ct., 1952-53; asso. firm Crowley, Barrett & Karaba, Chgo., 1953-60, partner, 1960-75, mng. partner, 1975—; dir. Am. Nat. Bank of South Chicago Heights, Citizens Nat. Bank of Downers Grove, A&R Printers, Inc., Caron Internat., Inc., O'Brien Corp.; Asst. counsel Emergency Commn. on Crime, Chgo. City Council, 1952. Pres. 7th Av. P.T.A., 1964-66; Bd. dirs. La Grange Little League, 1964-67, pres., 1968. Served with USNR, 1945-46. Mem. ABA, Ill. Bar Assn., Chgo. Bar. Assn. (bd. mgrs. 1962-63, chmn. grievance com. 1972—), Order of Coif. Presbyn. (elder). Clubs: Legal, Law. Home: 812 S Stone Ave La Grange IL 60525 Office: 111 W Monroe St Chicago IL 60603

KARAGHEUZOFF, THEODORE, city official; b. Bklyn., Mar. 2, 1935; s. Sarkis and Anne (Papasian) K.; m. Odette Mary Chambart, May 23, 1964; children: Patricia, Nicole, Steven, Christopher. B.C.E., CCNY, 1955, Northwestern U., 1956; LL.B., Bklyn. Sch. Law, 1961. Bar: N.Y. 1961; Registered profl. engr., N.Y. Traffic engr., asst. to dir. traffic signals N.Y.C. Traffic Dept., 1955-59, asst. dir. traffic signals, 1959-61, asst. to commr., 1961-63, dep. commr., chief engr., 1963-68, traffic commr., 1968-73, 74-78, commr. bldgs., 1973; asst. gen. supt. N.Y.C. Transit Authority, 1978-82, gen. supt., 1982—; Asst. prof. N.Y. U. Center for Safety Edn.; cons. engr. traffic problems. Mem. nat. com. for Uniform Traffic Laws. Recipient Outstanding Young Engr. award City Coll. Alumni Assn., 1969, Distinguished Service award Coll. City. N.Y., 1973, Pub. Service award Fund for N.Y.C., 1976; named Young Man of Year Bklyn. Jaycees, 1970. Mem. Inst. Transp. Engrs., Am. Soc. Municipal Engrs., Soc. Municipal Engrs. (Municipal Engr. Year), Am. Soc. C.E., Queens County Bar Assn., Chi Epsilon, Tau Beta Pi. Home: 85-03 Midland Pkwy Jamaica Estates NY 11432 Office: NYC Transit Authority 25 Jamaica Ave Brooklyn NY

KARAKASH, JOHN J., engineering dean, consultant; b. Istanbul, Turkey, June 14, 1914; came to U.S., 1936, naturalized, 1948; s. Joachim Theodore and Irene (Georges) K.; m. Marjorie Rutherford, June 21, 1945; 1 son, John Thomas. Student, Robert Coll., Istanbul, 1932-35; B.S., Duke, 1937; M.S. (Moore fellow), U. Pa., 1938; D.Engring. (hon.), Lehigh U., 1971. Registered profl. engr., Pa. Instr. U. Pa., 1938-40; project engr. Moore Sch. Elec. Engring., 1944-46; research engr. Am. TV Labs., Chgo., 1940-42; edn. dir. 6th Service Command Signal Corps Radar Sch., Chgo., 1942-44; asst. prof. elec. engring. Lehigh U., 1946-50, asso. prof., 1950-55, prof., head dept., 1955—, Distinguished prof., 1962—, dean, 1965—, project engr. UHF filters, 1950-54; project dir. active networks Signal Corps., 1954-60; cons. Bell Telephone Labs., Murray Hill, N.J., 1950-56, Dept. Edn. Commonwealth P.R., 1972, IBM, 1980; dir. Komline & Sanderson Engring. Corp. Author: Transmission Line and Filter Networks, 1950, also articles. Mem. Gen. State Authority Commonwealth of Pa., 1974—; trustee Wilkes Coll.; bd. dirs. Lehigh Valley Care Ctr. Recipient Alfred Nobel Robinson award for service to univ., 1948, Hillman award for distinguished service Lehigh, 1962, 81, Outstanding Tchr. award, 1968; Pa. Profl. Engring. award for distinction, 1965. Fellow I.E.E.E.; mem. Am. Soc. Engring. Edn., Engring. Council for Profl. Devel. (nat. accreditation com. for engring. 1970—), Franklin Inst., Pergamon Inst. (hon. adv. bd.), Phi Beta Kappa, Sigma Xi, Tau Beta Pi, Omicron Delta Kappa, Eta Kappa Nu, Iota Gamma Pi. Home: 1732 Chelsea Ave Bethlehem PA 18018 *In free societies, whenever rules and regulations, because of changing times, are in conflict with principles—it is the principles that need be conserved, and the conflicting rules and regulations summarily discarded.*

KARALEKAS, GEORGE STEVEN, advertising executive, political consultant; b. Boston, Nov. 26, 1939; s. Steven George and Sotiria (Sarris) K. B.S., Boston U., 1962. Vice-pres., assoc. media dir. Grey Advt., Inc., N.Y.C., 1962-70; dir. advt. services Can. Dry Corp., N.Y.C., 1970-72, dir. mktg. N.Y. ops., 1972-74; exec. v.p., dir. media and mktg., mgmt. account dir. deGarmo Advt., Inc., N.Y.C., 1974-80; sr. v.p., exec. dir. media, mgmt. dir. D'Arcy-MacManus & Masius, N.Y.C., 1980—; sr. v.p., exec. dir. media November Group, Pres. Nixon, N.Y.C., Washington, 1971-72; sr. v.p., spl. advt. cons. Campaign 76, Pres. Ford, N.Y.C., Washington, 1975-76; sr. v.p., exec. dir. media Campaign 80, Pres. Reagan, N.Y.C., Washington, 1979-80. Mem. Republican Nat. Com., 1970—. Mem. Internat. Radio and TV Soc., Am. Mgmt. Assn. Republican. Greek Orthodox. Home: Circle Dr Holliday Point Sherman CT 06784 Office: D'Arcy-MacManus & Masius Inc 360 Madison Ave New York NY 10017

KARALES, JAMES HARRY, photojournalist; b. Canton, Ohio, July 15, 1930; s. Harry and Mary (Fisher) K.; m. Eleanor Ann Cecilia Francis, Sept. 28, 1957; children: Joseph Harry, Jams Demetrios.; m. Monica Josephine Poltera; children: Alexandros Dimitrios, Andreas Marios. B.F.A., Ohio U., 1955. Asst. to W. Eugene Smith, 1955-58; free-lance, 1958-60, 71—; staff photographer Look mag., 1960-71. One-man exhbns. include, Limelight Gallery, N.Y.C., 1958, Leitz Gallery, N.Y.C., 1965, Leitz Gallery, Portland, Oreg., 1959, Nikon Gallery, 1971, Art Dirs. Club N.Y., 1975, Rizzoli Gallery, 1980; represented in permanent collection, Mus. Modern Art; important pictures include Rendville, Ohio, 1956; Logging, 1958, Gheel, Belgium, 1961, Vietnam, 1964, 65, 66, Turning Point for the Church, Selma, Ala., 1965. Recipient award Pictures of year, 1965; Page One citation Newspaper Guild N.Y., 1966; 2d award 35th nat. competition Inst. Outdoor Advt.; cert. of merit Art Dirs. Club N.Y., 1966, 68; medal, 1969; One-Show Merit award, 1973; 2d place award Overseas Press Club, 1970; Indsl. Arts Methods award, 1972; Creative Artist Pub. Service award, 1974; Art Dirs. Club N.J. award, 1974; Gubernatorial citation for Celebration of N.Y. in Color, 1979. Home: 217 Cleveland Dr Croton-on-Hudson NY 10520

KARAM, RAYMOND A., government official; b. Oct. 12, 1929. B.S., U.S. Mil. Acad., 1955; M.P.A., Harvard U., 1962; J.D., George Washington U., 1978. Bar: Va. 1978. Dep. asst. sec. budget and programs U.S. Dept. Transp., Washington. Office: Budget and Programs Office Dept Transportation 400 7th St SW Washington DC 20590

KARAN, DONNA (FASKE), fashion designer; b. Forest Hills, N.Y., Oct. 2, 1948; m. Mark Karan; 1 dau., Gabrielle. Ed., Parsons Sch. of Design. With Addenda Co., to 1968; with Anne Klein & Co., N.Y.C., 1968—, co-designer, 1971-74, designer, 1974—. Recipient Coty award, 1977, 81, Coty Hall of Fame Citation, 1984. Showed first complete collection for Anne Klein & Co. in 1974; collaborator on Anne Klein collections with Louis dell'Olio. Office: care Anne Klein & Co 205 W 39th St New York NY 10018

KARANIKAS, ALEXANDER, English language educator; b. Manchester, N.H., Oct. 5, 1916; s. Stephen and Vaia (Olgas) K.; m. Helen J. Karagianes, Jan. 2, 1949; children: Marianthe Vaia, Diana Christine, Cynthia Maria. Student, U. N.H., 1934-36; A.B. cum laude, Harvard, 1939; M.A., Northwestern U., 1950; Ph.D. in English, Northwestern U., 1953. With N.H. Writers Project, 1940-41; radio news commentator sta. WMUR, Manchester, 1946; grad. asst. Northwestern U., 1950-52; instr. Kendall Coll., Evanston, Ill., 1952-53, Northwestern U., 1953-54, 57-59; mem. faculty U. Ill. at Chgo. Circle Campus, 1954—, prof. English, 1968-82, prof. emeritus, 1982—; cons. in field. Author: When A Youth Gets Poetic, 1934, In Praise of Heroes, 1945, Tillers of a Myth: The Southern Agrarians as Social and Literary Critics, 1966 (Friends of Lit. award 1967), Elias Venezis, (with Helen Karanikas), 1969, Hellenes and Hellions: Modern Greek Characters in American Literature, 1981. Co-chmn. Nat. Bicentennial Symposium on the Greek Experience in Am., 1976; Publicity dir. N.H. Ind. Voters, 1946; sec. Manchester Vets. Council, 1946; Candidate for Congress, 1948. Served with USAAF, 1942-45. Mem. Modern Lang. Assn., Hellenic Profl. Soc. Ill., Modern Greek Studies Assn. (Midwest chmn. 1972—), Soc. Study So. Lit., Friends of Lit., Phi Eta Sigma, Order Ahepa (dist. sec. 1946). Mem. Greek Orthodox Ch. Home: 618 N Harvey Ave Oak Park IL 60302 Office: Univ of Ill at Chicago Chicago IL 60680

KARAS, DONALD A., publisher; b. Boston, Dec. 9, 1931; s. Murray and Leah (Shershow) K.; Feb. 1956; children: Jon, Robin, Steven, James. B.S., Northeastern U., Boston, 1954; student, Harvard Bus. Sch. With Bill Communications Co., N.Y.C., 1958—, publisher food service div., 1967—; pres. Restaurant Bus., Inc., 1969—, now sr. v.p. co.; chmn. exec. com., dir. Clabir Corp.; chmn., dir. Isaly Co.; dir. Hagen Communications Co., Bill Communications.; Bd. dirs. Knowledge Scis. Mem. Young Pres.'s Orgn., Chief Execs. Orgn., World Bus. Council, Met. Pres.'s Orgn. Clubs: Jockey, Palm Bay, Sunningdale Country, Union League. Home: 136 E 36th St New York NY 10016 Office: 633 3d Ave New York NY 10017

KARASZ, FRANK ERWIN, chemical engineer, educator; b. Vienna, Austria, July 23, 1933; came to U.S., 1961; s. Karl Franz and Katherina K.; m. Sarah Langdell, Apr. 10, 1982; children: by previous marriage: Alison, Hilary. B.Sc., U. London, 1954, D.Sc., 1972; Ph.D., U. Wash., 1957. Postdoctoral fellow U. Oreg., 1958, Nat. Phys. Lab., U.K., 1959-61; research chemist Gen. Electric Research Lab., Schenectady, N.Y., 1961-67; assoc. prof. U. Mass., Amherst, 1967-69, prof. polymer sci. and engring., 1969—, co-dir. materials research lab.; sr. vis. fellow, Japan, 1981; vis. prof. U. Zurich, 1973, U. Stockholm, 1976, U. London, 1975. Editor books; mem. editorial bd. several sci. jours.; contbr. articles to profl. publs. Recipient N. Am. Thermal Analysis Soc. Mettler award, 1975. Mem. Am. Chem. Soc., Am. Phys. Soc. (past chmn. polymer physics div., high polymer physics prize 1984). Club: Cosmos (Washington). Home: 85 Lessey St Amherst MA 01002 Office: U Mass Grad Research Ctr Amherst MA 01003

KARATZ, WILLIAM WARREN, lawyer; b. Benton Harbor, Mich., Aug. 9, 1926; s. Harry E. and Grace M. (Campbell) K. Ph.B. (La Verne Noyes scholar), U. Chgo., 1948; postgrad., Sch. Pol. Sci., 1949; LL.B. (Harlan Fiske Stone scholar), Columbia U., 1952. Bar: N.Y. State 1953, U.S. Supreme Ct. 1960. Asso. in law Columbia U. Sch. Law, N.Y.C., 1952-53; asso. firm Winthrop, Stimson, Putnam & Roberts, N.Y.C., 1953-62, partner, 1963—. Bd. editors: Columbia Law Rev, 1950-52. Served with USN, 1944-46. Fellow Am. Bar Found.; mem. Am. Bar Assn., Am. Law Inst., Bar Assn. City N.Y. (mem. exec. com. 1969-73, chmn. exec. com. 1972-73, v.p. 1973-74), N.Y. State Bar Assn. (mem. ho. of dels. 1972-77), Am. Coll. Trial Lawyers, Am. Judicature Soc., N.Y. County Lawyers Assn., Fed. Bar Council (trustee 1982—), Am. Arbitration Assn. (nat. panel arbitrators), N.Y. Legal Aid Soc. (chmn. criminal def. br. com. 1968-72). Clubs: Century Assn., Recess (N.Y.C.); Grand Officer and Grand Jurisconsulte Chevaliers du Tastevin. Home: 303 E 57th St New York NY 10022 Office: 40 Wall St New York NY 10005

KARAVOLAS, HARRY J(OHN), biochemist; b. Peabody, Mass., Feb. 21, 1936; s. John Louis and Maria (Kayavas) K.; m. Barbara A. Katsaras, Aug. 26, 1962; 1 son, Christian Mark. B.S., Mass. Coll. Pharmacy, 1957, M.S. (Am. Found. Pharm. Edn. fellow), 1959; Ph.D. (USPHS fellow), St. Louis U., 1963; postgrad., Harvard U., 1963-66. Research fellow in biol. chemistry Harvard U. Med. Sch., 1963-66, research asso., instr. biol. chemistry, 1966-68, vis. lectr. biol. chemistry, 1975; tutor biochemical scis. Harvard Coll., 1966-68; asst. prof. physiol. chemistry and endocrinology U. Wis., Madison, 1968-72, mem. endocrinology-reproductive physiology program, 1968—, asso. dir., 1974—, asso. prof. physiol. chemistry, 1972-75, prof., chmn. dept., 1975—; sect. head neuroendocrinology Waisman Center on Mental Retardation and Human Devel., 1972—; mem. study sect. biochem. endocrinology NIH, 1979—. Editorial bd.: Endocrinology, 1974-78; bd. reviewers: Federation Proceedings, 1972-77; contbr. sci. articles to profl. jours. Recipient Borden award; Merck award; Rexall award, 1957; Amoco Distinguished Teaching award U. Wis., 1977; Ford Found. research grantee, 1970; NICHD research career devel. awardee, 1972-75; NIH research grantee, 1972. Mem. Am. Assn. Biol. Chemists, Endocrine Soc., Soc. Neuroscience, AAAS, Sigma Xi. Home: 2 Regis Circle Madison WI 53711 Office: Univ Wisconsin 591 Med Scis Bldg 1215 Linden Dr Madison WI 53706

KARAWINA, ERICA, painter, stained glass designer; b. Ger., 1904; came to U.S., 1923, naturalized, 1937; d. Paul Wilhelm and Meta (Jaenecke) K.; m. Sidney C. Hsiao, June 21, 1938. Studied under, Charles J. Connick. One-woman shows, Grace Horne Gallery, Boston, 1933, U. N.H., 1936, Art Club, Lancaster, Pa., 1937, Wadsworth Atheneum, 1938, Colby (Maine) Coll., U. Dayton, Ohio, 1939, Okla. Art Center, Okla. Art Center, Grand Rapids Mich., 1940, Ferargil Galleries, 1947, Fitchburg Art Mus., 1949, Currier Gallery, Beaux Arts Gallery, Honolulu, 1952, Gima's, 1953, China. Inst., Taipei, 1956, The Gallery, Honolulu, 1957, Contemporary Arts Center, 1977, numerous stained glass commns., Hawaii; represented in permanent collections, Library of Congress, Washington, Boston Mus. Fine Arts, Met. Mus., Worcester (Mass.) Fine Arts Mus., Colorado Springs Art Center, Addison Gallery, Mus. Modern Art, N.Y.C., Honolulu Acad. Arts, Tennent Art Found. Recipient John Poole Meml. Prize, James C. Castle award Narcissus Festival of Arts, 1961. Fellow Internat. Inst. Arts; mem. Hawaii Artists League, Arts Council Hawaii, Stained Glass Assn. Hawaii. Address: 3529 Akaka Pl Honolulu HI 96822

KARAYANIS, PLATO, opera company director; b. Pitts., Dec. 26, 1928; s. Theodore and Thalia K.; m. Dorothy E. Krebill, Sept. 30, 1956. B.F.A. in Music, Carnegie-Mellon U., 1952, Curtis Inst. Music, 1956. Formerly an adminstr., asst. stage dir. Met. Opera Nat. Co.; adminstrv. position San Francisco Opera; staged opera prodns., Germany, U.S.; exec. v.p., treas. Affiliate Artists, Inc., 1967-77; gen. dir. The Dallas Opera, 1977—; scholarship mem. opera dept. Berkshire Music Festival. Sang as baritone in, Germany and Switzerland. Martha Baird Rockefeller Fund for Music grantee, Hamburg, Germany. Office: Dallas Opera Majestic Theatre 1925 Elm St Dallas TX 75201

KARAYANNIS, NICHOLAS MARIOS, chemist; b. Athens, Greece, May 30, 1931; came to U.S., 1965; s. Marios L. and Antiopi M. (Horsch) K.; m. Alexandra E. Manolakis, Oct. 1, 1955; children: Marios, Yannis. B.S., Nat. Tech. U., Athens, 1955; Ph.D., U. Coll., London, 1960. Sci. adviser Greek Nat. Def. Gen. Staff, Athens, 1961-62, Greek Ministry Coordination, 1962-65; fuels and lubricants tech. instr. Nat. Tech. U., Athens, 1963-65; research assoc. Johns Hopkins U., Balt., 1965-67, Drexel U., Phila., 1967-70; sr. research chemist Amoco Chem. Corp., Naperville, Ill., 1970-76, research assoc., 1976—. Patentee in field. Served with Greek Army, 1959-61. Research assoc. grantee NIH, 1965-67, U.S. Army Edgewood Arsenal, 1967-70. Mem. Am. Chem. Soc., N.Y. Acad. Scis., AAAS, Greek Tech. Chamber, Ramsay Soc. Chem. Engrs., Phi Lambda Upsilon. Club: Pebblewood Swim and Racquet. Home: 15 Pebblewood Trail Naperville IL 60540 Office: Amoco Chems Corp Naperville IL 60566

KARAYN, JAMES, JR., broadcasting executive; b. Los Angeles, Jan. 5, 1933; s. James and Edith Elsinora (Edwards) K.; m. Barbara Thompson, Mar. 1, 1964. B.A., U. So. Calif., 1956; postgrad., UCLA, 1956-58. News dir. Sta. KTLA-TV, Los Angeles, 1956-62; producer-writer NBC News, Washington, 1962-64; exec. producer, chief Washington bur. Nat. Ednl. TV, 1965-71; founder, pres. Nat. Public Affairs Center for TV, Washington, 1971-75; exec. dir. 1976 Presdl. Debates, LWV, Washington, 1975-76; pres., gen. mgr. Stas.-WHYY-TV and WUHY-FM, Phila. and Wilmington, Del., 1977-83; pres. Karayn & Co., Inc.; speaker USIA Dept. State. TV prodns. State of the Union, 1967, 68, The Warren Years, 1970, Watergate Coverage, 1974, Impeachment Hearings, 1974, In Performance at Wolf Trap, 1973, 74, Terrorism/The World at Bay, 1978, Every Four Years, 1980, Fabulous Philadelphians: From Ormandy to Muti, 1981; author: Campaign Debates '78 Study, 1977, The Case for Permanent Presidential Debates, 1979. Served with U.S. Army, 1952-54. Recipient Silver Gavel, ABA, 1970; Columbia-DuPont award Columbia U., 1972, 73, 74; Disting. Journalism Alumni award U. So. Calif., 1973; Peabody award, 1974, 76, 77; George Polk award L.I. U., 1973; Am. Film Inst. award, 1981. Mem. Acad. TV Arts and Scis. (Emmy award 1967, 68, 73, 76), Phila. Com. Fgn. Relation, Center for Study of Presidency, White House Corrs. Assn., Sigma Delta Chi, Phi Gamma Delta. Clubs: Washington Press, Sunday Morning Breakfast. Home: 115 Lombard St Philadelphia PA 19147 *I have spent my career in the last quarter century as a broadcast journalist seeking to heighten public awareness and understanding of the many vital, sensitive and challenging issues and concerns affecting our lives and the democracy of our country. I have tried to uphold tough and high standards for myself and those who have worked with me, admired the bold and the provocative, respected honesty, creativity and compassion.*

KARCHER, ALAN JOSEPH, state legislator, lawyer; b. New Brunswick, N.J., May 19, 1943; s. Joseph Timothy and Ellen Louise (Joseph) K.; m. Margaret Anne Taylor, Mar. 24, 1962; children: Elizabeth, Ellen, Timothy. B.A. cum laude, Rutgers U., 1964, J.D., 1967; LL.D., Georgian Ct. Coll., 1982; M.A. in L.S., New Sch., 1984. Bar: N.J. 1967, D.C. 1967, Fla. 1979. Exec. sec. to pres. N.J. Senate, Trenton, 1966-67; acting sec. to gov. of N.J., Trenton, 1968-70, sole practice, Sayreville, N.J., 1970—; mem. N.J. Gen. Assembly, 1974—, majority leader, 1979-81, speaker, 1982—; municipal atty. Borough of Sayresville, 1972—; dir. law City of Rahway, N.J., 1973—; acting gov. State of N.J., 1982, 83. Author: booklet What's Right with New Jersey, 1976; contbr. articles to mags. Chmn. Middlesex County Mental Health Bd.; bd. govs. South Amboy Meml. Hosp.; trustee N.J. State Opera, Opera Theatre N.J. Mem. N.J. Bar Assn., D.C. Bar Assn., Fla. Bar Assn. Democrat. Lodges: K.C.; Elks. Home: 76 Winkler Rd Sayreville NJ 08872 Office: Alan J Karcher PA 61-67 Main St Sayreville NJ 08872 (201) 257-1515

KARDAS, BARBARA JEAN, coll. dean; b. N.Y.C., Mar. 7, 1931; d. Robert Andrew and Helen Frances (MacNaughton) Cotil; m. Julian Kardas, Feb. 24, 1957; 1 dau., Janine. B.S., SUNY, Oswego, 1952; M.A., Hunter Coll., N.Y.C., 1956; Ph.D., Northwestern U., 1969. Tchr. elem. sch., 1952-67; mem. faculty Chgo. State U., 1967—, prof. edn., 1974—, dean, 1974—; proposal reader Nat. Endowment Humanities, 1979; pres. Chgo. Consortium Colls. and Univs., 1979—. Author: Teacher Aides, 1969; contgr. articles to profl. jours. Pres. Epis.

Ch. Women; mem. vestry Holy Nativity Ch. Recipient Disting. Alumnus award SUNY, Oswego, 1975. Mem. AAUP, Am. Assn. Colls. Tchr. Edn., Ill. Assn. Colls. Tchr. Edn. (exec. bd.), Nat. Council Adminstrv. Women (dir. Ella F. Young chpt.), Am. Assn. Higher Edn., Ill. Curriculum Council, Kappa Delta Pi, Phi Delta Kappa. Office: Chgo State Univ 95th and King Dr Chicago IL 60628

KARDON, JANET, museum director, curator; b. Phila.; d. Robert and Shirley (Drasin) Stolker; m. Robert Kardon, Nov. 19, 1949; children: Ross, Nina, Roy. B.S. in Edn., Temple U.; M.A. in Art History, U. Pa. Lectr. Phila. Coll. Art, 1968-75, dir. exhbns., 1975-78; dir. Inst. Contemporary Art, Phila., 1978—; cons., panel mem. Nat. Endowment for Arts, 1975—; vice chmn. visual arts panel Pa. Council on Arts, Phila., 1978—; U.S. commr. Venice Biennale, Venice, 1980. Created essays for 30 exhbns. Grantee Nat. Endowment for Arts, 1978. Mem. Assn. Art Mus. Dirs., Coll. Art Assn. Home: 56 Crosby Brown Rd Gladwyne PA 19035 Office: Inst Contemporary Art U Pa 34th and Walnut Sts Philadelphia PA 19104

KARDON, ROBERT, corp. exec.; b. Phila., Mar. 8, 1922; s. Morris and Sophie (Winkleman) K.; m. Janet Stolker, Nov. 19, 1949; children—Roy, Nina, Ross. Student, U. Miami (Fla.), 1940-42, Shriveham Am. U., Swindon, Eng., 1945-46. Chmn. bd. B.T. Babbitt Co., Inc., 1964-66, Pitts. Mortgage Corp., 1964-72, Murphree Mortgage Co., Nashville, 1966-72, Kardon Investment Co., 1945-75, Peoples Bond & Mortgage Co., Phila., 1950—; chmn. bd., v.p. United Container Co., Phila., 1938-75; pres., chief exec. officer Kardon Industries, Inc., 1974—; dir. Continental Bank Phila. Trustee Phila. Mus. Art, Hill Top Prep. Sch. Served with AUS, 1942-46. Mem. Young Pres. Orgn., World Bus. Council. Club: Locust (Phila.). Home: 56 Crosby Brown Rd Gladwyne PA 19035 Office: 1201 Chestnut St Philadelphia PA 19107

KARDOS, PAUL JAMES, ins. co. exec.; b. North Vandergrift, Pa., Mar. 20, 1937; s. Joseph and Mary K.; m. Paulette Laura Sobota, Oct. 29, 1966; children—Diane, Brian. B.S. in Math, Grove City Coll., 1962. With Life Ins. Co. of N. Am., until 1977, v.p., until 1977; sr. v.p. Horace Mann Educators, Springfield, Ill., 1977-78, exec. v.p., 1978-79, pres., 1979—; dir. INA Corp. subs. *

KAREKEN, FRANCIS A., lawyer; b. Buffalo, Mar. 30, 1930; s. Michael and Gertrude (Lang) K.; m. Margaret Holland, Sept. 10, 1958; children: Michael, Susan. B.A. magna cum laude, U. Buffalo, 1954; J.D. cum laude, U. Chgo., 1958. Bar: D.C. 1959, N.Y. 1961, Wash. 1968. Law clk. 2d U.S. Circuit Ct. Appeals, N.Y.C., 1958-59; atty. antitrust div. Dept. Justice, Washington, 1959-61; asso. firm Hughes, Hubbard & Reed, N.Y.C., 1961-68; gen. atty., then asst. gen. counsel Weyerhaeuser Co., Tacoma, 1968-75, v.p., gen. counsel, 1975-80; sr. v.p., gen. counsel Penn Central Corp., N.Y.C., 1980—. Mem. Am., Wash. bar assns., Bar Assn. City of N.Y., Assn. Gen. Counsel, Order of Coif., Phi Beta Kappa. Office: 500 W Putnam Ave Greenwich CT 06836

KAREL, FRANK, III, foundation executive; b. Orlando, Fla., Aug. 30, 1935; s. Frank and Helen (Pool) K.; m. Graciela Guerrero, Aug. 17, 1957; children: Elizabeth Ann, Barbara Ann. B.S. in Journalism, U. Fla., 161; M.P.A., NYU, 1983. Sci. writer Miami Herald, (Fla.), 1961-64; assoc. dir. pub. relations Johns Hopkins Med. Instns., Balt., 1964-67; pub. info. officer div. regional med. program HEW, Bethesda, Md., 1967; exec. assoc. The Commonwealth Fund, N.Y.C., 1968-70; dir. planning Nfat. Jewish Hosp. and Research Ctr., Denver, 1970-72; assoc. dir. Nat. Cancer Inst., HEW, Bethesda, 1972-74; v.p. for communications Robert Wood Johnson Found., Princeton, N.J., 1974—. Served with USAF, 1954-58. Mem. Pub. Relations Soc. Am. (bd. dirs. health sect.), Nat. Assn. Sci. Writers, AAAS, Communications Network in Philanthropy (founding chmn.). Home: 9 Springwood Dr Lawrenceville NJ 08648 Office: Johnson Found PO Box 2316 Princeton NJ 08540

KAREL, MARCUS, food science educator; b. Lwow, Poland, May 17, 1928; came to U.S., 1951, naturalized, 1962; s. David and Cila (Lipschutz) K.; m. Carolyn Frances Weeks, Aug. 26, 1958; children: Linda, Steven, Karen, Debra. Student, Technische Hochschule, Munich, Germany, 1947-50; A.B., Boston U., 1955; Ph.D., Mass. Inst. Tech., 1960. Tech. asst. dept. food tech. Mass. Inst. Tech., Cambridge, 1953-57, research asso., 1957-61, asst. prof. food engring., dept. nutrition and food sci., 1961-64, asso. prof., 1964-69, prof., 1969—, asso. dept. head, 1976—; Vis. prof. food engring., dept. food and bioengring. Technion, Haifa, Israel, 1971; cons. NASA/Manned Spacecraft Center, 1969-70; mem. Nat. Acad. Sci. Mission to Argentina, 1962-63; mem. adv. bd. on mil. personnel supplies Nat. Acad. Sci.-NRC, 1972-74. Contbr. articles to profl. jours. Recipient Food Engring. award and Gold medal Am. Soc. Agrl. Engrs./Food and Dairy Supply Industry Assn., 1978; named to Food Engring. Hall of Fame, 1978. Fellow Inst. Food Technologists (chmn. N.E. sect. 1966-67, William V. Cruess award 1970), Inst. Food Sci. and Tech. U.K.; mem. Am. Inst. Chem. Engrs. (dir. food and bioengring. div.), Research and Devel. Assos. for Armed Forces (dir. 1978—). Office: Room 16-315 Mass Inst Tech Cambridge MA 02139

KARGER, DELMAR WILLIAM, educator, consultant, author; b. Cape Girardeau, Mo., May 9, 1913; s. Ernest J. and Clara M. (Hellewege) K.; m. Paula E. Miller, July 5, 1935 (dec. Nov. 1958); children—Bonnie E., Karen R., Joyce P.; m. Edith Kennedy Loring, Jan. 11, 1962 (dec. Aug. 1969); m. Ruth Lounsberry Rivard, Oct. 31, 1970. Student, S.E. Mo. State Coll., 1931-32; B.S. in Elec. Engring, Valparaiso U., 1935; M.S. in Gen. Engring, U. Pitts., 1947. Registered profl. engr. Insp., surveyor C.E. U.S. Army, 1935; asst. chief electrician Internat. Harvester Co., 1935-41, asst. plant engr., 1941-42; hdqrs. mfg. engr. Westinghouse Electric Corp., 1942-45, mgr. coop. edn., 1945-47; plant mgr. Pa. Electric Coil Corp., Pitts., 1947-48; mgr. orgn. systems and procedures RCA, 1948-50; chief indsl. engr. RCA Service Corp., 1950-51; mgmt. cons. Booz, Allen & Hamilton, N.Y.C., 1951; chief plant and indsl. engr. Magnavox Co., 1951-56, mgr. new products devel., 1956-59; prof. mgmt. Rensselaer Poly. Inst., Troy, N.Y., 1959—, chmn. dept. mgmt. engring., 1959-68, dean, 1963-70, Ford Found. prof. mgmt., 1970-78; prof. mgmt. U. West Fla., 1978—; pres., dir. Randac Systems, Inc., Troy, 1961-63; dir. Fiber Glass Industries, Inc., Amsterdam, N.Y., Wellington Tech. Industries, Madison, Ga., Madison Co., Bunker Ramo Corp., Oak Brook, Ill., Scott & Fetzer Co., Lakewood, Ohio; ind. mgmt. cons. Author: (with F. Bayha) Engineered Work Measurement, rev. edit, 1966, 3d edit., 1977, The New Product, 1960, La Mesure Rationelle du Travail, 1962, (with R.G. Murdick) Managing Engineering and Research, rev. edit, 1969, 3d edit., 1980, (with A.B. Jack) Problems of Small Business in Developing and Exploiting New Products, 1963, (with R.G. Murdick) New Product Venture Management, 1972, How to Choose a Career, 1978, (with W.C. Hancock) Advanced Work Measurement, 1982, The Technical Approach to the Stock Market, 1984; contbr. numerous articles to profl. jours. Former mem. fin. com., bd. dirs. N.Y. div. Am. Cancer Soc.; past bd. dirs. Inst. Resource Mgmt., Bethesda, Md. Fellow Am. Inst. Indsl. Engrs. (past nat. v.p., dir. inter-soc. affairs), Soc. Advancement Mgmt. (regional v.p.), AAAS, Methods-Time Measurement Assn. Standards and Research (pres. 1958-60); mem. Acad. Mgmt. (past dir.), New Product Mgmt. and Devel. Assn. (v.p., dir.). Presbyn. Clubs: Masons, Santa Rosa (Fla.) Golf and Beach. Home: 506 Circle Dr DeFuniak Springs FL 32433

KARGON, ROBERT HUGH, educator; b. Bklyn., Oct. 18, 1938; s. Ira C. and Inez (Schulman) K.; m. Marcia Rose, July 14, 1962; children: Jeremy, Dina. B.S., Duke U., 1959; M.S., Yale U., 1960; Ph.D., Cornell U., 1964. Asst. prof. U. Ill., 1964-65; asst. prof. to prof. Johns Hopkins, Balt., 1965—, chmn. dept. history of sci., 1972-75, Willis K. Shepard prof. history of sci., 1979—. Author: Atomism in England, 1966, Maturing of American Science, 1974, Science in Victorian Manchester, 1977, The Rise of Robert Millikan, 1982; Co-editor: Victorian Science, 1970. Mem. History of Sci. Soc., Am. Hist. Assn. Home: 2407 Everton Rd Baltimore MD 21209 Office: Dept History of Sci Johns Hopkins Univ Baltimore MD 21218

KARINEN, ARTHUR ELI, educator; b. Comptche, Cal., Feb. 25, 1919; s. Eli and Anna (Koskelo) K.; m. Florence Irene Wickstrom, Apr. 12, 1946; children—Sandra Jean, Nancy Ruth (Mrs. Ronald Wallace Magnus), Patricia Anna (Mrs. Alan Stanley Hightman), Judith Riika. A.B., U. Cal. at Berkeley, 1944, M.A. in Geography, 1948, Ph.D., U. Md., 1958. Cartographer OSS, 1942-43; instr. Ohio State U., 1946-47; asst. prof. geography U. Md., 1948-59; prof. geography Calif. State U. at Chico, 1959—, chmn. dept., 1967-72; Fulbright lectr. U. Oulu, Finland, 1970; vis. prof. Helsinki (Finland) Sch. Econs., 1979-80. Author: (with others) California: Land of Contrast, 3d edit, 1977. Mem. Assn. Am. Geographers, Am. Congress Surveying and Mapping, Am. Geog. Soc., Cal. Council Geog. Edn. (pres. 1965-66), Finnish Geog. Soc. (corr.). Presbyn. Home: 834 Arbutus Ave Chico CA 95926 *In all actions that may have an effect on others I try to place myself in their position and ask how I would feel if this action were directed at me.*

KARK, ROBERT M., physician, educator; b. Cape Town, Union S. Africa, Aug. 29, 1911; came to U.S., 1938, naturalized, 1948; s. Ezekiel and Rebeccah (Kark) K.; m. Julia Rieck, Aug. 21, 1935; children—Pieter, John, Elizabeth. B.A., U. Cape Town, 1931; M.R.C.S., L.R.C.P., Guy's Hosp. Med. Sch., London, Eng., 1935. House physician Guy's Hosp., 1935-36; registrar, demonstrator pathology Guy's Hosp. Med. Sch., 1937-38; Adrian Stokes fellow Thorndike lab. Boston City Hosp., 1938, Rockefeller fellow, 1939; research fellow Harvard Med. Sch., 1938-41; asst. dir. Med. Nutriton Lab., Chgo., 1947-50; prof. medicine U. Ill., 1950—, Rush Med. Coll., Chgo., 1971-82, disting. emeritus prof. medicine, 1982—; physician Presbyn. Hosp., Chgo., 1951—; attending physician Cook County and U. Ill. Hosps., Chgo.; sect. chief geriatrics Hines VA Hosp. (Ill.), 1983; Harveian lectr., London, 1958; Pfizer lectr. Royal Australasian Coll. Physicians, 1959; FitzPatrick lectr. Royal Coll. Physicians London, 1983; spl. cons. to USPHS.; Mem. adv. com. medicine Office Surgeon Gen., U.S. Army; mem. food and nutrition bd. NRC. Mem. bd. Lawrence Hall, Chgo.; regent Am. Coll., 1976-82. Served to lt. col. M.C. Royal Canadian Army, 1941-46. Decorated Burma Star.; Guggenheim fellow, 1961-62, 74-75. Fellow Royal Coll. Physicians (London), A.C.P. (master, past gov. No. Ill.), Royal Soc. Medicine; mem. AMA, Am. Soc. Clin. Investigation, Assn. Physicians Gt. Britain and Ireland, Osler Soc. Club: Athenaeum. Home: 860 N Lake Shore Dr Chicago IL 60611 Office: 1753 W Congress Pkwy Chicago IL 60612

KARKOW, RICHARD ELLIS, diversified services company executive; b. Chgo., July 3, 1928; s. Conrad Hansen and Florence Marie (Ellis) K.; m. Ruth Margaret Ehrlin, Jan. 29, 1955; children: Catherine, Douglas. A.B., Kenyon Coll., Gambier, Ohio, 1948; M.B.A., Harvard U., 1950; J.D., Loyola U., Chgo., 1958. With No. Trust Co., Chgo., 1954-59, H.M. Byllesby & Co., 1959-60; treas. Pet Inc., St. Louis, 1960-63; v.p., treas. The Kroger Co., Cin., 1963-69; exec. v.p. Stirling Corp., Rochester, N.Y., 1969-70; v.p. fin. Ill. Tool Works, Chgo., 1973-73, Carlson Cos., Inc., Mpls., 1973—. Mem. Fin. Execs. Inst., Ill. Bar Assn. Home: 1542 Tamarack Dr Long Lake MN 55356 Office: Carlson Cos Inc 12755 State Hwy 55 Minneapolis MN 55441

KARL, BARRY DEAN, historian; b. Louisville, July 24, 1927; s. Aaron and Anne (Simons) K.; m. Alice Hideko Woodard, June 14, 1957; children: Elisabeth Mead, Sarah Anne. B.A., U. Louisville, 1949; M.A., U. Chgo., 1951; Ph.D., Harvard U., 1961. Asso. editor for humanities and history U. Chgo. Press, 1951-55; exec. sec. to com. on gen. edn. Harvard U., 1959-61; asst. prof. history Washington U., St. Louis, 1962-63, prof., 1963-68, Brown U., 1968-71; prof. Am. history U. Chgo., 1971—, Norman and Edna Freehling prof., 1977—, chmn. dept. history, 1976-79; fellow Charles Warren Center, Harvard U., 1965. Author: Executive Reorganization and Reform in the New Deal, 1963, Presidential Planning and Social Science Research, 1969, Charles E. Merriam and the Study of Politics, 1974, Executive Reorganization and Presidential Power, 1978, (with Stanley N. Katz) The American Private Philanthropic Foundation and the Public Sphere 1890-1930, 1981, The Citizen and the Scholar: Ships that Crash in the Night, 1982, Corporate Philanthropy: Historical Background, 1982, The Uneasy State: The U.S. from 1915 to 1945, 1983. Co-recipient Faculty prize for, 1962-63, Harvard U. Press. Mem. Am. Hist. Assn. Home: 4823 S Kimbark Ave Chicago IL 60615 Office: 1126 E 59th St Chicago IL 60637

KARL, FREDERICK BRENNAN, former state justice; b. Daytona Beach, Fla., May 14, 1924; s. Fred J. and Mary M. (Brennan) K.; m. Mercedes Jensen, Aug. 21, 1971; children: Cynthia Anne, Frederick Brennan, Mary Theresa, James B.; stepchildren: Debra Louise, Tami Sue. Student, U. Fla., 1942; LL.B., Stetson U., DeLand, Fla., 1949, J.D. (hon), 1977. Bar: Fla. 1950. Assoc. David L. Black (Esq.), Daytona Beach, 1950-54; partner firm Raymond, Wilson, Karl, Conway & Barr, Daytona Beach and Tallahassee, 1954-74; pvt. practice, Tallahassee, 1974-75; partner firm Karl, Harris, McConnaughhay & Weidner, Tallahassee, 1976; justice Fla. Supreme Ct., 1977-78; city atty., Ormond Beach, Fla., 1960-65, Daytona Beach, 1965-68; spl. master exec. suspensions Fla. Senate, 1972-74; atty. Fla. Bd. Optometry, 1973-76; pub. counsel Fla. Pub. Service Commn., 1974-75; counsel select com. jud. impeachment Fla. Ho. Reps., 1975; Mem. Fla. Ho. of Reps. from Volusia County, 1956-64, Fla. Senate from 14th Dist., 1968-72. Contbr. articles to legal publs. Mem. Fla. Bd. Ind. Colls. and Univs., 1974-76; past chmn. Fla. Cancer Crusade; past mem. bd. Fla. Mental Health Assn.; past trustee St. Leo Coll., Dade City, Fla.; past legis. mem., mem. legis. adv. council to chmn. So. Regional Edn. Bd. Served with AUS, 1942-46. Decorated Silver Star, Bronze Star, Purple Heart; recipient Good Govt. award Fla. Jr. C. of C., 1963; Sch. Bell award Fla. Edn. Assn., 1962; Ben C. Willard Meml. award Stetson Lawyers Assn., 1976; named Most Valuable Senator Fla. Corr. and Daily Newspaper Editors, 1970. Mem. Am., Tallahassee bar assns., Fla. Bar. Roman Catholic. Home: 2510 Killarney Way Tallahassee FL 32308 Office: PO Box 12069 Tallahassee FL 32317

KARL, JEAN EDNA, editor, publishing co. exec.; b. Chgo., July 29, 1927; d. William A. and Ruth (Anderson) K. B.A., Mt. Union Coll., 1949, LL.D., 1969. With Scott, Foresman & Co., Chgo., 1949-56; editor children's books Abingdon Press, 1956-61; dir. children's book dept. Atheneum Pubs., N.Y.C., 1961—, v.p., 1964—, also dir.; Mem. joint com. ALA-Children's Book Council, 1961-66; chmn., 1961-63; bd. dirs. Children's Book Council, 1963-66, 74-77, pres., 1965; bd. dirs. Children's Services div. ALA, 1971-74. Author: From Childhood to Childhood, 1970, The Turning Place, 1976, Beloved Benjamin is Waiting, 1978, But We Are Not of Earth, 1981. Trustee Mt. Union Coll., 1974-77, Christ United Methodist Ch., N.Y.C., 1972—; mem. freedom to read com. Assn. Am. Pubs., 1974-79, bd. dirs. gen. trade div., 1975-77. Home: 136 E 36th St New York NY 10016 Office: 597 Fifth Ave New York NY 10017

KARL, MAX HENRY, insurance company executive; b. Milw., Feb. 2, 1910; s. Louis and Bertha (Gindlin) K.; m. Anita Renee Davis, Nov. 28, 1946; children:Robert, Kenneth, Karen. B.A. in Econs, U. Wis., 1931, J.D., 1933; D.Comml.Sci. (hon.), U. Wis.-Milw., 1982; LL.D., Cardinal Stritch Coll., 1984. Bar: Wis. 1933. Practiced in, Milw., 1933-57; founder, chmn. exec. com. Mortgage Guaranty Ins. Corp., Milw., 1957—; chmn., chief exec. officer MGIC Investment Corp.; past pres. Mortgage Ins. Cos. of Am.; past mem. adv. com. Fed. Home Loan Mortgage Corp. Chmn. Gov.'s Council on Econ. Devel.; del. Pres.'s Econ. Conf., 1974; v.p. Milw. Redevel. Corp.; Past pres. Milw. Jewish Fedn.; bd. dirs. United Jewish Appeal, Milw. Symphony, United Performing Arts Center, Greater Milw. Com.; chmn. bd. dirs. Touro Coll.; bd. dirs. United Israel Appeal, United Hias Service, Council of Jewish Fedns. and Welfare Funds, N.Y.C., Hillel Acad., Milw., Am. Friends of Hebrew U.; trustee Mt. Sinai Hosp., Milw., Nat. Mutiple Sclerosis Soc., Milw.; trustee emeritus Marquette U. Served with USAAF, 1942-45. Recipient House and Home award as one of ten individuals contbg. most to Am. housing, 1962, Golda Meir award, 1973, Vocat. Service award Milw. Rotary Club, 1979, Disting. Service award Wis. Alumni Club of Milw., Gitelson medallion Alpha Epsilon Pi, Headliner of Yr. award Milw. Press Club, 1982; Jabotinsky award State of Israel, 1980; Disting. Service award Wis. Alumni Assn., 1981; Evan P. Helfaer award Wis. chpt. Nat. Soc. Fund Raising Execs., 1982. Mem. Am., Wis., Milw. bar assns., Nat. Assn. Home Builders (Housing Hall of Fame, Roundtable), Beta Gamma Sigma. Jewish. Clubs: Brynwood Country, University. Office: MGIC Plaza Milwaukee WI 53201

KARL, MICHAEL M., physician; b. Milw., Jan. 30, 1915; s. Louis and Bertha K.; m. Irene Stark, Sept. 1, 1940; children: Bonnie, Terry. B.S., U. Wis., 1936; M.D., U. Louisville, 1938. Diplomate: Am. Bd. Internal Medicine. Pvt. practice medicine specializing in internal medicine, mem. faculty Washington U. Sch. Medicine, St. Louis, now prof. clin. medicine; mem. nat. adv. com. White House Conf. Families, Inst. Medicine, Nat. Acad. Scis.; dir. med. service Jewish Hosp., St. Louis. Served to capt. AUS. Mem. A.C.P. (bd. govs.), Am. Assn. Study Liver Diseases, Am. Coll. Nephrology, Alpha Omega Alpha. Office: Washington Univ Sch of Medicine 660 S Euclid Ave St Louis MO 63110 *

KARLE, ISABELLA LUGOSKI, scientist; b. Detroit, Dec. 2, 1921; 1942; 3 children. B.S., U. Mich., 1941, M.S., 1942, Ph.D. in Phys. Chemistry (Rackham fellow), 1942-43, 1944; D.Sc. (hon.), 1976, 79. Asso. chemist U. Chgo., 1944; instr. U. Mich., 1944-46; physicist U.S. Naval Research Lab., Navy Dept., Washington, 1946-59, head X-ray sect., 1959—; Mem. U.S. Nat. Com. on Crystallography; adv. bd. Office Chemistry and Chem. Tech., NRC; mem. bd. on internat. orgns. and programs Nat. Acad. Scis., 1980-83; mem. exec. com. Am. Peptide Symposium, 1975—. Mem. editorial bd.: Polymers, 1975-81, Internat. Jour. Peptide and Protein Research, 1981—. Recipient Superior Civilian Service award Navy Dept., 1965, Ann. Achievement award Soc. Women Engrs., 1968; Hillebrand award, 1970; Fed. Woman's award, 1973; Dexter Conrad award Office of Naval Research, 1980. Mem. Nat. Acad. Scis., Am. Phys. Soc., Am. Biophys. Soc., Am. Crystallographic Assn. (pres. 1976), Am. Chem. Soc. (Garvan award 1976). Research in application of electron and x-ray diffraction to structure problems in chemistry and biology. Office: Naval Research Lab Laboratory for Structure of Matter Code 6030 Washington DC 20375

KARLE, JEROME, research physicist; b. N.Y.C., June 18, 1918; married, 1942; 3 children. B.S., CCNY, 1937; A.M., Harvard U., 1938; M.S., U. Mich., 1942, Ph.D. in Phys. Chemistry, 1943. Research asso. Manhattan project, Chgo., 1943-44, U.S. Navy Project, Mich., 1944-46; head electron diffraction sect. Naval Research Lab., Washington, 1946-58, head diffraction br., 1958, now head lab. for structure matter; mem. NRC, 1954-56, 67-75, 78—; chmn. U.S. Nat. Com. for Crystallography, 1973-75. Fellow Am. Phys. Soc.; mem. Am. Chem. Soc., Crystallograph. Assn. (treas. 1950-52, pres. 1972), Internat. Union Crystallography (exec. com. 1978—, pres. 1981—), Am. Math. Soc., AAAS, Nat. Acad. Scis. Research in structure atoms, molecules, crystals, solid surfaces. Office: US Naval Research Lab Lab for Structure of Matter Code 6030 Washington DC 20375 *There is too much administration of everything creative. It distorts our society and its character. The solution is to select competent, well-qualified people and give them freedom and support to pursue their creative gifts.*

KARLEN, GOTTFRIED EMANUEL, lumber company executive, distributor; b. Helena, Mont., Oct. 12, 1893; s. Gottfried and Emily Maude (Betchen) K.; m. Anastatia Baldwin, July 6, 1921 (dec. Apr. 1963); m. Ruth Estes Huber, Mar. 22, 1976. Ed. pub. schs., Long Prairie, Minn. Car loader Red River Lumber Co., Akeley, Minn., 1911-13; checker Internat. Lumber Co., International Falls, Minn., 1913, Shevlin-Clarke Co., Ft. Frances, Ont., Can., 1914; foreman, asst. supt. St. Paul & Tacoma Lumber Co., 1915-17; buyer J. E. Morris Lumber Co., Seattle, 1919-22; v.p. Schwager-Karlen Lumber Co., 1922-28; pres. Karlen-Davis Co., Tacoma, 1928-73; now hon. chmn.; sr. partner Eatonville Lumber Co., Wash., 1943-53; partner Tacoma Lumber Fabricating Co., 1945-51; pres. Timber Devel. Co., Inc., Tacoma, 1937-54, Orwaca Land Co., 1951—, Thunderbird Park, Inc., 1954-73; chmn. Fed. Home Loan Bank of San Francisco, 1958-61; adv. bd. Puget Sound Nat. Bank. Past campaign chmn. Tacoma Community Chest and Council.; Hon. dir. Tacoma Gen. Hosp.; hon. trustee U. Puget Sound; trustee Coll. of the Desert, Palm Springs, Calif., 1974—. Served with U.S. Army, 1917-19. Mem. Nat. Lumber Mfrs. Assn. (past dir., v.p.), W. Coast Lumbermen's Assn. (past pres.), Wash. Hist. Soc., Tacoma C. of C. Republican. Clubs: Masons, Shriners; Rotary, Rainier, Wash. Athletic (Seattle); Tacoma Country and Golf (past pres.), Tacoma, Tacoma Lumbermen's (past pres.), Arlington (Portland, Oreg.); Pacific-Union, Bohemian (San Francisco); Thunderbird Country (past pres.), Committee of Twenty-Five (Palm Springs, Calif.); Balboa (Mazatlan, Mexico); Eldorado Country (Indian Wells, Calif.); Pennask Lake Fishing and Game (Vancouver, B.C., Can.). Home: 404 N D Apt 12 Tacoma WA 98403 Office: Washington Bldg Tacoma WA 98401

KARLIN, MYRON D., motion picture co. exec.; b. Revere, Mass., Sept. 21, 1918; s. Joseph and Sadie (Greenfield) K.; m. Charlotte Siletzky, July 26, 1942; children—Cheryl Jo, Joyce Ann. B.A., UCLA, 1939, M.A., 1941. Gen. mgr. Metro-Goldwyn-Mayer, Ecuador, 1946-48, Venezuela, 1949-52, Germany, 1952-54, 56-57, Argentina, 1954-55, v.p., Europe, 1968-70; gen. mgr. United Artists, Italy, 1958-59; pres. Brunswick Internat. Corp., Chgo., 1960-68; v.p. Warner Bros., U.K., Europe, Middle East, Africa, London, 1970-72; pres. Warner Bros. Internat., Burbank, Calif., 1972—, also dir. Served with U.S. Army, 1943-46; ETO. Decorated Croix de Guerre, France; knight of Italian Republic; comdr. Italian Republic. Jewish. Office: 4000 Warner Blvd Burbank CA 91522

KARLINSKY, SIMON, Slavic languages educator; b. Harbin, Manchuria, Sept. 22, 1924; came to U.S., 1938, naturalized, 1944; s. Aron and Sophie (Levitin) K. B.A., U. Calif. at Berkeley, 1960, Ph.D., 1964; M.A., Harvard, 1961. Conf. interpreter, music student, Europe, 1947-57; teaching fellow Harvard, 1960-61; asst. prof. Slavic langs.

and lits. U. Calif. at Berkeley, 1963-65, prof., 1967—, chmn. dept., 1967-69; vis. asso. prof. Harvard, 1966. Author: Marina Cvetaeva: Her Life and Her Art, 1966, The Sexual Labyrinth of Nikolai Gogol, 1976; editor: The Bitter Air of Exile, 1977; editor, annotator: Anton Chekhov's Life and Thought, 1975, The Nabokov-Wilson Letters, 1979; contbr. articles to profl. jours. Served with AUS, 1944-46. Woodrow Wilson fellow, 1960-61; Guggenheim fellow, 1969-70, 77-78. Mem. Phi Beta Kappa. Office: U Calif Berkeley CA 94720

KARLOS, ANTHONY CHRIST, broadcasting executive, former retail grocery executive; b. Chgo., Sept. 24, 1912; s. Christ A. and Angeline (Simoulis) K.; m. Demetrea Ganos, June 11, 1944; children: Chris, Dean, Stephanie. Student pub. schs., Chgo. Mgr. family-owned business, 1930-37; with Gen. Foods Corp., 1937-43, Grocerland Co-op, Inc., Chgo., 1940—, gen. mgr., 1949—, vice chmn. bd., 1961-63, chmn. bd., chief exec. officer, 1963-78, ret.; exec. v.p., dir., a founder Century Broadcasting Corp.; a founder, officer, dir. O'Hare-Chgo. Corp., 1960—; a founder, vice chmn. bd., dir. Archer Nat. Bank Chgo.; past officer, dir. several corps.; partner several real estate enterprises; del. 1st Panhellenic Investment Conf., Athens, Greece, 1980. Chmn., co-chmn. numerous fund-raising drives.; Bd. dirs., hon. parish council mem. United Greek Orthodox Chs., Chgo.; nat. bd. trustees City of Hope, Duarte, Calif.; hon. trustee Am. Coll. of Greece, Athens. Recipient Golden Torch of Hope City of Hope, 1965, Million Dollar Club award, 1973-74; named Man of Year Ill. and Chgo. wholesale grocers assns., 1961. Mem. Chgo. Wholesale Grocers Assn. (dir., past pres.), Chgo. Natural History Mus. (life asso.), Art Inst. Chgo., Chgo. Symphony Soc., Chgo. Hort. Soc., Chgo. Council Fgn. Relations, Hellenic Assn. Commerce and Industry of Ill., Order of Ahepa. Clubs: Masons, Execs. (Chgo.). Home: 6747 Minnehaha Lincolnwood Towers IL 60646 Office: 875 N Michigan Ave Suite 4145 Chicago IL 60611

KARLOVITZ, LES ANDREW, uinversity dean, mathematician; b. Budapest, Hungary, July 31, 1936; came to U.S., 1947; s. Bela Kalovitz and Maria (Koenig) K.; m. Julie Mahoney, July 11, 1959; children: Maximillian, Leslie, Jenni. B.S., Yale U., 1959; Ph.D., Carnegie Inst. Tech., 1964. Mem. faculty Case Western Res. U., Cleve., 1963-66; mem. u. Md., College Park, 1966-78; research prof. Inst. Fluid Dynamics and Applied Math, U. Md., 1971-78; dir., prof. Sch Math. Ga. Inst. Tech., Atlanta, 1978-82, dean Coll. Scis. and Liberal Studies, 1982—; vis. prof. Carnegie-Mellon U., Pitts., 1974-75, U. Brasilia, (Brazil), 1974; program dir. math. NSF, 1976-77. Contbr. articles to profl. jours.; mem. editorial bd.: Jour. Math Anaylsis, Soc. Indsl. and Applied Math, 1973-82. Mem. Am. Math. Soc., Soc. Indsl. and Applied Math. Home: 1303 Briardale Ln Atlanta GA 30306 Office: Ga Inst Tech Coll Sci Liberal Studies 225 North Ave NW Atlanta GA 30332

KARLSON, ALFRED GUSTAV, microbiologist, educator; b. Virginia, Minn., Apr. 26, 1910; s. Knute John and Pauline Henrietta (Johnson) K.; m. Janice Ruth Stillians, June 24, 1938; children: Alfred Lennart, Karl John, Kathy Jean, Trudy Ann, Julie Kay. B.S., Iowa State U., 1934, D.V.M., 1935, M.S., 1938; Ph.D., U. Minn., 1942. Diplomate: pub. health and med. microbiology Am. Bd. Microbiology, Am. Coll. Vet. Pathologists (pres. 1949). Instr. bacteriology Iowa State U., 1935-38; fellow exptl. medicine Mayo Grad. Sch., U. Minn., 1938-39, faculty, 1946—, prof. comparative pathology, 1962—, prof. med. microbiology, 1971; cons. exptl. medicine Mayo Clinic, 1946-53, cons. microbiology, 1953—; Sec. Conf. Research Workers Animal Diseases, 1948-64; mem. Nat. Bd. Vet. Examiners, 1948-64. Sect. editor: Biol. Abstracts, 1940—; editorial bd.: Jour. Bacteriology, 1950, 56, Am. Jour. Vet. Research, 1952—, Applied Microbiology, 1967—; Contbr. articles to sci. jours. Served to lt. col. Vet. Corps AUS, 1941-45. Recipient Alumni Achievement award Iowa State U., 1965, Distinguished Achievement citation, 1976. Fellow Am. Acad. Microbiology, Am. Vet. Med. Assn.; mem. Am. Thoracic Soc., Soc. Am. Bacteriologists, Soc. Exptl. Biology and Medicine, Sigma Xi. Unitarian-Universalist. Home: 428 16th Ave SW Rochester MN 55902 Office: Mayo Clinic Rochester MN 55905

KARLSON, ESKIL LEANNART, biophysicist; b. Johnkoping, Sweden, Jan. 5, 1920; came to U.S., 1925, naturalized, 1933; s. John Benjamin and Matilda Johann (Green) K.; m. Vangalla K. Kapsalaki (dec.); children: John B., Paul L., Judith O.; m. Betty Ore, Dec. 1982. M.S., U. Pitts., 1949, D.Sc., 1977; D.Sc., U. St. Louis, 1977. Pres., owner Precision Research, Inc., Stamford, Conn., 1960-67; v.p. research and devel. Pollution Control Industries Inc., Stamford, 1967-71; pres. Life Support Systems, Inc., Stamford, 1971—; exec. v.p. research and devel. Iconex Systems, Inc., Stamford, 1976-77, chmn. bd., 1968—, pres., 1983—; cons. N.B.S., Northeast Utilities Co., Hartford, Conn.; pres. Karlson's Industries. Author. Served with USCGR, 1941-44. Research fellow U. Gannon, Erie, Pa. Mem. Optical Soc. Am., Instrument Soc. Am., Health Physics Soc., Am. Nuclear Soc., Internat. Ozone Inst., Sigma Xi. Club: Circumnavigators. Patentee medicine, radiation, pollution control, space sci., computers, continuous ion exchange system. Home: 4634 State St Erie PA 16509

KARLSON, KARL EUGENE, surgeon; b. Worcester, Mass., July 20, 1920; s. Karl Johann and Mabel Cecelia (Fisher) K.; m. Gloria E. Anderson, June 24, 1947; children—Karl, Peter, Nancy, Steven, James, Matthew. Student, Bethel Coll., 1938-39; B.S., U. Minn., 1943, M.D., 1944, Ph.D., 1952. Diplomate: Am. Bd. Surgery. Intern U. Minn., Mpls., 1944-45, resident in surgery, 1947-51; mem. faculty dept. surgery Downstate Med. Center SUNY, Bklyn., 1951-71, prof. surgery, 1959-71; prof. med. sci. Brown U., Providence, 1971—; surgeon-in-charge thoracic and cardiovascular surgery R.I. Hosp., Providence, 1971—; cons. in surgery Miriam Hosp., VA Hosp.; adj. prof. biomed. engring. U. R.I. Contbr. chpts. to med. books, articles to med. jours. Served with USN, 1945-46, 54-56. NIH fellow, 1950-51. Mem. Am. Surg. Assn., Soc. Univ. Surgeons, Soc. Clin. Surgery, Am. Assn. Thoracic Surgery, A.C.S., Soc. Thoracic Surgeons, Soc. Vascular Surgery, Am. Coll. Cardiology, Internat. Cardiovascular Soc., Société Internationale de Chirugie. Home: 252 Bowen St Providence RI 02906 Office: 110 Lockwood St Providence RI 02903

KARLSTROM, PAUL JOHNSON, art historian; b. Seattle, Jan. 22, 1941; s. Paul Isadore and Eleanor (Johnson) K.; m. Ann Heath, Dec. 29, 1964; 1 dau., Clea Heath. B.A. in English Lit, Stanford U., 1964; M.A., UCLA, 1969, Ph.D. (Samuel H. Kress fellow), 1973. Mem. staff J. Paul Getty Museum, Malibu, Calif., 1966; asst. curator Grunwald Center for Graphic Arts, UCLA, 1967-70; Samuel H. Kress fellow Nat. Gallery Art, Washington, 1970-71; instr. Calif. State U., Northridge, 1972-73; West Coast area dir. Archives Am. Art, Smithsonian Instn. at De Young Mus., San Francisco, 1973—; vis. instr. Calif. Coll. Arts and Crafts, Oakland, Calif., 1976. Guest curator, Hirshhorn Mus., Washington, 1977; Author: Venice Panorama, 1969, Americans Abroad: Painters of the Victorian Era, 1975, Louis M. Eilshemius, 1978, The United States and the Impressionist Era, 1979; contbr. articles to profl. jours. Mem. adv. bd. Center Mus. Studies, San Francisco; adv. com. UCLA Oral History Program. Recipient award for acad. distinction UCLA, 1974. Mem. Coll. Art Assn. Am. Office: Archives Am Art De Young Mus San Francisco CA 94118

KARLTON, LAWRENCE K., federal judge; b. Bklyn., May 28, 1935; s. Aaron Katz and Sylvia (Meltzer) K.; m. Mychelle Stiebel, Sept. 7, 1958. Student, Washington Sq. Coll.; LL.B., Columbia U., 1958. Bar: Fla. 1958, Calif. 1962. Acting legal officer Sacramento Army Depot, Dept. Army, Sacramento, 1959-60, civilian legal officer, 1960-62; individual practice law, Sacramento, 1962-64; mem. firm Abbott, Karlton & White, 1964, Karlton & Blease, until 1971, Karlton, Blease & Vanderlaan, 1971-76; judge Calif. Superior Ct. for Sacramento County, 1976-79, U.S. Dist. Ct., Sacramento, 1979—, now chief judge. Co-chmn. Central Calif. council B'nai B'rith Anit-Defamation League Commn., 1964-65; treas. Sacramento Jewish Community Relations Council, chmn., 1967-68. Mem. Am. Bar Assn., Sacramento County Bar Assn. Club: B'nai B'rith (past pres.). Office: 650 Capitol Mall Sacramento CA 95814 *

KARMEIER, DELBERT FRED, city transportation official; b. Okawville, Ill., Apr. 2, 1935; s. Wilbert and Ida (Harre) K.; m. Naomi Firnhaber, Oct. 10, 1958; children: Kenton Howard, Dianne Jill. B.S.C.E., U. Ill., 1957, M.S. in Transp. Engring. (Automotive Safety Found. fellow), 1959. Research assoc. U. Ill., 1958-59; traffic engr. St. Louis County (Mo.), 1959-65, traffic commr., 1965-69; dir. transp. City of Kansas City (Mo.), 1969-74, dir. aviation and transp., 1974—; mem. Nat. Com. on Uniform Traffic Control Devices, 1971—. Mem. Inst. Transp. Engrs. (pres. Missouri Valley sect. 1965-66), Airport Operator's Council Internat., Am. Rd. and Transp. Builder's Assn. (dir. 1973-83, chmn. pub. transit adv. council 1980-83), Transp. Research Bd., Beta Sigma Psi (nat. editor 1963-69, pres. Kansas City alumni 1981-82, Disting. Alumnus 1971). Lutheran. Home: 11615 Minor Dr Kansas City MO 64114 Office: 414 E 12th St Kansas City MO 64106

KARMEL, ROBERTA S., lawyer; b. Chgo., May 4, 1937; d. J. Herzl and Eva E. (Elin) Segal; m. Paul R. Karmel, June 9, 1957; children: Philip, Solomon, Jonathan, Miriam. B.A., Radcliffe Coll.; LL.B., NYU, 1962. With SEC, 1962-69, 77-80, asst. regional adminstr., until 1969, commr., Washington, 1977-80; asso. firm Willkie Farr & Gallagher, N.Y.C., 1969-72; partner firm Rogers & Wells, N.Y.C., 1972-77, 80—; adj. prof. law Bklyn. Law Sch., 1973-77, 82—; dir. Internat. Minerals & Chem. Corp., N.Y. Stock Exchange. Author: Regulation by Prosecution, 1982; Contbr. articles to legal publs. Mem. ABA, Assn. Bar City N.Y. (chmn. subcom. 1975-76), Am. Judicature Soc. Home: 26 Hopke Ave Hastings-on-Hudson NY 10706 Office: 200 Park Ave New York NY 10166

KARMIN, MONROE WILLIAM, journalist; b. Mineola, N.Y., Sept. 2, 1929; s. Stanley Albert and Phyllis Rae (Appelbaum) K.; m. Mayanne Sherman, Oct. 30, 1955; children: Paul Nance, Elizabeth Anne. B.A., U. Ill., 1950; M.S., Columbia U., 1953. Staff writer Wall St. Jour., N.Y.C. and Washington, 1953-74; profl. staff House Com. on Banking, Currency & Housing, 1974-76; staff Washington Bur., Chgo. Daily News, 1977-78; nat. econ. corr. Knight-Ridder Newspapers, 1978-81; sr. econ. writer U.S. News & World Report, 1981—. Served with USAF, 1951-52. Recipient Pulitzer prize for nat. reporting, 1967. Mem. Sigma Delta Chi (award for gen. reporting 1967). Clubs: Washington Press, Nat. Press, Fed. City. Home: 7011 Beechwood Dr Chevy Chase MD 20815

KARN, RICHARD WENDALL, civil engineer; b. Oakland, Calif., July 19, 1927; s. William Nathan and Agnes Pauline (Langren) K.; m. Margaret Jean Britto, Aug. 28, 1949; children: Pamela Joyce, Robert Alan. B.S.C.E., U. Calif.-Berkeley, 1950. Registered profl. engr., Calif. From asst. civil engr. to engring. mgr. Alameda County Flood Control and Water Conservation Dist., Haywood, Calif., 1950-66; ptnr., then pres. Bissell & Karn, Inc., San Leandro, Calif., 1966—. Mem. Haywood Environ. Quality Commn., 1975. Served with USNR, 1945-46; PTO. Mem. ASCE (pres. elect 1984), Bay Counties Civil Engrs. and Land Surveyors Assn. (pres. 1977). Republican. Mem. United Ch. of Christ. Lodge: San Leandro Rotary. Office: Bissell & Karn Inc 2551 Merced St San Leandro CA 94577

KARNAS, GEORGE JAMES, airline exec.; b. Duluth, Minn., Mar. 5, 1930; s. James George and Mary (Rozinka) K.; m. Lois Picconatto, Apr. 10, 1951; children—Kathryn, James, Michael, Darcy Ann. Student, Ariz. State U., 1948. Insp., Coolerator, Duluth, 1947-52; agt. North Central Airlines, Duluth, 1952-54, sr. agt., 1954-59, mgr. fleet service, 1959-73, v.p. inflight service, 1973-79; sr. v.p. inflight service Republic Airlines, 1979—; officer Airline Agts. Union, 1956-59, chmn., 1958-59; dir. Richfield Bank & Trust Co., Minn.; Treas. Richfield Sch. Bd., 1972, vice chmn., 1973-75, chmn., 1976-77; coach Am. Legion Baseball, 1969-79. Served with AUS, 1947-48, 50-51. Mem. Am. Legion, Nat. Restaurant Assn., Inflight Food Service Assn. (pres. 1977-78), Twin City Aviation Mgmt. Assn., Richfield C. of C. (pres. 1978, dir), Roman Catholic. Clubs: Decathlon, Athletic (v.p., dir.), Minn. Valley Country.). Home: 2921 Washburn Circle Richfield MN 55423 Office: 7500 Northliner Dr Minneapolis MN 55450

KARNES, WILLIAM MICHAEL, corporation financial executive; b. Chgo., Mar. 29, 1946; s. William F. and Bette Jean (Spehn) K.; m. Mary Alice Doyle, Feb. 8, 1975; children: Meg, W. Michael. B.B.A., U. Md., 1980, U. Notre Dame, 1968; M.B.A., Harvard U., 1970. Cons. Fry Cons., Chgo., 1970-72; v.p. Mgmt. Analysis Center, Chgo., 1972-75; v.p., treas. Macke Co., Cheverly, Md., 1975-80; treas. Playboy Enterprises, Chgo., 1980; now treas. Communication Satellite Corp., Washington. Mem. Nat. Investor Relations Inst., N. Am. Soc. Corp. Planning. Home: 7900 Old Falls Ct McLean VA 22102 Office: 950 L'Enfant Plaza Washington DC

KARNEY, JOE DAN, utility co. fin. exec.; b. Sulphur Springs, Tex., June 28, 1933; s. Dooley Dan and Thelma Rea (Vandever) K.; m. Gwendolyn Diane Kraatz, Dec. 29, 1972. B.B.A. in Acctg, So. Methodist U., 1961. C.P.A., Tex. Asst. treas. Dallas Power & Light Co., 1969-75, asst. treas., asst. sec., 1975-77, treas., asst. sec., 1977—. Served with U.S. Army, 1953. Mem. Fin. Execs. Inst., Am. Inst. C.P.A.'s, Tex. Soc. C.P.A.'s. Methodist. Club: Rotary. Home: 4001 Kerr Ct Dallas TX 75234 Office: 1506 Commerce Dallas TX 75201

KARNI, EDI, economics educator; b. Tel Aviv, Israel, Mar. 20, 1944; s. Eliezer and Sara (Vitis) K.; m. Barbara Shapiro, Mar. 16, 1980; children: Anat, Anna. B.A., Hebrew U., 1965, M.A., 1970, M.A., U. Chgo., 1970, Ph.D., 1971. Asst. prof. Ohio State U., Columbus, 1971-72; fellow Inst. for Advanced Studies/Hebrew U., Jerusalem, Israel, 1976-77; vis. prof. U. Chgo., 1977-79; assoc. prof. Tel Aviv U., 1972-81; prof. econs. Johns Hopkins U., Balt., 1981—. Contbr. articles to profl. jours. Mem. Am. Econ. Assn. Jewish. Home: 6511 Copper Ridge Baltimore MD 21209 Office: Dept Polit Economy Johns Hopkins U Baltimore MD 21218

KARNOVSKY, MORRIS JOHN, pathologist, biologist; b. Johannesburg, South Africa, June 28, 1926; came to U.S., 1955; s. Herman Louis and Florence (Rosenberg) K.; m. Shirley Esther Katz, Aug. 26, 1952; children; David Mark, Nina Jane. B.S., U. Witwatersrand, Johannesburg, 1946, M.B., B.Ch., 1950; diploma clin. pathology, U. London, 1954; M.A. (hon.), Harvard U., 1965. Prof. pathology Harvard U. Med. Sch., Boston, 1968-72, Shattuck prof., 1972—, chmn. program in cell and devel. biology, 1975—. Fellow Royal Microbiology Soc.; mem. Am. Soc. Cell Biology (pres. 1983-84), Am. Assn. Pathologists (co-pres. 1978-79, Rous-Whipple award 1981). Club: Harvard (Boston). Office: Harvard Med Sch 25 Shattuck St Boston MA 02115

KARNOW, STANLEY, journalist; b. N.Y.C., Feb. 4, 1925; s. Harry and Henriette (Koeppel) K.; m. Claude Sarraute, July 15, 1948 (div. 1955); m. Annette Kline, Apr. 21, 1959; children: Curtis Edward, Catherine Anne, Michael Franklin. B.A., Harvard U., 1947; student, U. Paris, France, 1948-49, Inst. d'Etudes politiques, 1949-50. Corr. Time mag., Paris, 1950-57; bur. chief North Africa Time-Life, 1958-59, Hong Kong, 1959-62; spl. corr. London Observer, 1961-65, Time, Inc., 1962-63; Far East corr. Sat. Eve. Post, 1963-65, Washington Post, 1965-71, diplomatic corr., 1971-72; spl. corr. NBC News, 1973-75; assoc. editor The New Republic, 1973-75; columnist Des Moines Register and Tribune Syndicate, 1975—, Le Point, Paris, 1976—; editor Internat. Writers Service, 1976—; chief corr. PBS series Vietnam: A Television History, 1983. Author: Southeast Asia, 1963, Mao and China: From Revolution to Revolution, 1972, Vietnam: A History, 1983 (citation as best book 1983); also articles, TV scripts. Served with USAAF, 1943-46. Neiman fellow Harvard, 1957-58; recipient citation Overseas Press Club, 1966, Ann. award for best newspaper interpretation of fgn. affairs, 1968; fellow Inst. Politics John F. Kennedy Sch. Govt.; also fellow East Asian-Research Center Harvard, 1970-71; vis. assoc. European Studies Center, 1976—. Mem. Council Fgn. Relations, White House Corrs. Assn., Signet Soc., Authors Guild. Clubs: Harvard (Washington); Shek-O (Hong Kong). Home: 10850 Springknoll Dr Potomac MD 20854 Office: 1163 Nat Press Bldg NW Washington DC 20045

KAROFSKY, SYDNEY BERNARD, wallcovering company executive, designer; b. Boston, Sept. 3, 1914; s. Harry and Mary (Hibel) K.; m. Sylvia Ruth Dulman, June 20, 1937; children: Peter, Paul. B.Arch., MIT, 1937. Chief designer Krokyn & Brown Architects, 1937-40; founder, chmn. Northeastern Wallpaper Corp., Boston, beginning, 1947, Northeastern Wallcoverings, Inc., beginning 1957, Walls Unltd., beginning 1961, Northeastern Wallpaper Corp. of Hartford, beginning 1957, Northeastern Wallpaper Corp. N.Y., Syracuse, beginning 1974, Northeastern Wallpaper Corp. Pa., Phila., beginning 1975; chmn. Dept. Commerce Nat. Bur. Standards for Vinyl Wallcovering; bd. mem. Inter Industry Com.; bd. dirs. Boston Indsl. Devel. Port of Boston; dir. Commonwealth Bank & Trust Co. Co-author: Procedures for Development of Voluntary Product Standards and Value Added Concept; dimentional Walls, 1957; exhibited watercolors in 3 one-man shows at, H.R.C.A. Gallery, Boston. Life trustee and past pres. B'nai B'rith Hillel House, Boston U.; trustee Hecht House Hosp. Assn.; hon. pres. Hebrew Rehab. Center for Aged.; sustaining fellow MIT. Recipient 1st Mentioned Pl. for Class of 1904 Prize at MIT, Adv. Carnation award. Mem. Nat. Wallcovering Distbrs. Assn. (past pres., Justin P. Allman award 1976), N.E. Wallcovering Distbrs. Assn. (past pres.), Nat. Assn. Wholesalers (trustee, officer, dir.), Internat. Assn. Artists, Copley Art Soc., Mus. Transp. of Boston (hon. mem. for life), M.I.T. Alumni Assn. (officer, trustee bus. men's council). Republican. Jewish. Clubs: M.I.T., Stein (past pres.), Charles River Yacht, Pinebrook Country (past dir.), Ocean Reef Country, Masons. Patentee. Office: 292 Summer St Boston MA 02210

KAROL, NATHANIEL H., lawyer, consultant; b. N.Y.C., Feb. 16, 1929; s. Isidore and Lillian (Orlow) K.; m. Liliane Leser, July 20, 1967; children: David, Jordan. B.S. in Social Sci, CCNY, 1949; M.A. (fellow), Yale U., 1950; LL.B., N.Y. U., 1957, LL.M., 1959, J.D., 1966. Bar: N.Y. 1957. Mgmt. trainee Curtiss Wright Corp., Wood-Ridge, N.J., 1956-57; practiced in, N.Y.C., 1957-58; contracting officer USAF, N.Y.C., 1958-62; chief contract mgmt. survey and cost adminstrn. Office of Procurement, NASA, Washington, 1962-64; asst. dir. cost reduction, 1964-66; dep. asst. sec. Grants Adminstrn., HEW, Washington, 1966-69; univ. dean City U. N.Y.; exec. dir. Research Found., 1969-73; v.p. Hebrew Union Coll., Cin., 1973-75; partner, nat. chmn. cons. services for edn. Coopers & Lybrand (C.P.A.s), Chgo., 1975-81; pres. Nathaniel H. Karol & Assocs. Ltd., 1981—; cons. to govt. agys. and ednl. instns., 1969—. Author: Managing the Higher Education Enterprise. Served with U.S. Army, 1953-56. Recipient Outstanding Performance award HEW, 1968, Superior Performance award, 1969. Mem. N.Y. Bar, Nat. Assn. Coll. and Univ. Bus. Officers, Nat. Assn. Coll. and Univ. Attys. Home: 1228 Cambridge Ct Highland Park IL 60035 Office: Nathaniel H Karol & Assos Ltd 1228 Cambridge Ct Highland Park IL 60035 *What one is, is as important as what one does. I regard as successful the man who is able to establish a set of values and to observe them consistently. If there is a single thing for which I would wish to be remembered, it is that I was a man whose word was his bond.*

KAROL, REUBEN HIRSH, civil engineer; b. Toms River, N.J., Aug. 25, 1922; s. Joel Benjamin and Molly K.; m. Sylvia Gross, Sept. 3, 1943; children: Diane, Leslie, Michael. B.S. in Civil Engring., Rutgers U., 1947, M.S., 1949. Lic. profl. engr., N.J. Asst. prof. civil engring. Rutgers U., New Brunswick, N.J., 1947-51, dir. Rutgers Ctr. Continuing Engring. Studies, 1967—, prof. civil engring., 1980—; design engr. Standard Oil Devel. Co., Linden, N.J., 1951-56; dir. Engring. Chem. Research Ctr. Am. Cyanamic Co., Princeton, N.J., 1956-67; pres. Darol-Warner, Inc., mfr. sci. instruments. Author: four coll. textbooks including Chemical Grouting, 1983; contbr. 25 articles to profl. jours.; U.S., fgn. patentee in field; exhibited wood sculpture in 4 one-man shows; commd. wood sculpture, Busch Student Ctr., Outdoor concrete sculpture, Civil Engring. Lab., Rutgers U. Served to 1st Signal Corps U.S. Army, 1943-46. Mem. ASCE (chmn. grouting com. 1976-82, Robert Ridgway award 1947), ASTM (chmn. grouting com. 1979—, Outstanding Achievement award 1982), Am. Soc. Engring. Edn., Nat. Soc. Profl. Engrs. Home: 261 S Adelaide Ave HighlandPark NJ 08904 Office: Dept Civil Engring Rutgers Unvi New Brunswick NJ 08903

KARON, BERTRAM PAUL, psychologist, educator; b. Taunton, Mass., Apr. 29, 1930; s. Harold Banny and Celia (Silverman) K.; m. Mary Kathryn Mossop, Oct. 17, 1957; 1 son, Jonathan Alexander. A.B., Harvard, 1952; M.A., Princeton, 1954, Ph.D. (USPHS fellow), 1957; grad., Council fellow, Dartmouth, summer 1953. Research fellow psychometrics Ednl. Testing Service and Princeton, 1952-55; intern in direct analysis John N. Rosen, M.D., Gardenville, Pa., 1955-56; sr. clin. psychologist Annandale (N.J.) Reformatory, 1958; psychologist, dir. research Akron (Ohio) Psychol. Cons. Center, 1958-59; research psychologist Phila. Psychiat. Hosp., 1959, USPHS fellow, 1959-61; practice clin. psychology, Phila., 1961-62; asst. prof. psychology Mich. State U., 1962-63, asso. prof., 1963-68, prof., 1968—; vis. lectr. Calif. Sch. Profl. Psychology, Los Angeles; vis. scholar Wright Inst., Los Angeles, 1979; Research cons. U.S. Naval Hosp., Phila., 1962, U. Pa., 1962; lectr. psychiatry Ypsilanti (Mich.) State Hosp., 1964-65; cons. VA Hosp., Allen Park, Mich., 1966-75, Ann Arbor, Mich., 1971-72. Author: The Negro Personality: A Rigorous Investigation of the Effects of Culture, 1958, rev. edit, Black Scars, 1975, (with others) Psychotherapy of Schizophrenia: The Treatment of Choice, 1981; contbg. author: Projective Techniques in Personality Assessment, 1968, Techniques for Behavior Change, 1971, The Schizophrenic Syndrome: An Annual Review, 1971, The Construction of Madness, 1976; Editor: Affects, Imagery, and Consciousness (Silvan S. Tomkins), vols. 1 and 2, 1962, 63; Contbr. numerous articles on schizophrenia to profl. jours. NIMH grantee, 1966-71. Fellow Am. Psychol. Assn. (div. psychotherapy, clin. psychology); mem. Soc. Psychotherapy Research, Am. Statis. Assn., Psychologists Interested in Study Psychoanalysis, Midwest, Mich. psychol. assns., Mich. Soc. Psychoanalytic Psychology (pres. 1983-84). Home: 420 John R St East Lansing MI 48823

KAROSEN, LEON, professional sports team executive. Chmn. bd. Kansas City Kings Basketball Team, Mo. Office: Kansas City Kings 1800 Genessee Suite 101 Kansas City MO 64101§

KARP, ABRAHAM JOSEPH, educator; b. Indura, Poland, Apr. 5, 1921; came to U.S., 1930, naturalized, 1930; s. Aaron and Rachel (Schor) K.; m. Deborah Burstein, June 17, 1945; children—Hillel J., David J. B.A. magna cum laude, Yeshiva U., 1942; Rabbi, Jewish Theol. Sem. of Am., 1945, M.H.L., 1949, D.D., 1971. Rabbi Beth Shalom Synagogue, Kansas City, Mo., 1951-56, Beth El, Rochester, N.Y., 1956-72; prof. history and religious studies U. Rochester, 1972—, Philip S. Bernstein prof. Jewish studies, 1976—; vis. prof. Dartmouth, 1967, Hebrew U., Jerusalem, 1970, Jewish Theol. Sem. Am., 1967-71, 75-76; corr. mem. Inst. Contemporary Jewry, Hebrew U., 1973—. Author: The Jewish Way of Life, 1962, The United Synagogue of America-A History, 1963, The Jewish Experience in America, 1971, Golden Door to America, 1976, To Give Life, 1980, The Jewish Way of Life and Thought, 1981; editor: Conservative Judaism-The Legacy of Solomon Schechter, 1965, Beginnings-Early American Judaica, 1976; translator: Five from the Holocaust, 1975; contbg. author: Jewish Art and Civilization, 1972. Fellow Herbert Lehman Inst. Ethics, Jewish Theol. Sem. Am.; Mem. Am. Jewish Hist. Soc. (pres., chmn. publs. com., Lee M. Friedman medal 1976), President's Historians Circle Jerusalem, Rabbinical Assembly, Assn. Jewish Studies, Phi Beta Kappa. Home: 240 Cobbs Hill Dr Rochester NY 14610 *On April 5, 1921, I was granted a loan: my life. On February 18, 1930, I was given a gift: Life in America, which has been for me a land of freedom and opportunity. All my family, all the friends of my youth who remained behind in Europe perished in the Holocaust. Years have been granted me to repay the loan. I seize each opportunity to return the gift.*

KARP, DAVID, writer; b. N.Y.C., May 5, 1922; s. Abraham and Rebecca (Levin) K.; m. Lillian Klass, Dec. 25, 1944; children—Ethan Ross, Andrew Gabriel. B.S.S., Coll. City N.Y., 1948. Continuity dir. radio sta. WNYC, N.Y.C., 1948-49; pres. Leda Prodns., Inc., 1968—; guest lectr. Coll. City N.Y., 1964. Free-lance writer for radio, mags., motion pictures, novels, 1949—; (recipient Emmy award for writing 1964-65, Ohio State U. award 1956, Look mag. award 1958, Mystery Writers Am. award 1960); Author: One, 1953, (under pseudonym) Platoon, 1953, The Day of the Monkey, 1955, All Honorable Men, 1956, Leave Me Alone, 1957, Enter, Sleeping, 1960, (with Murray D. Lincoln) Vice President In Charge of Revolution, 1960, The Last Believers, 1964. Served with AUS, 1943-46; PTO. Guggenheim fellow, 1956. Mem. Writers Guild Am. West (council 1967-74, pres. TV radio br. 1969-71), P.E.N., Nat. Acad. TV Arts and Scis. (editorial bd. TV Quar. 1965-78), Acad. Motion Picture Arts and Scis. Home: 1116 Corsica Dr Pacific Palisades CA 90272 Office: Leda Prodns Inc care Brown Kraft & Co 11940 San Vincente Blvd Los Angeles CA 90049 *People who wait for great moments to make their mark miss the point. Life is made up of thousands upon thousands of tiny marks. Like a sculptor who works in marble—you make your life in flakes and bits and chips and the scourings of marble dust. In the end you have created an image of yourself.*

KARP, HARVEY LAWRENCE, electrical and metal products manufacturing company executive; b. N.Y.C., Nov. 26, 1927; s. Harry and Sadie (Zimmerman) K.; m. Beverly Bailis, Nov. 24, 1955; children: David, Nicholas. B.A., Coll. City N.Y., 1949; LL.B., Yale U., 1952. Bar: N.Y. 1952, Calif. 1954. Lawyer Chesapeake Industries, Inc., N.Y.C., 1952-54; gen. counsel, v.p. Houston Fearless Corp., Los Angeles, 1955-60; founder, vice-chmn. bd. dirs., pres. Monogram Industries, N.Y.C., 1960—; dir. Craig Corp. Bd. dirs. Neuroscis. Research Found., Am. Health Found. Served with USNR, 1945. Clubs: Yale, Harmonie, Explorers. Home: PO Box 30 East Hampton NY 11937 Office: West End Rd East Hampton NY 11937

KARP, HERBERT RUBIN, neurologist, educator; b. Atlanta, Apr. 13, 1921; s. Louis and Sadie (Fischer) K.; m. Hazel Berman, June 16, 1948; children—Eleanor Beth, Miriam Sarah, Benjamin Chaim. B.A., Emory U., 1943, M.D., 1951. Diplomate: Am. Bd. Psychiatry and Neurology. Intern then resident in internal medicine Grady Meml. Hosp., 1951-54; resident in neurology Duke U. Med. Center, 1954-56; clin. and research fellow in neurology and neuropathology Harvard U.-Mass. Gen. Hosp., 1956-58; asst. prof. neurology Emory U., 1958-63, prof., 1963—, prof. medicine, 1983—, chmn. dept. neurology, 1974-83, dir. gerontology program dept. medicine, 1983—; dir. med. services Wesley Woods Geriatric Ctr., 1983—. Sec. bd. trustees Atlanta Symphony Orch., 1979-80; pres. Ahavath Achim Synagogue, 1980-81; bd. trustees Nat. Found. Jewish Culture, 1976—. Served with USNR, 1943-46. Spl. fellow Nat. Inst. Neurol. Diseases, 1956-58. Fellow Am. Acad. Neurology; mem. Am. Neurol. Assn. (mem. council), Assn. Univ. Profs. Neurology, Am. Heart Assn. (stroke council), Alpha Omega Alpha. Democrat. Home: 880 Somerset Dr NW Atlanta GA 30327 Office: 1365 Clifton Rd NE Atlanta GA 30322

KARP, MARSHALL WARREN, advt. exec.; b. N.Y.C., June 4, 1942; s. Benjamin and Beatrice (Ziffer) K.; m. Emily Shwartz, Nov. 9, 1969; children—Adam, Sarah. B.A. in English, Rutgers U., 1963. Direct mail copywriter Prentice-Hall, 1963-65; copywriter Warren, Muller, Dolobowsky, 1965-66; v.p., asso. creative dir. DKG Inc., N.Y.C., 1967-72; sr. v.p., asso. creative dir. The Marschalk Co., Inc., N.Y.C., 1972-77, exec. v.p., creative dir., 1977—, also dir. Author comedy: Squabbles, 1983. Recipient Clio award, 1975, 76, 77. Office: 1345 Ave of Americas New York NY 10105

KARP, MARTIN EVERETT, management consultant; b. N.Y.C., Apr. 30, 1922; s. Albert and Bessie (Orenstein) K.; m. Naomi Joslyn Kaplan, Mar. 14, 1948; children: Betsy Karp Davis, Leslie Karp Goldenberg, Jonathan. B.M.E., CCNY, 1942; student, Harvard U., 1944, MIT, 1945, Northeastern U., 1951-52. Lab. engr. Gen. Electric Co., Lynn, Mass., 1942-44; mgr. research and devel. Nat. Pneumatic Co., Boston, 1946-52; dir. product planning, engring. Remington Office Machine div. Sperry Rand Co., 1953-66, dir. mfg., 1966-68; staff asst. to office of pres. ITT, 1968-69, v.p., group gen. mgr., 1969-82, group exec., 1977-82, dir. product and mktg. strategy, 1980-82; mgmt. cons., 1982—; adj. assoc. prof. Pace Grad. Sch. Bus. Contbr. articles to tech. jours. Served as lt. (j.g.) USNR, 1944-46. Mem. ASME, Tau Beta Pi. Jewish (pres. congregation 1961-63). Patentee control systems. Home and Office: 127 Harvest Commons Westport CT 06880

KARP, NATHAN, political activitist; b. Bklyn., Apr. 25, 1915; s. Daniel and Sarah (Goldenzweig) K.; m. Anne Werthamer, June 19, 1937; children: Alan, Diane, Stanley. Student pub. schs., Vineland, N.J. Garment worker; mem. nat. exec. subcom. Socialist Labor Party, asst. to nat. sec., mem. hdqrs. staff, Palo Alto, Calif., 1964-68, nat. sec., 1969-80, fin. sec., 1980-82, candidate for office of mayor, N.Y.C., 1953; for gov. N.Y. State, 1954. Contbr.: numerous articles to Weekly People, ofcl. jour. Socialist Labor Party. Mem. Internat. Ladies Garment Workers Union. Home: 2330 California St Mountain View CA 94040 Office: 914 Industrial Ave Palo Alto CA 94303

KARP, RICHARD, advt. exec.; b. N.Y.C., Aug. 17, 1929; s. Harry and Jo Golden (Bosk) K.; m. Jane Hausman, Nov. 26, 1978; 1 son, David. B.S., B.A., N.Y. U., 1950; postgrad., Boston U. Publicist 20th Century Fox Film Corp., 1954-56; sr. writer Donahue & Coe Advt., N.Y.C., 1956-58; asso. creative dir., account supr. Reach, McClinton Advt., N.Y.C., 1958-63; exec. v.p., creative dir. Grey Advt., N.Y.C., 1963—; guest lectr. Baruch U., 1977-79. Author: monograph The Films of Buster Keaton, 1949. Served with AUS, 1950-51; Served with USAF, 1951-54. Decorated Commendation medal; recipient Clio award, 1978, Internat. Advt. award, 1967, Screen Advt. award, 1970, Copywriters Club award, 1959. Mem. Brit. Inst. Practitioners in Advt. Home: 455 E 57th St New York NY 10022 Office: 777 3d Ave New York NY 10017

KARP, RICHARD MANNING, computer scientist; b. Boston, Jan. 3, 1935; s. Abraham Louis and Rose (Nanes) K.; m. Diana Leigh Grand, Aug. 12, 1979. A.B., Harvard U., 1955, S.M., 1956, Ph.D., 1959. Research staff mem. IBM Research, Yorktown Heights, N.Y., 1959-68; prof. computer sci. and ops. research and math U. Calif., Berkeley, 1968—. Contbr. articles on computer sci., ops. research and applied math. to profl. jours. Recipient Lanchester prize, 1978, Fulkerson prize, 1979. Mem. Nat. Acad. Scis., N.Y. Acad. Scis. Office: 573 Evans Hall University of California Berkeley CA 94720

KARP, RUSSELL, former cable TV industry executive; b. N.Y.C., 1929; s. Max and Vivian (Segal) K.; m. Gloria Mindich, 1978; children: Andrew David, Susannah; stepchildren—Lauren, Nancy. B.A., Washington U., St. Louis, 1951; LL.B., Yale, 1954. Asso. Jaffe & Stern (attys.), 1954-57; with Screen Gems, Inc. div. Columbia Pictures Industries, Inc., 1957-68, sec., 1961, v.p., 1962, v.p., treas., 1965; v.p. corporate affairs Columbia Pictures Industries, Inc., 1968, v.p., treas., 1969-71; financial and mgmt. cons. entertainment and communications industries, 1972-74; pres., chief operating officer, dir. Teleprompter Corp., 1974-81; vice chmn. Westinghouse Broadcasting and Cable, 1982; fin. and mgmt. cons., 1982-83. Bd. dirs. Am.'s Watch, 1982—, N.Y.C. Ballet, 1983—. Home: 4725 Independence Ave Bronx NY 10471

KARP, THEODORE CYRUS, music history educator, consultant, researcher; b. N.Y.C., July 17, 1926; s. Charles M. and Henrietta (Steinhardt) K.; m. Judith Leah Schwartz, Aug. 18, 1973; 1 dau., Shira Tova. B.A., Queens Coll., 1947; piano diploma, Juilliard Sch. Music, 1945, postgrad., 1945-46; grad., U. Louvain, Belgium, 1950; Ph.D., NYU, 1960. Asst. prof. U. Calif.-Davis, 1963-67, assoc. prof., 1967-70, prof., 1970-73; prof. music history Northwestern U., Evanston, Ill., 1973—; music editor Grolier Soc., N.Y.C., 1962; music cons., 1964-70. Author: Dictionary of Music, 1973; contbr. articles to music publs. NEH sr. fellow, Paris, 1967; Inst. for Research in Humanities research fellow U. Wis., Madison, 1978. Mem. Am. Musicological Soc. (council 1967-69, chmn. No. Calif. chpt. 1970-72, chmn. Midwest chpt. 1980-82). Jewish. Home: 806 Chilton Ln Wilmette Il 60091 Office: Sch Music Northwestern U Clark St Evanston Il 60201

KARPATKIN, MARGARET, physician, medical center administrator; b. London, July 4, 1932; U.S., 1964; d. James Bonnell and Cecelia Florence (Poll) Howell; m. Simon Karpatkin, Dec. 26, 1965; children: David, Judith. Student, King's Coll., U. London, 1952-54; M.B. B.S., St. George's Hosp. Med. Sch., 1957, M.D., 1964. Diplomate: Am. Bd. Pediatrics. Resident house surgeon St. Peter's Hosp., Chertsey, Eng., 1957; resident house physician med. unit St. George's Hosp., London, 1957-58, resident clin. pathologist Teaching Group, 1958-59, pathology registrar, 1959-61, research asst., 1961-64; assoc. research scientist NYU, N.Y.C., 1964-67, assoc. prof. clin. pathology, 1968-70, asst. prof. pediatrics, 1970-72, assoc. prof., 1972-78, prof., 1978—; dir. pediatric hematology and oncology Med. Ctr.; research assoc. ARC Research Lab., N.Y.C., 1965-67; chairperson med. adv. council Met. chpt. Nat. Hemophilia Found., N.Y.C., 1982. Mem. Soc. Pediatric Research, Am. Soc. Hematology, Am. Pediatric Soc. Home: 200 East End Ave New York NY 10028 Office: NYU Med Ctr 550 1st Ave New York NY 10016

KARPATKIN, RHODA HENDRICK, consumer information organization executive, lawyer; b. N.Y.C., June 7, 1930; d. Charles and Augusta (Arkin) Hendrick; m. Marvin Karpatkin, June 16, 1951 (dec.); children: Deborah Hendrick, Herbert Isaac, Jeremy Charles. B.A., Bklyn. Coll., 1951; LL.B., Yale U., 1953. Bar: N.Y. State 1954. Pvt. practice law, 1954-74; partner firm Karpatkin & Karpatkin, 1958-61, Karpatkin, Ohrenstein & Karpatkin, N.Y.C., 1961-74; exec. dir. Consumers Union of U.S. Inc., Mt. Vernon, N.Y., 1974—; Spl. counsel for decentralization N.Y.C. Bd. Edn., 1969-70; adj. prof. dept. urban studies Queens Coll., 1972-74; bd. dirs. Nat. Resource Center for Consumers of Legal Services, 1976-83; mem. N.Y.C. Consumer Adv. Council, 1973-79; commr. Nat. Commn. on New Tech. Uses of Copyrighted Works, 1975-78; Mem. Local Sch. Bd. 5, N.Y.C., 1966-70, chmn., 1967-69; mem. Community Sch. Bd. 3, N.Y.C., 1970-71; mem. com. acad. freedom A.C.L.U., 1973—; bd. advisors Sch. Law, Columbia U. Center for Law and Econ. Studies, 1975—; mem. Commn. on Law and the Economy, Am. Bar Assn., 1976-79, Commn. to Reduce Ct. Costs and Delay, 1978—, Pres.'s Commn. for Nat. Agenda for the Eighties., 1979-80; Trustee Public Edn. Assn., 1972—. Contbg. author: Current School Problems, 1971, Consumer Education in the Human Services; Contbr. articles to profl. publs. Mem. Assn. Bar City N.Y. (com. consumer affairs 1969-80, chmn. 1974-79, com. on internat. human rights 1980—, audit com. 1982-83), Nat. Inst. for Dispute Resolution. Home: 280 Riverside Dr New York NY 10025 Office: 256 Washington St Mount Vernon NY 10550

KARPE, ROBERT WALTER, government official; b. Bakersfield, Calif., Nov. 3, 1930; s. Elmer Ferdinand Darpe and Florence Ann (Johnson) K.; m. Phyllis Jean Henning, Mar. 13, 1954; children: Robert Leslie, Sandra Lee, Raymond Elmer. B.S., U. Calif.-Berkeley, 1953. Realtor, Calif. Pres. Karpe Real Estate, Bakersfield, 1959-71, chmn. bd., 1976-81; commr. chief exec. officer Calif. Dept. Real Estate, Sacramento, 1971-75; pres. Govt. Nat. Mortgage Assn., Washington, 1981—. Trustee Calif. State Coll., Bakersfield, 1969-71; founding chmn. Nat. Realtors for Reagan Bush, Bakersfield, 1980. Named Young Man of Yr. Bakersfield Jr. C. of C., 1962, Calif. Realtor of Yr. Calif. Assn. Realtors, 1968, Headliner Man of Yr. Kern County Bd. Trade, Calif., 1968. Mem. Nat. Assn. Real Estate Lic. Law Ofcls. (v.p. 1974-75), Calif. Real Estate Assn. (pres. 1968), Lambda Alpha. Republican. Baptist. Clubs: Sutter (Sacramento); Comstock (San Francisco). Office: Govt Nat Mortgage Assn 451 7th St SW Washington DC 20410

KARPF, MICHAEL, physician; b. Poland, Apr. 16, 1945; came to U.S., 1945; s. Oscar and Anan (Kalkuna) K.; m. Ellen Strauss, July 16, 1967; children: Jason, Scott. B.S., U. Pa.-Phila, 1967; M.D., U. Pa.-Phila., 1971. Diplomate: Am. Bd. Internal Medicine. Asst. prof. U. Pa., Phila., 1977-78, U. Miami, 1978-79, U. Pitts., 1979-81, dir. gen. medicine, 1979—, assoc. prof., 1981—, Falk chmn. in gen. medicine, 1980. Active Am. Cancer Soc., Pitts. Served to lt. comdr. USPHS, 1972-74. Fellow ACP; mem. Soc. Research and Edn. in Primary Care Internal Medicine, Assn. Program Dirs. Internal Medicine, Am. Fedn. Clin. Research, Alpha Omega Alpha. Jewish. Clubs: Racquet (Fox Chapel); Interurban (N.Y.C.). Home: 201 W Chapel Ridge Rd Pittsburgh PA 15238 Office: Univ Pitts Sch of Medicine 3550 Terrace St Pittsburgh PA 15261

KARPLUS, WALTER J., educator; b. Vienna, Austria, Apr. 23, 1927; came to U.S., 1938; s. Robert and Garda K.; m. Takako Kohda, Feb. 8, 1969; children—Maya, Anthony. B.E.E., Cornell U., 1949; M.S., U. Calif. at Berkeley, 1951; Ph.D., U. Calif. at Los Angeles, 1955. Field engr. Sun Oil Co., 1949-50; research engr. Internat. Geophysics, Inc., Los Angeles, 1951-52; prof. engring. and applied sci., chmn. computer sci. dept. U. Calif. at Los Angeles, 1955—; Co-founder, chmn. bd. Torr Labs., Inc. Author or co-author: Analog Simulation, 1958, Analog Methods, 1959, High-Speed Analog Computers, 1961, On-Line Computing, 1967, Solution Des Equations Differentielles, 1968, Hybrid Computation, 1968, Digital Computer Treatment of Partial Differential Equations, 1981; Contbr. profl. jours. Served with USNR, 1945-46. Fulbright research fellow, 1961-62; Guggenheim fellow, 1968-69. Fellow IEEE; mem. Assn. Computing Machinery, Soc. Computer Simulation, Sigma Xi. Patentee in field. Home: PO Box 24673 Village Station Los Angeles CA 90024 Office: 3732 Boelter Hall U Calif Los Angeles CA 90024

KARPOWICZ, RAY ANTHONY, broadcasting executive; b. Madison, Ill., Feb. 6, 1925; s. Anthony and Mary (Pero) K.; m. Virginia Lee Mitchell, Aug. 9, 1952; children: Paul, James, Christy, Laurie, Lisa. B.S., U. Mo., 1949. Account exec. WTMV Radio, East St. Louis, Ill., 1949-51; account exec., sales mgr. WEW Radio, St. Louis, 1951-54; account exec. KTVI-TV, St. Louis, 1954-55, KSD-TV, 1955-61, sales mgr., 1961-69, gen. mgr., 1969—; gen. mgr., chief exec. Pulitzer Broadcast Stas., 1979—; pres., gen. mgr. WEVU-TV. Author: Effects of Wired Music, 1953. Served with USAAF, 1943-46; PTO. Decorated D.F.C., Air medal with 6 oak leaf clusters. Mem. St. Louis Advt. Club, Mo. Broadcasters Assn., Nat. Assn. Broadcasters, Nat. Acad. TV Arts and Sci., Media Club, Stadium Club St. Louis. Home: 5970 Pelican Bay Blvd Naples FL 33940 Office: 1111 Olive St St Louis MO 63101

KARR, JOHN F., sports exec.; b. Detroit, Apr. 13, 1929; s. Eino E. and Helen K.; (m), July 5, 1952; children—John E., Karen, Christopher, Susan. B.S., Wayne State U., 1952; M.B.A., Ind. U., 1953. Formerly with Burroughs Corp., Trane Co., Arthur D. Little, Inc., Goodyear Tire & Rubber Co.; with Cole Nat. Corp., Cleve., 1968-78, v.p. fin. and adminstrn., dir., to, 1978; pres., dir. Northstar Met Center/Mgmt. Corp., Bloomington, Minn., 1978—. Served in U.S. Army, 1946-48. Office: 7901 Cedar Ave Bloomington MN 55420 *

KARR, LLOYD, lawyer; b. Monticello, Iowa, May 19, 1912; s. Charles L. and Margaret E. (Houston) K.; m. Margaret E. Phelan, May 14, 1938; children—Janet A., Richard L. Bar: Iowa bar 1937. Since practiced in, Webster City; mem. firm Karr, Karr & Karr (P.C.); county atty., Hamilton County, 1940-48; Pub. Webster City Daily Freeman Jour., 1952-55, Winter Park (Fla.) Sun-Herald, 1959-65; Mem. adv. council naval affairs 6th Naval Dist., 1959-62. Contbr. articles to profl. publs. Served with AUS, 1943-45. Recipient Award of Merit Iowa Bar Assn., 1968. Fellow Am. Coll. Probate Counsel; mem. Am., Iowa State Bar Assn. (bd. govs. 1959-61, pres. 1962- 63), Iowa Acad. Trial Lawyers, DeMolay Legion of Honor, Sigma Delta Chi. Clubs: Mason, Elk. Home: 1420 Wilson Ave Webster City IA 50595 also 711 2d St Webster City IA 50595

KARR, NORMAN, association executive; b. N.Y.C., July 30, 1927; s. Arnold and Hilda (Horowitz) K.; m. Selma Butter, June 17, 1951; children: Arnold J., Joanne Karr Skop. B.A., CCNY, 1950. Textile reporter/editor Jour. of Commerce, 1950-55; editor Driver's Digest, 1955-56; public relations dir./asst. to pres. Am. Inst. Men's & Boy's Wear (renamed Men's Fashion Assn. of Am.), N.Y.C., 1956-66, exec. dir., 1966—; lectr. Phila. Coll. Textiles & Sci., Fashion Inst. Served with U.S. Army, 1945-46. Mem. Young Menswear Assn. (v.p.). Office: 240 Madison Ave New York NY 10016

KARRAKER, LOUIS RENDLEMAN, former appraisal company executive; b. Jonesboro, Ill., Aug. 2, 1927; s. Ira Oliver and Helen Elsie (Rendleman) K.; m. Patricia Grace Stahlheber, June 20, 1952; children: Alan Louis, Sharon Elaine. B.A., So. Ill. U., 1949, M.A., 1952; postgrad., U. Wis., Washington U., St. Louis. Asst. prof. history Augustana Coll., Sioux Falls, S.D., 1956-60, acting chmn. div. social scis., 1960-61, asst. to pres., 1962-64; personnel mgr. Parker Pen Co., Janesville, Wis., 1964-68, asst. to chmn., 1967-68, gen. asst. to chmn., 1968-69; with Am. Appraisal Assos., Inc., Milw., 1969-84, group v.p., then exec. v.p., 1974-79, pres., 1979-84, also dir.; ret., 1984; dir. Wis. Marine Bank. Served with USNR, 1952-53. Republican. Lutheran. Home: 3035 Applewood Ct Brookfield WI 53005 Office: 525 E Michigan St Milwaukee WI 53201

KARRAS, ALEX, former profl. football player, actor; b. Gary, Ind., July 15, 1935; (married). Player Detroit Lions, ret., 1971; host NFL Preview ABC-TV; after TV football program, Chgo. Appeared: Monday Night Football, ABC-TV; appearances: TV talkshows, TV movies including Mulligan's Stew, 1977, When Time Ran Out, 1980; numerous other TV appearances; movies include Win, Place or Steal, 1977, FM, 1978. Named All-Pro, 1960, 61, 63, 65; recipient Outland award, 1947 *

KARRER, EUGENE ROBERT, automobile co. exec.; b. Detroit, Sept. 17, 1925; s. Charles Peter and Marie Mary (Rinke) K.; m. Madeline M. Lauwerier, Nov. 10, 1945; children—Eugene, David, Patricia Ann, Charles, Nancy. B.S., Gen. Motors Inst., 1951; M.S. (Sloan fellow), Mass. Inst. Tech., 1959. Designer-engr. Ford Motor Co., Detroit, 1951-63, exec. engr. test, 1963-65, chief engr., 1965-69, v.p. Latin Am. ops., 1972-74, v.p. climate control div., 1975-77, v.p. elec. and electronics div., Dearborn, Mich., 1977—; chief engr. Philco Ford, Phila., 1969-70, v.p., gen. mgr. refrigeration div., Ind., 1970-72, exec. v.p. consumer ops., Phila., 1974-75. Served to lt. (j.g.) USNR, 1943-47. Mem. Am. Soc. Body Engrs. (pres. 1965), Soc. Automotive Engrs., Engring. Soc. Detroit. Roman Catholic. Clubs: Fairlane (Dearborn); Meadowbrook Country (Northville, Mich.); Stewart (Fla.) Yacht and Country. Home: 300 Knobbyview Dr Highland MI 48031 Office: American Rd Dearborn MI 48121

KARSAVINA, JEAN FATERSON, writer; b. Warsaw, Poland, Feb. 23, 1908; came to U.S., 1917, naturalized, 1934; d. Adam and Regina (Segal) Faterson; m. Monroe Schere, May 1, 1966. Student, Smith Coll., 1924-26; B.A., Barnard Coll., 1927. Editor The Soviet Rev. and Studies in Soviet Lit., N.Y.C., 1959-64; freelance fiction and article writer for mags., 1935—, tchr. fiction workshops, 1938-49; lectr. in field. Editor: Reprints from the Soviet Press, 1965—; author: novel Reunion in Poland, 1945 (Child Study Assn. award 1946); Tree By the Waters, 1948, White Eagle, Dark Skies, 1974 (Nat. Jewish Book Council Distinguished Fiction award 1975); (with Lukas Foss) opera libretto Jumping Frog of Calaveras County, 1950, (with Joseph Wagner) New England Sampler, 1965; English text The Duenna (Prokofiev), 1948; also N.Y. stage prodn., 1948, NBC-TV, Text of Pique Dame (Tchaikovsky), 1953; transls. from Polish and Russian, including War and Peace, 1956, Polish Cookery, Adaptation for Americans, 1960; ghost writer of med., how-to books; editorial cons. to pubs. Mem. Writers' Guild Am., Authors' League Am. Pub. Address: care Knox Burger 39 1/2 Washington Sq S New York City NY 10012 *Working at the writing trade—as distinguished from writing with no conception of markets and similar harsh realities - is invaluable discipline. If I had to do it over again, I would put a secure lock on the door of a room of my own, also, like Katherine Anne Porter, learn to say "No!" to all the demands which are considered priorities in a woman's daily life before she is allowed to get to her typewriter—demands which can, and do, wreck one's working day*

KARSCH, DANIEL SELWYN, advt. exec.; b. N.Y.C., Jan. 28, 1923; s. Samuel and Louise (Selwyn) K.; m. Shirley Sperans, Nov. 24, 1949; children—Andrew, Thomas. B.A., U. Va., 1942; postgrad., Princeton, 1942-43. With advt. dept. Warner Bros. Pictures, 1945-46; account exec. Ray Austrian & Assos., 1946-52; pres. Daniel & Charles, Inc., N.Y.C., 1952-70, chmn. exec. com., 1970—; exec. v.p., dir. Creamer Inc. Served with U.S. Army, 1942-45.

KARSEN, SONJA PETRA, Spanish educator; b. Berlin, Apr. 11, 1919; U.S., 1938, naturalized, 1945; d. Fritz and Erna (Heidermann) K. Titulo de Bachiller, 1937; B.A., Carleton Coll., 1939; M.A. (scholar in French), Bryn Mawr Coll., 1941; Ph.D., Columbia U., 1950. Instr. Spanish Lake Erie Coll., Painesville, Ohio, 1943-45; instr. modern langs. U. P.R., 1945-46; instr. Spanish Syracuse U., 1947-50, Bklyn. Coll., 1950-51; asst. to dep. dir. gen. UNESCO, 1951-52, Latin Am. Desk, asst. dept., 1952-53, mem. tech. asistance mission Costa Rica, 1954; asst. prof. Spanish Sweet Briar Coll., Va., 1955-57; assoc. prof., chmn. dept. Romance langs. Skidmore Coll., Saratoga Springs, N.Y., 1957-61, prof. Spanish, 1961—, chmn. dept. modern langs. and lits., 1961-79; Fulbright lectr. Free U., Berlin, 1968; mem. adv. and nominating com. Books Abroad, 1965-67. Author: Guillermo Valencia, Colombian Poet, 1951, Educational development in Costa Rica with UNESCO's Technical Assistance, 1951-54, 1954, Jaime Torres Bodet: A Poet in a Changing World, 1963, Selected Poems of Jaime Torres Bodet, 1964, Versos y prosas de Jaime Torres Bodet, 1966, Jaime Torres Bodet, 1971; editor: Lang. Assn. Bull., 1980-83; adv. bd.: Modern Lang. Studies; contbr. articles to profl. jours. Decorated chevalier dans l'Ordre des Palmes Academiques, 1964; recipient Leadership award N.Y. State Assn. Fgn. Lang. Tchrs., 1973, 79, Nat. Disting. Leadership award N.Y. State Assn. Fgn. Lang. Tchrs., 1979, Disting. Service award N.Y. State Asn. Fgn. Lang. Tchrs., 1983, Spanish Heritage award, 1981, Alumni Achievement award Carleton Coll., 1982; exchange student auspices Inst. Internat. Edn.l at Carleton Coll., 1938-39; Buenos Aires Conv. grantee for research in Colombia, 1946-47; faculty research grantee Skidmore Coll., summer 1959, 61, 63, 65, 67, 69, 70, 73. Mem. AAUP, MLA (del. assembly 1976-78), Am. Assn. Tchrs. Spanish and Portuguese, Nat. Assn. Self-Instructional Lang. Programs (v.p. 1981-82, pres. 1982-83), AAUW, Nat. Geog. Soc., Instituto Internacional de Literatura Iberoamericana, Asociacion Internacional de Hispanistas, UN Assn. U.S.A., Am. Soc. French Acad. Palms, Fulbright Alumni, Phi Sigma Iota. Office: Skidmore Coll Saratoga Springs NY 12866 *Perseverance, hard work and high ethical standards coupled with the opportunities for fulfilling one's potential, available in the United States to agreater extent than anywhere else in the world, have made my life what it is today.*

KARSH, BERNARD, sociology educator; b. Chgo., Aug. 25, 1921; s. David and Harriett (Pugach) K.; m. Annette Eleanor Shier, June 9, 1946; children: Paul I., Aaron N. Student, Roosevelt U., 1946; M.A., U. Chgo., 1948, Ph.D., 1953. Research asst., then asst. prof. U. Chgo., 1948-53; mem. faculty U. Ill. at Champaign, 1954—, prof. sociology, 1961—, head dept. sociology, 1973-79; assoc. dir. Inst. of Aviation, 1976-79; vis. lectr. U. Kan., 1951, U. Ind., 1952; vis. prof. Keio U., Tokyo, Japan, 1966; adj. prof. Fla. Atlantic U., 1972; cons. in field. Author: Diary of a Strike, 1957, Worker Views His Union, 1958, Workers And Employers In Japan, 1973; also articles. Served with USAAF, 1939-43. Fulbright scholar, 1960. Fellow Am. Sociol. Assn.; mem. Assn. Asian Studies, Indsl. Relations Research Assn., AAUP, Midwest Conf. Asian Studies (v.p. 1970-71, pres. 1971-72). Home: 1412 W William St Champaign IL 61820

KARSH, YOUSUF, photographer; b. Mardin, Armenia, Dec. 23, 1908; emigrated to Can., 1924; s. Amsih and Bahia K.; m. Estrellita Nachbar, Aug. 28, 1962. Pupil, John H. Garo; numerous hon. degrees including; LL.D., Queen's U., Kingston, Ont., Carleton U.; D.H.L., Dartmouth Coll., Ohio U., Mt. Allison U.; D.C.L., Bishop's U., Lennoxville, Que.; D.H.L., Emerson Coll.; B.Profl. Arts, Brooks Inst.; D.F.A., U. Mass., 1979, U. Hartford, 1980; M.F.A., Tufts U., 1981. Opened photog. studio, Ottawa, Ont., Can., 1932; vis. prof. photography Ohio U., Emerson Coll.; lectr in field. Author: Faces of Destiny, 1946, Portraits of Greatness, 1959, This Is the Mass, 1958, This Is Rome, 1959, This is the Holy Land, 1960, These are the Sacraments, 1962, In Search of Greatness (autobiography), 1962, The Warren Court, 1965, Karsh Portfolio, 1967, Faces of Our Time, 1971, Karsh Portraits, 1976, Karsh Canadians, 1978, Karsh: A Fifty-Year Retrospective, 1983; portrait photographer leading nat. and internat. statesmen, corporate execs., polit. and govtl. ofcls., religious leaders including royal families of, Eng., Monaco, Norway, Greece, Pope John Paul II, also leading intellectual and entertainment figures, first one-man show, Nat. Gallery Can., 1959, one man show, Men Who Make Our World, Expo 67, Internat. Ctr. Photography, N.Y.C., 1983, Mus. Photography, Bradford, Eng., Nat. Portrait Gallery, London, 1984, Nat. Portrait Gallery, Edinburgh, Scotland, exhibited throughout, Can., U.S., Europe, Australia, TV appearances, works represented in permanent collections, Mus. Modern Art, N.U.C., Met. Mus. Art, N.Y.C., Art Inst. Chgo., St. Louis Art Mus., George Eastman House, Rochester, N.Y., Nat. Portrait Gallery, London, Nat. Gallery Can., numerous others; photographer ann. poster child: Muscular Dystrophy Assn. Am; 12 photographs used on postage stamps in 12 countries. Decorated Order of Can., Centennial medal, Can. Council medal; recipient U.S. Presdl. citation for service to handicapped, 1971, Achievement in Life award Ency. Brit.; named Master Photog. Arts Profl. Photographers Assn. Can. Fellow Royal Photog. Soc. Gt. Britain; mem. Royal Can. Acad. Arts. Clubs: Dutch Treat, Century (N.Y.C.); Rideau (Ottawa). Office: Chateau Laurier Suite 660 Ottawa ON Canada K1N 8S7

KARSON, BURTON LEWIS, musician; b. Los Angeles, Nov. 10, 1934; s. Harry L. and Cecilia K. B.A., U. So. Calif., 1956, M.A., 1959, D.M.A., 1964. Instr. music Univ. Coll., U. So. Calif., Los Angeles, 1958-59, univ. chapel organist, 1960-61; instr. music Glendale (Calif.) Coll., 1960-65; asst. prof. music Calif. State U., Fullerton, 1965-69, assoc. prof., 1969-74, prof., 1974—; writer, critic Los Angeles Times, 1966-71. Founder, condr., artistic dir., Baroque Music Festival, Corona del Mar, Calif.; concert preview lectr., Los Angeles Philharm. Orch., Carmel Bach Festival, Pacific Chorale of Orange County, others; Editor: Festival Essays for Pauline Alderman, 1976; contbr. articles profl. publs. Pianist, harpsichordist; organist, ch. musician St. Joachim's Ch., Costa Mesa, Calif., 1974-82; organist, choirmaster St. Michael and All Angels Episcopal Ch., Corona del Mar, Calif., 1982—; choral condr., condr. Luth. Chorale of Los Angeles, 1979-83. Mem. Am. Musicol. Soc., Am. Guild Organists, Phi Mu Alpha Sinfonia (province gov.), Pi Kappa Lambda. Research on music history and criticism in early Calif., 17th-18th century music in Germany. Home: 404 De Sola Terr Corona del Mar CA 92625 Office: Dept of Music Calif State Univ Fullerton CA 92634

KARSON, SAMUEL, psychologist, educator; b. Balt., Jan. 3, 1924; s. Norman Jacobson and Annie (Raskin) K.; m. Dorothy Faye Liberty, Sept. 6, 1946; children—Linda, Michael. B.S., L.I. U., 1948; Ph.D., Washington U., St. Louis, 1952. Asst. prof. U. N.H., 1957-58; research asst. prof. dept. nursing U. Miami, Fla., 1959-62; chief psychologist, dir. research Dade County Child Guidance Clinic, Miami, 1958-62; spl. asst. for clin. psychology FAA, 1962-66, guest lectr. aviation med. examiner seminars, 1966—; prof., head dept. psychology Eastern Mich. U., 1966-77; cons. in field, 1966-77; chief psychologist Office Med. Services, U.S. Dept. State, Washington, 1977-81, cons., 1981—. Author: (with J. O'Dell) A Guide to the Clinical Use of the 16PF. Served with USAAF, 1942-45; Served with USAF, 1955-57. Fellow Am. Orthopsychiat. Assn., Am. Psychol. Assn.; mem. Soc. Multivariate Exptl. Psychology, Assn. Aviation Psychologists (pres. 1973-74), Sigma Xi, Psi Chi. Home: 6737 Fairfax Rd Chevy Chase MD 20815

KARSTEN, ORLO LOUIS, JR., ins. co. exec.; b. Mt. Pleasant, Iowa, Aug. 3, 1923; s. Orlo Louis and Leona May (Marvin) K.; m. Jacquelin Seay, Sept. 24, 1950; children—Kristine, Ellen. B.A., State U. Iowa, 1948, M.S., 1949. Actuarial asst. Northwestern Mut. Life Ins. Co., Milw., 1949-56, v.p. underwriting, 1963-77, v.p. policyowner services, 1977—; actuary Rio Grande Nat. Life Inst. Co., Dallas, 1956-59; v.p., actuary Gt. Am. Res. Ins. Co., Dallas, 1959-63. Bd. dirs. Blood Center S.E., Wis., Milw. Served with USAAF, 1943-46; CBI; Served with USAAF; ETO. Fellow Soc. Actuaries (mem. mortality com.); mem. Home Office Life Underwriters Assn. (pres.), Med. Info. Bur. (dir., treas.). Republican. Presbyterian. Home: 4640 N Woodburn St Milwaukee WI 53211 Office: Northwestern Mut Life Ins Co 720 E Wisconsin Ave Milwaukee WI 53202

KARSTEN, THOMAS LOREN, realtor, lawyer; b. Mpls., Sept. 4, 1915; s. H.A. and Ida D. (Karsten) K.; m. Marilyn R. Herst, Nov. 26, 1950; children—Lesley, Thomas, Liza, Timothy. A.B., U. Chgo., 1937, LL.D., 1939. Bar: Ill. bar 1938, N.Y. bar 1948. Exec. asst. to under sec. interior, 1942, naval aide to gov., P.R.; also lectr. adminstrv. law U. P.R. and; alternate mem. Anglo-Am. Caribbean Commn., 1943-45; assoc. prosecutor Internat. Mil. Tribunal, Nuremberg, Germany, 1945-46; mem. firm Schwartzreich & Mathias, N.Y.C., 1946-50; spl. counsel to Spl. Senate Com. to Investigate Organized Crime in Interstate Commerce, 1950; dir. consumer goods div. OPS, Washington, 1951-52; asst. to pres. Am. Trading & Prodn. Corp., Balt.; v.p. No. Properties, Inc.; v.p., dir. Blaustein Industries, Inc., Am. Trading Corp., Wilshire Properties, Inc., Atapco-Valley, Inc., Atapco-Valley Land Corp., Atapco-San Diego, Inc.; v.p. Charles St. Devel. Corp., 1953-68; exec. v.p. Ogden Devel. Corp.; also vice chmn. Greenwood Village, Inc., 1968-70; now pres. Thomas L. Karsten Assos., Kar Co.; chmn. Karsten Instl. Realty Advisers; dir. First Interstate Investment Services, Arden Group. Collaborating author: Handbook of Federal Indian Law, 1941. Mem. N.Y.C. Mayor's Com. on Puerto Rican Affairs, 1949-50; v.p. A Fair Deal for N.Y. County, 1949-50; commr. Balt. County Redevel. and Rehab. Commn.; v.p. Green Spring Valley Area Planning Council; exec. v.p., dir. Planned Parenthood Assn.; dir. Nat. Travelers Aid Assn.; commr. Md. Gambling Study Commn. Served to lt. comdr. USNR, 1942-46. Mem. UN Assn. (v.p., bd. dirs.). Clubs: Standard (Chgo.); Regency (Los Angeles). Home: 1521 Amalfi Dr Pacific Palisades CA 90272 Office: 10960 Wilshire Blvd Los Angeles CA 90024

KARTIGANER, JOSEPH, lawyer; b. Berlin, Germany, June 5, 1935; came to U.S., 1939; s. Harold and Lilly (Wolkowitz) K.; m. Cathleen Vaudine Noland, Apr. 20, 1968; children: Deborah Lynn, Alison Beth. A.B., CCNY, 1955; LL.B., Columbia U., 1958. Bar: N.Y. 1960. Assoc. White & Case, N.Y.C., 1960-69, ptnr., 1969—; lectr. law Columbia Law Sch., N.Y.C. Fellow Am. Coll. Probate Counsel (regent 1978—), Am. Coll. Tax Counsel; mem. ABA (real property, probate and trust law sect., DIV. DIR. 1983—), Am. Law Inst., Internat. Acad. Estate and Trust Law (academician), Internat. Acad. Estate and Law (exec. com. 1980—). Clubs: Board Room (N.Y.C.); Scarsdale Golf (Hartsdale, N.Y.). Home: 1040 Park Ave New York NY 10028 Office: White & Case 280 Park Ave New York NY 10017

KARTMAN, BEN, editor; b. Chgo., Mar. 8, 1901; s. Abraham and Etta (Landau) K.; m. Leah Affron, Jan. 11, 1927 (dec.); children—Keith Harris, Edwin Affron. A.B., U. Ill., 1923. Instr. English and journalism U. Ill., 1923-25; copyreader Chgo. Daily jour., 1925-26, Chgo. Daily News, 1926-28, make-up editor, 1928-44; asso. editor Coronet mag., 1945-52; editorial dir. Family Weekly, 1954-59, exec. editor, 1959-65; editorial writer Hollister Newspapers, 1964-66; prodn. editor Popular Mechanics Do-It-Yourself Ency., 1967-68; instr. Medill Sch. Journalism, Northwestern U., 1952-65; instr. mag. non-fiction Midwestern Writers Conf., 1945-54; lectr. humanities U. Chgo., 1952-53; Bd. govs. Midwestern Writers Conf.; Pres. Assn. Family Living, 1958-60. Editor: Disaster!, 1948, Wilmette: a History, 1976; editorial bd.: Viewpoint mag; Contbr. to: Ency. Brit. Book Year, 1945, Am. People's Ency. Yearbook, 1954, 55. Bd. dirs. Youth Orch. Greater Chgo., 1952-65, Lawson YMCA, 1964-71, Wilmette United Fund, 1973-76, Chgo. Hall of Fame, 1976; v.p. fine arts bd. Kendall Coll.; chmn. pub. relations com. Met. Chgo. YMCA; v.p. bd. dirs. Wilmette Vol. Pool; bd. dirs. Wilmette Community Concert Assn., 1974-79, pres., 1975-76; exec. com. Wilmette July 4th Celebration, 1974—. Named Wilmette Jaycees Man of Year, 1978. Mem. Soc. Midland Authors (v.p. 1955-57, pres. 1957-61), Phi Epsilon Pi (nat. v.p. 1925-27, nat. editor 1924-28), Sigma Delta Chi, Pi Delta Epsilon. Jewish. Home: 208 Golf Terr Wilmette IL 60091

KARZON, DAVID THEODORE, pediatrician, educator; b. N.Y.C., July 8, 1920; m. Allaire Urban, July 18, 1946; children—David Theodore, Elizabeth U. B.S., Ohio State U., 1940, M.S., 1941; M.D., Johns Hopkins, 1944. Diplomate: Am. Bd. Pediatrics (examiner 1982—), Am. Bd. Microbiology. Intern, then resident Johns Hopkins Hosp., 1944-45; resident N.Y.-Cornell Med. Center, 1950-52; mem. faculty State U. N.Y. at Buffalo Sch. Medicine, 1952-68, prof. pediatrics, 1963-68; asso. attending physician Children's Hosp., Buffalo, 1952-64, attending physician, 1964-68; prof. pediatrics, chmn. dept. Vanderbilt U. Sch. Medicine, 1968—; med. dir. Children's Hosp., Vanderbilt U., 1971—; cons. USPHS, NIH, Bur. Biologics FDA, 1972—; Mem. spl. adv. com. immunization practice to surgeon gen., 1964-70. Asso. editor: Am. Jour. Epidemiology, 1966-78; editorial bd.: Jour. Pediatrics, 1974—; Editorial bd. sect. on: Immunology Intervirology, 1972—. Served to capt. M.C. AUS, 1946-48. Lowell M. Palmer sr. fellow, 1952-54; Markle scholar, 1956-61; recipient Research Career award NIH, 1962-68. Mem. Am. Acad. Pediatrics, Soc. Pediatric Research, Assn. Med. Schs. Pediatric Dept. Chairmen, So. Soc. Pediatric Research, Am. Pediatric Soc., Am. Acad. Microbiologists, Am. Soc. Microbiology, Am. Epidemiological Soc., N.Y. Acad. Sci., Am. Assn. Immunologists, Soc. Exptl. Biology and Medicine, Fedn. Am. Socs. Experimental Biology, Infectious Diseases Soc. Am., Ambulatory Pediatric Assn., Phi Beta Kappa, Alpha Omega Alpha. Home: 1049 Overton Lea Rd Nashville TN 37220 Office: Dept Pediatrics Vanderbilt Univ Sch Medicine Nashville TN 37232

KASA, PAMELA DOROTHY, lawyer; b. Granite City, Ill., Oct. 10, 1943; d. William Anthony and Isabella Josephine (Ceva) K.; m. Thomas Haddaway Chibbaro, Dec. 30, 1975; children: Audrey Cara, Julie. B. Chem. Engring., Rensselaer Poly. Inst., Troy, N.Y., 1965; J.D., Georgetown U., 1968; LL.M., NYU, 1980. Bar: N.Y. 1969. Patents and trademark atty. GAF Corp., N.Y.C., 1968-69; investigating atty. City of N.Y., 1969-70; patent atty. Celanese Corp., N.Y.C., 1971-76; sr. atty. Bristol-Myers Co., N.Y.C., 1976-79, sec., counsel, 1982—; v.p., counsel Clariol Appliance div. Bristol-Myers Co., N.Y.C., 1979-82. Club: Board Room (N.Y.C.). Home: 42 Franklin Ave Staten Island NY 10301 Office: Bristol-Myers Co 345 Park Ave New York NY 10154

KASBEER, STEPHEN FREDERICK, university official; b. Princeton, Ill., Feb. 28, 1925; s. Virgil Sumner and Dorothy Marie (Uthoff) K.; m. Elizabeth Branning Royce, June 15, 1947 (div. 1978); children: Deborah Ann, William Royce.; m. Pamela Christine Rehm, Aug. 10, 1978. B.S., Northwestern U., 1945, M.A., 1951; J.D., John Marshall Law Sch., 1966. Bar: Ill. 1967, U.S. Dist. Ct. (no. dist.) Ill. 1967. Pres. Kasbeer Concrete Products, Princeton, Ill., 1948-49; sec., gen. counsel Harper-Wyman Co., Hinsdale, Ill., 1951-69; group v.p. Bell & Howell Co., Chgo., 1969-73; exec. v.p., chief operating officer Evang. Hosp. Assn., Oak Brook, Ill., 1973-81; v.p., asst. to pres. S & C Electric Co., Chgo., 1981; sr. v.p. Loyola U., Chgo., 1981—; health care cons. Equitable Life Assurance Soc. U.S., N.Y.C., 1980-81; dir. Evang. Hosp. Assn., Chgo., 1968-73. Trustee Village of Indian Head Park (Ill.), 1967-69, West Suburban YMCA, LaGrange, Ill., 1968-71. Served to lt. (j.g.) USN, 1943-46; PTO. Mem. Ill. Bar Assn., Chgo. Bar Assn., Human Resources Mgmt. Assn. Chgo. (pres. 1972), Am. Soc. Hosp. Attys., Econ. Club Chgo. Republican. Congregationalist. Clubs: University; Club Internat. (Chgo.). Home: 232 E Walton Pl Chicago IL 60611 Office: Loyola U Chgo 820 N Michigan Ave Chicago IL 60611

KASCH, RICK DARREL, hotel corporation executive; b. Sioux Falls, S.D., May 23, 1950; s. Albert Darrel and Phyllis Lorraine (Pederson) K.; 1 dau., Abigail Nicolle. B.S., U. S.D., 1972. C.P.A., Kans., Mo. Sr. acct. Arthur Andersen & Co., Kansas City, Mo., 1972-77; dir. audit div. John W. Meara & Co., Kansas City, 1977-79; chief fin. officer, treas., exec. v.p. Brock Hotel Corp., Irving, Tex., 1979—. Mem. Am. Inst. C.P.A.s. Office: Brock Hotel Corp 4441 W Airport Freeway Irving TX 75062

KASCHUB, WILLIAM JOHN, lawyer; b. Meriden, Conn., Nov. 21, 1942; s. Robert William and Agnes Wilkenson (Cooper) K.; m. Phyllis Linda Platz, Mar. 1, 1969; children: Diana Lynne, Kristen Sarah, Cynthia Elizabeth. A.B., Bowdoin Coll., 1964; LL.B., Boston Coll., 1968; postgrad., N.Y. U. Sch. Law. Bar: N.Y. With Gen. Electric Co., N.Y.C., 1969-71; labor atty. Internat. Paper Co., N.Y.C., 1971-73; gen. labor atty. GTE Service Corp., Stamford, Conn., 1979-81; also labor atty. (various subsidiaries in), Stamford and Northlake, Ill., 1973-81, v.p. human resources relations, Stamford, 1981—. Mem. Electronics Industry Assn. Republican. Lutheran. Club: Aspetuk Valley Country. Home: 38 Dan's Hwy New Canaan CT 06840 Office: GTE Service Corp One Stamford Forum Stamford CT 06904

KASDAN, LAWRENCE EDWARD, film director, screenwriter; b. Miami Beach, Fla., Jan. 14, 1949; s. Clarence Norman and Sylvia Sarah (Landau) K.; m. Meg Goldman, Nov. 28, 1971; children: Jacob, Jonathan. B.A., U. Mich., 1970, M.A. in Edn, 1972. Copywriter W.B. Doner & Co. (Advt.), Detroit, 1972-75, Doyle, Dane Bernbach, Los Angeles, 1975-77; freelance screenwriter, 1977-80, motion picture dir., screenwriter, Los Angeles, 1980—. Co-screenwriter: The Empire Strikes Back, 1980; screenwriter: Continental Divide, 1981, Raiders of the Lost Ark, 1981; writer, dir.: Body Heat, 1981; co-screenwriter: Return of the Jedi, 1982; co-screenwriter, dir., exec. producer: The Big Chill, 1983. Recipient Clio awards for advt., Writers Guild Am. award for the Big Chill, 1983. Mem. Writers Guild Am. W., Dirs. Guild Am. W. Address: care Peter Benedek 9601 Wilshire Blvd Suite 825 Beverly Hills CA 90210

KASDORF, DONALD LEE, mfg. co. exec.; b. Chgo., July 13, 1929; s. Harry Ernst and Frances Lillian (Granquist) K.; m. Carol Jean Gaebel, July 21, 1951; children—Leslie Lynne, Donna Lee. B.S.B.A., Northwestern U., 1960. Corp. controller Wells Mfg. Co., 1955-62; div. controller Lamb Industries, Milw., 1962-63; corp. controller Abbott Labs., North Chicago, Ill., 1963-71; sr. v.p. fin., treas. Modine Mfg. Co., Racine, Wis., 1971—. Mem. Racine Environ. Com.; chmn. adv. bd. Salvation Army, Racine, 1977—. Served with U.S. Army, 1951-53. Mem. Fin. Execs. Inst., Nat. Assn. Accountants, Am. Mgmt. Assn. Club: Racine Country. Home: 8 Pinewood Ct Racine WI 53402 Office: 1500 DeKoven Racine WI 53401

KASER, DAVID, librarian; b. Mishawaka, Ind., Mar. 12, 1924; s. Arthur Leroy and Loah (Steele) K.; m. Jane Jewell, Sept. 1, 1950; children: John Andrew, Kathleen Jewell. A.B., Houghton Coll., 1949; M.A., U. Notre Dame, 1950; A.M. in L.S., U. Mich., 1952, Ph.D., 1956. Serials librarian, instr. library sci. Ball State U., 1952-54; asst. in exchanges U. Mich. Library, 1954-56; chief acquisitions Washington U. Libraries, St. Louis, 1956-59, asst. dir., 1959-60; prof. library sci. Peabody Coll. and dir. libraries Vanderbilt U., 1960-68; dir. libraries Cornell U., 1968-73; prof. library sci. Ind. U., 1973—; fgn. assignments in, Ireland, 1960, Korea, 1965, 81, Laos, 1966, Taiwan, 1967, 79, 81,, SE Asia, 1969, Eng., 1971, France, 1972, Saudi Arabia, 1975-76, 83,, Nigeria, 1978, Indonesia, 1978. Author: Messrs. Carey & Lea of Philadelphia, 1957, Washington University Manuscripts, 1958, Cost Book of Carey & Lea, 1825-1838, 1963, Joseph Charless, Printer in the Western Country, 1963, Books in America's Past, 1966, Book Pirating in Taiwan, 1969, Library Development in Eight Asian Countries, 1969, Book for a Sixpence, 1980, Books and Libraries in Camp and Battle, 1984; Editor: Mo. Library Assn. Quar, 1958-60, College and Research Libraries, 1963-69. Guggenheim fellow, 1967. Mem. ALA (councilor 1965-69, 75-79), Bibliog. Soc. Am., Assn. Coll. and Research Libraries (pres. 1968-69), Assn. Southeastern Research Libraries (chmn. 1966-68), Tenn. Library Assn. (pres. 1968-69), Am. Antiquarian Soc., Phi Beta Kappa, Beta Phi Mu (internat. pres. 1975). Home: 2402 Rock Creek Dr Bloomington IN 47401

KASH, DON ELDON, political science educator; b. Macedonia, Iowa, May 29, 1934; s. Albert W. and Blanche Opal (Smith) K.; m. Beverly Ann Brendes, Aug. 17, 1958; children: Kelli Denise, Jeffrey Paul. B.A., U. Iowa, 1959, M.A., 1960, Ph.D., 1963. Instr. Tex. Technol. U., 1960-61; asst. prof. Ariz. State U., 1963-65, U. Mo. at Kansas City, 1965-66; asso. prof. Purdue U., 1966-70; prof. polit. sci. U. Okla., 1970—, George Lynn Cross research prof. polit. sci., 1975—; dir. Sci. and Pub. Policy Program, 1970-78; vis. asso. prof. Ind. U., 1969-70; chief conservation div. U.S. Geol. Survey, 1978-81; cons. Argonne U. Assn., Commn. on Govt. Procurement of U.S. Congress, NSF, Oak Ridge Nat. Lab., Office of Tech. Assessment, U.S. Congress; mem. Assembly Engring., marine bd. NRC. Author: The Politics of Space Cooperation, 1967, Energy Under the Oceans: A Technology Assessment of Outer Continental Shelf Oil and Gas Operations, 1973, North Sea Oil and Gas: Implications for Future U.S. Development, 1973, Energy Alternatives: A Comparative Analysis, 1975, Our Energy Future, 1976, U.S. Energy Policy: Crisis and Complacency, 1983; contbr. articles to profl. jours. Served with AUS, 1952-54. Recipient grants Kansas City Assn. Trusts and Founds., 1965, NSF, 1966, 67, 71, 73, 74, IMB, 1967. Mem. Am. Polit. Sci. Assn., AAAS, AAUP. Home: 2610 McGee Dr Norman OK 73069 Office: U Okla Room 432 601 Elm St Norman OK 73019

KASHA, LAWRENCE N., producer, director theatrical and film productions; b. Bklyn., Dec. 3, 1934; s. Irving and Rose (Katz) K. B.A., N.Y. U., 1954, M.A., 1955. Theatrical dir. and producer: Nat. Co. L'il Abner, 1958; nat. tour Camelot, 1963-64, Anything Goes; off-Broadway co., 1962; Broadway co. Bajour, 1964; nat. co. Funny Girl, 1965, London co., 1966, Show Boat revival, 1966, Cactus Flower, 1968, Star Spangled Girl, 1968; London co. Mame, 1969; Broadway co. Lovely Ladies, Kind Gentlemen, 1970; producer: off-Broadway prodn. Parade, 1960; Broadway prodn. She Loves Me, 1963, Hadrian VII, 1969, Applause, 1970, Father's Day, 1971, Inner City, 1972, Seesaw, 1973, No Hard Feelings, 1973, Heaven Sent, Los Angeles, 1978, Seven

Brides for Seven Brothers, 1978; CBS-TV spls. Applause, 1973, Another April, 1974, Rosenthal & Jones, 1975; TV series Busting Loose, 1977, Komedy Tonite, NBC, 1978 (Recipient Tony award 1970), NBC (Outer Critics Circle award 1973); Playwright: (with Hayden Griffin) The Pirate, 1968, (with Lionel Wilson) Where Have You Been, Billy Boy?, 1969, (with David S. Landay) Heaven Sent, 1978, Seven Brides for Seven Brothers, 1978, Woman of The Year, 1981. Mem. Dirs. Guild Am., Actors Equity Assn., Writers Guild West. Home: 2229 Gloaming Way Beverly Hills CA 90210

KASHDAN, ISAAC, chess master; b. N.Y.C., Nov. 19, 1905; s. Isadore and Molly (Friedl) K.; m. Hadassah Cohen, June 3, 1933; 1 son, Richard L. B.A., Coll. City N.Y., 1926. Mem. U.S. Chess Fedn., 1925—, life dir., 1945—, master, 1926—, internat. grandmaster, 1932—; trainer, capt. teams Olympics, 1928, 30, 31, 33, 37, non-playing capt., 1960, 64; chess editor Los Angeles Times, 1955—; internat. chess judge, 1948—; statistician Jacques Coe & Co., 1941-49. Adminstrv. officer Jewish Fedn. Council Los Angeles, 1949-67. U.S. Chess champion, 1938, 42, 47. Home: 2231 Overland Ave Los Angeles CA 90064 Office: Los Angeles Times Times Mirror Square Los Angeles CA 90053

KASHGARIAN, MICHAEL, physician; b. N.Y.C., Sept. 20, 1933; s. Toros and Arax (Almasian) K.; m. Jean Gaylor Caldwell, July 2, 1960; children: Michaele, Thea. A.B., N.Y. U., 1954; M.D., Yale U., 1958. Diplomate: Am. Bd. Pathology. Intern Barnes Hosp., St. Louis, 1958-59; asst. in medicine Washington U., St. Louis, 1958-59; asst. resident in pathology Yale New Haven Med. Center, 1959-61, resident in pathology, 1962-63; research fellow in renal physiology (U. Goettingen), Germany, 1961-62, practice medicine specializing in pathology, New Haven, 1962—; instr. Yale U., 1962-64, asst. prof., 1964-67, asso. prof., 1967-74, prof., 1974—, vice chmn. dept., 1976—; asso. pathologist Yale New Haven Hosp., 1964-66, asst. attending pathologist, 1966-69, attending pathologist, 1969—, pres. med. staff, 1983-84; cons. in pathology, 1962—. Author: (with J.P. Hayslett, B.H. Spargo) Renal Disease, 1974, (with G.N. Burrow) The Endocrine Glands; editorial bd.: Nephron, 1970—, Am. Jour. Pathology, 1975—, Am. Jour. Kidney Diseases; contbr. articles to med. jours. Chmn. ednl. adv. council North Haven Bd. Edn., 1971; chmn. Christian edn. com. Ch. of Christ, Yale, 1970. Served to 1st lt., M.C. USAR, 1954-65. USPHS fellow, 1963-65; research career devel. awardee, 1965-75. Fellow Am. Soc. Clin. Pathologists; mem. AMA, Am. Assn. Pathologists and Bacteriologists, Am. Soc. Nephrology, Internat. Acad. Pathology, Conn., New Haven County med. assns., Am. Assn. Pathologists, Conn. Soc. Pathologists (pres. 1945), Am. Heart Assn., AAAS, Am. Physiol. Soc., Sigma Xi, Alpha Omega Alpha, Alpha Kappa Kappa. Home: 22 Old Orhcard Rd North Haven CT 06473 Office: 310 Cedar St New Haven CT 06510

KASHIWA, SHIRO, judge; b. Kohala, Hawaii, Oct. 24, 1912; s. Ryuten and Yukiko (Matsubara) K.; m. Mildred Aiko, July 20, 1941; children: Gregg, Wendy. B.S., U. Mich., 1934, J.D., 1936. Bar: Hawaii 1937. Individual practice law, Honolulu, 1937-69; atty. gen. State of Hawaii, 1959-63; asst. U.S. atty. gen., head land and natural resources div. Dept. Justice, Washington, 1969-72; judge U.S. Ct. Claims, Washington, 1972-82, U.S. Ct. Appeals, fed. cir., 1982—. Home: 2510 Virginia Ave NW Washington DC 20037 Office: US Ct Appeals for Fed Circuit 717 Madison Pl NW Washington DC 20439

KASHIWAHARA, KEN, journalist. B.A. in Broadcasting, San Francisco State Coll., 1963. Anchorman, polit. reporter Sta.-KHVH-TV, Honolulu, 1969-71; anchorman, polit. editor Sta. KGMB-TV, 1971-72; polit. reporter Sta.-KABC-TV, Los Angeles, 1972-74; co-anchorman weekend edit. Eyewitness News and reporter weekday edit. ABC, Los Angeles, 1974-75; corr. SE Asia, 1975, chief news bur., Hong Kong, 1975-78, chief bur., San Francisco, 1978—. Contbr. articles to mil. and civilian press. Served as info. officer USAF, 1964-69. Office: care ABC News 277 Golden Gate San Francisco CA 94102 *

KASINOFF, BERNARD HERMAN, hosp. adminstr.; b. N.Y., Feb. 15, 1920; s. Max and Anna (Miller) K.; m. Helen Jaworski, Oct. 17, 1952; 1 dau., Jessica D. B.A., U. Va., 1942, M.D., 1946. Chief mental hygiene treatment group VA, N.Y.C., 1958-62; dir. Valley Mental Health Center, Staunton, Va., 1962-69; clin. dir. DeJarnette San., 1969-71; supt. Southwestern State Hosp., Marion, Va., 1971—; Pvt. practice neuropsychiatry. Pres. Am. Cancer Soc., Waynesboro, Va., 1970. Served to capt. M.C. AUS, 1947-49. Fellow Am. Geriatrics Soc; mem. Neuropsychiat. Soc. Va. (pres. 1973-74), Med. Soc. Va. (chmn. com. religion and medicine), AMA, Am. Psychiat. Assn., Assn. Med. Hosp. Supts. Club: Elk. Office: PO Box 917 Lebanon PA 17042

KASKE, ROBERT EARL, educator; b. Cin., June 1, 1921; s. Herman Charles and Ann (Laake) K.; 1 son by previous marriage, David Louis; m. Carol Margaret Vonckx, June 4, 1958; 1 son, Richard James. B.A., Xavier U., 1942; M.A., U. N.C., 1947, Ph.D., 1950. Instr. to asst. prof. Washington U., St. Louis, 1950-57; asst. prof. Pa. State U., 1957-58; assoc. prof. U. N.C.-Chapel Hill, 1958-61; prof. U. Ill.-Urbana, 1961-64; prof. English Cornell U., Ithaca, N.Y., 1964—, Avalon Found. prof. in humanities, 1975—. Contbg. author: Medieval Literature and Folklore Studies: Essays in Honor of Francis Lee Utley, 1970, Chaucer the Love Poet, 1973, Chaucer and Middle English Studies in Honor of Rossell Hope Robbins, 1974, The Wisdom of Poetry: Essays in Early English Literature in Honor of Morton W. Bloomfield, 1982, Dante, Petrarch, Boccaccio: Studies in the Honor of Charles S. Singleton, 1983; Chief editor: Traditio; editorial adv. com.: A Manual of the Writings in Middle English; adv. bd.: Speculum; Contbr. articles to profl. jours. Served to 1st lt. AUS, 1942-46. Sr. fellow Am. Council of Learned Socs., 1971-72, Cornell U. Soc. for Humanities, 1972-73; Guggenheim fellow, 1962-63, 77-78; Nat. Endowment for Humanities grantee, 1977-78; sr. fellow Southeastern Inst. Medieval and Renaissance Studies, 1979. Fellow Mediaeval Acad. Am. (councillor 1975-78); Mem. Modern Lang. Assn., Dante Soc. Am., Internat. Assn. Univ. Profs. of English, Acad. Lit. Studies (original). Home: 121 N Quarry St Ithaca NY 14850 Office: Dept English Goldwin Smith Hall Cornell U Ithaca NY 14853

KASKEL, HOWARD M., real estate company executive. Pres. Doral Hotels Corp., N.Y.C. Office: Doral Hotels Corp 500 Madison Ave New York NY 10022 *

KASKELL, PETER HOWARD, association executive, lawyer; b. Berlin, Germany, Mar. 29, 1924; s. Joseph and Lilo (Schaeffer) K.; m. Joan Folsom Macy, Nov. 30, 1968; stepchildren: Brenda, Alison. Grad., Horace Mann Sch., N.Y.C., 1940; B.A., Columbia U., 1943, LL.B., 1948. Bar: N.Y. 1948. Assoc. White & Case, N.Y.C., 1948-51; atty. Nat. Prodn. Authority, Washington, 1951-52, W.R. Grace & Co., N.Y.C., 1952-54; div. counsel Curtiss-Wright Corp., Buffalo, 1954-56; with Olin Corp., Stamford, Conn., 1956-83, v.p. legal affairs, 1971-83; sr. v.p. Center for Public Resources Inc., N.Y.C., 1983—; organizer, chmn. Lawyers Com. for the Conv. on Contracts for the Internat. Sale of Goods. Former trustee Aldrich Mus. Contemporary Art, Ridgefield, Conn., Boys' Athletic League, N.Y.C.; treas. Conn. Humanities Council; pub. dir. CARE. Served with Intelligence Ser. AUS, 1943-45; ETO. Decorated Bronze Star medal. Mem. Westchester-Fairfield Corporate Counsel Assn. (past pres., mem. exec. com.), ABA, Assn. Bar N.Y.C. (com. on legal edn.). Clubs: Wilton Riding (past gov.); Landmark (Stamford)). Home: 31 DeForest Rd Wilton CT 06897 Office: 120 Long Ridge Rd Stamford CT 06904

KASKOWITZ, EDWIN, management consulting company executive; b. St. Louis, May 15, 1936; s. Nathan and Fannie K.; children: Joy, Sara, Naomi. B.A., Washington U., St. Louis, 1958, M.S.W. (grad. scholar), 1961. Sr. social worker St. Louis County Health Dept., 1965-67; exec. dir. Gerontol. Soc., 1967-80; pres. Business Radio Corp., Atlanta, Ga., 1981-82; pres., chief exec. officer The Association Mgmt. Group, Chevy Chase, Md., 1982—; Pres. B'nai-B'rith-Habirah, Washington, 1974-75; adv. bd. Over Easy program sta. KQED-TV, 1977-81. Served with USAR, 1954-62. Fellow Royal Soc. Health; mem. Gerontol. Soc. Am., Am. Soc. Assn. Execs. Office: 4103 Edgevale Ct Chevy Chase MD 20815

KASLICK, RALPH SIDNEY, dentist, educator; b. Bklyn., Oct. 17, 1935; s. John J. and Dorothy K.; m. Jessica Hellinger, Oct. 24, 1976. A.B., Columbia U., 1956, D.D.S., 1959, cert. in periodontology, 1962. Instr. Fairleigh Dickinson U. Sch. Dentistry, Hackensack, N.J., 1965-67, asst. prof., 1967-70, asso. prof., 1970-74, prof., 1974—, asst. dean for acad. affairs, 1973-75, acting dean, 1975-76, dean, 1976—; cons. in field. Contbr. chpts. to textbooks, articles to profl. jours. Served to capt. U.S. Army, 1962-64. Recipient Stanley S. Bergen award for contbn. to dental edn. Seton Hall U., 1982. Fellow Am. Coll. Dentists, N.Y. Acad. Dentistry; mem. Council Deans Am. Assn. Dental Schs., Internat. Assn. Dental Research (past pres. N.J. sect.), Am. Acad. Periodontology, ADA, Sigma Xi, Omicron Kappa Upsilon. Office: 110 Fuller Pl Hackensack NJ 07601

KASLOW, ARTHUR LOUIS, physician; b. Omaha, Jan. 15, 1913; s. Hyman Y. and Hannah Rebecca (Cutler) Kazlowsky; m. Sally Powers, May 21, 1972; children by previous marriage: Harvey, A. Art, David, Jeremy, Harmon, Daniel. B.S., Creighton U., 1934, M.D., 1935; postgrad., Inst. Religion, Tex. Med. Center, 1966. Intern Hollywood Presbyn. Hosp., Los Angeles, 1935-36; resident San Mateo (Calif.) County Hosp., 1936-37; instr. student health physician Stanford, 1938-41; practice medicine, specializing in internal medicine, Los Angeles, 1946-50, specializing in gastro-enterology, 1950-65, specializing in family medicine and counseling, Solvang, Calif., 1966—; mem. staff Hollywood Presbyn. Hosp., Goleta Valley Community Hosp., Cottage Hosp. of Santa Barbara; founder Kaslow Med. Center for treatment of chronic degenerative diseases. Contbr. articles to profl. publs. Served to maj. M.C. USAAF, 1941-45. Fellow Internat. Coll. Applied Nutrition; mem. Am. Coll. Gastro-enterology, Am. Diabetes Assn., Am. Coll. Angiology, Internat. Acad. Metabology (pres.). Lodge: Rotary. Inventor stomach irrigation tube, oxygen mask, placement therapy; founder RPT methods of acupuncture treatment for multiple sclerosis; originator Non-Processed Carbohydrate Test Meal in diagnosis metabolic rejectivity syndrome. Home: 3175 Riley Rd Doxholm Solvang CA 93463 Office: 793 Alamo Pintado Rd Solvang CA 93463 also Kaslow Med Self-Care Center 1187 Coast Village Rd Montecito CA 93108 2740 S Bristol St Santa Ana CA 92704

KASPER, HERBERT, fashion designer; b. N.Y.C., Dec. 12, 1926; s. Samuel and Rose (Fogel) K. B.S., NYU, 1949; student, Parsons Sch. Design, N.Y.C., 1947-49. Free-lance designer, Paris, 1949-50; designer John Fredericks Inc., N.Y.C., 1951-52, Penart Fashion, 1952-54, Arnold & Fox Inc., 1954-64, Joan Leslie Inc., 1964—; critic Parsons Sch. Design; pres. Council Fashion Designers Am., 1977-79. Served with U.S. Army, 1945-46. Recipient Coty award, 1955, 70; recipient Cotton Fashion award, 1967, Fashion Sales Guild award, 1972; named to Coty Hall of Fame, 1976. Mem. Tau Epsilon Phi. Office: Casper for Joan Leslie Inc 530 7th Ave New York NY 10018

KASPER, RUSSELL RICHARD, hospital equipment supply company executive; b. Milw., Nov. 23, 1932; s. Bruno and Frances (Lisiecki) K.; m. Sandra J. Weston, July 9, 1960; children: Kathleen D., Robert R., Janet M. B.B.A., U. Wis., 1955. C.P.A., Wis. Auditor Arthur Young & Co. (C.P.A.s), Milw., 1955-61; controller James Mfg. Co., Ft. Atkinson, Wis., 1961-64, Marmon Group, Chgo., 1964-68; v.p. fin. Trane Co., LaCrosse, Wis., 1968-72, Calspan Corp., Buffalo, 1972-77; v.p. fin. and adminstrn. Diversified Industries, Inc., St. Louis, 1977-82, UHI Corp., Los Angeles, 1982—. Served with AUS, 1955-57. Mem. Am. Inst. C.P.A.s, Nat. Assn. Accountants. Home: 1419 Greenoaks Dr. Arcadia CA 91006 Office: 2464 Mariondale Ave Los Angeles CA 90032

KASRIEL, ROBERT HERMAN, educator, mathematician; b. Tampa, Fla., Oct. 18, 1918; s. David and Sophie (Kornblum) K.; m. Ernestine Moskowitz, Jan. 31, 1946; children—Sarita Gay, David A. B.S. in Edn. and Math, U. Tampa, 1940; M.A. in Math, U. Va., 1949, Ph.D., 1953. Coordinator war tng. courses U. Tampa, Fla., 1940-42; instr. math. U.S. Maritime Acad., Pass Christian, Miss., 1945-47; staff aero. research NACA, 1952-54; asst. prof. math. Ga. Inst. Tech., Atlanta, 1954-57, asso. prof., 1957-62, prof., 1962—; vis. faculty mem. U. Va., summer 1956, U. Wis., summer 1963—. Author: Undergraduate Topology, 1971. Served with AUS, 1942-45; to lt. (j.g.) U.S. Maritime Service, 1945-47. Mem. Am. Math. Soc., Math. Assn. Am., A.A.U.P., Sigma Xi (pres. Ga. Tech. chpt. 1966-67, M.A. Ferst research award 1962). Home: 926 Northcliffe Dr NW Atlanta GA 30318

KASS, ARTHUR, record company executive; b. Bklyn., Jan. 24, 1926; s. Charles and Kate K.; m. Lynn Kuhlthau, Dec. 3, 1973; 1 son, Merrill.; m. Carole Kranepool, June 23, 1983. B.B.A., CCNY, 1948. Vice pres. MGM Records, N.Y.C.; now pres. Buddah Records Inc., N.Y.C. Served with AUS. Mem. Records Industry Assn. Am. (dir.). Office: Buddah Records Inc 1790 Broadway New York NY 10019

KASS, BENNY LEE, lawyer; b. Chgo., Aug. 20, 1936; s. Herman and Ethel (Lome) K.; m. Salme Lundstrom, Aug. 30, 1963; children: Gale, Brian. B.S., Northwestern U., 1957; LL.B., U. Mich., 1960; LL.M., George Washington U., 1967. Bar: D.C. 1960. Atty. Maritime Adminstrn., 1960-61; counsel House Info. Subcom., 1962-65; asst. counsel Senate Adminstrv. Practice Subcom., Washington, 1965-69; pvt. practice law, Washington, 1969—; mem. firm Kass & Skalet; prof. communication law Am. U.; pub. mem. Nat. Advt. Rev. Bd., 1971—; commr. D.C. Conf. on Uniform State Laws. Columnist: Washington Post; Contbr. articles to profl. jours. Chmn. consumer affairs subcom. Mayors Econ. Devel. Com., 1968-70; chmn. Ad Hoc Com. on Consumer Protection, 1965—. Served with USAF, 1961-62. Am. Polit. Sci. Assn. Congl. fellow, 1966. Mem. Am., Fed. bar assns., Am. Polit. Sci. Assn., Sigma Delta Chi. Office: Kass & Skalet 1528 18th St NW Washington DC 20036

KASS, EDWARD HAROLD, physician; b. N.Y.C., Dec. 20, 1917; s. Hyman A. and Ann (Selvansky) K.; m. Fae Golden, 1943 (dec. 1973); children: Robert, James, Nancy; m. Amalie Moses Hecht, 1975; stepchildren: Anne, Robert, Thomas, Jonathan, Peter. A.B. with high distinction, U. Ky., 1939, M.S., 1941; Ph.D., U. Wis., 1943; M.D., U. Calif., 1947; M.A. (hon.), Harvard U., 1958; D.Sc. (hon.), U. Ky., 1962. Diplomate: Am. Bd. Pathology, Am. Bd. Microbiology, Am. Bd. Preventive Medicine. Grad. asst., instr. bacteriology U. Ky., 1939-41; research asst., instr. U. Wis. Med. Sch., 1941-43, immunologist dept. phys. chemistry, 1944, grad. asst. dept. pathology, 1944-45; intern Boston City Hosp., 1947-48, resident, 1948-49; research fellow Thorndike Meml. Lab., 1949-52; sr. fellow in virus diseases NRC, 1949-52; instr. in medicine Harvard Med. Sch., 1951-52, assoc. in medicine, 1952-55, asst. prof. medicine, 1955-58, assoc. prof. bacteriology and immunology, 1958-62, assoc. prof. medicine, 1968-69; asst. physician Thorndike Meml. Lab., 1951-58; assoc. dir. bacteriology Mallory Inst. Pathology, 1957-63; dir. Channing lab., dept. med. microbiology Boston City Hosp., 1963-77; dir. Channing lab. and physician Peter Bent Brigham Hosp., Boston, 1977—; prof. medicine Harvard U., 1969-73, William Ellery Channing prof. medicine, 1973—; Macy Faculty Scholar Oxford U., 1974-75; vis. prof. Hebrew U.-Hadassah Med. Sch., Jerusalem, 1974; vis. prof. community medicine St. Thomas Hosp., London, 1982-83; vis. prof. med. microbiology Royal Free Hosp., London, 1982-83; lectr. London Sch. Hygiene and Tropical Medicine, London; cons. in field. Author 8 books; editor: Jour. Infectious Diseases, 1968-79, Revs. Infectious Diseases, 1979—; mem. editorial bds. profl. jours.; contbr. articles to med. jours. Recipient Public Service award NASA; spl. award Nat. Heart, Lung and Blood Inst.; Pioneer in Antibiotic Therapy award. Fellow Am. Coll. Epidemiology, ACP (Rosenthal award), Coll. Am. Pathologists, Am. Heart Assn., N.Y. Acad. Scis., Am. Coll. Epidemiology, Royal Soc. Medicine (London), Royal Coll. Physicians (London); fellow Infectious Diseases Soc. Am. (sec. 1962-68, pres. 1970, Bristol award 1980); mem. Internat. Epidemiol. Assn. (treas. 1977-81), Internat. Congress for Infectious Disease (pres. 1983—), Mass. Soc. Pathologists, New Eng. Soc. Pathologists, Soc. Exptl. Biology and Medicine, Am. Acad. Arts and Scis., AAAS, Am. Epidemiol. Soc., Am. Fedn. Clin. Research, Pan Am. Infectious Disease Soc., AMA, Am. Pub. Health Assn., Am. Soc. Clin. Investigation, Am. Soc. Microbiology, Soc. Epidemiol. Research, Am. Soc. Nephrology, Am. Thoracic Soc., Assn. Am. Physicians, Infectious Disease Soc. Mex. (hon.), Pan Am. Infectious Diseases Soc. (hon.), Phi Beta Kappa, Sigma Xi, Alpha Omega Alpha. Jewish. Club: Harvard (Boston, N.Y.C.). Home: Todd Pond Rd Lincoln MA 01773 Office: 180 Longwood Ave Boston MA 02115

KASS, IRVING, physician, educator; b. Topeka, Kans., July 15, 1917; s. David and Sophia R. (Sherr) K.; m. Edythe Blackberg, May 9, 1948; children—Mark David, Sharlene Rondi, Philip Alan. B.A., U. Kans., 1939, M.A. in Bacteriology, 1944, M.D., 1944. Diplomate: Am. Bd. Internal Medicine. Intern Michael Reese Hosp., Chgo., 1944, resident, 1948-49, Nat. Jewish Hosp., Denver, 1947-48, New Eng. Med. Center, Boston, 1950-51; staff physician VA Center, Wadworth, Kans., 1951-55; asso. med. dir. Nat. Jewish Hosp., Denver, 1955-64; asst. prof. medicine U. Colo. Sch. of Medicine, 1956-64; asso. med. dir. Will Rogers Hosp., Saranac Lake, N.Y., 1964-66, dir. clin. research, 1964-66; asso. prof. internal medicine U. Nebr. Coll. Medicine, Omaha, 1966-69, prof., 1969-73, Margaret and Richard Larson prof. medicine, 1973—; chmn. pulmonary medicine U. Nebr. Med. Center, 1966-80, dir. research pulmonary div., 1980—; mem. nat. adv. council Tb., Center for Disease Control, Atlanta, Ga., 1970-73; cons. WHO, 1976, 79, Pan Am. Sanitary Bur., 1977, 79; chmn. pulmonary seminar 3d and 4th World Congresses, Internat. Rehab. Med. Assn., 1978, 82. Contbg.; author text on lung disease, 1979; contbr. numerous articles on pulmonary disease to profl. jours., to chemotherapy of asthma. Leader Denver council Boy Scouts Am., 1955-64; chmn. winter carnival, Saranac Lake, N.Y., 1966. Served with M.C. U.S. Army, 1945-47. Named Admiral Great Navy of State Nebr., 1968. Fellow A.C.P., Am. Coll. Chest Physicians (gov. Nebr. 1972-82); mem. Am. Lung Assn. (nat. bd. rep. dir. 1969-81, chmn. com. disability criteria 1978-82), Am. Lung Assn. Nebr. (pres. 1977-78, dir. 1980—, exec. com. 1966-80), AMA (co-chmn. respiratory com. 1980—), Sigma Xi, Phi Beta Kappa, Alpha Omega Alpha, Delta Sigma Rho. Jewish. Clubs: Rotary, B'nai B'rith. Research in treatment and drug therapy of Tb. Developer comprehensive program in pulmonary rehab. Home: 709 S 111th St Omaha NE 68154 Office: U Nebr Med Center 42d and Dewey Ave Omaha NE 68105 *Achievement is governed by many factors including depth of inner drive, capacity for patience, meticulous attention to detail, intelligence to know where one's knowledge ends and ignorance begins, and sufficient control over mood swings so as not to become too depressed by failure or too elated by success.*

KASS, JULIUS, lawyer; b. N.Y.C., Sept. 25, 1905; s. Max and Sarah Bessie (Schneider) K.; m. Eleanor L. Levine, June 18, 1931; children—Stephen L., Emily Kass Pedinielli. B.A., Rutgers U., 1926, LL.B., 1929. Bar: N.J. bar 1929, N.Y. bar 1946. Tchr., Perth Amboy, N.J., 1926-32, pvt. practice, Perth Amboy, 1929-42; partner firm Bandler & Kass, N.Y.C., 1947-77; chmn. Pan Am. Aluminum Corp., Miami, Fla., 1956—; counsel labor relations Mayor N.Y.C., 1946-48. Served to lt. col. USAAF, 1942-45. Mem. Am., N.Y. State bar assns., Assn. Bar City N.Y. Jewish. Address: 10205 Collins Ave Bal Harbour FL 33154

KASS, LEON RICHARD, educator; b. Chgo., Feb. 12, 1939; s. Samuel and Anna (Shoichet) K.; m. Amy Judith Apfel, June 22, 1961; children—Sarah, Miriam. B.S., U. Chgo., 1958, M.D., 1962; Ph.D. in Biochemistry, Harvard U., 1967. Intern Beth Israel Hosp., Boston, 1962-63; staff asso. Lab. Molecular Biology, Nat. Inst. Arthritis and Metabolic Diseases, NIH, Bethesda, Md., 1967-69, staff fellow, 1969-70, sr. staff fellow, 1970; exec. sec. com. on life scis. and social policy NRC-Nat. Acad. Scis., Washington, 1970-72; tutor St. John's Coll., Annapolis, Md., 1972-76; Joseph P. Kennedy Sr. research prof. in bioethics Kennedy Inst., Georgetown U., 1974-76; Henry R. Luce prof. liberal arts of human biology in coll. U. Chgo., 1976—, also mem. com. on social thought; founding fellow, bd. dirs. Inst. of Society, Ethics and Life Scis., 1969—. Contbr. articles to profl. jours. Served with USPHS, 1967-69. NIH postdoctoral fellow, 1963-67; John Simon Guggenheim Meml. Found. fellow, 1972-73; Nat. Endowment for Humanities grantee, 1973-74. Mem. AAAS, Phi Beta Kappa, Alpha Omega Alpha. Jewish. Home: 5811 S Dorchester Chicago IL 60637 Office: 1116 E 59th St Chicago IL 60637

KASSANDER, ARNO RICHARD, JR., research adminstrator; b. Carbondale, Pa., Sept. 10, 1920; s. Arno Richard and Elsa (Hausstein) K.; m. Sara Witmer Nollen, May 15, 1943; 1 dau., Helen Ann. B.A., Amherst Coll., 1941, Sc.D. (hon.), 1971; M.S., Okla. U., 1943; Ph.D., Ia. State U., 1950. Asst. geologist Tex. Co., 1941; research asst. Magnolia Petroleum Co., 1942; asst. prof. Ia. State U., 1950-54; asso. dir. Inst. Atmospheric Physics, U. Ariz., Tucson, 1954-56, dir., 1956-73, Water Resources Research Center, Tucson, 1965-72, v.p. for research, 1972-82; dir. div. indsl. cooperation U. Ariz. Found., 1982—; dir. Burr Brown Research Corp., 1st Interstate Bank Ariz.; mem. Pres.'s Sci. Adv. Com. Panel on Environment, 1969-72, Nat. Adv. Com. on Oceans and Atmosphere, 1976-77. Bd. dirs. Tucson Airport Authority. Served with AUS, 1943-46. Mem. AAAS, Ariz. Acad. Sci., Am. Meteorol. Soc., Sigma Xi, Theta Delta Chi. Club: Rotarian. Home: 3341 E 4th St Tucson AZ 85716

KASSAR, RAYMOND E., electronic games company executive; b. N.Y.C., Jan. 2, 1928; s. Edward and Elizabeth A. K. B.A., Brown U., 1948; M.B.A., Harvard U., 1952. With Burlington Industries, 1948-72, pres. and v.p. several divs., 1955-70, v.p. and exec. v.p., 1970-74; pres. R.E. Kassar Corp., 1974-78; chmn., chief exec. officer Atari, Inc. div. Warner Communications, Inc., Sunnyvale, Calif., 1978—. Bd. dirs. Am. Cancer Soc., 1975—, San Francisco Symphony, San Francisco Ballet, San Francisco Opera, Martha Graham Dance Co. Served with USAF, 1952-53. Roman Catholic. Office: 1265 Borregas Ave Sunnyvale CA 94086

KASSEBAUM, DONALD GENE, health sciences university administrator; b. Portland, Oreg., May 15, 1931; s. Arnold F. and

Isabel (Booth) K. B.A., Reed Coll., 1952; M.D., U. Oreg., 1956. Intern, resident, fellow in medicine and cardiology U. Oreg. Med. Sch., Portland, 1956-59; sr. research fellow div. cardiology U. Utah Coll. Medicine, Salt Lake City, 1960-62; from asst. prof. to prof. medicine U. Oreg. Med. Sch., Portland, 1962-70; chief medicine Oreg. Health Sci. U. Hosp., Portland, 1970-76, dir., 1975—; bd. dirs., exec. com. Northwest Oreg. Health Systems Agy., 1976—. Contbr. articles to profl. jours. Mem. emergency med. services adv. council State of Oreg., 1975-77; mem. Comprehensive Health Planning Assn., Portland, 1975-76. Fellow ACP; mem. Soc. for Critical Care Medicine, Western Soc. for Clin. Research, Am. Fedn. Clin. Research, Council of Teachnig Hosps., Assn. Am. Med. Colls., Alpha Omega Alpha. Republican. Presbyterian. Home: 4740 SW Fairhaven Dr Portland OR 97221 Office: Oreg Health Scis U 3181 SW Sam Jackson Park Rd Portland OR 97201

KASSEBAUM, NANCY LANDON, U.S. Senator; b. July 29, 1932; d. Alfred M. and Theo (Landon); m. Philip Kassebaum, 1955 (div. 1979); children: John Philip, Linda Josephine, Richard Landon, William Alfred. B.A. in Polit. Sci, U. Kans., 1952; M.Diplomatic History, U. Mich., 1956. Mem. Kans. Govtl. Ethics Commn., Kans. Com. for Humanities, Maize (Kans.) Sch. Bd.; mem. Washington staff Sen. James B. Pearson of Kans., 1975-76; v.p. KFH-KBRA-FM stas.; mem. U.S. Senate from Kans., 1979—, mem. Fgn. Relations Com., Commerce, Sci. and Transp. Com., Budget Com., Spl. Com. on Aging. Recipient Matrix award Women in Communications. Republican. Episcopalian. Office: 302 Russell Senate Office Bldg Washington DC 20510

KASSEL, VIRGINIA WELTMER, TV producer; b. Omaha; d. Tyler and Inez (Willard) Weltmer. B.A., Bryn Mawr Coll. Producer Sta. WGBH-TV, Boston, 1959-63; producer NET, N.Y.C., 1964-68, coordinator nat. programs, 1968-70; mgr. spl. projects, 1976-79, exec. producer humanities programs, 1979-81; sr. producer CBS Cable, N.Y.C., 1981-83; dir. devel. and prodn. East Coast Primetime Entertainment, Inc., 1983—. Creator, producer: The Adams Chronicles, Sta. WNET, N.Y.C., 1970-76; Contbr. articles to profl. publs. Recipient George Foster Peabody award, 1977, Ohio State award, 1977; Nat. Assn. Ednl. Broadcasters Spl. Achievement award, 1977. Mem. Nat. Acad. TV Arts and Sci. (recipient 4 awards), Writers Guild Am. Home: 4 E 89th St New York NY 10028 Office: Primetime Entertainment Inc 485 Madison Ave New York NY 10022

KASSING, DAVID BURTON, research co. exec.; b. Erie, Pa., July 1, 1933; s. Burton Leslie and Kathleen (Gruber) K.; children—Kim Leslie, Katherine Lisa, Kenneth Burton, Susan. B.A. in Liberal Arts, Beloit Coll., 1955; M.B.A. in Econs, Cornell U., 1957, postgrad., U. Chgo., 1957-60. Asst. prof. bus. adminstrn. Clarkson Coll. of Tech., 1961-62; staff anaylst Center for Naval Analyses, Arlington, Va., 1962-65; dir. Inst. of Naval Studies, 1968-71; exec. v.p. Center for Naval Analyses, 1972-73, pres., 1973—; dir. Naval Forces Div., office asst. sec. defense, systems analysis, 1966-68; dir. research President's Comm. on All-Vol. Armed Force, 1969-70. Contbr. article to publ. in field. Fellow Walgreen Found. for Study of Am. Instns., 1959-60; Ford Found. fellow, 1957-59. Mem. Am. Econ. Assn., Phi Kappa Phi, Beta Gamma Sigma. Home: 3516 Sterling Ave Alexandria VA 22304 Office: 2000 N Beauregard St Alexandria VA 22209

KASSMAN, HERBERT SEYMOUR, lawyer, management consultant; b. Binghamton, N.Y., June 13, 1924; s. Maurice Pincus and Clara (Wolkenstein) K.; m. Deborah Gordon Newman, Aug. 22, 1948; 1 dau., Judith Clare. A.B., Harvard U., 1947, LL.B., 1953. Bar: Mass. 1953. Engr., writer, editor Jackson & Moreland (cons. engrs.), Boston, 1948-50; with Polaroid Corp., Cambridge, Mass., 1953-72, asst. sec., 1961-65, sec., 1965-72; dir. Greater Boston Elderly Legal Services, 1979-82; mem. Chelsea adv. bd. Govt. Land Bank, 1975—. Bd. dirs., trustee Chorus Pro Musica, Boston, 1955—; trustee Met. Cultural Alliance, 1969—, Ford Hall Forum, 1978—; bd. dirs. Beneficent Soc. of New Eng. Conservatory of Music, 1976—, Concerned Boston Citizens for Elder Affairs, 1976—. Served to lt. (j.g.) USNR, 1943-46. Mem. ABA, Mass. Bar Assn., Boston Bar Assn. (chmn. pvt. internat. law com. 1977-81, co-chmn. internat. law sect. 1981—), Boston Patent Law Assn. Home: 5 Stonewall Rd Lexington MA 02173 Office: 33 Broad St Boston MA 02109

KASSOFF, EDWIN, state justice; b. Bklyn., July 15, 1924; s. Leo and Sarah (Steinberg) K.; m. Phyllis Brafman, Nov. 29, 1949; children—Mitchell Jay, Robert Stephen. B.B.A., CCNY, 1947; J.D., Bklyn. Law Sch., 1953; grad., U. Nev. Nat. Coll. State Judiciary, 1972. Bar: N.Y. State bar 1953, U.S. Supreme Ct. bar 1963. Practice law, N.Y.C., 1953-71; judge Civil Ct. N.Y.C., Queens, 1971-73; justice Supreme Ct. State N.Y., Jamaica, 1974—; instr. law Queens Coll., 1956-63; vis. lectr. law Columbia U., 1966-67; asst. prof. Pace U., 1964-70, asso. prof., 1970-74, prof., 1974—; co-counsel legis. com. N.Y. State Constl. Conv., 1967; research counsel majority party N.Y. State Assembly, 1968; asst. counsel Joint Legis. Com. Mass Transp., 1969; faculty adviser U. Nev. Nat. Coll. State Judiciary, 1973-74, mem. faculty, 1975—; Alt. del. Democratic Nat. Conv., 1968; sec. jud. conv. Queens County Dem. Party, 1969-71; chmn. Dem. Law Com. Queens County, 1969-71; Mem. Temp. State Commn. to Study Causes of Campus Unrest, 1970. Author: Business Law Text, 1964, Instructor's Manual for Business Law Text, 1964, Test Manual for Business Law Courses, 1964, Sales and Bailment Text, 1973, American Commercial Law Text, 1975, Advanced American Commercial Law Text, 1976. Served to lt. inf. AUS, 1943-46; ETO. Hon. Ky. col. Mem. Am. Bus. Law Assn. (pres. 1972), N.E. Regional Bus. Law Assn. (pres. 1964), Assn. Justices N.Y. State Supreme Ct. (sec. 1978, treas. 1979, 2d v.p. 1980, 1st v.p. 1981), Nat. Conf. State Trial Judges (del. N.Y. State 1977—, pres., mem. exec. com. 1983), Bd. Justices of State of N.Y. (chmn. publ. com., Bench Book com.), Queens County Bar Assn., Am. Bar Assn. (chmn. edn. com. 1979—), N.Y. State Bar Assn. (chmn. com. jud. conduct), Nat. Conf. State Tax Judges (treas.). Office: Supreme Ct State of NY 88-11 Sutphin Blvd Jamaica NY 11435

KASSON, JAMES MATTHEWS, electronics executive; b. Muncie, Ind., Mar. 19, 1943; s. Robert Edwin and Mary Louise K.; m. Betty Roseman, Aug. 14, 1977. B.S.E.E., Stanford U., 1964; M.S.E.E., U. Ill., 1965. Engring. mgr. Santa Rita Tech., Santa Clara, Calif., 1963-69; engring. sect. mgr. Hewlett-Packard, Palo Alto, Calif., 1969-73; v.p. tech. and advanced devel. ROLM Corp., Santa Clara, 1973—. Patentee in field. Mem. IEEE (citation for contbn. 1981). Home: 1080 Deanne Dr Menlo Park CA 94025 Office: ROLM Corp 4900 Old Ironsides Dr Santa Clara CA 95050

KAST, FREMONT ELLSWORTH, educator; b. Modesto, Calif., Jan. 27, 1926; s. Fremont Horace and Arlette Evelyn (Bradley) K.; m. Phyllis Jean Hames, June 20, 1948; children—Karen Ann, Cheryl Jean. B.A., San Jose State U., 1946; M.B.A., Stanford U., 1949; Ph.D., U. Wash., 1956. Instr. Syracuse (N.Y.) U., 1949-51; asst. prof. Univ. Wash., Seattle, 1951-56, asso. prof., 1957-61, prof. mgmt., 1961—, asso. dean, 1979—; Fulbright prof. Netherlands Sch. Econs., 1963; vis. prof. UCLA, 1973; cons. Boeing, Seattle, 1960-65, Air Force Inst. Tech., 1972-74, Sci. Research Assos., Palo Alto, Calif., 1972—. Author: (with Johnson and Rosensweig) Technology and Management, 1963, The Theory and Management of Systems, 3d edit, 1973, Contingency Views of Organization and Management, 1973, Organization and Management, 3d edit, 1979. Served to lt. (j.g.) USNR, 1944-47. Mem. Nat. Acad. Mgmt. (pres. 1976-77), Am. Sociol. Assn., AAUP, Am. Acad. Polit. and Social Sci. Home: 10749 Lakeside Ave NE Seattle WA 98125 Office: Grad Sch of Bus Adminstrn Univ of Washington Seattle WA 98195

KASTELIC, ROBERT FRANK, bank holding company executive; b. Granite City, Ill., July 17, 1934; s. Joseph and Anna Marie (Kries) K.; m. Patricia Ann Dalton, Apr. 8, 1961; children: Michael J., Constance A., Robert J., Kirsten S. B.S. in Acctg., U. Ill., 1956. Sr. acct. Price Waterhouse & Co. (C.P.A.s), St. Louis, 1956-63; v.p., comptroller Merc. Bancorp., St. Louis, 1963-72; exec. v.p., chief fin. officer Equimark Corp. and Equibank, Pitts., 1972-83, vice-chmn. bd., 1983—; pres., dir. Nottingham Corp., Pitts.; dir. Community Service Life Ins. Co., Equimark Comml. Fin. Co. Mem. rev. com. United Way, Pitts., 1977-78; chmn. Equimark Charitable Found., Pitts.; bd. dirs. St. Francis Hosp., Civic Light Opera. Served with U.S. Army, 1956-58. Mem. Am. Inst. C.P.A.s, Am. Mgmt. Assn., Am. Soc. Corp. Secs., Mo., Pa. insts. C.P.A.s, Bank Adminstrn. Inst., Fin. Execs. Inst., Nat. Investor Relations Inst., Health and Welfare Planning Assn. (dir.), Newcomen Soc. N.Am. Club: Duquesne. Home: 825 Fox Chapel Rd Pittsburgh PA 15238 Office: 2 Oliver Plaza Pittsburgh PA 15222

KASTEN, KARL ALBERT, artist, emeritus educator; b. San Francisco, Mar. 5, 1916; s. Ferdin and Barbara Anne K.; m. Georgette Gautier, Mar. 29, 1958; children: Ross, Lee, Beatrix, Cho-An. M.A., U. Calif., 1939; postgrad., U. Iowa, 1949; student, Hans Hofmann Sch. Fine Arts, 1951. Instr. Calif. Sch. Fine Arts, 1941, U. Mich., 1946-47; asst. prof. art San Francisco State U., 1947-50; prof. U. Calif., Berkeley, 1950—. Bibliography appears in: Etching (Edmondson), 1973, Assemblage and Collage (Meilach and Ten Hoor), 1973, Modern Woodcut Techniques (Kuraski), 1977; group shows include, San Francisco Mus. Art, 1939, Chgo. Art Inst., 1946, Whitney Mus., 1952, Sao Paolo Internat. Biennials, 1955, 61, Achenbach Found., 1976, World Print III Travelling Exhbn., 1980-83. Served to capt. U.S. Army, 1942-46. Decorated 4 battle stars; fellow Creative Arts Inst., 1964, 71; Tamarind Lithography Workshop, 1968, Regents Humanities, 1977. Mem. Calif. Soc. Printmakers, Univ. Art Mus. Council. Democrat. Clubs: Univ. Faculty, Univ. Arts. Home: 1884 San Lorenzo Ave Berkeley CA 94707 Office: U Calif Berkeley CA 94720

KASTEN, PAUL RUDOLPH, nuclear engr.; b. Jackson, Mo., Dec. 10, 1923; s. Arthur John and Hattie L. (Krueger) K.; m. Eileen Alma Kiehne, Dec. 28, 1947; children: Susan (Mrs. Robert M. Goebbert), Kim Patrick, Jennifer. B.S. in Chem. Engring, U. Mo. at Rolla, 1944, M.S., 1947; Ph.D. in Chem. Engring, U. Minn., 1950. Staff mem. Oak Ridge Nat. Lab., 1950—, dir. gas-cooled reactor and thorium utilization programs, 1970-78, dir. HTGR and GCFR programs, 1978—; guest dir. Inst. Reactor Devel., Nuclear Research Center, Jülich, W. Germany, 1963-64; faculty U. Tenn., Knoxville, 1953—, prof. nuclear engring., 1965—. Fellow A.A.A.S., N.Y. Acad. Scis.; mem. Nat. Soc. Profl. Engrs., Am. Nuclear Soc., Sigma Xi, Tau Beta Pi, Phi Lambda Upsilon. Lutheran. Research and publ. in role of thorium in power reactor devel. and high temperature gas-cooled reactors. Home: 341 Louisiana Ave Oak Ridge TN 37830 Office: Oak Ridge Nat Lab PO Box X Oak Ridge TN 37830

KASTEN, ROBERT W., JR., U.S. senator; b. Milw., June 19, 1942; s. Robert W. and Mary (Ogden) K. B.A., U. Ariz., 1964; M.B.A., Columbia U., 1966. With Genesco, Inc., Nashville, 1966-68; dir., v.p. Gilbert Shoe Co., Thiensville, Wis., 1968-75; mem. Wis. Senate, Madison, 1972-75, mem. joint fin. com., 1973-75, chmn. joint survey com. on tax exemptions, 1973-75; mem. 94th-95th congresses from 9th Wis. Dist., U.S. Senate, 1981—. Alt. del. Republican Nat. Conv., 1972, del., 1976; mem. Milw. Council on Alcoholism, Milw. Soc. for Prevention of Blindness; regional dir. Milw. Coalition for Clean Water. Served to 1st lt. USAF, 1967-72. Named Jaycee of Yr., 1972, Legis. Conservationist of Yr. Nat. Wildlife Fedn., 1973. Mem. Nat. Audubon Soc., Sigma Nu, Alpha Kappa Psi. Office: US Senate Room 110 Hart Senate Office Bldg Washington DC 20510 *

KASTEN, STANLEY HARVEY, sports association executive; b. Lakewood, N.J., Feb. 1, 1952; s. Nathan and Sylvia (Saltztreger) K.; m. Helen Weisz, Aug. 14, 1977; children: Alana Marie, Corey Richard. A.B., NYU, 1973; J.D., Columbia U., 1976. Exec. asst. Turner Broadcasting Co., Atlanta, 1976-77; in-house counsel Atlanta Braves, 1976-77; v.p., asst. gen. mgr. Atlanta Hawks, 1978-79, v.p., gen. mgr., 1980—, dir., 1980—; bd. govs. Nat. Basketball Assn., N.Y.C., 1978—. Bd. dirs. Police Athletic League, Atlanta, 1980-81. Mem. ABA, N.J. Bar Assn. Lodge: B'nai Brith Gate City (trustee 1982—). Office: Atlanta Hawks The Omni 100 Techwood Dr NW Atlanta GA 30303

KASTENMEIER, ROBERT WILLIAM, congressman; b. Beaver Dam, Wis., Jan. 24, 1924; s. Leo Henry and Lucille (Powers) K.; m. Dorothy Chambers, June 27, 1952; children: William, Andrew, Edward. LL.B., U. Wis., 1952. Bar: Wis. bar 1952. Dir. br. office claims service War Dept., P.I., 1946-48; practice in, Watertown, until 1959, justice of the peace, 1955-58; mem. 86th-98th congresses from 2d Dist. Wis.; mem. com. on judiciary, chmn. subcom. house jud. com., mem. com. on interior and insular affairs. Served from pvt. to 1st lt., inf. AUS, 1943-46. Home: 745 Pony Ln Sun Prairie WI Office: 119 Monona Ave Suite 505 Madison WI 53703 also 2232 Rayburn House Office Bldg Washington DC 20515 *

KASTER, BARBARA JEANNE, filmmaker; b. El Paso, Tex., June 27, 1934; d. James Jay and Louize (Beeman) K.; 1 dau., Kimberly Chris. A.B., Tex. Western Coll., 1957; M.A., U. Tex., 1967, Ph.D., 1970. Tchr. El Paso Pub. Schs., 1957-66; asst. prof. U. South Fla., 1967; teaching asst. Ind. U., 1968, U. Tex., 1968-70; asst. prof. Fla. Atlantic U., 1970-73; assoc. prof. communication Bowdoin Coll., Brunswick, Maine, 1973-75, Harrison King McCann prof., 1975—; pres. Dunster Films, Brunswick, 1970—; cons. audio visual dept. Maine Med. Center, 1976—; cons. Media Design, Inc., Portland, Maine, 1976—. Contbr. articles to profl. jours. and text books.; films include Making Policy, Not Coffee, 1972, Flo!, 1975, Green Seas, White Ice, 1978, Poggio Civitate, 1979, The Treasure, 1981, To Serve the Common Good, 1983. Bd. dirs. El Paso chpt. LWV, 1966; v.p. Palm Beach (Fla.) County chpt. NOW, 1972; mem. Palm Beach County Democratic Com., 1973. Grantee Mell Found., 1974; Ford Found., 1976. Mem. Nat., So., Eastern speech communication assns., Assn. Am. Film Inst. Democrat. Roman Catholic. Home: RFD 2 Box 2112 Brunswick ME 04011 Office: Bowdoin Coll Brunswick ME 04011

KASTIN, ABBA JEREMIAH, physician, endocrinologist; b. Cleve., Dec. 24, 1934; s. Isadore I. and Ruth (Urdang) K. A.B., Harvard U., 1956, M.D., 1960; hon. Dr., U. Nacional Federico Villerarreal, Lima, Peru, 1980. Intern Vanderbilt U. Hosp., Nashville, 1960-61, resident in gen. medicine, 1961-62; clin. assoc. USPHS, NIH, 1962-64; clin. investigator VA Hosp., New Orleans, 1965-68; chief endocrinology sect. VA Med. Ctr., 1968—; prof. dept. medicine Tulane U. Sch. Medicine, New Orleans, 1974—; mem. med. adv. bd. Nat. Pituitary Agy., 1974-77; cons. FDA, 1979. Editor-in-chief: Peptides, 1980—; mem. editorial bd.: Jour. Clin. Endocrinology and Metabolism, Brain Research Bull., Neurosci. and Biobehavioral Rev.; contbr. numerous articles to profl. jours. Mem. Civic Orch. of New Orleans, 1965—; trustee Jewish Fedn. Greater New Orleans, 1982—. Recipient Edward T. Tyler Fertility award Internat. Fertility Soc., 1975, Eagle award Fed. Bus. Assn., 1975, Copernicus medal Med. Facualty Krakow, Poland, 1979, William S. Middletown award VA, 1982. Mem. Endocrine Soc., Am. Physiol. Soc., Soc. Exptl. Biol. Medicine, Soc. Neurosci., Internat. Soc. Psychoneuroendocrinology, Internat. Soc. Neuroendocrinology, Internat. Pigment Cell Soc.; hon. mem. La Soc. de Chimie, Chilean Soc. Endocrinology; hon.mem. Phillippine Soc. Endocrinology and Metabolism; hon. mem. Peruvian Ob-Gyn Soc.; hon.mem. Peruvian Endocrine Soc.; hon. mem. Polish Endocrine Soc. Jewish. Home: 4400 Morales St Metairie LA 70002 Office: Endocrinology Sect VA Med Center 1601 Perdido St New Orleans LA 70146

KASTLER, BERNARD ZANE, natural gas company executive; b. Billings, Mont., Oct. 30, 1920; s. B.Z. and Elsie (Grossman) K.; m. Donna Irene Endicott, July 24, 1948; children: Lynn, Kerry Sue. Student, U. Colo., 1940-41; LL.B. summa cum laude, U. Utah, 1949. Bar: Utah 1949, Mont. 1948, U.S. Supreme Ct., also fed. cts. Practice law, Salt Lake City, 1949-52; atty. Mountain Fueld Supply Co., Salt Lake City, 1952—, sec., asst. treas., gen. counsel, 1958-68, v.p. fin., treas., 1968-72, pres., chief adminstrv. officer, 1972-74, 76-82, chief exec. officer, 1974-82, chmn. bd., 1976—, also dir.; chmn. bd. Entrada Industries Inc., Mountain Fuel Resources, Inc., Wexpro Co., Celsius Energy Co., Interstate Brick Co., Interstate Land Corp.; dir. Albertson's, Inc., Bonneville Internat. Corp., Intermountain Health Care, Inc., 1st Security Corp.; mem., chmn. Rocky Mountain regional council Conf. Bd.; mem. Utah Ho. of Reps., 1963-66. Contbr. articles to profl. jours. Bd. dirs. Mountain States Legal Found.; moderator Nat. Assn. Congl. Christian Chs., 1955; trustee Westminster Coll.; co-chmn. NCCJ; mem. Latter-day Saints Hosp.-Deseret Found.; trustee Youth Tobacco Adv. Council; mem. exec. adv. com. Jr. Achievement Greater Salt Lake. Served with USNR, World War II. Mem. ABA, Utah Bar Assn., Salt Lake County Bar Assn., Mont. Bar Assn., Fed. Power Bar Assn., Ind. Natural Gas Assn., Salt Lake City C. of C. (gov. 1967-78, v.p. govt. and pub. affairs council 1968—, pres. 1977-78), U. Utah Alumni Assn., Pacific Coast Gas Assn. (chmn. 1980), Am. Gas Assn. (past dir.), Rocky Mountain Oil and Gas Assn. (past dir. and mem. operating and exec. coms.), Zion Natural History Assn. (dir.), Hon. Cols. Corp., Order of Coif, Phi Kappa Phi, Phi Delta Phi. Congregationalist (former deacon and trustee). Lodges: Masons; Kiwanis. Office: Mountain Fuel Supply Co 180 East First South Salt Lake City UT 84139 also: PO Box 11368 Salt Lake City UT 84139

KASTOR, FRANK SULLIVAN, English educator; b. Evanston, Ill., Aug. 19, 1933; s. Herman Walker and Rebecca (Sullivan) K.; m. Sue Schurman (div. 1962); m. Sue Dirksen, Dec. 27, 1964 (div. 1974); m. Tina Bennett, Oct. 28, 1979; children: Jeffrey, Mark, Harlan, Kristina. B.A., U. Ill., 1955, M.A., 1956; Ph.D., U. Calif., Berkeley, 1963. Teaching asst. U. Ill., 1955-56, U. Calif., Berkeley, 1960-63; asst. prof. English U. So. Calif., 1964-66, 67-68; assoc. prof. English No. Ill. U., 1968-69; prof. English, Wichita State U., 1969—, chmn. dept., 1969-75. Contbr. to: The Milton Ency; author books, articles, revs., TV documentaries. Served with USAF, 1956-59. Research grantee U. Calif. at Berkeley, 1962, U. So. Calif., 1964, No. Ill. U., 1969, Wichita State U., 1970; Fulbright lectr., Spain, 1966-67; Kans. Com. for Humanities grantee, 1973, 74; recipient Nat. Endowment Humanities award, 1971. Mem. MLA, Philol. Assn. Pacific Coast (sec. chmn. 1969, 70, 72), Milton Soc. Am., Renaissance Soc. Am., Conf. on Christianity and Lit., AAUP, Phi Kappa Phi.

KASTOR, JOHN ALFRED, cardiologist, educator; b. N.Y.C., Sept. 15, 1931; s. Alfred Bernard and Ellen Voigt Bentley; m. Mae Belle Eisenberg, July 4, 1954; children: Elizabeth Mae, Anne Sarah, Peter John. B.A., U. Pa., 1953; M.D., N.Y. U., 1962. With NBC, N.Y.C., 1956-58; intern, asst. resident in medicine Bellevue Hosp., N.Y.C., 1962-64; chief resident physician N.Y. U. Hosp., N.Y.C., 1964-65; clin. and research fellow in medicine Mass. Gen. Hosp., Boston, 1965-68, clin. asst. and asst. in medicine, 1968-69; instr. in medicine Harvard Med. Sch., 1968-69; dir. med. intensive care unit Hosp. U. Pa., Phila., 1969-72, assoc. chief cardiovascular sect., 1972-77, chief, 1977-81; physician-in-chief U. Md. Hosp., 1984—; prof. medicine U. Pa. Sch. Medicine, Phila., 1976-83; Theodore E. Woodward prof. medicine U. Md. Sch. Medicine, 1984—. Editor: Internat. Jour. Cardiology; Contbr. numerous articles on cardiac electrophysiology and gen. cardiology to med. jour. Served with U.S. Army, 1953-55. Fellow Am. Coll. Cardiology, A.C.P., Council Clin. Cardiology Am. Heart Assn., Coll. Physicians Phila.; mem. Am. Fedn. Clin. Research, Am. Heart Assn. (gov. Southeastern Pa. chpt. 1975-81), Assn. Univ. Cardiologists, Assn. Profs. Medicine, Venezuelan Soc. Internal Medicine, Paul Dudley White Soc. (dir. 1977—), Alpha Omega Alpha. Home: 1001 Westview St Philadelphia PA 19119 Office: Univ of Md Hosp 22 S Greene St Baltimore MD 21201

KATARINCIC, JOSEPH ANTHONY, lawyer; b. Pitts., July 20, 1931; s. Joseph Julius and Mary Ann (Shutlic) K.; (m), July 29, 1961; m. Jean Rosemary Donaghue, July 29, 1961; children—Julia, Joseph Anthony, James. B.A. cum laude, Duquesne U., 1953; M.A., U. Pitts., 1958, LL.B., 1960. Bar: Pa. bar 1961, U.S. Supreme Ct. bar 1975. Law clk. to judge U.S. Ct. Appeals 3d Circuit, 1960-62; asso. firm Kirkpatrick, Lockhart, Johnson & Hutchison, Pitts., 1962-67, partner, 1967—; adj. prof. law Duquesne U., 1961-70; mem. Jud. Conf. of U.S. Ct. Appeals 3d Circuit. Mem. task force Kane Meml. Hosp., 1975; bd. dirs. Pontifical Assn. of Holy Childhood, Pitts., Fox Chapel Country Day Sch., Duquesne U.; bd. govs. U. Pitts. Sch. Law. Served to 1st lt. USAF, 1954-57. Named One of 100 Outstanding Grads. Duquesne U., 1978. Mem. Am. Law Inst., Acad. Trial Lawyers of Allegheny County, Am. Bar Assn., Allegheny County Bar Assn. Roman Catholic. Clubs: Pitts. Field, Duquesne. Home: 9 Old Timber Trail Pittsburgh PA 15238 Office: 1500 Oliver Bldg Pittsburgh PA 15222

KATAYAMA, ARTHUR SHOJI, lawyer; b. Los Angeles, June 10, 1927; s. Asaji and Teru (Mori) K.; m. Mie Nakamura, Dec. 20, 1976. A.B., Morningside Coll., 1951; LL.B., Pacific Coast U., 1956. Bar: Calif. bar 1959. With intelligence div. U.S. Treasury Dept., Los Angeles, 1953-58; with N. Am. Aviation, Los Angeles, 1958-59; practiced in, Los Angeles, 1959-60; mem. firm Mori & Katayama, Los Angeles, 1960-77; firm Nagata, Masuda & Katayama, 1980-83, Katayama & Nagata, 1983—; Mem. adv. bd. Sumitomo Bank of Calif., Los Angeles.; Mem. Cal. Democratic State Central Com., 1958-60. Served with AUS, 1945-47. Mem. Am., Los Angeles County, Orange County bar assns. Club: Mesa Verde/Costa Mesa Country. Home: 56 Ocean Vista Newport Beach CA 92660 Office: 333 S Grand Ave Suite 3700 Los Angeles CA 90071-1599

KATAYAMA, ROBET NOBUICHI, lawyer; b. Honolulu, Oct. 11, 1924; s. Sanji and Yuki (Kiriu) K.; m. Sachie Uyeno, June 8, 1974; children: Alyce A. Katayama Jenkins, Robert Nobuichi, Kent J. B.A., U. Hawaii, 1950; J.D., Yale U., 1955; LL.M., George Washington U., 1967; grad., Indsl. Coll. Armed Forces, 1971. Bar: Calif. 1956, Ill. 1973. Gen. counsel Overseas Mdse. Inspection Co., San Francisco, 1956-58; commd. 1st lt. JAGD U.S. Army, 1958, advanced through grades to col., 1973, ret., 1973; gen. counsel Army Contract Adjustment Bd., Washington, 1964-70; prof. law JAG Sch. U.Va., 1968-70; assoc., then ptnr. Baker & McKenzie, Chgo. and Tokyo, 1973-77, ptnr., 1978—; dir. SEH Am. Inc., Vancouver, Wash., SP Am., Inc., San Jose, Calif., Nikko Trading Corp., San Francisco. Named Real Dean U. Hawaii, Honolulu, 1950; Community Chest scholar Honolulu Community Chest, 1950. Mem. ABA, Internat. Lawyers

Assn., Japanese C. of C. of San Francisco (dir. 1979), Calif. Council Internat. Trade, Oakland, West Coast Coalition Internat. Investment, Am. Electronics Assn., Japanese Am. Soc. Legal Studies, Ret. Officers Assn. Democrat. Buddhist. Clubs: San Francisco Stock Exchange, Press of San Francisco. Lodge: Go for Broke Inc. (legal officer). Office: Baker & McKenzie Suite 2600 101 California St San Francisco CA 94111

KATCHADOURIAN, HERANT ARAM, university official and dean, psychiatrist; b. Iskenderun, Turkey, Jan. 23, 1933; came to U.S., 1958, naturalized, 1972; s. Aram Adour and Efronia (Nazarian) K.; m. Stina Lindfors, Aug. 30, 1964; children—Nina, Kai. B.A., Am. U., Beirut, 1954, M.D., 1958; postgrad., U. Rochester, 1958-61. Intern Am. U. Hosp., Beirut, 1958; resident Strong Meml. Hosp., Rochester, N.Y., 1958-61; univ. ombudsman Stanford U., 1969-70, univ. fellow, 1970-73, prof. psychiatry and behavioral scis., 1976—, vice provost, 1976—, dean undergrad. studies, 1976—; Mem. corp. vis. com. M.I.T.; trustee Haigazian Coll. Author: (with D. Lunde) Fundamentals of Human Sexuality, 1975, The Biology of Adolescence, 1977; editor: Human Sexuality: A Comparative and Developmental Perspective, 1979. Mem. Alpha Omega Alpha. Home: 956 Mears Ct Stanford CA 94305 Office: Bldg 1 Room 2B Stanford U Stanford CA 94305

KATEB, GEORGE ANTHONY, educator; b. Bklyn., Feb. 27, 1931; s. Anthony Francis and Victoria Anna (Mesnooh) K. A.B., Columbia U., 1952, A.M., 1953, Ph.D., 1960. Mem. faculty Amherst Coll., 1957, prof., 1967—, Kenan prof. polit. sci., 1974-78, Joseph P. Eastman prof. polit. sci., 1980—; vis. lectr. Mt. Holyoke Coll., 1958, Yale U., 1973; cons. Author: Utopia and Its Enemies, 2d edit, 1972, Political Theory: Its Nature and Uses, 1968, Utopia, 1971, Hannah Arendt: Politics, Conscience, Evil, 1983; editorial bd.: Mass. Rev, 1961-70, Polit. Theory, 1972—, Am. Polit. Sci. Rev, 1976—, Jour. History Ideas, 1976-81, Jour. Utopian Studies, 1977-80, Raritan, 1980—; cons. editor: Polit. Theory, 1983—. Nat. Endowment Humanities. Univ. fellow Columbia U., 1953-54; fellow Soc. Fellows, Harvard U., 1954-57; Guggenheim fellow, 1971-72. Mem. Am. Polit. Sci. Assn., New Eng. Polit. Sci. Assn. (exec. com. 1965-66, pres. 1978-79), Am. Soc. Polit. and Legal Philosophy (v.p. 1972-74), Conf. for Study of Polit. Thought, ACLU, AAUP, Phi Beta Kappa. Home: 99 Northampton Rd Amherst MA 01002 Office: Amherst Coll Amherst MA 01002

KATELL, SIDNEY, consulting cost engineer, retired educator; b. N.Y.C., Feb. 2, 1915; s. Aaron and Gusta (Ornstein) K.; m. Elvie League, July 4, 1948; children: Alan David, Barry Steven. B.Chem. Engring., NYU, 1941. Chem. engr. design U.S. Bur. Mines, Louisiana, Mo., 1948-53, chem. engr., Morgantown, W.Va., 1954-55, chief gas treating and testing sect., 1955-57, chief process evaluation group, Morgantown, 1957-76; prof. mineral resource econs. Coll. Mineral and Energy Resources, W.Va. U., 1976-82; pvt. cons., 1982—; chem. engr. Westinghouse Electric Co., Pitts., 1953-54. Contbr. articles to profl., govtl. jours. Mem. Am. Assn. Cost Engrs. (pres. 1970-71, award merit 1973), Am. Chem. Soc., Am. Inst. Chem. Engrs., Am. Gas Assn. (Operating Sect. award merit 1955), Morgantown C. of C. (chmn. pollution control com.), B'nai B'rith. Jewish (pres. congregation).

KATES, JOSEF, electronic consultant; b. Vienna, Austria, May 5, 1921; m. Lillian S. Kates; children: Louis, Naomi, Celina, Philip. B.A., U. Toronto, 1948, M.A., 1949, Ph.D. in Physics, 1951. With Imperial Optical Co., Toronto, 1942; spl. projects engr. Rogers Electronics Tubes, 1944-48; with Computation Center, U. Toronto, 1948-54; pres. Setak Computer Services Corp., Ltd. (formerly KCS Ltd.), Toronto, 1954—; dep. mng. partner Can. firm Kates, Peat, Marwick & Co., Can., 1967-68; pres. Josef Kates Assos., Inc., Toronto, 1974—, Teleride Corp., 1978—; chancellor U. Waterloo, 1979-85; chmn. Sci. Council Can., 1975-78; mem. Bd. dirs. Can. Weitzmann Inst. of Sci., Can. Technion Soc., New Mt. Sinai Hosp.; former mem. Nat. Research Council Adv. Com. on Computers. Fellow Engring. Inst. Can. (past chmn. mng. sec. Toronto region); mem. Can. Indsl. Traffic League (past chmn. ops. research com.), Ops. Research Soc. (past pres.), Can. Assn. Data Processing Service Orgns. (past v.p.), Ont. Inst. Mng. Cons. Designed and built first pilot model of electronic computer in Can., also first computer game playing machine. Office: 156 Front St W Toronto ON M5J 2L6 Canada

KATES, MORRIS, biochemist; b. Galati, Romania, Sept. 30, 1923; emigrated to Can., 1924, naturalized, 1944; s. Samuel and Toby (Cohen) K.; m. Pirkko Helena Sofia Makinen, June 14, 1957; children: Anna-Lisa, Marja Helena, Ilona Sylvia. Student, Parkdale Coll., 1936-41; B.A., U. Toronto, Ont., Can., 1945, M.A., 1946, Ph.D., 1948. Research asst. Banting Inst., U. Toronto, 1948-49; postdoctoral fellow Nat. Research Council Can., Ottawa, Ont., 1949-51, research officer bioscis. div., 1951-68; prof. chemistry U. Ottawa, 1968-69, prof. biochemistry, 1969—; vice-dean research Faculty Sci. and Engring., 1978—, chmn. dept. biochemistry, 1982—. Author: Techniques of Lipidology, 1972; editor: Metabolic Inhibitors, vols. II and IV, 1972, 73; co-editor: Can. Jour. Biochemistry, 1974—. Fellow Chem. Inst. Can., Royal Soc. Can.; mem. Can. Biochem. Soc., Am. Chem. Soc., Am. Soc. Biol. Chemists, Biochem. Soc. (London), Am. Oil Chemists' Soc., Am. Soc. Microbiologists, AAAS, Ottawa Biol. and Biochem. Soc. (Sci. prize 1977, pres. 1974-75). Research, numerous publs. on lipid biochemistry, 1948. Home: 1723 Rhodes Crescent Ottawa ON K1H 5T1 Canada Office: Dept Biochemistry U Ottawa 40 Somerset E Ottawa ON K1N 6N5 Canada

KATHERINE, ROBERT ANDREW, chemical company executive; b. Phila., May 26, 1941; s. John and Winifred Irene (Smith) K. B.S.Ch.E., Drexel Inst. Tech., 1964, M.B.A., 1968; P.M.D., Harvard Grad. Sch. Bus., 1977. Plant mgr. synthetic phenol plastics div. Allied Chem. Corp., 1964-66; asst. to dir. Far East sales Air Products & Chems., Phila., 1966-70; product group mgr. corp. devel. P.Q. Corp., 1970-72, div. sales mgr. splty. chems., 1972-74; bus. dir. polymers Hooker Chem. Corp., Burlington, N.J., 1974-78, v.p., gen. mgr. Ruco div., 1978-80, v.p., gen. mgr. fabricated products div., 1980-81; pres. McCloskey Varnish Co., 1981-83, chmn. bd., chief exec. officer, 1983—; instr. Villanova U., 1973-75; asst. prof. Phila. Coll. Textiles and Sci., 1969-75. Trustee Inter-Sci. Found., Hahnemann Hosp. and Med. Coll. Mem. Soc. Plastics Industry (chmn. vinyl film group, exec. com. plastic bottle inst.), Nat. Paint and Coatings Assn., Young Pres.' Orgn., Am. Chem. Soc., Am. Mgmt. Assn. (pres.' assn.), Pa. Soc. Republican. Baptist. Clubs: Harvard Bus. Sch. (Phila., N.Y.C.); Union League (Phila.); Aronimink. Home: 4102 Battles Ln Newton Square PA 19073 Office: McCloskey Corp 7600 State Rd Philadelphia PA 19136

KATHKIN, BURTON KENNETH, communications company executive, lawyer; b. N.Y.C., Aug. 8, 1932; s. Nathan and Rosalind (Davis) Katkin; m. Lemore Seif, Dec. 26, 1954; children: Faith, Julie, Paula, Jonathan. B.S., CCNY, 1954; J.D., Columbia U., 1959. Bar: N.Y., U.S. Supreme Ct., U.S. dist. ct. (no. and ea. dists.) N.Y., D.C., U.S. ct. appeals (2d cir.). Assoc. Baer & Marks, N.Y.C., 1959-67; atty. N.Y. Telephone Co., N.Y.C., 1967-72, gen. attn., 1972-76; atty. Am. Tel. & Tel., N.Y.C., 1976-77, gen. atty., 1977-82; v.p. regulatory N.Y. Telephone Co., N.Y.C., 1982-83; v.p. regulation and govt. regulations NYNEX Corp., White Plains, N.Y., 1983—. Vice chmn. N.Y. State Council on Econ. Edn., 1982; chmn. bd. Judith Harris Selig Meml. Fund, Inc., 1983; bd. dirs. William Alanson White Inst., 1981. Served to 1st lt. U.S. Army, 1954-56. Mem. ABA, N.Y. Bar Assn., Fed. communications Bar Assn., Assn. Bar City N.Y., Nat. Exchange Carrier Assn. (dir. 1983—). Home: 15 Deer Hill Ln Scarsdale NY 10583 Office: NYEX Corp 400 Westchester Ave White Plains NY 10604

KATIMS, MILTON, conductor, violist; b. Bklyn.; s. Harry and Caroline K.; m. Virginia Peterson Katims; children: Peter Michael, Pamela Artura. A.B., Columbia U.; Mus.D. (hon.), Whitworth Coll., 1959, Seattle U., 1974, Cornish Inst., 1976. Staff condr. NBC, 1944-54; mem. faculty Juilliard Sch. Music, 1946-54; artistic dir. Sch. Music, U. Houston, 1976-84; Mem. music adv. panel State Dept. Cultural Presentations, 1968. Violist, Budapest String Quartet, 1940-54; first violist under Arturo Toscanini, NBC Symphony, 1943-54; guest condr., NBC Symphony, Boston, Cleve., Phila., N.Y.C., Chgo., Paris, Brussels, Barcelona, Israel, 1947-54; also Hollywod Bowl,, London, Venezuela, Vancouver Festival; guest condr., Philharmonia Orch., London, 1961; mus. dir., condr., Seattle Symphony, 1954-76; condr., Seattle World's Fair Festival, 1962; mus. dir., Menton Festival, 1963, La Jolla (Calif.) Festival, summers 1964-68; guest condr., Mozart Festival at Lincoln Center, 1966, 74, 75, Japan Philharm., Tokyo, 1967, Helsinki, Finland, Oslo and Bergen, Norway, 1973, 75; Editor various viola works; contbr. articles to: Music Pubs. Jour., Columbia Records; Contbr. articles to Vox, RCA Victor Records, N.Y. Times Mag., Sat. Rev. of Lit., Pantheon Music Internat. Recipient Columbia U. medal, 1953, Alice M. Ditson Condr. award, 1963. *Whether I am conducting, playing my viola or talking about music, I have always tried to convey my own joy in making music.*

KATKIN, EDWARD SAMUEL, psychology educator; b. N.Y.C., Aug. 15, 1937; s. Nathan and Rosalind (Davis) K.; m. Felice Lapin, Aug. 10, 1958 (dec. 1961); m. 2d Wendy Sue Freedman, Fed. 3, 1963; children: Kenneth, Elizabeth. B.A., CCNY, 1958; Ph.D., Duke U., 1963. Asst. prof. SUNY, Buffalo, 1963-66, assoc. prof., 1966-70, prof. dept. psychology, 1970—. Fellow Am. Psychol. Assn.; mem. Soc. Psychophysiol. Research (pres. 1983-84), Am. Psychosomatic Soc., N.Y. Acad. Sci. Home: 195 Autumnview Rd Williamsville NY 14221 Office: Dept Psychology SUNY 4230 Ridge Lea Buffalo NY 14226

KATLEMAN, HARRIS L., TV broadcasting co. exec.; b. Omaha, Aug. 19; s. Michael and Bess (Levey) K.; children: Steven, Lisa, Michael. B.A., UCLA, 1950. Sr. exec. v.p., dir. Goodson-Todman Broadcasting, 1961—; pres. Four Star Entertainment; sr. v.p. MGM, Inc.; pres. MGM-TV; exec. producer Bennett, Katleman Prodns., 1977-80; chmn. bd. Twentieth Century Fox TV, 1980—; also dir. Twentieth Century Fox Film Co. (Recipient Emmy nomination Richard Boone Repertory Theatre.). Mem. bd. govs. Mcpl. League of Beverly Hills, Calif. Mem. Acad. TV Arts and Scis. (founding mem.). Republican. Jewish. Office: Twentieth Century Fox PO Box 900 Beverly Hills CA 90213

KATLIC, JOHN EDWARD, electric utility company executive; b. Washington, Pa., Nov. 3, 1928; s. Frederick John and Dorothy Ann (Gideon) K.; m. Nancy Jean Nicely, Aug. 26, 1950; children: Mark Richard, Kerry Leigh, Kevin Edward, Kathleen Diane, Nancy Ellen. B.S.E.M., W.Va. U., 1955, M.S.E.M., 1961. Mine surveyor Rochester & Pittsburgh Coal Co., Indiana, Pa., 1948-49; mine supt. Consolidation Coal Co., Morgantown, W.Va., 1959-62, gen. supt., 1962-66, v.p., Pitts., 1973-75; sr. mining engr. Eastern Assn. Coal, Pitts., 1967-68, div. mgr., 1969, v.p. personnel safety and indsl. relations, 1970; also dir.; v.p., gen. mgr. coal Allied Chem. Co., Morristown, N.J., 1970-73; exec. v.p. engring. and govt. relations Island Creek Coal Co., Lexington, Ky., 1975-83; sr. v.p. fuel supply Am. Electric Power Service Corp., 1983—; mem. negotiating team Nat. Bituminous Coal Wage Agreement, Joint Industry Devel. Com., 1978; bd. dirs. Colo. Sch. Mines Research Inst.; mem. bus. adv. group; research and devel. Purdue U.; mem. bus. adv. council Coll. Bus., Marshall U., 1978-79. Mem. Morgantown City Council, 1964-66, Marshall U. Found., 1979; bd. dirs. W.Va. Edn. Found.; mem. steering com. W.Va. U. Served with inf. U.S. Army, 1946-47; C.E., 1950-52; Japan; C.E.; Germany. Mem. W.Va. Coal Assn. (dir.), Ky. Coal Assn. (dir.), Va. Coal Assn. (dir.), Nat. Mine Rescue Assn., Mine Rescue Vets. of Pitts. Dist., Cave Run Sailing Assn. Republican. Methodist. Clubs: King Coal, Ky. Cols., Cherry River Navy. Lodges: Masons; Shriners. Patentee mining machine indicator, dust control in longwall mining. Home: 1233 Ridgewood Way NE Lancaster OH 43130 Office: PO Box 700 Lancaster OH 43130

KATO, TAIKI, banker; b. Tokyo, Japan, June 10, 1931; s. Yasunobu and Hata K.; m. Kumi Baba, Nov. 3, 1960; 1 son, Hiroo. B.A., Tokyo U., 1951, LL.M., 1953; student, Poitiers U., Paris, France, 1959. With Bank of Tokyo Ltd., 1953—, mgr. loans and discounts dept., 1970-71, with N.Y. agy., 1971-76, dep. gen. mgr., 1972-76, acting gen. mgr., Tokyo, 1976-78, gen. mgr., 1978-80; pres., dir. Bank of Tokyo Trust Co., N.Y.C., 1980—, also dir.; dir. Shimano Corp., Tohlease Corp., Bank of Tokyo Trust Co. (Cayman) Ltd. Clubs: Nippon (dir.), Wall Street.). Home: 400 E 56th St New York NY 10022 Office: 100 Broadway New York NY 10005

KATO, WALTER YONEO, physicist; b. Chgo., Aug. 19, 1924; s. Naotaro and Hideko (Kondo) K.; m. Anna Chieko Kurata, June 26, 1953; children—Norman, Cathryn, Barbara. B.S., Haverford (Pa.) Coll., 1946; M.S., U. Ill., 1949; Ph.D., Pa. State U., University Park, 1954. Research asso. Ordnance Research Lab., Pa. State U., 1949-52; research asso. Brookhaven Nat. Lab., Upton, N.Y., 1952-53, sr. nuclear engr., asso. chmn. dept. applied sci., 1975-77, asso. chmn. dept. nuclear energy, 1977-80, dep. chmn., 1980—; sr. physicist Argonne (Ill.) Nat. Lab., 1953-75; vis. prof. dept. nuclear engring. U. Mich., Ann Arbor, 1974-75; cons. Office Nuclear Regulatory Research, U.S. Nuclear Regulatory Commn., 1974—. Contbr. numerous articles to profl. jours. Bd. dirs. Naperville (Ill.) YMCA, 1966-74. Served with Ordnance Corps AUS, 1946-47. Fulbright Research fellow, 1958-59. Fellow Am. Nuclear Soc. (dir.), Argonne Univ. Assn. (Distinguished Appt. award 1974); mem. Am. Phys. Soc., A.A.A.S., Sigma Xi. Methodist. Home: 3 Chips Ct Port Jefferson NY 11777 Office: Dept Nuclear Energy Brookhaven Nat Lab Upton NY 11973

KATON, JOHN EDWARD, chemist, educator; b. Toledo, Ohio, Jan. 5, 1929; s. John Arnold and Doris Helen (Graf) K.; m. Jeanette Scott, May 28, 1955; children—Kent S., Linden L., Alison A. B.A., Bowling Green State U., 1951; M.S., Kans. State U., 1955; Ph.D., U. Md., 1958. Sr. research chemist Monsanto Co., Dayton, Ohio, 1958-61; research group leader Monsanto Research Corp., Dayton, 1961-68; asso. prof. chemistry Miami U., Oxford, Ohio, 1968-72, prof., 1972—. Editor: Organic Semiconducting Polymers, 1968; book rev. editor: Applied Spectroscopy; contbr. articles to profl. jours. Scoutmaster Dan Beard council Boy Scouts Am., 1974-75. Mem. Soc. Applied Spectroscopy (pres. 1976), Am. Chem. Soc. (Cin. sect. Outstanding Chemist award 1979), Optical Soc. Am., Coblentz Soc. (bd. mgrs. 1978-82), Fedn. Analytical Chemistry and Spectroscopy Socs. (chmn. 1981), Spectroscopy Soc. Pitts., Sigma Xi (Miami U. chpt. Outstanding Research award 1972), Phi Kappa Phi, Phi Lambda Upsilon. Mem. Assemblies of God Ch. Patentee in field. Home: 909 S Locust St Oxford OH 45056 Office: Dept Chemistry Miami U Oxford OH 45056

KATONA, PETER GEZA, biomedical engineer, educator; b. Budapest, Hungary, June 25, 1937; came to U.S., 1956, naturalized, 1962; s. Stephan and Irene (Renner) K.; m. Jaroslava Blanar, Aug. 27, 1966; children—Catherine Iris, Andrew George. B.S. in Elec. Engring, U. Mich., 1960; S.M. in Elec. Engring. (Sloan fellow, 1960-62), M.I.T., 1962, Sc.D., 1965. Asst. prof. elec. engring. M.I.T., 1965-69; assoc. prof. biomed. engring. Case Western Res. U., Cleve., 1969-78, prof., 1978—, chmn. dept., 1980—. Editorial bd.: American Jour. Physiology, 1975-81; contbr. articles on cardio-respiratory control to profl. jours. Mem. Am. Physiol. Soc., Biomed. Engring. Soc. (bd. dirs. 1977-80, pres. elect 1983-84), IEEE, Am. Soc. Engring. Edn. Home: 2886 Courtland Blvd Shaker Heights OH 44122 Office: Biomed Engring Dept Case Western Res Univ Cleveland OH 44106

KATOPE, CHRISTOPHER GEORGE, English educator; b. Lowell, Mass., Apr. 1, 1918; s. George and Bessie (Savas) K.; m. Marjorie Spencer King, June 6, 1942; children: Theodora (Mrs. Charles Rowland), Christopher Lawrence. Student, Ind. U., 1937-38, U. Louisville, 1939-41; M.A., U. Chgo., 1947; Ph.D., Vanderbilt U., 1954. Instr. English Westminster Coll., 1947-50; instr. English Allegheny Coll., 1952-54, asst. prof., 1954-62, asso. prof., 1962-69, prof. English, 1969-83, prof. emeritus, 1983—; vis. prof. Columbia, 1968. Author, editor: (with P. Zolbrod) Beyond Berkeley, 1966, Rhetoric of Revolution, 1970; Contbr.: articles to profl. jours. Rhetoric of Revolution. Served with USNR, 1941-45. Fulbright prof. Athens Coll., 1959-60, Anatolia Coll., Greece, 1960-61. Mem. Modern Greek Studies Assn. Home: 514 Euclid Ave Box 39 Saegertown PA 16433 Office: Allegheny College Meadville PA 16335

KATRITZKY, ALAN ROY, chemistry educator; b. London, Eng., Aug. 18, 1928; s. Frederick Charles and Emily Gertrude (Lane) K.; m. Agnes Juliane Dietlinde Kilian, Aug. 5, 1952; children: Margaret, Erika, Rupert, Freda. B.A., Oxford U., 1951, B.Sc., 1952, M.A., 1954, D.Phil., 1954; Ph.D., Cambridge U., 1958, Sc.D., 1963. ICI fellow U. Oxford, 1956-58; lectr. chemistry U. Cambridge, 1958-63; fellow Churchill Coll.; prof. chemistry U. East Anglia, 1963-80, dean, 1963-70, 76-80; Kenan prof. organic chemistry U. Fla., Gainesville, 1980—; cons. UNESCO, industry. Editor: Advances in Heterocyclic Chemistry, vols. 1-36, 1963-84; regional editor: Tetrahedron, 1980—. Fellow Royal Soc.; mem. Am., Brit., German, French, Swedish, Japanese, Swiss chem. socs.; hon. mem. Italian Chem. Soc. Home: 1221 SW 21st Ave Gainesville FL 32601 Office: Dept Chemistry U Fla Gainesville FL 32611

KATSAHNIAS, THOMAS GEORGE, steel company executive; b. Chgo., May 28, 1928; s. George George and Jenny (Gekas) K.; m. Ann Moudakes, Sept. 30, 1951; children: Jeneane Ann, George Thomas, Theodore John. A.A., North Park Coll., 1948; B.S., Ill. Inst. Tech., 1951; M.B.A., U. Chgo., 1960. Supt. galvanizing Inland Steel Co., East Chicago, Ind., 1964-65, supr. tin mill, 1965-67, mgr. cold mills, 1967-71, asst. gen. mgr. flat products, 1971-77, gen. mgr.-IHW, 1977-78, v.p. steel mfg., 1978—. Gen. campaign chmn. Lake Area United Way, Griffith, Ind., 1979-80; v.p. N.W. Ind. Assn. Commerce and Industry, Merrillville, 1979—; bd. dirs. Calumet Area Found. Health Care, Highland, Ind., 1981—. Mem. Ind. State C. of C. (dir. 1979—). Greek Orthodox. Home: 8227 Oakwood Ave Munster IN 46321 Office: Inland Steel Co 3210 Watling St East Chicago IN 46321

KATSH, ABRAHAM ISAAC, university president emeritus, educator; b. Poland, Aug. 10, 1908; came to U.S., 1925, naturalized, 1932; s. Reuben and Rachel (Maskilleison) K.; m. Estelle Wachtell, Feb. 20, 1943; children: Ethan, Salem, Rochelle. B.S., N.Y. U., 1931, A.M., 1932, J.D., 1936; postgrad., Princeton, 1941; Ph.D., Dropsie U., 1944, LL.D., 1976; D.H.L. (hon.), Hebrew Union Coll.-Jewish Inst. of Religion, 1964, Spertus Coll. of Jewish Studies, Chgo., 1968, D.D., Christian Theol. Sem., 1970, U. Dubuque, LH.D., Lebanon Valley (Pa.) Coll. Instr. Hebrew N.Y. U., 1934-37; founder, exec. dir. Jewish Culture Found., 1937-44, exec. chmn., 1944-67, instr. edn., 1937-44, asst. prof., 1944-45, asso. prof., 1945-47, prof. edn., 1947-66; prof. Hebrew and Near Eastern studies Grad. Sch. Arts and Scis., 1966-67; dir. Inst. Hebrew Studies, 1962-67, Arabic instr., 1942-43; founder, dir. Library Judaica and Hebraica, 1942, curator, 1952-67, chmn. dept. fgn. langs., 1953-54, chmn. dept. Hebrew culture edn., 1953—; dir. Hebrew lang. and lit. sect. Wash. Sq. Coll., 1957-66, N.Y. U. distinguished prof. research, 1967-68, prof. emeritus, 1976—; lectr. New Sch. Social Research; dir. Am. Workshop on Israel Life and Culture, held in Israel sponsored by N.Y. U., 1949-67; pres. Dropsie U., Phila., 1967-76, pres. emeritus, 1976—, Distinguished research prof. Hebraica, 1967—, Distinguished Research prof., 1976—; vis. scholar Oxford Center for Postgrad. Hebrew Studies, 1977-78; scholar Mishkenot Shaananim, 1978-79; lectr. at internat. congress and world congress; U.S. participant Congress Linguistics and Hebrew Scholarship, U. Vienna, 1976; Chmn. Nat. Bd. of License for Tchrs. and Colls. field Hebrew Studies, 1957—; spl. examiner N.Y.C. Bd. Edn. Author: Einstein's Theory of Relativity (Hebrew), 1937, Hebrew in American Higher Education, 1941, Hebraic Contributions to American Life, 1941, Krochmal and the German Idealists, 1948, Hebrew Language, Literature and Culture in American Institutions of Higher Learning, 1950, Education and Racial Prejudices, Democracy and Interfaith, Hebraic Backgrounds of American Democracy, 1951, Judaism in Islam, 1954, Judaic Backgrounds of Islam (Hebrew), 1957, The Bible and the Koran, 1962, The Antonin Genizah Collection in the USSR, 1963, Yiggal Hazon, 1964, The Scroll of Agony (Hebrew), 1964, (English), 1966, Megilat Yessurin (Hebrew), 1966, Chronique d'una Agonie (French), 1966, Dodens Dokument (Swedish), 1967, Buch der Agonie (German); Midrash David Hanagid (Hebrew), vol. I, 1967, vol. II, 1968, Ginze Mishna, 1971, Ginze Talmud, vol. I, 1976, vol. II, 1979; asst. editor charge: Modern Lang. Jour, 1949-74; mng. editor: Jour. Ednl. Sociology, 1948-51; editor-in-chief: Hebrew Abstracts, 1950-70; editor: Bar Mitzvah, 1955-76, Biblical Heritage of American Democracy, 1977; editorial com.: Nat. Study Jewish Edn, 1957; editor: (1978) Jewish Quar. Rev; chmn. editorial bd.: Jewish Apocryphal Literature, 1968—; Contbr. to jours. and encys. Trustee Dropsie U., A.S.O.R.; bd. govs. World Hebrew Acad. Recipient B'nai Zion Meritorius key, 1944; Founders citation N.Y. U. Chair Hebrew Culture Edn., 1953; B'rith Abraham Gold Medal, 1952; Tercentary citation Jewish Book Council Am., 1954; 1st prize Hebrew Acad. Am., 1956; Matz Found. prize, 1956; 1st prize Hebrew Acad. Histadruth Ivrith, 1957; Dropsie Coll. Jubilee citation, 1957; named Ky. Col., 1957; prof. chair named in honor N.Y. U., 1957; recipient Am. Assn. Jewish Edn. award, 1959; Ernest O. Melby award, 1962; Municipality of Haifa Scholarly prize, 1979; established in his honor Abraham I. Katsh prize Hebrew U. Jerusalem, 1981. Mem. N.Y. State Fedn. Fgn. Lang. Tchrs. (dir.), World Congress Hebrew Lang. and Culture (exec. com.), Jewish Book Council Am. (nat. com.), Zionist Orgn. Am. (nat. chmn. 1949-51), Nat. Council Jewish Edn. (exec. com.), Jewish Acad. Arts and Sci. (chmn. exec. bd., pres. 1981—), Nat. Assn. Profs. Hebrew in Am. Instns. Higher Learning (founder, pres. 1951-53, hon. pres. 1953—), Am. Assn. Jewish Edn. (nat. chmn. bd. licenses), Hadoar Assn. (exec. bd.), Inst. Internat. Edn., Modern Lang. Assn. (chmn. evaluation modern Hebrew materials), Am. Jewish Congress, World Hebrew Congress, Phi Delta Kappa. Home: 45 E 89th St New York NY 10128 *In pioneering the introduction of modern Hebrew language and culture in American colleges and universities, I hoped that our people too would be able to light the little spark our ancestors ignited, in order to better understand Western civilization and American democracy, so that we shall be considered contributors to civilization and not servants to humanity.*

KATTAWAR, GEORGE WILLIFORD, physicist, educator; b. Beaumont, Tex., Aug. 10, 1937; s. Williford John and Lily (Angelo) K.; m. Euginia Louise Lee, Oct. 21, 1961; children: George Jeffrey, Gregory Williford, Karen Lee. B.S., Lamar U., 1959; M.S., Tex. A&M U., 1961, Ph.D., 1964. Theoretical physicist Los Alamos Sci. Lab., 1963-64; research physicist Esso Prodn. Research Co., Houston, 1964-66; asst. prof. physics N. Tex. State U., 1966-68; asso. prof. physics Tex. A&M U., 1968-73, prof., 1973—; vis. scientist S.W. Center Advanced Study, summers 1966-68; cons. Naval Ocean R & D Activity. Contbr. articles to profl. jours. Grantee NSF, Army Research Office, Office Naval Research.; recipient AMOCO Disting. Teaching award, 1981. Fellow Optical Soc. Am.; mem. Am. Astron. Soc., Sigma Xi. Club: Masons. Home: Route 5 Box 1342 College Station TX 77840 Office: Tex A&M U College Station TX 77843

KATZ, ABRAHAM, fgn. service officer; b. Bklyn., Dec. 4, 1926; s. Alexander and Zina (Rabinowitz) K.; m. Edith Shakin, Dec. 27, 1974; children—Tamar, Jonathan, Naomi. B.A. cum laude, Bklyn. Coll., 1948; M.I.A., Columbia U., 1950; Ph.D., Harvard U., 1968. Commd. fgn. service officer Dept. State, 1951; 1st sec. U.S. missions to NATO, OECD, Paris, 1959-64; counselor Am. Embassy, Moscow, 1964-66; dir. office of OECD European Communities and Atlantic Polit. Econ. Affairs, Washington, 1967-74; dep. chief of mission OECD, Paris, 1974-78; dep. asst. sec. for internat. econ. policy and research Dept. Commerce, Washington, 1978-80, asst. sec. internat. econ. policy, 1980-81; U.S. rep., ambassador OECD, Paris, 1981—. Author: The Politics of Economic Reform in the Soviet Union, 1972. Mem. Assn. Advancement Slavic Studies, Am. Polit. Sci. Assn., Am. Fgn. Service Assn., Am. Assn. Comparative Econ. Studies. Clubs: Cosmos, B'nai B'rith. Office: US OECD APO New York NY 09777

KATZ, ADRIAN IZHACK, physician, educator; b. Bucharest, Romania, Aug. 3, 1932; came to U.S., 1965, naturalized, 1976; s. Ferdinand and Helen (Lustig) K.; m. Miriam Lesser, Mar. 31, 1965; children—Ron, Iris. M.D., Hebrew U., 1961. Research fellow Yale U., 1965-67, Harvard U., 1967-68; intern Belinson Med. Center, Israel, 1961, resident, 1962-65; practice medicine specializing in internal medicine and nephrology, New Haven, 1966-67, Boston, 1967-68, Chgo., 1968—; mem. attending staff Albert Merritt Billings Hosp., 1973-82; head nephrology sect., attending physician U. Chgo. Hosps., 1968—; asst. prof. medicine U. Chgo., 1968-71, asso. prof., 1971-74, prof., 1975—; Fogarty sr. internat. fellow, vis. scientist Lab Cell Physiology, Collège de France, Paris, 1977-78. Co-author: Kidney Function and Disease in Pregnancy; contbr. chpts. to books, articles to profl. jours. Fellow A.C.P.; mem. Am. Physiol. Soc., Am. Soc. Clin. Investigation, Assn. Am. Physicians, Am. Soc. Nephrology, Internat. Soc. Nephrology, Central Soc. Clin. Research, N.Y. Acad. Scis. Home: 1125 E 53d St Chicago IL 60615 Office: 950 E 59th St Chicago IL 60637

KATZ, ALEX, artist; b. Bklyn., July 24, 1927; s. Isaac and Ella (Marion) K.; m. Ada Del Moro, Feb. 1, 1958; 1 son, Vincent. Certificate, Cooper Union, 1949. One-man exhbns. include, Roko Gallery, N.Y.C., 1954, 57, Fischbach Gallery, N.Y.C., 1964, 65, 67, 68, 70, 71, Stable Gallery, N.Y.C., 1960-61, Tanager Gallery, N.Y.C., 1959, 62, Martha Jackson Gallery, N.Y.C., 1962, Grinnell Gallery, Detroit, 1964, Sun Gallery, Provincetown, Mass., 1958, 59, Pa. State Coll., 1957, Mili-Jay Gallery, Woodstock, N.Y., 1961, David Stuart Gallery, Los Angeles, 1966, Bertha Eccles Art Center, Ogden, Utah, 1968, Towson State Coll., Balt., Phyllis Kind Gallery, Chgo., 1969, 71, W.Va. U., 1969, Galerie Dieter Brusberg, Hanover, W.Ger., 1971, Thelen Galerie, Cologne, West Germany, Reed Coll., Portland, 1972, Sloan-O'Sickey Gallery, Cleve., Carlton Gallery, N.Y.C., 1973, Marlborough Gallery, N.Y.C., 1973, 75, 76, Whitney Mus. Am. Art, N.Y.C., 1974-75, Va. Mus. Fine Arts, Richmond, Santa Barbara (Calif.) Mus. Art, U. Minn., Indpls. Mus. Art, 1975, Marlborough Fine Art, London, Galerie Marguerite Lamy, Paris, Galerie Roger d'Amécourt, Paris, 1977, traveling show, Fresno Arts Center, Art Galleries Calif. State U., Seattle Art Mus., Vancouver Art Gallery, 1977-78, Marlborough Galerie, A.G., Zurich, 1977, Rose Art Mus., Brandeis, U., Waltham, Mass., Balt. Art Mus., 1978, Brooke Alexander Gallery, N.Y.C., 1979, others, retrospective exhbn. at, Utah Mus. Fine Arts, Salt Lake City, U. Calif. at San Diego, Mpls. Mus. Art, Wadsworth Atheneum, Hartford, Conn., 1971, Am. Found. Arts, Miami, Fla., 1976, group shows include, Pa. Acad., 1960, Va. Mus., Richmond, Whitney Mus., 1960, 67-68, 79, Art Inst. Chgo., 1961, 62, 64, 72, Yale Mus., 1962, Colby Coll., 1961, 63, 64, 70, Am. Fedn. Art., 1964-65, Mus. Modern Art, 1964, 65, 66, 68, 69, Milw. Arts Center, 1966, 69, 75, R.I. Sch. Design, 1966, Cin. Art Mus., 1968, Am. Acad. Design, U. Calif. at LaJolla, 1969, Whitney Ann., N.Y.C., 1972, Whitney Biennial, N.Y.C., 1973, N.Y. Acad. Design, N.Y.C., Marlborough Gallery, N.Y.C., 1976, Cleve. Mus. Art, 1974, DeCordova Mus., Mass., 1975, Mus. Fine Arts, St. Petersburg, 1975-76, U. Mo., 1979, numerous others; vis. critic, Yale U., 1960-63; rep. permanent collections, Whitney Mus., Mus. Modern Art, Met. Mus., Brandeis U., N.Y.U., Bowdoin Coll., Detroit Mus., Allentown (Pa.) Art Mus., Weatherspoon Gallery of Art, Greensboro, N.C., Tokyo (Japan) Gallery, Allen Meml. Art Mus., Oberlin, Ohio, numerous others. (Recipient award New Eng. Art, Provincetown, Mass. 1971), numerous others. (Profl. Achievement citation Cooper Union, alumni medal for achievement 1980), numerous others. (medal for achievement in painting Skowhegan Sch. 1980). Guggenheim fellow, 1972. Address: 435 W Broadway New York NY 10012

KATZ, ARNOLD MARTIN, med. educator; b. Chgo., July 30, 1932; s. Louis Nelson and Aline (Grossner) K.; m. Phyllis Beck, Apr. 18, 1959; children—Paul, Sarah, Amy, Laura. B.A. with honors, U. Chgo., 1952; M.D. cum laude, Harvard, 1956. Diplomate: Nat. Bd. Med. Examiners. Intern Mass. Gen. Hosp., Boston, 1956-57, asst. resident, 1959-60; asst. registrar Inst. Cardiology, London, Eng., 1960-61; research fellow dept. medicine U. Calif. at Los Angeles, 1961-64; asst. prof. physiology Columbia; also asst. physician Presbyterian Hosp., N.Y.C., 1963-67; asso. prof. medicine and physiology U. Chgo., 1967-69; Philip J. and Harriet L. Goodhart prof. cardiology Mt. Sinai Sch. Medicine, N.Y.C., 1969-77; also attending physician; cons. VA, 1970—; prof. medicine, head cardiology div. U. Conn., Farmington, 1977—. Author: Physiology of the Heart, 1977; Mem. editorial bd.: Am. Jour. Physiology, 1966-72, Jour. Applied Physiology, 1966-72; editorial bd.: Jour. Molecular and Cellular Cardiology, 1967-75; asso. editor, 1980—; editorial bd.: Am. Jour. Cardiology, 1970-75, Jour. Clin. Investigation, 1971-76, Am. Jour. Medicine, 1971-77, Jour. Mechanochemistry and Cell Motility, 1970—, Circulation Research, 1974-79, Physiol. Rev, 1976-79, Cardiology, 1980—, Cardiovascular Pharmacology, 1978—; reviewer several profl. jours.; Contbr. articles to profl. jours. Bd. dirs. N.Y. Heart Assn., 1971-74, 75-77, Greater Hartford chpt. Am. Heart Assn., 1977—, Conn. Heart Assn., 1979—. Served with USPHS, 1957-59. Moseley traveling fellow Harvard, 1960-61; Am. Heart Assn. advanced research fellow, 1961-63; established investigator, 1963-68; Humboldt fellow Alexander von Humboldt Found., W.Ger., 1975-76. Fellow Am. Coll. Cardiology, A.C.P.; mem. Am. Physiol. Soc., Harvey Soc., Cardiac Muscle Soc. (pres. 1969-71), Am. Soc. Pharmacology and Exptl. Therapeutics, Am. Soc. Clin. Investigation, Assn. Am. Physicians, Am. Physiol. Soc. (circulation group), Internat. Soc. Heart Research, Chgo. Soc. Internatl Medicine, N.Y. Heart Assn., Am. Soc. Biol. Chemists, Alpha Omega Alpha. Home: 4 Old Gate Ln Farmington CT 06032 Office: Dept Medicine U Conn Health Center Farmington CT 06032

KATZ, DANIEL, psychology educator; b. Trenton, N.J., July 19, 1903; s. Rudolph and Regina (Fleischer) K.; m. Christine Ross Braley, Sept 1, 1930; children: Joanna Braley, Jean Braley. A.B., U. Buffalo, 1925; A.M., Syracuse U., 1926, Ph.D., 1928. Instr. psychology Princeton U., 1928-31; asst. prof. Princeton, 1931-40, asso. prof., 1940-43; prof. psychology, chmn. dept. Bklyn. Coll., 1943-47; prof. psychology U. Mich., 1947—; program dir. Survey Research Center, 1947-50, research asso., 1950—; Research dir. surveys div. OWI, 1943-44; Fulbright fellow, Norway, 1951-52, NSF sr. fellow, 1957-58; fellow Center Advanced Study Behavioral Scis., 1960-61; vis. prof. U. Aarhus, 1971-72. Author: (with Floyd H. Allport) Students Attitudes, 1931, (with R.L. Schanck) Social Psychology, 1938, (with Henry Valen) Political Parties in Norway, 1964, (with R. L. Kahn) The Social Psychology of Organizations, 1966, 2d edit., 1978, (with R.L. Kahn, B. Gutek and E. Barton) Bureaucratic Encounters, 1975; Editor: (with Leon Festinger) Research Methods in the Behavioral Sciences, 1953, Public Opinion and Propaganda, 1954, (with Robert L. Kahn and J. Stacy Adams) The Study of Organizations, 1980; Editorial bd.: Pub. Opinion Quar, 1939-50, Jour. Conflict Resolution, 1957-70; editor: Jour. Abnormal and Social Psychology, 1962-64, Jour. Personality and Social Psychology, 1965-67; Contbr. articles profl. jours. Recipient Gold Medal award Am. Psychol. Found., 1977. Mem. Am. Psychol. Assn. (dir. 1960-63), Indsl. Relations Research Assn., Soc. Psychol. Study Social Issues (sec.-treas. 1945-48, pres. 1949-50), Phi Beta Kappa, Sigma Xi. Home: 1789 Country Club Rd Ann Arbor MI 48105

KATZ, DOLORES JEAN, reporter, journalist; b. Cleve., Oct. 2, 1945; d. Irving and Evelyn M. (Feldman) K. B.A., U. Wis., 1967; postgrad. (Lucius W. Nieman fellow), Harvard U., 1976-77. Asst. news editor Jour. Am. Hosp. Assn., Chgo., 1968-69; reporter Ill. State Register, Springfield, 1969-70; med. reporter Detroit Free Press, 1970—. Office: 321 W Lafayette St Detroit MI 48231

KATZ, DONALD LAVERNE, chemical engineering educator emeritus, consultant; b. nr. Jackson, Mich., Aug. 1, 1907; s. Gottlieb and Lucy (Schnackenberg) K.; m. Lila Maxine Crull, Sept. 17, 1932 (dec. 1965); children: Marvin LaVerne, Linda Maxine; m. Elizabeth Harwood Correll, Nov. 26, 1965; stepchildren: Richard, Steven, Jonathan H. B.S., U. Mich., 1931, M.S., 1932, Ph.D., 1933. Research engr. Phillips Petroleum Co., Bartlesville, Okla., 1933-36; asst. prof. chem. engring. U. Mich., Ann Arbor, 1936-42, assoc. prof., 1942-43, prof., 1943-66, Alfred H. White univ. prof. chem. engring., 1966-77, prof. emeritus, 1977—, chmn. dept. chem. and metall. engring., 1951-62; cons. engr., 1936—; mem. sci. adv. bd. EPA, 1976-79. Contbr. articles to profl. jours. Trustee Ann Arbor Pub. Schs., pres. bd. trustees, 1953-56; trustee Engring. Index, 1966-72. Recipient Hanlon award Natural Gasoline Assn. Am., 1950; named Mich. Engr. Yr. Mich. Soc. Profl. Engrs., 1959; recipient John Franklin Carll award Soc. Petroleum Engrs., 1964, Founders award Am. Inst. Chem. Engrs., 1964, Warren K. Lewis award, 1967, W.H. Walker award, 1968, Mineral Industry Edn. award AIME, 1970, Disting. Pub. Service award USCG, 1972, E.V. Murphree award Am. Chem. Soc., 1975, Nat. medal of Sci., 1983. Fellow AAAS, Am. Nuclear Soc., Am. Inst. Chem. Engrs. (dir. 1955-57, v.p. 1958, pres. 1959, sec. commn. engring. edn. 1962-64, Eminent Chem. Engr. 1983); mem. Am. Chem. Soc., AIME (Lucas medal 1979), ASME, Am. Soc. Engring. Edn., Am. Gas Assn. (Gas Industry Research award 1977), Am. Assn. Petroleum Geologists, Ann Arbor Council Chs. (pres. 1944-46), Nat. Soc. Profl. Engrs., Nat. Acad. Sci. (chmn. USCG com. on hazardous materials 1964-72, 77-79, mem. sci. and tech. communications com. 1967-69, chmn. com. air quality and power plant emissions 1974-75), Engrs. Council Profl. Devel. (dir., mem. exec. com. 1959-65, chmn. bd. trusteesm. 1969-72, chmn. council 1971-72), Nat. Acad. Engring., Sigma Xi, Tau Beta Pi, Phi Lambda Upsilon (hon.), Phi Kappa Phi, Alpha Chi Sigma. Methodist. Home: 2011 Washtenaw Ave Ann Arbor MI 48104 Office: Dept Chem Engring Univ Mich Dow Bldg Ann Arbor MI 48109

KATZ, EDWARD MORRIS, banker; b. Passaic, N.J., Apr. 18, 1921; s. David and Badane (Gubersky) K.; m. Phyllis Kushner, June 20, 1948; children—David, Alan, Michael. B.A., Bklyn. Coll., 1947; M.A., NYU, 1948. Auditor Amalgamated Bank N.Y., N.Y.C., 1951-55, cashier, 1955-73, v.p., 1957-61, sr. v.p., 1961-71, exec. v.p., 1971-78, pres., chief exec. officer, 1978—, dir., 1966—; dir. Urban Community Ins. Served with USAAF, 1941-45. Mem. Nat. Assn. Bank Auditors, Am., N.Y. State bankers assns. Home: 48 Windsor Rd Great Neck NY 11021 Office: 11-15 Union Square New York NY 10003

KATZ, HAROLD, weight loss firm executive; b. Phila., May 5, 1937; s. David and Sophie (Beck) K.; children: Marlene, Diane, David. Grad. high sch. Founder weight loss center, Willow Grove, Pa., 1972; now pres., chmn. bd. Nutri/System, Inc., Huntington Valley, Pa.; also acquired Fox Morris Personnel Cons., Tele-Cut Hair Salons; owner Phila. 76'ers (basketball team), 1981—. Bd. dirs., hon chmn. March of Dimes; active fund-raising Cystic Fibrosis of Phila. Named Sportsman of Yr. B'nai Brith, 1982; recipient Am. Spirit award Eastern Paralysis Vets. Assn. Mem. Internat. Franchise Assn. Republican. Jewish. Clubs: Golden Slipper, B'nai Brith, Jewish Basketball League. Office: 2655 Philmont Ave Huntingdon Valley PA 19006 *

KATZ, HAROLD AMBROSE, lawyer, former state legislator; b. Shelbyville, Tenn., Nov. 2, 1921; s. Maurice W. and Gertrude Evelyn (Cohen) K.; m. Ethel Mae Lewison, July 21, 1945; children: Alan, Barbara, Julia, Joel. A.B., Vanderbilt U., 1943; J.D., U. Chgo., 1948, M.A., 1958. Bar: Ill. 1948. Ptnr. Katz & Friedman, Chgo., 1948—; spl. legal cons. to Gov. of Ill., 1961-63; master-in-chancery, circuit ct., Cook County, Ill., 1963-67; mem. Ill. Ho. of Reps., 1965-83, chmn. judiciary com., co-chmn. rules com.; lectr. U. Coll., U. Chgo., 1959-64; Chmn. Ill. Commn. on Orgn. of Gen. Assembly, 1966-82; del. nat. Democratic conv., 1972. Author: (with Charles O. Gregory) Labor Law: Cases, Materials and Comments, 1948, Labor and the Law, 1979; editor: Improving the State Legislature, 1967; Contbr. articles to mags. Mem. ABA, Ill. Bar Assn. (chmn. labor law sect. 1979-80), Internat. Soc. for Labor Law and Social Legislation (U.S. chmn. 1961-67), Am. Trial Lawyers Assn. (chmn. workmen's compensation sect. 1963-64). Jewish. Home: 1180 Terrace Ct Glencoe IL 60022 Office: Katz Friedman Schur & Eagle 7 S Dearborn St Chicago IL 60603

KATZ, HENRY, ins. co. exec.; b. Bklyn., June 30, 1937; s. Bennie and Neti (Schloss) K.; m. Eileen Cohen, Sept. 6, 1959; children—Douglas, Ronald. A.B., N.Y. U., 1957, LL.B., 1960. Bar: N.Y. bar 1961. Atty. N.Y. State Ins. Fund, 1960-63; asso. counsel N.Y. State Ins. Dept., 1963-70; with Home Ins. Co., N.Y.C., 1970-78, gen. counsel, 1973-76, sr. v.p. charge govt. and industry affairs, 1977-78; v.p. govt. relations Hartford Ins. Group, Conn., 1978—. Mem. Am. Ins. Assn. (past chmn. law and legis. com.), Am. Bar Assn., Am. Arbitration Assn., Phi Delta Phi. Office: Hartford Plaza Hartford CT 06115

KATZ, HERBERT MARVIN, educator; b. Bklyn., Apr. 4, 1926; s. Abraham and Edna (Goldstein) K.; m. Evelyn Greene, July 1, 1954; children—Susan, Joel. B.Ch.E., CCNY, 1949; M.S., U. Cin., 1949, Ph.D., 1953. Asst. chem. engr. Argonne (Ill.) Nat. Lab., 1954-56; chem. engr. Brookhaven Nat. Lab., Upton, N.Y., 1957-66; prof. Howard U., 1968—, chmn. chem. engring., 1968-74. Treas. Human Relations Com. Eastern Suffolk County, N.Y., 1964-65, Alliance for Democratic Reform, Montgomery County, Md., 1969-70. Served with U.S. Army, 1944-46. Mem. Am. Inst. Chem. Engrs., Am. Chem. Soc., Sigma Xi. Patentee in field. Home: 1602 Sherwood Rd Silver Spring MD 20902 Office: Dept Chem Engring Howard U Washington DC 20001

KATZ, HERBERT MELVIN, publisher, editor; b. N.Y.C., Nov. 13, 1930; s. Dr. Charles and May (Tonkin) K.; m. Marjorie Phillis Pearle, Jan. 5, 1957 (div. May 1974); children—Daniel Seth, Nina Judith; m. Nancy Beth Jacobs, Aug. 15, 1974. B.A., N.Y.U., 1951; M.A., Columbia, 1952. Publicity writer Viking Press, 1952-53; editor-in-chief Pyramid Books, 1953-55; editorial dir. Funk & Wagnalls Co., also Wilfred Funk, Inc., 1955-61; editor G.P. Putnam's Sons, 1961-63; v.p., editor-in-chief M. Evans & Co., 1964—. Author: Love and Marriage, 1975, Nicolette, 1976; co-author: U.S.A.: A History and Guide, 1965, Museum Adventures: An Introduction to Discovery, 1969. Office: 216 E 49th St New York City NY 10017

KATZ, HILDA, artist; b. June 2, 1909; d. Max and Lina (Schwartz) K. Student, Nat. Acad. Design, 1940-41. Author (under pen name Hulda Weber) poems included numerous anthologies.; Contbr.: numerous poems, short stories to books and mags. including Humpty Dumpty's Mag. (publ. for children); One-woman exhbns. include, Bowdoin Coll. Art Mus., 1951, Calif. State Library, 1953, Print Club Albany, N.Y., 1955, U. Maine, 1955, 58, Jewish Mus., 1956, Pa. State Tchrs. Coll., Massillon Mus., 1957, Ball State Tchrs. Coll., Springfield (Mass.) Art Mus., Miami Beach (Fla.) Art Center, Richmond (Ind.) Art Assn., 1959, Old State Capitol Mus. La., other exhbns. include, Corcoran Bienniale Library of Congress, Am. in the War Exhbn, 26 museums, Am. Drawing anns. at, Albany Inst., Nat. Acad. Design, Conn. Acad. Fine Arts, Bklyn. Mus., Delgado Mus., Art-U.S.A., 1959, Congress for Jewish Culture, Met. Mus. Art., Springfield (Mo.) Art Mus., Children's Mus. Hartford, Conn., Miniature Printers, Peoria (Ill.) Art Center, Pa. Acad. Fine Arts, Originale Contemporate Graphic Internat., France, Bezalel Nat. Mus., Israel, Venice (Italy) Bienniale, Royal Etchers and Painters Exchange Exhibit, Eng., Bat Yam Mus., Israel, Paris, France, 1958, 59, Am.-Italian Print Exchange, numerous libraries, artists socs., invitational exhbns. include, Rome, Turin, Venice, Florence, Naples (all Italy), Nat. Academe Muse, France, Israel, USIA exhbns. in, Europe, S. Am., Asia, Africa; represented spl. collections, U.S. Nat. Mus., 1965, U. Maine, Library of Congress, 1965-71, Met. Mus. Art, 1965-66, 80, Nat. Gallery Art, 1966, Nat. Collection Fine Arts, 1966-71, 78, Nat. Air and Space Mus., 1970, N.Y. Pub. Library, 1971, 78, U.S. Mus. History and Tech., 1972, Naval Mus., Fort Lewis Coll., Durango, Colo., 1980-81, Boston Public Library, Israel Nat. Mus., Jerusalem, State Mus. Albany, N.Y., 1980; also represented in permanent collections, Balt. Mus. Art, Franklin D. Roosevelt, Fogg Mus., Harvard, Santa Barbara (Calif.) Art Mus., Syracuse U., Colorado Springs Fine Arts Center, Pennell Collection, Am. Artists Group Prize at Samuel Golden Coll., U. Minn., Calif. State Library, Pa. State Library, Bezalel Nat. Mus., Archives Am. Art, Smithsonian Instn., Archives and State Mus. Albany, N.Y., Newark Pub. Library, Addison Gallery Am. Art, Bat Yam Municipal Mus., Safed Mus., Israel, Pa. State Tchrs. Coll., Richmond Art Assn., Peoria (Ill.) Art Center, Boston Pub. Library, St. Margaret Mary Sch. Art, Musee National d'Art Modern, Archives of Am. Art at Smithsonian Instn., Washington. (Recipient award Miss. Art Assn. Internat. Water Color Club 1947, 51), Archives of Am. Art at Smithsonian Instn., Washington. (New Haven Paint and Clay Club), Archives of Am. Art at Smithsonian Instn., Washington. (purchase award Peoria Art Center 1950), Archives of Am. Art at Smithsonian Instn., Washington. (Print Club Albany 1962), Archives of Am. Art at Smithsonian Instn., Washington. (also Library of Congress), Archives of Am. Art at Smithsonian Instn., Washington. (U. Minn.), Archives of Am. Art at Smithsonian Instn., Washington. (Calif. State Library), Archives of Am. Art at Smithsonian Instn., Washington. (Met. Mus. Art), Archives of Am. Art at Smithsonian Instn., Washington. (Pa. State Tchrs. Coll.), Archives of Am. Art at Smithsonian Instn., Washington. (Art Assn. Richmond), Archives of Am. Art at Smithsonian Instn., Washington. (Ind.), Archives of Am. Art at Smithsonian Instn., Washington. (N.Y. Pub. Library), Archives of Am. Art at Smithsonian Instn., Washington. (Newark Pub. Library), Archives of Am. Art at Smithsonian Instn., Washington. (St. Margaret Mary Sch. Art Coll.), Archives of Am. Art at Smithsonian Instn., Washington. (landscape award Soc. Miniature Painters), Archives of Am. Art at Smithsonian Instn., Washington. (Gravers and Sculpture), Archives of Am. Art at Smithsonian Instn., Washington. (James Joyce award Poetry Soc. Am. 1975), Archives of Am. Art at Smithsonian Instn., Washington. (named Dau. of Mark Twain 1970), Archives of Am. Art at Smithsonian Instn., Washington. (life fellow Met. Mus. Art), Archives of Am. Art at Smithsonian Instn., Washington. (named to Exec. and Profl. Hall of Fame (plaque of honor 1966). Fellow Internat. Acad. Poets (founder 1977); mem. Soc. Am. Graphic Artists (group prize 1950), Print Club Albany (N.Y.), Boston Printmakers (award 1955), Washington Printmakers (exhbns.), Conn. Acad. Fine Arts, Am. Color Print Soc., Audubon Artists (group exhbns., award 1944), Phila. Water Color Club (group exhbns.), Nat. Assn. Women Artists (award 1945, 47), Print Council Am., Hunterdon Art Center, Internat. Platform Assn., Poetry Soc. Am., Artists Equity N.Y., Authors Guild, Inc., Accademia Di Scienze, Lettere, Arti (Consigliere), Milano, Italy (hon.). Address: 915 West End Ave Apt 5D New York NY 10025 *Along with his soul, the child is born with prescience of his life, completely apart from the hereditary and environmental. That is why genius manifests in the mundane. Soul and prescience remain unique to each individual. Today, the young call it "DOING YOUR OWN THING". For me... it was ART.*

KATZ, HILLIARD JOEL, physician; b. Stockton, Calif., May 26, 1918; s. Nelson and Pauline (Landman) K.; m. Jeanette Lillian Gordon, Aug. 18, 1946; children: Stephanie, Steven Nelson, Hilary. A.B., U. Calif. at Berkeley, 1939; M.D., U. Calif. at San Francisco, 1942. Diplomate: Am. Bd. Internal Medicine. Intern U. Calif. Hosps., San Francisco, 1942-43, asst. resident internal medicine, 1943-44, attending physician, electrocardiographer, 1948—, chief staff, 1964-66, physician charge CCU,, 1966-73; resident, sr. resident in internal medicine San Francisco VA Hosp., 1946-48; practice medicine specializing in cardiology, San Francisco; clin. instr. medicine U. Calif. Sch. Medicine, San Francisco, 1948-53, asst. clin. prof., 1953-61, asso. clin. prof., 1961-70, clin. prof. cardiovascular div., 1970—, coordinator for transpacific clin. programs, asst. to chancellor for spl. events, San Francisco, 1948—; chmn. Nat. Com. for Emergency Coronary Care, 1974-76; mem. med. adv. com. Calif. Wine Inst. Served to capt. M.C. AUS, 1944-46. Fellow Am. Coll. Cardiology, A.C.P., Am. Heart Assn. (fellow council clin. cardiology 1963, Distinguished Service award 1963, Service Recognition award 1964); mem. Calif. Heart Assn. (dir. 1956-71), San Francisco Heart Assn. (pres. 1955-57, Distinguished Service certificate 1959), Calif. Acad. Medicine (pres. 1965), U. Calif. Sch. Medicine Alumni-Faculty Assn. (pres. 1961-62), Soc. Med. Friends Wine (pres. 1968, bd. govs.), Berkeley Wine and Food Soc., Wine and Food Soc. San Francisco, Confrerie des Chevaliers du Tastevin, Commanderie de Bordeaux de San Francisco, Cercle de l'Union, Phi Beta Kappa, Alpha Omega Alpha. Club: Nautilus. Home: 223 Cherry St San Francisco CA 94118 Office: 450 Sutter St San Francisco CA 94108

KATZ, J. LAWRENCE, educator, biophysicist, biomedical engineer; b. Bklyn., Dec. 18, 1927; s. Frank and Rose (Eidenberg) K.; m. Gertrude Seidman, June 17, 1950; children: Robyn Laurie, Andrea Lee, Talbot Michael. B.S. in Physics, Poly. Inst. Bklyn., 1950, M.S., 1951, Ph.D., 1957. Teaching fellow physics, research fellow, instr.

math. Poly. Inst. Bklyn., 1950-56; mem. faculty Rensselaer Poly. Inst., Troy, N.Y., 1956—, prof. physics, 1967—, prof. biophysics and biomed. engring., 1971—, chmn. dept. biomed. engring., 1982, dir. Center for Biomed. Engring., 1974—; summer research asso. Wright Aero. Co., 1956; Summer research asso. Knolls Atomic Power Lab., Schenectady, 1957; hon. research asst. crystallography Univ. Coll., London, 1959-60; vis. prof. biomed. engring., oral biology U. Miami, Fla., 1969-70; vis. prof. biomechanics Chengdu U. Sci. and Tech., China; vis. scientist program Am. Assn. Physics Tchrs.-Am. Inst. Physics, 1970-72; vis. prof. orthopaedics and rehab. U. Miami, summer 1974; cons. in field, 1950—; dir. Bioanalytical Labs., Inc., Troy; adj. prof. orthopaedics Albany Med. Coll., 1972-77, prof. surgery, 1977—; vis. prof. dept. orthopedic surgery Harvard U. Med. Sch., 1978; vis. biophysicist Children's Hosp., Boston, 1978; E. Leon Watkins vis. prof. Wichita (Kans.) State U., 1978; vis. prof. biophysics and biomed. engring. Inst. de Fisica e Quimica de São Carlos, U. São Paulo, Nov. 1978; mem. engring. biology and medicine tng. com. NIH, 1968-71; mem. U.S. Standards Inst. Com. N44; chmn. subcom. diagnostic radiology; mem. VA sci. rev. and evaluation bd. for rehab. engring. research and devel., 1981-83. Editor: (with Robert Plonsey) Marcel Dekker Series on Biomedical Engineering and Instrumentation; contbr. papers to profl. lit., chpts. to books. Mem. organizing com. Black Arts Council, 1969-70; mem. exec. com. Schenectady County Liberal party, 1963—; chmn. 4th jud. dist. nominating conv. Liberal party, 1967-68; Liberal party candidate for U.S. Congress, 1968; committeeman Liberal party, 1968-71; asst. chmn. Schenectady County Liberal party, 1969-71; nat. bd. dirs. Ams. for Democratic Action, 1977—, N.Y. state bd. dirs., 1978—; sponsor tri-city div. United Negro Coll. Fund, 1967-68; mem. Schenectady Light Opera Co., 1964—. Served with USNR, 1946-48. NSF sci. faculty fellow, 1959-60; Guggenheim fellow, 1977-78. Fellow Am. Phys. Soc.; mem. Am. Crystallographic Assn. (chmn. crystal data com.), AIME (chmn. dental med. tech. com.), AAUP (pres. Rensselaer chpt. 1974-75), Biophys. Soc., Orthopaedic Research Soc. (mem. program com. 1973-75, chmn. 1975, exec. com. 1975), Internat. Assn. Dental Research, Am. Soc. Engring. Edn. (chmn. biomed. engring. div. 1978-79, chmn. elect and program chmn. 1977—), Soc. Biomaterials (v.p. 1977-78, pres. 1978-79), Biomed. Engring. Soc. (dir. 1981-84, pres. elect 1982-83, pres. 1983-84), ASTM (chmn. composites subcom. of com. med. implants and devices), IEEE (chmn. composites subcom. com. med. implants and devices), Fedn. Am. Scientists, Sigma Xi, Sigma Pi Sigma. Jewish (trustee temple 1962-63, 63-64, mem. social action com. 1968-69). Patentee pretensioned prosthetic device for skeletal joints. Home: 838 Maxwell Dr Schenectady NY 12309 Office: Rensselaer Poly Inst Troy NY 12181

KATZ, JAY, physician, educator; b. Zwickau, Germany, Oct. 20, 1922; came to U.S., 1940, naturalized, 1945; s. Paul and Dora (Ungar) K.; m. Esta Mae Zorn, Sept. 13, 1952; children: Sally Jean, Daniel Franklin, Amy Susan. B.A., U. Vt., 1944; M.D., Harvard U., 1949. Intern Mt. Sinai Hosp., N.Y.C., 1949-50; resident Northport (N.Y.) VA Hosp., 1950-51, Yale U., 1953-55, instr. psychiatry, New Haven, 1955-57, asst. prof., 1957-58, asst. prof. psychiatry and law, 1958-60, asso. prof. law, asso. clin. prof. psychiatry, 1960-67, adj. prof. law and psychiatry, 1967-79, prof., 1979—; tng. and supervising psychiatrist Western New Eng. Inst. for Psychoanalysis, 1972—; cons. to asst. sec. health and sci. affairs HEW, 1972-73, mem. artificial heart assessment panel, 1972-73. Author: (with Joseph Goldstein) The Family and the Law, 1964, (with Joseph Goldstein and Alan M. Dershowitz) Psychoanalysis, Psychiatry and Law, 1967, Experimentation with Human Beings, 1972, (with Alexander M. Capron) Catastrophic Diseases—Who Decides What?, 1975. Bd. dirs. Family Service of New Haven. Served to capt. M.C. USAF, 1951-53. John Simon Guggenheim Meml. Found. fellow, 1981. Fellow ACP (William C. Menninger award 1983), Am. Psychiat. Assn. (Isaac Ray award 1975), Am. Orthopsychiat. Assn., Am. Coll. Psychiatry, Center for Advanced Psychoanalytic Studies; mem. Inst. Medicine, Nat. Acad. of Scis., Group for Advancement of Psychiatry, Am. Psychoanalytic Assn. Jewish. Home: 27 Inwood Rd Woodbridge CT 06525 Office: 127 Wall St New Haven CT 06520

KATZ, JOSEPH JACOB, chemist, educator; b. Apr. 19, 1912; s. Abraham and Stella (Asnin) K.; m. Celia S. Weiner, Oct. 1, 1944; children—Anna, Elizabeth, Mary, Abram. B.Sc., Wayne U., 1932; Ph.D., U. Chgo., 1942. Research asso. chemistry U. Chgo., 1942-43, asso. chemist metall. lab., 1943-45; sr. chemist Argonne (Ill.) Nat. Lab., 1945—; Tech. adviser U.S. delegation UN Conf. on Peaceful Uses Atomic Energy, Geneva, Switzerland, 1955; chmn. AAAS Gordon Research Conf. on Inorganic Chemistry, 1953-54. Am. editor: Jour. Inorganic and Nuclear Chemistry, 1955—. Recipient Distinguished Alumnus award Wayne U., 1955, Profl. Achievement award U. Chgo. Alumni Assn.; Guggenheim fellow, 1956-57. Mem. Am. Chem. Soc. (award for nuclear applications in chemistry 1961, sec.-treas. div. phys. chemistry 1966-76), Nat. Acad. Scis., Am. Nuclear Soc., Phi Beta Kappa, Sigma Xi. Home: 1700 E 56th St Chicago IL 60637 Office: 9700 S Cass Ave Argonne IL 60439

KATZ, JOSEPH LOUIS, chemical engineer; b. Colon, Panama, Aug. 4, 1938; naturalized, 1970; s. Adolfo and Margarita (Eisen) K.; m. Liliane Capelluto, Apr. 10, 1965; children: Daniel P., Alan R. B.S., U. Chgo., 1960, Ph.D., 1963. Amanuensis U. Copenhagen Chem. Lab. III, 1963-64; mem. tech. staff N. Am. Aviation Sci. Center, Thousand Oaks, Calif., 1964-70; asso. prof. chem. engring. Clarkson Coll. Tech., Potsdam, N.Y., 1970-75, prof., 1975-79; prof. chem. engring. Johns Hopkins U., Balt., 1979—, chmn. dept., 1981—; dir. Energy Research Inst., 1981-83; prof. U. Aix-Marseille, France, 1976; vis. prof. M.I.T., Cambridge, 1977. Recipient John W. Graham Research prize, 1975, Md. Chemist of Yr. award, 1982; John Simon Guggenheim Meml. Found. fellow, 1976-77. Fellow Am. Phys. Soc., AAAS; mem. Am. Inst. Chem. Engrs., Am. Chem. Soc., Sigma Xi. Home: 5600 Greenspring Ave Baltimore MD 21209 Office: Dept Chem Engring Johns Hopkins U Baltimore MD 21218

KATZ, JOSEPH MORRIS, manufacturing company executive; b. Iampole, Russia, July 7, 1913; came to U.S., 1914; s. Samuel and Sarah (Averbach) K.; m. Agnes Roman, 1937; children—Marshall P., Andrea K. Plesset. Student, U. Pitts., 1931-34. Founder, chmn. bd. Papercraft Corp., Pitts., 1945-83, chmn. exec. com., 1983—. Mem. Gov.'s Fiscal Task Force, 1970-71; mem. Gov.'s Bus. Adv. Council Commonwealth Pa., State Planning Bd. Commonwealth Pa., 1973-78; trustee U. Pitts.; chmn. bd. visitors Faculty Arts and Scis.; mem. bd. visitors Grad. Sch. Bus.; trustee Katz Found., Montefiore Hosp.; bd. dirs. Am. Historic and Cultural Soc., Pitts. Symphony Soc., Civic Light Opera; bd. dirs., v.p. Allegheny Trails council Boy Scouts Am., City of Hope; trustee numerous others. Named Businessman of Yr., Pitts., 1965, Salesman of Yr., Pitts., 1969, Man of Yr. Herbert Lehman award, 1970; recipient Human Relations award Am. Jewish Com., 1972; Spirit of Life award City of Hope, 1982; Horatio Alger award, 1981. Clubs: Duquesne, Westmoreland Country, Concordia, Standard, Pitts. Athletic Assn. (Pitts.); Harmonie (N.Y.C.). Home: Gateway Towers Pittsburgh PA 15222 Office: Papercraft Corp Papercraft Park Pittsburgh PA 15238

KATZ, JULIAN, gastroenterologist, educator; b. N.Y.C., Apr. 3, 1937; s. Abraham M. and Fay (Sher) K.; m. Sheila Moriber, Aug. 18, 1963; children—Jonathan Peter, Sara Katherine. A.B., Columbia U., 1958; M.D., U. Chgo., 1962. Diplomate: Am. Bd. Internal Medicine. Intern U. Chgo. Hosps., 1962-63; resident in medicine Duke U., 1963-65; fellow in gastroenterology Yale U., 1965-67; practice medicine specializing in gastroenterology, internal medicine, Phila., 1969—; prof. medicine, lectr. in physiology and biochemistry Med. Coll. Pa., 1970—, also lectr. local and nat. groups; chief clin. gastroenterology Med. Coll. Pa. Editor profl. jours.; Contbr. articles to profl. jours. and books. Served with USN, 1967-69. Fellow ACP; mem. Am. Soc. Gastrointestinal Endoscopy, Am. Soc. Study Liver Disease, Am. Gastroenterological Assn., others. Home: 701 Dodds Ln Gladwyne PA 19035 Office: Gastrointestinal Specialists 555 City Ave Bala Cynwyd PA 19004

KATZ, KURT, capital equipment manufacturing company executive; b. Kassel, Ger., Aug. 1, 1932; came to U.S., 1938, naturalized, 1943; s. Siegfried and Blanche (Lowenstein) K.; m. Helen E. Grau, June 10, 1956; children—Beverly, Mark, Rachel, Brenda. B.Chem. Engring., Bklyn. Poly. Inst., 1954; M.Chem. Engring., N.Y. U., 1955; postgrad., U. Pitts., 1955-60. With Westinghouse Electric Co., Pitts., 1958-73, gen. mgr. water quality control div., 1968-73; v.p., dir. Peabody Internat. Corp., Darien, Conn., 1973-82, exec. v.p., chief operating officer, 1982—, pres., chief operating officer water/fluids group, 1974—. Pres. Pitts. PTA, 1965-67; bd. dirs. Hillel Acad., Pitts., 1968, Torah Acad., New Haven, 1977-79. Mem. Am. Chem. Soc., Am. Soc. Naval Architects and Marine Engrs., Water Pollution Control Fedn., Phi Lambda Upsilon. Jewish. Office: 4 Landmark Sq Stamford CT 06904

KATZ, LEON, paper company executive; b. Springfield, Mass., Aug. 27, 1921; s. Frederick and Sarah (Kirsner) K.; m. Blossom Shirley Zeidman, June 8, 1947; children: Stanley G., Barbara D., Nancy L. B.S., Trinity Coll., 1944; Ph.D. in Organic Chemistry, U. Ill., 1947. With GAF Corp., 1953-70; v.p. research and devel.; exec. v.p. Rockwood Industries, 1970-72; v.p. comml. devel. Polychrome Corp., 1972-73; v.p. research and devel. packaging div. Am. Can Co., 1973-80, v.p. gen. mgr. recovery systems and research and devel. fiber, 1980-82; sr. v.p. corp. research and devel. James River Corp., 1982. Contbr. articles to profl. jours. Served with AUS, 1943-44. Mem. Am. Chem. Soc., AAAS, N.Y. Research Dirs., Am. Mgmt. Assn., Sigma Xi, Pi Mu Epsilon, Phi Lambda Upsilon. Patentee in field. Office: James River Corp PO Box 6000 Norwalk CT 06856 *

KATZ, LEON, speech and drama educator; b. Bronx, N.Y., July 10, 1919; s. Bernard and Rachel (Koslow) K.; m. Sadell Kasmere, Oct. 9, 1942; children: Elia, Fredric. B.S.S., CCNY, 1940; M.A., Columbia, 1946, Ph.D., 1962. Instr. Cornell U., 1946-47, Hunter Coll., N.Y.C., 1947-49; asst. prof. Vassar Coll., 1949-58; lectr. Columbia, 1958-60; asso. prof. Manhattanville Coll., Purchase, N.Y., 1960-64; vis. asso. prof. Stanford, 1964-65; prof. San Francisco State Coll., 1965-68; Andrew Mellon vis. prof. Carnegie-Mellon U., Pitts., 1968-69, prof. drama dept., 1969-77; prof. dept. speech and theater arts U. Pitts., 1977-81; prof. Yale U., 1981—. Drama critic, sta. WQED-TV, San Francisco, 1966-68; film critic syndicated on radio, 1970-72; playwright TV writer.; Author: plays Three Cuckolds, 1958, Dracula: Sabbat, 1972, Making of Americans, 1973, Astapovo, 1982; TV dramas Confrontation, 1969; Necessity, 1972; Co-editor: QED and Other Early Writings by Gertrude Stein, 1970. Served to capt. USAAF, 1942-46. Nat. Endowment for Humanities Research grantee, 1972—; Ford Found. fellow, 1952-53. Mem. AAUP, AFTRA, Actors Equity. Jewish. Home: 59 Irving St New Haven CT

KATZ, LESLIE GEORGE, publisher; b. Balt., Nov. 22, 1918; s. Joseph and Kate (Kropman) K.; m. Jane Mayhall, June 4, 1940. Student, Black Mountain (N.C.) Coll., 1936-39, New Sch. for Social Research, N.Y.C., 1940-42. Pub. Eakins Press Found., N.Y.C., 1966—; Cons. Joseph Katz Co. (advt.), N.Y.C., 1950-58; Bd. dirs. Corp. of Yaddo, Saratoga Springs, N.Y. Author: Invitation to the Voyage, 1958; Contbr. fiction and essays to mags. Home: 15 W 67th St New York NY 10023 Office: 155 E 42d St New York NY 10017

KATZ, LEWIS, chemistry educator; b. Fond du Lac, Wis., Mar. 19, 1923; s. Alex and Rivka (Tabajovich) K.; m. Shirley Rita Robbins, Sept. 12, 1948; children: Susan Theresa, Deborah Ann. Student, N.D. State U., 1940-42; B.Chem., U. Minn., 1946, Ph.D., 1951. Instr. chemistry U. Conn., 1952-55, asst. prof., 1955-59, asso. prof., 1959-64, prof., 1964—, acting v.p. grad. edn. and research, 1981-83; guest scientist Weizmann Inst., U. Leyden, U. Stockholm, 1969. Contbr. articles profl. jours. Served with AUS, 1943-46. Postdoctoral fellow Calif. Inst. Tech., 1951-52; Nat. Sci. Found. sci. faculty fellow Cambridge U., 1961-62. Mem. Am. Chem. Soc., Am. Crystallog. Assn., Am. Assn. Univ. Profs., Phi Beta Kappa, Sigma Xi, Phi Lambda Upsilon. Home: 8 Eastwood Rd Storrs CT 06268

KATZ, LEWIS ROBERT, legal educator; b. N.Y.C., Nov. 15, 1938; s. Samuel and Rose (Turoff) K.; m. Jan Karen Daugherty, Jan. 14, 1964; children: Brett Elizabeth, Adam Kenneth, Tyler Jessica. A.B., Queens Coll., 1959; J.D., Ind. U., 1963. Bar: Ind 1963, Ohio 1971. Assoc. firm Snyder, Bunger, Cotner & Harrell, Bloomington, Ind., 1963-65; instr. U. Mich. Law Sch., Ann Arbor, 1965-66; asst. prof. Case Western Res. U. Law Sch., Cleve., 1966-68, assoc. prof., 1968-71, prof., 1971—, John C. Hutchins prof. law, dir. Center for Criminal Justice, 1973—; criminal justice agys. cons. Author: The Justice Imperative: Introduction to Criminal Justice, 1979, (with O.C. Schroeder, Jr.) Ohio Criminal Law, 1974, Justice Is The Crime, 1972. Nat. Defender Project of Nat. Legal Aid and Defender Assn. fellow, 1968. Mem. Am. Bar Assn. Home: 2873 N Park Blvd Cleveland Heights OH 44118 Office: Case Western Res U Law Sch Cleveland OH 44106

KATZ, MARSHALL PAUL, manufacturing company executive; b. Pitts., Sept. 17, 1939; s. Joseph M. and Agnes (Roman) K.; m. Wallis Fisk, June 13, 1965; 1 dau., Lauren Sarah. B.A., Cornell U., 1961. Mng. dir. Papercraft Internat. S.A., Baudour, Belgium, 1965-66; chmn., pres., chief exec. officer Papercraft Corp., Pitts., 1969—. Bd. dirs. Pitts. Opera, United Way, United Jewish Fedn.; trustee Montefiore Hosp. Served with USCGR. Mem. Young. Pres.'s Orgn. Clubs: Westmoreland Country (bd. dirs.), Duquesne, Concordia., Masons. Home: 6 Edgewood Rd Pittsburgh PA 15215 Office: Papercraft Park Pittsburgh PA 15238

KATZ, MARTIN HOWARD, lawyer; b. Bklyn., Jan. 21, 1931; s. Nathan and Sally K.; m. Theresa Victory, June 22, 1975; 1 son, Norman. B.A., Bklyn. Coll., 1952; J.D., Bklyn. Law Sch., 1955, LL.M., 1957. Sr. ptnr. firm Katz, Lubkin & Katz, Bklyn., 1955-68; gen. counsel AAMCO Industries, Inc., Bridgeport, Pa., 1968-74; sr. assoc. Blank, Rome, Comisky & McCauley, Phila., 1974-76; dep. atty. gen., chief antitrust div. Pa. Dept. Justice, 1978; v.p., corp. counsel Jewelcor Inc., Wilkes-Barre, Pa., 1978-82; gen. counsel U.S. Consumer Product Safety Commn., Washington, 1982—; lectr. bus. orgns. and mgmt. Pres. Long Beach (N.Y.) Civic Assn., 1965-68, Stonybrook Condominium Council, Norristown, Pa., 1976-78; Trustee Temple B'nai B'rith, Kingston, Pa. Recipient Pres.'s award Long Beach chpt. Nat. Cystic Fiborsis Found., 1967; Hero award United Way, 1978; Angel award, 1979. Mem. ABA, Fed. Bar Assn. Home: 838-102 Quince Orchard Blvd Gaithersburg MD 20878

KATZ, MAURICE HARRY, lawyer, educator; b. N.Y.C., Jan. 18, 1937; s. Milton and Florence (Davies) K.; m. Margery E. Rosenberg, May 6, 1962; children—Brian, Bradley, Andrew. A.B. cum laude, Columbia, 1958; LL.B., Harvard, 1961. Bar: Calif. bar 1963, N.Y. bar 1962, also U.S. Supreme Ct. bar 1962, U.S. Ct. Appeals bar 1962. Mem. firms Loeb and Loeb, Los Angeles, 1962-64, Freshman, Marantz and Comsky, Beverly Hills, Calif., 1964-66, Grobe, Reinstein, and Katz, Los Angeles, 1966-76, Katz and Weisman, 1976-78, Maurice H. Katz, 1978—; prof. U. San Fernando Sch. Law, Los Angeles, 1965-76, U. West Los Angeles, 1976—; judge pro tem Beverly Hills Mcpl. Ct., 1968-70, Los Angeles Municipal Ct., 1975—; hearing officer County of Los Angeles Civil Service Commn., 1976; arbitrator Los Angeles County Superior Ct., 1980—. Trustee Ennis-Brown House, 1980—; sec. Los Angeles-Bordeaux Sister City Com., 1981—; judge Los Angeles County Wine Fair, 1981—. Served with USMCR, 1961-62. Mem. State Bar Calif., Am., Los Angeles County, Beverly Hills bar assns., Hollywood Food and Wine Soc., Chaîne des Rôtisseurs, Phi Beta Kappa. Jewish. Home: 315 N McCadden Pl Los Angeles CA 90004 Office: 1880 Century Park E Los Angeles CA 90067

KATZ, MICHAEL, pediatrician, educator; b. Lwow, Poland, Feb. 13, 1928; came to U.S., 1946, naturalized, 1951; s. Edward and Rita (Gluzman) K. A.B., U. Pa., 1949, postgrad. (Harrison fellow), 1950-51; M.D., SUNY, Bklyn., 1956; M.S., Columbia U. Sch. Public Health, 1968. Intern UCLA Med. Center, 1956-57; resident Presbyterian Hosp. (Babies Hosp.), N.Y.C., 1960-62, dir. pediatric service, 1977—; hon. lectr. in pediatrics Makerere U. Coll., Kampala, Uganda, 1963-64; instr. in pediatrics Columbia U., 1964-65, prof. tropical medicine Sch. Public Health, 1971—, prof. pediatrics Coll. Physicians and Surgeons, 1972-77, Reuben S. Carpentier prof., chmn. dept. pediatrics, 1977—; asso. mem. Wistar Inst., Phila., 1965-71; asst. prof. pediatrics U. Pa., 1966-71; cons. WHO Regional Offices, Guatemala, Venezuela, Egypt, Yemen; mem. U.S. del. 32d World Health Assembly, Geneva, 1979; cons. UNICEF, N.Y.C. and Tokyo., USAID, Egypt, 1982. Contbr. articles to profl. jours.; author: (with others) Parasitic Diseases, 1982; editor: (with Volker ter Meulen) Slow Virus Infections of the Central Nervous System, 1977; editorial bd.: Med. Microbiology and Immunology, 1975—, Pediatric Infectious Diseases, 1981—, Vaccines, 1983—; also co-editor manuals. Served to lt. M.C., USNR, 1957-59. NIH grantee, 1968-76; WHO grantee, 1972-76; recipient Jurzykowski Found. award in Medicine, 1983. Fellow Infectious Diseases Soc. Am., AAAS, Am. Acad. Pediatrics; mem. Soc. Pediatric Research, Am. Pediatric Soc., Harvey Soc., Am. Soc. Microbiology, Deutsche Gesellschaft fur Neuropathologie und Neuroanatomie E.V. (corr.), Am. Soc. Tropical Medicine and Hygiene, N.Y. Soc. Tropical Medicine (pres. 1976-77), Royal Soc. Tropical Medicine and Hygiene (London), Inst. Medicine of Nat. Acad. Scis., Sigma Xi. Home: 930 Fifth Ave New York NY 10021 Office: Coll Physicians and Surgeons Columbia U 630 W 168th St New York NY 10032

KATZ, MILTON, legal educator, public official; b. N.Y.C., Nov. 29, 1907; s. Morris and Clara (Schiffman) K.; m. Vivian Greenberg, July 2, 1933; children: John, Robert, Peter. A.B., Harvard U., 1927, J.D., 1931; LL.D., Brandeis U., 1972. Bar: N.Y. 1932, Mass. 1959. Mem. anthrop. expdn. across Central Africa for Peabody Mus., Harvard, 1927-28; various ofcl. posts with U.S. Govt., 1932-39; prof. law Harvard, 1940; leaves of absence, 1941-46, 48-50, Henry L. Stimson prof. law, also dir. internat. legal studies, 1954-78, dir. internat. program in taxation, 1961-63; Sherman Fairchild Distinguished vis. scholar Calif. Inst. Tech., 1974; John Danz lectr., cons. program social mgmt. tech. U. Wash., 1974; Phi Beta Kappa distinguished vis. scholar, 1977-78; Disting. prof. law Suffolk U. Law Sch., 1978—; solicitor WPB, 1941-43; U.S. exec. officer Combined Prodn. and Resources Bd., 1942-43; with OSS, 1943-44; U.S. spl. rep. in, Europe; with rank AEP, 1950-51; chief U.S. del. Econ. Commn. for Europe, 1950-51; chmn. Def. Financial and Econ. Com. North Atlantic Treaty, 1950-51; v.p. Ford Found., 1951-54, cons., 1954-66; cons., asst. sec. edn. HEW, 1967; cons., chmn. energy adv. com. Office Tech. Assessment, 1974—, Nat. Endowment Humanities, 1974—; Pres. Cambridge Community Services, 1959-61; chmn. com. manpower White House Conf. Internat. Cooperation, 1965; chmn. com. on life scis. and social policy Nat. Acad. Sci.-NRC, 1968-75; mem. panel tech. assessment Nat. Acad. Sci., 1968-69. Author: Cases and Materials in Administrative Law, 1947, Government Under Law and the Individual, (with others), 1957, (with Kingman Brewster, Jr.) Law of International Transactions and Relations, 1960, The Things That Are Caesar's, 1966, The Relevance of International Adjudication, 1968, The Modern Foundation: Its Dual Nature, Public and Private, 1968, (with others) Man's Impact on the Global Environment, 1970, Assessing Biomedical Technologies, 1975, Technology, Trade and the U.S. Economy, 1978, strengthening Conventional Deterrence in Europe—A Proposal for the 1980s, 1983; also articles. Trustee Case Western Res. U., 1967-80, Brandeis U.; mem. corp. Boston Mus. Sci.; mem. vis. com. humanities Mass. Inst. Tech., 1970-73; mem. adv. bd. Energy Lab., 1974—; chmn. bd. trustees Carnegie Endowment Internat. Peace, 1970-78, Internat. Legal Center, 1971-78; trustee, mem. exec. com. World Peace Found.; pres. Citizen's Research Found., 1969-78; co-chmn. Am. Bar Assn.-AAAS Com. on Sci. and Law; mem. com. on tech. and internat. econ. and trade issues Nat. Acad. Engring. Served with USNR, 1944-46; MTO, ETO; lt. comdr. Res. Decorated Legion of Merit; comdr.'s cross Fed. Republic Germany)., Order of Merit. Fellow Am. Acad. Arts and Scis. (pres. 1979-82); mem. Harvard Alumni Assn. (dir. 1952-55). Home: 6 Berkeley St Cambridge MA 02138

KATZ, PAUL, educator, conductor; b. N.Y.C., Nov. 2, 1907; s. Nathan and Molly (Rothenberg) K.; m. Phyllis Margolis, July 29, 1934; 1 son, Nevin. Mus.B. in Theory, Cleve. Inst. Music, 1931; postgrad., Am. Conservatory of Music, Fountainbleau, France; student of, Sevcik, Ysaye, Auer, Boulanger; hon. degrees, U. Dayton, Central State U. Tchr., condr., chmn. orch. dept. Cin. Coll. Conservatory Music; lectr., tchr. U. Dayton, Wright State U. Condr., Dayton Philharmonic Orch., 1933—; Composer. Mem. Audubon Soc. Jewish. Home: 5100 Aquilla Dr Dayton OH 45415 *I have always thought music has the potential of bringing all people together. In all my music activities I strived to improve the quality of my community.*

KATZ, PHYLLIS POLLAK, magazine publisher; b. N.Y.C., Dec. 29, 1939; s. Henry Abraham and Rose (Chaiken) P.; m. Edward Katz, Sept. 12, 1971; children: Charles Daniel, Jacob Evan. B.A., Cornell U., 1961; postgrad., U. Pa., 1961-68, Am. Sch. Classical Studies, Athena, 1964-66. Dept. asst. Univ. Mus., U. Pa.; lectr. N.Y. U., 1970-71; asst. editor Archaeology mag., N.Y.C., 1968-72, editor, 1972—, pub., 1978—. Archaeol. excavations, Gordion, Turkey, 1965, Porto Cheli, Greece, Samothrace, Greece, 1966, Torre del Mordillo, Italy, 1967. Heinemann fellow, 1964-66. Mem. Archaeol. Inst. Am., Soc. Am. Archaeology, Soc. Hist. Archaeology, Am. Anthrop. Assn., Asia Soc. Jewish. Office: 53 Park Pl New York NY 10007 *

KATZ, ROBERT ARVIN, corp. exec., lawyer; b. Boston, Jan. 14, 1927; s. Morris Wolf and Freda (Cohen) K.; m. Tracy Oppenheimer, Dec. 28, 1952; children—Terry Alison, Robin Elizabeth, Wendy Arete, Michael Edward. A.B., Harvard, 1946, postgrad., 1947-48; LL.B., Boston U., 1954. Bar: Ill. bar 1954, Conn. bar 1960, N.Y. bar 1966. Practice in, Chgo., 1954-59; asso. firm Peebles, Greenberg & Keele (and predecessors), 1954-59; asst. sec. Revlon, Inc., N.Y.C., 1961-65; sec. Joseph E. Seagram & Sons, Inc., N.Y.C., 1965-69; chmn. exec. com., dir. Bevis Industries, Inc., Providence, 1969-72; individual practice law, N.Y.C., 1969-72, 75—; chmn. McGrath Services Corp.,

1973-74. Served to ensign USNR, 1944-46. Home: 200 E 58th St New York NY 10022 Office: 200 E 58th St New York NY 10022

KATZ, ROBERT LEE, business executive; b. San Francisco, Jan. 8, 1926; s. Adrian J. and Anne (Schallman) K.; m. Susan Goldsmith, June 14, 1953; children: Andrew, Peter, Jeffrey. A.B., U. Calif. at Berkeley, 1945; M.B.A., Stanford U., 1948; D.C.S., Harvard U., 1956. Asst. prof. Amos Tuck Sch. Bus. Adminstrn., Dartmouth Coll., 1953-56; asst. prof. Harvard, 1956-60; lectr. bus. mgmt. Stanford, 1960-68; prof. bus. mgmt. l'Inst. pour l'Étude des Méthodes de Direction de l'Enterprise, Lausanne, Switzerland, 1966-67; pres. Robert L. Katz and Assos., 1953—, U.S. Natural Resources, Inc., Menlo Park, Calif., 1969-72; chmn. bd. Yosemite Park & Curry Co., 1970-72; dir. Petro-Lewis Corp., Crosspoint Fin. Corp., Newell Cos., Caltex Investment Mgmt. Co., NPI Corp. Author: Cases and Concepts in Corporate Strategy, 1970, Management of the Total Enterprise, 1970, Organizational Behavior and Administration, 1961; Contbr. articles to profl. jours. Co-incorporator of town, 1st chmn. Planning Commn. Town of (Calif.) Portola Valley, 1964-66. Served to lt. (j.g.) USNR, 1945-46. Mem. Acad. Mgmt. Republican. Clubs: Harvard (N.Y.C.); Stanford Golf (Palo Alto, Calif.). Home: 155 Mapache Dr Portola Valley CA 94025

KATZ, RONALD LEWIS, physician, educator; b. Bklyn., Apr. 22, 1932; s. Joseph and Belle (Charnis) K.; m. Leah Katz; children by previous marriage—Richard Ian, Laura Susan, Margaret Karen. B.A., U. Wis.-Madison, 1952; M.D., Boston U., 1956; postgrad. in Pharmacology (NIH fellow), Coll. Physicians and Surgeons, Columbia U., 1959-60, Royal Postgrad. Med. Sch., U. London, 1968-69. Intern USPHS Hosp., S.I., 1956-57; resident Columbia-Presbyn. Med. Center, 1957-60; asst. prof. anesthesiology Coll. Physicians and Surgeons, Columbia U., 1960-66, asso. prof., 1966-70, prof., 1970-73; prof., chmn. dept. anesthesiology U. Calif. at Los Angeles, 1973—; Cons. NIH, FDA, numerous state agys. Author, editor: Muscle Relaxants, 1975; Contbr. numerous articles to profl. jours.; Mem. editorial bd.: Handbook of Anesthesiology, 1972—, Progress in Anesthesiology, 1973—. Mem. Am. Soc. Anesthesiologists, Am. Physiol. Soc., Am. Soc. Pharmacology and Exptl. Therapeutics, N.Y. Acad. Medicine. Inventor peripheral nerve stimulator. Home: 3063 Greentree Ct Bel Air CA 90024 Office: Dept Anesthesiology U Calif at Los Angeles Los Angeles CA 90024

KATZ, S. STANLEY, banker; b. Albany, N.Y., Oct. 21, 1928; s. Jacob and Rose K.; m. Cecilia Sigalowsky, June 19, 1955; children—Mitchell H., Raquel D. Student, Siena Coll., 1950-52; B.A., Syracuse U., 1954; M.A., Maxwell Grad. Sch., 1956; Ph.D., Am. U., 1966. Economist U.S. Bur. Budget, Devel. Loan Fund and AID, 1956-61, OECD, Paris, 1962-65, World Bank, 1966-67; dep. asst. sec. Dept. Commerce, Washington, 1968-78; v.p. Asian Devel. Bank, Manila, 1978—; lectr. George Washington U., 1974-78. Author: Foreign Assistance Contribution to Indian Economic Development, 1966; contbr. articles to profl. jours. Home: 2163 Paraiso St Dasmarinas Makati Manila Philippines Office: 2330 Roxas Blvd PO Box 789 Manila Philippines

KATZ, SAMUEL, educator; b. Berlin, Germany, Feb. 13, 1923; came to U.S., 1934, naturalized, 1940; s. Herman and Bertha (Low) K.; m. Jean Barbara Parker, July 10, 1953; children—David R., Daniel M., Miriam E. B.S., U. Mich., 1943; A.M., Columbia, 1947, Ph.D., 1955. With radiation lab. Mass. Inst. Tech., 1943-46; mem. sci. staff Lamont Geol. Obs., Columbia, 1948-53; sr. physicist Stanford Research Inst., 1953-57; mem. faculty Rensselaer Poly Inst., 1957—, prof. geophysics, 1962—, chmn. dept. geology, 1964-69. Contbr. articles in field to profl. jours. Mem. Am. Geophys. Union, Soc. Explorations Geophysicists, Seismol. Soc. Am., A.A.A.S., Sigma Xi. Home: 908 Karenwald Ln Schenectady NY 12309 Office: Rensselaer Poly Inst Troy NY 12181

KATZ, SAMUEL LAWRENCE, educator, physician; b. Manchester, N.H., May 29, 1927; s. Morris and Ethel (Lawrence) K.; m. Betsy Jane Cohan, June 27, 1950; children: Samuel Lawrence Jr. (dec.), John L., David L., Deborah Susan, William L., Susan Johanna, Penelope Jennifer; m. Catherine Minock Wilfert, July 23, 1971; stepchildren: Rachel Ann, Katie Claiborne. A.B. magna cum laude, Dartmouth Coll., 1949; M.D. cum laude, Harvard U., 1952. Intern Beth Israel Hosp., Boston, 1952-53; resident Children's Hosp., Boston, 1953-54, 55-56, Mass. Gen. Hosp., 1954-55; from research fellow to asst. prof. Harvard Med. Sch., 1956-68; prof., chmn. dept. pediatrics Duke Med. Sch., 1968—, Wilburt C. Davison prof., 1972—; mem. sci. adv. bd. St. Jude's Children's Research Hosp., Nat. Jewish Hosp., Denver; research virology, virus vaccines, immunization NIH, Am. Acad. Pediatrics, FDA. Contbr. to books, articles to profl. jours.; mem. editorial bd.: Revs. of Infectious Diseases. Served with USNR, 1945-46. Nat. Found. fellow, 1956-58; NIH research career devel. awardee, 1965-68. Mem. Am. Fedn. Clin. Research, Am. Soc. Clin. Investigation, Soc. Pediatric Research, Am., New Eng. pediatric socs., Infectious Diseases Soc. Am., Am. Assn. Immunologists, Am. Acad. Pediatrics (Grulee award 1975), Assn. Med. Sch. Pediatric Dept. Chmn. (pres. 1977-79), Inst. Medicine of Nat. Acad. Sci. Developer (with John F. Enders) attenuated live measles-virus vaccine. Home: Route 8 Box 40 Chapel Hill NC 27514 Office: Duke Med Center Durham NC 27710

KATZ, SANFORD NOAH, lawyer, educator; b. Holyoke, Mass., Dec. 23, 1933; m. Joan Raphael; children: Daniel, Andrew. B.A. with distinction in History, Boston U., 1955; J.D., U. Chgo., 1958; postgrad. (USPHS fellow), Yale U. Law Sch., 1963-64. Bar: D.C. 1959, U.S. Supreme Ct. 1963, Mass. 1970. Clk. to Hon. Marvin Jones, chief judge U.S. Ct. Claims, Washington, 1958-59; instr. Catholic U. Am. Sch. Law, 1959-60, asst. prof. law, 1960-62, assoc. prof., 1962-64, U. Fla., 1964-66, prof., 1966-68, Boston Coll., 1968—; vis. prof. U. Mich., summer 1967; lectr. in law and social work Smith Coll., summers, 1965-69; asso. Clare Hall, Cambridge (Eng.) U., 1973; mem. Faculty of Laws, 1973; vis. fellow Hampstead Child Therapy Clinic, London, 1973; del. White House Conf. on Children, 1970; mem. Spl. Adv. Com. to Atty. Gen. Mass., 1974, Joint Mass. House and Senate Commn. on Family, 1977, Mass. Jud. Nominating Commn., 1977-79. Author: books, the most recent being Adoptions Without Agencies: A Study of Independent Adoptions, 1978, (with Inker) Fathers, Husbands and Lovers—Legal Rights and Responsibilities, 1979; author: Child Snatching—The Legal Response to the Abduction of Children, 1981; Author: (with Weyrauch) American Family Law in Transition, 1983; author monographs, book introductions; contbr. articles, revs. to profl. publs.; editor: The Youngest Minority: Lawyers in Defense of Children, vols. I and II, 1974, (with John Eekelaar) Family Violence: An International and Interdisciplinary Study, 1978, Marriage and Cohabitation in Contemporary Societies, 1980; editor-in-chief: Family Law Quar., 1970-83; editorial bd.: Mass. Family Law Jour. Chmn. Lydia Rapoport Endowment Fund, Smith Coll.; bd. dirs. Boston Coll. Campus Sch. for Multi-handicapped Students. Chestnut Hill, Mass. Field Found. grantee, 1968-69; Grant Found. grantee, 1971-75; HEW grantee, 1973-78. Mem. Internat. Soc. Family Law (pres.), Mass. Bar Assn., Am. Bar Assn. (chmn. family law sect. 1980-81). Chief drafter HEW model acts; research on child abuse and neglect, marriage, child custody and divorce, model legislation, contract law. Office: 885 Centre St Newton Centre MA 02159

KATZ, SAUL MILTON, social scientist, educator; b. N.Y.C., Apr. 7, 1915; s. Charles L. and Malle (Salop) K.; m. Martha Marie Keller, Sept. 11, 1953; children: Charles, Jonathan, David, Mollie. B.S., Cornell U., 1940, M.S., 1943; M.A., Harvard U., 1949, M.P.A., 1950, Ph.D., 1953. Chief food, agr., forestry U.S. Mil. Govt., Germany, 1946-49; chief exports U.S. Dept. Agr., Washington, 1955-57, program coordinator Latin Am., 1957-59; mem. central planning staff AID, State Dept., Washington, 1960-61; asso. prof. econ. and social devel. U. Pitts., 1961-64, prof., 1964—, dir. programs in econ. and social devel., 1968-73, asso. dean, 1972-73; Cons. UN, 1969—, OAS, 1964—, AID, 1963—, various fgn. govts. and industry. Author: Research Guide to Cooperative Farming, 1941, Guide to Modernizing Administration for National Development (translated to Spanish 1965, to Chinese 1968), Systems Approach to Development Administration, 1965, Education for Development Administrators: Character, Form, Content and Curriculum, 1967, Administrative Capability and Agricultural Development, 1970, Quantitative Techniques for National Economic Development Planning, 1972, Striving for the Heavenly Society: The Tactics of Development, 1975, The Regional Organization and Management of Development, 1978, The Regional Organization and Management of Development in Israel, 1981, others. Bd. dirs. Inter-Univ. Consortium on Research and Instn. Bldg.; also chmn. com. systems of Comparative Adminstrn. Group, 1965—. Served to capt. AUS, 1942-47; ETO. Decorated Bronze Star, Purple Heart; Croix de Guerre avec aguille, France). Mem. Am. Econ. Assn., Am. Agr. Econ. Assn., Am. Soc. Pub. Adminstrn., Soc. Internat. Devel., Center Inter-Am. Relations, Sociedad Interamericana de Planificacion (Venezuela). Home: 1240 Malvern Ave Pittsburgh PA 15217 Office: 3R26 Forbes Quadrangle U Pitts Pittsburgh PA 15260

KATZ, SIDNEY, physician, educator, health service adminstr.; b. Cleve., Feb. 4, 1924; s. Leo and Ida (Hagler) K.; m. Beverly Suid, Mar. 17, 1946; children: Michael Jay, Lynne Meredith (Mrs. Dwight Gilbert), Kent Roger, James David. B.S., Case Western Res. U., 1945, M.D., 1948. Intern U. Hosps., Cleve., 1948-49, resident, 1948-50; fellow Case Western Res. U., 1950, mem. faculty depts. medicine and preventive medicine, 1952-71; assoc. dir. dept. community medicine, 1970-71, prof. preventive dept. medicine community medicine, 1970-71; prof. medicine and dir. Office Health Services Edn. and Research, Coll. Medicine, Mich. State U., East Lansing, 1971-77, chmn. dept. community health sci., 1971-83; assoc. dean medicine, dir. Gerontology Ctr. Brown U., 1983—; cons. HEW, 1965—; Trustee Med. Sch. Case Western Res. U., 1974-77. Author: Effects of Continued Care, 1972; editorial bd.: Med. Care, 1975-78; contbr. articles to profl. jours. Fellow Am. Cancer Soc., 1950. Served with AUS, 1951-52; Served with USNR, 1943-45. Decorated Bronze Star. Mem. Inst. Medicine of Nat. Acad. Scis., Am. Fedn. Clin. Research, Central Soc. Clin. Research, Assn. Tchrs. Preventive Medicine (dir. 1977-80), Gerontol. Soc., Internat. Epidemiol. Soc., Am. Epidemiol. Soc., Am., Mich. State, Ingham County med. socs., Sigma Xi, Alpha Omega Alpha, Phi Delta Epsilon, Phi Sigma Delta. Jewish. Home: 21 Twin Pond Rd East Greenwich RI 02818

KATZ, SOL, physician; b. N.Y.C., Mar. 29, 1913; s. Samuel and Bessie K.; m. Beatrice Guzewich Paul, Nov. 16, 1946; children—Paul, Rita, Judith. B.S. magna cum laude, CCNY, 1935, M.D., Georgetown U., 1939, Sc.D. (hon.), 1978. Diplomate: Am. Bd. Internal Medicine. Intern Georgetown U., Hosp., Washington, 1939-40; resident D.C. Gen. Hosp., Washington, 1940-42, pulmonary fellow, 1942-45, chief div. pulmonary diseases, 1946-59; chief med. service VA Hosp., Washington, 1959-70; dir. pulmonary disease div. Sch. Medicine, Georgetown U., Washington, 1970-78, prof. pulmonary medicine, 1978—; professorial lectr. in medicine Sch. Medicine, George Washington U.; hon. vis. cons. Brompton Hosp., London, 1974-75, vis. prof., 1981; cons. in pulmonary diseases NIH, Walter Reed Army Hosp. Asso. editor: American Family Physician; contbr. writings in field to profl. publs. Recipient commendation for outstanding med. achievement VA, 1962. Mem. A.C.P., Am. Coll. Chest Physicians, Am. Thoracic Soc., Brit. Thoracic Assn., Am. Fedn. Clin. Research, So. Soc. Clin. Investigation, Brompton Hosp. Assn., Internat. Union Against TB, Med. Soc. D.C. (Disting. Service award 1970), Phi Beta Kappa, Alpha Omega Alpha. Condr. research in chemotherapy of TB. Office: 3800 Reservoir Rd Washington DC 20007

KATZ, SOLOMON, history educator; b. Buffalo, June 10, 1909; s. Saul and Sophia (Gelber) K.; m. Marcia Geller, Sept. 6, 1931 (dec. 1976); children: Kenneth, Cynthia (Mrs. Robert Stern). A.B., Cornell U., 1930, Ph.D., 1933; student, Sorbonne, Paris, France, 1932-33. Asst. prof. Greek U. Oreg., 1935-36; mem. faculty U. Wash., 1936—, successively instr., asst. and assoc. prof., prof. history, 1936-79, chmn. dept., 1954-60, dean Coll. Arts and Scis., 1960-66, provost, 1965-75, v.p. acad. affairs, 1967-75, univ. historian, 1975—. Author: Jews in Visigothic and Frankish Kingdoms of Spain and Gaul, 1937, The Decline of Rome and the Rise of Medieval Europe, 1955; also articles. Del. 7th Internat. Congress Roman Frontier Studies, Israel, 1967; v.p. sect. 13th Internat. Congress Hist. Scis., USSR, 1970; Trustee Seattle Art Mus., Lakeside Sch., Ryther Child Center, PONCHO, United Arts Council; trustee; pres. Seattle Repertory Theatre.; mem. Seattle Arts Commn., Seattle Ctr. Adv. Commn., 5th Ave. Theatre Assn., Henry Gallery Assn. Served from 1st lt. to maj. USAAF, 1942-46. Decorated Bronze Star; George C. Boldt traveling fellow, Europe, 1932-33; Am. Council Learned Socs. fellow, Europe, 1934-35; Fulbright research scholar, France, 1952-53; Guggenheim fellow, Italy, 1953-54; Danforth grantee, Europe, 1970. Mem. Am. Hist. Assn. (pres. Pacific Coast br. 1968), Am. Philol. Assn., Archaeol Inst., Medieval Acad., AAUP, Phi Beta Kappa. Club: Rainier (Seattle). Home: 7708 56th Pl NE Seattle WA 98115

KATZ, SOLOMON HERTZ, anthropologist, educator; b. Beverly, Mass., July 22, 1939; s. Max and Rose (Hefferon) K.; m. Judith Kapustin, June 21, 1964; children: Noah, Rachel. B.A., Northeastern U., 1963; M.A. (NIH fellow), U. Pa., 1966, Ph.D., 1967. Research asst. Harvard U.-Mass. Gen. Hosp., Boston, 1961-63; research asst. Bermuda Biol. Sta., St. Georges, West Bermuda, 1963; NIH fellow U. Pa., 1968, asst. prof. anthropology, depts. pediatric dentistry and anthropology, 1968-72, asso. prof., 1972-76, prof., 1976—, curator phys. anthropology Univ. Museum, 1968—; sr. med. research scientist, dir. div. psychoendocrinology Eastern Pa. Psychiat. Inst., Phila., 1972-80; research prof. preventive and community medicine, dir. perinatal div. Eastern Pa. Psychiat. Inst. div. Med. Coll. Pa., Phila., 1981—; dir. W.M. Krogman Center for Research in Child Growth and Devel., Children's Hosp. of Phila.-U. Pa., 1972—; pres. Inst. Continuous Study of Man, 1974—. Editor: Biological Anthropology, 1975; corr. editor: Comments on Contemporary Psychiatry, 1972-74; asso. editor, co-chmn. joint publs. bd.: Zygon, 1975—; asso. and founding asso. editor: Human Ecology, 1972-74. Mem. Narberth Home and Sch. Bd., 1976-77. NIH-Nat. Inst. Dental Research grantee, 1963-67; Nat. Inst. Environ. Health Scis. grantee, 1975-79; Nat. Heart, Lung and Blood Inst. grantee, 1976-81, 82-85; NSF grantee, 1968-69; Smithsonian Instn. grantee, 1978-79; Grant Found. grantee, 1974-78; Internat. Research Exchange grantee, 1978; Wenner Gren Found. grantee, 1979. Mem. Am. Assn. Phys. Anthropologists, AAAS, Am. Heart Assn., Phila. Acad. Scis., Am. Anthrop. Assn., Am. Mammologist Soc., Inst. on Religion in an Age of Sci. (pres. 1977-79, 81-84). Home: 519 N Wynnewood Ave Narberth PA 19072 Office: Dept Anthropology Univ Museum 33d and Spruce St Philadelphia PA 19104

KATZ, STANLEY H., advertising executive; b. Newark, Jan. 2, 1923; s. Charles and Therese (Reif) K.; m. Vivienne Patricia Fox, Nov. 17, 1946; children: Robert N., Douglas D., William L. Student, N.Y. U., 1940-42. Vice-pres., dir. mktg. A. Hollander & Sons, N.Y.C., 1946-53; exec. v.p. Leber Katz Partners, N.Y.C., 1954-56, pres., chief exec. officer, 1956-80, chmn., chief exec. officer, 1980—; dir. U.S. Shoe Corp., Cin., 1978—. Contbr. articles to profl. jours. Served with USAAF, 1942-45. Mem. Am. Inst. Mgmt. (president's council 1972-78), Am. Assn. Advt. Agys. (gov. N.Y. council 1979—). Clubs: Friars, Lucullus Soc., Royal Danish Yacht. Office: Leber Katz Partners 767 Fifth Ave New York NY 10053 *

KATZ, STANLEY NIDER, history-law educator; b. Chgo., Apr. 23, 1934; s. William Stephen and Florence (Nider) K.; m. Adria Holmes, Jan. 16, 1960; children: Derek Holmes, Marion Holmes. A.B., Harvard U., 1955, M.A., 1959, Ph.D., 1961; LL.D. (hon.), Stockton State Coll., 1981. Asst. prof. history Harvard U., 1961-65, U. Wis., Madison, 1965-71; prof. legal history U. Chgo., 1971-78; Class of 1921 Bicentennial prof. history Am. law and liberty Princeton U., 1978—; vis. prof. law U. Pa., 1978—; mem. Oliver Wendell Holmes Devise, Washington, 1976—; bd. govs. Inst. European Studies, Chgo., 1976—; chmn. Council on Internat. Exchange Scholars, Washington, 1981—; mem. N.J. Supreme Ct. Com. on Model Rules of Profl. Conduct, 1982-83; vice chmn. ABA Commn. on Undergrad. Edn. in Law and Humanities, 1977-81. Author: Newcastle's New York, 1968; editor: The Case and Tryal of John Peter Zenger, 1963 (rev. edit. 1972); co-editor: Colonial America, 1971, 76, 83, Am. History: Promise and Progress, 1983; editor: Oliver Wendell Holmes Devise History of U.S. Supreme Ct., 1977—. Mem. N.J. Com. for Humanities, 1978—. Mem. Am. Soc. Legal History (pres. 1978-81), Inst. Early Am. History and Cultures (council 1974-76), Orgn. Am. Historians (exec. com. 1976-79), Am. Antiquarian Soc., Phi Beta Kappa. Democrat. Jewish. Clubs: Quadrangle (Chgo.); Princeton (N.Y.C.). Office: Woodrow Wilson Sch Princeton U Prospect St Princeton NJ 08544

KATZ, WILLIAM ARMSTRONG, library science educator; b. Seattle, July 6, 1924; s. Karl K. and Ruth M. (Armstrong) K.; m. Linda Sternberg, Dec. 11, 1970; children: Randy, Janet. B.A., U. Wash., 1947, M.A., 1955; Ph.D., U. Chgo., 1965. Newspaper reporter, 1948-55; librarian King County Pub. Library, Seattle, 1955-60; asst. to dir. publishing dept. ALA, 1960-63; asso. prof. U. Ky., 1963-66; prof. Sch. Library and Info. Sci., State U. N.Y., Albany, 1966—; cons. in field. Author: Introduction to Reference Work, 2 vols., 4th edit, 1982, Magazines for Libraries, 4th edit., 1982, Magazine Selection, 1971, Guide to Magazine and Serial Agents, 1975, Your Library-A Reference Guide, 1983, Reference and Information Services, 1982, Collection Development, 1980, Writer's Choice, 1983; Editor: Jour. Edn. for Librarianship, 1964-72, Reference Quar, 1963-73, Best of Library Lit, 1970—; editor mag. column: Library Jour, 1970—, The Reference Librarian, 1981; Contbr.: Ency. Brit., Yearbook, 1970—, 3ALA Yearbook, 1976—. Served with AUS, 1942-45. Decorated Bronze Star.; Recipient award merit Seattle Hist. Soc., 1965. Mem. ALA (Isadore G. Mudge citation 1973). Address: 135 Western Ave Albany NY 12222

KATZ, WILLIAM LOREN, author, publishing company executive; b. Bklyn., June 2, 1927; s. Bernard and Madeline (Simon) K. B.A., Syracuse U., 1950; M.A., N.Y. U., 1952. Tchr. am. history, N.Y.C., 1954-60, Hartsdale, N.Y., 1960-67, author, 1967—; cons. N.Y. State Edn. Dept., 1967-68, 83-84, USAF Schs. in Eng., Belgium and Holland, 1974-75; scholar in residence Tchrs. Coll. Columbia, 1971-73; tchr.Black history Tombs Prison, N.Y.C., 1973, N.Y. U. Afro-Am. Inst., 1973; faculty Inst. Urban and Minority Edn., Gen. Assistance Center, Tchrs. Coll. Columbia U., 1976; tchr. am. history New Sch. for Social Research, N.Y.C., 1977-83; pres. Ethrac Publs., 1971—. Author: Eyewitness: The Negro in American History, 1967 (Gold Medal award for non-fiction NCCJ), Teachers' Guide to American Negro History, 1968, (with Warren J. Halliburton) American Majorities and Minorities: A Syllabus of United States History for Secondary Schools, 1970, The Black West: A Documentary and Pictorial History, 1971, (with Warren J. Halliburton) A History of Black Americans, 1973, The Constitutional Amendments, 1974, Making Our Way: America at the Turn of the Century, 1975, Black People Who Made the Old West, 1977, Teaching Approaches to Black History in the Classroom, 1973, An Album of the Civil War, 1974, An Album of Reconstruction, 1974, Minorities in American History, Vols. I-VI, 1974-75, An Album of the Great Depression, 1978, An Album of Nazism, 1979; editor: The American Negro: His History and Literature, 147 vols, 1968-71, (with James M. McPherson) The Anti-Slavery Crusade in America, 69 vols, 1969, Minorities in America: Picture Histories, 1972—, Pamphlets in American History, 1977-82; editorial bd. jour.: Black Studies, 1970-73; editorial dir.: (with Henry Steele Commager and Arthur Schlesinger, Jr.) Vital Sources in American History for High School Students, 168 vols, 1980; Contbr. articles to Sat. Rev., Jour. Negro History, N.Y. Times, Jour. Negro Edn., Jour. Black Studies, Reader's Digest, Congl. Record, Others. Mem. exec. bd. Art Against Apartheid, 1984; mem. nat. council Nat. Emergency Civil Liberties Com, 1981—. Served with USNR, 1945-46. Home: 231 W 13th St New York NY 10011 *If you believe that a person has no history worth mentioning, it's easy to assume he has no humanity worth defending.*

KATZBERG, ALLAN ALFRED, anatomy educator; b. Orcadia, Sask., Can., July 6, 1913; came to U.S., 1949, naturalized, 1952; s. Frederick and Ida (Hoffman) K.; m. Betty Jeanne Bainbridge, Aug. 10, 1948; children: Allan Alfred, Susan Katzberg Foster, Mary Joanna, Elizabeth Lynne. B.Sc., U. Man., Can., 1943; M.S., Institutum Divi Thomae, Cin., 1949; Ph.D., U. Okla., 1956. Tchr. pub. schs., Sask., 1933-37; instr. anatomy U. Okla. Med. Center, Oklahoma City, 1949-56, asst. prof. anatomy, 1956-59; head cellular biology sect. U.S. Air Force Aerospace Med. Center, Brooks AFB, Tex., 1959-60, dep. chief astrobiology br., 1960-63; asso. prof. physiology U. Sask., Saskatoon, 1963-64; chmn. anatomy S.W. Found. for Research and Edn., San Antonio, 1964-68; asso. prof. biology Western Ill. U., Macomb, 1968-69; asso. prof. anatomy Ind. U. Med. Center, Indpls., 1969-77, prof., 1977—, acting chmn. anatomy dept., 1970-71; Dir. summer seminar Institutum Divi Thomae, Cin., 1961; mem. expdn. to collect primates of E. Africa, 1964; cons. U.S. Air Force Arctic Aero-Med. Lab., Fairbanks, Alaska, 1961, Cambridge U., Eng., 1964-65, S.W. Agrl. Inst., Tex., 1965, S.W. Research Inst., 1966, U. Utah, Purdue U., U. Calif., 1966, FAA, 1967, U.S. Air Force, 657st Aeromed. Research Lab., Holloman AFB, 1967, Ford Motor Co., 1967; project officer human studies on board Discoverer Satellites 17, 18, 29, 30, 35, 36. Contbr. articles to profl. jours. Deacon Bapt. Ch., 1955—. Recipient Ind. State Med. Assn. award, 1971, 72; Eli Lilly award, 1972. Mem. Am. Assn. Anatomists, Tex. Cell and Tissue Culture Assn. (pres. 1960-61), Pan Am. Assn. Anatomists (founder), Sociedad Mexicana de Anatomia (hon. mem.), Royal Microscopical Soc., Youth for Christ (pres. 1963). Home: 944 E Main St Carmel IN 46032 Office: Dept Anatomy Indiana University Medical Center Indianapolis IN 46202 *The great adventure as an educator began in a one room country school house at a salary of forty cents a day. The real pay came later, after introducing a student to the vast unknown. I could watch him enter his own frontier with a confident step, and could share his thrill as he reached up to touch the face of God.*

KATZELL, RAYMOND A., educator, psychologist; b. Bklyn., Mar. 16, 1919; s. Abraham and Fannie (Skoblow) K.; m. Florence Joyce Goldstein, Sept. 7, 1941; m. Mildred Engberg, May 11, 1953. B.S.,

N.Y. U., 1939, A.M., 1941, Ph.D., 1943; postgrad., Columbia, 1939. Diplomate: Am. Bd. Examiners in Psychology. Research asst. psychology NRC grant for research on selection and tng. pilots N.Y. U., 1939-42, instr. psychology, 1942-43, adj. asso. prof. psychology, 1951-53; instr. evenings Sch. Bus. Adminstrn., Coll. City N.Y., 1942-43; asst. prof. psychology U. Tenn., 1945-46, asso. prof., 1946-48; asso. prof. personnel psychology, dir. psychol. service center Syracuse (N.Y.) U., 1948-51; lectr. psychology Columbia, 1955-57; cons. personnel psychology in indsl. orgns., 1945—; v.p. Richardson, Bellows, Henry & Co., Inc., 1951-57, dir., 1947-68; prof. mgmt. engring. and psychology and dir. research center indsl. behavior N.Y. U., 1957-63, prof. psychology, 1963—, head dept., 1963-72; cons. N.Y.C. Dept. Personnel, 1967-72, U.S. Dept. Labor, 1968-80, HEW, 1968-70, U.S. Dept. Justice, 1969-79, Equal Employment Opportunities Commn., 1973; Chmn. Adv. Council Psychologists, N.Y. State, 1963-68; expert cons. USAF, 1950-51; personnel psychologist personnel research sect. Adj. Gen.'s office, U.S. War Dept., 1943-45. Co-author: Testing and Fair Employment, 1968, Work, Productivity and Job Satisfaction, 1975, Guide to Worker Productivity Experiments in the U.S, 1977; contbr. articles to profl. jours. Fellow Am. Psychol. Assn. (pres. div. indsl. psychology 1960-61), AAAS; former mem. Soc. Advancement Mgmt. (pres. Central N.Y. chpt. 1949-51), N.Y. State Psychol. Assn. (pres. 1958-59). Home: 1 Barry Dr Glen Cove NY 11542

KATZEN, JAY KENNETH, consultant; b. N.Y.C., Aug. 23, 1936; s. Perry and Minerva (Rich) K.; m. Patricia Anne Morse, May 30, 1963; children: John Timothy Rich, David Mark Nicholas, James Alexander Scott. B.A. magna cum laude, Princeton U., 1958; M.A., Yale U., 1959. Joined U.S. Fgn. Service, 1959; fgn. service officer Dept. State, Washington, 1959-60, 62-63, 66-69; consular-comml. officer Am. consulate gen., Sydney, Australia, 1960-62, econ. officer Am. embassy, Bujumbura, Burundi, 1963-64, labor attaché Am. embassy, Kinshasa, Zaire, 1964-66, polit. officer Am. embassy, Bucharest, Rumania, 1969-71, counselor of embassy Am. embassy, Bamako, Mali, 1971—73; adviser U.S. Mission to UN, N.Y.C., 1973-77; with Office of Vice Pres., Washington, 1977, Nat. War Coll., 1977; chargé d'affaires Am. embassy, Brazzaville, Congo, 1977-78; polit. adv. to U.S. del. World Adminstrv. Radio Conf., 1979; vis. prof. Boston U. Grad. Sch. Mgmt., 1977-78. Clubs: Princeton Quadrangle., Princeton of Washington, Army Navy. Address: 8021 E Boulevard Dr Alexandria VA 22308

KATZEN, LILA PELL, sculptor; b. Bklyn., Dec. 30, 1932; d. Harry and Rose (Schultz) Pell; m. Phillip Katzen, June 6, 1948; children: Denize-Fran, Hal-Zachary. Student, Arts Students League, N.Y.C., 1947, Hans Hofmann, N.Y.C. Provincetown, Mass., 1950-51; B.A., Cooper Union, N.Y.C., 1949. Prof. Md. Inst. Coll. Art, Balt., 1962-80; pres. Katzen Studio, Inc., N.Y.C., 1982—; lectr. New Sch. Social Research, N.Y.C., 1976; vis. prof. U. Tex., Arlington, 1977; commns. HUD, Miami, Fla., 1977-79, varied works for Royal Family, Saudi Arabia, 1979-82, GSA in Rodino Bldg., Newark, 1980-82, Brandeis U., Waltham, Mass., 1983. Fellow Tiffany Found., 1966; recipient grant Archtl. League N.Y., 1967, honor award Sao Paolo Biennale, 1970, Creative Arts award AAUW, 1974. Mem. Coll. Art Assn., Archtl. League N.Y., Sculptors Internat. Home: 345 W Broadway New York NY 10013

KATZEN, RAPHAEL, consulting chemical engineer; b. Balt., July 28, 1915; s. Isidor and Esther (Stein) K.; m. Selma M. Siegel, June 19, 1938; 1 dau., Nancy Katzen Riedel. B.Chem. Engring., Poly. Inst. Bklyn., 1936, M.Chem. Engring., 1938, D.Chem. Engring., 1942. Tech. dir. Northwood Chem. Co., Phelps, Wis., 1938-42; project mgr. Diamond Alkali Co., Painesville, Ohio, 1942-44; mgr. engring. Vulcan Engring. Div., Cin., 1944-53; mng. partner Raphael Katzen Assos., Cin., 1953-80; pres. Raphael Katzen Assos. Internat., Inc., 1956—. Contbr. articles to profl. jours. Mem. Cin. Air Pollution Bd., 1972-75. Recipient Distinguished Alumnus award Poly. Inst. Bklyn., 1970, Dedicated Alumnus award, 1977; Disting. Cons. award Ohio Assn. Cons. Engrs., 1978; Profl. Accomplishment, Disting. Engr. award Tech. and Sci. Socs. Council, 1978, 79; Poly. Inst. N.Y. fellow, 1981. Fellow Am. Inst. Chemists, Am. Inst. Chem. Engrs., Am. Cons. Engrs. Council; mem. Am. Chem. Soc., Nat. Soc. Profl. Engrs., TAPPI, Sigma Xi, Tau Beta Pi, Phi Lambda Upsilon. Clubs: Univ. (Cin.); Chemists (N.Y.C.); American (Miami, Fla.). Patentee in field. Home: 2868 Alpine Terr Cincinnati OH 45208 Office: 1050 Delta Ave Cincinnati OH 45208 *We are put on this earth to produce to the best of our ability and our talents should not be wasted through lack of effort, or misguided direction.*

KATZENBACH, NICHOLAS DEBELLEVILLE, computer corporation executive; b. Phila., Jan. 17, 1922; s. Edward Lawrence and Marie Louise (Hilson) K.; m. Lydia King Phelps Stokes, June 8, 1946; children—Christopher Wolcott, John Strong Minor, Maria Louise Hilson, Anne deBelleville. B.A., Princeton U., 1945; LL.B., Yale U., 1947, Balliol Coll., Oxford (Eng.) U., 1947-49. Bar: N.J. bar 1950, Conn. bar 1955, N.Y. bar 1972. With firm Katzenbach, Gildea & Rudner, Trenton, N.J., 1950; atty.-adviser Office Gen. Counsel Air Force, 1950-52, part-time cons., 1952-56; asso. prof. law Yale Law Sch., 1952-56; prof. law U. Chgo. Law Sch., 1956-60; asst. atty. gen. Dept. Justice, 1961-62, dep. atty. gen., 1962-64, acting atty. gen., 1964, atty. gen., 1965-66, under sec. state, 1966-69; sr. v.p., gen. counsel, dir. IBM Corp., 1969—. Author: (with Morton A. Kaplan) The Political Foundations of International Law, 1961; Editor-in-chief: Yale Law Jour, 1947; Contbr. articles to profl. jours. Served to 1st lt. USAAF, 1941-45. Decorated Air medal with three clusters; Ford Found. fellow, 1960-61. Mem. Am. Law Inst., Am. Bar Assn., Am. Judicature Soc. Democrat. Episcopalian. Home: 117 Library Pl Princeton NJ 08540 Office: IBM Corp Old Orchard Rd Armonk NY 10504

KATZMAN, DANIEL, developer, retired manufacturing company executive; b. Omaha, Aug. 24, 1924; s. Meyer and Nettie (Gerelick) K.; m. Ruth Goldberg, Aug. 24, 1947; children: Steven Edward, Saragail. B.S. in Bus. Adminstrn., U. Nebr., 1948. Hotel exec., 1948-52; co-founder Commodore Corp. (mobile home mfrs.), 1952, pres., after 1967, chmn. bd., 1977—, chmn. emeritus, 1983—; now developer mobile home parks, Fla.; dir. U.S. Nat. Bank, Omaha. Del. Reconstructed Assembly of Jewish Agy. Jerusalem, 1971. Trustee Omaha Jewish Fedn., Archbishop Bergen Meml. Hosp., Omaha; bd. dirs. nat. cabinet United Jewish Appeal, Am. Friends Hebrew U.; gen. chmn. New Jewish Community Center of Omaha Bldg. Project, 1972-73; trustee Daniel and Ruth Katzman Found.; bd. overseers Jewish Theol. Sem., 1973—. Served with AUS, 1943-46. Mem. Mobile Homes Mfrs. Assn. (treas., dir.). Home: 1211 Gulf of Mexico Dr Longboat Key FL 33548 Office: PO Box 3349 Sarasota FL 33578

KATZMAN, HERBERT HENRY, artist; b. Chgo., Jan. 8, 1923; s. Louis and Fay (Horowitz) K.; m. Judith Baker, Nov. 25, 1949; children: Nicholas, Steven, Anne.; m. Laurel Carroll, Oct. 25, 1982. Certificate, Sch. Art Inst. Chgo., 1946. Tchr. painting and drawing Sch. Visual Arts, N.Y.C., 1959—. Group shows include, Mus. Modern Art, N.Y.C., 1952, Whitney Mus., N.Y.C., 1954, Venice (Italy) Biennial, 1957, Pa. Acad. Fine Arts; represented in permanent collections, Art Inst. Chgo., Mus. Modern Art, Whitney Mus., Hirschorn Mus., Washington, U. Mass., U. Minn., W.Va., Wright State U., Dayton, Ohio. Served with USN, 1942-44. Nat. Acad. Arts and Letters grantee, 1958, Nat. Council Humanities, 1966; Guggenheim fellow, 1968. Assoc. mem. NAD. Home: 463 West St Apt 919C New York City NY 10014

KATZMAN, ROBERT, physician, educator; b. Denver, Nov. 29, 1925; s. Maurice and Leah (Schnitt) K.; m. Nancy Bernstein, Sept. 2, 1947; children: David Jonathan, Daniel Mark. B.S., U. Chgo., 1949, M.S., 1951; M.D. cum laude, Harvard, 1953. Diplomate: Nat. Bd. Med. Examiners, Am. Bd. Neurology and Psychiatry. Intern Boston City Hosp., 1953-54; chief resident neurologist Neurol. Inst., Columbia Presbyn. Hosp., N.Y.C., 1956-57; mem. faculty Albert Einstein Coll. Medicine, 1957—, prof. neurology, chmn. dept., 1964—, acting asso. dean for clin. affairs, 1972-73, prof. neurosci., 1974—; Mem. research rev. panel Nat. Multiple Sclerosis Soc., 1964-70, mem. adv. com. fellowships, 1970—; cons. Jewish Bd. Guardians, 1962-68; mem. clin. research adv. com. Nat. Found.-March Dimes, 1975-76; med. adv. bd. Dystonia Found., 1980-82. Author: (with others) Basic Neurochemistry, 1972, 3d edit., 1981, Brain Electrolytes and Fluid Metabolism, 1973, Alzheimer's Disease: Senile Dementia and Related Disorders, 1978, Congenital and Acquired Cognitive Disorders, 1979, Neurology of Aging, 1983; editorial bd.: Neurology, 1963-72, (with others) Brain Research, 1975—, Jour. Neurochemistry, 1975-80; editorial adv. bd.: Jour. Neuropathology and Exptl. Neurology, 1964-82. Recipient Borden undergrad. research award Harvard Med. Sch., 1953; sr. fellow neurophysiology USPHS, 1961-62; Career Research Devel. grantee, 1962-66; recipient ann. prize Neuropathology Soc., 1962; NATO sr. fellow, 1969. Fellow Am. Acad. Neurology (Weir Mitchell award 1960, chmn. neurochemistry sect. 1965-67); mem. Am. Assn. Neuropathology, Am. Neurol. Assn., Am. Electroencephalographic Soc., Am. Physiol. Soc. (cons. bd. 1968-71), Assn. Research Nervous and Mental Diseases (trustee 1976—, pres. 1977), N.Y. Neurol. Soc. (councillor 1968-69, pres. 1970-71), Am., Internat. socs. neurochemistry, Soc. Exptl. Biology and Medicine, Soc. Neurosci., Alzheimer's Disease and Related Disorders Assn. (chmn. med. adv. bd. 1979—), Tourette Syn. Assn. (med. adv. bd. 1976—), Inst. Medicine, Nat. Acad. Scis., Phi Beta Kappa, Sigma Xi, Alpha Omega Alpha. Address: 1300 Morris Park Ave New York NY 10461

KATZNELSON, IRA ISAAC, political science educator; b. N.Y.C., July 3, 1944; s. Ephraim and Sylvia (Rosenbaum) K.; m. Deborah Ruth Socolow, Jan. 14, 1967; children: Jessica, Zachary, Emma, Leah. B.A. summa cum laude, Columbia U., 1966; Ph.D. (Euretta J. Kellett fellow 1966-68, Danforth Found. fellow 1966-69), Cambridge (Eng.) U., 1969. Asst. prof., then asso. prof. polit. sci. Columbia U., 1969-74; mem. faculty U. Chgo., 1974-83, prof. polit. sci., 1979-83, chmn. dept., 1979-83; study dir. Nat. Opinion Research Center, 1978-83; Henry A. and Louise Loeb prof. polit. sci., dean Grad. Faculty New Sch. Social Research, 1983—. Author: Black Men, White Cities, 1973, City Trenches: Urban Politics and the Patterning of Class in the United States, 1981; co-author: The Politics of Power, 2d edit, 1979; Founding editor: Politics and Society, 1969-75; editorial bd., 1969—. Chmn. bd. B'nai B'rith Hillel Found., U. Chgo., 1978-81. German Marshall Fund fellow, 1978-79. Mem. Am. Polit. Sci. Assn., Caucus New Polit. Sci., Social Sci. History Assn., Phi Beta Kappa. Home: 211 Central Park W New York NY 10024 Office: Grad Faculty New School Social Research 66 W 12th St New York NY 10011

KAUDERER, BERNARD MARVIN, naval officer; b. Phila., July 21, 1931; s. Harry Thau and Anne Mae (Mandell) K.; m. Myra Frances Weissman, Mar. 21, 1954; children: Howard Todd, Heidi Susanne, Robin Beth. B.S. U.S. Naval Acad, 1953. Commd. ensign U.S. Navy, 1953, advanced through grades to vice adm., 1983; comdr. Submarine Group Five, 1977-79; dep. dir. research, devel., test and evaluation Office Chief Naval Ops., Navy Dept., Washington, 1979-81; comdr. submarine force U.S. Pacific Fleet, Pearl Harbor, Hawaii, 1981-83, Atlantic Fleet, Norfolk, Va., 1983—. Decorated Legion of Merit, Meritorious Service medal, Navy Commendation medal, Navy Expeditionary medal. Clubs: Mason, Shriner. Office: Comdr Submarine Force US Atlantic Fleet Norfolk VA 23511

KAUFFMAN, BRUCE WILLIAM, state supreme ct. justice; b. Atlantic City, Dec. 1, 1934; s. Joseph Bernard and Lilyan (Abraham) K.; m. Rita Marie Wisneski, Dec. 31, 1971; children—Bradley Leonard, Marjorie Beth, Robert Andrew, Lauri Ann, Christine Lynne. B.A., U. Pa., 1956; LL.B., Yale, 1959. Bar: N.J. bar 1960, Pa. bar 1961, U.S. Supreme Ct. bar 1965. Law clk. to judge N.J. Superior Ct., Trenton, 1959-60; asso. firm Dilworth, Paxson, Kalish, Levy & Kauffman, Phila., 1960-65, partner, 1966-80, chmn. litigation dept., 1975-80; justice Supreme Ct. of Pa., 1980—; mem. com. of censors U.S. Dist. Ct., Eastern Pa., 1976-80; Del. Pa. Constl. Conv., 1967-68; chmn. Montgomery County Govt. Study Commn., 1973-74; mem. Civil Service Commn., Lower Merion Twp., 1978-80; pres. Merion Park Civic Assn., 1966-68. Fellow Am. Coll. Trial Lawyers, Am. Law Inst.; mem. Am., Pa., Phila. bar assns., Am. Judicature Soc., Juristic Soc., Lawyers' Club Phila., Yale Law Sch. Assn., Pa. Soc., USCG Aux., Pi Sigma Alpha, Phi Gamma Mu, Phi Beta Kappa, Order of Coif. Clubs: Union League, Locust, Yale. Office: 515 Three Penn Center Philadelphia PA 19102 *Hard work, independence, integrity, and a strong desire to help others are the ingredients which I believe have led me to the Supreme Court of Pennsylvania. Without the rule of law, ordered society is impossible. As a Supreme Court Justice, I have devoted my best efforts toward achieving the fair and expeditious administration of justice in the Commonwealth of Pennsylvania.*

KAUFFMAN, DANIEL ERB, educational administrator; b. Hesston, Kans., June 19, 1922; s. James A. and Mable (Erb) K.; m. Edith L. Yoder, May 27, 1944; children: Daniel Eric, Deborah Ann (Mrs. Maurice Miller), Salome Elaine (Mrs. Joe Green), James David. B.A., Goshen Coll., 1946; M.A., Columbia, 1957. Bus. mgr. Hesston Coll., 1946-61; dir. stewardship Mennonite Ch., Scottdale, Pa., 1961-66; assoc. supt. Southmoreland (Pa.) Schs., 1966-71; dir. coll. relations Goshen (Ind.) Coll., 1971—; sect. dir. Goodville Mut. Casualty Co., New Holland, Pa., 1973—. Mem. Hesston City Council, 1955-61; Vice chmn. bd. Prairie View Hosp., Newton, Kans., 1956-61; chmn. bd. Kiowa County Hosp., Greensburg, Kans., 1954-61; pres. bd. Schowalter Found., Newton, 1971—; bd. dirs. Greencroft Retirement Home, Goshen, Ind., 1980—. Mennonite. Clubs: Lions, Exchange. Home: 62567 CR 17 Goshen IN 46526

KAUFFMAN, EWING MARION, pharmaceutical executive; b. Mo., Sept. 21, 1916; s. John S. and Effie May (Winders) K.; m. Muriel Irene McBrien, Feb. 28, 1962; children: Larry, Sue, Julia. Asso. in Sci., Kansas City Jr. Coll.; D.Sc., Union Coll., Schenectady. Founder, chmn. Marion Labs., Inc., Kansas City, Mo., 1950—; owner, chmn. Kansas City Royals Baseball Club, 1969—. Mem. Civic Council, Kansas City.; pres. Ewing M. Kauffman Found.; bd. dirs. Mayor's Corps Progress. Served to ensign USNR. Recipient Horatio Alger award Am. Schs. and Colls. Assn., Golden Plate award Am. Acad. Achievement, Mktg. Man of Year award Sales and Marketing Execs. Internat., Disting. Service award Fellowship Christian Athletes, Disting. Eagle award Boy Scouts Am. Mem. Kansas City C. of C. Clubs: Indian Hills Country, Kansas City, Eldorado Country. Home: 5955 Mission Dr Shawnee Mission KS 66208 Office: 10236 Bunker Ridge Rd Kansas City MO 64137

KAUFFMAN, FREDERICK CHARLES, pharmacologist; b. Chgo., July 9, 1936; s. Frederick Christlieb and Mathilda Margaret (Goeres) K.; m. Ella J. Smith, Aug. 5, 1961; children—Elizabeth M., Andrew F. B.A., Knox Coll., Galesburg, Ill., 1958; Ph.D., U. Ill., 1965. Postdoctoral fellow Washington U., St. Louis, 1965-68; asst. prof., then asso. prof. pharmacology SUNY, Buffalo, 1968-74; mem. faculty U. Md. Med. Sch., 1974—, prof. pharmacology, 1978—; cons. NIH; lectr. drug intervention and nutrition various hosps. Author numerous papers in field. Foreman Baltimore County Grand Jury, 1981. Mem. Am. Soc. Pharmacology and Exptl. Therapeutics, Soc. Neurosci., Am. Soc. Neurochemistry, Am. Chem. Soc. Lutheran. Home: Box 251 Falls Rd Cockeysville MD 21030 Office: Univ Md Med Sch 660 W Red Wood St Baltimore MD 21030

KAUFFMAN, GEORGE BERNARD, chemistry educator; b. Phila., Sept. 4, 1930; s. Philip Joseph and Laura (Fisher) K.; m. Ingeborg Salomon, June 5, 1952 (div. Dec. 1969); children: Ruth Deborah, Judith Miriam; m. Laurie Marks Papazian, Dec. 21, 1969; stepchildren: Stanley Robert Papazian, Teresa Lynn Papazian. B.A. with honors, U. Pa., 1951; Ph.D., U. Fla., 1956. Grad. asst. U. Fla., 1951-55; research participant Oak Ridge Nat. Lab., 1955; instr. U. Tex., Austin, 1955-56; research chemist Humble Oil & Refining Co., Baytown, Tex., 1956, Gen. Electric Co., Cin., 1957, 59; asst. prof. chemistry Calif. State U., Fresno, 1956-61, assoc. prof., 1961-66, prof., 1966—; guest lectr. coop. lecture tours Am. Chem. Soc., 1971; vis. scholar U. Calif., Berkeley, 1976, U. Puget Sound, 1978; dir. undergrad. research participation program NSF, 1972. Author: Alfred Werner—Founder of Coordination Chemistry, 1966, Classics in Coordination Chemistry, Part I, 1968, Part II, 1976, Part III, 1978, Werner Centennial, 1967, Teaching the History of Chemistry, 1971, Coordination Chemistry: Its History through the Time of Werner, 1977, Inorganic Coordination Compounds, 1981, The Central Sciences: Essays on the Uses of Chemistry, 1984; contbr. numerous articles to profl. publs.; contbg. editor: Jour. Coll. Sci. Teaching, 1973—, The Hexagon, 1980—, Polyhedron, 1983—; editor tape lecture series: Am. Chem. Soc, 1975-81. Named Outstanding Prof. Calif. State U. and Colls. System, 1973; recipient Coll. Chemistry Tchr. award Mfg. Chemists Assn., 1976; Dexter award in History of Chemistry, 1978; Research Corp. grantee, 1956-57, 57-59, 59-61; Am. Chem. Soc. Petroleum Research Fund grantee, 1962-64, 65-69; Am. Philos. Soc. grantee, 1963-64, 69-70; NSF grantee, 1960-61, 63-64, 67-69, 76-77; John Simon Guggenheim Meml. Found. fellow, 1972-73; grantee, 1975; Strindberg fellow Swedish Inst., Stockholm, 1983. Mem. AAAS, AAUP, United Profs. Calif., Assn. Univ. Pa. Chemists, History Sci. Soc., Soc. History Alchemy and Chemistry, Am. Chem. Soc. (chmn. div. history of chemistry 1969, exec. com. 1970, councilor 1976-78), Mensa, USSR Acad. Sci. (award 1976), Sigma Xi, Phi Lambda Upsilon, Phi Kappa Phi, Alpha Chi Sigma, Gamma Sigma Epsilon. Home: 3881 Pico Ave Fresno CA 93726 Office: Calif State U Dept of Chemistry Fresno CA 93740

KAUFFMAN, JOHN THOMAS, utility executive; b. Weehawken, N.J., Aug. 17, 1926; s. William Carl and Frances E. K.; m. Julia A. Crouch, Aug. 19, 1949; children: Anne E. Kauffman Zayaitz, Janet L. B.S. in Marine Engring, U.S. Mcht. Marine Acad., 1946, Purdue U., 1950. With Pa. Power & Light Co., 1950—; asst. v.p., then v.p. System Power & Engring., 1973-78, exec. v.p. ops., Allentown, 1978—, also dir.; chmn. bd. dirs. Pa. Mines Corp., Interstate Energy Co.; dir. affiliates and subsidiary cos. Mem. Electric Power Research Inst. (research adv. com.), ASME, Am. Nuclear Soc., Edison Electric Inst. (nuclear power exec. adv. com.), Pa. Electric Assn. (exec. com.), Pa. Indsl. and Profl. Council, Engrs. Club Lehigh Valley. Clubs: N.E. River Yacht; Brookside Country (Allentown). Home: 664 Spruce St Emmaus PA 18049 Office: 2 N 9th St Allentown PA 18101

KAUFFMAN, KENNETH MARK, govt. ofcl.; b. Sacramento, Mar. 24, 1930; s. Mark Gerard and Irma Tilly (Marks) K.; m. Pepita Lorraine Urbina, Aug. 26, 1957; children—Suzette, Laura, Kenneth, Hilary. B.A., U. Calif., 1952; M.A., Harvard, 1955, Ph.D., 1958. Teaching fellow econs. Harvard, 1955-57; instr. econs. Wellesley Coll., 1957-58, Harvard, 1958-61; chief economist U.S. AID Mission to India, 1961-66; sr. research fellow Council Fgn. Relations, N.Y.C., 1966-67; asst. dir. U.S. AID Mission to Turkey, 1967-71, dep. dir., 1971-73, counselor of embassy for internat. devel., 1972-73; dep. dir. AID Mission to Indonesia, 1973-76; asso. asst. adminstr. AID, Washington, 1976-77, dep. asst. adminstr. for internat. affairs, 1977-79; interdept. seminar in nat. and internat. affairs Dept. State, 1979-80; U.S. rep. to Devel. Assistance Com., minister counsellor U.S. Mission to OECD, Paris, 1980—; cons. Arthur D. Little, Inc., 1960. Author: (with J.I. Heller) Tax Incentives for Industrial Development in Less Developed Countries, 1963. Mem. Am. Econ. Assn. Home: 5524 5th St S Arlington VA 22204 Office: US Mission to OECD 19 rue de Franquerville 75016 Paris France

KAUFFMAN, MARK, photographer; b. Los Angeles, Sept. 3, 1922; s. Mitchell and Anna (Bearman) K.; m. Anita Jansson, May 18, 1948; children: Linda, Yvonne, Lenita, Sylvia Ann. Grad. vocational photography, John C. Fremont Sch., 1940. Photographer Life mag., Los Angeles, Chgo., 1941-46, Far East, China, 1946-47, London, 1948-49, Paris, 1950, Washington, 1950-57, London Bur. Time Life, 1957-61; photography editor Playboy mag., 1971-76, 78—. Winner first place U. Mo. Sch. Journalism News Pictures Contest, 1951; recipient Grand award Whitehouse Photographers Assn., 1953; 1st place award color photography Ency. Brit. and Nat. Press Photographers Assn., 1959; named Photographer of Year by U. of Mo. and Ency. Brit. Home: 444 28th Ave San Francisco CA 94121

KAUFFMAN, ROBERT CRAIG, painter, sculptor; b. Los Angeles, Mar. 31, 1932. Student, U. So. Calif. Sch. Architecture, 1950-52; B.A., UCLA, 1955, M.A., 1956. One-man shows, La Jolla Mus. Contemporary Art, Calif., 1981, Thomas Segal Gallery, Boston, 1982, group exhbns. include, Felix Landau Gallery, San Francisco Mus. Art, 1951, 52, 54, Los Angeles County Mus., 1960, 73, Dilexi Gallery, 1959, 60, 62, Ferus Gallery, 1963, 64, Pace Gallery, 1965, 70, Seattle Art Mus. Pavilion, Robert Fraser Gallery, London, 1966, U. Ill. Krannert Art Mus., Detroit Inst. Art, 1967, Whitney Mus. Am. Art, N.Y.C., 1967, 69, Albright-Knox Art Gallery, Buffalo, one-man shows include, Felix Landau Gallery, Los Angeles, 1953, one-man shows, Dilexi Gallery, San Francisco, 1958, 60, Ferus Gallery, Los Angeles, 1962, 65, 67, Pace Gallery, N.Y.C., 1967, 69, 70, Pasadena Art Mus., Calif., 1970, U. Calif.-Irving, Irving Blum Gallery, Los Angeles, 1972, Galerie Darthea Speyer, Paris, Mizuno Gallery, Los Angeles, 1975, Robert Elkon Gallery, N.Y.C., Comsky Gallery, Los Angeles, 1976, Arco Ctr. for Visual Art, Los Angeles, 1978, Blum Helman Gallery, N.Y.C., 1979, 82, Janus Gallery, Venice, Calif, 1979, Aldrich Mus. Contemporary Art, Ridgefield, Conn., 1969, Art Inst., Chgo., Jewish Mus., N.Y.C., Mus. Contemporary Art, Chgo., Joslyn Art Mus., Omaha, U. So. Calif., 1970, Govett-Brewster Art Mus., New Plymouth, N.Z., Laguna Beach Mus. Art, Fort Worth Art Mus., 1971, Mus. Modern Art, N.Y.C., Calif. Inst. Arts, Valencia, 1972, Whitney Mus. Am. Art, Art Inst. Chgo., Chgo., U. Calif.-Irvine, 1974, Santa Barbara Mus. Art, Calif., SUNY-Potsdam Brainerd Hall Art Gallery, 1975, Newport Harbor Art Mus., Calif., Indpls. Mus. Art, 1976, Salles de la Fondation Nationale des Arts Plastiques et Graphiques, Paris, Wash. State U. of Art, Pullman, Casat Gallery, La Jolla, 1977, Margo Leavin Gallery, Los Angeles, 1978, Whitney Mus. Am. Art, U. N.Mex. Fine Arts Ctr., Albuquerque, Crocker Art Mus., San Francisco, Calif. State U.-Fullerton, 1979, U. Hartford, Conn., 1980, Blum Helman Gallery, Am. Acad. Arts and Letters, N.Y.C., Los Angeles County Mus. Art, 1981; represented in permanent collections, Mus. Modern

Art, N.Y.C., Los Angeles County Mus. Art, Whitney Mus. Am. Art, Albright-Knox Art Gallery, Larry Aldrich Mus., Aldrich Mus., Pasadena Art Mus., U. Ariz.-Tucson, Tate Gallery, London, Milw. Art Ctr., Chgo. Art Inst., U. Sydney, Australia, Long Beach Mus., San Francisco Mus. Modern Art, Fort Worth Art Ctr. Mus., San Diego Mus. Art, Santa Barbara Mus. Art, Newport Harbor Art Mus., Bennington Coll. Art Collection, Vt. Recipient U.S. Govt. Fellowship for Arts, 1967, 69th Am. Exhibit 1st prize Art Inst. Chgo., 1970. Office: care Blum Helman Gallery 20 W 57th St New York NY 10019 *

KAUFFMAN, STEVEN KING, engineering and construction company executive; b. Los Angeles, Apr. 28, 1926; s. Frank Edgar and Frances Emily (Woods) K.; m. Teresa R. Natale, Nov. 6, 1970; children: Mark Keefe, John Kupferle. B.S., Tufts U., 1948; B.C.E., Rensselaer Poly. Inst., 1953; M.B.A., George Washington U., 1962. Commd. ensign U.S. Navy, 1948, advanced through grades to comdr., 1963; stationed, Korea, 1953-54, various assignments, U.S., 1954-64, asst. chief of staff, civil engring., Antarctica, 1964-66, public works officer and resident officer in charge of constrn., Roosevelt Rds., P.R., 1966-68, ret., 1968; sr. ops. analyst Stanford (Calif.) Research Inst., 1968-71; exec. asst. N.Y.C. Transit Authority, 1971-75; exec. officer Rapid Transit, 1975-79, gen. mgr., 1979-80; pres. Safety Elec. Equipment Corp., Wallingford, Conn., 1980-82; v.p. transp. Raymond Kaiser Engrs., Oakland, Calif., 1983—; dir. Stone Platt of Am., Safety Elec. Equipment Corp. Named N.Y.C. Transit Man of Yr., 1979. Mem. Am. Mgmt. Assn., Soc. Am. Mil. Engrs., Nat. Assn. Mfrs., N.Y. Railroad Club. Republican. Clubs: Army-Navy Country, New Haven Country, Quinnipiack. Mt. Kauffman in Antarctica named in his honor, 1967. Office: PO Box 23210 Oakland CA 94623

KAUFFMANN, HOWARD C., oil company executive; b. Tulsa, Feb. 25, 1923; s. Howard C. and Polly Ethyl (Myers) K.; m. Suzanne McMurray, Nov. 5, 1944; children: Craig, Robert Lane, Kristine, Douglas, Scott. B.M.E., U. Okla., 1943. Petroleum engr., prodn. mgr. Carter Oil Co., 1946-57; ops. mgr. Internat. Petroleum Co., Ltd., Peru and Colombia, 1958-62; asst. regional coordinator Latin Am. Exxon Corp., 1962-64; dir., v.p., then exec. v.p., pres. Internat. Petroleum Co. Ltd., Coral Gables, Fla., 1964-66; pres., dir. Esso Inter-Am., Inc., Coral Gables, 1966-68; exec. v.p., dir., then pres. Esso Europe, Inc., London, 1968-73; sr. v.p., dir. Exxon Corp., N.Y.C., 1974-75, pres., dir., 1975—; dir. Chase Manhattan Corp., Chase Manhattan Bank (N.A.), United Techs. Corp., Pfizer, Inc., Am. Petroleum Inst., Bus. Council State of N.Y.; mem. Emergency Com. for Am. Trade. Bd. dirs. United Way of N.Y.C., Econ. Devel. Council N.Y.C. Inc.; trustee Inst. for Advanced Study, Princeton; bd. dirs., mem. exec. com. Nat. Action Council for Minorities in Engring.; chmn. Nat. Adv. Council on Minority Engring.; corp. fund vice chmn. John F. Kennedy Ctr. for Performing Arts. Served. to lt. (j.g.) USNR, World War II. Mem. N.Y. Chamber Commerce and Industry (dir.), U.S. Internat. Council, Pi Gamma Delta, Tau Beta Pi, Sigma Tau, Pi Tau Sigma, Tau Omega. Baptist. Office: Exxon Corp 1251 Ave of the Americas New York NY 10020 *

KAUFFMANN, IVAN JOHN, church exec.; b. Minier, Ill., Nov. 5, 1922; s. John and Alma M. (Litwiller) K.; m. Lola M. Good, May 23, 1946; children—Paul, John, Joel, Mary, Ruth, James. B.A., Goshen Coll., 1949; Th.B., Goshen Bibl. Sem., 1958. Ordained to ministry Mennonite Ch., 1949; pastor Hopedale (Ill.) Mennonite Ch., 1949-69, 70-71; sec. info. services Mennonite Bd. Missions, Elkhart, Ind., 1969-70; gen. sec. Mennonite Ch. of Can. and U.S., Lombard, Ill., 1971—; pres. Menn Housing Aid, Inc. Home: 1835 N Luna Ave Chicago IL 60639 Office: 528 E Madison St Lombard IL 60148

KAUFFMANN, STANLEY JULES, author; b. N.Y.C., Apr. 24, 1916; s. Joseph H. and Jeannette (Steiner) K.; m. Laura Cohen, Feb. 5, 1943. B.F.A., NYU, 1935. Mem. Washington Sq. Players, 1931-41; asso. editor Bantam Books, 1949-52; editor-in-chief Ballantine Books, 1952-56; editor Alfred A. Knopf, 1959-60; film critic New Republic, N.Y.C., 1958-65, 67—, asso. lit. editor, 1966-67, theater critic, 1969-79, Saturday Rev., 1979—; drama critic N.Y. Times, 1966; condr. program The Art of Film, Channel 13, N.Y.C., 1963-67; vis. prof. drama Yale U., 1967-68, 69-73, 77—; Distinguished prof. City U. N.Y., 1973-76; vis. prof. drama City U. N.Y. Grad. Center, 1977—. Author: The Hidden Hero, 1949, The Tightrope, 1952, A Change of Climate, 1954, Man of the World, 1956, A World on Film, 1966, Figures of Light, 1971; Editor: (with Bruce Henstell) American Film Criticism: from the Beginnings to Citizen Kane, 1973, Living Images, 1975, Persons of The Drama, 1976, Before My Eyes, 1980, Albums of Early Life, 1980, Theater Criticisms, 1983. Recipient George Jean Nathan award for dramatic criticism, 1972-73, George Polk award for criticism, 1982; Ford Found. fellow for study abroad, 1964, 71; hon. fellow Morse Coll., Yale U., 1964; Guggenheim fellow, 1979-80. Address: 10 W 15th St New York NY 10011

KAUFMAN, ALAN JOEL, lawyer, publishing company executive; b. Harrisburg, Pa., Sept. 27, 1943; s. Irving and Evelyn (Gordon) K. B.A., Am. U., 1965, J.D., 1968; LL.M., NYU, 1969. Bar: N.Y. 1969, D.C. 1968. Counsel Ziff Davis Pub., N.Y.C., 1971-73; assoc. Sheldon Fogelman, N.Y.C., 1974-77; v.p., sec.,counsel New Am. Library, Inc., N.Y.C., 1978—; arbitrator Am. Arbitration Assn., N.Y.C., 1981—. Mem. Phi Alpha Delta. Home: 120 E 34th St New York NY 10016 Office: New Am Library Inc Times Mirror 1633 Broadway New York NY 10019

KAUFMAN, ALEX, plastics and chem. co. exec.; b. Lemburg, Poland, Sept. 9, 1924; came to U.S., 1950, naturalized, 1955; s. Isadore and Bronislava (Halpern) K.; m. Amalia Fuss, Sept. 6, 1951; children—Bernice, Irene, Mark. Grad. in Chemistry, Stuttgart (Ger.) Poly. Inst., 1950. With Hatco Chem. div. W. R. Grace & Co., Fords, N.J., 1961—, pres. parent co., N.Y.C., 1962-78, corp. v.p., 1967, exec. v.p., 1968-78, dir., 1969—; group exec. Hatco Group, 1968-78; pres. Grace Petrochems. Inc., P.R., 1969-78, Kalex Chem. Products, Inc., 1978—, Hatco Chem. Corp., 1978—. Bd. dirs. Raritan Bay Health Services Corp., 1979—; mem. nat. adv. bd. Multiple Sclerosis Soc. Mem. Soc. Plastics Industry, Chem. Mfrs. Assn., Soc. Chem. Industry, Woodbridge C. of C., Newcomen Soc. Home: 57 Century Ln Watchung NJ 07060 Office: King George Post Rd Fords NJ 08863

KAUFMAN, ANDREW LEE, legal educator; b. Newark, Feb. 1, 1931; s. Samuel and Sylvia (Meltzer) K.; m. Linda P. Sonnenschein, June 14, 1959; children: Anne, David, Elizabeth, Daniel. A.B., Harvard U., 1951, LL.B., 1954. Bar: N.J. 1954, D.C. 1954, Mass. 1979, U.S. Supreme Ct. 1961. Assoc. Bilder, Bilder & Kaufman, Newark, 1954-55; law clk. to Justice Felix Frankfurter U.S Supreme Ct., 1955-57; ptnr. Kaufman, Kaufman & Kaufman, Newark, 1957-65; lectr. in law Harvard U., Cambridge, Mass., 1965-66, prof., 1966-81, Charles Stebbins Fairchild prof. law, 1981—. Author: (with others) Commercial Law, 1971, Problems in Professional Responsibility, 1976. Treas. Shady Hill Sch., 1969-76, Hillel Found. Cambridge, Inc., 1977—. Mem. Mass. Bar Assn. Office: Law Sch Harvard U Cambridge MA 02138

KAUFMAN, ARNOLD, broadcast company executive; b. Oct. 12, 1916; m. Mary Arnold, July 22, 1977; 1 dau. by previous marriage, Ellen M. Feldman. B.S. in Civil Engring., Northeastern U., 1940; cert. advanced mgmt., Harvard U. Bus. Sch., 1956. Vice pres. RKO Gen., Inc., N.Y.C., 1947-59, sr. v.p., 1970—; v.p. NTA, Inc., N.Y.C., 1959-60; pres. Arnold Kaufman, Inc., N.Y.C., 1960-70; dir. Jeffrey Martin, Inc. Served to lt. (j.g.) USN, 1944-46; PTO. Named to Athletic Hall of Fame, Northeastern U., 1979. Clubs: Inwood Country; Friars (N.Y.C.). Home: 141 E 56 th St New York NY 10022 Office: RKO Gen Inc 1440 Broadway New York NY 10018

KAUFMAN, ARNOLD RICHARD, mfg. co. exec.; b. Ft. Wayne, Ind., Oct. 12, 1921; s. Albert Frederick and Elenora Wilamena (Meyer) K.; m. Pauline L. Werling, May 26, 1945; children—Michael J., Scott A. Student, Ball State Tchrs' Coll., 1939-41, Ill. Inst. Tech., 1944-45; B.S.E.E., Tri-State Coll., 1946. Sales engr. Gen. Electric Co., Chgo., 1944-45; sales mgr. Utah Radio Products Inc., Huntington, Ind., 1950-56; pres. Utrad Corp., Huntington, 1956-66, Triad Transformer Co., Venice, Calif., 1963-66; v.p. Litton Precision Products Co., Beverly Hills, Calif., 1964-68, Litton Industries Inc., Beverly Hills, 1968-71, now exec. v.p. Served with USAAF, 1941-42. Mem. Western Electronic Mfrs. Assn., I.E.E.E. Republican. Lutheran. Club: Bel Air (Calif.) Country. Home: 16081 Valleywood Rd Sherman Oaks CA 91403 Office: 360 N Crescent Dr Beverly Hills CA 90210

KAUFMAN, BEL, author, educator; b. Berlin, Germany; d. Michael J. and Lala (Rabinowitz) K.; (div.)children: Jonathan Goldstine, Thea Goldstine. B.A. magna cum laude, Hunter Coll.; M.A. with highest honors, Columbia U.; LL.D., Nasson Coll., Maine. Adj. prof. English CUNY; lectr. throughout country, also appearances on TV and radio.; Mem. Commn. Performing Arts. Editorial bd., Phi Delta Kappan.; Author: Up the Down Staircase, 1965, Love, etc, 1979; also short stories, articles, TV play, translations of Russian, lyrics for musicals. Bd. dirs. Shalom Aleichem Found.; adv. council Town Hall Found. Recipient plaque Anti-Defamation League; award and plaque United Jewish Appeal; Paperback of Year award; Bell Movie award; also ednl. journalism awards; named to Hall of Fame Hunter Coll. Mem. Author's Guild (council), Dramatists Guild, P.E.N. (membership com.), English Grad. Union, Phi Beta Kappa. Address: 1020 Park Ave New York NY 10028

KAUFMAN, CHARLES RUDOLPH, lawyer; b. Chgo., Dec. 25, 1908; s. Aaron C. and and Miriam (Eisenstaedt) K.; m. Violet-Page Koteen, Feb. 20, 1936 (dec.); children: Thomas H. (dec.), Constance Page Kaufman Dickinson), Christopher Lee. A.B., U. Mich., 1930; J.D. magna cum laude (Fay diploma), Harvard U., 1933. Bar: D.C. 1935, Ill. 1938, U.S. Supreme Ct. 1947. Legal sec. Judge Learned Hand, U.S. Ct. Appeals, 1933-34; supervising atty. SEC, Washington, 1934-37; pvt. practice Pope & Ballard, 1937-52, Vedder, Price, Kaufman & Kammholz, Chgo., 1952—. Legis. editor: Harvard Law Rev., 1932-33. Former mem. New Trier Twp. High Sch. Bd. Edn.; active in various charitable, civic and law sch. programs.; trustee Hadley Sch. for Blind; bd. dirs. Planned Parenthood Assn., Chgo. area. Mem. ABA, Ill. Bar Assn., Chgo. Bar Assn., Harvard Law Soc. Ill. (dir.), Chgo. Law Club. Home: 170 Westview Rd Winnetka IL 60093 Office: 115 S LaSalle St Chicago IL 60603

KAUFMAN, DONALD LEROY, aluminum company executive; b. Erie, Pa., May 9, 1931; s. Isadore H. and Lena (Sandler) K.; m. Estelle Friedman, Aug. 15, 1954; children: Craig Ivan, Susan Beth, Carrie Ellen. B.S. in Bus. Adminstrn, Ohio State U., 1953, LL.B., 1955. Bar: Ohio 1955. Pres. Alside, Inc. subsidiary U.S. Steel Corp., Akron, Ohio, 1974—. Mem. adv. com. U. Akron; trustee Jewish Welfare Fund, Akron, 1958-65, young leaders div., 1961-65, Akron City Hosp. Found.; bd. dirs. Akron City Hosp. Found. Served to 1st lt. USAF, 1955-57. Mem. Akron Bar Assn., Sigma Alpha Mu, Tau Epsilon Rho. Club: Rosemont Country. Home: 545 Hampshire Rd Akron OH 44313 Office: PO Box 2010 Akron OH 44309

KAUFMAN, FRANK ALBERT, U.S. district judge; b. Balt., Mar. 4, 1916; s. Nathan Hess and Hilda (Hecht) K.; m. Clementine Alice Lazaron, Apr. 22, 1945; children: Frank Albert, Peggy Ann (Mrs. Fred Wolf III). A.B. summa cum laude, Dartmouth Coll., 1937; LL.B. magna cum laude, Harvard U., 1940; LL.D. (hon.), U. Balt. Bar: Md. 1940. Atty. Offices Gen. Counsel Treasury, Lend Lease Adminstrn. and FEA, 1941-42, 45; lend lease rep., Turkey, 1942-43; bur. chief Psychol. Warfare Allied Forces Hdqrs. and SHAEF, 1943-45; asso. firm Frank, Bernstein, Conaway, Kaufman & Goldman (and predecessor), Balt., 1945-47, partner, 1948-66; U.S. dist. judge, Md., 1966—; lectr. U. Balt., 1948-62, U. Md., 1953-54. Mem. Gov. Md. Commns. Mgmt. and Labor Relations, 1960, Uniform Comml. Code, 1961, Health Problems, 1968; chmn. Gov. Md. Commn. Study Sentencing Criminal Cases, 1962-66; Officer and/or bd. dirs. Am. Jewish Com., 1960-70, Balt. chpt., 1948-70, Goucher Coll., 1957—, Md. Inst. Coll. Art, 1956-81, Park Sch., Balt., 1956-66, Sinai Hosp. Balt., 1957-75, Balt. chpt. NCCJ, 1950's, Balt Hebrew Congregation, 1940's, 50's, Balt. Jewish Council, 1954-66, Jewish Family and Children's Service, Balt., 1946-54; Assoc. Jewish Charities and Welfare Fund, Balt., 1953-54, Jewish Welfare Bd., Balt., 1965-67, Md. Partners of Alliance, 1965-72, Good Samaritan Hosp., Balt., 1967-73, Johns Hopkins Hosp. Nat. Forum on Medicine, Balt., 1983—, Harvard Law Sch. Assn. and Fund, 1945-60's. Mem. ABA (gov. 1982—), Fed., Md., Balt. bar assns., Am. Law Inst., Harvard Law Sch. Assn. Md., Order of Coif, Phi Beta Kappa. Jewish (dir. congregation 1947-48, 60-62). Clubs: Suburban (Balt.) (dir. 1941-42, 53-60, pres. 1956-60); Rule Day, Wranglers, Law Roundtable, Hamilton Street (Balt.). Home: Brooklandville MD Office: US Court House Baltimore MD 21201

KAUFMAN, FREDERICK, chemist, educator; b. Vienna, Austria, Sept. 13, 1919; came to U.S., 1940, naturalized, 1946; s. Erwin and Else (Pollack) K.; m. Klari Simonyi, Nov. 2, 1951; 1 son, Michael Stephen. Student, Vienna Technische Hochschule, 1937-38; Ph.D., Johns Hopkins, 1948. With Ballistic Research Labs., Aberdeen (Md.) Proving Ground, U.S. Army, 1948-64, chief phys. chemistry sect., 1951-60, chief chem. physics br., 1960-64; lectr. Johns Hopkins U., Balt., 1948-64; prof. chemistry U. Pitts., 1964—, chmn. dept., 1977-80, univ. prof. chemistry, 1980—, dir. space research coordination center, 1975—; mem. advisory bd. office of chemistry tech. Nat. Acad. Scis., 1975-77; cons. to govt. agys. and industry. Editorial bd.: Jour. Chem. Physics, 1971-74, Jour. Photochemistry, 1972—, Internat. Jour. Chem. Kinetics, 1976—, Jour. Phys. Chemistry, 1980—. Recipient Rockefeller Pub. Service award Woodrow Wilson Sch., Princeton, 1955; Kent award Ballistic Research Labs., 1958; Research and Devel. award U.S. Army, 1962. Fellow Am. Phys. Soc.; fellow AAAS; mem. Am. Chem. Soc. (Pitts. award 1977), Chem. Soc. Gt. Britain, Nat. Acad. Sci., Combustion Inst. (v.p. 1978-82, pres. 1982—), AAAS, Nat. Acad. Scis., Phi Beta Kappa, Sigma Xi. Home: 5854 Aylesboro Ave Pittsburgh PA 15217 Office: Dept Chemistry U Pitts Pittsburgh PA 15260

KAUFMAN, FREDERICK ALLEN, steel company executive; b. Ellwood City, Pa., Dec. 14, 1919; s. William Jackson and Clara (DeArment) K.; m. Martha C. Harlan, Nov. 20, 1948; children: Lynn Louise Van Raaphorst, Martha Elizabeth Christof. B.S., Grove City Coll., 1941, D.Sc., 1967. Mem. staff Mellon Inst. Indsl. Research, Pitts., 1944-46; v.p. McKay Co., 1946-58, Universal-Cyclops Corp., Bridgeville, Pa., 1958-65, gen. mgr., 1965-68, pres., 1959-68; also dir.; dir. Cyclops Corp.; v.p., group exec. Teledyne, Inc., Pitts., 1968—; chmn. Teledyne Vasco, Latrobe, Pa. Trustee Grove City (Pa.) Coll., Latrobe Hosp. Mem. Am. Inst. Iron and Steel (dir.), Am. Soc. Mining and Metall. Engrs. Presbyterian (trustee). Clubs: Masons (32 deg.), Shriners.). Home: 729 Laurel Dr Ligonier PA 15658 Office: Teledyne Inc Teledyne Vasco PO Box 151 Latrobe PA 15650

KAUFMAN, GERALD J., advertising executive; b. N.Y.C., May 22, 1933; s. Carl C. and Sonia (Efron) K.; m. Olivia Zane Bender, Dec. 26, 1965; children: Jason, Craig. B.B.A., CCNY, 1954. Creative dir. Smith & Dorian, Inc., N.Y.C., 1954-64; creative dir., sr. v.p. Ted Bates Advt., N.Y.C., 1964—. Commr. Larchmont Jr. Soccer League, 1980—. Recipient Annual Advt. award Advt. Age, 1976, Clio award, 1977, Silver medal V.I. Internat. Film Festival, 1978. Democrat. Jewish. Club: Sheldrake Yacht. Office: 1515 Broadway New York NY 10036

KAUFMAN, GORDON DESTER, educator, theologian; b. Newton, Kans., June 22, 1925; s. Edmund George and Hazel (Dester) K.; m. Dorothy Wedel, June 11, 1947; children: David W., Gretchen E., Anne Louisa, Edmund G. A.B. with highest distinction, Bethel (Kans.) Coll., 1947, L.H.D. (hon.), 1973; M.A. in Sociology, Northwestern U., 1948; B.D. magna cum laude, Yale, 1951; Ph.D. in Philos. Theology, Yale, 1955. Ordained to ministry Mennonite Ch., 1953; asst. prof. religion Pomona Coll., 1953-58; asso. prof. theology Vanderbilt U., 1958-63; prof. theology Harvard Div. Sch., 1963—, Edward MallincKrodt Jr. prof. div., 1969—; vis. prof. United Theol. Coll., Bangalore, India, 1976-77. Author: Relativism, Knowledge and Faith, 1960, The Context of Decision, 1961, Systematic Theology: a Historicist Perspective, 1968, God the Problem, 1972, An Essay on Theological Method, 1975, rev. edit., 1979, Nonresistance and Responsibility and other Mennonite Essays, 1979, The Theological Imagination: Constructing the Concept of God, 1981. Mem. Soc. for Values in Higher Edn., Am. Acad. Religion (pres. 1981-82), Metaphys. Soc. Am., Am. Theol. Soc. (pres. 1979-80). Democrat. Home: 6 Longfellow Rd Cambridge MA 02138 Office: 45 Francis Ave Cambridge MA 02138

KAUFMAN, HAROLD RICHARD, mechanical engineer and physics educator; b. Audubon, Iowa, Nov. 24, 1926; s. Walter Richard and Hazel (Steere) K.; m. Elinor Mae Wheat, June 25, 1948; children: Brian, Karin, Bruce, Cynthia. Student, Evanston Community Coll., 1947-49; B.S.M.E., Northwestern U., 1951; Ph.D., Colo. State U., 1971. Researcher in aerospace propulsion NACA, Cleve., 1951-58; mgr. space propulsion research NASA, Cleve., 1958-74; prof. physics and mech. engring. Colo. State U., 1974—, chmn. dept. physics, 1979—; cons. ion source design and applications. Served with USNR, 1944-46. Recipient James H. Wyld Propulsion award AIAA, 1969; NASA medal for exceptional sci. achievement, 1971. Asso. fellow AIAA; mem. Tau Beta Pi, Pi Tau Sigma. Pioneer electron—bombardment ion thruster, 1960, tech. of which is basis of most present broad-beam ion sources. Home: 401 Spinnaker Ln Fort Collins CO 80525 Office: Colorado State Univ Fort Collins CO 80523

KAUFMAN, HENRY, investment banker; b. Wenings, Ger., Oct. 20, 1927; came to U.S., 1937; s. Gustav and Hilda (Rosenthal) K.; m. Elaine Reinheimer, Sept. 15, 1957; children—Glenn, Craig, Daniel. B.A., N.Y. U., 1948, Ph.D., 1958; M.S., Columbia U., 1949. Asst. chief economist research dept. Fed. Res. Bank N.Y., 1957-61; with Salomon Bros., N.Y.C., 1962—, gen. partner, 1967—, mem. exec. com., 1972—, mng. dir., 1981—, also chief economist, charge bond market research, industry and stock research and bond portfolio analysis research depts.; pres. Money Marketeers, N.Y. U., 1964-65; dir. Phibro Corp., N.Y.C. Trustee Hudson Inst.; bd. govs. Tel-Aviv U. Mem. Am. Econ. Assn., Am. Fin. Assn., Conf. Bus. Economists, Econ. Club N.Y.C. (dir.), UN Assn. (dir.), Council Fgn. Relations. Address: Salomon Bros 1 New York Plaza New York NY 10004

KAUFMAN, HERBERT, political scientist, educator; b. N.Y.C., Sept. 21, 1922; s. Benjamin Harry and Gertrude (Meltzer) K.; m. Ruth L. Davis, Mar. 19, 1967. B.S.S., CCNY, 1942; M.A., Columbia U., 1946, Ph.D., 1950. Research analyst Pres.'s Com. Civil Rights, 1947; research asso. Inst. Pub. Adminstrn., N.Y.C., 1948-49; lectr. govt. CCNY, 1951-53; mem. faculty Yale U., 1953-69, prof. polit. sci., 1963-69, chmn. dept., 1964-67; sr. fellow Brookings Instn., Washington, 1969—; vis. scholar Russell Sage Found., N.Y.C., 1981-82; cons. U.S. Bur. Budget, Econ. Stblzn. Agy., Mayor N.Y.C. Com. Mgmt. Survey, State Com. to Study Orgnl. Structure Govt. N.Y.C., N.Y. State Health Dept., Mayor N.Y.C. Task Force City Personnel. Author: The Forest Ranger: A Study in Administrative Behavior, 1960, (with Wallace S. Sayre) Governing New York City, 1960, Politics and Policies in State and Local Government, 1963, The Limits of Organizational Change, 1971, Administrative Feedback, 1973, Are Government Organizations Immortal?, 1976, Red Tape: Its Origins, Uses, and Abuses, 1977, The Administrative Behavior of Federal Bureau Chiefs, 1981. Mem. New Haven Plan Commn., 1963-66, chmn., 1964-66; chmn. New Haven Housing Authority, 1966-67. Served with AUS, 1942-46. Fellow Center Advanced Study Behavioral Scis., 1959-60; co-recipient Fruin-Colnon award Nat. Municipal League, 1961; recipient Louis Brownlow Book award Nat. Acad. Pub. Adminstrn., 1982. Democrat. Jewish. Office: Brookings Institution 1775 Massachusetts Ave NW Washington DC 20036

KAUFMAN, HERBERT EDWARD, ophthalmologist, educator; b. N.Y.C., Sept. 28, 1931; s. Benjamin and Claire (Krinsky) K.; m. Maija H. Uotila; children: Stephen, Joshua, Claire. A.B. magna cum laude, Princeton U., 1952, M.D., Harvard U., 1956. Intern Mass. Gen. Hosp., Boston, 1956-57; resident Mass. Eye and Ear Infirmary, Boston, 1959-62; assoc. prof., chief div. ophthalmology Coll. Medicine, U. Fla., 1962-64, prof., chmn. dept., 1964-77, prof. pharmacology, 1970-77, acting dean, 1972; prof., head dept. ophthalmology La. State U. Med. Center, 1978—; med. dir. Eye and Ear Inst. La., 1978—; chmn. tng. com. Nat. Eye Inst., 1970-71, mem. nat. adv. council, 1978-82; Pocklington lectr. Royal Coll. Surgeons, 1979; Jackson Meml. lectr., 1979, Thorpe Meml. lectr., 1982, Dunphy Meml. lectr., 1983, Waldert Meml. lectr., 1983, Wohl Meml. lectr., 1983. Editorial bd.: Am. Jour. Ophthalmology; editor: Investigative Ophthalmology, 1972-77; Contbr. articles profl. jours. Served with USPHS, 1957-59. Recipient Lions Humanitarian award, 1968; named one of Ten Outstanding Young Men in Am., 1964. Fellow AAAS, A.C.S., Am. Coll. Clin. Pharmacology; mem Am. Assn. Immunologists, Am. Assn. Ophthalmology, Am. Fedn. Clin. Research, AMA, Am. Soc. Microbiology, Am. Soc. Clin Investigation, Assn. Research Vision and Ophthalmology (pres. 1975, Proctor medal 1978), Assn. U. Profs. Ophthalmology (trustee, pres. 1980), Pan Am. Assn. Ophthalmology (mem. council), Am. Acad. Ophthalmology and Otolaryngology, Eye Bank Assn. Am. (dir.), N.Y. Acad. Scis., Com. Study Nat. Needs for Biomed. and Behavioral Research Personnel, Contact Lens Assn. Ophthalmologists (pres. 1979), Soc. Exptl. Biology and Medicine, Royal Soc. Medicine, Sigma Xi. Office: La State U Eye Center 136 S Roman St New Orleans LA 70112

KAUFMAN, IRA JEFFREY, investment banker; b. Chgo., Mar. 4, 1928; s. Hy and Gertrude (Schwartz) K.; m. Audrey Becker, Jan. 12, 1969; children—Stephen, Stacy, Elizabeth, Jonathan. Student, Chgo. Mil. Acad., 1938-41, Northwestern Mil. and Naval Acad., 1941-45, U. Ill., 1945-46. With Rodman & Renshaw, Inc., 1958—, pres., 1969-79, chmn. bd., 1969—; past chmn. exec. com. Skyline Corp.; dir. emeritus Dan River Mills, Inc.; Mem. Chgo. Bd. Trade; mem. Chgo. Options Exchange, Midwest Stock Exchange; chmn. bd. Exchange Nat. Bank Chgo., 1979—, Exchange Internat. Corp., 1979—. Trustee, mem. exec. adv. bd. St. Joseph Hosp. Clubs: Standard, Chgo. Yacht, Attic

(Chgo.); Palm Bay (Miami, Fla.). Home: 2479 Woodbridge Ln Highland Park IL 60035 Office: 120 S LaSalle St Chicago IL 60603

KAUFMAN, IRVING, engr., educator; b. Geinsheim, Germany, Jan. 11, 1925; came to US., 1938, naturalized, 1945; s. Albert and Hedwig K.; m. Ruby Lee Dordek, Sept. 10, 1950; children—Eve Deborah, Sharon Anne, Julie Ellen. B.E., Vanderbilt U., 1945; M.S., U. Ill., 1949, Ph.D., 1957. Engr. RCA Victor, Indpls., Ind. and Camden, N.J., 1945-48; instr., research asso. U. Ill., Urbana, 1949-56; sr. mem. tech. staff Ramo-Woodridge & Space Tech. Labs., Calif., 1957-64; prof. engring. Ariz. State U., 1965—; dir. Solid State Research Lab., 1968-78; vis. scientist Consiglio Nazionale delle Ricerche, Italy, 1973-74; vis. prof. U. Auckland, N.Z., 1974; liaison scientist U.S. Office Naval Research, London, 1978-80; lectr. and cons. elec. engring. Contbr. articles to profl. jours. Sr. Fulbright research fellow, Italy, 1964-65, 73-74. Fellow IEEE; mem. Am. Phys. Soc., Sigma Xi, Tau Beta Pi, Eta Kappa Nu, Pi Mu Epsilon. Jewish. Patentee in field. Office: Dept Elec and Computer Engring Ariz State U Tempe AZ 85287

KAUFMAN, IRVING ROBERT, federal judge; b. N.Y.C., June 24, 1910; s. Herman and Rose (Spielberg) K.; m. Helen Ruth Rosenberg; children: James Michael, Richard Kenneth. LL.B., Fordham U., 1931; LL.D., Jewish Theol. Sem. Am., Fordham U., Oklahoma City U.; D.Litt. (hon.), Dickinson Sch. Law, D.C.L., N.Y. U. Bar: N.Y. bar 1932. Spl. asst. to U.S. Atty., So. Dist. N.Y.; asst. U.S. Atty.; spl. asst. to Atty. Gen. U.S. charge of lobbying investigation; established permanent lobbying unit for Dept. Justice; individual practice law, N.Y.C.; partner firm Noonan, Kaufman and Eagan; U.S. dist. judge So. Dist. N.Y., 1949-61; circuit judge U.S. Ct. Appeals (2d. circuit), 1961—, chief judge, 1973-80; Cardozo lectr. Assn. Bar City N.Y.; U.S. del. to 2d UN Congress Prevention Crime and Treatment Offenders, Conf. Anglo-Am. Legal Exchange, Ditchley, Eng., 1969, 77, 80; mem. exec. com. U.S. Jud. Conf., 1975-80, mem. com. standards jud. conduct, chmn. com. operation jury system, 1966-73, chmn. com. jud. branch, 1979—. Contbr. articles to profl. jours. Trustee Mt. Sinai Med. Center, Mt. Sinai Med. Sch., Mt. Sinai Hosp.; trustee emeritus Riverdale Country Sch. Recipient Achievement in Law award Fordham Coll. Alumni Assn.; Encaenia award Fordham Coll.; Chief Justice Harlan Fiske Stone award Assn. Trial Lawyers City N.Y. Fellow Inst. Jud. Adminstrn. (Silver Anniversary Vanderbilt award, pres. 1969-71, chmn. exec. com., chmn. juvenile justice standards project); mem. Am. Judicature Soc. (Herbert Harley award 1980), Am. Law Inst., Fed. Bar Assn., ABA, N.Y. Bar Assn., Assn. Bar City N.Y., Fordham Law Alumni Assn. (dir.), Tau Epsilon Phi (Man of Year citation), Phi Alpha Delta (hon.). Office: US Courthouse Foley Sq New York NY 10007

KAUFMAN, JANE, artist; b. N.Y.C., May 26, 1938; d. Herbert and Roslyn (Lesser) K. B.A., N.Y. U., 1960; M.A., Hunter Coll, 1965. Tchr. fine arts pub. high schs., N.Y.C., 1960-69; instr. fine arts Lehman Coll., Bronx, N.Y., 1969-70, Bard Coll., 1971-73, Bklyn. Mus. Art Sch., 1972-73; lectr. Queens Coll., N.Y., 1973-74; vis. artist Mich. State U., 1974, Syracuse U., 1974, Fla. Internat. U., U. Colo., Nova Scotia Coll. Art, 1975, Art Inst. Chgo., Wright State U., U. N.M., 1977, Calif. Inst. Arts, 1979, Cooper Union Sch. Art, 1981, 82, The N.Y. Feminist Art Inst., N.Y., 1981. One person shows, A.M. Sachs Gallery, N.Y.C., 1968,70, Whitney Mus. Am. Art, N.Y.C., 1971, Paley & Lowe Gallery, N.Y.C., 1972, Henri Gallery, Washington, 1973, Alessandra Gallery, N.Y.C., 1975,77, Belarca Gallery, Bogota, Colombia, 1976, Droll/ Kolbert Gallery, N.Y.C., 1978,80, group shows include, Westlerly Gallery, N.Y.C., 1966, Westmoreland County Mus., Greensburg, Pa., 1966,69, Dallas Mus. Fine Arts, 1969, Aldrich Mus., Ridgefield, Conn., 1970, Whitney Mus. Am. Art, N.Y.C., 1971-72, Columbus Gallery Fine Arts, 1971, Paley & Lowe Gallery, N.Y.C., Corcoran Gallery Art, Washington, 1972, Phila. Civic Center Mus., 1974, Alessandra Gallery, N.Y.C., 1975,76, Droll/Kolbert Gallery, 1977, Holly Solomom Gallery, N.Y.C., 1979, Va. Mus., Richmond, 1980, Miami Art Center, Sidney Janis Gallery, N.Y.C., 1981, Susan Caldwell Gallery, N.Y.C., numerous others; represented in permanent collections, Whitney Mus. Modern Art, Aldrich Mus., Worcester Art Mus., Mus. Modern Art of South Australia, Canberra, Bklyn. Mus., also numerous private collections. Guggenheim Found. fellow, 1974; Nat. Endowment for Arts grantee, 1979; N.Y. State Council Arts grantee, 1982. Home: 151 W 18th St New York NY 10011

KAUFMAN, JEROME J., aluminum company executive; b. Cleve., Nov. 27, 1917; s. Isadore and Lena (Sandler) K.; m. Janet Levine, Jan. 16, 1939; children—Jeffrey, James, Joel. Grad., Erie Acad. High Sch., 1935. Chmn. bd., chief exec. officer Alside, Inc. subs. U.S. Steel Corp., Akron, Ohio, 1974—, also dir.; dir. First Nat. Bank Akron, 1961—. Trustee Akron City Hosp., Rehab. Center Summit County, United Fund Summit County; adv. com. U. Akron. Served with inf. AUS, World War II. Recipient Kovod award United Jewish Appeal, 1956. Clubs: Rosemont Country (Akron) (dir.); Westview Country (Miami, Fla.); Tamarisk Country (Palm Springs, Calif.); Hillcrest Country (Los Angeles). Home: 1000 Quayside Terr Miami FL 33138 Office: 1201 Brickell Ave Suite 613 Miami FL 33131

KAUFMAN, JOHN E., association executive; b. New Orleans, Feb. 20, 1927; s. Harold B. and Fannye (Gonsenheim) K.; m. Betsy Joan Baer, Aug. 17, 1951; children: Gail Susan (Mrs. James W. Furgal), John Gilbert. B.E.E., Cornell U., 1949. Registered prof. engr., N.Y. Illuminating engr. Am. Electric Power Service Corp., N.Y.C., 1950-56; with Illuminating Engring. Soc., N.Y.C., 1956—, tech. dir., 1967—; dir. Camillus Cutlery Co., N.Y. Editor: IES Lighting Handbook, 3d-6th edits, 1959-81. Bd. dirs. Engring. Socs. Library, 1970-82. Served with USNR, 1945-46. Fellow Illuminating Engring. Soc., A.A.A.S. (council 1967-73); mem. IEEE, Council Ednl. Facility Planners (distinguished mem.), Internat. Commn. on Illumination (U.S. nat. com.), Chartered Instn. Bldg. Services. Home: 1752 Newfield Ave Stamford CT 06903 Office: 345 E 47th St New York NY 10017

KAUFMAN, JULIAN MORTIMER, broadcasting co. exec.; b. Detroit, Apr. 3, 1918; s. Anton and Fannie (Newman) K.; m. Katherine LaVerne Likins, May 6, 1942; children—Nikki (Mrs. Sam Garcia), Keith Anthony. Grad. high sch. Pub. Tucson Shopper, 1948-50; account exec. ABC, San Francisco, 1950-51; sta. mgr. KPHO-TV, Phoenix, 1951-54; gen. mgr., v.p. Bay City Television Corp., San Diego, 1954—; v.p. Jai Alai Films, Inc., San Diego, 1961—; dir. Spanish Internat. Broadcasting, Inc., Los Angeles. Contbr. articles to profl. jours. Mem. Gov.'s adv. bd., Mental Health Assn., 1958—; Bd. dirs. Francis Parker Sch., San Diego Conv. and Visitors Bur., World Affairs Council, Pala Indian Mission. Served with USAAF, 1942-46. Mem. San Diego C. of C., Advt. and Sales Club, Sigma Delta Chi. Club: University (San Diego). Home: 3125 Montesano Rd Escondido CA 92025 Office: 8253 Ronson Rd San Diego CA 92111

KAUFMAN, KARL LINCOLN, state official; b. Attica, Ohio, 1911; s. S.F. and I. (Huffman) K.; m. Mary Jo Rettig, 1936; children: Karl, James, Robert. B.Sc., Ohio State U., 1933; Ph.D., Purdue U., 1936. Instr., then asst. prof. Wash. State Coll., 1936-40; asso. prof. Med. Coll. Va., 1940-45, prof., head dept., 1945-49; cons. pharm. mfrs.; exec. officer Coll. Pharmacy, Butler U., Indpls., 1949-52, dean, 1952-76; pharm. dir. Ind. Dept. Mental Health, 1976—; project dir. several drug abuse edn. projects. Co-author: American Pharmacy, vol. I, 1945-48, Manual for Pharmacy Aides; Contbr. to: articles to profl. jours. World Book Ency. Past pres. Ind. Health Careers, Inc.; past pres. Comprehensive Health Planning Council, Marion County Heart Assn.; bd. dirs. Am. Cancer Soc.; past chmn. Internat. Sci. Fair Council; founder, sec.-treas. Ind. Sci. Edn. Fund, exec. dir., 1982—; former coordinator Ind. Regional Sci. Fairs; past pres. Ind. Interprofl. Health Council. Mem. Am., Ind. pharm. assns., Am. Soc. Hosp. Pharms., Am. Chem. Soc., Sigma Xi, Phi Sigma, Rho Chi. Republican. Episcopalian. Clubs: Mason (32), Internat. Torch (internat. past pres.). Home: 8616 W 10th St Apt 302 Indianapolis IN 46234

KAUFMAN, MARJORIE RUTH, English educator; b. Milw., May 24, 1922. B.S., Wis. State Tchrs. Coll., 1944; M.A., U. Wash., 1947; Ph.D., U. Minn., 1954. Tchr. high school, Wausau, Wis., 1944-46; from teaching asst. to teaching assoc. English U. Wash., 1946-67; instr. U. Minn., 1947-54; from instr. to assoc. prof. Mt. Holyoke Coll., South Hadley, Mass., 1954-71, prof., 1971-80, Emma B. Kennedy prof. English, 1980—. Author: Henry Jame's Comic Discipline, 1954; mem. editorial bd.: Mass. Rev., 1959-65; contbr. articles to profl. jours. Gladys Murphy Graham fellow AAUW, 1961-62; faculty fellow Mt. Holyoke Coll., 1968-69. Mem. Am. Studies Assn., MLA. Address: Dept English Mount Holyoke Coll South Hadley MA 01075 *

KAUFMAN, MERVYN DOUGLAS, editor, author; b. Los Angeles, Nov. 30, 1932; s. Max and Fannie Esther (Jackson) K.; m. Nancy Simon, Feb. 17, 1967; 1 dau., Amy. A.B., UCLA, 1954; M.S. (with honors), Columbia U., 1959. Staff writer Scholastic Mags., N.Y.C., 1959-61; asst. then asso. editor Horizon Caraval Books, N.Y.C., 1961-64; asso. then mng. editor Automobile Quar. mag., N.Y.C., 1964-66; sr. editor Illustrious Americans book series Silver Burdett Co., Morristown, N.J., 1966-68; staff editor Reader's Digest Gen. Books, N.Y.C., 1968-70; copy chief then mng. editor Am. Home mag., N.Y.C., 1971-76; mng. editor Woman's Day mag., N.Y.C., 1976-82; editorial dir. House Beautiful mag., N.Y.C., 1982—. Author: (juvenile sci. book) No Holidays for Honeybees, 1966; juvenile biographies Thomas Alva Edison, 1962, Christopher Columbus, 1963, The Wright Brothers, 1964, Louis Sullivan, 1969, Fiorello LaGuardia, 1972, Jesse Owens, 1973; co-author: The Making of a Musical: Fiddler on the Roof, 1971. Served with U.S. Army, 1955-56. Office: 1700 Broadway New York NY 10019

KAUFMAN, MICHAEL DAVID, management executive; b. Bklyn., Apr. 7, 1941; s. Abraham and Shirley (Blank) K.; m. Susan Gail Zipkis, June 30, 1962; children—Robert Jay, Craig Douglas. B.S.M.E., Poly. Inst. Bklyn., 1962, M.S. in Indsl. Mgmt, 1967. With Xerox Corp., Stamford, Conn., 1967-80, dir. corp. fin. planning, 1980-81; pres., chief operating officer Centronics Data Computer Corp., Hudson, N.H., 1980-81; partner Oak Mgmt. Corp., Westport, Conn., 1981—; chmn. bd. Interactive Images, Mass.; dir. Fla. Data Corp., Fingraph, others; instr. M.B.A. program U. Conn., 1977-78; mem. adv. bd. Imaging Scis. Inst., Poly. Inst. N.Y., 1980—. Bd. dirs. So. N.H. Bd. Commerce and Industry, 1980-81. Recipient award of distinction Poly. Inst. Bklyn., 1980. Mem. Am. Inst. Indsl. Engrs., ASME, Nat. Soc. Profl. Engrs., Poly. Inst. Bklyn. Alumni Assn. (dir.). Club: Nashawtuc Country. Office: 257 Riverside Ave Westport CT 06880

KAUFMAN, NATHAN, physician, educator; b. Lachine, Que., Can., Aug. 3, 1915; s. Solomon and Anna (Sabesinsky) K.; m. Rita Friendly, Sept. 10, 1946; children: Naomi, Michael, Miriam, Hannah, Judith. B.Sc., McGill U., Montreal, 1937, M.D., C.M., 1941. Mem. faculty Western Res. U. Med. Sch., 1948-60, asst. prof., 1952-54, asso. prof., 1954-60; pathologist-in-charge Cleve. Met. Gen. Hosp., 1952-60; prof. pathology Duke Sch. Medicine, 1960-67; prof. dept. pathology Queen's U. Med. Sch., Kingston, Ont., Can., 1967-81, prof. emeritus, 1981—, head dept., 1967-79; clin. prof. dept. humanities Med. Coll. Ga., Augusta, 1980—; pathologist-in-chief Kingston Gen. Hosp., 1967-79; past cons. Hotel Dieu Hosp., St. Mary's of the Lake Hosp., Kingston Clinic, Ont. Cancer Treatment and Research Found.; asso. editor Lab. Investigation Jour., 1952-66, editor, 1972-75, mem. editorial bd., 1975—; asso. editor Am. Jour. Pathology, 1967, mem. editorial bd., 1967-71; Mem. grants panel Med. Research Council Can., 1970-74, mem. council, 1971-77, exec. com., 1971-74; active coms. Ont. Council Health, 1968-79, chmn. provincial rev. ednl. subcom., 1972-75. Served to capt. M.C., Royal Can. Army, 1942-46. Decorated Order Brit. Empire; recipient Disting. Alumni award Duke U., 1975. Mem. Internat. Acad. Pathology (v.p. 1972-74, pres. elect 1974, pres. 1976-78, pres. U.S.-Can. div. 1973-75, sec.-treas. 1979—), Royal Coll. Physicians and Surgeons Can. (com. on exams. 1972), Cleve. Soc. Pathologists (past pres.), Am. Assn. Pathologists (editor Symposium series 1970-71), Soc. Exptl. Biology and Medicine, Am. Soc. Clin. Pathologists, Am. Assn. Cancer Research, Am. Soc. Cytology, AAAS, N.Y. Acad. Scis., Canadian Med. Assn., Can., Ont. assns. pathologists, Ont. Med. Assn., Can. Soc. Cytology, Sigma Xi. Office: 1003 Chafee Ave Augusta GA 30904

KAUFMAN, PAUL, physician, former naval officer, association executive; b. Bay Shore, N.Y., Mar. 24, 1923; s. Sam and Rose (Sinkoff) K.; m. Greta Maxine Konersman, Feb. 1, 1956; children: Barry W., Michael J., Bruce E. B.A., NYU, 1943; M.D., George Washington U., 1947; grad., Naval War Coll., 1962, Naval Command and Staff Course. Diplomate: Am. Bd. Pediatrics. Intern D.C. Gen. Hosp., 1947-48; resident in pediatrics Children's Hosp., Washington, 1948-50; practice medicine specializing in pediatrics, Arlington, Va., 1952-59; served as enlisted man U.S. Navy, 1943-45; med. officer active duty, 1950-52, commd. lt. j.g. M.C., 1947, advanced through grades to rear adm., 1973, chief pediatric service Naval Dispensary, Washington, 1959-61, dep. surgeon on staff Comdr. in Chief Pacific, 1962-65, asst., fleet med. office on staff Comdr. in Chief Pacific Fleet and Comdr. Service Forces, Pacific Fleet, 1962-65, dir. planning Bur. Medicine Surgery Navy Dept., Washington, 1965-70, dep. comdg. officer, dir. clin. services and grad. tng. Naval Hosp., Nat. Naval Med. Center, Bethesda, Md., 1970-72, comdg. officer, dir. Naval Regional Med. Center, Jacksonville, Fla., 1972-74, asst. chief Bur. Medicine Surgery for Planning ang Logistics, Washington, 1974-75, chmn. Def. Med. Materiel Bd., spl. asst. to vice chief of naval ops. for med. matters, dir. program planning and analysis, and asst. chief Navy's Bur. Medicine and Surgery for Materiel Resources, Washington, 1975-76, dep. surgeon gen. Navy Bur. Medicine and Surgery, 1976-77; med. exec. asst. Dept. Health and Rehabilitative Services, Jacksonville, 1977-78; asst. v.p. med. affairs Sci. and Tech. Div. Pharm. Mfrs. Assn., Washington, 1978-82, asst. v.p. Sci. and Tech. Div., 1982—. Contbr.: articles to Clin. Proc. Children's Hosp, Washington, 1949-50. Bd. dirs. N.E. Fla. Heart Assn., 1972-74, Health Planning Council of Greater Jacksonville Area, 1972-74, Emergency Med. Services Jacksonville, 1972-74. Decorated Joint Service Commendation medal with oak leaf cluster, Navy Commendation medal, Navy Achievement medal, Legion of Merit. Fellow Am. Acad. Pediatrics, A.C.P.; mem. Am. Acad. Family Physicians, George Washington U. Med. Alumni Assn., AMA, Arlington County (Va.) Med. Soc., Med. Soc. Va., No. Va. Pediatric Soc., Am. Heart Assn. Club: Order Eagles. Office: 1100 15th St NW Washington DC 20005

KAUFMAN, PHILLIP ALLEN, semiconductor company executive; b. Detroit, Apr. 19, 1942; s. Irving and Ruth (Seedman) K.; m. Molly Luke, May 30, 1965; children: Michelle Ilene, Matthew Douglas. B.S. in Elec. Engrin., U. Mich., 1964, M.S. in Elec. Engring., 1966. Sr. staff engr. Interstate Electronics Corp., Anaheim, Calif., 1966-70; tech. dir., dir. corp. product planning Computer Automation, Inc., Irvine, Calif., 1970-76; dir. systems engring.-corp. strategic staff Intel Corp., Santa Clara, Calif., 1976—. Office: Intel Corp 3065 Bowers Ave Santa Clara CA 95051

KAUFMAN, RAYMOND HENRY, physician; b. Bklyn., Nov. 24, 1925; s. Morris and Anne (Markewich) K.; m. Patricia Ann Judson, June 23, 1946; children: Susan Jo (Mrs. Edward B. Kahn), Wendy Beth (Mrs. Seth Katzman), Murri Ellen, Elisabeth Ann. Student, Coll. William and Mary, 1942-43, U. N.C., 1943-44; M.D., U. Md., 1948. Diplomate: Am. Bd. Obstetrics and Gynecology. Intern Beth Israel Hosp., N.Y.C., 1948-49, resident obstetrics and gynecology, 1949-53; fellow pathology Meth. Hosp., Houston, 1955-58; asst. prof. obstetrics, gynecology, pathology Baylor Coll. Medicine, Houston, 1959-65, asso. prof., 1965-72, acting chmn. dept., 1968-72, prof., chmn. dept. obstetrics and gynecology, 1973—, prof. pathology, 1973—. Author: (with H.L. Gardner) Benign Diseases of Vulva and Vagina, 1969, 80; contbr. articles to profl. jours. Served with USNR, 1943-45; to capt. USAF, 1953-55. Mem. Am. Coll. Obstetrics and Gynecology, A.C.S., Central Assn. Obstetrics and Gynecology (chmn. com. for cons. gynecol. pathology 1968—, pres. 1976), Am. Assn. Obstetrics and Gynecology, Tex. Assn. Obstetrics and Gynecology (v.p. 1971, 81, pres. 1983), Am. Gynecol. Soc., Houston Obstet. and Gynecol. Soc. (pres. 1971—), Soc. Gynecol. Oncology (v.p. 1983-84), Am. Cytology Soc., Am. Fertility Soc., Am. Soc. Colposcopy, Internat. Soc. Vulvar Disease (pres. 1978-79), Phi Delta Epsilon (nat. sec. 1970—). Home: 11002 Hunters Park Dr Houston TX 77024

KAUFMAN, ROBERT JULES, lawyer; b. N.Y.C., Jan. 21, 1921; s. Ernst B. and Gertrude S. (Popper) K.; m. Susan H. Sanger, Feb. 22, 1951; children—Peter S., James H. Student, Columbia Coll., 1942, Yale U. Law Sch., 1948. Bar: N.Y. bar 1949. Asso. firm Gale, Bernays, Falk & Eisner, N.Y.C., 1948-53; mem. firm Gale & Falk, asst. gen. counsel DuMont TV Network, 1953-55; with ABC, N.Y.C., 1955—, v.p., gen. atty. network govtl. regulation, 1968—; mem. internat. copyright panel Dept. State; guest speaker on radio and television matters at Practicing Law Inst. and N.Y. U. Law Sch. Served to lt. USN, 1942-46. Mem. Am. Bar Assn., Bar Assn. City N.Y. (com. on communications), Copyright Soc. U.S.A., Nat. Acad. TV Arts and Scis., Phi Beta Kappa. Home: 33 Clarendon Rd Scarsdale NY 10583 Office: 1330 Ave of Americas New York City NY 10019

KAUFMAN, ROBERT MAX, lawyer; b. Vienna, Austria, Nov. 17, 1929; came to U.S., 1939, naturalized, 1945; s. Paul M. and Bertha (Hirsch) K.; m. Sheila Seymour Kelley, Nov. 20, 1959. B.A. with honors, Bklyn. Coll., 1951; M.A., NYU, 1954; J.D. magna cum laude, Bklyn. Law Sch., 1957. Bar: N.Y. 1957, U.S. Supreme Ct. 1961. Successively jr. economist, economist, sr. economist N.Y. State Div. Housing, 1953-57; atty. antitrust div. U.S. Dept. Justice, 1957-58; legis. asst. to U.S. Senator Jacob K. Javits, 1958-61; asso. Proskauer Rose Goetz & Mendelsohn, N.Y.C., 1961-69, partner, 1969—; dir. Pirelli Cable Corp., chmn. bd., 1980-81, Pirelli Enterprises Corp.; dir. Pirelli Cable Systems, Inc., Haseg (S.A.), Roytex, Inc.; mem. N.Y. State Legislature Adv. Com. on Election Law, 1973-74; chmn. adv. com. N.Y. State Bd. Elections, 1974-78; chmn. N.Y. State Bd. Pub. Disclosure, 1981-82; mem. platform com. N.Y. Republican State Com., 1974; mem. jud. selection adv. coms. Senator Javits, 1972-80, and Senator Moynahan, 1977—; treas., mgr., counsel various polit. campaigns. Co-author: Congress and the Public Trust, 1970, Disorder in the Court, 1973. Bd. dirs. Lawrence M. Gelb Found., Inc.; bd. dirs., sec. Community Action for Legal Services, Inc., 1976-78; bd. dirs., exec. v.p. Ernest and Mary Hayward Weir Found.; presdl. appointee mem. bd. visitors U.S. Mil. Acad., 1977-79. Served with U.S. Army, 1957-58. Mem. Assn. Bar City N.Y. (past v.p.; chmn. com. on 2d Century; past chmn. exec. com., past chmn. com. profl. responsibility, past chmn. spl. com. on campaign expenditures, past chmn. com. civil rights, past vice chmn. com. grievances), N.Y. State Bar Assn. (ho. of dels. 1978), New York County Lawyers Assn. (past chmn. com. on civil rights). Office: 300 Park Ave New York NY 10022

KAUFMAN, RONALD PAUL, physician, school official; b. Hartford, Conn., Nov. 30, 1929; s. Louis Elliot and Saray K.; m. Beth Winkler, Dec. 28, 1968; children—Ronald Paul, Michael, Karyn, Leesa, Jennifer. B.S., Trinity Coll., 1951; M.D., U. Pa., 1955. Asst. dir. dept. medicine Hartford Hosp., 1966-70, dir. med. edn. dept., 1967-70; med. dir. George Washington U. Hosp., Washington, 1970-75; asso. dean clin. affairs. Univ. Med. Center, 1972-73, dean, 1973-77, acting v.p. for med. affairs, 1975-76, v.p. for med. affairs, 1976—, Walter A. Bloedorn prof. adminstrv. medicine, 1983—. Author: (with L. Gregory Pawlson) HMOs and the Academic Medical Center—A Reassessment. Mem. D.C. Med. Community com. Mayor's Panel on Human Resources Orgn. and Mgmt. of D.C., 1977. Served to capt. M.C. USAF, 1958-60. Mem. Am. Acad. Med. Dirs., A.C.P., AMA, Am. Soc. Internal Medicine, Assn., Acad. Health Centers, Assn. Am. Med. Colls., Assn. for Hosp. Med. Edn., D.C. Med. Soc., Med. Adminstrs. Conf., Nat. Bd. Med. Examiners, Am. Coll. Physician Execs., Nat. Acad. Med. Examiners, World Access Inc., Pan Am. Med. Assn., D.C. Consortium Univ. Health Sci. Centers, So. Med. Assn., D.C. Hosp. Assn., Assn. Vol. Trustees Not-for-Profit Hosps. (alternate). Office: Sch Medicine George Washington U 901 23d St NW Washington DC 20037

KAUFMAN, SANFORD PAUL, lawyer; b. N.Y.C., Jan. 4, 1928; s. Max and Rose (Kornitzky) K.; m. Bernice R. Sulkis, June 17, 1956; children—Leslie Keith, Brad Leigh, Rona Sheryl, Jeffrey Scott, Adam Ira. B.B.A. in Accounting, Coll. City N.Y., 1948; LL.B., N.Y. U., 1952, LL.M. in Taxation, 1957. Bar: N.Y. bar 1953, Calif. bar 1962. With firm Garey & Garey, N.Y.C., 1953-55; asst. gen. counsel Olympic Radio & TV, Long Island City, 1961-63; sec., gen. counsel Tel-Autograph Corp., Los Angeles, 1961-63; asst. gen. counsel Nat. Gen. Corp., Los Angeles, 1963-74; sec., gen. counsel Familian Corp., Los Angeles, 1974-77; individual practice law, 1977—. Bd. dirs. Temple Ner Tamid, S. Bay, Calif. Mem. Am. Soc. Corporate Secs., Los Angeles County Bar Assn., Beverly Hills Bus. Men's Assn. Club: K.P. (past chancellor). Home: 28412 S Golden Meadow Dr Palos Verdes CA 90274 Office: 11704 Wilshire Blvd Los Angeles CA 90025 *A person's finest attributes: honesty, integrity, loyalty, dependability and reliability, and the fear of God.*

KAUFMAN, SEYMOUR ALVIN, radiologist; b. Boston, Apr. 5, 1926; s. Frank S. and Ida K. (Ganick) K.; m. Charlotte F. Rothberg, Feb. 10, 1951; children—Lisa Nan, John Andrew, Peter Ross. M.D., Boston U., 1948. Intern Boston City Hosp., 1948-49, resident, 1949-50, Mass. Meml. Hosp., Boston, 1952-54; practice medicine specializing in radiology, Boston, 1963—; mem. staff Boston U. Hosp., Boston City Hosp., Northeastern U.; clin. prof. radiology Boston U. Contbr. numerous articles to profl. publs. Active in fund raising United Fund, Mus. Fine Arts Boston, Alumni funds, Combined Jewish Philanthropies; trustee New Eng. Sch. Keyboard Tech. Served to capt. M.C. USAF, 1950-52. Fellow Am. Coll. Radiology; mem. Radiol. Soc. N. Am., Am., New Eng. Roentgen ray socs., Mass. Radiologic Soc., AMA, Mass. Med. Soc. Clubs: St. Botolph, Wightman. Home: 64 Bishopsgate Rd Newton Center MA 02159 Office: 720 Harrison Ave Boston MA 02118

KAUFMANN, RALPH JAMES, educator; b. Grand Forks, N.D., Aug. 2, 1924; s. Ralph Jennings and Mary (Allyn) K.; m. Ruth Joan Hackett, June 30, 1944 (div.); children—James, Margaret, Mary and Sarah (twins); m. Leslie Delaney Connor, May 31, 1969; children—Christopher, Courtney. B.A., Grinnell (Iowa) Coll., 1947, L.H.D.,

1975; M.A., Princeton, 1949, Ph.D., 1953; postgrad., Univ. Coll., London, Eng., 1950-51. Instr. English Princeton, 1949-53; asst. prof. English Wesleyan U., Middletown, Conn., 1953-55; mem. faculty U. Rochester, 1955-69, prof. history, English, 1964-69, asso. dean, 1961-63, chmn. history dept., 1966-68; prof. English U. Tex., Austin, 1969-73, Stiles prof. humanities and comparative lit., 1973—, asso. dean, 1971-73, chmn. comparative studies, 1974-78; presdl. cons. Wesleyan U.; Asso. dir. Center Contemporary Cultural Studies, Birmingham, Eng. Author books and essays on Renaissance and modern culture. Bd. dirs. Nat. Humanities Faculty, 1972—. Served with USNR, 1943-46. Woodrow Wilson fellow, 1947-48; Fulbright fellow, 1950-51; Folger fellow, 1961; Guggenheim fellow, 1964-65; recipient Curtis prize for excellence in teaching U. Rochester, 1964; Harbison award for distinguished teaching Danforth Found., 1968; Liberal Arts prize outstanding teaching, 1982. Mem. Modern Langs. Assn. Am. Home: 1516 Forest Trail Austin TX 78703

KAUFOLD, LEROY, aerospace company executive; b. Blackwell, Okla., Sept. 16, 1924; s. Herbert L. and Nora (Johnston) K.; m. Patricia Swanson, Apr. 17, 1943; children: Kim, Mark, Robert. Student, UCLA, 1948-50, U. So. Calif., 1950-52, M.I.T., 1970. With Northrop Avionics, Hawthorne, Calif., 1948-74, chief engr., v.p., and gen. mgr., until 1974; pres. Northrop-Wilcox Electric Co., Kansas City, Mo., 1974-80; corporate v.p. Northrop Co., Century City, Calif., 1975—; mgmt. cons., 1980—. Served with USN, 1942-45. Patentee in field. Home: PO Box 10742 Eugene OR 97440

KAUFTHAL, ILAN, corp. exec.; b. Czechoslovakia, Aug. 20, 1947; s. Leo and Edith K.; m. Linda S., Jan. 30, 1971; children—Joshua, David, Daniel. B.S.E.E., Columbia U., 1969; M.B.A., N.Y. U., 1971. Dir. mergers and acquisitions NL Industries, N.Y.C., 1973-79, treas., 1979—, v.p., 1981—. Office: NL Industries Inc 1230 Ave of Americas New York NY 10020

KAULA, WILLIAM MASON, educator, geophysicist; b. Sydney, Australia, May 19, 1926; s. Edgar Louis and Edna (Mason) K.; m. Denise Bouche, June 11, 1949; children: Anne, Jacqueline, Charles, Marie; m. Gene Hurley, July 22, 1978. B.S., U.S. Mil. Acad., 1948; M.S. in Geodesy, Ohio State U., 1953; D.Sc. (hon.), 1975. Commd. 2d lt. C.E. U.S. Army, 1948; advanced through grades to capt., 1953, resigned, 1957; geodesist U.S. Army Map Service, 1957-60; researcher orbital dynamics and planetary structure NASA, 1960-63; prof. geophysics UCLA, 1963—. Author: Theory of Satellite Geodesy, 1966, Introduction to Planetary Physics, 1968; Contbr. papers to profl. lit. Fellow Am. Geophys. Union. Home: 1262 S Barrington Ave Los Angeles CA 90025 Office: Dept Earth and Space Scis U Calif Los Angeles CA 90024

KAULAKIS, ARNOLD FRANCIS, management consultant; b. Lewiston, Maine, Oct. 6, 1916; s. Frank Kulakis and Amelia (Vicaniskis) K.; m. Marguerite Marie Adams, Oct. 18, 1940; children: Bernadette, Robert, Michael, Marguerite. B.S. in Chem. Engring., MIT, 1938. V.p., dir. Exxon Research & Engring. co., Linden, N.J., 1961-66; dep. refining coordinator Exxon Corp., N.Y.C., 1966-68; exec. chmn., chief exec. officer BOC-Airco Cryogenic Plant Ltd., London, 1968-71; mng. dir. Cryoplants Ltd., London, 1971-72; v.p. energy devel. The Pittston Co., Greenwich, Conn., 1972-81; chmn. bd., chief exec. officer Pittston Petroleum Inc., Montvale, N.J., 1977-83; mgmt. cons. Afkay Assocs., Chatham, N.J., 1983—. Patentee in field; contbr. articles to profl. jours. Mem. Welding Research Council (vice chmn. exec. com. 1964-68), Jr. Engring. Tech. Soc. (dir. 1962-68), Am. Petroleum Inst., Am. Mining Congress (synthetic fuels com.). Address: 187 Washington Ave Chatham NJ 07928

KAUPER, THOMAS EUGENE, lawyer, educator; b. Bklyn., Sept. 25, 1935; s. Paul Gerhardt and Anna Marie (Nichlas) K.; m. Shirley Yvonne Worrell, Dec. 27, 1958; children—Karen Yvonne, Krista Diane. A.B., U. Mich., 1957, J.D., 1960. Bar: Ill. bar 1962. Law clk. to Justice Potter Stewart, U.S. Supreme Ct., Washington, 1960-62; asso. firm Sidley & Austin, Chgo., 1962-64; asst. prof. Law Sch., U. Mich., Ann Arbor, 1964-67, asso. prof., 1967-69, prof. law, 1969—; on leave as dep. asst. atty. gen. Office Legal Counsel, Dept. Justice, Washington, 1969, asst. atty. gen. antitrust div., 1972-76. Contbr. articles to legal publs. Mem. Am., Ill. bar assns., Order of Coif, Phi Beta Kappa. Lutheran. Home: 1125 Fair Oaks Ave Ann Arbor MI 48104 Office: Law Sch U Mich Ann Arbor MI 48104

KAUS, OTTO MICHAEL, judge; b. Vienna, Austria, Jan. 7, 1920; came to U.S., 1939, naturalized, 1942; s. Otto F. and Gina (Wiener) K.; m. Peggy A. Huttenback, Jan. 12, 1943; children: Stephen D., Robert M. B.A., UCLA, 1942; LL.B., Loyola U., Los Angeles, 1949. Bar: Calif. 1949. Pvt. practice, Los Angeles, 1949-61; judge Superior Ct. Calif., 1961-64; assoc. justice Calif. Ct. Appeal (2d appellate dist., div. 3), Los Angeles, 1965-66, presiding justice, 1966-81; assoc. justice Supreme Ct. Calif., San Francisco, 1981—; mem. faculty Loyola U. Law Sch., 1950-75, U. So. Calif., 1974-77. Served with U.S. Army, 1942-45. Mem. Am. Law Inst., Phi Beta Kappa, Order of Coif. Office: Supreme Court 350 McAllister St San Francisco CA 94102

KAUSLER, DONALD HARVEY, educator; b. St. Louis, July 16, 1927; s Charles Richard and Pauline Ann (Svejkovsky) K.; m. Martha Blanche Roeper, Oct. 25, 1952; children—Rene, Donald Harvey, Jill, Barry. A.B., Washington U., St. Louis, 1947, Ph.D., 1951. Research psychologist USAF, Mather AFB, Cal., 1951-55; asst. prof., then asso. prof. U. Ark., 1955-60; asso. prof., then prof. St. Louis U., 1960-71, chmn. dept. psychology, 1963-71; prof. psychology U. Mo.-Columbia, 1971—. Author: Psychology of Verbal Learning and Memory, 1974, Experimental Psychology and Human Aging, 1982; Editor: Readings in Verbal Learning; Contemporary Theory and Research, 1966—; Contbr. articles to profl. jours. Mem. Am. Psychol. Assn., Am. Assn. U. Profs., Phi Beta Kappa, Sigma Xi. Home: 3905 Faurot Dr Columbia MO 65201

KAUTZ, JAMES CHARLES, investment banker; b. Cin., Mar. 3, 1931; s. Paul Daniel and Marie M. (Fisher) K.; m. Caroline Miller, June 15, 1957; children: Leslie Barnes, Daniel Paul. A.B., U. Cin., 1953; M.B.A., U. Pa., 1957. Staff asst. Procter & Gamble Co., Cin., 1957-59; corp. sec. Main Supply, Cin., 1959-66; gen. ptnr. Goldman, Sachs & Co., N.Y.C., 1966—. Trustee Vassar Coll.; hon. trustee U. Cin. McMicken Found.; mem. fin. com. Greater N.Y. council Boy Scouts Am., 1979—. Served with U.S. Army, 1953-55. Club: Bond (N.Y.C.). Home: 251 Oak Ridge Ave Summit NJ 07901 Office: 85 Broad St New York NY 10004

KAUTZ, LYNFORD ENGLISH, institution consultant; b. West Chester, Pa., Apr. 5, 1915; s. Jacob R. and Martha S. (Sharples) K.; m. Jacqueline Jean Paul, Jan. 24, 1950; children: Jill Louise, Jacqueline Jean. Teaching certificate, West Chester State Coll., 1936-37, Jourdan Sch. Publicity and Promotion, Phila., 1945-46, Am. TV Inst., Chgo., 1947-48. Instr. Booth Sch., Rosemont, Pa., 1939-41; promotional dir. Black Hills Passion Play Am., Spearfish, S.D., 1947-49; dir. funds Chgo. office NCCJ, 1949-52; regional dir. Nat. Fund Med. Edn., Chgo., 1952-54; dir. devel. and pub. relations Northwestern U., 1954-62; v.p. devel. Boston U., 1962-67; dir. resources Fletcher Sch. Law and Diplomacy, 1967-69; dir. office devel. Smithsonian Instn., 1969-75; cons. Smithsonian and other non-profit instns., 1975-77; nat. dir. planning and devel. Am. Youth Hostels, Delaplane, Va., 1977-78; instl. cons., 1978—; cons. Washington Center for Learning Alternatives, 1978-79; dir. devel. and public affairs Nat. Center for State Cts., 1980-82; mgr. univ. campaigns Va. Tech. U., 1982. Trustee Arden Shore Assn., Lake Bluff, Ill. Served with inf. AUS, 1941-45; ETO. Decorated Purple Heart. Mem. Am. Pub. Relations Assn., Pub. Relations Soc. Am., Pith Helmut Soc. Presbyn. Clubs: Chicago, Economic (Chgo.); Longwood Cricket (Chestnut Hill, Mass.); Algonquin (Boston). Home: 1002 Abbey Way McLean VA 22101

KAUTZ, RICHARD CARL, chemical and feed company executive; b. Mucatine, Iowa, Aug. 1, 1916; s. Carl and Leah (Amlong) K.; m. Mary Elda Stein, Dec. 24, 1939; children: Linda, Judith Kautz Curb, John Terry, Thomas R., Susan E. Kautz Teeple, Sarah J. Kautz Aavang, Mary Catherine Kautz Huff, Jennifer W. Kautz Kreger. Student, U. Ariz., 1936-37; B.S. with high distinction, U. Iowa, 1939; D.H.L., George Williams Coll., 1973. Supr. in fin. dept. Gen. Electric Co., 1939-43; with Grain Processing Corp. and Kent Feeds, Inc., Muscatine, 1943—, chmn. bd., dir., mem. exec. com., 1966—; mem. adv. com. Export-Import Bank U.S., 1984—. Mem. U. Iowa Pres.'s Club; mem. citizens com. Rock Island dist. U.S. Army Engrs.; chmn., pres. bd. trustees, mem. Herbert Hoover Presdl. Library Assn., 1976—; chmn. nat. bd. YMCA, 1970-73, now mem., mem. exec. com. and bd.; mem. exec. com. World Alliance YMCA's, 1973—, mem. pres.'s com., exec. com.; mem. Bd. Trustees YMCA's; trustee YMCA Retirement Fund, Center for Study of Presidency, 1977—; bd. dirs., mem. exec. com., chmn. Bus.-Industry Polit. Action Com., 1977—. Mem. NAM (dir., chmn. exec. com. 1977, chmn. fin. com. 1978, vice chmn. 1975, chmn. 1976), Iowa Mfrs. Assn. (dir.), Muscatine C. of C., DeMolay Legion of Honor, Beta Gamma Sigma (dirs. table), Sigma Chi (named Significant Sig.). Presbyn. Clubs: Mason (Shriner), Elk, Rotarian., Union League (Chgo.); Met., Capitol Hill (Washington); Marco Polo, Met., Canadian (N.Y.C.); University Athletic (Iowa City); Des Moines, Lincoln (Des Moines). Home: Rural Route 4 Box 201 Muscatine IA 52761 Office: 1600 Oregon St Muscatine IA 52761

KAUVAR, ABRAHAM J., gastroenterologist, medical administrator; b. Denver, May 8, 1915; s. Charles Hillel and Belle Gertrude (Bluestone) K.; m. Jean Bayer, Aug. 22, 1943; children: Kenneth B., Jane Kauvar Athens, Lawrence, David. B.A., U. Denver, 1935; M.D., U. Chgo., 1939; Sc.D. (hon.), Hawthorne Coll., 1981. Diplomate: Am. Bd. Internal Medicine. Intern Billings Hosp., U. Chgo., 1939-40; resident Peter Bent Brigham Hosp., Boston, 1940-41, Mayo Clinic, Rochester, Minn., 1941-42; practice medicine specializing in gastroenterology, Denver, 1946-74; mgr., chief exec. officer Health and Hosps. Agy., City and County of Denver, 1974-80; pres. Health and Hosp. Corp., N.Y.C., 1980-81; internist-gastroenterologist Denver Clinic, 1981—; spl. cons. Med. Care and Research Found., Denver; pres. Mackinaw Health Systems, Inc.; prof. medicine U. Colo. Med. Sch.; health cons. govts., Ireland, Israel; mem. Social Security Appeals Council, Dept. Health and Human Services; pres. med. staffs Colo. Gen. Hosp., 1954-55, Rose Meml. Hosp., 1955-56; dir. Nat. Jewish Hosp., 1957—; pres. Tchrs. Award Found., 1957. Contbr. articles to profl. jours.; lectr.: hypoglycemia Am. Lecture Series, 1954. Bd. dirs. Salvation Army, 1957—. Served to maj. U.S. Army, 1942-46. Recipient Disting. award Denver Med. Soc., 1975; Disting. Humanitarian award U. Chgo. Alumni Assn., 1981. Mem. Am. Fedn. Clin. Research, ACP, Am. Gastroent. Assn., Am. Endoscopic Soc., Am. Geriatric Soc., Soc. Med. Adminstrs., Am. Coll. Gastroenterology (v.p. 1976-77). Jewish. Clubs: Denver, Denver Tennis, Rotary. Home: 70 S Ash St Denver CO 80222 Office: 1565 Clarkson St Denver CO 80203

KAUZMANN, WALTER JOSEPH, chemistry educator; b. Mt. Vernon, N.Y., Aug. 18, 1916; s. Albert and Julia Maria (Kahle) K.; m. Elizabeth Alice Flagler, Apr. 1, 1951; children: Charles Peter, Eric Flagler, Katherine Elizabeth Julia. B.A., Cornell U., 1937; Ph.D., Princeton U., 1940. Westinghouse research fellow Westinghouse Mfg. Co., E. Pittsburgh, Pa., 1940-42; mem. staff Explosives Research Lab., Bruceton, Pa., 1942-44, Los Alamos Lab., 1944-46; asst. prof. Princeton U., 1946-51, asso. prof., 1951-60, prof. chemistry, 1960-82, chmn. dept., 1964-68, David B. Jones prof. chemistry, 1963-82, chmn. biochem. sci. dept., 1980-81; vis. scientist Atlantic Research Lab., NRC Can., 1983; vis. lectr. Kyoto U., 1974; vis. prof. U. Ibadan, 1975. Author: Quantum Chemistry, 1957, Kinetic Theory of Gases, 1966, Thermal Properties of Matter, 1967, (with D. Eisenberg) Structure and Properties of Water, 1969. Jr. fellow Soc. Fellows, Harvard, 1942; Guggenheim fellow, 1957, 74-75; Recipient Linderstrom-Lang medal, 1966. Fellow Am. Acad. Arts and Scis.; mem. Nat. Acad. Scis., Am. Soc. Biol. Chemists, Am. Chem. Soc., Am. Phys. Soc., A.A.A.S., Fedn. Am. Scientists, Sigma Xi. Home: 4 Newlin Rd Princeton NJ 08540 Frick Chem Lab Princeton NJ 08540

KAVALEK, LUBOMIR, chess expert; b. Prague, Czechoslovakia, Aug. 9, 1943; came to U.S., 1970; s. Lubomir and Stepanka (Kavalkova) K.; m. Irena Koritsanska, Nov. 24, 1971. Student, Faculty of Transp., U. Zilina, 1960-65, Faculty of Journalism, Charles U., Prague, 1967-68, George Washington U., 1970-71. Journalist Voice of Am., USIA, 1971-72; cons. editor RHM Chess Pub., Great Neck, N.Y., 1973—; Mem. German chess team, Solingen, 1969-76; mem. U.S. chess team in chess Olympiad, 1972, 74, 76, 78, 82. Mem. Internat. Assn. Chess Journalists, U.S. Chess Fedn. German chess team champion, 1969, 71, 72, 73, 74, 75, 80, 81, Dutch Open champion, 1969, Czechoslovakian champion, 1962, 68, Internat. Grandmaster, 1965—, U.S. co-champion, 1972, 73; U.S. champion, 1978, European Club champion, 1976. Home: 11002 Saffold Way Reston VA 22090 *In the eternal battle between logic and creativity the winner fights the artist in chess. It is not a recovery from a split personality, but trying to find a balance between those two - that is what keeps me going.*

KAVANAGH, KEVIN PATRICK, insurance company executive; b. Brandon, Man., Can., Sept. 27, 1932; s. Martin and Katherine Power K.; m. Elisabeth M. Mesman, July 1963; children: Sean K., Jennifer T. B.Comm., U. Man., 1953. With Great-West Life Assurance Co., 1953—, v.p. mktg. (U.S.), Denver, 1973-75, v.p. group ops., head office, Winnipeg, Man., 1975-78, sr. v.p. group ops., 1978, pres., 1978—, chief exec. officer, 1979—. Former bd. dirs. Man. div. Can. Cancer Soc.; bd. govs. Man. Mus. Man and Nature; bd. dirs. Winnipeg Symphony Orch. Mem. Men's Club Winnipeg (exec. com.), Conf. Bd. Can. Clubs: Manitoba, Winnipeg Winter., Toronto. Office: 60 Osborne St N Winnipeg MB R3C 3A5 Canada

KAVANAGH, PRESTON BRECKENRIDGE, utility executive; b. Washington, Aug. 15, 1932; s. Preston Breckenridge and Mary Lucille (Day) K.; m. Lois Lapham, Feb. 10, 1956; children: Katherine, Preston III, Evan. B.A., Princeton U., 1954; S.T.B., Harvard U., 1960. Ordained to ministry United Ch. of Christ, 1961; parish minister inner city, Cleve., 1960-61; minister Chgo. City Missionary Soc., 1961-63; with Commonwealth Edison Co., Chgo., 1963—, sec., 1970-73, div. v.p., 1973-76, mgr. customer service, 1976, gen. purchasing agt., 1976-79, mgr. purchasing, 1979-80, v.p., 1980—. Contbr. articles to profl. jours. Bd. dirs. United Way of Chgo., Evang. Health Services, Welfare Services Com. Cook County Dept. Public Aid, First Non-Profit Risk Pooling Trust, Jr. Achievement. Served with USN, 1954-57. Mem. Nat. Assn. Purchasing Mgrs. Mem. United Ch. of Christ. Club: Princeton (Chgo.). Home: 620 Exmoor Ave Kenilworth IL 60043 Office: PO Box 767 Chicago IL 60690

KAVANAGH, RALPH WILLIAM, physics educator; b. Seattle, July 15, 1924; s. Ralph W. and Esther (Weken) K.; m. Joyce Eberhart, July 31, 1948; children: Kathleen, Janet, Stephanie, Linda, William Leonard. B.A., Reed Coll., 1950; M.A., U. Oreg., 1952; Ph.D., Calif. Inst. Tech., 1956. Mem. faculty Calif. Inst. Tech., Pasadena, 1956—, assoc. prof. physics, 1965-70, prof., 1970—; research assoc. Centre de Recherches Nucleaires, U. Strasbourg, France, 1967-68; research assoc. Sch. Physics U. Melbourne, Australia, 1983. Contbr. articles to profl. jours. Served with USNR, 1942-46. Fellow Am. Phys. Soc. Home: 450 S Bonita Ave Pasadena CA 91107

KAVANAGH, THOMAS GILES, state justice; b. Bay City, Mich., Aug. 14, 1917; m. Mary Mahoney, 1939; children: Joseph Hayes, Kathleen Kavanagh Doherty, Thomas Giles, Kervin Pedraic. A.B., U. Notre Dame, 1938; LL.B. cum laude, U. Detroit, 1943. Judge Mich. Ct. Appeals, 1964-68; justice Mich. Supreme Ct., 1968—. Bd. dirs. Cardinal Newman Found., Wayne State U. Mem. State Bar Mich., Oakland, Detroit bar assns., Catholic Lawyers Soc., Notre Dame Law Assn. Roman Catholic. Office: Law Bldg PO Box 30052 Lansing MI 48909 *

KAVANAUGH, EVERETT EDWARD, JR., trade association executive; b. New Haven, June 9, 1941; s. Everett Edward and Marion (Gallagher) K.; m. Martha Gamble Murphy, Feb. 23, 1963; 1 son, Brett Michael. A.B., Georgetown U., 1963; M.B.A., George Washington U., 1970; J.D., Am. U., 1978. Bar: D.C. Sales rep. Northwestern Mut. Ins. Co., Washington, 1963-68; asst. to exec. offices U.S. C. of C., Washington, 1970-72; pres. Cosmetic, Toiletry and Fragrance Assn., Washington, 1972—. Mem. Am. Soc. Assn. Execs. Roman Catholic. Club: Congl. Country (Bethesda, Md.). Home: 4915 Jamestown Rd Bethesda MD 20816 Office: Cosmetic Toiletry and Frangrance Assn 1110 Vermont Ave NW Washington DC 10005

KAVESH, ROBERT ALLYN, economist, educator; b. N.Y.C., Sept. 12, 1927; s. Samuel and Pearl (Berlin) K.; m. Ruth Freidson, June 24, 1951 (div. 1980); children: Richard, Laura, Andrew, Joseph. B.S., N.Y. U., 1949; A.M., Harvard U., 1950, Ph.D., 1954. Asst. prof. econs. Dartmouth Coll., 1953-56; bus. economist Chase Manhattan Bank, N.Y.C., 1956-58; prof. econs. and finance Grad. Sch. Bus. Adminstrn., NYU, 1958-74, Marcus Nadler prof. finance and econs., 1974—, chmn. dept. econs., 1968-83; dir. Western Pacific Industries Inc., Del Labs., Inc., Greater N.Y. Mut. Ins. Co., Ins. Co. Greater N.Y.; trustee Apple Savs. Bank; mem. Savs. Banks Econ. Forum, 1975—; mem. econ. adv. bd. U.S. Dept. Commerce, 1968-70; mem. investment adv. com. N.Y. State Comptroller, 1976—; pres. The Money Marketeers, 1983-84. Author: Businessmen in Fiction, 1955, How Business Economists Forecast, 1966, Methods and Techniques of Business Forecasting, 1974; also articles.; Asso. editor: Bus. Economics, 1965—. Bd. dirs. Thomas A. Edison Coll. N.J., 1973-78. Served with U.S. Navy, World War II. Recipient Danforth Found. prize disting. teaching, 1968, Madden Meml. award for profl. achievement NYU, 1979, Gt. Tchr. award, 1983. Fellow Nat. Assn. Bus. Economists (council 1973-76); mem. Am. Fin. Assn. (exec. sec.-treas. 1961-79), Regional Sci. Assn. (past sec.), Am. Econ. Assn. Home: 110 Bleecker St New York NY 10012 Office: 100 Trinity Pl New York NY 10006

KAWALEK, THADDEUS P., college president; b. Chgo., Aug. 22, 1921; s. Peter John and Anastasia (Wojtas) K.; m. Lorraine A. Wielgos, June 18, 1949; children: Paul Edward, Nadine Ann, Nina Marie. B.E., No. Ill. U., 1942; M.A., U. Chgo., 1951, Ph.D., 1959. Tchr., dir. instrumental music Tobin Grade Sch., Oak Lawn, Ill., 1942; tchr. music Marshall and Harrison high schs., 1945-46; part-time tchr., dir. instrument music O.W. Holmes Sch., Oak Park, Ill., 1946-47; counselor maladjusted children, Oak Park, 1947-51; prin. Horace Mann Sch., Oak Park, 1952; supt. schs. Sch. Dist. 152 1/2, Hazel Crest, Ill., 1952-58; instr. DePaul U. Grad. Sch., winter 1961; supt. Sch. Dist. 95, Brookfield, Ill., 1958-62; prof. Roosevelt U. Grad Sch., Chgo., 1960-62; asst. supt. schs., Gary, Ind., 1962-64; dean faculties, prof. edn. adminstrn. Roosevelt U., 1963-66; v.p., dean Columbia Coll., Chgo., 1966-67; pres. Chgo. Coll. Osteo. Medicine, 1967—; dir. various programs in field, also dir. sch. property tax assessment surveys. Bd. dirs. S.E. Chgo. Commn. Served with AUS, 1942-45. Mem. Am. Osteo. Assn., Am. Assn. Higher Edn., Am. Assn. Colls. Osteo. Medicine (pres.). Clubs: Edgewood Valley Country, Execs., Union League (Chgo.); Olympia Fields Country. Office: 5200 S Ellis Ave Chicago IL 60615 *

KAWANA, KOICHI, educator, artist; b. Asahikawa, Kokkaido, Japan, Mar. 16, 1930; came to U.S., 1952, naturalized, 1971; s. Kiichi and Toki (Takeda) K. B.S., Yokohama Mcpl. U., (Japan), 1951; A.B., UCLA, 1955, M.A., 1959, M.F.A., 1964; Ph.D., Pacific Western U., 1979. Lectr. landscape design, Japanese art history UCLA, 1962—, univ. research artist, 1964-66, lectr. art, 1966, asst. prof. art in residence, 1966, sr. artist dept. architects and engrs., 1968-70, design cons., archtl. assoc., 1970-73, prin. archtl. assoc., 1973—; pres. Environ. Design Assocs., 1966—; v.p. Kapa Co., 1969—. Contbr. articles to profl. jours. Recipient Seikyoju rank award Adachi-shiki Sch. Floral Design, 1961, Design award Progressive Architecture, 1972, Gold medal Accademia Italia della Arti de del Lavoro; winner Nat. Soc. Interior Designers competition, 1961; decorated Order of Merit, Mil. and Hospitaller Order St. Lazarus of Jerusalem. Mem. Am. Soc. Interior Designers, So. Calif. Hort. Inst., Japan Am. Soc. So. Calif. (council 1965—, Disting. Service award 1965, Victor H. Carter Diamond award 1980), Los Angeles County Mus. Art, Far Eastern Art Council, Pi Gamma Mu, Pi Sigma Alpha. Sumi paintings include in collections White House, Washington, Grunwald Graphics Arts Found., garden design for Wattles Park, Los Angeles, Mo. Bot. Garden, St. Louis, Chgo. Hort. Soc. Bot. Garden, Glencoe, Ill., Denver Bot. Gardens, others. Home: 633 24th St Santa Monica CA 90402 Office: U Calif 601 Westwood Plaza Los Angeles CA 90024

KAWANO, WALTER MASAO, investment banker; b. Honolulu, Jan. 26, 1929; s. Isomatsu and Hanayo (Kenjo) K.; m. Florence Kikuye Sugimura, June 18, 1955; children—Cathy, Sandra. B.B.A., U. Hawaii, 1952. Certified financial planner. Registered rep. H. Kawano & Co., Inc., Honolulu, 1952-54, accountant, 1954-58, v.p., office mgr., 1958-63, exec. v.p., 1963-72, pres., 1972—; sec.-treas. Hawaii Research & Investment Inc., Honolulu, 1965—; dir. H.R.I. Properties, Ltd., Programmed Ins. Agy., Inc. Mem. Mutual Fund Council Million Dollars Producers, Internat. Assn. Financial Planners, St. Louis Alumni Assn., Japanese Jr. C. of C. Home: 1573 Kanalui Pl Honolulu HI 96816 Office: Room 700 1149 Bethel St Honolulu HI 96813

KAY, ALAN FRANCIS, business executive; b. Newark, Oct. 28, 1925; s. Harry and Ceil K.; m. Pamela Whitcher, Dec. 31, 1964; children—Joshua, Roger, Benjamin, Max. B.S., Mass. Inst. Tech., 1948; Ph.D., Harvard U., 1952. Vice pres. TRG, Inc., 1954-65; pres. AutEx, Inc., Wellesley, Mass., 1966-75, chmn. bd., 1975-76, Itel-AutEx, Inc. (subs. Itel Corp.), Wellesley, 1976-79; founder, developer AutEx Block Trading Info. System; chmn. bd. Participation Systems Inc., Winchester, Mass.; sustaining fellow, guest Inst. at MIT; advisor orgns. in nat. security field. Contbr. articles to profl. jours. Mem. IEEE (chmn. antennas and propagation group Boston chpt. 1966-67), Soc. Indsl. and Applied Math. Patentee in field. Home: 67 Byron Rd Weston MA 02193 Office: E40-293 MIT Cambridge MA 02139 *The number one problem is the likelihood of nuclear war.*

KAY, ALBERT, ret. govt. ofcl.; b. Bklyn., Apr. 3, 1914; s. Herman and Tillie (Handmaker) K.; m. Lucie Breyer, June 20, 1942; children—Jeffrey Albert, Carol Ann. A.B., Columbia, 1935, grad. work econs, 1935-36, 38-40. Econ. analyst Office Adminstr., Nat. Housing Agency, 1946-47; econ. analyst, material div. Exec. Office Sec., Navy Dept., 1947-48; chief manpower div. Munitions Bd., Office Sec. Def., 1948-51; dep. dir. Office Manpower Supply, Office Asst. Sec. Def., 1951-53, dir., 1953-70. Served to capt. AUS, 1941-46. Mem. Phi Beta Kappa. Club: Westwood Country. Home: 204 E Columbia St Falls Church VA 22046

KAY, BERNARD MELVIN, osteopathic pediatrician, educational adminstrator; b. San Diego, July 13, 1932; s. Harry and Bessie (Katz) K.; m. Judith L. Gee, Jan. 23, 1973; children: Mark, Jeff, Randy, Terri, Lisa, Kevan. Student, U. Detroit, 1950-53; D.O., Coll. Osteo. Medicine and Surgery, Des Moines, 1957. Intern Flint Osteo. Hosp., Mich., 1957-58; resident in pediatrics Coll. Hosp., Des Moines, 1958-60; practice osteo. medicine specializing in pediatrics, Westland, Mich., 1960-74; chmn. dept. pediatrics Garden City Hosp., Mich., 1960-74; prof., chief div. pediatrics Mich. State U. Hosp., East Lansing, 1974-79, mem. univ. faculty, 1974—, chmn. dept. pediatrics, 1979—, acting assoc. dean clin. affairs, 1983—; cons. on primary care HHS, Hyattsville, Md., 1980-81, Mich. Bd. Mental Health, Lansing, 1981—; chmn. subcom. on alternate reimbursement Mich. Task Force on Medicaid, 1983. Fellow Am. Coll. Osteo. Pediatricians (Watson Meml. lectr. 1980, pres. 1983-84). Office: Dept Pediatrics Fee Hall A-306 Mich State U East Lansing MI 48824 *I have never been afraid to make a mistake. I fear only that I become so comfortable that I'm afraid to change.*

KAY, CYRIL MAX, biochemist; b. Calgary, Alta., Can., Oct. 3, 1931; s. Louis and Fanny (Pearlmutter) K.; m. Faye Bloomenthal, Dec. 30, 1953; children: Lewis Edward, Lisa Franci. B.Sc. in Biochemistry with honors (J.W. McConnell Meml. scholar), McGill U., 1952; Ph.D. in Biochemistry (Life Ins. Med. Research Fund fellow), Harvard U., 1956; postgrad., Cambridge (Eng.) U., 1956-57. Phys. biochemist Eli Lilly & Co., Indpls., 1957-58; asst. prof. biochemistry U. Alta., Edmonton, 1958-61, asso. prof., 1961-67, prof., 1967—, co-dir. Med. Research Council Group on Protein Structure and Function, 1974—; Med. Research Council vis. scientist in biophysics Weizmann Inst., Israel, 1969-70, summer vis. prof. biophysics, 1975, summer vis. prof. chem. physics, 1977, 80; mem. biochemistry grants com. Med. Research Council, 1970-73; mem. Med. Research Council Can., 1982—; Can. rep. Pan Am. Assn. Biochem. Socs., 1971-76; mem. exec. planning com. XI Internat. Congress Biochemistry, Toronto, Ont., Can., 1979. Contbr. numerous articles to profl. publs.; asso. editor: Can. Jour. Biochemistry, 1968—; editor-in-chief: Pan Am. Assn. Biochem. Socs. Revista, 1971-76. Recipient Ayerst award in biochemistry Can. Biochem. Soc., 1970. Fellow N.Y. Acad. Scis., Royal Soc. Can.; mem. Can. Biochem. Soc. (council 1971—, v.p. 1976-77, pres. 1978-79). Home: 9408-143d St Edmonton AB T5R 0P7 Canada Office: Med Scis Bldg Dept Biochemistry U Alta Edmonton AB T6G 2H7 Canada

KAY, DEAN, music publishing company executive; b. Oakland, Calif., June 21, 1940; s. James Alvin and Muriel Edna Thompson; m. Belgina Michelle Janes, Aug. 19, 1967; 1 dau., Lisa Renee. Ed., San Jose State U., 1958-62. Profl. mgr. Welk Music Group, Santa Monica, Calif., 1971-73, gen. mgr., 1973-74, v.p., gen. mgr., 1974-79, exec. v.p., gen. mgr., 1979—; dir. Teleklew Prodns., Inc.; Mem. Calif. Copyright Conf. Featured entertainer: Tennesee Ernie Ford TV Show, 1961-63; producer radio and TV commls., Erwin Wasey Advt., Inc., 1964-66; freelance songwriter and entertainer, 1967-71; Writer: mus. composition That's Life. Mem. Nat. Acad. Rec. Arts and Scis., Country Music Assn. (dir.), Am. Fedn. Musicians, Am. Fedn. TV and Rec. Artists, ASCAP, Music Pubs. Assn., Nat. Music Pubs. Assn. (dir.). Office: 1299 Ocean Ave Suite 800 Santa Monica CA 90401 *

KAY, DOUGLAS CASEY, leasing co. exec.; b. Pueblo, Colo., July 2, 1932; s. Cecil Harmon and Nadine (Casey) K.; m. Ann Jeffrey, Dec. 28, 1953; children—Fredrick Charles, Lynn Kay Peters, Balfour Jeffrey. A.B., U. Kans., 1954; M.B.A., Harvard, 1959. Asst. treas. U.S. Leasing Corp., San Francisco, 1959-62, asst. to pres., 1963-66, treas., 1966-67, v.p., Cleve., 1967-69, sr. v.p., San Francisco, 1969-72; asst. v.p. Laurentide Financial Corp., San Francisco, 1962-63; 1st v.p. leasing White, Weld & Co., San Francisco, 1972-73; chmn. bd. Matrix Leasing Internat., Inc., San Francisco, 1973-74; sr. v.p. GATX Leasing Corp., San Francisco, 1974-78, exec. v.p., 1978—. Served with USAF, 1954-57. Home: 723 W Poplar Ave San Mateo CA 94402 Office: 4 Embarcadero Center San Francisco CA 94111

KAY, HERBERT, natural resources company executive; b. Johnsonburg, Pa., Mar. 19, 1924; s. Alexander S. and Carla Z. K.; m. Rita Inge Schmidt, May 4, 1956; children: Peter, Darcy, Philip. B.S. in Chem. Engring., Pa. State U., 1944; S.M., MIT, 1947; postgrad., Sloan Sch., 1968. Process engr. Stanolind Oil & Gas Co., Tulsa, 1947-49; group supr. Consolidation Coal Co., Library, Pa., 1949-55; sr. v.p. Climax Molybdenum Co., N.Y.C., 1955-77; v.p. Amax, Inc., Greenwich, Conn., 1977—, also dir. U.K., Holland, Italy, France, Japan. Mem. vis. acad. com. NYU, U. Conn., U. Bridgeport. Served with USNR, 1944-45. Mem. Am. Inst. Chem. Engrs., Am. Chem. Soc., AIME, Am. Mining Congress (coal and synfuels coms.), Madison C. of C. Clubs: Univ., Chemist's (N.Y.C.). Patentee in field. Home: 141 Old Church Rd Greenwich CT 06830 Office: Amax Center Greenwich CT 06830

KAY, HERMA HILL, legal educator; b. Orangeburg, S.C., Aug. 18, 1934; d. Charles Esdorn and Herma Lee (Crawford) Hill. B.A., So. Meth. U., 1956; J.D., U. Chgo., 1959. Bar: Calif. 1960. Law clk. to Justice Roger Traynor, Calif. Supreme Ct., 1959-60; asst. prof. law U. Calif., Berkeley, 1960-62, asso. prof., 1962, prof., 1963—, dir. family law project, 1964-67; co-reporter uniform marriage and div. law Nat. Conf. Commrs. on Uniform State Laws, 1968-70; vis. prof. U. Manchester, Eng., 1972, Harvard U., 1976; mem. Gov.'s Commn. on Family, 1966. Contbr. articles to profl. jours; contbg. author: Law in Culture and Society, 1969; author: Text, Cases and Materials on Sex-Based Discrimination, 1981, Conflict of Laws; Cases, Comments, Questions, 3d edit, 1981. Trustee, chmn. bd. Russell Sage Found., N.Y.; trustee Rosenberg Found., Calif.; mem. Equal Rights Advs. Calif., chmn., 1976-83. Fellow Center Advanced Study in Behavioral Scis., Palo Alto, Calif., 1963-64. Mem. Calif. Bar Assn., Bar U.S. Supreme Ct., Calif. Women Lawyers (bd. govs. 1975-77). Democrat. Club: Zonta (Berkeley) (pres. 1980-81). Office: School of Law University of California Berkeley CA 94720

KAY, JACK GARVIN, chemist, educator; b. Scott City, Kans., July 11, 1930; s. Albert Edward and Ellamay (Garvin) K.; m. Gloria Patricia Johnson, June 4, 1952; children: Morris Martin, Maren Patricia. A.B. (NROTC fellow), U. Kans., 1952, Ph.D., 1960. Research asst. U. Kans., 1956-59, Monsanto research fellow, 1958-59; instr. chemistry U. Ill., Urbana, 1959-62, asst. prof., 1962-66; prof. chemistry U. Toledo, 1966-69, chmn. dept. chemistry, 1966-68, dir. chemistry Ph.D. program devel., 1966-68; prof., head chemistry dept. Drexel U., Phila., 1969—; v.p. Chem. Edn. Projects, Inc., 1973-82, pres., 1974-83, bd. govs., 1976-77; vis. research chemist Bell Telephone Labs., Inc., Murray Hill, N.J., summer 1961, Sandia Corp., Albuquerque, summer 1964; cons. Chemotronics, Inc., AVCO, Inc.; Prin. investigator U.S. AEC, 1960-69. Contbr. articles to profl. jours. Trustee Research Fund of Phila. Gen. Hosp., 1976-80. Served from ensign to lt. (j.g.) USNR, 1952-55. Fellow Am. Inst. Chemists; mem. Am. Chem. Soc. (alt. councilor 1980, Councilor 1982—, chmn. Phila. sect.), Am. Phys. Soc., Faraday Soc., AAAS, Sigma Xi, Alpha Chi Sigma, Lambda Chi Alpha (Wilbur N. McMullan Meml. award), Sigma Pi Sigma, Phi Lambda Upsilon. Presbyn. (elder). Club: Mason. Home: 132 Valley Rd Ardmore PA 19003 Office: Dept Chemistry Drexel U Philadelphia PA 19104

KAY, JEROME HAROLD, cardiac surgeon; b. St. Cloud, Minn., Mar. 17, 1921; m. Adrienne Levin, June 15, 1950; children: Gregory Louis, Stephen Paul, Karen Lynne, Cathy Ann, Robert Michael, Richard Keith. A.A., UCLA, 1941; A.B., U. Calif., San Francisco, 1943, M.D., 1945. Diplomate: Am. Bd. Surgery, Am. Bd. Thoracic Surgery. Intern San Francisco County Hosp., 1945-46; asst. resident surgeon VA Hosp., McKinney, Tex., 1946-49, resident surgeon, 1949-50; fellow in surgery Johns Hopkins Sch. Medicine, Balt., 1950-52, asst. resident surgeon, 1952-53, resident surgeon, 1953-54, instr., 1953-54; instr. surgery U. So. Calif. Sch. Medicine, Los Angeles, 1956, asst. clin. prof., 1958, asso. prof. surgery, 1958-80, clin. prof., 1982—; prof. surgery Charles R. Drew Postgrad. Med. Sch., 1982—; pres. Los Angeles Heart Inst., 1980—. Producer of 9 motion pictures in field of open heart surgery; co-author 13 chpts. in med. textbooks; contbr. articles to med. jours in field of cardiopulmonary diseases and surgery. Served to maj. USPHS, 1954-56. Recipient 1st ann. Heart Research award Children's Heart Found. So. Calif., 1966. Fellow A.C.S., Am. Coll. Cardiology, Am. Coll. Angiology, Am. Heart Assn.; mem. Am. Assn. Thoracic Surgery, AMA, Los Angeles County Med. Assn., Pan Pacific Surg. Assn. (v.p. 1975-78), Am. Fedn. Clin. Research, Assn. Advancement Med. Instrumentation, Am. Coll. Chest Physicians (gov. So. Calif. area 1970-73), Internat. Cardiovascular Soc., Soc. Thoracic Surgeons (founding mem.), John Paul North Surg. Soc. (past pres.), Los Angeles County Heart Assn., Med. Research Assn. Calif. (past v.p., dir.), numerous others. Inventor Kay-Anderson Heart Lung Machine, 1958, Kay-Shiley disc valve, 1965, Kay muscle guard, 1967. Office: 123 S Alvarado St Los Angeles CA 90057

KAY, JOEL PHILLIP, lawyer; b. Corsicana, Tex., Aug. 27, 1936. B.S. in Econs., Wharton Sch., U. Pa., 1958; LL.B., U. Tex., 1961; LL.M., Georgetown U., 1967. Bar: Tex. 1961. Trial atty. tax div. Dept. Justice, 1963-67; asst. U.S. atty. So. Dist. Tex., 1967-69; partner Sheinfeld, Maley & Kay, Houston, 1969—. Served with AUS, 1961-63. Mem. ABA, Tex. Bar Assn. (dir. 1979-81, chmn. bd. 1981-82), Houston Bar Assn., Tex. Bar Found. (trustee 1983—). Address: 3700 First City Tower Houston TX 77002

KAY, JOHN FRANK, materials engineer; b. Bklyn., Aug. 15, 1950; s. John Frank and Agnes Mary (MaKoske) K. B.S., Rensselaer Poly. Inst., 1972, M.S., 1974, Ph.D., 1977. Postdoctoral assoc. Rensselaer Poly. Inst., Troy, N.Y., 1978; sr. engr., advanced composites systems Owens Corning Fiberglas Corp., Granville, Ohio, 1978—. Contbr. articles to field to profl. jours. Mem. Am. Chem. Soc., Soc. Biomaterials, Soc. Advancement Materials and Process Engrs., Am. Helicopter Soc., AIAA, Am. Def. Preparedness Assn., Sigma Xi. Home: 1572 Lonsdale Rd Columbus OH 43227 Office: Tech Ctr Owens Corning Fiberglas Corp Granville OH 43023

KAY, JOHN STEPHEN, agro-industrialist; b. Rhinelander, Wis., Jan. 27, 1933; s. John Stephen and Dorothea Eva (Ott) K.; m. Claudia E. Escalante, Jan. 16, 1976; children by previous marriage: Julie M., John S., Sarah A., Susan E., Anthony J., Andrew W., Paul J., Daniel T., Mary K. B.C.E., U. Wis., 1954; student, UCLA, 1964. Sr. v.p. land devel. and tourism C. Brewer & Co., Ltd., Honolulu, 1970-73; pres. Administration, Inc., Honolulu, 1968—, Kay Investments Inc.; also chmn. bd. Administration, Inc., Honolulu; dir. Pacific Aquaculture; pres., dir. Convention Services Internat. Clubs: Pacific., Plaza, Honolulu. Home: 43-360 Holokuku Kaneohe, Oahu HI 96734 Office: Grosvenor Ctr Suite 1765 Honolulu HI 96813

KAY, ROBERT LEO, chemistry educator; b. Hamilton, Ont., Can., Dec. 13, 1924; s. Norman Robert and Elizabeth (Blatz) K.; m. Ann Donata Morrow, Sept. 20, 1952; children: David Robert (dec.), Theresa Ann, Joanne Frances, Robert Leo. B.A., U. Toronto, 1949, M.A., 1950, Ph.D., 1952. With Rockefeller Inst. for Med. Research, N.Y.C., 1952-56; asst. prof. chemistry Brown U., Providence, 1956-63; sr. fellow Mellon Inst., Pitts., 1963-67; prof. chemistry Carnegie-Mellon U., Pitts., 1967—, acting dir. Center Spl. Studies, 1973-74, head dept. chemistry, 1974-83; Mem. Council Gordon Research Confs., 1974-78. Contbr. articles to sci. jours.; Editor: Jour. Solution Chemistry, 1971—; editorial bd.: Jour. Phys. Chemistry, 1973-81. Served with Canadian Army, 1943-46. Merck of Can. Postdoctoral fellow, 1952; research grantee Research Corp., 1957-59, NSF, 1959-60, 72—, AEC, 1959-63, Office Saline Water, U.S. Dept. Interior, 1963-70, NIH, 1972-74. Mem. Biophys. Soc., AAAS, Am. Chem. Soc., Pitts. Chemists Club. Home: 221 Parkway Dr Pittsburgh PA 15228

KAY, SAUL, pathologist; b. N.Y.C., Feb. 13, 1914; s. Wolf and Rose (Savitzky) Kossovsky; m. Grace Calef, Aug. 31, 1940; 1 dau., Deborah. B.A., N.Y. U., 1936; M.D., N.Y. Med. Coll., 1939. Intern Harlem Hosp., N.Y.C., 1939-41; resident Fordham Hosp., 1941-42, N.Y. Postgrad. Med. Sch. and Hosp., 1946-48, Columbia Presbyn. Med. Center, 1948-50; practice medicine specializing in pathology, Richmond, Va., 1950—; prof. dept. surg. pathology Med. Coll. Va., 1952-78, emeritus prof., 1978—. Served to maj. AUS, 1942-45. Decorated Bronze Star. Mem. Coll. Am. Pathology, Va. Acad. Sci., Richmond Acad. Medicine, Am. Soc. Clin. Pathology, Internat. Acad. Pathology, Am. Assn. Pathologists, Am. Soc. Cytology, AMA, Va. Path. Soc. Home: 322 Charmian Rd Richmond VA 23226 Office: Med Coll Va Richmond VA 23298

KAY, STEPHEN BALL, investment banking firm executive; b. Scranton, Pa., Nov. 21, 1934; s. Barney Lawrence and Florence (Levy) K.; children: Jacqueline Holtz, Julie Florence. B.A. cum laude, Harvard U., 1956, M.B.A., 1958. Treas. Kays-Newport & Co., Inc., Providence, 1958-65; with Goldman, Sachs & Co., Boston, 1965—, v.p. securities sales dept., 1970-73, v.p., resident mgr. Boston office, 1973-75, ptnr., 1975—; trustee Brookline Savs. Bank. Chmn. New Eng. region B'nai B'rith Antidefamation League; mem. vis. com. Boston U. Grad. Sch. Mgmt.; mem. com. on univ. resources Harvard U. Mem. Soc. Preservation New Eng. Antiquities (trustee), Harvard Bus. Sch. Assn. Greater Boston (pres.). Office: Goldman Sachs & Co One Boston Pl Boston MA 02108

KAY, ULYSSES, composer, educator; b. Tucson, Jan. 7, 1917; s. Ulysses Simpson and Elizabeth (Davis) K.; m. Barbara Harrison, Aug. 20, 1949; children: Virginia, Melinda, Hillary. B.Mus., U. Ariz., 1938; M.Mus., Eastman Sch. Music, 1940; postgrad., Yale U., 1941-42, Columbia U., 1946-49; Mus. D., Lincoln Coll., 1963, Bucknell U., 1966, U. Ariz., 1969, Dickinson Coll., Carlisle, Pa., 1978; D.H.L., Ill. Wesleyan U., 1969, U.Mo.-Kansas City, 1981. Editorial adviser Broadcast Music, Inc., N.Y.C., until 1968; prof. music Herbert H. Lehman Coll., CUNY, 1968—, disting. prof., 1972—; vis. prof. Boston U., 1965, UCLA, 1966-67; Mem. 1st ofcl. del. U.S. composers to USSR Dept. State Cultural Exchange Program, 1958; guest condr. N.Y. Little Symphony, Tucson Symphony, Phila. Orch., 1979. Commd. by, Louisville Symphony Orch., Koussevitzky Music Found., DePaur Inf. Chorus, Quincy (Ill.) Fine Arts Soc.; Composer: operas Jubilee, Frederick Douglass; ballet Danse Calinda; Concerto for Orchestra, Three Pieces after Blakefor soprano and orch., Serenade for Orchestra; male chorus Triumvirate; cantata Song of Jeremiah, Inscriptions from Whitman; other orch., choral, band, chamber music works. Served with USNR, 1942-46. Recipient award 3d Ann. Gershwin Contest, 1947, Rome prize in Composition, 1949-50, 51-52; Alice M. Ditson fellow, 1946; Julius Rosenwald fellow, 1948; Fulbright fellow, Italy, 1950-51; Guggenheim fellow, 1964-65; recipient ABC prize, 1946. Mem. Corp. of Yaddo, Am. Fedn. Musicians, League of Composers, Am. Inst. Arts and Letters, Phi Mu Alpha-Sinfonia. Club: Federal City (Washington). Home: 1271 Alicia Ave Teaneck NJ 07666 Address: care Music Dept Herbert H Lehman Coll Bedford Park Blvd W Bronx NY 10468

KAY, WILLIAM GEMMILL, JR., private investment company executive; b. Phila., May 5, 1930; s. William Gemmill and Margaret Wentworth (Leech) K.; m. Sanford Peyton Stallworth, Apr. 19, 1958; children: Peyton S., William Gemmill, III, Caroline Wentworth. A.B. in English, Dartmouth Coll., 1952; M.S. in Indsl. Mgmt. (Alfred P. Sloan fellow), M.I.T., 1963. Mktg. mgr. Campbell Soup Co., 1956-62; v.p. mktg. Pepperidge Farm, Inc., 1963-67; also dir.; exec. v.p. Asso. Products, Inc., 1967-72; also dir.; group v.p. consumer products Ill. Central Industries, Chgo., 1972-75; pres. Standard Brands Foods, Standard Brands, Inc., N.Y.C., 1975-76; exec. v.p., office of chief exec. Sun Co., Inc., Radnor, Pa., 1976-82, also dir.; pres. Wentworth Mgmt. Group, Radnor, 1982—; dir. Provident Nat. Corp., Provident Nat. Bank. Bd. dirs. Phila. Orch. Assn., 1978—; v.p., trustee Phila. Acad. Music, 1978—. Served with USCG, 1953-55. Republican. Episcopalian. Clubs: Merion Cricket, Merion Golf, Racquet. Home: 922 Mount Pleasant Rd Bryn Mawr PA 19010 Office: Two Radnor Corp Center 100 Matsonford Rd Radnor PA 19087

KAYE, DANNY, actor, comedian, baseball executive; b. N.Y.C., Jan. 18, 1913; s. Jacob and Clara (Nemerovsky) Kaminski; m. Sylvia Fine, Jan. 3, 1940; 1 dau., Dena. L.H.D., Colgate U. Founder, mng. ltd. partner Seattle Mariners baseball team, 1976—. Appeared on stage in: Straw Hat Revue, Ambassador Theatre, N.Y.C., 1939, Lady in the Dark, 1940, Let's Face It, 1941; on screen with, Samuel Goldwyn, Inc., 1943-48; motion pictures include Up In Arms, 1943, Wonder Man, 1944, Kid from Brooklyn, 1945, Secret Life of Walter Mitty, 1946, A Song is Born, 1947, The Inspector General, 1948, On The Riviera, 1950, Hans Christian Anderson, 1952, Knock on Wood, 1954, White Christmas, 1954, The Court Jester, 1955, Merry Andrew, 1957, Me and the Colonel, 1958, The Five Pennies, 1959, On the Double, 1961, The Man from the Diner's Club, 1962, The Madwoman of Chaillot, 1969; star: TV show The Danny Kaye Show; other TV appearances include Look In at Met. Opera, 1975, Pinocchio, 1976, Skokie, 1981, Live from Lincoln Center, 1981; Broadway play Two by Two, 1970-71. Ofcl. permanent ambassador-at-large UNICEF. Recipient Spl. Acad. award, 1954; Emmy award for Danny Kaye Show, 1963; Best Children's Spl., 1975; George Foster Peabody award for Danny Kaye Show, 1963; award Internat. Distinguished Service UN Children's Fund; Scopus Laureate; Wateler Peace Prize Carnegie Found., 1981. Home: Beverly Hills CA Office: PO Box 750 Beverly Hills CA 90213

KAYE, DONALD, physician, educator; b. N.Y.C., Aug. 12, 1931; s. Morris and Rose (Hirschtritt) K.; m. Janet Miriam Sovitsky, June 26, 1955; children: Kenneth Marc, Karen Lynne, Kendra Beth, Keith Steven. A.B., Yale, 1953; M.D., N.Y. U., 1957. Diplomate: Am. Bd. Internal Medicine (subsplty. bd. on infectious disease). Intern N.Y. Hosp., 1957-58, resident, 1958-60; practice medicine, specializing in internal medicine and infectious diseases, N.Y.C., 1961-69, Phila., 1969—; asso. attending physician N.Y. Hosp., 1961-69; physician-in-chief Hosp. Med. Coll. Pa., 1969—; instr. medicine Cornell U. Med. Coll., 1961-63, asst. prof., 1963-66, asso. prof., 1966-69; prof., chmn. dept. medicine Med. Coll. Pa., Phila., 1969—; cons. Phila. VA Hosp., 1969—; Mem. revision com. U.S. Pharmacopeia, 1975—; mem. VA Merit Rev. Bd. in Infectious Diseases, 1976-78; mem. com. on infectious diseases Am. Bd. Internal Medicine, 1976-84. Author: Urinary Tract Infection and Its Management, 1972, Infective Endocarditis, 1976, Fundmentals of Internal Medicine, 1983, Internal Medicine for Dentists, 1983; editorial bd.: Am. Jour. Medicine; contbr. articles to profl. jours. Recipient Distinguished Teaching award Lindback Found., 1972; NIH grantee, 1967-76, 82—; Pharm. Industry grantee, 1965—. Fellow A.C.P. (gov. elect Eastern Pa. 1982-83); mem. AMA, N.Y. State, Pa., Phila. County med. socs., Am. Soc. Microbiology, Am. Soc. Tropical Medicine and Hygiene, Soc. Exptl. Biology and Medicine, Am. Fedn. Clin. Research, Am. Soc. Clin. Investigation, Assn. Am. Physicians, Infectious Disease Soc. Am., Phi Beta Kappa, Alpha Omega Alpha. Home: 1535 Sweet Briar Rd Gladwyne PA 19035 Office: 3300 Henry Ave Philadelphia PA 19129

KAYE, EVELYN PATRICIA (EVELYN PATRICIA SARSON), author, journalist; b. London, Oct. 1, 1937; U.S., 1963; d. Max and Florence (Wright) K.; m. J. Christopher Sarson, Mar. 25, 1963; children: Katrina May, David Arnold. Advanced level gen. certificate of edn. in English and French, North London Collegiate Sch., Edgware, Middlesex, Eng., 1956. Sec., publicity asst. Elek Books Ltd., London, 1957-58; gen. reporter Southend Times, Southend-on-Sea, Eng., Willesden Citizen, London, East London News Agy., 1958-61; staff reporter Reuters News Agy., Paris, 1961-62; reporter, feature writer The Guardian, Manchester, Eng., 1962-63; co-founder, pres. Action for Children's TV, Newtonville, Mass., 1969-71, exec. dir., 1971-73, dir. publs., 1973-74; studied in, Jerusalem, Israel, 1959-60; speaker and media cons. on children's TV and broadcasting. Author: Family Guide to Childrens Television: What To Watch, What To Miss, What To Change and How To Do It, 1974, rev. edit., 1979, The Family Guide to Cape Cod: What to Do When You Don't Want To Do What Everyone Else Is Doing, 1976, Crosscurrents: Children Families and Religion, 1980, How To Treat TV with TLC: The ACT Guide to Children's television, 1979; co-author: coll. textbook Relationships in Marriage and Family, 1984; corr.: The Record (N.J.), 1984—; contbr. articles on media, travel, children's TV and the arts to nat. mags. Mem. Am. Soc. Journalists and Authors (exec. v.p., pres. 1984-85), Authors Guild, Soc. Profl. Journalists. Home and Office: 223 Tenafly Rd Englewood NJ 07631

KAYE, GEORGE MARVIN, bus. exec.; b. Newark, N.J., Sept. 7, 1931; s. Samuel and Sally (Falk) K.; children—Deborah, Jennifer, Edward A. B.S., Rutgers U., 1952; M.B.A., 1958. Partner J.H. Cohn & Co. (C.P.A.'s.), Newark, N.J., 1955-67; exec. v.p. Sterling Communications, Inc., N.Y.C., 1967-68; v.p. Felsway Corp., Totowa, N.J., 1968-73, sr. v.p., 1973-78, pres., 1978—. Served to lt. comdr. USCG, 1953-55. Mem. Fin. Execs. Inst., Volume Footwear Retailers Am. (dir.), Beta Gamma Sigma. Club: Berkeley Tennis. Home: 83 Lloyd Rd Montclair NJ 07042 Office: 994 Riverview Dr Totowa NJ 07512

KAYE, GORDON ISRAEL, pathologist, educator; b. N.Y.C., Aug. 13, 1935; s. Oscar Swarz and Rebecca (Schachman) K.; m. Nancy Elizabeth Weber, June 4, 1956; children: Jacqueline Elizabeth, Vivienne Rebecca. A.B., Columbia U., 1955, A.M., 1957, Ph.D., 1961. Research asst. cytology Columbia U., 1953-55, asst. zoology, 1955; research and teaching asst. cytology Rockefeller Inst., 1957-58; asst. anatomy Columbia U., 1958-61, research assoc. dept. anatomy, 1961-63, assoc. surg. pathology, dir. F. Higginson Cabot Lab. Electron

Microscopy, div. surg. pathology Coll. Physicians and Surgeons, 1963-66, asst. prof. surg. pathology, dir. F. H. Cabot Lab., 1966-70, asso. prof. surg. pathology, dir. F. H. Cabot Lab., 1970-76; prof., chmn. dept. anatomy Albany (N.Y.) Med. Coll., 1976—, prof. pathology, 1981—; cons. electron microscopy dept pathology N.Y. VA Hosp., 1965—; mem. Wenner-Gren Found. Seminar on Creative Process, 1964-65. Editor: Current Topics in Cellular Anatomy, 1981; asso. editor: The Anat. Record, 1972—; editorial reviewer: Exptl. Eye Research, 1964—, Cancer, 1972—, Investigative Ophthalmology, 1973—, Gastroenterology, 1969—. Trustee Palisades Free Library, 1965-71; mem. Citizens Adv. Com., Sparkill Palisades Fire Dist., 1968-69; pres. Palisades Free Library, 1969-71; trustee Orangetown Public Library, 1971-73; mem. citizens adv. com. Title III Program, S. Orangetown Central Sch. Dist., 1972-75; trustee Rockland Country Day Sch., 1974-78. Recipient Charles Huebschman prize in Zoology Columbia U., 1954; Research Career Devel. award Nat. Inst. Arthritis and Metabolic Diseases, NIH, USPHS, 1972-76; Ford Found. scholar, 1951-55; NSF predoctoral fellow, 1955-56; Nat. Inst. Neurol. Diseases and Blindness predoctoral fellow, 1959-61. Mem. Assn. Anatomy Chairmen (pres. 1980-81), Assn. Am. Med. Colls. (rep. council acad. socs. 1979—), Am. Assn. Anatomists, Electron Microscope Soc. Am., Am. Soc. Cell Biology, Harvey Soc., Assn. Career Scientists Health Research Council, Internat. Soc. Eye Research, N.Y. Acad. Scis., N.Y. Soc. Electron Microscopists (dir. 1964-67), Sigma Xi. Club: Waquoit Bay Yacht (Waquoit, Mass.). Office: Albany Med Coll Dept Anatomy 47 New Scotland Ave Albany NY 12208

KAYE, JEROME R., engineer and construction company executive; b. Newark, June 3, 1928; s. Benjamin and Lillian (Chusid) K.; m. Beverly Glasgal, Dec. 21, 1952; children: Michael, Richard, Janet, Sharon. A.B., Columbia U., 1949; LL.B., Harvard U., 1952. Bar: N.Y. 1953, N.J. 1968. Atty., then dept. counsel Office Gen. Counsel, Navy Dept., Bklyn., 1955-62; with The Lummus Co., Bloomfield, N.J., 1962—, asst. sec., 1966-70, sec., asst. counsel, 1970—, v.p., 1982—. Councilman, Matawan Twp., N.J., 1966-69; mem. Matawan Twp. Municipal Utilities Authority, 1968-70. Served with AUS, 1952-54. Mem. Fed. Bar Assn. Home: 19 Slayton Dr Short Hills NJ 07078 Office: The Lummus Co 1515 Broad St Bloomfield NJ 07003

KAYE, JEROME SIDNEY, cell biologist; b. Hartford, Conn., June 15, 1930; s. Samuel and Rebecca (Eisenberg) K.; m. Rachel Donald McMaster, Sept. 23, 1955 (dec.); m. Susan Allison, Feb. 27, 1982. A.B., Columbia U., 1952, A.M., 1954, Ph.D., 1957. Instr. zoology UCLA, 1958-59; mem. faculty dept. biology U. Rochester, N.Y., 1960—, assoc. prof., 1965-73, prof. biology, 1974—. Lalor Found. fellow, 1958; Fondation pour la Recherche Medicale fellow, 1983-84. Mem. Am. Soc. for Cell Biology, Electron Microscope Soc. Am. Office: Dept Biology U Rochester Rochester NY 14627

KAYE, NORA (NORA KOREFF), choreographer, dancer, ballet co. artistic adminstr.; b. N.Y.C.; m. Herbert Ross, 1959. Studied with, Michael Fokine, Met. Opera Ballet Sch. Ballet debut with, Met. Opera's children's ballet; joined, Am. Ballet Theatre, N.Y.C., 1939; with, N.Y.C. Ballet, 1951-54; returned to, Am. Ballet Theatre, 1954-60; asso. artistic dir., 1977—; co-founder, prima ballerina, Ballet of the Two Worlds, 1959-60; ret. as dancer, 1961; asst. to Herbert Ross on: films, including The Sunshine Boys; prodn. asso.: film The Turning Point (Recipient Award of Distinction, Dance Mag. 1980). Office: care Am Ballet Theatre 90 Broadway New York NY 10003

KAYE, NORMAN JOSEPH, business educator; b. Milw., Apr. 24, 1923; s. Bernard Joseph and Marie (Barczykowski) K.; m. Margaret Ann Biedermann, Aug. 16, 1947; children—John, Mary Kaye Gembolis, James, Paul, Elizabeth Kaye Buchholtz, William, Robert, Laurence. B.S. cum laude, Marquette U., 1948; M.B.A. with distinction, U. Mich., 1951; Ph.D., U. Wis., 1956. Mem. faculty Marquette U., Milw., 1949—, prof., 1966—, chmn. indsl. mgmt. dept., 1969-71; Cons. statis. and communication areas. Author: Elementary Quantitative Techniques for Business Problem Solving, 1969; also articles. Served with AUS, 1943-45. Decorated Purple Heart, Combat Inf. badge.; Recipient Teaching Excellence award Coll. Bus. Adminstrn., Marquette U., 1964; Ford Found. fellow Harvard, 1959, Carnegie Inst. Tech., 1962. Mem. Assn. Social Economics, Am. Inst. Decision Scis., Am. Statis. Assn. (pres. Milw. chpt. 1965, 78, dir. 1953-73), Beta Alpha Psi, Beta Gamma Sigma. Home: 3137 S 30th St Milwaukee WI 53215

KAYE, STEPHEN RACKOW, lawyer; b. Nyack, N.Y., May 4, 1931; s. Edward and Florence (Karp) K.; m. Judith Smith, Feb. 11, 1964; children: Luisa Marian, Jonathan Mackey, Gordon Bernard. A.B., Cornell U., 1952, LL.B. with honors, 1956. Bar: N.Y. 1956, U.S. Supreme Ct. 1961. Assoc. Sullivan & Cromwell, N.Y.C., 1956-63, Proskauer Rose Goetz & Mendelsohn, 1964-68, ptnr., 1968—, mng. ptnr., 1978—. Mng. editor: Cornell Law Quar.; contbr. to profl. publs. Served to 1st lt. AUS, 1952-54; Korea. Mem. ABA, N.Y. State Bar Assn., Assn. Bar City N.Y., N.Y. County Lawyers Assn., Order of Coif, Phi Kappa Phi. Republican. Office: Proskauer Rose Goetz & Mendelsohn 300 Park Ave New York NY 10022

KAYE, SYLVIA FINE, producer, lyricist, composer; b. N.Y.C., Aug. 29; d. Samuel and Bessie Fine; m. Danny Kaye, Jan. 3, 1940; 1 dau., Dena. Adj. prof. U. So. Calif., Yale U. (Recipient Emmy award for children's spl. 1975-76); Broadway shows include Let's Face It, Straw Hat Revue; film scores include On the Riviera, Up in Arms, Wonder Man, Secret Life of Walter Mitty; co-producer: film scores Court Jester, General, Knock on Wood; producer, writer several TV spls.; popular songs include Moon is Blue, Man with the Golden Arm; spl. songs for Danny Kaye include Lullaby in Ragtime, Starislavsky, Pavlova, Melody in 4f, Anatole of Paris, Eileen, Five Pennies; exec. producer: Danny Kaye's Look-In at the Met. Opera. Mem. ASCAP.

KAYE, WALTER, financial executive; b. Bklyn., Aug. 22, 1927; s. Jack and Ida (Shapiro) K.; m. Bernice Glatzer, May 6, 1952; children: Steven Mark, Russell Stewart. Student, CCNY, 1950-53; postgrad. (fellow), N.Y. Inst. Credit, 1956. Credit mgr., treas. A. Steinam Co., Inc., N.Y.C., 1951-68; v.p. Ambassador Factors Corp., N.Y.C., 1968-74; sr. v.p. Congress Factors Corp., N.Y.C., 1974—. Served with U.S. Army, 1944-46. Recipient Yitzhak rabin award B'nai B'rith, 1982, Plaque Manhattan Credit, 1979. Mem. N.Y. Inst. Credit, N.Y. Credit and Fin. Mgmt. Clubs: Manhattan Credit (pres. 1978-79), Empire Credit (pres. 1971-74), The Financemen's). Home: 61 Bramblebrook Rd Ardsley NY 10502 Office: 1133 Ave of the Americas New York NY 10036

KAYNOR, SANFORD BULL, lawyer; b. Waterbury, Conn., Nov. 24, 1926; s. Warren Fox and Margaret (Smith) K.; m. Laura Sanford, June 6, 1953; children: Laura Smith, Sanford Bull, Frederick Kirk. B.S., Yale U., 1949; LL.B., Columbia U., 1952. Bar: N.Y. 1953, Conn. 1982. Asso. firm Havens, Wandless, Stitt & Tighe, N.Y.C., 1952-58; exec. v.p., gen. counsel, sec. U.S. Industries, Inc., N.Y.C. Served with AUS, 1945-46. Republican. Episcopalian. Clubs: Yale of N.Y.C.; Tokeneke (Darien, Conn.); Sankaty Head (Sciasconset, Nantucket). Home: 14 East Trail Darien CT 06820 Office: One Cummings Point Rd PO Box 10207 Stamford CT 06904

KAYNOR, WILLIAM AKIN, lawyer; b. Waterbury, Conn., Apr. 18, 1923; s. Warren Fox and Margaret (Smith) K.; m. Irene Roberte Moullin, June 20, 1964; children: William Akin, Robert Moullin. B.A., Yale U., 1945; LL.B., Harvard U., 1952. Bar: N.Y. 1953. Ptnr. Davis Polk & Wardwell, N.Y.C., 1961—; dir. Americana Hotels & Realty Corp., Chgo., Il., 1982—, Interactive Systems Corp., Santa Monica, Calif., 1979—. Office: Davis Polk & Wardell One Chase Manhattan Plaza New York NY 10005

KAYREBCE, MARGARET, author; b. Neepawa, Man., Can., July 18, 1926; d. Robert Harrison and Margaret Cambell (Simpson) Wemyss; m. John Fergus Laurence, 1947 (div. 1969); 2 children. B.A., United Coll. now U. Man., 1947; D. Litt., McMaster U., 1971, Trent U., 1971, U. Toronto, 1971, Carleton U., 1974, U. Brandon, 1974, Mt. Allison, 1976, U. York, 1980, LLD., Dalhousie U., 1971; B.F.A., Kansas City Art Inst., 1964. Writer in residence U. Toronto, 1969-70, U. Western Ont., 1973; chancellor Trent U., Peterborough, Ont., Can. Author: book A Tree for Poverty, 1960, This Side Jordan, 1960, The Prophet's Camel Bell, 1963, The Tomorrow-Tamer, 1963, The Stone Angel, 1964, A Jest of God, 1966 (Gov. Gen. award for Fiction), Long Drums and Cannons essays on Nigerian lit., 1968, The Fire Dewllers, 1969, Jason's Quest children's fiction, 1969, A Bird in the House, 1970, The Diviners, 1974, Heart of a Stranger essays, 1976, Six Darn Cows children's, 1980; contbr.: short stories Prism, Tamarack Rev., Saturday Evening Post, Ladies Home Journal, Chatelaine, Atlantic Monthly, Argosy, Winter's Tales; articles Holiday mag. Decorated companion Order of Can.; recipient Beta Sigma Phi award for Best First Novel by a Canadian, 1960, Pres. Medal for Best Canadian Short Story U. Western Onst., 1961, 62, 64, Molson award, 1975, Periodical Distributor's award, 1977, Binai Birith Woman of the Yr. award, 1976, award of Merit City of Toronto, 1978. Office: Office of the Chanecellor Trent Univ Peterborough ON Canada K9J 7B8 *

KAYS, WILLIAM MORROW, university administrator, mechanical engineer; b. Norfolk, Va., July 29, 1920; s. Herbert Emery and Margaret (Fechteler) K.; m. Alma Campbell, Sept. 14, 1947 (dec. June 1982); children: Nancy, Leslie, Margaret, Elizabeth.; m. Judith Adams, July 1983. A.B., Stanford U., 1942, M.S., 1947, Ph.D. in Mech. Engring., 1951. Asst. prof. mech. engring. Stanford U., 1951-54, assoc. prof., 1954-57, prof., 1957—, chmn. dept. mech. engring, 1961-72, dean engring., 1972-84; dir. Acurex Corp.; cons. to numerous firms. Author: Compact Heat Exchangers, 1964, Convective Heat and Mass Transfer, 1966; Hon. editorial adv. bd.: Internat. Jour. Heat and Mass Transfer. Served with U.S. Army, 1942-46. Fulbright fellow, 1959-60; NSF sr. postdoctoral fellow, 1966-67. Fellow ASME (Heat Transfer Div. Meml. award 1965); mem. Am. Soc. Engring. Edn., Nat. Acad. Engring. Home: 108 Peter Coutts Circle Stanford CA 94305 Office: Sch Engring Stanford U Stanford CA 94305

KAYSEN, CARL, economist; b. Phila., Mar. 5, 1920; s. Samuel and Elizabeth (Resnick) K.; m. Annette Neutra, Sept. 13, 1940; children—Susanna, Laura. A.B., U. Pa., 1940; Ph.D., Harvard U., 1954. Researcher Nat. Bur. Econ. Research, 1940-42; economist OSS, 1942; mem. faculty Harvard U., 1946-66, jr. fellow, 1947-50, asst. prof. econs., 1950-55, asso. prof., 1955-57, prof., 1957-66, Lucius N. Littauer prof. polit. economy, 1964-66, asso. dean, 1960-66; dir. Inst. Advanced Study, Princeton, N.J., 1966-76, prof., 1966-77; David W. Skinner prof. polit. economy M.I.T., 1977—, dir., 1981—; clk. to Judge E. E. Wyzanski, U.S. Dist. C., 1950-52; dep. spl. asst. to Pres. Kennedy for nat. security affairs, 1961-63; mem. Carnegie Commn. on Higher Edn.; vice chmn., dir. research Sloan Commn. on Govt. and Higher Edn.; faculty lectr. London Sch. Econs., 1956; Haynes lectr. Calif. Inst. Tech., 1966; Stafford Little lectr. Princeton U., 1968; Oliver W. Holmes lectr. Harvard Law Sch., 1969; Paley lectr. Hebrew U., Jerusalem, 1970; Godkin lectr. Harvard U., 1976; dir. Polaroid Corp., United Parcel Service. Mem. editorial bd.: Fgn. Affairs. Life trustee U. Pa.; trustee German Marshall Fund, Russell Sage Found. Served to capt. air intelligence AUS, 1942-45. Fulbright scholar London Sch. Econs., 1955-56; Guggenheim fellow, 1955-56; Ford Found. fellow, Greece, 1959-60. Mem. Am. Philos. Soc., Am. Acad. Arts and Scis., Phi Beta Kappa. Club: Century (N.Y.C.). Office: Program in Science Tech and Soc MIT Cambridge MA 02139

KAYSER, ELMER LOUIS, educator, historian; b. Washington, Aug. 27, 1896; s. Samuel Louis and Susie Brown (Huddleston) K.; m. Margery Ludlow, Féb. 11, 1922; 1 dau., Katherine Ludlow (Mrs. Arthur Hallett Page III) (dec.). B.A., also Bachelor's Diploma in Edn., George Washington U., 1917, M.A., 1918, LL.D. (hon.), 1948; Ph.D., Columbia, 1932; L.H.D., Mount Vernon Coll., 1975. Asst. in history George Washington U., 1914-17, instr., 1917-20, asst. prof., 1920-24, asso. prof., 1924-32, prof., 1932-67, emeritus, 1967—, asst. librarian, 1917-18, recorder, 1918, sec., 1918-29, dir. summer sch., 1925-29, dir univ. students, 1930-34, dean, 1934-62, dean emeritus, 1967—, univ. historian, 1962—, asso. chmn. sch. of govt., 1957-58; radio commentator on world affairs, 1940-45. Author: The Grand Social Enterprise, 1932, A Manual of Ancient History, 1937, The George Washington U., 1821-1966, 1966, Washington's Bequest to a National University, 1965, Luther Rice, Founder of Columbian Coll, 1966, Bricks Without Straw, 1970, A Medical Center, 1973; co-author: Contemporary Europe, 1941; Past mem. bd. editors: World Affairs. Sec.-treas. Gen. Alumni Assn., George Washington U., 1918-24, v.p., 1945-50, pres., 1950-53; vice-chmn. bd. trustees Mt. Vernon Sem., 1946-66; hon. bd. dirs. Mt. Vernon Coll., 1966—; past chmn. com. improvement Adminstrn. Justice D.C.; historian Nat. Capital Sesquicentennial Commn., 1950; past bd. govs. Nat. Cathedral Sch.; past chmn. sec. navy's adv. com. naval history.; Historian Nat. Capital Sesquicentennial Commn., 1950. Served with F.A. O.T.S., World War I; Camp Zachary Taylor, Ky. Recipient Alumni Achievement award George Washington U., 1941, Alumni Service award, 1962, George Washington award, 1977; comdr. Nat. Order of Merit, Ecuador). Mem. Inst. Jud. Adminstrn., Am. Hist. Assn. (treas. 1957-73), Columbia Hist. Soc. (v.p.), AAUP (council 1952-54), Am. Peace Soc. (dir.), Sigma Phi Epsilon (citation for distinguished service 1965), Pi Gamma Mu, Omicron Delta Kappa, Delta Phi Epsilon, Gate and Key. Club: Cosmos (past bd. mgrs.). Home: 2921 34th St NW Washington DC 20008 Office: George Washington U Washington DC 20052

KAYSER, THOMAS ARTHUR, art museum director; b. Milw., Oct. 4, 1935; s. Arthur John and Lilian (Graf) K.; m. Janet Dalzin, Apr. 28, 1962; children: Cynthia, Erik. Student, Layton Sch. Art, 1954-58, Cranbrook Acad. Art, 1958-59. Asst. display mgr. Dersey Advt., Milw., 1959-60; designer K.C.S. Co., Milw., 1960-62, Display Corp., 1962-65; asst. dir. Flint Inst. Art, Mich., 1965-78; exec. dir. Kalamazoo Inst. Art, 1978—; chmn. museums com. Mich. Council for the Arts, Detroit, 1979—. Served with U.S. Army, 1957-58. Mem. Am. Assn. Museums, Art Museums Assn., Midwest Museums Assn., Mich. Museums Assn. Methodist. Club: Porsche (Detroit) (dir. 1977-78). Home: 2132 Rambling Rd Kalamazoo MI 49008 Office: Kfalamazoo Inst Arts 314 S Park St Kalamazoo MI 49007

KAZ, NATHANIEL, sculptor; b. N.Y.C., Mar. 9, 1917; s. I. Rudolph and Ida (Elkan) K.; children: Naomi Della, Eric Justin. Student, Art Students League. Tchr. Art Students League, N.Y.C. One-man shows, Downtown Gallery, 1939, Asso. Am. Artists, 1946, Grand Central Moderns, 1954, Joan Avnet Gallery, 1965, exhbns., Whitney Mus., Met. Mus. Art, Bklyn. Mus., Art Inst. Chgo., U. Nebr., Phila. Mus. Fine Arts, Mus. Modern Art, N.Y. and San Francisco world's fairs; represented in permanent collections, Bklyn. Mus., Whitney Mus., Met. Mus., pvt. collections; designed and executed 10 ft. carving in limestone for, Fine St. Temple, Nashville, 6 ft. bronze for, Pub. Sch. 59, Bklyn.; exhibited 4 ritual works, Grand Central Moderns, 1957, Temple of Beth Emeth, Albany, N.Y., 1965; designed and executed two 7 ft. colored aluminum reliefs of Thespians-Tragedy and Comedy for, Jr. High Sch. 164, Queens, New York, 1958. Recipient Mich. Sculpture award, 1929, Sect. Fine Arts award, 1940, Artists for Victory award, 1942, Audubon Artists 6th ann. award, 1947, Medal of Honor, 1960, Bklyn. Soc. Artists 32d ann. award, 1952, Sculpture prize Bklyn. Mus., 1952, Alfred G. B. Steel prize 148th ann. exhibit Pa. Acad. Fine Arts, 1953, Winner nat. competition UN monument design Nat. Council U.S. Art, Merit award NAD, 1976; grantee Nat. Inst. Arts and Letters, 1976. Mem. Sculptors Guild. Studio: 160 W 73rd St New York NY 10023 *

KAZAN, ELIA, theatrical, motion picture dir. and producer, author; b. Constantinople, Turkey, Sept. 7, 1909; s. George and Athena (Sismanoglou) K.; m. Molly Day Thacher, Dec. 2, 1932 (dec.); children: Judy, Chris, Nick, Katharine; m. Barbara Loden, June 5, 1967 (dec.); m. Frances Rudge, June 28, 1982. A.B., Williams Coll., 1930; postgrad., Yale U., 1930-32; M.F.A., Wesleyan U., Middletown, Conn., 1955. Co-founder Actors Studio. Actor with, Group Theatre, 1932-39; dir. stage plays, 1940-55, including, Skin of Our Teeth, Harriet, Jacobowsky and the Colonel, All My Sons, Deep Are the Roots, A Streetcar Named Desire, Death of a Salesman, Camino Real, Tea and Sympathy, Cat on a Hot Tin Roof, The Dark at the Top of the Stairs, J.B (Antoinette Perry award for direction 1958), Sweet Bird of Youth, After the Fall, But for Whom Charlie, The Changeling; numerous motion pictures, 1944—, including; A Tree Grows in Brooklyn, Boomerang, Gentlemen's Agreement (Acad. award for best direction 1947), Pinky, Panic in the Streets, A Streetcar Named Desire, Zapata, Man on a Tight Rope, On the Waterfront, (1954 Acad. Award for best direction), East of Eden, Baby Doll, A Face in the Crowd, Wild River, Splendor in the Grass, America, America, The Arrangement, The Visitors, The Last Tycoon; Author: America, America, 1962, The Arrangement, 1967; producer, dir. film, 1968, The Assassins, 1972, The Understudy, 1974, Acts of Love, 1978, The Anatolian, 1982.

KAZAN, LAINIE (LAINIE LEVINE), singer; b. Bklyn., May 15, 1942. B.A., Hofstra U. Singer, actress, rec. artist, MGM Records.; Appeared in: motion picture Romance of a Horsethief, 1971, One From the Heart, 1981.

KAZANJIAN, HOWARD, motion picture producer; b. Pasadena, July 26, 1942; s. Harry and Rose (Khazoyan) K.; m. Carol Eskilian, May 29, 1970; children: Peter, Noah. B.S., U. So. Calif., 1964. Producer More Am. Graffiti, 1978-79; exec. producer Raiders of the Lost Ark, 1980-81; producer Return of the Jedi, 1981-83; producer film documentary The Making of Raiders of the Lost Ark, 1982. Bd. dirs Cinema Circulus, U. So. Calif., 1983; mem. screening com. bd. Asst. Dirs. Tng. Program, Los Angeles, 1970-79. Recipient Emmy award for The Making of the Raiders of the Lost Ark, 1982. Mem. Dirs. Guild Am. (council 1970-79). Office: Lucasfilm Ltd PO Box 2009 San Rafael CA 94912

KAZARINOFF, NICHOLAS D., educator; b. Ann Arbor, Mich., Aug. 12, 1929; s. Donat Konstantinovich and Rosalind (Yeska) K.; m. Margaret Louise Koning, July 17, 1948; children—Michael N., Nicholas N., Katherine T., Paul Donat, Alexander N., Dimitri N. B.S., U. Mich., 1950, M.S., 1951; Ph.D., U. Wis., 1954. Instr. math. Purdue U., 1953-55, asst. prof., 1955-56; mem. faculty U. Mich., Ann Arbor, 1956-71, asso. prof., 1960-64, prof., 1964-71; prof., chmn. dept. State U. N.Y. at Buffalo, 1971-75, Martin prof. math., 1972-77; vis. mem. Army Research Center, U. Wis., Madison, 1959-60; exchange prof. Steklov Math. Inst., Moscow, USSR, 1960-61, 65; vis. prof. Center Nat. Research, Italy, 1978, 80; mng. editor Mich. Math. Jour., 1961-65; cons. editor Math. Revs., 1966-69; Mem. at large Conf. Bd. Math. Scis., 1972-75. Author 4 books; contbr. to profl. jours. Mem. city council, Ann Arbor, 1969-71. Recipient Distinguished Undergrad. Teaching award, 1968. Mem. Am. Math. Soc., Math. Assn. Am., AAAS, Sigma Xi, Phi Beta Kappa, Pi Mu Epsilon. Democrat. Unitarian (past local pres.). Home: 157 Sherbrooke Ave Williamsville NY 14221 Office: 221 Diefendorf Hall Buffalo NY 14214

KAZAZIS, KOSTAS, linguist, educator; b. Athens, Greece, July 15, 1934; came to U.S., 1957; m. Maria Enckell, May 14, 1958; children—Marina, Silvia. Licence ès sciences politiques, U. Lausanne, Switzerland, 1957; M.A. in Polit. Sci, U. Kans., 1959; Ph.D. in Linguistics, Ind. U., 1965. Instr. linguistics U. Ill., Champaign-Urbana, 1964-65; asst. prof. linguistics U. Chgo., 1965-70, asso. prof., 1971-77, prof., 1977—. Author: (with F.W. Householder and Andreas Koutsoudas) Reference Grammar of Literary Dhimotiki, 1964; contbr. articles to profl. jours. Recipient Am. Council Learned Socs. fellowship and grants. Mem. Linguistic Soc. Am. (life), Modern Greek Studies Assn., Albanian Studies Assn., Am. Assn. for S.E. European Studies, Soc. for Romanian Studies. Home: 6019 S Ingleside St Chicago IL 60637 Office: Dept Linguistics U Chgo 1010 E 59th St Chicago IL 60637

KAZEMI, HOMAYOUN, physician, medical educator; b. Teheran, Iran, Sept. 28, 1934; came to U.S., 1953, naturalized, 1970; s. Parviz and Irandokht K.; m. Katheryne McNulty, June 7, 1958; children: Paul, Laili. B.A., Lafayette Coll., 1954; M.D., Columbia U., 1958. Diplomate: Am. Bd. Internal Medicine. Intern M.I. Bassett Hosp., Cooperstown, N.Y., 1958-59; resident in medicine Mass. Gen. Hosp., Boston, 1963, chief pulmonary unit, 1967—; asso. prof. medicine Harvard U., 1971-78, prof., 1979—; bd. dirs. Boston Tb Assn; vis. prof. U. Ghent, 1975-76; dir. U.S. Beryllium Case Registry, 1968-78. Author: Disorders of the Respiratory System, 1976, (with L.G. Miller) Manual of Pulmonary Medicine, 1982—; mem. editorial bd.: New Eng. Jour. Medicine, 1981—. Am. Heart Assn. spl. fellow, 1961-63. Fellow A.C.P.; mem. Am. Fedn. Clin. Research, Am. Thoracic Soc. (pres. Eastern sect. 1974-75), Am. Lung Assn. Boston (dir.), Mass. Med. Soc., Am. Physiol. Soc., Am. Heart Assn. Cardiopulmonary Council (exec. com. 1979—), Am. Soc. Clin. Investigation, Soc. Occupational and Environ. Health. Office: Mass Gen Hosp Boston MA 02114

KAZEMZADEH, FIRUZ, history educator; b. Moscow, Oct. 27, 1924; U.S., 1944, naturalized, 1955; s. Kazem and Talieh (Yevseyev) K.; m. Caterina Bosio, Jan. 5, 1959; children: Tatiana, Allegra, Monireh. B.A., Stanford U., 1946, M.A., 1947; Ph.D., Harvard U., 1951. Research fellow Hoover Inst., Stanford, Calif., 1949-50; cons. publs. State Dept., 1951-52; head Soviet affairs unit, information dept. Radio Free Europe, 1952-54; research fellow Russian Research Center, Center Middle Eastern Studies, Harvard, 1954-56, instr. history and lit., 1955-56; mem. faculty Yale U., 1956—, prof. history, 1967—, chmn. council Russian and East European studies, 1968-69, chmn. com. Middle Eastern studies, 1979—, dir. grad. studies in history Middle Eastern studies, 1975-76; master Davenport Coll., 1976-81. Editor: World Order, Baha'i Mag, 1966—; Author: The Struggle for Transcaucasia, 1917-1921, 1952, Russia and Britain in Persia, 1864-1914; A Study in Imperialism, 1968. Morse fellow, 1958-59; Ford fellow internat. studies, 1966. Mem. Baha'i Faith and Nat. Spiritual Assembly Baha'is of U.S. Office: Dept History Yale U New Haven CT 06520

KAZEN, ABRAHAM, JR., congressman; b. Laredo, Tex., Jan. 17, 1919; m. Consuelo Raymond; children: Abraham, Norma Kazen Dillman, Christina Kazen Attal, Catherine, Jo-Betsy. Student, U. Tex., 1937-40, Cumberland Law Sch., Lebanon, Tenn., 1941. Bar: Tex. bar 1942. Mem. firm Raymond, Alvarado & Kazen, Laredo, 1946-55; mem. Tex. Ho. of Reps., 1947-52, Tex. Senate, 1952-66, pres. pro tempore, 1959; acting gov., Tex., 1959; mem. 90th-98th congresses 23d Dist. Tex.; mem. armed services com., interior com. Served to capt. USAAF, World War II; ETO, CBI. Mem. Tex., Laredo bar assns., Am. Legion, V.F.W., Air Force Assn., U. Tex. Ex-Students Assn. Democrat. Club: K.C. Home: Laredo TX 78040 Office: 2408 Rayburn Bldg Washington DC 20515

KAZIN, ALFRED, writer; b. Bklyn., June 5, 1915; s. Charles and Gita (Fagelman) K.; m. Caroline Bookman, May 23, 1947 (div.); 1 son, Michael; m. Ann Birstein, June 26, 1952 (div.); 1 dau., Cathrael; m. Judith Dunford, May 21, 1983. B.S.S., CCNY, 1935; A.M., Columbia U., 1938; Litt.D., Adelphi U., 1965, U. New Haven, 1976, Hebrew Union Coll., 1982. Lit. editor New Republic, 1942-43, contbg. editor, 1943-45, Fortune Mag., 1943-44; lectr. Black Mountain Coll., fall 1944; vis. prof. U. Minn., summer 1946, 50; lectr. Harvard U., 1953; William Allan Neilson research prof. Smith Coll., 1954-55; Berg prof. lit. NYU, 1957; prof. Am. studies Amherst Coll., 1955-58; vis. prof. CCNY, 1962; Beckman prof. U. Calif., 1963; Disting. prof. English, SUNY-Stony Brook, 1963-73; Disting. prof. English Hunter Coll., CUNY, 1973-78, 79—; William White prof. English, U. Notre Dame, 1978-79. Writer-in-residence, Am. Acad. in Rome, 1975; Author: On Native Grounds, 1942, A Walker in the City, 1951, The Inmost Leaf, 1955, Contemporaries, 1962, Starting Out in the Thirties, 1965, Bright Book of Life, 1973, New York Jew, 1978, An American Procession, 1984; co-author: Introduction to the Works of Anne Frank, 1959; General Introduction to Dell Edition of the Novels of Theodore Dreiser, 1960; others.; editor: The Viking Portable William Blake, 1946; Editor: F. Scott Fitzgerald, The Man and His Work, 1951, Moby-Dick, 1956, Introduction to Selected Stories of Sholem Aleichem, 1956, The Open Form: Essays For Our Time, 1961, The Selected Short Stories of Nathaniel Hawthorne, 1966; Co-editor: The Stature of Theodore Dreiser, 1955; co-editor: Emerson: A Modern Anthology, 1958; The Ambassadors (James), 1969; contbr. articles to newspapers, mags. Guggenheim fellow, 1940, 1947; Rockefeller fellow study of trade-union and Army popular edn. movements in Gt. Britain, 1945; NEH sr. fellow Ctr. Advanced Study Behavioral Scis., Stanford, 1977-78; Recipient George Polk Meml. award for criticism, 1966; Brandeis U. Creative Arts award, 1973; Hubbell medal MLA, 1982. Mem. Nat. Inst. Arts and Letters, Am. Acad. Arts and Scis. Office: English Dept City U NY 33 W 42d St New York NY 10036

KAZMAYER, ROBERT HENDERSON, bus. analyst, publisher; b. Rush, N.Y., Nov. 1908; s. Jacob and Viola (Darron) K.; m. Clara V. Rapp., July 29, 1936 (div.); 1 son, Robert L.; m. Ida L. Wright, Nov. 18, 1955 (dec. Nov. 1970). Student, U. Rochester, 1929-31, Colgate-Divinity Sch., 1931-34; LL.D., Salem Coll., Salem. W.Va., 1956. Ordained deacon M.E. Ch., 1932; ordained elder, 1934, held pastorates at, Indian Falls, 1930-31; Lewiston M.E. Ch., Rochester, N.Y., 1931-34, Monroe Av M.E. Ch., 1934-38; left ministry to devote full time to writing, lecturing, 1939, travelled annually in, Central and South Am., Australia, Far East, Eng., much of continental Europe, Russia, 1929-41; in 22 months following Pearl Harbor, travelled numerous states addressing over 400 audiences, lecturing on Germany, Russia, Japan, internat. politics; originator and for two years moderator of Rochester Town Hall of the Air, WHEC; three years as radio ch. editor WSAY; originator of Kazmayer Seminar Tours; Lectured throughout, U.S., Can., Europe, the East; mem. bd. lectrs. Freedoms Found. Valley Forge. Publishes: news letter for U.S., Brit. bus. men Watch For; bimonthly travel letters.; Author: Out of the Clouds, 1944, New Strength for America; speeches; Contbr.: We Believe in Prayer; Conducted: Pastor's Exchange in Christian Advocate, 1935-36. Recipient L'Accueil De Paris Conseil Municipal Paris, 1956; George Washington Honor medal Freedoms Found., 1961. Life mem. Acad. Polit. Sci., 1952; charter mem. Anglo-Am. Goodwill Assn. (Brit.), Authors League; mem. Am. Acad. Polit. and Social Sci. Methodist. Clubs: Mason (33 deg., Shriner), Rotarian., Union League (Chgo.); Adventurers (Chgo., N.Y., London); Overseas Press (N.Y.C.). Home: Kendall NY 14476 also 5270 New Tampa Hwy Lakeland FL 33801 Office: 84 Rand St Rochester NY 14615 *Working Principle: Nothing is ever being done so well it can't be done better.*

KEACH, STACY, SR., producer, director; b. Chgo., May 29, 1914; s. Walter Edmund and Dora (Stacy) K.; m. Mary Cain Peckham, June 18, 1937; children—Stacy, James. B.S., Northwestern U., 1935; M.A., 1936. Prof. theatrical prodns. Northwestern U., Evanston, Ill., 1935-36, Armstrong Coll., Savannah, Ga., 1936-41, Pasadena (Calif.) Playhouse, 1941-42; pres. Stacy Keach Prodns., North Hollywood, Calif., 1948—, Kaydan Record Corp., North Hollywood, 1957—, Verdict Film Corp., Hollywood, 1972—. Producer, dir., Universal Studios, Universal City, Calif., 1941-46, RKO Studios, Hollywood, Calif., 1946-48; producer, 1948-50, NBC, Hollywood, 1950-53, Columbia Pictures, Hollywood, 1952-54; appears as Clarence Birds Eye on Birds Eye Frozen Food commls., 1981—. Recipient Rockefeller Found. award, 1941, Freedom Found. award (2), award Los Angeles City Council, 1973. Mem. Information Film Producers Assn., Sigma Alpha Epsilon. Club: Rotarian. Office: 5216 Laurel Canyon Blvd North Hollywood CA 91607 *There is nothing in life more precious than the love of one to another. It is the solution for securing happy families, good friends and lasting peace on earth.*

KEACH, STACY, JR., actor, director, producer, writer; b. Savannah, Ga., June 2, 1941; s. Stacy and Mary Cain (Peckham) K.; m. Jill Donohue, 1981. A.B. in English and Drama, U. Calif. at Berkeley, 1963; student, Yale Drama Sch., 1963-64, London Acad. Dramatic Art, 1964-65. Asso. prof. drama Yale, 1967-68; Pres. Positron Prodns. Ltd. Contbr. articles to newspapers and mags.; Broadway debut in Indians, 1969; appeared in: Broadway prodn. Deathtrap, 1979; off-Broadway appearances in Macbird, 1966-67; The Niggerlovers, 1967, Peer Gynt, 1969, Henry IV, 1 and 2, 1968, Hamlet, 1972, King Lear, 1968, Long Day's Journey Into Night, 1971, Cyrano de Bergerac, 1978, Hughie, London; off-Broadway appearances in Barnum, 1978, 82; mem., Lincoln Center Repertory Co., also, Long Warf Theatre; film appearances include: The Heart is a Lonely Hunter, 1968, End of the Road, 1969, Doc, 1970, The Traveling Executioner, 1970, The New Centurions, 1971, Fat City, 1971, Brewster McCloud, 1970, Luther, 1972, The Dion Brothers, 1973, Conduct Unbecoming, 1974, Jesus of Nazareth, 1976, The Killer Inside Me, 1974, The Squeeze, 1976, Gray Lady Down, 1976, The Greatest Battle, 1977, Two Solitudes, 1977, Cheech & Chong's Up in Smoke, 1977, The Ninth Configuration, 1978, The Long Riders, 1979, Road Games, 1980, Butterfly, 1980, Cheech & Chong's Nice Dreams, 1981, That Championship Season, 1982, Butterfly, 1982; TV appearances in: Orville and Wilbur, 1971, Particular Men, 1972, Classics for Today, 1972, Man of Destiny, 1973, all Public Broadcasting System, All the Kind Strangers, 1974, Caribe, 1974-75, both ABC, The Michener Dynasty, NBC, 1975; TV appearances in NBC, 1975; TV appearances in: A Rumor of War, CBS, 1979; TV appearances in CBS, 1979; TV appearances in: The Blue and the Gray, 1981, Wait Until Dark, 1982, Murder Me, Murder You, 1983; TV appearances include: Princess Daisy, 1983; TV appearances in: More than Murder, 1983, Mickey Spillane's Mike Hammer series, 1983; dir.: Pullman Car Hiawatha, 1964-65, The Stronger, 1964-65, The Maids, 1964-65, The Repeater, 1971 (Cine Golden Eagle award, London Film Festival outstanding film), Incident at Vichy, 1974, Six Characters in Search of an Author, 1976; screen writer, producer The Long Riders, 1979. Spokesman Am. Cleft Palate Assn., United Indian Devel. Assn.; mem. Nat. Citizens Communications Lobby. Fulbright award, 1964-65; Best Actor award U. Calif., 1963; Best Actor award Oreg. Shakespeare award, 1963; Obie award, 1967; Vernon Rice Drama Desk award, 1967, 72; Sat Rev. award, 1967. Address: Positron Productions Ltd 9000 Sunset Blvd Suite 1115 Los Angeles CA 90069 *The fundamental virtue of success is that it allows you to know the true significance of what it means to have the freedom to make your dreams come true.*

KEADY, GEORGE CREGAN, JR., judge; b. Bklyn., June 16, 1924; s. George Cregan and Marie (Lussier) K.; m. Patricia Drake, Sept. 2, 1950; children: Margaret Keady Zehner, Marie E., George Cregan, Catherine A., Kathleen V. Student, U. Kans., 1943-44; B.S., Fordham U., 1949; J.D., Columbia U., 1950; LL.D., Western New Eng. Coll., 1973. Bar: Mass. 1950. Since practiced in, Springfield, Mass.; asso. firm Ganley & Crook, 1950-53; assoc. firm Peter D. Wilson, 1953-57; partner firm Wilson, Keady & Ratner, 1958-79; justice Dist. Ct., Springfield, 1979-82; assoc. justice Superior Ct., Springfield, 1982—; dean Western New Eng. Coll. Law Sch., 1970-73; dir. Western Mass. Bar Rev., 1956-63, Western New Eng. Coll. Bar Rev., 1965-72; chmn. Mass. Continuing Legal Edn., Inc., 1977-80. Active United Fund, Springfield, 1950-72, Joint Civic Agys., Springfield; chmn. fund drive Am. Cancer Soc., Springfield, 1962; selectman, Longmeadow, Mass., 1958-68, chmn. selectmen, 1960-61, 63-64, 66-68, moderator, 1968-73; vice chmn. Rep. Town Com., Longmeadow, 1956-60; alt. del. Rep. Nat. Conv., 1960, del., 1964; pres. Hampden Dist. Mental Health Clinic, Inc., 1968-71, Child Guidance Clinic, Springfield, 1962-64; corporator, trustee, sr. vice-chmn. Baystate Med. Center; trustee Western New Eng. Coll., Baypath Jr. Coll. Served with AUS, 1943-46. Decorated Bronze star. Mem. ABA, Mass. Bar Assn., Hampden County Bar Assn. (exec. com. 1960-79, pres. 1965-67), Phi Delta Phi. Roman Catholic. Club: Longmeadow Country. Home: 16 Meadowbrook Rd Longmeadow MA 01106 Office: 50 State St Springfield MA 01103

KEADY, WILLIAM COLBERT, judge; b. Greenville, Miss., Apr. 2, 1913; m. Dorothy Clark Thompson, July 31, 1935; children—William Colbert, Peggy Anne. J.D., Washington U., 1936. Bar: Miss. bar 1936. Practiced in, Greenville, 1936-68; chief judge U.S. Dist. Ct. for Miss. No. Dist., Greenville, 1968—. Mem. Miss. Ho. of Reps., 1940-43, Miss. Senate, 1940-45; former mem. Delta Council, Miss. Econ. Council; mem. Jud. Conf. U.S., 1977-80; trustee William Percy Meml. Library, 1946-49, Greenville Pub. Schs., 1947-51; chmn. bd. Greenville Pub. Schs., 1950-51; past pres. Greenville Indsl. Foundl; past bd. dirs. Kings Daus. Hosp., Washington County YMCA. Mem. Am., Fed., Washington County bar assns., Miss. State Bar (commr. for 4th circuit 1954-55, pres.-elect 1968), Am. Coll. Trial Lawyers, Am. Judicature Soc. Presbyterian.

KEAGY, ANN, designer, educator; b. Cleve., June 10, 1921; m. J. Rodman Keagy, Nov. 17, 1951; 1 dau., Wendy. Grad., Pratt Inst., 1941; student, Cleve. Inst. Art, 1942, U. Mex., 1943, Columbia U., 1943. Dir. fashion dept. Briarcliff Jr. Coll., 1941-44; costume designer, Hollywood, 1944, owner custom shop, Briarcliff Manor, N.Y., 1944-47; designer Rea Mfg. Co., 1947-53; dir. fashion design dept. Parsons Sch. Design, N.Y.C., 1947-53, chmn. fashion design dept., 1953-83; mem. adv. bd. Moore Inst. Art, Phila., 1953—, Stephens Coll., Columbia, Mo., 1954—, R.I. Sch. Design, 1958—, Shenkar Coll., Tel Aviv, 1970—, Akashi Coll., Kobe, Japan, 1971-72, Inst. Design and Merchandising, Los Angeles, 1972—; hon. bd. advisors Silverman-Rogers project Kent State U., Ohio, 1983—; ednl. cons. Pratt Inst., 1956, Ryerson Poly. Inst., Toronto, 1960—, LaSalle Coll., Montreal, 1975, Morocco, 1975; judge art exhibition Scholastic Art Awards Program, 1960-76. Coordinator: film Norman Norell, 1972; contbg. author: Careers and Opportunities in Fashion, 1968. J.C. Penney Co. grantee, 1975, 78; Arthur Houghton Found., 1971; recipient Parsons Medal for Distinguished Achievement, 1977. Mem. Fashion Group (bd. govs. 1973-75), Fashion Group Found. (gov. 1980—), Fashion Inner Circle. Home: 134 Lambert Rd New Canaan CT 06840

KEALA, FRANCIS AHLOY, security executive; b. Honolulu, June 1, 1930; s. Samuel Louis and Rose (Ahloy) K.; m. Betty Ann Lyman, Nov. 28, 1952; children—Frances Ann, John Richard, Robert Mark. B.A. in Sociology, U. Hawaii, 1953. Patrolman Honolulu Police Dept., 1956-62, detective, 1962-65, lt., 1965-68, capt., 1968-69, chief of police, 1969-83; dir. security Hawaiian Telephone Co., 1983—. Bd. dirs. Aloha council Boy Scouts Am., Hawaii chpt. ARC, Muscular Dystrophy, Honolulu; bd. dirs. St. Louis High Sch., Palama Settlement, Sex Abuse Treatment Center; mem. civilian adv. group U.S. Army. Served with AC U.S. Army, 1953-55. Mem. Internat. Assn. Chiefs of Police, Hawaii State Law Enforcement Ofcls. Assn., FBI Nat. Acad. Assos. Club: Rotary (Honolulu). Office: 1177 Bishop St Honolulu HI 96813

KEALEY, THOMAS ROBERT, civil engineer; b. Phila., Feb. 16, 1921; s. Thomas and Amy Roger (Jennings) K.; m. Rita Ruth Rice, Dec. 3, 1950; children: James Thomas, Carol Ann Kealey Steckbeck. B.S. in Civil Engring, Drexel Inst. Tech., 1942, M.S., Mass. Inst. Tech., 1947. Instr. civil engring. Drexel Inst. Tech., Phila., 1946; design engr. Modjeski & Masters, Harrisburg, Pa., 1947-59, partner, 1960-70, mng. partner, 1971—. Prin. works include Theodore Roosevelt Bridge, Washington, Girard Point Bridge, Phila., Robert Moses Bridge, Fire Island, N.Y., Newburgh-Beacon Bridges, N.Y., I-10 Mississippi River Bridge, Baton Rouge., 1st and 2d Greater New Orleans Bridge, I-310 Mississippi River Bridge, Luling, La. Pres. Lenker Manor Civic Assn., Harrisburg, 1954-55; trustee Paxton Presbyterian Ch., Harrisburg, 1969-72; leader Boy Scouts Am., 1959-68; mem. Wormleysburg Planning Commn., 1979—. Served with C.E. AUS, 1942-46. Fellow ASCE; mem. ASTM, Nat. Soc. Profl. Engrs., Am. Ry. Engrs. Assn., Internat. Bridge, Tunnel and Turnpike Assn., Am. Cons. Engrs. Council, Post Tensioning Inst., Research Council on Structural Connections, Harrisburg Civil War Round Table, Confederate Stamp Alliance, Ky. Rifle Assn. Republican. Clubs: Execs., Masons. Home: 25 W Lawn Circle Wormleysburg PA 17043 Office: 4713 Carlisle Pike Mechanicsburg PA 17055

KEALY, WILLIAM JAMES, investment executive; b. N.Y.C., Apr. 21, 1940; s. William F. and Regina Maura (Kerwin) K.; m. Ellen Mary O'Keefe, Apr. 20, 1963; children: William K., Maureen E., Daniel M. B.B.A., St. John's U., 1963; postgrad., NYU, 1964-67. Cert. fin. analyst. Analyst Equitable Life, N.Y.C., 1958-64, Lionel D. Edie, 1964-67; dir. research Goldman Sachs & Co., N.Y.C., 1967—; dir. N.Y. Soc. Security Analysts, 1982—. Trustee, treas. St. Luke's Sch. Bd., N.Y.C., 1976—. Served fwith USMC, 1960-67. Republican. Roman Catholic. Club: Downtown Athletic. Office: 85 Broad St New York NY 10004

KEAN, BENJAMIN HARRISON, physician; b. Chgo., Dec. 2, 1912; s. Harrison and Tillie (Rhodes) K.; m. Collette B. Touey, Dec. 26, 1975. A.B., U. Calif., 1933; M.D., Columbia, 1937. Diplomate: Am. Bd. Pathology, Am. Bd. Microbiology. Intern Gorgas Hosp., C.Z., 1937-39; pvt. practice medicine, N.Y.C., 1946—; clin. prof. emeritus tropical medicine and public health Cornell U. Med. Coll.; attending physician N.Y., Drs. hosps.; dir. parasitology lab. N.Y. Hosp.; mem. sci. adv. com. tropical diseases program WHO, 1978-80; med. cons. Gen. Motors, Internat. Travelers Health Inst. Author: (with Breslau) Parasites of the Human Heart, 1964, (with Tucker) Traveler's Health Guide, 1965, Traveler's Medical Guide for Physicians, 1966; also chpts. in books, articles.; co-editor: Tropical Medicine and Parasitology: Classic Investigations, 1978. Served to lt. col. M.C., AUS, 1942-46. Recipient Presdl. award of Golden Heart Philippine Govt., 1968; Egyptian Order of Merit, Govt. of United Arab Republic, 1980. Fellow ACP, Coll. Am. Pathologists; mem. AMA, Royal Soc. Tropical Medicine and Hygiene, Am. Soc. Clin. Pathology, Am., N.Y. socs. tropical medicine, Am. Assn. Pathology and Bacteriology. With Dr. Edward I. Goldsmith developed surg. procedure for extracorporeal hemofiltration; research in toxoplasmosis, malaria, amebiasis, diarrhea in travelers, other tropical diseases. Home: 435 E 70th St New York NY 10021 Office: 912 Fifth Ave New York NY 10021

KEAN, JOHN, utility company executive; b. N.Y.C., Oct. 28, 1929; s. John and Mary Alice (Barney) K.; m. Joan E. Jessup, June 25, 1952; children: Mary Lita, John, Katharine, Susan. B.A., Harvard U., 1953; student, N.Y. Inst. Fin., 1954-55. Security analyst Kean, Taylor & Co., N.Y.C., 1953-55; comml. and gas cadet Pub. Service Elec. & Gas Co., Newark, 1955-56, adminstrv. asst., 1956-59, v.p. sales and pub. relations, 1959-63; pres. Elizabethtown (N.J.) Gas Co., 1963-80, chmn. bd., chief exec. officer, 1980—; pres., dir. Nat. Utilities & Industries Corp., Elizabeth, N.J., 1969—; v.p. Internat. Gas Union (sci. and tech. fedn. representing 41 countries); dir. City Fed. Savs. & Loan Assn., Elizabethtown Water Co., Nat. Computer Utility Co., Nat. Energy Leasing Co., Nat. Exploration Co., Utility Propane Co. Mayor, Bedminster Twp., N.J., 1962-69, committeeman, 1970—; pres. N.J. State League of Municipalities, 1969-70, mem. exec. com., 1962—; Hon. chmn. bd. dirs. Deborah Hosp.; trustee Kean Coll. N.J., Pingry Sch., Rippel Found., St. Mark's Sch., Christodora House. Served with USMCR, 1948-50. Mem. Am. Gas Assn. (dir. 1967-80, chmn. bd. 1978-79), N.J. Gas Assn. (pres. 1962), N.J. Utilities Assn. (dir.). Club: Mason. Home: Klines Mill Rd Box 62 Bedminster NJ 07921 Office: 1 Elizabethtown Plaza Elizabeth NJ 07207

KEAN, JOSEPH ANDREW, lawyer; b. Grimes, Iowa, July 10, 1915; s. Edward Michael and Grace W. (Williams) K.; m. Ann Dorner, Nov. 12, 1951; children—Andrew, Joann, Patricia, Janet. B.A., U. Iowa, 1937, J.D., 1941. Bar: Calif. bar 1947. Partner firm Kean & Engle, Los Angeles, 1947—; vip., dir. Pacific Air Products Co. Served to lt. comdr. USCGR, 1942-46. Republican. Roman Cath. Clubs: Los Angeles Country, Pauma Valley Country. Home: 234 Muirfield Rd Los Angeles CA 90004 Office: 3600 Wilshire Blvd Los Angeles CA 90010

KEAN, NORMAN, producer, theatre owner, manager; b. Colorado Springs, Colo., Oct. 14, 1934; s. Barney B. and Flora (Bienstock) K.; m. Gwyda DonHowe, Oct. 12, 1958; 1 son, David. Student, U. Denver, 1952-54. Pres. Norman Kean Prodns., Inc., 1966—, Edison Theatre, N.Y.C., 1970—, Edison Enterprises, Inc., 1974—; owner, mgr. E. 74th St. Theater, N.Y.C., 1966-69; lectr. N.Y. U. Sch. Continuing Edn. Stage mgr.: Johnny Johnson, N.Y.C. and on tour, 1956, Orpheus Descending, 1957, The Waltz of the Toreadors, 1957-58, A Touch of the Poet, 1958-59, Camino Real, 1960, Laurette, 1960; gen. mgr.: The Pleasure of His Company, 1960, Bayanihan Philippine Dance Co., 1961, General Seeger, 1961, The Matchmaker, 1962, Tiger, Tiger, Burning Bright, Phoenix Theatre, N.Y.C., 1962, Laterna Magika from Prague, 1963, APA-Phoenix, APA Repertory Company, N.Y.C., 1964-69, Oh! Calcutta!, 1969; producer: Max Morath at the Turn of the Century, N.Y., U.S., Can., 1969-70; gen. mgr., assoc. producer: Happy Birthday, Wanda June, N.Y.C., 1970-71; gen. mgr., asso. producer: Orlando Furioso from Rome, N.Y.C., 1970, Don't Bother Me, I Can't Cope, N.Y.C., Chgo., Los Angeles, 1972-74; producer: Hosanna, N.Y.C., 1974; gen. mgr.: Sizwe Banzi is Dead, 1974-75, The Island, 1974-75; producer: Me and Bessie, 1975-78, Oh! Calcutta!, 1976, By Strouse, 1978, A Broadway Musical, 1978, The Guardsman, 1983. Trustee Am. Acad. Dramatic Arts. Served with U.S. Army, 1954-55. Mem. League N.Y. Theatres and Producers (officer). Jewish. Club: Century (Denver). Home: 280 Riverside Dr New York NY 10025 Office: Edison Theatre Bldg 240 W 47th St New York NY 10036

KEAN, ROBERT WINTHROP, JR., water company executive; b. Hewlitt, N.Y., Aug. 18, 1922; s. Robert Winthrop and Elizabeth (Stuyvesant) K.; m. Luz Maria Silverio (div. May 1975); children—Robert Winthrop, Peter Stuyvesant, Alexander Livingston, Nicholas, Christopher; m. Sandra Johnson, Mar. 28, 1976 (div. 1981); m. Katherine Tobeason, Nov. 4, 1982. B.A. in Psychology, Princeton U., 1943. Chmn. bd., chief exec. officer Elizabethtown Water Co., Elizabeth, N.J., 1950—; dir. Elizabethtown Gas Co.; dir., vice-chmn. N.J. Bus. Industry Assn.; dir. Nat. Utilities & Industries Corp., Nat. State Bank, Hackensack Water Co.; mem. Surgeon Gen.'s Water Task Force for India, 1967, Northeastern U.S. Water Supply Advisory Com., 1967—. Mem. Citizens Com. for Higher Edn. in N.J., 1966-67; mem. Republican State Finance Com., 1970-75; trustee Elizabeth Gen. Hosp., Fisk U., Nashville. Served to capt. F.A. AUS, 1943-46. Decorated D.F.C., Air medal with oak leaf cluster; named Citizen of Year N.J. Soc. Profl. Engrs., 1965. Mem. Nat. Assn. Water Cos. (dir., past pres.), N.J. Utilities Assn. (dir., past pres.), N.J. C. of C. (dir.). Home: 390 E Mt Pleasant Ave Livingston NJ 07039 Office: 1 Elizabethtown Plaza Elizabeth NJ 07207

KEAN, THOMAS H., gov. N.J.; b. N.Y.C., Apr. 21, 1935; m. Deborah Bye; children: Thomas, Reed, Alexandra. A.B., Princeton; M.A., Columbia. Tchr. history and govt.; mem. N.J. Assembly, 1967-77, speaker, 1972, minority leader, 1974; acting gov., 1973, gov., 1981—. Office: Care Carl Golden Rm 112 State Hse Trenton NJ 08625

KEANE, BIL, cartoonist; b. Phila., Oct. 5, 1922; s. Aloysius William and Florence Rita (Bunn) K.; m. Thelma Carne, Oct. 23, 1948; children: Gayle, Neal, Glen, Christopher, Jeff. Student pub. schs., Phila. Staff artist, Phila. Bull., 1945-58; syndicated cartoonist, Register & Tribune Syndicate, Des Moines, 1954—; creator, cartoonist: Channel Chuckles, from 1954, Family Circus, 1960—; author numerous books of cartoon collections; cartoonist: Stars and Stripes, 1945. Served with AUS, 1942-45; PTO. Mem. Nat. Cartoonists Soc. (Best Syndicated Panel award 1967, 71, 74), Newspaper Comics Council, Cartoonists Guild. Office: care Register & Tribune Syndicate 715 Locust St Des Moines IA 50304 *

KEANE, EDWARD WEBB, lawyer; b. Detroit, Sept. 18, 1930; s. Lee A. and Florette (Webb) K.; m. Mary Burdell, 1954; children: Edward Webb, Jennie K., Matthew K. A.B., Harvard U., 1952, J.D., 1957. Bar: D.C. 1957, N.Y. 1960, U.S. Supreme Ct. 1965. Law clk. to Justice William J. Brennan, Jr. U.S. Supreme Ct., 1957-58; assoc. Sullivan & Cromwell, N.Y.C., 1958-65, ptnr., 1966—. Mem. ABA, N.Y. State Bar Assn., N.Y. County Bar Assn., Assn. Bar City N.Y., Am. Judicature Soc. Home: 1 Lexington Ave New York NY 10010 Office: Sullivan & Cromwell 125 Broad St New York NY 10004

KEANE, GUSTAVE ROBERT, architect, cons.; b. Vienna, Austria, Jan. 7, 1914; s. Robert Kien and Frances (Partl) K.; m. Constance van Lennep, Jan. 30, 1940; children—Robert van Lennep, John Francis. Archtl. engr., State U. Czechoslovakia, 1937. Designer Harvey Wiley Corbett, N.Y.C., 1940-43; with Eggers Partnership, N.Y.C., 1945—, partner, 1963-73; archtl.-engring. cons., tech. adviser to attys. in def. of malpractice litigation against design professions; mgmt. cons. archtl. and engring. firms, 1973—; guest lectr. Bd. dirs. Bldg. Research Inst., Washington, Nat. Bd. Accreditation in Concrete Constrn. Prin. works include Am. Embassy, Ankara, Turkey, U.S. Naval Hosp, P.R., N.J. Coll. Medicine and Dentistry, Lafayette Hosp, N.Y. Times Printing Plant, BASF Corporate Hdqrs. N.J; Contbr. to books, jours. Past chmn. architects com. United Hosp. Fund. Fellow A.I.A., Am. Soc. Testing Materials; mem. Am. Assn. Hosp. Planning. Home and office: 7 Harmony Rd Huntington NY 11743

KEANE, MARK EDWARD, consultant; b. Chgo., Sept. 10, 1919; s. Fred J. and Mary E. (Sullivan) K.; m. Carolyn Mims, Sept. 12, 1942 (dec. Aug. 1977); children: Mark Edward, Daniel, Dennis, Brian, Mary, Peter, Barry; m. Judith Whirley Mohr, Mar. 28, 1981. B.S. in Pub. Service Engring., Purdue U., 1941. Intern, Nat. Inst. Pub. Affairs, Washington, 1941-42; staff cons. Pub. Adminstrn. Service, Chgo., 1945-48; asst. to city mgr., Wichita, Kans., 1948-49, city mgr., Shorewood, Wis., 1950-53, Oak Park, Ill., 1953-62, Tucson, 1962-66; dir. land and facilities devel. adminstrn. HUD, Washington, 1966-67; exec. dir. Internat. City Mgmt. Assn., Washington, 1967-83; cons., 1983—. Served to maj. AUS, 1942-45. Mem. Nat. Acad. Pub. Adminstrn. Home: 1026 16th St NW Washington DC 20036

KEANEY, JOHN JOSEPH, educator; b. Boston, May 8, 1932; s. Bartley and Bridget (Greene) K.; m. Edwina Marie Tonelli, Sept. 7, 1957; children—Anne M., John J., Paul M. A.B., Boston Coll., 1953; A.M., Harvard U., 1955, Ph.D., 1959. Instr. to prof. dept. classics Princeton U., 1959—. Mem. Am. Philol. Assn. (editor publs. 1970-72). Roman Catholic. Home: 60 The Western Way Princeton NJ 08540 Office: 103 E Pyne Princeton Univ Princeton NJ 08544

KEAR, BERNARD HENRY, materials scientist; b. Port Talbot, South Wales, July 5, 1931; came to U.S., 1959, naturalized, 1965; s. Herbert and Catherine Ann (Rees) K.; m. Jacqueline Margaret Smith, Aug. 22, 1959; children: Andrew, Gareth, Edward, Gwyneth. B.Sc., U. Birmingham, 1954, Ph.D., 1957, D.Sc., 1970. With Tube Investments Ltd., Eng., 1957-59; staff scientist Franklin Inst., Phila., 1959-63; with United Technologies Corp., East Hartford, Conn., 1963-81, sr. cons. scientist, 1977-81; sci. adv. Exxon Research and Engring. Co., 1981—; adj. prof., research supr. U. Conn. Editor 5 books in field; contbr. 117 articles to profl. jours.; holder 20 patents. Bd. dirs., pres. Interfaith Housing for Elderly Project, Madison, Conn., 1974-79. Recipient Mathewson gold medal Am. Inst. Metall. Engrs., 1971. Fellow Am. Soc. Metals (Howe medal 1970); mem. Nat. Acad. Engring., Metall. Soc., Electron Microscopy Soc. Am. Office: Exxon Research and Engring Co Route 22 E Annandale NJ 08801

KEARL, BRYANT EASTHAM, university administrator; b. Paris, Idaho, Sept. 21, 1921; s. Chase and Hazel Loveless K.; m. Ruth Warr, Sept. 5, 1941; children: Susan DeJongh-Kearl, Richard B., Kathryn Dammon, Robert. Student, U. Idaho, 1936-37; B.S., Utah State U., 1941; M.S., U. Wis., 1942; Ph.D., U. Minn., 1951. Instr. agrl. journalism U. Wis., 1944-46, asst. prof., 1947-49, asso. prof., 1950-51, prof., 1952—, asso. dean, 1963-67, vice chancellor, 1967-70, acting chancellor, 1968, vice chancellor academic affairs, 1978—; vis. prof. Friedrich Wilhelms U., Bonn., 1961-62; sr. planning officer U. East Africa, 1964-65; exec. dir. Asia office Agrl. Devel. Council, 1970-74; mem. com. on weather info. systems NRC, 1979-80; cons. FAO World Conf. on Agrarian Reform and Rural Devel., 1979; mem. study team for CGIAR Rev. of Internat. Agrl. Research Centers, 1980-81. Mem. Midwest Univs. Consortium Bd., 1965-70, 74—, vice chmn., 1976—; trustee U. Wis. Hosps., 1977—; mem. council Elvehjem Art Mus., 1978—. Served with USN, 1944-46. Decorated Bronze Star. Mem. Assn. Edn. Journalism, Am. Agrl. Coll. Editors (past pres.), AAUP, AAAS, Alpha Zeta, Epsilon Sigma Phi. Mormon. Home: 2807 Ridge Rd Madison WI 53705 Office: 150 Bascom Hall University of Wisconsin Madison WI 53706

KEARL, WAYNE, communications consultant; b. nr. Edmonton, Alta., Can., Oct. 26, 1918; s. Stanley Brandon and Mabel (Stoddard) K.; m. Dorothy Hatch, May 14, 1941; children: Stanley, Edward, Robert. Student, Brigham Young U., 1937-40. News dir., salesman KSL, Salt Lake City, 1947-52; sales mgr., sta. mgr. KGMB-TV, Honolulu, 1952-54; gen. mgr. KENS-TV, San Antonio, 19S4—; pres. Harte-Hanks Television Group, 1975—; v.p. Harte-Hanks Communications, Inc., 1978-79, sr. v.p., pres. broadcasting and entertainment, 1979-82, spl. cons., 1982—; chmn. Television Code Rev. Bd., 1974-76; dir. CBS Affiliates Bd., 1974-78; instr. broadcast mgmt. U. Tex., 1965, Trinity U., 1982—. Announcer/copywriter, KOVO, Provo, Utah, 1941-43. Home: 207 Chichester St San Antonio TX 78209 Office: Harte-Hanks Inc PO Box 269 San Antonio TX 78291

KEARNEY, HUGH FRANCIS, historian, educator; b. Liverpool, Eng., Jan. 22, 1924; s. Hugh and Martha (Thomas) K.; m. Catherine Mary Murphy, June 18, 1956; children: Martha, Hugh, Peter. M.A., U. Cambridge, Eng., 1947; Ph.D., Univ. Coll., Dublin, Ireland, 1955. Lectr. Univ. Coll., Dublin, 1950-62; reader U. Sussex, Eng., 1962-70; Pares prof. U. Edinburgh, Scotland, 1970-75; Amundson prof. U. Pitts., 1975—. Author: Strafford in Ireland, 1959, Scholars and Gentlemen, 1970, Science and Change, 1971; editor: Origins of Scientific Revolution, 1964. Office: U Pittburgh Dept History Pittburgh PA 15260

KEARNEY, JOHN JOSEPH, JR., utility executive; b. Bklyn., June 28, 1924; s. John Joseph and Kathryn Virginia (Diamond) K.; m. Regina C. Welsh, Feb. 21, 1952; children: John J., David W., Elizabeth L., Peter A. B.S., Coll. of Holy Cross, 1945; J.D., Bklyn. Law Sch., 1957. Bar: N.Y. 1958; C.P.A., N.Y. Accountant J.K. Lasser & Co., David Fields & Co., N.Y.C., 1945-51; tax accountant Charles Pfizer & Co., Bklyn., 1951-56; asst. div. controller IBM, N.Y.C., 1956-59; sec., gen. auditor L.I. Lighting Co., Mineola, N.Y., 1959—. Trustee St. Joseph's Coll., 1976—; trustee, faculty advisor SUNY, Farmingdale. Served with USNR, 1942-44. Mem. Am. Soc. Corporate Secs., Inst. Internal Auditors, Am. Inst. C.P.A.s, N.Y. State Soc. C.P.A.s, Shareholder Relations Soc. N.Y. Club: Cherry Valley (Garden City, N.Y.). Home: 35 Russell Rd Garden City NY 11530 Office: 250 Old Country Rd Mineola NY 11501

KEARNEY, JOHN WALTER, sculptor, painter; b. Omaha, Aug. 31, 1924; m. Lynn Haigh, June 2, 1951; children: Daniel Raymond, Jill Ann. Student, Cranbrook Acad. Art, 1946-48. Tchr., 1948—, co-founder, 1950; since dir. Contemporary Art Workshop Chgo.; Adv. bd. Art Inst. Chgo., A.R.S.G., Fine Arts Work Center, Provincetown, Mass., Chgo. Council on Fine Arts. Sculptor, painter, 1946—; (Recipient prizes for sculpture and painting 1952, 53, 60, 61, 64, 76, 77), one-man shows in, N.Y.C., 1964, 69, 72, 74, 76, 79, Rome, 1964, 68, Chgo., 1966, 81, 84, Ft. Wayne (Ind.) Mus., 1966, A.C.A. Gallery, 1964, 69, 72, 74, 76, 79, Galleria Schneider, Rome, 1969, Ill. Inst. Tech., 1976, Ulrich Mus. Art, Wichita State U., Dirksen Fed. Bldg., Chgo., 1979, Cherrystone Gallery, Wellfleet, Mass., 1980, Contemporary Art Workshop, 1981, 84, 2-person show, Art Inst. Chgo., A.R.S.G., 1977; represented in permanent collections, Mundelein Coll., Chgo., Chrysler Art Mus., Norfolk (Va.) Art Mus., Ulrich Mus. Art of Wichita State U., Canton Art Inst., Detroit Children's Mus., Ft. Wayne Art Mus., Minn. Mus., St. Paul, New Sch. Social Research, N.Y.C., City of Chgo. Park Dist., Northwestern U., Roosevelt U., Chgo., U. Wyo. Art Mus., St. Lawrence U., Canton, N.Y., Wichita Art Mus., 4th Fin. Center, Wichita, Peace Mus., Chgo., Chgo. Mus. Sci. and Industry, Lincoln Park Zoo, Chgo., also pvt. collections including, John D. Rockefeller IV collection, Robert Mayer collection, spl. sculpture in bronze and silver, steel bumpers sculpture. Trustee Ill. Com. for Handgun Control. Served with USN, World War II; PTO. Named Man of Year in Arts in Chgo., 1963; Fulbright grantee, 1963-64; Italian Govt. grantee, 1963-64; grantee Nat. Found. Arts and Humanities, 1968. Mem. Provincetown Art Assn. (former v.p. and trustee). Home: 830 W Castlewood Terr Chicago IL 60640 Studio: 542 W Grant Pl Chicago IL 60614 Studio: 638 Commercial St Provincetown MA 02657

KEARNEY, JOSEPH LAURENCE, athletic conference administrator; b. Pitts., Apr. 28, 1927; s. Joseph L. and Iva M. (Nikirk) K.; m. Dorothea Hurst, May 13, 1950; children: Jan Marie, Kevin Robert, Erin Lynn, Shawn Alane, Robin James. B.A., Seattle Pacific U., 1952, LL.D., 1979; M.A., San Jose State U., 1964; Ed.D., U. Wash., 1970. Tchr., coach Paradise (Calif.) High Sch., 1952-53; asst. basketball coach U. Wash., 1953-54; coach, tchr. Sunnyside (Wash.) High Sch., 1954-57; prin. high sch., coach Onalaska (Wash.) High Sch., 1957-61; prin. Tumwater (Wash.) High Sch., 1961-63; asst. dir. Wash. High Sch. Activities Assn., 1963-64; athletic dir., asso. dir. U. Wash., 1964-76; athletic dir. intercollegiate athletics Mich. State U., East Lansing, 1976-80, Ariz. State U., Tempe, 1980; commr. Western Athletic Conf., Denver, 1980—. Pres. Community Devel. Assn., 1957-61. Served with USNR, 1945-47. Recipient Disting. Service award Mich. Assn. Professions, 1979. Mem. Nat. Football Found., Nat. Collegiate Athletic Assn., Nat. Assn. Collegiate Dirs. Athletics. Home: 7361 S Monroe Ct Littleton CO 80122 Office: Western Athletic Conf 14 W Dry Creek Circle Littleton CO 80120

KEARNEY, LESTER T., JR., former banker, retired air force officer; b. Sweetwater, Tex., Jan. 9, 1924; s. Lester T. and Mildred (Hendricks) K.; m. Jonnie Mae King, Dec. 8, 1980; children: Kathleen Lynn, Jamie Kearney Endahl, Leslie Ann. Student, San Angelo (Tex.) Coll., 1942; grad., Air Command and Staff Coll., 1959, Nat. War Coll., 1966. Commd. 2d lt. USAAF, 1944; advanced through grades to maj. gen. USAF, 1973; service in ETO, Korea, Panama and U.S., chief of staff Mil. Airlift Command, Scott AFB, Ill., 1973, comdr. 21st Air Force, McGuire AFB, N.J., 1973-75, vice dir. J-5, plans and policy Office Joint Chiefs Staff, Washington, 1975-77, ret., 1977; former v.p. Southwest Bank, San Angelo, Tex.; tech. cons. Lockheed-Ga. Mem. polit. affairs com. Bd. City Devel.; mem. City Planning Commn. Decorated D.S.M. (2), Legion of Merit (2), Air medal (6), Joint Service Commendation medal, Air Force Commendation medal. Mem. Daedialians (life). Club: Rotary. Home: 2559 Lindenwood St San Angelo TX 76901

KEARNEY, LOUISA DANIELS, magazine publisher; b. N.Y.C., Dec. 19, 1950; d. Henry and Virginia M. (Kaboolian) Daniels; m. Stephen M. Kearney, June 1, 1973. B.A., Queen's Coll.-CUNY, 1972. Asst. controller Harper's Mag., N.Y.C., 1972-76, adminstrv. coordinator, 1976-79, assoc. pub., 1980-82; pub. Harper's Mag., 1982—; treas. Harper's Mag. Found.; fin. analyst Charter Pub., N.Y.C., 1980. N.Y. Bd. Regents scholar, 1968; recipient Nat. Council Women citation accomplishment, 1982. Office: Harper's Mag 2 Park Ave New York NY 10016

KEARNEY, RICHARD DAVID, lawyer; b. Dayton, Ky., Jan. 3, 1914; s. David Richard and Mary (Manouge) K.; m. Margaret Helen Murray, Nov. 22, 1944. A.B., Xavier U., 1935; LL.B., U. Cin., 1938. Bar: Ohio 1938. Asst. gen. counsel U.S. High Commr., Germany, 1949-50; dep. U.S. mem. Validation Bd. for German Dollar Bonds, 1953-56; asst. legal adviser European affairs Dept. State, 1956-62, prin. dep. legal adviser, 1962-67; mem. with personal rank of ambassador UN Internat. Law Commn., 1967-77, 1st v.p. commn., 1970, pres. commn., 1972-73, spl. rapporteur for internat. rivers, 1974-78; chmn. Sec. State's Adv. Com. Pvt. Internat. Law, 1964-78; head U.S. del. Conf. Uniform Internat. Sales Law, 1964, The Hague Conf. Pvt. Internat. Law, 1964, 68, 76, conf. on Enforcement Fgn. Judgements, 1966, UN Conf. on Law of Treaties, 1968-69, Inter-Am. Conf. on Human Rights, 1969, UN Conf. on State Succession; pres. Washington Conf. Internat. Wills, 1973; sr. adviser, v.p., mem. exec. com. Am. Soc. Internat. Law, 1978-81; Mem. governing council Internat. Inst. for Unification of Pvt. Law, 1968—. Served to maj. AUS, 1942-46; ETO. Recipient Carr medal State Dept., 1978. Mem. Am. Acad. Polit. Sci., Am. Bar Assn., Fgn. Service Assn., Order of Coif. Democrat. Roman Catholic. Clubs: Landsdowne (London, Eng.); Annapolis Yacht. Home: 167 Friar Tuck Hill Sherwood Forest MD 21405

KEARNS, DAVID TODD, duplicating machine mfg. co. exec.; b. Rochester, N.Y., Aug. 11, 1930; s. Wilfred M. and Margaret May (Todd) K.; m. Shirley Virginia Cox, June 1954; children—Katherine, Elizabeth, Anne, Susan, David Todd, Andrew. B.S., U. Rochester, 1952. With IBM Corp., 1954-71, v.p. mktg. ops., data processing div., until 1971; with Xerox Corp., Stamford, Conn., 1971—, group v.p. for info. systems, 1972-75; group v.p. charge Rank Xerox and Fuji Xerox, 1975-77, exec. v.p. internat. ops., 1977, pres., chief exec. officer, 1977—, also dir.; dir. Rank Xerox Ltd., Time Inc., Fuji Xerox.; mem. Pres.'s Commn. on Exec. Exchange; mem. adv. council Grad. Sch. Bus., Stanford U. Bd. visitors Grad. Sch. Bus., Duke U.; chmn. bd. trustees U. Rochester; trustee Stamford Hosp., Inst. Aerobics Research; chmn. nat. bd. dirs. Jr. Achievement; bd. dirs. Nat. Urban League, Nat. Action Council for Minority Engrs. Served with USNR, 1952-54. Address: Xerox Corp Stamford CT 06904

KEARNS, FRANCIS EMNER, bishop; b. Bentleyville, Pa., Dec. 9, 1905; s. George Verlinda and Jennie Mae (McCleary) K.; m. Alice Margaret Thompson, Sept. 1, 1933; children—Rollin Thompson, Margaret (Mrs. Richard E. Baldwin), Francis Emner II. A.B., Ohio Wesleyan U., 1927, D.D., 1954; S.T.B., Boston U. Sch. Theology, 1930; postgrad., U. Berlin, Germany, U. Edinburgh, Scotland, 1930-31; Ph.D., U. Pitts., 1939; LL.D., Mt. Union Coll., 1965; L.H.D., Ohio No. U., 1965; Pd.D., Baldwin-Wallace Coll., 1966. Ordained to ministry Meth. Ch., 1931; pastor, Dravosburg, Pa., 1931-32; asso. pastor Christ Meth. Ch., Pitts., 1932-35, Ben Avon Meth. Ch., 1935-40, Asbury Meth. Ch., Uniontown, Pa., 1940-45, Wauwatosa (Wis.) Meth. Ch., 1945-64; bishop United Meth. Ch., 1964—; Mem. gen. bd. evangelism, 1965-68, vice chmn. gen. bd. edn., 1968-72, chmn. div. curriculum resources, 1968-72, mem. program council, 1968-72; mem. Meth. Corp., 1968-72; mem. gen. assembly Nat. Council Chs.; pres. Ohio Council Chs., 1969-71; mem. gen. bd. Global Ministries of United Meth. Ch., 1972-76, vice-chmn. div. health and welfare ministries, 1972-76; mem. gen. bd. Ch. and Soc. of United Meth. Ch., 1972-76; chmn. Meth. Interbd. Com. on Christian Vocations, 1964-68, Faith and Order Commn., Ohio Council Chs., 1965-69; mem. Meth. Interbd. Commn. on Town and Country, 1964-68, North Central Jurisdictional Council, 1972-76. Author: The Church is Mine, 1962; Contbr. articles profl. jours. Trustee Baldwin-Wallace Coll., Mt. Union Coll., Ohio No. U., Ohio Wesleyan U., Meth. Theol. Sch. in Ohio, Otterbein Coll., United Theol. Sem. Mem. Phi Beta Kappa. Clubs: Mason (33 deg.), Rotarian. Home: 290 Cotswold Dr Delaware OH 43015 *In early life I had an experience of Christ. I have sought to be a faithful servant of his. This has enabled me to set high goals and to give myself wholeheartedly to their realization. The central motivation for my ministry has been love and concern for persons kindled by the love and compassion of Christ.*

KEARNS, HENRY, international finance and business consultant; b. Salt Lake City, Apr. 30, 1911; s. Henry A. and Mary (Orilla) K.; m. Marjorie Harriett Prescott, Aug. 30, 1938; children: Patricia Kearns Hitchcock, Henry Timothy, Michael and Mary Kearns Rohe (twins). Student, U. Utah Sch. Engring., 1929-31; grad., Internat. Corr. Schs., 1935; D.Bus. Adminstrn. (hon.), Woodbury Coll., 1960, D.Econs., Chung Aug U., Seoul, Korea, 1971. Salesman, Loesch & Osborne Motor Co., Pasadena, Calif., 1933-34; service sta. salesman Shell Oil Co., 1934-35; new car salesman Uptown Chevrolet Co., Pasadena, 1935-37, new car sales mgr., 1937-38, gen. sales mgr., 1938-39; partner David H. Lane Chevrolet Co., Pasadena, 1939-41; organizer, v.p., gen. mgr. Victory Mfg. Co., Los Angeles, 1942-43, pres., gen. mgr., 1943-46, established plastic devel. sect., 1943-47; asst. sec. internat. affairs U.S. Dept. Commerce, 1957-60, 60-69; now cons. internat. trade and finance; owner Kearns Car Rental, Orange Oaks Ranch; pres. San Gabriel Valley Motors, Rio Hondo Devel. Co., Policyholders Ins., Co., Sharder Water Co., Kearns Internat., Am. Capital Corp.; v.p., dir. Pike Corp. Am., 1966-67; pres., chmn. Export Import Bank U.S., 1969-73; pres. Kearns Internat., 1973-75, chmn., 1975—; pres. Fin. Services Corp., Panama, 1975—; pres. Nat. Sci. Engring. Co., 1966-67; adviser to bd. dirs. Philippine Investment Mgmt. Inc., Manila, 1964-66; dir., chmn. bd., chmn. adv. bd. Am. Asian Bank, San Francisco, 1974-79, chmn., 1979—; dir. FMC Corp., Am. Internat. Group, Inc., Washington Fin. Center, 1977-78; mem. adv. council Brazil Inter Part, 1980—; mem. Nat. Adv. Com. on Internat. Monetary and Fiscal Policy, 1969-73. Vice pres., dir. C. of C. U.S.; pres. Alhambra C. of C.; mem. nat. council cons. SBA; mem. spl. Pasadena War Meml. Com.; chmn. Pasadena Freedom Train Com.; exec. bd., com. for Young Men in Govt.; vice chmn. Task Force Intelligence Activities, Hoover Commn., 1965-66; Republican central committeeman Los Angeles County; pres. Pasadena Rep. Club, Pasadena Rep. Assembly; chmn. Eisenhower-Nixon campaign, So. Calif., 1956; mem. exec. com. Calif. Rep. Central Com.; vice-chmn. Rep. Nat. Finance Com.; trustee Pasadena Boys Club; Trustee Hazel Hurst Found. Blind; bd. dirs. Pasadena Civic Music Assn., Am. Soc. Internat. Execs., Internat. Execs. Service Corps; trustee Woodbury U., Los Angeles. Decorated knight grand cross Most Exalted Order of White Elephant, Thailand; grand officer de l'Ordre Nat., Republic Ivory Coast; comandador de Mesma Ordem Nacional do Cruxeiro do Sul, Brazil; Order Brillant Star, Republic of China; Diplomatic Order Merit, Korea; knight comdr. Ct. of Honor; recipient Disting. Service award City of Pasadena, 1943; capt. Robert Dollar award Nat. Fgn. Trade Council, 1971; award Phila. Fgn. Traders Assn., 1972; Disting. Service award San Francisco World Trade Club, 1973; Emeritus award U. Utah, 1976; Merit Honor award. Fellow AIM; mem. So. Calif. Sales Mgrs. Council (past pres.), Tournament of Roses Assn. (pres. 1966-67), Korean-Am. C. of C. (bd. dirs.), Nat. Indsl. Info. Com. Clubs: Masons, San Francisco Golf, Bohemian (San Francisco); Stock Exchange of San Francisco (pres., dir.); Burning Tree (Washington); St. Francis Yacht. Home: 1960 Vallejo St San Francisco CA 94123 Office: 155 Sansome St San Francisco CA 94104 *Those who have learned to use the moments of life ordinarily wasted by the average person will rise above the masses. Each moment of life is so fleeting that it must be seized, wrung dry of opportunity, and filed for future reference.*

KEARNS, JAMES JOSEPH, artist; b. Scranton, Pa., Aug. 7, 1924; s. David Joseph and Ann Mary (Keller) K.; m. Betty Ione Hough, June 19, 1948; children: David, Diane, Mark, Aaron, Lisa. B.F.A., Sch. Art Inst. Chgo., 1950. Instr. Sch. Visual Arts, N.Y.C., 1960—, Skowhegan (Maine) Sch. Painting, summers 1961-64. Illustrator: Can These Bones Live (E. Dahlberg), 1962, The Heart of Beethoven (S. Rodman), 1969; One-man shows include, Grippi Gallery, N.Y.C., 1956, 57, 60, 62, 68, Bloomfield (N.J.) Coll., 1967, 72, Sculpture Center, N.Y.C., 1973, Caldwell (N.J.) Coll., 1976, Trenton (N.J.) State Mus., 1984, group shows include, Whitney Mus. Am. Art, 1959, 60, 61, 80, Am. Fedn. Art, Art Inst. Chgo., 1979, traveling exhbns., Pa. Acad. Fine Arts, Phila., 1964, 65, Butler Inst. Am. Art, Youngstown, Ohio, 1964, Monmouth (N.J.) Mus., 1969, Squibb Gallery, Princeton, N.J., 1974, sculpture, Schenectady Mus., 1976, 35th Audubon Artists, N.Y.C., 1977, Whitney Mus. Am. Art, N.Y.C., 1980; represented in permanent collections, Mus. Modern Art, N.Y.C., Whitney Mus. Am. Art, Newark Mus. Art, Montclair (N.J.) Mus., Topeka Pub. Library, Smithsonian Nat. Collection Fine Arts, Washington, Hirshhorn Mus., Washington, also numerous pvt. collections. Served with U.S. Army, 1943-46. Nat. Inst. Arts and Letters grantee, 1959.

KEARNS, JANET CATHERINE, mfg. co. sec.; b. Chgo., Oct. 29, 1940; d. Casimir J. and Eleanor (Galus) Kubik; m. Edward P. Kearns, May 4, 1975. Grad., Madonna High Sch., 1958. Legal sec. Seyfarth, Shaw, Fairweather & Geraldson, Chgo., 1960-66; sec. to pres. Bowey's, Inc., Chgo., 1966-69, Sealy, Inc., 1969—, corp. sec., 1977—. Democrat. Roman Catholic. Office: 525 W Monroe St 21st Floor Chicago IL 60606

KEARNS, JEROME BARTON, banker; b. Ft. Wayne, Ind., Apr. 28, 1939; s. Bernard T. and Dolores Ann (Krouse) K.; m. Judith L. Christie, Aug. 25, 1962; children—Margaret Christie, Sean Barton, Ann Maureen. B.S. in Finance, U. Notre Dame, 1961. Credit analyst to sr. credit analyst Nat. Bank Detroit, 1961-64; asst. v.p. comml. loans St. Joseph Bank & Trust Co., South Bend, Ind., 1964-65, v.p., 1965-68, sr. v.p., 1968-70, exec. v.p., 1970-72, pres., 1972-74, vice chmn. bd., 1974-75; pres., owner Edmore, Inc. (distbr. apparel and footwear), 1975-80; pres., dir. Am. Nat. Bank & Trust Co., South Bend, 1980-83; pres. Capital Credit Corp.; dir. Sun Metal Products, Inc., Warsaw, Ind. Adv. council Ind. Small Bus. Adminstrn., 1969. Div. chmn. United Way, 1971, group chmn., 1972, campaign v.p., 1973, gen. chmn., 1974; mem. Mid-Am. regional task force United Way Am., 1973—; Bd. dirs. Cath. Social Service, 1968—, pres., 1969; bd. dirs. Citizens for Decent Lit., Model Neighborhood Planning Agy., Urban Coalition St. Joseph County, Urban League St. Joseph County, United Way St. Joseph County, Goodwill Industries of Michiana. Recipient Commendation and Recognition award Gov. Ind., 1975; named Outstanding Young Man South Bend Jr. C. of C., 1974. Mem. No. Ind. Group Robert Morris Assos. (past dir.), South Bend-Mishawaka Area C. of C. (dir., mem. exec. com.), Nat. Alliance Businessmen (dir.), Nat. Assn. Accountants (past dir.), Ind. Assn. Credit Mgmt., Am., Ind. bankers' assns. Clubs: Notre Dame of St. Joe Valley (past pres., dir.), South Bend Country, Indiana, Knollwood Country (South Bend). Home: 54387 Old Bedford Terr Mishawaka IN 46544

KEARNS, WILLIAM MICHAEL, JR., investment banker; b. Orange, N.J., June 26, 1935; s. William Michael and Doris Mae (Hodgkinson) K.; m. Patricia Anne Wright, Aug. 17, 1957; children: William Michael III, Susan Elizabeth, Kathleen Anne, Michael Patrick, Elizabeth Anne. A.B., U. Maine, 1957; postgrad., Boston Coll. Law Sch., 1957-58; A.M., NYU, 1960; student, Grad. Sch. Bus. Adminstrn., 1960-64. With Chase Manhattan Bank, 1958-59; security analyst Hayden, Stone & Co., Inc., N.Y.C., 1960-62; asso. instl. sales and syndicate dept. Kuhn, Loeb & Co., N.Y.C., 1962-64, asst. v.p., 1964-66, v.p., 1966-68, sales mgr., 1968-69, gen. partner, 1970-77; mng. dir. Lehman Bros. Kuhn Loeb Inc., 1977-84, Lehman Bros., Shearson Lehman/Am. Express Inc., N.Y.C., 1984—; chmn. fin. com., dir. SRI Corp.; dir. N.J. Realty Co., Gibson Greetings, Inc.; mem. faculty Fairleigh Dickinson U. Coll. Bus. Adminstr., 1959-68; instr. security analysis N.Y. Inst. Finance, 1961-67; adj. prof. Grad. Sch. Bus. Adminstrn., N.Y. U., 1971-72. Trustee Drumthwacket Found., Inc., Morris Mus. Arts and Sci., 1968—, Rider Coll., 1981—, Morristown-Beard Sch., Tri-County Scholarship Fund; mem. N.J. Republican Fin. Com. Served with USMCR, 1955-61. Mem. Investment Assn. N.Y., Nat. Assn. Security Dealers (corp. fin. com. 1976-80), Securities Industry Assn. (minority capital com. 1978—, exec. com. N.Y. dist. 1970—, vice chmn. 1973, chmn. 1974—), New Eng. Soc., Knights of Malta, Beta Theta Pi, Kappa Beta Phi, Kappa Phi Kappa. Roman Catholic. Clubs: Down Town Assn., University (trustee 1978-81), Bond, Economic (N.Y.C.); Morris County Golf (Convent Station, N.J.) (gov. 1976-82, treas. 1978-82); Skytop (Pa.); Monday, Twin Oaks (Morristown). Home: Village Rd New Vernon NJ 07976 Office: 55 Water St New York NY 10041

KEARSE, AMALYA LYLE, judge; b. Vauxhall, N.J., June 11, 1937; d. Robert Freeman and Myra Lyle (Smith) K. B.A., Wellesley Coll., 1959; J.D. cum laude, U. Mich., 1962. Bar: N.Y. State 1963, U.S. Supreme Ct. 1967. Assc. firm Hughes Hubbard & Reed, N.Y.C., 1962-69, partner, 1969-79; judge U.S. Ct. of Appeals, 2d Circuit, 1979—; lectr. evidence N.Y. U. Law Sch., 1968-69. Author: Bridge Conventions Complete, 1975, 2nd edit., 1984, Bridge at Your Fingertips, 1980; translator, editor: Bridge Analysis, 1979; editor: Ofcl. Ency. of Bridge, 3d edit, 1976; Mem., Charles Goren Editorial Bd., 1974—. Bd. dirs. NAACP Legal Def. and Endl. Fund, 1977-79, Nat. Urban League, 1978-79; trustee N.Y.C. YWCA, 1976-79, Am. Contract Bridge League Nat. Laws Commn., 1975—; mem. Pres.'s Com. on Selection of Fed. Jud. Officers, 1977-78. Mem. Am. Law Inst., Assn. Bar City N.Y., Am. Bar Assn., Lawyers Com. for Civil Rights Under Law. Nat. Womens Pairs Bridge Champion, 1971, 72. Office: US Ct Appeals Foley Sq New York NY 10007

KEATING, CHARLES H., JR., construction company executive. Chmn., pres. Am. Continental Corp., Phoenix, Ariz. Office: Am Continetnal Corp 2735 E Camelback Rd Phoenix AZ 80516§

KEATING, CORNELIUS FRANCIS, record company executive; b. Boston, Aug. 3, 1925; s. Cornelius Francis and Mary (Grey) K.; children: Cecily, Gregory, David, Christopher, Elisabeth. A.B., Harvard U., 1947, LL.B., 1950. Bar: N.Y. 1951. Atty. Thayer & Gilbert, N.Y.C., 1951-53, Life Ins. Assn. Am., 1953-55, Columbia Records, 1955-57, gen. atty., 1957-58; gen. mgr. Columbia Record Club, 1958-60, v.p., gen. mgr., 1960-67; pres. CBS Direct Marketing Services (div. CBS), N.Y.C., 1967-70, Columbia House div., 1970-79, CBS/Columbia Group, 1979-80; sr. v.p. CBS/Records Group, 1980—; dir. Nat. Bus. Lists. Trustee Rheedlen Found. Served to ensign USNR, 1943-46. Mem. 3d Class Mail Assn. (dir., chmn. bd. 1968-72), Direct Mktg. Assn., Harvard Law Sch. Assn. N.Y., Confrerie des Chevaliers du Tastevin, Commanderie de Bordeaux. Club: Harvard (New Canaan). Home: 1161 Ponus Ridge New Canaan CT 06840 Office: 1211 Ave of Americas New York NY 10036

KEATING, EUGENE KNEELAND, animal scientist; b. Liberal, Kans., Feb. 15, 1928; s. Arthur Hitch and Nilie Charlotte (Kneel) K.; m. Iris Louise Myers, Aug. 12, 1951; children—Denise Keating Schnagl, Kimberly Alan. B.S., Kans. State U., 1953, M.S., 1954; Ph.D., U. Ariz., 1964. Owner, mgr. ranch, Kans., 1954-57; instr., farm mgr. Midwestern U., Wichita Falls, Tex., 1957-60; research asst. U. Ariz., Tucson, 1960-64; prof. animal sci. Calif. State Poly. U., Pomona, 1964—, chmn. dept., 1971-78. Contbr. articles to profl. jours. Bd. dirs. Los Angeles County Jr. Livestock Fair, 1971—, chmn., 1975. Served with USAAF, 1946-49. Mem. Nat. Intercollegiate Rodeo Assn. (West Coast regional faculty dir. 1972-76), Am. Soc. Animal Sci., Am. Soc. Lab. Animal Sci., Brit. Soc. Animal Protection, Sigma Xi, Phi Lambda Upsilon, Gamma Sigma Delta, Alpha Zeta.; Fellow Am. Inst. Chemists. Republican. Presbyterian. Clubs: Block and Bridle, Ind. Order Foresters. Home: 149 Loretto Ct Claremont CA 91711 Office: 3801 Temple Ave W Pomona CA 91768

KEATING, LOUIS CLARK, language educator; b. Phila., Aug. 20, 1907; s. Louis Alcloma and Blanche Augusta (DeYoung) K.; m. Lucille Elizabeth Tate, July 23, 1936; children: Richard Clark, Geoffrey Tate, Anne Elizabeth. A.B., Colgate U., 1928; A.M., Harvard U., 1930, Ph.D., 1934; postgrad., Sorbonne, 1932-33, Middlebury Spanish Sch., summers 1928, 29, Heidelberg U., summer 1931, Centro de Estudios Historicos, summer 1933. Saltonstall travelling scholar Harvard U., 1932-33; instr. Romance langs. Colgate U., 1928-29; asst. prof. Spanish Macalester Coll., 1934-36; asst. prof. Romance langs. Monticello Coll., 1936-37; assoc. Romance langs. U. Ill., 1937-39; asst. prof. Romance langs. George Washington U., 1939-40, assoc. prof., 1940-46, prof., exec. officer dept. Romance langs., 1946-57; vis. prof. U. Tenn., summer 1947; resident dean U. Md. Grad. Fgn. Study Center, Paris, 1949-50; head dept. Romance langs. U. Cin., 1957-60; edn. adviser USOM, Peru, 1960-62; prof. Romance langs. U. Ky., Lexington, 1962—, chmn. dept. modern fgn. langs., 1963-66; vis. prof. U. Calgary, Alta., Can., 1969-70; staff Chapman Coll. World Campus Afloat, spring 1967, fall 1974. Author: Studies on the Literary Salon in France, 1550- 1615, 1941, Critic of Civilization, Georges Duhamel, 1965, Andre Maurois, 1969, Du Bellay, 1971, Etienne Pasquier, 1972, Audubon, The Kentucky Years, 1976; articles, revs. in lang. jours.; also translator. Mem. Arlington County (Va.) Sch. Bd., 1953-57, chmn. bd., 1956-57. Served to capt., Signal Corps AUS, 1943-46. Decorated officier d'Academie, France). Mem. AAUP, MLA, Am. Assn. Tchrs. French, Fed. Schoolmens Club, Phi Beta Kappa. Presbyn. Home: 608 Raintree Rd Lexington KY 40502

KEATING, LOUIS JEREMIAH, lawyer; b. Chgo., Jan. 1, 1930; s. Louis Joseph and Catherine Rita (Dowd) K.; m Mary B. English, June 30, 1956; children: Moira, Celeste, Brian, Thomas, Christopher. J.D., DePaul U., 1952. Bar: Ill. 1952. Assoc. Kirkland & Ellis, Chgo., 1954-62, ptnr., 1954-62; dir. Peoria Jour. Star, Inc., 1983; asst. prof. Northwestern U., fall 1977. Served to lt. j.g. USN, 1952-54. Mem. Chgo. Bar Assn., Ill. State Bar Assn., ABA, Inter-Am. Bar Assn., Phi Gamma Mu. Club: Flossmoor Country.

KEATING, STEPHEN FLAHERTY, retired business executive; b. Graceville, Minn., May 6, 1918; s. Luke J. and Blanche (Flaherty) K.; m. Mary E. Davis, Dec. 14, 1945; children: Stephen, Elizabeth, Thomas, Mary. B.S., U. Minn., 1940, J.D., 1942. Bar: Minn. 1942. Spl. agt. FBI, Norfolk, Va., Detroit, 1942-43; asso. Otis, Faricy & Burger, St. Paul, 1946-48; mgr. mil. contracts, aero div. Mpls. Honeywell Regulator Co., 1948-54, divisional v.p., 1954-56, v.p., 1956-61, exec. v.p., 1961-65; pres. Honeywell Inc., 1965-74, chmn., 1974-78, vice-chmn., 1978-80, also dir.; chmn. exec. com., dir. Toro Co.; dir. Gen. Mills, Inc., PPG Industries, Donaldson Co., Econs. Lab., Inco Ltd. Mem. Minn. State Arts Bd.; 1st v.p. Minn. Landscape Arboretum Found. Served as air combat intelligence officer USNR, 1943- 46. Mem. Order of Coif. Clubs: Minneapolis, Woodhill. Home: 688 Hillside Dr Wayzata MN 55391 Office: 1930 Midwest Plaza Bldg Minneapolis MN 55402

KEATING, THOMAS ARTHUR, football player; b. Chgo., Sept. 2, 1942; s. James William and Margret (Touhy) K. B.A., U. Mich., 1965. Player with Buffalo Bills, 1964-65; player Oakland (Calif.) Raiders, 1966-72, player rep., 1967-73; player Pitts. Steelers, 1973-74, Kansas City Chiefs, 1974—. Named All A.F.L., 1966, 1967, 1969, All Pro Nat. Football League, 1970. Mem. Nat. Football League Players Assn. (mem. exec. com., mem. negotiating com., v.p.). Home: 706 Pacific St Alameda CA 94501 Office: Kansas City Chiefs Kansas City MO

KEATING, WILLIAM CLEVELAND, JR., psychiatrist, county official; b. Sacramento, May 17, 1920; s. William Cleveland and Vern (Francis) K.; m. Verna E. Carlson, May 17, 1942; children: Karen, William Cleveland III, Robert L. Student, U. Calif. at Berkeley, 1938-39; B.S., St. Mary's Coll., Moraga, 1942; M.D., Tulane U., 1947; certificate, Menninger Found. Sch. Psychiat. Hosp. Adminstrn., 1957. Intern, resident surgeon Sacramento County Hosp., 1947-49; practice medicine specializing in psychiatry, Sonoma, Calif., 1949-60, Vacaville, Calif., 1960—; ward physician, dir. outpatient and preadmission dept. Sonoma State Hosp., 1949-56, acting asst. supt., then asst. supt., 1957-60; supt. Calif. Med. Facility, 1960-66; asst. dep. dir. Calif. Dept. Mental Hygiene, 1966-71, dep. dir., 1971-73; program chief Mental Disabilities program, 1973-74; asst. dep. dir. Calif. Dept. Health, 1974-77; program chief Ventura County (Calif.) Mental Health Services, Ventura, 1977—. Served with AUS, 1942-44; to capt. M.C., 1952-54. Home: 854 Via Ondulando Ventura CA 93003 Office: 300 N Hillmont Ventura CA 93003

KEATING, WILLIAM JOHN, newspaper executive, former congressman; b. Cin., Mar. 30, 1927; s. Charles H. and Adele (Kipp) K.; m. Nancy Nenninger, Sept. 22, 1951; children: Nancy C. Keating Roe, William J., Michael K., Daniel N., Susan M. Keating Lame, Thomas J., John S. B.B.A., U. Cin., 1950, J.D., 1950, LL.D., 1975. Bar: Ohio 1950. Asst. atty. gen. Ohio, 1957-58; judge Cin. Mcpl. Ct., 1958-65, presiding judge, 1962-63; judge Ct. Common Pleas, Hamilton County, Ohio, 1965-67; mem. Cin. City Council, 1967-70; majority leader, chmn. finance com.; mem. 92d-93d congresses from Ohio, 1970-74; pres., pub. Cin. Enquirer, Inc., 1973-84; pres. Gannett Central Newspaper Group, 1979-84; sr. v.p., pres. newspaper div. Gannett Co., Inc., Washington, 1984—; dir. Fifth Third Bank, AP. Bd. dirs. Kenton County Airport. Served with USNR, World War II. Mem. Ohio Newspaper Assn., Newspaper Advt. Bur., Greater Cin. C. of C. (dir., chmn. 1981), Am. Newspaper Pubs. Assn., Am. Soc. Newspaper Editors, Former Mems. Congress, Am. Legion, Sigma Chi. Office: PO Box 7850 Washington DC 20044

KEATINGE, RICHARD HARTE, lawyer; b. San Francisco, Dec. 4, 1919; m. Betty West, Apr. 20, 1944; children: Richard West, Daniel Wilson, Nancy Elizabeth (Mrs. Michael Tronick). A.B. with honors, U. Calif., Berkeley, 1939; M.A., Harvard U., 1941; J.D., Georgetown U., 1944. Bar: D.C. 1944, N.Y. 1945, Calif. 1947, U.S. Supreme Ct. 1964. Sr. economist, sr. indsl. specialist WPB, Washington, 1941-44; practice law, N.Y.C., 1944-45, Washington, 1945-47, Los Angeles, 1947—; sr. ptnr. Keatinge, Pastor & Mintz (and predecessor firms), 1948-79, Reavis & McGrath, 1979—; spl. asst. atty. gen., State of Calif., 1964-68; public mem. Adminstrv. Conf. of U.S., 1968-74. Mem.: Georgetown Law Jour, 1943-44. Mem. Calif. Law Revision Commn., 1961-68, chmn., 1965-67; trustee Coro Found., 1965-73; v.p. U. Calif. Berkeley Found., 1978—, chmn. bd. trustees, 1983—. Fellow (life) Am. Bar Found.; mem. ABA (bd. govs. 1978-79, mem. ho. of dels. 1974-82, 82—, mem. council 1961-64, 65-69, 74-78, 82—, chmn. adminstrv. law sect. 1967-68, mem. standing com. on resolutions 1973-74, chmn. com. on sales, exchanges and basis taxation sect. 1963-65, mem. council econs. of law practice sect. 1974-75, mem. commn. on law and economy 1976-78, vice chmn. 1977-78, mem. spl. com. on housing and urban devel. law 1968-73, vice chmn. adv. commn. on housing and urban growth 1974-77, nat. sec. Jr. Bar Conf. 1949-50), State Bar Calif. (del. conf. of dels. 1966-67, 77—, mem. exec. com. public law sect. 1976-78), Los Angeles County Bar Assn. (chmn. taxation sect. 1966-67, mem. fair jud. election practices com. 1978-79, mem. exec. com. law office mgmt. sect. 1977—, mem. housing and urban devel. law com. 1971-80, mem. arbitration com. 1974—, mem. new quarters com. 1979-80), Assn. Bus. Trial Lawyers (bd. govs. 1974-79, pres. 1978-79), Inter-Am. Bar Assn., Internat. Bar Assn., Am. Judicature Soc., Am. Law Inst., Am. Arbitration Assn. (nat. panel of arbitrators 1950—), Com. to Maintain Diversity Jurisdiction, Lawyers Club Los Angeles, Phi Beta Kappa. Home: 1141 S Orange Grove Blvd Pasadena CA 91105 Office: 700 S Flower St 6th Fl Los Angeles CA 90017

KEATLEY, ROBERT LELAND, journalist, newspaper publisher; b. Astoria, Oreg., Feb. 14, 1935; s. R.L. and Eva S. (Poysky) K.; 1 son, Eric Leland.; m. Catharine De Williams; 1 dau., Heather Eva Margaret. B.A., U. Wash., 1956; M.A., Stanford U., 1959. Mem. staff Wall St. Jour., 1959—, Asian bur. chief, Hong Kong, 1964-68, diplomatic corr., Washington, 1968-77, fgn. editor, N.Y.C., 1978; editor Asian Wall St. Jour., Hong Kong, 1979—, pub., 1983—; columnist Wall St. Jour., 1981—. Co-author: China—Behind the Mask, 1973. Served as officer USNR, 1956-58. Clubs: Ladies Recreation, Hong Kong (Hong Kong). Address: 22 Old Peak Rd Hong Kong

KEATON, DIANE, actress; b. Calif. Student, Neighborhood Playhouse, N.Y.C., 1968. Appeared on: New York stage in Hair, 1968, Play It Again Sam, 1971, The Primary English Class, 1976; appeared in: numerous films, including Lovers and Other Strangers, 1970, Play It Again Sam, 1972, The Godfather, 1972, Sleeper, 1973, The Godfather Part 2, 1974, Love and Death, 1975, I Will-I Will-For Now, 1975, Harry and Walter Go To New York, 1976, Annie Hall, 1977 (Acad. award, Brit. Acad. award Best Actress, N.Y. Film Critics Circle award, Nat. Soc. Film Critics award), Looking for Mr. Goodbar, 1977, Interiors, 1978, Manhattan, 1979, Reds, 1981, Shoot the Moon, 1982; accomplished artist and singer.; Author: book of photographs Reservations, 1980; editor: (with Marvin Heiferman) Still Life, 1983. Recipient Golden Globe award, 1978. Office: care Stan Kamen William Morris Agy 1350 Ave of Americas New York NY 10019 *

KEATON, HARRY JOSEPH, lawyer; b. Prague, Czechoslovakia, June 8, 1925; came to U.S., 1947, naturalized, 1953; s. Fred G. and Nina (Ordner) K.; m. Minto E. Hannus, Dec. 21, 1952; children—Elizabeth, Deborah, Janette, Juliana. Student, San Francisco City Coll., 1947-48; B.A. with highest honors, U. Calif., Berkeley, 1950, J.D., 1953. Bar: Calif. bar 1954, U.S. Supreme Ct. bar 1963. Law clk. and atty. Dept. Justice, Washington; spl. asst. to U.S. Atty. for D.C., 1953-55; asso. firm Loeb & Loeb, Los Angeles, 1955-60, partner, 1960-66; partner, head dept. labor law firm Rutan & Tucker, Los Angeles And Santa Ana, Calif., 1966-72, Mitchell, Silberberg & Knupp, Los Angeles, 1972—; lectr. U. So. Calif. Law Center, 1962-66; mem. adv. bd. 21st Region, NLRB; nat. panelist Am. Arbitration Assn. Contbr. articles to profl. jours.; revising editor: Calif. Law Rev, 1952-53. Mem. Calif. Republican Central Com., 1961-74, mem. exec. com., chmn. labor com., 1961-64, chmn. atty.'s com., 1973-74; pres. Young Reps. of Calif., 1962-63; v.p. Los Angeles County, Calif. Rep. Assembly, 1964; exec. v.p. Calif. Rep. League, 1966-68, bd. dirs., 1964—; pres. Pacific S.W. regional bd. Anti-Defamation League, 1975-77, chmn. exec. com., 1973-75, nat. commr., 1976—, chmn. nat. com. on discrimination, 1976—, mem. nat. exec. com., 1980—; mem. San Francisco Regional panel White House Fellowships Program, 1976-80; vice chmn. community relations com. Jewish Fedn. Council Greater Los Angeles, 1978—; chmn. Commn. on Jewish Security, 1980—. Fellow Am. Bar Found.; mem. Los Angeles County Bar Assn. (trustee 1969-71, chmn. labor law com. 1974-75), Calif. Bar Assn., Am. Bar Assn. (chmn. com. on insts. and meetings 1980—, chmn. subcom. com. on developing labor law sect. labor law 1975-80), Am. Judicature Soc., Indsl. Relations Research Assn., Order of Coif, Phi Beta Kappa, Phi Alpha Delta. Clubs: Chancery, Mountain Gate Tennis. Office: 1800 Century Park E Los Angeles CA 90067

KEATS, DONALD HOWARD, composer, educator; b. N.Y.C., May 27, 1929; s. Bernard and Lillian (Katz) K.; m. Eleanor Steinholz, Dec. 13, 1953; children: Jeremy, Jennifer, Jeffrey, Jocelyn. Mus.B., Yale U., 1949; M.A., Columbia U., 1951; Ph.D., U. Minn., 1962; Fulbright scholar, Staatliche Hochschule fur Musik, Hamburg, Germany, 1954-56. Teaching fellow Yale U. Sch. Music, 1948-49; instr. music theory U.S. Naval Sch. Music, Washington, 1953-54; post music dir., Ft. Dix, N.J., 1956-57; faculty Antioch Coll., Yellow Springs, Ohio, 1957-76, prof., 1967-76, chmn. music dept., 1967-71; vis. prof. music U. Wash. Sch. Music, 1969-70, Lamont Sch. Music, U. Denver, 1975-76, prof. music, composer-in-residence, 1976—, Phipps Prof. in the humanities, 1982-85. Pianist concerts of own music, London, 1973, Tel Aviv, Jerusalem, N.Y.C., 1975, Denver, 1984; Composer: Divertimento For Winds and Strings, 1949, The Naming of Cats, 1951, The Hollow Men, 1952, String Quartet 1, 1952, Concert Piece for Orchestra, 1952, Variations for Piano, 1955, First Symphony, 1957, Piano Sonata, 1961, An Elegiac Symphony, 1962, Anyone Lived in a Pretty How Town, 1965; ballet New Work, 1966; Polarities for Violin and Piano, 1968-70, String Quartet 2, 1969, A Love Triptych, 1970, Dialogue for Piano and Winds, 1973, Diptych for Cello and Piano, 1975, Upon the Intimation of Love's Mortality, 1975, Branchings for Orch, 1976, Epithalamium for Violin, Cello and Piano, 1977, Four Puerto Rican Love Songs: Tierras del Alma for soprano, flute and guitar, 1978, Musica Instrumentalis I for chamber group, 1980. Served with U.S. Army, 1952-54. Recipient ASCAP awards, 1964—; awards from Ford, Danforth and Lilly founds., Nat. Endowment for Arts; winner Rockefeller Found. Symphonic Competitions, 1965, 66; Guggenheim fellow, Europe, 1964-65, 72-73; Nat. Endowment for Arts grantee, fellow, 1975. Mem. ASCAP, Coll. Music Soc., Am. Music Center, Am. Soc. Univ. Composers., Phi Beta Kappa. Home: 9261 E Berry Ave Englewood CO 80111 Office: Lamont Sch Music U Denver Denver CO 80208

KEATS, HAROLD ALAN, corp. exec.; b. Bridgeport, Conn., Oct. 25, 1913; s. Abraham and Jeannette (Boges) C.; m. Charleen Turner, Dec. 19, 1953; children—Candace, Harold Alan. Student, University Sch., Bridgeport, Conn., 1928-31, Washington U., 1932-33. Owner Harold A. Keats Constrn. Co., Fort Lauderdale, 1936, Keats S.S. & Tourist Agy.; pres. Indian Citrus Groves, Inc., Fla. Sunshine Groves, Inc., Harold A. Keats Investment Co., Inc., Englewood Mailing Lists, Inc.; partner Keats, Allen & Keats; pres. Rocking K Ranch Inc., Gulf & Eastern Devel. Corp.; Nat. vice comdr. Amvets, 1947, nat. comdr., 1948-49; liaison officer to White House, 1949—; counselor Amvets Nat. Service Found., 1949—; U.S. commr. Am. Battle Monuments Commn., 1950-53; hon. consul Republic of Honduras in Ft. Lauderdale, 1980—. Past nat. chmn. Vets. Democratic com.; dir. vets. div. Nat. Dem. Com. Served with USNR, 1942-45, 51; commd. lt., intelligence Pub. Information, 1949. Mem. Mil. Order World Wars, Past Nat. Comdrs. Orgn. (nat. chmn.), Am. Yachtsmen's Assn. (nat. pres.), Charolais Cattlemen's Assn. Fla. (state pres.), Knights Round Table Assn. (pres.). Clubs: Mason (32 deg., Shriner), African Safari of Fla. (pres.), Safari Internat. (dir.). Home: 777 Bayshore Dr Ft Lauderdale FL 33304 Office: 512 Galleria Profl Bldg 915 Middle River Dr Fort Lauderdale FL 33304

KEATS, MARTIN MERRILL, dentist; b. Bklyn., Jan. 12, 1909; s. Samuel and Ida (Kaplan) K.; m. Judy Stein, Sept. 24, 1931; children: Andrew Terry, Ronald Stuart. Student, Colby Coll., 1924-26; D.M.D., Harvard, 1930. Pvt. practice dentistry, N.Y.C., 1930—, practice devoted to rehab. prosthesis. Served to capt. AUS, 1944-46. Fellow Acad. Gen. Dentistry; Mem. N.Y. Acad. Dentistry, Am. Acad. Periodontology, Am. Equilibration Soc., Am. Acad. Gnathologic Orthopedics, Am. Dental Assn., N.Y. State, First Dist. dental socs., Fedn. Dentaire Internationale, Am. Prosthodontic Soc., N.Y. Acad. Scis., Internat. Acad. Gnathology, North Eastern Gnathological Soc., Alpha Omega. Clubs: One Hundred, Harvard, Fenway. Home: 2 W Devonia Ave Mount Vernon NY 10552 Office: 18 E 48th St New York NY 10017

KEATS, THEODORE ELIOT, physician, educator; b. New Brunswick, N.J., June 26, 1924; m. Margaret E. McNamara, Aug. 27, 1949 (dec.); children—Matthew Mason, Ian Stuart B.; m. Patricia L. Hart, Mar. 30, 1974. B.S., Rutgers U., 1945; M.D., U. Pa., 1947. Diplomate: Am. Bd. Radiology (trustee). Intern U. Pa. Hosp., Phila., 1947-48; resident U. Mich. Hosp., Ann Arbor, 1948-51; instr. U. Calif. Sch. Medicine, San Francisco, 1953-54, asst. prof., 1954-56; asso. prof. U. Mo. Sch. Medicine, Columbia, 1956-59, prof. radiology, 1959-63; prof., chmn. dept. radiology U. Va. Sch. Medicine, Charlottesville, 1963—; vis. prof. Karolinska Hosp., Stockholm, 1963-64; mem. adv. council Greenbrier Clinic. Author: (with Lee B. Lusted) Atlas of Roentgenographic Measurement, 5th edit., 1983, An Atlas of Normal Roentgen Variants that May Simulate Disease, 1973, 3d edit., 1983, Self-Assessment of Current Knowledge in Diagnostic Radiology, 2d edit, 1980, (with Thomas H. Smith) An Atlas of Normal Developmental Roentgen Anatomy, 1978; editor-in-chief: Current Problems in Diagnostic Radiology, 1981; editor: Radiology for Emergency Physicians, 1983; asst. Am. editor: Skeletal Radiology; editorial bds.: Yearbook of Diagnostic Radiology. Served with AUS, 1943-47; to capt., M.C. AUS, 1951-53. Fellow Am. Coll. Radiology; mem. A.M.A., Am. Roentgen Ray Soc., Radiol. Soc. N.Am., Soc. Chmn. Acad. Radiology Depts., Assn. U. Radiologists, Soc. Pediatric Radiology, So. Med. Assn., Internat. Skeletal Soc., Phi Beta Kappa, Sigma Xi, Alpha Omega Alpha. Home: 421 Key West Dr Charlottesville VA 22901

KEAVENY, DENIS JAMES, food co. exec.; b. Bklyn., Apr. 22, 1946; s. James Michael and Catherine Theresa (Murphy) K.; m. Sharon M. Conwell, May 18, 1968; children—Glenn, Sean, Keri. B.B.A., Manhattan Coll., 1967. Sr. auditor Arthur Andersen & Co., N.Y.C., 1967-71; mgr. internat. auditing Hershey Foods Corp., Pa., 1971-75; comptroller Hershey Chocolate Co., 1975-79, v.p. fin. and adminstrn., 1979-81; v.p. fin., treas. Penn Dairies, Inc., Lancaster, Pa., 1981—. Mem. Fin. Execs. Inst. Home: 717 Hilltop Ln Hershey PA 17033 Office: 1801 Hempstead Rd PO Box 7007 Lancaster PA 17604

KEBABIAN, PAUL BLAKESLEE, librarian; b. Watch Hill, R.I., July 24, 1917; s. John Couzu and Edith Jennie (Blakeslee) K.; m. Justine Richardson, Nov. 21, 1942; children: Jean Edith, Ann Ruth, Helen Jane. B.A., Yale U., 1938; B.S., Columbia U., 1948. Cataloger, supr. exchanges Yale U. Library, New Haven, 1939-42, 46-47; chief cataloger preparation div. N.Y. Pub. Library, 1949-61, 62-63; Ford Found. program specialist Library of U. Baghdad, Iraq, 1961-62; asso. dir. libraries U. Fla., Gainesville, 1963-66; dir. libraries U. Vt., Burlington, 1966-82; asso. prof. library sci. U. Fla., 1963-66; cons. in field. Author: American Woodworking Tools, 1978; co-editor, contbr.: Tools and Technologies—America's Wooden Age, 1979; contbr. articles to profl. jours. Served with USAAF, 1942-46. Mem. ALA, New Eng., Vt. library assns., Assn. Coll. and Research Libraries, Early Am. Industries Assn. (past pres., dir. 1970-82, editor 1982—), Vt. Hist. Soc. Democrat. Home: 11 Scotsdale Rd South Burlington VT 05401

KEBBLISH, JOHN BASIL, coal company executive; b. Gray, Pa., Jan. 14, 1925; s. Joseph and Catherine (Benya) K.; m. Ruth L. Mueller, Oct. 14, 1955; children: John J., Heather R. B.S. in Mining

Engring., Pa. State U., 1947, 1948. With Consol. Coal Co. (and subs. cos.), various locations, 1948-71, pres., Bluefield, W. Va., 1966-70, v.p., Pitts., 1970-71; exec. v.p. The Pittston Co., N.Y.C., 1971-73; pres., chief exec. officer Ashland Coal, Inc. (Ky.) (subs. Ashland Oil, Inc.), 1974—; v.p., exec. officer Ashland Oil, Inc., 1976—. Served with AUS, 1944-46. Home: 243 Bellefonte Circle Ashland KY 41101 Office: PO Box 6300 Huntington WV 25771

KECECIOGLU, DIMITRI BASIL, mechanical engineering educator; b. Istanbul, Turkey, Dec. 26, 1922; came to U.S., 1946, naturalized, 1956; s. Basil C. and Mary (Melayios) K.; m. Lorene June Legan, Dec. 22, 1951; children: Zoe Diana, John Dimitri. B.S., Robert Coll., Istanbul, 1942; M.S., Purdue U., 1948, Ph.D., 1953. Asst. instr. Purdue U., Lafayette, Ind., 1943-47, instr., 1947-52; engring. scientist in charge mech. research labs. Allis-Chalmers Mfg. Co., Milw., 1952-57, asst. to dir. mech. engring. industries group, 1957-60, cons. engr. industries group, 1960-63, dir., chmn. corp. reliability program, 1960-63; prof. aerospace and mech. engring. U. Ariz., Tucson, 1963—; reliability and maintainability engring. cons., Tucson, 1963—; dir. Reliability Engring. Inst., 1963—; reliability cons. Northrop Space Labs., Gen. Elec. Co., Center for Mgmt. and Indsl. Devel., Rotterdam, Netherlands, Delco Radio div. Gen. Motors Corp., Aerojet-Gen. Corp., Westinghouse Elec. Co., U.S. Army Mgmt. Engring. Tng. Agy.; Fulbright lectr. Nat. Tech. U., Athens, 1971-72. Author: Bibliography on Plasticity, 1950, Introduction to Probabilistic Design for Reliability, 1975, Manual of Product Assurance Films and Videotapes, 1980; contbr. over 100 articles to profl. jours. Recipient Presidency award Milw. Tech. Council, 1962; Automotive Industries Author award, 1963; Ralph E. Teetor Outstanding Engring. Educator award Soc. Automotive Engrs., 1977. Mem. ASME (chmn. Milw. sect. 1960), Soc. Mfg. Engrs., IEEE, Soc. Exptl. Stress Analysis (chmn. Milw. sect. 1957), Am. Soc. Engring. Edn., AAAS, Am. Soc. Quality Control (Reliability Edn. Advancement award 1980, Allen Chop award for outstanding contbns. to reliability 1981), Soc. Reliability Engrs. (pres. chpt. 1974-77), Hellenic Ops. Research Soc. Greece, Sigma Xi, Tau Beta Pi. Patentee in field. Home: 7340 N La Oesta Ave Tucson AZ 85704

KECK, JAMES COLLYER, physicist, educator; b. N.Y.C., June 11, 1924; s. Charles and Anne (Collyer) K.; m. Margaret Ramsey, Sept. 6, 1947; children—Robert Lyon, Patricia Anne. B.A., Cornell U., 1947, Ph.D., 1951. Research asst. Cornell U., 1951-52; sr. research fellow Calif. Inst. Tech., 1952-55; prin. scientist Avco-Everett Research Lab., Everett, Mass., 1955-65, dep. dir., 1960-64; Ford prof. engring. Mass. Inst. Tech., Cambridge, 1965—. Served with AUS, 1944-46. Fellow Am. Acad. Sci.; mem. Am. Phys. Soc., Combustion Inst., Phi Beta Kappa, Sigma Xi, Phi Kappa Phi. Research high energy photonuclear reactions, theory of chem. reaction rates, high temperature gas dynamics, combustion, air pollution, thermionics. Office: Mass Inst Tech Cambridge MA 02139

KECK, JAMES MOULTON, advertising and marketing executive, retired air force officer; b. Scranton, Pa., Sept. 4, 1921; s. Righter L. and Helen Louise (Walker) K.; m. Barbara Brown Fleck, June 2, 1943; children: Bonnilyn B., Thomas J., Allison S. B.S., U.S. Mil. Acad., 1943. Commd. 2d lt. USAAF, 1943; advanced through grades to lt. gen. USAF, 1972; pilot, ETO, 1943-45; dep. dir. ops. Office Dept. Chief Staff Plans and Ops., Hdqrs. USAF, 1970-71, dir. plans, 1971-72; comdr. 2d Air Force, Barksdale AFB, La., 1972-73, vice comdr. in chief SAC, Offutt AFB, Nebr., 1973-77, ret., 1977; sr. v.p. corporate affairs Bozell & Jacobs Internat., Omaha, 1977—. Chmn. bd. dirs. St. Joseph Hosp.; pres. Josslyn Art Mus., United Way Midlands; bd. dirs. Western Heritage Mus., Omaha Community Playhouse, Omaha Safety Council, YMCA; mem. Mid-Am. council Boy Scouts Am.; councillor AK-Sar-Ben; sr. warden St. Andrews Episc. Ch.; Republican candidate for U.S. Senate from Nebr., 1982. Decorated D.S.M., Legion of Merit with oak leaf cluster, D.F.C. with oak leaf cluster, Air medal with 3 oak leaf clusters. Mem. Air Force Assn., Order Daedalians, West Point Soc. Home: 911 S 113 St Omaha NE 68154 Office: Regency Circle Omaha NE 68114

KECK, LEANDER EARL, divinity school dean; b. Washburn, N.D., Mar. 3, 1928; s. Jacob S. and Elizabeth (Klein) K.; m. Janice Osborn, Sept. 7, 1956; children: Stephen Lee, David Alderson. B.A., Linfield Coll., McMinnville, Oreg., 1949, D.Lit. (hon.), 1980; B.D., Andover Newton Theol. Sch., Newton, Mass., 1953; Ph.D., Yale U., 1957; S.T.D. (hon.), Bethany Coll., W. Va., 1975, D.H.Lett., Atlantic Christian Coll., Wilson, N.C., 1980, D.D., Tex. Christian U., 1980. Ordained to ministry Christian Ch. (Disciples of Christ), 1952; instr. Wellesley Coll., 1957-59; from asst. prof. to prof. N.T. Vanderbult U. Div. Sch., Nashville, 1959-72; prof. N.T. Candler Sch. Theology, Emory U., Atlanta, 1972-79; vis. prof. Union Theol. Sem., Manila, spring 1971; Winkley prof. Bibl. theology, dean Yale U. Div. Sch., 1979—. Author: Taking The Bible Seriously, 1962, Mandate to Witness, 1964, A Future For the Historical Jesus, 1975, The Bible in the Pulpit, 1978, Paul and His Letters, 1979; editor numerous books; editorial council: Interpretation, 1976-82; editorial bd.: Quarterly Review, 1980—; contbr. articles, essays profl. publns. Research fellow Assn. Theol. Schs., 1964-65, 76. Mem. Soc. Bibl. Lit. (editor monograph series 1972-78), Assn. Theol. Schs. (exec. com. 1980-86), Studiorum Novi Testamenti Societas. Democrat. Office: 409 Prospect St New Haven CT 06510

KECK, ROBERT CLIFTON, lawyer; b. Sioux City, Iowa, May 20, 1914; s. Herbert Allen and Harriet (McCutchen) K.; m. Ruth P. Edwards, Nov. 2, 1940; children: Robert, Laura E. Simpson, Gloria E. Sauser. A.B., Ind. U., 1936; J.D., U. Mich., 1939; L.H.D., Nat. Coll. Edn., 1973. Bar: Ill. 1939. Since practiced in Chgo.; mem. firm Keck, Mahin & Cate, 1939—, partner, 1946—; sec., dir. Methode Electronics, Inc.; dir. First Ill. Corp., Union Spl. Corp., Schwinn Bicycle Co., Ill. Bank of Evanston. Chmn. bd. trustees Nat. Coll. Edn., 1955—; trustee Sears Roebuck Found., 1977-79. Served with USNR, 1943-45. Fellow Am. Coll. Trial Lawyers; mem. Am., Fed., Ill., Chgo. assns., Bar Assn. Seventh Fed. Circuit (past pres.), Phi Gamma Delta. Republican. Methodist. Clubs: Mason., Westmoreland Country (Wilmette); Executives, Economic, Chicago, Metropolitan (Chgo.); Biltmore Forest Golf (Asheville, N.C.); Glen View (Golf, Ill.). Home: 1043 Seneca Rd Wilmette IL 60091 Office: Sears Tower 83d Floor Chicago IL 60606

KECK, WILLIAM, architect; b. Watertown, Wis., Dec. 1, 1908; s. Fred George and Amalie (Henze) K.; m. Stella M. McLeish, Oct. 23, 1937; 1 dau., Margaret M. Student, Northwestern Coll., 1926-27; B.S., U. Ill., 1931. Draftsman, specifications writer, Chgo., 1931-42; site planner, specifications writer U.S. C.E., Chgo., 1942-43; partner George Fred Keck & William Keck (architects), Chgo., 1946—; Cons. regional office Housing and Urban Devel., also Ill. Housing Devel. Authority; dir. Hyde Park-Kenwood Community Conf., Chgo., 1953-55, mem. planning com., 1952—, Housing Code Modernization Met. Housing and Planning Council. Prin. works include Kunstadter House, Highland Park, Ill., 1953, Prairie Cts. Housing Project, Chgo., Blair House, Lake Bluff, Ill., 1958, Hirsch House, Highland Park, 1963, Child Care Center, Chgo., Harper Sq. Housing project, Chgo., 1970. Bd. dirs. Hyde Park Neighborhood Club, S.E. Chgo. Commn. Served as lt. USNR, 1943-46. Honored at 4th Ann. Conf. of Am. sect. Internat. Solar Energy Soc., 1979; recipient 1st Ill. medal in architecture U. Ill., 1980. Fellow AIA; mem. Alpha Rho Chi. Home: 5551 University Ave Chicago IL 60637 Office: 612 N Michigan Ave Chicago IL 60611

KEDDY, WAYNE RICHARD, hospital administrator; b. Moncton, N.B., Can., July 9, 1945; m. Daphne Keddy; children: Scott, Caroline, Matthew. B. Commerce, Acadia U. Dir. hosp. services North York Gen. Hosp., Toronto, Ont., Can., 1970-73; asst. exec. dir. Stratford Gen. Hosp., 1973-75; assoc. adminstr. Hamilton Gen. Hosp., Ont., 1975-77; assoc. exec. dir. McMaster U. Med. Centre, Hamilton, 1977-79; adminstr. McMaster div. Chedore-McMaster Hosp., Hamilton, 1979—; preceptor, lectr. M.B.A. program McMaster U., Hamilton, 1977—; surveyor Can. Council on Hosp. Accreditation, Ottawa, 1983—. Mem. Can. Coll. Health Service Execs., Am. Soc. Law and Medicine, Hamilton Med.-Legal Soc., Can. Hosp. Assn. (faculty 1973—), Ont. Hosp. Assn.-various subcoms. Mem. United Ch. of Canada. Lodge: Rotary. Office: McMaster Div Chedoke-McMaster Hosps MPO Box 2000 Hamilton ON Canada 18N 3Z5

KEE, HOWARD CLARK, religion educator; b. Beverly, N.J., July 28, 1920; s. Walter Leslie and Regina (Corcoran) K.; m. Janet Burrell, Dec. 15, 1951; children: Howard Clark III, Christopher Andrew, Sarah Leslie. A.B., Bryan (Tenn.) Coll., 1940; Th.M., Dallas Theol. Sem., 1944; postgrad., Am. Sch. Oriental Research, Jerusalem, 1949-50; Ph.D. (Two Bros. fellow), Yale, 1951. Instr. religion and classics U. Pa., 1951-53; from asst. prof. to prof. N.T. Drew U., 1953-68; Rufus Jones prof. history of religion, chmn. dept. history of religion Bryn Mawr (Pa.) Coll., 1968-77; William Goodwin Aurelio prof. Biblical studies, chmn. grad. div. religious studies Boston U., 1977—; vis. prof. religion Princeton U., 1954-55; mem. archaeol. teams at, Roman Jericho, 1950, Shechem, 1957, Mt. Gerizim, 1966, Pella, Jordan, 1967, Ashdod, Israel, 1968; chmn. Council on Grad. Studies in Religion. Author: Understanding the New Testament, 4th edit., 1983, Making Ethical Decisions, 1958, The Renewal of Hope, 1959, Jesus and God's New People, 1959, Jesus in History, 1970, 2d edit., 1977, The Origins of Christianity: Sources and Documents, 1973, The Community of the New Age, 1977, Christianity: An Historical Approach, 1979, Christian Origins in Sociological Perspective, 1980, Miracle in the Early Christian World, 1983, The New Testament in Context: Sources and Documents, 1984; editor: Biblical Perspectives on Current Issues, 1976—; librettist: New Land, New Covenant (Howard Hanson), 1976; contbr.: Interpreter's Dictionary of the Bible, 1962, supplement, 1976. Bd. mgrs. Am. Bible Soc., 1956, chmn. transls. com.; bd. dirs. Mohawk Trail Concerts, Inc., Charlemont, Mass.; mem. adv. bd. Yale U. Inst. Sacred Music. Am. Assn. Theol. Schs. fellow, Germany, 1960; Guggenheim fellow, Israel, 1966-67; Nat. Endowment Humanities grantee, Eng., 1984. Mem. Soc. Values in Higher Edn., Columbia U. Seminar in N.T., Am. Acad. Religion, Soc. Bibl. Lit., Bibl. Theologians, Studiorum Novi Testamenti Societas, New Haven Theol. Discussion Group. Presbyterian. Home: 121 Pinckney St Boston MA 02114 Office: Boston U 745 Commonwealth Ave Boston MA 02215 *Life is a gift from the Creator. It is mediated to us through parents, family, friends, teachers. It is conveyed through love and learning, through challenge and conflict, through accomplishment and disappointment. The gift must be shared, not jealously guarded or proudly prized. By sharing life, we can approach others with candor and honesty, with joy and sympathy, with wonder and understanding. The shared gift brings gratitude and fulfillment.*

KEE, WALTER ANDREW, former government official; b. Phila., July 12, 1914; s. Walter Leslie and Regina Veronica (Corcoran) K.; m. Genevieve O'Hair, Dec. 2, 1943; children: Kathleen, Sheila. B.S., Purdue U., 1949; M.L.S., Columbia U., 1950. Engring. and phys. sci. librarian N.Y. U., N.Y.C., 1950-51; librarian E.I. DuPont de Nemours, Savannah River Lab., Aiken, S.C., 1951-55; head library and documents sect. Martin Co., Balt., 1955-59; chief library br. AEC, Washington, 1959-74; librarian ERDA, Washington, 1975-76, asst. to dir. div. adminstrv. services, 1976-77, also Freedom of Info. and Privacy Act officer, 1975-77; dir. div. publs. mgmt. Dept. Energy, 1977-78. Contbr.: chpt. to Special Librarianship: A New Reader (Eugene Jackson), 1980. Asst. to chief So. Shores Fire Dept.; sec. Dare County Firemen's Assn., 1980-83; historian So. Shores Civic Assn. Served with USNR, 1942-45. Mem. Fed. Library Com., Com. on Sci. and Tech. Info., Spl. Libraries Assn. (cons.), Am. Soc. Info. Sci. Home: 6101 Albatross Dr New Nem NC 28560

KEECH, RICHMOND B., U.S. judge; b. Washington, Nov. 28, 1896; s. Leigh R. and Anne L. (Contee) K.; m. Alice Cashell Berry, Sept. 24, 1957. LL.B., Georgetown U., 1922, LL.M., 1923. Practice law, Washington, 1922-25, asst. corp. counsel, D.C., 1925-30, people's counsel, 1930-34; law mem. and vice chmn. Pub. Utilities Commn., 1934-40, corp. counsel, gen. counsel, 1940-45; adminstrv. asst. to Pres. U.S., 1945-46; judge U.S. Dist. Ct. D.C., 1946-66, chief judge, 1966, sr. dist. judge, 1967—. Served in transp. service USN, World War I; capt. J.A.G. Res. Mem. Bar Assn. D.C., Am. Legion, Barristers, Masters of Foxhounds Assn. Am., Phi Alpha Delta. Episcopalian (jr. warden emeritus). Clubs: Rotary, Lawyers, Nat. Press, Potomac Hunt, Lawyers, Metropolitan (Washington); Chevy Chase (Md.); American Foxhound, Virginia Foxhound. Home: 12930 Travilah Rd Potomac MD 20854 Office: US Dist Ct for DC Washington DC 20001

KEEDICK, ROBERT LEE, lecture bureau executive; b. N.Y.C., Dec. 2, 1919; s. Lee and Mabel (Ferris) K.; m. Harriet Byrnes, May 29, 1958; children: Theodore Lee, Lauri Lynne. B.A., Brown U., 1941. With Keedick Lecture Bur., N.Y.C., 1941—, pres., 1957—; v.p. Keedick Press. Served to lt. USNR, 1942-46. Clubs: Dutch Treat (dir.), Explorers, Brown U. (N.Y.C.); Aspetuck Valley Country., Naples Bath and Tennis. Home: 23 Edgemarth Hill Rd Westport CT 06880 Office: 521 Fifth Ave New York NY 10017

KEEFE, DONALD FORAN, lawyer; b. New London, Conn., Mar. 12, 1917; s. Arthur T. and Mabel (Foran) K.; m. Kate Stevens Hemingway, Apr. 8, 1942; children—Sarah, Nicholas, Thomas. B.A., Yale U., 1938, LL.B. cum laude, 1946; postgrad., King's Coll., Cambridge (Eng.) U., 1938-39. Bar: Conn. bar. Since practiced in, New Haven; partner firm Tyler, Cooper, Grant, Bowerman & Keefe (and predecessor), 1949—; dir. Colonial Bancorp Inc., Blue Cross and Blue Shield Conn., Inc. Pres. United Fund Greater New Haven, 1964-66, bd. dirs., 1961-67; mem. sch. bd. Cath. Archdiocese Hartford, 1966-69; Mem. adv. bd. Albertus Magnus Coll., New Haven. Served to comdr. USNR, 1941-45. Decorated knight St. Gregory. Mem. Am., Conn., New Haven County bar assns., Am. Judicature Soc., New Haven C. of C. (dir. 1966-72, v.p. 1971-72). Republican. Roman Catholic. Clubs: Quinnipiac, Lawn (New Haven). Home: 30 Old Orchard Rd North Haven CT 06473 Office: 205 Church St New Haven CT 06509

KEEFE, HARRY VICTOR, JR., banking executive; b. Boston, Apr. 9, 1922; s. Harry V. and Catherine T. (Dennis) K.; children: Kathleen K., Harry Victor. B.A., Amherst Coll., 1943; postgrad., Boston U., 1946. Analyst R.L. Day & Co., Boston, 1946-52, ptnr., 1952-56, Tucker Anthony & R.L. Day, N.Y.C., 1956-62; chmn. Keefe Mgmt. Services, N.Y.C., 1962—; founder, chief exec. officer, dir., chmn. Keefe, Bruyette & Woods, Inc., N.Y.C., 1973—; dir. Bay State Milling Co., Boston. Author: Banking, A Vital and Stable Industry. Trustee Lafayette Coll., Easton, Pa., Brunswick Sch., Boston. Served with USNR, 1942-56. Roman Catholic. Clubs: Fairfield County Hounds (master), Greenwich Country, John's Island, Amherst Alumni Assn. (pres. 1955-56). Home: Aiken Rd Greenwich CT 06830 Office: Keefe Bruyette & Woods Inc One Liberty Plaza New York NY 10006

KEEFE, JOHN WEBSTER, curator; b. Mt. Kisco, N.Y., Apr. 23, 1941; s. Webster W. and Josephine Jayne (Metcalf-Lewis) K.; m. Katharine Caecilia Lee, Oct. 3, 1970 (div. 1976). B.A., Yale U., 1963, M.A., 1965. Ford Found. mus. curatorial tng. intern, Toledo, 1965-67; asst. and asso. curator Toledo Mus. Art, 1967-70; asst. curator European decorative arts Art Inst. Chgo., 1970-73, curator, 1973-79; chief curator Grand Rapids Art Mus., 1981-83; curator decorative arts New Orleans Mus. Art, 1983—; guest lectr., vis. curator U. Chgo., 1980. Contbr. articles to profl. jours.; author various mus. handbooks and exhbn. catalogues. Trustee Chgo. Architecture Found., 1976-80. Decorated chevalier French Order Arts and Letters; Heritage Found. fellow, summer 1962; recipient honor cert. Univ. Med. Centre Hadassah Book of Builders, Jerusalem, 1979, Pioneer Women of Israel, Chgo., 1977, 78. Mem. Am. Ceramic Circle (founding), Internat. Wedgwood Seminar (trustee 1973-76), Art Inst. Chgo. Profl. Mus. Assn. (v.p. 1974-76), Chgo. Sch. Architecture Found. (trustee 1974-81, v.p. aux. bd. 1976-80), Decorative Arts Soc. (nat. adv. bd.), Soc. Archtl. Historians, Furniture History Soc. Gt. Brit., Victorian Soc. Am., Friends of Cast Iron Architecture, Paperweight Collectors Assn., Am. Assn. Mus., Assn. Mich. Mus. (trustee 1982-84). Presbyterian. Clubs: Casino, Yale, Arts of Chgo. Home: 2450 Burgundy St Faubourg Marigny New Orleans LA 70117 Office: PO Box 19123 City Park New Orleans LA 70179

KEEFE, ROGER MANTON, former banker, financial consultant; b. New London, Conn., Feb. 26, 1919; s. Arthur T. and Mabel (Foran) K.; m. Ann Hunter, June 4, 1949; children: Christopher Hunter, Matthew Foran and Michael Devereux (twins), Susan Ann, Robin Mary, Victoria Morrill. Student, Coll. St. Gregory, Downside Abbey, Eng., 1936-37; B.A. in History and Internat. Relations, Yale, 1941. With Chase Manhattan Bank, N.Y.C., 1945-71, sr. v.p. charge div. financing devel. and tech. services, 1966-71; exec. v.p. Conn. Bank & Trust Co., Hartford, 1971-76, vice chmn., 1976-80, CBT Corp., Darien, Conn., 1976—, chmn. exec. com., 1980-83, Conn. Bank & Trust Co., 1980-83; pres. R.M. Keefe Assocs., Inc., 1983—; dir. Callahan Mining Co. Mem. exec. council Yale Class of 1941, 1962—, treas., 1966-71; mem. bd. edn., Norwalk, Conn.; mem. Nat. Republican Finance Com., 1961—, also treas. adv. finance com.; mem. N.Y. State Rep. Finance Com., 1961-69; trustee St. Thomas More Corp., 1962—, treas., 1964-69; trustee Greens Farms Acad., 1978, Am. Shakespeare Theatre, 1974—, Fairfield U., 1982—; bd. dirs. St. Joseph's Hosp., 1978. Served to maj. AUS., World War II; ETO. Decorated Silver Star, Bronze Star with cluster, Purple Heart., Knight of St. Gregory. Mem. Fin. Execs. Inst., Assn. Res. City Bankers, Am. Arbitration Assn., Southwestern Area Commerce and Industry Assn. (dir. 1978). Clubs: Yale (N.Y.C.); Wee Burn Country, Landmark, Harbor, Norwalk Yacht; Internat. (Washington). Home: Nathan Hale Rd Wilson Point South Norwalk CT 06854

KEEFE, WILLIAM JOSEPH, educator; b. Piper City, Ill., Nov. 28, 1925; s. Joseph and Elfreda (Huxtable) K.; m. Martha Maria Schroeder, Dec. 22, 1948; children—Kathryn, Robert, Nancy, Mary Jo, John. B.S., Ill. State U., 1948; M.A., Wayne State U., 1949; Ph.D., Northwestern U., 1951. Asst. prof. polit. sci. U. Ala., 1951-52; mem. faculty Chatham Coll., Pitts., 1952-68, asso. prof., 1955-61, prof., 1961-68; prof. dept. polit. sci. U. Pitts., 1968—, chmn. dept., 1968-75; Mem. adv. com. Eagleton Inst. Politics, Rutgers U., 1965—. Author: (with Morris Ogul) The American Legislative Process: Congress and the States, 5th edit, 1981, Parties, Politics, and Public Policy in America, 1972, 4th edit., 1984, Congress and the American People, 1980, 2d edit., 1984, American Democracy, 1983; contbr. to profl. jours. Del. Democratic Nat. Conv., 1976. Served with USNR, 1944-46. Mem. Am. Polit. Sci. Assn. (chmn. program com. 1975—, chmn. Congl. program 1968-75, chmn. Woodrow Wilson award com. 1977, treas. 1981, trustee trust and devel. bd. 1981—). Office: Dept Polit Sci U Pitts Pittsburgh PA 15260

KEEFER, WILLIAM W., industrial parts manufacturing executive; b. Chgo., 1925; married. Grad., U. Chgo., 1950; postgrad., MIT, U. Copenhagen. Fin. exec. U.S. Steel Corp., 1950-55; cons. A.T. Kearney Co., Chgo., 1955-57; with Warner Electric Brake & Clutch Co., South Beloit, Ill., 1957—, controller, 1958-60, v.p., controller, 1960-62, v.p. adminstrn., 1962-65, exec. v.p., 1965-67, pres., 1967—, chmn., 1984—, also dir.; dir. Heritage Bank-Beloit, Heritage Wis. Corp., Franklin Electric Co. Trustee Beloit Coll. Office: 449 Gardner St South Beloit IL 61080

KEEFRIDER, HARRY JOSEPH, business executive; b. Phila., Dec. 4, 1921; s. Harry E. and Priscilla Cecelia (Connolly) K.; m. Helen Marie Linsley, Jan. 16, 1944; children: Harry, Christopher, Robert, Stephen, John. B.S. in Econs., Villanova U., 1943. C.P.A., Pa. Staff sr. Peat, Marwick, Mitchell & Co., 1946-49; with Woodward & Dickerson, Inc., Phila., 1949—, asst. sec., 1960-63, treas., 1963-64, sec.-treas., dir., 1964-82, v.p., sec., dir., 1982—. Mem. Crime Commn. of Phila. Served with USN, 1942-46; PTO. Mem. Am. Inst. C.P.A.s, Pa. Assn. C.P.A.s., Soc. Preservation and Encouragement of Barbershop Quartet Singing in Am. Democrat. Roman Catholic. Home: 727 Fitzwatertown Rd North Hills PA 19038 Office: 937 Haverford Rd Bryn Mawr PA 19010

KEEGAN, KENNETH DONALD, oil company executive; b. Buffalo, N.Y., Apr. 29, 1927; s. Walter James and Lillian Frances K.; m. Elizabeth Lillian Peyer, Dec. 17, 1955; children: K. Brian, Karen Lynn. B.S. in Fgn. Service, Georgetown U., 1947; M.B.A., N.Y. U., 1964. Mgr. fin. Texaco Inc., N.Y.C., 1966-68; dir. fin. Texaco Services (Europe) Ltd., Brussels, Belgium, 1968-80; v.p., treas. Texaco Can., Inc., Don Mills, Ont., 1980—; dir. Texaco Chems. Can., Ltd., 1980—, Oilship Ltd., 1980—. Mem. Conf. Bd. Can. (fin. exec. council), Fin. Execs. Inst. Republican. Roman Catholic. Club: Donalda (Don Mills). Office: 90 Wynford Dr Don Mills ON M3C 1K5 Canada

KEEGAN, RICHARD JOHN, advt. agy. exec.; b. New Haven, May 10, 1924; s. Richard Joseph and Katherine Veronica (Shea) K.; m. Joan Elizabeth Noden, Oct. 17, 1953; children—Stephen J., Janet C. Student, Pomona Coll., 1943-44; B.A., Cornell U., 1949; postgrad., Harvard Bus. Sch., 1974. Product mgr. Vick Chem. Co., N.Y.C., 1949-52; account supr. Sherman Marquette Advt. Agy., N.Y.C., 1952-54; sr. v.p. Bryan Houston, Inc., N.Y.C., 1954-60; v.p. Young & Rubicam Inc. Advt. Agy., N.Y.C., 1960-70; sr. v.p., dep. dir. Needham Harper & Steers Inc., N.Y.C., 1972-76; group sr. v.p. Doyle Dane Bernbach Advt. Inc., N.Y.C., 1976—, also dir.; Cons. Magic Mountain, Vt. Chmn. United Way Drive; rep. Greenwich Town Govt. Served to 1st lt. U.S. Army, 1943-46. Decorated Purple Heart, Silver Star. Mem. Am. Assn. Advt. Agys., Proprietary Assn. U.S., Alpha Tau Omega. Republican. Roman Catholic. Clubs: Cornell (N.Y.C.); Stanwich (Greenwich). Home: 179 N Maple Ave Greenwich CT 06830 Office: 437 Madison Ave New York NY 10022

KEEHN, SILAS, banker; b. New Rochelle, N.Y., June 30, 1930; s. Grant and Marjorie (Burchard) K.; m. Marcia June Lindquist, Mar. 26, 1955; children: Elisabeth, Britta, Peter. A.B., Hamilton Coll., Clinton, N.Y., 1952; M.B.A. in Fin, Harvard U., 1957. With Mellon Bank N.A., Pitts., 1957-80, v.p., then sr. v.p., 1967-78, exec. v.p., 1978-79, vice chmn., 1980; v.p. Mellon Nat. Corp., 1979-80, vice chmn.,

1980; chmn. bd. Pullman, Inc., Chgo., 1980; pres. Fed. Res. Bank Chgo., 1981—. Charter trustee Hamilton Coll.; trustee Rush-Presbyn.-St. Luke's Med. Center; mem. Northwestern U. Assocs.; bd. dirs. United Way of Chgo. Served with USNR, 1953-56. Mem. Chgo. Council on Fgn. Relations (dir.), Chgo. Assn. Commerce and Industry (dir.). Clubs: Chgo.; Commercial, Economic (Chgo.); Fox Chapel Golf (Pitts.); University (Chgo.); Links (N.Y.C.); Rolling Rock (Ligonier, Pa.); Bankers, Indian Hill. Office: 230 S LaSalle St Chicago IL 60690

KEELAN, KEVIN ROBERT, clergyman; b. Elizabeth, N.J., Mar. 4, 1921; s. Patrick Joseph and Ellen Cecelia (McNesby) K. Student, Seton Hall U., 1940-42; B.A., St. Francis Coll., 1945; S.T.L., Cath. U. Am., 1949; Ph.L., St. Thomas U., Rome, Ph.D., 1951. Joined Third Order Regular of St. Francis, 1942; ordained priest Roman Catholic Ch., 1949; instr. philosophy, dean students St. Francis Coll., Loretto, Pa., 1951-53, pres., 1956-59; asst. prof. philosophy, dean U. Steubenville, Ohio, 1953-56, pres., 1959-62, chmn. bd. trustees, exec. v.p., 1966-69, pres., 1969-74; minister provincial Province Most Sacred Heart Jesus, 1962-66; pastor St. John the Evangelist Ch., Pitts., 1977—. Vice chmn., mem. fin. com. bd. trustees Southside Cath. Schs. Consolidation, Pitts. Recipient Porter W. Averill award Thomas Jefferson High Sch., 1955; Poverello medal Founders Assos. Coll. of Steubenville, 1975. Mem. Nat. Cath. Edn. Assn., South Side C. of C., K.C.; mem. Ancient Order Hibernians. Home: St John the Evangelist Friary 54 S 14th St Pittsburgh PA 15203

KEELE, HAROLD M., lawyer; b. Monticello, Ill., Aug. 26, 1901; s. Frederick W. and Delta (Parsons) K.; m. Caryl Dunham, 1960. A.B. cum laude, U. Ill., 1923, LL.B., 1927. Bar: Ill. bar 1928. Mem. English faculty U. Ill., 1924-25, U. Mont., 1925-26; since practiced in, Chgo.; asst. U.S. atty. No. Dist. Ill., 1928-29; asst. states atty., Cook County, Ill., 1929-32; partner firm Greenberg, Keele, Lunn & Aronberg (and predecessors), Chgo., 1938—; Gen. counsel Select Com. to Investigate Tax Exempt Founds., 82d Congress, 1952. Co-editor: vol. on founds. in Greenwood Ency. of Am. Instns; contbr. articles to profl. publs. Served to maj. USAAC, 1942-45. Mem. Am., Ill. bar assns., Phi Beta Kappa, Phi Delta Phi, Zeta Psi, Alpha Alpha Alpha, Delta Sigma Rho. Republican. Presbyn. Clubs: Casino, Tavern. Home: 200 E Pearson St Chicago IL 60611 Office: Suite 4500 One IBM Plaza Chicago IL 60611

KEELER, RUBY, actress; b. Halifax, N.S., Can., Aug. 25, 1910; d. Ralph and Elnora (Leahy) K.; m. Al Jolson, 1928 (div. 1939); 1 son; m. John Lowe, Oct. 29, 1941; 1 son, 3 daus. D.F.A. (hon.), Providence Coll., 1971, Saint John's U., 1974. Debut in, N.Y.C.; in chorus The Rise of Rosy O'Reilly, 1923; later appeared in: Bye-Bye, Bonnie, 1927, Lucky, 1927, The Sidewalks of New York, 1927, Show Girl, 1929, all N.Y.C., Hold Onto Your Hats, Chgo., 1940; appeared in: films including 42nd Street, 1933, Gold Diggers of 1933, Footlight Parade, 1933, Dames, 1934, Flirtation Walk, 1934, Go Into Your Dance, 1935, Shipmates Forever, 1935, Colleen, 1936, Ready, Willing and Able, 1937, Mother Carey's Chickens, 1938, Sweetheart of the Campus, 1941; star: No No Nanette!, 1970; appeared on: TV in The Greatest Show on Earth, Jackie Gleason Show, This is Your Life, Jerry Lewis Show. Mem. Actors Equity Assn., Screen Actors Guild. Address: care Gloria Safier 667 Madison Ave New York NY 10021 *

KEELEY, EDMUND LEROY, English and creative writing educator, author; b. Damascus, Syria, Feb. 5, 1928; came to U.S., 1939; s. James Hugh and Mathilde (Vossler) K.; m. Mary Stathatos-Kyris, Mar. 18, 1951. B.A., Princeton U., 1949; D. Phil., Oxford (Eng.) U., 1952. Fulbright tchr. English Am. Farm Sch., Salonika, Greece, 1949-50; Woodrow Wilson fellow, 1950-51; instr. English Brown U., 1952-53; Fulbright lectr. Salonika U., 1953-54; instr. English Princeton U., 1954-57, asst. prof., 1957-63, assoc. prof., 1963-70, prof. English and creative writing, 1970—, co-chmn. program in comparative lit., 1964-65, dir. creative arts program, 1966-71, dir. program creative writing and theatre, 1971-73, dir. creative writing program, 1974-81, mem. Hellenic studies com., 1979—; lectr. dept. Byzantine and Modern Greek Oxford (Eng.) U., 1960; vis. lectr. Writers Workshop, U. Iowa, 1962-63. Writer in residence, Knox Coll., spring 1963; Author: The Libation, 1958, (with Philip Sherrard) Six Poets of Modern Greece, 1960, George Seferis: Collected Poems, 1924-1955, 1967, C.P. Cavafy: Selected Poems, 1972, C.P. Cavafy: Collected Poems, 1975, Angelos Sikelianos: Selected Poems, 1979, The Dark Crystal, Voices of Modern Greece, 1981, George Seferis: Collected Poems, 1981, The Gold-Hatted Lover, 1961, (with Mary Keeley) The Plant, the Well, the Angel (V. Vassilikos), 1964, The Impostor, 1970, (with George Savidis) C.P. Cavafy: Passions and Ancient Days, 1971, Odysseus Elytis: The Axion Esti, 1974, Voyage to a Dark Island, 1972, Cavafy's Alexandria, 1976, Ritsos in Parentheses, 1979, A Conversation with Seferis, 1982, Modern Greek Poetry: Voice and Myth, 1984; Editor: (with Peter Bien) Modern Greek Writers, 1972; editor: (with Philip Sherrard) Odysseus Elytis: Selected Poems, 1981; Bd. editorial direction: Princeton Alumni Weekly, 1964-77; adv. bd.: Princeton Essays in the Arts, 1974-78; editorial bd.: Byzantine and Modern Greek Studies, 1974-83, Translation Rev, 1978—, Jour. Modern Greek Studies, 1983—. Mem. scholarship fund com. Am. Farm Sch., Salonika, Greece, 1955-60, trustee, 1978—; chmn. McCarter Theatre Com., 1969, trustee, 1983—; Mem. nat. bd. Translation Center, Columbia, 1975-77, dir., 1977—; mem. translation jury Nat. Book Awards, 1977. Served with USNR, 1945-46; with USAF, 1953-56. Jr. fellow Council Humanities, 1956-57; Rome prize fellow Am. Acad. Arts and Letters, 1959-60; Guggenheim fellow, 1959-60, 73; McCosh faculty fellow, 1969-70; Recipient Columbia Translation Center-PEN award, 1975; Ingram Merrill Found. fellow, 1977-78; Nat. Endowment for Humanities grantee, 1977-78; Harold Morton Landon Translation award Acad. Am. Poets, 1980; fellow Nat. Endowment Arts, 1981; Rockefeller Found. scholar, Bellagio Study Ctr., Italy, 1982; PEN/NEA fiction syndicate award, 1983. Mem. Authors Guild, Comparative Lit. Assn., Soc. Fellows Am. Acad. Rome (exec. com. 1975-77), MLA, Am. Lit. Translators Assn. (exec. bd. 1983—), P.E.N. (membership com. 1978-83, program com. 1979—, exec. bd. 1980—), Modern Greek Studies Assn. (pres. 1969-73, 80-82), Poetry Soc. Am. (v.p. 1977-78, 81-83), Phi Beta Kappa. Home: 140 Littlebrook Rd Princeton NJ 08540

KEELEY, GEORGE PAUL, investment consultant; b. Phila., Feb. 7, 1930; s. George A. and Elizabeth G. (Nunan) K.; m. Lois M. Mailloux, Feb. 6, 1960; children: Elizabeth Gaynor, Sarah Anne, George Paul. B.A. in Economics, Haverford Coll., 1956; M.B.A., Harvard U., 1958. With Am. Cement Corp., 1958-69; v.p., gen. mgr. east coast ops. div. Hercules Cement Co., Phila., 1963-67; pres. Land & Leisure Group, Los Angeles, 1967-69; founder, prin. Keeley, Park & Co., Haverford, Pa., 1970-74; mng. prin. Victor Palmieri & Co., Inc., Los Angeles, 1974-79; pres. Keeley Mgmt. Co., 1979—; chmn., prin. PX Imaging Corp., Plymouth Meeting, 1981—; chmn. U.S. Bus. Press, Inc.; adv. bd. Century IV Ptnrs.; dir. PQ Corp., Valley Forge., Bryn Mawr Trust Co., Am. Video Accessories, Integrated Techs., Inc. Bd. mgrs. Haverford Coll. Served with USAF, 1951-52. Mem. Harvard Bus. Sch. Club. Clubs: Merion Cricket (Haverford, Pa.); Aronimink Golf (Newtown Square, Pa.); Sunday Breakfast, Union League of Phila.; Johns Island (Vero Beach, Fla.). Home: 805 Parkes Run Ln Villanova PA 19085 Office: Two Radnor Corp Center Radnor PA 19087

KEELEY, JOHN LEMUEL, surgeon; b. Streator, Ill., Apr. 12, 1904; s. John William and Mary Catherine (Fife) K.; m. Mary Edith Schneider, Oct. 14, 1937; children—John Lemuel, George William, James Michael. B.S., Loyola U., Chgo., 1927, M.D., 1929. Diplomate: Am. Bd. Surgery, Am. Bd. Thoracic Surgery. Asst. physician dept. student health U. Wis., 1931-33; resident surgery Wis. Gen. Hosp., Madison, 1933-36; Arthur Tracy Cabot fellow in surgery Harvard, 1936-37; Harvey Cushing fellow surgery, research fellow surgery, acting resident urology Peter Bent Brigham Hosp., Boston, 1937-38; instr. surgery La. State U., 1938-40, asst. prof., 1940-41; vis. surgeon Charity Hosp., New Orleans, 1938-41; asst. clin. prof. surgery Loyola U. Sch. Medicine, Chgo., 1941-43, asso. clin. prof., 1943-54, prof. surgery, 1954—, asst. chmn. dept., 1954-58, chmn., 1958-69; asso. attending surgeon Cook County Hosp., Chgo., 1941-52, attending surgeon, 1952—; sr. attending surgeon Mercy Hosp. Chgo., 1941—, chmn. dept., 1958-67; chmn. dept. surgery Loyola U. Hosp., 1968-69; attending gen. and thoracic surgeon West Side VA Hosp., 1953-63; surg. cons. Hines VA Hosp., 1963—, Woodlawn, South Shore, Little Company of Mary hosps. Author articles surg. subjects. Fellow A.C.S.; mem. Chgo. Med. Soc., Chgo. Surg. Soc., Am., Central, Western surg. assns., Am. Assn. for Thoracic Surgery, Am. Coll. Chest Physicians, Soc. for Vascular Surgery, Am. Acad. Pediatrics (surg. affiliate), Phi Chi, Alpha Omega Alpha. Roman Catholic. Clubs: University (Chgo.); Edgewood Valley Country (La Grange, Ill.). Home: 2900 S Lincoln Ave North Riverside IL 60546 Office: Loyola U Med Center 2160 S 1st Ave Maywood IL 60153

KEELEY, ROBERT VOSSLER, diplomat; b. Beirut, Sept. 4, 1929; s. James Hugh and Mathilde Julia (Vossler) K.; m. Louise Schoonmaker, June 23, 1951; children: Michael M., Christopher J. A.B., Princeton U., 1951, postgrad., 1951-53; postgrad. (Princeton fellow in pub. affairs), 1970-71, Stanford U., 1965-66. With Fgn. Service, Dept. State, Washington, 1956—; officer in charge Congo (Leopoldville) external affairs, Washington, 1963-64, officer-in-charge Congo (Brazzaville), Rwanda and Burundi affairs, 1964-65, polit. officer, Athens, Greece, 1966-70; detailed Woodrow Wilson fellow Princeton U., 1970; dep. chief mission, Kampala, Uganda, 1971-73, alt. dir. E. African affairs, Washington, 1974, dep. chief mission, Phnom Penh, Khmer Republic, 1974-75; dep. dir. Interagency Task Force for Indochina Refugees, 1975-76; ambassador, Mauritius, 1976-78; dep. asst. sec. for African Affairs Dept. State, Washington, 1978-80; ambassador to, Zimbabwe, 1980-84; sr. fellow Ctr. for Study Fgn. Affairs, Fgn. Service Inst., Washington, 1984—. Served to lt. (j.g.) USCGR, 1953-55. Mem. Am. Fgn. Service Assn. Home: 3814 Livingston St NW Washington DC 20015 Office: M/FSI/CSFA SA3 Dept State Washington DC 20520

KEELY, GEORGE CLAYTON, lawyer; b. Denver, Feb. 28, 1926; s. Thomas and Margaret (Clayton) K.; m. Jane Elisabeth Coffey, Nov. 18, 1950; children: Margaret Clayton, George C. (dec.), Mary Anne, Jane Elisabeth, Edward Francis, Kendall Anne. B.S. in Bus, U. Colo., 1948; LLB., Columbia U., 1951. Bar: Colo. 1951. Partner firm Fairfield & Woods, Denver, 1951—; v.p., dir. Silver Corp., East Wash. Ry. Co., 1965-79; mem. exec. com. Timpte Industries, Inc., 1970-78, now dir.; dir. Hugh M. Woods Co., T.L.R. Leasing Co. Mem. Colo. Commn. Promotion Uniform State Laws, 1967—; regional planning adv. com. Denver Regional Council Govts., 1972-74; Bd. dirs. Bow Mar Water and Sanitation Dist., 1970-74; trustee Town of Bow Mar, 1972-74; trustee, v.p. Silver Found.; mem. exec. bd. Denver Area council Boy Scouts Am. Served with USAAF, 1944-47. Fellow Am. Bar Found., Colo. Bar Found.; mem. Am. Bar Assn. (ho. of dels. 1977-79), Denver Bar Assn. (award of merit 1979), Colo. Bar Assn., Nat. Conf. Commrs. Uniform State Laws (sec. 1971-75, exec. com. 1971—, chmn. exec. com. 1975-77, pres. 1977-79), Am. Law Inst., Cath. Lawyers Guild of Denver (dir. 1965-67), Phi Delta Phi, Beta Theta Pi, Beta Gamma Sigma. Clubs: U. Denver (dir. 1966-75, pres. 1973-74), Law of Denver (pres. 1966-67), Denver, Pinehurst Country. Home: 5220 Longhorn St Littleton CO 80120 Office: Colorado National Bldg Denver CO 80202

KEEN, CHARLOTTE ELIZABETH, marine geophysicist, researcher; b. Halifax, N.S., Can., June 22, 1943; d. Murray Alexander and Elizabeth Randell (Cobb) Davidson; m. Michael J. Keen, May 11, 1963 (div.). B.Sc. with 1st class honors, Dalhousie U., Halifax, 1964, M.Sc., 1966; Ph.D., Cambridge U., (Eng.), 1970. Research scientist Atlantic Oceanographic Lab., Energy, Mines, Resources, Dartmouth, N.S., 1970-74, Geol. Survey of Can., Atlantic Geosci. Centre, Dartmouth, 1972—; chmn. Can. Nat. Com. Lithosphere; mem. Can. Nat. Com. Internat. Union Geol. Scis., Geodesy and Geophysics, Iternat. Commn. Marine Geology. Contbr. articles to sci. jours. Recipient Young Scientist medal Atlantic Provinces Inter-Univ. Commn. Sci., 1977. Fellow Royal Soc. Can., Geol. Assn. Can. (past pres.'s medal 1979); mem. Am. Geophys. Union, Can. Geophys. Union. Anglican. Home: Box 48 Site 5 RR1 Porters Lake NS Canada B0J 2S0 Office: Atlantic Geosci Centre Bedford Inst Oceanography PO Box 1006 Dartmouth NS Canada

KEEN, CONSTANTINE, mfg. co. exec.; b. N.Y.C., Jan. 1, 1925; s. Andrew and Sophie (Findani) K.; m. Kally Carajikis, Sept. 23, 1951; children—Katherine, Andrew. B.A., N.Y. U., 1952. Asst. treas. Sandz Indsl. Corp., N.Y.C., 1951-55; with Fedders Corp., Edison, N.J., 1955—, asst. credit mgr., 1955-57, credit mgr., 1957-60, dir. credit, 1960-68, v.p., dir. credit, 1968-75, v.p., dir. distbr. relations, 1975-77, v.p., treas., 1977—; dir. Interclissa Corp., Madrid, Spain, 1977—. Served with USAAF, 1942-45. Decorated D.F.C., Air Medal. Greek Orthodox. Clubs: Ahepa, Masons. Home: 10 Merrivale Rd Great Neck NY 11021 Office: Fedders Corp Woodbridge Ave Edison NJ 08817

KEEN, MICHAEL JOHN, geophysicist, educator; b. Sussex, Eng., Jan. 1, 1935; emigrated to Can., 1961, naturalized, 1967; s. John and Susannah (Bedwell) K.; B.A., Univ. Coll., Oxford, 1957; Ph.D., Cambridge U., 1961. Successively asst., asso., prof. geology Dalhousie U., Halifax, N.S., Can., 1961-69, chmn. dept., 1968-72, 76-77, asst. dean faculty arts and sci., 1972-75; dir. Atlantic Geosci. Centre, Geol. Survey Can., 1977—. Author: Introduction to Marine Geology, 1968; also articles on marine geology and geophysics. Fellow Royal Soc. Can.; Mem. Geol. Assn. Can. (v.p. 1973-74, pres. 1974-75), Can. Geophys. Union (pres. 1981-83), Am. Geophys. Union, Geol. Soc. Am. Research in marine geology and geophysics. Home: 1591 Chestnut Halifax NS B3H 3S9 Canada Office: Atlantic Geosci Centre Geol Survey Can Bedford Inst Oceanography Dartmouth NS B2Y 4A2 Canada

KEENAN, BOYD RAYMOND, political science educator; b. Parkersburg, W.Va., June 29 1928; s. Claude Joseph and Lillie (Sayre) K.; m. Donna May Booth, June 9, 1951; children: Kevin Lee, Karen Ruth. A.B., U. Ky., 1949, M.A., 1957; Ph.D., U. Ill., 1960. Reporter Parkersburg News, 1949-50; state editor Lexington (Ky.) Herald, 1950-52; news editor U. Ky., 1952-55, dir. news bur., 1955-57; teaching asst. U. Ill., 1957-58, Charles E. Merriam fellow polit. sci., 1958-59; asst. to dir. Com. Instl. Coop., 1959-60; asst. prof. polit. sci. Marshall U., Huntington, W.Va., 1960-62; vis. prof. polit. sci. Purdue U.; assoc. dir. Com. Instl. Coop., 1962-64, prof. polit. sci., head dept., 1964-67; prof. polit. sci. U. Ill. at Chgo., 1967—; Dep. dir. Ill. Bd. Higher Edn.; chmn. Ill. Sci. Adv. Council; sci. adviser Ill. Gov., 1970-71; mem. Ill. Energy Resources Commn., 1974-79; cons. UNESCO, 1975, EPA, 1976; co-dir. Ohio River Basin Energy Study, 1976-80; sr. fellow Inst. for Humanities, 1982-83. Editor, contbr.: Science and the University, 1966; Contbr. articles profl. jours. Mem. Am. Polit. Sci. Assn., Midwest Conf. Polit. Scientists, Am. Soc. Pub. Adminstrn. Home: 271 Boyd Ave Elmhurst IL 60126 Office: Box 4348 U Ill Chicago IL 60680

KEENAN, CHARLES WILLIAM, chemistry educator; b. Fort Worth, Apr. 10, 1922; s. Charles Joseph and Mary Catherine (Markey) K.; m. Elizabeth Alden Pabody, Feb. 3, 1945; children: John Markey, Emily Spence. B.S., Centenary Coll. Iowa, 1943; Ph.D., U. Tex., 1949. Asst. prof. chemistry U. Tenn., Knoxville, 1949-54, asso. prof., 1954-58, prof., 1958—. Author: (with D.C. Kleinfelter and J.H. Wood) General College Chemistry, 1957, rev. edit., 1980, (with W.E. Bull and J.H. Wood) Fundamentals of College Chemistry, 1963, rev. edit., 1972. Served with USNR, 1945-46. NSF fellow Cambridge (Eng.) U., 1957-58, 64-65. Mem. Am. Chem. Soc., AAUP, AAAS, Sigma Xi, Phi Beta Kappa, Phi Kappa Phi. Unitarian. Home: 4501 Appleby Ridge Knoxville TN 37920 Office: U Tenn Chemistry Dept Knoxville TN 37996

KEENAN, EDWARD LOUIS, history educator; b. Buffalo, May 13, 1935; s. Edward Louis and Emma (Boudiette) K.; m. Joan Glasser, Nov. 25, 1961; children: Edward, Christopher, Nicholas, Matthew (dec.). A.B., Harvard, 1957, M.A., 1962, Ph.D., 1966; postgrad., Leningrad State U., 1959-61. Teaching fellow Harvard, Cambridge, Mass., 1962-63, instr., 1965-68, lectr., 1968-70, prof. history, 1970—, asso. dir. Russian Research Center, 1971-76, dir., 1976-77, master North House, 1970-75, dean Grad. Sch. Arts and Scis., 1977—; lectr. Slavic Workshop, Ind. U., 1962-64; Bd. govs. Reza Shah Kabir U., 1975—; bd. dirs. (Center for Middle Eastern Studies), 1981-83. Author: The Kurbskii-Groznii Apocrypha, 1972; Contbr. articles to profl. jours. Guggenheim fellow, 1970. Democrat. Office: University Hall 17 Cambridge MA 02138

KEENAN, JAMES GEORGE, educator; b. N.Y.C., Jan. 19, 1944; s. George F. and Cecelia Ann (Schmidt) K.; m. Ann Frances O'Rourke, Mar. 18, 1967; children: James, Kathleen, Kevin, Kenneth, Mary. A.B., Holy Cross Coll., 1965; M.A., Yale U., 1966, Ph.D., 1968. Asst. prof. Classics U. Calif., Berkeley, 1968-73; assoc. to full prof. Classics Loyola U. of Chgo., 1973—, chmn. classics, 1978—. Co-editor: edition of Greek papyri: The Tebtunis Papyri, vol. IV, 1976. Fellow Nat. Endowment for Humanities, 1973-74; travel grantee Am. Council Learned Scos., 1974, Am. Council Learned Socs., 1983. Mem. Am. Philological Soc., Am. Soc. Papyrologists (dir.), Classical Assn. Midwest and South, Assn. International des Papyrologues, Egypt Exploration Soc. Roman Catholic. Home: 6956 N Ridge Blvd Chicago IL 60645 Office: Dept Classical Studies Loyola U of Chgo 6525 N Sheridan Rd Chicago IL 60626

KEENAN, MICHAEL EDGAR, advertising agency executive; b. Columbus, Ohio, Mar. 15, 1934; s. Edgar Charles and Kathryn Ellen (Dowden) K.; children: Margaret, Matthew, Emily, Jennifer, Andrew, Martha. A.B., Duke U., 1955. Research, Compton Advt., N.Y.C., 1957-60; mktg. Foote, Cone & Belding, 1960-62, Lennen & Newell, 1962-64; v.p., dir. consumer products div. Fuller, Smith & Ross, 1964-70; chmn., chief exec. officer Keenan & McLaughlin Inc., N.Y.C., 1970-82; chmn. plans bd. Stan Merritt, Inc., N.Y.C., 1983—; mgr. Media Gen., Inc., N.Y.C., 1984—; lectr. mktg. NYU, 1960-64. Served with CIC, AUS, 1955-57. Mem. Am. Assn. Advt. Agys. (chmn. N.Y. council). Club: Thursday (past pres.). Home: 630 3d Ave New York NY 10128 Office: 630 3d Ave New York NY 10017

KEENAN, ROBERT ANTHONY, insurance company executive, educator, consultant; b. Jersey City, July 25, 1930; s. Anthony A. and Anne (McCartin) K.; m. Ann Louise Wallenberger, Sept. 12, 1959; children: Jeanne, Robert, Mary, Elizabeth, Paul. B.B.S. in Fin., Pace U., N.Y.C., 1958, postgrad, 1959-60; postgrad., NYU, 1967-68. C.P.A., N.Y., N.J. Gen. auditor Johnson & Johnson, New Brunswick, N.J., 1966-68; v.p. ops. and fin. Ortho Pharm., Raritan, N.J., 1968-72; v.p. fin. Johnson & Johnson Internat., New Brunswick, N.J., 1972-76; pres. Fgn. Credit Ins. Assocs., N.Y.C., 1977—; dir. N.Y.-N.J. World Trade Group, 1978—; prof. Grad. Sch., Monmouth Coll.; mem. mgmt. com. Internat. Credit Ins. Assn., Berne, Switzerland, 1983. Contbg. author: Operational Auditing, 1968-69, International Financial Handbook, 1983. Mem. adv. council Middlesex Coll., Raritan, 1978—; mem. planning commn. Holmdel, N.J.; active Republican Party. Served with USN, 1948-52. Recipient Alumnus Pace U., 1973. Mem. Fin. Execs. Inst. N.J. (dir. 1970-83, pres. 1980-81), Am. Inst. C.P.A.'s, N.Y. State Soc. C.P.A.'s, N.J. Soc. C.P.A.'s, Internat. C. of C. Roman Catholic. Club: Union League (N.Y.C.). Lodge: Atlantic Indians. Home: 126 Crawfords Corner Rd Holmdel NJ 07733 Office: Fgn Credit Ins Assoc 40 Rector St New York NY 10006

KEENAN, TERRANCE, found. exec.; b. Phila., Feb. 1, 1924; s. Peter Joseph and Marie (Sloupova) K.; m. Joette Kathryn Lehan, Oct. 20, 1979. A.B., Yale U., 1950; J.D. (hon.), Alderson-Broaddus Coll., Philippi, W.Va., 1973. Asst. headmaster Thomas Jefferson Sch., St. Louis, 1950-55; writer Merrill Lynch Pierce Fenner & Smith, N.Y.C., 1955-56; asst. editor office reports Ford Found., N.Y.C., 1956-65; sr. exec. asso. Commonwealth Fund, N.Y.C., 1965-72; v.p. Robert Wood Johnson Found., Princeton, N.J., 1972—. Vice chmn. bd. trustees Solebury Sch., New Hope, Pa.; v.p., trustee Eden Inst., Princeton. Served with USNR, 1943-46. Mem. Pub. Relations Soc. Am., Phi Beta Kappa. Democrat. Roman Catholic. Clubs: Yale (N.Y.C.); Nassau (Princeton). Home: 20 Farmington Place Newtown PA 18940 Office: Box 2316 Princeton NJ 08540

KEENE, CHRISTOPHER, conductor, author; b. Berkeley, Calif., Dec. 21, 1946; s. James Phillip and Yvonne San Jule Yvette (Cyr) K.; m. Sara Frances Rhodes, Dec. 21, 1967; children: Anthony Alexander, Nicholas Patrick. Ed., U. Calif. at Berkeley, 1963-67. With, Spoleto Festival, 1968, 69, 71; gen. dir., 1973; music dir., 1976; mus. dir., Am. Ballet Co., 1969-70; with, Santa Fe Opera, 1971, Covent Garden, 1973, N.Y. City Opera, Met. Opera, 1971, Chgo. Symphony, 1976, Berlin Opera; music dir., N.Y.C. Opera, 1983—; numerous guest appearances opera cos., maj. symphony orchs., 1972—; mus. dir., Artpark, 1975—, Syracuse Symphony Orch., L.I. Philharmonic, 1979—; Author: libretto Duchess of Malfi; Transl.: others. El Cimarron. Home: 650 West End Ave New York NY 10024

KEENE, CLIFFORD HENRY, medical administrator; b. Buffalo, Jan. 28, 1910; s. George Samuel and Henrietta Hedwig (Yeager) K.; m. Mildred Jean Kramer, Mar. 3, 1934; children—Patricia Ann (Mrs. William S. Kneedler), Martha Jane (Mrs. William R. Sproule), Diane Eve (Mrs. Gordon D. Simonds). A.B., U. Mich., 1931, M.D., 1934, M.S. in Surgery, 1938; D.Sc., Hahnemann Med. Coll., 1973; LL.D., Golden Gate U., 1974. Diplomate: Am. Bd. Surgery, Am. Bd. Preventive Medicine (occupational medicine). Resident surgeon, instr. surgery U. Mich., 1934-39; cons. surgery of cancer Mich. Med. Soc. and Mich. Dept. Health, 1939-40; pvt. practice surgery, Wyandotte, Mich., 1940-41; med. dir. Kaiser-Frazer Corp., 1946-53; instr. surgery U. Mich., 1946-54; med. adminstrv. positions with Kaiser Industries and Kaiser Found., 1954-75, v.p., 1960—; v.p., gen. mgr. Kaiser Found. Hosps. and Kaiser Found. Health Plan, 1960—; med. dir. Kaiser Found. Sch. Nursing, 1954—; dir. Kaiser Found. Research Inst., 1958—; pres. Kaiser Found. Hosps. Health Plan, Sch. Nursing, 1968-75, dir., 1960—; chmn. editorial bd. Kaiser Found. Med. Bull., 1954-65; lectr. med. econs. U. Calif. at Berkeley, 1956—; mem. vis. com. Med. Sch. Stanford, 1966-72, Harvard, 1967-71, 79-81, U. Mich., 1973-78; Mem. Presdl. Panel Fgn. Med. Grads. (Nat. Manpower

Commn.), 1966—. Contbr. papers to profl. lit. Bd. visitors Harvard Bus. Adv. Council, 1972, Charles R. Drew Postgrad. Med. Sch., 1972-79; trustee Amman Civil Hosp., Jordan, 1973, Community Hosp. of Monterey Peninsula, 1983—. Served to lt. col. M.C. AUS, 1942-46. Recipient Distinguished Service award Group Health Assn. Am., 1974; Distinguished Alumnus award U. Mich. Med. Center, 1976. Fellow A.C.S.; mem. Am. Assn. Indsl. Physicians and Surgeons, Nat. Acad. Scis., Inst. Medicine, Calif. Acad. Medicine, Frederick A. Coller Surg. Soc., Calif., Am. med. assns., Alpha Omega Alpha. Home: Whitman Ln PO Box 961 Pebble Beach CA 93953 Office: Kaiser Center 300 Lakeside Dr Oakland CA 94666

KEENE, J. RANDSDELL, lawyer; b. 1947. B.A., U. Southwestern La.; J.D., La. State U. Bar: La. 1972, U.S. Dist. Ct. (we. dist.)La., U.S. Ct. Appeals, U.S. Supreme Ct. U.S. atty., ptnr. firm Evans, Feist, Auer & Keene. Mem. ABA, La. Bar Assn., Shreveport Bar Assn., Am. Trial Lawyers Assn., Real Estate Securities and Syndication Inst. Affiliate. Office: PO Box 1784 Shreveport LA 71166 *

KEENE, THOMAS VICTOR, JR., aerospace company executive; b. Indpls., July 15, 1923; s. Thomas Victor and Marion (Craig) K.; m. Doris Dennis, June 16, 1950; children—Thomas Victor III, Dennis Malcolm. B.S., Harvard Coll., 1945, M.B.A., 1947. With Eli Lilly Co., 1945-46, Ford Motor Co., 1947-49; with Hughes Aircraft Co., Culver City, Calif., 1949-54, 1971—; sr. v.p. fin.; with Litton Industries, 1954-68; self-employed cons., 1969-71. Mem. Fin. Execs. Inst. Club: Bel-Air Bay. Office: Hughes Aircraft Co 200 N Sepulveda Ave El Segundo CA 90245

KEENER, BRUCE, III, retired naval officer; b. Knoxville, Tenn., Nov. 6, 1924; s. Bruce, Jr. and Eleanor (Lloyd) K.; m. Kathryn Marie Bateman, June 10, 1947; children—Bruce, IV, Kathryn Eleanor Keener Lafferty. B.S., U.S. Naval Acad., 1947; B.E.E., Naval Postgrad. Sch., 1955, M.S., 1956. Enlisted in U.S. Navy, 1943, commd. ensign, 1947, advanced through grades to rear adm., 1975; service in (Atlantic and Pacific fleets), comdr., 1973-74, 1975-77, dir. ship aquisition div., 1977-81, pres., N.Y.C., 1981—. Contbr. to mil. publs. Decorated Legion of Merit, Bronze Star, Meritorious Service medal with 3 stars. Mem. U.S. Naval Inst. Episcopalian. Home: 21 Maria Pl Ponte Vedra Beach FL 32082

KEENEY, EDMUND LUDLOW, physician; b. Shelbyville, Ind., Aug. 11, 1908; s. Bayard G. and Ethel (Adams) K.; m. Esther Cox Loney Wight, Mar. 14, 1950; children: Edmund Ludlow, Eleanor Seymour (Mrs. Cameron Leroy Smith). A.B., Ind. U., 1930; M.D., Johns Hopkins U., 1934. Diplomate: Am. Bd. Internal Medicine. Intern Johns Hopkins Hosp., 1934-37, vis. physician, instr. internal medicine, 1940-48; practice medicine, specializing internal medicine, San Diego, 1948- 55; dir. Scripps Clinic and Research Found., La Jolla, 1955-67, pres., 1967-77, pres. emeritus, 1977—; med. cons. Sheraton Corp., Crocker Nat. Bank, Aerojet Gen. Corp.; dir. research on fungus infections OSRD, 1942-46; cons. U.S. Navy, 1948—, VA, 1954—. Author: Practical Medical Mycology, 1955, Medical Advice for International Travel; Contbr. articles on allergy, immunology and mycology to med. jours. Bd. dirs. U. San Diego, Allergy Found. Am. Fellow A.C.P.; mem. A.M.A., Am. Soc. Clin. Investigation, Am. Acad. Allergy (pres. 1964), Western Assn. Physicians, Cal. Med. Assn., Western Soc. Clin. Research, Phi Beta Kappa, Alpha Omega Alpha, Beta Theta Pi. Republican. Presbyn. Clubs: Rotary, El Dorado Country., La Jolla Country, Fox Acres Country. Home: 338 Via del Norte La Jolla CA 92037 Office: 10666 N Torrey Pines Rd La Jolla CA 92037 *The great use of a lifetime is to spend it for something that outlives it.*

KEENEY, NORWOOD HENRY, JR., chemical engineering educator; b. Hartford, Conn., July 10, 1924; s. Norwood Henry and Edith (Gocher) K.; m. Phyllis R. Mottram, June 15, 1946; 1 son, Norwood Henry III. B.S., Trinity Coll., 1948; M.S., U. Maine, 1950; Ph.D., U. Manchester, Eng., 1962. Paper chemist Fram Corp., Providence, 1950-53; mem. faculty U. Lowell, Mass., 1953—, assoc. prof. chem. engring., 1956-64, prof., 1964—, chmn. dept., 1976—. Del. N.H. Rep. Conv., biannually, 1964—, N.H. Constl. Conv., 1974. Served with USAF, 1943-45. Decorated Air medal with cluster. Mem. TAPPI, Am. Inst. Chem. Engrs., N.H. Soc. Profl. Engrs., Nat. Soc. Profl. Engrs., V.F.W., Sigma Xi. Home: 152 Wason Rd Hudson NH 03051 Office: Dept Chem Engring U of Lowell Lowell MA 01854

KEENY, SPURGEON MILTON, JR., govt. ofcl.; b. N.Y.C., Oct. 24, 1924; s. Spurgeon Milton and Amelia (Smith) K.; m. Sheila Spear, May 3, 1952; children—Christopher Spear, Christy Virginia, Spurgeon Milton III. B.A., Columbia, 1944, M.A. in Physics, 1946; postgrad., Sch. Internat. Affairs and Russian Inst., 1946-47. With Directorate of Intelligence, Hdqrs. USAF, 1950-55; mem. staff Panel on Peaceful Uses Atomic Energy, Joint Congl. Com. Atomic Energy, Washington, 1955-56; chief atomic energy div. Office of Asst. Sec. Def. for Research and Engring., Washington, 1956-57; mem. Gaither security resources panel Exec. Office of Pres., 1957; tech. asst. to President's Sci. Adviser, Washington, 1958-69; sr. staff mem. Nat. Security Council, 1963-69; asst. dir. for sci. and tech. U.S. Arms Control and Disarmament Agy., Washington, 1969-73, dep. dir., 1977-81; scholar-in-residence Nat. Acad. Scis., Washington, 1981—; dir. policy and program devel. Mitre Corp., McLean, Va., 1973-77; Mem. U.S. delegation to Geneva Conf. Experts on Nuclear Test Detection, 1958; to Geneva Conf. on Discontinuance of Nuclear Weapons Tests, 1958-60; chief U.S. delegation U.S./Soviet Talks on Theater Nuclear Forces, 1980; mem. adv. com. Program Sci. and Internat. Affairs, Harvard, 1973-77; dep. chmn. com. environ. decision making Nat. Acad. Scis., 1974-77; chmn. Nuclear Energy Policy Study Ford Found., 1975-77; mem. com. on internat. security and arms control Nat. Acad. Scis., 1981—. Co-author: Nuclear Power Issues and Choices, 1977. Served to 1st lt. USAF, 1948-50. Recipient Rockefeller Pub. Service award, 1970; Disting. Honor award U.S. Arms Control and Disarmament Agy., 1981. Fellow Am. Acad. Arts Scis.; mem. Council on Fgn. Relations, Am. Phys. Soc. (mem. study group on light-water reactor safety 1974-75), Phi Beta Kappa. Home: 3600 Albemarle St NW Washington DC 20008 Office: Nat Acad Scis 2101 Constitution Ave Washington DC 20418

KEEP, JOHN L(ESLIE) H(OWARD), historian; b. Keston, Kent, Eng., Jan. 21, 1926; emigrated to Can., 1970; s. Norman M.H. and Phyllis M.R. (Austin) K.; m. Ann E. Keep, Dec. 8, 1948. B.A., U. London, 1950, Ph.D., 1954. Research officer Fgn. Office, London, 1953-54; lectr. Russian history U. London, 1954-66, reader, 1966-70; asso. prof. U. Wash., Seattle, 1964-65; prof. history U. Toronto, Ont., Can., 1970—. Author: The Rise of Social Democracy in Russia, 1963, The Russian Revolution: A Study in Mass Mobilization, 1976, The Debate on Soviet Power. . . 1917-1918, 1979; editorial bd.: Slavonic and East European Rev, 1963-70, Can. Slavonic Papers, 1979—. Served to capt. Brit. Army, 1943-47. Guggenheim fellow, 1978-79. Mem. Am. Assn. Advancement Slavic Studies, Can. Assn. Slavists. Office: Dept History U Toronto Toronto ON M5S 1A1 Canada

KEEPIN, GEORGE ROBERT, JR., physicist; b. Oak Park, Ill., Dec. 5, 1923; s. George Robert and Erlene Marie (Bennett) K.; m. Madge Mary Twomey, June 13, 1948; children: Robert, William, Ardis, Mavis, Denice. Ph.B, U. Chgo., 1943; B.S., MIT, 1946, M.S., 1947; Ph.D. in Physics, Northwestern U., 1949. Teaching fellow dept. physics MIT, Cambridge, Mass., 1947; postdoctoral fellow U. Calif.-Berkeley, 1950-52; instr. dept. physics U. Minn., Mpls., 1950-52; research physicist Los Alamos Sci. Lab., 1952-63, group leader nuclear safeguards research, 1966-76, dir. nuclear safeguards program, 1976-80; head physics div. IAEA, Vienna, Austria, 1963-65, spl. adviser to dep. dir. gen. nuclear safeguards, 1982—; mem. U.S. del. UN Atoms-for-Peace Conf., Geneva, 1955, 71, IAEA tech. adviser, 1964. Author: Progress in Nuclear Energy-Delayed Neutrons, 1956, Physics of Nuclear Kinetics, 1965; editor: Nuclear Analysis R and D; patentee in field. Fellow Am. Phys. Soc., Am. Nuclear Soc. (exec. com. 1967-69); mem. Fedn. Am. Scientists (chpt. chmn. 1957-58), Inst. Nuclear Materials Mgmt. (nat. chmn. 1978-80), Sigma Xi. Office: IAEA DDGISG PO Box 200 Vienna Austria A-1400

KEER, LEON MORRIS, engineering educator; b. Los Angeles, Sept. 13, 1934; s. William and Sophia (Bookman) K.; m. Barbara Sara Davis, Aug. 18, 1956; children: Patricia Renee, Jacqueline Saundra, Harold Neal, Michael Derek. B.S., Calif. Inst. Tech., 1956, M.S., 1958; Ph.D., U. Minn., 1962. Mem. tech. staff Hughes Aircraft Co., Culver City, Calif., 1956-59; research fellow, instr. U. Minn., Mpls., 1959-62; asst. prof. Northwestern U., Evanston, Ill., 1964-66, assoc. prof., 1966-70, prof. engring., 1970—; preceptor Columbia U., N.Y.C., 1963-64. Co-editor: monograph Solid Contact and Lubrication, 1980; contbr. articles to profl. jours. NATO fellow, 1962; Guggenheim Found. fellow, 1972. Fellow Am. Acad. Mechanics (sec. 1981—); mem. ASME, ASCE, Acoustical Soc. Am., Sigma Xi, Tau Beta Pi. Home: 2801 Harrison St Evanston IL 60201 Office: Dept Civil Engring Northwestern U Evanston IL 60201

KEESEE, THOMAS WOODFIN, JR., financial consultant; b. Helena, Ark., Feb. 11, 1915; s. Thomas Woodfin and Sarah Gladys (Key) K.; m. Patricia Peale, Apr. 7, 1940 (div. Dec. 1951); m. Patricia Hartford, June 26, 1953; children: Allen P.K., Thomas Woodfin, III, Anne H. B.A., Duke U., 1935; J.D., Harvard U., 1938. Bar: N.Y. bar 1939. Asso. firm Simpson, Thacher & Bartlett, N.Y.C., 1938-42; asst. to pres. Sperry Gyroscope Co., Inc., Gt. Neck, N.Y., 1942-46; with Bessemer Securities Corp., N.Y.C., 1946-80, pres., chief exec. officer, 1970-76, dir., 1976-80; dir. Inversiones Cremerca (C.A.), Caracas, Venezuela, ITT Corp., N.Y.C., Codepesa S.A., Caracas, Phipps Houses, N.Y.C., Am. Guarantee & Liability Ins. Co., Chgo., Jamaica Water Properties, Inc., (N.Y.); U.S. adv. bd. Zurich Ins. Co. Chmn. endowment investment com. Duke U., also trustee; trustee Arthur W. Butler Meml. Sanctuary, Bedford, N.Y.; chmn. pres.'s council Nat. Audubon Soc. Mem. N.Y. State Bar Assn., Harvard Law Sch. Assn., Pilgrims Soc., Phi Beta Kappa, Sigma Chi. Episcopalian. Clubs: Harvard, Knickerbocker, Racquet and Tennis, Board Room (N.Y.C.) (pres.); Bedford Golf and Tennis; Clove Valley Rod and Gun (Millbrook, N.Y.); Cosmos (Washington). Home: RD 3 Sarles St Mount Kisco NY 10549

KEESEY, ULKER TULUNAY, ophthalmology and psychology educator; b. Turkey, Oct. 18, 1932; d. Cemal and Mubeccel Tulunay. B.A., Mt. Holyoke Coll., 1955; Ph.D., Brown U., 1959. Asst. prof. U. Wis., 1963, now prof. depts. ophthalmology and psychology, 1975—; cons. Nat. Eye Inst., 1972-76. Contbr. articles to profl. jours. Fellow Optical Soc. Am.; Mem. Assn. Research Vision and Ophthalmology. Home: 102 Pine Ridge Trail Madison WI 53717 Office: Dept Ophthalmology U Wis Madison WI 53706

KEESHAN, BOB, television producer-actor; b. N.Y.C., June 27, 1927; s. Joseph and Margaret (Conroy) K.; m. Anne Jeanne Laurie, Dec. 30, 1950; children: Michael Derek, Laurie Margaret, Maeve Jeanne. Student, Fordham U., 1946-49, D.F.A., 1975; Pd.D., R.I. Coll., 1969; D.H.L., Alfred U., 1969, L.I.U., 1977, Coll. of New Rochelle, (N.Y.), 1980, LeMoyne Coll., 1983; H.H.D., Dartmouth Coll., 1975, Bucknell U., 1981; Litt.D. (hon.), Ind. State U., 1978; LL.D., Elmira U. (N.Y.), 1980; D.L., Marquette U., 1983. Pres. Robert Keeshan Assocs., 1955—; dir. Marvin Josephson Assocs. Inc., N.Y.C., 1969-77, Bank of Babylon, N.Y., 1973-79, Anchor Savs. Bank, 1976—. Appeared as Clarabell on: Howdy Doody Show, NBC-TV, 1947-52; as Corny the Clown on: Time for Fun, ABC-TV, 1953-55; producer, also appeared as Tinker the Toymaker on: Tinker's Workshop, ABC-TV, 1954-55; producer, appearing as Captain Kangaroo on: Captain Kangaroo, CBS-TV, 1955—; commentator: Subject is Young People, CBS Radio, 1980-82, Up to the Minute, CBS News, 1981-82, CBS Morning News, 1982—; producer, appeared as Mr. Mayor and The Town Clown on: Mr. Mayor, CBS-TV, 1964-65; Author: juvenile She Loves Me. . .She Loves Me Not, 1963. Mem. bd. edn. West Islip, N.Y., 1953-58; pres. Suffolk County Hearing and Speech Center, 1966-71, Suffolk County Police Athletic League, 1973-77; mem. Suffolk County council Boy Scouts Am.; bd. dirs. Nat. Assn. Hearing and Speech Agys., 1969-71, United Fund L.I., 1967-68, Good Samaritan Hosp., West Islip, N.Y., 1969-78; pres. Good Samaritan Hosp., 1978-79, chmn. exec. com., 1979-80; chmn. bd. trustees Coll. New Rochelle, N.Y., 1974-80; chmn. Council of Governing Bds., 1979-80. Served with USMCR, 1945-46. Recipient Sylvania award, 1956, Peabody award, 1958, 72, 79, Jr. Membership award Calif. Fedn. Women's Clubs, 1961, 62, Freedom Found. award, 1962, 72, Page One award, 1965, Ursula Laurus award Coll. New Rochelle, 1958, Ohio State award, 1973, DeWitt Carter Reddick award U. Tex., 1978, Sadie award U. Ala., 1978, Am. Edn. award Edn. Industries Assn., 1978, Disting. Achievement award Ga. Radio and TV Inst.-Pi Gamma Kappa, 1978, Emmy award for outstanding children's entertainment series Nat. Acad. TV Arts and Scis., 1978, 81, 82, Emmy award as outstanding performer in children's programming, 1982, Gabriel award cert. of merit, 1978, 82; James E. Allen Meml. award for disting. service to edn., Albany, N.Y., 1981; Disting. Service to Children award Parents Without Partners, 1981; named TV Father of Yr., 1980; recipient Nat. Edn. award, 1982, award Mass. Soc. for Prevention Cruelty to Children, 1982, Suffolk Early Childhood Edn. Council, 1983, Abe Lincoln awards So. Bapt. Radio and TV Commn., 1983, Phi Alpha Tau award Emerson Coll., 1983, award N.Y. Elem. Sch. Prins. Assn., 1983. Clubs: L.I. Yacht (Babylon) (commodore 1964-65); Friars (N.Y.C.); Southward Ho Country (Bay Shore N.Y.). Office: 524 W 57th St New York NY 10019

KEESLING, FRANCIS VALENTINE, JR., lawyer, management consultant; b. San Francisco, Mar. 3, 1908; s. Francis Valentine and Haidee (Grau) K.; m. Mary Heath, Mar. 20, 1937; 1 son, Francis Valentine III. Grad., Phillips Acad., Andover, Mass.; A.B., Yale U., 1930; LL.B., Stanford U., 1933. Bar: Calif. 1934. Practice in, San Francisco, 1934-55; with West Coast Life Ins. Co., San Francisco, 1936-77, pres., 1963-68, chmn. bd., 1968-73, dir., 1954-77; gen. counsel, dir. Hexol Inc., 1973—; cons. Met. Parking Corp., 1980—; Chief liaison and legis. officer nat. hdqrs. SSS, Washington, 1940-45, spl. adv. to dir., 1945-65; Washington rep. City and County of San Francisco, 1948-55. Mem. welfare com. City and County of San Francisco, 1946-47; mem. San Francisco Bay Area Council; past chmn. task force alcohol and drugs Gov.'s Com. on Traffic Safety; past mem. adv. com. on alcoholism Calif. Dept. Pub. Health; sr. council, past pres. San Francisco YMCA; bd. dirs., past pres. Calif. Traffic Safety Found. Served from lt. to col. U.S. Army. Decorated D.S.M. Mem. Assn. Life. Ins. Counsel (exec. com., pres. 1956-57), Am. Life Conv. (legal sect., past state v.p., del. ho. dels. Am. Bar Assn. 1962-63, past v.p. Calif. and Nev.), Health Ins. Assn., Am., Calif., San Francisco bar assns., San Francisco Art Assn. (past pres.), Calif. Ins. Fedn. (past pres.), Chi Psi, Phi Delta Phi. Clubs: Masons., Stock Exchange, Bankers, Pacific Union (San Francisco); Capitol Hill (Washington); Villa Taverna. Home: 60 San Rafael Ave Belvedere CA 94920 Address: 1000 California St San Francisco CA 94108

KEESOM, PIETER HENDRIK, physicist; b. Leiden, Netherlands, Feb. 10, 1917; came to U.S., 1948, naturalized, 1965; s. Wilhelmus Hendrikus and Anna-Maria (Moorman) K.; m. Cecilia A. Zantman, Nov. 4, 1946; children—Cecilia M., William H., Hendrick J., Peter S. Ph.D., U. Leiden, 1948. Engr. State Mines of the Netherlands, 1946-48; vis. prof. physics Purdue U., West Lafayette, Ind., 1948-50, asst. prof., 1950-53, asso. prof., 1953-57, prof., 1957—. Contbr. articles to profl. jours. Guggenheim fellow, 1960. Fellow Am. Phys. Soc. Roman Catholic. Home: 1113 Hillcrest West Lafayette IN 47906 Office: Physics Dept Purdue U West Lafayette IN 47907

KEETON, KATHY, publisher; b. South Africa, Feb. 14, 1939; d. Keith and Queenie K. Student, Royal Ballet Sch., London. Pres. Omni mag., N.Y.C.; vice chmn. Penthouse Internat. Office: Omni Mag 1965 Broadway New York NY 10023 *

KEETON, MORRIS TEUTON, educational organization administrator; b. Clarksville, Tex., Feb. 1, 1917; s. William Robert and Ernestine (Tuten) K.; m. Ruth Urice, Jan. 9, 1944; children: Gary KaDel, Scot, Gerlinde Joan. B.A., So. Meth. U., 1935, M.A., 1936; M.A., Harvard U., 1937, Ph.D., 1938; L.H.D. (hon.), Thomas A. Edison Coll., 1982, U. Md., 1983. Instr. philosophy and social sci. So. Meth. U., 1938-41; ednl. sec. Brethren Civilian Pub. Service, 1942-45; ordained to ministry Meth. Ch., 1946; mem. faculty Antioch Coll., 1947-77, prof. philosophy and religion, 1956-77, coll. pastor, 1947-60; dir. Carnegie study Antioch ednl. program, 1956-60, dean faculty, 1963-66, acad. v.p., 1966-72, provost, v.p., 1972-77, acting pres., 1975-76; exec. dir. Council Advancement Exptl. Learning, 1977-79, pres., 1979—; Coll. examiner North Central Assn. Colls. and Secondary Schs., 1960-77; mem. exec. bd. Commn. Instns. Higher Edn., 1973-77; chmn. commn. on higher edn. and the adult learner Am. Council on Edn., 1981—; mem. bd. edn. Yellow Springs Exempted Village Sch. Dist., 1961-65; head mission in, Germany, Am. Friends Service Com., 1953-55, chmn. internat. confs. and seminars program com., 1959-63, chmn. diplomats conf., Clarens, Switzerland, 1961, chmn. mission to, Germany, 1963; chairperson steering com. Coop. Assessment Exptl. Learning, 1974-77. Author: The Philosophy of Edmund Montgomery, 1950, Values Men Live By, 1960, Shared Authority on Campus, 1971, Models and Mavericks—A Profile of Liberal Arts Colleges, 1971; co-author: Journey Through a Wall, 1964, Ethics for Today, 4th edit., 1967, 5th edit., 1972, Struggle and Promise: A Future for Colleges, 1969, Experiential Learning, 1976, Learning by Experience-What, Why, How, 1978; editor: (with Harold Titus) The Range of Ethics, 1966; co-editor: Sourcebooks on New Directions in Experiential Learning, 1978-83. Guggenheim fellow, 1946. Fellow Soc. Religion Higher Edn.; mem. Am. Philos. Assn. (sec.-treas. Western div. 1959-61, chmn. Carus Lectures com. 1965-69), AAUP, Am. Assn. Higher Edn. (exec. com. 1965-66, dir. campus governance program 1966-69, pres. 1972-73). Democrat. Home: 10989 Swansfield Rd Columbia MD 21044

KEETON, ROBERT ERNEST, federal judge; b. Clarksville, Tex., Dec. 16, 1919; s. William Robert and Ernestine (Tuten) K.; m. Betty E. Baker, May 28, 1941; children: Katherine, William Robert. B.B.A., U. Tex., 1940, LL.B., 1941; S.J.D., Harvard U., 1956; LL.D. hon., William Mitchell Coll., 1983. Bar: Tex. 1941, Mass. 1955. Assoc. firm Baker, Botts, Andrews & Wharton (and successors), Houston, 1941-42, 45-51; assoc. prof. law So. Meth. U., 1951-54; Thayer teaching fellow Harvard U., 1953-54, asst. prof., 1954-56, prof. law, 1956-73, Langdell prof., 1973-79; assoc. dean Harvard, 1975-79; judge Fed. Dist. Ct., Boston, 1979—; Commr. on Uniform State Laws from Mass., 1971-79; trustee Flaschner Jud. Inst., 1979—; dir. Nat. Inst. Trial Advocacy, 1973-76; ednl. cons., 1976-79. Author: Trial Tactics and Methods, 1954, 2d edit., 1973, Cases and Materials on the Law of Insurance, 1960, 2d edit., 1977, Legal Cause in the Law of Torts, 1963, Venturing To Do Justice, 1969, (with Jeffrey O'Connell) Basic Protection for the Traffic Victim—A Blueprint for Reforming Automobile Insurance, 1965, After Cars Crash—The Need for Legal and Insurance Reform, 1967, (with Page Keeton) Cases and Materials on the Law of Torts, 1971, 2d edit., 1977, Basic Text on Insurance Law, 1971; also articles. Served to lt. comdr. USNR, 1942-45. Recipient Wm. B. Jones award Nat. Inst. Trial Advocacy, 1980, Leon Green award U. Tex. Law Rev., 1981, Francis Rawle award Am. Law Inst.-ABA, 1983, Samuel E. Gates litigation award Am. Coll. Trial Lawyers, 1984. Fellow Am. Bar Found., mem., Am. Acad. Arts and Scis., Am. Bar Assn., Mass. Bar Assn., State Bar Tex., Am. Law Inst., Am. Risk and Ins. Assn., Chancellors, Friars, Order of Coif, Beta Gamma Sigma, Beta Alpha Psi, Phi Delta Phi, Phi Eta Sigma. Home: 26 Bailey Rd Watertown MA 02172 Office: US Dist Ct McCormack Post Office and Courthouse Bldg Boston MA 02109

KEEVIL, NORMAN BELL, JR., mining company executive; b. Cambridge, Mass., Feb. 28, 1938; s. Norman Bell and Verna Ruth (Bond) K.; m. Nancy J. Brown, 1957; children: Scott, Laura, Jill, Norman; m. Catherine E. Taylor, July 5, 1970. Ph.D., U. Calif.-Berkeley, 1964. Registered profl. engr., Ont. V.p. exploration Teck Corp., Vancouver, B.C., Canada, 1962-68, exec. v.p., Vancouver, B.C., 1968-81, pres., chief exec. officer, 1981—; dir. Lornex Mines, Vancouver, Southam Inc., Toronto. Mem. Soc. Exploration Geophysicists. Mem. Can. Inst. Mining, Mining Assn. Can. (bd. dirs.). Clubs: Vancouver; Slaughnessy (Vancouver). Home: 4706 Drummond Dr Vancouver BC Canada V6T 1B4 Office: Teck Corp 1199 W Hastings St Vancouver BC Canada V6E 2K5

KEFAUVER, WELDON ADDISON, publisher; b. Canal Winchester, Ohio, Apr. 3, 1927; s. Ross Baker and Virginia Marie (Burtner) K. B.A., Ohio State U., Columbus, 1950. Mem. faculty Columbus Acad., 1956-58; mng. editor Ohio State U. Press, 1958-64, dir., 1964—; dir. Am. Univ. Press Services, Inc., 1971-72, 76-79; mem. U.S. del. 2d Asian Pacific Conf. Publs., Taiwan, 1978. Author: Scholars and their Publishers, 1977; editorial adv. bd.: Scholarly Publishing. Served with AUS, 1945-46. Recipient citation Ohioana Library Assn., 1974. Mem. Assn. Am. Univ. Presses (v.p. 1971-72, dir. 1971-72, 76-79, pres. 1977-78), Soc. Scholarly Pub., Nathaniel Hawthorne Soc., AAUP. Clubs: Torch, Crichton, Ohio State U. Faculty (Columbus). Home: 675 Eastmoor Blvd Columbus OH 43209 Office: 1050 Carmack Rd Columbus OH 43210

KEGEL, WILLIAM GEORGE, mining company executive; b. Pitts., Mar. 15, 1922; s. William G. and Gertrude (Holl) K.; m. Jacqueline Treacy, Feb. 17, 1942; children: Kathy, Danyele, Janice, Jacqueline, William, Madeline, Colleen, Lisa, Brian. Student elec. engring, U. Pitts., 1940-43. Mgr. mech. and elec. depts. Lee Norse Co., 1941-50; with Jones & Laughlin Steel Corp., Pitts., 1950-76, gen. mgr. raw materials and traffic, 1975-76; pres. Cerro Marmon Coal Group, 1976-79; chief exec. officer Rochester & Pitt. Coal Co., Indiana, Pa., 1979—; dir. Savs. & Trust Co. Pa., Indiana. Mem. Indiana (Pa.) Airport Authority, 1980; bd. dirs. Brownsville Gen. Hosp., 1964-71; mem. Centerville Borough Council, 1952-60. Mem. Pitts. Coal Mining Inst., Coal Mining Inst. Am., Am. Mining Congress (dir.), AIME. Republican. Roman Catholic. Clubs: Duquesne Indiana Country, Laurel Valley Golf. Home: 1 Daugherty Dr Indiana PA 15701 Office: 655 Church St Indiana PA 15701

KEGELES, GERSON, biochemistry educator; b. New Haven, Apr. 23, 1917; s. Alex and Jennie (Wilder) K.; m. Bertha Webber, Apr. 16, 1944; children: Winifred, Lawrence, Stanley, Gloria, Joyce. B.S. in Chemistry, Yale U., 1937, Ph.D., 1940, postgrad., 1940-41; postdoctoral research, U. Wis., 1945-47. Research phys. chemist Nat. Cancer Inst., 1947-51; mem. faculty Clark U., Worcester, Mass., 1951-68, prof. chemistry, 1956-68, chmn. dept., 1960-63; prof. biophys. chemistry U. Conn., Storrs, 1968-82, prof. emeritus, 1982—; cons. to industry, 1954—. Contbr. articles to profl. jours., sects. to books. Served with AUS, 1941-45. Mem. Am. Acad. Arts and Scis., Am. Chem. Soc., Biophys. Soc. Home: 6 Oakwood Dr RFD 2 Stafford Springs CT 06076 Office: U-125 U Conn Storrs CT 06268

KEGERREIS, ROBERT JAMES, university president; b. Detroit, Apr. 2, 1921; s. Irl George and Adah Marguerite (Merry) K.; m. Katherine Louise Falknor, Oct. 30, 1943; children: Robert Duncan, Melissa Ann. B.A. in Econs, Ohio State U., 1943, B.Sc. in Fgn. Trade, 1943, M.B.A. in Mktg. Mgmt, 1947, Ph.D. in Bus. Adminstrn, 1968; LL.D. (hon.), Central State U., Wilberforce, Ohio, 1977. Sr. researcher Fed. Res. Bank Cleve., 1947-49; market researcher Donald R.G. Cowan Agy., Cleve., 1949; partner Kegerreis Stores, Woodsfield, Ohio, 1950-60; v.p., treas. KBK Devel. Corp., Woodsfield, 1954-60; pres. KV Stores, Inc., 1960-69; mgmt. cons., 1966—; dir. Robbins & Myers, Inc., Systems Research Labs., Inc., Dayton Power & Light Co., Ranco, Inc., Progressive Industries Corp.; asso. prof. bus. adminstrn., chmn. dept. Ohio U., Athens, 1967-69; prof. mktg., dean (Coll. Bus. and Adminstrn.), 1969-71, v.p., dir. adminstrn., 1971-73; pres. Wright State U., Dayton, 1973—. Author articles. Trustee Dayton Art Inst., Dayton-Miami Valley Consortium, Meth. Theol. Sch. Ohio; trustee Univ. Regional Broadcasting Co. Served as officer USNR, 1943-46. Mem. AAUP, Assn. Consumer Research, Am. Inst. Decision Scis., Am. Psychol. Assn., Am. Mktg. Assn., Acad. Mgmt., Ohio Coll. Assn., Sphinx, Beta Gamma Sigma, Phi Delta Kappa, Delta Tau Delta. Methodist. Clubs: Dayton Rotary, Moraine Country., Bicycle. Office: Office of President Wright State U Dayton OH 45435

KEGLEY, CHARLES WILLIAM, former philosophy educator; b. Chgo., Feb. 17, 1912; s. Charles R.W. and Orpha M. (Koch) K.; m. Elizabeth Meck, 1940; children: Charles William II and John Franklin (twins); m. Jacquelyn Ann Kovacevic, June 12, 1965. B.A., Northwestern U., 1933, M.A., 1937, Ph.D., 1943; B.D., Chgo. Luth. Sem., 1936. Ordained to ministry Luth. Ch., 1937; pastor St. Paul's Luth. Ch., Evanston, Ill., 1940-45; chmn. univ. bd. religion and dir. John Evans Religious Center, Northwestern U., 1944-46; lectr. philosophy Northwestern U., 1946-50; prof. philosophy religion and ethics, dean Grad. Sch., Chgo. Luth. Theol. Sem., Chgo., 1945-50; prof. philosophy Wagner Coll., N.Y.C., 1949-69; prof. philosophy, chmn. dept. philosophy and religious studies Calif. State Coll., Bakersfield, 1970-80; Rockefeller vis. prof. philosophy U. Philippines, 1965-67; Condr. study tours, Europe, Far East, 1939—; del. XIII Internat. Congress Aesthetics, 1964, XIV Congress, 1968; chmn. Am. Luth. delegation World Conf. Christian Youth, Amsterdam, 1939; lectr. Internat. Congress, Philosophy, Brussels, 1953, Venice, 1958, Athens, 1960, Mexico, 1963, Amsterdam, 1967, Uppsala, 1970. Author: Protestantism in Transition, 1965, Politics, Religion and Modern Man, 1968; co-author: Religion in Modern Life, 1956, Existence Today, 71957, (with wife) Introduction to Logic, 1978; founder, editor: Library of Living Theology; editor: The Theology of Paul Tillich, 1952, enlarged edit., 1983, Reinhold Niebuhr—His Religious, Social and Political Thought, 1956, enlarged edit., 1984, The Theology of Henry Nelson Wieman, 1963, The Theology of Emil Brunner, 1966, The Theology of Rudolph Bultmann, 1970, The Philosophy and Theology of Anders Nygren, 1970; asso. editor: USA Today. Mem. Am. Philos. Assn., Am. Soc. Reformation Research, European Soc. Culture, Am. Soc. Ch. History, Omicron Delta Kappa. Clubs: Rich County Country (N.Y.C.); University (Chgo.); Bakersfield (Calif.); Racquet. Home: 7312 Kroll Way Bakersfield CA 93309 *The aim of my life, as I think it should be for everyone: to be inspired by love and guided by reason.*

KEHOE, PAUL JOSEPH, food products company executive; b. Ottawa, Ont., Canada, 1925; married. B.Sc. in Engring., Queens U., 1951. With Kellogg Co. of Can. Ltd., 1951-53, Kellogg Co., Battle Creek, Mich., 1954—, v.p. mfg. services, 1972-77, sr. v.p. mfg., 1977-81, exec. v.p. corp. tech., 1981—. Office: Kellogg Co Inc 235 Porter St Battle Creek MI 49016

KEHRL, HOWARD HARMON, automotive executive; b. Detroit, Feb. 2, 1923; s. Howard and Martha Sophy (Horlacher) K.; m. Mary Katherine Maloney, June 29, 1946; children: John Howard, Howard Richard, David James, Kathleen Mary. B.S., Ill. Inst. Tech., 1944; M.S. in Mech. Engring., U. Notre Dame, 1948; S.M. (Sloan fellow 1959-60), M.I.T., 1960; D.Sc. in Indsl. Mgmt. (hon.), Lawrence Inst. Tech., 1977. Registered profl. engr., Mich. With Gen. Motors Corp., Detroit, 1948—; v.p., gen. mgr. Oldsmobile, 1972, charge car and truck group, 1973-74, exec. v.p. corp., 1974-81, vice chmn. charge tech. staffs, operating staffs and public affairs groups, also dir., mem. exec. com., 1981—; dir. Dayton-Hudson Corp.; adv. council U. Notre Dame Coll. Engring.; mem. Sloan chair fellows com. M.I.T. Bd. dirs. United Found., Detroit; trustee Harper-Grace Hosps., Detroit. Served with USNR, 1943-46. Recipient Honor award U. Notre Dame, 1977, Corp. Leadership award M.I.T., 1980. Mem. Soc. Automotive Engrs., Automotive Orgn. Team, Mich. Soc. Profl. Engrs. (hon. life), Engring. Soc. Detroit, Tau Beta Pi. Office: Gen Motors Corp 3044 W Grand Blvd Detroit MI 48202 *

KEIDAN, FRED HANNAN, lawyer; b. Detroit, Nov. 16, 1931; s. Harry Benjamin and Katherine Marian (Levenson) K.; children by previous marriage: Laura Ruth, Mimi Rosalind. B.A., U. Mich., 1952, LL.B., 1955. Bar: Mich. 1956. Mem. firm Watson, Wunsch & Keidan, Detroit, 1955-56, 58-76; of counsel to Morris, Rowland, Regan & Prekel, 1976-77; partner firm Morris, Rowland, Prekel, Paquette & Keidan, Troy, Mich., 1978—. Pres. jr. div. Jewish Welfare Fedn., Detroit, 1961. Served with AUS, 1956-58. Mem. State Bar Mich., ABA, Detroit Bar Assn. (sec. young lawyers sect. 1962, chmn. family law sect. 1976-77), Oakland County Bar Assn., Maritime Law Assn., Propeller Club (dir. Port Detroit 1974-77), Econ. Club Detroit, Troy C. of C., Zeta Beta Tau, Phi Alpha Delta. Club: Rotary. Home: 2330 Dorchester St Troy MI 48084 Office: 3001 W Big Beaver Rd Suite 504 Troy MI 48084

KEIL, ALFRED ADOLF HEINRICH, engineering educator; b. Konradswaldau, Germany, May 1, 1913; came to U.S., 1947, naturalized, 1954; s. Kurt Alfred and Marie (Berger) K.; m. Ursula Leppelt, Oct. 15, 1943; children: Michael G., Juergen G. Dr. nat. sc., U. Breslau, Germany, 1939. Research asst. U. Breslau, 1939-40; research asso. Chem.-Phys. Research Establishment, Kiel, Germany, 1940- 45; chief scientist underwater explosive research div. Norfolk Naval Shipyard, Portsmouth, Va., 1947-59; tech. dir. structural mech. lab. David Taylor Model Basin, 1959-63, tech. dir. basin, 1963-66; prof., head dept. naval architecture and marine engring. MIT, 1966-71, dean Sch. Engring., 1971-77, Ford prof. engring., 1977-78, prof. emeritus, 1978—; Mem. Nat. Adv. Com. on Oceans and Atmosphere, 1977-79. Contbr. articles profl. jours. Served with German Army, 1939-40. Recipient Civilian Distinguished Service award Navy Dept., 1963; Gibbs Bros. gold medal for naval architecture Nat. Acad. Scis., 1967. Mem. Nat. Acad. Engring., Am. Soc. Naval Engrs. (Gold Medal award 1964), Verein Deutscher Ingenieure (corr. mem.), Soc. Naval Architects and Marine Engrs., Marine Tech. Soc. (Lockheed award 1979). Home: 39 Hillside Terr Belmont MA 02178 Office: Mass Inst Tech Cambridge MA 02139

KEIL, JOHN MULLAN, advertising agency executive; b. Rochester, N.Y., Dec. 30, 1922; s. Alvin Richard and Elizabeth (Mullan) K.; m. Barbara Louise Miller, Sept. 16, 1950; children—Peter Mullan, Nicholas John, Elizabeth Jane. B.A., U. Rochester, 1946. Copywriter advt. dept. Armstrong Cork Co., Lancaster, Pa., 1946-48, Wendell P. Colton Advt., N.Y.C., 1948-51, Needham & Grohmann, Inc., 1951-55, v.p., account exec., 1955-60; v.p., creative dir. Dancer, Fitzgerald, Sample, Inc., N.Y.C., 1960-64, copy group head, 1964-67, v.p., 1967-70, sr. v.p., creative dir., 1970—, dir., 1971—, exec. v.p., 1975—, chmn. creative planning con., 1973, exec. creative dir., 1983—; lectr. Amos Tuck Sch. Dartmouth Coll. Contbr.: articles to Jour. Advt. Vice chmn. Zoning Bd. Appeals, Grandview-on-Hudson, N.Y., 1961-71; Pres., trustee Rockland Country Day Sch.; mem. trustees council U. Rochester. Served with USAAF, 1943-45. Decorated D.F.C., Air medal with two oak leaf clusters. Mem. Alpha Delta Phi. Clubs: Princeton, Nyack (N.Y.) Field, Upper Nyack Tennis. Home: 251 River Rd Grandview-on-Hudson NY 10960 Office: 405 Lexington Ave New York NY 10017

KEIL, KLAUS, geology educator, consultant; b. Hamburg, Ger., Nov. 15, 1934; s. Walter and Elsbeth K.; m. Rosemarie, Mar. 30, 1961; children: Kathrin R., Mark K. M.S., Schiller U., Jena, Ger., 1958; Ph.D., Gutenberg U., Mainz, W.Ger., 1961. Research assoc. Mineral. Inst., Jena, 1958-60, MaxPlanck-Inst. Chemistry, Mainz, 1961, U. Calif.-San Diego, 1961-63; research scientist Ames Research Center NASA, Moffett Field, Calif., 1964-68; prof. geology, dir. Inst. Meteoritics, U. N.Mex., Albuquerque, 1968—; cons. Sandia Labs., others. Contbr. over 350 articles to sci. jours. Recipient Apollo Achievement award NASA, 1970, George P. Merrill medal Nat. Acad. Scis., 1970, Exceptional Sci. Achievement medal NASA, 1977, Regents Meritorious Service medal U. N.Mex., 1983, numerous others. Fellow Meteoritical Soc., AAAS, Mineral. Soc. Am.; mem. Am. Geophys. Union, German Mineral. Soc., others. Office: Dept Geology U N Mex Albuquerque NM 87131

KEIL, ROBERT MATTHES, chemical company executive; b. Bloomefield, N.J., Apr. 5, 1926; s. Wiiliam August and Myra (Maguire) K.; m. Betty Jane Apgar, May 3, 1952; children: Barbara Lynn, Nancy Lee. B.S., Syracuse U., 1948. Gen. mgr. olefin plastics Dow Chem. U.S.A., Midland, Mich., 1969-76, v.p. consumer goods and services, 1976-78, v.p. mktg., 1978-79, exec. v.p., 1979-80; fin. v.p. Dow Chem. Co., Midland, Mich., 1980-82, exec. v.p., 1982—, dir., 1981—; dir. Dowell Schlumberger, Houston, Dow Corning Corp., Midland, Mich., Comerica bank, Midland; chmn. Dow Chem. Que. Ltd., 1978-82. Pres. Midland Community Ctr., 1976-77. Served to lt. U.A. Army, 1943-46, 51-52. Office: Dow Chem Co 2030 Dow Center Midland MI 48640

KEILL, STUART LANGDON, psychiatrist; b. Binghamton, N.Y., Oct. 5, 1927; s. Kenneth and Dorothy B. (Langdon) K.; m. Joanne Veness, Sept. 2, 1950; children: Elinor Anne Moran, Patricia J., Brian S., Victoria M. B.A., Princeton U., 1947; M.A., Cornell U., 1948; M.D., Temple U., 1952. Intern Highland Hosp., Rochester, N.Y.; resident in psychiatry N.Y. State Psychiat. Inst., Presbyn. Hosp., Columbia U., N.Y.C., 1955-58; dir. edn., dir. West Side Community Mental Health Ctr., N.Y.C., 1958-71, Roosevelt Hosp., 1958-71; regional dir. N.Y. State Dept. Mental Health, 1971-75; prof. clin. psychiatry SUNY, Stony Brook, 1975-80; chmn. dept. psychiatry Nassau County Med. Ctr., East Meadow, N.Y., 1975-80; clin. prof. psychiatry SUNY, Buffalo, 1980—; chief psychiat. service VA Med. Ctr., Buffalo, 1981—; counselor Advocates Coalition for Psychiat. Patients, 1980—; mem. com. on pub. social policy Fedn. Protestant Welfare Agys., 1974-77; cons. USPHS, Adamaha, 1977-80; mem. faculty NIMH Staff Coll., 1979. Mem. editorial bd.: Social Work and Health Care, 1975—; assoc. editor: Gen. Hosp. Psychiatry Jour., 1981—. Chmn. Nassau council Health Systems Agy., 1977-80; mem. adv. com. Dr. Glory's Children's Theatre, N.Y.C., 1977-80. Served with USN, 1953-55. Recipient Julius T. Marcus award dept. psychiatry SUNY, Stony Brook, 1980. Fellow Am. Coll. Psychiatrists, Am. Psychiat. Assn. (chmn. com. adminstrv. psychiatry); mem. MEDIPP Psychiatry Council (dist. chmn. 1981—), Am. Assn. Psychiat. Adminstrs. (pres. 1981-82), Am. Hosp. Assn. (chmn. psychiat. services sect.), N.Y. State Psychol. Assn., Am. Assn. Gen. Hosp. Psychiatrists (v.p.), N.Y. Soc. Clin. Psychiatry (pres. 1974-75, chmn. pub. psychiatry com.). Office: VA Med Ctr 3495 Bailey Ave Buffalo NY 14215

KEILLOR, GARRISON EDWARD, writer, radio announcer; b. Anoka, Minn., Aug. 7, 1942; s. John P. and Grace R. (Denham) K.; m. Mary Guntzel, Sept. 6, 1965; 1 son, Jason. B.A., U. Minn., 1966. Author: Happy to Be Here, 1982; contbr. articles to profl. jours., articles to New Yorker mag.; author: radio show Prairie Home Companion, 1974—. Democrat. Plymouth Brethren. Address: 45 E 8th St Saint Paul MN 55101

KEILSON, JULIAN, statistics educator; b. Bklyn., Nov. 19, 1924; s. Jonas I. and Sarah (Eimer) K.; m. Paula Lyman, Mar. 3, 1954; children: Julia, David. B.S. in Physics, Bklyn. Coll., 1947; M.A., Harvard U., 1948, Ph.D., 1950. Research fellow electronics Harvard U., Boston, 1950-52; scientist Lincoln Lab., Boston, 1952-56; vis. lectr. MIT, Boston, 1962; research fellow U. Birmingham, Eng., 1963; sr. scientist Sylvania Applied Research Labs., 1956-66; prof. stats. U. Rochester, N.Y., 1966—; cons. CNA, 1975—, GTE, 1980—. Author: Green's Function Methods in Probability Theory, 1965, Markov Chain Models - Rarity and Exponentiality, 1979; assoc. editor: Jour. Applied Probability, 1976—; editor: Stochastic Processes and Their Applications, 1973-79. Fellow Inst. Math Stats., Royal Statis. Soc.; mem. Internat. Statis Inst., IEEE, Ops. Research Soc. Home: 95 Rowland Pkwy Rochester NY 14610 Office: U Rochester Grad Sch Mgmt Wilson Blvd Rochester NY 14627

KEIM, ROBERT PHILLIP, advertising executive; b. Ridgewood, N.Y., Jan. 28, 1920; s. William John and Josephine (Becht) K.; m. Gloria Kathleen Smith, Jan. 24, 1943; children: William Gary, Barbara Kathleen. B.A. magna cum laude, Queens Coll.; student, Grad. Sch. Internat. Relations, U. Md., 1950-51. Trainee Compton Advt., N.Y.C., 1942; campaigns mgr. Advt. Council, Inc., N.Y.C., 1954-61, pres., 1966—; also dir.; 2d v.p. marketing service Chase Manhattan Bank, N.Y.C., 1962-66; Cons. supt. USAF Acad., 1958; Mem. Air Force Res. Policy Com., 1961-63; del. White House Conf. Edn., 1956, White House Conf. Inflation, 1974; mem. Pres.'s Com. Traffic Safety, 1957-62, Nat. Adv. Council on Minority Bus. Enterprise; mem. exec. com. Air Force Acad. Found. for Falcon Stadium Fund, 1960-61. Author: Air Force Academy Cadet Procurement Study, 1958, Reserve Forces Utilization Study, 1962; writer, prod.: Air Force Hour, 1946-49, Armed Forces Hour, 1949-50; Adv. bd.: Public Relations News, 1977-81. Bd. visitors Ithaca Coll. Sch. Communications, 1974; bd. dirs. Bus. Council for Internat. Understanding; mem. exec. com. James Webb Young Meml. Fund, U. Ill., 1976-81; mem. Pres.'s Council on Energy Efficiency, 1980. Served to col. USAF, 1942-54. Decorated Legion of Merit, Commendation ribbon; elected fellow R.I. Sch. Design, 1982; scholar Queens Coll., 1941; recipient Dept. English 1st in class award, 1942, Ann. award Internat. Advt. Assn., 1982. Methodist (elder, past steward). Clubs: Union League (N.Y.C.); Wheatley Hills Golf. Address: 46 Orchard Dr East Williston NY 11596

KEIM, WAYNE FRANKLIN, agronomy educator, plant geneticist; b. Ithaca, N.Y., May 14, 1923; s. Franklin David and Alice Mary (Voigt) K.; m. Ellen Joyce Neumann, Sept. 6, 1947; children: Kathryn Louise Keim Logsdon, David Wayne, Julie Ann Keim Hughes. B.S. with distinction, U. Nebr., 1947; M.S., Cornell U., 1949, Ph.D., 1952. Instr., then asst. prof. Iowa State U., Ames, 1952-56; from asst. prof. to prof. Purdue U., West Lafayette, Ind., 1956-75; vis. prof., NSF sci. faculty fellow U. Lund, (Sweden), 1962-63; vis. prof. Colo. State U., Fort Collins, 1971-72, prof., head dept. agronomy, 1975—. Recipient Best Tshr. award Sch. Agr., Purdue U., 1965, 68. Fellow Am. Soc. Agronomy (agronomic edn. award 1971); mem. Crop Sci. Soc. Am. (pres. 1983-84), Genetics Soc. Am., Soil Sci. Soc. Am., Soil Conservation Soc. Am., Am. Inst. Biol. Sci., Council Agrl. Sci. and Tech., AAAS, Am. Genetics Assn. Home: 1441 Meeker Dr Fort Collins CO 80524 Office: Dept Agronomy Colo State U Fort Collins CO 80523

KEISER, BERNHARD EDWARD, engineering company execuitve, consulting electrical engineer; b. Richmond Heights, Mo., Nov. 14, 1928; s. Bernhard and Helen Barbara Julia (Buerkle) K.; m. Florence Evelyn, Jan. 22, 1955; children: Sandra, Carol, Nancy, Linda, Paul. B.S.E.E., Washington U., St. Louis, 1950, M.S.E.E., 1951, D.Sc.E.E., 1953. Registered profl. engr., Va., Md., D.C. Mgr. plans and programs RCA, Cape Canaveral, Fla., 1964-67, adminstr. advanced system planning, Moorestown, N.J., 1967-69; v.p., tech. dir. Page Commuincation Engring., Washington, 1969-70; dir. advanced engring. Atlantic Research Corp., Alexandria, Va., 1971-72; dir. anaylsis Fairchild Space & Electronics Co., Germantown, Md., 1972-75; pres. Keiser Engring., Inc., Vienna, Va., 1975—. Author: EMI Control in Aerospace Systems, 1979, Principles of Electro-magnetic Compatibility, 1979. Fellow IEEE (chmn. No. Va. sect. 1980-81), Washington Acad. Scis., Radio Club Am. Republican. Lutheran.

KEISER, EDMUND DAVIS, JR., educator; b. Appalachia, Va., Feb. 18, 1934; s. Edmund Davis and Ora Elizabeth (Wade) K.; m. Alice Sue Tucker, Sept. 10, 1982; children—Mark Edmund, Julie Ann, stepchildren: Louis King, Jennifer King. B.A., So. Ill. U., 1956, M.S., 1961; Ph.D. in Zoology, La. State U., 1967. Tchr. sci. Kinmundy (Ill.) High Sch., 1956-57, Mt. Vernon (Ill.) Twp. Sch. Dist., 1957-58; dist. sci. coordinator Freebury Sch. Dist. 70, Freeburg, Ill., 1958-62; instr. biology La Salle-Peru-Oglesby Jr. Coll., La Salle, Ill., 1962-64; teaching asst. La. State Univ., Baton Rouge, 1964-66; asst. prof. U. Southwestern La., Lafayette, 1966-70, asso. prof., 1970-75, prof., 1976, mem. council grad. coordinators, 1973-76; chmn., prof. biology U. Miss., University, 1976—; Mem. Atchafalaya River Basin Research Council, 1972-74; mem. exec. council La. Acad. Scis., 1972-74, state dir. sci. teaching, 1972-74; research asso. Gulf South Research Inst., 1972-74; dir. Lafayette Natural History Mus. and Planetarium, 1973, U.S. Fish and Wildlife Service Atchafalaya River Basin Herpetofaunal Study, 1973-76; mem. exec. council Gopher Tortoise Soc., 1979-81; commr. Miss. Dept. Wildlife Conservation, 1978-79; mem. Govs. Select Com. Radioactivity and Radioactive Waste Depository, 1979-80; commr. Commn. Miss. Dept. Wildlife Conservation, 1980—, chmn. Commn., 1983-84. Mem. Miss. Wildlife Heritage Com., 1980—. Served with USMC, 1957. Recipient numerous grants; Disting. Prof. award U. Southwestern La., 1973; Govs. Meritorious Service award State of Miss., 1979; citation for outstanding sci. teaching Nat. Sci. Tchrs. Assn.-Ill. Supt. Public Instrn., 1962. Mem. Am. Soc. Ichthyologists and Herpetologists, Brit. Herpetol. Soc., Md. Herpetological Soc., Phila. Herpetological Soc., La. Acad. Sci., Assn. de Ictiologos e Herpetologos de Latino-Americana, Soc. for Study Amphibians and Reptiles, Miss. Acad. Sci., Herpetologists League, Herpetological Assn. Africa, Caribbean Inst. Sci., Gopher Tortoise Soc., Sigma Xi (chpt. pres. 1976, 79-80), Beta Beta Beta, Phi Eta Sigma, Phi Kappa Phi. Clubs: Explorers (fellow); Civitan (Lafayette, La.) (mem. exec. com.); National Exchange (Oxford, Miss.)). Home: 211 St Andrews Circle Oxford MS 38655 Office: Dept of Biology Univ Mississippi University MS 38677

KEISER, HARRY ROBERT, physician; b. Chgo., Aug. 9, 1933; s. Harry Rudolph and Anna Mae (Hungerford) K.; m. Linda Lee Hallsten, June 11, 1965; children: Harry Rudolph, Robert Hungerford. B.A., Northwestern U., 1955, M.D., 1958. Diplomate: Nat. Bd. Med. Examiners, Am. Bd. Internal Medicine. Intern Phila. Gen. Hosp., 1958-59; resident in internal medicine VA Research Hosp., Chgo., 1959-60; clin. asso. Nat. Heart Inst., NIH, Bethesda, Md., 1960-63; resident in internal medicine U. Calif. Hosp., San Francisco, 1963-64; sr. investigator, then acting chief exptl. therapeutics br. Nat. Heart Inst., 1964-73; dep. chief hypertension-endocrine br. Nat. Heart, Lung and Blood Inst., 1974—, clin. dir. inst., 1976—; clin. asst. prof. medicine Georgetown U. Med. Sch., 1965—; commd. officer USPHS, 1960—, med. dir., 1972—. Author articles on causes of hypertension. Fellow ACP; mem. Am. Fedn. Clin. Research, Am. Soc. Pharmacology and Exptl. Therapeutics, Am. Heart Assn., Sierra Club, Izaak Walton League. Home: 6132 Lux Ln Rockville MD 20852 Office: Bldg 10 Room 8C-103 Nat Heart Lung and Blood Inst Bethesda MD 20205

KEISER, JOHN HOWARD, university president; b. Mt. Olive, Ill., Mar. 12, 1936; s. Howard H. and Lorraine G. K.; m. Nancy Peterka, June 27, 1959; children: John, Sam, Joe. B.S. in Edn, Eastern Ill. U., 1958; M.A., Northwestern U., 1960, Ph.D. in History, 1964. Prof. history Westminster Coll., Fulton, Mo., 1963-65, Eastern Ill. U., Charleston, 1965-71; v.p. acad. affairs Sangamon State U., Springfield, Ill., 1971-78, acting pres., 1978; pres. Boise (Idaho) State U., 1978—. Author: Building for the Centuries, Illinois, 1865-1898, 1977, Illinois Vignettes, 1977. Bd. dirs. Abraham Lincoln council Boy Scouts Am., Springfield, Ore-Ida Council, Boise. Recipient Harry E. Pratt Meml. award Jour. Ill. History, 1970, 72; award of merit Ill. State Hist. Soc., 1980, Am. Assn. State and Local History, 1980. Mem. Orgn. Am. Historians, Am. Hist. Soc., Labor History Soc., Boise C. of C. Roman Catholic. Club: Rotary. Office: President's Office 1910 University Blvd Boise ID 83725

KEISER, NORMAN MICHAEL, securities company executive; b. Binghamton, N.Y., Sept. 15, 1919; s. Norman George and Helen Elizabeth (Clinton) K.; m. Louise Knight Belcher, June 26, 1943; children: Michael Lewis, Bruce Norman, Thomas Clinton, Stephen Knight. B.S., Wharton Sch., U. Pa., 1941. Mem. sales staff Armstrong Cork Co., Lancaster and Buffalo, Pa., 1941-42, 45-47; with George D.B. Bonbright Co., Buffalo, 1947-50; exec. v.p. Hugh Johnson & Co., Buffalo, 1950-69, pres., 1969-74, vice chmn., 1974-76; v.p. First Albany Corp., Buffalo, 1977—; exec. v.p., dir. Johnson's Charts, Buffalo, 1949—; pres. Binghamton Credit Corp., N.Y., 1951-80, also dir. Served as aviator USNR, 1942-45. Decorated Navy Cross, Silver Star, D.F.C. (3), Air medal (3). Mem. Beta Gamma Sigma, Phi Gamma Delta. Republican. Presbyn. (elder). Club: Bond (Buffalo). Home: 39 Hillcrest Rd East Aurora NY 14052 Office: 69 Delaware Ave Buffalo NY 14202

KEITEL, HARVEY, actor; b. Bklyn., 1947. Studied with, Lee Strasberg, Frank Corsaro at Actors Studio. Motion picture performances include Who's That Knocking at My Door?, 1968, Mean

Streets, 1973, Alice Doesn't Live Here Anymore, 1975, Taxi Driver, 1976, Mother Jugs and Speed, 1976, Buffalo Bill and the Indians, 1976, Welcome to L.A, 1977, Blue Collar, 1978, The Duellists, 1978, Fingers, 1978, Bad Timing, 1980, The Border, 1982, Exposed, 1983; stage appearances include Hurlyburly, 1984; numerous TV appearances including drama A Memory of Two Mondays, 1971; movie The Virginia Hill Story, 1974, Eagle's Way, 1979, Saturn 3, 1980, Bad Timing, 1980; appeared on stage in: Hurlyburly, 1984. *

KEITER, WILLIAM EDWARD, insurance company executive; b. Orange, N.J., Dec. 7, 1929; s. Ernest R. and Florence H. (Reineke) K.; m. Jeanne D. Flauss, May 16, 1953; children: Nancy, John, Susan. B.A., Muhlenberg Coll., 1951; M.B.A., U. Pa., 1952. With N.Y. Life Ins. Co., N.Y.C., 1954—, 2d v.p., 1964-67, v.p., 1967-74, sr. v.p. in charge investment dept., 1974-79, exec. v.p., 1979—. Trustee Episcopalian Diocesan Investment Trust, Newark, Muhlenberg Coll., United Student Aid Funds. Served with fin. corps AUS, 1952-54. Office: NY Life Ins Co 51 Madison Ave New York NY 10010 *

KEITH, BRIAN MICHAEL, actor; b. Bayonne, N.J., Nov. 14, 1921; s. Robert Lee and Helena (Shipmen) K.; m. Victoria Lei Aloha Young, 1968; children: Michael, Mimi, Bobby, Daisy. Student pub. schs., L.I., N.Y. Pres. Miguel Prodns., Inc. (TV prodn., real estate, agr., and minerals co.). Appeared in summer stock, Broadway, films and TV, 1945—; on stage in Da, 1979; films Arrowhead, 1952, Alaska Seas, 1953, Violent Men, 1954, Bamboo Prison, 1955, Five Against the House, 1955, Storm Center, 1956, Run of the Arrow, 1957, Dino, 1957, Nightfall, 1957, Sierra Baron, 1958, The Young Philadelphians, 1959, With Six You Get Eggroll, 1960, The Deadly Companions, 1961, Savage Sam, 1963, The Parent Trap, 1961, Moon Pilot, 1962, The Raiders, 1964, Those Calloways, 1965, A Tiger Walks, 1964, The Hallelujah Trail, 1965, Rare Breed, 1966, The Russians Are Coming, 1966, Nevada Smith, 1966, Reflections in a Golden Eye, 1967, Krakatoa, East of Java, 1968, Gaily, Gaily, 1969, Suppose They Gave a War and Nobody Came, 1969, Mckenzie Break, 1970, Scandalous John, 1971, Something Big, 1972, The Yakuza, 1975, The Wind and the Lion, 1975, Joe Panther, 1976, Nickelodeon, 1976, Hooper, 1978, Meteor, 1979, The Mountain Men, 1980, Charlie Chan and The Curse of the Dragon Queen, 1981, Sharkey's Machine, 1982; TV series include Crusader, 1955-56, The Westerner, 1960, Family Affair, 1966-71, The Little People, 1972-73, The Brian Keith Show, 1973-74; TV appearances include How the West Was Won, 1978, Centennial, 1978, The Seekers, 1979, Power, 1979, Moviola, 1980. Chmn. Hawaii unit Am. Lung Assn. Served with USMC, 1941-45; PTO. Decorated Navy Air medal. Mem. Actor's Equity Assn., Screen Actors Guild, AFTRA, Dirs. Guild Am. Roman Catholic. Club: Outrigger Canoe (Honolulu). Office: care James McHugh Agy 8150 Beverly Blvd Suite 206 Los Angeles CA 90048 *

KEITH, DAMON JEROME, judge; b. Detroit, July 4, 1922; s. Perry A. and Annie L. (Williams) K.; m. Rachel Boone, Oct. 18, 1953; children: Cecile Keith, Debbie, Gilda. S.B., W.Va. State Coll., 1943; LL.B., Howard U., 1949; LL.M., Wayne State U., 1956; hon. degrees, U. Mich., Howard U., Wayne State U., Mich. State U., N.Y. Law Sch., Detroit Coll. Law, W.Va. State Coll., U. Detroit, Atlanta U., Lincoln U. Bar: Mich. 1949. Atty. Office Friend of Ct., Detroit, 1952-56; sr. ptnr. firm Keith, Conyers Anderson, Brown & Wahls, Detroit, 1964-67; mem. Wayne County Bd. Suprs., 1958-63; chief U.S. judge Eastern Dist. Mich., 1967-77; judge U.S. Ct. Appeals for 6th Circuit, Detroit, 1977—; Mem. Wayne County (Mich.) Bd. Suprs., 1958-63; chmn. Mich. Civil Rights Commn., 1964-67; pres. Detroit Housing Commn., 1958-67; commnr. State Bar Mich., 1960-67; mem. Mich. Com. Manpower Devel. and Vocat. Tng., 1964, Detroit Mayor's Health Advisory Com., 1969. Contbr. to legal jours. Trustee Med. Corp. Detroit, Interlochen Arts Acad., Cranbrook Sch.; mem. Citizen's Advisory Com. Equal Ednl. Opportunity Detroit Bd. Edn.; vice pres. United Negro Coll. Fund Detroit; 1st v.p. emeritus Detroit chpt. NAACP; mem. com. mgmt. Detroit YMCA, Detroit council Boy Scouts Am., Detroit Arts Commn. Served with AUS, World War II. Recipient Alumni citation Wayne State U., 1968, Citizen award Mich. State U., numerous others; Spingarn medalist, 1974; named 1 of 100 Most Influential Black Ams. Ebony Mag., 1971, 77. Mem. Am. (council sect. legal edn. and admission to bar), Nat., Mich., Detroit bar assns., Nat. Lawyers Guild, Am. Judicature Soc., Alpha Phi Alpha. Baptist (deacon). Club: Detroit Cotillion. Office: US Ct Appeals 240 Fed Bldg Detroit MI 48226 *

KEITH, DONALD RAYMOND, army officer; b. Mason County, Mich., Jan. 31, 1927; s. John Daniel and Agnes Elizabeth (Miller) K.; m. Erika Krausse, Apr. 11, 1953; 1 son, Michael Thomas. B.S., U.S. Mil. Acad., 1949; M.A., Columbia U., 1957. Commd. 2d lt. U.S. Army, 1949, advanced through grades to gen., 1981; asst. prof. chemistry U.S. Mil. Acad., 1958-61; asst. sec. gen. staff Dept. Army, Washington, 1964-66; comdg. officer 5th Bn., 73d Arty., 1967-68, 36th Field Arty. Group, 1969-70; exec. to chief research and devel. Dept. Army, Washington, 1970-71; dir. research and analysis CORDS, Mil. Assistance Command, Vietnam, 1971-73; dir. devels. Office Chief Research and Devel., Dept. Army, Washington, 1973-74; dir. Weapons Systems Office Dep. Chief Staff for Research and Devel. and Acquisition Dept. Army, Washington, 1974-76; comdg. gen. U.S. Army Field Arty. Center, Ft. Sill, Okla., 1976-77; dep. chief staff research, devel. and acquisition Dept. Army, 1977-81; comdr. U.S. Army Materiel Devel. and Readiness Command, 1981—. Co-author: Management of Defense Research and Development, 1967. Decorated Legion of Merit with 2 oak leaf clusters, Bronze Star, Meritorious Service medal, Army Commendation medal with oak leaf cluster, Vietnamese Distinguished Service Order. Home: Quarters 7 Fort McNair Washington DC 20024 Office: Comdr USA DARCOM 50001 Eisenhower Ave Alexandria VA 22333

KEITH, JENNIE, anthropology educator, author; b. Carmel, Calif., Nov. 15, 1942; d. Paul K. and Romayne Louise (Fuller) Hill; m. Marc Howard Ross, Aug. 25, 1968 (div. 1978); 1 son, Aaron Elliot Ross; m. Roy Gerald Fitzgerald, July 19, 1980; 1 dau., Kate Romayne Keith-Fitzgerald. B.A., Pomona Coll., 1964; M.A., Northwestern U., 1966, Ph.D., 1968. NIMH fellow, Paris, 1968-70; asst. prof. anthropology Swarthmore Coll., 1970-76, assoc. prof., 1976-82, prof., 1982—; mem. research edn. rev. com. NIMH, Washington, 1979-82; co-dir. workshop on age and anthropology Nat. Inst. Aging, Washington, 1980-81, task group leader, nat. research plan on aging, 1981. Author: Old People, New Lives, 1977, 2d paperback edit., 1982 (Am. Jour. Nursing Book of Yr. 1978), Old People as People, 1982; co-editor: New Methods for Old-Age Research, 1980; editorial bd.: Gerontologist, 1981—; assoc. editor: Research on Aging, 1981—. Bd. dirs. Sr. Community Services, Polsom, Pa., 1980—, Inst. Outdoor Awareness, Swarthmore, Pa., 1980—. Conf. grantee Nat. Inst. Aging, 1980, research grantee, 1982-84. Fellow Am. Anthrop. Assn., Geronthol Soc. Am.; mem. Assn. Anthropology and Gerontology (founder, sec. 1980-81). Office: Dept Anthropology Swarthmore Coll Swarthmore PA 19081 *Developement of my own potential through a combination of discipline and creativity, with goals of both utility and elegance, and with out harm to others—these are my goals in brief.*

KEITH, ROBERT EMERSON, JR., banker; b. Phila., Dec. 15, 1945; s. Robert E. and Hazel (Marscher) K.; m. Margot Wallace, Aug. 27, 1965; children: Robert Emerson III, Leslie. B.A., Amherst Coll., 1963; J.D., Temple U., 1966. Bar: Pa. 1967. Investment officer Fidelity Bank, Phila., 1970-72, sr. investment officer, 1972-73, asst. v.p., 1973-75, v.p., 1975-78, sr. v.p., 1979—; dir. Globe Ticket Co., N.Y.C., WaWa, Inc. Bd. dirs. Assoc. Day Care of Phila., 1980—, Old Phila. Devel. Corp., 1983—. Office: Fidelity Bank Broad and Walnut Sts Philadelphia PA 19109

KEITH, WARREN GRAY, engring. educator; b. Anamosa, Iowa, Sept. 16, 1908; s. Roy Theo and Jessie (Gray) K.; m. Fannie Luella Bare, Aug. 22, 1937; children—James Warren, Carolyn Luella. B.S. in Civil Engring, Iowa State U., 1934, M.S., U. Mo., 1948. Registered profl. engr., Ala., Miss. Engr., Chisago County, Minn., 1937-41; stress analyst Goodyear Aircraft Corp., Akron, Ohio, 1943-45; mem. faculty U. Ala., 1941-43, 45—, prof. civil engring., head dept., 1964-68, prof. emeritus, 1974—, dir. engring. tech. programs, 1972-74; partner Woodman-Keith Engring. Co., cons. engring., 1949—. Mem. Am. Soc. Civil Engrs. (pres. Ala. 1954), Am. Soc. Engring. Edn., Nat., Ala. socs. profl. engrs., Chi Epsilon (nat. council 1958-69, nat. pres. 1964-66). Home: 1611 27th Ave East Tuscaloosa AL 35404

KEITH, WILLIAM JOHN, English literature educator; b. London, Eng., May 9, 1934; naturalized, 1974; s. William Henry and Elna Mary (Harpham) K.; m. Hiroko Teresa Sato, Dec. 26, 1965. B.A., Jesus Coll., Cambridge U., 1958; M.A., U. Toronto, 1959, Ph.D., 1961. Lectr. English McMaster U., 1961-62, asst. prof., 1962-66; asso. prof. English U. Toronto, 1966-71, prof., 1971—. Author: Richard Jefferies, 1965, Charles G. D. Roberts, 1969, The Rural Tradition, 1974, The Poetry of Nature, 1980, Epic Fiction, 1981; Editor: U. Toronto Quar, 1976—. Served with RAEC, 1953-55. Fellow Royal Soc. Can.; mem. Richard Jefferies Soc. (hon. pres. 1974—), Assn. Canadian Univ. Tchrs. English. Home: 142 Hilton Ave Toronto ON M5R 3E9 Canada Office: University Coll U Toronto Toronto M5S 1A1 Canada

KEITHLEY, GEORGE FREDERICK, writer; b. Chgo., July 18, 1935; s. James Balliet and Helen (Stuart) K.; m. Mary Zoe Marhoefer, Nov. 5, 1960 (div. 1980); children: Elizabeth, Clare, Christopher. A.B., Duke, 1957; postgrad., Stanford, 1957-58; M.F.A., U. Iowa, 1960, 1960-62. Mem. faculty dept. English Calif. State U., Chico, 1962—, prof., 1973—; judge Masefield award Poetry Soc. Am., 1972, Hemley award, 1973, Dickinson award, 1976, Ames award, 1978, Acad. Am. Poets prizes for Calif. State U., Northridge, 1970-71, Beloit Coll., 1974; editorial cons. Harcourt Brace Co., W.W. Norton Co., Univ. Ky. Press. Author: epic poem The Donner Party, 1972 (Western Heritage award 1972, Book of Month Club alt.), stage adaptation, Sacramento Civic Theater, 1973, Sacramento Bicentennial, 1975, opera, 1979, 82; Song in a Strange Land, 1974 (co-recipient di Castagnola award 1973); verse play The Best Blood of the Country (winner Duke Players Playwriting award 1977), (Leighton Rollins award 1977, DramaRama 82 1st Prize 1982), Lyric Poetry (Boyle award New Eng. Poetry Club 1980); represented in: anthology 19 New American Poets, 1984; editor: (with Charles V. Genthe) Themes in American Literature, 1972; guest editor: Flume Press Chapbook Series, 1984. Recipient Outstanding Educator Am. citation, 1973; Chancellor's Leave Creative Work grantee, 1966; Outstanding Prof. award Calif. State U., Chico, 1977-78. Mem. Poetry Soc. Am., New Eng. Poetry Club, Assoc. Writing Programs, Dramatists Guild, Alpha Tau Omega. Democrat. Home: 1302 Sunset Ave Chico CA 95926 *There is in all life a rhythm to be felt, to be sensed, and brought into our consciousness by art. To sense these rhythms in harmony with the movement of his own spirit is a task which the poet gladly undertakes. Often people wish to give voice to this inner urgency of life, even to give it flesh and blood, in the shape of our human drama. They hope to create in language the theatre of the spirit, where a troop of awful and honorable and comical characters give speech and gesture to our souls. This is my hope, too.*

KEITH-SPIEGEL, PATRICIA COSETTE, educator, researcher, author; b. Glendale, Calif.; d. Boyd E. and Barbara (Halsey) Keith; 1 son, Gary Brian. B.A. cum laude, Occidental Coll., 1961; M.A. (NDEA predoctoral fellow), Claremont Grad. Sch., 1964, Ph.D., 1968. Psychology research asst. Brentwood VA Hosp., 1964-66; asst. prof. psychology Calif. State U., Northridge, 1966-69, asso. prof., 1969-73, prof., 1973—. Author: Outsiders U.S.A, 1973; sect. editor: Internat. Ency. of Psychiatry, Psychoanalysis, Psychology and Neurology; contbr. articles to profl. jours. Recipient Superior Performance award VA, 1965, Vol. Service awards, 1967-68. Fellow Am. Psychol. Assn. (council reps. 1975-78, ethics com. 1975-80), Western Psychol. Assn. (dir. 1975-78, pres. 1981); mem. Calif. Psychol. Assn. (dir. 1975-78, Outstanding Humanitarian award 1977, Silver Psi award 1978), Los Angeles Psychol. Assn. (dir. 1971-75), San Fernando Valley Psychol. Assn. (dir.), Psi Chi (nat. v.p. Western region 1977-80), Beta Phi Delta. Home: 9951 Calvin Ave Northridge CA 91324

KEKES, JOHN, philosopher, educator; b. Budapest, Hungary, Nov. 22, 1936; came to U.S., 1965, naturalized, 1977; s. Eugene and Anna (Borsodi) K.; m. Jean Justilliano, May 6, 1967. B.A., Queen's, Kingston, Ont., Can., 1961; M.A., Queen's, Kingston, Ont., Can., 1962; Ph.D., Australian Nat. U., 1965. Instr. to assoc. prof. philosophy Calif. State U., Northridge, 1965-71; prof. U. Sask., Regina, 1971-74, SUNY-Albany, 1974—, chmn. dept. philosophy, 1974-77, prof. philosophy and pub. policy, 1974—. Author: A Justification of Rationality, 1976, The Nature of Philosophy, 1980. Fellow Rockefeller Found. Humanities, 1980-81, Earhart Found., 1983; resident scholar Rockefeller Found. Stud Ctr., Bellagio, Italy, 1982. Mem. Am. Philos. Assn., Mind Assn., Royal Inst. Philosophy. Home: 114 S Pine Ave Albany NY 12208 Office: Dept Philosophy SUNY Albany NY 12222

KELALIS, PANAYOTIS, pediatric urologist; b. Nicosia, Cyprus, Jan. 17, 1932; came to U.S., 1960, naturalized, 1969; s. Peter and Julia (Petrides) K.; m. Barbara Wilson, Apr. 8, 1970. Student, U. Edinburgh, 1950-51; M.B.B.Ch., U. Dublin, 1957; M.S. in Urology, Mayo Grad. Sch. Medicine, 1964. Resident in urology Mayo Grad. Sch. Medicine, Rochester, Minn., 1960-64; asst. to staff Mayo Clinic, 1964, cons. urology, 1965—, head sect. pediatric urology and chmn. dept. urology, 1975—; prof. urology Mayo Med. Sch., 1975—. Editor: Clinical Pediatric Urology, 2 vols., 1976; contbr. numerous sci. articles to profl. jours., chpts. in books. Hon. consul Republic of Cyprus. Recipient Edward J. Noble Found. award, 1964; decorated knight Order of St. Andrew. Fellow ACS; mem. Am. Assn. Genito-Urinary Surgeons, Internat. Soc. Urology, Am. Urol. Assn., Soc. Pediatric Urology, Am. Acad. Pediatrics (chmn. urology sect.), Soc. Univ. Urologists, Sociedad Latino Americana de Urologia Infantile (hon.), Royal Soc. Medicine, Assn. Francaise d'Urologie (hon.), Sociedad Argentine de Urologia (corr.), Sigma Xi. Office: Mayo Clinic Rochester MN 55901

KELB, NORMAN ERNEST, indsl. exec.; b. Toledo, Apr. 2, 1893; s. Frank F. and Theresa (Himmelmann) K.; m. Carrie Bernice Schill, Aug. 15, 1917 (dec. 1948); 1 son, Edwin D.; m. Zelma Bird, 1952 (dec. 1975). Student pub. schs. With France Stone Co., 1913-29; sec.-treas., mgr. Erie Stone Co., 1929-39; pres., dir. High Point Oil Co., 1925—, Refiners Transport, Inc., Cumberland Quarriers, Inc., 1940—; pres. Ayrshire Collieries Corp., 1957-70. Served with U.S. Army, World War I. Mem. Nat. Coal Assn., Nat. Crushed Stone Assn. (pres. 1956, 57), Ind., Indpls. chambers commerce. Clubs: Mason (Shriner), Columbia (Indpls.); Woodland Country. Home: 4420 Cranbrook Dr Indianapolis IN 46250 Office: 7921 Castleway Dr PO Box 50854 Castleton Br Indianapolis IN 46250

KELCH, DAVID ERDMAN, utility exec.; b. New Orleans, July 19, 1928; s. Raymond Ellsworth and Norma (Erdman) K.; m. Maxyne Jones, Oct. 16, 1949; children—Mary Louise, David Carter. Asst. chief accountant Zia Co., Los Alamos, 1951-55; with Tex. Electric Service Co., Ft. Worth, 1955—, sec., asst. treas., 1966-73, sec.-treas., 1973-79, v.p., treas., 1979—; dir. subsidiary Old Ocean Fuel Co. Home: 2101 Yosemite Ct Fort Worth TX 76112 Office: 115 W 7th St Fort Worth TX 76102

KELCH, RAY ALDEN, educator; b. Logan, Ohio, Sept. 13, 1923; s. Albert Robison and Clara (Lindsey) K. A.B., Ohio State U., 1947, M.A., 1949, Ph.D., 1955. Mem. faculty Stephens U., Columbia, Mo., 1953-57; mem. faculty San Francisco State Coll., 1957—, prof. history, 1964—, chmn. dept., 1964-70; vis. prof. Ariz. State U., Tempe, 1970-71. Served with AUS, 1943-46. Mem. Am. Hist. Assn., Conf. Brit. Studies, Am. Assn. U. Profs. Democrat. Protestant Episcopalian. Home: 171 Melrose Ave San Francisco CA 94127

KELCH, ROBERT PAUL, pediatric endocrinologist; b. Detroit, Dec. 3, 1942; s. Paul and Iona Bertha (Schmidt) K.; m. Jeri Anne Parker, Aug. 17, 1963; children: Randall Paul, Julie Marie. Ph.B. (Gen. Motors Co. Nat. Merit scholar 1960), Wayne State U., Detroit, 1964; M.D. (univ. merit scholar 1963, Rollo E. Mccotter award 1964), U. Mich., Ann Arbor, 1967. Intern in pediatrics, then Wyeth pediatric residency fellow U. Mich. Med. Center, 1967-70, research fellow, 1969-70, mem. faculty, 1972—, prof. pediatrics, 1977—, acting chmn. dept., 1979-80, chmn. dept., 1981—; physician-in-chief C.S. Mott Children's Hosp. U. Mich., 1983—; NIH trainee pediatric endocrinology U. Calif. Med. Center, San Francisco, 1970-72. Co-author: A Practical Approach to Pediatric Endocrinology, 1975; contbr. articles med. jours. Served with USNR. Fellow Am. Acad. Pediatrics; mem. Soc. Pediatric Research, Endocrine Soc., Am. Fedn. Clin. Research, Central Soc. Clin. Research, Lawson Wilkins Pediatric Endocrine Soc., Midwest Soc. Pediatric Research. (pres. 1983-84). Methodist. Home: 3525 Charter Pl Ann Arbor MI 48105 Office: F2125 C S Mott Hosp Ann Arbor MI 48109

KELEHAN, JAMES LAWRENCE, management consultant; b. Mpls., Oct. 30, 1914; s. James H. L. and Sadie (Moran) K.; m. Mary Donahue, Jan. 3; children: Catherine M. Kelehan, Paul J. B.S., U. Minn., 1936, J.D., 1938. Asso. dir. Defense Plant, RFC, Washington, 1946-48; asst. gen. mgr. AEC, 1954-56; asst. to v.p. Boiler div. Babcock & Wilcox, 1957-60; pres., dir. Air Preheater Co., Inc., Wellsville, N.Y., 1961-64; v.p. mfg. Cumbustion Engring., Inc., Windsor, Conn., 1964-67, v.p. indsl. group, 1967-74; pres. James L. Kelehan and Assos., 1975—; adv. com. Conn. Bank & Trust Co. Chmn. bd. trustees Hartford Grad. Center. Recipient Outstanding Service award AEC, 1956. Mem. Mfrs. Assn. Hartford County (past pres., dir.). Club: El Conquistador Country (Bradenton, Fla.) (pres., dir.). Home: 6419 Sun Eagle Ln Bradenton FL 33507

KELEMEN, PÁL, archeologist, art historian; b. Budapest, Hungary, Apr. 24, 1894; came to U.S., 1932, naturalized, 1939; s. Joseph and Jenny (Gratt) K.; m. Elisabeth Hutchings Zulauf, May 2, 1932. Ed. univs., Budapest, Munich and Paris, Budapest, Vienna, Florence, London, Madrid, Seville; L.H.D., U. Ariz. Made 10 survey trips, Latin Am., since 1933; 2 for cultural div. Dept. State, to, Mexico, Guatemala, Honduras, El Salvador, Nicaragua, Panama, Colombia, Ecuador, Peru, Bolivia; survey and lecture trip for Dept. State to, Portugal, Spain, Switzerland, Hungary, Czechoslovakia, Belgium, 1948; lecture tour univs., mus. in, Southwest, Pacific coast, Can., 1952; vis. prof. U. Tex., 1953, Columbia, 1968; survey, Mex., 1953, 63, 64, 67, research, Portugal, Italy, Sicily, 1954, Eng., Switzerland, Italy and Spain, 1959; lectr. Nat. Gallery Art, Washington, Met. Mus. Art, N.Y.C.), and other univs. and mus.; U.S. specialist lecture tour for Dept. State to, Portugal, Spain, Italy, also Istanbul, Athens, Thessaloniki, London, 1956. Author: Battlefield of the Gods, Essays on Mexican Art, History and Exploration (travel book of the month; transl. Hungarian and German), 1937, Medieval American Art, 2 vols, 1943, 44, 46, 67, Baroque and Rococo in Latin America, 1951, 68, Medieval American Art, Masterpieces of the New World before Columbus, 1 vol, 1956, El Greco Revisited; Candia, Venice, Toledo, 1961, Spanish edit., 1965, El Greco Revisited: His Byzantine Heritage, 1962; paperbacks ancient, colonial art of Ams., Dutch, 1962, German, 1964, French, 1965, Spanish, 1967, Portuguese, 1969; Art of the Americas: Ancient and Hispanic, 1969, paperback, 1970, Hungarian edit., 1981, Peruvian Colonial Painting, 1971, Hussar's Picture Book, 1972, Folk Baroque in Mexico, 1974, The Painter in Europe and in Viceregal Spanish America, 1976, Vanishing Art of the Americas, 1977, Stepchild of the Humanities: Art of the Americas Observed, 1979, Colonial Organs of Latin Am., Swiss edit, 1981, Is Maya Art Primitive?, 1982, Icon and Santo, 1983; contbr. to: Ency. Brit., Stauffacher's World Art History; also contbr. leading periodicals in, Europe, U.S., Latin Am. Hon. presbiter First Magyar Ref. Ch., N.Y. Officer, 4 yrs., World War I; mem. Commn. for Protection and Salvage of Artistic and Historic Monuments in War Areas, World War II; trustee Kodaly Center Am. Decorated comdr. Order of Merit, Ecuador. Fellow Royal Anthrop. Inst.; mem. various sci. socs. in U.S., Latin Am., Europe. From consideration of early Christian art, turned since coming in U.S. to pre-Colombian and colonial art in Latin Am. Address: 1241 Silverado St La Jolla CA 92037

KELL, GEORGE CLYDE, broadcaster, former professional baseball player; b. Swifton, Ark., Aug. 23, 1922; s. M. C. and Alma (Perrin) K. Third baseman Phila. Athletics, Am. League, 1943-46, Detroit Tigers, Am. League, 1946-52; thrid baseman Boston Red Soc, Am. League, 1952-54; third baseman Chgo. White Sox, Am. League, 1954-56, Balt. Orioles, 1956-57; broadcaster CBS-TV Game of the Week, 1958; radio broadcaster Detroit Tigers, 1959-64; TV broadcaster Sta.-WDIV, 1965—. Inductee Baseball Hall of Fame, 1983; named to Am. League All-Star Team (6 times). Office: Detroit Tigers Tiger Stadium Detroit MI 48216

KELLAM, RICHARD B., judge; b. 1909. Bar: Va. bar 1934. Chief judge U.S. Dist. Ct. for Va. Eastern Dist., Norfolk. *

KELLAMS, DARRELL FRANK, educator; b. Salina, Kans., July 1, 1926; s. Perry C. and Ruth K.; m. Elizabeth Marie Lincoln, Feb. 7, 1947; children—David Michael, John Keith, Robert Andrew. B.S. in Edn, Emporia (Kans.) State U., 1951; M.Ed., U. Kans., 1955, Ed.D., 1964. From elem. sch. tchr. to jr. high sch. prin., Shawnee Mission, Kans., 1951-64; mem. faculty U. Nebr., Omaha, 1965—, prof. ednl. adminstrn., chmn. dept., 1968—. Contbr. articles to profl. jours. Served with AUS, 1944-46. Profl. Devel. fellow U. Nebr. System, 1979. Mem. Am. Assn. Sch. Adminstrs., Nat. Assn. Core Curriculum, NEA, Nebr. Council Sch. Adminstrs., Nebr. Schoolmasters Club, Am. Legion, Phi Delta Kappa (Nebr. area coordinator). Lutheran. Office: U Nebr 60th and Dodge Sts Omaha NE 68182 *

KELLAR, EDWARD PETER, information resource management executive; b. Adams, Mass., Sept. 25, 1925; s. Peter P. and Antonia M. (Lubas) K.; m. Doris Parker, Nov. 24, 1955; children: Elizabeth, Robert, Joan, Peter, David. B.S., U. Pa., 1955; M.B.A., Northeastern U., 1960. Prodn. control Gen. Electric Co., Pittsfield, Mass., 1943-51; engr. Sprague Electric Co., North Adams, Mass., 1952-53; financial mgmt. trainee, various managerial positions safety razor div., mgr. adminstrn. Gillette Industries Ltd., U.K.; corp. controller, v.p. Fin.

Office, Gillette Co., Boston, 1955-83; v.p. info. resource mgmt. Beth Israel Hosp., Boston. Mem. Financial Execs. Ins. Club: Duxbury Yacht. Home: PO Box 1519 Duxbury MA 02332 Office: Beth Israel Hosp 330 Brookline Ave Boston MA 02215

KELLAR, LORRENCE THEODORE, food retail and manufacturing executive; b. Burlington, Iowa, Aug. 10, 1937; s. William Paul and Grace Alberta (Matthews) K.; m. Susan Stewart, Aug. 10, 1958 (div. 1976); children: Kevin, Katherine, Nicholas; m. 2d Barbara Ann Weeks, Aug. 26, 1977; 1 dau., Ainsley. B.S., U. Iowa, 1958; M.B.A., U. Va., 1962. With 3M Corp., St. Paul, 1962-65, Kroger Co., Cin., 1965—, beginning as mgr. fin. planning, successively asst. treas., v.p. corp. devel., v.p. capital mgmt., 1965-82, v.p., treas., 1982—. Pres., chmn. bd. Cin. Ballet Co., 1976—; bd. dirs. WCET Pub. TV, Cin., 1982—, Cin. Charterd Com., 1970-78; pres. Queen City Assn., 1969. Recipient Corbett award in fine arts Cin. Post, 1983. Mem. Fin. Execs. Inst. Clubs: Cin. Country; Quenn City (Cin.). Office: Kroger Co 1014 Vine St Cincinnati OH 45201

KELLAWAY, ROGER WARREN, composer, pianist; b. Waban, Mass., Nov. 1, 1939; s. Ralph Willard and Alice (Parker) K.; m. Jorjana McIntosh, Nov. 11, 1965; 1 son, Colin. Student, New Eng. Conservatory of Music. Pianist, music arranger; composer: musical scores for motion pictures including The Extraordinary Adventures of the Mouse and His Child; animated cartoon Silent Scream, 1980; ballet music for George Balanchine, Pamtgg; arranger: music for Roger Kellaway Cello Quartet; piano accompanist, producer various singers and artists. Address: care Haber & Ehrlich 16255 Ventura Suite 710 Encino CA 91436 *

KELLEHER, HERBERT DAVID, lawyer, airline executive; b. Camden, N.J., Mar. 12, 1931; s. Harry and Ruth (Moore) K.; m. Joan Negley, Sept. 9, 1955; children—Julie, Michael, Ruth, David. B.A. cum laude (Olin scholar), Wesleyan U., 1953; LL.B. cum laude (Root Tilden scholar), N.Y. U., 1956. Bar: N.J. bar 1957, Tex. bar 1962. Clk. N.J. Supreme Ct., 1956-59; assoc. firm Lum, Biunno & Tompkins, Newark, 1959-61; ptnr. firm Matthews, Nowlin, Macfarlane & Barrett, San Antonio, 1961-69; sr. ptnr. firm Oppenheimer, Rosenberg, Kelleher & Wheatley, Inc., San Antonio, 1969—; founder, gen. counsel, pres. chmn., dir. S.W. Airlines Co., Dallas, 1967—; dir. May Petroleum, Inc., Dallas., Mercantile Tex. Corp. Chmn. adv. bus. council Trinity U., San Antonio; vice chmn. bus. adv. council U. Tex. Sch. Bus.; campaign coordinator Connally for Gov., 1961, 63, 65; Bexar County dir. Bentsen for Senator, 1970, 76, state co chmn., 1975-76; chmn. Senate Dist. 19 Democratic Com., 1968-70; del. Dem. Nat. Conv., 1964, 68; mem. state steering com. Bentsen for Pres., 1975-76; pres. bd. trustees St. Mary's Hall, San Antonio; pres. Travelers Aid Soc., San Antonio. Named Chief Exec. Officer of Year The Fin. World, 1982, Best Chief Exec. Regional Airline Industry Wall St. Transcript, 1982; Recipient Fin. Mgmt. award Air Transport World, 1982. Fellow Tex. Bar Found. (life); mem. Am., San Antonio, N.J. bar assns., State Bar Tex., San Antonio C. of C. (dir.), Order of Alamo, Tex. Cavaliers. Home: 144 Thelma Dr San Antonio TX 78212 Office: 711 Navarro St Suite 620 San Antonio TX 78205

KELLEHER, PATRICK JOSEPH, art historian; b. Colorado Springs, Colo., July 26, 1917; s. Patrick and Mary (Devaney) K.; m. Marion Mackie, Mar. 14, 1948; 1 dau., Maria. A.B., Colo. Coll., 1939; M.F.A., Princeton, 1942, Ph.D. (Procter fellow), 1947; postgrad. fellow, Am. Acad. in Rome, 1947-49. Chief curator art Los Angeles County Mus., 1949; lectr. U. Buffalo, 1950-51; curator collections Albright-Knox Art Gallery, Buffalo, 1950-54; curator European art Nelson Gallery-Atkins Mus., Kansas City, Mo., 1954-59; dir. Art Mus., Princeton, 1960-72, prof. art and archeology, 1960-73. Served to maj. AUS, 1942-46. Mem. Phi Beta Kappa. Home: 176 Parkside Dr Princeton NJ 08540

KELLEHER, ROBERT JOSEPH, judge; b. N.Y.C., Mar. 5, 1913; s. Frank and Mary (Donovan) K.; m. Gracyn W. Wheeler, Aug. 14, 1940; children: R. Jeffrey, Karen Kathleen. A.B., Williams Coll., 1935; LL.B., Harvard U., 1938. Bar: N.Y. 1939, Calif. 1942, U.S. Supreme Ct 1942. Atty. War Dept., 1941-43; Asst. U.S. atty. So. Dist. Calif., 1948-50; pvt. practice, Beverly Hills, 1951-71, U.S. dist. judge, 1971—. Mem. So. Calif. Com. Olympic Games, 1964; capt. U.S. Davis Cup Team, 1962-63; treas. Youth Tennis Found. So. Calif., 1961-64. Served to lt. USNR, 1942-45. Mem. So. Calif. Tennis Assn. (v.p. 1958-64, pres. 1983—), U.S. Lawn Tennis Assn. (pres. 1967-68), Delta Kappa Epsilon., Harvard of So. Calif., Williams (N.Y.C.), La Jolla (Calif.), Beach and Tennis. Home: 15 St Malo Oceanside CA 92054 Office: US Courthouse 312 N Spring St Los Angeles CA 90012

KELLEHER, THOMAS F., justice R.I. Supreme Ct.; b. Providence, Jan. 4, 1923; m. Mary Frances. Grad., Boston U. Sch. Law, 1948. Bar: R.I. bar. Practice law, probate judge, solicitor, Smithfield, R.I.; now justice R.I. Supreme Ct.; Mem. Gov.'s Task Force Mental Health, 1963; chmn. Com. on Juvenile Delinquency, 1961. Mem. R.I. Ho. of Reps., 1955-66, dep. majority leader, 1965. Served with USN, 1942-46; capt. USAR ret. Mem. Res. Officers Assn. Home: 381 Nayatt Rd Barrington RI 02806 Office: State Supreme Court Providence RI 02903

KELLEN, STEPHEN MAX, investment banker; b. Berlin, Germany, Apr. 21, 1914; came to U.S., 1936, naturalized, 1944; s. Max and Leonie (Marcuse) Katzenellenbogen; m. Anna-Maria Arnhold, Mar. 7, 1940; children: Marina Kellen Gundlach, Michael. Grad., Royal French Coll., Berlin, 1932. With Berliner Handels-Gesellschaft, Berlin, 1932-35, Lazard Bros. Ltd., London, Eng., 1936, Loeb, Rhoades & Co., N.Y.C., 1937-40; with Arnhold and S. Bleichroeder, Inc., N.Y.C., 1940—, pres., 1955—; dir. Pittway Corp., Siemens Western Fin. N.Y.; mem. adv. com. N.Y. Stock Exchange. Mem. trustees council Nat. Gallery Art,, Washington; trustee Trust for Cultural Resources City of N.Y., Carnegie Hall Soc.; mem. trustees council Nat. Gallery Art, Washington. Mem. Investment Bankers Assn. Am. (bd. govs. 1969-71, chmn. fgn. investment com. 1967-72), Securities Industry Assn. (bd. govs. 1972-73, chmn. internat. finance com. 1972-73). Clubs: Bond, Wall Street, Metropolitan (N.Y.C.). Home: 784 Park Ave New York NY 10021 also Ridgefield CT Office: 30 Broad St New York NY 10004

KELLER, ALEX STEPHEN, lawyer; b. Vienna, Austria, Mar. 18, 1928; came to U.S., 1940, naturalized, 1945; s. Frederick O. and Fanny (Margo) K.; m. Gloria G. MacMillan, Aug. 5, 1949; children: Susan Lynn, Stephen Eric. B.A., U. Denver, 1948, LL.B., 1950. Bar: Colo. 1950. Since practiced, Denver; mem. firm Carl Cline, 1950-54, Early & Keller, 1954-69, Keller & Dunievitz, 1969-76, Keller, Dunievitz & Johnson, 1976—; vets. counselor U. Denver, 1948-50. Contbr. articles to legal jours. Pres. Young Democrats Colo., 1953; alternate del. Dem. Nat. Conv., 1952. Served as spl. agt. CIC, 1945-47. Mem. Am. Coll. Trial Lawyers, Am. Acad. Trial Lawyers, Am. Bar Assn., Colo. Bar Assn. (Award of Merit 1978, bd. govs. 1972-74, exec. council 1974), Denver Bar Assn. (trustee 1978-81), Arapahoe County Bar Assn., Internat. Soc. Barristers (pres. 1978-79). Lutheran. Club: Sports Car Am. (chmn. bd. 1969-72, 74, 75). Home: 4357 S Yosemite Ct Englewood CO 80111 Office: 950 17th St Suite 935 Denver CO 80202 *I have had the good fortune to be able to come to the United States. Because of that fact I have learned that self-discipline, hard work, honesty and common sense, sprinkled with a sense of humor, will inevitably result in success. At least that is true in this country and very few, if any, others. Man's purpose is clearly to serve his brothers and sisters on this planet and to leave it a little better than it would have been without him. The pursuit of wealth for its own sake is a waste of time.*

KELLER, CHARLES WALTER, civil engineer; b. Mpls., Nov. 27, 1925; s. Charles Walter and Rowena Rita (Bidwell) K.; m. Sydney Jerrems, Nov. 8, 1945; children: Chick, Jerry, Bill. B.S. in Civil Engring, U. Kans., 1945. Registered profl. engr., 26 states. With Black & Veatch (cons. engrs.), Kansas City, Mo., 1946—, partner, 1964—, exec. partner, head mgmt. services div., 1974—; chmn. bd. Moore, Gardner & Assocs., Inc. (cons. engrs.), Asheboro, N.C., Bank of Waverly, Mo., Higginsville (Mo.) State Bank; dir. Boatmen's Bank of Kansas City. Contbr. to profl. publs. Bd. govs. Am. Royal Horseshow. Served with C.E. USNR, 1943-46, 51-53. Fellow Am. Cons. Engrs. Council, ASCE; mem. Nat. Soc. Profl. Engrs., Am. Waterworks Assn., Water Pollution Control Fedn., Cons. Engrs. Council Mo. (pres. 1968), Sigma Chi. Methodist. Clubs: Kansas City, Missouri Yacht, Mission Hills Country, Saddle and Sirloin (pres. 1983), Rotary, Shriners. Home: 2601 W 70th St Mission Hills KS 66208 Office: PO Box 8405 1500 Meadowlake Pkwy Kansas City MO 64114

KELLER, CHRISTOPH, JR., bishop; b. Bay City, Mich., Dec. 22, 1915; s. Christoph and Margaret Ely (Walter) K.; m. Caroline P. Murphy, June 22, 1940; children: Caroline, Cornelia, Cynthia, Kathryn, Christoph, Elisabeth. Grad., Lake Forest (Ill.) Acad., 1934; B.A., Washington and Lee U., 1939, D.D., 1973; student, Grad. Sch. Theology, U. South, 1954, D.D., 1968; certificate spl. work, Gen. Theol. Sem., N.Y.C., 1957, S.T.D. (hon.), 1968. Planter, Alexandria, La., 1940—; pres. Deltic Farm & Timber Co., El Dorado, Ark., 1948-51; exec. v.p. Murphy Corp., El Dorado, 1951-54, dir., 1948—; ordained priest P.E. Ch., 1957; rector, Harrison, Ark., also charge missions in, Eureka Springs and Mountain Home, Ark., 1957-61; rector St. Andrews Episcopal Ch., Jackson, Miss., 1962-67; dean St. Andrews Cathedral, Jackson, until 1967; bishop coadjutor Diocese of Ark., 1967-70, diocesan bishop, 1970-81; exec. council Episc. Ch., 1976-82; chmn. Episcopal Ch. Bldg. Fund, 1982—; Dep. Gen. Conv. P. E. Ch., 1958, 61, 64, 67. Pres. La. Aberdeen Angus Breeders Assn., 1947, La. Delta Council, 1950; chmn. United Fund, El Dorado, 1952; Mem. Madison Parish (La.) Sch. Bd., 1952-53; Trustee All Saints Jr. Coll., Vicksburg, Miss., 1949-51, 67-81, U. South, 1973-77, Washington and Lee U., Lexington, Va., 1981—, Gen. Theol. Sem., N.Y.C., 1981—. Served as officer USMCR, World War II. Home: Inglewood Plantation Route 2 Box 53D Alexandria LA 71302

KELLER, DAVID COE, department store executive; b. Warren, Ohio, Jan. 30, 1921; s. David Claude and Minnie Corlin (Furgerson) K.; m. Gladys Marie Carstens, Jan. 6, 1945; 1 dau., Anne Marie (Mrs. Scot McCormick). B.B.A., Cleve. State U., 1943. Staff acct. Touche Ross & Co., Cleve., 1946-49; asst. controller M. O'Neil Co. (dept. store), Akron, Ohio, 1950-56; controller, treas., dir. F.N. Arbaugh Co. (dept. store), Lansing, Mich., 1956-59; v.p., treas., dir. Wurzburg Co. (dept. store), Grand Rapids, Mich., 1959-72; chief financial officer, v.p., treas. Wieboldt Stores Inc., Chgo., 1972-82, pres., chief exec. officer, 1982—. Bd. dirs. Jr. Achievement Grand Rapids, 1961-69; dir. Civic Fedn., Chgo., 1974—. Served with USMCR, 1943-45. Named Grand Rapids Boss of Year Am. Woman's Clubs, 1969. Mem. Ill. Retails Mchts. Assn. (treas. 1977—, bd. dirs., exec. com.), State St. Council (tax com.), Tau Kappa Epsilon. Club: Mason (Shriner). Office: Wieboldt Stores Inc 1 N State St Chicago IL 60602

KELLER, DONALD JOHN, food company executive; b. Chgo., Feb. 14, 1932; s. Philip F. and Gertrude (Rice) K.; m. Virginia Wilson, July 22, 1955; children: Ann Keller (Mrs. R.C. Springborn), Edward Wilson, Amy Margaret. A.B., Princeton U., 1954; M.B.A., Northwestern U., 1958. Account exec. Leo Burnett Co., Chgo., 1958-63; with Gen. Foods Corp., White Plains, N.Y., 1963—, group v.p., 1977-79, exec. v.p., 1979—, dir., 1981—. Mem. bd. visitors The Fuqua Sch. Bus., Duke U., 1979—. Served with AUS, 1954-56. Presbyterian (ruling elder). Club: Riverside (Conn.) Yacht. Office: 250 North St White Plains NY 10625 *

KELLER, EDWARD CLARENCE, JR., ecologist, statistician, geneticist, educator; b. Freehold, N.J., Oct. 8, 1932; s. Edward Clarence and Pauline (Van Sickle) K.; m. Helen Elizabeth Baylor, July 7, 1950; children: Edward Clarence III, Kim Lorie. B.Sc., Pa. State U., 1956, M.Sc., 1959, Ph.D., 1961; Sc.D., Salem Coll., 1978. Faculty Pa. State U., 1956-61, NIH fellow, 1959-60; NIH fellow, research asso. U. N.C. med. Sch., 1961-64; asso. prof. U. Md., College Park, 1964-67; mgr. data systems and biostatistics biol. systems div. NUS Corp., Hawthorne, Calif., 1967-68; prof. biology W.Va. U., Morgantown, 1968—, chmn. dept. biology, 1969-74; vis. prof. sci. edn. U. Md., 1980; v.p. Ecometrics, Inc., Morgantown, 1973-80; cons. various industry groups, various govtl. agys.; sec. Found. for Sci. and Handicapped, 1977—. Co-author books and lab. manuals; contbr. articles to profl. jours.; reviewer fed. agys. and sci. jours. Mem. AAAS, Am. Inst. Biol. Sci., Ecol. Soc. Am., Sci. Tchrs. Assn., Am. Statis. Assn., Nat. Marine Educators Assn. (chmn. com. handicapped), Coastal Soc., W.Va. Acad. Sci. (pres. 1975-76, editor procs., Nat. Found. alumnus of year 1965), Handicapped and Sci. Assn., Assn. Sci. for the Handicapped, Coll. Sci. Tchrs. Assn., Sigma Xi, Gamma Sigma Delta, Phi Epsilon Phi, Phi Sigma, Beta Beta Beta. Home: 236 Grand St Morgantown WV 26505 Office: Dept Biology W Va U Morgantown WV 26506

KELLER, EDWARD LOWELL, elec. engr.; b. Rapid City, S.D., Mar. 6, 1939; s. Earl Lowell and E. Blanche (Oldfield) K.; m. Carole Lynne Craig, Sept. 1, 1963; children—Edward Lowell, Craig, Morgan. B.S., U.S. Naval Acad., 1961; Ph.D., Johns Hopkins U., 1971. Mem. faculty U. Calif., Berkeley, 1971—, asso. prof. elec. engring., 1977-79, prof., 1979—; sr. scientist Smith Kettlewell Inst.Visual Scis., San Francisco, 1980—. Contbr. articles to sci. jours. Served with USN, 1961-65. Sr. Von Humboldt fellow, 1977-78. Mem. AAAS, Assn. Advancement Research in Vision and Ophthalmology, IEEE, Soc. Neurosci. Research on primate oculomotor system and math. modelling of nervous system. Home: 6 Duncan St Orinda CA 94115 Office: Dept Elec Engring U Calif Berkeley CA 94720

KELLER, ELIOT AARON, broadcast executive; b. Davenport, Iowa, June 11, 1947; s. Norman Edward and Millie (Morris) K.; m. Sandra Kay McGrew, July 3, 1970; 1 dau., Nicole. B.A., U. Iowa, 1970; M.S., San Diego State U., 1976. Corr. Sta. WHO-AM/FM/TV, Des Moines, 1969-70; newsman Sta. WSUI, Iowa City, Iowa, 1967-68, 68-69, 69-70, corr., 1968-69, 69-70; newsman Sta. WHBF-AM/FM/TV, Rock Island, Ill., 1969, Sta. WOC-AM/FM/TV, Davenport, 1970; freelance newsman and photographer, Iowa City, 1969-77; pres. KRNA, Inc., Iowa City, 1971—, mem. exec. com., 1982—; gen. mgr. Sta. KRNA, 1974—; dir. Sta. KRNA, Inc., 1971—. Mem. Radio-TV News Dirs. Assn., Broadcast Fin. Mgmt. Assn. Jewish. Home: 609 Keokuk Ct Iowa City IA 52240 Office: 1027 Hollywood Blvd at Broadway Iowa City IA 52240 *The chance only comes once.*

KELLER, GEORGE MATTHEW, oil executive; b. Kansas City, Mo., Dec. 3, 1923; s. George Matthew and Edna Louise (Mathews) K.; m. Adelaide McCague, Dec. 27, 1946; children: William G., Robert A., Barry R. B.S. in Chem. Engring., MIT, 1948. Mem. engring. dept. Standard Oil Calif., San Francisco, 1948-63, fgn. ops. staff, 1963-67, asst. v.p., asst. to pres., 1967-69, v.p., 1969-74, dir., 1970—, vice-chmn., 1974-81, chmn., chief exec. officer, 1981—; dir. First Interstate Bancorp., First Interstate Bank Calif., Boeing Co. Trustee, MIT; Trustee Notre Dame Coll., Belmont, Calif., Am. Enterprise Inst. Served to 1st lt. USAAF, 1943-46. Mem. M.I.T. Club No. Calif. (dir. 1972—), Am. Petroleum Inst. (dir.), Council Fgn. Relations, World Affairs Council No. Calif. (trustee 1972-79). Clubs: Peninsula Golf and Country (San Mateo, Calif.); World Trade, Bankers, Stock Exchange (San Francisco). Home: San Mateo CA Office: 225 Bush St San Francisco CA 94104

KELLER, HAROLD KEFAUVER, major league baseball executive; b. Middletown, Md., July 7, 1927; s. Charles Ernest and Naomi Sheffer (Kefauver) K.; m. Marietta Catherine McKee, Aug. 2, 1946 (div. Mar. 1965); children: Harold Kefauver, Jo Ann Lee, John David, Patricia Lu, Jan McKee; m. Dorothy Carol Mims, Mar. 27, 1965; 1 son, William Nevin. B.S., U. Md., 1953. Baseball player, 1948-54; tchr. Frederick (Md.) High Sch., 1954-59; asst. farm dir. Washington Senators (later Minn. Twins), 1959-60; farm dir. Wash. Senators-Tex. Rangers, 1961-62, 64-78; Eastern scouting supr. Minn. Twins, 1963-64; dir. player devel. Seattle Mariners, 1979—. Served with AUS, 1947-49. Mem. Assn. Profl. Baseball Players of Am. Republican. Club: Am. Contract Bridge League (pres. Ft. Western unit 1977-78). Home: 2018 245th Ave SE Issaquah WA 98027 Office: PO Box 4100 Seattle WA 98104

KELLER, JOHN FRANCIS, wine company executive; b. Mt. Horeb, Wis., Feb. 5, 1925; s. Frank S. and Elizabeth K. (Meier) K.; m. Barbara D. Mabbott, Feb. 18, 1950; children: Thomas, Patricia, Daniel, David, John. B.B.A. in Accounting, U. Wis., 1949; M.B.A., U. Chgo., 1963; grad., Exec. Program, Stanford U., 1978. C.P.A., Wis., Ill. Mgr. statis. control and gen. accounting Miller Brewing Co., Milw., 1952-58; controller Maremont Corp., 1958-68; v.p. finance Hamm's Brewing Co., 1968-70; v.p. finance, dir. United Vintners, Inc., San Francisco, 1970-80, chmn. bd., chief exec. officer, dir., 1980—; v.p. Wines group Heublein Wines, 1980—; dir. Madera Glass Co.; lectr./asso. prof. Calif. State U. at Hayward Grad. Sch. Bus. and Econs. Mem. Jr. Achievement; Active local Boy Scouts Am., Community Chest; pres. parish council St. Bartholomew Catholic Ch.; dir. Serra High Sch. Bd.; bd. dirs. Big Bros. San Francisco, 1971-75, Hill High St., St. Paul, 1969-70. Served to 2d lt. 82d Airborne div. AUS, 1944-46; ETO. Mem. Financial Execs. Inst., Wis., Calif. socs. C.P.A.s, Am. Mgmt. Assn., Am. Inst. C.P.A.s, Nat. Assn. Accountants, Assn. Corp. Growth, U.S., San Francisco chambers commerce, VFW, Pi Kappa Alpha (past treas., dir.). Home: 785 Tournament Dr Hillsborough CA 94010 Office: 1 Maritime Plaza San Francisco CA 94111

KELLER, JOSEPH BISHOP, mathematician, educator; b. Paterson, N.J., July 31, 1923; s. Isaac and Sally (Bishop) K.; m. Evelyn Fox, Aug. 29, 1963 (div. Nov. 17, 1976); children—Jeffrey M., Sarah N. B.A., N.Y.U., 1943, M.S., 1946, Ph.D., 1948. Prof. math. Courant Inst. Math. Scis., N.Y.U., 1948-79; chmn. dept. math. Univ. Coll. Arts and Scis. and Grad. Sch. Engring. and Sci., 1967-73; prof. math. and mech. engring. Stanford U., 1979—. Contbr. articles to profl. jours. Mem. Nat. Acad. Scis., Am. Acad. Arts and Scis., Am. Math. Soc., Am. Phys. Soc., Soc. Indsl. and Applied Math. Home: 820 Sonoma Terr Stanford CA 94305 Office: Dept Math Stanford U Stanford CA 94305

KELLER, KENNETH HARRISON, chemical engineering educator; b. N.Y.C., Oct. 19, 1934; s. Benjamin and Pearl (Pastor) K.; June 2, 1957 (div.); children: Andrew Robinson, Paul Victor; m. Bonita F. Sindelir, June 19, 1981; 1 son, Jesse Daniel. A.B., Columbia U., 1956, B.S., 1957; M.S. in Engring., Johns Hopkins U., 1963, Ph.D., 1964. Asst. prof. dept. chem. engring. U. Minn., Mpls., 1964-68, asso. prof., 1968-71, prof., 1971—, asso. dean Grad. Sch., 1973-74, acting dean Grad. Sch., 1974-75, head dept. chem. engring. and materials sci., 1978-80, v.p. acad. affairs, 1980—; cons. in field, mem. cardiology adv. com. NIH. Editor chem. engring. sect.: Jour. Bioengring, 1975-79. Mem. adv. com. program for Soviet emigre scholars, 1974-82; bd. govs. Argonne Nat. Lab.; bd. dirs. Walker Art Ctr. Served from ensign to lt. USNR, 1957-61. NIH Spl. fellow, 1972-73. Mem. Am. Soc. Artificial Internal Organs (pres. 1980-81), Am. Inst. Chem. Engrs. (Food and Bioengring. award 1980), Internat. Soc. Artificial Organs, N.Y. Acad. Scis., Am. Council for Emigrés in the Professions (dir. 1972-80), Phi Beta Kappa, Sigma Xi (nat. lectr. 1978-80). Office: 213 Morrill Hall U Minn 100 Church St SE Minneapolis MN 55455

KELLER, LEROY, newspaper broker; b. Longmont, Colo., Aug. 31, 1905; s. Samuel Ashby and Vinnie Alice (Howard) K.; m. Winifred Cora Allen, Mar. 31, 1935; children: John Pierce, Lynn Keller Andrews. A.B., U. Colo., 1929. Joined United Press Assns., 1929, staff writer, 1929-33, syndicate rep., 1933-35, bus. rep., 1936-45, asst. bus. mgr., 1945-48, gen. sales mgr., 1948- 64, v.p., 1952—, dir. client relations, 1959-64, v.p., gen. mgr. internat. divs., 1964-71; newspaper broker, 1971—; v.p. United Features Syndicate, 1958-65; Adv. com. World Press Inst., ANPA-World Press Achievement Awards. Mem. Inter-Am. Press Assn., Internat. Press Inst., Sigma Alpha Epsilon. Clubs: University (N.Y.C.); Scarsdale Golf, Fox Meadow Tennis (Scarsdale). Home: 133 Pondfield Rd Bronxville NY 10708 Office: Suite 902 405 Park Ave New York NY 10022 *It is ironic that, having spent most of my life fighting for competition in the news business, the end result is that most daily newspapers in the United States have done away with competition in their markets. Nonetheless, I still believe that competition in all business activities best serves the free enterprise society on which our democracy is founded. A final thought: I believe that large groups should not go public because that forces management to put too much emphasis on the bottom line.*

KELLER, MARTHE, actress; b. Basel, Switzerland, 1945. Attended, Munich Stanislavsky Sch. Mem., Schiller Theatre Group, Berlin, E. Ger.; film debut in Devil by the Tail, 1968; appeared in films TV and theatre in France; including film And Now My Love, 1974; Am. films, including Marathon Man, 1976, Black Sunday, 1977, Bobby Deerfield, 1977, Fedora, 1979, The Formula, 1980, The Amateur, 1982. Office: care William Morris Agency 151 El Camino Beverly Hills CA 90212 *

KELLER, PAUL, advertising agency executive; b. Mainz, Germany, Sept. 23, 1921; came to U.S., 1937, naturalized, 1942; s. Bernard and Johanna (Metzger) K.; m. Ruth Ettinghouse, Dec. 25, 1948; children: Steven A., Richard M., Susan F. B.A., NYU, 1948; M.A., Columbia U., 1949. Research analyst N.W. Ayer, N.Y.C., 1950-55; media research dir. Bryan Houston, N.Y.C., 1955-57; dir. media and research Reach McClinton, N.Y.C., 1957-69; assoc. research di. Ted Bates Advt., N.Y.C., 1969-80, research dir., 1980—; mem. faculty Hofstra U., Hempstead, N.Y., 1974-78; univ. guest lectr. Contbr. articles to profl. jours. Served with U.S. Army, 1942-45; PTO. Decorated Bronze Star, Purple Heart. Mem. Radio-TV Research Council, Phi Beta Kappa. Office: 1515 Broadway New York NY 10036

KELLER, REED T., physician, educator; b. Aberdeen, S.D., May 26, 1938; s. Emil T. and Maybelle K.; m. Mary Ann Larsen, June 14, 1959; children—Kristen, Laura, Julie. B.A., U. N.D., 1959, B.S., 1961; M.D., Harvard U., 1963. Asst. prof. Case Western Res. Sch. Medicine, 1970-73; chief medicine U. N.D., Rehab. Hosp., Grand Forks, 1973—; prof., chmn. dept. medicine U. N.D. Med. Sch., Grand Forks, 1973—. Contbr. articles to profl. jours. Served with USAF, 1968-70. Fellow Am. Coll. Gastroenterology, A.C.P.; mem. Soc. Exptl. Biology and Medicine, N.D. Commn. on Med. Edn., Assn. Profs. Medicine, Am. Soc. Gastrointestinal Endoscopy, AMA, Phi Beta Kappa, Alpha Omega Alpha. Office: Dept Medicine U ND Grand Forks ND 58202

KELLER, RICHARD CHARLES, banker; b. Buffalo, Apr. 12, 1937; s. Walter F. and Katherine D. K.; m. Diane M. Henry, June 30, 1962; 2 children. B.S., U. Buffalo, 1969. With Marine Midland Bank, N.A., 1959—, exec. v.p. money mgmt., chmn. asset-liability com., now sr. exec. v.p. fin. markets sector. Served with USAF, 1961-62. Mem. Treasury Securities Luncheon Group, Bond Club of N.Y.C. Club: City Midday (N.Y.C.). Office: Marine Midland Bank 140 Broadway New York NY 10015

KELLER, ROBERT ALEXANDER, III, soft drink co. exec., lawyer; b. Oklahoma City, Apr. 12, 1930; s. Robert Alexander and Martha Ezelle (Barrett) K.; children—Susan L., Stephen B., Christopher D., Jennifer P. B.B.A., U. Okla., 1951; J.D., Stanford U., 1958. Bar: Calif. bar 1958. Asso. firm Orrick, Herrington, Rowley & Sutcliff, San Francisco, 1958-65; asst. dean Stanford U. Law Sch., 1965-70, mem. bd. visitors, 1979-81; mem. firm Munger, Tolles & Rickershauser, Los Angeles, 1971-72; atty. Coca-Cola Co., Atlanta, 1972—, v.p., gen. counsel, 1975-79, sr. v.p., gen. counsel, 1979—. Mem. Calif. Gov.'s Commn. on Adminstrv. Procedures, 1961; bd. dirs. San Francisco chpt. ACLU, 1966-68; mem. Palo Alto (Calif.) Human Relations Council, 1967-68. Served to lt. USNR, 1951-55. Mem. Am. Bar Assn., Calif. Bar Assn., So. Center Internat. Studies. Office: PO Drawer 1734 Atlanta GA 30301

KELLER, ROBERT JOHN, educator; b. White Bear Lake, Minn., May 25, 1913; s. John Joseph and Lillie (Olson) K.; m. Alice Maurine Fawcett, Dec. 29, 1943; children: Janet Maurine, Marilyn Jean. B.E., Winona (Minn.) State Tchrs. Coll., 1937; M.A., U. Minn., 1940, Ph.D., 1947; LL.D., Yonsei U., Seoul, Korea, 1973. Rural sch. tchr., 1931-32, tchr., prin., Ramsey County, Minn., 1932-38, high sch. tchr., N. St. Paul, Minn., 1938-40; teaching research asst. U. Minn., 1940-42, 45-46; civilian research psychologist, 1946-47; asst. prof. U. Minn., Mpls., 1947, assoc. prof., 1948, prof. edn., 1951-82, prof. emeritus, 1982—; dir. Univ. High Sch., 1956-64; dean Coll. Edn., U. Minn., 1964-70; Carnegie vis. prof. U. Hawaii, 1957-58, vis. prof., 1970-71; AID higher edn. cons. Ministry Edn., Republic Korea, 1971-73, 74, 77. Author: (with Ruth Eckert) A University Looks at its Program, 1954, Minnesota's Stake in the Future, Higher Education 1956-70, 1957, Higher Education for Our State and Times, 1959, (with Otto Domian) Comprehensive Educational Survey of Kansas, Vol. I-V, 1960, Educational Survey for Wisconsin Evangelical Lutheran Synod, Vols. I-II, 1962, (with R.C. Gibson, A.O. Pfnister) Expansion and Coordination of Higher Education in Missouri, 1962, Higher Education in Korea, 1974, The Korean Higher Education Reform Project in Transition, 1975, Higher Education and National Development in Southeast Asia, 1977; contbr. to: Innovation in Higher Education, 1973, The Pursuit of Excellence in Higher Education, 1980. Assoc. dir. Bur. Instnl. Research, 1947-50, dir., 1950-54; chmn. Senate Com. on Instnl. Relationships, 1948-64; dir. Gov.'s Com. on Higher Edn., 1956-57, Legislative Interim Commn. on Higher Edn., 1958-59, Kans. Study Higher Edn., 1959-60; trustee Coll. Entrance Exam. Bd., 1964-67; mem. exec. bd., commn. instns. higher edn. N. Central Assn., 1967-71, bd. dirs. assn., 1970-77; v.p. Am. Assn. Higher Edn., 1968-69, pres., 1969-70. Served with USAAF, 1942- 45. Decorated Dong Baeg medal; Order of Merit, Republic of Korea. Fellow AAAS; mem. Am. Psychol. Assn., Am. Ednl. Research Assn., Psychometric Soc., NEA, Am. Assn. Jr. Colls., Phi Delta Kappa, Kappa Delta Pi. Home: 1989 W Shryer Ave Saint Paul MN 55113 Office: 275 Peik Hall U Minn Minneapolis MN 55455

KELLER, ROY ALAN, educator; b. Davenport, Iowa, Feb. 5, 1928; s. Leo Roy and Mable Dorothy (Daebelliehn) K.; m. Anne Gibson Reinhart, June 29, 1952 (div.); children—Douglas Bruce, Neal Scott, Eric Steven, Travis Reed; m. Sabra Bowman Black, Sept. 22, 1979. B.Sc., U. Ariz., 1950, M.S., 1952; Ph.D., U. Utah, 1956. Instr. chemistry U. Ariz., 1952-53, asst. prof., 1956-65, asso. prof., 1965-68; prof., dept. chemistry State U. N.Y. at Fredonia, 1968—, chmn. dept., 1968-74; vis. prof. U. Utah, 1976-77. Editor: (with J. Calvin Giddings) Advances in Chromotography, 1965-74; editor: Jour. Chromatographic Sci, 1968-79. Founding trustee Prescott (Ariz.) Coll. Recipient Internat. award Petroleum Research Fund of Am. Chem. Soc., 1962. Mem. Am. Chem. Soc., Phi Beta Kappa, Sigma Xi, Phi Kappa Phi, Phi Lambda Upsilon, Sigma Pi Sigma, Pi Mu Epsilon. Home: Fredonia NY 14063

KELLER, THOMAS FRANKLIN, management science educator; b. Greenwood, S.C., Sept. 22, 1931; s. Cleaveland Alonzo and Helen (Seago) K.; m. Margaret Neel Query, June 15, 1956; children: Thomas Crafton (dec.), Neel McKay, John Caldwell. A.B., Duke U., 1953; M.B.A., U. Mich., 1957, Ph.D., 1960. C.P.A., N.C. Mem. faculty Grad. Sch. Bus. Adminstrn., Duke, 1959—, assoc. prof., 1962-67, prof., 1967-74, R.J. Reynolds Industries prof., 1974—, also vice provost, 1971-72, dean grad. sch. bus. adminstrn., 1974—, chmn. dept. mgmt. scis., 1974—; editorial bd. Duke Univ. Press, 1970—; vis. assoc. prof. Carnegie Mellon U., 1966-67, U. Wash., 1963-64; cons. govt., industry; Fullbright-Hays lectr., Australia, 1975; dir. Health Care Systems, Inc., Pennwalt, Inc., Ladd Furniture Inc. Author: Accounting for Corporate Income Taxes, 1961, Intermediate Accounting, 1963, 68, 74, Advanced Accounting, 1966, Financial Accounting Theory vol. 1, 1965, 73, vol. 2, 1970, Earnings or Cash Flows: An Experiment on Functional Fixation and the Valuation of the Firm, 1979; editor: monographs Financial Information Needs of Security Analysts, 1977, The Impact of Accounting Research on Practice and Disclosure, 1978; Contbr. articles to profl. jours. Served with AUS, 1953-55. Mem. Am. Accounting Assn. (v.p. 1967-68, editor jour. 1972-75), N.C. Assn. C.P.A.s, Am. Inst. C.P.A.s, Financial Execs. Inst., Phi Kappa Sigma, Beta Gamma Sigma, Alpha Kappa Psi. Presbyn. (elder). Home: 1024 W Markham Ave Durham NC 27701

KELLER, WILLIAM FRANCIS, publishing consultant; b. Meyersdale, Pa., May 22, 1922; s. Lloyd Francis and Dorothy Marie (Shultz) K.; m. Frances Jane Core, Mar. 31, 1944. A.A., Potomac State Coll. of W.Va. U., 1941; B.S., U. Md., 1943, M.S., 1945. Ednl. rep. Blakiston Co. Med. Pub. Co., 1945-51, asso. editor, 1951-54; editor coll. div. McGraw Hill Book Co., N.Y.C., 1954-56, editor-in-chief, 1956-65, gen. mgr. div., 1965-68; pres. Year Book Med. Publs., Chgo., 1968-81, chmn. bd., 1968-82; pub. cons., Crystal Lake, Ill., 1982—. Served with U.S. Army, 1945-46. Office: 7916 W Hillside Rd Crystal Lake IL 60014

KELLER, WILLIAM HALL, JR., cable television executive; b. Greenville, Ga., June 16, 1924; s. William Hall and Martha Nettie (Turner) K.; m. Dorothy Louise Moore, Apr. 17, 1948; children: William, Richard, Scott. Student, Ga. Tech. Inst., 1945-46, Carson Newman Coll., 1946, U. Ill., 1946. Lic. radiotelephone operator, FCC. Chief engr., then pres. Dee Rivers Broadcast Group, Decatur, Ga., 1947-55; broadcast equipment sales RCA, Atlanta, 1955-56; owner Stas. WGOV and WCRY, Valdosta and Macon, Ga., 1956-64; with Group W Cable, Valdosta, 1964—, pres., 1974—. Pres. PTA, 1959; chmn. adv. bd. Salvation Army, Valdosta, 1959-62; mem. Valdosta City Council, 1964-72; bd. dirs. officer Boy's Club, ARC, Youth Ctr., United Fund. Served with USN, 1943-45. Mem. Ga. Cable TV Assn. (pres. 1978-79), So. Cable TV Assn. (pres. 1981-82), UP Broadcasters Assn. (dir.), Ga. Assn. Broadcasters (past dir.), Valdosta Jaycees (v.p. 1959). Democrat. Methodist. Club: Valdosta Country (dir. 1960-64). Home: 905 Pineridge Dr Valdosta GA 31602 Office: Group W Cable Castle Park Valdosta GA 31602

KELLER, WILLIAM MARTIN, corporate executive; b. Wilkes-Barre, Pa., Oct. 26, 1916; s. Roy S. and Alice (Obrien) K.; m. Mary Anne Davis, Oct. 25, 1939; chiildren: Anne Elizabeth Hufford, William Martin III. A.B., Syracuse U.; grad., Harvard U. Bus. Sch.; LL.D. in Internat. Relations, U. Liberia, W. Africa. Indsl. engr. Montgomery Ward & Co., Armstrong Cork Co., Inc.; mgr. indsl. engring., plant mgr., gen. factories mgr., v.p. mfg., v.p. mktg., v.p., gen. mgr. reinforced plastics div., v.p. internat. Owens-Corning Fiberglas Corp., N.Y.C.; U.S. Dept. State Diplomatic rep. to Liberia; dir. Marianne Rd., Inc.; pres. W.M. Keller Assos.; bus. cons. Former chmn. bd. trustees Cherry Lawn Sch., Darien; trustee Council Chs. and Synagogues. Decorated Star of Africa, Republic of Liberia). Mem. Pa. Soc. Clubs: Mason (Shriner), Elk, Kiwanian., Pinnacle, N.Y. Athletic (N.Y.C.) (life); Harvard Business (Denver); Kissing Camels Golf, Garden of Gods (Colorado Springs, Colo.); Metropolitan (Washington). Home: 2221 Hill Circle Rd Colorado Springs CO 80904

KELLERMAN, KARL FREDERIC, engineer; b. Washington, May 11, 1908; s. Karl Frederic and Gertrude (Hast) K.; m. Margaret Phillips, June 2, 1934; 1 son, Karl Frederic II. Student, Friends Sch., Washington, 1917-21; E.E., Cornell, 1929; grad. study in bus. law, management; C.L.U., Am. Coll. Life Underwriters, 1938, Northwestern U. Inst. Mgmt., 1961. Registered profl. engr. Communications engr. N.Y. Tel. Co., 1929-36; asst. br. mgr. and cons. on bus. ins. and taxation N.Y. Life Ins. Co., N.Y.C., 1936-42; charge tech. product sales devel. Aircraft Radio Corp., Boonton, N.J., 1946-47; exec. dir. com. on guided missiles Research and Devel. Bd., Washington, 1947-49; mgr. Washington office for Brush Devel. (electronics), 1949-53; pres. Kellerman & Co. (cons. engrs.), 1953-55; asso. dir. systems planning Bendix Aviation Corp., 1955-57, asst. v.p. engring., 1957-60, asst. to exec. v.p., 1960-62; pres. Microwave Devices, Inc. (subs. Bendix Co.), Rockville, Md., 1962-64; sci. adviser USAF Systems Command, 1964-73; pres. Low Country Guild, Inc., Bluffton, S.C., 1973-78, Guild Park, Inc., 1973—, Kellerman & Assos., Inc. (cons. engrs.), 1977—; Pvt. pilot; golfer (former sect. champion); pres. D.C. Golf Assn., 1959, Middle Atlantic Golf Assn., 1972. Writer, speaker on airborne electronics, measurements and guided missiles. Mem. council Cornell U., 1954-60. Served to comdr. USNR, World War II; head electronics coordination br. engring div., Bur. Aeros. Recipient ofcl. Navy commendation for initiation and supervision electronic test equipment standardization program, 1945. Life mem. I.E.E.E.; mem. Cornell Soc. Engrs., A.A.A.S., Aircraft Owners and Pilots Assn., Sigma Xi, Tau Beta Pi, Eta Kappa Nu, Delta Upsilon. Clubs: Cosmos, Columbia Country (Washington); Cornell (N.Y.C.); Sea Pines Golf (South Carolina); Three Score and Ten (Pinehurst, S.C.). Initiated establishment new radio frequency standards lab. at Nat. Bur. Standards, 1944. Home and Office: 300 Woodhaven Dr Apt 1301 Hilton Head Island SC 29928

KELLERMAN, SALLY CLAIRE, actress; b. Long Beach, Calif., June 2, 1937; d. John Helm and Edith Baine (Vaughn) K.; m. Richard Edelstein, Dec. 19, 1970; 4 step-daus.; m. Jonathan Krane, 1980. Student, Los Angeles City Coll., Actor's Studio, N.Y.C. Stage appearances include Singular Man, N.Y.C., Breakfast at Tiffany's; films include A Little Romance, Mash, Brewster McCloud, Last of the Red-Hot Lovers, Foxes, Reflection of Fear, Slither, Lost Horizon, The Big Bus, Head On, Rafferty and the Gold Dust Twins, The Boston Strangler, Loving Couples, The April Fools, Welcome to L.A., Serial; also TV roles Chrysler Theatre, Mannix, It Takes a Thief; TV film Verna: USO Girl, 1978 (Nominee Acad. and Golden Globe awards for M). Mem. Actor's Equity, AFTRA. Home: 7944 Woodrow Wilson Rd Los Angeles CA 90368 Office: care Creative Artists Agy 1888 Century Park E Suite 1400 Los Angeles CA 90067 *

KELLETT, WILLIAM HIRAM, JR., architect, engineer, educator; b. Bryan, Tex., Oct. 15, 1930; s. William Hiram and Elizabeth (Minsky) K.; m. Christina Maria Binsch, Feb. 2, 1962 (div.); children: Elizabeth Julia, Rene Janine, Kira Lorraine; m. 2d Ann Robertson Wilkins, Dec. 11, 1971; children: Robert Lynn, Patricia Ann. A.A., Victoria Coll., 1954; B. Arch., Tex. A&M U., 1960, M.Arch., 1967. Registered architect, engr. Elec. technician W.E. Kutzschbach Co., Bryan, 1950-51; engring. technologist Johnston & Davis, Victoria, Tex., 1952-54; mech. elec. systems designer Hall Engring. Co., Bryan, 1955-62, Environments, Inc., 1962-74; pres. Mech. & Elec Cons., Bryan, 1974-76; owner, operator William H. Kellett, Cons. Engrs., Bryan, 1976—; prof. environ. design, architecture and bldg. constrn. Tex. A&M U., College Station, 1962—. Vice chmn. City Charter Com., Bryan, 1969; chmn. Bd. Equalization, 1969-70. Mem. AIA, Illuminating Engr. Soc., AAUP, ASHRAE, Refrigeration Engrs. and Tech. Assn., Nat. Soc. Profl. Engrs., Tex. Soc. Profl. Engrs., Phi Theta Kappa, Tau Beta Pi, Tau Sigma Delta. Home: 1000 Esther Blvd Bryan TX 77801 Office: Coll Architecture and Environ Design Tex A&M U Coll Station TX 77840

KELLEY, ALBERT BENJAMIN, institute administrator; b. N.Y.C., May 15, 1936; s. Hubert Williams and Anna Alberta (Davis) K.; m. Ziba A. Jurenas, June 16, 1979; children: Sumako Chongyol, Hubert Chongsu. Student, Def. Lang. Inst., 1955, Naganuma Inst., Tokyo, 1957-58, Sophia U., Tokyo, 1957, Harvard U. Bus. Sch., 1972. News editor Shipping and Trade News, Japan, 1957-60; Washington transp. corr. N.Y. Jour. Commerce, 1960-63; policy adviser ICC, 1963-65; mgr. transp. and communications dept. U.S. C. of C., 1966-67; dir. pub. affairs Fed. Hwy. Adminstrn., 1967-69; sr. v.p. Ins. Inst. Hwy. Safety, Washington, 1969—; guest lectr. Johns Hopkins Sch. Pub. Hygiene and Pub. Health, 1974—, U. So. Calif., 1974, U. Fla., 1972, UCLA, 1970, U. Calif., Davis, 1977; bd. dirs. Center Auto Safety, 1975—. Author: The Pavers and The Paved, 1971; author-narrator: Boobytrap!, 1971, Cars That Crash and Burn, 1973, Crashes That Need Not Kill, 1976; also articles. Served with AUS, 1954-57. Recipient Golden Eagle award Council Internat. Nontheatrical Events, 1971, 73, 76; 1st prize Zagreb (Yugoslavia) Film Festival, 1973, 75; Bronze Venus Medallion Virgin Islands Internat. Film Festival, 1976. Mem. Internat. Transp. Research Forum (past dir.), Nat. Safety Council, Am. Assn. Automotive Medicine, Washington Oratorio Soc. (dir.). Office: Watergate 600 Suite 300 Washington DC 20037

KELLEY, ALBERT JOSEPH, management executive; b. Boston, July 27, 1924; s. Albert Joseph and Josephine (Sullivan) K.; m. Virginia Marie Riley, June 7, 1945; children: Mark, Shaun, David. B.S., U.S. Naval Acad., 1945, MIT, 1948; Sc.D. in Instrumentation and Control Engring., MIT, 1956; postgrad., U.S. Naval Postgrad. Sch., 1953-54. Commd. ensign USN, 1945, advanced through grades to comdr.; fire control officer U.S.S. Rochester, 1946-47; carrier squadron pilot, electronics officer USN Carrier Air Group 2, 1950-51; exptl. test pilot, project dir. U.S. Naval Air Test Center, Patuxent River, Md., 1951-53; asst. head guided missile guidance br. Bur. Weapons, 1956-58, project dir. Eagle missile system Bur. Weapons, 1958- 60; program mgr. Agena launch vehicle NASA, 1960-61, dir. electronics and control, 1961-64; dep. dir. Electronics Research Center, Cambridge, Mass., 1964-67; dean Sch. Mgmt., Boston Coll., 1967-77; pres. Arthur D. Little Program Systems Mgmt. Co., 1977—; cons. Dept. Def.; dir. LFE Corp., State St. Bank and Trust, State St. Fin Corp., Perini Corp., Nat. Space Inst., C.S. Draper Lab. Author: Venture Capital, A Guidebook for New Enterprises, New Dimensions of Project Management. Mem. space applications bd. NRC. Recipient NASA Exceptional Service medal, 1967. Fellow AIAA, IEEE; mem. Internat. Acad. Astronautics, Sigma Xi, Tau Beta Pi, Eta Kappa Nu, Sigma Gamma Tau, Beta Gamma Sigma. Home: 351 Atherton St Milton MA 02187 Office: Arthur D Little Inc Acorn Park Cambridge MA 02140

KELLEY, ALLEN CHARLES, economist; b. Everett, Wash., Sept. 5, 1937; s. Charles Edward and Velma L. (Allen) K.; m. Patty Ann Cochran, June 20, 1959; children: Brian Allen, Mark Andrew, Michael Charles. Student, Linfield Coll., 1955-57; A.B., Stanford U., 1959, Ph.D., 1964. Vis. research fellow Australian Nat. U., 1962-63; cons. Rand Corp., 1962-67; acting asst. prof. Stanford U., 1963-64; faculty U. Wis., Madison, 1964-72, prof., 1970-72; prof. econs. Duke U., Durham, N.C., 1972—, chmn. dept., 1973-80; asso. dir. Center for Demographic Studies, 1973—; vis. prof. Monash U., Melbourne, Australia, 1970-71; Esmee Fairbairn research prof. Herriot Watt U., Edinburgh, Scotland, 1978; research scholar Internat. Inst. Applied Systems Analysis, Laxenburg, Austria, 1979. Author: Dualistic Economic Development, 1972, (with J.G. Williamson) Lessons from Japanese Development - An Analytical Economic History, 1974, The Professor's Guide to TIPS, 1975, (with R.M. Schmidt) The User's Guide to TIPS, 1975, TIPS Program Manual, 1976, (with J.G. Williamson) Modeling Urbanization and Economic Growth, 1980; Editorial bd.: Jour. Econ. Edn, 1973—; Contbr. articles, revs. to profl. jours. Scholar, fellow Weyerhaeuser Co., 1955-59, Ford Found., 1961-62, Earhart Found., 1959-61, Social Sci. Research Council, 1962-63; grantee Carnegie Found., 1964-65, Exxon Edn. Found., 1965-67, 68-70, 71-74, Ford Found., 1973-79, Nat. Inst. Edn., 1974-75, NSF, 1966-68, Rockefeller Found., 1967-69, Sloan Found., 1969-73, 79—; co-recipient Arthur Cole prize Econ. History Assn., 1972. Mem. Am. Econ. Assn. (chmn. com. econ. edn. 1978—), So. Econ. Assn. (v.p. 1981-82), Internat. Union for Sci. Study Population, Population Assn. Am., Joint Council on Econ. Edn. (trustee 1978—, exec. com. 1978—), Phi Beta Kappa. Home: 4607 Chicopee Trail Durham NC 27707 Office: Econs Dept Duke U Durham NC 27706

KELLEY, ALOYSIUS PAUL, priest, university president; b. Carlisle, Pa., Oct. 4, 1929; s. Aloysius Paul and Teresa (Barron) K. A.B., St. Louis U., 1955, M.A., 1956, Ph.L., 1956; S.T.L., U. Innsbruck, Austria, 1963; Ph.D., U. Pa., 1968. Joined S.J., 1949; ordained priest Roman Catholic Ch., 1962; chmn. dept. classics Georgetown U., 1969-71, asst. acad. v.p., 1971-72, acting acad. v.p., 1972-74, exec. v.p. for acad. affairs and provost, 1974-79; pres. Fairfield (Conn.) U., 1979—. Trustee Georgetown Prep. Sch., 1969-72, Loyola Coll., Balt., 1971-75, Scranton U., 1974-80, Bridgeport Area C. of C., 1979-82, St. Joseph's U., Phila., 1980—, Georgetown U., 1982—, Conn. Grand Opera, 1980—; mem. D.C. Commn. Postsecondary Edn., 1974-79; vice chmn. Conn. Conf. Ind. Colls., 1980-81, chmn., 1981-83. Fulbright-Hayes fellow, 1971. Mem. Am. Philol. Assn., Assn. Univ. Adminstrs., AAUP, Am. Assn. Higher Edn., Am. Assn. Univ. Adminstrs. Democrat. Clubs: Algonquin (Bridgeport, Conn.); Patterson (Fairfield, Conn.); University (N.Y.C.). Home and Office: Fairfield U Fairfield CT 06430

KELLEY, DANIEL FRANCIS, JR., lawyer; b. San Juan, P.R., Oct. 5, 1919; s. Daniel Francis and Consuelo (Porrata-Doria) K.; m. Katherine Joan MacKenzie, May 2, 1953; children: Brenda, Jean, Robin. Grad., Loomis Sch., 1937; A.B., Cornell U., 1941; Indsl. Adminstr., Harvard, 1943; LL.B., Yale, 1947. Bar: N.Y. 1949, P.R. 1951, D.C. 1978. Asso. firm Sullivan & Cromwell, N.Y.C., 1947-49, Charles R. Hartzell, San Juan, P.R., 1949-54; sr. partner McConnell, Valdes, Kelley, Sifre, Griggs & Ruiz-Suria, Hato Rey, P.R., 1954—. Served to capt. AUS, 1943-46. Clubs: Ewanok Country (Manchester, Vt.); Sakonnet Golf (Little Compton, R.I.); La Gorce Country (Miami Beach, Fla.); St. Botolph (Boston); Board Room, Yale (N.Y.C.); Dorado Beach Golf. Home: Dorado Villa 3011 Dorado Beach Hotel Dorado PR 00646

KELLEY, DANIEL MCCANN, publisher; b. Boston, Dec. 3, 1925; s. Joseph A. and Frances (McCann) K.; m. Lilyan Lotrecchiano, Nov. 17, 1956; children: Virginia, Betsy, Catherine, Margaret. B.S., Mass. Inst. Tech., 1946. Editorial supr. McGraw-Hill Book Co., N.Y.C., 1947-51; asst. editor Archtl. Record, F.W. Dodge Corp., N.Y.C., 1954-56; advt. sales rep. McGraw-Hill Publs. Co., N.Y.C., 1956-62; advt. sales mgr., then pub. McGraw-Hill Health/Edn. Publs. Co., Chgo., 1962-76; pub. Postgrad. Medicine/Sportsmedicine, McGraw-Hill Publs. Co., Mpls., 1976—. Bd. dirs. Health Industries Assn., 1973-74, Nat. Coll. Edn., 1974-83; v.p., bd. dirs. Minn. chpt. Leukemia Soc. Am., 1982—. Served with USNR, 1943-47, 52-53. Mem. Pharm. Mfrs. Assn., Pharm. Advt. Club, Midwest Pharm. Advt. Club, Nat. Wholesale Druggists Assn., Assn. Ind. Clin. Publs. (dir. 1984—). Roman Catholic. Home: 5505 Lakeview Dr Edina MN 55424 Office: 4530 W 77th St Minneapolis MN 55435

KELLEY, DAVID LEE, oil company executive, petroleum engineer; b. San Antoni, Apr. 24, 1936; s. Buster Arnold and Magdalene Edna (Sherpherd) K.; m. Suzanne Elizabeth Simons, Nov. 26, 1960; children: Leah Elizabeth, Travis David. B.S. in Petroleum Engring., U. Tex., 1959, M.S. in Petreum Engring., 1966. Jr. gas engr. Mobil Oil Corp., Enda, Tex., 1959-60; petroleum engr. Continental Oil Co., Sweetwater, Tex., 1960-64; research petoleum engr. Tex. Petroleum Research Comm., Austin, 1964-66; petroleum engr. Monsanto Co., Houston, 1966-68; exec. v.p. MacRae Consol. Oil & Gas Corp. and subs., Houston, 1968-79; pres., chief exec. officer MacRae Consol. Oil & Gas Corp. and subs, Houston, 1979-83; chmn. bd., chief exec. officer Kelley Oil Corp., 1983—. Served with U.S. Army, 1960. Mem. AIME; MEM. Ind. Petroleum Assn. Am.; mem. Am. Soc. Profl. Engrs., Sigma Gamma Epsilon, Pi Epsilon Tau. Republican. Methodist. Club: Champions Golf. Home: 14114 Bonney Brier Houston TX 77069 Office: 1100 Dresser Tower Houston TX 77002

KELLEY, DEAN MAURICE, clergyman, church association administrator; b. Cheyenne, Wyo., June 1, 1926; s. Mark M. and Irena (Lancaster) K.; m. Maryon M. Hoyle, June 9, 1946; 1 dau., Lenore Hoyle. A.B., Denver U., 1946; Th.M., Iliff Sch. Theology, Denver, 1949; postgrad., Columbia U., 1949-50. Ordained to ministry Methodist Ch., 1946; pastor in, Oak Creek, Colo., 1946-49, East Meadow, N.Y., 1950-52, Westhampton Beach, N.Y., 1952-55, Queens, N.Y., 1955-56, Bronx, N.Y., 1957-60; exec. dir. religious liberty Nat. Council Chs., 1960—; Co-dir. project on ch., state and taxation NCCJ, 1980—. Author: Why Conservative Churches Are Growing, 1972, Why Churches Should Not Pay Taxes, 1977; editor: Government Intervention in Religious Affairs, 1982. Home: Melville NY 11747 Office: 475 Riverside Dr New York NY 10027

KELLEY, DONALD E., judge; b. McCook, Nebr., Jan. 29, 1908; s. Charles W. and Elsie (Asten) K.; m. Georgia E. Pyne, June 21, 1930; children: John Michael, Donald Pyne. LL.B., U. Nebr., 1930. Gen. practice law, McCook, 1930-38, asst. atty. gen. Nebr., Lincoln, 1939-41, county atty., Red Willow County, Nebr., 1942-44, gen. practice law, Denver, 1945-53, 61-67, U.S. atty., Dist. Colo., 1953-59; city atty. City and County of Denver, 1959-61; state senator, Colo., 1963-67; justice Colo. Supreme Ct., Denver, 1967-79, dep. chief justice, 1970-77; of counsel firm Krendl & Netzorg, P.C., Denver, 1981—; v.p., sec. treas. Disputes Settlement, Inc. Writer, producer: film A Judicial Nominating Commission Interview. Hon. life mem. Colo. div. Am. Cancer Soc. Mem. Am. Law Inst., ABA, Colo. Bar Assn. (past bd. govs.), Denver Bar Assn. (hon. life, past trustee), Nat. Inst. Municipal Law Officers (regional v.p. 1959-61), Am. Judicature Soc. (dir. 1970-74), Phi Delta Phi, Delta Upsilon. Clubs: Mason (32 deg., KCCH),

Rotarian.). Home: 3144 S Columbine Denver CO 80210 Office: 1410 Grant St C-308 Denver CO 80203

KELLEY, DONALD HAYDEN, lawyer; b. Denver, May 29, 1929. B.S. in Law, U. Nebr., 1950, LL.B., 1952. Bar: Nebr. bar 1952, Fla. bar 1967. Trial atty. U.S. Dept. Justice, Washington, 1955; tax trial atty. Office of Regional Counsel, IRS, Dallas, 1956; practiced in, North Platte, Nebr., 1956—; partner firm Kelley, Wallace, Scritsmier, Moore & Byrne (and predecessors), 1979—; lectr. in field. Comment editor: Nebr. Law Rev, 1951-52; contbr. articles to legal jours. Mem. ABA, Fla. Bar Assn., Nebr. Bar Assn. (chmn. sect. on real estate probate and trust law 1973-75), Am. Coll. Tax Counsel, Am. Bar Found., Am. Coll. Probate Counsel, Internat. Acad. Estate and Trust Law, Am. Law Inst. Home: 2002 Sunset Dr North Platte NE 69101 Office: 221 W 2d St North Platte NE 69101

KELLEY, DONALD REED, historian; b. Elgin, Ill., Feb. 17, 1931; s. Walter Louis and Helen Lenore (Davis) K.; m. Bonnie Gene Sullivan, June 30, 1979; 1 son, John Reed. B.A., Harvard Coll., 1953; M.A., Columbia U., 1956, Ph.D., 1962; postgrad., U. Paris, 1958-59. Instr. Queens Coll., 1960-63; asst. prof. So. Ill. U., 1963-65, SUNY, 1965-68, asso. prof., 1968-70, prof., 1970-72; vis. prof. Harvard U., 1972-73; prof. U. Rochester, N.Y., 1973—. Author: Foundations of Modern Historical Scholarship, 1970, François Hotman, 1973, The Beginning of Ideology, 1981; editor: The Monarchy of France (Claude de Seyssel), 1981; mem. editorial bd.: Jour. History of Ideas, 1978—, French Hist. Studies, 1981—. Served with U.S. Army, 1953-55. Fulbright fellow, 1958-59; Newberry library fellow, 1965; Am. Council Learned Socs. fellow, 1967-68; Folger Library fellow, 1970; mem. Inst. for Advanced Study, 1969-70, 77-78; Guggenheim fellow, 1974-75, 81-82; Nat. Endowment Humanities fellow, 1977-78. Fellow Am. Acad. Arts and Scis.; mem. Am. Hist. Assn., Renaissance Soc. Am., Medieval Acad. Home: 312 Wilmot Rd Rochester NY 14618 Office: Dept History U Rochester Rochester NY 14627

KELLEY, DONALD WILLIAM, artist, educator; b. Tulsa, Okla., July 20, 1939; s. William Lel and Dorothy Ann (Gumaer) K.; m. Margaret Elizabeth Tomshany, Apr. 4, 1961; children: Lydia Anne, Megan Brooks. B.A., U. Tulsa, 1962; M.F.A., Claremont Grad. Sch., 1966; postgrad., U. N.Mex., 1966. Mem. faculty dept. art Santa Ana (Calif.) Coll., 1965-66, Calif. State Coll., Fullerton, 1968, Otis Art Inst., Los Angeles, 1968-69; mem. faculty dept. art U. Cin., 1969—, now assoc. prof. and chmn. dept. fine arts. One man exhbns. include, U. Tulsa, 1972, Not in N.Y. Gallery, Cin., 1974, Cin. Art Mus., 1975, Antioch Coll., Miami U., Oxford, Ohio, group exhbns. include, Cin. Art Mus., 1970, Contemporary Art Center, Cin., 1972, U. Akron, 1976, Tampa Bay Art Center, Louisville Sch. Art, 1977, Massilon (Ohio) Mus. Art; represented in permanent collections, Art Inst. Chgo., Cin. Art Mus., La Jolla Mus. Art, Los Angeles County Mus. Art, Mus. Modern Art, N.Y.C., Pasadena Art Mus., San Diego Fine Arts Gallery. Tamarind Lithography Workshop, printer fellow, 1966-69. Mem. AAUP., Cin. Graphic Arts Forum, Cin. Art Mus., Contemporary Arts Ctr. Home: 3168 Pond Run Rd New Richmond OH 45157 Office: Dept Fine Arts Coll of Design Architecture and Art Univ of Cin Cincinnati OH 45221

KELLEY, ESTEL WOOD, foods company executive; b. Sharpsville, Ind., Mar. 24, 1917; s. Floyd and Maude (Wood) K.; m. Wilma E. Lippert, June 17, 1939; children: E. Wood, Wayne L., Karen. B.A., Ind. U., 1939, LL.D., 1971; postgrad., Northwestern U., 1940. C.P.A., Ind. Controller, treas., dir., mem. exec. com. R.H. Macy & Co., Kansas City, Mo., 1951-56; successively gen. mgr. distbn.-sales, treas., gen. mgr. Birds Eye div., corp. v.p. Gen. Foods Corp., White Plains, N.Y., 1956-64; exec. v.p., dir., mem. exec. com. Heublein, Inc., Hartford, 1964-68; corp. v.p. Gulf and Western Industries, Inc.; pres. Consumer Products group; pres., chief exec. officer, dir. Fairmont Foods Co., N.Y.C., 1974-82; mng. gen. ptnr. Kelley & Partners, Ltd.; chmn., pres. Kelley, Inc.; chmn., chief exec. officer, dir. Steak n Shake, Inc.; chmn., chief exec. officer, pres., dir. Fairmont Products, Inc.; chmn., dir. King Cola, Inc., King Cola Midwest, Inc.; dir. So. Guaranty Corp., Continental Steel Corp.; instr. mktg., mfg. cost Columbia.; Co-founder Prickett Chair; founder E.W. Kelley Mktg. Founder Fin. and Accounting Fund, Ind. U.; Mayor, Leawood, Kans., 1955-56; bd. dirs. Ind. U. Found.; dean's adv. council Ind. U. Sch. Bus., mem. pres.'s priorities coordinating com.; chmn. YMCA Internat. Div. Com. Recipient Silver Beaver award Boy Scouts Am. Mem. Nat. Assn. Accountants, Fin. Execs. Inst. (dir.), Acad. Alumni Fellows, Am. Mgmt. Assn., Beta Gamma Sigma (dirs. table). Quaker. Clubs: Metropolitan (N.Y.C.); Kokomo Country; Lake Region Yacht and Country, Fla. Citrus (Winter Haven); Kokomo (Ind.) Country, Masons (32 deg.). Office: 777 Third Ave New York NY

KELLEY, EUGENE JOHN, educator, university dean; b. N.Y.C., July 8, 1922; s. Eugene Lawrence and Agnes Regina (Meskill) K.; m. Dorothy M. Kane, Aug. 3, 1946; 1 dau., Sharon A. B.S., U. Conn., 1945; M.B.A., Boston U., 1949, M.Ed., 1948; Ph.D., N.Y. U., 1955. Instr. mktg. Babson Inst., 1947-49; dir. div. bus. adminstrn. Clark U., 1949-56, asst. prof., 1949-54, asso. prof., 1954-56; vis. lectr. Harvard U. Bus. Sch., 1956-57; asst. prof. Mich. State U., 1957-58, asso. prof., 1958-59; prof. mktg., asst. dean Grad. Sch. Bus. Adminstrn. N.Y. U., 1959-60, prof., asso. dean, 1960-64; research prof. bus. adminstrn. Coll. Bus. Adminstrn. Pa. State U., 1963—, dean, 1973—; dir. Central Counties Bank; mem. nat. adv. Council SBA; mem. Commn. on Edn. for Bus. Professions of Nat. Assn. State Univs. and Land Grant Colls.; cons. GAO, N.J. Bd. Higher Edn. Author: Marketing Planning and Competitive Strategy, 1972, Managerial Marketing: Policies, Strategies and Decisions, 1973, Social Marketing: Perspectives and Viewpoints, 1973; Editor: Jour. Mktg, 1967-73. Served with USAAF, 1942-43. Mem. Am. Mktg. Assn. (pres. 1982-83, dir.), Acad. Mgmt., Am. Assembly Collegiate Schs. of Bus. (dir., chmn. govtl. relations com.). Home: 468 Sierra Ln State College PA 16801 Office: 106 Bus Adminstrn Bldg University Park PA 16802

KELLEY, EVERETTE EUGENE, retail company executive; b. Hartford, Kan., July 27, 1938; s. Joseph Leo and Lelia Elizabeth (Hartenbower) K.; m. Peggy Lou Clapham, Apr. 25, 1959; children: Kimaley Kay, Barbara Lynn, Janet Marie. B.S., Kans. State Tchrs. Coll., 1960. C.P.A., Ill. Auditor Arthur Andersen & Co. (C.P.A.s), Chgo., 1960-69; financial v.p. Cunningham Drug Stores, Detroit, 1969-71; controller City Products Corp., Chgo., 1971-75; sr. asst. controller Household Finance Corp., Chgo., 1975-76; exec. v.p. finance Moore Handley, Inc., Birmingham, Ala., 1976—. Mem. Am. Inst. C.P.A.s, Fin. Execs. Inst. (pres. Birmingham chpt. 1982-83). Home: 3533 S Brookwood Rd Mountain Brook AL 35223 Office: PO Box 2607 Birmingham AL 35202

KELLEY, FRANK, state legislator; b. Mercer, Mo., Sept. 17, 1923; s. Olin Francis and Ada Marie (Davis) K.; m. Sandra Marlene Doyle; children: Sandra, Michael, Patrick, Timothy, Daniel, Christopher. B.S. in Journalism, U. Kans., 1951. Reporter Salina (Kans.) Jour., 1951-53; reporter, editor Hutchinson (Kans.) News, 1953-56; editor, pub. Hutchinson Record, 1956-60; exec. dir. Ariz. Republican Party, 1961-63; exec. Stephen Shadegg Assos., Phoenix, 1963-65; cons. Samaritan Health Service, Phoenix, 1965—; mem. Ariz. Ho. of Reps. from 26th Dist., 1965—, majority whip, 1973-76, speaker, 1977—. Del. Rep. Nat. Conv., 1976. Served as pilot USAAF, 1943-45. Congl. fellow, 1955-56. Mem. Am. Soc. Hosp. Pub. Relations, Am. Legion, Sigma Delta Chi. Baptist. Clubs: Phoenix Press, Tempe Rep. Men's, Kiwanis, Elks. Home: 5819 E Thomas Rd Scottsdale AZ 85251 Office: 1700 W Waahington St Phoenix AZ 85007

KELLEY, FRANK J., manufacturing conglomerate executive; b. San Francisco, Sept. 5, 1923; s. Frank J. and Elizabeth Taylor (Frank) K.; m. Mary Fenley, June 28, 1945; children: Mary Lewis, Elizabeth Kelley Johnson, Pamela Kelley Renchard, Susan Frank, Frank J., Iva Wickliffe. B.S., U.S. Naval Acad., 1945. With CompuDyne Corp., Chgo., 1966—, now chmn., pres., treas. Served as ensign USN, 1945-47. Office: CompuDyne Corp 100 S Wacker Dr Suite 2038 Chicago IL 60606

KELLEY, FRANK JOSEPH, state government official; b. Detroit, Dec. 31, 1924; s. Frank Edward and Grace Margaret (Spears) K.; m. Nancy Courtier; children: Karen Ann, Frank Edward II, Jane Francis. Pre-law certificate, U. Detroit, 1948, J.D., 1951. Bar: Mich. 1952. Gen. practice law, Detroit, 1952-54, Alpena, 1954-61, atty. gen. Mich., Lansing, 1962—; Instr. econs. Alpena Community Coll., 1955-56; instr. pub. adminstrn., Alpena County, 1956; atty. city real estate law U. Mich. Extension, 1957-61. Mem. Alpena County Bd. Suprs., 1958-61; pres. Alpena Community Services Council, 1956; chmn. Gt. Lakes Commn., 1971; Founding dir., 1st sec. Alpena United Fund, 1955; founding dir., 1st pres. Northeastern Mich. Child Guidance Clinic, 1958; pres., bd. dirs. Northeastern Mich. Cath. Family Service, 1959. Mem. ABA, 26th Jud. Circuit Bar Assn. (pres. 1956), State Bar Mich., Nat. Assn. Attys. Gen. (pres. 1967), Internat. Movement Atlantic Union, Alpha Kappa Psi., K.C. (4 deg., past legal adv.). Office: Office of Atty Gen Law Bldg Capitol Complex Lansing MI 48913 *

KELLEY, FREDERICK WARREN, naval officer; b. Jamestown, N.J., Sept. 5, 1930; s. Federick and Celia Josephine (Johnson) K.; m. Marilyn Ann Heffner, Feb. 19, 1956; children: Linda Ann, Douglas Brewster, Birchard Warren, Jim Jong. A.B., Naval Res. Officer's Tng. Corp., Brown U., 1952; student, Submarine Sch., 1954, Advanced Nuclear Power Sch., 1957, Nat. Reactor Testing Sta., 1958, Guided Missile Sch., 1964. Commd. lt. j.g. U.S. Navy, 1952, advanced through grades to rear adm., 1978; served with USS Skipjack, 1958-60; engring. officer USS Theodore Roosevelt, 1961-62; dir. dept. nuclear propulsion Naval Submarine Sch., 1962-65; exec. officer USS George Washington, 1965-67; comdg. officer USS Kamehameha, 1967-70; comdr. Submarine Squadron 15, Hawaii, 1970-71, Submarine Div. 12, 1972; comdg. officer USS Woodrow Wilson, 1972; asst. chief of staff Submarine Force Pacific, 1972-75; comdr. Submarine Group 7, 1975-77; comdg. officer Naval Base, Pearl Harbor, Hawaii, 1977-78; comdg. 13th Naval Dist., Seattle, from 1978; now dir. Undersea and Strategisc Warfare Devel. div., Washington. Bd. dirs. Evergreen Safety Council, Seattle, 1978, Seafair Council, Seattle, 1978, Seattle Council Boy Scouts Am., 1978. Decorated Legion of Merit, Meritorious Service medal with gold star, Navy Commendation medal. Mem. Navy League (Scroll of Honor), Navy Relief Soc., United Service Orgn., Naval Inst., Nat. Def. Transp. Assn. (bd. dirs. 1979—). Episcopalian. Clubs: Seattle Yacht, Wash. Athletic, Seattle C. of C. Pres.'s. Lodge: Rotary. Office: Undersea and Strategic Warfare Devel Div Navy Dept Washington DC 20350

KELLEY, GEORGE WALTER, educator, biologist; b. Winfield, Kans., Dec. 5, 1921; s. George Walter and Lela (Bonewell) K.; m. Ava Bargar, Dec. 25, 1942; children: James Alan, Kathy Ann, Jeanne Margaret. B.S., U. Nebr., 1947; M.S., U. Ky., 1950; Ph.D., U. Nebr., 1953. Asst. parasitologist U. Ky., 1948-50; parasitologist Nebr. Health Dept., 1950-53; asso. prof. U. Nebr., Lincoln, 1953-64; mktg. specialist Eli Lilly Internat. Corp., Indpls., 1964-67; chmn. dept. biology, prof. Youngstown (Ohio) State U., 1967—; spl. coop. agt. Dept. Agr., 1954-57; tech. cons. pharm. firms. Chmn. com. higher edn. for Crossroads Resource Conservation and Devel., Youngstown, 1970—; evaluator, cons. N. Central Assn. Colls. and Secondary Schs. Contbr. numerous articles on parasitic diseases of livestock to profl. jours. Served with AUS, 1942-45; ETO. Decorated Bronze Star, Purple Heart. Mem. Am. Soc. Parasitologists, Am. Inst. Biol. Scis., AAAS, Sigma Xi, Phi Kappa Phi. Home: Rural Route 2 Box 700 Spencer IN 47460 Office: Dept Biol Sci Youngstown State Univ Youngstown OH 44555

KELLEY, GERALD, linguistics educator; b. Boston, June 24, 1928; s. Jeremiah Lowney and Harriet Alberta (Tirrell) K.; m. Helen Delaney, Mar. 8, 1956; 1 dau., Nora Tirrell. B.A., St. John's Sem., 1949; M.A., Boston Coll., 1950; Ph.D., U. Wis., 1955. Rockefeller Found. fellow U. Wis., 1957-59, asst. prof., 1959-63, Cornell U., 1963-65, asso. prof., 1965-69, prof. linguistics and Asian studies, 1969—; chmn. modern lang. and linguistics, 1971-77, dir. South Asia program; cons. in field. Contbr. articles on linguistics, sociolinguistics, Hindi and Telugu to profl. jours. Served with U.S. Army, 1955-57. Mem. Linguistic Soc. Am., Am. Inst. Indian Studies (exec. com., trustee). Democrat. Clubs: Statler (Ithaca, N.Y.); Secunderabad (Hyderabad, India). Home: 117 Renwick Dr Ithaca NY 14850 Office: Morrill Hall Cornell U Ithaca NY 14853

KELLEY, GLENN E., state supreme court justice; b. St. Edward, Nebr., Apr. 25, 1921; m. Margaret A. Kelley, July 25, 1946; children: Glenn A., David P., Anne L. B.S., No. State Coll., 1944; LL.B., U. Mich., 1948. Bar: Minn. 1948. Sole practice, 1948-69; judge Minn. Dist. Ct. 3d Jud. Dist., Winona, Minn., 1969-81; assoc. justice Minn. Supreme Ct., St. Paul, 1981—. Served to 1st lt. USAAF, 1942-45. Mem. Nat. Assn. R.R. Trial Counsel, Am. Judicature Soc., Minn. Bar Assn., ABA. Office: 230 State Capitol Saint Paul MN 55155 *

KELLEY, HAROLD HARDING, educator; b. Boise, Idaho, Feb. 16, 1921; s. Harry H. and Maude M. (Little) K.; m. Dorothy J. Drumm, Jan. 4, 1942; children—Ann R. Kelley Rodnick, Harold S., Laura Megan, Kelley Emory. A.B., U. Calif.-, Berkeley, 1942, M.A., 1943; Ph.D., MIT, 1948. Study dir. in group dynamics U. Mich., Ann Arbor, 1948-50; asst. prof. psychology Yale U., New Haven, 1950-55; asso. prof., then prof. U. Minn., Mpls., 1955-61; prof. psychology UCLA, 1961—; Bd. dirs. Social Sci. Research Council, 1975-77. Author: (with C.I. Hovland & I.L. Janis) Communication and Persuasion, 1953, (with J.W. Thibaut) The Social Psychology of Groups, 1959, Interpersonal Relations, 1978, (with others) Attribution: Perceiving the Causes of Behavior, 1972, Personal Relationships, 1979, (with others) Close Relationships, 1983. Served with USAAF, 1943-46. Center for Advanced Study in Behavioral Sci. fellow, 1956-57. Fellow Nat. Acad. Scis., Am. Acad. Arts and Scis., Am. Psychol. Assn. (pres. personality and social psychology div. 1965-66, Disting. Sci. Contribution award 1971). Home: 21634 Rambla Vista St Malibu CA 92065 Office: Dept Psychology U Calif Los Angeles CA 90024

KELLEY, HELEN, orgn. ofcl.; b. Cedar Rapids, Iowa, May 21, 1925; d. William John and Frances Jane (Heenan) K. B.A., Immaculate Heart Coll., Los Angeles, 1949; M.A., St. Louis U., 1954, Ph.D., 1958. Tchr. grammar sch., Visalia, Calif., 1947-48; tchr. history Immaculate Heart High Sch., Los Angeles, 1948-55; tchr. sociology Immaculate Heart Coll., Los Angeles, 1958-63, pres., 1963-77; also trustee; dep. asso. dir. ACTION, Washington, 1977-81, dir. older Ams. vol. program, 1977-81; edn. dir. People for the Am. Way, Washington, 1981—. Contbr. articles to profl. jours. Fellow Radcliffe Inst., 1963. Mem. Am. Sociol. Assn., Soc. Sci Study Religion, Assn. Higher Edn., Nat. Cath. Ednl. Assn. Democrat. Roman Catholic. Home: 1615 Q St NW Washington DC 20009

KELLEY, JACKSON DEFOREST, actor; b. Atlanta, Jan. 20, 1920; s. Ernest David and Clora (Casey) K.; m. Carolyn Meagher Dowling, Sept. 7, 1945. Student public schs., Decatur, Ga. Appeared in: motion pictures Fear in the Night, 1946, The Men, 1950, Tension at Tablerock, 1956, Gunfight at OK Corral, 1956, Law and Jake Wade, 1958, Raintree County, 1957, Warlock, 1959, Where Love Has Gone, 1964, Star Trek—The Motion Picture, 1979, Star Trek: The Wrath of Khan, 1981, Star Trek: The Search for Spock, 1984; appeared as Dr. McCoy in TV series: Star Trek, 1966-69. Served with USAAF, World War II. Mem. Screen Actors Guild, Acad. Motion Picture Arts and Scis., Am. Film Inst. Office: care Blake Agy 409 N Camden Dr Beverly Hills CA 90210

KELLEY, JOHN DENNIS, librarian; b. Nov. 3, 1900; s. John H. and Nora J. (Mullen) K.; m. Mary Agnes Barry, June 29, 1940; children—John H., Thomas B., Dennis J., David B. A.B., Boston Coll., 1922; M.B.A., N.Y.U., 1927. Shoe buyer Nat. Cloak & Suit Co., N.Y.C., 1922-27; mdse. mgr. Gilchrist Co., Boston, 1928-31; office mgr. Carew & McGreenery (investments), 1932-37; librarian, dir. Somerville (Mass.) Pub. Library.; Pres., dir. Central Coop. Bank; corporator Somerset Savs. Bank.; Commr. Div. Pub. Libraries Mass., 1950—. Trustee Somerville Hosp. Mem. ALA, Mass. Library Assn. (past pres.). Clubs: Rotarian., Boston Review. Home: 39 Juniper Ave Wakefield MA 01880 Office: Highlands Ave and Walnut St Somerville MA 02143

KELLEY, JOHN JOSEPH, JR., lawyer; b. Cleve., June 17, 1936; s. John Joseph and Helen (Meier) K.; m. Gloria Hill, June 20, 1959; children: John Joseph III, Scott MacDonald, Christopher Taft, Megan Meredith. B.S. cum laude in Commerce, Ohio U., 1958; LL.B., Case Western Res. U., 1960. Bar: Ohio bar 1960. Clk. firm Walter & Haverfield, Cleve., 1957-60; asso. firm Walter, Haverfield, Buescher & Chockley, Cleve., 1960-66, partner, 1967-72; chief exec. officer Fleischmann Enterprises, Cin., 1972-77; individual practice law, Cin., 1977—; chmn. bd. Basic Packaging Systems, Inc.; dir. Orgamac Leasing Ltd; pres. Naples Devel., Inc., Yankee Leasing Co. Mem. Lakewood (Ohio) City Council, 1965-72, pres., 1972; mem. exec. com. Cuyahoga County (Ohio) Republican Central Com., 1965-72; mem. Hamilton County (Ohio) Rep. Policy Com.; Ohio chmn. Robert Taft, Jr. Senate Campaign Com., 1970, 76; bd. govs. Case Western Res. U., 1961. Mem. Assn. Ohio Commodores, ABA, Ohio State Bar Assn., Cleve. Bar Assn., Cin. Bar Assn. Clubs: Cleve. Athletic, Cin. Country, Queen City, Naples Bath and Tennis. Home: 3575 Bayard Dr Cincinnati OH 45208 Office: 4001 Carew Tower Cincinnati OH 45202

KELLEY, JOHN PAUL, tire and rubber company executive; b. Columbus, Ohio, May 12, 1919; s. John Adrian and Josephine (Nash) K.; m. Dorothy Rose Peters, July 31, 1942; children: John M., Ann P., Daniel O., Peter D. B.S. in Journalism, Ohio State U., 1941; M.B.A., Harvard U., 1946. Mgr. sales promotion Seiberling Rubber Co., Akron, Ohio, 1946-48; account supr. Batten, Barton, Durstine & Osborn, Cleve., 1948-51; mgr. consumer advt. Monsanto Chem. Co., St. Louis, 1951-54; pres. Mumm, Mullay & Nichols, Columbus, 1954-59; v.p. advt. Goodyear Tire and Rubber Co., Akron, 1959—. Served to 1st lt AUS, 1943-46. Mem. Assn. Nat. Advertisers (past chmn.), Advt. Council (past chmn., dir.). Republican. Roman Catholic. Club: Portage Country (Akron). Home: 333 N Portage Path Akron OH 44303 Office: Goodyear Tire and Rubber Co 1144 E Market St Akron OH 44316

KELLEY, MAURICE LESLIE, JR., physician; b. Indpls., June 29, 1924; s. Maurice Leslie and Martha (Daniel) K.; m. Carol J. Povec, Feb. 11, 1967; children: Elizabeth Ann, Mary Sarah. Stuoent, U. Vt.; student, Va. Ply. Inst.; stuoent, Princeton U., 1943-45; M.D., U. Rochester, 1949. Intern, resident Strong Meml. Hosp., Rochester, N.Y., 1949-51, Bixby fellow in medicine, 1953-56; fellow in gastroenterology Mayo Clinic, Rochester, Minn., 1957-59; asst. prof. medicine U. Rochester, 1959-64, asso. prof., 1964-67; practice medicine specializing in gastroenterology, Rochester, N.Y., 1959-67; asso. prof. clin. medicine Dartmouth Med. Sch., 1967-74, prof. clin. medicine, 1974—; chmn. sect. internal medicine Hitchcock Clinic, 1972-74, chmn. sect. gastroenterology, 1974; mem. staff Strong Meml. Hosp., Hitchcock Clinic, Mary Hitchcock Meml. Hosp.; cons. Canandaigua VA, Rochester Gen., Genesee hosps., VA. Med. Center, White River Junction. Contbr. articles to profl. jours., chpts. to books. Served with AUS, 1942-45; M.C. USAF, 1951-53. Fellow A.C.P. (gov. for N.H. 1974-78), Am. Gastroenterol. Assn.; mem. Am. Soc. Gastrointestinal Endoscopy, AMA (chmn. sect. gastroenterology 1970-71), Am. Physiol. Soc., Alpha Omega Alpha. Home: 15 Ledge Rd Hanover NH 03755 Office: 2 Maynard St Hanover NH 03755

KELLEY, RICHARD GILBERT, banker; b. Hyannis, Mass., Sept. 3, 1931; s. Gilbert S. and Mary B. (Jack) K.; m. Denise A. Williston, June 8, 1952; children: Kathryn Gretchen, Richard Gilbert. B.S. in Bus. Adminstrn, Quinnipiac Coll., 1966; postgrad., Stonier Grad. Sch. Banking, Rutgers U., 1975. Exec. v.p. Citizens First Nat. Bank N.J., Ridgewood, 1973-79, pres., 1979-80, chmn. bd., chief exec. officer, 1980—; mem. faculty Nat. Comml. Lending Grad. Sch., U. Okla., Norman, 1980—, Stonier Grad. Sch. Banking, Rutgers U., New Brunswick, N.J., 1981. Treas. Bergen Comml. Blood Bank. Served with USN, 1951-55. Mem. N.J. Bankers Assn. (chmn. fed. legis. com.). Club: Ridgewood Country. Lodge: Rotary. Office: 208 Harristown Rd Glen Rock NJ 07452 *

KELLEY, ROBB BEARDSLEY, insurance company executive; b. Des Moines, Jan. 21, 1917; s. Lawrence Elam and Susan Josephine (Gunn) K.; m. Winifred Elizabeth Murray, June 21, 1951; children: Bruce Gunn, Carolyn Robb, Sarah Gordon. B.A., Dartmouth Coll., 1938. With Employers Mut. Casualty Co., 1939—, pres., chief exec. officer, treas., Des Moines, 1963-83, chmn., chief exec. officer, treas., 1983—; pres., chief exec. officer, treas. Emcasco Ins. Co., 1963-83, chmn., chief exec. officer, treas., 1983—; pres., chief exec. officer, treas. Employers Modern Life Co., 1963-83, chmn., chief exec. officer, treas., 1983—; chmn. bd., treas. Union Mut. Ins. Co.; chmn. Dakota Fire Ins. Co., Ill. Emcasco Ins. Co.; dir. Bankers Trust Co., Des Moines; dir., treas. Iowa Bus. Devel. Credit Corp.; chmn. Am. Mut. Ins. Alliance, 1976-77; bd. dirs., past chmn. Mut. Reins. Bur.; bd. govs., exec. com. Ins. Inst. Am. and Am. Inst. Property and Liability Underwriters. Past chmn., now mem. exec. com. Drake U., Des Moines; trustee Iowa Methodist Med. Center, pres., 1974-78. Served with AUS, 1942-44. Recipient Brotherhood award NCCJ, 1967; Des Moines Community award Distinguished Community Service, 1970. Mem. Soc. Chartered Property and Casualty Underwriters (pres.). Republican. Presbyterian. Club: Shriners. Home: 4321 Greenwood Dr Des Moines IA 50312 Office: 717 Mulberry St Des Moines IA 50309

KELLEY, ROBERT E., air force officer; b. Albany, N.Y., Nov. 3, 1933; s. Frank Benedict and Helen Marie (Parker) K.; m. Margaret Elizabeth Odell, June 30, 1956; children: Patrick (dec.), Michael, Christopher, Karen, Kathleen, Robert E. (dec.), Diana, Colleen. B.S., Rutgers U., 1956; M.S., George Washington U.; grad., Nat. War Coll.; D.Sc. hon., U. Nev.-Las Vegas, 1983. Commd. officer U.S. Air Force, advanced through grades to lt. gen.; vice comdr. Tactical Air Weapons Ctr., Englin AFB, Fla., 1977-78; comdr. 836 Air Div., Davis-Monthan AFB, Ariz., 1978-79, U.S. Air Force Tactical Fighter Weapons Ctr., Nellis AFB, Nev., 1979-81; supt. U.S. Air Force Acad. Found., Colorado Springs, Colo., 1981—; dir. Air Force Acad. Found.,

Colorado Springs, 1981—; chmn. F-16 Multinat. Test and Eval. Exec. Com., Washington. Mem. Colo. Gov.'s Task Force on Drunk Driving, 1982—, Nev. Gov.'s Commn. on Cancer, 1980-81; chmn. Nev. Combined Fed. Campaign, Las Vegas, 1979-80. Mem. Order of Daedalians, Mil. Order World Wars, Air Force Assn., U.S. Squash Racquets Assn., Fed. Execs. Assn. Nev. (pres. 1980-81), Chi Psi. Roman Catholic. Club: Las Vegas Country. Mem. Washington Squash Racquets Fitzgerald Cup team, 1975-76; capt. Air Force Woodruff Cup Squash Racquet team, 1974, 75, 76; vet. champion Washington Area Squash Racquets, 1976. Office: US Air Force Acad Colorado Springs CO 80840 *

KELLEY, ROBERT LLOYD, history educator; b. Santa Barbara, Calif., June 2, 1925; s. Loyd and Berta Lee (Winniford) K.; m. Madge Louise Haskin, June 10, 1972; children by previous marriage—Sandra Lee (Mrs. Thomas Gory), Brian Michael, Alison Gail (Mrs. William Eason), Dorcas Louise; stepchildren—Christopher John, Lisa Ann Naumchik. B.A., U. Calif.-Santa Barbara, 1948; M.A., Stanford U., 1949, Ph.D., 1953. Historian Air Def. Command, Colorado Springs, Colo., 1953-54; instr. history Santa Barbara City Coll., 1954-55; prof. history U. Calif., Santa Barbara, 1955—, asst. to chancellor, 1960-62, chmn. Grad. Program Public Hist. Studies, 1975-81; vis. prof. U. Mich., Ann Arbor, 1969-70; Fulbright prof. Moscow U., 1979; cons. to state agys. on water problems of Sacramento Valley. Author: Gold vs Grain: The Hydraulic Mining Controversy in California's Sacramento Valley, 1959, The Transatlantic Persuasion: The Liberal-Democratic Mind in the Age of Gladstone, 1969, The Shaping of the American Past, 3d edit, 1982, The Sounds of Controversy: Crucial Arguments in the American Past, 1975, The Cultural Pattern in American Politics: The First Century, 1979, Transformations: UC Santa Barbara 1909-1979, 1981; cons. editor: The Public Historian, 1978—; Bicentennial essayist: Am. Hist. Rev, 1977; contbr. articles to profl. jours. Mem. Calif. commn. for Tchr. Preparation and Licensing, 1973-74; dir. seminar Nat. Endowment for Humanities, 1978, 81. Served to capt. USAF, 1943-46, 51-53. Recipient Harold J. Plous Meml. award U. Calif., Santa Barbara, 1962; Louis Knott Koontz prize Pacific Coast br. Am. Hist. Assn., 1965; NEH fellow, 1975-76; Woodrow Wilson Internat. Center fellow, 1982-83; Guggenheim fellow, 1982-83. Mem. Am. Hist. Assn., Orgn. Am. Historian (program chm. ann. meeting 1974, mem. exec. bd. 1980-83). Democrat. Episcopalian.

KELLEY, TIMOTHY EDWARD, lawyer; b. Bay City, Mich., Jan. 11, 1924; s. Joseph E. and Florence (Baumgarten) K.; m. Margaret Ann Pearsall, Aug. 20, 1948; children: Marcia Kelley Leachman, Barbara Kelley Charlebois, Stacey Kelley Smith, Laura. B.A. magna cum laude, U. Notre Dame, 1948; LL.B., Yale, 1951. Bar: Tex. bar 1952. Partner firm Thompson, Knight, Simmons & Bullion, Dallas, 1951-73; pres. Timothy E. Kelley (P.C.), Dallas, 1973—; lectr. So. Methodist U., Dallas, 1975-76. Pres. Dallas Legal Services, 1969; chmn. Dallas Alliance for Shaping Safer Cities, 1972-73, Fair Campaign Practices Com., 1972—; coordinator Common Cause, 1972-75. Served with AUS, 1943-46. Mem. ABA, Dallas Bar Assn. (dir. 1965, 69, 70, 73, chmn. bd. 1966, pres. 1971), State Bar Tex. (dir. 1973-76), Tex. Bar Found., Am. Bd. Trial Advocates, Am. Assn. Trial Attys. (v.p. 1971-72). Club: Univ. Home: 4529 Bobbitt Dr Dallas TX 75229 Office: 5440 Harvest Hill Suite 250 Dallas TX 75230

KELLEY, VERNE FRANCIS, JR., management consultant, social psychologist; b. Oak Park, Ill., July 29, 1928; s. Verne F. and Irene (Plamondon) K.; m. Lois Phillips, Nov. 25, 1954. B.A., U. Notre Dame, 1950; M.A. with distinction, DePaul U., 1980; postgrad., U. Ill., 1979. Sales, mdsg. exec. Procter & Gamble, 1951-52; pub. relations exec. United Air Lines, 1952-53; TV writer/producer, account exec. Ruthrauff & Ryan, Inc., 1953-57; v.p. advt. and pub. relations Greyhound Corp., 1957-66; v.p. creative services, dir. Anderson, Metzger & Kelley, 1966-68; sr. v.p. Daniel J. Edelman, Inc., 1969-72; pres. Kelleyco, 1973-79, Kelley & Keller, 1979—. Author articles on mktg. Mem. Am. Sociol. Assn., Clin. Social Psychology Assn., Pi Gamma Mu. Home: 441 A Grant Pl Chicago IL 60614 Office: 2444 N Clark St Chicago IL 60614 *We are what we are through our relationships with others.*

KELLEY, VINCENT CHARLES, pediatrician; b. Tyler, Minn., Jan. 23, 1916; s. Charles Enoch and Stella May (Ross) K.; m. Dorothy Jean MacArthur, Sept. 5, 1942; children: Nancy Jean, Thomas Vincent, Richard Charles, William MacArthur, Robert Kenneth, Jean Elizabeth, James Joseph. B.A., U. N.D., 1934, M.A., 1935; B.S. in Edn, U. Minn., 1936; Ph.D. in Biochemistry, U. Minn., 1942; B.S. in Medicine, U. Minn., 1944, M.B., 1945, M.D., 1946. Diplomate: Am. Bd. Pediatrics. Prof. chemistry Emory and Henry Coll., 1941; Rockefeller research fellow U. Minn., 1941-42, Swift fellow in pediatrics, 1948-50, intern in pediatrics, 1945-46, instr., 1949-50; asst. prof. organic chemistry Coll. St. Thomas, 1942-43; asso. prof. pediatrics U. Utah, 1950-58; prof., head div. endocrinology, metabolism and renal disease dept. pediatrics U. Wash., 1958—; dir. Utah State Heart Labs., 1953-58. Contbr. numerous articles on biochemistry, pediatrics and endocrinology to profl. jours.; editor: Metabolic, Endocrine and Genetic Disorders of Children, 3 vols., 1974, Practice of Pediatrics, 10 vols., 1958-83; editorial bd.: Audio Digest, 1956-72, Med. Digest, 1956-75, Am. Jour. Diseases Children, 1958-69, Internat. Med. Digest, 1960-71. Served with U.S. Army, 1943-45; M.C. USAAF, 1946-48. Recipient E. Mead Johnson award for pediatric research, 1954, Ross Pediatric Edn. award, 1971. Mem. Am. Acad. Pediatrics, AAAS, AAUP, Am. Inst. Biol. Scis., Am. Heart Assn., AMA, Am. Pediatric Soc., Am. Rheumatism Assn., Am. Soc. Nephrology, Internat. Endocrine Soc., N.Y. Acad. Scis., Pan-Am. Med. Assn., Soc. Exptl. Biology and Medicine, Endocrine Soc., Soc. Pediatric Research, Western Soc. Clin. Research, Western Soc. Pediatric Research, Phi Beta Kappa, Sigma Xi, Phi Lambda Upsilon, Phi Eta Sigma, Kappa Kappa Psi. Office: Dept Pediatrics RD-20 U Wash Seattle WA 98195

KELLEY, WALTER BERNARD, communications co. exec.; b. Boston, Oct., 31, 1919; s. Walter T. and Mary R. (Gallagher) K.; m. Kathleen Harrington, Dec. 20, 1943; children—Joseph, Robert, Paul, John. B.S. in Civil Engring, Northeastern U., 1941; M.S. (Alfred P. Sloan fellow), Mass. Inst. Tech., 1952. Engr. Met. Dist. Water Supply Commn. of Mass., 1937-41; with AT&T, 1941—; v.p. ops. AT&T Long Lines, N.Y.C., 1970-76, v.p. tariffs and costs parent co., 1976—; dir. New Eng. Tel. & Tel. Co. Bd. dirs. nat. council Northeastern U. Served to lt. comdr. USN, 1942-45; PTO. Home: 346 Algonquin Rd Franklin Lakes NJ 07417 Office: 195 Broadway Room 2640 New York NY 10007

KELLEY, WAYNE PLUMBLEY, JR., magazine publisher; b. Rochester, N.Y., May 23, 1933; s. Wayne Plumbley and Elspeth Barbour (Moore) K.; m. Margaret Mary Ruikka, June 22, 1964; children: Wayne Plumbley, Richard Daniel. B.A., Vanderbilt U., 1955. City editor, state capitol reporter Chronicle, Augusta, Ga., 1960-65; Washington corr., reporter Atlanta Jour., 1965-69; assoc. editor Congl. Quar. Inc., Washington, 1969-72, mng. editor, 1972-74, exec. editor, 1974-80, pub., 1980—, exec. v.p., 1984—; dir. St. Petersburg Times Co. Served with U.S. Army, 1956-57. Nieman fellow Harvard U., 1963-64. Mem. Am. Polit. Sci. Assn. (Congl. fellowship adv. com. 1975—). Clubs: Washington Press, Federal City. Office: Congressional Quaterly 1414 22d St NW Washington DC 20037

KELLEY, WENDELL J., utilities executive; b. Champaign, Ill., May 2, 1926; s. Victor W. and Erma (Dalrymple) K.; m. Evelyn Kimpel, June 12, 1947; children: Jeffrey, David, Alan, Stephen, John. B.S. in Elec. Engring, U. Ill., 1949. Registered profl. engr., Ill. With Ill. Power Co., Decatur, 1949—, mgr. personnel, 1959-61, v.p., 1961-66, pres., 1966-76, chmn. and pres., 1976—, also dir.; dir. Millikin Nat. Bank, Decatur, Electric Energy, Inc., Millikin Mortgage Co., Franklin Ins. Co., Springfield. Chmn. Mid-Am. Interpool Network, 1969-71, vice chmn., 1975-77, now mem. exec. com.; bd. dirs. Edison Electric Inst., Washington, 1974-77, 80-83; past trustee Nat. Electric Reliability Council, vice chmn., 1975-77, chmn., 1978-80; past mem. Ill. Council on Econ. Edn.; mem. citizens com. U. Ill.; past mem. U. Ill. Found.; past mem. adv. council St. Mary's Hosp., Decatur, pres., 1972-73; past mem. Shults-Lewis Children's Home, Valparaiso, Ind. Served with USAAF, 1944-45. Recipient Alumni Honor award Coll. Engring., U. Ill., 1974, Alex Van Praag, Jr. Disting. engring. award, 1983. Fellow IEEE (past chmn. central Ill. sect., Centennial medal and cert. 1984); mem. Elec. Engring. Alumni Assn. U. Ill. (past pres., Disting. Alumnus award 1973), Ill. State C. of C. (chmn. 1973-74, past dir.), U. Ill. Alumni Assn. (past dir.), Nat., Ill. socs. profl. engrs., Eta Kappa Nu. Mem. Ch. of Christ (elder). Home: 65 Dellwood Dr Decatur IL 62521 Office: 500 S 27th St Decatur IL 62525

KELLEY, WILLIAM FREDERICK, ednl. adminstr.; b. Madison, Wis., Feb. ll, 1914; s. William and Elizabeth Anne (Harrington) K. A.B., St. Louis U., 1936, Ph.L., 1938, M.A., 1939, S.T.L., 1945; Ph.D., U. Minn., 1950. Joined Soc. of Jesus, 1931; ordained priest Roman Catholic Ch., 1944; instr. English, speech St. Louis U. High Sch., 1938-41; asst. to pres. Creighton U., Omaha, 1950- 51, dean coll. arts and scis., 1951-58, acad. v.p., 1958-62, asst. to pres., 1967—; pres. Marquette U., 1962-65; dir. Study Am. Jesuit Higher Edn., Washington, 1965-67; Mem. Father Marquette Tercentenary Commn.; mem. commn. on colls. and univs. N. Central Assn.; commn. on tchr. edn. Assn. Am. Colls.; vice chmn. State Commn. for Acad. Facilities, 1964; mem. Wis. Indsl. Research Council; sponsor Atlantic Council U.S.; vice chmn. Assn. Urban Univs., 1964. Bd. dirs. Coll. Entrance Exam. Bd. Mem. N.E.A., Jesuit Ednl. Assn., Nat. Cath. Edn. Assn. (chmn. Midwest sect. 1961, nat. exec. com. higher edn. sect.), Nat. Jesuit Deans' Inst., Am. Council on Edn., Am. Conf. Acad. Deans (exec. com. 1956), Phi Delta Kappa. Address: Creighton U Omaha NE 68178

KELLEY, WILLIAM LEWIS, engineering company executive; b. Seattle, June 4, 1932; s. Lewis Philips and Sarah Maurine (Middleton) K.; m. Mae Lee Brown, Feb. 17, 1955; children: Michael W., Katherine M., Patrick L. B.S. in C.E., U. Wash.-Seattle, 1955, 1955; M.S. in C.E., Stanford U., 1962. Registered profl. engr., Calif. Wash. Resident engr. Seattle City Light, Seattle, 1965-68; project mgr. Tippetts, Abbott McCarthy Stratton, Morocco, 1968-71; regional mgr. Internat. Engring. Co., Inc., San Francisco, 1972-74, v.p., 1974-81, exec. v.p., 1981—. Patentee apparatus and method for schedule monitoring and control. Mem. Nat. Soc. Profl. Engrs., ASCE, U.S. C. of C., Tau Beta Pi. Republican. Methodist. Club: Engineers of San Francisco. Home: 8 Candlestick Rd Orinda CA 94563

KELLEY, WILLIAM NIMMONS, physician, educator; b. Atlanta, June 23, 1939; s. Oscar Lee and Will Nimmons (Allen) K.; m. Lois Faville, Aug. 1, 1959; children: Margaret Paige, Virginia Lynn, Lori Ann, William Mark. M.D., Emory U., 1963. Intern in medicine Parkland Meml. Hosp., Dallas, 1963-64, resident, 1964-65; sr. resident medicine Mass. Gen. Hosp., Boston, 1967-68; clin. asso., sect. on human biochem. genetics NIH, 1965-67; teaching fellow medicine Harvard U. Med. Sch., 1967-68; asst. prof. to prof. medicine, asst. prof. to asso. prof. biochemistry, chief div. rheumatic and genetic diseases Duke U. Sch. Medicine, 1968-75; Macy faculty scholar Oxford U., 1974-75; prof., chmn. dept. internal medicine, prof. dept. biol. chemistry U. Mich. Med. Sch., Ann Arbor, 1975—; mem. bd. sci. advisers NICHD, NIH, 1975; chmn. arthritis center study sect. NIH, 1978, metabolism study sect., 1798-81; Bd. govs. Am. Bd. Internal Medicine, 1978—, chmn.-elect, 1984-85; mem. exec. com. Am. Bd. Med. Spltys., 1980-82. Author: (with J.B. Wyngaarden) Gout and Hyperuricemia, 1976, (with I.M. Weiner) Uric Acid, 1979, (with Harris, Ruddy and Sledge) Textbook of Rheumatology, 1981, 2d edit., 1985; contbr. articles to med. jours. Recipient C.V. Mosby award, 1967, John D. Lane award USPHS, 1969, Geigy Internat. prize rheumatology, 1969, Research Career Devel. award, 1972-75, Heinz Karger Meml. Found. prize, 1973; Mead Johnson scholar, 1967; Clin. scholar Am. Rheumatism Assn., 1969-72; Josiah Macy Found. scholar, 1974-75. Fellow ACP (trustee Mich. chpt. 1975—); mem. Am. Soc. Clin. Investigation (editorial bd. 1974-79, pres.-elect 1982-83, pres. 1983-84), So. Soc. Clin. Investigation, Central Soc. Clin. Research, Am. Soc. Biol. Chemists (editorial bd. 1976-81), Am. Fedn. Clin. Research (nat. council 1977-80, exec. com. 1975-80, nat. sec.-treas. 1976-78, pres. 1979-80, chmn. publs. com. Clin. Research 1976-78), Assn. Am. Physicians, Assn. Profs. Medicine (nominating com. 1978-79), Am. Rheumatism Assn. (chmn. membership com., program com., research com., dir. 1975-76, exec. com. 1976—, editorial bd. 1972-78, sec.-treas. 1982—), AAAS, Am. Soc. Human Genetics, Am. Soc. Nephrology, Am. Soc. Internal Medicine (trustee Mich. chpt.), Central Rheumatism Soc. (pres. 1978-79), N.Y. Acad. Scis., Sigma Xi, Alpha Omega Alpha. Home: 521 Hillspur Rd Ann Arbor MI 48105 Office: D3105 SACB Dept Internal Medicine U Mich Med Center Ann Arbor MI 48109

KELLEY, WILLIAM THOMAS, emeritus marketing educator; b. Jersey City, Feb. 4, 1917; s. William Scholes and Elsie (Thomas) K.; m. Barbara Bacher, June 23, 1945; 1 son, Thomas Bacher. B.A., U. Toronto, 1939; M.B.A., Wharton Sch., U. Pa., 1941, Ph.D., 1951. Assoc. economist U. S.C., 1941-42; chief sect. War Shipping Adminstrn., 1942-43; mem. faculty U. Pa., Phila., 1946—, prof. bus. adminstrn., 1974-82, emeritus prof. mktg., 1982—; cons. to govt. and industry, 1953—; vis. prof. U. Lancaster, Eng., 1965-66; vis. fellow Ashridge (Eng.) Mgmt. Coll., 1977. Author: Management of Promotion, 1963, Marketing Intelligence, 1968, The New Consumerism, 1973, The Elderly Consumer, 1980, also articles, monographs; editor: Mktg. Abstracts, 1953-61; editorial bd.: Jour. Mktg, 1966-76. Served to 1st lt. AUS, 1944-46. Ford Found. fellow, 1963. Mem. Am. Mktg. Assn., Am. Econ. Assn., Am. Council Consumer Interests, Greater Phila. C. of C. (past officer). Quaker. Home: 608 Spruce Ln Villanova PA 19085 Office: Mktg Suite Dietrich Hall 36th and Spruce Sts Philadelphia PA 19104

KELLIHER, PETER MAURICE, lawyer, arbitrator; b. Chgo., Dec. 23, 1912; s. Edward J. and Catherine (Rooney) K.; m. Virginia Dowdle, Jan. 28, 1942; children—Diane, Peter. A.B., U. Chgo., 1935, J.D., 1937. Bar: Ill. bar 1938. Spl. asst. corp. counsel City Chgo., 1940-41; U.S. commr. conciliation, 1941-42, arbitrator-umpire labor disputes, 1945—; pres. Kelliher Co., Inc.; developer Hemingway House, Huntington Hills, Algonquin Indsl. Park, One East Superior Office Bldg.; impartial referee Inland Steel Co., Youngstown Sheet & Tube. Past commr. Chgo. Urban Renewal Commn.; bd. dirs. Greater North Michigan Ave. Assn.; mem. fin. com. Holy Name Cathedral. Served to capt. AUS, 1942-45. Recipient Heritage of Liberty award Am. Jewish Com. Mem. Nat. Acad. Arbitrators (pres. 1964), Indsl. Relations Research Assn., Wine and Food Soc. Clubs: Tavern, One Hundred (Chgo.); Beach (Palm Beach). Home: 109 E Bellevue Pl Chicago IL 60611 Office: 77 W Washington St Chicago IL 60602

KELLISON, JAMES BRUCE, lawyer; b. Richmond, Va., June 18, 1922; s. John Ray and Clara (Cato) K.; m. Audrey Cresswell, May 5, 1962; children: Bruce, Jr., Elizabeth, Julia. B.A., U. Richmond, 1943; J.D., George Washington U., 1948. Bar: D.C. 1948. Asso. partner Hogan & Hartson, Washington, 1954-73; partner Altmann Kellison & Siegler, Washington, 1973-83; Mem. adv. com. on rules of probate procedure Superior Ct., 1972—. Pres., bd. trustees Louise Home, 1971—; trustee, sec. Columbia Lighthouse for the Blind, 1969-76; trustee Audubon Naturalist Soc., 1968-71; chmn. bd. trustees Washington Found., 1978—. Served with USNR, 1943-46. Fellow Am. Coll. Probate Counsel; mem. Am., D.C. bar assns., Am. Judicature Soc., Nat. Grange, Omicron Delta Kappa, Lambda Chi Alpha, Phi Delta Phi. Republican. Clubs: Metropolitan, Barristers, St. Albans Tennis (Washington); Chevy Chase (Md.); Lawyers, Siasconset (Mass.) Casino. Home: 4518 Klingle St NW Washington DC 20016 Office: 1616 H St NW Washington DC 20006

KELLISON, STEPHEN GEORGE, professional association executive, actuary; b. Ord., Nebr., Mar. 20, 1942; s. Orin Albian and Sarah Viola (Crouch) K.; m. Chery Le Wagner, June 14, 1963 (div. Jan. 1970); m. 2d Erica Elizabeth Bowers, Jan. 27, 1978. A.B., U. Nebr.-Lincoln, 1963, M.S., 1967. Actuarial supr. Occidental Life Ins. Co., Los Angeles, 1963-65; actuary Lincoln Liberty Life Ins. Co., Lincoln, Nebr., 1965-66; prof. U. Nebr., 1965-75; consulting actuary G.V. Stennes & Assocs., Dallas, 1975-76; exec. dir. Am. Acad. Actuaries, Washington, 1976—; cons. Nebr. Legislature, Nebr. Ins. Dept. Author: The Theory of Interest, 1970, Fundamentals of Numerical Analysis, 1975. Fellow Soc. Actuaries (dir. 1973-75); mem. Am. Acad. Actuaries (dir. 1975-76), Phi Xeta Kappa. Clubs: Nebr. Actuaries (pres. 1970-71), Mid Atlantic Actuarial). Home: 9931 Great Oaks Way Fairfax VA 22030 Office: Am Acad Actuaries 1835 K St NW Suite 515 Washington DC 20006

KELLN, ALBERT LEE, naval officer; b. Shattuck, Okla., Dec. 17, 1929; s. David and Eva (Meier) K.; m. Prudence Jane Lamb, June 19, 1954; children—Deborah, Melinda, David, Elizabeth. Student, U. Okla., 1947-48; B.S., U.S. Naval Acad., 1952. Commd. ensign U.S. Navy, 1952, advanced through grades to rear adm., 1974; mem. precommissioning crew (U.S.S. Skate), 1957-59, commissioning crew engr., exec. officer, 1959-62, exec. officer, 1962-63, engring. officer, 1963-65, comdg. officer, 1966-69, comdr., 1969-70, program mgr. nuclear power personnel, head sub-marine/nuclear power distbn. control br., Washington, 1970-71, comdr., Scotland, 1972-74, Charleston, S.C., 1974-75, dir. Strategic Submarine div., Trident program coordinator, Washington, 1975-78, dep. dir. strategic and gen. ops., 1978-79, dep. dir., 1979-80, ret., 1980; def. system cons., 1980—. Decorated Def. D.S.M., Legion of Merit (2), Meritorious Service medal, Navy Commendation medal (3). Home: 8621 Woodward Ave Alexandria VA 22309

KELLNER, IRWIN L., economist; b. N.Y.C., Oct. 4, 1938; s. Philip and Mildred (Isaacson) K.; m. Ann Heimann, Jan. 22, 1961; children—Lori, Shari. B.A., Bklyn. Coll., 1960, M.A., 1964; Ph.D. in Econs, New Sch. Social Research, 1973. Research analyst Philip Morris, Inc., 1960-63; sr. research analyst William Esty Co., Inc., 1963-66; asst. bus. outlook editor Bus. Week Mag., 1966-70; asso. economist Mfrs. Hanover Trust Co., N.Y.C., 1970-72, v.p., 1972-78, dep. chief economist, 1973-78, sr. v.p., 1978—, chief economist, 1980—; dir. Riegel Textile Corp.; vis. lectr. colls.; appeared on TV and radio; speaker bus. and community groups. Author: monthly Econ. Report; contbr. numerous articles on bus. and banking to profl. jours; commentaries to Fin. Digest. Mem. Port Washington (N.Y.) Planning Bd. Recipient award for tobacco econs. Tobacco Mchts. Assn., 1978. Mem. Conf. Bd. (mem. Econ. Forum), Forecasters Club N.Y. (past pres.), Money Marketeers (past gov.), N.Y. Assn. Bus. Economists (past pres.), Am. Econ. Assn., Am. Statis. Assn., Bus. Economists Council, Downtown Economists Luncheon Group, Nat. Assn. Bus. Economists. Office: Manufacturers Hanover Trust Co 270 Park Ave New York NY 10017

KELLOGG, ALFRED LATIMER, educator; b. Cleve., Apr. 24, 1915; s. Alfred Noah and Clara Florence (Beck) K.; m. Ellen Carlisle Cushman, June 7, 1941 (dec. Dec. 1977); children—Marion Lewis Kellogg Fisher, Alfred Cushman. A.B., Western Res. U., 1937; Ph.D., Yale U., 1941. Instr. English Yale U., 1941-42, 45-47, Cornell U., 1942; asst. prof. English Rutgers U., New Brunswick, N.J., 1947-51, asso. prof., 1951-61, prof., 1961—; mem. Inst. for Advanced Study, Princeton U., 1951-52. Author: Chaucer, Langland, Arthur, 1972; contbr. articles to scholarly jours. Served with Signal Intelligence AUS, 1942-45; ETO. Am. Philos. Soc. Penrose Fund grantee, 1965, 77; Ford fellow, 1951-52; Guggenheim fellow, 1953-54; Rutgers Faculty fellow, 1976-77, 80-81. Mem. Medieval Acad. Am., MLA, Dante Soc., Modern Humanities Assn., Internat. Arthurian Soc., Internat. Assn. U. Profs. English, Phi Beta Kappa. Home: 224 Lawrence Ave Highland Park NJ 08904 Office: 222 Scott Hall Rutgers Univ New Brunswick NJ 08903

KELLOGG, HERBERT HUMPHREY, educator, metallurgist; b. N.Y.C., Feb. 24, 1920; s. Herbert H. and Gladys (Falding) K.; m. Jeanette Halstead, July 20, 1940; children—Thomas Bartlett, Jane Falding, David Humphrey, Elizabeth Ann. B.S., Columbia, 1941, M.S., 1943. Asst. prof. mineral preparation Pa. State U., State Coll., 1942-46; faculty Columbia, N.Y.C., 1946—, Stanley-Thompson prof. chem. metallurgy, 1968—; Chmn. titanium adv. com. Office Def. Mblzn., 1954-58. Research; contbr. numerous articles to publs. Recipient Best Paper award extractive metals div. Am. Inst. Mining., Metall. and Petroleum Engrs.; James Douglas Gold medal Am. Inst. Mining, Metall. and Petroleum Engrs., 1973. Fellow Am. Inst. Mining, Metall. and Petroleum Engrs. (chmn. extractive metallurgy div. 1958), Metall. Soc., Instn. Mining and Metallurgy (London); mem. Am. Chem. Soc., Nat. Acad. Engrs., Sigma Xi, Tau Beta Pi. Home: Closter Rd Palisades NY 10964 Office: Columbia New York City NY 10027

KELLOGG, MARION KNIGHT, lawyer, educator; b. Bowling Green, Ky., July 24, 1904; s. Robert Marion and Nelle (Willis) K.; m. Virginia Dryden, Oct. 3, 1931. B.A., Va. Mil. Inst., 1925; LL.B, Yale, 1928. Bar: N.Y. bar 1929, Mich. bar 1932, Va. bar 1961. Practiced in, N.Y.C., 1928-32, Detroit, 1932-56, Charlottesville, 1956—; asso. firm Chadbourne, Hunt, Jaeckel & Brown, Cravath, de Gersdorf, Swaine & Wood, 1928-32; pvt. practice, 1932-56; mem. firm Kellogg, Fulton & Donovan, 1942-46; lectr. law Sch. U. Va., 1956-64, prof. law, 1964-75, emeritus, 1975; exec. dir. Law Sch. Found., 1964-73. Pres. Charlottesville-Albermarie United Givers Fund, 1964; mem. Charlottesville Community Relations Com., 1964-65; mem. steering com. United Negro Coll. Fund, Shenandoah Area, 1966—. Served to lt. col., Q.M.C. AUS, 1942-45. Mem. Am., N.Y., Mich., Va., Charlottesville-Albermarle, Detroit, Fed., Inter-Am. bar assns., Internat. Law Assn., Am. Law Inst., Charlottesville Com. Fgn. Relations (past pres.), Order of Coif (hon.), Phi Delta Phi. Presbyn. Clubs: Farmington Country, Farmington Hunt, Commonwealth (Richmond, Va.); Nat. Lawyers (Washington); Torch (past pres.), Colonnade (Charlottesville); Yale (N.Y.C.); Graduate (New Haven). Home: Farmington PO Box 3755 University Station Charlottesville VA 22903

KELLOGG, RALPH HENDERSON, physiologist; b. New London, Conn., June 7, 1920; s. Edwin Henry and Constance Louise

(Henderson) K. B.A., U. Rochester, N.Y., 1940, M.D., 1943; Ph.D., Harvard U., 1953. Intern, Univ. Hosps., Cleve., 1944; investigator physiology U.S. Naval Med. Research Inst., Bethesda, Md., 1946; teaching fellow physiology Harvard Med. Sch., Boston, 1946-47, instr., 1947-53; asst. prof. physiology U. Calif.-Berkeley, 1953-58, U. Calif.-San Francisco, 1958-59, asso. prof., 1959-65, prof., 1965—, lectr. history of health scis., 1978—, acting chmn. physiology, 1966-70; mem. physiology study sect. NIH, 1966-70; physiology test com. Nat. Bd. Med. Examiners, 1966-73, chmn., 1969-73; com. respiration nomenclature Internat. Union Physiol. Scis., 1970-77, commn. respiratory physiology, 1975-81; editorial com. U. Calif. Press, 1972-76. Physiology editor: Stedman's Med. Dictionary, 1972—; joint editorial bd.: Am. Jour. Physiology and Jour. Applied Physiology, 1962-66; editorial bd.: Jour. Applied Physiology, 1977-79; contbr. articles to profl. publs.; contbg. author books on physiology of saline and urea diuresis, respiration, high-altitude acclimatization, history of physiology. Served with M.C., USNR, 1943-46. Sr. research fellow Harvard U., 1962-63; vis. fellow Corpus Christi Coll. Univ. Lab. Physiology, Oxford (Eng.) U., 1970-71; vis. scientist Laboratoire de Physiologie Respiratoire, Centre National de la Recherche Scientifique, Strasbourg, France, 1977; NIH research grantee, 1962-76. Mem. AAAS, Am. Physiol. Soc., AAUP, Am. Assn. History of Medicine, History of Sci. Soc., Phi Beta Kappa, Sigma Xi, Alpha Omega Alpha. Clubs: Roxburghe, Harvard. Home: 601 Noriega St San Francisco CA 94122 Office: Dept Physiology U Calif San Francisco CA 94143

KELLOGG, ROBERT LELAND, English educator, university dean; b. Ionia County, Mich., Sept. 2, 1928; s. Charles Edwin and Lucille Jeanette (Reasoner) K.; m. Joan Alice Montgomery, Apr. 4, 1951; children: Elizabeth Joan, Jonathan Montgomery, Stephen Robert. B.A., U. Md., 1950; M.A., Harvard U., 1952, Ph.D., 1958. Mem. faculty U. Va., 1957—, prof. english, 1967—, chmn. dept., 1974-78, dean Coll. Arts and Scis., 1978—. Author: (with Robert Scholes) The Nature of Narrative, 1966; contbr. profl. jours. Served with USAR, 1954-56. Am.-Scandinavian Found. fellow, 1956-57; Guggenheim fellow, 1968-69. Mem. Medieval Acad. Am., Modern Lang. Assn., South Atlantic Modern Lang. Assn. (pres. 1974-75), Raven Soc., Phi Beta Kappa (pres. local chpt. 1981). Democrat. Club: Colonnade. Home: Pavilion IX West Lawn Charlottesville VA 22903 Office: Garrett Hall U Va Charlottesville VA 22903

KELLOGG, TOMMY NASON, reinsurance corporation executive; b. Ava, Mo., Mar. 29, 1936; s. Charles Roy and Bessie May (Robertson) K.; m. Louise Marie Howard, Dec. 21, 1957 (div. 1960); 1 son, Larry J.; m. Sandra Lee Weydt, Jan. 28, 1965 (div. 1983); children: Todd T., Christopher C. B.A., Drury Coll., 1958; M.S., Mich. State U., 1961; J.D., DePaul U., 1970. Bar: Ill. Instr. econs. Mich. State U., East Lansing, 1960-61; underwriter Employers Ins. of Wasau, Chgo., 1961-68; with Gen. Reins. Corp., 1968—, v.p., Greenwich, Conn., 1974-78, sr. v.p., 1978—; v.p., dir. Gen. Re Services, Ltd.; dir. Gen. Re Services Corp., Greenwich, Herbert Clough, Inc.; chmn. United Fin. Ins. Co., Bermuda, North Star Excess Lines, Greenwich. Served with USAR, 1960-68. Edn. research grantee Mich. State U., 1958. Mem. Am. Soc. C.P.C.U.s, Omicron Delta Kappa, Lambda Chi Alpha. Republican. Baptist. Home: 12 Lincoln Ave Old Greenwich CT 06870 Office: Gen Reins Corp 600 Steamboat Rd Greenwich CT 06830

KELLOGG, WILLIAM WELCH, meteorologist; b. New York Mills, N.Y., Feb. 14, 1917; s. Frederick S. and Elizabeth (Walcott) K.; m. Elizabeth Thorson, Feb. 14, 1942; children: Karl S., Judith Liebert, Joseph W., Jane K. Holien, Thomas W. B.A., Yale U., 1939; M.A., U. Calif. at Los Angeles, 1942, Ph.D., 1949. With Inst. Geophysics, U. Calif. at Los Angeles, 1946-52, asst. prof., 1950-52; with Rand Corp., Santa Monica, Calif., 1947-64, head planetary scis. dept., 1959-64; asso. dir. Nat. Center Atmospheric Research, Boulder, Colo., also dir. lab. atmospheric scis., 1964-73, sr. scientist, 1973—; Mem. earth satellite panel IGY, 1956-59; mem. space sci. bd. Nat. Acad. Scis., 1959-68, mem. com. meteorol. aspects of effects of atomic radiation, 1956-58, mem. com. atmospheric scis., 1966-72, mem. polar research bd., 1972-77; mem. Rocket and Satellite Research Panel, 1957-62; mem. adv. group supporting tech. for operational meteorol. satellites NASA-NOAA, 1964-72; rapporteur meteorology of high atmosphere, commn. aerology World Meteorol. Orgn., 1965-71; chmn. internat. commn. meteorology upper atmosphere Internat. Union Geodesy and Geophysics, 1960-67, mem., 1967-75; mem. internat. com. climate Internat. Assn. Meteorology and Atmospheric Physics, 1978—; mem. sci. adv. bd. USAF, 1956-65; chmn. meteorol. satellite com. Advanced Research Projects Agy., 1958-59; mem. panel on environment President's Sci. Adv. Com., 1968-72; mem. space program adv. council NASA, 1976-77; chmn. meteorol. adv. com. EPA, 1970-74, mem. nat. air quality criteria adv. com., 1975-76, air pollution transport and transformation adv. com., 1976-78; mem. council on carbon dioxide environ. assessment Dept. Energy, 1976-78; adv. to sec. gen. on World Climate Program, World Meteorol. Orgn., 1978-79; dir. research Naval Environ. Prediction Research Facility, Monterey, Calif., 1983-84. Served as pilot-weather officer USAAF, 1941-46. Co-recipient spl. award pioneering work in planning meteorol. satellite Am. Meteorol. Soc., 1961; recipient Risseca award contbn. human relations in scis. Jewish War Vets. U.S.A., 1962-63; Exceptional Civilian Service award Dept. Air Force, 1966. Fellow Am. Geophys. Union (pres. meteorol. sect. 1972-74), Am. Meteorol. Soc. (council 1960-63, pres. 1973-74); mem. AAAS (chmn. atmospheric and hydrospheric sect. 1984), Sigma Xi. Club: Cosmos (Washington). Research on meteorology, dynamics and turbulence of upper atmosphere, use rockets and satellites for atmospheric research; prediction radioactive fallout and dispersal; applications of infrared techniques; atmospheres of Mars and Venus; theory of climate and causes of climate change. Home: 445 College Ave Boulder CO 80302 Office: Nat Center Atmospheric Research Boulder CO 80307 *If there is anything that generally characterizes a gratifying and successful career in science, it is the challenge of diversity. The really important problems of the universe, and especially of society, involve several disciplines, and we are compelled to work at these discipline interfaces. Pigeon holes are for pigeons, not scientists*

KELLSTROM, FRANCIS S., construction company executive; b. 1913; married. Grad., Am. Sch. Elec. Engring. With Fischbach Corp., N.Y.C., 1950—, v.p., 1952-61, exec. v.p., 1961-66, pres., 1966-80, chmn. bd., 1980-84, dir. Served with USN, 1942-49. Office: Fischbach Corp 485 Lexington Ave New York N.Y. 10007 *

KELLY, ALONZO HYATT, JR., automotive engineering company executive; b. Richlands, Va., Sept. 30, 1922; s. Alonzo Hyatt and Amanda Dalby (Torbert) K.; m. Marilee Z. Diamond, Dec. 29, 1949; children: Alonzo Hyatt, III, Elizabeth, Amanda, Ted. Student, Emory and Henry Coll., 1940-42; diploma in meteorology, UCLA, 1944; B.S.E., Auburn U., 1947; M.S., U. Mich., 1949. Registered profl. engr., Mich. Research engr. U. Mich., Ann Arbor, 1949-54; with Gen. Motors Corp., 1954—; mgr. Gen. Motors Proving Grounds facilities and ops., 1978-82; asst. dir. engring. analysis Gen. Motors Tech. Center, Warren, Mich., 1982—. Served with USAAF, 1943-46. Mem. Soc. Automotive Engrs., Nat. Rifle Assn., Airplane Owners and Pilots Assn., Exptl. Aircraft Assn. Republican. Methodist. Clubs: Huron Valley Swim., Ann Arbor Golf and Outing. Office: Gen Motors Tech Center Warren MI 48090

KELLY, ANNE M., lawyer, pharmaceutical company executive; b. Union City, N.J., Sept. 22, 1928; d. Joseph and Anna K. (Boos) K. B.S., Fordham U., 1952; J.D., Seton Hall Sch. Law, 1977. With Warner-Lambert Co., Morris Plains, N.J., 1964—, info. sci., lit. sci., patent trainee, 1964-68, patent agt., 1968-77, sr. patent atty., 1978, sr. atty., corp. staff, 1978-79, corp. sec., 1980—. Mem. ABA, N.J. Bar Assn., N.J. Patent Law Assn., Am. Chem. Soc., Am. Soc. Corp. Secs. Roman Catholic. Office: 201 Tabor Rd Morris Plains NJ 07950 *

KELLY, ANTHONY ODRIAN, carpet mfg. co. exec.; b. Dublin, Ireland, June 12, 1935; s. John Peter and Delia Mary (Finnegan) K.; m. Sheila Josephine Clancy, Sept. 4, 1963; children—Barbara Anne, Adrienne Elizabeth, Damian Anthony. Grad., Coll. Commerce, Dublin, 1958; M.B.A., Columbia U., 1965, doctoral degree, 1971. Adj. asst. prof. Columbia U., N.Y.C., 1968-69; dir. econ. studies Sperry & Hutchinson Co., 1969-71, asst. to pres. furnishings div., 1975; dir. mktg. Irish Agrl. Devel. Co., 1971-74; sr. v.p. mktg. Bigelow-Sanford, Inc., Greenville, S.C., 1976-79, exec. v.p., chief operating officer, 1979—; chmn. bd. Bigelow-Can. Ltd. Ford Found. fellow; Samuel Bronfman fellow. Mem. Inst. Cost and Mgmt. Accts., Beta Gamma Sigma. Club: Greenville Country. Office: Bigelow Sanford Inc PO Box 3089 Greenville SC 29602 *

KELLY, AUREL MAXEY, judge; b. Cleve., Apr. 24, 1923; d. Chester Collins and Elnora (Campbell) Maxey; m. Thomas F. Kelly, May 29, 1943; children—Shannon, Keven. A.B. cum laude, Whitman Coll., 1943; J.D., Columbia U., 1947. Bar: Wash. State Bar 1949, Colo. bar 1961. Continuity acceptance MBS, N.Y.C., 1947; asst. editor Baker-Voorhis Pub. Co., 1947-48; practiced in Walla Walla, Wash., 1949-60; dep. pros. atty., Walla Walla County, 1955-56; justice of peace Walla Walla precinct, 1956-59; asso. firm Roepnack & Orahood, 1961-62; partner firm Kelly & Kelly, 1962-74; spl. asst. atty. gen. State of Colo., 1963-68; sr. asst. atty. gen., 1968-74, chief criminal div., 1971-74; judge Colo. Ct. Appeals, Denver, 1974—; Vice pres. State Fedn. Young Republicans, 1952-54, nat. committeewoman, 1954-56; vice chmn. Walla Walla County Rep. Central Com., 1954-55; mem. Colo. Commn. on Status of Women, 1969-74; bd. overseers Whitman Coll., 1977—. Mem. Am., Wash., Colo., Colo. Women's, 1st Dist, Denver bar assns., Am. Judicature Soc., Nat. Assn. Women Judges, Las Mujeres de Lulac, Kappa Kappa Gamma. Office: 2 E 14th St Denver CO 80203

KELLY, BURTON VINCENT, banker; b. Woodstock, N.B., Can., June 16, 1932; s. Burton Murrant and Harriet Ann (Murphy) K.; m. Mary Pamela Ludford Taylor, Aug. 31, 1957; 1 son, John B.V. B.Comm., Sir George Williams U. Joined Bank at Woodstock, 1950, numerous postings, Latin Am. and Caribbean; exec. dir., sr. rep. Orion Banking Group and Orion Multinat. Services Ltd., London; mng. dir. Orion Banking Group and Orion Multinational Services Ltd., 1975-77, asst. gen. mgr. for Latin Am. and Caribbean, Montreal, 1977-78, v.p. and gen. mgr., 1978-79, sr. v.p. internat., 1979-83, exec. v.p. world corp. banking div., Toronto, 1983—; dir. RoyWest Holdings Ltd., RoyWest Investments Ltd., RoyWest Trust Corp. Ltd., Nassau, Bahamas. Mem. Inst. Can. Bankers (asso.). Clubs: Royal Montreal Curling, Royal Montreal Golf, St. James's, Royal Nassau Sailing, Granite. Home: 9 Peebles Ave Don Mills ON M3C 2N9 Canada Office: Royal Bank Canada 200 Bay St Toronto ON M5J 2J5 Canada

KELLY, CHARLES J., JR., investment company executive; b. June 10, 1929; s. Charles J. and Margaret (Grimes) K.; m. Marguerite Stehli, Dec. 23, 1962; children: Karen Grimes, Marguerite Grace, Lisa Stehli. B.A., Stanford U., 1951; LL.B., Yale U., 1954. Bar: N.Y., U.S. Supreme Ct. Asso. atty. Chadbourne, Parke, Whiteside & Wolff, N.Y.C., 1957-58; spl. counsel CAB, 1959-60; spl. asst. to Sec. Comm., Washington, 1960-61; with Reynolds & Co., 1961-62; partner Kelly, Grimes & Winston, 1962-69; pres., dir. Meridian Investing and Devel. Co., N.Y.C., 1969-72, pres., chief exec. officer, 1972-74; pres. Capital Strategy, Inc.; dir. Big Sky of Mont., Inc., 1970-74; trustee The Hotel Investors, 1970-77; dir. KTCA-TV, Mpls., 1978—. Author: The Sky's The Limit: The History of the Airlines, 1962; repub. with introduction by Charles A. Lindbergh, 1972. Bd. dirs. Charles A. Lindbergh Fund. Served to 1st Lt. USAF, 1954-56. Clubs: Raquet & Tennis, Yale (N.Y.C.); Minneapolis; Woodhill Country (Wayzata, Minn.). Office: 431 Lake St Wayzata MN 55391

KELLY, CROSBY MOYER, business executive; b. Hinsdale, Ill., Mar. 23, 1918; s. Thomas Cowen and Mary Emma (Moyer) K.; m. Willah Mary Smith, Mar. 12, 1951. B.A., U. Ariz., 1939; postgrad., U. Mexico, 1939-40. With Ford Motor Co., 1941-48; dir. advt. and pub. relations Rapid Standard Co., Inc., Grand Rapids, Mich., 1949; exec. dir. Chgo. Fair of, 1950; sales rep. Central Services, Inc., Kansas City, Mo., 1951; owner-mgr. importing-distbg. co., Havana and Camaguey, Cuba, 1952-55; v.p., dir. advt. and pub. relations, asst. to chief exec. officer Litton Industries, Inc., Beverly Hills, Calif., 1955-65; chmn. bd. Crosby M. Kelly Asso. Ltd., 1965-73; chmn. Pres. Advt. Measurements, Inc., 1965-70; sr. v.p. Litton Industries, Inc., 1973-76; v.p. communications Rockwell Internat., 1976-78; chmn. bd. Crosby M. Kelly Assos. Ltd., Pitts., 1978—; pres. Sage Inst., Portland, Oreg., 1980-83; dir. Western World Ins. Co., Crested Butte Silver Mining, Inc.; chmn. bd. Performance Measurements Co., Detroit, 1968-70; Cons., insp. gen. Fgn. Assistance, Dept. State, 1962; guest lectr. European Inst. Bus. Adminstrn. Fontainebleau, France, 1966; instr. U. Pitts. Grad. Sch. Bus., 1978. Head Am. delegation Internat. Congress Air Force Assns., Turin, Italy, 1964; del. UN Indsl. Devel. Orgn. 1st World Symposium, 1967; Trustee Albertus Magnus Coll., 1970-73, Mercy Hosp., Pitts., 1977-80. Decorated commendatore Order of Merit Republic Italy, 1969. Clubs: Los Angeles Country; Univ. (N.Y.C.). Home: 2221 SW 1st Ave Portland OR 97201 Butternut Brook Farm Litchfield CT 06759

KELLY, DAVID AUSTIN, consumer products and chemical company executive; b. Mt. Kisco, N.Y., June 24, 1938; s. William Andrew and Katharine Elizabeth (Barrett) K.; m. Judith Boesel, June 18, 1966; children: Carolyn Boesel, Douglas Austin. B.A., Lafayette Coll., 1962; M.B.A., U. Chgo., 1964. Chartered fin. analyst. Asst. v.p. investment mgmt. group First Nat. City Bank, N.Y.C., 1964-69; portfolio mgr., v.p. J.M. Hartwell & Co., Inc., N.Y.C., 1969-72; dir., pres. P/H Mgmt. Corp., Pitts., 1972-74; asst. treas. Gulf Oil Corp., Pitts., 1974-80; v.p., treas. Borden, Inc., N.Y.C., 1980—. Past councilor N.Y. Soc., Order of Founders and Patriots Am.; mem. fin. policy com. Lafayette Coll., Easton, Pa., 1976-79. Served with U.S. Army, 1957-59. Mem. Fin. Analysts Fedn., N.Y. Soc. Security Analysts, Soc. Internat. Treas., NAM (chmn. auditing com. 1983-84). Clubs: Duquesne (Pitts.); Milbrook, Stanwich (Greenwich, Conn.). Home: 303 Overlook Dr Greenwich CT 06830 Office: 277 Park Ave New York NY 10172

KELLY, DONALD PHILIP, holding company executive; b. Chgo., Feb. 24, 1922; s. Thomas Nicholas and Ethel M. (Healy) K.; m. Byrd M. Sullivan, Oct. 25, 1952; children: Patrick, Laura, Thomas. Student, Loyola U., Chgo., 1953-54, De Paul U., 1954-55, Harvard U., 1965. Mgr. tabulating United Ins. Co. Am., 1946-51; mgr. data processing A.B. Wrisley Co., 1951-53, Swift & Co., 1953-65, asst. controller, 1965-67, controller, 1967-68, v.p. corporate devel., controller, 1968-70, fin. v.p., dir., 1970-73, Esmark, Inc., Chgo., 1973, pres., chief operating officer, 1973-77, pres., chief exec. officer, 1977-82, chmn., pres., chief exec. officer, 1982—, also dir.; dir. G. D. Searle & Co., Harris Bankcorp., Inc., Harris Trust & Savs. Bank, Inland Steel Co., McGraw-Edison Co. Trustee Michael Reese Hosp. and Med. Center, Chgo., St. Norbert Coll., De Pere, Wis., Com. for Econ. Devel., Washington, Mus. Sci. and Industry, Chgo.; mem. citizens bd. U. Chgo.; mem. Conf. Bd. N.Y.; mem. exec. com. adv. council Coll. Bus. Adminstrn., U. Notre Dame. Served in USNR, 1942-46. Mem. Fin. Execs. Inst. Clubs: Chgo., Comml., Econ. (Chgo.). Office: 55 E Monroe St Chicago IL 60603

KELLY, DOROTHY ANN, college president; b. Bronx, N.Y., July 26, 1929; d. Walter David and Sarah (McCauley) K. B.A., Coll. New Rochelle, 1951; M.A., Catholic U., Washington, 1958; Ph.D., U. Notre Dame, 1970; Litt.D. (hon.), Mercy Coll., Dobbs Ferry, N.Y., 1976, LL.D., Nazareth Coll. of Rochester, N.Y., 1979; D.H.L. (hon.), Coll. St. Rose, 1981, Manhattan Coll., 1979. Mem. faculty Coll. New Rochelle (N.Y.), 1957—; chmn. dept. history Coll. New Rochelle, 1965-67, acad. dean, 1967-72, acting pres., 1970-71, pres., 1972—; trustee, vice chmn. Commn. Ind. Colls. and Univs. State of N.Y., 1977-78, chmn. bd. trustees, 1978-80, mem. govt. relations com., 1980—; chmn. Com. Higher Edn. Opportunity, 1977; mem. commr. edn. Adv. Council on Higher Edn. for N.Y. State, 1975-77, subcom. on postsecondary occupational edn., 1975-77; exec. com. Empire State Found. Ind. Liberal Arts Colls., 1975—, vice chmn., 1977-81, chmn., 1981—; trustee, mem. exec. com. Assn. Colls. and Univs. State of N.Y., 1976—; mem. exec. com. Assn. Colls. Mid-Hudson Area, 1976—, pres., 1979-81; mem. com. on purpose and identity Assn. Cath. Colls. and Univs., 1975-80; mem. Neylon Conf. steering com., 1978—, mem. bishops and pres. com., 1979—; mem. adv. council on fin. aid to students Office Edn., HEW, 1978—; chmn. Women's Coll. Coalition, 1981-83; trustee United Student Aid Funds, 1980—; chmn. govt. relations adv. com. Nat. Assn. Ind. Colls. and Univs., 1981-82; bd. dirs. Westchester County Assn., 1980—. Mem. AAUP, Am. Hist. Assn., AAUW, Nat. Fedn. Bus. and Profl. Women, Am. Assn. Higher Edn., Nat. Assembly Women Religious. Address: Coll New Rochelle New Rochelle NY 10801

KELLY, DOUGLAS, JR., retired agricultural chemical company executive, consultant; b. Huntsville, Ala., Jan. 25, 1915; s. Douglas and Roberta (Bradford) K.; m. Francenia Irwin, June 18, 1937; children: Douglas, III, William Laird. B.B.A., Tulane U., 1936; postgrad., U. Pa., 1947. Sales rep. Allied Chem. Corp., 1936-49; dist. mgr. Monsanto Co., 1949-67; v.p. Riverside Industries, Marks, Miss., 1967-72; pres. Riverside Chem. Co., Memphis, 1972—; v.p. Cook Industries, Memphis, 1972—, Terra Chem. Internat., Inc., 1979—, cons., 1981—; chmn. bd. Riverside Chem. Co., 1979-81; cons. Cook Internat. (Palm Beach), Fla. Active local Boy Scouts Am. Served to lt. USNR, 1943-47. Mem. Natl. Agrl. Chems. Assn. (dir.), Southeastern Agrl. Chems. Assn. (dir.). Methodist. Clubs: Chickasaw Country, Summit, Rotary. Home: 752 Eventide Dr Memphis TN 38119 Office: 871 Ridgeway Loop Rd Memphis TN 38117

KELLY, EAMON MICHAEL, university president; b. N.Y.C., Apr. 25, 1936; s. Michael Joseph and Kathleen Elizabeth (O'Farrell) K.; m. Margaret Whalen, June 22, 1963; children—Martin (dec.), Paul, Andrew, Peter. B.S., Fordham U., 1958; M.S., Columbia U., 1960, Ph.D., 1965. Officer in charge Office of Social Devel., Ford Found., N.Y.C., 1969-73, officer in charge program related investments, 1974-79; exec. v.p. Tulane U., New Orleans, 1979-81, pres., 1981—; dir. policy formulation div. Econ. Devel. Adminstrn., Dept. Commerce, Washington, 1968; spl. asst. to adminstr. SBA, Washington, 1968-69; spl. counselor to sec. Dept. Labor, 1977. Contbr. articles to profl. jours. Pres. city council, councilman-at-large City of Englewood, N.J., 1974-77; trustee So. Coop. Devel. Fund, Inc.; bd. dirs. Nat. Urban Coalition; trustee Coop. Assistance Fund, Witherspoon Devel. Corp.; council trustee Gulf South Research Inst. Mem. AAUP., Nat. Assn. Ind. Colls. and Univs. (dir.), Am. Council Edn. (dir.). Democrat. Roman Catholic. Home: 2 Audubon Pl New Orleans LA 70118 Office: Tulane U New Orleans LA 70118

KELLY, EDMUND JOSEPH, lawyer; b. Mt. Vernon, N.Y., May 18, 1937; s. Hugh Joseph and Catherine (Rice) K.; m. Joan Anne Fee, Nov. 18, 1961; children: Kathleen Anne, Edmund Murphy, Thomas More, Mary Fee, Michael McNaboe. A.B. cum laude, Coll. of Holy Cross, 1959; J.D. (James Kent scholar), Columbia U., 1962. Bar: N.Y. 1962. Gen. counsel Office of Sec. of Air Force, Pentagon, Washington, 1962-65; assoc. firm White & Case, N.Y.C., 1965-70, mem., 1971-84; vice chmn. Dominick & Dominick Co., N.Y.C., 1984—; dir. Chgo. Pneumatic Tool Co., N.Y.C., Fed. Paper Bd. Co., Inc., Montvale, N.J.; lectr. Practicing Law Inst., Am. Mgmt. Assn. Editor: Columbia Law Rev, 1961-62; Contbr. articles to legal jours. Air Force mem. Armed Services Procurement Regulation Com., 1964-65. Clubs: The Board Room (N.Y.C.); Scarsdale Golf. Home: 48 Hampton Rd Scarsdale NY 10583 Office: 90 Broad St New York NY 10004

KELLY, EDWARD JAMES, lawyer; b. Des Moines, Nov. 23, 1911; s. Edward J. and Mary Elizabeth (O'Donnell) K.; m. Mary Elizabeth Nolan, May 1, 1946; children—Edward James, Mary Elizabeth, Brian Francis, Anne Nolan. B.A., State U. Iowa, 1934, J.D., 1936. Bar: Iowa bar 1936. Partner Whitfield, Musgrave, Selvy, Kelly & Eddy, Des Moines, 1946—. Pres. Des Moines Jr. C. of C., 1940-41; Chmn. bd. edn. St. Joseph Acad., Des Moines, 1970-72; chmn. hosp. com. Health Planning Assembly of Polk County, Iowa, 1971-72; mem. bd. edn. Dowling High Sch., Des Moines, 1971-72; Iowa del. Republican Nat. Conv., 1956; pres. Des Moines Health Center, Des Moines Soc. for Crippled Children and Adults; bd. dirs. Def. Research Inst., Inc., Polk County Legal Aid Soc., N.W. Community Hosp., Inc. Served to maj. USAAF, 1942-46; ETO. Decorated Bronze Star; Croix de Guerre with silver star, France; Croix de Guerre with palm, Belgium). Mem. Am., Iowa, Polk County bar assns., Iowa Def. Counsel Assn. (pres.), Internat. Assn. Ins. Counsel (pres. 1971-72), Des Moines C. of C., VFW, Am. Legion, Delta Upsilon, Phi Delta Phi. Roman Catholic. Clubs: K.C. (4 deg.), Des Moines, Pioneer of Iowa, Des Moines Optimist (past pres.); Union League (Chgo.)). Home: 5309 Harwood Dr Des Moines IA 50312 Office: 1400 United Central Bank Bldg Des Moines IA 50309

KELLY, ELLSWORTH, painter, sculptor; b. Newburgh, N.Y., May 31, 1923. Student, Boston Mus. Fine Arts Sch., Ecole des Beaux-Arts, Paris, 1946-48. Works exhibited, Salon de Realities Nouvelles, Paris, 1950, 51, Carnegie Inst., 1958, 61, 64, 67, Sao Paulo Biennial, 1961, Tokyo Internat., 1963, Documenta III, Germany, 1964, Documenta IV, 1968, Venice Biennale, 1966, Guggenheim Internat., 1967, Corcoran Ann., Washington, 1979, others, one man shows, Galerie Arnaud, Paris, 1951, Galerie Maeght, Paris, 1958, 64, Sidney Janis Gallery, N.Y.C., 1965, 67, 68, 71, Betty Parsons Gallery, N.Y.C., 1956, 57, 59, 61, 63, Tooth Gallery, London, 1962, Washington Gallery Modern Art, 1964, Inst. Contemporary Art, Boston, Dayton's Gallery 12, Mpls., 1971, Albright Art Gallery, 1972, Leo Castelli Gallery, N.Y.C., 1973, 75, 77, 81, Irving Blum Gallery, Los Angeles, 1965-68, 73, Greenberg Gallery, St. Louis, 1973; work exhibited one-man shows, Whitney Mus. Am. Art, N.Y.C.; works exhibited, St. Louis Mus. Art, 1983, one man shows, N.Y. Mus. Modern Art, 1973, 78, Pasadena (Calif.) Mus. Modern Art, 1974, Walker Art Mus., Mpls., Detroit Inst. Fine Arts, Ace Gallery, Venice, Calif., 1975, Janie Lee Gallery, Houston, Blum/Helman Gallery, N.Y.C., 1975, 77, 79, 81, Met. Mus., N.Y.C., 1979, Stedelijk Mus., Amsterdam, Hayward Gallery, London, 1980, Mus., Baden Baden, others, represented in permanent collections, Mus. Modern Art, Met. Mus., Whitney Mus.,

Carnegie Inst., Albright Art Gallery, Buffalo, Chgo. Art Inst., Worcester Mus., Toronto (Can.) Mus., Tate Gallery, London, Walker Art Center, Mpls., Guggenheim Mus., N.Y.C., Los Angeles County Mus., Phila. Mus., Musée National d'Art Moderne, Paris, Stedlijk Mus., Amsterdam, Kroller-Mueller Mus., Otterlo, Holland, Munster Mus., Germany, UNESCO, Paris, others, sculpture in lobby, Transp. Bldg., Phila. (Recipient Brandeis painting award 1963), Transp. Bldg., Phila. (Edn. Minister award Tokyo Internat 1963), Transp. Bldg., Phila. (Carnegie Inst. 4th prize 1962), Transp. Bldg., Phila. (painting prize 1964), Transp. Bldg., Phila. (painting prize Chgo. Art Inst. 1964, 74), Transp. Bldg., Phila. (R.I. Sch. Design 1980), Transp. Bldg., Phila. (Skowhegan 1981). Mem. Nat. Inst. Arts and Letters.

KELLY, EUGENE WALKER, JR., university administrator, educator; b. Charleston, S.C., June 26, 1936; s. Eugene Walter and Beverly Mae (Nugent) K.; m. Betty Joyce Ledford, Dec. 28, 1968 (div.); children: David, Amy, Julia, Jeanne; m. 2d Joan Frances Hardy, Feb. 28, 1981. B.A., Josephinum Coll., Worthington, Ohio, 1958, M.Div., 1962; M.Ed., U. S.C., Columbia, 1969, Ph.D., 1971. Diplomate: lic. psychologist, Va., profl. counselor, Va., ordained priest Roman Catholic Ch. Priest Diocese of Charleston, S.C., 1962-68; tchr., counsel Bishop English High Sch., Charleston, 1962-65; tchr., counselor Cardinal Newman High Sch., Columbia, S.C., 1965-66; asst. prof. counselor edn. Old Dominion U., Norfolk, Va., 1971-76, assoc. prof., 1976-79, dept. chmn., 1976-79; dean Sch. Edn. and Human Devel. George Washington U., 1979, prof., 1979—. Author: Beyond Schooling: Education in a Broader Context, 1982, Interpersonal Communication, 1977. Mem. tng. and edn. com. Nat. Capital YMCA, Washington, 1982—. Recipient Career Service award Nat. capitol Personnel & Guidance Assn., 1981. Mem. Am. Assn. Colls. for Tchr. Edn., Am. Assn. Counseling and Devel., Am. Assn. Marriage & Family Therapy, Hampton Rds. Personnel and Guidance Assn. (pres. 1975-76), Phi Delta Kappa. Democrat. Episcopalian. Home: 5031 Filmore Ave #204 Alexandria VA 22311 Office: Sch Edn and Human Devel George Washington Univ 2201 G St NW Washington DC 20052

KELLY, FRANCIS DANIEL, lawyer; b. Des Moines, Aug. 9, 1909; s. Maximus Vincent and Mary Ellen (Feeney) K.; m. Jane E. Keogh, Dec. 5, 1947; children: Jeremiah F., Mark D., Daniel K., James K. A.B., Marquette U., 1931, J.D., 1933. Bar: Wis. 1933. With Jour. Co., Milw., 1927-78, sr. v.p., bus. mgr., 1973-77, exec. v.p., 1977-78, ret., 1978; counsel firm Maier and Fitzpatrick Ltd., Milw., 1978—; Mem. pres.'s exec. senate Marquette U.; mem. adv. council St. Michael Hosp. Found., Milw. Mem. regional bd. NCCJ.; former mem. bd. Cardinal Stritch Coll. Served as lt. comdr. USNR, 1942-45. Named 1 of 3 honorees Regional NCCJ, 1973. Mem. Am. Bar Assn., Wis. Bar Assn., Milw. Bar Assn., Wis. Newspaper Assn. (Golden Mem.). Roman Catholic. Club: Milw. Athletic. Home: 113 W Fox Dale Rd Milwaukee WI 53217 Office: 161 W Wisconsin Ave Milwaukee WI 53203

KELLY, GENE CURRAN, dancer, actor, director; b. Pitts., Aug. 23, 1912; s. James Patrick Joseph and Harriet (Curran) K.; m. Betsy Blair, Sept. 22, 1941 (div. 1957); 1 dau., Kerry; m. Jeanne Coyne, Aug. 6, 1960; children: Timothy, Bridget. A.B., U. Pitts., 1933. Appeared in: N.Y. prodns. Leave It To Me, 1938, Time of Your Life, 1940, One for the Money, 1939, Pal Joey, 1941; staged: Billy Rose's Diamond Horseshoe, 1940, Best Foot Forward, 1941; dir.: dances for motion pictures Anchors Aweigh, 1944, The Pirate, 1948, Living in a Big Way, 1947; appeared: in films Me and My Girl, 1942, the Pirate, 1948, The Three Musketeers, An American in Paris, 1950, The Devil Makes Three, 1952, Brigadoon, 1954, Inherit the Wind, 1960; others including Les Girls, 1957, Marjorie Morningstar, 1958, Let's Make Love, 1960, What A Way to Go, 1964, The Young Girls of Rochefort, 1968, Forty Carats, 1973, Viva Knievel, 1977, Xanadu, 1980; co-dir.: On the Town, 1949, Singing in the Rain, 1951, It's Always Fair Weather, 1955; dir.: Invitation to the Dance, 1953, Hello Dolly!, 1970, Tunnel Of Love, 1960, Gigot, 1962, A Guide for the Married Man, 1967; dir. live action: That's Entertainment, Part II, 1976; producer, dir.: The Happy Road, 1956, Flower Drum Song, 1958, The Cheyenne Social Club, 1970; co-narrator: That's Entertainment, 1974 (Cecil B. DeMille award 1981); Author: Take Me Out to the Ball Game, 1948. Served as a lt. (j.g.) USNR, 1944-46. Recipient Kennedy Center Honors, 1982. Mem. Chgo. Dance Masters Assn., Screen Actors Guild (v.p.), Phi Kappa. Address: care Chasin-Park-Citron Agy 9255 W Sunset Blvd Los Angeles CA 90069

KELLY, GEORGE ANTHONY, author, clergyman, eduator; b. N.Y.C., Sept. 17, 1916; s. Charles W. and Bridget (Fitzgerald) K. M.A. in Social Sci., Catholic U Am., 1943, Ph.D., 1946. Ordained priest Roman Catholic Ch., 1942, elevated to msgr., 1960; pastor St. Monica's Parish, N.Y.C., 1945-56; dir. Family Life Bur., 1955-65, Family Consultation Service, 1955-65; dir. dept. edn. Archdiocese N.Y.C., 1966-70; dir. Inst. Advanced Studies in Cath. doctrine, St. John's U., Jamaica, N.Y., 1975—; exec. sec. Fellowship of Cath. Scholars, 1976; consultor Archdiocese N.Y., Congregation for the Clergy, Rome, 1984; sec. bd. trustees St. Joseph's Sem.; sec. adv. bd. Pastoral Life Conf.; co-chmn. Archdiocesan Common Parish, 1966-70. Author: books, the most recent being Who Should Run the Catholic Church?, 1976, The Battle for the American Church, 1979, The Crisis of Authority: John Paul II and the American Bishops, 1981, The New Biblical Theorists: Raymond E. Brown and Beyond, 1983. Recipient first Cardinal Wright award Friends of the Fellowship of Cath. Scholars, 1979. Mem. AAUP, Am. Sociol. Assn., Am. Cath. Sociol. Soc., Assn. for Sociology of Religion, Am. Cath. Hist. Soc., Am. Cath. Theol. Soc. Office: Saint John's U Jamaica NY 11439

KELLY, HENRY ANSGAR, educator; b. Fonda, Iowa, June 6, 1934; s. Harry Francis and Inez Ingebord (Anderson) K.; m. Marea Tancred, June 18, 1968; children—Sarah Maria, Dominic Tancred. A.B., St. Louis U., 1959, A.M., 1961, Ph.L., 1961; Ph.D., Harvard U., 1965. Asst. prof. English UCLA, 1967-69, asso. prof., 1969-72, prof., 1972—. Author: The Devil, Demonology and Witchcraft, 1968, 1974, Divine Providence in the England of Shakespeare's Histories, 1970, Love and Marriage in the Age of Chaucer, 1975, The Matrimonial Trials of Henry VIII, 1976; co-editor: Viator, 1970—. Guggenheim fellow, 1971-72; Nat. Endowment Humanities fellow, 1980-81. Mem. Medieval Acad. Am. Roman Catholic. Home: 1123 Kagawa St Pacific Palisades CA 90272 Office: Dept English UCLA 405 Hilgard St Los Angeles CA 90024

KELLY, HUGH PADRAIC, physics educator; b. Boston, Sept. 3, 1931; s. Hugh Patrick and Katherine Mary (Donahue) K.; m. Zita Jean Stanislawski, Apr. 30, 1955; children: Timothy, Matthew, Mary, Teresa, Dominic, Anne, Patricia, Caroline, Lillian. A.B., Harvard U., 1953; M.S., UCLA, 1954; Ph.D., U. Calif.-Berkeley, 1963. Elec. engr. Hughes Aircraft Co., Culver City, Calif., 1952-54; research asst. prof. U. Calif.-San Diego, La Jolla, 1963-65; successively asst. prof., assoc. prof., prof. U. Va., Charlottesville, 1965-77, chmn. physics dept., 1974-78, commonwealth prof., 1977—. Contbr. articles to physics jours. Served to 1st lt. USMC, 1954-57. Fellow Am. Phys. Soc. (chmn. Southeastern sect. 1981-82, vice-chmn. div. electron and atomic physics 1983-84); mem. Phi Beta Kappa. Home: 2807 Noethfields Rd Charlottesville VA 22901 Office: Dept Physics U Va McCormick Rd Charlottesville VA 22901

KELLY, JACK RICHARD, JR., business executive; b. Atlanta, June 29, 1934; s. Jack Richard and Gladys L. (Murphy) K.; m. Patricia Ann Carter, May 1, 1953; children: Sharon Ann, Richard Earl. B.S. in Physics, Ga. State U., 1964; grad. program mgmt. devel., Harvard U., 1968. Tech. asst., then research asst. Engring. Expt. Sta., Ga. Inst. Tech., 1952-58, now industry adv.; with Sci.-Atlanta, Inc., 1958-83, exec. v.p., chief operating officer, dir., to 1983; gen. ptnr. Noro-Mosley Ptnrs., Atlanta, 1983—; dir. Gladwin, Inc. Mem. com. minority bus. devel. Leadership Atlanta, 1971; trustee, past pres. So. Tech. Found. Presbyterian. Club: Atlanta Athletic. Office: 100 Galleria Pkwy NW Atlanta GA 30339 *

KELLY, JAMES, artist; b. Phila., Dec. 19, 1913; s. James Alphonsus and Mabel (Witzel) K.; m. Sonia Gechtoff, June 23, 1953; children—Susannah, Miles. Student, Pa. Acad. Fine Arts, 1938, Barnes Found., 1941; diploma in painting, Calif. Sch. Fine Arts, 1954. Lectr. painting and drawing U. Calif., Berkeley, 1957. (Recipient painting awards San Francisco Mus. Art, Phoenix Art Mus.), One-man shows include, San Francisco Art Assn., 1956, Stryke Gallery, N.Y.C., 1963, East Hampton (N.Y.) Gallery, 1965, 69, Albright Coll., Reading, Pa., 1966, LI. (N.Y.) U., 1968, Westbeth Galleries, N.Y.C., 1971-72, group shows include, Pa. Acad. Fine Arts, Phila., 1951, San Francisco Mus. Art, 1955, 56, 57, 58, 65, Los Angeles County Mus., 1968, Phoenix Art Mus., 1975, Smithsonian Instn., Washington, 1977; represented in permanent collections, San Francisco Mus. Modern Art, Los Angeles County Mus., U. Mass., Oakland (Calif.) Mus. Art, Mus. Modern Art, N.Y.C., Westinghouse Corp. Served with USAF, 1941-45. Ford Found. grantee Tamarind Lithography Workshop, Los Angeles, 1963; Nat. Endowment for Arts fellow, 1977. Mem. Artists Equity Assn. Home: 463 West St Apt 936 New York NY 10014

KELLY, JAMES BARTON, engineering company executive, lawyer; b. St. Louis, Feb. 12, 1927; s. James Christopher and Hazel Jean (Barton) K.; m. Eileen Mary Redling, Oct. 16, 1949; children—James Patrick, Stephen Robert, Michael Matthew, Daniel Joseph. B.S., U.S. Mcht. Marine Acad., 1949; LL.B., St. Johns U., 1954; LL.M., N.Y. U., 1957. Bar: N.Y. State bar 1954, U.S. Supreme Ct. bar 1964. Engr. Combustion Engring., Inc., Stamford, Conn., 1949-56, asst. sec., 1956-63, sec., 1963-73, corp. v.p., 1967—, pres. indsl. products group, 1973—; dir. Ga. Kaolin Co., Basic Inc., Unimin Corp. Bd. dirs. Stamford Mus. Recipient Alumni award for outstanding profl. achievement U.S. Mcht. Marine Acad., 1964. Mem. Am., N.Y. State bar assns., Assn. Bar City N.Y. Clubs: Canadian, Duquesne, Landmark, Mid-Ocean, Seaview, Waccabuc Country. Office: 900 Long Ridge Rd Stamford CT 06904

KELLY, JAMES FRANCIS, dept. store exec.; b. Mt. Vernon, N.Y., Nov. 7, 1906; s. Hugh and Elizabeth (Dunne) K.; m. Ruth Wellington Dee, Oct. 19, 1935; children—Barbara (Mrs. John G. Ryden), Hampton Merrill (stepson). LL.B., St. John's U., 1930. Bar: N.Y. bar 1940. With Asso. Dry Goods Corp., 1934—, sec., 1956-71, also v.p., dir. Club: Dunes Golf (Myrtle Beach, S.C.). Home: 310 73d Ave #3A Myrtle Beach SC 29577 Office: 417 Fifth Ave: New York City NY 10016

KELLY, JAMES H., business executive; b. 1923; married. Grad., Rutgers U., 1951. C.P.A., N.J. Auditor, C.P.A., Puder & Puder (C.P.A.s), 1946-49; credit mgr., chief acct., auditor L. Bamberger & Co., 1950-57; v.p. Lit Bros., Phila., 1957-64; with Sperry and Hutchinson Co., N.Y.C., 1964—, v.p. adminstrn., 1968-72, group v.p. adminstrn., 1972-74, sr. v.p. fin., 1974-77, exec. v.p. corp. staff, 1977-83, chmn., chief exec. officer, 1983—. Served with USAAF, 1943-46. Office: Sperry and Hutchinson Co 330 Madison Ave New York NY 10017 *

KELLY, JAMES PATRICK, JR., engineering and construction executive; b. Bklyn., July 19, 1933; s. James Patrick and Marion Rita (Gleason) K.; m. Nancy Karen Sather, June 10, 1967; children: Kathryn, Mark, Lisa Angelique, Trevor, Lisa, James. B.S. in Engring, U.S. Naval Acad., 1955; postgrad., U. Houston. Registered profl. engr., Calif. Asst. site mgr. Pathfinder; reactor Allis Chalmers Mfg. Co., Sioux Falls, S.D., 1963-67; nuclear project mgr. Brown & Root, Houston, 1967-69; constrn. project mgr., then asst. v.p. Gibbs & Hill, Omaha and N.Y.C., 1969-75; pres. Dravo Lime Co., Pitts., 1975-77; group v.p. natural resources Dravo Corp., Pitts., 1976-81, sr. v.p., 1981—, sr. v.p. engring. and constrn., domestic and internat., 1982—; dir. So. Industries, Inc. Bd. dirs. S.D. Mental Health Assn., 1966-67, Western Pa. Sch. Blind Children, 1978—; mem. Sioux Falls Bd. Edn., 1965-66, Assn. Retarded Citizens Pitts., 1970—. Served as officer USN, 1955-63. Mem. Nat. Soc. Profl. Engrs., Am. Nuclear Soc., Am. Iron and Steel Inst., Western Pa. Engrs. Soc., Mensa, Sierra Club, Newcomen Soc. Club: Duquesne (Pitts.). Home: 2778 Beechwood Blvd Pittsburgh PA 15217 Office: 1 Oliver Plaza Pittsburgh PA 15222

KELLY, JOHN, labor union official. Pres. Office and Profl. Employees Internat. Union. Office: 265 W 14th St Suite 610 New York NY 10011§

KELLY, JOHN BRENDEN, JR., constrn. company executive, sports association executive; b. Phila., May 24, 1927; s. John Brenden and Margaret (Majer) K.; m. Sandra Worley, May 28, 1981; children: Ann, Susan, Maura, Elizabeth, John Brenden III, Margaret. Grad., U. Pa., 1950. With John B. Kelly, Inc. of Pa., Phila., 1950—, former pres., chmn. bd., 1979—; pres., dir. Phila. Athletic Co.; dir. Phila., Geriatrics & Med. Centers, Inc.; Pres. Amateur Athletic Union, 1970-72; chmn. Greater Phila. Olympic Com., 1964-68, 72-76; v.p. U.S. Olympic Com., 1972—. Mem. Phila. City Council, 1968-70; Bd. dirs. Hero Scholarship Fund Police Athletic League Phila.; pres. John B. Kelly Found., 1961—. Recipient Sullivan award Amateur Athletic Union, 1947, Phila. Zionist award, 1964; named Outstanding Young Man of Year Phila. Jr. C. of C., 1960, Pa. Jr. C. of C., 1961. Mem. VFW, Phila. Pres.'s Orgn., Schuylkill Navy Phila. (commodore 1963-64), Kappa Sigma (Man of Year 1975). Clubs: Phila. Country, Urban, Phila. Athletic (pres.), Vesper Boat (treas.), N.Y. Athletic; Seaview Country (Atlantic City). Office: 1720 Cherry St Philadelphia PA 19103

KELLY, JOHN FALLON, lawyer; b. St. Paul, July 22, 1938; s. Leon Fallon and Mary (Batchelder) K.; m. MaryAnn Kelly, Aug. 27,1960; children: Michelle, John, Shannon. B.A., St. Thomas Coll., 1961; J.D., William Mitchell Coll., 1965. Bar: Minn., U.S. Dist. Ct. Minn. Sole practice Burnsville, Minn., 1965-74; v.p., gen. counsel ITT Indsl. Credit Co., St. Paul, 1974—, also dir., 1974—. Bd. dirs. Minn. chpt. Cystic Fibrosis, 1977—. Mem. Minn. State Bar Assn., ABA.

KELLY, JOHN PATRICK, educator; b. Sigourney, Iowa, Sept. 30, 1924; s. John Walter and Vena (Wraight) K.; m. Jean Ann Donohue, June 14, 1947 (dec. 1971); children: Michael, Camilla, Carol; m. Gretchen Louise Bullington, Jan. 6, 1979. B.A., U. Iowa, 1948, M.A., 1953, Ph.D., 1959; B.Mortuary Sci., Coll. Mortuary Sci., St. Louis, 1950. Mem. faculty U. Nev., Reno, 1955—, prof. elem. edn., 1968-83, prof. emeritus, 1983—. Co-editor: Basic Reading; Contbr. articles to profl. jours. Served with USNR, 1943-46. William H. Carpenter fellow, 1950; Kellogg Found. fellow, 1965. Mem. Nat. Council Tchrs. English, Internat., Western Region Coll. reading assns., Am. Radio Relay League, Sierra Nevada Amateur Radio Soc., Amateur Radio Emergency Services, Sagebrush Radio Relay Services, Phi Delta Kappa, Phi Delta Theta. Clubs: Elks, K.C. Home: 790 Brookfield Dr Reno NV 89503

KELLY, JOSPEH E., banker; b. S.I., N.Y., Dec. 15, 1937; s. Joseph E. and Elizabeth M. (Kaufman) K.; m. Carol A. Pilkowskas, June 30, 1962; children: Lori, Debbie, Janette, Joseph Adam. B.S., Fordham U., 1962. C.P.A., N.Y.; C.P.A., Ga. Audit mgr. Price Waterhouse & Co., N.Y.C., 1962-72; v.p., dir. acctg. Chem. Bank, N.Y.C., 1972-79; exec. v.p., comptroller C & S Ga. Corp., Atlanta, 1979—. Vice pres. parish council St. Ann's Catholic Ch., Atlanta, 1982-83. Mem. Am. Inst. Banking (v.p. fin., mem. exec. com. Atlanta chpt. 1983), Assn. Bank Holding Cos., Bank Adminstrn. Inst., Fin. Execs. Inst., Mgmt. Acctg. Exchange Group. Republican. Club: Commerce (Atlanta). Home: 2605 Hearthstone Circle Chimney Springs Atlanta GA 30062 Office: C & S Georgia Corp 35 Broad St Atlanta GA 30399

KELLY, KEVIN, author; b. Boston, Aug. 5, 1934; s. St. Clair and Joan (Sinnott) K. A.A. (New Eng. Scholastic Press Assn. scholar), Boston U., 1950, B.A., 1952, M.A., 1953. Mem. staff Boston Globe, 1958—, drama critic, 1962—, critic-at-large, 1966—, film critic, 1969-76; theatre critic TV show Look, 1982-83; mem. nominating com. Tony Awards, 1980-83; local theatre critic for Show Bus. Illus., 1960-62; speaker in field, mem. drama com. Pulitzer Prize, 1983-84. Contbr. to mags. Recipient Boston Globe award, 1946, 47; Herbert Bayard Swope award for excellence in journalism, 1980; named Collegium of Distinction, Coll. Liberal Arts, Boston U., 1974. Hon. mem. Phi Beta Kappa. Home: 39 Mount Hope Norwell MA 02061 Office: 135 Morrissey Blvd Boston MA 02107

KELLY, LEO MICHAEL, lawyer; b. Boston, Feb. 4, 1925; s. Thomas Joseph and Rose Anne (McKenna) K.; m. Helen Marie Clune, May 9, 1953; children: Leo Michael, Daniel J., Maureen H., John V., Kathleen M. B.S. in Physics, Boston Coll., 1949, LL.B., 1961. Bar: Mass. 1961. Aerodynamicist Bur. Standards, Washington, 1948-50; insp. FDA, 1950-56; patent atty., then asst. gen. counsel EG&G Inc., Wellesley, Mass., 1957-78, asst. clk., 1965-78, gen. counsel, clk., since 1978—, v.p., gen. counsel, clk., 1982—. Past bd. dirs. Quincy (Mass.) Youth Hockey Assn. Served with USAAF, 1942-45. Mem. Am. Soc. Corp. Secs., Mass. Bar Assn. Home: 50 Windy Hill Cohasset MA 02025 Office: 45 William St Wellesley MA 02181

KELLY, LUCIE STIRM YOUNG, nursing educator; b. Stuttgart, Germany, May 2, 1925; came to U.S., 1929; d. Hugo Karl and Emilie Rosa (Engel) Stirm; m. J. Austin Young, Aug. 30, 1946 (div. Feb. 1971); m. Thomas Martin Kelly, 1972; 1 dau. by previous marriage, Gay Aleta (Mrs. Donald Meyer). B.S., U. Pitts., 1947, M.Litt., 1957, Ph.D. (HEW fellow), 1965; D. Nursing Edn. (hon.), U. R.I., 1977, L.H.D., Georgetown U., 1983. Instr. nursing McKeesport (Pa.) Hosp., 1952-57; asst. prof. nursing U. Pitts., 1957-64, asst. dean, 1965; asst. adminstr. nursing McKeesport Hosp., 1966-69; prof., chmn. nursing dept. Calif. State U., Los Angeles, 1969-72; co-project dir. curriculum research Nat. League for Nursing, 1973-74; project dir. patient edn., office consumer health edn. Coll. Medicine and Dentistry N.J., also adj. asso. prof. community medicine Coll. Medicine and Dentistry N.J.-Rutgers Med. Sch., 1974-75; prof. nursing Sch. Pub. Health and Sch. Nursing, Columbia, N.Y.C., 1975—; acting head div. health adminstrn. Sch. Pub. Health, 1980-81; on leave as exec. dir. Mid-Atlantic Regional Nursing Assn., 1981-82; cons. U. Nev., Las Vegas, 1970-72, Ball (Ind.) State U., 1971, Long Beach (Calif.) Naval Hosp., 1971-72, Travis AFB, Calif., 1972, Comprehensive Health Planning, Los Angeles, 1970-72, Brentwood VA Hosp., 1971-72, Central Nursing Office VA, Washington, 1971—, N.J. Dept. Higher Edn., 1974—, John Wiley Pub., 1974-76, Sch. Nursing Am. U. Beirut; mem. spl. med. adv. group VA Dept. Medicine and Surgery, Washington, 1980—; cons. nursing com. AMA, 1971-74, Citizen's Com. for Children, N.Y.C.; v.p. Pa. Health Council, 1968-69; sec. Allegheny County (Pa.) Comprehensive Health Planning, 1969; mem. adv. com. physicians assts. Calif. Bd. Med. Examiners, 1970-72; mem. adv. com. Cancer Soc., Los Angeles, 1970-72; com. nursing VA, Washington, 1971-74, regional med. programs, Pa., 1967-69, Calif., 1970-72; mem. spl. adv. council on med. licensure and profl. conduct N.Y. State Assembly, 1977-79; mem. nat. adv. com. Encore (nat. YWCA post-mastectomy group rehab. project), 1977—; lectr., cons., guest (Beijing Med. Coll. (China), 1982, nat. and internat. lectr. Author: Dimensions of Professional Nursing, 4th edit, 1981; Contbg. editor: Jour. Nursing Adminstrn, 1975-82; mem. editorial bd.: Nurse Practioner, 1976-82; columnist: Nursing Outlook; editor-in-chief, 1982—; bd. advs.: Nurses Almanac, 1978, Nurse Manager's Handbook, 1979; mem. editorial adv. bd.: Am. Health, 1981—; contbr. articles to profl. jours. Bd. dirs. ARC, Los Angeles, 1971-72, Vis. Nurse Service N.Y., 1980—, Concern for Dying, 1983—; trustee Calif. State Coll. Los Angeles Found., 1971-72; mem. health services com. Children's Aid Soc., N.Y., 1978—; v.p. Am. Nurses Found., 1980—; mem. nat. adv. council on nurse tng. HRA, 1981-85. Named Outstanding Alumna U. Pitts. Sch. Nursing, 1966; recipient Disting. Alumna award, 1981; named Pa. Nurse of Year, 1967. Fellow Am. Acad. Nursing, mem. (dir. 1978—), Pa. (pres. 1966-69) nurses assns), Nat. League Nursing, U. Pitts. Sch. Nursing Alumni (pres. 1959), Am. Hosp. Assn. (com. chmn. 1967-68), Altrusa Internat., Assn. Grad. Faculty Community Health/Public Health Nursing (v.p. 1980-81), Sigma Theta Tau (sr. editor jour. Image 1978-81, pres.-elect 1981-83, pres 1983—), Pi Lambda Theta, Alpha Tau Delta (certificate of merit). Collection papers in Mugar Library, Boston U. Home: 6040 Blvd E West New York NJ 07093 Office: 600 W 168th St New York NY 10032

KELLY, LUTHER WRENTMORE, JR., physician, educator; b. Charlotte, N.C., June 9, 1925; s. Luther Wrentmore and Charlotte (Abbott) K.; m. Susan F. Bowman, Dec. 1, 1956; children: Abbott Bowman, Mary Luther. Student, U. N.C., 1942-44; certificate of medicine, Sch. Medicine, 1946; M.D., Harvard U., 1948; research fellow, Western Res. U. Sch. Medicine, 1954. Diplomate: Am. Bd. Internal Medicine (in endocrinology), Am. Bd. Nuclear Medicine. Intern, then resident medicine Univ. Hosps., Cleve., 1948-53; staff physician Nalle Clinic, Charlotte, N.C., 1955—; chmn. dept. medicine Charlotte Meml. Hosp., 1964-68; clin. asst. prof. medicine U. N.C. Sch. Medicine, 1966-69, clin. assoc. prof., 1969-72, clin. prof. medicine, 1972—; Mem. adv. com. aging Family Service Assn. Am., 1961-62; Bd. dirs. Family and Childrens Service Mecklenburg County, 1955-61, pres., 1958-61; v.p. Am. Group Practice Assn., 1977, pres., 1979-80; bd. dirs. N.C. Council Human Relations, 1955-60; Pres. Community Health Assn., Charlotte, 1972, Nalle Clinic Corp., 1976-78; project dir. diabetes cons. and edn. service N.C. Regional Med. Program, 1971-73; bd. dirs. Charlotte Drug Edn. Center, pres. bd. dirs., 1983-84; mem. med. alumni council U. N.C. Sch. Medicine. Author articles thyroid and adrenal gland function. Served with USNR, 1950-52. Recipient Disting. Service award U. N.C. Sch. Medicine Alumni Assn. Fellow A.C.P.; mem. Endocrine Soc., Am. Diabetes Assn., N.C. Diabetes Assn. (pres. 1968-69), Am. Soc. Internal Medicine, Charlotte Soc. Internal Medicine (past pres.), Am. Acad. Med. Dirs. (dir. 1975-77), Soc. Nuclear Medicine, Am. Coll. Nuclear Physicians. Home: 2510 Forest Dr Charlotte NC 28211 Office: 1350 S Kings Dr Charlotte NC 28201

KELLY, MATTHEW EDWARD, assn. exec.; b. Parkersburg, W.Va., Apr. 15, 1928; s. Matthew Glenn and Lillian (Schottler) K.; m. Mildred Joan Flasch, June 6, 1953. B.A., Marietta Coll., 1952. Asst. mgr. Twin Cities Area C. of C., Benton Harbor, Mich., 1955-62; exec.

v.p. Oshkosh (Wis.) C. of C., 1962-69, Springfield (Mo.) Area C. of C., 1969-76, Elgin (Ill.) C. of C., 1977—. Dir. Ill. Polit. Action Com., 1980—, N. Kane County PIC; trustee N.W. Suburban Mass Transit Dist. Served with AUS, 1946-47. Mem. Am. Chamber Commerce Execs. (dir.), Inst. for Orgnl. Mgmt. (past dir., mem. nat. bd. regents). Club: Rotarian. Home: 480 Arlington Ave Elgin IL 60120 Office: Elgin C of C PO Box 648 Elgin IL 60120

KELLY, MICHAEL ANTHONY, computer company executive; b. Bury, Lancashire, U.K., Dec. 23, 1934; s. Daniel Cuthbert and Cicely Ann (Brunton) K.; m. Elizabeth Ann Nock, Oct. 10, 1959; children: Simon Francis, Paul Xavier, Emma Siobhan, James Dominic. Grad., Royal Mil. Acad., Sandhurst, 1956. Sales exec. IBM (U.K.) Ltd., Newcastle, 1964-69; mng. dir. Memorex (U.K.) Ltd., Hounslow, 1976-78; v.p. Memorex Corp., Brussels, 1978-80; pres. Gen. Automation Europe, Slough, U.K., 1980-82, Sparrow Computer B.V. Ltd., Slough, 1982—; v.p. Gen. Automation Inc., Anaheim, Calif., 1980-82. Served to capt. Brit. Army, 1954-64. Roman Catholic. Home: Forge Cottage Greys Green Henley on Thames England RG9 4QH Office: Sparrow Computer 45 Ledger's Rd Slough Berkshire England SL1 2PQ *Attitude is more than fifty percent of the game. The right attitude allied to healthy respect for cash and profit is the formula for success in modern business.*

KELLY, MICHAEL JOHN, university dean; b. Des Moines, Aug. 10, 1937; s. Dennis Hughes and Aileen (Carney) K.; m. Narindar Uberoi, Feb. 4, 1967; children: Kieran, Sean. B.A., Princeton U., 1959; Ph.D., King's Coll., Cambridge U., 1964; LL.B., Yale U., 1967. Legis. asst. Congressman Neal Smith of Iowa, Washington, 1964; with The Rouse Co., Columbia, Md., 1967-70; counsel Office Mayor of Boston, 1970; asst. Mayor of Balt., 1970-72; asst. prof. law U. Md. Law Sch., Balt., 1972-74, asso. prof., 1974-75, dean, 1975—; cons. Police Found. Chmn. Balt. Housing Authority, 1977—, Balt. City Bd. Ethics, 1975—. Trustee Enoch Pratt Free Library, 1977—, Princeton U., 1980-84. Nat. Inst. Law Enforcement fellow Washington, 1974-75. Mem. Am. Bar Assn., Md. State Bar Assn., Bar Assn. Balt. City, Am. Law Inst. Home: 4407 Norwood Rd Baltimore MD 21218 Office: 500 W Baltimore St Baltimore MD 21201

KELLY, PATRICK F., federal judge; b. Wichita, Kans., June 25, 1929; s. Arthur J. and Reed (Skinner) K.; m. Joan Y. Cain, Jan. 3, 1953; children: Deanna Kelly Riepe, Patrick F. B.A., Wichita U., 1951; LL.B., Washburn Law Sch., 1953. Bar: Kans. Individual practice law Dunn & Hamilton, 1955; from asso. to partner firm Kahrs & Nelson, 1955-59; partner firm Frank & Kelly, 1959-68, Render, Kamas & Kelly, 1968-76; individual practice law Patrick F. Kelly (P.A.), Wichita, 1976-80; judge U.S. Dist. Ct., Dist. of Kans., Wichita, 1980—. Trustee Wichita State U., 1969-74, chmn., 1972-74; chmn. Midway chpt. ARC, 1967. Served with JAGC USAF, 1953-55. Fellow Am. Coll. Trial Lawyers; mem. Am. Bar Assn., Kans. Bar Assn., Kans. Trial Lawyers Assn., Am. Arbitration Assn. (arbiter), Internat. Soc. Barristers, Am. Bd. Trial Advocates. Home: 14 Linden Dr Wichita KS 67206 Office: 232 Federal Bldg Wichita KS 67202 *

KELLY, PAUL EDWARD, metals company executive; b. Phila., May 11, 1912; s. Edward A. and Katherine (McKeegan) K.; m. Margaret Mary Krull, Nov. 23, 1940 (dec. Feb. 1969); children: Judith (Mrs. John Shea), Christine (Mrs. Peter Kiernan), Janet (Mrs. Gustavo Escobar), Paul Edward, Peter; m. Margaret Mary Walsh, Aug. 4, 1970 (dec. Sept. 1980); m. Adeline Cook Galbally, May 30, 1981. B.S., St. Josephs Coll., Phila., 1934. Acct. Lybrand, Ross Brothers & Montgomery, Phila., 1935; with Superior Tube Co., Wynnewood, Pa., 1936—, treas., 1943-52, dir., 1951—, v.p., 1952-67, pres., 1967-83, chmn. bd., chief exec. officer, 1983—, Cawsl Corp.; dir. Williams & Co., Pitts., Swepco Tube Corp., Clifton, N.J., Lease Fin. Corp., Radnor, Pa., Western Pneumatic Tube Corp., Kirkland, Wash., Tubesales, Inc., Los Angeles., Greenwich Capital Markets (Conn.), Johnson & Hoffman Mfg. Co., Carle Place, N.Y., Drever Corp., Huntington Valley, Pa., Anchor/Darling, Inc., Radnor; Mem. Eastern div. Gov. Pa. Economy League, 1952—. Trustee Superior-Pacific Fund; chmn. bd. trustees St. Joseph's Univ. Sch.; bd. dirs. Merry Cath. Med. Ctr. Mem. Welded Steel Tube Inst., Cleve. (dir.). Clubs: Merion Golf, Philadelphia Country, Fourth Street. Office: Wynnewood PA 19096

KELLY, PAUL KNOX, investment banker; b. Boston, Feb. 18, 1940; s. Thomas Joseph and Rita Patricia K.; m. Nancy Lee Belden, July 17, 1978; 1 dau., 3 stepdaus. A.B in English, U. Pa., 1962; M.B.A. in Fin, Wharton Sch., 1964. Investment analyst bond dept. Prudential Ins. Co. Am., 1964-65; asst. treas. Comml. Credit Co., 1965-68; v.p. First Boston Corp., N.Y.C., 1968-75; partner, mem. mgmt. com. Prescott, Ball & Turben, Cleve., 1975-77; also dir.; sr. v.p. Butcher & Singer, Inc., Cleve., 1977-78; also dir.; exec. v.p., mem. exec. com. Blyth Eastman Dillon & Co., N.Y.C., 1978-80; also dir.; mng. dir. Merrill Lynch White Weld Capital Markets Group, N.Y.C., 1980-82; exec. v.p., dir. Dean Witter Reynolds, Inc., 1982-84; pres., dir. Quadex Securities Corp., 1984—; dir. Porta Systems Corp. Clubs: Union of Cleve., Chagrin Valley Hunt, Princeton of N.Y. Home: 16 Edgemarth Hill Rd Westport CT 06880 Office: 645 Fifth Ave New York NY 10022 *It is my belief that, in order to be outstanding in any endeavor, one must understand the true nature of risk and be willing to assume a greater degree of risk than complete security permits.*

KELLY, PAUL L., corporate executive; b. Salem, Mass., May 7, 1939; s. Lawrence J. and Edith (Rioux) K.; m. Grace Anita Doyle, Dec. 24, 1966; children: Paul Lance, Maria Christina. Student, Phillips Acad., Andover, Mass., 1956-58; B.A., Yale U., 1962, LL.B., 1965. Bar: Tex. 1965. Atty. firm Fulbright & Jaworski, Houston, 1965-67; asst. sec. Anderson, Clayton & Co., Houston, 1967-69; sec. Zapata Corp., Houston, 1969, v.p. adminstrn., sec., 1970-72, v.p. adminstrn., 1972-77, sr. v.p. corp. affairs, 1977-79, sr. v.p., gen. counsel, 1979-80, v.p. corp. affairs, 1980—; v.p. industry and govt. relations Rowan Cos., Inc., 1982—; mem. nat. coastal zone mgmt. adv. com. U.S. Dept. Commerce, 1979-82; mem. outer continental shelf policy com. U.S. Dept. Interior, 1981—. Mem. ABA, State Bar of Tex., Internat. Assn. Drilling Contractors (dir. 1977—), Alaska Oil and Gas Assn. (dir. 1981—), Nat. Ocean Industries Assn. (dir. 1978—), Am. Oceanic Orgn. (dir. 1982—), U.S. C. of C. (natural resources com. 1981—). Home: 6122 San Felipe Rd Houston TX 77057 Office: 2470 First City Tower 1001 Fannin St Houston TX 77002

KELLY, PRESTON WEST, publishing company executive; b. Chgo., June 2, 1936; s. Henry George K. and Elizabeth (West) kelly; m. Lois Van Dyke, Feb. 7, 1965; 1 dau., Susan Elizabeth. B.S., Carleton Coll., 1957; postgrad., U. Iowa, 1957, U. Chgo., 1958-60. Exec. sci. editor Scott, Foresman & Co., Chgo., 1958-65; dir. research and news media Holt, Rinehart & Winston, N.Y.C., 1965-72, v.p., gen. mgr. film div., 1972-73; v.p. corp. mktg. services CBS-Holt, N.Y.C., 1973-74; sr. v.p. planning and devel. McGraw-Hill Book Co., 1975-84, sr. v.p. bus. systems devel., tech. and research, 1984—. Mem. Phi Beta Kappa. Home: 106 Mansfield Ave Darien CT 06820 Office: McGraw-Hill Book Co 1221 Ave of the Americas New York NY 10020

KELLY, RAYMOND FRANCIS, commodity company executive; b. Middleboro, Mass., Aug. 11, 1939; s. John James and Elizabeth (Gilbride) K.; July 11, 1964; children: Kevin, Lisa. B.B.A., Loyola Marymount U., Los Angeles. Acct., Price Waterhouse & Co., Los Angeles, 1961-69; with Baker Commodities, Inc., Los Angeles, 1969—, now exec. v.p., dir.; dir., sec. Can. Pac Agri Products Ltd. C.P.A., Calif. Mem. Am. Inst. C.P.A.s, Calif. Assn. C.P.A.s. Roman Catholic. Club: Jonathan. Office: Baker Commodities Inc 4020 Bandini Blvd Los Angeles CA 90023 *

KELLY, RICHARD SMITH, lawyer; b. Chgo., Jan. 18, 1925; s. Frank Brazzil and Adelaide (Smith) K.; m. Nancy G. Kelly, Aug. 26, 1950; children—Richard Smith, Mark F., David G., Peter M., Anne M., John T., Paul T. B.A., U. Mich., 1948; J.D., Northwestern U., 1951. Bar: Ill. bar 1951. Ptnr. firm Springer, Bergstrom & Crowe, Chgo., 1951-55; with firm McDermott, Will & Emery, Chgo., 1955-60; atty. Container Corp. Am., Chgo., 1960-67, asst. gen. counsel, 1967-69, gen. counsel, 1969-71, v.p., gen. counsel, 1971-77, sr. v.p., gen. counsel, 1977-83, dir., 1975-83; ptnr. Keck, Mahin & Cate, Chgo., 1983—; sec., asst. gen. counsel Marcor Inc., Chgo., 1968-71, sec., gen. counsel, 1971-78, dir., 1976-78; mem. adv. bd. Southwestern Legal Found. Served with AUS, 1943-46. Mem. Am., Ill., Chgo. bar assns. Clubs: Law, University, Michigan Shores, Economic (Chgo.). Home: 423 Laurel Ave Wilmette IL 60091 Office: 8200 Sears Tower Chicago IL 60606

KELLY, ROBERT, poet, educator; b. Bklyn., Sept. 24, 1935; s. Samuel Jason and Margaret Rose (Kane) K. A.B., CCNY, 1955; postgrad., Columbia U., 1955-58. Translator, treas. Continental Transl. Service, N.Y.C., 1955-58; lectr. English Wagner Coll., 1960-61; prof. English Bard Coll., 1961—; dir. poetry Avery Grad. Sch. Arts, 1981—; vis. prof. SUNY, Buffalo, 1964; vis. prof. modern poetry Tufts U., 1966-67; dir. Fed. Writers Project, N.Y., 1967—; participant N.Y. Writer's Conf., 1967; poet-in-residence Calif. Inst. Tech., 1971-72, U. Kans., 1975, Dickinson Coll., 1976. Author: numerous books of poetry, the latest being Sonnets, 1969, Songs I-XXX, 1969, The Common Shore, 1969, Kali Yuga, 1970, Flesh Dream Book, 1971, Ralegh, 1972, The Pastorals, 1972, Reading her notes, 1972, The Tears of Edmund Burke, 1973, The Mill of Particulars, 1973, The Loom, 1975, Sixteen Odes, 1976, The Lady Of, 1977, The Convections, 1978, The Book of Persephone, 1978, The Cruise of the Pnyx, 1979, Kill the Messenger Who Brings Bad News, 1979, Sentence, 1980, The Alchemist to Mercury, 1981, Spiritual Exercises, 1981, Mulberry Women, 1982, Under Words, 1983; books of fiction The Scorpions, 1967, Cities, 1971, A Line of Sight, 1974, Wheres, 1978; book of essays In Time, 1971; Editor: (with Paris Leary) anthology A Controversy of Poets, 1965; editor: book of essays Chelsea Rev, 1957-60, Trobar mag. and Trobar Books, 1960-65, Matter, 1964—; contbg. editor: Caterpillar, 1966-72, Alcheringa, 1977—, Sulfur, 1981—. Home: Lindenwood House Annandale-on-Hudson NY 12504 Office: Bard Coll Annandale-on-Hudson NY 12504

KELLY, ROBERT EMMETT, physicist, educator; b. Cape Girardeau, Mo., Nov. 26, 1929; s. Robert Emmett and Gladys (Admas) K.; m. Sarah Grace Combs, June 6, 1962; children: Katelyn, Frank, Tara. B.S., S.E. Mo. State U., 1950; M.S., U. Mo., 1952; Ph.D., U. Conn., 1959. Physicist E.I. DuPont de Nemours & Co., Inc., Aiken, S.C.; mem. faculty dept. physics U. Miss., University, 1959—, prof., 1966—; mem. research staff Los Alamos, Boeing, Gen. Electric Co., Am. Optical Co., Lawrence Radiation Lab., Woods Hole Oceanographic Inst., Hanford Lab., Marshall Space Flight Center; cons. Los Alamos Sci. Lab., Lawrence Livermore Lab. Contbr. articles to profl. jours.; woodwind performer various civic symphonies, concert bands. Served with AUS, 1954-56. AEC fellow, 1965; NASA fellow, 1970-71. Mem. Am. Radio Relay League, Acoustical Soc. Am., Am. Geophys. Union, Am. Fedn. Musicians, Benton Lit. Soc., Chamber Music Players, Chemistry, German, Amateur Radio clubs, Sigma Xi, Pi Mu Epsilon, Omicron Delta Kappa, Sigma Pi Sigma. Methodist. Home: PO Box 493 University MS 38677

KELLY, ROBERT THOMAS, publisher; b. Des Plaines, Ill., Aug. 8, 1924; s. Frank J. and Florence M. (Gelling) K.; m. Vivian S. Houser, Aug. 8, 1945; children: David, Christine, Timothy. B.S., U. Ill., 1954. Lic. profl. engr., Calif. With Boeing Airplane Co., 1954-55, Elgin Nat. Watch Co., 1955-57, Honeywell Co., 1957-63, Bell Helicopter Co., 1963-64; with Hitchcock Publishing Co. (subs. ABC), Wheaton, Ill., 1964—; pub., editorial dir., v.p. Assembly Engring. mag., 1975—; Mem. sch. bd. Hoffman Estates, Ill., 1959-61. Served as pilot USAAF, 1943-45. Sr. mem. Am. Inst. Indsl. Engrs., Soc. Mfg. Engrs.; mem. I.E.E.E., Antique Airplane Assn., Exptl. Aircraft Assn. Office: Hitchcock Bldg Wheaton IL 60187

KELLY, THOMAS JOSEPH, III, photojournalist; b. Hackensack, N.J., Aug. 8, 1947; s. Thomas J. and Severina (Augenti) K.; m. Patricia Lee Moulder, May 3, 1975; children: Danielle Marie, Devon Lee, Thomas Joseph. Student public schs., Woodbury and North Bergen, N.J. Maps and records clk. Phila. Electric Co., Plymouth Meeting, Pa., 1967-71; free lance photographer, Norristown, Pa., 1969-71; chief photographer Today's Post, King Of Prussia, Pa., 1971-74; photography supr. The Mercury, Pottstown, Pa., 1974—; instr. photography Pa. Press Inst.; chmn. photography jury Pulitzer Prize Com., 1983. Contbr.: photographs to Newsweek, Life, Time, Am. Photographer, others. Mem. Phila. Speakers Bur. Served with U.S. N.G., 1966-72. Recipient numerous state, regional and nat. photog. awards including nat. citation AP, 1978, 79, Pulitzer prize for news photography, 1979; Robert F. Kennedy Journalism award, 1980. Mem. Nat. Press Photographers Assn. (Region 3 Photographer of Yr. 1975, 76, 79), Pa. Press Photographers Assn. (past pres., Pa. Photographer of Yr. 1976), 1st Amendment Coalition of Pa. Roman Catholic. Office: The Mercury Hanover and King Sts Pottstown PA 19464

KELLY, THOMAS PAINE, JR., lawyer; b. Tampa, Fla., Aug. 29, 1912; s. Thomas Paine and Beatrice (Gent) K.; m. Jean Baughman, July 25, 1940; children: Carla (Mrs. Henry Dee), Thomas Paine III, Margaret Jo. A.B., U. Fla., 1935, J.D., 1936. Bar: Fla. 1936. Since practiced in, Tampa; jr. partner McKay, Macfarlane, Jackson & Ferguson, 1939-48; partner Macfarlane, Ferguson, Allison & Kelly, 1948—. Chmn. Tampa Com. 100, 1960-61; pres. Tampa Citizens' Safety Council, 1961-62; Bd. dirs. Tampa chpt. ARC, 1955-62, pres., 1958-59; bd. dirs. Boys Clubs Tampa, 1956-67, pres., 1966-67. Served to col. F.A. AUS, 1940-45. Decorated Silver Star. Fellow Am. Coll. Trial Lawyers, Internat. Acad. Trial Lawyers; mem. Am. Bar Assn., Bar Assn. Hillsborough County, Fla. Bar (chmn. com. profl. ethics 1953-58, chmn. com. ins. and negligence law 1962-63, chmn. fed. rules com. 1969-70). Democrat. Episcopalian. Home: 5426 Lykes Ln Tampa FL 33611 Office: 215 Madison St Tampa FL 33601

KELLY, THOMAS WILLIAM, army officer; b. Phila., Nov. 16, 1932; s. Vincent de Paul and Mary Gertrude K.; m. Dorothy Mary Bursak, Apr. 27, 1957; children: Vincent de Paul, Francis Xavier, Elisabeth Anne. B.S., Temple U., 1956; postgrad., U.S. Army War Coll., 1967, U.S. Army Command and Gen. Staff Coll., 1973. Commd. 2d lt., armor U.S. Army, 1956, advanced through grades to brig. gen.; comdr. cav. troops, tank bns. and 194th Armored Brigade, U.S., Europe and Asia; asst. chief to staff for plans and policy Allied Forces So. Europe, Italy; cons. Decorated Legion of Merit with 2 oak leaf clusters, D.F.C., Bronze Star with V and 4 oak leaf clusters, Air medal with V and 31 oak leaf clusters, Purple Heart, numerous others. Mem. Assn. U.S. Army, Armor Assn., Smithsonian Assocs., Hon. Order Ky. Cols. Roman Catholic. Office: AFSOUTH Box 138 FPO New York NY 09524 *

KELLY, WILLIAM ALOYSIUS, lawyer; b. Phila., Nov. 20, 1923; s. William A. and Helen M. (Kitchen) K.; m. Grace Neuman, June 24, 1954; children: Kevin W., Michael E. B.S. in Econs., U. Pa., 1949, J.D., 1952. Bar: Pa., U.S. Supreme Ct. Ptnr. Folz, Bard, Kamsler, Goodis & Greenfiels, Phila., 1961-66, Dechert Price & Rhoads, 1968—; lectr. tax law subjects. Contbr. articles to tax jours. Served with inf. AUS, 1943-45; ETO. Fellow Am. Coll. Tax Councils; mem. ABA (taxation sect. council 1980-83), Phila. Bar Assn., Nat. Assn. Real Estate Investment Trusts (bd. dirs.), Friendly Sons of St. Patrick, St. Thomas More Soc. Republican. Roman Catholic. Clubs: Union League; Golf and Country (Oreland, Pa.); Manufacturers; Penn. (Phila.) (dir.). Home: 1040 Church St Abington PA Office: Dechert Price & Rhoads 3400 Centre Sq W 1500 Market St Philadelphia PA 19102

KELLY, WILLIAM CLARK, science administrator; b. Braddock, Pa., Mar. 18, 1922; s. Clark William and Alma (Wilhelm) K.; m. Gertrude Clark Blackwood, Sept. 8, 1947; children—Emily Clark, William Blackwood. B.S., U. Pitts., 1943, M.S., 1946, Ph.D., 1951. From asst. physics to asso. prof. U. Pitts., 1943-58; Ford faculty fellow, 1954-55; dir. dept. edn. and manpower Am. Inst. Physics, 1958-65; dir. fellowships NRC, Washington, 1965-67; dir. Office Sci. Personnel, 1967-74; exec. dir. Commn. on Human Resources, 1974-82, Office Sci. and Engring. Personnel, 1982-83; Sec. Internat. Commn. Physics Edn., Internat. Union Pure and Applied Physics, 1966-72, chmn., 1972-75; mem. com. on teaching of sci. Internat. Council Sci. Unions, 1975-78; Mem. Nat. Manpower Adv. Com.'s Subcom. on Profl., Scientific and Tech. Manpower, 1971-73. Author: with others General Physics, 4th edit, 1973, High School Physics, rev. edit, 1958, (with T.D. Miner) Physics for High School, 1967. Mem. Conf. Bd. Assoc. Research Councils, 1969-83. Recipient Disting. Service award Nat. Acad. Sci., 1980. Fellow AAAS; mem. Am. Assn. Physics Tchrs. (Distinguished Service citation 1959), Am. Phys. Soc., Sigma Xi. Club: Cosmos (Washington). Home: 9320 Renshaw Dr Bethesda MD 20817

KELLY, WILLIAM HAROLD, physics educator; b. Rich Hill, Mo., July 2, 1926; s. George Samuel and Ola Lorena (Ayers) K.; m. Altabelle Dougherty, Sept. 1, 1950; children: Douglas Scott, Linda Sue, Brian Patrick. A.A., Graceland Coll., 1948; B.S.E., U. Mich., 1950, M.S., 1951, Ph.D., 1955. Eastman Kodak predoctoral fellow in physics U. Mich., 1954-55; asst. prof. physics and astronomy Mich. State U., 1955-61; physicist U.S. Naval Research Lab., Washington, 1956, Lawrence Radiation Lab., Berkeley, Cal., 1961-62; asso. prof. physics Mich. State U., 1961-67, prof. physics, 1967-79, asso. chmn. undergrad. programs, 1968-76, chmn. dept. physics, 1976-79; dean Coll. Letters and Sci., prof. physics Mont. State U., Bozeman, 1979-83; dean Coll. Scis. and Humanities, dir. Scis. and Humanities Research Inst., prof. physics Iowa State U., Ames, 1983—; summer research participant Oak Ridge (Tenn.) Nat. Lab., 1964; physicist Lawrence Radiation Lab., Berkeley, Calif., 1967-68. Trustee Graceland Coll., 1978—. Served with USNR, 1944-46. Fellow Am. Phys. Soc.; mem. AAAS, Am. Assn. Physics Tchrs. (pres. 1981-82), Mich. Physics Tchrs., Am. Soc. Engring. Edn. (sec.-treas. physics div. 1978-80), Am. Inst. Physics (governing bd. 1980-83, exec. com. 1981-83), Tau Beta Pi, Sigma Xi, Phi Kappa Phi.; Mem. Reorganized Ch. Jesus Christ of Latter Day Saints (high priest 1971—, elder 1956—). Research, articles nuclear structure physics, gamma ray spectroscopy, physics pedagogy, nuclear physics instrumentation. Home: 1133 Oklahoma St Ames IA 50010 Office: Coll Scis and Humanities Iowa State U Ames IA 50011

KELLY, WILLIAM R., employment agency executive. Chmn. Kelly Services, Inc., Troy, Mich. Office: Kelly Services Inc 999 W Big Beaver Rd Troy MI 48084§

KELLY, WILLIAM WATKINS, educational association executive; b. Asheville, N.C., Sept. 21, 1928; s. John Jackson and Trula (Watkins) K.; m. Lura Jane Kelly, Feb. 14, 1953 (div. Jan. 14, 1983); children: William Watkins, Robert Jackson, Blair Massey, Gregory Clark.; m. Catherine Messer Penney, Jan. 22, 1983. B.A., Va. Mil. Inst., 1950; A.M., Duke U., 1955, Ph.D., 1957. Commandant cadets, tchr. English John Marshall High Sch., Richmond, Va., 1950-52; instr. English Va. Mil. Inst., 1952-53, English Air Force Acad., 1957-58, asst. prof., 1958-60, English Va. Mil. Inst., 1960-62; asst. prof. Am. thought and language Mich. State U., 1962-65, assoc. prof., 1965-69; assoc. dir. The Honors Coll., 1965-68, dir., 1968-69; pres. Mary Baldwin Coll., 1969-76, Transylvania U., Lexington, Ky., 1976-81; sr. assoc. Univ. Assos., 1981-82; exec. v.p. L.Q.C. Lamar Soc., 1981-82; pres. Ala. Assn. Ind. Colls. and Univs., 1982—; Mem. Va. Commn. on Status Women, 1973-76, Ky. Commn. on Women, 1977-81; chmn. Ky. Rhodes Scholar Selection Com., 1978-79; pres. Council Ind. Ky. Colls. and Univs., 1978-80; bd. dirs. Com. for Humanities in Ala., 1983—. Author: Ellen Glasow: A Bibliography, 1964. Bd. dirs. Ky. State C. of C., 1980—. Served with USAF, 1957-60; lt. col. Res. Danforth fellow, 1953-57; Duke scholar, 1954-55; Ellis L. Phillips Found. intern Rutgers U., 1964-65. Mem. MLA, Am. Studies Assn., Soc. Values in Higher Edn., Am. Assn. Higher Edn., Ellen Glasgow Soc. (pres. 1973-75), English Speaking Union, Newcomen Soc. N.Am., Phi Beta Kappa, Omicron Delta Kappa. Lodge: Rotary. Home: 1820 Mountain Laurel Ln Birmingham AL 35244 Office: 6 Office Park Circle Suite 112 Birmingham AL 35223

KELM, GEORGE, coal company executive, lawyer; b. Chgo., July 28, 1928; s. George A. and Lillian A. K.; m. Jean A. McConahay, June 30, 1956; children: Bruce, Robert, Nancy. B.S., Northwestern U., 1951, J.D., 1954. Bar: Ill. bar 1955. Asso. firm Hopkins & Sutter, 1954-63, partner, 1964-72, mng. partner, 1973-78; pres. Sahara Coal Co., Inc., Chgo., 1978—; v.p. Woods Charitable Fund, Inc.; dir. Lincoln Telecommunications Co., AM Internat., Inc. Trustee Village of Deerfield, 1967-75, Lawrence U., Appleton, Wis., 1980—, Newberry Library, Chgo., 1979—. Served with USN, 1946-48. Mem. Chgo. Bar Assn., Ill. Bar Assn., Am. Bar Assn., Law Club Chgo., Legal Club Chgo., Econ. Club Chgo. Clubs: Chgo., Univ., Comml. (Chgo.). Home: 510 Brierhill Rd Deerfield IL 60015 Office: Three First Nat Plaza Suite 3050 Chicago IL 60602

KELMAN, ARTHUR, educator, plant pathologist; b. Providence, Dec. 11, 1918; s. Philip and Minnie (Kollin) K.; m. Helen Moore Parker, June 22, 1949; 1 son, Philip Joseph. B.S., U. R.I., 1941, D.Sc. (hon.), 1977; M.S., N.C. State U., 1946; Ph.D., 1949; postgrad., U. Wis., 1947-48. Faculty N.C. State U., Raleigh, 1948-65, prof., 1957-65, W.N. Reynolds distinguished prof. plant pathology, 1961-65; chmn. dept. plant pathology U. Wis., Madison, 1965-75, L.R. Jones disting. prof., 1975—, prof. bacteriology, 1977—; vis. investigator Rockefeller Inst., 1953-54; vis. lectr. Am. Inst. Biol. Sci., 1961-62; chmn. div. biol. sci. Assembly Life Sci. NRC, 1980-82. Author: The Bacterial Wilt Caused by Pseudomonas solanacearum, 1953. Chmn. div. biol. scis. NRC, 1979-82; chmn. sect. applied biology Nat. Acad. Scis., 1981—. Served with AUS, 1942-45. NSF sr. postdoctoral fellow Cambridge (Eng.) U., 1971-72. Fellow Am. Phytopath. Soc. (chmn. sourcebook com., councilor-at-large, v.p. 1965-66, pres. 1966-67), AAAS; mem. Internat. Soc. Plant Pathology (v.p. 1968-73, pres. 1973-78), Nat. Acad. Scis. (chmn. sect. applied biology 1981-83), Am. Acad. Arts and Scis., Soc. Gen. Microbiology, Am. Soc. Microbiology, Am. Inst. Biol. Sci., Sigma Xi, Alpha Zeta, Gamma Sigma Delta, Phi Kappa Phi, Phi Sigma, Xi Sigma Pi. Home: 234 Carillon Dr Madison WI 53705

KELMAN, HERBERT CHANOCH, psychology educator; b. Vienna, Austria, Mar. 18, 1927; came to U.S., 1940, naturalized, 1950; s. Leo and Lea (Pomeranz) K.; m. Rose Brousman, Aug. 23, 1953. B.A., Bklyn. Coll., 1947, L.H.D. (hon.), 1981; B.H.L., Sem. Coll. Jewish Studies, N.Y.C., 1947; M.S., Yale U., 1949, Ph.D., 1951; A.M. (hon.), Harvard U., 1969; diploma, U. San Martin de Porres, Peru, 1979; L.H.D. (hon.), Hofstra U., 1983. Research asst. Yale U., 1947-51; research fellow Johns Hopkins U., 1 951-54; fellow Center Advanced Study Behavioral Scis., 1954-55, 67; research psychologist NIMH, 1955-57; lectr. social psychology Harvard U., 1957-62; fellow Inst. Social Research, Oslo, Norway, 1960-61; prof. psychology U. Mich., 1962-69, chmn. doctoral program social psychology, 1966-67; research psychologist Center for Research on Conflict Resolution, 1962-69; Richard Clarke Cabot prof. social ethics Harvard U., 1968—; exec. com. Center for Internat. Affairs, 1976—; vis. fellow Battelle Seattle Research Center, 1972-73; disting. vis. prof. Am. U., Cairo, 1977; fellow Woodrow Wilson Internat. Center for Scholars, 1980-81; chmn. internat. conf. social-psychol. research in developing countries U. Ibadan, Nigeria, 1966. Author: A Time to Speak: On Human Values and Social Research, 1968; co-author: Cross-National Encounters, 1970; Editor, co-author: International Behavior—A Social-Psychological Analysis, 1965; co-editor: The Ethics of Social Intervention, 1978; Contbr. articles to profl. jours. Mem. adv. com. govt. programs behavioral sci. NRC-Nat. Acad. Sci., 1966-68; nat. field rep. Congress Racial Equality, 1954-60; nat. adv. council War Resisters League, 1952-71; bd. sponsors SANE, Citizens Orgn. for a Sane World, 1966—; nat. com. Center for War/Peace Studies, 1972—; exec. council Nat. Peace Acad. Campaign, 1977—; mem. psychology tng. rev. com. NIMH, 1969-73. Recipient Socio-Psychol. prize AAAS, 1956; Western Behavioral Scis. Inst. fellow, 1964; Guggenheim fellow, 1980-81; recipient N.Y. Acad. Sci. award, 1982, Mass. Psychol. Assn. award, 1983. Fellow Soc. Psychol. Study Social Issues (pres. 1964-65, Kurt Lewin Meml. award 1973), Am. Psychol. Assn. (com. on sci. and profl. ethics and conduct 1968-71, council 1968-71, dir. 1971-75, pres. div. on personality and social psychology 1970-71, bd. social and ethical responsibility 1972-74, award for disting. contbn. to psychology in pub. interest 1981), Inst. Soc. Ethics and Life Scis. (dir. 1969-72); mem. Soc. Exptl. Social Psychology, Am. Sociol. Assn. (chmn. social psychology sect. 1977-78), Internat. Studies Assn. (pres. 1977-78), Internat. Peace Research Assn., Internat. Assn. Cross-Cultural Psychology, Internat. Assn. Applied Psychology, Interam. Soc. Psychology (gov. 1972-73, pres. 1976-79, Interam. Psychology award 1983), Internat. Soc. Polit. Psychology (Sanford award 1983, pres.-elect 1984-85), Peace Sci. Soc. (pres. 1975-76), Internat. Soc. Ednl. Cultural Scientific Interchanges (Fourth Annual award 1976), Council Fgn. Relations. Home: 984 Memorial Dr Cambridge MA 02138

KELMAN, WOLFE, rabbi; b. Vienna, Austria, Nov. 27, 1923; came to U.S., 1946, naturalized, 1962; s. Hersh Leib and Mirl (Fish) K.; m. Jacqueline Levy, Mar. 2, 1952; children: Levi Yehuda, Naamah Kathrine, Abigail Tobie. B.A., U. Toronto, Ont., Can., 1946; M.H.L., Jewish Theol. Sem. Am., 1950, D.D. (hon.), 1973. Rabbi various congregations; vis. rabbi West London Congregation Brit. Jews, London, Eng., 1957-58; exec. v.p. Rabbinical Assembly, 1951—; dir. joint placement commn. Rabbinical Assembly, United Synagogue Am. and Jewish Theol. Sem. Am., 1951-66; vis. prof. homiletics Jewish Theol. Sem. Am., 1966-73, adj. asst. prof. history, 1973—. Mem. governing council World Jewish Congress, 1968—, chmn. cultural commn., 1975-77, co-chmn. interreligious affairs, 1979—; Pres. Com. Neighbors Concerned for Elderly, Their Rights and Needs, 1971—; bd. dirs., exec. com. Hebrew Immigrant Aid Soc., 1974—. Served with RCAF, 1943-45. Home: 845 West End Ave New York NY 10025 Office: 3080 Broadway New York NY 10027 *My personal and public attitudes are informed by the principles of the legitimacy of pluralism and reverence for diversity. Although born in central European pre-Hitler Vienna, my basic education and attitudes were formed in Canada. The synthesis between Anglo-Saxon emphasis on personal liberty and the suprememcy of conscience, and the hallowed Jewish traditional emphasis on justice tempered by compassion and great reverence for tradition have shaped my perceptions and, hopefully deeds.*

KELMENSON, LEO ARTHUR, advertising executive; b. N.Y.C., Jan. 3, 1927; s. Joseph A. and Ruth (Rothberg) K.; (div.)children: Todd-Arthur, Joel Adam; m. Barbara Dauphin, Feb. 20, 1973. B.S., Columbia U., 1951; postgrad., Grad. Sch. Bus., 1952. From TV prodn. to sr. v.p., asst. to pres. Lennen & Newell, 1951-65; exec. v.p., mem. exec. com. Norman Craig & Kummel, 1965-66; sr. v.p., dir., mem. exec. com. Kenyon & Eckhardt, 1967-68; pres. Kenyon & Eckhardt Advt. Inc., 1968—; pres., chief exec. officer, chmn. exec. com. Kenyon & Eckhardt Inc. (C.P.V.), 1970—; pres. Kelmenson Funds Ltd.; dir. Locations Unltd.; lectr. New Sch. Social Research.; Adviser communications office U.S. Atty. Gen., 1960-63; spl. project officer Dept. State, 1952-64; v.p., dir. African Med. and Research Found., 1957—. Author: poetry Epilogue, 1964; also short stories. Mem. pub. relations com. Nat. Cancer Found., 1958—; adv. com. Nat. Cultural Center, 1962; pres. Shoes for Little Souls, 1960, Remsenburg Assn., 1968; bd. dirs. ASPCA; mem. pres.'s adv. council Am. Diabetes Assn., 1977-78. Served with USMCR, World War II. Recipient Theodore Roosevelt Man of Year award, 1955; Silver Quill Poetry award, 1955; Res. Officers Assn. award, 1965; Guggenheim World Peace award, 1951. Mem. U.S. Olympic Com., N.Y. Advt. Club, Soc. Am. Businessmen Club, Sigma Phi Epsilon. Clubs: Sands Point (N.Y.) Yacht, L.I. Polo. Office: 200 Park Ave New York NY 10017

KELNE, NATHAN, editorial and public relations consultant; b. Rochester, N.Y., Sept. 21, 1918; s. Morris and Rose (Mondschein) K.; m. Esther Tein, Sept. 7, 1946; 1 dau., Elizabeth Rose. B.S., N.Y. U., 1942. Sr. editor Printers' Ink Pub. Co., N.Y.C., 1946-56; mgr. editorial planning N.Y. Stock Exchange, N.Y.C., 1956-61; v.p. Barkas & Shalit, Inc., N.Y.C., 1963-66; with N.Y. Life Ins. Co., N.Y.C., 1966—, asst. v.p., 1970-71, 2d v.p., 1971-74, v.p., 1974-83; editorial, pub. relations cons., 1983—. Trustee Village of East Hills, N.Y., 1967-71. Served with USAAF, 1942-46. Decorated D.F.C., Air medal with oak leaf clusters; recipient Jesse Neal Outstanding Editorial Achievement award Nat. Conf. Bus. Paper Editors, 1956. Mem. Am. Arbitration Assn., Pub. Relations Soc. Am., Pub. Relations Seminar. Home: 58 Tara Dr East Hills NY 11576 Office: 51 Madison Ave New York City NY 10010

KELSEY, CLYDE EASTMAN, JR., educator; b. Wadena, Minn., Mar. 30, 1924; s. Clyde Eastman and Lorraine (Lamb) Bagley) K.; m. Betty Jean Williams, Apr. 1, 1949; children: Becky Kelsey Marcin, Nancy. B.A., U. Tex., El Paso, 1948; M.A., U. Tulsa, 1951; Ph.D., U. Denver, 1960; hon. degree, U. de Oriente, Venezuela, 1969. Dir. counseling bur. U. Tex., El Paso, 1951-61, prof., head dept. philosphy, psychology, 1961-62; dean students, dir. Inter-Am. Inst., 1962-66; program adv., Venezuela, Ford Found., 1966-69; vice chancellor public affairs U. Denver, 1969-72; v.p. devel. and univ. relations Tex. Tech U., Lubbock, 1972-81, prof. edn, 1981-82; sr. research fellow Nat. Center Higher Edn. Mgmt., 1983—; lectr. 4th Army U.S., 1961-65; cons. U.S. Dept. State, Peace Corps, 1961-66; mem. adv. bd. Kans. Wesleyan Coll., 1969-71; v.p. Colo. Partners of Alliance, 1971-73. Contbr. articles to profl. jours. Bd. dirs. El Paso Mental Health Assn., 1951-58, pres., 1953-55; Bd. dirs. El Paso Sch. Retarded Children, 1952-57, pres., 1953-55; bd. dirs. Lubbock Goodwill Industries, 1972—, v.p., 1973-77, pres., 1978-80. Served with USNR, 1942-45. Decorated Order San Carlos Republic Colombia; recipient Disting. Alumni Service award U. Denver, 1972; Fulbright scholar Colombia, 1960-61. Fellow Tex. Acad. Sci.; mem. Am. Psychol. Assn., S.W. Psychol. Assn., Tex. Psychol. Assn., AAAS, Am. Ednl. Research Assn. Home: 3307-A 74th St Lubbock TX 79423 Office: PO Box 4650 Lubbock TX 79409

KELSEY, FLOYD LAMAR, JR., architect; b. Colorado Springs, Colo., Jan. 2, 1925; s. Floyd Lamar and Myrtice (Graves) K.; m. Ruth Ann Witty, June 22, 1946; children—Patricia Ann, Carol Susan. Student, Colo. Coll., 1942-44; B.S. in Architecture with honors, U. Ill., 1947. Partner Bunts & Kelsey (architects), Colorado Springs, 1952-66; prin. Lamar Kelsey Assos.; cons. design rev. bd. U. Colo., 1969-70; adv. panel, region 8 Gen. Services Adminstrn., 1969-70; vis. lectr. U. Colo., 1960, U. Denver, 1958. Author: Schools for America, 1967, Open Space Schools, 1971; Contbr. to profl. jours. Recipient design awards AIA, Am. Inst. Steel Constrn., Am. Assn. Sch. Adminstrs., Nation's Schs. mag. Fellow AIA (former mem. nat. coms. on ednl. facilities, edn., architecture for arts and recreation); mem. Colorado Springs C. of C. (past dir.), Gargoyle Archtl. Hon. Soc., Phi Delta Theta. Methodist. Clubs: El Paso, Winter Night (pres. 1976), Broadmoor Golf (Colorado Springs)). Home: 10 Briarcrest Pl Colorado Springs CO 80906 Office: 430 N Tejon St Colorado Springs CO 80903

KELSEY, FRANCES OLDHAM (MRS. FREMONT ELLIS KELSEY), govt. ofcl.; b. Cobble Hill, Vancouver Island, C., Can., July 24, 1914; came to U.S., 1936, naturalized, 1956; d. Frank Trevor and Katherine (Stuart) Oldham; m. Fremont Ellis Kelsey, Dec. 6, 1943; children—Susan Elizabeth, Christine Ann. B.Sc., McGill U., 1934; M.Sc., 1935; Ph.D., U. Chgo., 1938, M.D., 1950. Instr., asst. prof. pharmacology U. Chgo., 1938-50; editorial asso. AMA, Chgo., 1950-52; asso. prof. pharmacology U. S.D., 1954-57; med. officer FDA, Washington, 1960—, dir. div. sci. investigations, 1967—. Author: (with F.E. Kelsey, E.M.K. Geiling) Essentials of Pharmacology, 1960. Recipient Pres.'s award for Distinguished Fed. Civilian Service (refusal to approve coml. distbn. thalidomide in U.S.), 1962. Mem. Am. Soc. Pharmacology and Exptl. Therapeutics, Soc. Exptl. Biology and Medicine, Am. Med. Writers Assn., N.Y. Acad. Scis., Teratology Soc., Sigma Xi. Home: 5811 Brookside Dr Chevy Chase MD 20015 Office: FDA 5600 Fishers Ln Rockville MD 20857

KELSEY, JOHN LOVELAND, investment banker; b. Long Branch, N.J., May 20, 1925; s. James Edward and Frieda Louise K.; children—Grayson Lee, Jonathan Combs. B.S. in Bus, Ind. U., 1949; M.B.A. in Fin, U. Pa., 1950. Fgn. exchange analyst treas.'s office Standard Oil of N.J., N.Y.C., 1950; instl. salesman Union Securities Co. (merged with Eastman Dillon & Co. 1956), Union Securities Co. (name changed to Eastman Dillon, Union Securities & Co.), Union Securities Co. (merged with Blyth & Co.), Union Securities Co. (named changed to Blyth Eastman Dillon & Co., Inc.), Union Securities Co. (merged with Paine Webber 1980), Union Securities Co. (name changed to Blyth Eastman Paine Webber, Inc.), N.Y.C., 1951-56; gen. partner Blyth Eastman Paine Webber, Inc., 1960—, exec. v.p., 1972—, mng. dir., 1980—; dir. Papercraft Corp., Fed. Paper Bd. Co., Standard Motor Products Inc. Served with USAAF, 1943-46. Mem. Bond Club of N.Y., N.Y. Soc. Security Analysts. Republican. Clubs: Univ., Wharton Grad. Sch. (N.Y.C.); Rumson Golf and Country, Deal Golf and Country, Pine Valley Golf. Office: 1221 Ave of the Americas New York NY 10020

KELSEY, MYRON PLOUGH, agricultural economist; b. Clyde, N.Y., Sept. 2, 1931; s. F. Wayne and Julia Atchison (Plough) K.; m. Joan Thostesen, Apr. 18, 1954; children: Catherine, Timothy. B.S., Cornell U., 1953, M.S., 1956; Ph.D., Purdue U., 1959. Prof. dept. agrl. econs. Mich. State U., East Lansing, 1959—. Served in U.S. Army, 1953-55. Mem. Am. Agrl. Econs. Assn., Am. Soc. Farm Mgrs. and Rural Appraisers. Methodist. Home: 1879 Cahill Dr East Lansing MI 48823 Office: Dept Agrl Econs Mich State U East Lansing MI 48824

KELSO, ALEC JOHN (JACK KELSO), anthropologist, educator; b. Chgo., Dec. 5, 1930; s. Alexander Joseph and Collette Mary (Scanlon) K.; m. Mary Gemeny, Dec. 29, 1951; children: Colette, William. B.S., No. Ill. U., 1952; M.A., Ph.D., U. Mich., 1958. Instr. Wayne State U., Detroit, 1957; faculty U. Colo., Boulder, 1958—, prof. anthropology, 1967—, chmn. dept., 1963-68, 71-74, 77-81; dir. Summer Inst. Anthropology, 1961-62, 64, 68-70, acad. dir. semester at sea, 1978-79, vis. lectr. semester at sea, 1983; vice chancellor Colorado Springs campus, 1975-77; dir. residential acad. program Farr and Hall, 1983—; vis. prof. dept. genetics U. Hawaii, 1965-66; Disting. vis. prof. Oreg. State U., 1971; keynote speaker Internat. Assn. Pediatrics, Tokyo, 1981. Author: Introduction to Physical Anthropology Laboratory Manual, 1962, Physical Anthropology, 1970, 2d edit., 1974; Editor: Yearbook of Physical Anthropology, 1962, 63. Mem. Am. Anthrop. Assn. (exec. bd. 1974-77), Am. Assn. Phys. Anthropoligists (exec. com. 1961-64, v.p. 1972—), Internat. Assn. Human Biologists, World Soc. for Ekistics, Sigma Xi (chpt. pres. 1973—). Address: 2305 Kenwood Dr Boulder CO 80303 *I used to think that knowing was most important. Then I thought understanding was most important. Now I suspect that not knowing is more important than either.*

KELSO, JOHN HODGSON, government official; b. Iowa City, June 16, 1925; s. Edward Lewis and Eliza (Hodgson) K.; m. Marian Louise Towers, Aug. 22, 1948; 1 son. B.A., State U. Iowa, 1949, M.A., 1950. John T. Occupational research analyst Bur. Naval Personnel, Dept. Navy, Washington, 1951-55; orgn. and methods examiner Agr. Research Services, Dept. Agr., Washington, 1955-57; mgmt. analyst mgmt. adv. br. Bur. State Services, USPHS, HEW, Washington, 1957-58, chief survey group, 1958-60, chief mgmt. adv. br., 1960-62, asst. exec. officer, 1962-66, exec. officer, Bethesda, Md., 1966-68; asso. adminstr. mgmt. Health Services and Mental Health Adminstrn., 1968-73; dir. office regional operations USPHS, Office Asst. Sec. for Health, HEW, 1973-76; dep. adminstr. Health Services Adminstrn., 1976-81, acting adminstr., 1981-82; dep. adminstr. Health Resources and Services Adminstrn., 1982—. Served with AUS, 1943-46. Recipient Superior Service award USPHS, 1969, Distinguished Service award HEW, 1972, Meritorious Rank award, 1983. Mem. Sigma Alpha Epsilon. Methodist. Home: 2332 N Early St Alexandria VA 22302 Office: 5600 Fischer's Ln Rockville MD 20852

KELSO, JOHN MORRIS, physicist; b. Punxsutawney, Pa., Mar. 12, 1922; s. John Claude and Helen Alverta (Kurtz) K.; m. Nancy Jane Weaver, Jan. 6, 1945; 1 dau., Jean Susan Kelso Roseborough. B.A. in Physics, Gettysburg Coll., 1943; M.S., Pa. State U., 1949, Ph.D., 1949. Asso. prof. elec. engring. Pa. State U., State College, 1949-54; evaluation specialist Glenn L. Martin Co., Balt., 1954-55; head space physics (fields) sect. Space Tech. Labs., Inc., Redondo Beach, Calif., 1955-62; v.p., dir. research ITT Electrophysics Lab., Inc., Columbia, Md., 1962-76; cons. Office of Telecommunications Policy, Washington, 1976-78; chief scientist Signal Analysis Center, Honeywell, Inc., Annapolis, Md., 1978—; vis. asso. prof. Chalmers U. Tech., Gothenburg, Sweden, 1951-52; mem. Nat. Acad. Scis. com. adv. to Central Radio Propagation Lab. U.S. Bur. Standards, 1963-65; mem. evaluation panel Nat. Astronomy and Ionosphere Ctr., Arecibo, P.R., 1965-68. Author: Radio Ray Propagation in the Ionosphere, 1964; author articles. Fellow IEEE; mem. Am. Phys. Soc., Am. Geophys. Union, Internat. Union Radio Sci. (chmn. U.S. Commn. G 1972-75), Am. Mensa. Home: 2596 Timber Cove Annapolis MD 21401 Office: Signal Analysis Center Honeywell Inc PO Box 391 Annapolis MD 21404

KELSO, LOUIS ORTH, investment banker, economist; b. Denver, Dec. 4, 1913; s. Oren S. and Nettie (Wolfe) K.; m. Betty Hawley (div.); children: Martha Jennifer Kelso Brookman, Katherine Elizabeth von Stein; m. Patricia Hetter. B.S. cum laude, U. Colo., 1937, LL.B, 1938; D.Sc., Araneta U., Manila, 1962. Bar: Colo. 1938, Calif. 1946, practice law, Denver 1938-42, San Francisco 1946-75. Asso. Pershing Bosworth, Dick & Dawson, 1938-42; partner Brobeck, Phleger & Harrison, 1946-59; sr. partner Kelso, Cotton, Seligman & Ray, 1959-70; mng. dir. Louis O. Kelso, Inc., San Francisco, 1970-75; chmn. chief exec. Kelso & Co., Inc. (mcht. bankers), San Francisco, 1975—, also dir.; asso. prof. law U. Colo., 1946; Pres. Inst. Study Econ. Systems, San Francisco. Author: (with Mortimer J. Adler) The Capitalist Manifesto, 1958, The New Capitalists, 1961, (with Patricia Hetter) Two-Factor Theory The Economics of Reality, 1968, (with Patricia Hetter Kelso) Social Capitalism, 1984; Editor-in-chief: Rocky Mountain Law Rev, 1938; Contbr. articles to profl. jours. Bd. dirs. Inst. Philos. Research, Chgo.; founding trustee Crystal Springs Sch. Girls, Hillsborough, Calif. Served to lt. USNR, 1942-46. Mem. Am., Calif., San Francisco bar assns., San Francisco Com. Fgn. Relations. Clubs: Pacific-Union, Bohemian, Bankers, Villa Taverna (San Francisco); Chgo. Three Embarcadero Center Suite 1760 San Francisco CA 94111

KELSO, ROBERT CHARLES, lawyer; b. New Salem, Ind., Nov. 13, 1916; s. Rayburn and Amy (Hargitt) K.; m. Evelinne M. Bursch, Nov. 8, 1941; children—Robinne Sue Kelso Hornbaker, Margaret Anne Kelso Gerard. Student, U. Ill., 1934-37; J.D. cum laude, John Marshall Law Sch., 1942; postgrad. law, Goethe U., Frankfurt, Germany. Bar: Ill. bar 1942, Ariz. bar 1948, D.C. bar 1960. Asst. states atty., Rockford, Ill., 1945-47; city atty. Springerville and Eagar, Ariz., 1948-51; practice in, Springerville, 1948-51; spl. counsel European and internat. law Dept. Def., 1951-56; sr. partner firm Lewis and Roca, Phoenix, 1959—; asso. prof. internat. comml. law Am. Inst. Fgn. Trade, 1958-68; Mem. Regional Export Expansion Council, 1962-70; chmn. Ariz.-Mexican Trade Commn., 1965-67; del. Internat. Congress Jurists, Hamburg, Germany, 1953; hon. consul Fed. Republic Germany, 1961-73. Author: Legal Problems Arising Out of Industrial Use of Atomic Energy, 1956, International Law of Commerce, 1961; co-author: International Trade Handbook, 1963, also articles. Bd. govs. Ill. Young Republicans, 1946-47; del. Ill. Rep. Conv., 1946; chmn. Apache County (Ariz.) Rep. Com., 1950; del. Ariz. Rep. Com., 1950. Named to Order John Marshall, 1942; awarded Bundes Verdienst Kreuz, erste Klasse, West Germany, 1972. Mem. Am., Ill., Ariz., Am., Internat. bar assns., Fedn. Ins. Counsel, Theta Chi. Elder Presbyterian Ch. in Am. Clubs: Rotary, Ariz. (Phoenix). Home: 5342 Ouesta Tierra Dr Phoenix AZ 85012 Office: 100 W Washington St Suite 2300 Phoenix AZ 85003

KELSON, ALLEN HOWARD, writer, editor, dining critic; b. Chgo., May 4, 1940; s. Ben and Esther Mae (Ashkin) K.; m. Carla S. Lipson, Aug. 18, 1966; children: David Lauren, Melina Elisabeth. Student, U. Ill., Chgo., 1957, 1958; B.A. in English, Roosevelt U., Chgo., 1965. Catalog copywriter Sears, Roebuck & Co., Chgo., 1962-64, sales promotion writer, 1964-67, spl. projects dir., catalog advt. div., 1967-68; editor-in-chief WFMT Guide, Chgo. Guide, Chgo. mag. WFMT, Inc., Chgo., 1968—; pub. relations and advt. mgr. WFMT, Inc., 1968-70, v.p., dir., 1974—; asso. pub. Chgo. mag., 1977—; Prin. Kelson Kapuler Advt., 1962-68; editor Chgo. GuideBook, 1972-73; lectr. Nat. Retail Mchts. Assn., 1973, Nat. Restaurant Assn., 1975; judge Ill. Women's Press Assn., 1976, Les Turner ALS Found. Cook-Off, 1982, 83, Nat. Restaurant Assn. Great Menu competition, 1978. Author: Guide to Chicago, 1983, 100 Menus, 1984. Mem. adv. staff Walt Disney Magnet Sch., Chgo. Bd. Edn., 1974-77; Mem. adv. council Internat. Visitors Center, Chgo.; bd. dirs. Byline mag. Northwestern U.; bd. regents Roosevelt U. Alumni Assn. Recipient Merit award Chgo. Advt. Club, 1965, Designer awards Chgo. 4, 1973, 74; hon. mem. Duncan Hines Meml. Fellowship, 1971; Am. Inst. Graphic Arts award, 1976; Chgo. '76 Show award, 1976; TV comml. direction and writing awards N.Y. Art Dirs. Club, 1979; Chicago '80 award, 1980. Mem. Am. Soc. Mag. Editors. Club: East Bank (Chgo.). Office: Three Illinois Center Chicago IL 60601

KELTNER, RAYMOND MARION, JR., surgeon, educator; b. Springfield, Mo., Apr. 15, 1929; s. Raymond Marion and Othello Mary (Forgey) K.; m. Carla Ann Clark, May 10, 1974; children from previous marriage: Aintre B., Raymond M., Merl K., Albert D., Gisela W. B.S., Drury Coll., 1950, U. Mo., 1955; M.D., Washington U., St. Louis, 1957. Practice medicine specializing in surgery, Houston, 1962-63, Houghton, Mich., 1966-68; mem. faculty Washington U., 1963-66; asst. prof. surgery St. Louis U. Sch. Medicine, 1968-71, assoc. prof., 1971-76, prof., 1976—; attending surgeon St. Louis U. Hosp., 1968—; chief of surgery St. Louis City Hosp. Contbr. articles to surg. jours. Fellow Am. Coll. Surgeons; mem. AMA (Service Recognition award), Western Surg. Assn. Home: 3901 Flora Pl Saint Louis MO 63110 Office: 1325 S Grand Ave Saint Louis MO 63104

KELTON, JOHN T., lawyer; b. Bay City, Mich., Mar. 12, 1909; s. Frank P. S. and Jessie Eleanor (Tremain) K.; m. Carol E. Copeland, July 9, 1935; children: Carol E.M., Joy T. Student, Culver (Ind.) Mil. Acad., 1925-28; B.S. in Chem. Engring, Mass. Inst. Tech., 1932; LL.B., Harvard U., 1935. Bar: N.Y. 1935. Practiced patent law as asso. and mem. Watson, Bristol, Johnson & Leavenworth, N.Y.C., 1935-40, 46-49; mem. Watson, Johnson, Leavenworth & Blair, 1950-53, Watson, Leavenworth, Kelton & Taggart, 1954-81, Darby & Darby (P.C.), 1981—. Served from 2d lt. to lt. col. AUS, 1940-46. Mem. ABA, N.Y. State Bar Assn., Assn. Bar City N.Y., Am. Patent Law Assn. (bd. mgrs. 1964-67, pres. 1973), N.Y. Patent Law Assn. (pres. 1967). Congregationalist. Clubs: Harvard, Union League (N.Y.C.). Home: Nutmeg Ln Westport CT 06880 Office: 405 Lexington Ave New York NY 10174

KEM, LAWRENCE R., publishing executive; b. Sikeston, Mo., Apr. 22, 1935; s. Louis R. and Rosa M. (Bohannon) K.; m. Barbara Hope, Sept. 1, 1956; children—Elizabeth, Laura. B.S. summa cum laude, S.E. Mo. State U., 1956. Mgr. dept. mfg. and distbn. Procter & Gamble, St. Louis, S.I., N.Y., 1958-64; partner McKinsey & Co., Cleve. and London, 1964-72; group v.p., gen. mgr. spl. products ops. Gen. Cable Corp., Greenwich, Conn., 1972-74; chmn., dir., chief exec. officer Am. Appraisal Assocs., Inc., Milw., 1974-82; pub. Johnson Hill Press, Inc., Ft. Atkinson, Wis., 1982—; dir. Sta-Rite Industries, Inc., Milw.; also dir. Johnson Hill Press, Inc., Ft. Atkinson, Wis. Served to lt. (j.g.) USNR, 1956-58. Mem. Young Pres. Orgn. Clubs: Town, Milw., Univ. (Milw.); Union League (N.Y.C.). Home: 8425 N River Rd Milwaukee WI 53217 Office: 1233 Jonesville Ave Ft. Atkinson WI 53538

KEM, RICHARD SAMUEL, army officer; b. Richmond, Ind., Aug. 9, 1934; s. Charles Edward and Janice Allene (Beard) K.; m. Ann Callahan, May 7, 1960; children: Michelle, John Samuel, Steven Edward. B.S., U.S. Mil. Acad., 1956; M.S., U. Ill., 1962, George Washington U., 1972; postgrad., Naval War Coll., 1972, Northwestern U., 1979. Commd. 2d lt. U.S. Army, 1956, advanced through grades to brig. gen., 1979; comdg. officer 577th Engr. Bn., Vietnam, 1968-69; staff, faculty U.S. Mil. Acad., West Point, N.Y., 1969-71; staff officer Mil. Personnel Center, 1972-73, Office Army Chief Staff, 1974-75;

chief public affairs Office Chief Engrs., 1975-76; comdg. engr. 7th Brigade, Ger., 1976-78; chief installations and constrn., Europe, 1978-79, dep. asst. chief engrs., 1979-80; dep. dir. civil works Office Chief Engrs., 1980; comdr., div. engr. Ohio River div., 1981—; bd. engrs. Rivers and Harbors, 1982—. Decorated Legion of Merit with oak leaf cluster, Bronze Star. Mem. ASCE, Soc. Mil. Engrs., Internat. Nav. Congress. Episcopalian. Office: Fed Bldg 550 Main St Cincinnati OH 45201

KEMBLE, CHARLES ROBERT, university president; b. Oskaloosa, Iowa, Aug. 17, 1925; s. Roy H. and Pauline (Hoover) K.; m. Helen Elizabeth Elfstrom, July 3, 1949; children: Christopher, Keith Eilene, Cynthia Kemble Lawshe, Geoffrey, Carol Lynn. Student, Kans. U., 1943, Cornell U., 1945; B.S., U.S. Mil. Acad., 1949; M.A., U. Pa., 1956; Ph.D., George Washington U., 1966. Commd. 2d lt. U.S. Army, 1949, advanced through grades to col., 1970; asst. prof. U.S. Mil. Acad., 1956-60; exec. asst. dir. ops. Joint Chiefs of Staff, 1961-64; assoc. prof. English, dir. Am. studies U.S. Mil. Acad., 1966-72, ret., 1972; pres. N.Mex. Mil. Inst., 1972-77, Lamar U., Beaumont, Tex., 1977—; dir. 1st Security Nat. Bank, Beaumont. Author: The Image of the American Army Officer, 1973; co-editor: John Brown's Body (Benet), 1968. Decorated Legion of Merit, Bronze Star, others. Mem. Am. Studies Assn., MLA, Assn. U.S. Army, Ret. Officers Assn., Beaumont C. of C. (bd. dirs.). Lodge: Rotary. Home: 102 Redbird St Beaumont TX 77710 Office: Office of Pres Lamar U Beaumont TX 77710

KEMBLE, ERNEST DELL, psychology educator; b. Memphis, Dec. 19, 1935; s. Clarence Dell and Lillian Mae (Swett) K.; m. Darolis Cathryn Spencer, Aug. 31, 1963; 1 dau., Katrina Coleen. B.A. cum laude, Memphis State U., 1962; M.A., Vanderbilt U., 1965, Ph.D., 1968. Mem. faculty U. Minn., Morris, 1966—, asso. prof. psychology, 1970-76, prof., 1976—. Contbr. articles to profl. jours. U. summer research fellow, 1969, 75; U. grantee, 1969, 70, 74, 77, 78, 80, 81; Research assoc. Wis. Regional Primate Center, 1967; NIMH; postdoctoral fellow, 1969-70; recipient Horace T. Morse award, 1977. Mem. Animal Behavior Soc., Psychonomic Soc., Am. Psychol. Assn. (disting. teaching award Div. 2 1983), Internat. Soc. Research on Aggression, Midwestern Psychol. Assn., Sigma Xi. Research on functions of limbic system of brain. Home: 105 E 9th St Morris MN 56267 Office: U Minn Dept Psychology Morris MN 56267

KEMELMAN, HARRY, author; b. Boston, Nov. 24, 1908; s. Isaac and Dora (Prizer) K.; m. Anne Kessin, Mar. 29, 1936; children—Ruth (Mrs. George Rooks), Arthur Frederick, Diane (Mrs. Murry Rossant). A.B., Boston U., 1930; M.A., Harvard, 1931. Tchr. Boston pub. schs., 1935-41, eve. div. Northeastern U., 1938-41; chief job analyst and wage adminstr. Boston Port Embarkation, 1942-49; free-lance writer, 1949-63; tchr. Franklin Inst., Boston, 1963-64, State Coll., 1964—. Author: Friday the Rabbi Slept Late, 1964, Saturday the Rabbi Went Hungry, 1966, The Nine Mile Walk, 1967, Sunday the Rabbi Stayed Home, 1969, Commonsense in Education, 1970, Monday the Rabbi Took Off, 1972, Tuesday, the Rabbi Saw Red, 1973, Wednesday, The Rabbi Got Wet, 1976, Thursday, The Rabbi Walked Out, 1978, Conversations with Rabbi Small, 1981. Recipient Edgar award for best first novel, 1965; Faith and Freedom Communications award, 1967. Mem. Author's League, Mystery Writers Assn. Address: PO Box 674 Marblehead MA 01945

KEMENY, JOHN GEORGE, educator; b. Budapest, Hungary, May 31, 1926; came to U.S., 1940, naturalized, 1945; s. Tibor and Lucy (Fried) K.; m. Jean Alexander, Nov. 5, 1950; children: Jennifer M., Robert A. B.A., Princeton U., 1947, Ph.D., 1949, LL.D., 1971; D.Sc., Middlebury Coll., 1965, Boston Coll., 1973, U. Pa., 1975, Bard Coll., 1978, Dickinson Coll., 1981; LL.D., Columbia U., 1971, U. N.H., 1972, Colby Coll., 1976, Lafayette Coll., 1976, Brown U., 1980, Dartmouth Coll., 1981. Asst. theoretical div. Los Alamos Project, 1945-46; asst. teaching and research Princeton, 1946-48; Fine instr. Office Naval Research fellow math., 1949-51, asst. prof. philosophy, 1951-53; research asst. to Dr. Albert Einstein, Inst. Advanced Study, 1948-49; prof. math. Dartmouth Coll., 1953-70, 81—, adj. prof. math, 1972-81, chmn. math. dept., 1955- 67, Albert Bradley 3d Century prof., 1969-72, pres., 1970-81; coordinator ednl. plans and devel., 1967-69, lectr. in, Austria, Israel, India, Japan, 1964-65, Vanuxem lectr., Princeton U., 1974; Cons. Rand Corp., Santa Monica, Calif., 1953-69; mem. Nat. Commn. Libraries and Info. Sci., 1971-73; mem. regional dir.'s adv. com. HEW, 1971-73. Author: Man and the Computer; co-author: Finite Mathematics with Business Applications: Denumerable Markov Chains; Basic Programming, 1967; Contbr. to Ency. Brit., articles to profl. jours.; Cons. editor: Jour. Symbolic Logic, 1950-59; assoc. editor: Jour. Math. Analysis and Applications, 1959-70. Chmn. U.S. Commn. on Math. Instrn., 1958-60; mem. NRC, 1963-66; chmn. Pres.'s Commn. on Accident at Three Mile Island, 1979; mem. Hanover Sch. Bd. (N.H.), 1961-64; Trustee Found. Center, 1970-76, Carnegie Found. Advancement Teaching, 1972-78; bd. dirs. Council for Fin. Aid to Edn., 1976-79; chmn. Consortium on Financing Higher Edn., 1979-80. Served with AUS, 1945-46. Recipient Priestley award, 1976. Mem. Assn. Symbolic Logic, Math. Assn. Am. (chmn. New Eng. sect. 1959-60, bd. govs. 1960-63, chmn. panel biol. and social scis. 1963-64), Am. Math. Soc., Am. Philos. Assn., Am. Acad. Arts and Scis., Phi Beta Kappa, Sigma Xi (nat. lectr. 1967). Club: Century Assn. Office: Dept Math Dartmouth Coll Bradley Hall Hanover NH 03755

KEMMERER, DONALD LORENZO, economics educator; b. Manila, Dec. 24, 1905; s. Edwin Walter and Rachel (Dickele) K.; m. Mirjane Strong, Nov. 27, 1934; children: Jane S., Edwin Walter II. A.B., Princeton U., 1927, A.M., 1931, Ph.D., 1934. Asst. sec. to fin. adv. commns. to Chile, 1925, Asst. sec. to financial adv. commns. to, Poland, 1926, China, 1929; instr. econs. Lehigh U., 1934-37; asso. econ. U. Ill., 1937-39, asst. prof., 1939-45, asso. prof., 1945-49, prof. econs., 1949-73, emeritus, 1973—, dir. Center for Econ. Edn., 1981-83; vis. prof. NYU, summer 1952, U. Melbourne, Australia, 1958; cons. Kabul (Afghanistan) U., 1959; Fulbright prof. U. Montpellier, France, 1960, U. Munich, 1964; econ. adviser Pa. R.R., 1945, Investors Mgmt. Co., 1950-57; dir. mutual funds Anchor Corp., 1957-75; chmn. bd. Univ. Fed. Savs. and Loan Assn., 1972-75; Cons. European Productivity Agy., 1955; v.p. Economists Nat. Com. Monetary Policy, 1957-67, pres., 1967-70; mem. U.S. Assay Com., 1967. Author: Path to Freedom, 1940, (with E.L. Bogart) Economic History of American People, 1942, rev., 1947, (with E.W. Kemmerer) ABC of Federal Reserve System, 12th edit., 1950, (with R.H. Blodgett) Comparative Economic Development, 1956, (with C.C. Jones) American Economic History, 1957, rev. edit., 1959, John E. Rovensky, Banker and Industrialist, 1977; contbr. articles to profl. jours. Econ. adviser Republican platform planning com., 1944; pres. Lincoln Ednl. Found., 1958-84; bd. dirs. Am. Econ. Found., 1977-83, Am. Inst. Econ. Research, 1977-79, 81—. Mem. Midwest Econ. Assn. (2d v.p. 1950), Am. Econ. Assn., Am. Hist. Assn., Orgn. Am. Historians, Bus. History Conf. (pres. 1976), Econ. Hist. Assn., Com. Monetary Research and Edn. (pres. 1970-80), Univ. Profs. for Acad. Order (pres. 1972, treas. 1978-84), Phi Beta Kappa. Clubs: Mont Pelerin, Am. Alpine, Champaign Country; Princeton (N.Y.C., Chgo.). Lodge: Rotary. Home: 1006 W Armory Ave Champaign IL 61821 Office: 110 David Kinley Hall Urbana IL 61801

KEMMERER, JOHN L., JR., mining company executive. Chmn. Kemmerer Resources Corp.; dir. Bralorne Resources Ltd., Kimbark Oil & Gas Co., Steel Heddle Mfg. Co., Unette Corp., Faber-Castell Corp.; Former officer Nat. Coal Assn., also Bituminous Coal Research Assn., Washington. Address: 120 Broadway New York NY 10271

KEMMIS, DANIEL ORRA, state legislator, lawyer; b. Fairview, Mont., Dec. 5, 1945; s. Orra Raymond and Lilly Samantha (Shidler) K.; m. Jeanne Marie Koester, June 9, 1978; children: Abraham, Samuel; children by previous marriage: Deva Fall, John Orra. B.A., Harvard U., 1968; J.D., U. Mont., 1978. Bar: Mont. 1978. State rep. Mont. Ho. of Reps., Helena, 1975—, minority leader, 1981-82, Speaker of House, 1983-84; ptnr. Morrison, Jonkel, Kemmis & Rossbach, Missoula, 1978-80, Jonkel & Kemmis, 1981—; cons. No. Lights Inst., Helena. Contbg. author (to profl. publs.). Mem. Friends of U. Mont. Library, Missoula, 1980—; bd. dirs. Freeman Meml. Com., Missoula; candidate for chief justice Mont. Supreme Ct. Named Disting. Young Alumnus U. Mont, 1981—. Mem. State Bar Mont., Mont. Trail Lawyers Assn. Democrat. Roman Catholic. Home: 504 Blaine St Missoula MT 59801 Office: PO Box 8687 Missoula MT 59807

KEMP, ARTHUR, emeritus economics educator; b. Buffalo, Jan. 29, 1916; s. Arthur and Caroline (Durk) K.; m. Helene Morlock, Aug. 23, 1940. B.A., U. Buffalo, 1939; M.B.A., Northwestern U., 1940; Ph.D., N.Y. U., 1949; D.Social Scis. (hon.), Francisco Marroquin U., Guatemala, 1981. Instr. Yale, 1941-43; asst. prof. NYU, 1946-53; prof. Claremont (Calif.) McKenna Coll., 1953—, now emeritus prof. money and credit; dir. dept. econ. research AMA, 1959-60; research asst. to chmn. Hoover Commn., 1947-49. Author: The Legal Qualities of Money, 1956, The Role of Government in Developing Peaceful Uses of Atomic Energy, 1960, The Role of Gold, 1963. Served to 1st lt. USAAF, 1943-46. Recipient citation of merit U. Buffalo, 1962. Mem. Am., Western econ. assns., Am. Fin. Assn., Econ History Assn., Mont Pelerin Soc. (past treas., dir.), NAM (past v.p.), Phila. Soc. (past pres., dir.). Home: 1541 Lafayette Rd Claremont CA 91711

KEMP, DANIAL SCHAEFFER, chemistry educator, consultant; b. Portland, Oreg., Oct. 20, 1936; s. Paul Daniel and Lovie Ellen (Schaeffer) K. B.A., Reed Coll., 1958; Ph.D., Harvard U., 1964. Mem. faculty MIT, Cambridge, 1964—, prof. chemistry, 1974—; cons. Pfizer Research Labs., Groton, Conn., 1967—. Author: Organic Chemistry, 1980; contbr. numerous articles to profl. jours. Mem. Am. Chem. Soc. Home: 226 Commonwealth Ave Boston MA 02116 Office: Dept Chemistry Room 18-027 MIT Cambridge MA 02139

KEMP, EDGAR RAY, JR., retail executive; b. Corsicana, Tex., Sept. 15, 1924; s. Edgar Ray and Earla Mae (Brennan) K.; m. Margaret Ellen Letzig, Sept. 17, 1949; children: William R., Daniel B., Ellen C., Michael E. B.B.A., U. Ark., 1948. C.P.A., Ark. Pvt. C.P.A. practice, 1948-58; treas. M. M. Cohn Co., 1958-63; vice chmn. Dillard Dept. Stores, Inc., Little Rock, 1963—, also vice chmn., chief adminstrv. officer.; Chmn. Little Rock br. Fed. Res. Bank of, St. Louis. Served with USAAF, 1943-45; Served with USAF, 1951-52. Mem. Am. Inst. Accts., Nat. Assn. Accts., Sigma Chi, Alpha Kappa Psi. Roman Catholic. Office: 900 W Capitol St Little Rock AR 72201 *

KEMP, EMORY LELAND, educator; b. Chgo., Oct. 1, 1931; s. Emory Lel and Anita (Hucker) K.; m. Janet Karen Dodd, July 26, 1958; children—Mark, Alison, Geoffrey. B.Sc. with high honors, U. Ill., 1952, Ph.D., 1962; M.Sc. in Engring, U. London, 1958; Diploma (Fulbright fellow), Imperial Coll. Sci. and Tech., London, Eng., 1955. Registered profl. engr., W. Va.; chartered civil and structural engr., U.K. Asst. engr. Ill. State Water Survey, Urbana, 1952; asst. engr. research and devel. lab. U.S. Army, Fort Belvoir, Va., 1952-54; structural engr. Sir Bruce White Wolfe Barry & Partners & Ove Arup & Partners, London, 1956-59; fellow and instr. dept. theoretical and applied mechanics U. Ill., Urbana, 1959-62; asso. prof. dept. civil engring. W. Va. U., Morgantown, 1962-66, prof., 1966—, chmn. dept., 1967-74, dir. program for history sci. and tech., 1975. Served with U.S. Army, 1952-54. Fellow Inst. Civil Engrs., Am. Soc. C.E., Am. Concrete Inst.; mem. Inst. Structural Engrs., Soc. Indsl. Archeology, Soc. for History of Tech., Newcomen Soc., Phi Kappa Phi, Tau Beta Pi, Chi Epsilon. Methodist. Home: 429 Riley St Morgantown WV 26505

KEMP, FRANCIS BOLLING, III, banker; b. Greensboro, N.C., Sept. 10, 1940; s. Francis B. and Billie (Stocks) K.; m. Virginia Wadsworth Millner, Aug. 15, 1964; children: Francis Bolling IV, Elizabeth R. A.B. cum laude, Davidson Coll., 1963; M.B.A., Harvard U., 1967. Credit analyst NCNB Nat. Bank of N.C., Charlotte, 1967-68, fin. services officer nat. div., 1968-69, asst. v.p., 1969-71, v.p., 1971-72, sr. v.p., 1972-75, exec. v.p., 1975-83, corp. banking group exec., 1975-77, N.C. banking group exec., 1977—, pres., 1983—; corp. exec. v.p. NCNB Corp., 1983—; dir. VISA, U.S.A., Inc.; Chmn. NCNB Community Devel. Corp., 1978—. Mem. bd. visitors Davidson Coll., 1978-81; trustee N.C. Symphony, 1978—, pres., 1979-80, vice chmn., 1980-81; bd. dirs. Spirit Sq. Performing Arts Center, 1980—, pres., 1982-83; bd. dirs. Charlotte Uptown Devel. Corp., 1981—; pres. Arts and Scis. Council, 1983-84; bd. dirs., exec. com. Arts and Scis. Council of Charlotte-Mecklenburg, Inc.; bd. dirs. Gov.'s Council on Arts and Humanities, 1983—, Univ. Research Park, 1983—; trustee Charlotte Country Day Sch., 1983—. Served to 1st. lt. U.S. Army, 1963-65. Mem. Charlotte C. of C., Robert Morris Assocs., Assn. Res. City Bankers, Phi Beta Kappa, Beta Theta Pi. Republican. Presbyterian. Clubs: Charlotte City, Country of N.C., Quail Hollow Country. Office: One NCNB Plaza Charlotte NC 28255

KEMP, HARRIS ATTERIDGE, architect; b. Kewanee, Ill., July 3, 1912; s. John Edward and Pauline (King) K.; m. Carol Western, Sept. 18, 1937; children: David Anders, Peter Alan, Constance Susan. B.S., U. Ill., 1934, M.S., 1935; M.Arch., Mass. Inst. Tech., 1937. Francis J. Plym fellow in architecture to, Europe, 1937-38; designer Wis. State Architects Office, 1938-40; supr. plant layout dept. N.Am. Aviation Corp., 1940-44; asso., chief designer George L. Dahl—Architects and Engrs., Dallas, 1944-55; partner Harper & Kemp Architects, Dallas, 1955-75, Harper, Kemp, Clutts and Parker, Architecture/Planning, 1975—; Dir. Dallas Central Bus. Dist. Assn., 1968—. Important works include Office, Dallas Municipal Adminstrn. Center, Denton State Sch., Dallas Livestock Coliseum, Gt. Am. of Dallas Bldg., 2355 Stemmons Bldg., Catalogue Order Warehouse, Sears Roebuck & Co., Dallas, Collins Radio Group Hdqrs. Mem. pub. adv. panel GSA, Region 7, 1969-72. Fellow A.I.A. (pres. Dallas chpt. 1957); mem. Tex. Soc. Architects (dir. 1964-67), Phi Delta Theta. Presbyn. (elder). Club: Dallas Country. Lodge: Kiwanis. Home: 5328 Waneta Dr Dallas TX 75209 Office: 1st Internat Bldg Suite 720 Dallas TX 75270

KEMP, J. ROBERT, beef industry consultant, food company executive; b. Seattle, Nov. 4, 1920; s. S.H. and Bertha (Bankhead) K.; m. Mary M. Filer, Sept. 23, 1942; children: Kandace, Kathy, Karen, Kay. B.S. in Agr, U. Idaho, 1943. With Armour and Co., 1946-62, plant mgr., various locations, 1955-62; v.p., gen. plant mgr. Iowa Beef Processors Inc., Fort Dodge, 1962-63, v.p. sales, mem. exec. com., 1963-68, exec. v.p., Dakota City, Nebr., 1968-70, co-chmn. bd., 1970-75; also dir.; pres. Columbia Foods Inc., 1975-78, Northwest Feeders Inc., 1978—. Served with USAAF, 1943-46; PTO. Phi Delta Theta. Clubs: Elks, Kiwanis, Arid. Home: 8 Mesa Vista Dr Boise ID 83705 Office: PO Box 2724 Boise ID 83701

KEMP, JACK F., Congressman; b. Los Angeles, July 13, 1935; m. Joanne Main; children: Jeffrey, Jennifer, Judith, James. B.A., Occidental Coll., 1957; postgrad., Long Beach State U., Calif. Western U. Spl. asst. to gov., Calif., 1969; mem. 92d-98th Congresses from 31st Calif. N.Y., N.Y.; profl. football player for 13 years; pub. relations officer Marine Midland Bank, Buffalo. Mem. Pres.'s Council on Phys. Fitness and Sports. Recipient Disting. Service award N.Y. State Jaycees; Outstanding Citizen award Buffalo Evening News. Mem. Nat. Assn. Broadcasters, Engrs. and Technicians, Buffalo Area C. of C., Sierra Club, Am. Football League Players Assn. (co-founder, pres. 1965-70, exec. com., player pension bd.). Republican. Address: 2252 Rayburn House Office Bldg Washington DC 20515

KEMP, JAMES BRADLEY, JR., lawyer; b. New Orleans, Apr. 10, 1932; s. James Bradley and Honora Arlene (Pickren) K.; m. Marguerite Bradburn Freret, Sept. 6, 1952; children: James, Randolph, Ann, Robert. B.B.A., Tulane U., 1953, J.D., 1958. Bar: La. 1958, U.S. Ct. Customs and Patent Appeals 1969, U.S. Supreme Ct. 1970, U.S. Ct. Internat. Trade 1981, U.S. Ct. Appeals (5th, 7th, 11th cirs.). Internat. admiralty atty. Phelps, Dunbar, Marks, Claverie & Sims, New Orleans, 1958—, ptnr., 1964—; speaker Southeastern Admiralty Law Inst., 1975, bd. govs., 1977—, chmn., 1981; speaker U. New Orleans Maritime Seminar, 1977; mem. met. area com. Bur. Govtl. Research. Solicitor United Fund, New Orleans, 1963-68, Heart Fund, New Orleans, 1975; chancellor Greater New Orleans Fedn. Chs., 1981-83; mem. religious activities policy com. La. World Expn., 1984. Served to 1st lt. U.S. Army, 1953-55. Mem. ABA (chmn. subcom. maritime financing 1983—), Maritime Law Assn. (mem. various coms.), Fed. Bar Assn., La. Bar Assn. (bar admissions com. 1978—), New Orleans Bar Assn., Internat. Bar Assn., Marine Tech. Soc. (com. marine law and policy 1979—), Def. Research Inst., Propeller Club U.S., Internat. House, New Orleans Def. Counsel Assn., La. Def. Counsel Assn., Fgn. Relations Assn. New Orleans, Average Adjusters Assn., Phi Delta Phi. Republican. Presbyterian. Clubs: So. Yacht, Plimsoll, Whitehall, Bienville, City, Mariners of the Port New Orleans, U.S. Yacht Racing Union. Home: 241 Bellaire Dr New Orleans LA 70124 Office: Phelps Dunbar Marks Claverie & Sims 1300 Hibernia Bank Bldg 313 Carondelet St New Orleans LA 70112

KEMP, JOHN DANIEL, biochemist, educator; b. Mpls., Jan. 20, 1940; s. Dean Dudly and Catherine Georgie (Treleven) K.; m. Sharon Margaret Kvalheim, May 3, 1975 (div. 1984); children: Todd, Cristine, Laura. B.A. in chemistry, UCLA, 1962, Ph.D, 1965. NIH postdoctoral fellow U. Wash., Seattle, 1965-68; mem. faculty U. Wis., Madison, 1968—; prof. plant pathology U. Wash., Madison; head microbiology Agrigenetics Corp., Madison. Author papers on plant molecular genetics. Grantee NSF, Dept. Agr. Mem. Sigma Xi. Office: Dept Plant Pathology U Wis Madison WI 53706 Office: Agrigenetics Corp 5649 E Buckeye Rd Madison WI 53716

KEMP, PATRICK SAMUEL, accountant, educator; b. Galveston, Tex., Aug. 2, 1932; s. Samuel Herbert and Florence (Moor) K.; m. Carol Margaret Boren, Aug. 22, 1959; children—Robert Wade, Cathleen Anne. B.A., Rice U., 1953; M.P.A., U. Tex., 1956; Ph.D., U. Ill., 1959. Staff accountant Arthur Young & Co., Houston, 1954-55; instr. U. Ill., Urbana, 1956-59; asst. prof. acctg. Emory U., 1959-61, asso. prof., 1961-62, U. Richmond, 1962-65, prof., 1965-68, Va. Poly. Inst. and State U., 1968-74; prof., chmn. dept. acctg. Oreg. State U., 1974—. Author: Accounting For The Manager, 1970. Mem. Am. Acctg. Assn., Am. Inst. C.P.A.'s, Nat. Assn. Accountants, Oreg. Soc. C.P.A.'s (instr. continuing profl. edn. program), Alpha Kappa Psi, Beta Alpha Psi, Beta Gamma Sigma. Office: Sch Bus Oreg State U Corvallis OR 97331

KEMP, ROBERT, banker; b. Jamaica, N.Y., Nov. 15, 1936; s. Robert and Ada Kathleen (Freeman) K.; m. Margaret Charlotte Brown, June 13, 1964; children—Victoria Alexandra, Alicia Kathleen. Certificate, Am. Inst. Banking, 1959; B.S. cum laude, N.Y. U., 1964; grad. student, Queens Coll., 1970-75. With Jamaica Savs. Bank, 1954—, dep. auditor, 1970-71, auditor, 1971-80, v.p., auditor, 1980—. Mem. Savs. Banks Assn. N.Y. State, Orgn. Am. Historians, Nat. History Soc., Navy Records Soc., Areopagus, Beta Gamma Sigma. Lutheran. Club: Mason. Home: 253-26 87th Dr Bellerose NY 11426 Office: 303 Merrick Rd Lynbrook NY 11564

KEMP, ROBERT GRANT, biochemist; b. Massillon, Ohio, Feb. 12, 1937; s. Arthur Henry and Evelyn Annie (Grant) K.; m. Marilyn Ann Baranowski, Dec. 30, 1967 (div.); children: Suzanne Louise, Kathryn Therese. B.A., Coll. of Wooster, 1959; Ph.D., Yale U., 1964. Research assoc. U. Wash., Seattle, 1964-66; asst. prof. Med. Coll. of Wis., Milw., 1966-70, assoc. prof., 1970-75, prof., 1975-76; prof., chmn. dept. U. Health Scis./Chgo. Med. Sch., North Chicago, Ill., 1976—; investigator Am. Heart Assn., 1968-73. Co-author: Biochemical Problems and Calculations, 1975; contbr. articles in field to profl. jours. NIH predoctoral fellow, 1960-63; Wash. State heart fellow, 1965-66; Fulbright fellow, Valdivia, Chile, 1971. Mem. Am. Chem. Soc., Am. Soc. Biol. Chemists, AAAS. Home: 828 Lavergne Wilmette IL 60091 Office: 3333 Green Bay Rd North Chicago IL 60064

KEMP, WALTER HORACE, III, mag. pub., poet; b. Greenfield, Mass., Aug. 10, 1925; s. Howard M. and Mary Louise (West) K.; m. Marilyn Jean Hanback, Dec. 20, 1957 (div.); children—Mary Louise, William Bradley MacLaren, Karolyn Kirsten; children by previous marriage—Kerry Britten, John Robert Owen. B.S., Northwestern U., 1949. Writer-editor Armour Research Found., Chgo., 1950; editor A.M.A., Chgo., 1951-52; sales mgr. Am. Family Physician, Kansas City, Mo., 1953-56; mng. editor, 1957-71, pub., 1971—; cons. pharm. industry. Poetry; contributed to, Sat. Eve. Post. Served with AUS, 1943-45. Decorated Purple Heart, Bronze star. Mem. Am. Soc. Assn. Execs., Pharm. Mfg. Assn., Pharm. Advt. Club, Sigma Delta Chi. Club: Kansas City Press. Home: 3506 W 83d St Prairie Village KS 66208 Office: 1740 W 92d St Kansas City MO 64114

KEMPE, LLOYD LUTE, chemical engineering educator; b. Pueblo, Colo., Nov. 26, 1911; s. Henry Edwin and Ida Augusta (Pittelkow) K.; m. Barbara Jean Bell, June 27, 1938; 1 dau., Marion Louise (Mrs. Steven Sanford Palmer). B.S. in Chem. Engring, U. Minn., 1932, M.S., 1938, Ph.D., 1948. Registered profl. engr., Minn., Mich. Research asst. in soils U. Minn., 1934-35, research asso., 1940-41, asst. in chem. engring., 1946-48; asst. san. engr. Minn. Dept. Health, 1935-40; instr. bacteriology U. Mich., Ann Arbor, 1948-49, asst. prof., 1949-50, asst. prof. chem. engring. and bacteriology, 1952-55, asso. prof., 1955-58, prof., 1958-60, prof. chem. engring. and san. engring., 1960-64, prof. chem. engring., 1964-67, prof. chem. engring. and microbiology, 1967—; asst. prof. food tech. U. Ill., 1950-52. Mem. editorial bd.: Biotech. and Bioengring, 1959-70, Applied Microbiology, 1964—, Food Tech, 1967-69, Jour. Food Sci, 1967-69. Mem. adv. com. on food irradiation Am. Inst. Biol. Scis./AEC; adv. com. on microbiology of foods Nat. Acad. Scis./NRC; adv. com. on botulism hazards HEW/FDA; adv. com. on mil. environ. research Nat. Acad. Scis./NRC. Served to col. AUS, 1941-45. Decorated Bronze Star. Mem. Am. Inst. C.E., Am. Chem. Soc., Am. Soc. Microbiology, Inst. Food Technologists, A.A.A.S., Am. Acad. Environ. Engrs., Water Pollution Control Fedn., Soc. Indsl. Microbiology, Sigma Xi, Phi Lambda Upsilon, Tau Beta Pi, Alpha Chi Sigma. Club: Mason. Home: 3020 Exmoor St Ann Arbor MI 48104 Office: Dept Chem Engring U Mich Ann Arbor MI 48104

KEMPER, ALBERT STRAYER, JR., lawyer; b. Port Republic, Va., Mar. 20, 1901. LL.B., U. Va., 1927. Bar: Va. bar 1925, W.Va. bar 1927. Mem. firm Richardson, Kemper & Hancock (and predecessor), Bluefield, W.Va., 1929-50, 70-75, of counsel, 1971—; chmn. bd. Rish Equipment Co., Bluefield; house counsel, officer Tierney Interests, Bluefield, 1950-69. Asso. editor: Va. Law Rev, 1925-26. Mem. W.Va. Commn. Constnl. Revision, 1958-64; mem. adv. bd. W.Va. Dept. Commerce, 1961-68; Chmn. fund dr. ARC, Bluefield, 1950. Mem. Am. Bar Assn., Va. Bar Assn. (hon.), Mercer County Bar Assn. (pres. 1940), W.Va. Bar Assn. (pres. 1947), W.Va. State Bar, Va. State Bar. Office: 602 Law & Commerce Bldg Bluefield WV 24701 *

KEMPER, DAVID WOODS, II, banker; b. Kansas City, Mo., Nov. 20, 1950; s. James Madison and Mildred (Lane) K.; m. Dorothy Ann Jannarone, Sept. 6, 1975; children: John W., Elizabeth C. B.A. cum laude, Harvard U., 1972; M.A. in English Lit., Oxford, Worcester Coll., 1974; M.B.A., Stanford U., 1976. With Morgan Guaranty Trust Co., N.Y.C., 1975-78; v.p. Commerce Bank of Kansas City (Mo.), 1978-79, sr. v.p., 1980-81; pres. Commerce Banchshares, Inc, 1982—; dir. Commerce Bancshares, Inc.; dir. BMA, Kansas City, Mo., 1982. Contbr. articles on banking to profl. jours. Bd. dirs. St. Luke's Hosp., Kansas City, Mo., 1981, Kansas City Trust & Founds., 1982; mem. exec. com. Kansas City Area Econ. Devel. Mem. Assn. Res. City Bankers. Clubs: Kansas City Country; University, River (Kansas City). Office: Commerce Bancshares Inc 720 Main St Kansas City MO 64199

KEMPER, JAMES MADISON, JR., banker; b. Kansas City, Mo., Oct. 10, 1921; s. James M. and Gladys (Grissom) K.; m. Mildred Lane, Mar. 30, 1948; children: Laura Lane, David Woods, Jonathan McBride, Julie Ann. B.A., Yale, 1943. With Commerce Trust Co. (now Commerce Bank of Kansas City), Kansas City, 1946—, asst. cashier, 1946-49, v.p., dir., 1949-55, exec. v.p., 1955, pres., 1955-64, chmn., 1964; chmn. bd., pres. Commerce Bank of Kansas City, 1964-66, chmn. bd., 1966-83, dir., 1983—; chmn., pres. Commerce Bancshares, Inc., Kansas City, Mo., 1966-83, chmn., chief exec. officer, 1983—; pres., chmn. Tower Properties, Inc.; dir. Owens-Corning Fiberglas Corp., Toledo. Trustee Com. Econ. Devel., Washington. Office: Executive Plaza Bldg PO Box 13686 720 Main St Kansas City MO 64199

KEMPER, JAMES SCOTT, JR., insurance company executive; b. Chgo., Apr. 8, 1914; s. James Scott and Mildred (Hooper) K.; m. Joan Hoff, Dec. 27, 1960; children: James Scott III, Linda Kemper White, Stephen H., Judith (Mrs. Harrie Lewis), Robert C. A.B., Yale U., 1935; LL.B., Harvard U., 1938. Bar: N.Y., Ill., Calif. With Antitrust div. Justice Dept.; pvt. practice law, N.Y.C., Chgo., Los Angeles; past pres. Lumbermens Mut. Casualty Co.; now chmn. bd.; past pres. Kemper Corp., Long Grove, Ill. Dir. Am. Mut. Ins. Alliance; trustee The Conf. Bd., Inc.; Bd. dirs. Nat. Council on Alcoholism, Boys Clubs of Am., Chgo. Boys Club, Lyric Opera of Chgo.; pres., trustee J.S. Kemper Found.; trustee Kemper Ednl. and Charitable Fund, Northwestern Meml. Hosp., Chgo., Ill., Inst. Tech.; mem. adv. com. Drug Abuse and Alcoholism Program of Citizens Conf. on State Legislatures; mem. adv. bd. Chgo. Met. Council on Alcoholism, Inc. Served to lt. comdr. USNR, World War II. Recipient award Freedoms Found., at Valley Forge, 1968, Alpha Kappa Psi Found. award for distinguished service to higher edn., 1973, William H. Spurgeon award Nat. Exploring Div., Boy Scouts Am., 1973, Coll. of Humanities award, 1973, Gold Key award Nat. Council on Alcoholism, 1974. Mem. Econ. Club of Chgo., Alpha Sigma Phi. Clubs: Chicago, Glen View; Bohemian (San Francisco); Pauma Valley Country; Ironwood Country (Palm Desert, Calif.). *

KEMPER, JOHN DUSTIN, mechanical engineering educator; b. Portland, Oreg., May 29, 1924; s. Clay Wallace and Leona Bell (Landis) K.; m. Barbara Jeanne Lane, June 28, 1947; 1 dau., Kathleen Lynne. B.S., UCLA, 1949, M.S., 1959; Ph.D., U. Colo., 1969. Chief mech. engr. Telecomputing Corp., North Hollywood, Calif., 1949-55, H.A. Wagner Co., Van Nuys, Calif., 1955-56; v.p. engring. Marchant div. SCM Corp., Oakland, Calif., 1956-62; faculty U. Calif., Davis, 1962—, prof. engring., 1967—, dean coll. Engring., 1969-83. Author: The Engineer and His Profession, 1967, 2d edit., 1975, 3d edit., 1982. Served with USAF, 1944-46. Fellow ASME (chmn. San Francisco sect. 1962-63), AAAS; mem. Am. Soc. Engring. Edn., Nat. Soc. Profl. Engrs. Office: Dept Mech Engring U Calif Davis CA 95616

KEMPER, RUFUS CROSBY, JR., banker; b. Kansas City, Mo., Feb. 22, 1927; s. Rufus Crosby and Enid (Jackson) K.; m. Mary Barton Stripp; children: Rufus Crosby III, Pamela Warrick Gabrovsky, Sheila Kemper Dietrich, John Mariner, Mary Barton; stepchildren—Alexander Charles McPherson, Heather Christian McPherson. Grad., Phillips Acad., Andover, Mass., 1942; student, U. Mo.; LL.D. (hon.), William Jewel Coll., Westminster Coll. Chmn., chief exec. officer, dir. United Mo. Bancshares, Inc., Kansas City, Mo., United Mo. Bank of Kansas City N.A., Mo.; dir. City Bank and Trust Co., Kansas City, Mo.; pres., dir. Kemper Realty Co., Kansas City, Mo., Pioneer Service Corp.; v.p., dir. Kemper Investment Co., Kansas City; adv. dir. United Mo. Bank of Brookfield, Boonville, Overland Park Bancshares, Inc., Kans., Overland Park Bank and Trust Co.; dir. United Mo. Bank of St. Joseph; chmn. bd., dir. City Bancshares, Inc., Kansas City, Mo.; dir United Kans. Bancshares, Inc., City Nat. Bank, Atchison, Kans., Chgo. Title Ins. Co., Kansas City, Mo., United Mo. Mortgage Co., Commonwealth Theatres, Inc., Kansas City So. Industries, Mo.; mem. mfrs. adv. bd. Lumbermen's Mut. Ins. Co., Chgo. Mem. adv. com. Research Med. Center; trustee Freedom's Found. Valley Forge, Kansas City Art Inst.; hon. trustee YWCA.; bd. dirs. Kansas City Indsl. Found., Heart of Am.; council Boy Scouts Am., Kansas City Hist. Found., Heart of Am. United Way, Mid-Am. Arts Alliance, Starlight Theatre; hon. bd. dirs. Albrecht Art Mus., St. Joseph, Mo.; mem. nat. com. Whitney Mus. Am. Art, N.Y.C.; commr. Nat. Mus. Am. Art, Washington. Served with USNR, World War II. Recipient Key Man Kansas City Jr. C. of C., 1952, Distinguished Service, 1964; Man of Yr. award Kansas City Press Club, 1974; Outstanding Kansas Citian award Native Sons Kansas City, 1975, 82; 1st Advocacy award Mid-Continent Ind. Small Bus. Assn., 1980; named Banker Advocate of Yr. SBA, 1981; recipient Lester Milgram Humanitarian award, 1982, Man of Yr. award Downtown, Inc., 1982, Pirouette award Kansas City Ballet Guild and Kansas City Tomorrow Alumni Assn., 1983. Mem. Beta Theta Pi (Man of Yr. 1974). Republican. Episcopalian. Clubs: River, Carriage, Kansas City Country, Kansas City, 1021, Mo., Stage Harbor Yacht, Chathan, Mass. Home: 9975 W 179th St Bucyrus KS 66013 Office: United Mo Bank of Kansas City 10th and Grand Ave Kansas City MO 64141

KEMPER, VICTOR JAY, cinematographer; b. Newark, Apr. 14, 1927; s. Louis and Florence K.; m. Claire Kellermann, May 24, 1953; children: Jan, Steven, Florence. B.S., Seton Hall U. Engr., TV Channel 13, Newark, 1949-54; tech. supr. E.U.E. Screen Gems, N.Y.C., 1954-56; v.p. engring. Gen. TV Network, N.Y.C., 1956-57; pres. V.J.K. Prodns., Hollywood, Calif. Latest films include Slapshot, 1977, Coma, 1978, And Justice for All, 1979, The Jerk, 1979, The Final Countdown, 1980, Xanadu, 1980. Served with USN, 1944-45. Mem. Am. Soc. Cinematographers, Acad. Motion Pictures Arts and Scis. Office: 10313 W Pico Blvd Los Angeles CA 90064

KEMPF, CECIL JOSEPH, naval officer; b. Maud, Okla., Nov. 20, 1927; s. John Joseph and Sylvia Lorene (Moody) K.; m. Theodosia Ann Suman, Dec. 20, 1950; children: Charles John, David Fuller, Suzanne Ellen. B.S., U.S. Naval Acad., 1950, Naval Postgrad. Sch., 1956; M.S., Mass. Inst. Tech., 1957. Commd. ensign U.S. Navy, 1950, advanced through grades to rear adm., 1976, designated naval aviator, 1951; comdg. officer U.S.S. Dubuque, 1972-74, U.S.S. Tripoli, 1974-75; dep. mgr. anti-submarine warfare systems project Naval Material Command, 1975-76; comdr. anti-submarine warfare wing U.S. Pacific Fleet, 1976-78; dir. aviation programs div. Office Chief Naval Ops., 1978-79; vice comdr. Naval Air Systems Command, 1979-81; asst. dep. chief naval ops. for air warfare Navy Dept., Washington, 1981-81, dir. Naval Res., Office Chief of Naval Ops., 1983—. Mem. Naval Acad. Alumni Assn., Assn. Naval Aviation. Episcopalian. Home: 88 Westover Ave Bolling AFB Washington DC 20336 Office: Dir Naval Res Office Chief Naval Ops Navy Dept Washington DC 20350

KEMPF, PAUL STUART, optics company executive; b. Dubuque, Iowa, Apr. 25, 1918; s. Fred Ferdinand and Vera Content (Smith) K.; m. Dorothea Ruth Guenther, Dec. 16, 1943 (div. June 1966); 1 son, Karlton Guenther; m. Pilar M. Moreno, Dec. 1967; children: Karlos Alberto, Karla Pilar. Student, Iowa State Coll., 1936-37; B.A. cum laude, U. Iowa, 1941; M.B.A. with distinction, Harvard U., 1947. Asst. to mgr. indsl. relations Inland Steel Co., 1947-51; mgr. indsl. relations Inland Steel Products Co., 1951-54; dir. indsl. relations Pacific Mercury Electronics, 1954-56, Hoffman Electronics, 1956-57; v.p. personnel and indsl. relations Crane Co., 1957-59; dir. corp. indsl. relations Hughes Aircraft Co., 1959-64; pres. Western Optics, Inc., 1964-72, Metron Optics Inc., 1972—, Metron Marker Co., 1977—; instr. U. Calif. at, Los Angeles, 1957. Served to lt. USNR, 1942-45. Recipient award for unusual and valuable contbn. to personnel adminstrn. Los Angeles Mchts. and Mfrs. Assn., 1956. Mem. Am. Chem. Soc., Soc. Photo-optical Instrumentation Engrs., Harvard Bus. Sch. Assn., Phi Beta Kappa, Theta Xi. Republican. Methodist. Office: PO Box 690 Solana Beach CA 92075

KEMPFER, HOMER, association executive; b. Prairie Home, Mo., Mar. 9, 1911; s. John and Anna (Hertzig) K.; m. Helen Friend Allion, Dec. 31, 1955; children—Margaret Deane, Norma Bernadine. B.S. in Edn, Central Mo. State Coll., 1933, M.A., U. Mo., 1935; Ed.D., Tchrs. Coll., Columbia U., 1941. Tchr., prin., supt. various pub. schs. in, Mo., 1929-40; supr. adult edn. N.Y. State Dept. Edn., Buffalo, 1941-47; specialist gen. adult and post-high sch. edn. U.S. Office Edn., Washington, 1947-52; exec. dir. Nat. Home Study Council, Washington, 1952-58; with AID, New Delhi, India and, Washington, 1958-66; exec. dir. Nat. Assn. Trade and Tech. Schs., Washington, 1965-66; dir. literacy div., dep. dir. Dept. Adult Edn. and Youth Activities, UNESCO, Paris, 1966-67; dir. U.S. Armed Forces Inst., Madison, Wis., 1967-69; mem. accrediting commn. Nat. Assn. Trade and Tech. Schs., Washington, 1967-76; dir. Inst. Ind. Study, various locations, 1969—, Cosmetology Accrediting Commn., 1969-70, Reston Area Office, Va. Poly. Inst. and State U. Profs. Edn., 1970-72; cons. accreditation Am. Assn. Med. Assts., 1971-76; cons. Adminstrn. Aging, Dept. HEW, Washington, 1972-73; exec. dir. Capital Area Gy. Aging, Richmond, Va., 1974, Council Noncollegiate Continuing Edn., 1974—. Author: Adult Education, 1955, The Growing Edge, 1976—, Adult Education Ideas, 1948-52. Recipient Margaret Hoe fellowship, 1940-41; Disting. Service award Nat. Home Study Council, 1958. Mem. NEA (life), Indian Adult Edn. Assn. (life), Am. Soc. Tng. and Devel., Am. Soc. Assn. Execs. Home: 1609 Westover Hills Blvd Richmond VA 23225 *I sought adventure and found it.*

KEMPH, JOHN PATTERSON, physician; b. Lima, Ohio, Dec. 17, 1919; s. Emil and Nell (Patterson) K.; m. Kytja K.S. Voeller, July 13, 1975; children: Patricia, Judith, Jeffrey, Bonnie. A.B., Ohio No. U., 1947; B.Sc., Ohio State U., 1947, M.Sc., 1948, M.D., 1953. Research fellow dept. physiology Ohio State U., 1948-51, research asso., 1951-55; intern Mt. Carmel Hosp., Columbus, Ohio, 1953-54; resident Columbus State Hosp., 1954-55, U. Mich. Med. Center, 1955-57, 60-61; practice medicine, specializing in psychiatry, Ann Arbor, Mich., 1962-64, Bklyn., 1968-72, Toledo, 1972—; instr. dept. psychiatry U. Mich. Med. Center, 1960-62, asst. prof., asso. prof., 1960-68; prof., dir. div. psychiatry SUNY at, Buffalo, 1968-72; prof., chmn. dept. psychiatry Med. Coll. Ohio, Toledo, 1972-74; v.p. acad. affairs, dean Med. Faculty, 1974—; cons. VA Hosp., Ann Arbor, 1960-68, Peace Corps, 1964-66; mem. Liaison Com. on Med. Edn., 1975-81. Contbr. articles to sci. jours. Served with AUS, 1942-46. Research and tng. grantee NIH, 1973-79, NIMH, 1968-72. Fellow Am. Psychiat. Assn., Am. Acad. Child Psychiatry (editorial bd. Jour.), Am. Orthopsychiat. Assn., Am. Coll. Psychiatrists; mem. AMA, Am. Group Psychotherapy Assn., Am. Assn. Mental Deficiency, Am. Psychosomatic Soc., N.Y. Council on Child Psychiatry, Soc. Profs. Child Psychiatry, Am. Assn. Chmn. Depts. Psychiatry, Am. Assn. Med. Colls. (council of deans), Sigma Xi, Nu Sigma Nu. Methodist. Office: Med Coll Ohio Caller Service No 10008 Toledo OH 43699

KEMPLE, JOSEPH NEPHI, leasing and transportation company executive; b. Ontario, Calif., Mar. 14, 1921; s. William H. and Eva (Kaminar) K.; m. Roberta Williams, June 17, 1945; children—Kathleen, Steven. B.S. in Engring, Stanford U., 1948. With Columbia-Geneva div. (now Western operations) U.S. Steel Corp., San Francisco, 1947-57, product mgr., 1952-57; with Page Steel & Wire div. Am. Chain & Cable Co., Inc., Monessen, Pa., 57-62, gen. mgr., 1959-62; exec. v.p. Warner Co., Phila., 1962-63; pres. Guiberson div. Dresser Industries, Inc., Dallas, 1963-66; exec. v.p. mktg. Dresser Oil Tool div., Dallas, 1966-68; pres., dir. Marion Power Shovel Co., Inc., 1968-73; pres. Flexible Co., Loudonville, Ohio, 1973-75; pres., dir. Scope Leasing, Inc., Columbus, Ohio, 1975—; dir. Richland Trust Co., Mansfield, Ohio, Fahey Bank, Marion., Ohio. Mem. Tau Beta Pi. Home: 8005 Wood Ln Worthington OH 43085 Office: Scope Leasing Inc 150 E Wilson Bridge Rd Columbus OH 43085

KEMPNER, ISAAC HERBERT, III, sugar company executive; b. Houston, Aug. 28, 1932; s. Isaac Herbert and Mary (Carroll) K.; m. Helen Hill, July 1, 1967. Grad., Choate Sch., 1951; B.A., Stanford U., 1955, M.B.A., 1959. Asst. v.p. Tex. Nat. Bank, Houston, 1959-64; v.p., sec.-treas., mgr. raw sugar Imperial Sugar Co., Sugarland, Tex., 1964-71, chmn. bd., 1971—; dir. Capital Bank, Houston, Merc. Tex. Corp.; chmn. bd. SLT Communication Inc.; pres. Foster Farms Inc. Trustee H. Kempner Trust Assn., Meth. Hosp., Houston, Houston Arts Commn., Houston Ballet Found. Served to 1st lt. USMCR, 1955-57. Mem. U.S. Cane Sugar Refiners Assn. (chmn.), Sugar Club (pres. 1978-79). Clubs: Tejas, Bayou, Houston Country (Houston); Camden Ale and Quail (Camden, Tex.). Office: PO Box 9 Sugarland TX 77478

KEMPNER, JACK JULIAN, educator; b. Ridgefield Park, N.J., Jan. 5, 1917; s. Emanuel and Sylvia (Wald) K.; m. Marjorie H. Vale, Sept. 17, 1941; children—Kenneth, Roger, Clifford. B.S., N.Y.U., 1947; M.S., U. Colo., 1953; Ph.D., Ohio State U., 1956. C.P.A., Mont. Chief accountant, office mgr. Columbia Lithographing Corp., N.Y.C., 1939-41; asst. prof. naval sci. Columbia, 1944-45; asso. prof. accounting Cal. Western U., San Diego, 1947-51; asst. prof. naval sci. U. Colo., 1951-53; grad. instr. accounting Ohio State U., 1953-56; prof. Sch. Bus. Adminstr., U. Mont., Missoula, 1956-81, prof. emeritus, 1981—, also chmn. dept. acctg.; vis. prof. Mich. State U. at, São Paulo, Brazil, 1962-64; pvt. practice auditor, tax adviser. Contbr. articles to profl. jours. Treas., bd. dirs. Missoula Crippled Childrens Assn. Served to comdr. USNR, 1941-46. Named CPA of Year, Mont., 1970. Mem. Am. Inst. C.P.A.'s, Mont. Soc. C.P.A.'s (past pres.), Am. Accounting Assn. (Outstanding Educator of Year 1976), Nat. Assn. Accountants, Beta Gamma Sigma, Alpha Kappa Psi, Beta Alpha Psi. Presbyterian (elder). Clubs: Rotarian, Elk. Home: 440 King St Missoula MT 59801

KEMPNER, JOSEPH, engineering educator; b. Bklyn., Apr. 25, 1923; s. Arthur and Anna (Richman) K.; m. Carol F. Brown, Jan. 12, 1947; children—Robert M., Marien A. B.Aero. Engring. summa cum laude, Poly. Inst. Bklyn., 1943, M.Aero. Engring., 1947, Ph.D. in Applied Mechanics, 1950. Registered profl. engr., N.Y. Research fellow Poly. Inst. Bklyn., 1944, mem. faculty, 1947—, prof. applied mechanics and aerospace engring., 1957—, chmn. undergrad. aerospace studies, asst. dir. research, 1962-63, dir. applied mechanics, 1964-76, head dept., 1966-76; aero. engr. NASA, 1944-47; cons. indsl. and govt. research labs. Mem. adv. group II, ship structural design procedure and analysis, ship research com. Maritime Transp. Research Bd., Nat. Acad. Scis.-NRC; also mem. com. basic research, adv. to Army Research Office, 1973-76, 81—; prin. investigator research contracts Office Naval Research and Air Force Office Sci. Research. Contbr. articles to profl. jours. Recipient citation distinguished research Poly. chpt. Sigma Xi, 1973; named Outstanding Educator Am., 1973, 74-75. Fellow N.Y. Acad. Scis. (I.B. Laskowitz Gold medal 1973), Am. Acad. Mechanics; asso. fellow Am. Inst. Aeros. and Astronautics; mem. ASME, Am. Soc. Engring. Edn., Sigma Xi, Tau Beta Pi, Sigma Gamma Tau. Home: 1163 E 13th St Brooklyn NY 11230 Office: 333 Jay St Brooklyn NY 11201

KEMPNER, MAXIMILIAN WALTER, lawyer; b. Berlin, Feb. 27, 1929; U.S., 1939; s. Paul H. and Marga Marie (von Mendelssohn) K.; m. Barbara Paige Mooney, July 5, 1952; children—Paul C., Elizabeth Daphne, Emily M. B.A., Harvard U., 1951, LL.B., 1954; LL.M., Columbia U., 1957. Bar: N.Y. bar 1954. With firm Webster & Sheffield, N.Y.C., 1957—, partner, 1963—; lectr. law Columbia U. Law Sch.; co-chmn. Lawyers Com. for Civil Rights Under Law; mem. exec. com. Joint Conf. on Legal Edn., in State of N.Y.; mem. vis. com. Columbia U. Law Sch. Dir. Council on Library Resources, Inc., The John & Mary R. Markle Found., Am. Council on Germany. Served with U.S. Army, 1954-56. Mem. Am. Law Inst., Am. Bar Assn. (chmn. sect. of legal edn. and admissions to bar), Assn. Bar City N.Y., N.Y. State Bar Assn., Council Fgn. Relations, Inc. Presbyterian. Clubs: Century Assn., Harvard of N.Y.C. Office: 1 Rockefeller Plaza New York NY 10020

KEMPNER, ROBERT MAX WASILII, lawyer, political scientist; b. Freiburg, Germany, Oct. 17, 1899; came to U.S., 1939; s. Walter K. and Lydia (Rabinowitsch) K.; m. Ruth Lydia Hahn (Benedicta Maria); children: Lucian Walter, André Franklin. Student of law, polit. sci., pub. adminstrn., criminology, univs. of Berlin, Breslau, Freiburg (Germany), U. Pa. Asst. to state atty., Berlin, 1926, judge municipal ct., 1927, superior govt. counselor; Ministry of Interior, Berlin, judge civil service tribunal, 1928-33; lectr. German Acad. Politics Sch. Social Work, Police Inst., Berlin, 1926-33; counselor internat. law and migration problems, 1934-35; Pres. and prof. polit. sci. Fiorenza Coll., Florence, Italy, and Nice, France, 1936-39; research asso. and asst. Inst. Local and State Govt., U. Pa. (research on machinery of European dictatorships under Carnegie and Carl Schurz grants), 1939-42; expert to Fed. courts, espionage and fgn. agt. trials; expert cons. Dept. Justice, OSS and to sec. of War on legal, polit., police and intelligence techniques of European dictatorships and fgn. orgns. in, U.S., 1942-45; U.S. staff prosecutor in Nuremberg trials against Goering, Frick et al; research dir. U.S. prosecution, 1945-46; dep. U.S. chief of counsel for war crimes, chief prosecutor of German Reich cabinet mems., state secs. and diplomats Nuremberg investigation of Holocaust, 1946-49; expert cons. in internat. law; atty. indemnification matters and prosecution of war criminals, 1951—; cons. Reichstag fire trial, 1960; cons. to Israel Govt. in Eichmann case, 1961; vis. prof. U. Erlangen; prof. (hon.) U. Berlin; lectr. schs., colls., univs. and pvt. orgns. Author several books, primarily on Germany, 1931—, The Judgment in The Wilhelmstrassen Case, 1950, German Police Administration, 1953, Eichmann and Accomplices, 1961, SS Under Crossexamination, 1964, 80, The Warren Report in German Language, 1964, Edith Stein and Anne Frank-Two of Hundred thousand, 1968, The Third Reich under Crossexamination, 1969, The Murder of 35,000 Berlin Jews, 1971, American Courts in Germany; Memoirs, 1983; Contbr. to profl. jours. Decorated German Grand Cross of Merit with star, Cross of Polonia Restituta.; Recipient medal Charles U., Prague, Carl von Ossietzky medal, Wilhelm Leuschner medal. Fellow U. Jerusalem.; Mem. Am. Polit. Sci. Assn., Am. Soc. for Internat. Law, German Bar. Home: 112 Lansdowne Ct Lansdowne PA 19050 *All out for justice!*

KEMPNER, WALTER, physician; b. Berlin, Germany, Jan. 25, 1903; came to U.S., 1934, naturalized, 1941; s. Walter and Lydia (Rabinowitsch) K. M.D., U. Heidelberg, Germany, 1926. Intern medicine U. Heidelberg, 1926-27; research asst. and asso. to Dr. Otto Warburg, Kaiser Wilhelm Inst. for Cellular Physiology, 1927-28, 33-34; asst. physician dept. medicine Berlin U. Sch. Medicine, 1928-33; with Duke Sch. Medicine, 1934—, asso., then asst. prof., asso. prof., 1934-51, prof., 1952-72, prof. emeritus, 1972—. Contbr. articles to profl. jours. Trustee Walter Kempner Found. Recipient Ciba award Am. Heart Assn., 1975. Fellow A.C.P.; mem. Am. Physiol. Soc., A.M.A. Originator rice diet in treatment hypertensive and arteriosclerotic vascular disease, heart and kidney disease, vascular retinopathy, diabetes mellitus and obesity. Office: Duke U Med Center Durham NC 27710

KEMPSTER, NORMAN ROY, journalist; b. Sacramento, Jan. 4, 1936; s. Roy Dixon and Viola Alice (Cox) K.; m. Jane Leon, June 30, 1957; children: Jill Suzanne, David Norman. B.A., Calif. State U., 1957. Reporter U.P.I., 1957-73, Washington Star-News, 1973-76; Reporter Washington Bur. Los Angeles Times, 1976-80, Reporter Jerusalem Bur., 1981—; Joe Alex Morris meml. lectr. Harvard U., 1983. Served with AUS, 1959-61. Profl. Journalism fellow, 1967; recipient Gerald Loeb award for disting. journalism, 1980. Mem. Fgn. Press Assn. in Israel (v.p. 1982-83), White House Corrs. Assn. (dir. 1974-75). Episcopalian. Club: Washington Press. Home and office: 3 Diskin Apt 21 Jerusalem Israel

KEMPTER, CHARLES PRENTISS, chemist, materials scientist; b. Burlington, Vt., Feb. 12, 1925; s. Rudolph Harbison and Marjorie A. (Prentiss) K.; m. Anke Margreeth Smit, Apr. 10, 1953 (div.); children—Colin, Eric, Reid; m. Judith Anne Hardison, Aug. 16, 1977. Student, U. Vt., 1942-43, 46-48, U. N.H., 1943-44; B.S., Stanford U., 1949, M.S., 1950, Ph.D., 1956. Cert. profl. chemist. Teaching asst. phys. scis. Stanford U., 1949-50; Owens-Ill. research fellow chem. dept. Stanford, 1953-56; physiochemist research and devel. Dow Chem. Co., Pittsburg, Calif., 1950-53; staff mem. nuclear propulsion div. Los Alamos Sci. Lab., U. Calif. at Los Alamos, 1956-63, 64-71; participant Kiwi-A test, Project Rover, 1958-59, sci. cons., 1971-73; tech. dir. Kempter-Rossman Internat., Washington, 1973-75, sci. advisor, 1975—; thesis adviser Los Alamos Grad. Center, U. N.Mex., 1959-71; adviser N.Mex. State Crime Lab., 1971-73; vis. scientist Inst. Phys. Chemistry, U. Vienna, Austria, 1963-64. Contbr. numerous articles on solid state sci. and high temperature materials in sci. to profl. publs.; contbg. author: Plutonium, 1960. Served with AUS, 1943-46; ETO; res. col., 1971—. Recipient Scroll of Honor U.S.

Holocaust Meml. Council, 1981. Life fellow, hon. fellow Am. Inst. Chemists (adviser to pres. 1969-72, mem. new activities com. 1962-64, nat. membership com. 1962-68, hon. membership com. 1969-71, long range planning com. 1971-72); mem. Internationale Planseegesellschaft für Pulvermetallurgie, N.Mex. Inst. Chemists (councillor 1969-72), Am. Chem. Soc., AAAS, Union Concerned Scientists, Res. Officers Assn., Sigma Xi, Sigma Phi. Clubs: Stanford of San Diego., Admiral Kidd. Patentee in field.

KEMPTON, GEORGE ROGER, manufacturing and transportation company executive; b. N.Y.C., Jan. 21, 1934; s. Thomas John and Gertrude I. (Dempster) K.; m. Joyce H. Graichen, Aug. 1954; children: Terry, Laurie. B.A., Andrews U., 1955. With Clark Equipment Co., Jackson, Mich., 1955-78, v.p. sales, 1971-73, v.p., gen. mgr., 1973-78; pres., chief operating officer Kysor Indsl. Corp., Cadillac, Mich., 1978—, dir., bd. dirs. Mem. Soc. Automotive Engrs., Farm and Indsl. Equipment Inst., Jackson C. of C. (bd. dirs. 1974-78). Home: 1126 Sunnyside St Cadillac MI 49601 Office: One Madison St Cadillac MI 49601

KEMPTON, JAMES MURRAY, journalist; b. Balt., Dec. 16, 1918; s. James Branson and Sally (Ambler) K.; m. Mina Bluethenthal, June 11, 1942; children: Sally Ambler, James Murray (dec.), Arthur Herbert, David Llewellyn; m. 2d Beverly Gary; 1 son Christopher. B.A., Johns Hopkins U., 1939. Publicity dir. Am. Labor Party, 1941-42; reporter N.Y. Post, 1942-43, asst. to labor columnist, 1947-49, labor columnist, 1959-63; reporter Wilmington Morning Star, N.C., 1946-47; editor New Republic, 1963-64; columnist N.Y. World Telegram, 1964-66, N.Y. Post, 1966-69, N.Y. Rev. Books, 1969-71; commentator CBS, 1970-77; fellow Adlai Stevenson Inst., 1972-73; columnist N.Y. Post, 1977-81, Newsday, N.Y.C., 1981—. Author: Part of Our Time, 1955, America Comes of Middle Age, 1962, The Briar Patch, 1973. Del. Democratic nat. conv., 1968. Served as cpl. U.S. Army, 1943-45; PTO. Recipient Sydney Hillman Found. award for reporting, 1950, Page Oneaward Newspaper Guild, 1958, 60, 82, George Polk Meml. award, 1966, Nat. Book award for contemporary affairs, 1973, Acad.-Inst. award Am. Acad. and Inst. Arts and Letters, 1978. Office: Newsday 1500 Broadway New York NY 10036

KEMSLEY, WILLIAM GEORGE, JR., publisher; b. Detroit, Apr. 11, 1928; s. William G. and Verna (Smith) K.; m. Marcella Bennis Myers, Sept. 10, 1966; children: Diane Amelia (from previous marriage), Molly O., Katie, William George, Andrew, Maggie. Student, Columbia U., 1948-49, Wayne State U., 1949-52; B.A., Charter Oak Coll., 1984. Adminstrv. dir. Archives of Am. Art, Detroit, 1958-60; freelance writer, cons., 1961-64; asst. to pres. Detroit Bolt & Nut Co., 1960-61; exec. v.p. Corp. Ann. Reports, Inc., N.Y.C., 1964-68; propr. WKA Corp. Graphics, N.Y.C., 1968-79; exec. editor, pub. Backpacker mag., 1972-80; pres. Foot Trails Publs., Inc., Greenwich, Conn., 1980—; treas., ptnr. AMG Energy, Inc., Hackensack, N.J., 1983—. Contbr. articles on travel and sports to mags. and newspapers. Served with USNR, 1945-46. Mem. Explorers Club, Sierra Club, Nat. Audubon Soc., Appalachian Mountain Club, Am. Hiking Soc. (founder). Episcopalian. Home: Bedford Rd Greenwich CT 06830 Office: 100 W Franklin St Hackensack NJ 06701

KENDALL, GEORGE PRESTON, insurance company executive; b. Seattle, Aug. 11, 1909; s. George R. and Edna (Woods) K.; m. Helen A. Hilliard, Sept. 30, 1933; children—Goerge Preston, Thomas C., Helen R. B.S., U. Ill., 1931. With Washington Nat. Ins. Co., Evanston, Ill., 1931-75, sec., 1950-56, exec. v.p., 1956-68, dir., 1948—, pres., 1962-67, chmn. bd., chief exec. officer, 1968-75; chmn. bd., dir. Washington Nat. Corp., 1968-82. Dir. State Nat. Bank Evanston.; Bd. dirs. Evanston Hosp. Corp., 1975—. Served from 2d lt. to 1st lt., inf. AUS, 1942-45. Decorated Purple Heart. Mem. Theta Chi. Clubs: Mason (K.T., Shriner), Univ. (Evanston); Westmoreland Country (Wilmette); Bankers (Chgo.). Office: 1630 Chicago Ave Evanston IL 60201

KENDALL, GLEN RICHARD, computer software corporation executive; b. Grand Junction, Colo., Jan. 13, 1942; s. Richard S. and Maydell (Hallar) K.; m. Belinda Burwell Laird, Dec. 12, 1975; 1 stepdau., Virginia Lynn Osborn. A.B., Dartmouth Coll., 1964, M.B.A. with high distinction, 1971. Spl. asst. to Sec. of Interior, Washington, 1971-72; dir. policy planning EPA, Washington, 1972-74; v.p. Energy Resources Co., Cambridge, Mass., 1974-75; founder, pres. Kendall Assos. (also Terradata), San Francisco, 1975—; founder Terrascis., 1982. Served with U.S. Army, 1964-69; Vietnam. Mem. Econ. Roundtable Calif. (pres. 1979), Amos Tuck Alumni Assn. No. Calif. (pres.). Office: 609 Mission 400 San Francisco CA 94105

KENDALL, JOHN PLIMPTON, business executive; b. Boston, June 26, 1928; s. Henry Plimpton and Evelyn (Way) K.; m. Nancy Nichols Feick, Oct. 8, 1955; children: Andrew Way, Sarah Louise, David Feick. Grad., Amherst Coll., 1951, LL.D., 1976; M.B.A., Harvard U., 1953; LL.D., Washington and Jefferson Coll., 1971. With Kendall Co., Boston, 1956—, mgr. European operations, 1966-68, v.p., 1968-70, chmn. bd., 1970-72, also dir.; pres. Faneuil Hall Assos., Inc., Boston, 1973—; dir. Nat. Shawmut Bank, Boston, Colgate-Palmolive Co. Pres. Henry P. Kendall Found.; chmn. bd. trustees Hampshire Coll., Amherst, Mass., 1974-80, trustee, 1980-82; trustee Boston U., Dexter Sch., Brookline, Mass., Kendall Whaling Museum, Marine Biol. Lab.; pres. Franklin Found., 1974-80, mem., 1980—. Served with USNR, 1946-47; USMCR, 1953-55. Home: 29 Water St Marion MA 02738 Office: One Boston Pl Boston MA 02108

KENDALL, JOHN SEEDOFF, college president, educator; b. Rockford, Ill., Aug. 28, 1928; s. Leonard and Gerda (Seedoff) K.; m. Joanne E. Milton, June 19, 1953; children: Mary, Peter J., David M. B.A., Gustavus Adolphus Coll., 1949; M.A., U. Minn., 1951, Ph.D., 1959; B.D., Lutheran Sch. Theology, Chgo., 1954. Diplomate: lic. cons. psychologist, Minn. Research fellow U. Minn., Mpls., 1957-59; asst. prof. psychology Gustavus Adolphus Coll., St. Peter, Minn., 1958-65, prof., 1968-81, pres., 1981—; dean Augustana Coll., Sioux Falls, S.D., 1965-68; cons. Minn. Dept. Pub. Welfare, 1959-81. Bd. dirs. Luth. Social Service Minn., 1975-81; trustee Minn. Pvt. Coll. Fund, 1981—, Gustavus Adolphus Coll., 1981—. Mem. Am. Psychol. Assn., AAAS, Minn. Hist. Soc., Am.- Scandinavian Found. Lutheran. Clubs: Mpls.; Decatholon (Mpls.). Home: Route 1 Box 12 Saint Peter MN 56082 Office: Gustavus Adolphus Coll Saint Peter MN 56082

KENDALL, KATHERINE ANNE, social worker; b. Muir-of-Ord, Scotland, Sept. 8, 1910; came to U.S., 1920, naturalized, 1940; d. Roderick and Annie Scott (Walker) Tuach; m. Willmoore Kendall, June 22, 1935 (div. Apr. 1950). B.A., U. Ill., 1933; M.A., La. State U., 1939; Ph.D., U. Chgo., 1950; D.Public Service honoris causa, Syracuse U., 1981. Asst. prof. Richmond Sch. Social Work, 1941-42; asst. dir. home service A.R.C., 1942-44; lectr. U. Chgo. Sch. Social Service Adminstrn., 1944-45; asst. dir., tng. supr. Inter-Am. and Internat. Tng. units U.S. Children's Bur., 1945- 47; social affairs officer UN Secretariat, 1947-50; exec. sec. Am. Assn. Schs. Social Work, 1950-52; ednl. sec. Council on Social Work Edn., 1952-58, assoc. dir., 1958-63, exec. dir., 1963-66, dir. internat. edn., 1966-71; Carnegie vis. prof. U. Hawaii, 1960-61; Mem. exec. bd. Internat. Assn. Schs. Social Work, 1954-66, sec.-gen., 1966-78, hon. pres., 1978—; ofcl. non-govtl. rep. UN, 1954—; Moses prof. Hunter Coll. Social Work, 1983-84; dir. Internat. Conf. on Social Work Edn., Population and Family Planning, East-West Center, Hawaii, 1970. Author: Reflections on Social Work Education, 1950-1978; UN reports International Exchange of Social Welfare Personnel, 1949, Training for Social Work: First International Survey, 1950; Editor: Social Work Values in an Age of Discontent, 1970, Population Dynamics and Family Planning: A New Responsibility for Social Work Education, 1971, World Guide to Social Work Edn., 1984; compiler: Social Casework—Cumulative Index 1920-1979, 1981. Mem. UN Internat. meeting experts on social work tng., Munich, 1956; faculty mem. UN Seminar, Keeru, Finland, 1952; assignment by UN mission social work edn., Guatemala, 1949, UN, Brazil, 1952, Paraguay, 1954; dir. 1st seminar Schs. Social Work in Central Am., 1963. Mem. Mortar Bd., Nat. Assn. Social Workers, Nat. Conf. Social Welfare, Internat. Assn. Schs. Social Work, Council on Social Work Edn., Internat. Council on Social Welfare, Phi Beta Kappa, Chi Omega. Home: 350 1st Ave New York NY 10010

KENDALL, LEON THOMAS, insurance company executive; b. Elizabeth, N.J., May 20, 1928; m. Nancy O'Donnell; 6 children. B.S. magna cum laude in Accounting, St. Vincent Coll., 1949; M.B.A. in Mktg, Ind. U., 1950; D.B.A. in Econs, Ind. U., 1956. Teaching asso. Ind. U. Sch. Bus., 1950-53; economist Fed. Res. Bd., Atlanta, 1956-58, U.S. Savs. and Loan League, Chgo., 1958-64; v.p., economist N.Y. Stock Exchange, 1964-67; pres. Assn. Stock Exchange Firms, 1967-72, Securities Industry Assn., 1972-74; chmn., dir. Mortgage Guaranty Ins. Corp., Milw., 1974—; vice chmn. MGIC Investment Corp., 1980—; vice chmn. MGIC Mortgage Mktg. Corp.; dir. Fed. Res. Bank Chgo.; commr. N.J. Mortgage Study, 1971-72. Author: (with Miles Colean) Who Buys the Houses, 1958, The Savings and Loan Business: Its Purposes, Functions and Economic Justification, 1962, Anatomy of the Residential Mortgage, 1964, Readings in Financial Institutions, 1965, The Exchange Community in 1975, 1965; Editor: Thrift and Home Ownership: Writings of Fred T. Greene, 1962; Contbr.: chpt. to American Enterprise: The Next Ten Years, 1961, The World Capital Shortage, 1977. Mem. adv. com. on broker/dealer reporting SEC, 1972; mem. adv. com. alternative mortgage instruments Fed. Home Loan Bd.; Bd. visitors U. Wis. Sch. Bus.; mem. deans adv. council Ind. U. Sch. Bus.; mem. adv. bd. Fed. Home Loan Mortgage Corp. Served with USAF, 1954-56. Grad. fellow Ind. U., 1950-53; Found. for Econ. Edn. fellow Pitts. Plate Glass Co., 1952. Mem. Am. Econ. Assn., Bond Club New York, Nat. Assn. Bus. Economists (council), Am. Finance Assn., Acad. Alumni Fellows Ind. U. Sch. Bus., Lambda Alpha, Delta Epsilon Sigma, Beta Gamma Sigma. Address: MGIC Investment Corp MGIC Plaza Milwaukee WI 53201

KENDALL, PETER LANDIS, television news executive; b. Toledo, Oct. 8, 1936; s. Roy Cline and Edythe Mae (Kindy) K.; m. Beate Margit Fritz, June 11, 1966; children: Adrian Peter, Stefanie Karin. B.A., U. Cin., 1959; B.S. cum laude, U. Ill., Urbana, 1960. News producer-writer Voice of Am., Washington, 1961-64; corr. Deutsche Welle, Bonn, W. Germany, 1964-66; morning news producer CBS News, Washington, 1971-74, producer, London, 1974-77, bur. chief, 1977-82, sr. producer-asst. bur. mgr., Washington, 1982—. Producer: London, The Royal Wedding, CBS 1981, Iranian Hostages Return, Frankfurt, W. Germany, 1980, Moscow Olympics 1980, Econ. Summits, London, 1977, Bonn. 1978, Versailles, 1982; numerous presdl. visits to Europe. Recipient Emmy award for Senate and Watergate coverage Nat. Acad. TV Arts and Scis., 1974. Mem. Am. Corrs Assn. (exec. bd. London 1977-80), Sigma Delta Chi. Espiscopalian. Club: Tamesis Sailing (London). Home: 4955 Quebec St NW Washington DC 20016 Office: CBS News 2020 M St NW Washington DC 20036

KENDALL, ROBERT MCCUTCHEON, chemical engineer, corporation executive; b. Pasadena, Calif., Dec. 29, 1931; s. Jackson Warner and Marjorie Harper (McCutcheon) K.; m. Angela Rose Heine, Sept. 1, 1957; children: Thomas Robert, Kathleen Renee, John Erwin, Patricia Lynne. B.S. with distinction, Stanford U., 1952, M.S., 1953; Sc.D., M.I.T., 1959. Lab. researcher Petroleum Inst. France, Rueil-Malmaison, 1956; thermodynamic specialist Gen. Electric Co., Danville, Calif., 1957-60; sr. scientist Vidya, Inc., Palo Alto, Calif., 1960-65; founder, sr. v.p., dir. Aerotherm div. mgr. Acurex Corp., Mountain View, Calif., 1965-82; founder, pres. Alzeta Corp., 1982—; cons. prof. chem. engring. Stanford U. Contbr. articles to profl. jours. Mem. Combustion Inst., Am. Inst. Chem. Engrs., Sigma Xi, Tau Beta Pi. Republican. Lutheran. Patentee in field. Home: 1097 Enderby Way Sunnyvale CA 94087

KENDALL, WILLIAM DENIS, medical electronic equipment company executive; b. Halifax, Yorkshire, Eng., May 27, 1903; came to U.S., 1923, naturalized, 1957; s. Joe Willie and Sarah Alice (Fell) K.; m. Margaret Burden, May 22, 1952. Student, Halifax Tech. Coll., 1966-69; Ph.D., Calif. Western U., 1974. Chartered engr. Asst. chief insp. Budd Mfg. Co., 1929; dir. mfg. Citroen Motor Co., Paris, France, 1929-38; mng. dir. Brit. Mfg. & Research Co., mfr. aircraft cannons and shells, Grantham, Eng., 1938-45; cons. to Pentagon on high velocity small arms, 1940-45; exec. v.p. Brunswick (N.J.) Ordnance Plant, 1952-56; dir., v.p. operations Mack Trucks Co., 1952-55; pres., dir. Am. Marc, Inc., Los Angeles, 1955-61; pres. Dynapower Systems and Dynapower Medonics, Los Angeles, 1961-73; chmn., chief exec. Kendall Med. Internat., Inc., Los Angeles, 1973—; chmn. Steron Products Inc., 1983—; partner rheumatoid arthritis clinic, London; dir. A.M. Byers Co., Pitts. Mem. Churchill's War Cabinet Gun Bd., 1941-45, M.P., Grantham div. Kesteven and Rutland, 1942-50; councillor Grantham Town Council, 1945-52; Bd. govs. Kings Sch., Grantham, 1942-52. Served with Royal Fleet Aux., 1919-23. Decorated chevalier Oissam Alouite Cherifien; freeman City of London, 1942—; mem. Worshipful Co. Clockmakers. Fellow Royal Soc. Arts (London), Inst. Mech. Engrs., Inst. Automotive Engrs. Mem. Religious Soc. Friends (Quaker). Clubs: Mason (Pacific Palisades, Cal.) (32 deg., Shriner); Riviera Country (Pacific Palisades, Cal.); United British Service, Royal Norfolk and Suffolk Yacht (Lowestoft, Eng.). Patentee in field. Home: 1319 N Doheny Dr Los Angeles CA 90069 also 159 Abbotts Rd Mitcham Surrey England Office: 127 E Liberty St Reno NV 89501 also 10 Manstone Rd London NW2 England

KENDE, ANDREW STEVEN, chemistry educator; b. Budapest, Hungary, July 17, 1932; came to U.S., 1941, naturalized, 1951; s. George and Elizabeth (Barinkai) K.; m. Frances Boothe, Sept. 4, 1954; 1 son, Mark. A.B., U. Chgo., 1951; M.S., Harvard, 1954, Ph.D., 1957. Sr. research scientist Lederle Labs., Am. Cyanamid Co., Pearl River, N.Y., 1957-63, cons., 1968—; research asso. Lederle Labs., 1963-66, research fellow, 1966-68; vis. prof. State U. N.Y., Buffalo, 1967, Mich. State U., East Lansing, 1968; prof. chemistry U. Rochester, N.Y., 1968—, chmn., 1979—, Charles Frederick Houghton prof. chemistry, 1981—; vis. prof. U. Genève, 1974; vis. scholar Stanford, 1975; Cons. medicinal chem. study sect. NIH, 1972-76, chmn., 1974-76, cons. chem. pathology study sect., 1979-81; cons. Dow Chem. Co., 1975—. Bd. editors: Organic Reactions, 1968-83; editor-in-chief, 1983—; Bd. editors: Chem. Reviews, 1973-76, Organic Syntheses, 1978—, Synthetic Communications, 1981—. Am. Cancer Soc. fellow Glasgow (Scotland) U., 1956-57; Guggenheim fellow, 1978-79. Mem. Am. Chem. Soc. (exec. bd. Rochester sect. 1970—, chmn. organic chem. div. 1978-79), Chem. Soc. (London). Home: 19 Larchwood Dr Pittsford NY 14534 Office: Dept Chemistry River Campus University of Rochester Rochester NY 14627

KENDE, HANS JANOS, plant physiology educator; b. Szekesfehervar, Hungary, Jan. 18, 1937; came to U.S., 1965, naturalized, 1970; s. Istvan and Katalin (Grosz) K.; m. Gabriele F. Guggenheim, May 15, 1960; children: Benjamin R., Michael, Judith N. Nat. Ph.D., U. Zurich, Switzerland, 1960. Research Council fellow, Ottawa, Can., 1960-61; research fellow Calif. Inst. Tech., Pasadena, 1961-63; plant physiologist Negev Inst. of Arid Zone Research, Beersheva, Israel, 1963-65; assoc. prof. Mich. State U.-Dept. Energy Plant Research Lab., East Lansing, 1965-69, prof., 1969—; vis. prof. Swiss Fed. Inst. Tech., Zurich, 1972-73, 79-80. Mem.: editorial bd. Plant Physiology, 1969—, Biochemie und Physiologie der Pflanzen, 1975—, Plant Molecular Biology, 1981—, Planta, 1982—; (editorial bd.) Jour. Plant Growth Regulation, 1988—; Contbr. articles to profl. jours. Mem. adv. panel for devel. biology NSF, 1974-77. Guggenheim fellow, 1972-73. Mem. AAAS, Am. Soc. Plant Physiologists. Home: 805 Virginia Ave East Lansing MI 48823 Office: Plant Research Lab Mich State U East Lansing MI 48824

KENDER, WALTER JOHN, horticulturist; b. Camden, N.J., Dec. 20, 1935; s. Walter and Martha K.; m. Carole Holm, May 26, 1957; 1 son, David. B.S., Del. Valley Coll., 1957; M.S., Rutgers U., 1959, Ph.D., 1962. Asst. prof., then asso. prof. horticulture U. Maine, Orono, 1962-69; mem. faculty Cornell U., N.Y. State Agrl. Expt. Sta., Geneva, 1969-82, prof. pomology, 1975-82, head dept. pomology and viticulture, 1972-82; chmn. dept. pomology Cornell U., Ithaca, N.Y., 1975-82; prof., dir. citrus research and edn. ctr. U. Fla., Lake Alfred, 1982—; co-chmn. task force fruit research N.E. U.S. Dept. Agr. State Expt. Stas., 1973—; sec. Internat. Working Group Juvenility Woody Plants, 1974—; disting. scientist Agrl. U., Wageningen, Netherlands, 1974. Contbg. author: Blueberry Culture, 1966; contbr. profl. jours. Fellow Am. Soc. Hort. Sci. (dir. 1975-79); Mem. N.Y. State Hort. Soc., Internat. Soc. Hort. Sci., Internat. Citriculture Soc. (corr.), Am. Pomological Soc., Am. Soc. Enologists, Council Agrl. Sci. and Tech., Fla. State Hort. Soc., N.Y. State Fruit Testing Assn. (sec.-treas. 1972-82), Sigma Xi (past chpt. pres.). Home: 40 Club Ct Haines City FL 33844 Office: Citrus Research and Edn Ctr 700 Experiment Station Rd Lake Alfred FL 33850

KENDERDINE, JOHN MARSHALL, retired army officer, petroleum engineer; b. Ft. Worth, Dec. 6, 1912; s. Robert Leonard and Caroline (Raab) K.; m. Su Anne Carroll, Feb. 26, 1937; children—James Marshall, Su Carroll. B.S. in Petroleum Engring, Tex. A. and M. Coll., 1934; grad., Army War Coll., 1953, Advanced Mgmt. Program, Harvard, 1959, Exec. Decision Inst., 1961. Registered profl. engr., Tex. Petroleum engr. Gulf Oil Corp., 1934-37; br. mgr. Norvell-Wilder Supply Co., Midland, Tex., 1938-41; commd. 1st lt. AUS, 1941, advanced through grades to brig. gen., 1962; mil. logistician in, France, Germany and U.S., World War II; spl. asst. to administr. War Assets Adminstrn., 1946; mil. staff and command assignments, 1947-60, joint petroleum officer, Europe, 1961; exec. dir. supply operations Def. Supply Agy., 1962-65; comdr. Def. Indsl. Supply Center, Phila., 1965-66, Def. Personnel Support Center, 1966-67; ret.; v.p. Scott Paper Co., 1967-70; chmn. C.F. Adams, Inc., Ft. Worth, 1970—; pres. Black Jack Oil Co. Contbr. articles to profl. jours. Decorated Legion of Merit, Commendation ribbon with 3 oak leaf clusters, D.S.M. Mem. Am. Logistics Assn., Assn. U.S. Army, Flight Safety Found., Armed Forces Communications and Electronics Assn. (dir. 1965), Commerce and Industry Council Phila., Phila. C. of C. (dir. 1966), Airline Passengers Assn. (adv. bd.). Clubs: Union League, Petroleum, Century II. Home: 3212 Chapparral Ln Fort Worth TX 76109 Office: C F Adams Inc PO Box 253 Fort Worth TX 76101

KENDIG, EDWIN LAWRENCE, JR., physician, educator; b. Victoria, Va., Nov. 12, 1911; s. Edwin Lawrence and Mary McGuire (Yates) K.; m. Emily Vigina Parker, Mar. 22, 1941; children: Anne Randolph Kendig Young, Mary Emily Corbin Kendig Rankin. B.A. magna cum laude, Hampden-Sydney Coll., 1932, B.S., 1933, D.Sc. hon., 1971; M.D., U. Va., 1936. House officer Med. Coll. Va. Hosp., Richmond, Bellevue Hosp., N.Y.C., Babies Hosp., Wilmington, N.C., Johns Hopkins Hosp., Balt., 1936-40; instr. pediatrics Johns Hopkins U., 1944; pratice medicine specializing in pediatrics, Richmond, 1940—; dir. child chest clinic Med. Coll. Va., 1944—, prof. pediatrics, 1958—; mem. staff St. Mary's Hosp., Richmond, 1966—, chief of staff, 1966-67; mem. staff Chippenham Hosp., Jonston Willis Hosp., Stuart Circle Hosp., Richmond Meml. Hosp.; cons. dieases of chest in children; William P. Buffum orator Brown U., 1979; Abraham Finkelstein Meml. lectr. U. Md., 1983. Lectr., throughout the world; contbr. numerous articles, editorial abstracts and diseases of chest in children to profl. publs.; editor: Disorders of Respiratory Tract in Children, 1967, 72, 77, (with V. Chernick) Disorders of Respiratory Tract in children, 4th edit., 1983, (with C.F. Ferguson) Pediatric Otolaryngology, 1967; contbg. editor: books Current Pediatric Theory, 9 edits., Antimicrobial Therapy, 3 edits., Pratice of Pediatrics (Kelley), Practice of Pediatrics (Maurer), Allergic Diseases of Infancy, Childhood and Adolescence. Chmn. Richmond Bd. Health, 1961-69; bd. vistors U. Va., 1961-72; former mem. bd. dirs. Va. Hosp. Service Assn.; former ofcl. examiner Am. Bd. Pediatrics; mem. White House Conf. on Children and Youth, 1960; dir. emeritus Dominion Nat. Bank; pres. alumni adv. com. U. Va. Sch. Medicine, Charlottesville, 1974-75; bd. dirs. Maymont Found., Richmond. Recipient resolution of recognition Va. Health Commr., 1978, Obici award Louise Obici Hosp., 1979. Mem. Am. Acad. Pediatrics (pres. Va. sect., chmn. sect. on diseases of chest, mem. exec. bd. 1971-78, nat. pres. 1978-79), Va. Bd. Medicine (pres.), Richmond Acad. Medicine (pres. 1962, chmn. bd. trustees 1963), Va. Pediatric Soc. (past pres.), Am. Pediatric Soc., AMA, So. Med. Assn., So. Soc. Pediatric Research, Internat. Pediatric Assn. (standing com.), Med. Soc. Va. (editor Va. Med. Jour. 1982, resolution of recognition 1978), Soc. of Cincinnati, Raven, Phi Beta Kappa, Alpha Omega Alpha, Tau Kappa Alpha, Kappa Sigma, Omicron Delta Kappa. Episcopalian. Clubs: Commonwealth, Conutry of Va.; Farmington (Charlottesville). Home: 5008 Cary St Rd Richmond VA 23226 Office: 5801 Bremo Rd Richmond VA 23226

KENDIG, ELLSWORTH HAROLD, JR., lawyer; b. Toledo, Jan. 3, 1922; s. Ellsworth Harold and Ellen Katherine (Owen) K.; m. Donita Rae Porter, Dec. 29, 1972; children by previous marriage: Susan (Mrs. William Willen), Robert E., Richard C., Margaret E. A.B., U. Mich., 1943; postgrad., Wayne State U. Law Sch., 1949. Bar: Calif. bar 1950. With firm Herlihy & Herlihy, Los Angeles, 1950-57; mem. firm Kendig, Stockwell & Gleason (and predecessor firms), Los Angeles, 1957-82, Von Mizener & Kendig, 1982—. Served with USNR, 1943-46; PTO. Mem. Am. Bar Assn., Internat. Assn. Ins. Counsel, Nat. Audubon Soc., Los Angeles Audubon Soc. (v.p.), Nat. Wildlife Fedn., Nature Conservancy, Am. Arbitration Assn. (arbitrator). Methodist. Club: Los Angeles Country. Home: 603 S McCadden Pl Los Angeles CA 90005 Office: 2067 S Atlantic Blvd Los Angeles CA 90040

KENDIG, PERRY FRIDY, former college president; b. Mountville, Pa., July 7, 1910; s. Calvin Miles and Blanche (Fridy) K.; m. Virginia Gantt, Apr. 17, 1947; children: Beth Roberts, John Gantt, William Calvin. A.B., Franklin and Marshall Coll., 1932; A.M., U. Pa., 1936, Ph.D., 1947. Prin., East Drumore Twp. High Sch., Lancaster County, Pa., 1932-34; asst. instr. English, U. Pa., 1936-38; spl. instr. English, Drexel U., 1937-38; from instr. to prof., head dept. English, dean students Muhlenberg Coll., 1938-52; dean coll., prof. English, Roanoke Coll., 1952-63, pres., 1963-75; past pres. Council Lutheran Ch. in Am. Colls.; former pres. Va. Found. Ind. Colls., Assn. Va. Colls. Author: Trinity Reformed Church: An Historical Sketch, 1938, The Poems of St. Columban Translated into English Verse, 1949, (by Jesse

Lynch Holman, 1810) Some Notes on a Little Known American Novel: The Prisoners of Niagara or Errors of Education, 1956. Mem. Gov.'s Bi-racial Com. Higher Edn.; bd. dirs. Roanoke Valley Arts Council, Valley Roofing Found. Served to lt. comdr. USNR, 1942-46. Mem. MLA, Hawk Mountain Sanctuary Assn., AAUP, Va. Soc. Ornithology, Nat. Audubon Soc., Roanoke Valley Bird Club, English Speaking Union, Blue Key, Phi Beta Kappa (past pres. Roanoke area), Phi Sigma Kappa, Omicron Delta Kappa, Delta Sigma Rho-Tau Kappa Alpha, Eta Sigma Phi, Alpha Kappa Alpha, Sigma Delta Pi, Alpha Psi Omega. Lutheran. Lutheran (past exec. bd. Va. Synod). Clubs: University (Washington); Commonwealth (Richmond, Va.); Shenandoah (Roanoke); Town (Salem). Home: 831 C Duke of Gloucester St SW Roanoke VA 24014

KENDLE, JOHN EDWARD, historian, educator; b. London, Apr. 14, 1937; emigrated to Can., 1948, naturalized, 1957; s. Arthur and Sybil Violet Mary (Jordan) K.; m. Judith Ann Halsey, Aug 3, 1963; children—John Stephen, Andrew Bruce, Nancy Elizabeth. B.A., U. Man. (Can.), 1958; Ph.D. (Can. Council fellow), U. London, 1965. Asst. prof. history U. Man., 1965-70, asso. prof., 1970-75, prof., 1975—, chmn. dept. history, 1982—; vis. research fellow Australian Nat. U. and Auckland U., 1967-68. Author: The Colonial and Imperial Conferences 1887-1911, 1967, The British Empire-Commonwealth, 1897-1931, 1972, The Round Table Movement and Imperial Union, 1975, John Bracken: A Political Biography, 1979. Can. Council fellow, 1967-68, 71-72, 78-79; recipient Research award Can. Council, 1975-76. Mem. Canadian Hist. Assn. (pres. 1981-82), Am. Com. Irish Studies, Royal Commonwealth Soc. Home: 149 The Glen Winnipeg MB R2M 0B5 Canada Office: Saint John's College University of Manitoba Winnipeg MB R3T 2M5 Canada

KENDLER, BERNHARD, editor; b. Cin., Jan. 28, 1934; s. Harry Harlan and Mildred (Black) K.; m. Jill Ferguson, Dec. 12, 1975. B.A. in English, NYU, 1955; M.A. in Comparative Lit, U. Mich., 1956. Research asst. Calif. Tchrs. Assn., 1958-60; editor A.S. Barnes & Co., Inc., N.Y.C., 1960-62; copy editor J.B. Lippincott Co., Phila., 1962-63; mng. editor, editor Cornell U. Press, Ithaca, N.Y., 1963—. Mem. Am. Studies Assn., Phi Beta Kappa. Home: 47 Sheraton Dr Ithaca NY 14850 Office: 124 Roberts Pl: Ithaca NY 14851

KENDLER, HOWARD H., educator, psychologist; b. N.Y.C., June 9, 1919; s. Harry H. and Sylvia (Rosenberg) K.; m. Tracy Seedman, Sept. 20, 1941; children—Joel Harlan, Kenneth Seedman. A.B., Bklyn. Coll., 1940; M.A., U. Iowa, 1941, Ph.D., 1943. Instr. U. Iowa, 1943; research psychologist OSRD, 1944; asst. prof. U. Colo., 1946-48; asso. prof. N.Y. U., 1948-51, prof., 1951-63; chmn. dept. Univ. Coll., 1951-61; prof. U. Calif., at Santa Barbara, 1963—, chmn. dept. psychology, 1965-66; project dir. Office Naval Research, 1950-68, USAAF, 1951-53; Mem. adv. panel psycholobiology NSF, 1960-62; tng. com. Nat. Inst. Child Health and Human Devel., 1963-66; cons. Dept. Def., Smithsonian Instn., 1959-60, Human Resources Research Office, George Washington U., 1960; vis. prof. U. Calif. at, Berkeley, 1960-61, Hebrew U. Jerusalem, 1974-75; chief clin. psychologist Walter Reed Gen. Hosp., 1945-46. Author: Basic Psychology, 1963, 2d edit., 1968, 3d edit., 1974, Basic Psychology: Brief Version, 1977, Psychology: A Science in Conflict, 1981; co-author: Basic Psychology: Brief Edition, 1970; Co-editor: Essays in Neobehaviorism: A Memorial Volume to Kenneth W. Spence; asso. editor: Jour. Exptl. Psychology, 1963-65; Contbr. to profl. jours., books. Served as 1st lt. AUS. Fellow Center for Advanced Studies in Behaviorial Scis., Stanford, Calif., 1969-70; NSF grantee, 1954-76. Mem. Am. psychol. assn. (pres. div. exptl. psychology 1964-65, pres. div. gen. psychology 1967-68), Western psychol. assn. (pres. 1970-71), Soc. Exptl. Psychologists (exec. com. 1971-73), Psychonomic Soc. (governing bd. 1963-69, chmn. 1968-69), Sigma Xi. Home: 4596 Camino Molinero Santa Barbara CA 93110

KENDRICK, DAVID ANDREW, economist; b. Gatesville, Tex., Nov. 14, 1937; s. Andrew Green and Nina Alice (Murray) K.; m. Gail Tidd, July 4, 1964; children—Ann, Colin. B.A., U. Tex., 1960; Ph.D. (Woodrow Willson fellow 1961-62), M.I.T., 1965. Asst. prof. Harvard U., Cambridge, Mass., 1966-70; vis. scholar Stanford (Calif.) U., 1969-70; vis. prof. M.I.T., Cambridge, 1978-79; prof. econs. U. Tex., Austin, 1970—. Author: (with A. Stoutiesdijk) The Planning of Industrial Investment Programs, 1978, (with P. Dixon and S. Bowles) Notes and Problems in Microeconomic Theory, 1980, Stochastic Control for Economic Models, 1981. Served with U.S. Army, 1960-61. Ford faculty fellow, 1969-70. Mem. Econometric Soc., Am. Econs. Assn., Soc. Econ. Dynamics and Control. (pres. 1980). Home: 7209 Lamplight Ln Austin TX 78731 Office: Dept Econs GSB4112c U Tex Austin TX 78712

KENDRICK, HERBERT SPENCER, JR., lawyer; b. Brownfield, Tex., Nov. 16, 1934; s. Herbert Spencer and Elsie Kathryn (Woosley) K.; m. Carol Ann Puckett, Sept. 6, 1958; children: Herbert Spencer III, Kathryn Gene. B.B.A., So. Methodist U., 1957, LL.B., 1960; LL.M., Harvard, 1961. Bar: Tex. 1960. Trial atty. tax div. Justice Dept., 1961-65; pvt. practice, Dallas, 1965—; sr. partner firm Akin, Gump, Strauss, Hauer & Feld; dir. Capital Bank, Dallas; adj. prof. taxation So. Meth. U. Law Sch., 1966—. Co-author: Texas Transaction Guide, 10 vols, 1972, 73. Mem. Am., Tex., Dallas bar assns., Sigma Alpha Epsilon, Phi Alpha Delta. Presbyterian. Clubs: Dallas, Salesmanship of Dallas, Masons, Shriners, Brook Hollow Golf. Home: 4421 Larchmont St Dallas TX 75205 Office: 2800 Republic Bank Dallas Bldg Dallas TX 75201

KENDRICK, JAMES BLAIR, JR., university official, research scientist; b. Lafayette, Ind., Oct. 21, 1920; s. James Blair and Violet (McDonald) K.; m. Evelyn May Henle, May 17, 1942; children: Janet Blair, Douglas Henle. B.A., U. Calif. at Berkeley, 1942; Ph.D., U. Wis., 1947. Mem. staff, faculty U. Calif. at, Riverside, 1947-68, prof. plant pathology and plant pathologist, 1961-68, chmn. dept., 1963-68; v.p. agrl. scis. U. Calif., 1968-77, v.p. agr. and univ. services, 1977—; dir. agrl. expt. sta., 1973-80, dir. coop. extension, 1975-80; Participant 10th Internat. Bot. Congress, Edinburgh, Scotland, 1964; mem. Calif. Bd. Food and Agr., 1968—, U.S. Agrl. Research Policy Adv. Com., 1976; Mem. governing bd. Agrl. Research Inst., 1974-76. Contbr. articles to profl. jours. Bd. dirs. Guide Dogs for Blind, San Rafael, Calif., 1983—. Served with AUS, 1944-46. NSF sr. postdoctoral fellow U. Cambridge (Eng.) and Rothamsted (Eng.) Exptl. Sta., 1961-62. Fellow AAAS (chmn. sect. O 1978); mem. Am. Phytopath. Soc. (editorial bd. jour. 1965-68, councilor at large 1968-70), Internat. Soc. Plant Pathology (council 1968-73), Am. Inst. Biol. Scis., Calif. C. of C. (agrl. com. 1968—), Nat. Assn. State Univs. and Land Grants Colls. (chmn. div. agr. 1972-73, exec. com. 1974-76), Western Assn. State Agrl. Expt. Sta. Dirs. (chmn. 1975), Phi Beta Kappa, Sigma Xi. Congregationalist. Club: Commonwealth of Calif. (San Francisco). Spl. research diseases vegetable crops. Home: 615 Spruce St Berkeley CA 94707

KENDRICK, JOHN JESSE, JR., lawyer; b. Brownfield, Tex., Nov. 22, 1943; s. John Jessie and Irma Ione (Smith) K.; m. Leanne Johanson, Mar. 18, 1967; children: John Jesse, III, Kristin Lee. B.B.A., So. Methodist U., 1965, J.D., 1968. Bar: Calif. 1969, Tex. 1970. Auditor Peat, Marwick, Mitchell & Co., C.P.A.s, Dallas, 1965; asso. firm Nossaman, Waters, Scott, Krueger & Riordan, Los Angeles, 1968-69; asso. corporate finance dept. Bache & Co. Inc., N.Y.C., 1969-70; partner firm Kendrick & Kendrick, Dallas, 1970-76, Jenkens & Gilchrist, 1976-78, Johnson & Swanson, 1978—; dir. Capital Bank, Dallas; lectr. in field. Editor: Texas Transaction Guide, 12 vols, 1972; case note editor: Southwestern Law Jour, 1968; Contbr. legal jours. Mem. Am., Dallas bar assns., Order of Coif. Episcopalian. Clubs: Dallas, Brook Hollow Golf, Calyx. Home: 4800 Drexel Dr Dallas TX 75205 Office: 4700 Interfirst Two Dallas TX 75270

KENDRICK, JOSEPH TROTWOOD, former foreign service officer, writer, cons.; b. Pryor, Okla., Feb. 5, 1920; s. Joseph Trotwood and Anne (Williams) K.; m. Elise Fleager Simpkins, Aug. 20, 1955 (div. 1977); children—Pamela York, Drew Trotwood (dec. 1970), Juliette Simpkins, Katherine Mary. Student, U. Okla., 1938-40; B.S., Georgetown U., 1948; M.A., Columbia, 1951; Ph.D., George Washington U., 1979. Joined U.S. Fgn. Service, 1941; assigned, Nicaragua, Poland, USSR, Germany, 1941-54; spl. asst. to dir. Office Eastern European Affairs, U.S. Dept. State, 1954-57, pub. affairs adviser, 1958; 2d sec., consul, Kabul, 1959-61; dep. polit. adviser SHAPE, Paris, 1962-64; polit. counselor, Oslo, Norway, 1964-68; dep. dir. Office Atomic Energy and Aerospace, U.S. Dept. State, 1968-70, dir., 1970-71; spl. asst. to dir. Bur. Pol. Mil. Affairs, 1971-72; detailed to Dept. Def., 1972-73; dean, center for area and country studies Fgn. Service Inst., Dept. State, 1974-75; writer, cons., 1975—. Author: Executive-Legislation Consultation on Foreign Policy: Strengthening Executive Branch Procedures. Served to lt. (jg.) USNR, 1944-46. Recipient Outstanding Civilian Service medal Dept. Army, 1974. Mem. Am. Assn. Advancement Slavic Studies, Am. Fgn. Service Assn., Am. Polit. Sci. Assn., Inst. Strategic Studies (London), Delta Chi. Home: PO Box 3499 Vail CO 81657

KENDRICK, PETER MURRAY, pay TV co. exec.; b. Winchester, Mass., Oct. 8, 1936; s. Wallace Dolloff and Esther (Burke) K.; m. Grace Terry, June 17, 1967; children—Caroline, Timothy. B.S.B.A., Babson Coll., 1962. Office mgr. Am. Hosp. Supply Corp., Chgo. and Charlotte, N.C., 1962-65; registered rep. Hayden, Stone & Co., 1966-69; gen. mgr. Continental Cablevision, Concord, N.H. and Jackson, Mich., 1969-74; pres. New Eng. Cablevision, Portland, Maine, 1974-79, chmn. bd., 1980; pres. Home Theater Network, Portland, 1977—. Served with USAF, 1956-59. Recipient Highest Programming award Cable TV Nat. Assn., 1973. Mem. New Eng. Cable TV Assn. (v.p. 1972, pres. 1975), Mich. Cable TV Assn. (v.p. 1973). Home: Landing Woods Ln Falmouth Foreside ME 04105 Office: 465 Congress St Portland ME 04101

KENDRICK, WILLIAM BRYCE, biology educator; b. Liverpool, Eng., Dec. 3, 1933; s. William and Lillian Maud (Latham) K.; m. Laureen Carscadden, Dec. 1977; children: Clinton, Kelly. B.Sc. hons, U. Liverpool, 1955, Ph.D., 1958, D.Sc., 1980. NRC postoctoral fellow, 1958-59; research officer Plant Research Inst. Can. Agrl. Ministry, Ottawa, Ont., 1959-65; asst. prof. biology U. Waterloo, 1965-66, assoc. prof., 1966-71, prof., 1971—. Author articles, handbooks, textbooks; editor anthologies, handbooks. Guggenheim fellow, 1979-80. Fellow Royal Soc. Can.; mem. Mycol. Soc. Am., Can. Bot. Assn., Brit. Mycol. Soc. Home: 331 Daleview Pl Waterloo ON N2L 5M5 Canada Office: Dept Biology U Waterloo Waterloo ON N2L 3G1 Canada

KENDZIERSKI, LOTTIE HENRYKA, philosophy educator; b. Milw., July 23, 1917; d. Stanislaus and Leocadia (Cywinski) K. B.A., Marquette U., 1937, M.A., 1938; Ph.D., Fordham U., 1944. Instr. Mt. St. Mary Coll., Hooksett, N.H., 1940-41, Coll. New Rochelle, N.Y., 1941-42; instr. Marquette U., 1946-51, asst. prof. philosophy, 1951-54, asso. prof., 1954-64, prof., 1964-75, prof. emeritus, 1975—. Author: (with G. Smith) The Philosophy of Being, 1961, (with F.C. Wade) Cajetan: Commentary on Being and Essence, 1964, St. Thomas Aquinas: On Charity, 1960. Mem. Am. Cath. Philos. Assn. Home: 3038 S 60th St Milwaukee WI 53219

KENEFICK, JOHN COOPER, railroad executive; b. Buffalo, Dec. 26, 1921; s. John L. and Charlotte (Cooper) K.; m. Helen Walker Ryan, Aug. 19, 1973; 1 dau., Mary; stepchildren: Elizabeth, John, Mary, Nancy Ryan. B.S., Princeton U., 1943. With U.P.R.R., Omaha, 1947-52, v.p. ops., then exec. v.p., 1968-70, chief exec. officer, 1970-71, pres., 1971—, chmn. bd., chief exec. officer, 1982—; dir. U.P. Corp.; with N.Y. Central R.R., 1946, 54-68, Denver Rio Grande & Western R.R., 1952-54; dir. Omaha Nat. Corp., Western Electric Co., 1st Security Corp. Bd. dirs. Creighton U., Omaha, Clarkson Hosp., Omaha; trustee Princeton U. Served to lt. (j.g.) USNR, 1943-46. Mem. Omaha C. of C. (past pres.). Clubs: Omaha Country, Omaha; Links, Sky (N.Y.C.); California; Log Cabin (St. Louis). Home: 410 Fairacres Rd Omaha NE 68132 Office: 1416 Dodge St Omaha NE 68179

KENEFICK, JOHN HENRY, JR., consultant, retired engineering company executive; b. Meriden, Conn., Aug. 5, 1921; s. John Henry and Ellen Gertrude (Hourrigan) K.; m. Stephanie Maria Lesobey, Dec. 15, 1945; children: John Henry, III, Kathleen, Brian, Timothy, Stephen, Eileen, Thomas. B.S. in Chem. Engring, Purdue U., 1945. With Pullman Kellogg Co., 1974-80, sr. v.p. worldwide engring. and constrn., Houston, 1978-80; pres. Pullman Swindell Co., Pitts., 1980-81; sr. v.p. subsidiary ops. M.W. Kellogg, Houston, 1981-82, sr. v.p., asst. to pres., 1982-83; pvt. cons., 1983—; dir. Pullman Swindell Mexicana. Author. Mem. Am. Inst. Chem. Engrs., Houston C. of C., Sigma Xi. Republican. Clubs: Petroleum, Inwood Golf (Houston); Duquesne (Pitts.). Pantentee in field. Home: 12411 Cobblestone Dr Houston TX 77024

KENELLY, JOHN WILLIS, JR., mathematician, educator; b. Bogalusa, La., Nov. 22, 1935; s. John Willis and Erma (Whittom) K.; m. Charmaine Voss, Aug. 12, 1956; children: Deidre Ammie, John Trent. B.S., Southeastern La. U., 1957; M.S., U. Miss., 1957; Ph.D., U. Fla., 1961. Instr. U. Fla., 1959-61; asst. prof. U. Southwestern La., 1961-63; asso. prof. Clemson (S.C.) U., 1963-68, prof. math., 1969—, head dept., 1969-77; prof. math., chmn. dept. U. New Orleans, 1968-69; vis. prof. U.S. Mil. Acad., 1982-83; research investigator NASA; mem. com. undergrad. programs Math. Consultant's Bur., 1968—; chief reader advanced placement program in math. Ednl. Testing Service, 1975-79; chmn. calculus devel. com. Coll. Bd., 1979—, mem. math. adv. com., 1981—; dir. Clemson area 1st Nat. Bank. Author: Informal Logic, 1967; Contbr. articles to profl. jours.; referee: Pacific Jour. Math. Mem. Math. Assn. Am. (vis. lectr. 1969—), Am. Math. Soc., Nat. Council Tchrs. Math., Ops. Research Soc. Am., Inst. Mgmt. Sci. Pres., Clemson Unitarian Fellowship. Lodge: Rotary. Home: 327 Woodland Way Clemson SC 29631

KENEN, PETER BAIN, educator, economist; b. Cleve., Nov. 30, 1932; s. Isaiah Leo and Beatrice (Bain) K.; m. Regina Horowitz, Aug. 21, 1955; children: Joanne Lisa, Marc David, Stephanie Hope, Judith Rebecca. A.B., Columbia U., 1954; M.A., Harvard U., 1956, Ph.D., 1958. Mem. faculty Columbia U., 1957-71, prof. econs., 1964-71, chmn. dept., 1967-69, provost univ., 1969-70, adviser to pres., 1970-71; prof. econs. and internat. finance, dir. internat. finance sect. Princeton U., 1971—; cons. Council Econ. Advisers, 1961, U.S. Treasury, 1962-68, 77-80, Bur. Budget, 1964-68. Author: British Monetary Policy and the Balance of Payments (1951-57), 1960, Giant Among Nations, 1960, (with A.G. Hart and A. Entine) Money, Debt and Economic Activity, 1969, (with R. Lubitz) International Economics, 3d edit, 1971, A Model of the U.S. Balance of Payments, 1978; author: (with P.R. Allen) Asset Markets, Exchange Rates, and Economic Integration, 1980; Editor: International Trade and Finance, Frontiers for Research, 1975, Essays in International Economics, 1980; editor: (with R. Lawrence) The Open Economy, 1968, (with others) The International Monetary System under Flexible Exchange Rates, 1982; Contbr. articles to profl. jours. Recipient David A. Wells prize Harvard, 1958-59; Univ. medal Columbia U., 1977; Fellow Center Advanced Study Behavioral Scis., 1971-72; John Simon Guggenheim Found. fellow, 1975-76. Mem. Am. Econ. Assn., Royal Econ. Soc., Econometric Soc., Council Fgn. Relations, Group of Thirty. Research on econ. basis for internat. trade, internat. financial theory and policy. Home: 15 Forester Dr Princeton NJ 08540

KENISTON, KENNETH, educator, psychologist; b. Chgo., Jan. 6, 1930; s. Hayward and Roberta (Cannell) K.; m. Ellen Uviller, June 6, 1960 (div. July 1975); children—Ann Rogers, Sarah Hayward; m. Suzanne Berger, Jan. 10, 1976; 1 son, Daniel Eben. B.A., Harvard U., 1951; D. Phil., Oxford (Eng.) U., 1956. Fellow Harvard Soc. Fellows, 1953-56; research asso. Lab. Human Relations; dept. social relations Harvard, 1956-62, lectr. clin. psychology, 1960-62; mem. faculty Yale Med. Sch., 1962—, asso. prof., asso. dir. social and community psychiatry tng. program, 1966-69, prof. psychiatry, 1971—; dir. Behavioral Scis. Study Center, 1969-72; chmn., exec. dir. Carnegie Council Children, 1972-78; Andrew Mellon prof. human devel. Mass. Inst. Tech., 1976—; Mem. Carnegie Commn. Higher Edn. Bd. overseers Harvard, 1973-79. Author: The Uncommitted: Alienated Youth in American Society, 1965, Young Radicals: Notes on Committed Youth, 1968, Youth and Dissent, 1971, Radicals and Militants, 1973, All Our Children: the American Family Under Pressure, 1977. Mem. Am. Acad. Arts and Scis., Council Fgn. Relations, Phi Beta Kappa, Sigma Xi. Office: E51-210 Mass Inst Tech Cambridge MA 02139

KENKEL, ROBERT AUGUST, automotive parts manufacturer; b. Defiance, Iowa, Aug. 20, 1934; s. Nicholas and Mary (Eckerman) K.; m. Bernice A. Donohue, June 15, 1957; children: Gregory, Kurt, Matthew, Therese, Karen, Vincent, Amy, Robert. B.S.M.E., Iowa State U., 1956. Registered profl. engr., Ind. Pres. Gravely div. McGraw-Edison, Winston-Salem, N.C., 1957-80, Internat. Metal Products div. McGraw-Edison, Phoenix, 1980-82, Wagner div. McGraw-Edison, Parsippany, NJ, 1982—. Served with AUS, 1957. Mem. Nat. Soc. Profl. Engrs. Republican. Roman Catholic. Home: 1 Colonial Way Madison NJ 07940 Office: 100 Misty Ln Parsippany NJ 07054

KENLY, F. CORNING, JR., financial consultant; b. Lake Forest, Ill., Feb. 21, 1915; s. F. Corning and Ruth (Farwell) K.; m. Miriam Little, May 21, 1941; children: M.B. Kenly Earle, David F., F. Corning, III. B.S., Harvard U., 1937; postgrad., Harvard U. Bus. Sch., 1964. Loan adminstr. Harris Trust & Savs. Bank, Chgo., 1938-39; fin. exec. Household Finance Corp., Chgo., 1940-41; sr. v.p. investments New Eng. Mut. Life Ins. Co., Boston, 1948-80; v.p., dir. NEL Equity Fund, Inc., NEL Growth Fund, Inc., NEL Retirement Equity Fund, Inc., 1970-80; pres., dir. NEL Income Fund, Inc., NEL Cash Mgmt. Account, NEL Tax Exempt Bond Fund, 1970-80; mem. real estate adv. com. Citibank (N.A.), N.Y.C.; mem. adv. bd. Boston Bay Capital Co., Boston; bd. assos. R.T. Madden Co., N.Y.C. Trustee Cardigan Mountain Sch.; mem. corp. Boston Mus. Sci.; mem. alumni exec. com. Thacher Sch. Served to lt. comdr. USNR, 1941-46. Mem. Boston Security Analysts Soc., Harvard Bus. Sch. Assn. of Boston. Clubs: Somerset, Economic, Union (Boston); Manchester (Mass.) Yacht; Essex County (Manchester); Birnam Wood (Santa Barbara, Calif.). Home and Office: PO Box 400 Spy Rock Hill Manchester MA 01944

KENLY, GRANGER FARWELL, marketing consultant, college official; b. Portland, Oreg., Feb. 15, 1919; s. F. Corning and Ruth (Farwell) K.; m. Suzanne Warner, Feb. 7, 1948 (div. Nov. 1977); children: Margaret Farwell, Granger Farwell; m. Stella B. Angevin, Oct. 8, 1978. A.B. cum laude, Harvard U., 1941. Adminstrv. asst. to v.p. Poole Bros., Inc., Chgo., 1941-42; asst. advt. mgr. Sunset Mag., San Francisco, 1946-47; pub. relations, sales promotion mgr. Pabco Products, Inc., San Francisco, 1947-51; v.p. mgmt., supr. Needham, Louis & Brorby, Inc., Chgo., 1951-60; mgr. marketing plans dept. Pure Oil Co., Palatine, Ill., 1961-62, v.p. pub. relations, personnel, 1962-66; v.p. pub. affairs Abbott Labs., North Chicago, Ill., 1966-71; v.p. corporate and investor relations IC Industries, Inc., Chgo., 1972-83; exec. dir. career planning and placement Lake Forest Coll., Ill., 1984—; Mem. 22d Ann. Global Strategy Conf. U.S. Naval War Coll., 1970. Bd. dirs. Evanston Hosp., 1963-82; trustee Ill. Soc. Prevention Blindness, 1958-64, Lawson YMCA, Chgo., Off the Street Boys Club, Chgo. Served to maj. USAAF, 1942-46; ETO. Mem. Pub. Relations Soc. Am., Chgo. Assn. Commerce, Newcomen Soc. N.Am. Republican. Episcopalian. Clubs: Chicago, University, Economic (Chgo.); Glen View (Golf, Ill.); Onwentsia (Lake Forest, Ill.); Harvard (N.Y.C.). Home: 1160 N Sheridan Rd Lake Forest IL 60045 Office: Lake Forest College Sheridan and College Rds Lake Forest IL 60045

KENNA, EDGAR DOUGLAS, manufacturing company executive; b. Summit, Miss., June 11, 1924; s. Edgar Douglas and Norma Catchings (Carruth) K.; m. Jean Cruise, June 12, 1945; children: Edgar Douglas III, Marilyn, Susan, Michael. Student, U. Miss., 1941-42; B.S., U.S. Mil. Acad., 1945. Pres. Fuqua Industries, Atlanta, 1968-70, Robert B. Anderson, Ltd., N.Y.C., 1970-73, Nat. Assn. Mfrs., Washington, 1973-77; pres. Carrier Corp., Syracuse, 1978-81; partner G.L. Ohrstrom Co., N.Y.C., 1981—; chmn. Ropex Corp.; dir. Phillips Petroleum Co., Carlisle Corp., Fleet Fin. Group, Vinnell Corp., Harrow Corp., Corona Clipper Corp., Vistan Corp., Leach Corp. Trustee U.S. Mil. Acad., George C. Marshall Found. Served with AUS, 1942-49. Recipient Freedom Found. award, 1976. Republican. Congregationalist. Clubs: Lost Tree (Palm Beach); Met., Univ. (N.Y.C.); Congressional (Washington). Developed reentry systems for Apollo, Atlas, Titan, and Minuteman missile systems. Home: 11216 Turtle Beach Rd North Palm Beach FL 33408 Office: G L Ohrstrom & Co 540 Madison Ave New York NY 10022

KENNAMER, LORRIN GARFIELD, JR., univ. dean; b. Abilene, Tex., Dec. 20, 1924; s. Lorrin Garfield and Ruie Lee (Hart) K.; m. Laura Helen Durham, Dec. 22, 1948. A.B., Eastern Ky. State Coll., 1947; M.S., U. Tenn., 1949; Ph.D., Vanderbilt U./George Peabody Coll., 1952. Tchr. Oak Ridge High Sch., 1947-49; from instr. to asso. prof., chmn. dept. geography and geology East Tex. State Coll., Commerce, 1952-56; mem. faculty U. Tex., 1956-67, prof. geography, 1961-67, chmn. dept., 1961-67, asso. dean arts and scis., 1961-67; dean arts and scis. Tex. Tech. U., 1967-70; dean U. Tex. Coll. Edn., Austin, 1970—; vis. summer prof. U. Vt., 1959, Mich. State U., 1961, U. Wash., 1967; Bd. examiners Tex. Edn. Agy., 1964-71; mem. com. exams. Coll. Entrance Exam. Bd., 1965-71, trustee, 1970—, vice-chmn., 1972-74, chmn., 1974-76; pres. Tex. Council Deans Edn., 1973. Author: (with Bowden, Hoffman) Geography Worktext Series, 4th edit, 1979, (with S. Arbingast) Atlas of Texas, rev. edit, 1976, (with W. Chambers) Texans and Their Land, 1964, (with James Reese) Texas-Land of Contrast, 1972, rev., 1978. Served to lt. (j.g.) USNR, World War II. Recipient Distinguished Service award Nat. Council Geog. Edn., 1972. Hon. life fellow Tex. Acad. Sci.; mem. Nat. Council Geog. Edn. (exec. bd. 1958-65, sec. 1958-64, pres. 1967), Assn. Am. Geographers (exec. council 1962-64, 68-71), Am. Geog. Soc., Southwestern Social Sci. Assn. (pres. 1972-73), Sigma Xi, Omicron Delta Kappa, Pi Gamma Mu, Phi Delta Kappa, Phi Kappa Phi. Unitarian. Home: 2704 San Pedro St Austin TX 78705

KENNAN, ELIZABETH TOPHAM, college president; b. Phila., Feb. 25, 1938; d. Frank and Henrietta (Jackson) Topham; m. Martin L. Budd, July 26, 1977; 1 son by previous marriage, Frank Alexander Kennan. B.A. summa cum laude, Mt. Holyoke Coll., 1960; M.A. (Hon. Woodrow Wilson fellow, Marshall scholar), St. Hilda's Coll., Oxford (Eng.) U., 1962; Ph.D., U. Wash., 1966; L.H.D. (hon.), Trinity Coll., Washington, 1978, Amherst Coll., 1980, Oberlin Coll., 1983, St. Mary's Coll. Asst. prof. history Catholic U. Am., 1966-70, asso. prof., 1970-78, dir. medieval and Byzantine studies program, 1970-78, dir. program in early Christian humanism, 1974-78; pres. Mt. Holyoke Coll., 1978—; lectr. in field; dir. Summer Inst. for Basic Skills, 1974; dir. Andrew W. Mellon Fellowships in Early Christian Humanism, 1974-78; mem. bd. advs. Hill Monastic Microfilm Library, 1976-78; mem. bd. cons. Nat. Endowment for Humanities, 1975—; dir. Bank of New Eng. West, Springfield, Mass., N.E. Utilities, Hartford, Conn., Berkshire Life Ins. Co., Pittsfield, Mass.; cons. to colls.; dir. Council on Library Resources, 1982—; mem. Pres.'s Emergency Adv. Bd. on Univ. Fin., 1976-77, Consortium on Financing Higher Edn., 1980—, chmn., 1982-83. Translator, author: (with John D. Anderson) introduction and notes On Consideration (St. Bernard of Clairvaux), 1976; contbr. articles to profl. publs. Bd. dirs. Assn. Am. Colls., 1980—; chmn. com. on govtl. relations Am. Council on Edn., 1979-82; Bd. dirs. Women's Coll. Coalition, 1979—. Named Tchr. of Year Cath. U. Am., 1977. Mem. Mediaeval Acad. Am. (chmn. com. on centers and regional assns. 1975—, dir. books-out-of-print project 1976-77, mem. council 1984—), Phi Beta Kappa., Council on Fgn. Relations. Home: Pres's House Mt Holyoke Coll South Hadley MA 01075 Office: Pres's Office Mt Holyoke Coll South Hadley MA 01075

KENNAN, GEORGE FROST, former ambassador, educator; b. Milw., Feb. 16, 1904; S. Kossuth Kent and Florence (James) K.; (Annelise Sorensen), 1931; children: Grace, Joan E., Christopher, Wendy. A.B., Princeton U., 1925, LL.D. (hon.), 1956, Yale U., 1950, Dartmouth Coll., 1950, Colgate U., 1951, U. Notre Dame, 1953, Kenyon Coll., 1954, New Sch. Social Research, 1955, U. Mich., 1957, Northwestern U., 1957, Brandeis U., 1958, U. Wis., 1963, Harvard U., 1963, Rutgers U., 1966, Denison U., 1966, Ripon Coll., 1968, Marquette U., 1972, Cath. U. Am., 1976, Duke U., 1977, Dickinson Coll., 1979, Lake Forest Coll., 1982, Clark U., 1983, Oberlin Coll., 1983, D.C.L., Oxford U., 1969. Vice consul, Hamburg, Germany, 1927, Tallinn, Finland, 1928, 3d sec., Riga, Kovno, and Tallinn, 1929, lang. officer, Berlin, Germany, 1929, 3d sec., Riga, 1931; accompanied Ambassador Bullitt to, Moscow, 1933, 3d sec., 1934; consul, Vienna, Austria, 1935, 2d sec., Moscow, USSR, 1935, Prague, Czechoslovakia, 1938, consul, 1939, 2d sec., Berlin, 1939, 1st sec., 1940, counselor legation, Lisbon, Portugal, 1942; counsellor Am. delegation European Adv. Commn., London, Eng., 1944; minister-counselor, Moscow, 1945; dep. for fgn. affairs Nat. War Coll., Washington, 1946; dir. policy planning staff Dept. State, 1947; dept. counselor, chief long range adviser to sec. state, 1949-50; mem. Inst. for Advanced Study, 1950-52; U.S. ambassador to, USSR, 1952; ret. from Fgn. Service, 1953; mem. Inst. for Advanced Study, Princeton, 1953, permanent prof., 1956-74, prof. emeritus, 1974—; Stafford Little lectr., 1954; George Eastman vis. prof. Oxford (Eng.) U., 1957-58; ambassador to, Yugoslavia, 1961-63; U. fellow Harvard, 1965-70. Author: American Diplomacy 1900-1950 (Freedom House award 1951), Realities of American Foreign Policy, 1954, Das Amerikanisch Russische Verhältnis, 1954, Russia Leaves the War, vol. I of Soviet-American Relations 1917-20, 1956 (Bancroft prize 1956, Nat. Book award, Francis Parkman prize, Pulitzer prize 1957), Decision to Intervene, vol. 2, 1958, Russia, The Atom and The West, 1958, Russia and the West Under Lenin and Stalin, 1961, On Dealing with the Communist World, 1964, Memoirs, 1925-1950, 1967 (Pulitzer prize 1968, Nat. Book award), From Prague after Munich, 1968, Democracy and the Student Left, 1968, The Marquis de Custine and His Russia in 1839, 1971, Memoirs 1950-63, 1972, The Cloud of Danger: Current Realities of American Foreign Policy, 1977, The Decline of Bismarck's European Order: Franco-Russian Relations, 1875-1890, 1979, The Nuclear Delusion: Soviet-Am. Relations in the Atomic Age, 1982. Fellow All Souls Coll., Oxford U., 1969; Woodrow Wilson Internat. Center Scholars Smithsonian Instn., Washington, 1974-75; Recipient Albert Einstein Peace prize, 1981, Grenville Clark prize, 1981, Peace Prize German Book Trade, 1982, Union medal Union Theol. Sem., 1982, Gold Medal in History Am. Acad. and Inst. Arts and Letters, 1984. Mem. Nat. Inst. Arts and Letters (pres. 1964-67, dir.), Am. Acad. Arts and Letters (pres. 1967-71), Am. Philos. Soc., Royal Soc. Arts (Benjamin Franklin fellow 1968), Order of Pour le Merite for Arts and Scis. Club: Century (N.Y.C.). Address: Inst for Advanced Study Princeton NJ 08540

KENNAN, KENT WHEELER, composer, educator; b. Milw., Apr. 18, 1913; s. Kossuth Kent and Sara Louise (Wheeler) K. Student, U. Mich., 1930-32; B.Mus. in Composition and Theory, Eastman Sch. of Music U. Rochester, 1934, M.Mus., 1936, Royal Acad. of Santa Cecilia, Rome, 1938. Mem. faculty Kent (Ohio) State U., 1939-40; tchr. composition, orchestration, counterpoint and theory U. Tex.-Austin, 1940-42, 45-46, 49-83; tchr. theory Ohio State U., 1947-49; tchr. composition, orchestration Eastman Sch. of Music, summers 1954, 56. (Orchestral works have been performed under Toscanini, Ormandy, Hanson, Stokowski, others, by N.Y. Philharm. Symphony, Phila. Orch., Chgo., Houston, Detroit and San Antonio Symphonies, others); Composer: Night Soliloquy, 5 Preludes for Piano; Sonata for Trumpet and Piano, also vocal music; Author: (with Donald Grantham) Technique of Orchestration, 3d revised edit, 1983, Counterpoint, revised edit., 1972. Served with USAAF, 1942-46. Recipient Prix de Rome in Music, 1936. Mem. ASCAP, Nat. Assn. Composers U.S.A., Delta Tau Delta, Phi Mu Alpha, Pi Kappa Lambda. Address: 1513 Westover Rd Austin TX 78703

KENNARD, KENNETH CLIFTON, educator; b. Easton, Pa., July 10, 1923; s. Harold Jones and Flossie (Doan) K.; m. Marilyn Aileen Salstrom, Aug. 19, 1949; children—Kenneth M., Ruth I. Student, Bryan Coll., 1941-42, Ga. Sch. Tech., 1943; A.B., Wheaton (Ill.) Coll., 1948, M.A., 1949, Northwestern U., 1952, Ph.D., 1966. Instr. philosophy, dean men The King's Coll., Briarcliff, N.Y., 1951-53; instr. Wheaton Coll., 1953-58, asst. prof., 1959-66, also acting dir. philosophy, 1964-65; asso. prof., chmn. dept. philosophy U. So. Colo., 1966-68; prof. dept. philosophy Ill. State U., 1968—, chmn. dept., 1968-75. Served with USAAF, 1943-46. Wheaton Coll. faculty research grantee, 1962. Mem. Am. Philos. Assn., Ill. Philos Assn. (v.p. 1968-70, pres. 1973-75), Phi Sigma Tau. Home: 101 Veronica Way Normal IL 61761

KENNEDY, ADRIENNE LITA, playwright; b. Pitts., Sept. 13, 1931; d. Cornell Wallace and Etta (Haugabook) Hawkins; m. Joseph C. Kennedy, May 15, 1953 (div. 1966); children—Joseph C., Adam. B.S., Ohio State U., 1953; student creative writing, Columbia U., 1954-56; playwrighting, New Sch. Social Research, Am. Theatre Wing, Circle in the Sq. Theatre Sch., 1957, 58, 62. Mem. playwriting unit Actors Studio, N.Y.C., 1962-65; Yale lectr. Yale, 1972-74; CBS fellow Sch. Drama, 1973; lectr. Princeton U., 1977; vis. asso. prof. Brown U., 1979-80; Internat. Theatre Inst. rep. to conf., Budapest, 1978. (Recipient Obie award 1964); Author: plays Funnyhouse of a Negro, 1964, Cities in Bezique, 1965, A Rat's Mass, 1966, A Lesson in Dead Language, 1966, The Lennon Play; adaptation, 1968, Sun; commd., Royal Ct., London, 1968, Lancashire Lad; commd. by, Empire State Youth Inst., 1979, Onestes, Electra, Juilliard Sch. Music, 1980, Black Children's Day, Rites and Reason, Brown U., 1980; Represented in numerous anthologies. Guggenheim fellow, 1968; Rockefeller fellow, 1967-69; Nat. Endowment Arts grantee, 1973; Rockefeller grantee, 1974; Creative Artists Pub. Service grantee, 1974; Yale fellow, 1974-75. Mem. P.E.N. (bd. dirs. 1976-77). Address: 172 W 79th St New York NY 10021 *I believe in listening to one's inner voices.*

KENNEDY, ANTHONY M., judge; b. Sacramento, July 23, 1936. A.B., Stanford U., 1958; student, London Sch. Edons.; LL.B., Harvard U., 1961. Bar: Calif. bar 1962, U.S. Tax Ct. bar 1971. Former partner firm Evans, Jackson & Kennedy; prof. constl. law McGeorge Sch. Law, U. of Pacific, 1965—; now judge U.S. Ct. Appeals, 9th Circuit, Sacramento.; Mem. bd. student advisors Harvard Faculty, 1960-61. Mem. Am., Sacramento County bar assns., State Bar Calif., Phi Beta Kappa.

KENNEDY, BARTON *See* **MC LANATHAN, RICHARD**

KENNEDY, BERENICE CONNOR (MRS. JEFFERSON KENNEDY, JR), mag. exec.; b. Phila.; d. William J. and Ethel N. (Waltman) Connor; m. Jefferson Kennedy, Jr., Oct., 1963. A.B., U. Pa., 1947. Account exec. Geare-Marston, Inc. (advt.), Phila., 1948-50; dir. radio and TV, Buckley Orgn., Phila., 1950-51; dir. editorial promotion Ladies' Home Jour., Phila., 1951-60, asso. editor, N.Y.C., 1961-62; sr. editor McCall Corp., N.Y.C., 1962-66; pres. Feminine Forecast, Inc., 1966—; editor Talk mag., 1969-79; pres., dir. Donovan Communications, Inc., 1976-79; editorial dir. Service Publs., 1980—. Named Phila. Advt. Woman of the Year Phila. Advt. Clubs, 1960; recipient award for creative design Phila. Art Dirs. Club, 1955; Salute to Women award Rep. Women in Bus. and Industry, 1966. Mem. Am. Soc. Mag. Editors, Phila. Club Advt. Women (dir. 1953-55), Fashion Group (dir. 1957-59), Advt. Women N.Y. (dir. 1962-64), Advt. Fedn. Am., Delta Delta Delta. Club: Overseas Press. Home: 200 E 66th St New York NY 10021

KENNEDY, BERNARD JOSEPH, utility executive; b. Niagara Falls, N.Y., Aug. 16, 1931; s. Edward J. and Frances (Coyle) K.; m. Geraldine Drexelius, Sept. 20, 1958; children: Mary Kathleen, Maureen Jean, Patricia, Colleen, Joseph B. B.A., Niagara U., 1953; LL.B., U. Mich., 1958. Bar: N.Y. bar 1960. Legal asst. Iroquois Gas Corp., Buffalo, 1958-63, gen. atty., 1963-67, sec., gen. counsel, 1967—; v.p., gen. counsel Nat. Fuel Gas Distbn. Corp., 1975-77, sr. v.p., 1977—; exec. v.p. Nat. Fuel Gas Co., 1976—; pres. Nat. Fuel Gas Supply Corp., 1978—, Penn-York Energy Corp., 1978—, Seneca Resources Corp., 1978—, Empire Exploration, 1983—; dir. AEGIS Ltd., Bermuda, Marine Midland Banks, Cellular Systems Corp. Pres. Assn. Retarded Children, Erie County, 1970-72; Chmn. bd. advisers Erie County Dept. Social Welfare; chmn. council Bus. Sch., Canisius Coll.; Bd. dirs. Erie County chpt. A.R.C.; chmn. Cath. Charities Appeal, 1981. Served to 1st lt. AUS, 1953-55. Mem. ABA (vice chmn. gas com.), Erie County Bar Assn., N.Y. Bar Assn. (chmn. pub. utilities com. 1973), Fed. Power Bar Assn., Am. Gas Assn. Home: 33 Ruskin Rd Eggertsville NY 14226 Office: 10 Lafayette Sq Buffalo NY 14203

KENNEDY, BRUCE R., airline executive; b. Denver, Oct. 11, 1938; s. Roger W. and Jean (Converse) K.; m. Karleen Isaacson, Nov. 21, 1965; children: Kevin, Karin. B.B.A., U. Alaska, 1963. Corp. sec. Alaska Continental Devel. Corp., Fairbanks, 1959-64, v.p., 1964,-67, pres., 1967-72, chmn., 1972; dir. Alaska Airlines, Inc., Seattle, 1972, sr. v.p. properties, 1973-78, pres., chief operating officer, 1978—, chmn., 1979—. Served to 1st lt. U.S. Army, 1965-67. Mem. Air Transport Assn. (dir.). Republican. Presbyterian. Office: PO Box 68900 Seattle WA 98188

KENNEDY, BURT RAPHAEL, film director; b. Muskegon, Mich., Sept. 3, 1922; s. Thomas James and Gertrude Amelia (O'Hagen) K.; m. Sheila Theresa Foster, July 11, 1973; children: Susan, Bridget. Grad. high sch. Writer, dir., producer films for all major motion picture cos. in, Hollywood, 1948—; Writer, dir., producer films: Mail Order Bride, 1964, The Rounders, 1965, The Money Trap, 1966, Return of the Seven, 1966, The War Wagon, 1967, Support Your Local Sheriff, 1969, Young Billy Young, 1969, Support Your Local Gunfighter, 1971, Hannie Caulder, 1972, The Train Robbers, 1972; wrote, produced, directed TV series: Combat, 1962-67; dir. TV movie: All Kind of Strangers, 1974, The Honor Guard, 1977, Wild Wild West Revisited, 1979; wrote TV movie: Concrete Cowboys, 1980, Seven Brides for Seven Brothers, 1981-82; dir. TV movie: Simon and Simon, 1983, Magnum P.I., 1983; wrote TV movie: The Littlest Horse Thieves, 1976. Served with U.S. Army, 1942-46. Decorated Silver Star medal, Bronze Star medal, Purple Heart with oak leaf cluster. Mem. Dirs. Guild Am., Writers Guild Am., Producers Guild. *

KENNEDY, CHRISTOPHER ROBIN, ceramist; b. Ottawa, Ont., Can., June 25, 1948; s. Robert Alvin and Ruth Christina (Downie) K.; m. Christine Willa Wayman, Jan. 28, 1978; children: Scott Wayman, Stuart James. B.S., Rutgers U., 1969; M.S., Pa. State U., 1971, Ph.D., 1974. Asst. ceramist Argonne Nat. Lab., Ill., 1974-79, ceramist, 1979-82; staff engr. Exxon Research and Engring. Co., Florham Park, N.J., 1982-83, sr. staff engr., group leader materials devel. group, 1984—. Contbr. articles to profl. jours. Mem. Am. Ceramic Soc., Nat. Inst. Ceramic Engrs., Keramos, Sigma Xi. Home: 6 Carroll Dr Brookside NJ 07926 Office: PO Box 101 Florham Park NJ 07932

KENNEDY, CORNELIA GROEFSEMA, judge; b. Detroit, Aug. 4, 1923; d. Elmer H. and Mary Blanche (Gibbons) Groefsema; m. Charles S. Kennedy, Jr.; 1 son, Charles S. III. B.A., U. Mich., 1945, J.D. with distinction, 1947; LL.D. (hon.), No. Mich. U., 1971, Eastern Mich. U., 1971, Western Mich. U., 1973, Detroit Coll. Law, 1980. Bar: Mich. bar 1947. Law clk. to Chief Judge Harold M. Stephens, U.S. Ct. of Appeals, Washington, 1947-48; asso. Elmer H. Groefsema, Detroit, 1948-52; partner Markle & Markle, Detroit, 1952-66; judge 3d Judicial Circuit Mich., 1967-70; dist. judge U.S. Dist. Ct., Eastern Dist. Mich., Detroit, 1970-79, chief judge, 1977-79; circuit judge U.S. Ct. Appeals, 6th Circuit, 1979—. Recipient Sesquicentennial award U. Mich. Fellow Am. Bar Found.; mem. ABA, Mich. Bar Assn. (past chmn. negligence law sect.), Detroit Bar Assn. (past dir.), Fed. Bar Assn., Am. Judicature Soc., Nat. Assn. Women Lawyers, Am. Trial Lawyers Assn., Mich. Assn. of Professions, Nat. Conf. Fed. Trial Judges (past chmn.), Phi Beta Kappa. Office: 744 Federal Bldg and US Courthouse Detroit MI 48226

KENNEDY, CORNELIUS BRYANT, lawyer; b. Evanston, Ill., Apr. 13, 1921; s. Millard Bryant and Myrna Estelle (Anderson) K.; m. Anne Martha Reynolds, June 20, 1959; children: Anne Talbot, Lauren Asher. A.B., Yale U., 1943; J.D., Harvard U., 1948. Bar: Ill. bar 1949, D.C. bar 1965. Asso. firm Mayer Meyer Austrian & Platt, Chgo., 1949-54, 55-59; asst. U.S. atty. Dept. Justice, Chgo., 1954-55; counsel to Minority Leader, U.S. Senate, 1959-65; sr. mem. firm Kennedy & Webster, Washington, 1965-82; of counsel Armstrong, Teasdale, Kramer & Vaughan, Washington, 1983—; public mem. Adminstrv. Conf. U.S., 1972-82, sr. conf. fellow, 1982—, chmn. rulemaking com., 1973-82. Contbr. articles to law jours. Fin. chmn. Lyric Opera Co., Chgo., 1954; chmn. young adults group Chgo. Council Fgn. Relations, 1958-59; pres. English Speaking Union Jrs., Chgo., 1957-59; trustee St. John's Child Devel. Center, Washington, 1965-67, 75—, pres., 1983—. Served to 1st lt., AC U.S. Army, 1942-46. Fellow Am. Bar Found.; mem. Am. Law Inst., ABA (council sect. adminstrv. law 1967-70, chmn. sect. 1976-77), Fed. Bar Assn. (chmn. com. adminstrv. law 1963-64), Legal Club Chgo. Clubs: Met. (Washington); Chevy Chase (Md.); Sailing of the Chesapeake (Annapolis, Md.); Explorers (N.Y.C.); Adventurer's (Chgo.); Capitol Hill (Washington). Home: 7720 Old Georgetown Pike McLean VA 22102 Office: 888 17th St NW Washington DC 20006

KENNEDY, DAVID MICHAEL, historian, educator; b. Seattle, July 22, 1941; s. Albert John and Mary Ellen (Caufield) K.; m. Judith Ann Osborne, Mar. 14, 1970; children: Ben Caufield, Elizabeth Margaret, Thomas Osborne. B.A., Stanford U., 1963; M.A., Yale U., 1964, Ph.D., 1968. Asst. prof. history Stanford U., 1967-72; asso. prof., 1972-80, prof., 1980—, chmn. program in internat. relations, 1977-80, asso. dean, 1981—; vis. prof. U. Florence, Italy, 1976-77; lectr. Internat. Communications Agy., Denmark, Finland, Turkey, Italy, 1976-77, Ireland, 1980. Author: Birth Control in America: The Career of Margaret Sanger, 1970, Over Here: The First World War and American Society, 1980, (with Thomas A. Bailey) The American Pageant: A History of the Republic, 7th edit, 1983. Mem. nat. planning group Am. Issues Forum, 1974-75; bd. dirs. CORO Found., 1981—. Recipient Bancroft prize, 1971; John Gilmary Shea prize, 1970; Am. Council Learned Socs. fellow, 1971-72; John Simon Guggenheim Meml. Found. fellow, 75-76. Mem. Am. Hist. Assn., Orgn. Am. Historians, Soc. Am. Historians, Am. Studies Assn. Democrat. Roman Catholic. Office: Dept History Stanford U Stanford CA 94305

KENNEDY, DONALD, university president; b. N.Y.C., Aug. 18, 1931; s. William Dorsey and Barbara (Bean) K.; m. Jeanne Dewey, June 11, 1953; children: Laura Page, Julia Hale. A.B., Harvard U., 1952, A.M., 1954, Ph.D., 1956; D.Sc., Columbia U., Williams Coll., U. Mich. Mem. faculty Syracuse U., 1956-60; mem. faculty Stanford U., 1960-77, prof. biol. scis., 1965-77, chmn. dept., 1965-72; sr. cons. Office Sci. and Tech. Policy, Exec. Office of Pres., 1976; commr. FDA, 1977-79; v.p., provost Stanford U., 1979-80, pres., 1980—; Bd. overseers Harvard, 1970-76. Author: (with W. H. Telfer) The Biology of Organisms, 1965; also articles.; Editor: The Living Cell, 1966, From Cell to Organism, 1967; editorial bd.: Jour. Exptl. Zoology, 1965-71, Jour. Comparative Physiology, 1965-76, Jour. Neurophysiology, 1969-75, Science, 1973-77. Fellow Am. Acad. Arts and Scis., AAAS; mem. Nat. Acad. Scis., Am. Physiol. Soc., Soc. Gen. Physiologists, Am. Soc. Zoologists, Soc. Exptl. Biology (U.K.). Home: 623 Mirada Ave Stanford CA 94305 Office: Office of President Stanford U Stanford CA 94305

KENNEDY, EDWARD MOORE, U.S. senator; b. Boston, Feb. 22, 1932; s. Joseph Patrick and Rose (Fitzgerald) K.; children: Kara Anne, Edward Moore, Patrick Joseph. A.B., Harvard U., 1956; student, Internat. Law Sch., The Hague, Netherlands, 1958; LL.B., U. Va., 1959. Bar: Mass. 1959, U.S. Supreme Ct. 1963. Asst. dist. atty., Suffolk County, Mass., 1961-62, U.S. senator from, Mass., 1962—; chmn. Judiciary Com., 1979-81; ranking Dem. Labor and Human Resources Com., 1981—. Author: Decisions for a Decade, 1968, In Critical Condition: The Crisis in America's Health Care, 1972, Our Day and Generation, 1979, (with Mark O. Hatfield) Freeze: How You Can Help Prevent Nuclear War, 1979 1982. Pres. Joseph P. Kennedy, Jr. Found., 1961—; trustee Children's Hosp. Med. Center, Boston, John F. Kennedy Library, Boston Symphony, John F. Kennedy Center for Performing Arts, Robert F. Kennedy Meml. Found., Boston Coll., Mass. Gen. Hosp. Served with AUS, 1951-53. Named one of 10 outstanding young men U.S. Jaycees, 1967. Office: Senate Office Bldg Washington DC 20510

KENNEDY, EUGENE CULLEN, psychologist, author; b. Syracuse, N.Y., Aug. 28, 1928; s. James Donald and Gertrude Veronica (Cullen) K.; m. Sara Charles. A.B., Maryknoll Coll., 1950; S.T.B., Maryknoll Sem., 1953, M.R.E., 1954; M.A., Catholic U. Am., 1958, Ph.D., 1962. Ordained priest Roman Catholic Ch., 1955; instr. psychology Maryknoll Sem., 1955-56, prof. psychology, 1960-69, Loyola U., Chgo., 1969—; cons. Menninger Found., 1965-67; mem. profl. adv. bd. Chgo. Dept. Mental Health. Author 35 books, 1965—; including: Himself! The Life and Times of Richard J. Daley, 1978, Free to be Human, 1979, Father's Day, 1981, Crisis Counseling, 1981, On Being a Friend, 1982, Queen Bee, 1982. Trustee U. Dayton, Ohio. Recipient Nat. Cath. Book award for Fashion Me A People, 1967, Nat. Cath. Book award for Comfort My People, 1968; Thomas More medal Thomas More Assn., 1972, 78; Carl Sandburg award for Himself, 1978; Carl Sandburg award for Father's Day, 1982; Soc. of Midwest Authors award, 1982; Friends of Lit. award, 1982. Fellow Am. Psychol. Assn. (pres. div. 36 1975-76); Mem. Soc. Sci. Study Religion, Authors Guild. Democrat. Home: 1300 Lake Shore Dr Chicago IL 60610 Office: 6525 N Sheridan Rd Chicago IL 60626 *My principal goal in all my work is to try to understand and to try to help others understand what is so human about all of us.*

KENNEDY, EUGENE FRANCIS, JR., architect; b. Bklyn., Jan. 31, 1904; s. Eugene Francis and Anna Teresa (Lee) K.; m. Carol Fox, Apr. 10, 1928 (dec. 1975); children—Roselyn, Peter, Michael, Maura; m. Jayne McGuire, Jan. 15, 1976. Student, Boston Archtl. Center, 1920-24, Ecole des Beaux Arts, Paris, 1925, Am. Acad., Rome, 1926. Draftsman Maginnis and Walsh, Boston, 1926-40, chief designer, 1940-51; partner Maginnis and Walsh and Kennedy (Architects), 1951-69, Kennedy and Kennedy (Architects), Boston, 1969—. Prin. works include: Nat. Shrine of Immaculate Conception, Washington, Cathedral of Mary Our Queen, Balt., Carney Hosp, Dorchester, Mass. Named Knight of St. Gregory the Great Pope Paul VI; Rotch travelling scholar, 1924-26. Fellow AIA; mem. Boston Soc. Architects, Mass. State Assn. Architects, Nat. Acad. Design. Roman Catholic. Home: 241 Perkins St J-502 Jamaica Plain MA 02130

KENNEDY, EUGENE PATRICK, educator; b. Chgo., Sept. 4, 1919; s. Michael and Catherine (Frawley) K.; m. Adelaide Majewski, Oct. 27, 1943; children—Lisa Kennedy Helprin, Sheila, Katherine. B.Sc., De Paul U., 1941; Ph.D. (Nutrition Found. fellow), U. Chgo., 1949; Sc.D. (hon.), U. Chgo., 1977, A.M., Harvard, 1960. Research chemist chem. research dept. Armour & Co., 1941-47; postdoctoral fellow Am. Cancer Soc., U. Calif. at Berkeley, 1949-50; with Ben May Lab. Cancer Research, dept. biochemistry U. Chgo., 1950-56, prof. biochemistry, 1956-60; sr. postdoctoral fellow NSF, Oxford (Eng.) U., 1959-60; Hamilton Kuhn prof. biol. chemistry Harvard Med. Sch., 1960—, head dept., 1960-65; Macy scholar Cambridge, 1976. Recipient Glycerine research award, 1955; Am. Oil Chemist Soc. Lipid Research award, 1970; Gairdner Found. award, 1976; Ledlie prize, 1976. Mem. Am. Chem. Soc. (Paul Lewis award 1958), Nat. Acad. Sci., Am. Soc. Biol. Chemists (pres. 1970-71), Am. Acad. Arts and Scis. Home: 63 Buckminster Rd Brookline MA 02146 Office: Dept Biol Chemistry Harvard Med Sch Boston MA 02115

KENNEDY, EUGENE RICHARD, microbiologist, univ. dean; b. Scranton, Pa., July 3, 1919; s. Thomas A. and Margaret (Culkin) K.; m. Marjorie Giblin, July 24, 1945; children—Anne, Michael, Christine. B.A., U. Scranton, 1941; M.S., Cath. U., 1943; Ph.D., Brown U., 1949. Diplomate: Am. Bd. Microbiology. Serologist Walter Reed Army Med. Center, Washington, 1942; instr. bacteriology and immunology R.I. Hosp. Sch. of Nursing, Providence, 1946-48, Brown U., 1946-48; instr. Cath. U. Am., Washington, 1949-51, asst. prof., 1951-55, asso. prof., 1956-66, prof. microbiology, 1966—, dean,

1973—. Contbr. articles to profl. jours. Served to capt. Med. Service Corps U.S. Army, 1943-46. Mem. Am. Soc. for Microbiology, AAAS, Sigma Xi, Phi Beta Kappa. Home: 11804 Saddlerock Rd Silver Spring MD 20902 Office: McMahon Hall Cath U Washington DC 20064

KENNEDY, FRANCES MIDLAM (MRS. JOSEPH CONRAD KENNEDY), advt. exec.; b. Wilmington, Del., Feb. 26, 1913; d. Edward West and Annie (Bullen) Midlam; m. Joseph Conrad Kennedy, Sept. 4, 1937; children—Edward Carter, Stephen Dandridge, Katharine Conrad (Mrs. David C. Treadway). Student pub. schs. Writer Compton Advt., N.Y.C., 1939-47; v.p., copy chief Dancer-Fitzgerald-Sample, Inc., Chgo., 1947-62, v.p., creative group head, mem. creative rev. com., N.Y.C., 1962-69, sr. v.p., creative dir., chmn. creative/mgmt. rev. bd., 1969-81, exec. v.p., chmn. creative rev. bd., 1981—. Recipient Emma Proetz award, 1954; Golden 30 award Chgo. Copywriters Club, 1958; named Chgo. Advt. Woman of Year Advt. Women Chgo., 1960. Episcopalian. Club: Cosmopolitan. Home: 517 E 84th St New York NY 10028 Office: 405 Lexington Ave New York NY 10017

KENNEDY, FRANK ROBERT, legal educator; b. Strafford, Mo., July 27, 1914; s. David Rolland and Maida Mary (Appleby) K.; m. Patricia Harvey, Aug. 26, 1939; children: Candace (Mrs. V.P. Gottschall), Robert Mitchell, Diane (Mrs. William Bulger), David Harold. A.B., S.W. Mo. State U., 1935; LL.B., Washington U., 1939; J.S.D., Yale U., 1953, 1939-40. Bar: Mo. 1939, Iowa 1961. Tchr., forensic coach Lebanon (Mo.) High Sch., 1935-36; instr. law State U. Iowa, 1940-41, asst. prof. law, 1941-46, assoc. prof., 1946-49, prof., 1949-61; prof. law U. Mich., Ann Arbor, 1961-78, Thomas M. Cooley prof., 1979—; on leave as exec. dir. Commn. on Bankruptcy Laws U.S., Washington, 1971-73; Acting chief counsel to indsl. user unit, rationing div. OPA, Washington, 1942-43; vis. prof. U. Pa., 1966; Reporter adv. com. bankruptcy rules Jud. Conf. U.S., 1960-76; reporter uniform exemptions act Nat. Conf. Commrs. for Uniform State Laws, 1974-76, reporter uniform fraudulent conveyance act, 1983-84. Co-author: Collier on Bankruptcy, 14th edit., vols. 4, 4A, 4B, 1942, 54, 59; Contbr. articles to legal, tech. jours. Served from ensign to lt. comdr. USNR, 1943-46; comdr. Res., ret. Mem. Am. Bar Assn., AAUP, Nat. Bankruptcy Conf., Am. Law Inst., Order of Coif, Delta Theta Phi, Omicron Delta Kappa, Pi Sigma Alpha. Club: Rotarian. Home: 2515 Manchester Rd Ann Arbor MI 48104

KENNEDY, FREDRICK C., supermarket executive. Head produce dept. Loblaw Grocerteria Co., Toronto, Ont., Can., 1937-39; produce clk. Great Atlantic & Pacific Tea Co. of Can., Ltd., 1939-40, head produce dept., 1940-43, store mgr., 1943-44, asst. sales mgr. Toronto office, 1944-51, sales and purchasing rep. Montreal office, 1951-66, v.p., 1966-69, gen. supt., 1969-70, pres. Can. div., then chmn. bd., 1970-75, corp. pres., 1975—; v.p., gen. mgr. Great Atlantic & Pacific Tea Co. of Can., Inc., Montvale, N.J., 1970-81, exec. v.p., 1981—, also dir.; pres., dir. A & P Properties Ltd., A & P Drug Mart Ltd. Office: Great Atlantic & Pacific Tea Co Inc 2 Paragon Dr Montvale NJ 07645 *

KENNEDY, G. DONALD, civil engineer; b. South Lyon, Mich., Jan. 25, 1900; s. John and Elizabeth (Bridson) K.; m. Ora L. Wood, June 2, 1928; children: David Donald, John T., Ann E. Kennedy Drucker, Patrick W., Michael J. B.S., U. Mich., 1921. Former registered profl. engr., Mich., Calif., Va., Oreg., Wash., Nebr., Kans., Ohio, Miss., Ill., N.Mex., D.C. Mem. survey party on housing project Dupont Engring. Co., Flint, Mich., 1919; asst. civil engr. Hoad and Decker, cons. engrs., Ann Arbor, Mich., 1921-24; design engr. and city engr., Jackson, Mich., 1925-26; with City of Pontiac, Mich.; on spl. mcpl. problems, including water supply and airport devel., 1927-32; bus. mgr., cons. engr., dep. commr. and commr. Mich. State Hwy. Dept., 1933-42; past v.p. charge hwy. devel. Automotive Safety Found., Washington; with Portland Cement Assn., Chgo., 1950-67, successively cons. engr., asst. to pres., v.p., exec. v.p., pres., 1950-67; cons. post war planning com. U.S. Senate, 1943-44; cons. to legis. interim coms., Calif., Wash., Oreg., Kans., Nebr., Miss., Ohio, 1945-49; Bd. dirs. ACTION, Inc.; former bd. cons. The Eno Found.; former mem. adv. com. Transp. Center, Northwestern U.; State hwy. commr., Mich., 1940-42; ex officio mem. state adminstrv. bd., state bd. aeronautics, state planning commn.); chief Emergency Pub. Works Div.; mem. hwy. traffic adv. com. War Dept., 1942-45; vice chmn. Roosevelt interregional hwy. com. (interstate system plan), 1941-44; mem. adv. bd. Pub. Works Task Force; Commn. on Orgn. of Exec. Br. of U.S. Govt. (Hoover Commn.), 1948-49; mem. hwy. research bd. NRC, 1952-60, chmn., 1954-55; pres. Am. Assn. State Hwy. Ofcls., 1942; bd. govs. Met. Housing and Planning Council, Chgo., 1964-78; vice chmn., mem. exec. com. Automotive Safety Found., 1943-50; mem. Chgo. Citizens Traffic Safety Bd., 1955-62; Attended Internat. Concrete Road Congress, Rome, 1959, Symposium on Concrete Pavements, Buenos Aires, 1960, Internat. Road Fedn. Meeting, Madrid, 1962; mem. Tech. Mission to Japan, 1963. Recipient George S. Bartlett Award for outstanding contbn. to hwy. progress, 1948. Fellow ASCE (life; chmn. hwy. div. 1953), Inst. Transp. Engrs. (life mem.); mem. Am. Pub. Works Assn. (life), Am. Planning Assn. (life), Engring. Soc. Detroit (charter), Am. Road Builders Assn. (life). Club: Cosmos (Washington). Home: 1630 Sheridan Rd Apt 6K Wilmette IL 60091

KENNEDY, GEORGE, actor; b. Feb. 18, 1926. Films include Jolly Pink Jungle, The Ballad of Josie, Cool Hand Luke, 1967 (Acad. award for best supporting actor), Bandolero, Boston Strangler, Guns of the Magnificent Seven, Gaily Gaily, The Good Guys and The Bad Guys, Airport, Tick... tick...tick, False Witness, Fool's Parade, Thunderbolt and Lightfoot, Earthquake, Airport '75, The Eiger Sanction, The Human Factor, The New Blue Knight, Airport '77, Mean Dog Blues, Brass Target, Death on the Nile, Hotwire, 1980, Modern Romance, 1981, Search and Destroy, 1981; TV movies include The Priest Killer, 1971, Deliver Us from Evil, 1973, A Cry in the Wilderness, 1974, The Blue Knight; appeared in: TV series the Blue Knight, 1975-76. Served with U.S. Army, 16 years. Address: care Charter Mgmt 9000 Sunset Blvd Los Angeles CA 90069

KENNEDY, GEORGE ALEXANDER, classicist, educator; b. Hartford, Conn., Nov. 26, 1928; s. George and Ethel (Hall) K.; m. Mary Lee Hunnicutt, Mar. 25, 1955; 1 dau., Claire Alexandra. B.A., Princeton U., 1950; M.A., Harvard U., 1952, Ph.D., 1954. Instr. Harvard U., 1955-58; asst. prof. classics Haverford (Pa.) Coll., 1958-63, asso. prof., 1963-65; prof. U. Pitts., 1965-66, U. N.C., Chapel Hill, 1966-72, chmn. dept. classics, 1966-76, Paddison prof. classics, 1972—; chmn. U. N.C. Press, Nat. Humanities Council, 1980—. Author: The Art of Persuasion in Greece, 1963, Quintilian, 1969, The Art of Rhetoric in the Roman World, 1972, Classical Rhetoric and its Christian and Secular Tradition, 1980, Greek Rhetoric under Christian Emperors, 1983. Fulbright fellow, 1964-65; Guggenheim fellow, 1964-65; Nat. Endowment Humanities fellow, 1979-80; Dumbarton Oaks fellow, 1979-80. Fellow Am. Acad. Arts and Scis.; mem. Am. Philol. Assn. (award of merit 1975, pres. 1979), Speech Communication Assn. (Golden Anniversary award 1972, Wichelns-Winans award 1980), Renaissance Soc. Am., Ry. and Locomotive Hist. Soc., Inst. Early Am. History and Culture (council 1975—), Internat. Soc. for History of Rhetoric (v.p. 1981—), Phi Beta Kappa. Home: 303 Estes Dr Chapel Hill NC 27514

KENNEDY, GEORGE D., chemical company executive; b. Pitts., May 30, 1926; s. Thomas Reed and Lois (Smith) K.; m. Valerie Putis; children: Charles Reed, George Danner, Jamey Kathleen, Susan Patton, Timothy Christian. B.A., Williams Coll., 1947. With Scott Paper Co., 1947-52, Champion Paper Co., 1952-65; pres. Brown Co., 1965-71; also dir.; exec. v.p. Internat. Minerals & Chem. Corp., Northbrook, Ill., 1971-78, pres., 1978—, dir., 1975—, chief exec. officer, 1983; dir. Brunswick Corp.; dir., mem. exec. com. Kemper Corp. Mem. exec. bd. N.E. Ill. council Boy Scouts Am.; chmn. Children's Meml. Hosp.; trustee Chgo. Symphony; mem. Chgo. Com., Mid-Am. Com.; mem. bus. adv. council Carnegie-Mellon U. Grad. Sch. Indsl. Adminstrn. Mem. Chgo. Assn. Commerce and Industry (dir.), Chgo. Council Fgn. Relations (dir.). Clubs: Board Room, N.Y. Athletic (N.Y.C.); Larchmont (N.Y.) Yacht; Sleepy Hollow Country (Scarborough, N.Y.); Skokie Country (Glencoe, Ill.); Commercial (Chgo.). Office: 2315 Sanders Rd Northbrook IL 60062

KENNEDY, GRACE HARLAN, interior designer; b. Seattle, May 23, 1908; d. Paul Kinney and Josephine Belle (Smith) Harlan; m. Leo Raymond Kennedy, June 8, 1931 (dec. May 1978); 1 dau., Paula Lee. Student, Omaha U., 1928-29; Ph.B., Duchesne Coll., 1931; postgrad., Creighton U., 1930-31, Chgo. Art Inst., 1930, Chgo. U., 1932, Nebr. U., 1932-33, Washington U., 1939. Tchr. art Omaha U., 1933, Duchesne Coll., 1934, Milw. Art Inst., 1935-37; artist advt. dept. Gimbels Inc., 1943-47; interior designer Orchard and Wilhelm Co., Omaha, 1948-68, J.L. Brandeis & Sons, 1968—. One-woman shows of paintings and textiles, St. Louis Pub. Library, 1944, Milw. City Club, 1945, Regency-5 Apt. Complex, Omaha, 1976, group shows, Joslyn Mus., Omaha, 1931-76, Nat. Assn. Women Artists, N.Y.C., 1944-46, Wis. Painters and Sculptors, Milw., 1945, Kansas City Art Inst., 1947, Internat. Textile Exhbn., Greensboro, N.C., 1946, pictures of interior designs published in nat. mags. Treas. St. Louis LWV, 1941-42; Donor trust fund to Jesuit Community, Creighton U., 1977. Fellow Am. Inst. Interior Designers; mem. Am. Soc. Interior Designers (nat. v.p. 1965-67, Designer of Distinction award Nebr.-Iowa chpt. 1982). Home: 662 S 84th St Omaha NE 68114 Office: 8001 Dodge St Omaha NE 68114

KENNEDY, HARRY SHERBOURNE, bishop; b. Bklyn., Aug. 21, 1901; s. David K. and Ida (Hargreaves) K.; m. Katharine Kittle, July 27, 1927; children—Bruce H., David K., Paul S., Joel and Mark (twins). Student, Colo. State Coll., 1922-26; A.B., St. John's Theol. Sem., 1926; postgrad., U. So. Calif., 1931; D.D., Seabury-Western Theol. Sem., 1943; S.T.D., Ch. Div. Sch. Pacific, 1944; D.D., Trinity Coll., 1957; L.H.D., Colo. Coll., 1967. Ordained to ministry Episcopal Ch., 1926; clergyman P.E. Ch., 1926-44, bishop of, Honolulu, 1944—. Served to capt. as chaplain AUS, 1942-43. Decorated comdr. Order Brit. Empire, 1964. Address: 1001 Wilder Ave Honolulu HI 96822

KENNEDY, HARVEY EDWARD, science information publishing executive; b. Goldsboro, N.C., Oct. 2, 1928; s. Robert H. and Zilphia E. (Taylor) K.; m. Dorothy Childress, Aug. 18, 1951; children: Connie Grayce, Jeffrey Reynolds. B.A., Atlantic Christian Coll., 1948; M.S., N.C. State Coll., 1952, Ph.D., 1954. Research scientist N.C. Santoriam, U.N.C. Med. Ctr., Chapel Hill, 1954-58; asst. prof. Ohio State U., Columbus, 1958-61; dir. product devel. Vetco div. Johnson & Johnson, New Brunswick, N.J., 1961-67; dir. sci. affairs BioScience Info. Services, Phila., 1967-75, exec. dir., 1975-80; pres. BioSciences Info. Services, Phila., 1980—. Editor: (spl. series) International Communication for Biomedical Research, 1980. Mem. Internat. Fedn. Sci. Editors (interim bd., v.p. 1980-83), Am. Soc. Info. Sci., Am. Inst. Biol. Scis. (exec. com.), Council Biology Editors (pres. 1978-79), Am. Soc. Microbiology (chmn. com. info. sci. 1976-79). Club: Cosmos (Washington). Home: 205 Haverford Ave Swarthmore PA 19081 Office: BioScience Information 2100 Arch St Philadelphia PA 19103

KENNEDY, JACK LELAND, lawyer; b. Portland, Oreg., Jan. 30, 1924; s. Earnest E. and Lera M. (Talley) K.; m. Clara C. Hagans, June 5, 1948; children: James M., John C. Grad., Southwestern U., Los Angeles; J.D., Lewis and Clark Coll., 1951. Bar: Oreg. 1951. Since practiced in, Portland; partner firm Kennedy, King Zimmer & O'Malley, 1971—; trustee Northwestern Coll. Law, Portland; dir. Profl. Liability Fund, 1979—. Contbr. articles to legal jours. Bd. overseers Lewis and Clark Coll. Served with USNR, 1942-46. Fellow Am. Coll. Trial Lawyers; mem. ABA, Oreg. State Bar (bd. govs. 1976-79, pres. 1978-79), Multnomah Bar Assn. Republican. Clubs: City (Portland); Columbia River Yacht. Home: 1281 SW Davenport St Portland OR 97201 Office: 1410 One Main Pl Portland OR 97204

KENNEDY, JAMES ROSS, chemical manufacturer; b. Kearny, N.J., July 31, 1911; s. James Ruddick and Mary (Ross) K.; m. Doris Ritti, Jan. 15, 1947; children: James R., John, Karen. B.A., U. Wis., 1935. With Home Fire Ins. Co., 1935-40, Peat, Marwick, Mitchell & Co., 1940-44; with Celanese Corp., 1944—, exec. v.p., 1960-67, vice chmn., 1967-76; also dir.; chief fin. officer, dir. ARA Services, Inc., 1978—; dir. United Student Aid Funds Inc., Sealy, Inc. Hon. trustee Com. Econ. Devel. Clubs: Princeton, Essex Fells (N.J.) Country. Home: Old Chester Rd Essex Fells NJ 07021 Office: ARA Services Inc Independence Sq W Philadelphia PA 19106

KENNEDY, JAMES WAITE, advertising executive, consultant; b. Belding, Mich., Sept. 23, 1937; s. Lloyd Weston and Lois (Waite) K.; m. Katherine McCloud, Aug. 25, 1961; children: David, Sarah, Polly. B.A., Stanford U., 1959; P.M.D., Harvard Bus. Sch., 1969. With Foote, Cone & Belding, San Francisco and Chgo., 1959-66, Gen. Foods Corp., White Plains, N.Y., 1966-79; dir. human resources J. Walter Thompson Co., N.Y.C., 1979-83; pres. Mgmt. Team Cons., Inc., New Canaan, Conn., 1983—. Served with USAR, 1960. Mem. N.Y. Human Resources Planning Soc., Harvard Bus. Sch. Club N.Y.C. Office: 199 Elm St New Canaan CT 06840

KENNEDY, JOHN FISHER, engineering educator; b. Farmington, N.Mex., Dec. 17, 1933; s. Angus John and Edith Wilma (Fisher) K.; m. Nancy Kay Grogan, Nov. 21, 1959; children: Suzanne Marie, Sean Grogan, Brian Matthew Fisher, Karen Lynn. B.S. in Civil Engring., U. Notre Dame, 1955; M.S., Calif. Inst. Tech., 1956, Ph.D., 1960. Research fellow Calif. Inst. Tech., Pasadena, 1960-61; asst. prof. MIT, Cambridge, 1961-64, asso. prof., 1964-66; dir. Iowa Inst. Hydraulic Research; prof. fluid mechanics U. Iowa, Iowa City, 1966—; chmn. div. energy engring. U. Iowa, 1974-76; Fulbright scholar, vis. prof. U. Karlsruhe, Germany, 1972-73; Erskine fellow U. Canterbury, Christchurch, N.Z., 1976; cons. to govt. agys., indsl. firms, engring. cons. offices, 1960—; vis. asso. in hydraulics Calif. Inst. Tech., 1977; ASCE Hunter Rouse lectr., 1981. Served to 2d lt. C.E., U.S. Army, 1957. Recipient J.C. Stevens award ASCE, 1959; W.L. Huber Research prize, 1964; Karl Emil Hilgard Hydraulic prize, 1974, 78; Engring. Honor award U. Notre Dame, 1978; Corning Glass Works fellow, 1959-60. Mem. Nat. Acad. Engring., ASCE, ASME, Am. Soc. Engring. Edn., Internat. Assn. Hydraulic Research (mem. council 1972-76, v.p. 1976-80, pres. 1981—), Sigma Xi, Chi Epsilon (hon.), Tau Beta Pi. Roman Catholic. Home: 2 Ashwood Dr Iowa City IA 52240 *Half of being a good sculptor is knowing when to stop carving.*

KENNEDY, JOHN JOSEPH, educator; b. Cortland, N.Y., Sept. 13, 1914; s. John Austin and Anna Gertrude (Ryan) K.; m. Elizabeth Carol Riordan, Aug. 19, 1942; children—John Christian, Kathryn Kennedy Bueno. B.A., U. N.Mex., 1936; A.M., Columbia U., 1938, Ph.D., 1954. Liaison officer internat. activities Pub. Adminstrn. Clearing House, Chgo., 1938-41; regional specialist Latin Am., Dept. State, Washington, 1941-42, 46-48; vis. prof. U. P.R., 1949-50; asst. prof. polit. sci. U. Notre Dame, 1951-56, asso. prof., 1956-59; prof. U. Va., Charlottesville, 1959-64; prof., dir. Latin Am. studies program Notre Dame (Ind.) U., 1964—; vis. prof. Coll. City N.Y., 1960; cons. Ford Found., Peru and Chile, 1964; Rockefeller Found.; affiliate, vis. prof. U. del Valle, Colombia, 1968-71, cons., 1978-80. Author: Catholicism, Nationalism and Democracy in Argentina, 1958, Over All Development in Chile, 1969. Served to lt. comdr. USNR, 1942-46. Nat. Council on Religion in Higher Edn. fellow, 1937; postdoctoral fellow Council on Fgn. Relations N.Y., 1958-59. Mem. Am. Polit. Sci. Assn. Democrat. Roman Catholic. Home: 1937 Inglewood Pl South Bend IN 46616 Office: Box 201 Notre Dame IN 46556

KENNEDY, JOHN RAYMOND, pulp and paper company executive; b. N.Y.C., Sept. 21, 1930; s. John Raymond and Ethel R. (Leavy) K.; m. Elizabeth C. Calogerakis, Oct. 24, 1974; children: John Raymond III, James, Andrew, Paula; 1 stepson, Nicholas. B.S., Georgetown U., 1952. With Fed. Paper Bd. Co., Inc., Montvale, N.J., 1952—; pres. Fed. Paper Bd. Co, Inc., Montvale, N.J., 1966—; chief exec. officer Fed. Paper Bd. Co., Inc., Montvale, N.J., 1975—, also dir.; dir. Am. Mut. Liability Ins. Co., Am. Policyholders Ins. Co., Chgo. Pneumatic Tool Co., First Nat. Stage Bancorp., West Chem. Porducts, Inc. Pres. Bergen-Passaic Assn. Retarded Citizens; bd. dirs. Georgetown U.; trustee New Canaan Inn Retirement Home, (Conn.), Low-Heywood Thomas Sch., Stamford, Conn. Mem. Am. Paper Inst. Republican. Roman Catholic. Clubs: Devon Yacht, Maidstone, Blind Brook, Nat. Golf Links Am., Woodway Country, Fairfield County Hunt, University. Home: 223 Michigan Rd New Canaan Ct 06840 Office: Federal Paper Board Company Inc 75 Chestnut Ridge Rd Montvale NJ 07645

KENNEDY, JOHN WESLEY, arbitrator, former university official, economics educator; b. Spencer, N.C., Oct. 9, 1920; s. John Quincy and Willie (Huffman) K.; m. Melva Pearce Dail, Aug. 21, 1942; children: John Wesley, Marcia Frances, Melva Ann. A.B., Duke, 1942, A.M., 1947; Ph.D., U. N.C. at Chapel Hill, 1951. Asst. prof. econs., bus. adminstrn. U. Fla., 1949-52; asso. prof., prof. Auburn U., 1952-56; mem. faculty U. N.C. at Greensboro, 1956—, dean, 1964-71, prof. econs., 1956—, prof. emeritus, 1984—, vice chancellor for grad. studies, 1971-84; Labor arbitrator, 1954—. Author: (with others) Economics—Principles and Applications, 9th edit, 1978, A Problem Manual in Economic Theory, 6th edit, 1974; Contbr. articles to profl. jours. Pres. Greensboro Assn. Retarded Children, 1958-60. Served to lt. USNR, 1942-45. Mem. Indsl. Relations and Research Assn., Nat. Acad. Arbitrators. Baptist (deacon 1966-70). Home: 2505 Fairway Dr Greensboro NC 27408

KENNEDY, KEITH FURNIVAL, packaging company executive, lawyer; b. New London, Conn., Nov. 1, 1925; s. Joseph Reilly and Madeleine (Mason) K.; m. Joan Ruth Canfield, Feb. 11, 1956; children: Joseph Keith, Austin Robert, Thomas Canfield, Richard Furnival. B.S., Yale U., 1949; LL.B., Harvard U., 1953. Bar: N.Y. 1955. Atty. Vick Chem. Co., 1953-54, 58- 60; sec., dir. personnel J.T. Baker Chem. Co., 1955-58; with Riegel Paper Corp., 1960-71, sec., 1961-69, gen., atty., 1964-69, v.p. finance and law, counsel, 1969-71; sr. v.p. Rexham Corp., 1972—, also dir.; dir. Laminex, Inc., Schiller Industries, Inc., Brittains-Riegel Indsl., Ltd. Active Scarsdale Vol. Fire Co. 3; bd. dirs. Adoption service Westchester, pres., 1971-73; mem. pres.'s adv. council Coll. New Rochelle, 1973-77; bd. dirs. Calvary Hosp., N.Y.C., 1977—, vice chmn., N.Y.C., 1982—. Served to 1st lt. AUS, 1943-46, 51-52. Mem. Assn. Bar City N.Y., Am. Soc. Corp. Secs., St. Andrews Soc. N.Y., Chi Phi. Roman Catholic. Clubs: Union League, Economic of N.Y., Yale (N.Y.C.); Larchmont (N.Y.) Yacht, Niantic Bay (Conn.) Yacht. Office: 90 Park Ave New York NY 10016

KENNEDY, LAWRENCE ALLAN, engineering educator; b. Detroit, May 31, 1937; s. Clifford Earl and Emma Josephine (Muller) K.; m. Valaree J. Lockhart, Aug. 3, 1957; children: Joanne, Julie, Janet, Raymond, Jill, Brian. B.S., U. Detroit, 1960; M.S., Northwestern U., 1962, Ph.D., 1964. Registered profl. engr., N.Y. Chmn. dept., prof. mech. and aero. engring. SUNY-Buffalo, 1964-83; chmn. dept. mech. engring., prof. Ohio State U., Columbus, 1983—; vis. assoc. prof. mech. and aero. engring. U. Calif.-San Diego, 1968-69, VonKarman Inst., Rhode-St. Genese, Belgium, 1971-72; Goebel vis. prof. mech. and aero. engring. U. Mich., Ann Arbor, 1980-81; cons. Cornell Aero. Lab., Buffalo, 1968-72, Tech. Adv. Service, Fort Washington, Pa., 1969—, Ashland Chem. Corp., Dublin, Ohio, 1980-81, Mech. Engring. Sci. and Application, Buffalo, 1972-83. Contbr. numerous articles on engring. to profl. jours.; editor: Progress in Astronautics and Aeros., Vol. 58, 1978. NATO fellow, 1971-72; Agard lectr., 1971-72; NSF fellow, 1968-69; W.P. Murphy fellow, 1960-63. Fellow AIAA (assoc.); mem. ASME, Am. Phys. Soc., Combustion Inst. Roman Catholic. Home: 1020 Ravine Ridge Worthington OH 43085 Office: Dept Mech Engring Ohio State U Columbus OH 43210

KENNEDY, LEROY ERRETT, insurance executive; b. Nortonville, Ky., Mar. 13, 1924; s. Albert Roy and Bessie Mae (Oldham) K.; m. Lois Helen Carroll, Aug. 9, 1946 (div. July 1979); children: Karen Ruth Kennedy Howick, Martha Ann. A.B., Louisville U., 1949; J.D., Stetson U., 1951. Bar: Fla. 1951, Ky. 1951. Claim rep. State Farm Mut. Ins. Co., Mayfield, Ky., 1951-53; regional claim mgr. Allstate Ins. Co., Jackson, Miss., 1953-59; home office claim mgr. Gen. Mut. Ins., Birmingham, Ala., 1959-61; v.p. Celina Ins. Group, Ohio, 1961-69, Northwestern Nat. Inc. Co., Milw., 1969-81; pres. Northwestern Nat. Ins. Co., Milw., 1981—, dir., 1976—; dir. Underwriters Salvage Co., Chgo.; bd. govs., exec. com. Improved Risk Muts., 1982—. Bd. dirs. Wis. Heritages, Inc., Milw., 1982—, DePaul Rehab. Hosp., Milw., 1983. Served to 1st lt. U.S. Army, 1943-56; ETO. Mem. Central Claim Execs. Assn. (pres. 1974-75), Ohio Ins. Info. Service (trustee 1962-69), Def. Research Inst., Internat. Assn. Ins. Counsel, Fedn. Ins. Counsel, ABA. Club: Milw. Athletic. Home: 1818 E Shorewood Blvd 110 Shorewood WI 53211 Office: Northwestern Nat Ins Co 731 N Jackson St Milwaukee WI 53201

KENNEDY, MARC J., lawyer; b. Newburgh, N.Y., Mar. 2, 1945; s. Warren G. K. and Frances F. (Kennedy); m. Mahvash Rezvan, June 10, 1980; m. Carol Feldstein, May 9, 1968 (div. 1978). B.A. cum laude, Syracuse U., 1967; J.D., U. Mich., 1970. Bar: N.Y. 1971. Assoc. Davies, Hardy, Ives & Lawther, N.Y.C., 1971-72, London, Buttenweiser & Chalif, 1972-73, Silberfeld, Danziger & Bangser, 1973; counsel Occidental Crude Sales, Inc., N.Y.C., 1974-75; v.p., gen. counsel Internat. Ore & Fertilizer Corp., N.Y.C., 1975-82; asst. gen. counsel Occidental Chem. Corp., Houston, 1982; v.p., gen. counsel Occidental Chem. Co., Tampa, Fla., 1982—; faculty mentor Columbia Pacific U., Mill Valley, Calif., 1981—. Trustee Bar Harbor Festival Corp., N.Y.C., 1974—; bd. dirs. Am. Opera Repertory Co., N.Y.C., 1982—; mem. com. planned giving N.Y. Foundling Hosp., 1977—; Explorer post advisor Boy Scouts Am., 1976-78. Mem. ABA (vice-chmn. com. internat. law, liaison young lawyers sect. 1974-75), Internat. Bar Assn., Am. Soc. Internat. Law, Maritime Law Assn., N.Y. State Bar Assn., Assn. Bar City N.Y. (admiralty law com. 1982—). Home: 690 Island Way 201 Clearwater FL 33515 Office: Occidental Chem Co 5404 Cypress Center Dr Tampa FL 33609

KENNEDY, MARGARET SWIERZ, magazine editor; b. Milford, Mass., Oct. 19, 1941; d. Mitchell Martin and Jennie (Novack) Swierz;

m. Eugene Martin Kenndedy Jr., Nov. 7, 1964; 1 son, Eugene Martin. A.B., Clark U., 1963. Sec. Conde Nast. Publs., N.Y.C., 1963—; also asst. editor House and Garden Mag., N.Y.C., editor furniture and design projects; exec. editor House Beautiful Mag., N.Y.C., 1981—; guest editor Mademoiselle Mag., 1962. Mem. N.Y. Home Fashions League, Phi Beta Kappa. Roman Catholic. Home: 46 E 91st St New York NY 10128 Office: House Beautiful 1700 Broadway New York NY 10019

KENNEDY, MATTHEW WASHINGTON, educator, pianist; b. Americus, Ga., Mar. 10, 1921; s. Royal Clement and Mary (Dowdell) K.; m. Anne Lucille Gamble, May 23, 1956; 1 dau., Nina Gamble. Diploma, Juilliard Inst. Mus. Art, 1940; A.B., Fisk U., 1946; M.S., Juilliard Sch. Music, 1950; postgrad., George Peabody Coll. for Tchrs. Faculty Fisk U., Nashville, 1947-48, 54—, asso. prof., 1967—, chmn. music dept., 1975-77; summer piano faculty Mich. All State Piano Inst. Nat. Music Camp, Interlochen, 1973. Dir. univ., Jubilee Singers, 1957-68, 71-73, 75—; pianist-accompanist, throughout world, 1946-47, 50-54; solo pianist, 1958—; arranger spirituals. Mem. resource panel Tenn. Arts Commn.; bd. dirs. John W. Work III Meml. Found., Nashville Symphony Assn. Served with AUS, World War II; ETO. Recipient Disting. Service award Nat. Assn. Negro Musicians, 1980. Mem. Sigma Upsilon Pi, Omega Psi Phi. Baptist (deacon). Club: Nashville Fine Arts. Home: 2417 Gardner Ln Nashville TN 37207

KENNEDY, RICHARD JEROME, writer; b. Jefferson City, Mo., Dec. 23, 1932; s. Donald and Mary Louise (O'Keefe) K.; m. Lillian Elsie Nance, Aug. 3, 1960; children: Joseph Troy, Matthew Cook. B.S., Portland State U., 1958. Author: 17 children's books including The Parrot and the Thief, 1974, Song of the Horse, 1981. Served with USAF, 1951-54. Address: 415 W Olive Newport OR 97365

KENNEDY, RICHARD THOMAS, government official; b. Rochester, N.Y., Dec. 24, 1919; s. Thomas Roderick and Anastasia Louise (O'Brien) K.; m. Jean Drew Martin, Mar. 29, 1947. B.A., U. Rochester, 1941; M.B.A., Harvard U., 1953; postgrad., Nat. War Coll., Washington, 1964-65. Commd. 2d lt. U.S. Army, 1942, advanced through grades to col., 1965; planning and fin. mgmt. adv. to, Iran, 1959-61; with Army Gen. Staff, Washington, 1962; internat. security affairs Office Asst. Sec. Def., 1965-69; sr. mem. staff NSC, 1969-71; ret., 1971; dir. staff planning and coordination NSC, Washington, 1971-72; dep. asst. to pres. for NSC planning, 1973-75; commr. U.S. Nuclear Regulatory Commn., 1976-80; undersec. for mgmt. Dept. State, Washington, 1981-82, ambassador-at-large for nuclear non-proliferation affairs, 1983—; v.p., treas., dir. Potomac Plaza Apts., Inc., 1965-69, pres. bd., 1967-69; alt. U.S. rep. gen. conf. IAEA, 1975, 77, U.S. rep. to, 1981—; U.S. mem., v.p. OECD Nuclear Energy Agy., 1983—; v.p., dir. Watergate East, Inc., 1976-79. Decorated D.S.M., Legion of Merit, Bronze Star, Army Commendation medal. Mem. Assn. U.S. Army, Am. Nuclear Soc. (internat. adv. com. 1977—), Ret. Officers Assn., DAV, Sigma Chi. Roman Catholic. Clubs: Harvard Bus. Sch., Army-Navy, Army-Navy Country, Capitol Hill. Home: 2510 Virginia Ave NW Washington DC 20037 Office: Dept State 2201 C St NW Washington DC 20520

KENNEDY, ROBERT EMMET, retired newspaperman; b. Cin., June 6, 1910; s. Robert Emmet and Amelia (Garnier) K.; m. Rosetta Vinson, Oct. 27, 1933; children: Jeanne Colleen (Mrs. Theodore Lamb), Robert Emmet. Student, DePaul U., 1928. Police reporter, later asst. city editor City News Bur., 1929-35; asst. city editor, polit. editor Washington corr., editorial page editor Chgo. Times, 1935-48; editorial writer Chgo. Sun-Times, 1948-50, chief editorial writer, 1950-65, asso. editor, 1965-74; pres. Sea Breeze West Condominium, Inc., Marco Island, Fla., 1974-75. Contbr. to: Marco Island Eagle, 1976—. Mem. Am. Soc. Newspaper Editors, Nat. Conf. Editorial Writers (chmn. 1958), Sigma Delta Chi. Club: Chgo. Press (pres. 1963). Home: 1850 S Inlet Dr Marco Island FL 33937

KENNEDY, ROBERT EUGENE, advertising agency executive; b. N.Y.C., June 2, 1942; s. John David and Katherine Patricia K.; m. Roseanne C. McNeill, June 26, 1965; children—Noelle, Stephen, Elizabeth, Kristen. Student, Iona Coll., 1961-68. With Dancer-Fitzgerald-Sample Inc., N.Y.C., 1961—, asst. controller, 1969-72, v.p., controller, 1972-76, sr. v.p., 1976—, treas., 1977—, exec. v.p., chief fin. officer, 1979—; also dir., also chmn. subs. Program Syndicated Services, Inc., 1979—; vice chmn. DFS Internat., Inc., 1981—; vice chmn., chief fin. officer DFS Holdings Inc., 1982—. Served with USMC, 1965. Mem. Advt. agy. Fin. Mgmt. Group, Fin. Execs. Inst., Pascack Valley Hosp. Assn. Clubs: Arcola Country (Paramus, N.J.); Pinacle, Union League (N.Y.C.). Office: 405 Lexington Ave New York NY 10017

KENNEDY, ROBERT NORMAN, architect; b. Louisville, Sept. 29, 1932; s. Charles Fleming and Roberta (Dunn) K.; m. Sheila Simkin Suess, Mar. 2, 1980; children: Kevin Elizabeth, Kelly Eileen. B.S. in Architecture, U. Cin., 1956. Architect, firms in, Indpls., 1954—; partner Kennedy Brown & Assos., 1961-81, Archonics Partners, 1981—; mem. Ind. Archtl. Registration Bd., 1972—. Prin. works include Market Sq. Arena, Indpls., 1975, Edn. Center, Indpls., 1964, Robinson (Ill.) Public Library, 1976, Eagle Creek Park master plan, Indpls., 1976. Dir. Indpls. Dept. Met. Devel., 1976-81; bd. dirs. Commn. Downtown Indpls., 1977—, Indpls. Met. YMCA. Recipient Good Govt. award Indpls. Jr. C. of C. Fellow AIA (founder Indpls. chpt. 1965); mem. Ind. Soc. Architects (dir. 1965-72, Edward D. Pierre award 1977), Nat. Council Archtl. Registration Bds. Republican.

KENNEDY, ROGER GEORGE, foundation executive, Museum executive; b. St. Paul, Aug. 3, 1926; s. Walter J. and Elisabeth (Dean) K.; m. Frances Hefren, Aug. 23, 1958; 1 dau., Ruth. Grad., St. Paul Acad., 1944; B.A., Yale, 1949; LL.B., U. Minn., 1952. Bar: Minn. bar 1952, D.C. bar 1953. Atty. Justice Dept., 1953; corr. NBC, 1954-57; dir. Dallas Council World Affairs, 1958; spl. asst. to sec. Dept. Labor, 1959; successively asst. v.p., v.p., chmn. exec. com., dir. Northwestern Nat. Bank St. Paul, 1959-69; v.p. finance, exec. dir. Univ. Found., Minn., 1969-70; v.p. financial affairs Ford Found., N.Y.C., 1970-78, v.p. arts, 1978-79; dir. Nat. Mus. History and Tech., Smithsonian Instn., Washington, 1979—; spl. asst. to sec. HEW, 1957, cons. to sec., 1969. Author: Minnesota Houses, 1967, Men on a Moving Frontier, 1969; NBC radio and TV Today; Am. Churches, 1982, others, 1954-57; Contbr. articles to mags., profl. jours. Served with USNR, 1944-46. Office: Nat Mus Am History 14th and Constitution Ave NW Washington DC 20560

KENNEDY, ROSE FITZGERALD (MRS. JOSEPH P. KENNEDY), b. Boston, July 22, 1890; d. John Francis and Josephine Mary (Hannon) Fitzgerlad; m. Joseph P. Kennedy, Oct. 7, 1914 (dec. 1969); children: Joseph (dec.), John Fitzgerald, (Pres. U.S. 1961-63; dec.) Rosemary, Kathleen (dec.), Eunice (Mrs. Robert Sargent Shriver), Patricia Kennedy Lawford, Robert Francis (dec.), Jean (Mrs. Stephen Smith), Edward M. Ed., New Eng. Conservatory, Convent of Sacred Heart, Boston, Manhattanville Coll. Sacred Heart, Blumenthal Acad., Valls, The Netherlands; LL.D., Manhattanville Coll., Georgetown U., 1977. Author: Times to Remember, 1974. Named Papal Countess Pope Pius XII. Roman Catholic. Address: Hyannis MA 02647 *

KENNEDY, THOMAS JAMES, JR., assn. exec.; b. Washington, June 24, 1920; s. Thomas James and Ruth Elizabeth (Norris) K.; m. F. Elaine Godtfring, Sept. 30, 1950; children—Thomas James III, Ann Elizabeth, Joan Frances, Paul Edward, Christopher Alan. B.S., Cath. U. Am., 1940; M.D., Johns Hopkins, 1943. Diplomate: Am. Bd. Internal Medicine. Intern med. service Peter Bent Brigham Hosp., Boston, 1944; research fellow, research service 3d med. div. Goldwater Meml. Hosp., N.Y.C., 1945-47, resident physician, research service 1st med. div., 1947-50; research fellow N.Y. U. Coll. Medicine, 1945-47; asst. medicine Columbia Coll. Phys. and Surg., 1948-50; joined USPHS, 1950; asst. surgeon gen.; asso. medicine George Washington U. Sch. Medicine, 1951-65; investigator lab. kidney and electrolyte metabolism Nat. Heart Inst., 1950-60, attending physician, responsible physician, 1953-60; asst. to dir. labs. and clinics Office Dir., NIH, 1960-62, spl. asst. to dir. for sci. communications, 1962-65, dir. div. research facilities and resources, 1965-68, asso. dir. for program planning and evaluation, office of dir., 1968-74; exec. dir. Assembly Life Scis., NRC-Nat. Acad. Scis., 1974-76; dir. dept. planning and policy devel. Assn. Am. Med. Colls., Washington, 1976—. Served to capt. AUS, 1944-47. Mem. Am. Fedn. Clin. Research, Am. Physiol. Soc. Home: 10703 Weymouth St Garrett Park MD 20896 Office: One Dupont Circle Suite 200 Washington DC 20036

KENNEDY, THOMAS LEO, investment mgmt. co. exec.; b. Medina, N.Y., Mar. 27, 1936; s. John Patrick and Agnes (Kinn) K.; m. Mary Ellen Reynolds, Nov. 26, 1959; children—Patrick Thomas, Michael Joseph. B.S., Coll. Holy Cross, 1958; M.B.A., Babson Coll., 1966; postgrad., Mgmt. Devel. Program, Harvard, 1976. Sr. systems analyst New England Merchants Nat. Bank, Boston, 1967-68, asst. sec., 1968-69, auditor, 1969-78, v.p., 1972, comptroller, 1978-80; v.p., asst. treas. Pioneer Group, Inc., Boston, 1980—; instr. Am. Inst. Banking. Mem. Milton (Mass.) Town Meeting, 1967—; mem. Milton Fin. Com., 1978-81. Served with USNR, 1959-62. Mem. Am. Inst. C.P.A.'s, Mass. Soc. C.P.A.'s (investment co. com.). Home: 19 Westvale Rd Milton MA 02186 Office: Pioneer Group Inc 60 State St Boston MA 02109

KENNEDY, WILBERT KEITH, agronomy educator; b. Vancouver, Wash., Jan. 4, 1919; s. Wilbert Parsons and Gracie Evelyn (Woolf) K.; m. Barbara Josephine Barber, Dec. 9, 1941; children: Wilbert Keith, James Clayton. B.S., Wash. State U., 1940; M.S. in Agr, Cornell U., 1941, Ph.D., 1947. Asst. prof., asst. agronomist Wash. State Coll., 1947-48, asso. prof., asso. agronomist, 1948-49; prof. agronomy Cornell U., Ithaca, N.Y., 1949—; asso. dir. research N.Y. State Coll. Agr., Cornell U.; also asso. dir. Cornell U. Agr. Exptl. Sta., 1959, dir. research and dir. expt. sta., 1959-65; asso. dean N.Y. State Coll. Agr., 1965-67, vice provost univ., 1967-72, dean, 1972-78, provost univ., 1978—; cons. Kasetsart U., Thailand, 1968, Ford Found., Malaysia, 1970. Contbr. articles to profl. jours. Mem. sch. bd., Dryden, N.Y., 1953-55; exec. com. Louis Agassiz council Boy Scouts Am., 1955-70; active local Community Chest. Served to maj. AUS, 1942-46. Guggenheim fellow; Fulbright Scholar, 1956-57; Recipient N.Y. Farmers award, 1958; Merit Certificate award Am. Grassland Council, 1964. Fellow Am. Soc. Agronomy, A.A.A.S.; mem. Sigma Xi, Phi Kappa Phi, Alpha Zeta. Lodge: Rotary. Home: 3 Sandra Pl Ithaca NY 14850 Office: Day Hall Cornell U Ithaca NY 14853

KENNEDY, WILLIAM, newspaper editor; s. Richard and Pearl (Anderson) K.; (married); 1 son, Victor; children by previous marriage: Patricia, Ross. A.A., U. Minn., 1947; B.A. in Journalism, U. Calif. at Berkeley, 1950. Columnist-reporter Times-Star, Alameda, Calif., 1950, News-Observer, San Leandro, Calif., 1950-51; patrolman Berkeley (Calif.) Police Dept., 1951; reporter Duluth (Minn.) Tribune, 1954-55, Watsonville (Calif.) Register-Parjaronian, 1955-60; editor Cupertino (Calif.) Courier, 1960-62; reporter Southwest Times Record, Ft. Smith, Ark., 1962-63, polit. editor, 1964-69, editor, 1971-75, Hawaii Tribune-Herald, Hilo, 1975-77, Vista (Calif.) Press, 1977—; Washington bur. chief Donrey Media Group, 1969-71; tchr. article writing and short story Monterey Peninsula Coll., 1957-58, Foothills Coll., Los Altos Hill, Calif., 1959-60. Author novels, short stories, articles. Served with USMCR, 1943-46. Newspaper recipient Pulitizer Service award, 1956. Mem. Am. Soc. Newspaper Editors, Sigma Delta Chi. Club: Nat. Press (Washington). Home: PO Box 221 Marble City OK 74545 *If I could choose but a single possession, it would be integrity, for without it life is worthless. If I could choose but a single rule by which to live, it would be the Golden Rule, for it is the only one that assures joy of living. If I could correct deficiency in my past life, it would be to learn early to be tolerant of others' shortcomings. If I could offer but a single piece of advice, it would be to live each day to the fullest, always mindful of the rights, feelings and needs of others.*

KENNEDY, WILLIAM BEAN, theology educator; b. Spartanburg, S.C., Oct. 18, 1926; s. Leland McDuffie and Elizabeth Fleming (Bean) K.; m. Frances Barron Harris, July 9, 1952; children: Katharine Fleming, William Bean, Jane Harris, Emmily Pou. B.A., Wofford Coll., 1947, LL.D. (hon.), 1970; M.A., Duke U., 1948; B.D., Union Theol. Sem., Richmond, Va., 1954; Ph.D., Yale U., 1957. Ordained to ministry Presbyterian Ch. in U.S., 1954. Tchr. Spartanburg High Sch., 1948-49; instr. Emory U. at Oxford, 1949-51; minister of edn. First Congl. Ch., West Haven, Conn., 1954-57; asst. prof. Christian edn. Union Theol. Sem., Richmond, 1957-59, assoc.prof., 1959-65; sec. edn. Bd. Christian Edn., Presbyn. Ch. U.S., Richmond, 1965-69; dir. office edn. World Council Chs., Geneva, 1969-75; dir. Atlanta Assn. Internat. Edn., 1976-79, prof. religion and edn., 1979-81; Skinner and McAlpin prof. practical theology Union Theol. Sem., N.Y.C., 1981—; mem. task force on world hunger Presbyn. Ch. U.S., Atlanta, 1976-82; cons. hunger program Nat. Council Chs., N.Y.C., 1981. Author: Into Covenant Life, 1963, Shaping of Protestant Education, 1965; contbr. numerous articles, revs. to profl. jours.; internat. editor: Religious Edn., 1984—. Served with USN, 1945-46. Moore fellow, 1954; recipient issues research grant Assn. Theol. Schs., Vadalia, Ohio, 1982. Mem. Nat. Council Chs. (pres. profs. and research sect. 1961-62), Religious Edn. Assn. (dir. 1981—), Assn. Profs. and Researchers in Religious Edn. (dir. 1983—), Phi Beta Kappa. Democrat. Presbyterian. Home: 99 Claremont Ave Apt 601 New York NY 10027 Office: Union Theol Sem 3041 Broadway New York NY 10027

KENNEDY, WILLIAM JESSE, III, insurance company executive; b. Durham, N.C., Oct. 24, 1922; s. William Jesse, Jr. and Margaret Lillian (Spaulding) K.; m. Alice Charlene Copeland, Jan. 29, 1949; 1 son, William Jesse IV. B.S. in Bus. Adminstrn, Va. State Coll., 1942; M.B.A., U. Pa., 1946, N.Y. U., 1948. With N.C. Mut. Life Ins. Co., Durham, 1950—, financial v.p., 1966-69, sr. v.p., 1969-72, pres., chief exec. officer, 1972—, chmn., 1979—; dir. J.A. Jones Constrn. Co., Charlotte, N.C., Mechanics & Farmers Bank, Durham, Urban Nat. Corp., Boston, Pfizer, Inc., Mobile Corp., N.Y.C., Quaker Oats, Chgo. Mem. Durham Com. Negro Affairs, NAACP, Durham Bus. and Profl. Chain; bd. dirs. N.C. Central U. Found., N.C. Citizens Assn.; trustee Triangle Univs. Center Advanced Studies; bd. overseers Wharton Sch., N.Y. U. Grad. Sch. Bus.; bd. visitors Fuqua Sch. Bus., Duke; trustee United Student Aid Funds, N.Y.C. Served with AUS, 1943-45. Charles E. Merrill Found. fellow Stanford Exec. Program, 1971. Mem. Durham C. of C., Conf. Bd., N.C. Soc. Fin. Analysts, Omega Psi Phi. Baptist (trustee 1950—). Club: Kiwanian. Office: NC Mut Life Ins Co Mutual Plaza Durham NC 27701 *

KENNEDY, WILLIAM JOSEPH, educator, novelist; b. Albany, N.Y., Jan. 16, 1928; s. William Joseph and Mary Elizabeth (McDonald) K.; m. Ana Daisy Dana Segarra, Jan. 31, 1957; children: Dana Elizabeth, Katherine Anne, Brendan Christopher. B.A., Siena Coll., 1949; L.H.D. hon, Russell Sage Coll., 1980. Asst. sports editor, columnist Glens Falls Post Star, N.Y., 1949-50; reporter Albany Times-Union, N.Y., 1952-56, spl. writer, 1963-70; asst. mng. editor, columnist P.R. World Jour., San Juan, 1956; reporter Miami Herald, Fla., 1957; corr. Time-Life Publs. in P.R., 1957-59; reporter Knight Newspapers, 1957-59; founding mng. editor San Juan Star, 1959-61; lectr. SUNY, Albany, 1974-82, prof. English, 1983—; vis. prof. Cornell U., Ithaca, N.Y., 1982-83. Author: novel The Ink Truck, 1969, Legs, 1975, Billy Phelan's Greatest Game, 1978, Ironweed, 1983; non-fiction O Albany!, 1983, (with Francis Ford Coppola) The Cotton Club, 1983; contbr. short stories and articles to profl. jours. and mags. Served with U.S. Army, 1950-52. MacArthur Found. fellow, 1983; Nat. Endowment for Arts fellow, 1981. Office: SUNY 1400 Washington Ave Albany NY 12222

KENNEDY, X.J. (JOSEPH KENNEDY), writer, educator; b. Dover, N.J., Aug. 21, 1929; s. Joseph Francis and Agnes (Rauter) K.; m. Dorothy Mintzlaff, 1962; children: Kathleen, David, Matthew, Daniel, Joshua. B.Sc., Seton Hall U., 1950; M.A., Columbia U., 1951; certificate, U. Paris, France, 1956. Teaching fellow U. Mich., Ann Arbor, 1956-60, instr. English, 1960-62; faculty English dept. Woman's Coll., U. N.C., Greensboro, 1962-63; asst. prof. English Tufts U., Medford, Mass., 1963-67, assoc. prof., 1967-73, prof., 1973-79; Vis. lectr. Wellesley Coll., 1964, U. Calif. at Irvine, 1966-67. Author: Nude Descending a Staircase, 1961, Introduction To Poetry, 1966, 5th edit., 1982, Growing into Love, 1969, Breaking and Entering, 1971, Emily Dickinson in Southern California, 1974, Celebrations After the Death of John Brennan, 1974, (with J.E. Camp, Keith Waldrop) Three Tenors, One Vehicle, 1975, One Winter Night in August, 1975, Introduction to Fiction, 1976, 3d edit., 1983, Literature, 1976, 2d edit., 1979, 3d edit., 1983, The Phantom Ice Cream Man, 1979, (with Dorothy M. Kennedy) The Bedford Reader, 1982, 2d edit., 1985, Did Adam Name the Vinegarroon?, 1982, Knock at a Star: a Child's Introduction to Poetry, 1982, The Owlstone Crown, 1983, The Forgetful Wishing-Well, 1985, Cross Ties: Selected Poems, 1985; Poetry editor: Paris Rev, 1961-64; Editor: (with J.E. Camp) Mark Twain's Frontier, 1963, (with J.E. Camp, Keith Waldrop) Pegasus Descending, 1971, Messages, 1973, Tygers of Wrath: poems of hate, anger and invective, 1981; Editor, pub.: (with Dorothy M. Kennedy) Counter/Measures mag, 1971-74. Judge Nat. Council on Arts poetry book selections, 1969, 70. Served with USN, 1951-55. Recipient Lamont Poetry award Acad. Am. Poets, Bess Hokin prize Poetry Mag., 1961; grant Nat. Council Arts and Humanities, 1967-68; Shelley Meml. award, 1970; Bread Loaf fellow in poetry Middlebury Coll., 1960; Guggenheim fellow, 1973-74; Bruern fellow in Am. civilization U. Leeds, 1974-75. Mem. John Barton Wolgamot Soc., P.E.N., MLA, Nat. Council Tchrs. English, Children's Lit. Assn., Authors Guild, Phi Beta Kappa.

KENNEL, CHARLES FREDERICK, physicist, educator; b. Cambridge, Mass., Aug. 20, 1939; s. Archie Clarence and Elizabeth Ann (Fitzpatrick) K.; m. Deborah Susan Bochner, Aug. 21, 1964; children: Matthew Bochner, Sarah Alexandra. A.B. (Nat. scholar 1955-59), Harvard U., 1959; Ph.D. in Astrophys. Scis. (W.C. Peyton Advanced fellow 1962-63), Princeton U., 1964. Prin. research scientist Avco-Everett Research Lab., Mass., 1960-61, 64-67; vis. scientist Internat. Center Theoretical Physics, Trieste, Italy, 1965; mem. faculty U. Calif., Los Angeles, 1967—, prof. physics, 1971—, chmn. dept., 1983—; mem. Inst. Geophysics and Planetary Physics, 1972—, acting asso. dir. inst., 1976-77; mem. space sci. bd. Nat. Acad. Scis.-NRC, 1977-80, chmn. com. space physics, 1977-80; cons. in field. Co-author: Matter in Motion, The Spirit and Evolution of Physics, 1977; co-editor: Solar System Plasma Physics, 1978. Bd. dirs. Los Angeles Jr. Ballet Co., 1977—, pres., 1979-80. NSF postdoctoral fellow, 1965-66; Sloan fellow, 1968-70. Fellow Am. Geophys. Union, Am. Phys. Soc.; mem. Am. Astron. Soc., Internat. Union Radio Sci. Club: Cosmos (Washington). Address: Inst Geophysics and Planetary Physics U Calif Los Angeles CA 90024

KENNELLY, BARBARA BAILEY, congresswoman; b. Hartford, Conn., July 10, 1936; d. John Moran and Barbara (Leary) Bailey; m. James J. Kennelly, Sept. 26, 1959; children—Eleanor Bride, Barbara Leary, Louise Moran, John Bailey. B.A. in Econs, Trinity Coll., Washington, 1958; grad., Harvard-Radcliffe Sch. Bus. Adminstrn., 1959; M.A. in Govt, Trinity Coll., Hartford, 1971. Mem. Hartford Ct. of Common Council, 1975-79; sec. of state State of Conn., Hartford, 1979-83; mem. 98th Congress, 1st Dist. Conn.; Hartford rep., sec. exec. com. Capitol Region Council of Govts., 1975-79; mem. exec. com. Eastern Regional Conf., Council of State Govts.; dir. Conn. Bank & Trust Co. Bd. dirs. Hartford Architecture Conservancy; mem. Conn. bd. dirs. Catholic Family Services, Inc. Mem. Internat. Inst. Mcpl. Clks., Nat. Assn. of Secs. of State. Democrat. Roman Catholic. Home: 95 Scarborough St Hartford CT 06105 Office: Longworth House Office Bldg Rm 1228 Washington DC 20515

KENNELLY, ROBERT ANDREW, educator, geographer; b. Jamestown, N.D., Oct. 6, 1919; s. Patrick James and Helena (Rotering) K.; m. Martha Mullan, Sept. 7, 1946; children—Robert Andrew, Barbara Jane, Donald James. Student, N.D. State Sch. Sci., 1936-38; B.A., State U. Iowa, 1948, M.A., 1950, Ph.D., 1952, Nat. U. Mexico, summer 1950. Grad. asst. State U. Iowa, 1948-51, part-time instr., 1951; faculty Long Beach (Calif.) State Coll., 1952-71, prof. geography, 1961-71, coordinator dept. social scis., 1957-58, chmn. div. social scis., 1958-64; cons. chancellor's office, asso. dean acad. planning, trustees Calif. State Univs. and Colls., 1964-67; v.p. adminstrn. Calif. State U. at Hayward, 1967—; Vis. summer prof. Central Wash. State Coll., Ellensburg, 1962, 63, U. Idaho, 1964. Editor: Cal. Geographer, 1959-69; Contbr. articles to profl. jours. Served as pilot USAAF, World War II; ETO; lt. col. Res. (ret.). Decorated D.F.C. Mem. Assn. Am. Geographers, Pacific Coast Geographers, Pacific Coast Council Latin Am. Studies, Calif. Council Geog. Tchrs., Sigma Nu. Home: 17869 Almond Rd Castro Valley CA 94546

KENNER, WILLIAM HUGH, educator, author; b. Peterborough, Ont., Can., Jan. 7, 1923; s. Henry Rowe Hocking and Mary I. (Williams) K.; m. Mary Josephine Waite, Aug. 30, 1947 (dec. Dec. 1964); children: Catherine, Julia, Margaret, John, Michael; m. Mary Anne Bittner, Aug. 13, 1965; children: Robert, Elizabeth. B.A., U. Toronto, 1945, M.A., 1946; Ph.D., Yale U., 1950; D.H.L., Chgo. U., 1976, Trent U., 1977. Asst. prof. Assumption Coll., Windsor, Ont., 1946-48; instr. U. Calif. at Santa Barbara, 1950-51, asst. prof., 1951-56, asso. prof., 1956-58, prof. English, 1958-73, chmn. dept. English, 1956-62; prof. English Johns Hopkins, 1973-75, Andrew W. Mellon prof. in humanities, 1975—, chmn. dept. English, 1980—; vis. prof. U. Mich., summer 1956, U. Chgo., summer 1962, U. Va., fall 1963, U. Calif., Berkeley, 1981. Author: Poetry of Ezra Pound, 1951, Dublin's Joyce, 1956, The Invisible Poet, T.S. Eliot, 1958, Samuel Beckett, 1961, The Stoic Comedians, 1963, The Counterfeiters, 1968, The Pound Era, 1971, Bucky: A Guided Tour of Buckminster Fuller, 1973, A Readers Guide to Samuel Beckett, 1973, A Homemade World, 1975, Geodesic Math and How to Use It, 1976, Joyce's Voices, 1978, Ulysses, 1980, A Colder Eye, 1983. Guggenheim fellow, 1956, 64. Home: 103 Edgevale Rd Baltimore MD 21210

KENNERLY, DAVID HUME, photographer; b. Roseburg, Oreg., Mar. 9, 1947; s. Orlie Alden and Joanne (Hume) K.; m. Mel Harris,

Oct. 30, 1983; 1 son, Byron Hume. Student, Portland State Coll., 1965-66. Photographer Oreg. Jour., 1966, The Oregonian, 1967, UPI, Los Angeles, 1967-68, N.Y.C., 1968-69, Washington, 1969-70, Saigon, 1971-72; contract photographer Life Mag., S.E. Asia, 1972; photographer Time mag., S.E. Asia, 1973, Washington, 1973-74, contract photographer, 1977—; personal photographer Pres. of U.S., Washington, 1974-77. Author: SHOOTER, 1979. Recipient Pulitzer Prize for feature photography in, Vietnam, 1972; 2 1st place awards for photos of, Cambodia, World Press Photo, 1976; Spl. citation Nat. Press Photographers, 1976; 1st pl. color feature White House Press Photographers, 1984. Mem. White House Press Photographers. Address: 3332 P St NW Washington DC 20007

KENNETT, WILLIAM ALEXANDER, Canadian government official; b. Toronto, Ont., Can., Sept. 4, 1932; s. Horace and Lena (Thorburn) K.; m. Valerie Cosby Spence, Jan. 25, 1958; children: Steven A., Brenda. B.A. in Polit. Sci. and Econs., Toronto U., 1955; M.S., London Sch. Econs., 1957. With Dept. Trade and Commerce Govt. of Can., Ottawa, 1957—, with Dept. Fin., 1960—, inspector gen. of banks, 1977—; dir. Can. Deposit Ins. Corp., 1977—, Royal Can. Mint. V.p. Ottawa YM-YWCA, Inst. of Citizenship, Ottawa. Home: 395 Huron Ave Ottawa ON Canada K1Y 0X2 Office: Dept Finance 160 Elgin St Ottawa ON Canada K1A 0G5

KENNEY, FRANK DEMING, lawyer; b. Chgo., Feb. 20, 1921; s. Joseph Aloysius and Mary Edith (Deming) K.; m. Virginia Stuart Banning, Feb. 12, 1944; children: Claudia Kenney Carpenter, Pamela Kenney Voetberg, Sarah Kenney Swanson, Stuart. A.B., U. Chgo., 1948, J.D., 1949. Bar: Ill. 1948, U.S. Dist. Ct. (no. dist.) Ill. 1949. Assoc. J.O. Brown, Chgo., 1948-49; assoc., ptnr. Winston & Strawn, and predecessors, Chgo., 1949—. Nat. housing fin. commr. Kappa Sigma Fraternity, U.S. and Can., 1959—; mem. adv. com. Civic Fedn., Chgo., 1959—. Served to 1st lt. AUS, 1942-46; CBI, PTO. Mem. Chgo. Bar Assn. (chmn. real property law com. 1982-83), Ill. State Bar Assn., ABA, Law Club of Chgo. Republican. Roman Catholic. Clubs: Spring Creek Basset Hunt (master 1977—), Fox River Valley Hunt (Barrington, Ill.)). Home: 50 Hart Rd PO Box 581 Barrington IL 60010 Office: Winston & Strawn One First Nat Plaza Chgo IL 60603

KENNEY, H(ARRY) WESLEY, JR., producer, director; b. Dayton, Ohio, Jan. 3, 1926; s. Harry Wesley and Mimi (Keeton) K.; children by previous marriage: Nina, H. Wesley, III, Kara; m. Heather North, May 22, 1971; 1 son, Kevin. B.F.A., Carnegie Inst. Tech., 1950. Mem. staff Dumont Network, 1950-56. Free-lance producer, dir. for: TV, including Rocky King Detective, 1953-56, Omnibus Plays of Week, 1954-56, Night Beat, 1957-58, True Story, 1959-61, The Doctors, 1964-65, All in the Family, 1974-75, My Favorite Martin, 1966, Gidget, 1966; exec. producer: Days of Our Lives (Emmy for Best Daytime Series 1978), Corday Prodns, Burbank Studios, Calif., 1974—; dir. pilot: The Jeffersons, 1974, Filthy Rich, 1981; dir.: pilot and series Ladies Man, 1980-81; exec. producer: TV series The Young and the Restless, 1982-83 (Emmy award for best daytime series 1983); producer, dir. for: theatre, including King and I, 1960, My Three Angels, 1953, Twelfth Night, 1961; (Recipient Emmy award for Best Dir. of Daytime Spl. 1974, for Best Dir. of Yr.-Daytime 1974), others (Merit award Carnegie Mellon U. 1978). Served with USN, 1943-46. Mem. Dirs. Guild Am., Producers Guild Am., Actors Equity, Omega Delta Kappa. *I recognize myself as an "average guy" with an average intelligence and talent and more than average patience and luck. An awareness of this fact has allowed me to accept the success I have had, always working for something better, but recognizing those shortcomings that have at times made me fail. Also because of this—thank God—I have had more than my share of happiness.*

KENNEY, HOWARD WASHINGTON, physician; b. Tuskegee Institute, Ala., Oct. 4, 1917; s. John A. and Frieda (Armstrong) K.; m. Gwendolyn Persley, July 31, 1943; children—Diane Elizabeth, Linda Harper, Phyllis Armstrong, Howard Washington. B.S., Bates Coll., 1940; M.D., Meharry Med. Coll., 1944. Diplomate: Am. Bd. Internal Medicine. Intern Syndenham Hosp., N.Y.C., 1944; resident internal medicine Freedmen's Hosp., Washington, 1945-46; fellow internal medicine Howard U. Med. Sch., 1946-47, research fellow cardiovascular disease, 1947-48; staff physician VA Hosp., Tuskegee, 1948-49; pvt. practice, Newark, 1949-51, Tuskegee, 1953-55, 65-69; mem. staff Tuskegee VA Hosp., 1955-62, hosp. dir., 1959-62, cons., 1953-55; dir. VA Hosp., E. Orange, N.J., 1962-65; med. dir. Tuskegee Inst., 1965-69; regional med. dir., region I VA, 1969-73, asso. dep. chief med. dir. for policy and planning, 1973-74, asso. dep. chief med. dir. for operations, 1974-75; pvt. practice gen. internal medicine, Silver Spring, Md., 1975—; asst. clin. prof. medicine Georgetown U. Med. Sch., 1978—; cons. internal medicine Community Hosp., Newark, 1949-51, John A. Andrew Meml. Hosp., Tuskegee Institute, 1953-55; Mem. rev. com., div. regional med. programs for heart disease, cancer, stroke and related diseases NIH, 1967-70; mem. adv. com. for sickle cell disease HEW, 1971-75; chmn. med. adv. com. Macon County chpt. Nat. Found., 1953-55. Contbr. articles to profl. jours. Mem. Bd. Police Commrs., East Orange, 1963-65; mem. bd. of rev. Md. Dept. Health and Mental Hygiene, 1981—; bd. dirs. Albert Schweitzer Fellowship, 1970-74. Served to capt. M.C. AUS, 1943-44, 51-53. Fellow A.C.P.; mem. Am., Nat. med. assns., John A. Andrew Clin. Soc. (pres. 1958, sec. 1965-69), Med. Soc. D.C., Montgomery County (Md.) Med. Soc. (affiliate), Alpha Omega Alpha, Kappa Pi. Episcopalian (past vestryman). Home: 3604 East West Hwy Chevy Chase MD 20015 Office: 1111 Spring St Silver Spring MD 20910

KENNEY, JAMES FRANCIS, lawyer; b. Bridgeport, Conn., June 29, 1921; s. Michael J. and Rose G. (Spaine) K.; m. Marie E. Henninger, Apr. 26, 1947; children—James Francis, Maureen E. A.B., Catholic U. Am., 1942; J.D., Georgetown U., 1948. Bar: D.C. bar 1948, Conn. bar 1949. Ins. adjuster INA Cos., Washington, 1946-48; asso. firm Berge, Fox & Arent, Washington, 1948-50; sr. partner firm McNamara, Clancy & Kenney (and predecessor firms), Bridgeport, Conn., 1950—; mem. Jud. Council Conn., 1957-71; lectr. comml. law Warren Inst., Bridgeport, 1950-54; legal counsel Welfare Dept., Bridgeport, 1950-52; trial atty., City of Bridgeport, 1952-58. Author: A Guide for Medical-Legal Relations for the Greater Bridgeport Area, 1961, rev., 1975. Mem. Bridgeport Charter Revision Commn., 1968-72; mem. Bridgeport Democratic Town Com., 1966-74, legal counsel, 1974-75; bd. dirs. Boys and Girls Clubs of Bridgeport, 1954—, v.p., 1958-74; bd. dirs. Archbishop Shehan Center; incorporator Met. Zool. Soc. Served to lt. USNR, 1942-46. Recipient Distinguished Alumnus award Cath. U. Am., 1967. Mem. Am., Conn., Greater Bridgeport bar assns., Am. Judicature Soc., Fedn. Ins. Counsel, Internat. Assn. Ins. Counsel, Assn. Trial Attys. Am., Cath. U. Alumni Assn. (nat. pres. 1955-57), Blue Key, Delta Theta Phi. Roman Catholic. Clubs: K.C. (4 deg.), Algonquin (Bridgeport) (pres. 1965-66); Patterson Country (Fairfield) (sec. 1970-71); Conn. Golf (Easton)). Home: 27 Far Horizons Dr Easton CT 06612 Office: 955 Main St Bridgeport CT 06604

KENNEY, JOHN R., insurance corporation executive, lawyer; b. Hinsdale, Ill., Jan. 1, 1927; s. John Harvery and Catherine Margo (Foster) K.; m. Joan Tilton, June 17, 1949 (div. 1973); children: Elizabeth Kenney Fisher, Ann Kenney Elstad, Rebecca, Ellen, Catherine; m. Alice Katz, Dec. 30, 1973. B.A., Yale U., 1949, LL.B., 1952. Bar: Conn. Assoc. Taft, Stettinius & Hollister, Cin., 1952-55; assoc. gen. counsel Travelers Ins. Cos., Hartford, Conn., 1969—, corp. sec., 1981—. Mem. Assn. Life Ins. Counsel, Am. Soc. Corp. Secs., ABA, Conn. Bar Assn., Phi Beta Kappa. Democrat. Home: 22 Charter Oak Pl Hartford CT 06106 Office: Travelers Corp 1 Tower Sq Hartford CT 06115

KENNEY, JOHN WILLIAM, banker; b. Redwood Falls, Minn., Oct. 6, 1918; s. Charles Hockett and Mary Ellen (Peavoy) K.; m. Kathryn Dodds, Jan. 3, 1942; children—Nancy Delight (Mrs. Stanley Evans), Janice Louise Kindred. B.S. in Bus. Adminstrn, U. So. Calif., 1941; grad., Pacific Coast Sch. Banking, U. Wash., 1954. With United Calif. Bank, Los Angeles, 1945-66, v.p., mgr., 1955-66, exec. v.p., Los Angeles, 1968-69, San Francisco, 1969-72, vice chmn., 1972-74, Los Angeles, 1976—; chmn., chief exec. officer So. Ariz. Bank & Trust Co., Tucson, 1966-67, pres., chief exec. officer, 1967-68; dir. Western States Bankcard Assn. Bd. dirs. Calif. Traffic Safety Found.; chmn. 1975 campaign United Way of Bay Area, also bd. dirs., trustee; bd. dirs. Bay Area Council. Served to lt. comdr. USNR, 1942-48; ETO, PTO. Mem. Assn. Res. City Bankers, Kappa Sigma, Alpha Kappa Psi. Clubs: California, Los Angeles Country (Los Angeles); San Francisco Golf, Villa Taverna, Pacific-Union (San Francisco). Office: 707 Wilshire Blvd Los Angeles CA 90017 *

KENNEY, LOUIS AUGUSTINE, librarian; b. Dorchester, Nebr., Feb. 28, 1917; s. Frank J. and Amelia (Peter) K.; m. Josephine Signer, July 17, 1950; children—Martin, Bonita, Philip, Douglas. A.B., Nebr. State Tchrs. Coll., 1939; B.L.S., U. Ill., 1940, M.S., 1947; postgrad., U. Zurich, Switzerland, 1949-50; Ph.D., U. Md., 1960. Asst. librarian Engring. Library, U. Ill., 1940-41, 46, bibliographer acquisition dept., 1947-48, serials cataloger, 1955-57; acquisition librarian U. Notre Dame, 1948-54; chief tech. services Ill. State Library, 1957-59; chief librarian Air Force Inst. Tech., 1959-60; univ. librarian San Diego State U., 1961-80, univ. librarian emeritus, 1981—. Mem. San Diego Opera Assn., San Diego Symphony Assn.; mem. Friends of Malcolm A. Love Library, San Diego State U.; Mem. A.L.A., Calif. Library Assn. (dist. pres. 1965), San Diego State U. Alumni Assn., Phi Alpha Theta.

KENNEY, NEIL PATRICK, radiologist; b. Dodge, Nebr., Mar. 17, 1932; s. Bernard Vincent and Irene (Chapman) K.; m. Helen Hall, Sept. 29, 1956; children—Joellen, Kathy, Patricia, Steven, John. M.D., Creighton U., 1956. Intern U.S. Naval Hosp., Oakland, Calif., 1956-57; resident in radiology U. Minn., 1960-64; mem. faculty dept. radiology Creighton U. Sch. Medicine, Omaha, 1964—, prof., 1972—, chmn. dept. radiology, 1971—. Served with U.S. Navy, 1956-60. Fellow Am. Coll. Radiology; mem. AMA, Nebr. Med. Assn., Radiol. Soc. N. Am. Democrat. Roman Catholic. Home: 9720 Brentwood Rd Omaha NE 68114 Office: 601 N 30th St Omaha NE 68131

KENNEY, RAYMOND JOSEPH, JR., lawyer; b. Boston, Aug. 3, 1932; m. Claire L. Ducey; children: Marianne L., Raymond J. III, Stephen V., John M. A.B. cum laude, Boston Coll., 1953, J.D., 1958. Bar: Mass. 1958, U.S. Dist. Ct. 1959, 1st Circuit Ct. of Appeals 1969. Mem. firm Martin, Magnuson, McCarthy & Kenney (and predecessor firms), Boston, 1958—; instr. law Mass. Dept. Edn., Univ. Extension, 1958-60, Boston U., 1961-66; corporator Winchester Savs. Bank, 1973—; lectr. continuing legal edn. Mem.; Winchester (Mass.) Fin. Com., 1967-70, chmn., 1970-71; moderator Town of Winchester, 1972-77; chmn. Mass. Jud. Nominating Commn., 1975-77; mem. standing com. on civil rules Supreme Jud. Ct., 1977—; vice chmn. Mass. Clients Security Bd., 1979—. Author: Mass. Practice series (West); asso. editor: Mass. Law Quar, 1965-72; editor-in-chief, 1973-76; contbr. article to legal jour. Bd. dirs. Winchester chpt. ARC, 1968-71; pres. Mass. Continuing Legal Edn., 1980-83. Fellow Am. Coll. Trial Lawyers, Am., Mass. (trustee) bar founds.; mem. ABA (del. 1976-78), New Eng. Bar Assn. (pres. 1980-81), Mass. Bar Assn. (pres. 1977-78), Middlesex Bar Assn. (Lowell Bar Assn.), Internat. Assn. Ins. Counsel, Am. Judicature Soc. (dir. 1978-81), Boston Coll. Alumni Assn. (pres. 1983-84). Home: 5 Salisbury St Winchester MA 01890 Office: 73 Tremont St Boston MA 02108 *The continued well-being of society is dependent upon maintaining vitality in the law. The law must, and does, contain within itself the means to attain its own advancement, thereby preserving and enhancing that vitality. One of life's great privileges is to have been afforded the opportunity to labor in a profession which so reaches the very essence of human relationships.*

KENNEY, RICHARD ALEC, educator; b. Coventry, Eng., Oct. 4, 1924; came to U.S., 1967; s. Alec and Dorothy Ada (Cooke) K.; m. Bette Gladys Green, Aug. 8, 1959; 1 son by previous marriage, Michael Alec. B.Sc. with honors, U. Birmingham, Eng., 1945, Ph.D., 1947. Lectr. physiology U. Leeds, Eng., 1947-51; with Colonial Research ser., Nigeria, 1951-54; staff mem. WHO, S.E. Asia Region, 1955-60; chmn. physiology U. Singapore, 1960-65; reader physiology U. Melbourne, Australia, 1965-67; prof. physiology George Washington U. Med. Center, 1968—, chmn. dept., 1970—; tutor physiology Royal Australian Coll. Surgeons, 1965-67. Author: Physiology of Aging; Contbr. articles to profl. jours. Mem. Physiol. Soc. (London), Am. Physiol. Soc., Renal Assn. (London), Internat. Nephrol. Soc. Club: Cosmos (Washington). Home: 4424 Reservoir Rd NW Washington DC 20007 Office: 2300 I St NW Washington DC 20037

KENNEY, RICHARD LAWRENCE, financial executive; b. Waltham, Mass., July 21, 1927; s. Francis John, Sr. and Margaret Veronica (Mahan) K.; m. Jean R. Christoforo, Aug. 14, 1982; children: Leona A., Richard Lawrence, Margaret-Mary D., Michael L. B.B.A. with high honors, Northeastern U., 1958. Tax mgr., internal auditor Warren Bros. Co., Cambridge, Mass., 1951-62; mgr. finance and taxation Stop and Shop, Inc., Boston, 1962-69; asst. treas., tax mgr. 1st Nat. Stores, Inc., Somerville, Mass., 1969-70, controller, 1970-72, v.p., 1972, treas., 1974-, sr. v.p. fin., 1976-77, sr. v.p. adminstrn., 1977-78, exec. v.p., 1978-79; v.p. fin. and adminstrn. Healthco, Inc., Boston, 1979—; tax cons. Served with USAAF, 1945-47. Mem. Tax Execs. Inst. (past pres. New Eng. chpt.), Nat. Assn. Pub. Accountants, Sigma Epsilon Rho. Home: 20 Mill Ln Hingham MA 02043 Office: 25 Stuart St Boston MA 02116

KENNEY, THOMAS FREDERICK, broadcasting executive; b. Dearborn, Mich., Sept. 25, 1941; s. Charles B. and Grace M. (Wilson) K.; m. Beth H. Rockwood, Aug. 22, 1964; children: Sean, Blair. B.S., Mich. State U., 1964. Program mgr. Sta. KFMB-TV, San Diego, 1973-75; program dir., then dir. broadcasting ops. Sta. KHOU-TV, Houston, 1975-79; v.p., gen. mgr. KHOU-TV, 1979—; chmn. Arbitron TV Ratings Adv. Council. Bd. dirs. Houston Salvation Army, Ft. Bend County Mcpl. Utility Dist. 42. Clubs: Houstonian, Kingwood Country. Home: 3106 Little Bear Dr Kingwood TX 77339 Office: 1945 Allen Pkwy Houston TX 77019

KENNEY, THOMAS MICHAEL, publisher; b. Melrose, Mass., Mar. 4, 1947; s. James Edward and Agnes Ruth (Courtney) K.; m. Erica Marie Rizzo, June 6, 1970; 1 dau., Alexandra Beth. A.B., Dartmouth Coll., 1969; postgrad., N.Y. U. Bus. Sch. With Time Inc., 1972-76; asst. circulation dir. Time mag., 1975-76; circulation dir. Sports Illustrated mag., 1976; with Charter Publishing Co., 1976-82; pub. Redbook, 1978-79; gen. mgr. Redbook, Ladies Home Jour., Sport and Discount Merchandiser mags., 1979-80, corp. pres., 1980-82; v.p., gen. mgr. CBS Publs., N.Y.C., 1983—; dir. Select Mags., Inc., 1976-82, chmn. bd., 1981-82. Served to capt. USMCR, 1969-72. Decorated Navy Commendation medal with combat V. Club: Yale (N.Y.C.). Home: 2 Crows Nest Rd Bronxville NY 10708 Office: 1515 Broadway New York NY 10036

KENNEY, VINCENT PAUL, physicist, educator; b. N.Y.C., Sept. 15, 1927; s. Vincent Thomas and Marguerite Claire (Cox) K.; m. Margaret Campbell Dennison, Oct. 16, 1954; children: Ann Marguerite, Charles Dennison, John Belden, Mary Elizabeth. A.B., Iona Coll., 1948; M.S., Fordham U., 1950, Ph.D., 1956. Predoctoral research asso. Brookhaven Nat. Lab., Upton, N.Y., 1953-55; mem. faculty U. Ky., 1955-63, U. Notre Dame, South Bend, Ind., 1963—, prof. physics, 1966—; vis. research staff, cons. Oak Ridge Nat. Lab., 1955-63, Lawrence Radiation Lab., 1959-61, Cern, 1961-63, 82-84, Brookhaven Nat. Lab., 1957—, Argonne (Ill.) Nat. Lab., 1963—, Nat. Accelerator Lab., 1969—; Disting. Sci. lectr. U. Notre Dame, 1981; sr. vis. fellow Cavendish Lab. Cambridge U., 1982-83. Served to 1st lt. USAF, 1951-53. Max Planck fellow Inst. for Physics and Astrophysics, Munich, Germany, 1961-62, 72; recipient Alumni Achievement award Iona Coll., 1966; assoc. fellow Clare Hall, Cambridge U., 1983—. Fellow Am. Phys. Soc.; mem. AAAS, Sigma Xi. Roman Catholic. Club: Odd Couples. Research boson spectroscopy, high energy multiparticle interactions. Home: 1329 N St Joseph South Bend IN 46617

KENNEY, W. JOHN, lawyer; b. Oklahoma City, June 16, 1904; s. Franklin R. and Nelle (Torrence) K.; m. Elinor Craig, Jan. 17, 1931; children: Elinor Kenney Farquhar, John F., Priscilla Kenney Streator, David T. A.B., Stanford U., 1926; LL.B., Harvard U., 1929. Practiced law, San Francisco, 1929-36; chief oil and gas unit SEC, 1936-38; practice law, Los Angeles, 1938-41; spl. asst. to under sec. navy, gen. counsel and chmn. Price Adjustment Bd., Navy Dept., 1941-46; asst. sec. Dept. Navy, 1946-47, undersec., 1947-49; head ECA, Eng., 1949-50; dep. dir. for mut. security, 1952; mem. Sullivan, Shea & Kenney, Washington, 1950-70; ptnr. Cox, Langford & Brown, Washington, 1971-73, Squire Sanders & Dempsey, 1973—; dir. Riggs Nat. Bank, 1958-81, Mchts. Fund Inc., both Washington. Chmn. Democratic Central Com. D.C., 1960-64; Chmn. bd. D.C. chpt. ARC, 1968-71; trustee, mem. exec. com. George Marshall Ednl. Found.; adv. council Johns Hopkins Sch. Advanced Internat. Study. Mem. ABA. Democrat. Clubs: Calif. (Los Angeles); Alibi, Met., Chevy Chase (Washington). Home: 2700 Calvert NW Washington DC 20008 Office: 1201 Pennsylvania Ave NW Washington DC 20004

KENNEY, WILLIAM RICHARDSON, law association executive; b. Mineola, N.Y., Sept. 17, 1922; s. George Churchill and Alice Stewart (Maxey) K.; m. Rev. Marguerite Anne Shirley, Apr. 20, 1943; children: George, James, Charles, Anne, John, Thomas. Student, U. Cin., 1941-43; LL.B. cum laude, U. Balt., 1950; grad., Air Command and Staff Coll., 1951, Nat. Coll. State Trial Judges, 1970. Bar: Md. bar 1950, U.S. Supreme Ct. bar 1956. Enlisted in USAAF, 1943, advanced through grades to col.; combat navigator, S.W. Pacific, World War II; legal officer, 1950-73, assigned, Alaska, 1965-68, 1968-73, ret. as chief judge, 1973; bd. dirs. Potomac Sch. Law, 1975-82; v.p., mem. faculty Mil. Law Inst., 1970—; dir. retiree affairs U.S. Air Force, Washington area, Bolling AFB, D.C., 1978-83; with Fed. Bar Assn., Washington, 1983—. Editor legal jours. Dir. Friendly Citizens Assn., 1975-77. Decorated Legion of Merit, Air medal, Joint Services Commendation medal, Air Force Commendation medal. Mem. ABA, Fed. Bar Assn. (pres. St. Louis chpt. 1958-59, The Pentagon 1964-65, Anchorage, Alaska 1965-66, nat. council 1962—, nat. pres. 1975-76), Nat. Conf. Fed. Trial Judges (chmn. com. mil. judges 1971-72), Judge Adv. Assn. (dir. 1962—, nat. pres. 1979-80), Air Force Assn. Episcopalian (vestryman 1967-68, chancellor 1968-83). Club: Nat. Lawyers (Washington). Home: 800 Little John Ct Virginia Beach VA 23455 Office: Fed Bar Assn 1815 H St NW Washington DC 20006

KENNICK, WILLIAM ELMER, philosophy educator; b. Lebanon, Ill., May 28, 1923; s. Samuel Arthur and Dorothy (Campbell) K.; m. Anna Perkins Howes, June 25, 1949; children: Christopher Campbell, Justin Howes, Sylvia Bowditch. B.A., Oberlin Coll., 1945; M.A. (hon.), Ahmherst Coll., 1962; Ph.D., Cornell U., 1952. Instr. philosophy Oberlin Coll., 1947-48, Boston U., 1950-51; mem. faculty Oberlin Coll., 1951-56, asst. prof. philosophy, head dept., 1953-56; mem. faculty Amherst Coll., 1956—, prof. philosophy, 1962-, G. Henry Whitcomb prof. philosophy, 1976—, William F. Kenan, Jr. prof., 1978-80, acting dean of faculty, 1980; dir. Amherst Inn Corp., 1980—; Mem. commn. on instns. higher edn. New Eng. Assn. Schs. and Colls., 1973-76, chmn. bd., 1976—. Author: Art and Philosophy, 1964, 2d revised edit., 1979, (with Morris Lazerowitz) Metaphysics: Readings and Reappraisals, 1966; Mem. editorial bd.: Mass. Rev., 1962-72; bd. dirs., 1962—; Contbr. articles to profl. jours. Trustee Amherst Acad., 1974—. Served with M.C. AUS, 1946-47. Mem. Am. Philos. Assn., Phi Beta Kappa. Home: 415 Shays St Amherst MA 01002

KENNY, DOUGLAS TIMOTHY, univ. pres.; b. Victoria, C., Can., Oct. 20, 1923; s. John Ernest and Margaret Julia (Collins) K.; m. Lucille Rabowski, Apr. 18, 1950 (dec.); children—John, Kathleen; m. Margaret Lindsay Little, June 5, 1976. Student, Victoria Coll., 1941-43; B.A., U. B.C., 1945, M.A., 1947; Ph.D., U. Wash., 1950. Lectr. U. B.C., Vancouver, 1950-54, asst. prof. psychology, 1954-57, asso. prof., 1957-64, prof., 1965—, head dept. psychology, 1965-69, acting dean of arts, 1969-70, dean of arts, 1970-75, pres., 1975—; vis. asso. prof. Harvard. Cons. editor: Can. Jour. Psychology; Contbr. articles to profl. jours. Mem. research com. Can. Mental Health Assn.; mem. adv. com. Youth Counselling Centre; mem. Canada Council, World Fedn. Mental Health, Can. Council for Christians and Jews, Social Sci. and Humanities Research Council; trustee Monterey Inst. Internat. Studies. Nat. NRC grantee; Pres.'s Research Fund grantee; recipient Can. Council award. Mem. Can. Psychol. Assn., B.C. Psychol. Assn. (pres. 1951-52), Am. Psychol. Assn., Wash. State Psychol. Assn., Vancouver Inst. (pres. 1973-74), U. B.C. Faculty Assn. (pres. 1961-62). Clubs: Vancouver, Univ. (Vancouver). Office: Univ BC 107-6328 Memorial Rd Vancouver BC V6T 2B3 Canada

KENNY, EDMUND JOYCE, lawyer; b. Salem, Mass., Jan. 17, 1920; s. Jeremiah C. and Jane (Donovan) K.; m. Elizabeth Young, June 5, 1943 (div. 1968); children: Joyce, William, Janet, Robert; m. 2d Joan Shea, Cot. 13, 1973. B.A., Boston Coll., 1940, J.D., 1946; LL.M., Harvard U., 1946. Bar: Mass. 1946, Ill. 1947. Mem. firm Winston & Strawn, Chgo., 1950—. Home: 325 Sunset Dr Northbrook IL 60062 Office: Winston & Strawn One First Nat Plaza Chicago IL 60603

KENNY, HERBERT ANDREW, author; b. Roxbury, Mass., Dec. 22, 1912; s. Herbert A. and Mary (Conroy) K.; m. Teresa E. Flaherty, Sept. 16, 1939; children: Ann Gonzalez, Herbert A.P., Susan R. Carroll. A.B., Boston Coll., 1934. Mem. staff Boston Post, 1933-56, night city editor, 1953-56; editorial writer Boston Globe, 1956-62, editor arts and books, 1962-67, book editor, 1967-74; editor-in-chief X Press: Pubs., Manchester, Mass., 1976—; lectr. Suffolk U., 1947-50, Boston Coll., 1977-78. Curator: Oral Archives of Irish Heritage in Am. Politics, Boston U. Sch. Public Communication, 1979—; author: (with G.P. Keane) A Catholic Quiz Book, 1947; Author: Sonnets to the Virgin Mary, 1955; (poetry) Twelve Birds, 1964, Suburban Man, 1965, Dear Dolphin, 1967, Alistare Owl, 1969; Cape Ann: Cape America, 1971, Literary Dublin: A History, 1974, A Boston Picture Book, 1974, (with Barbara Westman) The Secret of the Rocks: The Boris Photographs, 1977; contbr.: Nat. Book Critics Jour., 1977-79. Mem. Gov. Mass. Arts Council, 1965-66, 77-80; mem. appeals bd., Manchester, Mass., 1950-79, chmn., 1960-79. Robert Frost fellow poetry Bread Loaf Writers Conf., 1956. Mem. Harvard Musical Assn., Eire Soc., Poetry Soc. Am., New Eng. Poetry Club, Mass. Hist. Soc. Roman Catholic. Clubs: Tavern (Boston); St. Botolph. Home: 804 Summer St Manchester-by-the-Sea MA 01944 *I have found journalism and marriage make for a very enjoyable life.*

KENNY, MICHAEL H., bishop; b. Hollywood, Calif., June 26, 1937. Ed., St. Joseph Coll., Mountain View, Calif., St. Patrick's Sem., Menlo Park, Calif., Cath. U. Am. Ordained priest Roman Cath. Ch., 1963; ordained bishop of, Juneau, Alaska, 1979—. Office: 419 6th St Juneau AK 99801 *

KENNY, ROBERT WAYNE, history educator, artist; b. San Angelo, Tex., Oct. 4, 1932; s. Jack and Ava (Henry) K.; m. Shirley Elise Strum, July 22, 1956; children: David, Joel, Daniel, Jonathan, Sarah. A.A., Tarleton State Coll., Stephenville, Tex., 1951; B.J., U. Tex., 1954; M.A., U. Minn., 1958; Ph.D., U. Chgo., 1963. Instr. journalism U. Tex., Austin, 1958-59; asst. prof. history Washinton and Lee U., Lexington, Va., 1961-62, George Washington U., Washington, 1962-66, assoc. prof., 1966-71, prof., 1971—, chmn. dept., 1971-73, 75-76, 82-83. Author: Elizabeth's Admiral, 1970; editor: Law of Freedom in a Platform, 1973, (with others) Letters and Papers of Sir Nathaniel Bacon, 1979. Fellow NEH, 1968. Mem. Am. Hist. Assn., Conf. Brit. Studies, Am. Assn. Environ. History. Home: 8616 Old Dominion Dr McLean VA 22101 Office: George Washington University Washington DC 20052

KENNY, ROGER MICHAEL, executive search consultant; b. N.Y.C., Oct. 3, 1938; s. Michael F. and Mary T. (Glynn) K.; m. Carole Ann Smith, Oct. 3, 1959; children: Glynn Scott, Lynn Marie. B.B.A., Manhattan Coll., 1959; M.B.A., N.Y. U., 1961. With Port Authority of N.Y. and N.J., 1959-67, mgr. bus. ops., 1965-67; asso. Spencer Stuart & Assos., 1967-70, v.p. West Coast ops., 1970-71, N.Y.C., 1971-77, sr. v.p., partner, 1977—; ptnr. Kenny, Kindler & Hunt, 1982—; Supt. adv. com. Bd. of Edn., White Plains, N.Y., 1977-79. Contbg. author: Harvard Bus. Rev, 1976; Contbr. articles to profl. jours. Served with U.S. Army, 1961-63. Mem. Nat. Assn. Corp. and Profl. Recruiters, Am. Soc. Public Adminstrs. Roman Catholic. Clubs: Board Room, Economic, Westchester Country. Home: 892 North St White Plains NY 10605 Office: Park Ave Plaza New York NY 10055 *People who are willing to experiment seem to be the most successful, at least in terms of their achievements. A completely empirical approach to life is impossible. First of all, the necessary facts aren't always available and too frequently the wrong conclusions are derived from too much empiricism.*

KENNY, THOMAS HENRY, inventor, artist, cons., realty corp. exec.; b. Bridgeport, Conn., Jan. 12, 1918; s. T. Henry and Marie E. (Sorgi) K.; m. Stella Wasylkoski, Aug. 9, 1941; children—Thomas Henry, Michael A., Lisa, Lee Ann. M.F.A., Knox Coll., 1942. Pres., dir. Kenny Realty Co., Roslyn, N.Y., 1952—; dir. Rainy Lake Mining Ltd., 1958-62; v.p., dir. Kenny Devel. Corp., 1954—; pres. K-P Records, 1960-62. Author: numerous books including Confucius Speaks, 1972, Garlic, The Enduring Miracle, 1976, Coffee the Deadly Brew, 1976, Mining Guide to San Diego County, 1980, Imperial County Mining Guide, 1981; mus. group shows include Kenny-Retrospect, Mus. Modern Art, Miami, Fla., 1970, 246 Years of Am. Art, New Brit. Mus., 1970, Internat. Graphics Neue Galerie der Stadt Linz, Austria, New Acquisitions Mus. Arte Modern Rio de Janeiro, Brazil, 1971, others; represented in permanent collections numerous museums including, Met. Mus. Art, N.Y., Phila. Mus. Art, Stedelijk Mus., Amsterdam, Mus. Modern Art, Mexico City, others. Served with USAAC, 1942-46; ETO. Fellow Royal Soc. Art (London); mem. Coll. Art Assn., Inst. Contemporary Arts (London), Am. Fedn. Arts, Gold Prospectors Assn. Republican. Roman Catholic. *Be satisfied with success in even the smallest task, for by gaining success in small matters you will acquire the ability to be successful in greater undertakings.*

KENRICH, JOHN LEWIS, chemical executive, lawyer; b. Lima, Ohio, Oct. 17, 1929; s. Clarence E. and Rowena (Stroh) Katterheinrich; m. Betty Jane Roehll, May 26, 1951; children: John David, Mary Jane, Kathryn Ann, Thomas Roehll, Walter Clarence. B.S., Miami U., Oxford, Ohio, 1951; LL.B., U. Cin., 1953. Bar: Ohio 1953, Mass. 1969. Asst. counsel B.F. Goodrich Co., Akron, Ohio, 1956-65; asst. sec., counsel W.R. Grace & Co., Cin., 1965-68; corp. counsel, sec. Standard Internat. Corp., Andover, Mass., 1969-70; v.p. Splty. Products Group div. W.R. Grace & Co., Cin., 1970-71; v.p., sec. Chemed Corp., Cin., 1971-82, sr. v.p., gen. counsel, 1982—; dir. Chemed Corp., Omnicare, Inc., Arocom Inc., Elson T. Killam Assos. Inc., Dubois Chemie GmbH, Germany, DuBois Mexicana, DuBois Chemicalien BV, Netherlands. Trustee Better Bus. Bur. Cin., 1981—; Mem. City Planning Commn., Akron, 1961-62. Served to 1st lt. JAGC, AUS, 1954-56. Mem. Am., Ohio, N.Y. bar assns., Beta Theta Pi, Omicron Delta Kappa, Delta Sigma Pi, Phi Eta Sigma. Republican. Presbyterian. Clubs: Queen City, Bankers (Cin.). Home: 423 Compton Rd Cincinnati OH 45215 Office: 1200 DuBois Tower Cincinnati OH 45202

KENSHALO, DANIEL RALPH, psychologist, educator; b. West Frankfort, Ill., July 27, 1922; s. Daniel Ralph and Edith (Schroeder) K.; m. Mary Janice Gordon, Aug. 28, 1970; children: Daniel Ralph, Rebecca Carolyn, Mark Hoyt, Janice Machelle. A.B., Washington U., 1947, Ph.D., 1953. Faculty physiol. psychology Fla. State U., 1950—, prof., 1959—, Distinguished prof., 1975—; vis. prof. physiology U. Marburg, Germany, 1969, U. Claude Bernard, Lyon, France, 1973. Cons. editor: Handbook of Perception, vol. 3, 1974, Perception and Psychophysics, 1973; Contbr. numerous articles to sci., profl. jours. Served as officer USNR, World War II. NSF grantee, 1955-57, 1964—; NASA grantee, 1961-64; NIH grantee, 1961—. Fellow Am. Psychol. Assn., AAAS, N.Y. Acad. Scis., Internat. Neuropsychology Soc., Soc. Neurosci.; mem. So. Soc. Philosophy and Psychology (sec. 1959-62, pres. 1963), Am. Physiol. Soc., Eastern Psychol. Assn. Psychonomic Soc., Sigma Xi, Psi Chi. Home: 2414 Delgado Dr Tallahassee FL 32304

KENSIL, JAMES LEWIS, athletics association executive; b. Phila., Aug. 19, 1930; s. Lewis Martin and Kathryn Beatrice (Rush) K.; m. Catherine Tighe, Jan. 2, 1954; children: Michael, Joseph, Mary Jo, Daniel. B.A., U. Pa., 1952. Newsman AP, N.Y.C., 1952, Columbus, Ohio, 1954-56, sports writer, N.Y.C., 1956-61; dir. pub. relations Nat. Football League, N.Y.C., 1961-67, exec. dir., 1968-77; pres. N.Y. Jets Football Club, Inc., 1977—. Served with AUS, 1952-54. Office: NY Jets Football Club 598 Madison Ave New York NY 10022

KENSING, HENRY VINCENT, metals company executive, lawyer; b. Mt. Kisco, N.Y., June 1, 1933; s. Howard George and Susan Antonia (O'Brien) K.; m. Eileen Mary Murphy, Sept. 6, 1969; children: Brian Christopher, Edward Henry, Sean Michael. A.B., Fordham Coll., 1955; LL.B. cum laude, Harvard, 1960. Bar: N.Y. 1960. Assoc. atty. firm Seward & Kissel, N.Y.C., 1960-71; atty. Howmet Corp., Greenwich, Conn., 1971-73, gen. counsel, sec., 1973-75; v.p., gen. counsel, sec. Pechiney Ugine Kuhlman Corp., Greenwich, 1976—; trustee Village of Mt. Kisco, N.Y., 1963-67, mayor, 1967-81; dir. Dynamics Corp. Am., Greenwich. Trustee No. Westchester Hosp. Center, Mt. Kisco, 1974-81. Served to 1st. lt. arty. AUS, 1955-57. Mem. Ancient Order Hibernians. Roman Catholic. Clubs: K.C., Elk. Home: 60 Orchard Rd Mount Kisco NY 10549 Office: 475 Steamboat Rd Greenwich CT 06830

KENSLER, CHARLES JOSEPH, cons. co. exec.; b. N.Y.C., Jan. 21, 1915; s. Joseph and Bertha (Bruns) K.; m. Diane Seyfort-Ruegg, Apr. 18, 1959; 1 son, Thomas Wells. A.B., Columbia U., 1937, M.A., 1938; Ph.D., Cornel U. Med. Coll., N.Y.C., 1947. Asso. prof. Cornell U. Med. Coll., 1953-54; head biology sect. Arthur D. Little, Cambridge, Mass., 1954-57, mgr. life scis. div., 1960-73, sr. v.p. profl. ops., 1973—; lectr. in pharmacology Harvard U. Med. Sch., Cambridge, Mass., 1954-57; prof., chmn. dept. pharmacology and exptl. therapeutics Boston U. Sch. Medicine, 1957-60; now prof.; vis. prof. M.I.T.; past pres. Mass. Health Research Inst., Boston; past chmn. bd. trustees Gordon Research Confs., Kingston, R.I.; traveling fellow Oxford (Eng.) U., 1949-50. Contbr. numerous articles on biochemistry, pharmacology, toxicology to profl. publs. Served with U.S. Army, 1943-46. USPHS fellow, 1947-48; NRC fellow, 1948-49; Sloan Found. scholar, 1951-54. Mem. Environ. Mutagen Soc. (council), Soc. Toxicology (council), Am. Soc. Pharmacology and Exptl. Therapeutics, Am. Cancer Research Soc. Clubs: St. Botolph's, Harvard (Boston). Home: Woodland Rd Ryegate North Hampton NH 03862 Office: 25 Acorn Park Cambridge MA 02140

KENT, ALLEN, educator; b. N.Y.C., Oct. 24, 1921; s. Samuel and Anna (Begun) K.; m. Rosalind Kossoff, May 24, 1943; children: Merryl Frances Kent Samuels, Emily Beth Kent Yeager, Jacqueline Diane Kent Maryak, Carolyn May Kent Hall. B.S. in Chemistry, CCNY, 1942. Sci. editor Intersci. Pubs., 1946-51; Research assoc. Center Internat. Studies, MIT, 1951-53; prin. documentation engr. Battelle Meml. Inst., Columbus, Ohio, 1953-55; asso. dir. Center for Documentation and Communication Research; prof. library sci. Western Res. U., 1955-63; dir. office communications programs, chmn. interdisciplinary doctoral program info. sci., prof. library sci., edn. and computer sci. U. Pitts., 1963-76, Univ. Disting. prof. library and info. sci. and asso. dean, 1976—; mem. mgmt. info. com. Health and Welfare Assn. Allegheny County, N.H., 1972—; dir. Marcel Dekker, Inc., N.H., 1978—. Author: (with others) Machine Literature Searching, 1956, (with J. W. Perry) Documentation and Information Retrieval, 1957, Tools for Machine Literature Searching, 1958, Centralized Information Services, 1958, Mechanized Information Retrieval, 1962, 2d edit., 1966; also fgn. transls. Specialized Information Centers, 1965; Information Analysis and Retrieval, 1971, Resource Sharing in Libraries, 1977, On-Line Revolution in Libraries, 1978, Structure and Governance of Library Networks, 1979, Use of Library Materials, 1979, Information Technology, 1982; editor, co-editor numerous books in field; exec. editor: Ency. Library and Info. Sci, 1968—, Ency. Computer Sci. and Tech, 1972—. Chmn. bd. Interuniv. Communications Council Inc. Served with USAAF, 1942-46. Recipient Info. Tech. Merit award Eastman Kodak Co., 1968. Fellow Am. Inst. Chemists, AAAS; mem. Assn. Computing Machinery, ALA, Am. Soc. Info. Sci. (recipient award of merit 1977, award for best info. sci. book of yr. 1980). Club: Cosmos (Washington). Home: 89 Mayfair Dr Mount Lebanon PA 15228 Office: U of Pitts Office of Communications Program Pittsburgh PA 15260 *My goal has been to be useful. This entails service, dedication to my profession and to the institution which supports my work, and absolute standards of honesty.*

KENT, CALVIN ALBERT, business educator; b. Kansas City, Kans., Sept. 8, 1941; s. Homer C. Wright; m. Nita Sue Davis, Aug. 23, 1963; children: Nita Christine, Anna Elaine. B.A., Baylor U., 1963; M.A., U. Mo., 1965, Ph.D., 1967; postgrad., U. Va., 1967, Wichita State U., 1972, U. Chgo., 1975. Instr. econs. U. Mo., Columbia, 1963-64; instr. social scis. Stevens Coll., Columbia, 1964-67; faculty U. S.D., Vermillion, 1967-78, prof. econs., 1973-78, dir. public fin. studies, 1971-78; Herman W. Lay prof. pvt. enterprise, dir. Center Pvt. Enterprise and Entrepreneurship, Baylor U., Waco, Tex., 1978—; exec. dir. S.D. Council on Econ. Edn., 1969-78; chief economist taxation coms. S.D. Legislature; cons. S.D. Dept. Rev. Alderman, Vermillion, 1972-78; mem. Pres.'s Adv. Com. Entrepreneurship Edn., 1983—. Author: Indian Poverty, 1969, Taxation of Cooperative Enterprise, 1970, Death Taxes in the American States, 1974, Municipal Regulation and Franchising, 1975, Encyclopedia of Entrepreneurship, 1981, The Environment for Entrepreneurship, 1984; contbr. articles to profl. jour. Pres. City Council, 1974-78; Vice chmn. S.D. Mcpl. League, Dist. 2, 1972-74. Named Outstanding Tchr., U. S.D., 1970-72, Outstanding Prof., Baylor U., 1983; NSF awardee, 1974; named Outstanding Young Religious Leader, 1976; Disting. Prof., Baylor Sch. Bus., 1981; recipient Freedoms Found. at Valley Forge award for excellence in pvt. enterprise edn., 1980. Mem. AAUP, Nat. Assn. Econ. Educators (pres. 1978-80), Assn. Pvt. Enterprise Edn. (sec.-treas. 1982—). Republican. Presbyterian. Clubs: Rotary, Masons, Shriners. Home: 10013 Shadowcrest Waco TX 76710 Office: Baylor U Waco TX 76798

KENT, DAVID GUILD, arts management consultant; b. Seattle, Sept. 3, 1931; s. Clarence Guild and Hannah (Tarang) K.; m. Elaine Johnson, Feb. 24, 1962; children: Stephanie Jo, Richard Guild. Student, Pacific Luth. Coll., 1949-52; B.B.A., U. Wash., 1958. With Seattle Symphony, 1958; subscription and Tanglewood bus. office mgr. Boston Symphony, 1958-62; mgr. R.I. Philharm., 1962-65, Hartford Symphony, 1965-68; gen. mgr. Denver Symphony, 1968-75; fundraising and mgmt. cons., 1975-77; gen. mgr. Fla. Philharm., 1977-78; exec. v.p., gen. mgr. Kansas City (Mo.) Philharm., 1978-82; arts mgmt. and fundraising cons., 1982—. Served with AUS. Mem. Major Symphony Orch. Mgrs. Assn., Mo. Citizens for Arts, Kansas City Arts Council, Am. Symphony Orch. League. Lutheran. Club: Rotary. Home: 203 Woodbridge Ln Kansas City MO 64145 Office: 8400 W 110th St Suite 600 Overland Park KS 66210

KENT, EDGAR ROBERT, JR., investment banker; b. Balt., May 28, 1941; s. E. Robert and Marian (Meuller) K.; children: E. Robert, Josephine Townsend, Louise Daniel. B.S., Princeton U., 1963; M.B.A., Columbia U., 1966; J.D., U. Md., 1975. Chartered fin. analyst. Assoc. Joel Dean Assoc., N.Y.C., 1966-68; ptnr. Alex Brown & Sons, Balt., 1968—; dir. Devel. Credit Corp. of Md., Balt., Kemp Co., Md. Blue Sky Adv. Com. Trustee Calvert Sch., Balt. Republican. Home: 4303 Keswick Rd Baltimore MD 21210 Office: Alex Brown & Sons 135 E Baltimore St Baltimore MD 21202

KENT, FREDERICK HEBER, lawyer; b. Fitzgerald, Ga., Apr. 26, 1905; s. Heber and Juanita (McDuffie) K.; m. Norma C. Futch, Apr. 25, 1929; children: Frederick Heber, Norma Futch K. Lockwood, John Bradford, James Cleveland. J.D., U. Ga., 1926. Bar: Ga. 1926, Fla. 1926. Since practiced in, Jacksonville, Fla.; sr. partner firm Kent, Watts, Durden, Kent, Nichols & Mickler; chmn. bd. Kent Theatres, Inc.; pres. Kent Enterprises, Inc.; dir. Fla. 1st Nat. Bank of Jacksonville, Fla. Nat. Banks of Fla., Inc. Chmn. local ARC, 1934, 1950; pres. Jacksonville's 50 Years of Progress Assn., 1951; bd. dirs. YMCA, pres., 1946-50; bd. dirs. Jacksonville Community Chest-United Fund, 1955-59, pres., 1958-59; chmn. Fla. State Plant Bd., 1955-56; bd. control (regents) Fla. Instns. of Higher Learning, 1953-58, chmn., 1955-56; bd. dirs. Riverside Hosp. Assn., 1956-76, pres., 1964-65; chmn. State Jr. Coll. Council, 1962-72; mem. adv. com. Fla. Higher Edn. Facilities Act, 1963, 64; chmn. bd. trustees Fla. Jr. Coll., Jacksonville, 1965-71; mem. Select Council on Post High Sch. Edn. in Fla., 1967, Fla. Gov.'s Commn. for Quality Edn., 1967; trustee Bolles Sch., Jacksonville, 1954-65, Theatre Jacksonville, 1966-76; chmn. Fla. Quadricentennial Commn., 1962-65; mem. Jacksonville City Council, 1933-1937; chmn. Fla. Democratic Exec. Com., 1938-40. Served as lt. USNR, 1942-45. Recipient Distinguished Service award U.S. Jr. C. of C., 1933, Ted Arnold award Jacksonville C. of C., 1961; Fred H. Kent campus Fla. Jr. Coll. at Jacksonville named in his honor, 1974. Mem. Internat. Bar Assn., ABA, Fla. Bar Assn., Jacksonville Bar Assn., Jacksonville C. of C., Am. Judicature Soc., Newcomen Soc. N.Am., Am. Legion, Sigma Alpha Epsilon, Delta Sigma Pi. Republican. Clubs: Rotary (pres. 1958-59), Timuquana Country, Florida Yacht, Seminole, Friars, Ye Mystic Revellers, Ponte Vedra, River, Sawgrass Country, Highlands (N.C.) Country, Blowing Rock (N.C.) Country. Home: 2970 St Johns Ave Apt 12-A Jacksonville FL 32205 Office: 850 Edward Ball Bldg Jacksonville FL 32202 *Never commit oneself to a project or a position until satisfied that all ascertainable facts are known. Reserve the right to change if justified by new information. When committed, stay put and exert one's best efforts to live up to that commitment.*

KENT, GEOFFREY, physician; b. Amsterdam., Netherlands, Jan. 30, 1914; came to U.S., 1953, naturalized, 1958; s. Jacob and Nelly (Friedlander) K.; m. Katharine M. Ruscoe, Sept. 22, 1944; children: Jonathan H., Simon R., Paul A., Helen J. M.D., U. Amsterdam, 1939; Ph.D., Northwestern U., 1957. Resident, chem. pathologist Royal Infirmary, Manchester, Eng., 1939-43; chief med. asst., asst. dir. dept. clin. investigation and research U. Manchester, 1944; sr. registrar Chase Farm Hosp., Middlesex, Eng., also London Hosp., 1947-50; dir. labs. Gen. and Providence Hosp., Moose Jaw, Sask., Can., 1950-53; sr. pathologist, asso. dir. pathology Cook County Hosp., Chgo., 1953-57; dir. labs West Suburban Hosp., Oak Park, Ill., 1958-69; chmn. dept. pathology Chgo. Wesley Meml. Hosp., 1969-73; pathologist in chief, dir. labs. Northwestern Meml. Hosp., Chgo., 1973-76; prof. pathology Northwestern U., 1969—. Served to capt. Royal Army M.C., 1944-47. Home: 78 Brinker Rd Barrington Hills IL 60010 Office: Dept Pathology Northwestern U Med Sch 303 E Chicago Ave Chicago IL 60611

KENT, GEORGE CANTINE, JR., zoology educator; b. Kingston, N.Y., July 25, 1914; s. George Cantine and Charlotte (Delamater) K.; m. Lila Carringer, June 8, 1937; 1 dau., Susan Carolyn. B.A., Maryville (Tenn.) Coll., 1937; M.A., Vanderbilt U., 1938, Ph.D., 1942. Asst. biology Maryville Coll., 1935-37; teaching fellow Vanderbilt U., 1937-42; research assoc. Cornell U., summer 1941; instr. embryology Vanderbilt U., summer 1942; vis. prof. zoology Northwestern State Coll., Natchitoches, La., summer 1955; mem. faculty La. State U., 1942—, prof. zoology, 1956-79, Alumni prof., 1967-79, prof. emeritus, 1979, chmn. dept. zoology, physiology and entomology, 1960-64; cons. bur. Commn. Undergrad. Edn. Biol. Scis.; vis. lectr. sci. insts. Vice chmn. bd. govs. Center Research in Coll. Instrn. Sci. and Math., Fla. State U., 1966-70. Author: Comparative Anatomy of the Vertebrates, 5th rev. edit, 1983; also numerous articles. Pres. Young Men's Bus. Club Baton Rouge, 1948; Mem. La. State Guard, 1942-46. Recipient Nat. Council Scholarship medal Phi Sigma, 1970. Fellow AAAS; mem. Am. Inst. Biol. Scis., Am. Soc. Zoologists, Soc. Exptl. Biology and Medicine, Endocrine Soc., N.Y. Acad. Scis., La. Acad. Sci. (pres. 1959, editor proc. 1945-55), Assn. S.E. Biologists (pres. 1956), Soc. Study Reprodn., Sigma Xi, Alpha Epsilon Delta (life), Omicron Delta Kappa, Phi Sigma (hon.). Home: 482 Stanford Ave Baton Rouge LA 70808 *I prefer being wrong part of the time to never being wrong for the reason that I cannot decide what might be right.*

KENT, HARRY CHRISTISON, educator; b. Los Angeles, May 20, 1930; s. Harry and Florence (Christison) K.; m. Sheila Marie Kelly, Aug. 18, 1956; children—Colleen Marie, Bruce Kelly. Geol. Engr., Colo. Sch. Mines, 1952; M.S., Stanford, 1953; Ph.D., U. Colo., 1965. Geologist The California Co., Fla. and La., 1953-56; mem. faculty Colo. Sch. Mines, Golden, 1956—, asso. prof., 1967-69, prof., 1969—, head geology dept., 1969-75; dir. Potential Gas Agy., 1976—. Bd. mgrs. Jeffco br. YMCA, Denver. Fellow Geol. Soc. Am.; mem. Am. Assn. Petroleum Geologists, Soc. Econ. Paleontologists and Mineralogists, Sigma Xi. Democrat. Home: 5131 Jellison Ct Arvada CO 80002 Office: Potential Gas Agy Colo Sch Mines Golden CO 80401

KENT, JAMES A., engr., university dean; b. New Britain, Conn., Feb. 10, 1922; m. Anita C. Barbe, Feb. 20, 1943; children: James, David, Nicholas, Edward, Joseph. B.S. in Chem. Engring, W.Va. U., 1943, Ph.D., 1950. Research engr. Dow Chem. Co., Midland, Mich., 1950-52; research group leader Mansanto Chem. Co., Nitro, W.Va., 1952-54; prof. chem. and nuclear engring. W.Va. U., 1954-67, asso. dean engring., 1963-67; dean coll. engring. Mich. Tech. U., Houghton, 1967-78; dean Coll. Engring. and Sci., U. Detroit, 1978—. Editor: Handbook of Industrial Chemistry, 1974; Contbr. articles to profl. jours. Prin. developer radiation-processed wood-plastic combinations. Mem. Gov's Adv. Com. on State Tech. Services, W. Va., 1966-67, Artificial Heart Com., Nat. Heart and Lung Inst., 1968-73; adv. com. materials program Office of Tech. Assessment, 1975-77; adv. com. Mich. Transp. Research Program, 1976—; chmn. Mich. Gov.'s Planning Com. on Hazardous/Toxic Wastes, 1977-79; mem. Mich. Gov.'s Com. to Develop State Hazardous Waste Mgmt. Plan. Served to 1st lt. C.E. Aus, 1943-46. Recipient Meritorious Achievement award Pitts. sect. Am. Nuclear Soc., 1966; numerous awards engring. and sci. hon. socs. Fellow Am. Inst. Chemists; mem. Am. Inst. Chem. Engrs., Sigma Xi, Tau Beta Pi. Club: Rotarian. Home: 411 S Woodward Apt 619 Birmingham MI 48011 Office: Coll Engring and Sci U Detroit Detroit MI 48221

KENT, JAMES HOWARD, grain processing company executive; b. Des Moines, July 25, 1923; s. Gage A. and Mildred (Johnson) K.; m. Irene Kemp, June 19, 1949; children: Katheine I., Gage A. Student, U. Iowa, 1941-43, Simpson Coll., 1942, No. State Coll., 1944, Manchester Coll. of Tech., (Eng.), 1945; Dr. Sci. (hon.), Iowa Wesleyan Coll., 1981. Distillery operator Grain Processing Corp., Muscatine, Iowa, 1946; prodn.-sales br. mgr. Kent Feeds Inc., Muscatine and Sioux City, 1947-50; mgr. Lone Tree Grain & Feed Co., Lone Tree, Iowa, 1951-54; exec. v.p. Kent Feeds Inc., 1954-66; pres. Grain Processing Corp.-Kent Feeds Inc., 1966—. Trustee Simpson Coll., 1973—, Judson Coll., 1981—; mem. adv. council Iowa State U. Engring. Coll., Ames, 1974—. Served with U.S. Army, 1943-46; ETO. Mem. Muscatine C. of C. (bd. dirs.). Republican. Am. Baptist. Clubs: Union League (Chgo.); (Des Moines). Lodges: Masons; Elks. Office: 1600 Oregon St Muscatine IA 52761

KENT, LINDA GAIL, dancer; b. Buffalo, Sept. 21, 1946; d. Jerol Edward and Dorismae (Kohler) K. B.S., Juilliard Sch., 1968. Dancer Alvin Ailey Am. Dance Theater, 1968-74, then prin. dancer, 1970-74; prin. dancer Paul Taylor Dance Co., N.Y.C., 1975—. Mem. Am. Guild Mus. Artists, Actors Equity. Democrat. Unitarian. Home: 175 W 92d St New York NY 10025 Office: 550 Broadway New York NY 10012

KENT, RAYMOND DENNIS, speech scientist; b. Red Lodge, Mont., Dec. 12, 1942; s. Armas Matthew and Sylvia Josephine K.; m. Jane E. Finley, Dec. 28, 1972; children: Laurel, Jason. B.A. with honors, U. Mont., 1965; M.A., U. Iowa, 1969, Ph.D., 1970. Fellow MIT, 1970-71; prof. communication disorders U. Wis., Madison, 1971-79, prof. and chmn. communication disorders, 1983—; sr. research assoc. Boys Town Inst. for Communication Disorders in Children, Omaha, 1979-82. Author: (with L.D. Shriberg) Clinical Phonetics, 1981; editor: Jour. of Speech and Hearing Research, 1977-81; contbr. articles in field. Nat. Inst. Neurologic and Communicative Disorders and Stroke grantee; recipient editors awards Jour. Speech Hearing Research, 1972-74, Jour. Speech Hearing Disorders, 1979. Mem. Acoustical Soc. Am., Am. Speech Lang. Hearing Assn., Am. Assn. Phonetic Scis., N.Y. Acad. Sci., Sigma Xi. Home: 1 Kingsbury Ct Madison WI 53711 Office: Dept Communication Disorders U Wis Madison WI 53706

KENT, RICHARD TRAVIS, pharm. co. exec.; b. Bronxville, N.Y., Nov. 7, 1926. B.S. in Bus. Adminstrn, Northwestern U., 1949. With Bank of the Manhattan Co., 1949-54; asst. treas. McKesson & Robbins, N.Y.C., 1954-65; treas. REA Express, N.Y.C., 1965-68; v.p., treas. Bristol-Myers Co., N.Y.C., 1969—; dir. Excelsior Income Shares, Inc. Served with USN, 1944-46. Clubs: Treas. (N.Y.C.); Mill Reef (Antigua, B.W.I.). Home: 108 E 82d St New York NY 10028 Office: 345 Park Ave New York NY 10154

KENT, ROBERT BRYDON, law educator; b. Lowell, Mass., Dec. 2, 1921; s. Silas Stanley and Madeleine (Brydon) K.; m. Barbara Tuttle, Mar. 31, 1951; children: Robert Brydon, Dorothy Clarke, Elizabeth Montgomery, Hugh Clarke. A.B., Harvard Coll., 1943; LL.B., Boston U., 1949. Bar: Mass. 1948. Individual practice law, Ware, Mass., 1948-50; instr. Sch. Law, Boston U., 1950-52, asst. prof., 1952-54, prof., 1954-81; prof. law, dean Sch. Law, U. Zambia, 1970-72; dir. Law Practice Inst., Zambia, 1970-71; part-time vis. prof. Law Sch., Harvard U., 1973-74; vis. prof. Cornell Law Sch., 1980-81, prof., 1981—, assoc. dean, 1982—; Ford fellow in law teaching Harvard Law Sch., 1960-61; hon. vis. fellow Trinity Coll., Oxford U., 1976; reporter com. on civil rules supreme, superior, dist. cts., R.I., cons. criminal procedure. Author: (with Austin W. Scott) Cases and Other Materials on Civil Procedure, 1967, Rhode Island Practice: Civil Rules with Commentaries, 1969. Moderator Town of Lexington, Mass., 1965-70, selectman, 1977-81; vice chmn. Civil Liberties Union of Mass., 1966-69; exec. com. Law Assn. of Zambia, 1970-72; trustee Kimball Union Acad., pres., 1973-76. Served with U.S. Army, 1943-46. Mem. Am. Law Inst. Democrat. Unitarian. Home: 619 Cayuga Heights Rd Ithaca NY 14850 Office: Cornell U Law Sch Myron Taylor Hall Ithaca NY 14853

KENT, ROBERT WARREN, lawyer; b. Oceanside, N.Y., July 8, 1935; s. Meredith L. and Ruth W. K.; m. Sally Anne Macnair, Aug. 24, 1957; children: Robert W., William M., Richard M., Deborah K. A.B., Princeton U., 1957; J.D., Harvard U., 1960; postgrad., Advanced Mgmt. Program. Asso. firm Breed, Abbott & Morgan, N.Y.C., 1960-67; asso. counsel Armco Inc., Middletown, Ohio, 1967-69, asst. counsel, 1969-73, counsel, 1973-78, asst. gen. counsel, 1978-81, corp. v.p. law, gen. counsel, sec., 1981—. Pres. Moundbuilders Area council Boy Scouts Am., 1980-81. Mem. Ohio Mfrs. Assn. (v.p. 1977—), Am. Bar Assn. Episcopalian. Office: 703 Curtis St Middletown OH 45043

KENT, STEVEN ROBERT, insurance company executive; b. Des Moines, Dec. 28, 1943; s. Robert J. and Delores Elizabeth (Kurt) K.; m. Barbara Sue Prior, June 16, 1973; children: Patricia, Linda, Kathleen. Student, St. Louis U., 1962-64; B.S., Drake U., 1966. Fin. examiner to spl. asst. to commr. Iowa Ins. Dept., Des Moines, 1966-72; asst. to pres., asst. sec. Nat. Aviation Underwriters, Inc., St. Louis, 1972-74; asst. sec. Houston Gen. Ins. Group, 1974; asst. v.p., asst. sec. Equitable Gen. Ins. Group, Ft. Worth, 1975, v.p., sec., 1976-80; sr. v.p., sec., treas. Houston Gen. Ins. Co., Ft. Worth, 1981—, also dir.; dir. Tarrant Bank. Bd. dirs., treas. Symphony Soc. Tarrant County. Home: 4405 Hillside Ct Fort Worth TX 76132 Office: 4100 Equitable Dr Tower II Fort Worth TX 76113

KENTERA, CHRIS WILLIAM, univ. press exec.; b. Memphis, Aug. 20, 1925; s. Chris William and Clara Belle (Williams) K.; m. Carla Della Roach, June 5, 1949; children—Gregory Owen, Marc Alan. B.A., B.S., U. Mo., 1950. From field rep. to sr. editor Prentice-Hall, Inc., Englewood Cliffs, N.J., 1950-64; editorial dir. The Free Press, N.Y.C., 1964-65; exec. editor Addison-Wesley Pub. Co., Reading, Mass., 1965-67; dir. N.Y. U. Press, 1967-73, Pa. State U. Press, University Park, 1973—; dir. Am. Univ. Pubs. Group Ltd., London, Eng., Penn State Press Ltd., London; pub. cons., mem. adv. council Papers of Martin Van Buren. Bd. dirs. U.S. Gymnastics Safety Assn., Washington. Served with U.S. Army, 1944-46; ETO. Mem. Am. Assn. Univ. Presses, Am. Polit. Sci. Assn., Am. Econ. Assn., Coll. Art Assn., MLA, Beta Gamma Sigma. Club: Toftrees Country. Home: 721 Cricklewood Dr State College PA 16801 Office: Pa State Univ Press University Park PA 16802

KENTERA, GEORGE RICHARD, newspaperman; b. Humboldt, Tenn., July 15, 1922; s. Chris William and Clara Belle (Williams) K.; m. Eileen Ruth Kohler, Dec. 18, 1945; children: Gale Lynn Kentera Waldron, Jean Anne. B.J., U. Mo., 1943. Mem. staff Newark Evening News, 1947-71, Washington corr., 1959-65, mng. editor, 1965-70, exec. editor, 1970-71; mem. staff Washington bur. Detroit News, 1971-75; asst. mng. editor Phila. Bull., 1975—, mng. editor, 1975-78; asst. news editor Washington bur. Knight-Ridder Newspapers, 1978—. Mem. Nat. Press Club. Home: 7808 Accotink Pl Alexandria VA 22308 Office: 1195 National Press Bldg Washington DC 20045

KENTON, GLENN C., government official; b. Washington, Dec. 21, 1943; s. William and Jean K. A.B., Swarthmore Coll., 1965; J.D., Georgetown U., 1968. Bar: Del. bar. Asso. firm Brown Shiels & Barros, Dover, Del., 1969-71; counsel Del. Ho. of Reps., Dover, 1969-71; to Congressman Pierre S. du Pont, 1971-76; sec. state Del., 1977—. Mem. Del. Bar Assn. Republican. Office: Townsend Bldg Dover DE 19901 *

KENWORTHY, CARROLL H., newspaperman; b. Kokomo, Ind., May 10, 1904; s. Murray S. and Ida Lenora (Holloway) K.; m. Mary Lowes, Jan. 1, 1932; children-Thomas L., David K. (dec.), Lee Hadley. A.B., Earlham Coll., Richmond, Ind., 1925; student, Hartford (Conn.) Sem., 1926; A.M., Columbia, 1927. Reporter Hartford Courant, 1926, Japan Advertiser, Tokyo, 1927-29; corr. for newspapers in, U.S. and China from Tokyo, 1927-29; with Washington Bur. of Wall Street Jour., 1929; diplomatic reporter for Washington Bur. of United Press, 1930-40, White House corr., 1929-67, editor fgn. dept., Washington, 1941-67. Trustee Earlham Coll., 1954-63. Mem. Overseas Writers (twice pres.), Nat. Press Club. Home: 13 Kendal Kennett Square PA 19348

KENYON, CARLETON WELLER, librarian; b. Lafayette, N.Y., Oct. 7, 1923; s. Herbert Abram and Esther Elizabeth (Weller) K.; m. Dora Marie Kallander, May 21, 1948; children: Garnet Eileen, Harmon Clark, Kay Adelle. A.B., Yankton Coll., 1947; M.A., U. S.D., 1950, J.D., 1950; A.M. in L.S, U. Mich., 1951. Bar: S.D. 1950. Asst. law librarian, head catalog librarian U. Nebr., 1951-52; asst. reference librarian Los Angeles County Law Library, 1952-54, head catalog librarian, 1954-60; law librarian State of Calif., Sacramento, 1960-69; became cons. Library of Congress, Washington, 1963, asso. law librarian, 1969-71, law librarian, 1971—; cons. county law libraries; lectr. legal bibliography and research. Author: California County Law Library Basic List Handbook and Information of New Materials, 1967; compiler: Calif. Library Laws; assisted in compiling checklists of basic: Am. publs. and subject headings; contbr. articles and book revs. to law revs., library jours. Served with USAAF, 1943-47. Mem. Am., Fed. bar assns., State Bar S.D., Internat. Assn. Law Librarians, Am. Assn. Law Librarians (chmn. com. on cataloging and classification 1969-71, mem. staff Law Library Inst. 1969, 71), Law Librarians Soc. Washington. Home: 11407 Grago Dr Fort Washington MD 20744 Office: 101 Independence Ave Washington DC 20540

KENYON, CHARLES MOIR, publishing co. exec.; b. Pawtucket, R.I., Nov. 6, 1916; s. Archibald and Jessie Maria (Griffiths) K.; m. Muriel Vanderbilt, Feb. 5, 1943; children—Richard, Ann, Barbara (Mrs. Ferdinand Engel), Robert, Elizabeth. A.B., Brown U., 1937, M.A., 1939, postgrad., 1939-41; postgrad., U. Mich., 1940-41. Instr. English Brown U., 1939-41, 45-46; mng. editor Chilton Co., Phila., 1946-53; pub. relations exec. Gray & Rogers, Phila., 1953-56; accounts supr., mgr. direct mail advt. J. Walter Thompson Co., N.Y.C., 1956-67; dir. marketing Am. Edn. Publs., Middletown, Conn., 1967, pres., 1967-72; chmn. Everyweek Edn. Press, Rickmansworth, Eng., 1968-71; v.p. Xerox Edn. Group, 1967-72; pres. Kenbrook Co., Essex, Conn., 1972—; asso. dir. Conn. Bank & Trust Co. Author: First Voyage Out, 1967. Chmn. Essex Zoning Commn. Served to capt. USNR, 1941-45. Clubs: Essex Boat; Pettipaug Yacht (Essex). Home: River Rd Essex CT 06426

KENYON, EDWARD TIPTON, lawyer; b. Summit, N.J., Jan. 27, 1929; s. Theodore S. and Martha (Tipton) K.; m. Dolores Cetrule, July 11, 1953; children: David S., James N., Jonathan W., Theodore H. A.B., Harvard U., 1950; LL.B., Columbia U., 1953. Bar: N.Y. 1956, N.J. 1957. Asso. firm Thacher, Proffitt, Prizer, Crawley & Wood, N.Y.C., 1955-56; law clk. to U.S. Dist. Judge Reynier J. Wortendyke, Newark, 1956-57; asso. firm Jeffers, Mountain & Franklin, Morristown, N.J., 1957-59, Bourne, Noll and Kenyon (and predecessor), Summit, 1959-62, partner, 1962—. Trustee Summit Art Center, 1960-72, Trinity-Pawling Sch., Pawling, N.Y., 1977—, Pingry Sch., Hillside, N.J., 1970—; deacon Central Presbyterian Ch., Summit, 1960-65, trustee, 1965-72, pres., 1970-72; trustee Overlook Hosp., Summit, 1964-72, chmn., 1970-72; trustee Overlook Hosp. Found., 1975—, sec., 1977-80, v.p., 1980-81, pres., 1981—. Served with M.C. U.S. Army, 1953-55. Mem. Summit Bar Assn. (pres. 1983—), Union County (N.J.) Bar Assn., N.J. Bar Assn., N.Y. State Bar Assn., ABA, N.J. Soc. Hosp. Attys., Am. Soc. Hosp. Attys., Am. Coll. Probate Counsel, Am. Law Inst. Republican. Clubs: Beacon Hill (trustee 1977-81, pres. 1979-81), Harvard of N.Y.C., Harvard of N.J. (trustee 1958-69), Harvard of N.J. (pres. 1968-69). Home: 80 Bellevue Ave Summit NJ 07901 Office: 382 Springfield Ave Summit NJ 07901

KENYON, HEWITT, mathematician, educator; b. Marysville, Calif., Aug. 31, 1920; s. Frederick Newcomb and Inez (Hewitt) K.; m. Barbara Elise Vernon, July 19, 1947; children—Charity, Emily; m. Linda Root, June 17, 1961; children—Amos, Rachel, Leah, Miriam, Naomi. B.S. in Chemistry, U. Calif. at Berkeley, 1942, Ph.D. in Math, 1954. Instr. U. Rochester, N.Y., 1952-55, asst. prof., 1955-61, George Washington U., Washington, 1961-63, asso. prof., 1963-66, prof. math., 1967—, chmn. dept., 1967-71; vis. asso. prof. U. Calif. at Berkeley, 1966-67. Served with USNR, 1942-46. Mem. Am. Math. Soc., Math. Assn. Am., AAUP, Sigma Xi. Home: 1611 Kennedy Pl NW Washington DC 20011

KENYON, RICHARD ALBERT, college dean; b. Syracuse, N.Y., Apr. 8, 1933; s. Albert Rees and Marjorie Ellen (Robinson) K.; m. Barbara Louise Kibbe, June 12, 1954; children: Alan Richard, David Lewis, Steven Arthur. B.M.E., Clarkson Coll., 1954; M.S., Cornell U., 1956; Ph.D., Syracuse U., 1965. Registered profl. engr., N.Y. Instr. mech. engring. Cornell U., 1954-56; instr. Clarkson Coll. Tech., Potsdam, N.Y., 1956-58, asst. prof., 1958-62, asso. prof., 1962-70, head dept. mech. engring., 1968-69, asso. dean, 1966-68, asso. dir. div. research, 1966-68; prof., head dept. mech. engring. Rochester (N.Y.) Inst. Tech., 1970-71, dean Coll. Engring., 1971—; mem. N.Y. State Bd. Engring. and Land Surveying, 1981—. Author: Priniciples of Fluid Mechanics, 1960, Fundamentals of Thermodynamics, 1962, Fluid Mechanics, 1980. Exec. council St. Lawrence council Boy Scouts Am., 1967-68. NSF sci. faculty fellow Syracuse U., 1962-64. Fellow ASME (regional v.p. 1978-82, sr. v.p. 1982-84); mem. Rochester Engring. Soc. (v.p. 1973, pres. 1974-75), Am. Soc. Engring. Edn., Assn. Engring. Colls. N.Y. State (sec.-treas. 1972-78, v.p. 1978-80, pres. 1980-84), Sigma Xi, Tau Beta Pi, Pi Tau Sigma. Home: 57 Old Forge Ln Pittsford NY 14534 Office: 1 Lomb Meml Dr Rochester NY 14623

KENYON, RICHARD DUANE, army officer; b. Buffalo, Apr. 11, 1936; s. Duane Eugene and Jane Elaine (Fraser) K.; m. virginia Louise Mix, June 4, 1957; children: Michael, Susan, Steven. B.S., U.S. Mil. Acad., 1957; M.S. in Aero. Engring., Princeton U., 1964. Commd., officer U.S. Army, 1957, advanced through grades to maj. gen., aviation duty, W. Germany, 1959-62, with helicopter unit, Vietnam, 1964-65; instr. U.S. Mil. Acad., 1966-67; bn. comdr. U.S. Army, Vietnam, 1969-70, project mgr. blackhawk Helicopter, 1976-79; dep. comdg. gen. Army Aviation Sch., Ft. Rucker, Ala., 1979-81; dir. weapon systems Hdqrs. Dept. Army, Washington, 1981-83, asst. dept. chief staff for research, devel. and acquisition, 1984—. Decorated Legion of Merit, Bronze Star, Air medal (11). Mem. Army Aviation Assn. Am., Helicopter Soc. Am. (v.p.), Am. Helicopter Soc. Roman Catholic. Home: 6710 Coachman Dr Springfield VA 22152

KENYON, WILLIAM HOUSTON, JR., lawyer; b. Lakeville, Conn., Aug. 23, 1899; s. William Houston and Maria Wellington (Stanwood) K.; m. Mildred Adams, Jan. 2, 1935 (dec. Nov. 1980); m. Harriet Hardy, Nov. 26, 1983. A.B., Harvard U., 1921, LL.B., 1924. Bar: N.Y. 1925. With firm Kenyon & Kenyon (patent attys.), N.Y.C., 1924-25, partner, 1929-43, 46-78, of counsel, 1979—; spl. asst. U.S. atty. So. Dist. N.Y., 1925-27; spl. asst. U.S. atty. gen., N.Y.C. and Washington, 1927-29; lectr. law NYU Law Sch., 1928-36; chief patent counsel procurement War Dept., 1943-45; counsel Pres. Truman's Com. Survey Patent System, 1945-46; vis. lectr. Yale Law Sch., 1948-62. Contbr. articles to legal jours. N.Y. area agt. Harvard Law Sch. Fund, 1947-70; chmn. gift com. Harvard Class of 1921 Reunion, 1961, 66, 71, 76; co-chmn. Class of 1921 com. Harvard Campaign, 1980-84; Com., 1971—; trustee Kenyon Prize Fund, CCNY, 1934—. Served with ARC, 1918; Italy. Recipient commendation and medal exceptional civilian service Sec. War, 1945. Mem. Am. Patent Law Assn., N.Y. Patent Law Assn. (bd. govs. 1949-58, v.p. 1954-56, pres. 1956-57, chmn. com. profl. ethics and grievances 1969-72), Am. Law Inst., ABA, N.Y. County Lawyers Assn. (chmn. com. fed. legislation 1946-49), Assn. Bar City N.Y. (chmn. com. on patents 1968-71). Clubs: Harvard (N.Y.C.); Metropolitan (Washington). Home: One Broadway New York NY 10004 Office: 59 Maiden Ln New York NY 10038

KENZIE, ROSS BRUCE, banker; b. Prattsburg, N.Y., Sept. 22, 1931; s. J. Frederick K. and Ruth (Wemett) Woodruff; m. Langley Hoge, June 4, 1953; children: Rachel L., Mary L. B.S. in Civil Engring., U.S. Mil. Acad., West Point, N.Y., 1953. With Merrill Lynch Pierce Fenner & Smith, Inc., Boston, Akron, Cleve., 1957-79, met. regional dir., 1973-79; pres., chief operating officer Buffalo Savs. Bank, 1979-80; chmn., chief exec. officer Goldome Bank, 1980—; dir. Nat. Council Savs. Instn., Washington, 1981—, Savs. Bank Trust Co., N.Y.C., Instn. Investors Mutual Fund, Inc., Instn. Securities Corp., Merchants Ins. Group, Buffalo. Contbr. articles in field to profl. jours. Bd. dirs. Millard Fillmore Hosp., Buffalo, 1981—; bd. dirs. coll. council State Coll. Buffalo, 1981—; gen. chmn. United Way of Buffalo and Erie County, 1982; trustee Canisius Coll., Buffalo, 1982—. Served to lt. U.S. Army, 1953-57. Recipient John Peter Medaille award Medaille Coll., 1983, Exec. of Yr. award SUNY Sch. Mgmt. Buffalo, 1983. Home: 109 Brantwood Rd Snyder NY 14226 Office: Goldome Bank 1 Fountain Plaza Buffalo NY 14203

KEOGH, JAMES, journalist; b. Platte County, Nebr., Oct. 29, 1916; s. David James and Edith (Dwyer) K.; m. Verna Pedersen, May 17, 1940; children—Kevin, Katherine Ann (Mrs. Peter O. Crouse). Ph.B., Creighton U., 1938. Reporter Omaha World-Herald, 1938-48, city editor, 1948-51; contbg. editor Time mag., 1951-52, asso. editor, 1952-56, sr. editor, 1956-61, asst. mng. editor, 1961-68, exec. editor, 1968; spl. asst. Pres. U.S., 1969-70; freelance writer, 1971-72; dir. USIA, 1973-77; exec. dir. The Business Roundtable, 1977—. Author: This is Nixon, 1956, President Nixon and the Press, 1972. Recipient Distinguished Nebraskan award, 1972. Clubs: Belle Haven (Greenwich, Conn.) (pres.-commodore 1967-68); Sky (N.Y.C.)). Home: Byram Dr Belle Haven Greenwich CT 06830 Office: 200 Park Ave New York NY 10166

KEOHANE, NANNERL OVERHOLSER, college president, political science educator; b. Blytheville, Ark., Sept. 18, 1940; d. James Arthur and Grace (McSpadden) Overholser; m. Patrick Henry III, Sept. 16, 1962 (div. May 1969); 1 son, Stephan; m.2d. Robert Owen Keohane, Dec. 18, 1970; children: Sarah, Jonathan, Nathaniel. B.A., Wellesley Coll., 1961, Oxford U., Eng., 1963; Ph.D., Yale U., 1967. Lectr. Swarthmore Coll., Pa., 1967-69, asst. prof., 1969-73, Stanford U., Calif., 1973-78, assoc. prof., 1978-81; fellow Ctr. for Advanced Study in the Behavioral Scis.-Stanford U., 1978-79; pres., prof. polit. sci. Wellesley Coll., Mass., 1981—; mem. adv. council on history sci. Rockefeller Commn. on the Humanities, 1979-80. Author: Philosophy and the State in France: The Renaissance to the Enlightenment, 1980; assoc. editor: Signs Mag., 1980—; co-editor: Feminist Theory: A Critique of Ideology, 1982. Trustee WGBH Ednl. TV Found., 1981—; corp. mem. Woods Hole Oceanographic Instn. Marshall scholar, 1961-63; Sterling fellow, 1966-67; AAUW dissertation fellow. Mem. Council on Fgn. Relations, Phi Beta Kappa. Democrat. Presbyterian. Clubs: Cosmopolitan (N.Y.C.); Saturday, Commercial (Boston). Office: Wellesley Coll Office of the Pres Wellesley MA 02181

KEOUGH, DONALD RAYMOND, beverage and entertainment company executive; b. Maurice, Iowa, Sept. 4, 1926; s. Leo H. and Veronica (Henkels) K.; m. Marilyn Mulhall, Sept. 10, 1949; children: Kathleen Anne, Mary Shayla, Michael Leo, Patrick John, Eileen Tracy, Clarke Robert. B.S., Creighton U., 1949, LL.D., 1982. With Butter-Nut Foods Co., Omaha, 1950-61, Duncan Foods Co., Houston, 1961-67; v.p., dir. mktg. foods div. The Coca-Cola Co., 1967-71, pres. div., 1971-73; exec. v.p. Coca-Cola USA, Atlanta, 1973-74, pres., 1974-76; exec. v.p. Coca-Cola Co., 1976-79, sr. exec. v.p., 1980-81, pres., chief operating officer, dir., 1981—; dir. IBM World Trade Americas/ Far East Corp. Mem. pres.'s council Creighton U.; trustee U. Notre Dame, Spelman Coll., The Lovett Sch., Agnes Scott Coll. Served with USNR, 1944-46. Clubs: Capital City, Piedmont Driving Commerce (Atlanta). Office: 310 North Ave NW PO Drawer 1734 Atlanta GA 30301

KEOUGH, FRANCIS PAUL, librarian; b. Brookline, Mass., Apr. 2, 1917; s. John Joseph and Annie (O'Malley) K.; m. Helen D. Drews, May 13, 1954; children—David D., Ann, Jeffrey. Adj. in Arts, Harvard, 1940; B.S. in L.S, Columbia, 1947. With Boston Pub. Library, 1934-39; asst. Harvard Archives, 1939-42; reference asst. Coll. Library, 1947-51; archivist radiation lab. Mass. Inst. Tech., 1945-46; library dir. Framingham (Mass.) City Library, 1951-64; dir. Springfield (Mass.) Pub. Library, 1964-78; exec. dir. Springfield Library and Museums Assn., 1971-76; public library bldg. cons., 1962—; lectr. communications Simmons Coll. Sch. Library Sci., 1958, 60, 1961-62; lectr. information resources and techniques Mass. Dept. Edn., 1958; chmn. adv. com. certification, mem. spl. adv. com. personnel standards for regional personnel Adv. Com. Title III and IV, L.S.C.A. Mem. planning com. Mass. Library Assn., Springfield Adult Edn. Council; exec. bd. Western Mass. Regional Adv. Council. Served with AUS, 1942-45. Mem. ALA, Mass. Library Assn. (past pres., chmn. coms.), New Eng. Library Assn., Western Mass. Library Club, Men's Librarian Club. Club: Harvard (Springfield). Home: 16 Oxford St Springfield MA 01108

KEPECS, JOSEPH GOODMAN, physician, educator; b. Phila., Oct. 8, 1912; s. Jacob and Mary (Goodman) K.; m. Joan A. Epstein, Oct. 17, 1944; children—Susan, Jonathan. B.S., U. Chgo., 1935, M.D., 1937; grad., Inst. for Psychoanalysis, Chgo., 1949. Intern Cook County Hosp., Chgo., 1938-39; resident St. Elizabeth's Hosp., Washington, 1940-41; practice medicine, specializing in psychiatry, Madison, Wis., 1965—; attending physician dept. psychiatry Michael Reese Hosp., Chgo., 1950-65; prof. psychiatry U. Wis., 1965—; lectr. Chgo. Inst. for Psychoanalysis, 1957-60, mem. faculty, 1974—; professorial lectr. dept. psychiatry U. Chgo., 1960-65. Served with AUS, 1941-46. Mem. Am. Psychoanalytic Assn., Wis. Psychoanalytic Study Group (pres. 1979-80), Am. Psychosomatic Soc., Am. Psychiat. Assn., Chgo. Psychoanalytic Soc. (pres. 1964-65). Home: 3580 Lake Mendota Dr Madison WI 53705 Office: 600 Highland Ave Madison WI 53706

KEPES, GYORGY, artist, phographer, educator, author; b. Selyp, Hungary, Oct. 4, 1906; came to U.S., 1937, naturalized, 1956; s. Ferene and Ilone (Fai) K.; m. Juliet Appleby, Nov 3, 1937; children: Juliet, Imre. M.A., Royal Acad. Fine Arts, Budapest, 1928. Ind. painter and filmmaker, assoc. with Munka Art Group, Budapest, 1929-30; exhbn., stage and graphic designer, Berlin, 1930-32, 34-36; designer studio of Laszlo Monoly-Nagy, London, 1936-37; head light and color dept New Bauhaus, Chgo., 1937-38, Inst. Design, 1938-43; designer exhbn. Arts of UN, Art Inst. Chgo., Chgo., 1944; designer introduction room Expn. Dest Techniques Americaines de l'Habitation et de L'Urbanisme, Paris, 1945; prof. design North Tex. State Coll., Denton, 1943-45, Bklyn. Coll.; prof. visual design MIT, Cambridge, from 1946, dir., founder Ctr. Advanced Visual Studies, 1967-70, inst. prof., 1970-74; vis. instr. Art Dirs. Club, Chgo., 1939; vis. prof. Harvard U., Cambridge, 1965; vis. lectr. UCLA, 1969; vis. artist U. Hawaii, Honolulu, 1970; painter-in-residence Am. Acad., Rome, 1974; Bicentennial prof. U. Utah, Salt Lake City, 1975; Andrew Mellon prof. Rice U., Houston, 1975; artist-in-residence Dartmouth Coll., Hanover, N.H., 1977; disting. vis. Louis D. Beaumont prof. Washington U., St. Louis, 1978; Kern Inst. prof. communications Rochester Inst. Tech., N.Y., 1981. One-man shows, Art Inst. Chgo., Katherine Kuh Gallery, San Francisco Mus. Art, Mus. Modern Art, N.Y.C., Mus. Modern Art, Cleve., Phila. Mus. Fine Arts, Houston Mus. Fine Arts, Dallas Mus. Fine Arts, Hayden Gallery, MIT, 1978, Saidenberg Gallery, N.Y.C., 1982, Rome, Boston, London, also other cities, exhibited in group shows, Galleria del Levante, Munich, W.Ger., 1978, New Gallery Comtemporary Art, Cleve., 1979 (toured through 1980), San Francisco Mus. Art (toured U.S.), 1981-82; represented in permanent collections, Mus. Modern Art, N.Y.C., Whitney Mus., N.Y.C., R.I. Sch. Design, Providence, Mus. Fine Arts, Boston, Fogg Art Mus., Harvard U., MIT, Art Inst. Chgo., San Francisco Mus. Modern Art, Bauhaus Archiv, Berlin, Nat. Mus. Fine Arts, Budapest; author: Lauguage of Vision, 1944, The New Landscape, 1956; editor: Visual Arts Today, 1960, Vision and Value Series, 6 vols., 1965; contbr. articles to profl. jours. Recipient Typog. Arts award Am. Inst. Graphic Art, 1947, Silver medal Archtl. League, 1961, Fine Arts award AIA, 1968; Guggenheim fellow, 1960-61. Fellow Am. Acad. Arts and Scis.; mem. Nat. Inst. Arts and Letters, NAD (academician), Arts Dirs. Club N.Y. (Hall of Fame). *

KEPETS, HUGH MICHAEL, artist; b. Cleve., Feb. 6, 1946; s. Nathan and Frances K. B.F.A., Carnegie Mellon U., 1968; M.F.A., Ohio U., 1972. One-man shows include, Fischbach Gallery, N.Y.C., 1974, 75, 78, Vick Gallery, Phila., 1974, 76, 77, Michael Berger Gallery, Pitts., 1975, G.W. Einstein Co., Inc., N.Y.C., 1976, Graphics 1, Graphics 2, Boston, 1976, 79, Rubicon Gallery, Los Altos, Calif., 1977, New Gallery, Cleve., 1978, Women's City Club, Cleve., A.J. Wood Gallery, Phila., Carnegie-Mellon U., Pitts., 1979, Orion Editions, N.Y.C., 1980, Houghton (N.Y.) Coll., Galerie 99, Bay Harbor Islands, Fla., 1981, Michael Berger, Pitts., 1982, Cumberland Gallery, Nashville, 1983, Mattingly Baker, Dallas, Marcus/Gordon, Pitts., 1981; exhibited in group shows including, Cleve. Mus. Art, 1968, 71-79, Bklyn. Mus., 1972, 76, Asso. Am. Artists, N.Y.C., 1972, 74, Butler Inst. Am. Art, 1972, U. Pa., Phila., Espace Cardin, Paris, Michael Berger Gallery, Yale U. Art Gallery, Tyler Art Gallery, Phila., 1973, New Gallery, 1973, 74, 79, Akron (Ohio) Art Inst., 1974, Virginia Mus. Art, Richmond, Vick Gallery, 1974, Boston Mus. Fine Arts, 1975-77, 82, Phila. Print Club, Westmoreland County Art Mus., Skidmore Coll., 1975, Queens Mus., N.Y.C., Albion Coll., Lehigh U., Indpls. Mus. Art, Grand Palais-Paris, McNay Art Inst. of San Antonio, U. Mo., Kansas City, 1976, Glassboro (N.J.) State Coll., Library of Congress, 1977, Yale U. Art Gallery, 1978, Am. Acad. Arts and Letters, N.Y.C., 1978, 79, 80, Hunt Inst. for Bot. Documentation, Pitts., 1979, Md. Inst. Coll. Art, Balt., 1980, Hudson River Mus., Yonkers, N.Y., 1982, U. Pitts., 1983, Pratt Graphics Ctr., N.Y.C.; represented in permanent collections, Met. Mus. Art, N.Y.C., Cleve. Mus. Art, Phila. Mus. Fine Arts, Library of Congress, Del. Mus. Art, Indpls. Mus. Art, Harvard U.'s Fogg Mus., N.Y. Public Library, Worcester (Mass.) Art Mus., Yale U. Art Gallery, Minn. Mus. Art, St. Paul, R.I. Sch. Design Mus. Art, Art Inst. Chgo., U. N.C. at Chapel Hill Ackland Art Center, Utah State U., Brandeis U., Middlebury (Vt.) Coll., Kresge Art Gallery, others, also various banks and corps. including, Atlantic-Richfield Corp., N.Y.C., Johns Manville Corp., N.Y.C., FMC Corp., Chgo., AT&T, IBM, Xerox Corp., RCA, Princeton, N.J., Amarada Hess Corp., N.Y.C., Citicorp, N.Y.C., Prudential Ins. Co. Am., N.Y.C., Commerce Bancshares, Kansas City, Mo., Bank of Am., San Francisco, Gen. Mills Co., N.Y.C., Westinghouse Electric Corp., Pitts., Oliver Realty, Pitts., Gen. Electric Co., N.Y.C., Chem. Bank, N.Y.C., Rockwell Internat., Pitts., Lehman Bros., N.Y.C. Nat. Endowment for Arts grantee, 1976; Creative Artists Public Service grantee, 1975, 79-80; recipient Purchase awards Davidson Nat. Print and Drawing Competition Fashion Inst. Tech., 1976, Phila. Print Club, 1975, Cleve. Arts prize Women's City Club, 1979. Home: 39 Gramercy Park N New York NY 10010

KEPHART, A. EVANS, lawyer; b. Ebensburg, Pa., Dec. 21, 1905; s. John William and Florence M. (Evans) K.; m. Ruth Bond Hill, 1929; children: Susan Hill (Mrs. Howard K. Simpson), Katherine Evans (Mrs. Christopher Barnes); m. Marie Elizabeth Kenny, June 16, 1949; children: Samuel Robinson,, James William. A.B., Princeton U., 1927; LL.B., Harvard U., 1930. Bar: Pa. bar 1930. Since practiced in, Phila.; legal sec. Supreme Ct. Pa., 1930-32; asst. city solicitor, Phila., 1930-37; examiner Pa. Bd. Law Examiners, 1932-54; mem. Pa. Senate, 1939-54; partner firm Stassen & Kephart, 1959-68; state ct. adminstr. Supreme Ct. Pa., 1968-74. Recipient Good Citizenship award S.A.R. Mem. Pa., Phila. bar assns., Mil. Order Loyal Legion. Clubs: Union League, Clover (Phila.); Philadelphia Country (Gladwyne, Pa.); Tucson Nat. Mason. Home: Apt 301 Benson House 930 Montgomery Ave Bryn Mawr PA 19010 also 8321 N Rose Marie Ln Tucson AZ 85741 also Bar N Ranch West Yellowstone MT 59758

KEPHART, WILLIAM MILTON, sociologist, educator, author; b. Phila., Mar. 30, 1918; s. William John and Reba Isabel (Criswell) K.; m. Ann Kulousek, Dec. 6, 1947; 1 dau., Janis Lynn. A.B., Franklin and Marshall U., 1941; M.A., U. Pa., 1948, Ph.D., 1951. Instr. Franklin and Marshall Coll., 1946-47; instr. to prof. sociology U. Pa., Phila., 1947—, assoc. chmn. dept. sociology, 1960-70. Author: Divorce, 1951, Racial Factors and Law Enforcement, 1960, (with M. Bressler) Career Dynamics, 1961, Liberal Education and Business, 1963, Extraordinary Groups, The Sociology of Unconventional Life Styles, 1981, The Family, Society and the Individual, 1982; Mem. editorial bd.: Jour. of Comparative Family Studies, 1970—. Mem. City of Phila. Police Adv. Bd., 1960-65; research adv. Greenfield Center for Human Relations, 1960-70; Bd. dirs. Nat. Council on Family Relations, 1965-70. Served to 1st lt. AUS, 1941-46. Recipient Alumni medal Franklin and Marshall Coll., 1976. Mem. Am. Sociol. Assn. (chmn. marriage and divorce sect.), Eastern Sociol. Assn., Pa. Sociol. Soc. (pres.), Franklin and Marshall Alumni Soc. (pres.), Phi Beta Kappa, Pi Gamma Mu. Home: 691 Meadowbrook Ln Moylan PA 19065 Office: Sociology Dept U Pa Philadelphia PA 19174

KEPLER, RAYMOND GLEN, physicist; b. Long Beach, Calif., Sept. 10, 1928; s. Glen Raymond and Erma Martina (Larsen) K.; m. Carol Flint, Apr. 19, 1953; children: Julianne, Linda, Russell B., David L. B.S., Stanford U., 1950; M.S., U. Calif.-Berkeley, 1955, Ph.D., 1957. Mem. tech. staff central research dept. E.I. duPont de Nemours & Co., 1957-64; div. supr. Sandia Nat. Labs., Albuquerque, 1964-69, dept. mgr., 1969—. Fellow Am. Phys. Soc. (chmn. edn. com.); mem. AAAS, Sierra Club, Sigma Xi. Home: 9004 Bellehaven NE Albuquerque NM 87112 Office: Sandia Labs Albuquerque NM 87185

KEPLEY, JAMES SPENCER, aquarist; b. Pitts., Oct. 28, 1942; s. Amos Burton and Lea (Clayton) K.; m. Joanne Marie Anderson, June 8, 1968; children: Marie Elizabeth, Amanda Lea. Student, A & M Coll. Tex., 1961-62, U. N.C., 1963-64, Carnegie-Mellon U., 1966-68. Aquarist Pitts. Aquazoo, 1967-70; dir., curator Aquarium of Cape Cod, W. Yarmouth, Mass., 1970-71; curator Sealand of Cape Cod, W. Brewster, Mass., 1971-73; curator of fishes Sea World, Inc., Aurora, Ohio, 1973-78; exec. dir. Nat. Aquarium in Balt., 1978-82; adminstr. Sea World Shark Inst., Long Key, Fla., 1982—. Author numerous papers in field. Served with U.S. Army, 1962-66. Am. Assn. Zool. Parks and Aquariums profl. fellow, 1974—. Mem. Am. Soc. Ichthologists and Herpetologists, Am. Fisheries Soc., Internat. Assn. Aquatic Animal Medicine, The Oceanic Soc., World Mariculture Soc., Cleve. Saltwater Enthusiasts (dir. 1976-78), Am. Legion. Roman Catholic. Lodge: Rotary. Home: Route 1 153C Grassy Key Marathon FL 33050 Office: PO Box 968 Long Key FL 33001

KEPLEY, THOMAS ALVIN, government official; b. Salisbury, N.C., May 28, 1928; s. Thomas Albert and Frances Roena (Lowder) K.; m. Pauline Blair, Oct. 26, 1956; children: Alleen Jan, Vickie Lynn, Carolyn Sue, Linda Leigh, Kaye Frances. B.S., N.C. State U., 1950; postgrad., George Washington U., 1967-70. Registered profl. engr., Mass. Asst. dir. trainee VA Center, Martinsburg, W.Va., 1972-73, asst. dir., Marion, Ind., 1973-76, Northport, N.Y., 1976-79, dir., Chillicothe, Ohio, 1979-81; dep. dir. dept. medicine and surgery Gt. Lakes region VA, Washington, 1981—; clin. asso. Sch. Allied Health Professions, Ithaca (N.Y.) Coll., 1979-81. Mem. Ross County Health Adv. Com., Chillicothe, 1979-80; mem. Ohio Statewide Health Coordinating Council, 1980. Served with U.S. Army, 1950-52. Mem. Am. Coll. Hosp. Adminstrs., Assn. Mil. Surgeons U.S., Tau Kappa Epsilon. Lutheran. Clubs: Rotary, Elks. Home: 2507 Kittery Ln Bowie MD 20715 Office: 810 Vermont Ave NW Washington DC 20420

KEPNER, WOODY, public relations executive; b. Millersburg, Pa., June 30, 1920; s. E. Elwood and Charlotte (Dressler) K.; m. Palma M. Brown, Feb. 10, 1943; children: Linda Louise Kepner Henke, Dawn Annette Kepner Kendrick, Tana Lee Kepner Tracy. Student pub. schs. Freelance reporter Williamsport Grit, Harrisburg Telegraph, Harrisburg Patriot-News, Harrisburg Sunday Courier, 1935-41; reporter, feature and spl. events writer, photo editor, news editor, news bur mgr. Miami (Fla.) Publicity Dept., 1945-53, dir., 1953-57; pres., owner Woody Kepner Assos. Inc., Miami, 1957—. Vice pres. United Fund Dade County, 1963—. Served with USN, 1942-45. Mem. Fla. Pub. Relations Assn., Pub. Relations Soc. Am., Greater Miami C. of C. Clubs: Bankers, Cricket. Home: 6901 SW 120th St Miami FL 33156 Office: 9200 S Dadeland Blvd Suite 300 Miami FL 33156

KEPPEL, FRANCIS, organization executive; b. N.Y.C., Apr. 16, 1916; s. Frederick Paul and Helen Tracy (Brown) K.; m. Edith Moulton Sawin, July 19, 1941; children: Edith Tracy, Susan Moulton. A.B., Harvard U., 1938. With Harvard Coll., 1939-41; sec. of Joint Army and Navy Com. on Welfare and Recreation, Washington, 1941-44; asst. to provost Harvard, 1946-48, dean faculty edn., 1948-62; U.S. commr. edn., 1962-65; asst. sec. edn. HEW, 1965-66; chmn. bd. Gen. Learning Corp., N.Y.C., 1966-74; sr. fellow Aspen Inst. for Humanistic Studies, N.Y.C., 1974—; sr. lectr. Harvard U., 1977—; chmn. Nat. Student Aid Coalition, 1980—; Vice chmn. bd. higher edn. City U. N.Y., 1967-71; bd. overseers Harvard U., 1967-73. Author: The Necessary Revolution in American Education, 1966. Trustee Am. Trust for Brit. Library, 1981—, Carnegie Corp., 1970-79; vice chmn. Lincoln Center for Performing Arts; bd. govs. Internat. Devel. Research Centre in Ottawa, 1980—; mem. Nat. Commn. Libraries and Info. Sci., 1978-83. Served to 1st lt. AUS, 1944-46. Fellow Am. Acad. Arts and Scis.; mem. Phi Beta Kappa. Clubs: Cosmos (Washington); Century Assn. (N.Y.C.); St. Botolph (Boston). Home: 984 Memorial Dr Cambridge MA 02138

KEPPEL, GEOFFREY, psychology educator; b. Oakland, Calif., Mar. 17, 1935; s. Charles William and Rollande (Auger) K.; m. Sheila Geering, Sept. 1, 1956; children: Melissa Eaton, Peter Charles. B.A., U. Calif. at Berkeley, 1957; M.S., Northwestern U., 1961, Ph.D., 1963. Asst. prof. U. Calif., Berkeley, 1963-66, assoc. prof., 1966-70, prof., 1970—, chmn. dept. psychology, 1972-77, dir. Inst. Human Learning, 1977-80, dean social scis., 1980—. Author: (with L. Postman) Verbal Learning and Memory, 1969, Norms of Word Association, 1970, Design and Analysis: A Researcher's Handbook, 1973, (with W.H. Saufley, Jr.) Introduction to Design and Analysis: A Student's Handbook, 1980, Design and Analysis: A Researcher's Handbook, 2d edit, 1982. Served with AUS, 1957-59. Mem. Council Grad. Depts. Psychology (chmn. 1974-76). Home: 6494 Benvenue Ave Oakland CA 94618 Office: Dept Psychology Coll Letters and Science U Calif Berkeley CA 94720

KEPPEL, JOHN, writer; b. Quogue, L.I., N.Y., Aug. 21, 1917; s. David and Dorothy (Vickery) K.; m. Grace Marjorie Wood, June 7, 1952; 1 son, David. A.B. cum laude, Harvard, 1940; spl. student, Johns Hopkins, 1967-68. Fgn. service officer, 1947-70; tng. Russian lang. Fgn. Service Inst.; 3d sec., vice consul, Moscow, 1947-50, 2d sec., consul, 1953-55, assigned, Frankfurt, 1950, 2d sec., vice consul, Seoul, Korea, 1951-52, consul, 1952, assigned, Regensberg, 1952, 2d sec., Rome, 1955-56, 1st sec., 1957; dep. chief div. research and analysis, USSR, Eastern Europe Dept. of State, Washington, 1958, chief bloc internat. polit. activities div., 1959-61; dep. dir. office of research and analysis for Sino-Soviet bloc, 1961; fellow Center for Internat. Affairs, Harvard, 1961-62; counsellor of embassy polit. affairs, Rio de Janeiro, 1962-64; sr. tng. officer Fgn. Service Inst., Dept. of State, Washington, 1965-66, chmn. div. polit. studies, 1966-67; spl. student Johns Hopkins, 1967-68; dep. spl. asst. to sec. state, 1968-69; chief operations staff UN Fund for Population Activities, 1969-72, asst. dir., 1972-74. Served from pvt. to capt., inf. AUS, 1941-46. Decorated Bronze Star medal with clusters; Croix de Guerre, France). Mem. U.S. Assn. for The Club of Rome. Home: 22 N Main St Essex CT 06426

KEPPLER, HERBERT, publishing co. exec.; b. N.Y.C., Apr. 21, 1925; s. Victor and Josephine T. (Windmann) K.; m. Louise M. Lyman, July 7, 1956; children—Kathryn Louise, Thomas Victor. B.A., Harvard, 1945. Reporter N.Y. Sun, 1948-49; with Modern Photography, N.Y.C., 1950—, editorial dir., pub., 1967—; v.p. photog. pub. div. ABC Leisure Mags. Inc. div. ABC, N.Y.C., 1974-78, sr. v.p. photog. pub. div., 1978—. Author: Official 35mm Camera Rating Guide, 1957, Keppler on the Eye-Level Reflex, 1960, How to Make Better Pictures in Your Home, 1962, 124 Ways to Test Cameras, Lenses and Equipment, 1962, The Pentax Way, 1966, The Nikon-Nikkormat Way, 1976. Served to ensign USNR, 1945-46. Mem. Rolls-Royce Owners Club. Home: 119 N Highland Pl Croton-on-Hudson NY 10520 Office: 825 7th Ave New York NY 10019

KEPPLER, WILLIAM EDMUND, multi-national company executive; b. N.Y.C., June 12, 1922; s. Louis and Amelia (Koszut) K.; m. Natalie E. Lang, July 15, 1944; children: Gail, William Edmund, Jean. B.S. in Chem. Engring, Pratt Inst., 1943, M.S., N.Y. U., 1944. Vice pres. Merck Sharp & Dohme, West Point, Pa., 1965-71, Squibb Corp., Holmdel, N.J., 1971-73; pres. Bell Mgmt., Blue Bell, Pa., 1973-74, Engel Industries, St. Louis, 1974-75; sr. v.p. tech. ops./mgmt. systems Schering-Plough Corp., Kenilworth, N.J., 1975—; tchr. chem. engring. Cooper Union, N.Y. U., U. Bd. dirs. Phila. chpt. Am. Cancer Soc., 1979; pres. Montour County (Pa.) Cerebral Palsy, 1953-57. Fellow Am. Inst. Chem. Engrs.; mem. Am. Mgmt. Assn. Episcopalian. Club: Whitemarsh Valley Country (Lafayette, Pa.). Home: 773 Midway Ln Blue Bell PA 19422 Office: 2000 Galloping Hill Rd Kenilworth NJ 07033

KERAN, MICHAEL WILLIAM, banker, economist; b. Mpls., Sept. 9, 1931; s. William, Jr. and Leone (Jorgenson) K.; m. Helene Fachtmann, Aug. 17, 1967; children: Michael W., Patrick. B.B.A., U. Minn., 1955, M.A., 1958, Ph.D., 1966. Asst. v.p., economist Fed. Res. Bank, St. Louis, 1965-73, sr. v.p., dir. research, San Francisco, 1973—; sr. econ. advisor U.S. Treasury Dept., 1971-72; asst. fin. attache U.S. Embassy, Tokyo, 1962-65; internat. economist U.S. Treasury, Washington, 1960-62; instr. U. Minn., 1958-60. Contbr. articles to profl. jours. Dir. Pacific Heritage Mus., 1982; chmn. Triburon Ctr. Environ. Studies, San Francisco State U., 1978-81. Served to cpl. U.S. Army, 1950-52; Korea. Mem. Am. Econ. Assn., Western Econ. Assn. (exec. com. 1975-78). Republican. Roman Catholic. Home: 3215 Paradise Dr Tiburon CA 94920 Office: Fed Res Bank 101 Market St San Francisco CA 94105

KERANS, GRATTAN, state legislator; b. Washington, Jan. 2, 1941; s. Edwin Grattan and Anne Frances (Kelley) K.; m. Janet Raye Holsclaw, 1965; 1 son, Timothy. Student, Montgomery Coll., U. Oreg. Mem. Oreg. Ho. of Reps., 1975—, majority whip, 1977, majority leader, 1979-83, house speaker, 1983—. Roman Catholic. Office: Office of Speaker State Capitol Salem OR 97310 *

KERBER, LINDA KAUFMAN, historian, educator; b. N.Y.C., Jan. 23, 1940; d. Harry Hagman and Dorothy (Haber) Kaufman; m. Richard Kerber, June 5, 1960; children: Ross Jeremy, Justin Seth. A.B. cum laude, Barnard Coll., 1960; M.A., NYU, 1961; Ph.D., Columbia U., 1968. Instr., asst. prof. history Stern Coll., Yeshiva U., N.Y.C., 1963-68; asst. prof. history San Jose State Coll., (Calif.), 1969-70; vis. asst. prof. history Stanford U., (Calif.), 1970-71; asst. prof. history U. Iowa, Iowa City, 1971-75, prof., 1975—. Author: Feralists in Dissent: Imagery and Ideology in Jeffersonian America, 1970, (paperback edit.) Feralists in Dissent: Imagery and Ideology in Jeffersonian America, 1980, Women of the Republic: Intellect and Ideology in Revolutionary America, 1980; co-editor: Women's America: Refocusing the Past, 1982; mem. editorial bd.: Jour. Am. History, Signs: Jour. Women in Culture and Society; contbr. articles and book revs. to profl. jours. Danforth Found. fellow; Barnard Coll. fellow; NEH fellow, 1976, 83-84; grantee Am. Philos. Soc., 1971, Am. Bar Found., 1975, Am. Council Learned Socs., 1975. Mem. Orgn. Am. Historians, Am. Hist. Assn., Am. Studies Assn., Am. Soc. for Le4gal History, Berkshire Conf. Women Historians. Jewish. Office: Dept History U Iowa Iowa City IA 52242

KERBIS, GERTRUDE LEMPP, architect; m. Walter Peterhans (dec.); m. Donald Kerbis (div. 1972); children: Julian, Lisa, Kim. B.S., U. Ill.; M.A., Ill. Inst. Tech.; postgrad., Grad. Sch. Design, Harvard, 1949-50. Archtl. designer Skidmore, Owings & Merrill, Chgo., 1954-59, C.F. Murphy Assocs., 1959-62, 65-67; pvt. practice architecture, Chgo., 1967—; lectr. U. Ill., 1969; prof. William Rainey Harper Coll., 1970—, Washington U., St. Louis, 1977, 82; archtl. cons. Dept. Urban Renewal, City of Chgo.; mem. Northeastern Ill. Planning Commn., Open Land Project, Mid-North Community Orgn., Chgo. Met. Housing and Planning Council, Chgo. Mayor's Commn. for Preservation Chgo.'s Hist. Architecture; bd. dirs. Chgo. Sch. Architecture Found., 1972-76; trustee Glessner House Found., Inland Architect Mag.; lectr. Art Inst. Chgo., U. N.Mex., Ill. Inst. Tech., Washington U., St. Louis, Ball State U., Muncie, Ind., U. Utah, Salt Lake City. Prin. archtl. works include, U.S. Air Force Acad. dining hall, Colo., 1957, Skokie (Ill.) Pub. Library, 1959, Meadows Club, Lake Meadows, Chgo., 1959, O'Hare Internat. Airport 7 Continents Bldg, 1963; prin. developer and architect: Tennis Club, Highland Park, Ill., 1968, Watervliet, Mich. Tennis Ranch, 1970, Greenhouse Condominium, Chgo., 1976; represented in: permanent archtl. drawings collection, Art Inst. Chgo. Fellow AIA (dir. Chgo. chpt. 1971-75, chpt. pres. 1980, mem. nat. com. architecture arts and recreation 1972-75, com. on design 1975—, head subcom. inst. honors nomination); mem. AAUP, ACLU, U. Ill., Ill. Inst. Tech. alumni assns., Art Inst. Chgo., Chgo. Council Fgn. Relations, Chgo. Women in Architecture (founder), Planned Parenthood Assn., Chgo. Network, Lincoln Park Zool. Soc., Chgo. Arts Club., Lambda Alpha. Office: 172 W Burton Pl Chicago IL 60610

KERBY, PHILIP PEARCE, journalist; b. Pueblo, Colo., Dec. 24, 1911; s. William Bunyan and Olive Burdette (Hinton) K.; m. Elizabeth Josephine Poe, Feb. 12, 1953; 1 son, David Hinton. Student pub. schs., Pueblo. Reporter, editorial writer Pueblo-Chieftain Star-Jour., 1931-42; reporter Denver Post, 1942-45; radio news editor Sta. KGHF, Pueblo, 1946-47; editor Rocky Mountain Life, Denver, 1948; founding editor Frontier (polit. monthly), Los Angeles, 1949-67; asso. editor The Nation, 1967-71; editorial writer, columnist Los Angeles Times, 1971—; lectr. U. So. Calif., U. Calif., Los Angeles. Editorials and articles anthologized in textbooks. Recipient Pulitzer prize for editorial writing, 1976. Office: Los Angeles Times 202 W 1st St Los Angeles CA 90053

KERCHEVAL, KEN, actor; b. Wolcottville, Ind., July 15, 1935; s. John Marine and Christine (Reiber) K.; (div.)children: Aaron, Liza, Caleb. Student, Ind. U., 1953-55, U. Pacific, 1956, Neighborhood Playhouse, N.Y.C., 1956-58. Broadway appearances in Father's Day; also off-Broadway prodns.; TV appearances in The Patricia Neal Story; numerous others; film appearances include Network; appearance as Cliff Barnes in: TV series Dallas. Mem. Screen Actors Guild, Actors Equity, AFTRA. Club: Masons. Office: care Two Century Plaza Suite 2060 2049 Century Park E Los Angeles CA 90067

KERESTER, CHARLES J., lawyer; b. Youngstown, Ohio, Feb. 6, 1927; s. John J. and Mary K.; m. Eleanor H. Kerester, Mar. 29, 1952; children: Alison, Scott, Brian, Dale. B.S. summa cum laude, Ohio State U., 1949, J.D., 1952. Bar: Ohio, D.C. Assoc. Jones, Day, Reavis & Pogue, Cleve., 1952-57, 60-61, ptnr., 1961—; atty., staff. joint com. on internal revenue taxation U.S. Congress, Washington, 1961—; mem. adv. bd. Tax Mgmt. Inc., div. Bur. Nat. Affairs, Washington, 1961—. Author: Tax Treatment of Reapture of Depreciation, 1964, Tax Treatment of Executive Compensation, 1972; portfolios in field. Mem. law rev. Ohio State U. Coll. Law, 1952. Mem. ABA, Internat. Fiscal Assn.(U.S. Br.), Ohio State Bar Assn., Bar Assn. Greater Cleve., Tax Club of Cleve (pres. 1976-77), Order of Coif. Clubs: Pymatuning Yacht (Youngstown) (bd. dirs. 1982—); Saturday Night Dance (Cleveland Heights) (pres. 1976-77). Home: 2986 Falmouth Rd Shaker Heights OH 44122 Office: Jones Day Reavis & Pogue 1700 Huntington Bldg Cleveland OH 44115

KERFOOT, H(UBERT) POTTER, missiles and space company executive; b. Shawnee, Okla., Aug. 15, 1922; s. Hubert Potter and Laura Etta K.; m. Helen Clara Bendall, July 2, 1949; children: Roberta Jean Kerfoot Clinkinbeard, Daniel Mark, Kathleen Diane Kerfoot McCallum. B.E., U. So. Calif., 1948, M.A., 1949, Ph.D., 1953. Specialist in aerospace labs., supr. flight control systems Missile div. N.Am. Aviation, Downey, Calif., 1953-60; mgr. flight scis. Lockheed Missiles & Space Co., Van Nuys, Calif., 1960, dir. resource allocation, dir. engring., Sunnyvale, Calif., 1961-72; v.p., asst. gen. mgr. research and devel. div., 1972-75, v.p., gen. mgr. advanced systems div., 1975—. Served with U.S. Army, 1943-46. Mem. AIAA, AAAS, Am. Def. Preparedness Assn., Am. Oceanic Orgn., Assn. U.S. Army, Sigma Xi. Home: 630 Nandell Ln Los Altos CA 94022 Office: PO Box 504 Sunnyvale CA 94086

KERINS, FRANCIS JOSEPH, college president; b. N.Y.C., Mar. 23, 1927; s. John and Ellen (Mulrooney) K.; m. Mary Elizabeth Costigan, June 2, 1951; children: Mary Ellen Kerins Walker, Donna (Mrs. Joseph Zelinski), John, Edward, Francis, Joseph, James. A.B., St. Francis Coll., 1949; A.M., St. Louis U., 1951; Ed.D., U. Denver, 1959; L.H.D., Coll. Idaho, 1983. Prof., adminstr. Loretto Heights Coll., 1952-68; prof. higher edn. U. Denver, 1968-69; pres. Coll. St. Francis, Joliet, Ill., 1969-74, Carroll. Coll., Helena, Mont., 1974—; mem. Nat. Commn. on Higher Edn. Issues; chmn. Western Ind. Colls. Fund; cons. colls. and univs.; chmn. bd. Bank of Mont.; bd. dirs. Am. Council on Edn., Council Ind. Colls.; chmn. Commn. on Colls. Northwest Assn. Contbr. articles to profl. jours. Chmn. Lewis and Cark County Bicentennial Com., 1975—; trustee Loretto Heights Coll., 1961-67, Coll. St. Francis. 1969-74, Carroll Coll., 1974—; pres. Helena Symphony Soc., 1981—; bd. dirs. Helena YMCA, United Way; mem. Helena Airport Bd. Served with AUS, 1950-52. Fellow Am. Council Edn.; mem. Mont. Com. for Humanities (past chmn.); Assn. Cath. Colls. and Univs. vice chmn.; mem. Helena C. of C. (dir.). Roman Catholic. Club: Rotary (past pres.). Office: Carroll College Helena MT 59601

KERKER, MILTON, chemistry educator, college dean; b. Utica, N.Y., Sept. 25, 1920; s. Samuel and Sarah (Cohen) K.; m. Reva Stemerman, June 16, 1946; children: Ruth Ann, Martin Joseph, Susan Lee, Joel Leon. A.B., Columbia U., 1941, M.A., 1947, Ph.D., 1949; D.Sc., Lehigh U., 1975. Mem. faculty Clarkson Coll. Tech., Potsdam, N.Y., 1949—, prof. chemistry, 1956—, Thomas S. Clarkson prof., 1974—, also chmn. dept., 1960-64, dean Sch. Arts and Sci., 1964-74, dean Sch. Sci., 1981—; Unilevr vis. prof. U. Bristol, Eng., 1967-68; vis. prof. Hebrew U., 1974-75; Welch Found. lectr., 1965; Langmuir lectr. Am. Chem. Soc., 1980. Author: Electromagnetic Scattering, 1963, The

Scattering of Light and Other Electromagnetic Radiation, 1969; also articles.; Editor-in-chief: Jour. Colloid and Interface Sci, 1965—. Ford Found. fellow, 1952-53. Fellow Optical Soc. Am.; mem. Am. Chem. Soc. (chmn. div. colloid and surface chemistry 1965-66, Kendall award 1971), Internat. Union Pure and Applied Chemistry (sec. Commn. on Colloids 1977-83), History Sci. Soc., AAAS. Home: 4 Hillcrest Dr Potsdam NY 13676

KERKORIAN, KIRK, former motion picture company executive, consultant; b. Fresno, Calif., June 6, 1917; s. Ahron and Lily K.; m. Hilda Schmidt, Jan. 24, 1942 (div. 1951); m. Jane Maree Hardy, Dec. 5, 1954; children: Tracy, Linda. Student pub. schs., Los Angeles. Comml. airline pilot, from 1940; founder Los Angeles Air Service (later Trans Internat. Airlines Corp.), 1948, Internat. Leisure Corp., 1968; controlling stockholder Western Airlines, 1970; chief exec. officer Metro-Goldwyn-Mayer, Inc., Culver City, Calif., 1973-74, chmn. exec. com., vice-chmn. bd., 1974-79; controlling stockholder MGM/UA Entertainment Co.; cons., 1979—. Served as capt. Transport Command RAF, 1942-44. Office: MGM Inc 10202 W Washington Blvd Culver City CA 90230 *

KERLEY, JAMES JOSEPH, chemical company executive; b. Phila., Nov. 20, 1922; s. Philip William and Jane Veronica (Touey) K.; m. Dorothea Long Ickler, Oct. 24, 1944; children: Janet, James, Doris Ann, Suzanne. B.S. magna cum laude, Temple U., 1944; M.A., U. Pa., 1949, postgrad., 1949-51; LL.D., Temple U., 1969. Trainee Smith, Barney & Co., Phila., 1946-47; instr. finance Temple U., 1947-51; with Ford Motor Co., 1951-58; v.p., div. controller Crosley div. Avco Co., 1958-60; v.p., controller Ling-Temco-Vought Co., Dallas, 1960-62; v.p. finance Trans World Airlines, N.Y.C., 1962-65, sr. v.p., 1965-68, mem. exec. com., 1964-68; also dir.; fin. v.p. I.U. Internat. Corp., 1968-69; sr. v.p. fin. Lone Star Industries, Inc., 1969-70; former exec. v.p. Monsanto Co., chmn. fin. com., to 1980, also dir.; dir. Merc. Trust Co., Merc. Bancorp., both St. Louis, Mo. Pacific Corp., Rohr Industries, Inc., Assos. Corp. N.Am. Trustee St. Louis U. Served to 1st lt. USMCR, 1943-46; PTO. Mem. Beta Gamma Sigma. Home: 816 S Hanley Rd Saint Louis MO 63124 Office: 800 N Lindbergh Blvd Saint Louis MO 63166

KERLINGER, FRED NICHOLS, educational psychology educator; b. N.Y.C., July 4, 1910; s. George Edward and Lotte (Fisher) K.; m. Betty Jane McCue, Dec. 16, 1946; children: Paul N., Stephen C. B.S., NYU, 1942; M.A., U. Mich., 1951, Ph.D., 1953. Civilian edn. officer U.S. Army, Japan, 1946-50; research asst. U. Mich., 1951-53; asst. prof. ednl. sociology and psychology Wayne State U., Detroit, 1953-55; asso. prof., then prof. ednl. psychology N.Y. U., 1955-75, head div. behavioral scis., 1968-71; prof. psychology U. Amsterdam, Netherlands, 1975-80; prof. ednl. psychology U. Oreg., Eugene, 1980—; summer vis. prof. U. Ind., 1953, Columbia U. Tchrs. Coll., 1955, U. Calif., Berkeley, 1968; vis. prof. U. Amsterdam, 1972-73. Author: Foundations of Behavioral Research, 2d edit, 1973 (trans. into Spanish, Japanese, German, Czechoslovakian and Italian), (with E. Pedhazur) Multiple Regression in Behavioral Research, 1973, Behavioral Research: A Conceptual Approach, 1979; also articles.; Rev. editor: Am. Ednl. Research Jour, 1967-69; editor: Rev. Research in Edn, 1973-75. Mem. bd. edn., Hartsdale, N.Y., 1960-63. Recipient Outstanding Achievement award U. Mich., 1982. Fellow Am. Psychol. Assn.; mem. Am. Ednl. Research Assn. (pres. 1976-77), AAAS. Office: U Oreg Coll Edn Eugene OR 97403

KERMAN, ARTHUR KENT, physicist, educator; b. Montreal, May 3, 1929; s. Samuel and Ida (Birn) K.; m. Enid Ehrlich, Dec. 21, 1952; children: Ben, Daniel, Elizabeth, Melissa, James. B.Sc., McGill U., 1950; Ph.D., MIT, 1953. Mem. faculty dept. physics MIT, Cambridge, 1956, prof., 1964—, dir. Ctr. Theoretical Physics, 1976—, dir. lab. nuclear scis., 1983—; vis. prof. SUNY-Stony Brook, 1970-71; adj. prof. Brklyn. Coll., 1971-75; cons. Argonne Nat. Lab., 1961—, Brookhaven Nat. Lab., 1965-81, Lawrence Berkeley Lab., 1975, Lawrence Livermore Lab., 1964—, Los Almos Sci. Lab, 1961—, Nat. Bur. Standards, 1970-81; mem. adv. com. to Office Sci. and Tech. White House Sci. Council, 1982—; mem. adv. com. Woods Hole Sub-panel of U.S. Dept. Energy, 1982—. Assoc. editor: Rev. Modern Physics 1968-71. NRC fellow Calif. Inst. Tech., 1953-54, Niels Bohr Inst., Copenhagen, 1954-55; Guggenheim fellow U. Paris, 1961-62. Fellow Am. Phys. Soc., Am. Acad. Arts and Scis.; mem. N.Y. Acad. Scis. Office: MIT Dept Physics 6-305 Cambridge MA 02139

KERN, BERNARD DONALD, educator, physicist; b. New Castle, Ind., Oct. 31, 1919; s. William Bernard and Cecile (Hudson) K.; m. Nedda Wisler Burdsall, Aug. 20, 1946; children—Richard B., Jonathan K., Arthur R. B.S., Ind. U., 1942, M.S., 1947, Ph.D., 1949. Physicist Signal Corps and Manhattan Project, Chgo., 1942-43; sr. physicist Oak Ridge Nat. Lab., 1949-50; mem. faculty U. Ky., 1950—, prof. physics, 1958—, chmn. dept. physics and astronomy, 1967-69; physicist U.S. Naval Radiol. Def. Lab., San Francisco, 1957-58, cons., 1957-69; prof. Inst. Teknologi Bandung (Indonesia), U Ky., State Dept. Ednl. Assistance Program, 1961- 62. Author articles on nuclear physics. Served to lt. (j.g.) USNR, 1943-46. Fellow Am. Phys. Soc.; mem. Am. Inst. Physics, Am. Assn. Physics Tchrs. Office: Dept Physics and Astronomy U Ky Lexington KY 40506

KERN, EDITH, Romance languages and literature educator; b. Dusseldorf, Germany, Feb. 7, 1912; d. L.G. Berg and J. Bison. B.A., Bridgewater Coll., 1942; M.A., Johns Hopkins U., 1944, Ph.D. in Romance Lang. and Lit, 1946. Instr. to asst. prof. modern langs. U. Md., U. Kans.; dir. TV project U. Pa., 1946-60; prof. French Grad. Sch., St. Johns U., N.Y.C., 1960-65; prof. Romance lit. and comparative lit. U. Wash., Seattle, 1965-72; D. Silbert prof. humanities, chmn. comparative lit. Smith Coll., Northampton, Mass., 1972-77; John Cranford Adams prof. Hofstra U., 1977—; vis. prof. UCLA, 1962, SUNY-Buffalo, 1965, Stanford U., 1970, U. Warwick, Eng., 1978, Brandeis U., fall 1978, State U. N.Y. at Binghamton, spring 1979; dir. NEH Summer Seminar, 1975, 79, NEH Seminar for Coll. Tchrs., 1977-78. Author: Sartre, 1962, Existential Thought and Fictional Technique, 1970, The Absolute Comic, 1980; contbg. author: Disciplines of Criticism, 1968, Boccaccio, 1974, Beckett, 1978; mem. editorial bd.: Twentieth Century Lit, 1972—; founding editor: Dada/Surrealism; Contbr. articles to profl. jours. Bollingen Found. fellow, 1967; Nat. Endowment for Humanities fellow, 1972; Guggenheim fellow, 1975-76; Radcliffe-Harvard Fellow, 1975-76; Rockefeller Found. Fellow, 1982. Mem. MLA (v.p. 1975-76, pres. 1977-78), Comparative Lit. Assn. (nat. exec. council 1973—), Nat. Soc. Lit. and Arts, Internat., Am. comparative lit. assns., PEN. Home: 1025 Fifth Ave New York NY 10028

KERN, FRANKLIN LORENZ, banker; b. Frankenmuth, Mich., Aug. 22, 1932; s. Ruben William and Regina (Bernthal) K.; m. Loretta L. Gehrke, Apr. 22, 1962; children: Andrew James, Sara Beth. B.A., Mich. State U., 1954; diploma, Bank Adminstrn. Inst. and Northwestern U., 1963, Bank Adminstrn. Inst. and U. Wis., 1971. Asst. to controller Second Nat. Bank, Saginaw, Mich., 1963-65, auditor, 1965—. Sec.-treas. Frankenmuth Community Band, 1967-72; chmn. Student Aid Fund St Lorenz Lutheran Congregation, 1964-74, elder, 1974-80; sec. 125th anniversary com., Frankenmuth, Mich., 1969; Bd. dirs., treas. Saginaw Civic Symphony Assn., 1971-73, Luth. Homes of Mich., Inc., 1983—. Mem. Bank Adminstrn. Inst. (pres. Eastern Mich. chpt. 1968-69), Mich. State U. Alumni Assn., Frankenmuth High Sch. Alumni Assn. (past sec.-treas.). Address: Second Nat Bank of Saginaw 101 N Washington Saginaw MI 48607

KERN, FRED, JR., educator, physician; b. Montgomery, Ala., Sept. 9, 1918; s. Fred and Rose (Helburn) K.; m. Bernie Cronheim, June 17, 1942; children: Katherine, Patricia, David. B.A., U. Ala., 1941; M.D., Columbia, 1943. Diplomate: Am. Bd. Internal Medicine (chmn. subsplty. bd. gastroenterology 1969-72). Intern Grady Hosp., Atlanta, 1943-44, resident, 1946-48; instr. medicine Cornell U., 1950-51; asst. prof. preventive medicine and pub. health U. Colo., Denver, 1952-54, asst. prof. medicine, 1954-55, asso. prof. medicine, 1955-65, head div. gastroenterology, 1959-82, prof. medicine, 1965—; pres. Digestive Diseases Info. Center, 1978; mem. exec. com., adv. bd. Nat. Coop. Crohn's Disease Study, 1972-81; mem. adv. bd. Nat. Coop. Gallstone Study, 1973—; mem. Nat. Arthritis, Metabolism and Digestive Diseases Adv. Council, 1978-81. Author: (with K.R. Hammond) Teaching Comprehensive Medical Care, 1959, (with R.B. Hill) The Gastrointestinal Tract, 1976; also articles on gastrointestinal and hepatic physiology and biochemistry and clin. gastroenterology.; Editorial bd.: Gastroenterology, 1964-70; chmn., 1978-83; editorial bd.: Annals of Internal Medicine, 1975-78. Served with AUS, 1944-46. Mem. Nat. Found. Ileitis and Colitis (adv. bd. 1970, chmn. grants rev. com. 1978-81), Digestive Disease Found. (adv. bd. 1971), Am. Fedn. Clin. Research, Am. Coll. Physicians, Am. Inst. Nutrition, Am. Gastroent. Assn. (v.p. 1973-74, pres. 1975-76), Gastroent. Soc. Australia (hon.), Internat. Assn. Study of Liver, Central Soc. Clin. Research, AAAS, Assn. Am. Physicians, Western Assn. Physicians, Soc. Exptl. Biology and Medicine, Am. Assn. for Study Liver Disease, Am. Clin. and Climatol. Assn., Alpha Omega Alpha. Home: 740 Krameria St Denver CO 80220

KERN, GEORGE CALVIN, JR., lawyer; b. Balt., Apr. 19, 1926; s. George Calvin and Alice (Gaskins) K.; m. Joan Shorell, Dec. 22, 1962; 1 child, Heath. B.A., Princeton U., 1947; LL.B., Yale U., 1952. Bar: N.Y. 1952. Chief U.S. Info. Ctr., Mannheim, W.Ger., 1947-48; dep. dir. pub. info. Office U.S. Mil. Govt. for Germany, Berlin, Nurmberg, 1948-49; assoc. Sullivan & Cromwell, N.Y.C., 1952-60, ptnr., 1960—; dir. Allied Stores Corp., N.Y.C., 1971—, Soltex Polymer Corp., Houston, 1976—. Served to lt. USN, 1944-46. Clubs: India House; Sky (N.Y.C.). Home: 830 Park Ave New York NY 10021 Office: Sullivan & Cromwell 125 Broad St New York NY 10004

KERN, HARRY FREDERICK, editor; b. Denver, July 7, 1911; s. Harry F. and Alice (Robertson) K.; m. Janet Campbell Mackenzie, Dec. 27, 1939; children—Rosemary Annand, Nathaniel Robertson. Student, Harvard, 1930-35. Joined Newsweek, 1935, became asst. editor, 1937, asso. editor, 1941, war editor, 1942; sr. editor internat. affairs Newsweek mag., N.Y.C., 1950-56, also editor-in-chief internat. edits., 1950-56; pres. Fgn. Reports, 1956. Decorated Order Sacred Treasure, Japan; Order of Merit, Lebanon). Mem. Council Fgn. Relations. Clubs: Knickerbocker (N.Y.C.); Met. (Washington); Travellers (Paris). Home: Lloyd Ln Huntington NY 11743 Office: 818 18th St NW Suite 540 Washington DC 20006

KERN, IRVING JOHN, retired food company executive; b. N.Y.C., Feb. 10, 1914; s. John and Min (Weitzner) Kleinberger; m. Beatrice Rubenfeld, June 22, 1941; children—John A., Arthur H., Robert M. B.S., N.Y. U., 1934, student Grad. Sch. Art and Sci., 1960-65; D.H.L., Mercy Coll., Dobbs Ferry, N.Y., 1980. Asst. buyer Bloomingdale's Dept. Store, N.Y.C., 1934-40; with Dellwood Foods, Inc., Yonkers, N.Y., 1945-82, pres., 1966-77, chmn. and chief exec. officer, 1977-82; dir. Scarsdale Nat. Bank. Mem. Community Mental Health Services Bd. of Westchester County, 1954-59; mem. bd. dirs., sec. Westchester County Assn., 1950-57, 76—; exec. bd. Westchester County Better Bus. Bur., 1970-73; bd. dirs. Westchester Coalition, 1972—, Westchester Minority Bus. Assistance Orgn., 1973-75, Milk Industry Found., 1976-82, Nat. Dairy Council, 1979-81; bd. dirs., vice chmn. Westchester Pvt. Industry Council, 1979—. Served to lt. col. AUS, 1940-45. Decorated Bronze Star. Mem. N.Y. Milk Bottlers Fedn. (pres., dir.), Met. Dairy Inst. (exec. v.p., dir.), Phi Beta Kappa, Tau Epsilon Phi. Office: 170 Sawmill River Rd Yonkers NY 10701

KERN, MARTIN H(AROLD), supermarket chain executive; b. Jersey City, Apr. 3, 1941; s. William Kern Harriett and Arendt K. Student, Rutgers U. Vice pres. frozen food T-A Shop Rite Supermarkets div. Wakefern Food Corp., Elizabeth, N.J., 1959-65, v.p. dairy-deli, 1965-70; sr. v.p. mktg. Wakefern Food Corp., Elizabeth, N.J., 1970-80; pres., chief exec. officer Jetro Holdings, N.Y.C., 1980-82; exec. v.p. Gt. Atlantic & Pacific Tea Co., Montvale, N.J., 1982—; asst. prof. Kingsboro Community Coll. Contbr. numerous articles on food mktg. and distbn. to profl. jours. Active Park East Synagogue, N.Y.C., Israel Bonds Assn.; mem. Deborah Hosp.; bd. dirs. Mercox Landing Assn., Water Mill, N.Y. Served with USAFR, 1959-65. Recipient awards from trade assns., schs., 1965—. Mem. Young Pres. Orgn., Eastern Daily Deli Assn. (bd. dirs. 1970—, pres.), Eastern Frozen Food Assn. (dir. 1963-71), les Amis de Escoffier Soc. Home: 60 Sutton Pl S New York NY 10022 home: Water Mill NY Office: Gt Atlantic & Pacific Tea Co 2 Paragon Dr Montvale NY 07645

KERN, OTTO, mfg. co. exec.; b. Switzerland, Feb. 11, 1927; s. Ernst and Hedwig (Eberle) K.; m. Maria Schwegler; 1 dau., Tanja. Grad., Juventus, Switzerland, 1949. Gen. mgr. Excello Gmb, W. Ger., 196670, European ops. mgr., 1970-74, v.p. internat., 1974-78; group v.p. Excello Corp., Troy, Mich., 1978—. Mem. Soc. Mfg. Engrs. Republican. Office: 2855 Coolidge St Troy MI 48084

KERNAN, ALVIN BERNARD, educator; b. Manchester, Ga., June 13, 1923; s. Alvin Berbanks Peters and Jimmie Katherine (Fletcher) P.; m. Suzanne Scoble, Dec. 13, 1949; children—Geoffrey, Katherine, Marjorie, Alvin. B.A., Williams Coll., 1949, Oxford (Eng.) U., 1951; Ph.D., Yale, 1954. Instr. English Rensselaer Poly. Inst., Troy, N.Y., 1953-54; instr. Yale, 1954-59, asst. prof. English, 1959-63, asso. prof., 1963-66, prof., 1966-73; asso. provost, 1965-68, acting provost, 1970, dir. div. humanities, 1970-73; prof. English, dean Grad. Sch. Princeton, 1973-77, Andrew Mellon prof. humanities, 1977—. Author: The Cankered Muse, 1959, The Plot of Satire, 1965, The Revels History of the Drama in English, 1576-1613, Vol. III, 1975, The Playwright as Magician, 1979, The Imaginary Library, 1982. Served with USN, 1941-45. Decorated Navy cross, D.F.C., Air medal; Moody fellow, 1949-51; Morse fellow, 1957-58; Am. Council Learned Socs. fellow, 1961-62; Nat. Endowment Humanities sr. scholar fellow, 1968-69, 81-82. Mem. Phi Beta Kappa. Home: 76 Battle Rd Princeton NJ 08540

KERNAN, RICHARD W., photographic processing company executive. Pres., chief operating officer Fotomat Corp., St. Petersberg, Fla. Office: Fotomat Corp 205 Ninth St N St Petersberg FL 33701§

KERNEL, WALTER GLENN, beverage company executive; b. Hermitage, Tenn., Nov. 2, 1932; s. Walter L. and Ethel (Turner) K.; m. Joan Wade, Jan. 30, 1951; children: Carol Hand, Barbara. B.S. in Acctg., Bowling Green U., Ky., 1954. With Minute Maid Co., Plymount Orlando, Fla., 1954-60, Minute Maid Div., Orlando, 1961; fiscal mgr. Minute Maid Internat. subs. Coca-Cola Export Corp., Geneva, Switzerland, 1961-64, asst. controller Minute Maid Div., Orlando, 1964-68; v.p., asst. controller Coca-Cola Co., Atlanta, 1968—. Mem. Fin. Exec. Inst. Office: Coca-Cola Co 310 North Ave Atlanta GA 30313

KERNER, FRED, book publisher, author; b. Montreal, Can., Feb. 15, 1921; s. Sam and Vera (Goldman) K.; m. Jean Elizabeth Somerville, July 17, 1945 (div. Apr. 1951); 1 son, Jon Fredrik; m. Sally Dee Stouten, May 18, 1959; children: David, Diane. B.A., Sir George Williams U., Montreal, 1942. Asst. sports editor Montreal Gazette, 1942-44; news editor Canadian Press, Montreal, Toronto, N.Y.C., 1944-50; asst. night city editor A.P., N.Y.C., 1950-57; editor Hawthorn Books, Inc., N.Y.C., 1957-58, pres., 1965-68; exec. editor Crest-Premier Books, Fawcett World Library, N.Y.C., 1958-63, editor-in-chief, 1963-65; pres. Centaur House, Inc. (pubs.), 1964-80, Paramount Securities Corp., 1965-67, Veritas Internat. Pubs., 1976—, Fred Kerner/Pub Projects, 1967—; editorial dir. book and ednl. divs. Reader's Digest, Can., 1969-75; v.p., pub. dir. Harlequin Enterprises Ltd., 1975-83, editor emeritus, sr. cons. editor, 1984—; v.p. Publitex Internat. Corp. (pubs.), 1968-75; pres. Athabaska House, 1975-77; dir. Nat. Mint, Inc.; panelist various profl. confs. Chmn. Internat. Affairs Conf. Coll. Editors, 1965. Author: (with Leonid Kotkin) Eat, Think and be Slender, 1954, (with Walter M. Germain) The Magic Power of Your Mind, 1956, (with Joyce Brothers) Ten Days to a Successful Memory, 1957, Stress and Your Heart, 1961; pseudonym Frederick Kerr: Watch Your Weight Go Down, 1962, (with Walter M. Germain) Secrets of Your Supraconscious, 1965, (with David Goodman) What's Best for Your Child and You, 1966, (with Jesse Reid) Buy High, Sell Higher, 1966; pseudonym M.H. Thaler: It's Fun to Fondue, 1968, (with Ion Grumeza) Nadia, 1977; Contbg. author: Successful Writers and How They Work, 1958, Words on Paper, 1960, Overseas Press Club Cookbook, 1964, Chamber's, Ency; Editor: Love is a Man's Affair, 1958, Treasury of Lincoln Quotations, 1965. Mem. local sch. bd., N.Y.C., 1968-69; chmn. sch. com. Westmount High Sch., 1970-72; mem. sch. com. Roslyn Sch., 1973; chmn. pubs. com. Edward R. Murrow Meml. Fund; judge Dr. William Henry Drummond Nat. Poetry Contest.; Trustee Gibson Lit. Awards, C.A.A. Lit. Awards, Benson & Hedges Lit. Awards; bd. govs. Concordia U., 1975-79; bd. dirs. Can. Book Pubs. Council, Can. Copyright Inst.; founding chmn. Fund to Develop Can. Writers, 1983—. Mem. Orgn. Canadian Authors and Pubs. (founding dir.), Canadian Authors Assn. (v.p. 1972-80, founding dir. Lit. Luncheons, pres. Montreal br. 1974-75, nat. pres. 1982-83), Mystery Writers Am., Canadian Soc. Profl. Journalists, Authors Guild, Authors League Am., Am. Acad. Polit. and Social Sci., Can. Assn. Restoration of Lost Positives (pres.), Alumni Assn., Sir George Williams U. (exec. com. 1970-75, pres. 1971-73), Sigma Delta Chi. Clubs: Advertising, Deadline, Overseas Press, Dutch Treat (N.Y.C.); Toronto Men's Press; Author's (London, Eng.). Home: 25 Farmview Crescent Willowdale ON Canada M2J 1G5 Office: PO Box 952 Station B Willowdale ON Canada M2K 2T6

KERNOCHAN, JOHN MARSHALL, lawyer, educator; b. N.Y.C., Aug. 3, 1919. A.B., Harvard U., 1942; J.D., Columbia U., 1948. Bar: N.Y. bar 1949. Asst. dir. Legis. Drafting Research Fund Columbia U., N.Y.C., 1950-51, acting dir., 1951-52, dir., 1952-69, lectr. law, 1951-52, asso. prof., 1952-55, prof., 1955-77, Nash prof. law, 1977—, exec. dir., 1956-59, co-chmn., 1960-62; chmn. bd. Galaxy Music Corp.; cons. Temporary State Commn. to Study Organizational Structure of Govt. N.Y.C., 1953. Contbr. articles to profl. jours. and textbooks. Mem. civil and polit. rights com. Pres.'s Commn. on Status of Women, 1962-63; Bd. dirs. Vol. Lawyers for the Arts, Am. Symphony Orch. League; mem. legal and legis. com. Internat. Confedn. Socs. Authors and Composers. Mem. Assn. Bar City N.Y. Home: 16 Highgate Rd Riverside CT 06878 Office: Columbia U Sch Law 435 W 116th St New York NY 10027

KERNODLE, RIGDON WAYNE, educator, sociologist; b. Greensboro, N.C., 1919; s. William Edgar and Lena Florence (McClain) K.; m. Ruth Granbery Lynch, Feb. 22, 1945; children—Michael Wayne, Kathryn Ruth. A.A., Brevard Jr. Coll., 1941; B.A., U. N.C., 1943, M.A., 1945, Ph.D., 1949. Instr. sociology Coll. William and Mary, 1945-47, chmn., prof. dept. sociology, 1952—, Heritage prof., 1968; teaching staff residency tng. program in psychiatry Eastern State Hosp. Author: (with C.F. Marsh) Hampton Roads Communities in World War II, 1951, Last of Rugged Individualist, 1960, Unsolved Issues in American Society, 1960; Editor: The Sixth Decade of Our Century, 1959, Values, Decisions and the American Economy, 1961, Nonmedical Leaves From a Mental Hospital, 1966, The Aegelic Tennis Stroke, 1968, Three Family Placement Programs in Belgium and The Netherlands, 1972, Commentary on Why People Fall In and Out of Love Romantically, 1973, Comparison of Social Networks of Black and White Elderly, 1979, Family Life of Older Americans, 1980, Leisure Perspectives of Older Persons, 1980. Coordinator William and Mary Elderhostel. Recipient Thomas Jefferson award Coll. William and Mary, 1976. Mem. Am. Sociol. Soc., So. Sociol. Soc. (2d v.p.), Nat. Council Family Relations, Internat. Congress on Social Psychiatry, Am. Gerontol. Soc. Home: 108 Governors Dr Williamsburg VA 23185

KERR, A(RTHUR) STEWART, lawyer; b. Knoxville, Tenn., Aug. 12, 1915; s. John Thomas and Eunice Miller (Bruner) K.; m. Jennie Ilene Veen, Nov. 29, 1968; children by previous marriage: Katherine (Mrs. David F. Campbell), A. Stewart Jr., Bruce B. B.A., U. Tenn., Chattanooga, 1936; J.D., U. Va., 1938. Bar: D.C. and Tenn. 1939, Mich. 1947, U.S. Supreme Ct. 1952. Spl. asst. to U.S. Atty. Gen., Washington, Chgo. and Detroit, 1938-47; partner Kerr, Russell & Weber (and predecessors), Detroit, 1947-; dir. various corps.; mem. Atty. Gen.'s Nat. Com. to Study Antitrust Laws, 1953-55, 68. Bd. cons.: Antitrust Bull. Pres. Children's Aid Soc., 1972—; bd. dirs., pres. Met. Detroit Council Chs., 1981-82. Mem. ABA (past council antitrust sect.), Inter-Am. Bar Assn., Fed. Bar Assn., Mich. Bar Assn. (past chmn. antitrust sect. and adminstrv. law sect.), Detroit Bar Assn. Home: 557 Robert John Rd Grosse Pointe Woods MI 48236 Office: 2100 Comerica Bldg Detroit MI 48226

KERR, BAINE PERKINS, oil company executive; b. Rusk, Tex., Aug. 24, 1919; s. James Herman and Myrta Blake (Perkins) K.; m. Mildred Pickett Caldwell, June 13, 1942; children: Baine Perkins, John Caldwell, James Robinson, Mary Blake. B.A., LL.B., U. Tex. at Austin, 1942. Bar: Tex. 1942. Practiced in, Houston, 1945-77; partner firm Baker & Botts, 1955-77; dir. Pennzoil Co., Houston, 1964—, chmn. exec. com., 1972—, pres., 1977—. Bd. govs. (adv.) William Marsh Rice U., Houston; adv. bd. Marine Mil. Acad., Harlingen, Tex.; trustee Interferon Found.; mem. adv. council Coll. Natural Scis. Found., U. Tex. at Austin. Served with USMCR, 1942-45. Mem. Chancellors, Order of Coif, Phi Beta Kappa, Phi Eta Sigma, Phi Delta Theta, Phi Delta Phi. Office: PO Box 2967 Houston TX 77001

KERR, BYRON THOMAS, consulting civil engineer; b. Campbellton, N.B., Can., Dec. 28, 1924; s. Thomas F. and Myrtle (Balter) K.; m. Shirley B. Bulmer, Dec. 27, 1947; children: Peter Thomas, Patricia Ann, Susan Winifred. B.Engring. with honors, N.S. Inst. Tech., Halifax, 1947. Resident engr. Shawinigan Engring. Co., Que., Can., 1947-50; pres., dir. Purdy Henderson Ltd. (constrn. co.), Montreal, Que., 1951-55, Warnock Hersey Co., Ltd. (cons. co.), Montreal, 1955-70, Warnock Hersey Mgmt. Cons. Ltd., 1955-70, Warnock Hersey Appraisal Co. Ltd., 1955-70, Kerr, Crippen, Roy & Assos., 1970—, Warnock Hersey Carribean Ltd., Kingston, Jamaica, 1972—, North Am. Trust, Montreal, 1966-69; mgmt. cons., 1969-72; mgmt. cons., gen. mgr. Engring. Inst. Can., 1972-78; pres., chief exec.

officer Warnock Hersey Profl. Services Ltd., 1978—, Byron T. Kerr & Assos. Ltd. (mgmt. cons.), 1981—; dir. various Canadian cos. Alderman City of St.-Lambert, Que., 1957-61, mayor, 1961-64. Served with Royal Canadian Navy, 1942-46. Fellow Am. Inst. Mgmt.; mem. Engring. Inst. Can., Order Engrs. Que., assns. profl. engrs. Ont., N.S., Alta., Newcomen Soc. Clubs: Mt. Stephen (Montreal); Cercle Universitaire (Ottawa, Ont.). Home: 240 1st St Saint-Lambert PQ J4R 1B5 Canada

KERR, CHESTER BROOKS, publisher; b. Norwalk, Conn., Aug. 5, 1913; s. Chester M. and Mary (Seymour) K.; children by previous marriage: John Seymour II, Philip, Alexander, Chester Brooks; m. Joan Paterson Mills, 1964; stepchildren: Edwin S. Mills, Hilary Paterson Mills, Alison Mills. B.A., Yale U., 1936; L.H.D. hon., Johns Hopkins U., 1978. Editor Harcourt, Brace & Co., 1936-40; dir. Atlantic Monthly Press, 1940-41; acting. dir. U.S. Internat. Book Assn., 1946; v.p. Reynal & Hitchcock, 1947; dir. Survey of Am. Univ. Pressses, 1948-49; sec. Yale U. Press, New Haven, 1949-59, dir., 1959-79; fellow Berkeley Coll. Yale U., 1950-75; pres. Ticknor & Fields, a Houghton Mifflin Co., N.Y.C., 1979—; mem. adminstrv. bd. Papers of Benjamin Franklin, 1954-77; dir. Franklin Book Program, 1971-74; cons. univ. presses pub. program Ford Found., 1956-63, 65-67; chief book div. OWI, 1942-45; cons. to asst. sec. state for info., 1951; cons. Library of Congress, 1976-77; mem. exec. com. Nat. Book Com., 1968-75; dir. Nat. Enquiry, 1975-78. Author: A Report on American University Presses, 1949. Vice chmn. Conn. Vols. for Stevenson, 1952; co.-chmn. New Haven McCarthy for Pres. Com., 1968; trustee New Haven Free Pub. Library, 1953-70. Mem. Assn. Am. Univ. Presses (sec.-treas. 1957-59, pres. 1965-67, dir. 1967-68), Am. Book Pubs. Council (dir. 1966-69), Am. Pubs. Assn. (dir. 1975-78, sec. 1976-77), Internat. Assn. Scholarly Pubs. (pres. 1977-80, Curtis Benjamin prize as outstanding pub. 1978). Clubs: Yale, Publishers Lunch, Grolier (N.Y.C.); Mory's, Graduate, Elizabeth (New Haven). Home: 421 Humphrey St New Haven CT 06511 Office: Ticknor & Fields 52 Vanderbilt Ave New York NY 10017

KERR, CLARENCE WILLIAM, univ. adminstr.; b. Greenfield, Ohio, June 19, 1923; s. Clarence Ware and Genevieve (Meyers) K. B.A., Princeton U., 1947; M.A. (Woodrow Wilson fellow), Harvard U., 1949; Ph.D. (Frederick Sheldon fellow), Harvard U., 1957. Instr. to asst. prof. history Kenyon Coll., 1956-59; asst. prof. history Wesleyan U., Middletown, Conn., 1959-64, lectr., 1964-73, adj. prof., 1973—, asst. to provost, 1963-65, asst. provost, 1965-68, asso. provost, 1968-69, acting provost, 1969-70, provost, 1970—. Mem. AAUP, Renaissance Soc. Am., New Eng. Assn. Schs. and Colls. (sec.-treas.), Psi Upsilon. Democrat. Presbyterian. Clubs: Quadrangle (Princeton); Signet (Harvard); Princeton (N.Y.C.). Home: 101 High St Middletown CT 06457 Office: Office of the Provost Wesleyan U Middletown CT 06457

KERR, CLARK, educator; b. Stony Creek, Pa., May 17, 1911; s. Samuel William and Caroline (Clark) K.; m. Catherine Spaulding, Dec. 25, 1934; children—Clark E., Alexander W., Caroline M. B.A., Swarthmore Coll., 1932, LL.D., 1952; M.A., Stanford, 1933; postgrad., London Sch. Econs., 1936, 39; Ph.D., U. Calif., 1939; LL.D., Harvard, 1958, Princeton, 1959, others. Traveling fellow Am. Friends Service Com., 1935-36; instr. econs. Antioch Coll., 1936-37; teaching fellow U. Calif., 1937-38; Newton Booth fellow, 1938-39; acting asst. prof. labor econs. Stanford, 1939-40; asst., later asso. prof. U. Wash., 1940-45; asso. prof., prof., dir. Inst. Indsl. Relations, U. Calif. at Berkeley, 1945-52, chancellor, 1952-58, pres., 1958-67, pres. emeritus, 1974—; chmn. Carnegie Commn. on Higher Edn., 1967-73, Carnegie Council Policy Studies in Higher Edn., 1974-79; Vice chmn. divs. War Labor Bd., 1943-45; nat. arbitrator Armour Co. and United Packing House Workers, 1945-52; impartial chmn. Waterfront Employers, Pacific Coast and Internat. Longshoremen's and Warehousemen's Union, 1946-47; pub. mem. Nat. WSB, 1950-51; various arbitrations in pub. utilities, newspaper, aircraft, canning, oil, local transport and other industries, 1942—; Adv. panel Soc. Sci. Research, NSF, 1953-57; chmn. Armour Automation Com., 1959-79. Author: (with E. Wight Bakke) Unions, Management and the Public, rev. edit, 1960, (with Dunlop, Harbison, Myers) Industrialism and Industrial Man, rev. edit, 1964, The Uses of the University, rev. edit, 1972, Labor and Management in Industrial Society, 1964, Marshall, Marx and Modern Times, 1968, Labor Markets and Wage Determination: The Balkanization of Labor Markets and Other Essays, 1977, Education and National Development: Reflections from an American Perspective during a Period of Global Reassessment, 1979; Contbr.: Rev. Econs. and Statistics. Trustee Rockefeller Found., 1960-76; bd. mgrs. Swarthmore Coll., 1972—. Mem. Am., Royal, Western econ. assns., Am. Acad. Arts and Scis., Indsl. Relations Research Assn., Nat. Acad. Arbitrators, AAUP, Phi Beta Kappa, Kappa Sigma. Mem. Soc. of Friends. Home: 8300 Buckingham Dr El Cerrito CA 94530 Office: Inst of Indsl Relations U Calif Berkeley CA 94720

KERR, DEBORAH, actress; b. Helensburgh, Scotland, Sept. 30, 1921; emigrated to U.S., 1947; d. Arthur Kerr-Trimmer; m. Anthony C. Bartley, Nov. 28, 1945 (div. 1959); children—Melanie, Francesca; m. Peter Viertel, July 23, 1960. Student, Helensburgh schs., Northumberland House Sch., Bristol. Began: motion picture career in England in Major Barbara, 1940; appeared in: I See a Dark Stranger; Black Narcissus (N.Y. Critics award), The Hucksters, Edward, My Son, King Solomon's Mines, Quo Vadis, Thunder in the East, Prisoner of Zenda, Julius Caesar, Dream Wife, Young Bess, From Here to Eternity, The End of the Affair, 1955, Proud and Profane, 1956, The King and I, 1956, Heaven Knows Mr. Alison, 1956 (N.Y. Critics Award), Bonjour Tristesse, 1958, Count Your Blessings, 1959, The Journey, 1959, Beloved Infidel, 1959, The Grass is Greener, 1960, The Sundowners, 1960 (N.Y. Critics award), The Naked Edge, 1961, Chalk Garden, 1964, Night of the Iguana, 1964, Marriage on the Rocks, 1965, Casino Royale, 1967, The Gypsy Moths, The Arrangement; appeared: on stage in Heartbreak House, 1943, Gaslight (for Brit. troops in Europe), 1945, Tea and Sympathy, 1954-55, The Day After the Fair, London, 1972-73, U.S. tour, 1973—; appeared in: U.S. tour of Seascape, 1975, Long Day's Journey into Night, Los Angeles, 1977, Candida, London, 1977, The Last of Mrs. Cheney, U.S. and Can., 1978-79, The Day After the Fair, Australia, 1979; appeared on: London stage in Overheard, 1981 (Recipient Sarah Siddons award as Chgo. actress of the year.). Office: care Jess S Morgan 6420 Wilshire Blvd 19th Floor Los Angeles CA 90048

KERR, DONALD MACLEAN, JR., physicist; b. Phila., Apr. 8, 1939; s. Donald MacLean and Harriet (Fell) K.; m. Alison Richards Kyle, June 10, 1961; 1 dau., Margot Kyle. B.E.E. (Nat. Merit scholar), Cornell U., 1963, M.S., 1964, Ph.D. (Ford Found. fellow, 1964-65, James Clerk Maxwell fellow 1965-66), 1966. Staff Los Alamos Nat. Lab., 1966-76, group leader, 1971-72, asst. div. leader, 1972-73, asst. to dir., 1973-75, alt. div. leader, 1975-76; dep. mgr. Nev. ops. office Dept. Energy, Las Vegas, 1976-77, acting asst. sec. def. programs, Washington, 1978, dep. asst. sec. def. programs, 1977-79, dep. asst. sec. energy tech., 1979; dir Los Alamos Nat. Lab., 1979—; mem. Navajo Sci. Com., 1974-77; mem. sci. adv. panel U.S. Army, 1975-78; mem. engring. advs. bd. U. Nev.-Las Vegas, 1976-78; chmn. com. research and devel. Internat. Energy Agy., 1979; mem. nat. security adv. council SRI Internat., 1980—; mem. adv. bd. U. Alaska Geophys. Inst., 1980—; Mem. sci. adv. group Joint Strategic Planning Staff, 1981—; Mem. Naval Research Adv. Com., 1982—; adv. bd. Georgetown U. Center Strategic and Internat. Studies, 1981—; Mem. corp. Charles Stark Draper Lab., 1982—. Mem. AAAS, Am. Phys. Soc., Am. Geophys. Union, Southwestern Assn. Indian Affairs, Sigma Xi, Tau Beta Pi, Eta Kappa Nu. Club: Cosmos (Washington). Research, publs. on plasma physics, microwave electronics, ionospheric physics, energy and nat. security policy. Office: Los Alamos Sci Lab Los Alamos NM 87545

KERR, DOROTHY MARIE BURMEISTER, publishing company executive; b. Chgo., Oct. 1, 1935; d. Edwin Charles and Dorothy Gladys (Braithwaite) Burmeister; m. James Robert Kerr, Aug. 27, 1955 (div. Jan. 1970); 1 dau., Kathryn Elizabeth; m. James Mullinix, Apr. 20, 1978; 1 son, Mark Edwin Mullinix. B.A., Cornell U., 1956. Publicity dir. United chpts. Phi Beta Kappa, Washington, 1957-62; dir. circulation and promotion The Am. Scholar, Washington, 1957-62; pres., creative dir. Dorothy Kerr & Assos., Inc., Washington, 1962-79, sec.-treas., 1979—; circulation mktg. mgr. U.S. News and World Report, 1979—; cons. Annenberg Sch. Communication, U. Pa., Phila., 1973-75; lectr. George Washington U., 1974-76, adv. bd. editing and pub. program. Bd. dirs. Florence Crittenton Home, Washington, 1968-71; bd. dirs. Better Bus. Bur., mem. exec. com., 1978-83; bus. adv. com. Washington Tech. Inst., 1976; Washington adv. council SBA, 1976-78. Recipient Man of Year award Mail Advt. Club, 1971. Mem. Direct Mktg. Assn., Nat. Soc. Arts and Letters (treas. 1979-83), Assn. Direct Mktg. Agys. (dir., exec. v.p. 1978-79), Kappa Delta. Clubs: Advt. (dir., pres. 1979-80), Capital Speakers (v.p. 1971), Direct Mktg. (pres. 1965), Nat. Press (Washington)). Home: 3106 Cleveland Ave NW Washington DC 20008 Office: 2300 N St NW Washington DC 20037 *Much of what must be done in life is neither exciting nor glamorous, but one should be willing to do whatever is needed; any task worth doing is worth doing well.*

KERR, EWING THOMAS, U.S. dist. judge; b. Bowie, Tex., Jan. 21, 1900; s. George N. and Ellen H. (Wisdom) K.; m. Ellen Irene Peterson, Feb. 22, 1933; children—Hugh Neal, Judith Ann. B.A., U. Okla., 1923; B.S., Central Coll., Okla., 1923; postgrad., U. Colo., 1925. Bar: Wyo. bar 1927. Prin. jr. high sch., Hominy, Okla., 1923-25, Cheyenne Pub. Schs., 1925-27; practice at, Cheyenne, 1927-29, asst. U.S. dist. atty. for, Wyo., 1930-33, atty. gen., 1939-43; atty. for Wyo. Senate, 1943; U.S. dist. judge Dist. Wyo., Cheyenne, 1955—. Served as maj. AUS; with Allied Commn.; in Italy; head legal div. in area; reorganized civilian cts. in, 1945; Austria. Mem. Wyo. Bar Assn., Cheyenne C. of C. Republican. Presbyn. Clubs: Mason (past master lodge, past grand master lodge, 33 deg.), Rotarian.). Home: 2951 Spruce Dr Cheyenne WY 82001 Office: Post Office Bldg Cheyenne WY 82001

KERR, FRANK JOHN, astronomer, university provost; b. St. Albans, Eng., Jan. 8, 1918; s. Frank Robison and Myrtle Constance (McMeekin) K.; m. Maureen Parnell, Jan. 7, 1966; children: Gillian Wheeler, Ian Kerr, Robin Lowry. B.Sc., U. Melbourne, Australia, 1938, M.Sc., 1940, D.Sc., 1962; M.S., Harvard U., 1951. Research scholar U. Melbourne, 1939-40; mem. staff radiophysics lab. Commonwealth Sci. and Indsl. Research Orgn., Sydney, Australia, 1940-68; vis. prof. U. Md., 1966-68, prof., 1968—, dir. astronomy program, 1973-78, acting provost div. math. phys. scis. and engring., 1978-79, provost, 1979—; vis. scientist Leiden U., 1957; vis. prof. U. Tex., 1964, U. Tokyo, 1967; Mem. NSF Adv. Panel Astronomy, 1969-72, chmn., 1971-72. Co-editor: Procs. Internat. Astron. Union Symposia, 1963, 73; Contbr. numerous articles to profl. jours. Trustee Asso. Univs. Inc., 1981-84. Fulbright travel grantee, 1950-51; Leverhulme fellow, 1967; NSF research grantee, 1967-83; Guggenheim fellow, 1974-75. Mem. Internat. Astron. Union (pres. commn. 33 1976-79), Am. Astron. Soc. (councillor 1972-75, v.p. 1980-82). Club: Cosmos (Washington). Home: 12601 Davan Dr Silver Spring MD 20904 Office: MPSE Div U Md College Park MD 20742

KERR, GERALD WAYNE, government official; b. Villisca, Iowa, Feb. 23, 1931; s. Harlan A. and Loraine (Owen) K.; m. Elynor Ann Anderson, June 21, 1958; children: David Owen, Janet Christine, Roger Alan. B.A., Peru State Coll., 1955; postgrad., U. Rochester, 1955-56; M.A., Trinity Coll., 1960. Diplomate: Am. Bd. Health Physics. Indsl. hygienist Pratt & Whitney Aircraft, Middletown, Conn., 1956-61; health physicist U.S. AEC, Washington, 1961-75; chief agreements and export br. U.S. Nuclear Regulatory Comm., Washington, 1975-76, asst. dir. office state programs, 1976-80, dir. office state programs, 1980—. Served with USMC, 1951-54. Mem. Health Physics Soc. Republican. Methodist. Home: 509 Lynch St Rockville MD 20850 Office: US Nuclear Regulatory Commn 4550 Montgomery Ave Washington DC 20555

KERR, HUGH THOMSON, author, emeritus theology educator; b. Chgo., July 1, 1909; s. Hugh Thomson and Olive May (Boggs) K.; m. Dorothy DePree, Dec. 28, 1938; 1 son, Stephen T. A.B., Princeton U., 1931; B.D., Western Theol. Sem., Pitts., 1934; M.A., U. Pitts., 1934; Ph.D., U. Edinburgh, Scotland, 1936. Ordained to ministry Presbyn. Ch., 1934; from instr. to prof. doctrinal theology Louisville Presbyn. Theol. Sem., 1936-40; prof. systematic theology Princeton Theol. Sem., 1940-74, Benjamin B. Warfield prof. theology emeritus, 1974—; mem. univ. chapel com., 1960-63, nat. council com. on ch. architecture, 1960-62; dir. Gallahue Conf. Quo Vadis, 1968, Westminster Found., 1954-65, Westminster Found. of univ., 1954—; Del. for N.Am., World Alliance Reformed Chs., 1945-60; mem. commn. on women World Council Chs., 1950-54, del. faith and order conf., 1957; chmn. com. curriculum Council Theol. Edn., 1949-53; mem. coms. marriage and divorce, ordination of women Presbyn. Ch., 1955-57. Editor: Theology Today quar, 1950; Author: A Compend of Calvin's Institutes, 1938 (in Japanese 1958), Compend of Luther's Theology, 1963, Positive Protestantism: An Interpretation of the Gospel, 1960 (in Japanese 1954), Mystery and Meaning in the Christian Faith, 1958, What Divides Protestants Today, 1958, By John Calvin, 1960, Readings in Christian Thought, 1966, Our Life in God's Life, 1979, Protestantism, 1979, (with J.M. Mulder) Conversion, 1983; also films Protestantism, multi-media presentations, articles, chpts. in books.; Editor: Sons of the Prophets, 1963. Guggenheim fellow, 1960. Mem. Am. Theol. Soc., Soc. Bibl. Lit., Am. Acad. Religion, Am. Assn. Univ. Profs., Am. Ch. History Soc. Home: 707 Rosedale Rd Princeton NJ 08540 Office: Box 29 Princeton NJ 08540

KERR, JAMES ALLEN, finance company executive; b. Elizabeth, N.J., May 30, 1920; s. James and Ann (Allen) K.; m. Dorothy Margaret Jordan, Feb. 1, 1942; children: James Allen, Dorothy Allyson Kerr Pilcher. Accounting degree, Armed Forces Inst.; student, Columbia U. and City Coll. N.Y., 1946-49. Estimator trainee Methodist Pub. House, Dobbs Ferry, N.Y., 1938-40; with Walter E. Heller & Co., Inc., N.Y.C., 1946—, v.p., 1961-68, sr. v.p., 1968-73, exec. v.p., 1973—; sr. v.p., dir., mem. exec. com. Walter E. Heller Internat. Corp.; pres., charge ops. Northeastern div. Walter E. Heller & Co. of N.Y., Inc.; also dir.; pres., dir. Heller Hawaiian Corp.; pres. Walter E. Heller of New Eng., Inc.; dir. Walter E. Heller Industries, Inc.; Past mem. Dept. Commerce Regional Expansion Council. Served with USN, 1941-45. Mem. AIM, Nat. Conf. Comml. Receivable Cos., New York Inst. Credit (trustee), Newcomen Soc., New Canaan Hist. Soc. Republican. Episcopalian. Club: La Coquille (Palm Beach, Fla.). Home: 159 Lost District Dr New Canaan CT 06840 Office: 101 Park Ave New York NY 10017

KERR, JAMES W., pipe line company executive; b. Hamilton, Ont., Can., Mar. 11, 1914; s. George Robert and Helen Robertson (Bews) K.; m. Ruth Eleanor Marrs, Oct. 5, 1940; children: David, Barbara. B.Sc., U. Toronto. Various positions with Canadian Westinghouse Co., 1937-58, v.p., gen. mgr. apparatus products group, 1956-58; pres., chief exec. officer TransCan. PipeLines, Toronto, 1958-61, chmn. bd., pres., 1961-68, chmn., chief exec. officer, 1968-79, cons. and dir., 1979—; dir. Bell Can. Enterprises, Canadian Imperial Bank Commerce, Bell Canada, Lehndorff Corp., Maple Leaf Mills Ltd., Internat. Minerals & Chem. Corp. (Can.) Ltd.; dir. emeritus Gt. Lakes Gas Transmission Co.; Hon. pres. Internat. Gas Union. Bd. govs. Queen Elizabeth Hosp., Toronto; bd. dirs. McMaster U. Med. Centre Found.; chmn. Salvation Army Territorial Adv. Bd. Exec. Served as squadron leader RCAF, 1942-45. Mem. Bd. Trade Met. Toronto (past pres.), Am. Gas Assn., Can. Gas Assn. (past pres.), Engring. Inst. Can., Assn. Profl. Engrs. Province Ont. Clubs: York, Toronto, Hamilton, Rosedale Golf, Rideau, Mount Royal.

KERR, JEAN, writer; b. Scranton, Pa., July 1923; d. Thomas J. and Kitty (O'Neill) Collins; m. Walter Kerr, Aug. 16, 1943; children—Christopher, John and Colin (twins), Gilbert, Gregory, Katharine. M.F.A., Cath. U. Am., 1945; L.H.D., Northwestern U., 1962, Fordham U., 1965. Author: play Jenny Kissed Me, 1949, Touch and Go, 1950, (with Eleanor Brooke) King of Hearts, 1954, Please Don't Eat the Daisies, 1957, The Snake Has All the Lines, 1960, Mary, Mary, 1961, Poor Richard, 1964, Penny Candy, 1970, Finishing Touches, 1973, How I Got to Be Perfect, 1978, Lunch Hour, 1980. Recipient Campion award, 1971; Laetare medal, 1971. Mem. Nat. Inst. Arts and Scis. Democrat. Roman Catholic. Home: 1 Beach Ave Larchmont NY 10538

KERR, JOHN FAY, educator, poet; b. Monette, Ark., May 28, 1930; s. Felix Washington and Mary Florence (Fay) K. B.A., Ark. State U., 1953; M.A., U. Mich., 1956; postgrad., U. Iowa, 1956, U. Mo., Columbia, 1957-58; Ph.D., U. Tex., Austin, 1965. Tchr. speech and journalism Kennett (Mo.) High Sch., 1954-55; asst. prof. Am. lit. and fiction writing Westminster Coll., Fulton, Mo., 1956-57; instr. English U. Mo., Columbia, 1957-58, U. Tex., Austin, 1958-63; asst. prof. Am. lit. and fiction writing La. State U., Baton Rouge, 1965-67; asst. prof. English Calif. Poly. State U., San Luis Obispo, 1967-69, asso. prof., 1969-74, prof., 1974—, dir. grad. studies English, 1973-76; lectr., reader poetry, Calif. Author: Hemingway's Use of Physical Setting and Stage Props in His Novels: A Study in Craftsmanship, 1965; asso. editor: Calif. State Poetry Quar, 1977-80; contbr. poetry to mags. and anthologies. Served with USMC, 1946-49. Recipient excellence in teaching award U. Tex., Austin, 1961, award for humorous poetry Calif. Fedn. Chaparral Poets. Mem. Calif. State Poetry Soc. (pres. 1975). Democrat. Home: 245-D N Oak Park Blvd Grover City CA 93433 Office: Dept of English California Polytechnic State University San Luis Obispo CA 93407 *My successes in life have come when I've had the pride to keep trying, the humility to seek advice, and sufficient interest and leisure to daydream about the undertaking. Perhaps most important is the daydreaming.*

KERR, THOMAS JEFFERSON, IV, foundation executive; b. Columbus, Ohio, Oct. 8, 1933; s. Thomas Jefferson and Ruth Glenora (Powell) K.; m. Donna Jean Lawton, June 11, 1955; children: Thomas Jefferson V, Cheryl Lee, Kathleen Anne. B.S., Cornell U., 1956; M.A., U. Buffalo, 1959; Ph.D. (univ. fellow), Syracuse U., 1965. Asst. prof., then prof. history Otterbein Coll., Westerville, Ohio, 1963-71, acting acad. dean, 1969-70, pres., 1971-84, Grant Hosp. Devel. Found., Westerville, 1984—; Chmn. Assn. Ind. Colls. and Univs., Ohio, 1976-78, Ohio Found. Ind. Colls., 1978-80. Mem. Greater Columbus Arts Council, 1975-78; trustee Blue Cross Central Ohio, 1978-84, Grant Hosp., 1975—; mem. Franklin County Draft Bd., 1969-71. Recipient Cokesbury Grad. Coll. Teaching award, 1963. Mem. Am. Assn. Higher Edn., Phi Kappa Phi, Kappa Phi Kappa, Omicron Chi Epsilon, Phi Eta Sigma. Republican. Methodist. Clubs: Mason, Rotarian., Torch. Home: 4890 Smoketalk Ln Westerville OH 43081

KERR, WALTER F., drama critic, author; b. Evanston, Ill., July 8, 1913; s. Walter Sylvester and Esther (Daugherty) K.; m. Jean Collins, Aug. 16, 1943; children—Christopher, Colin, John, Gilbert, Gregory, Katharine. B.S. in Speech, Northwestern U., 1937, M.A., 1938, L.H.D., 1962; LL.D., St. Mary's, Notre Dame; D.Litt., LaSalle, 1956, Fordham U., 1965, Notre Dame U., 1968, U. Mich., 1972. Instr. speech and drama Cath. U., Washington, 1938-45, asso. prof. drama, 1945-49; drama critic Commonweal, 1950-52, N.Y. Herald Tribune, 1951-66, N.Y. Times, 1966—; specialist drama theory, criticism. Dir.: profl. theatre Sing Out, Sweet Land, 1944, Touch and Go (George Abbott), King of Hearts (Elaine Perry); Author: (plays) Touch and Go; (books) How Not to Write a Play, 1955; Criticism and Censorship, 1957, Pieces at Eight, 1958, The Decline of Pleasure, 1962, The Theatre in Spite of Itself, 1963, Tragedy and Comedy, 1967, Thirty Plays Hath November, 1969, God on the Gymnasium Floor, 1971, The Silent Clowns, 1975, Journey to the Center of the Theater, 1979; also articles. Recipient George Jean Nathan award, 1964; Dineen award Nat. Cath. Theatre Conf., 1966; Iona award, 1970; Campion award, 1971; Laetare medal, 1971; award Nat. Inst. Arts and Letters, 1972; Pulitzer prize for criticism, 1978; elected to Theater Hall of Fame, 1982. Mem. N.Y. Critics' Circle (pres. 1955-57). Club: Players (hon.). Home: 1 Beach Ave Larchmont Manor NY 10538 Office: 230 W 41st St New York NY 10018

KERR, WILLIAM, nuclear engineering educator; b. Sawyer, Kans., Aug. 19, 1919; s. William and Maria Louise (Gill) K.; m. Ruth Duncan, Apr. 28, 1945; children: William Duncan, John Gill, Scott Winston. B.S. in Elec. Enging, U. Tenn., 1942, M.S., 1947; Ph.D., U. Mich., 1954. Instr., then asst. prof. U. Tenn., 1942-44, 46-48; mem. faculty U. Mich., Ann Arbor, 1948—, prof. nuclear engring., 1958—, chmn. dept., 1961-74, acting dir. Mich. Meml.-Phoenix Project, 1961-65, dir., 1965—, dir. Office Energy Research, 1977—, project supr. AID Nuclear Energy Project, 1956-65; Cons. Atomic Power Devel. Assos., 1954—, Argonne Nat. Lab., Colo. Commn. on Higher Edn.; chmn. nuclear engring. edn. com. Asso. Midwest Univs., 1961-62, pres., 1966-67, bd. dirs., 1965-67; trustee Argonne Univs. Assn., 1965-71; adv. com. reactor safeguards Nuclear Regulatory Commn., 1972—. Mem. Am. Soc. Engring. Edn., IEEE, Am. Nuclear Soc., Sigma Xi, Eta Kappa Nu, Phi Kappa Phi, Tau Beta Pi. Home: 2009 Hall St Ann Arbor MI 48104

KERR, WILLIAM A., glass manufacturing company exective. Chmn. Kerr Glass Mfg. Corp., Los Angeles. Office: Kerr Glass Mfg Corp 501 S Shatto Pl Los Angeles CA 90020§

KERR, WILLIAM TURNBULL, communications company executive; b. Seattle, Apr. 17, 1941; adopted son of Rose Agnes (Bradshaw) K.; m. Mary Carley Lang, Oct. 15, 1966; 1 dau., Susannah Gaskill. B.A., U. Wash., 1963; B.A., M.A., Oxford U., 1965; postgrad., Harvard U., 1965-67, M.B.A., 1969. Vice pres. Dillon, Read Overseas Corp., London, 1969-73; cons. McKinsey & Co., Inc., N.Y.C., 1973-79; v.p. The New York Times Co., N.Y.C., 1979—. Rhodes scholar, 1963-65. Roman Catholic. Clubs: Westhampton (N.Y.) Country; Reform (London). Office: 229 W 43rd St New York NY 10036

KERREBROCK, JACK LEO, aeronautics and astronautics engineering educator; b. Los Angeles, Feb. 6, 1928; s. Oscar A. and Florence (Hoy) K.; m. Bernice Veverka, Apr. 11, 1953; children:

Christopher, Nancy, Peter. Student, U. Oreg., 1946-47; B.S., Oreg. State Coll., 1950; M.S., Yale, 1951; Ph.D., Calif. Inst. Tech., 1956. Aero. research scientist Lewis Lab., NASA, Cleve., 1951-53; research fellow Calif. Inst. Tech., 1955-56; engring. leader Oak Ridge Nat. Lab., 1956-58; sr. research fellow Calif. Inst. Tech., 1958-60; mem. faculty M.I.T., 1960—, Richard C. Maclaurin prof. aeros. and astronautics, 1975—, dir. Gas Turbine and Plasma Dynamics Lab., 1969-78, head div. energy conversion and propulsion Gas Turbine and Plasma Dynamics Lab., 1970-81, head dept. aeros. and astronautics, 1978-81, 83—; asso. adminstr. Office Aeros. and Space Tech., NASA, Washington, 1981-83; cons. to govt., industry, 1957—; Mem. Air Force Sci. Adv. Bd., 1972—; mem. NASA Research and Tech. Adv. Com., 1975-77, Aeros. and Space Engring. Bd., NRC, 1976—; mem. aero. adv. com. NASA, 1978—. Recipient Gas Turbine Power award ASME, 1971. Fellow AIAA; mem. Nat. Acad. Engring., Am. Acad. Arts and Scis. Home: 108 Tower Rd Lincoln MA 01773 Office: 33-207 MIT Cambridge MA 02139

KERREY, BOB, governor of Nebraska; b. Lincoln, Nebr., Aug. 27, 1943; s. James and Elinor K.; children: Benjamin, Lindsey. B.S. in Pharmacy, U. Nebr., 1965. Owner, founder, developer outlets in Omaha and Lincoln Grandmother's Skillet restaurant, Omaha, 1972-75; owner, founder fitness enterprises, including Sun Valley Bowl and Wall-Bankers Racquetball Club and Fitness Ctr., Lincoln, Nebr.; gov. State of Nebr., Lincoln, 1983—. Bd. dirs. Lincoln Ctr. Assn., Nebr. Easter Seal Soc. Served to ensign USN, 1967-69; Vietnam. Decorated medal of Honor, Bronze Star, Purple Heart. Mem. Am. Legion, VFW, DAV, Lincoln C. of C., Phi Gamma Delta. Congregationalist. Lodges: Sertoma; Lions.

KERRIDGE, ROBERT LOUIS, trade assn. exec.; b. New London, Conn., July 7, 1910; s. Philip Markham and Agnes (Briggs) K.; m. Margaret Green, Oct. 3, 1938; children—David Tate, James Gordon, Julie Thorburn. A.B., Dickinson Coll., 1932. With Riegel Paper Corp., 1934-68, dir. marketing, 1960-68, v.p., 1953-68; also dir.; mgr. Pulp, Paper and Paper Bd., Export Assn. U.S., 1969—. Home: RD D 1 Riegelsville PA 18077 Office: 528 N New St Bethlehem PA 18018

KERRIGAN, JOSEPH MICHAEL, lawyer; b. Haverhill, Mass., Sept. 29, 1919; s. James A. and Anna M. (Murphy) K.; m. Jean M. Dooley, Nov. 20, 1943; children—Joseph Michael, Kathleen Ann, Patricia, Timothy, Matthew. A.B., Holy Cross Coll., 1939; J.D., Harvard U., 1942, I.A. Bus. Sch, 1943. Bar: Mass. bar 1947, N.H. bar 1951, Fed. bar 1951. Trial atty. Hartford Accident & Indemnity Co., Boston, 1947-51; asso. firm Sullivan & Gregg, Nashua, N.H., 1951-55; partner firm Hamblett & Kerrigan, Nashua, 1955—, sr. partner, 1975—; sec., counsel Rivier Coll., 1970—; mem. First Circuit Jud. Nominating Panel, 1979—. Mem. Nashua Planning Bd., 1956-61, chmn., 1960-61. Served with USAAF, 1944-46. Fellow Am. Coll. Trial Lawyers, Am. Bar Found.; mem. Nashua Bar Assn. (pres. 1970-71), N.H. Bar Assn. (pres. 1975-76), New Eng. Bar Assn. (pres. 1976-77), Am. Bar Assn., Am. Law Inst., N.H. Bar Found. (trustee 1977—, pres. 1979—). Republican. Roman Catholic. Club: Twenty Assos. Home: 125 Lille Rd Nashua NH 03062 Office: 4 Water St Nashua NH 03060

KERRIGAN, (THOMAS) ANTHONY, poet, editor, translator; b. Winchester, Mass., Mar. 14, 1918; s. Thomas Aloysius and Madeline (Flood) K.; m. Elaine Gurevitch, Sept. 11, 1951; children—Michael, Antonia, Camilo Jose, Patrick, Elie, Malachy. Licenciado en filosofia y letras, U. Habana, Cuba, 1945, U. Paris, 1952, U. Barcelona, Spain, 1951. Mem. faculty U. Fla., Gainesville, 1950-51; grantee Bollingen Found., 1961-75; editor, translator Princeton U. Press, 1969-75; vis. prof. English State U. N.Y., Buffalo, 1974; vis. prof. Spanish U. Ill., 1977-78; faculty fellow Center Study Man in Contemporary Soc., U. Notre Dame, 1979—. Editor, translator: 40 books including 7 vols. the Selected Works of Miguel de Unamuno; Author 3 books poetry. Served with Mil. Intelligence U.S. Army, World War II. Winner Nat. Book award, 1975; finalist, 1974; Translation Center Columbia U. fellow, 1977-78. Fellow Am. Acad. Learned Socs.; mem. Internat. Council of the Translation Center. Address: 47 Fitzwilliam Square Dublin 2 Ireland Office: Center Study Man U Notre Dame Notre Dame IN 46556 *In the belief that the blood family (and eventually the clan) is the basic unit of society, I strive for family. The passion to persist inspires any worthwhile endeavor. From support of family, one goes on to support the preservation of the Old Stones of achieved building, authentic music ("classical"), incandescent writing and thought, images of divinity. Therein lies immortal morality. God does not weave a loose web.*

KERRY, JOHN FORBES, lieutenant governor Massachusetts; b. Denver, Dec. 11, 1943; s. Richard John and Rosemary (Forbes) K.; m. Julia Stimson Thorne, May 22, 1970; children: Alexandra, Vanessa. B.A., Yale U., 1966; J.D., Boston Coll., 1976. Bar: Mass. 1976. Nat. coordinator Vietnam Vets. Against The War, 1969-71; asst. dist. atty. Middlesex (Mass.) County, 1976-79; ptnr. firm Kerry & Sragow, Boston, 1979-82; lt. gov. State of Mass., 1983—. Author: The New Soldier, 1971. Democratic candidate for Congress from, 5th Mass. Dist., 1972; bd. vistors Walsh Sch. Fgn. Service, Georgetown U. Served to lt. (j.g.) SUNR, 1966-69. Decorated Silver Star, Bronze Star with oak leaf cluster, Purple Hearts (3). Roman Catholic. Office: State House Boston MA 02110 *

KERSCHNER, LEE R(ONALD), educational administrator; b. May 31, 1931; m. Helga Koller, June 22, 1958; children: David, Gabriel, Riza. B.A. in Polit. Sci. (Univ. fellow), Rutgers U., 1953; M.A. in Internat. Relations (Univ. fellow), Johns Hopkins U., 1958; Ph.D. in Polit. Sci. (Univ. fellow), Georgetown U., 1964. From instr. to prof. polit. sci. Calif. State U., Fullerton, 1961-69; state univ. dean Calif. State Univs. and Colls. Hdqrs., Long Beach, 1969-71, asst. exec. vice chancellor, 1971-76, vice chancellor for adminstrv. affairs, 1976-77; exec. dir. Colo. Commn. on Higher Edn., Denver, 1977-83, Nat. Assn. Trade and Tech. Schs., 1983—; cons. in field. Mem. exec. com. Am. Jewish Com., Denver, 1978—. Served with USAF, 1954-58; col. Res. Mem. State Higher Edn. Exec. Officers Assn., Am. Council on Edn. Home: 13206 Chestnut Oak Dr Gaithersburg MD 20878 Office: 2021 K St NW Washington DC 20878

KERSH, BERT YARBROUGH, educator; b. Ft. Sam Houston, July 16, 1927; s. Henry Leonard and Ruth (Scott) K.; m. Barbara Jean Brown, Jan. 29, 1950; children—Todd, Pamela, Lee, Scott. B.A., U. Calif. at Santa Barbara, 1950; M.A., U. Calif. at Berkeley, 1953, Ph.D., 1955. Asst. prof. edn. U. Oreg., 1955-59; human factors scientist System Devel. Corp., Santa Monica, Calif., 1959-60; from asso. to full research prof., asso. dir. teaching research div. Oreg. State System Higher Edn., Monmouth, 1960-67; dean faculty Oreg. Coll. Edn., Monmouth, 1967-78, prof. edn., dir. research, 1978-81, prof. edn. and psychology, 1981—; mem. evaluation bds. Nat. Council Accreditation Tchr. Edn., 1970-73; mem. exec. com. Nat. Center for Higher Edn. Mgmt. Systems, Western Interstate Commn. for Higher Edn., 1969-72; cons. for fed. and pvt. ednl. agys. Contbr. articles profl. jours., tech. reports. Served with AUS, 1946-48, 50-51. NDEA research grantee. Mem. Am. Ednl. Research Assn., Oreg. Ednl. Research Assn. (pres. 1981-82). Democrat. Presbyterian. Home: 260 Sacre Ln N Monmouth OR 97361

KERSH, KENNETH GEORGE, college president; b. Fort Smith, Ark., Mar. 20, 1928; s. George R. and Georgia Ann (Hicks) K.; m. Nancy Lou Graham, Dec. 1, 1953; children: Graham, Richard, Kimberly, Georgia, Nana. A.B., Ark. Inst. Tech., 1954; M.Ed., U. Ark., 1959, Ed.D., 1966. Tchr., adminstr. pub. schs., Ark., Tex., Ariz., 1955-61; assoc. prof., dean of mem. chmn. edn. and psychology div., dean of univ., dir. grad. studies, prof. Pembroke State U., N.C., 1961-71; prof., chmn. dept. edn. Hendrix Coll., Ark., 1971-73; pres. Ark. Tech. U., Russellville, 1973—; chmn. Ark. Council of Presidents, Nat. Council for Accreditation of Tchr. Edn. Evaluation Teams; chmn. agrl. com. Am. Assn. State Colls. and Univs. Served with USAF, 1946-50. Mem. NEA, Ark. Edn. Assn., Phi Delta Kappa. Lodges: Masons; Shriners; Rotary. Home: 1313 N Arkansas St Russellville AR 72801 Office: Office of Pres Ark Tech U Russellville AR 72801

KERSHAW, JOSEPH, meat packing company executive; b. Hazleton, Pa., June 29, 1927; s. Edwin Lees and Eva A. (Gabler) K.; m. Ruth Mary Finlayson, Sept. 10, 1949; children: Nancy Jo, Joan E., Sharon R., Pamela A., Kristine W. Cert. of proficiency in acctg., U. Pa. Wharton Evening Sch. of Accounts and Fin., 1955. With Medford's Inc., Chester, Pa., 1947-66, office mgr., 1953-56, purchasing agt., 1956-66; purchasing mgr. Schluderberg-Kurdle Co., Inc., Balt., 1966-74, v.p. purchasing, 1974-77, exec. v.p., 1977-81, pres., 1981—, also dir. Mem.adv. bd. Salvation Army, Chester, 1958-59; mem. Citizens Council for Urban Renewal, Chester. Served to sgt. USAAF, 1945-47. Recipient Disting. Service award, named Outstanding Young Man of Yr. Chester Jaycees, 1961. Republican. Presbyterian. Home: 2315 Foxley Rd Timonium MD 21093 Office: 3800 E Baltimore St Baltimore MD 21203

KERSHAW, JOSEPH ALEXANDER, economist, educator; b. Bala-Cynwyd, Pa., Apr. 21, 1913; s. Isaac and Caroline (Alexander) F.; m. Mary Anna Nettleton, Oct. 8, 1936; children: David N., Stephen A. A.B., Princeton, 1935; A.M., N.Y. U., 1938; Ph.D., Columbia, 1947. Asst. prof. econs. Hofstra Coll., 1936-42; dir. ration banking br. OPA, 1942-47; asst., also head econs. dept. Rand Corp., 1948-62; prof. econs., provost Williams Coll., Williamstown, Mass., 1962-68, prof. econs., 1970-76, provost, 1971-74, prof. emeritus, 1976—, acting v.p. and treas., 1980-81; comptroller Sterling and Francine Clark Art Inst., 1976-80; asst. dir. Office Econ. Opportunity, 1965-66; program officer Ford Found., 1968-70; Bd. advisers Inst. for Research on Poverty, U. Wis., 1966-68; mem. acad. council Marlboro Coll., 1975-83; exec. dir. Temporary N.Y. State Commn. on Post-Secondary Edn., 1976-77. Author: History of Ration Banking, 1947, (with R. McKean) Teacher Shortages and Salary Schedules, 1962, Government Against Poverty, 1970, The Very Small College, 1976. Trustee So. Vt. Coll., 1978-84. Home: 80 Jerome Dr Williamstown MA 01267

KERSHAW, KENNETH ANDREW, biology educator; b. Morcambe, Eng., Sept. 5, 1930; emigrated to Can., 1969, naturalized, 1977; s. Andrew and Margaret K.; m. Ellen Catherine Bruce, Apr. 1, 1967; children: Daniel Kenneth, Andrew Duncan, Matthew Alexander. B.Sci. with honors in Biology, Manchester (Eng.) U., 1952; Ph.D., Univ. Coll. North Wales, Bangor, 1957, D.Sc., 1966. Lectr. dept. biology Imperial Coll., London, 1957-62; faculty Ahmadu Bello U., Zaria, Nigeria, 1962-64; prof. biology McMaster U., Hamilton, Ont., Can., 1969—. Author: Quantitative and Dynamic Plant Ecology, 1964, 73, Physiological Ecology of Lichens, 1983. Fellow Royal Soc. Can. Home: 601 Old Dundas Rd Ancaster ON L9G 3J3 Canada Office: Dept Biology McMaster U Hamilton ON Canada

KERSHNER, HOWARD ELDRED, author, found. exec.; b. Tescott, Kans., Nov. 17, 1891; s. Isaiah and Cora (Lett) K.; m. Gertrude Elizabeth Townsend, July 6, 1915 (dec. Sept. 1976); children: Wendell Townsend, Margaret Lynette (Mrs. Stephen C. Weber), Mary Linaford (Mrs. Glenn C. Bassett, Jr.); m. Lenore Bowers, Sept. 10, 1978 (dec. Feb. 1981). Grad., Fowler (Kans.) Friends' Acad., 1910; A.B., Friends' U., Wichita, Kans., 1914, LL.D. (hon.), 1948; grad. student, Harvard, 1923-24; L.H.D. (hon.), Washington and Jefferson Coll., 1941; Litt.D., Grove City (Pa.) Coll., 1957; D.D., George Fox Coll., 1969; H.H.D., Northwood Inst., 1970. With Boston real estate office, 1914-16; editor pub. Dodge City (Kans.) Daily Jour., 1917-18; asst. to chief newspaper sect. War Industries Bd., Washington, 1918; real estate operator in, Boston, Kans. and Fla., 1919-27; publisher Nat. Am. Soc., N.Y.C., 1927-38; dir. relief in Europe for American Friends Com., 1939-42; exec. vice pres., dir. Internat. Commn. Child Refugees, 1939-52; dir. child feeding (Spanish Civil War), 1939-40, 1940-42; mem. bd. Save the Children Fedn., 1950—, vice chmn., 1945-50, sec., 1959-69; radio-TV commentator, 1952-68; prof. current econ. problems Northwood Inst., 1974—; prof. econs. Fuller Theol. Sem., Winona Lake, Ind., summers 1961-63; also editor newsletter Answers to Economic Problems. Author: The Menace of Roosevelt and his Policies, 1936, William Squire Kenyon, 1931, One Humanity, 1943, Brit. edit., 1944, Quaker Service in Modern War, 1950, God, Gold and Government, 1956, Diamonds, Persimmons and Stars, 1964, Dividing the Wealth-Are You Getting Your Share?, 1970, A Saga of America, 1976, How to Stay in Love with One Woman for 70 Years, 1977; also chpts. in books.; Edited and arranged: Air Pioneering in the Arctic, 1928, James W. Ellsworth, a biography, 1929, Lincoln Ellsworth, 1930; Founder, editor-in-chief: monthly jour. Christian Economics, 1950-72; Narrator for: film Children of Tragedy, 1945, and Reconstruction Begins, 1946; Author five hundred papers, 9 thousand editorials; syndicated column Its Up to You, Howard Kershner's Commentary on the News, 1952-79; sermonettes pub. semimonthly in Christian Economics and used in church calendars of 1600 chs. Mem. Am.-African Affairs assn., Nat. Tax Reform Com., Am. Emergency com. Panama Canal, Com. to Unite Am., council advisers, Com. to Restore Constn.; sponsoring com. For Am.; adv. bd. Supreme Ct. Amendment League; mem. Am. Conservative Union; nat. adv. bd. SCALE; sr. adv. bd. Youth for Decency; exec. com. Nat. Com. Food Small Democracies, 1942-49; former dir. CARE; founder, chmn. Temp. Council on Food for European Children, 1943-45; diplomatic mission to principal Latin-Am. capitals, seeking grants for Internat. Children's Fund of UN, 1947-48; one of founders Christian Freedom Found., Inc., pres., 1950-72, chmn. bd., 1972-74; mem. N.Y. bd. dirs. Community Devel. Found.; mem. com. for monetary research and edn. U. Oreg., Eugene.; Mem. Mont Pelerin Soc. Decorated chevalier Order of Leopold, Belgium; Medaille d'Honneur d'Argent des Affaires Etrangers, France; Ordre de Merit Union Internationale de Protection de l'Enfants, Geneva, Switzerland; chevalier Legion of Honor, France; Freedoms found. medal, 1952-57, 59-61, 65, 67, 71-72; recipient citation City of Los Angeles, 1971, and State of Calif., 1973. Mem. Internat. Platform Assn. Republican. Mem. Soc. of Friends (clk. N.Y. yearly meeting of Friends 1945-51). Made more than 300 radio addresses about condition of children in Europe; also weekly news commentator on 325 radio stas., called Howard Kershners Commentary on the News, 1957-75. Donor personal archives U. Oreg., Eugene; co-founder Center for Bus. and Econs., George Fox Coll., Newberg, Oreg. and donor library and personal effects. Home and Office: Box 58 Northwood Inst Cedar Hill TX 75104

KERSHNER, IRVIN, motion picture director; b. Phila., Aug. 29, 1923. Student fine arts, Temple U., U. So. Calif. Documentary film maker USIS, Middle East, 1950-52; now dir., producer; dir., producer, writer Ophito Prodns., Lantana Prodns. Dir., cameraman: TV documentary Confidential File, 1953-55; dir.: movies including Stakeout on Dope Street, Young Captives, Hoodlum Priest, The Luck of Ginger Coffey, The Film-Flam Man, Up the Sandbox, Loving, Spy, The Return of a Man Called Horse, Raid on Entebbe; TV films including Naked City, The Rebel. Office: Tuck Silverberg Mitchel Silverberg and Knupp 1800 Century Park E Los Angeles CA 90067

KERSLAKE, KENNETH ALVIN, art educator, printmaker; b. Mt. Vernon, N.Y., Mar. 8, 1930; s. Archibald and Cecilia fox (Gotterson) K.; m. Sarah Jane Allen, Aug. 25, 1956; children: Scott Paul, Katherine Rachael. Student, Pratt Inst., 1950-53; B.F.A., U. Ill., 1955, M.F.A., 1957. Grad. asst. U. Ill.-Champaign, 1955-57, interim instr., 1957-58; instr. U. Fla., Gainesville, 1958-60, asst. prof. art, 1961-68, assoc. prof., 1969-74, prof., 1974—; workshop lectr. U. Alaska-Fairbanks, 1982, No. Ariz. U., Flagstaff, 1982; artist-in-residence U. Mo.-Columbia, 1980; invited faculty U. Ga. Studies Abroad Program, Cortona, Italy, 1982. Exhibitor one-man shows, Oxford Gallery, Eng., 1978, U.N.D., Grand Forks, 1979, Mint Mus. Gallery, Charlotte, N.C., 1981, U. Alaska-Fairbanks, 1982, U.S. Embassy, Belgrade, Yugoslavia, 1983, group shows, Bklyn. Mus., 1977, Bradford (Eng.) Mus., 1979, So. Graphics Council, 1981, Pratt Graphic Ctr., N.Y.C., 1983; represented in permanent collections, Library of Congress and Nat. Collection, Washington, Bklyn Mus., High Mus., Atlanta, Johnson Wax Collection, Racine, Wis. Recipient Joseph Pennell award Library of Congress, 1975, Associated Am. Artist award Associated Am. Artist Gallery, 1979, Disting. Faculty award Fla. Blue Key-U. Fla., 1979, grantee, Tamarind Found. Inc., 1964. Mem. Soc. Am. Graphic Artists, Boston Printmakers, Print Club Phila., So. Graphic Council, Los Angeles Printmakers Soc. Democrat. Episcopalian. Home: 1114 NW 36th Dr Gainesville FL 32605 Office: FAC 317 Dept Art Coll Fine Arts U Fla Gainesville FL 32611

KERST, DONALD WILLIAM, physicist, educator; b. Galena, Ill., Nov. 1, 1911; s. Herman Samuel and Lilian (Wetz) K.; m. Dorothy Birkett, Aug. 1940; children: Marilyn Elizabeth, Stephen Marshall. B.A., U. Wis., 1934, Ph.D., 1937, D.Sc., 1961; D.Sc., Lawrence Coll., 1942; Dr. honoris causa, U. São Paulo, Brazil. Instr. physics U. Ill., 1938-40, asst. prof., 1940-42, assoc. prof., 1942-43, prof., 1943; war work, Los Alamos, 1943-45; tech. dir. Midwestern Univs. Research Assn., 1953-57; with John Jay Hopkins Lab. for Pure and Applied Sci., Gen. Atomic div. Gen. Dynamics Corp., 1957-62; E.M. Terry prof. physics U. Wis., 1962—. Winner Comstock prize Nat. Acad. Scis. for devel. betatron, 1945, John Scott award, 1946, John Price Wetherill medal Franklin Inst. for devel. of betatron, 1950. Mem. Nat. Acad. Scis., Am. Phys. Soc. (chmn. plasma physics div. 1972), AAAS, Inst. Nav. Home: 1506 Wood Ln Madison WI 53705 also 425 Date Palm Rd Vero Beach FL 32960

KERSTEN, MERLE EUGENE, manufacturing company executive; b. Logan, Iowa, Nov. 18, 1925; m. Billie E. Burgess, June 22, 1947; children: Randall, Jeri, Janet, Vanessa. B.S., Northwestern U., 1946, B.S.C.E., 1948. Mgr. steelform dept. The Ceco Corp., Oak Brook, Ill., 1959-67, gen. mgr. sales, 1967-68, v.p. sales, 1968-70, group v.p., 1970-83, sr. v.p., 1983—; pres. Concrete Reinforcing Steel Inst., Schaumburg, Ill., 1982—. Club: Union League. Home: 1009 E Elizabeth St Naperville IL 60540 Office: 1400 Kensington Rd Oak Brook IL 60521

KERSTING, EDWIN JOSEPH, university dean; b. Ottawa, Ohio, Nov. 4, 1919; s. Alphonse A. and Mary F. K.; m. Billy Kate Walker, Mar. 23, 1946; children: Karl W., Ann L. D.V.M., Ohio State U., 1952; M.S., U. Conn., 1964. Pvt. practice vet. medicine, Charleston, W.Va. and Columbus, Ohio, 1951-62; research asst. U. Conn., Storrs, 1961-62, asst. prof. clin. vet. medicine, state extension veterinarian, 1962-65, asst. dean resident instrn., dir., 1965-66, dir. internat. programs in agr., 1965—, dean, 1966—, dir., 1966—, prof. clin. vet. medicine, dept. pathobiology, 1966—, acting dean designate proposed Sch. Vet. Medicine, 1975-81; mem. adv. bd. to U.S. Sec. Agr. Animal Health Scis. Research Program; bd. overseers Sch. Vet. Medicine, U. Pa.; assoc. mem. univ. bd. trustees, mem. adv. council Coll. Vet. Medicine, Cornell U.; cons. dept. surg. research, adj. mem. research com. Hartford (Conn.) Hosp.; mem. research rev. com. Assn. Northeastern Dirs. Agrl. Experiment Stas.; adv. com. Northeastern Research Center for Wildlife Diseases; cons. Ministry Agr., Belize; adv. com. Conn. Soil Conservation Service; ex-officio bd. overseers Bartlett Arboretum. Contbr. articles to profl. publs. Pres. Conn. Lung Assn., 1977-79; exec. com. Eastern States Expn., 1968—. Served with U.S. Army and Am. Field Service, 1942-44. Mem. AAAS, AVMA, N.Y. Acad. Scis., Conn. Vet. Med. Assn., Royal Soc. Health, Sigma Xi, Alpha Zeta, Epsilon Sigma Phi, Gamma Sigma Delta, Phi Zeta, Phi Kappa Phi. Congregationalist. Home: 97C Sycamore Ln Manchester CT 06040 Office: Coll Agr and Natural Resources U Conn Storrs CT 06268

KERTESZ, ANDRE, photographer; b. Budapest, Hungary, July 2, 1894; came to U.S., 1936, naturalized, 1944; s. Leopold and Ernestine (Hoffman) K.; m. Elizabeth Sali, June 17, 1933. Grad., Hungarian Acad. Commerce, Budapest, 1912; self-taught in photography. Photography, 1912—; accounts clk. Budapest Stock Exchange, 1912-14, 18-25; free-lance photographer for Franfurt Illustrierie, Berliner Illustrierte, Uhu, Strasburger Illustrierte, Le Nazionale de Fiorenza, Vu, Sourier, The Times (London), also others, Paris, 1925-35; contract photographer Keystone Studios, N.Y.C., 1936-37; free-lance mag. photographer Harper's Bazaar, Vogue, Town and Country, Am. Mag., Collier's Coronet, Look, also others, N.Y.C., 1937-49; contract photography Conde Nast Publs., N.Y.C., 1949-62, free-lance photographer, 1962—. Contbr. photographs to Am. and European mags.; one-man shows include, Sacre du Printemps, Paris, 1927, Art Inst. Chgo., 1946, Bibliotheque Nationale, Paris, 1963, IV Mostra Biennale Internazionale della Fotografia, Venice, Italy, 1964, Mus. Modern Art, N.Y.C., Serpentine Gallery, London, 1979, Salford U. (Eng.), 1980, Galerie Wilde, Cologne, W.Ger., 1981, Jane Corkin Gallery, Toronto, Ont., Can., E. Houk Gallery, Chgo., 1982, Chrysler Mus., Norfolk, Va., 1983, exhibited in group shows including, Hayward Gallery, London, 1978, Gallerie Zabriskie, Paris, 1979, Centre Culturel, Boulogne-Billancourt, France, 1981, Deja Vue Galleries, Toronto, Kestner-Gesellschaft, Hanover, W.Ger., 1982, Art Inst. Chgo.; represented in permanent collections, Mus. Modern Art, N.Y.C., Internat. Mus. Photography, George Eastman House, Rochester, N.Y., Smithsonian Instn., Washington, Carpenter Ctr., Harvard U., Cambridge, Mass., Detroit Inst. Arts, Art Inst. Chgo., Ctr. Creative Photography, U. Ariz., Tucson, Musee d'Art Moderne, Paris; author: Enfants, 1933, Paris Vu Par Andre Kertesz, 1934, Nos Amies Les Betes, 1936, Les Cathedrales du Vin, 1937, Day of Paris, 1945, Andre Kertesz, Photographer, 1964, On Reading, 1972, Sixty Years of Photography, 1973, J'Aime Paris, 1974, Washington Square, 1975, Of New York, 1976, Distortions, 1976. Decorated comdr. Order Arts and Letters (France); recipient photography competition prize Borsszem Janko mag., Budapest, 1916, Silver medal Expn. Coloniale, Paris, 1930, Gold medal 4th Mostra Biennale Internazionale della Fotografia, Venice, 1963, N.Y.C. Mayor's award of honor for arts and culture, 1977, award U. Salford (Eng.), 1980; Guggenheim fellow, 1974. Mem. Am. Soc. Mag. Photographers (mem. of honor). Office: 2 Fifth Ave New York NY 10011 *

KERTESZ, LOUIS, food company executive; b. Bekesszentandras, Hungary, Aug. 20, 1936; s. Lajos and Maria (Taschler) K.; m. Magdolna Percza, Dec. 5, 1959; children: Magdolna Ava, Louis M. B.S. in Chem. Engring., U. Vienna, 1958; B.A. in Bus., U. Wis., 1966. Produce dir. Kohl Corp., Milw., 1970-75; regional dir. A&P, Indpls., 1975-77, v.p. produce, Montevale, N.J., 1977-80; pres. M.K. Inernat. Food Inc., Montevale, 1983—. Bd. dirs. Am. Hungarian Found.; cons. Am. Soccer Assn. Recipient M. V. P. European Soccer Cup, Madrid, 1977, Outstanding Performer A&P, 1979, Outstanding Achievement

Dept. of Citrus, 1980, Produce Marketer of Yr., 1980; named Ky. col. Mem. Produce Mktg. Assn. (chmn.), United Fresh Fruit and Vegetable Assn. (dir.). Home: 124 Deer Trail N Ramsey NJ 07446 Office: M K Internat Food Inc 1 Paragon Dr Montevale NJ 07645

KERTH, LEROY T., physics educator; b. Visalia, Calif., Nov. 23, 1928; s. Lewis John and Frances (Niccolls) K.; m. Ruth Lorraine Littlefield, Nov. 19, 1950; children: Norman Lewis, Randall Thomas, Christine Jane, Bradley Niccolls. A.B. in Physics, U. Calif., Berkeley, 1950, Ph.D., 1957. Mem. staff Lawrence Berkeley Lab, U. Calif., Berkeley, 1950-59, sr. scientist, 1959-61; asso. prof. physics U. Calif., Berkeley, 1961-65, prof., 1965—, asso. dean Coll. Letters and Scis., 1966-70, spl. asst. to chancellor, 1970-71, assoc. dir. for computing div. Fellow Am. Phys. Soc. Home: 5 Los Conejos St Orinda CA 94563 Office: Physics Dept U Calif Berkeley CA 94701

KERTTULA, JALMAR, state senator; b. Milw., Apr. 6, 1928; m. Helen Joyce Kerttula; 2 children. Mem. Alaska Ho. of Reps., 5 terms; speaker of the house 6th Legislature; mem. Alaska State Senate, Juneau, 1972—, Senate pres., 1980—. Former mem. Dept. Agr. Nat. Soils and Water Conservation Bd.; former bd. dirs. U. Alaska Alumni Bd.; mem. Alaska Investment Adv. Bd., Gov.'s Pipeline Commn. Democrat. Office: Alaska Senate State Capitol Juneau AK 99811 *

KERTZ, HUBERT LEONARD, telephone co. exec.; b. San Francisco, July 11, 1910; s. Hubert J. and Laura V. (Seavey) K.; m. Justine Jankowsky, July 28, 1934; children—Brenda L., Pamela. A.B., Stanford, 1934, E.E., 1936. With Pacific Tel. & Tel. Co., 1926-42, 46-61, asst. v.p., 1953-58, v.p., 1958-61; asst. v.p. AT&T, 1961-64, v.p., 1964-75; pres., mng. dir. Am. Bell Internat. Inc., 1975—. Bd. dirs. Hwy. Users Fedn., Hwy. Safety Found. Served from lt. (j.g.) to comdr. USNR, 1942-46; PTO. Decorated Bronze Star. Fellow I.E.E.E.; mem. Armed Forces Communication Assn., Am. Mgmt. Assn., Calif. C. of C., Soc. Calif. Pioneers. Club: Econ. (N.Y.C.). Office: 5000 Hadley Rd South Plainfield NJ 07080

KERWIN, JOSEPH PETER, physician, former astronaut; b. Oak Park, Ill., Feb. 19, 1932; m. Shirley Ann Good; children: Sharon, Joanna, Kristina. B.A., Coll. Holy Cross, 1953; M.D., Northwestern U., 1957. Flight surgeon U.S. Navy, 1958—; capt. naval aviator, 1962-65, astronaut, 1965-83; dir. Space and Life Scis., 1983—. Mem. Skylab I and II crews. Address: NASA Lyndon B Johnson Space Center Space and Life Scis Office Code SA Houston TX 77058 *

KERWIN, LARKIN, physics educator; b. Quebec, Que., Can., June 22, 1924; s. Timothy and Catherine (Lonergan) K.; m. Maria G. Turcot, June 10, 1950; children: Lupita, Alan, Larkin, Terrence, Rosa Maria, Gregory, Timothy, Guillermina. B.S., St. Francis Xavier U., 1944, LL.D., 1970; M.S., M.I.T., 1946; D.Sc., Laval U., 1949, U. B.C., 1973, McGill U., 1974, Meml. U. Nfld., 1978, U. Ottawa, 1981, Royal Mil. Coll., Kingston, 1982, LL.D., U. Toronto, 1973, U. Alta., 1983, Dalhousie U., 1983; D.L., Concordia U., 1976; D.C.L. (hon.), Bishop's U., 1978. Asst. prof. physics Laval U., 1948-51, assoc. prof., 1951-56, prof., 1956—, chmn. dept., 1961-67, vice-dean faculty scis., 1967-69, vice-rector, 1969-72, rector, 1972-77; v.p. Natural Scis. and Engring. Council Can., 1978-80; pres. Nat. Research Council Can., 1980—; dir. Cape Breton Devel Corp.; research physicist Geotech. Corp., Cambridge, 1945-46. Author: Atomic Physics, an Introduction, 1963; also articles. Decorated Lt. Gov.'s medal, 1941; Gov. Gen. medal, 1944; Pariseau medal, 1965; Centenary medal, 1967; Prix David, 1951; Jubilee medal, 1977; knight comdr. Equestrian Order Holy Sepulchre Jerusalem; also knight grand cross; officer Order of Can.; also companion; Laval Alumni medal, 1978; Gold Medal Can. Council Profl. Engrs., 1982. Fellow Royal Soc. Can. (pres. 1976), Royal Soc. Arts, AAAS, Am. Inst. Physics; mem. Internat. Union Pure and Applied Physics (sec.-gen.), Assn. Canadienne-Francaise pour l'avancement des sciences, Assn. Univs. and Colls. Can. (pres. 1974-75), Am. Phys. Soc., Corp. Profl. Engrs. Quebec, Sociedad Mexicana Fisica, Canadian Assn. Physicists (pres. 1955, medal 1969), Sigma Xi. Club: Cercle Universitaire (Quebec). Home: 2166 Parc Bourbonniere Sillery PQ G1T 1B4 Canada

KERWIN, WILLIAM JAMES, electrical engineering educator, consultant; b. Portage, Wis., Sept. 27, 1922; s. James William and Nina Elizabeth (Haight) K.; m. Madolyn Lee Lyons, Aug. 31, 1947; children: Dorothy E., Deborah K., David W. B.S., U Redlands, 1948; M.S., Stanford U., 1954, Ph.D., 1967. Aero. research scientist NACA, Moffett Field, Calif., 1948-59; chief measurements research br. NASA, Moffett Field, Calif., 1959-62, chief space tech. br., 1962-64, chief electronics research br., 1964-70; head electronics dept. Stanford Linear Accelerator Ctr., 1962; prof. elec. engring. U. Ariz., Tucson, 1969—; cons. Burr-Brown Research Corp., Los Alamos Nat. Lab. Author: (with others) Active Filters, 1970, Handbook Measurement Science, 1982; contbr. articles to profl. jours.; patentee in field. Served to capt. USAAF, 1942-46. Recipient Invention NASA, 1969, 70, fellow NASA, 1966-67. Fellow IEEE. Republican. Episcopalian. Home: 1981 Shalimar Way Tucson AZ 85704 Office: U Ariz Dept Elec and Computer Engring Tucson AZ 85721

KERXTON, ALAN SMITH, lawyer; b. Balt., Mar. 19, 1938; s. Benjamin and Eva (Smith) K.; m. Leslie Lurie, Aug. 2, 1961; children—Amy Lynn, Susan Deborah, Katherine Diane. B.A., Ohio State U., 1960, J.D., 1962. Bar: D.C. bar 1963. Atty. corporate reorgn. br. SEC, 1963-66; pvt. practice, Washington, 1966—; prin. firm Levitan, Ezrin, West & Kerxton (Chartered), 1976—; lectr. Cath. U. Am. Law Sch., fall 1973. Served with AUS, 1962-63. Mem. Am., D.C., Montgomery County bar assns. Home: 11815 Beekman Pl Potomac MD 20854 Office: 7315 Wisconsin Ave Bethesda MD 20014

KESEY, KEN, writer; b. La Hunta, Colo., Sept. 17, 1935; s. Fred and Geneva (Smith) K.; m. Norma Faye Haxby, May 20, 1956; children: Shannon, Zane, Jed, Sunshine. B.S., U. Oreg., 1957; postgrad., Stanford U., 1958-59. Pres. Intrepid Trips, Inc., 1964; editor, pub. mag. Spit in the Ocean, 1974—. Author: One Flew Over the Cuckoo's Nest, 1962, Sometimes a Great Notion, 1964, Garage Sale, 1973. Address: 85829 Ridgeway Rd Pleasant Hill OR 97455

KESLER, ALONZO PRATT, lawyer; b. Salt Lake City, Apr. 26, 1905; s. Alonzo Pratt and Donnette (Smith) K.; m. Ellen Tourssen, June 30, 1939; children: Pamela, John Tourssen. Student, U. Liege, Belgium, 1926-27; A.B., U. Utah, 1930, J.D., 1933. Bar: Utah 1933. Since practiced in, Salt Lake City; mem. firm Callister Kesler & Callister; city pros. atty., Salt Lake City, 1935-40, asst. city atty., 1942-52, former atty. gen., Utah, U.S. atty. Dist., 1953-61; commr. Utah State Tax Commn.; Mem. Nat. Conf. Commrs. Uniform State Laws, 1957; chmn. Utah Commn. on Uniform State Laws. Mem. exec. com. Community Welfare Council, 1957-59; Pres. emigration league Western Baseball Assn.; chmn. speakers com. A.R.C., 1945, Nat. Found. Infantile Paralysis campaign, 1950; chmn. state, county campaigns Am. Cancer Soc.; Pres. Young Republicans, 1937-38; Rep. candidate for atty. gen. Utah, 1944-48; chmn. Utah Rep. Com., 1950-53; mem. Rep. Nat. Com., 1952-53; chmn. state del. Rep. Nat. Conv., 1952; Bd. dirs. Legal Aid Soc., Salt Lake City, 1934-71, pres., 1964-66. Recipient Merit of Honor award U. Utah Emeritus Club, 1978. Mem. Utah State Bar (pres. 1959-60, chmn. jud. council 1966—), ABA (mem. jr. bar council 1937-39, vice chmn. 1940, mem. spl. com. on jud. conduct code 1974-75, mem. council gen. practice sect., mem. ho. of dels., mem. spl. com. sponsored Keog Bill), Fed. Bar Assn. (pres. Utah chpt. 1970-71, nat. 1st v.p. 1976-77), Salt Lake County Bar Assn. (pres. 1945-46) bar assns), Pi Kappa Alpha. Clubs: Salt Lake Country, Alta, Kiwanis. Home: 910 Donner Way Apt 601 Salt Lake City UT 84108 Office: Kennecott Bldg Salt Lake City UT 84133

KESLER, CLYDE ERVIN, engineering educator; b. Dewey, Ill., May 7, 1922; s. Roy Francis and Helen (Deffenbaugh) K.; m. Mary Anne Kirk, July 20, 1947; children: Philip Roy, David Clyde. B.S. in Civil Engring., U. Ill., 1943, M.S. in Structural Engring., 1946. Engr. aide I.C.R.R., Champaign, Ill., 1946-47; faculty U. Ill., Urbana, 1947—, prof. mechanics and civil engring., 1962—; pres. Am. Concrete Inst., Detroit, 1967-68; cons. concrete and reinforced concrete problems to pvt. cos., govt. agys., 1949—. Author: (with Taylor, Corten and Wetenkamp) Mechanical Behavior of Solids, 1959; also articles. Served to maj. C.E., U.S. Army, 1943-46. Recipient Alfred E. Lindau award Am. Concrete Inst., 1970, Halliburton Engring. Edn. Leadership award U. Ill., 1982. Fellow ASCE, Ill. Acad. Engring. Anglers; mem. Am. Soc. Engring. Edn., ASTM (Sanford E. Thompson award 1958), Wire Reinforcing Inst. (hon.), Am. Concrete Inst. (hon.), Nat. Acad. Engring., Chi Epsilon, Tau Beta Pi, Phi Kappa Phi, Sigma Xi. Home: RFD 3 Box 314 Champaign IL 61820 Office: Newmark Lab Civil Engring 208 N Romine St U Ill Urbana IL 61821

KESSEL, BRINA, educator, ornithologist; b. Ithaca, N.Y., Nov. 20, 1925; d. Marcel and Quinta (Cattell) K.; m. Raymond B. Roof, June 19, 1957 (dec. 1968). B.S. (Albert R. Brand Bird Song Found. scholar), Cornell U., 1947, Ph.D., 1951; M.S. (Wis. Alumni Research Found. fellow), U. Wis.-Madison, 1949. Student asst. Patuxent Research Refuge, 1946; student teaching asst. Cornell U., 1945-47, grad. asst., 1947-48, 49-51; instr. biol. sci. U. Alaska, summer 1951, asst. prof. biol. sci., 1951-54, assoc. prof. zoology, 1954-59. prof. zoology, 1959—, head dept. biol. scis., 1957-66, dean, 1961-72, curator terrestrial vertebrate mus. collections, 1972—, adminstrv. asso. for acad. programs, grad. and undergrad., dir. acad. advising, office of chancellor, 1973-80; project dir. U. Alaska ecol. investigation for AEC Project Chariot, 1959-63; ornithol. investigations NW Alaska pipeline, 1976-81, Susitna Hydroelectric Project, 1980-83. Contbr. articles to profl. jours. Fellow AAAS, Am. Ornithologists Union (v.p. 1977), Arctic Inst. N.Am.; mem. Wilson, Cooper ornith. socs., Pacific Northwest Bird and Mammal Soc., Pacific Seabird Group, Sigma Xi (pres. U. Alaska 1957), Phi Kappa Phi, Sigma Delta Epsilon. Home: Box 80211 College AK 99708

KESSEL, JOHN HOWARD, educator, polit. scientist; b. Dayton, Ohio, Oct. 13, 1928; s. Arthur V. and Helen (Hopkins) K.; m. Margaret Sarah Wagner, Aug. 22, 1954; children—Robert Arthur, Thomas John. Student, Purdue U., 1946-48; B.A., Ohio State U., 1950; Ph.D., Columbia, 1958. Instr. Amherst and Mt. Holyoke colls., 1957-58; instr., asst. prof. Amherst Coll., 1958-61; asst. prof. U. Wash., 1961-65; Arthur E. Braun prof. polit. sci. Allegheny Coll., Meadville, Pa., 1965-70; prof. polit. sci. Ohio State U., Columbus, 1970—; vis. prof. U. Calif., San Diego, 1977, U. Wash., 1980, Am. U., 1980; vis. scholar Am. Enterprise Inst., 1980-82. Author: The Goldwater Coalition: Republican Strategies in 1964, 1968, The Domestic Presidency, 1975, Presidential Campaign Politics: Coalition Strategies and Citizen Response, 1980; Co-editor: Micropolitics-Individual and Group Level Concepts, 1970; editor: Am. Jour. Polit. Sci, 1974-76; Contbr. articles to profl. jours. Mem. exec. council Inter-Univ. Consortium for Polit. Research, 1964-65, 67-68; Exec. dir. Nixon-Lodge Vols. Mass., 1960; dir. arts, scis. div. Republican Nat. Com., 1963-64. Served with USNR, 1950-53. Mem. Am. Polit. Sci. Assn. (exec. council 1969-71), Midwest Polit. Sci. Assn. (pres. 1978-79). Home: 516 E Schreyer Pl Columbus OH 43214

KESSELHAUT, ARTHUR MELVYN, financial consultant; b. Newark, May 18, 1935; s. Harry and Rela (Wolk) K.; m. Nancy Slater, June 17, 1956; children—Stuart Lee, Amy Beth. B.S. in Bus. Adminstrn, Syracuse (N.Y.) U., 1958; postgrad., N.Y. U. With Coopers & Lybrand, N.Y.C., 1958-64; treas., sr. v.p. Anchor Group, Elizabeth, N.J., 1964-79, also Anchor Capital Fund, Anchor Daily Income Fund, Inc., Anchor Growth Fund, Inc., Anchor Income Fund, Inc., Anchor Spectrum Fund, Inc., Fundamental Investors, Inc., Westminster Fund, Washington Nat. Fund, Inc., Anchor Pension Mgmt. Co.; sr. v.p. corp. devel. USLIFE Corp., N.Y.C., 1979-82, exec. v.p.; chief adminstrv. officer, 1982—. Served with AUS. Decorated Commendation medal. Address: 47 Nance Rd West Orange NJ 07052

KESSELMAN, JONATHAN RHYS, economics educator, public policy researcher; b. Columbus, Ohio, Mar. 17, 1946; s. Louis C. and Jennie K.; m. Sheila Kaplan, Mar. 12, 1973. B.A. withhonors, Oberlin Coll., 1968; Ph.D. in Econs., MIT, 1972. Asst. prof. econs. U. B.C., Vancouver, Can., 1972-76, assoc. prof., 1976-81, prof., 1981—; research assoc. Inst. for Research on Poverty, Madison, Wis., 1974-75; vis. scholar Delhi Sch. Econs., New Delhi, 1978-79; cons. econs., 1973-81. Author: Financing Canadian Unemployment Insurance, 1983; editorial bd.: Can. Taxation: Jour. of Policy, 1979-82; contbr. numerous articles on taxation, income security, employment policy to profl. jours. Bd. dirs. Tibetan Refugee Aid Soc., Vancouver, 1980-82; mem. adv. panel Can. Minster of Employment and Immigration, Ottawa, Ont., 1982-83. Sr. scholar Oberlin Coll., 1967-68; NSF fellow, 1968-70; grantee U.S. Dept. Labor, 1971-72; leave fellow Can. Council, (locat.) New Delhi, 1978-79; grantee Social Sci. and Humanities Research Council Can., 1983-84. Mem. Am. Econ. Assn., Can. Econs. Assn., Can. Tax Found. Home: 3330 W 23d Ave Vancouver BC Canada V6S 1K3 Office: Dept Econs U BC 997-1873 E Mall Vancouver BC Canada V6T 1Y2

KESSELMAN, MARK JONATHAN, political science educator, writer; b. N.Y.C., Aug. 27, 1938; ss. Paul and Anne (Price) K. B.A., Cornell U., 1959; M.A., U. Chgo., 1963. From asst. prof. to assoc. prof. Columbia U., N.Y.C., 1965-72, prof., 1972—. Author: The Ambiguous Consus, 1967, (with others) The Politics of Power, 1979, French Politics and Public Policy, 1980; editor: The French Workers Movement, 1984. Fellow Guggenheim Found., 1975, Rockefeller Found., 1980. Mem. Am. Polit. Sci. Assn., Phi Beta Kappa. Office: Columbia U 420 W 118th St New York NY 10027

KESSELMAN, THEODORE LEONARD, banker; b. Youngstown, Ohio, May 1, 1932; s. Leonard and Clara (Brailovsky) K.; m. Shirley Hope Cohen, June 14, 1953; children: Suzanne Lynn, Stuart Jonathan. A.B. magna cum laude, Harvard U., 1954, LL.B., 1957. With Bankers Trust Co., N.Y.C., 1957—, sr. corp. trust adminstr., asst. sec. trust dept., asst. v.p. banking ops., 1957-66, head adminstrv. services banking ops., 1965-66, v.p. in charge securities ops., 1966-68, asst. to exec. v.p., 1969-70, asst. to office of chmn., 1970-72, v.p., head strategic analysis div., 1972-73, 1st v.p., head corp. devel. dept., 1973-74, sr. v.p., 1974-79, exec. v.p., 1979—; dir. BT Leasing Corp., BT Leasing Services, Inc.; mem. panel of arbitrators N.Y. Stock Exchange, N.Y. Futures Exchange. Bd. dirs. Arts and Bus. Council; trustee Mus. Am. Folk Art; trustee, mem. exec. com. Youth Symphony Orch. N.Y. Mem. Am. Bankers Assn. (exec. com. corp. planning), ACLU, Harvard Alumni Assn. N.Y., Harvard Law Sch. Assn., Phi Beta Kappa. Jewish. Home: 193-40 McLaughlin Ave Holliswood NY 11423 Office: 280 Park Ave New York NY 10017

KESSEN, WILLIAM, educator, psychologist; b. Key West, Fla., Jan. 18, 1925; s. Herman Lowry and Maria Angela (Lord) K.; m. Marion Lord, June 10, 1950; children: Judith, Deborah, Anne, Peter Christopher, Andrew Lord, John Michael. B.S., U. Fla., 1948; Sc.M., Brown U., 1950; Ph.D., Yale U., 1952. Postdoctoral fellow Child Study Center, Yale U., 1952-54, faculty depts. psychology and pediatrics, 1954-76, Eugene Higgins prof. psychology, 1976—, chmn. dept. psychology, 1977-80, prof. pediatrics, 1978—, acting univ. sec., 1980-81; mem. intellective processes research com. Social Sci. Research Council, 1959-63, chmn., 1961-63. Author: (with G. Mandler) The Language of Psychology, 1959, The Child, 1965, Childhood in China, 1975, (with M.H. Bornstein) Psychological Development from Infancy, 1979; editor: Mussen's Handbook of Child Psychology, vol. 3, 1983; contbr. articles to profl. jours. Mem. Carnegie Council on Children, 1973-77. Fellow Center Advanced Study Behavioral Sciences, 1959-60; Guggenheim fellow, 1970-71. Fellow AAAS, Am. Psychol. Assn. (pres. div. 7 1979-80); mem. Soc. Research Child Devel., Soc. Exptl. Psychologists. Home: 30 Halstead Ln Branford CT 06405 Office: Dept Psychology Yale U Box 11A Yale Sta New Haven CT 06520

KESSLER, EDWIN, meteorologist, nat. lab. adminstr.; b. N.Y.C., Dec. 2, 1928; s. Edwin and Marie Rosa (Weil) K.; m. Lottie Catherine Menger; children: Austin Rainier, Thomas Russell. A.B., Columbia Coll., 1950; S.M., MIT, 1952, Sc.D., 1957. Research scientist USAF Cambridge Research Labs., Bedford, Mass., 1954-61; dir. atmospheric physics div. Travelers Research Center, Hartford, Conn., 1961-64; dir. Nat. Severe Storms Lab., Norman, Okla., 1964—; adj. prof. U. Okla., 1964—; vis. prof. M.I.T., 1975-76. Past asso. editor: Jour. Applied Meteorology; Contbr. articles to profl. jours. Served with U.S. Army, 1947-48. Recipient award for outstanding authorship NOAA, 1971. Fellow Am. Meteorol. Soc. (past pres. Greater Boston br., nat. councilor 1966-69, past mem. com. on severe local storms, past chmn. com. on weather radar, cert. cons. meteorologist), AAAS; mem. Royal Meteorol. Soc. (fgn.), Weather Modification Assn., Am. Geophys. Union, Sigma Xi. Office: 1313 Halley Circle Norman OK 73069

KESSLER, GEORGE WILLIAM, mfg. co. cons.; b. St. Louis, Mar. 1, 1908; s. William Henry and Blanche M. (Pougher) K.; m. Alice Mae Maxwell, July 28, 1951; children—Judith Ann Green, William Clarkson. B.S. in Mech. Engring, U. Ill., 1930. With Babcock & Wilcox Co., Barberton, Ohio, 1930—, v.p. power generation group, 1961—. Contbr. articles to profl. jours. Fellow ASME; mem. Am. Standards Assn. (dir.), Soc. Naval Architects and Marine Engrs. (Joseph H. Linard award 1949), Am. Soc. Naval Engrs., Franklin Inst., Nat. Acad. Engring., Welding Research Council, Tau Beta Pi, Phi Eta Sigma, Sigma Tau, Pi Tau Sigma, Alpha Sigma Phi. Clubs: Propeller, Cornell (N.Y.C.). Patentee in field. Home: 720 Williams Dr Winter Park FL 32789

KESSLER, HERBERT LEON, art historian, educator; b. Chgo., July 20, 1941; s. Ben and Bertha K.; m. Johanna Zacharias, Apr. 24, 1976; 1 dau., Morisa. A.B., U. Chgo., 1961; M.F.A., Princeton U., 1963, Ph.D., 1965. Asst. prof. U. Chgo., 1965-68; asso. prof., 1968-73, prof., 1973-76, chmn. dept. art, univ. dir. fine arts, 1973-76; prof., chmn. dept. art Johns Hopkins U., 1976—. Author: The Illustrated Bibles from Tours, 1977, French and Flemish Illuminated Manuscripts, 1969. Sr. fellow Dumbarton Oaks, Washington.; Woodrow Wilson fellow; Inst. Advanced Study fellow; Am. Council Learned Socs. fellow; Am. Philos. Soc. fellow. Mem. Coll. Art Assn., Medieval Acad. Am., Phi Beta Kappa. Home: 2430 20th St NW Washington DC 20009 Office: Johns Hopkins U Baltimore MD 21218

KESSLER, IRVING ISAR, epidemiologist; b. Chelsea, Mass., Mar. 22, 1931; s. Haim Mordecai and Annie (Lown) K.; m. Laure Aurelian, Nov. 25, 1970; children: Abigail Eve, Amalia Deborah. A.B., N.Y. U., 1952; M.A., Harvard U., 1955, Dr.P.H., 1966; M.D., Stanford U., 1960; M.P.H., Columbia U., 1962. Diplomate: Nat. Bd. Med. Examiners, Am. Bd. Preventive. Medicine. Intern USPHS Hosp., N.Y.C., 1960-61; resident in preventive medicine Harvard U., 1962-64; asst. in medicine Peter Bent Brigham Hosp., Boston, 1962-64; instr. environ. medicine, clin. fellow in surgery SUNY Downstate Med. Center, Bklyn., 1964-66; asst. prof. chronic diseases Johns Hopkins U., Balt., 1966-69, asso. prof., 1969-72, prof. epidemiology, 1973-78; prof., chmn. dept. epidemiology and preventive medicine U. Md., Balt., 1978—; sci. adv. com. Am. Cancer Soc., 1978-82; mem. med. bd. U. Md. Hosp.; bd. dirs. Md. Med. Research, Inc.; cons., vis. prof. Univs. Heidelberg, Oxford, London, Zagreb, Jerusalem, Karachi, Lahore, Madras, New Delhi, Tokyo, Kyoto, Osaka, Caracas, Mexico City, Laval; cons. WHO, Internat. Agy. Research in Cancer; panel mem. Nat. Cancer Plan, 1972-75. Author: The Community as an Epidemiologic Laboratory, 1970, Cancer in the United States, 1972, Cancer Control: Advances in Screening, Diagnosis and Therapy, 1980; asso. editor: Am. Jour. Epidemiology, 1973—; contbr. articles to sci. jours., chpts. to books. Bd. dirs. Israel Cancer Research Found., Gov.'s Council on Toxic Substances. Served with U.S. Army, 1948-49; med. dir. (res.) USPHS, 1948-49. Recipient Faculty Research award Am. Cancer Soc., 1972-77. Fellow Am. Coll. Preventive Medicine, Am. Epidemiol. Soc., N.Y. Acad. Sci., AAAS; mem. Am. Soc. Preventive Oncology (dir.), Assn. Tchrs. of Preventive Medicine (dir.), Md. Inst. Public Health Research, Soc. of Hygiene (pres. 1977-78), Md. Gerontological Assn. (pres. 1984-85), Phi Beta Kappa, Sigma Xi. Jewish. Research on cancer, diabetes mellitus, Parkinson's disease, congenital malformations, health care evaluation, gerontology, health info. mgmt., phys. impairment. Home: 3404 Bancroft Rd Baltimore MD 21215 Office: 655 W Baltimore St Baltimore MD 21201 *Epidemiology is the scientific discipline underlying preventive medicine which bridges the gap between medical science and human health. In an era of escalating health costs and diminishing faith in the medical care system, my professional career has been dedicated to the development of preventive medicine as an academic discipline and instrument of public health policy. Of equal concern to me is the enhancement of preventive medicine as a rewarding career for the finest of our nation's young physicians.*

KESSLER, JACQUES ISAAC, gastroenterologist, educator; b. Rousse, Bulgaria, May 23, 1929; emigrated to Can., 1963, naturalized, 1966; s. Isaac Joseph and Liza Leah (Schwartz) K.; m. Roslyn Norma Sobcov, Nov. 21, 1965; children: Liza Daphna, Linda Ruth, Audrey Joan, Joseph Isaac. Student, Nat. U., Sofia, Bulgaria, 1947-50; M.D., Hadassah Med. Sch., Hebrew U., Jerusalem, 1955. Cert. specialist in internal medicine and gastroenterology Royal Coll. Physicians, Can. Intern Beilinson Hosp., Petach Tikva, Israel, 1954-55, resident in internal medicine, 1955-59; resident, research fellow in gastroenterology and metabolism Mt. Sinai Hosp., N.Y.C., 1959-63; resident internal medicine and gastroenterology Jewish Gen. Hosp., Montreal, Que., Can., 1963-67; sr. physician, dir. div. gastroenterology Royal Victoria Hosp., Montreal, 1967—; prof. medicine McGill U., Montreal, 1972—; cons. to hosps. Asso. editor: Can. Jour. Physiology and Pharmacology, 1968-73; contbr. numerous articles to profl. jours., chpts. to books. Recipient L. Doljansky Gold medal Hebrew U., 1955, Med. Research Council Can. research asso., 1968—, grantee, 1964—; USPHS grantee, 1967-70; Queen Elizabeth II Silver Jubilee medal Gov. Gen. Can., 1977. Fellow Royal Coll. Physicians Can., Am. Coll. Gastroenterology; mem. Am. Soc. Clin. Investigation, AAAS, Am. Fedn. Clin. Research, Am. Gastroenterol. Assn., Can. Soc. Clin. Investigation, Can. Med. Assn., Can. Assn. Gastroenterology. Jewish.

Home: 624 Carleton Ave Westmount PQ H3Y 2Y2 Canada Office: One Westmount Sq Westmount PQ H3Z 2P9 Canada

KESSLER, JOHN OTTO, physicist, educator; b. Vienna, Austria, Nov. 26, 1928; came to U.S., 1940, naturalized, 1946; s. Jacques and Alice Blanca (Neuhut) K.; m. Eva M. Bondy, Sept. 9, 1950; children: Helen J., Steven J. A.B., Columbia U., 1949, Ph.D., 1953. With RCA Corp., Princeton, N.J., 1952-66, sr. mem. tech. staff, 1960-66, mgr. grad. recruiting, 1964-66; prof. physics U. Ariz., Tucson, 1966—; Vis. research asso. Princeton, 1962-64; sr. vis. fellow, vis. prof. physics U. Leeds, Eng., 1972-73; vis. prof. Technische Hogeschool Delft, Netherlands, spring 1979; Fulbright fellow dept. applied math. and theoretical physics Cambridge U., Eng., 1983-84. Contbr. articles to tech. jours. Fellow AAAS; mem. Am. Phys. Soc., Phi Beta Kappa. Patentee in field. Home: 2740 E Camino La Zorrela Tucson AZ 85718 Office: Physics Dept PAS Bldg U Ariz Tucson AZ 85721

KESSLER, JOHN WHITAKER, real estate consultant; b. Cin., Mar. 7, 1936; s. Charles Wilmont and Elisabeth (Whitaker) K.; m. Charlotte Hamilton Power, Aug. 8, 1964; children: Catherine, Elizabeth, Jane. B.S., Coll. Bus. Adminstrn. Ohio State U., 1958. Mem. sales dept. Armstrong Cork Co., Lancaster, Pa., 1958-59; mgr. spl. products div. M & R Dietetics Labs., Columbus, Ohio, 1959-62; co-founder, mng. partner Multicon, Columbus, 1962-70; pres. Multicon Communities div. Multicon Properties, Inc., 1970-72; prin. John W. Kessler Co., Columbus, 1972—; pres. Marsh & McLennan Real Estate Advs., Inc., 1980—; dir. Ltd. Stores, Inc., TriSouth Investments Inc., Rax Restaurants, Inc.; Mem. Fed. Res. Bd. Cleve. Pres. Children's Hosp. Research Found; bd. dirs. Columbus Mus. Art; pres. Spoleto USA, Charleston, S.C.; chmn. bd. Ohio State U. Devel. Fund. Mem. Columbus C. of C. (chmn.). Office: John W Kessler Co 100 E Broad St Suite 1501 Columbus OH 43215

KESSLER, KARL GUNTHER, physicist; b. Hamburg, Germany, Aug. 21, 1919; came to U.S., 1926, naturalized, 1933; s. Gunther and Anna (Schneider) K.; m. Elizabeth Louise Kefgen, June 28, 1944; children—Heidi Ann, Susan Mary. A.B., U. Mich., 1941, M.S., 1942, Ph.D. in Physics, 1947. Asst., instr., research physicist U. Mich., 1942-48; physicist Nat. Bur. Standards, 1948—, chief spectroscopy sect., 1959-62, chief atomic physics div., 1962-70, chief optical physics div., 1970-77, dir. Center for Absolute Phys. Quantities, 1977—. Recipient Exceptional Service award Dept. Commerce, 1962. Fellow Am. Phys. Soc., Optical Soc. Am. (pres. 1969); mem. Am. Astron. Soc., Internat. Astron. Union, AAAS, Acad. Sci. Washington, Philos. Soc. Washington, Phi Beta Kappa, Sigma Xi. Home: 5927 Anniston Rd Bethesda MD 20817 Office: Nat Bur Standards Washington DC 20234

KESSLER, MILTON, English language educator, poet; b. Bklyn., May 9, 1930; s. Arthur and Elizabeth (Racow) K.; m. Sonia Berer, Aug. 24, 1952; children: David Lawrence, Paula Nan, Daniel Solomon. B.A. magna cum laude, U. Buffalo, 1957; M.A., U. Wash., 1962; postgrad., Ohio State U., 1959-63. Lectr. in English Queens Coll., City U. N.Y., 1963-65; mem. faculty State U. N.Y. at Binghamton, 1965—, prof. English, 1974—, dir. creative writing program, 1973-75, 78-79; host 1st SUNY writers' festival, 1977; vis. prof. English U. Negev, Beersheva, Israel, 1971-72; vis. lectr., U. Haifa, Israel, 1973, vis. prof., 1981, U. Hawaii, 1975; vis. lectr. Keio U., Tokyo, 1978—; vis. poet Black colls. Miss., and pub. schs., Pitts., Ann Arbor, Mich., Tacoma, also N.Y., 1967-82. Guest poet, Antioch Internat. Summer Writing Seminars, Oxford, Eng., 1977-78; vis. poet Inst. Internat. Studies, Japan, 1978, also poetry readings.; Author: A Road Came Once, 1963, Called Home, 1967, Woodlawn North, 1970, Sailing Too Far, 1973, Everyone Loves Children: A Long Poem, 1982; translator: (with Gerald E. Kadish) Love Songs and Tomb Songs of Ancient Egypt in Alcheringa, 5, 1973, (with Tateo Imamura) Random Talks of Deibutsu (Kosho Shimizu), 1979; co-editor: (with John Logan) Choice: A Mag. of Poetry and Graphics, 1972—. Robert Frost fellow in poetry Bread Loaf Conf., 1961; MacDowell Found. fellow, 1966, 79; Yaddo fellow, 1965-76; Nat. Endowment for Arts grantee, 1967; Distinguished fellow in Fine Arts State U. N.Y. Research Found., 1969; Internat. fellow Keio U., Tokyo, 1978; Millay Found. fellow, 1979. Mem. PEN, Phi Beta Kappa. Jewish. Home: 25 Lincoln Ave Binghamton NY 13905 Office: English Dept State U NY Binghamton NY 13901

KESSLER, NATHAN, manufacturing company executive; b. St. Louis, Aug. 19, 1923; s. Isadore Harry and Esther (Becker) K.; m. Sara Ellen Potashnick, June 21, 1947; children—Joy Sandra, Gail Sue, Margie Ann. B.S., M.S. in Chem. Engring. (White-Rodgers fellow), Washington U., St. Louis, 1944. Registered profl. engr., Ill.; Cert. energy Mgr. With A.E. Staley Mfg. Co., Decatur, Ill., 1944—, plant supt., 1962-63, gen. supt., 1963-67, v.p., 1967—, group v.p. tech., 1970—, also dir., mem. exec. com.; pres. Ill. Jets. Mem. exec. com. of steering com. for formation Jr. Coll. Central Ill., 1972-74; Bd. dirs. U. Ill. Indsl. Research Adv. Bd., 1982—; mem. engring. adv. council Rice U., 1970-73; dir., past pres. bd. United Fund Decatur.; Past bd. dirs. Planned Parenthood of Decatur, Jr. Achievement of Decatur; bd. dirs. Progress Resources, 1975—, v.p., 1978. Mem. Am. Assn. Energy Engrs. (charter), Tech. Transfer Soc. (dir.), Am. Inst. Chem. Engrs., Scientists and Engineers for Secure Energy, Am. Oil Chemists Soc., Nat. Soybean Processors Assn. (past chmn. plant ops. symposium), Corn Refiners Assn. (past chmn. pollution control com.), Air, Water pollution control assns., Ill. C. of C., Decatur Assn. Commerce., B'nai B'rith (past pres. Decatur). Home: 49 Allen Bend Dr Decatur IL 62521 Office: A E Staley Mfg Co Decatur IL 62525

KESSLER, PAUL THOMAS, JR., electrical construction company executive; b. Zion, Ill., Aug. 18, 1918; s. Paul Thomas K. and MaryBeulah (Kessler); m. Beatrice B. Sisson, Apr. 16, 1983. B.S., Northwestern U., 1939, M.B.A., 1940; J.D., Loyola U., Chgo., 1943. C.P.A., Ill. Asst. chief acct. Alien Property Custodian, Chgo., 1942-43; tax mgr. Arthur Andersen & Co., Chgo., 1943-47; ptnr. Winston & Strawn, Chgo., 1947-66; exec. v.p. Beatrice Foods Co., Chgo., 1966-76; chmn., pres., chief exec. officer L.E. Myers Co. Group, Chgo., 1982—, dir.; chmn. L.E. Myers Co. Internat. Ltd., Barcelona, Spain; dir. Chgo Milw. Corp. Mem. ABA, Chgo. Bar Assn. Republican. Episcopalian. Clubs: Chgo.; Met. (Chgo.); Bath & Racquet (Sarasota, Fla.). Home: 5207 Cape Leyte Dr Sarasota FL 33581 Office: The L E Myers Co Group 547 W Jackson St Chicago IL 60606

KESSLER, RICHARD CALLIE, motel executive; b. Savannah, Ga., May 28, 1946; s. Callie Whitfield and Mildred K.; m. Martha Jane Wilson, June 1970; children: Mark, Laura. B.S. in Indsl. Engring., Ga. Inst. Tech., 1969, M.S., 1970. Asst. to Cecil B. Day Days Inns of Am., Inc., 1970; founder, devel. ptnr. Day Realty of Orlando, Inc., 1972—, Day Realty of Savannah, Day Realty of Richmond, Day Realty of Albany, Day Realty of Fla., 1972; pres., chief exec. officer, chmn. bd. Days Inns of Am., Inc., Atlanta, 1979—. Bd. dirs. Ga. Tech. Exec. Roundtable, Day Co. Found., Easter Seal Soc. Ga.; mem. mgmt. adv. council dept. mgmt. U. Ga. Mem. Ga. Bus. in Industry Assn. (adv. council). Lutheran. Lodge: Kiwanis. Office: Days Inn of Am Inc 2751 Buford Hwy NE Atlanta GA 30324

KESSLER, RICHARD HOWARD, physician; b. Paterson, N.J., Dec. 15, 1923; s. Mitchell Richard and Rae (Levin) K.; m. Marian Judith Singer, May 14, 1944; children—William Samuel, Peter Bernard, John Robert. B.S., Rutgers U., 1948; M.D., N.Y. U., 1952. From instr. to asso. prof. Cornell U. Med. Sch., 1955-68; prof. Northwestern U. Med. Sch., Chgo., 1968-77; also asso. dean; cons. physician Northwestern Meml. Hosp., 1972-77; sr. v.p. profl. and acad. affairs Michael Reese Hosp., 1977—, attending physician, 1977—; prof. medicine Pritzker Sch. Medicine, U. Chgo., 1978—; attending physician N.Y. Hosp., 1965-68, VA Research Hosp., Chgo., 1968-71; cons. health econs. Nat. Bur. Econ. Research; cons. edn. service VA, Washington. Cons. editor: Ency. Brit, 1973-79; contbr. articles to profl. jours. Vice pres. Kidney Found. Ill., 1974-77; bd. dirs. Cook County Grad. Sch. Medicine; mem. exec. com. Anti-Defamation League of B'nai B'rith, Ill. Regional Med. Program, 1972-77; commr. Health and Hosp. Governing Com. of Cook County, 1974-76, Health Systems Agy., City of Chgo., 1980—; mem. exec. com. Ill. Cancer Council, 1981—. Served with AUS, 1942-46. Life Ins. Med. Research fellow, 1955-56; sr. fellow Nathan Hofheimer Found., 1957-62; Fellow Hastings Inst. Soc., Ethics and Life Scis., A.C.P. Mem. Am. Physiol. Soc., Am., Internat. socs. nephrology, Harvey Soc., Central Soc. for Clin. Research, Am., Ill., Chgo. heart assns., Am. Soc. Clin. Pharmacology and Therapeutics (editorial bd. 1966—), Hosp. Research and Ednl. Trust (editorial bd. 1975-78), AAAS, Alpha Omega Alpha. Home: 3240 Lake Shore Dr Chicago IL 60657 Office: 29th St and Ellis Ave Chicago IL 60616

KESSLER, ROBERT CLARENCE, physician; b. Roscoe, N.Y., May 9, 1923; s. Clarence L. and Florence McCall (Eells) K.; m. Shirley Mason, Mar. 23, 1946; children—Karen M., Bruce P., William M., Barbara J. Student, Union Coll., Schenectady, 1940-43; M.D., Albany Med. Sch., 1947. Diplomate: Am. Bd. Preventive Medicine. Intern Nat. Naval Med. Center, Bethesda, Md., 1947-48; resident U.S. Naval Hosp., Portsmouth, Va., 1948-49, Chelsea, Mass., 1952-54; staff physician Eastman Kodak Co., Rochester, N.Y., 1954-72, asst. med. dir., 1973-74, med. dir., 1974—; Vice chmn. health services adv. com. U.S. CD Council, 1964-72. Served with M.C. USN, 1947-54. Mem. AMA, Med. Soc. State N.Y., Med. Soc. County of Monroe, Am. Acad. Occupational Medicine, Am. Occupational Medicine Assn. (pres. 1983-84), Indsl. Med. Assn. Upstate N.Y. (pres. 1974). Republican. Presbyterian. Home: 99 Penfield Crescent Rochester NY 14625 Office: 1669 Lake Ave Rochester NY 14650

KESSLER, ROBERT JACK, publisher; b. N.Y.C., Dec. 1, 1933; s. Frank and Sonya (Stimer) K.; m. Pamela Udis, June 4, 1960 (div. Mar. 1974); 1 dau., Amanda Udis; m. 2d Janet Elizabeth Lincoln, Oct. 15, 1977. B.A., Queen's Coll., 1956. Freelance song writer, lyricist, N.Y.C., 1956-77; mng. editor, pres. Pendragon Press, N.Y.C., 1977—. Mem. ASCAP. Office: Pendragon Press 162 W 13th St New York NY 10011

KESSLER, RONALD BOREK, newspaper reporter; b. N.Y.C., Dec. 31, 1943; s. Ernest Borek and Minuetta K.; m. Pamela Johnson Whitehead; children: Greg, Rachel. Student, Clark U., Worcester, Mass., 1962-64. Reporter Worcester Telegram, 1964; investigative reporter, editorial writer Boston Herald-Traveler, 1964-68; N.Y. bur. reporter Wall St. Jour., 1968-70; investigative reporter Washington Post, 1970—. Author: The Life Insurance Game, 1984. Recipient public affairs reporting award Am. Polit. Sci. Assn., 1965; citation Freedoms Found., 1966; 1st prize in newswriting UPI, 1967; Sevellon Brown Meml. award AP, 1967; sci. writers award ADA, 1968; 1st place in public service award Md.-Del.-D.C. Press Assn., 1972; outstanding series award AAUW, 1972; Bill Pryor Meml. Reporting award, 1973; Front Page award Washington-Balt. Newspaper Guild, 1973; H George Polk Meml. award for community service, 1973; for nat. reporting, 1979; named Washingtonian of Yr. Washington Mag., 1972; Dow Jones Inc Newspaper Fund intern, 1964. Office: 1150 15th St NW Washington DC 20071

KESSLER, STANTON A., lawyer; b. Chgo., Mar. 27, 1934; s. Louis I. and Blanche K.; m. Eslee Schreeger, July 20, 1969 (div.); children: Alexis, Louis; m. Susan Getzendanner, Feb. 18, 1983. B.A., Amherst Coll., 1955; LL.B., Harvard U., 1958. Bar: Ill. 1958, D.C. 1964. Atty. Office of Chief Counsel, IRS, Washington, 1959-64; assoc. Mayer, Brown and Platt, Chgo., 1964-68, ptnr., 1969—. Served with USMC, 1958-59. Mem. Chgo. Council Lawyers, Internat. Fiscal Assn. Office: Mayer Brown and Platt 231 S LaSalle St Chicago Il 60604

KESSLER, WILLIAM HENRY, architect; b. Reading, Pa., Dec. 15, 1924; s. Frederick H. and Lucia W. (Kline) K.; m. Margot Walbrecker, May 11, 1946; children: Tamara Kessler Wagner, Chevonne Kessler Patten. B.A. in Architecture, Inst. Design, Chgo., 1948; M.Arch., Harvard U., 1951. Chief designer Yamasaki, Leinweber & Hellmuth, Detroit, 1951-55; prin. William Kessler and Assos., Inc., Detroit, 1955—; adj. prof. U. Mich. Coll. Architecture. Prin. works include Center Creative Studies, Detroit, Harvard U. Sch. Pub. Health, Boston, Grand Valley State Coll, Allendale, Mich., Detroit Sci. Center, Wayne County Community Coll.-Taylor (Mich.) core, New Detroit Gen. Hosp.-Wayne State U. Health Care Inst, Detroit. Councilman, Grosse Pointe Park, Mich., 1966-67. Served with USAAF, 1943-46. Recipient over 75 archtl. design awards. Fellow AIA (Gold medal Detroit chpt. 1974), Mich. Soc. Architects (Gold medal 1976). Home: 1013 Cadieux Rd Grosse Pointe Park MI 48230 Office: 733 Saint Antoine St Detroit MI 48226

KESTER, JOHN GORDON, lawyer; b. Oshkosh, Wis., June 18, 1938; s. Gordon John and Frances Ruth (Polk) K.; m. Mary Elizabeth Foust, June 17, 1961 (div. 1972); children—Robert Gordon, Charles Forrest. B.A., U. Wis., 1959; Fulbright scholar, U. d'Aix-Marseille, France, 1959-60; LL.B. magna cum laude, Harvard, 1963. Bar: D.C. bar 1964, U.S. Ct. Mil. Appeals bar 1965, U.S. Supreme Ct. bar 1968. Law clk. to Justice Black, Washington, 1963-65; asso. firm Steptoe & Johnson, Washington, 1968; asst. prof. law U. Mich., 1968-69; dep. asst. sec. manpower and res. affairs Army Dept., Washington, 1969-72; partner firm Williams, Connolly & Califano, Washington, 1972-77; spl. asst. to sec. and dep. sec. Def., 1977-78; partner firm Williams & Connolly, Washington, 1979—. Contbr. articles to legal jours.; Pres.: Harvard Law Rev, 1962-63. Mem. bd. visitors USAF Acad.; mem. adv. bd. U.S. Naval Acad. Served to capt. AUS, 1965-68. Recipient Disting. Civilian Service award Army Dept., 1971; medal for Disting. Public Service Dept. Def., 1979. Mem. Am. Bar Assn., Am. Soc. Internat. Law, Council Fgn. Relations, Phi Beta Kappa. Home: 4317 Forest Ln NW Washington DC 20007 Office: Hill Bldg Washington DC 20006

KESTER, LENARD, artist; b. N.Y.C., May 10, 1917; s. Human and Yetta (Kalfus) K. Student pub. schs. Exhibited one-man shows, art galleries and museums, U.S., maj. nat. exhbns.; executed: Mayo Clinic mural, 1953; paintings in permanent collections, Bklyn., Toledo, Boston, Denver, Balt., Springfield, Mo. museums, U. Miami, also, Calif. State Fair, Everson Mus.; pvt. collections.; Designer stained glass window, Billy Rose Mausoleum. Recipient numerous prizes, awards; awarded Life mag. commn., 1947, Albert Dorne award, 1964, Mario Cooper award, 1966; Tiffany Found. fellow, 1949. Mem. Am. Watercolor Soc. (Windsor and Newton award 1959), Soc. Western Artists; asso. N.A.D. (Obrig prize 1959, Saltus gold medal). Studio: 1117 N Genesee Ave Los Angeles CA 90046 *I Think the most important function an artist can serve in the society in which he lives, and to himself in particular, is to report faithfully the life around and within him in such a manner that it is communicable to the other inhabitants of our world, first during our time and then for the peoples and times of the future.*

KESTER, RANDALL BLAIR, lawyer; b. Vale, Oreg., Oct. 20, 1916; s. Bruce R. and Mabel M. (Judd) K.; m. Rachael L. Woodhouse, Oct. 20, 1940; children: Laura, Sylvia, Lynne. A.B., Willamette U., 1937; J.D., Columbia U., 1940. Bar: Oreg. 1940. Assoc., then partner firm Maguire, Shields, Morrison & Bailey, Portland, 1940-57; justice Oreg. Supreme Ct., 1957-58; partner Maguire, Shields, Morrison, Bailey & Kester, 1958-66, Maguire, Kester & Cosgrave, 1966-71, Cosgrave & Kester, Portland, 1972-78, Cosgrave, Kester, Crowe, Gidley & Lagesen, 1978—; instr. Northwestern Coll. Law, 1947-56; gen. solicitor northwestern dist. U.P. R.R., 1958-79; sr. counsel UPRR Co., 1978-81. Past v.p. Portland area council Boy Scouts of Am.; past pres. Mountain Rescue and Safety Council Oreg.; past trustee Willamette U.; past bd. dirs. Oreg. Symphony Soc. Recipient Silver Beaver award Boy Scouts Am. Mem. ABA, Multnomah Bar Assn. (past pres.), Oreg. State Bar, Am. Law Inst., Inst. Jud. Adminstrn., Nat. Ski Patrol, Mt. Hood Ski Patrol (past pres.), Mazamas (past pres., climbing chmn.), Wy'east Climbers, Portland C. of C. (pres. 1973, chmn. bd. 1974), Phi Delta Phi, Beta Theta Pi, Tau Kappa Alpha. Clubs: Arlington, City (past v.p.), University, Multnomah Athletic (Portland). Home: 10075 SW Hawthorne Ln Portland OR 97225 Office: 901 The 1515 Bldg 1515 SW 5th Ave Portland OR 97201

KESTER, STEWART RANDOLPH, banker; b. Bronxville, N.Y., July 30, 1927; s. Robert Livingston, Jr. and Mae Anna (Jones) K.; m. Marion Fay Syrett, Sept. 23, 1950; children: Cheryl, Stewart Randolph, Valerie, Marcia. B.A., Colgate U., 1949. Sales rep. Procter & Gamble Co., N.Y.C., 1949-55; mng. partner Kester Bros., Pompano Beach, Fla., 1955—, R. & S. Properties, Pompano Beach, 1956—; pres. Fla. Coast Banks, Inc., Pompano Beach, 1973-75, vice chmn. bd., 1975-84; chmn. exec. com., dir. Fla. Coast Bank. Vice mayor, commr., Pompano Beach, 1964-66, mayor, Pompano Beach, 1966-67; mem. Broward County Charter Commn., 1974-75; pres. United Way of Broward County, 1978-79; chmn. bd. trustees Pompano Police Edn. Fund, Inc.; mem. exec. com. Broward chpt. NCCJ, 1983—; bd. dirs. Ft. Lauderdale Symphony, Broward Workshop, Inc., 1981-83. Served with AUS, 1946-47. Named Outstanding Young Man Pompano Beach Jaycees, 1962; recipient Service award Ft. Lauderdale C. of C., 1975, Silver medallion 1984. Mem. S.R. (dir.), S. Fla. Coordinating Council (pres.), Pompano Beach Hist. Soc., Greater Pompano Beach C. of C. (past dir.). Republican. Presbyterian. Clubs: Pompano Beach Exchange (past pres., charter mem.; Book of Golden Deeds award 1976), Lighthouse Point Yacht and Tennis.). Office: 1101 E Atlantic Blvd PO Box 91 Pompano Beach FL 33061

KESTERSON, DAVID BERT, english educator; b. Springfield, Mo., Feb. 19, 1938; s. Homer Russell and Dorothy (Mace) K.; m. Linda Marie Houston, Apr. 12, 1963; children: A. Todd, Chad Russell. B.S.E., S.W. Mo. State U., 1959; M.A., U. Ark., 1961, Ph.D., 1961. Grad. teaching asst. U. Ark., Fayetteville, 1962-64; asst. prof. English N.C. State U., Raleigh, 1964-68; from asst. prof. to prof. English North Tex. State U., Denton, 1968—, disting. Alumni prof., 1979, chmn. dept. English; cons. various pressess on manuscripts in Am. lit. Author: Josh Billings, 1973, Bill Nye, 1980; monograph Bill Ney: The Western Writings, 1976; editor: Studies in the Marble Faun, 1971, Critics on Poe, 1973, Critics on Mark Twain, 1973; founding editor: Hawthorne Soc. Newsletter, 1974-82; assoc. editor: Studies in the Novel, 1970—, Nathaniel Hawthorne Jour., 1980-82. Served with USAR, 1956-60. NDEA fellow, 1959-62; recipient Mortar Bd. Outstanding Educator award, 1980. Mem. Nathaniel Hawthorne Soc. (co-founder, 1st pres. 1974-76), Am. Humor Studies Assn. (pres. 1980-81), South Central Modern Lang. Assn. (exec. com. 1976-77), MLA (del. assembley 1976-79, 84—), Melville Soc., Poe Studies Assn., Soc. Study So. Lit., South Atlantic Modern Lang. Assn. Office: Dpt English N Tex State U Denton TX 76203

KESTIN, JOSEPH, mechanical engineer, educator; b. Warsaw, Poland, Sept. 18, 1913; came to U.S., 1952, naturalized, 1960; s. Paul and Leah K.; m. Alicja Wanda Drabienko, Mar. 12, 1949; 1 dau., Anita Susan. Dipl. Ing., Engring., U. Warsaw, 1937; Ph.D., Imperial Coll., London, 1945; M.A. ad eundem, Brown U., 1955; D.Sc., U. London, 1966; Dr. h.c., Universite Claude Bernard (Lyon I). Sr. lectr. dept. mech. engring. Polish U. Coll., London, 1944-46, dept. head, 1947-52; prof. engring., dir. Center for Energy Studies, Brown U., Providence, 1952—; vis. prof. Imperial Coll., London, 1958, Summer Sch. in Jablonna, Warsaw Polish Acad. Scis., 1973; professeur associe U. Paris, 1966, Université Claude Bernard (Lyon I) and Ecole Centrale de Lyon, 1974; Fulbright lectr. Instituto Superior Tecnico, Lisbon, 1972; spl. lectr. Norges Tekniske, Hogskole, Trondheim, Norway, 1963, 71; lectr. Nobel Com. Berzelius Symposium, 1979; fellow Inst. Advanced Studies, West Berlin; spl. adv. on engring. edn. to Chancellor of U. Tehran, Iran, 1968; chmn. NRC Eval. Panel for Office of Standard Ref. Data of Nat. Bur. Standards, 1976-80; mem. Eval. Panel for Nat. Measurement Lab. of Nat. Bur. Standards, 1978-80, Numerical Data Adv. Bd., Nat. Acad. Scis., 1976-80; cons. Nat. Bur. Standards, NATO, Rand Corp.; Mem. vis. com. U. Va., Charlottesville, 1964; mem. exec. com. Nat. Bur. Standards Evaluation Panels, 1974-78. Author 3 books on thermodynamics; editor-in-chief: Dept. Energy Sourcebook on Production of Electricity from Geothermal Energy; tech. editor: Jour. Applied Mechanics, 1956-71; mem. editorial bd.: Internat. Jour. Heat and Mass Transfer, 1961-71, Heat Transfer-Soviet Research, 1968—, Heat Transfer-Japanese Research, 1972—, Mechanics Research Communications, 1973—, Jour. Non-Equilibrium Thermodynamics, 1976—, Revue Generale de Thermique, 1975, Physica A, 1978—, Internat. Jour. Thermophysics, 1979—, Jour. Chem. and Engring. Data, 1980—; contbr. articles to profl. jours. Fellow Inst. Mech. Engrs. (London) (Water Arbitration prize 1949), ASME (task group on energy 1974-76, applied mechanics div. 1967-78, chmn. 1978, nat. nominating com. 1976-78, Centennial medals for research achievements and disting. service, James Harry Potter Gold medal 1981); mem. Am. Soc. Engring. Edn. (chmn. Curtis W. McGraw Research award com. 1976-78), Internat. Assn. Properties of Steam (U.S. del. exec. com. 1954—, chief of del. 1972—, pres. 1974-76), Internat. Union Pure and Applied Chemistry (chmn. subcom. transport properties 1981—), U.S. Acad. Engring., Sigma Xi (pres. Brown U. chpt. 1979—), Tau Beta Pi. Clubs: Univ., Faculty Brown U. (Providence). Home: 140 Woodbury St Providence RI 02906 Office: Brown U Providence RI 02912

KESTING, THEODORE, mag. editor; b. Mont Clare, Pa., Aug. 27, 1918; s. Theodore F. and Pauline (Hechler) K.; m. Jean M. Hoffman, Jan. 6, 1945 (dec.); children—Virginia Joan, Frederic, Kristin, David; m. Lorraine Williams, Mar. 4, 1968. Student, Girard Coll., 1928-36, Pa. Sch. Indsl. Arts, 1937-39, Charles Morrice Price Sch., 1940-41. Editor Curtis Pub. Co., 1936-45; editor, v.p. Sports Afield Pub. Co., Mpls., 1945-53; editor, pub. Am. Boy, 1950-53; editor Sports Afield, Hearst mags., 1956-70, Rod and Gun, 1969-70; editor at large Sports Afield, 1971—. Author: The Outdoor Encyclopedia, 1957. Home: Beaver Dam Farm Hume VA 22639 Office: 250 W 55th St New York City NY 10019

KESTNBAUM, ALBERT S., advertising executive; b. N.Y.C., Apr. 21, 1939; s. Nathan and Marian (Lanxner) K.; m. Roberta Anne; children: Ellen, Suzanne, Amy, David. B.A., NYU, 1959; postgrad., CCNY, 1961. Vice pres. mktg. devel. J.B. Williams Co., N.Y.C., 1968-70, v.p. mktg., 1970, sr. v.p., 1970—; pres. Parkson Advt. Agy., N.Y.C., 1972—, chmn. bd., 1977—; pres. Chestnut Communications, 1980—. Mem. pub. info. com. Am. Cancer Soc. Mem. Dirs. Guild Am. Acad.

TV Arts and Scis. Home: 18 Tomney Road Greenwich CT 06830 Office: 60 Arch St Greenwich CT 06830 *The best opportunities for success come from thorough, audacious and determined effort, in areas where your skills are most substantial, and where the potential reward is great. Often, ironically, the key ingredient to success is giving yourself permission to fail.*

KESTNER, NEIL RICHARD, educator; b. Milw., Dec. 11, 1937; s. Louis George and Erna (Sander) K.; m. Arlene Katherine Schweigerdt, June 10, 1967. B.S., U. Wis., 1960; M.S., Yale U., 1962, Ph.D., 1964. Postdoctoral fellow U. Chgo., 1963-64; asst. prof. dept. chemistry Stanford U., 1964-66; asso. prof. La. State U., Baton Rouge, 1966-71, prof., 1971—, also dir. freshman chemistry, 1973-76, chmn., 1976-81. Author: (with H. Margenau) Theory of Intermolecular Forces, 1969, 71, (with J. Jortner) Electrons in Fluids, 1973. Alfred P. Sloan Found. fellow, 1967-71; NSF grantee, 1965-72; Dept. Energy grantee, 1976—. Mem. Am. Chem. Soc., Am. Phys. Soc., Sigma Xi. Clubs: Pelican Yacht (New Roads, La.); U.S. Power Squadron (Baton Rouge). Home: 11655 Highland Rd Baton Rouge LA 70810 Office: Dept Chemistry La State U Baton Rouge LA 70803

KETCHAM, ALFRED SCHUTT, educator, surgeon; b. Newark, N.Y., Oct. 7, 1924; s. Colston Esty and Ellen (Schutt) K.; m. Elsie Jane Chase, July 13, 1946; children—Sue Ellen, Wendy Jane, Sally Lin, Jill Ann, Jeff Terry, Dana Kay. B.S., Hobart Coll., 1945, Sc.D., 1970; M.D., U. Rochester, 1949. Diplomate: Am. Bd. Surgery. Intern U.S. Naval Med. Center, Bethesda, Md., 1949-50; surg. resident USPHS Hosp., San Francisco, 1950-52, Seattle, 1952-55; chief surgery USPHS Indian Hosp., Talihina, Okla., 1955-57; sr. investigator Nat. Cancer Inst., NIH, Bethesda, 1957-62, chief surgery, 1962-74, clin. dir., asso. sci. dir. for clin. research, 1970-74; prof. surgery, chief div. oncology, dept. surgery U. Miami Sch. Medicine, 1974—, Am. Cancer Soc. prof. clin. oncology, 1974—; Cons. oncology Walter Reed Army Med. Center, Washington, Nat. Naval Med. Center; mem. breast cancer task force Am. Cancer Soc. Asso. editor: Am. Jour. Surgery; cons. editor: Jour. BREAST; editorial bd.: Internat. Advances in Surg. Oncology; contbr. articles to profl. publs. Recipient Meritorious Service medal HEW, 1970. Mem. AMA, USPHS Clin. Soc., European Soc. Cancer Research, Soc. Head and Neck Surgeons (past pres.), James Ewing Soc., Am. Surg. Assn., So. Surg. Soc., A.C.S., Am. Radium Soc. (past pres.), Am. Assn. Cancer Research, Soc. Pelvic Surgeons, Am. Fedn. Clin. Oncologic Socs. (pres. bd. govs.), Am. Soc. Clin. Oncology, Theta Delta Chi. Home: 1120 San Pedro Ave Coral Gables FL 33156 Office: Dept Surgery Div Oncology U Miami Sch Medicine PO Box 016310 Miami FL 33101

KETCHAM, CHARLES BROWN, educator, clergyman; b. Oberlin, Ohio, Mar. 5, 1926; s. Charles Burgess and Lucile (Brown) K.; m. Joyce Alene Parker, June 29, 1950; 1 son, Merrick Scott. B.A. magna cum laude, Mt. Union Coll., Alliance, Ohio, 1949; Fulbright scholar philosophy, U. Edinburgh, Scotland, 1949-50; div. student, New Coll., 1950-51, U. Zurich, Switzerland, 1951; B.D. magna cum laude, Drew U., 1953; Ezra Squire Tipple fellow, St. Mary's Coll., U. St. Andrews, Scotland, 1953, Ph.D., 1956; postdoctoral fellow, Harvard Div. Sch., 1970. Ordained to ministry Methodist Ch., 1952; minister, Rockaway Valley, N.J., 1955-57; lectr. philosophy Drew U., 1957; mem. faculty Allegheny Coll., 1957—, chaplain, 1957-63, James M. Thoburn prof. religion, chmn. dept. religion and philosophy, 1966—; vis. scholar Union Theol. Sem., N.Y.C., 1963-64; vis. prof. U. Kent, Eng.; chmn. com. higher edn. Western Pa. conf. Meth. Ch., 1962-67; del World Meth. Ecumenical Conf., Oxford, Eng., 1962. Author: The Search for Meaningful Existence, 1968, Federico Fellini, 1976, A Theology of Encounter, 1978; co-author, editor: Faith and Freedom, 1969; Contbr. to jours. Div. vice chmn. local United Fund, 1965-70; Bd. dirs. Meadville Multiracial Com., 1966-70, Meadville chpt. NAACP, 1963—; chmn. bd. trustees Meadville Public Library, 1980—. Served with AUS, 1944-46. Recipient Allegheny Coll. award for teaching excellence, 1983. Mem. Danforth Assos. (regional selection chmn. 1975—), Am. Acad. Religion, Psi Kappa Omega. Home: 369 Henry St Meadville PA 16335

KETCHAM, HENRY KING, cartoonist; b. Seattle, Mar. 14, 1920; s. Weaver Vinson and Virginia Emma (King) K.; m. Alice Louise Mahar, June 13, 1942 (dec.); 1 son, Dennis L.; m. Jo Anne Stevens, July 1, 1959 (div.); m. Rolande Praeprost, June 9, 1970; children: Dania, Scott Henry. Student, U. Wash., 1938. Animator, Walter Lantz Prodns., Universal Studios, Hollywood, Calif., 1938-39, Walt Disney Prodns., 1939-41; free lance cartoonist, 1946-51; creator: (distributed by) Dennis the Menace, Field Newspaper Syndicate, 1951; also creator: Half Hitch, 1971-75; Donor: Hank Ketcham Collection, Boston U. Libraries.; Author: Dennis the Menace cartoon book collections, 1954—, I Wanna Go Home, 1965, Well, God, I Goofed Again, 1975, Someone's in the Kitchen with Dennis, 1978; designer: Dennis The Menace Playground, Monterey, Calif. Served as chief photographer specialist USNR, 1941-45; creative work Navy War Bond, Tng. Film Program, 1942-45. Recipient Billy de Beck Award for outstanding cartoonist of yr., 1952. Mem. Nat. Cartoonists Soc., Phi Delta Theta. Clubs: Mill Reef (Antigua); Golf Club de Geneva; Old Baldy (Saratoga, Wyo.); Cypress Point Golf (Pebble Beach); Royal and Ancient Golf (St. Andrews, Scotland); Old Capital. Address: PO Box 800 Pebble Beach CA 93953

KETCHAM, ORMAN WESTON, lawyer, former judge; b. Bklyn., Oct. 1, 1918; s. Walter Seymour and Arline May (Weston) K.; m. Anne Phelps Stokes, Dec. 22, 1947; children: Anne Weston, Helen Phelps Ryan, Elizabeth Miner Mercogliano, Susan Stokes. B.A., Princeton U., 1940; postgrad., Yale U., 1940-41, LL.B., 1947, J.D., 1971. Bar: D.C. 1948. With firm Covington & Burling, Washington, 1948-53; asst. gen. counsel Fgn. Ops. Adminstrn., Washington, 1953-55; trial atty. antitrust div. Justice Dept., 1955-57; judge Juvenile Ct. D.C., 1957-71, Superior Ct. D.C., 1971-77; sr. staff atty. Nat. Center State Cts., 1977-81; sr. fellow Washington Coll. Law Inst., 1981—; adj. prof. law Georgetown U., 1963-67, U. Va., 1971-77, William and Mary Coll., 1978-80, Am. U., 1981—; mem. council of judges Nat. Council on Crime and Delinquency, 1959-75, bd. dirs., 1974—; mem. U.S. del. UN Congress on Crime, Stockholm, 1965, Geneva, 1975; mem. Nat. Com. on Secondary Edn., 1970-74; chmn. adv. council to Select Com. on Crime, Ho. of Reps., 1969-70. Author: (with others) Justice for the Child, 1961, Changing Faces of Juvenile Justice, 1978, (with Monrad G. Paulsen) Cases and Materials Relating to Juvenile Courts, 1967. Washington rep. Fund for the Republic, 1953; mem. vis. com. Brookings Instn., 1971-76. Served as lt. comdr. USNR, 1941-46. Mem. ABA, Bar Assn. D.C., Am. Law Inst., Nat. Council Juvenile and Family Ct. Judges (pres. 1965-66), Internat. Assn. Youth Magistrates (v.p. 1966-74). Congregationalist. Clubs: Cosmos, Princeton (N.Y.C.); Chevy Chase. Home: 2 E Melrose St Chevy Chase MD 20015 Office: 4400 Massachusetts Ave NW Washington DC 20016

KETCHLEDGE, RAYMOND WAIBEL, electrical engineer; b. Harrisburg, Pa., Dec. 8, 1919; s. Raymond A. and Sophie (Waibel) K.; m. Janet M. Bell, Sept. 16, 1970; children: Raymond, Carol, Bruce, William Bell, Kevin Bell, David, Randy Bell, Richard, Robin. B.S., Mass. Inst. Tech., 1941, M.S., 1942. With Bell Telephone Labs., 1942-82, exec. dir. electronic switching div., Naperville, Ill., 1966-75, exec. dir. mil. systems div., 1975-82; dir. Naperville Bank & Trust Co., 1967-76. Fellow IEEE (Alexander Graham Bell medal 1976); mem. Nat. Acad. Engring. Patentee in field. Home: 1785 Chadwick Rd Englewood FL 33533

KETCHUM, ALTON HARRINGTON, retired advertising executive; b. Cleve., Oct. 8, 1904; s. Wesley H. and Velma M. (Davis) K.; m. Robyna Neilson, Apr. 27, 1940; 1 dau., Deborah (Mrs. Harvey Lambert). B.A., Western Res. U., 1926. Spl. corr. United Press, 1926-27; editorial, advt. work Penton Pub. Co., Powers-House Co., Nesbitt Service Co., 1927-33; with McCann-Erickson, Inc., 1934-62, beginning as copy writer, successively copy group head, v.p., creative supr. internat. div., 1948-62; v.p. Infoplan div. Interpublic, Inc., 1962-64; corporate adminstrv. staff Interpublic, 1964-69; mng. dir. Harrington's Hist. Resources, 1970—; Spl. asst. Petroleum Adminstrn. for War, 1943-44; supr. nat. campaign to explain Am. econ. system sponsored by Advt. Council, 1948-51; spl. rep. USIA, India, 1954, cons., 1956—, mem. exec. res., 1957-60. Designed: People's Capitalism exhibit, 1956, Golden Key Exhibit for, Dept. of Commerce, 1956; Author: Follow the Sun, 1930, The Miracle of America, 1948, The March of Freedom, 1951, Let Freedom Ring, 1952, Uncle Sam: The Man and The Legend, 1959, The Green Bough, 1984; editor: Bull. Inst. Mktg. Communications, 1965-69, Principles and Practices of Marketing Communications, 1966; Mem. internat. editorial bd.: World Govt. News, 1949-52. Organizer Westchester-Fairfield (Conn.) com. Am. Assn. for UN, 1946; mem. Historic Dist. Commn., Greenwich.; Mem. Greenwich (Conn.) Aux. Police. Recipient awards Freedoms Found., 1949, 61, award of merit USIA, 1956; medal for outstanding service to advt. Advt. Fedn. Am., 1961; Ohio Gov.'s award for achievement, 1965. Mem. Assn. Am. Geographers, Am. Acad. Polit. and Social Sci., Am., Greenwich hist. socs., India-Am. League (pres. 1960-64), Hist. Assn. Gt. Britain, Nat. Planning Assn., S.A.R., Company Mil. Historians. Gave original designs for baton and badge of marshals of France to French people, 1953. Home: 333 Cognewaug Rd Cos Cob CT 06807

KETCHUM, CARLTON GRISWOLD, retired public relations executive; b. Yankton, S.D., Feb. 17, 1892; s. Lester and Luna L. (Beard) K.; m. Mildred Caroline Storey, Oct. 8, 1914; 1 son, David Storey. Student, Oberlin Coll., 1910-11; B.S. in Econs, U. Pitts., 1916. Various positions, 1900-12; asst. to dir. univ. extension U. Pitts., 1912-14, asst. registrar, 1914-16, publicity, asso. campaign dir., campaign dir., 1916-19; pres., dir. Ketchum, Inc. (campaign direction, pub. relations), Pitts., 1919-66, chmn., 1966-78. Bd. dirs. YMCA; v.p., bd. dirs. Assn. for Improvement the Poor; v.p. 100,000 Pennsylvanians.; Finance dir. Republican Nat. Com., 1937-41, 49-57; mem. Rep. finance coms. Served from pvt. to 2d lt. U.S. Army, 1917-19; Served to 2d col. USAAF, 1942-45. Mem. Am. Legion (past comdr.), Western Pa. Hist. Soc. (exec. com. 1971—, v.p., dir.), Omicron Delta Kappa. Presbyterian (nat. exec. com. Presbyn. Lay Com.). Clubs: Duquesne, Univ. (Pitts.); Masons. Home: 530 Glen Arden Dr Pittsburgh PA 15208 Office: 314 Chatham Center Pittsburgh PA 15219

KETCHUM, DAVID STOREY, retired fund-raising executive; b. Pitts., Sept. 28, 1920; s. Carlton G. and Mildred (Storey) K.; m. Sally Louise Doerschuk, Jan. 14, 1950; children: Louise Anne, Laura Jean. A.B., Cornell U., 1941. Sales rep. IBM Corp., 1941-42; pres., dir. Ketchum, Inc., Pitts., 1945-82, chmn. bd., 1978-82, chmn. emeritus, 1983—. Pres. Hist. Soc. Western Pa.; Past pres. Children's Home Pitts.; trustee Presbyn.-Univ. Hosp., Pitts., Shadyside Presbyterian Ch., Pitts.; former trustee Pitcairn-Crabbe Found., Pitts., Winchester-Thurston Sch., Pitts.; past v.p. Council Chs. Pitts.; past pres. Am. Assn. Fund Raising Counsel; mem. Cornell U. Council. Served to capt. USAAF, 1942-45. Decorated Soldier's medal, Bronze Star. Mem. Pitts. Bibliophiles, Sigma Alpha Epsilon. Clubs: Duquesne, Univ., Fox Chapel Racquet (Pitts.). Home: 131 Yorkshire Rd Pittsburgh PA 15208 Office: Chatham Center Pittsburgh PA 15219

KETCHUM, EZEKIEL SARGENT, banker; b. Louisville, Apr. 28, 1935; s. Paul A. and Elizabeth (Sargent) K.; m. Barbara J. Frank, June 13, 1959; children: Allison, Randolph, Sarah, Clayton. B.A. in Econs, Harvard U., 1957; postgrad., U. Pitts., 1959-60. With Mellon Bank N.A., Pitts., 1958-78, v.p. credit policy mgmt., 1976-78; exec. v.p. banking group Am. Bank & Trust Co. Pa., Reading, 1978—; dir. Nat. Forge Co., Irvine, Pa., 1974—. Bd. dirs. Reading Hosp. and Med. Center, 1978—, Reading Area Community Coll. Found.; council sustaining membership chmn. Hawk Mountain council Boy Scouts Am., 1979—, v.p. adminstrn.; bd. dirs. United Way Berks County, 1980. Served with USAR, 1957. Mem. Am. Bankers Assn., Robert Morris Assn. Address: 35 N 6th St Reading PA 19601

KETCHUM, GARDNER MASON, educator; b. Phila., Oct. 20, 1919; s. Harold Bostwick and Bertha (Mason) K.; m. Marion Stanford, Mar. 19, 1949; 1 son, Richard Gardner. S.B., Mass. Inst. Tech., 1941, S.M., 1944, Sc.D., 1949. Registered profl. engr., N.Y. Asst., then instr. Mass. Inst. Tech., 1941-48; devel. engr. Gen. Electric Co., 1948-53; mem. faculty Union Coll., Schenectady, 1953—, prof. mech. engring., 1956—, chmn. dept., 1962-74; cons. indsl. cos. U.S. Army. Fellow ASME; mem. Am. Soc. Engring. Edn., Sigma Xi, Tau Beta Pi. Home: 1307 Glenwood Blvd Schenectady NY 12308

KETCHUM, HARRY WILBUR, govt. ofcl.; b. Colorado Springs, Colo., May 10, 1910; s. John Henry and Arial (Harkrader) K.; m. Sybil Mae Leuty, June 8, 1935; children—Harry Wilbur, Lynne Anne. A.B., U. Denver, 1933; M.B.A., Harvard Grad. Sch. Bus. Adminstrn., 1935. Instr. econs. U. Conn., 1935-36; asst. prof. bus. adminstrn. Judson Coll., Marion, Ala., 1936-39; chmn. dept. statistics, prof. econs., dean undergrad. div., dir. Sch. Social Sci. and Pub. Affairs, Am. U., 1939-47; asst. chief marketing div., chief distbn. cost sect. Office Industry and Commerce, U.S. Dept. Commerce, 1947-50; charge alumnium task force, light metals div. NPA, 1950-51; dir. program rev. staff and dir. program coordination and review div. Office Civilian Requirements, 1951-52, chief emergency flood mission, Mo.-Miss. river basins, 1952, dep. asst. adminstr. for civilian requirements, 1952, dep. to asst. dir. and dir. distbn. costs div., 1952-53; dir. office distbn. Bus. and Def. Services Adminstrn., 1952-63, dir. mktg. info. div., 1963-64; economist Office Chems. and Consumer Products, 1964-68; dir. mktg. info. staff div. Bus. and Def. Services Adminstrn., 1968-71; spl. detail Office Emergency Planning, 1971; dir. Office Exceptions Review Price Commn., 1971-73; financial economist Office Bus. Research and Analysis, Bur. Competitive Analysis, U.S. Dept. Commerce, 1973-75; bus. mgr. House of Ruth, Inc., 1975—. Contbr. articles to profl. jours. Mem. Pi Kappa Alpha. Club: Masons. Home: 906 La Grande Rd Silver Spring MD 20903

KETCHUM, JAMES ROE, curator; b. Rochester, N.Y., Mar. 15, 1939; s. George Roe and Mary Louise (Frantz) K.; m. Barbara M. Van Ness, Aug. 18, 1962; children: John Van Ness, Sarah Graham, Timothy Roe, Chester Arthur. A.B., Colgate U., 1960; postgrad., Georgetown U., 1960-61, George Washington U., 1961-62. Staff historian Dept. Interior, Washington, 1960-62; registrar The White House, Washington, 1962-63, curator, 1963-70, U.S. Senate, Washington, 1970—. Editor: The White House: An Historic Guide, 1962-70; contbr. numerous articles to profl. jours. and encys. Mem. Com. Preservation of White House, 1964-70; trustee U.S. Capitol Hist. Soc., 1971-79; alt. mem. Fed. Council Arts and Humanities, 1974—; trustee Woodrow Wilson Birthplace Found., 1980—. Member Am. Assn. Museums, City Mus. Washington, Nat. Trust Historic Preservation, Theta Chi. Home: 209 11th St SE Washington DC 20003 Office: S 411 US Capitol Bldg Washington DC 20510

KETCHUM, MARSHALL DANA, economics educator; b. Buffalo, Dec. 16, 1905; s. Dorr Mason and Maude (Moore) K.; m. Clara Louise Whitten, Sept. 1, 1931; children: Marshall Dorr, Richard Jennings. B.S., Syracuse U., 1928, M.S., 1929; Ph.D., U. Chgo., 1937. Registrar Syracuse U., 1929-30; instr. Duke, 1931-32; asst. prof., then asso. prof., prof. Utah State U., 1932-38, U. Ky., 1938-46; professorial lectr. Grad. Sch. Bus., U. Chgo., 1945, mem. faculty, 1946—, asso. prof., 1946-51, prof., 1951-71, prof. emeritus, professorial lectr., 1971—; lectr. exec. devel. program U. Mich., 1954-63; Dir., bd. regents Life Officers Investment Seminar, 1948-74, Fin. Analysts Seminar, 1956-81; dir., chmn. exec. com. Conf. Savs. and Residential Financing, 1958-67; editoral adv. in fin. Houghton Mifflin Co., 1960-71. Author: The Fixed Investment Trust, 1937, (with Ralph R. Pickett) Investment Principles and Policy, 1954; Co-editor: (with Leon Kendall) Readings in Financial Institutions, 1965; Contbr. articles to profl. jours. Mem. Am. Econ. Assn., Am. Fin. Assn. (past pres., editor Jour. Finance 1946-55, chmn. bd. dirs., chmn. adv. com., chmn. editorial bd., mem. adv. com. 1957-61), Am. Real Estate and Urban Econs. Assn., AAUP. Club: Quadrangle (Chgo.). Home: 5805 Dorchester Ave Chicago IL 60637

KETCHUM, MICHAEL JEREMY, health insurance company executive; b. Lansing, Mich., Sept. 3, 1932; s. Jay C. and Lola M. (Power) K.; m. Simmey Lynn Dietrich; children—Sarah, Julie. B.S., Mich. State U., 1959. Enrollment rep. Mich. Hosp. Service (Blue Cross), 1959-61; hosp. relations dir. Ill. Hosp. and Health Service (Blue Cross), 1961-63; enrollment mgr., project planning mgr., competition and distbn. analyst Mich. Med. Service (Blue Shield), 1963-66; with Ohio Med. Indemnity Mut. Corp. (Blue Shield), 1966—, sr. v.p., 1969-72, pres., 1972—; dir., mem. exec. com. BCS Fin. Corp., Chgo.; dir. Ins. Fedn. Ohio; chmn. bd., dir. Community Life Ins. Co.; sec., dir. Mid-Ohio Health Care Assn.; treas., dir. Mid-Ohio Health Care Plan. Mem. Devel. Com. Greater Columbus.; bd. dirs. United Way of Franklin County, Columbus. Served with USNR, 1952-56. Mem. Columbus, Worthington (Ohio) chambers commerce. Clubs: Dublin-Worthington Rotary, Ohio State U. Pres.'s. Office: 6740 N High St Worthington OH 43085

KETCHUM, MILO SMITH, civil engineer; b. Denver, Mar. 8, 1910; s. Milo Smith and Esther (Beatty) K.; m. Gretchen Allenbach, Feb. 28, 1944; children: David Milo, Marcia Anne, Matthew Phillip, Mark Allen. B.S., U. Ill., 1931, M.S., 1932; D.Sc. (hon.), U. Colo., 1976. Asst. prof. Case Sch. Applied Sci., Cleve., 1937-44; engr. F.G. Browne, Marion, Ohio, 1944-45; owner, operator Milo S. Ketchum (Cons. Engr.), Denver, 1945-52; partner, prin. Ketchum, Konkel, Barrett, Nickel & Austin (Cons. Engrs. and predecessor firm), Denver, 1952—; prof. civil engring. U. Conn., Storrs, 1967-78, emeritus, 1978—; mem. Progressive Architecture Design Awards Jury, 1958, Am. Inst. Steel Constrn. Design Awards Jury, 1975, James F. Lincoln Arc Welding Found. Design Awards Jury, 1977; Stanton Walker lectr. U. Md., 1966. Author: Handbook of Standard Structural Details for Buildings, 1956; Editor-in-chief: Structural Engineering Practice; Contbr. engring. articles to tech. mags. and jours. Recipient Disting. Alumnus award U. Ill., 1979. Fellow Am. Concrete Inst. (dir., Turner medal 1966), ASCE (pres. Colo. sect., hon.), Instn. Structural Engrs. (London), Am. Cons. Engrs. Council; mem. Nat. Acad. Engring., Am. Soc. Engring. Edn., Internat. Assn. Shell and Space Structures, Structural Engrs. Assn. Colo. (pres.), Cons. Engrs. Council Colo. (pres.), Old Saybrook (Conn.) Hist. Soc., Sigma Xi, Tau Beta Pi, Chi Epsilon, Phi Kappa Phi, Alpha Delta Phi. Club: North Cove Yacht. Home: 13527 W 67th Way Arvada CO 80004 *Everyone makes mistakes. The more you do, the more mistakes you make. The important thing is what you do with your mistakes. If you disregard them and say they do not exist, then you are in trouble. You must follow through until the problem caused by the mistake is solved.*

KETCHUM, MORRIS, JR., architect, writer; b. N.Y.C., May 5, 1904; s. Morris and Jane H. (Gillet) K.; m. Isabella Stiger, Apr. 28, 1934. B.Arch., Columbia U., 1928; diploma, Sch. Fine Arts, Fontainebleau, France, 1928; chevalier, Chevalier des Arts et des Lettres, France, 1966. Prin. ptnr. Morris Ketchum, Jr. & Assocs., N.Y.C., 1928-74, ret., 1974; vice chmn. Landmarks Preservation Commn., N.Y.C., 1973-79. Author: Blazing a Trial, 1982, Shops and Stores. Recipient cert. of appreciation City of N.Y., 1979, cert. of excellence N.Y. State Assn. Architects, 1963, Ann. Archtl. award N.Y. State Council on Arts, 1973. Fellow AIA (nat. pres. 1965, 1st honor award 1950, award of merit 1950, 70, Medal of Honor N.Y. chpt. 1966). Club: Century Assn. (N.Y.C.). Home and Office: Pennswood Village Newton Pa 18940

KETCHUM, RALPH DOUGLAS, manufacturing company executive; b. Binghamton, N.Y., May 6, 1926; s. Melvin Robert and Elizabeth Corine (Chauncey) K.; m. Vera Beatrice Tajchman, June 26, 1947; children: Rebecca, Mark, John, Paul, R David. B.Naval Scis., Tufts U., 1945, B.S. in Mech. Engring, 1947; postgrad., Oklahoma City U. With Gen. Electric Co., 1947—, v.p. lighting group, 1976-79, sr. v.p., group exec., Cleve., 1979—. Vice pres. United Way Services Cleve., 1979; pres., bd. dirs. Associated Industries Cleve., 1978; bd. dirs. Clevel. Growth Assn., 1979, Cleve. Tomorrow, 1982; trustee Cleve. Orch., 1980. Served to lt. (j.g.) USNR, 1943-47. Republican. Roman Catholic. Club: Pepper Pike (Ohio) Country. Office: Gen Electric Co Nela Park Cleveland OH 44112

KETCHUM, ROBERT GLENN, photographer, print maker; b. Los Angeles, Dec. 1, 1947; s. Jack Burson and Virginia (Moorhead) K. B.A. cum laude, UCLA, 1970; M.F.A., Calif. Inst. Arts, 1974. Founder, tchr. photography workshops Sun Valley Center for Arts and Humanities, 1971-73; tchr. photography Calif. Inst. Arts, 1975; curator photography Nat. Park Found., Washington, 1979—; trustee Los Angeles Center Photog. Studies, 1975-81, pres., 1979-81, v.p., 1981. Author and contbr.: photographs American Photographers and the National Parks, 1981; One-man shows, Nikon House Gallery, N.Y.C., 1979, Smithsonian Instn. travelling exhbn., 1980-84, Silver Image Gallery, Seattle, 1980, H.I.A. Gallery, Venice, Calif., 1981, Hunter Mus. Art, Tenn., 1983, Asheville Art Mus. (N.C.), 1984, group shows include, Sheldon Meml. Art Gallery, N.B., 1984, Los Angeles County Mus. Art, 1978, The White House, Washington, 1979, Mcpl. Art Gallery, Los Angeles, 1980, Friends of Photography Calif. Ciba-Geigy research grantee, 1979; Nat. Park Found. research grantee, 1978, 79. Mem. Friends of Photography, Sierra Club, Phi Delta Theta. Home: 696 Stone Canyon Rd Los Angeles CA 90077 Office: PO Box 57473 Washington DC 20037

KETELSEN, JAMES LEE, diversified industry executive; b. Davenport, Ia., Nov. 14, 1930; s. Ernest Henry and Helen (Schumann) K.; m. Joan Velde, Feb. 22, 1953; children—James V., Lee. B.S., Northwestern U., 1952. C.P.A., Tex., Ill. Accountant Price Waterhouse & Co. (C.P.A.s), Chgo., 1955-59; v.p. finance, treas. J.I. Case Co., Racine, Wis., 1962-68, pres., chief exec. officer, 1968-72; exec. v.p. Tenneco Inc., Houston, 1972—, chmn. bd., chief exec. officer, 1978—, also dir.; dir. Morgan Guaranty Trust Co., Consol. Foods Corp. Bd. dirs. Am. Petroleum Inst.; trustee Northwestern U., Conf. Bd. Served to lt. USNR, 1952-55. Mem. Chi Psi. Clubs: River Oaks Country, Petroleum (Houston). Office: 1010 Milam St Houston TX 77001

KETNER, KENNETH LAINE, philosophy educator; b. Mountain Home, Okla., Mar. 24, 1939; s. Louis Elaine and Johnnie Lucille (Hannah) K.; m. Berti Gabriella Zehetmeier, Aug. 24, 1964; 1 son, Kenneth Laine. B.A. in Philosophy, Okla. State U., 1961, M.A., 1967; M.A. in Folklore, UCLA, 1968; Ph.D., U. Calif., Santa Barbara, 1972. Part-time instr. Okla. State U., 1964-67; teaching asst. U. Calif., Santa Barbara, 1969-70; mem. faculty Tex. Tech U., Lubbock, 1971—, prof. philosophy, 1977—, chmn. dept., 1979-81; founder, dir. Inst. Studies in Pragmaticism, 1972—; Charles Sanders Peirce prof philosophy, 1981—. Author: A Critical Study of Stephen C. Pepper's Approach to Metaphysics, 1967, An Essay on the Nature of World Views, 1972, An Emendation of R. G. Collingwood's Doctrine of Absolute Presuppositions, 1973, also articles; editor, compiler: Charles Sanders Peirce: Contributions to The Nation, 3 parts, 1975, 78, 79, Comprehensive Bibliography of Works of C.S. Peirce, 1977. Asst. prof. philosophy and folklore UCLA, summers 1972, 74; co-organizer C.S. Peirce Bicentennial Internat. Congress, Amsterdam, Netherlands, 1976. Served to capt. USAR, 1962-64. Grantee NSF, Nat. Endowment Humanities, Am. Council Learned Socs. Fellow Am. Anthrop. Assn., Charles S. Peirce Soc. (pres. 1978, co-founder, co-editor Peirce Studies 1979); mem. Am. Philos. Assn., Am. Folklore Soc., Folklore Soc. Eng., Calif. Folklore Soc., Semiotic Soc. Am. (editorial bd. jour.), Deutsche Gesellschaft für Semiotik, Tau Kappa Epsilon. Democrat. Taoist. Home: PO Box 65135 Lubbock TX 79464 Office: Dept Philosophy PO Box 4530 Tex Tech Univ Lubbock TX 79409

KETNER, RALPH WRIGHT, retail food company executive; b. Salisbury, N.C., Sept. 20, 1920; s. George Robert and Effie Viola (Yost) K.; m. Anne Blizzard, Mar. 22, 1980; children—Linda, Robert. Student, Tri-State Coll., 1937-39. Gen. mgr. Excel Grocery, Salisbury, 1950-56; head grocery buyer Winn Dixie Co., Raleigh, N.C., 1956-57; pres., treas. Food Town Stores Inc., Salisbury, 1957-81, chmn. bd., chief exec. officer, treas., 1981—; vp. Save-Rite, Inc.; dir. Security Bank and Trust Co., Rose's Inc. Holder copyright on inventory form. Mem. adv. bd. Salvation Army; mem. N.C. Job Tng. Coordinating Council; past bd. dirs. Rowan County (N.C.) Vocat. Rehab.; mem. adv. com. distbrv. edn., N.C., mem. N.C. adv. bd.; hon. life mem. DECA; mem. N.C. Devel. Fund, 4-H Clubs. Served with U.S. Army, 1942-46. Recipient N.C. Grocery of Yr. award, 1972-73; named N.C. Retailer of Yr., 1977; Paul Harris fellow. Mem. Salisbury-Rowan C. of C. (past dir.), N.C. Food Dealers (past pres., dir.), Mchts. Assn. (past pres.), Am. Legion. Presbyterian (elder). Clubs: Asparagus, Rotary, Elks, Moose. Home: 333 Richmond Rd Salisbury NC 28144 Office: PO Box 1330 Harrison Rd Salisbury NC 28144

KETNER, WAYNE MITCHELL, glass company executive; b. Toboso, Ohio, Dec. 10, 1920; s. George A. and Nellie (Irwin) K.; m. Frances Elizabeth Berry, Sept. 3, 1944; children: Gary Wayne, Pamela Ann. B.S., Ohio U., 1942; postgrad., Harvard Grad. Sch. Bus. Adminstrn., 1942-43. With Owens-Corning Fiberglas Corp., Toledo, 1943—, asst. comptroller, 1964-65, comptroller, 1965-68, v.p., controller, 1969-76, v.p. planning, 1976-78, sr. v.p. planning, 1978—. Mem. Planning Execs. Inst., Assn. Corp. Growth, N.Am. Soc. Corp. Planning, Delta Tau Delta. Methodist. Clubs: Masons, Inverness (Toledo). Office: Fiberglas Tower Toledo OH 43659

KETO, JOHN EDWIN, cons. engr.; b. Maynard, Mass., June 9, 1909; s. Wayne and Tynne Jameson (Stein) K.; m. Evelyn Camburn, Apr. 29, 1936; children—Martha Sharron, John Wayne. E.E., U. Cin., 1932, M.S., 1935; D.Sc. (hon.), Bradley U., Peoria, Ill., 1961. Teaching fellow elec. engring. U. Cin., 1933-35; research physicist propagation and high frequency phenomena Signal Corps, U.S. Army and Air Force, Wright Field, Dayton, Ohio, 1935-41, br. chief and chief engr., 1941-46, chief, 1946-51, tech. dir., 1951-52; became tech. dir. Wright air devel. div. Air Research and Devel. Command, 1952; then chief scientist aero. systems div. Air Force Systems Command, 1957-69; cons., 1969—; Mem. exec. com. Ohio Research and Devel. Found., 1963-65; mem. radar panel, research and devel. bd. Nat. Mil. Establishment, 1947-51; USAF mem. Dept. Def. Com., Sr. Sci. and Engring. Service, 1957; Air Force mem. exec. com. U.S. nat. com. Internat. Sci. Radio Union, 1957-69. Trustee Wright State U., Dayton, 1965-79. Recipient Presdl. Medal for Merit, 1946; scholarship Am. Mgmt. Assn., 1956, Exceptional Civilian Service award USAF, 1959. Fellow I.R.E. (chmn. Dayton sect. 1946-47); mem. Profl. Group Aero. and Navigational Electronics, Profl. Group Mil. Electronics, Armed Forces Communications and Electronics Assn. (dir. Dayton sect. 1954-56), Am. Assn. Common Clubs, Sigma Xi, Tau Beta Pi, Eta Kappa Nu. Home: 829 Laurelwood Rd Dayton OH 45419

KETTEL, LOUIS JOHN, internist, educator; b. Chgo., Nov. 4, 1929; s. Alfred C. and Elanora E. (Stroud) K.; m. Lois Mary Bornemeier, June 23, 1951; children—Linda Kettel Owen, Louis Michael, Laura Beth. B.S., Purdue U., 1951; M.D., Northwestern U., 1954, M.S. (USPHS fellow), 1958. Diplomate: Am. Bd. Internal Medicine. Intern Passavant Meml. Hosp., Chgo., 1954-55; resident Northwestern U. Hosps., Chgo., 1955-56, fellow in internal medicine, 1956-57; practice medicine specializing in internal medicine, Tucson, 1968—; mem. staff Univ. Hosp., VA Med. Ctr., Phoenix, chmn. Dean's Com., 1977—, mem. staff, Tucson, chmn. Dean's Com., 1977—; instr. dept. internal medicine Northwestern U., 1960-62, assoc., 1962-65, asst. prof., 1965-68; asso. prof. U. Ariz. Coll. Medicine, Tucson, 1968-73, prof., 1973—, asso. dean, 1974-77, dean, 1977—; chmn. Joint Bd. Med. and Osteo. Examiners of Medicine and Surgery, 1977—. Guest editor: Chest, 1968-78, Am. Rev. Respiratory Disease, 1974-78, The Med. Letter, 1974—; abstractor: Am. Rev. Respiratory Disease, 1969-73; contbr. chpts. to books, articles and revs. to med. jours. Gov.'s observer White House Conf. on Aging, 1981; chmn. health adv. com. Ariz. Corrections System, 1979—; chmn. Ariz. Statewide Health Coordinating Council, 1982—, Ariz. State Health Planning Adv. Council, 1982—; chmn. working group on education Health Policy Agenda for the Am. People, mem. steering com., 1982—; Chmn. Calvary Lutheran Ch. Bd. Edn., 1969-72, ch. pres., 1975-77, 79-80; bd. dirs. Luth. Campus Bd., 1974-80, Westberg Inst., 1982—, Weizmann Inst., Tuscon chpt., 1983—; pres. Switchboard, Inc., 1976-78; mem. guidelines com. United Way of Tucson, 1974. Served to capt. M.C. U.S. Army, 1958-60. USPHS cardiovascular trainee, 1960-62; VA research grantee, 1975-79. Fellow Am. Coll. Chest Physicians, A.C.P.; mem. AMA (sec. med. sch. sect. 1981—), Am. Thoracic Soc. (chmn. Sci. Assembly on Clin. Problems in Respiratory Disease 1971-72, rep. councilor 1972-75), Am. Fedn. Clin. Research, Ariz. Med. Assn. (dist. dir. 1981—), Pima County Med. Soc. (dir. 1981—), AAAS, Assn. Am. Med. Colls. (exec. council, mem. adminstrn. bd., council of Deans 1982—), Ariz. Lung Assoc. (exec. com. 1980—). Office: 1501 N Campbell Ave Tucson AZ 85724

KETTELKAMP, DONALD BENJAMIN, surgeon, educator; b. Anomosa, Iowa, Jan. 21, 1930; s. Enoch George and Elsie (Norden) K.; m. Alice June Mencke, Dec. 30, 1954; children: Karen June, Lisa Marie, Suzanne D., Jonathan B. B.A., Cornell U., Mt. Vernon, Iowa, 1952; M.D., U. Iowa, 1955, M.S., 1960. Diplomate: Am. Bd. Orthopaedic Surgery. Intern Thomas D. Dee Meml. Hosp., Ogden, Utah, 1955-56; resident orthopedic surgery U. Iowa, Iowa City, 1958-61; practice medicine specializing in orthopaedic surgery, Anchorage, 1961-64; asst. prof. Albany (N.Y.) Med. Coll., 1964-66, asso. prof., 1966-68, U. Iowa, Iowa City, 1968-71, prof., 1971; prof., chmn. dept. orthopaedic surgery U. Ark., Little Rock, 1971-74, Ind. U., Indpls., 1974—. Asso. editor: Clin. Orthopaedics; contbr. articles to profl. jours. Mem. AMA, A.C.S., Am. Acad. Orthopaedic Surgeons, Orthopaedic Research Soc., Russell Hibbs Soc., Continental Orthopaedic Soc., Am. Soc. Surgery of Hand, Am. Orthopaedic Assn., Assn. Orthopaedic Chairmen (pres. 1981), Internat. Soc. of the Knee. Office: Ind U Sch Medicine Dept Orthopaedic Surgery 1100 W Michigan St Indianapolis IN 46223

KETTELL, RUSSELL WILLARD, banker; b. Boston, Feb. 2, 1944; s. Prescott Lowell and Wilhelmina (Schurrman) K.; m. Carol Bailey, Oct. 27, 1973; 1 son, Alexander. B.A. in Econs., Middlebury Coll.; M.B.A., U. Chgo. Sr. v.p., treas. World Savs. and Loan Corp., Oakland, Calif. Home: 440B Ballera Alameda CA 94501 Office: World Savs and Loan Corp 1970 Broadway Oakland CA 94501

KETTER, ROBERT LEWIS, engineering educator, former university president; b. Welch, W.Va., Dec. 7, 1928; s. E. F. and Ella Louise (Drummn) K.; m. Lorelei Zimmerman, Dec. 22, 1948; children: Katharyn K. Ross, Susannah K. White, Mary, Michael. B.S. in Civil Engring., U. Mo., 1950, M.S., Lehigh U., 1952, Ph.D., 1956, D.Eng., 1981; D.Sc., Kyungpook Nat. U., Taegu, Korea, 1973; Engring.D., Lehigh U., 1982. From research asst. to research asst. prof. civil engring. Lehigh U., 1950-58; prof. civil engring., chmn. dept. U. Buffalo, 1958; acting dean Grad. Sch., SUNY, Buffalo, 1964-65, dean, 1965-66, v.p. univ., 1966-69, pres., 1970-82, prof. engring., 1982—; dir. Marine Midland Bank-Western. Author: (with G.C. Lee and S.P. Prawel Jr.) Structural Analysis and Design, 1979, (with G.C. Lee and L.T. Shu) The Design of Single Story Rigid Frames, 1981; also articles in field and in edn. Chmn. bd. trustees Western N.Y. Nuclear Research Center, Inc., 1970-76; chmn. bd. Comprehensive Health Planning Council of Western N.Y., Inc., 1970-71; mem. N.Y. State Com. Electric Power Research, 1973-78; Bd. mgrs. Buffalo and Erie County Hist. Soc.; bd. visitors Roswell Park Meml. Inst., 1970-80; bd. dirs. Greater Buffalo Devel. Found.; trustee Univs. Research Assn., 1977-83, chmn. pres.'s council, 1981-82; bd. dirs. Sierra Research Corp., 1978-82; mem. N.Y. State Commn. Jud. Nomination, 1978. Recipient Adams Meml. award Am. Welding Soc., 1968; Disting. Service in Engring. award U. Mo., 1971. Mem. ASCE (dir. Niagara Frontier sect., chmn. several nat. coms.), Structural Stability Research Council Found. (chmn. tech. coms.), Internat. Inst. Welding (ofcl. expert rep. U.S. on commn. X), Internat. Assn. Bridge and Structural Engrs., Am. Welding Soc., Nat. Assn. State Univs. and Land Grant Colls. (legal affairs com. 1978—), Buffalo Fine Arts Acad., Buffalo Soc. Natural Scis., Sigma Xi, Tau Beta Pi, Phi Eta Sigma, Omicron Delta Kappa, Pi Mu Epsilon, Chi Epsilon. Office Suny at Buffalo Sch of Engineering Buffalo NY 14260

KETTERING, GORDON HOWARD, forest products company executive; b. Dayton, Ohio, Dec. 8, 1923; s. Howard Arthur and Ila Vesta (Carpenter) K.; m. Majorie Anne Smith, Sept. 7, 1947; children: Robert, Lori. B.C.E., Ohio State U., 1949. Registered profl. eng., Ohio, Wis. Various positions Mead Corp., Chillicothe, Ohio, 1949-70, Kingsport, Tenn., 1949-70; pres. Gilbert Paper Co. Div., Menasha, Wis., 1970-73, corp. v.p. research and engring., Dayton, Ohio, 1973-78, corp. v.p. personnel, 1978-79, corp. v.p. operating services, 1979-81, corp. v.p. pres. Chillichothe div., 1981-83, part-time cons., 1938—. Pres. Western Mich. U. Paper Tech. Found., Kalamazoo, 1981-83, bd. dirs., Kalamazoo, 1975-81. Served to lt.(j.g.) USN, 1943-45; PTO. Mem. TAPPI. Republican. Presbyterian. Club: Rotary. Home: 4 Shadewood Ln Hilton Head Island SC 29928

KETTLER, MILTON ELLSWORTH, home builder; b. Washington, May 31, 1923; s. Clifford Ellsworth and Elsie Belle (Weaver) K.; m. Barbara Elizabeth Walker, Oct. 4, 1947; children—Ellen Luise, Robert Charles, Peter Brookes. B.A., U. Mich., 1945. Real estate salesman Phillips, Canby & Fuller, Washington, 1945-49; real estate broker C.H. Hillegeist Co., Washington, 1949-52; chmn. bd., dir. Kettler Bros., Inc., Washington and Gaithersburg, Md., 1952—; dir. C&P Telephone Co., First Am. Bank N.A., Washington. Trustee Am. U. Served to ensign USNR, 1945. Mem. Nat. Assn. Home Builders (hon. life dir., Bill Molster Nat. Mktg. award 1970), Md. Inst. Home Builders (pres. 1971-72), Met. Washington Home Builders Assn. (pres. 1969-70), Suburban Md. Home Builders Assn. (pres. 1974-75), Inst. Residential Mktg. (charter), Theta Chi, Lambda Alpha. Methodist. Clubs: Masons, Columbia Country, Montgomery Village Golf, Burning Tree Golf, Cove Creek, Annapolis Yacht, Potomac Squash, Pisces. Home: Cove Creek Club Stevensville MD 21666 Office: 19110 Montgomery Village Ave PO Box 2127 Gaithersburg MD 20760

KETY, SEYMOUR S(OLOMON), physiologist, psychobiologist, emeritus educator; b. Phila., Aug. 25, 1915; s. Louis and Ethel (Snyderman) K.; m. Josephine R. Gross, June 18, 1940; children: Lawrence Philip, Roberta Frances. A.B., U. Pa., 1936, M.D., 1940, Sc.D. (hon.), 1965, Loyola U., 1969, U. Ill., 1981, M.D., U. Copenhagen, 1979. NRC fellow Harvard, 1943-44; from instr. to asst. prof. pharmacology U. Pa. Sch. Medicine, 1943-48; prof. clin. physiology Grad. Sch. Medicine, 1948-51; scientific dir. Nat. Insts. Mental Health and Neurol. Diseases and Blindness, 1951-56; chief Lab. Clin. Sci., NIMH, 1956-61, 62-67; Henry Phipps prof., dir. dept. psychiatry Johns Hopkins Sch. Medicine, 1961-62; prof. psychiatry Harvard Med. Sch., 1967-83, prof. neurosci. in psychiatry, 1983, prof. emeritus, 1983—; dir. psychiat. research labs. Mass. Gen. Hosp., Boston, 1967-77, Mailman Research Center (McLean Hosp.), Belmont, Mass., 1977—; Thomas Dent Mütter lectr., 1951, Eastman lectr., 1957, NIH lectr., 1960, Thomas William Salmon lectr., 1961, Alvarenga Prize lectr., 1961; Acad. lectr. Am. Psychiat. Assn., 1961; Saul Korey lectr., 1964, James Arthur lectr., 1966, 3d Mental Health Research Fund. lectr., London, 1965, Benjamin Musser lectr., 1970, Edward Mapother lectr., London, 1974, George Bishop lectr., 1975, Harvey lectr., 1975, Grass Found. lectr., 1975; Henry Maudsley lectr. Editor-in-chief: Jour. Psychiat. Research, 1959-82; contbr. sci. articles to profl. publs. Organizing com. Internat. Neuro-chem. Symposia, 1952-60; sci. advisory com. Mass. Gen. Hosp., 1956-60; dir. Found. Fund Research in Psychiatry, 1962-65; assoc. Neuroscis. Research Found., 1962—; trustee Rockefeller U., 1976—. Recipient Theobold Smith award AAAS, 1949, Max Weinstein award, 1954; Distinguished Service award HEW., 1958; Stanley Dean award, 1962; McAlpin award Nat. Assn. for Mental Health, 1972; Intra-Sci. award, 1975; William C. Menninger award A.C.P., 1976; Fromm-Reichman award, 1978; Founds. Fund award, 1979; Passano award, 1980. Disting. fellow Am. Psychiat. Assn. (Disting. Service award 1980); hon. fellow Royal Coll. Psychiatrists; mem. Nat. Acad. Scis. (Kovalenko award 1973), Am. Acad. Arts and Scis., Am. Philos. Soc., Assn. Research Nervous and Mental Disease (trustee, pres. 1965, 80, Research Achievement award 1980), Am. Psychopath. Assn. (pres. 1965, Paul Hoch award 1973), Soc. for Psychiat. Research, Am. Soc. Clin. Investigation, Am. Soc. Pharmacology and Exptl. Therapeutics, Soc. for Neurosci. (Grass Found. award 1975), Phi Beta Kappa, Sigma Xi, Alpha Omega Alpha. Office: Mailman Research Center McLean Hosp Belmont MA 02178

KEULEGAN, GARBIS HOVANNES, hydraulician; b. Sebastia, July 12, 1890; s. Hovannes Garabed and Emma Marguerite (Klein) K.; m. Nellie Virginia Moore, Sept. 15, 1928; 1 dau., Emma Pauline. A.B., Anatolia Coll., 1910; B.A., Ohio State U., 1914, M.A. (Univ. fellow), 1915; Ph.D., Johns Hopkins U., 1928. Research engr. Westinghouse Electric & Mfg. Co., East Pittsburgh, Pa., 1919-21; physicist Nat. Bur. Standards, Washington, 1921-62; cons. in hydraulics U.S. Waterways Expt. Sta., Vicksburg, Miss., 1963—. Contbr. articles on hydraulics to profl. jours. Served with inf. U.S. Army, 1918-19. Recipient Gold Medal award for exceptional service Dept. Commerce, 1962, Achievement award Dept. Army, 1969, Meritorious Civilian Service award, 1972. Mem. ASCE (hon.), Nat. Acad. Engring., Washington Acad. Scis., Sigma Xi. Democrat. Roman Catholic. Home: 215 Buena Vista Dr Vicksburg MS 39180 Office: PO Box 631 Vicksburg MS 39180

KEULER, ROLAND LEO, shoe company executive; b. Kiel, Wis., Aug. 28, 1933; s. Joseph N. and Christina (Woelfel) K.; m. Shirley A. Johst, June 22, 1957; children: Suzanne Marie, Catherine Ann, David Richard, Carolyn Marie, Brian John and Barbara Jean (twins). B.A., Marquette U., 1959. C.P.A., Wis. Acct. Arthur Andersen & Co. (C.P.A.'s), Milw., 1959-65; sec.-treas. Napco Graphic Arts, Inc., Milw., 1965-70; controller Weyenberg Shoe Mfg. Co., Milw., 1970-72, treas., 1972-; project bus. cons., 1977—. Served with AUS, 1954-56. Mem. Am., Wis. insts. C.P.A.s, Beta Gamma Sigma, Beta Alpha Psi. Home: 720 W Fairfield Ct Glendale WI 53217 Office: PO Box 1188 Milwaukee WI 53201 also 234 E Reservoir Ave Milwaukee WI 53212

KEULKS, GEORGE WILLIAM, university dean, chemistry educator; b. East St. Louis, Ill., Apr. 2, 1938; s. George and Meta June (Krug) K.; m. JoAnn Marco, Aug. 27, 1960; children: Gavin Wade, Catherine Danielle, Amy Elizabeth, Laura Ashley. B.A., Washington U., St. Louis, 1960; M.S., U. Ark., 1962; Ph.D., Northwestern U., 1964. Chemist Monsanto Co., summers, 1959-60; research chemist Gulf Research and Devel. Co., Pitts., 1964-65; mem. summer session faculty Johns Hopkins U., 1966; asst. prof. chemistry U. Wis., Milw., 1966-71, assoc. prof., 1971-74, prof., 1974—, chmn. dept. chemistry, 1972-74, assoc. dean natural scis., 1974-75, acting dean Grad. Sch., 1975-76, dean Grad. Sch., 1976—; cons. in chemistry. Contbr. articles to profl. jours. NSF grantee, 1974-83. Mem. AAAS, Am. Chem. Soc., Catalysis Club Chgo., Catalysis Soc. N.Am., Nat. Council Univ. Research Adminstrs., Nat. Assn. State Univs. and Land-Grant Colls., Sigma Xi, Phi Lambda Upsilon. Methodist. Home: 4492 N Maryland Ave Milwaukee WI 53211 Office: Graduate School PO Box 340 U Wis Milwaukee WI 53201

KEUPER, JEROME PENN, technical university president; b. Ft. Thomas, Ky., Jan. 12, 1921; s. Clarence J. and Aileen (Miller) K.; m. Natalie Packard Snow, Apr. 17, 1948; children—Melanie, Philip. B.S., MIT, 1948; M.S., Stanford U., 1949; Ph.D., U. Va., 1952; D.Sc. (hon.), High Point (N.C.) Coll., 1975; hon. degrees, Bridgeport Engring. Inst., 1976, Eastern Ky. U., Richmond, 1977, Jacksonville (Fla.) U., 1978, U. de los Andes, Bogotá, Colombia, 1978. Research asso. Carnegie Instn., 1949-50; instr. U. Va., 1951-52; sr. research physicist Remington Arms Co., Bridgeport, Conn., 1952-58; prof., chmn. math. dept. Bridgeport (Conn.) Engring. Inst., 1955-58; sr. scientist, mgr. systems analysis RCA, 1958-64; chmn., dir. Jacksonville br. Fed. Res. Bank Atlanta; founder, 1958; since pres. Fla. Inst. Tech., Melbourne, also trustee.; Mem. commn. colls., also vis. com. So. Assn. Colls. and Schs., 1969; exec. com. Fla. Assn. Colls. and Univs., 1973; past pres. Ind. Colls. and Univs. Fla.; mem. S.E. adv. bd. Ins. Internat. Edn. Mem. Fla. Council 100, Fla. Nuclear and Space Commn.; chmn. bd. F.I.T. Aviation; pres. Fla.-Colombia Ptnrs., Fla. Ind. Colls. Found.; mem. adv. council Nat. Energy Found.; chmn. bd. Hawthorne Coll., Antrim, N.H. Served to 1st lt. OSS AUS, World War II. Recipient Silver Seal award Nat. Council State Garden Clubs, 1972; named Man of Week Orlando Sentinel, 1962, Silver Knight Mgmt., Nat. Mgmt. Assn., 1972, Ky. col., 1965; named to U.S. Army Field Arty. OCS Hall of Fame, 1981; Frank G. Brewer trophy Nat. Aero. Assn., 1981; Jerome P. Keuper Sch. established in, Bogota, Colombia, 1971. Sr. mem. I.E.E.E.; charter mem. Missile, Space and Range Pioneers; mem. Am. Phys. Soc., Am. Soc. Computing Machinery, Marine Tech. Soc., Ops. Research Soc. Am., Am. Soc. Tech. Writers and Pubs., Nat. Assn. Partners of the Alliance (exec. com.), Palm Soc. (past pres.), Sigma Xi, Pi Kappa Alpha. Mason (Shriner). Home: 201 Oak St Melbourne Beach FL 32951 Office: PO Box 1150 Melbourne FL 32901

KEVAN, DOUGLAS KEITH MCEWAN, entomologist, educator; b. Helsinki, Finland, Oct. 31, 1920; s. Douglas K. and Gwynneth M. (Paine) K.; m. Kathleen Edith Luckin, Sept. 11, 1943; children—Peter G., Martin K., Simon M. B.Sc. with 1st class honours in Zoology, U. Edinburgh, Scotland, 1941; Associateship, Imperial Coll. Tropical Agr. (now U. W.I.), Trinidad, 1943; Ph.D., U. Nottingham, Eng., 1956. Entomologist H.M. Colonial Service, Trinidad, 1941-43, Kenya Dept. Agr., 1943-48; acting sr. entomologist Uganda Dept. Agr., 1945; Brit. mil. adminstr., civilian locust-liaison officer, Somalia, 1946-47; 1st head zoology sect. U. Nottingham Sch. Agr., 1948-58; prof. entomology Macdonald Campus, McGill U., 1958—, chmn. dept. entomology and plant pathology, 1958-64; chmn. entomology Macdonald Coll. Campus, McGill U., 1964-72; chmn. Lyman Entomol. Mus. Com., 1960—; dir. Lyman Entomol. Mus. and Research Lab., 1972—. Author: Soil Animals, 1962, 2d edit., 1968, Land of the Grasshoppers, 1974, Land of Locusts I, 1978, Orthopterorum Catalogus 15 and 16, 1977, The Orthopteroid Insects of the Bermudas, 1980, Land of Locusts II, 1983; also more than 400 articles.; Co-author: Orthopteroid Insects of Quebec and the Atlantic Provinces of Canada, 1974; also monograph; Editor, contbg. author: Soil Zoology, 1955. Fellow Royal Soc. Edinburgh, Royal Entomol. Soc. London, Entomol. Soc. Can. (pres. 1972-73, Achievement award and Gold medal 1981), Entomol. Soc. Finland (hon.); mem. Pan-Am. Acridolog. Soc. (hon.), Inst. Biology, Entomol. Soc. Am., Entomol. Soc. Que., Can. Soc. Zoologists, Entomol. Soc. Can., Am. Entomol. Soc., Can. Assn. Univ. Tchrs., Systematics Assn., McGill Assn. Univ. Tchrs., Soc. Systematic Zoology, Assn. Applied Biologists, Am. Acarological Soc., Assn. Tropical Biology, Soc. Bibliograph Natural History, Watsonian Club (life, pres. Montreal br. 1973—), Sigma Xi. Research on Orthopteroids, especially taxonomy of Pyrgomorphidae and Gryllidae, soil fauna especially smaller arthropods, insect poetry; ethnoentomology. Home: 20 Woodridge Crescent Beaconsfield PQ H9W 4G7 Canada Office: Dept Entomology Macdonald Coll Campus of McGill U 21111 Lakeshore Dr Ste Anne de Bellevue PQ H9X 1C0 Canada

KEVILL, DENNIS NEIL, chemistry educator; b. Walton-Le-Dale, Eng., May 27, 1935; came to U.S., 1960, naturalized, 1966; s. Henry and Freda Margaret (Cater) K.; m. Gundula Martina Solis; children: Heide Denise, Peter Frederic. B.Sc., Univ. Coll., London, 1956, Ph.D., 1960. Asst. lectr. Univ. Coll., 1959-60; research asso. U. Nebr., 1960-63; mem. faculty No. Ill. U., DeKalb, 1963—, prof. chemistry, 1970-; vis. lectr. U. W.I., Jamaica, 1968-69; vis. prof. Univ. Coll., London, 1975-76, U. Tübingen, (W.Ger.), 1983; Nat. Acad. Scis. exchange participant with Yugoslavia, 1983, cons. to industry. NATO sr. fellow in sci., 1974. Contbr. articles to profl. jours. Mem. Am. Chem. Soc. (chmn.-elect and program, chmn. Rock River sect. 1980-81, chmn. sect. 1981-82), Chem. Soc. (London), Sigma Xi, Phi Lambda Upsilon. Home: PO Box 383 DeKalb IL 60115

KEVORKIAN, JIRAIR, mathematics, aeronautics and astronautics educator; b. Jerusalem, Israel, May 14, 1933; came to U.S., 1952; s. Leon and Araxie (Kalemkerian) K.; m. Seta Tabourian, Mar. 8, 1980. B.S., Ga. Tech. Inst., 1955, M.S., 1956; Ph.D., Calif. Tech. Inst., 1961. Aerodynamicist Convair, Fort Worth, 1956-57, Calif. Inst. Tech., Pasadena, 1961-64; asst. prof. U. Wash., Seattle, 1964-66, assoc. prof., 1966-71, prof. applied math., aeros. and astronautics, 1971—; cons. Los Alamos Nat. Lab., N. Mex., 1974—; vis. prof. U. Paris, 1971-72.

Co-author: Perturbation Methods in Applied Mathematics, 1981. Fulbright-Hayes vis. lectr., 1975-76. Mem. Soc. for Indsl. and Applied Math. Home: 3730 W Commodore Way Seattle WA 98199 Office: Applied Math Program FD-20 U Wash Seattle WA 98195

KEY, CHAPIN, health cons.; b. Lincoln, Eng., Mar. 6, 1922; emigrated to U.S., 1923, naturalized, 1974; s. Archibald Frederick and Lillian Hannah (Moodey) K.; m. Edna Muriel Brown, Sept. 24, 1949; children: Susan, Brian Chapin. B.Sc., U. Alta., 1941, M.D., 1945; certificate in gen. surgery, Royal Coll. Physicians and Surgeons Can., 1951; M.H.A., U. Minn., 1968. Intern Royal Alexandra Hosp., Edmonton, Alta., 1944; resident City Gen. Hosp., Sheffield, Eng., 1947-49, Gen. Hosp., Nottingham, Eng., 1950-51; practice medicine specializing in surgery, Langley, B.C., Can., 1951-66; adminstrv. resident Palo Alto-Stanford Hosp. Centre, 1967-68; asst. dir. med. services Vancouver (B.C.) Gen. Hosp., 1968-69, dir. med. services, 1969-73, adminstr., 1973, exec. dir., 1973-77, pres., 1977; exec. dir. health programs, Province B.C., 1977-78, dep. minister of health, 1978-81; asst. prof. U. B.C., 1974-76, asso. clin. prof., 1976-78, hon. prof., 1978—; health services cons., 1981—. Mem. tech. subcom. Greater Vancouver Regional Hosp. Dist., 1972-74; mem. Greater Vancouver Met. Mental Health Adv. and Planning Com., 1972-74; preceptor Program in Hosp. Adminstrn. U. Minn., 1974-77; preceptor adminstrn. Canadian Hosp. Assn., 1974-77; chmn. bldg. com. Langley Meml. Hosp., 1954-65; Chmn. Langley Bd. Trade, 1963-64; mem. Langley City Planning Commn., 1956-64. Fellow Royal Coll. Surgeons Can.; mem. Am. Coll. Hosp. Adminstrs., Canadian Coll. Health Care Execs., B.C. Hosp. Assn. (v.p. 1974-77, pres. 1977), B.C. Surg. Soc. Clubs: Vancouver, Royal Vancouver Yacht, Vancouver. Home: 4101 Yew St Apt 410 Vancouver BC Canada V6L 3B7 Office: Chambers in the Station 400 W Cordova Vancouver BC Canada V6B 1G1

KEY, DAVID MCKENDREE, former fgn. service officer; b. Tokyo, Feb. 4, 1900; s. Albert Lenoir and Grace (Condit-Smith) K.; m. Marjorie Wright, Feb. 7, 1925; children—Albert Lenoir II, David McKendree, Marjorie. Student, The Groton Sch., Mass., 1912-18; A.B., Harvard, 1922; postgrad., Gonville and Caius Coll., Cambridge, Eng., 1922-23, Georgetown Sch. Fgn. Service, Washington, 1923-24. Detailed to Dept. State, 1925; vice consul of career at Antwerp, Belgium, 1926; 3d sec. embassy, Berlin, 1927, London, Eng., 1929; attended Disarmament Conf., Geneva, Switzerland, 1932, London Econ. Conf., 1933; asst. chief Div. Current Info., 1934; consul, 2d sec., Ottawa, Ont., 1936, 1st sec. embassy, Rome, 1940; asst. liaison officer Dept. State, 1941-44; consul gen., Barcelona, Spain, 1944-45, counselor of embassy, Rome, 1945-46, Rio do Janeiro, Brazil, 1947-49, ambassador to, Burma, 1950-52; Far Eastern adviser U.S. del. 6th, 7th, 8th gen. assemblies UN, 1952-53; asst. sec. state internat. orgn. affairs, 1953-55; gen. mgr. Am. Fgn. Service Assn., 1957-61; pres. Diplomatic and Consular Officers Ret. Inc., 1957-58. Chmn. nat. com. Am. Med. Center for Burma, 1959-64. Served with USMC, World War I. Clubs: Alibi, Dacor House (Washington). Home: Mountain Lake Lake Wales FL 33853

KEY, DONALD, art critic; b. Iowa City, Jan. 30, 1923; s. Philip R. and Lola (Diehl) K.; m. Patricia Anne Miller, May 11, 1947; 1 son, Theodore Allen. B.A. in Journalism, U. Iowa, 1950. Asst. to editor, fine arts columnist Cedar Rapids (Ia.) Gazette, 1950-59; art editor Milw. Jour., 1959-72. Author: Future Unknown; Contbr. articles to profl. jours. Served with AUS, 1942-46; ETO. Mem. Theta Xi, Sigma Delta Chi. Club: Milwaukee Press. Home: 7519 N Crossway Rd Milwaukee WI 53217

KEY, JACK DAYTON, librarian; b. Enid, Okla., Feb. 24, 1934; s. Ernest Dayton and Janie (Haldeman) K.; m. Virgie Ruth Richardson, Aug. 12, 1956; children—Toni, Scot, Todd. B.A., Phillips U., Enid, Okla., 1958; M.A., U. N.Mex., 1960; M.S., U. Ill., 1962. Staff supr. Grad. Library U. Ill., 1960-62; pharmacy librarian U. Iowa, 1962-64; med. librarian Lovelace Found. for Med. Edn. and Research, Albuquerque, 1965-70; librarian Mayo Clinic, Rochester, Minn., 1970—; cons. in field; participant Naval War Coll. Conf., 1979; Alberta A. Brown lectr. Western Mich. U., 1979. Author: The Origin of the Vaccine Inoculation by Edward Jenner, 1977, William Alexander Hammond (1828-1900), 1979; editor: Library Automation: The Orient and South Pacific, 1975, Automated Activities in Health Sciences Libraries, 1975-78, Classics and Other Selected Readings in Medical Librarianship, 1980, A Devil Visits Arabela: An Unusual Encounter with Radix Pedis Diaboli, 1980; contbr. articles to profl. jours. Served with USN, 1952-55. U. N.Mex. fellow, 1958-59; N.Mex. Library Assn. Marion Dorroh Meml. scholar, 1960; Rotary Paul Harris fellow, 1979; recipient Outstanding Hist. Writing award Minn. Medicine, 1980; decorated knight Icelandic Order of Falcon. Mem. Med. Library Assn., Am. Inst. History Pharmacy, Am. Assn. History Medicine, Am. Med. Writers Assn., Am. Osler Soc. Republican. Mem. Disciples of Christ. Clubs: Alcuin Soc., Ampersand, Rotary. Home: 624 23d St NE Rochester MN 55901 Office: Mayo Clinic Rochester NM 55901

KEY, JOE LYNN, plant biochemist; b. Troy, Tenn., Sept. 10, 1933; m. Connie Clark, Sept. 8, 1956; children: Diana, Debra. B.S., U. Tenn., 1955; M.S., U. Ill., Ph.D., 1959. NSF postdoctoral fellow U. Calif., Davis, 1959-60, asst. prof. botany, 1960-62; asso. prof. Purdue U., West Lafayette, Ind., 1962-66, prof., 1966-69; research prof. U. Ga., Athens, 1969—, chmn. div. biol. scis., 1972-83; on leave as dir. Competitive Research Grants Office (U.S. Dept. Agr.), 1978-79; half-time leave with Agrigenetics Corp., Boulder, Colo., 1983-84. Contbr. articles to profl. jours. Mem. Am. Soc. Biol. Chemists, Internat. Soc. Plant Molecular Biology, Am. Soc. Plant Physiologists (pres. 1977), Developmental Biology Soc. Am. Home: 129 Beaver Trail Athens GA 30605 Office: Botany Dept U Ga Athens GA 30602

KEY, MARCUS M(ALVIN), physician, educator; b. Lakeland, Fla., Mar. 2, 1924; s. Marcus M. and Annabelle (Farish) K.; m. Dorothy Elizabeth McTeigue, Aug. 23, 1952; children: Marianne, Robert F., James T., Dorothy E., Marcus M., Margaret S. B.A., Columbia U., 1949, M.D., 1952; M.D., M.Indsl. Health, Harvard U., 1954. Diplomate: Am. Bd. Dermatology, Am. Bd. Preventive Medicine. Intern USPHS Hosp., Boston, 1952-53; resident Presbyterian Hosp., N.Y.C., 1954-56; fellow Cin. Gen. Hosp., 1956-58; asst. chief sect. dermatology Div. Occupational Health, USPHS, Cin., 1960-65, chief sect. dermatology, 1965-67; chief clin. services occupational health program Nat. Center Urban and Indsl. Health, Cin., 1967-68; dep. dir. Bur. Occupational Safety and Health, Environ. Control Adminstrn., Cin., 1968-69; dir. Bur. Occupational Safety and Health, Rockville, Md., 1969-71, Nat. Inst. Occupational Safety and Health and asst. surgeon gen., Rockville, 1971-74; asso. prof. public health and preventive medicine W.Va. U., 1967-74; asso. clin. prof. dermatology U. Cin., 1971-74, asso. clin. prof. environ. health, 1971-74; prof. occupational medicine Sch. Public Health U. Tex. Health Sci. Ctr., Houston, 1975—, prof. family practice and community medicine, prof. dermatology Sch. Medicine, 1982; interim dir. Houston Health Dept., 1982—; dir. Tex. Occupational Safety and Health Ednl. Resource Center, Houston, 1977-82. Editor: (with others) Pulmonary Reactions to Coal Dust, 1971, Occupational Diseases, A Guide to Their Recognition, 1977; bd. editors: Cutis, 1965-74, Archives Environ. Health, 1976-79. Ex-officio mem. Nat. Commn. on State Workmen's Compensation Laws, 1971-72; expert cons. WHO, 1973—; mem. med. resources adv. panel Tex. Air Control Bd., 1977—; mem. Pres.'s Com. on Health and Ecol. Effects of Increased Coal Utilization, 1977. Served as capt. USAAF, 1943-47. Decorated Air medal; recipient Meritorious Service medal USPHS, 1970, Meritorious Achievement award Am. Conf. Govtl. Indsl. Hygienists, 1972. Fellow Am. Occupational Med. Assn., Am. Acad. Occupational Medicine (pres. 1978-79); mem. Am. Conf. Govtl. Indl. Hygienists (chmn. 1969-70), Am. Indsl. Hygiene Assn. (dir. Gulf Coast chpt. 1978-81), Am. Acad. Dermatology, Tex. Med. Assn., Harris County (Tex.) Med. Soc., Royal Soc. Medicine (hon.). Democrat. Roman Catholic. Club: Army and Navy. Home: 614 Wellesley St Houston TX 77024 Office: 1115 N MacGregor Houston TX 77030

KEY, MARY RITCHIE (MRS. AUDLEY E. PATTON), linguist, author, educator; b. San Diego, Mar. 19, 1924; d. George Lawrence and Iris (Lyons) Ritchie; children: Mary Helen Key Ellis, Harold Hayden Key, Thomas George Key. Student, U. Chgo., summer 1954, U. Mich., 1959; M.A., U. Tex., 1960, Ph.D., 1963; postgrad., UCLA, 1966. Asst. prof. linguistics Chapman Coll., Orange, Calif., 1963-66; asst. prof. linguistics U. Calif., Irvine, 1966-71, assoc. prof., 1971-78, prof., 1978—, chmn. program linguistics, 1969-71, 75-77; cons. Am. Indian langs., Spanish, in Mexico, 1946-55, S.Am., 1955-62, English dialects, 1968-74, Easter Island, 1975, Calif. Dept. Edn., 1966, 70-75, Center Applied Linguistics, Washington, 1967, 69; lectr. in field. Author: numerous books, including Comparative Tacanan Phonology, 1968; Male/Female Language, 1975, Paralanguage and Kinesics, 1975, Nonverbal Communication, 1977, The Grouping of South American Indian Languages, 1979, The Relationship of Verbal and Nonverbal Communication, 1980, Catherine the Great's Linguistic Contribution, 1980, Polynesian and American Linguistic Connections, 1983; founder, editor: newsletter Nonverbal Components of Communication, 1972-76; mem. editorial bd.: Forum Linguisticum, 1976—, Lang. Scis., 1978—, La Linguistique, 1979—; contbr. articles to profl. jours. Recipient Friends of Library Book award, 1976; U. Calif. Regent's grantee, 1974; Fulbright-Hays grantee, 1975. Mem. AAUW, Linguistic Soc. Am., Am. Dialect Soc. (exec. council; regional sec. 1974—), Internat. Reading Assn. (dir. 1968-72), Delta Kappa Gamma (local pres. 1974-76). Office: Program in Linguistics U Calif Irvine CA 92717

KEY, ROBERT EDWARD LEE, judge; b. Evergreen, Ala., Feb. 2, 1917; s. Robert Edward Lee and Ellen Winifred (Weaver) K.; m. Marjorie Virginia Yeatman, Dec. 11, 1941; 1 dau., Elizabeth Ann (Mrs. H. Eldon Scott III). A.B., George Washington U., 1947; LL.B., U. Ala., 1949. Bar: Ala. bar 1949. Practiced in, Evergreen, 1949-52; circuit solicitor 21st Jud. Circuit of Ala., 1952-65; circuit judge 35th Jud. Circuit of Ala., 1965—; dir. 1st Ala. Bank of Conecuh County, Evergreen. Chmn. Charles Ballard McInnis Trust Com., 1972—; trustee Samford U., 1979—. Mem. Ala. Assn. Circuit Judges (pres. 1981-82), Phi Delta Phi. Clubs: Mason (Shriner, K.T. Home: 308 Rural St Evergreen AL 36401 Office: Conecuh County Courthouse Evergreen AL 36401

KEY, TED, cartoonist; b. Fresno, Calif., Aug. 25, 1912; s. Simon Leon and Fanny (Kahn) K.; m. Anne Elizabeth Wilkinson, Sept. 30, 1937; children—Stephen Lewis, David, Peter. A.B., U. Calif. at Berkeley, 1933. Asso. editor Judge, 1937. Writer, cartoonist: others This Week; radio script writer, J. Walter Thompson Co., for CBS, NBC; radio play The Clinic; pub. in: anthology Best Broadcasts of, 1939-40; creator: cartoon features Diz and Liz, Jack and Jill mag, 1961; Author, creator of: Hazel appearing in Sat. Eve. Post, 1943-69, King Features Syndicate, 1969—; book Hazel, 1946, Here's Hazel, Many Happy Returns, 1950, If You Like Hazel, 1952, So'm I, 1953, Hazel Rides Again, 1955, Fasten Your Seat Belts, 1956, Phyllis, 1957, All Hazel, 1958, The Hazel Jubilee, 1959, The Biggest Dog in the World, 1960, Hazel Time, 1962, Life With Hazel, 1965, Diz and Liz, 1965, Squirrels in the Feeding Station, 1967, Hazel Power, 1971, Right On Hazel, 1972, Ms. Hazel, 1972; screenplay Million Dollar Duck; movie story Gus; Creator: Hazel TV Show, NBC-TV; author: movie story and screenplay The Cat from Outer Space; creator: Positive Attitude Posters, 1965—, Sales Bullets, 1960—. Served with Signal Corps AUS, 1944-46. Mem. Nat. Cartoonists Soc., Writers Guild Am. West. Jewish. Club: Players (N.Y.C.). Address: 1694 Glenhardie Rd Wayne PA 19087

KEYDEL, FREDERICK REID, lawyer; b. Detroit, May 8, 1928; s. Oscar Frederick, Jr. and Miriam Powers (Reid) K.; m. Roberta Wells Latzer, Mar. 15, 1952; children: Janet Powers Keydel Lawson, William Latzer, Thomas Mason. B.A., Yale U., 1949; J.D., U. Mich., 1952. Bar: Mich. 1952. Asso. firm Joslyn, Joslyn & Dean, Detroit, 1954-59, partner, 1959-64, Joslyn, Keydel, Wallace & Joslyn, Detroit, 1964—; dir. Miami Oil Producers, Inc., 1975—; dir., sec. Pointe Aux Barques, Inc., 1961—; vis. adj. prof. U. Miami Sch. Law LL.M. Program in Estate Planning, 1975—. Contbr. articles to profl. jours. Served with USAF, 1952-54. Mem. Am. Coll. Probate Counsel (regent 1980—), Internat. Acad. Estate and Trust Law (mem. exec. council 1980—), Am. Bar Assn. (sec., mem. council sect. real property, probate and trust law 1977-81, sec. 1980-81), Am. Law Inst., Am. Coll. Tax Counsel. Episcopalian. Clubs: Detroit, Detroit Athletic, Country Club of Detroit, Pointe Aux Barques. Home: 157 Kenwood Rd Grosse Pointe Farms MI 48236 Office: 2211 Comerica Bldg Detroit MI 48226

KEYE, WILLIAM R., business exec.; b. St. Paul, 1921; married. B.S. in Elec. Engring, U. Minn., 1943. With UNIVAC div. Remington Rand, 1953-57; founder, officer Control Data Corp., Mpls., 1967—, sr. v.p. ops., 1967-69, exec. v.p. ops., 1969-70, chmn. exec. com., exec. v.p., 1970-73, vice chmn. bd., 1973—, also dir. Office: Control Data Corp 8100 34th Ave S Bloomington Minneapolis MN 55420 *

KEYES, ARTHUR HAWKINS, JR., architect; b. Rutland, Vt., May 26, 1917; s. Arthur Hawkins and Blanche (Emery) K.; m. Lucile Sheppard, Mar. 29, 1941; children: Arthur S., Spencer S., Janet S. A.B. cum laude, Princeton U., 1939; M.Arch., Harvard U., 1942. Partner Keyes, Lethbridge and Condon, Washington, 1956-75; partner Keyes Condon Florance (Architects), Washington, 1975-80, pres., 1980—, Sea Ridge Devel. Corp.; Pres. Washington Bldg. Congress, 1964-65; chmn. alumni adv. council Sch. Architecture, Princeton U., 1965-73. Served with USNR, 1942-46. Fellow AIA (spl. presdl. citation 1982); mem. Soc. Archtl. Historians, Nat. Trust Hist. Preservation, Com. of 100 on the Fed. City. Republican. Clubs: Cosmos, Chevy Chase. Home: 2605 31st St NW Washington DC Office: 1320 19th St NW Washington DC 20036

KEYES, DANIEL, author; b. N.Y.C., Aug. 9, 1927; s. William and Betty (Alicke) K.; m. Aurea Georgina Vazquez, Oct. 14, 1952; children—Hillary Ann, Leslie Joan. B.A. in Psychology, Bklyn. Coll., 1950, M.A. in English, 1961. Asso. fiction editor Magazine Mgmt. Co., N.Y.C., 1950-52; v.p. Fenko and Keyes Photography, Inc., 1952-53; tchr. English N.Y.C. Bd. Edn., 1955-62; instr. English Wayne State U., Detroit, 1962-66; mem. faculty Ohio U., Athens, 1966—, prof. English and creative writing, 1972—. Author: novels Flowers for Algernon (Hugo award 1959), 1966 (Nebula award 1966), The Touch, 1968, The Fifth Sally, 1980; non-fiction The Minds of Billy Milligan, 1981 (Spl. award Mystery Writers Am.). Served with U.S. Maritime Service, 1945-47. Mem. PEN, Authors' Guild, Dramatists' Guild, Assoc. Writing Programs., Authors' League Am. Office: Ohio U Athens OH 45701

KEYES, EDWARD LAWRENCE, JR., electric company executive; b. N.Y.C., Apr. 19, 1929; s. Edward Lawrence and Emily (Shepley) K.; 1 dau., Elisabeth Elliott. B.A. cum laude, Princeton, 1951. Asst. to pres. Emerson Electric Co., St. Louis, 1961-64, asst. v.p. adminstrn., 1964-66, v.p. adminstrn., 1966-67, exec. v.p., dir., 1967-70, pres., 1970, 1970-71, 1971-73, dir. div., group v.p. corporate, 1973-74, exec. v.p. ops., 1974-77, pres. co., 1977—, chief operating officer, 1978—, corp. dir., 1973—, also dir.; dir. 1st Nat. Bank Clayton, Central Trust (Jefferson City), Mo. Served to 1st lt. USAF, 1951-56. Republican. Roman Catholic. Clubs: Cottage (Princeton); St. Louis Country, Racquet (St. Louis); Log Cabin. Home: 33 Deerfield Rd Saint Louis MO 63124 Office: 8000 W Florissant Ave Saint Louis MO 63136

KEYES, FENTON, inst. adminstr.; b. N.Y.C., Jan. 26, 1915; s. Harold Brown and Elsie Louise (Fenton) K.; m. Elizabeth Dortch Dix, Nov. 18, 1944; children—Charles Fenton, Janet Bayard. B.A., Yale U., 1937, Ph.D., 1942. Instr. sociology Colgate U, 1940-42; supr. records Hdqrs. 2d Service Command M.I., Governors Island, N.Y., 1942-43; analyst Dept. Justice, Washington, 1943; asst. prof. sociology, asst. to pres. Skidmore Coll., 1946-47, bus. mgr., 1947-53, v.p., 1953-56; dean coll., dean grad. sch. Tex. State Coll. for Women, 1956-57, Tex. Woman's U., dean faculty and grad. studies, 1957-60; pres. Coker Coll., Hartsville, S.C., 1960-68; lab. mgr. behavioral and social scis. lab. Franklin Inst. Research Labs., Phila., 1968-70; dir. acad. affairs Coll. Allied Health Scis., Thomas Jefferson U., 1970-72; pvt. cons., 1973—, free lance writer, 1973—. Author: Aim for a Job in Allied Health, 1973, A Definitive Study of Your Future in Social Work, 1975, A Definitive Study of Your Future in Mental Health, 1976, Opportunities in a Psychiatric Career, 1977, A Definitive Study of Your Future as a Paramedic, 1979, Exploring Careers for the Gifted, 1981; Contbr. articles to profl. jours. Chief historian Staff Comdg. Gen. China Theater, 1944-46. Served to capt. U.S. Army, 1943-46. Decorated Bronze Star with oak-leaf cluster. Fellow Am. Sociol. Assn. Democrat. Home: 643 Addison St Philadelphia PA 19147 (summer) Chelmsford North Litchfield Beach Box 221 Pawley's Island SC 29585

KEYES, GORDON LINCOLN, history educator; b. Kearney, Ont., Can., Mar. 5, 1920; s. Arthur Beverley and Edna (File) K.; m. Mary Ferguson, June 9, 1945; children: Katherine Mary, John Thomas David. B.A., U. Toronto (Ont.), 1941, M.A., 1942; Ph.D., Princeton U., 1944. Lectr. in Greek McMaster U., Hamilton, Ont., 1941-42; asst. prof. Birmingham-So. Coll., Ala., 1945-47; faculty Victoria Coll., U. Toronto, 1947—, prof. Greek and Roman history, 1963—, Nelles prof. ancient history, 1967—, also chmn. combined depts. classics, 1967-69, chmn. dept. classics, 1971-75; prin. Victoria Coll., 1976-81. Author: Christian Faith and the Interpretation of History: A Study of St. Augustine's Philosophy of History, 1966. Can. Council sr. research fellow, 1959-60. Mem. Soc. Promotion Roman Studies, Am. Philol. Assn., Classical Assn. Can., Mediaeval Acad. Am. Home: 122 Orchard Dr Thornbury ON N0H 2P0 Canada

KEYES, JAMES HENRY, corporation financial executive; b. LaCrosse, Wis., Sept. 2, 1940; s. Donald M. and Mary M. (Nodolf) K.; m. Judith Ann Carney, Nov. 21, 1964; children: James Patrick, Kevin, Timothy. B.S., Marquette U., 1962; M.B.A., Northwestern U., 1963. Instr. Marquette U., Milw., 1963-65; c.p.a. Peat. Marwick & Mitchell, Milw., 1965-66; with Johnson Controls, Inc., Milw., 1967—, mgr. systems dept., 1967-71, div. controller, 1971-73, 1971-73, corp. controller, treas., 1973-77, v.p., chief fin. officer, 1977—. Active Milw. Symphony Orch., 1980—. Mem. Fin. Execs. Inst., Am. Inst. C.P.A.s, Wis. Inst. C.P.A.s. Office: Johnson Controls Inc 5757 N Green Bay Ave Milwaukee WI 53209

KEYES, MARGARET NAUMANN, educator; b. Mt. Vernon, Iowa, Mar. 4, 1918; d. Charles Reuben and Sarah (Naumann) K. B.A., Cornell Coll., Mt. Vernon, 1939, L.H.D., 1976; M.S., U. Wis., 1951; Ph.D. (Ellen H. Richards grad. fellow), Fla. State U., 1965; H.H.D., Coe Coll., 1977. Tchr. home econs. Stanley (Iowa) High Sch., 1939-42, Washington Jr. High Sch., Clinton, Iowa, 1942-44, Clinton High Sch., 1944-50; instr. related art U. Iowa, Iowa City, 1951-57, asst. prof. related art dept. home econs., 1957-68, asso. prof., 1968-75, prof., 1975—; research prof. U. Iowa Found., 1971-74. Author: Nineteenth Century Home Architecture Iowa City, 1967; mem. editorial bd., Home Econs. Research Jour; contbr. articles to periodicals. Mem. Terr. Hill Planning Commn. for Iowa, Terr. Hill Authority for Iowa; mem. design rev. bd. Iowa City Urban Renewal Commn.; dir. research Old Capitol Restoration Com., 1971-75; dir. Old Capitol, 1975—; mem. Iowa State Hist. Bd. Mem. Am. Home Econ. Assn. (exec. bd., chmn. art sect.), Iowa Home Econs. Assn., AAUP, Soc. Archtl. Historians, Am. Soc. Interior Designers, Interior Design Educators Council, Iowa Soc. Preservation Hist. Landmarks (dir. 1970-75), Cornell Coll. Alumni Assn. (dir. 1970-73), Nat. Trust Hist. Preservation (bd. advs. 1974-77), Internat. Fedn. Home Econs. (individual), Victorian Soc. Am. (v.p., dir. 1974-80), P.E.O., Phi Beta Kappa, Omicron Nu, Omicron Delta Kappa. Democrat. Presbyterian. Club: Altrusa (pres. 1969-70).

KEYES, ROBERT WILLIAM, physicist; b. Chgo., Dec. 2, 1921; s. Lee P. and Katherine K.; m. Sophie Skadorwa, June 4, 1966; children—Andrew, Claire. B.S., U. Chgo., 1942, M.S., 1949, Ph.D., 1953. With Argonne Nat. Lab., 1946-50; staff mem. Westinghouse Research Lab., Pitts., 1953-60; mem. research staff IBM Research Lab., Yorktown Heights, N.Y., 1960—; vis. physicist Am. Phys. Soc. Vis. Indsl. Physicists Program, 1974-75, 77; vice chmn. Gordon Conf. on High Pressure Physics, 1970; chmn. Gordon Conf. on Chemistry and Physics of Microstructure Fabrication, 1976, Nat. Materials Adv. Bd. (ad hoc com. on ion implantation as a new surface treatment tech.), 1978; mem. Nat. Acad. Scis.-NAE-NRC evaluation panel Nat. Bur. Standards, 1970-73; cons. physics survey com., mem. statis. data panel Nat. Acad. Sci.-NRC Council Physics Survey Com., 1972; mem. data and info. panel Nat. Acad. Sci.-NRC Com. on Survey of Materials Sci. and Engring., 1974. Editor: Revs. Modern Physics, 1976—; corr.: Comments on Solid State Physics, 1970—. Served with USN, 1944-46. Recipient Outstanding Contbn. award IBM, 1963. Fellow Am. Phys. Soc., IEEE (chmn. subcom. cultural and sci. relations 1976, mem. del. to USSR 1975, W.R.G. Baker prize 1976); mem. Nat. Acad. Engring. Asso. Office: IBM PO Box 218 Yorktown Heights NY 10598

KEYS, SAMUEL ROBERT, educator; b. New Castle, Ind., July 11, 1922; s. John B. and Pearl (Smith) K.; children: Carol, Bryan, Dana, Scott. Student, Earlham Coll., 1942-43; B.A., Olivet Nazarene Coll., 1948; M.A., U. Mo. at Kansas City, 1950; Ph.D., U. Minn., 1959. Tchr., counselor Kansas City (Mo.) pub. schs., 1949-53; asst. prof. No. Ill. U., DeKalb, 1958-60; asso. curriculum coordinator, State of Ill., 1960-61; asso. prof. N.Y.U., 1961-67; asso. dean Coll. Edn., U. Mo., 1967-69; prof., dean Coll. Edn., Kansas State U., Manhattan, 1969-76; on leave of absence serving as spl. adv. to U.S. Commr. Edn.; also dep. commr. U.S. Office Edn., Washington, 1976-78; prof. Kans. State U., Manhattan, 1978—; dir. higher edn. program, past chmn. exec. com., pres. corp. Mid-Continent Regional Ednl. Lab.; past mem. standards adv. bd. Kans. Dept. Edn. Dem. candidate for Congress, 1980. Served with USNR, 1942-45. Fellow Fund Advancement Edn., 1953-54. Mem. AAUP, Assn. Supervision and Curriculum Devel., Assn. Higher Edn., Phi Delta Kappa. Club: Rotary. Home: 1422 McCain Ln Manhattan KS 66502

KEYS, THOMAS EDWARD, medical library consultant; b. Greenville, Miss., Dec. 2, 1908; s. Thomas Napoleon and Margaret (Boothroyd) K.; m. Elizabeth Schaack, Nov. 2, 1934; children: Thomas Frederick, Charles Edward (dec.). A.B., Beloit Coll., 1931, Sc.D., 1972; M.A., U. Chgo., 1934. Order asst. Newberry Library, Chgo., 1931-32; asst. librarian Mayo Clinic, 1934-35, reference librarian, 1935-42, librarian, 1946-69, sr. library cons., 1969-72; prof. Mayo Found. Grad. Sch. Medicine, 1969-72, emeritus, 1972—; cons., lectr. in field. Author: (with others) Cardiac Classics (later Classics of Cardiology), 1941, 61, 83, History of Surgical Anesthesia, 1945, 63, 78, (with A. Faulconer) Foundations of Anesthesiology, 1965, (with Jack Key) Classics of Medical Librarianship, 1980; others; contbr. numerous articles to profl. jours. Bd. regents Nat. Library of Medicine, 1959-62. Recipient numerous awards. Fellow Med. Library Assn., Mayo Found. Soc. for History of Medicine; mem. Internat. Soc. History Medicine, Am. Soc. Anesthesiologists (hon.), Am. Soc. History of Anesthesia (hon.), Doctors Mayo Soc., Am. Osler Assn., Phi Beta Kappa, Beta Phi Mu, Pi Kappa Alpha. Episcopalian. Home and Office: 1224 S Peninsula Dr Apt 108 Daytona Beach FL 32018

KEYSER, FRANK RAY, JR., former governor Vermont; b. Chelsea, Vt., Aug. 17, 1927; s. Frank Ray and Ellen L. (Larkin) K.; m. Joan Friedgen, July 15, 1950; children—Christopher Scott, Carol Ellen, Frank Ray III. Student, Tufts Coll., 1946-49, LL.D., 1961; LL.B., Boston U., 1952; LL.D., Norwich U., 1962. Bar: Vt. bar 1952. Practiced in, Chelsea, 1952-65; mem. Vt. Ho. of Reps., 1955-59, speaker, 1959-60; gov., Vt., 1961-63; mem. law firm Wilson & Keyser, 1952-65; chmn. law firm Keyser Crowley Banse Akel & Faley, Inc.; chmn., dir. White Pigment Corp., Proctor Trust Co.; chmn. dir. Vt. Bancorp.; dir. Keystone Custodian Funds, Inc., Mass. Cos., Inc., Union Mut. Ins. Co., Central Vt. Ry., Grand Trunk Corp., Central Vt. Public Service Corp., Sherburne Corp., Yankee Nuclear Power Corp. Served with USNR, World War II. Named Outstanding Young Vermonter Vt. Jr. C. of C., 1959; One of 10 Outstanding Young Men in Nation, 1961, Nat Jr. C. of C. Mem. ABA, Vt. Bar Assn., Assoc. Industries of Vt. (dir., v.p.), Farm Bur., Am. Legion. Republican. Mason. Address: 64 Warner Ave Proctor VT 05765

KEYSER, SAMUEL JAY, linguistics educator; b. July 7, 1935; s. Abraham L. and Sabina (Shaplen) K.; m. Margaret Joan Horridge, Mar. 10, 1959; children: Rachel Suzanne, Beth Rebecca, Benjamin Jay Kendall. B.A., George Washington U., 1956; B.S. hons, Oxford (Eng.) U., 1958, M.A., 1962, Yale U., 1960, Ph.D., 1962. Staff research lab. Mass. Inst. Tech., 1961-62, faculty, 1977—, Brandeis U., 1965-71, Univ. Coll. London, 1971-72, U. Mass. at Amherst, 1972-77. Author: English Stress: Its Form, Its Growth and Its Role in Verse, 1971, Beginning English Grammar, 1973, CV Phnology, 1983; Editor: Linguistic Inquiry, 1970—, Current Studies in Linguistics, 1972, Linguistic Inquiry Monograph Series, 1976. Served with USAF, 1962-65. Fulbright scholar, 1956-57, 57-58; sr. Fulbright, 1971-72. Mem. Linguistic Soc. Am., Linguistic Soc. Gt. Britain, Philol. Soc., Phi Beta Kappa. Home: 4 Ames St Cambridge MA 02139 Office: 18 Vassar St Room 20D-213 Cambridge MA 02139

KEYSERLING, LEON H., economist, lawyer; b. Charleston, S.C., Jan. 22, 1908; s. William and Jennie (Hyman) K.; m. Mary Dublin, Oct. 4, 1940. A.B., Columbia U., 1928; LL.B., Harvard U., 1931; D.Bus. Sci. hon., Bryant Coll., 1965, L.H.D., U. Mo., 1978. Bar: N.Y., D.C., U.S. Supreme Ct. Asst. dept. econs. Columbia U. (teaching), 1932-33; atty. AAA, 1933; sec., legis. asst. to Senator Robert F. Wagner, 1933-37; top expert Senate Com. Banking and Currency, 1935-37; gen. counsel U.S. Housing Authority, 1937-38, dep. adminstr. and gen. counsel, 1938-42; acting adminstr. U.S. Housing Authortiy, 1941-42; acting commr. Fed. Pub. Housing Authority, 1942; gen. counsel Nat. Housing Agy., 1942-46; vice chmn. Pres.'s Council Econ. Advisers (Employment Act 1946), 1946-50, chmn., 1950-53, de facto mem. Cabinet and Nat. Security Council; cons., economist and practicing atty. working with various nat. firms, orgns. and individuals in U.S. and at times cons. to govts. of France, Israel and P.R., 1953-71, vol. pub. service U.S. economy and policies, 1971—; hon. mem. faculty Indsl. Coll. Armed Forces, 1966—; cons. U.S. Senate and Ho. of Reps., 1942-46, 53—; founder, pres. Conf. on Econ. Progress, 1954—; pres. Nat. Com. for Labor Israel, 1969-73; dir. cos. Author: (with Rexford G. Tugwell) Redirecting Education, 1934, Toward Full Employment and Full Production, 1954, Inflation-Cause and Cure, 1959, The Federal Budget and the General Welfare, 1959, Key Policies for Full Employment, 1962, (with Benjamin A. Javits), The Peace by Investment Corporation, 1961, Poverty and Deprivation in the U.S., 1962, Taxes and the Public Interest, 1963, Two Top Priority Programs to Reduce Umemployment, 1963, The Toll of Rising Interest Rates, 1964, Progress or Poverty, 1964, Agriculture and the Public Interest, 1965, The Move toward Railroad Mergers, 1965, The Role of Wages in a Great Society, 1966, A Freedom Budget for All Americans, 1966, Goals for Teachers Salaries in Our Public Schools, 1967, Achieving Nationwide Educational Excellence, 1968, Israel's Economic Progress, 1968, Taxiation of Whom and for What?, 1969, More Growth with Less Inflation or More Inflation without Growth?, 1970, Wages, Prices, and Profits, 1971, The Coming Crisis in Housing, 1972, The Scarcity School of Economics, 1973, Full Employment without Inflation, 1975, 'Liberal" and 'Conservative" National Economic Policies and Their Consequences, 1919-1979, 1979, Money, Credit, and Interest Rates: Their Gross Mismanagement by the Federal Reserve System, 1980, The Economics of Discrimination, 1981, How to Cut Unemployment to 4 Percent and End Inflation and Deficits by 1987, 1983; co-author: numerous pub. reports Council Econ. Advisers, 1946-53. Winner $10,000 prize Pabst Postwar Employment Contest, 1944; award Centennial of Fiorello H. LaGuardia, 1983. Mem. Am. Econ. Assn., Am. Polit. Sci. Assn., Phi Beta Kappa. Clubs: Cosmos, Harvard; Columbia U. (Washington). *

KEYT, DAVID, philosophy and classics educator; b. Indpls., Feb. 22, 1930; s. Herbert Coe and Hazel Marguerite (Sissman) K.; m. Christine Harwood Mullikin, June 25, 1975; children by previous marriage: Sarah, Aaron. A.B., Kenyon Coll., 1951; M.A., Cornell U., 1953, Ph.D., 1955. Instr. dept. philosophy U. Wash., 1957-60, asst. prof., 1960-64, assoc. prof., 1964-69, prof., 1969—, adj. prof. classics, 1977-79, acting chmn. dept. philosophy, 1967-68, 70, chmn. dept., 1971-78; vis. asst. prof. dept. philosophy UCLA, 1962-63; vis. assoc. prof. Cornell U., 1968-69; dir. Nat. Endowment for Humanities summer seminar, 1979. Contbr. articles in field to profl. jours. Served with U.S. Army, 1955-57. Inst. for Research in the Humanities fellow U. Wis., 1966-67; Center for Hellenic Studies fellow, 1974-75; Inst. for Advanced Study mem., 1983-84. Mem. Am. Philos. Assn., Soc. Ancient Greek Philosophy. Home: 12032 36th Ave NE Seattle WA 98125 Office: Dept Philosophy Univ Wash Seattle WA 98195

KEYWORTH, A. L., lumber and building supplies company executive. Chmn., pres. Beaver Lumber Co., Ltd., Willowdale, Ont., Can. Office: Beaver Lumber Co Ltd 245 Fairview Mall Dr Willowdale ON Canada M2J 4T1§

KEYWORTH, GEORGE ALBERT, III, Physicist; b. Boston, Nov. 30, 1939; s. Robert Allen and Leontine (Briggs) K.; m. Polly Lauterbach, July 28, 1962; children: Deirdre Anne, George Albert II. B.S., Yale U., 1963; Ph.D., Duke U., 1968; D.Sc. (hon.), Rensselaer Poly. Inst., 1982, D.Eng., Mich. Tech. Inst., 1984. Staff Los Alamos Nat. Lab., 1968-74, group leader neutron physics, 1974-78, div. leader, 1978-81; sci. adviser to Pres., dir. U.S. Office Sci. and Tech. Policy, Washington, 1981. Mem. Vice Pres.'s Task Force on Regulatory Relief, Pres.'s Commn. on Indsl. Competitiveness. Recipient Chmn.'s award Am. Assn. Engring. Socs., 1982. Fellow Am. Phys. Soc.; mem. AAAS, Sigma Xi. Republican. Club: Cosmos (Washington). Office: Office of Sci and Tech Policy Washington DC 20506

KEZDI, PAUL, medical educator, cardiologist; b. Monor, Hungary, Nov. 13, 1914; came to U.S., 1951, naturalized, 1957; s. Walter and Anna (Buday) Konig; m. Anita Bournakis, Apr. 29, 1965; children—Melinda Griesman, Ann Radcliffe, Laura J., Paula C., Chris. M.D. cum laude, U. Budapest, 1942. Diplomate: Am. Bd. Internal Medicine. Intern Meth. Hosp., Madison, Wis., 1952; resident Northwestern U. Hosp., Chgo., 1953-54; asst. prof. medicine, then asso. prof. Northwestern U. Med. Sch., 1958-65; prof. medicine Ind. U. Sch. Medicine, 1965-72; clin. prof. Ohio State U. Sch. Medicine, 1965-75; asso. dean research affairs, prof. medicine Wright State U. Sch. Medicine, 1976—; dir. Cox Heart Inst., Dayton, Ohio, 1965—; Mem. program project com. Nat. Heart Inst., 1965-68; cons. Nat. Center Health Services Research and Devel., 1968-69. Author: You and Your Heart, 1977; Editor: Baroreceptor and Hypertension, 1967; editorial bd.: Jour. Electrocardiology, 1968-73, Am. Jour. Physiology, 1970—. Trustee Kettering (Ohio) Med. Center, 1971-76. Fellow Am. Coll. Cardiology, Am. Coll. Chest Physicians; mem. A.M.A., Am. Heart Assn. (fellow council clin. cardiology, med. adv. bd. council high blood pressure research pres. Miami Valley chpt. 1974-75), Central Soc. Clin. Research. Home: 1712 Ladera Trail Dayton OH 45459

KEZDY, FERENC J., biochemist, educator; b. Budapest, Hungary, July 28, 1929; came to U.S., 1961, naturalized, 1969; s. Janos V. and Maria (Avar) K.; m. Marie T. Colas, Apr. 8, 1958; children: John, Pierre, Andre. Dr.Sci., U. Catholique de Louvain, Belgium, 1957. Asst. U. Catholique de Louvain, 1957-61; research asso. Northwestern U., 1961-65; prof. biochemistry U. Chgo., 1970—; cons. in field. Contbr. articles to profl. jours. Recipient Prix Stas-Spring Belgian Acad. Scis. Mem. AAAS, Am. Chem. Soc., Soc. Chimique de France, Am. Soc. Biol. Chemists, Soc. African Insect Scientists, Sigma Xi. Roman Catholic. Home: 645 Wesley Ave Evanston IL 60202 Office: 920 E 58th St Chicago IL 60637

KHACHADURIAN, AVEDIS, physician; b. Aleppo, Syria, Jan. 6, 1926; s. Khachadur and Aznive (Demirjian) K.; m. Laura Hadidian, July 27, 1961; children: Cynthia, Linda. B.A., Am. U. of Beirut, 1949, M.D., 1953. Resident internal medicine Am. U. of Beirut, 1953-56; fellow Postgrad. Sch. Medicine, London, 1956-57, Harvard Med. Sch., 1957-59; asst. prof. biochemistry and medicine Am. U. of Beirut, 1959-64, asso. prof., 1964-71, prof., 1971; prof. pediatrics, dir. Clin. Research Center, Northwestern U. Med. Sch., 1971-73; prof. medicine, head div. endocrinology and metabolism Coll. Medicine and Dentistry N.J.-Rutgers Med. Sch., Piscataway, N.J., 1973; mem. staff pediatrics Children's Meml. Hosp., Chgo.; cons. U. Chgo. Sch. Medicine. Mem. Lebanese Endocrine Soc., Am. Diabetes Assn., N.Y. Acad. Sci., Internat. Conf. Biochemistry Lipids (nat. rep. Lebanon), Acad. Medicine of N.J., Am. Fedn. Clin. Research, Am. Heart Assn., Am. Inst. Nutrition, Endocrine Soc., N.Y. Acad. Sci., N.Y. Lipid Research Club, Soc. Exptl. Biology and Medicine, Sigma Xi, Alpha Omega Alpha. Research genetics; natural history, pathogenesis and treatment of hereditary hyperlipidemias; diabetes; studies on various inborn errors of metabolism; metabolism of depot adipose tissue. Home: 22 Philip Dr Princeton NJ 08540

KHACHIGIAN, KENNETH LARRY, public affairs consultant; b. Visalia, Calif., Sept. 14, 1944; s. John and Elizabeth (Kizirian) K.; m. Meredith Jane Ford, July 18, 1964; children—Merissa, Kristina Elise. B.A., U. Calif., Santa Barbara, 1966; J.D., Columbia U., 1969. Bar: Calif. bar 1970. Dep. spl. asst. to Pres. U.S., White House, Washington, 1970-74; spl. asst. to sec. Dept. Agr., Washington, 1974-75; editorial cons. and asst. to former pres. Richard Nixon, San Clemente, Calif., 1975-79; cons. public affairs, San Clemente, 1979—; spl. cons. to Pres. U.S., White House, 1981; Cons. Reagan for Pres. Campaign, 1979-80; chief speech writer Presdl. Campaign tour, 1980; cons. to Presdl. Transition, 1980-81; sr. adviser, cons. Deuk Mejian for Gov. Calif., 1981-82; spl. cons. Gubernatorial Transition, 1982—; mem. adv. bd. Nat. Inst. Justice, 1982. Mem. Calif. Bar Assn. Republican. Presbyterian. Office: 209 Avenida Del Mar Suite 203 San Clemente CA 92672

KHADDURI, MAJID, international studies educator; b. Mosul, Iraq, Sept. 27, 1909; came to U.S., 1947, naturalized, 1954; s. Khadduri Q. and Latifa (Saati) K.; m. Majdia Dawaff, Dec. 9, 1942; children: Farid, Shirin. B.A., Am. U., Beirut, 1932; Ph.D., U. Chgo., 1938. Prof. higher tchrs. and law colls., Baghdad, 1938-47; vis. prof. Ind. U., 1947-48, U. Chgo., 1948-49; prof. Sch. Advanced Internat. Studies, Johns Hopkins, 1949—, distinguished research prof., 1970—; dir. research and edn. Middle East Inst., Washington, 1950—, bd. govs. Author: book War and Peace in the Law of Islam, 1955, Independent Iraq, 1951, Islamic Jurisprodence, 1961, Arab Contemporaries, 1973, others. Mem. Iraq del. UN Conf., San Francisco, 1945. Recipient Rockefeller research grant for book on Islamic Law of Nations, 1963; Decorated Order of Rafidain, Iraq, Order of Merit, Egypt). Mem. Am. Polit. Sci. Assn., Am. Soc. Internat. Law, Shaybani Soc. Internat. Law of Washington (pres.), P.E.N. (sec. Baghdad Center 1940-47, mem. N.Y. Center 1968—), Acad. U. Arabic Lang. (corr. 1983). Club: Cosmos (Washington). Home: 4454 Tindall St Washington DC 20016 Office: 1740 Massachusetts Ave Washington DC 20036

KHAN, AMANULLAH, physician; b. Jullundhar, India, Mar. 2, 1940; came to U.S., 1964; s. Ahmad Ali and Qamar (Nisa) K.; m. Fran Elise Austin, Dec. 9, 1972; children: Roxanna, Sabrina, Shireen. Licentiate state med. faculty, West Pakistan Med. Sch., 1959; M.B.B.S., King Edward Med. Coll., Lahore, 1963; Ph.D., Baylor U., 1968. Diplomate: Am. Bd. Allergy and Immunology, Am. Bd. Lab. Immunology. Rotating intern Samaritan Hosp., Troy, N.Y., 1965-66; fellow in hematology and oncology Wadley Insts. of Molecular Medicine, Dallas, 1966-69, chief research fellow, 1969-70, chmn. dept. immunotherapy, 1970—; mem. staffs Morton Cancer and Research Hosp., Dallas, Brookhaven Hosp., Doctor's Hosp.; adj. prof. Tex. Woman's U., 1975—, N. Tex. State U., 1975—. Author: Immune Regulators in Transfer Factor, 1979, Interferon: Properties and Clinical Uses, 1980, Experimental Hematology Today, 1980, Human Lymphokinea, 1982; editor: Jour. Clin. Hematology and Oncology, 1971—; mem. editorial bd.: Exptl. Hematology, 1973-75; contbr. articles to sci. jours. Fellow ACP, Am. Coll. Allergists; mem. Am. Assn. Immunologists, Am. Soc. Clin. Oncology, Am. Soc. Hematology, AMA, Dallas County Med. Soc., Tex. Med. Assn., King Edward Med. Coll. Alumni Assn. (pres. 1971-75, 78-79), Assn. Pakistani Physicians N. Am. (pres. 1983-84). Home: 4035 High Summit Dr Dallas TX 75234 Office: Wadley Insts Molecular Medicine 9000 Harry Hines Dallas TX 75235

KHAN, MOHAMMAD ASAD, geophysicist, educator; b. Aima, Lahore, Pakistan, Aug. 13, 1940; came to U.S., 1964, naturalized, 1975; s. Ghulam Qadir and Hajira (Karim) K.; m. Tahera Pathan, Jan. 4, 1974; 1 dau., Shehzi Samira. B.S., U. Punjab, Lahore, Pakistan, 1957, M.S., 1963; postgrad., Harvard U., 1964-65; Ph.D. (East West Center scholar), U. Hawaii, 1967. Forecaster Pakistan Meteorol. Dept., Lahore, 1958-63; lectr. in geophysics U. Punjab, 1963-64; asst. prof. geophysics and geodesy U. Hawaii, 1967-71, asso. prof., 1971-74, prof., 1974—; geophysicist, geodesist Hawaii Inst. Geophysics, 1967—; NSF and NASA fellow Summer Inst. Dynamical Astronomy at Mass. Inst. Tech., 1968-69; sr. vis. scientist geodynamics Goddard Space Flight Center NASA, Greenbelt, Md., 1972-74; sr. scientist Computer Scis. Corp., Silver Spring, Md., 1974-76, sr. cons., 1976-77; diplomatic minister/adviser Resource Survey and Devel. Pakistan, 1974-76; sr. resident asso. Nat. Acad. Scis., 1972-74; leader Am. Asian Studies and Contemporary Social Problems Seminar Series, Honolulu, 1968-69. Contbr. articles to profl. publs. Chmn. East and West: A Perspective for the 80's; mem. Hawaii Environ. Council, 1979—, chmn. exec. com., 1979—, vice chmn., 1981—; chmn. Pakistan Relief Fund, Honolulu, 1971. Fellow Explorers Club; mem. Geol. Soc. U. Punjab (pres. 1962-63), Am. Geophys. Union, Pakistan Assn. Advancement Sci., Am. Geol. Inst., Am. Geophys. Union, East West Center Alumni Assn. (dir. 1976—), Internat. Alumni of East West Center (exec. com., chmn. 1977-80). Research in geophys., geodetic and oceanographic applications of satellites, geodynamics, planetary interiors, global tectonics, global correlations, core-mantle boundary problems, gravity, isostasy, satellite altimetry, geodesy, earth models, geophys. exploration, charting and hydrography, ocean dynamics. Office: Hawaii Inst Geophysics U Hawaii 2525 Correa Rd Honolulu HI 96822 *Most men stand the test of adversity quite well, but if you really want to test the character of a man, give him power.*

KHANZADIAN, VAHAN, tenor; b. Syracuse, N.Y., Jan. 23, 1939; s. Avedis Sarkis and Araxey (Youghian) K. B.S., U. Buffalo, 1962; postgrad., Curtis Inst. Music, Phila., 1961-63. Mem. voice faculty Acad. Vocal Art, Phila. Debut as Ruggero in La Rondine, San Francisco Spring Opera, 1968; leading roles in Lucia di Lammermoor, Wozzeck, Fra Diavolo, Les Troyens, Madama Butterfly, Lucia Di Lammermoor; appeared throughout U.S., Can.; appeared with all major opera cos., and opera festivals, including San Antonio, Ravinia, Tanglewood, Saratoga, Opera de Colombia; numerous solo recitals throughout N.Am.; appeared with symphony orchs., including Chgo., Boston, Phila., Cleve., Minn., Indpls., St. Louis, Milw., Pitts.; TV appearances include Gheraman in Tchaikovsky's Queen of Spades; soloist in world premier of Menotti's Landscapes and Remembrances, PBS, 1976. Served with U.S. Army, 1964-65. Sullivan Found. grantee, 1971-74; Rockefeller Found. grantee, 1971-73. Address: 3604 Broadway Apt 2N New York NY 10031 *My ethnic background, Armenian, with its strong Christian influence was instrumental in projecting the importance of family, religion, education, and culture. The strength and knowledge attained in this environment guided me in the arts, where I was fortunate to have had the discipline and the opportunity to pursue my goal of making a contribution in serving music.*

KHAYATT, SHAKER ALBERT, investment banker; b. Alexandria, Egypt, Dec. 5, 1935; came to U.S., 1957, naturalized, 1970; s. Albert George and Winnifred (Shaker) K.; m. Edith Louise Yuengling, Feb. 4, 1963; children: Samiha, Djenan, Shaker Albert, Shafika. B.S., Alexandria U., 1957; S.M., Mass. Inst. Tech., 1961; M.B.A., Harvard U., 1963. Sr. asso. H.N. Whitney, Goadby & Co., N.Y.C., 1966-69; exec. v.p. Coggeshall & Hicks, Inc., N.Y.C., 1970-73, Laidlaw Adams & Peck Inc., 1973-79; pres. Khayatt & Co. Inc., 1979—; pres. Equipco Khayatt Inc.; dir. Mitchell Energy & Devel. Corp., Houston, Am. Capital Mgmt., Inc., N.Y.C. Mem. Egyptian Am. Profls. Soc., Egyptian-Am. C. of C., N.Y. Soc. Security Analysts. Clubs: Madison Sq. Garden, Harvard, City Midday (N.Y.C.); Pottsville (Pa.); Edgartown Yacht (Mass.); Ox Ridge Hunt (Conn.). Home: 137 Doubling Rd Greenwich CT 06830 Office: 50 Broad St New York NY 10004

KHEEL, THEODORE WOODROW, lawyer, labor arbitrator and mediator; b. N.Y.C., May 9, 1914; s. Samuel and Kate (Herzenstein) K.; m. Ann Sunstein, July 1, 1937; children: Ellen Margaret (Mrs. Arnold S. Jacobs), Robert Jeffrey, Constance Elizabeth, Martha Louise, Jane Meredith, Katherine Emily. A.B., Cornell U., 1935, LL.B., 1937. Bar: N.Y. 1937. Partner firm Battle, Fowler, Jaffin & Kheel, 1949-82, of counsel, 1982—; dir. Athlone Industries, Inc., Western Union Telegraph Co.; Pres. Center for Non-Broadcast TV, Inc.; adminstr. Inst. Collective Bargaining and Group Relations Inc.; mem. Presdl. bds. various labor disputes, 1962-66; spl. cons. Pres.'s Com. Equal Employment Opportunity, 1962-63; mem. Pres.'s Maritime Adv. Com., 1964-66, Pres.'s Nat. Citizens Com. for Community Relations, 1964-68; pres. Nat. Urban League, 1956-60. Author: Transit and Arbitration, 1960, Pros and Cons of Compulsory Arbitration, 1961, How Race Relations Affect Your Business, 1963, Guide to Fair Employment Practices, 1964, Kheel on Labor Law, 1974—. Mem. Am. Arbitration Assn. (dir.). Home: 407 W 246th St Bronx NY 10471 Office: 280 Park Ave New York NY 10017

KHERDIAN, DAVID, author; b. Racine, Wis., Dec. 17, 1931; s. Melkon and Veron (Dumehjian) K.; m. Kato Rozeboom, 1968 (div. 1970); m. Nonny Hogrogian, Mar. 17, 1971. B.S in Philosophy, U. Wis., 1960. Lit. cons. Northwestern U., 1965; founder/editor Giligia Press, 1966-72; rarebook cons. Fresno (Calif.) State Coll., 1968-69, lectr., 1969-70; ofcl. poet-in-the-schs., State of N.H., 1971; editor Ararat mag., 1971-72; dir. Two Rivers Press, Aurora, Oreg., 1978—; poetry judge, lectr., reader of own poetry. Author: On The Death of My Father and Other Poems, 1970, Homage to Adana, 1970, Looking Over Hills, 1972, The Nonny Poems, 1974, Any Day of Your Life, 1975, Country, Cat: City, Cat, 1978, I Remember Root River, 1978, The Road From Home: The Story of an Armenian Girl (Lewis Carroll Shelf award, Boston Globe/Horn Book award, Newbery Honor Book award, Jane Addams Book award), 1979 (Banta award), The Farm, 1979, It Started With Old Man Bean, 1980, Finding Home, 1981, Taking the Soundings on Third Avenue, 1981, The Farm: Book Two, 1981, Beyond Two Rivers, 1981 (Friends of Am. Writers award), The Song in the Walnut Grove, 1982, Place of Birth, 1983, Right Now, 1983, The Mystery of the Diamond in the Wood, 1983, Root River Run, 1984, The Animal; also bibliographies.; Editor: Visions of America by the Poets of Our Time, 1973, Settling America: The Ethnic Expression of 14 Contemporary Poets, 1974, Poems Here and Now, 1976, Traveling America with Today's Poets, 1976, The Dog Writes on the Window with His Nose and Other Poems, 1977, If Dragon Flies Made Honey, 1977, I Sing the Song of Myself, 1978; co-editor: Down at the Santa Fe Depot: 20 Fresno Poets, 1970; Translator: The Pearl: Hymn of the Robe of Glory, 1979, Pigs Never See the Stars: Armenian Proverbs, 1982. Served with AUS, 1952-54. Mem. PEN. Address: Box 626 Aurora OR 97002 *The poet understands that everything is connected and all is one. This is all he really knows. But knowing this he is permitted to speak—but briefly, quietly, disturbing nothing, removing nothing, revealing only the new-old relationships he has been given to see.*

KHO, JAMES WANG, computer scientist; b. Manila, Philippines, Sept. 6, 1944; came to U.S., 1966, naturalized, 1973; s. Eng-Too Lao and Lour-Chii Lim (Wang) K.; m. Joanne Jane Chan, June 22, 1976. M.S., U. Wis., 1968, Ph.D., 1972. Project and research specialist U. Wis., Madison, 1966-71; prof. computer sci. Wayne State U., Detroit, 1971-73, Calif. State U., Sacramento, 1973—, chmn. dept., 1977—; computer sci. cons., State of Calif., 1975—, lectr. in field for univs.; cons.; owner, operator import bus. Contbr. articles to profl. jours. Mem. Assn. Computing Machinery, Am. Inst. Decision Scis., Soc. Computer Simulation, Soc. Gen. Systems Research, Ops. Research Soc. Am., Data Processing Mgmt. Assn., Beta Gamma Sigma, Phi Kappa Phi, Pi Gamma Mu. Office: 6000 Jay St Sacramento CA 95819

KHORANA, HAR GOBIND, chemist, educator; b. Raipur, India, Jan. 9, 1922; s. Shri Ganpat Rai and Shrimati Krishna (Devi) K.; m. Esther Elizabeth Sibler, 1952; children: Julia, Emilie, Dave Roy. B.S., Punjab U., 1943, M.S., 1945; Ph.D., Liverpool (Eng.) U., 1948; D.Sc., U. Chgo., 1967. Head organic chemistry group B.C. Research Council, 1952-60; vis. prof. Rockefeller Inst., N.Y.C., 1958—; prof. co-dir. Inst. Enzyme Research, U. Wis., Madison, 1960-70, prof. dept. biochemistry, 1962-70, Conrad A. Elvehjem prof. life scis., 1964-70; Alfred P. Sloan prof. biology and chemistry MIT, Cambridge, 1970—; vis. prof. Stanford U., 1964; mem. adv. bd. Biopolymers. Author: Some Recent Developments in the Chemistry of Phosphate Esters of Biological Interests, 1961; Mem. editorial bd.: Jour. Am. Chem. Soc, 1963—. Recipient Merck award Chem. Inst. Can., 1958, Gold medal Profl. Inst. Pub. Service Can., 1960, Dannie-Heinneman Preiz, Göttingen, Germany, 1967, Remsen award Johns Hopkins U., 1968, Am. Chem. Soc. award for creative work in synthetic organic chemistry, 1968, Louisa Gross Horwitz prize, 1968, Lasker Found. award for basic med. research, 1968, Nobel prize in medicine, 1968; elected to Deutsche Akademie der Naturforscher Leopoldina, HalleSaale, Germany, 1968; Overseas fellow Churchill Coll., Cambridge, Eng., 1967. Fellow Chem. Inst. Can., Am. Acad. Arts and Scis.; mem. Nat. Acad. Sci. Research and numerous publs. on chem. methods for synthesis of nucleeotides, coenzymes and nucleic acids; elucidation on the genetic code, lab. synthesis of genes, biol. membrane, light-transducing pigments. Office: Dept Biology and Chemistry MIT Cambridge MA 02139

KHOSLA, VED MITTER, oral and maxillo-facial surgeon, educator; b. Nairobi, Kenya, Jan. 13, 1926; s. Jagdish Rai and Tara V. K.; m. Santosh Ved Chabra, Oct. 11, 1952; children: Ashok M., Siddarth M. Student, U. Cambridge, 1945; L.D.S., Edinburgh Dental Hosp. and Sch., 1950, Coll. Dental Surgeons, Sask., Can., 1962. Prof. oral surgery, dir. postdoctoral studies in oral surgery U. Calif. Sch. Dentistry, San Francisco, 1968—; chief oral surgery San Francisco Gen. Hosp.; lectr. oral surgery U. of Pacific, VA Hosp.; vis. cons. Fresno County Hosp. Dental Clinic.; Mem. planning com., exec. med. com. San Francisco Gen. Hosp. Contbr. articles to profl. jours. Examiner in photography and gardening Boy Scouts Am., 1971-73, Guatemala Clinic, 1972. Granted personal coat of arms by H.M. Queen Elizabeth II, 1959. Fellow Royal Coll. Surgeons (Edinburgh), Internat. Assn. Oral Surgeons, Internat. Coll. Applied Nutrition, Internat. Coll. Dentists, Royal Soc. Health, AAAS, Am. Coll. Dentists; mem. Brit. Assn. Oral Surgeons, Am. Soc. Oral Surgeons, Am. Dental Soc. Anesthesiology, Am. Acad. Dental Radiology, Omicron Kappa Upsilon. Club: Masons. Home: 1525 Lakeview Dr Hillsborough CA 94010 Office: U Calif Sch Dentistry Oral Surgery Div 3d and Parnassus Aves San Francisco CA 94122 *It is part of the cure to wish to be cured. With God all things are possible.*

KHOURI, FRED JOHN, political science educator; b. Cranford, N.J., Aug. 15, 1916; s. Peter and Mary (Rizk) K.; m. Catherine McLean, June 24, 1964. Student, Union Jr. Coll., Roselle, N.J., 1934-36; B.A., Columbia U., 1938, M.A., 1939, Ph.D., 1953. Instr. Brownsville Jr. Coll. and High Sch., Tex., 1939-40; instr. polit. sci. U. Tenn., 1946-47, U. Conn., 1947-50; asst. prof. Villanova U., Pa., 1951-61, prof., 1964—; vis. prof. Am. U. of Beirut, Lebanon, 1961-64; mem. Brookings Instn. Middle East Study Group, 1975-76; sr. fellow Middle East Ctr U. Pa., 1978-79, 80-81; lectr. in field. Author: The Arab States and the UN, 1954, The Arab Israeli Dilemma, 1968, (2d edit.) The Arab Israeli Dilemma, 1976; assoc. editor: Jour. South Asian and Middle Eastern Studies; contbr. to books and profl. jours. Served with U.S. Army, 1941-45. Decorated Order of Cedars, Lebanon. Fellow Middle East Studies Assn.; mem. Middle East Inst., Am. Polit. Sci. Assn., Am. Soc. Internat. Law, Internat. Studies Assn., Am. Acad. Polit. and Social Sci., World Affairs Council, Phi Kappa Phi. Democrat. Roman Catholic. Home: 1209 W Wynnewood Rd Apt 310 Wynnewood PA 19096 Office: Villanova Univ Villanova PA 19085 *Man's most desperate need is for lasting peace. Thus, ever since my military discharge in 1945, my life's aim has been to be whatever I could to promote that deeper and clearer understanding in the U.S. and elsewhere is so essential to the peaceful resolution of the world's major conflicts.*

KHURI, NICOLA NAJIB, educator, physicist; b. Beirut, Lebanon, May 27, 1933; came to U.S., 1959, naturalized, 1970; s. Najib N. and Odette (Joujou) K.; m. Elizabeth Anne Tyson, Dec. 9, 1955; children: Suzanne Odette, Najib Nicholas. B.A with high distinction, Am. U. Beirut, 1952; Ph.D., Princeton U., 1957. Asst. prof. Am. U. Beirut, 1957-58, 60-61, assoc. prof., 1961-62; mem. Inst. Advanced Study, Princeton U., 1959-60, 62-63; vis. assoc. prof. Columbia, 1963-64; assoc. prof. Rockefeller U., 1964-68, prof., 1968—; Cons. Brookhaven Nat. Lab., 1963-73; mem. Carnegie Panel on U.S. Security and Arms Control, 1981-83. Contbr. articles to profl. jours. Trustee Am. U. Beirut, Brearley Sch., N.Y.C. Fellow Am. Phys. Soc.; mem. Council on Fgn. Relations. Club: Century (N.Y.C.). Home: 4715 Iselin Ave Riverdale NY 10471 Office: Rockefeller U New York City NY 10021

KIAM, VICTOR KERMIT, II, diversified manufacturing company executive; b. New Orleans, Dec. 7, 1926; s. Victor Kermit and Nanon (Newman) K.; m. Ellen Lipscher, Nov. 26, 1956; children: Lisa, Victor Kermit, Robin. B.S., B.A., Yale U., 1948; student, Sorbonne, Paris, 1949; M.B.A., Harvard U., 1951. Salesman, dist. mgr., product mgr. cosmetics div. Lever Bros., 1951-53, supr., dist. mgr., 1954-55; mktg. dir. woman's wear div. Internat. Latex Corp., 1955-58; v.p. marketing, women's wear gen. mgr. div. Sarong, Inc., v.p. mktg., parent co., 1960-68; pres. Benrus Corp. (watch, jewelry and indsl. products mfg.), 1968-78, chief exec. officer, 1971—, chmn. bd., 1973-78, cons., 1978-80; chmn. bd. PIC Design Corp., 1968-77; pres. 630 Park Ave. Corp.; chmn. Friendship Collection, Inc., 1977—; chmn., pres., chief exec. officer Remington Products, Inc., Bridgeport, Conn., 1979—; vice chmn. Remington Japan Ltd., 1980—; chmn. China Publs., Inc., 1980, First Tchr., Inc., 1980—, Remington Leather Products, Inc., 1981—, Remington Trading Co., Japan, 1982—, Hong Kong, 1982—, Pace Equities Corp.; dir. Remington Consumer Products Ltd., London, Remington Omar, Inc., Can. Mem. adv. com. Norwalk Community Coll.; mem. corp. and found. com. Colgate U.; trustee U. Bridgeport, Hillside Hosp.; bd. dirs. Child Welfare League Am. Served with USNR, 1944-47. Mem. Inst. Dirs. (London), Young Pres.'s Orgn., U.S. Tennis Assn. Clubs: Century Country, Regency Whist; St. James (London). Home: 119 Wire Mill Rd Stamford CT Office: 60 Main St Bridgeport CT 06602

KIBBE, MILTON HOMER, physician, hosp. adminstr.; b. West Stafford, Conn., Aug. 14, 1911; s. Harlow Lawton and Queerie (Avery) K.; m. Elizabeth Alderman; children—Jill (Mrs. Joseph McNamara), Barry, Dennis, Karen, Vickie. B.S., U. Mass., 1934; M.D., Tufts U., 1938; postgrad., Columbia, Harvard, Yale. Diplomate: Am. Bd. Neurology and Psychiatry. Intern Muhlenberg Hosp., 1938-39, Somerset Hosp., 1939-40; practice medicine specializing in neurology and neurosurgery, Plainfield, N.J., 1940-41, psychiatry and neurology, Springfield, Mass., 1946-58, Radford, Va., 1973—; clin. dir. Lynchburg (Va.) Tng. Sch. Hosp., 1958-60; then supt. Peterburg (Va.) Tng. Sch. and Hosp., Central State Hosp.; staff psychiatrist St. Albans Psychiat. Hosp., Radford, 1973—; asso. clin. prof. psychiatry Med. Coll. Va. Bd. dirs. Chesapeake dist. Found. Mentally Retarded and Physically Handicapped. Served to maj. M.C. AUS, 1941-46. Recipient Christian P. Sorensen award Civitan Internat., 1963. Fellow Am. Psychiat. Assn. (life). Clubs: Mason (Shriner), Civitan (pres. Peterburg 1966-67). Spl. research brain injuries, electroencephalography. Home: 2011 7th St Radford VA 24141 Office: 117 3d Ave Radford VA 24141

KIBEL, THOMAS WILLIAM, construction company executive; b. Pitts., Dec. 23, 1946; s. Earl William and Helen (Rice) K.; m. Margaret Lee Byers, June 28, 1980. Student, Robert Morris Jr. Coll., 1964-66; B.S. in Bus. Adminstrn., Gannon Coll., 1968. C.P.A., Pa. Staff acct. gen. audit dept. Price Waterhouse & Co., Pitts., 1968-71, sr. acct., 1971-74, audit mgr., dept. specialized services, 1971-76; sec.-treas. Mellon-Stuart Co., Pitts., 1976—. Mem. fin. com. Our Lady of Most Blessed Sacrament Ch. Parish Council, 1976—. Mem. Am. Inst. C.P.A.s, Pa. Inst. C.P.A.s., Nat. Acctg. Assn. Democrat. Club: Pitts. Athletic Assn. Home: 3971 Murry Highlands Circle Murrysville PA 15668 Office: One North Shore Center Pittsburgh PA 15212

KIBLER, DAVID BURKE, III, lawyer; b. Lakeland, Fla., Feb. 5, 1924; s. David Burke, Jr. and Bessie (Dew) K.; m. Nell Idalene Bryant, Sept. 26, 1945; children: David Burke IV, Thomas Bryant, Jacquelyn, Nancy Dew. B.A. cum laude, U. Fla., 1947, J.D., 1949. Bar: Fla. bar 1949. Since practiced in, Lakeland; partner firm Holland & Knight (and predecessors), 1964—; chmn., dir. Kibler Agrl. Corp.; dir. (Sikes Corp.), Fla. First Service Corp., St. Petersburg, First Petersburg Service Corp.; mem. Lakeland bd. Fla. Fed. Savs. & Loan Assn.; atty. Fla. Citrus Com., 1961-65; Past pres., bd. dirs., exec. com., Lakeland United Fund; mem. Fla. Bd. Regents, 1967-75, chmn., 1969-72; past chmn., bd. dirs. Fla. Council 100; mem., chmn. Fla. Postsecondary Edn. Com.; mem., vice chmn. Fla. Postsecondary Edn. Planning Commn.; bd. dirs., v.p. U. South Fla. Found.; bd. dirs. Am. Found. Served to 1st lt. AUS, 1943-46; ETO. Decorated Bronze Star with V, Purple Heart with oak leaf cluster. Mem. Am., 10th Jud. Circuit bar assns., Am. Judicature Soc., Southeastern Legal Found. (legal adv. bd.), Fla. Bar, Am. Legion, Fla. Blue Key, Alpha Tau Omega, Phi Delta Phi. Democrat. Presbyterian. Clubs: Ponte Vedra (Fla.); Lakeland Yacht and Country, ImperiaLakes Country, Lone Palm Golf (Lakeland); Tower, Univ. (Tampa, Fla.); Elks. Home: 2113 Fairmont Ave Lakeland FL 33803 Office: 92 Lake Wire Dr Lakeland FL 33802

KIBRE, PEARL, educator, historian; b. Phila.; d. Kenneth and Jane (du Plone) K. Student, UCLA, 1920-22; A.B., U. Calif. at Berkeley, 1924, M.A., 1925; Ph.D., Columbia, 1936. Instr. history Pasadena (Calif.) Jr. Coll., 1925-28; research asst. Columbia, 1929-37; instr. history Bklyn., 1937-38; mem. faculty Hunter Coll., City U. N.Y., 1938—, prof. history, 1957-71, prof. grad. sch., 1964-71, prof. emeritus, 1971—; co-chmn. Columbia Seminar in History of Legal and Polit. Thought, 1972-74. Author: The Library of Pico della Mirandola, 1936, (with Lynn Thorndike) A Catalogue of Incipits of Mediaeval Scientific Writings in Latin, 1937, 2d edit., 1963, The Nations in the Mediaeval Universities, 1948, Scholarly Privileges in the Middle Ages, 1962 (Haskins gold medal 1964), Hippocrates Latinus: Repertorium of Hippocratic Writings in the Latin Middle Ages, 1975-82; Co-editor: Osiris, vol. XI, 1954; Contbr. to books, profl. jours. Research fellow N.Y. Acad. Medicine, Nyon, Switzerland, 1938-39; Guggenheim fellow, 1950-51. Fellow Mediaeval Acad. Am. (3d v.p. 1964-67, pres. of fellows 1975-78); mem. History Sci. Soc., AAUP, Medieval Club N.Y.C., Am. Hist. Assn., Renaissance Soc., Phi Beta Kappa; corr. mem. Acad. Internationale d'Histoire des Sciences. Home: 1100 Madison Ave New York NY 10028

KIBRICK, ANNE, nursing educator; b. Palmer, Mass., June 1, 1919; d. Martin and Christine (Grigas) Karlon; m. Sidney Kibrick, June 16, 1949; children: Joan, John. R.N., Worcester (Mass.) Hahnemann Hosp., 1941; B.S., Boston U., 1945; M.A., Columbia Tchrs. Coll., 1948; Ed.D., Harvard U., 1958; L.H.D. (hon.), St. Joseph's Coll., Windham, Maine, 1973. Asst. edn. dir. Cushing VA Hosp., Framingham, Mass., 1948-49; asst. prof. nursing Simmons Coll., Boston, 1949-55; dir. grad. div. Boston U. Sch. Nursing, 1958-63, dean, 1963-68, prof., 1968-70; chmn. dept. nursing, Boston Coll. Grad. Sch. Arts and Sci, 1970-74; chmn. sch. nursing Boston State Coll., 1974-82; dir. Sch. Nursing U. Mass., Boston, 1982—; Cons. div. nursing USPHS, 1964-68; nat. adv. council nurse tng. USPHS, NIH, 1968-73; cons. Hebrew U.-Hadassah Med. Orgn., Jerusalem, 1971—; mem. Inst. Medicine of Nat. Acad. Scis., 1972—, mem. steering com. costs of edn. of health professions, 1972-74; mem. Nat. Med. Audiovisual Tng. Center, 1972-76, Gov.'s Com. and Area Bd. Mental Health and Mental Retardation, Nat. Commn. for Study Nursing and Nursing Edn., 1970-73; mem. faculty com., regent's external degree program in nursing SUNY, 1974-82; mem. hosp. mgmt. bd. U. Hosp., U. Mass., 1976-81; dir. Medic Alert, Am. Jour. Nursing Co. Mem. editorial bd.: Mass. Jour. Community Health. Bd. dirs. Brookline Mental Health Assn., Met. chpt. ARC. Fellow Am. Acad. Nursing; mem. Nat. (pres. 1971-73), Mass. leagues nursing, Am. Nurses Assn., Mass. Nurses Assn. (dir. 1982—), Sigma Theta Tau, Pi Lambda Theta. Home: 381 Clinton Rd Brookline MA 02146

KICE, JOHN LORD, educator; b. Colorado Springs, Colo., Feb. 18, 1930; s. William Branson and Ruth (Lord) K.; m. Mary Ellen Bass, June 15, 1953; children—Virginia C., Joanne E. A.B., Harvard, 1950, M.A., 1953, Ph.D., 1954. Asst. prof. chemistry U. S.C., Columbia, 1956-59, asso. prof., 1959-60, Ore. State U., Corvallis, 1960-65, prof., 1965-70; prof., chmn. dept. chemistry U. Vt., Burlington, 1970-75; prof. chemistry Tex. Tech U., Lubbock, 1975-81, chmn. dept., 1975-81, assoc. v.p. research, 1982—. Author: Modern Principles of Organic Chemistry, 1966, 2d edit., 1974; Mem. editorial bd.: Internat. Jour. Sulfur Chemistry, 1969-76, Phosphorus and Sulfur, 1976-81; Contbr. articles to profl. jours. Recipient outstanding teaching award Ore. State U., 1962; Alfred P. Sloan Found. fellow, 1957-61; NIH spl. fellow, 1968-69. Mem. Am. Chem. Soc. (chmn. Ore. 1966-67), Phi Beta Kappa, Sigma Xi. Home: 5609 80th St Lubbock TX 79424

KICHER, THOMAS PATRICK, mechanical engineer, educator; b. Johnsonburg, Pa., Oct. 20, 1937; s. William Milton and Mary Elizabeth (Divany) K.; m. Janet Mary Logan, July 28, 1962; children: Rita Ann, Paul Thomas, Laura Lynn. B.S. in Engring. Sci., Case Inst. Tech., 1959, M.S. in Engring. Mechanics, 1962, Ph.D., 1965. Design engr. Douglas Aircraft, 1964-65; asst. prof. Case Western Res. U., Cleve., 1965-68, asso. prof., 1968-78, prof. mech. engring., 1978—; asso. dean sci. and engring. Cast Inst. Tech. of Case Western Res. U., 1974-79; cons. Union Carbide Corp., Medtronics Inc., Chase Brass & Copper Co., Stouffer Foods Corp., Westinghouse, Brunswick. Designed Mark X bowling ball for Brunswick Corp., 1980. Mem. ASME, AIAA, Soc. Exptl. Stress Analysis, Sigma Xi, Theta Tau (hon.). Office: 10900 Euclid Ave Cleveland OH 44106

KICKLIGHTER, CLAUDE MILTON, army officer; b. Glennville, Ga., Aug. 22, 1933; s. Claude Wilton and Ruby Dell (Drake) K.; m. Elizabeth Exley, Apr. 24, 1954; children: Elizabeth Jane, Claude M., Richard Van. A.B., Mercer U.; M.A., George Washington U.; grad. Nat. and Internat. Security Program, Harvard U., 1981, grad. Sr. Mgrs. in Govt. Program, 1982. Commd. officer U.S. Army, 1955, advanced through grades to maj. gen.; staff Dept. Army, 1968-70; with 101st Airborne Div., Vietnam; comdr. 1st Bn. 21st Field Arty., Ft. Carson, Colo., 1972-73; staff Office Joint Chief of Staff, 1974-75, Office Sec. Def., 1975-76; comdr. 24th Inf. Div. Arty., Ft. Stewart, Ga., 1976-78; asst. div. comdr., 1978-79; asst. chief staff logistics Allied Forces Central Europe, The Netherlands, 1979-81; gen. Security Assistance Center, Alexandria, Va., 1981-83; chief of staff U.S. Army Materiel Devel. and Readiness Command, Alexandria, 1983—. Contbr. article to mil. jours. Decorated Legion of Merit (4), Bronze Star, Air medal (2), others. Methodist. Home: 59 Fairfax Dr Fort Belvoir VA 22060 Office: 5001 Eisenhower Ave Alexandria VA 22333

KIDD, CHARLES VINCENT, educator; b. Paulsboro, N.J., Jan. 22, 1914; s. Walter Stephen and Nettie (Sparks) K.; m. Blanche Facer Hoover, Aug. 27, 1938; children: David, Stephen. A.B., Princeton U., 1935; M.A. Princeton U., 1937, Harvard U., 1957. Economist War Manpower Commn., Office War Moblzn. and Reconversion, Council Econ. Advisers, 1944-46; exec. sec. Pres.'s Sci. Research Bd., 1947; chief research planning NIH, Bethesda, Md., 1948-60, asso. dir., 1960-64; exec. sec. fed. council sci. and tech. Office Sci. and Tech., 1964-69; exec. sec., dir. council on fed. relations Assn. Am. Univs., 1969-77; research prof. pub. policy George Washington U., 1978—; cons. Pan-Am. Health Orgn., 1964-74, WHO, 1958-68, Ford Found., 1960-73, UN, 1969-73, State Dept., 1970-75, NSF, 1972—, Nat. Acad. Scis., 1979—. Author: American Universities and Federal Research, 1959; also other books and articles on sci. and ednl. policy. Mem. U.S. del. to UN Conf. Sci. and Tech., 1964, to UNESCO Conf. Sci. Policy, Karlovy Vary, 1966, to OAS Conf. Edn., Sci. and Culture, Maracay, 1968; head U.S. delegation to Castasia Conf., New Delhi, 1968; mem. Milbank Commn. for Study Higher Edn. for Pub. Health, 1973-76, U.S.-USSR Joint Group Experts in Field of Sci. Policy, 1974-77, Sci. Manpower Commn., 1975-78, Commn. Human Resources, Nat. Acad. Sci., 1975-78; Adv. com. Woodrow Wilson Sch. Princeton, 1965-67. Served as lt. (j.g.) USNR, 1944-46. Recipient Rockefeller Pub. Service award, 1955; Distinguished Service award Dept. HEW, 1964. Fellow AAAS. Clubs: Princeton (Washington); Cosmos. Home: 3900 Connecticut Ave Washington DC 20008 Office: George Washington U Library Suite 714 2130 H St Washington DC 20052

KIDD, MICHAEL, choreographer, dir.; b. Bklyn., Aug. 12; m. Mary Heatter; 2 daus.; m. Shelah Hackett; 1 son, 1 dau. Student, Coll. City of N.Y.; scholarship, Sch. of Am. Ballet. Choreography includes Hello Dolly; dir., producer: Li'l Abner; dir.: Cyrano; producer: (with N. Richard Nash) Wildcat, 1960, Here's Love, 1963, Ben Franklin in Paris, 1964; appeared: in films Movie-Movie (Recipient Antoinette Perry award for choreography Finian's Rainbow, Guys and Dolls, Destry Rides Again, Li'l Abner, Can-Can.). Address: care William Morris Agy 151 El Camino Beverly Hills CA 90212 *

KIDD, PAUL JAMES GARLAND, lawyer, corporation executive; b. Kingston, Ont., Can., June 25, 1913; s. Charles Edward and Mary (Youngson) K.; m. Elizabeth Dixon, May 23, 1940; children: Virginia E., Ruth M. B.A., Queens U., 1932, Osgoode Hall Law Sch., 1936; spl. course, Columbia, 1955. Bar: Called to Ont. bar 1936. Created Queen's counsel, 1954; dir. Hiram Walker-Gooderham & Worts, Ltd., Hiram Walker-Resources Ltd., Liquid Carbonic Inc. Mem. Delta Chi. Presbyterian. Home: 7080 Riverside Dr E Windsor ON N8S IC3 Canada Office: Walkerville Box 2518 Windsor ON N8Y 4S5 Canada

KIDD, ROY WALTER, banker; b. Rockhold, Ky., June 8, 1922; s. Arthur and Effie (Steele) K.; m. Tommie Elizabeth Fuller, Sept. 13, 1943; children—Lynda (Mrs. Bernard L. Greer, Jr.), Elaine (Mrs. Phillip B. Powell), Roy Walter. Student, Eastern Ky. State U., 1940-43; LL.B., U. Memphis, 1949; grad., Central States Sch. Banking, 1959. Bar: Tenn. bar 1949. With First Tenn. Bank N.A. (formerly First Nat. Bank), Memphis, 1946—, v.p. mortgage loan, 1959-68, sr. v.p., 1968—, mgr. mortgage loan div., 1961-74, mgr. loan and project adminstrn. dept., 1974-79, mgr. community devel. div., 1980—; v.p. Hobbitt's Glen Devel. Corp., 1975—. Trustee 1st Memphis Realty Trust, 1970-76, Pres. Civitan Club, East Memphis, 1960-61. Served to lt. (j.g.) USNR, 1943-46; ETO. Mem. Am. Bankers Assn. (adv. council housing and real estate fin. div. 1969-74), Mortgage Bankers Assn. Am., certified). Mem. Christian Ch. Club: Univ. (Memphis). Home: 211 Alexander St Memphis TN 38111 Office: 165 Madison Ave Memphis TN 38103

KIDD, WILLIAM CAUGHEY, management consultant; b. Cleve., July 5, 1914; s. Caughey C. and Hazel (Maskey) K.; m. Elaine Lacroix, Apr. 24, 1943; children: Sally C., Susan G. A.B., Oberlin Coll., 1936; M.B.A., Harvard U., 1938. Mem. staff Arthur Andersen & Co. (C.P.A.s), Chgo., 1938-41; with S.C. Johnson & Son, Inc., Racine, Wis., 1946-65, treas., 1955-62, v.p., regional dir., Europe, 1962-65; with Western Pub. Co., Racine, 1965-71, pres., 1967-71, chmn., 1971; sec. Wis. Dept. Bus. Devel., 1972-76; mgmt. cons., 1976—. Mem. region VII com. Boy Scouts Am., 1958-72; pres. Wis. area, 1974-77; chmn. Racine Environment Commn., 1967-69, 71-73; mem. Wis. Arts Bd., 1973-79; curator Wis. Hist. Soc., 1978—, pres., 1982—. Served as aviator USNR, 1941-45; comdr. Res. (Ret.). Recipient Silver Beaver and Antelope awards. Clubs: Madison; Racine Country, Somerset (Racine); Boston (New Orleans); American (London). Home: 3752 N Bay Dr Racine WI 53402 Office: 312 6th St Racine WI 53403

KIDDER, GEORGE HOWELL, lawyer; b. Boston, June 14, 1925; s. Henry Purkitt and Julia Edwards (Howell) K.; m. Ellen Windom Warren, Aug. 17, 1946 (dec. May 1956); children: Susan Warren, George Howell, Stephen Wells; m. Priscilla Peele Hunnewell, Sept. 3, 1958; children: Priscilla Hunnewell, Timothy Hurd, Peter Arnold. Grad., St. Mark's Sch., Southborough, Mass., 1943; student, Williams Coll., 1943-44; B.Naval Sci., Tufts Coll., 1945; LL.B., Harvard, 1950. Bar: Mass. 1951. With Office Gen. Counsel, CIA, 1952-54; practice in, Boston, 1951-52, 54—; mem. firm Hemenway & Barnes, 1956—; Dir. State St. Boston Corp., State St. Bank & Trust Co. Pres. bd. trustees St. Mark's Sch.; trustee Fenn Sch., Concord, 1956-77, pres. bd., 1960-73; bd. dirs. Episcopal Ch. Found.; trustee Concord Acad., 1963-78, pres. bd., 1971-78; trustee Boston Symphony Orch., Children's Med. Center and Children's Hosp. Corp., Wellesley Coll., 1962-80; trustee emeritus Wellesley Coll., 1980—; bd. dirs. Greater Boston Legal Services; pres. bd. trustees Episcopal Divinity Sch., Cambridge, Mass. Fellow Am. Coll. Probate Counsel; mem. Am. Law Inst., Internat. Acad. Estate and Trust Law; Mem. Tau Beta Pi. Home: 110 Spencer Brook Rd Concord MA 01742 Office: 60 State St Boston MA 02109

KIDDER, JAMES HUGH, surgeon; b. N.Y.C., Jan. 7, 1902; s. Hugh and Ann Elizabeth (Jordan) K. Student, Columbia, 1919-20; A.B., Fordham U., 1924; M.D., Cornell U., 1928. Intern Peck Meml. Hosp., Bklyn., 1928, French Hosp., N.Y.C., 1929-30, cons. surgeon, N.Y., Elmhurst Gen., St. Barnabas hosps.; clin. prof. surgery N.Y. Med. Coll.; dean Fordham U. Coll. Pharmacy, 1932, now emeritus. Pres. Interallied Confedn. Med. Res.-NATO, 1976-78. Ordered to active duty as Res. Officer, capt. M.C. U.S. Army, 1941; advanced to brig. gen.; past exec. officer 7th Evacuation Hosp.; So. Pacific; comdg. officer 134th Evacuation Hosp.; ETO.; Cons. to Army Surgeon Gen.; spl. asst. to Surgeon Gen. Fellow AAAS, AMA, A.C.S., Royal Soc. Health; mem. Am. Pharm. Assn., N.Y. State Pharm. Assn., N.Y. Acad. Medicine, N.Y. Acad. Pharmacy, N.Y. Acad. Sci., Assn., U.S. Army, Res. Officers Assn. (pres. D.C. Army chpt.), VFW, Am. Legion (comdr. Caduceus post), Mil. Order World Wars, Soc. Cons. to Armed Forces, Assn. Mil. Surgeons U.S. (nat. pres. 1967), Chi Gamma Iota, Phi Chi, Alpha Sigma Phi. Home: 4545 Connecticut Ave NW Washington DC 20008

KIDDER, MARGOT, actress; b. Yellow Knife, Can., Oct. 17, 1948; m. Tom McGuane (div.); 1 dau., Maggie; m. John Heard. Attended, U. B.C. Began career in Can. theater and TV; film debut in Gaily,

Gaily, 1969; other films Quackser Fortune Has a Cousin in the Bronx, 1970, Sisters, 1972, Gravy Train, 1974, The Great Waldo Pepper, 1975, The Reincarnation of Peter Proud, 1975, 92 in the Shade, 1977, Superman, 1978, The Amityville Horror, 1979, Superman II, 1981, Some Kind of Hero, 1981; starred in: TV series Nichols, 1972; other TV appearances include Mod Squad; starred in: TV movie Honky Tonk, 1974 *

KIDDER, MICHAEL GEORGE, managing editor; b. Des Moines, 1941; s. George Henry and Mary Kay (Scott) K.; m. Lois Elaine Mohr, Nov. 25, 1967; children: David, Sandy. B.A. in Journalism, Drake U., 1964. Asst. city editor Sacramento Bee, 1970-73, exec. sports editor, 1973-76, night editor, 1976, med. editor, 1976, mng. editor, 1980—; exec. editor Modesto (Calif.) Bee, 1977-80; juror Pulitzer Prize nominating jury, Columbia U., 1983, 84. Mem. Am. Soc. Newspaper Editors, Calif. Soc. Newspaper Editors (bd. dirs.), Sigma Delta Chi. Methodist. Home: 1633 McClaren Carmichael CA 95608 Office: Sacramento Bee PO Box 15779 Sacramento CA 95852

KIDDER, PRISCILLA, fashion designer, clothing mfr.; b. Quincy, Mass., Dec. 14, 1916; m. James Kidder. Student, New Eng. Art Sch. Asst. buyer White's Dept. Store, Boston; founder bridal shop, Boston, 1945, Priscilla of Boston, N.Y.C., 1950—. Office: care Priscilla of Boston 498 7th Ave New York NY 10018 *

KIDDLE, LAWRENCE BAYARD, educator; b. Cleve., Aug. 20, 1907; s. Bayard Taylor and Emma Melvina (Volmar) K.; m. Allene Cornelia Houglan, June 29, 1932; children: Sue (Mrs. Loche Van Atta), Mary Ellen. B.A. magna cum laude, Oberlin (Ohio) Coll., 1929; M.A., U. Wis. at Madison, 1930, Ph.D., 1935. Teaching asst. Spanish and French U. Wis., 1929-35; instr. U. N.Mex., Albuquerque, 1935-37, asst. prof., 1937-38; instr. Spanish Princeton, 1938-40; asst. prof. Romance langs. Tulane U., New Orleans, 1940-41, asso. prof., 1941-43; asst. prof. Spanish, Romance linguistics U. Mich., Ann Arbor, 1947-48, asso. prof., 1948-54, prof., 1954-78, prof. emeritus, 1978—; Fulbright prof. linguistics Instituto Caro y Cuervo, Bogota, Colombia, 1963-64. Editor: (with J.E. Englekirk) Los de Abajo (Mariano Azuela), 1939, Veinte Cuentos Hispanoamericanos del Siglo Veinte, 1956, El Libro de Las Cruzes (Alfonso El Sabio), 1961, Cuentos Americanos y Algunos Poemas, 1970, La Barraca (Blasco Ibanez), 1961. Served to lt. comdr. USNR, 1943-47. Decorated comandante Orden Militar De Ayacucho, Peru). Mem. Hispanic Soc. Am. (corr.), Modern Lang. Assn. Am., Am. Assn. Tchrs. Spanish and Portuguese (pres.), Linguistic Soc. Am. Democrat. Home: 2654 Englave Dr Ann Arbor MI 48103

KIDDOO, RICHARD C., oil company executive; b. Wilmington, Del., Aug. 31, 1927; s. William Richard and Nellie Louise (Bounds) K.; m. Catherine Schumann, June 25, 1950; children: Jean L., William R., Scott F., David B. B.Chem. Engring., U. Del., 1948. With Esso Standard Oil and Esso Internat. Inc., Md., N.J., N.Y., 1948-66; internat. sales mgr. Esso Europe Inc., London, 1966-67; mng. dir., chief exec. officer Esso Pappas Indsl. Co., Athens, Greece, 1967-71; pres. Esso Africa Inc., London, 1971-72; v.p. Esso Europe Inc., London, 1973-81; v.p. mktg. Exxon Co., U.S.A., Houston, 1981—; vice chmn. mktg. com. Am. Petroleum, Washington, 1983; bd. dirs. Hwy. Users Fedn., Washington. Served with USMC, 1945-46. Decorated Cross of King George I, Greece. Mem. Am. Inst. Chem. Engrs., Am. Petroleum Inst., Wings Club. Clubs: NYAC, Naval and Mil. (London); Petroleum (Houston); Gibson Island (Md.); Circumnavigators (N.Y.). Home: 9061 Briar Forest Houston TX 77024 Office: Exxon Co USA 800 Bell Ave Houston TX 77002

KIDENEY, JAMES WILLIAMS, architect; b. Pitts., Apr. 25, 1899; s. William W. and Ada J. (Porter) K.; m. Isabel Houck, Aug. 15, 1930. B.S., U. Mich., 1921; student, Europe, 1922-23. Licensed architect, N.Y.; certificate Nat. Council Archtl. Registration Bds. With archtl. offices, Buffalo, 1921-26, entered practice, 1926; partner Paul Hyde Harbach, 1929-42; pvt. practice, specializing in design schs., instnl. bldgs. and housing, Buffalo, 1942-50; as James Wm. Kideney & Assocs., 1950-58, firm Kideney, Smith, Fitzgerald & Partners, 1958-74; cons. Community Planning Assistance Center, others. Architect: dormitory and student Union bldg, N.Y. State Tchrs. Coll., Buffalo, Lockport, Tonawanda and Syracuse office bldgs., N.Y. Telephone Co. (various design awards). Mem. adv. council on sch. bldgs., grounds N.Y. State Edn. Dept., 1941-43, panel community planning cons., 1945-47; cons. architect N.Y. Joint Legislative Com. on Investigating Sch. Costs, 1941; chmn. com. architects, engrs. and landscape architects of Buffalo for post war constrn.; mem. N.Y. Gov.'s vol. com. on housing and constrn.; mem. airport adv. bd., Buffalo, 1950-52; mem. N.Y. State Bd. Examiners for Architects, 1949-56, chmn., 1953. Citation as outstanding citizen Buffalo Evening News, 1964; award for vol. services Community Planning Assistance Center, 1976. Fellow AIA (chmn. com. state and municipal pub. works 1942-46, chmn. com. local pub. bldgs. 1947-49), mem. C. of C., Buffalo Fine Arts Acad. (life), Buffalo Pub. Library (life), N.Y. State Assn. Architects (pres. 1938-42, Sidney L. Strauss award 1951, Award of Merit 1949, Award of Merit for N.Y. Telephone Co. offices), Alpha Rho Chi. Clubs: Buffalo, Rotary. Home: 56 Soldiers Pl Buffalo NY 14222

KIDERA, GEORGE J., surgeon; b. Chgo., Apr. 29, 1913; s. Edward J. and Marie (Nadherny) K.; m. Marie A. Cuchna, Aug. 1938 (dec. Feb. 1973); children: George Peter, Kristina Alice; m. Jean Allen, Aug. 16, 1975. Student, Northwestern U., 1930-31, Crane Jr. Coll., 1931-33; B.S., U. Ill., 1935, M.D., 1937; postgrad., Sch. Aviation Medicine, 1942, Cook County Hosp. Post Grad. Sch., 1948. Diplomate: Am. Bd. Preventive Medicine. Intern, resident West Suburban Hosp., Oak Park, Ill., 1937-38, then mem. surg. staff; pres. W. Suburban Hosp. Interns Alumni Assn., 1949-51; regional med. dir. United Air Lines, Chgo., 1938, 46-51, med. dir., 1951-72, v.p. med. services, 1972-78, cons. to chmn., 1978—; cons. Dart Industries, 1979—; cons. life scis. com. NASA, 1970—. Contbr. articles to med. jours. Served to lt. col., flight surgeon USAAF, 1942-46. Recipient Pres. award United Air Lines, 1950., Theodore C. Lyster award Am. Coll. Preventive Medicine, 1970. Fellow Aerospace Med. Assn. (pres. 1960, mem. exec. council 1963, Howard D. Edwards award 1960); mem. AMA, Airline Med. Dirs. Assn. (mem. exec. council 1950-51, pres. 1955), Ill. Med. Soc., Am. Assn. Indsl. Physicians and Surgeons, Chgo., Des Plaines (sec.), med. socs., Am. Med. Writers Assn., Internat. Air Transport Assn., Internat. Acad. Aviation and Space Medicine (chancellor 1972-77, 1st v.p. 1977—). Home: 19927 W Grand Ave Lake Villa IL 60046 Office: United Air Lines PO Box 66100 Chicago IL 60666

KIDERA, ROBERT A(NTHONY), college president; b. Hartland, Ill., Feb. 14, 1918; s. Joseph I. and Gertrude Ann (Bloner) K.; m. Helen Behling, Aug. 23, 1947; children: Robert, David, Geralyn, Judith, Thomas, Patricia. A.B., Marquette U., 1939, M.A., 1947; L.H.D. (hon.), Bridgeport Engring. Inst., 1974. Asst. prof. journalism Marquette U., 1948-51, asso. prof., 1951-56, prof., 1956-61, dir. public relations, 1959-61; asst. to pres. Cornell U., 1961-65; v.p. Fordham U., 1965-69, Tamblyn & Brown, N.Y.C., 1969-71; pres. Sacred Heart U., Bridgeport, Conn., 1971-76, Nazareth Coll., Rochester, N.Y., 1976—. Author: Fundamentals of Journalism, 1956. Trustee, mem. exec. com. Rochester Area Colls.; dir. Commn. Ind. Colls. and Univs.; mem. regional adv. council Gen. Valley; trustee Mfrs. Hanover Bank; Bd. dirs. Rochester Assn. UN; bd. govs. Genesee Hosp. Served to 1st lt. USAAR, 1942-46. Mem. Sigma Delta Chi. Roman Catholic. Clubs: Univ., Oak Hill Country, K.C., Rotary. Office: 4245 East Ave Rochester NY 14610

KIDMAN, ROY L., university librarian; b. Redondo Beach, Calif., July 25, 1925. B.S. in Chemistry, UCLA, 1951; M.S.L.S., U. So. Calif., 1953. Cataloger UCLA Law Sch., 1953-54; sci. librarian U. Kans., 1954-59; acting dir. library Tulane U., 1959-60; asst dir. U. Calif., 1960-62, biomed. librarian, San Diego, 1963-68; librarian Rutgers U., 1968-71, U. So. Calif., Los Angeles, 1971—. Mem. ALA, Calif. Library Assn., Beta Phi Mu. Club: Zamorano. Office: Univ Library U Southern Calif Los Angeles CA 90007

KIDNAY, ARTHUR JOSEPH, engineering educator; b. Milw., Apr. 4, 1934; s. Arthur J. and Margaret (Beck) K.; m. Joan Anne Dillon, Dec. 26, 1960; children: Elizabeth, Brian, Mary. B.S. in Chem. Engring., Colo. Sch. Mines, 1956, D.Sc., 1968, M.S., U. Colo., 1960. Registered profl. engr., Colo. Engr. Monsanto Corp., Springfield, Mass., 1956-58; research engr. Nat. Bur. Standards, Boulder, Colo., 1959-68; asst. prof. chem. engring. Colo. Sch. Mines, Golden, 1958-71, assoc. prof., 1971-75, prof., head dept., 1975—; cons. Nat. Bur.Standards, 1968—. Author: Equilibrium Properties of Fluid Mixtures, 1982. Served to 1st lt. U.S. Army, 1956-57. Mem. Am. Inst. Chem. Engrs. Home: 6141 Van Gordon St Arvada CO 80004 Office: Colorado School of Mines Golden CO 80401

KIDWELL, WAYNE LEROY, government official; b. Council, Idaho, June 15, 1938; s. John A. and Irene E. (Konkle) K.; m. Shari Linn, July 25, 1963; children: Vaughn, Blair. B.A., U. Idaho, 1960, J.D., 1964. Bar: Idaho 1964, Hawaii 1981. With firm Moffatt, Thomas, Barrett & Blanton, Boise, Idaho, 1965-66; pros. atty., Ada County, Idaho, 1966-68, individual practice law, Boise, 1968-74, atty. gen., State of Idaho, 1975-79, Marshall Islands, 1981; ptnr. Hoddick, Reinwald, O'Connor, Marrack, Honolulu, 1983; of counsel firm Runft and Longeteig, Boise, 1979-81; chmn. Western Regional Conf. Attys. Gen., 1977-78. Author: Prosecuting Attorneys Handbook, 1967. Mem. Idaho Senate, 1969-72, majority leader, 1971-72; chmn. Idaho Citizens for Reagan, 1976; co-chmn. Idaho President Ford Com., 1976, Nat. Citizens for Reagan, 1980. Served with AUS, 1960-62. Mem. Nat. Assn. Attys. Gen. (exec. com. 1975-76, chmn. environmental control com. 1977-78), Am. Trial Lawyers Assn., Am. Judicature Soc., Nat. Dist. Attys. Assn., Phi Alpha Delta. Methodist. Club: Shriners. Home: 6714 Kennedy Ln Falls Church VA 22042 Office: Dept Justice 10th St and Constitution Ave NW Washington DC 20530

KIECHLIN, ROBERT JEROME, coal company executive; b. N.Y.C., Nov. 2, 1919; s. Henry, Jr. and Lydia C. (Bergmann) K.; m. Regina W. Kolakowski, Oct. 6, 1951; children: Robert Jerome, Regina, William. B.S. in Acctg., NYU, 1940. C.P.A., N.Y., Mo. With Paisley & Conroy (C.P.A.s), N.Y.C., 1945-52; with N.J. Zinc Co., 1952—, asst. comptroller, 1957-61, comptroller, 1961-66, treas. and comptroller, 1966-71; controller Peabody Coal Co., St. Louis, 1971-79; v.p., controller, treas. R.L. Burns Corp., Evansville, Ind., 1979—; controller, treas. Pyro Energy Corp., Evansville, Ind., 1981—. Served with USNR, 1942-45; PTO. Decorated Navy Cross. Mem. N.Y. State Soc. C.P.A.s, Am. Inst. C.P.A.s, Nat. Assn. Accts., Fin. Execs. Inst. Home: Route 8 Box 145C Evansville IN 47711 Office: 653 S Hebron Evansville IN 47715

KIEFFER, JAMES MILTON, lawyer; b. Newark, May 22, 1921; s. Alonzo Michael and Mae (St. Germaine) K.; m. Eleanor Jane Van Atta, Sept. 7, 1946; children—Michael J., Laura J. Cufari, Andrew V., Elizabeth A. Sullivan. A.B., Hamilton Coll., 1946; LL.B., Cornell U., 1949. Bar: N.Y. bar 1949, Fla. bar 1976. Since practiced in, Rochester; asso., then partner Remington, Gifford, Willy & Williams, 1949-60; staff asst. to pres. Pfaudler Permutit, Inc., 1960-61, house counsel, 1961-63, sec., counsel, 1963-65, Ritter Pfaudler Corp. (now Sybron Corp.), 1965-68, v.p., sec., counsel, 1968-73, v.p., gen. counsel, 1973-79, sr. v.p., gen. counsel, 1980-81, sr. v.p., 1982-83, vice chmn. bd., 1983—. Served to 1st lt. USAAF, 1943-46. Mem. Am., Fla. bar assns., Rochester C. of C., Order of Coif, Psi Upsilon, Phi Delta Phi. Republican. Roman Catholic. Clubs: Rochester Country, Univ. (Rochester). Home: 52 Green Valley Rd Pittsford NY 14534 Office: 1100 Midtown Tower Rochester NY 14604

KIEFFER, JAROLD ALAN, policy and management consultant; b. Mpls., May 5, 1923; s. Charles O. and Edith Ida (Feinberg) K.; m. Frances Clarfield, Aug. 13, 1949; children: Edith Charlotte, Charles Edward, Philip William. B.A., U. Minn., 1947, Ph.D., 1950. Teaching asst. polit. sci. dept. U. Minn., 1949, Teaching asst. social sci. program, 1950-51; research asst., world affairs program Mpls. Star, 1949-50; exec. sec. def. moblzn. manpower coms., staff asst. to exec. sec. Office Def. Moblzn., Exec. Office of Pres., 1951-52, staff sec., 1952, asst. to exec. officer, exec. sec. borrowing authority review bd., 1953, spl. asst. to dir., 1955-56, acting dep. asst. dir. nat. security affairs, 1956-57, cons., 1958; exec. asst. to dir. orgn. and personnel, exec. sec. personnel adv. com. AEC, 1952-53; asst. to Arthur S. Flemming, mem. 2d Hoover Commn., 1953-55; liaison Task Force on Personnel and Civil Service, 1953-55; asst. to chmn. com. Pres.'s Adv. Com. on Govt. Orgn., 1953-61, cons., 1958; asst. to Meyer Kestnbaum, spl. asst. to Pres. for Hoover Commn. and intergovtl. relations commn. matters, The White House, 1955-56; adviser to Meyer Kestnbaum, 1956-57; asst. to Nelson Rockefeller, 1957-58; cons. HEW, Washington, 1958, asst. to sec., 1958-59, asst. to sec. for program analysis, 1959-61; sec. bd. trustees Nat. Cultural Center, 1959-63, exec. dir., 1961-63; renamed John F. Kennedy Center for Performing Arts; asso. prof. polit. sci. U., Oreg., 1963-67, acting chmn. polit. sci. dept., 1964, asst. to pres., 1963-67; chmn. public affairs and adminstrn. programs, prof. public policy and adminstrn. Sch. Community Service and Pub. Affairs, 1967-69; dir. Macalester Found. for Higher Edn., 1969-70; exec. officer bd. trustees Macalester Coll., 1970-71, also adj. prof. polit. sci., 1969-71; dir. Office Internat. Tng., AID, State Dept., 1971-72, asst. adminstr. for population and humanitarian assistance, 1972-75; adj. prof. internat. relations Am. U., Washington, 1975; staff dir. Pres.'s Panel on Biomed. Research, 1975-76. Dep. commr. social security HEW, 1976-77; dir. Task Force on House Adminstrv. System, Commn. on Adminstrv. Rev., U.S. Ho. of Reps., 1977; staff dir. Nat. Com. on Careers for Older Ams., 1978-80, Acad. Ednl. Devel., Inc., 1978-80, White House Conf. on Aging, 1980-82; policy and mgmt. cons., 1982—; vice chmn. Gov.'s Planning Council Arts and Humanities, State Oreg., 1965-67; chmn. Project 70's Task Force On State Govt. Reorgn., Oreg., 1968-69; cons. Office High Speed Ground Transp., U.S. Dept. Transp., 1969-70, U.S. Office Edn., 1971; officer, mem. exec. com. Lane County Auditorium Assn., Oreg., 1963-69. Served with AUS, 1942-46. Mem. Am. Polit. Sci. Assn., Am. Soc. Pub. Adminstrn., Advanced Transit Assn. (dir., chmn.). Home: 9019 Hamilton Dr Fairfax VA 22031

KIEFFER, RICHARD WILLIAM, banker; b. Milw., Nov. 19, 1937; s. Raymond Urban and Ruth (Sisson) K.; m. Lorna Coates, Jan. 29, 1963; children: Steven Richard, Kimberly Ann, Douglas Alan. Student, pub. schs., Cin. Vice pres. 1st Interstate Bancorp. and predecessor Western Bancorp., Salt Lake City, 1971-74, v.p., cashier, 1974-77, sr. v.p., cashier, 1977-81, exec. v.p., 1981—, bd. dirs. Past pres. South Davis Youth Soccer Assn., 1977. Mem. Salt Lake Bank Officers Assn. (pres. 1974-75), Am. Bankers Assn., Bank Adminstrn. Inst., Intermountain Automated Clearing House Assn. (dir., officer 1980-81), Salt Lake Clearing House Assn. (pres. 1983), Salt Lake City C. of C. Republican. Mormon. Clubs: Alta; Petroleum (Salt Lake City). Home: 2787 Oakwood Dr Bountiful UT 84010 Office: 1st Interstate Bank of Utah NA 175 S Main St Salt Lae City UT 84111

KIEFFER, STEPHEN AARON, radiologist, educator; b. Mpls., Dec. 20, 1935; s. Julius Hyman and Anita Elaine (Brudnick) K.; m. Cyrile Frada Kaplan, Dec. 21, 1958; children—Alisa, Mitchell, Stuart, Paula. B.A. summa cum laude, U. Minn., 1956, M.D., 1959. Diplomate: Am. Bd. Radiology. Intern Wadsworth VA Hosp., Los Angeles, 1959-60; resident in radiology U. Minn. Hosps., Mpls., 1960-62, 64-65; NIH fellow in neuroradiology, 1966-68; instr. U. Minn. Med. Sch., Mpls., 1966-67, asst. prof., 1967-68, asso. prof., 1968-72, prof., 1972-74; chief radiology service Mpls. VA Hosp., 1968-74; prof., chmn. dept. radiology SUNY-Upstate Med. Center, Syracuse, 1974—; cons. Syracuse VA Med. Center, Crouse-Irving-Meml. Hosp. Co-author: Introduction to Neuroradiology, 1972; co-editor: An Atlas of Cross-sectional Anatomy, 1979; contbr. numerous articles to profl. jours., also chpts. to books; editorial adv. bd.: Radiology, 1980—; cons. editorial bd.: Am. Jour. Neuroradiology, 1980—; asso. editor: Yearbook of Radiology, 1981—. Chmn. tech. adv. subcom. on computed tomography Central N.Y. Health Systems Agy., 1979-80; mem. tech. adv. com. on computed tomography N.Y. State Office Health Systems Mgmt., 1981; Bd. Dirs. Syracuse Jewish Fedn., 1975-81. Served to capt., M.C. U.S. Army, 1962-64. Nat. Heart Inst. trainee, 1961-62; Nat. Inst. Neurol. Diseases and Blindness fellow, 1966; James Picker Found. scholar, 1966-68. Fellow Am. Coll. Radiology (com. computed tomography); mem. Am. Roentgen Ray Soc. (pubs. com.), Am. Soc. Neuroradiology (pres. 1978-79), AMA, Assn. Univ. Radiologists, Central N.Y. Radiol. Soc. (chmn. program com. 1979-82, Med. Soc. N.Y. State), Minn. Radiol. Soc. (sec. 1974), Neurosurg. Soc. Am., Onondaga County Med. Soc., Radiol. Soc. N. Am. (refresher course com. 1977-82), Soc. Chairmen Acad. Radiology Depts., Phi Beta Kappa, Alpha Omega Alpha. Jewish. Home: 503 Standish Dr Syracuse NY 13224 Office: 750 E Adams St Syracuse NY 13210

KIEFFER, WILLIAM FRANKLINN, educator; b. Trenton, N.J., Mar. 16, 1915; s. William Miles and Carrie Jeanette (Halfpenny) K.; m. Elaine Steele, June 22, 1940; children—Richard William, Lois Jeanette. B.A., Wooster Coll., 1936; M.Sc., Ohio State U., 1938; Ph.D. (Jesse Metcalf fellow 1939-40), Brown U., 1940. Instr. chemistry Coll. Wooster, Ohio, 1940-42, prof. chemistry, 1946-80, prof. emeritus, 1980—, chmn. dept. chemistry, 1968-77; asst. prof. chemistry Western Res. U., 1942-46; Vis. prof. U. Wash., summer 1955; research participant radiation chemistry Oak Ridge Nat. Lab., 1951-52; vis. scientist in chemistry NSF, 1957-73; Sci. Faculty fellow Mass. Inst. Tech., 1963-64; vis. scholar Stanford U., 1969-70, U. Calif., Santa Cruz, 1974-75; vis. prof. U.S. Naval Acad., 1981; chmn. adv. com. for NBC prodn. Author: The Mole Concept in Chemistry, 1961, Chemistry, A Cultural Approach, 1971, Chemistry Today, 1976; Editor: Selected Readings in General Chemistry, 1958, Selected Readings for Chemical Bond, 1960, Selected Readings in Inorganic Chemistry, 1962, Selected Readings in History of Chemistry, 1965, Jour. Chem. Edn, 1955-67; Contbr. numerous articles to profl. jours. Continental Classroom of Am. Chem. Soc. (councillor 1956-75, chmn. local sect. 1949, recipient award in chem. edn. 1968), N.Y., Ohio acads. sci., AAAS, AAUP, Mfg. Chemists Assn. (teaching award 1965), Phi Beta Kappa, Sigma Xi. Presbyn. (elder, trustee). Club: Rotarian. Home: 1873 Golden Rain Rd Apt 3 Walnut Creek CA 94595

KIEFT, LESTER, chemist; b. Grand Haven, Mich., Sept. 18, 1912; s. Martin and Dena (Rossien) K.; m. Norma Elaine Richenbacher, June 28, 1941; children: John Martin, Richard, James. A.B., Hope Coll., 1934; M.S., Pa. State Coll., 1936, Ph.D., 1939. Asst. Pa. State Coll., 1934-37; asst. prof. chemistry Pa. State Jr. Coll., 1937-42, Bucknell U., 1942-44, prof. and head chemistry dept., 1944-81, prof. emeritus, 1981—; summer lectr., engring. (sci. and mgmt. war tng. program), 1941; dir. Inst. High Sch. Sci. Tchrs., Bucknell U., 1957—, Inst. for High Ability Secondary Students. Pres. Lewisburgh Borough Council, 1962-65; In charge Lewisburg (Pa.) Youth Activities, 1944-51; pres. Eastern Union County United Fund. Recipient Distinguished Service award Jr. C. of C., 1977; Good Citizenship award SAR, 1979. Mem. Am. Chem. Soc. (analytical subcom. on exams. and tests for soc. coop. chemistry test, vice chmn. central Pa. sect. 1954, chmn. 1955, chmn. Susquehanna Valley sect. 1958-59), AAAS, Pa. Sci. Tchrs. (dir. 1958—), Nat. Sci. Tchrs. Assn., Blue Key, Sigma Xi, Alpha Chi Sigma, Phi Eta Sigma, Sigma Xi, Phi Lambda Upsilon. Republican. Mem. United Ch. Christ (ch. council 1944—). Clubs: Lions (dist. gov. 1956-57, chmn. Sight Conservation and Eye Research Found. 1957—. Home: 319 Buffalo Rd Lewisburg PA 17837

KIELY, ROBERT JAMES, educator; b. N.Y.C., July 10, 1931; s. John V. and Mary C. (Caporal) K.; m. Jana Moravkova, 1962; children—Anne, Jan, Christina, Maria. A.B. magna cum laude, Amherst Coll., 1953; Ph.D. in English (Dexter prize English studies 1960, Samuel S. Fels fellow 1961), Harvard U., 1962. Mem. faculty Harvard U., 1962—, prof. English, 1968—, asso. dean faculty arts and scis., 1972-75; master Adams House, 1973—; vis. fellow St. Edmund's House, Cambridge U., 1970-71, 76-77. Author: Robert Louis Stevenson and the Fiction of Adventure, 1964, Man and Nature, 1966, The Romantic Novel in England, 1972, Beyond Egotism: The Fiction of James Joyce, Virginia Woolf and D.H. Lawrence, 1980. Served to lt. USNR, 1953-56. Mem. Modern Lang. Assn., Phi Beta Kappa. Home: 10 Linden St Cambridge MA 02138

KIER, PORTER MARTIN, paleontologist; b. Pitts., Oct. 22, 1927; s. Samuel Martin and Mary (Kebler) K.; m. Mary Ellen Lavely, Sept. 9, 1950; children—William McKee, Elizabeth Lavely. B.S., U. Mich., 1950, M.S., 1951; Ph.D., Cambridge (Eng.) U., 1954, Sc.D., 1973. Asst. prof. U. Houston, 1956-57; curator Smithsonian Instn., Washington, 1957-67, chmn. dept. paleobiology, 1967-72; dir. U.S. Nat. Mus. Natural History, 1973-80, sr. scientist, 1980—. Fulbright scholar, 1951-52; Guggenheim fellow, 1968. Fellow AAAS, Geol. Soc. Am., Geol. Soc. London; mem. Paleontol. Soc. (past pres.). Research and publs. in systematics of fossil echinoids and living habits of recent echinoids. Home: 5104 Bradford Dr Annandale VA 22003 Office: Smithsonian Instn Washington DC 20560

KIERAN, JAMES, physician; b. Yonkers, N.Y., Feb. 9, 1920; s. John and Alma (Boldtmann) K.; children: Anne Kieran Westerman, James, Margaret, Jane, John, Robert; m. Sonya Mansfield. A.B., Yale U., 1941; M.D., Columbia U., 1944. Intern and resident Bellevue Hosp., N.Y.C., 1944-49; pvt. practice medicine, Oakland, Calif., 1950-59, Berkeley, Calif., 1959—; clin. prof. medicine U. Calif. Sch. Medicine, San Francisco, 1959—; dir. pulmonary disease service Stanford Sch. Medicine, 1957-60. Served to capt. M.C., USAAF, 1945-47. Mem. Am. Thoracic Soc. (pres. 1971-72), Calif. Thoracic Soc. (pres. 1961-62), Am. Lung Assn. (pres. 1976-77), Calif. Lung Assn. (pres. 1969-70). Club: Rotary. Address: 2340 Ward St Berkeley CA 94705

KIERNAN, EDWARD J., labor union official. Pres. Internat. Union Police Assn. Office: 412 First St SE Washington DC 20003 *

KIERNAN, EDWIN A., JR., lawyer, corporation executive; b. N.Y.C., Aug. 2, 1926; s. Edwin A. and Helen M. (Clarke) K.; m. Ellen Mary Irving, Feb. 18, 1952; children: Robert Clarke, Katherine Waters. A.B., Columbia, 1947, J.D., 1950; LL.M., NYU, 1957. Bar: N.Y. 1950. Asso. Simpson Thacher & Bartlett, N.Y.C., 1950-52, 54-55, Wickes,

Riddell, Bloomer, Jacobi & McGuire, 1956-59; atty. Western Electric Co., Inc., 1959-60, Interpublic Group of Cos., Inc., N.Y.C., 1960-64, mng. atty., 1964-68, asst. gen. counsel, 1968-79, sec. and gen. counsel, 1980—, v.p., 1973-81, sr. v.p., 1981—; sec. McCann-Erickson, Inc., N.Y.C., 1962-79. Served to lt. (j.g.) USNR, 1944-46, 52-54. Mem. Am. Bar Assn., Assn. Bar City N.Y., Phi Beta Kappa. Home: 544 1st St Brooklyn NY 11215 Office: 1271 Ave of Americas New York NY 10020

KIERNAN, OWEN BURNS, educational consultant; b. Randolph, Mass., Mar. 9, 1914; s. Thomas Francis and Elizabeth (Burns) K.; m. Esther Harriet Thorley, July 13, 1940; children: Joan Ann, Nancy Elizabeth, John Albert. B.S., Bridgewater (Mass.) State Coll., 1935; M.Ed., Boston U., 1940, Sc.D. (hon.), 1968; Ed.D., Harvard U., 1950; L.H.D. (hon.), Lesley Coll., 1956; LL.D., Northeastern U., 1961; Litt.D. (hon.), Stonehill Coll., 1965, Ped.D., R.I. Coll., 1966. Prin. Henry T. Wing High Sch., Sandwich, Mass., 1938-44; supt. schs., Wayland and Sudbury, Mass., 1944-51, Milton, 1951-57, commr. edn., State of Mass., 1957-68; exec. dir. Nat. Assn. Secondary Sch. Prins., 1969-79; dir. sch. div. McManis Assos., Inc., 1980-82; cons. Washington, 1983—; Past chmn. Mass. Bd. Edn., Mass. Bd. Vocat. Edn.; corp. mem. MIT. Trustee U. Mass., Lowell Tech. Inst., Mus. Fine Arts, Mus. Sci. Boston, Boston U.; bd. dirs. Atlantic Council U.S.; chmn. edn. com. Atlantic Treaty Assn., 1968—; gov. bd. Atlantic Info. Centre for Tchrs., London, 1968—; exec. com. U.S. People-to-People Program. Mem. Am. Assn. Sch. Adminstrs., New Eng., Mass. supts. assns., Council Chief State Sch. Officers (pres. 1967), Phi Delta Kappa. Home: 12301 Delevan Dr Herndon VA 22071

KIERNAN, RICHARD FRANCIS, publisher; b. N.Y.C., Apr. 17, 1935; s. James J. and Grace (Nolan) K.; m. Jane Eickmeyer, Dec. 29, 1962; children: Christopher, Peter, Kathy Lynn. B.S., U. Conn., 1961. Pub., RN Mag., also asso. pub. Med. Econs. and gen. mgr. product devel. Litton Publs., 1963-73; pres. CPC Corp. div. Cliccott Pub. Co., Greenwich, Conn., 1973-74; pub. Physicians Mgmt., N.Y.C., 1974-76, Drug Update, 1976—; group v.p. Biomed. Info. Corp., N.Y.C., 1974-79; pub. office and hosp. edits. Drug Therapy, N.Y.C., 1979—; pres. Hosp. Publs., 1979—; Treas. Pharm. Adv. Council, 1979-81, pres., 1981. Served with AUS, 1958-63. Mem. Assn. Ind. Clin. Publs. (dir. 1979—). Roman Catholic. Clubs: Pharm. Advt. (dir.), Midwest Pharm. Advt., Ridgewood Country, N.Y. Athletic. Home: 153 Hamilton Rd Ridgewood NJ 07450 Office: 90 Park Ave New York NY 10016

KIESCHNICK, WILLIAM FREDERICK, petroleum company executive; b. Dallas, Jan. 5, 1923; s. William Frederick and Effie Elizabeth (Meador) K.; m. Betty Jane Camp, Sept. 25, 1948 (dec.); children—Michael Frank, Meredith Jane; m. Keithann Chapman Allen, Apr. 21, 1979. B.S., Rice U., 1947; Certificate Physics/Meteorology, U. Calif. at Los Angeles, 1943; postgrad., Scripps Inst., 1943. Research engr. Atlantic Richfield Co., Dallas, 1947-59, asst. to gen. mgr. exploration, 1959-61, dist. mgr. prodn. and exploration, Lafayette, La., 1961-63, regional mgr. dists. exploration and prodn., Dallas, 1963-67, v.p. synthetic fuel and mineral ops., 1967-69; v.p. ARCO Chem. Co., Phila., 1970-72, v.p. corp. planning, Los Angeles, 1972-73, exec. v.p., 1973-75, group exec. v.p. chem., fuels and transp. divs., 1975-78, vice chmn. bd., in charge of ops., 1979-81, pres., chief operating officer, 1981—; also dir., dir. Coldwell Banker Co., Los Angeles; also dir.; trustee Elderhostel, Inc. Contbr. articles to profl. jours. Adv. com. White House Conf. Aging; bd. dirs. So. Calif. region NCCJ; mem. exec. com. United Way; trustee Mus. Contemporary Art. Served to capt. USAAF, 1943-46. Decorated Bronze Star; fellow Aspen Inst. Humanistic Studies. Mem. Am. Petroleum Inst. (bd. dirs.), Los Angeles Area C. of C. (dir.). Office: Atlantic Richfield Co 515 S Flower St Los Angeles CA 90071

KIESER, ELLWOOD E., clergyman, television producer; b. Phila., Mar. 27, 1929. B.A., LaSalle Coll., 1950; M.A., St. Paul's Coll., 1953; Ph.D., Grad. Theol. Union, Berkeley, Calif., 1973. Ordained to priesthood, 1956. Creator, exec. producer TV series Insight. Pres. Humanitas Prize. Recipient Faith and Freedom award, 1972, Emmy award for outstanding achievement in religious series, 1972, Emmy award for religious spl. Address: 17575 Pacific Coast Hwy Pacific Palisades CA 90272

KIESLER, CHARLES ADOLPHUS, psychologist, university administrator; b. St. Louis, Aug. 14, 1934; (div.)children: Tina, Thomas, Eric, Kevin. B.A., Mich. State U., 1958, M.A., 1960; Ph.D. (NIMH fellow), Stanford U., 1963. Asst. prof. psychology Ohio State U., Columbus, 1963-64; asst. prof. psychology Yale U., New Haven, 1964-66, asso. prof., 1966-70; prof., chmn. psychology U. Kans., Lawrence, 1970-75; exec. officer Am. Psychol. Assn., Washington, 1975-79; Walter Van Dyke Bingham prof. psychology Carnegie Mellon U., Pitts., 1979—, head psychology, 1980-82, acting dean, 1981-82, dean Coll. Humanities and Social Scis., 1983—. Author: (with B.E. Collins and N. Miller) Attitude Change: A Critical Analysis of Theoretical Approaches, 1969, (with S.B. Kiesler) Conformity, 1969, The Psychology of Commitment: Experiments Linking Behavior to Belief, 1971, (with N. Cummings and G. Vanden Bos) Psychology and National Health Insurance: A Sourcebook, 1979. Served with Security Service USAF, 1952-56. Fellow Am. Psychol. Assn., AAAS; mem. AAUP, Eastern Psychol. Assn., Soc. Exptl. Social Psychology, Midwestern Psychol. Assn., Assn. for Advancement of Psychology, Psychonomic Soc., Council Applied Social Research, Sigma Xi, Psi Chi, Phi Kappa Phi. Office: Office of Dean Coll Humanities and Social Scis Carnegie Mellon U Pittsburgh PA 15213

KIESLER, SARA BETH, educator, psychologist; b. Washington, Sept. 20, 1940; d. Lawrence M. and Gaynelle (Silverman) Greene; children: Eric Joseph, Kevin Michael. B.S., Simmons Coll., 1961; M.A., Stanford U., 1963; Ph.D., Ohio State U., 1965. Asst. prof. Yale U., New Haven, 1965-66, Conn. Coll., New London, 1965-70; prof. U. Kans., Lawrence, 1970-75; study dir. NRC, Washington, 1975-79; prof. social scis Carnegie-Mellon U., Pitts., 1979—; cons. NIH, 1979-82; mem. faculty Robotics Inst., Pitts., 1983—. Author: (with C. Kiesler) Conformity, 1969, Intrpersonal Procsses, 1975; editor: Aging, 3 vols., 1980. Woodrow Wilson fellow, 1962; USPHS fellow, 1963-65; NSF grantee, 1966, 79, 80—. Fellow Am. Psychol. Assn.; mem. Soc. Exptl. Social Psychology, AAAS. Home: 665 College Ave Pittsburgh PA 15232 Office: Carnegie-Mellon U Porter Hall 319 Pittsburgh PA 15213

KIESLING, ERNST WILLIE, civil engineering educator; b. Eola, Tex., Apr. 8, 1934; s. Alfred William and Louise (Kern) K.; m. Juanita Haseloff, Aug. 25, 1956; children: Carol, Chris, Max. B.S. in Mech. Engring, Tex. Tech. Coll., 1955; M.S. in Applied Mechanics, Mich. State U., 1959, Ph.D., 1966. Registered profl. engr. Asst. prof. Tex. Tech. Coll., 1959-63; sr. research engr. S.W. Research Inst., San Antonio, 1966-69; prof., chmn. civil engring. dept. Tex. Tech U., Lubbock, 1969—. Tex. NSF faculty fellow, 1963-64. Mem. ASCE, Nat. Assn. Home Builders, Tex. Soc. Profl. Engrs. (Engr. of Yr. award South Plains chpt. 1974), Am. Underground Space Assn., Tex. Solar Energy Soc., Sigma Xi., Tau Beta Pi. Home: 7012 Nashville Dr Lubbock TX 79413 Office: Civil Engring Dept Tex Tech U Lubbock TX 79409

KIESLING, HERBERT JOHN, economist; b. St. Louis, Oct. 6, 1934; s. Herbert Charles and Alice Antoinette (Alt) K.; m. Iris Fabius, Feb. 5, 1966; children: Scott Fabius, Stephanie Ann. B.A., Washington U., St. Louis, 1956, M.A., 1961; Ph.D. in Econs., Harvard U., 1965. Asst. prof. econs. Ind. U., 1965-68, asso. prof., 1968-76, prof. econs. and public-environ. affairs, 1976—; mem. research staff Rand Corp., 1970; mem. sr. research staff Urban Inst., Washington, 1972-74; cons. Rand Corp. Author: (with others) How Effective is Schooling?, 1974; contbr. articles to profl. publs. Served with arty. U.S. Army, 1956-58. Mem. Am. Econ. Assn., Public Choice Soc., Internat. Soc. Public Fin., Soc. Preservation and Encouragement Barbershop Quartet Singing Am. Unitarian. Home: 2217 Wimbleton Ln Bloomington IN 47401 Office: Ballantine Hall Ind U Bloomington IN 47405

KIGER, JOSEPH CHARLES, educator; b. Kenton County, Ky., Aug. 19, 1920; s. Carl C. and Genevieve (Hoelscher) K.; m. Jean Myrick Moore, Mar. 27, 1947; children: Carl A., John J. A.B., Birmingham-So. Coll., 1943; M.A., U. Ala., 1947; Ph.D., Vanderbilt U., 1950. Teaching fellow Vanderbilt U., 1948-50; instr. history U. Ala., summer 1950, Washington U., St. Louis, 1950-51; dir. research select com. to investigate founds. U.S. Ho. of Reps., 1952; staff asso. Am. Council Edn., Washington, 1953-55; asst. dir. So. Fellowships Fund, Chapel Hill, N.C., 1955-58; asso. prof. history U. Ala., 1958-61; prof. history U. Miss., 1961—, chmn. dept. history, 1969-74; cons. non-profit orgns., also govt., 1954—. Author: Operating Principles of the Larger Foundations, 1954, (with others) Sponsored Research Policy of Colleges and Universities, 1954, American Learned Societies, 1963, A History of Mississippi, 1973; Editor: Research Institutions and Learned Societies, 1982. Served to capt. USMCR, 1942-46. Guggenheim fellow, 1960; grantee Russell Sage Found., 1953, Rockefeller Found., 1961, Am. Philos. Soc., 1964, Am. Council of Learned Socs., Nat. Acad. Scis., 1980. Mem. Am. Hist. Assn., So. Hist. Assn. (life), Am. Studies Assn. Home: Country Club Rd Oxford MS 38655 Office: Dept History Univ Miss University MS 38677

KIGHT, ALONZO BARNARD, manufacturing company executive; b. N.Y.C., Apr. 24, 1915; s. Alonzo Barnard and Florence (Cox) K.; m. Audrey Anne, Mar. 13, 1971; 1 dau., Jean Pirie. A.B., Harvard U., 1936; LL.B., Columbia U., 1940; M.B.A., U. Chgo., 1954. Bar: D.C. 1941, Ill. 1944, U.S. Supreme Ct 1944, others 1944. Patent atty. fgn. patent dept. Western Electric Co., 1946-48; with Borg-Warner Corp., 1949-69; v.p. Borg-Warner Internat., 1955-61, pres., dir., 1961-69, v.p. parent corp., 1962-69, pres.; v.p.-internat. Rockwell Internat. Corp., Pitts., to 1980; pres. Audlon Corp.; dir. N. Am. Biol. Corp., Instrumentation Lab., Inc. Bd. dirs. Pitts. Dance Council. Served with USNR, 1944-46. Mem. Beta Gamma Sigma, Phi Delta Phi. Clubs: Duquesne (Pitts.); Field. Home: 2346 NW Britt Ct Stuart FL 33494

KIGHT, EDWARD HILL, office equipment manufacturing company executive; b. Hagerstown, Md., Dec. 9, 1935; s. Linwood Starr and Evelyn Lindsay (Hill) K.; m. Margaret Ann Adkins, Feb. 1, 1964; children—Thomas Adkins, Daniel Hill. Student, U. Va., 1953-56. Various sales and mktg. positions SCM Corp., 1961-63, Bell & Howell, 1963-64, Dura Bus. Machines, 1964-69; v.p., gen. mgr. Edityper Corp., Washington, 1969-72; mktg. mgr. Sperry Univac Co., Phila., 1972-74, A.B. Dick Co., Chgo., 1974-77, exec. v.p. mktg. and services, 1977-81; pres. Stenograph Corp., 1981—. Mem. Internat. Word Processing Assn. Club: Sunset Ridge Country (Chgo.). Home: 1311 Wildwood Northbrook IL 60062 Office: 7300 Niles Center Rd Skokie IL 60077

KIKER, RALPH DOUGLAS, JR., journalist; b. Griffin, Ga., Jan. 7, 1930; s. Ralph Douglas and Nora Ellen (Bunn) K. A.B., Presbyn. Coll., 1952, Litt.D., 1973. Reporter Spartanburg (S.C.) Herald, 1950-51; reporter Atlanta Jour., 1959-62; ofcl. U.S. Peace Corps, 1962-63; White House corr. N.Y. Herald Tribune, 1963-66; news corr. NBC, Washington, 1966—; Washington editor Atlanta Monthly, 1966-67. Author: The Southerner, 1957, Strangers on the Shore, 1959; Contbr. articles to profl. jours. Served to lt. USNR, 1952-59. Recipient George Foster Peabody Broadcasting award, 1971. Mem. Pi Kappa Phi. Episcopalian. Home: 4020 Reno Rd NW Washington DC 20008 Office: 4001 Nebraska Ave NW Washington DC 20016

KIKKAWA, YUTAKA, physician; b. Oita City, Japan, Jan. 30, 1932; s. Watari and Chika K.; m. Helen M. Zak, June 27, 1964; children—Rita Marie, Denise Sumiko, James Makoto, Carol Jean. B.S., U. Tokyo, 1953, M.D., 1957. Intern Sacred Heart Hosp., Spokane, Wash., 1958-59; resident in pathology Albert Einstein Coll. Medicine, N.Y.C., 1959-63, asst. prof., 1965-70, asso. prof., 1970-74, prof., 1974-76; prof. pathology, chmn. dept. N.Y. Med. Coll., Valhalla, N.Y., 1976—. Contbr. articles to med. jours. Mem. Nat. Heart Lung and Blood Adv. Council, NIH, 1972-76. Mem. Am. Thoracic Soc. (councillor 1975-78), Am. Assn. Pathologists, Internat. Acad. Pathology, Assn. Pathology Chmn. Club: Scarsdale Golf. Home: 78 Greenacres Ave Scarsdale NY 10583 Office: Dept Pathology Basic Sci Bldg NY Med Coll Valhalla NY 10595

KILBERG, WILLIAM JEFFREY, lawyer; b. Bklyn., June 12, 1946; s. Jack and Jeanette Constance (Beck) K.; m. Barbara D. Greene, Sept. 27, 1970. Student, Bklyn. Coll., 1963-64; B.S., Cornell U., 1966; J.D., Harvard U., 1969. Bar: N.Y. 1970, D.C. 1972. White House fellow, spl. asst. to sec. Labor, Washington, 1969-70; gen. counsel Fed. Mediation and Conciliation Service, 1970-71; asso. solicitor U.S. Dept. Labor, 1971-73, solicitor, 1973-77; dep. team leader Dept. Labor, Reagan-Bush transition, 1980-81; partner firm Breed, Abbott and Morgan, 1977-80, Gibson, Dunn & Crutcher, 1980—; dir. Palmer Nat. Bank. Contbg. editor: The Lessons of Victory, 1969, Instead of Revolution, 1971; Contbr. articles to profl. jours. Bd. dirs. D.C. chpt. Anti-Defamation League of B'nai B'rith, mem. nat. civil rights com., 1972—; mem. legal affairs adv. com. Republican Nat. Com., 1977-80; class rep. Harvard Law Sch. Fund, 1973-74. Recipient Man of Year award Lafayette High Sch., 1970; League United Latin Am. Citizens award for outstanding service to Spanish-speaking, 1973; Arthur S. Flemming award, 1975; Judge Groat award, 1977; Father William J. Kelly scholar, 1964-66; N.Y. State scholar, 1963-66. Mem. Am., Fed., N.Y., D.C. bar assns., Am. Judicature Soc., Ripon Soc., Cornell, Harvard alumni assns., White House Fellows Assn. (1st v.p. 1981-82, pres. 1982-83). Jewish. Office: 1875 Eye St NW Washington DC 20006

KILBORNE, WILLIAM SKINNER, business consultant; b. Stockbridge, Mass., Sept. 1, 1912; s. Robert Stewart and Katharine (Skinner) K.; m. Elizabeth Briggs, June 25, 1935; children: William Skinner, Benjamin Briggs, Allerton Wright, Katharine Skinner Kilborne Cornwell.; m. Virginia G. Wylie, June 29, 1974. B.A., Yale U., 1935; M.B.A., Harvard U., 1937. With William Skinner & Sons, 1937-53, v.p., 1942-53, trustee, 1947-61; dir. Lexington Lumber Co., 1938-43, Internat. Silk Assn., 1948-53, v.p., 1951-53; spl. asst. to Sec. of Commerce, 1953-57; bus. research B.F. Goodrich Co., 1958-60; v.p. Casey & Kilborne, Inc., N.Y.C., 1960-62; pres. William S. Kilborne, Inc., 1962-74; v.p. John Moynahan & Co., Inc., 1963-66; chmn. Harkil Corp., 1969-75; bus. cons., corp. growth, 1975—. Mem. Nat. Def. Exec. Res., 1958-70; Vice pres. 15th Assembly District Republican Club, N.Y.C., 1939-41; mem. N.Y. County Rep. Com., 1940-41, Mercer County Rep. Com., 1978; bd. dirs. Nat. Fedn. Settlements, 1941-42, 44-46; trustee N.Y. Sch. Social Work, 1952-53, hon. trustee, 1953-59; bd. dirs. Lenox Hill Neighborhood Assn., 1939-50, pres., 1941-46; bd. dirs. Morningside Community Center, 1945-53, hon. dir., 1953-60; bd. dirs. Union Settlement, 1966-80. Mem. Mayflower Soc., Assn. Corp. Growth. Presbyn. Clubs: Yale of Princeton (pres. 1978-83), Yale of N.Y.C.). Home and Office: 164 Moore St Princeton NJ 08540

KILBOURNE, EDWIN DENNIS, virologist, educator; b. Buffalo, July 10, 1920; s. Edwin I. and Elizabeth (Alward) K.; m. Joy Schmid, Dec. 20, 1952; children: Edwin Michael, Richard Schmid, Christopher Norton, Paul Alward. A.B., Cornell U., 1942, M.D., 1944. Asst. Rockefeller Inst., 1948-51; mem. faculty Tulane U., 1951-55, Cornell U. Med. Coll., N.Y.C., 1955-68, prof. pub. health, dir. div. virus research, 1961-68; prof., chmn. dept. microbiology Mt. Sinai Sch. Medicine, City U. New York, 1968—. Author: (with Wilson G. Smillie) Human Ecology and Public Health, 4th edit, 1968; Editor: The Influenza Viruses and Influenza, 1975. Mem. Health Research Council N.Y.C., 1968-75. Recipient R.E. Dyer Lectureship award NIH, 1973, Borden award Assn. Am. Med. Colls., 1974, Dowling Lectureship award, 1976, Thomas Francis Lectureship award, 1976; Harvey Lectureship award, 1978; award of distinction Cornell U. Med. Alumni Assn., 1979; academy medal N.Y. Acad. Medicine. Fellow N.Y. Acad. Scis.; mem. Nat. Acad. Sci., Harvey Soc., So. Soc. Clin. Research, Central Soc. Clin. Research (emeritus), AAAS, Am. Assn. Immunologists, Am. Acad. Microbiology, Soc. Exptl. Biology and Medicine, Am. Soc. Clin. Investigation (emeritus), N.Y. Acad. Medicine, Am. Pub. Health Assn., Assn. Am. Physicians, Am. Soc. Microbiology, Infectious Diseases Soc. Am. Research and publs. on hormonal influences, genetic studies and exptl. transmission of viruses, recombinant virus vaccines especially influenza. Home: 446 Hillcrest Rd Ridgewood NJ 07450 Office: City U New York Mt Sinai Sch Medicine Dept Microbiology Fifth Ave at 100th St New York NY 10029

KILBRIDGE, MAURICE D., educator, university dean; b. Chgo., June 2, 1920; s. Joseph T. and Lillian (Volker) K.; m. Helen R. Hereley; children: Peter, Anthony, Christopher, Joshua. B.S. in Mathematics, Loyola U., Chgo., 1942, M.S., 1947; M.S. in Indsl. Engring, Ill. Inst. Tech., 1950; Ph.D., State U. Iowa, 1953; M.A. (hon.), Harvard U., 1967. Registered profl. engr., Iowa. Asst. prof. math. Loyola U., Chgo., 1947-48; exec. tng. dir. Spiegel, Inc., Chgo., 1948-51; asst. prof., then asso. prof., prof. indsl. engring. Ill. Inst. Tech., 1951-57, dir. dept. indsl. engring, 1953-58, coordinator research, 1956-58; prof. mgmt. Grad. Sch. Bus., U. Chgo., 1958-63; asst. dir. U.S. AID Mission to India, 1963-65; faculty research fellow dept. social relations Harvard U., 1960-61, prof. bus. adminstrn. Grad. Sch. Bus. Adminstrn.,, 1965-69, prof. urban systems Grad. Sch. Design,, 1969-70, dean Grad. Sch. Design,, 1970—; mem. Harvard U. adv. mission to Nat. Planning Bd., Govt. of Pakistan, 1954-56. Author: Productive Uses of Nuclear Energy, 1958, Productivity and the Work-Pay Exchange, 1959, Urban Analysis, 1970. Served as lt. USNR, World War II. Mem. Inst. Mgmt. Sci., Am. Soc. Planning Ofcls., Internat. Acad. Law and Sci. Home: 5 Forest St Lexington MA 02173

KILBURN, EDWIN ALLEN, lawyer; b. Wenatchee, Wash., Apr. 5, 1933; s. Howard L. and Dorothy M. (Allen) K.; m. Penelope P. White, Feb. 7, 1964; children: Penelope Allen, Nancy Kitchen. B.A. with highest honors, Wash. State U., 1955; J.D. cum laude, NYU, 1958. Bar: N.Y. 1958, U.S. Supreme Ct. 1963. Assoc. Cravath, Swaine & Moore, N.Y.C., 1958, 62-68; staff, sr., sr. group counsel ITT, N.Y.C., 1968-74, asst. gen. counsel, 1975-80, assoc. gen. counsel, 1981—, v.p., dir. corp. policy compliance, 1982—. Served to capt. JAGC U.S. Army, 1959-62. Root Tilden Scholar. Mem. ABA (antitrust adminstrv. law sect.), Phi Beta Kappa. Episcopalian. Clubs: Navesink (Middletown, N.J.); Internat. (Bolton, Mass.). Home: 18 Bellevune Ave Rumson NJ 07760 Office: ITT Corp 320 Park Ave New York NY 10022

KILBY, JACK ST. CLAIR, inventor; b. Jefferson City, Mo., Nov. 8, 1923; s. Hubert St. Clair and Vina (Freitag) K.; m. Barbara Annegers, June 27, 1948; children: Ann, Janet Lee. B.S. in Elec. Engring, U. Ill., 1947; M.S., U. Wis., 1950. Program mgr. Globe-Union, Inc., Milw., 1948-58; asst. v.p. Tex. Instruments, Inc., Dallas, 1958-70; self-employed inventor, Dallas, 1970—; disting. prof. elec. engring. Tex. A & M U., 1978—; inventor monolithic integrated circuit, others; cons. to govt. and industry. Served with AUS, 1943-45. Recipient Nat. Medal Sci., 1969; Ballentine medal Franklin Inst., 1967; Distinguished Alumni award U. Ill., 1974; named to Holley medal ASME, 1982, Nat. Inventors Hall of Fame U.S. Patent Office, 1981. Fellow IEEE (Sarnoff medal 1966, Brunetti award 1978); mem. Nat. Acad. Engring. (Zworkin medal 1975). Home: 7723 Midbury St Dallas TX 75230 Office: 5924 Royal Ln Suite 150 Dallas TX 75230

KILBY, PETER, economics educator; b. Buffalo, May 4, 1935; s. John Homer and Katherine (Killeen) K.; m. Marianne Baer, Feb. 16, 1960; children: Damian, Christopher, Karen. B.A., Harvard U., 1957; M.A., Johns Hopkins U., 1959; D.Phil., Oxford U., Eng., 1967. Economist U.S. AID, Lagos, 1960-62; asst. prof. dept. econ. Wesleyan U., Middletown, Conn., 1965-70; assoc. prof. Weselyan U., Middletown, Conn., 1970-75; prof. Wesleyan U., Middletown, Conn., 1975—, chmn. dept. econs., 1982—; cons. World Bank, 1978—, Internat. Labour Office, Geneva, 1964-77, U.S. AID, Washington, 1968—, Govt. Malaysia, Kula Lumpur, 1973. Author: The Nigerian Bread Industry, 1965, Industrialization in an Open Economy, 1969; editor: Entrepreneurship and Economic Development, 1971; co-author: Agriculture and Structural and Transformation, 1975. Mem. Ciskei Commn., S. Africa, 1978-80, Regional Sch., Killingworth, Conn., 1977-80, planning and zoing com., Killingworth, Conn., 1971-73, ILO Mission to Tanzania, East Africa, 1977. Fulbright fellow, 1959-60; Ford Found. fellow, 1962-65; East-West Center fellow, Honolulu, 1973. Democrat. Roman Catholic. Home: 295 Route 80 Killingsworth CT 06417 Office: Wesleyan U Dept Econs Middletown CT 06457

KILCARR, ANDREW JOSEPH, lawyer; b. N.Y.C., Jan. 28, 1932; s. Patrick Joseph and Mary Catherine (Finnan) K.; m. Barbara Anne Puhala, Aug. 21, 1954; children: Theresa, Patrick. B.S., Manhattan Coll., 1953; J.D., Georgetown U., 1959. Bar: D.C. 1960. Atty. antitrust div. U.S. Dept. Justice, Washington, 1959-64; atty. Donovan, Leisure, Newton & Irvine, Washington, 1964—. Served to 1st lt. USMCR, 1953-55. Mem. ABA, D.C. Bar Assn. Clubs: International (Washington); Washington Golf and Country (Arlington, Va.). Home: 7003 Duncraig Ct McLean VA 22101 Office: Donovan Leisure Newton & Irvine 1850 K St NW Washington DC 20006

KILCLINE, THOMAS JOHN, naval officer; b. Detroit, Dec. 9, 1925; s. Frank I. and Helene F. (Burns) K.; m. Evelyn Dornell Thompson, July 1, 1950; children: Tom, Patrick, Kathleen, Mary. B.S., U.S. Naval Acad., 1949, U.S. Naval Postgrad. Sch., 1955; M.S., Mass. Inst. Tech., 1956. Commd. ensign U.S. Navy, 1949, advanced through grades to vice adm., 1975; test pilot, 1962-65, comdr. carrier based jet squadron, Vietnam, 1966-67, legis. liaison, 1970-72; officer for personnel distbn. and devel. Bur. Naval Personnel, 1974-75; comdg. officer Naval Air Sta., Patuxent River, Md., 1972-74; comdr. Naval Base, Subic Bay, Philippines, 1975-78; chief legis. affairs Navy Dept., Washington, 1978-81; comdr. Naval Air Forces, U.S. Atlantic Fleet, Norfolk, Va., 1981-83; ret., 1983. Decorated Disting. Service medal, Legion of Merit with 3 gold stars, Bronze Star. Mem. Phi Delta Theta. Roman Catholic. Office: 1600 Walden Dr McLean VA 22101

KILDEE, DALE E., congressman; b. Flint, Mich., Sept. 16, 1929; s. Timothy Leo and Norma Alicia (Ullmer) K.; m. Gayle Heyn, Feb. 27,

1965; children: David, Laura, Paul. B.A., Sacred Heart Sem., 1952; tchr.'s certificate, U. Detroit, 1954; M.A., U. Mich., 1961; postgrad. (Rotary Found. fellow), U. Peshawar, Pakistan, 1958-59. Tchr. U. Detroit High Sch., 1954-56, Flint Central High Sch., 1956-64; mem. Mich. Ho. of Reps. from 81st Dist., 1964-74, Mich. Senate (from 29th Dist.), 1975-76, 95th-98th Congresses from (7th Mich. Dist.). Mem. Am. Fedn. Tchrs., Urban League, Phi Delta Kappa. Lodges: K.C.; Optimists. Home: 1434 Jane St Flint MI 48506 Office: 2432 Rayburn House Office Bldg Washington DC 20515

KILEY, DANIEL URBAN, landscape architect, planner; b. Boston, Sept. 2, 1912; s. Louis James and Louise (Baxter) K.; m. Anne Lothrop Sturges, June 11, 1942; children: Kathleen, Kor, Christopher, Antonia, Timothy, Christina, Aaron Alcott, Caleb. Student, Harvard Grad. Sch. Design, 1936-38. From apprentice to asso. Warren Manning (landscape design and regional planning), Cambridge, Mass., 1932-38; planning technician Concord (N.H.) City Plan Bd., 1938; architect Nat. Park Service, 1939, U.S. Housing Authority, 1940; assoc. Town Planning, Washington, 1940; pvt. practice as landscape architect, site planner, architect, 1940—; lectr., critic Balt. Mus., 1949, Worcester (Mass.) Mus., 1950, La. State U., 1950, Cornell U., 1957, Met. Mus., 1959, N.C. State Coll., 1958, Rensselaer Poly. Inst., 1960, Harvard U., 1962-63, Clemson Coll., 1963, also univs. Ill., Minn., Pa., Syracuse, Va., Wash., Tokyo, Kyoto, Hiroshima, Fukuoka, Yale U., U. Calif., Berkeley, U. Utah, Salt Lake City, Harvard U., Archtl. Assn. London, Dallas Inst. Forum, Beijing, China, Nanking, Shanghai, Hongchow, also Osaka U. (Japan); Graham Found. lectr., Chgo., 1976; mem. design rev. panel Redevel. Land Agy., Washington. Author articles.; prin. works include, Kitimat, B.C., Can. new city, 1951, Rockefeller Inst., N.Y., 1956, Union Carbide & Carbon, Westchester, N.Y., 1957, Reynolds Metals Co., Richmond, Va., 1958, Fountain Place, Dallas, Lincoln West, N.Y.C., Marine World Park, San Francisco, Candlestick Park, San Francisco, prin. works include, Independence Mall, 3d block, Phila., 1959-60, U. Minn., Mpls., 1960, Lincoln Center, N.Y., Yale U., 1961, Dulles Internat. Airport, Washington, 1961-63, Nat. Acad. Sci., Washington, 1961, Cummins Engine Plant, Columbus, Ind., 1962, Chrysler-Cummins Plant, Darlington, Eng., Burr-McManus Plaza, Hartford, Conn., 1962, Rochester Inst. Tech., Armstrong Cork Co., Lancaster Pa., 1956, Oakland (Calif.) Mus., 1962, U.S. Air Force Acad., Colorado Springs, Colo., Nat. Center Atmospheric Research, Boulder, Colo., 1963, New Eng. States Worlds Fair, Fredonia (N.Y.) State Coll., Potsdam (N.Y.) State Coll., U. Lagos, Nigeria, Central Filtration Plant, Chgo., Chgo. Art Inst., 1963, Washington Mall and Tidal Basin, 1968, 10th St. Overlook, Washington, 1970, Ft. Lawton Park, Seattle, 1972, La Defense, Paris, Victorian Garden, Smithsonian Instn., 1976, N.Y. Bot. Garden master plan, Riverside Park, Springfield, Mass., Eastwing Nat. Gallery Art, Washington, 1977, interior ct., Yale Center Brit. Art, 1977, Coco-Cola World Hdqrs. master plan, Atlanta, Woodruff Park, Atlanta, John and Mabel Ringling Bros. Mus. Park, Sarasota, Fla., Cary Arboretum, Millbrook, N.Y., N.Y. Bot. Garden, Bronx, 1978, campus plan, Gallaudet Coll. for Deaf, Washington, J.F. Kennedy Library, Boston, 1978, Am. Transit Union, Washington, Cummins Brussels, Belgium, Belle Isle Park, Detroit, Detroit Art Inst., 1979, Dallas Art Mus., 1980, London Standard Chartered Bank, San Antonio Art Mus., 1981, Brit. Rys., London, Bank of Korea, Seoul, Philbrook Art Center, Tulsa, Okla., 1982, Stamford (Conn.) Atrium, 1983, others. Mem. BiState Planning Commn., Lake Champlain Basin Region, 1959-63; mem Pres.'s Adv. Council Planning Pennsylvania Av., Washington, 1962-65; mem. Vt. Bd. Architects Registration, 1963; jury S.W. Redevel. Area, Washington, Boston Redevel. Authority, 1963, Nat. Honor Awards, Urban Redevel. Authority; also FHA, Washington, 1964; mem. tech. rev. com. on state land use plan State of Vt., 1975; design adv. group Cambridge (Mass.) Redevel. Bd., 1978. Served to capt. AUS; World War II. Decorated Legion of Merit; co-recipient 1st prize Jefferson Nat. Expansion Meml. Competition, 1947; winner U. N.H. Student Union Bldg. Competition, 1951; AIA honor awards Concordia State Coll., Ft. Wayne, Ind., 1960, Stiles and Morse Colls., Yale U., 1963, Dulles Airport, Washington, 1963, Ind. Bell Telephone Co., Columbus; hon. mention Chgo. Tribune Better Homes for Family Living, 1947; award of merit House and Home mag., 1957; 1st prize Progressive Architecture mag., 1961; award of merit Am. Soc. Landscape Architects, 1962; gold medal Phila. chpt. AIA; Gov.'s Design award State of Calif., 1966; Bard awards N.Y.C. Ford Found. Ct., 1968, N.Y.C. Lincoln Center North Ct., 1967; Allied Profession medal AIA, 1971; Architects Collaborative award AIA, 1972. Mem. NAD. Club: Century. Address: Castle Forest Charlotte VT 05445

KILEY, RICHARD KIM, securities analyst; b. Cambridge, Mass., June 4, 1949; s. Augustine Charles K. and Lillian (Wright) kiley; m. Marie Louise Colangelo, Oct. 6, 1973 (div. 1982). B.A., Harvard U., 1971, M.B.A., 1974. Grant mgr. U.S. Dept. Justice, Boston, 1971-72; securities analyst Brown Bros., Harriman, N.Y.C., 1974-77, Gen. Am. Investors Co., Inc., 1977—. Mem. N.Y. Soc. Security Analysts. Home: 425 Park Ave S Apt 17D New York NY 10016 Office: Gen Am Investors Co Inc 330 Madison Ave New York NY 10017

KILEY, RICHARD PAUL, actor; b. Chgo., Mar. 31, 1922; s. Leo Joseph and Leonore (McKenna) K.; m. Mary Bell Wood, May 5, 1948 (div. 1967); children: David, Michael, Kathleen, Dorothea, Erin, Dierdre; m. Patricia Ferrier. Student, Loyola U., 1940, Barnum Dramatic Sch., Chgo., 1941-42. Actor, radio broadcasts, Chgo., 1941; Actor: stage appearance touring co. of Street Car Named Desire; TV appearances in other shows; Misalliance, 1953 (Theatre World award); appeared Broadway plays including No strings (musical), 1962-63, Her First Roman (based on Shaw's Caesar and Cleopatra), 1968, The Incomparable Max, Voices, Absurd Person Singular, 1974, The Heiress, 1976; toured in Coward in Two Keys, 1976; other stage appearances include Guilty Conscience; motion picture appearances include Phenix City Story; also Endless Love; played Man of La Mancha (Drama Critics award, Drama Guild award), 1966 (Antoinette Perry award), London, 1969, Lincoln Center, 1972; also revival, tour, 1977-79; PBS one-man show: Verse Person Singular. Served with USNR; World War II. Recipient Antoinette Perry award as best actor in a musical for Redhead, 1958. Address: care Stephen Draper 37 W 57th St New York NY 10019

KILGARLIN, WILLIAM WAYNE, state supreme court justice; b. Houston, Nov. 29, 1932; s. William and Juanita Lillian (Lawther) K.; m. Margaret Rose Kruppa, Dec. 28, 1963. B.S., U. Houston, 1954; LL.B., U. Tex., 1962. Bar: Tex. Sole practice, Houston, 1962-78; mem. Tex. House of Reps., Houston, 1959-61; chmn. Harris County Democratic Party, Houston, 1962-66; judge 215th Dist. Ct. Tex., Houston, 1978-82; justice Supreme Ct. Tex., 1982—. Served to 1st lt. U.S. Army, 1955-57. Methodist. Office: Supreme Court Texas PO Box 12248 Capitol Station Austin TX 78711 *

KILGORE, EDWIN CARROLL, govt. ofcl.; b. Coeburn, Va., Jan. 24, 1923; s. Cecil Abram and Elizabeth Delle (Horne) K.; m. Ann Hitch, Dec. 30, 1944; children—Ashby Caroline, Elizabeth Cato. B.S. in Mech. Engring, Va. Inst. Poly., 1944, 1969. With NASA (and predecessor), 1944—; dep. asso. adminstr. ops. Langley (Va.) Research Center, 1975-76, dir. mgmt. ops., 1976-79, asso. adminstr. mgmt. ops., Washington, 1979—. Recipient Outstanding Leadership award NASA, Disting. Service medal, Apollo Spl. Achievement award, Lunar Orbiter Spl. Achievement award, Solid Propellant Spl. Achievement award; Roger Jones award Am. U. Mem. AIAA, Pi Tau Sigma. Methodist. Club: Hampton Kiwanis (pres. 1969). Office: Office Asso Adminstr Mgmt Ops NASA Washington DC 20546 *

KILGORE, EUGENE STERLING, JR., surgeon; b. San Francisco, Feb. 3, 1920; s. Eugene Sterling and Mary (Kirkpatrick) K.; m. Marilynn Wines; 1 son, Eugene Sterling. B.S., U. Calif.-Berkeley, 1941; M.D., U. Calif.-San Francisco, 1949. Intern in medicine Harvard service Boston City Hosp., 1949-50; intern in surgery Roosevelt Hosp., N.Y.C., 1950-51, resident gen. surgery, reconstructive hand surgery, 1951-55; practice medicine specializing in reconstructive hand surgery, San Francisco, 1955—; asso. clin. prof. surgery U. Calif.-San Francisco, 1955-75, clin. prof., 1975—; chief hand surgery dept. surgery U. Calif. Hosp., also San Francisco Gen. Hosp., 1965—; chief hand service Ft. Miley Vets. Hosp., San Francisco, 1965—, Martinez (Calif.) Vets. Hosp., 1970—, Livermore (Calif.) Vets. Hosp., 1965—; chief hand service plastic surgery tng. service St. Francis Meml. Hosp., 1965—, chief of surgery, 1979—; cons. hand surgery numerous pvt. hosps., San Francisco, 1955—. Author numerous publs. in field. Served to lt. col., inf. AUS, 1941-45. Decorated Bronze Star; recipient Gold Headed Cane, AOA medal; Kaiser award for excellence in teaching U. Calif.-San Francisco Sch. Medicine, 1976. Mem. AMA, ACS, Am. Assn. Surgery of Trauma, Am. Trauma Soc., Am. Soc. Surgery of Hand, Carribean Hand Soc., San Francisco Surg. Soc. (pres. 1979-80), Pacific Coast Surg. Assn. Clubs: Rotary; Bohemian (San Francisco). Office: 450 Sutter St San Francisco CA 94108 *The road to success lies in meeting responsibility with an open, inquisitive mind and hard work, tempered with humility, kindness, time for play as well as a good laugh. The lasting measure of success is how much remains after you have gone that continues to be of value to others.*

KILGORE, JOE MADISON, former congressman, lawyer; b. Brown County, Texas, Dec. 10, 1918; s. William Henry and Myrtle (Armstrong) K.; m. Jane Redman, July 28, 1945; children: Mark, Dean, Bill, Shannon. Student, Trinity U., 1935-36, U. Tex., 1936-41. Bar: Tex. 1946. Practiced, Edinburg, Tex., 1946-54; mem. Tex. Ho. of Reps., 1946-55, 84th to 88th Congresses, 15th Dist. Tex.; now mem. firm McGinnis, Lochridge & Kilgore, Austin, Tex.; chmn. bd. Republic Bank, Austin; dir. McAllen State Bank (Tex.), Republic Bank Corp.; Regent U., Tex., 1967-73; council Adminstrv. Conf. U.S., 1968-72; mem. U. Tex. Centennial Commn., 1981—. Bd. visitors M.D. Anderson Hosp. and Tumor Inst., 1975-78; chmn. adv. com. Tex. Legis. Conf., 1975-80; mem. investment com. Meth. Home; bd. dirs. Southwestern Legal Found., 1981—, Scott and White Hosp., 1983—, Scott, Sherwood and Brindley Found., 1983—; bd. dirs., exec. com. Tex. Research League, 1981—, exec. com.; bd. dirs. Scott and White Hosp., Scott, Sherwood and Brindley Found.; active numerous other civic orgns. Served as lt. col. USAAF., World War II; maj. gen. Res. Decorated Silver Star, Legion of Merit, D.F.C., Air medal with 2 oak leaf clusters, 4 personal citations. Fellow Am., Tex. bar founds.; mem. Am., Travis County bar assns., State Bar Tex., Delta Theta Phi. Democrat. Methodist. Home: 3311 River Rd Austin TX 78703 Office: Texas Bank Bldg 900 Congress Ave Austin TX 78701

KILGORE, JOE RAY, advertising executive; b. Bayton, Tex., Nov. 24, 1947; s. William Henry and Dorothy (Ortego) K.; m. Mary Coke, June 29, 1968; children: Heather M., Sean J., Lauren M. B.A., U. Houston, 1971. Copywriter McCann Erickson, Houston, 1968-75; exec. creative dir. Ogilvy & Mather, Houston, 1975—. Recipient Clio award, 1981. Mem. Houston Advt. Fedn. (dir., Grand Prix award 1979-82). Roman Catholic. Clubs: Houston Metro Racquet; One Copywriters and Art Dirs N.Y. (One Show award) (1983). Office: One Allen Center Houston TX 77459 *I have this nagging suspicion my life is going to be too short.*

KILGORE, JOHN EDWARD, JR., bus. exec.; b. Wichita Falls, Tex., Jan. 12, 1921; s. John Edward and Lillian (Amery) K.; m. Constance M. Brewer, May 1947; m. Emilie Smith Gilbreath, Nov. 1965; children—John Edward III, Constance Pritchett, Ralph Amery, Robert Monell, Alexander Gray; 1 stepson, Cabanne deM. Gilbreath. A.B., Amherst Coll., 1941; LL.B., Harvard, 1944. Bar: Tex. bar 1948. Partner Kilgore & Kilgore, Dallas, 1948-57, J. H. Whitney & Co., N.Y.C., 1957-68, John E. Kilgore & Co., 1968—; founder, chmn. Cambridge Royalty Co., Petroleum Royalties Ireland Ltd., 1973-80; founder, mng. dir. Cambridge Petroleum Royalties Ltd., U.K., 1972-80; dir. Paine Webber Inc., also various other corps. Trustee German Marshall Fund of U.S., 1978—. Served with USNR, 1942-45. Mem. Phi Beta Kappa. Clubs: Links, Union (N.Y.C.); Maidstone (East Hampton, N.Y.); Coronado, Bayou (Houston); Brooks (London). Office: 1200 San Jacinto Bldg Houston TX 77002

KILGORE, WILLIAM JACKSON, philosophy educator; b. Dallas, Apr. 30, 1917; s. Rather Bowlin and Clara (Cole) K.; m. Barbara Schmickle, Dec. 4, 1943; 1 dau., Barbara (Sally). A.B., Baylor U., 1938; Ph.D., U. Tex., 1958; student, Columbia U., 1949. Prof. philosophy Baylor U., 1949—, chmn. dept., 1959-, J. Newton Rayzor, Sr. Disting. prof. philosophy, 1976—; asst. prof. philosophy U. Tex., summer 1958; organizer, pres. Centennial Symposium on Ortega y Gasset World Congress of Philosophy, 1983. Author: Alejandro Korn's Interpretation of Creative Freedom, 1958, Una evaluación crítica de la philosofía de Alejandro Korn, 1961, One America, Two Cultures, 1965, An Introductory Logic, 1968, 2d edit., 1979; also articles in English, Portuguese and Spanish.; Translator An Introduction to the Philosophy of Understanding of Andrés Bello, 1983. Pres. sect. on ethics and problems of freedom XIII Internat. Congress of Philosophy, Mexico City, 1963; pres. sect. on art and communication Inter-Am. Congress of Philosophy, Brazilia, 1972. Grantee Danforth Found., 1957-58, Am. Council Learned Socs., 1961. Mem. Am. Philos. Assn., Southwestern Philos. Assn. (pres. 1963- 64), Am. AAUP (2d v.p. 1968-70, nat. council 1962-65, 68-70, pres. Tex. conf. 1965), Am. Philos. Assn., Tex. Philos. Soc., Inter-Am. Soc. Philosophy (exec. com. 1977—, pres. 1981-85), Interam. Soc. Psychology, Soc. for Iberian and Latin Am. Thought (pres. 1976—). Home: 305 Guittard Ave Waco TX 76706

KILGOUR, FREDERICK GRIDLEY, librarian; b. Springfield, Mass., Jan. 6, 1914; s. Edward Francis and Lillian Bess (Piper) K.; m. Eleanor Margaret Beach, Sept. 3, 1940; children: Christopher Beach, Martha, Alison, Meredith. A.B., Harvard U., 1935; student, Columbia Sch. Library Service, summers 1939-41; LL.D., Marietta Coll., 1980, Coll. of Wooster, 1981; D.H.L., Ohio State U., 1980, Denison U., 1983. Staff Harvard Coll. Library, 1935-42, OSS, 1942-45; dep. dir. office of intelligence collection and dissemination U.S. Dept. State, 1946-48; librarian Yale Med. Library, 1948-65; asso. librarian for research and devel. Yale U. Library, 1965-67; mng. editor Yale Jour. Biology and Medicine, 1949-65; lectr. in history of sci. Yale U., 1950-59, lectr. history of tech., 1961-67; fellow Davenport Coll., 1950-67; pres., exec. dir. Online Computer Library Ctr., OCLC, Inc., 1967-80, vice chmn. bd. trustees Online Computer Library Ctr.,, 1981-83; founder, chmn. bd. trustees, pres. Applied Info. Techs. Research Ctr., 1984—. Author: Library of the Medical Institution of Yale College and Its Catalogue of 1865, 1960; co-author: Engineering in History, 1956; author: Collected Papers, 2 vols., 1984; editor: Book of Bodily Exercises, 1960, Jour. Library Automation, 1968-71; contbr. to scholarly jours. Served as lt. (j.g.) USNR, 1943-46; overseas duty; Served as lt. (j.g.) USNR, 1944-45; overseas duty. Decorated Legion of Merit; recipient Margaret Mann citation in cataloging and classification, 1974, Melvil Dewey medal, 1978; Acad./Research Librarian of Year, 1979; Library Info. Tech. award, 1979. Mem. ALA, Am. Soc. Info. Sci. (Merit award 1979), Library Assn. (U.K.), Soc. for History of Tech. Club: Cosmos (Washington). Home: 1415 Kirkley Rd Columbus OH 43221 Office: 6565 Frantz Rd Dublin OH 43017

KILIAN, MICHAEL D., journalist, columnist, author; b. Toledo, July 16, 1939; s. D. Frederick and Laura Casmere (Dulski) K.; m. Pamela H. Reeves, Oct. 17, 1970; children: Eric, Colin. Student, New Sch. Social Research, N.Y.C., 1957-58, U. Md., 1964. Writer Sta. KNTV, San Jose, Calif., 1960-63; reporter City News Bur., Chgo., 1965-66; reporter, asst. polit. editor Chgo. Tribune, 1966-71, editorial writer, 1971-74, editorial page columnist, 1974-78, Washington columnist, 1978—; adv. Ency. Brit.; commentator CBS Radio, Sta. WBBM., 1973-82, WTTW Channel 11, 1975-78, Nat. Pub. Radio, 1978-79. Author: Who Runs Chicago?, 1979, The Valkyrie Project, 1981, Who Runs Washington?, 1982, Northern Exposure, 1983, Blood of the Czars, 1984. Bd. dirs. Fund for Animals, 1976—. Capt. USAF CAP.; Served with U.S. Army, 1963-65. Recipient Humor Writing award UPI, 1971. Mem. White House Corrs. Assn., Nat. Aero. Assn., Air Force Assn., Soaring Soc. Am. Presbyterian. Club: Nat. Press. Office: 1707 H St Washington DC *I am grateful to those who have taught me that no man was ever ill-served by a sense of honor or a sense of humor. I would hope that my work might in some way serve to remind my fellow man of the fraility of this planet and our civilization, and of the constant effort required to maintain both.*

KILKENNY, JOHN FRANCIS, U.S. judge; b. Heppner, Oreg., Oct. 26, 1901; s. John Sheridan and Rose Ann (Curran) K.; m. Virginia Brannock, Oct. 14, 1931; children—John Michael, Karen Margaret. LL.B. cum laude, U. Notre Dame, 1925. Bar: Oreg. bar 1926. And practiced in, Pendleton; partner Kilkenny & Fabre (and predecessors), 1926-59; judge U.S. Dist. Ct. of Oreg., 1959-69, U.S. Ct. Appeals, 1969-, now sr. judge.; Pres., dir. Happy Canyon Co., 1939-40. Author: Shamrocks and Shepherds. Mem. Oreg. Bd. Bar Examiners, 1951, 52; Trustee Oreg. State Library, Umatilia County Library; trustee U. Portland. Fellow Am. Bar Found., Am. Coll. Trial Lawyers; mem. ABA, Oreg. Bar Assn. (pres. 1943-44), Am. Judicature Soc., Am. Irish Hist. Soc. (v.p.), Oreg. Hist. Soc. (dir.), Oreg. Geog. Names Bd., Knight Malta. Republican. Catholic. Clubs: University, Arlington. Home: 821 SW Davenport Portland OR 97201 Office: Pioneer Courthouse Portland OR 97204 *

KILKER, CLARENCE CHRISTIAN, mgmt. cons.; b. Le Mars, Iowa, July 13, 1905; s. Chris A. and Lena (Hinz) K.; m. Edna D. Spiecker, July 10, 1932; children—Wallace Jay, Karen Kay (Mrs. Harold G. Brown). B.A., Westmar Coll., 1927; B.S., Morningside Coll., 1931; M.A., U. Nebr., 1938; postgrad., U. So. Calif., summer 1934, Columbia, 1941, U. Kans., 1942. Tchr. Onslow (Iowa) High Sch., 1927-28; prin. Newburg (Mo.) High Sch., 1928-30, South Sioux City (Nebr.) Jr. High Sch., 1931-37, South Sioux City High Sch., 1937-39, Manhattan (Kans.) Jr. High Sch., 1939-44; summer instr. U. Kans., 1942, Kans. State U., 1943; mgr. Manhattan C. of C. and Credit Bur., 1944-48; exec. v.p. Kans. C. of C., Topeka, 1949-70; registered rep. Seltsam, Hanni & Co., Topeka, 1970-76; summer instr. S.W. Inst. Orgn. Mgmt., 1947-48, U. Colo., 1959, 64; Sec. Manhattan Viking Co., Inc., 1945-48; pres. Lil' Duffer Restaurants of Nebr. and S.D., Inc., 1966-78; lectr. coll., univ. workshops on econ. edn. for tchrs., summers 1959-71, profl. speaker community devel., mgmt., pvt. enterprise econs. Trustee Kans. Council Econ. Edn., 1973-76. Recipient Distinguished Alumnus award Westmar Coll., 1977. Mem. Council of State C. of C.'s (exec. com. 1953, sec. 1961), Kans. Assn. Orgn. Mgrs. (pres. 1948), Asso. Credit Burs. Kans. (pres. 1946-47), Alpha Kappa Psi (hon.), Phi Kappa Delta. Presbyterian (trustee, deacon). Home: 1316 Campbell Ave Topeka KS 66604 Office: 1316 Campbell Ave Topeka KS 66604

KILL, LAWRENCE, lawyer; b. N.Y.C., Apr. 11, 1935; s. Bernard and Dora (Laskin) K.; m. Karyl Klein, Oct. 21, 1962; children—Debra, Andrea and Brenda. B.B.A., CCNY, 1957; LL.B. cum laude, Fordham U., 1960. Bar: N.Y. 1961. Trial atty. antitrust div. U.S. Dept. Justice, Washington, 1961-66; asso. firm Chadbourne, Parke, Whiteside & Wolff, N.Y.C., 1966-72; mem. firm Anderson, Russell, Kill & Olick (P.C.), N.Y.C., 1972—. Editor-in-chief: Fordham Law Rev, 1959-60. Served with U.S. Army, 1960-61. Mem. Assn. Bar City N.Y., ABA, N.Y. State Bar assn. Home: 29 Queens Ln Manhasset Hills NY 11040 Office: 666 3d Ave New York NY 10017

KILLAM, EVA KING, pharmacologist; b. N.Y.C., Nov. 16, 1921; d. Charles H. and Louise C. (Richter) King; m. Keith F. Killam, Jr., May 12, 1955; children: Anne Louise, Paul Fenton, Melissa Helen. A.B., Sarah Lawrence Coll., 1942; A.M., Mt. Holyoke Coll., 1944; Ph.D. in Pharmacology, U. Ill., 1953. Pharmacologist Army Chem. Center, Md., 1948-51; jr. pharmacologist to asso. pharmacologist UCLA Med. Sch., 1953-59; research asso. Stanford U. Med. Sch., 1959-68; prof. physiology U. Calif., Davis, 1968-72, prof. pharmacology, 1972—; epilepsy adv. com. NIH, 1976-80; study sect. preclin. pharmacology NIMH, 1972-76. Co-editor: Handbook of Electroencephalography, Vol. 7, 1977; editor-in-chief: Jour. Pharmacology and Exptl. Therapeutics, 1978—; editorial bd.: Soc. Exptl. Biology and Medicine, 1957-58, Internat. Jour. Neuropharmacology, 1962-68, Exptl. Neurology, 1980-83; contbr. articles to sci. jours. Fellow Am. Coll. Neuropsychopharmacology (counselor 1980-84); mem. Am. Soc. Pharmacology and Exptl. Therapeutics (counselor 1972-75, Abel award 1954), Western Pharmacology Soc. (pres. 1984), AAAS, Epilepsy Soc. Am., Sigma Xi. Office: Dept Pharmacology School of Medicine University of California Davis CA 95616

KILLEBREW, GWENDOLYN, opera singer; b. Phila. Student, Temple U., Juilliard Sch. Music. Formerly music tchr., social worker, music therapist. Operatic debut in Walkuere, Met. Opera, N.Y.C., 1967; mem.: Deutsche Oper am Rhein, Düsseldorf, W. Ger., 1976, appeared with, Salzburg Festival, Austria, Grand Theatre Municipal, Bordeaux, France, Theatre Municipal, Nancy, France, Theatre de l'Opera, Nice, France, Oper der Stadt Koeln, Cologne, W.Ger., Munich Gaertnerplatz, Germany, Grand Theatre de Geneve, Geneva, Conn. Opera, Hartford, N.Y.C. Opera, St. Paul Opera, Met. Opera, N.Y.C., San Francisco Opera, Zurich Opera, Bayreuth Festival, 1978, 79, others, appears with symphony orchs. and in solo recitals, rec. artist, Cambridge Records, Inc. Named Outstanding Alumna Temple U. Office: care Columbia Artists Mgmt Inc 165 W 57th St New York NY 10019 *

KILLEBREW, JAMES ROBERT, architect, engineer; b. Okmulgee, Okla., Dec. 10, 1918; s. Robert Herman and Edith (Tyler) K.; m. Prebel Lee Thompson, Nov. 14, 1966; children: Linda Gayle, Debra Lee, Tod Nenian; 1 dau. by previous marriage, Laura Janice. B.S. in Archtl. Engring., U. Tex., 1948. Registered architect, Tex.; registered profl. engr., Tex. Chmn. bd. Killebrew-Rucker and Assos., Inc. (Architects Planners Engrs.), Wichita Falls, Tex., 1954—; dir. Tex. Bank & Trust. Prin. archtl. works include Gen. Hosp. Plainview, Tex., Vernon (Tex.) Hosp., Vernon Geriatrics Psychiat. Hosp., Wichita Gen. Hosp., Gen. Hosp. Nocona (Tex.), Sci. Bldg., Phys. Edn. Bldg., Midwestern State U., Teenage Drug Addiction Center, Vernon, Fine Arts Bldg. at Midwestern State U., AC Spark Plug Ceramics Complex-Gen. Motors Corp., Parker Sq. Savs. and Loan, Wichita Falls, Sprague Electric Co., Howmet Turbine, Wichita Clutch Corp., G.H. Foster Plant, Family YMCA, SW Nat. Bank Tower. Served to lt. comdr. USN, 1940-45; PTO; Lic. capt. Res. (ret.). Fellow AIA (pres. Wichita

Falls chpt. 1966-67, 81); mem. Nat. Soc. Profl. Engrs., Tex. Soc. Profl. Engrs. (pres. N. Tex. chpt. 1960-61), Am. Soc. Archtl. Engrs. (charter mem.), ASHRAE, Wichita Falls C. of C. (chmn. various coms.), Navy League (pres. 1967-68), Fine Art Soc. Tex. (pres. 1970, chmn. bd. 1973). Mem. Christian Ch. (elder 1979-81). Club: Rotary (pres. 1983-84). Home: 1559 Hanover St Wichita Falls TX 76302 Office: 600 Petroleum Bldg Wichita Falls TX 76302 *The practice of architecture requires the efforts of many talented professionals and personnel aspiring to be professionals. No longer does one man act as master builder (or designer). If I have attained a notable degree of success, it is due to the combined efforts through many years, of all the excellent associates with which I have been fortunate to know.*

KILLEFER, TOM, banker; b. Los Angeles, Jan. 7, 1917; s. Wade and Dorothy (Parks) K.; m. Carolyn Clothier, Apr. 17, 1948; children: Wade II, Caroline, Gail, Anne. A.B. cum laude, Stanford U.; J.D., Harvard U., 1942; B.C.L., Oxford U., 1947. Bar: Calif. 1946, U.S. Supreme Ct. 1953, D.C. 1954, Mich. 1966. With Lillick, Geary, Wheat, Adams & Charles, Calif. and Washington, 1947-59, partner, 1956-59; staff U.S. High Commn. for Germany, 1951-52; exec. dir. Com. Am. Steamship Lines, 1959-60; 1st v.p., vice chmn., dir. Export-Import Bank of Washington, 1960-62; U.S. exec. dir. Inter-Am. Devel. Bank; spl. asst. to Sec. of Treasury, 1962- 66; exec. asst. to v.p. legal affairs Chrysler Corp., Detroit, 1966-67, v.p. finance, 1967, v.p. finance, gen. counsel, 1968-75, exec. v.p., 1975-76; pres. U.S. Trust Co., N.Y., 1976, chmn., pres., 1976-79, chmn. bd., 1976-82, chief exec. officer, 1979-80; dir. Gt. No. Nekoosa Corp., Northrop Corp., Saudi-U.S. Trust; past chmn. bd. dirs. Detroit br. Fed. Res. Bank of Chgo.; Sr. adviser, mem. U.S. del. 1st and 2d ann. meetings Inter-Am. Econ. and Social Council. Mem. exec. com., bd. dirs., fin. com. Overseas Devel. Council., Atlantic Council U.S.; trustee Protestant Episcopal Cathedral Found., Com. Econ. Devel., Internat. Mgmt. and Devel. Inst.; trustee, mem. vis. com. on internat. studies Stanford U.; mem. council Rockefeller U.; trustee Naval Aviation Mus. Found.; bd. visitors in East Asian Studies U. Mich.; trustee U.S. Trust Co. N.Y. Served to lt. (s.g.) USNR, 1941-46. Decorated D.F.C. Navy, Air medal, Purple Heart; Order of Merit, Peru; recipient nat. award of medal Am. Assn. Coll. Baseball Coaches; Disting. Achievement medal Stanford U. Athletic Bd. Mem. San Francisco Com. on Fgn. Relations, Assn. Gen. Counsel (emeritus), Assn. Rhodes Scholars, Ruffed Grouse Soc. N.Am. (dir.), Phi Beta Kappa, Zeta Psi. Episcopalian (vestryman 1960-65). Clubs: Alibi, Alfalfa, Metropolitan (Washington); Pacific Union (San Francisco); Links, River, Economic (N.Y.C.); Eastward Ho (Chatham, Mass.). Office: 45 Wall St New York NY 10005

KILLEN, ROBERT BURTON, utility executive; b. Dayton, O., July 13, 1913; s. Leo C. and E. Myrle (Clark) K.; m. Amber Heintzelman, June 24, 1939; children: Kathleen (Mrs. Richard A. Currence), Timothy, Constance (Mrs. Charles W. Smith, Jr.), Calvin. E.E., U. Cin., 1936. With Dayton Power & Light Co., 1933—, group v.p., 1968-70, exec. v.p., 1970-71, pres., 1971-73, chmn. and pres., 1973-75, chmn. and chief exec. officer, 1975-78, chmn., 1978-82, dir., 1982—; dir. Winters Nat. Bank & Trust Co., Bank One Dayton N.A. Office: Kettering Tower Dayton OH 45423

KILLEN, WILLIAM D. (BUDDY KILLEN), music publishing company executive; b. Florence, Ala., Nov. 13, 1932; s. Willie Lee and Minnie Jane (Sharp) K.; children: Linda Gale, Robin Killen Smith. Grad., high sch. Joined Tree Pub. Co., Nashville, 1953, exec. v.p., co-owner, 1957—, pres., chief exec. officer, owner, 1980—; dir. Commerce Union Bank Trust, Investors Savs. & Loan Assn. Bass player, Grand Ole Opry, 1950—, traveled with country artists, 1950-53; active songwriter and producer for numerous artists.; Songs include Ain't Goinna Bump No More. Chmn., co-host Easter Seal Telethon, Nashville, 1981-85; bd. dirs. Am. Inst. for Pub. Service, Washington; mem. Tenn. Film Commn., 1981, Nashville Symphony, 1973—; pres. W.O. Smith Community Music Sch.; chmn. WPLN Radio Ednl. Found. Recipient gold and platinum records for artists produced various labels; award Broadcast Music Inc. Mem. Country Music Assn. (v.p. 1977, treas. 1983-84), Nashville Songwriters Assn., ASCAP (dir. 1983-84), Nashville Music Assn., Nat. Music Pubs. Assn. (dir. 1983-84), Nat. Acad. Rec. Arts and Scis. (pres. chpt. 1969), Acad. Country Music, Gospel Music Assn., Nashville Area C. of C. (dir. 1983-84). Baptist. Club: Nashville City. Home: 2805 Lealto Ct 37214 Office: 8 Music Sq W Nashville TN 37205

KILLENBERG, GEORGE ANDREW, newspaper consultant, former newspaper editor; b. St. Clair County, Ill., Mar. 30, 1917; s. George W. and Lavina (Ruhl) K.; m. Therese Murphy, June 3, 1943; children: George M., Mary C., John A., Terry M., Susan M. B.S., St. Louis U., 1954, M.A., 1958. Engaged in pub. relations, 1935-41; mem. staff St. Louis Globe-Democrat, 1941—, city editor, 1956-66, mng. editor, 1966-79, exec. editor, 1979-84; past chmn., now dir. Mid-Am. Press Inst. Bd. dirs. Boys Town Mo., 1960—. Served with AUS, 1942-46. Mem. Sigma Delta Chi. Roman Catholic. Clubs: Press (pres. 1964), Media (St. Louis); Mo. Athletic. Home: 3042 Hatherly Dr Bel-Nor MO 63121

KILLGORE, ANDREW IVY, former ambassador; b. Greensboro, Ala., Nov. 7, 1919. B.S., Livingston U., 1943; J.D., U. Ala., 1949, Arab language tng. Fgn. Service Inst., 1955-57. Bar: Ala. bar. Selector-analyst U.S. Displaced Persons Commn., 1949-50, displaced populations officer, Frankfurt, W.Ger., 1950-51; visa officer Am. embassy, London, 1951-53; evaluator Dept. State, 1953-55; polit. officer, Beirut, Lebanon, 1956-57, Jerusalem, 1957-59, Amman, Jordan, 1959-61; internat. relations officer Dept. State, 1961-62; officer-in-charge Iraq-Jordan affairs, 1962-65; pub. affairs officer USIA, Baghdad, Iraq, 1965-67; polit. officer, Dacca, E.Pakistan (now Bangladesh), 1967-70; polit.-econ. officer Arab Region North Directorate, 1970-72; counselor polit. affairs, Tehran Iran, 1972-74, prin. officer, Manama, Bahrain, 1974, dep. chief mission, Wellington, N.Z., 1974-77, ambassador to Qatar, Doha, 1977-80, ret., 1980; pres. The Amrok Corp., Washington, 1980—. Co-chmn. Am. Citizens Overseas Polit. Action Com.; bd. dirs. Am. sect. Musa Al-Alami of Jericho Found. Served as lt. (j.g.) USN, 1943-46. Office: 2550 M St NW Suite 275 Washington DC 20037

KILLIAM, E.J., manufacturing company executive; b. 1920; married. With Nat. Gypsum Co., 1948—, prodn. mgr., 1964-65, dir. mfg. Huron Cement div., 1965-67, v.p. mfg., 1967-68, asst. to chmn. bd, 1968-73, v.p. mfg. ops. bldg. products div., pres. Bldg. Products div., 1973-78, corp. group v.p., 1978-82, pres., chief operating officer, also dir., 1982—. Office: Nat Gypsum Co 1st International Bldg Dallas TX 75270 *

KILLIAN, GEORGE ERNEST, association executive; b. Valley Stream, N.Y., Apr. 6, 1924; s. George and Reina (Moeller) K.; m. Janice E. Bachert, May 26, 1951; children: Susan E., Sandra J. B.S. in Edn., Ohio No. U., 1949; Ed.M., U. Buffalo, 1954. Tchr.-coach Wharton (Ohio) High Sch., 1949-51; insp. USN, Buffalo, 1951-54; dir. athletics Erie County (N.Y.) Tech. Inst., Buffalo, 1954-69, asst. prof. health, phys. edn., recreation, 1954-60, asso. prof., 1960-62, prof., 1962-69; exec. dir. Nat. Jr. Coll. Athletic Assn., Hutchinson, Kans., 1969—. Editor: Juco Rev., 1960—. Served with AUS, 1943-45. Recipient Bd. Trustees award Hudson Valley C. of C., 1969, Erie County Tech. Inst., 1969, Service award Ohio No. U. Alumni, 1972, Lysle Rishel Post, Am. Legion, 1982; named to Ohio No. U. Hall of Fame, 1979. Mem. U.S. Olympic Com. (dir.), Am. Legion, Phi Delta Kappa, Delta Sigma Phi. Clubs: Masons, Rotary. Home: 2401 Sand Dunes Dr Hutchinson KS 67502 Office: Nat Jr Coll Athletic Assn PO Box 1586 Hutchinson KS 67501

KILLIAN, JAMES R., JR., former college president; b. Blacksburg, S.C., July 24, 1904; s. James Robert and Jeannette (Rhyne) K.; m. Elizabeth Parks, Aug. 21, 1929; children: Carolyn (Mrs. Paul Staley), Rhyne Meredith. Student, Trinity Coll. Duke U., 1921-23, LL.D. (hon.), 1949; B.S., Mass. Inst. Tech., 1926; Sc.D. (hon.), Middlebury Coll., 1945; hon. degrees, Bates Coll., 1950, U. Havana, Cuba, 1953, Notre Dame U., 1954, Lowell Tech. Inst., 1954, Columbia, Coll. Wooster, Oberlin Coll., 1958, U. Akron, 1959, Worcester Poly. Inst., 1960, U. Me., 1963; LL.D., Union Coll., 1947, Bowdoin Coll., Northeastern U., 1949, Boston U., Harvard, 1950, Williams Coll., Lehigh U., U. Pa., 1951, U. Chattanooga, 1954, Tufts U., 1955, U. Cal., Amherst Coll., 1956, Coll. William and Mary, 1957, Brandeis U., 1958, Johns Hopkins, N.Y. U., 1959, Providence Coll., Temple U., 1960, U. S.C., 1961, Meadville Theol. Sch., 1962; D.Applied Sci., U. Montreal, 1958; D.Eng., Drexel Inst. Tech., 1948, U. Ill., 1960, U. Mass., 1961; Ed.D., R.I. Coll., 1962; H.H.D., Rollins Coll., 1964; D.P.S., Detroit Inst. Tech., 1972. Asst. mng. editor Technology Rev., 1926-27, mng. editor, 1927-30, editor, 1930-39; exec. asst. to pres. Mass. Inst. Tech., 1939-43, exec. v.p., 1943-45, v.p., 1945-48, pres., 1948-59, chmn. corp., 1959-71, hon. chmn., 1971-79; dir. Polaroid Corp., IBM, 1959-62, Gen. Motors Corp., 1959-75, Cabot Corp., 1963-75, AT & T, 1963-77, Ingersoll-Rand Co., 1971-76. Chmn. Carnegie Commn. on Ednl. TV, 1965-67; bd. dirs. Corp. for Pub. Broadcasting, 1968-75, chmn., 1973-74; Mem. Pres. Communication Policy Bd., 1950-51, President's Com. on Mgmt., 1950-52; mem. sci. adv. com. ODM, 1951-57; chmn. Army Sci. Adv. Panel, 1951-56, Pres.' Bd. Cons. on Fgn. Intelligence Activities, 1956-57; spl. asst. to Pres. U.S. for sci. and tech., 1957-59; chmn. Pres.' Sci. Adv. Com., 1957-59, mem., 1957-61, cons., 1961-73; pres. Atoms for Peace Awards, 1955-58, 59-69; mem. Adv. Council on State Depts. Edn., U.S. Office Edn., 1965-68; chmn. President's Fgn. Intelligence Adv. Bd., 1961-63; mem. gen. adv. bd. U.S. Arms Control and Disarmament Agy., 1969-74; Bd. visitors U.S. Naval Acad., 1953-55; moderator Am. Unitarian Assn., 1960-61; Trustee Nutrition Found., 1954-70, Washington U., 1966-70, Mt. Holyoke Coll., 1962-72, Alfred P. Sloan Found., 1954-77, Boston Mus. Fine Arts, Mitre Corp.; chmn., 1967-69; bd. dirs. Nat. Merit Scholarship Corp., 1960-63, Winston Churchill Found. U.S. Ltd.; mem. Mass. Bd. Edn., 1962-65. Recipient President's Certificate of Merit, 1948, Certificate of Appreciation Dept. of Army, 1953; Exceptional Civilian Service award Dept. of Army; Pub. Welfare medal Nat. Acad. Scis., 1957; George Foster Peabody Broadcasting Spl. Edn. awards, 1968, 76; decorated Croix d'officer, Legion of Honor France, 1957; Hoover medal, 1963; Sylvanus Thayer award U.S. Mil. Acad., 1978; Vannevar Bush award Nat. Sci. Bd., 1980; others. Fellow Am. Acad. Arts and Scis.; mem. Nat. Acad. Engring., Am. Soc. Engring. Edn. (hon.), Sigma Chi, Phi Beta Kappa (hon.), Tau Beta Pi (hon.). Clubs: St. Botolph (Boston); Century (N.Y.C.). Address: care Mass Inst Technology Cambridge MA 02139

KILLIAN, LEWIS MARTIN, sociology educator; b. Darien, Ga., Feb. 15, 1919; s. Lewis Martin and Edith (Robinson) K.; m. Katharine Newbold Goold, Apr. 11, 1942; children: Katharine Newbold, Lewis Martin, John Calhoun. A.B., U. Ga., 1940, M.A., 1941; Ph.D., U. Chgo., 1949. Asst. prof. sociology U. Okla., 1949-52; asso. prof. sociology Fla. State U., 1952-57, prof., 1957-68, chmn. dept. sociology, 1966-68; prof., head dept. sociology U. Conn., 1968-69; prof. U. Mass., Amherst, 1969—; vis. prof. UCLA, 1965-66, U. Hawaii, 1972; vis. lectr. Thames Poly., London, 1980-81. Author: (with Ralph H. Turner) Collective Behavior, 1957, rev. edit., 1972, (with Charles M. Grigg) Racial Crisis in America, 1963, The Impossible Revolution, 1968, White Southerners, 1970, The Impossible Revolution: Phase II, 1974. Cons. com. disaster studies NRC, 1952-57; cons. to atty. gen. of Fla., 1954-55. Col. USAR; ret.). Guggenheim fellow, 1975-76. Mem. Am., Eastern sociol. socs., Phi Beta Kappa, Omicron Delta Kappa, Kappa Alpha. Home: 19 Hickory Ln Amherst MA 01002

KILLIAN, ROBERT KENNETH, former lt. gov. Conn.; b. Hartford, Conn., Sept. 15, 1919; s. Edward F. and Annie (Nemser) K.; m. Evelyn Farnan, Dec. 7, 1942; children—Robert Kenneth, Cynthia Elaine. B.A., Union Coll., 1942; LL.B., U. Conn., 1948; LL.D., Sacred Heart U., Bridgeport, Conn., 1976, Union Coll., Schenectady, 1978. Bar: Conn. bar 1948. Since practiced in, Hartford; partner firm Gould, Killian & Wynne, asst. corp. counsel, City of Hartford, 1951-54; atty. gen., State of Conn., 1967-75, lt. gov., 1975-79; chmn. Hartford Dem. Town Com., 1963-67, Hartford Civic Center and Coliseum Commn., 1980—. Trustee Nat. Jewish Hosp. and Research Center, Denver. Served with inf. AUS, 1942-46. Decorated Purple Heart; recipient numerous citations by civic and pub. service orgns. Mem. Am., Conn., Hartford County bar assns. Roman Catholic. Clubs: K.C., Elks. Home: 234 Terry Rd Hartford CT 06105 Office: 37 Lewis St Hartford CT 06103

KILLIN, CHARLES CLARK, lawyer; b. Peoria, Ill., June 12, 1923; s. Thomas James and Marie (Clark) K. A.B., U. Mich., 1947, LL.B., 1950. Bar: Okla. 1950. Since practiced in Tulsa; partner Conner, Winters, Ballaine, Barry & McGowen (and predecessor), 1958—. Served with AUS, 1943-46. Fellow Am. Coll. Probate Counsel; mem. Am., Okla., Tulsa County bar assns., Theta Chi, Phi Alpha Delta. Republican. Presbyterian. Club: Rotary. Home: 2130 E 59th St Tulsa OK 74105 3483 Gulf Shore Blvd Apt 401 Naples FL 33940 Office: First Nat Tower Tulsa OK 74103

KILLINGER, GEORGE GLENN, psychologist, criminologist; b. Marion, Va., Mar. 13, 1908; s. James Peter and Lena (Kelly) K.; m. Grace Davis, June 29, 1935; children: Robert Peter, Evangeline, George Evan. A.B., Wittenberg Coll., 1930, LL.D., 1953; Ph.D., U. N.C., 1953. Diplomate: in clin. psychology Am. Bd. Examiners in Profl. Psychology. Research asst. Mooseheart Lab. for Child Research, summers 1929-31; instr. psychology U. N.C., 1930-33; asst. personnel dir. Mathieson Alkali Works, 1933-34; psychologist and spl. asst. to personnel dir. TVA, Knoxville, 1934-36; dir. out-patient and social service Southwestern State Hosp., Marion, Va., 1936-37; psychologist USPHS, Fed. Reformatory, Chillicothe, Ohio, 1937-38; supr. edn. U.S. Penitentiary, Atlanta, 1938-40, asst. asso. warden, 1940-41; supr. edn. U.S. Bur. Prisons, Washington, 1941-43; chief psychobiol. activites War Shipping Adminstrn., 1943-47; chmn. clemency and parole bd. Office of Sec. Army, Washington, 1947-48; chmn. U.S. Bd. of Parole, Dept. Justice, Washington, 1948-53, mem., 1953-60; Lectr. George Washington U., 1953-54; prof. dept. criminology and corrections Fla. State U., 1960-65; dir. Inst. Contemporary Corrections and Behavioral Scis., Sam Houston State U., Huntsville, 1965-77, Piper Distinguished prof., 1968; chmn. Tex. Bd. Pardons and Paroles, 1977-80, vice chmn., 1980—. Author: Personality Disorders, 1946, Prison Work as a Post-War Career, 1946, The Psychobiological Program of the War Shipping Administration, 1947, Penology, The Evolution of the American Correctional System, 1973, 2d edit., 1979, Corrections in the Community, 1974, 2d edit., 1978, Issues in Law Enforcement, 1975, Probation and Parole, 1976, 2d edit., 1983, Corrections and Administration, 1976, Introduction to Juvenile Delinquency, 1977; cons. editor Criminal Justice series Harcourt Brace Jovanovich, Inc, 1978—; Contbr. numerous sci. articles to tech. and professional publs. Mem. Tex. Commn. on Law Enforcement Standards and Edn., Nat. Task Force on Corrections; mem. Tex. Bd. Pardons and Paroles, Austin, 1977—. Served as lt. comdr., commd. officer USPHS, 1943-47; scientist dir. USPHS Res. Recipient E.R. Cass Achievement award Am. Correctional Assn., 1980; U.S. Dept. labor research grantee, 1966. Fellow Am. Psychol. Assn., AAAS; mem. Am. Prison Assn., Am. Assn. Adult Edn., USPHS Res. Officers Assn., Ednl. Found., Inc., Nat. Probation Parole Assn. (adv. council 1952-54), Wittenberg Alumni Assn. (past pres. Washington), Am. Legion, Alpha Psi Delta, Phi Mu Delta, Psi Chi, Pi Kappa Alpha, Alpha Kappa Delta. Democrat. Lutheran. Clubs: Kiwanis, Advt. (N.Y.C.); Kenwood Golf and Country, Touchdown, Univ. (Washington); Warwick (Houston); Huntsville (Tex.). Home: 6504 E Hill Dr Austin TX 78731

KILLINGSWORTH, CHARLES CLINTON, economist; b. Webb City, Mo., Jan. 1, 1917; s. James Ray and Genevieve Theresa (Beahan) K.; m. Beverly Hannah Kritzman, Feb. 6, 1943 (dec. Aug. 1970); children—Mark Robert, Charlotte Eve; m. Jacqueline Brown Schrecengost, June 19, 1971; children—Tammy Kay, Randi Patricia. A.B., Mo. State U., 1938; A.M., Okla. State U., 1939; Ph.D., U. Wis., 1946. Instr. polit. economy Johns Hopkins, 1941-45; chief, analytical studies unit Social Security Adminstrn., 1945-46; panel chmn. and spl. hearing officer Nat. War Labor Bd., 1943-46; mem. faculty Mich. State U., 1947—, prof. and head dept. econs., 1949-57; dir. Labor and Indsl. Relations Center, 1956-59, Univ. prof., 1960—; Arbitrator labor-mgmt. disputes since, 1943; permanent umpire Bethlehem Steel Co. and United Steel Workers Am., 1947- 52; nat. umpire U.S. Rubber Co., Rubber Workers Union, 1953-55, Ford Motor Co. and UAW, 1955-58, Goodyear Tire & Rubber Co. and United Rubber Workers, 1959-61; cons. to WSB, 1951; chmn, 1952-53; permanent umpire Youngstown Sheet & Tube Co. and Steelworkers, 1963-67; permanent arbitrator Firestone Tire & Rubber Co. and Rubber Workers, 1971—, Crucible Steel Co. and Steelworkers, 1971-80; mem. various presdl. labor dispute bds., 1962—. Author: State Labor Relations Acts, 1948; co-author: Trade Union Publns. 1851-1941 (3 vols.), 1944-45, Jobs and Income for Negroes, 1968, also articles in field of econs. Mem. panel arbitrators Am. Arbitration Assn., Fed. Mediation and Conciliation Service; mem. Nat. Council on Employment Policy (formerly Nat. Manpower Policy Task Force), 1964—, chmn., 1975-77. Mem. Nat. Acad. of Arbitrators (v.p. 1958-60, bd. govs. 1952-55, pres. 1968), Indsl. Relations Research Assn. (exec. bd. 1956-58, pres. 1978). Home: 4584 Sequoia Trail Okemos MI 48864

KILLIPS, DANFORTH, investment adviser; b. Chgo., Oct. 22, 1918; s. Andrew F. and Ruth D. (Patrick) K.; m. Leslie Parker, Apr. 5, 1947; children: Bruce Danforth, John Mitchell. B.S.L., Northwestern U., 1941, LL.B., 1947. Bar: Ill. bar 1947. With firm Seago, Pipin, Bradley & Vetter, Chgo., 1946-48, Parker & Carter, 1948-52; v.p., dir. Looart Press, Inc., Colorado Springs, Colo., 1952-60, dir., 1968-83; with Growth Research, Inc., Chgo., 1960-69, v.p., 1961, pres., 1961-69; also dir.; dir. Growth Industry Shares, Inc., Chgo., 1960-77, v.p., 1962-76; investment mgr. William Blair & Co., Chgo., 1969-73. Bd. dirs. Colorado Springs chpt. A.R.C., 1958-60, Colorado Springs YMCA, 1958-60, Vascular Disease Research Found., Chgo., 1964—; adv. bd. Chgo. Salvation Army, 1966-73. Served to capt. USAAF, 1941-45. Mem. Sigma Chi, Phi Delta Phi. Conglist. Clubs: Lit. (Chgo.); Anciente and Secret Order of Quiet Birdmen; Exchange (North Tucson). Home: 3208 E 3d St Tucson AZ 85716 Office: 2929 E 6th St Room 144 Tucson AZ 85716

KILLOUGH, JAMES STUART, banker; b. Phila., Mar. 5, 1940; s. Stuart K. and Doris (McFarland) K.; m. MaryAnn Kaiser, Apr. 18, 1964. B.A., U. Pa., 1956. With Heritage Bank, Cherry Hill and Jamesburg, N.J., 1964—, exec. v.p., cashier, 1964—. Bd. dirs. United Way Camden County, 1982-83. Served with U.S. Army. Office: Heritage Bank One Heritage Plaza Jamesburg NJ 08831

KILLOUGH, LARRY NEIL, accounting educator; b. Little Rock, Dec. 28, 1932; m. Irene Ruth Keefe, Nov. 29, 1952; children: Margaret Ruth, Gregory Neil. B.S., U. Tenn., 1955, Temple U., Phila., 1966; Ph.D., U. Mo., Columbia U., 1969. C.P.A., Ohio, Pa. Auditor Arthur Young & Co. (C.P.A.s), N.Y.C., 1958-60; auditor, procedures analyst Fairmont Foods Co., Phila., 1960-64; asst. prof. acctg. Temple U., 1966; instr. U. Mo., 1967-69; mem. faculty Va. Poly. Inst. and State U., Blacksburg, 1969—, prof. acctg., 1975—; vis. prof., Poland, Singapore. Co-author: Decision Making, 1977, C.P.A. Review, 1978, Governmental Accounting, 1983, Cost Accounting, 1984. Served with U.S. Army, 1955-57. Mem. Am. Inst. C.P.A.s, Nat. Assn. Accts, Am. Acctg. Assn., Va. Soc. C.P.A.s. Methodist. Club: Visa Yacht. Home: 213 Pine Dr Blacksburg VA 24060 Office: Dept Acctg Va Poly Inst and State Univ Blacksburg VA 24061

KILLPACK, JAMES ROBERT, banking exec.; b. Persia, Iowa, Aug. 11, 1922; s. James Marion and Dorothy (Divelbess) K.; m. Norma Hewett, June 11, 1949; children—James, John, Steven. B.S., Miami U., Oxford, Ohio, 1946. C.P.A., Ohio. With Peat, Marwick, Mitchell & Co., Cleve., 1946-58; treas. Ferro Corp., Cleve., 1958-66; fin. v.p. Island Creek Coal Co., Cleve., 1966-68; dir.corp. planning Eaton Corp. (formerly Eaton Yale & Towne Inc.), Cleve., 1968-69, v.p. corp planning, 1969, v.p. adminstrn., 1970, v.p. fin., 1970-78, exec. v.p. fin. and adminstrn., 1978-79; pres., dir. Nat. City Bank, Cleve., 1979—, Nat. City Corp., 1980—; dir. Sherwin-Williams Co., Weatherchem Corp. Served with AUS, 1942-45. Mem. Fin. Execs. Inst. (dir. Cleve. chpt., pres. 1970-71), Am. Inst. C.P.A.'s. Mem. Christian Ch. Clubs: Tavern, Union (Cleve.); Shaker Country (Shaker Heights, Ohio); Pepper Pike. Home: 13901 Shaker Blvd Suite 1-B Cleveland OH 44120 Office: National City Center Tower 1900E 9th St Cleveland OH 44114

KILLPACK, LARRY MOVELL, businessman, ret. air force officer; b. Huntington, Utah, Nov. 9, 1925; s. Jonathan Movell and Flora Catherine (Leonard) K.; m. Joann Alston, June 16, 1949; children—Larry Steven, Lorraine, Kevin Ray. B.S., U. Utah, 1949; M.B.A., Harvard, 1961; M.S., George Washington U., 1966; grad., Indsl. Coll. Armed Forces, 1965. Commd. 2d lt. USAAF, 1950; advanced through grades to maj. gen. USAF, 1974; maintenance officer, squadron comdr., Nellis AFB, Nev., 1959-64, chief, L.G. Hanscom AFB, Mass., 1964-67; mem. air staff Pentagon, 1967; dir. cost analysis (Air Force Systems Command), Andrew AFB, Washington, 1968, vice comdr., MacDill AFB, Fla., 1969, comdr., Vietnam, 1970, Ubon, Thailand, 1971, asst. comptroller, comdr., Denver, 1974, vice comdr., Bergstrom AFB, Tex., 1975, Randolph AFB, Tex., 1977-78; asst. DCS/personnel Hdqrs. USAF, Pentagon, 1978-79; ret., 1979; pres. Internat. Security Group Inc., San Antonio, 1979; group v.p. devel. Church's Fried Chicken, Inc., San Antonio, 1980—. Decorated D.S.M., Legion of Merit with 2 oak leaf clusters, D.F.C., Air medal with 15 oak leaf clusters, Air Force Commendation medal, Republic of Vietnam Gallantry Cross with palm. Mem. Am. Soc. Mil. Comptrollers, Air Force Assn., Order Daedalians, Scabbard and Blade, Tau Beta Phi. Mormon. Home: 518 Candleglo San Antonio TX 78239 Office: 302 Spencer Ln PO Box BH001 San Antonio TX 78284

KILLPATRICK, JAMES CARL, journalist; b. Hillsboro, Ill., Nov. 25, 1931; s. Carl Leon and Wanna (Sears) K.; m. Frances Eleanor Van Cleave, Oct. 17, 1959; children: Amy Ruth, Patrick Emerson. Student, U. Ill., 1949-50, So. Ill. U., 1954-55. News editor So. Illinoisan, Carbondale, 1956-61; night city editor, news editor Comml. Appeal, Memphis, 1961-71; sr. corr. Reuters News Service, N.Y.C., 1972-74; chief bureaus, sr. editor U.S. News and World Report, Washington,

1974—. Served with CIC, U.S. Army, 1952-54. Presbyterian. Home: 2117 Paul Spring Rd Alexandria VA 22307 Office: 2400 N St NW Washington DC 20037

KILMAN, JAMES WILLIAM, surgeon, educator; b. Terre Haute, Ind., Jan. 22, 1931; s. Arthur and Irene (Piker) K.; m. Priscilla Margaret Jackson, June 20, 1968; children: James William, Julia Anne, Jennifer Irene. B.S., Ind. State U., 1956; M.D., Ind. U., 1960. Intern Ind.U. Med. Ctr., Indpls., 1960-61; resident surgery Ind.U. Med. Center, 1961-66, asst. prof., 1966-69, assoc. prof., 1969-73; prof. surgery Ohio State U. Coll. Medicine, 1973-; chmn. dept. thoracic surgery Children's Hosp.; attending surgeon Univ. Hosp., Columbus, Ohio; attending staff Children's Hosp., Columbus, pres. staff, 1978; attending staff Grant Hosp., Riverside Hosp.; cons. surgeon VA Hosp., Dayton; pres. Columbus Acad. Medicine, 1977. Trustee Central Ohio Heart Assn., Acad. Medicine Edn. Found., Children's Hosp., 1978—. Served with USNR, 1951-55. USPHS Cardiovascular fellow, 1963-64. Mem. Columbus Surg. Soc. (pres. 1973-74), Columbus Acad. Medicine (council 1971-73), Am. Surg. Assn., Soc. U. Surgeons, Am. Assn. Thoracic Surgery, Am., Central, Western surg. assns., Soc. Vascular Surgery, Internat. Cardiovascular Soc., Internat. Soc. Surgeons, Chest Club, Cardiovascular Surgery Club, Sigma Xi, Alpha Omega Alpha. Research, articles infant cardiopulmonary bypass and surgery for congenital heart lesions. Home: 4231 Jackson Pike Grove City OH 43123 Office: 410 W 10th Ave Columbus OH 43210

KILMANN, RALPH HERMAN, business educator; b. N.Y.C., Oct. 5, 1946; s. Martin Herbert and Lilli (Loeb) K.; m. Audrey Ann Sabol, July 7, 1977; children: Catherine Mary, Christopher Martin. B.S., Carnegie-Mellon U., 1970, M.S., 1970; Ph.D., UCLA, 1972. Instr. Grad. Sch. Bus. U., Pitts., 1972; asst. prof. Grad. Sch. Bus., U. Pitts., 1972-75, assoc. prof., 1975-79, prof., 1979—, coordinator organizational studies group, 1981—, dir. program in corp. culture, 1983—; pres. Organizational Design Cons., Inc., Pitts., 1975—. Author: Social Systems Design: Normative Theory and the MAPS Design Technology, 1977, Corporate Culturing: A Complete Program for Managing Change, 1984; co-author: Methodological Approaches to Social Science: Integrating Divergent Concepts and Theories, 1978, Corporate Tragedies: Why the Worst is Happening to Business and What Can Be Done About It, 1984, The Management of Organization Design: Vols. 1 and II, 1976, Producing Useful Knowledge for Organizations, 1984; editorial bd.: Jour. Mgmt., 1983—; contbr. chpts. to books, articles to profl. jours. Mem. Eastern Acad. Mgmt. (treas. 1975-76, dir. 1983—), Am. Phychol. Assn., Inst. Mgmt. Scis. (1st prize Nat. Coll. Planning competition 1976), Beta Gamma Sigma. Developed Kilmann Insight Test, Learning Climate Questionnaire, Thomas-Kilmann Conflict-Mode Instrument in Ednl. Testing Service, MAPS Design Tech. for Social Systems Design, Kilmann-Saxton Culture-Gap Survey. Home: 110 Weir Dr Pittsburgh PA 15215 Office: Grad Sch Bus U Pitts Roberto Clements Dr Pittsburgh PA 15260 *Some live only for themselves, some sacrifice their lives for others. The space between is enjoying one's life while contributing to society. No one should have the full responsibility for saving the world, nor the complete freedom to ignore the future.*

KILMARTIN, EDWARD JOHN, educator, theologian; b. Portland, Maine, Aug. 31, 1923; s. Patrick Joseph and Elizabeth Gertrude (Sullivan) K. A.B., Boston Coll., 1947, M.A. in Philosophy, 1948, S.T.L., 1955; M.S. in Chemistry, Holy Cross Coll., 1950; S.T.D., Gregorian U., Rome, 1958. Joined S.J., Roman Catholic Ch., 1941; ordained priest Roman Cath. Ch., 1954; tchr. chemistry Fairfield (Conn.) Prep. Sch., 1950-51; prof. sacramental theology Weston Coll., Sch. Theology, Boston Coll., 1958-77, dean sch., 1960-62; prof. liturg. theology U. Notre Dame, 1977—, dir. grad. program in liturg. studies, 1980—. Editor: New Testament Abstracts, 1959-67; Author: The Eucharist in the Primitive Church, 1965; also articles on N.T. Mem. Cath. Theol. Soc. Am., Cath. Bibl. Assn. Office: U Notre Dame Notre Dame IN 46556

KILMER, FORREST JUNIOR, editor; b. Seneca, Ill., Feb. 3, 1921; s. William Albert and Anne Margaret (Arthur) K.; m. Jeannette Delores Etzel, Oct. 10, 1947; children: David Martin, Jeanene Ann, Mark Charles. Ed. pub. schs. Reporter Davenport (Iowa) Democrat, from 1939; later mng. editor Davenport Morning Democrat; exec. editor Quad City Times (name formerly Times-Democrat), Davenport, editor, 1970—; First chmn. Lee Editorial Bd. Former chmn. Scott County (Iowa) Juvenile Adv. Commn.; former mem. adv. council Iowa SBA; mem. Iowa Council on Crime and Delinquency.; Former trustee Davenport Pub. Library.; past pres. Iowa Freedom of Info. Council; mem. Gov.'s Task Force on Iowa Open Records Law. Served with AUS, World War II. Decorated Bronze Star. Mem. Am. Soc. Newspaper Editors, Iowa Freedom of Info. Council. Lutheran. Home: 512 4th St Bettendorf IA 52722 Office: 124 E 2d St Davenport IA 52801

KILPATRICK, CHARLES OTIS, newspaper editor, publisher; b. Fairview, Okla., June 16, 1922; s. John E. and Myrtle (Arant) K.; m. Margie Ada Partin, June 3, 1944; children: Kent Fairles, Millicent Kye, Mark Kevin. B.A., Stephen F. Austin State Coll., 1942. With daily newspapers, Nacogdoches, Tex., 1940-42; with Daily Sentinel, Nacogdoches, 1946-48, Courier-Times, Tyler, Tex., 1948-49; regional editor Tyler Morning Telegraph, 1949, mng. editor, 1949-50; mem. staff Evening News, San Antonio, 1950-51; Sunday Editor San Antonio Express, 1951-54; asst. mng. editor Evening News, 1954-55, mng. editor, 1955-56; asst. exec. editor San Antonio Express and San Antonio News, 1957-58, exec. editor, 1958, v.p., 1971; pub. San Antonio Express, 1971-72, San Antonio Express and News, 1972—. Bd. dirs. San Antonio Symphony, United Way, Goodwill Rehab. Services, San Antonio Indsl. Found., Tex. Council on Crime and Delinquency; trustee Southwest Research Center. Served as comdg. officer 14th Inf. Bn. USMCR; lt. col. Res. Pulitzer prize journalism juror, 1963, 64, 67, 71, 75. Mem. Tex. A.P. Mng. Editors Assn. (pres. 1963), Tex. Daily Newspaper Assn., San Antonio C. of C. (dir.), Am. Soc. Newspaper Editors. Episcopalian. Office: Express-News Corp Ave E at 3d St San Antonio TX 78206

KILPATRICK, GEORGE H., banker; b. Denver, Apr. 20, 1936; s. George Harrington and Margaret M. (Wall) K.; m. Dorothy Ray Winter, June 13, 1959; children—Robin, Jeffrey. B.S. in Finance with honors, U. Colo., 1959. Credit analyst, gen. banking officer Interfirst Bank Dallas, N.A., 1960-70, asst. cashier, 1962-64; asst. v.p. 1st Nat. Bank, 1964-67, v.p., 1967-70, sr. v.p., 1970-73, div. head loan adminstrn., 1970-71, group head gen. banking services, 1971-73; exec. v.p., chief operating officer, dir. Interfirst Bank Houston N.A. (N.A.), 1973-79; pres. 1st Internat. Bank in Houston (N.A.), 1973-79; exec. v.p. Interfirst Corp., 1979—. Bd. mgrs. Harris County Hosp. Dist., 1975-79. Mem. Young Presidents Orgn., Am. Bankers Assn., Am. Inst. Banking, Robert Morris Assos. (bd. regents loan mgmt. seminar 1973, 74), Beta Gamma Sigma, Sigma Chi. Methodist. Clubs: Houston Country, Dallas Country, Coronado, City. Office: 1201 Elm St Dallas TX 75283

KILPATRICK, JAMES JACKSON, JR., newspaperman; b. Oklahoma City, Nov. 1, 1920; s. James Jackson and Alma Mia (Hawley) K.; m. Marie Louise Pietri, Sept. 21, 1942; children: Michael Sean, Christopher Hawley, Kevin Pietri. B.J., U. Mo., 1941. Reporter Richmond (Va.) News Leader, 1941-49, chief editorial writer, 1949-51, editor, 1951-67; writer nat. syndicated column; asso. Nat. Rev., 1964-68, contbg. editor, 1968-82; TV commentator; pres. Op Ed Inc. Pres. Beadle Bumble Fund, 1954—. Author: The Sovereign States, 1957, The Smut Peddlers, 1960, The Southern Case for School Segregation, 1962, The Foxes' Union, 1977, (with Eugene J. McCarthy) A Political Bestiary, 1978, (with William Bake) The American South: Four Seasons of the Land, 1980, The American South: Towns and Cities, 1982, The Writer's Art, 1984; Editor: We the States, 1964; co-editor: The Lasting South, 1957. Vice chmn. Va. Com. on Constl. Govt., 1962-68; chmn. Va. Magna Carta Com., 1965. Recipient medal of honor for distinguished service in journalism U. Mo., 1953; ann. award for editorial writing Sigma Delta Chi, 1954; William Allen White award U. Kans., 1979; named to Okla. Hall of Fame, 1978. Fellow Sigma Delta Chi; mem. Nat. Conf. Editorial Writers (chmn. 1955-56), White House Corrs. Assn., Va. Ornithology Soc., Black-Eyed Pea Soc. Am. (No. 1 Pea, pro-tem. 1965—). Whig. Episcopalian. Club: Gridiron. Address: Woodville VA 22749

KILPATRICK, ROBERT DONALD, insurance company executive; b. Fairbanks, La., Feb. 5, 1924; s. Thomas David and Lula Mae (Crowell) K.; m. Faye Hines, May 29, 1948; children: Robert Donald, Kathleen Spencer, Lauren Douglas, Tracy Crowell, Thomas David. B.A., U. Richmond, 1948; postgrad., Harvard U. Grad. Sch. Bus., 1973. With Conn. Gen. Life Ins. Co., Hartford, 1954—, asst. sec., 1961-66, dir. orgn. and systems, 1966-68; v.p., chief adminstrv. officer Aetna Ins. Co. (affiliate), 1968-73; sr. v.p. group ins. ops. Conn. Gen., 1973-76, former pres., chief exec. officer, now chmn., 1976—; pres., chief exec. officer Conn. Gen. Corp.; dir. Fed. Res. Bank Boston, Scovill Inc. of Waterbury, Conn. Bd. dirs., mem. exec. com. Conn. Bus. Industry Assn.; bd. dirs. United Way; trustee Conn. Pub. Expenditure Council, Inc., U. Richmond, S.S. Huebner Found. Ins. Edn. of Wharton Sch. of U. Pa.; corporator Hartford Hosp., Inst. Living, Hartford; bd. regents U. Hartford. Served with USN, 1942-46, 50-54. Mem. Health Ins. Assn. Am. (dir.), U.S. C. of C. (dir.), Greater Hartford C. of C. (dir., mem. exec. com.), Bus. Roundtable (chmn. com. on fed. budget, policy com.), Council on Fgn. Relations. Club: Economic (N.Y.C.). Office: Conn Gen Life Ins Co Hartford CT 06152 *

KILPATRICK, S. JAMES, JR., educator, biostatistician; b. Belfast, No. Ireland, Apr. 24, 1931; came to U.S., 1965, naturalized, 1970; s. Samuel J. and Mary (Maginnis) K.; m. Mary Coyne Brown, Feb. 6, 1957; children: Mark Duncan, Sara Ellen. B.Sc. with honours, Queens U., Belfast, 1954, M.Sc., 1957, Ph.D., 1960. Asst. lectr. social preventive medicine Queens U., 1954-58, lectr., 1958-61; postdoctoral fellow statistics USPHS, Iowa State U., 1960-61; lectr. statistics Aberdeen (Scotland) U., 1961-65; prof. biostatistics Med. Coll. Va., Va. Commonwealth U., Richmond, 1965—, chmn. dept., 1965-83, prof. family practice, 1979-83; also mem. Cancer Center; mem. oral biology and medicine study sect. NIH, 1979-81; chmn. Va. Health Statistics Adv. Council, Va. Health Interview Council; ad hoc reviewer, site visitor Nat. Heart, Lung and Blood Inst., Nat. Cancer Inst. Vestryman St. Peter's Episcopal Ch., Richmond. Hon. research fellow Royal Coll. Gen. Practitioners, 1973-74. Mem. Biometric Soc., Va. Acad. Sci., Internat. Epidemiol. Assn., Sigma Xi. Home: 7808 Ardendale Rd Richmond VA 23225

KILROY, JAMES FRANCIS, educator; b. Chgo., Sept. 7, 1935; s. John Patrick and Nora (Joyce) K.; m. Mary Elizabeth Carroll, July 1, 1961; children—Maurya, James Dennis, Mark Justin. B.A., DePaul U., 1957; M.A., U. Iowa, 1961; Ph.D., U. Wis., 1965. Tchr. Pub. High Schs., Chgo., 1957-61; asst. prof. Vanderbilt U., 1965-69, asso. prof., 1969-77, prof., 1977—, chmn. dept. English, 1979—, asso. dean, 1973-76. Author: James Clarence Mangan, 1970, The Playboy Riots, 1971, The Modern Irish Drama (3 vols.), 1975, 76, 78, The Playboy as Poet, 1969, The Chiastic Structure of Tennyson's In Memoriam, 1977; co-editor: Lost Plays of the Irish Renaissance, 1970; mem. editorial bd.: Soundings. Am. Council Learned Socs. fellow, 1967-68; Nat. Endowment Humanities fellow, 1968. Mem. Modern Lang. Assn., Soc. for Values in Higher Edn. Roman Catholic. Home: 113 Carnavon Pkwy Nashville TN 37205 Office: Dept English Vanderbilt U Nashville TN 37235

KILROY, JOHN MUIR, lawyer; b. Kansas City, Mo., Apr. 12, 1918; s. James L. and Jane Alice (Scurry) K.; m. Lorraine K. Butler, Jan. 26, 1946; children: John Muir, William Terence. Student, Kansas City Jr. Coll., 1935-37; A.B., U. Kansas City, 1940; LL.B., U. Mo., 1942. Bar: Mo. 1942. Practice in, Kansas City, 1946—; ptnr. Shughart, Thomson & Kilroy, 1946—, pres., 1977—; instr. med. jurisprudence Kansas City Coll. Osteopathy, 1973—; Panelist numerous med.-legal groups A.C.S., Mo. Med. Assn., Kans. U. Med. Sch., S.W. Clin. Soc. Contbr. articles to profl. jours. Chmn. bd. dirs. Kansas City Heart Assn. Served to capt. AUS, 1942-46. Fellow Am. Coll. Trial Lawyers; mem. Internat. Assn. Barristers, Internat. Assn. Ins. Counsel, Am. Coll. Legal Medicine, Am. Bd. Profl. Liability Attys., Fedn. Ins. Counsel, Lawyers Assn. Kansas City (pres.), ABA, Mo. Bar Assn. (chmn. med. legal com.), Kansas City C. of C. Home: 6860 Tomahawk Rd Shawnee Mission KS 66208 Office: Commerce Bank Bldg 922 Walnut St Kansas City MO 64106

KILROY, RICHARD IGNATIUS, labor union executive; b. Texas, Md., July 31, 1927; s. Joseph Michael and Mary Ann (Schultheis) K.; m. Betty Lee Willis, Apr. 8, 1950; children: Margaret Mary, Mary Catherine, Richard I, Anne Marie, Mary Patricia; 1 stepson, A. Earl Hines. Student, pub. schs., Balt. Block operator Pa. R.R. Co., Balt., 1951-59; local chmn., asst. gen. chmn., dir., gen. chmn., v.p. Order of R.R. Telegraphers (named changed to Transp. Communication Employees, merged with Brotherhood of Ry. & Airline Clks.), Phila., 1956-67, local chmn., asst. gen. chmn., chmn., dir., gen. chmn., v.p., St. Louis, 1968; internat. v.p. Order of R.R. Telegraphers (named changed to Transp. Communication Employees, merged with Brotherhood of Ry. & Airline Clks., St. Louis, 1969-81; internat. pres. Brotherhood of Ry., Airlines & S.S. Clks., Freight Handlers, Express & Sta. Employees, Rockville, Md., 1981—; dir. African-Am Labor Ctr., Washington, 1982, Asian-Am. Free Labor Inst., 1982; v.p. AFL-CIO, Washington, 1981. Served with AUS, 1945-48. Mem. Ry. Labor Execs. Assn. (exec. sec.-treas. 1982). Democrat. Roman Catholic. Office: Brotherhood Ry Airline & Steamship Clks Freight Handlers Express & Sta Employees 3 Research Pl Rockville MD 20850 *

KILTY, JEROME TIMOTHY, playwright, stage director, actor; b. Balt., June 24, 1922; s. Harold Joseph and Irene (Zellinger) K.; m. Cavada Humphrey, May 11, 1956. B.A., Harvard, 1949. Vis. prof. drama U. Okla., Norman, 1971, U. Tex., Austin, 1972, U. Kans., Lawrence, 1973; apptd. to O'Conner Chair of Lit., Colgate U., Hamilton, N.Y., 1974-75; instr. drama Harvard U., Cambridge, Mass., 1983—. Co-founder, dir., actor, Brattle Theatre Co., Cambridge, Mass., 1948-52; actor N.Y.C. stage and TV, 1952-57, including, Relapse, 1951, Quadrille, 1952, Misalliance, 1953; played: Falstaff, Iago, City Centre, 1954; writer, actor: Dear Liar, Chgo. and London, 1957; dir.: revival Dear Liar, Paris, 1974, 80, Rome, 1975, for TV, Hallmark Hall of Fame, 1981; writer, dir.: Ides of March, London, 1963; writer, dir. for TV: Long Live Life, San Francisco, 1967; writer, dir. for TV, San Francisco, 1967; dir. Marie Bell, Elisabeth Bergner, Maria Casares, Pierre Brasseur in: French, German, Italian prodn. Long Live Life, 1962-65; assoc. dir., Am. Conservatory Theatre, San Francisco, 1966-68, Am. Shakespeare Co., Stratford, Conn., 1965-68; dir.: Possibilities, N.Y.C., 1968, Sarah Ferrati in Mrs. Warren's Profession (in Italian), Rome, 1976; writer, dir.: Don't Shoot Mable It's Your Husband, 1968; writer, actor: Dear Love, Boston, 1969, London, 1973; writer, dir.: The Laffing Man, 1975; writer: The Little Black Book, N.Y.C., 1972, Look Away, N.Y.C., 1973; musicals What the Devil, 1977, Barnum, 1978; play Hey Marie!, 1979; dir.: Julius Caesar, San Diego Nat. Shakespeare Festival, 1979, Love's Labor's Lost, 1980, Misalliance, Denver, 1980, I, James McNeill Whistler, Hartford Stage Co.; appeared in: A Month in the Country, N.Y.C., 1979-80; mem., Hartman Theatre Co., 1981-82; dir.: Tammy Grimes in The Millionairess; star: The Magistrate; mem., Am. Repertory Theatre Co., Cambridge, Mass., 1983—; created role: The King in Big River, 1983; co-star: A Moon for the Misbegotten, Cort Theatre, N.Y.C., 1984. Served to capt. USAAF, 1942-46; ETO. Decorated D.F.C., Air Medal with seven clusters. Mem. Signet Soc. Club: Players (N.Y.C.). Home: PO Box 1074 Weston CT 06883

KIM, CHIN-WU, linguist, educator; b. Chungju, Korea, Mar. 22, 1936; came to U.S., 1961, naturalized, 1983; s. Hyong-gi and Kyong-ok K.; m. Beverly Jean Kircher, June 14, 1964; children: Joseph H., Daniel H. B.A. in English, Yonsei U., Seoul, Korea, 1958, Wash. State U., 1962; M.A., UCLA, 1964; Ph.D. in Linguistics, UCLA, 1966. Asst. prof. linguistics U. Ill., Urbana, 1967-69, asso. prof. linguistics and speech, 1969-72, prof., 1972—, chmn. dept. linguistics, 1972-79; vis. prof. linguistics U. Hawaii, 1972-73; vis. prof. English Yongei U., Korea, 1983-84; adj. prof. U. Tehran, Iran, 1974-76. Author works in field. Served with Korean Air Force, 1958-61. Am. Council Learned Socs. fellow, 1965-66. Mem. Linguistic Soc. Am., Linguistic Soc. Korea, Internat. Circle Korean Linguistics (pres. 1978-80). Home: 1921 B Melrose Dr Champaign IL 61820 Office: Dept Linguistics U Ill 707 S Mathew St Urbana IL 61801 *I grew up in an economically poor and politically oppressive and unstable environment (Japanese colonial rule, World War II, Korean War). The educational system mirrored such a society (books were scarce, pencils were used down to the one-inch length, and classes were often cancelled), but I was determined to learn, as I did not want to let the poor environment be an excuse for ignorance. Now in the States, it saddens me to see many people not realize and make use of excellent opportunities they have, for I believe that in the presence of excellence, mediocrity is a sin.*

KIM, CHUNG WOOK, educator; b. Hiroshima, Japan, Jan. 8, 1934; s. Chan S. and Yoon S. (Rho) K.; m. Young Ja Kang, July 25, 1960; 1 dau., Janet. Ed., U. Notre Dame; Ph.D., Ind. U., 1963. Research asso. U. Pa., 1963-66; prof. physics Johns Hopkins U., 1966—. Contbr. articles to profl. jours. Mem. Am. Phys. Soc. Home: 1006 Timber Trail Rd Baltimore MD 21204 Office: Dept Physics Johns Hopkins U Baltimore MD 21218

KIM, EARL, composer; b. Dinuba, Calif., Jan. 6, 1920; s. Sung Kwon and Sarah (Kang) Kwon; m. Nora Philipsborn, 1947; 1 dau., Shawna; m. Miriam Odza, 1958; m. Martha Potter, Aug. 25, 1977; 1 dau., Eva. Student, UCLA, 1940-41; M.A., U. Calif., Berkeley, 1952. Asso. prof. music Princeton U., 1952-67; prof. Harvard U., 1967—, James Edward Ditson prof. music, 1971—. Condr., Ariel Chamber Ensemble, Cambridge, Mass., 1977-81; compositions include Bagatelles for Piano, 1952; Letters Found Near a Suicide, 1954, Dialogues for Piano and Orchestra, 1959, Exercises En Route, 1970, Narratives, 1976, Violin Concerto, 1979, 15 Caprices for Solo Violin, 1980; one-act opera Footfalls, 1981; Now and Then, 1981, Where Grief Slumbers, 1982, Cornet, 1984; guest composer-in-residence, Princeton U. Seminar in Advanced Studies in Music, 1960, Hartt Coll., 1963, Brandeis U., 1966, Marlboro Music Festival, Dartmouth Festival of Arts, 1971, Tanglewood, 1972, Marlboro Music Festival, 1982; Commns., Fromm Found., 1958, 60, Ingram Merrill Found., 1965, Koussevitsky Found., 1973, Walter W. Naumberg Found., 1976, U. Chgo., 1981, Hartford Symphony, 1984; recs. include: Violin Concerto. Served to capt. USAAF, 1942-46. Recipient Prix de Paris U. Calif., Berkeley, 1947-49, Nat. Inst. Arts and Letters award, 1965, Creative Arts award Brandeis U., 1971, Mark Horblit award Boston Symphony, 1983; Guggenheim Found. fellow, 1956-57; Nat. Endowment for Arts fellow, 1975, 77, 79, 81, 83. Office: Paine Hall 22 Music Dept Harvard U Cambridge MA 02138

KIM, ILPYONG JOHN, educator; b. Seoul, Korea, Aug. 15, 1931; came to U.S., 1954, naturalized, 1964; s. Suk Dae and Ui-Bong K.; m. Hyunyong Chung, June 22, 1963; children—Irene, Katherene. M.A. (NDEA fellow), Columbia U., 1962, Ph.D. (Internat. Devel. fellow), 1968. Asst. prof. govt. Ind. U., 1965-69; asso. prof. polit. sci. U. Conn., Storrs, 1970-75, prof., 1976—; Fulbright prof. internat. relations U. Tokyo, 1976—. Author: The Politics of Chinese Communism, 1973, Communist Politics in North Korea, 1975; editorial bd.: Asian Thought and Soc, 1973-75. Served with UN Forces, 1950-54; Korea. Decorated Bronze Star. Mem. Am. Polit. Sci. Assn., Assn. Asian Studies, Internat. Studies Assn., New Eng. Assn. Asian Studies (v.p. 1977-78, pres. 1978-79), Pi Sigma Alpha. Home: 61 Hollyndale Rd Storrs CT 06268 Office: Dept Polit Sci U Conn Storrs CT 06268

KIM, JAEGWON, educator; b. Taegu, Korea, Sept. 12, 1934; came to U.S., 1955, naturalized, 1966; s. Yongkyu and Hakjo (Lee) K.; m. Sylvia Hughes, June 18, 1961; 1 son, Justin Lee. A.B., Dartmouth Coll., 1958; Ph.D., Princeton U., 1962. Instr. philosophy Swarthmore Coll., 1961-63; asst. prof. philosophy Brown U., 1963-67, vis. prof., 1975; asso. prof. U. Mich., 1967-70, prof., 1971—, chmn. dept. philosophy, 1979—; asso. prof. Cornell U., 1970-71; prof. Johns Hopkins U., 1977-78; vis. prof. Stanford U., 1967. Contbr. numerous articles to profl. publs.; editor: (with Alvin I. Goldman) Values and Morals, 1978. Fellow, Am. Council Learned Socs, 1980-81; NSF grantee, 1977-79. Mem. Am. Philos. Assn. (chmn. com. on status and future of profession 1976-81, bd. officers 1976-81), Philosophy of Sci. Assn. (governing bd. 1979-81), Council Philos. Studies, Phi Beta Kappa. Home: 2019 Seneca Ave Ann Arbor MI 48104 Office: Dept Philosophy U Mich Ann Arbor MI 48109

KIM, JAI SOO, physics educator; b. Taegu, Korea, Nov. 1, 1925; came to U.S., 1958, naturalized, 1963; s. Wan Sup and Chanam (Whang) K.; m. Hai Kyou Kim, Nov. 2, 1952; children: Kami, Tomi, Kihyun, Himi. B.Sc. in Physics, Seoul Nat. U., Korea, 1949, M.S., U. Sask., Can., 1957, Ph.D., 1958. Asst. prof. physics Clarkson Coll. Tech., Potsdam, N.Y., 1958-59; asst. prof. physics U. Idaho, Moscow, 1959-62, assoc. prof., 1962-65, prof., 1965-67; prof. atmospheric sci. and physics SUNY, Albany, 1967—, chmn. dept. atmospheric sci., 1969-76, rep. Univ. Corp. for Atmospheric Research, 1970-76; dir. Korean Studies Program SUNY, Stony Brook, 1983—; vis. prof. Advanced Inst. Sci. and Tech., Seoul, Korea, 1983; cons. U.S. Army Research Office, 1978-79, Battelle Meml. Inst., 1978-81, Environ. One Corp., 1978—, N.Y. State Environ. Conservation Dept., 1976-82, Norlite Corp., 1982—. Contbr. articles to profl. jours. Mem. Am. Inst. Physics, Am. Geophys. Union, Sigma Xi. Home: 33 Folmsbee Dr Menands NY 12204 Office: 1400 Washington Ave Albany NY 12222

KIM, JAMES JOO-JIN, electronics company executive; b. Seoul, Korea, Jan. 8, 1936; came to U.S., 1955, naturalized, 1971; s. Hyang-Soo and Seung-Ye (Oh) K.; m. Agnes Chungsook Kil, Dec. 30, 1961; children—Susan, David, John. Student, Seoul Nat. U. Coll. Law, 1954-55; B.S., U. Pa., 1959, M.A., 1961, postgrad., 1961-63. Instr. Pa. Mil. Coll. (now Widener Coll.), Chester, 1960; teaching fellow Wharton Sch., U. Pa., Phila., 1961-63; asst. prof. econs. Villanova (Pa.) U.,

1964-70; founder, pres. AMKOR Electronics, Inc., Valley Forge, Pa., 1970-80, chmn., chief exec. officer, 1980—; dir. The Electronics Boutique, Inc., VLSI Tech., Inc. Active Korean Assn. Greater Phila., 1973-79, trustee, 1977; chmn. Korean Catholic Community, Shipley Sch. Ann. Giving Fund, 1978. Recipient award Pres. Park/Chung Hee, Korea, 1979. Roman Catholic. Club: Wharton. Office: AMKOR Electronics Inc PO Box 801 Valley Forge PA 19482

KIM, MOON HYUN, physician, educator; b. Seoul, Korea, Nov. 30, 1934; s. Jae Hang and Kum Chu (Choi) K.; m. Yong Cha Pak, June 20, 1964; children: Peter, Edward. M.D., Yonsei U., 1960. Diplomate: Am. Bd. Ob-Gyn. (examiner 1979—). Sr. instr. Ob-Gyn Yonsei U., Seoul, 1967-68; intern Md. Gen. Hosp., Balt., 1961-62; resident in Ob-Gyn Cleve. Met. Gen. Hosp., 1962-66; fellow in reproductive endocrinology U. Wash., Seattle, 1966-67, U. Toronto, Ont., Can., 1968-70; asst. prof. Ob-Gyn, also chief endocrinology and infertility U. Chgo., 1970-74; asso. prof. Ob-Gyn Ohio State U., Columbus, 1974-78, prof., 1978—, chief div. reproductive endocrinology, 1974—, vice chmn. dept. ob-gyn. Contbg. author books; contbr. articles to profl. jours. Recipient McClintock award U. Chgo., 1975; named Prof. of Yr. Ohio State U., 1976; recipient Clin. Teaching award, 1980. Fellow Am. Coll. Ob-Gyn; mem. Korean Med. Assn., Am. Fertility Soc., Chgo. Gynecol. Soc., Endocrine Soc., Soc. Study Reprodn., Soc. Gynecol. Investigation. Home: 4331 Donington Rd Columbus OH 43220 Office: 410 W 10th Ave N-613 Columbus OH 43210

KIM, RICHARD E., author, English language educator; b. Hamhung City, Korea, Mar. 13, 1932; naturalized, 1964; s. Chan-Doh and Ok-Hyun (Rhee) K.; m. Penelope Ann Groll, 1960; children: David, Melissa. Student, Middlebury (Vt.) Coll., 1955-59; M.A., Johns Hopkins U., 1960; M.F.A., State U. Iowa, 1962; M.A., Harvard, 1963. Instr. English Long Beach (Calif.) State Coll., 1963-64; asst. prof. English U. Mass. at Amherst, 1964-68, assoc. prof., 1968-69, adj. assoc. prof., 1969-; vis. prof. Syracuse U., 1970-71, San Diego State U., 1975-77. Author: The Martyred, 1964, The Innocent, 1968, Lost Names, 51970. Served to 1st lt. Republic of Korea Army, 1950-54. Ford Found. fellow, 1962; Guggenheim fellow, 1965; Nat. Endoment Arts fellow, 1978; Fulbright scholar Seoul Nat. U., 1981-83. Address: Leverett Rd Shutesbury MA 01072

KIM, SUNG-HOU, chemistry educator, biophysical and biological chemist; b. Taegu, Korea, Dec. 12, 1937; s. Yong-Tai and Ok-Kum (Choi) K.; m. Rosalind Yuan, July 27, 1968; children: Christopher Sang Jai, Jonathan Sang-Joon. B.S., Seoul Nat. U., 1960, M.S., 1962; Ph.D., U. Pitts., 1966. Teaching asst. in chemistry Seoul Nat. U., 1960-62; lectr. chemistry Kun-Kook U., Seoul, 1960-62; research asst. dept. crystallography U. Pitts., 1963-66; research assoc. MIT, Cambridge, 1966-70, sr. research scientist, 1970-72; asst. prof. Duke U., Durham, N.C., 1972-73, assoc. prof., 1974-78, Miller research prof., 1983-84; faculty sr. scientist Lawrence Berrkeley Lab., 1979—; exchange prof. Peking U., 1982; mem. adv. group biophysics and biophys. chemistry A Study sect. NIH, 1976-80; co-chmn. nucleic acids Gordon Research Conf., 1983; chmn. curriculum planning com. U.S. Nat. Com. for Crystallography, 1983-84. Contbr. numerous articles to sci. jours.; mem. editorial bd.: Jour. Biol. Chemistry, 1979-83, Nucleic Acid Research, 1983—. Recipient Sidhu award Pitts. Diffraction Conf., 1970, Research Career Devel. award NIH, 1976-79; Woo-Nam scholar Woo-Nam Found., Korea, 1959; Fulbright fellow, 1962; Lansdown scholar U. Victoria, 1980. Mem. Am. Soc. Biol. Chemists, Am. Chem. Soc., Am. Crystallographic Assn., AAAS, Korean Scientists and Engrs. in Am. Home: 1100 Larch Ave Moraga CA 94556 Office: Dept Chemistry U Calif Berkeley CA 94720

KIM, THOMAS KUNHYUK, coll. pres.; b. Shanghai, China, Feb. 18, 1929; came to U.S., 1948, naturalized, 1960; s. Hong Suh and Chong (Kim) K.; m. Martha Alice Zoellers, June 4, 1958; children—Lawrence Thomas, Catherine Ann. B.A., Berea Coll., 1952; M.B.A., Ind. U., 1954; Ph.D., Tulane U., 1961; L.H.D., Southwestern U., 1973. Asst. prof. econs. U. Akron, O., 1961-62; asso. prof. Baker U., Baldwin, Kans., 1962-65; prof. Tex. Tech. U., Lubbock, 1965-70; pres. McMurry Coll., Abilene, Tex., 1970—. Author: Introductory Mathematics for Economic Analysis, 1971. Mem. Phi Kappa Phi, Omicron Delta Epsilon. Methodist (del. gen. conf. 1972). Office: S 14th and Sayles Blvd McMurry Station Abilene TX 79697 *

KIM, WAN HEE, engineering educator; b. Osan, Korea, May 24, 1926; came to U.S., 1953, naturalized, 1962; s. Sang Chul and Cuck Hyung (Chong) K.; m. Chung Sook Noh, Jan. 23, 1960; children: Millie, Richard K. B.E., Seoul Nat. U., 1950; M.S. in Elec. Engring, U. Utah, 1954, Ph.D., 1956. Research asst. U. Ill. at Urbana, 1955-56; research staff IBM Research Center, Poughkeepsie, N.Y., 1956-57; asst. prof. Columbia U., N.Y.C., 1957-59, asso. prof., 1959-63, prof. elec. engring., 1963-78; Chmn. Tech. Cons., Inc., N.Y.C., 1962-69; chmn. KOMKOR Am., Inc., N.Y.C., 1970-72; Spl. cons. for Govt. Korea, 1967-69; adviser Korea Advanced Inst. Sci., Seoul, 1971-73; chmn. Korea Inst. Electronics Tech., 1977—; mem. bd. Korea Telecommunication Electric Research Inst., 1977—; pres. WHK Engring. Corp. Am., 1982—, WHK Electronics Inc., 1982—; chmn., chief exec. officer Industries Assn. Electronic Korea, 1978-81; chmn. KONTEC Corp., 1984—; pres. Asian Electronics Union, 1979-83; pub. Electronic Times of Korea, 1982—; cons. The World Bank, Washington, other indsl. orgns. Author: (with R.T. Chien) Topological Analysis and Synthesis of Communication Networks, 1962, (with M. Kawakami) Active Networks-Theory and Applications, 1969, (with H.E. Meadows) Modern Network Analysis, 1970; also numerous articles. U.S. rep. on U.S.-Japan Scientists Coop. Program.; trustee U.S.-ASIA Inst., Washington, 1984—. Served with Korean Army, 1950-53. Decorated Bronze Star.; Guggenheim grantee, 1964; NSF research grantee, 1958—. Fellow IEEE, Union Radio Scientifique Internat. (mem. U.S. nat. com. Commn. Band C 1963-78), Sigma Xi, Tau Beta Pi. Called the father of Korean electronics industry for his contbrn. to promotion of industry. Home: 282 Woodland St Tenafly NJ 07670 Home: 459 Homer Ave Palo Alto CA 94301 Office: Yoido PO Box 614 Seoul Korea *Be prepared five minutes earlier than others.*

KIM, YONG CHOON, philosopher, educator; b. Kyongju, Korea, June 1, 1935; came to U.S., 1958, naturalized, 1972; s. Chang Ho and Chung Ja (Choe) K.; m. Joyce Chungja Whang, Dec. 18, 1965; 1 dau., Grace. B.A., Belhaven Coll., Jackson, Miss., 1960; Th.M., Westminster Theol. Sem., Phila., 1964; Ph.D., Temple U., 1969. Asst. prof. Asian studies York Coll., Pa., 1969-70; asst. prof. philosophy and religion Cleve. State U., 1970-71; asst. prof. plhilosophy U. R.I., Kingston, 1971-74, assoc. prof., 974-79, prof., 1979—; founder, dir. Korean-Am. Christian Studies Inst., 1981—. Author: Oriental Thought, 1973, The Ch'ondogyo Concept of Man: An Essence of Korean Thought, 1978. Korean Culture and Arts Found. grantee, 1977. Mem. Assn. Asian Studies, Am. Acad. Religion, Soc. for Asian and Comparative Philosophy, Internat. Soc. Study of Korean Thought, AAUP. Home: 58 Parkwood Dr Kingston RI 02881 Office: Dept Philosophy Univ RI Kingston RI 02881 *Faith in God, hope for better future, intelligent application of talent, dilligence, and dedication forthe good of mankind are some of the principles, ideas, and goals of my life.*

KIM, YOON BERM, immunologist, educator; b. Soon Chun, Korea, Apr. 25, 1929; s. Sang Sun and Yang Rang (Lee) K.; m. Soon Cha Kim, Feb. 23, 1959; children: John, Jean, Paul. M.D., Seoul Nat. U., 1958; Ph.D., U. Minn., 1965. Intern Univ. Hosp. Seoul Nat. U., 1958-59; mem. faculty U. Minn., Mpls., 1960-73, assoc. prof. microbiology, 1970-73; mem., head lab. ontogeny of immune system Sloan Kettering Inst. Cancer Research, Rye, N.Y., 1973-83; prof. immunology Cornell U. Grad. Sch. Med. Scis., N.Y.C., 1973-83, chmn. immunology unit, 1980-82; prof. microbiology, immumology and medicine, chmn. dept. micorbiology and immunology U. Health Scis., Chgo. Med. Sch., 1983—; m. Lobund adv. bd. U. Notre Dame, 1977—. Contbr. numerous articles on immunology to profl. jours. Recipient research career devel. award USPHS, 1968-73. Mem. Assn. Gnotobiotics (pres.), Am. Assn. Immunologists, Am. Soc. Microbiology, Am. Assn. Pathologists, AAAS, Korean Med. Assn. Am., N.Y. Acad. Scis., Reticuloendothelial Soc., Internat. Soc. Devel. Comparative Immunology, Harvey Soc., Sigma Xi. Research on ontogeny and regulation of immune system, immunochemistry and biology of bacterial toxins, host-parasite relationships and gnotobiology. Home: 313 Weatherford Ct Lake Bluff IL 60044 Office: 3333 Green Bay Rd North Chicago IL 60064

KIMATIAN, STEPHEN H., lawyer, broadcasting executive, writer; b. N.Y.C., Oct. 19, 1941; s. Eli P. and Lucille (Ourganian) K.; m. Janet G.Serabian, June 21, 1964; children: Stephen, Ellen. A.B., Princeton U., 1963; J.D., Cornell U., 1966. Bar: N.Y. 1966, Md. 1978. Asso. firm O'Donnell & Schwartz, N.Y.C., 1967-70; dir. employee and labor relations Westinghouse Broadcasting Learning and Leisure Time Co., 1970-75; exec. adminstr. Sta. WJZ-TV, Balt., 1975-76, v.p., gen. mgr., 1976-78, area vice chmn., 1978-79; practice law, 1979—; partner Hooper Kiefer & Cornell, 1981—; trustee U.S. Bankruptcy Ct., Dist. Md.; health claims arbitrator, State of Md.; sec. Westinghouse Broadcasting Co., Inc. Bd. dirs., vice chmn. Balt. Urban League; chmn. bd. Balt. Broadcast Skills Bank; bd. dirs. Balt. area council Boy Scouts Am., Health and Welfare Council Central Md., Balt. Goodwill Industries, NCCJ; chmn. bd. trustees Community Coll. Balt.; judge Md. Humanities Journalism Award; pres. Md. Pub. Broadcasting Found. Mem. Bar Assn. City of Balt. (exec. council). Armenian Orthodox. Home: 215 Northway Baltimore MD 21218 Office: 343 N Charles St Baltimore MD 21201 *If you can state the problem, you can solve it.*

KIMBALL, ALLYN WINTHROP, educator; b. Buffalo, Oct. 2, 1921; s. Allyn Winthrop and Ethel (Manson) K.; m. Evelyn Marie Lay, June 16, 1944; children—Keith Allan, Lynn Ellen. B.S., U. Buffalo, 1943; postgrad., Mass. Inst. Tech., 1943; Ph.D., N.C. State Coll., 1950. Exptl. statistician USAF Sch. Aviation Medicine, Randolph Field, Tex., 1948-50; chief statistics sect., mathematics panel Oak Ridge Nat. Lab., 1950-60; prof. statistics and biostatistics Johns Hopkins, 1960—, chmn. dept. biostatistics, 1960-66, dean faculty arts and scis., 1966-70. Contbr. papers sci. lit. Trustee Asso. Univ., Inc., 1962—. Served from ensign to lt. USNR, 1943-46. Fellow A.A.A.S., Am. Statis. Assn.; mem. Biometric Soc., Am. Math. Soc., Inst. Math. Statistics. Home: 1106 Hampton Garth Towson MD 21204 Office: Johns Hopkins U Baltimore MD 21205

KIMBALL, AUBREY PIERCE, biochemistry educator; b. Lufkin, Tex., Oct. 20, 1926; s. Aubrey Joseph and Eula Bernice (Pixley) K.; m. Kay Tabor, Mar. 29, 1975; children by previous marriage: Kathleen, Erin, Lisa. B.S., U. Houston, 1958, Ph.D., 1961; postdoctoral, Stanford Research Inst., 1961-62. Research biochemist Stanford Research Inst., 1962-67; asso. prof. biochemistry U. Houston, 1967-72, prof., 1972—, planning dir. central campus cancer program, 1976—, chmn. dept. biophys. scis., 1977-78. Editor: (with J. Oro) Prebiotic and Biochemical Evolution, 1972; contbr. articles to sci. jours. Served with USNR, 1944-46, 50-52. Roche fellow, 1952-54; Robert A. Welch grantee, 1968—; NIH grantee, 1969—; recipient SW Lit. award for fiction, 1958. Fellow Am. Inst. Chemists, N.Y. Acad. Scis.; mem. Tex. Inst. Chemists (pres.), Am. Chem. Soc., Am. Assn. Cancer Research, Soc. Exptl. Biology and Medicine, Am. Soc. Biol. Chemists, S.W. Sci. Forum (dir. 1976—, pres. 1981-82, vice chmn. sci. and pub. policy), AAAS, Sigma Xi (pres. U. Houston chpt. 1981-82). Home: 1501 Bonnie Brae Houston TX 77006 *The goal of my research has always been directed to the development of anti-cancer drugs for the cure of childhood leukemias. This goal has been largely achieved where there is a 50-70% cure rate at present.*

KIMBALL, DAVID TENNEY, manufacturing company executive; b. Williams, Ariz., July 31, 1927; s. George W. and Marguerite (Vadeboncoeur) K.; m. Patricia Louise Brown, Sept. 8, 1948; children: Mary Lynette, Lori Ann, Leslie Sue, Caryn Louise. B.S., U. N.M., 1950; student exec. program, U. Calif. at Los Angeles, 1961-62. Supervisory engr. N. Am. Aviation, Downey, Calif., 1950-59; v.p., gen. mgr. Telecomputing Corp., Los Angeles, 1959; v.p., group exec. Whittaker Corp., Los Angeles, 1966-68; pres., dir. Tasker Industries, Los Angeles, 1968-73; pres., chief exec. officer, dir. Leeds & Northrup, 1973-79; pres., chief operating officer, dir. Gen. Signal Corp., 1980—; dir. Moore McCormack Resources, Inc., Pitney Bowes, Inc.; Mem. exec. com. Machinery and Allied Products Inst., 1974—. Mem. Defense Sci. Bd. Task Force on Export U.S. Technology, 1974—. Served with USNR, 1944-46. Recipient Balfour nat. award Sigma Chi, 1950. Mem. Phi Kappa Phi, Sigma Tau, Kappa Mu Epsilon, Sigma Chi. Republican. Roman Catholic. Clubs: Seaview Country, Shorehaven Golf, Ironwood Golf. Home: Point Rd Wilson Point Norwalk CT 06854 Office: High Ridge Park Stamford CT 06904

KIMBALL, EDWARD LAWRENCE, legal educator, lawyer; b. Safford, Ariz., Sept. 23, 1930; s. Spencer Woolley and Camilla (Eyring) K.; m. Evelyn Bee Madsen, June 9, 1954; children: Christian Edward, Paula, Mary, Miles Spencer, Jordan Andrew, Joseph Ellsworth, Sarah Camilla. B.S., U. Utah, 1953; LL.B., 1955; LL.M., U. Pa., 1959, S.J.D., 1962. Bar: Utah 1955, Wis. 1971. Law clk. Utah Supreme Ct., 1955; mem. faculty U. Mont., 1956-62, asso. prof. law, 1960-62; mem. faculty U. Wis. at Madison, 1962-73, prof. law, 1967-73, Brigham Young U., Provo, Utah, 1973—, Wilkinson prof. law, 1982—. Author: (with others) Criminal Justice Administration, 1969, rev. edit., 1982, Spencer W. Kimball, 1977, Programmed Materials on Problems in Evidence, 1978, Camilla, 1980, The Teachings of Spencer W. Kimball, 1982; Editorial bd.: Brigham Young U. Studies, 1970-75, The Carpenter, 1969-73. Mem. spl. rev. bd. Wis. Dept. Health and Social Services, 1970-73; mem. Utah Bd. Pardons and Paroles, 1979-83; dist. committeeman Four Lakes council Boy Scouts Am., 1965-72. Bicentennial fellow U. Pa., 1955-56; Rockefeller fellow U. Wis., 1961-62. Mem. Utah Bar Assn., Order of Coif, Phi Beta Kappa, Phi Kappa Phi, Lambda Delta Sigma, Delta Phi Kappa, Phi Delta Phi. Mem. Ch. Jesus Christ Latter-day Saints (bishop). Address: Brigham Young U Law School Provo UT 84602

KIMBALL, HAROLD GUFFEY, government official; b. Detroit, Nov. 28, 1931; s. Hugh J. and Agnes (Guffey) K.; m. Carolyn Amm, Mar. 24, 1979; children: Kimberly Anne, David Wayne, Douglas Harold; 1 stepdau., Carol Lynn. B.S. in Elec. Engring, Wayne State U., Detroit, 1955; M.S., U. Ill., Urbana, 1958. Civilian engr. USAF, Wright-Patterson AFB, Ohio, 1961-62; elec. engr. Electromagnetic Compatibility Analysis Center, Ill. Inst. Tech. Research Inst., Annapolis, Md., 1962-72; with Office of Telecommunications, Dept. of Commerce, Washington, 1972-78; dir. communications and data systems div. Office Space Tracking and Data Systems, NASA, 1978—; mem. industry/govt. adv. council on telecommunication George Washington U.; internat. vice chmn. CCIR study group 2 on space research; internat. radio cons. com. Internat. Telecommunications Union, U.S. del. Plenipotentiary Conf., 1982; chmn. U.S. study group 2, U.S. nat. com. CCIR; U.S. del. World Adminstrv. Radio Conf., 1979. Served as officer USAF, 1955-61. Recipient Creative Mgmt. award NASA, 1979, Outstanding Leadership medal, 1980. Mem. AIAA, Armed Forces Communications and Electronics Assn. Home: 1627 Comanche Rd Arnold MD 21012 Office: Hdqrs NASA Code TS Washington DC 20546

KIMBALL, LINDSLEY FISKE, retired foundation executive; b. Bklyn., N.Y., Nov. 27, 1894; s. Francis Tappan and Susie (Williams) K.; m. Maude Ryder Kouwenhoven, Sept. 9, 1926; children—Richard T., Dean F. A.B., Columbia U., 1917; Ph.D., N.Y. U., 1930; LL.D., Hobart and William Smith Colls., 1959, Xavier U., 1968; D.Sc., Rockefeller U., 1976. Asst. to v.p. Underwood Typewriter, 1919-24, Boy Scouts Am., 1924-38; dir. corps and spl. gifts Greater N.Y. Fund, 1938-42; cons. to pres. United Service Orgn., 1942-43, adminstrv. v.p., 1943-45, pres., 1945-49, 51-52; v.p. Rockefeller Found., 1949-53, exec. v.p., 1953-60; trustee Rockefeller U., 1947-71, treas., 1959-65, asst. to chmn. bd., 1971-75; v.p., dir. Gen. Edn. Board, Bd., 1959-60; mem. distbn. com. N.Y. Community Trust.; Cons. Nat. Indsl. Conf. Bd.; Mem. Wartime Joint Army and Navy Com. on Welfare and Recreation. Assoc. with Rockefeller Bros. Fund; trustee Nat. Urban League, Inc., 1959-68; pres. Nat. Urban League, 1964-68; trustee Sealantic Fund; mem. exec. bd. A.R.C. Greater N.Y.; v.p., mem. exec. com. Community Blood Council of Greater N.Y.; chmn. devel. com. N.Y. Blood Center and Lindsley F. Kimball Research Inst., 1st. v.p., 1964—; dir., mem. exec. com. United Negro Coll. Fund; vice chmn. N.AM. adminstrv. com. World Council of Christian Edn; bd. dirs. Vets. Hosp. Camp Shows; trustee Sleepy Hollow Restoration; chmn. civilian com. on welfare and recreation Dept. Def., 1948; vice chmn. dirs., finance com. Council on Founds.; trustee, treas. States Urban Action Center; mem. adv. com. Urban America; mem. Pres.'s Com. Religion Welfare in Armed Forces. Awarded Joint Army and Navy citation; Presdl. award of Medal for Merit, 1946. Republican. Conglist. Clubs: Century Association, Rockefeller Center Luncheon, Hemisphere (N.Y.C.); Sands Point Bath and Tennis. Inventor math. device used by USN. Home: Fell 102 Pennswood Village Newtown PA 18940

KIMBALL, PENN TOWNSEND, II, educator, journalist; b. New Britain, Conn., Oct 12, 1915; s. Arthur G. and Effie (Smallen) K.; m. Janet Evelyn Fraser, Apr. 8, 1947; 1 dau., Elisabeth K. Carlson. B.A., Princeton U., 1937; B.A., M.A., Balliol Coll., Oxford (Eng.) U., 1939, 46; postgrad., Yale U., 1950-51, Columbia, 1951-58. Reporter U.S. News and World Report, 1939-40, PM Newspaper, 1940-41; contbg. editor Time mag., 1945-46; sr. editor New Republic, 1947; adminstrv. asst. to Gov. Bowles of Conn., 1948-49; exec. sec. U.S. Senator Benton, 1949-50; asst. to Sunday editor N.Y. Times, 1951-54; with TV Radio Workshop, Ford Found., 1954-55; sr. editor Colliers, 1955-56; partner Louis Harris & Assos., N.Y.C., 1957-58; adminstrv. asst. to Gov. Harriman of N.Y., 1958; prof. Columbia Grad. Sch. Journalism, 1959—; mem. adminstrv. bd. Bur. Applied Social Research, 1963-67; cons. editor Harris Survey, 1963-74; faculty Salzburg (Austria) Seminar in Am. Studies, 1967; vis. lectr. Dartmouth, U. Calif. at Berkeley, U. Conn. Author: Bobby Kennedy and The New Politics, 1968, The Disconnected, 1972, The File, 1983; also articles in nat. magazines.; Bd. editors: Columbia Journalism Rev, 1963—. Sec. com. on appropriations Conn. Gen. Assembly, 1949, mem. citizens commn., 1968-69; mem. bd. finance, Westport, Conn., 1953-55, mem. charter commn., 1957, justice of peace, 1959-60, rep. town meeting, 1959-63; mem. Conn. Constl. Conv., 1965; faculty Nat. Urban Fellows summer program Yale, 1969-70; dir. pub. affairs Urban Devel. Corp., State N.Y., 1971-72; mem. nat. adv. com. election systems project Nat. Municipal League-League Women Voters, 1971-73; asst. dir. S. Bronx Devel. Office, 1979-80. Served to capt. USMCR, 1941-45; PTO; maj. Res. (ret.). Rhodes Scholar, 1937-39. Mem. Am. Assn. Pub. Opinion Research, Phi Beta Kappa. Democrat. Conglist. Club: National Press (Washington). Home: Box 240 Chilmark MA 02535 Office: Columbia Sch Journalism 116th and Broadway New York NY 10027

KIMBALL, RAYMOND ALONZO, commercial association executive; b. Kanosh, Utah, Apr. 1918; s. Abraham A. and Mary Jane (Gardner) K.; m. Adrus Hansen, Sept. 30, 1943; children: Kristine Kimball Harris, Diane Kimball Wilcox, Teo Kimball Winterrose, Colette Kimball Rolandelli, Melanie Kimball Shaha. Student, So. Utah State Coll., 1939; B.S., Utah State U., 1941; M.S., (Sloan fellow), U. Denver, 1946; postgrad., Stanford U., 1951-52. Research dir. Colo Pub. Expenditure Council, Denver, 1948-53; exec. dir. Colo. Pub. Expenditure Council, Denver, 1954-58; asst. tax commr. Colo Fuel & Iron c; asst. to pres. Denver Dry Goods Co., 1965-65; pres. Colo. Assn. Commerce and Industry, Denver, 1965—. Mem. White House Conf. Edn., 1956; mem. Com. Equality Ednl. Opportunity Denver pub. schs., 1963-64; stake patriarch Ch. of Jesus Christ of Latter-day Saints, 1965; pres. Littleton Stake, (Colo.), 1975-81; bd. dirs. Vis. Nurses Assn. Colo. Served to lt. USNR, 1942-45. Recipient Civis Princeps award Regis Coll., 1974, Disting. Service Alumnus award U. Denver, 1975; named Outstanding Citizen Denver Civitan Club, 1979. Mem. council Western Retail Assn. (pres. 1971-72), Mountain States Assn. (dir. 1967-68), Colo. C.of C. Execs. (pres. 1974-75), Colo. Soc. Assn. Execs. (pres. 1952-53). Club: City of Denver (pres. 1953-54). Lodge: Rotary. Home: 3228 E Fremont Dr Littleton CO 80122 Office: Colo C of C 1390 Logan St Suite 308 Denver CO 80203

KIMBALL, ROBERT ERIC, author; b. N.Y.C., Aug. 23, 1939; s. Morris Harold and Eve (Schulman) K.; m. Abigail Leon Kuflik, May 23, 1972; children: Philip Zachary, Miranda Erica. B.A., Yale U., 1961, LL.B., 1967. Carnegie teaching fellow Am. history Yale, 1961-62; legis. asst. to Rep. John V. Lindsay, 17th Congl. Dist. N.Y., 1962-63; dir. Republican Legis. Research Assn., 1963-64; curator Yale Collection of Lit. Am. Mus. Theatre, 1967-71; lectr. Am. studies Yale, 1970, 74; music, dance reviewer N.Y. Post, 1973-, Nat. Broadcasting Co., 1975-77; sr. research fellow, vis. prof. music Inst. for Studies in Am. Music, Bklyn. Coll., City U. N.Y., 1974-75; lectr. drama N.Y. U., 1979-80; lectr. music Yale U., 1980-81; cons. Goodspeed Opera House, 1974-75, 82—. Co-producer: Black Broadway, N.Y.C., 1979, 80; Author: Cole, 1971, (with William Bolcom) Reminiscing With Sissle and Blake, 1973, (with Alfred Simon) The Gershwins, 1973, The Unpublished Cole Porter, 1975, The Complete Lyrics of Cole Porter, 1983; Contbr. articles and revs. to periodicals and profl. jours.; (with Alfred Simon) liner notes for recs. Grove's Dictionary of Music. Prin. asst. to Republicans in U.S. Congress during passage of Civil Rights Act, 1964; v.p. Alwyn Ct. Tenants Assn. Mem. AFTRA, Theatre Library Assn., Phi Alpha Delta. Clubs: Dutch Treat, Elihu (v.p. 1979-80), Elihu (pres. 1980-82), Elizabethan of Yale, Freighter Travel of Am. Address: 180 W 58th St New York City NY 10019 *In striving to survive as a generalist in our increasingly specialized world, I have been guided and encouraged by these words from the Roman playwright Terence: "Homo sum; humani nil a me alienum puto"—I am a man, and consider nothing human alien to me.*

KIMBALL, ROLAND BALDWIN, educator; b. Manchester, N.H., Apr. 12, 1921; s. Richard Henry and Frieda Clara (Obst) K.; m. Charlotte Buecher, Apr. 12, 1943; children: Thomas Lloyd, Kenneth David, Scott Roland. B.S. in Math, U. N.H., 1942, M.Ed., 1949; Ed.D. (Charles Eliot scholar 1952-53), Harvard, 1958; John Hay fellow humanities, Williams Coll., 1960. Meteorologist Am. Airlines, Inc., 1946-47; tchr. math. Concord (N.H.) High Sch., 1947-54; dir.

secondary sch. services N.H. Dept. Edn., 1955-58, chief div. instrn., 1959-62; asso. prof. Stanford Sch. Edn., 1962-63; prof. edn. U. N.H., 1963—, chmn. dept., 1963-72, 78—, asst. dean, 1973-74, faculty fellow, 1977-78, interim dean, 1981—; cons. Nat. Endowment for Humanities, 1968, U.S. Dep. Schs., European Theater, 1968-70; adv. com. on tchr. edn. New Eng. Regional Commn., 1968-69; mem. Nat. Humanities Faculty, 1971—; Chmn. N.H. Comm. Maths. and Sci., 1957-60, N.H. Com. Improvement Instrn. in English, 1960-62; bd. govs. New Eng. Ednl. Data System, 1961-69; trustee N.H. Higher Edn. Assistance Found., 1963-68; bd. dirs. N.H. Council Better Schs., 1962-69, 72-75, Eastern Ednl. TV Network, 1961; chmn. N.H. Council for Tchr. Edn., 1965-68; state liaison rep. Am. Assn. Colls. Tchr. Edn., 1983—. Co-author: Education for Effective Thinking, 1960; Contbr. profl. jours. Mem. adv. com. on edn. N.H. Charitable Fund, 1966-70; mem. Gov.'s Com. on Econ. Opportunity, 1965-69; bd. dirs. Corp. Council on Critical Skills, 1983—. Served with USAAF, 1942-46; mem. Res. (ret.). Decorated Air Force Commendation ribbon. Mem. Com. Profs. Secondary Sch. Adminstrn. and Supervision, Am. Ednl. Research Assn., Phi Kappa Phi, Kappa Delta Pi, Phi Delta Kappa. Home: Riverview Rd Durham NH 03824 Office: Dept Edn Univ New Hampshire Durham NH 03824

KIMBALL, SPENCER WOOLLEY, clergyman; b. Salt Lake City, Mar. 28, 1895; s. Andrew and Olive (Woolley) K.; m. Camilla Eyring, Nov. 17, 1917; children: Spencer LeVan, Olive Beth (Mrs. Grant M. Mack), Andrew Eyring, Edward Lawrence. Student, Gila Jr. Coll., 1910-14, Brigham Young U., 1917, U. Ariz., 1917; LL.D., Brigham Young U., 1969. Mem. Council of Twelve Apostles of the Ch. of Jesus Christ of Latter-day Saints, 1943—, now pres.; on mission, Mo., 1914-16; pres. Seventies Quorum, stake clk., Thatcher, Ariz., 1918-38; counselor St. Joseph Stake Presidency, 1924-36; pres. Mt. Graham Stake, 1938-43; teller, clk. later asst. cashier Ariz. Trust & Sav. Bank, Safford, 1918-23; Bank of Safford, 1923-26; pres., mgr. Kimball Greenhalgh Ins. & Realty Co., Safford, Ariz., 1927-43; sec. Gila Valley Irrigation Co., 1935-43; organizer, part owner Gila Broadcasting Co., Safford, 1935—. Mem. Ariz. Assn. Tchrs. Retirement Bd., Thatcher and Safford (Ariz.) city councils; bd. dirs. A.R.C., Safford; chmn. war fund drives; trustee Gila Coll.; Mem. Boy Scouts Am. Clubs: Rotary Internat. (dist. gov.); Rotary (Safford) (pres.). Office: 50 E North Temple St Salt Lake CIty UT 84150 *

KIMBALL, WARREN FORBES, history educator; b. Bklyn., Dec. 24, 1935; s. Cyril Steere and Carolyn Shepley (Forbes) K.; m. Jacqueline Sue Nelson; children: Paula Marie, Thomas Patrick, Donna Grace. B.A., Villanova U., 1958; M.A., Georgetown U., 1965, Ph.D., 1968. Instr. U.S. Naval Acad., 1961-65; asst. prof. Georgetown U., 1965-67, U. Ga., 1967-70; assoc. prof. history Rutgers U., 1970-75, prof., 1975—. Author: The Most Unsordid Act: Lend-Lease, 1969, The Complete Churchill-Roosevelt Correspondence, 3 vols., 1984. Served with USNR, 1958-65. Fulbright sr. lectr. U. Madrid, Spain, 1975-76. Mem. Am. Hist. Assn., Orgn. Am. Historians, Soc. for Historians Am. Fgn. Relations. Home: 19 Larsen Rd Somerset NJ 08873 Office: Dept History Rutgers U Newark NJ 07102

KIMBERLING, JOHN FARRELL, lawyer; b. Shelbyville, Ind., Nov. 15, 1926; s. James Farrell and Phyllis (Casady) K. Student, Purdue U., 1945-46; A.B., Ind. U., 1947, J.D., 1950. Bar: Ind. 1950, Calif. 1954. Practiced in, Muncie, Ind., 1950-51, Los Angeles, 1953—; asso. firm Bracken, Gray, DeFur & Voran, 1950-51, Lillick McHose & Charles, and predecessor firms, 1953—, partner, 1963—; Dir. Mitsui Bank of Calif. Served from ensign to lt. (j.g.) USNR, 1951-53. Fellow Am. Coll. Trial Lawyers; mem. Am. Bar Assn., Los Angeles Bar Assn., State Bar Calif., Maritime Law Assn. U.S., Los Angeles Jr. C. of C. (past pres.), Beta Theta Pi, Phi Delta Phi. Republican. Clubs: California, Chancery. Home: 2127 Beech Knoll Rd Los Angeles CA 90046 Office: 707 Wilshire Blvd Los Angeles CA 90017 *My goal in life is and has been to do the very best of which I am capable in my professional life and in helping to make my community a better place in which to work and live.*

KIMBLE, GREGORY ADAMS, educator; b. Mason City, Iowa, Oct. 21, 1917; s. Howard and Iola (Adams) K.; m. Lucille Laird, Dec. 30, 1943; children: Jeffrey Laird, Judith Elisabeth. A.B., Carleton Coll., 1940; M.A., Northwestern U., 1942; Ph.D., State U. Iowa, 1945. Instr. to asst. prof. psychology Brown U., 1945-50; asst. prof. psychology Yale U., 1950-52; asso. prof. to prof. psychology Duke U., 1952-68, prof., chmn. dept. psychology, 1978—, U. Colo., 1968-75, prof. psychology, 1975-77; Chmn. exptl. psychology research review com. NIMH, 1968-71. Author: (with Dr. Norman Garmezy and Edward Zigler) Principles of General Psychology, 1956, 63, 68, 74, 80, 84, Conditioning and Learning, 1961, Foundations of Conditioning and Learning, 1967, How to Use (and Misuse) Statistics, 1978; Editor: Psychol. Monographs, 1962-65, Jour. Exptl. Psychology, 1975-83. Fellow AAAS, Am. Psychol. Assn. (past pres. div. exptl. psychology, div. gen. psychology, past chmn. policy and planning bd., mem. publs. bd. 1973-74, dir. 1980—); mem. Psychonomic Soc. (governing bd. 1963-67, 72-78), Soc. Exptl. Psychologists (sec.-treas. 1976-79), Eastern Psychol. Assn., Southeastern Psychol. Assn., Midwestern Psychol. Assn., Rocky Mountain Psychol. Assn. (past pres.), Sigma Xi, Phi Beta Kappa.

KIMBLE, WILLIAM EARL, lawyer; b. Denver, May 4, 1926; s. George Wilbur and Grace (Fick) K.; m. Jean M. Cayia, Dec. 27, 1950; children: Mark, Cary, Timothy, Stephen, Philip, Peter, Michael. LL.B., U. Ariz., 1951. Bar: Ariz. 1951. Spl. agt. FBI, 1951-52; practice in, Bisbee, 1952-60, Tucson, 1962—; judge Superior Ct. Ariz., 1960-62; partner firm Kimble, Gothreau, Nelson & Cannon, 1962—; Commr. Ariz. Oil and Gas Commn., 1958-60; adj. prof. law U. Ariz. Coll. Law, 1962—; spl. asst. atty. gen., Ariz., 1963-. Author: The Consumer Product Safety Act, 1973, Products Liability, 1977; Sr. editor: Consumer Products Alert newsletter, 1980-81. Republican nominee Ariz. atty. gen., 1956, U.S. Congress, 1964. Served with USNR, 1944-46. Mem. Sigma Chi, Phi Alpha Delta. Home: 95 Camino Miramonte Tucson AZ 85716 Office: 5151 E Broadway Tucson AZ 85712

KIMBREL, MONROE, banker; b. Miller County, Ga., Aug. 4, 1916; s. Charlie C. and Effie (Folds) K.; m. Nita Matlock, Apr. 17, 1941; children: Jenny Wood (Mrs. James Bunn III), Charles Daniel. B.S., U. Ga., 1936; grad., Stonier Grad., Sch. Banking, Rutgers U., 1949. With Farm Credit Adminstrn., Columbia, S.C., 1936-46; with First Nat. Bank, Thomson, Ga., 1946-65, chmn. bd., 1961-65; dir. Fed. Res. Bank, Atlanta, 1960-65, 1st v.p., 1965-68, pres., 1968-80; pres. Thomson Oak Flooring Co., Ga., 1979—; vice chmn. First R.R. & Banking Co. Ga., Augusta, 1980—. Mem. Am. Bankers Assn. (pres. 1962-63), Ga. Bankers Assn. (pres. 1956-57), U. Ga. Alumni Assn. (pres. 1970-73). Club: Rotarian (past dist. gov.). Home: Route 1 Box 6 Thomson GA 30824

KIMBRELL, HORACE WARREN, lawyer; b. Lees Summit, Mo., Apr. 19, 1916; s. Raymond Benefiel and Ruberta Katherine (Magers) K.; m. Ethel Young, Aug. 5, 1956. A.B., U. Kansas City, Mo., 1936, LL.B., 1939; L.H.D. (hon.), City U., Bellevue, Wash., 1982. Bar: Mo. 1939. Since practiced in, Kansas City; mem. staff U.S. atty. Western Dist. Mo., 1953-61; asst. gen. counsel Kansas City Life Ins. Co., 1961-72, asst. v.p., exec. adminstr. public affairs, 1972-76, asso. dir. public relations, 1976-78; public speaker and lectr., 1979—. Pres. Goodwill Industries Greater Kansas City, 1952-66, chmn. bd., 1966-76; pres. Goodwill Industries Am., Inc., 1961-66, chmn. bd., 1966-68, nat. ambassador, 1968—; sec. trustees U. Kansas City, 1949—; founder, trustee St. Paul Sch. Theology Methodist, Kansas City, 1958—. Served USNR, 1942-46. First recipient President's award U. Mo. System, 1982; recipient Chmn.'s award for outstanding vol. service Goodwill Industries Am., 1983. Mem. ABA, Fed. Bar Assn. (pres. Kansas City 1958, Earl Kintner award 1981), 8th circuit Bar Assn. (nat. v.p. 1965-67, mem. nat. council 1967—), Kansas City Bar Assn., Kansas City Lawyers Assn., Mo. Bar, Am. Judicature Soc., Nat. Lawyers Club (charter), Am. Soc. Internat. Law, Internat. Platform Assn., Navy League, State Hist. Soc. Mo. (life), World Order Through Law Center (charter). Republican. Methodist (ofel. bd., Sunday sch.(tchr.). Home and Office: 5900 E 129th St Grandview MO 64030

KIMBRELL, ODELL CULP, JR., physician; b. Spartanburg, S.C., May 2, 1927; s. Odell Culp and Leona (Nicholas) K.; children from former marriage: Odell Culp, Cynthia Anne. A.B., Duke U., 1947; M.D., U. Pa., 1951. Diplomate: Am. Bd. Internal Medicine. Intern Med. Coll. Va., Richmond, 1951-52, resident in internal medicine, 1954-56, VA Hosp., Phila., 1956-57; practice medicine specializing in internal medicine and endocrinology Gallipolis, Ohio, 1957-60, Raleigh, N.C., 1960—; mem. staff Wake County Hosp. System, Rex Hosp.; clin. prof. medicine U.N.C. Med. Sch., 1970—; med. dir. Occidental Life Ins. Co. N.C., Raleigh, 1967—. Contbr. articles to med. jours. Trustee Wake County Hosp. System Inc., Raleigh, 1971-81; sec. Wake County Hosp. System. Inc., Raleigh, 1973-74; pres. Wake County Hosp. System Inc., Raleigh, 1974-76; bd. dirs. Wake Health Facilities and Service Inc., 1975-81, pres., 1975-76; chmn. Wake County Heart Fund, 1961; deacon Hudson Meml. Presbyn. Ch., Raleigh, 1971-73. Served with USAF, 1952-54. Fellow ACP; mem. AMA, N.C. Med. Soc., Wake County Med Soc., Am. Soc. Internal Medicine, N.C. Soc. Internal Medicine, Raleigh Acad. Medicine, Assn. Life Ins. Med. Dirs. Am., Mid-Atlantic Med. Dirs. Club (pres. 1979-80). Democrat. Lodge: Lions. Home: 905 Hunting Ridge Rd Raleigh NC 27609 Office: Dr Odell Kinbrell 40 Bryan Bldg Raleigh NC 27605 *Serving through devoted application of mind, body and spirit.*

KIMBROUGH, EMILY (EMILY KIMBROUGH WRENCH), writer; b. Muncie., Ind., Oct. 23, 1899; d. Hal Curry and Charlotte Emily (Wiles) K.; m. John Wrench, Dec. 31, 1926; children—Margaret Achsah and Alis Emily (twins). B.A., Bryn Mawr Coll., 1921; student, The Sorbonne, Paris, 1922. Editor: Fashions of the Hour, Marshall Field & Co., Chgo., 1922-27; fashion editor: Ladies' Home Jour, 1927; mng. editor, 1927-29; writer, 1932—; Author: (with Cornelia Otis Skinner) Our Hearts Were Young and Gay, 1942, We Followed Our Hearts to Hollywood, 1943, How Dear to My Heart, 1944, It Gives Me Great Pleasure, 1948, The Innocents from Indiana, 1950, Through Charley's Door, 1952, Forty Plus and Fancy Free, 1954, So Near and Yet So Far, 1955, Water, Water Everywhere, 1956, And a Right Good Crew, 1958, Pleasure by the Busload, 1961, Forever Old, Forever New, 1964, Floating Island, 1968, Now and Then, 1972, Time Enough, 1974, Better Than Oceans, 1976. Home: 11 E 73d St New York NY 10021

KIMBROUGH, EMORY CALLOWAY LANDON, JR., educator, sociologist; b. Clarksville, Tenn., Nov. 15, 1934; s. Emory Calloway Landon and Martha (Beaumont) K. A.B., Davidson Coll., 1957; M.A. (Nat. Woodrow Wilson fellow), U. N.C., 1959; Ph.D. (So. fellow), U. N.C., 1963. Teaching fellow U. N.C, 1960-62; instr. sociology Washington and Lee U., Lexington, Va., 1962-63, asst. prof., 1963-66, asso. prof., 1966-69, prof., 1969—, chmn. dept. sociology and anthropology, 1967—. Fellow Am. Sociol. Assn.; mem. So. Sociol. Soc., Phi Beta Kappa, Beta Gamma Sigma, Alpha Tau Omega. Episcopalian. Home: 17 University Pl Lexington VA 24450

KIMBROUGH, ROBERT ALEXANDER, III, educator; b. Phila., June 26, 1929; s. R. A. and Agnes May (McComb) K.; m. Gertrude Bolling Alfriend, July 11, 1953 (div. Apr. 1976); children: Elisabeth, Robert, John; m. Phyllis Rose Woloshin, Mar. 20, 1977. B.A. with honors in English, Williams Coll., 1951; M.A., Stanford U., 1955; Ph.D., Harvard, 1959. Acting instr. Stanford (Calif.) U., 1954-55; teaching fellow and tutor Lowell House, Harvard, Cambridge, Mass., 1956-59; instr. U. Wis., Madison, 1959-60, asst. prof., 1960-64, asso. prof., 1964-68, prof., 1968—, departmental grad. adviser, 1961-68, chmn. dept. integrated liberal studies, 1970-75; pres. AFT Local 223. Author: Shakespeare's Troilus and Cressida and its Setting, 1964, Sir Philip Sidney, 1971; editor: Joseph Conrad, Heart of Darkness: An Authoritative Text, 1963, rev. edit., 1971, Henry James, The Turn of the Screw, 1966, Sir Philip Sidney: Selected Prose and Poetry, 1969, 2d edit., 1983; contbr. numerous articles and book reviews to scholarly jours. Served with USMCR, 1951-54; Korea; col. ret. Decorated Purple Heart, Bronze Star. Fellow Inst. Research in Humanities; mem. MLA, Renaissance Soc. Am., Shakespeare Assn. Am. Home: 3206 Gregory St Madison WI 53711 Office: Dept English Univ Wis 6181 Helen C White Hall Madison WI 53706

KIMBROUGH, WILLIAM ADAMS, JR., lawyer; b. Selma, Ala., July 21, 1935; s. William Adams and Elizabeth (Bradford) K.; m. Kay Lindsey, Dec. 28, 1958; children: Mary Elizabeth, William Adams. B.A. (Union Carbide scholar), U. of South, 1957; LL.B., U. Ala., 1961. Corr. Nat. Carbon Co., Chgo., 1957-58; mem. firm Lindsey & Christopher, Butler, Ala., 1961; asst. U.S. atty., 1962-65; gen. atty. Gulf, Mobile & Ohio R.R. Co., Mobile, Ala., 1965-70; mem. firm Stockman, Bedsole & Kimbrough, Mobile, 1970-76, Adams, Adams & Kimbrough, Grove Hill, Ala., 1976-77; U.S. atty. So. Dist. Ala., Mobile, 1977-81; mem. firm Turner, Onderdonk & Kimbrough, Chatom and Mobile, 1981—. Mem. Ala. State Democratic Exec. Com., 1966-70. Served with U.S. Army, 1958, 61-62. Mem. ABA, Ala., Mobile County, Clarke County bar assns., ICC Practitioners Assn., Omicron Delta Kappa. Methodist. Clubs: Bienville, Country of Mobile. Home: 4675 Old Shell Rd Mobile AL 36608 Office: PO Box 2821 Mobile AL 36652

KIMBROUGH, WILLIAM JOSEPH, librarian; b. Bowling Green, Ky., Apr. 21, 1930; s. William Joseph and Mary Alice (Sexton) K.; m. Ann Cecil Cornett, Nov. 25, 1954; children: Charles Madison, Howard David. A.B., Western Ky. U., 1952; M.A., Ind. U., 1956. Reference asst. Grosse Pointe (Mich.) Pub. Library, 1956-58; head librarian Sturgis (Mich.) Pub. Library, 1958-60; supr. adult services Lansing (Mich.) Pub. Library, 1960-65, chief librarian, 1965-69; asst. librarian, dir. pub. service Denver Pub. Library, 1970-75; dir. Mpls. Pub. Library and Information Center, 1975—. Editor: (with others) Requiem for the Card Catalog, 1979. Served to 1st lt. AUS, 1952-54. Mem. A.L.A. (past pres. library adminstrn. div.), Mich. Library Assn. (past pres.), Minn. Library Assn., Minn. Assn. Continuing and Adult Edn. (past pres.). Address: Mpls Pub Library 300 Nicollet Mall Minneapolis MN 55401

KIMEL, WILLIAM ROBERT, engineering educator; b. Cunningham, Kans., May 2, 1922; s. Chester LeRoy and Klonda Florence (Hart) K.; m. Mila D. Brown, Aug. 14, 1952. B.S.M.E., Kans. State U., 1944, M.S.M.E., 1949; Ph.D. in Engring. Mechanics (WARF fellow), U. Wis., 1956. Registered profl. engr., Kans., Mo. Research asso. Argonne (Ill.) Nat. Lab., 1957-58; engr. Boeing Airplane Co., summer 1953, Westinghouse Electric Co., summer 1954, U.S. Forest Products Lab., 1955-56; from instr. to asso. prof. mech. engring. Kans. State U., Manhattan, 1946-58; prof., head nuclear engring. dept., 1958-68; dean, dir. engring. expt. sta., prof. nuclear engring. U. Mo., Columbia, 1968—; Mem. Kans. Gov.'s Adv. Com. on Atomic Energy, 1961-68, chmn., 1966-68; mem. Mo. AEC, 1974-79, Argonne Nuclear Engring. Edn. Com., 1959—, chmn., 1966-67; cons. N.Y. Regents External Degree Program for Nuclear Tech. Contbr. articles to profl. jours. Mem. Columbia Area Indsl. Devel. Commn., 1970—, chmn., 1973-76; mem. adv. com. to Office of Civil Def., 1964-70, chmn., 1969-70; bd. dirs. Engring. Colls. Consortium for Minorities, 1974-80, v.p., 1974-75; bd. dirs. Jr. Engring. Tech. Soc., 1976—, chpt. pub. relations com. chmn., 1976-78, pres., 1980-81; mem. Gen. Public Utilities Rev. Com. to evaluate operator-accelerated retraining program, TMI, 1979-80; mem. task force to establish training, edn. and accreditation requirements for nuclear plant operators Inst. Nuclear Power Ops., 1981-82, mem. accreditation bd., 1982—; mem. Mo. Gov.'s Task Force on Low-Level Radioactive Waste, 1981—. Recipient Disting. Service award in engring. Kans. State U., 1972; Faculty Alumni award U. Mo., Columbia, 1979, Bliss award Am. Soc. Mil. Engrs., 1982; Disting. Service citation U. Wis. Coll. Engring., 1982. Fellow Am. Nuclear Soc. (chmn. edn. devel. com. 1963-66, 67-69, mem. exec. com. for tech. group edn. 1964-66, mem. planning com. 1966-75, chmn. 1970-74, mem. nominating com. 1969-70, 72-73, chmn. 79-80, exec. com. edn. div. 1968, chmn. edn. div. 1970-71, vice chmn. edn. div. 1969-70, dir. 1973-76, 77-81, exec. com. 1974-76, 77-79, mem. honors and awards com. 1975-78, engring. edn. and accreditation com. 1970-76, chmn. 1973, Governance award 1976, 77, 78, 79, 80, v.p and pres.-elect 1977-78, pres. 1978-79, mem. public policy com. 1979-80, mem. blue ribbon coms. 1976-78), ASME; mem. Am. Soc. Engring. Edn. (chmn. nuclear engring. div. 1963-64, chmn. awards policy com. 1977-78, energy com. 1981-84, mem. steering com. council of tech. divs. 1964-65, mem. com. on relations with AEC 1964, 67—, chmn. nuclear engring. brochure com. 1966-68, engring. coll.'s council 1975-77), Engrs. Council for Profl. Devel. (dir. 1971-77, chmn. admissions com. 1973-76, mem. com. to evaluate advanced level accreditation 1975-77, exec. com., program chmn. 1972), Nat. Soc. Profl. Engrs. (student profl. devel. com. 1973-75, edn. com. 1983-84), Profl. Engrs. in Edn. (chmn. N.C. region 1984—), Mo. Soc. Profl. Engrs. (mem. edn. adv. bd. 1968—, chmn. 1969-70, 73-74, 76-78, treas. 1978-79, sec. 1979-80, v.p. 1981-82, pres. 1983-84, profl. engrs. in edn. rep. to Nat. Soc. Profl. Engrs. polit. action com.), Columbia C. of C. (dir. 1968—, v.p. econ. devel. 1977—). Clubs: Rotary (v.p. pres.-elect Columbia 1977-79, pres. 1981-82. Home: 900 Yale St Columbia MO 65201 *We can never contribute adequately to repay those who preceded us, but we can try; evidently education is such a profession in that its practitioners labor for the current generation and for posterity.*

KIMELMAN, HENRY L., ambassador; b. N.Y.C., Jan. 21, 1921; s. Sigmund A. and Caroline (Hanenson) K.; m. Charlotte R. Kessler, Sept. 26, 1943; children: Donald Bruce, Susan Kimelman Edwards, John David. B.S., N.Y. U., 1943; postgrad., Harvard Grad. Sch. Bus. Adminstrn., 1944. Vice pres. Ozark Mountain Distilling Co., Joplin, Mo., 1945-48, pres., 1949-50; pres., treas. V.I. Hotel and V.I. Realty, St. Thomas, 1950-61; commr. commerce, V.I., 1961-64; chmn. bd. Island Block Corp. and Henry Elliot, Ltd., St. Thomas, 1964-67; asst. to sec. interior, Washington, 1967-69; pres., chmn. bd. West Indies Corp., St. Thomas, 1969-80; U.S. ambassador to, Haiti, 1980-81; dir. W.I. Bank & Trust Co., Am. Hotel Assn., Diners Club, Inc., Leeward Islands Transport, Antigua, W.I. Chmn. Econ. Devel. Bd. of V.I., 1961-64, V.I. Rum Council, 1961-64; V.I. adminstr. for U.S. Area Redevel. Adminstrn., Washington, 1961-64; dir. U.S. Nat. Parks Found., 1968-72; mem. adv. com. on arts J.F. Kennedy Center Performing Arts, 1979—; chmn. McGovern for Pres. Com., 1971-72; dep. chmn., finance chmn. Church for Pres., 1976; Bd. dirs. Psychiat. Inst. Found., 1974—; chmn. child devel. adv. bd. Child Devel. Asso. Consortium; chmn. V.I. fund drive Boy Scouts Am., 1978-79. Served to lt. (j.g.), Supply Corps USNR, 1942-46. Recipient Distinguished Service award State of Israel Bonds, 1959, also Interfaith Movement award, 1961; Disting. Beverage Alcohol Wholesaler award Time mag., 1980; Grand Cross of Nat. Order of Honor and Merit Republic of Haiti, 1983. Mem. Young Pres.'s Orgn. (pres. Caribbean chpt. 1964-66), World Bus. Council, Chief Execs. Forum. Club: Mason. Home: Windrush PO Box 8240 St Thomas VI 00801 Office: PO Box 8240 St Thomas VI 00801

KIMERER, NEIL BANARD, SR., psychiatrist, educator; b. Wauseon, Ohio, Jan. 13, 1918; s. William and Ruby (Upp) K.; m. Ellen Jane Scott, May 23, 1943; children: Susan Leigh, Neil Banard, Brian Scott, Sandra Lynn. B.S., U. Toledo, 1941; M.D., U. Chgo., 1944; postgrad. (fellow), Menninger Sch., 1947-50. Diplomate: Am. Bd. Psychiatry. Intern Emanuel Hosp., Portland, Oreg., 1944; resident psychiatry Winter VA Hosp., Topeka, 1947-50; asst. physician Central State Hosp., Norman, Okla., 1950, cons., 1955—; chief out-patient psychiat. clinic U. Okla. Sch. Medicine, Oklahoma City, 1951-53, instr. dept. psychiatry, neurology and behavioral scis., 1953-61, assoc. prof., 1961-69, clin. prof., 1969—; practice medicine specializing in psychiatry, Oklahoma City, 1953—; med. dir. Oklahoma City Mental Health Clinic, 1953-68; chmn. dept. psychiatry Bapt. Med. Ctr. Okla., 1979—; cons., spl. lectr. dept. psychology U. Okla., Norman, 1951-58; Mem. Comprehensive Health Survey Com., Oklahoma City, 1961—. Author: To Get and Beget, 1971; Contbr. articles in field to profl. jours. Mem. exec. com. Okla. Family Life Assn., 1958-60; bd. dirs. Oklahoma City Jr. Symphony Soc., 1959. Served as pfc ASTP, 1943-44; to capt. M.C. AUS, 1945-47. Fellow Am. Psychiat. Assn. (life); mem. Am., Okla. State med. assns., Oklahoma County Med. Soc., Oklahoma City Clin. Soc., Mid-Continent Psychiat. Soc., AAAS, Alpha Kappa Kappa (pres. Nu chpt. 1943). Club: Rotarian. Home: 2800 NW 25th St Oklahoma City OK 73107 Office: 2600 NW Hwy Oklahoma City OK 73112

KIMMEL, CAESAR PAUL, entertainment-communications company executive; b. Newark, July 19, 1926; s. Emanuel and Pauline (Polk) K.; m. Nancy Officer, Nov. 27, 1948; children: John Clark, Karen Lisa. Ed., Rutgers U. Exec. v.p. Kinney System, N.Y.C., 1949-61; v.p. Kinney Service, N.Y.C., 1961-71; exec. vp. Warner Communications, Inc., N.Y.C., 1971—. Served with USMCR, 1944-46. Clubs: Mason., City Athletic, Hollywood Golf. Office: Warner Communications Inc 75 Rockefeller Plaza New York NY 10019 *

KIMMEL, CAROL FRANCES, civic worker; b. Dongola, Ill., Sept. 22, 1917; d. Clyde and Grace (Kerr) Karraker; m. Walter G. Kimmel, Aug. 21, 1938; children—Walter J., Carol Ann, Ralph Grear. Student, Bethel Women's Coll., 1937; LL.D., Ill. State U., 1977. Tchr. music, Alto Pass, Ill., 1937-38; Pres. Audubon Sch. PTA, Rock Island, Ill., 1954-56; 1st v.p. Ill. PTA, 1964-66, pres., 1966-68; mem. bd. edn., Rock Island, Ill., 1963-72, pres., 1971-72; mem. exec. com. Nat. PTA, 1971-73, 1st v.p., 1973-75, pres., 1975-77; chmn. PTA Commn. on TV Violence, 1976-77; mem. Ill. Bd. Higher Edn. Task Force to Study Tchr. Edn., 1975—, Ill. Bd. Higher Edn. Task Force to Study Governance of Univs., 1974-75, Ill. Advisory Com. on Media Services, 1974, U.S. Office Edn. Community Edn. Natl. Advisory Council, 1976-79, advisory com. for sci. edn. NSF, 1976-79, Nat. Task Force on Responsible Decisions About Alcohol, 1974-77. Trustee So. Ill. U., Carbondale, 1977-83; mem. advisory council Nat. Orgn. Corp. for Pub. Broadcasting, 1975-77; mem., sec. Ill. Sch. Problems Commn., 1969-73; mem. Ill. Advisory Com. on Right to Read, 1973-75, Ill. Advisory Com. on Edn. for Gifted, 1974-75; mem. fin. advisory com. Nat. Advisory Com. Intergovtl. Relations, 1972-73, Western Ill. Advisory Com. on Edn., 1970-75; mem. Nat. Inst. Edn. Panel to Rev. Ednl. Research Labs. and Centers, 1977—, Ill. commr. Edn. Commn. of States, 1978—; trustee March of Dimes Birth Defects Found.,

1979—; chmn. Nat. Coalition for Parental Involvement in Edn., 1980—. Named Ill. Mother of Yr., 1977; Lay Educator of Yr. Phi Delta Kappa, 1981; recipient presdl. awards Ill. Assn. Sch. Adminstrs., 1975; citation Natl. Center for Voluntary Action, 1975; recognition by Univs. Ill., 1957. Mem. 3Delta Kappa Gamma (hon.), Alpha Delta Kappa (hon.). Republican. Presbyterian. Home: 1715 25th St Rock Island IL 61201 Office: Nat Congress of Parents and Teachers 700 N Rush St Chicago IL 60611 *The words that have constantly urged me on are ones I read long ago, "Our first responsibility to our children is to help them to live effectively in the world in which they find themselves—not the world I have known or would prefer."*

KIMMEL, HARVEY, business executive, accountant; b. Phila., May 2, 1943; s. Abe and Esther (Cohen) K.; m. Virginia L. Gross, Sept. 8, 1968; children: Jennifer, Sara. B.S., Pa. State U., 1964; M.A., Ohio State U., 1966. C.P.A., Ill. Auditor Arthur Young & Co., Chgo., 1965-69; controller Automated Mktg. Systems, Chgo., 1969-72; v.p. fin. W. Braun Co., Chgo., 1972-75; div. controller, dir. planning Beatrice Foods Co., Chgo., 1975-77; sr. v.p., treas. Edward Don Co., Oakbrook, Ill., 1977-81; pres., treas. Edward Don Co. N.J., Mt. Laurel, 1981—. Fellow Planning Execs. Inst.; mem. Am. Inst. C.P.A.s. Office: 820 E Gate Dr Mt Laurel NJ 08054

KIMMEL, JOE ROBERT, biochemist, educator; b. DuQuoin, Ill., May 3, 1922; s. Maurice Edward and Roberta (Pyatt) K.; m. Jean Howell, Apr. 3, 1947; children—Philip H., Lynn, Ellen, Bruce E. A.B., DePauw U., 1943; M.D., Johns Hopkins, 1947; Ph.D., U. Utah, 1954. Intern Salt Lake City Gen. Hosp., 1947-49; resident U.S. Naval Hosp., Oakland, Calif., 1950-52; research instr. biochemistry U. Utah Coll. Medicine, 1954-55, asst. research prof. biochemistry, 1955-59, asso. research prof. biochemistry, 1959-60, asso. prof. biochemistry, 1960-62, asso. prof. biochemistry and pediatrics, 1962-64; prof. biochemistry, dir. McIlvain Labs., Kans. U. Med. Center, 1964—. Served with USNR, 1950-52. Recipient Career Devel. award USPHS, 1960; Henry Strong Denison scholar Johns Hopkins, 1946-47. Mem. Am. Soc. Biol. Chemists, Endocrine Soc., AAAS, AAUP, Alpha Omega Alpha. Home: 6219 W 61st Terrace Shawnee Mission KS 66202 Office: Rainbow Blvd at 39th St Kansas City KS 66103

KIMMELL, LEE HAROLD, investment banker; b. Fort Worth, Jan. 21, 1950; s. Sam and Rowena (Ginsburg) K.; m. Barbara Marcus Kimmell, Aug. 16, 1975; children: David Marcus, Barbara Elizabeth. B.S. in Econs., U. Pa., 1972, M.B.A., 1974. Assoc. Smith, Barney & Co., N.Y.C., 1974-75, Salomon Bros., 1976, v.p., 1978, mng. dir., 1982—. Bd. dirs. N.Y. Service for Handicapped, N.Y.C., 1982—. Jewish. Office: 1 New York Plaza New York NY 10004

KIMMEY, JAMES RICHARD, JR., educator, consultant; b. Boscobel, Wis., Jan. 26, 1935; s. James Richard and Frances Dale (Parnell) K.; m. Sarah Webster Eastman, June 21, 1958; children—Elisabeth Webster, James Richard III. B.S., U. Wis., 1957, M.S., 1959, M.D., 1961; M.P.H., U. Calif. at Berkeley, 1967. Diplomate: Am. Bd. Preventive Medicine. Intern Univ. Hosps., Cleve., 1961-62; med. resident Univ. Hosp., Madison, 1962-63; served from surgeon to med. dir. USPHS, 1963-68, chief kidney disease br., 1964-66, regional health dir., N.Y., 1967-68; exec. dir. Community Health Inc., N.Y.C., 1968-70, Am. Pub. Health Assn., 1970-73; sec. Health Policy Council Wis., 1973-75; pres. James R. Kimmey Assos., Inc., 1975—; dir. Midwest Center for Health Planning, 1976-79; exec. dir. Inst. Health Planning, 1979—; adj. assoc. prof. Columbia Sch. Public Health, 1968-75; adj. prof. N.Y. U., 1968-70; lectr. Johns Hopkins, 1971-73; clin. instr. U. Wis., 1974—. Editor: The Nation's Health, 1972-73; mng. editor: Am. Jour. Pub. Health, 1970-73; editorial adv. bd.: Health Cost Mgmt., 1983—; Contbr. articles to profl. jours. Pres. World Fedn. Pub. Health Assns., 1972-73; bd. dirs. Internat. Union Health Edn., 1970-73; mem. sci. adv. bd. Gorgas Inst., 1970-73. Decorated USPHS Commendation medal, 1968. Fellow Am. Pub. Health Assn. (governing council 1978—, chmn. community health planning sect. 1979-80), Am. Coll. Preventive Medicine; mem. Am. Health Planning Assn. (dir. 1974-75, 77—, corp. sec. 1977—, pres. 1980-81, Richard H. Schlesinger award 1978), Phi Eta Sigma, Alpha Omega Alpha, Delta Omega. Democrat. Episcopalian. Home: 233 Carillon Dr Madison WI 53705 Office: 702 N Blackhawk Dr Madison WI 53705

KIMMINS, WARWICK CHARLES, biology educator; b. Isleworth, Eng., July 20, 1941; s. Horace Charles and Eileen May (Beck) K.; m. Ruth Willcock, July 28, 1964; children: Eliot, Sarah. B.Sc. with honors, London U., 1962, Ph.D., 1965. Cons. library research dept. Ency. Britannica, 1963-65; asst. prof. biology Dalhousie U., 1965-69, asso. prof., 1969-73, prof., 1973—, chmn. dept. biology, 1981—; Canadian rep. to Internat. Assn. Plant Physiology, 1981—. Contbr. chpts. to books, articles to profl. jours. Co-founder, chmn. E. Coast Community Sch.; v.p., ward council leader Cub Scouts of Can.; pres. Le Marchant Home and Sch. Assn.; bd. dirs. Can. Cancer Soc., Halifax. NRC grantee, 1965-69, 69-72, 73-79, 80-84. Mem. Can. Soc. Plant Physiologists (nat. exec.), Assn. Applied Biologists, Soc. Exptl. Biology, Soc. Gen. Microbiology, Can. Soc. Phytopathology, Am. Soc. Phytopathology. Unitarian. Club: Waegwoltic. Home: 1684 Edward St Halifax NS Canada B3H 3J3 Office: Dalhousie U Halifax NS Canada

KIMNACH, MYRON WILLIAM, botanist, horticulturist; b. Los Angeles, Dec. 26, 1922; s. Elmer Edward and Ida (Johnson) K.; m. Maria Jaeger, Nov. 17, 1961. Grad. high sch. Asst. mgr. U. Calif. Botanic Garden, Berkeley, 1951-62; curator Huntington Bot. Gardens, San Marino, 1962—; Bd. dirs. Internat. Succulent Inst., Orinda, Calif. Contbr. articles profl. jours. Pres., bd. dirs. Palm Soc., 1976-78. Served with USCGR, 1943-46. Fellow Cactus and Succulent Soc. Am. (pres. 1970-71, dir. 1968-74), Internat. Orgn. Succulent Plant Study. Home: 1600 Orlando Rd San Marino CA 91108 Office: 1151 Oxford Rd San Marino CA 91108

KIMPEL, BENJAMIN FRANKLIN, emeritus philosophy educator, author; b. Racine, Wis., May 9, 1905; s. Benjamin F. and Agnes (Beltz) K. B.A., U. Wis., 1926; fellow anthropology, U. Nebr., 1927-28; Ph.D. (Tew fellow), Yale U., 1932. Ordained to ministry Am. Unitarian Assn., 1937; mem. faculty Kans. Wesleyan U., 1933-36, prof. philosophy, 1935-36, Drew U., 1938-72, prof. emeritus, 1972—. Author: Religious Faith, Language, and Knowledge, 1952, Faith and Moral Authority, 1953, Symbols of Religious Faith, 1954, Moral Principles in the Bible, 1956, Language and Religion, 1957, Principles of Moral Philosophy, 1960, Kant's Critical Philosophy, 1964, Hegel's Philosophy of History, 1964, Nietzsche's Beyond Good and Evil, 1964, Schopenhauer's Philosophy, 1965, Philosophy of Zen Buddhism, 1966, Philosophies of Life of the Ancient Greeks and Israelites: An analysis of their parallels, 1981, Emily Dickinson as Philosopher, 1981, A Philosophy of the Religion of Ancient Greeks and Israelites, 1983, Stoic Moral Philosophies: Their Counsel for Today, 1984, Moral Philosophies in the Plays by Shakespeare, 1984. Mem. AAUP, Am. Philos. Assn., Beta Beta Beta, Kappa Pi, Pi Gamma Mu, Psi Chi, Phi Sigma Tau, Sigma Phi. Home: North Bennington VT 05257 *I have gradually learned, not without disbelief and doubt, that the goodness of living increases as the delight in substantial learning increases. If only we could believe this when our opportunities to learn are the most alert—what a world of worth we might carry with us in which we might live and breathe and have our being.*

KIMURA, YURIKO, modern dancer. Prin. dancer Martha Graham Gance Co., N.Y.C. Office: care Martha Graham Dance Co 316 E 63d St New York NY 10021§

KINARD, HARGETT YINGLING, financial consultant; b. York, Pa., May 29, 1912; s. Henry B. and Edith R. (Yingling) K.; m. Pearl E. Greenhill, Aug. 20, 1932; children: Joan S. (Mrs. Edward J. Mercado), Lois E. (Mrs. Jerry Branch), Gail E. (Mrs. Joseph R. Eastburn). Student, Drexel Inst., Phila., 1928-29; grad., Rider Coll., Trenton, N.J., 1933. C.P.A., Pa. Asso. firm Lybrand, Ross Bros. & Montgomery, Phila., 1933-51; with Electric Storage Battery Co., Phila., 1951-55, comptroller, 1952-55; v.p., treas. Maule Industries, Inc., 1955-58; v.p. finance, 1958-59, financial cons. to various internat. firms, 1959-60; v.p., comptroller First Union Nat. Bank of N.C., Charlotte, 1960-63, sr. v.p., comptroller, 1963-65, exec. v.p., comptroller, 1965-71; sr. v.p., treas. 1st Union Nat. Bank Corp., 1968-71; free lance financial cons., 1971—. Asst. commr. motor vehicles, State of N.C., 1974; asst. sec. N.C. Dept. Transp., 1974-77; Trustee N.C. State Tchrs. and Employees Retirement Fund, 1974-77. Mem. Am., Pa. insts. C.P.A.s, N.C. Assn. C.P.A.s, Fin. Execs. Inst, Service Corps Ret. Execs., Internat. Execs. Service Corps., Clearwater C. of C. Presbyn. Clubs: Kiwanian, Good Fellow., Carmel Country, Charlotte Executives. Home: 5825 Lansing Dr Charlotte NC 28226 also 2079 Broadway Clearwater FL 33515 Office: 5825 Lansing Dr Charlotte NC 28226

KINARIWALA, BHARAT, electrical engineer, educator; b. Ahmedabad, India, Oct. 14, 1926; came to U.S., 1951, naturalized, 1963; s. Jamnadas and Hiralaxmi (Shodhan) K.; m. Marva Schor, Apr. 23, 1953; children: Neela, Maya. B.S., Benares Hindu U., 1950; M.S., U. Calif. at Berkeley, 1954, Ph.D., 1957. Elec. engr. Cosmos India Rubber Works, Ltd., Bombay, India, 1950-51; acting asst. prof. U. Calif. at Berkeley, 1956-57; mem. tech. staff Bell Telephone Lab., N.J., 1957-66; prof. U. Hawaii, 1966—, chmn. dept. elec. engring., 1969-75, 78—. Author: (with Kuo and Tsao) Linear Circuits and Computation, 1973; author: (with Van Valkenburg) Linear Circuits, 1982; Assoc. editor: IEEE Trans. Circuit Theory, 1967-69. Fellow I.E.E.E. (chmn. symposium on circuit theory 1969, adminstrv. com. 1968, 69); mem. Sigma Xi. Research synthesis active RC networks, 1959; timing problem in high speed digital communication, 1961-64; theory distributed networks, 1964-66; computing algorithms, 1966; database systems, 1978. Home: 581 Kamoku St 2104 Honolulu HI 96826

KINCADE, ARTHUR WARREN, banker; b. Chillicothe, Mo., Aug. 14, 1896; s. John Albert and Flora (Dilley) K.; m. Mary Josephine Igou, Aug. 22, 1917; children—Arthur Warren, Imogene, Patricia Josephine. Ed. high sch. and coll., 1 year. Officer varous banks in, Okla. and Tex., 1915-31, pres. W. Tex. Mortgage Loan Co. and its subsidiaries, Amarillo, also v.p. First Nat. Bank, Amarillo, 1931-37; exec. v.p. Fourth Nat. Bank, Wichita, Kans., 1937-40, pres., 1940-69, chmn. bd., chief exec. officer, 1969—; chmn. bd. emeritus, cons. Fourth Financial Corp., Wichita. Author articles. Mem. Am. Petroleum Inst., Newcomen Soc., Alpha Kappa Psi (hon.). Club: Mason (K.T.; 32; Shriner). Home: PO Box 1090 Wichita KS 67202 Office: Fourth Nat Bank Wichita KS 67202

KINCAID, HUGH REID, lawyer; b. Fayetteville, Ark., Sept. 30, 1934; s. Hugh Z. and Mary (Gose) K.; children: William Reid, Kathryn Lea. B.S., U. Ark., 1956, J.D., 1959. Bar: Ark. 1959. Practice in Fayetteville, 1963—; trial atty. U.S. Dept. Justice, 1961-63; city atty., Fayetteville, 1965-69; mem. firm Kincaid, Horne & Trumbo, 1968—; lectr. bus. law Coll. Bus. Adminstn., U. Ark., 1963—. Pres. N.W. Ark. Community Concert Assn., 1969-71; bd. dirs. Fayetteville Pub. Schs., 1969-72, 76—, v.p., 1980—; bd. dirs. Washington County chpt. ARC, 1967-71, Northwest Ark. Symphony Soc., 1976-80, Arts Center of Ozarks, 1978-79; mem. Ark. Ho. of Reps., 1971-75. Served to 1st lt. JAGC, U.S. Army, 1959-61. Mem. ABA, Ark. Bar Assn., Washington County Bar Assn. (past pres.), Am. Trial Lawyers Assn., Ark. Trial Lawyers Assn. (bd. govs. 1979-82), Fayetteville C. of C. (dir. 1973-76). Methodist. Club: Lion. Home: 520 Lakeridge Dr Fayetteville AR 72701 Office: 207 W Center St Fayetteville AR 72701

KINCAID, JOHN FRANKLIN, scientist; b. Blackwell, Mo., Feb. 27, 1912; s. John Randall and Rose (Rich) K.; m. Nancy Virginia Ange, June 28, 1938 (dec.); children: James Randall, John Peter, Thomas Franklin (dec.); m. Marguerite Belair Hull, Oct. 30, 1971. A.B., Central Coll., Fayette, Mo., 1934; M.A., George Washington U., 1936; Ph.D., Princeton, 1938. Instr. chemistry U. Rochester, 1938-42; div. head explosives research lab. Carnegie Inst. Tech., 1942-45; research scientist Gen. Electric Co., 1945-46; head high pressure research dept. Rohm & Haas Co., 1946-49, research supr., 1949-58; head gen. sci. br., adv. research project div. Inst. Def. Analysis, 1958-59, dep. dir. advanced research projects div., 1959-60, dir. research and engring. support div., 1960-62; ind. cons., 1962-63; v.p. research and devel. Internat. Minerals and Chem. Corp., 1963-67; asst. sec. Dept. Commerce, 1967-69; cons., 1969-71; sr. scientist Applied Physics Lab., Johns Hopkins, 1971—. Author articles. Recipient Naval Ordnance Devel. award, 1945, Presdl. cert. merit, 1948. Mem. AIAA (Wyld Propulsion award 1981), AAAS, Am. Def. Preparedness Assn. Clubs: Cosmos (Washington); Aviation (Princeton, N.J.). Inventor or co-inventor mil. and indsl. processes and products. Home: 2111 Jefferson Davis HwyApt 109-s Arlington VA 22202

KINCAID, KEITH WILLIAM, news agency executive; b. Toronto, Ont., Can., Jan. 4, 1935; s. Frank S. and Vera I. (Lubbock) K.; m. Noreen A. Lumsden, Dec. 27, 1958; children: Kerry, Peter, Andrew. B.A. with honors in Journalism, U. Western Ont., 1958. With Canadian Press, 1958—, gen. exec., 1973-78, gen. mgr., chief exec. officer, Toronto, 1978—, pres., 1982—; chief exec. officer Broadcast News Ltd., Press News Ltd. Trustee Nat. Newspaper Awards. Recipient Merit award U. Western Ont., 1958; Media award N. Am. Assn. Alcoholism Programs, 1969. Mem. Commonwealth Press Union, Internat. Press Inst., Inst. Assn. Execs., Met. Toronto Bd. Trade. Anglican. Club: University (Toronto). Home: 95 Airdrie Rd Toronto ON M4G 1M4 Canada Office: 36 King St E Toronto ON M5C 2L9 Canada

KINCHEN, ROBERT PRESTON, library director; b. New Orleans, Mar. 12, 1933; s. Edward Preston and Ann Lou (Sutton) K.; m. Christine Rogers, Nov. 19, 1973. B.A., Northwestern State Coll. La., 1956; M.S., La. State U., 1966. Public service librarian Enoch Pratt Free Library, Balt., 1960-69, asst. to asso. dir., 1969-72; assoc. dir. Rochester (N.Y.) Public Library, 1972-76; dir. Onondaga Public Library, Syracuse, N.Y., 1976—. Trustee Laubach Literacy Internat. Served to 1st lt. U.S. Army, 1956-60. Mem. N.Y. Library Assn. (pres. public libraries sect. 1981), ALA. Home: 100 Burlington Dr Manlius NY 13104 Office: 327 Montgomery St Syracuse NY 13202

KIND, PHYLLIS, art dealer. B.A., U. Pa.; M.F.A., U. Chgo. Owner, dir. Phyllis Kind Gallery, Chgo., 1967—, N.Y.C., 1975—. Home: 136 Greene St New York NY 10012 Office: 313 W Superior St Chicago IL 60610 Office: 136 Greene St New York NY 10012

KINDEL, JAMES HORACE, JR., lawyer; b. Los Angeles, Nov. 8, 1913; s. James Horace and Philipina (Butte) K.; children: William, Mary, Robert, John. A.B., UCLA, 1934; LL.B., Loyola U., Los Angeles, 1940. Bar: Calif. 1941; C.P.A., Calif. Pvt. legal practice Kindel & Anderson, Los Angeles and Newport Beach, Calif., 1945—; ret. partner Coopers-Lybrand; officer, dir., part-owner R.J. Noble Co. (road and asphalt contractors), Orange, Calif., 1950—; dir. Bear Creek Corp.; part-owner sand and gravel and poultry bus., Guatemala; part owner Sunnymead Poultry Ranch, Calif., Tex. Trustee, UCLA. Mem. Am., Los Angeles, Orange County bar assns, State Bar Calif., Am. Inst. C.P.A.s, Phi Delta Phi, Theta Xi. Clubs: Chancery, California (Los Angeles). Home: 800 W 1st 2405 Los Angeles CA 90012 Office: 555 S Flower St Los Angeles CA 90071 also 4000 MacArthur Blvd Newport Beach CA 92660

KINDER, HAROLD M., corp. ofcl.; b. Pitts., Feb. 22, 1911; s. O. W. and Mary (Parsons) K.; m. Eva C. Korocz, Apr. 3, 1948. Student public schs., Flint, Mich., Northwestern Traffic Inst., 1940. Transp. supt. Kirby-Butler Co., Flint, 1928-36; police exec., Flint, 1936-42, traffic engr., 1946-47, police chief, 1947-48, city mgr., 1948-52; bus. mgr. Mich. Liquor Control Commn., 1952-54; Ohio mgr. Nat. Distillers Products Co., 1954-61, v.p., 1961-68, control states div. mgr., v.p., mgr. nat. brands div., N.Y.C., 1968-77; owner, mgr. Kinder Importing Co., Ft. Lauderdale, 1977—; Industry com. Nat. Alcoholic Beverage Control Assn. Author: Circumstantial Evidence-Bah. Mem. Red Feather Fund of Flint. Commd. 2d lt. U.S. Army; adv. to maj., 1946; service in; N. Africa; service in; Sicily; service in; Italy; service in; France; service in; Germany; service in; Greece; disch. as major, Corps. Mil. Police, O.R.C., 1946. Recipient Gold medal Nat. Distillers, 1962; decorated Order Brit. Empire, 1945; Legion of Merit; Bronze Star; Army Commendation ribbon; Corono de Italy; Morocco-Sultan's medal; E.A.M.E. campaign ribbon with 5 battle stars. Mem. Internat. Assn. Chiefs of Police, Fraternal Order Police, Nat. Safety Council (mem. program com.). Clubs: Marine Tower Yacht, Lago Mar (Ft. Lauderdale, Fla.); Univ. (Jackson, Miss.); 60 East (N.Y.C.); Elks; Capitol Hill (Washington). Home: Marine Tower Apt 602 2500 E Las Olas Blvd Fort Lauderdale FL 33301

KINDER, JAMES S., educator, author; b. Millersville, Mo., Oct. 19, 1895; s. Robert F. and Emily (Runnels) K.; m. Mary Clare Lett, Sept. 11, 1919 (dec. 1964); m. Lynn Sheridan Jackson, Sept. 26, 1972. B.S., Southeast Mo. State Coll., 1921; student, Univ. Coll. (Aberystwyth) Wales, 1919, U. Mo., 1922; A.M., Columbia Tchrs. Coll., 1923, Ph.D., 1934. Pub. sch. tchr. and adminstr., Bertrand, Mo., Oak Ridge, Mo., Marysvale, Utahand Sullivan, Mo., and Sullivan, Mo.; mem. faculty Chatham Coll., 1923-53, prof. edn., head dept. edn., dir. film service, 1938—; prof. edn. San Diego State U., 1953-, now prof. emeritus.; Vis. prof. summers Geneva Coll., U. Pitts., U. Wyo., Mich. State U., Southwestern La. Inst., San Diego State U., 1950, U. Va., 1951, Pa. State U., 1952. Author: The Internal Administration of the Liberal Arts College, 1934, Audio-Visual Materials and Techniques, 1950, 1959, Educational Tests for Use in Institutions of Higher Learning, (with C.W. Odell), 1930, (with F. Dean McClusky) Audio-Visual Reader, 1954, 1954, Using Audio-Visual Material in Education, 1965, Using Instructional Media, 1973; author: (with M.D. Alcorn and J.R. Schunert) Better Teaching in Secondary Schs, 1964, rev. edit., 1970; producer: (with Dana Gibson) (motion picture) Duplicating by the Spirit Method, 1957; Co-producer: motion pictures Mimeographing Techniques, 1958; contbr.: Sociological Foundation of Education, 1942; also 13 articles on travel to La Jolla Nite Life Revue. Served with AEF, 1917-18; France; instr. A.S.T.P., 1944; asst. adminstr., engring. sci. mgmt. War Tng. Program, 1941-45; Western Pa. area. Mem. Assn. Ednl. Communications and Tech., Ednl. Film Library Assn. (an organizer and mem. first bd. dirs.), Phi Delta Kappa (pres. Xi chpt. 1945-47). Clubs: Masons, Circumnavigators, La Jolla Country. Home: 1126 Skylark Dr La Jolla CA 92037

KINDIG, FRED EUGENE, educator, arbitrator; b. York, Pa., Sept. 5, 1920; s. Fred E. and Hattie (Keller) K.; m. Marie M. Doyle (dec. 1971); children: Pamela M., Bonita K., Gretchen A., Suzanne J.; m. Grace L. Mathison, Aug. 19, 1972 (dec. 1979); m. Susan S. Friend, Mar. 16, 1980. B.S., Pa. State U., 1942; M.S., U. Pitts., 1947, Ph.D., 1951. Indsl. engr., supr. Westinghouse Electric Corp., Pitts., 1942-51; asst. to exec. v. p. Phoenix Glass, Monaca, Pa., 1951-53; asst. and asso. prof. U. Pitts., 1953-62; prof., coordinator quantitative methods Ohio State U., Columbus, 1962-81, prof. emeritus, 1981—; labor mgmt. arbitrator, 1953—. Author: Fundamentals of Statistical Controls and Fundamentals of Linear Programming, 1956; Contbr. articles to profl. jours. Pres. PTA, various times; mem. Franklin County 648 Bd., 1979-82; trustee Columbus Tech. Inst., 1982—. Mem. Am. Inst. Decision Scis. (v.p. 1969-71), Am. Arbitration Assn., Nat. Acad. Arbitrators, Am. Soc. Quality Control, Inst. Math. Stats., Am. Statis. Assn., Ops. Research Soc. Am., Alpha Sigma Phi, Tau Beta Pi, Beta Gamma Sigma. Clubs: Brookside Country, Univ. Home: 213 St Antoine Worthington OH 43085 Office: 207 St Jacques Worthington OH 43085 *Although fate plays an important role, perseverance, absolute honesty, basic integrity, and the highest of moral standards make for an unbeatable combination.*

KINDL, FRED HENRY, engineering company executive; b. Los Angeles, July 4, 1920; s. Frederick Henry and Flora Ethel (Kellett) K.; m. Catherine Quinlan, Sept. 4, 1943; children: Jean Marie, Rosemary, Ellen, Patrice. B.S., Carnegie Inst. Tech., 1942. Engr. Gen. Electric Co., Schenectady, N.Y., 1946-50; pres. Ballston Mech. Products, 1950-55; with Gen. Electric Co., 1955-73, mgr. engring., 1969-73; pres. Encotech, Inc., Schenectady, 1973—. Served to capt. USAAF, 1942-46. Fellow ASME; mem. Am. Soc. Metals, ASTM, Am. Petroleum Inst., Schenectady C. of C. Republican. Clubs: Lake George, Mohawk. Patentee in field. Home: 14 N Church St Schenectady NY 12305 Office: 207 State St Schenectady NY 12301

KINDLEBERGER, CHARLES P., II, economist, emeritus educator; b. N.Y.C., Oct. 12, 1910; s. E. Crosby and Elizabeth Randall (McIlvaine) K.; m. Sarah Bache Miles, May 1, 1937; children: Charles P., Richard S., Sarah, E. Randall. A.B., U. Pa., 1932; A.M., Columbia U., 1934, Ph.D., 1937; Dr. h.c., U. Paris, 1966, U. Ghent, 1975. Research in internat. trade and fin. Fed. Res. Bank N.Y., 1936-39, Bank Internat. Settlements, 1939-40, Bd. Govs. FRS, 1940-42; Am. sec. Joint Econ. Com. U.S. and Can., 1941-42; served with OSS, Washington, 1942-44, 45; chief div. German and Austrian Econ. Affairs, Dept. State, Washington, 1945-48; asso. prof. econs. M.I.T., 1948-51, prof., 1951-76, prof. emeritus, 1976—, chmn. faculty, 1965-67; vis. prof. econs. Brandeis U., 1983—. Author: International Short-Term Capital Movements, 1937, The Dollar Shortage, 1950, International Economics, 1953, rev. edits., 1973, 78, The Terms of Trade, 1956, Economic Development, 1958, rev. edits., 1965, 77, Foreign Trade and the National Economy, 1962, Economic Growth of France and Britain, 1851-1950, 1964, Europe and the Dollar, 1966, Postwar European Growth, 1967, American Business Abroad, 1969, Power and Money, 1970; Editor: The International Corporation, 1970, The World in Depression, 1929-39, 1973, Economic Response, 1978, Manias, Panics and Crashes, 1978, International Money, 1981, A Financial History of Western Europe, 1984, Multinational Excursions, 1984. Intelligence officer 12th Army Group, 1944-45; disch. rank of maj., Gen. Staff Corps. Decorated Legion of Merit, Bronze Star; recipient Harms prize Institut für Weltwirtschaft, Kiel, 1978. Fellow Am. Econ. Assn. (Disting. fellow; v.p. 1966, pres.-elect 1983); mem. Am. Acad. Arts and Scis., Phi Beta Kappa, Delta Psi. Episcopalian. Home: Bedford Rd Lincoln MA 01773

KINDNESS, THOMAS NORMAN, congressman; b. Knoxville, Tenn., Aug. 26, 1929; s. Norman Garden and Christine (Gunn) K.; m. Ann Gifford Hosman, Sept. 15, 1951; children: Sharon L., David T.,

Glen J., Adam B.; m. Averil J. Stoneback, Jan. 7, 1984. A.B., U. Md., 1951; LL.B., George Washington U., 1953. Bar: D.C. 1954. Practiced in, Washington, 1954-57; asst. counsel legal dept. Champion Internat. Corp., Hamilton, Ohio, 1957-73; mayor, Hamilton, 1964-67, mem. city council, 1968-69; mem. Ohio Ho. of Reps. from 58th Dist., 1971-75; coordinator House Republican Campaign Com., 1973-74; mem. 94th-98th Congresses from 8th Ohio Dist. Office: 2417 Rayburn House Office Bldg Washington DC 20515

KINDSVATER, CARL EDWARD, water resources engineer; b. Hoisington, Kans., Aug. 1, 1913; s. John Alexander and Catherine Elisabeth (Michel) K.; m. Ruth Margaret Goodwin, Dec. 8, 1935; children—Kenneth Carl, Carol Ruth, Paul Edward. B.S. in Civil Engring, U. Kans., 1935; M.S. in Hydraulic Engring, State U. Iowa, 1937. Hydraulic engr. T.V.A., 1937-43, U.S. Corps Engrs., 1943-45; asso. prof. Ga. Inst. Tech., 1945-49, prof., 1949-55, Regents' prof., 1955-73, emeritus, 1973—; dir. Water Resources Center, 1963-70, Environmental Resources Center, 1970-72; staff scientist U.S. Geol. Survey, Reston, Va., 1972-76, Menlo Park, Calif., 1976-77, Reston, 1978-82; cons. water resources engr., 1946—. Author tech. research papers. Fellow ASCE (hon. mem., life mem., Collingwood prize 1945, Rickey medal 1955, Norman medal 1956, 60, Julian Hinds award 1979, dir. 1963-66); mem. Internat. Water Resources Assn., Internat. Assn. Hydraulic Research, Sigma Xi, Tau Beta Pi, Phi Kappa Phi, Chi Epsilon, Omicron Delta Kappa. Home: 10139 Flint St Overland Park KS 66214

KINERSON, KENDALL SCOTT, educator; b. Peacham, Vt., Mar. 8, 1921; s. Charles Raymond and Elizabeth (Scott) K.; m. Shirley Laighton, May 25, 1943; children—Nancy (Mrs. Dennis M. Dwyer), Linda (Mrs. Peter S. Stewart), Margaret Louise (Mrs. Jon W. Robertson), Katherine Scott. B.S., U. N.H., 1943; M.S., Rensselaer Poly. Inst., 1953; Ph.D., Mich. State U., 1957. Instr. physics U. Mass., Ft. Devens, 1946-48; instr. physics and math. to prof. physics and math., chmn. dept. math. Russell Sage Coll., Troy, N.Y., 1948—; cons. N.Y. State Dept. Edn., Bur. Secondary Curriculum Devel., Div. Evaluation of Higher Edn., Rensselaer Poly, Inst. Author: (with Parsegian, Meltzer and Luchins) Introduction to Natural Science, 1968, Laboratory and Mathematics Supplement to Introduction to Natural Science, 1968. Served to capt. AUS, 1943-46. Danforth tchr., 1955. Mem. Am. Assn. Physics Tchrs., Math. Assn. Am., AAUP. Presbyn. (elder, trustee). Club: Mason (32 deg., Shriner). Home: 451 Pinewoods Ave Extension Troy NY 12180

KING, ALAN, entertainer; b. Bklyn., Dec. 26, 1927; s. Bernard and Minnie (Solomon) K.; m. Jeannette Sprung, Feb. 1, 1947; children: Bobby, Andrew. Ed. pub. schs., Bklyn. Appeared, Catskill Mountains and burlesque, also U.S. Army camps, cafes and vaudeville, U.S. and Eng., Dominion Theatre, London, 1957, Palace Theatre, London, 1959, (with Judy Garland), Palace Theatre, N.Y.C., 1958, Met. Opera House, 1960, also Waldorf Astoria Hotel; TV appearances include Garry Moore Show, Ed Sullivan Show, Perry Como Show, also panel shows; TV producer: Return to Earth, 1976; numerous appearances in TV spls. and series, royal command performance for, Queen Elizabeth II, Glasgow, Scotland, 1958; produced: play The Lion in Winter, 1966; stage appearances include The Impossible Years, 1965, The Investigation, 1966, Dinner at Eight, 1966, Something Different, 1967; appeared in: movie Anderson Tapes, 1971, Bye, Bye Braverman, 1968, Just Tell Me What You Want, 1979, Lovesick, 1983; Co-author of: Anybody Who Owns His Own Home Deserves It, 1962; Help. I'm a Prisoner in a Chinese Bakery, 1964; also mag. articles. Club: The Friars (N.Y.C.) (monitor). Office: Wm Morris Agy Inc 151 E Camino Beverly Hills CA 90212 *

KING, ALGIN BRADDY, college dean, marketing educator; b. Latta, S.C., Jan. 19, 1926; s. Dewey Algin and Elizabeth (Braddy) K.; m. Joyce Heisick, Aug. 21, 1976; children: Drucilla Ratcliff, Martha Louise. B.A. in Retailing and Polit. Sci. (W.T. Grant Retailing scholar) cum laude, U. S.C., 1947; M.S., NYU, 1953; Ph.D., Ohio State U., 1966. Exec. trainee Sears, Roebuck & Co., 1948-48; instr. retailing U. S.C., 1948-51; chief econ. analysis br. dist. OPS, 1951-53; exec. dir. Columbia (S.C.) Mchts. Assn., 1953-54; asst. prof. Tex. A&M U., 1954-55; mem. faculty Coll. William and Mary, 1955-72, prof. bus. adminstrn., 1959-72, dir., 1959-63, assoc. dean, 1968-72; prof., dean Sch. Bus., Central Conn. State Coll., Avon, 1972-73; prof., head dept. bus. and econs. James Madison U., 1973-74; prof., dean Sch. Bus., Western Carolina U., Cullowhee, 1974-76; prof. mktg. and mgmt. Christopher Newport Coll., Newport News, Va., 1976—, dean sch. bus. adminstrn. and econs., 1977—; pres. Algin B. King & Assos., Ltd. (mgmt. and mktg. cons.); teaching asst. Ohio State U., 1963-64; professorial lectr. George Washington U.; mgmt. cons. CSC, U.S. Army. Author: (with others) Hampton Waterfront Economic Study, 1967, The Source Book of Economics, 1973, Management Perceptions, 1976; also chpts. in books, articles. Mem. finance resource group Conn. Council Higher Edn., 1972-73; mem. U.S. Senatorial Bus. Adv. Bd. Mem. U.S. Sales and Mktg. Execs. Club, Am. Marketing Assn., Acad. Mgmt., Am. Inst. Decision Scis., Phi Beta Kappa. Independent. Methodist. Clubs: Mason, Rotarian. Home: 103 N Will Scarlet Ln Williamsburg VA 23185

KING, ALLEN DEAN, former association executive; b. Oakhill, Kans., Sept. 27, 1925; s. Charles Clayton and Anna Marie (Binder) K.; m. Joanne E. Hughes, Oct. 8, 1950; 1 son, Edward Allen. Student, Naval Air Tech. Sch., 1945-46, Kans. State U., 1946-48. Rural carrier, Oakhill, 1948-75, Clay Center, Kans., 1975—; mem. bd. Nat. Rural Letter Carriers Assn., Washington, 1970-81, v.p., 1977-79, pres., 1979-81; dir. Nat. Gen. Ins. Co., St. Louis. Served with AC USN, 1944-46. Mem. Am. Legion. Presbyterian. Clubs: Elks, Country. Office: PO Box 84 Clay Center KS 67432

KING, ANDRE RICHARDSON, architectural graphic designer; b. Chgo., July 30, 1931; s. Earl James and Margie Verdetta (Doyle) K.; m. Jan Maria Cyrus, Jan. 28, 1961 (div. Dec. 1977); children: Jandra Maria, Andre Etienne; m. Sally M. Ryan, Sept. 19, 1980. Student, Chgo. Tech. Coll., 1956-57, U. Chgo., 1956-59; B.A.E., Art Inst. Chgo., 1959. With Skidmore, Owings & Merrill, Chgo., 1956-82; freelance archtl. graphic designer and cons., Chgo., 1982—, ind. designer, cons., 1982—. Served with USAF, 1951-55. Recipient Design award Art Inst. Chgo., 1959, DESI award, 1982; Hon. consul of, Barbados, W.I., 1971—. Mem. Soc. Environ. Graphic Designers, Soc. Topographic Arts, Chgo. Soc. Communicating Arts, Art Dirs. Club of Chgo. (pres. 1979-80, 80-82), Art Inst. Chgo. Alumni (bd. dirs.), Arts Club of Chgo., Consular Corps of Chgo., Sigma Pi Phi, Beta Boule. Home: 6700 South Oglesby Ave Chicago IL 60649 Office: 202 S State St Suite 806 Chicago IL 60604 *To provide creative excellence for the future through my works.*

KING, ARNOLD KIMSEY, educator; b. Hendersonville, N.C., Dec. 3, 1901; s. William Fanning Pinckney and Julia (Anderson) K.; m. Edna Coates, Aug. 31, 1929 (dec. Mar. 1978); children: Arnold Kimsey, William Dennis, Mary Ann; m. Louise Tunstall, Apr. 7, 1979. A.B., U. N.C., 1925; A.M., U. Chgo., 1927, Ph.D., 1951; LL.D., N.C. Central U., 1983. Instr. edn. U. N.C., Chapel Hill, 1925-26, asst. prof. teaching history, 1927-39, assoc. prof. edn., 1939-43, prof. edn., 1943—; adviser Gen. Coll., 1942-45, assoc. dean Grad. Sch., 1945-58, dir. summer session, 1958-64; v.p. inst. research Consol. U. N.C., 1964-72, spl. asst. to pres., 1972—; chmn. ednl. adv. com. NASA Ednl. Programs Br., 1963-74; Local coordinator U. N.C. participation in Coop. Study Teacher Edn. of Commn. on Tchr. Edn., 1939-43; chmn. region 6 Woodrow Wilson fellowship program Assn. Am. Univs., 1952-55. Editor: (with W. Carson Ryan and J. Minor Gwynn) Secondary Education in the South, 1946, Research in Progress, vols. 27-35 in U. N.C. Record Series, 1949-57, Planning for the Future, 1958, Long Range Planning, 1969. Trustee N.C. Wesleyan Coll., 1957—. Recipient Hugh McEniry award for contbns. to higher edn., 1972; Gen. Edn. Bd. fellow U. Chgo., 1933-34; Henry Milton Wolf fellow history, 1935-36. Mem. NEA, Assn. for Instl. Research, Phi Beta Kappa, Phi Delta Kappa, Lambda Chi Alpha. Democrat. Methodist (del. to gen. conf. Dallas 1968, St. Louis 1970, Atlanta 1972). Club: Kiwanian. Home: 512 Dogwood Drive Chapel Hill NC 27514

KING, B.B. (RILEY B. KING), singer, guitarist; b. Itta Bena, Miss., Sept. 16, 1925. L.H.D. (hon.), Tougaloo (Miss.) Coll., 1973, D.Mus., Yale U., 1977. Began teaching self guitar, 1945; later studied, Schillinger System; past disc jockey and singer Memphis radio stas., internat. appearances throughout world, recs. on, RPM, Crown, Bullet, Kent, ABC Records, ABC/Dunhill Records.; Founding mem., John F. Kennedy Performing Arts Center, 1971; toured, Russia, 1979 (Recipient more than 25 awards as best singer and/or guitarist, including Grammy award 1970); Subject, collabortor: B.B. King, 1970, B.B. King Blues Guitar, 1970, B.B. King Songbook, 1971, B.B. King, The World's Greatest Living Blues Artist, Blues Guitar, A Method by B.B. King, 1973. Co-chmn. Found. Advancement Inmate Rehab. and Recreation, 1972—. Humanitarian award Fed. Bur. Prisons, 1972, B'nai B'rith Music and Performance Lodge, N.Y.C., 1973; Gallery of Greats and Best Blues Guitarist, 1974; Artist of the Decade and Humanitarian award Record World mag., 1974; Best Blues Singer Nat. Assn. TV and Radio Announcers, 1974; Hall of Fame and Best Blues Vocalist and Guitarist Ebony mag., 1974. Address: care Sidney A Seidenberg 1414 Ave of Americas New York NY 10019 *I would say to all people, but maybe to young people especially—black and white or whatever color—follow your own feelings and trust them; find out what you want to do and do it, and then practice it and practice it every day of your life and keep becoming what you are, despite any hardships and obstacles you meet.* *

KING, BENJAMIN CHAMBERLIN, lawyer; b. New Iberia, La., May 14, 1915; s. Henry Allen and Sue (Chamberlin) K.; m. Luise Haessler, July 26, 1947; children—Katherine, Margaret, Ben, Sue. B.A., Tulane U., 1935, J.D., 1938. Bar: La. bar 1938. Practice in, New Iberia, 1938-41, Shreveport, 1946—; sr. partner Cook, Clark, Egan, Yancey & King, 1946—. Served to lt. col. USAAF, 1941-46. Decorated D.F.C., Air medal with 2 oak leaf clusters. Mem. ABA, La. Bar Assn., Shreveport Bar Assn. (pres. 1974), Delta Kappa Epsilon, Phi Delta Phi. Episcopalian. Home: 4524 Fairfield Ave Shreveport LA 71106 Office: Commercial Bank Bldg Shreveport LA 71107

KING, BENJAMIN FRANKLIN, III, banker; b. Nashville, Aug. 9, 1928; s. Benjamin Franklin, Jr. and Katherine (Herbert) K.; m. Lois Anne Jones, Nov. 22, 1950; children: Katherine Olivia, Benjamin Franklin IV. B.S., Ga. Inst. Tech., 1950. Clk. comptroller dept. First Nat. Bank, Mobile, Ala., 1950-56, asst. comptroller, 1956, auditor, 1957-67, v.p., cashier, 1967—; Instr. Am. Inst. Banking. Mem., pres. Allied Arts Council, 1974-75; chmn. Mobilian of Year Com., 1967—; chmn. budget com. Community Chest and Council, 1970-71; Bd. dirs. Met. YMCA, Child Day Care Assn.; pres., bd. dirs. Vis. Nurses Assn. Served to 1st lt. USAF, 1951-53. Mem. Am. Inst. Banking, Ala. Bankers Assn. (past chmn. bank ops. com.), Bank Adminstrn. Inst. (past pres. Tri-State Gulf chpt.), Mobile Clearing House Assn. (past pres.), Mardi Gras Mystic Socs., Beta Theta Pi. Baptist (chmn. bd. deacons). Clubs: Mobile Country (past pres.), Bienville., Civitan (pres. 1966). Home: 3929 Pembrocke Ave Mobile AL 36608 Office: 31 N Royal St Mobile AL 36621

KING, BILLIE JEAN MOFFITT, profl. tennis player; b. Long Beach, Calif., Nov. 22, 1943; d. Willard J. Moffitt; m. Larry King, Sept. 17, 1965. Student, Calif. State U. at Los Angeles, 1961-64. Amateur tennis player, 1958-67, profl., 1968—; mem. Tennis Challenge Series, 1977, 78; host Colgate women's sports TV spl. The Lady is a Champ, 1975; co-founder, dir. Kingdom, Inc., San Mateo, Calif.; sports commentator ABC-TV, 1975-78; mem. U.S. Team which won Fedn. Cup, 1976; co-founder, pub. WomenSports mag., 1974—. Author: Tennis to Win, 1970, (with Kim Chapin) Billie Jean, 1974. Named Sportsperson of Yr. Sports Illustrated, 1972, Woman Athlete of Yr. A.P., 1967, 73; Top Woman Athlete of Year, 1972; Woman of Yr. Time mag., 1976; One of 10 Most Powerful Women in Am. Harper's Bazaar, 1977; One of 25 Most Influential Women in Am. World Almanac, 1977. Singles champion tournaments Wimbledon, 1966-68, 72, 73, 75, U.S. Open, Forest Hills, N.Y., 1967, 71, 72, 74, U.S. Hardcourt, 1966, Italian Open, 1970, West German Open, 1971, Australian Open, 1968, South African Open, 1966, 67, 69, U.S. Indoor, 1966-68, 71, U.S. Clay Court, 1971, French Open, 1972, Avon, 1980; doubles champion at Wimbledon, 1961, 62, 65, 67, 68, 70-73, U.S. Open, 1965, 67, 74, 80, French, 1972, Italian, 1970, South African, 1967-70, Bridgestone, 1976, Va. Slims, 1974, 76; mixed double champion at Wimbledon, 1967, 71, 73, U.S. Open, 1967, 71, 73, French, 1967, 70, South African, 1967, Australian, 1968; winner 29 Va. Slims singles titles, 1970-77, 4 Colgate titles, 1977, Fedn. Cup, 1963-67, 76-79, Wightman cup, 1961-67; 70, 77, 78; World Tennis Team All-Star, 3 times. Address: care US Tennis Assn 51 E 42d St New York NY 10017 *

KING, CARL B., tool company executive; b. 1942; married. B.A., U. Tex., 1965, LL.B., 1966; M.B.A., Wharton Sch. Bus., U. Pa., 1968. Counsel corp. planning Exxon Corp., 1968-74; counsel Cameron Iron Works, Inc., Houston, 1974-75, v.p. corp. services, 1975-81, sr. v.p., sec., 1981—. Office: Cameron Iron Works Inc 13013 Northwest Freeway Box 1212 Houston TX 77251 *

KING, CAROLE, composer, singer; b. Bklyn., Feb. 9, 1942; m. Gerry Goffin; m. Charles Larkey; m. Rick Evers; m. Rick Sorensen, 1982; children—Louise, Sherry, Molly, Levi. Student, Queens Coll. Co-writer (with Gerry Goffin) numerous songs, 1960-68, including Will You Love Me Tomorrow?, He's a Rebel, Go Away, Little Girl, Up on the Roof, Natural Woman, the Locomotion, Take Good Care of My Baby, It's Too Late; solo recs. include Tapestry, 1971 (4 Grammy awards). Address: Free Flow Prodns Inc 1209 Baylor St Austin TX 78703

KING, CARY JUDSON, III, chemical engineer, educator; b. Ft. Monmouth, N.J., Sept. 27, 1934; s. Cary Judson and Mary Margaret (Forbes) K., Jr.; m. Jeanne Antoinette Yorke, June 22, 1957; children: Mary Elizabeth, Cary Judson IV, Catherine Jeanne. B. Engring., Yale, 1956; S.M., Mass. Inst. Tech., 1958, Sc.D., 1960. Asst. prof. chem. engring. Mass. Inst. Tech., Cambridge, 1959-63; dir. Bayway Sta. Sch. Chem. Engring. Practice, Linden, N.J., 1959-61; asst. prof. chem. engring. U. Calif. at Berkeley, 1963-66, asso. prof., 1966-69, prof., 1969—, vice chmn. dept. chem. engring., 1967-72, chmn., 1972-81, dean Coll. Chemistry, 1981—; cons. Procter & Gamble Co., 1969—, CPC Internat., 1982—. Author: Separation Processes, 1971, 80, Freeze Drying of Foods, 1971; Contbr. numerous articles to profl. jours. Active Boy Scouts Am., 1947—; pres. Kensington Community Council, 1972-73, dir., 1970-73. Named Inst. Lectr. Am. Inst. Chem. Engrs., 1973, Food, Pharm. and Bioengring. Div. award, 1975, William H. Walker award, 1976. Mem. Nat. Acad. Engring., Am. Inst. Chem. Engrs., Inst. Food Tech., Am. Soc. Engring. Edn. (George Westinghouse award 1978), Am. Chem. Soc., AAAS. Patentee in field. Home: 7 Kensington Ct Kensington CA 94707 Office: Coll Chemistry U Calif Berkeley CA 94720

KING, CHARLES EVERETT, biologist; b. Oak Park, Ill., May 8, 1934; s. Everett Smith and Marian (Earl) K.; children—Jennifer, Andrew. A.B., Emory U., 1958; M.S., Fla. State U., 1960; Ph.D., U. Wash., 1965. Postdoctoral fellow U. Wash., Seattle, 1965; instr. biology Yale U., 1965-66, asst. prof. biology, 1968-72; asst. prof. zoology U. Ill., 1966-68; asso. prof. biology U. South Fla., 1972-75, prof., 1975-77; prof., chmn. dept. zoology Oreg. State U., 1977—; cons. Com. on Environ., U.S. Congress. Served with U.S. Army, 1955-56. NSF grantee; USPHS Nat. Inst. on Aging grantee. Fellow AAAS; mem. Am. Soc. Naturalists, Genetics Soc. Am., Ecol. Soc. Am., Soc. Study Evolution. Home: 3415 NW Hayes Corvallis OR 97330 Office: Dept Zoology Oreg State U Corvallis OR 97331

KING, CHARLES GLEN, chemist; b. Entiat, Wash., Oct. 22, 1896; s. Charles Clement and Mary (Bookwalter) K.; m. Hilda Bainton, Sept. 11, 1919; children—Dorothy, Robert Bainton, Kendall Willard. B.S., Wash. State Coll., 1918; M.S., U. Pitts., 1920, Ph.D., 1923; postgrad., Columbia, 1926-27, Cambridge (Eng.) U., 1929-30; D.Sc., Wash. State Coll., 1950, U. Pitts., 1950, Drexel Inst., 1955; Dr. Pub. Service, Denison U., 1961. By-products specialist, State of Wash., 1918-19; instr. chemistry U. Pitts., 1920-26, asst. prof., 1926-30, prof., 1930-43; research asst. Columbia, 1926-27, vis. prof. chem., 1942-46, prof., 1946-62, emeritus; asso. dir. Inst. Nutrition Sci., 1963-66; spl. lectr., 1967-73; dir. grants mgmt. St. Luke's Hosp. Center, 1966-67; sci. dir. Nutrition Found., 1942-55, exec. dir., 1955-61, pres., 1961-63, trustee, 1963—; cons. Rockefeller Found., 1963-66; mem. sci. adv. bd. Robert A. Welch Found., 1954-63; Agrl. Research Policy Com. U.S. Dept. Agr., 1950-57; mem. exec. bd. U.S. com. UNICEF, 1968-69; Cons. Office of Surgeon Gen., AUS, 1940-66; NIH Study Sect. Chmn., 1946-51, Office Surg. Gen., USPHS, 1940-66. Trustee Boyce Thompson Inst., 1957-75, Food Law Inst., 1950-62; pres. 5th Internat. Congress on Nutrition, 1960; Mem. Food and Nutrition Bd., 1940-70. Served as pvt. 12th Inf. Machine Gun Co., 1918. Recipient Pa. Award of Merit, 1938, Pa. Pub. Health Assn. award, 1939, Pitts. award, 1943, G.M.A. award, 1944, John Scott award, 1949; Nicholas Appert award Inst. Food Technologists Chgo. sect., 1955; Charles Spencer award Am. Chem. Soc., 1963; Conrad A. Elvehjem award Am. Inst. Nutrition, 1966; Purkinje Gold medal Acad. Scis., Czechoslovakia, 1969. Mem. Internat. Union Nutritional Scis. (pres. 1966-69, hon. pres. 1972—), N.Y. Acad. Medicine, Am. Chem. Soc., Am. Soc. Biol. Chemists (pres. 1954-55), Inst. Food Technologists, Nat. Acad. Scis. (exec. com. internat. council sci. unions 1966-69), Am. Forestry Assn., AAAS, Am. Inst. Nutrition (pres. 1949-50), Am. Pub. Health Assn. (treas. 1949-60, pres. 1961-62), Royal Soc. Health (Eng.), Harvey Soc., Nutrition Soc. (Eng.), Finland Soc. Biochemistry, Biophysics and Microbiology (hon.), Phi Beta Kappa, Sigma Xi, Omicron Delta Kappa. Quaker. Clubs: Century (N.Y.C.); Cosmos (Washington). Isolated vitamin C, 1932. Home: 192 Kendal at Longwood Kennett Square PA 19348 Office: Inst Human Nutrition Columbia U New York City NY 10032

KING, CHESTER HARDING, lawyer; b. Syracuse, N.Y., Mar. 30, 1913; s. Chester Harding and Kathleen (Comstock) K.; m. Mary Ellen Crapon de Caprona, Dec. 18, 1948; children: Chester Harding III, Eleanor Mather, Charles Noel, Peter Denys Sedgwick. Grad., Kent (Conn.) Sch., 1930; A.B., Harvard U., 1934, LL.B., 1937. Bar: N.Y. 1938. Since practiced in, Syracuse; partner firm Bond, Schoeneck & King, 1952—. Mem. Episcopal Found. Central N.Y. Served to capt., inf. U.S. Army, 1941-45. Decorated Bronze Star with oak leaf cluster. Mem. ABA, N.Y. State Bar Assn. (chmn. com. estate gift taxation 1968-70), Onondaga County Bar Assn., Am. Judicature Soc., Am. Coll. Probate Counsel. (bd. regents 1982—). Home: 32 Albany Street Cazenovia NY 13035 Office: 1 Lincoln Center Syracuse NY 13202

KING, CLYDE RICHARD, journalism educator, writer; b. Gorman, Tex., Jan. 14, 1924; s. Clyde Stewart and Mary Alice (Neill) K. A.S., John Tarleton State Coll., 1943; B.A., U. Okla., 1948, M.A., 1949; Ph.D., Baylor U., 1962. Dir. news service, instr. journalism Mary Hardin-Baylor Coll., Belton, Tex., 1950; asst. prof. English Tarleton State Coll., Stephenville, Tex., 1951; dir. news service, instr. journalism East Tex. State Coll., Commerce, 1952-56; asst. prof., assoc. prof. U. Tex., Austin, 1956-62, prof. journalism, 1965—; mem. faculty adv. com. U. Tex. Press, 1977—; freelance writer, 1948—. Author: Ghost Towns of Texas, 1953, Wagons East, 1965, Mañana with Memories, 1964, Watchmen of the Walls, 1967, Susanna Dickinson; Messenger of the Alamo, 1976, A Birthday in Texas, 1980, We Sing Their Harvest Songs, 1980, The Lady Cannoneer, 1981; editor: Letters from Fort Sill, 1886-1887, 1971, Victorian Lady on the Texas Frontier, 1971, Brit. edit., 1972, Fred Gipson: Before Old Yeller, 1980. Mem. Winedale Adv. Com., 1969-72; pres. bd. Stephenville Hist. House Mus., 1976-79, 83; mem. adminstrv. bd. Stephenville First Meth. Ch. Served with AUS, 1943-45; ETO. Research grantee U. Tex., 1960, U.S. Ednl. Found. in India, 1980. Mem. Tex., West Tex. hist. assns., Stephenville C. of C., Gross Timbers Fine Arts Assn., Sigma Delta Chi, Sigma Phi Epsilon. Methodist. Club: Masons (32d deg. Scottish Rite). Home: 830 Alexander Rd Stephenville TX 76401

KING, COLBERT ISAIAH, banker; b. Washington, Sept. 20, 1939; s. Isaiah and Amelia (Colbert) K.; m. Gwendolyn Ann Stewart, July 3, 1961; children: Robert, Stephen, Allison. B.A., Howard U., 1961, postgrad., 1969. Dir. govt. relations Potomac Electric Power Co., Washington, 1976-77; legis. asst. to Senator Charles McMathias, Jr. of Md., 1972-76; chief policy and program devel. ACTION/VISTA, 1971-72; spl. asst. to under sec. HEW, 1970-71; dep. asst. sec. of treasury Dept. Treasury, Washington, 1977-79; U.S. exec. dir. World Bank, 1979-81; sr. v.p. Riggs Nat. Bank, Washington, 1981—; attache Dept. State, 1964-69. Alternate mem. Nat. Capital Planning Comm., 1973-75; mem. D.C. Mayor's Internat. Adv. Council; bd. dirs. Center for Study Social Policy, U. Chgo.; adv. com. office univ. relations Howard U.; research adv. council Joint Center Polit. Studies. Served with U.S. Army, 1961-63. Named to Outstanding Young Men of Am. U.S. Jaycees, 1974; recipient spl. citation Nat. Rehab. Assn., 1975, Ser. award Howard U. Center for Sickle Cell Disease, 1975. Mem. NAACP, PTA, Kappa Alpha Psi. Democrat. Episcopalian. Office: Riggs National Bank Washington DC 20220

KING, CORETTA SCOTT (MRS. MARTIN LUTHER KING, JR), lecturer, writer, concert singer; b. Marion, Ala., Apr. 27, 1927; d. Obidiah and Bernice (McMurray) Scott; m. Martin Luther King, Jr., June 18, 1953 (dec. Apr. 1968); children: Yolanda Denise, Martin Luther III, Dexter Scott, Bernice Albertine. A.B., Antioch Coll., 1951; Mus.B., New Eng. Conservatory Music, 1954, Mus.D., 1971; L.H.D., Boston U., 1969, Marymount-Manhattan Coll., 1969, Morehouse Coll., 1970; H.H.D., Brandeis U., 1969, Wilberforce U., 1970, Bethune-Cookman Coll., 1970, Princeton U., 1970; LL.D., Bates Coll., 1971. Voice instr. Morris Brown Coll., Atlanta, 1962; commentator Cable News Network, Atlanta, 1980—; lectr., writer. Author: My Life With Martin Luther King, Jr, 1969; Contbr. articles to mags.; Concert debut, Springfield, Ohio, 1948, numerous concerts, throughout U.S., concerts, India, 1959, performances, Freedom Concert. Del. to White House Conf. Children and Youth, 1960; sponsor Com. for Sane

Nuclear Policy, Com. on Responsibility, Moblzn. to End War in Viet Nam, 1966, 67, Margaret Sanger Meml. Found.; mem. So. Rural Action Project, Inc.; pres. Martin Luther King, Jr. Found.; chmn. Commn. on Econ. Justice for Women; mem. exec. com. Nat. Com. Inquiry; co-chmn. Clergy and Laymen Concerned about Vietnam, Nat. Com. for Full Employment, 1974; pres. Martin Luther King Jr. Center for Social Change; co-chairperson Nat. Com. Full Employment; mem. exec. bd. Nat. Health Ins. Com.; active YWCA; bd. dirs. So. Christian Leadership Conf., Martin Luther King, Jr. Found. Gt. Britain; trustee Robert F. Kennedy Meml. Found., Ebenezer Bapt. Ch. Recipient Outstanding Citizenship award Montgomery (Ala.) Improvement Assn., 1959, Merit award St. Louis Argus, 1960, Distinguished Achievement award Nat. Orgn. Colored Women's Clubs, 1962, Louise Waterman Wise award Am. Jewish Congress Women's Aux., 1963, Myrtle Wreath award Cleve. Hadassah, 1965, award for excellence in field human relations Soc. Family of May, 1968, Universal Love award Premio San Valentine Com., 1968, Wateler Peace prize, 1968, Dag Hammarskjold award, 1969, Pacem in Terris award Internat. Overseas Service Found., 1969, Leadership for Freedom award Roosevelt U., 1971, Martin Luther King Meml. medal Coll. City N.Y., 1971, Internat. Viareggio award, 1971, numerous others; named Woman of Year Utility Club N.Y.C., 1962, Nat. Assn. Radio and TV Announcers, 1968. Mem. Nat. Council Negro Women (Ann. Brotherhood award 1957), Women Strike for Peace (del. disarmament conf. Geneva, Switzerland 1962, citation for work in peace and freedom 1963), Women's Internat. League for Peace and Freedom, NAACP, United Ch. Women (bd. mgrs.), Alpha Kappa Alpha (hon.). Baptist (mem. choir, guild adviser). Club: Links (Human Dignity and Human Rights award Norfolk chpt. 1964). Address: care Press Relations Cable News Network 1050 Techwood Dr NW Atlanta GA 30318 *

KING, DONALD, company executive; b. Liverpool, Eng., Feb. 9, 1936; m. Maureen Rita; children: Phillip Hamilton, Mitchell Donald, Kerry Anne. Chartered acct. Price Waterhouse, U.K. and Can., 1959-73; with Marathon Realty Co., Ltd., Toronto, Ont., 1973—, pres., chief exec. officer, 1983—, dir. Pres. Ont. March of Dimes, 1981-83; dir. Canadin Rehab. Council for Disabled. Fellow Inst. Chartered Accts. Eng. and Wales; mem. Inst. Chartered Accts. Ont., Internat. Council Shopping Centres, Ont. C. of C. Home: 2431 Jarvis St Mississauga ON Canada L5C 2P7 Office: Marathon Realty Company Ltd Royal Trust Tower 1650 PO Box 375 Toronto ON Canada M5K 1K8

KING, DONALD BERNARD, ret. coll. dean; b. Bristol, Conn., Sept. 3, 1913; s. John and Kathryn (Jones) K.; m. Louise F. Dupraz, June 11, 1938; children—Judith, John, Peter, Jeremy, Robert, Kathryn. B.A., Dartmouth, 1935; Ph.D., Princeton, 1938. Instr. classics Dartmouth, 1938-39; mem. Soc. of Fellows of Harvard, 1939-41; asst. prof. English composition Pa. State U., 1941-43; asso. prof. classics and history Beloit (Wis.) Coll., 1946-51; prof. classics and English Coll. Mt. St. Joseph on-the-Ohio, 1961-67; dean of the coll. St. Norbert Coll., West DePere, Wis., 1967-79; Examiner, cons. North Central Assn., 1959—, commr. colls. and univs., 1968-71. Author: Erasmus' On Copia of Words and Ideas, 1963; Contbr. articles to profl. jours. Served to lt. USNR, 1943-46. Mem. Am. Assn. Univ. Profs., Am. Assn. Higher Edn., Classical Assn. Middle West and South, Conf. Acad. Deans. Home: RFD 1 Box 98 Perkinsville VT 05151

KING, DONALD C., psychologist; b. Albion, Ind., Oct. 8, 1930; s. Russell B. and Grace Edith (Butz) K.; m. Patricia Ann Grover, June 8, 1952; children—Laura Jean, John Grover, Joseph Russell, Jeffrey Gerald. B.S. with highest distinction, Purdue U., 1952, M.S., 1955, Ph.D., 1957. Mem. faculty Purdue U., 1956—, prof. adminstrv. sci., mgmt. and psychology, 1965—, asst. dean, 1963-66, chmn. adminstrv. scis. policy com., 1978—; dir. profl. programs Krannert Grad. Sch., 1968-71; cons. in field, 1957—. Author papers in field, chpts. in books. Served with AUS, 1952-54. Mem. Acad. Mgmt., Am. Psychol. Assn., Internat. Assn. Applied Social Scientists, Nat. Tng. Labs. Inst. Applied Behavioral Scis., Midwestern Psychol. Assn., Sigma Xi, Omicrom Delta Kappa. Home: 179 Blueberry Ln West Lafayette IN 47906 Office: Krannert Grad Sch Mgmt Purdue Univ West Lafayette IN 47907

KING, DONALD WEST, educational administrator, pathology educator; b. Cochranton, Pa., June 30, 1927; s. Donald W. and Leila (Fronds) K.; m. Mary Elizabeth Dickason, May 30, 1952; children: Donald III, Katherine, David. Student, Syracuse U., 1944-45, M.D., 1949. Diplomate: Am. Bd. Pathology. Intern Presbyn. Hosp., N.Y.C., 1949-50, resident, 1950-51; instr. dept. pathology Columbia U., 1951-52; fellow dept. chemistry Carlesberg Lab., Carlesberg, Denmark, 1955-56; asst. prof. pathology dept. Yale U., New Haven, 1956-61; prof., chmn. dept. pathology U. Colo., Denver, 1961-67; Delafield prof., chmn. dept. pathology Columbia U., N.Y.C., 1967-82; dir. Given Inst. Patholobiology, Aspen, Colo., 1967—; dean div. biol. scis. and Pritzker Sch Medicine, v.p. Med. Ctr. U. Chgo., 1983—. Served to 1st lt. M.C. U.S. Army, 1952-54. Mem. Am. Assn. Pathologists, N.Y. Path. Soc., Am. Soc. Exptl. Biology, Harvey Soc., Am. Soc. Human Genetics. Home: 999 N Lake Shore Dr Chicago Il 60611 Office: Div Biol Scis and Pritzker Sch Medicine U chgo 950 E 59th St Box 417 Chicago Il 60637

KING, DONALD WEST, JR., pathologist, medical school administrator; b. Cochranton, Pa., June 30, 1927; m., 1952; 3 children. M.D., Syracuse U., 1949. Resident, instr. pathology Columbia U. Coll. Physicians and Surgeons, N.Y.C., 1949-52, Delafield prof. pathology, chmn. dept., 1967-82; prof., chmn. dept. U. Colo., Denver, 1961-67; assoc. prof. pathology Grace-New Haven Med. Ctr., 1956-61, also asst. prof.; v.p. U. Chgo. Med. Ctr.; dean div. biol. scis. Pritzer Sch. Medicine Grace-New Haven Med. Ctr., 1983—. Served as lt. M.C. AUS, 1952-54. USPHS fellow U. Chgo., 1954-55, Carlsberg Lab., 1955-56. Mem. Am. Soc. Exptl. Pathology, Soc. Cell Biology, Human Genetics Soc., Am. Assn. Pathologists and Bacteriologists, Am. Soc. Clin Pathology. Office: Office Vice Pres U. Chgo Med Ctr Chicago IL 60637 *

KING, E. W., utility resource development company executive. Pres., chief exec. officer Can. Utilities, Ltd., Edmonton, Alta. Office: Can Utilities Ltd 10040-104th St Edmonton AB Canada T5J 2V6 *

KING, EDWARD DUNHAM, university press executive, designer; b. Greenville, S.C., Jan. 21, 1929; s. John Smith and Ruth Elizabeth (Dunham) K.; m. Lois Catherine Thayer, Nov. 24, 1954; children: Edward Thayer, Stuart Hildt, Mary Elizabeth, Charles Ward. Comml. design certificate, Sch. Practical Art, Boston, 1950; B.F.A. in Painting, U. Ala., 1955. Art editor Quar. Rev., Air U., Montgomery, Ala., 1955-57; asst. prodn. mgr. George Braziller (pub.), 1957-59; with Kiplinger Book Club, Washington, 1959-60; design and prodn. mgr. Johns Hopkins U. Press, Balt., 1960-69; asso. dir. U. Mo. Press, Columbia, 1969-73, dir., 1974—; Design cons. Hillside Studio, 1962-81; publs. adv. com. Am. Geol. Soc. One-man show, Hicks Street Gallery, Brooklyn Heights, N.Y., 1960; exhibited in group shows, Am. Inst. Graphic Arts, 1969-76, Assn. Am. U. Presses, 1969, 70, 72-76, 78-82, Leipzig Schonste Bucher Aus Aller Welt, 1969, 72 (Gold medal 1976), Internat. Bi-Ann. Art Book Competition, 1972, Mid-Western Ann. Book Show, 1969-76, 79-82, Chgo. Book Clinic, 1961, 67-68, 70-76, 78-82, Balt. Art Dirs. Show, 1962, 63, 65-67, Kansas City Art Dirs. Show, 1969, 70, 72-76, 79, St. Louis Art Dirs. Show, 1969—, N.Y. Type Dirs. Show, 1969, 70, Printing Industries Am., 1970, 76, 78, The One Show, 1973, N.Y. Art Dirs., Univ. and College Designers Assn., 1972, 74-75, 9th and 10th Southeastern Ann. Exhbns., Atlanta, 1954, 55, Birmingham Art Assn., Miss. Watercolor Soc., 1954, Ala. Art Assn., Forum Gallery, N.Y.C., 1955, Hicks St. Gallery, 1959. Served with AUS, 1946-48, 50-51. Mem. Am. Inst. Graphic Arts, Assn. Am. Univ. Presses (bd. dirs. 1979-81), St. Louis Soc. Communicating Arts. Democrat. Office: 200 Lewis Hall University of Mo Columbia MO 65201

KING, EDWARD LOUIS, chemistry educator; b. Grand Forks, N.D., Mar. 15, 1920; s. Edward Louis and Beatrice (Nicholson) K.; m. Joy Kerler, Dec. 20, 1952; children: Paul, Marcia (dec.). Student, Long Beach (Calif.) Jr. Coll., 1938-41; B.S., U. Calif., Berkeley, 1942, Ph.D., 1945. Research chemist Manhattan Project, U. Cal., Berkeley, 1942-46; mem. chemistry faculty Harvard, 1946-48, U. Wis., 1948-62, U. Colo., Boulder, 1963—, chmn. dept. chemistry, 1970-72. Author: How Chemical Reactions Occur, 1963, Chemistry, 1979; Editor: Inorganic Chemistry, 1964-68. Guggenheim fellow, 1957-58. Mem. Am. Chem. Soc., Phi Beta Kappa, Sigma Xi. Office: Dept Chemistry U Colo Boulder CO 80309

KING, EDWARD WILLIAM, transportation executive; b. North Fork, W.Va., Jan. 29, 1923; s. Edward Ward and Myrtle (Charlton) K.; m. Mary Elizabeth Preston, Oct. 31, 1947 (div. 1976); children: Edward William, Elizabeth King Griffin, Mary King Sullivan; m. Martha Lee Corns Mather, Apr. 7, 1977. Edn., Va. Poly. Inst., Washington and Lee U., U. Tenn.-Knoxville. Pres., treas. Mason & Dixon Lines, Inc., Kingsport, Tenn., until 1974, chmn. bd., treas., 1974—; pres., treas. Crown Enterprises, Inc.; treas. Mason & Dixon Tank Lines, Inc.; chmn. Regular Common Carrier Conf., 1966-67; dir. Kingsport Nat. Bank, Kingsport Fed. Savs. & Loan. Seal sale chmn. Sullivan County TB Assn.; mem. Kingsport Bd. Edn.; dir., sec.-treas. Holston Valley Hosp., 1956-79; trustee East Tenn. State U. Found. Named Young Man of Yr. Kingsport Jaycees, 1958. Mem. Am. Trucking Assn. (Tenn. v.p., trustee, ATA Found.), Trucking Employers, Tenn. Motor Transport Assn. (pres. 1957-58), Kingsport C. of C. (v.p.). Presbyterian. Clubs: Ridgefields Country (Kingsport); Kingsport Civitan (pres.). Office: Mason & Dixon Lines Inc Hwy 11W E Kingsport TN 37660

KING, ELMER RICHARD, physician, educator; b. Logan County, Ohio, May 15, 1916; s. John Oliver and Clara (Yoder) K.; m. Marie Hutchings Pace, Mar. 29, 1941; children—Marsha Ann, John Michael, Suzanne. B.A., Ohio State U., 1939, M.D., 1941; AEC fellow, Duke, 1948-49; postgrad. tng., Oak Ridge Inst. Nuclear Studies, 1949-50, Mayo Found., 1953. Diplomate: Am. Bd. Radiology, Am. Bd. Nuclear Medicine (founder). Commd. lt. (j.g.), M.C. U.S. Navy, 1941, advanced through grades to capt., 1961; intern U.S. Naval Hosp., Pensacola, Fla.; with atomic def. div. Bur. Medicine and Surgery, 1946-47; sr. scientist Operation Sandstone, Eniwetok Atoll, 1947; resident radiology U.S. Naval Hosp., Bethesda, Md., 1950-53; dir. div. nuclear medicine U.S. Naval Med. Center, Bethesda, 1954-61, chief radiology, 1958-61; ret., 1961; mem. faculty Med. Coll. Va., 1961—, prof. radiology, 1965—, chmn. dept. radiology, 1965-73; chmn. div. radiation therapy and onchology, 1973-76; Mem. Am. Bd. Med. Specialists. Author: (with T. G. Mitchell) Laboratory Guide to Nuclear Medicine, 1960; also numerous papers.; Editor: (with Charles Behrens) Atomic Medicine, 1969. Recipient certificate of merit Sec. Navy, 1947, Surgeon Gen. U.S., 1961; Alumni Achievement award Ohio State U., 1966. Fellow Am. Coll. Radiology (Gold medal 1979); mem. Radiol. Soc. N.Am., Am. Radium Soc., Am. Roentgen Ray Soc., Soc. Nuclear Medicine, Am. Soc. Therapy Radiology, AMA, Va Med. Soc., Va. Radiol. Soc., Nu Sigma Nu. Republican. Methodist Episcopalian. Clubs: Willow Oaks, Stone Henge (Richmond). Home: 641 Farnham Dr Richmond VA 23235

KING, ERIC MICHAEL, sports association executive; b. Mansfield, Nottinghamshire, Eng., Nov. 1, 1937; emigrated to Can., 1957; s. George Frederick and Olive Mary (Kempin) K.; m. Shirley Pryor, Sept. 29, 1962; children: Lisa Jean, Michelle Marie. B.A., U. Sask., 1968, B.Ed., 1969. Lab technician Govt. Can., Saskatoon, Sask., Can., 1959-65; exec. dir. Canadian Soccer Assn., Ottawa, Ont., Can., 1968—. Office: Canadian Soccer Assn 333 River Rd Ottawa ON Canada K1L 8H9

KING, FREDERICK ALEXANDER, neuroscientist, educator; b. Paterson, N.J., Oct. 3, 1925; s. James Aloysius and Louise Bisset (Gallant) K.; children: Alexander Karell, Elizabeth Gallant. A.B., Stanford, 1953; A.M. (John Carrol Fulton scholar 1953-55), Johns Hopkins, 1955, Ph.D., 1956. Instr. psychology Johns Hopkins U., 1954-56; asst. prof. psychiatry Ohio State U., 1957-59; mem. faculty Coll. Medicine, U. Fla., 1959-78, asst., then asso. prof., then prof. neurosurgery, 1965-69, prof., chmn. dept. neurosci., 1969-78; dir./co-dir. Center Neurobiol. Scis., 1964-78; dir. Yerkes Primate Center, prof. anatomy, asso. dean Sch. Medicine Emory U., Atlanta, 1978—; Mem. adv. com. Primate Research Centers, NIH, 1969-73; mem. psychobiology adv. panel, biol. and med. scis. div. NSF, 1963-67, cons. med. and biol. scis., 1967-70; mem. research scientist devel. rev. com. NIMH, 1969-70, 75-78, chmn. com. for coordination and communication for dirs. in biol. research tng. programs, 1972—; sec.-treas. Fla. Anat. Bd., 1969-71; vice chmn. bd. sci. advisers Yerkes Regional Primate Research Center, 1974-78; mem. brain scis. com. NRC-Nat. Acad. Scis., 1974-78. Gen. editor: Handbook of Behavioral Neurobiology, 5 vols, 1972—; Contbr. articles to profl. jours. Served with USNR, 1943-46, 51. Research fellow NIH, 1955-56; spl. fellow NIMH, Inst. Physiology, U. Pisa (Italy) Faculty Medicine, 1961-62. Mem. Internat. Neuropsychology Soc. (sec.-treas.), Soc. Neurosci. (chmn. com. on edn.), Am. Psychol. Assn. (chmn. membership com. div. physiol. and comparative psychology, chmn. com. for animal research and experimentation). Home: 2681 Galahad Dr Atlanta GA 30329 Office: Yerkes Primate Research Center Emory U Atlanta GA 30322

KING, GEORGE SMITH, JR., univ. athletic dir.; b. Charleston, W.Va., Aug. 16, 1928; s. George Smith and Margret F. (Nichols) K.; m. Jeanne Greider, June 18, 1949; children—George, Kristy (Mrs. Gary Danielson), Kathy, Kerry, Gordon. B.S., Morris Harvey Coll., 1950; M.A., W.Va. U., 1958. Basketball coach Morris Harvey Coll., 1955, W.Va. U., 1958-65; basketball coach Purdue U., 1965-71, dir. athletics, 1971—. Named to W.Va. Hall of Fame. Home: 1210 Tuckahoe Ln West Lafayette IN 47906 Office: Mackey Arena Purdue U West Lafayette IN 47907

KING, GERALD WILFRID, chemistry educator; b. West Hartlepool, Eng., Jan. 22, 1928; s. Wilfrid James and Doris Amelie K.; m. Gwyneth Jones, Mar. 27, 1954; children: Richard James, Juliette Mary, Jennifer Wyn, Gillian Clare. B.Sc., U. London, 1949, Ph.D., 1952, D.Sc., 1970. Sci. officer Atomic Weapons Research Establishment, Aldermaston, Eng., 1952-54; lectr. Univ. Coll., London, 1954-57; asst. prof. chemistry McMaster U., Hamilton, Ont., Can., 1957-59, asso. prof., 1959-64, prof., 1964—, chmn. dept. chemistry, 1979-82. Author: Spectroscopy and Molecular Structure, 1964; editor: Can. Jour. Chemistry, 1974-79; Contbr. numerous articles on chem. physics to profl. jours. Fellow Chem. Inst. Can., Royal Soc. Chemistry, Royal Soc. Can. Home: 674 Northland Ave Burlington ON L7T 3J7 Canada Office: Dept Chemistry McMaster U Hamilton ON L8S 4M1 Canada

KING, HANFORD LANGDON, JR., ret. bishop; b. Worcester, Mass., Sept. 18, 1921; s. Hanford Langdon and Hephizibah Vernon (Hopkins) K.; m. Helen R. Knospe, May 31, 1947; children—Deborah, Judith, Hanford Langdon. B.A., Clark U., 1943; S.T.B., Episcopal Theol. Sch., 1946; Ph.D., Columbia U., 1950; postgrad., Sch. of Prophets, San Francisco, 1952, 54, Coll. Preachers, Washington, 1958, Boston Theol. Inst., 1969, Grad. Theol. Union Calif., 1968, Aspen Inst. Humanistic Studies, 1964. Certified profl. ski instr., 1962. Ordained deacon Episcopal Ch., 1946, priest, 1947, consecrated bishop of, Idaho, 1972—, now ret.; lay vicar chs., Mass., 1944-46; mem. staff St. James Ch., N.Y.C., 1946-47; rector chs., N.Y.C., 1947-50, Bozeman, Mont., 1951-60, Rapid City, S.D., 1960-72; dep. gen. conv. Episc. Ch., 1958, 61, 64, 67, 70; mem. com. evangelism, 1970, bishop's com. evangelism, 1974, com. on ministry, 1974—; mem. Nat. Joint Commn. on Ch. in Small Communities, 1974; mem. exec. council Diocese of Mont., 1951-53, 60, chmn. dept. youth, 1952-54, dept. promotion, 1953-55; chmn. budget dept. Diocese of S.D., 1962-68, chmn. resources and devel., 1966-68. Author: Doctrine of Conscience in Contemporary Anglo-Catholic Theology; contbr. articles to mags. Pres. Rapid City (S.D.) Bd. Edn., 1970; weightlifting commr. AAU, 1959-61; trustee St. Luke's Hosp., Boise, 1972—, Mountain States Tumor Inst., Boise, 1972—, Ch. Div. Sch. Pacific, 1978—. Mem. Internat. Platform Assn. Home: 1203 Highland View Dr Boise ID 83702

KING, HAROLD TAFT, lawyer; b. Angleton, Tex., Mar. 3, 1909; s. Clarence and Harriett (Chappelle) K.; m. Thelma Owen, Aug. 9, 1933; 1 dau., Diane. Student, Northwestern U., 1925-26; J.D., U. Colo., 1930. Bar: Colo. 1930, U.S. Supreme Ct. 1947. Individual practice law, Denver, 1930—; ret. chmn. bd. Columbia Savs. & Loan Assn.; dir. Capitol Life Ins. Co., Columbia Savs. & Loan Assn.; Spl. rep. of State Dept. to Am. embassies, London, Dublin, Ireland, 1974; bd. visitors Air Force Acad.; del. Republican Nat. Conv., 1948, 68; chmn. del. UNESCO, Paris, 1970-72; mem. U.S. del. to, Egypt, 1976, U.S. econ. del. to, Israel, 1977; mem. adv. bd. Center for Study of Presidency; bd. dirs. Pub. Mems. Assn. U.S. State Dept.; asso. Fgn. Service Orgn., U.S. State Dept.; sr. adviser Dept. State, Mexico City, 1982. Cordier fellow Sch. Internat. Affairs, Columbia U., N.Y.C.; recipient Significant Sig award Sigma Chi. Mem. ABA, Colo. Bar Assn. (gov.), Denver Bar Assn., Downtown Denver Assn. (dir.). Clubs: Denver Country, Petroleum, Law, Mile High (Denver). Home: 31 Polo Club Circle Denver CO 80209 Office: 900 Pennsylvania St Denver CO 80201 *My goal in life has been to obtain the ultimate in happiness for my family by achieving financial security, the highest recognition in my profession, continued good health for them as well as myself and a mutual love between one for the other. To obtain all this I have practiced the Golden Rule.*

KING, HENRY HAYES, JR., business executive; b. Shreveport, La., July 12, 1932; s. Henry Hayes and Vashti Estell (Bullock) K.; m. Beverly Ann Farmer, June 16, 1956; children: Beverly Lynn, Thomas Bradford, David Earl. B.A., La. State U., 1956; postgrad., South Tex. Coll. Law, 1962; grad., Advanced Mgmt. Program, Harvard U. Grad. Sch. Bus., 1976. With Tex. Eastern Transmission Corp., Houston, 1958-76, dir. employee relations, 1971-72, dir. public relations, 1972-73, gen. mgr. human relations, 1973-74, gen. mgr. corp. adminstrv. staff, 1974, v.p. corp. adminstrv. staff, 1974-76; v.p. adminstrn. Tex. Eastern Corp., Houston, 1976-80, sr. v.p., chief adminstrv. officer, 1980-82, exec. v.p., 1982—. Bd. dirs. Jr. Achievement, Greater Houston Conv. and Visitors Council, Tex. Research League. Served to capt., inf. U.S. Army, 1956-58. Mem. Am. Compensation Assn., Am. Gas Assn., Am. Mgmt. Assn., Am. Soc. Personnel Adminstrn., Houston Personnel Assn., Houston World Trade Assn., Interstate Natural Gas Assn. Am., Nat. Assn. Corp. Dirs., Public Relations Soc. Am. Republican. Methodist. Clubs: Astrodome, Columns, Houston, Houston Center, Houston Racquet. Office: 1 Houston Center PO Box 2521 Houston TX 77252

KING, HENRY LAWRENCE, lawyer; b. N.Y.C., Apr. 29, 1928; s. H. Abraham and Henrietta (Prentky) K.; m. Barbara Hope, 1949 (dec. May 1962); children: Elizabeth Hope King Robertson, Patricia Jane King Cantlay, Matthew Harrison.; m. Alice Mary Sturges, Aug. 1, 1963 (div. 1978); children: Katherine Masury, Andrew Lawrence, Eleanor Sturges; m. Margaret Gram. A.B., Columbia U., 1948; LL.B., Yale U., 1951. Bar: N.Y. 1952, U.S. Supreme Ct., other fed. cts. 1952. Mem. firm Davis Polk & Wardwell, N.Y.C., 1951—, partner, 1961—; Pres. Assn. Alumni Columbia Coll., 1966-68, Alumni Fedn. Columbia U., 1973-75. Mng. editor: Yale Law Jour., 1951. Chmn. Columbia Coll. Fund, 1972-73; bd. dirs. Berkshire Farm Center and Services for Youth, Legal Aid Soc.; bd. dirs., exec. com. Yale Law Sch. Assn.; trustee Columbia U., Columbia U. Press, Chapin Sch.; trustee, mem. exec. com. Lawyers Com. Civil Rights Under Law. Recipient Columbia Alumni medal for conspicuous service, 1968. Fellow Am. Coll. Trial Lawyers; mem. Am. Law Inst., ABA, N.Y. State Bar Assn. (v.p., exec. com., chmn. antitrust law sect. 1979-80, mem. ho. of dels.), Assn. Bar City N.Y., N.Y. County Lawyers Assn., Am. Judicature Soc. Clubs: Fishers Island (N.Y.) Country, Hay Harbor (Fishers Island); Century Assn., River, Anglers, Pilgrims, Downtown Assn., Wall St. (N.Y.C.); Metropolitan (Washington). Home: 960 Park Ave New York NY 10028 also Fishers Island NY 06390 Office: 1 Chase Manhattan Plaza New York NY 10005

KING, HUGER SINKLER, corp. exec.; b. Darlington, S.C., June 15, 1907; s. C. Coker and Mary Simons (Sinkler) K.; m. Mary Lynn Carlson, May 21, 1932; children—Huger S., L. Richardson, Laurinda C., Michael Lowndes. Student, The Citadel, 1923-25; J.D., U. S.C., 1928. Bar: N.C. bar 1928. Practiced in, Greensboro, 1928-58; sr. partner King, Adams, Kleemeier & Hagan, 1955-58; chmn. Richardson Corp., Piedmont Financial Co. Inc. of N.Y.; vice chmn. Piedmont Mgmt. Co., Inc.; dir. Reins. Corp. of N.Y., Lexington Mgmt. Co., Richardson-Merrell, Inc., Piedmont Adv. Corp. Past pres. Greensboro Community Chest; chmn. Empty Stocking Fund.; Mayor, Greensboro, 1940-42; Trustee Davidson Coll., 1963-68; trustee, v.p. Richardson Found. Served as lt. comdr. USNR, 1942-45. Mem. Greensboro C. of C. (past pres.). Presbyn. (elder). Clubs: Univ. (N.Y.C.); Mchts. and Mfrs., Greensboro Country (Greensboro) (past pres.). Home: 610 Woodland Dr Greensboro NC 27408 Office: One Southern Life Center Greensboro NC 27401 also 99 John St New York NY 10038

KING, IMOGENE MARTINA, educator, nurse; b. West Point, Iowa, Jan. 30, 1923; d. Daniel A. and Mary (Schroeder) K. Diploma, St. John's Hosp., 1945; B.S. in Nursing, St. Louis U., 1948, M.S., 1957; Ed.D., Columbia U., 1961; Ph.D. (hon.), So. Ill. U., 1980. Instr. med.-surg. nursing St. John's Hosp., St. Louis, 1947-58; asst. prof. nursing Loyola U, Chgo., 1961-66, prof. grad. program in nursing, 1972-80; prof. U. South Fla., Tampa, 1980—; asst. chief research Grants br. div. nursing HEW, Washington, 1966-68; prof., dean sch. nursing Ohio State U., Columbus, 1968-72; mem. def. adv. com. on women in the services Dept. Def., 1972-75; cons. VA Hosp. Alderman Ward 2, Wood Dale, Ill., 1975-79, chmn. fin. com. Author: A Theory for Nursing: Systems, Concepts, Process; Contbr. articles in nursing to profl. jours., chpts. to books. Recipient recognition of contbns. to nursing edn. award Columbia U. Tchrs. Coll. Mem. Am. Nurses Assn.,

Fla. Nurses Assn. (recipient highest recognition award 1975), Ill. Nurses Assn., 19th Dist. Assn., Sigma Theta Tau, Alpha Tau Delta. Democrat. Roman Catholic. *Develop a healthy self-concept and know thyself. Practice the Golden Rule. Be honest and sincere in working with individuals and groups. Live each day to the best of your ability.*

KING, IVAN ROBERT, astronomy educator; b. Far Rockaway, N.Y., June 25, 1927; s. Myram and Anne (Franzblau) K.; m. Alice Greene, Nov. 21, 1952; children: David, Lucy, Adam, Jane. A.B., Hamilton Coll., 1946; A.M., Harvard U., 1947, Ph.D., 1952. Instr. astronomy Harvard U., 1951-52; mathematician Perkin-Elmer Corp., Norwalk, Conn., 1951-52; methods analyst U.S. Dept. Def., Washington, 1954-56; with U. Ill., 1956-64; assoc. prof. astronomy U. Calif. at Berkeley, 1964-66, prof., 1966—, chmn. astronomy dept., 1967-70. Contbr. numerous articles to sci. jours. Served with USNR, 1952-54. Mem. Soc. of Fellows Harvard, 1947-51. Mem. Nat. Acad. Scis.; Mem. Am. Acad. Arts and Scis., Am. Astron. Soc. (councillor 1963-66, chmn. div. dynamical astronomy 1972-73, pres. 1978-80), AAAS (chmn. astronomy sect. 1974), Internat. Astron. Union. Study of stellar systems. Office: Dept Astronomy U Calif Berkeley CA 94720

KING, JAMES AMBROS, tenor; b. Dodge City, Kans., May 22, 1925; s. Howard Willis and Hettie Lenora (Shaffer) K.; m. Marieluise Nagel; children: David, Daniel, Ruth, Thomas, Elisabeth. Mus.B., La. State U., 1950; M.A., U. Kansas City, Mo., 1952; Litt.D. (hon.), U. Ky., 1978, L.H.D., U. Mo., 1980; voice studies with, Dallas Draper, Martial Singher, Max Lorenz, William Hughes. Prof. music U. Ky., Lexington, 1952-61. Debut, Deutsche Oper, Berlin, 1962, Salzburg (Vienna) Festival, Bayreuth Festival, 1965, Vienna State Opera, 1963, Met. Opera, 1966, appearances, Kammersanger, Hamburg, Berlin, Munich, Zurich, and Vienna state operas, LaScala, Milano, Opera de Paris, Bolshoi Theater, Moscow, San Francisco Opera, Salzburg Festival, Covent Garden, London, Tokyo Opera, Met. Opera, N.Y.C., Deutsche Oper Berlin, Teatro Colón, Buenos Aires, Chgo. Opera, Stuttgart Opera, others; leading roles in: German film prodns. of operas and Fidelio; various appearances, European TV, 25 major recs., including 14 complete operas. Served with AC USN, 1943-45. Winner Am. Opera Auditions, Cin., 1961; named Alumnus of Yr. La. State U., 1979, 80; awarded title of Kammersänger cities of West Berlin, Munich, and Vienna. Mem. Phi Mu Alpha Sinfornia, Omicron Delta Kappa. Baptist. Office: care Shaw Concerts Inc 1995 Broadway New York NY 10023 *

KING, JAMES B., government official; b. Ludlow, Mass., Mar. 27, 1935; married; 5 children. B.A., Am. Internat. Coll., 1960. Tchr. Ludlow Jr. High Sch., 1961-62; Investigator fraudulent securities Securities div. Dept. Public Utilities, Mass., 1963-64, supr. investigators, 1964-65; jr. community action technician, sr. community technician, asso. commr. Commonwealth Service Corps, 1965; dir. Holyoke Program for Aging, 1966-67; spl. asst. Office Senator Edward M. Kennedy, Boston, 1967-75; fellow J.F. Kennedy Sch. Govt., Harvard U., 1972-73; dir. mktg. and community affairs Mass. Bay Transp. Authority, Boston; spl. asst. to Pres. for Personnel White House, Washington, 1977; mem. Nat. Transp. Safety Bd., Washington, 1977-78, chmn., 1978; now assoc. v.p. dept. govt. and community affairs Harvard U.; tchr. Ludlow Jr. High Sch., 1961-62. Office: Harvard U Dept of Govt & Community Affairs 2 Garden St Cambridge MA 02138

KING, JAMES BRUCE, newspaper editor; b. Enterprise, Oreg., Oct. 30, 1922; s. Oscar Lawrence and Julia Etta (Bruce) K.; m. Betty Ruth Berkley, June 27, 1944; 1 son, James Bruce. Student, Lower Columbia Community Coll., 1941-43, Whitman Coll., 1943-44; B.A. in Journalism, U. Wash., 1948. With Seattle Times, 1948—, beginning as reporter, successively copy editor, asst. news editor, news editor, asst. mng. editor, 1948-75, mng. editor, 1975-77, exec. editor, 1977—, v.p. news and editorial, 1980—; Vis. com. U. Wash. Sch. Communications, 1971-77. Mem. Community Devel. Round Table Seattle; former cons. self-improvement group McNeil Island Fed. Penitentiary. Served to lt. comdr. USNR, 1943-46; PTO. Mem. AP Mng. Editors (dir. 1977-83), Am. Soc. Newspaper Editors (dir. 1982—), U. Wash. Alumni Assn., Soc. Profl. Journalists, Sigma Delta Chi, Beta Theta Pi. Episcopalian. Clubs: Wash. Athletic, Rainier, Blue Ridge Community. Home: 10003 Vinton Ct NW Seattle WA 98177 Office: Seattle Times PO Box 70 Seattle WA 98111

KING, JAMES CECIL, educator; b. Uniontown, Pa., Sept. 14, 1924; s. Joseph Herbert and Eliza Ann (Kelley) K.; m. Diana Hanbury, Sept. 5, 1952 (div. Apr. 1958); children—Christopher Hanbury, Sheila Anne. B.A., George Washington U., 1949, M.A., 1950, Ph.D., 1954. Master for French, German and Latin St. Albans Sch. for Boys, Washington, 1952-55; asst. prof. German George Washington U., 1955-60, asso. prof., 1960-65, prof., 1965—; researcher Langs.-of-the-World Archives, 1960-61. Editor (with Petrus W. Tax); series Die Werke Notkers des Deutschen, 1972—. Served with U.S. Army, 1943-46. German Acad. Exchange Service grantee, 1963. Mem. Linguistic Soc. Am., Medieval Acad. Am., Am. Assn. Tchrs. German, MLA, Am. Goethe Soc., AAUP, Phi Beta Kappa. Anglican. Club: Cosmos (Washington). Home: 9296 Bailey Ln Fairfax VA 22031 Office: Dept Germanic Langs and Lits George Washington U Washington DC 20052

KING, JAMES CLAUDE, physicist; b. St. Joseph, Mo., Oct. 2, 1924; s. Oppie Irl and Isla Dessie (Wertenberger) K.; m. Martha Helene Dawson, Sept. 10, 1949; children: Elizabeth D., Kathleen I., Helen D., Robert S. B.A., Amherst Coll., 1949; M.S., Yale U., 1950, Ph.D., 1953. Research asst. Franklin Inst., Phila., summers 1947-49; dept. mgr. Bell Telephone Labs., Whippany, N.J. and Allentown, Pa., 1953-65; mgr. radiation physics dept. Sandia Labs., Albuquerque, 1965-68, dir. applied research, Livermore, Calif., 1968-71, dir. electrochem. components and measurement systems, Albuquerque, 1971-77, dir. weapons elec. subsystems, 1977—. Contbr. articles to physics jours. and IEEE Trans. Trustee Sandia Prep. Sch. Served to 1st lt. USAAF, 1943-46. Recipient C.B. Sawyer award for research in quartz crystals, 1973. Fellow Am. Phys. Soc.; Mem. Phi Beta Kappa, Sigma Xi, Phi Kappa Psi, Phi Alpha Psi. Patentee in field. Home: 7832 Academy Trail NE Albuquerque NM 87109 Office: Sandia Labs Albuquerque NM 87185

KING, JAMES M., JR., real estate cons.; b. Joliet, Ill., Jan. 22, 1910; s. James M. and Sallie (Tobey) K.; m. Helen Lucette Prichard, Oct. 27, 1939; children—Celeste (dec.), Helen Justine, Deborah Angell (dec.), Timothy Winans. Student, Amherst Coll., 1929-31, Northeastern U., 1941, Am. Inst. Banking, 1931-40. Asst. treas. Newport (R.I.) Trust Co., 1931-47; sec. to Robert R. Young, 1947-49; spl. asst. C. & O. Ry., N.Y.C., 1947-52, America Corp. (formerly Chesapeake Industries, Inc.), 1949-50, treas., 1950-52; pres. Television Center, 1951-52; sr. partner Francis I. duPont & Co., 1952-71; v.p. duPont Glore Forgan, Inc., N.Y.C., 1971-72, Harris Upham & Co. Inc. (now Smith Barney, Harris Upjohn & Co., Inc.), 1972-76; ret.; with Shields Model Roland, Inc., 1977; cons. comml. real estate Cushman & Wakefield, Inc., N.Y.C., 1978—. Mem. Alpha Delta Phi. Episcopalian. Club: The Brook (N.Y.C.). Home: Wood St Katonah NY 10536 Office: 100 Wall St New York NY 10005

KING, JOHN CHARLES PETER, editor; b. Vancouver, B.C., Can., Dec. 13, 1949; s. Charles Frederick Michael and Pauline Ida (Trueb) K.; m. Jane Louise Rubinski, Aug. 21, 1970; 1 dau., Sheila Louise. B.A., York U., 1973. Mem. staff The Globe and Mail Ltd., Toronto, 1970—, night city editor, 1973-75, bur. chief, Ottawa, Ont., Can., 1975-78, nat. editor, Toronto, 1978-81, bur. chief, Washington, 1981-84; assoc. editor Report on Bus., Toronto, 1984—. Home: 18 Oakwood Ave N Port Credit ON Canada L5G 3L7 Office: 444 Front St W Toronto ON Canada M5V 259

KING, JOHN F., banker. Grad., U. So. Calif., NYU. With Mfrs. Hanover Trust Co., 1958-73, Union Bank, 1973-75; v.p. 1st Interstate Bank Calif., 1975-76, sr. v.p., 1976-78, exec. v.p., 1978-80, pres., 1980—, dir. Office: First Interstate Bank Calif 707 Wilshire Blvd Los Angeles CA 90017 *

KING, JOHN FRANCIS, lawyer; b. Waynesboro, Pa., Apr. 23, 1925; s. Thomas Henry and Victoria Walker (Beaver) K.; m. Linda L. Meding; children—John Francis, Anne Lee, Margaret P. B.A., Dickinson Coll., 1949; J.D., Georgetown U., 1951. Bar: Md. bar 1952. Since practiced in, Balt.; partner firm Anderson, Coe & King, Balt., 1957—; Instr. comml. law McCoy Coll., Johns Hopkins, 1954-74. Pres. Arthritis Found. Md., 1970, City-County Democratic Club, 1963; Bd. dirs. Lawyers' Com. for Civil Rights, Balt., 1963-70, Med.-Legal Found. Md., 1968—, Md. Conf. Social Concern, 1970-72, ACLU Md., 1971—. Mem. Am., Md. State bar assns., Am. Coll. Trial Lawyers, A.M.A. (affiliate), Johns Hopkins Faculty Club, Am. Judicature Soc. Clubs: Elkridge (Md.); L'Hirondelle. Home: 214 E Montgomery St Baltimore MD 21230 Office: 800 Fidelity Bldg Baltimore MD 21201

KING, JOHN GORDON, educator, physicist; b. London, Eng., Aug. 13, 1925; came to U.S., 1928, naturalized, 1931; s. Gordon Allan and Sara (Merrick) K.; m. Elisabeth Sleck, June 11, 1949; children—Alan, Andrew, James, Charles, Martha, David, Benjamin, Matthew. B.S., Mass. Inst. Tech., 1950, Ph.D., 1953; Sc.D. (hon.), U. Hartford, 1972. Technician underwater sound lab. Harvard U., 1943-45; mem. faculty dept. physics Mass. Inst. Tech., 1953—, prof., 1965—, Francis L. Friedman prof. physics, 1974-; asso. dir. Research Lab. Electronics, 1973-76; cons. Avco Corp., 1955-58. Author papers in field. Served with AUS, 1944; Served with USNR, 1944-46. Recipient Sloan award Sloan Found., 1956; E. Harris Harbison award Danforth Found., 1971. Mem. Am. Phys. Soc., Am. Assn. Physics Tchrs. (Millikan award 1965). Home: Barley Neck Woolwich ME 04579 Office: Mass Inst Tech Cambridge MA 02139

KING, JOHN HUGH, broadcasting co. exec.; b. Sondheimer, La., Sept. 29, 1933; s. Charles Hughes and Hazel Mildred (Ezell) K.; m. Betty Marie Taylor, July 7, 1961; children—Karolyn Marie, Kathryn Marie. B.A. in Speech and English, N. Tex. State U., 1956. Claims examiner Crawford & Co. (Ins. Adjusters), Dallas, 1958-59, Millers Mut. Fire Ins. Co., Ft. Worth, 1959-62; asst. mgr. Sta. KGRT, Las Cruces, N.Mex., 1962-63; v.p. Holsum, Inc.; and program dir. Sta. KBIM-TV, Roswell, N.Mex., 1963-71; gen. mgr. KBIM-AM/FM Radio, Roswell, 1971-81; pres., gen. mgr. King Broadcasting Co., Inc., KBIM-AM/FM Radio and MUZAK, Roswell, 1981—; dir. Chaves County Savs. and Loan Assn. Bd. dirs. Roswell Community Concert Assn., 1971-81, Roswell YMCA, 1969. Served with U.S. Army, 1956-58. Mem. Roswell C. of C. Pres.'s Club (pres. 1979-80), Nat. Assn. Broadcasters, N.Mex. Broadcasters Assn., Delta Sigma Phi. Republican. Mem. Disciples of Christ. Clubs: Kiwanis, Roswell Country, Roswell Chess (pres.), Masons (Roswell)). Home: 2713 Riverside Dr Roswell NM 88201 Office: 214 N Main St Roswell NM 88201

KING, JOHN LANE, lawyer; b. Bellefontaine, Ohio, Oct. 24, 1924; s. John D. and Mabel L. (Nipken) K.; m. Eileen R. Hickey, Oct. 28, 1950; children: Sara R., John Lane, Mary L. King Olenick, Anne E. B.S., Ohio State U., 1947; J.D., U. Mich., 1950. Bar: Mich. 1951, Ohio 1950. Asst. atty. gen., State of Ohio, Columbus, 1950; staff Office of Regional Counsel, IRS, Detroit, 1950-53; mem. firm Berry, Moorman, King, Cook & Hudson,, Detroit, 1953—. Councilman, City of Grosse Pointe (Mich.), 1967-71, mayor, 1971-79; pres., bd. dirs. United Community Services Detroit; bd. dirs. World Med. Relief Inc., Bon Secours Hosp., Sacred Heart Rehab. Center; trustee Herbert Pointing Found., Clarence and Grace Chamberlin Found, Adele T. Groesbeck Found. Mem. Am., Mich., Detroit bar assns., Phi Alpha Delta. Clubs: Detroit Athletic, Detroit Country, Cardinal, Indian Village Tennis, Cooley. Home: 15 Wellington Pl Grosse Pointe MI 48230 Office: 2600 Detroit Bank and Trust Bldg Detroit MI 48226

KING, JOHN QUILL TAYLOR, college president; b. Memphis, Sept. 25, 1921; s. John Q. Taylor and Alice (Woodson) Johnson; m. Marcet Hines, June 28, 1942; children: John Q. Taylor, Clinton Allen, Marjon Alicia, Stuart Hines. B.A., Fisk U., 1941, L.H.D. (hon.), 1980; grad., Landig Coll. Mortuary Sci., 1942; B.S., Huston-Tillotson Coll., 1947; M.S., DePaul U., 1950; Ph.D., U. Tex., 1957; LL.D. (hon.), Southwestern U., 1970, St. Edward's U., 1976, L.H.D., Austin Coll., 1978. Mortician King-Tears Mortuary, Inc., Austin, Tex., 1946—; with Huston-Tillotson Coll., 1947—, prof. math., 1952-65, dean, 1960-65, pres., 1965—; mem. exec. council Ind. Colls. and Univs. Tex., 1965-82; vis. scientist Tex. Acad. Sci., 1960-67; mem. coop. writing com. Pitman Pub. Corp., 1956, 58, 60, 62; dir. Tex. Commerce Bank, Austin. Author: (with wife) The Story of Twenty-Three Famous Negro Americans, 1967, Famous Black Americans, 1975; booklet Mary McLeod Bethune: A Woman of Vision; contbr. numerous articles to religious and profl. jours., also booklet. Div. officer Boy Scouts Am., 1956-60, 78—; peace edn. com. Am. Friends Service Com., 1959-66; mem. Austin com. USO, 1960-72, Austin-Bergstrom AFB Community Council; mem. gen. bd. edn. United Meth. Ch., 1960-72; mem. Tex. Conf. Chs., 1963-76; exec. com. South Central Jurisdictional Bd. Christian Social Concerns, 1968-72; pres. Gen. Council on Ministries, 1972-80; del. Meth. Gen. and Jurisdictional Confs., 1956, 60, 64, 66, 67, 68, 70, 72, 76, 80, 84; chmn. Austin-Travis County Community Relations Council; bd. dirs. Wesley Found., U. Tex., 1953-69, Texas So. U., 1960-69, Tex. Conf. Chs., 1963-78, Child and Family Service, 1964-70, Tex. Mental Health Assn., 1955-67, Austin chpt. NCCJ, Tex. Meth. Student Movement, 1960-70, Community Council of Austin and Travis County, 1966-72, Eden Home for the Aged, 1967-74, Travis County unit Am. Cancer Soc., 1963-69, United Fund of Austin and Travis County, 1965-70; trustee Austin Coll., 1979—; mem. Tex. Statewide Health Coordinating Council, 1978-80, Austin CSC, 1975-81; chmn. Austin CSC, 1978-81; mem. Gov.'s Com. Aging, 1971-78; adv. bd. Big Bros. of Austin; adv. com. Perkins Sch. Theology, So. Meth. U., Regional Med. Program Tex.; bd. dirs. Amistad Research Center, 1972—; trustee Fisk U., 1965-77; mem. adv. com. Command and Gen. Staff Coll., 1977-80, chmn., 1980; mem. Centennial Commn., U. Tex., Austin. Served to capt. AUS, 1942-46; maj. gen. AUS (ret.). Recipient Carl Bredt award U. Tex. Coll. Edn., 1970; Distinguished Service award Tex. Luth. Coll., 1976; Martin Luther King humanitarian award, 1983. Mem. Am. Statis. Assn., Nat. Assn. for Industry-Edn. Cooperation (dir. 1980—), Nat. Inst. Sci., Philos. Soc. Tex., Austin C. of C. (v.p., dir. 1966-69, vice chmn. 1968-69), Austin Council Fgn. Affairs (trustee), Phi Beta Kappa, Sigma Pi Phi, Delta Pi Epsilon, Alpha Phi Alpha, Phi Delta Kappa, Alpha Kappa Mu. Methodist. Clubs: Masons (33 deg.), Shriners, Kiwanis. Home: 2400 Givens Ave Austin TX 78722

KING, JOHN WILLIAM, judge; b. Manchester, N.H., Oct. 10, 1918; s. Michael J. and Anna (Lydon) K.; m. Anna MaLaughlin, Oct. 13, 1945. A.B., Harvard, 1938; M.A., Columbia, 1941, LL.B., 1943; LL.D.; M.A. (hon.), Dartmouth Coll., St. Anselm's Coll., U. N.H., Columbia U.; Dr. Civil Laws (hon.), New Eng. Coll.; Dr. Pub. Adminstrn., Franklin Pierce Coll., Suffolk U. Bar: N.Y. bar 1942, N.H. bar 1945. Pvt. practice, N.Y.C., 1943- 48; former sr. partner King, Nixon, Christy & Tessier (attys.); now asso. justice Superior Ct. of N.H., 1969-79; asso. justice Supreme Ct. N.H., 1979—; instr. bus. law St. Anselm's Coll., Manchester, 1948—; mem. N.H. Constl. Conv., 1956; chmn. Manchester delegation N.H. Legislature, 1957; mem. sub-com. legislative counsel, 1957, minority leader, 1959-62, gov., N.H., 1963-69. Editor: N.H. Bar Jour, 1958-69. Mem. N.H. ballot law commn., 1952-54; sec. charter revision commn., Manchester, 1954-55, mem. salary adjustment commn., 1957—, chmn. ward line commn., 1957—; chmn. N.H. Accreditation Commn. on Cts., 1971—, Council of State Ct. Reps. of Nat. Center for State Cts., 1975, 76; Past pres. J.F. McElwain Manchester Employees' Credit Union, 1956—; bd. dirs. N.H. Tb. Soc.; trustee St. Anselm's Coll. Mem. Am., N.Y. State, N.H., Manchester bar assns., Bar Assn. City N.Y., Am. Judicature Society (dir. N.H.). Clubs: Elk., Eagle, K.C., Canadian, Raphael, Manchester Press, Belgium, Manchester Turnverein (Manchester). Home: Connemara Farm Kennedy Hill Rd Goffstown NH 03045 Office: 922 Elm St Manchester NH 03101

KING, JONATHAN, architect, educator; b. N.Y.C., Dec. 31, 1925; s. Gordon Congdon and Carol Therese (Weiss) K.; m. Cynthia Bregman. B.A., Columbia U., 1949. Assoc. editor G.P. Putnam's Sons, N.Y.C., 1949-52; staff assoc. Fund Advancement Edn. Ford Found., 1952-58; sec. treas. Ednl. Facilities Labs., Inc., N.Y.C., 1958-67, v.p., treas., 1967-70; sr. v.p. in charge systems bldg. Caudill Rowlett Scott (architects, engrs., planners), Houston, 1970-76; adj. prof. architecture Rice U., Houston, 1973-76; prof. architecture, dir. archtl. research lab. U. Mich., Ann Arbor, 1976—; Chmn. Archtl. Research Centers Consortium; mem. council Cornell U. Coll. Architecture, Art and Planning., 1970-74. Prin. author, project dir.: The Michigan Courthouse Study, 7 vols., 1981-82; Contbr.: articles to Sat. Rev. Archtl. Design; others Harvard Bus. Rev.; others. Served with AUS, 1943-46; PTO. Recipient Am. Builder Mag. award for innovations in bldg., 1965; Fulbright lectr. Royal Danish Acad. Fine Arts, 1983. Mem. Soc. Coll. and U. Planning, AIA (hon.). Home: 2659 Englave Dr Ann Arbor MI 48103 Office: U Mich Coll Architecture and Urban Planning Ann Arbor MI 48109

KING, JONATHAN ALAN, molecular biology educator; b. Bklyn., Aug. 20, 1941; m. Jacqueline Dee. B.S. in Zoology, magna cum laude with high honors, Yale U., 1962; Ph.D., Calif. Inst. Tech., 1968. Brit. Med. Research Council postdoctoral fellow Cambridge (Eng.) U., 1970; asst. prof. MIT, Cambridge, 1971-73, assoc. prof., 1974-78, prof. molecular biology, 1979—, dir. biology electron microscope facility, 1971—. Contbr. numerous articles to sci. jours. Chmn. Nat. Jobs with Peace Campaign. Gen. Motors Nat. scholar, 1958-62; Jane Coffin Shields Fund fellow, 1968-70; recipient U.S. Antarctic Service medal, 1968; Woodrow Wilson fellow, 1962-63; NIH fellow, 1963-67. Mem. Genetics Soc. Am., Am. Soc. Microbiology, Biophysics Soc., Teratology Soc., Soc. Occupational and Environ. Health, Am. Pub. Health Assn. Home: 114 Charles River Rd Watertown MA 02172 Office: MIT Dept Biology Cambridge MA 02139

KING, JOSEPH BERTRAM, architect; b. Greenville, S.C., Sept. 14, 1924; s. Joseph A. and Bertram (Kerns) K.; m. Julia Nelson Hipps, Aug. 2, 1945; children: Allen, David, Thomas. Student, Memphis State Coll., 1943; B.Arch. with honors, N.C. State U., 1949. Prin. J. Bertram King, Asheville, N.C., 1952—; Chmn. Planning and Zoning Commn., Asheville, 1966—; vice chmn. Met. Planning Bd., 1966-74. Prin. works include Humanities, Social Sci., Art and Mgmt. bldgs., residence hall, student center, U. N.C.-Asheville, occupational edn. bldg, Asheville High Sch., Bank of Asheville, Madison County High Sch, City-County Central Library Bldg, Reynolds High Sch, Sealtest Dairies. Bd. dirs. United Fund, N.C. Design Found.; mem. N.C. Design Found., 1983—; trustee Aston Park Hosp., 1966-73. Served with USAAF, 1942-45; ETO. Decorated Air medal with 2 oak leaf clusters.; Recipient various archtl. honor awards. Fellow A.I.A. (pres. N.C. chpt. 1973); mem. N.C. Bd. Architecture (past pres.), Asheville C. of C. (past pres. 1972), Tau Beta Pi, Sigma Pi Alpha, Phi Kappa Phi. Home: 222 Country Club Rd Asheville NC 28804 Office: 351 Merrimon Ave Asheville NC 28804

KING, KENDALL WILLARD, educator, biochemist; b. Pitts., Feb. 20, 1926; s. Charles Glen and Hilda (Bainton) K.; 1947 (div. 1976); children—Virginia King Cavanagh, Russell Glen. B.S., Va. Poly. Inst., 1949, M.S., 1950; Ph.D., U. Wis., 1952. Mem. faculty Va. Poly. Inst., 1953-68, prof. biochemistry, 1959-68, head dept. biochemistry and nutrition, 1966-68; asst. v.p.-grants Research Corp., program dir., 1968-77, v.p. grants, 1977—; research asso. Columbia, 1959-60; Adviser protein adv. group WHO/FAO/UNICEF/Pan Am. Health Orgn.; mem. sci. adv. com. Helen Keller Internat.; indsl. cons. enzymes Remick Assos.; mem. coms. Nat. Acad. Sci. NRC; also mem. com. internat. nutrition programs; mem. com. on pre-sch. child devel. Internat. Union Nutrition Scis.; also mem. U.S. Com., grants com. U.S. Dept. Agr. Served with AUS, 1944-46. Awarded Ordre de Travaux, Republic Haiti; recipient certificate of recognition Instituto de Nutricion de Centro America y Panama. Mem. Am. Inst. Nutrition, Am. Soc. Biol. Chemists, Am. Chem. Soc., AAAS, Inst. Food Tech., Am. Public Health Assn., Am. Inst. Chemists, Am. Inst. Nutrition, N.Y. Acad. Sci., Am. Assn. Cereal Chemists, Sociedad Latinamericano de Nutricion, Soc. Nutrition Edn., Sigma Xi (pres. elect 1967), Phi Lambda Upsilon, Phi Sigma. Baptist. Spl. research mode of action of cellulases, intermediary metabolism amino acids, nutrition edn. in emerging societies. Home: 3 Lakeshore Close North Tarrytown NY 10591 Office: Research Corp 405 Lexington Ave New York NY 10174 *How brilliant we are is no source of credit; nor should our innate limitations cause embarrassment. Our goodness, though, is our own achievement as are our lapses in ethical living. In them we earn legitimate praise or shame. The vogue to set goals and master excellence is often misdirected in that the merit of the goals themselves is seldom dealt with and the excellence focuses on competitive advantage rather than on self-mastery.*

KING, KENNETH TYLER, financial consultant; b. Hanford, Calif., Nov. 16, 1925; s. William Franklin and Faith B. (Tyler) K.; m. Virginia Lee Landon, June 16, 1946; children: Janine Virginia, Andrew Landon, Bruce Tyler. B.B.A., Woodbury Coll., 1949; postgrad., Stanford U., 1969-70. With Horace Mann Ins. Co., Springfield, Ill., 1949-51, Continental Casualty Co., Chgo. and Los Angeles, 1951-58; pres. Fireman Fund Am., San Francisco, 1958-72; chmn. bd. Capitol Life & Affiliates, Denver, 1972-82, Providence Washington Ins. Co. & Affiliates, R.I., 1972-82; pres. Providence Capitol Corp., N.Y.C., 1972-82; pvt. practice fin. cons., Denver, 1982—; dir. Fin. Programs, Inc., Denver, Striker Petroleum Corp., W. & G. Meyer & Co., San Francisco. Bd. dirs. Presbyn. Med. Center, Denver, 1976—, S.W. Outward Bound Sch., Santa Fe, 1975—; hon. consul of, Norway, 1979. Served with USMC, 1942-46. Decorated Purple Heart, Bronze Star. Mem. Health Ins. Assn. Am. (dir. 1960-64), Am. Council Life Ins. (dir. 1973-76). Clubs: Bohemian (San Francisco); Denver Country. Home: 3125 E Exposition Ave Denver CO 80209 Office: 1600 Sherman St Denver CO 80201

KING, KERRYN, corporation executive; b. Dallas, Oct. 15, 1917; s. Oswin Kerryn and Naiad Isobel (Keedy) K.; m. Carol Fritz, Nov. 11, 1939 (div.); children: Steven, Valerie King Steinhauer, Wyldon King Fishman, Zoe King Jacobie; m. Shirley L. Maytag, Dec. 16, 1967. B.S., So. Meth. U., 1939, LL.D. (hon.), 1966. Asst. to v.p. Tex. Power & Light Co., 1939-42; publns. editor Consol. Vultee Aircraft Corp., 1942-43; with Hill & Knowlton, Inc., 1943-52, v.p., 1947-52; dir. pub. relations Texaco Inc., 1953-57, gen. mgr. pub. relations and personnel, 1957-58, v.p., 1958-60, v.p., asst. to chmn. bd., 1960-63, v.p. charge ops., Latin Am., 1963-65, v.p. pub. relations and personnel, 1965-71, sr. v.p. world wide sales, pub. relations and personnel, 1971-72, sr. v.p. pub. affairs, 1972-82, pub. affairs cons., 1983—; Chmn. civilian pub. relations adv. com. U.S. Mil. Acad.; mem. Pub. Relations News Editorial Adv. Bd., chmn., 1977-80. Trustee Found. Public Relations Research and Edn.; mem. adv. bd. Met. Opera Assn.; hon. trustee Horace Mann Sch.; bd. dirs. Allergy Found. Am., Eye-Bank for Sight Restoration, Inc. Mem. Internat. Public Relations Assn., Public Relations Soc. Am. (pres. 1979), Sigma Delta Chi. Clubs: River (N.Y.C.); N.Y. Yacht; Am. Yacht (Rye, N.Y.). Home: 141 E 72d St New York NY 10021

KING, LARRY L., author, actor; b. Putnam, Tex., Jan. 1, 1929; s. Clyde Clayton and Cora Lee (Clark) K.; m. Barbara Sue Blaine, May 6, 1978; children—Cheryl King McGetrick, Kerri Lee King Grandey, Bradley Clayton, Lindsay Allison. Student, Tex. Tech. U., 1949-50; neiman fellow, Harvard U., 1969-70; Duke fellow communications, Duke U., 1976. Newsman papers in, N.Mex. and Tex., 1950-55, congl. asst., 1955-64; contbg. editor Harper's mag., 1966-71, Tex. Monthly mag., 1973—, New Times mag., 1974-77; pres. Texhouse Corp., Washington, 1980—; Ferris prof. journalism and polit. sci. Princeton U., 1973-76. Author: The One-Eyed Man, 1966, ...And Other Dirty Stories, 1968, Confessions of a White Racist, 1971, The Old Man and Lesser Mortals, 1974, Wheeling and Dealing, 1978, Of Outlaws, Con Men, Whores, Politicians and Other Artists, 1980, The Whorehouse Papers, 1981; plays The Best Little Whorehouse in Texas, 1978, The Kingfish, 1979; also numerous articles; starred in: The Best Little Whorehouse in Texas on Broadway, 1979. Served with AUS, 1946-49. Recipient Stanley Walker Journalism award 1973. Mem. Authors Guild, PEN, Writers Guild East, Tex. Inst. Letters, Actors Equity Assn. Democrat. *I have always avoided strong drink and evil companions.*

KING, LAWRENCE PHILIP, lawyer, educator; b. Schenectady, N.Y., Jan. 16, 1929. B.S.S., CCNY, 1950; LL.B., NYU, 1953; LL.M., U. Mich., 1957. Bar: N.Y. 1954, U.S. Supreme Ct. 1963. Atty. Paramount Pictures Corp., N.Y.C., 1955-56; asst. prof. law Wayne State U., 1957-59; asst. prof. NYU, 1959-61, asso. prof., 1961-63, prof., 1963—, Charles Seligson prof. law, 1979—, asso. dean Sch. Law, 1973-77; asso. reporter adv. com. on bankruptcy rules U.S. Jud. Conf., 1968-76, reporter, 1979-83, mem. adv. com. bankruptcy rules, 1983—. Author: (with R. Duesenberg) Sales and Bulk Transfers under the U.C.C., 1966; contbr. articles, books revs. to legal jours.; editor-in-chief: Collier On Bankruptcy, 1964, 15th edit., 1979—. Trustee Village of Saltaire (N.Y.), 1980-84, mayor, 1984—. Recipient NYU Law Alumni Achievement award, 1976, NYU Law Alumni 25-Yr. Faculty Service award, 1984, award Bankruptcy Lawyers div. UJA-Fedn., 1984. Mem. Nat. Bankruptcy Conf., Am. Law Inst., Am., N.Y. State bar assns., Assn. Bar City N.Y., Comml. Law League Am. (Man of Year award 2d Dist. 1969). Office: NY U Sch Law 40 Washington Square S New York NY 10012

KING, LELAND W., architect; b. Battle Creek, Mich., Dec. 17, 1907; s. Leland Wiggins and Elizabeth Gale (Arnold) K.; m. Hametia Fielder, Nov. 29, 1934; children: Sheryl Letia, Louisa Sands. Student, Ga. Sch. Tech., 1927, Armour Inst. Tech., (Chgo. Art Inst., Beaux Arts Design), 1928-29. Registered architect, Colo., Ariz., N.Y., Calif., Nat. Council Archtl. Registration Bds. Archtl. draftsman, designer indsl., sch., hosp. and residential projects, Ga., Ill., Mich., Wis., 1925-32; supr. architect's office U.S. Treasury, 1935-37; field insp. diplomatic and consular bldgs. Dept. State, 1937-40, in Scandinavia, Balkans, Europe, Middle East, C. and S. Am., asso. chief Fgn. Bldg. Ops., 1941-51; dir. and supervising architect, 1952-54; in charge U.S. diplomatic and consular bldg. design and constrn., worldwide; cons. Bd. Edn. White Fish Bay, Milw., 1931-32; tech. adviser to U.S. del. UNESCO Hdqrs. Bldg., Paris, 1952-53; exec. sec. Fgn. Service Bldgs. Com., U.S. Congress, 1952-54; gen. archtl. and indsl. design as asso. Norman Bel Geddes, 1954-55; asso. with James Gordon Carr (Architect), 1956; v.p., dir. architecture Pereira and Luckman, 1956-59; supervising archt. Ampex Corp., 1959-62; pvt. archtl. practice, 1961—, as Leland King, FAIA, Cons. Architect, Bodega Bay, Calif., 1983—; sr. partner King/Reif & Assos. (architecture and planning), Menlo Park, Calif.; Chmn. archtl. and constrn. engrng. panel research, adv. council to postmaster gen., 1967, 68; supervising architect U.S. Embassy projects, Stockholm, Paris, 1953; architect Memorex project, Santa Clara, Calif. Works exhibited, Mus. Modern Art, N.Y.C., 1953, Octagon, 1954, San Jose Mus., 1980. Receiving honor award AIA, 1955, 56, McGraw-Hill Top Ten Plants award, 1971; and AIA chpt. award, 1974. Fellow AIA; mem. Calif. C. of C. Clubs: Cosmos (Washington); Stanford University Golf. Home: 21218 Heron Dr Bodega Harbor Bodega Bay CA 94923 Office: 555 Hwy One Suite B Bodega Bay CA 94923

KING, LEON, banking and insurance executive; b. Phila., 1921; s. Abraham and Ethel (Walton) K.; m. Diane Averbach, Nov. 30, 1946; children: Cheryl, Elliot, Louis. B.S. in Econs, Wharton Sch., U. Pa., 1945. C.P.A., Pa. Public acct., 1946-52; controller hotel div. Bankers Securities Corp., 1952-57; controller Sun-Ray Drug Co., 1957-60, Bellevue Stratford Hotel, 1960-64; with Indsl. Valley Bank and Trust Co., Phila., 1964-83, exec. v.p., 1973-83; with Indsl. Valley Title Ins. Co., Phila., 1964—, chmn. bd., chief exec. officer, 1983—; chmn. bd. Am. Acceptance Corp., Mobile Field Office Co.; dir. Central Mortgage Co., Dist. Realty Title Ins. Co., Continental Title Ins. Co. Mem. Bank Adminstrn. Inst. (acctg. commn. 1976-80), Am. Inst. C.P.A.s, Pa. Inst. C.P.A.s. Clubs: Urban (Phila.); Masons. Home: 4030 Woodruff Rd Lafayette Hill PA 19444 Office: Indsl Valley Title Ins Co IVB Bldg Philadelphia PA 19103

KING, LESLIE JOHN, geography educator; b. Christchurch, New Zealand, Nov. 10, 1934; s. Lawrence Charles and Phyllis Ivy (Walter) K.; m. Doreen Mercia Brown, Oct. 22, 1960; children—Loren A., Andrew Brett. B.A., U. New Zealand, 1955, M.A., 1957; Ph.D., U. Ia., 1960. Lectr. U. New Zealand, 1960-62; asst. prof. McGill U., Montreal, Que., 1962-65; prof. geography Ohio State U., 1964-70; prof. geography, acad. v.p. McMaster U., Hamilton, Ont., Can., 1970—. Author: Readings in Economic Geography, 1968, Statistical Analysis in Geography, 1969, Cities, Space and Behavior, 1978. Mem. Hamilton Urban Renewal Com., 1970—. Recipient Fulbright travel award, 1957. Mem. Assn. Am. Geographers (Distinguished Service award 1976), Regional Sci. Assn. Home: Rural Route 3 Dundas ON Canada Office: McMaster U Hamilton ON Canada

KING, LOUIS DELWIN, college dean emeritus; b. Walhalla, S.C., July 31, 1917; s. Henry Louis and Zoie (Bond) K. B.S. magna cum laude, U. S.C., 1949; M.S., U. Fla., 1951; Ph.D., 1953. Drug clk., Walhalla, 1935-42; registered pharmacist Bells Drug Store, Walhalla, 1949-50; teaching asst. U. Fla., 1950-51; mem. faculty Rutgers U., 1953-81, prof. pharmacy, asso. dean, 1966-81, emeritus, 1981—. Contbr. profl. and sci. jours. Served with AUS, 1942-46. Mem. Am. Pharm. Assn., S.C. Pharm. Assn., Sigma Xi, Rho Chi, Kappa Psi. Lodge: Lions. Home: PO Box 557 Walhalla SC 29691

KING, LOWELL RESTELL, pediatric urologist; b. Salem, Ohio, Feb. 28, 1932; s. Lowell Waldo and Vesta Ethylwin (Snyder) K.; m. Mary Elizabeth Hill, July 9, 1960; children—Andrew Restell, Erika Lillie. B.A., Johns Hopkins U., 1953, M.D., 1956. Intern Johns Hopkins Hosp., Balt., 1956-57, resident in urology, 1957-62; asst. prof. urology Johns Hopkins U., 1962-63, Northwestern U., 1963-67, asso. prof., 1967-70, prof., 1970-81, prof. surgery, 1974-81; prof. urology and pediatrics Duke U., Durham, N.C., 1981—; prof., chmn. dept. urology Presbyn.-St. Luke's Hosp., 1968-70; surgeon-in-chief Children's Meml. Hosp., Chgo., 1974-80. Author: (with P.P. Kelalis) Clinical Pediatric Urology, 1976; editor profl. jours.; contbr. articles sci. jours. Vestryman, sr. warden Ch. of Our Savior, 1974-80; bd. dirs. Gads Hill Settlement House, 1969-73. Mem. Am. Urol. Assn., Am. Acad. Pediatrics (sec. sect. urology 1972-76), Soc. Pediatric Urology (pres. 1983), Chgo. Urol. Assn. (pres. 1972-73), AMA, Chgo. Med. Soc., N.C. Med. Soc. Republican. Episcopalian. Club: Chgo. Athletic. Home: 3915 St Marks Rd Durham NC 27707 Office: Duke U Med Center PO Box 3831 Durham NC 27710

KING, LUTHER JEFFERSON, railroad exec.; b. Chaffee, Mo., Jan. 1, 1925; s. Luther J. and Bertha (Francis) K.; m. Vonda M. Woodyard, Jan. 1, 1943; children—David, Joe, Brad. Student, S.E. Mo. Coll., 1942. With St. Louis San Francisco R.R., 1942-68, asst. supt., 1957-58, supt., 1958-63; with No. Pacific R.R., St. Paul, 1968-78, asst. v.p. ops., 1972-78; pres. Terminal R.R. Assn. St. Louis, 1978—. Served with AUS, 1943-46. Decorated Croix de Guerre. Mem. Regional Commerce and Growth Assn., Nat. Freight Transp. Assn., Traffic Club St. Louis. Methodist. Clubs: Glen Echo Country, Mo. Athletic Assn., Masons, Shriners. Office: Terminal RR Assn St Louis 906 Olive St Saint Louis MO 63101

KING, MARCIA, library director; b. Lewiston, Maine, Aug. 4, 1940; d. Daniel Alden and Clarice Evelyn (Curtis) Barrell; m. Howard P. Lowell, Feb. 15, 1969 (div. 1980); m. Richard G. King, Jr., Aug. 1980. B.S., U. Maine, 1965; M.S.L.S., Simmons Coll., 1967. Reference, field advisory and bookmobile librarian Maine State Library, Augusta, 1965-69; dir. Lithgow Pub. Library, Augusta, 1969-72; exec. sec. Maine Library Adv. Com., Maine State Library, 1972-73; dir. Wayland (Mass.) Free Pub. Library, 1973-76; state librarian (State of Oreg.), Salem, 1976-82, dir., 1982—. Mem. allocations com. United Way. Mem. ALA, Oreg., Pacific N.W. library assns., Chief Officers of State Library Agys., Pub. Library Assn., Ariz. State Library Assn., Oreg. Hist. Soc., Assn. Specialized and Coop. Library Agys., AAUW., Exec. Women's Council So. Ariz., Tucson C. of C. Unitarian. Home: 7130 N Camino de los Caballos Tucson AZ 85743 Office: Tucson Pub Library PO Box 27470 City Hall Annex Tucson AZ 85726

KING, MARIAN, author; b. Washington; d. Joseph and Jeannette (Michel) K. Student, Miss Maderia's Sch., Greenway, Va.; studied abroad. Author: ABC Game Book, 1928, The Mirror of Youth, 1928, ABC Game Cards, 1930, Kees, 1930 (Jr. Lit. Guild selection), The Story of Athletics, 1931, The Dutch Mother Goose, 1931, Amon, A Lad of Palestine, 1932, Skeeta, 1933, The Golden Cat Head, 1933, Kees and Kleintje, 1934 (Jr. Lit. Guild Selection), A Boy of Poland, 1934, Sean and Sheela, 1937, It Happened in England, 1939, Piccolino, 1939, Elizabeth: The Tudor Princess, 1940, Young King David, 1948, The Coat of Many Colors, 1951, Life of Christ, 1953, Young Mary Stuart: Queen of Scots, 1954, Portraits of Children in the National Gallery Art, 1954-55 (filmed and won 2 Emmy awards), A Gallery of Children, 1955, rev. edit., 1967, Portrait of Jesus (King James version and Douay version, separate vols.), 1956, rev. edit., 1970, A Gallery of Mothers and their Children, 1958, What Would You Do?, 1962, A Gallery of Children, 1967, Mary Baker Eddy Child of Promise, 1968, The Star of Bethlehem, 1968, The Ageless Story of Jesus, 1970, Mico and Piccolino, 1972, Adventures in Art: The National Gallery, Washington, 1978 (filmed for TV) (Cine Golden Eagle cert.); children's book editor: The Nat. Observer; contbr. to: Highlights mag. for children, 1972—; Selected: Bible Text (King James Version) for Paintings Depicting the Life of Christ for the, Nat. Gallery of Art Folder No. 2.; Contbr. to books of several sch. book pubs., also various periodicals.; Researcher: TV film U.S. One. Served with Brit. Supply Missions, Washington, 1940-45; mem. White House Conf. Children, 1970; historian, book cons. Hospitality Information Services for Diplomats, Washington. Mem. Authors Guild, Nat. Council Women, Childrens Book Guild, Authors Book Guild Am., Am. Newspaper Women's Club. Home: 4501 Connecticut Ave Washington DC 20008

KING, MORGANA, jazz vocalist; b. Pleasantville, N.Y., 1930. Began singing professionally at age 15, performed in N.Y.C., N.J., L.I., nightclubs originally, then throughout country. Albums include Gemini Changes, I Know How It Feels to be Lonely, Miss Morgana King, More Morgana, Wild Is Love, With a Taste of Honey, Everything Must Change, Higher Ground, Stretchin' Out, Looking Through the Eyes of Love; appeared: as actress in films Mania Carleone in The Godfather, Godfather-Part II as Mrs. Sabatino in Nunzio. Office: care Muse Records 160 W 71st St New York NY 10023 *

KING, MORRIS KENTON, dean med. sch.; b. Oklahoma City, Nov. 13, 1924; s. C. Willard and Lenore (Miesse) K.; m. June Ellen Greenfield, June 21, 1953; children—Michael, Douglas, John, David, Thomas. B.A., U. Okla., 1947; M.D., Vanderbilt U., 1951. Intern Barnes Hosp., St. Louis, 1951-52, resident, 1954-55, Vanderbilt U. Hosp., 1953-54; mem. faculty preventive medicine Washington U., St. Louis, 1958—, prof., 1967—, dean, 1965—. Served with USNR, 1943-46. Mem. Central Soc. Clin. Research, Infectious Diseases Soc. Am. Home: 7017 Kingsbury St Saint Louis MO 63130 Office: 660 S Euclid St Saint Louis MO 63110

KING, NINA DAVIS, journalist; b. Coco Solo, Panama, May 7, 1941; d. James White and Ruth (Steele) Davis. B.A. in French, U. N.C., 1963, M.A. in Comparative Lit. (Chancellors fellow), 1967; Ph.D. in English, Wayne State U., 1973. Lectr. Queens Coll., 1970-73; copy editor Newsday, L.I., N.Y., 1973-76, asst. news editor, 1976-77, asst. book rev. editor, 1977-79, book rev. editor, 1979—. Mem. Nat. Book Critics Circle, Carteret County Humane Soc., Phi Beta Kappa. Home: 99 12th Ave Sea Cliff NY 11579 Office: Newsday Long Island NY 11747

KING, ORDIE HERBERT, JR., oral pathologist; b. Memphis, Aug. 11, 1933; s. Ordie Herbert and Hazel (Eaton) K.; children by previous marriage—Anna LaVelle, Ordie Herbert III; m. Violette Papagianis, Mar. 21, 1974; children—Catherine Ann, Alexander Carlos. B.S., Memphis State U., 1957; D.D.S., U. Tenn., 1959, Ph.D., 1965. Diplomate: Am. Bd. Oral Pathology. USPHS postdoctoral fellow U. Tenn., 1960-62; resident oral pathology U. Tenn. and City of Memphis Hosps., 1962-63; research asso. dept. pathology U. Tenn., 1963-65, asst. prof. pathology, 1965, Northwestern U., 1966; asso. prof., chmn. dept. oral pathology St. Louis U., 1967-69, prof., chmn. dept. oral pathology, 1969-70; acting chmn., vis. asso. prof. dept. oral pathology Washington U., St. Louis, 1969-70; prof. oral pathology, asso. prof. pathology W.Va. U., Morgantown, 1970-74, prof. pathology, 1974, So. Ill. U., Edwardsville, 1974—, chmn. dept. diagnostic specialties, 1979—; dental cons. to chief med. examiner, State of Tenn., 1963-65; mem. med. staff W.Tenn. Cancer Clinic, 1962-65; chmn. dept. dentistry St. Louis U. Hosps., 1967-70; dir. So. Ill. Pathology Lab., Ltd., Godfrey, Ill., 1977—; cons. cancer control program Nat. Center for Chronic Disease Control, USPHS, 1967-70. Contbr. articles to profl. jours. Bd. dirs. W.Va. div. Am. Cancer Soc., 1972-74. Fellow Am. Acad. Oral Pathology; mem. Am. Soc. Cytology, ADA, Am. Hereford Assn., Delta Sigma Delta, Kappa Alpha, Phi Rho Sigma, Omicron Kappa Upsilon. Home: 6111 Vollmer Ln Godfrey IL 62035

KING, PATRICIA MILLER, library administrator, historian; b. Bklyn., July 26, 1937; d. Donald Knox and Amy Beatrice (Heyliger) Miller; m. Samuel W. Stein, Jan. 2, 1978; 1 dau. by previous marriage, Victoria Elizabeth King. A.B., Radcliffe Coll., 1959, A.M., 1961; Ph.D., Harvard U., 1970. Teaching asst. Harvard U., 1965-70; asst. prof. Wellesley Coll., Mass., 1970-71; dir. research Haney Assocs., Concord, Mass., 1971-73; dir. Schlesinger Library, Radcliffe Coll., 1973—, dir. projects. Contbr. articles to profl. jours. Mem. adv. bd. The Women's Resource Ctr.; mem. New England Med. Ctr., Tufts U. Sch. Medicine, Boston, 1982—; mem. sci. and edn. consortium adv. com. Harvard Med. Sch., 1983—; mem. Database Task Force, Nat. Council for Research on Women, N.Y.C., 1983—; mem. community adv. com. Women's Network Exchange, Boston, 1983—. Grantee in field. Mem. Mass. Hist. Soc., Am. Antiquarian Soc., Orgn. Am. Historians, Am. Hist. Assn., ALA, Berkshire Conf. of Women Historians. Home: 3 Whittier St Cambridge MA 02140 Office: Schlesinger Library Radcliffe Coll 10 Garden St Cambridge MA 02138

KING, PAUL HAMILTON, environ. engr.; b. Bklyn., July 14, 1936; s. Marchant A. and Grace M. (Hamilton) K.; m. Patricia Irene Horner, June 20, 1959; children—Deborah May, Stephen Hamilton. B.S., Calif. Inst. Tech., Pasadena, 1957, M.S., 1961; Ph.D., Stanford U., 1966. San. engr. USPHS, Chgo., 1957-59, Brown and Caldwell (cons. engrs.), San Francisco, 1959-60; asst. prof. U. Ky., Lexington, 1961-63; mem. faculty Va. Poly. Inst., Blacksburg, 1966-79, Charles P. Lunsford prof. civil engring., 1976-79; prof., head dept. civil engring. U. Ariz., Tucson, 1979—; cons. in water quality mgmt. to industry. Author tech. papers. Mem. ASCE (Walter Huber research prize 1976), Ariz. Water and Pollution Control Assn., Assn. Environ. Engring. Profs. (pres. 1976), Am. Water Works Assn., Water Pollution Control Fedn., Am. Soc. Engring. Edn., Sigma Xi. Home: 2002 W Magic Circle Tucson AZ 85704 Office: U Ariz Tucson AZ 85721

KING, PETER COTTERILL, corporate executive; b. White Plains, N.Y., Aug. 23, 1930; s. Robert Cotterill and Ruth (McKeown) K.; m. Nancy English, June 28, 1958; children: Margot E., Philip M., Sabrina P. B.S., U.S. Mil. Acad., 1952; M.B.A., U. Pa., 1958; seminar certificate, Harvard, 1968. Commd. 2d lt. U.S. Army, 1952, advanced through grades to 1st lt., 1956; resigned, 1956, col.; systems engr. IBM Research Center, Yorktown Heights, N.Y., 1958-62; v.p. Security Bank & Trust Co., Lawton, Okla., 1962-69; pres. Security Broadcasting Corp., Lawton, 1964-69; adminstr. Southwestern Power Adminstrn., Dept. Interior, 1969-77; pres. EDG Energy Mgmt., Inc., Tulsa, 1977-80; assoc. The Dorchester Cos., Tulsa, 1980-82; chmn. First State Bancorp., Tulsa, 1982—. Chmn. United Way campaign, Lawton, 1968; chmn. Okla. Arts and Humanities Council, 1970-72; Mem. Lawton City Council, 1968-69; Bd. dirs. Tulsa Arts and Humanities Council; trustee Nat. Electric Reliability Council, 1975-77. Mem. Tulsa C. of C. Republican. Episcopalian. Home: 1123 E 18th St Tulsa OK 74120 Office: 2250 E 73d St Tulsa OK 74136

KING, PETER JOSEPH, JR., gas company executive; b. Concord, N.H., Aug. 5, 1921; s. Peter Joseph and Helen (Hallinan) K.; m. Louise L. Lynch, Sept. 11, 1948; children: Anne, Peter, Joseph. B.S., Georgetown U., 1942; LL.B., Harvard U., 1948, postgrad. Advanced Mgmt. Program, 1966. Bar: N.H. 1949, Mass. 1950, Colo. 1963. Practice law, N.H., 1948-51; with AEC, 1952-53, Colo. Interstate Gas Co., Colorado Springs, 1953—, pres., 1976—, chief operating officer, 1977—, dir.; dir. Colorado Springs Nat. Bank, 1971—. Bd. dirs. Myron Stratton Home, Colorado Springs, 1974. Served to 1st lt. AUS, 1942-45, 51-52. Mem. Interstate Natural Gas Assn. Roman Catholic. Clubs: Garden of the Gods, El Paso, Denver Petroleum, Broadmoor Golf. Home: 7 Chase Ln Colorado Springs CO 80906 Office: Colorado Interstate Gas Co PO Box 1087 Colorado Springs CO 80944

KING, PRESTON CLOUD, JR., lawyer; b. Washington, July 30, 1904; s. Preston C. and Sally (Myers) K.; m. Kathryn M. Larcombe, Aug. 15, 1929; 1 dau., Barbara (Mrs. Bruce Allan Reichelderfer). J.D., Georgetown U., 1927. Bar: D.C. 1927, Md. 1933, Ill. 1940. Asso. law firm Adkins & Nesbit, Washington, 1927-29; ptnr. Pope, Ballard & Loos, Washington, 1929-80, Holland & Knight, 1980—; former chmn. admission and grievance com. U.S. Dist. Cts. for D.C. Past pres. Potomac Democratic Club. Mem. Jud. Conf. D.C. Circuit, Md. Hist. Soc. Methodist (trustee). Clubs: Lawyers (past pres.), Barristers (past pres.), Metropolitan (Washington); Potomac (Md.); Hunt; Chevy Chase (Md.). Home: Rexholm Farm 12630 Travilah Rd Potomac MD 20854 Office: 600 Maryland Ave SW Washington DC 20024 22 W Jefferson St Rockville MD 20850

KING, RAY JOHN, educator, electrical engineer; b. Montrose, Colo., Jan. 1, 1933; s. John Frank and Grace (Rankin) K.; m. Diane M. Henney, June 20, 1964; children: Karl V., Kristin J. B.S. in Electronic Engring., Ind. Inst. Tech., 1956, 1957; M.S., U. Colo., 1960, Ph.D., 1965. Instr. Ind. Inst. Tech., 1956-58, asst. prof., 1960-62, acting chmn. dept. electronics, 1960-62; research asso. U. Colo., 1962-65, U. Ill., 1965; asso. prof. elec. engring. U. Wis., Madison, 1965-69, prof., 1969-82, asso. dept. chmn. for research and grad. affairs, 1977-79; staff research engr. Lawrence Livermore Nat. Lab. (Calif.), 1982—; vis. Erskine fellow U. Canterbury, N.Z., 1977; guest profl., Fulbright scholar Tech. U. Denmark, 1973-74. Author: Microwave Homodyne Systems, 1978; contbr. articles to profl. jours. NSF Faculty fellow, 1962-65. Mem. IEEE, Internat. Sci. Radio Union, Sigma Xi, Iowa Tau Kappa, Sigma Phi Delta. Patentee in field. Home: 5782 San Antonio St Pleasanton CA 94566 Office: Mail Code L-156 Lawrence Livermore Nat Labs Livermore CA 94550

KING, RICHARD ADAMS, educator, agricultural economist; b. Worcester, Mass., July 2, 1922; s. Philip and Eleanor Foster (Adams) K.; m. Alfreda May Smedberg, June 10, 1944; children: Philip Austin, Sara Foster, Deborah Shattuck, Susan Chamberlain. B.S., U. Conn., 1946; M.S., U. Calif. at Berkeley, 1947; M.P.A. (Littauer fellow 1947-48), Harvard, 1948, Ph.D., 1951; postdoctoral fellow polit. economy, U. Chgo., 1955-56. Field asst. farm mgmt. and statis. clk. U. Conn., 1943-46; grad. asst. Giannini Found. Agrl. Econs., U. Calif. at Berkeley, 1946-47; asst. prof. agrl. econs. U. Conn., 1948-50; mem. faculty N.C. State U. of Raleigh, 1951—, asso. prof. agrl. econs., 1951-55, prof. agrl. econs., 1956—, M.G. Mann prof., 1957—; coordinator agrl. econs. N.C. agrl. mission to Peru; also vis. prof. faculty social scis. U. Agraria, La Molina, Lima, Peru, 1964-65; vis. prof. agrl. econs. U. Calif. at Berkeley, 1969; Vis. lectr. Grad. Sch. Bus. Adminstrn., U. Va., 1961-63; Cons. Ford Found., Research Triangle Inst. Author: Interregional Competition Research Methods, 1965, (with A.J. Coutu) The Agricultural Development of Peru, 1969, (with R.G. Bressler, Jr.) Markets, Prices and Interregional Trade, 1970. Bd. dirs. Franklinton Center, 1960-76, chmn., 1968. Served with USAAF, 1943. Fellow Am. Agrl. Econs. Assn. (pres. 1979); mem. Am., So. econs. assns., So. Agrl. Econs. Assn. (pres. 1976). Mem. United Ch. of Christ (dir. So. Conf.

1972-76, Bd. Homeland Ministries 1974-81, dir. 1975-81). Home: 2108 Buckingham Rd Raleigh NC 27607

KING, RICHARD ALLEN, lawyer, state official; b. St. Joseph, Mo., July 4, 1944; s. Allen Welden and Lola (Donelson) K.; m. Charlotte Proett, Nov. 27, 1964; children: Mary, Suzanne, Allen. B.A., U. Mo., Columbia, 1966, J.D. cum laude, 1968. Bar: Mo. 1968. Law clk. Office of Chief Counsel, IRS, 1967; partner Constance, Slayton, Stewart & King, Independence, Mo., 1971-80, Cockran, Kramer, Kapke, Willerth & King, Independence, 1980-81; exec. asst. to gov. Mo., Jefferson City, 1981-82, dir. revenue State of Mo., 1982—; asst. city counselor, Independence, 1968-69, mayor, 1974-78; vice chmn. Nat. Conf. Republican Mayors, 1975-77; chmn. Mo. Gov.'s Task Force on Community Crime Prevention, 1975-76; pres. Good Govt. League, Independence, 1972-73; mem. Mo. Commn. Human Rights, 1973-74. Bd. dirs. Am. Cancer Soc., Independence, 1973-79, chmn. crusade, 1973; bd. dirs. Independence Boys Club, 1972-79, Independence Community Assn. Arts, 1973-76, Independence Sanitarium and Hosp., 1974-78, Jefferson City Meml. Hosp., 1981—, NE Jackson County Mental Health Center, 1978-80, Greater Kansas City Nat. Council on Alcoholism, 1978—; v.p., dir. Am. Legion Boys State Mo., 1975-81; pres. Friends U. Mo. Truman Campus, 1979-80; trustee Harry S. Truman Scholarship Found., 1975-78, Kansas City U., 1979-80. Served with U.S. Army, 1969-72. Recipient Outstanding Young Man of Mo. award Mo. Jaycees, 1975, award Mo. Inst. Pub. Adminstrn., 1983. Mem. Am., Mo., Eastern Jackson County bar assns., Independence C. of C. (pres. 1980—), Order of Coif, Phi Delta Phi, Beta Theta Pi. Republican. Methodist. Club: Rotary. Home: 816 Primrose St Jefferson City MO 65101 Office: Exec Office State of Mo PO Box 720 Jefferson City MO 65101 *There is nothing in life as important as living. "Success" is an objective which all too often deprives its pursuer of the satisfaction he seeks. That satisfaction lies in meaningful personal relationships, sensitivity in spiritual communion with a Higher Power, and appreciation for the deepest meaning and purpose of life.*

KING, RICHARD HARDING, food processing company executive; b. Louisville, Oct. 19, 1925; s. Harvey M. and Margaret (Farley) K.; m. Marjorie R. Jones, Feb. 19, 1959; children: Ronald Craig, David Malcolm. B.B.A., Tulane U., 1946; M.B.A., Northwestern U., 1948. With Winchester div. Olin-Mathieson Chem. Corp., New Haven, 1947-53; instr. evenings New Haven Jr. Coll., 1948-53; with Ford div. Ford Motor Co., 1953-59; mgr. profit analysis and control Chrysler Internat. (S.A.), Geneva, Switzerland, 1959-61; financial cons. corp. controllers dept. Raytheon Co., 1961-62; with Glidden Co., 1962-67; (co. merged with SCM Corp. 1967), v.p. corp. planning, 1967-68, controller Internat. Milling Co., 1968-69; v.p. finance Internat. Multifoods Corp. (name changed 1970), 1970—; speaker in planning field, 1965—; dir. Lamalie Assos., Inc. Mem. steering com. Minn. Gov.'s Loaned Exec. Action Program, 1972; Bd. dirs. Goodwill Industries of Mpls., 1970-76, vice chmn., 1975-76; bd. govs. Methodist Hosp., mem. exec. com., 1980—; bd. dirs. Meth. Hosp. Found.; trustee Layman's Ministerial Endowment Fund, v.p., bd. dirs., 1978—, pres., 1979-82. Mem. Am. Mgmt. Assn., Nat. Indsl. Conf. Bd., Financial Execs. Inst., World Future Soc., Beta Gamma Sigma, Omicron Delta Kappa. Methodist. Clubs: Minneapolis, Interlachen Country, Six O'Clock, Tower. Home: 4705 Annaway Dr Edina MN 55436 Office: Box 2942 Multifoods Tower Minneapolis MN 55402

KING, RICHARD HOOD, newspaper executive; b. Boston, Jan. 24, 1934; s. Gilbert and Frances (Hood) K.; m. Reta Schoonmaker, July 25, 1959; children: D. Whitney, Richard H. Jr., Nanci A. A.B., Harvard U., 1955, M.B.A., 1961. Mgr. acctg. Hitchiner Mfg. Co., Inc., Milford, N.H., 1963-68, div. controller, Wallingford, Conn., 1968-71; sec., treas. Smyth Mfg. Co., Inc., Bloomfield, Conn., 1971-72; v.p. fin. Progressive Trade Corp., Glastonbury, Conn., 1972-73; v.p., treas. Hartford Courant Co. (Conn.), 1973—. Treas. Hartford Courant Found., 1974—; v.p., treas., bd. dirs. Camp Courant. Inc., 1980—; v.p., sec., bd. dirs. Better Bus. Bur., Hartford, 1978; bd. dirs. Hartford Chamber Orch. Served to lt. (j.g.) USN, 1955-57; PTO. Mem. Inst. Newspaper Controllers and Fin. Officers (dir. 1981-83), Fin. Execs. Inst. (treas. Hartford chpt. 1980-81, sec. 1981-82, v.p. 1982-83, pres. 1983-84). Club: Chapoquoit Yacht (West Falmouth, Mass.) (treas. 1973-74). Home: 616 Goodale Hill Rd Glastonbury CT 06033 Office: Hartford Courant Co 285 Broad St Hartford CT 06115

KING, ROBERT AUGUSTIN, engineering company executive; b. Marion, Ind., Sept. 3, 1910; s. Roy Melvin and Estella Bernice (Sheron) K.; m. Johanna A. Akkerman, July 19, 1975; children: Robert Alexander, Sharon Johanna, Estella Regina; children by previous marriage: Hugh Melbourne, Mary Elizabeth. B.S. in Chem. Engring, U. Okla., 1935. Chief chemist Phillips Petroleum Co., Borger, Tex., 1935-43; sr. process engr. E. B. Badger & Sons, N.Y.C. and London, 1944-53; dist. mgr. Stone & Webster, N.Y.C., 1954-56; mng. dir. Badger Co., The Hague, Netherlands, 1957-64; pres. King-Wilkinson, Inc., Houston, 1965—, also dir. Mem. Am. Inst. Chem. Engrs., Am. Chem. Soc., Inst. Petroleum (London). Democrat. Episcopalian. Clubs: Petroleum (Houston); Chemists (N.Y.C.); Univ. (Washington). Home: 11026 Braes Forest Houston TX 77071 Office: 5718 Westheimer St Suite 2000 Houston TX 77057

KING, ROBERT BAINTON, physician; b. Pitts., Aug. 26, 1922; s. Charles G. and Hilda (Bainton) K.; m. Molly Gibbs, Aug. 26, 1951; children: Nancy, Susan, Kimberly. Student, U. Pitts., 1940-42, U. Mich., 1942-43; M.D., U. Rochester, 1946. Diplomate: Am. Bd. Neurol. Surgery (mem. 1974-80, sec. 1974-76, chmn. 1976-78, adv. council 1980—). Intern Barnes Hosp., St. Louis, 1946-47, fellow, 1947-49, asst. resident, 1949; clk. neurology and neuropathology Nat. Hosp., London, 1952-53; practice medicine specializing in neurosurgery, St. Louis, 1957, Syracuse, N.Y., 1957—; instr. neurosurgery Washington U., St. Louis, 1951-52, asst. prof., 1952-57, asso. prof., 1957; prof. neurol. surgery Upstate Med. Center, Syracuse, 1957—, chmn. dept. neurosurgery, 1966—; attending State Univ. Hosp., Crouse-Irving Meml. Hosp.; cons. Syracuse VA Hosp., Syracuse Psychiat. Hosp., Taylor Brown Meml. Hosp.; cons. to Surgeon Gen., U.S. Army, 1968—. Contbr. numerous articles on neurosurgery to profl. jours.; contbr. chpts. to med. books. Deacon Dewitt Community Ch., 1972—. Served with M.C. U.S. Army, 1949-51. Named Neurosurgeon of Year Am. Acad. Neurol. Surgery, 1979. Fellow A.C.S. (chmn. surg. forum com. 1976-80, com. grad. edn. 1976—); mem. World Fedn. Neurosurg. Socs., Congress Neurol. Surgeons (chmn. joint com. edn. 1976-79), Soc. Neurol. Surgeons (pres. 1977-78), Neurosurg. Soc. Am. (coms.), Am. Assn. Neurol. Surgeons (pres. 1980-81), Am. Assn. Neurol. Surgery (chmn. exec. council research found.), Am. Acad. Neurol. Surgeons (pres. 1979-80), Am. Council Grad. Med. Edn. (exec. council), Am. Neurol. Assn., Scandinavian Neurosurg. Soc., N.Y. State Neurosurg. Soc. (pres. 1973-74, dir. 1973-77), Am. Bd. Med. Spltys. (exec. council), Research Soc. Neurol. Surgeons, AMA, Royal Soc. Medicine, N.Y. Acad. Scis. Club: Century. Home: 408 Maple Dr DeWitt NY 13066 Office: 750 E Adams St Syracuse NY 13210

KING, ROBERT BRUCE, chemistry educator; b. Rochester, N.H., Feb. 27, 1938; s. Samuel Joshua and Frances Katherine (Shelly) K.; m. Jane Hermine Kempner, June 20, 1960; children—Robert Bruce, David Samuel. B.A., Oberlin Coll., 1957; Ph.D., Harvard, 1961. Research chemist E.I. duPont de Nemours, Wilmington, Del., 1961-62; fellow Mellon Inst., Pitts., 1962-64, sr. fellow, 1964-66; research asso. prof. chemistry U. Ga., 1966-68, research prof., 1968-73, regents' prof., 1973—, acting head chemistry dept., 1980-82; cons. in field. Author: Organometallic Syntheses, 1965, Transition Metal Organometallic Chemistry: An Introduction, 1969; editor: Inorganic Compounds with Unusual Properties, 1976, 2d edit., 1979, (with R.R. Hautala and C. Kutal) Solar Energy: Chemical Conversion and Storage, 1979; regional editor: Jour. Organometallic Chemistry, 1981; editorial bd.: Chem. Revs, 1970-72, Jour. Organometallic Chemistry, 1966—, Organometallics in Chem. Syntheses, 1969-73, Jour. Coordination Chemistry, 1970-81. Alfred P. Sloan Found. fellow, 1967-69; NATO sr. fellow, 1978; Japan Soc. for Promotion of Sci. fellow, 1981; named Ga. Scientist of Year, 1972. Mem. Am. Chem. Soc. (recipient award 1971), Chem. Soc. (London), Sigma Xi. Unitarian Universalist. Club: Athens Country. Home: 185 Holly Falls Dr Athens GA 30606

KING, ROBERT CHARLES, biologist, educator; b. N.Y.C., June 3, 1928; s. Charles James and Amanda (McCutchen) K. B.S., Yale U., 1948, Ph.D., 1952. Scientist biology dept. Brookhaven Nat. Lab., 1951-55; mem. faculty Northwestern U., 1956—, prof. biology, 1964—; chmn. 8th Brookhaven Symposium in Biology, 1955; vis. investigator, fellow Rockefeller U., 1959; NSF sr. postdoctoral fellow U. Edinburgh, Scotland, 1958, Commonwealth Sci. and Indsl. Research Orgn. Div. Entomology, Canberra, Australia, 1963, Sericultural Expt. Sta., Tokyo, Japan, 1970. Author: Genetics, 2d edit., 1965, A Dictionary of Genetics, 2d edit., 1972, Ovarian Development in Drosophila melanogaster, 1970; also numerous papers.; editor: Handbook of Genetics Series, 5 vols., (with H. Akai) Insect Ultrastructure, 2 vols., 1982. Fellow AAAS; mem. Am. Soc. Zoologists, Histochem. Soc., Am. Soc. Cell Biology (treas. 1972-75), Electron Microscopy Soc. Am., Genetics Soc. Am., Am. Soc. Naturalists, Soc. Devel. Biology, Entomol. Soc. Am., Genetics Soc. Can., Genetics Soc. Korea, Sigma Xi (pres. Northwestern U. chpt. 1966-67). Home: 3313 Harrison St Evanston IL 60201 Office: Dept Ecology and Evolutionary Biology Northwestern Univ Evanston IL 60201

KING, ROBERT COTTON, association executive; b. Mpls., Jan. 8, 1931; s. George Herbert and Helen (Morse) K.; m. Arlene Catherine Wortman, May 23, 1955; children: Robert Cotton, Mary Louise, Katharine Ann. B.A., U. Minn., 1954; grad. Advanced Mgmt. Program, Harvard Bus. Sch., 1974. Mgr. Morris (Minn.) C. of C., 1957-59, Fergus Falls (Minn.) C. of C., 1959-62; editor Fergus Falls Daily Jour., 1962-65; editorial writer Mpls. Tribune, 1965-67; asst. mng. editor Mpls. Star, 1967-68, mng. editor, 1969-72, editor, 1972-75, v.p. advt., 1975-79; pres. Info. Pubs., Inc., Mpls., 1979-80; group v.p. Mpls. Star and Star Tribune Co., 1980-82; exec. v.p. Downtown Council of Mpls., 1983—. Bd. dirs. Edina (Minn.) Little League Baseball, 1969—, Downtown YMCA, 1977-79, Minn. Better Bus. Bur., 1978—; bd. dirs. Catholic Bull., 1978—, treas., 1979—. Served to 1st lt. AUS, 1955-57. Profl. Journalism fellow Stanford, 1968. Mem. Minn. A.P. (pres. 1973), Minn. Advt. Fedn. (dir. 1978-79), Sigma Delta Chi. Episcopalian. Clubs: Mpls., Kiwanis (pres. 1978). Home: 5809 Oaklawn Ave Edina MN 55424 Office: 425 Portland Ave Minneapolis MN 55415

KING, ROBERT DESMOND, educational administrator, educator; b. Hattiesburg, Miss., Nov. 25, 1936; s. Martin Desmond and Cornelia Marguerite (Rhymes) K.; m. Karen Ann Russell, June 9, 1973; children: Irene, Kevin, Michael. B.S., Ga. Tech., 1959, M.S., 1959; M.A., U. Wis., 1962, Ph.D., 1965. Mathematician IBM, Cape Canaveral, 1959-60; asst. prof. German and linguistics U. Tex., Austin, 1965-69, assoc. prof. linguistics, 1969-73, prof., 1973—, dean, 1976-79, 1979—; vis. asso. prof. U. Toronto, summer 1968; vis. prof. linguistics U. N.C., Chapel Hill, summer 1972, U. Oreg., summer 1974. Author: Historical Linguistics and Generative Grammar, 1969; contbr. articles to profl. jours. Mem. Institut fur deutsche Sprache, Linguistic Soc. Am., Linguistic Soc. S.W. Home: 2800 Vance Ln Austin TX 78746 Office: Coll Liberal Arts Univ Tex Austin TX 78712

KING, ROBERT ELWIN, manufacturing company executive; b. Lafayette, Ind., Feb. 5, 1923; s. Franklin George and Mary Lulu (Rose) K.; m. Mary Lee Mehlope, Nov. 27, 1947; children: Kathryn Rose, Debra Lee, Scott Robert. B.S.E.E., Purdue U., 1946. Comml. v.p. products Square D. Co., Palatine, Ill., 1970-71, v.p. products, 1971-76, v.p. DE group, 1976-79, v.p. mfg., 1979-81, exec. v.p., 1981-82, pres. elec. group, 1981—. Patentee bus duct hanger and circuit breaker trip device. Curator Transylvania U., Lexington Ky, 1976—. Served to 1st lt. U.S. Army, 1942-46; Philippines. Mem. IEEE, Tau Beta Pi, Sigma Psi. Disciples of Christ Ch. Club: Rolling Green Country (Arlington Heights, Ill.). Home: 8 Bridgeton on Asbury Rolling Meadows Il 60008 Office: Square D Co 1415 S Roselle Rd Palatine Il 60067

KING, ROBERT HOWARD, publisher; b. Excelsior Springs, Mo., June 29, 1921; s. Howard and Nancy Eaton (Henry) K.; m. Marjorie Kerr, Feb. 26, 1966; children—John McFreeley, Mary Nan, Sarah Ann. Student, Kenyon Coll., Gambier, Ohio, 1942. Vice pres. sales Ency. Brit., Chgo., 1946-61; pres. Spencer Internat. Press, Chgo., 1961-66; v.p. Dill Clitherow & Co., Palatine, Ill., 1966-68; pres. Time-Life Libraries, Palatine, 1968-79; chmn. bd., chief exec. officer World Book-Childcraft Internat., Inc., Chgo., 1979—; Chmn. bd. Direct Selling Ednl. Found. Served to capt. AUS, 1942-46. Mem. Direct Selling Assn. (past chmn. bd., chmn. nominating com.), World Fedn. Direct Selling Assns. (chmn. bd.), Sales and Mktg. Execs. Internat., Internat. Trade Club. Clubs: Meadow, Chgo.; Lighthouse Point Yacht (Fla.); Ocean Reef (Key Largo, Fla.). Home: 155 Harbor Point Chicago IL 60603 Office: 510 Merchandise Mart Plaza Chicago IL 60654

KING, ROBERT JAMES, psychologist; b. Logansport, Ind., May 8, 1932; s. William John and Margaret Patricia (Valley) K.; m. Jane Kemper, Oct. 17, 1959; children: Robert, David, Jane, Micheal, John. B.S., Loyola U., 1955, M.S., 1961; Ph.D., Ill. Inst. Tech., 1973. Registered psychologist, Ill., Ariz. Asst. personnel mgr. Gen. Foods Corp., Chgo., 1958-60; personnel mgr. Kaiser Engrs., Chgo., 1960-61; employment mgr. Motorola, Inc., 1961-63, personnel mgr., 1963-65, corp. mgr. personnel testing, 1965-73, corp. dir. human resources, 1973—; lectr. U. Mich. Indsl. Relations Bur., Loyola U. Grad. Sch. and Inst. Indsl. Relations, Ill. Inst. Tech. Grad. Sch. Psychology; lectr., cons. Midwest Indsl. Relations Assn. Mem. Am. Psychol. Assn., Ill. Psychol. Assn., Ariz. Psychol. Assn., Indsl. Relations Assn. Chgo. Extensive research in psychometric testing and orgn. planning and devel. Home: 1521 S Prospect Ave Park Ridge IL 60068 Office: Motorola Ctr 1303 E Algonquin Rd Schaumburg IL 60196

KING, ROBERT JOHN, banker; b. Holyoke, Mass., Oct. 20, 1935; s. John Steven and Doris H. (Gosselin) K.; m. Anita Louise Cunningham, Sept. 24, 1960; children: Robin Ann, Robert John. B.A., Amherst Coll., 1957; M.B.A., Fordham U., 1975. Mgr. N.Y. Telephone Co., N.Y.C., 1957-60; dir. adminstrv. services Reader's Digest Assn., Pleasantville, N.Y., 1960-71; v.p. adminstrn. Griswold, Heckel & Kelly Assos., N.Y.C., 1971-76; sr. v.p. adminstrn. J. Walter Thompson Co., N.Y.C., 1976-83; adminstrv. v.p. Marine Midland Bank, N.Y.C., 1983—. Bd. dirs. Mt. Kisco (N.Y.) Boys Club, 1970—. Mem. Nat. Assn. Corp. Real Estate Execs.; Mem. Real Estate Bd. N.Y., Westchester County Assn., Mt. Kisco C. of C. (past dir.). Republican. Roman Catholic. Club: Mt. Kisco Country. Home: 77 Croton Ave Mount Kisco NY 10549

KING, ROBERT LEONARD, physician; b. Pearisburg, Va., Feb. 4, 1904; s. Clarence L. and Katharine (Oglesby) K.; m. Phoebe E. Edmunds, Dec. 29, 1936; children—Robert Leonard, Phoebe Ann (Mrs. Malcolm A. Moore), John Edmunds, Margaret C. (Mrs. F. Christian Killien), George R., Henry E. Student, Washington and Lee U., 1920-22; M.D., U. Va., 1928, B.S., 1931. Diplomate: Am. Bd. Internal Medicine, Nat. Bd. Med. Examiners. Intern U. Va. Hosp., 1928-29, resident, 1929-31; instr., 1926-31; partner Mason Clinic, Seattle, 1939-69, chief sect. cardiology, 1946-67, chief internal medicine, 1958-69, emeritus chief medicine, 1969—; chief med. service Virginia Mason Hosp., 1950-65, emeritus, 1969—, chief profl. services, 1966-69, trustee, 1946—; instr. U. Va., 1926-31; clin. asst. prof. U. Wash., 1947-53, clin. asso. prof. medicine, 1948—, honoree Robert L. King chair of cardiovascular research, 1957; cons. internal medicine and cardiology 0Seattle Med. Surg. Clinic, 1969-80; cons. VA Hosp.; former sr. cons. Harborview Hosp.; mem. staff Drs. Hosp., Providence Hosp., Overlake Meml. Hosp., Bellevue, Wash., St. Frances Xavier Cabrini Hosp., Swedish Hosp.; Mem. adv. bd. at large Seattle Trust and Savs. Bank.; Mem. Sommer Meml. Lectures Adv. Com., 1966-76; cons. in cardiology Alaska Dept. Health, 1950-55; mem. hosp. chaplain adv. bd. Episcopal Diocese of Seattle. Former editor-in-chief: Cardiology Digest; Contbr. articles to med. jours. Trustee Virginia Mason Research Center, Seattle, Inst. Research and Med.; mem. Seattle Found. Served to lt. col., M.C. AUS, 1942-46. Fellow A.C.P., Am. Fedn. Clin. Research, Am. Coll. Cardiology (gov. Wash. 1966-69); mem. Wash. State Med. Assn., King County Med. Soc., A.M.A.; Mem. Osgoode Soc.; mem. Am. Heart Assn. (pres. 1952-53, dir. 1947-56, chmn. policy com. 1965—, trustee, hon. mem. council clin. cardiology, Distinguished Service award, Gold Heart award 1960), Wash. Heart Assn. (founder, pres. 1947-50, trustee 1948—, chmn. research policy com. 1954—, Distinguished Service award 1956), Seattle Acad. Internal Medicine (pres. 1941-45), North Pacific Soc. Internal Medicine (sec.-treas. 1947-52), Am. Rheumatism Assn., Pacific Interurban Club (chmn. 1967-69), Paul D. White Soc., S.R. (pres. 1969), Raven Soc., Srs. N.W. Golf Assn., Sigma Phi Epsilon, Iota Sigma, Nu Sigma Nu, Alpha Omega Alpha. Episcopalian (former vestryman). Clubs: Rotarian., University, Seattle Golf (Seattle); Overlake Golf and Country (Bellevue). Home: 834 Hillside Dr E Seattle WA 98112 Office: Mason Clinic 1100 9th Ave Seattle WA 98101

KING, ROBERT LEROY, business administration educator; b. Decatur, Ga., Jan. 22, 1931; s. John Todd and Charlotte (Stringer) K.; m. Helen Butler Leaptrott, Mar. 25, 1956; children: Robert Todd, Keith Alan, John Christopher. B.B.A., U. Ga., 1952; M.A., Mich. State U., 1953, Ph.D., 1960. Asst. instr. Mich. State U., 1955-57; asst. prof., then asso. prof. U. S.C., 1957-65; mem. faculty Va. Poly. Inst. and State U., 1965-82, prof. bus. adminstrn., 1965-82, head dept., 1969-76, assoc. dean Grad. Sch., 1968-69; prof., chmn. dept. bus. adminstrn. the Citadel, 1982—; exchange prof. Acad. Econs., Wroclaw, Poland, 1978-82, Warsaw Tech. U., 1981; Fulbright lectr. Indsl. Mgmt. Inst., Kabul, Afghanistan, 1978; cons. in field. Editor: Marketing and the New Science of Planning, 1968, An Annotated Index of the Proceedings of American Marketing Association Conferences, 1955-65, 1966, 66-72, 1973, 1976-79, also articles. Served with AUS, 1953-55; maj. Res. Ford fellow, 1956-57, 64-65; fellow Found. Econ. Edn., 1963. Mem. Am. Marketing Assn. (editor bibliographies series 1968—, chmn. collegiate chpt. and student activites com. 1967—), So. Marketing Assn. (2d v.p. 1970, 1st v.p. 1971, pres. 1972-73), Am. Acad. Advt., Acad. Mktg. Sci., Assn. for Consumer Research, Acad. Internat. Bus., Am. Assn. Advancement Slavic Studies, Delta Sigma Pi, Omicron Delta Epsilon, Omicron Delta Kappa, Beta Gamma Sigma. Home: 639 McCutchen St Charleston SC 29412

KING, ROBERT WILSON, chemical company executive; b. Denver, Sept. 26, 1918; s. Leon Wilson and Nellie Sanford (Kellogg) K.; m. Eleanor E. Knight, July 1, 1941 (div.); children: Cynthia King Betts, Sara King Gervasio, John, Mary King Braley, William, Susan DeVoge, Deborah Dunn; m. Virginia Mae Armstrong, Dec. 18, 1965. B.S. in Chem. Engring, U. Denver, 1940; M.S., M.I.T., 1942. Dir. engring. Union Carbide Chemicals Co., 1959-62; gen. mgr. functional products Union Carbide, 1962-65; v.p. (Linde div.), N.Y.C., 1965-72, sr. v.p., 1972-77, pres. Med. Products div., N.Y.C., 1977—. Ruling elder Fifth Ave Presbyterian Ch., N.Y.C. Mem. U. Denver Alumni Assn. (pres. N.Y.C.), Internat. Oxygen Mfg. Assn. (past pres.), Am. Inst. Chem. Engrs. Clubs: Pine Valley Golf, Beta Theta Pi. Office: 270 Park Ave New York NY 10017

KING, RONOLD WYETH PERCIVAL, educator; b. Williamstown, Mass., Sept. 19, 1905; s. James Percival and Edith Marianne Beate (Seyerlen) K.; m. Justine Merrell, June 22, 1937; 1 son, Christopher Merrell. A.B., U. Rochester, 1927, S.M., 1929; Ph.D., U. Wis., 1932; student, U. Munich, Germany, 1928-29, Cornell U., 1929-30. Asst. in physics U. Rochester, 1927-28; Am.-German exchange student, 1929-30; White fellow in physics Cornell U., 1929-30; U. fellow in elec. engring. U. Wis., 1930-32, research asst., 1932-34; instr. physics Lafayette Coll., 1934-36, asst. prof., 1936-37; Guggenheim fellow, Berlin, Germany, 1937-38; with Harvard U., 1938—, successively instr., asst. prof., asso. prof., 1938-46, prof. applied physics, 1946-72, prof. emeritus, 1972—; cons. electromagnetics and antennas, 1972—. Author: Electromagnetic Engineering, Vol. 1, 1945, 2d edit, Fundamental Electromagnetic Theory, 1963, Transmission Lines, Antennas and Wave Guides, (with A.H. Wing and H.R. Mimmo), 1945, 2d edit., 1965, Transmission-Line Theory, 1955, 2d edit., 1965, Theory of Linear Antennas, 1956, (with T.T. Wu) Scattering and Diffraction of Waves, 1959, (with R.B. Mack and S.S. Sandler) Arrays of Cylindrical Dipoles, 1968, (with C.W. Harrison, Jr.) Antennas and Waves: A Modern Approach, 1969, Tables of Antenna Characteristics, 1971, (with G.S. Smith et al) Antennas in Matter, 1981; also articles in field. Guggenheim fellow, Europe, 1958. Fellow Am. Acad. Arts and Scis., Am. Phys. Soc., AAAS, IEEE; mem. Internat. Sci. Radio Union, AAUP, Bavarian Acad. Sci. (contbg. mem.), Phi Beta Kappa, Sigma Xi. Home and office: 92 Hillcrest Pkwy Winchester MA 01890

KING, RUFUS, lawyer; b. Seattle, Mar. 25, 1917; s. Rufus Gunn and Marian (Towle) K.; m. Janice L. Chase, June 15, 1941 (div. June 1951); children: Rufus III, Agnes S.; m. Elvine R. Rankine. A.B., Princeton U., 1938; postgrad., Stanford U., 1940-41; J.D., Yale U., 1943. Bar: N.Y. 1944, D.C. 1948, Md. 1953. Instr. Princeton, 1938-39; partner Rice & King, Washington, 1953-64; pvt. practice, Washington, 1964-75; partner King & Newmyer, Washington, 1977-83; of counsel Berliner & Maloney, Washington, 1983—; counsel Senate Crime Com., 1951, also other congl. coms.; cons. Nat. Commn. Law Enforcement and Adminstrn. Justice.; Chmn. joint com. on narcotic drugs Am. Bar Assn. and AMA, 1956—. Author: Gambling and Organized Crime, 1968, The Drug Hangup, 1971; Contbr. articles to profl. and popular jours. Pres. Montgomery County Community Psychiat. Clinic. Mem. ABA (chmn. criminal law sect. 1957-60, sec. 1954-57, mem. ho. of dels. 1960-66, chmn. spl. com. atomic attack 1962—, del. sect. individual rights, mem. spl. com. on standards for adminstrn. criminal justice), N.Y. State Bar Assn., Md. Bar Assn., Bar Assn. D.C., Am. Law Inst. (life). Episcopalian. Clubs: Princeton (N.Y.C.); Metropolitan (Washington); American (Miami). Home: 3524 Williamsburg Ln NW Washington DC 20008 Office: 1100 Connecticut Ave NW Washington DC 20036

KING, SAMUEL PAILTHORPE, judge; b. Hankow, China, Apr. 13, 1916; s. Samuel W. and Pauline (Evans) K.; m. Anne Van Patten Grilk, July 8, 1944; children—Samuel Pailthorpe, Louise Van Patten, Charlotte Lelepoki. B.S., Yale, 1937, LL.B., 1940. Bar: D.C., Hawaii bars 1940. Practiced law, Honolulu, 1941-42, 46-61, 70-72, Washington, 1942; atty. King & McGregor, 1947-53, King & Myhre, 1957-61; judge 1st Circuit Ct. Hawaii, 1961-70, Family Ct., 1966-70, U.S. Dist. Ct. for Hawaii, 1972—, chief judge, 1974—; Faculty Nat. Coll. State Judiciary, 1968-73, Nat. Inst. Trial Advocacy, 1976. Co-translator, co-editor: (O. Korschelt) The Theory and Practice of Go, 1965. Served with USNR, 1941-46; capt. Res. ret. Fellow Am. Bar Found.; mem. ABA, Hawaii Bar Assn. (pres. 1953), Order of Coif. Republican (chmn. Hawaii central com. 1953-55, nat. com. 1971-72). Episcopalian. Home: 1717 Mott-Smith Dr Honolulu HI 96822 Office: PJKK Federal Bldg Honolulu HI 96850

KING, SHELDON SELIG, medical center administrator, educator; b. N.Y.C., Aug. 28, 1931; s. Benjamin and Jeanne (Fritz) K.; m. Ruth Arden Zeller, June 26, 1955; children: Tracy Elizabeth, Meredith Ellen, Adam Bradley. A.B., NYU, 1952; M.S., Yale U., 1957. Adminstrv. intern Montefiore Hosp., N.Y.C., 1952-53, 55; adminstrv. asst. Mt. Sinai Hosp., N.Y.C., 1957-60, asst. dir., 1960-66, dir. planning, 1966-68; exec. dir. Albert Einstein Coll. Medicine-Bronx Municipal Hosp. Center, Bronx, N.Y., 1968-72; asst. prof. Albert Einstein Coll. Medicine, N.Y.C., 1968-72; dir. hosps. and clinics Univ. Hosp., assoc. clin. prof. U. Calif., San Diego, 1972-81, acting head div. health care scis., dept. community medicine, 1978-81; exec. v.p., dir. Stanford Univ. Hosp.; assoc. v.p. Stanford U. Med. Center, 1981—; clin. assoc. prof. dept. community, family and preventive medicine Stanford U.; mem. adminstrv. bd. Council Teaching Hosps., 1982—; preceptor George Washington U., Ithaca Coll., Yale, U. Mo., City U. N.Y.; Chmn. health care com. San Diego County Immigration Council, 1974-77; adv. council Calif. Health Facilities Commn., 1977—. Mem. editorial adv. bd.: Who's Who in Health Care, 1977; mem. editorial bd.: Jour. Med. Edn, 1979—. Bd. dirs. Hosp. Council San Diego and Imperial Counties, 1974-77, treas., 1976—, pres., 1977—; bd. dirs. United Way San Diego, 1975-80, Brith Milah Bd. Served with AUS, 1953-55. Fellow Am. Coll. Hosp. Adminstrs., Am. Pub. Health Assn., Royal Soc. Health; mem. Am. Hosp. Assn., Calif. Hosp. Assn. (trustee 1978-81). Home: 989 Cottrell Way Stanford CA 94305 Office: Stanford Univ Hosp C-204 Stanford CA 94305

KING, SOL, architect; b. Poland, July 19, 1909; came to U.S., 1923, naturalized, 1925; s. Lester and Celia (Sarna) K.; m. Jennie Lifshitz, Apr. 14, 1935; children—Phyllis D. (Mrs. Samuel P. Weiner) (dec.), Susan M. (Mrs. Ralph Ryback). Student, U. Detroit, 1929-31; B.S. in Architecture, U. Mich., 1934. With Albert Kahn Assos. (architects and engrs.), Detroit, 1935—, dir. architecture, 1956-75, pres., 1958-74, chmn., 1974-75; propr. Sol King (architect), Detroit, 1958—; Pub. adv. panel archtl. services GSA, 1967-69; mem. Mich. Bd. Registration Architects, 1972-75, chmn., 1974—; mem. Mich. Bd. Registration Profl. Engrs., 1972-75; pres. Sci. and Engring. Fair Met. Detroit, 1974. Prin. works include Willow Run (Mich.) Bomber Plant, 1942, assembly plant, Ford Motor Co., St. Louis, 1948, main office bldg, Ford div. Ford Motor Co., Dearborn, Mich., 1957, Nat. Bank Detroit hdqrs. bldg, 1959, physics and astronomy bldg, U. Mich., 1963, Gen. Motors Futurama Bldg, N.Y. World's Fair, 1964, lab. and office bldg, Avon Products, Inc., Springdale, Ohio, 1965, Woodhaven (Mich.) Stamping plant, Ford Motor Co., 1965, Southeastern br. facilities, Avon Products, Inc., Atlanta, 1969, Houston Chronicle printing plant, 1970, Washington Post printing facilities, 1971, hosp. and parking structure, Children's Hosp. Mich., 1971, Appliance Park-East, Gen. Electric Co., Columbia, Md., 1972, classroom and office bldg. and Sch. Pub. Health at, U. Mich., Ann Arbor, 1973. Mem. founders Soc. Detroit Inst. Arts, 1950—; bd. dirs., sec., treas., v.p. Jewish Community Center, Detroit, 1946-56; trustee Thomas Alva Edison Found.; mem. grad. scholarship com. Coll. Architecture and Design, U. Mich., 1956—, chmn. alumni adv. com., semi-centennial celebration, 1956; sponsor fgn. student exchange Program Assn. Collegiate Schs. Architecture, 1963-64, 65-67; sponsor grad. scholarship Albert Kahn Assos., 1956—. Recipient Sesquicentennial award U. Mich., 1967; Sol King award for excellent teaching in architecture U. Mich, 1969; Wisdom award of honor Wisdom Hall of Fame, 1970. Fellow AIA (dir., v.p. Detroit chpt. 1969-70, mem. various coms. 1962—), Mich. Soc. Architects (Gold medal award 1967, dir. 1951-56, chmn. task force on a uniform fed. archtl.-engring. contract com. 1969), Engring. Soc. Detroit (v.p. 1968, pres. 1969-70, bd. dirs., chmn. 1976, chmn. Coll. Fellows 1976, Disting. Service award 1976); mem. Newcomen Soc. N.Am, Soc. Archtl. Historians, Technion Soc., Bldg. Ofcls. Conf. Am., Bldg. Research Inst., O.R.T. Jewish (bd. govs. Congregation Shaarey Zedek 1966—, Temple Emanuel P.B. 1977—). Clubs: Economic of Detroit (dir. 1971-79); President's (U. Mich.); Palm Beach (Fla.) Country. Home: 2860 S Ocean Blvd Palm Beach FL 33480 Office: PO Box 1115 Palm Beach FL 33480

KING, STEPHEN EDWIN, novelist; b. Portland, Maine, Sept. 21, 1947; s. Donald and Nellie Ruth (Pillsbury) K.; m. Tabitha Jane Spruce, Jan. 2, 1971; children: Naomi, Joe Hill, Owen. B.S., U. Maine, 1970. Tchr. English, Hampden (Maine) Acad., 1971-73; writer in residence U. Maine at Orono, 1978-79. Novels include Carrie, 1974, Salem's Lot, 1975, The Shining, 1976, The Stand, 1978, Firestarter, 1980, Danse Macabre, 1981, Cujo, 1981, Different Seasons, 1982, The Dark Tower: The Gunslinger, 1982, Christine, 1983, Pet Sematary, 1983; short story collection Night Shift, 1978; author numerous other short stories. Mem. Author's Guild Am., Screen Artists Guild, Screen Writers of Am., Writer's Guild. Democrat. Office: Press Relations Viking Press 625 Madison Ave New York NY 10022

KING, STEPHEN SCOTT, lawyer; b. Duluth, Minn., Oct. 9, 1937; s. Louis H. and Harriet Mildred (Rosen) K.; (div.)children—Rori Nicole, Ian Mitchell. B.S., UCLA, 1959, J.D., 1962. Bar: Calif. bar 1963. Asso. King & Seligsohn (and predecessor firms), Los Angeles, 1963-64, partner, 1964—; asst. sec., dir. Kings Restaurants, Inc., Los Angeles, 1970—; Lectr. continuing edn. bar program U. Calif.; lectr. law Southwestern U. Law Sch., Los Angeles, 1967-71; prof. law Mid-Valley Coll. Law, Encino, Calif., 1973-74; Mem. dean's council UCLA Law Sch., 1968—. Mem. ABA, Los Angeles County Bar Assn. (chmn. family law sect. 1975-76), Wilshire Bar Assn., Hollywood Bar Assn., Am. Arbitration Assn. (nat. panel arbitrators), Lawyers Club Los Angeles, Los Angeles Trial Lawyers Assn. Home: 3424 Woodcliff Rd Sherman Oaks CA 91403 Office: 3550 Wilshire Blvd Suite 1518 Los Angeles CA 90010

KING, SUSAN BENNETT, govt. ofcl.; b. Sioux City, Iowa, Apr. 29, 1940; d. Francis Moffatt and Marjorie (Rittenhouse) Bennett; m. Rufus G. King III, June 22, 1968 (div. July 1975). B.A. in Polit. Sci, Duke U., 1962; postgrad. in law, Columbus Sch. Law Cath. U., 1975-77. With Adminstrv. Office of U.S. Cts., Washington, 1962-63; legis. asst. to U.S. Senate Subcom. on Juvenile Delinquency, Washington, 1963-66; Washington dir. Nat. Com. for Effective Congress, 1967-73; exec. dir. Center for Public Financing of Elections, Washington, 1973-75; exec. asst. to chmn. Fed. Election Commn., Washington, 1975-77; chmn. U.S. Consumer Product Safety Commn., Washington, 1978-81; fellow Inst. of Politics, J.F.K. Sch. Govt., Harvard U., 1981; mem. J.F.K. Inst. Study Group on Election Reform. Co-founder, bd. dirs. Women's Campaign Fund, Washington, 1973-75; mem. legis com. Nat. Women's Polit. Caucus; bd. dirs. Nat. Assn. for So. Poor, 1975—; bd. visitors Duke U. Inst. Policy Scis. and Public Affairs. Mem. Am. Polit. Sci. Assn., Phi Beta Kappa.

KING, THOMAS ALLEN, association executive; b. Indpls., Mar. 6, 1942; s. Ben Allen and Mildred Ruth (Waters) K.; m. Verletta Sue Jackson, July 3, 1965; children: Brian, Scott, Greg. B.A., Butler U., 1966. Public relations asst. Indpls. Newspapers, Inc., 1963-66; with Indpls. C. of C., 1970—, pres., 1979—. Bd. dirs. Big Bros. Indpls., Jr. Achievement Greater Indpls., Indpls. Area Red Cross, Goodwill Industries Indpls., '500' Festival Assocs. Served with USAF, 1966-70. Mem. Am. C. of C. Execs. Assn. Republican. Methodist. Home: 8080 Broadway Indianapolis IN 46240 Office: 320 N Meridian St Indianapolis IN 46204

KING, THOMAS AUSTIN, naval officer; b. Greenwich, Conn., May 27, 1920; s. Walter John and Catharine H. (Austin) K. B.S., U.S. Mcht. Marine Acad., 1942, M.S. Commd. 2d lt. U.S. Mcht. Marines, advanced through grades to rear adm., with Maritime Adminstrn. as fgn. rep. in India, Gulf coast dir., New Orleans, Eastern region dir., 1970-80; supt. U.S. Mcht. Marine Acad., Kings Point, N.Y., 1980—. Active Nat. Cargo Bur., United Seamen's Service, Am. Mcht. Marine Library, Life-Saving Benevolent Assn.; pres. Am. Mcht. Mariners Meml. Corp. Served to capt. USNR, 1983—. Address: US Merchant Marine Acad Kings Point NY 11024

KING, THOMAS BURNESS, educator; b. Motherwell, Scotland, Apr. 27, 1923; came to U.S., 1953, naturalized, 1959; s. Robert Dick and Mary Ann Forbes (Burness) K.; m. Helen Z. Scott, Apr. 3, 1950; children—Lesley Helen, Anne Scott, Robert Alan, Edith Burness. B.Sc., Glasgow U., 1945, Ph.D., 1950. Metallurgist Clyde Alloy Steel Co., Scotland, 1940-41, research metallurgist, 1945-46; asso. lectr. metallurgy Royal Coll. Sci. and Tech., Glasgow, 1948-50, lectr., 1950-52; mem. faculty Mass. Inst. Tech., 1953—, prof. metallurgy, 1961—, head dept., 1962-72. Fellow Am. Acad. Arts and Scis.; mem. Am. Inst. Mining, Metall. and Petroleum Engrs. (fellow Metall. Soc.), Am. Soc. Metals, Iron and Steel Inst., Sigma Xi. Home: 23 Jefferson Rd Winchester MA 01890 Office: Mass Inst Tech Cambridge MA 02139

KING, THOMAS CREIGHTON, thoracic surgeon, educator; b. Salt Lake City, Apr. 10, 1928; s. Creighton G. and Alice (Edwards) K.; m. Joan Peters, Aug. 23, 1952; children—John Creighton, Elizabeth, Patrick Edward. B.S., U. Utah, 1952, M.D., 1954; M.A. in Ednl. Psychology, U. Mo., Kansas City, 1963. Diplomate: Am. Bd. Surgery, Am. Bd. Thoracic Surgery. Intern Columbia-Presbyn. Hosp., N.Y.C., 1954-55; resident U. Utah Hosps., 1955-59; asst. prof. surgery U. Kans., 1960-64; asso. chief staff, dir. research labs. Kansas City Vets. Hosp., 1962-64; asso. prof. surgery U. Ill., 1964-66, Asso. prof. ednl. psychology, 1964-66, chief of tng., 1964-66; attending surgeon U. Ill. Research and Edn. Hosp., 1964-66; asso. attending surgeon Cook County Hosp., Chgo., 1964-66; asso. prof. surgery, asso. dean Coll. Medicine, U. Utah, Salt Lake City, 1966-68, acad. v.p., 1968-69, provost, 1969-73, prof. surgery, 1969-73, v.p. health affairs, 1970-73; staff surgeon U. Utah Med. Center, 1968-73; chief thoracic surgery VA Hosp., Salt Lake City, 1968-73; prof. surgery Columbia Coll. Physicians and surgeons, 1973—; attending surgeon Presbyn. Hosp., N.Y.C., 1973—; Cons. med. edn. WHO; mem. Utah Bd. Health, 1967-73. Contbr. articles to profl. jours. Mem. A.C.S., Am. Ednl. Research Assn., Am. Fedn. Clin. Research, Soc. U. Surgeons, Western Surg. Assn., Assn. Am. Med. Colls., Am. Assn. Thoracic Surgery, Am. Surg. Assn. Home: 211 Central Park W New York NY 10024

KING, THOMAS JOSEPH, biologist, university official; b. N.Y.C., June 4, 1921; s. Thomas Joseph and Sarah Ann (Donovan) K.; m. Marion F. Emerson, Dec. 21, 1946; 1 dau., Deborah Ann King Kurz. B.S., Fordham U., 1943; M.S., NYU, 1949, Ph.D., 1953; Sc.D. (hon.), Med. Coll. Pa., 1971. Instr. dept. physiology Hunter Coll., 1947; teaching fellow dept. biology NYU, 1947-50, Damon Runyon lectr., 1966; research fellow Inst. Cancer Research, Phila., 1950-53, assoc. mem. and chmn. dept. embryology, 1953-56, sr. mem., chmn. dept. embryology, 1960-67; prof. biology Georgetown U., 1967-72, professorial lectr. dept. Ob-gyn, 1971-72; dir. Kennedy Inst. Ethics, 1980—; assoc. dir. for research programs Nat. Cancer Inst., NIH, Bethesda, Md., 1972-74, acting dir. div. cancer research resources and centers, 1974-75, dir. div. cancer research resources and centers, 1975-80; Disting. lectr. Yale U., 1965; instr. Marine Biology Lab., Woods Hole, Mass., 1964-66. Editor: (with others) Advances in Morphogenesis, 1966, 2d. rev. edit., 1972, Developmental Aspects of Carcinogenesis and Immunity, 1974. Mem. sci. adv. com. Damon Runyon/Walter Winchell Cancer Research Found., 1971-74. Served to 1st lt. Med. Adminstrn. Corps U.S. Army, 1943-46. Recipient Achievement award in sci. Fordham Coll. Alumni Assn., 1961, Achievement award in edn. Fordham Coll. Alumni Assn., 1981, Charles Leopold Mayer prize Academic de Science, Institut de France; Nat. Cancer Inst. grantee, 1950-67; Am. Cancer Soc. grantee, 1959-63. Mem. Am. Soc. Zoologists, Soc. Devel. Biology (pres. 1973), Am. Soc. Naturalists, Am. Assn. Cancer Research (dir. 1978—), Internat. Inst. Embryology, Am. Soc. Cell Biologists, AAAS, Internat. Soc. Cell Biology, Phi Beta Kappa, Sigma Xi. Democrat. Roman Catholic. Club: Cosmos (Washington). Office: Kennedy Inst Ethics Georgetown U Washington DC 20057

KING, THOMAS WILLIAM, food chain exec.; b. Huntington Beach, Calif., Jan. 27, 1931; s. Frank Leroy and Hattie (Dyson) K.; m. Betty June Mayberry, Nov. 22, 1950; children—Michael, Patrick. Student, Orange Coast Coll., 1949. With Alpha Beta Co., La Habra, Calif., 1950-80, sr. v.p. operating services, 1973-76, exec. v.p., 1976-80; pres., chief exec. officer Acme Markets, Inc., 1980—. Mem. Nat. Assn. Food Chains (past chmn), Warehousing and Transp. Clinic, Western Assn. Food Chains (pres.). Club: Elks. Office: 124 N 15th St Philadelphia PA 19101

KING, WILLARD FAHRENKAMP (MRS. EDMUND LUDWIG KING), educator; b. Roswell, N.M., July 13, 1924; d. W. F. and Willard (Pickerill) Fahrenkamp; m. Edmund Ludwig King, Jan. 29, 1951. Student, Tex. Christian U., 1940-41; B.A., U. Tex., 1943, M.A., 1946; Ph.D., Brown U., 1957. Instr. Spanish U. Tex., 1946-47, 49-50; instr. Spanish Brown U., 1950-51, Bryn Mawr (Pa.) Coll., 1958-60, asst. prof., 1960-64, asso. prof., 1964-70, prof. Spanish, 1970—, chmn. dept. Spanish, 1964—, dir. Hispanic studies program, 1971—; Bd. dirs. Internat. Inst. in Spain. Author: Prosa novelística y academias literarias en el siglo XVII, 1963; also articles.; Editor, translator: Lope de Vega, El Caballero de Olmedo, 1972; translator: Américo Castro, The Spaniards, 1970. Guggenheim fellow, 1965-66. Mem. Modern Lang. Assn., Renaissance Soc. Am., Phi Beta Kappa. Democrat. Home: 171 Western Way Princeton NJ 08540 Office: Thomas Library Bryn Mawr Coll Bryn Mawr PA 19010

KING, WILLIAM BRUCE, lawyer; b. Boston, June 3, 1932; s. Gilbert and Frances (Hood) K.; m. Sheila Malone, July 9, 1955; children: Stephen Bruce, Rachel Creath, Christopher Bruce. A.B., Harvard U., 1954, LL.B., 1959. Bar: Mass. 1959. Assoc. firm Goodwin, Procter & Hoar, Boston, 1959-68, ptnr., 1968—; prin. William B. King P.C., 1981—; mem. bd. investment, trustee, corporator Cambridge Savs. Bank; sec. Bradley Real Estate Trust, Mytec Inc.; trustee, pres. Cambridge Heritage Trust, 1984—. Trustee Buckingham Browne and Nichols Sch., 1970-76, sec., 1970-73, vice chmn., 1974-76; vice chmn. Cambridge Hist. Commn., (Mass.), 1973—; pres. Cambridge Civic Assn., 1963-65; bd. govs. Nat. Assn. Real Estate Investment Trusts, 1982—. Served with USN, 1954-56. Mem. ABA, Mass. Bar Assn., Boston Bar Assn., Cambridge-Arlington-Belmont Bar Assn. (pres. 1974-75). Home: 25 Hurlbut St Cambridge MA 02138 Office: 28 State St Boston MA 02109

KING, WILLIAM COLLINS, oil company executive; b. Pitts., Aug. 11, 1921; s. William Raffington and Anne Blatchford (Collins) K.; m. Carolyn Ottilie Thorne, Sept. 1, 1951; children: William R., John Thorne, Louise R., Andrew C. B.S. in Chem. Engring., Carnegie-Mellon U., 1943, M.S., MIT, 1948. With Gulf Research & Devel. Co. div. Gulf Oil Corp., Pitts., 1948-55, with chems dept., 1955-57, dir. market research and econ. planning chems. dept., 1957-63, world wide coordinator chem. ops., 1963-67, v.p. chem. ops. in Europe and Middle East, 1967-72, dir. corp. policy analysis, 1972-80, v.p. corp. planning, 1980—; dir. Fertiberia, S.A., Spain, Rio Gulf Petrolquimica, S.A.; speaker, 1975—, participant nat. and local programs, participant local radio programs. Contbr. articles to profl. publs. Bd. dirs. Hist. Soc. Western Pa., 1977—; v.p., bd. dirs. Civic Light Opera Co., Pitts., 1978—. Fellow Am. Chem. Soc. Mem. N.Am. Soc. Corp. Planning (dir. chpt. 1982—), Strategic Mgmt. Soc., Council Planning Execs. (conf. bd.), Am. Inst. Chem. Engrs. Clubs: Duquesne; Fox Chapel Racquet (Pitts.). Office: Gulf Oil Corp PO Box 1166 Pittsburgh PA 15230

KING, WILLIAM EMERY, ins. exec.; b. Glendive, Mont., Aug. 13, 1912; s. William S. and Gertrude L. (Emery) K.; m. Florence Tousley, Dec. 26, 1936; children—Judith, Winifred, Robert; m. Lois Schmidt Hagstrom, Feb. 13, 1971. B.S., Hamline U., 1934; LL.B., St. Paul Coll. Law, 1939. Bar: Minn. bar 1939. Ins. claim adjuster Employers Liability Assurance Corp., 1935-41; practice of law, St. Paul, 1939-45; claim atty. St. Paul Fire & Marine Ins. Co., 1941-48, asst. sec., 1948-52, sec., 1952-54, v.p., 1954—, also dir.; dir. St. Paul Fire & Marine Ins. Co., St. Paul Mercury Indemnity Co., St. Paul Mercury Ins. Co., Comml. State Bank, St. Paul. Bd. dirs. St. Paul chpt. A.R.C.; pres. bd. trustees Hamline U. Mem. Hamline U. Alumni Assn. (pres. 1956-57), St. Paul C. of C. (bd. 1963-66). Clubs: Minnesota, Somerset (St. Paul). Home: 2365 Delaware Ave St Paul MN 55118

KING, WILLIAM RICHARD, business educator, consultant; b. McKeesport, Pa., Dec. 24, 1938; s. Dewey Clark and Cambria Edith (Jones) K.; m. Fay Eileen Bickerton, June 20, 1958; children—James David, Suzan Lorain. B.S. with honors, Pa. State U., 1960; M.S. Case Inst. Tech, 1962; Ph.D., 1964. Indsl. engr. Pitts. Steel Co., 1960; instr., research fellow, research asst. Case Inst. Tech., 1960-64; asst. prof. ops. research, 1964-65; asst. prof. stats. and ops. research Air Force Inst. Tech., 1965-67; asso. prof. bus. adminstrn. U. Pitts., 1967-69, prof., 1969—, dir. doctoral program, 1971-74, dir. Strategic Mgmt. Inst., 1980—; on leave as profl. staff mem. U.S. Senate Budget Com., 1976-77; vis. scholar Va. Poly. Inst. and State U., 1971; v.p., dir. Cleland-King, Inc.; mgmt. cons. Author: Quantitative Analysis for Marketing Management, 1967, Probability for Management Decisions, 1968, (with David Cleland) Systems Analysis and Project Management, 1968 (McKinsey Found. award 1969), 3d edit., 1983), Management: a Systems Approach, 1972, Marketing Management Information Systems, 1977, (with David Cleland) Strategic Planning and Policy, 1978, (with John Grant) The Logic of Strategic Planning, 1982; also articles in profl. jours.; Editor: (with David Cleland) Systems, Organizations, Analysis, Management, 1969, Project Management Handbook, 1983, (with Gerald Zaltman) Marketing Scientific and Technical Information, 1979; asso. editor: Mgmt. Science; Sr. editor: MIS Quar, 1983—; area editor: Internat. Jour. Policy and Info.; mem. editorial adv. bd.: Ency. of Econs. and Bus. Active YMCA, YMHA; v.p., dir. Pitts. Commerce Inst., 1971-80; Bd. dirs. Western Pa. Montessori Sch., 1968-71, pres., 1968-69. Served to 1st lt. USAF, 1965-67. Ford Found. Systems research fellow, 1960-62; Travelers Ins. Co. research fellow, 1963-64. Fellow AAAS; mem. Ops. Research Soc. Am., Acad. Mgmt., Strategic Mgmt. Soc., Inst. Mgmt. Scis., N. Am. Soc. Corp. Planning, Am. Mktg. Assn., Soc. for Info. Mgmt., Am. Inst. Decision Scis., World Future Soc., Tau Beta Pi, Beta Gamma Sigma, Alpha Pi Mu, Sigma Tau. Office: Grad Sch Bus U Pitts Pittsburgh PA 15260

KING, WOODIE, JR., producer, actor, dir. A founder, Concept-East Theatre; founder, dir., New Federal Theatre at Henry St. Settlement, N.Y.C.; dir.: cultural arts program Moblzn. for Youth in N.Y; producer: plays For Colored Girls Who Have Considered Suicide When Rainbow Is Enuf; Author, editor: Present Condition. Address: 417 Convent Ave New York NY 10031

KING, WOODS, JR., machinery company executive; b. Cleve., Aug. 5, 1928; s. Woods and Louise Alexander (Baldwin) K.; m. Beverly Holden Bailey, Feb. 4, 1956; children: Woods III, Kerry Baldwin, Michelle Louise, Beverly Dana. B.A., Yale U., 1950; LL.B., U. Va., 1953. Bar: Ohio 1953. Assoc. Hauxhust, Inglis, Sharp & Cull, Cleve., 1954-56, 58-60; counsel, asst. sec. Gabriel Co., 1960-63, Clevite Corp., 1963-69; v.p., gen. counsel Warner & Swasey, Cleve., 1969-83; group ops. counsel Bendix Corp., Cleve., 1983—; dir. Prodn. Finishing Co. Team capt. Cleve. United Torch, 1974; Councilman Village of Hunting Valley, Ohio, 1967-75; Trustee, sec. Cleve. Mus. Natural History; trustee Central Sch. Practical Nursing., Govtl. Research Inst. Served to 1st lt. USAF, 1956-58. Mem. Am., Ohio, Cleve. bar assns. Clubs: Union, Chagrin Valley Hunt. Home: Cedar Rd Gates Mills OH 44040 Office: 11000 Cedar Ave Cleveland OH 44106

KINGDON, HENRY SHANNON, physician, biochemist, educator; b. Puunene, Maui, Hawaii, July 2, 1934; s. Robert Wells and Anna Catherine (McCune) K.; m. Mary Lee Colman, June 22, 1957; children: Holly, Catherine, Henry Colman. A.B. in Chemistry, Oberlin Coll., 1956; M.D., Western Res. U., 1963, Ph.D. in Biochemistry, 1963; postgrad., U. Wash., 1962-63. Intern Univ. Hosp., Seattle, 1963-64; resident U. Wash. Affiliated Hosps., Seattle, 1964-65; practice medicine specializing in internal medicine, Chgo., 1967-72, Chapel Hill, N.C., 1973-81; asst. prof. medicine and biochemistry U. Chgo., 1967-71, asso. prof., 1971-73, acting chmn. dept. medicine, summer 1971, dir. med. internship program, 1971-72; prof. medicine and biochemistry U. N.C., Chapel Hill, 1973-81; med. dir. Hyland Therapeutics div. Travenol Labs., Glendale, Calif., 1981—, v.p., 1984—. Contbr. articles on mechanisms of blood coagulation, primary structure of proteins, and on regulation of anabolic nitrogen metabolism to profl. jours. Served with USPHS, 1965-67. Guggenheim Meml. Found. fellow, 1972-73; NIH grantee, 1957-59, 69-81. Mem. Am. Soc. Biol. Chemists, Am. Soc. Hematology, Internat. Soc. Thrombosis and Haemostasis, Central Soc. Clin. Research, So. Soc. Clin. Research, Phi Beta Kappa, Sigma Xi. Home: 1545 Lancashire Pl Pasadena CA 91103 Office: 444 W Glenoaks Blvd Glendale CA 91202

KINGDON, ROBERT MCCUNE, historian, educator; b. Chgo., Dec. 29, 1927; s. Robert W. and Anna Catherine (McCune) K. A.B., Oberlin Coll., 1949; M.A., Columbia U., 1950, Ph.D., 1955; postgrad, U. Geneva, 1951-52. Instr., asst. prof. history U. Mass., 1952-57; asst. prof., asso. prof., prof. history State U. Iowa, Iowa City, 1957-65; prof. history U. Wis., Madison, 1965—; mem. Inst. Research Humanities, 1974—, dir., 1975—; vis. instr. Amherst (Mass.) Coll., 1953-54; vis. prof. Stanford U., 1964, 80; Bd. dirs. Center Reformation Research, St. Louis, pres., 1967—. Author: Geneva and the Coming of the Wars of Religion in France, 1555-1563, 1956, Geneva and the Consolidation of the French Protestant Movement, 1564-1572, 1967, The Political Thought of Peter Martyr Vermigli, 1980; editor: (with J.F. Bergier) Registres de la Compagnie des Pasteurs de Genève au temps de Calvin, 1962—, The Sixteenth Century Journal, 1973—; contbr. articles to profl. jours. Mem. Am. Soc. Reformation Research (v.p. 1970, pres. 1971), Am. Soc. Ch. History (pres. 1980), Central Renaissance Conf., Renaissance Soc. Am. (exec. bd. 1972—), Internat. Fedn. Socs. and Insts. for Study of Renaissance (sec.-treas. 1967—). Home: 4 Rosewood Circle Madison WI 53711

KINGERY, WILLIAM DAVID, educator, ceramist; b. N.Y.C., July 7, 1926; s. Lisle B. and Margaret (Reynolds) K.; m. Gertrude Phillips, Nov. 22, 1965; children—William David, Peter (dec.), Rebekah, Andrew. Grad., Taft Sch., Watertown, Conn., 1943; S.B., MIT, 1950, Sc.D., 1952; Dr. (hon.), Tokyo Inst. Tech., 1982. Mem. faculty MIT, 1951—, prof. ceramics, 1960—, Orton lectr., 1980; vis. prof. Ecole Poly. Fed. de Lausanne, Switzerland, 1980; Mem. materials adv. bd. Nat. Acad. Sci., 1960-68. Author: Property Measurements at High Temperatures, 1959, Introduction to Ceramics, 1960, 2d edit., 1976; Editor: Ceramic Fabrication Process, 1958, Kinetics of High-Temperature Process, 1959, Ice and Snow, 1963; editor-in-chief: Cerammgia Internat, 1976—; Contbr. profl. jours. Chmn. Marion-Bermuda Cruising Yacht Race, 1977-79; chmn. bd. trustees, 1980—; treas. East Marion Steamship Authority. Fellow Am. Ceramic Soc (Ross Coffin Purdy award 1952, John Jeppson award 1958, outstanding service award New Eng. sect. 1957, 1st Distinguished Sosman Meml. lectr. 1973, A.V. Bleininger award 1976, F.H. Norton award 1977, hon. life mem. 1983), Keramos (hon.), Am. Chem. Soc., Glaciological Soc.; mem. Nat. Acad. Engring. Home: Allens Point Rd Marion MA 02738 Office: 77 Massachusetts Ave Cambridge MA 02139

KINGET, G. MARIAN, educator, psychologist; b. Belgium, June 2, 1910; came to U.S., 1948, naturalized, 1957; d. Rene Jules Henri and Elisa (Declercq) K. Ph.D. summa cum laude, U. Louvain, Belgium, 1948; postdoctoral, N.Y. U., 1948-49, Columbia U., 1949-50. With U. Chgo., 1950-52; asst. prof. psychology Mich. State U., East Lansing, 1952-55, asso. prof., 1955-66, prof., 1966-81, emeritus prof., 1981—. Author: On Being Human, 1975, Psychotherapie et Relations Humaines (transl. Spanish and Portuguese), Vol. II, 1962, The Drawing-Completion Test, 1952, (with Carl R. Rogers) Psychotherapie et Relations Humanes (transl. Spanish, Italian and Portuguese), Vol. I, 1962, Psychotherapie en Menselijke Verhoudingen, 1959; contbr. chpts. to books. Mem. Am., Midwestern, Mich. psychol. assns., AAUP. Home: 4583 Nakoma Dr Okemos MI 48864 Office: Mich State U East Lansing MI 48823

KINGHAN, CHARLES ROSS, artist; b. Anthony, Kans., Jan. 18, 1895; s. Robert E. and Sarah Frances (Edwards) K; m. Ruth F. Weidler, Sept. 13, 1927; children: Donald Earl, Charles Bruce. Student, Acad. Fine Arts, Am. Acad. Art, Art Inst., Audubon Sch. Art, all Chgo. Asso. Stevens, Sundblom & Henry Studios, Chgo., 1926-30; free-lance, 1950-51; tchr. Am. Acad. Art, 1933-35; co-owner Huguenot Sch. Art, 1949-53; with Maxon Advt. Agy., 1952-53; art work Batten, Barton, Durstine & Osborn Advt. Agy., N.Y.C., 1954; now tchr. pvt. class in water color, mem. juries of award and selection Am. Watercolor Soc., Allied Artists. Represented permanent collections, Smithsonian Instn., Washington, Phila. Mus. Art, U. Maine, also pvt. collections.; Author: Rendering Techniques for Commercial Art and Advertising, 1957, Ted Kautzky and How He Painted, 1959; also contbr. articles to art mags. Recipient gold medal All Ill. Soc. Arts, 1933, Ernest Quantrel award Hudson Valley Art Assn., 1951; 1st prize New Rochelle Woman's Club, 1951, 53, Westchester Woman's Club, Bronxville, N.Y., 1954; 1st prize watercolor Westchester Fedn. Women's Clubs, 1956; Emily Lowe award Am. Watercolor Soc., 1957; John Newton Howitt award Hebrew Vets. Assn., 1959; Rudolph Lesch award, 1965; others. Mem. Am. Watercolor Soc. (v.p. 1969, 71), Phila. Watercolor Club, Allied Artists Hudson Valley Art Assn. (dir.), New Rochelle Art Assn. (past pres.), NAD, Allied Artists of Am., Hebrew Vets. Assn. (v.p. 1969), Salmagundi Club. Home: 551 Gibson Ave Pacific Grove CA 93950

KINGMAN, ALTON (HAYWARD), JR., banker; b. Brockton, Mass., May 6, 1922; s. Alton Hayward and Ethel (Wales) K.; m. Mary Ellen Stavely, Oct. 7, 1945; children: Joan, Dan, Mary Lou. Student, Lehigh U., 1940-43; grad., Pacific Coast Banking Sch., U. Wash., 1969. With First Interstate Bank of Calif., San Francisco, 1949—, sr. v.p. br. adminstrn., 1971-74, sr. v.p., mgr. personal bank, 1974-76, exec. v.p. and sr. adminstrv. officer No. Calif., 1976—; dir. Master Card Internat. Pres. Ind. Colls. No. Calif.; bd. dirs., mem. adv. bd. Jr. Achievement of Bay Area Inc.; bd. dirs. NCCJ, San Francisco, YMCA, San Francisco, United Way, Bay Area, Bay Area Council; mem. exec. bd. San Francisco Bay Area council Boy Scouts Am. Served to 1st lt. USAAF, 1942-45. Mem. Western States Bankcard Assn. (chmn. bd. dirs.), Robert Morris Assos., San Francisco Clearing House Assn., San Francisco Conv. and Visitors Bur. (dir.). Clubs: Bankers of San Francisco, Sequoyah Country, Stock Exchange of Los Angeles, Pacific Union, Masons. Home: 81 Graeagle Oakland CA 94605 Office: 405 Montgomery St San Francisco CA 94104

KINGMAN, DAVID ARTHUR, professional baseball player; b. Pendleton, Oreg., Dec. 21, 1948. Attended, Harper Coll., U. So. Calif. Baseball player San Francisco Giants, 1971-74, N.Y. Mets, 1975-77, San Diego Padres, 1977, Calif. Angels, 1977, N.Y. Yankees, 1977, Chgo. Cubs, 1978-81, N.Y. Mets, 1981-84, Oakland A's, 1984—; mem. Nat. League All-Star Team, 1976, 79, 80. Office: care Oakland A's Oakland-Alameda Coliseum Oakland CA 94621 *

KINGMAN, DONG, artist, educator; b. Oakland, Calif., Apr. 1, 1911; s. Dong Chuan-Fee and Lew Shee K.; m. Wong Shee, Sept. 1929 (dec. June 1954); children—Eddie, Dong Kingman Jr.; m. Helena Kuo, Sept. 1956. Student, Lingnan, Hong Kong, 1924-26. Tchr. art San Diego Art Gallery, 1941-43; tchr. Famous Artists Schs., Westport, Conn., Columbia U., Hunter Coll.; Lectr. tour around world sponsored by internat. cultural exchange program Dept. State, 1954. (Recipient award Chgo. Internat. Watercolor Exhbn. 1944, gold medal of honor Audubon Artist Exbn. 1946, winner $300 prize award, Am. award Met. Spl. Watercolor Exhibit 1952); Represented in permanent collections, Whitney Mus. Am. Art, Am. Acad. Arts and Letters, Bklyn. Mus., Toledo Mus. Art, Joslyn Art Mus., Omaha, Mus. Fine Arts, Boston, Met. Mus. Art, Mus. Modern Art, N.Y.C., U. Nebr., Wadsworth Atheneum, Bloomington (Ill.) Art Assn., San Francisco Mus., Mills Coll., De Young Mus., Albert Bender Collection, Eleanor Roosevelt Collection, Chgo. Art Inst., N.Y. State Tchrs. Coll., Springfield (Ill.) Art Assn., Cranbrook Acad. Art, Butler Art Inst., Ft. Wayne Mus., Addison Gallery, U.S. Dept. State, many others; executed murals, Bank of Calif., San Francisco, N.Y. Hilton Hotel, R.H. Macy & Co., Franklin Sq., N.Y., Boca Raton Hotel, Fla., Hyatt Regency Hotel, Hong Kong, Ambassador Hotel, Kowloon, Hong Kong, Lincoln Savs. Bank, N.Y.C.; Illustrator: The Bamboo Gate (Vanya Oakes), 1946, China's Story (Enid LaMonte Meadowcroft), 1946, Nightingale (Andersen), 1948, Johnny Hong in Chinatown (Clyde Robert Bulla), 1952, Caen's and Kingman's San Francisco (Herb Caen), 1964, City on the Golden Hill (Herb Caen), 1967; author: (with Helena Kuo Kingman) Dong Kingman's Watercolors, 1980; Painted: title paintings for 55 Days at Peking. Served in U.S. Army. Guggenheim fellow, 1942, 43. Home: 21 W 58th St New York NY 10019 Office: care Hammer Galleries 33 W 57th St New York NY 10019

KINGMAN, HENRY SELDEN, JR., banker; b. Mpls., Feb. 23, 1922; s. Henry Selden and Josephine (Woodward) K.; m. Marilyn Eastman, Apr. 26, 1947; children: Katharine Richards, Sally Hornig, David, Woodward. B.A., Amherst Coll., 1943. With Gen. Mills, 1946-57; pres. Farmers & Mechanics Savs. Bank, Mpls., 1969—, chmn. bd., 1975—, also chief exec. officer, trustee; dir. Title Ins. Co. Minn., N.Am. Life & Casualty Co. Trustee Mpls. Found.; bd. dirs. Abbott-Northwestern Hosp., Mpls. Office: 90 S 6th St Minneapolis MN 55480 *

KINGMAN, JOSEPH RAMSDELL, III, banker; b. Mpls., Dec. 8, 1927; s. Joseph Ramsdell and Margaret Perry (Morris) K.; m. Kathleen Popesh, Aug. 4, 1977; children: James B., Kate P. B.A., Amherst Coll., 1949. With 1st Nat. Bank of Mpls., 1950-61, Imperial Fin. Services, 1962-63; with 1st Nat. Bank of Mpls., 1963-82, vice chmn., to 1982; pres. Am. Nat. Bank & Trust Co., St. Paul, 1983—. Bd. dirs. Met. Econ. Devel. Assn., Center for Humanism, Awareness and Research Tng., St. Paul Chamber Orch. Served with U.S. Army, 1950-52. Mem. Am. Bankers Assn. Clubs: Minneapolis, St. Paul Athletic, Minnesota. Office: Am Nat Bank 5th and Minnesota St Saint Paul MN 55101 *

KINGMAN, WILLIAM LOCKWOOD, financial consultant; b. Medford, Mass., Aug. 21, 1930; s. Henry Eugene and Helen Elizabeth (Crandell) K.; m. Nancy Barbara Dean, Mar. 27, 1954; children—Lawrence Eugene, Celena Elizabeth. Grad., Middlesex Sch., Concord, Mass., 1949; B.A. in Econs, Yale U., 1953. With Franklin Mgmt. Corp., Boston, 1956—, v.p., 1960-66, exec. v.p., 1966-68, vice chmn., 1968-71, chmn., 1971—, also dir.; with, N.Y.C., 1959-71, v.p., dir., 1960-71; audit com. Middlesex Instn. Savs., 1959—, trustee, 1961—. Trustee New Eng. Fund (now Sigma Trust), 1961-73; dir. Sigma Capital, 1969-73; Mem. Acton Republican Com., Actdn Fin. Com., 1972-77; Mem. corp. Emerson Hosp., Concord, Mass., 1960-76, trustee, 1961-71; trustee The Fenn Sch., Concord, Mass., 1967-77, treas., 1969-77; mem. bd. mgmt., trustee Charlestown (Mass.) Armed Services YMCA, 1978—; bd. dirs. Boston Port, Seaman's Aid Soc., 1981—. Served to lt. (j.g.) USNR, 1953-56; lt. (s.g.) Res. Mem. Navy League U.S. Clubs: Union, Wardroom (Boston); Cumberland (Portland, Maine); Nashoba Valley Hunt, Old Northbridge Hounds. Home: 65 Esterbrook Rd RFD 1 Acton MA 01720 Office: 222 Lewis Wharf Boston MA 02110

KINGMAN, WOODWARD, bank executive; b. Mpls., Sept. 5, 1925; s. Henry Selden and Josephine (Woodward) K. B.A. cum laude, Amherst Coll., 1949; M.B.A., Harvard U., 1951. Budget analyst Cowles Mag. Inc., N.Y.C., 1951-56; loan officer First Nat. City Bank, N.Y.C., 1956-66; asst. to exec. v.p. fin. ITT, N.Y.C., 1967-69; pres. Govt. Nat. Mortgage Assn.; dep. commr. FHA, HUD, Washington, 1969-74; acting asst. sec. housing prodn. and mortgage Credit HUD, 1973-74; exec. v.p. for trust investment and fiduciary services Crocker Nat. Bank, San Francisco, 1974—; dir. Lomas & Nettleton Fin. Corp., Dallas, Pacific Securities Depository Trust Co., San Francisco, Bishop Trust Co., Honolulu. Mem. N.Y.C. Council, 1966; pres. San Francisco Planning and Urban Research, 1980-82; treas. Calif. Assn. Am. Conservatory Theatre, 1978—, San Francisco Conservatory Music, 1979—; bd. dirs. Spring Opera Theater, San Francisco, 1980-81; vice chmn. Republican Nat. Fin. Com., 1979—. Served to 2d lt. inf. AUS, 1943-46. Recipient cert. merit HUD, 1974. Mem. Res. City Bankers Assn. Congregationalist. Clubs: Racquet and Tennis, Am. Alpine, Harvard (N.Y.C.); Chevy Chase (Md.); Burlingame Country (Hillsborough, Calif.); Pacific Union, Bankers (San Francisco); California (Los Angeles). Home: 1010 Francisco St San Francisco CA 94109 Office: 111 Sutter St 20 San Francisco CA 94104

KINGON, ALFRED HUGH, government official; b. N.Y.C., May 11, 1931; s. Nathan N. and Grace J. (Linde) K.; m. Jacqueline J. Goldwyn, June 24, 1962; 1 son, Michael. B.S., Union Coll., 1953; postgrad., N.Y. U., 1955-61. Asso. investment advisory dept. Burnham & Co., N.Y.C., 1963-67; v.p., research dir. Scheinman, Hochstin & Trotta, N.Y.C., 1967-70; v.p., portfolio mgr. The Businessman's Fund, N.Y.C., 1970-71; exec. v.p. Macro Communications, N.Y.C., 1971-82; editor in chief Financial World, 1973-83, Saturday Review, 1980-82; asst. sec. commerce for internat. econ. policy Dept. Commerce, Washington, 1983—; mem. Pres.'s Nat. Productivity Adv. Com., President's Pvt. Sector Survey on Cost Control, 1982. Author: The New Deal, The Fair Deal, The Coming Ordeal, 1971. Trustee Mannes Coll. Music, 1981-83, Little Red Schoolhouse, 1977-81. Mem. N.Y. Soc. Security Analysts. Republican. Home: 2 Primrose St Chevy Chase MD 20815 Office: Room 3864 Dept Commerce 14th St betweem E St and Constitution Ave Washington DC 20230

KINGREY, BURNELL WAYNE, coll. dean; b. Worthington, Minn., Sept. 12, 1921; s. Harold Raymond and Iva (Goodrich) K.; m. Patricia Abbott, June 3, 1945; children—Michael, Jean, Karel. A.A., Worthington Jr. Coll., 1941; D.V.M., Iowa State U., 1944, M.S., 1955. Diplomate: Am. Coll. Vet. Internal Medicine. Pvt. practice vet. medicine, Lena, Ill., 1944-53; faculty Iowa State U., 1953-63, prof., head dept. vet. medicine and surgery, 1955-63; dir. clinics Vet. Research Council, 1958-63; dean Sch. Vet. Medicine, U. Mo., 1963-73, dean emeritus, 1977—; pres. Double Crown Ranches, Inc., 1973—; dir. vet. edn. and services program Old West Regional Commn., Billings, Mont., 1977—; ICA cons. to, Argentina and Chile, 1961; AID cons. to San Carlos U., Guatemala, 1962, India, 1968; cons. Sch. Vet. Medicine, Bogotá, Colombia, 1969, U. Wis. Bd. Regents, 1973; chmn. Bd. of Scientific Advisors Merck Inst., 1974—; chmn. external examiners Miss. State U., 1979—; mem. N. Central Coll. and Univ. Accreditation Team, 1976. Mem. Lena Sch. Bd., 1952-63. Recipient Disting. Service award U. Mo., 1976; Strange award Iowa State U., 1979. Mem. AMVA (adv. manpower study 1977-78), Wyo. Vet. Med. Assn., Am. Assn. Vet. Clincians, Am. Acad. Sci., Am. Legion, Phi Kappa Phi, Delta Psi Omega, Gamma Sigma Delta, Phi Zeta, Alpha Zeta, Sigma Xi. Clubs: Rotarian, Mason. Home: Box 545 Douglas WY 82633

KINGSBERG, HAROLD JOSEPH, investment management company executive; b. N.Y.C., Aug. 29, 1927; s. Malcolm and Rebecca (Berkowitz) K.; m. Ruth Joel, Aug. 6, 1950; children: Robert, Alan, Sally. B.A., Harvard U., 1949, M.B.A., 1951. With Central Nat. Corp., N.Y.C., 1953-63, asst. v.p., 1956-60, v.p., 1960-63, Gen. Am. Investors, 1963-78, exec. v.p., 1978—. Home: 47 E 88th St New York NY 10128 Office: Gen Am Investors 330 Madison Ave New York NY 10017

KINGSBERY, WALTON WAITS, JR., accountant; b. Evergreen, Ala., June 25, 1928; s. Walton Waits and Alpha Lee (Eaton) K.; m. Helen Elizabeth Clayton, Mar. 21, 1953; children: Walton Waits, III, J. Clayton, Peter C. B.S. with honors, U. Ala., 1950. C.P.A., Ohio, N.J., N.Y., Calif. With Price Waterhouse & Co., 1950—, mng. partner, Cleve., 1977—, mem. policy bd., 1979—, mng. ptnr. Western area, Los Angeles, 1982—. Author booklets, papers in field. Chmn. Shrewsbury (N.J.) Planning Bd., 1972; bd. dirs. Greater Cleve. Growth Assn., 1978—; trustee Beech Brook, 1979, Cleve. Playhouse, 1980; clk. Village of Hunting Valley, Ohio. Served with AUS, 1950-53. Mem. Am. Inst. C.P.A.s, Nat. Assn. Accountants, Ohio Soc. C.P.A.s, N.J. Soc. C.P.A.s, N.Y. Soc. C.P.A.s, Calif. Soc. C.P.A.s, Bluecoats, Newcomen Soc. N.Am. Clubs: Cleve. Country, Union, Cleve. Racquet; Duquesne (Pitts.).

KINGSBURY, ARTHUR FRANCH, III, newspaper publishing executive; b. Middletown, Conn., May 20, 1948; s. Arthur Franch and Mary Etta (Siteman) K.; children: Kristen, Mary, Elizabeth. B.S.B.A., Babson Coll., 1969. C.P.A., Mass. Staff acct. Arthur Andersen & Co., Boston, 1969-72; asst. controller Globe Newspaper Co., Boston, 1972-78, controller, 1978-81; treas. Globe NewspaperCo., Boston, 1981-82; v.p., treas. Globe Newspaper Co., Boston, 1982—; dir. Vinfen Corp., Boston, 1979—. Mem. Conservation Commn., Sandwich, Mass., 1979-80, Bd. Appeals, Sandwich, 1980-82. Served with U.S. Army, 1969-75. Mem. Am. Inst. C.P.A.s, Mass. Soc. C.P.A.s. Republican. Roman Caltholic. Club: Business Associates (Boston) (treas. 1982—). Home: 165 Quincy Shore Dr Qunicy MA 02107 Office: Globe Newspaper Co. 135 Morrissey Blvd Boston MA 02107

KINGSBURY, FREDERICK HUTCHINSON, JR., banker; b. Scranton, Pa., May 21, 1907; s. Frederick H. and Hope (MacIntosh) K.; m. Charlotte Meyer Beresford, Apr. 27, 1934 (div. May 1962); children: Hope MacIntosh Costikyan, Frederick H. III; m. Eleanor Bried O'Donnell, Oct. 3, 1962. Student, The Hill Sch., 1923-25; A.B., Princeton U., 1929. With Brown Bros. Harriman & Co., 1929—, partner, 1949—; chmn. bd. Prudential Ins. Co. Gt. Britain, N.Y., 1957-73; dep. chmn. Brown Harriman & Internat. Banks Ltd., London, 1972-77; dir. Hudson Ins. Co., Hudson Life Reassurance Corp., Skandia Am. Reins. Corp., Skandia Corp., Am. European Reins. Corp., chmn. bd., 1974-82; dir. Interpace Corp., 1952-79, Bangor Punta Corp., 1956-79; mem. internat. adv. com. Am. Bankers Assn., 1962-65. Mem. alumni council Princeton, 1949-54; trustee St. Barnabas Hosp., N.Y.C. Decorated Officer Order Oranje-Nassau, Netherlands). Presbyn. (trustee 1968-71). Clubs: University, Links, India House (N.Y.C.); University Cottage (Princeton); Pine Valley Golf (Clementon, N.J.); Blooming Grove Hunting and Fishing (Hawley, Pa.). Home: 655 Park Ave New York NY 10021 Office: 59 Wall St New York NY 10005

KINGSBURY, JOHN MERRIAM, boitanist, educator; b. Boston, July 4, 1928; s. Willis Albert and Constance Elizabeth (Merriam) K.; m. Louise Arnold Gerken, June 6, 1956; 1 dau., Joanna Merriam. B.S., U. Mass., 1950; A.M., Harvard U., 1952, Ph.D., 1954. Instr. Brandeis U., Waltham, Mass., 1953-54; mem. faculty N.Y. State Coll. Agr. and Life Scis., Cornell U., Ithaca, N.Y., 1954—, prof. botany, 1970—; prof. clin. scis. Coll. Vet. Medicine, Cornell U., Ithaca, N.Y., 1978—, dir. arboretum and bot. garden, 1982—; founding dir. Shoals Marine Lab., 1972-79; adj. prof. U. N.H., 1976-78; cons. Upstate Med. Ctr., Syracuse, N.Y., 1977—. Author: Poisonous Plants of the United States and Canda, 1964, Deadly Harvest—A Guide to Common Poisonous Plants, 1965, Seaweeds of Cape God and the Islands, 1969, The Rocky Shore, 1970, Oil and Water—The New Hampshire Story, 1975. NSF faculty fellow, 1958; Fulbright sr. scholar, 1980. Fellow Am. Coll. Vet. Toxicologists (hon.); mem. Bot. Soc. Am., Sea Edn. Assn. (trustee 1977—, pres. 1982—), Soc. Econ. Botany, Am. Soc. Limnology and Oceanography, Am. Assn. Poison Control Ctrs., Marine Biol. Lab. Office: Plant Sci Bldg Cornell U Ithaca NY 14853

KINGSBURY-SMITH, JOSEPH, journalist; b. N.Y.C., Feb. 20, 1908; s. William Barstow and Maria (Jordan) S.; m. Eileen King, July 20, 1940; children: Eileen Jordan, Diane. Ed. privately and at, St Francis Xavier, N.Y.C., 1918, St. Joseph's Sch., 1923, Friend's Prep. Sch., Poughkeepsie, N.Y., 1926, U. London, 1928. Copy boy, cub reporter Internat. News Service, 1924-26; with fgn. cable desk United Press, 1926-27; reporter London Bur. Internat. News Service, 1927-31, covered, 1931-32, 1932-36, mgr., 1936, exec. asst. dir. fgn. service, 1940, 1941-44; European gen. mgr. Internat. News Service and Internat. News Photos, 1944-55; v.p., dir. Hearst Corp.; gen. mgr. Internat. News Service, Internat. News Photos; v.p., dir. Hearst Consol. Pubs., Inc., 1955-58; pub. N.Y. Jour.-Am., 1959-66; v.p., European dir. Hearst Corp.; chief fgn. writer Hearst Newspapers and King Features Syndicate, 1966-76; nat. editor Hearst Newspapers, 1976—; v.p., dir. Washington office Hearst Corp.; Washington rep. Hearst Founds. Trustee Fordham U., Hearst Estate. Decorated officer Legion of Honor; knight comdr. Order St. Denis of Zante; recipient George R. Holmes Meml. award, 1941-49, Nat. Headliners' Club award, 1941, 47, 50, Distinguished Service award Sigma Delta Chi, 1949, George Polk award L.I. U., 1950, Pulitzer prize for distinguished internat. reporting, 1956, U.S. Govt. Disting. Service award, 1961. Mem. Am. Soc. Newspaper Editors. Clubs: Knight of Malta., Brook., Metropolitan. Office: 1701 Pennsylvania Ave NW Washington DC 20006

KINGSLEY, BEN, actor; b. Scarborough, Eng., Dec. 31, 1943; s. Rehimtulla Harji and Anna Lyna (Goodman) Bhanji; m. Gillian Alison Macaulay Sutcliffe, July 1, 1978; 1 son, Edmund William MacAulay. Assoc. artist Royal Shakespeare Co., Eng., 1968—; actor. Play include Hamlet, 1975-76; films include Gandhi, 1981 (Acad. 1982), Betrayal, 1982. Recipient Padma Shri award Govt. of India, 1984; named Best Actor and Best Newcomer Brit. Acad. Film and TV Arts, 1982, Standard Film Awards, London, 1983. Mem. Brit. Acad. Film and TV Arts, Acad. Motion Picture Arts and Scis. Quaker. Address: care ICM Ltd 388 396 Oxford St London England W1

KINGSLEY, DANIEL THAIN, public relations executive; b. Portland, Oreg., Oct. 1, 1932; s. George Archibald and Jane (Powers) K.; m. Nancy C.; children by previous marriage: Daniel, Clay, Blake, Christopher, Elizabeth, Reed B. A.B. cum laude, Princeton U., 1954. Sales mgr. Kingsley Lumber Co., Portland, 1959-62, pres., 1962-68; commr. GSA, Washington, 1969-71; spl. asst. White House Office, Exec. Office of Pres., 1971-74; exec. v.p., gen. mgr. Deaver & Hannaford, Inc. (pub. relations), 1977-83; exec. dir. Nat. Venture Capital Assn. and propr. Daniel T. Kingsley pub. affairs cons., 1983—; asso. adminstr. ops. SBA, 1975-77. Vice pres. Parry Center for Children, Portland, 1966-68; trustee Bishop Dagwell Hall, Episcopal Boys Sch., Portland, 1966-68. Served with AUS, 1954-56. Republican. Episcopalian. Clubs: Multnomah Athletic (trustee), Racquet (Portland); Congressional Country (Potomac, Md.); Georgetown (Washington). Home: 10705 Stanmore Dr Potomac MD 20854 Office: 1225 19th St Suite 750 Washington DC 20036

KINGSLEY, JAMES GORDON, college president; b. Houston, Nov. 22, 1933; s. James Gordon and Blanche Sybil (Payne) K.; m. Martha Elizabeth Sasser, Aug. 24, 1956; children: Gordon Alan, Craig Emerson. A.B., Miss. Coll., 1955; M.A., U. Mo., 1956; B.D., Th.D., New Orleans Bapt. Theol. Sem., 1960, 65; H.H.D., Mercer U., 1980; postgrad., U. Louisville, 1968-69, Nat. U. Ireland, 1970, Harvard U., 1976. Asst. prof. Miss. Coll., 1956-58; instr. Tulane U., 1958-60; asst. prof. William Jewell Coll., Liberty, Mo., 1960-62, prof. lit. and religion, 1969—, dean, 1976-80, pres., 1980—; asso. prof. Ky. So. Coll., Louisville, 1964-67, prof., 1967-69. Author: A Time for Openness, 1973, Frontiers, 1983; contbr. articles to profl. jours. LaRue fellow, 1976. Mem. English Speaking Union, Am. Assn. Higher Edn., Bapt. Hist. Soc. Baptist. Clubs: Rotary, Kansas City Univ. Home: 510 E Mississippi St Liberty MO 64068 Office: William Jewell Coll Liberty MO 64068

KINGSLEY, JOHN MCCALL, JR., manufacturing company executive; b. Berlin, Germany, Dec. 1, 1931; s. John McCall and Elizabeth (Curry) K.; m. Ines Hinckeldeyn, 1967; children—John M.

III, Kate Alexandra. B.A., Yale, 1953; M.B.A., Harvard, 1955. C.P.A., N.Y. Sr. staff acct. Price Waterhouse & Co. (C.P.A.'s), N.Y.C., 1957-62; asso. Dillon, Read & Co., Inc., N.Y.C., 1962-65; v.p. finance Gen. Host Corp., N.Y.C., 1966-69; v.p. corporate finance F.S. Smithers & Co., Inc., 1970-71; exec. v.p., dir. Sturm, Ruger & Co., Inc., 1971—; dir. Black Hawk Oil Co. Trustee Bridgeport (Conn.) Hosp., Pkwy. U.S. Govt. Bond Fund and Pkwy. Cash Fund. Served with AUS, 1955-57. Mem. Am. Inst. C.P.A.'s, N.Y. State Soc., C.P.A.'s. Republican. Episcopalian. Clubs: Round Hill (Greenwich, Conn.); Maidstone (East Hampton, N.Y.). Home: Will Merry Ln Greenwich CT 06830 Office: Lacey Pl Southport CT 06490

KINGSLEY, NATHAN, journalist; b. N.Y.C., Nov. 20, 1926; s. Joseph H. and Bess (Miller) K.; m. Cynthia Jean Kirkpatrick, June 20, 1950; 1 dau., Alexandra Marjorie. B.S. with honors (Commencement award), CCNY, 1948; M.A. in Polit. Sci, Columbia U., 1978. With N.Y. Herald Tribune, 1943-65, mng. editor, Paris, 1959-64, asso. mng. editor fin. and nat. coverage, N.Y.C., 1964-65; news dir. Radio Free Europe, 1965-72; dep. dir. programming Voice of Am., 1972-74; dir. Office Press, Broadcast and Public Affairs, Dept. State, 1974-76; v.p., sec. Radio Free Europe/Radio Liberty, 1976-80; sr. editor U.S. News & World Report, Washington, 1980—; freelance corr. CBS Radio News, W. Ger., 1968-72; chmn. bd. Parkway Communications Corp., 1981—. Served with USNR, 1944-46. Recipient Radio/TV Spot Coverage award Overseas Press Club, 1972; Poynter fellow in journalism Yale U., 1979. Mem. Sigma Delta Chi, Soc. Profl. Journalists, Radio TV News Dirs. Assn. Clubs: Nat. Press, Nat. Broadcasters, Federal City (Washington); Overseas Press (N.Y.C.); Lansdowne (London). Office: 2300 N St NW Washington DC 20037

KINGSLEY, ROBERT, judge; b. Cedar Falls, Iowa, Oct. 8, 1903; s. Frank Amos and Angeline (Van Niman) K.; m. Doris Field Forbes-Manson, June 12, 1937; m. Ninon Michelle Hogan, July 3, 1976. A.B., U. Minn., 1923, A.M., 1923, LL.B., 1926; S.J.D., Harvard, 1928; LL.D., U.S. Internat. U., San Diego, 1973. Bar: Minn. Bar 1926, Calif. bar 1934. Instr. law U. Minn., 1926-27; Thayer teaching fellow sch. law Harvard, 1927-28; asst. prof. law U. So. Calif., 1928-30, prof. law, 1930-63, vice dean sch. law, 1947-51, asso. dean, 1951-52, dean, 1952-63; vis. prof. law U. Chgo., 1930, U. N.C., 1955, Hastings Coll. Law, 1956; vis. lectr. U. Witwatersrand, Johannesburg, South Africa, 1958; judge Calif. Dist. Ct. Appeal, 2d Appellate Dist., Div. 4, 1963—. Mem. Am. Bar Assn., Los Angeles County Bar Assn., Los Angeles Civic Light Opera Assn. (chmn.), Order of Coif, Phi Beta Kappa, Delta Sigma Rho, Delta Theta Phi. Clubs: Nat. Lawyers (Washington); Los Angeles County Lawyers, University (Los Angeles). Home: 231 S Citrus Ave Los Angeles CA 90036 Office: Room 430 3580 Wilshire Blvd Los Angeles CA 90010

KINGSLEY, SIDNEY, playwright; b. N.Y.C., Oct. 22, 1906; s. Dr. Robert and Sonia (Kirshner) K.; m. Madge Evans, July 25, 1939. Student, Townsend Harris Hall, 1920-24; B.A., Cornell, 1928; D.Litt., Monmouth Coll., 1978, Ramapo State Coll., 1978. Chmn. N.J. Motion Picture and TV Authority, 1976—. Author: plays Men in White, 1934, The Patriots, 1943; author, dir.: Dead End, 1936, Ten Million Ghosts, 1937, The World We Make, 1939, Detective Story, 1949, Darkness at Noon, 1951, Lunatics and Lovers, 1954, Night Life, 1962; (Awarded Pulitzer prize for best American play 1934, Theater Club medal for best play 1934, 36, 43, Drama Critics Circle award for best play 1943, 51, N.Y. Newspaper Guild front page award 1943, Page One Citation 1949, Federated Women's Club award, Cath. Dial award 1943, Edgar Allen Poe award for play, film 1949, Donaldson award for outstanding achievement in theater, Am. Acad. Arts and Letters award of merit medal for outstanding drama 1951, Yeshiva U. award achievement in theatre 1965). Mem. Dramatists Guild (pres. 1961-69). Address: care Dramatists Guild Inc 234 W 44th St New York NY 10036

KINGSLEY, THOMAS DROWNE, economist; b. Rutland, Vt., Oct. 12, 1916; s. Percy Morgan and Fanny (Drowne) K.; m. Martha Bush Clark, Nov. 8, 1943 (dec. 1977); children: Martha Clark Kingsley Goshen, Mary Lee Kingsley Johnson. A.B., Yale U., 1940; student, Fletcher Sch. Law and Diplomacy, 1940-41, Universidad Nacional de Buenos Aires, Argentina, 1942, Grad. Sch. Pub. Adminstrn., Harvard, 1955-56. Joined U.S. Fgn. Service, 1943; assigned successively, Montevideo, Uruguay, Caracas, Venezuela, Asuncion, Paraguay, Dusseldorf, Germany, 1943-55; staff Operations Coordinating Bd., Exec. Office Pres., Washington, 1956-58; 1st sec. embassy, Lisbon, Portugal, 1958-62; chief air transport relations Aviation div. Dept. State, 1962-63; chief econ. affairs Office Brazil Affairs, 1963-66; chief econ. affairs and consul Am. consulate gen., Sao Paulo, Brazil, 1966-69; sr. economist for Latin Am., Export-Import Bank U.S., Washington, 1969-82. Mem. Am. Fgn. Service Assn., Diplomatic and Consular Officers Ret., SAR, U.S. Dressage Fedn., Am. Horse shows Assn., U.S. Combined Tng. Assn. Episcopalian. Clubs: Washington Bridle Trails Assn., Harvard, Yale (Washington). Home: 5105 Battery Ln Bethesda MD 20014

KINGSLEY, WALTER INGALLS, TV executive; b. N.Y.C., Oct. 20, 1923; s. Samuel and Esther (Schenker) K.; m. Betty Jane Bower, Oct. 14, 1944; children: Samuel John, James Oliver, Thomas Andrew; m. Patricia Ann Ratchford, Apr. 1, 1966; 1 dau., Janis Susan. Grad., Phillips Andover Acad., 1942; B.A., Amherst Coll., 1947. Sales exec. Cowles Broadcasting Co., Boston, 1948-50; gen. sales mgr. Ziv Television, N.Y.C. and Los Angeles, 1950-58; pres. Independent Television Corp., N.Y.C., 1958-61; exec. v.p. Wolper Prodns., Metromedia Producers Corp. div. Metromedia, N.Y.C., 1966-71; pres. Kingsley Co., 1972-83, Am. Film Inst., 1983—; faculty Interracial Council for Bus. Opportunity, N.Y.C. Co-founder, bd. dirs. Big Bros. Greater Los Angeles; bd. dirs. Big Bros./Big Sisters Am. Served with AUS, 1943-46. Home: 11750 Sunset Blvd Los Angeles CA 90049 Office: 9777 Wilshire Blvd Beverly Hills CA 90212

KING-SMITH, DICK, author; b. Bitton, Eng., Mar. 27, 1922; m. Myrle England, Feb. 6, 1943; children: Juliet, Liz, Giles. B.Ed., Bristol U., Eng., 1975. Farmer, Gloucestershire, Eng., 1947-67; tchr. Farmborough Primary Sch., 1975-82. Author: (children's books) The Fox Busters, 1978, Daggie Dogfoot, 1980, The Mouse Butcher, 1981, Magnus Powermouse, 1982, The Queen's Nose, 1983, The Sheep-Pig, 1983. Served to lt. Grenadier Guards, 1941-46. Address: Diamond's Cottage Queen Charlton Keynsham AvonUnited Kingdom BS18 2SJ Office: Fiking Jr Books 40 W 23d St New York NY 10010

KINGSTON, FREDERICK TEMPLE, college administrator; b. Toronto, Ont., Can., Dec. 30, 1925; s. George Frederick and Florence (Brown) K.; m. Pauline Boyd Smith, June 15, 1951; children: G. Frederick, Elizabeth, Paul W.T., Rebecca. B.A. in Philosophy and English, Trinity Coll., U. Toronto, 1947, M.A., 1950, L.Th., 1950, B.D., 1952; D.Phil., Christ Ch. Coll., Oxford (Eng.) U., 1954. Ordained priest Anglican Ch. Can., 1950; prof. theology Anglican Coll., Vancouver, B.C., Can., 1953-59; prof. philosophy Canterbury Coll., U. Windsor, Ont., Can., 1959—, prin. coll., 1965—; Mem. corp. Trinity Coll., Toronto, 1965—; vis. prof. Laval U., 1983. Author: French Existentialism: A Christian Critique, 1961, On the Importance of Residence Life to Higher Education, 1977; Editor: Anglicanism and Principles of Christian Unity, 1972, Anglicanism and Contemporary Social Issues, 1973, The Church and Industry, 1974, The Church and Ethics in Public Life, 1975, The Church and the Arts, 1977, Anglicanism and the Lambeth Conferences, 1978, Anglicanism and the Essentials of the Facts, 1978, Living Christian Spiritually, 1979, The Reality of God in the Contemporary World, 1982. Served as chaplain Can. Navy, 1950-51. John H. Moss Meml. scholar, 1947; Can. Council leave fellow, 1968-69; mem. cultural exchange program to France, 1974; Can. Council research grantee, France, 1975; research leave U. Paul Valery, Montpelier, France, 1978-79; participant Que.-Ont. exchange program Laval U., 1980-81. Mem. Anglican Ch. Can. Home: 833 Kildare Rd Windsor ONN8Y 3H3 Canada

KINGSTON, MAXINE HONG, author; b. Stockton, Calif., Oct. 27, 1940; d. Tom and Ying Lan (Chew) Hong; m. Earll Kingston, Nov. 23, 1963; 1 son, Joseph Lawrence. B.A., U. Calif., Berkeley, 1962. Tchr. English, Sunset High Sch., Hayward, Calif., 1965-66, Kahuku (Hawaii) High Sch., 1967, Kahaluu (Hawaii) Drop-In Sch., 1968, Kailua (Hawaii) High Sch., 1969, Honolulu Bus. Coll., 1969, Mid-Pacific Inst., Honolulu, 1970-77; asst. prof. English, vis. writer U. Hawaii, Honolulu, 1977—. Author: The Woman Warrior: Memoirs of a Girlhood Among Ghosts, 1976 (Nat. Book Critics Circle award for non-fiction; cited by Time mag., N.Y. Times Book Rev. and Asian Mail as one of best books of yr.), China Men, 1981 (Am. Book award; nominated for Pulitzer prize and Nat. Book Critics Circle award); contbr.: short stories, articles and poems to mags. and jours., including Iowa Rev. Recipient Mademoiselle Mag. award, 1977, Anisfield-Wolf Race relations award, 1978; Stockton (Calif.) Arts Commn. award, 1981; Hawaii award for Lit., 1982; NEA writing fellow, 1980; Guggenheim fellow, 1981; named a Living Treasure of Hawaii, 1980. Office: English Dept U Hawaii Honolulu HI 96822

KINGSTON, ROBERT CHARLES, army officer; b. Brookline, Mass., July 16, 1928; s. John James and Mary (Shehan) K.; m. Josephine Rae, Aug. 14, 1956; stepchildren—George R. Cody, Leslie C. Reiman. B.A., U. Omaha, 1965; M.A., George Washington U., 1969; postgrad., Armed Forces Staff Coll., 1966, Nat. War Coll., 1969, Advanced Mgmt. Program, U. Pitts., 1972. Commd. 2d lt. U.S. Army, 1949, advanced through grades to lt. gen., 1981, comdr. 1st and 3d brigades, 1st Cavalry div., Vietnam, 1969-70, dep. sec. of gen. staff Office of Chief of Staff, 1970-72, comdr. Joint Casualty Resolution Center, Thailand, 1973, asst. div. comdr. 1st Inf. div., Ft. Riley, Kans., 1974-75, comdg. gen. John F. Kennedy Center for Mil. Assistance, comdt. U.S. Army Inst. for Mil. Assistance, Fort Bragg, N.C., 1975, chief of staff UN Command U.S. Forces in Korea, 1977-79, comdr. 2d Info. Div., Korea, 1979-81, comdr. Rapid Deployment Joint Task Force, MacDill AFB, Fla., 1981—. Decorated D.S.C., D.S.M., Silver Star with 1 oak leaf cluster, Bronze Star, others. Mem. Co. Mil. Historians, Assn. U.S. Army, Spl. Forces Assn. (hon. pres.), Uniformed Services Benefit Assn. (bd. govs.), Airlift Assn. (dir.), Am. Legion, VFW. Roman Catholic. Office: Comdr in Chief US Central Command MacDill AFB FL

KINGSTON, ROBERT HILDRETH, physicist; b. Somerville, Mass., Feb. 13, 1928; s. Alexander Haddon and Martha (Aitcheson) K.; m. Ruth Marilyn Ahara, Apr. 19, 1952; children—Robert E., Susan E., Margaret J., Katherine A. B.S., M.S., M.I.T., 1948, Ph.D., 1951. Mem. tech. staff Bell Labs., Murray Hill, N.J., 1951-52; staff mem. M.I.T. Lincoln Lab., Lexington, 1952-59, leader optics and infrared group, 1961-69, head optics div., 1969-72, leader infrared radar group, 1972-77, sr. staff mem., 1977—; vis. asso. prof. Stanford U., 1964-65; lectr. dept. elec. engring. and computer sci. M.I.T., 1975. Author: Detection of Optical and Infrared Radiation, 1978; Editor: Semiconductor Surface Physics, 1957. Chmn. United Fund, Lexington, 1963, Lexington chpt. ARC, 1970-71, Capital Expenditures Com., Lexington, 1972-73; mem. Town Meeting, Lexington, 1958-77. Fellow Am. Phys. Soc., IEEE (editor Jour. Quantum Electronics 1965-70), Optical Soc. Am. Club: Lexington Bicentennial Band. Office: MIT Lincoln Lab Lexington MA 02173

KINIGSTEIN, JONAH, painter; b. N.Y.C., June 26, 1923; s. Jacob and Yetta (Zelman) K.; m. Barbara Stein, May 17, 1952; children—Noah, Lisa. Student, Cooper Union Art Sch., 1941-43, La Grande Chaumiere, Paris, France, 1947-51, Belle Arte, Rome, Italy, 1953-54. One man shows include, Les Impressions D'Art, Paris, 1948, Galleries Breteau, Paris, 1950, Alan Gallery, N.Y.C., 1954, 55, Stembab Gallery, Boston, 1959, Werbin Gallery, Detroit, 1957, ACA Gallery, N.Y., 1959, 68, Grippi Gallery, N.Y.C., 1962, Kinematic art at Nordness Gallery, 1964, Rittenhouse Gallery, Phila., 1975; 82, one man shows include, Washington Irving Gallery, N.Y.C., 1982, group shows include, Salon d'Automn, Paris, 1949, 50, Salon De Mai, Paris, 1949-50, Salon de Moine de Trente, Paris, 1949, 50, Whitney Mus. Young Am. exhbn., 1957, Bklyn. Mus., 1956, Nat. Acad. Arts and Letters, 1958, Butler Art Inst., 1956, Lehigh U., 1974, Brainard Hall Art Gallery, 1976, Root Art Center, Hamilton Coll., Canton, N.Y., 1977; rep. premanent collections, Whitney Mus., Mus. Modern Art, Albright Art Gallery, Butler Art Inst., Nelson Galley Art, Washington Mus., Brandeis Coll., U. Ill., U. Ariz., Ain Herod Mus. in Tel Aviv, also pvt. collections. Fulbright scholar, Italy, 1953-54; grantee Nat. Acad. Arts and Letters, 1958; recipient 2d prize Butler Art Inst., 1956, purchase prize U. Ill., 1959, Louis Comfort Tiffany Found. award, 1962, 1st prize Silvermine Guild, 1959, Perkins-Elmer prize, 1962. Address: 105 E 9th St New York NY 10011

KINKLE, GEORGE PHILLIP, JR., lawyer; b. Louisville, Jan. 19, 1925; s. George Phillip and Mary Murray (McClarty) K.; m. Caroline Jennings Moore, June 23, 1949; children—Christi Ann, George Randolph, Cary Murray. Bar: Calif. bar 1951. Since practiced in, Los Angeles; mem. firm Kinkle, Rodiger, Graf, Dewberry & Spriggs, Los Angeles, 1959—. Pres. 5th Assembly, Republican Coordinating Council, 1972-74; mem. Calif. Rep. State Central Com., 1972—. Served as ensign USNR, 1943-46. Mem. Calif., Los Angeles bar assns., So. Calif. Def. Council, Am. Bd. Trial Advs. Clubs: Annandale Golf, University. Home: 1156 Oxford Rd San Marino CA 91108 Office: Kinkle Rodiger & Spriggs 621 Sunset Blvd Los Angeles CA 90012

KINNAIRD, CHARLES ROEMLER, lawyer; b. Indpls., July 21, 1932; s. Wayne Davis and Marjorie Goetz (Roemler) K.; m. Susan Wiltshire Stempfel, May 28, 1955; children—James R., Christine S., Robert G., Edward W., Keith D. A.B., Princeton U., 1954; LL.B., Harvard, 1961. Bar: Mich. bar 1962. Since practiced in, Detroit; asso. firm Long, Preston, Kinnaird & Avant, 1961-69, partner, 1969—. Contbr. articles to legal jours. Trustee Edward C. and Hazel L. Stephenson Found. Served to lt. USNR, 1954-58. Mem. Mich., Detroit, Am. bar assns., Am., Mich. socs. hosp. attys. Clubs: Detroit, Country of Detroit; Belvedere Golf (Charlevoix, Mich.); Princeton of Mich. Home: 104 Moran Rd Grosse Pointe Farms MI 48236 Office: 4300 Penobscot Bldg Detroit MI 48226

KINNAIRD, LAWRENCE, educator; b. Williamstown, W.Va., July 9, 1893; s. John Asher and Virginia May (Hall) K.; m. Lucia Fuller Burk, Aug. 3, 1929. A.B., U. Mich., 1915; postgrad., U. Grenoble, France, 1919; M.A., U. Calif., 1927, Ph.D., 1928. Asst. and asso. prof. history San Francisco State Coll., 1932-36; asst. prof. U. Calif., Coll. Agr., 1936-37; asst. and asso. prof. history U. Calif., 1937-48, prof. history, 1948-60; vis. prof. Chatham Coll., 1962-63, U. Calif. at Santa Barbara, 1960-62, 63-66; Acting dir. Bancroft Library, 1954-55; Cultural attaché U.S. Embassy, Santiago, Chile, 1942-45; chmn. U.S. del. to 4th Inter-Am. Congress Tchrs., Santiago, 1943. Editor and author: Spain in the Mississippi Valley, 3 vols, 1945, The Frontiers of New Spain, 1766-1768, 1958; Author: History of the Golden Gate (for Nat. Park Service), 1962, History of the Greater San Francisco Bay Region, 2 vols, 1966; Mem. bd. editors: Pacific Hist. Rev, 1956-59; Contbr. to hist. pubs. Mailing. Served as 1st lt., pilot U.S. Army, 1917-20; with Air Service. Mem. Am. Hist. Assn., Orgn. Am. Historians, Western History Assn. (hon.), Calif. Hist. Soc., Alpha Sigma Phi. Address: PO Box 3973 Carmel CA 93921 Office: Dept History U California Berkeley CA 94720

KINNAMON, KENETH, English educator; b. Dallas, Dec. 4, 1932; s. David Ernest and Gladys Lucile (Page) K.; m. Francisca Guillen; children: John Homer, Louis Alexander, Theodore Antony. Student, North Tex. State Coll., 1950-51; B.A. with high honors, U. Tex., 1953, postgrad., 1954-55; A.M., Harvard U., 1954, Ph.D., 1966. Instr. in English Boston Conservatory Music, 1956, Tex. Tech. Coll., 1956-62; instr. English, U. Ill., Urbana-Champaign, 1965-66, asst. prof., 1966-70, asso. prof., 1970-73, prof., 1973-82, head dept. English, 1973-82; Ethel Pumphrey Stephens prof. English, U. Ark.-Fayetteville, 1982—; chmn. dept. U. Ark-Fayetteville, 1983—; manuscript referee for various pubs. and jours.; promotion referee for Yale U., U. N.Mex., CCNY; proposal referee Guggenheim Found., Nat. Endowment for Humanities; asso. U. Ill. Center for Advanced Study, 1974. Author: The Emergence of Richard Wright, 1972; editor: James Baldwin: A Collection of Critical Essays, 1974, (with Richard K. Barksdale) Black Writers of America, 1972. Recipient summer stipend Nat. Endowment for Humanities, 1969; U. Ill. summer faculty fellow, 1968, 70. Mem. MLA, Coll. Lang. Assn., Am. Studies Assn., Coll. English Assn. Socialist. Home: 1661 Boston Pl Fayetteville AR 72701 Office: 333 Communications Center U Ark Fayetteville AR 72701

KINNARD, WILLIAM JAMES, JR., pharmacology educator; b. Wilmington, Del., Apr. 18, 1932; s. William J. and Helen F. (Ossenkemper) K.; m. Dolores F. Malia, July 18, 1959. B.S., U. Pitts., 1953, M.S., 1955; Ph.D., Purdue U., 1957. From instr. to prof. U. Pitts., 1957-68; prof. pharmacology, dean Sch. Pharmacy, U. Md., Balt., 1968—; dean Grad. Sch., U. Md., 1976-79; Chmn. bd. U.S. Pharmacopeial Conv., 1975—. Contbr. jours. in field. Fellow Am. Found. Pharm. Edn., 1954-57; recipient Honors Achievement award Angiology Research Fedn., 1960-65, Distinguished Alumnus award U. Pitts. Sch. Pharmacy, 1973. Fellow Am. Coll. Clin. Pharmacology, AAAS, Acad. Pharm. Sci.; mem. Am. Soc. Pharmacology and Exptl. Therapy, Am. Pharm. Assn., Inst. Medicine of Nat. Acad. Scis., Am. Assn. Coll. of Pharmacy (pres. 1976-77), Rho Chi. Lutheran. Home: 4000 N Charles St Baltimore MD 21218

KINNARD, WILLIAM VADEN, JR., physician, hospital administrator; b. Albany, N.Y., May 16, 1930; s. William Vaden and Lydia Adele (Grattage) K.; Aug. 1, 1953; children: David Randall, Susan Anne, William Vaden. A.B., Middlebury Coll., 1952; M.D., Albany Med. Coll., 1956; postgrad., Rensselear Poly. Inst. Grad. Sch. Mgmt., 1968. Med. tng. in internal medicine and cardiology, 1959-62, pvt. practice medicine, 1962-64; in adminstrv. positions Albany Med. Center Hosp., 1964-75; pres. Buffalo Gen. Hosp., 1975—; asso. clin. prof. medicine SUNY, Buffalo; dir. Blue Cross Western N.Y., Liberty Nat. Bank, Buffalo; mem. N.Y. State Hosp. Rev. and Planning Council. Served with USNR, 1957-59. Recipient various plaques, citations from med. staff, adminstrv. groups. Mem. Western N.Y. Hosp. Assn. (officer), N.Y. State Hosp. Assn. (trustee), Am. Hosp. Assn. (ho. of dels.). Office: 100 High St Buffalo NY 14203

KINNE, FRANCES BARTLETT, university president; b. Story City, Iowa, May 23; d. Charles Morton and Bertha (Olson) Bartlett; m. Harry L. Kinne, Jr., June 24, 1948. Student edn., U. No. Iowa, 1936; B.Mus.Edn., Drake U., 1940, M. Mus. Edn., 1944, D.F.A. (hon.), 1981; Ph.D. cum laude, U. Frankfurt, Germany, 1957; L.H.D. (hon.), Wagner Coll., S.I., N.Y. Tchr. music Kelley (Iowa) Consol. Sch., 1936-37; music supr. Boxholm (Iowa) Consol. Sch., 1937-40, Des Moines pub. schs., 1940-43; sr. hostess Camp Crowder, Mo., 1943-46; recreation dir. VA, Wadsworth, Kans., 1946-48; lectr. music, English, also Western culture Tsuda Coll., Tokyo, 1949-50; music cons. U.S. Army Gen. Hdqrs., Tokyo, 1950-51; mem. faculty Jacksonville U., 1958—, prof. music and humanities, 1963—, dean, 1961—, interim pres., 1979, pres., 1979—; Disting. Univ. prof., 1961-62; Mem. public relations com. Ind. Colls. and Univs. of Fla.; mem. adv. council Nat. Soc. Arts and Letters; mem. orgn. ad hoc com. Assembly Nat. Art Edn.; dir. Barnett Banks of Fla. Author: A Comparative Study of British Traditional and American Indigenous Ballads, 1958, Music, Moon and Man, 1970; contbr. chpt. to book, articles to profl. jours. Bd. dirs. Assn. Am. Colls., Jacksonville Symphony Women's Guild; bd. dirs., trustee Drake U.; hon. bd. dirs. Jacksonville Symphony Assn.; trustee Greater Jacksonville Com. Found., Ballet Repertory Group of Jacksonville; mem. bd., exec. com. Found. for Sight; resource mem. Heritage Found.; mem. Bus. Arts Adv. Com., Commn. on Recreation and Culture, City of Jacksonville; bd. govs. Gator Bowl Assn. Recipient hon. awards Bus. and Profl. Women's Clubs, 1962; Disting. Service award Drake U., 1966; 1st Fla. Gov.'s award for achievement in arts, 1972; EVE award in edn., 1973; Arts Assembly Individual award, 1978-79; Roast award Soc. for Prevention of Blindness, 1980; Brotherhood award NCCJ, 1981; Top Mgmt. award Jacksonville Sales and Mktg. Execs., 1981; Alumni Achievement award U. No. Iowa; Ann. Burton C. Bryan award; Key to City City of Lake City (Fla.); named Eve of the Decade, 1970-80, hon. mem. 3d Armored Div., U.S. Army; Day named in her honor Women's Club of Jacksonville and other orgns.; named to Internat. Inner Wheel; Paul Harris fellow Rotary Found. Mem. AAUW, Nat., Fla. music tchrs. assns., Music Educators Nat. Conf., Fla. Music Edn. Assn. (past dir.), Assn. Am. Colls. (bd. dirs., exec. com.), Friday Musicale, Fla. Coll. Music Edn. Assn. (past pres., v.p.), Delius Assn. of Fla., Fla. Council of Arts, Nat. Assn. Schs. Music (past chmn. region 7), Jacksonville C. of C. (dir., speakers bur., past gov., chmn. fine arts com., mem. com. of 100), Internat. Council Fine Arts Deans (past chmn., chmn. fed. liaison com.), P.E.O., Green Key (hon.), Alpha Xi Delta, Mu Phi Epsilon (Elizabeth Mathias award, Judge internat. music edn. award), Alpha Psi Omega (hon.), Alpha Kappa Pi (hon.), Alpha Kappa Psi (hon.). Clubs: St. John's Dinner (past pres.), Women's of Jacksonville (program com.). Lodge: Order Eastern Star. Home: 7304 Arrow Point Trail S Jacksonville FL 32211

KINNE, MORRIS Y., JR., lawyer, business exec.; b. Webster City, Iowa, Dec. 18, 1928; s. Morris Y. and Gladys (Shirley) K.; m. Katherine Ann Spencer, June 6, 1957; children—Michael, Douglas, Cathryn, Patricia. Student, Iowa State U., 1947-49; B.A. in Gen. Sci, State U. Iowa, 1955; J.D., 1958. Bar: Iowa bar 1958. Mem. tax dept. Peat, Marwick, Mitchell & Co. (C.P.A.'s), Des Moines, Iowa, 1958-59; asso. firm Dickinson, Throckmorton, Parker, Mannheimer & Raife, Des Moines, 1959-64; sec. Rath Packing Co., Waterloo, Iowa, 1964-75; Western regional counsel Gen. Host Corp., N.Y.C., 1975-78, v.p. corp. staff services, Stamford, Conn., 1978—; v.p., gen. counsel, sec. Bar-S Foods Co., Phoenix, 1981—. Served with USAF, 1951-54. Mem. Am. Bar Assn., Am. Meat Inst. Home: 9025 N Arroya Grande Phoenix AZ 85028

KINNEAR, JAMES WESLEY, III, petroleum company executive; b. Pitts., Mar. 21, 1928; s. James Wesley and Susan (Jenkins) K.; m. Mary Tullis, June 17, 1950; children—Robin Wood (Mrs. David Bruce Anderson), Susan, James Wesley IV, William M. B.S. with distinction, U.S. Naval Acad., 1950. With Texaco, Inc., 1954—, sales mgr., Hawaii, 1959-63, div. sales mgr., Los Angeles, 1963-64, asst. to vice chmn. bd.,

N.Y.C., 1964-65, asst. to chmn. bd., gen. mgr. marine dept., 1965, v.p. supply and distbn., 1966-70, sr. v.p. strategic planning, 1970-71, sr. v.p. worldwide refining, petrochems., supply and distbn., 1971-72, sr. v.p. world wide mktg. charge internat. marine ops. and petrochems., 1972-76, sr. v.p. internat. marine and aviation sales petrochem. dept., marine dept., mktg. and refining in Europe, 1976-78, exec. v.p., 1978-83, dir., 1977—; pres. Texaco U.S.A., 1982—; dir. Am. Petroleum Inst., Corning Glass Works. Pres. bd. trustees St. Paul's Sch., Concord, N.H. Served to lt. comdr. USNR, 1950-54. Mem. U.S. Naval Inst. Episcopalian. Clubs: Round Hill (Greenwich, Conn.); Verbank Hunting, Brook (N.Y.C.); Iron City Fishing (Parry Sound, Ont.). Home: 2929 Buffalo Speedway Houston TX 77002 Office: 1111 Rusk St Houston TX 77002

KINNEARY, JOSEPH PETER, U.S. judge; b. Cin., Sept. 19, 1905; s. Joseph and Anne (Mulvihill) K.; m. Byrnece Camille Rogers, June 26, 1950. B.A., U. Notre Dame, 1928; LL.B., U. Cin., 1935. Bar: Ohio 1935, U.S. Supreme Ct 1960. Pvt. practice in, Cin. and Columbus, 1935-61, asst. atty. gen., Ohio, 1937-39, 1st asst. atty. gen., 1949-51, spl. counsel to atty. gen., 1959-61; U.S. atty. So Dist. Ohio, 1961-66; judge U.S. Dist. Ct., So. Dist. Ohio, 1966—, chief judge, 1973-75; lectr. law trusts Coll. Law, U. Cin., 1948. Delegate Democratic Nat. Conv., 1952. Served to capt. AUS, World War II. Decorated Army Commendation ribbon. Mem. Phi Delta Phi. Roman Catholic. Home: 2440 Northwest Blvd Columbus OH 43221 Office: 319 US Courthouse 85 Marconi Blvd Columbus OH 43215

KINNEAVY, JAMES LOUIS, English language educator; b. Denver, June 26, 1920; s. James and Mary T. (Peila) K.; m. Geri Weaver, 1958 (div. 1959); m. Gloria Mitchell, Feb. 17, 1961; children: Janice Lynn, Kathleen Diane. B.A., Coll. Santa Fe, 1941; M.A., Cath. U. Am., 1951, Ph.D., 1956; D.H.L. (hon.), St. Edward's U., 1980. Tchr. English pub. schs., Bernalillo, N.Mex., 1941-44, various cities, La., 1944-49; dean students Coll. Santa Fe, 1955-58; prof. English Western State Coll., Gunnison, Colo., 1958-63; prof. U. Tex., Austin, 1963-83, Joan and Roland Blumberg Centennial prof. English, 1982—, dir. composition, 1975-82, dir. grad. rhetoric program, 1979—, sec. faculty senate, 1973-74, sec. gen. faculty, 1974-75. Author: A Theory of Discourse, 1971, A Study of Three Theories of The Lyric, 1956; contbr. articles to profl. jours. Recipient grant Fund for Improvement of Post-Secondary Edn. Dept. Edn., 1980—. Mem. AAUP, MIA, Coll. Composition and Communications. Democrat. Roman Catholic. Home: 6929 Scenic Brook Dr Austin TX 78736 Office: Dept English U Tex Austin TX 78712

KINNEBERG, ARTHUR HEMPTON, copper mining company executive; b. Cass County, Minn., July 12, 1921; s. Andrew and Dorothy (Hempton) K.; m. Marjory Jane Dugan, June 6, 1945; children—Joan, Bruce, Eric, William. B.Sc. in Gen. Engring, U.S. Naval Acad., 1945. With Kennecott Copper Corp., McGill, Nev., 1948-50, Braden Copper Co., Caletones, Chile, 1951-57; with Phelps Dodge Corp., 1958—, gen. mgr., Douglas, Ariz., 1977—, sr. v.p., 1978—, dir., 1980—; pres. Phelps Dodge Merc. Co., Tucson, Cornelia and Gila Bend R.R. Co.; dir. Apache Powder Co. Mem. Douglas Sch. Bd., 1963-68, pres., 1967-68. Served with U.S. Navy, 1945-48. Mem. AIME, Mining and Metall. Soc. Am., Ariz. Mining Assn. (dir.), Ariz. C. of C. (dir.), U. Ariz. Found. Republican. Episcopalian. Clubs: Phoenix Country, Old Pueblo, Plaza, Shriners, Elks. Home: 511 W Flynn Ln Phoenix AZ 85013

KINNELL, GALWAY, writer; b. Providence, Feb. 1, 1927; s. James Scot and Elizabeth (Mills) K.; m. Inès Delgado de Torres; children—Maud Natasha, Fergus. A.B., Princeton U., 1948; M.A., U. Rochester, 1949. Author: poems What a Kingdom It Was, 1960, Flower Herding on Mount Monadnock, 1964; translation The Poems of Francois Villon, 1965; novel Black Light, 1966; poems Body Rags, 1968; translation On The Motion and Immobility of Douve, 1968, The Lackawanna Elegy, 1970; poems First Poems, 1971, The Book of Nightmares, 1971, The Avenue Bearing the Initial of Christ into the New World, 1974; interviews Walking Down the Stairs, 1978; rev. translation The Poems of Francois Villon, 1977; poems Mortal Acts, Mortal Words, 1980, Selected Poems, 1982. Guggenheim fellow, 1963-64, 74-75; recipient award Nat. Inst. Arts and Letters, 1962, Medal of Merit, 1975; Longview Found. award, 1962; Rockefeller Found. grant, 1968; Amy Lowell traveling scholarship, 1969; Cecil Hemley poetry prize, 1969; Brandeis U. creative arts award, 1969. Mem. Nat. Acad. and Inst. Arts and Letters. Address: Sheffield VT 05866

KINNEY, ALDON MONROE, JR., business executive, lawyer; b. Cin., May 19, 1921; s. Aldon Monroe and Elsie Marguerite (Griffin) K.; m. Marjorie Ann Aszman, June 13, 1942; children: Gael Maureen Kinney Coleman, Roxanne Kinney Wiley, Aldon Monroe, III. Student, Denison U., 1939-41; A.B., U. Cin., 1943, J.D., 1948, LL.M., 1953. Bar: Ohio bar 1949, U.S. Supreme Ct. bar 1952. Partner firm Jenings & Kinney, Cin., 1949-53; individual practice law, Cin., 1953-70; counsel, adminstrv. asst. to chmn. A. M. Kinney, Inc., Cin., 1953-66, chmn., 1966—, Processes Research, Inc., Cin., 1966—, Design Art Corp., 1966—, Kinlab, Inc., 1966—, Kinvernon Corp., 1966—, A. M. Kinney Assos., Inc., Chgo., 1966—, Kintech Services, Inc., Cin., 1969—, Walter Kidde Constructors, Inc., N.Y.C., 1973—, Walter Kidde Engrs. Internat., Inc., 1973—, Vulcan Cin., Inc., 1975—, Kinnair, Inc., Cin., 1977—; solicitor, City of Madeira, Ohio, 1953-70; dir. Bank One of Milford, 1961—. Mem. Newtown (Ohio) Bd. Edn., 1955-57; bd. dirs. Contemporary Arts Center, Cin., 1971-76. Served to sgt. USAAF, 1943-46. Mem. Cin. Bar Assn., Lawyers Club, Engring. Soc. Cin. Clubs: Queen City, Bankers. Office: 2900 Vernon Pl Cincinnati OH 45219 *Obedience to God is the first principle of life. Duty to man is the second. Happiness as a goal is a poor third. Competitive success achieved by breaking the rules of the game is humiliating.*

KINNEY, DOUGLAS MERRILL, geologist; b. Los Angeles, Feb. 24, 1917; s. Douglas Mudge and Elisabeth Brier (Stratton) K.; m. Jeanette Elizabeth Dawless, Mar. 21, 1942; children—Douglas M., Frederick D., Deborah J. B.A., Occidental Coll., 1937; M.S., Yale, 1942, Ph.D., 1951. Geologist Union Oil Co., Calif. and Rocky Mountain states, 1937-40; geologist U.S. Geol. Survey, Ark., Mo., Utah, Calif. and Colo., 1942-78, geologic map editor, Reston, Va., 1956-80; pres. Geol. Survey Assos., Inc., Bethesda, Md., 1980—; N.Am. v.p. Commn. Geol. Map of World. Fellow Geol. Soc. Am.; mem. Geol. Soc. Washington (pres. 1973), Am. Assn. Petroleum Geologists, Phi Beta Kappa, Sigma Xi. Home and Office: 5221 Baltimore Ave Bethesda MD 20816

KINNEY, EARL ROBERT, food executive; b. Burnham, Maine, Apr. 12, 1917; s. Harry E. and Ethel (Vose) K.; m. Margaret Velie Thatcher, Apr. 23, 1977; children: Jeanie Elizabeth, Earl Robert, Isabella Alice. A.B., Bates Coll., 1939; postgrad., Harvard U. Grad. Sch., 1940. Founder, North Atlantic Pack Co., Bar Harbor, Maine, 1941, pres., 1941-42, treas., dir., 1941-64; with Gorton Corp. (became subs. Gen. Mills, Inc. 1968), 1954-68, pres., 1958-68; v.p. Gen. Mills, Inc., 1968-69, exec. v.p., 1969-73, chief fin. officer, 1970-73, pres., chief operating officer, 1973-77, chmn. bd., 1977-81; pres., chief exec. officer Investors Group of Cos., Mpls., 1982—; dir. Nashua Corp., CPT Corp., Deluxe Check Printers, Inc., Hannaford Bros. Co., Portland, Maine, Union Mut. Life Ins. Co., Portland Jackson Lab., 11 Sun Co. Trustee Bates Coll., also chmn. alumni drives, 1960-64; bd. dirs., exec. com. Mpls. YMCA. Office: 1000 Roanoke Bldg Minneapolis MN 55402

KINNEY, GILBERT FORD, chemical engineer, educator; b. Judsonia, Ark., Dec. 29, 1907; s. Gilbert Earle and Mabel (Ford) K.; m. Martha Turquand Stinson, Sept. 6, 1934; children—Abbott Hart (Mrs. Robert Hall), Gilbert Ford. A.B., Ark. Coll., 1928; M.S., U. Tenn., 1930; Ph.D., N.Y. U., 1935; student, Mass. Inst. Tech., 1938. Operator radio sta. WNBZ, 1930-32; head inst. chemistry Pratt Inst., 1935-42; safety radiologist Operation Crossroads, 1946; prof. chem. engring. Naval Postgrad. Sch., 1946-71, chmn. material sci. and chemistry dept., 1963-69, disting. prof. emeritus, 1971—; sr. scientist Naval Weapons Center, China Lake, Calif., 1972—; cons. in field, 1952—. Author: Engineering Thermodynamics, 1953, Plastics, 1958, Explosive Shocks, 1962. Served to capt. USNR, 1942-64. Recipient Distinguished Prof. Medallion Naval Postgrad. Sch., 1967. Mem. Am. Chem. Soc., Am. Assn. U. Profs., Ret. Officers Assn., Sigma Xi, Alpha Chi Sigma, Alpha Lambda Tau. Home: 1116 Sylvan Rd Monterey CA 93940 *God was our manufacturer, but Jesus is our test pilot.*

KINNEY, HARRY EDWIN, mechanical engineer, building contractor; b. Trinidad, Colo., June 7, 1924; s. Oliver Earl and Opal (Sanger) K.; m. Carol N. Roberts, Aug. 30, 1970; children: Charlotte Jean, Donald Bruce. B.S. in Mech. Engring, U. N.Mex., 1945. Staff mem. Sandia Labs., 1956-73; commr., City of Albuquerque, 1966-73, vice chmn., 1970-71, chmn., 1971-73, mayor, Albuquerque, 1974-77, gen. contractor, residential constrn., 1977-81; commr. Bernalillo County, N.Mex., 1956-58, 61-65. Chmn. Middle Rio Grande Council Govts. of N.Mex., 1970-72; mem. U.S. Adv. Commn. on Intergovtl. Relations, 1975-77; mem. adv. bd. U.S. Conf. Mayors, 1975-77, 82—, chmn., 1977; Pres. Albuquerque-Bernalillo County Econ. Opportunity Bd., 1964-66, N.M. Council Social Welfare, 1965-67; chmn. City-County Joint Alcoholism Bd., 1969-72; pres. Ams. for Rational Energy Alternatives, 1980—; v.p. Chapparal council Girl Scouts U.S.A., 1978-81; bd. dirs. Met. YMCA, 1977-81; Spl. asst. to U.S. senator, 1973-74. Served with USNR, 1943-46, 50-52. Mem. ASME, Naval Res. Assn., Kappa Sigma. Episcopalian. Address: 3006 Vista Grande NW Albuquerque NM 87120 *Since my junior high school days I have consistently had an extreme interest in government. I have concentrated my efforts and involvement in local government because I felt the potential for the greatest participation existed there. I believed then that local government provided an avenue for more input which would directly improve our quality of life. I still believe this.*

KINNEY, JOHN FRANCIS, clergyman; b. Oelwein, Iowa, June 11, 1937; s. John F. and Marie B. (McCarty) K. Student, St. Paul Sem., 1957-63, N.Am. Coll., Rome, 1968-71; J.C.D., Pontifical Lateran U., 1971. Ordained priest Roman Catholic Ch., 1963. Assoc. pastor Ch. of St. Thomas, Mpls., 1963-66; vice chancellor of St. Paul and Mpls. Diocese, 1966-73; assoc. pastor Cathedral, St. Paul, 1971-74, chancellor, 1973; pastor Ch. of St. Leonard, St. Paul, 1974—; aux. bishop Archdiocese of St. Paul and Mpls., 1977—. Mem. Canon Law Soc. Am. Roman Catholic. Office: 226 Summit Ave Saint Paul MN 55102

KINNEY, JOHN (JACK) FRANCIS, lawyer, public service company executive; b. Omaha, Nov. 6, 1921; s. John Francis and Josephine Marie (Kelley) K.; m. Virginia Ann Roach, June 9, 1945; children: Michael Francis, Susan Margaret Kinney Wieland, Mary Virginia Kinney Clouse, John Charles, Jeanne Elizabeth Kinney Buser, Molly Ann Kinney Campbell, Matthew Joseph, Teresa Louise Kinney Miller, Stephen Patrick, Eileen Patricia. J.D., Creighton U., 1950. Bar: Nebr. 1950, Iowa 1950. Gen. counsel Iowa Pub. Service Co., Sioux City, 1968-73, v.p., gen. counsel, 1973-76, sr. v.p., gen. counsel, 1976-82, sr. v.p., chief operating officer, 1982—, dir.; dir. Cimmred, Inc., Sioux City, Energy Reserves, Inc., Centennial Coal, Inc. Served to capt. USAF, 1943-46. Decorated D.F.C., Air medal (5). Mem. Iowa Bar Assn., Nebr. Bar Assn., Fed. Energy Bar Assn. Republican. Roman Catholic. Lodges: Kiwanis (Sioux City); K.C. (Sioux City). Home: 3014 Pierce St Sioux City IA 51104 Office: Iowa Public Service Company 401 Douglas St Sioux City IA 51102

KINNEY, SAMUEL MARKS, JR., lawyer, industrialist; b. Jenkintown, Pa., July 10, 1925; s. Samuel Marks and Margaret R. (Rennie) K.; m. Kathryn Clouser, Sept. 21, 1946; children: Lee K. Anthony, Samuel Marks III, Brian Scott. Grad., Lawrenceville Sch., 1942; student, Allegheny Coll., 1942-43; B.A., Pa. State U., 1946; J.D., Rutgers U., 1948. Bar: N.J. 1949, U.S. Supreme Ct. 1949. Asso. atty. Martin & Reiley, Newark, 1949-51; counsel, mgr. army contracts Daystrom Instrument div. Daystrom, Inc., Murray Hill, Pa., 1951-54; asst. sec., counsel Daystrom, Inc., 1954-57, sec., counsel, 1957-59, asst. v.p. finance, 1959-61, v.p., gen. counsel, 1961-62; sec. Union Camp Corp., 1962-72, v.p., 1962-69, sr. v.p., 1969-70, exec. v.p., 1970-72, pres., 1972-77, mem. exec. com., 1972-79, vice chmn. bd., 1977-79; also dir.; of counsel Hannoch, Weisman, Stern, Besser, Berkowitz & Kinney, 1979—; dir. 1st Nat. State Bancorp., 1st Nat. State Bank N.J., Can. Cement Lafarge Ltd., Montreal, Que., Lafarge Corp., Dallas; mem. internat. adv. bd. Lafarge (S.A.), France. Contbr. papers to profl. jours. Chmn. Union County (N.J.) Young Republican Club, Inc., 1951-52; mem. Westfield Town Council, 1961-67, chmn. finance and laws and rules coms.; mem. bus. exec. research com. Bus. Execs. Research Center, Rutgers U., 1957-58; trustee Overlook Hosp., C. F. Mueller Scholarship Found.; bd. overseers Rutgers U. Found.; mem. Pa. State U. Alumni Council. Served with USMCR, 1943-45. Recipient Disting. Alumnus award Pa. State U., 1977. Mem. Am. Bar Assn. Episcopalian (vestryman). Clubs: Echo Lake Country (Westfield) (trustee); Baltusrol Golf (Springfield, N.J.); Essex (Newark); Seaview Country (Absecon, N.J.); Union League, Economic (N.Y.C.). Home: 109 Golf Edge Westfield NJ 07090 Office: 744 Broad St Newark NJ 07102

KINNEY, WILLIAM RUDOLPH, accounting educator, researcher; b. Okmulgee, Okla., Aug. 13, 1942; s. William R. and Beulah M. (Timberlake) K.; m. Carolyn K. Dreessen, Oct. 11, 1959; children: Kristi, Jeff, Robert. B.S., Okla. State U., 1963, M.S., 1965; Ph.D., Mich. State U., 1968. C.P.A., Okla. Auditor Arthur Young & Co., Oklahoma City, 1963-65; asst. prof. Okla. State U., Stillwater, 1967-68; John F. Murray prof. acctg. U. Iowa, Iowa City, 1969—. Assoc. editor: The Acctg. Rev., 1980—. Mem. Am. Inst. C.P.A.'s (auditing standards bd.), Am. Acctg. Assn., Am. Statis. Assn. Home: 2605 Rochester Ave Iowa City IA 52240 Office: Inst Acctg Research U Iowa Iowa City IA 52242 Dept History Iowa State U Ames 50011

KINNISON, WILLIAM ANDREW, university president; b. Springfield, Ohio, Feb. 10, 1932; s. Errett Lowell and Audrey Muriel (Smith) K.; m. Lenore Belle Morris, June 11, 1960; children—William Errett, Linda Elise, Amy Elisabeth. A.B., Wittenberg U., 1954, B.S. in Edn, 1955; M.A., U. Wis., 1963; Ph.D. (1st Flesher fellow), Ohio State U., 1967; postgrad., Harvard Inst. Ednl. Mgmt., 1970; LL.D., Calif. Luth. Coll., 1983; Th.D., John Carroll U., 1983. Asst. dean admissions Wittenberg U., Springfield, 1958-65, asst. to pres., 1967-70, v.p. for univ. affairs, 1970-73, v.p. adminstrn., 1973, pres., 1974—. Author: Samuel Shellabarger: Lawyer, Jurist, Legislator, 1969, Building Sullivant's Pyramid: An Administrative History of the Ohio State University, 1970, Concise History of Wittenberg University, 1976, An American Seminary, 1980; also articles. Asst. to dir. Sch. Edn., Ohio State U., Columbus, 1965-67; past chmn. Assn. Ind. Colls. and Univs. Ohio.; Chmn. standing com. Lutheran World Ministries, 1976—; mem. exec. council Luth. Ch. in Am., 1978—; mem. Commn. New Luth. Ch., 1982—; mem. bd. dirs. Am. Assn. Colls., 1981—. Served with U.S. Army, 1956-58. Mem. Clark County Hist. Soc. (trustee 1963—), Am. Assn. for Higher Edn., Orgn. Am. Historians, Blue Key, Phi Beta Kappa, Phi Delta Kappa, Kappa Phi Kappa, Pi Sigma Alpha, Tau Kappa Alpha, Delta Sigma Phi, Omicron Delta Kappa. Clubs: Cosmos, Harvard of N.Y., Rotary. Home: 644 N Wittenberg Ave Springfield OH 45504

KINO, GORDON STANLEY, electrical engineering educator; b. Melbourne, Australia, June 15, 1928; came to U.S., 1951, naturalized, 1967; s. William Hector and Sybil (Cohen) K.; m. Dorothy Beryl Lovelace, Oct. 30, 1955; 1 dau., Carol Ann. B.Sc. with 1st class honours in Math, London (Eng.) U., 1948, M.Sc. in Math, 1950; Ph.D. in Elec. Engring, Stanford U., 1955. Jr. scientist Mullard Research Lab., Salford, Surrey, Eng., 1947-51; research asst., then research asso. Stanford U., 1951-55, research asso., 1957-61, mem. faculty, 1961—, prof. elec. engring., 1965—; mem. tech. staff Bell Telephone Labs., 1955-57; cons. to industry, 1957—. Author: (with Kirstein, Waters) Space Charge Flow, 1968; also numerous papers on microwave tubes; electron optics, plasma physics, bulk effects in semiconductors, acoustic surface waves, acoustic imaging, non-destructive testing. Guggenheim fellow, 1967-68. Fellow IEEE, Am. Phys. Soc., Nat. Acad. Engring., AAAS. Inventor Kino electron gun, 1959. Home: 867 Cedro Way Stanford CA 94305

KINSELLA, JOHN EDWARD, food science and chemistry researcher, educator, administrator; b. Wexford, Ireland, Feb. 22, 1938; came to U.S., 1963; s. John and Mary (Cullen) K.; m. Ruth Ann De Angelis, July 10, 1965; Children: Sean, Helen, Kathryn, Kevin. B.S. in Biology and Agrl. Sci., U. Dublin, 1961, M.S., Pa. State U., 1965, Ph.D. in Food and Biochemistry, 1967. Asst. prof. food biochemistry Cornell U., Ithaca, N.Y., Eng., 1967-73, assoc. prof. food chemistry, Ithaca, N.Y., 1973-77, prof. food chemistry, chmn. food sci. dept., 1977—, Liberty Hyde Bailey prof. food sci., 1981—, dir. Inst. Food Sci., Ithaca, N.Y., Eng., 1980—; research chemist U.S. Dept. Agr., 1973-74; cons. U.S. Food industry, World Bank; cons NSF, Brazil, Govt. Indonesia. Contbr. numerous articles to profl. jours; patentee protein tech. and plant cell culture. Recipientttterson Found. fellow Borden Award Borden Found., 1976; research Grantee NSF, NIH, U.S. Dept. Agr., various industry assns. Mem. Am. Chem. Soc., Inst. Food Technologists (mem. com. on research needs 1966—, exec. com. 1982-85, Am. Inst. Nutrition), AAAS, Am. Dairy Sci. Assn., Am. Oil Chem. Soc. Democrat. Roman Catholic.

KINSELLA, JOHN JAMES, advertising agency executive; b. Joliet, Ill., Jan. 1, 1929; s. John Jules and Eileen (Baskerville) K.; m. Jeanette Cullinane, June 15, 1963; children: Jeanette, Mary Catherine, Eileen, Margaret, John. B.A. in Polit. Sci., Notre Dame U., 1950; M.B.A., DePaul U., 1952. With McCann-Erickson, Chgo., 1954-59, account supr., 1955-59; with Leo Burnett Co., Inc., Chgo., 1959—, pres., 1972—, chief exec. officer, 1981—, chmn. bd., 1983—, also dir. Bd. dirs. Santa for the Very Poor, Chgo., Chgo. Central Area Com.; trustee DePaul U.; prin. Chgo. United; publicity chmn. Chgo. Com. Econ. Devel. Mem. Am. Assn. Advt. Agys. (bd. dirs.), Am. Advt. Fedn. (council of judges 1983). Roman Catholic. Clubs: Westchester Country (Rye, N.Y.); Saddle and Cycle, Irish Fellowship, Tavern, Racquet (Chgo.); Shore Acres Country (Lake Forest, Ill.). Home: 166 Sheridan Rd Winnetka IL 60093 Office: Prudential Plaza Chicago IL 60601

KINSELLA, THOMAS J., business executive; b. Newburgh, N.Y., Mar. 14, 1909; s. John P. and Rose A. (Dillon) K.; m. Sally H. McGarry, Sept. 10, 1938. B.S., SUNY, Albany, 1930; M.A., Clark U., 1931, Ph.D., 1938. Fellow asst. Clark U., 1930-32; asst. prof. commerce SUNY, Albany, 1937-41; price exec., div. dir. OPA, Washington, 1941-46; asst. to pres. Barrett div. Allied Chem. & Dye Corp., 1947-51, v.p., 1951, exec. v.p., 1952, pres., 1952—; pres Barrett Co., Ltd., 1952-60, Plastics and Coal div. Allied Chem. Corp., 1958-61; gen. mgr. Corporate Comml. Devel., 1961-63; regional v.p. Mobil Chem. Co., 1964-67; v.p., dir. Mobil Chem. Internat., 1964-67; dir. Mobil China Allied Chem. Ltd., 1963-67; v.p., dir. Mobil Sekiyukk, Tokyo, 1964-67; gen. rep. Gulf Petroleum (S.A.), 1967-72; chmn. China Gulf Plastics Corp., 1967-72; also dir.; dir. Taiwan VC Industries Corp., 1967-72; pres. King Investments, 1972—; gen. rep. and adviser to the pres. The Badger Co., Inc., 1974—; mem. war procurement policy com. War Prodn. Bd. Mem. Am. Econ. Assn., Armed Forces Chem. Assn., Am. Ordnance Assn., Kappa Phi Kappa, Pi Gamma Mu. Home: 2201 Vails Gate Heights Dr New Windsor NY 12550 Office: One Broadway Cambridge MA 02142

KINSEY, JAMES LLOYD, chemist, educator; b. Paris, Tex., Oct. 15, 1934; s. Lloyd King and Elaine Mills K.; m. Berma McDowell, July 28, 1962; children: Victoria, Samuel, Adam. B.A., Rice U., 1956, Ph.D., 1959; NSF fellow, U. Uppsala, Sweden, 1959-60; postdoctoral fellow, U. Calif., Berkeley, 1960-62. Asst. prof. dept. chemistry M.I.T., 1962-67, asso. prof., 1967-74, prof., 1974—, chmn. dept., 1977-82; cons. Los Alamos Sci. Labs.; Miller Research fellow, 1960-62; mem. Nat. Acad. Scis.-NRC Bd. Chem. Scis., 1980-83, co-chmn., 1981-83; mem. com. on recommendations U.S. Army Basic Sci. Research-NRC, 1981—. Asso. editor: Jour. Chem. Physics, 1981-84; contbr. articles to profl. jours. Alfred P. Sloan fellow, 1964-68; Guggenheim fellow, 1969-70. Fellow Am. Phys. Soc.; mem. AAAS, Am. Chem. Soc. (vice-chmn. div. phys. chemistry 1983), Sigma Xi. Home: 44 Lombard St Newton MA 02158 Office: Mass Inst Tech Cambridge MA 02139

KINSINGER, JACK BURL, chemist, educator; b. Akron, Ohio, June 23, 1925; s. William Franklin and Idelle (Althaus) K.; m. Addie Jean Parker, Sept. 2, 1946; children: Paul Craig, Amy Jo. B.A., Hiram Coll., 1948; M.S., Cornell U., 1951; Ph.D., U. Pa., 1958. Group leader research Rohm & Haas Co., Phila., 1951-56; asst. prof. Mich. State U., East Lansing, 1957-61, assoc. prof., 1961-66, prof. chemistry, 1966-82, assoc. chmn. dept. chemistry, 1965-69, chmn. dept., 1969-75, asst. v.p. research and devel., 1977, assoc. provost, 1977-82; prof. chemistry Ariz. State U., Tempe, 1982—, v.p. acad. affairs, 1982—; cons. Union Carbide Co., 1958-80, vice chmn. div. polymer chemistry, 1966-68, chmn., 1969; dir. chemistry div. NSF, 1975-77. Editor: Computer Symposium, 1968; Contbr.: chpt. Ency. Polymer Chemistry, 1971. Served to 2d lt. USAAF, 1943-45. Mem. Am. Chem. Soc., Council Chem. Research (vice chair exec. com. 1980-81), Am. Phys. Soc., AAAS. Home: 8208-E Voltaire Ave Scottsdale AZ 85260 Office: Ariz State Univ Tempe AZ 85287

KINSINGER, ROBERT EARL, executive; b. Chgo., Aug. 5, 1923; s. Elmer John and Frances Louise (Ballenger) K.; m. Sylvia Kading, May 20, 1950; children: William, Candace, Lisa. A.B., Stanford U., 1948, M.A., 1951; Ed.D., Columbia U., 1958; LL.D., Simpson Coll., 1977; L.H.D., Hahnemann U. Staff mem. U.S. del. 3d Gen. Assembly UN, Paris, France, 1948; regional field rep., mgr. chpt. and regional blood center ARC, Boise, Ida., 1949-56; lectr. Columbia U., 1956, Queens Coll., 1957; ednl. cons. Nat. League Nursing, 1957-60; dir. health careers project SUNY, 1960-66; program dir. W.K. Kellogg Found., Battle Creek, Mich., 1966-70, v.p., 1970-83; chmn. Ednl. Services for the Professions, Inc., 1983—; pres. Kinland Properties; cons. in field. Vice chmn. adv. council Mich. Comprehensive Health Planning Bd.; chmn. Commn. on Physicians Assts.; Bd. dirs. Highlands, Inc.; dir. Jossey-Bass Inc., Pubs. Author: Education for Health Technicians-An Overview, 1965; co-author: Clinical Nursing Instruction by Television, 1965; Editor: Career Opportunities for Health Technicians, 1971. Served to lt. USNR, World War II. Recipient commn. of honor SUNY, Farmingdale, 1970; Man of Yr. award Nat. Council Community Services, 1971; Honors of Soc. award Am. Soc. Allied

Health Professions. Mem. AAAS, Am. Assn. Higher Edn., Am. Dietetic Assn. (chmn. adv. com.). Club: Battle Creek Country. Home: 290 Contidene Rd Twain Harte CA 95383 Office: 13613 Tuolumne Rd Sonora CA 95370

KINSLEY, WILLIAM BENTON, literature educator; b. Montpelier, Vt., Sept. 11, 1934; emigrated to Can., 1965; s. Benton Rufus and Ann Megdalene (Finnegan) K.; m. Therese Huang, Dec. 20, 1964; children: Anne-Marie, Claire, Eliane. Student, Wesleyan U., 1952-55; B.A., U. Toronto, (Ont., Can.), 1958; postgrad., U. Lyon, France, 1959; Ph.D., Yale U., 1965. Instr. St. Michael's Coll., Winnoski, Vt., 1958-59, U. Rochester, N.Y., 1963-64; asst. prof. English lit. U. Montreal, Que., Can., 1964-71, assoc. prof., 1971-81, prof., 1981—, chmn. dept. etudes anglaises, 1970-71, 75-79. Editor: Contexts 2: The Rape of the Lock, 1979. Warden St. Pascal-Baylon Catholic Ch., Montreal, 1981-84. Can. council fellow, 1972-73. Mem. MLA, Am. Soc. Eighteenth Century Studies (pres. English 1974-75), Assn. Can. Univ. Tchrs. English, Can. Comparative Lit. Assn. Home: 3782 Kent Ave Montreal PQ Canada H3S 1N3 Office: Etudes Anglaises U Montreal Case postale 6128 Sta A Montreal PQ Canada H3C 3J7

KINSMAN, ROBERT DONALD, art museum administrator; b. Bridgeport, Conn., Sept. 13, 1929; s. Cummings Sanborn and Sarah Elizabeth (Barton) K.; m. Patricia Ann Mulreed, Oct. 3, 1953. B.S., Columbia U., 1958, M.A. in Art History, 1966, A.B.D. Asst. curator Nat. Gallery Art, Washington, 1961-62; instr. art history Mary Washington Coll., U. Va., Fredericksburg, 1962-63; curator contemporary art Detroit Inst. Arts, 1963-65; asst. prof. art history and dir. duPont Art Galleries, Mary Washington Coll., 1966-68; asst. prof. art history SUNY, Albany, 1968-77; dir. Sheldon Swope Art Gallery, Terre Haute, Ind., 1978—. Contbr. articles to profl. jours. Bd. dirs. Arts Illiana, Inc., 1981—. Served with U.S. Army, 1951-53. Mem. Am. Assn. Museums, AAUP, Coll. Art Assn. Am. Home: 4951 Dixie Bee Rd Terre Haute IN 47802 Office: 25 S 7th St Terre Haute IN 47807

KINSOLVING, CHARLES LESTER, clergyman, journalist; b. N.Y.C., Dec. 18, 1927; s. Arthur Barksdale and Edith (Lester) K.; m. Sylvia Alice Crockett, Dec. 18, 1953; children: Laura Louise, Thomas Philip, Kathleen Susan. Student, U. Pa., 1947-49, Johns Hopkins U., 1951-52; grad., Ch. Div. Sch. of Pacific, 1955. Ordained to ministry Episcopal Ch., 1955, Anglican Cath. Ch., 1979; Protestant chaplain's asst. San Quentin Prison, 1955-56; founder, seminarian and minister, Rodeo-El Sobrante, Calif., 1953-57, Pasco, Wash., 1957-61, New London, N.H., 1961-62, Clayton Valley and Pittsburg, Calif., 1962-64, Salinas, Calif., 1964-66; legislative asst. to Bishop James A. Pike, 1964-66; rector St. Thomas' Anglican Ch., Silver Spring, Md., 1978-79, St. Charles The Martyr Ch., Annapolis, Md., 1982—; supply priest Diocese of Mid Atlantic States, 1979—; religion writer, columnist San Francisco Chronicle, 1966-71, San Francisco Examiner, 1971-73; White House and State Dept. corr., religion and polit. columnist Nat. Newspaper Syndicate, 1973-76, McNaught Syndicate, 1976-80, Globe Syndicate, 1980—; commentator WAVA News, 1974-77; polit. editor Sta. WEAM, Falls Church, Va., 1979-80, Sta. WJOK, 1983—; commentator Va. Network, 1980; editor Washington Weekly, 1977-80; media columnist Pittsburgher, other city mags., 1978—; nat. editor Washington Guide. Contbr. articles to profl. and religious jours. Mem. Monterey County (Calif.) Democratic Central Com., 1965-66; mem. Calif. Gov.'s Population Study Commn., 1964; Bd. dirs. Am. League to Abolish Capital Punishment. Served with AUS, 1946, 51. Recipient awards Anti-Defamation League of B'nai B'rith, Hadassah, Com. to Bring Nazi War Criminals to Justice; Radio Editorial award A.P. Broadcasters, 1975. Mem. Newspaper Guild, AFTRA, White House Corrs. Assn., Delta Kappa Epsilon. Address: 1517 Beulah Rd Vienna VA 22180

KINSTLER, EVERETT RAYMOND, artist; b. N.Y.C., Aug. 5, 1926; s. Joseph E. and Essie K.; m. Lea C. Nation, June 23, 1958; children: Katherine G., Dana C. Ed., Art Students League, N.Y.C., 1943-45; hon. doctorate, Rollins Coll., 1983. Started career as illustrator, N.Y.C., 1943, began specializing in portraiture, 1955; instr. Art Students League, N.Y.C., 1969-74. Portraits include over 25 U.S. cabinet officers ofcl. White House portrait former President Gerald R. Ford; J. Edgar Hoover, Richard K. Mellon, Mrs. Irenee duPont, Jr., Herbert Lehman, gov. of N.Y. State, Kurt Waldheim, sec.-gen. UN, Gen. Mark W. Clark, Casper Weinberger, sec. of def., Cyrus Vance, sec. of state, Astronaut Alan B. Shepard, Jr., William Bowen, pres. Princeton U., George W. Ball, undersec. of state, James Cagney, John D. Rockefeller III, Byron Nelson, Frank Cary, pres. IBM, Charles Scribner, Jr., John Wayne, John Kemeny, pres. Dartmouth Coll., William Simon, sec. Treasury, Elliot Richardson, ambassador to Gt. Britain, James P. Hodgson, ambassador to Japan, Tennessee Williams, John Connally, gov. of Tex.; began specializing in portraiture: portraits include over 25 U.S. cabinet officers, ofcl. White House portrait Katharine Hepburn, Pres. Richard M. Nixon; Bartlett Gramatti, pres. Yale U., also numerous others; represented in permanent collections, Mus. City N.Y., Met. Mus. Art, N.Y.C., The Pentagon, Am. Embassy, Paris, Carnegie Mus., N.Y. Stock Exchange, Bklyn. Mus., White House, Smithsonian Instn., numerous colls., univs., bus. firms; Author: Painting Portraits, 1971, Painting Faces, Figures, Landscapes, 1981. Mem. Allied Artists Am. (dir. 1958-60), Artists Fellowships, Inc. (pres. 1967-70), Portraits Inc., Am. Watercolor Soc. (dir.), Pastel Soc. Am., Audubon Artists, NAD. Clubs: Century Assn., Lotos (life), Nat. Arts (v.p.), Dutch Treat (N.Y.C.); Players (life). Address: National Arts Club 15 Gramercy Park New York NY 10003

KINTNER, EARL WILSON, lawyer; b. Corydon, Ind., Nov. 6, 1912; s. Lee and Lillie Florence (Chanley) K.; m. Valerie Patricia Wildy, May 28, 1948; 1 son, Christopher Earl Mackelcan; children by previous marriage: Anna Victoria, Jonathan M., Rosemary Jane (dec.). A.B., De Pauw U., 1936, LL.D. (hon.), 1970; J.D., Ind. U., 1938. Bar: Ind. 1938, U.S. Supreme Ct. 1945, D.C. 1953. Practice law, Princeton, Ind., 1938-44, city atty. Princeton, 1939-42; pros. atty. 6th Ind. Jud. Circuit, 1943-48; dep. U.S. commr. UN War Crimes Commn., 1945-48; sr. trial atty. FTC, 1948-50, legal adviser, 1950-53, gen. counsel, 1953-59, chmn., 1959-61; adj. prof. NYU Sch. Law, 1958; del., chmn. com. hearing officers Pres.'s Conf. on Adminstrv. Procedure, 1953-54; mem. panel on invention and innovation U.S. Dept. Commerce, 1965-66; mem. U.S. Adminstrv. Conf., 1972-76, 78—; mem. adv. com. on civil rules U.S. Jud. Conf., 1971-82. Author: An Antitrust Primer, 1964, 73, Robinson-Patman Primer, 1970, 79, A Primer on the Law of Deceptive Practices, 1971, 78, A Merger Primer, 1973; co-author: An Intellectual Property Primer, 1975, An International Anti-trust Primer, 1975, Anti-trust Legislation, 11 vols., 1977, An Anti-trust Treatise, Vols. 1-6, 1984; editor: The United Nations War Crimes Commission and Development of the Laws of War, 1948, The Hadamar Trial, 1948, FTC staff legal manual, 1952. Bd. dirs. D.C. Legal Aid Soc., 1963—, pres., 1973-76; bd. visitors Ind. U. Law Sch., 1964—, chmn., 1973. Served from ensign to lt. USNR, 1944-46. Recipient Disting. Service award Ind. U., 1960, Disting. Alumni award DePauw U., 1965, 75. Mem. Fed. Bar Assn. (pres. 1956-57, 58-59), ABA (chmn. adminstrv. law sect. 1959-60, council antitrust law sect. 1958-61), N.Y. Bar Assn. (exec. com antitrust sect.), Fed. Bar Found. (pres. 1959—), Fed. Bar Bldg. Corp. (pres. 1959—), Bar Assn. D.C. (dir. 1972-74), Am. Judicature Soc. (dir. 1961-64), Am. Legion, DAV, Sigma Delta Chi, Phi Delta Phi (pres. Province II 1962-67), Pi Sigma Alpha, Delta Sigma Rho, Lambda Chi Alpha. Republican. Episcopalian. Clubs: Cosmos, National Lawyers (pres. 1959—), Capitol Hill (Washington); Union League (N.Y.); Coral Beach and Tennis (Bermuda); Masons (32 deg.), Shriners). Home: 3220 Idaho Ave NW Washington DC 20016 1050 Connecticut Ave NW Washington DC 20036

KINTNER, WILLIAM ROSCOE, political science educator; b. Lock Haven, Pa., Apr. 21, 1915; s. Joseph Jennings and Florence (Kendig) K.; m. Xandree M. Hyatt, June 15, 1940; children: Kay Kintner Asip, Jane Kintner Hogan, Gail Kintner Markou, Carl H. B.S., U.S. Mil. Acad., 1940; Ph.D., Georgetown U., 1949. Commd. 2d lt. U.S. Army, 1940, advanced through grades to col., 1956; inf. bn. co., Korean War; mem. sr. staff CIA, 1950-52; mem. planning staff NSC, 1954; mem. staff spl. asst. to Pres., 1955; cons. Pres.'s Com. to study U.S. Assistance Program (Draper Com.), 1959; chief long-range plans strategic analysis sect. Coordination Group, Chief of Staff, U.S. Army, 1959-61; ret., 1961; prof. polit. sci. Wharton Sch., U. Pa., Phila., 1961—; dep. dir. Fgn. Policy Research Inst., Phila., 1961-69, dir., 1969-73, pres., 1976; Am. ambassador to Thailand, 1973-75; cons. Dept. Def., NSC, Stanford Research Inst.; fellow Hudson Inst.; sr. adviser Ops. Research Office, Johns Hopkins U., 1956-57; mem. acad. bd. Inter-Am. Def. Coll., 1967-72; mem. bd. Fgn. Scholarships, 1970-73; civilian faculty adv. com. Nat. War Coll., 1970-72. Author: The Front is Everywhere, 1950, (with George C. Reinhardt) Atomic Weapons in Land Combat, 1953, The Haphazard Years, 1960, (with others) Forging a New Sword, 1958, Protracted Conflict, 1959, A Forward Strategy for America, 1961, Building the Atlantic World, 1963, (with Joseph Z. Kornfeder) The New Frontier of War, 1962, Peace and the Strategy Conflict, 1967, (with Harriet Fast Scott) The Nuclear Revolution in Soviet Military Affairs, 1969, (with Wolfgang Klaiber) Eastern Europe and European Security, 1971, (with Harvey Sicherman) Technology and International Politics, 1975, (with John F. Copper) A Matter of Two Chinas: The China-Taiwan Issue in U.S. Foreign Policy, 1979; editor: Orbis, 1969-73, 76—; editor, contbr.: Safeguard: Why the ABM Makes Sense, 1969; contbr. articles to profl. jours. Trustee Freedom House, N.Y.C.; mem. bd. Gen. Ch. of New Jerusalem, Bryn Athyn, Pa.; mem. adv. com. World Affairs Council, Phila. Decorated Legion of Merit with oak leaf cluster, Bronze Star with oak leaf cluster. Mem. Council Fgn. Relations, Am. Polit. Sci. Assn., Pa. Soc., Council Am. Ambassadors. Home: 2259 Pennypack Ln Bryn Athyn PA 19009 Office: U Pa Philadelphia PA 19104

KINTZELE, JOHN A., lawyer; b. Denver, Aug. 16, 1936; s. Louis Richard and Adele H. K.; m. Shirley Ann Asklof, June 25, 1965; children—John A., Marcia A., Elizabeth A. B.S. in Bus, U. Colo., 1958, LL.B., 1961. Bar: Colo. bar 1961. Asso. James B. Radetsky, Denver, 1962-63; individual practice law, Denver, 1963—; corp. officer, dir. Kintzele, Inc. Chmn. Colo. Lawyer Referral Service, 1978—; Election commr., Denver, 1975—. Served to 1st lt. U.S. Army, 1965-68. Mem. Am., Colo., Denver bar assns., Am. Judicature Soc. Democrat. Roman Catholic. Home: 2040 Clermont St Denver CO 80207 Office: 1317 Delaware St Denver CO 80204

KINTZLE, GERALD WILLIAM, b. Monticello, Iowa, Oct. 15, 1941; s. Irvin John and Agnes Catherine (Meyer) K.; m. Marsha Lou Elliott, July 14, 1969; children: Jill Ann, Cynthia Jo. B.S. in Fin., 1963. Pharm. rep. Pfizer Lab., Denver, 1967-69; investment officer First Nat. Bank, Denver, 1969-70; sr. v.p. Stern Bros. & Co., Denver, 1970—. Served to lt. comdr. USN, 1963-67; Far East, Italy. Republican. Roman Catholic. Office: Stern Bros & Co 1100 Main St Kansas City MO 64199

KINZEL, AUGUSTUS BRAUN, technical executive; b. N.Y.C., July 26, 1900; s. Otto and Josephine (Braun) K.; 1927 (div.); children: Carol (Mrs. Charles Uht) (dec.), Doris (Mrs. Richard Campbell), Augustus F., Angela (Mrs. John W. Talbot), Helen (Mrs. William Murray Hawkins, Jr.); m. Marie MacClymont, May 3, 1945 (dec. Nov. 1973). A.B., Columbia U., 1919; B.S., M.I.T., 1921, D.Metall. Engring., 1922; D.Sc., U. Nancy, France, 1933, D.hon. caucsa, 1963; D.Eng., N.Y. U., 1955; D.Sc., Clarkson Coll. Tech., 1957; D.Engr., Rensselaer Inst., 1965, Worcester Poly. Inst., 1965, U. Mich., 1967; LL.D., Queens U., 1966; D.Sc., Northwestern U., 1969, Poly. Inst. N.Y., 1981. Metallurgist Gen. Electric Co., Pittsfield, Mass., 1919-20, 22-23, Henry Disston & Sons, Inc., Phila., 1923-26; lectr., inst. extension courses in advanced metallurgy Temple U., 1925-26; research metallurgist Union Carbide & Carbon Research Labs., Inc., N.Y.C., 1926-28, group leader, 1928-31, chief metallurgist, 1931-45, v.p., 1945-48, pres., 1948-65, v.p., 1944-54; dir. research Union Carbide Corp., 1954-55, v.p., research, 1955-65; pres., chief exec. officer Salk Inst. Biol. Scis., La Jolla, Calif., 1965-67; trustee Systems Devel. Found., Palo Alto, Calif., 1961—, v.p., 1979—; past dir. Menasco Mfg. Co., Sprague Electric Co.; chief cons. in metallurgy Manhattan Dist. and AEC, 1943-65; chmn. Naval Research Adv. Com., 1954-55, mem., 1951-79; Regent's lectr. U. Calif., San Diego, 1971; chmn. adv. bd. The Energy Center, U. Calif., San Diego, 1976—; Chmn. governing council Courant Inst. Math. Scis., N.Y. U.; trustee Calif. Inst. Tech.; chmn. Engring. Found. Bd., N.Y.C., 1945-48; bd. dirs. Scripps Meml. Hosp., 1971-77; v.p., dir. Berkshire Farm Research Inst., 1950—; Howe Meml. lectr. Am. Inst. Mining and Metall. Engrs., 1952; Sauveur lectr. Am. Soc. Metals, 1952. Sr. author: Alloys of Iron and Chromium, vols. 1 and 2, 1937, 40; mem. editorial adv. bd.: Energy mag, 1977—; contbr. articles on metallurgy and engring. to tech. publs. Recipient Morehead medal Internat. Acetylene Assn., 1955; Stevens Inst. Tech. Powder Metallurgy medal award, 1959; Indsl. Research Inst. medal, 1960; James Douglas gold medal award AIME, 1960; Wisdom award of honor, 1973; Miller medal Am. Welding Soc., 1953. Fellow N.Y. Acad. Scis., Royal Soc. Arts, Am. Inst. Chemists, Metall. Soc., Am. Soc. Metals (Campbell lectr. 1947, Burgess Meml. lectr. 1956, past chmn. N.Y. sect.), Metall. Soc.; mem. Eurospace (hon.), Engrs. Joint Council (hon. pres. 1960-61), Am. Philos. Soc., Soc. Chem. Industry, Nat. Acad. Engring. (founding pres.), Nat. Acad. Scis., AIME (hon. mem., past pres.), Am. Welding Soc. (dir., Adams lectr. 1944), Internat. Inst. Med. Electronics and Biomed. Engring., ASTM, Soc. Automotive Engrs., Am. Iron and Steel Inst., Internat. Inst. Welding (v.p., elector Hall of Fame). Clubs: La Jolla (Calif.); Beach and Tennis; Cosmos (Washington); University Chemists (N.Y.C.). Patentee metallurgy and engring. Address: 1738 Castellana Rd La Jolla CA 92037 *Early in my career I learned two behavioural guides. First, choose a field of endeavor that you enjoy. If you enjoy your work you will be successful. Second, any transaction must benefit all parties thereto. Otherwise, it just isn't worthwhile.*

KINZER, DONALD LOUIS, historian; b. Kent, Wash., Nov. 9, 1914; s. Addison Louis and Lois Minerva (Fay) K.; m. Kathryn Jane Tipton, Aug. 20, 1955; 1 son, William Tipton. B.A., Western Wash. Coll., 1942, U. Wash., 1947, M.A., 1948, Ph.D., 1954. Instr. U. Wash., 1954-55, U. Del., 1955-58; asso. prof. Trenton State Coll., 1958-66, Ind. U.-Purdue U., Indpls., 1966-70, prof., 1970—, chmn. dept., 1970-80. Author: An Episode in Anti-Catholicism: The American Protective Association, 1964. Served with USAAF, 1942-46. Mem. Am. Hist. Assn., Orgn. Am. Historians, Ind. Hist. Soc., AAUP. Home: 5610 Central Ave Indianapolis IN 46220 Office: Dept History Cavanaugh Hall Ind Purdue U Indianapolis IN 46202

KINZER, JAMES RAYMOND, pipeline co. exec.; b. Pampa, Tex., Sept. 14, 1928; s. William Graham and Leota (Gott) K.; m. Billy June Chesher, June 30, 1956; children—Mark William, Kandia Ann, Karen June, Kourtney Margaret, John Richard. B.B.A., So. Methodist U., 1950, LL.B., 1952. Bar: Tex. bar 1952. Asso. firm Locke, Purnell, Boren, Laney & Neely, Dallas, 1955-59; counsel Tex. Industries, Inc., 1960-63; atty. Mobil Oil Corp., 1964-65; asst. gen. counsel Mobil Pipe Line Co., Dallas, 1966-70, gen. counsel, 1970—. Served with AUS, 1952-55. Mem. Am. Bar Assn., Fed. Energy Bar Assn., Assn. Oil Pipe Lines, Am. Petroleum Inst., Southwestern Legal Found., State Bar Tex., Dallas Bar Assn. Roman Catholic.

KIONKA, EDWARD JAMES, lawyer; b. Oak Park, Ill., Feb. 18, 1939; s. Edward Frederick and Antoinette (Harcus) K.; m. Sandra Sellers, Aug. 17, 1958 (div. Apr. 1974); children: Thomas Edward, Meridith Ann, David James.; m. Debra Ann Kosydor, Dec. 31, 1981. B.S., U. Ill., 1960, J.D., 1962; LL.M. (Krulewitch fellow), Columbia U., 1974. Bar: Ill. 1962, Mo. 1977. Asso. Leibman, Williams, Bennett & Baird (now Sidley & Austin), Chgo., 1962-64; instr. U. Mich. Law Sch., 1964-65; exec. dir. Ill. Inst. Continuing Legal Edn., Springfield, 1965-67; asst. dean, asst. prof. law U. Ill. Coll. Law, 1967-71; cons. atty., Ill., 1971-72, 74-75, part-time, 1973—; asso. prof. law So. Ill. U., Carbondale, 1973-75, 76-77, prof., 1977—; spl. counsel gen. govt. com. 6th Ill. Constl. Conv., 1970; cons. to lawyers on civil trials, appeals; mem. com. rules of evidence Ill. Supreme Ct., 1976-79, reporter com. jury instructions in civil cases, 1979—; bd. dirs. Ill. Inst. Continuing Legal Edn., 1967-72, 73—, mem. exec. com., chmn. curriculum com., 1967-71, treas., 1980-82, vice-chmn., 1982-83, chmn., 1983-84. Author: Torts: Injuries to Persons and Property in a Nutshell, 1977, Practitioner's Handbook for Appeals to the Illinois Supreme and Appellate Courts, 1978, 80; co-author: Materials for the Study of Evidence, 1983; asso. editor-in-chief: U. Ill. Law Forum, 1961-62; editor: Illinois Civil Practice After Trial, 1970. Mem. ABA, Ill. Bar Assn. (publs. com. 1979—, sec. 1981-82, vice-chmn. 1982—), Chgo. Bar Assn., Assn. Trial Lawyers Am., Appellate Lawyers Assn. (treas. 1974-75, sec. 1975-76, v.p. 1976-77, pres. 1977-78), Am. Judicature Soc., Order of Coif, Scribes, Phi Delta Phi. Home: 1201 Carter St Carbondale IL 62901

KIOSKI, JANET IRENE, editor; b. Ontonagon, Mich., Dec. 10, 1945; d. Edward Frances and Irene Mary (Jones) Wolfe; m. James E. Kioski, July 13, 1968. B.A., No. Mich. U., 1968; M.A., Central Mich. U., 1975. Photo editor Saturday Evening Post, Indpls., 1978, assoc. editor, 1979, sr. editor, 1980, cons. editor, 1981—; tchr. communications Lockyear Coll., Indpls., 1979. Mem. Am. Assn. Bus. and Profl. Women. Republican. Methodist. Office: 100 Waterway Blvd Indianapolis IN 46202 *

KIPARSKY, PAUL, linguistics educator; b. Helsinki, Jan. 28, 1941; U.S., 1961; s. Valentin and Dagmar (Jaatinen) K.; m. Carol Acker, Aug. 13, 1966. M.A., U. Minn., 1962; Ph.D., MIT, 1965. Asst. prof. linguistics MIT, Cambridge, Mass., 1965-68, assoc. prof., 1968-72, prof., 1972—. Author: Panini as a Variationist, 1979 (Rishi prize 1981), Explanation in Phonology, 1982, Theoretical Problems on Panini's Grammar, 1982. Home: 103 Ocean St Dorchester MA 02124 Office: MIT Cambridge MA 02139

KIPLINGER, AUSTIN HUNTINGTON, editor, publisher; b. Washington, Sept. 19, 1918; s. Willard Monroe and Irene (Austin) K.; m. Mary Louise Cobb, Dec. 11, 1944; children: Todd Lawrence, Knight Austin. A.B., Cornell U., 1939; postgrad., Harvard U., 1939-40; LL.D. (hon.), Union Coll., 1977, D.A.M., Embrey Riddle Aero. U., 1980, D.H.L., Bryant Coll., 1982. Reporter Kiplinger Washington Letter, 1939, San Francisco Chronicle, 1940-41; exec. editor Kiplinger mag., Changing Times, 1945-48; columnist Chgo. Jour. of Commerce, 1949-50; news commentator ABC, Chgo., 1951-55, NBC, 1955-56; exec. v.p. The Kiplinger Washington Editors, 1956-59, pres., 1959—; editor Kiplinger Washington Letter, 1961—; pub. Changing Times Mag., 1959-79, editor-in-chief, 1979—. Author: (with W. M. Kiplinger) Boom and Inflation Ahead, 1958, (with Knight A. Kiplinger) Washington Now, 1975, (with Arnold B. Barach) The Exciting '80s, 1979. Pres. Juvenile Protective Assn. Chgo., 1955-56; chmn. Mayor's Adv. Com. on Youth Welfare, Chgo., 1956; vice chmn. Nat. Capital Health and Welfare Council, 1960-67; Trustee Landon Sch., 1960-63; trustee Cornell U., 1960—, chmn. univ. council, 1965-68; trustee Fed. City Council, Greater Washington Ednl. Telecommunications Assn., 1967-77, Washington Journalism Center, 1967—; pres. Nat. Symphony Orch. Assn., 1978-80. Served as naval aviator aboard carriers, 1942-45; PTO. Mem. Telluride Assn., Assn. Radio and TV News Analysts, Phi Beta Kappa, Delta Upsilon, Sigma Delta Chi. Unitarian. Clubs: Metropolitan, National Press, Overseas Writers (Washington); Commonwealth (Chgo.); Cornell (N.Y.); Potomac Hunt, Chevy Chase. Home: Montevideo 16801 River Rd Poolesville MD 20837 Office: 1729 H St Washington DC 20006

KIPNIS, DAVID MORRIS, physician, educator; b. Balt., May 23, 1927; s. Rubin and Anna (Mizen) K.; m. Paula Jane Levin, Aug. 16, 1953; children—Lynne, Laura, Robert. A.B., Johns Hopkins U., 1945, M.A., 1949; M.D., U. Md., 1951. Intern Johns Hopkins Hosp., 1951-52; resident Duke Hosp., Durham, N.C., 1952-54, U. Md. Hosp., 1954-55; asst. prof. medicine Washington U. Sch. Medicine, St. Louis, 1958-63, asso. prof., 1963-65, prof., 1965—, Busch prof., chmn. dept. medicine, 1973—; asst. physician Barnes Hosp., 1958-63, asso. physician, 1963-72, physician-in-chief, 1973—; Chmn. endocrine study sect. NIH, 1963-64, mem. diabetes tng. program com., 1970—; chmn. Nat. Diabetes Adv. Bd. Editor: Diabetes, 1973; Asso. editor: Am. Jour. Medicine, 1973; Editorial bd.: Am. Jour. Med. Scis; Contbr. articles to profl. jours. Served with AUS, 1945-46. Markle scholar in med. scis., 1957-62; Banting lectr. Brit. Diabetes Assn., 1972. Mem. Am. Soc. Clin. Investigation, Assn. Am. Physicians, Am. Fedn. Clin. Research, Am. Diabetes Assn. (Lilly award 1965, Banting medal 1977, Best medal 1981), Endocrine Soc. (Oppenheimer award 1965), Am. Soc. Biol. Chemists, Am. Acad. Arts and Scis., Inst. Medicine of Nat. Acad. Scis., Nat. Acad. Scis. Home: 7200 Wydown Blvd Clayton MO 63105 Office: 660 S Euclid St Box 8121 Dept Medicine St Louis MO 63110

KIPNIS, IGOR, harpsichordist; b. Berlin, Germany, Sept. 27, 1930; s. Alexander and Mildred (Levy) K.; m. Judith Robison, Jan. 6, 1953; 1 son, Jeremy Robison. Student, Westport (Conn.) Sch. Music, 1941-48; A.B., Harvard U., 1952. Tchr. baroque performance practice Berkshire Music Center, Tanglewood, Mass., summers 1964-67, chmn. baroque dept., 1965-67; asso. prof. fine arts Fairfield (Conn.) U., 1971-75, artist-in-residence, 1975-77; faculty Festival Music Soc. Early Music Inst., Indpls., summers 1974—; vis. tutor Royal No. Coll. Music, Manchester, Eng., 1982—; v.p. Conn. Early Music Festival, 1983—. Rec. artist, Nonesuch, Angel, Columbia, Epic, Odyssey, London, Golden Crest, Kapp, Vanguard, Decca, Intercord, Grenadilla records; music critic: Mus. Courier, 1961, Notes, 1961, N.Y. Post, 1962, N.Y. Herald Tribune, 1961-62, others, 1955—; record reviewer: Am. Record Guide, 1955-61; contbg. editor: Stereo Review, 1961-83; host of: weekly radio program Age of Baroque, WQXR, N.Y., 1966-68; Editor: A First Harpsichord Book, 1970, Dussek: The Sufferings of the Queen of France, 1975, Telemann: Overture in E Flat Major, 1978, Krebs: Six Preludes, 1984; Debut, radio sta. WNYC, 1959, solo recital debut, N.Y.C. Hist. Soc., 1962, N.Y. Philharmonic, Chgo. Symphony, 1975, debut as fortepianist, Festival Mus. Soc. Indpls., 1981, concerts, recitals, throughout U.S. and Can., 1962—, tours, Europe, 1967, 69, 70, 75, 76, 77, 79, 80, 81, 82; mem. adv. bd., Keyboard Mag.; tours, S.Am., 1968, 75, 76, Israel, 1969, Australia, 1971, 79, Hawaii, 1971, Soviet

Union, 1983. Served with AUS, 1952-54. Recipient nominations Nat. Acad. Recording Arts and Scis., 1964, 71, 72, 77, 79; Martha Baird Rockefeller Fund for Music, Inc. grants, 1966, 68; Deutsche Schallplatten Preis, 1969; Stereo Review Record of Year award, 1971, 72, 75; Best Harpsichordist award Contemporary Keyboard Mag. Poll, 1978, 79, 80; Best Classical Keyboardist award Contemporary Keyboard Mag. Poll, 1982. Mem. Am. Musicol. Soc., Dolmetsch Found., Galpin Soc., ASCAP, Am. Fedn. Musicians, Performers of Conn. (hon.), Am. Mus. Instrument Soc., Grainger Soc., New Bach Soc., Stokowski Soc., Riemenschneider Bach Inst. (hon.), Barbirelli Soc., Phi Beta Kappa (hon.). Club: Bohemians (N.Y.C.). Home: 20 Drummer Ln RFD 2 West Redding CT 06896

KIPNISS, ROBERT, artist; b. N.Y.C., Feb. 1, 1931; s. Sam and Stella Anita K.; m. Jean Elizabeth Prutton, July 6, 1954; children: Max, Ivan, Ruby, Benjamin. Student, Wittenberg Coll., 1948-50; B.A., U. Iowa, 1952, M.F.A., 1954; Ph.D. (hon.), Wittenberg U., 1980. One man exhbns. include, Museo de Arte Moderno, Cali, Columbia, 1977, Kalamazoo Art Inst., Canton Art Inst.; represented in permanent collections, Chgo. Art Inst., Whitney Mus. Am. Art, N.Y.C., Yale U. Art Gallery, Nat. Collection Fine Arts, Library of Congress, Los Angeles County Mus., Detroit Inst. Art, Cleve. Mus., N.Y. Public Library, Butler Art Inst., De Young Mus., Indpls. Mus. Art, Portland Mus. Art. Served with U.S. Army, 1956-58. Recipient Ralph Fabri prize in lithography Nat. Acad. Design, 1976; James R. Marsh Meml. award in lithography Audubon Artists, 1978; Charles M. Lea prize Print Club Phila., 1978; prize for lithography Soc. Am. Graphic Artsts, 1979; Medal of Honor in Graphics Audubon Artists, 1983. Mem. Audubon Artists (dir. graphics), Boston Printmakers, Print Club Phila. Office: 26 E 33d St New York NY 10016

KIPP, DEAN CARL, educator, physician; b. Manhattan, Kans., Apr. 27, 1918; s. Carl Louis and Ethel (McKean) K.; m. Mary Elizabeth Davis, May 28, 1943; children—Karen Dean (Mrs. Donald R. McCann, Jr.), Jan Kendree (Mrs. Larry McElwain); Crane Davis. Student, St. Benedict's Coll., 1935-37; B.S., Kans. State U., 1939; M.D., Kans. U., 1943. Diplomate: Am. Bd. Plastic Surgery. Intern Ohio State U. Hosp., 1943-44, resident surgery, 1947-49; resident pathology Barnes Hosp., St. Louis, 1946-47; clin. asso. prof. surgery Southwestern br. U. Tex. Med. Sch., Dallas, 1962—; chief dept. plastic surgery Baylor U. Med. Center, 1965-79. Served with M.C. USNR, World War II; PTO. Fellow A.C.S.; mem. Am., Tex., Dallas med. assns., Am. Soc. Plastic Surgeons, Internat. Fedn. Plastic Surgeons, Tex. Surg. Soc., Tex. Soc. Plastic Surgeons. Home: 8600 Skyline #1000 Dallas TX 75243

KIPP, LYMAN, sculptor, educator; b. Dobbs Ferry, N.Y., Dec. 24, 1929; s. Lyman E. and Edna G. (Steenwerth) K.; children: Lisa, Keith, Alison, Ian. Student, Pratt Inst., 1950-52, Cranbrook Acad. Art, 1952-54. Mem. faculty art Bennington (Vt.) Coll., 1960-63, Pratt Inst., Bklyn., 1962-63; vis. artist Dartmouth Coll., 1966; mem. faculty dept. art Hunter Coll., N.Y.C., 1963-68, prof. art, 1978—, chmn. dept. art, 1975-78; prof. dept. art Lehman Coll., Bronx, N.Y., 1968-75. One-man shows sculpture, Laguna Gloria Mus., Austin, Tex., 1976, Art Center, Waco, Tex., Nielson Meml. Mus., Amarillo, Tex., 1977, U. Ala., Huntsville, Max Hutchinson Gallery, N.Y.C., Construct, Chgo., 1978, 80, Calvin Coll., Grand Rapids, Mich., 1979, numerous others, numerous groups shows, latest being, Aldrich Mus., Conn., 1978, 79, Hamilton Gallery, N.Y.C., 1978, U. Wis., Oshkosh, 1979, Patterson State Coll., N.J., Grant Park, Chgo., Fine Arts Mus. L.I., Hempstead, N.Y., Shidoni Gallery, Tesuque, N.Mex., 1980, Arts Festival Atlanta, SUNY, Buffalo, Navy Pier, Chgo., 1980, 81, 82, 83, U. Rochester, N.Y., 1980, U. N.D., Grand Forks, Martha Jackson/David Anderson Gallery, N.Y.C., Ianuzzi Gallery, Phoenix, 1982, Met. Mus. Art, Miami, 1983; represented in permanent collections, Albright-Knox Art Gallery, Buffalo, High Mus. Art, Atlanta, Pa. State U., Phila., M.I.T., Cambridge, Nat. Collection Fine Art, Washington, Fed. Office Bldg., Van Nuys, Calif., Grosse Pointe (Mich.) Library, Whitney Mus. Am. Art, N.Y.C., Fort Worth Mus., Salem (Mass.) State Coll., N.Y. Bank Savs., N.Y.C., univs. Ky., Mich. and Nebr. Guggenheim fellow, 1965; Fulbright fellow, 1965; recipient City U. Faculty research award, 1970, 75. Mem. Artists Equity Assn. Home: Route 100 Somers NY 10589

KIPP, RAYMOND JOSEPH, univ. dean; b. Ossian, Iowa, Dec. 7, 1922; s. William and Pauline (Giesing) K.; m. Margaret D. Bradley, Aug. 29, 1949; children—Jerry, Carole. B.C.E., Marquette U., 1951; M.C.E., U. Wis., 1957, Ph.D., 1965. Diplomate: Am. Acad. Environ. Engrs. With N.Am. Aviation, Los Angeles, 1951; asst. city engr., City of Los Angeles, 1952; mem. faculty Marquette U., Milw., 1953—, chmn. dept. civil engring., 1965-71, dean, 1971—; cons. engr. Chmn. Met. Sewerage Dist., 1974-81. Served with USNR, 1942-47. Decorated Air medal with 3 oak leaf clusters. Mem. Engrs. Soc. Milw. (Engr. of Year 1972). Home: 1050 Pilgrim Pkwy Elm Grove WI 53122 Office: 1515 W Wisconsin Ave Milwaukee WI 53233

KIPP, ROBERT ALMY, redevelopment executive; b. Lincoln, Nebr., May 21, 1932; s. Harold Lyman and Constance (Almy) K.; m. Deborah Yvonne Graves, Apr. 29, 1956; children: Steven, David. B.C.E., U. Kans., 1952, M. Pub. Adminstrn. in City Mgmt, 1956. Instr. Sch. Engring., U. Kans., 1954-55; planning dir., City of Newton, Kans., 1955-56, asst. city mgr., city planner, City of Lawrence, Kans., 1956-60, city mgr., City of Vandalia, Ohio, 1960-63, Fairborn, Ohio, 1963-70, mem. staff, City of Kansas City, 1970—, dir. adminstrn., 1973-74, city mgr., 1974-83; pres. Crown Ctr. Redevel., Kansas City, 1983—. Bd. dirs. Ohio Municipal League. Served with USAF, 1952-54. Recipient Disting. Service award U. Kansas, 1980, Nat Pub. Service award Am. Soc. Pub. Adminstrn.-Nat. Acad. Pub. Adminstrn., 1983. Mem. Internat. City Mgmt. Assn. (pres. 1977-79). Club: Rotary. Office: 414 E 12th St Kansas City MO 64106 *

KIPPENHAN, CHARLES JACOB, educator, mech. engr.; b. Middle Amana, Iowa, Nov. 8, 1919; s. Adam John and Emilia (Heinemann) K.; m. Jane Elizabeth Munsinger, Dec. 18, 1941; children—Judith Evans (Mrs. James R. Halstead II), Kurt Alfred. B.S. in Mech. Engring, State U. Iowa, 1940, M.S., 1946, Ph.D., 1948. Instr. mech. engring. State U. Iowa, 1941-42; from asst. prof. mech. engring. to prof., head dept. Washington U., St. Louis, 1948-64; prof. mech. engring. U. Wash., Seattle, 1963—, chmn. dept. mech. engring., 1964-73, adj. prof. architecture, 1973—; cons. to industry, 1949—. Contbr. profl. jours. Served to lt. USN, 1942-46. AEC-Am. Soc. Engring. Edn. fellow nuclear energy seminar Cornell U., summer 1959, direct energy conversion U. Ill., summer 1963; NSF sci. tchr. fellow TH Munich, Germany, 1960-61. Mem. ASHRAE, Am. Soc. Engring. Edn., ASME, Sigma Xi, Theta Tau, Pi Tau Sigma, Tau Beta Pi. Unitarian. Home: 3908 NE 38th St Seattle WA 98105

KIRBO, CHARLES HUGHES, lawyer, former presidential adviser; b. Bainbridge, Ga., Mar. 5, 1917; s. Ben and Ethel (West) K.; m. Margaret LeGette, May 20, 1951; children: Charles Hughes, Susan Ray, Betsy Anne, Katherine. LL.B., U. Ga., 1939. Bar: Ga. 1939. Ptnr. firm King & Spalding, Atlanta, 1960—; chief of staff Ga. Gov. Jimmy Carter, 1970-74; adviser to Pres. Jimmy Carter. Served to maj. U.S. Army, World War II. Home: 10705 Stroup Rd Roswell GA 30075 Office: 2500 Trust Company Tower Atlanta GA 30303

KIRBY, ALLAN PRICE, JR., investment company executive; b. Wilkes Barre, Pa., June 18, 1931; s. Allan Price and Marian (Sutherland) K.; children: Jessie Ann, Allan Price III, Slater Baran, Coray Sutherland, Milan Stanton. Grad., Morristown Sch., 1949; B.A., Lafayette Coll., 1953. Pres. Liberty Sq., Inc., Morristown, N.J.; dir., chmn. exec. com. Alleghany Corp.; bd. mgrs. IDS Life Variable Annuity Fund A and B; mem. East Side adv. bd. Chem. Bank. Bd. dirs., v.p. F.M. Kirby Found.; trustee Fred M. and Jessie A. Kirby Episcopal House; trustee, treas. Angeline Elizabeth Kirby Meml. Health Center. Served as lt. (j.g.) USNR, 1953-55. Mem. Delta Kappa Epsilon. Clubs: Mendham (N.J.) Golf and Tennis; Morris County Golf (Convent, N.J.); Yale (N.Y.C.); Black River Fish and Game (Pottersville, N.J.). Office: 14 E Main St PO Box 90 Mendham NJ 07945

KIRBY, CHARLES WILLIAM, JR., dancer, choreographer; b. Little Rock, Apr. 28, 1926; s. Charles William and Eva Rose (Horton) K. A.A., Little Rock Jr. Coll., 1945. Adv. bd. George Brown Coll. Tech., Toronto; exec. com. Canadian Actors Equity Assn.; pres. Southeastern Regional Ballet Festival Assn., 1965; co-founder, co-owner Abundance Restaurant, Toronto, 1980—. Prin. soloist, Ballet Soc. Ark., 1947; asso. dir., Acad. Ballet Arts, Little Rock, 1948-50; prin. dancer, Ark. State Musicals, 1949, Memphis Open Air Theatre, 1950; co-dir., Acad. Dance Arts, Memphis, 1950-65; prin. dancer, costume designer, choreographer, Front St. Theatre, Memphis, 1954-64; choreographer, Memphis Opera Theatre; performer, Dallas Summer Musicals, 1964; co-organizer, choreographer ballets, Memphis Civic Ballet, 1953-65; mem., Nat. Ballet Can., 1965-72; soloist, 1972-76; prin. dancer, 1976—; appeared: CBC TV spls. Swan Lake, 1967, Cinderella, 1968 (Emmy award), Sleeping Beauty, 1972 (Emmy award), Giselle, 1975, La Fille Mal Gardee, 1979; choreographer: CBC opera prodn. La Rondine, 1971, Maurice Ravel Centennial Concert, 1975, summer opera festivals, Nat. Arts Centre Can., Canadian Opera Co.; co. mgr., Dance Repertory Co., N.Y.C., 1972; author, dir., choreographer, narrator: spl. ednl. program Spectrum: A Retrospective Look at Dance, 1973. Served with AUS, 1944. Recipient key to City of Little Rock, 1965. Mem. Assn. Canadian TV and Radio Artists. Episcopalian.

KIRBY, EMILY BARUCH, psychologist, college official; b. N.Y.C., Apr. 16, 1929; d. Paul Ludwig and Aimee Augusta (Mayer) Baruch; m. Frank Eugene Kirby, Aug. 17, 1952; children: Russell Steven, Nicholas Quentin, Paula Rachel, Nathaniel Benedict. B.A., N.Y. U., 1952, M.A., 1953; Ph.D., Northwestern U., 1974. Instr. psychology Elmhurst (Ill.) Coll., 1965-68, asst. prof., 1968-74; dir. instnl. research Central YMCA Community Coll., Chgo., 1974-77; dir. instructional research and evaluation Oakton Community Coll., Morton Grove, Ill., 1977-80; v.p. faculty and acad. affairs Hudson Valley Community Coll., Troy, N.Y., 1980—; adj. faculty Women's Mgmt. Program, Mundelein Coll., Chgo., 1977-79; cons. on law enforcement, group and individual therapy, also assertiveness tng.; bd. dirs. Hudson Mohawk Consortium of Colls. and Univs., Latham, N.Y., 1980-83; Mem. subcom. on employment and pensions Ill. Commn. on Status of Women.; mem. region IV N.Y. planning bd. Bd. Coop. Ednl. Services, 1981-83. Contbr. articles to profl. jours., also popular publs. Bd. dirs. North Shore Ecology Center, Highland Park, Ill., 1977-80. Mem. Am. Psychol. Assn. (chmn. com. on ednl. psychologists in community colls. 1978—), AAAS, Am. Ednl. Research Assn. (chairperson newsletter editorial com., spl. interest group com. for North Central region 1978-79, spl. interest group community coll. research), Assn. Instnl. Research, Antioch Coll. Alumni Assn., Kappa Delta Pi, Phi Delta Kappa. Democrat. Unitarian. Clubs: Northwestern (Chgo.); Altrusa (chmn. internat. relations Albany chpt. 1982-83). Home: 2000 Greenbriar Ln Riverwoods IL 60015 *Nothing is wasted; every experience is useful. Life's main challenge is synthesize, then integrate ideas and events, adding large dollops of humor*

KIRBY, FRED MORGAN, II, corporation executive; b. Wilkes Barre, Pa., Nov. 23, 1919; s. Allan P. and Marian G. (Sutherl) K.; m. A. Walker Dillard, Apr. 30, 1949; children: Alice, Fred Morgan III, Dillard, Jefferson. Grad., Lawrenceville Sch., 1938; A.B., Lafayette Coll., Easton, Pa., 1942; postgrad., Harvard Grad. Sch. Bus. Adminstrn., 1947. Vice pres., then pres., dir. Allan Corp., 1953-75; pres., chmn. Filtration Engrs.; Inc., 1951-56; dir. Alleghany Corp., 1958-61, v.p., 1961, exec. v.p., 1963-67, chmn., 1967—, pres., 1968-77; dir. mem. exec. com. Pittston Co., U.S. Industries, Inc., F.W. Woolworth Co. Trustee Fred M. and Jessie A. Kirby Episcopal House, Inc.; pres., dir. F.M. Kirby Found., Inc. Served to lt. (s.g.) USNR, 1942-46. Mem. Zeta Psi. Clubs: Westmoreland (Wilkes Barre, Pa.); Morris County (N.J.) Golf, Racquet and Tennis, World Trade (N.Y.C.); Spring Valley (N.J.) Hounds; Tower (Mpls.). Office: 17 DeHart St Morristown NJ 07960

KIRBY, JAMES CORDELL, JR., educator; b. Macon County, Tenn., June 19, 1928; s. James Cordell and Beulah (Russell) K.; m. Barbara Glenn Eggleston, Mar. 22, 1955. B.A., Vanderbilt U., 1950; student Law Sch., 1950- 51; LL.B., LL.M., N.Y.U., 1954. Bar: Tenn. bar 1954, Ill. bar 1966, Ohio bar 1971, N.Y. State bar 1975, also U.S. Supreme Ct 1975. With firm Waller, Davis & Lansden, Nashville, 1954-55, 57-61; chief counsel judiciary subcom. constl. amendments U.S. Senate, 1961-63; asso. prof., then prof. law Vanderbilt U. Law Sch., 1963-65; prof. law Northwestern U. Law Sch., 1965-68, N.Y. U., 1968-70, 74-79, v.p., gen. counsel, sec., 1974-75; dir. Appellate Judges Seminar, 1975-77; dean coll. law Ohio State U., 1970-74; vis. prof. U. Tenn. Coll. Law, 1978-79, prof. law, 1979—, acting dean, 1980-81; mem. panels Am. Arbitration Assn., also Fed. Mediation and Conciliation Service; research dir. spl. study congl. ethical standards Assn. Bar City N.Y., 1967-70; mem. Ohio Ethics Commn., 1973-74, chmn., 1974. Served as 1st lt. AUS, 1955-57. Mem. Am. Bar Assn. (spl. commn. presdl. inability and vice presdl. vacancy 1964, spl. comm. electoral coll. reform 1966), Order of Coif, Phi Beta Kappa, Phi Kappa Sigma, Omicron Delta Kappa. Democrat. Episcopalian. Club: Century Assn. (N.Y.C.). Home: 3636 Taliluna Ave Apt 314 Knoxville TN 37919

KIRBY, JAMES EDMUND, JR., educator, theologian; b. Wheeler, Tex., June 24, 1933; s. James Edmund and Mamie (Helton) K.; m. Patty Ray Boothe, July 22, 1955; children: David Edmund, Patrick Boothe. B.A. cum laude, McMurry Coll., 1954; B.D., Perkins Sch. Theology, 1957, S.T.M., 1959; Ph.D., Drew U., 1963; postgrad., Cambridge (Eng.) U., 1957-58. Ordained to ministry Methodist Ch., 1959; pastor First Methodist Ch., Roby, Tex., 1958-59, Milford (Pa.) Meth. Ch., 1960-61; asst. prof. Bible, McMurry Coll., Abilene, Tex., 1959-60; asst. prof. religion Sweet Briar Coll., Va., 1963-67; prof. religion, head dept. religion Okla. State U., Stillwater, 1967-70; head Sch. Humanistic Studies, 1970-76; dean Sch. Theology, Drew U., Madison, N.J., 1976-81, Perkins Sch. Theology, So. Meth. U., Dallas, 1981—; teaching asst. Drew Theol. Sem., Madison, N.J., 1960-61; cons. bd. missions United Meth. Ch., South Africa, 1968. Contbr. articles to profl. jours.; pres. bd. dirs. Wesley Works Editorial Project. Bd. dirs. United Fund, Stillwater. John M. Moore fellow, 1957-58; Dempster fellow, 1962. Mem. Am. Acad. Religion, Soc. Values in Higher Edn., Am. Soc. Ch. History, Assn. United Meth. Theol. Schs. (pres.), Alpha Chi, Omicron Delta Kappa. Home: 9235 Windy Crest Dallas TX 75243 Office: Perkins Sch Theology 200 Kirby Hall Southern Meth U Dallas TX 75275

KIRBY, KENT BRUCE, artist; b. Fargo, N.D., Dec. 31, 1934; s. Harold Ely and Vida Nicola (Vennerstrom) K.; m. Lynn Rennetha Schutte, Sept. 1, 1956 (div. 1981); children: Kalin Louise, Jeffrey Bruce, Kirstin Beth. B.A., Carleton Coll., 1956; M.A., U. Dakota, 1959; M.F.A., U. Mich., 1970. Tchr. Benjamin Franklin Jr. High Sch., Fargo, 1956-59; instr. in art, acting head dept. art Muskingum Coll., 1959-61; instr. Wilkes Coll., 1961-62; faculty art Alma (Mich.) Coll., 1962—, prof., 1971—, chmn. dept. art and design, 1962—, chmn. div. fine arts, 1973-75, Charles A. Dana prof. art, 1976. One man shows, Saginaw (Mich.) Art Mus., 1976, Carleton Coll., Northfield, Minn., 1972, U. N.Mex., 1980, Ctr. for Creative Studies, Detroit, 1982, group shows include, Mich. Printmakers Biennial Exhbn., Detroit Inst. Arts, 1977, 20th N.D. Ann. Print and Drawing Exhbn., Grand Forks, 2d Internat. Exhbn. Prints and Drawings, Wesleyan U., 1982, Color Print U.S.A., Tex. Tech. U., Lubbock, 1983; represented in permanent collections, Guggenheim Mus., N.Y.C., Chgo. Art Inst., Met. Mus. Art, N.Y.C., Detroit Art Inst. Chmn. museums com., council mem. Mich. State Council for Arts, 1966-68. Research fellow Newberry Library, 1974; Mich. Council for Arts grantee, 1975, 78; Nat. Endowment for Arts grantee, 1976. Mem. AAUP, Coll. Art Assn., Nat. Council Art Adminstrs. Home: 4100 Riverview St Alma MI 48801 Office: 614 W Superior St Alma MI 48801

KIRBY, MAURICE HELM, JR., banker; b. St. Petersburg, Fla., Oct. 20, 1926; s. Maurice Helm and Louise (Richardson) K.; m. Janice C. Champion, June 25, 1949; children: Karen (Mrs. Thomas R. Clark), Maurice Helm III. Student, Emory U., 1944, U. Calif., Berkeley, 1944-45; B.S., Purdue U., 1947; M.B.A., Ind. U., 1948. Supr. Internat. Harvester Co., Evansville, Ind., 1948-55; asst. plant mgr. Bucyrus Erie Co., Evansville, 1955-57; plant supt. Reynolds Metals Co., Louisville, 1957-59; underwriter Ohio Co., Columbus, 1959-62; sr. v.p. First Nat. Bank of Cin., 1962—; dir. Hamilton Mut. Ins. Co., Stevenson Photo Color Co., Crosset Co., Kennedy Mfg. Co., Ohio Nat. Fund, Inc., Wadsworth Electric Mfg. Co., Inc. Served with USNR, 1944-47. Mem. Newcomen Soc. N.Am., Greater Cin. C. of C., Bankers Club. Clubs: Kiwanian., Queen City (Cin.); Coldstream Country. Home: 6726 Farmbrook Dr Cincinnati OH 45230 Office: First Nat Bank 5th and Walnut Sts Cincinnati OH 45202

KIRBY, ROBERT STEPHEN, lawyer; b. Rochelle, Ill., Aug. 4, 1925; s. Stephen F. and Eulalia E. (Coleman) K.; m. Carolyn C. Clark, June 10, 1950; children: Kathleen, Robert, James, Thomas, Julie. B.S., U. Ill., 1948; postgrad., U. Wis.-Madison, 1948; J.D., U. Ill., 1950. Bar: Ill. 1950, U.S. Dist. Ct. (no dist.) Ill. 1950, U.S. Ct. Appeals (7th cir.) 1953, U.S. Supreme Ct. 1956. Ptnr. Frisch & Fox, Chgo., 1950-52; with Ill. Central R.R. Co., Chgo., 1952-69, gen. atty., 1961-66, asst. gen. solicitor, 1966-69; with IC Industries, Inc., Chgo., 1969—, sr. v.p., gen. counsel, sec., 1981—; dir. Chgo. Community Ventures, Chgo., IC Products Co., LaSalle Properties, Inc. Bd. govs. Henrotin Hosp., Chgo., 1962—. Served with USMC, 1943-45. Mem. Chgo. Bar Assn., Delta Kappa Epsilon, Phi Delta Phi. Clubs: Mid-America (Chgo.); Skokie Country (Glencoe, Ill.); Quail Ridge (Boynton Beach, Fla.). Office: IC Industries Inc 111 E Wacker Dr Chicago IL 60601

KIRBY, WILLIAM JOSEPH, corporation executive; b. Balt., Sept. 23, 1937; s. William J. and Marjorie M. (Wagner) K.; M. Catherine Gordon Craig, June 17, 1961; William Joseph III, Andrew Craig, Daivd Francis. B.A., Pa. State U., 1959; M.A. in Indsl. and Labor Relations, Cornell U., 1961; A.M.P., Harvard U., 1981. Mgmt. trainee Bell Telephone of Pa., Phila., 1961; employee benefits staff asst. Avisun Corp., Phila., 1961-62; recruiting mgr. Am. Viscose Corp., Phila., 1962-64; personnel mgr. FMC Film & Packaging, Fredericksburg, Va., 1964-69; dir. personnel adminstrn. FMC Machinery Group, Chgo., 1969-72; dir. personnel FMC Corp., Chgo., 1972-76, v.p. personnel, 1976—. Trustee Village of Golf, Ill.; pres. bd. INROADS, Inc., Chgo.; bd. dirs. Chgo. Econ. Devel. Corp.; adv. com. Inst. for Humanities U. Ill., Chgo., 1982. Mem. Human Resources Mgmt. Assn. Chgo. (dir. 1978-81), Machinery and Allied Products Inst. (human resources council), U.S. C. of C. (employee benefits com.), Labor Policy Assn. Republican. Episcopalian. Clubs: Mid-Am., Harvard, Glen View, Chgo. Athletic Assn. Office: FMC Corp 200 E Randolph Dr Chicago IL 60601

KIRBY, WILLIAM MURRAY MAURICE, medical educator; b. Springfield, S.D., Nov. 21, 1914; s. William McLeod and Era R. (Keeling) K.; m. Georgiana H. Dole, Apr. 12, 1944; children: Barbara Dole, Philip Keeling, Richard Murray. B.S., Trinity Coll., Hartford, Conn., 1936; M.D., Cornell U., 1940. Diplomate: Am. Bd. Internal Medicine (bd. 1961-67). Intern N.Y. Hosp., 1940-41; resident in medicine Stanford Hosp., 1941-44; instr. medicine Stanford Sch. Medicine, 1947-49; mem. faculty U. Wash. Med. Sch., 1949—, prof. medicine, 1955—; Mem. med. adv. bd. FDA, 1964—. Author chpts. in textbooks on infectious diseases, also numerous articles. Served with U.S. Army, 1944-47. Mem. A. Soc. Clin. Investigation, Assn. Am. Physicians. Home: 5656 NE Keswick Dr Seattle WA 98105 Office: Dept Medicine RG-20 U Wash Sch Medicine Seattle WA 98195

KIRCH, MAX SAMUEL, modern language educator; b. Phila., Mar. 28, 1915; s. Isadore and Clara (Hirsch) K; m. Louise Catherine Zirpoli, May 28, 1939; children—Patricia Ann, Thomas Edward. B.A., U. Pa., 1934, M.A., 1949, Ph.D., 1951. Instr. German U. Pa., 1946-53; instr. modern langs. U. Del., 1953-54, asst. prof., 1954-60, asso. prof., 1960-64, prof., 1964—, chmn. dept. langs. and lit., 1963-71; dir. Nat. Def. Edn. Act. Insts., 1960-62; Mem. German achievement test com. Coll. Entrance Exam Bd., 1963-67. Author: Einfluss des Niederdeutschen auf die Hochdeutsche Schriftsprache, 1952, Functional German, revised edit., 1967; also articles. Served with AUS, 1945-46. Decorated officier de l'Ordre des Palmes Academiques, France). Mem. Linguistic Soc. Am., Am. Council Teaching Fgn. Langs., Am. Assn. Tchrs. German, Modern Lang. Assn. Am., Middle States Assn. Modern Lang. Tchrs. (pres. 1971, 77), Nat. Fedn. Modern Lang. Tchr. Assns. (exec. bd. 1973, v.p, pres. 1979-81), Niederdeutscher Verein für Sprachforschung. Home: 731 Swarthmore Dr Newark DE 19711

KIRCHHEIMER, ARTHUR EDWARD, lawyer, business executive; b. N.Y.C., June 26, 1931; s. Arthur and Lena K.; m. Esther A. Jordan, Sept. 11, 1965. B.A., Syracuse U., 1952, LL.B., 19S4. Bar: N.Y. 1954, Calif. 1973. Individual practice law, Syracuse, 1954-70; corp. counsel Norwich Pharmacal Co., N.Y., 1970-72; sr. v.p. Wickes Cos., Inc., San Diego, 1972-84, spl. counsel, 1984—; sole practice law, 1984—; sec., dir. Corp. Fin. Council San Diego, 1975. Pres. Mental Health Assn. Onondaga County, 1970; chmn. Manilus (N.Y.) Planning Commn., 1969-72. Mem. Am., Fed., Calif., N.Y., Los Angeles, San Diego bar assns., Am. Soc. Corp. Secs. Home: 2876 Palomino Circle La Jolla CA 92037 Office: 1670 Wells Fargo Bank Bldg San Diego CA 92101

KIRCHHOFF, DONALD JOSEPH, former food company executive; b. St. Louis, June 29, 1925; s. Joseph V. and Freida (Kruger) K.; m. Bluette Hartman, Mar. 24, 1947; children: Susan Lee, Barbara Ann, Karen Mari. B.S., Miami U., Oxford, Ohio, 1948; M.B.A., Harvard U., 1949. With Kroger Co., Detroit, 1949-51, Nat. Tea Co., 1951-54; successively mgr. ops. analysis, asst. to pres., v.p., mgr. Honduras div., exec. v.p., pres. Standard Fruit & Steamship Co., New Orleans, 1964-69; exec. v.p. Castle & Cooke, Inc., Honolulu, 1970-73, pres., chief operating officer, 1973-75, pres., chief exec. officer, 1975-82, also dir. Served to lt. USNR, 1943-48, 51-53. Recipient Am. Eagle award

Invest-in-Am. Council, Inc., 1980. Clubs: Pacific-Union; Villa Taverna (San Francisco). Office: PO Box 2629 San Francisco CA 94126

KIRCHMAYER, LEON KENNETH, electrical engineer; b. Milw., July 24, 1924; s. Henry F. and Clara (Zenker) K.; m. Olga Temoshok, Dec. 2, 1950; children: Karyn, Kenneth. B.E.E., Marquette U., 1945; M.S. in Elec. Engring. (Univ. fellow 1945-46), U. Wis., 1947; Ph.D. in Elec. Engring. (Tau Beta Pi fellow 1947-48), U. Wis., 1950; grad. sr. exec. program, M.I.T., 1975. Lab. instr. and research asst. Marquette U., 1944-45; exptl. research engr. Cutler-Hammer, Inc., Milw., 1945-46; instr. elec. engring. U. Wis., Madison, 1946-48; with Gen. Electric Co., Schenectady, 1948—, mgr. system generation analytical engring., 1958-63, mgr. system planning and control, 1963-77, mgr. advanced system tech. and planning, 1977—. Author: Economic Operation of Power Systems, 1958, Economic Control of Interconnected Systems, 1959, (with D.N. Ewart, H.J. Fiedler and H.H. Happ) Modern Dispatch Techniques of Interconnected Power Systems, 1969; co-editor: (with W. Morsch) Technology Trends: Communications, Computers, Electric Energy, Electric Components, Instrumentation, 1975, A Technology Assessment Primer, 1975; assoc. editor: (with W. Hafele) Modeling of Large-Scale Energy Systems, 1981; contbr. articles to profl. jours. Bd. dirs. Schenectady Light Opera Co., 1952-57, pres. co., 1955-56. Recipient Disting. Service citation U. Wis., 1972; Mgmt. award Gen. Electric Co., 1951. Fellow IEEE, ASME; mem. Nat. Soc. Profl. Engrs. (Schenectady chpt. Engr. of Yr. 1965), Schenectady Gen. Electric Engring. Assn., Internat. Fedn. Automatic Control, Am. Automatic Control Council, Ops. Research Soc. Am., Conf. Internat. des Grands Reseaux Electriques à Haute Tension, Nat. Acad. Engring., Marquette U. Alumni Assn., U. Wis. Alumni Assn., Sigma Xi, Tau Beta Pi (Fellow 1946-47), Pi Mu Epsilon, Eta Kappa Nu. Clubs: Glen Hills Swimming, Mohawk, Mayfield Yacht. Patentee in field. Home: 11 Rivercrest Dr Rexford NY 12148 Office: 1 River Rd Schenectady NY 12345

KIRCHNER, DON F., marketing educator; b. Detroit, Sept. 28, 1931; s. Ralph T. and Frances I. (Schriener) K.; m. Cecile Dumas. A.B., Mich. State U., 1953; M.B.A., U. Detroit, 1959; Ph.D., UCLA, 1969. Research analyst Maxon, Inc., Detroit, 1950-53; mgr. merchandising Security Cos., Detroit, 1956; v.p. Richardson-Shaw, Inc., Detroit, 1956-62; chmn. dept. mktg. Calif. State U., Northridge, 1962—. Served with USAF, 1954-56. Mem. AAUP, Am. Mktg. Assn., Advt. Club Los Angeles (dir. 1977-81), So. Mktg. Assn., Assn. Consumer Research, Western Mktg. Educators Assn., Valley Internat. Trade Assn. (v.p.), Sierra Club, Nature Conservancy, Audubon Soc. Roman Catholic. Office: Dept Mktg Calif State U Northridge CA 91330

KIRCHNER, EDWIN JAMES, retired food company executive; b. Keokuk, Iowa, July 4, 1924; s. Edwin William and Gertrude Ann (Breheny) K.; m. Wilma Bernice Johnson, Apr. 21, 1944; children: Linda Kirchner Hurley, Karen Ann Kirchner Porreca, Patrick Adam. Grad. high sch. Accounting Union Electric Power Co., Keokuk, 1942-48; with Hubinger Co., Keokuk, 1948-83, adminstrv. asst. to v.p. finance, 1960-67, asst. v.p., asst. treas., asst. sec., 1967-69, treas., 1969-76, asst. sec., 1969-73, v.p., 1973-79, mgr. spl. projects, 1979-83, ret., 1983, also dir., 1969-76; sec.-treas. Keokuk Grain Inspection Service, 1970-72, v.p., 1972-75, also dir. Mem. Keokuk Cath. Sch. Bd., 1972-78, pres., 1972-75, mem. long range planning com., 1977—; Bd. dirs. South Lee County (Ia.) chpt. ARC, 1965-71, chpt. chmn., 1969-71; mem. exec. com. lay adv. bd. St. Joseph Hosp., 1972-75; trustee Keokuk Area Hosp., 1975-77; trustee, treas. Tri-State Health Care Found., 1982—; commr. Low Rent Housing Authority, 1981—. Served with USAAF, 1943-46; ETO; Served with USAAF; MTO. Clubs: K.C. (treas. 1965-72), Elk.). Home: 2 Wahkonsa Heights Keokuk IA 52632

KIRCHNER, ISABELLE LORETTA, insurance company executive; b. Bklyn.; b. John Joseph and Julia Loretta (O'Leary) Morrissey; m. William L. Kirchner, Jr., Jan. 3, 1959; children: William, Joan (stepchildren), John. B.A., St. John's U., Bklyn., 1950, LL.B., 1952; L.H.D. (hon.), Caldwell (N.J.) Coll., 1972. Bar: N.Y. 1952, N.J. 1961. With Prudential Ins. Co. Am., Newark, 1952-59, 64—, asst. sec., 1971, v.p., sec., 1971—; with firm Lum, Biunno & Tompkins, Newark, 1961-64. Bd. dirs., chmn. triennial fund raising Interracial Council Bus. Opportunity N.J., now co-chmn.; bd. regents, mem. exec. com., chmn. student affairs com., sec. of univ. Seton Hall U., South Orange, N.J.; trustee, mem. fin. com., joint adv. com., chmn. ins. subcom., mem. personnel com., budget com. Overlook Hosp., Summit, N.J.; trustee, vice chmn. N.J. State Sch. for Arts; trustee, v.p. Puerto Rican Latino Scholarship Fund.; trustee The Advocate, Cath. Sunday newspaper; mem. Archbishop's Com. of Laity. Recipient Papal medal Pro Ecclesia et Pontifice, 1983. Mem. ABA, N.J. Bar Assn. (past chmn. corp. law sect.), Essex County Bar Assn., Am. Soc. Corp. Secs., N.J. Assn. Corp. Gen. Counsel (sec.), Greater Newark C. of C., LWV. Home: 29 Pine Ct New Providence NJ 07974 Office: Prudential Plaza Newark NJ 07101

KIRCHNER, JOHN ALBERT, educator; b. Waynesboro, Pa., Mar. 27, 1915; s. Francis Edward and Jessie Cecilia (Cameron) K.; m. Aline Legault, Oct. 11, 1947; children—John C., Thomas L., Paul E., Marie Cecile, Christine A. M.D., U. Va., 1940; M.S. (hon.), Yale U., 1952. Intern Charity Hosp., New Orleans, 1940-41; resident otolaryngology Johns Hopkins Hosp., 1946-50; mem. faculty Yale Sch. Medicine, 1951—, prof. otolaryngology, 1962—; cons. in research NIH, 1966—; spl. research pathology and physiology of larynx and pharynx. Editor: Yearbook Ear, Nose and Throat, 1969-75. Served to capt. AUS, 1942-46. Decorated Bronze Star.; Recipient Harris P. Mosher award research Am. Trilogical Soc., 1958; Fellow Silliman Coll., Yale U., 1977—. Fellow A.C.S.; mem. Am. Laryngol. Assn. (pres. 1979-80, Casselberry award 1966, Newcomb award 1969), Am. Acad. Otolaryngology (v.p. 1978-79), Am. Laryngol., Rhinol. and Otol. Soc. (pres. 1981-82), New Eng. Otolaryngol. Soc. (pres. 1965-66), Am. Assn. Head and Neck Surgery (pres. 1977-78), Collegium Oto-Rhino-Laryngologicum Amicitae Sacrum, Sigma Xi. Home: 12 Rimmon Hill Rd Woodbridge CT 06525 Office: 333 Cedar St New Haven CT 06510

KIRCHNER, LEON, composer, pianist; b. Bklyn., Jan. 24, 1919; s. Samuel and Pauline K.; m. Gertrude Schoenberg, July 8, 1949; children: Paul, Lisa. A.B., U. Calif.-Berkeley, 1960. Faculty Mills Coll., Oakland, Calif., 1952-61, Luther B. Marchant prof. music, 1954-61; prof. music Harvard, 1961-66, Walter B. Rosen Prof. music, 1966—. Composer: Piano Sonata, 1948, Piano Suite 49, 1949, Sinfonia, 1951, Sonata Concertante, 1952, Piano Concerto, 1953, Trio for Piano, Violin and Cello, 1954, Toccata for Strings, Solo Winds and Percussion, 1955, String Quartet 2, 1958, Concerto for Violin, Cello, 10 Winds and Percussion, 1960, Piano Concerto No. 2, 1962, Words from Wordsworth for chorus, 1966, String Quartet No. 3, 1966 (Pulitzer prize 1967), Music for Orch, 1969; also recs. Recipient Prix de Paris, 1942; N.Y. Music Critics award, 1950, 60; Naumburg award for composition Library Congress, 1954; award Am. Acad. Arts and Letters.; Guggenheim fellow, 1948-50. Mem. ASCAP, Internat. Soc. Contemporary Music, League Am. Composers, Nat. Inst. Arts and Letters, Am. Acad. Arts and Scis., AAUP. Address: Dept Music Harvard U Cambridge MA 02138

KIRGIS, FREDERIC L., retired lawyer; b. Chicago Heights, Ill., Sept 25, 1907; s. Frederic and Anne (Smith) K.; m. Kathryn Burrows, June 30, 1933 (dec. Apr. 1980); children: Frederic L., Jerry B. (dec.), Ann Patricia. A.B., U. Ill., 1929, J.D., 1931; J.S.D., Yale, 1936. Bar: Colo. bar 1941. Instr. law U. Ill., 1931-32; Sterling teaching fellow in law Yale, 1932-33; asst. solicitor U.S. Dept. Interior, 1933-36, first asst. solicitor, 1936-40; spl. asst. to U.S. Atty. Gen., 1941-45; partner Gorsuch, Kirgis, Campbell, Walker & Grover, Denver, 1945-79, of counsel, 1979—; Mem. adv. council U.S. Pub. Land Law Rev. Commn., 1965-7O. Mem. ABA (chmn. sect. administv. law 1965-66), Colo. Bar Assn., Denver Bar Assn., Order of Coif, Phi Beta Kappa Clubs. Clubs: Denver Country, Denver; Law. Home: 1200 Humboldt St Denver CO 80218 Office: 1401 17th St Suite 1100 Denver CO 80202

KIRJASSOFF, GORDON LOUIS, cons., civil engineer; b. Phila., Dec. 5, 1922; s. Louis Solomon and Belle (Gordon) K.; m. G. Enid Newfield, Oct. 22, 1944 (dec. Oct. 1963); children: Kim, David; m. Constance Tumen Lovenstein, June 12, 1965; children: Janet (Mrs. Robert Springborn), Linda. B.S. in Civil Engring, Drexel U., 1944. Registered profl. engr., Mass., R.I., Conn., Vt., N.J., Maine, N.Y., N.H., Va., W.Va., Ill., Minn., Kans., Mo., Ariz. Project engr. Edwards and Kelcey, Newark, 1947-53, asso., 1953-58, partner, 1958—; exec. v.p. Edwards and Kelcey, Inc., Boston, 1959-78, chmn. bd., pres., 1978—, Edwards and Kelcey Engrs., Inc., Livingston, N.J., 1978—. Served with U.S. Maritime Service, 1944-46. Mem. ASCE, ASME, Nat. Soc. Profl. Engrs., Am. Council Cons. Engrs. Home: Claridge House II Verona NJ 07044

KIRK, ALAN GOODRICH, II, utilities executive; b. Rosemont, Pa., Dec. 15, 1926; s. William Thompson and Edith Graves (Ely) K.; m. Patricia Joan Carr, Apr. 20, 1953; children: Augustus, Jennifer, William, Alison. A.B., Princeton U., 1950; LL.B., U. Pa., 1956. Bar: Pa. 1956. Assoc. firm Dechert, Price & Rhoads, Phila., 1956-58; asst. dean U. Pa. Law Sch., 1958-62; gen. counsel, asst. sec. William H. Rorer Co., Ft. Washington, Pa., 1962-69; assoc. solicitor (water) Dept. Interior, Washington, 1969, asst. to sec., 1969-70, asst. to solicitor, 1970-71; dep. gen. counsel EPA, Washington, 1971-72, asst. adminstr. for enforcement, gen. counsel, 1973-75; gen. counsel Potomac Electric Power Co., Washington, 1975, v.p., gen. counsel, 1976-81, sr. v.p., gen. counsel, 1981—. Served with U.S. Mcht. Marine, 1944-46; Served with AUS, 1950-53. Mem. Am., Fed., D.C. bar assns. Clubs: Ivy (Princeton, N.J.); Metropolitan, Burning Tree (Washington). Office: Potomac Electric Power Co 1900 Pennsylvania Ave NW Washington DC 20068

KIRK, ALEXIS VEMIAN, designer; b. Los Angeles, Dec. 29, 1938; s. Paul A. and Araxie J. Hopkins (Vemian) K.; children: Lisa Vemian, Alexia Vemian. Student, Boston Mus. Fine Arts Sch., R.I. Sch. Design, Harvard U. Staff designer Design Research Inc., Cambridge, Mass., 1961-64; pres. D.D. Inc., Newport, R.I., 1964-68; chief designer El Greco Inc., N.Y.C., 1968-69, Hattie Carnegie Inc., 1969-70; pres. Alexis Kirk Inc., N.Y.C., 1970—. Jewelry design, tech. dir. film Black Sunday, 1977; Set design, actor film The Garden, 1978 (Acad. award nominee); costume and jewelry design, actor film Seizure, 1978. Recipient Automotive Design award Gen. Motors Corp., 1955; Gold medal Boston Mus. Fine Arts, 1956; Swarovski award Austria, 1972-73; Coty award, 1970; Gt. Am. Design award I. Magnin Co., 1974; Frederick Atkins award, 1975; City of Hope Humanitarian of Yr., 1984. Mem. Design Am., Council Fashion Designers Am., N.Y. Fashion Council. Republican. Episcopalian. Home: 309 E 49th St #16-B New York NY 10017 Office: 385 Fifth Ave New York NY 10016

KIRK, COLLEEN JEAN, conductor, educator; b. Champaign, Ill., Sept. 7, 1918; d. Bonum Lee and Anna Catherine (Hoffert) K. B.S. with high honors, U. Ill., 1940, M.S., 1945; Ed.D., Columbia U., 1953. Tchr. music public schs., Danvers, Ill., 1940-44, Watseka, Ill., 1944-45; instr. Univ. High Sch., Urbana, Ill., 1945-49; asst. prof. edn. and music U. Ill., 1949-58, asso. prof., 1958-64, prof., 1964-70, Fla. State U., Tallahassee, 1970—, condr. choral union, 1970—; choral clinician, condr., adjudicator. Dir. music, Wesley United Meth. Ch., Urbana, 1947-70; dir. jr. chorus, Ill. Summer Youth Music, Urbana, 1963-71; co-dir., Fla. Honors Choral Ensemble, Tallahassee, 1980-81; dir., Fla. Jr. High Sch. Choral Ensemble, Tallahassee, 1983; Author: (with others) Modern Methods in Elementary Education, 1959; frequent contbr. to: The Choral Jour. Mem. Am. Choral Dirs. Assn. (pres. So. div. 1971-75, nat. pres. 1981-83), Am. Choral Found., Inc., Music Educators Nat. Conf., Assn. Profl. Vocal Ensembles, Fla. Music Educators Assn., Internat. Fedn. Choral Music, AAUP, Coll. Music Soc., Fla. Vocal Assn., Fla. Coll. Music Educators Assn., Pi Kappa Lambda, Kappa Delta Pi, Sigma Alpha Iota. Office: Sch Music Fla State U Tallahassee FL 32306 *

KIRK, DANIEL LEE, physician, cons.; b. Alliance, O., Aug. 1, 1919; s. John Lee and Olive (Strine) K.; m. Betty Kathryn Blair, Sept. 9, 1942; children—Daniel Lee, Nancy Jayne. Student, Gettysburg Coll., 1940; M.D., George Washington U., 1943; certificate in Clin. Psychiatry, U. Pa., 1955, U. Wis., 1963. Intern Harrisburg (Pa.) Hosp., 1943-44; resident psychiatry Harrisburg State Hosp., 1944-45; practice medicine, specializing in psychiatry, Waynesboro, Pa., 1945-50; staff physician Elwyn (Pa.) Sch., 1950-52, clin. dir., 1952-57; asst. supt. Pennhurst State Sch. and Hosp., Spring City, Pa., 1957-59; supt. Selinsgrove (Pa.) State Sch. and Hosp., 1959-68; former med. dir., research chmn. South Mountain (Pa.) Restoration Center; cons. in geriatric medicine; adj. prof. dept. spl. edn. Pa. State U., 1965—; adviser Smith Kline & French film Toymakers; cons. Comprehensive Mental Health/Mental Retardation Program Region IV. Contbr. articles med. jours. Served with M.C. AUS, 1945. Fellow Am. Geriatrics Soc., Am. Assn. Mental Deficiency, N.Y. Acad. Scis., Nat. Bd. Med. Examiners; mem. AMA, Pa. Med. Soc., Med. Club Phila., Assn. Med. Supts. Mental Hosps., Nat., Pa. assns. retarded children. Clubs: Mason, Rotarian. Home: 201 N Church St Waynesboro PA 17268

KIRK, DONALD, journalist; b. New Brunswick, N.J., May 7, 1938; s. Rudolf and Clara (Marburg) K.; m. Susanne Smith, May 31, 1965. A.B., Princeton U., 1959; M.A., U. Chgo., 1965; postgrad. (Ford Found. fellow), Columbia U., 1964-65. Reporter Chgo. Sun-Times, 1960-61, N.Y. Post, 1961-64; corr., writer, various newspapers and mags., 1965—; Asia corr. Washington Star, 1967-70; Far East corr. Chgo. Tribune, 1971-74, N.Y. corr., 1975-76; world editor USA Today, 1982—. Author: Wider War: The Struggle for Cambodia, Thailand and Laos, 1971, Tell It To the Dead: Memories of a War, 1975; Contbg. author books.; Contbr. articles to mags., jours. Recipient Page One award Chgo. Newspaper Guild, 1960; citations Overseas Press Club, 1967, 72, 73; OPC award for best article on Asia, 1974; George Polk Meml. award for fgn. reporting, 1975; Fulbright scholar, New Delhi, India, 1962-63; Edward R. Murrow fellow Council Fgn. Relations, N.Y.C., 1974-75. Mem. Am. Soc. Journalists and Authors, Sigma Delta Chi. Clubs: Nat. Press (Washington); Overseas Press (N.Y.C.); Fgn. Corrs. (Hong Kong); Princeton (N.Y.C.). Address: 7 Pomander Walk NW Washington DC 20007 care Fgn Corrs Club Japan 1-7-1 Yurakucho Chiyoda-Ku Tokyo 100 Japan

KIRK, DONALD JAMES, accountant; b. Cleve., Nov. 28, 1932; s. John James and Helen Anna (Pilskaln) K.; m. Tara Collins, May 30, 1975; children: J. Alexander, Bruce D.; stepchildren: John Needham, Elizabeth Needham. B.A., Yale U., 1959; M.B.A., NYU, 1961; LL.D. (hon.), Lycoming Coll., 1979. Acct., Price Waterhouse & Co., N.Y.C., London and Washington, 1959-73, partner, 1967-73; mem. Fin. Acctg. Standards Bd., Stamford, Conn., 1973-78, chmn., 1978—. Officer, bd. dirs. Urban League of Southwestern Fairfield County, Conn., 1971-77; mem. Greenwich (Conn.) Rep. Town Meeting, 1971-77, Greenwich Bd. of Estimate and Taxation, 1977; bd. dirs. Nat. Arts Stabilization Fund, 1983—. Served as aviator USN, 1953-57. Recipient Alumni Achievement award NYU Grad. Sch. Bus. Adminstrn., 1980. Mem. Am. Inst. C.P.A.s. Club: Stanwich (Greenwich) (officer, dir.). Office: Fin Acctg Standards Bd High Ridge Park Stamford CT 06905

KIRK, DUDLEY, sociologist, educator; b. Rochester, N.Y., Oct. 6, 1913; s. William and Margaret Louise (Dudley) K.; m. Ruth Louise Avelar, Nov. 21, 1947; children: Margaret Louise, John Dudley, Deborah Avelar. A.B., Pomona Coll., 1934; M.A., Fletcher Sch. Law and Diplomacy, Tufts U., 1935, Harvard U., 1938, Ph.D., 1946; student, U. Mexico, 1930, London Sch. Econ. and Polit. Sci., 1936. Tutor sociology Harvard U., 1937-39; research asst., later research asso. Office Population Research, Princeton U., 1939-47, asst. prof. sociology at univ., 1945-47; demographer Office Intelligence Research, State Dept., 1947-51, chief div. research, Near East, South Asia and Africa, 1952, chief planning staff for research and intelligence, 1952-54; staff mem. Pres.'s Com. Immigration and Naturalization, 1951; demographic dir. Population Council, N.Y.C., 1954-67; prof. demography Food Research Inst. and dept. sociology Stanford U., 1967—, Morrison prof. population studies, 1971—, chmn. dept. sociology, 1975-76; vis. sr. research demographer Princeton U., 1978; coordinator Courses by Newspaper, NEH, 1981-82; mem. U.S. Nat. Com. on Health and Vital Stats., 1961-65; mem. research adv. com. AID, 1968-72. Author: (with others) The Future Population of Europe and the Soviet Union, 1944, Europe's Population in the Interwar Years, 1946, The Principles of Political Geography, 1957, (with Ellen K. Eliason) Food and People, 1982. Fellow Center Advanced Study in the Behavioral Scis., 1964-65. Fellow AAAS, Am. Sociol. Assn., Am. Statis. Assn., Inter-Am. Statis. Inst.; mem. Am. Soc. Study Social Biology (dir., chmn. editorial bd. Social Biology, pres. 1969-72), Am. Acad. Polit. and Social Sci., Internat. Union Sci. Study Population, Population Assn. Am. (pres. 1959-60), Sociol. Research Assn. Home: 854 Lathrop Dr Stanford CA 94305

KIRK, EDGAR LEE, musician, educator; b. Harrisburg, Pa., May 28, 1923; s. Arthur Lee and Bertha Mae (Berthel) K.; m. Ellen Calhoun Gray, June 18, 1947; children: Arthur Lee, Douglas Gray. B.M., Eastman Sch. Music, U. Rochester, 1947, M.M., 1948, Ph.D., 1957. Mem. faculty Mich. State U., 1948—, prof. bassoon, chmn. applied music, 1973—, asst. chmn. grad. studies, 1978—, dir. admissions dept. music, 1982; prof. bassoon Eastman Sch. Music, U. Rochester, summers, 1954-65; instr. bassoon Interlochen Arts Acad., 1975-79. Bassoonist, Rochester (N.Y.) Philharmonic Orch., 1946-47, 54-55; staff bassoonist, radio sta. WHAM, Rochester, 1947-48; 1st bassoonist, Lansing (Mich.) Symphony Orch., 1960-73; mem., Richards Woodwind Quintet, 1965—; Rec. artist: Wind Quintets of Peter Muller, Crystal Records, Anton Reicha, Wind Quintets Opus 99, No. 2 and Opus 100, No. 6, Mus. Heritage Soc. Served with U.S. Army, 1943-46. Mem. Internat. Double Reed Soc. (pres. 1973-74). Home: 1281 Scott Dr East Lansing MI 48823 Office: Music Dept Mich State U East Lansing MI 48824

KIRK, GRAYSON LOUIS, educator; b. Jeffersonville, Ohio, Oct. 12, 1903; s. Traine C. and Nora (Eichelberger) K.; m. Marion Louise Sands, Aug. 17, 1925; 1 son, John. Mem. B.A., Miami (Ohio) U., 1924, LL.D., 1950; M.A., Clark U., 1925; Ph.D., U. Wis., 193O; postgrad., Ecole Libre des Sciences Politiques, Paris, 1928-29; hon. degrees from over 35 U.S. and fgn. colls. and univs., 1950—. Faculties U. Wis., Columbia, 1929-40, prof. govt., 1943-47, provost, 1949-50, v.p., provost, 1950-51, pres., trustee univ., 1953-68, pres., trustee emeritus, 1968—, Bryce prof. history internat. relations, 1959-72, emeritus, 1972—; dir. Bullock Fund, Ltd., Bullock Tax-Free Shares, Inc., High Income Shares, Inc., Nation-Wide Securities Co., Dividend Shares, Inc., Money Shares, Inc., Monthly Income Shares Inc.; mem. adv. bd. IBM; trustee emeritus Greenwich Savs. Bank. Author of several works in internat. relations field.; Editor: (with R.P. Stebbins) War and National Policy: a Syllabus, 1942; Contbr. to: Yale Law Rev. Trustee emeritus Asia Found.; trustee, v.p. Tinker Found.; trustee emeritus Inst. Internat. Edn.; trustee French Inst.; bd. dirs., chmn. Acad. Polit. Sci.; bd. dirs. Am. Soc. French Legion of Honor (chmn.), Belgium Am. Edn. Found., Inc., Lycée Francais N.Y.; Fellow Social Sci. Research Council, 1936-37; mem. secretariat staff Dumbarton Oaks Conf., 1944; exec. officer 3d Commn., San Francisco Conf., 1945. Named comdr. Order Orange-Nassau, Netherlands, 1952; hon. knight comdr. Order Brit. Empire, 1955; grand officer Legion of Honor, 1956; Grand Ufficialato dell Ordine al Merito della Repubblica, Italy, 1956; Asso. Knight Order of Hosp. of St. John Jerusalem, 1959; medal Order of Taj, Iran, 1961; cross of grand officer Order George I, Greece; Order Sacred Treasure, 1st class, Japan; commandeur de 1er Ordre des Palmes Academiques, France). Mem. Am. Philos. Soc., Council Fgn. Relations, Acad. Arts and Scis., Pilgrims (v.p.), Phi Beta Kappa, Phi Kappa Tau. Clubs: University, Century (N.Y.C.); Bohemian (San Francisco). Home: 28 Sunnybrook Rd Bronxville NY 10708 Office: Columbia U 225 Broadway New York NY 10007

KIRK, JAMES CURTIS, oil co. exec.; b. Hubbard, Tex., May 10, 1921; s. James Floyd and Edna Pearl (Windham) K.; m. Robin R. Hartness, Oct. 23, 1977; children by previous marriage—James Lee, Carol Lyn, Steven Thomas, Gilbert Paul, Kathryn Ann K. Stromberg. B.S., Baylor U., 1944; Ph.D., Ohio State U., 1949. Analytical chemist Pan Am. Refining Corp., Texas City, Tex., 1944-46; with Continental Oil Co., Ponca City, Okla., 1949-57, 60—, research chemist, supervising research chemist, 1949-57, gen. mgr. research and devel., 1967-75, v.p. research and devel., 1975—; mgr. research Petroleum Chems. Inc., Lake Charles, La., 1957-60. Vice-chmn. Okla. Air Pollution Adv. Council, 1967-71; mem. Sch. Bd. for Kay County Vo-Tech. Sch., 1971-77; chmn. Airport Mgmt. Bd., 1974—; bd. dirs. Kaw Lake Assn., 1975—. Mem. Am. Chem. Soc. (past sect. chmn.), Soap and Detergent Assn. (past com. chmn.), Soc. Petroleum Engrs. Republican. Office: Drawer 1267 Ponca City OK 74601

KIRK, JAMES LAWRENCE, II, accountant, broadcasting executive; b. Thomaston, Ga., June 9, 1926; s. Elmer Edison and Alberta Kathryn (Bennett) K.; m. Joyce Oneita Sheffield, Mar. 27, 1970; children: Marsha, Warren, Melissa, Vicki, Pamela, Randy. B.S., Fla. So. Coll., 1949. C.P.A. Gen. mgr. Mississippi Valley Telephone Co., Carthage, Ill., 1949-50; pub. accountant, Tampa, Fla., 1951-54; chief accountant Sta. WTVT, Tampa, 1955; v.p. Consol. Telephone Co., Moultrie, Ga., 1956-61; pub. accountant, Moultrie, 1962—; pres. Kirk Broadcasting, Inc., including So. Melody, Inc. (Muzak), Atlanta, 1964—. Mem. Moultrie Sch. Bd., 1967-69; active Moultrie Colquitt County Library; chmn. bd. trustees Colquitt County Meml. Hosp., 1981-83. Served with USN, 1944-46. Mem. Am., Fla. insts. C.P.A.s, Ga. Soc. C.P.A.s, Ga. Hosp. Assn. (trustee 1983), VFW. Club: Elks. Home: 904 S Main St Moultrie GA 31768 Office: Box 707 130 1st St SE Moultrie GA 31768

KIRK, JOHN MALCOLM, army officer; b. Seattle, Nov. 23, 1933; s. Charles Gilbert and Evelyn Elizabeth (Canfield) K.; m. Margaret Mary Burns, July 15, 1956; children: Duncan Ronald, Margaret Stacy, Malcolm Stuart, Suzanne. B.A. in Engring., U.S. Mil. Acad., 1956; postgrad., Command and Gen. Staff Coll., 1969, Armed Forces Coll., 1974, Army War Coll., 1975. Commd. 2d lt. U.S. Army, 1956, advanced througn grades to brig. gen., 1980, exec. officer 2d tng.

Brigade, Ft. Ord, Calif., 1971, commdr. 3d Bn. ed Tng. Brigade, 1971-73; faculty adivsor Armed Forces Staff Coll., Norfolk, Va., 1973-74, asst. chief staff G3, 1st Armored div, Europe, 1975-77, chief staff G3 1st Armored div., Norfolk, 1977, comdr. 1st Brigade, 1977-79, chief staff 1st Brigade, 1979-80, asst. div. comdr. 5th Inf. div., Ft. Polk, La., 1980—. Mem. Assn. U.S. Army, Armor Assn. Asst Div Commander HQ 5th Infantry Div Ft Polk LA 71459

KIRK, JOHN WILLIAM, law publisher; b. Toronto, Ont., Can., June 9, 1915; s. William Joseph and Mae Elizabeth (Johnston) K.; m. Mary Violet Pegg, June 20, 1942 (dec. Mar. 1983); children: Mary Louise, John William, Rosemary, Paul, Betty-Anne, Kathleen, Michael. Student, St. Augustine's Sem., 1933-39, No. Vocat. Sch., 1939-40. Sec. to gen. mgr. and pres. Beardmore & Co., Acton, Ont., Can., 1940; asst. purchasing agt. Def. Industries, Ltd., Ajax, Ont., 1941-45; tax editor, mng. editor, asst. v.p. CCH Can., Ltd., Toronto, 1950-62, v.p., 1962-63, dir., 1963—, pres., chief exec. officer, 1969-80; chmn. bd. Formules Municipales Ltd., Farnham, Que., Capital Communications, Ltd.; dir. C.T. Corp. System (Can.), Ltd. Mem. Can. Tax Found., Can. Mfrs. Assn., Can. Law Info. Council, Can. Law Pubs. Assn., Que. C. of C., Toronto C. of C., Toronto Bd. Trade. Clubs: Knights Holy Sepulchore of Jerusalem (lt. Eastern Can.), K.C. (past grand knight), Serra of Hamilton). Home: 256 North Shore Blvd E Burlington ON L7T 1W9 Canada

KIRK, MICHAEL, artist, educator; b. N.Y.C., Oct. 31, 1947; s. Alfred and Ann (Letzter) K.; m. Renee Rockoff, June 25, 1978. B.A. in Art History, Rutgers U., 1969; postgrad., SUNY, Buffalo, 1969-70; M.F.A., Pratt Inst., 1973. Instr. printmaking Parsons Sch. Design, N.Y.C., 1973—. One-man exhbns. include, Marilyn Meyers Gallery, Chevy Chase, Md., 1978, Print Club, Phila., 1975, Picker Art Gallery, Colgate U., Gimpel and Weitzenhoffer, N.Y.C., 1975, 77, 80, Keuka (N.Y.) Coll., 1981, Ctr. Music, Dance & Art, Lake Placid, N.Y., 1982, Murrsony-Williams-Proctor Mus., Utica, N.Y., Gallery 34, Community Coll. Finger Lakes, group exhbns. include, Graphica Creativa/75, Jyvaskyla, Finland, 1975, Nat. Print Show, Potsdam, N.Y., 1976, Bienale Internat. de la gravure, Krakow, Poland, Manscape Okla. Art Center, 1977, Jane Haslen Gallery, Washington, Primera Bienal de Gradado de Am., Maracaibo, Venezuela, 1978, Mitchell Mus., Mt. Vernon, Ill., 1979, Ramapo Community Coll., Snug Harbor Mus., S.I., 1980, Fine Arts Gallery, Parsons Sch. Design, N.Y.C., Bklyn. Mus., Cooper Union, N.Y.C., 1982, Toronto U., 1983; represented in permanent collections, Library of Congress, Pa. State U., Nat. Collection Fine Arts, Phila. Mus. Art, Bklyn. Mus., U. N.D., U. Minn., Colgate U., also corp. collections. Ednl. Professions Devel. Act grantee, 1970. Mem. Soc. Am. Graphic Artists. Home: 307-9 Canal St New York NY 10013 Office: 2 W 13th St New York NY 10011

KIRK, ROBERT L., aerospace company executive; (m). B.S., Purdue U. With Litton Industries, Inc., Washington and, Switzerland, 1959-67, v.p. until, 1967; v.p. def. systems avionics, then v.p. Internat. Tel. & Tel. Corp., N.Y.C., 1967-77; pres., chief exec. officer Vought Corp., Dallas, 1977—; group v.p. LTV Corp. Office: PO Box 225907 Dallas TX 75265

KIRK, ROGER, foreign service officer; b. Newport, R.I., Nov. 2, 1930; s. Alan Goodrich and Lydia Selden (Chapin) K.; m. Madeleine Elizabeth Yaw, Apr. 24, 1954; children: Marian, Sarah, Julia, Alan. A.B., Princeton U., 1952; postgrad., Johns Hopkins U. Sch. Advanced Internat. Studies, 1953. Joined Fgn. Service, 1955; adminstrv. asst. Am. embassy, Moscow, USSR, 1949-50, 51; mem. staff Exec. Secretariat, Dept. State, Washington, 1955-57; staff asst. Office Sec. State, 1960-61, Office Soviet Affairs, 1962-63; polit. officer, Rome, Italy, 1957-59, Moscow, 1963-65, New Delhi, India, 1965-67, Saigon, Vietnam, 1968-69; internat. relations officer Bur. East Asian Affairs, 1969-71; assigned Sr. Seminar, 1971-72; dep. asst. dir. Internat. Relations Bur., ACDA, 1972-73; ambassador to, Somalia, Mogadiscio, 1973-75; dep. dir. Bur. Intelligence and Research, Dept. State, 1975-78; resident rep. U.S. Mission to IAEA, 1978-83; permanent U.S. rep. to UN Indsl. Devel. Orgn., 1980-83; sr. dep. asst. sec. Bur. Internat. Orgn. Affairs, Dept. State, 1983—. Served to lt. USAF, 1952-55. Episcopalian. Office: IO Dept State Washington DC 20520

KIRK, ROGER MANN, consultant; b. Chgo., Feb. 24, 1917; s. Roger Mann and Frances (Shell) K.; m. Ruth M. Cook, Sept. 14, 1940; children—John, Harvey. B.S., U. Ill., 1940; postgrad. in mktg., Northwestern U. Dir. mktg. John H. Dulany & Sons, Inc., Fruitland, Md., 1949-54; mdsg. mgr. Nabisco, N.Y.C., 1954-56; v.p. sales and advt. Cook Chem. Co., Kansas City, Mo., 1956-59; with Lehn & Fink Products Co. div. Sterling Drug Inc., Montvale, N.J., 1959-75, pres., 1970-75; exec. v.p. Sterling Drug Inc., N.Y.C., 1975-77, dir., 1970—; pres. Brown and Williamson Tobacco Corp., Louisville, 1977-79, vice chmn., 1979-81, cons., 1981—. Trustee, mem. fin. com. Children's Asthma Research Inst. and Hosp., Denver, 1970-78; found. chmn. Louisville Mus. History and Sci. Served to lt. USNR; World War II. Recipient Humanitarian award Children's Asthma Research Inst. and Hosp., 1971. Mem. Grocery Mfrs. Assn. (award for contbns. as chmn. mktg. com. 1972), N.Y. Sales Execs. Club (v.p., dir. 1970—), Cosmetic Toiletry and Fragrance Assn. (past dir.). Clubs: N.Y. Yacht, Corinthians, Pendennis, Owl Creek Country. Office: Batus Inc 2000 Citizens Plaza Louisville KY 40202

KIRK, RUSSELL AMOS, author, lecturer; b. Plymouth, Mich., Oct. 19, 1918; s. Russell Andrew and Marjorie (Pierce) K.; m. Annette Yvonne Courtemanche, Sept. 19, 1964; 4 daus. B.A., Mich. State U., 1940; M.A., Duke U., 1941; D.Litt., St. Andrews U., Scotland, 1952; hon. degrees include; Litt.D., Boston Coll., St. John's U., Loyola Coll., Balt., Gannon Coll., Central Mich. U., Albion Coll., Grand Valley Coll.; LL.D., Park Coll., Niagara U.; L.H.D., Le Moyne Coll.; D.Journalism, Olivet Coll., 1977. Pres., Ednl. Reviewer Found., 1960—, Marguerite Eyer Wilbur Found., 1979—; vis. prof. various univs.; dir. social sci. program Ednl. Research Council Am., 1979—. Contbr. to scholarly and popular publs., U.S., Can., Gt. Britain, Australia, Italy, Norway, Austria, including, Sewanee Rev., Fortnightly Rev., Dublin Rev., Yale Rev., Jour. History of Ideas, Annals of Am. Acad., N.Y. Times mag., Fortune, Wall St. Jour., History Today, Gen. Edn., The Critic, Kenyon Rev., Nat. Rev., The Month, S.W. Rev., Commonweal, Christianity Today, Queen's Quar., America, Contemporary Rev., Analysis, Center mag.; founder quar. jour.: Modern Age; editor quar.: Univ. Bookman; Author: John Randolph of Roanoke, 1951, 64, 78, The Conservative Mind, 1953, 73, 78, St. Andrews, 1954, A Program for Conservatives, 1954, Academic Freedom, 1955, Beyond the Dreams of Avarice, 1956, The Intelligent Woman's Guide to Conservatism, 1957, The American Cause, 1957, Old House of Fear, 1961, The Surly Sullen Bell, 1962, Confessions of a Bohemian Tory, 1963, The Intemperate Professor, 1965, A Creature of the Twilight, 1966, Edmund Burke, 1967, Political Principles of Robert A. Taft, 1967, Enemies of the Permanent Things, 1969, Eliot and His Age, 1972, Roots of American Order, 1974, The Princess of All Lands, 1979, Decadence and Renewal in Higher Learning, 1979, Lord of the Hollow Dark, 1979, Portable Conservative Reader, 1982, Reclaiming a Patrimony, 1983, Watchers at the Strait Gate, 1984; also critical intros. and prefaces to reprints standard scholarly works. Guggenheim fellow.; Sr. fellow Am. Council Learned Socs. Address: Piety Hill Mecosta MI 49332

KIRK, SAMUEL ALEXANDER, psychologist, educator; b. Rugby, N.D., Sept. 1, 1904; s. Richard B. and Nellie (Boussard) K.; m. Winifred Eloise Day, June 25, 1933; children: Jerome Richard, Nancy Lorraine. Ph.B., U. Chgo., 1929, M.S., 1931; Ph.D., U. Mich., 1935; L.H.D., Lesley Coll., 1969, U. Ill., 1983. Research psychologist Wayne Country Tng. Sch., Northville, Mich., 1931-34, mental hygienist, 1934-35; dir. div. edn. for exceptional children State Tchrs. Coll., Milw., 1935-42, 46; chmn. grad. sch. vis. lectr. U. Mich, 1942; prof. edn. and psychology U. Ill., 1947-68, prof. emeritus, 1968—; dir. Inst. Research Exceptional Children, 1952-68; prof. spl. edn. U. Ariz., Tucson, 1968—. Author: (with Hegge and Kirk) Remedial Reading Drills, 1936, Teaching Reading to Slow-Learning Children, 1940, (with Johnson) Educating the Retarded Child, 1951, (with Karnes and Kirk) You and Your Retarded Child, 1955, Early Education of the Mentally Retarded, 1958, Educating Exceptional Children, 2d edit, 1972, 4th edit. (with Galagher), 1983, (with Wiener) Behavior Research on Exceptional Children, 1964, (with McCarthy and Kirk) The Illinois Test of Psycholinguistic Abilities, 1968, (with Kirk) Psycholinguistic Learning Disabilities, 1971, (with Lord) Exceptional Children: Resources and Perspectives, 1974, (with McCarthy) Learning Disabilities, 1975, (with Kleibahn and Lerner) Teaching Reading to Slow and Disabled Readers, 1978; Contbr. articles to profl. publs. Served as maj. AUS, 1942-46. Recipient 1st internat. award for profl. service in mental retardation Joseph P. Kennedy Jr. Found., 1962; J.E. Wallace Wallin ann. award Council for Exceptional Children, 1966; recognition award for early childhood edn., 1981; ann. award Assn. Children with Learning Disabilities, 1966, Caritas Soc., 1966; Internat. Milestone award Internat. Fedn. Learning Disabilities, 1975; Distinguished Service award Am. Assn. Speech and Hearing, 1976; Distinguished Citizen award U. Ariz. Alumni Assn., 1977; award for outstanding leadership Ill. Council Exceptional Children, 1980; recognition award Pa. Assn. Children with Learning Disabilities, 1980; Ariz. Div. Developmental Disability, 1980; Helen T. Devereaux Meml. award, 1981. Fellow Am. Psychol. Assn., Am. Assn. for Mental Deficiency (award 1969); mem. Internat. Council Exceptional Children (pres. 1941-43), Nat. Soc. Study Edn. (chmn. 1950 yearbook com), Brit. Assn. Spl. Edn. (hon. v.p. 1962), Sigma Xi. Home: 9500 Morrill Way Tucson AZ 85715 *The satisfaction derived from service to mankind is a manifestation of the idealism of America.*

KIRK, SHERWOOD, librarian; b. Kermit, W.Va., July 12, 1924; s. James Douglas and Magdalene (Elkins) K.; m. Ora Ward, Jan. 9, 1958; children: Diana, James Sherwood, Philip Lindsey. Student, Mich. State U., 1944; A.B., U. Ky., 1949; postgrad., U. Ill., 1949-50. Student asst. U. Ky., 1946-49; circulation asst. U. Ill., 1949-51; head reference and circulation Marshall U., 1951-52; sr. asst., agrl. librarian U. Neb., 1952-54; spl. project asst. Nat. Agr. Library, Washington, 1954-55; reference asst., liaison loan div. Library of Congress, 1955-56, catalog asst., 1956-57; coordinator pub. library services Ky. Dept. Libraries, Frankfort, 1957-63, asst. state librarian, 1963-69; state librarian Fla., 1969-71; assoc. dir. library ops. Ill. State Library, Springfield, 1971-82; exec. dir. Western Ill. Library System, Monmouth, 1982—; planning cons. Perry County (Ky.) Pub. Library, 1966-69; Mem. Ky. Gov.'s Planning Com. on Libraries, 1968; chmn. Fla. Sec. of State's Com. Library Service to State Govt., 1970; adv. com. library services and constrn. Fla. State Library; bd. dirs. Friends of Lincoln Library, Springfield, Ill., 1977—; sec. Resource Sharing Alliance West Central Ill.; mem. Adv. Com. on Edn. in Ill. Author publs. Recipient plaque for outstanding librarian Ky. Library Trustee Assn., 1968. Mem. A.L.A. (council 1967-69), Ky. Library Assn. (pres. 1965-66), Fla. Library Assn., Ill. Library Assn. (chmn. local arrangement 1974, conv., mem. Bicentennial, com. 1974—), Assn. State Library Agys. Methodist (adminstrv. bd.). Clubs: Mason (Shriner), Optimist (Frankfort); Springfield Literary (pres. 1972). Home: 6 Edwardian Ct Monmouth IL 61462 Office: 58 West Side Sq Monmouth IL 61462

KIRK, THOMAS GARRETT, JR., librarian; b. Phila., Aug. 2, 1943; s. Thomas Garrett and Bertha (C.) K.; m. Elizabeth B. Walter, Aug. 29, 1964; children: Jennifer E., Cynthia M., Kristen A. B.A., Earlham Coll., Richmond, Ind., 1965; M.A., Ind. U., 1969. Sci. librarian Earlham Coll., 1965-79; acting dir. libraries U. Wis., Parkside, Kenosha, 1979-80; library dir. Berea (Ky.) Coll., 1980—; vis. instr. Ind. U. Library Sch., summers 1977, 78; bd. dirs. SOLINET, 1981-84, treas., 1982-84. Author: Library Research Guide to Biology, 1978; editor: Course-related Library and Literature Instruction, 1979. Mem. ALA, Assn. Coll. Research Libraries, Southeastern Library Assn., Ky. Library Assn. Quaker. Office: Hutchins Library Berea Coll Berea KY 40404

KIRKBRIDE, CHALMER GATLIN, consulting engineering firm executive; b. nr. Tyrone, Okla., Dec. 27, 1906; s. Zachariah Martin and Georgia Anna (Gatlin) K.; m. Billie Lucille Skains, Apr. 13, 1939; 1 son, Chalmer Gatlin. B.S.E., U. Mich., 1930, M.S.E., 1930; Sc.D., Beaver Coll., 1959; Eng. D., Drexel U., 1960, Widener U., 1970. Chem. engr. research dept. Standard Oil Co., Whiting, Ind., 1930-34; dir. tech. service Am. Oil Co., Texas City, Tex., 1934-41; chief chem. engring. devel. Mobile Oil Co., Dallas, 1942-44; Disting. prof. dept. chem. engring. Tex. A&M U., 1944-47, cons. chem. engr., 1944-47; sci. cons. to sec. of War Bikini atomic bomb tests, 1946; v.p. charge research and devel. Houdry Process Corp., Marcus Hook, Pa., 1947-52, pres. and chmn. bd., Phila., 1952-56, dir., 1948-62, Catalytic Constrn. Co., 1952-56; exec. dir. comml. devel., research, engring. and patent depts. Sun Oil Co., Phila., 1956-60, v.p. comml. devel., research, engring. and patents, 1960-70, dir., 1963-70; now pres. Kirkbride Assocs., Inc., Washington; pres. Avisun, Phila., 1959-60, dir., 1959-68, Sunolin Chem. Co., 1957-68; exec. producer motion picture The Seeds of Evil, 1972; Dir. Coordinating Research Council, 1958-70; pres. Coordinating Research Council, 1965-67; Mem. Pres. Nixon's Task Force on Oceanography, 1969; mem. adv. panel on sea grant programs NOAA Dept. Commerce, 1970-74; petroleum specialist Fed. Energy Agy., 1974-75; sci. adviser to adminstr. ERDA, 1975-77, cons. engr., 1978—; pres. Kirkbride Assocs. Inc., 1979—. Author: Chemical Engineering Fundamentals, 1947; Contbr. articles to profl. jours. Trustee Widener U., Chester, Pa., 1956-72, emeritus, 1972—; vice chmn. bd. trustees, 1959-71; chmn. bd. dirs. Riddle Meml. Hosp., 1965-67, dir., 1965-71. Served as 2d lt. Chem. Warfare Res., 1935-40. Recipient Disting. Pub. Service award U.S. Navy, 1968; Engring. Centennial medal Widener U., 1970; George Washington award Phila. Engring. Club, 1971; Kirkbride Hall of Sci. and Engring. at Widener Coll. dedicated 1965; elected to Nat. Acad. Engring., 1967. Fellow Am. Inst. Chem. Engrs. (pres. 1954, Profl. Progress award 1951, Founders award 1967, Fuels and Petrochem. award 1976, named Eminent Chem. Engr. 1983); mem. Am. Chem. Soc., Am. Petroleum Inst., Alpha Chi Sigma, Phi Lambda Upsilon, Tau Beta Pi. Clubs: Army-Navy, Capitol Hill (Washington). Patentee in field of catalysis, chemicals, plastics and petroleum refining. Office: 4000 Massachusetts Ave NW Suite 805 Washington DC 20016

KIRKBY, MAURICE ANTHONY, oil company executive; b. Southwell, Notts, U.K., Apr. 12, 1929; emigrated to came to Can., 1983; s. George Sydney and Rose (Marson) K.; m. Muriel Beatrice Longmire, 1954; children: Peter Michael, Susan Margaret. B.A. with 1st class honors in Mech. Sci., King's Coll., Cambridge, Eng., 1952, M.A., 1955. Chief petroleum engr. Brit. Petroleum Co. p.l.c., London, 1969-74, gen. mg. exploration and prodn. dept., 1976-80, dirs.' support staff, 1982-83; gen. mgr. BP Petroleum Devel., Aberdeen, Scotland, 1974-76; sr. v.p. oil and gas Standard Oil Co., Cleve., 1980-82; pres., chief exec. officer, dir. BP Resources Can. Ltd., Calgary, Alta., Can., 1983—. Contbr. articles to profl. jours. Mem. Bus. Council on Nat. Issues, Ottawa, Ont., Can., 1983. Served with RAF, 1947-49. Fellow Inst. Mining and Metallurgy (dir. 1980), Inst. Petroleum; mem. Inst. Mech. Engrs., Soc. Petroleum Engrs. (dir. 1980, 81-83). Clubs: Petroleum, Ranchmen's (Calgary). Office: BP Resources Can Ltd 333 5th Ave SW Calgary AB Canada T2P 3B6

KIRKENDALL, WALTER MURRAY, physician, educator; b. Louisville, Mar. 31, 1917; s. Charles Allen and Margaret C. (Caplinger) K.; m. Margaret Jane Allen, Mar. 31, 1948; children—William Charles, James Allen, Matthew John, Thomas Murray, David Edward, Nancy Jane, Mary Margaret, Kathryn Ann, Joseph Howard, Michael Bruce. M.D., U. Louisville, 1941. Diplomate: Am. Bd. Internal Medicine and Nephrology. Intern Univ. Hosps., Iowa City, 1941-42, resident internal medicine, 1946-49; jr. asst. resident internal medicine Gen. Hosp., Louisville, 1945-46; research asst. anatomy U. Louisville Coll. Medicine, 1938-39; staff mem. State U. Iowa Hosps., 1949-72; asst. dept. internal medicine U. Iowa Coll. Medicine, 1949-50, asso., 1950-51, asst. prof., 1951-52, clin. asso. prof., 1952-58, asso. prof., 1958-59, prof., 1959-72, dir. cardiovascular research labs., 1958-70, dir. renal-hypertension-electrolyte div., 1970-72; chief med. service VA Hosp., Iowa City, 1952-58, cons. in medicine, 1958-72; prof. medicine U. Tex. Med. Sch., Houston, 1972—, chmn. dept. internal medicine, 1972-76; dir. med. service Hermann Hosp., 1972-76, dir. hypertension div., 1976—; mem. med. adv. bd. Council High Blood Pressure Research, Am. Heart Assn., chmn., 1967-69; mem. exec. com. Undergrad. Cardiology Tng. Programs, Nat. Heart Inst., 1969-72. Contbr. articles to profl. jours. Served from 1st lt. to maj., M.C. U.S. Army, 1942-46. Decorated Army Commendation medal; recipient Bierring award Iowa Tb and Health Assn., 1966; named Internist of Year Iowa Soc. Internal Medicine, 1971; Louis Mark lectr. Am. Coll. Chest Physicians, 1963. Fellow A.C.P., Am. Coll. Cardiology; mem. AMA, AAUP, AAAS, Central Clin. Research Club, Am. Fedn. Clin. Research (counselor Midwestern sect. 1955-57), Central Soc. Clin. Research, Am. Coll. Chest Physicians (gov. Iowa 1964), Internat., Am. socs. nephrology, Internat. Soc. Cardiology, Am. Clin. and Climatol. Assn., Soc. Exptl. Biology and Medicine, So. Soc. Clin. Investigation, N.Y. Acad. Scis., Assn. Profs. Medicine, Am., Houston socs. internal medicine, Nat. Kidney Found., Am. Coll. Pharmacology and Chemotherapy, Am. Soc. Pharmacology and Exptl. Therapeutics, Tex. Med. Assn., Harris County Med. Soc., Sigma Xi, Alpha Omega Alpha, Phi Chi. Home: 5203 Del Monte Houston TX 77056 Office: PO Box 20708 Houston TX 77025

KIRKHAM, DON, soil physicist, educator; b. Provo, Utah, Feb. 11, 1908; s. Francis Washington and Martha Alzina (Robison) K.; m. Mary Elizabeth Erwin, Sept. 2, 1939; children: Victoria, Mary Beth, Don Collier. Clarinetist diploma, McCune Sch. Music and Art, Salt Lake City, 1926; student, U. Utah, 1925-27; A.B. with honors in physics, Columbia U., 1933, A.M. in Physics, 1934, Ph.D., 1938; Erediplom, U. Ghent, Belgium, 1958; D.Agrl. Scis. (hon.), Royal Agrl. U., Ghent, 1963. Asst. in physics Columbia U., 1934-38; instr., asst. prof. math. and physics, also asso. Agrl. Expt. Sta., Utah State U., 1937-40; hydraulic engr. Soil Conservation Service, Dept. Agr., 1940; civilian physicist Bur. Ordnance, U.S. Navy, 1940-46; asso. physics George Washington U., 1946; faculty Iowa State U., 1946—, Curtiss Disting. prof. agr., prof. agronomy and physics, 1959-78, prof. emeritus, 1978—; Fulbright prof., The Netherlands, 1950-51, Guggenheim fellow, Belgium, 1957-58; lectr. U. Vienna, Austria, 1958, Ireland, 1960, Göttingen (Germany) U., 1974; land reclamation adviser Turkish Govt., 1959; Ford Found. land reclamation cons. UAR; also lectr. Alexandria (Egypt) U., 1961; guest prof. Hohenheim-Stuttgart U., 1982; sect. chmn. Internat. Soil Structure Symposium, Belgium, 1958; panelist IAEA, Vienna, 1960; lectr., Yugoslavia, Bulgaria, 1964; mem. U.S. AID Univ. Study Team, Argentina, summer 1965; panelist on land reclamation FAO, Egypt, 1974-77; council Internat. Sodic Soil Symposium, Budapest, 1964; soil physics del. to internat. congresses and symposia, Armenia, 1969, Moscow, 1971, New Delhi, 1971, Belgium, 1973, Madras, India, 1973; sect. chmn. 7th congress Internat. Soil and Tillage Orgn., Uppsala, Sweden, 1976. Author: (with W.L. Powers) Advanced Soil Physics; contbr. numerous articles to books, sci. jours.; assoc. editor: Jour. Water Resources Research, 1965-71; cons. editor: Soil Science. Dir. Iowa Water Resources Research Council, 1964-73; Active Boy Scouts Am.; mem. Utah N.G., 1925-27. Co-recipient Internat. Wolf prize in Agr., Israel. Fellow Am. Phys. Soc., Am. Soc. Agronomy; mem. Am. Geophysics Union (award most meritorious paper sci. hydrology 1952), Soil Sci. Soc. Am. (chmn. soil physics 1950, Stevenson award 1951, 25th anniversary honor lect. 1961, del. to internat. meetings in Bucharest 1964, hon. mem.), Am. Math. Assn., Netherlands Soc. Agrl. Research, Internat. Soil Sci. Soc. (U.S. v.p. 1957-59), Iowa Acad. Soc. (most meritorious paper math. 1948, physics 1949), Internat. Soil Tillage Orgn. (hon. 1982), S.A.R. (v.p. Iowa 1966), Sigma Xi (honor lectr. U. Iowa chpt. 1959), Phi Kappa Phi, Gamma Sigma Delta. Republican. Mem. Ch. of Jesus Christ of Latter-Day Saints (missionary Germany 1927-30, pres. Hamburg dist. 1930). Patentee. Home: 2109 Clark Ave Ames IA 50010 *My career has been based on these guidelines: Do don't stew. Keep moving. Persist. Don't take yourself too seriously.*

KIRKHAM, FRANCIS ROBISON, lawyer; b. Fillmore, Utah, Aug. 23, 1904; s. Francis W. and Alzina (Robison) K.; m. Ellis Musser, July 9, 1929; children: James F., Elizabeth (Mrs. James Stillman, Jr.), Katherine (Mrs. Geoffrey Hallam Movius), Eugene R. A.B., George Washington U., 1930, LL.B., 1931. Bar: D.C. 1931, Calif. 1936. Law clk. Chief Justice Charles E. Hughes, 1933-35; with firm Pillsbury, Madison & Sutro, San Francisco, 1936—, partner, 1940—; gen. counsel Standard Oil Co., Calif., 1960-70; Mem. atty. gen.'s nat. com. to study antitrust laws, 1953-55, mem. commn. on Revision Fed. Ct. Appellate System, 1973. Author: (with Reynolds Robertson) Jurisdiction of the Supreme Court of the U.S. Drafted for Supreme Court Revision of General Orders in Bankruptcy, 1936, 39. Recipient Alumni Achievement award; George Washington U., 1970; Alumni Merit Honor award U. Utah, 1976. Fellow Am. Coll. Trial Lawyers, Am. Bar Found.; mem. ABA (chmn. anti-trust law sect. 1961), San Francisco Bar Assn., State Bar Calif., Am. Law Inst., Am. Judicature Soc., Am. Soc. Internat. Law, Order of Coif, Delta Theta Phi. Clubs: Pacific Union, Bohemian, San Francisco Golf, Stock Exchange (San Francisco). Home: 3245 Pacific Ave San Francisco CA 94118 Office: Standard Oil Bldg San Francisco CA 94104

KIRKHAM, JAMES FRANCIS, lawyer; b. Washington, May 14, 1933; s. Francis Robison and Ellis (Musser) K.; m. Katherine Drury Dibblee, June 17, 1960; children: Lila Haliday, James Dibblee. B.A., Yale U., 1954; LL.B., U. Calif.-Berkeley, 1957. Bar: Calif. 1957. Assoc. Pillsbury, Madison & Sutro, San Francisco, 1960-65, ptnr., 1966—. Co-author: Assassination and Political Violence, 1970. Served with U.S. Army, 1957-59. Mem. State Bar Calif. (exec. com. 1982—), ABA (antitrust sect., litigation sect.). Clubs: Bohemian; Pacific Union (San Francisco). Home: 2239 Green St San Francisco CA 94123 Office: Pillsbury Madison & Sutro 225 Bush St San Francisco CA 94104

KIRKHAM, PETER GILBERT, banker; b. Red Deer, Alta., Can., Oct. 24, 1934; s. Norman K. and Marjorie K.; m. Theresa Burghardt, 1962. Diploma engring., Royal Mil. Coll. Can., Kingston, 1957; B.A.Sc. in Engring, U. B.C., 1958; M.B.A., U. Western Ont., 1963;

M.A. in Econs, U. Western Ont., 1964, Ph.D., Princeton U., 1970. Mem. faculty U. Western Ont., 1969-73; asst. dep. minister for statistics Can., Ottawa, 1973-75, dep. minister, chief statistician, 1975-80; sr. v.p., chief economist Bank of Montreal, Que., Can., 1980-82, sr. v.p. human resources, 1982—. Served to capt. Canadian Army, 1953-61. Address: Rural Route 3 Carp ON K04 1L0 Canada

KIRKLAND, BRYANT MAYS, clergyman; b. Essex, Conn., May 2, 1914; s. Henry Burnham and Helen Josephine (Mays) K.; m. Bernice Eleanor Tanis, Aug. 19, 1937; children: Nancy Tanis (Mrs. Tom L. Thompson), Elinor Ann (Mrs. Anthony Landrum Hite), Virginia Lee (Mrs. Laird James Stuart). A.B., Wheaton Coll., 1935; Th.B., Princeton Theol. Sem., 1938; Th.M., Eastern Bapt. Theol. Sem., Phila., 1946; D.D. (hon.), Beaver Coll., 1949, Lafayette Coll., 1962, Denison U., 1964; LL.D., U. Tulsa, 1962; S.T.D., Parson Coll., 1966; Litt.D., Washington and Jefferson Coll., 1968; L.H.D., Lebanon Valley Coll., 1983. Ordained to ministry Presbyn. Ch., 1938; pastor, Pa., 38-46, N.J., 1946-57, Tulsa, 1957-62, Fifth Ave. Presbyn. Ch., N.Y.C., 1962—; Vis. lectr. homiletics Princeton Theol. Sem., 1951-56, 64-83; overseas guest lectr. U.S. Armed Forces, U.S. Army Chaplain Sch., 1965, 68, 71, 74, 81; Berger lectr., 1968, Swartley lectr., 1969, T.J. and Inez Raney lectr., 1969, Logan lectr., 1974, Royster lectr., 1976, 80, Staley lectr., 1978, 81, B. Cobb lectr., 1982, George A. Buttrick lectr., 1983, Otis lectr., 1984, B. Cobb lectr., 1982; mem. Commn. Ecumenical Mission and Relations, Presbyn. Ch., 1949-62, Commn. on Continuing Edn., 1967; mem. council Nat. Presbyn. Ch. Center, Washington, 1962-65. Author: Growing in Christian Faith, 1963, Home Before Dark, 1965, Living in a Zig Zag Age, 1972, Experiencing God in Unexpected Ways, 1978, Pattern For Faith, 1982; contbg. author: Evangelical Sermons of Our Day, 1959, Year of Evangelism in Local Church, 196O. Trustee Beaver Coll., U. Tulsa; pres. bd. trustees Princeton Theol. Sem. Named Clergyman of Year Religious Heritage Am., 1975. Mem. Am. Bible Soc. (trustee). Clubs: Rotarian., Tulsa; University, Princeton (N.Y.C.); Nassau. Home: 1158 Fifth Ave New York NY 10029 Office: 7 W 55th St New York NY 10019

KIRKLAND, GELSEY, dancer; b. Bethlehem, Pa., 1953. Student, Sch. Am. Ballet. With N.Y.C. Ballet, 1968-74, soloist, 1969-72, prin. dancer, 1972-74; ballerina Am. Ballet Theatre, 1974-81, 82—. Appeared: TV show The Nutcracker, 1977; created roles in ballets, including: Firebird, 1970, The Goldberg Variations, Scherzo fantastique, An Evening's Waltzes, The Leaves are Fading, Hamlet, The Tiller in the Field, Four Bagatelles, Stravinsky Symphony in C, Song of the Nightingale; Connotations, others; guest dancer, Royal Ballet, London, 1980, 81, Stuttgart Ballet, 1980. Office: care Press Relations Am Ballet Theatre 890 Broadway New York NY 10003 Office: care Dube Zakin Mgmt Inc 1841 Broadway New York NY 10023 *

KIRKLAND, JOHN DAVID, oil and gas company executive; b. McAllen, Tex., June 6, 1933; s. O.D. and Daisy (Donohoe) K.; m. Ann Wales, June 15, 1957; children: David, Solace, Robert. B.A., Yale U., 1955, LL.B., 1958. Bar: Tex. 1958. Atty. Baker, Botts, Shepherd & Coates, Houston, 1958-67; v.p. in charge fin. Pennzoil Co., Houston, 1967-73, exec. v.p., dir., 1973-78; dir. exec. edn. Jones Sch. Mgmt. and Adminstrn., Rice U., 1978-79; vice chmn., dir. Sandefer Oil & Gas, Inc., Houston, 1980; exec. v.p., dir. Roy M. Huffington, Inc. (internat. petroleum operators), Houston, 1980—; mem. exec. com.; dir. Mesa Petroleum Co., 1967-73; dir. Jupiter Corp., 1962-67, Downtown Bank, 1965-70, Pogo, Inc., 1970-77, Plato, Inc., 1973-78. Pres. Houston Ballet Found., 1972-74, chmn. bd. trustees, 1979—; treas., chmn. fin. com. United Way of Houston, 1983—. Mem. Am., Tex. bar assns., Order of Coif. Home: PO Box 4455 Houston TX 77210 Office: PO Box 4455 Houston TX 77210

KIRKLAND, JOSEPH LANE, labor union official; b. Camden, S.C., Mar. 12, 1922; s. Randolph Withers and Louise (Richardson) K.; m. Irena Neumann, Jan. 19, 1973. Student, Newberry (S.C.) Coll., 1940; grad., U.S. Mcht. Marine Acad., 1942; B.S., Georgetown U. Sch. Fgn. Service, 1948; LL.D. (hon.), Duke U., Princeton U., Dartmouth Coll. Deck officer U.S. Merchant Marine, 1941-46; nautical scientist Hydrographic Office Navy Dept., 1947-48; mem. research staff AFL, 1948-53; asst. dir. dept. social security AFL-CIO, 1953-58; dir. research and edn. Internat. Union Operating Engrs., 1958-60; exec. asst. to pres. AFL-CIO, 1961-69, sec.-treas., 1969-79, pres., 1979—; Mem. U.S. del. ILO, 1958, 69, 70, 75, 76, 80-83; Mem. Blue Ribbon Def. Panel.; mem. Commn. on Founds. and Pvt. Philanthropy, 1969-70, Pres.'s Commn. CIA Activities Within U.S., 1975, Nat. Commn. on Productivity, 1971-74; mem. gen. adv. com. ACDA, 1974; mem. Presdl. Commn. on Fin. Structure and Regulation, 1970-72. Bd. dirs. Am. Council Germany, African-Am. Free Labor Inst., Am. Arbitration Assn., Am. Inst. Free Labor Devel., Rockefeller Found., Maritime Inst. Research and Indsl. Devel., Council Fgn. Relations.; chmn. bd. dirs. Human Resources Devel. Inst. Recipient Distinguished Pub. Service medal Dept. Def. Mem. Internat. Orgn. Masters, Mates and Pilots., Nat. Planning Assn. Office: 815 16th St NW Washington DC 20006

KIRKLIN, JOHN WEBSTER, surgeon; b. Muncie, Ind., Aug. 5, 1917; m. Margaret Katherine; 3 children. B.A. summa cum laude, U. Minn., 1938; M.D. magna cum laude, Harvard U., 1942, U. Munich, Germany, 1961, D.Sc., Hamline U., 1966, U. Ala., Birmingham, 1978, Ind. U., Bloomington, 1983; hon. degree, U. Bordeaux, France, 1982, Universidad de la República, Uruguay, 1982. Diplomate: Am. Bd. Surgery, Am. Bd. Thoracic Surgery (mem. exam. and tng. programs coms.). Intern Hosp. U. Pa., 1942-43; resident in surgery Mayo Clinic and Mayo Grad. Sch. Medicine, Rochester, Minn., 1943-44, 46-48, first asst. in surgery, 1949-50, chmn. dept. surgery, 1964-66; asst. resident in surgery Children's Hosp., Boston, 1948-49; surgeon Mayo Clinic, 1950-66, instr. surgery, 1951-53, asst. prof., 1953-57, asso. prof., 1957-60, prof., 1960-66, bd. govs., 1965-66; surgeon-in-chief U. Ala., Birmingham, 1966-82; Fay Fletcher Kerner prof. surgery U. Ala.-Birmingham Sch. Medicine and Med. Ctr., 1966—; assoc. chief staffy U. Ala.-Birmingham Hosps., 1966—; chmn. dept. surgery U. Ala.-Birmingham Sch. Medicine and Med. Ctr., 1966-82, dir. div. cardiothoracic surgery, dir. Congenital Heart Disease Research and Tng. Ctr., 1982—; mem. task force on prevention and treatment of cardiovascular disease in the young Nat. Heart, Lung and Blood Inst., 1977-78; mem. policy adv. bd. for coronary artery surgery, mem. adv. com. crippled children services regional program NIH. Author: (with R.B. Karp) The Tetralogy of Fallot from a Surgical Viewpoint, 1970, (with others) Cardiac Surgery and the Conduction System, 1983; contbr. articles to profl. publs.; editorial bd.: Am. Heart Jour, 1964-76, Am. Jour. Cardiology, 1974-80, Circulation, 1967-78, Jour. Thoracic and Cardiovascular Surgery, 1971-83, Year Book Cardiovascular Medicine and Surgery; corr. mem. editorial bd.: European Jour. Intensive Care Medicine, 1974—; former editorial bd.: Jour. French Soc. Thoracic Surgery. Served to capt. U.S. Army, 1944-46. Hon. fellow Royal Australasian Coll. Surgeons, Royal Coll. Surgeons (Ireland), Royal Coll. Surgeons (Edinburgh), Royal Coll. Surgeons (Eng.); mem. Ala. Acad. Sci., Ala. Heart Assn., Am. Acad. Pediatrics, Am. Assn. Thoracic Surgery (pres. 1978-79), AAUP, Am. Coll. Cardiology (v.p. bd. govs. 1973-74), A.C.S., Am. Heart Assn., AMA, Am. Soc. Artificial Internal Organs, Am. Soc. Critical Care Medicine, Am. Surg. Assn. (recorder 1967-71), Assn. Surgeons Gt. Brit. and Ireland (hon. fellow), Birmingham Surg. Soc., Cardiac Soc. Australia and N.Z. (corr.), Deutsche Gesellschaft Fur Chirurgie, Harvard Med. Alumni Assn., Internat. Surg. Group, Jefferson County Med. Soc., Mayo Found. Alumni Assn., Nat. Acad. Scis., N.Y. Acad. Scis., Royal Soc. Medicine (affiliate), Soc. Clin. Surgery, Soc. Critical Care Medicine, Soc. Surg. Chairmen, Soc. Thoracic Surgeons, Soc. Univ. Surgeons, Soc. Vascular Surgery, So. Soc. Clin. Investigation, So. Surg. Assn., Surg. Biology Club; hon. mem. European Soc. Cardiovascular Surgery, Mexican Soc. Cardiology, N.Y. Soc. Thoracic Surgery. Office: Dept Surgery Univ Sta Birmingham AL 35294

KIRKORIAN, ROY, telecommunications executive; b. Fresno, Calif., Aug. 5, 1945; s. Berge and Jessie Elizabeth (Koesheyan) K.; m. Gayle Jacquelyn Jones, Mar. 27, 1971; children: Nicole, Gina, Adam. Student, U. Uppsala (Sweden), 1965-66; B.S., Calif. State Poly. Coll., 1967; J.D., Hasting Coll. Law, 1970. Bar: Calif. 1970. With firm Conron, Heard & James, Bakersfield, Calif., 1971-74, Cahill Gordon & Reindel, N.Y.C., 1974-75; asst. v.p. legal Continental Telephone Corp., Atlanta, 1975-78; v.p. legal and sec. Continental Telecom Inc., Atlanta, 1978-83; pres. Texocom (formerly Contel Suppply and Service, Atlanta, 1983—. Bd. dirs. Metro Arts, Atlanta, 1983. Mem. Am. Soc. Corp. Secs, ABA, Calif. Bar Assn. Club: Capital City (Atlanta). Home: 3980 E Brookhaven Dr Atlanta GA 30319 Office: Texocom 2580 Cumberland Pkwy W Atlanta GA 30339

KIRKPATRICK, ANDREW BOOTH, JR., lawyer; b. Asheville, N.C., Jan. 16, 1929; s. Andrew Booth and Gertrude Elizabeth (Ingle) K.; m. Frances Gordon Cone, Oct. 9, 1954; children: Christine, Melissa, Charles. B.S. cum laude, Davidson Coll., 1949; LL.B. magna cum laude, Harvard U., 1954. Bar: Del. 1954. Law clk. U.S. Ct. Appeals 3d Circuit, 1954-55; assoc. firm Morris, Nichols, Arsht & Tunnell, Wilmington, Del., 1955-58, partner, 1958—; chmn. censor com. Supreme Ct. Del., 1970-78. Trustee U. Del.; Trustee, pres. Unidel Found., Inc.; Active Young Republicans of New Castle County, 1957-58, Kennett Pike Assn., Wilmington, 1967-68; chmn. Gov.'s Commn. on Organized Crime, 1972-73; trustee Tatnall Sch., Inc., 1972-82. Served to 1st lt. inf. U.S. Army, 1951-53. Fellow Am. Coll. Trial Lawyers; mem. Am. Bar Assn., Del. Bar Assn. (pres. 1978-79), Am. Law Inst., Phi Beta Kappa. Presbyterian. Clubs: Wilmington, Wilmington Country (bd. dirs.), Vicmead Hunt). Home: 9 Barley Mill Dr Wilmington DE 19807 Office: Morris Nichols Arsht & Tunnell 12th and Market Sts Wilmington DE 19899

KIRKPATRICK, CLAYTON, former newspaper executive; b. Waterman, Ill., Jan. 8, 1915; s. Clayton Matteson and Mable Rose (Swift) K.; m. Thelma Marie De Mott, Feb. 13, 1943; children: Pamela Marie Kirkpatrick Foy, Bruce, Eileen Bea Kirkpatrick Sipos, James Walter. A.B., U. Ill., 1937. Reporter City News Bur., Chgo., 1938; mem. staff Chgo. Tribune, 1938—, day city editor, 1958-61, city editor, 1961-63, asst. mng. editor, 1963-65, mng. editor, 1965-67, exec. editor, 1967-69, editor, 1969-79; v.p. Chgo. Tribune Co., 1967-77, exec. v.p., 1977-79, pres., 1979-81, chmn., 1981; ret., 1981; U.S. del. 19th Gen. Conf., UNESCO, Nairobi, 1976. Served with USAAF, 1942-45. Decorated Bronze Star medal; recipient Elijah Parish Lovejoy award Colby Coll., 1978; William Allen White award U. Kans., 1977; Fourth Estate award Nat. Press Club, 1979. Mem. Phi Beta Kappa, Sigma Delta Chi. Republican. Methodist. Clubs: Chicago, Tavern, Commercial, Glen Oak Country, Butler Nat. Golf. Home: 156 Sunset Ave Glen Ellyn IL 60137 Office: 435 N Michigan Ave Chicago IL 60611

KIRKPATRICK, EVRON MAURICE, publisher, editor; b. nr. Raub, Ind., Aug. 15, 1911; s. Omer and Lenna Mae (Hain) K.; m. Jeane D. Jordan, Feb. 20, 1955; children: Thomas Reed (dec.), Mary Ellen, Ann Maureen, Douglas J., John E., Stuart A. B.A. with high honors, U. Ill., 1932, A.M., 1933; Ph.D. (Cowles fellow in govt. 1933-35), Yale U., 1939; LL.D., Ind. U., 1977. Instr. polit. sci. U. Minn., 1935-39, asst. prof., 1939-43, asso. prof., 1943-48, prof., 1948, chmn. social sci. div., 1944-48; asst. research dir. research and analysis br. O.S.S., 1945; asst. research dir. and projects control officer research and intelligence Dept. State, 1946, intelligence program adviser, 1947, chief, external research staff, 1948-52, chief, psychol., intelligence and research staff, 1952-54; dep. dir. Office of Intelligence Research, 1954; exec. dir. Am. Polit. Sci. Assn., 1954-81; editorial advisor in polit. sci. Henry Holt & Co., 1952-60, Holt Rinehart, and Winston, 1960-68; chmn. Heldref Publs., 1970—; editor, chmn. bd. editors World Affairs; chmn. bd. trustees Orgn. for Pub. Research Inc., 1955—; lectr. Howard U., 1957-61; cons. Nat. Ednl. Television, 1963-65; professorial lectr. Georgetown U., 1959—. Author: The People, Politics, and the Politician, 1941, American Government, 1942, Survey of American Government, 1943, Running the Country, (with A. N. Christensen), 1946, Target: The World Communist Propaganda Activities in 1955, 1956, Elections - USA, (with Jeane Kirkpatrick), 1956, Year of Crisis: An analysis of Communist Propaganda Activities in 1956, 1957; editor: World Affairs, 1980—; contbr.: to Man and Society, 1938, Essays on the Behavioral Study of Politics, 1962, Perspectives, 1963, Foundation of Political Science, 1978, The Past and Future of Presidential Debates, 1978, International Handbook of Contemporary Development in Political Science, 1981; articles to profl. jours. Mem. Pres.'s Commn. on Registration and Voting Participation, 1963-64, Commn. on Presdl. Campaign Debates, 1963-64, Presdl. Task Force on Career Advancement, 1966; Trustee Nat. Center Edn. Politics; trustee Helen Dwight Reid Ednl. Found., 1960—, treas., 1964-72, pres., 1972—; dir. Govtl. Affairs Inst., 1954-64; mem. adv. com. on fgn. affairs So. Regional Edn. Bd., 1952-56; chmn. trustees Inst. Am. Univs., France, 1958—. Recipient Com. on Status of Blacks in Profession award, 1980; Pi Sigma Alpha award Nat. Capital Area Polit. Sci. Assn., 1981. Mem. Nat. Arbitration Assn. (bd. arbitrators 1943-47), Internat. Polit. Sci. Assn. (mem. council 1955-67, exec. com. 1958-64), Am. Polit. Sci. Assn. (Charles E. Merriam award 1980), Nat. Acad. Scis. (mem. div. behavioral scis. NRC 1963-66, mem. com. internat. relations in behavioral NRC 1966-70), Am. Peace Soc. (pres.), Phi Beta Kappa, Pi Sigma Alpha (mem. exec. com. 1958-82, pres. 1974-76). Home: 6812 Granby St Bethesda MD 20817 Office: 4000 Albemarle St NW Washington DC 20016

KIRKPATRICK, FORREST HUNTER, management consultant; b. Galion, Ohio, Sept. 4, 1905; s. Arch M. and Mildred (Hunter) K. Student, U. Dijon, 1926; A.B., Bethany Coll., 1927, LL.D., 1949; A.M., Columbia U., 1931, profl. diploma, 1934, 36; postgrad., U. London, U. Pitts., U. Pa., U. Cambridge, U. Oxford; LL.D., Coll. Steubenville, 1958, Drury Coll., 1968; Hum.D. (hon.), Wheeling Coll., 1981. Dean, prof. Bethany Coll., 1927-40, 46-52; gen. mgr. personnel adminstrn. RCA, 1941-46, edn. cons., 1946-53; vis. prof. or lectr. N.Y. U., U. Pitts., Columbia U., U. Akron, U. Wis., Cornell U., 1938-54; asst. to chmn. Wheeling-Pitts. Steel Corp., 1952-64, v.p., 1964-70; vis. prof. W.Va. U., 1970-80; adj. prof. Bethany Coll., 1970-85; dir. Blue Cross W.Va., Inc., Sharon Tube Co., Banner Fibreboard Co.; Cons. Am. Council on Edn., 1938-45, War Manpower Com., 1942-44, Dept. State, 1944, U.S. Civil Service, 1945, Post Office Dept., 1953, HEW, 1970; mem. ednl. program com. USAF, 1948-51; mem. mission to Sweden Dept. Labor, 1962, mem. manpower adv. com., 1963-68. Author research reports and articles on mgmt. and labor econs. Mem. W.Va. Commn. Higher Edn., 1964-70, W.Va. Com. Humanities and Pub. Policy, 1972-77, Edn. Com. of the States, 1973-77; mem. W.Va. Water Resources Bd., 1975-83; Bd. govs. W.Va. U., 1957-69; bd. dirs. Wheeling Symphony Soc., Inc., 1950-81, Wheeling Country Day Sch., 1953-64, 70-73, Wheeling Coll., 1957—, Northern Panhandle Behavioral Health Center, 1974-84; trustee Ohio Valley Med. Center, Inc., Wheeling, 1954—. Mem. Am. Econ. Assn., Indsl. Relations Research Assn. (life), Nat. Assn. Mfrs. (dir. 1965-70), Acad. Polit. Sci. (life), Am. Personnel and Guidance Assn. (life), NEA (life), AAUP (emeritus), Am. Mgmt. Assn. (emeritus), Nat. Vocat. Guidance Assn., Nat. Alliance Businessmen (met. chmn. 1971-72), Beta Gamma Sigma, Beta Theta Pi, Alpha Kappa Psi, Kappa Delta Pi, Phi Delta Kappa. Clubs: University (N.Y.C. and Pitts.); Fort Henry, Wheeling Country (Wheeling); Duquesne (Pitts.); Soc. Friends of St. George (Windsor). Home: Tally Ho Apts 931 National Rd Wheeling WV 26003 Office: PO 268 Wheeling WV 26003

KIRKPATRICK, HAROLD LLEWELLYN, educator; b. Pomona, Calif., May 16, 1919; s. Webster LeRoy and Grace (Colwell) K. B.A., U. of Am., 1952; M.A., U. Calif. at Berkeley, 1954, Ph.D., 1962. Mem. faculty U. Nev., 1960-73; dean Coll. Arts and Scis., 1970-72; prof. history and internat. relations, dean U. of Americas, 1973-75, adminstrv. v.p., 1976—; gen. mgr. Kirk Assos., Reno, 1966—. Dir. YMCA Camps, 1944, 1952, 56-60; dir. recreation dept., Sparks, Nev., 1961-65; pres. Nev. Recreation and Parks Assn., 1965-66; commr. Title III Nev. Dept. Edn., 1973. Served to lt. AUS, 1944-49. Ford Found. fellow, 1955-56, 56-57, 58-59. Mem. AAUP, Nat. Soc. Profs., Am. Assn. Advancement Slavic Studies, Western Slavic Assn., Phi Kappa Phi, Phi Alpha Theta, Alpha Mu Gamma, Sigma Psi. Republican. Conglist. Audio-visual taping: Origins of the Medieval City, 1966. Home: Apto 185 Sta Catarina Mártir (Pue) Mexico

KIRKPATRICK, JAMES C., secretary state Missouri; b. Braymer, Mo., June 15, 1905; s. Ray N. and Lena L. (Rea) K.; m. Jessamine Elizabeth Young, Aug. 18, 1927; 1 son, Don W. Student, Central Mo. State Coll., L.H.D. (hon.), U. Mo. Sch. Journalism. Editor Warrensburg (Mo.) Daily Star-Jour., Jefferson City (Mo.) Post-Tribune, Capital News, Jefferson City; pub. Windsor (Mo.) Rev., 1954-72; co-pub. Lamar (Mo.) Daily Democrat, 1972-74; adminstrv. asst. to gov. Mo.; sec. state Mo., 1965—; campaign dir. Missourians for Progress, 1962; mem. Mo. Gov's Com. Commerce and Indsl. Devel., 1961-65. Bd. dirs. Mo. 4-H Found.; trustee, pres., bd. regents Central Mo. State Coll. Recipient honor scroll Mo. Good Rds. and Sts. Assn., 1968; Honor medal U. Mo. Sch. Journalism, 1969; Achievement award Nat. Notary Assn., 1980; Harry S. Truman Spl. Recognition award pub. service, 1983; Chancellor's medal U. Mo.-Rolla, 1984. Mem. Mo. Acad. Squires, Warrensburg and Windsor C. of C. Democrat. Clubs: Rotary, Lions. Office: Office Sec State 209 Capitol Bldg Jefferson City MO 65102

KIRKPATRICK, JAMES RALPH HILBORN, judge; b. Kitchener, Ont., Can., Dec. 26, 1916; s. James Ralph and Bessie Clare (Hilborn) K.; m. Winifred N. Burston, Apr. 12, 1942. Grad. with honors, Royal Mil. Coll., 1938, Osgoode Hall Law Sch., 1947. Bar: Called to Ont. bar. Barrister, solicitor Shannon & Kirkpatrick, 1947-50; magistrate, judge juvenile and family courts County of Waterloo, 1950-68; sr. judge provincial ct. criminal div. Province of Ont., Kitchener, 1968—. Past pres. Juvenile and Family Ct. Judges Ont., Waterloo Regional Police Commn.; hon. pres. Kitchener-Waterloo Big Bros. Assn., Kitchener-Waterloo, South Waterloo naval assns. Served with Canadian Navy, 1939-45. Decorated D.S.C. Anglican. Clubs: Univ. of Toronto, Hillsboro, Westmount Golf and Country, Caledon Ski, Overseas League. Home: Rural Route 3 Kitchener ON N2G 3W6 Canada Office: 200 Frederick St Suite 1000 Kitchener ON N2H 6P1 Canada

KIRKPATRICK, JEANE DUANE JORDAN, political scientist, government official; b. Duncan, Okla., Nov. 19, 1926; d. Welcher F. and Leona (Kile) Jordan; m. Evron M. Kirkpatrick, Feb. 20, 1955; children: Douglas Jordan, John Evron, Stuart Alan. A.A., Stephens Coll., 1946; A.B., Barnard Coll., 1948; M.A., Columbia U., 1950, Ph.D., 1967; postgrad. (French govt. fellow), U. Paris Inst. de Sci. Politique, 1952-53; L.H.D. (hon.), Mt. Vernon Coll., 1978, Georgetown U., 1981, U. Pitts., 1981, U. West Fla., 1981, U. Charleston, 1982, St. Anselm's, 1982, Hebrew U., 1982, Betheny Coll., 1983, Colo. Sch. Mines, 1983, St. John's U., 1983. Research analyst Dept. State, 1951-53; research asso. George Washington U., 1954-56, Fund for the Rep., 1956-58; asst. prof. polit. sci. Trinity Coll., 1962-67; assoc. prof. polit. sci. Georgetown U., Washington, 1967-73, prof., 1973—; Leavey prof. in founds. Am. freedom, 1978— (on leave); resident scholar Am. Enterprise Inst. for Pub. Policy Research, 1977— (on leave); mem. cabinet U.S. permanent rep. to UN, 1981—; co-chmn. task force presdl. election process 20th Century Fund; cons. Am. Council Learned Socs., Dept. State, HEW, Dept. Def., intermittently 1955-72; vice chmn. com. on v.p. selection Democratic Nat. Com., 1972-74, mem. nat. commn. party structure and presdl. nomination, 1975—; mem. credentials com. Dem. Nat. Conv., 1976; mem. internat. research council Center for Strategic and Internat. Studies, Georgetown U. Author: Foreign Students in the United States: A National Survey, 1966, Mass Behavior in Battle and Captivity, 1968, Leader and Vanguard in Mass Society: The Peronist Movement in Argentina, 1971, Political Woman, 1973, The Presidential Elite, 1976, Dismantling the Parties: Reflections on Party Reform and Party Decomposition, 1978, The Reagan Phenomenon, 1982, Dictatorships and Doublestandards, 1981; Editor, contbr.: Elections USA, 1956, Strategy of Deception, 1963, the New Class, 1978, The New American Political System, 1978; Contbr.: articles to Publius; others. Trustee Helen Dwight Reid Ednl. Found., 1972—, Robert A. Taft Inst. Govt., 1978—; mem. bd. curators Stephens Coll. Recipient Distring. Alumna award Stephens Coll., 1978; Earhart fellow, 1956-57. Mem. Internat. Polit. Sci. Assn. (exec. council), Am. Polit. Sci. Assn., So. Polit. Sci. Assn. Home: 6812 Granby St Bethesda MD 20817 Office: 799 UN Plaza New York NY 10017 *My experience demonstrates to my satisfaction that it is both possible and feasible for women in our times to successfully combine traditional and professional roles, that it is not necessary to ape men's career patterns,—starting early and keeping one's nose to a particular grindstone, but that, instead, one can do quite different things at different stages of one's life. All that is required is a little luck and a lot of work.*

KIRKPATRICK, JOHN ELSON, oil company executive; b. Oklahoma City, Feb. 13, 1908; s. Elmer Elsworth and Claudia (Spencer) K.; m. Eleanor Blake, June 20, 1932; 1 dau., Joan Elson. Student, U.S. Mil. Acad., 1925-26; B.S., U.S. Naval Acad., 1931; postgrad., Harvard U. Grad. Sch. Bus. Adminstrn., 1935-36; LL.D., Oklahoma City U., 1963; Dr. Humanities, Bethany Nazarene Coll., 1967. Founder, v.p., treas. Allied Steel Products Corp., Tulsa, 1936-41; v.p., treas. Kirkpatrick & Bale Oil Co., Oklahoma City, 1945-50; owner Kirkpatrick Oil Co., Oklahoma City, 1950—; hon. chmn. bd., dir. mem. exec. com. Liberty Nat. Bank and Trust Co.; adv. bd. Liberty Mut. Ins. Co.; partner Kirkpatrick Oil & Gas Co.; adv. dir. Union Bank & Trust Co., Oklahoma City, United Okla. Bank, NCCJ. Hon. consul Republic Korea, 1974—; Life trustee Okla. Zool. Soc.; mem., trustee, also donor bldg. Okla. Art Center; bd. dirs. Okla. Heritage Assn., Allied Arts Found.; bd. dirs., past pres. Oklahoma City Symphony Soc.; hon. dir. Okla. State Fair; adv. com. Last Frontiers; council Boy Scouts Am.; sr. adv. bd. Frontiers of Sci. Found.; hon. trustee Mercy Hosp., Oklahoma City, Bus. Com. for Arts, Inc.; trustee, chmn. bd. Okla. Sci. and Arts Found.; past pres. Presbyn. Homes; founder, past pres. Oklahoma City Community Found.; chmn. bd. Lyric Theatre Okla.; hon. life trustee Nat. Cowboy Hall Fame and Western Heritage Center, Water Devel. Found. Okla.; exec. com. United Appeal Greater Oklahoma City, campaign chmn., 1961; chmn. bd. Okla. Theater Center; treas., mem. exec., finance, adminstrv. and devel. coms. of bd. trustees Oklahoma City U.; also donor Kirkpatrick Auditorium at univ., 1965; chmn. Oklahoma City Performing Arts Indsl. and Cultural Devel.; Trust; sec. Oklahoma City Indsl. and Cultural Devel.; Trust Okla. Natural Heritage Found.; bd. dirs. Ballet Okla.; life bd. dirs. Conf. S.W. Founds., Inc.; pres., chmn. bd. Okla. Center for Sci. and Arts, Inc. Served from ensign to capt. USN, 1931-35, 41-45; rear adm. ret. Decorated Bronze Star with V; recipient Distinguished Service award Okla. U., 1959; Nat. Brotherhood citation NCCJ, 1962; AIA award, 1963; Outstanding Okla. Oil Man award Okla. Petroleum Council, 1974; Merit award Okla. Hosp. Assn., 1974; Esquire/Bus. Com. for the Arts award, 1974, 75; named to Okla. Hall of Fame, 1962; donor bldg. Okla. Center Sci. and Arts, 1978. Mem. Ind. Petroleum Assn. (past dir.), Oklahoma City C. of C. (life dir.), Oklahoma Petroleum council (dir.), Okla. Hist. Soc. (life), Harvard Area Group. Clubs: Economic, Men's Dinner, Rotary, Oklahoma City Petroleum (pres. 1959-60). Home: 1800 W Wilshire Blvd Oklahoma City OK 73116 Office: 1300 N Broadway Oklahoma City OK 73103

KIRKPATRICK, JOHN GILDERSLEEVE, lawyer; b. Toronto, Ont., Can., Jan. 28, 1917; s. Herbert Rutherfoord and Edna (Nelles) K.; m. Irena Groten, June 24, 1944; children—Xenia, Kathleen, Patricia. B.Sc., McGill U., 1939, B.C.L., 1942. Bar: Que. bar 1943, created Queen's Counsel 1961. Partner firm Ogilvy, Renault (and predecessors), Montreal, 1942—; Chmn., dir. Anaconda-Ericsson Communications Inc., Ludvig Svensson (Can.) Ltd.; trustee Roy Fund Income Trust; dir. Domtar Inc., Volvo Can. Ltd., RoyFund (Equity) Ltd., Canron Inc., Krupp Can. Ltd. Anglican. Home: 1321 Sherbrooke St W Montreal PQ H3G 1J4 Canada Office: 1981 McGill College Ave Suite 1100 Montreal PQ H3A 3C1 Canada

KIRKPATRICK, RICHARD BOGUE, newspaperman, lawyer; b. Van Buren, Ind., Dec. 16, 1912; s. Otto L. and Magnolia (Bogue) K.; m. Carolyn Ann Hawkins, Dec. 12, 1943 (dec. Sept. 1960); 1 son, Thomas Hawkins; m. Kay Poch Lynch, Aug. 26, 1971; children—Kip Michael, Kimberly Lisa; 1 stepdau., Vicki Lynch Porter. J.D., U. Cin., 1952. Bar: Ohio bar 1952, Ky. bar 1952, U.S. Supreme Ct 1963, D.C., bar 1968. With editorial dept. Cin. Enquirer, 1934-68, polit. columnist, 1948-68, head bur., Frankfort, Ky., 1948-56, Columbus, O., 1956-61, bur. chief, Washington, 1961-68; partner Ansary, Kirkpatrick & Rosse, Washington, 1968-69; sec. dir. Campbell Music Co., Inc., 1968-69; asst. minority counsel U.S. House Ways and Means Com., 1969-70; aide U.S. senator Paul J. Fannin, 1970; staff asst. criminal div. Justice Dept., Washington, 1970—; Cons. NASA, 1968-69; mem. scholarships adv. com. Am. Polit. Sci. Assn. Served to lt. col. AUS, 1941-45, 46-47. Mem. Am., Ohio, Ky., D.C. bar assns., Sigma Delta Chi. Methodist (trustee 1953-55). Club: Nat. Press (Washington). Home: 5006 Westport Rd Chevy Chase MD 20815 Office: Justice Dept Washington DC 20530

KIRKPATRICK, WILLIAM ALEXANDER, steel co. exec.; b. Pitts., May 11, 1923; s. Harlow Barton and Elizabeth (Hillman) K.; m. Jo Anne McCollough, Aug. 20, 1945; children—Carolin Gaylord, William Alexander. A.B., Yale, 1944. With Allegheny Ludlum Industries, Inc., Pitts., 1946—, statistician, 1950-51, asst. to controller, 1951-54, mgr. budgets and statistics, 1954-55, asst. controller, 1955-60, controller, 1960-68, v.p. finance, 1968-73, v.p. adminstrn., 1973-79, v.p. corp. devel., 1979—. Served to 2d lt. AUS, 1943-46. Mem. Am. Iron and Steel Inst., Financial Execs. Inst. Clubs: Duquesne, Harvard-Yale-Princeton, Chartiers Country (Pitts.). Home: Winthrop Rd Rosslyn Farms Carnegie PA 15106 Office: Two Oliver Bldg Pittsburgh PA 15222

KIRKSEY, CHARLEY DARWIN, educator; b. Gilliland, Tex., May 6, 1916; s. Jesse Gardner and Jessie (Patterson) K.; m. Blanche Elizabeth Ashley, June 2, 1941; children—Dara (Mrs. Jerry Leland Carlton), Dale Glen. B.S., N. Tex. U., 1940, M.S., 1947; Ph.D., U. Tex., 1957. Tchr. high sch., Friendswood, Tex., Westminster, Tex., 1940-42; mem. faculty Lamar U., Beaumont, Tex., 1946—, prof. bus. adminstrn., 1960—. Contbr. articles to profl. jours. Served with USNR, 1942-46. Mem. Am. Inst. Decision Scis., Adminstrv. Mgmt. Soc., Tex. Assn. Coll. Tchrs., Delta Sigma Pi, Pi Omega Pi. Democrat. Baptist. Home: 925 Thomas Rd Beaumont TX 77706

KIRKSEY, ROBERT EDWARD, naval officer; b. Atlanta, Aug. 5, 1930; s. Lester Lynn and Florence Ester (Bearden) K.; m. Viola Marie Kaikkonen, July 7, 1953; children: Jennifer Lynn, Robert Edward, Gregg Alan, Andrew Jon. B.A., U.S. Naval Postgrad. Sch., 1966; M.S., George Washington U., 1970. Commd. ensign, naval aviator U.S. Navy, 1953, advanced through grades to rear adm., 1976; dir. carrier programs div. Navy Dept., Washington, 1976-78; comdr. Carrier Group Three, Alameda, Calif., 1978-79, Carrier Group Five, Cubi Point, Philippines, 1979-81; dir. strategy, plans and policy div. Dept. Navy, Washington, 1981-83; dir. plans and policy Comdr. Pacific, Camp Smith, Hawaii, 1983—. Decorated D.S.M., Silver Star, Legion of Merit, D.F.C., Air medal. Mem. Assn. Naval Aviators, Tailhool Assn. Naval Aviators, Lambda Chi Alpha. Home: 33 Makalapa Dr Honolulu HI 96818 Office: Office of Comdr Pacific Honolulu HI 96818

KIRKWOOD, DAVID HERBERT WADDINGTON, government official; b. Toronto, Ont., Can., Aug. 8, 1924; s. William Alexander and Mossie May (Waddington) K.; m. Diana Thistle Gill, June 6, 1953; children: Peter H. A., Gill D. W., Melissa M. T., John R. W. B.A., U. Toronto, 1945, M.A., 1950. Research physicist Can. Atomic Energy Program, Chalk River, Ont., Canada, 1945-48; fgn. service officer Can. Dept. External Affairs, Ottawa, Ont., 1950-69; asst. sec. to cabinet Privy Council Office, Ottawa, 1969-72; asst. dep. minister Dept. Nat. Def., Ottawa, 1972-75; sr. asst. dep. minister Dept. Transport, Ottawa, 1975-78; chmn. Anti Dumping Tribunal, Ottawa, 1978-80; dep. minister service Dept. Supply and Services, Ottawa, 1980-83; dep. minister Can. Dept. Nat. Health and Welfare, Ottawa, 1983—. Home: 572 Manor Ave Ottawa ON Canada K1M 0J7 Office: Dept Nat Health and Welfare Jeanne Mance Bldg Ottawa ON Canada K1A 0K9

KIRKWOOD, GENE, motion picture producer; b. Bronx, N.Y., Apr. 21, 1945; s. David and Helen Stein; m. Shelley Steinberg, Sept. 10, 1977. Student pub. schs., New Rochelle, N.Y. Appeared in: Hot Rods to Hell, 1966, Riots on the Sunset Strip, 1967; producer: films Rocky (Acad. award as Best Picture 1976, Gold and Platinum record awards for soundtrack), New York, New York, 1977, Comes a Horseman, 1978, The Idolmaker, 1981, The Pope of Greenwich Village; partner, Koch-Kirkwood Prodns., 1978—. Recipient Fgn. Press award, 1977; Golden Globe award, 1976; Los Angeles Film Critics award, 1976 (all for Rocky). Office: care Koch-Kirkwood Entertainment 10201 W Pico Blvd Los Angeles CA 90035 *

KIRKWOOD, GORDON MACDONALD, classics educator; b. Toronto, Ont., Can., May 7, 1916; came to U.S., 1946, naturalized, 1960; s. George Leslie MacKay and Gertrude Erie (Marlatt) K.; m. Patricia Marie Frueh, Sept. 16, 1940; children: Michael John, David Hoyt. Sr. B.A., Trinity Coll., U. Toronto, 1938; M.A., Cornell U., 1939; Ph.D., Johns Hopkins U., 1942. Latin master Lower Can. Coll., Montreal, Que., 1945-46; lectr. in Latin U. Sask., Can., summer, 1946; mem. faculty Cornell U., 1946—, asst. prof. classics, 1948-54, asso. prof., 1954-59, prof., 1959—, chmn. dept. classics, 1963-72, Frederic J. Whiton prof. classics, 1974—. Author: A Study of Sophoclean Drama, 1958 (Am. Philo. Assn. award of merit 1959), Short Guide to Classical Mythology, 1959, Early Greek Monody, 1974; contbr. numerous articles, revs. to profl. jours.; editor: Poetry and Poetics, Studies in Honor of James Hutton, 1975. Served to lt. Royal Can. Vol. Res., 1943-45; Can. Navy. Recipient Clark Disting. Teaching award Cornell U., 1979; Ford faculty fellow, 1953-54; Guggenheim fellow, 1956-57; Am. Council Learned Socs. fellow, 1962-63; Nat. Endowment for Humanities fellow, 1977. Mem. Am. Philol. Assn. (pres. 1983), Classical Assn. Atlantic States, AAUP, Phi Beta Kappa. Office: Dept Classics Goldwin Smith Hall Cornell U Ithaca NY 14853

KIRKWOOD, JAMES, author, playwright, actor; b. Los Angeles, Aug. 22, 1930; s. James and Lila (Lee) K. Grad. high sch. Appeared in: Broadway plays Wonderful Town, Dallas, N.Y.C., Panama Hattie, Dallas, Welcome Darlings, on tour, Oh Men, Oh Women, Buck's County, Pa., and on summer tour, The Tender Trap, Buck's County and summer tour, The Rainmaker, summer tour, Never Too Late, on South African tour; appeared on: numerous TV shows, including as Mickey Emerson on Valiant Lady, CBS-TV, for 4 years, Garry Moore Show, CBS-TV, for 2 years; appeared with, Jim Kirkwood and Lee Goodman comedy-satire team in nightclubs, Number One Fifth Avenue, Bon Soir, Le Ruban Bleu, Cafe Soc., Downtown, Blue Angel, Mocambo, Hollywood, Calif., Embassy Club, London, Eng., Tic-Toc, Montreal, Ont., Can.; radio performances include Kirkwood-Goodman Show, WOR, N.Y.C., 2 years, Teenagers Unlimited, Mut. Network, 26 weeks, Henry Aldrich, Theatre Guild of the Air.; (Recipient Tony award for best book of a musical 1975-76, Pulitzer prize in drama 1976 (both for A Chorus Line); Author: There Must Be A Pony!, 1961, Good Times/Bad Times, 1968, American Grotesque, 1970, P.S. Your Cat Is Dead!, 1972, Some Kind of Hero, 1975, also screenplay, 1982, Hit Me with A Rainbow, 1980; playwright: UTBU (prod. on Broadway), 1966, P.S. Your Cat Is Dead! (prod. on Broadway Golden Theatre), 1975, off-Broadway revival, 1978, (with Nicholas Dante) A Chorus Line, 1975; opened, Newman Theatre, 1975; then prod. at, Shubert Theatre, N.Y.C. (Drama Critics award for Best Musical 1975). Served with USCGR, 3 years. Mem. Screen Actors Guild, Actors Equity Assn., A.F.T.R.A., Dramatist Guild, Am. Guild Variety Artists. Home: 58 Oyster Shores Rd East Hampton NY 11937 also 1023 Catherine St Key West FL 33040 *Life has got to be one huge joke. To my knowledge nobody has ever come up with a logical explanation that fits any other alternative. But as long as we've been placed on the joke-board, there's nothing to do but play along with as much high humor as possible. Regards any life hereafter—express right on up to Heaven. I mean, haven't we been tortured enough here? They surely couldn't have any other form of hell that would be half as perverse lying in wait as a surprise. Or could they?*

KIRKWOOD, JOHN HARRISON, steel company executive; b. Pitts., July 3, 1934; s. Harrison John and Sara Teresa (Montgomery) K.; m. Adeline Veronica Zeto, Nov. 26, 1960; children: Kimberly Margaret, Koleen Sara, Kelly Lynn. A.B., Brandeis U., 1956; M.B.A., Duquesne U., 1963, J.D., 1967. Bar: Pa. Indsl. engr., dir. personnel Jessop Steel, Washington, Pa., 1960-65; mgr. labor relations Crucible Steel, Pitts., 1966-68; with Jones & Laughlin Steel, Pitts., 1968—, labor atty., dir. employee services, dir. salary personnel and orgn., gen. mgr. personnel, v.p. personnel, form 1967, v.p. indsl. relations; pvt. practice cons. various mfg. cos. Contbr. articles to profl. jours. Past bd. dirs. Jr. Achievement S.W. Pa., Psychol. Service Pitts. Recipient Sec. Labor Symposium award Labor Mgmt. Coop.; mem. Indsl. Relations Honor Soc. W.Va. U. Mem. Am. Iron and Steel Inst. (vice chmn. labor relations sect., chmn. steering com.), Pa. Bar Assn. Republican. Roman Catholic. Clubs: Duquesne, Pitts. Field. Home: 106 Shadow Ridge Dr Pittsburgh PA 15238 Office: Jones & Laughlin Steel Corp 3 Gateway Center Pittsburgh PA 15263

KIRKWOOD, MAURICE RICHARD, banker; b. Tipton, Ind., Dec. 24, 1920; s. Walter Bryan and Lettie (Cooper) K.; m. Anne Elizabeth Smith, Aug. 30, 1942; children—Candace Lynn, Susan Kay. B.S. with distinction, Ind. U., 1942, M.S., 1943. Instr. Ind. U., 1942-43; gen. mgr. Stars & Stripes, Darmstadt, Germany, 1946-52; v.p. Fidelity Bank & Trust Co., Indpls., 1952-59; v.p., cashier, sec. to bd. Am. Fletcher Nat. Bank and Trust Co., Indpls., 1959—; sec., dir. 101 Monument Corp., 1966-70; guest lectr. Ind. U. Bus. Sch., 1954—; v.p., sec. Am. Fletcher Corp., 1975—; sec. Indpls. Clearing House, 1956-57; dir. instr. Am. Inst. Banking, 1959-61; Sec., dir. Ind. Dept. Financial Instns., 1965—; sec. to adv. com. of banking comptroller of the currency. Author: National Bank and the Future, 1962. Treas. Muscular Dysthrophy Assn., 1959-64; treas. P.T.A., 1958-60; dist. chmn. United Fund, 1957; mem. regional adv. com. to Comptroller Currency, 1970-72; Bd. dirs. Meth. Home for Aged, Franklin, Ind.; bd. dirs., sec. Am. Fletcher Found. Served to 1st lt. AUS, 1943-46. Recipient Meritorious Civilian Service award Dept. Army, 1952; award of appreciation Office Comptroller of Currency, 1962. Mem. Robert Morris Assos. (bd. dirs. 1965-69, chmn. bd. regents Comml. Lending Sch. 1968—, pres. Ohio Valley chpt. 1963-64, Distinguished Service award 1974), Ind. U. Sch. Bus. Alumni Assn. (dir. 1965-69), Nat. Assn. Accountants, Indpls. C. of C., Ind. Traffic Safety Found., Indpls. Civic Progress Assn., Ind. Credit Men's Assn., Sigma Nu, Beta Gamma Sigma, Phi Eta Sigma, Delta Sigma Pi. Methodist. Clubs: Hillcrest Country, Ind. U. Varsity, Ind. U. Men's, Columbia (Indpls.). Home: 5214 Nob Ln Indianapolis IN 46226 Office: 101 Monument Circle Indianapolis IN 46277

KIRMAN, CHARLES GARY, educational administrator; b. Chgo., Feb. 2, 1949; s. Irving A. and Sylvia Lea K.; m. Heidemarie Mocker, Nov. 15, 1976; children: Christian, Courtney. B.S. in Profl. Photography, Rochester (N.Y.) Inst. Tech., 1972. Staff photographer Chgo. Sun-Times, 1972-81; pres. European Beauty Culture Coll., Phoenix, 1982—. Served with USNR, 1966-68. Recipient Nat. Headliner award for spot news photography, 1977; named Ill. Press Photographer of Year, 1975, Chgo. Press Photographer of Year, 1974. Mem. Ill. Press Photographers Assn., Chgo. Press Photographers Assn., Nat. Headliner Club. Home: 14024 N 49th St Scottsdale AZ 85254 Office: European Beauty Culture Coll 4404 N Central Ave Phoenix AZ

KIRMSER, PHILIP GEORGE, educator; b. St. Paul, Dec. 17, 1919; s. Philip and Helen Juliana (Mendler) K.; m. Jeune Ethel Blomquist, June 12, 1942; children—Lawrence Philip, Sandra Jeune. B.Chem. Engring., U. Minn., 1939, M.S. in Math, 1944, Ph.D., 1958. Registered profl. engr., Kans. Instr. Kan. State U., 1942-44; mech. engr. U.S. Naval Ordnance Lab., 1946-48; instr. U. Minn., 1948-54; asso. prof. Kans. State U., 1954-58, prof., 1958—, head applied mechanics dept., 1962-75, prof. engring. and math., 1975—; Vis. scientist Institut Battelle, Geneva, Switzerland, 1970; vis. prof. dept. math. Ecole Polytechnique Federale, Lausanne, Switzerland, 1978; pres. Invenxco, Inc.; cons. Phillips Petroleum Co., 1961-64, Boeing Co., 1966, J.B. Ehrsam Co., 1964, Bayer McElrath (mgmt. consultants), 1965—, Karagozian & Case (structural engrs.), 1974; Dir. Midwest Mechanics Conf. Contbr. articles to tech. jours. Served to lt. (j.g.) USNR, 1944-46. Fulbright scholar to Netherlands, 1951-52; cited by USN for work at Bikini atomic tests, 1946. Mem. Am. Soc. for Engring. Edn. (pres. Kans.-Nebr. sect. 1961-62, chmn. mechanics div. 1972-73), Soc. Indsl. and Applied Math. (vis. lectr. 1972-73, 74-75), Am. Math. Assn., Am. Math. Soc., Soc. het Koninklijk Instituut van Ingenieurs, Sigma Xi, Phi Lambda Upsilon, Phi Kappa Phi, Pi Mu Epsilon. Patentee heated melt recyle responsive to temperative differential of crystal mass, method and apparatus for reproducing ideographs. Home: 1009 Michael Rd Manhattan KS 66502

KIRMSS, FRANK, JR., holding co. exec.; b. Bklyn., Aug. 20, 1935; s. Frank Joseph and Eleanor Catherine (Cross) K.; 1 dau., Natalie Dawn. B.S., U. Omaha, 1962; grad., Advanced Mgmt. Program, Harvard U., 1975; M.B.A., So. Meth. U., 1978. Jet. pilot SAC, 1958-65; pilot Am. Airlines, 1965-72; chmn., chief exec. APO Internat., Dallas, 1972—; pub. Road Test mag., Dallas, 1979—. Mem. So. Meth. U. M.B.A. Assn. Patentee gas saving devices. Home: 6987 Helsem Way Dallas TX 75230 Office: 5201 S Hampton Rd Dallas TX 75232

KIRSCH, ARTHUR WILLIAM, banker, human resources executive; b. Bklyn., Jan. 22, 1941; s. Joseph and Helen (Silverstein) K.; m. Isabel Leader, Sept. 20, 1965 (div. 1980); children: Deborah Beth, Gabrielle; m. Denise McLaughlin, May 15, 1982. B.A., Washington Sq. Coll., NYU, 1962; postgrad., Grad. Sch. Pub. Adminstrn., NYU, 1962-68. Program budget dir. N.Y.C. Human Resources Adminstrn., 1966-68; sr. assoc. E.F. Shelley & Co., N.Y.C., 1968-73; v.p. Citibank, N.A., N.Y.C., 1973-80; exec. v.p. Marine Midland Bank, N.A., N.Y.C., 1980—; pres., dir. Kirsch Bros., Inc., Bklyn., 1978—, K & N, Inc., 1978—. Author: (with William Crinler and Don Cooke) Climbing the Job Ladder, 1968, (with Cooke) Upgrading the Work Force, 1971. Served with U.S. Army, 1962-65. Office: Marine Midland Bank NA 140 Broadway New York NY 10015

KIRSCH, EDWIN JOSEPH, educator, microbiologist; b. Hoboken, N.J., Aug. 25, 1924; s. Max and Lena (Lessing) K.; m. Kathleen Marie Willington, Aug. 10, 1945; children—Glenn Edward, Lee Edwin, Paul Willington. B.S., Mich. State U., 1949; M.S., Purdue U., 1955, Ph.D., 1958. Research biologist Lederle Labs., Am. Cyanamid Co., 1950-53, sr. scientist, 1957-63; asso. prof. Purdue U., 1963-69, prof., 1969—; cons. NASA Apollo project, 1968-69; cons. biol. waste-treatment and waste-reuse, 1965—. Contbr. articles profl. jours. Served with M.C. USAAF, 1943-45. Mem. Am. Soc. Microbiology, Soc. Indsl. Microbiology, Water Pollution Control Fedn., Ind. Water Pollution Control Assn., Sigma Xi. Club: Fortnightly Literary (Lafayette). Home: 1616 Sheridan Dr West Lafayette IN 47906

KIRSCHBAUM, THOMAS HARRY, obstetrician and gynecologist; b. Mpls., Apr. 22, 1929; s. Murray M. and Ella A. (Anderberg) K.; children—Steven, Kristin. B.A., U. Minn., 1949, B.S., 1951, M.D., 1953. Intern U. Minn. Hosps., Mpls., 1953-54; resident in obstetrics and gynecology U. Minn. Hosp., 1956-59; asst. prof. U. Utah Med. Sch., 1959-64; asso. prof., then prof. U. Calif. Med. Sch., Los Angeles, 1964-71; prof. obstetrics and gynecology, chmn. dept. Mich. State U. Med. Sch., East Lansing, 1971—; cons. RAND Corp., 1964-71; spl. expert Reproductive Service Br. Center Population Research NICHD, 1983—. Co-editor: Seminars in Perinatology, 1977—. Served with USNR, 1954-56. Mem. Am. Coll. Obstetricians and Gynecologists, Perinatal Research Soc., Soc. Gynecol. Investigation, Am. Gynecol. Soc., Residency Rev. Com. Obstetrics and Gynecology, Central, Pacific Coast obstet. and gynecol. socs., Phi Beta Kappa, Alpha Omega Alpha. Home: 4974 Sentinel Dr #101 Bethesda MD 20816 Office: NICHD-CPR/RSB Landow Bldg 7910 Woodmont Ave Bethesda MD 20205

KIRSCHEN, BORELL, insurance company executive; b. Trenton, N.J., Aug. 7, 1937; s. Sidney and Nady (Berkowitz) K.; m. Janet Johnson, Aug. 28, 1973; 1 dau., Diane Constance Winthrop. B.A. with honors, Williams Coll., 1959; J.D., Yale U., 1962. Bar: D.C. 1962, Calif. 1963. Contract negotiator/adminstr. N. Am. Aviation Co., El Segundo, Calif., 1962-64; partner firm Gill & Kirschen, Pacific Grove, Calif., 1964-69; dep. dist. atty., Monterey County, Calif., 1969-71; asso. counsel, then asst. gen. counsel Fireman's Fund Ins. Co., San Francisco, 1971-77, sr. v.p., gen. counsel, 1977—; dir. Am. Ins. Co., San Francisco Reins. Co., Assoc. Indemnity Co. Chmn. Pacific Grove Art Center, 1970-71, Gateway Center for Retarded, Seaside, Calif., 1966-67; pres. World Affairs Council Monterey Peninsula, 1970-71; bd. dirs. Monterey Peninsula Mus. Art, 1968-70; trustee Marin Civic Ballet, 1983—. Mem. ABA, Am. Ins. Assn. (chmn. law and regulation com. 1979—), Calif. Bar Assn., San Francisco Bar Assn. Clubs: Williams, Yale (N.Y.C.); San Francisco Comml., San Francisco Rugby. Office: 777 San Marin St Novato CA 94998

KIRSCHENBAUM, JULES, artist; b. N.Y.C., Mar. 25, 1930; s. Louis and Anna B. (Citlitz) K.; m. Cornelia Ruhtenberg, July 18, 1956; 1 son, Matthew. Student, Bklyn. Mus. Art Sch., 1948-51. Prof. art Drake U., Des Moines, Iowa; vis. prof. art Temple U., Phila., 1972-73. Exhibited, Met. Mus., Chgo. Art Inst., Corcoran Gallery, Mus. Modern Art, Whitney Mus., Pa. Acad. Arts and Letters, Nat. Acad. Design, Rome, Florence, Italy, Spoleto, Italy; represented permanent collections, Whitney Mus., Everhard Mus., Scranton, Pa. Recipient Dana medal Pa. Acad., 1953, 1st prize Butler Art Inst., 1957, Hallgarten prize NAD, 1953, I. Maynard award, 1954, Wallace Truman prize, 1955, 1st prize in figure painting, 1960; Fulbright scholar, 1956. Home: 2829 Forest Dr Des Moines IA 50312

KIRSCHNER, STANLEY, chemist; b. N.Y.C., Dec. 17, 1927; s. Abraham and Rebecca K.; m. Esther Green, June 11, 1950; children—Susan Joyce, Daniel Ross. B.S. magna cum laude, Bklyn. Coll., 1950; A.M., Harvard U., 1952; Ph.D., U. Ill., 1954. Research chemist Monsanto Chem. Co., Everett, Mass., 1951; teaching asst. in chemistry Harvard U., 1950-52, U. Ill., Urbana, 1952-54; mem. faculty dept. chemistry Wayne State U., Detroit, 1954—, prof., 1960—; vis. prof. U. London, 1963-64, U. Florence, Italy, 1976, U. Sao Paulo, Brazil, 1969, Tohoku U., Sendai, Japan, 1978. Author: Advances in the Chemistry of Coordination Compounds, 1961, Coordination Chemistry, 1969; Contbr. articles to profl. jours. Served with USNR, 1945-46. Recipient Pres.'s award for excellence in teaching Wayne State U., 1979; Fulbright fellow, 1963-64; NSF fellow, 1963-64; Ford Found. fellow, 1969-70; recipient Heyrovsky medal Czechoslovak Acad. Scis., 1978. Fellow AAAS, Am. Inst. Chemists, N.Y. Acad. Scis.; mem. Am. Chem. Soc., Chem. Soc. (London), AAUP, Brazilian Acad. Scis., Phi Beta Kappa, Sigma Xi (research award 1974), Phi Lambda Upsilon, Alpha Phi Omega, Alpha Chi Sigma. Home: 25615 Parkwood Dr Huntington Woods MI 48070 Office: Dept Chemistry Wayne State Univ Detroit MI 48202

KIRSCHSTEIN, RUTH LILLIAN, physician; b. Bklyn., Oct. 12, 1926; d. Julius and Elizabeth (Berm) K.; m. Alan S. Rabson, June 11, 1950; 1 son, Arnold. B.A. magna cum laude, L.I. U., 1947; M.D., Tulane U., 1951. Intern Kings County Hosp., Bklyn., 1951-52; resident pathology VA Hosp., Atlanta, Providence Hosp., Detroit, Clin. Center, NIH, Bethesda, Md., 1952-57; fellow Nat. Heart Inst., Tulane U., 1953-54; mem. staff NIH, Bethesda, 1957-72, 74—, asst. dir. div. biologics standards, 1971-72; dep. dir. Bur. Biologics, FDA, 1972-73, dep. asso. commr. sci., 1973-74; dir. Nat. Inst. Gen. Med. Scis., 1974—; bd. dirs. Found. Advanced Edn. Scis.; chmn. grants peer rev. study team NIH. Recipient Superior Service award HEW, 1971, 78, Presdl. Meritorious Exec. award, 1980. Mem. Am. Assn. Immunologists, Am. Assn. Pathologists, Am. Soc. Microbiology. Home: 6 West Dr Bethesda MD 20814 Office: Nat Inst Gen Med Scis NIH Bethesda MD 20014

KIRSHNER, DON, entertainment co. exec.; b. Bronx, N.Y., Apr. 17, 1934; s. Gilbert and Belle (Jaffe) K.; m. Sheila Carol Grod, Sept. 20, 1959; children—Ricky, Daryn. Student, City Coll. N.Y., 1951-52; B.B.A., Upsala Coll., 1956. Pres. Aldon Music Co., N.Y.C., 1959-63; pres. screen gems-TV music div. Columbia Pictures, N.Y.C., 1963-67; chmn. bd. Kirshner Entertainment Corp., N.Y.C., 1968—, dir., 1968—; formed Don Kirshner Prodns., 1973; exec. producer TV series Don Kirshner's Rock Concert. Publisher: Born Free (Academy Award 1966), Lawrence of Arabia, (Acad. award 1962), Love Will Keep Us Together, (Song of Yr. 1975). Hon. bd. dirs. Juvenile Diabetes Assn., 1976—. Named Publisher of Year Broadcast Music Inc., 1976, Man of Year Deborah Hosp., 1968, Trendsetter of the Year Billboard Mag., 1972; recipient Creative Achievement award B'nai Brith, 1975. Jewish. Clubs: Friars, Village. *

KIRSHNER, NORMAN, pharmacologist, researcher, educator; b. Wilkes-Barre, Pa., Sept. 21, 1923; s. Samuel and Marie (Frank) K.; m. Annette Grossman, Feb. 14, 1963; children: Naomi Lynn, Susan Laura, Miriam Amy. B.S., U. Scranton, 1947; M.S., Pa. State U., 1951, Ph.D., 1952. Asst. prof. pharmacology Duke U., 1957-66, assoc. prof., 1966-70, prof., 1970—, chmn. dept. pharmacology, 1977—; mem. study sect. NIH, Washington; cons. Roche Inst., Nutley, N.J. Contbr. numerous articles to profl. jours.; editor: Molecular Pharmacology, 1978-82. Served with U.S. Army, 1943-45; ETO, PTO. NIH grantee, 1957—; NSF grantee. Mem. Am. Soc. Biol. Chemists, Am. Soc. Pharmacology and Exptl. Therapeutics, Am. Soc. Neurochemistry. Democrat. Jewish. Office: Dept Pharmacology Duke U Durham NC 27710

KIRSNER, JOSEPH BARNETT, physician, educator; b. Boston, Sept. 21, 1909; s. Harris and Ida (Waiser) K.; m. Minnie Schneider, Jan. 6, 1934; 1 son, Robert S. M.D., Tufts U., 1933; Ph.D. in Biol. Scis., U. Chgo., 1942. Intern Woodlawn Hosp., Chgo., 1933-34, resident, 1934-35; asst. in medicine U. Chgo., 1935-37, mem. faculty, 1937—, asso prof., 1946-51, prof., 1951—, Louis Block Distinguished Service prof. medicine, 1968—, chief of staff, also dep. dean for med. affairs, 1970-76; Cons. NIH, 1956-69; hon. pres. Gastrointestinal Research Found., 1961—; Mem. drug efficacy adv. com. to NRC; chmn. adv. group Nat. Commn. on Digestive Diseases, 1978; chmn. emeritus sci. adv. com. Nat. Found. Ileitis and Colitis. Author: also 650 articles. Gastrointestinal Exfoliative Cytology; Editorial bd.: Médecine et Chirurgies Digestives. Served with M.C. AUS, 1943-46; ETO; PTO. Recipient Julius Friedenwald medal disting. work gastroenterology, 1975; Horatio Alger award, 1979; hon. Gold Key for Disting. Service U. Chgo. Med. Alumni Assn., 1979. Mem. Am. Assn. Physicians, ACP (master, John Phillips award), Am. Gastroent. Assn. (past pres., governing bd.), Am. Gastroscopic Soc. (past pres.), Am. Soc. Gastrointestinal Endoscopy (Rudolf Schindler award), Am. Soc. Clin. Investigation, Central Soc. Clin. Research, Chgo. Soc. Internal Medicine (past pres.), Inst. Medicine Chgo. (George H. Coleman medal). Research in gastrointestinal disorders, inflammatory disease of gastrointestinal tract. Home: 5805 Dorchester Ave Chicago IL 60637 *We need a return to higher standards, and not to equate opportunity with a decline in quality. Striving for personal excellence and achievement is the best approach to the attainment of universal excellence and peace.*

KIRSNER, ROBERT, educator; b. nr. Ukmerge, Lithuania, July 9, 1921; came to U.S., 1935, naturalized, 1943; s. Samuel and Anna (Levine) K.; m. Mildred Dorothy Warshofsky, Apr. 11, 1947; children: Steven and David (twins), Barbara, Kenneth, Tamara. A.B., U. Cin., 1943, M.A., 1945; M.A., Princeton U., 1947, Ph.D., 1949. Instr. Princeton, 1945-49; from asst. prof. to prof. Romance langs. and lit. U. Cin., 1949-64; prof. Spanish U. Miami, Fla., 1964—, chmn. dept. fgn. langs., 1965-73; vis. prof. Johns Hopkins, summer 1948, Nat. U. Guatemala, summer 1951, Tulane U., summer 1957; NDEA Lang. Inst. San Francisco State Coll., summer 1959, NDEA Lang. Inst., Mich. State U., 1961, U. Ariz., summer 1964, U. Calif. at Berkeley, summer 1966; resident dir. Rollins Coll. in Bogota, 1963-64. Author: (with Brent) Cuentos espanoles, 1950, (with Irving) Paisajes del Sur, 1954, (with Kinne) A Repasar, 1954, (with Brent) Bibliography of America Castro's Writings, 1956, New Bibliography of Castro's Writings, 1964, The Novels and Travels of Camilo Jose Cela, 1964, La Catira, novela américo-hispanoj, 1965, Historia de Una Escalera: A Play in Search of Characters, 1965, Four Colombian Novels of La Violencia, 1966, La Ironia del Bien en Misericordia, 1970, Cela's Quest, 1970, La Tesis de Nancy, una Lección para los Exilados, 1973, La Suspensión de Mito en Algunas obras Representativas de la Nueva Novela Hispanoamericana, 1975, Hondradez, Matrimonio y Cortesanía en Fortunata y Jacinta, 1976, De doña Bárbara a Luisiana: feminismo refinado, 1976, Desde Cervantes, 1977, Camilo José Cela: La conciencia Literania de su Sociedad, 1978, La Nueva Novela Hispanica: Un Mundo de Héroes Desarraigados, 1979, Irreductible Identy: A Quixotic Question, 1979, Veinte Anos de Matrimonio en la Novela de Galdos; also articles.; Asso. editor: Caribe. Mem. Princeton Admissions Com.; So. Fla. Mem. Jewish Community Relations Council Cin., 1954-64; Bd. dirs. Hillel Found., U. Cin., 1953-59. Served with AUS, 1943-44. Mem. Am. Assn. Tchrs. Spanish and Portuguese (chmn. lit. sect. 1951, exec. com. 1959-61, pres. So. Ohio chpt. 1950-52), Modern Lang. Assn. Am. (chmn. bibliog. com. Spanish contemporary lit. sect. 1951-54, chmn. 18th-19th centuries sect. 1962), AAUP (pres. U. Cin. chpt. 1962-63, pres. Fla. conf. 1983-85), Central States MLA, So. Atlantic MLA (v.p. 1976-77, pres. 1977-78), Ohio Modern Lang. Tchrs. Assn. (pres. 1960-61), Inst. de Lit. Iberoamericana., B'nai B'rith (v.p. Cin. 1953-54), AAUP (v.p. Fla. conf. 1979-81). Club: Princeton (So. Fla.) (v.p.). Home: 500 Alminar Coral Gables FL 33146 *I believe success should always be in the future. A completed task should be the beginning for a new venture-one that will be less imperfect, hopefully, than the one just completed.*

KIRSTEIN, LINCOLN, ballet promoter; b. Rochester, N.Y., May 4, 1907; s. Louis E. and Rose (Stein) K.; m. Fidelma Cadmus, Apr. 1941. B.S., Harvard, 1930. Founder Hound and Horn (lit. Periodical), 1927, editor, 1927-34; established Sch. Am. Ballet, N.Y.C., 1933, now pres. Dir., N.Y. City Ballet Co.; dir. gen., Am. Ballet.; Author: Dance: A Short History of Theatrical Dancing, 1935, Blast at Ballet, 1938; poems Low Ceiling, 1935; Ballet Alphabet, 1939, Ballet: Bias of Belief, 1983; pub.: Pavel Tchelitchew Drawings, 1947, Elie Nadelman Drawings, 1949, The Classic Ballet, 1952, Rhymes & More Rhymes of a Pfc, 1965, Movement and Metaphore: Four Centuries of Ballet, 1969, Elie Nadelman, 1973, New York City Ballet, 1973, Nijinsky Dancing, 1975. Recipient Presdl. Medal of Freedom, 1984, N.Y. State Gov.'s Arts award, 1984. Address: Sch Am Ballet 144 W 66th St New York NY 10023

KIRSTEN, DOROTHY, opera singer; b. Montclair, N.J., July 6, 1919; d. George W. and Margaret (Beggs) K.; m. John D. French, July 18, 1955. Mus. tng., U.S., France and Italy; Mus.D., Ithaca Coll.; D.F.A., Santa Clara U. Debut as Mimi in: La Boheme, Chgo. Opera Co., Nov. 1940; Debut as Musetta in: debut La Boheme, Met. Opera Co., Dec., 1945; has sung roles of Violetta; Cho Cho San; Juliet; Marguerite; Manon Lescaut; Nedda; Micaela; Louise; Fiora; Tosca; Mimi; Massanet Manon; Cressida; Girl of Golden West and many operettas; also appeared: films Mr. Music, The Great Caruso. Episcopalian. Address: care Met Opera Lincoln Center New York NY 10023

KIRSTEUER, ERNST KARL EBERHART, biologist; b. Vienna, Austria, Sept. 28, 1933; came to U.S., 1965; s. Ernst and Barbara (Reichhalter) K.; m. Erika Stepnitz, Jan. 18, 1958. Ph.D. (research fellow 1958-60), U. Vienna, 1961. Instr. U. Vienna, 1961-62; prof. marine biology U. Cumana, Venezuela, 1963-65; asst. curator Am. Mus. Natural History, N.Y.C., 1965-70, asso. curator, 1970-75, chmn., curator, 1975—; corp. mem. Bermuda Biol. Sta. for Research, 1979—. Contbr. articles in field to profl. jours. NSF grantee, 1968-71. Mem. Am. Soc. Zoologists, Soc. Systematic Zoology, Internat. Assn. Meiobenthologists, Internat. Oceanographic Found., Biol. Soc. Washington. Club: West Side Rifle and Pistol. Office: Central Park W 79 th St New York NY 10024

KIRWAN, THOMAS M., television network executive; b. Passaic, N.J., Feb. 22, 1940; s. Raymond F. and Gertrude (G.) K.; m. Gloria E. Schnabel, June 18, 1966; children: Gloria, Kristen, Thomas. B.S., Providence Coll., 1962; M.B.A., Fairleigh Dickenson U., 1969. C.P.A. With Price Waterhouse & Co., N.Y.C., 1965-68; asst. to treas. and controller Elgin Nat. Industries, N.Y.C., 1969-72, v.p. fin., 1972-74, Holt Rinehart & Winston div. CBS, N.Y.C., 1974-76; pres. W.B. Saunders Co. div. CBS, Phila., 1976-78; v.p. fin., chief fin. officer CBS, Inc., N.Y.C., 1978-81, Sr. v.p., 1981; pres. CBS Columbia Group, 1981—. Served to lt. U.S. Army, 1963-65. Mem. Am. Inst. C.P.A.s, N.J. Soc. C.P.A.s. Republican. Roman Catholic. Office: CBS 51 W 52d St New York NY 10019

KIRWAN, WILLIAM ENGLISH, II, mathematics educator, university official; b. Louisville, Apr. 14, 1938; s. Albert Dennis and Elizabeth (Heil) K.; m. Patricia Ann Harper, Aug. 27, 1960; children: William English, III, Ann Elizabeth. B.A., U. Ky., 1960; M.S. (NDEA fellow 1960-63), Rutgers U., 1962, Ph.D., 1964. Instr. Rutgers U., 1963-64; mem. faculty U. Md., 1964—, prof. math., 1972—, chmn. dept., 1977-81, vice chancellor for acad. affairs, 1981—; vis. lectr. London U., 1966-67; program dir. NSF, 1975-76. Contbr. articles to profl. jours. Mem. adv. bd., Montgomery County (Md.), 1975—. Mem. Am. Math. Soc. (council 1980—, editor Proc. 1980—), Math. Assn. Am., Phi Beta Kappa, Sigma Xi, Omicron Delta Kappa. Office: Dept Math Univ Md College Park MD 20742

KISBANY, JACKIE EDITH, business executive; b. Lakewood, Ohio, Nov. 17, 1928; d. Sidney Walter and Della N. (Korver) Jackson; m. Frederick N. Kisbany; 1 dau., by previous marriage, Deborah Downs Cottingham Dryer. B.S. cum laude, Miami U., Oxford, Ohio, 1950. Sec. (to Henry Laribee) Laribee & Cooper (Lawyers), Medina, Ohio, 1955-69; to Baya M. Harrison Harrison, Greene, Mann, Davenport (et al, Lawyers), St. Petersburg, Fla., 1970-72; corp. sec., sec. to chmn. bd. Jack Eckerd Corp., Clearwater, Fla., 1972—. Mem. Beta Gamma Sigma., Delta Zeta. Republican. Home: 601 Clearwater Point 830 S Gulfview Blvd Clearwater Beach FL 33515 Office: PO Box 4689 Clearwater FL 33518

KISELEWSKI, JOSEPH, sculptor; b. Browerville, Minn., Feb. 16, 1901; s. Blasius and Sophie (Wollney) K.; m. Adeline Peters, June 20, 1931. Ed., Mpls. Sch. Art, 1918-21, N.A.D., 1921-23, Beaux Arts Inst. Design, 1923-25. Works: statue of Gen. Pulaski, Milwa., fishery pediment for the, U.S. Dept. of Commerce Bldg., Washington; exterior and interior work on George Rogers Clark Meml, Vincennes, Ind.; groups at entrance of, Bronx County Courthouse, N.Y.C., figure of John Wesley, Winston-Salem, N.C., Katherine Ely Tiffany sun dial, Bryn Mawr (Pa.) Coll., Madonna and Child, Rosary Coll., River Forest, Ill., Sea horse fountain, Huntington Mus., Brookgreen, S.C., 3 medallions for, Lyman Ellyn Mus., New London, Conn., meml. to Jessir L. Eddy, Tarrytown, N.Y., two life size statues for garden at, St. Joseph's Ch., Browerville, Minn., giant sundial, Bus. Systems Bldg., and, four fountains for, RCA Bldg., New York World's Fair, 1939, 11 works for, Met. Housing Project, N.Y.C.; heroic figure of Christ for Bishop's Monument, Fargo, N.D., Good Conduct Medal for, U.S. War Dept., World Peace Medal for, Soc. of Medalists, N.Y.C.; bronze statue of Our Lady of the Mountains, Covington, Ky.; 4 plaques for, House Chamber of Capitol Bldg., 2 reliefs for, Gen. Accounting Bldg., Washington, heroic statue of John Peter Zenger, Bronx, N.Y., World War II meml. Vets, Cemetary Holland, Justice; large limestone panel, N.Y.C. Cts. Bldg., Moses for, Syracuse U. Law Sch., 1966, Harold Vanderbilt bronze statue, U. Nashville, 1965, Sylvanus Thayer bronze bust for, Hall of Fame for Great Ams., N.Y.U., 1966, Gilmore D. Clarke bust, NAD; medals John F. Kennedy; others. (Awarded Prix de Rome 1926-29, Beaux Arts Paris prize 1925-26, Elizabeth N. Watrous gold medal 1937, silver medal, Archtl. League, N.Y.C.). Asso. fellow Am. Acad. in Rome.; Mem. NAD, Archtl. League of N.Y., Nat. Sculpture Soc. Roman Catholic. Club: Century Assn. Home: PO Box 93 Browerville MN 56438

KISER, CLYDE VERNON, retired demographer; b. Bessemer City, N.C., July 22, 1904; s. Augustus Burton and Minnie May (Carpenter) K.; m. Louise Venable Kennedy, Feb. 24, 1934 (dec. Mar. 1954). A.B. (Mangum medal 1925), U. N.C., 1925, A.M., 1927; Ph.D. (Richard W. Gilder fellow 1930-31), Columbia, 1932. Research fellow Milbank Meml. Fund, N.Y.C., 1931-33, research asso., mem. tech. staff, 1933-62, sr. mem. tech. staff, 1962-69, v.p. for tech. affairs, 1969-70; statis. cons. USPHS, 1936; vis. research asso., sr. research demographer Office Population Research, Princeton, 1942-75; adj. prof. sociology N.Y. U., 1945-56; Cons. Pan Am. Health, 1967; Mem. Census Adv. Com., 1965-71, Nat. Com. on Vital and Health Statistics, 1965-69; chmn. local arrangements com. N.Y.C., Internat. Population Conf., 1961; mem. standing com. Pub. Health Conf. Records and Statistics, Div. Vital Statistics, Dept. Health, Edn. and Welfare, 1958- 64, chmn. subcom. fertility measurement, 1963, chmn. subcom. on population dynamics, 1968-69. Author: Sea Island to City: A Study of St. Helena Islanders in Harlem and Other Urban Centers, 1932, Group Differences in Urban Fertility, 1942, (with Grabill and Whelpton) The Fertility of American Women, 1958, (with Grabill and Campbell) Trends and Variations in Fertility in the United States, 1968, The Milbank Memorial Fund: Its Leaders and Its Work, 1905-74, 1975; Editor: Research in Family Planning, 1962, (with Whelpton) Social and Psychological Factors Affecting Fertility, vols. I- V, 1946-58, Estudios de Demografía, 1967, Forty Years of Research in Human Fertility, 1971, (with A. L. Kiser) Kiser-Carpenter Chronicle, 1983. Bd. dirs. Gallaudet Coll., 1968-81. Recipient Grant Squires prize Columbia, 1940. Fellow Am. Statis. Assn.; mem. Am. Eugenics Soc. (pres. 1963-69), Population Assn. Am. (pres. 1952-53), Eastern Sociol. Soc. (v.p. 1959-60, chmn. com. social statistics 1960-68), Internat. Union Sci. Study Population (chmn. U.S. nat. com. 1958-61), Am. Pub. Health Assn. (com. on vital and health statistics monographs), Am. Sociol. Assn. Democrat. Lutheran. Home: 605 N 14th St Bessemer City NC 28016 *In youth time often drags and ones perception of a lifetime is that of virtual eternity. In retirement the years speed by like mad and one is awed by the shortness of man's allotted time on earth.*

KISER, JACKSON L., federal judge; b. June 24, 1929; m. Carole Gorman; children: Jackson, William, John Michael, Elizabeth Carol. B.A., Concord Coll., 1951; J.D., Washington and Lee U., 1952. Bar: Va. Asst. U.S. atty. Western Dist. Va., 1958-61; assoc., then ptnr. R.R. Young, Young, Kiser, Haskins, Mann, Gregory & Young P.C., Danville, Va., 1961; now judge U.S. Dist. Ct. (we. dist.) Va. Mem. Martinsville City Sch. Bd., 1971-77. Served with JAGC, U.S. Army, 1952-54; served to capt. USAR, 1955-61. Mem. ABA, Am. Coll. Trial Lawyers (state com.), Va. Bar Assn. (exec. com.), Va. State Bar, Va. Trial Lawyers Assn., 4th Cir. Jud. Conf. (permanent mem.), Martinsville-Henry County Bar Assn., Order of Coif. Office: US Dist Ct PO Box 3326 Danville VA 24541 *

KISER, JAMES WEBB, banker, lawyer; b. Belmont, N.C., Aug. 16, 1934; s. Walter Webb and Lottie (Bumgardner) K.; m. Nancy Lee Howard, Feb. 9, 1963; children: James Leland, Robert Howard, Kenneth Webb. B.S., Davidson Coll., 1956; J.D. with honors, U. N.C., 1959. Bar: N.C., U.S. Supreme Ct. Asso. firm Ervin, Horack, Snepp & McArtha, Charlotte, N.C., 1962-64; asst. city atty., Charlotte, 1964-65, acting city atty., 1965-66, city atty., 1966-68; v.p., gen. counsel, corp. sec. N.C. Nat. Bank, Charlotte, 1968—, sr. v.p., 1974—; v.p., sec., gen. counsel NCNB Corp., 1968-74, sr. v.p., sec., gen. counsel, 1974—; sec. NCNB Properties, 1968—, NCNB Mortgage Corp., 1969. Editor-in-chief: N.C. Law Rev, 1958-59. Served to capt. JAGC AUS, 1959-62. Decorated Commendation medal. Mem. Am., N.C., 26th Jud. Dist. bar assns., N.C. State Bar, Am. Soc. Corp. Secs., Order of Coif. Methodist. Clubs: Charlotte Country, Charlotte City. Home: 1316 Biltmore Dr Charlotte NC 28207 Office: One NCNB Plaza Charlotte NC 28255

KISER, ROBERT WAYNE, chemistry educator; b. Rock Island, Ill., Apr. 26, 1932; s. Jay Clifford and Margaret W.M. (Lutz) K.; m. Barbara Marie Hatje, May 29, 1954; children: Mark David, Scott Alan, Ann Marie. B.A., St. Ambrose Coll., 1953; M.S., Purdue U., 1955, Ph.D., 1958. Mem. faculty Kans. State U. at Manhattan, 1957-67, assoc. prof. chemistry, 1962-66, prof., 1966-67; mem. faculty U. Ky., Lexington, 1967-80, prof., 1967—, chmn. dept., 1968-72; dir. Mass Spectrometry Center, 1967—, dir. grad. study chemistry, 1968-72; Cons. Batelle Meml. Inst., Columbus, O., 1963-68, Midwest Research Inst., Kansas City, Mo., 1967—. Author: Problems and Experiments in Instrumental Analysis, 1963, Introduction to Mass Spectrometry and Its Applications, 1965; Contbr. articles to profl. jours. Named hon. citizen Louisville, 1970. Mem. Alumni Assn. St. Ambrose Coll. (merit award 1971), Am. Chem. Soc., Am. Phys. Soc., Royal Soc. Chemistry, Am. Soc. Mass Spectrometry, Mass Spectrometry Soc. Japan, Sigma Xi, Alpha Chi Sigma. Home: 781 Glendover Rd Lexington KY 40502

KISH, GEORGE, geographer, educator; b. Budapest, Hungary, Nov. 24, 1914; came to U.S., 1939; m. Elvina Anger, 1949; 1 dau. A.B. cum laude, Ecole Libre des Scle. Politiques, Paris, 1935; M.A. in Geography and History, U. Paris, Sorbonne, 1937; M.S., U. Budapest, 1938, D.Sc., 1939; Ph.D., U. Mich., 1945. Vol. Hungarian Ctr. for Tariff Policy, 1933; asst. sec. Hungarian Assn. Textile Industries, 1936-39; asst. dept. geography U. Mich., 1939-40, teaching fellow, 1940-43, instr. dept. history, 1942, instr. dept. geography, 1943-46, asst. prof., 1946-50, assoc. prof., 1950-56, prof., 1956—, William Herbert Hobbs prof., 1981—, curator maps Clements Library, 1945-46; vis. prof. Northwestern U., 1946; vis. assoc. prof. U. Minn., 1953, James Ford Bell lectr., 1966; Carnegie Disting. vis. prof. U. Hawaii, 1957; Eva Germaine Rivington Taylor Lectr. Royal Geog. Soc., London, 1968; Kenneth Nebenzahl lectr. Newberry Library, Chgo., 1980. Author: Le Probleme de la Population au Japon, 1936, Land Reform in Italy: Observations on the Changing Face of the Mediterranean, 1966, History of Cartography, 1973, A Source Book in Geography, 1978, Bibliography of International Geographical Congresses: 1871-1976, 1979, La Carte, Image des Civilisations, 1980, (12 books) Around the World Series, 1956-66; contbr. articles to encys. and profl. jours. Pres. Ann Arbor (Mich.) Symphony Orch., 1972-74, Mich. Orch. Assn., 1977-79. Served with OSS, 1942-45. Recipient Andree plaque for Polar Studies Swedish Geog. Soc., 1973, Greater Linaeus Silver medal History of Scis. Royal Swedish Acad. Scis., 1973, Jomard prize Paris Geog. Soc., 1981, Honors award Assn. Am. Geographers, 1979. Mem. Hungarian Geog. Soc. (hon.), Paris Geog. Soc. (hon.), Italian Geog. Soc., Assn. Am. Geographers, Medieval Acad. Am., Am. Assn. Advancement of Slavic Studies (exec. bd. 1961-71), Internat. Geog. Union (chmn. U.S. nat. com. 1966-73, sec.-treas. Working Group on Old Maps 1964—). Office: Geography Program U Mich Ann Arbor MI 48109 *Born and raised in Europe, it has been my good fortune to have been able to continue my professional career in the United States. As a teacher and practioner of geography, I have had the privilege of contributing to the knowledge of other lands and peoples in our own country, as well as training professional geographers.*

KISH, LESLIE, emeritus educator, research statistician; b. Poprad, Hungary, July 27, 1910; came to U.S., 1926, naturalized, 1936; s. Albert and Serena (Spiegel) Kiss; m. Rhea Helen Kuleske, Mar. 3, 1947; children: Carla Elene, Andrea Stefanie. B.S. in Math cum laude, CCNY, 1939; M.A. in Math. Statistics, U. Mich., 1948; Ph.D. in Sociology, U. Mich., 1952. Sect. head U.S. Bur. Census, 1940-41; statistician Dept. Agr., 1941-47; mem. faculty U. Mich., 1951—, prof. sociology, 1960-81, prof. emeritus, 1981—, Henry Russel lectr., 1981, sampling head of the, 1951—; program dir., research scientist Inst. Social Research, 1963—, dir. sampling program fgn. statisticians, 1962-81; vis. prof. in statistics London Sch. Econs., 1965, 69, 72-73; cons. World Fertility Survey. Author: Survey Sampling, 1965; contbr. numerous articles to profl. jours., chpts. to books. Served with USAAF, 1942-45. Recipient Distinguished faculty award U. Mich., 1975. Fellow Am. Statis. Assn. (v.p. 1973-75, pres. 1977), Internat. Statis. Inst., Internat. Assn. Survey Statisticians (v.p. 1977-79, pres. 1983-85), Am. Sociol. Assn., Royal Statis. Soc. (hon. fellow), AAAS, Am. Acad. Arts and Scis.; mem. Population Assn. Am., Inter-Am. Statis. Inst., Internat. Union Sci. Study Population, Phi Beta Kappa, Sigma Xi. Home: 702 Sunset Rd Ann Arbor MI 48103 Office: Inst Social Research U Mich Ann Arbor MI 48106 *Survey sampling uses chance to achieve statistical representation with randomized selection of samples from defined populations. In social research we perceive populations as composed of groups and communities, and hope that we contribute toward a better, safer, more predictable future.*

KISHI, TOYOHISA, banker; b. Kanonji, Kagawa Prefecture, Japan, June 3, 1929; came to U.S., 1977; s. Toru and Mieko (Yokoyama) K.; m. Yoko, Nov. 9, 1957; children: Hitoshi, Tetsuro. Edn., Kyoto U., Japan. Dep. gen. mgr. Fuji Bank, Ltd., Tokyo, 1973-76, dep. chief mgr. internat. div., 1976-77; pres. Fuji Bank and Trust Co., N.Y.C., 1977-81, chmn., 1981—; dir., gen. mgr. Fuji Bank, Ltd., N.Y.C., 1981—. Home: 117 E 57th St New York NY 10022 Office: Fuji Bank Ltd 1 World Trade Ctr New York NY 10048

KISHIMOTO, YASUO, neurology educator, neurochemist; b. Osaka, Japan, Apr. 11, 1925; came to U.S., 1962; s. Yasuichi and Ohiyono (Sugimura) K.; m. Miyoko Nishikawa, May 12, 1949; children: Tsutomu, Yoriko, Takashi, Momoko Anne. B.S., Kyoto U., Japan, 1948, Ph.D., 1956. Assoc. research biochemist U. Mich., Ann Arbor, 1967; sr. investigator G.D. Searle & Co., Skokie, Ill., 1967-69, Eunice Kennedy Shriver Ctr., Waltham, Mass., 1969-76; assoc. biochemist Mass. Gen. Hosp., Boston, 1969-76; assoc. Harvard U. Med. Sch., 1969-76; dir. Biochem. Research John F. Kennedy Inst., Balt., 1976—; prof. neurology Johns Hopkins U., Balt., 1976—; cons. grant revs. NIH, 1981—, NSF. Author: Methods of Neurochemistry: Research Methods in Neurochemstry, Vol. 3, 1978, Handbook of Neurochemistry, 1983, The Enzymes, Vol. 16, 1984; contbr. numerous articles in field to profl. jours. Recipient The Moore award Am. Soc. Neuropathology, 1976; grantee NIH, 1969, NSF, 1981—. Mem. Am. Soc. Biol. Chemists, Am. Soc. Neurochemistry, Internat. Soc. Neurochemistry, AAAS, Japanese Soc. Biochemistry, Japanese Biochem. Soc., Internat. Soc. Glycoconjugates. Home: 4506 Roland

Ave Baltimore MD 21210 Office: Johns Hopkins Univ 707 N Broadway Baltimore MD 21205

KISLIK, LOUIS A., mktg. co. exec.; b. N.Y.C., Apr. 18, 1931; s. Louis Krimont and Isabelle (Deutelbaum) K.; m. Sheila Ann Cohn, Aug. 4, 1954; 1 son, Harold Alan. B.A., Swarthmore Coll., 1952; M.B.A., U. Pa., Phila., 1954. Salesman data processing div. I.B.M. Corp., Garden City, N.Y., 1958-62; controller Pubs. Clearing House, Port Washington, N.Y., 1962-67, exec. mgr., 1967-69, pres., 1969-78, cons., 1978—; dir. Abilities, Inc., Albertson, N.Y., 1970—. Bd. dirs. Five Towns Community Center, Inc., 1970-74; bd. mgrs. Swarthmore Coll., 1976-80; bd. dirs. Mobilized Community Resources, 1977-80; mem. Comprehensive Planning Commn., Nassau County Youth Bd., 1978-80. Served to lt. USCGR, 1954-58. Mem. Direct Mail and Mktg. Assn. (dir. 1967-76, chmn. 1972-74), Asso. 3d Class Mail Users (dir. 1971-78). Club: Inwood (N.Y.) Country. Home and Office: 1552 Pebble Ln Hewlett NY 11557

KISLIK, RICHARD WILLIAM, publishing executive; b. N.Y.C., Oct. 31, 1927; s. Louis K. and Isabelle (Deutelbaum) K.; m. Audrey Gerber, June 19, 1949; children: Nancy J., Andrew R., Laurie S., Wendy J. A.B., Harvard U., 1948, M.B.A., 1949. Research asst. Harvard Bus. Sch., 1949-50; asst. controller Maidenform Brassiere Co., 1950-54; controller Doubleday & Co., Inc., 1954-60; treas., dir. Ziff-Davis Pub. Co., 1960-61; v.p. finance, dir. Random House, Inc., 1961-68; cons., 1968; v.p. Intext Ednl. Pubs., Inc., 1968-69, pres., 1969—; exec. v.p. Intext, Inc., 1970-71, pres., 1971-77, chmn. bd., chief exec. officer, 1972-80, cons., 1980; pres., dir. W.H. Smith Pubs. Inc., 1981—; dir. Lin Broadcasting Corp. Home: 940 Park Ave New York NY 10028 Office: 112 Madison Ave New York NY 10016

KISNER, RONALD HARRIS, consumer products executive, lawyer; b. New Bedford, Mass., Nov. 11, 1948; s. Samuel and Selma (Harris) K.; m. Ellen Schwartz, June 3, 1973; children: Jamie Lauren, Tracy Jaclyn. B.A., Syracuse (N.Y.) U., 1970; J.D., Washington Coll. Law, 1973. Bar: N.Y. 1974. With APL Corp., Gt. Neck, N.Y., 1973—, v.p., dir., 1974 —; dir., sec., treas. Standard-bred Pacers and Trotters, Inc. Vice pres., mem. exec. com. men's div. Children's Med. Center N.Y. Fund. Mem. Am., N.Y. State bar assns. Address: 1 Linden Pl Suite 311 Great Neck NY 11021

KISOR, HENRY DU BOIS, editor, critic, columnist; b. Ridgewood, N.J., Aut. 17, 1940; s. Manown and Judith (Du Bois) K.; m. Deborah A. Abbott, June 24, 1967; children: Colin, Conan. B.A., Trinity Coll., 1962; M.S. in Journalism, Northwestern U., 1964. Copy editor Wilmington News-Jour. (Del.), 1964-65, Chgo. Daily News, 1965-73, book editor, 1973-78, Chgo. Sun-Times, 1978—; adj. prof. Medill Sch. Journalism Northwestern U., Evanston, Ill., 1979-82. Bd. dirs. Chgo. Hearing Soc., 1975-76. Nat. Endowment for Humanities seminar fellow, 1978; recipient Pulitzer prize nominatio in criticism Columbia U., 1981, Stick-o-Type award Chgo. Newspaper Guild, 1981, Outstanding Achievement award Ill. UPI, 1983. Mem. Nat. Book Critics Circle. Office: Chicago Sun-Times 401 N Wabash Ave Chicago IL 60611

KISOR, MANOWN, JR., banker; b. Flushing, N.Y., May 23, 1936; s. Manown and Judith (Dubois) K.; m. Margaret Ayres Leonard, Sept. 5, 1960; children: Anne, Judith, William. B.A. cum laude, Trinity Coll., 1958; postgrad., Northwestern U., 1958-60; M.B.A., N.Y. U., 1963. Asst. sec. Bank of N.Y., 1960-64; v.p. Standard Stats. Co., 1965-66; sr. v.p. Paine Webber Jackson & Curtis, 1967-77, Comerica Bank-Detroit, 1977—, officer in charge trust investments, 1977—. Woodrow Wilson fellow, 1958-59. Mem. Am. Fin. Assn., Nat. Assn. Bus. Economists, N.Y. Soc. Security Analysts., Fin. Analysts Soc. Detroit. Clubs: Detroit, Metamora, Metamora Hunt. Office: 211 W Fort St Detroit MI 48232

KISSANE, JAMES DONALD, educator; b. Pocatello, Idaho, June 21, 1930; s. Donald P. and Leedice Irene (McAnelly) K.; m. Nancy Jane Duke, June 8, 1952; children—Alan, John, Peter, Emily. B.A., Grinnell Coll., 1952; Ph.D., Johns Hopkins, 1956. Asst. prof. Grinnell (Iowa) Coll., 1956-60, asso. prof., 1960-65, prof. English, 1965—, Carter-Adams prof. lit., 1972—; vis. prof. English U. Ky., 1971-72. Author: (with S.P. Zitner and M.M. Liberman) A Preface to Literary Analysis, 1964, The Practice of Criticism, 1966, Alfred Tennyson, 1970; Contbr.: articles to various publs. Alfred Tennyson. Mem. Modern Lang. Assn., Phi Beta Kappa. Office: Dept English Grinnell Coll Grinnell IA 50112

KISSEBERTH, PAUL BARTO, publisher; b. Tiffin, Ohio, July 5, 1932; s. Roscoe Paul and Mary Margaret (Barto) K.; m. Ann Capps Grinton, June 26, 1954; children: Mary, Katharine, Michael, John. B.A., Ohio Wesleyan U., 1954. With McGraw Hill Inc., 1956—; Western field sales mgr. Fleet Owner Mag. and Nat. Petroleum News Mag., Chgo., 1974-76; advt. sales mgr. Fleet Owner Mag., N.Y.C., 1976-78, pub., 1978—; chmn. McGraw-Hill pubs. com., 1981-82. Lay leader First United Methodist Ch., Stamford, Conn., 1980-83. Served to 1st lt. USAF, 1954-56. Mem. Nat. Hwy. Users Fedn., Motor Equipment Mfrs. Assn., Associated Bus. Publs., Truck Trailer Mfrs. Assn., Western Hwy. Inst., Beta Theta Pi. Home: 39 Happy Hill Rd Stamford CT 06903 Office: 1221 Ave of the Americas New York NY 10020

KISSEL, JAMES W., lawyer; b. Hartford, Wis., Dec. 5, 1915; s. Adolph P. and Lillian (Schuppert) K.; m. Katherine M. Vakos, July 22, 1939; children—Peter James, Jonathan James. B.A., U. Wis., 1938; J.D., John Marshall Law Sch., 1942; postgrad., Harvard Grad. Sch. Bus. Adminstrn., 1943-44. Bar: Ill. bar 1942. Asso. firm Sidley, McPherson, Austin & Burgess, Chgo., 1942-56; partner firm Sidley & Austin, Chgo., 1956—; lectr. Northwestern U. Sch. Law, Ill. Inst. Continuing Legal Edn. Contbr. articles to profl. jours. Served as lt. USNR, 1942-45. Recipient Disting. Service award John Marshall Law Sch. Mem. Chgo. Bar Assn. (pres. 1973-74), Am. Coll. Trial Lawyers, Soc. Trial Lawyers, Nat. Assn. R.R. Trial Counsel, Am. Bar Found., Chgo. Bar Found. (dir.). Republican. Methodist. Home: 1739 de L'Ogier Dr Glenview IL 60025 Office: 1 First Nat Plaza Chicago IL 60603

KISSICK, W. NORMAN, chemical company executive; b. Toronto, Ont., Can., Oct. 3, 1930; s. William John and Evelyn E. K.; m. Lois E. Caddell; children: James Stephen, John David, William Peter. B.A. Sc., U. Toronto, 1952. Process enge. Dominion Tar and Chems., Toronto, Ont., 1952-53; process engr. Dominion Tar. and Chems., Montreal, 1953-54; dept. head Carbide Chem. Co., Montreal, 1955-61; head olefins dept. Carbide Chem, Co., Montreal, 1961-63; area supr. olefins Union Carbide Can. Ltd., Montreal, 1963-65, asst. plant mgr., 1965-69, bus. mgr. chems., Toronto, 1969-73, gen. bus. mgr., 1973-75, v.p., dir., 1975-81, pres., chief operating officer, dir., 1981-83—, chmn. bd. chief exec. officer, 1983—; dir. Gt. Lakes Forest Products Ltd., Petrosar Ltd., Toronto-Dominion Bank. Mem. Ont. Bus. Adv. Council. Mem. Can. Chem. Producers Assn. (dir.), Corps. of Engrs. Que., Can. Soc. Chem. Engring., Soc. Chem. Industries Can., Can. Mfrs. Assn. (dir.). Office: 123 Eglinton Ave E Toronto ON Canada M4P 1J3

KISSICK, WILLIAM LEE, physician, educator; b. Detroit, July 29, 1932; s. William Leslie and Florence (Rock) K.; m. Priscilla Harriet Dillingham, June 16, 1956; children: William, Robert-John, Jonathan, Elizabeth. B.A., Yale U., 1953, M.D., 1957, M.P.H., 1959, Dr.P.H., 1961. Intern Yale-New Haven Med. Center, 1957-58; resident Montefiore Hosp. and Med. Center, N.Y.C., 1961-62; dir. Office Program Planning Evaluation, Office of Surgeon Gen., USPHS, 1966-68; exec. dir., nat. adv. commn. health facilities Office of the Pres., Washington, 1968; prof., chmn. dept. community medicine Sch. Medicine U. Pa., 1968-71, George S. Pepper prof. public health and preventive medicine, 1971—, prof. research medicine, 1976—, prof. health care systems Wharton Sch., 1971—, chmn. interdisciplinary health policy and planning curriculum, 1980—, dir. Center for Health Policy Research, Analysis and Planning, 1981—; fellow, mem. exec. com. Nat. Center for Health Care Mgmt.; dir. health policy and planning program Leonard Davis Inst. Health Econs.; vis. prof. community medicine Guy's Hosp. Med. Sch.; vis. prof. dept. social sci. and adminstrn. London Sch. Econs. and Polit. Scis.; vis. prof. Inst. European Health Services Research, Leuven U., 1974-75; cons. N.C. Dept. Planning, Nat. Center Health Services Research, Health Resources Adminstrn., Benedum Found., WHO, Appalachian Regional Commn.; mem. Accrediting Commn. on Edn. for Health Services Adminstrn., 1980—; chmn. com. on med. affairs Yale U. Council, 1980—. Editor: Dimensions and Determinants of Health Policy, 1968. Bd. dirs. Met. Collegiate Center Germantown, Yale Alumni Fund; trustee Appalachian Regional Hosps., 1969-76. Served with USPHS, 1962-68. Mem. AAAS, Am. Coll. Preventive Medicine, Am. Public Health Assn., Pa., Phila. County med. socs., Phila. Coll. Physicians. Clubs: Yale, Sydenham Coterie (Phila.). Home: Ellet Ln Philadelphia PA 19119

KISSILOFF, WILLIAM, indsl. designer; b. N.Y.C., Jan. 11, 1929; s. Carl and Rose (Ruchelman) K.; m. Gertrud Nachtigall, May 4, 1963; 1 son, Ari. Grad. in Indsl. Design, Pratt. Inst., 1949. Creative dir. Design Built Inc., Long Island City, N.Y., 1951-63; pres. Kissiloff & Wimmershoff Inc., N.Y.C., 1963-75; chief exec. officer Kissiloff Assos. subs. Benton & Bowles, Inc., N.Y.C., 1975-80; pres. Kissiloff Assos., Inc., N.Y.C., 1980—; lectr. in field. Spl. design projects include U.S. govt. pavillions at internat. expositions in, Thailand, 1964, Japan, 1968, Yugoslavia, 1969, Rumania, 1974, IRS Visitors Center, 1969, others, mus. exhbns. include, Nat. Park Service, 1971, NSF, 1972, Hall of Sci. City of N.Y., 1973, N.Y. State Div. for Historic Preservation, 1975, Bicentennial exhbns., Rockefeller Center, Inc., N.Y.C., Kennedy Space Center, Fla., mus. design, Nat. Baseball Hall of Fame, 1980. Recipient awards Communication Arts Assn., 1967, Art Dirs. Club, Washington, 1975, 1979, Fed. Design Council, 1975. Mem. Indsl. Designers Soc. Am., Am. Inst. Graphic Arts (award 1965), Am. Assn. Museums, Assn. Sci.-Tech. Centers. Home: 215 E 68th St New York NY 10021 Office: 212 Fifth Ave New York NY 10010

KISSINGER, HAROLD ARTHUR, army officer; b. Elkhart Lake, Wis., Apr. 7, 1922; s. Arthur Philip and Lillian (Becker) K.; m. Marilyn Hope Lueke, July 26, 1944; children: Mark Donald, Greg W. B.S., U. Wis., 1956, M.B.A., 1958; grad., Command and Gen. Staff Coll., 1961, Indsl. Coll. Armed Forces, 1964. Commd. 2d lt. U.S. Army, 1944, advanced through grades to lt. gen., 1974; staff officer Office Chief of Staff of U.S. Army, 1962-63; politico-mil. adviser Office Asst. Sec. of Def., Washington, 1965-68; dep. comdg. gen. U.S. Army Electronics Command, Ft. Monmouth, N.J., 1968-70; comdg. gen. Cam Ranh Bay Qui Nhon Support Command, U.S. Army, Vietnam, 1970-72; dir. Joint Service Tactical Communications Office, Office Sec. Def., Ft. Monmouth, N.J., 1972-74; dep. dir. gen. NATO Integrated Communication System Mgmt. Agy., Brussels, Belgium, 1974—; prof. mil. sci. and tactics Wash. State U., 1946-49; Pres., dir. The Kiscan Corp., Wis. Author: Automation in Manufacturing and Supply Management Systems, 1958, The Computer Comes of Age, 1964. Decorated D.S.M. (2), Legion of Merit (4), Army Commemdation medal (3); Mil. Order Merit, Korea; Army Distinguished Service Order 1st Class, Vietnam). Mem. Assn. U.S. Army, Armed Forces Communications and Electronics Assn., Wis. Alumni Assn., Pi Kappa Alpha. Club: Mason. Home: RFD 1 Stone Lake WI 54876

KISSINGER, HENRY ALFRED, former secretary of state; b. Fuerth, Germany, May 27, 1923; came to U.S., 1938, naturalized, 1943; s. Louis and Paula e6(Stern) K.; m. Ann Fleischer, Feb. 6, 1949 (div. 1964); children—Elizabeth, David; m. Nancy Maginnes, Mar. 30, 1974. A.B. summa cum laude, Harvard U., 1950, M.A., 1952, Ph.D., 1954. Exec. dir. Harvard Internat. Seminar, 1951-69, lectr. dept. govt., 1957-59, dir. def. studies program, 1958-69, asso. prof. govt., 1959-62, prof., 1962-69; faculty Center Internat. Affairs, Harvard U., 1960-69; asst. to Pres. for Nat. Security Affairs, 1969-75; sec. of state, 1973-77; faculty Georgetown U., 1977—; contbg. analyst ABC News, 1983—; chmn. Nat. Bipartisan Commn. on Central Am., 1983-84; mem. internat. adv. com. Chase Bank.; sr. fellow Aspen Inst., 1977—; Study dir. nuclear weapons and fgn. policy Council Fgn. Relations, 1955-56; dir. spl. studies project Rockefeller Bros. Fund, Inc., 1956-58; cons. Ops. Research Office, 1950-61; cons. to dir. Psychol. Strategy Bd., 1952; cons. Ops. Coordinating Bd., 1955, cons. weapons systems evaluation group, 1959-60; cons. NSC, 1961-62, ACDA, 1961-68, Dept. State, 1965-69. Author: Nuclear Weapons and Foreign Policy, 1957, A World Restored: Castlereagh, Metternich and the Restoration of Peace, 1812-22, 1957, The Necessity for Choice: Prospects of American Foreign Policy, 1961, The Troubled Partnership: A Reappraisal of the Atlantic Alliance, 1965, White House Years, 1979, For the Record, 1981, Years of Upheaval, 1982; Editor: Problems of National Strategy: A Book of Readings, 1965, Confluence, An Internat. Forum, 1951-58; Contbr. to profl. jours. Trustee Met. Mus. Art, N.Y.C., 1978—. Served with AUS, 1943-46. Recipient citation Overseas Press Club, 1958; Woodrow Wilson prize for best book fields of govt., politics, internat. affairs, 1958; Distinguished Pub. Service award Am. Inst. Pub. Service, 1973; Nobel Peace prize, 1973; Presdl. Medal of Freedom, 1977; Guggenheim fellow, 1965-66. Mem. Am. Polit. Sci. Assn., Council Fgn. Relations, Am. Acad. Arts and Scis., Phi Beta Kappa. Clubs: Cosmos, Federal City, Metropolitan (Washington); Century, River (N.Y.C.). Office: Suite 400 1800 K St NW Washington DC 20006

KISSINGER, J(OHN) PETER, transportation official; b. Reading, Pa., Oct. 19, 1947; s. John Richard and Bertha Mary (Oshman) K.; m. Barbara A. Williams, July 11, 1970. B.S. in Engring., U.S. Coast Guard Acad., 1969; M.S. in Ops. Research, George Washington U., 1975. Engr. U.S. Coast Guard, New Bedford, Mass., 1969-71, Norfolk, Va., 1971-72, safety engr., 1972-77; transp. safety specialist Nat. Transp. Safety Bd., Washington, 1977-79, spl. asst., 1979-81, mng. dir., 1981—. Served to lt. comdr. USCGR, 1969-83. Recipient Coast Guard Achivement medal U.S. Coast Guard, 1977. Mem. Washington Mgmt. Sci. and Ops. Research Council. Office: Nat Transp Safety Bd 800 Independence Ave SW Washington DC 20594 *My career goal is to foster continued safety improvements in the transportation system by applying a systems approach to risk management.*

KISSINGER, WALTER BERNHARD, automotive test and service equipment manufacturing company executive; b. Furth, Germany, June 21, 1924; came to U.S., 1938, naturalized, 1939; s. Louis and Paula (Stern) K.; m. Eugenie Van Drooge, July 4, 1958; children: William, Thomas, Dana Marie, John. B.A., Princeton U., 1951; M.B.A., Harvard U., 1953. Asst. to v.p. fgn. operations Gen. Tire & Rubber Co., Akron, Ohio, 1953-56; pres. Advanced Vacuum Products Co., Stamford, Conn., 1957-62; exec. v.p., dir. Glass-tite Industries, Providence, 1960-62; v.p., gen. mgr. Harman- Kardon, Inc., Plainview, N.Y.; asst. to pres. Jerrold Corp., 1963-64; exec. v.p., Chmn. exec. com., dir. Jervis Corp., Hicksville, N.Y., 1964-68; chmn., pres., chief exec. officer Allen Group Inc., Melville, 1969—; mem. adv. bd. Mfrs. Hanover Trust Co.; bd. dirs. Nat. Council for U.S.-China Trade. Mem. adv. council dept. history Princeton U.; mem. exec. bd. Suffolk County council Boy Scouts Am. Served to capt. AUS, 1943-46, 50. Decorated Commendation medal. Club: Princeton of New York. Home: Lower Dr Huntington Bay NY 11743 Office: 534 Broad Hollow Rd Melville NY 11747

KISSLINGER, CARL, educator, geophysicist; b. St. Louis, Aug. 30, 1926; s. Fred and Emma (Tobias) K.; m. Millicent Ann Thorson, Mar. 27, 1948; children: Susan, Karen, Ellen, Pamela, Jerome. B.S., St. Louis U., 1947, M.S., 1949, Ph.D., 1952. Faculty St. Louis U., 1949-72, prof. geophysics, geophys. engring., 1961-72, chmn. dept. earth and atmostpheric scis., 1963-72, prof. geophysics, 1972—; dir. Coop. Inst. Research in Environ. Scis., U. Colo., Boulder, 1972-79, Systems, Sci. and Software, Inc., LaJolla, Calif., 1976-78; UNESCO expert in seismology, chief tech. adviser Internat. Inst. Seismology and Earthquake Engring., Tokyo, 1966-67; chmn. com. seismology NRC-Nat. Acad. Scis., 1970-72; mem. U.S. Geodynamics Com., 1975-78; U.S. nat. corr. Internat. Assn. Seismology and Physics of Earth's Interior, 1970-72; mem. U.S. nat. com. for Internat. Union Geodesy and Geopnysics, 1974—, Gov.'s Sci. Adv. Council, State of Colo., 1973-77; mem. bur. Internat. Union Geodesy and Geophysics, 1975—; mem. com. scholarly communication with People's Republic of China, Nat. Acad. Scis., 1977-81. Recipient Alumni Merit award St. Louis U., 1976; Alexander von Humboldt Found. Sr. U.S. Scientist award, 1979. Fellow Am. Geophys. Union (bd. dirs. sect. seismology 1970-72, fgn. sec. 1974—), Geol. Soc. Am., Assn. Exploration Geophysics (India), AAAS; mem. Soc. Exploration Geophysicists, Seismol. Soc. Am. (dir. 1968-74, pres. 1972-73), Austrian Acad. Sci. (corr.), Phi Beta Kappa, Sigma Xi. Home: 4165 Caddo Pkwy Boulder CO 80303

KISSLINGER, LEONARD SOL, educator, physicist; b. St. Louis, Aug. 15, 1930; s. Fred and Emma (Tobias) K.; m. Margaret V. Hampton, Sept. 1, 1956; children: Stephen A., Benjamin L., Paul W. B.S., St. Louis U., 1951; M.A., Ind. U., 1952, Ph.D. (NSF fellow), 1956. Faculty Case Western Res. U., 1956-69, assoc. prof., 1960-63, prof. physics, 1963-69, Carnegie-Mellon U., Pitts., 1969—; vis. prof. U. Paris-Sud, Orsay, France, 1973-74; cons. Los Alamos Nat. Lab., 1977—; researcher Niels Bohr Inst., Copenhagen, 1958-59, Weizmann Inst. Sci., Rehovoth, Isreal, 1962-63, MIT, 1966-67; vis. prof. U. Wash., 1981-82. Contbr. articles to profl. jours.; Assoc. editor: Zeitschrift für Physik, 1976-81. Research Corp. fellow, 1958-59; Weizmann Meml. fellow, 1962-63. Fellow Am. Phys. Soc. (exec. com. div. nuclear sci. 1980-82); mem. AAAS, AAUP, Sigma Xi, Pi Mu Epsilon. Home: 4785 Wallingford St Pittsburgh PA 15213

KISTER, JAMES MILTON, educator, mathematician; b. Cleve., June 29, 1930; s. James Leonard and Katherine Alice (Sherrick) K.; m. Susan Spence, 1956; 1 dau., Karen Lynn; m. Jane Bridge; 1978. B.A., Wooster (Ohio) Coll., 1952; M.A., U. Wis., 1956, Ph.D., 1959. Research asst. Los Alamos Sci. Lab., 1953-55; mem. faculty U. Mich., Ann Arbor, 1959—, prof. math., 1966—, chmn. dept., 1971-73; asso. Office Naval Research, U. Va., 1960-61; mem. Inst. Advanced Study, Princeton, N.J., 1962-64; vis. prof. UCLA, 1967; vis. fellow Clare Hall, Cambridge (Eng.) U., 1970; vis. mem. Institut des Hautes Etudes Scientifique, 1974; vis. prof. U. Calif. at Berkeley, summer 1975; vis. fellow Wolfson Coll., Oxford U., 1977. Asso. editor: Duke Math. Jour, 1972-75; asso. editor: Mich. Math. Jour, 1976-78; mng. editor, 1978, 82—. Mem. Am. Math. Soc. Office: Dept Math U Mich Ann Arbor MI 48109

KISTLER, ALAN LEE, educator; b. Laramie, Wyo., Nov. 26, 1928; s. John Cornelius and Lynn (Isaacson) K.; m. Ingeborg Magdalene Busemann, May 15, 1955; children—Stephen, Lynn, Eva. B.Engring., Johns Hopkins, 1950, M.S. in Aero, 1952, Ph.D., 1955. Research engr. jet propulsion lab. Cal. Inst. Tech., Pasadena, 1957-61, mgr. fluid physics sect., 1965-68; asso. prof. mech. engring. Yale, 1961-65; dir. continuum mechanics lab. Northrop Corp., 1968-69; prof. mech. engring. Northwestern U., Evanston, Ill., 1969—; Mem. fluid mechanics research adv. com. NASA, 1966-68. Bd. editors: The Physics of Fluids jour, 1973; Contbr. articles to profl. jours. Served with AUS, 1955-57. Mem. Am. Phys. Soc., Am. Inst. Aeros. and Astronautics (tech. com. fluid dynamics), AAAS. Unitarian-Universalist. Home: 3241 Park Pl Evanston IL 60201

KISTLER, DARCI ANNA, ballet dancer; b. Riverside, Calif., June 4, 1964; d. Jack B. and Alicia (Kinner) K. Student, Profl. Children's Sch., N.Y.C., Sch. Am. Ballet, N.Y.C.; studied with, Irma Kosmouska, Los Angeles. Mem. N.Y.C. Ballet, 1980—, soloist, 1981-82; prin. dancer, 1982—; role Andantino, Gershwin Concerto, Valse-Scherzo, Piano-Rag Music, Pastorale, Suite for Histoire du Soldat; appearance PBS TV series, Dance in Am. Home: 55 W 73d St New York NY 10023 Office: New York City Ballet New York State Theater New York NY 10023 *To be good is not enough when you dream of being great.*

KISTLER, WILLIAM ARTHUR, JR., equipment manufacturing company executive; b. Wichita Falls, Tex., 1926; married. B.S., U. Houston, 1950; M.S., Rice U., 1953. Lab. technician devel. engring. Hughes Tool Co., Houston, 1947-58, field engr., 1958-60, asst. v.p. mfg., product mgr., 1960-66, v.p. mfg., 1966-75, exec. v.p. ops., 1975-79, corp. exec. v.p.; pres. Drilling Tools & Equipment Group, 1979—, pres., chief exec. officer parent c., 1982—, also dir.; v.p., dir. Hughes Tool Co. S.A.C.I.F.I, Hughes de Mex., Hughes Tool Co. de Mex., Hughes Tool Co. DISC; dir. Hughes Tool Co., Ltd., London, Hughes Tool S.A.F., Gt. Southern Life Ins. Co., Tex. Commerce Greenway Bank. Served to lt. (j.g.) USNR, 1943-47. Mem. NAM (bd. dirs.). Office: Hughes Tool Co 5425 Polk Ave Houston TX 77023 *

KISTNER, DAVID HAROLD, biology educator; b. Cin., July 30, 1931; s. Harold Adolf and Hilda (Gick) K.; m. Alzada A. Carlisle, Aug. 8, 1957; children—Alzada H., Kymry Marie Carlisle. A.B., U. Chgo., 1952, B.S., 1956, Ph.D., 1957. Instr. U. Rochester, 1957-59; instr., asst. prof. Calif. State U., Chico, 1959-64, asso. prof. biology, 1964-67, prof., 1967—; research asso. Field Mus. Natural History, 1967—, Atlantica Ecol. Research Sta., Salisbury, Zimbabwe, 1970—; dir. Shinner Inst. Study Interrelated Insects, 1968-75. Author: (with others) Social Insects, Vols. 1-3; editor: Sociobiology, 1975—; contbr. articles to profl. jours. Recipient Outstanding Prof. award Calif. State Univs. and Colls., Los Angeles, 1976; John Simon Guggenheim Meml. Found. fellow, 1965-66; NSF grantee, 1960—; Am. Philos. Soc. grantee, 1972. Fellow Explorers Club; mem. Entomol. Soc. Am., Pacific Coast Entomol. Soc., Kans. Entomol. Soc., AAUP, AAAS, Soc. Study of Evolution, Am. Soc. Naturalists, Am. Soc. Zoologists, Soc. Study of Systematic Zoology, Chico State Coll. Assos. (charter), Council Biology Editors. Research trips to Africa, Orient, Europe, S. Am., Australia, China. Home: 3 Canterbury Circle Chico CA 95926

KIT, SAUL, educator, biochemist; b. Passaic, N.J., Nov. 25, 1920; s. Isadore and Minnie (Darvick) K.; m. Dorothy Anken, Sept. 28, 1945; children: Sally, Malon, Gordon. A.B., U. Calif.-Berkeley, 1948, Ph.D., 1951. Post-doctoral fellow U. Chgo., 1951-52; research chemist, asst. biochemist U. Tex.; M.D. Anderson Hosp. and Tumor Inst., Houston, 1952-57, asso. biochemist, 1957-60, biochemist, chief sect. nucleo protein metabolism, 1961-62; prof. biochemistry, head div. biochem.

virology Baylor Coll. Medicine, Houston, 1962—; Am. Acad. Microbiology vis. prof. Instituto Venezolano, Caracas, Venezuela, 1971; vis. prof. U. Buenos Aires, Argentina, 1971; Cons. NIH, 1970—, chmn. pathobiol. chemistry study sect., 1975-79; cons. Nat. Cancer Inst.; sci. adv. bd. Am. Genetics Internat. Inc., Novagene Inc. Mem. editorial bd.: Intervirology; Contbr. articles to profl. jours. Served with AUS, 1942-46. Recipient Research Career award NIH, 1962. Mem. Am. Soc. Cell Biology (treas. 1965-68, pres. 1971), Am. Assn. Cancer Research, Am. Soc. Biol. Chemists, Am. Chem. Soc., Am. Soc. Microbiology., Am. Soc. Virology, Argentine Soc. Virology (corr.). Home: 11935 Wink St Houston TX 77024

KITAJ, R.B., artist; b. Chagrin Falls, Ohio, 1932; s. and Jeanne Brooks; children: Lemuel, Dominie Lee. Diploma, Ruskin Sch., U. Oxford, 1960; grad., Royal Coll. Art, London, 1962; hon. doctorate, U. London. Vis. lectr. Slade Sch., U. London; vis. prof. U. Calif., Berkeley, UCLA. Exhibited one man shows at, Marlborough Fine Art, London, 1963, 70, 77, 80, Marlborough Fine Art, N.Y.C., 1965, 73, 79, Marlborough Fine Art, Zurich, 1977, Angeles County Mus., 1965, Stedelijk Mus., Amsterdam., 1967, Cleve. Mus., U. Calif., Berkeley, 1968, retrospective exhbns., Hirshhorn Mus., Washington, Cleve. Mus., Kunsthalle, Dusseldorf, W. Ger.; rep. in permanent collections in museums in U.S. and Europe. Mem. U.S. InstiArts and Letters. Home: care Marlborough Fine Art Ltd 6 Albemarle St London W1 England

KITCH, PAUL RICHARD, lawyer; b. Marion, Kans., June 18, 1911; s. Charles A. and Anna (Haun) K.; m. Josephine Pridmore, Jan. 25, 1936; children: Edmund, Paul Richard, Thomas, James, David; m. Diana Parlette, Apr. 1, 1974; 1 dau., Mary. A.B., Southwestern Coll., Winfield, Kans., 1932; J.D., U. Chgo., 1935. Bar: Kans. 1935. Assoc. Brooks, Brooks & Fleeson, Witchita, Kans., 1935-42, mem., 1942; with Fleeson, Gooing, Coulson & Kitch, Wichita, 1942—, sr. ptnr., 1957—; dir. Kans. State Bank & Trust Co., Wichita. Pres. Wichita Bd. Edn., 1947. Mem. Wichita Area C. of C. (pres. 1961). Home: 8316 E Central Wichita KS 67206 Office: Wichita Plaza Bldg Wichita KS 67201

KITCHEL, DENISON, ret. lawyer, writer; b. Bronxville, N.Y., Mar. 1, 1908; s. William Lloyd and Grace (Wheeler) K.; m. Naomi Margaret Douglas, Apr. 22, 1941; children—James Douglas, Harvey Denison. A.B., Yale U., 1930; J.D., Harvard U., 1933. Bar: Ariz. bar 1934. Asso. Ellinwood & Ross, Phoenix, also Bisbee, 1934-38, mem. firm, 1938-46, Evans, Kitchel & Jenckes, Phoenix, 1946-70, of counsel, 1970—; former counsel Phelps Dodge Corp., Am. Smelting & Refining Co., So. Pacific Co., Motorola, Am. Airlines, Borden Co.; Chmn. com. labor relations Am. Mining Congress, 1957-63; spokesman mining industry Congressional Com. on Labor Legislation, 1953-63; mem. Ariz. Copper Tariff Bd., 1967-76, 78—, chmn., 1973-76, 78—; mem. U.S. del. tripartite tech. meeting on mines ILO, Geneva, 1957; mem. adv. panel on labor-mgmt. U.S. Senate, 1959-60. Author: Too Grave a Risk-The Connally Amendment Issue, 1963, The Truth About the Panama Canal, 1978. Gen. counsel Ariz. Republican State Com., 1957-63; gen. dir. Goldwater for Pres. Com., 1963-64, Rep. presdl. Campaign, 1964. Served from 1st lt. to lt. col. USAAF, 1942-45. Mem. Am., Maricopa County bar assns., State Bar Ariz., AIME, Free Soc. Assn. (pres. 1965-69), Mont Pelerin Soc. Episcopalian. Home: 9735 Vereda Solana Pinnacle Peak Heights Scottsdale AZ 85255

KITCHELL, RALPH LLOYD, veterinarian, educator; b. Waukee, Iowa, July 9, 1919; s. John J. and Josephine (Gutshall) K.; m. Mary Clare Murray, Mar. 27, 1947; children—Margaret Anne, Michael John, Martha Marie. D.V.M., Iowa State Coll., 1943; Ph.D., U. Minn., 1951. Instr. bacteriology Kans. State Coll., 1943; research fellow Animal Diagnostic Lab. U. Minn., 1946-47, instr. sect. vet. anatomy, 1947-51, asso. prof., 1951-54, acting head sect., 1948-51, head div. vet. anatomy, 1951-64; asst. dean Coll. Vet. Medicine (U. Minn.), 1960- 63, asso. dean. Coll. Vet. Medicine, 1963-64; dean Coll. Vet. Medicine Kans. State U., 1964-65; dean, dir. Coll. Vet. Medicine Iowa State U., Ames, 1966-71; prof. vet. medicine Coll. Vet. Medicine, Iowa State U., 1966-72; vis. prof. anatomy Sch. Vet. Medicine, U. Calif. at Davis, 1971-72, prof., 1972—. Contbr. articles on vet. neurology to sci. jours. Served to maj. U.S. Army, 1943-46; CBI. Recipient Faculty Recognition award U. Minn., 1952, 54; Disting. Tchr. award, 1980; USPHS spl. research fellow, Stockholm, London, 1957-58. Mem. Am. Assn. Anatomists, Internat. Assn. Study Pain, Am. Assn. Vet. Anatomists (past pres.), Am. Vet. Neurol. Assn. (pres.), Am. Vet. Med. Assn. Home: 2206 Butte Pl Davis CA 95616

KITCHEN, HYRAM, veterinarian, educator; b. Oakland, Calif., Sept. 24, 1932; s. Samuel Earl and Clara (Peak) Scribner; m. Yvonne Saasta, Feb. 2, 1958; children: Diane, Michael. B.S., U. Calif., Davis, 1954, D.V.M., 1956; Ph.D., U. Fla., 1965. Practice vet. medicine, Los Altos, Calif., 1957-58; research asso. Coll. Medicine, U. Fla., 1960-63, fellow in cardiology, 1963-65, instr. dept. biochemistry and medicine, 1965-66, asst. prof., 1966-69; asso. prof. Coll. Vet. Medicine, Mich. State U., 1969-73, prof., 1973-74; acting dir. Center Lab. Animal Resources, 1974; prof., head dept. environ. practice Coll. Vet. Medicine, U. Tenn., Knoxville, 1974-80, dean, 1980—. Contbr. articles to profl. jours. Served to capt. U.S. Army, 1958-60. Recipient Outstanding Faculty award Tenn. Vet. Med. Assn., 1982; Kiwanis scholar, 1950; Peter J. Shield scholar, 1951-52; Chancellor's research scholar, 1982. Mem. Am. Soc. Biol. Chemists, Am. Assn. Zoo Vets., Am. Assn. Vet. Med. Colls., Am. Soc. Human Genetics, Am. Soc. Vet. Clin. Pathologists, AAAS, AVMA, Am. Hampshire Sheep Assn., Tenn., Internat. Arabian horse assns., Tenn. Farm Bur., Tenn. Sheep Breeders Assn., Sigma Xi, Phi Zeta, Sigma Alpha Epsilon, Phi Kappa Phi, Gamma Sigma, Alpha Zeta. Lutheran. Home: Box 186 Route 3 Hines Valley Rd Loudon TN 37774 Office: U Tenn PO Box 1071 Knoxville TN 37901 *Diversity, curiosity, sensitivity, and the imaginative use of comparative biological approach are strong pillars of scientific investigation in veterinary medicine.*

KITCHEN, JOHN MARTIN, historian, educator; b. Nottingham, Eng., Dec. 21, 1936; s. John Sutherland and Margaret Helen (Pearson) K. B.A. with honors, U. London, 1963, Ph.D., 1966. Mem. Cambridge Group Population Studies, Eng., 1965-66; mem. faculty Simon Fraser U., Burnaby, B.C., Can., 1966—. Author: The German Officer Corps 1890-1914, 1968, A Military History of Germany, 1975, Fascism, 1976, The Silent Dictatorship, 1976, The Political Economy of Germany 1815-1914, 1979, The Coming of Austrian Fascism, 1980, Germany in the Age of Total War, 1981. Fellow Inter-Univ. Seminar on Armed Forces and Soc. Fellow Royal Hist. Soc., Royal Soc. Can. Office: Simon Fraser Univ History Dept Burnaby BC Canada V5A 1S6 *

KITCHEN, JOHN MILTON, lawyer; b. Indpls., Apr. 15, 1912; s. William Burrette and Edith (Scott) K.; m. Jane Rauch, Apr. 8, 1939; children: Jeanne, Marjorie, John, Louise. Grad., Wabash Coll., 1933; J.D., Harvard U., 1937. Bar: Ind. 1936, U.S. Supreme Ct. 1950. Practiced in, Indpls., 1937—; faculty Ind. U. Sch. Law, 1939-41; partner firm Rauch, Chase & Kitchen, 1946-72; counsel Dutton, Kappes & Overman, 1972—; pres. John M. Kitchen Agy., Inc., 1955—; gen. counsel, dir. Permanent Magnet Castings, Inc., 1948-70, Permanent Magnet Co., 1970-75; v.p., sec., dir. Crooked Stick Devel. Corp., 1975-81; Gen. counsel U.S. Auto Club, 1959-69; sec., dir., gen. counsel, mem. exec. com. U.S. Auto Club Benevolent Found., 1959—; gen. counsel, exec. com. Nat. Clay Cts. Championship, 1969-75; gen. counsel Indpls. Sesquicentennial Commn., 1970-72; gen. counsel, exec. com. Western Clay Cts. Championship, 1946-68, U.S. Open Clay Cts. Championship, 1969-73; Chmn. Gov. Ind. Commn. Jud. Reform, 1969-71; mem. Mayor's Task Force on Pub. Safety, 1971—; staff contbr. sports Indpls. Newspapers, Inc., 1959—. Author: Legal Aspects of Procurement Terminations and Renegotiation, 1952, Capital Gain v. Ordinary Income, 1958, A Lawyer's Life, 1969, The Lawyer's Position in Society, 1971. Pres. Green Hill Found., 1954-58; trustee Indpls. Bar Found., 1969—, pres., 1969-72; trustee Tudor Hall Sch., Inc., 1952-70, pres., 1962-65; bd. dirs., treas. Indpls. Lawyers Commn., 1969-74; mem. presidents club Children's Mus. Indpls., 1977—; policy steering com. Central State Hosp., 1977—. Served to capt. AUS, 1942-46. Fellow Am. Bar Found., Ind. Bar Found. (disting. charter fellow), Indpls. Bar Found. (disting. charter fellow); mem. ABA (ho. dels.), Ind. Bar Assn. (ho. dels.), Indpls. Bar Assn. (pres. 1969-70), Indpls. Assn. Wabash (pres. 1950-52), Ind. Conf. Bankers and Lawyers (chmn., dir. 1973—), Mil. Order Loyal Legion (Ind. judge adv. gen. 1975—), Phi Beta Kappa (chmn., trustee Alpha chpt. 1977-83, pres. 1980-83). Clubs: Univ. (v.p., dir. 1971-73), Dramatic, Woodstock (pres. 1972-73), Woodstock (dir. 1971-74), Contemporary (pres. 1964-66), Trader's Point Hunt, Little Harbor, Birchwood Estate. Home: 99 Highland Manor Ct Indianapolis IN 46208 Office: Guaranty Bldg Monument Circle Indianapolis IN 46204

KITCHEN, LAWRENCE OSCAR, aircraft/aerospace corporation executive; b. Ft. Mill, S.C., June 8, 1923; s. Samuel Sumpter and Ruby Azalee (Grigg) K.; m. Brenda Lenhart, Nov. 25, 1978; children by previous marriage: Brenda, Alan, Janet. Ed., Foothill Coll. Aero. engr. U.S. Navy Bur. Aeronautics, Washington, 1946-58, staff asst. to asst. chief bur., 1958; with Lockheed Missiles & Space Co., Sunnyvale, Calif., 1958-70, mgr. product support logistics, 1964-68, dir. fin. controls, 1968-70; v.p.-fin. Lockheed-Ga. Co., Marietta, 1970-71, pres., 1971-75, Lockheed Corp., Burbank, Calif., 1975—, chief operating officer, 1976—; mem. internat. bd. Security Pacific Nat. Bank, 1976—. Mem. bd. visitors Emory Inst.; mem. founders bd. Hollywood Presbyn. Hosp.; mem. nominating com. Aviation Hall of Fame. Served with USMC, 1942-46. Mem. Nat. Def. Transp. Assn., AIAA, Nat. Assn. Accountants, Navy League, Am. Def. Preparedness Assn., Soc. Logistics Engrs., Air Force Assn., Assn. U.S. Army. Clubs: Lakeside Golf, Wings. Office: PO Box 551 Burbank CA 91520

KITT, EARTHA MAE, actress, singer; b. North, S.C., Jan. 26, 1928; d. John and Anna K.; m. William McDonald, June 1960 (div.); 1 dau. Grad. high sch. Soloist with, Katherine Dunham Dance Group, 1948; night club singer, 1949—; appearing in, France, Turkey, Greece, Egypt, N.Y.C., Hollywood, Las Vegas, London, Stockholm; stage appearances in Dr. Faustus, Paris, 1951, New Faces of 1952, N.Y.C., Mrs. Patterson, N.Y.C., 1954, Shinbone Alley, N.Y.C., 1957, Timbuktu, 1978; motion pictures include New Faces, 1953, Accused, 1957, Anna Lucasta, 1958, Mark of the Hawk, 1958, St. Louis Blues, 1957, Saint of Devil's Island, 1961, Synanon, 1965, Up The Chastity Belt, 1971; also 2 French films; star: documentary film All By Myself, 1982; rec. artist for, RCA Victor, numerous television appearances.; Author: Thursday's Child, 1956, A Tart Is Not a Sweet, Alone With Me, 1976. Named Woman of Year Nat. Assn. Negro Musicians, 1968. Address: care Internat Creative Mgmt 40 W 57th St New York NY 10019 *

KITTELL, DONALD DAVENPORT, investment firm executive; b. Jamaica, N.Y., Sept. 21, 1937; s. Donald D. and Dorothy (R.) K.; m. Mary D. West, June 23, 1962; children: Reid W., Robert W., Andrew W. B.A., Hamilton Coll., 1959; M.B.A., Harvard U., 1962. With Gen. Motors Corp., 1962-67; with IBM Corp., 1967-77; sr. v.p. fin. and adminstrn. N.Y. Stock Exchange, 1977-78, sr. v.p. market ops., 1978-80, exec. v.p. trading services and fin., 1980-82; exec. v.p. adminstrn. Dean Witter Reynolds, 1982—; dir. Nat. Stock Clearing Corp. Mem. Fin. Execs. Inst. Office: 130 Liberty St New York NY 10006

KITTLE, CHARLES FREDERICK, surgeon; b. Athens, Ohio, Oct. 24, 1921; s. Frederick F. and Ida (Falls) K.; m. Jeane Mignon Groenier, 1945; children: Candace Mignon, Bradley Dean, Leslie Jeane, Brian David; m. Ann Catherine Bates, 1981. A.B. with honors, Ohio U., Athens, 1944, LL.D., 1967; M.D. with honors, U. Chgo., 1945; M.S. in Surgery, U. Kans., 1950. Diplomate: Am. Bd. Surgery, Am. Bd. Thoracic Surgery (mem. bd. 1967—, chmn. 1973—). Intern U. Chgo. Clinics, 1945-46; resident gen. and thoracic surgery U. Kans. Med. Center, 1948-52; spl. tng. radio-isotopes for med. use Oak Ridge Inst. Nuclear Studies, 1950, cons. med. div., 1950-55; mem. faculty U. Kans. Sch. Medicine, 1950-66; asso. prof. surgery, lectr. history medicine, 1959-66; cons. thoracic surgery VA Hosp., Wadsworth, Kans., 1954-57, cons. gen. surgery, 1957-60; attending gen. surgery VA Hosp., Kansas City, Mo., 1954-66, Wichita, Kans., 1955-62; prof. surgery, head sect. thoracic and cardiovascular surgery U. Chgo. Clinics, 1966-72; prof. surgery, dir. thoracic surgery sect. Rush Med. Sch. and Presbyn.-St. Luke's Hosp., 1973-78; dir. Rush Cancer Center, 1978—; attending surgery Cook County Hosp., 1966—; cons. Municipal Tb Sanatorium, Chgo., 1968-74, Hines VA Hosp., Maywood, Ill., 1973—; spl. research cardiovascular surgery, control of blood flow. Served as lt. (j.g.) USNR, 1946-48. Clin. fellow; Am. Cancer Soc., 1950-52; Markle scholar med. scis., 1953-58. Mem. AAAS, Am. Assn. History Medicine, Am. Assn. Thoracic Surgery, Am. Coll. Cardiology (bd. govs. Kans. 1963-66, Ill. 1968—), Chgo. Surg. Soc. (pres. 1972-73), A.C.S. (bd. govs. 1965-68), Am. Heart Assn. (chmn. program com. cardiovascular surgery 1965-68, exec. com. cardiovascular surgery council 1962—, chmn. council 1972-74), Am. Physiol. Assn., Central Surg. Soc., Chgo. Med. Soc., Am. Surg. Assn., Internat. Cardiovascular Soc. (sec. 1965-71), Internat. Soc. Surgery, N.J. Thoracic Surgery Soc., Ill. Thoracic Surgery Soc. (pres. 1983-84), Soc. Clin. Surgery, Soc. Surg. Oncology, Soc. Vascular Surgery, Soc. Univ. Surgeons (pres. 1966-67), Soc. Thoracic Surgery, Phi Beta Kappa, Sigma Xi, Alpha Omega Alpha. Home: 856 S Laflin Chicago IL 60607 Office: 1725 W Harrison St Chicago IL 60612

KITTLE, RALPH WADE, paper company executive; b. Ringgold, Ga., July 19, 1920; s. John Patrick and Effie (Gordy) K.; m. Cornelia Kittle, June 28, 1947; children: Cornelia, Cary, Ralph. Student, Mercer U., 1937-39, U. Chattanooga, 1940-42, Chattanooga Coll. Law, 1940-42; J.D., U. Va., 1948. Bar: N.Y., D.C., Va. Assoc. Davis Polk and Wardwell, N.Y.C., 1948-53; counsel to U.S. Senate, Washington, 1953; atty., v.p. Internat. Paper Co., N.Y.C., 1954-72, Washington, 1972—; mem. adv. com. on women to Sec. Labor, 1973-75; spl. cons. EEOC/Dept. Labor, Washington, 1971; mem. temp. state commn. on water resources planning State N.Y., 1962-65; participant Nat. Conf. on AIr Pollution, Washington, 1966, Nat. Water Quality Criteria Conf., Norman, Okla., 1966. Mem. mng. bd.: Va. Law Rev.; editor-in-chief: Va. Spectator Mag., U. Va. Reading Guide; mem. editorial bd.: U. Va. Newspaper. Chmn. bd. trustees Mary Baldwin Coll., Staunton, Va., 1970-80, Lees Coll., Jackson, Ky., 1972-82; mem. exec. com. Forest Industries Com. on timber evaluation and taxation; bd. dirs. Am. Council for Capital Formation; mem. adv. com. Am. Enterprise Inst., 1981-83; mem. Bus.-Govt. Relations Council, Washington, Pres.' Com. on Employment of Handicapped, Washington; active Nat. Multiple Sclerosis Soc.; past vice chmn. govt. relations com. Bus. Roundtable; mem. adv. council Women's Inst. Am. U. Served to capt. USAAF, 1942-45. Decorated D.F.C., Air medal, Purple Heart. Mem. Nat. Assn. Mfrs. (pub. affairs com.), Nat. Forest Products Assn. (past chmn. govt. affairs com.). Clubs: Kewsick Hunt (Va.); Internat.; Nat. Lawyers (Washington); Wings (N.Y.). Home: Route 2 PO Box 10 Keswick VA 22947 Office: Internat Paper Co 1620 Eye St NW Suite 700 Washington DC 20006

KITTLESON, HENRY MARSHALL, lawyer; b. Tampa, Fla., May 13, 1929; s. Edgar O. and Ardath (Ayers) K.; m. Barbara Clark, Mar. 20, 1954; 1 dau., Laura Helen. B.S. with high honors, U. Fla., 1951, J.D., 1953. Bar: Fla. 1953. Partner Holland & Knight, Lakeland and Bartow, Fla., 1955—; dir. Bartow Fed. Savs. & Loan Assn., 1959-74, chmn. bd., 1971-72; mem. adv. bd. Fla. Fed. Savs. & Loan Assn.; dir. Am. Bank of Lakeland, 1973-80; mem. Fla. Law Revision Commn., 1967-76, vice chmn., 1969-71; mem. Gov.'s Property Rights Study Commn., 1974-75, Nat. Conf. Commrs. Uniform State Laws, 1982—. Mem. Bartow Zoning Bd. Adjustment, 1963-64; mem. council U. Fla. Law Center, 1974-77. Served to maj. USAF, 1953-55. Fellow Am. Bar Found.; mem. Am. Law Inst., Am. Coll. Real Estate Lawyers, ABA (chmn. standing com. on ethics and profl. responsibility 1980-81), Fla. Bar (chmn. standing com. profl. ethics 1965-66), ABA (chmn. 1965-66), Blue Key, Sigma Phi Epsilon, Phi Delta Phi, Phi Kappa Phi, Beta Gamma Sigma. Democrat. Presbyterian. Clubs: Lakeland Yacht and Country., Tampa. Home: 5334 Woodhaven Ln Lakeland FL 33803 Office: 92 Lake Wire Dr Lakeland FL 33802

KITTLITZ, RUDOLF GOTTLIEB, JR., chemical engineer; b. Waco, Tex., Apr. 19, 1935; s. Rudolf Gottlieb and Lena Hulda (Landgraf) K.; m. Linda Ann Watkins, Nov. 24, 1966; children: Lenell, Theresa, Liesel, Rolf. B.S. in Chem. Engring, U. Miss., 1957. Engr., polychems. research E.I. du Pont de Nemours & Co., Wilmington, Del., 1957-60, engr., textile fibers dept., Seaford, Del., 1960-62, sr. engr., textile fibers dept., Seaford, 1962-67, Chattanooga, 1967-68, sr. research engr., 1968-83, sr. research engr. textile fibers, Seaford, 1983—; lectr. in field.; adj. prof. U. Tenn.-Chattanooga, 1980-82. Vice chmn. Community Action Com., Seaford, 1966. Fellow Am. Soc. Quality Control (cert. quality and reliability engr., chmn. Chattanooga sect. 1975-76, councilor region 11 chem. div. 1975-80); Mem. Am. Statis. Assn., AAAS. Democrat. Baptist. Club: Seaford Golf and Country. Home: 917 N Atlactic Circle Seaford DE 19973 Office: Box 400 Sussex Ave Seaford DE 19973

KITTO, GEORGE BARRIE, educator; b. Wellington, N.Z., July 31, 1937; U.S., 1962; s. George H. and Acushla Meta (Benjamin) K.; m. Mary B. Scully, June 16, 1962; children: David J., Robyn A., John Michael. B.Sc., Victoria U., 1961, M. Sc. with 1st class honors, 1962; Ph.D., Brandeis U., 1966. Asst. prof. U. Tex., Austin, 1966-70, assoc. prof., 1970-77, prof., 1977—; cons. Swiss Fed. Research Inst., 1978-79, Greece Govt., UN, 1978—. Faculty advisor YMCA, Austin, 1980—; bd. dirs. Environ. Resource & Info. Center, Austin, 1974; cons. KPFT-Pacifica Radio, Houston, 1975—. Recipient Award for Teaching Excellence U. Tex., Austin, 1981; Durkee grad. fellow, 1962-66. Fellow Chem. Soc. London; mem. Royal Soc. N.Z., AAAS, Internat. Oceanographic Found., Am. Chem. Soc., Am. Soc. Biol. Chemists. Club: S.W. Speakers Exchange. Home: 5102 Crestway St Austin TX 78731 Office: U Tex Chemistry Dept. Austin TX 78712

KITTREDGE, JOHN KENDALL, insurance company executive; b. Pitts., July 7, 1927; s. Richard Carlyle and Velma (Null) K.; m. Elizabeth Delo, May 26, 1951; children—Amy, Carol. B.A., Williams Coll., 1948. With Prudential Ins. Co. Am., 1948—, v.p., 1965-73, sr. v.p., 1973-77, exec. v.p., 1977—; chmn. Prudential Property and Casualty Co., 1978-82, Prudential Reins. Co., 1978—. Mem. N.J. Bd. Higher Edn., 1971-73; mem. public issues com. Am. Cancer Soc., 1978-82; bd. dirs. Mental Health Assn., Essex County, 1968-72; trustee Coll. Medicine and Dentistry N.J., 1970-79, chmn., 1971-78. Fellow Soc. Actuaries; mem. Am. Acad. Actuaries, Inst. of Medicine, Phi Beta Kappa. Home: 90 Druid Hill Rd Summit NJ 07901 Office: Prudential Plaza Newark NJ 07101

KITTREDGE, ROBERT BRIGGS, lawyer; b. Boston, Nov. 14, 1920; s. Elwyn H. and Evelyn M. (Doyle) K.; m. Jane Pierce, Mar. 10, 1945; children: Diane (Mrs. Philip G. Rettig), Lucia, Robert Briggs, Emily, Deborah. A.B., Williams Coll., 1943; LL.B., Harvard U., 1948. Bar: Mass. 1948. Since practiced in, Boston; partner firm Ely, Partlett, Brown & Proctor (later Gaston Snow & Ely Bartlett), Boston, 1948-62; v.p. Loomis, Sayles & Co. Inc., Boston, 1962—; also dir.; pres. Loomis-Sayles Mutual Fund Inc., Boston, 1973—, Loomis-Sayles Capital Devel. Fund Inc., 1971—; trustee Winchester Savs. Bank. Bd. dirs. Winchester (Mass.) Hosp., 1958-77, pres., 1969-74. Served to lt. USNR, 1943-45. Mem. Investment Counsel Assn. Am. (chmn. exec. com.), Investment Co. Inst. (bd. govs.). Clubs: Winchester Country; Union (Boston). Home: 27 Everett Ave Winchester MA 01890 Office: 225 Franklin St Boston MA 02110

KITTROSS, JOHN MICHAEL, communications educator; b. N.Y.C., Apr. 25, 1929; s. John H. and Lucile S. (Vossen) K.; m. Sally Sprague, Dec. 27, 1951; children—David M., Julia A. A.B., Antioch Coll., 1951; M.S., Boston U., 1952; Ph.D., U. Ill., 1960. Various positions broadcasting, summer stock, motion picture prodn., 1946-52; research asst. U. Ill. Inst. Communications Research, Urbana, 1955-59; from instr. to assoc. prof. dept. telecommunications U. So. Calif., 1959-68; prof. communications Temple U., 1968—, asst. dean, 1971-73, assoc. dean, 1973-80. Author: Television Frequency Allocation Policy in the United States, 1979; co-author: Stay Tuned: A Concise History of American Broadcasting, 1978; editor: Free and Fair: Courtroom Access and the Fairness Doctrine, 1970, Jour. Broadcasting, 1960-72, Documents in American Telecommunications Policy, 1977, Administration of American Telecommunications Policy, 1981; compiler: Bibliography of Theses and Dissertations in Broadcasting, 1920-1973, 1978; contbr. articles to profl. jours. Trustee Upper Moreland Free Pub. Library, 1976-82. Served with AUS, 1952-54. Mem. Broadcast Edn. Assn., Assn. Edn. in Journalism and Mass Communication, Internat. Communications Assn., Internat. Inst. Communications, Radio-TV News Dirs. Assn., AAUP, ACLU, Sigma Delta Chi Soc. Profl. Journalists. Unitarian (trustee ch. 1966-68). Home: 2318 Fairway Rd Huntingdon Valley PA 19006 Office: Sch Communications and Theater Temple U Philadelphia PA 19122

KITTS, DEAN CARSON, lawyer, mfg. co. exec.; b. Matheson, Ont., Can., Dec. 9, 1934; s. James and Evelyn (Carson) K.; m. Elizabeth Ann Brawley, May 24, 1958; children—Dean, Robert, Mary. B.Sc. in Chem. Engring, U. Toronto, 1958; LL.B., Osgoode Hall, 1963. Bar: Called to Ont. bar 1963, named Queen's counsel 1979. Asso. firm Cavanagh & Norman (patent agts.), Toronto, Ont., 1963-64; corp. counsel John Labatt Ltd., London, Ont., 1966-81, v.p., 1971-81, sec., 1971—, v.p. adminstrn., gen. counsel, 1981—. Mem. Assn. Profl. Engrs. Ont., Canadian, Am. bar assns., Patent and Trade Mark Inst. Can. Clubs: London, St. Thomas Golf and Country. Home: 18 Applewood Crescent Saint Thomas ON N5R 1H2 Canada Office: 451 Ridout St N London ON N6A 4M3 Canada

KITTS, EMMETT HARRY, consumer finance company executive; b. Bluefield, W.Va., Oct. 31, 1920; s. James Walter and Ella (Hewson) K.; m. Montrial Conn, July 12, 1941; children: Darlene, Leslie Ann. Student, Northwestern U., 1970. With Gen. Finance Corp., Evanston, Ill., 1946—, v.p. ops., then sr. v.p., div. gen. mgr., 1962-69, exec. v.p., 1970-81, pres., 1981—, also dir., mem. exec. com. Served to capt. AUS, 1942-46. Decorated Bronze Star. Methodist. Clubs: Westmoreland Country (Wilmette, Ill.); Shriners. Home: 669 Carriage Hill Dr Glenview IL 60025 Office: 1301 Central St Evanston IL 60201

KITZ, RICHARD JOHN, anesthesiologist, educator; b. Oshkosh, Wis., Mar. 25, 1929; s. Edward G. and Lona M. (Schneider) K.; m. Jeanne Hogan, Feb. 27, 1954; 1 dau., Anne Mary. B.S., Marquette U., 1951, M.D., 1954; M.A. (hon.), Harvard U. Med. Sch., 1969. Diplomate: Am. Bd. Anesthesiology (dir.). Intern in surgery, Columbia U., 1954-55, resident in surgery, 1957-58, resident in anesthesiology, 1958-60, instr. in anesthesiology, 1960-61, NIH spl. research fellow, 1961-62, asst. prof. anesthesiology, 1962-66, assoc. prof., 1966-69; prof. Harvard U. Med. Sch., 1969—, Henry Isaiah Dorr prof. anaesthesia, 1970—; prof. research and teaching in anesthesia Harvard U.-M.I.T.; anaesthetist-in-chief Mass. Gen. Hosp., Boston, 1969—; cons. FDA; prin. investigator Harvard Anaesthesia Research and Research Tng. Center. Contbr. numerous articles, revs. to profl. publs.; editor: (with E. M. Papper) Uptake and Distribution of Anesthetic Agents, 1963, (with M. B. Laver) Scientific Basis of Anesthesia; Editorial bd.: Anesthesia Rev. Served with M.C. USN, 1955-57. Fellow. Coll. Anesthesiologists; mem. AMA, Assn. Univ. Anesthetists, Am. Soc. Anesthesiologists, Mass. Soc. Anesthesiologists. Roman Catholic. Clubs: Harvard of Boston, Beverly Yacht, Blue Water Sailing. Home: 6 Pond Rd Dover MA 02030 Office: Dept Anesthesia Mass Gen Hosp Boston MA 02114

KITZKE, EUGENE DAVID, research management executive; b. Milw., Sept. 2, 1923; s. Leo R. and Regina R. (Tomczyk) K.; m. Lorraine Grace Shummon, Sept. 2, 1946; children: Mary Victoria, Paul Simon, Patrice Lynn, Jerome Peter. B.S., Marquette U., 1945, M.S., 1947. Instr. microbiology St. Mary's Sch. Nursing, Grand Rapids, Mich., 1946-47; assoc. prof. Aquinas Coll., 1947-51; lab researcher S.C. Johnson & Son, Inc., Racine, Wis., 1951-57, research mgr., 1957-76, v.p. corp. research and devel., 1976-81; pres. Oak Crete Block Corp., South Milwaukee, Wis., 1980—; asst. clin. prof. dept. environ. medicine Med. Coll. Wis., Milw., 1973-81; owner Danel enterprise, South Milwaukee; dir. Argentine Johnson, Brazil Johnson, Microgen Corp. Patentee (in field); contbr. articles to tech. jours., fiction and poetry to mags. Mem. Pres.' Council Alverno Coll., 1979-81. Mem. Chem. Spltys. Mfrs. Assn. (exec. bd.), Palm Soc. (exec. bd., past pres.), Am. Genetic Assn., AAAS, Sigma Xi, Phi Sigma, Sigma Tau Delta. Roman Catholic. Home: 616 Aspen South Milwaukee WI 53172 Office: Box 413 South Milwaukee WI 53172 Office: 7101 S PennsylvaniaAve Oak Creek WI 53154

KIVES, RAYMOND, lawyer; b. Winnipeg, Man., Can., May 13, 1942; s. Joseph and Rose K.; m. Barbara Rosenfield, June 29, 1969; children—Sari, Stephanie, Reagan, Michael David. LL.B., U.Man., 1967. Bar: Called to Man. bar 1968. Mem. firm Simkin Gallagher, Winnipeg, 1963-67; exec. v.p. K-Tel Internat., Winnipeg, 1967-77, 1977—; pres. K-Tel Europe, London, 1977-81. Bd. dirs. Winnipeg Jewish Child and Welfare Services, 1975-76; bd. dirs. Winnipeg Jewish Community Council, 1976-77, Ramah Hebrew Sch., 1975-76, Big Bros., Winnipeg, 1974-75. Mem. Law Soc. Man. Jewish. Club: B'nai B'rith. Home: 221 Park Blvd Winnipeg MB R3P 0G6 Canada Office: 1670 Inkster Blvd Winnipeg MB R2X 2W8 Canada

KIVETT, MARVIN F., anthropologist; b. Nebr., Mar. 10, 1917; s. Thomas and Murl (Mark) K.; m. Caroline Ritchey, Sept. 12, 1941; 1 son, Ronald Lee. A.B., U. Nebr., 1942, M.A., 1951. Archeologist Smithsonian Instn., 1946-49; mus. dir. Nebr. Hist. Soc., Lincoln, 1949-63, adminstrv. dir., 1963—. Editor: Nebr. History, 1963—; Contbr. articles to profl. jours. Served with AUS, 1942-46. Home: 5425 Franklin St Box 82554 Lincoln NE 68501 Office: 1500 R St Lincoln NE 68508

KIVETTE, RUTH MONTGOMERY, English educator; b. Union City, N.J., Jan. 10, 1926; d. Joseph and Margaret Eliza (Ditty) Montgomery; m. Everett McNeill Kivette, Oct. 23, 1954. A.B., Bernard Coll., 1948; A.M., Columbia U., 1950, Ph.D., 1960; B.D., Union Theol. Sem., N.Y.C., 1954. Asst. prof. Davis and Elkins Coll., Elkins, W.Va., 1950-52; lectr. Barnard Coll., N.Y.C., 1952-55, 57-61, asst. prof., 1961-67; assoc. prof. Bernard Coll., N.Y.C., 1967-74; prof. English Barnard Coll., N.Y.C., 1974—. Kent fellow, 1954; Lilly postdoctoral fellow in religion, 1963; folger Library fellow, 1966; Mellon grantee, 1983. Mem. AAUP, AAUW, Law and Humanities Inst., Milton Soc. Am., MLA, Renaissance Soc. Am. Office: Barnard Coll New York NY 10027

KIWITT, SIDNEY, motion picture executive; b. Bklyn., Jan. 16, 1928; s. Rudolph John Albert and Dora (Alexandrov) K.; m. Paris Ratner, Mar. 10, 1972; children: Wendy, Peter David. B.B.A., U. N.Mex., 1950. With Peat Marwick Mitchell & Co., N.Y.C., 1950-60; exec. v.p. Warner Bros., Inc., N.Y.C., 1960-83; pres. K-Films, Inc., N.Y.C., 1983—. Served with USNR, 1945-46. Mem. Am. Inst. Public Accts., U.S. Yacht Racing Union., Parrot Soc. of Bedford (Eng.). Republican. Jewish. Office: 630 Fifth Ave Suite 862 New York NY 10020

KIZER, CAROLYN ASHLEY, poet, educator; b. Spokane, Wash., Dec. 10, 1925; d. Benjamin Hamilton and M. (Ashley) K.; m. Stimson Bullitt, Jan., 1948 (div.); children—Ashley Ann, Scott, Jill Hamilton; m. John Marshall Woodbridge, Apr. 11, 1975. B.A., Sarah Lawrence Coll., 1945; postgrad. (Chinese govt. fellow in comparative lit.), Columbia, 1946-47; studied poetry with, Theodore Roethke U. Wash., 1953-54. Specialist in lit. U.S. Dept. State, Pakistan, 1964-65; first dir. lit. programs Nat. Endowment for Arts, 1966-70; poet-in-residence U. N.C. at Chapel Hill, 1970-74; Hurst Prof. Lit. Washington U., St. Louis, 1971; lectr. Spring Lecture Series Barnard Coll., 1972; acting dir. grad. writing program Columbia, 1972; McGuffey Lectr. Poet-in-residence, Ohio U., 1974; vis. poet Iowa Writer's Workshop, 1975; Participant Internat. Poetry Festivals, London, Eng., 1960, 70, Yugoslavia, 1969, 70, Pakistan, 1969, Rotterdam, Netherlands, 1970, Knokke-le-Zut, Belgium; Author: The Ungrateful Garden, 1961, Knock Upon Silence, 1965, Midnight Was My Cry, 1971; Founder, editor: Poetry N.W, 1959-65; Contbr. poems, articles to Am., Brit. jours. Mem. ACLU, Amnesty Internat., P.E.N., Poetry Soc. Am., Acad. Am. Poets. Episcopalian. Address: 120 4th St SE Washington DC 20003

KIZER, ROBERT F., concrete products company executive; b. 1934; married. B.A., Hillsdale Coll., Mich., 1959. Dir. mktg. Huron Portland Cement Co., 1959-65; v.p. Medusa Corp., 1965-77; exec. v.p. Gen. Portland, Inc., 1977-78; exec. v.p. cement and constrn. materials group Lone Star Industries, Inc., Greenwich, Conn., 1978-79, v.p. domestic ops., 1979—; dir. Portland Cement Co. of Utah, Lone Star LaFarge, Lone Star Cement, Inc. Office: Lone Star Industries Inc 1 Greenwich Plaza Greenwich CT 06830 *

KIZZIAR, JANET WRIGHT, psychologist, author, lecturer; b. Independence, Kans.; d. John L. and Thelma (Rooks) Wright; m. Mark Kizziar. B.A., M.A., Ed.D., U. Tulsa. Sch. psychologist Tulsa Pub. Schs., 1966-68; pvt. practice psychology, Tulsa, 1969-78, Bartlesville, Okla., 1978—. Co-host: Psychologists' Corner program, Sta. KOTV, Tulsa.; Author: (with Judy W. Hagedorn) Gemini: The Psychology and Phenomena of Twins, 1975, Search for Acceptance: The Adolescent and Self Esteem, 1979. Sponsor Youth Crisis Intervention Telephone Center, 1972-74; Bd. dirs. March of Dimes, Child Protection Team, Women and Children in Crisis, United Fund, YMCA Fund, Mental Health of Washington County., Alternative High Sch. Named Disting. Alumni U. Tulsa, Outstanding Young Woman of Okla. Mem. Am. Psychol. Assn., Tulsa Psychol. Assn. (past pres.), NOW, Am. Women in Radio and TV, Am. Assn. Sex Educators, Counselors and Therapists, Internat. Twins Assn. (pres. 1976-77). Home: 2503 SE Glynnwood Dr Bartlesville OK 74006 Office: 1740 SE Washington Suite G Bartlesville OK 74003

KJAR, JOSEPH A., broadcasting executive; b. Salt Lake City, June 13, 1920; s. Joseph E. K. and Effie (Morris) Ashron; m. Noma Robers, Nov. 30, 1945; children: Joseph Gregory, Kristin, William Scott, Susan, Kevin Richard. Student, U. Utah, 1937-41, Columbia U., 1943, Harvard U., 1944. Staff announcer, program dir., gen. sales mgr., gen. mgr., v.p. KSL-AM and KSL Inc., div. Bonneville Internat. Corp., Salt Lake City, 1946-72, exec. v.p., 1972-80, exec. v.p., chief operating officer, 1980—; vice chmn., dir.-at-large CBS. Radio Affiliates Bd., 1968-69; conv. chmn. CBS Radio Affiliates Bd., 1959-70, bd. chmn., 1970-71; mem. Salt Lake Regional bd. Zion's First Nat. Bank. Mem. adv. council Weber State Coll.; mem. nat. adv. council Brigham Young U. Sch. Mgmt., 1981-82; chmn. Scouters conv., 1968; chmn. bd. Salt Lake United Fund, 1973. Recipient Broadcasters Disting. Service award U. Utah, 1964, Meritorious Service award Brigham Young U. Dept. Communication, 1975. Mem. Nat. Assn. Broadcasters, Radio Advt. Bur. (mem. bd. 1979-82), Utah Broadcasters Assn. (1968), Rocky Mountain Broadcasters Assn. (mem. bd.), Nat. Assn. FM Broadcasters (Bd. dirs., exec. com.), Clear Channel Broadcasters Service (pres. 1976-78). Republican. Mormon. Home: 525 E 100 N Centerville UT 84014 Office: Bonneville Internat Corp 36 S State St Suite 2100 Salt Lake City UT 84111

KJELDAAS, TERJE, JR., educator; b. Oslo, Norway, Oct. 24, 1924; came to U.S., 1940; s. Terje and Mimi Helene (Hansen) K.; m. Sigrid Seland Moeller, June 17, 1950; children—Ingrid, John. B.S., Poly. Inst. Bklyn., 1948; A.M., Columbia, 1949; Ph.D., U. Pitts., 1959. Research engr. Westinghouse Elec. Research Labs., Churchill Boro, Pa., 1950-59; prof. physics Poly. Inst. N.Y., 1959—, head dept., 1977-80; cons. Contbr. articles to profl. jours. Served with USAAF, 1943-46. Mem. Am. Phys. Soc. Home: 50 Fort Pl Staten Island NY 10301 Office: 333 Jay St Brooklyn NY 11201

KJELLAND, ROLAND ARTHUR, former steel executive; b. Valley City, N.D., June 19, 1925; s. Ole H. and Hilda G. (Larsen) K.; m. Helen E. Walters, Nov. 23, 1955; children: Deanna L., Janice M., James P. B.B.A., U. Mich., 1950. Controller stamping div. Kaiser-Frazer Co., 1950-58; adminstrv. asst. to pres. Willys Overland do Brasil (S.A.), Sao Paulo, 1958-63; v.p., controller Kaiser Steel Corp., 1963-70, v.p., Oakland, Calif., 1970-72, exec. v.p., 1977-80, pres., chief exec. officer, 1980-81; dir., exec. v.p. Kaiser Resources, Ltd., 1972-73; v.p. Kaiser Industries Corp., Oakland, 1970-76; pres., chief exec. officer Nat. Steel & Shipbldg., San Diego, 1976-77. Served with USN, 1944-46. Recipient Disting. Alumnus award Valley City State Coll., 1978. Clubs: Orinda Country, World Trade. Office: PO Box 58 Oakland CA 94604

KLAAS, NICHOLAS PAUL, chemical company executive; b. Kieler, Wis., June 25, 1925; s. Paul Francis and Ida (Schroeder) K.; m. Ruth Elizabeth Barry, Nov. 5, 1949; children: Paul, Patricia, Kathleen, James. B.A., Loras Coll., 1945; Ph.D., U. Notre Dame, 1948. Product mgr. Rohm & Haas Co., Phila., 1948-52; mgr. research and devel. 3M Co., St. Paul, 1952-65; exec. v.p., dir. Wyomissing Corp., West Reading, Pa., 1965-71; group v.p. chems. GAF Corp., N.Y.C., 1971-77; gen. mgr. splty. chems. Ga. Pacific Corp., Portland, Oreg., 1977; pres. J.T. Baker Chem. Co., Phillipsburg, N.J., 1977—; chmn. bd. J.T. Baker B.V., Deventer, Netherlands, 1978—. Patentee in field; contbr. articles to profl. jours. Trustee St. Joseph Hosp., Reading, Pa., 1968-71; bd. regents Loras Coll., Dubuque, Iowa, 1974-76. Mem. Synethic Organic Chem. Mfg. Assn. (dir. 1974-77), Asphalt Roofing Mfrs. Assn. (dir. 1974-77), Am. Chem. Soc., AAAS, Soc. Chem. Industry, N.Y. Acad. Sci. Club: Smoke Rise. Home: 410 Gravel Hill Rd Kinnelon NJ 07405 Office: JT Baker Chem Co 222 Red School Ln Phillipsburg NJ 08865

KLABUNDE, CHARLES SPENCER, artist; b. Omaha, Oct. 1, 1935; s. Otto H. and Susannah A. (Rohrbough) K.; m. Sandra Sue Schmitt, May 23, 1964; children—Noah Robert, Jedediah McKenzie. B.F.A., U. Nebr., Omaha; M.F.A., U. Iowa, Iowa City. Profl. painter and printmaker, N.Y.C., 1967—; adj. prof. art Cooper Union, 1968-75. Illustrator: spl. collectors edit. The Lost Ones (Samuel Beckett), 1984; rep. permanent collections, Mus. Modern Art, N.Y.C., Met. Mus. Art, Whitney Mus. Am. Art, Bklyn. Mus., Art Inst. Chgo., Mpls. Inst. Art, Phila. Mus. Art, Library of Congress, Nat. Gallery. Served with U.S. Army, 1958-59. Guggenheim fellow, 1971. Home: 68 W 3d St New York NY 10012 Office: 16 Waverly Pl New York NY 10003

KLACSMANN, JOHN ANTHONY, ret. chem. co. exec.; b. West New York, N.J., Oct. 6, 1921; s. Joseph J. Klacsmann and Anna Elizabeth (Schmiedeberg) Goessling; m. Betty Birdsey, Sept. 23, 1944; children—Steven B., Peter G., John Anthony. B.S., Yale U., 1942, M.A., 1944, Ph.D., 1947. Asst. to lab. dir. Union Carbide Corp., Oak Ridge, 1944-46; with E.I. duPont de Nemours & Co., 1947—, v.p., gen. mgr. fabrics and finishes dept., 1973-75; v.p., gen. mgr. internat. dept., 1975-78, v.p. internat., Wilmington, Del., 1978-81, ret., 1981; dir. DuPont Can. Inc. Mem. Am. Chem. Soc., AAAS, Conf. Bd. (internat. council), Council Americas and World Affairs Council (trustee), U.S.-USSR Trade and Econ. Council (alt. dir.), Egypt-U.S. Bus. Council, Philippine-Am. C. of C., Spain-U.S. C. of C., U.S.-W. German Trade and Econ. Council, Internat. Mgmt. and Devel. Inst., Adv. Council on Japan-U.S. Econ. Relations, Stanford Research Inst., Sigma Xi. Republican. Clubs: Wilmington, Wilmington Country. Home: 62 Village Walk Dr Sawgrass Ponte Vedra Beach FL 32082

KLAERNER, CURTIS MAURICE, former oil company executive; b. Fredericksburg, Tex., Sept. 7, 1920; s. Elgin and Irene (Wagner) K.; m. Aileen E. Eitt, Sept. 4, 1942; children: Sherilyn Kay, Curtis Elgin. B.S. in Chem. Engring, U. Tex., 1942; grad. program sr. execs., Mass. Inst. Tech., 1956. Process engr., then chief process engr. Magnolia Petroleum Co., 1942-53; refinery mgr., then mgr. Eastern region mfg. Socony Mobil Oil Co., 1953-59; regional exec., then regional v.p. Mobil Internat. Oil Co., 1959-61; pres. Mobil Inner Europe, Geneva, Switzerland, 1962-65; corp. v.p. charge marine transp. and internat. sales Socony Mobil Oil Co., 1965-69; exec. v.p. internat. div. Mobil Oil Corp., 1969-72, pres., 1972-79; also exec. v.p., dir., mem. exec. com. corp.; vice chmn., dir. Commonwealth Oil Refining Co., San Antonio, 1979, pres., chief operating officer, 1979-83; ret., 1983; vice chmn. Weed Instrument Co.; dir. Belgian Refining Corp., W.I. Oil Corp., Nat. Petroleum Ltd.; Bd. dirs. Nat. Fgn. Trade Council.; mem. adv. council Engring. Found., U. Tex., Austin. Recipient Disting. Grad. award Coll. Engring., U. Tex., 1983. Mem. Council Fgn. Relations, Brit. Am. Soc. (dir.), Internat. C. of C. (trustee U.S. chamber), German-Am. C. of C. (dir., vice chmn.), Phi Eta Sigma, Omega Chi Epsilon, Phi Kappa Sigma. Republican. Episcopalian. Clubs: Union League, Pinnacle, Circumnavigators (N.Y.C.); Oak Hills Country, Optimists (San Antonio). Home: 144 Cas Hills Dr San Antonio TX 78213

KLAGES, ROY ARTHUR, educator; b. Cape Girardeau, Mo., Aug. 31, 1916; s. Arthur F. and Mary (Ulrich) K.; m. Dorothy M. Cole, Dec. 23, 1941 (dec. 1952); 1 dau., Mary Frances Klages Kinley; m. Ida Cook Parr, Dec. 23, 1955; stepchildren—Frances V. Parr (Mrs. Ronald Bradow), Laurence L. Parr. B.S., Mo. State U., 1938; postgrad., Northwestern U., 1939; M.B.A., U. Tex., Austin, 1945, Miss. State U., 1950, Washington U., St. Louis, 1953; Ph.D., St. Louis U., 1959. Sales rep. S.E. Missourian Newspaper, Cape Girardeau, 1932-38; mgr. bookstore Mo. State U., 1934-38; supt., tchr. Belgrade (Mo.) Consol. Schs., 1938-42; instr. Cape Girardeau Pub. Schs., 1942-43; asst. prof. Southwestern Coll., Winfield, Kans., 1943-45; asso. prof., head div. mktg. Miss. State U., State College, 1945-55; grad. asst. St. Louis U., 1955-59; asso. prof. U. Detroit, 1959-64; prof., chmn. dept. mktg. State U. N.Y. at Albany, 1964—; cons. in field. Bd. dirs. Advt. Inst., St. Louis, 1957-58. Mem. Am. Mktg. Assn., AAUP, Nat. Fgn. Trade Council, Am. Collegiate Retail Assn., Sales, Mktg. Execs. Assn. Eastern N.Y. (pres. 1970-71), Sales and Mktg. Execs. Internat. (vice chmn. coll. relations 1969-72), Nat. Retail Mchts. Assn., Acad. Internat. Bus., Am. Econ. Assn. Methodist. Club: Masons. Home: PO Box 306 102 Okara Dr Guilderland NY 12084 Office: State U NY 1400 Washington Ave Albany NY 12222

KLAGSBRUNN, HANS ALEXANDER, lawyer; b. Vienna, Austria, Apr. 28, 1909; U.S., 1912; s. Hugo and Lili (Brandt) K.; m. Elizabeth Mapelsden Ramsey, Jan. 27, 1934. Student, Vienna Gymnasium, 1922-25; B.A., Yale U., 1929, LL.B., 1932; postgrad., Harvard U. Law Sch., 1932-33. Bar: D.C., U.S. Supreme Ct 1935. Asso. RFC (and affiliates), 1933-45; exec. v.p., gen. counsel, dir. and mem. exec. com. Def. Plant Corp.; surplus property dir. and asst. gen. counsel RFC; RFC mem. Hancock Contract Settlement Bd. and Clayton Surplus Property Bd. in Office War Mblzn.; dep. dir. Office War Mblzn. and Reconversion, The White House, 1945-46; mem. Army Chem. Corps Reorgn. Com., 1955-56; sr. mem. Klagsbrunn & Hanes (attys.), 1946-68; counsel to successor firm, 1969—; Mem. Jud. Conf. D.C. Circuit, 1964-66; chmn. com. criminal indigents; mem. U.S. Ct. Appeals Com. on Admissions and Grievances, 1967-74, chmn., 1972-74; mem. task force on U.S. energy policy Twentieth Century Fund, 1976-77; Mem. Health and Welfare Council, bd. dirs., 1958-73, pres., 1961-63; mem. Loudoun County Sanitation Authority, 1959-68, vice chmn., 1965-68; mem. Piedmont (Va.) Environ. Council, 1975-76. Bd. dirs. Friendship House, 1957-68, pres., 1959-68; bd. dirs. Columbia Hosp. for Women, 1964-74, sec., 1966-67, 1st v.p., 1967-68. Recipient Health and Welfare Council Community Service awards, 1961, 63. Mem. Am. Bar Found., Fed. Bar Assn., Am. Arbitration Assn. (nat. panel), Bar Assn. D.C. (chmn. U.S. Ct. Appeals com. 1966-67), Am. Bar Assn. (past chmn. coms.), Nat. Planning Assn., A.I.M., Am. Judicature Soc., Newcomen Soc., Phi Beta Kappa, Order of Coif, Phi Beta Kappa Assos., Nat. Symphony Orch. Assn. Clubs: Metropolitan, Yale, Nat. Press, City Tavern. Home: 3420 Q St N W Washington DC 20007 also Salem Farm R F D 1 Purcellville VA 22132 Office: 3420 Que St NW Washington DC 20007

KLAGSTAD, ROBERT EDGAR, fin. exec.; b. Detroit, Mar. 10, 1923; s. Harold L. and Ione (Hatch) K.; m. Shirley E. Weemhoff, Apr. 3, 1948; children—Karen Ione, Robert J., Richard H. Student, Mass. Inst. Tech., 1941-42; B.B.A. in Accounting, U. Mich., 1949. C.P.A., Wis. With Price, Waterhouse & Co. (C.P.A.s), Chgo., 1949-53; v.p., comptroller Lake Shore Nat. Bank, Chgo., 1953-63; treas. Marine Corp., Milw., 1963-75; controller I.D.I. Corp., Milw., 1975-77; treas. Empire Generator Corp., Germantown, Wis., 1978—. Served to 1st lt. USAAF, 1942-45; ETO. Mem. Exptl. Aircraft Assn., Internat. Aerobatic Club, Delta Kappa Epsilon. Republican. Mem. Reformed Ch. Address: 11424 N Spring Ave Mequon WI 53092

KLAHR, SAULO, scientist, educator; b. Santander, Colombia, June 8, 1935; came to U.S., 1961, naturalized, 1970; s. Herman and Raquel (Konigsberg) K.; m. Carol Declue, Dec. 29, 1965; children—James Herman, Robert David. B.A., Colegio Santa Librada, Cali, Colombia, 1954; M.D., U. Nat., Bogota, Colombia, 1959. Intern Hosp. San Juan de Dios, Bogota, 1958-59; resident U. Hosp., Cali, 1959-61; mem. faculty Washington U. Sch. Medicine, St. Louis, 1966—, prof. medicine, 1972—, dir. renal div., 1972—; asso. physician Barnes Hosp., 1972-75, physician, 1975—; established investigator Am. Heart Assn., 1968-73; mem. adv. com. artificial kidney chronic uremia program USPHS, 1971—; bd. dirs. Eastern Mo. Kidney Found., 1973-75, chmn. med. advisory bd., 1973-74; research com. Mo. Heart Assn., 1973-80, chmn., 1980-81; sci. adv. bd. NKF, 1978—; mem. gen. medicine B study sect. USPHS, 1979-83, chmn. gen. medicine B study sect., 1981-83; chmn. NKF Research and Fellowship Com., 1979-81. Author articles, chpts. in books; editor: Contemporary Nephrology; editorial bd.: Am. Jour. Nephrology, The Kidney and Body Fluids in Health and Disease; assoc. editor: Jour. Clin. Investigation. USPHS postdoctoral fellow, 1961-63. Fellow ACP; mem. Am. Soc. Nephrology (sec.-treas. 1981—), Am. Soc. Clin. Investigation, Am. Physiol. Soc., Biophys. Soc., N.Y. Acad. Scis., Central Soc. Clin. Research, Soc. Exptl. Biology and Medicine, Sigma Xi. Home: 11544 Ladue Rd Saint Louis MO 63141

KLAMAN, SAUL B., economist; b. Boston, Jan. 18, 1920; s. Jacob and Martha (Benjamin) K.; m. Hannah Bell, Sept. 12, 1948; 1 son, Mark Lewis. B.S., U. Mass., 1941; M.A., Mich. State U., 1942; Ph.D., N. Y. U., 1961. Econ. analyst OPA, 1942-43; agrl. economist USDA, 1943; economist Bd. Govs. FRS, Washington, 1946-58; sr. staff mem. Nat. Bur. Econ. Research, N.Y.C., 1956; economist Nat. Assn. Mut. Savs. Banks, N.Y.C., 1958, dir. research, 1959-66, v.p., chief economist, 1966-75, dep. exec. v.p., 1975-76, exec. v.p., 1976-77, pres., 1977-83, Nat. Council Savs. Instns., 1983—; dir. Bradford Trust Co., Bradford Nat. Corp., J. I. Kislak Co., Nat. Bur. Econ. Research, Inc.; adj. prof. econs. and fin. Baruch Coll., CUNY, 1966-76; econ. adv. bd. to sec. commerce, 1972-76; mem. Pres.'s Task Force on Met. and Urban Problems, 1964-65, Pres.'s; Task Force on Low-Income Housing, 1969-70, Pres.'s Commn. on Mortgage Interest Rates, 1968-69; mem. bus. adv. council U. Mass., 1969-82, task force on future, 1971-72. Author: The Postwar Residential Mortgage Market, 1961; Contbr. articles to profl. jours. Served from ensign to lt. (j.g.) USNR, 1943-46. Mem. Am. Econ. Assn., Am. Finance Assn. (dir. 1975-77, instl. chmn. 1973-77), Am. Real Estate and Urban Econs. Assn., Nat. Assn. Bus. Economists (v.p. 1970-71, mem. council 1967-74, pres. 1971-72), Conf. Bus. Economists, Forecasters (pres. 1969-70). Clubs: Sky (N.Y.C.); Cosmos, University (Washington). Home: Nathan Hale Dr Stamford CT 06902 Office: 1101 15th St NW Washington DC 20005

KLAMON, LAWRENCE PAINE, diversified company executive; b. St. Louis, Mar. 17, 1937; s. Joseph Martin and Rose (Schimel) K.; m. Jo Ann Karen Beatty, Nov. 1957 (div. Feb. 1974); children: Stephen Robert, Karen Jean, Lawrence Paine; m. Frances Ann Estes, Mar. 1980. A.B., Washington U., St. Louis, 1958; J.D., Yale U., 1961. Bar: N.Y. bar 1964. Confidential asst. Office Sec. Def., Washington, 1961-62, spl. asst. to gen. counsel, 1962-63; asso. Cravath, Swaine & Moore, N.Y.C., 1963-67; v.p., gen. counsel Fuqua Industries, Inc., Atlanta, 1967-73, sr. v.p. fin. and adminstrn., 1971-81, pres., 1981—. Bd. editors: Yale Law Jour, 1959-61. Mem. Am. Bar Assn., Assn. Bar City N.Y., Am. Soc. Corp. Secs., Phi Beta Kappa, Order of Coif, Omicron Delta Kappa. Home: 2665 Dellwood Dr NW Atlanta GA 30305 Office: First Atlanta Tower Atlanta GA 30383

KLAPINSKY, RAYMOND JOSEPH, investment company executive; b. Beaver Meadows, Pa., Dec. 7, 1938; s. Michael and Sophia Ann (Soroko) K.; m. Dorothea Eva Kakauas, July 15, 1961; children: Jennifer Rae, Christopher James. B.A., U. Del., 1960; J.D., George Washington U., 1967. Bar: D.C. 1967, Pa. 1970, U.S. Supreme Ct. 1976, U.S. Ct. Appeals (D.C. cir.) 1967, U.S. Dist. Ct., D.C. 1967. Trial atty. U.S. SEC, Washington, 1967-69; assoc. counsel, corp. sec. Wellington Mgmt. Co., Phila., Valley Forge, Pa., 1969-75; v.p., counsel, corp. sec. The Vanugard Group Investment Cos., Valley Forge, Pa., 1975—. Served to capt. USMC, 1960-64. Mem. Fed. Bar Assn., Pa. Bar Assn., D.C. Bar Assn., Phila. Bar Assn. Republican. Roman Catholic. Home: 180 Woodhill Ln Media PA 19063 Office: The Vanguard Group of Investment Cos 1300 Morris Dr PO Box 876 Valley Forge PA

KLAPPERICH, FRANK LAWRENCE, JR., investment banker; b. Oak Park, Ill., Oct. 11, 1934; s. Frank Lawrence and Marjorie (Doan) K.; m. Margaret Monroe Touborg, Mar. 9, 1957; children: Margaret Friis, Susan Doane, Frank Lawrence III, Elizabeth Monroe. A.B., Princeton U., 1956; M.B.A., Harvard U., 1961. With Kidder, Peabody & Co., Inc., Chgo., 1961—, v.p., 1964—, dir., 1972—; dir. Charter Fin. Corp., Chgo. Bd. dirs. Chgo. Theatre Group of Chgo. Art Inst. Served with USN, 1956-59; lt. comdr. Res. Mem. Investment Analysts Soc. Chgo., Securities Industry Assn., Inst. Chartered Fin. Analysts, Harvard Bus. Sch. Assn. Chgo. Clubs: Princeton (N.J.); Charter; Princeton (N.Y.C.); Chicago, University, Mid Day, Bond (pres. 1983-84), Econ., Chicago, Executive, Princeton (pres. 1970-71), Harvard (Chgo.); Indian Hill (Winnetka). Home: 345 Woodley Rd Winnetka IL 60093 Office: 125 S Wacker Dr Chicago IL 60606

KLAPPERT, PETER, poet, educator; b. Rockville Center, N.Y., Nov. 14, 1942; s. Herman Emil and Grace Barbara (Rupp) K. B.A., Cornell U., 1964; M.A., U. Iowa, 1967, M.F.A., 1968. Instr. English Rollins Coll., Winter Park, Fla., 1968-71; Briggs-Copeland lectr. English Harvard U., 1971-74; vis. lectr. New Coll., Sarasota, Fla., 1972, asst. prof., 1977-78, George Mason U., Fairfax, Va., 1978-81, assoc. prof., 1981—, dir. creative writing, 1979-80; resident fellow Yaddo, 1972, 73, 75, 81, MacDowell Colony, 1973, 75, Fondation Karolyi, 1976, Millay Colony, 1981, Va. Center for Creative Arts, 1978, 79, 81. (Winner Yale Series of Younger Poets Competition 1970); writer-in-residence, Coll. William and Mary, 1976-77; (Nat. Endowment for Arts fellow 1973, 79, recipient Lucille Medwick award 1977); Author: poems Lugging Vegetables to Nantucket, 1971; essay/anthology After The Rhymers Guild, 1971; poems Circular Stairs, Distress in the Mirrors, 1975, Non-Sequitur O'Connor, 1977, The Idiot Princess of the Last Dynasty, 1984. Mem. Assoc. Writing Programs, Poetry Soc. Am., Washington Ind. Writers., Writers' Ctr. of Bethesda (Md.). Address: Dept English Coll George Mason U Fairfax VA 22030

KLARE, GEORGE ROGER, psychology educator; b. Mpls., Apr. 17, 1922; s. George C. and Lee (Launer) K.; m. Julia Marie Price Matson, Dec. 24, 1946; children: Deborah, Roger, Barbara. Student, U. Nebr., 1940-41, U. Minn., 1941-43, U. Mo., 1943; B.A., U. Minn., 1946, M.A., 1947, Ph.D., 1950. Instr. U. Minn., 1948-50; staff psychologist Psychol. Corp., N.Y.C., 1950-51; research asso. U. Ill., 1952-54; asst. prof. dept. psychology Ohio U., Athens, 1954-57, asso. prof., 1957-62, prof., 1962-79, disting. prof., 1979—, chmn. dept., 1959-63, acting dean Coll. Arts and Sci., 1965, dean, 1966-71, media coordinator, 1972-75; research asso. Harvard U., 1968-69; vis. prof. State U. N.Y. at Stony Brook, 1971-72, U. Iowa, 1979-80; staff mem. N.Y.C. Writers Conf., 1956-57; cons., lectr. Nat. Project Agr. Communication, 1957-59, Com. on World Literacy and Christian Lit., 1958-62; exec. asst., sr. research engr. Autonetics, 1960-61; cons. Resources Devel. Corp., 1962-65, Boston Pub. Sch., 1968, D.C. Heath Co., 1971, Western Electric, 1973, Westinghouse, 1975, Human Resources Research Orgn., 1978-79, U.S. Navy, 1975, Armed Services Readability Research, 1975, Center for Ednl. Experimentation, Devel. and Evaluation, 1978-79, 81, U.S. Army, 1979, Bell System Center for Tech. Edn., 1975-80, Time, Inc., 1977-79, AT&T, 1979-81; lectr. Open Univ., Eng., 1975, NATO Conf. Visual Presentation of Info., The Netherlands, 1978. Author: (with Byron Buck) Know Your Reader, 1954, The Measurement of Readability, 1963, (with Paul A. Games) Elementary Statistics: Data Analysis for the Behavioral Sciences, 1967, A Manual for Readable Writing, 1975, 4th edit., 1980; editorial bd.: Info. Design Jour, 1979—, Instructional Science, 1975—, Reading Teacher, 1981-82. Served to 1st lt. USAAF, 1943-45. Decorated Air medal, Purple Heart; Fulbright travel grantee U.S.-U.K. Ednl. Commn. to Open U., 1977-81. Fellow Am. Psychol. Assn.; mem. Nat. Reading Conf. (invited address 1975, Oscar Causey award for outstanding contbns. to reading research 1981), Internat. Reading Assn., Am. Ednl. Research Assn., Delta Phi Lambda, Psi Chi, Phi Delta Kappa. Home: 5 Pleasantview Dr Athens OH 45701

KLARE, MICHAEL THOMAS, political scientist; b. N.Y.C., Oct. 14, 1942; s. Charles and Mildred (Smith) K. B.A., Columbia Coll., 1963, M.A., 1968; postgrad., Yale U., 1963-65; Ph.D., Union Grad. Sch., 1976. Instr. Parsons Sch. Design, N.Y.C., 1967-70; research dir. N. Am. Congress on Latin Am., Berkeley, Calif., 1970-76; vis. lectr. Tufts U., 1973; vis. fellow Center of Internat. Studies, Princeton U., 1976-77; sr. fellow Inst. Policy Studies, Washington, 1977—; contbg. editor Pacific News Service, 1980—; def. corr. The Nation, 1983—; cons. in field. Author: War Without End, 1972, Supplying Repression, 1978, Beyond the Vietnam Syndrome, 1981. Compton fellow, 1976-77; Field Found. grantee, 1975-77, 77-80. Mem. Am. Polit. Sci. Assn., Inter-Univ. Seminar on Armed Forces and Society. Home: 205 West End Ave New York NY 10023 Office: 1901 Q St NW Washington DC 20009

KLARMAN, HERBERT ELIAS, educator, economist; b. Chmielnik, Poland, Dec. 21, 1916; came to U.S., 1929, naturalized, 1929; s. Morris Louis and Helen (Klarman) K.; m. Mary A. Monk, 1967; children: Seth Andrew, Joseph Michael. A.B., Columbia U., 1939; M.A., U. Wis., 1941, Ph.D., 1946. Asst., then asso. dir. Hosp. Council Greater N.Y., 1949-51, 52-62; asst. dir. N.Y. State Hosp. Study, Columbia U., 1948-49; asst. prof. econs. Bklyn. Coll., 1947-48; economist nat. income div. Dept. Commerce, 1946-47; med. economist Nat. Security Resources Bd., 1951-52; mem. faculty Johns Hopkins U., 1962-69, prof. public health adminstrn. and polit. economy, 1965-69; prof. environ. medicine and community health Downstate Med. Center, SUNY, 1969-70; prof. econs. Grad. Sch. Public Adminstrn., N.Y. U., N.Y.C., 1970-82; Michael Davis lectr. U. Chgo., 1981; mem. health services research study sect. NIH, 1962-66; chmn. planning com. 2d Conf. on Econs. Health, 1967-69; mem. U.S. Nat. Com. on Vital and Health Stats., 1967-71, N.Y. State Health Adv. Council, 1976-83; mem. spl. med. adv. group VA, 1977-81; mem. Inst. Medicine, Nat. Acad. Scis., 1971. Author: Hospital Care in New York City, 1963, Economics of Health, 1965; also articles, chpts. in books.; Editor: Empirical Studies in Health Economics, 1970. Served to capt. AUS, 1942-46. Recipient first Norman A. Welch Meml. award, 1965; Guggenheim fellow, 1976-77. Fellow AAAS, Am. Public Health Assn.; mem. Am. Econ. Assn., Am. Statis. Assn., Royal Econ. Soc., Phi Beta Kappa. Home: 1 E University Pkwy Baltimore MD 21218

KLASS, MORTON, anthropology educator, consultant; b. Bklyn., June 24, 1927; s. David A. and Millie (Fisher) K.; m. Sheila Solomon, May 2, 1953; children: Perri Elizabeth, David Arnold, Judith Alexandra. B.A., Bklyn. Coll., 1955; Ph.D., Columbia U., 1959. Mem. faculty Bennington Coll., Vt., 1959-64; vis. asst. prof. Columbia U., N.Y.C., 1962-65; assoc. prof. Barnard Coll., N.Y.C., 1965-69, prof. anthropology, 1969—; dir. So. Asian Inst. Columbia U., N.Y.C., 1982—; vis. lectr. Fgn. Service Inst., Dept. State, Washington, 1966-76. Author: East Indians in Trinidad, 1961, From Field to Factory, 1978, Caste: The Emergence of the South Asian System, 1980, (with H. Helman) The Kinds of Mankind, 1971. Served with U.S. Mcht. Marines, 1945-48. Am. Council Learned Socs. grantee, 1971-72; Social Sci. Research Council fellow, 1957-58; recipient Clark F. Ansley Columbia U. Press, 1959. Fellow Am. Anthropol. Assn.; mem. Royal Anthrop. Inst. Gt. Brit. and Ireland, Assn. Asian Scholars, North-Eastern Anthrop. Assn. Democrat. Jewish. Club: Players Guild (Leonia, N.J.) (trustee 1977-78). Office: Anthropology Dept Barnard Coll Columbia U New York NY 10027

KLATELL, JACK, dentist; b. N.Y.C., July 15, 1918; s. Meyer and Jennie (Merin) Klatsky; m. Arline Bragin, Aug. 9, 1944; children: Robert E., David A. Dental. B.S., Coll. City N.Y., 1938; D.D.S., Columbia U., 1941. Intern Mt. Sinai Hosp., N.Y.C., 1941-42; sr. resident dental and oral surgery Seaview Hosp., S.I., N.Y., 1942-43; pvt. practice dentistry, N.Y.C., 1943—; dir. dept. dentistry, dentist-in-chief Mt. Sinai Hosp., 1965—; asso. clin. prof. N.Y.U. Coll. Dentistry, 1967—; prof. dentistry Mt. Sinai Sch. Medicine, 1966—, also chmn. dept.; cons. Bronx VA Hosp., 1972—, Goldwater Meml. Hosp., 1974-80. Contbr. profl. jours. Served to capt. Dental Corps AUS, 1943-46. Fellow Acad. Gen. Dentistry, Internat. Coll. Dentists, Am. Coll. Dentists; mem. ADA, Am. Acad. Oral Pathology, N.Y. Inst. Clin. Oral Pathology, Met. Conf. Hosp. Dental Chiefs, Am. Assn. Hosp. Dentists, Phi Beta Kappa, Omicron Kappa Upsilon, Alpha Omega. Home: 8 E 83d St New York NY 10028 Office: 59 E 54th St New York NY 10022

KLATELL, ROBERT EDWARD, lawyer, electronics corp. exec.; b. Tampa, Fla., Dec. 11, 1945; s. Jack S. and Arla M. (Bragin) K.; m. Penelope E. Manegan, June 14, 1970; children—Christopher J., James M., Jeremy N. B.A., Williams Coll., 1968; J.D., N.Y. U., 1971. Bar: N.Y. bar 1972. Asso. mem. firm Kramer, Lowenstein, Nessen, Kamin & Soll, N.Y.C., 1970-76; gen. counsel Arrow Electronics, Inc., Greenwich, Conn., 1976—, v.p., 1979—. Mem. Am. Bar Assn., Assn. Bar of City of N.Y., Westchester-Fairfield County Corp. Counsels Assn. Office: Arrow Electronics Inc 600 Steamboat Rd Greenwich CT 06830

KLATSKIN, BERTRAM, oral surgeon; b. N.Y.C., Feb. 11, 1916; s. Archibald and Celia (Golubowski) K.; m. Ruth Weiner, Nov. 20, 1941; children: Andrew, Lois Klatskin Kolstad, Beth Klatskin Sidebotham. A.B. with honors, Cornell U., 1937; D.D.S., Columbia U., 1941. Diplomate: N.Y. State Bd. Oral Surgery. Intern in oral surgery Morrisania City Hosp., Bronx, N.Y., 1941-42; resident Sea View Hosp., S.I., N.Y., 1942-43; gen. practice dentistry, S.I., 1943-61, practice oral surgery, 1961—; mem. staff Sea View Hosp., 1943—, chief oral surgery, 1950—, dir. dental services, 1973—, also mem. exec. bd., v.p. med.-dental staff and med. bd., 1976-80, pres., 1980-84, dep. dir. med. affairs, 1979—; asso. attending oral surgeon S.I. Hosp., 1970-72, attending oral surgeon, 1972—, mem. exec. bd., 1974-77; also mem. tumor bd., asst. attending oral surgeon Columbia-Presbyn. Med. Center, 1972-74, asso. attending oral surgeon, 1974—; oral surgery staff Columbia U. Dental Sch., 1943—, St. Vincents Med. Center, Richmond Meml. Hosp.; clin. prof. oral surgery Columbia U., 1976—; lectr. community and profl. groups; malpractice cons. N.Y. State Supreme Ct.; mem. dist. bd. Health Systems Agy.; dental cons. nursing homes.; mem. Emergency Med. Service Com., N.Y.C. Health and Hosps. Corp. Council of Med. Bd. Pres., 1980-84. Contbr. articles to profl. jours. Mem. Sea View Community Adv. Bd.; mem. exec. bd. S.I. unit Am. Cancer Soc., 1967—, vice chmn., 1975-77, honoree, 1978. Served as maj. AUS, 1953-55. Fellow Am. Coll. Dentists, Internat. Assn. Oral Surgeons, Royal Soc. Health, Am. Assn. Oral and Maxillofacial Surgeons; mem. Am. Dental Soc., N.Y. State Second Dist. Dental Soc. (trustee 1964), Richmond County Dental Soc. (pres. 1963, Man. of Yr. 1984), N.Y. State Soc. Oral Surgeons, Am. Dental Soc. Anesthesiology, Met. Conf. Hosp. Dental Chiefs, Am. Assn. Hosp. Dentists, Clin. Soc. Sea View Hosp. (pres. 1975-80), Cornell Club, Columbia Dental Alumni Assn., Omicron Kappa Upsilon, Alpha Omega (pres. 1968-70). Club: Masons. Home: 202 Merrill Ave Staten Island NY 10314 Office: Sea View Hosp 460 Brielle Ave Staten Island NY 10314

KLATT, ALBERT ARTHUR, communications cons.; b. Chgo., June 15, 1920; s. Albert August and Bertha (Bach) K.; m. Carolyn Taylor, May 7, 1949; children—Kenneth, Gordon, Kurt, Kristin. B.A., Central YMCA Coll., 1942. Writer Leo Burnett Co., Chgo., 1947-53; copy supr. Needham, Harper and Steers, Inc., Chgo., 1953-56, copy chief, 1956-63, creative dir., 1963-66, chmn. plans bd., 1966-73, gen. mgr., 1973-80; communications cons., 1980—. Served with USNR, 1942-46; PTO; Served with USNR; ETO. Presbyterian. Home: 122 Harding Ct Vernon Hills IL 60061

KLATTE, EUGENE CARL, physician, educator; b. Indpls., Mar. 19; s. Ernest William and Catherine Mae (Ladd) K.; m. Barbara Ann Lyntton, Aug. 26, 1950; children—Susan, Constance, Kathryn, Jeanette, Teresa. B.S., Ind. U., 1949, M.D., 1952. Diplomate: Am. Bd. Radiology (trustee). Resident in radiology U. Calif., 1955-57; Picker scholar in radiation research Ind. U., 1957-59, instr., 1957-58, asst. prof. radiology, 1958-59, asso. prof., 1959-62, prof., chmn. dept. radiology, 1971—; now disting. prof.; prof., chmn. dept. radiology Vanderbilt U., 1962-71. Contbr. numerous articles to profl. jours. Served to capt. USAF, 1953-55. Fellow Am. Coll. Radiology, Am. Coll. Chest Physicians; mem. AMA, Assn. Univ. Radiologists, Phi Beta Kappa, Alpha Omega Alpha. Office: Ind U Med Center Indianapolis IN 46223 *

KLAUER, RAYMOND LOUIS, department store chain executive; b. Spokane, Wash., Sept. 23, 1931; s. Raymond George and Florence Elizabeth (Volinger) K.; m. JoAnn Lorraine Roy, Mar. 21, 1953; children: Judy, Susan, James, Kathleen, John. Bus. degree, Mdse. Inst., 1955; A.A., Los Angeles Coll., 1957. With May Co., Los Angeles, 1949-75, pres., Cleve., 1975-76, pres., chief exec. officer, Los Angeles, 1976-78, 80-83, chmn., chief exec. officer, 1983—, corp. group exec., 1978; vice chmn. bd. May Dept. Stores Co., St. Louis, 1978—. Vice pres. Los Angeles Mchts. Club for City of Hope, 1973-75; bd. dirs. Boys Club of Los Angeles, 1973-75; bd. dirs., mem. exec. com. Greater Cleve. Growth Assn., 1976-77; mem. exec. com. So. Calif. Bldg. Funds, 1978-81, bd. dirs., 1981—; bd. govs. Performing Arts Council Music Ctr. Los Angeles County, 1982—; mem. council nat. trustees Nat. Jewish Hosp./Nat. Asthma Ctr., 1983—; bd. dirs. So. Calif. region NCCJ, 1981—. Served with USAF, 1950-54. Mem. Fraternity of Friends of Music Center-Los Angeles. Clubs: Bel Air Country, Los Angeles Athletic., Regency, Long Beach Yacht. Office: 10738 W Pico Blvd Los Angeles CA 90064 *If there is one thing that I have learned over the years, it is that you just can't do it all alone—and for that I am grateful to a lot of people.*

KLAUS, ELMER ERWIN, educator, chemical engineer; b. Neffsville, Pa., Apr. 19, 1921; s. Elmer Ernest and Esther (Graver) K.; m. Jean Rebecca Hartswick, Sept. 22, 1945; children—Dennis Richard, Diane Gail. B.S., Franklin and Marshall Coll., 1943; M.S., Pa. State U., 1946, Ph.D., 1952. Research asst. Pa. State U., 1943-46, instr., 1946-52, asst. prof., 1952-56, assoc. research prof., 1956-66, prof. chem. engring., 1966-82, M.R. Fenske faculty fellow in chem. engring., 1979-82, prof. emeritus and M.R. Ferske fellow emeritus, 1983—; cons. Nat. Bur. Standards, 1983—; chmn. Am. Soc. Lubrication Engrs. ASME Lubrication Conf., 1967; chmn. Gordon Research Conf. Friction Lubrication and Wear, 1976; mem. steering com. for wear and corrosion Office Tech. Assessment, 1976; mem. NRC Com. U.S. Army Basic Research, 1977-80. Co-editor: Boundary Lubrication—An Appraisal of World Literature, 1969; asso. editor: Jour. Lubrication Technology, 1968-79; Contbr. articles to profl. jours. Exec. bd. Juniata Valley council Boy Scouts Am., 1965—. Recipient Pentathalon award Franklin and Marshall Coll., 1943; Outstanding Achievement in research award Pa. State U. Coll. Engring., 1972; Silver Beaver award Juniata Valley council Boy Scouts Am., 1973; ASLE nat. award, 1976; ASLE Capt. Alfed E. Hunt medal, 1980; ASME Mayo D. Hersey award, 1982. Fellow Am. Inst. Chemists, Am. Soc. Lubrication Engrs. (hon. mem.; dir. 1966-72); mem. Am. Chem. Soc., Am. Inst. Chem. Engrs., ASME (research com. on lubrication, mem. council mech. failures prevention group 1971, chmn. 1976-81), Sigma Xi, Alpha Chi Sigma, Phi Lambda Upsilon, Sigma Pi Sigma. Mem. United Ch. of Christ. Club: Mason (Shriner). Home: 221 Nimitz Ave State College PA 16801 Office: Fenske Labs Pa State U University Park PA 16802

KLAUSEN, RAYMOND, TV art director; b. Jamaica, N.Y., May 29, 1939; s. Jens and Ane Kathrine (Jensen) K. B.A., Hofstra U., 1961; M.A. in Art, N.Y. U., 1963; M.F.A. in Theatre Design, Yale U., 1967. Theatrical set designer, 1967—; freelance TV art dir., 1970—; designer sets for numerous TV series, individual specials,, nat. tours for Lionel Richie, Kenny Rogers; Hello, Hollywood, Hello!, MGM, 1978, Jubilee!, MGM, 1981, exhbns. include, Multiple Gallery, N.Y.C., 1971, McKenzie Gallery, Los Angeles, 1970-73, Gallery Moos, Toronto, Can., 1973, Upstairs Gallery, Long Beach, Calif., 1974, Dirks Perri Gallery, Studio City, Calif., 1976-77. Served with AUS, 1962-63. Bates Travel fellow, Europe, 1967; recipient 3 Nat. Acad. TV Arts and Sci. Emmy awards for Cher series, 1976, nominations for 1980 Acad. Awards and Lynda Carter's Celebration, 1981, Acad. award, 1982, 83. Address: 363 S Las Palmas Ave Los Angeles CA 90020

KLAUSLER, ALFRED PAUL, journalist, clergyman; b. Hankinson, N.D., Feb. 22, 1910; s. Joseph Paul and Amanda (Hunziker) K.; m. Signe Fox, June 28, 1934; children—Peter M., Paula S., Thomas A. Diploma, Concordia Coll., St. Paul, 1929, Concordia Sem., St. Louis, 1932; student, Columbia, U., Chgo.; M.A., Loyola U., Chgo., 1961; Litt.D., Valparaiso U. Ordained to ministry Luth. Ch., 1934; pastor Our Savior's Luth. Ch., Glendive, Mont., 1934-42; exec. sec. dept. communications Walther League, 1946-66; exec. sec. Asso. Ch. Press, 1961-74; religion editor Westinghouse Broadcasting, 1969—; instr. Valparaiso U., 1950-52, Concordia Tchrs. Coll., River Forest, Ill., 1954; lectr. Wartburg Sem., Kent State U., Concordia Sem.; asst. pastor St. Philip Luth. Ch. Author: fiction Midnight Lion, 1957, Growth in Worship, 1957, Christ, and Your Job, 1958, Meditations for Youth, 1959, Censorship and Obscenity, 1966; also mag. articles.; Co-editor: The Journalist's Prayer Book, 1972; editor at large: Christian Century, 1974—; editorial cons.: Christian Ministry, 1974—. Served as chaplain AUS, 1942-46; col. Res.; staff command chaplain, 322d Logis. Command, 1961-62; Fort Lee. Decorated Army Commendation medal with oak leaf cluster; recipient Lipphard award for disting. service in religious journalism, 1974. Mem. Nat. Religious Publicity Council (pres. Chgo. 1958-59), Chgo. Bible Soc. (bd. mgrs. 1961-74), Luth. Human Relations Assn. Am. (dir.), Alpha Lambda Phi, Pi Gamma Mu, Sigma Delta Chi. Clubs: Headline, Press (Chgo.). Home: 2520 S 60th Ct Chicago IL 60650 Office: 407 S Dearborn St Chicago IL 60605

KLAUSMEIER, HERBERT JOHN, psychologist, educator; b. Boonville, Ind., Nov. 4, 1915; s. Henry P. and Catherine E. (Heilmann) K.; m. Iyla T. Johnson, Aug. 18, 1946; children—Thomas Wayne, Connie Alice. B.S., Ind. State U., 1940, M.S., 1947; Ed.D., Stanford, 1949. Sch. tchr., 1936-38, 40-41, 46-47; asst. prof., asso. prof. psychology and edn. U. No. Colo., 1949-52; asst. prof. ednl. psychology U. Wis., Madison, 1952-54, asso. prof., 1954-57, prof., 1958—, V.A.C. Henmon prof. ednl. psychology, 1968—; asso. dir. Wis. Research and Devel. Center for Cognitive Learning, 1964-67, dir., 1967-72, also originator individually guided edn. Author: Analyses of Concept Learning, 1966, Teaching in the Secondary School, 3d edit, 1968, Teaching in the Elementary School, 4th edit, 1974, Conceptual Learning and Development: A Cognitive View, 1974, Individually Guided Motivation, 1975, Learning and Human Abilities: Educational Psychology, 4th edit, 1975, cognitive Development of Children and Youth: A Longitudinal Study, 1978, Cognitive Learning and Development: Information-Processing and Piagetian Perspectives, 1979, Learning and Teaching Concepts: A Strategy for Testing Applications of Theory, 1980; adv. editor: Jour. Ednl. Psychology, 1968—; editor: Leadership Series in Individually Guided Education, 1976, 77. Served with USNR, 1941-46. Recipient Alumni Disting. Service award Ind. State U., 1962, Distinguished Research award Wis. Edn. Research Assn., 1976; Leadership award Assn. Individually Guided Edn., 1976. Fellow Am. Psychol. Assn. (pres. Rocky Mountain br. 1951-52, pres. ednl. psychology div. 1970-71); mem. Am. Edn. Research Assn., others. Home: 10 Colony Circle Madison WI 53717

KLAUSNER, SAMUEL ZUNDEL, sociologist, educator; b. Bklyn., Dec. 19, 1923; s. Edward Solomon and Bertha (Adler) K.; m. Bracha Turgeman, Oct. 26, 1948 (div. 1960); children: Rina Ellen Klausner Spence, Jonathan David; m. Madeleine Suringar, Feb. 20, 1964 (div. 1982); children: Daphne, Tamar. B.S., NYU, 1947; M.A., Columbia U., 1951, Ed.D., 1952, Ph.D., 1963. Cert. psychologist, N.Y., D.C. Lectr. in edn. CCNY, 1951-52, 55-57; lectr. in sociology Columbia U., 1957-63; instr. in psychology Hebrew U., Jerusalem, 1952-53; lectr. religion and psychiatry Union Theol. Sem., 1961-63; asso. prof. to prof. sociology U. Pa., 1967—; dir. Center for Research on the Acts of Man, 1971—; clin. psychologist Govt. Mental Hosp., Jerusalem, 1954-55; program dir. Bur. Applied Social Research, Columbia U., 1956-61; sr. research asso. Bur. Social Sci. Research, Washington, 1964-67; exec. sec. Soc. for Sci. Study Religion, 1964-70; cons. U.S. Dept. Commerce, 1968-69, U.S. Naval Chaplains Sch., 1973—, Nat. Library Medicine, 1969, NRC, 1967-81, others; vis. prof. Al Mansoura U., Egypt, 1983. Author: Psychiatry and Religion, 1964, The Quest for Self-Control, 1965, The Study of Total Societies, 1967, Why Man Takes Chances, 1968, Society and Its Physical Environment, 1970, On Man in His Environment, 1971, Eskimo Capitalists, 1981; author also articles. Served with USAAC, 1943-45; Served with Israel Air Force, 1947-48. Ford Found. area research fellow, 1952-53. Mem. Am. Sociol. Assn., Am. Psychol. Assn., Assn. Sociol. Study of Jewry, Soc. Sci. Study of Religion, AAAS. Jewish. Home: 2201 Bryn Mawr Ave Philadelphia PA 19131 Office: Dept Sociology Univ Pa Philadelphia PA 19104 *My ideals of social conduct have not been designed to assist in attaining professional success. Judaism is a central guiding reference and though I may deviate from its principles in my daily behavior for reasons of good sense and self interest, they remain normative. My professional station arises from an obsession with the requirements of scholarship. A willingness to be critical of current social institutions has brought social attention but not professional advancement.*

KLAW, BARBARA VAN DOREN, author, editor; b. N.Y.C., Sept. 17, 1920; d. Carl and Irita (Bradford) Van Doren; m. Spencer Klaw, July 5, 1941; children: Joanna Klaw Schultz, Susan Klaw Del Tredici, Rebecca Klaw Feldman, Margaret Klaw Metcalfe. B.A., Vassar Coll., 1941. Writer-researcher OWI, Washington, 1942-43; reporter N.Y. Post, 1943-45; free lance editor, writer, 1945-63; editor Am. Heritage mag., N.Y.C., 1963—. Author: One Summer, 1936, One Winter, 1938, A Pony Named Nubbin, 1939, Joan and Michael, 1941, all under pseudonym Martin Gale; under pseudonym Eleanor Benton: The

Complete Book of Etiquette, 1956, Camp Follower, 1944; editor folklore anthology, 1960. Home: 118 Riverside Dr New York NY 10024 Office: 10 Rockefeller Plaza New York NY 10020

KLAW, SPENCER, writer, editor, educator; b. N.Y.C., Jan. 13, 1920; s. Alonzo and Alma (Ash) K.; m. Barbara Van Doren, July 5, 1941; children—Joanna Klaw Schultz, Susan Klaw Del Tredici, Rebecca Klaw Feldman, Margaret Klaw Metcalfe. A.B., Harvard U., 1941. Reporter San Francisco Chronicle, 1941; Washington corr. Raleigh (N.C.) News and Observer, and United Press, 1941-43; reporter United Press, N.Y.C., 1946, The New Yorker, 1947-52; asst. to Sunday editor New York Herald Tribune, 1952-54; asso. editor Fortune, 1954-60; free-lance writer, 1960—; lectr. in journalism U. Calif., Berkeley, 1968-69, Grad. Sch. Journalism, Columbia U., N.Y.C., 1970—; editor Columbia Journalism Rev., 1980—. Author: The New Brahmins: Scientific Life in America, 1968, The Great American Medicine Show, 1975; contbr. to publs. including, American Heritage, Esquire, Fortune, Natural History, Playboy, Harper's, The Reporter. Home: 118 Riverside Dr New York NY 10024 Office: 700 Journalism Bldg Columbia U New York NY 10027

KLAWANS, HAROLD LEO, neurologist, author; b. Chgo., Nov. 1, 1937; s. Harold Leo and Blanche (Rosenberg) K.; m. Paula Barkan, Aug. 23, 1959; children: Deborah, Rebecca, Jonathan. Student, U. Mich., 1955-58; M.D., U. Ill., 1962. Intern Presbyn. St. Luke's Hosp., Chgo., 1962-63; resident in neurology U. Minn., Mpls., 1963-64, Presbyn. St. Lukes Hosp., 1966-68; practice medicine specializing in neurology, Highland Park, Ill., 1968—; instr. U. Ill. Med. Coll., Chgo., 1968-70; asst. prof. neurology Rush Med. Sch., Chgo., 1971-72, asso. prof., 1972-74, prof. neurol. sci. and pharmacology, 1977—, asso. chmn. dept. neurol. scis., 1977—; prof. medicine U. Chgo. Pritzker Sch. Medicine, 1974-76; med. adv. Midwest chpt. Com. to Combat Huntington Disease, 1970—, Tourette Syndrome Assn., 1977—; chmn. med. adv. bd. United Parkinson Found., 1972—; stroke com. Chgo. Heart Assn., 1972-76, chmn., 1974-75. Author (novel): Sin of Commission, 1982; Author (essays): Medicine of History, 1982; Editor: Clin. Neuropharmacology, 1974—; assoc. editor: Handbook of Clin. Neurology, 1972-81; editor, 1982—; contbr. numerous articles to profl. jours. Served with U.S. Army, 1964-66. United Parkinson Found. grantee, 1968—; Boothroyd Found. grantee, 1975—; State Ill. Dept. Mental Health grantee, 1978-80. Fellow Am. Acad. Neurology; mem. Am. Neurol. Assn., Am. Coll. Neuropharmacology, Internat. Coll. Neuropharmacology, Soc. Neurochemistry, Soc. Biol. Psychiatry, World Fedn. Neurology, Research Group on Huntington Chorea (sec. 1977—). Jewish. Home: 1888 McCraren St Highland Park IL 60035 Office: 1725 W Harrison Ave Chicago IL 60612

KLAYF, BERNARD SPENCER, department store executive; b. N.Y.C., Apr. 9, 1921; s. Abraham and Ella (Davis) K.; m. Betty Louise Buchbinder, Aug. 15, 1945 (dec. Nov. 1950); 1 dau., Barbara Lynn; m. Aurelia Dixon McIntyre, Nov. 30, 1951; 1 dau., Martha Spencer. Ph.B., U. Wis., 1942. With WPB, Washington, 1942-43; with Federated Dept. Stores, Inc., 1946—, v.p. for personnel and operations, Cin., 1947-55, v.p., gen. mdse. mgr., 1956-62, exec. v.p., Miami, Fla., 1962-65, v.p. parent co., Cin., 1965-69, sr. v.p., 1970-75, exec. v.p., 1975—, also dir.; dir., mem. exec. com. Associated Merchandising Corp., West Shell Realty, Cin. Equitable Ins. Co.; dir. Kreidler Shell. Served to capt. USAAF, 1943-46. Clubs: Queen City, Whist, Losantiville Country (Cin.). Home: 1 Grandin Pl Cincinnati OH 45208 Office: 7 W 7th St Cincinnati OH 45202

KLEBAN, EDWARD LAWRENCE, composer, lyricist; b. N.Y.C., Apr. 30, 1939; s. Julian Milton and Sylvia K. B.A., Columbia Coll., 1960. Mem. BMI Mus. Theater Workshop under Lehman Engel, 1966—. Producer, CBS Records, Hollywood, Calif., 1961-65, CBS Records, N.Y.C., 1965-68; free lance composer lyricist for theater, TV, films and recordings, 1968—; (Recipient 3 Recording Industry Assn. Am. Gold Records 1964, 65, 78, Nat. Acad. Recording Arts Scis. Grammy nominations 1967, 68, 75, 79, N.Y. Drama Critics award 1975, Antoinette Perry award 1976, Pulitzer prize for drama Drama Desk 1976, Obie award Theater World 1975-76, Wedgie award London 1977, Los Angeles Drama Critics award 1977); Composer and/or lyricist: A Little Bit Different, 1960, The Refrigerators, 1971, The Revue, 1972, Irene, 1973, The Desert Song, 1973, Free to Be You and Me k2(TV), 1974, Feelin' Good k2(TV), 1974, A Chorus Line, 1975, The Hindenberg; film, 1975. Order of Arrow Boy Scouts Am., 1952. Mem. Dramatists Guild, Am. Fedn. Musicians, Broadcast Music, Inc.

KLEBBA, ROBERT HAROLD, medical corporation executive; b. Mt. Vernon, Ill., Dec. 1, 1928; s. Benny A. K. and Lucille (Overby) Morgan; m. Lois JoAnn McGuire, Nov. 16, 1950; 1 son, Robert Steven. Student, Glendale City Coll., 1951-52. Exec. v.p., dir. U.S. Mfg. Co., Pasedena, Calif., 1951-78, Durr-Fillauer Med., Inc., Chattanooga, 1978—. Home: 9219 Magic Mountain Dr Chattanooga TN 37421 Office: Durr-Fillauer Med Inc 218 Commerce St Montgomery AL 36192

KLEBERG, JACK CARL, gen. mgmt. and mktg. exec.; b. Chgo., July 22, 1930; s. Carl W. and Margaret (Johnson) K.; m. Bonnie Seidel, June 14, 1952; children—Bonnie Beth, Wendy Kathleen, Craig Charles, Jacquelyn Suzanne. B.S., U.S. Mil. Acad., 1952; student, Xavier U., Cin., 1962-63; M.B.A., Wayne State U., 1966. Commd. 2d lt. U.S. Army, 1952, advanced through grades to 1st lt., 1956; resigned, 1956; with Gen. Motors Corp., 1958-64, Master Consol., Inc., 1964-67; spl. asst. to pres. Dunhill Internat., 1967-68; v.p. marketing Goerlich's, Inc., Toledo, 1968-69, pres., 1969-72; also dir.; pres. Questor Edn. Products Co., Bronx, N.Y., 1971-72; group v.p. automotive replacement parts group Questor Corp., 1972-73, v.p. corp. devel., 1973-74; group v.p. Papercraft Corp., Pitts., 1974-78; mgmt. cons., 1979-80; sr. v.p. Drake Beam Morin, Inc., Pitts., 1980—. Decorated Army Commendation ribbon. Mem. West Point Grad. Assn. Home: 114 Shannon Dr Pittsburgh PA 15238 Office: 300 Porter Bldg 601 Grant St Pittsburgh PA 15219

KLEE, VICTOR LA RUE, JR., mathematician, educator; b. San Francisco, Sept. 18, 1925; s. Victor La Rue and Mildred (Muller) K.; m. Elizabeth Bliss, June 10, 1945; children—Wendy Pamela (m. Paul James Wehrenberg), Barbara Christine, Susan Lisette, Heidi Elizabeth. B.A., Pomona Coll., 1945, D.Sc., 1965; Ph.D., U. Va., 1949. Asst. prof. U. Va., 1949-53; NRC fellow Inst. for Advanced Study, 1951-52; asst. prof. U. Wash., Seattle, 1953-54, asso. prof., 1954-57, prof. math., 1957—, adj. prof. computer sci., 1974—, prof. applied math., 1976—; vis. asso. prof. UCLA, 1955-56; vis. prof. U. Colo., 1971, U. Victoria, 1975, U. Western Australia, 1979; cons. IBM Watson Research Center, 1972; cons. to industry. Contbr. articles to profl. jours. Recipient Research prize U. Va., 1952, Vollum award for disting. accomplishment in sci. and tech. Reed Coll., 1982; NSF sr. postdoctoral fellow Sloan Found.; fellow U. Copenhagen, 1958-60, Center Advanced Study in Behavioral Scis., 1975-76; Guggenheim fellow; Humboldt award U. Erlangen-Nürnberg, 1980-81. Fellow AAAS (chmn. sect. A 1975); mem. Am. Math. Soc. (asso. sec. 1955-58, mem. exec. com. 1969-70), Math. Assn. Am. (pres. 1971-73, L.R. Ford award 1972, Disting. Service award 1977, C. B. Allendoerfer award 1980), Soc. Indsl. and Applied Math. (mem. council 1966-68), Assn. Computing Machinery, Ops. Research Soc. Am., Math. Programming Soc., Stereological Soc., Phi Beta Kappa, Sigma Xi (nat. lectr. 1969). Home: 13706 39th Ave NE Seattle WA 98125

KLEEMANN, RONALD A., artist; b. Bay City, Mich., July 24, 1937. B.S., U. Mich., 1961. One-man shows include, French & Co., N.Y.C., 1971, Louis K. Meisel Gallery, N.Y.C., 1974, 76, 79, 83, Reed Coll., Portland, Oreg., 1976, Indpls. Mus. Art, 1977; exhibited in group shows, San Francisco Mus. Modern Art, 1961, Galerie 99, Bay Harbor Island, Fal., 1970, Emily Lowe Gallery, Hofstra U., N.Y., SUNY, Potsdam, Mus. Contemporary Art, Chgo., N.Y. Cultural Center, 1971, Aldrich Mus., Ridgefield, Conn., U. Mass., Amherst, Warren Benedek Gallery, N.Y.C., 1972, Galerie des 4 Mouvements, Paris, Galerie Isy Brachot, Brussels, Katonah (N.Y.) Gallery, Shorewood Graphics Gallery, N.Y.C., De Cordova Mus., Lincoln, Mass., 1973, Hedendaagse Kunst, Utrecht, Netherlands, Palais van Schone Kunsten, Brussels, Basel, Switzerland, Tokyo Met. Mus., Kyoto (Japan) Mcpl. Mus., Aichi Perfectual Art Mus., Nagoya, Japan, Galerie Francois Petit, Paris, Moos Gallery, Montreal and Toronto, Can., Wadsworth Atheneum, Hartford, Conn., Indpls. Mus. Art, Randolph-Macon Coll., Lynchburg, Pa., Taft Mus. and Contemporary Art Center, Cin., Butler Inst. Am. Art, Youngstown, Ohio, 1974, Sidney Janis Gallery, N.Y.C., Morgan Gallery, Shawnee Mission, Kans., Edwin A. Ulrich Mus. Art, Wichita (Kans.) State U., Louis K. Meisel Gallery, 1975, Robert McDougall Art Gallery, Christchurch, Acad. Fine Arts and Nat. Gallery, Wellington, Denedin Public Art Gallery, Govett-Brewster Art Gallery, New Plymouth, Waikato Art Mus., Hamilton (all New Zealand), 1975-76, Young Hoffman Gallery, Chgo., Grand Palais, Paris, Washington Internat. Art Fair, 1976, Squibb Gallery, Princeton, N.J., 1983, Terra Mus. Am. Art, Evanston, Ill., Byer Mus. Arts, Evanston, 1984, Morgan Gallery, Kansas City, Mo., 1983, travelling exhbn., Vancouver Centennial Mus., Glenbow Alta. Inst., Calgary, Mendel Art Gallery, Saskatoon, Sask., Winnepeg (Man.) Art Gallery, Edmonton (Alta.) Art Gallery, Meml. U. Art Gallery, St. John's, Nfld., Confedn. Art Gallery, Charlottetown, P.E.I., Mus. Contemporary Art, Montreal, Que., Dalhousie U. Art Gallery, Halifax N.S., Windsor (Ont.) Art Gallery, London Art Gallery and, McIntosh Meml. Art Gallery, Ont. (all Can.), 1976-78, Jacksonville (Fla.) Art Mus., Shore Gallery, Boston, Montclair (N.J.) State Coll., 1977, traveling exhbn. various museums, Australia, 1977-78, Fling (Mich.) Inst. Arts, Okla. Art Center, Gallery 700, Milw., Monmouth (N.J.) Mus., Palm Springs (Calif.) Art Fair, Arts and Crafts Center, Pitts., Thomas Segal Gallery, Boston, U. Nebr., Lincoln, 1978, others; represented in permanent collections, Mus. Modern Art, N.Y.C., Guggenheim Mus., N.Y.C., Indpls. Mus., Va. Mus., Byer Mus. Arts, Evanston, Ill.; illustrator: (1980) book Photorealism (Louis K. Meisel); works included in books, articles, newspapers.; ofcl. artist, Indpls. 500, 1977, 78, 79, Superbowl, 1982-83. Office: Louis K Meisel Gallery 141 Prince St New York NY 10012 *My purpose in making art is to representationally chronicle events American in interpretation & subcultural in content. The recorded events may run the gamut of the artist as observer or as actual creator of the event or events chronicled*

KLEIMAN, ALAN BOYD, artist; b. Bklyn., Feb. 20, 1930; s. Louis and Alfreda (Belosky) K.; m. Audrey Barbara Code, Feb. 9, 1963; 1 dau., Andrea Kristin. B.F.A., Va. Commonwealth U., 1951; M.F.A., Cranbrook Acad. Art, 1953. Asst. publicity dir. Artist Tenents Assn., 1960-67; v.p. Grand St. Artist Group, 1970-75; chmn. Soho Artifacts, 1971-75. Author: Investigations into the Light of Red Color, 1968, Light, Dazzle and Glow, 1970; Group shows include, Nexus Gallery, Boston, 1959, Betty Parsons Gallery, N.Y.C., 1961, 79, Sun Gallery, 1962, New Gallery, Provincetown, Mass., 1961-62, Marino, N.Y.C., 1966, Warren Benedek, N.Y.C., 1972, Landmark Gallery, N.Y.C., 1975-76, Renaissance Soc., Chgo., 1979, Art U.S.A. '80, U.S., Can., Sweden, Siegel Gallery, N.Y.C., 1983, Queensborough Coll., N.Y.C.; represented in permanent collections, Mus. Modern Art, Whitney Mus. Am. Arts, Met. Mus. Art, N.Y.C., Carnegie Mus., Pitts., Boston Mus. Fine Arts, William Patterson Coll., Wayne, N.J. Served with U.S. Army, 1953-55. Recipient 1st prize Boston Arts Festival, 1954.; N.Y. State Council Arts grantee, 1977-78; Curtral Council Found. awardee, 1978. Mem. Theatre of Artists League (v.p. 1972), Orgn. Ind. Artists, Am. Abstract Artists. *My creative drive has at times thrived on procrastination, anger, jealousy, rage, talent and plain hard work. Balancing emotion and intelligence make the tension expressed in my painting. I want to make more and better art.*

KLEIMAN, BERNARD, lawyer; b. Chgo., Jan. 26, 1928; s. Isadore and Pearl (Wikoff) K.; m. Lenore Silver, April 27, 1959; children—Leslie, David. B.S., Purdue U., 1951; J.D., Northwestern U., 1954. Bar: Ill. bar 1954. Practice law in assn. with Abraham W. Brussell, 1957-60; dist. counsel United Steel Workers Am., 1960-65, gen. counsel, 1965—; partner Kleiman, Cornfield & Feldman, Chgo., 1960-75; prin. B. Kleiman (P.C.), 1976-77, Kleiman and Whitney (P.C.), 1978—; Mem. collective bargaining coms. for nat. labor negotiations in basic steel, aluminum and can mfg. industries. Contbr. articles to legal jours. Served with U.S. Army, 1946-48. Mem. Am., Ill., Chgo., Allegheny County bar assns. Office: 1 E Wacker Dr Chicago IL 60601 also 5 Gateway Center Pittsburgh PA 15222

KLEIMAN, DAVID HAROLD, lawyer; b. Kendallville, Ind., Apr. 2, 1934; s. Isador and Pearl (Wikoff) K.; m. Meta Dene Freeman, July 6, 1958; children: Gary, Andrew, Scott, Matthew. B.S., Purdue U., 1956; J.D., Northwestern U., 1959. Bar: Ind. 1959. Assoc. firm Bamberger & Feibleman, Indpls., 1959-61; partner firm Bagal, Talesnick & Kleiman, Indpls., 1961-73, Dann, Pecar, Newman, Talesnick & Kleiman, 1973—; dep. pros. atty., 1961-62; counsel Met. Devel. Commn., 1965-75; Ind. Heartland Coordinating Commn., 1975-81. Editor: Jour. of Air, Law and Commerce, 1958-59. Chmn. Young Leadership Council, 1967; v.p. Indpls. Hebrew Congregation, 1973; pres. Jewish Community Center Assn., 1972-75, Jewish Welfare Fedn., 1981—; v.p. United Way of Greater Indpls., 1982—. Recipient Young Leadership award, 1968. Mem. Am., Ind., Indpls. bar assns., Comml. Law League Am. Clubs: Columbia, B'nai B'rith. Office: 1600 Market Sq Center Indianapolis IN 46204

KLEIMAN, JOSEPH, life sciences company executive; b. Grand Rapids, Mich., Oct. 1, 1919; s. Jacob and Bessie (Targowitch) K.; m. Shirley Ruth Present, Aug. 30, 1942; children: Richard Neil, Robert, William. B.S. in Engring, U. Mich., 1941, M.S., 1942. Engr. Reeves Instrument Corp., N.Y.C., 1946-51; v.p., gen. mgr. Belock Instrument Corp., College Point, N.Y., 1951-58, Whittaker Gyro (div. Telecomputing Corp.), Los Angeles, 1958-59, exec. v.p. corp., 1959-64; v.p. corp. devel. Whittaker Corp., 1964-67, sr. v.p., 1967—, also dir.; dir. Yardney Elec. Corp., Diagnostic Products Corp. Vice pres. Am. Soc. for Technion-Israel Inst. Tech.; vice chmn. Union Am. Hebrew Congregations, 1975-79. Mem. Nat., Calif. socs. profl. engrs., Sigma Xi, Phi Lambda Upsilon, Iota Alpha. Jewish. Home: 11240 Chalon Rd Los Angeles CA 90049 Office: 10880 Wilshire Blvd Los Angeles CA 90024

KLEIMAN, STEVEN LAWRENCE, mathematics educator; b. Boston, Mar. 31, 1942; s. Macklen and Ida (Kleiman); m. Beverly Klostergaard, Nov. 6, 1969; children: Deborah Britt, Alexander Bjørn. S.B. M.I.T, 1961; M.A., Harvard U., 1962, Ph.D. (NSF fellow 1961-64, Univ. final yr. fellow 1964-65), 1965. Instr. Columbia U., 1965-66, asst. prof. math., 1966-68, assoc. prof., 1968-69, M.I.T., 1969-76; prof., 1976—; vis. prof. U. Paris, Orsay, France, 1970, U. Aarhus, Denmark, 1972, U. Calif., San Diego, winter, spring 1974, Irvine, winter 1976, U. Aarhus, 1970; vis. fellow Institut des Hautes Etudes Sci., Paris, France, 1966-67, 70, U. Copenhagen, 1976, 82-83; lectr. speaker in field, Internat. Congress Math., 1970. Editor: Communications in Algebra, 1977—. NATO postdoctoral fellow, 1966-67; A.P. Sloan fellow, 1968-72; J.S. Guggenheim fellow, 1979-80. Mem. Am. Math. Soc., Soc. Math. France, Math. Assn. Am. Office: 2-278 MIT Cambridge MA 02139

KLEIN, ARTHUR LUCE, theatrical co. exec.; b. Carbondale, Pa., Mar. 31, 1916; s. Joseph and Jennie (Kallish) K.; m. Luce Weill-Kinsbourg, Oct. 8, 1946; children—Judith, Florence, Joel, Rosine. B.A., U. Mich., 1939, M.A., 1940, Ph.D., 1948; postgrad., Sorbonne, is, 1947. Asst. prof. dept. dramatic art U. Calif. at Berkeley, 1948-50; producer Royal Acad. Dramatic Art, London, Eng., 1950-52; founder Spoken Arts, Inc., New Rochelle, N.Y., 1956, pres., 1956—; lectr. Am. theatre for Dept. State in Europe, 1954. Dir.: Bruno and Sidney at Watergate, Phoenix Theatres, London, 1952; tour: Glass Menagerie, on Continent and throughout Scandinavia, 1953, Skits & Sketches, in Europe, 1954-55; Co-translator: Anouilh's Medea, 1949, The Rendezvous at Senlis, 1949, Cecile or School for Fathers; Translator: Puss in Boots, 1970. Bd. dirs. Boys Clubs, New Rochelle; mem. pres.'s adv. com. Coll. of New Rochelle. Served to capt., Signal Corps AUS, 1942-45; ETO. Democrat. Jewish religion. Home: 95 Valley Rd New Rochelle NY 10801 Office: Spoken Arts Bldg: 310 North Ave New Rochelle NY 10801

KLEIN, BERNARD, publishing company executive; b. N.Y.C., Sept. 20, 1921; s. Joseph J. and Anna (Wolfe) K.; m. Betty Stecher, Feb. 17, 1946; children: Cheryl Rona, Barry Todd, Cindy Ann. B.A., CCNY, 1942. Founder, pres. U.S. List Co., N.Y.C., 1946—; founder, pres., chief editor B. Klein Publs., Inc., Coral Springs, Fla. and; Rye, N.Y., 1953—; cons. direct mail advt. and reference book pub. to pubs., industry, 1950—. Author: all biennials Ency. of American Indian, 1954—; Guide to American Directories. Served with AUS, 1942-45; ETO. Mem. Direct Mail Advt. Assn. Club: Masons. Home: 7309 Corkwood Terr Tamarac FL 33321 Office: PO Box 8503 Coral Springs FL 33065

KLEIN, BURTON HAROLD, economics educator; b. Mpls., Oct. 16, 1917; s. Joseph Harry and Ethel Anna (Figen) K.; m. Cecelia Katz, Jan. 29, 1955; children—Roger, Jon, Margaret Ann. B.A., Harvard Coll., 1940, Ph.D., 1953. Staff mem. Council Econ. Advisors, Washington, 1948-52; with Rand Corp., Santa Monica, Calif., 1952-67, head econs. dept., 1963-67; spl. asst. to Sec. Def., Washington, 1963-65; prof. econs. Calif. Inst. Tech., Pasadena, 1967—; vis. prof. Harvard U., 1961, Hebrew Univ., Jerusalem, 1963, M.I.T., 1981. Author: Germany's Economic Preparations for War, 1956, Dynamic Economics, 1977, Wages, Prices, and Business Cycles, 1983. Served with A.C. U.S. Army, 1942-46. Recipient David Wells Prize Harvard U., 1953. Mem., Phi Beta Kappa. Jewish. Home: PO Box 28446 San Diego CA 92128 Office: Dept Econs California Inst Tech Pasadena CA 91109

KLEIN, CALVIN RICHARD, designer; b. N.Y.C., Nov. 19, 1942; s. Leo and Flore (Stern) K.; m. Jayne Centre, Apr. 26, 1964 (div. 1974); 1 dau., Marci. A.A., Fashion Inst. Tech., 1962. Pres., designer Calvin Klein, N.Y.C., 1969—; Critic Parsons Sch. Design; critic, cons. Fashion Inst. Tech., dir., 1975—. Recipient Coty award, 1973, 74, 75; named Outstanding Am. talent in women's fashion design Council Fashion Designers of Am., 1983. Mem. Council Fashion Designers, Mus. Modern Art, Met. Mus. Art, Whitney Mus., Guggenheim Mus. Office: 205 W 39th St New York NY 10018

KLEIN, CHARLES, judge; b. Atlantic City, Sept. 16, 1900; s. Samuel and Esther (Grun) K.; m. Rosalie S. Benson, June 30, 1933; 1 son, Richard Benson. LL.B., Temple U., 1921, LL.D., 1949; postgrad., Villanova U. Extension Sch., 1922; LL.D., Franklin and Marshall Coll., 1959, U. Pa., 1967, La Salle Coll., 1968; L.H.D., Dickinson Coll., 1960; J.D., St. Joseph's Coll., 1961; D.C.L., Bucknell U., 1963. Bar: Pa. bar 1921. Since practiced in, Phila.; spl. counsel Pa. Dept. Banking, 1927-31; spl. dep. atty. gen., 1931-34; judge Orphans Ct., Phila., 1934-52, pres. judge, 1952—; North lectr. Franklin and Marshall Coll., 1940; acting dean Temple U. Sch. Law, 1941-42; gov.'s counsel Pub. Service Commn. Investigation; counsel Joint Legis. Com. investigating milk industry in Pa.; spl. asst. OPA; spl. adviser Republic of Cuba. Past pres. Jewish Hosp., Am. Jewish Com., Jewish Family Welfare Council; past v.p. Albert Einstein Med. Center; former dir. many philanthropic and civic orgns.; trustee, hon. chancellor Temple U. Recipient U. Distinguished Alumni award; Robert L. Johnson award; Lucien Moss Home award; Clair Post Am. Legion Honor award; B'nai B'rith Mid-City Lodge Civic award. Clubs: Caveat, Socialegal, Midday (Phila.). Law sch. bldg. Temple U. named in his honor. Home: 916 River Park Apts Philadelphia PA 19131 Office: City Hall Philadelphia PA 19107

KLEIN, DAVID, foreign service officer; b. N.Y.C., Sept. 2, 1919; s. Sam and Fannie H. (Falk) K.; m. Anne L. Cochran, Mar. 14, 1953; children—Peter S., Steven C., John W., Barbara J., Richard L., Suzanne G. B.A., Bklyn. Coll., 1939; M.B.A., Harvard U., 1947; M.A., Columbia U., 1952; postgrad., U. Md., 1964-66; grad., Nat. War Coll., 1966. Fgn. service officer, 1947—, vice consul, Lourenco Marques, 1947-49, 3d sec., econ. officer, Rangoon, Burma, 1949-51; Russian lang. and area studies Dept. State, 1951-52; 2d sec., consular/econ. officer, Moscow, 1952-54, Regensburg-Soviet studies, 1954-55, polit./econ. officer, Berlin, 1955-57, 1st sec., polit. officer, Bonn, Germany, 1957-60; Soviet desk Dept. State, 1960-62; sr. mem. for European affairs Nat. Security Council, 1962-65; counselor econ. affairs, Moscow, 1966-67, counselor polit. affairs, 1967-68, polit. adviser, Berlin, 1968-71, U.S. minister to, 1971-74; asst. dir. ACDA, Washington, 1974-75; exec. dir. Am. Council on Germany, 1975—, dir., 1978—; exec. dir. John J. McCloy Fund, 1975—; pres. German Am. Partnership Program, 1976—; instr. govt. and politics U. Md., 1969-71; chmn. bd. Zeiss Avionics, Calif. Author: The Basmachi, a Study in Soviet Nationalities, 1952. Bd. dirs. Deutsches Haus, N.Y. U., 1977—; vice chmn. bd. trustees Mercer County Community Coll., West Windsor, N.J. Served to col. AUS, 1941-46. Decorated Legion of Merit; recipient superior service award Dept. State, 1964. Mem. Harvard Bus. Club (v.p. Washington 1965-66), Am. Fgn. Service Assn., Council on Fgn. Relations. Unitarian. Clubs: Century, Univ. (N.Y.). Home: 6 Greenhouse Dr Princeton NJ 08540 Office: 680 Fifth Ave New York NY 10019

KLEIN, DONALD FRANKLIN, scientist, psychiatrist, educator; b. N.Y.C., Sept. 4, 1928; s. Jesse and Rose K.; m. Rachel Gittelman, Dec. 29, 1968; children: Beth, Geri, Hilary, Michelle, Erika. B.A. magna cum laude, Colby Coll., Waterville, Maine, 1947; M.D., SUNY, Bklyn., 1952. Rotating intern USPHS Hosp., S.I., N.Y., 1952-53; resident in psychiatry Creedmoor State Hosp., 1953-54, 56-58; dir. research and evaluation, dept. psychiatry L.I. Jewish-Hillside Med. Center, 1972-76; prof. psychiatry SUNY Med. Sch., Stony Brook, 1972-76; dir. research N.Y. State Psychiat. Inst., 1976—; attending psychiatrist Presbyn. Hosp., N.Y.C., 1977—; prof. psychiatry Columbia U. Coll. Physicians and Surgeons, 1978—; chmn. clin. psychopharmacology study sect. NIMH, 1973-75; Served as sr. asst. surgeon USPHS, 1954-56. Co-author: Diagnosis and Drug Treatment of Psychiatric Disorders: Adults and Children, 2d edit., 1980, Mind, Mood and Medicine, 1981; co-editor: Critical Issues in Psychiatric

Diagnosis, 1978, Anxiety: New Research and Changing Conceptions, 1980; contbr. articles to med. jours. Recipient A.E. Bennett neuropsychiat. research award, 1964. Fellow Psychiat. Research Soc. (past pres.), Am. Psychopath. Assn. (past pres., Hamilton award 1980), Am. Coll. Neuropsychopharmacology (life fellow; past pres.), Royal Coll. Psychiatry (founding mem.). Home: 1016 Fifth Ave New York NY 10028 Office: 722 W 168th St New York NY 10032

KLEIN, EDMUND, dermatologist; b. Vienna, Austria, Oct. 22, 1921; s. David and Helen (Bibelman) K.; m. Martha Alice Doble, Oct. 25, 1952; children: Lawrence E., Judith S., Peter S., Rene L., Amy K. B.A., U. Toronto, 1947, M.D., 1951. Research fellow Harvard U., 1951-52; research asso. Children's Med. Center, Boston, 1952-58; clin. and research fellow, resident dept. dermatology Mass. Gen. Hosp. and Harvard Med. Sch., 1956-59; asst. prof. depts. medicine and dermatology Tufts U. Sch. Medicine, 1959-61; mem. staff Roswell Park Meml. Inst., Buffalo, 1961—, dir. tumor immunology treatment and research center, 1972—, chief dept. dermatology, 1961-75, asso. chief, 1975—; research prof. dermatology State U. N.Y. Med. Sch., Buffalo, 1970—; cons., chief skin cancer service Sidney Farber Cancer Center, Harvard Med. Sch., 1977—; cons. viral carcinogenesis br., div. cancer cause and prevention, viral oncology Nat. Cancer Inst. Contbr. articles to med. publs. Recipient Founders award in cancer immunology Cancer Research Inst., N.Y.C., 1975; 1st prize originality research Internat. Soc. Hematology, 1956; Albert and Mary Lasker award clin. research cancer chemotherapy and immunology, 1972; also numerous acad. awards. Mem. Am. Acad. Dermatology, Am. Assn. Cancer Research, AMA, Toronto, Buffalo acads. medicine, Soc. Investigative Dermatology, N.Y. State, Erie County med. socs., Alpha Omega Alpha. Home: 262 Brompton Rd Williamsville NY 14221 Office: Dept Dermatology Roswell Park Meml Inst Buffalo NY 14203 also Office: Dept Dermatology SUNY-Buffalo Sch Medicine Buffalo NY 14214 1331 N Forest Rd Williamsville NY 14221

KLEIN, EDWARD ELKAN, clergyman; b. Newark, May 25, 1913; s. Benjamin and Elsa (Elkan) K.; m. Ruth Anne Strauss, Sept. 11, 1940; children—Barbara Anne Klein Hillman, Stephen Alan. B.A. magna cum laude, N.Y. U., 1934; M.H.L., Rabbi, Hebrew Union Coll.-Jewish Inst. Religion, 1940, D.D., 1965. Rabbi, 1940; asst. rabbi Stephen Wise Free Synagogue, N.Y.C., 1940-42, rabbi, 1943-81, rabbi emeritus, 1981—; dir. Hillel Found., U. Calif., Berkeley, 1942-43; vis. lectr. homiletics Hebrew Union Coll.-Jewish Inst. Religion, N.Y.C., 1966—. Co-chmn. League of West Side Orgns., 1952—; mem. N.Y.C. Mayor's Appeal Bd. for Fair Housing Practices, 1958-62, N.Y.C. Mayor's Adv. Com. on Higher Edn., 1966-68; mem. nat. adv. com. Religious Action Center, Washington; mem. social action commn. Union Am. Hebrew Congregations, 1960—; past chmn. ch. and state com. Central Conf. Am. Rabbis; chmn. bd. Lincoln Sq. Community Council; bd. dirs. Am. Found. on Nonviolence.; Fellow Nat. Council on Religion in Higher Edn. Mem. Phi Beta Kappa. Home: 10 W 66th St New York NY 10023 Office: 30 W 68th St New York NY 10023

KLEIN, EDWARD JOEL, editor, author, lecturer; b. Yonkers, N.Y., Oct. 19, 1936; s. Meyer I. and Gertrude (Axelrod) K.; m. Emiko Oshikiri, June 25, 1963 (div. 1975); children: Karen, Alec; m. Tessa Namuth, Mar. 20, 1978 (div. 1981). B.S., Columbia U., 1960, M.S., 1961. Copy boy, feature writer N.Y. Daily News, N.Y.C., 1957-60; reporter World Telegram & Sun, N.Y.C., 1960-61; reporter, editor Japan Times, Toyko, 1961-63; fgn. corr. UPI, Tokyo, 1963-64; editor The Shipping and Trade News, Toyko, 1964-65; assoc. editor Newsweek Mag., N.Y.C., 1965-69, fgn. editor, 1969-76, asst. mng. editor, 1976-77; editor N.Y. Times Mag., N.Y.C., 1977—. Author: (with Robert Littell and Richard Chesnoff) If Israel Lost the War, 1969, The Parachutists, 1981. Mem. Council Fgn. Relations. Office: NY Times 229 W 43d St New York NY 10028

KLEIN, EUGENE VICTOR, football exec.; b. N.Y.C., Jan. 29, 1921; s. Benjamin and Sadie (Olsen) K.; m. Joyce Fay Finberg, Feb. 10, 1976; children by previous marriage—Randee, Michael Gary. Student, N.Y. U., 1939-40. Automobile dealer, Calif., 1946-55, automobile distbr., 1955-60; chmn. bd. Columbia Savs. & Loan Assn., Los Angeles, 1955-65; pres., dir. Nat. Theatres & TV, Inc., 1955-59; chmn. bd., pres. Nat. Gen. Corp., 1961-73; pres., gen. partner San Diego Chargers Football Club, 1966—; dir. City Nat. Bank, Zenith Nat. Ins. Co. Active local civic groups and orgns. Recipient Medallion of Valor State of Israel, 1969. Office: San Diego Stadium PO Box 20666 San Diego CA 92120 *

KLEIN, GEORGE DEVRIES, geologist; b. Den Haag, Netherlands, Jan. 21, 1933; came to U.S., 1947, naturalized, 1955; s. Alfred and Doris (deVries) K.; m. Chung Sook Kim Chung, May 23, 1982; children: Richard L., Roger N. B.A., Wesleyan U., 1954; M.A., U. Kans., 1957; Ph.D., Yale U., 1960. Research sedimentologist Sinclair Research Inc., 1960-61; asst. prof. geology U. Pitts., 1961-63; asst. prof. to assoc. prof. U. Pa., 1963-69; prof. U. Ill., Urbana, 1970—; vis. fellow Wolfson Coll. Oxford U., 1969; vis. prof. geology U. Calif., Berkeley, 1970; vis. prof. oceanography Oreg. State U., 1974, Seoul Nat. U., 1980, U. Tokyo, 1983; CIC vis. exchange prof. geophys. sci. U. Chgo., 1979-80; chief scientist Deep Sea Drilling Project Leg 58, 1977-78; continuing edn. lectr.; asso. Center Advanced Studies U. Ill., 1974, 83. Author: Sandstone Depositional Models for Exploration for Fossil Fuels, 2d edit, 1980, Clastic Tidal Facies, 1977, Holocene Tidal Sedimentation, 1975; asso. editor: Geol. Soc. Am. Bull., 1975-81; cons. editor: McGraw-Hill Ency. of Sci. and Yearbook, 1977—; chief cons. adv. editor: CEPCO div. Burgess Pub. Co, 1979-81; series editor: Geol. Sci. Monographs. Recipient Outstanding Paper award Jour. Sedimentary Petrology, 1970; Erasmus Haworth Disting. Alumnus award in geology U. Kans., 1980; Outstanding Geology Faculty Mem. award U. Ill. Geology Grad. Student Assn., 1983; NSF grantee. Fellow AAAS, Geol. Soc. Am., Geol. Assn. Can.; mem. Am. Geophys. Union, Am. Inst. Profl. Geologists, Soc. Exploration Geophysicists, Soc. Econ. Paleontologists and Mineralogists, Internat. Assn. Sedimentologists, Am. Assn. Petroleum Geologists, Netherlands Geol. and Mining Soc., Sigma Xi. Office: Dept Geology Univ Ill 245 Natural History Bldg 1301 W Green St Urbana IL 61801

KLEIN, HAROLD PAUL, microbiologist; b. N.Y.C., Apr. 1, 1921; Alexander and and Lillyan (Pal) K.; m. Gloria Nancy Dolgov, Nov. 14, 1942; children—Susan Ann, Judith Ellen. B.A., Bklyn. Coll., 1942; Ph.D., U. Calif., Berkeley, 1950. Am. Cancer Soc. fellow Mass. Gen. Hosp., Boston, 1950-51; instr. microbiology U. Wash., Seattle, 1951-54, asst. prof., 1954-55; asst. prof. biology Brandeis U., Waltham, Mass., 1955-56, asso. prof., 1956-60, prof., 1960-63, chmn. dept. biology, 1956-63; vis. prof. bacteriology U. Calif., Berkeley, 1960-61; div. chief exobiology, dir. life scis. Ames Research Center, NASA, Mountain View, Calif., 1963—; mem. U.S.-USSR Working Group in Space Biology and Medicine, 1971—; leader biology team Viking Mars Mission, 1976. Mem. editorial bd.: Origins of Life, 1970—. Served with U.S. Army, 1943-46. NSF Sr. Postdoctoral fellow, 1963; grantee NIH, 1955-63; NSF, 1957-63. Mem. Am. Soc. for Microbiology, Am. Soc. Biol. Chemists, Internat. Astronautical Fedn., Am. Chem. Soc., AAAS, Phi Beta Kappa. Home: 1022 N California Ave Palo Alto CA 94303 Office: 200-7 Ames Research Center NASA Mountain View CA 94035

KLEIN, HENRY, architect; b. Cham, Germany, Sept. 6, 1920; came to U.S., 1939; s. Fred and Hedwig (Weiskopf) K.; m. Phyllis Harvey, Dec. 27, 1952; children: Vincent, Paul, David. Student, Inst. Rauch, Lausanne, Switzerland, 1936-38; B.Arch., Cornell U., 1943. Registered architects, Oreg., Wash. Designer Office of Peitro Belluschi, Architect, Portland, Oreg., 1948-51; architect Henry Klein Partnership, Architects, Mt. Vernon, Wash., 1952—; bd. dirs. Washington Parks Found., Seattle, 1977—. Bd. dirs. Shaw Island Found, Wash., 1979. Served with U.S. Army, 1943-46. Recipient Louis Sullivan Internat. Union Bricklayers and Allied Craftsmen, 1981. Fellow AIA. Jewish. Home: 1957 Little Mountain Rd Mount Vernon WA 98273 Office: Henry Klein Partnership Architects 205 Matheson Bldg Mount Vernon WA 98273

KLEIN, HERBERT SANFORD, historian; b. N.Y.C., Jan. 6, 1936; s. Emil Aaron and Florence (Friedman) K.; m. Harriet E. Manelis, Sept. 3, 1956; children—Rachel, Daniel, Jacob. A.B., U. Chgo., 1957, M.A., 1959, Ph.D., 1963. Instr. dept. history U. Chgo., 1962-63, asst. prof. history, 1963-67, asso. prof., 1967-69, Columbia U., 1969-71, prof., 1971—; vis. prof. U. Calif., Berkeley, 1968, U. Toronto, Ont., Can., 1974-75, Oxford (Eng.) U., 1975, U. de la Republica, Montevideo, Uruguay, 1978, U. Federal de Parana, Brazil, 1977, Hebrew U. of Jerusalem, 1983. Author: Slavery in the Americas, A Comparative History of Cuba and Virginia, 1967, Parties and Political Change in Bolivia, 1880-1952, 1969, The Middle Passage: Comparative Studies in the Atlantic Slave Trade, 1978, Bolivia, The Evolution of a Multi-Ethnic Society, 1982; co-author: Evolution and the Rebirth of Inequality, 1981; contbr. numerous articles, revs. to profl. jours. Recipient Socio-Psychol. prize AAAS, 1978; Social Sci. Research Council grantee, 1971-72, 79-80; Am. Council Learned Socs. grantee, 1973; NSF grantee, 1974-76; Nat. Endowment for Humanities grantee, 1975-77; Am. Philos. Soc. grantee, 1978; Tinker Found. grantee, 1975-77; Guggenheim and Woodrow Wilson fellow Smithsonian Instn., 1980-81. Mem. Conf. Latin Am. Historians, Am. Hist. Assn. Jewish. Office: Dept History Columbia U New York NY 10027

KLEIN, JOAN DEMPSEY, judge; b. San Jose, Calif., Aug. 18, 1924; d. Edward Joseph and Estelle (Kottinger) Dempsey; m. Donrad Lee Klein, Mar. 16, 1963; children—Marc Dempsey Gross, Brad Hunter Gross; stepchildren—Karen Beth Klein, Susan Linda Klein, Amy Ellen Klein. B.A., San Diego State Coll., 1948; LL.B., UCLA, 1955. Bar: Calif. bar, Supreme Ct. bar 1965. Teaching fellow UCLA, 1949-50; dept. atty. gen., trial lawyer State of Calif., 1955-63; judge Los Angeles Mcpl. Ct., 1963-75, presiding judge, 1974; mem. Los Angeles Superior Ct., 1974-78; presiding justice Calif. Ct. Appeals, Los Angeles, 1978—; prof. jud. adminstrn. U. So. Calif., 1974-75; mem. Calif. Council on Criminal Justice, 1970-74, Jud. Criminal Justice Planning Com., 1974-76; del. Nat. Adv. Commn. on Criminal Justice Standards and Goals, Washington, 1973; chmn. adv. com. Calif. Hwy. Patrol, 1976; participant S. Am. lecture tour Internat. Communication Agy. Mem. adv. bd. Girl's Week, Los Angeles City Schs., Gifted Children's Assn., San Fernando Valley; Vol. League San Fernando Valley. Named Alumna of Yr. UCLA Law Sch., 1963, Angel of Distinction Los Angeles Central City Assn., 1969, Woman of Achievement Calif. Fedn. Bus. and Profl. Women's Club, 1973, Mcpl. Ct. Judge of Yr. Calif. Trial Lawyers Assn., 1973, Woman of Yr. Los Angeles Times, 1975; recipient Profl. Achievement award UCLA Alumni Assn., 1975, Myrtle Wreath award Hadassah, 1977, Community Woman of Achievement award Big Sisters of Los Angeles, 1979, cert. of merit from Gov. Brown, 1979; Portrait in Excellence award B'nai B'rith Women. Mem. Internat. Fedn. Women Lawyers, Nat. Assn. Women Judges (founding and current pres.), Calif. Women Lawyers (pres. 1975), Calif. Judges Assn., Los Angeles County Bar Assn., Women Lawyers Assn., Los Angeles, Bus. and Profl. Women's Club, Legion Lex U. So. Calif., UCLA Law Sch. Alumni Assn. (past pres.). Democrat. Office: Ct of Appeals 3580 Wilshire Blvd Los Angeles CA 90010 *

KLEIN, JOSEPH, musical director; b. Sharon, Mass., July 16, 1936; (married); 3 sons. Grad., Columbia, Tanglewood, Mass.; pupil of Nadia Boulanger, Paris, France. Formerly chmn. music dept. Horace Mann Sch., N.Y.C. Formerly arranger-pianist for, CBS radio and TV; mus. coach for, Crosby family for Hollywood Palace TV Show; mus. dir., Seagram Liquor, McDonald's Hamburgers, Toyota, indsls.; active in Calif. star-system theatres including, Ben Kapen's Melodyland, Hyatt Music Theatre, Circle Star Theatre, Carousel Theatre, also Los Angeles Civic Light Opera; mus. dir. nat. co.: Man of La Mancha, 1967-70; condr.: on Broadway Johnny Johnson, 1971, Lost in the Stars, 1972, Man of La Mancha, 1972, Cyrano, 1973, Over Here, with The Andrew Sisters, 1974, Sacramento Music Circus, 1975, 76, 78, 79, 80, Pippin, 1977, On The Twentieth Century, 1979, Jones Beach, 1981; musical dir.: Radio City Music Hall, N.Y.C., 1982-83; dir.: Columbia Univ. Bands, N.Y.C., 1984—; music faculty: Trinity Sch., N.Y.C., 1984—. Mem. Am. Fedn. Musicans, Actors Equity, Soc. Stage Dirs. and Choreographers. Address: 28 W 87th St New York NY 10024

KLEIN, JOSEPH MARK, mining company executive; b. N.Y.C., Nov. 9, 1921; s. Erwin Wolffe and Ada (Black) K.; m. Betty Evelyn Northington, Dec. 24, 1948; children: Kathryn Ann, Elizabeth Ellen, Joseph Mark, Timothy Northington. Certificate in fgn. trade, Am. Grad Sch. Internat. Mgmt., 1946. Vice pres. internat. ops. Clary Corp., San Gabriel, Calif., 1948-60, dir., 1967-70; dir. internat. ops. Remington Rand Corp., N.Y.C., 1961-62; pres. NBC Internat. Ltd.; v.p. NBC News, N.Y.C., 1962-66; exec. v.p., dir. Cyprus Mines Corp., Los Angeles, 1966-79; chmn. bd. Hawaiian Cement Corp., 1969-79; pres., dir. Pluess-Staufer Industries, Inc., Los Angeles, 1979—; dir. Mission Ins. Group, Inc.; mem. Pres.'s Export Expansion Council, 1971-74; Vice-chmn. bd. trustees Am. Grad. Sch. Internat. Mgmt., 1975-83, chmn. bd. trustees, 1983—. Served to capt. U.S. Army, 1940-46. Decorated Silver Star, Bronze Star, Purple Heart; recipient Jonas B. Mayer Outstanding Alumni Assn. award Am. Grad. Sch. Internat. Mgmt., 1974, So. Calif. Alumni Assn. award, 1974. Mem. Am. Inst. Mining Engrs., Am. Mgmt. Assn., Newcomen Soc., Town Hall, Nat. Parks Assn., Ret. Officers Assn., Mil. Order Purple Heart (Ariz. comdr. 1949-50). Republican. Presbyterian. Clubs: California, Riviera Country, Elks. Home: 1071 Villa View Dr Pacific Palisades CA 90272 Office: 4818 Lincoln Blvd Marina del Rey CA 90291

KLEIN, LAWRENCE ROBERT, economist, educator; b. Omaha, Sept. 14, 1920; s. Leo Byron and Blanche (Monheit) K.; m. Sonia Adelson, Feb. 15, 1947; children: Hannah, Rebecca, Rachel, Jonathan. B.A., U. Calif.-Berkeley, 1942; Ph.D., MIT, 1944; M.A., Lincoln Coll., Oxford U., 1957; LL.D. (hon.), U. Mich., 1977, Dickinson Coll., 1981, Sc.D., Widener Coll., 1977, Elizabethtown Coll., 1981, Ball State U., 1982, Technion, 1982, U. Nebr., 1983; Dr. honoris causa, U. Vienna, 1977; Dr.Ed., Villanova U., 1978; Dr. (h.c.), Bonn U., 1974, Free U. Brussels, 1979, U. Paris, 1979, U. Madrid, 1980. Faculty U. Chgo., 1944-47; research assoc. Nat. Bur. Econ. Research, 1948-50; faculty U. Mich., 1949-54; research assoc. Survey Research Center, 1949-54, Oxford Inst. Stats., 1954-58; faculty U. Pa., Phila., 1958—, prof., 1958—, Univ. prof., 1964—, Benjamin Franklin prof., 1968—; vis. prof. Osaka U., 1960, U. Colo., 1962, City U. N.Y., 1962-63, 82, Hebrew U., 1964, Princeton U., 1966, Stanford U., summer 1968, U. Copenhagen, 1974; Ford vis. prof. U. Calif. at Berkeley, 1968, Inst. for Advanced Studies, Vienna, 1970, 74; cons. Canadian Govt., 1947, UNCTAD, 1966, 67, 75, 77, 80, McMillan Co., 1965-74, E.I. du Pont de Nemours, 1966-68, State of N.Y., 1969, AT&T, 1969, Fed. Res. Bd., 1973, UNIDO, 1973-75, Congl. Budget Office, 1977—, Council Econ. Advisers, 1977-80; chmn. bd. trustees Wharton Econometric Forecasting Assocs., Inc., 1969-80, chmn. profl. bd., 1980—; trustee Maurice Falk Inst. for Econ. Research, Israel, 1969-75; adv. council Inst. Advanced Studies, Vienna, 1977—; chmn. econ. adv. com. Gov. of Pa., 1976-78; mem. com. on prices Fed. Res. Bd., 1968-70; prin. investigator econometric model project Brookings Instn., 1963-72, Project LINK, 1968—; sr. adviser Brookings Panel on Econ. Activity, 1970—; mem. adv. com. Inst. Internat. Econs., 1983; coordinator Jimmy Carter's Econ. Task Force, 1976; mem. adv. bd. Strategic Studies Center, Stanford Research Inst., 1974-76. Author: The Keynesian Revolution, 1947, Textbook of Econometrics, 1953, An Econometric Model of the United States, 1929-1952, 1955, Wharton Econometric Forecasting Model, 1967, Essay on the Theory of Economic Prediction, 1968, An Introduction to Econometric Forecasting and Forecasting Models, 1980; Author-editor: Brookings Quar. Econometric Model of U.S.; Ecometric Model Performance, 1976, Lectures in Econometrics, 1983; Editor: Internat. Econ. Rev, 1959-65; asso. editor, 1965—; Editorial bd.: Empirical Econs, 1976—. Recipient William F. Butler award N.Y. Assn. Bus. Economists, 1975; Golden Slipper Club award, 1977; Pres.'s medal U. Pa., 1980; Alfred Nobel Meml. prize in econs., 1980. Fellow Econometric Soc. (past pres.), Am. Acad. Arts and Scis., Nat. Assn. Bus. Economists; mem. Am. Philos. Soc., Nat. Acad. Scis., Social Sci. Research Council (fellow 1945-46, 47-48, com. econ. stability, dir. 1971-76), Am. Econ. Assn. (John Bates Clark medalist 1959, exec. com. 1966-68, pres. 1977), Eastern Econ. Assn. (pres. 1974-76). Office: U Pa Philadelphia PA 19104 *

KLEIN, SISTER M. ROSALIE, university dean; b. Milw. B.S. in Nursing, Marquette U., 1952, M.S., 1960; M.Med. Sci., Tulane U., 1968, D.Sc., 1970. Nursing supr. St. Francis Hosp., Cape Girardeau, Mo., 1952-54; nursing supr. St. Michael Hosp., Milw., 1954-56, dir. nursing service, 1956-59; instr. Marquette U., Milw., 1959-62, asst. prof., 1962-67, coordinator basic program in nursing, 1965-67, dean, 1970—; Bd. dirs. St. Joseph's and St. Michael Hosp., Racine, Wis., Marion Catholic Home, health facility for aged. Mem. Wis. (past pres.), Nat. leagues nursing, Am. Assn. Colls. Nursing, Wis. Assn. Colegiate Schs. Nursing (pres. 1978—), Am. Nurses Assn., Am. Public Health Assn., Am. Assn. Higher Edn., Western Soc. Research in Nursing, Milw. Dist. Nurses Assn. Office: Marquette U Coll Nursing 510 N 16th St Milwaukee WI 53233

KLEIN, MARION ANN, health and beauty aid company executive; b. Mt. Carmel, Pa., Oct. 20, 1926; d. Daniel and Florence (Buckley) K. B.A., Douglass Co., 1948; M.B.A., NYU, 1954. Econ. research analyst Mt. Life Ins. Co., N.Y.C., 1948-54; market research mgr. Food Mfrs., Inc., Hackettstown, N.J., 1954-59; ptnr. Sounding Bd. Research Co., Bloomfield, N.J., 1959-62; market research mgr. Colgate Palmolive Co., N.Y.C., 1962-65; various mktg. and market research positions Bristol-Myers Co., N.Y.C., 1965-81, v.p. market research, 1981—; trustee Market Sci. Inst., Cambridge, Mass., 1978-81. Mem. mktg. research com. Proprietary Assn., Washington, 1977—. Recipient Alumna Club NYU Alumna Club, Tribute to Women in Internat. Industry Nat. YWCA, Acad. of Women Achievers, N.Y.C. Mem. Am. Mktg. Assn., Advt. Research Found., Market Research Council. Home: 85 Belgrade Ave Clifton NJ 07013 Office: Bristol-Myers Co 345 Park Ave New York NY 10154

KLEIN, MARTIN JESSE, physicist, educator; b. N.Y.C., June 25, 1924; s. Adolph and Mary (Neuman) K.; m. Miriam June Levin, Oct. 28, 1945 (div. 1973); children: Rona F. (Mrs. Andrew Glass), Sarah M. (Mrs. Joseph Zaino), Nancy R.; m. Linda L. Booz, Oct. 8, 1980. A.B., Columbia, 1942, M.A., 1944; Ph.D., Mass. Inst. Tech., 1948. With OSRD for USN, 1944-45; research asso. physics Mass. Inst. Tech., 1946-49; instr. physics Case Inst. Tech., 1949-51, asst. prof., 1951-55, asso. prof., 1955-60, prof., 1960-67, acting dept. head, 1966-67; prof. history of physics Yale, 1967-74, Eugene Higgins prof. history of physics and prof. physics, 1974—, chmn. dept. history sci., 1971-74; Van der Waals guest prof. U. Amsterdam, 1974; vis. prof. Rockefeller U., 1975, adj. prof., 1976-79. Author: Paul Ehrenfest, Vol. I: The Making of a Theoretical Physicist, 1970; Editor: Collected Scientific Papers of Paul Ehrenfest, 1959; editorial adviser: Ency. Brit, 1956-76; Translator: Letters on Wave Mechanics, 1967; Contbr. articles to profl. jours. NRC fellow Dublin (Ireland) Inst. Advanced Studies, 1952-53; Guggenheim fellow, Leyden, Netherlands, 1958-59, Yale, 1967-68. Fellow Am. Acad. Arts and Scis., Am. Phys. Soc., AAAS; mem. Nat. Acad. Scis., History of Sci. Soc., Am. Assn. Physics Tchrs., Am. Hist. Assn., AAUP, Académie Internationale d'Histoire des Sciences (corr.), Phi Beta Kappa, Sigma Xi. Address: Dept Physics Box 2036 Yale U Station New Haven CT 06520

KLEIN, MAURICE J., lawyer; b. Phila., Aug. 23, 1908; s. Joseph A. and Raye (Blum) K.; m. Fay Clearfield, Jan. 7, 1934 (dec.); children—Raymond, Jerome. LL.B., Temple U., 1932. Bar: Pa. 1932. Practice in, Phila., 1932-72; sr. partner Abrahams & Loewenstein, 1944-72. Nat. vice chmn. bd. trustees Union of Am. Hebrew Congregations, 1967-72, nat. bd. mem., 1961-81, hon. life trustee, 1981—, chmn. nat. rules com., 1969-73, mem. nat. commn. congl. rabbinic affairs, 1970—; exec. com. Pacific S.W. council, 1972—; pres. Council Reform Synagogues of Pa., 1964-68, Phila. Fedn. Reform Synagogues, 1961-63, Congregation Judea, Philadelphia, 1955-57; hon. life trustee Congregation Judea, 1957—; trustee Jewish Community Relations Council, 1961-65, N.E. High Sch. Found., 1970—; mem. Temple U. Assos., 1970; mem. adv. com. Sch. Jewish Communal Service, Hebrew Union Coll., 1974—; bd. dirs., ex-officio Temple Emanuel, Beverly Hills, 1973—. Named Man of Year N.E. High Sch., 1969. Mem. Phila. Bar Assn., Alumni Assn. N.E. High Sch., Phila. (pres. 1965-67, hon. life trustee 1967—), Am. Jewish Hist. Soc. (nat. exec. council 1973—), Lambda Sigma Kappa. Home: 1250 S Beverly Glen Blvd Los Angeles CA 90024

KLEIN, MELVYN NORMAN, lawyer, business executive; b. Chgo., Dec. 27, 1941; s. Harry and Bertha M. (Gleicher) K.; m. Annette Lorraine Grossman, Mar. 26, 1976; children: Jacqueline Anne, Jenna Katherine. A.B. with highest honors in Econs., Colgate U., 1963; J.D., Columbia U., 1966. Bar: D.C. 1968, Tex. 1980. Legis. asst. Rep. Sidney Yates, Washington, 1966; mem. firm McKinsey & Co., Washington, 1967-68; mem. staff Vice Pres. Hubert Humphrey's Presdl. Campaign, 1968; sr. v.p. Donaldson, Lufkin and Jenrette, Inc., N.Y.C., 1969-77; counsel Brownstein, Zeidman & Schomer, Washington, 1978; pres., chief exec. officer, chmn. exec. and fin. coms., dir. Altamil Corp., Corpus Christi, 1977-84; dir., chmn. fin. com. Playboy Enterprises, Inc.; dir. Victorio Co., Phoenix, Levitz Furniture Corp., Keith Barish Prodns.; dir., mem. exec. com. Sparkman Energy Corp., RSR Holding Corp.; dir. First City Bank of Corpus Christi, DLJ Capital Corp. Chmn. Corpus Christi Bus. Devel. Comm., 1979—; chmn. bd. govs. Art Mus. South Tex.; bd. dirs. S. Tex. Ednl. Broadcasting System, 1978-79; mem. exec. com. Pres.'s Pvt. Sector Study of Cost Control in Fed. Govt. Mem. Am. Bus. Conf. (founding mem., chmn. capital formation and tax policy com. 1980—), ABA, D.C. Bar Assn., State Bar Tex., Young Pres. Orgn. Clubs: Rotary, Corpus Christi Yacht, Corpus Christi Country; Standard (Chgo.); City Mid-Day (N.Y.C.). Office: 1940 First City Bank Tower Corpus Christi TX 78477

KLEIN, MILTON MARTIN, history educator; b. N.Y.C., Aug. 15, 1917; s. Edward and Margaret (Greenfield) K.; m. Margaret Gordon, Aug. 25, 1963; children: Edward Gordon, Peter Gordon. B.S.S.,

M.S. in Edn., 1939; Ph.D., Columbia U., 1954. AAF, 1944-47; tchr. N.Y.C. pub. schs., 1947-57; vis. bia U., summers 1959, 60, lectr. history, 1954-58; prof. nn. dept. L.I. U., 1958-62, dean Coll. Liberal Arts and Sci., 1962-, dean grad. studies and research SUNY-Fredonia, 1966-69; prof. history U. Tenn., 1969—, alumni disting. service prof., 1977—, Lindsay Young prof., 1980—; Walter E. Meyer vis. prof. N.Y. U. Law Sch., 1976-77; chmn. Columbia U. Faculty Seminar on Early Am. History and Culture, 1971-72. Author: Social Studies for the Academically Talented Student, 1960, The Politics of Diversity: Essays in the History of Colonial New York, 1974, New York in the American Revolution: A Bibliography, 1974; also numerous articles.; editor: Independent Reflector (William Livingston), 1963; Editor: A History of the American Colonies, 13 vols, 1973—, New York-The Centennial Years, 1676-1976, 1976, Courts and Law in Early New York, 1978; mem. editorial bd.: Am. Jour. Legal History, 1970-76, N.Y. History, 1973—, U. Tenn. Press, 1972-75; adv. editor: Eighteenth-Century Studies, 1975—; adv. bd.: America: History and Life, 1982—. Served to lt. col. USAF Res. Recipient Outstanding Teaching award U. Tenn. Alumni, 1974, Kerr History prize N.Y. State Hist. Assn., 1975, Articles prize Am. Soc. Eighteenth Century Studies, 1976; Fulbright lectr. U. Canterbury, Christchurch, N.Z., 1962; Ford Found. travelling fellow, 1955-56; Lilly Found.-Clements Library fellow, 1961; Am. Philos. Soc. grantee, 1973. Mem. Am. Hist. Assn., Conf. on Brit. Studies, Orgn. Am. Historians, Am. Soc. 18th Century Studies (articles prize 1976), Southeastern Am. Soc. 18th Century Studies (dir. 1978-81, v.p. 1982-84), AAUP (nat. council 1978-80), Am. Soc. Legal History (chmn. membership com. 1969-74, dir. 1971-76, sec. 1975-77, v.p. 1978-80, pres. 1980-82), Phi Beta Kappa, Sigma Alpha Mu, Phi Alpha Theta, Phi Kappa Phi, Omicron Delta Kappa, Mortar Bd, Golden Key. Home: 8124 Kingsdale Dr Knoxville TN 37919

KLEIN, MORTON, industrial engineer, educator; b. N.Y.C., Aug. 9, 1925; s. Norbert and Lottie (Wigdor) K.; m. Gloria Ritterband, July 31, 1949; children: Lisa, Melanie. B.S.M.E., Duke U., 1946; M.S., Columbia U., 1952, D.Engring. Sci., 1957. Engr. Picatinny Arsenal, Dover, N.J., 1950-54; instr. Sch. Engring and Applied Sci., Columbia U., N.Y.C., 1956, asst. prof., 1957-61, asso. prof., 1961-69, prof. ops. research, 1969—, chmn. dept. indsl. engring. and ops. research, 1982—; cons. to industry, govt. Author: (with Cyrus Derman) Probability and Statistical Inference for Engineers, 1959; editor: Management Science, 1960-77. Served with USN, 1943-46. Mem. Ops. Research Soc. Am. Inst. Mgmt. Scis., Am. Inst. Indsl. Engrs., Pi Tau Sigma, Alpha Pi Mu, Omega Rho. Office: 301 A SW Mudd Columbia Univ New York NY 10027

KLEIN, MORTON JOSEPH, chemist; b. Chgo., Feb. 26, 1928; s. Isador J. and Rose (Tiger) K.; m. Ruth Blum, June 16, 1953; children—Gayle Susan Klein Collins, Mitchell Jay, Ronald David. Student, Ill. Inst. Tech., 1945-46, Ph.D., 1953; B.S., U. Ill., 1948. Mem. staff IIT Research Inst., Chgo., 1953—, asst. dir. chemistry, 1962-65, dir. applied chemistry, 1965-67, dir. chemistry research, 1967-75, dir. chemistry and chem. engring. research, 1975-77, v.p. research ops., 1977—; Mem. Ill. com. CARE, 1962-64; chmn. N.Am. exec. com., internat. pres. Internat. Ozone Inst. Commr. Skokie Environ. Commn.; Trustee Mt. Sinai Med. Center. Recipient award sci. merit IIT Research Inst., 1957. Mem. Am. Chem. Soc., Am. Inst. Chemists, Am. Inst. Aeros. and Astronautics, Sigma Xi, Phi Lambda Upsilon. Clubs: Chemists (N.Y.C.); Internat. (Chgo.). Home: 9021 Sleeping Bear Rd Skokie IL 60076 Office: 10 W 35th St Chicago IL 60616

KLEIN, NORMA, author; b. N.Y.C., May 13, 1938; d. Emanuel and Sadie (Frankel) K.; m. Erwin Fleissner, July 27, 1963; children: Jennifer, Katherine. B.A., Barnard Coll., 1960; M.A. in Slavic Langs., Columbia U., 1963. Author: short stories Love and Other Euphenisms, 1972, Sextet in A Minor, 1982; novels Give Me One Good Reason, 1973 (Book of Month Club alternate), Girls Turn Wives, 1976 (Lit. Guild alternate), Domestic Arrangements, 1981, Wives and Othger Women, 1982, It's Okay if You Don't Love Me, 1977, Love is One of the Choices, 1978, Beginner's Love, 1983, The Swap, 1983; teenage fiction Mom, the Wolf Man and Me, 1972, It's Not What You Expect, 1973, Taking Sides, 1975, What It's All About, 1975, Confessions of an Only Child, 1973, Tomboy, 1978, A Honey of A Chimp, 1980, Robbie and the Leap Year Blues, 1981, Hiding, 1976, Breaking Up, 1980, The Queen of the What Ifs, 1982, French Postcards, 1979; juvenile fiction Naomi in the Middle, 1974, Blue Trees, Red Sky, 1975, Girls Can Be Anything, 1973 (Jr. Lit. Guild alternate), If I Had My Way, 1974, A Train for Jane, 1974, Dinosaur's Housewarming Party, 1974, Visiting Pamela, 1979. Home: 27 W 96th St New York NY 10025

KLEIN, OSCAR ROY, JR., actuary; b. Osawatomie, Kans., June 4, 1927; s. Oscar Roy and Josephine Henrietta (Bliesner) K.; m. Betty Freeman Nichols, Apr. 16, 1949; children—David, Thomas, William, Cynthia. A.B., Washburn U., 1949; M.A., U. Mich., 1951. With Bus. Men's Assurance Co. Am., Kansas City, Mo., 1951—, beginning in actuarial dept., successively supr. valuation sect., supr. group actuarial, actuarial asst., asst. actuary, actuary, v.p. and actuary, v.p. and chief actuary, 1951-73, exec. v.p., chief actuary, 1973-80, exec. v.p. tech. services, 1980—, also dir.; dir. BMA Properties. Bd. dirs. United Way; mem. Kansas City Sports Commn. Served with USNR, 1945-46. Fellow Soc. Actuaries, Canadian Inst. Actuaries; mem. Am. Acad. Actuaries. Club: Indian Hills Country. Home: 8600 Wenonga Ln Leawood KS 66206 Office: BMA Tower Kansas City MO 64141

KLEIN, PAUL LESTER, media analyst; b. Bklyn., Nov. 6, 1928; s. Sydney and Kate (Silver) K.; m. Janet Barbara Goldstein, Dec. 20, 1959; children: Adam Daniel, Molly R. B.A., Bklyn. Coll., 1954. Dir. research Doyle-Dane-Bernbach, N.Y.C., 1956-60; v.p. audience measurement NBC, N.Y.C., 1961-70; chmn. bd., pres. Computer TV, Inc., N.Y.C., 1970-75; exec. v.p. programs NBC TV Network, N.Y.C., 1976-79; pres. PKO TV Ltd., N.Y.C., 1979—, Playboy Video Corp., Los Angeles, 1982—; cons. PBS, Ford Found., 1970-75, ABC, NCAA, Time, Inc. Contbg. editor: New York Mag.; author: TV Guide; producer: TV prodn. People vs. Jean Harris. Served with AUS, 1946. Recipient award for "Holocaust" B'nai Sholom, 1978. Mem. Nat. Assn. TV Arts and Scis., Friars Club. Jewish. Home: 9400 Lloydcrest Dr Beverly Hills CA 90210 Home: 420 E 54th St New York NY 10022 Office: Playboy Video Corp 8560 Sunset Blvd Los Angeles CA 90069 *The most disappointing yet exhilarating experience is to wake up one day to discover you know nothing and neither does anyone else: most, if not everything that will happen is random, that you will live a life of mistakes. . .an it ain't so bad.*

KLEIN, PETER MARTIN, lawyer, transportation company executive; b. N.Y.C., June 2, 1934; s. Saul and Esther (Goldstein) K.; m. Ellen Judith Matlick, June 18, 1961; children: Amy Lynn, Steven Ezra. A.B., Columbia U., 1956, J.D., 1962. Bar: N.Y. 1962, D.C. 1964, U.S. Supreme Ct. bar 1966. Asst. proctor Columbia U., 1959-62; asst. counsel Mil. Sea Transp. Service, Office Gen. Counsel, Dept. Navy, Washington, 1962-65; trial atty. civil div. Dept. Justice, N.Y.C., 1966-69; gen. atty. Sea-Land Service, Inc., Menlo Park, N.J., 1969-76, v.p., gen. counsel, sec., 1976-79, Sea-Land Industries, Inc., Menlo Park, 1979-84; asso. gen. counsel R.J. Reynolds Industries, Inc., Winston-Salem, N.C., 1978-84; sr. v.p., gen. counsel, sec. Sea-Land Corp., Menlo Park, Calif., 1984—; dir. Sea-Land Industries Investments, Inc., 1981-84, Reynolds Leasing Corp., 1981—; mem. adv. com. on pvt. internat. law Dept. State, 1974—; mem. U.S. delegation UN Conf. on Trade and Devel., UN Commn. on Internat. Trade Law, 1975-76. Trustee Jewish Edn. Assn. Met. N.J., 1973-76; trustee Temple B'nai Abraham of Essex County, N.J., 1973—, v.p., 1976-81, pres., 1981-83. Served with USN, 1956-59; Antarctica. Mem. Am. Maritime Assn. (dir., chmn. coms. on law and legis. 1974-78), Am. Polar Soc., ABA, Navy League U.S. (life mem.), Fed. Bar Assn., N.Y. State Bar Assn., D.C. Bar Assn., Internat. Bar Assn., Maritime Law Assn., U.S. Club, Nat. Press. Home: 42 Billingsley Dr Livingston NJ 07039 Office: PO Box 800 Iselin NJ 08830

KLEIN, ROBERT, manufacturing executive; b. Phila., Dec. 3, 1924; s. Julius and Eleanor (Arons) K.; m. Judith Auritt, June 30, 1946; children: William J., Sally G., Anne L. B.A., Pa. State U., 1948. From indsl. engr. to pres. Caloric Corp., Topton, Pa., 1948-69; pres. Samuel Klein Corp., Alburtis, Pa., 1969-74, AllianceWall Corp., Atlanta, 1963-78, chmn. bd., 1978—, Eichler Wood Products Co., Laury's Station, Pa., 1971-78, John M. Spiegel Co., Allentown, Pa., 1972-78; mng. dir. Alliance Europe, Genk, Belgium, 1971—; dir., v.p. Nat. Bank Topton, 1960-67; mng. dir. Alliance Pentagon, Odense, Denmark, 1972—; dir. BVG Vineyards, N.Y.C. and Listrac, France, Broomall Industries, Inc., Pa. Chmn. adv. com. Good Shepherd Home Workshop, 1967—; pres. bd. assos. Muhlenberg Coll., 1969-70, trustee, 1970-82, life trustee, 1982; trustee Jewish Fedn., Allentown, 1970-74, 78-81; bd. dirs. Porcelain Enamel Inst., 1974—, Nat. Foundry Assn.; pres. alumni trustees, sec. Coll. Bus. Adminstrn., Pa. State U., 1977—, also mem. alumni council. Served with USMCR, 1943-45. Decorated Purple Heart; recipient Alumni Achievement award Muhlenberg Coll., 1976, Pa. State U., 1978; Alumni fellow Pa. State U., 1981. Home: 2720 Allen St Allentown PA 18104 Office: Suite 204 512 Hamilton St Allentown PA 18101 *Work hard, think smart, and work with and encourage your associates. Always remember that every decision you make includes and affects people. This should not decrease aggressiveness but instead make your decisions "people sensitive."*

KLEIN, ROBERT, comedian, actor; b. N.Y.C., Feb. 8, 1942; s. Benjamin and Frieda (Moskowitz) K.; m. Brenda Boozer, Apr. 29, 1973. B.A., Alfred (N.Y.) U., 1962; student, Yale U. Sch. Drama, 1962-63. Mem. Second City Theatrical Co., Chgo., 1965-66. Broadway appearances include The Apple Tree, 1966, New Faces of, 1968, Morning, Noon and Night, 1969; film appearances include The Bell Jar, Hooper, Nobody's Perfekt, The Last Unicorn (voice); records include Child of the Fifties, 1973, Mind Over Matter, 1974, New Teeth, 1975; frequent guest and host on TV numerous concert appearances throughout U.S. Mem. Actors Equity Assn., Screen Actors Guild, AFTRA, Am. Guild Variety Artists, Writers Guild. *

KLEIN, ROBERT MICHAEL, lawyer; b. Detroit, Nov. 19, 1939; s. Victor Walter and Ruth Virginia (Arie) K.; m. Carlyn Ashley Anderson, May 10, 1975. B.A., Williams Coll., 1962; LL.B., U. Mich., 1965, LL.M., 1966. Bar: Mich. bar 1966. Since practiced, Detroit; partner firm Butzel, Long, Gust, Klein & Van Zile, Detroit, 1966—; Mem. lawyers' adv. com. U.S. Brewers Assn. Contbr. articles to legal jours. Trustee William G. Beaumont Hosp. Mem. Williams Coll. Alumni Assn. (sec. Mich. 1972), Cranbrook Alumni Assn. (v.p. 1975), Am., Mich., Detroit bar assns. Home: 756 Williamsbury Birmingham MI 48010 Office: Butzel Long Gust Klein & Van Zile 1881 1st Nat Bldg Detroit MI 48226

KLEIN, RONALD LLOYD, elec. engr., educator; b. Bloomington, Ill., Apr. 26, 1939; s. Frank Samuel and Lila Mabel (Sharp) K.; m. Nancy Ann Jones, Aug. 20, 1961; children—Laura, Karla. B.S., U. Ill., 1962, M.S., 1963; Ph.D. in E.E, U. Iowa, 1969. Mem. tech. staff Bell Telephone Labs., North Andover, Mass., 1963-67; elec. engr. Ill. Bell Telephone Co., Chgo., 1967; asst. prof. U. Kans., 1969-74, asso. prof., 1974-78, prof. elec. engring., 1978-79; prof. elec. engring., chmn. dept. W.Va. U., Morgantown, 1979—. Contbr. articles to profl. jours. U.S. Air Force research grantee, 1975-77; NSF research grantee, 1973-75. Mem. IEEE. Home: 124 Poplar Dr Baker's Ridge Morgantown WV 26505 Office: Room 825 Engring Scis West Va Univ Morgantown WV 26506

KLEIN, SAMI WEINER, librarian; b. Worcester, Mass., July 6, 1939; d. Phillip and Barbara Rose (Ginsberg) Weiner; m. Eugene Robert Klein, Oct. 22, 1961; children: Pamela, Jeffrey, Elizabeth. B.A., Simmons Coll., 1961; M.L.S., U. Md., 1973; postgrad., Johns Hopkins U., 1976-78. Chemist Hercules, Wilmington, Del., 1961-62, FDA, Washington, 1965-66; librarian NSWC, White Oak, Md., 1973-78; chief hqrs. library EPA, Washington, 1978-82; chief info services Nat. Bur. Standards Library, Gaithersburg, Md., 1982—; cons. in field; mem. librarians exec. council Met. Washington Council of Govts., 1981-82. Mem. sec. Harpers Choice PTA, Columbia Md., 1961. Recipient Gold medal Am. Soc. Chemists, 1961. Mem. Spl Libraries Assn. (treas. info.-tech. group 1982-84), ALA (sec.-treas. Fed. Librarians Roundtable 1983-84), Am. Soc. for Info. Sci., D.C. Law Librarians Soc., Beta Phi Mu. Democrat. Jewish. Home: 11041 Wood Elves Way Columbia MD 21044 Office: Nat Bur Standards Route 270 Gaithersburg MD 20234

KLEIN, VERLE WESLEY, naval officer; b. Stickney, S.D., Apr. 7, 1933; s. Albert and Kate (Noteboom) K.; m. Marlene June Hargens, Dec. 19, 1954; children—Pamela Louise, Janice Lynn. B.S., U.S. Naval Postgrad. Sch., 1962; M.B.A., George Washington U., 1975. Commd. ensign U.S. Navy, 1954, advanced through grades to rear adm., 1980; assigned to (Patrol Squadron 22), 1955-58, flight instr., Corpus Christi, Tex., 1958-60, with, 1963-65, test pilot, Patuxent River, Md., 1967-69, comdg. officer, 1969-70, ops. officer, 1971-72, asst. aviation comdr. detailer, 1972-74, head major procurement programs and budgeting br., 1975-76, exec. asst. and naval aide to asst. sec., 1976-78, comdr., Patuxent River, 1978-80, dep. dir. Office Budgets and Reports, also fiscal mgmt. div., 1980—. Decorated Silver Star, Legion of Merit with two gold stars, D.F.C., Air medal with two gold stars, Navy Commendation medal, Gallantry Cross, Republic Vietnam, numerous others. Mem. Am. Soc. Mil. Comptrollers. Home: 3301 Miller Heights Rd Oakton VA 22124 Office: OP-92D Room 4C560 Pentagon Washington DC 20350

KLEIN, WALTER CHARLES, agroindustry executive; b. N.Y.C., May 11, 1918; s. Joseph Charles and Charlotte (Fleischman) K.; m. Mary Kennard Eddy, Apr. 5, 1941; children: Walter Charles, John E., Margaret K. A.B., Harvard Coll., 1939. Asst. v.p. Bunge Corp., N.Y.C., 1947-52, v.p., 1952-59, dir., 1955—, pres., chief exec. officer, 1959—; adv. bd. Chem. Bank. Overseer Exec. Council Fgn. Diplomats, Washington; bd. dirs. U.S.-USSR Trade and Econ. Council. Republican. Congregationalist. Clubs: Orange Lawn Tennis (South Orange, N.J.) (gov. 1959-62); Short Hills (N.J.) (bd. dirs., pres. 1984); Knickerbocker, India House, Downtown Assn. (N.Y.C.); Baltursrol Golf (Springfield, N.J.). Office: Bunge Corp 1 Chase Manhattan Plaza New York NY 10005

KLEIN, WILLIAM EUGENE, army officer; b. Clarksdale, Miss., Dec. 29, 1931; s. Johl William and Louise Marchant (Larcade) K.; m. Carolyn Purdue, May 7, 1955; children: Katherine Sills, Carolyn Rhoads, William Marchant, Richard Pace, Johl Kelly. Student, U. Ala., 1949-50; B.S., U.S. Mil. Acad., 1954; M.S., U. So. Fla., 1972. Commd. 2d lt. U.S. Army, 1954, advanced through grades to brig. gen.; exec. officer, comdr.-in chief Strike Command, 1969-72; brigade comdr. 25th Inf. Div., 1976-79, chief of staff, 1978-79, SVIII Airborne Corps, 1979-80; asst. div. comdr. 82d Airborne Div., Ft. Bragg, N.C., 1981—. Bd. govs. Fayetteville USO, N.C. Decorated Silver Star with 3 oak leaf clusters, D.F.C., Bronze Star with 4 oak leaf clusters. Republican. Episcopalian. Office: Asst Div Comdr 82d Airborne Div Fort Bragg NC 28307 *

KLEIN, WILLIAM KENNETH, consultant, former hospital administrator; b. Mpls., Sept. 9. 1916; s. Kenneth O. and Lenora (Bye) K.; m. Mariam Ott, May 18, 1940; children: Kenneth William, Henry Alexander, Marianne. B.B.A., U. Minn., 1938. Dir. services and supplies, also asst. dir. U. Minn. Hosps., 1942-47; dir. Hurley Hosp., Flint, Mich., 1947-53, L.I. Coll. Hosp., 1953-66, exec. dir., 1966-77, ret., 1977; pres. William Klein Cons., Inc., 1978—; dir. Group Health Inc., Health Providers Service Co., Med. Centers Asso., L.I. Coll. Hosp. Nursing Home Co., Cobble Hill Nursing Home Co., Health Providers Ins. Co., Hosp. Underwriters Mut. Ins. Co.; dir., chmn. Hosp. Assurance, Ltd.; cons. Health and Mental Hygiene Facilities Improvement Corp. Fellow Am. Coll. Hosp. Adminstrs.; mem. Am. Hosp. Assn., Hosp. Assn. N.Y. State (past trustee), Greater N.Y. Hosp. Assn. (past pres.), Alpha Delta Phi (past chmn. nat. exec. council). Home and Office: 9 Plum Beach Point Dr Port Washington NY 11050

KLEINBERG, HOWARD J., newspaper editor; b. N.Y.C., Oct. 23, 1932; s. Benjamin and Ruth (Wile) K.; m. Natalie Bernstein, Feb. 22, 1953; children—Linda Kleinberg Landy, Eliot, Eileen, David. Student pub. schs. Mem. staff Miami (Fla.) News, 1950-65, 66—, mng. editor, 1968-76, editor, 1976—; pub. relations exec. Hank Meyer Assos., Miami, 1965-66. Served with AUS, 1953-55; Korea. Recipient 1st place Page One Makeup Fla. AP, 1962, Fla. Sportswriters Assn., 1959. Mem. Am. Soc. Newspaper Editors, AP Mng. Editor's Assn., Inter-Am. Press Assn., Sigma Delta Chi. Home: 14520 SW 79th Ct Miami FL 33158 Office: Box 615 Miami News Miami FL 33152

KLEINBERG, JACOB, educator, chemist; b. Passaic, N.J., Feb. 14, 1914; s. William and Rebecca (Sirota) K.; m. Jane L. Crawford, June 11, 1942; children: Judith Ann, Mary Jill. B.S., Randolph-Macon Coll., 1934; M.S., U. Ill., 1937, Ph.D., 1939. Asst. prof. James Millikin U., 1940-43, U. Ill. Coll. Pharmacy, 1943-46; mem. faculty U. Kans., 1946—, prof. chemistry, 1951—, chmn. dept., 1963-70. Author: Unfamiliar Oxidation States, 1950, (with L.F. Audrieth) Non-Agueous Solvents, 1953, (with W.J. Argersinger, Jr. and E. Griswold) Inorganic Chemistry, 1960, (with J.C. Bailar, Jr. and T. Moeller) University Chemistry, 1965, (with M. Kahn) Radiochemistry of Iodine, 1977, (with J.C. Bailar, Jr., T. Moeller, C.O. Guss, M.E. Castellion and C. Metz) Chemistry, 1978, 2d edit., 1984, Chemistry with Inorganic Qualitative Analysis, 1980, 2d edit., 1984; Editorial bd.: Chem. Revs, 1951-53, Inorganic Chemistry, 1961-64, Jour. Inorganic and Nuclear Chemistry, 1955—. Mem. Am. Chem. Soc., Phi Beta Kappa, Sigma Xi. Spl. research unfamiliar oxidation states of metals, non-aqueous solvents. Home: 9 Winona Ave Lawrence KS 66044

KLEINBERG, LAWRENCE, manufacturing executive; b. N.Y.C., Dec. 20, 1943; s. Paul and Gertrude (Voron) K.; m. Lois Helene Kass, June 10, 1967; children: Brian Andrew. B.A. in Econs., Adelphi U., 1965, M.B.A., 1969. Analyst, Pfizer, Inc., N.Y.C., 1965-69; various fin. mgmt. positions Beech-Nut, Inc., N.Y.C., 1969-73; v.p., controller Life Savers, Inc., N.Y.C., 1973-79, sr. v.p. fin., 1979-83, exec. v.p., 1983, pres., 1984—, also dir.; dir. Life Savers Mfg., Inc. Office: 625 Madison Ave New York NY 10022

KLEINBERG, MARVIN H., patent lawyer; b. N.Y.C., Aug. 17, 1927; s. Herman and Lillian (Grossman) K.; m. Irene Aertker, July 7, 1962; children—Sarah Elizabeth, Ethan Chaim, Joel Victor. B.A. in Physics, U. Calif. at Los Angeles, 1949; J.D., U. Calif. at Berkeley, 1953. Bar: Calif. bar 1954, also U.S. Patent Office, U.S. Supreme Ct. bars 1954. Since practiced law, Los Angeles, dep. pub. defender, Los Angeles County, 1954; patent atty. RCA, Camden, N.J., 1955-57, Litton Industries, Inc., Beverly Hills, Calif., 1957-61; patent counsel Modal Systems Inc., La Jolla, Calif., 1961-63; mem. firm Golove & Kleinberg, Los Angeles, 1963-70, Golove, Kleinberg & Morganstern, 1970-72, Kleinberg, Morganstern & Scholnick, 1973-76, Kleinberg, Morganstern, Scholnick & Mann, Beverly Hills, 1976-79; individual practice law as Marvin Kleinberg, Inc., Beverly Hills, 1979—; adj. lectr. patent law, mem. Innovation Clinic Adv. Council Franklin Pierce Law Center, Concord, N.H., 1975—; adv. council PTC Research Found., 1981—; dir., sec. Digem, Inc., Los Angeles. Active YMCA Indian Guides, 1974-79; pres. Opportunity Houses Inc., Riverside, Calif., 1973-76, UCLA Class of '49, 1979—; co-chairperson Sholem Ednl. Inst., Los Angeles, 1974-75; chief referee Region 58, Am. Youth Soccer Orgn., 1976—. Served to sgt. AUS, 1946-47. Mem. Los Angeles Patent Law Assn., Am., Los Angeles County bar assns., Zeta Beta Tau. Home: 3901 Cody Rd Sherman Oaks CA 91403 Office: 2049 Century Park E Suite 2400 Los Angeles CA 90067

KLEINDIENST, RICHARD GORDON, lawyer; b. Winslow, Ariz., Aug. 1923; s. Alfred and Gladys (Love) K.; m. Margaret Dunbar, Sept. 3, 1948; children: Alfred Dunbar, Wallace Heath, Anne Lucile, Carolyn Love. A.B. magna cum laude, Harvard U., 1947, LL.B., 195O; LL.D., Susquehanna U. Bar: Ariz. 1950. Sr. partner firm Shimmel, Hill, Kleindienst & Bishop, Phoenix, 1958-69; dep. atty. gen. Dept. Justice, 1969-72, atty. gen., 1972-73; partner firm Lesher, Kimble & Rucker, Tucson, from 1979; now partner successor firm Lesher, Clausen & Borodkin, P.C., Tucson; Past mem. bd. Small Bus. Devel. Center, Office Econ. Opportunity. Mem. Ariz. Ho. of Reps. from Maricopa County, 1953-54; chmn. Ariz. Young Republican League, 1955, Ariz. Rep. Com., 1956-60, 61- 63; mem. Rep. Nat. Com., 1956-60, 61, 63; nat. dir. field operations Goldwater Pres. com., 1964; candidate for gov. Ariz., 1964; nat. dir. field operations Nixon for Pres. Com., 1968; gen. counsel Rep. Nat. Com., 1968; Past mem. local Am. Legion, V.F.W., Urban League, Goodwill Industries, Ariz., Am. heart assns., Phoenix Day Nursery, Phoenix Symphony Assn., Nat. Symphony Orch. Served to lt. USAAF, World War II. Mem. Fed. Bar Assn. (pres. 1974—), Phi Beta Kappa, Sigma Alpha Epsilon. Clubs: Thunderbirds, Arizona (Phoenix); Burning Tree. Office: Lesher Clausen & Borodkin 3773 E Broadway Tucson AZ 85716

KLEINE, HERMAN, economist; b. N.Y.C., Mar. 6, 1920; s. Max and Fannie (Schechter) K.; m. Paula Stein, June 16, 1962; children—Joseph, Michael. B.S., State U. N.Y. at Albany, 1941; M.A., Clark U., 1942, Ph.D., 1951. Researcher for Nat. Indsl. Conf. Bd., 1946; instr. to asst. prof. Worcester Poly tech. Inst., 1946-49; economist ECA, Mut. Security Agy., The Hague, Netherlands, 1949-53; internat. relations and econs. FOA, ICA, Washington, 1953-57; dir. U.S. Ops. Mission to Ethiopia, ICA, 1957-59, asst. dep. dir. for ops., 1959-61; Nat. War Coll., 1961-62; AID adviser U.S. Mission to UN, N.Y.C., 1962-64; dep. asst. adminstr. for Africa AID, Washington, 1964-67; dep. dir. U.S. AID mission to Brazil, 1967-69; asso. U.S. coordinator Alliance for Progress, 1969-70; dep. U.S. coordinator, asst. adminstr. Latin Am. Bur. AID, Washington, 1971-76; advisor to controller Interam. Devel. Bank, 1976—; Mem. U.S. delegation UN Gen. Assembly, 1962, 63. Served from pvt. to capt. USAAF, 1942-46. Recipient AID Distinguished honor award, 1973, Adminstrs. Distinguished Career Service award, 1976, Superior Honor award Dept. State, 1976; Distinguished Alumnus award State U. N.Y. at Albany, 1977; duPont fellow, 1948. Mem. Kappa Phi Kappa. Jewish. Home: 7305 Burdette

Ct Bethesda MD 20817 Office: IDB 808 17th St NW Washington DC 20006

KLEINER, RICHARD ARTHUR, writer, editor; b. N.Y.C., Mar. 9, 1921; s. Israel Simon and Alma (Kempner) K.; m. Hortensia Rivas, Aug. 7, 1954; children—Katherine Evert, Cynthia Smetana, Peter. Litt.B., Rutgers U., 1942. With Newspaper Enterprise Assn., Cleve., 1947-49, N.Y.C., 1949-64, Los Angeles, 1964—, sr. editor, 1977—; West Coast dir. United Media Prodns., 1982—; mem. journalism faculty Calif. State Coll., Long Beach, 1975-77, UCLA, 1977-82. Author: books, including E.S.P. And The Stars, 1970, Index of Initials and Acronyms, 1971, Take One, 1974, The Two Of Us, 1976, Hollywood's Greatest Love Stories, 1976, Please Don't Shoot My Dog, 1981; contbr. numerous articles to mags. Served with U.S. Army, 1942-46. Office: 1665 N Beverly Dr Beverly Hills CA 90210

KLEINERT, HAROLD EARL, hand surgeon; b. Sunburst, Mont., Oct. 7, 1922; s. Amil and Christine K.; children: Harold, Robert, Christine, James, Jeanne. Student, No. Mont. Coll., 1941, U. Mich., 1941-43; M.D., Temple U., 1946. Diplomate: Am. Bd. Surgery, 1955. Rotating intern Grace Hosp., Detroit, 1946-47, resident in surgery, 1949-53; instr. in surgery U. Louisville, 1954-57, asst. prof. surgery, 1957-62, asso. prof., 1962-69, clin. prof., 1969—; asso. prof. Ind. U., 1967-73, clin. prof., 1973—; nat. cons. to Surgeon Gen. U.S. Air Force, 1973—; mem. staff Jewish Hosp., Louisville, 1955—, pres., 1972; mem. staff Sts. Mary and Elizabeth Hosp., Norton-Kosair-Children's Hosp., Methodist Hosp., Baptist Hosp., Suburban Hosp., Baptist East Hosp., St. Anthony Hosp., Clark County Meml. Hosp., Floyd County Meml. Hosp., North Clark Community Hosp.; Cons. to hosps. Contbr. numerous articles to profl. publs.; author profl. movies, videotapes. Served with USAAF, 1947-49; with Air N.G., 1953-65. Fellow A.C.S.; mem. Am. Soc. Surgery of the Hand (pres. 1976), AMA (Sci. Achievement award 1980), Am. Assn. Surgery of Trauma, Am. Soc. Plastic and Reconstructive Surgeons, Am. Acad. Orthopedic Surgeons, Am. Assn. Plastic Surgeons (Hon. Award medal 1980), Ohio Valley Soc. Plastic and Reconstructive Surgery, Am. Rheumatism Assn., So. Med. Assn., Ky. Med. Assn., So. Surg. Assn., Am. Trauma Soc., Jefferson County Med. Soc., Aerospace Med. Assn., French Soc. Surgery of Hand, Italian Soc. for Surgery of Hand, Can. Soc. for Surgery of Hand, Colombia Soc. for Surgery of Hand, Louisville Surg. Soc. (pres. 1972), Ky. Surg. Soc. Club: Rotary. Research in microsurgery. Inventor microsurgery instruments, tendon instruments. Office: 250 E Liberty St Louisville KY 40202

KLEINERT, ROBERT WILLIAM, telephone company executive; b. Phila., Apr. 6, 1923; s. Edward and Eleanor (Achtermann) K.; m. E. Jane Bass, June 24, 1950; children: Richard W., Robert A., John C. B.S. in Elec. Engring, Drexel U., Phila., 1951; LL.D. (hon.), Rider Coll., Trenton, N.J., 1976. With Bell Telephone System, 1940—; pres. N.J. Bell, 1970-78, AT&T Long Lines, Bedminster, N.J., from 1978; now pres., chief operating officer AT&T Communications, Basking Ridge, N.J.; dir. Fidelity Union Trust Co., Newark, N.J.; Mfrs. Ins. Co., Am. Bell Internat. Trustee Drexel U., Phila. Served with AUS, 1943-46. Recipient Brotherhood award NCCJ, 1974; Americanism award Anti-Defamation League, 1976; Silver Antelope award N.E. region Boy Scouts Am., 1981; named N.J. Bus. Statesman of Year Sales Execs. Club, 1975. Mem. N.J. C. of C. (dir.). Office: AT&T Communications 295 N Maple Ave Rm 4342L1 Basking Ridge NJ 07920 *

KLEINFELD, ERWIN, mathematician, educator; b. Vienna, Austria, Apr. 19, 1927; came to U.S., 1940; s. Lazar and Gina (Schönbach) K.; m. Margaret Morgan, July 2, 1968; children—Barbara, David. B.S., City Coll., N.Y., 1948; M.A., U. Pa., 1949; Ph.D., U. Wis., 1951. Instr. U. Chgo., 1951-53; asst. prof. Ohio State U., 1953-56, asso. prof., 1957-60, prof., 1960-62; prof. math. Syracuse U., 1962-67, U. Hawaii, 1967-68, U. Iowa, 1968—; vis. lectr. Yale, 1956-57; cons. Nat. Bur. Standards, summer 1953; research specialist U. Conn., summer 1955; research mathematician Bowdoin Coll., summer 1957; research asso. Cornell U., summer 1958, U. Calif. at Los Angeles, summer 1959, Stanford, summer 1960, Inst. Def. Analysis, summer 1961, 62, AID-India, summer 1964, 65; vis. prof. Emory U., 1976-77. Editorial bd.: Jour. Algebra-Academic Press; cons. editor, Merrill Pub. Co.-Div. Bell & Howell.; Contbr. articles research jours. Served with AUS, 1945-46. Recipient Wis. Alumni Research Found. fellowship, 1949-51; U.S. Army Research Office grantee, 1955-70; NSF grantee, 1970-75. Mem. Am. Math. Soc., Sigma Xi. Office: Math Dept Univ of Iowa Iowa City IA 52242

KLEINFIELD, SONNY RICHARD, journalist; b. Paterson, N.J., Aug. 12, 1950; s. Nat and Lillian K. Student, Clark U., 1968-69; B.A. cum laude in Journalism, N.Y. U., 1972. Reporter Wall Street Jour., 1972-77; reporter N.Y. Times, 1977—. Author: A Month at the Brickyard, 1977, The Hidden Minority, 1979, The Biggest Company on Earth, 1981, The Traders, 1983; contbr. articles to mags. Recipient Meyer Berger award Columbia U., 1974, Easter Seal Communication award, 1978, Gerald Loeb award UCLA Grad. Sch. Bus., 1979, Amos Tuck Media award for Econ. Understanding, 1979. Mem. Authors League, Authors Guild. Home: 150 Mercer St New York NY 10012 Office: 229 W 43d St New York NY 10036

KLEINHOLZ, FRANK, artist; b. Bklyn., Feb. 17, 1901; s. Herman and Bessie K.; m. Leah Schwartz, June 18, 1927 (dec. Oct. 2, 1945); m. Lidia Brestovan, Apr. 22, 1946 (dec. Sept. 1981); children—Lisa, Marco, Anna. Ed. pub. schs. and high sch., Bklyn.; student, Bedford YMCA Prep Sch., 1916-18, Colby Coll., Waterville, Me., 1918-19, Fordham Law Sch., N.Y.C., 1920-23, Alex Dobkin, 1938, Sol Wilson, Am. Artists Sch., N.Y.C., 1939; D.F.A., Colby Coll., 1965. Practicing lawyer, 1924-36. Attention to painting, 1936—; Exhibited, Am. Artists Sch., 1940; painting Abstractionists, Directions in Am. Painting Exhbn., Carnegie Inst., Pitts., 1941; purchased by Carnegie acting dir., John O'Connor, Pa. Acad. of Fine Art, Phila., 1942, Va. Biennial, Richmond; 2 paintings Bargain Counter, Artists for Victory Exhbn., Met. Mus., N.Y.C., 1942 (Back Street awarded 6th purchase prize); also rep., Bklyn., Newark and other large mus., One-man show, Asso. Am. Artists Galleries, N.Y.C., 1942-43, also shows, 1944—; exhibited, Akron (Ohio) Art Inst., 1965, ACA Gallery, Rome, Italy; Represented in, Met. Mus. and, pvt. collections of, Mr. and Mrs. Otto Spaeth and, Mr. John O'Connor.; Author: Frank Kleinholz, a Self Portrait, 1965, Ilse De Brehat, The Flowering Rock. Home: 21 2d Ave Port Washington NY 11050 Office: care ACA Gallery 100 E 71st St New York NY 10021

KLEINHOLZ, LEWIS HERMANN, educator; b. N.Y.C., May 18, 1910; s. Jacob Karl and Fannie (Geller) K. B.S., Colby Coll., 1930, Sc.D., 1963; M.A., Harvard U., 1935, Ph.D., 1937; diploma, Army Sch. Aviation Medicine, 1942, R.A.F. Sch. Air-Sea Rescue, 1944. Instr. Colby Coll., 1930-33; teaching fellow Harvard, 1934-35, instr., tutor, 1940-41; research investigator Marine Biol. Lab., Woods Hole, Mass., 1935-68, summer instr., 1948-66, dir. invertebrate zool. staff, 1949-53; asst. Radcliffe Coll., 1936-37; research investigator Marine Biol. Lab., St. George's, Bermuda, 1936, Plymouth, Eng., 1937, Naples, Italy, 1937, 51- 52; instr. Cambridge Jr. Coll., 1938-42; research investigator Marine Biol. Lab., Cold Spring Harbor, N.Y., 1940; project engr. Aero-Med. Research Lab., Wright Field, O., 1945; asst. prof. Reed Coll., 1946-47, asso. prof., 1947-50, prof., 1950—, chmn. dept. biology, 1955-61; research investigator Marine Biol. Lab., Plymouth, Eng., 1960, Kristinebergs Zoologiska Sta., Sweden, 1960, 61, Stazione Zoologica, Naples, 1960, Station Biologique de Roscoff, France, 1962; vis. research prof. Med.-Kem. Inst., U. Lund, Sweden, 1961-62; U.S. rep. Internat. Sci. Symposium, Paris, 1947, Naples, 1953; NRC Adv. Com. on Naples, Italy, Research Station, NSF Symposium, Selection of Sci. Personnel, 1954, Biol. Research in Liberal Arts Coll., 1954, Found. Fund for Advancement of Edn., Western Selection Com., 1954; mem. internat. symposium on recent advances in physiology invertebrates U. Oreg., 1955; mem. examining com. basic sci. Oreg. Bd. Higher Edn., 1949-60; mem. cell biology sect., div. research grants NIH; cons. U.S. Office Edn., 1975. Author: (with Brown et al) Selected Invertebrate Types, 1950, Recent Advances in the Physiology of Invertebrates, (with Scheer et al), 1957, Physiology of Crustacea, (with Waterman et al), 1959, The Functional Organization of the Compound Eye, (with Bernhard et al), 1966; Contbr. to profl. jours.; Mem. internat. bd. editors: Pubblicazioni della Stazione Zoologica di Napoli, 1959; bd. editors: Biol. Bull, 1962-66, Gen. and Comparative Endocrinology, 1972—, Internat. Jour. Invertebrate Reproduction, 1979—. Dir. Portland Jr. Symphony Soc., 1950-58; trustee Marine Biol. Lab., Woods Hole, 1950. Served as observer RAF, 1944; capt. USAAF, 1945. Guggenheim Found. fellow, 1945-46; State Dept. Fulbright fellow, 1951- 52; sci. faculty fellow NSF, 1958-59; fellow N.Y. Acad. Sci., 1958—. Mem. Am. Inst. Biol. Scis. (steering com. for biol. scis. curriculum study 1958-60), Marine Biol. Assn. of U.K., Marine Biol. Assn. India, Am. Soc. Zoologists (exec. com. 1959-62), Oreg., N.Y. acads. sci., Nat. Conf. Pre-Med. Edn., Internat. Soc. Cell Biology, Soc. Gen Physiologists, Phi Beta Kappa, Sigma Xi, Gamma Alpha. Address: Reed Coll Portland OR 97202

KLEINKNECHT, KENNETH SAMUEL, aerospace company executive, former NASA ofcl.; b. Washington, July 24, 1919; s. Christian Frederick and Nell May (Barr) K.; m. Patricia Jean Todd, May 24, 1947; children—Linda May, Patricia Ann, Frederick William. B.S.M.E., Purdue U., 1942. Project engr. NACA Lewis Research Center, Cleve., 1942-51; aero. research scientist NASA Flight Research Center, 1951-59, successively mgr. Mercury Project, dep. mgr. Gemini Program, mgr. command and service modules, 1959-70, mgr. Skylab program, 1970-74, dir. flight ops., Houston, 1974-76, asst. mgr., 1976-77, dep. asso. adminstr. for space transp. systems (European ops.) to European Space Agy., Paris, Washington, 1977-79, head constrn. space shuttle orbiter, 1979-81; mgr. program engring. Martin Marietta Aerospace, Denver div., 1981—. Exec. bd. Sam Houston Area council Boy Scouts Am., Houston, 1972-77. Recipient (with others) Group Achievement award for Mercury Project NASA, 1962, NASA medal for outstanding leadership Pres. of U.S., 1963, 81, John J. Montgomery award San Diego chpt. Nat. Soc. Aerospace Profls., 1963, with others) Group Achievement award for X-15 Research Airplane Flight Test Orgn., 1964, for Gemini Program, 1966, NASA Exceptional Service medal, 1969, NASA Disting. Service medal, 1969, 73. Fellow Am. Astron. Soc. (W. Randolph Lovelace II award 1975), AIAA (asso.), Internat. Acad. Astronautics (corr.). Club: Masons. Home: 825 Front Range Rd Littleton CO 80120 Office: Martin Marietta Aerospace Denver Div PO Box 179 Denver CO 80210 *As a member of the team that made lunar and space shuttle missions successes, I believe that my "formula for success" is one part high goal and one hundred parts persistence. I have always believed in establishing principles, high ideals of conduct as structures to direct our lives. It is voluntary total dedication to valid ideals and attention to detail that will bring success on every level. To reach beyond one's present grasp is to assure ever higher attainments in the future.*

KLEINMAN, ARTHUR MICHAEL, medical anthropologist, psychiatrist, educator; b. N.Y.C., Mar. 11, 1941; s. Marcia F. (Kaplan) K.; m. Joan Andrea Ryman, Mar. 20, 1965; children: Peter John, Anne Simone. A.B., Stanford U., 1962, M.D., 1967; M.A., Harvard U., 1974. Diplomate: Nat. Bd. Med. Examiners, Am. Bd. Neurology and Psychiatry. Med. intern Yale-New Haven Hosp., 1967-68; surgeon USPHS, Bethesda, Md., Taiwan, 1968-70; resident in psychiatry Mass. Gen. Hosp., Boston, 1972-75; assoc. prof. U. Wash., Seattle, 1976-79, prof. psychiatry and anthropology, 1979-82; prof. med. anthropology and psychiatry Harvard U., Cambridge, Mass., 1982—. Author: Patients and Healers in the Context of Culture, 1980 (Wellcome medal Royal Anthrop. Inst.); co-editor: Relevance of Social Science for Medicine, 1981; editor-in-chief: Culture, Medicine and Psychiatry: A Jour. of Internat. Cross-Cultural Research, 1976—. Recipient Research award NIMH, 1977-79, Nat. Acad. Scis., 1980, Rockefeller Found., 1983, Social Sci. Research Council, 1983. Mem. Inst. Medicine of Nat. Acad. Scis., Am. Psychiat. Assn., Am. Anthrop. Assn., Royal Anthrop. Inst. Home: 44 Larchwood Dr Cambridge MA 02138 Office: Harvard U 330 William James Hall Kirkland St Cambridge MA 02138

KLEINMAN, LEONARD, educator; b. N.Y.C., July 25, 1933; s. Leo and Ann (Paolo) K.; m. Faye Millar, July 3, 1957; children—Julie Ann, Paul. B.A., UCLA, 1955, M.S., 1956; Ph.D., U. Calif., Berkeley, 1960. Research asso. U. Chgo., 1960-61; asst. prof. physics U. Pa., Phila., 1961-64; asso. prof. U. So. Calif., 1964-67; prof. U. Tex., Austin, 1967—. Contbr. articles to profl. jours. NSF grantee, 1973—. Fellow Am. Phys. Soc.; mem. Phi Beta Kappa. Home: 7207 West Rim Dr Austin TX 78731 Office: Department of Physics University of Texas Austin TX 78712

KLEINMAN, LOU, university dean, educator; b. N.Y.C., Apr. 25, 1924; s. Samuel and Tillie (Weinberg) K.; m. Joan Marcia Walerstein, Aug. 30, 1953; children: Beth Ann, Steven Howard, Marci Irene. B.S., NYU, 1948, Ed.D., 1959; M.A., Harvard U., 1949. Cert. social studies and math, tchr., sch. adminstr., N.Y.; cert. social studies and math tchr., N.J. Tchr. Fair Lawn (N.J.) High Sch., 1949-52; mem. faculty Oneonta State Coll., 1952-53; prof. adminstrn. and supervision NYU, 1953-55, 60-74, assoc. dean, 1967-74; assoc. prof., dir. Camden div. Rutgers U., New Brunswick, N.J., 1955-60; prof. edn., dean Sch. Edn. and Allied Professions U. Miami, Coral Gables, Fla., 1974—. Author: (with F. Lutz and S. Evans) Grievances and Their Resolution, 1967. Div. chmn. United Jewish Appeal, N.Y.C., 1967; mem. edn. com. Fedn. Jewish Philanthropies, Miami, Fla., 1976—; bd. dirs. Hillel, Miami, 1976—. Served with USAAF, 1943-46. Recipient Inside-Out award U. Miami, 1979, Disting. Alumni Achievement award NYU, 1980. Mem. Am. Assn. Colls. Tchr. Edn., Fla. Assn. Colls. Tchr. Edn. (pres. 1981-82). Office: Sch Edn U Miami Coral Gables FL 33124 *The fullest development of each individual is the key to all human progress.*

KLEINPELL, ROBERT MINSSEN, educator, paleontologist, geologist; b. Chgo., Sept. 13, 1905; s. William Ernst and Alma Louise (Wilke) K.; m. Dariel Shively, Dec. 29, 1934 (dec.); m. Mildred Knapp, Aug. 4, 1972. A.B., Occidental Coll., Los Angeles, 1926; A.M., Stanford, 1928, Ph.D., 1934. Field geologist Richfield Oil Co., 1928-31; asst. geologist U.S. Geol. Survey, 1931-33; cons. geologist and paleontologist Cal. petroleum industry, 1933-39; stratigrapher petroleum survey Nat. Devel. Co., P.I., 1939-45; instr. systematic biology and hist. geology, coll. curriculum Santo Tomas and Los Banos Internment Camps, P.I., 1942-45; mem. faculty U. Calif. at Berkeley, 1946-73, prof. paleontology, 1947-73, emeritus, 1973—; cons. paleontologist, geologist, 1945—; vis. prof. micropaleontology Calif. Inst. Tech., 1939-41; acting dir. Mus. Paleontology, U. Calif. at Berkeley, 1958-60; mem. bd. adv. editors geol. sci. U. Calif. Press, 1964-73. Editor: Cushman Found. for Foraminiferal Research, 1962-65; asst. editor, 1965-70; Author: Miocene Stratigraphy of California, 1955, The Miocene Stratigraphy of California Revisited, 1981; Contbr. articles to profl. jours. Fellow Geol. Soc. Am., Am. Geog. Soc., A[illegible] Calif. Acad. Sci., Paleontol. Soc. (chmn. Pacific Coast sect., counc[illegible] 1963-64, nat. v.p., councilor 1964-65); mem. Am. Assn. Petroleu[illegible] Geologists (Distinguished lectr. 1960, hon. life mem. Pacific sect. and nat.), Soc. Econ. Paleontologists and Mineralogists (hon. life mem. Pacific sect., nat. v.p., councilor 1961-62, councilor for paleontology 1967-68), Am. Mus. Natural History (bd. adviser dept. micropaleontology 1945-48), Am. Acad. Polit. Scis., Far Eastern Assn., Biosystematists, LeConte Soc., Phi Beta Kappa, Sigma Xi, Theta Tau, Alpha Tau Omega. Mem. Am. Party. Lutheran. Home: 5900 Encina Rd 3 Goleta CA 93117

KLEINROCK, LEONARD, computer scientist; b. N.Y.C., June 13, 1934; s. Bernard and Anne (Schoenfeld) K.; m. Stella Schuler, Dec. 1, 1967; children—Nancy S., Martin C. B.S. in Elec. Engring, CCNY, 1957; M.S., MIT, 1959, Ph.D., 1963. Asst. elec. engr. Photobell Co. Inc., 1951-57; research engr. Lincoln Labs., M.I.T., 1957-63; mem. faculty UCLA, 1963—, prof. computer sci., 1970—; pres. Linkabit Corp., 1968-69, Tech. Transfer Inst., 1976—; cons. in field, prin. investigator govt. contracts. Author: Queueing Systems, Vol. I, 1975, Vol. II, 1976, Communication Nets: Stochastic Message Flow and Delay, 1964, Solutions Manual for Queueing Systems, Vol. I, 1982; also articles. Recipient Paper award ICC, 1978, Leonard G. Abraham paper award Communications Soc., 1975, Outstanding Faculty Mem. award UCLA Engring. Grad. Students Assn., 1966, Townsend Harris medal CCNY, 1982, L.M. Ericsson Prize Sweden, 1982; Guggenheim fellow, 1971-72. Fellow IEEE; mem. Nat. Acad. Engring., Ops. Research Soc. Am. (Lanchester prize 1976), Assn. Computing Machinery, Internat. Fedn. Info. Processes Systems, Amateur Athletic Union. Jewish. Office: Boelter Hall 3732 UCLA Los Angeles CA 90024

KLEINROCK, LEWIS JAMES, investment company executive; b. Scranton, Pa., May 26, 1932; s. Harry and Mary (Ryan) K.; m. Judith Mae Powell, Mar. 14, 1952; children: David (dec.), Linda (dec.), James. B.A., Williams Coll., 1953; postgrad., Law Sch., Yale U., 1953-54; M.B.A., Harvard U., 1959. Systems analyst Esso Standard Oil Co., Bayonne, N.J., 1959-60; investment counselor, Lehman, Pa., 1960-62; investment asso. Utilities and Industries Corp., N.Y.C., 1962-63; dep. dir. investment research Chase Investors Mgmt. Corp., N.Y.C., 1963-73; dir. investment research John Hancock Mut. Life Ins. Co., Boston, 1973-79, sr. v.p., head portfolio mgmt., 1980-82; pres., chief exec. officer Independence Investment Assocs., 1982—; dir., chmn. fin. com. John Hancock Variable Life Ins. Co., 1981-82. Served with USMC, 1954-57, summer 1958. Mem. Boston, N.Y. Soc. Security Analysts, Fin. Analysts Fedn., Inst. Chartered Fin. Analysts. Home: 76 Hallett Hill Rd Weston MA 02193 Office: One Liberty Sq Boston MA 02109 *For me, "getting the job done" has been a whole lot easier and more gratifying when I have acknowledged that what other people want to do is get their job done and be supported in doing so.*

KLEINSCHROD, WALTER ANDREW, publishing company executive, editor; b. Long Island City, N.Y., Jan. 1, 1928; s. Max Joseph and Martha (Forst) K.; m. Patricia Rita Corbett, Sept. 22, 1951; children: Kathy (Mrs. Robert Thompson), Linda (Mrs. Michael Dietrich), Mary (Mrs. Gerald Coy), Jeanne, Carol. B.A. in Journalism, Washington Square Coll. NYU, N.Y.C., 1951. With Geyer-McAllister Publs. Inc., N.Y.C., 1952—; assoc. editor Office Mgmt. mag., 1952-53; editor Gifts & Decorative Accessories mag., 1953-61, v.p., editorial dir., 1961-82; editor Office Adminstrn. and Automation mag., 1983—; sr. v.p. Gifts & Decorative Accessories mag., 1978—; editor Adminstrv. Mgmt. mag., 1961—; pub.-editor Info. & Word Processing Report newsletter, 1972—; editor Word Processing World mag., 1973-79; pub. Corp. Public Issues newsletter, 1978-80; Editor newsletter, communications counsel Union Free Sch. Dist. 2, Uniondale, N.Y., 1967-69. Co-author: Selling Gifts and Decorative Accessories, 1965, Word Processing: Operations, Applications, and Administration, 1979, Word/Information Processing: Administration and Office Automation, 1983; author: Word Processing, 1974, Management's Guide to Word Processing, 1975; contbg. author: Handbook of Business Administration, 1967, The Computer Sampler, 1968, Ency. of Management, 2d Edit, 1973, International Handbook of Automatic Data Processing, 1976; Editorial advisor: Handbook of Modern Office Management and Administrative Services, 1972. Pres. Hempstead (N.Y.) Democratic Club, 1974-76; chmn. alumni communications com. N. Y. U., 1978-80. Served to sgt. USAAF, 1946-47. Mem. Hempstead Commuter Assn. (founding pres. 1967-73, dir.), Adminstrv. Mgmt. Soc., Assn. Info. Systems Profls., N.Y. Bus. Press Editors Inc. (charter), Am. Bus. Press (chmn. editorial exec. com. 1962-64, chmn. judges com. J.D. Crain award 1969-70, chmn. govt. affairs com. 1977-80), Sierra Club, Kappa Tau Alpha, Sigma Delta Chi. Mem. Christian Ch. Club: Overseas Press of Am. Home: 177 Rutland Rd Hempstead NY 11550 Office: 51 Madison Ave New York NY 10010

KLEINSMITH, BRUCE JOHN *See* **NUTZLE, FUTZIE**

KLEINSMITH, LEWIS JOEL, cell biologist, educator; b. Detroit, Apr. 13, 1942; s. Ralph Louis and Sylvia (Raphael) K.; m. Cynthia Weinstein, June 14, 1964; children: Alyssa Jan, Francesca Lynn. B.S., U. Mich., 1964; Ph.D., Rockefeller U., 1968. Asst. prof. dept. zoology U. Mich., Ann Arbor, 1968-71, assoc. prof., 1971-74, prof. div. biol. scis., 1975—; Vis. prof. biochemistry U. Fla. Med. Sch., Gainesville, 1974-75. Editor: Chromosomal Proteins and Their Role in the Regulation of Gene Expression, 1975; Contbr. chpts. to books, articles to profl. jours. Recipient Henry Russel award, 1971; Distinguished Service award U. Mich., 1971; Guggenheim fellow, 1974-75. Fellow AAAS; Mem. N.Y. Acad. Scis., Am. Soc. Biol. Chemists, Am. Soc. for Cell Biology, Am. Inst. Biol. Scientists, Phi Beta Kappa, Sigma Xi. Home: 2642 Essex Rd Ann Arbor MI 48104

KLEINZELLER, ARNOST, physician, educator; b. Ostrava, Czechoslovakia, Dec. 6, 1914; s. Arnold and Josefa (Schongut) K.; m. Lotte Reuter, Apr. 2, 1943; children: Anna, Jana. M.D., U. Brno, Czechoslovakia, 1938; Ph.D., U. Sheffield, Eng., 1939-41; Rockefeller fellow, U. Cambridge, Eng., 1942; D.Sc., U. Prague, 1959; M.A., U. Pa., 1973. Head lab. cell metabolism State Inst. Health, Prague, Czechoslovakia, 1945-48; mem. faculty Tech. U., Prague, 1948-52, Charles U., 1952-55; head lab. cell metabolism Czechoslovak Acad. Sci., Prague, 1956-66; vis. prof. dept. physiology U. Rochester (N.Y.) Sch. Medicine and Dentistry, 1966-67; prof. physiology U. Pa. Med. Sch., 1967—; vis. prof. dept. biochemistry U. Cambridge, Eng., 1980; mem. exec. com. Internat. Cell Research Orgn., 1962-67, chmn. panel IV, 1962-68; mem. U.S. nat. com. Internat. Union Physiol. Scis., 1975-81, sec., 1975-78. Author: (with Vrba and Malek) Manometric Methods, 1954, Membrane Transport and Metabolism, 1961, (with Malek, Longmuir, Cerkasov and Kovac) Manometric Methods, 1964; editor: Biophysics. Med. Research Council fellow, 1943-44. Fellow Phila. Coll. Physicians; mem. Internat. Soc. Cell Biology (exec. com. 1964-68), Czechoslovak Nat. Com. Biol. Scis. (hon. sec. 1961-66), Biochem. Soc. Gt. Britain, Am. Physiol. Soc., Soc. Gen. Physiology (councillor 1977-79), Biophys. Soc., Am. Soc. Cell Biology, Academia Leopoldina, Gt. Britain Physiol. Soc. (asso.), AAAS (com. sci. freedom and responsibility 1982—). Research in metabolic processes in cells and tissues; mechanism of fatty acid formation in yeast cells; transport of electrolytes and sugar across cell membranes. Home: 9 University Mews Philadelphia PA 19104

...T WILLIAM, agricultural engineer, educator; b. ... Nov. 30, 1925; s. Roy Harry and Marguerite E. ...; m. Beatrice M. Heinze, Dec. 26, 1948; children: ..., Pamela Sue. B.S. in Agr. Engring., Mich. State Coll., ..., 1951; Ph.D., Mich. State U., 1957. Registered profl. engr., ...s., Nebr. Instr. agrl. engring. Mich. State Coll., 1949-51; from ... to asst. profl. agrl. engring., also head electrification and processing sect. U. Ill., 1951-56; prof. agrl. engring., head dept. U. Mass., 1957-66; prof., chmn. dept. agrl. engring. U. Nebr., 1966-67, asso. dir. agrl. expt. sta., 1967-76, dean internat. programs, 1976—; spl. appointments (U. Calif.), 1963, U. Md., 1965; Chmn. Great Plains Agrl. Council.; Mem. New Eng. Council Econ. Devel. Contbr. profl. jours., books. Served with AUS, 1944-46. Fellow Am. Soc. Agrl. Engrs. (mem. cabinet, chmn. electric power and processing div. 1963-64); mem. Am. Soc. Engring. Edn., Engrs. Joint Council (nat. planning com. 1961), Engrs. Council Profl. Devel., Engring Alumni Assn. Mich. State U. (dir.), Agrl. Expt. Sta. Dirs. Assn. (chmn. 1973-74), U.S. Univs. Dirs. Internat. Programs (chmn. 1981-83), Farmhouse, Sigma Xi, Tau Beta Pi, Phi Lambda Tau, Pi Mu Epilon, Gamma Sigma Delta, Alpha Epsilon. Methodist. Lodges: Masons, Shriners; Rotary. Home: 6520 Sumner Lincoln NE 68506

KLEISER, JOHN RANDAL, motion picture director; b. Lebanon, Pa., July 20, 1946; s. John Raymond and Harriet Kelly (Means) K. B.A., U. So. Calif., 1964, M.A., 1974. Dir.: films Grease, 1978, The Blue Lagoon, 1980, Summer Lovers, 1982, Grandview U.S.A., 1984; TV shows All Together Now, 1975, Dawn: Portrait of a Teenage Runaway, 1976, The Boy in the Plastic Bubble, 1977, The Gathering, 1978; short subjects Foot Fetish, 1974; Peege, 1973, Portrait of Grandpa Doc, 1977 (Recipient Emmy nomination Best Dir. for The Gathering 1978). Office: Randal Kleiser Prodns 3050 Runyan Canyon Rd Los Angeles CA 90046

KLEISNER, GEORGE HARRY, former retail executive; b. Chgo., Apr. 20, 1909; s. John and Marie (Frey) K.; m. Mary Cecilia Wetzel, Aug. 28, 1937 (dec. 1967); children: Patricia, Pamela, Kerry, Kim; m. Catherine Orlando, Oct. 12, 1974; children: Geoffrey, Christopher. B.S., Northwestern U., 1930. Mng. editor W. L. Johnson Pub. Co., 1930-33; with Montgomery Ward & Co., 1933-64, beginning as mdse. trainee, Chgo., successively asst. div. mgr., N.Y.C., buyer, div. mgr. hosiery and accessories, asst. soft lines mdse. mgr., soft lines mdse. mgr., 1943-52, charge, 1952-58, v.p., 1955-57, mdse. mgr., 1958-64; assoc. mgmt. cons. Wendell C. Walker & Assos., 1964-65; v.p. charge N.Y. office Bear Brand Hosiery Co., 1965-80; cons. Americal Corp., Henderson, N.C., 1980—. Served as 2d lt. Q.M.C. U.S. Army Res., 1938-43. Mem. Northwestern U. Alumni Assn. (dir. 1931-33), Holy Name Soc., Wool Club N.Y.C., Theta Xi, Sigma Delta Chi. Republican. Roman Catholic. Club: Scarsdale (N.Y.) Golf. Home: 52 Barry Rd Scarsdale NY 10583

KLEMA, ERNEST DONALD, educator, nuclear physicist; b. Wilson, Kan., Oct. 4, 1920; s. William W. and Mary Bess (Vopat) K.; m. Virginia Clyde Carlock, May 23, 1953; children: Donald David, Catherine Marion. A.B. in Chemistry, U. Kans., 1941, M.A. in Physics, 1942; postgrad., Princeton U., 1942, U. Ill., 1946-49; Ph.D. in Physics, Rice U., 1951. Staff scientist Los Alamos Sci. Lab., 1943-46; sr. physicist Oak Ridge Nat. Lab., 1950-56, prin. physicist, 1958; asso. prof. nuclear engring. U. Mich., 1956-58; prof. nuclear engring. Northwestern U., 1959-68, chmn. dept. engring. scis., 1960-66; prof. engring. sci. Tufts U., 1968—, dean Coll. Engring., 1968-73, adj. prof. internat. politics Fletcher Sch. Law and Diplomacy, 1973—; Chmn. subcom. on neutron standards and measurements NRC, 1958-62; del. Internat. Atomic Energy Agy. symposium neutron detection, dosimetry and standardiazation, Harwell, Eng., 1962; cons. Oak Ridge Nat. Lab., Argonne Nat. Lab. Author articles fission cross-sects., gamma-gamma angular correlations, empirical nuclear models, thermal neutron measurements, semi-conductor radiation detectors. Fellow Am. Phys. Soc., Am Nuclear Soc.; mem. IEEE (sr.), Phi Beta Kappa, Sigma Xi, Pi Mu Epsilon, Alpha Chi Sigma. Clubs: Harbor (Seal Harbor, Me.); Princeton (N.Y.C.). Patentee purification hydrogen-argon mixtures. Home: 53 Adams St Medford MA 02155 Office: Tufts U Medford MA 02155

KLEMENS, PAUL GUSTAV, physicist, educator; b. Vienna, Austria, May 24, 1925; came to U.S., 1959, naturalized, 1968; s. Walter and Ida (Klug) K.; m. Ruth Hannah Wiener, July 30, 1950; children: Michael Walter, Susan Margaret. B.Sc., U. Sydney, 1946, M.Sc., 1948; Ph.D., Oxford U., 1950. With Nat. Standards Lab., Sydney, Australia, 1950-59, research officer, 1950-52, sr. research officer, 1952-57, prin. research officer, 1957-59; physicist Westinghouse Research Lab., Pitts., 1959-64, mgr. transport properties of solids dept., 1964-67; prof. physics U. Conn., 1967—, head dept. physics, 1967-74; vis. prof. Leiden (Netherlands) U., 1963-64; mem. adv. bd. on heat Nat. Bur. Standards, 1967-70, adv. bd. on cryogenics, 1974-79; mem. governing bd. Internat. Thermal Conductivity Confs., 1973—; mem. adv. bd. NRC Associateship Program, 1983—; mem. standing com. on accreditation Conn. Bd. Higher Edn., 1980—. Contbr. articles to sci. jours. Fellow Am. Phys. Soc., Inst. Physics (Eng.); mem. Conn. Acad. Sci. and Engring. Clubs: Cosmos (Washington); Explorers (N.Y.C.). Home: 21 Timber Dr Storrs CT 06268 Office: Dept Physics U Conn Storrs CT 06268

KLEMENT, VERA, painter; b. Danzig, Poland, Dec. 14, 1929; d. Klement and Rose (Rakovckik) Shapiro; (div.) 1 son, Max Klement Shapey. Cert. in fine arts, Cooper Union Sch. Art and Architecture, 1950. Asso. prof. art U. Chgo., 1969—. One woman shows, RoKo Gallery, N.Y.C., 1958, 60, One woman shows, Bridge Gallery, N.Y.C., 1965, Artemisia Gallery, Chgo., 1974, Chicago Gallery, 1976, Festival Gallery, 1978, Marianne Deson Gallery, 1979, 81, Goethe Inst., 1981, CDS Gallery, N.Y.C., Roy Boyd Gallery, Chgo., 1983, group shows include, Mus. Modern Art, N.Y.C., 1954, 55, Bklyn. Mus., 1950-60, Dallas Mus. Fine Arts, 1954, Tate Gallery, London, 1956, Museo de Arte Moderno, Barcelona, Spain, 1955, Musee d'Arte Moderne, Paris, U. Ky., 1959, Art Inst. Chgo., 1967, Walker Art Center, Mpls., 1977, U. Mo., 1978, Detroit Inst. Arts, Ukranian Inst. Art, Chgo., Kunstverein, Munich, Germany, 1979, many others; represented in permanent collections, Mus. Modern Art, N.Y.C., Phila. Mus. Art, Print Club, Phila., Ill. State Mus., Springfield, U. Tex., also private collections. Louis Comfort Tiffany Found. fellow, 1954; Guggenheim fellow, 1981-82; recipient numerous awards, prizes. Address: 727 S Dearborn St Chicago IL 60605

KLEMKE, ELMER DANIEL, philosophy educator; b. St. Paul, July 29, 1926; s. Daniel and Matilda (Gutsche) K. B.A. magna cum laude (scholar, asst.), Hamline U., 1950; postgrad. (asst.), U. Minn., 1953-55; M.A. (fellow), Northwestern U., 1959; Ph.D. (teaching asst.), Northwestern U., 1960. Mem. faculty Kendall Coll., Evanston, Ill., 1957-59, DePauw U., Greencastle, Ind., 1959-64; mem. faculty Roosevelt U., Chgo., 1964—, chmn. dept. philosophy, 1965-74; prof. philosophy, asso. dean Coll. Scis. and Humanities, Iowa State U., Ames, 1974-76, prof. philosophy, 1976—. Author: The Epistemology of G.E. Moore, 1969, Reflections and Perspectives: Essays in Philosophy, 1973, Studies in the Philosophy of Kierkgaard, 1976; Editor: Essays on Frege, 1968, Studies in the Philosophy of G.E. Moore, 1969, Essays on Bertrand Russell, 1970, Essays on Wittgenstein, 1971, Readings in Semantics, 1973, Ontological Turn, 1973, Introductory Readings in the Philosophy of Science, 1980, The Meaning of Life, 1981, Philosophy: The Basic Issues, 1982, Contemporary Analytic and Linguistic Philosophies, 1983; contbr. articles to profl. jours. Trustee Roosevelt U., 1973-74. Named Best Tchr., DePauw U., 1962, Top Prof., Roosevelt U., 1965. Mem. Am. Philos. Assn. (sec.-treas. Western div. 1969-72), AAUP. Home: 111 Lynn Ave Apt 804 Ames IA 50010

KLEMME, CARL WILLIAM, banker; b. Ft. Wayne, Ind., Sept. 11, 1928; s. Ludwig and Marianne (Rupil) K.; m. Ann Elise Wichman, Sept. 11, 1954; children—Ellen Elise, Sarah Ann, Carl Andrew. B.S., Yale U., 1950; M.B.A., N.Y. U., 1956; postgrad., Advanced Mgmt. Program Harvard U., 1971. With Morgan Guaranty Trust Co., N.Y.C., 1950-80, v.p., 1961-70, sr. v.p., 1970-72, exec. v.p., 1972-80, Russell Reynolds Assos., Inc., N.Y.C., 1981-82, Nat. Bank N.Am., 1982—; dir. Depository Trust Co. Mem. Millburn Bd. Edn., 1967-73; trustee Howard U., Millburn (N.J.) Public Library, 1979—, Wittenberg U., 1983—; bd. dirs. Downtown-Lower Manhattan Assn., 1972-80, Bank Adminstrn. Inst., 1975-81; chmn. Bank Adminstrn. Inst., 1979-80. Served with U.S. Army, 1950-52. Mem. Phi Beta Kappa. Republican. Episcopalian. Home: 35 Woodfield Dr Short Hills NJ 07078 Office: 44 Wall St New York NY 10005

KLEMME, HOWARD CHARLES, lawyer; b. Boulder, Colo., Mar. 18, 1930; s. Claude Chase and Freda Lena (Vernold) K.; m. Barbara Faith Brichacek, June 9, 1952; children: Cynthia, Amelia, Valerie, Paul, Andrea. B.A., U. Colo., 1952, LL.B., 1954; LL.M., Yale U., 1960. Bar: Colo. 1954. Teaching and research asst. Ohio State U. Coll. Law, 1954-55, vis. asst. prof. law, 1955-56; asst. prof., law librarian Colo. U., 1956-59, asst. prof., 1960-61, asso. prof., 1961-63; prof. U. Colo., 1963—. Reporter, editor: Colo. Civil Jury instrns, 1965—, 1st edit., 1969, 2d edit., 1980. Bd. dirs. Boulder Inter-Faith Housing, Inc.; mem. Boulder City Council, 1963-70, Boulder Public Housing Authority, 1968-73, Boulder County Planning Commn., 1973—. Recipient William Lee Knous award U. Colo. Law Sch. Alumni Bd., 1974. Mem. Colo. Bar Assn., Am. Law Inst., Order of Coif, Phi Beta Kappa. Office: Sch of Law Box 401 U Colo Boulder CO 80309

KLEMT, CALVIN CARL, sem. librarian; b. Louisville, Aug. 19, 1925; s. William Walter and Emma (Bach) K.; m. Bette Mae Bartlett, June 7, 1951; children—Kristin Elizabeth, Paul William. Student, U. Ky., 1946-49; B.A., Heidelberg Coll., 1950; M.Div., Union Theol. Sem., N.Y.C., 1953; A.M. in L.S, U. Mich., 1962. Ordained to ministry Evang. and Ref. Ch., 1953; pastor Suffield (Ohio) Evang. and Ref. Ch., 1953-58, Big Rapids (Mich.) United Ch. of Christ, 1959-61; librarian Central Luth. Theol. Sem., Fremont, Nebr., 1962-66, Austin (Tex.) Presbyn. Theol. Sem., 1966—. Served with AUS, 1943-46. Mem. Am. Theol. Library Assn. Home: 4804 Broken Bow Pass Austin TX 78745

KLEPPE, JOHN ARTHUR, electrical engineering educator, business executive; b. Oakland, Calif., Feb. 21, 1939; s. Arthur William and Musa (Anderson) K.; m. Julianna Marie Galli, Aug. 12, 1961; children: John Frederick, Johanna Beth, Judith Anne. B.S. in Elec. Engring., U. Nev., 1961, M.S., 1967; Ph.D., U. Calif.-Davis, 1970. Registered profl. engr., Nev., Calif. Prof. elec. engring. U. Nev., Reno, 1970—, dir. Engring. Research and Devel., 1976—; pres., research cons. Sci. Engring. Instruments, Inc., Reno, 1968—; pres. Klepco, Inc., 1976—; cons.; chief engr. NSF weather expdn. to Antarctica, 1977; del. White House Conf. Small Bus., 1980. Contbr. articles, papers to publs. and confs. in U.S., Switzerland, Eng., Holland, 1964. Served to lt. C.E. USN, 1961-65. Recipient Outstanding Engring. Achievement award for Nev., 1981. Mem. IEEE, N.Y. Acad. Scis., Nev. Innovation and Tech. council (pres. 1981—), Sigma Xi, Tau Beta Pi. Home: 2425 Greensboro Dr Reno NV 89509 Office: SEI 1275 Kleppe Ln 14 Sparks NV 89431

KLETSCHKA, HAROLD DALE, cardiovascular surgeon, biomedical company executive; b. Mpls., Aug. 26, 1924; s. Herbert Leland and Emma Elizabeth (Kopf) K. A.S., Brainerd (Minn.) Jr. Coll., 1943; B.S., U. Minn., 1946, M.B., 1947, M.D., 1948; LL.B., Blackstone Sch. Law, Ill., 1970; grad, Air War Coll., 1972. Diplomate: Am. Bd. Surgery, Am. Bd. Thoracic Surgery. Intern Kings County Hosp., Bklyn., 1947-49; asst. resident surgery Univ. Hosp., Ann Arbor, Mich., 1950-51; resident gen. surgery State U. N.Y. Downstate Med. Center, 1953-54, chief resident thoracic surgery, 1952-53, 54-55; thoracic and gen. surgeon Bratrud Clinic, Thief River Falls, Minn., 1951-52; asst. chief, acting chief neurosurgery 3275th and 2349th USAF hosps., Parks AFB, Calif., 1955-56, asst. chief thoracic surgery, 1956, chief thoracic surgery, 1956-57; founder, chief USAF Cardiovascular Research Center, 1957-58; practice medicine specializing in thoracic and cardiovascular surgery, San Francisco and San Jose, Calif., 1958-59; thoracic surgeon VA Hosp., Syracuse, N.Y., 1959-60; chief thoracic surgery, 1960-67; asst. prof. surgery SUNY Upstate Med Center, Syracuse, 1959-67, cons. thoracic surgery, 1959-67, USAF med service liaison officer for surgeon gen., 1964-67; dep. comdr., chief hosp. services 102d TAC Hosp., Phalsbourg Air Base, France, 1961-62; mil. cons. to surgeon gen. USAF; surgeon Hdqrs. Command USAF, 1965-73; aerospace med. cons. to dir. Aerospace Med. Services, Malcolm Grow USAF Med. Center, 1965-73; thoracic surgeon VA Hosp., Houston, 1967-68, Montgomery, Ala., 1968-72, dir. cardiopulmonary labs., 1970-72; co-founder, incorporator, 1st chmn. bd., pres., chief exec. officer Bio-Medicus, Inc., Minnetonka, Minn., 1972—; mem. Nat. council on U.S.-USSR Health Care, Citizen Exchange Corps, N.Y.C., 1976—; mem. exec. com. Council for U.S.-USSR Health Exchange, Boston, 1976—. Contbr.: chpt. to Progress in Surface and Membrane Science, 1973; Bd. editors: Minn. Medicine, 1960-82; editor charge spl. issue, 1966; contbr. articles to profl. jours.; collaborator liturg. mus. composition dedicated to Cardinal Spellman: Pater Noster, 1961, internat. TV performance, 1962. Campaign mgr. Ind. Republican candidate Dist. 43B, Minn. Ho. of Reps.; mem. nat. adv. bd. Am. Security Council.; mem. Reagan-Bush '84 Election Com., Reagan Presdl. Campaign Task Force, Reagan Nat. Adv. Bd.; spl. advisor U.S. Congl. Adv. Bd. Recipient Bausch & Lomb Hon. Sci. award, 1941, IR-100 award for devel. Rafferty-Kletschka artificial heart, 1972, Worldwide Symbolic grad. Air War Coll., 1973, 1st pl. award Med./Analytical div. Plastics World, 1976, 1st prize in Med. div. 8th Bachner award competition, 1976; Named to Wisdom Hall of Fame, 1979. Fellow A.C.S.; mem. Am. Heart Assn. (council on basic scis., council on cardiovascular surgery), Am. Med. Writers Assn., Internat. Platform Assn., AAUP, Air Force Assn., U. Minn. Alumni Assn., Am. Soc. Artificial Internal Organs, Twin City Thoracic and Cardiovascular Surg. Soc., VFW, U. Minn. Alumni Club. Club: K.C. (4 deg.). Patentee in field; co-inventor Kletschka/Rafferty Blood Pump, heart assist device and artificial heart; pioneer non-pulsatile blood flow field with contbns. of discoveries and devices; discoverer medical spallation phenomenon; pioneer Kletschka-Levowitz fracture; performed world's 1st clin. use of constrained force vortex artificial heart blood pump. Home: 1925 Noble Dr Minneapolis MN 55422 *In the beginning, be disposed interiorly so as to be receptive to the whispers of God regarding His plans. Listen attentively until those designs are clearly perceived, and then follow them. Truth is the indispensable guiding beacon for life's journey. Be fearless in making decisions based on independent personal judgements, honestly founded on trying to be right. Failure is not to be feared. Success is measured by a dedicated effort without compromising truth, honesty, and fairness in the process.*

KLETT, GORDON A., savings and loan association executive; b. Galva, Iowa, Apr. 29, 1925; s. Ernest and Frieda (Gutknecht) K.; m. Edna Mae Klett, June 11, 1950; children: Joel G., Kristin F., Andrea E. B.A., Valparaiso U., 1949; M.A., UCLA, 1951. With U.S. Weather Bur., St. Paul, 1941-42; vis. lectr. U. Ceylon, Colombo, 1951-52; fgn. service officer U.S. Dept. State, Mex., 1956-58; with Glendale (Calif.) Fed. Savs. and Loan Assn., 1953-56, 59—, pres., chief operating officer, 1980—; dir. Wilshire Mortgage Corp., Wilshire Diversified, Inc. Served with USAAF, 1943-46. Office: 700 N Brand Blvd Glendale CA 91203

KLEY, JOHN ARTHUR, banker; b. Jericho, N.Y., Oct. 24, 1921; s. John and Annie (Upton) K.; m. Florence Elizabeth Cannon, Sept. 1, 1945 (dec. Apr. 1983); 1 dau., Martha Anne. Grad., Stonier Grad. Sch. Banking, Rutgers U., 1952; B.P.S., Pace U., 1974. With Washington Irving Trust Co. (and successor County Trust Co.), White Plains, N.Y., 1937-76, asst. treas., asst. v.p., v.p., 1947-57, exec. v.p., 1957-60, pres., 1960-72, chmn. bd., 1972-76; v.p. Bank N.Y. Co., 1968-74, vice chmn., 1974-77; dir. Bank of N.Y., 1973-77, vice chmn., 1976-77. Past chmn. bd. trustees, trustee emeritus Westchester Community Coll.; past pres., chmn. Westchester Community Coll. Found.; past pres. Legal Aid Soc. West County; past chmn. bd. regents Stonier Grad. Sch. Banking, Rutgers U. Served from pvt. to maj. USAAF, 1942-46; lt. col. Res. Recipient Leffingwell medal, 1960. Mem. N.Y. State Bankers Assn. (pres. 1969-70). Episcopalian. Clubs: Imperial Golf (Naples, Fla.); Country of Naples; Whippoorwill (Armonk, N.Y.). Home: 1900 Gulf Shore Blvd N Naples FL 33940

KLIBAN, B(ERNARD), cartoonist; b. Jan. 1, 1935. Ed., Pratt Inst., Cooper Union. Cartoonist: books Cat, 1975, Never Eat Anything Bigger Than Your Head and Other Drawings, 1976, Whack Your Porcupine and Other Drawings, 1977, Tiny Footprints and Other Drawings, 1978, Playboy's Kliban, 1979, Two Guys Fooling Around with the Moon and Other Drawings, 1982, Luminous Animals and Other Drawings, 1983; artist and cartoonist for posters, calendars, greeting cards. Office: care Workman Pub Co Inc 1 W 39th St New York NY 10018 *

KLIEBHAN, M(ARY) CAMILLE, college president; b. Milw., Apr. 4, 1923; d. Alfred Sebastian and Mae Eileen (McNamara) K. Student, Cardinal Stritch Coll., Milw., 1945-48; B.A., Cath. Sisters Coll., Washington, 1949; M.A., Cath. U. Am., 1951, Ph.D., 1955. Joined Sisters of St. Francis of Assisi, Roman Catholic Ch., 1945; legal sec. Spence and Hanley (attys.), Milw., 1941-45; instr. edn. Cardinal Stritch Coll., 1955-62, asso. prof., 1962-68, prof., 1968—, head dept. edn., 1962-67, dean students, 1962-64, chmn. grad. div., 1964-69, v.p. for acad. and student affairs, 1969-74, pres., 1974—, bd. dirs., 1974—. Bd. dirs. Goals for Milw. 2000, 1980-83; mem. coordinating bd. Nat. Council Accreditation Tchr. Edn., 1981-83; treas. Wis. Found. Ind. Colls., 1974-79, v.p., 1979-81, pres., 1981-83; bd. dirs. DePaul Rehab. Hosp., 1982—, Sacred Heart Sch. Theology, 1983—, Holy Redeemer Coll., Waterford, Wis., 1984—; mem. community edn. com. Mental Health Assn. Milwaukee County, 1983—; mem. TEMPO, 1982—. Mem. Am. Psychol. Assn., Wis. Assn. Tchr. Educators, Phi Delta Kappa, Delta Epsilon Sigma, Psi Chi, Delta Kappa Gamma. *It is because of my faith that I can meet every condition with courage.*

KLIEWER, EDWARD ALBERT, JR., lawyer; b. Electra, Tex., Dec. 21, 1914; s. Edward Albert and Edith Genevieve (Green) K.; m. Ozelle Everitt, Aug. 8, 1940; children—Edward Albert III, Nancy Kliewer Dunlap. Student, Tyler Jr. Coll., 1931-32; LL.B., U. Tex., 1937. Asso. firm Blalock, Lohman & Blalock, Marshall, Tex. and Houston, 1937-41; partner firm Blalock, Lohman & Kliewer, Houston, 1945-49, Kliewer & Hood, Dallas, 1950—; dir. Delta Drilling Co., Pauley Petroleum Inc., Delta Marine Drilling Co. Served to maj. JAG Corps U.S. Army, 1942-45. Mem. State Bar Tex., Am., Dallas bar assns. Republican. Methodist. Home: 7015 Azalea Lane Dallas TX 75230 Office: 2000 Northtower Southland Center Dallas TX 75201

KLIGER, MILTON RICHARD, shipping co. exec.; b. N.Y.C., Sept. 26, 1922; s. David and Sadie (Zelikow) K.; m. Ruth Salkind, Jan. 30, 1944; children—Alan, Sandra (Mrs. Norton A. Elson). B.B.A., Baruch Coll., 1947. With Maritime Overseas Corp., N.Y.C., 1953—, v.p., treas., 1962-67, sr. v.p., 1967-78, exec. v.p., 1978—; v.p., treas. Overseas Shipholding Group, N.Y.C., 1969-74, sr. v.p., treas., 1974—. Home: 169 E 69th St New York NY 10021 Office: 511 Fifth Ave New York NY 10017

KLIGERMAN, MORTON M., radiologist; b. Phila., Dec. 26, 1917; s. Samuel and Dorothy (Medvene) K.; m. Barbara C. Coleman, Mar. 14, 1956; children—Hilary, Thomas A., Valli á Court. B.S., Temple U., 1934, M.D., 1941, M.Sc., 1948; M.A. (hon.), Yale U., 1958. Instr. radiology Temple U., Phila., 1947-48, Columbia U., N.Y.C., 1948-50, asst. prof. radiology, 1950-53, assoc. prof., 1953-58; Robert E. Hunter prof. radiology, chmn. dept. radiology Yale U., New Haven; also radiologist-in-chief Yale-New Haven Hosp., 1958-72; dir. Cancer Research and Treatment Center U. N.Mex., Albuquerque, 1972-80, prof. radiology, 1972-80; asst. dir. for radiation therapy Los Alamos Sci. Lab., 1972-80; chief div. radiation oncology Bernalillo County Med. Center, Albuquerque, 1972-80; prof. radiation therapy U. Pa., Phila., 1980—; cons. on staff Presbyn. Hosp., Lovelace-Bataan Med. Center, St. Joseph Hosp., VA Hosp., all Albuquerque, Los Alamos Med. Center. Contbr. articles to profl. jours. Bd. dirs. Opera Assn. N.Mex., 1975-80, nat. council, 1980—; bd. dirs. Santa Fe Opera Found., 1976-80, also pres.; bd. dirs. N.Mex. div. Am. Cancer Soc., 1972-76. Served with M.C. U.S. Army, 1944-47. Recipient Disting. Alumni award Temple U., 1964; Silver Medallion Columbia U., 1967; Grubbe Gold Medal award Chgo. Med. Soc.-Chgo. Radiol. Soc., 1976. Fellow Am. Coll. Radiology; mem. Pa. Med. Soc., Philadelphia County Med. Soc., Am. Assn. Cancer Research, Am. Radium Soc. (v.p. 1976-77, pres. 1982-83, Janeway medal 1981), Am. Soc. Therapeutic Radiologists (pres. 1968-69, Gold medal 1982), Am. Legion. Home: 2122 Delancey Pl Philadelphia PA 19103 Office: Hosp of U Pa 3400 Spruce St Philadelphia PA 19104

KLIGLER, SEYMOUR H., lawyer; b. N.Y.C., June 24, 1920; s. Harry and Clara (Kisilew) K.; m. Gloria Blackin, Oct. 19, 1942; children—Cheryl, Roger. B.S., Coll. City N.Y., 1941; J.D., Harvard, 1948. Bar: N.Y. bar 1948. Since practiced in, N.Y.C.; asso. firm Herman Goldman, 1948-65; partner firm Brauner Baron Rosenzweig Kligler & Sparber, 1965—; chief legal officer Bd. Coop. Ednl. Services Nassau County, N.Y. Trustee bd. edn. Union Free Sch. Dist. 17, Hempstead, N.Y., 1955-64, pres., 1959-64; trustee bd. edn. central high sch. dist. 2, Hempstead and N. Hempstead, N.Y., 1959-64, chmn. commn. vocat. spl. edn., Nassau County, 1962-65; Candidate Dem. party N.Y. State Assembly, 1965; Trustee Herman Goldman Found., 1973—. Served to 2d lt. AUS, 1941-45. Mem. Am. Bar Assn., N.Y. Sch. Bd. Attys. Assn., Maritime Law Assn. U.S. Club: Shelter Rock Tennis. Home: 49 Peach Dr Roslyn NY 11576 Office: 120 Broadway New York NY 10005

KLIMAS, ANTANAS, linguist, educator; b. Pelekonys, Lithuania, Apr. 17, 1924; came to U.S., 1948, naturalized, 1959; s. Vincas and Marija (Siugzdinis) K.; m. Dana Liormanas, June 19, 1954; children: Tadas, Ruta, Paulius, Lina. Student, Tchrs. Tng. Coll., Kaunas, Lithuania, 1941-42, U. Kaunas, 1941-43, Baltic U., Hamburg, Germany, 1946-47; M.A., U. Pa., 1950, Ph.D., 1956. Asst. instr. German U. Pa., 1950-56, instr., 1956-57; asst. prof. U. Rochester, N.Y., 1957-62, asso. prof., 1962-70, prof., 1970—. Author: (with William R. Schmalstieg and Leonardas Dambriunas) Introduction to

Modern Lithuanian, 1966, 3d edit., 1980, Lithuanian Reader for Self-Instruction, 1967, (with William Schmalstieg) A Glossary of Lithuanian Linguistic Terminology, 1972; editor: Lituanus; contbr. articles on linguistics to profl. jours. Mem. Linguistic Soc. Am., Assn. Advancement Baltic Studies, Am. Tchrs. German, Lithuanian Cath. Acad. Sci., Delta Phi Alpha. Home: 533 Winton Rd S Rochester NY 14618 Office: Univ of Rochester Coll Arts and Sci Rochester NY 14627

KLIMCZAK, ERNEST JOSEPH, paper co. exec.; b. Chgo., Aug. 3, 1924; s. John and Angeline (Niadek) K.; m. Bernice Owsiany, May 15, 1965. B.S., Ill. Inst. Tech., 1945; M.B.A., U. Chgo., 1958, diploma exec. program, 1959. Registered profl. engr., Ill. With Ahlberg Bearing Co., Chgo., 1943-58, v.p., gen. mgr., dir., 1955-58; exec. v.p., dir. Braden Winch Co., Tulsa, 1958; gen. mgr. Arrow Gear Co., Tulsa, 1958-59; v.p. Motor Products Corp., Detroit, 1959-60; pres., dir. Allied/Egry Bus. Systems Co., Dayton, Ohio, 1960-64; Egry Continuous Forms, Ltd., Toronto, Ont., Can., 1960-64; pres. Allied Paper Corp., Chgo., 1964-73; v.p. SCM Corp., Kalamazoo, 1973—; pres. Allied Paper Inc., 1964—. Office: 2030 Portage St Kalamazoo MI 49001

KLIMENT, STEPHEN ALEXANDER, architect, editor; b. May 24, 1930; s. Felix and Sophia (Baltinester) K.; m. Felicia Drury, Dec. 24, 1957; children: Pamela Drury, Jennifer Anne. Student, Ecole Speciale d'Architecture, Paris, 1948-49; B.Arch., M.I.T., 1953; M.F.A., Princeton U., 1957. Draftsman Jean Labatut, Princeton, N.J., 1957; designer Skidmore, Owings & Merrill, N.Y.C., 1957-59, Reeb-Draz Assos., Cleve., 1959-60; editor Archtl. and Engring. News, 1961-69; v.p. Caudill Rowlett Scott, N.Y.C., 1969-72; architect, cons., 1972—; editor-in-chief Advt. & Pub. News, 1978-80; sr. editor Whitney Library of Design, 1981—; lectr. U. Oreg., Tex. A&M U., Carnegie-Mellon U., Pa. State U., Lawrence Inst. Tech., Yale U., Harvard U. Author: Creative Communications for a Successful Design Practice, (with R.H. McNulty) Neighborhood Conservation. Bd. dirs. Bldg. Research Inst., 1969-71; chmn. adv. Council Princeton Sch. Architecture and Urban Planning, 1973—; mem. governing bd. Assn. Princeton Grad. Alumni, 1972-75. Served with AUS, 1953-55. Fellow AIA (dir. N.Y. chpt. 1966-68, sec. 1976-78). Episcopalian. Club: Univ. (N.Y.C.). Home: 120 E 81st St New York NY 10028 Office: care Whitney Library Design 1515 Broadway New York NY 10036

KLIMISCH, RICHARD LEO, chemist; b. Yankton, S.C., Jan. 1, 1938; s. Andrew R. and Opal (Haley) K.; m. Virginia Jenkinson, Sept. 15, 1962; children: Kurtis D., Erik R. B.S., Loras Coll., 1960; Ph.D., Purdue U., 1964. Research chemist DuPont Co., Wilminton, Del., 1964-67, Gen. Motors Co. Research Labs., Warren, Mich., 1967-70, asst. dept. head, 1970-75, head environ. sci. dept., 1975-83, exec. dir. environ. activities staff, 1983—. Mem. environ., engring. and med. adv. coms. Coordinating Research Council. Mem. AAAS, Am. Chem. Soc., Sigma Xi. Office: Environ Activities Staff Gen Motors Warren MI 48090

KLINCK, HAROLD RUTHERFORD, educator; b. Gormley, Ont., Can., Sept. 24, 1922; s. Roscoe Franklin and Olive Ila (Jennings) K.; m. Isabel Penelope Gilchrist, June 30, 1951; children: John Rutherford, Thomas Daniel, Harold Robert, Margaret Elizabeth, David Roscoe. B.S.A., Ont. Agrl. Coll., U. Toronto, 1950; M.Sc., McGill U., 1952, Ph.D., 1955. Grad. asst. McGill U., Montreal, Que., 1950-54, lectr. agronomy, 1954-56, asst. prof., 1956-65, asso. prof., 1965-71, prof. agronomy, 1971—, acting dean, 1971-72, acting vice prin., 1971-72. Contbr. articles to profl. jours. Decorated Commandeur del'Ordre du Mérite Agronomique; Recipient Nuffield Found. travel grant to study at Cambridge, Eng., 1961, Commonwealth Found. sci. exchange travel grant to visit, Malawi, Africa, 1972. Fellow Agrl. Inst. Can.; mem. Can. Seed Growers Assn. (hon. life), Que. Seed Growers Assn. (hon. life), Master Brewers Assn. (hon.). Home: 12 Maple Ave Ste Anne de Bellevue PQ H9X 2E4 Canada Office: Macdonald Coll McGill U Ste Anne de Bellevue PQ H9X 1C0 Canada

KLINCK, PATRICIA EWASCO, state ofcl.; b. Albany, N.Y., May 13, 1940; d. Albert C. and Mary Ann (Sopko) Ewasco; m. C. Hoagland Klinck, Jr., Sept. 12, 1970; 1 dau., Natalie Childs. B.A. in History, Smith Coll., 1961; M.S. in L.S, Simmons Coll., Boston, 1963; postgrad. in edn., State U. N.Y. at Albany, 1964-67. Young adult worker Boston Pub. Library, 1961-63; library dir. Colonie Central High Sch., Albany, 1963-67; librarian Library/U.S.A., U.S. Pavilion, N.Y. World's Fair, summer 1965; library dir. Simon's Rock Coll., Gt. Barrington, Mass., 1967-70; regional dir. N.W. Regional Library, Vt. Dept. Libraries, Montpelier, 1970-72, dir. extension services div., 1972-73, 73-74, acting asst. state librarian, 1973, asst. state librarian, 1974-77, state librarian, 1977—; Chmn. New Eng. Library Bd., 1979-81; bd. dirs. Chief Officers State Library Agys., 1978-80, vice chmn., 1978-80, chmn., 1981-82. Mem. Am., New Eng., Vt. library assns. Home: 47 Brewer Pkwy South Burlington VT 05401 Office: 111 State St Montpelier VT 05602

KLINE, BILLY DAN, gas co. fin. exec.; b. Shreveport, La., Aug. 7, 1935; s. Daniel Michael and Jewell Alelia (Lovin) K.; m. Nancy Sue Tubbs, June 7, 1957; children—Michael, Kevin, Kimberly, Kenneth. B.S. in Acctg, La. Tech. U., 1957. With Arkansas La. Gas Co., Shreveport, 1957—, asst. mgr. dept. tax and ins., 1973-75, treas., 1975-81, sec.-treas., 1979—. Active United Way, Jr. Achievement. Served with USAF, 1957-58. Mem. Shreveport C. of C. Mem. Churches of Christ. Club: YMCA. Home: 1743 Willow Point Dr Shreveport LA 71119 Office: Arkla Bldg 525 Milam St Shreveport LA 71151

KLINE, CLAIRE BENTON, JR., philosophy educator; b. Pitts., May 13, 1925; s. Claire Benton and Wilma S. (Huot) K.; m. Mary C. Hicks, June 6, 1950; children: John B., Mary M. B.A., Coll. Wooster, 1944; B.D., Princeton Theol. Sem., 1948, Th. M., 1949; Ph.D., Yale U., 1961. Ordained to ministry Presbyn. Ch. U.S.A., 1948; asst. instr. philosophy Yale, 1950-51; interim supply pastor, Bklyn., 1950-51; asst. prof. philosophy Agnes Scott Coll., 1951-61, asso. prof., 1961-62, prof., 1962-68, chmn. dept., 1957-63, dean faculty, 1957-68, vis. prof., 1969-71, 76—; vis. prof. theology Columbia Theol. Sem., Decatur, Ga., 1964-65, prof. theology, 1969—, dean faculty, 1969-71, pres., 1971-76; vis. asst. prof. philosophy Emory U., summers 1952-54, 56; sr. assoc. Westminster Coll., Cambridge U. (Eng.), 1982-82. Mem. Decatur Bd. Edn., 1972-80; Bd. dirs. Pastoral Counseling Service, Urban Tng. Orgn., Ga. Assn. Pastoral Care, Council on Theology and Culture of Presbyn. Ch. Mem. Phi Beta Kappa. Democrat. Home: 717 Lake Dr SW Lithonia GA 30058

KLINE, DANIEL L., educator; b. Phila., Dec. 25, 1917; s. Emanuel and Hettie (Salkowe) K.; m. Vivian Bass, Apr. 25, 1945; children—Katherine, Elizabeth, Emily. B.S., Purdue U., 1942; Ph.D. in Physiology, Columbia, 1946. Instr. physiology Columbia Coll. Phys. and Surg., 1945; from asst. prof. to asso. prof. physiology Yale Med. Sch., 1949-66; prof. physiology, chmn. dept. Cin. Coll. Medicine, 1966—. Mem. editorial bd.: Am. Jour. Physiology, 1965-70, Jour. Applied Physiology; cons. editor: Science. Recipient Lamport award N.Y. Acad. Sci., 1979; Guggenheim fellow, 1957-58. Mem. Am. Physiol. Soc., Soc. Exptl. Biology and Medicine, Assn. Am. Med. Colls., Am. Fedn. Scientists, AAAS, Sigma Xi. Home: 933 Avondale Ave Cincinnati OH 45229

KLINE, DAVID GELLINGER, neurosurgery educator; b. Phila., Oct. 13, 1934; s. David Francis and Lois Ann (Gellinger) K.; m. Carol Anne Loewen, Mar. 1, 1958 (div.); children: Susan, Robert, Nancy. A.B. in Chemistry, U. Pa., 1956, M.D., 1960. Diplomate: Am. Bd. Neurol. Surgery (sec.-treas. 1978-83, chmn. 1983-84). Intern U. Mich., Ann Arbor, 1960-61, resident in gen. surgery, 1961-62, teaching assoc. in neurosurgery, 1964-67; research investigator Walter Reed Army Inst. Research and Walter Reed Gen. Hosp., 1962-64; instr. La. State U. Med. Sch., New Orleans, 1967-68, asst. prof., 1968-70, assoc. prof., 1970-73, prof., 1973—, chmn. dept. neurosurgery, 1971—; cons. USPHS Health Center Hosp., New Orleans VA Hosp., Kessler AFB Hosp.-Lederle Labs.; vis. investigator Delta Regional Primate Center, Covington. Contbr. articles to sci. jours. Served with M.C. AUS, 1962-64. Recipient Frederick Coller Surg. prize, 1967; numerous grants. Mem. Am. Acad. Neurol. Surgery, Soc. Neurol. Surgeons, So. Neurol. Surgery Soc. (sec. 1976-79, pres. elect), Am. Assn. Neurol. Surgeons, Soc. Univ. Neurosurgeons, Congress Neurol. Surgeons, Assn. Acad. Surgery, Soc. Univ. Surgeons, A.C.S., Nerve Study Group (pres. 1981), Phi Beta Kappa, Kappa Sigma, Phi Chi. Episcopalian (vestry and lay reader). Home: 307 Fairway Dr New Orleans LA 70124 Office: Med Center La State U 1542 Tulane Ave New Orleans LA 70112 *Success, whether defined by the individual who believes he or she has achieved it or "granted" by others has little meaning unless it is accompanied by happiness. To have both, one must not only enjoy his or her life's work but also life as a whole and particularly people and specifically working hard with and interacting well with others. Honesty about one's own efforts as well as those of others, a large measure of perseverance, a sense of humor, and a degree of courage as well as a certain amount of realistic optimism are very necessary to survive let alone flourish.*

KLINE, ELLIOT HOWARD, university dean, business educator; b. Denver, July 16, 1940; s. Morris and Sadie (Uswalk) K.; m. Linda Sue Newman, May 18, 1964; children: James, Edward. B.A., U. Colo., 1963, M.P.A., 1966, Ph.D., 1971. Instr. Tex. A&M U., College Station, 1966-67; lectr. U. Colo., Colorado Springs, 1968-69; asst. prof. U. Denver, 1968-70; dir., asso. prof. Inst. Public Affairs and Adminstrn. Drake U., Des Moines, 1970-77; dean, prof. Sch. Bus. and Pub. Adminstrn. U. Pacific, Stockton, Calif., 1977—; planning cons. State Savs. and Loan Assn., Stockton, 1979; dir. adminstrv. analysis Office City Clk., Indianola, Iowa, 1975; lectr. Brookings Instn., 1982, 83; vis. lectr. Washington Sem. Program, Am. U., 1982; cons. various orgns., 1973—; vis. lectr. Washington Sem. Program, Am. U., 1982. Guest editor: The Stockton Record, 1980—; contbr. articles to various publs. Served with USCGR, 1960, 1960-65. Recipient Grad. Sch. Research grants Drake Univ., 1972, 74. Mem. C. of C., Acad. Mgmt., Am. Assn. Higher Edn., Am. Mgmt. Assn., Am. Soc. Public Adminstrn. (mem. nat. council 1976-79), Calif. Assn. Public Adminstrn., Edn., Internat. Personnel Mgmt. Assn., No. Calif. Polit. Sci. Assn. (mem. exec. bd. 1981—), Western Govtl. Research Assn. (exec. com. 1981—), Western Assn. Collegiate Schs. Bus. (exec. bd. 1981—). Office: Sch Bus and Pub Adminstrn Univ of Pacific Stockton CA 95211

KLINE, EUGENE R., steel company executive; b. Lewistown, Pa., Apr. 26, 1931; s. Russell E. and C. Pauline (Knepp) K.; m. Anne E. Rogan, Aug. 20, 1955; children: Timothy Russell, Betsy Anne. B.A., Gettysburg Coll., 1953; M.B.A., U. Pa., 1957; P.M.D., Harvard U. Bus. Sch., 1973. With Bethlehem Steel Corp., (Pa.), 1957—, asst. to v.p. pub. affairs dept., 1970-77, asst. v.p., 1977-79, v.p. pub. affairs dept., 1979—. Trustee St. Luke's Hosp., Bethlehem, 1977—, Allentown Coll. of St. Francis de Sales, 1979—, Gettysburg Coll., 1980. Served as lt. U.S. Army, 1953-55. Mem. Am. Iron and Steel Inst. (com. pub. relations), Pub. Afairs Council (vice-chmn. 1982—), Machinery and Allied Products Inst. (pub. affairs council 1980—), Conf. Bd. (pub. affairs research council 1979—), Pa. C. of C. (dir. 1978—). Club: Saucon Valley Country. Office: Bethlehem Steel Corp Bethlehem PA 18016

KLINE, GEORGE LOUIS, philosophy educator, author; b. Galesburg, Ill., Mar. 3, 1921; s. Allen Sides and Wahneta (Burner) K.; m. Virginia Harrington Hardy, Apr. 17, 1943; children: Brenda Marie, Jeffrey Allen, Christina Hardy (Mrs. Francis C. Hanak). Student, Boston U., 1938-41; A.B. with honors, Columbia U., 1947, M.A., 1948, Ph.D., 1950. Instr. philosophy Columbia, 1950-52, 53-54, asst. prof., 1954-60; vis. asst. prof. U. Chgo., 1952-53; asso. prof. philosophy and Russian Bryn Mawr Coll., 1960-66, prof. philosophy, 1966—, Milton C. Nahm prof. philosophy, 1981—, chmn. dept., 1977-82. Author: Spinoza in Soviet Philosophy, 1952, 81, Religious and Anti-Religious Thought in Russia, 1968; co-author: Continuity and Change in Russian and Soviet Thought, 1955, Marx and the Western World, 1967, Phenomenology and Existentialism, 1967, rev. edit., 1969, Hegel and the Philosophy of Religion, 1970, Sartre: A Collection of Critical Essays, 1971, Hegel and the History of Philosophy, 1974, Dissent in The USSR: Politics, Ideology, and People, 1975, Speculum Spinozanum, 1977, Western Philosophical Systems in Russian Literature, 1979, Vico and Marx: Affinities and Contrasts, 1983; Translator: History of Russian Philosophy (V.V. Zenkovsky), 2 vols, 1953, Boris Pasternak: Seven Poems, 1969, 2d edit., 1972, Joseph Brodsky: Selected Poems, 1973; co-translator: A Part of Speech (Joseph Brodsky), 1980; Editor: Soviet Education, 1957, Alfred North Whitehead: Essays on his Philosophy, 1963; editor, contbr.: European Philosophy Today, 1965; co-editor, contbr.: Russian Philosophy, 3 vols, 1965, 2d edit., 1969, reprint, 1976, Explorations in Whitehead's Philosophy, 1983; Co-editor: Jour. Philosophy, 1959-64; cons. editor, 1964-78, Ency. Philosophy, 1962-67, Studies in Soviet Thought, 1962—, Jour. Value Inquiry, 1967—, Process Studies, 1970—, Soviet Union, 1975-80, Philosophy Research Archives, 1975—, Jour. History of Ideas, 1976—, Slavic Review, 1977-79; cons. editor philosophy: Current Digest of Soviet Press, 1961-64. Served with USAAF., 1942-45. Decorated D.F.C; Cutting traveling fellow, Paris, 1949-50; Fulbright fellow, Paris, 1950, 79; Ford fellow, Paris, 1954-55; Rockefeller fellow, USSR and East Europe, 1960; Nat. Endowment for Humanities sr. fellow, 1970-71; Guggenheim fellow, 1978-79. Mem. Am. Philos. Assn., Soc. Ancient Greek Philosophy, Metaphys. Soc. Am. (councillor 1969-71, 78-82), Internat. Soc. Metaphysics, Philosophy Edn. Soc. (pub. Rev. Metaphys., dir. 1966—), Soc. Phenomenology and Existential Philosophy, Am. Assn. Advancement Slavic Studies (dir. 1972-75), Hegel Soc. Am. (councillor 1968-70, 74-78, v.p. 1971-73), Internationale Hegel-Vereinigung, Soc. Advancement Am. Philosophy, Soc. Study History of Philosophy, P.E.N., Soc. Philosophy of Creativity (chmn. Eastern div. 1976-78), Phi Beta Kappa. Home: 632 Valley View Rd Ardmore PA 19003 Office: Thomas Library Bryn Mawr Coll Bryn Mawr PA 19010

KLINE, GORDON MABEY, chemist, editor; b. Trenton, N.J., Feb. 9, 1903; s. Manuel Kuhl and Florence (Campbell) K.; m. Dorothy Beard, Mar. 15, 1926; 1 dau., Ann Linthicum (Mrs. Robert True Cook). A.B., Colgate U., 1925; M.S., George Washington U., 1926; Ph.D., U. Md., 1934. Research chemist N.Y. State Dept. Health, 1926-27; research chemist Picatinny Arsenal, 1928-29; chemist, phys. sci. adminstr. Nat. Bur. Standards, Washington, 1929-69, chief organic plastics sect., 1935-51, chief div. polymers, 1951-63, cons., 1964-69; tech. editor Modern Plastics Mag.; editorial dir., cons. Modern Plastics Ency., 1936—; tech. investigator with U.S. Army, ETO, 1945; Chmn. tech. com. on plastics Internat. Standardization Orgn., ann. meetings, N.Y.C., 1951, Turin, Italy, 1952, Stockholm, 1953, Brighton, Eng., 1954, Paris, 1955, The Hague, Netherlands, 1956, Burgenstock, Switzerland, 1957, Washington, 1958, U.S. del., Munich, 1959, Prague, 1960, Turin, 1961, Warsaw, 1962, London, 1963, Buda[illegible] Bucharest, 1965, Stockholm, 1966, Phila., 1968, Prague, 19[illegible] 1970, Moscow, 1971, Baden-Baden, 1972, Montreux, 1973, [illegible] 1974, Pugnochiuso, Italy, 1975, Ottawa, 1976, London, 1977, Ma[illegible] 1978, Budapest, 1980, Orlando, Fla., 1981; sec. div. plastics a[illegible] polymers Internat. Union Pure and Applied Chemistry, 1951-59, vice chmn., 1959-63, chmn., 1963-67, mem. macro-molecules div., 1967-75; observer for ISO, 1976—; plastics adv. council, Princeton, 1957-65. Editor: Analytical Chemistry of Polymers, Part 1, 1959, Parts 11 and 111, 1961; Contbr. articles profl. jours. Recipient Honor award Am. Inst. Chemists, Washington sect., 1952, Exceptional Service Gold medal Dept. Commerce, 1953, award Standards Engrs. Soc., 1964, Rosa award Nat. Bur. Standards, 1965; charter mem. Plastics Hall of Fame, 1973. Mem. ASTM (award of merit 1954), Am. Chem. Soc., Am. Inst. Chemists, Soc. Plastics Engrs., Soc. Plastics Industry, Soc. Plastics Pioneers, Phi Beta Kappa, Sigma Xi. Clubs: Cosmos (Washington); Chemists (N.Y.C.). Home: 1 N Golfview Apt 602 Lake Worth FL 33460 Office: 1221 Ave of Americas New York NY 10020

KLINE, J. ANTHONY, state court justice; b. N.Y.C., Aug. 17, 1938; s. Harry and Bertha (Shapiro) K.; m. Fiona Fleming, Dec. 7, 1968 (div. 1977); m.2d. Susan Sward, Nov. 25, 1982. B.A., Johns Hopkins U., 1960; M.A., Cornell U., 1962; LL.B., Yale U., 1965. Bar: Calif. 1966, N.Y. 1967, U.S. Supreme Ct. 1971. Assoc. atty. Davis Polk & Wardwell, N.Y.C., 1966-69; staff atty. OEO Legal Services Program, Berkeley, Calif., 1969-70; mng. atty. Pub. Advocates Inc., San Francisco, 1970-75; legal affairs sec. to gov. of Calif. Sacramento, 1975-80; judge Superior Ct., San Francisco, 1980-82; presiding justice Calif. Ct Appeals. 1st appellate dist. div., 1982—; bd. dirs. San Francisco Lawyers Commn. Urban Affairs, 1972-74; mem. legal com. ACLU of No. Calif., San Francisco, 1972-74. Contbr. articles to legal jours. Bd. dirs. Am. Jewish Congress of No. Calif., San Francisco, 1983; pres. San Francisco Com. for Log Cabin Ranch, 1983; chmn. bd. dirs. San Francisco Conservation Corps, 1984—. Alfred P. Sloan fellow Cornell U., 1960-62; recipient Ambrose Gherini prize and Sutherland Cup. Yale U., 1965. Mem. Calif. Judges Assn., San Francisco Pvt. Industry Council. Democrat. Jewish. Office: Calif Ct of Appeals State Bldg 350 McAllister St San Francisco CA 94102

KLINE, JACOB, biomedical engineering educator; b. Boston, Aug. 3, 1917; s. Joseph and Jennie (Goldman) K.; m. Barbara Fine, Dec. 22, 1957; children: David, Jonathan, Pamela. B.S., MIT, 1942, M.S., 1951; Ph.D. (NSF fellow), Iowa State U., 1962. Electronics engr. Internat. Tel. & Tel. Co., Newark, 1942-46; chief video sect. optical research lab. Boston U., 1946-48; research asst. MIT, 1948-51, research engr., 1951-52; mem. faculty U. R.I., Kingston, 1952-66, asso. prof. engring., 1956-60, dir. bio-med. engring. program, 1962-66; prof. biomed. engring., dir. biomed. engring. program U. Miami, Coral Gables, Fla., 1966—, chmn. dept. biomed. engring., 1979—; cons. in field. Contbr. articles to profl. jours. NASA/Am. Soc. Engring. Edn. fellow, summers, 1965, 66. Fellow Am. Acad. Dental Electrosurgery, AAAS; mem. IEEE (dir. 1943—), Am. Soc. Artificial Organs, Am. Assn. Advancement Med. Instrumentation. (chmn. bd. trustees AAMI Found. 1982—). Patentee myocardial prosthetic device. Home: 1445 Trillo Ave Coral Gables FL 33146 Office: U Miami Coll Engring Coral Gables FL 33124

KLINE, JAMES EDWARD, lawyer; b. Fremont, Ohio, Aug. 3, 1941; s. Walter J. and Sophia Cecelia K.; m. Mary Ann Bruening, Aug. 29, 1964; children: Laura Anne, Matthew Thomas, Jennifer Sue. B.S. in Social Sci, John Carroll U., 1963; J.D., Ohio State U., 1966. Bar: Ohio 1966. Asso. firm Eastman & Smith (formerly Eastman, Stichter, Smith & Bergman), Toledo, 1966-70; partner Eastman, Stichter, Smith & Bergman, 1970—; corp. sec. Sheller-Globe Corp., 1977—; mem. securities adv. com. Ohio Div. Securities, 1979—. Trustee Kidney Found. of Northwestern Ohio, Inc., 1972-81, pres., 1979-80; bd. dirs. Crosby Gardens, Toledo, 1974-80, pres., 1977-79; trustee Toledo Symphony Orch., 1981—; bd. dirs. Toledo Zool. Soc., 1983—. Fellow Ohio Bar Found.; mem. Am. Bar Assn., Ohio State Bar Assn. (corp. law com. sec. 1973-76, vice chmn. 1977-82, chmn. 1983—), Toledo Bar Assn., Nat. Assn. Corp. Dirs., Toledo Area C. of C. Roman Catholic. Clubs: Rotary, Inverness, Toledo. Home: 5958 Swan Creek Dr Toledo OH 43614 Office: 800 United Savs Bldg Toledo OH 43604

KLINE, JOHN WILLIAM, retired air force officer, management consultant; b. Zanesville, Ohio, June 26, 1919; s. Gerry William and Lillian Elizabeth (Scheiderer) K.; m. Katherine Edmond Winton, Oct. 24, 1942; children: Susan Isabel (Mrs. John Farris Morehead), Flora Edmond (Mrs. Richard Crandall Creighton), Elizabeth Gerry. Student, Ohio U., 1937-40; grad., Primary, Basic and Advanced Flying Schs., 1941, Air Command and Staff Sch., 1949, Air War Coll., 1959; B.A., La. Tech. U., 1971. Commd. 2d lt. USAAF, 1941; advanced through grades to maj. gen. USAF, 1965; comdr. (2d Bomb Wing), Hunter AFB, Ga., 1961-63, Dow AFB, Maine, 1963-64; dir. operations, chief staff Hdqrs. 8th Air Force, Westover AFB, Mass., 1964-66; vice comdr. 3d Air Div., Andersen AFB, Guam, 1966-68; asst. dep. chief staff ops. Hdqrs. SAC, Offutt AFB, Nebr., 1968-69; vice-comdr. 2d Air Force, Barksdale AFB, La., 1969-72; ret., 1972; v.p., mgmt. cons. Paul R. Ray, Inc., Ft. Worth, 1972—; pres. Mapotec, Inc., Daytona Beach, Fla., 1974, Precision Aerial Surveys, Inc., 1975—; v.p. ops. Aero Service, Houston, 1976-80, v.p. new ventures and planning, 1980-82. Decorated D.S.M., Legion of Merit with 3 oak leaf clusters, Air medal with oak leaf cluster, Air Force Commendation medal; Air Force Distinguished Service Order Republic Vietnam). Mem. Beta Theta Pi. Presbyterian. Club: Champions Golf (Houston). Home: 1038 Town Pl Houston TX 77057

KLINE, KEVIN DELANEY, actor; b. St. Louis, Oct. 24, 1947; s. Robert Joseph and Peggy (Kirk) K. B.A. in Speech and Theatre, Ind. U.; adv. program diploma, Juliard Sch. Drama Div., N.Y.C., 1972. Founding mem. The Acting Co., N.Y.C., 1972-76. Actor: Broadway prodns. On the Twentieth Century, 1978 (Tony award 1978); (Broadway prodns.) Loose Ends, 1979; Broadway prodns. Pirates of Penzance, 1980 (Tony award 1980); off-Broadway Richard III, 1983; film Sophie's Choice 1982, Pirates of Penzance 1982, The Big Chill, 1983. Club: Players (N.Y.C.). Office: DHKPR Agy 165 W 46th St New York NY

KLINE, LEE B., architect; b. Renton, Wash., Feb. 2, 1914; s. Abraham McCubbin and Pearl (Davidson) K.; m. Martha Myers, Aug. 29, 1936; children—Patricia, Joanne Louise Kline Kresse. B.Arch., U. So. Calif., 1937. Draftsman, designer, 1937-43, pvt. archtl. practice, Los Angeles, 1943—; instr. engring. extension U. Calif., 1947-53; mem. panel arbitrators Am. Arbitration Assn., 1964—. Pres. LaCanada Irrigation Dist., 1966—, dir., 1963—; Bd. dirs. Foothill Mcpl. Water Dist., 1980—, LaCanada br. ARC, 1959-81. Recipient Disting. Service citation Calif. council AIA, 1960, honor awards AIA, 1957, 59, Sch. of Month awards Nation's Schools, 1964, 71. Fellow AIA (pres. Pasadena chpt. 1957, pres. Calif. council 1959). Home: 5160 Oakwood Ave LaCanada CA 91011 Office: 963 W Colorado Blvd Los Angeles CA 90041

KLINE, L(EONARD) PATTON, insurance executive; b. Kansas City, Mo., Nov. 6, 1928; s. Leonard Charles and Ruth Carr (Patton) K.; m. Jean Caruthers Lysle, Dec. 29, 1950; children: Leonard Patton, Charles L., Laura F. B.S. in Applied Econs., Yale U., 1950. With Mann-Kline, Inc., Kansas City, Mo., 1950-69, pres., 1968-72, Mann-Kline, Inc. (co. merged with Marsh & McLennan Inc.), N.Y.C., 1969;

..., exec. v.p., 1974-75, pres., chief exec. officer, 1975-78, ...ef exec. officer, 1978-80; dir. Marsh & McLennan Cos., ..., 1981—; dir. Beech Aircraft Corp., Charter Corp., PHH ...ine Bros. Land Devel. Co. Chmn. bd. dirs. N.Y. Heart ...ustee Coll. Ins. N.Y. Served as officer Security Command, ... 1951-53. Mem. SAR, Kingsley Trust Assn. Episcopalian. ...: Kansas City Country, River (Kansas City); Sky, Economic, ...quistadores del Cielo, River (N.Y.C.); Misquamicut, Watch Hill ...acht, Links, Blind Brook. Home: 840 Park Ave New York NY 10021 also Browning Rd Watch Hill RI 02891 Office: 1221 Ave of the Americas New York NY 10020

KLINE, RAYMOND ADAM, govt. ofcl.; b. New Ringgold, Pa., Sept. 14, 1926; s. Raymond Adam and Helen Marie (Herb) K.; m. Jeanelle Batley, Apr. 26, 1958; children—Robin Jeanelle, Raymond Ashley. A.B., Lebanon Valley Coll., 1950; LL.B., George Washington U., 1957. Bar: D.C. bar 1958. Mgmt. analyst Army Missile Command, Huntsville, Ala., 1958-61; chief mgmt. devel. office Marshall Space Flight Center, Huntsville, 1961-66; asst. asso. adminstr. for systems mgmt. NASA Hdqrs., Washington, 1967-75, asst. adminstr. instl. mgmt., 1975-77; asso. adminstr. mgmt. ops, 1977-79; dep. adminstr. GSA, 1979—; instr. in polit. sci. U. Ala., 1958-63. Served with U.S. Army, 1944-46, 50-51. Mem. D.C. Bar, Phi Delta Phi, Pi Gamma Mu. Home: 15432 Carrolton Rd Rockville MD 20853 Office: GSA Bldg 19th and F Sts NW Washington DC 20405

KLINE, ROBERT REEVES, educator, clergyman; b. Williamsport, Pa., Dec. 27, 1918; s. George F. and Gertrude (Thibodeau) K. B.A., Mt. St. Mary's Coll., Emmitsburg, Md., 1941; student, Mt. St. Mary's Sem., Emmitsburg, 1941-45; M.A., Georgetown U., 1951, Ph.D., 1959. Ordained priest Roman Catholic Ch., 1945, created domestic prelate, 1962; parish priest Diocese of Scranton, Pa., 1945-47; asst. dean mem. Mt. St. Mary's Coll., 1947-53, chaplain, 1953-57, St. Joseph Coll. Women, Emmitsburg, 1957-61, lectr., 1947—; chmn. dept. philosophy Mt. St. Mary's Coll. and Sem., 1952-62, pres., 1961-67, pres. emeritus, 1983—, chmn. dept. psychology and sociology, 1969-80, trustee, 1951-68, chmn. bd. trustees, 1961-67; Prosynodal judge Matrimonial Tribunal, Archdiocese of Balt., 1971-77. Author: The Present State of Axiology in the United States, 1959. Mem. Am. Cath. Philos. Assn., Acad. Religion and Mental Health, Monsignor Tierney Honor Soc., Delta Epsilon Sigma. Address: Mt St Mary's Coll and Sem Emmitsburg MD 21727

KLINE, STEPHEN JAY, mechanical engineer; b. Los Angeles, Feb. 25, 1922; s. Eugene Field and Sheda (Lowman) K.; m. Naomi Jeffries, July 11, 1977; children: David M., Mark D., Carolyn R. B.A., Stanford U., 1943, M.S., 1949; Sc.D., M.I.T., 1952. Research analyst N. Am. Aviation, 1946-48; mem. faculty Stanford (Calif.) U., 1952—, prof. mech. engring., 1961—, chmn. thermoscis. div., 1961-73, prof. values, technology and society, 1970—; cons. Gen. Electric, Gen. Motors, United Technology, DuPont, Brown Boveri. Author: Similitude and Approximation Theory, 1965, Computation of Turbulent Boundary Layers, 1968; editor: Evaluation of Complex Turbulent Flows, 1981. Served with AUS, 1943-46. Recipient Melville medal ASME, 1959, Fluids Engring. award, 1975, Centennial award, 1980; George Stephenson medal Inst. Mech. Engrs. Britain; Bucraino medal Italian Film Soc., 1965. Fellow ASME (past chmn. fluid mechanics com. Fluids Engring. Div.); mem. Nat. Acad. Engring. Office: Dept Mech Engring Stanford U Stanford CA 94305 *Since I was young, I have been intrigued with increasing understanding of physical nature and human sociotechnical systems particularly where the results are important in real life matters. It is this combination of interests that led me to a career in engineering research, and later, to extend my interest to explicity study of the interaction of technology with individual humans, social systems and ecologies.*

KLINEFELTER, JAMES LOUIS, lawyer: b. Los Angeles, Oct. 8, 1925; s. Theron Albert and Anna Marie (Coffey) K.; m. Joanne Wright, Dec. 26, 1957 (div.); children—Patricia Anne, Jeanne Marie, Christopher Wright; m. Mary Lynn S. Klinefelter, Aug. 19, 1971; 1 dau., Mary Katherine. B.A., U. Ala., 1949, LL.B., 1951. Bar: Ala. bar 1951. Regional claims rep. State Farm Mut. Auto Ins. Co., Anniston, Ala., 1951-54; partner firm Burnham, Klinefelter, Halsey & Love, Anniston, 1954—; Dir. So. Plating and Mfg. Co., Citibanc of Ala., Anniston.; Mem. adv. com. Supreme Ct. Ala. Mem., chmn. Ala. and Calhoun County Democratic Exec. Com., 1964—. Served to lt. (j.g.) USNR, 1943-46. Mem. Am., Ala., Calhoun County bar assns., Phi Kappa Sigma, Phi Alpha Theta. Clubs: Kiwanis (past pres.), Anniston Country (Anniston)). Home: 1412 Christine Ave Anniston AL 36201 Office: First Nat Bank Bldg P O Box 1618 Anniston AL 36202 *When obligations or obnoxious tasks are accepted gratefully as opportunities, one's life can be turned about, and bitterness and resentment changed into joyful satisfaction. Hard tasks are the food of growth.*

KLING, MERLE, political scientist, univ. ofcl.; b. Russia, June 15, 1919; came to U.S., 1921, naturalized, 1927; s. Saul and Dina (Hoffman) K.; m. Sandra Perlman, Aug. 26, 1978; 1 son, Arnold Saul. A.B., Washington U., St. Louis, 1940, M.A., 1941, Ph.D., 1949. Mem. faculty Washington U., 1946—, asst. prof. polit. sci., 1950-54, asso. prof., 1954-61, prof., 1961—, dean, 1966-69, 73-76, provost, 1976—, acting chmn. dept. polit. sci., 1970-71; vis. prof. U. Ill., 1961; research asso. Center Internat. Studies, Princeton U., 1964-65. Author: The Soviet Theory of Internationalism, 1952, A Mexican Interest Group in Action, 1961; contbr. articles to profl. jours. Served with AUS, 1942-45. Mem. Am. Polit. Sci. Assn. (council 1967-69), Midwest Polit. Sci. Assn. (editor jour. 1965-66, pres. 1969-70), Phi Beta Kappa, Alpha Kappa Delta, Omicron Delta Kappa. Home: 20 N Kingshighway Saint Louis MO 63108 Office: Box 1080 Washington U Lindell and Skinker Sts Saint Louis MO 63130

KLING, WILLIAM, consultant, retired foreign service officer; b. N.Y.C., May 8, 1915; s. Irving and Sophie (Kling) K.; m. Suzanne Kaufman (M.D.), June 28, 1940; children: Robert Irving, Michael Paul, Virginia Airini Susan. B.S., CCNY, 1937; M.S., Mass. State Coll., 1938; Ph.D., Clark U., 1943. Grad. asst. Mass. State Coll., 1937-38, Clark U., 1938-39; instr. Coll. City N.Y., 1939-40; agrl. economist Dept. Agr., also War Food Adminstrn., 1940-45; agrl. attache, Bucharest, Rumania, Budapest, Hungary, Belgrade, Yugoslavia, Sofia, Bulgeria, Tirana, Albania, 1945-47; first sec., consul Am. embassy, London, 1948-54, 1st sec., consul, Wellington, New Zealand, 1954-60; assigned Dept. of State, Washington, 1960-68, chief div. of functional intelligence, 1961-63, dep. dir. and acting dir. Office of Functional and External Research, 1962-63, econ. adviser to asst sec. for African Affairs, 1963-66, dep. dir. econ. affairs Office Inter African Affairs, 1966-68; dir. govt. affairs Uniroyal, Inc., Washington, 1968-73; Washington rep. Am. Soybean Assn., 1973-79; prin. William Kling Assos. (consultants), Falls Church, Va., 1979—; cons. Japanese Fedn. Agrl. Coop. Assns., 1979; dir. econs. and div. Distilled Spirits Council U.S., Inc., Washington, 1979—; Mem. Nat. Def. Exec. Res., 1970—; cons. to Office Emergency Preparedness, Exec. Office of Pres., 1970—, GSA, 1973—; mem. export policy task force U.S. C. of C., 1978-79, mem. multilateral trade negotiation task force and chmn. agr. subgroup, 1978-79. Contbr. to profl. jours.; Editor: DISCUS UPC News. Recipient Meritorious Honor award State Dept., 1968. Mem. Am. Fgn. Service Assn., Soc. Internat. Devel., Soc. Govt. Economists., Diplomatic and Consular Officers Ret. Clubs: Nat. Economists, Internat. Economists. Home: 6434 Lakeview Dr Lake Barcroft Falls Church VA 22041 Office: 425 13th St NW Suite 1132 Washington DC 20004

KLING, WILLIAM HUGH, broadcasting executive; b. St. Paul, Apr. 29, 1942; s. William Conrad and Helen A. (Leonard) K.; m. Sarah Margaret Baldwin, Sept. 25, 1976. B.A. in Economics, St. John's U., 1964; postgrad., Boston U., 1964-66. Dir. broadcasting St. John's U., Collegeville, Minn., 1966-70; asst. dir. radio activities Corp. Pub. Broadcasting, Washington, 1970-72; pres. Minn. Pub. Radio, Inc., St. Paul, 1972—; founding dir. Nat. Pub. Radio, 1968-70, dir., 1977—; chmn. bd. Assn. Pub. Radio Stas., 1973-77; founding chmn. bd. dirs. Am. Pub. Radio, 1982, pres., 1983; mem. Temporary Commn. on Alt. Financing for Pub. Broadcasting. Recipient Edward R. Murrow award, 1981. Club: Minnesota. Office: 45 E 8th St Saint Paul MN 55101

KLINGBERG, WILLIAM GENE, pediatrician; b. Wichita, Kans., Sept. 17, 1916; s. Harry R. and Ethel (Martin) K.; m. Barbara Jean Hendrickson, June 18, 1941; children: William Gene, Judith Jean, Susan Jane, John David. A.B., Municiple U. of Wichita, 1938; M.D., Washington U., 1943. Diplomate: Am. Bd. Pediatrics. Intern St. Louis Children's Hosp., 1943, resident, 1944-46; asst. prof. to assoc. prof. Washington U. Sch. Medicine, St. Louis, 1947-60; prof. pediatrics W.Va. U., Morgantown, 1960—, chmn. dept. pediatrics, 1960-82; vis. prof. Ankara U., (Turkey), 1957-58. Chmn., campus ministry Westminster Found., Inc., Morgantown, 1973—. Served to capt. M.C. U.S. Army, 1945-47. Named Outstanding Tchr. W.Va. U., 1976, Disting. West Virginian State of W.Va., 1982. Fellow Am. Acad. Pediatrics; mem. Am. Hematology Soc., Va. Med. Assn., AMA, Alpha Omega Alpha. Presbyterian. Home: 636 Bellaire Dr Morgantown WV 26505 Office: Dept Pediatrics W Va U Morgantown WV 26506

KLINGES, DAVID HENRY, shipbuilding company executive; b. Wilkes-Barre, Pa., July 22, 1928; s. David Jerome and Aida Edythe (DiGuisto) K.; m. Jean Lennox Reeve, Mar. 6, 1954; children: Katherine Reeve, David Henry, Peter Christian, John Hamilton. A.B. in Govt, Franklin and Marshall Coll., 1950; LL.B., Yale U., 1953. Assoc. firm Haight, Gardner, Poor & Havens, N.Y.C., 1956-61; with Bethlehem Steel Corp. (and Subsidiaries), N.Y.C., 1961—, gen. mgr. sales shipbldg., Bethlehem, Pa., 1972-75, asst. v.p., 1975-78, v.p., 1978—. Mem. alumni council Franklin and Marshall Coll., 1963-67; mem. alumni bd. Yale U., 1953—; trustee Webb Inst. Naval Architecture, 1979—, Franklin & Marshall Coll., 1982—. Served with USN, 1953-56. Mem. Am. Bar Assn., Am. Bur. Shipping, Lloyd's Register of Shipping, Am. Iron and Steel Inst., Marine Index Bur., Maritime Law Assn., Pa. Soc., Navy League U.S., Propeller Club of U.S., Soc. Naval Architects and Marine Engrs., Shipbuilders Council Am. (chmn. bd. 1983—), Transp. Inst. Republican. Roman Catholic. Club: Saucon Valley Country. Home: Route 4 Saucon Valley Rd Bethlehem PA 18015 Office: Martin Tower Bethlehem PA 18016

KLINGLER, EUGENE HERMAN, cons. engr., educator; b. Ft. Wayne, Ind., Sept. 3, 1932; s. Herman and Helen (Gerhardstein) K.; m. Rosemary Racht, Dec. 27, 1954; children—Eugenie Marie, Theodore, Roxane, Sidney Ann, Georgia Kay, Fritz James. B.S., Ind. Inst. Tech., 1953; M.S., N.Mex. State U., 1957; Ph.D., Carnegie Inst. Tech., 1961. Registered profl. engr., Mich., Ind. Eng. Servomechanisms Lab., Wheatfield Plant, Bell Aircraft Corp., Buffalo, 1953-55; mem. faculty N.Mex. State U., 1957; weapons systems analyst Westinghouse Air Arm div., Balt., 1957; instr. Ind. Inst. Tech., Ft. Wayne, 1958, chmn. dept. elec. engring., 1965-69; project engr. dept. elec. engring. Carnegie Inst. Tech., 1957-61; staff engr. inertial equipment lab. Space Tech. Labs., Redondo Beach, Calif., 1961-62; chief electronics engr. spl. products div. Fairchild Camera & Instrument Corp., Los Angeles, 1962; sr. mem. tech. staff, staff to dir. space systems lab. Northrop Space Labs., Hawthorne, Calif., 1962-63; mgr. hide research lab. N.Am. Aviation, Inc., Tulsa, 1963-65; prof., chmn. dept. elec. engring. U. Detroit, 1969-75; tchr. U. So. Calif., 1961-62, U. Tulsa, 1964; pres., chmn. bd. Eugene Klingler, Inc., 1968—. Served with U.S. Army, 1955-57. Ford fellow Carnegie Inst. Tech., 1959-61. Mem. Nat. Soc. Profl. Engrs., IEEE (group chmn., bd. dirs. Mich.), Engring. Soc. Detroit, Sigma Xi, Tau Beta Pi, Sigma Pi Sigma, Eta Kappa Nu. Patentee and numerous publs. in field. Home: 5045 Charing Cross Rd Bloomfield Hills MI 48013

KLINGMAN, DARWIN DEE, business and computer science educator, consultant; b. Dickinson, N.D., Feb. 5, 1944; s. Virgil Wayne and Ethel Lara (Forester) K.; m. Brenda Mabel Sargent, Aug. 29, 1964 (div. Mar. 1974). B.A. in Math., Wash. State U., 1966, M.A., 1967; Ph.D. interdisciplinary, U. Tex., 1969. Asst. prof. bus. and computer sci. U. Tex., Austin, 1969-71, assoc. prof., 1972-75, prof., 1976—; dir. Ctr. Bus. Decision Analysis U. Tex, Austin, 1982—; Bruton Centennial prof. U. Tex., Austin, 1983—; vis. prof. computer sci. Free U., Berlin, 1975; vis. prof. math. Wash. State U., Pullman, 1977. Contbr. numerous articles to profl. jours., 1969-82; editor Network Models and Associated Applications, 1982. Recipient Outstanding Grad. Tchr. award U. Tex., 1983, Outstanding Research award Golden Key Nat. Honor Soc., 1983; Alexander von Humboldt fellow, Bonn, W. Ger., 1974. Mem. Inst. Mgmt. Sci. (v.p. at large 1981-82), Math. Assn. Am. (1977-81), Assn. Computing Machinery, Math. Programming Soc. (charter), Ops. Research Soc. Am., Naval Research Logistics Quar. Soc. Office: Analysis Research and Computation U Tex 3701 N Lamar Suite 201 Austin TX 78765

KLINGSBERG, DAVID, lawyer; b. N.Y.C., Feb. 4, 1934; s. Samuel S. and Dorothy (Wecker) K.; m. Fran Sue Morganstern, Aug. 16, 1959; children—Ethan, Jordan, Matthew. LL.B., Yale U., 1957; B.S., N.Y. U., 1954. Bar: N.Y. bar 1957. Law clk. to U.S. Dist. Judge, N.Y., 1957-58; atty. U.S. Dept. Justice, Office Dep. Atty. Gen., Washington, 1958-59; asst. U.S. atty. criminal div. So. Dist. N.Y., 1959-61; chief appellate atty. U.S. Atty. Office, N.Y., 1961-62; asso. firm Kaye, Scholer, Fierman, Hays and Handler, N.Y.C., 1962-65, partner, 1966—; trial practice faculty, continuing legal edn. program Columbia Law Sch., 1977—. Contbg. author: White Collar Crime, 1980; contbr. articles to legal jours.; editorial bd.: Yale Law Jour, 1956-57. Trustee Beth El Synagogue, New Rochelle, N.Y. Fellow Am. Coll. Trial Lawyers; mem. Am. Bar Assn., Assn. of Bar of N.Y.C., N.Y. State Bar Assn., Fed. Bar Council. Office: 425 Park Ave New York NY 10022

KLINK, FREDRIC J., lawyer; b. N.Y.C., Oct. 4, 1933; s. Frederick Carl and Sophia Adelaide (Wolf) K.; m. Sandra Scott Morehouse, 1979; children—Christopher, Charles. A.B., Columbia U., 1955, LL.B., 1960. Bar: N.Y. 1960. Practiced in, N.Y.C.; ptnr. firm Schwartz Klink & Schreiber and predecessor, 1978—. Editor: Columbia U. Law Rev, 1959-60. Served as lt. (j.g.) USNR, 1955-57. Mem. Am. Law Inst., Am., N.Y. C. bar assns. Home: Pond Hill Wilson Point Norwalk CT 06854 Office: 666 3d Ave New York NY 10017

KLINMAN, NORMAN RALPH, immunologist; b. Phila., Mar. 23, 1937; s. William and Miriam (Ralph) K.; m. Linda A. Sherman, June 18, 1978; children—Andrew, Douglas. A.B., Haverford (Pa.) Coll., 1958; M.D., Jefferson Med. Coll., Phila., 1962; Ph.D. (Helen Hay Whitney Found. research fellow 1963-66), U. Pa., 1965. Fellow in immunology U. Pa. Med. Sch., 1962-66, Weizman Inst., Tel Aviv, 1966-67, Nat. Inst. Med. Research, London, 1967-68; mem. faculty U. Pa. Med. Sch., 1968-78, prof. pathology, 1975-78; mem. dept. immunopathology Scripps Clinic and Research Found., La Jolla, Calif., 1978—; adj. prof. U. Calif., San Diego; cons. NIH, 1975-78. Author articles in field, chpts. in books; asso. editor: Jour. Immunology, 1972-76, Immunochemistry, 1970-74; adv. editor: Jour. Exptl. Medicine; editor: B Lymphocytes in the Immune Response. Am. Cancer Soc. research scholar, 1966-68; recipient USPHS Career Devel. award, 1970-75, Parke-Davis award, 1976. Mem. Am. Assn. Immunologists, Am. Assn. Exptl. Pathologists. Home: 5811 Box Canyon Rd La Jolla CA 92037 Office: 10666 N Torrey Pines Rd La Jolla CA 92037

KLINTWORTH, GORDON KENNETH, pathologist, educator; b. Fort Victoria, Rhodesia, Aug. 4, 1932; came to U.S., 1962, naturalized, 1967; s. John George and Iveagh Irene (Gordon) K.; m. Felicity Helen Tait, Dec. 14, 1957; children: Susan, John, Sandra. B.Sc., U. Witwatersrand, South Africa, 1954, M.B., B.Ch., 1957, B.Sc. with honors, 1961, Ph.D., 1966. Diplomate: Am. Bd. Pathology. Intern, resident Johannesburg (S. Africa) Gen. Hosp.; faculty Duke U., 1964—, prof. pathology, 1973—, prof. ophthalmology, 1981—; vis. prof. U. London Inst. Ophthalmology, 1970, Victor Kark scholar, 1961-62. Author: (with B.F. Fetter, W.S. Hendry) Mycoses of the Central Nervous System, 1967, (with M.B. Landers, III) The Eye: Structure and Function in Disease; editor: (with A. Garner) Pathobiology of Ocular Disease: A Dynamic Approach; contbr. articles to med. jours. USPHS fellow, 1962-64; Louis B. Mayer scholar, 1972-73; Recipient Research Career Devel. award Nat. Eye Inst., 1971-76. Mem. Am. Assn. Pathologists, Internat. Soc. Neuropathologists, N.Y. Acad. Sci., Internat. Acad. Pathology, Am. Assn. Neuropathologists, AAAS, Verhoeff Soc., Assn. Research in Vision and Ophthalmology, Tissue Culture Assn., Am. Assn. Ophthal. Pathology, Eastern Ophthalmic Pathology Soc., Nat. Geog. Soc., Sigma Xi. Home: 2718 Spencer St Durham NC 27706

KLION, STANLEY RING, management consultant; b. N.Y.C., May 9, 1923; s. Samuel M. and Henrietta (Ring) K.; m. Janet Tucker, Dec. 16, 1951; children: Catherine B., Emily J., Jenny T. A.B., Rutgers U., 1942. C.P.A., N.Y. State, D.C. With Peat, Marwick, Mitchell & Co., 1955—, ptnr., Phila., Boston and N.Y.C., 1960-75, vice chmn. mgmt. cons. dept., dir., N.Y.C., 1975-81; exec. vice chmn. Peat Marwick Internat., 1981—; exec. v.p., dir. IRC Inc., Phila., 1967-68; mem. audit adv. com. to sec. Navy, Washington, 1972-75; adj. prof. mgmt. Grad. Sch. Bus., N.Y. U., 1978-81. Pres. Citizens Council on City Planning, Phila., 1965-67; mem. Wilson Council, Washington, 1981—. Served as maj. U.S. Army, 1942-46. Mem. Am. Inst. C.P.A.'s (council 1979-80, chmn. MAS exec. com. 1975-78), N.Y. State Soc. C.P.A.'s, AAAS, Phi Beta Kappa. Republican. Jewish. Clubs: Economic, Sunningdale Country, Harmonie, Board Room (N.Y.C.). Home: 25 Bailiwick Rd Greenwich CT 06830 Office: 345 Park Ave New York NY 10154

KLIPPER, STUART DAVID, artist; b. Bronx, N.Y., Aug. 27, 1941; s. George J. and Raye S. K. B.A., U. Mich., 1962. Instr. photography Mpls. Coll. Art and Design, 1970, 72, 74, Blake Sch., Mpls., 1975-76; instr. photography studio arts dept. U. Minn., Mpls., 1974, asst. prof., summer 1975; vis. artist Colo. Coll., 1978-80; guest curator Macalaster Coll. Gallery, 1978; cons. in field, guest lectr. art centers, vis. artist art schs. and colls. Contbr. photographs mags., books.; one-man photog. exbhns. include, Mpls. Inst. Arts, 1964-70, JCC Gallery, Mpls., Suzanne Kohn Gallery, St. Paul, 1972-74, Peter M. David Gallery, Mpls., 1975-77, Walker Art Center, Mpls., 1978, Minn. Mus. Art, 1980, Land Mark Center, St. Paul, Chgo. Art Inst., group exhbns. include, Nelson-Atkins Gallery, Kansas City, Mo., 1974, Mpls. Inst. Arts, 1975, 76, 78, Minn. Mus. Art, 1976, John Michael Kohler Art Center, Sheboygan, Wis., 1978, Art Inst. Chgo., 1980, George Eastman House, 1981, Walker Art Center, 1974, 81; rep. permanent collections, Mus. Modern Art, N.Y.C., Mpls. Inst. Arts, Minn. Mus. Art, U. Minn. Gallery, Walker Art Center, Art Inst. Chgo., Exchange Nat. Bank, Chgo., David and Reva Logan Found. collection, Chgo., U. Kans. Mus. Art, Chase Manhattan Art Program, Fermi Nat. Accelerator Lab. Fellow Guggenheim Found., 1979, Nat. Endowment Arts, 1979; grantee Minn. Arts Bd., 1973, 75, NEA, 1977; visual arts fellow Bush Found., 1980. Address: 614 W 27th St Minneapolis MN 55408

KLIPPSTATTER, KURT L., conductor, music dir.; b. Graz, Austria, Dec. 17, 1934; s. Karl and Karoline K.; m. Mignon Dunn, July 22, 1972. Guest faculty mem. Memphis State U., 1973-76; dir. orchestral activities Hartford (Conn.) Coll. Music, 1977—. Condr., music coach numerous theatres, orchs., Austria, West Germany, 1954-72; artistic dir., Memphis Opera Theatre, 1973-76; music dir., Ark. Symphony, Little Rock, 1973-80; Music columnist: Ark. Democrat, 1979—. Mem. Central Opera Service, Am. Symphony Orch. League.

KLIR, GEORGE JIRI, systems science educator; b. Prague, Czechoslovakia, Apr. 22, 1932; came to U.S., 1966, naturalized, 1972; s. Jan and Emilie (Pritasilova) K.; m. Milena Reholova, Jan. 26, 1962; children: Jane, John. M.S.E.E., Czech Inst. Tech., Prague, 1957; Ph.D., Czechoslovak Acad. Scis., Prague, 1964. Research fellow Inst. Computer Research, Prague, 1960-64; lectr. U. Baghdad, Iraq, 1964-66, UCLA, 1966-68; assoc. prof. Fairleigh Dickinson U., 1968-69, Sch. Advanced Tech., SUNY, Binghamton, 1969-72, prof. systems sci., 1972—, chmn. dept. systems sci., 1977—; dir. Internat. Conf. Gen. Systems Research, 1977. Author: Cybernetic Modelling, 1967, An Approach to General Systems Theory, 1969, Methodology of Switching Circuits, 1972; author, co-author or editor 10 other books; contbr. numerous articles to profl. jours.; editor-in-chief: Book Series on Basic and Applied General Systems Research, 1978-82; Book Series on Frontiers in Systems Science: Implications for the Social Sciences, 1978-84; Internat. Jour. Gen. Systems, 1974—; editorial bds. other profl. jours. Recipient award for outstanding contbns. Austrian Soc. Cybernetics, 1976, Netherland Soc. Systems Research, 1976; IBM research fellow, 1969; Netherlands Inst. Advanced Studies fellow, 1975-76, 82-83; Japan Soc. for Promotion of Sci. fellow, 1980. Mem. IEEE, AAUP, Philosophy of Sci. Assn., Assn. Computing Machinery, Soc. Gen. Systems Research (mng. dir., v.p. 1978-80), Gen. Systems Research (pres. 1980-81), Internat. Fedn. for Systems Research (pres. 1980-83). Home: 916 Murray Hill Rd Binghamton NY 13903 Office: Thomas J Watson Sch Engring Applied Sci and Tech SUNY Binghamton NY 13901 *The main force behind my intellectual development has been my passion for discovery and integration in science and technology. The most precious values in professional life are for me scientific honesty and tolerance.*

KLITGAARD, GEORGINA, artist; b. N.Y.C., July 3, 1893; d. John Austen and Georgina (Berrian) Berrain; m. Kaj. Klitgaard, 1919; children—Peter, Wallace. B.A., Barnard Coll., 1912. Gave first one-man exhbn. of paintings, N.Y.C., 1927, Concoran Gallery, Washington, 1941, Rehn Galleries, 6 shows, 1930—, St. Gaudens Meml., 1948, St. Gaudens Meml., Woodstock, N.Y., 1955, 64; prin. works: exhbt. View of Kingston, Pitts. Internat., Chgo., San Francisco and N.Y. world's fairs, Corcoran Gallery, Washington, murals for, Goshen, N.Y., Poughkeepsie, N.Y. and, Pelham, Ga.; represented in, Met. Mus. Art, Whitney Mus. Am. Art, Newark Mus., Dayton Art Inst., New Brit. Art Inst., Bklyn. Mus. Recipient awards Carnegie Internat. Exhbn., Pa. Acad., Art Inst. Chgo., Pan Am. Exhbn., San Francisco, others.; Fellow Huntington Hartford Found., 1965-65, Guggenheim Found.; Helene Wurlitzer Found. N.M. grantee, 1967-69. Mem. Am. Soc. Painters, Sculptors and Engravers, Audubon Artists, Am. Recorders Soc. Address: Rehn Galleries 655 Madison Ave New York NY 10021 *

KLITZKE, THEODORE ELMER, arts consultant, former college dean; b. Chgo., Nov. 4, 1915; s. John Frederick and Edith (Bachman) K.; m. Margaret Bridget Gaughan, Feb. 23, 1946; children: Annetta, Margaret. B.F.A., Chgo. Art Inst., 1940; B.A., U. Chgo., 1941, Ph.D., 1953; D.F.A. (hon.), Kansas City Art Inst., 1980, Md. Inst., Coll. Art, 1982. Instr. art history U. Chgo., 1946-47; edn. adviser U.S. Armed Forces in Germany, Nurnberg, 1948-51; asst. prof. art history N.Y. State Coll. Ceramics, SUNY, Alfred, 1953-59; prof. art history, chmn. dept. U. Ala., 1959-68; v.p. acad. affairs, dean Md. Inst., Coll. Art, 1968-82, dean emeritus, 1982—, acting pres., 1977-78; mem. accessions com. Balt. Mus. Art, 1979-82. Contbr. articles to profl. jours. Bd. dirs. Ala. chpt. ACLU, 1965-68; bd. dirs. S.W. Ala. Self-Help Housing, 1966-68. Served with AUS, 1942-46. Recipient First Annual Peace and Freedom award Democratic Student Orgn., U. Ala., 1968; citation Civil Liberties Union Ala. Mem. Southeastern Coll. Art Conf. (pres. 1961-62), AAUP, Coll. Art Assn., Nat. Assn. Schs. Art (dir. 1971-74, mem. commn. on accreditation 1975-78, treas. 1980-82, fellow 1981), Print and Drawing Soc. of Balt. Mus. Art (pres. 1974-76), Union Ind. Colls. Art (chmn. planning com. 1977-80). Home: 7918 Sherwood Ave Baltimore MD 21204

KLOCK, JOSEPH PETER, JR., lawyer; b. Phila., Mar. 14, 1949; s. Joseph Peter and Mary Dorothy (Fornace) K.; m. Susan Marie Girsch, Mar. 17, 1979; children: 1 dau., Susan Elizabeth. B.A., LaSalle Coll., 1970; J.D., U. Miami, Fla., 1973. Bar: Fla. 1973, Pa. 1973, D.C. 1978. Ptnr. Steel, Hector & Davis, Miami, Fla., 1977—; adj. prof. U. Miami Law Sch., 1974—. Bd. dirs. YMCA Camp Fla., 1974-79; trustee The Carrollton Sch. Mem. ABA, Fla. Bar (chmn. civil procedure rules com. 1979—), Pa. Bar Assn., D.C. Bar Assn., Dade County Bar Assn., Monroe County Bar Assn., Palm Beach County Bar Assn., Bar Assn. City N.Y., Am. Law Inst., Iron Arrow Soc., Phi Alpha Delta, Phi Kappa Phi, Omicron Delta Kappa. Democrat. Roman Catholic. Clubs: Surf; Bath (Miami Beach, Fla.). Home: 1237 S Alhambra Circle Coral Gables FL 33146 Office: Steel Hector & Davis 4000 Southeast Fin Center Miami FL 33131

KLOMBERS, NORMAN, podiatrist, association executive; b. N.Y.C., Jan. 28, 1923; s. Moe and Lillian K.; m. Gloria Evelyn Piatek, Jan. 16, 1955; children: Lee Alan, Robin Sheri. Grad., Coll. Arts and Scis., L.I. U., 1942; D.P.M. cum laude, N.Y. Coll. Podiatric Medicine, 1944. Diplomate: Am. Bd. Podiatric Orthopedics. Practice podiatric medicine, N.Y.C., 1944-68; dir. profl. services Podiatry Soc. N.Y., 1968-78; dir. dept. sci. affairs Am. Podiatry Assn., Washington, 1978-80, exec. dir., 1980—; faculty N.Y. Coll. Podiatric Medicine, 1944-78. Fellow Am. Coll. Foot Orthopedists. Office: 20 Chevy Chase Circle NW Washington DC 20015

KLONGLAN, GERALD EDWARD, sociology educator; b. Nevada, Iowa, Apr. 1, 1936; s. Bernie R. and Willene Rebecca (Maland) K.; m. Donna Eileen Becvar, June 29, 1960; children: Jason, Suzanne. B.S., Iowa State U., 1958, M.S., 1962, Ph.D., 1963. Mem. faculty Iowa State U., Ames, 1963—, prof. sociology, 1972—, chmn. dept. sociology and anthropology, 1976—; evaluation researcher AID, Malawi, 1967, project cons., Ghana, 1976; ednl. cons. Kind Saud U., Saudi Arabia, 1981-83; project implementor U. Zambi, Lusaka, 1982-83. Author: Social Indicators, 1972; (research monographs) Adoption Diffusion of Ideas, 1967; Creating Interorganizational Coordination, 1975, Communication Policy, 1983. Vol. scientist Am. Cancer Soc., 1969—; bd. dirs. Luth. Campus Ministry, Ames, 1972-78, chmn. bd., Ames, 1974-76. Recipient Wilton Park award Iowa State U., 1983. Mem. Rural Sociol. Soc. (council 1974-76, v.p. 1977-78), Midwest Sociol. Soc. (tng. com. 1975-78), Sigma Xi (pres. Iowa State U. chpt. 1983-84). Home: 1622 Maxwell Ave Ames IA 50010 Office: Dept Sociology and Anthropology 103 East Hall Iowa State U Ames IA 50011

KLONIS, STEWART, artist, retired educator; b. Naughatuck, Conn., Dec. 24, 1901; s. Michael and Constance (Wren) K.; m. Charlotte O. Leal, June 26, 1931 (div. 1959); m. Laura Palumbo, Oct. 1959; 1 dau., Laura Maddalena. Student, N.Y. U., 1924-26, Art Students League N.Y., 1927-31. Mem. of Artists Aid Com., 1932-36; acting treas. Artists Coop. Market, 1933; mem. bd. control Art Students League N.Y., 1934, treas., 1935-36, pres., 1937-45, exec. dir., 1946-80, hon. mem., 1952—; v.p. Am. Fine Art Soc. N.Y., 1939-41, pres., 1941-82, ret., 1982; trustee Edward MacDowell Traveling Scholarship Fund, 1934-45; instr. Queens Coll., 1940-45; dir. at large Artists Equity Assn., 1952—; mem. advisory council N.Y.C. Center Gallery, 1954—, chmn., 1954; mem. arts com. Fulbright Awards, 1949-57, chmn., 1953-55, 57; mem. advisory com. for arts Inst. Internat. Edn., 1961—. Bd. dirs. MacDowell Colony, 1970-79; trustee Nat. Arts Mus. of Sports, 1963—. Recipient Gari Melchers award Artists Fellowships, Inc., 1975; gold medal of honor Nat. Arts Club Art Student League N.Y., 1977; citation for outstanding contbn. to art edn. in U.S. Artists Equity of N.Y., 1977. Benjamin Franklin fellow Royal Soc. Arts (hon. corr. mem. for N.Y. State 1975-78, hon. sr. corr. mem. for U.S. 1979—); mem. Mcpl. Art Soc., Nat. Acad. Design (assoc.). Democrat. Club: Century Association. Home: 19 Upper Commons Woodbury CT 06798 *My life has been devoted to providing an opportunity to develop young and gifted individuals in the visual fine arts, on whom depends the future for cultural development.*

KLONOFF, HARRY, psychologist; b. Winnipeg, Man., Can., July 29, 1924; s. Abraham and Ida (Aronovitch) K.; m. Mary Plosker, Aug. 16, 1948; children: Hillary, Pamela, Melanie. B.A., U. Man., 1949; M.A., U. Toronto, 1951; Ph.D. (research fellow), U. Wash., 1954. Head dept. psychology Shaughnessy Vets. Hosp., Vancouver, B.C., Can., 1955-61, Shaughnessy Hosp., 1961-77; head div. psychology dept. psychiatry U. B.C., Vancouver, 1961-82, prof., 1970—; head dept. psychology Health Scis. Centre Hosp., 1981-82; head sect. psychology Vancouver Gen. Hosp., 1970-78. Contbr. articles on psychology and psychiatry to sci. publs., chpts. in books. Served with AUS, 1944-46. Nat. Health Med. Research Council grantee, 1968—. Mem. Am. Psychol. Assn., Can. Psychol. Assn., Western Psychol. Assn., B.C. Psychol. Assn. (pres. 1957-58), AAAS, Internat. Neuropsychology Soc., Gerontol. Soc., Assn. Am. Med. Colls., Can. Mental Health Assn. Home: 1415 W 39th Ave Vancouver BC Canada V6M 1I2 Office: 7-2255 Westbrook Mall University of British Columbia Vancouver BC Canada V6T 2A1

KLOOSTER, JUDSON, university dean, dentist; b. La Combe, Alta., Can., Dec. 24, 1925; s. Henry J. and Evelyn Mae (Eglin) K.; m. Arlene Jean Madsen, Nov. 28, 1948; children: Cherylin Klooster Peach, Lynette Carol, Terrill Ann Klooster McClanahan. Student, Andrews U., Berrien Springs, Mich., 1942-43, Pacific Union Coll., Angwin, Calif., 1943-44; D.D.S., U. Pacific, San Francisco, 1947; M.M.S., Tulane U., 1968. Pvt. practice dentistry, San Francisco, 1947-49, Escondido, Calif., 1949-67; mem. faculty U. Pacific Sch. Dentistry, 1947-49; part-time mem. faculty Loma Linda U. Sch. Dentistry, 1956-67, prof. restorative dentistry, 1967—, dir. continuing edn., 1968-72, dean, 1971—; cons. USPHS, VA. Author chpt. in book. Served to lt. Dental Corps, USNR, 1953-55. Fellow Am., Internat. (dist. regent) colls. dentists; mem. ADA, Calif. Dental Assn. (chmn. council dental edn. 1972-75), Tri-County Dental Soc. (ex officio dir. 1971—, pres. elect 1978-79, pres. 1979-80), Xi Psi Phi. Republican. Mem. Seventh-day Adventist Ch. (elder 1969—). Club: Rotarian (pres. San Bernardino South club 1977-78). Home: 25131 Crestview Dr Loma Linda CA 92354 Office: Dean's Office Loma Linda U Sch Dentistry Loma Linda CA 92350

KLOPFENSTEIN, PHILIP ARTHUR, financial development officer, historical researcher; b. Lake Odessa, Mich., Apr. 28, 1937; s. Glendull Carl and Bernice (Shumway) K.; m. Anna Jo Davis, Aug. 24, 1960. B.A., Mich. State U., 1961; M.A., Western Mich. U., 1964; arts adminstrn. cert., Harvard U., 1970. Cert. tchr., Mich. Faculty mem. U. Ark., Little Rock, 1965-68; tchr. Ark. Ednl. TV, Conway, 1969-70; dir. Southeast Ark. Arts and Scis. Ctr., Pine Bluff, 1970-76, Augusta Richmond County Mus., (Ga.), 1977-79, Montgomery Mus. Fine Arts, (Ala.), 1979-82; v.p., devel. officer Found. Hist. Research and Reclamation, Montgomery, Ala., 1982—; mgmt. cons. Endright Services, Inc., 1983—. Served with U.S. Army, 1957-59. USIA grantee, 1980. Mem. Am. Assn. Mus., Assn. Art Mus. Dirs., Ala. Mus. Assn., Southeastern Mus. Conf., Ark. Mus. Assn. (pres. 1976-77). Lodge: Rotary Internat., Montgomery, Ala. (newsletter editor 1981-82). Home: 2155 Kingsbury Dr Montgomery AL 36106 Office: Found Hist Research and Reclamation Inc PO Box 11578 Montgomery AL 36111

KLOPMAN, WILLIAM ALLEN, manufacturing executive; b. 1921; married. Grad., Williams Coll. With Burlington Industries, Inc., 1946—; pres. Klopman Mills div., 1963-71, group v.p. parent co., Greensboro, N.C., 1971-72, exec. v.p., 1972-74, pres., mem. exec. fin. com. and mgmt. policy com., 1974-76, pres., 1976-78, chmn. bd., chief exec. officer, 1976—, also dir. Served with USNR, 1942-45. Office: Burlington Industries Inc PO Box 21207 Greensboro NC 27420

KLOPP, RICHARD PACKARD, engineering company executive; b. Reading, Pa., Mar. 11, 1921; s. Adam V. and Dorothy (Packard) K.; m. Louise Henry, Jan. 6, 1945; children: Deborah A., John R. B.S. in Chem. Engring, Cornell U., 1943. Registered profl. engr., Fla., La., Pa. Chem. engr. The Tex. Co., Lawrenceville, Ill. and Westville, N.J., 1946-52; with Catalytic, Inc., Phila., 1952—, now chmn. bd., chief exec. officer.; dir. First Pa. Bank, First Pa. Corp., UMI Group, Inc., Mut. Fire, Marine and Inland Ins. Co. Trustee Drexel U.; co-chmn. Phila. Area Labor Mgmt. Com.; chmn. Jr. Achievement Delaware Valley; bd. mgrs. Franklin Inst., Franklin Research Ctr. Served to 1st lt. U.S. Army, 1943-46. Mem. Am. Inst. Chem. Engrs., Am. Petroleum Inst., Greater Phila. C. of C. (exec. com., chmn.), Nat. Soc. Profl. Engrs., World Affairs Council Phila. (dir.). Republican. Clubs: Phila. Country (pres.), Union League, Seaview Country, Sunday Breakfast. Office: Catalytic Inc Centre Sq West 1500 Market St Philadelphia PA 19102

KLOPPENBURG, RALPH H., architect; b. Davenport, Iowa, Nov. 9, 1903; s. Louis and Alvina (Haase) K.; m. Bernyce Schlichting, 1926; children—Jack Ralph, Robert K., Jerry King, Sally (Mrs. David F. Conley). B.Arch., U. Ill., 1926. Instr. U Ill., 1926-28; practice as Ralph Kloppenburg, 1931-59, Kloppenburg & Kloppenburg, Milw., 1959—; Mem. Wis. Registration Bd. Architects and Engrs., 1946-65. Prin. works include schs., Menomonee Falls, Wis., 1948-68, West Bend Mut. Ins. Co, Wis., Milw. Downer Sem, River Hills, 1961, Zoology Research Bldg, U. Wis., Madison, 1961, Badger Meter Mfg. Co, Milw., Phys. Edn. and Bus. Econs. bldgs, Whitewater U., 1966-67, Univ. Sch, Milw., 1970, Germantown (Wis.) Schs, 1969-71, New Berlin (Wis.) Schs, 1969-70, Grafton (Wis.) High Sch, 1971-73, Weyenberg Library, Mequon, Wis., 1971-73, others. Fellow A.I.A. (pres. Wis. chpt. 1945-47). Republican. Episcopalian. Clubs: Rotarian, Milwaukee, University, Milwaukee Country. Home: 708 E Green Tree Rd Milwaukee WI 53217 Office: 5856 Port Washington Rd Milwaukee WI 53217

KLOSKA, RONALD FRANK, financial executive; b. Grand Rapids, Mich., Oct. 24, 1933; s. Frank B. and Catherine (Hilaski) K.; m. Mary F. Minick, Sept. 7, 1957; children—Kathleen Ann, Elizabeth Marie, Ronald Francis, Mary Josephine, Carolyn Louise. Student, St. Joseph Sem., Grand Rapids, Mich., 1947-53; Ph.B., U. Montreal, Que., Can., 1955; M.B.A., U. Mich., 1957. Staff accountant Lybrand Ross Bros. & Montgomery, Niles, Mich., 1957, staff to sr. accountant, 1960-63; treas., v.p. Skyline Corp., Elkhart, Ind., 1963-67, exec. v.p. finance, treas., 1967-74, pres., 1974—, also dir.; dir. Midwest Commerce Banking Co., Elkhart. Mem. adv. bd. Salvation Army, Elkhart.; Bd. dirs. Stanley Clark Sch., South Bend, Ind. Served to 1st lt. AUS, 1957-60. Mem. Am. Inst. C.P.A.s, Mich., Ind. assns. C.P.A.s. Roman Catholic. Club: South Bend Country. Home: 1329 E Woodside St South Bend IN 46614 Office: 2520 By Pass Rd Elkhart IN 46514

KLOSNER, JEROME MARTIN, educator; b. N.Y.C., Mar. 23, 1928; s. Morris and Minnie (Gotchkofsky) K.; m. Naomi Beth Certner, May 31, 1965; children—Michael Robert, Lise Helaine, Marc Alexander. B.C.E., Coll. City N.Y., 1948; M.S., Columbia, 1950; Ph.D., Poly. Inst. Bklyn., 1959. Sr. structures engr. Republic Aviation Corp., Farmingdale, N.Y., 1952-56; sr. scientist Avco Research & Advanced Devel. Div., Wilmington, Mass., 1956, cons., 1956-67; research asso. Poly. Inst. Bklyn., 1956-59, asst. prof., 1959-62, asso. prof., 1962-67, prof. applied mechanics, 1967—; cons. Gen. Applied Sci. Labs., Inc., L.I., N.Y., 1959, FTC, Washington, 1963, Ingersoll-Rand Corp. Research Center, Princeton, N.J., 1966, Technautics Corp., N.Y.C., 1968-69, Weidlinger Assos., 1976—; vis. mem. Courant Inst. Math. Scis., N.Y.U., 1966-67; Mem. Nat. Research council com. on Recommendations for U.S. Army Basic Sci. Research, 1976-79. Reviewer, contbr. articles profl. jours. Fellow Am. Inst. Aeros. and Astronautics (asso.), ASCE; mem. ASME, Soc. Rheology, AAUP, Sigma Xi, Sigma Gamma Tau. Office: 333 Jay St Brooklyn NY 11201

KLOSS, GENE (MRS. PHILLIPS KLOSS, ALICE GENEVA GLASIER), artist; b. Oakland, Calif., July 27, 1903; d. Herbert P. and Carrie (Hefty) Glasier; m. Phillips Kloss, May 19, 1925. A.B., U. Calif., 1924; student, Calif. Sch. Fine Arts, 1924-25. Illustrator: The Great Kiva (Phillips Kloss), 1980; One-man shows, Sandzen Meml. Gallery, Lindsborg, Kans., Albany Inst. History and Art, 1953, Albany Inst. History and Art, Tulsa, Scottsdale, Ariz., Albuquerque, 1956, Findlay Galleries, Chgo., 1957, Mus. N.Mex., 1960, W. Tex. Mus., 1964, Mus. Arts and Scis., Grand Junction, Colo., 1967, Mus. Okla., 1970, Brandywine Galleries, Albuquerque, 1971, Bishop's Gallery, 1972, Gallery A, Taos, N.Mex., 1973, Gallery Graphics, Carmel, Wichita (Kans.) Art Assn., 1974, Pratt Graphic Center, N.Y.C., 1976—, Muckenthaler Cultural Center, Los Angeles, 1980; exhibited in, Three Centuries Art U.S., Paris, 1938; exhibited 3-man show, Pratt Graphic Center, N.Y., 1975; represented in collections, Library Congress, Carnegie Inst., Smithsonian Instn., N.Y. Pub. Library, Met. Mus., Pa. Acad. Fine Arts, Chgo. Art Inst., San Francisco Mus., Honolulu Acad. Fine Arts, Dallas Mus., Mus. N.Mex., Tulsa U., Kans. State Coll., Pa. U. John Taylor Arms Meml., Met. Mus., Peabody Mus., Mus. Tokyo, Auchenback Found. for Graphic Arts, San Francisco, Nat. Gallery, U. N.Mex. Mus., Copley Library, La Jolla, Calif., others; executed 1953 membership prints for, Albany Print Club and for Soc. Am. Graphic Artists, gift plate for, Print Makers of Calif., 1956; exhibited with, Audubon Soc., 1955; etcher, painter in oil, watercolor. Recipient Eyre Gold medal Pa. Acad. Fine Arts, 1936; asso. mem. award Calif. Soc. Etchers, 1934; honorarium Cal. Soc. Etchers, 1940, 41, 44; 3d award oils Oakland Art Gallery Ann., 1939; Purchase prize Chgo. Soc. Etchers, 1940; best black and white Tucson Fine Arts Assn., 1941; 1st prize Print Club, Phila., 1944; Purchase prize Library Congress, 1946; 1st prize prints N.Mex. State Fair, 1946; Ann. Exhibit, Meriden, Conn., 1947; Open award Calif. Soc. Etchers, 1949-51; Henry B. Shope prize Soc. Am. Etchers, 1951; hon. mention, 1953; 1st prize prints Arts and Crafts Assn., Meriden, Conn., 1951, Chgo. Soc. Etchers, 1952; Phila. Sketch Club prize, 1957; Fowler purchase prize Albany Print Club, 1959; purchase prize, 1961; Annoymous prize NAD, 1961. N.A. Mem. NAD, Soc. Am. Graphic Artists, Print Club of Albany, Phila. Water Color Club, MBLS (adv.). Subject of book Gene Kloss Etchings (Phillips Kloss), 1981.

KLOSS, JOHN ANTHONY, fashion designer; b. Detroit, June 13, 1937; s. Frank Joseph and Lillian Joan (Ostrawski) Klosowski. Grad., Traphagen Sch. Fashion, 1958. Designer, pres. studio, Henri Bendel, N.Y.C., 1965-69; owner, John Kloss, Inc., N.Y.C., 1965—; designer, Cira, Lily of France, 1972—, Butterick Fashion Mktg. Co., John Kloss Sportswear, 1977—; exhibited, Met. Mus., Pratt Retrospective, Glamour Hours of Hollywood (Recipient Coty Am. Fashion Critic's award for lingerie 1971, 74, Fashion award for lingerie 1975). Crystal Ball award; Calla award, 1975. Home: 76 Ridge Brook Dr Stamford CT 06903 Sea Ranch Club 5100 N Ocean Blvd Fort Lauderdale FL 33308 Office: SLC Corp 149 Madison Ave New York NY 10016 *As a designer of women's wear, I design with the man in mind. If men like what I do, women will buy it.*

KLOSSON, MICHAEL, foreign service officer; b. Washington, Aug. 22, 1949; s. Boris Hansen and Harriet Fraser (Cheston) K.; m. Ellen Chereskin, June 5, 1976. B.A., Hamilton Coll., 1971; M.P.A., Woodrow Wilson Sch., Princeton U., 1974; M.A., Princeton U., 1975. Asst. lectr. Hong Kong Baptist Coll., 1971-72; commd. fgn. service officer Dept. State, 1975, staff asst. to asst. sec. of state for East Asian affairs, Washington, 1975-77; Chinese Lang. trainee Fgn. Service Inst., Taichung, Taiwan, 1977-78; polit. officer Am. embassy, Taipei, Taiwan, 1978-80; polit. officer office Japanese affairs Dept. State, Washington, 1980-81, spl. asst. to sec. of state, 1981—. Herbert H. Lehman fellow, 1971; Winston Churchill fellow, 1972-74. Mem. Am. Fgn. Service Assn., Phi Beta Kappa. Office: Dept State 2201 C St NW Washington DC 20520

KLOSTER, BURTON JOHN, JR., credit corporation executive, lawyer; b. Hackensack, N.J., Oct. 27, 1931; s. Burton John and Myra C. (Young) K.; m. Hildegrad Sobek, July 6, 1957; children: Doris, John. B.A., Cornell U., 1953, LL.B., 1957. Bar: N.Y. 1958, Ky. 1961. Mem. legal staff Gen. Electric Co., 1957-76; v.p., gen. counsel, sec. Gen. Electric Credit Corp., Stamford, Conn., 1976—. Served to 1st lt. QMC U.S. Army, 1954-56. Mem. ABA, N.Y. State Bar Assn., Ky. Bar Assn. Republican. Congregationalist. Home: 30 Quail Ridge Rd Georgetown CT 06829 Office: Gen Electric Credit Corp 260 Long Ridge Rd Stamford CT 06904

KLOSTER, FRANK ELLIS, cardiologist, educator; b. Forest City, Iowa, Dec. 27, 1929; s. Bert Helmer and Ethel Mae (Brooker) K.; m. Darlene M. Passer, July 21, 1950; children: Peter, Kurt, Mark, Carol, Thomas. B.S., Iowa State U., 1955; M.D., State U. Iowa, 1958. Intern Mountain View Gen. Hosp., Tacoma, Wash., 1958-59; gen. practice medicine, Osage, Iowa, 1959-61; resident in medicine U. Oreg., Portland, 1961-63, fellow in cardiology, 1963-65, instr., 1965-66, asst. prof., 1966-70, assoc. prof., 1970-74, prof., 1974—, dir. cardiology labs., 1968-73, head div. cardiology, 1973—, vice chmn. dept. medicine, 1982—, acting chmn. dept. medicine, 1983—; cons. VA Hosp., Portland; vis. prof. Erasmus U., Rotterdam, Netherlands, 1972-73, U. Göteborg, (Sweden), 1982. Author numerous sci. publs. Mem. med. adv. com. YMCA. Served with USN, 1948-52. Fisher Found. scholar, 1956-57; NIH spl. fellow, 1972-73; recipient Physician Recognition award AMA. Fellow Am. Coll. Cardiology, Council Clin. Cardiology (Am. Heart Assn.); mem. Oreg. Heart Assn. (dir. 1969-72, 79-85, exec. com. 1970-72, 79-81), Am. Fedn. Clin. Research, Western Soc. Clin. Research, Western Assn. Physicians, Assn. Univ. Cardiologists, Soc. Critical Care Medicine, Alpha Omega Alpha. Lutheran. Home: 5608 SW Orchid St Portland OR 97219 Office: 3181 SW Sam Jackson Park Rd Portland OR 97201

KLOSTERMEIER, WALTER R., banker; b. St. Louis, May 14, 1919; s. Henry W. and Edna (Pohlman) K.; m. Mary Stuart Conzelman, Sept. 4, 1948; children: Debra Anne, Robert Stuart. B.S. in edn, Washington U., 1949, certificate in personnel adminstrn, 1951. Asst. to dir. indsl. relations Granite City Steel Co., Ill., 1948-63; v.p., personnel dir. Centerre Bank, St. Louis, 1963-70, sr. v.p., 1971—. Served to lt. USNR, 1941-45. Mem. Asso. Industries Mo. (indsl. relations exec. com.), Am. Soc. Personnel Adminstrn., St. Louis Indsl. Relations Club, Am. Bankers Assn., Phi Delta Theta. Republican. Lutheran. Clubs: Mo. Athletic, Algonquin Golf (St. Louis). Home: 14 Granada Way Saint Louis MO 63124 Office: 510 Locust St Saint Louis MO 63101

KLOTMAN, ROBERT HOWARD, music educator; b. Cleve., Nov. 22, 1918; s. Louis and Pearl (Warshawsky) K.; m. Phyllis Helen Rauch, Apr. 4, 1943; children: Janet Lynn, Paul Evan. B.S. in Music Edn., Ohio No. U., 1940, M.A., Case-Western Res. U., 1950; Ed.D., Columbia U., 1956; D.F.A. (hon.), Ohio No. U., 1984. Supr. music pub. schs., Dola, Ohio, 1940-42, tchr. instrumental, vocal music pub. schs., Euclid, Ohio, 1942, 46, tchr. instrumental music pub. schs., Cleveland Heights, Ohio, 1946-59, dir. music edn. pub. schs., Akron, Ohio, 1959-63, divisional dir. music edn. pub. schs., Detroit, 1963-69; prof., chmn. dept. music edn. Ind. U., Bloomington, 1969—; ednl. dir. firm Scherl & Roth (string importers), Cleve., 1956-70; mem. adv. bd. Contemporary Music Project, Ford Found., 1964-65; ednl. cons. Summy-Birchard Co. (music pubs.); mem. bicentennial com. J. C. Penney Co., 1974-75. Condr., Akron Youth Symphony Orch., 1959-63, Bloomington Youth Symphony Orch., 1969-75; Author: Learning to Teach Through Playing: String Techniques and Pedagogy, 1971, The School Music Administrator and Supervisor: Catalysts for Change in Music Education, 1973, (with others) Humanities Through the Black Experience, Foundations of Music Education, 1983; contbg. author: Ency. of Edn., 1971; editor: Orch. News, 1959-70; editorial bd.: Music Educators Jour., 1962-64, Instrumentalist, 1974—; editor: (with others) Scheduling Music Classes, 1968; editor, contbg. author: Music Performance Trust Funds Guide; composer: Action with Strings, 1962, Renaissance Suite, 1964, String Literature for Expanding Technique, 1973. Bd. dirs., sec. Ind. U. Credit Union, 1974—. Served with inf. AUS, 1942-46; ETO, PTO. Recipient citation Nat. Assn. Negro Musicians Inc., 1966, Black Music Caucas, 1978. Mem. Am. String Tchrs. Assn. (pres. 1962-64), Music Educators Nat. Conf. (chmn. commn. on tchr. edn. 1968-72, pres. 1976-78), Phi Mu Alpha Sinfonia, Phi Delta Kappa. Home: 2740 Spicewood Ln E Bloomington IN 47401 Office: Sch of Music Ind U Bloomington IN 47401

KLOTS, ALLEN TRAFFORD, publishing company executive; b. N.Y.C., Mar. 31, 1921; s. Allen Trafford and Mary (FitzBrown) K. B.A., Yale, 1943. Editor Dodd, Mead & Co., Inc., N.Y.C., 1948-66, sec., exec. editor, 1966-82, sr. editor, 1982—. Chmn. Young Friends of City Center, 1968-72; Bd. dirs. City Center of Music and Drama, 1962-75; co-chmn. 30th anniversary com., 1973-74; bd. dirs. Contemporary Music Soc., 1975-79; bd. dirs., sec. Friends of French Opera, 1978-81. Served to lt. USNR, 1943-46. Clubs: Century, Dutch Treat. Home: 333 E 68th St New York NY 10021 Office: 79 Madison Ave New York NY 10016

KLOTTER, JOHN CHARLES, legal educator; b. Louisville, Nov. 6, 1918; s. John J. and Lillie R. (Fischer) K.; m. Jane Riddle, Nov. 2, 1954 (dec.); children: James C., Douglas A., Ronald L. A.B., Western Ky. U., 1941; J.D., U. Ky., 1948. Bar: Ky. bar 1948, U.S. Supreme Ct. bar 1967. Tchr. pub. schs., Louisville, 1941-42; spl. agt. FBI, 1948-50; legal officer Ky. State Police, 1951-52; dir. div. probation and parole

State of Ky., Frankfort, 1952-56; asso. dir. So. Police Inst., U. Louisville, 1957-71; dir. So. Police Inst., prof., dean, 1971-81; Editorial dir. criminal justice text series W.H. Anderson Co., 1970-76; chmn. Louisville-Jefferson County Criminal Justice Commn., 1974-76; mem. Ky. Crime Commn., 1971-75, Ky. Law Enforcement Council, 1971—, Atty. Gen.'s Prosecutors Adv. Council, 1970—. Author: Techniques for Police Instructors, 1963, (with Kanovitz) Constitutional Law, 1968, 75, 77, 80, Criminal Evidence, 1971, 75, 81, Legal Guide for Police, 1978, Criminal Justice Instructional Techniques, 1979, Legal Aspects of Private Security, 1981, Criminal Law, 1983. Served to capt. U.S. Army, 1942-46. Ford Found. grantee, 1968. Mem. Ky., Louisville bar assns., Res. Officers Assn., Soc. Former Spl. Agts. FBI, Internat. Assn. Chiefs Police. Home: 2103 Starmont Rd Louisville KY 40207 Office: Sch Justice Adminstrn U Louisville Louisville KY 40292

KLOTZ, ARTHUR PAUL, physician, educator; b. Milw., Sept. 28, 1913; s. Paul Oscar and Christine (Kratt) K.; m. Margaret Pollard, Mar. 16, 1941; children: Stephen Arthur, Suzanne Ruth, John Haven, Peter Paul. Student, Marquette U., 1931-33; B.S., U. Chgo., 1938, M.D., 1938. Intern Cin. Gen. Hosp., 1938-39; resident Aspinwall VA Hosp., Pitts., 1946-49; asst. medicine, instr. gastroenterology U. Chgo., 1949-54; chief div. gastroenterology U. Kans. Med. Center, Kansas City, 1954-75, prof. medicine, 1962-75; staff Boswell Meml. Hosp., Sun City, Ariz., 1975—, dir. gastrointestinal lab., 1977—. Editorial bd.: Am. Jour. Digestive Diseases, 1963-67; editor: Boswell Hosp. Proc, 1980—; Contbr. articles to profl. jours. Served to capt., M.C. AUS, 1942-45. Decorated Bronze Star. Mem. AMA (rep. sci. exhibits in gastroenterology), A.C.P., Am. Assn. Study Liver Diseases, Am. Gastroenterol. Assn., Central Soc. Clin. Research, Am. Fedn. Clin. Research, Am. Geriatrics Soc. (gov. western div. 1982-83). Home: PO Box 26 Sun City AZ 85372 Office: 10503 Thunderbird Blvd Suite 22 Sun City AZ 85351

KLOTZ, BILL W., civil engineer; b. Goose Creek, Tex., Oct. 9, 1925; s. Louis and Lucy Elizabeth (Sampson) K.; m. Dorothy Brubaker, Jan. 31, 1945; children: Linda Ann Klotz, Mary Louis Klotz McClung, David Wayne, Susan Kay Klotz Struzick, William Louis. B.S. in Civil Engring., Tex A&M U., 1948. Registered profl. engr., Tex., Okla., Alaska, La., Miss. With Lockwood, Andrews & Newman, Inc., Houston, 1948—, pres., 1974—. Contbr. articles on engring. to profl. jours. Trustee Victoria Ind. Sch. Dist., Tex., 1967-68; vice chmn. bd. commrs. Victoria Pub. Housing Authority, 1960-68; pres. Jr. Achievement Victoria, 1961-63; bd. dirs. Victoria United Fund, 1965-69; adv. bd. Victoria Salvation Army, 1962-68. Served to 2d lt. USAAF, 1943-44. Fellow ASCE; mem. Nat. Soc. Profl. Engrs., Tex. Soc. Profl. Engrs. (Engr. of Yr. award Victoria chpt.), Am. Cons. Engrs. Council, Cons. Engrs. Council Tex. (pres.), City Planners Assn. Tex., Houston Engring. and Sci. Soc., South Tex. C. of C. (past bd. dirs.), Victoria C. of C. (past pres.), Houston C. of C. (transp. com.), Tau Beta Pi. Lodge: Rotary. Home: 415 Southchester St Houston TX 77079 Office: 1500 City West Blvd Houston TX 77042

KLOTZ, FLORENCE, costume designer; b. N.Y.C.; d. Philip K. and Hannah Koltz. Student, Parsons Sch. Design, 1941. Designer: Broadway shows Superman, 1960, Never Too Late, 1960, Nobody Loves An Albatross, Owl and The Pussycat, Broadway Broadway, Dancin' In The Streets, 1982, Take Her She's Mine, 1960, Side By Side By Sondheim, 1975, Legends, Follies, 1971 (Tony award), A Little Night Music, 1973 (Tony award), Pacific Overtures, 1976 (Tony award), On the 20th Century, 1978 (Drama Desk award); N.Y.C. Ctr. prodns. Carousel, 1956, Oklahoma, 1956, Annie Get Your Gun, 1956, 4 Baggatelle, Astaire Variations, 1983; movies Something for Everyone, 1969, A little Night Music, 1976; ice shows John Curry's Ice Dancing, 1979. Democrat. Home: 1050 Park Ave New York NY 10028

KLOTZ, HARRY RICHARD, elec. equipment mfg. co. exec.; b. Phila., Nov. 21, 1926; s. Harry Warren and Kathryn (Christman) K.; m. Mary Ellen Scheffler, July 28, 1951; children—Sandra Leigh, Richard Wayne. B.A., Pa. State U., 1948. C.P.A., Pa. With Price Waterhouse & Co. (C.P.A.'s), Phila., 1948-56, sr. auditor, 1953-56; with Campbell Soup Co., Camden, N.J., 1956-72, dir. finance internat. div., 1966-72; v.p. finance, sec.-treas. Admiral Internat. Enterprises Corp., Rosemont, Ill., 1972-74; v.p. sales and licensing Admiral Internat. div. Rockwell Internat. Corp., 1974-75; v.p. fin. dept., dir. internat. fin. Motorola, Inc., Schaumberg, Ill., 1975—. Treas. Cinnaminson Twp. Sewerage Authority, 1964-72; scoutmaster Montgomery County council Boy Scouts Am., 1948-49; bd. dirs. Safer Found. Served with USNR, 1945-46. Mem. Pa. Inst. C.P.A.'s, Fin. Execs. Inst., Sigma Phi Epsilon. Presbyterian (elder). Home: 375 Briarwood Ln Palatine IL 60067 Office: 1303 E Algonquin Rd Schaumburg IL 60196

KLOTZ, HERBERT WERNER, professional services company executive; b. Berlin, Germany, Feb. 24, 1917; came to U.S., 1937, naturalized, 1944; s. Herbert and Gertrud (Koppel) K.; m. Patricia Radford Hopkins, Apr. 3, 1954; childrenRadford Werner, Leslie Ritchie, James Taylor. B.A., Zuoz (Switzerland) Coll., 1935; postgrad., U. Zurich, Switzerland, 1935-36. With Smith, Barney & Co. (and predecessor), N.Y.C., 1937-42, W.E. Hutton & Co., 1946-48; engaged in mgmt. personal investments, 1949-52; with Winslow, Douglas & McEvoy, N.Y.C., 1953-54; pres., treas. Tex. Securities Corp., N.Y.C., 1954-57; with Alex Brown & Sons, Washington, 1957-60; spl. asst. to sec. commerce, 1961, dep. to sec. commerce, 1961-62, asst. sec. commerce adminstrn., 1962-65; exec. v.p. Am. Growth Investment Co., 1966-67; dir. Govt. Systems Center, Kurt Salmon Assos., Inc., 1968-69; pres., dir. Quest Research Corp., 1970-81, chmn. bd., 1981—, Dynamic Engring., Inc., 1976—, DHR, Inc., 1978—, Engring. Resources, Inc., 1978—; pres., chmn. bd. QuesTech, Inc., 1981—. Asso. dir. Nat. Com. Bus. and Profl. Men and Women for Kennedy-Johnson, 1960; bd. dirs. Washington Internat. Horseshow Assn., 1969-83. Served to 1st lt. AUS, 1942-45; maj. Res. ret. Democrat. Episcopalian. Clubs: 1925 F Street, Metropolitan, Federal City (Washington); Warrenton Hunt, Fauquier (Warrenton, Va.). Home: 1401 Langley Pl McLean VA 22101 Office: 6858 Old Dominion Dr McLean VA 22101

KLOTZ, IRVING MYRON, educator, scientist; b. Chgo., Jan. 22, 1916; s. Frank and Mollie (Nasatir) K.; m. Mary Sue Hanlon, Aug. 7, 1966; children: Edward, Audie Jeanne, David. B.S., U. Chgo., 1937, Ph.D., 1940. Research asso. in chemistry Northwestern U., 1940-42, instr., 1942- 46, asst. prof., 1946-47, asso. prof., 1947-50, prof., 1950-63, Morrison prof. chemistry, 1963—; Lalor fellow Marine Biol. Lab., Woods Hole, Mass., 1947-48, corp. mem., 1947—, trustee, 1957-65. Author: Chemical Thermodynamics, 3d rev. edit., 1972, Energies in Biochemical Reactions, rev. edit., 1967; articles sci. jours. Recipient Army-Navy cert. of appreciation for wartime research, 1948. Fellow Royal Soc. Medicine, Am. Acad. Arts and Scis.; mem. Nat. Acad. Scis., Am. Soc. Biol. Chemists, Am. Chem. Soc. (Eli Lilly award 1949, Midwest award 1970), AAAS, Phi Beta Kappa, Sigma Xi, Phi Lambda Upsilon, Alpha Chi Sigma. Home: 2515 Pioneer Rd Evanston IL 60201

KLOTZ, JOHN WESLEY, electronics consultant; b. Pitts., May 2, 1919; s. E. I. and Lydia (Banse) K.; m. Norma E. Faust, June 27, 1964; children: Donald, Cheryl. Student, Capital U., 1937-39; B.S. in Physics, Ohio State U., 1942, student Grad. Sch., 1942. Research engr. Naval Research Lab., 1942-47; adminstrv. engr. Research and Devel. Bd., Office Sec. Def., 1948-53, dir. electronics, 1954-57, dir. defensive missiles, 1957-59, dep. asst. dir. def. research and engring., 1959-63, chmn. research group on fed. aviation, 1963-75, asst. dir., tactical command and surveillance systems, 1965-69, asst. dir. combat support, 1970-75; electronics cons. to govt. and industry, 1975—; Adv. mem. exec. com. Radio Tech. Com. for Aeros., 1971—; mem. tech. adv. com. FAA, 1975. Recipient Meritorious Civilian Service award Sec. of Def., 1975. Mem. AIAA, IEEE, Am. Def. Preparedness Assn., Springfield (Va.) Civic Assn. (v.p. 1955), Sigma Pi Sigma. Presbyterian. Club: Brookville Swimming. Home: 3401 Saylor Pl Alexandria VA 22304

KLOTZBACH, ROBERT JAMES, manufacturing company executive; b. N.Y.C., Aug. 27, 1922; s. Charles James and Mary Agnes (Reilly) K.; m. Myrtle Anna Byrd, Oct. 26, 1946; 1 son, Robert Byrd. B.S., Fordham U., 1943; postgrad. Chem. Engring, N.Y. U., 1943-44. Chem. engr. Manhattan Dist. Linde Co., Tonawanda, N.Y., 1944; project engr. Clinton Labs., Oak Ridge, 1945-46; dir. long range planning chem. tech. Oak Ridge Nat. Lab., 1946-55; dir. engring. nuclear div. Union Carbide Co., N.Y.C., 1955-65, Niagara Falls, N.Y., 1965-72, dir. tech., div. metals, 1973-84; dir. tech. UMETCO Minerals Corp., 1984—. Election commr. City of Oak Ridge, 1950. Served with U.S. Army, 1943-46. Mem. Niagara Frontier Research Dirs., AAAS. Republican. Roman Catholic. Clubs: Niagara, Niagara Falls Country. Home: 5140 Dana Dr Lewiston NY 14092 Office: 4625 Royal Ave Niagara Falls NY 14302

KLOTZMAN, DOROTHY ANN, musical educator; b. Seattle, Mar. 24, 1937; d. Henry and Irva (Graham) Hill. B.S., Juilliard Sch., 1958, M.S., 1960. Prof., chmn. music Bklyn. Coll., 1971-81; dir. Conservatory Music, 1981—. Condr., Bklyn. Coll. Symphonic Band, 1970-81, Symphony Orch., 1980—; 1st woman condr., Goldman Band, 1973-75, 77; bd. dirs., Goldman Band, 1979; guest condr., Guggenheim Concerts Band, 1980-83; bd. dirs., Guggenheim Concerts Band, 1980—; Composer: symphonic band Good Day Sir Christmas; soprano solo, chorus and instrumental ensemble Divertimento; chamber orch. Concerto; saxophone and orch. Chimera; ballet Variations; orch. Overture for a Dedication; arranger: Slavonic Dance No. 12 (Dvorak); editor: Richard Franko Goldman: Selected Essays and Reviews, 1948-1968. Mem. citizens adv. bd. WNCN, 1976; Bd. dirs. Bklyn. Ctr. for Performing Arts at Bklyn. Coll., 1983—; trustee Bklyn. Coll. Found, 1981—. Recipient N.Y. Philharmonic Young Composers' Contest 1st prize, 1953-54; Benjamin award in composition, 1955, 58; Fromm prize composition Aspen Music Sch., 1960; Danforth Found. E. Harris Harbison award, 1972. Mem. Am. Music Center, Am. Musicol. Soc., Coll. Music Soc., Music Library Assn., Am. Soc. Composers and Performers. Home: 543 E 24th St Brooklyn NY 11210

KLUGE, JOHN WERNER, broadcasting and advt. exec.; b. Chemnitz, Germany, Sept. 21, 1914; s. Fritz and Gertrude (Donj) K.; children—Samantha, Joseph B. Student, Wayne U.; B.A. (4 year honor scholar), Columbia, 1937. Vice pres., sales mgr. Otten Bros., Inc., Detroit, 1937-41; pres., dir. radio sta. WGAY, Silver Spring, Md., 1946-59, St. Louis Broadcasting Corp., Brentwood, Mo., 1953-58, Pitts. Broadcasting Co., 1954-59; pres., treas., dir. Capitol Broadcasting Co., Nashville, 1954-59, Asso. Broadcasters, Inc., Ft. Worth-Dallas, 1957-59; partner Western N.Y. Broadcasting Co., Buffalo, 1957-60; pres., dir. Washington Planagraph Co., 1956-60, Mid.-Fla. Radio Corp., Orlando, 1952-59; treas., dir. Mid-Fla. Television Corp., 1957-60; owner Kluge Investment Co., Washington, 1956-60; partner Nashton Properties, Nashville, 1954-60, Texworth Investment Co., Ft. Worth, 1957-60; chmn. bd. Seaboard Service System, Inc., 1957-58; pres. New Eng. Fritos, Boston, 1947-55, N.Y. Inst. Dietetics, N.Y.C., 1953-60; chmn. bd., pres., dir. Metromedia, Inc., N.Y.C.; chmn. bd., treas., dir. Kluge, Finkelstein & Co. (food brokers), Balt.; chmn. bd., treas. Tri-Suburban Broadcasting Corp., Washington, Kluge & Co.; chmn. bd., pres., treas. Washington, Silver City Sales Co., Washington; dir. Marriott-Hot Shoppes, Inc., Chock Full O' Nuts Corp., Nat. Bank Md., Waldorf Astoria Corp., Just One Break, Inc., Belding Heminway Co., Inc.; mem. adv. council Mfrs. Hanover Trust Co.; Mem. Washington Bd. Trade. Bd. dirs. Brand Names Found., Inc., Shubert Found.; v.p., bd. dirs. United Cerebral Palsy Research and Ednl. Found., 1972—; trustee Strang Clinic Miliken U.; bd. govs. N.Y. Coll. Osteo. Medicine. Served to capt. U.S. Army, 1941-45. Mem. Nat. Food Brokers Assn., Washington Food Brokers Assn. (pres. 1958), Grocery Wheels Washington, Grocery Mfrs. Reps. Washington, Advt. Club Washington, Nat. Assn. Radio and Television Broadcasters, Advt. Council N.Y.C., Nat. Sugar Brokers Assn. Clubs: Army and Navy, University, Figure Skating, National Capital Skeet and Trap, Broadcasters (Washington); Metropolitan, Columbia Associates, University (N.Y.C.); Olympic (San Francisco); Marco Polo (N.H. gov.). Office: Metromedia Inc 1 Harmon Plaza Secaucus NJ 07094 *

KLUGER, RICHARD, author, editor, critic; b. Paterson, N.J., Sept. 18, 1934; s. David and Ida (Abramson) K.; m. Phyllis Schlain, Mar. 23, 1957; children—Matthew Harold, Leonard Theodore. A.B. cum laude, Princeton, 1956. Copy editor Wall St. Jour., 1956-57; editor, pub. County Citizen, New City, N.Y., 1958-60; staff writer N.Y. Post, 1960-61; asso. editor Forbes mag., 1962; gen. books editor N.Y. Herald Tribune, 1962-63, book editor, 1963-66; editor Book Week, 1963-66; sr. editor Simon and Schuster, 1966-68, mng. editor, 1968, exec. editor, 1968-70; editor-in-chief Atheneum Pubs., 1970-71; pres., pub. Charterhouse Books, 1971-73. Author: When the Bough Breaks, 1964, National Anthem, 1969, Simple Justice, 1976, Members of the Tribe, 1977, Star Witness, 1979, Un-American Activities, 1982; author: (with Phyllis Kluger) Good Goods, 1982. Home: Back Brook Rd Ringoes NJ 08551

KLUGMAN, JACK, actor; b. Phila., Apr. 27, 1922; s. Max and Rose K.; m. Brett Somers, 1966 (; (separated), 1966; children: David, Adam. Student, Carnegie Inst. Tech., Am. Theatre Wing, N.Y.C. Film appearances include Timetable, 1956, Twelve Angry Men, 1957, Cry Terror, 1958, Days of Wine and Roses, 1962, Act One, 1963, Yellow Canary, 1963, Hail, Mafia, 1965, The Detective, 1968, The Split, 1968, Goodbye Columbus, 1969, Who Says I Can't Ride a Rainbow, 1971, Two Minute Warning, 1976; TV series Harris Against the World, 1964-65, The Odd Couple, 1970-75, Quincy, 1976—; other TV appearances include Naked City; TV movies Fame is the Name of the Game, 1966, The Underground Man, 1974, One of My Wives is Missing, 1976; N.Y. stage debut in Stevedore, Equity Library Theatre, 1949; Broadway debut in Golden Boy, 1952; other stage appearances include The Sudden and Accidental Re-education of Horse Johnson; appears in summer stock. Winner Emmy award, 1963, 71, 73. Mem. AFTRA, Actors Equity, Screen Actors Guild. Office: care Universal Studio Universal City CA 91608

KLUGMAN, STEPHAN CRAIG, newspaper editor; b. Fargo, N.D., May 11, 1945; s. Theodore and Charlotte Jean (Olson) K.; m. Julia Sue Terpening, Sept. 18, 1971; children: Joshua Theodore, Carolyn Randolph. B.A., Ind. U., 1967. Copy editor Chgo. Sun-Times, 1967-68, asst. telegraph editor, 1968-73, telegraph editor, 1973-74, city editor, 1974-76, asst. mng. editor features, 1976-78; asst. prof. journalism Northwestern U., 1978-82, dir. undergrad studies, 1979-82; editor Ft. Wayne Jour.-Gazette (Ind.), 1982—. Office: 600 W Main St Fort Wayne IN 46802

KLUMPP, THEODORE GEORGE, physician, bus. exec.; b. N.Y.C., May 15, 1903; s. Charles and Marie (Hayo) K.; m. Virginia R. Morgan, Aug. 3, 1934; children—Virginia-Ann, Karla-Marie, Kathleen Morgan, Maralys, Russell Allan, Theodore George. B.S., Princeton U., 1924; M.D., Harvard U., 1928; LL.D. (hon.), U. Chattanooga, 1960, D.Sc., Phila. Coll. Pharmacy and Sci., 1943, New Eng. Coll. Pharmacy, 1961, Albany Med. Coll., 1964. Intern Peter Bent Brigham Hosp., Boston, 1929-30; asst. resident physician Lakeside Hosp., Cleve., 1930-32; instr. and asst. clinic prof. Yale U Med. Sch., 1932-36; chief Drug Div., FDA, Washington, 1936-41; adj. clin. prof. medicine George Washington U., Washington, 1940-41; dir. drugs, food and phys. therapy and sec. council on pharmacy and chemistry AMA, Chgo., 1941-42; pres. Winthrop Labs. div. Sterling Drug Inc., 1942-70, chmn., 1970-73, also dir. parent co., 1960-75; pres., dir. Winthrop Products, Inc., N.J., 1947-51; cons. surgeon C. & O. Ry.; dir. Sterwin Chem., Inc.; mem. adv. council Sr. Med. Cons.'s, 1976—; v.p. U.S. Pharmacopoeia, 1950-70, del. at large conv., 1975—; chmn. Task Force on Handicapped, ODM, 1951; med. cons. Pres.'s Council Phys. Fitness and Sports, 1973—; Bd. dirs. World Med. Assn., N.Y. Heart Assn., Nat. Soc. Med. Research, 1973-77; mem. com. rehab. Am. Heart Assn., 1956-63; bd. govs. Sterling-Winthrop Research Inst., 1946-60; chmn. bd. govs. Nat. Vitamin Found., 1947-49; chmn. Nat. Pharm. Council, 1953-55, mem. exec. com., 1953-64; v.p. Nat. Health Council, 1955-57; chmn. med. service task force Hoover Commn. on Orgn. Exec. Br. Gov., 1953-55; mem. Commn. on Drug Safety, 1962-64, Gov.'s Council on Rehab., 1959—, N.Y. Vocat. Rehab. Planning Council, 1967—; mem. planning bd. Village Sands Point, 1958-78; mem. com. on ecology, Town of North Hempstead, N.Y., 1971-77. Cons. editor: Med. Times, 1973-75; asso. editor, 1975—; Contbr. articles on therapeutics, food, drug, and cosmetic act, also various med. subjects. Mem. vis. com. Harvard Sch. Public Health, 1958-64, Harvard Med. Sch. and Sch. Dental Medicine, 1964-70; bd. dirs. sec. Nat. Fund Med. Edn., 1968-69, pres., 1969-71, chmn., 1971-75; v.p., 1975—; Trustee Bklyn. Coll. Pharmacy, L.I. U., 1968-77, chmn., 1974-77; trustee Affiliated Colls and Univs., Inc., 1972—, Human Resources Sch., Albertson, N.Y., 1974—, Arnold and Marie Schwartz Coll. Pharmacy and Health Sci., 1977—. First recipient Spl. award for Distinguished Service Am. Pharm. Mfrs. Assn., 1955. Fellow A.C.P., N.Y. Acad. Medicine, AAAS, Am. Soc. Clin. Investigation; mem. Pharm. Mfrs. Assn. (pres. 1948-50, dir. 1958-72, v.p. 1958), Am. Hosp. Assn. (hon.), AMA (mem. com. exercise and phys. fitness 1964-72), Am. Pharm. Assn., New Haven County Med. Soc., Academia de Ciencias Medicas, Fisicas y Naturales de La Habana, Nat. Health Assembly, Nat. Assn. Human Devel. (chmn. bd. 1974—), Sigma Xi, Alpha Kappa Alpha. Methodist. Clubs: Princeton, Chemists (N.Y.C.); Manhasset Bay Yacht; Farmington Country (Charlottesville, Va.). Home: 9 Harbor View Rd Port Washington NY 11050 Office: 90 Park Ave New York City NY 10016 *There is so much to be done in a lifetime that it is important to keep busy, to accept responsibilities and not run away from them, and to regard challenges as opportunities rather than as threats. Life is so full of many things that it is a calamity to waste any part of the one and only life we have to live. It is a biological law that nature tends to eliminate those who have relinquished their functional usefulness, and this applies to man as well as all living things. Reciprocally, nature tends to protect and prolong the lives of those who use their mental, emotional and physical functions to their fullest capacities.*

KLURFELD, JAMES MICHAEL, journalist; b. N.Y.C., May 15, 1945; s. Herman and Jeanette (Garfield) K.; m. Judith E. Freiband, July 23, 1967; children: Jennifer, Jason. B.A., Syracuse U., 1967. Tchr. N.Y. Bd. Edn., 1967-68; reporter Newsday, Melville, N.Y., 1968-73, Albany bur. chief, 1973-76, Washington bur. chief, 1981—. Recipient Pulitzer prize, 1969, award for nat. corr. Sigma Delta Chi, 1983. Office: Newsday 1301 Pennsylvania Ave NW Washington DC 20001

KLUSS, WILFRED MARTIN, shipping company executive; b. Waterloo, Iowa, June 19, 1921; s. Fred John and Harriet Maude K.; m. Mary Munro Crandon; children: Stewart Radford, Annette Elizabeth, Suzanne Caroline. S.B., Harvard U., 1942; B.A., New Coll., Oxford U. (Eng.), 1949, M.A., 1949. Specialist in overseas devel. ECA, Paris, 1949-50; statistician Morgan Stanley & Co., N.Y.C., 1950-51; asst. loan officer IBRD, Washington, 1951-54; with Middle East affairs and marine depts Mobil Oil Co., N.Y.C., 1954-71; chmn. Mobil Shipping Co., London, 1966-69, mgr. internat. ops., 1969-71; with Concoco, Inc., Stamford, Conn., 1971-79, Houston, 1979-81, v.p., 1975-81; vice chmn., dir. Robert E. Derecktor RI Inc.; with Shaarup Tankers, Inc., Greenwich, Conn. Mem. exec. com. European Republican Com., London, 1968; bd. govs. New Rochelle Hosp. Med. Ctr. (N.Y.), 1977-78, treas., 1978; active ELISSA Restoration Galveston Hist. Found., 1979—. Served to lt. comdr. USNR, 1943-46. Decorated Bronze Star; Rhodes scholar, 1947-49. Mem. Soc. Naval Architects and Marine Engrs., Am. Bur. Shipping, Oil Cos. Internat. Marine Forum (exec. com. 1977-81), Fedn. Am. Controlled Shipping, Am. Petroleum Inst. Episcopalian. Clubs: Larchmont Yacht (commodore 1973-76), Storm Trysail, Cruising Am., Royal Ocean Racing, N.Y. Yacht, Circunmavigators. Home: 19 White Fox Rd Stamford CT 06903 Office: Skaarup Tankers Inc 66 Field Point Rd Greenwich CT 06830

KLUSZEWSKI, THEODORE BERNARD, profl. baseball coach; b. Argo, Ill., Sept. 10, 1924; s. John and Josephine (Guntarski) K.; m. Eleanor Rita Guckel, Feb. 9, 1946. Student, Ind. U., 1944-46. Profl. baseball player with Cin. Reds, Pitts. Pirates, Chgo. White Sox and Calif. Angels, 1946-61; profl. baseball coach, 1961—; coach Cin. Reds, 1969—; v.p. United County Life Ins. Co. Ohio. Active Multiple Sclerosis Soc. Named to Cin. Reds Hall of Fame, 1962, Ohio Baseball Hall of Fame, 1977. Mem. Greater Cin. Safety Council, Fraternal Order Police, Ind. U. Alumni Assn., Ballplayers of Yesterday, Ind. I Men's Assn. Club: Harper's Point Racquet. Home: 8353 Island Ln Maineville OH 45039 Office: 100 Riverfront Stadium Cincinnati OH 45202

KLUTZNICK, PHILIP M., former government official; b. Kansas City, Mo., July 9, 1907; s. Morris and Minnie (Spindler) K.; m. Ethel Riekes, June 8, 1930; children: Bettylu, Richard (dec.), Thomas Joseph, James Benjamin, Robert, Samuel. Student, U. Kans., 1924-25, U. Nebr., 1925-26; LL.B., Creighton U., Omaha, 1929; LL.D. (hon.), Creighton U., Omaha, 1957, D.H.L., Dropsie Coll., 1954, Hebrew Union Coll.-Jewish Inst. Religion, 1957, Coll. Jewish Studies, 1968, LL.D., Wilberforce (Ohio) U., 1959, Chgo. Med. Sch., 1968, Yeshiva U., 1974, Brandeis U., 1974, Roosevelt U., 1981, U. Ill.-Chgo., 1983, L.H.D., Governor's State U., 1983. U.S. commr. Fed. Pub. Housing Authority, 1944-46; ltd. partner Saloman Bros.; adv. com. Urban Investment and Devel. Co.; hon. dir. Mortgage Guaranty Ins. Corp., Milw.; Mem. U.S. dels. to UN, 1957, 61, 62; U.S. rep., rank of ambassador, to ECOSOC, 1961-63; mem. President's Adv. Com. on Indo-Chinese Refugees; sec. commerce, Washington, 1980-81. Bd. dirs. Nat. Jewish Welfare Bd.; founder Inst. Jewish Policy Planning; nat. council Boy Scouts Am.; chmn. exec. com. Dearborn Park; trustee Eleanor Roosevelt Inst.; bd. dirs. Creighton U., Roosevelt U., Lyric Opera Chgo.; trustee Com. Econ. Devel.; pres. emeritus World Jewish Congress, 1977—. Recipient Ralph Bunche peace award, 1981. Mem. UN Assn. U.S.A. (gov.; sr. dir.), Chgo. Assn. Commerce and Industry (adv. com.), Lambda Alpha, Zeta Beta Tau (hon.), B'nai B'rith (hon. internat. pres.). Clubs: Cosmos, Army-Navy (Washington); Standard,

Carlton, Commercial. Office: 875 N Michigan Ave Suite 4044 Chicago IL 60611

KLUTZNICK, THOMAS JOSEPH, real estate executive; b. Omaha, Apr. 19, 1939; s. Philip Morris and Ethel K.; m. Ellen Diengott, Aug. 3, 1960; children: Karen, John, Daniel, Katherine. B.A., Oberlin (Ohio) Coll., 1961. With Draper & Kramer, Chgo., 1961-63, Klutznick Enterprises/KLC Ventures Ltd., 1963-68; exec. v.p., then pres., chief exec. officer Urban Investment & Devel. Co., Chgo., 1968-78, chmn. bd., chief exec. officer, 1978-82; mng. ptnr. Miller, Klutznick, Davis, Gray Co., Chgo., 1982—; dir. Datapoint Corp. Bd. dirs. Jewish Fedn. Met. Chgo.; mem. Chgo. exec. com. Anti-Defamation League; bd. mgrs. YMCA Met. Chgo.; trustee Oberlin Coll., Nat. Jewish Hosp., Denver, Rush-Presbyn.-St. Luke's Med. Center, Chgo.; bd. overseers Grad. Sch. Fine Arts, U. Pa.; mem. U. Chgo. Citizens Bd., Northwestern U. Assos.; pres.'s council Museum Sci. and Industry, Chgo. Mem. Assn. Commerce and Industry Chgo. (officer), Internat. Council Shopping Centers, Met. Housing and Planning Council, Urban Land Inst., Econ. Club Chgo., Execs. Club Chgo., Lambda Alpha. Clubs: Carlton, Metropolitan, Whitehall, Standard. Office: Miller Klutznick Davis Gray Co 875 N Michigan Ave Suite 1360 Chicago IL 60611 *

KLUWIN, JOHN A., lawyer; b. Oshkosh, Wis., Sept. 16, 1907; s. Fred R. and Nellie (McCarthy) K.; m. Noreta Roemer, Sept. 29, 1934; children: Mary Ann, John A., Robert J., William J., Thomas N., Michael G. LL.B., Marquette U., 1930. Bar: Wis. 1930. Since practiced in, Milw.; lectr. in law Marquette U. Law Sch., part-time 1945-51; Pub. panel mem. WLB, 1944-45. Contbr. to: Marquette Law Rev. Named Disting. Law Alumnus Marquette U., 1983. Fellow Am. Bar Found.; mem. Internat. Assn. Ins. Counsel (past pres.), ABA (gov.), Wis. Bar Assn. (past pres.), Bar Assn. Milw., past pres.), Am. Arbitration Assn., Am. Coll. Trial Lawyers (regent 1964-68), Marquette U. Alumni Assn. (pres. 1964-65). Roman Catholic. Clubs: Kiwanis, Milw. Athletic, M, Marquette U. Home: 9325 Hickory Dr Kewaskum WI 53040 Office: 788 N Jefferson St Milwaukee WI 53202

KMETZ, DONALD R., university dean. Dean Sch. Medicine, U. Louisville. Office: Office of Dean Sch Medicine U Louisville Louisville KY 40292 *

KNAB, DONALD RALPH, insurance company executive; b. Cin., June 4, 1922; s. Chester Don and Edna Katherine (Spatz) K.; m. Janet Elaine Scheid, June 1, 1946; children: Pamela E., Michael F. B.A., U. Cin., 1946, J.D., 1947. With Prudential Ins. Co. Am., Newark, 1947—, sr. v.p. real estate, 1970—; dir. Deansbank Inc. Mem. exec. com. bd. dirs. Regional Plan Assn., 1971—; trustee Urban Land Inst., 1983—. Served with U.S. Army, 1943-45. Decorated Purple Heart. Mem. Beta Theta Pi. Episcopalian. Clubs: Cance Brook Country (Short Hills, N.J.); Ponte Vedra (Jacksonville, Fla.); Baltusrol Golf (Springfield, N.J.). Office: Prudential Ins Co Prudential Plaza Newark NJ 07101

KNAGGS, NELSON STUART, chemical company executive; b. Hagerstown, Md., Mar. 31, 1907; s. John Nelson and Carolynn (Pagenheardt) K.; m. Esther Aneshansel, July 19, 1929 (dec. May 1964); children—Nelson S., James F., David R.; m. Marielle Seidel, Nov. 23, 1976. Student, Davis and Elkins Coll., 1925-27, LL.D., 1956, U. Cin., 1928-29, 33-34, L.H.D., 1971. Research chemist Hilton-Davis Chem. Co., Cin., 1933-41, dir. fgn. div., 1941-48, v.p. marketing and advt., 1948-71, sr. v.p., 1971-72; pres. Knaggs/World Enterprises, Inc., Cin., 1972—; v.p. Thomassett Color Co., Cin., 1954-72; chmn. bd. Nikko Inn, Inc., Ohio, 1962-80; dir. Spectrum Exploration & Mining Co., South Africa. Author: Adventures in Man's First Plastic, 1947, The Romance of Natural Waxes, 1947, Dyestuffs of the Ancients, 1953, Lost in the Amazon, 1965, Journey to Nepal, 1968, The Rediscovery of John J. Audubon's White Wolf, 1970, also articles profl. jours. Trustee Davis and Elkins Coll., 1970-76; bd. dirs. Cin. Mus. Natural History, v.p., 1948—; bd. dirs., v.p. Cin. Council World Affairs; v.p. Internat. Visitors Center, Cin. Mem. Am. Chem. Soc., Engring. Soc. Cin., Cin. Lit. Soc. Clubs: Queen City (bd. govs. 1978—), Cin. Travel (dir. 1947—), Cin. Travel (pres. 1947-50, 73-77), Fgn. Trade (Cin.) (pres. 1943-45); Explorers (N.Y.C.) (dir. 1959-61). Patentee carbon paper. Expdns. to Amazon River Basin, C.Am., Mexico, India, Kingdom of Nepal, Cambodia, Seychelles Islands; diamond exploration South Africa, 1975, 76, 77. Home: 3130 Ferguson Rd Cincinnati OH 45211

KNAKE, ELLERY LOUIS, weed science educator; b. Gibson City, Ill., Aug. 26, 1927; s. Louis Franz and Wilhelmina Dorthea (Behrens) K.; m. Colleen Mary Wilken, June 23, 1951; children: Gary Louis, Kim Paul. B.S., U. Ill., 1949, M.S. (Wright fellow), 1950, Ph.D., 1960. Tchr. vocat. agr. Barrington (Ill.) Consol. High Sch., 1950-56; instr. vocat. agr. service U. Ill., Urbana, 1956-60, asst. prof. dept. agronomy, 1960-64, asso. prof., 1964-69, prof. weed sci., 1969—; 2d v.p. N. Central Weed Control Conf., 1969, 1st v.p., 1970, pres., 1971, hon. mem., 1979; UNDP cons., Yugoslavia, 1976; participant East-West Center Confs., Honolulu, 1976, 77. Editor: Weeds Today mag., 1978-82; asso. editor: Agronomy Jour., 1976-78; contbr. articles to profl. jours. Served with AUS, 1945-46. Recipient Ciba-Geigy award for outstanding contbns. to agr., 1972; Educator award Midwest Agr. Chem. Assn., 1975; Funk award Coll. Agr., U. Ill., 1978; Superior Service award U.S. Dept. Agr., 1983. Fellow Am. Soc. Agronomy (Crops and Soils mag. Best Article award 1967, extension edn. award 1978), Weed Sci. Soc. Am. (v.p. 1972, pres.-elect 1973, pres., chmn. bd. 1974, Outstanding Extension Worker award 1972, editorial bd. Herbicide Handbook); mem. Am. Agrl. Editors Assn., Iroquois County Hist. Soc. (charter life), Nabor House, Sigma Xi, Phi Eta Sigma, Alpha Tau Alpha, Alpha Zeta, Phi Kappa Phi, Gamma Sigma Delta, Epsilon Sigma Phi. Roman Catholic. Club: K.C. Home: 511 W Main St Urbana IL 61801 Office: N323 Turner Hall Univ of Ill 1102 S Goodwin Urbana IL 61801 *Two of my favorite quotations best express the principles that guide my life. "Die when I may, I want it said of me by those who knew me best, that I plucked a thistle and planted a flower wherever I thought a flower would grow"—Abraham Lincoln. "The purpose of life is to accomplish something that outlives you" —anonymous.*

KNAPLUND, PAUL WILLIAM, former bus. machines co. exec., cons.; b. Madison, Wis., Aug. 19, 1928; s. Paul Alexander and Dorothy Alice (King) K.; m. Virginia Joan Samp, Sept. 27, 1951; children-Paul Alexander, Kristine Samp, Justin King, Eric Colbert. A.B., Harvard, 1949; M.A., U. Wis., 1950. With IBM, 1950-80, v.p., 1964-80; dir. Scarsdale Nat. Bank. Trustee Nat. Rowing Found. Club: Am. Yacht. Home: 5 Pinecrest Rd Scarsdale NY 10583

KNAPP, BETTINA LIEBOWITZ, educator; b. N.Y.C., May 9, 1926; d. David and Emily (Gresser) Liebowitz; m. Russell S. Knapp, Aug. 28, 1949; children: Albert, Charles. B.A., Barnard Coll., 1947; M.A., Columbia U., 1949, Ph.D., 1956; cert., Sorbonne, 1947. Lectr. Columbia U., 1952-60; prof. Hunter Coll., 1961—, Grad. Center CUNY, 1961—; lectr. in field. Author: numerous books including Louis Jouvet, Man of the Theatre, 1957, That Was Yvette. A Biography of Yvette Guilbert, 1964, Aristide Bruant, A Biography, 1968, Jean Cocteau. A Critical Study of his Writings, 1970, Georges Duhamel. A Critical Study of his Writings, 1972, Off-Stage Voices, 1975, Dream and Image, 1977, Fernand Crommelynck, 1978, Anais Nin, 1978, The Prometheus Syndrome, 1979, Gerard de Nerval The Mystic's Dilemma, 1980, Emile Zola, 1980, Theatre and Alchemy, 1980, Sacha Guitry, 1981, Paul Claudel, 1982; contbr. articles in field. Guggenheim fellow, 1973-74; Am. Philos. Soc. grantee, 1975-76; recipient Alliance Francaise medal, 1948, Shuster award, 1981. Jewish. Office: Hunter Coll Dept Romance Langs 695 Park Ave New York NY 10021

KNAPP, CHARLES B., economist, educator; b. Ames, Iowa, Aug. 13, 1946; s. Albert B. and Anne Marie (Taft) K.; m. Lynne Vickers, Aug. 25, 1967; 1 dau., Amanda. B.S., Iowa State U., 1968; M.A., Ph.D., U. Wis., 1972. Asst. prof. econs., research assoc. Center for Study of Human Resources, U. Tex., Austin, 1972-76; spl. asst. to Sec. of Labor, Dept. Labor, Washington, 1977-79, dep. asst. sec. labor, 1979-81; assoc. prof. public policy George Washington U., 1981-82; sr. v.p., assoc. prof. econs. Tulane U., New Orleans, 1982—. Contbr. articles to profl. jours. NDEA fellow, 1968-71; Ford Found. fellow, 1971-72. Mem. Am. Econ. Assn. Democrat. Roman Catholic. Office: Tulane U 218 Gibson Hall New Orleans LA 70118

KNAPP, CHARLES WILLIAM, financial corporation executive; b. Honolulu, Oct. 14, 1934; s. George Clarence and Miriam (Waddoups) K.; m. Nancie Brooke, Dec. 5, 1968; children: Elyse, Evan. Student, U. Hawaii, 1951-53; B.A., U. Utah, 1955; postgrad., Hastings Sch. Law, U. Calif., 1951-58. First v.p. Shearson, Hammill & Co., San Francisco, 1964-69; gen. partner Cumberland Assos., San Francisco, 1969-71; pres. Shapell Industries, Beverly Hills, Calif., 1971-72, Trafalgar Assos., Los Angeles, 1972—; vice chmn. Fin. Corp. Am., Los Angeles, 1973-75, chmn., chief exec. officer, 1975—; chmn. bd. dirs. Budget Capital Corp., State Savs. & Loan, Century Bank. Served with U.S. Army, 1953-55, 56-58. Republican. Mormon. Clubs: St. Francis Yacht, San Francisco Golf, Bel Air Country, LaQuinta Country, Lake Region Yacht and Country. Office: 6420 Wilshire Blvd Suite 1500 Los Angeles CA 90048

KNAPP, CLEON T., publisher; b. Los Angeles, Apr. 28, 1937; s. Cleon T. and Sally (Brasfield) K.; m. Elizabeth Ann Wood, Mar. 17, 1979; children: Jeffrey James, Brian Patrick, Aaron Bradley, Laura Ann. Student, UCLA, 1955-58. With John C. Brasfield Pub. Corp. (purchased co. in 1965, changed name to Knapp Communications Corp. 1977); now pub. Bon Appetit mag., Archtl. Digest, Home mag., and GEO mag., Los Angeles, 1958—, chief exec. officer, 1965—, chmn. bd.; chmn. Knapp Press, Rosebud Press; owner Wilshire Mktg. Corp.; organizer, dir. Wilshire Bancorp. Trustee UCLA Found.; bd. dirs. Damon Runyon-Walter Winchell Cancer Fund. Mem. Mag. Pubs. Assn. (bd. dirs.). Office: 5900 Wilshire Blvd Los Angeles CA 90036

KNAPP, DANIEL C., former association executive; b. Peoria, Ill., June 19, 1915; s. Christian and Nina (Fernsler) K.; m. Ruth Weinberger, Dec. 18, 1948; children: Theresa L., Karen D. B.A., Bradley U., 1937; M.A., U. Ill., 1938; postgrad., Ohio State U., 1944-45; grad., Advanced Mgmt. Program, Harvard U., 1962. Govt. intern Nat. Inst. Pub. Affairs, Washington, 1938-39; adminstrv. aide Social Security Bd., 1939-42; chief, dept. recruitment and placement VA, 1946-51; exec. officer Dept. Army, Washington and Okinawa, 1951-62; joined U.S. Fgn. Service, 1962; dep. chief career devel. staff State Dept., 1962-64, chief manpower resources staff, 1964-66; dir. manpower planning program, 1966-68; dir. personnel environmental health service HEW, Washington, 1968-70; chief personnel policy U.S. EPA, Washington, 1970-74; dir. operating programs Nat. Inst. for Automotive Service Excellence, Washington, 1974-82; ret., 1982. Contbr. articles to profl. jours. Served to 1st lt. AUS, 1942-46. Mem. Am. Soc. Pub. Adminstrn., Internat. Personnel Mgmt. Assn., Pi Gamma Mu. Home: 15421 Carrolton Rd Rockville MD 20853

KNAPP, DAVID CURTIS, univ. pres.; b. Syracuse, N.Y., Nov. 13, 1927; s. Clifford Raymond and Alma Isobel (Curtis) K.; m. Rita Kyllikki Roschier, Aug. 31, 1964; children—Karl M., Eric J. A.B., Syracuse U., 1947; M.A., U. Chgo., 1948, Ph.D., 1953. Asst. prof. to prof. govt. U. N.H., 1953-62, dean, 1961-62; asso. dir. Study of Am. Colls. of Agr., College Park, Md., 1963-65; dir. Inst. of Coll. and Univ. Adminstrs., Am. Council on Edn., 1965-68; dean N.Y. State Coll. Human Ecology, Cornell U., Ithaca, N.Y., 1968-74, provost, 1974-78; pres. U. Mass., 1978—. Author: (with C.E. Kellogg) The College of Agriculture: Science in the Public Service, 1964. Served with U.S. Army, 1950-52. Fulbright research scholar, Finland, 1959-60; Bullard fellow Grad. Sch. Pub. Adminstrn., Harvard, 1962-63. Mem. Am. Polit. Sci. Assn., Am. Soc. for Pub. Adminstrn., Phi Beta Kappa. Home: 17 Bald Pate Hill Rd Newton Center MA 02159

KNAPP, DAVID HEBARD, banker; b. N.Y.C., May 22, 1938; s. Alfred John and Doris (Hebard) K.; m. Letitia Lykes, Aug. 18, 1959; children—Genevieve, Christopher, Breckenridge. B.A., Williams Coll. With Rotan, Mosle, Houston, 1960-62; asst. cashier, mgr. credit dept. Fannin Bank, Houston, 1962-64, asst. v.p. comml. loans, 1964-66, v.p. comml. loans, 1968-70, vice chmn. bd., 1970-82; co-chmn. exec. com. Interfirst Bank Fannin, 1982—; devel. loan officer AID, Rio de Janeiro, Brazil, 1966-68; pres. Penta Internat., Inc., Houston, 1979—; dir. Lykes Bros. Inc., Tampa, Fla., Bank of Clearwater, Fla., Oceanonics, Inc., Houston, Walter P. Moore & Assos., Interocean Steamship Co., Tampa, Fla., South Coast Terminals, Inc., Houston., Lykes Bros. Steamship Co., New Orleans. Trustee St. Lukes Episcopal Hosp., Houston, St. John's Sch., Houston, Urban Affairs Corp., Houston; trustee Armand Bayou Nature Center, Pasadena, Tex., pres., 1977-79. Clubs: Houston Country, Tejas (Houston). Home: 3023 Chevy Chase Houston TX 77019 Office: PO Box 20008 Houston TX 77025

KNAPP, DENNIS RAYMOND, judge; b. Buffalo, W.Va., May 13, 1912; s. Amon Lee and Ora Alice (Forbes) K.; m. Helen Ewers Jordan, June 1, 1935; children—Mary F., Margaret Ann, Dennis Raymond. A.B., W.Va. Inst. Tech., 1932, LL.D., 1972; A.M., W.Va. U., 1934, LL.B., 1940. Bar: W.Va. bar 1940. High sch. tchr., Putnam County, W.Va., 1932-35, supt. schs., 1935-37, practiced in, Nitro, 1940-56; judge Ct. of Common Pleas, Kanawhe County, W.Va., 1957-70; U.S. dist. judge for So. Dist. W.Va., Charleston, 1970—; Vice pres., dir. Bank of Nitro, 1949-70; v.p. Hygeia, Inc., 1968-70. Bd. dirs. Goodwill Industries, Inc., 1968-70; adv. bd. Marshall U., Huntington, W.Va. Served with AUS, 1944-46. Named Alumnus of Year W.Va. Inst. Tech., 1967. Mem. Am., W.Va. bar assns., W.Va. Jud. Assn., W.Va. Tech. Coll. Alumni Assn. (pres. 1968). Republican. Methodist. Home: 2109 21st St Nitro WV 25143 Office: US Courthouse Charleston WV 25320

KNAPP, DONALD OGDEN, museum director; b. Cleve., Mar. 17, 1947; s. Frederick Allen and Ethel Ricketts (Ogden) K.; m. Christine Ann Wentz, Aug. 12, 1972; children: Eileen Marie, Benjamin Ogden. B.S., Ind. U., 1970, M.S., 1978. Planetarium coordinator Bartholomew Consol. Sch. Corp., Columbus, Ind., 1972-79; planetarium dir. Schenectady Mus., N.Y., 1979-81, exec. dir., 1981—. Mem. Fedn. Hist. Services (trustee, sec. 1982-83), Am. Assn. Museums, Am. Assn. State and Local History, Internat. Planetarium Soc., Middle Atlantic Planetarium Soc. Office: Schenectady Mus and Planetarium Nott Teer Heights Schenectady NY 12308

KNAPP, EDWARD ALAN, government administrator; b. Salem, Oreg., Mar. 7, 1932; s. Gardner and Lucille (Moore) K.; m. Jean Elaine Hartwell, June 27, 1954; children: Sandra, David, Robert, Mary. A.B., Pomona Coll., 1954; Ph.D., U. Calif.-Berkeley, 1958. With Los Alamos Sci. Lab., U. Calif., 1958-82, dir. accelerator tech. div., 1977-82; asst. dir., then dir. Nat. Sci. Found., Washington, 1982—; cons. in field. Contbr. articles to profl. jours. Fellow Am. Phys. Soc.; mem. IEEE, AAAS, Sigma Xi. Methodist. Office: Nat Sci Found 1800 G St NW Washington DC 20550 *

KNAPP, GEORGE FRANCIS, communications co. exec.; b. N.Y.C., Sept. 6, 1931; s. George F. and Annette R. (McCabe) K.; m. Ann Eileen Stanley, Jan. 9, 1954; children—Eileen, Kathleen, George, Margaret, Richard. B.E.E., Manhattan Coll., 1953; M.B.A., N.Y. U., 1964; grad., Advanced Mgmt. Program, Harvard, 1974. Registered profl. engr., N.Y. Engr. Westinghouse Elec. Corp., Pitts., 1953; div. engr. N.Y. Telephone Co., 1956-58, various mgmt. positions, 1961-65; engr. Bell Telephone Labs., 1959-60; dir. ops. Chilean Telephone Co., Santaiago; 966-68; pres. P.R. Telephone Co., San Juan, 1969-74; chmn. ITT Worldcom Inc., N.Y.C., 1978—, ITT Am. Cable & Radio Corp., 1975—; v.p. ITT Corp., 1976—; chmn. bd. and/or pres., dir. ITT telecommunications subs. Bd. dirs. Greater N.Y. council Boy Scouts Am.; trustee Manhattan Coll. Served with AUS, 1954-56. Mem. Armed Forces Communications and Electronics Assn. (bd. dirs.), IEEE. Republican. Roman Cath. Clubs: Metopolitan (N.Y.C.); Hackensack (N.J.) Golf. Home: 661 Shawnee Dr Franklin Lakes NJ 07417 Office: 67 Broad St New York NY 10004

KNAPP, GEORGE GRIFF PRATHER, insurance company executive; b. New Rochelle, N.Y., June 26, 1923; s. Griff Prather and Lucy Chadbourne (Norvell) K.; m. Eva Witte, May 30, 1953; children: Edward, Wesley, Helen, Elizabeth. B.A., Harvard U., 1945; postgrad., Law Sch., 1946. With Chubb & Son, N.Y.C., 1947—, mgr. personal lines dept., 1966-73, asst. to pres., 1973, Can. zone officer, 1974-78, N.Y. zone officer, 1978—, sr. v.p., 1968—, Fed. Ins. Co., 1968—, dir., 1970—. Gov. Lawrence Hosp., 1968-75. Served with U.S. Army, 1943-46. Republican. Roman Catholic. Clubs: Down Town Assn., Harvard (N.Y.C.); Bronxville Field. Home: 22 Elm Ln Bronxville NY 10708 Office: 100 William St New York NY 10038

KNAPP, GEORGE LAWRENCE, JR., outdoor advt. exec.; b. Shawnee, Okla., Sept. 10, 1915; s. George Lawrence and Edna Lois (Chitty) K.; m. Mary Elizabeth Lambert, Feb. 18, 1939; children—Nancy Gail, Dorothy Jeanne. Grad., Okla. Mil. Acad., 1935; B.A., Okla. U., 1937. Former pres. Knapp Outdoor Advt. Corp., Knapp Neon & Plastic Sign Co.; now v.p. Marden Outdoor Advt. Co.; dir. Farmers & Mchts. Bank & Trust co., Tulsa. Mem. President's Adv. Council for Traffic Safety, President's Com. on Physically Handicapped.; past chmn. Okla. Wild Life Commn.; Bd. dirs. Asso. Industries Okla., Better Bus. Bur. Tulsa, Advt. Council, Tulsa Cancer Soc., Goodwill Industries; mem. pres.'s council U. Okla.; mem. exec. bd., fund chmn. Arthritis Fedn. Eastern Okla. Served to lt. (j.g.) USNR, 1943-46. Mem. Outdoor Advt. Assn. Am. (dir. at large, past pres., chmn. bd.), Advt. Fedn. Am. (dir.), Execs. Assn. (past pres.), Izaak Walton League of Tulsa, Izaak Walton League of Okla. (past pres.), Tulsa C. of C., Beta Theta Pi. Clubs: Rotarian., Tulsa, Southern Hills Country, Okla. Green Country. Home: 2300 Riverside Dr Tulsa OK 74114

KNAPP, JOHN J., lawyer, government official; b. N.Y.C., 1934; 2 Sons. B.S., Manhattan Coll., 1958; J.D., Fordham U., 1961. Bar: N.Y. 1961. Law clk. to judge U.S. Dist. Ct. (so. dist.), N.Y., 1961; assoc. Paul, Weiss, Rifkind, Wharton and Garrison, N.Y.C., 1968-71; asst. sec. Textron Inc., Providence, 1971-81; v.p., gen. counsel, sec. Nat. Kinney Corp., N.Y.C., 1981; gen. counsel HUD, Washington, 1981—. Office: Office Gen Counsel HUD 451 7th St SW Washington DC 20410

KNAPP, JOHN MERRILL, educator; b. N.Y.C., May 9, 1914; s. John Harold and Lillian (Merrill) K.; m. Elizabeth-Ann Campbell, Feb. 21, 1944; children—Joan, Phoebe. A.B., Yale, 1936; M.A., Columbia, 1941; Mus.D., Westminster Choir Coll., 1970. Tchr. history Thacher Sch., Ojai, Calif., 1936-38; asst. dir. Yale Glee Club, 1938-39; mem. faculty Princeton, 1941-42, 46—, prof. music, 1961—, dir., 1941-42, 46-52, asst. dean coll., 1955-58, dean, 1961-66. Author: The Magic of Opera, 1972; Editor: Selected List of Music for Mens Voices, 1952, (Handel) Amadigi, 1972. Former trustee Hun Sch., Westminster Choir Coll., Hotchkiss Sch. Served with USNR, 1942-46. Mem. Internat., Am. musicol. socs., Coll. Music Soc., AAUP, Halle Händel Soc. (exec. bd.), Göttingen Handel Soc. (exec. com.). Home: Rosedale Ln Princeton NJ 08540

KNAPP, RICHARD BRUCE, anesthesiologist; b. N.Y.C., Oct. 17, 1933; s. John J. and Hilda K. (Appel) K.; m. Harriett Hollister Boynton, June 1, 1953; children—Laurie (dec.), Carolyn, Pamela, Richard Benjamin. A.B., Columbia U., 1955; M.D., N.Y. Med. Coll., 1959. Diplomate: Am. Bd. Anesthesiology. Intern C.V. Meml. Hosp., Johnstown, Pa., 1959-60; resident in anesthesiology N.Y. Hosp., Cornell Med. Center, 1960-62, chief resident, 1962; anesthesiologist Robert Packer Hosp., Guthrie Clinic, Sayre, Pa., 1964-66, chmn. sect. anesthesiology, 1965-66; anesthesiologist Greenwich (Conn.) Hosp., 1966-74; prof., chmn. dept. anesthesiologist W.Va. U. Med. Center, Morgantown, 1974—; clin. instr. Cornell Med. Coll., 1960-62; asst. clin. prof. N.Y. Med. Coll., 1968-72, asso. clin. prof., 1972-74. Served to lt. M.C. USNR, 1962-64. USPHS fellow, 1959-60. Fellow Am. Coll. Anesthesiology, Am. Coll. Chest Physicians; mem. Assn. Univ. Anesthetists, AMA, N.Y. Acad. Scis. Club: Lakeview Country. Home: Box 15 Harewood Morgantown WV 26505 Office: WVa U Med Center Morgantown WV 26506

KNAPP, RICHARD C., transportation company executive; b. 1923. Student, U. Detroit Coll. Engring. Chmn. bd. Anchor Motor Freight Inc., 1955-80; exec. v.p. auto group Leaseway Transp. Corp., Cleve., 1980—. Served to lt. USNAC, 1942-46. Address: Leaseway Transportaiton Corp 3700 Park East Dr Cleveland OH 44122 *

KNAPP, RICHARD JOSEPH, coast guard officer; b. Passaic, N.J., Feb. 14, 1929; s. Joseph and Anne K.; m. Pamela Hancock Pelham, Apr. 30, 1960; children: Joseph, Marc, Nancy, Richard. B.S. in Engring., U.S. Coast Guard Acad., 1951; M.B.A., George Washington U., 1962; student, Mcht. Marine Indoctrination Sch., 1958. Commd. officer U.S. Coast Guard, 1951; advanced through grades to rear adm.; asst. to comptroller Coast Guard Hdqrs., 1963-66; chief staff officer Coast Guard Squadron One, Vietnam, 1965-66; comdg. officer Coast Guard Cutter Acushnet, 1967-68; chief cost analysis br., budget div. Coast Guard Hdqrs., 1968-72; comdg. officer Coast Guard Cutters Southwind and Edisto, 1972-73; chief ocean ops. div. Coast Guard Hdqrs., 1974-76, dep. chief personnel, 1977-78, comptroller, 1978-80; comdr. 17th Coast Guard Dist., Juneau, Alaska, 1980—. Decorated Legion of Merit with combat distinciton device, Meritorious Service medal, Coast Guard Commendation medal. Episcopalian. Lodge: Rotary. Office: PO Box 3-500 Juneau AK 99802

KNAPP, RICHARD MAITLAND, assn. exec.; b. Hartford, Conn., July 23, 1941; s. Maitl K.; m. Elizabeth Burgoyne, Apr. 1969; children—Heather, Peter. B.A., Marietta (Ohio) Coll., 1963; M.A., U. Iowa, 1965, Ph.D. in Hosp. and Health Adminstrn, 1968. Project dir. Teaching Hosp. Info. Center, Council of Teaching Hosps., Assn. Am. Med. Colls., Washington, 1968-69, dir. div. teaching hosps., 1969-73, dir. dept. teaching hosps., 1973—; preceptor dept. health systems mgmt. Sch. Public Health and Tropical Medicine, Tulane U., New Orleans, 1980-82; mem. adv. com. ambulatory dental services program Robert Wood Johnson Hosp., 1978—. Contbr. articles to profl. jours. Mem. vestry St. Anne's Episcopal Ch., Reston, Va., 1979—; bd. dirs. No. Va. Vis. Nurses Assn., 1981—. USPHS trainee, 1964-65. Mem. Am. Hosp. Assn. (adv. panel voluntary cost containment 1978—, council research and devel. 1978-81, council fed. relations 1980—), Assn. Univ. Programs in Health Adminstrn., Delta Upsilon. Home: 11778 Indian Ridge Rd Reston VA 22091 Office: 200 One Dupont Circle NW Washington DC 20036

KNAPP, ROBERT CHARLES, physician; b. N.Y.C., Jan. 19, 1927; s. Jack and Hilda (Knapp); m. Miriam Hermanos, Nov., 1955; children: Louise, Jennifer, Michael. A.B., Columbia U., 1949; M.D., SUNY Downstate Med. Center, Bklyn., 1953; M.A., Harvard U., 1983. Diplomate: Am. Bd. Ob-Gyn. Intern Kings County Hosp., Bklyn., 1953-54, resident, 1954-58; instr. ob-gyn SUNY, Bklyn., 1958-62, Am. Cancer Soc. fellow, 1962-63, asst. prof. ob-gyn, 1962-63; asst. prof. Cornell U., 1963-69, asso. prof., 1969-70; chmn. dept. ob-gyn Nassau County Med. Center, East Meadow, N.Y., 1967-70; asso. prof. ob-gyn Harvard U., 1970-75, William H. Baker prof. gynecology, 1975; asso. chief of staff Boston Hosp. for Women, 1975-80; dir. gynecology surgery and oncology Brigham and Women's Hosp., Boston, 1980—; dir. gynecology Sidney Farber Cancer Inst., 1975—. Served with U.S. Army, 1944-46. Fellow Am. Coll. Obstetricians and Gynecologists, A.C.S.; mem. Am. Soc. Clin. Oncology, Am. Fedn. Clin. Research, AAAS, Obstet. Soc. Boston, Am. Radium Soc., Boston Surg. Soc., Soc. Gynecologic Oncologists, Am. Assn. for Cancer Research, Soc. Surg. Oncologists. Home: 160 Laurel Rd Chestnut Hill MA 02167 Office: 75 Francis St Boston MA 02115

KNAPP, THOMAS EDWIN, sculptor, painter; b. Gillette, Wyo., Sept. 28, 1925; s. Chester M. and Georgia Mabel (Blankenship) K.; m. Dorothy Wellborn; children: Gordon, Kathy, Dan, Kent, Keith. Student, Santa Rosa Jr. Coll., 1952-53; A.A., Calif. Coll. Arts and Crafts, 1953-54; student, Art Ctr. Sch., Los Angeles, 1954-55. Animation artist Walt Disney Studios, Burbank, Calif., 1954-56, Portrait & Hobby Camera Shops, WyoFoto Studies, Cody, Wyo., 1956-64; owner Rocky Mountain Land Devel. Corp., Cody, Wyo., 1965-66; comml. artist Mountain States Telephone Co., Albuquerque, 1966-69; lectr. at art seminars. Exhibited one-man shows, Cody County Art League, 1968, Jamison Gallery, Santa Fe, 1969, Mesilla Gallery, 1971, Inn of Mountain Gods, Mescalero Apache Reservations, N.Mex., 1978, Mountain Oyster Club, Tucson, Dos Pajaros Gallery, El Paso, (with Dorothy Wellborn) joint shows, Rosquist Gallery, Tucson, 1975, 77, Colony House, Roswell, N.Mex., 1974, 75, (with Michael Coleman), Zantman Gallery, Palm Desert Calif., 1977, group shows, Saddleback Inn, Santa Ana, Calif., 1968-77, Zantman Gallery, Carmel, Calif., 1975, 76, 77, Borglum Meml. Sculpture Exhbn. Nat. Cowboy Hall of Fame, Oklahoma City, 1975-76, Maxwell Gallery, San Francisco, 1975; represented permanent collections, Whitney Gallery Western Art, Cody, Senator Quinn Meml. Auditorium, Spencer, Mass., Heritage Mus., Anchorage, Indpls. Mus. Art, Mescalero Tribe, N.Mex.; works include Dance of the Mountain Spirits (Blue Ribbon award 1976), Laguna Eagle dancer (spl. award 1974), Blue Ribbon los Angeles Indian Art Show, 1975-76, Santa Clara Buffalo dancer (Spl. award San Antonio Indian Nat. show 1974, Spl. award Los Angeles Indian show 1976), Mandan chieftan (Spl. award San Diego Indian show 1974, Spl. award Los Angeles Indian show 1976); mem. adv. bd.: Quar. Jour. Mus. Native Am. Cultures, Spokane, Wash. Active Boy Scouts Am., 1947-68. Served with USN, World War II; Korea. Decorated Air medal; recipient Order Arrow award Boy Scout Am., 1968. Mem. Am. Foundrymen's Soc., N.Mex. Amigos. Club: Safari Internat. Homeand Office: PO Box 510 Ruidoso Downs NM 88346

KNAPP, WHITMAN, U.S. judge; b. N.Y.C., Feb. 24, 1909; s. Wallace Percy and Carolina Morgan (Miller) K.; m. Ann Fallert, May 17, 1962; 1 son, Gregory Wallace; children by previous marriage—Whitman Everett, Caroline (Mrs. Edward M. W. Hines), Marion Elizabeth. Grad., Choate Sch., 1927; B.A., Yale, 1931; LL.B., Harvard, 1934. Bar: N.Y. bar 1935. With firm Cadwalader, Wickersham & Taft, N.Y.C., 1935-37; dep. asst. dist. atty., N.Y.C., 1937-41; with firm Donovan, Leisure, Newton & Lumbard, N.Y.C., 1941; mem. staff dist. atty., N.Y.C., 1942-50, chief, appeal bur., 1944-50; partner firm Barrett Knapp Smith Schapiro & Simon (and predecessors), 1950-72; U.S. dist. judge So. Dist. N.Y., 1972—; spl. counsel N.Y. State Youth Commn., 1950-53; Waterfront Commn. N.Y. Harbor, 1953-54; Mem. temp. commn. revision N.Y. State penal law and criminal code, 1964-69; chmn. Knapp Commn. to Investigate Allegations of Police Corruption in N.Y.C., 1969-72; gen. counsel Urban League Greater N.Y., 1962-72. Editor: Harvard Law Rev, 1933-34. Sec. Community Council Greater N.Y., 1952-58; pres. Dalton Schs., N.Y.C., 1950-53, Youth House, 1967-68; Trustee Univ. Settlement, 1945-64, Moblzn. for Youth, 1965-70. Mem. Am. Law Inst., Am. Bar Assn., Am. Bar Found., Am. Coll. Trial Lawyers, Assn. Bar City N.Y. (sec. 1946-49, chmn. exec. com. 1971-72). Home: 134 Greene St New York NY 10012 Office: US Courthouse Foley Sq New York NY 10007

KNAPPENBERGER, PAUL HENRY, JR., sci. mus. adminstr.; b. Reading, Pa., Sept. 5, 1942; s. Paul Henry and Kathryn (Medrick) K.; m. Peggy Ann Witmyer, Aug. 31, 1963; children—Paul Charles, Timothy Alan. A.B. in Math, Franklin and Marshall Coll., 1964; M.A. in Astronomy (NASA fellow), U. Va., 1966, Ph.D., 1968. Astronomer Fernbank Sci. Center, Atlanta, 1968-72; instr. Emory U. and Ga. State U., Atlanta, 1970-72; dir. Sci. Mus. of Va., Richmond, 1973—; asst. prof. Va. Commonwealth U., U. Richmond; bd. dirs. Assn. Sci. and Tech. Centers; instr. astronomy Yellowstone Inst.; Former pres. Windsor Forest Community Assn.; former v.p. Midlothian Athletic Assn. Co-author: Adventures on a Dark Night, 1981. NSF Sci. Edn. grantee, 1971-72; grantee Nat. Endowment Humanities, Inst. Mus. Services. Mem. Am. Astron. Soc., AAAS, Internat. Planetarium Soc., Southeastern Planetarium Assn., Va. Acad. Sci., Richmond Astron. Soc., Assn. Sci. and Tech. Centers, Am. Assn. Museums. Lutheran. Club: Richmond Rotary. Home: 11760 Heathmere Crescent Midlothian VA 23113 Office: 2500 W Broad St Richmond VA 23220

KNAUB, DONALD EDWARD, museum director; b. York, Pa., Dec. 18, 1936; s. Harry N. and Mary (Kenney) K.; m. Karen Palmer, June 21, 1970; children: Zackary Daniel, Andrea Rachael. A.B. in Liberal Arts, Elizabethtown Coll., 1959; M.A., Boston U., M.F.A., 1962; cert. arts adminstrn., Harvard U., 1975. Info. asst. N.Y. Public Library System, 1962-68; civic arts dir., City of Davis, Calif., 1973-78; exec. dir. Muckenthaler Cultural Ctr., Fullerton, Calif., 1978-79; dir. Huntsville (Ala.) Mus. Art, 1979—; chmn. fine arts com. Orange County Spl. Mus. Task Force, 1978-79; mem. com. arts and lectures U. Calif., Davis, 1972-78. Mem. Am. Assn. Museums, Southeastern Museum Conf. Internat. Com. for Fine Arts., Internat. Council on Museums, Assn. Art Mus. Dirs. (external affairs com.). Home: 902 Kennamer St Huntsville AL 35801 Office: 700 Monroe St Huntsville AL 35801

KNAUER, GEORG NICOLAUS, classical philologist; b. Hamburg, Germany, Feb. 26, 1926; came to U.S., 1975; s. Georg A. and Ilse M. (Groothoff) K.; m. Elfriede Regina Overhoff, Aug. 3, 1951; 1 son, Georg Lorenz. Dr. phil., U. Hamburg, 1952. Research asst. Thesaurus Linguae Latinae, Munich, Germany, 1952-54; Assistent Freie U., Berlin, 1954-61, Privatdozent, 1961-64, assoc. prof., 1964-66, prof., 1966-74; prof. classical studies U. Pa., Phila., 1975—; Brit. Council scholar U. London, 1957-58; vis. prof. Yale U., 1965-66; Nellie Wallace lectr. Oxford (Eng.) U., 1969; mem. Inst. Advanced Study, Princeton, N.J., 1973-74; vis. prof. Columbia U., fall 1976; mem. Notgemeinschaft für eine freie Universität, Berlin.; Mem. Fed. Com. of Bund Freiheit der Wissenschaft, Bonn, Germany; mem. Internat. Council on Future of Univ., N.Y.C. Author: Psalmenzitate in Augustins Konfessionen, 1955, Die Aeneis und Homer, 1964. Served with German Army, 1944-45. Guggenheim fellow, 1979-80; vis. scholar Am. Acad., Rome. Mem. Am. Philol. Assn., Renaissance Soc. Am. Home: Apt 1505 3600 Conshohocken Ave Philadelphia PA 19131 Office: Dept of Classical Studies 720 Williams Hall Univ of Pennsylvania Philadelphia PA 19104

KNAUER, VIRGINIA HARRINGTON WRIGHT (MRS. WILHELM F. KNAUER), government official; b. Phila., Mar. 28, 1915; d. Herman Winfield and Helen (Harrington) Wright; m. Wilhelm F. Knauer, Jan. 27, 1940; children: Wilhelm F., Valerie H. (Mrs. I. Townsend Burden III). B.F.A., U. Pa., 1937, LL.D. (hon.); grad., Pa. Acad. Fine Arts, 1937; postgrad., Royal Acad. Fine Arts, Florence, Italy, 1938-39; LL.D., Phila. Coll. Textiles and Sci., Allentown Coll. St. Francis de Sales, Widener Coll., Chester, Pa., Tufts U.; Litt.D., Drexel U.; L.H.D., Russell Sage Coll., Pa. Coll. Podiatric Medicine. Dir. Pa. Bur. Consumer Protection, 1968-69; spl. asst. consumer affairs to U.S. pres. White House, 1969-77, 81-83, spl. adv. on consumer affairs to U.S. pres., 1983—; dir. U.S. Office Consumer Affairs, 1971-77, 81—; pres. Virginia Knauer & Assos., Inc., Washington, 1977-81; chmn. Council for Advancement of Consumer Policy, 1979-81; U.S. rep., vice chmn. consumer policy com. OECD, 1970-77; mem. Council Wage and Price Stability, 1974-77; Councilman-at-large, Phila., 1960-68; vice-chmn. Philadelphia County Rep. Com., 1958-77; pres. Phila. Congress Rep. Women's Councils, 1958-77; dir. Pa. Council Rep. Women, 1963-80; founder N.E. Phila. Council Rep. Women, pres., 1956-68. Bd. dirs. Hannah Penn House, 1956—, v.p., 1971; former trustee Pa. Coll. Podiatric Medicine; co-founder Knauer Found. Historic Preservation. Recipient Gimbel-Phila. award, Ind. Achievement in Govt. award Soc. Consumer Affairs Profls., 1983; named Disting. Dau. Pa., 1969. Mem. Nat. Trust Historic Preservation, Zeta Tau Alpha, Kappa Delta Epsilon (hon.). Episcopalian. Office: US Office Consumer Affairs Washington DC 20201

KNAUSS, EARL L., financial executive; b. Ottawa, Kans., July 27, 1933; s. Earl L. and Nina (Hood) K.; m. Karen Rollins, 1974; children: Sharon, Michelle. Student, Kans. U., 1951-55. With Farmland Industries, Inc., Kansas City, Mo., 1955—, now fin. v.p., treas.; dir. Coop. Farm Chem. Assn.; pres., dir. Coop. Service Co.; treas., dir. Coop. Fin. Assn.; vice chmn. Farmland Foods, Inc.; sec.-treas., dir. Farmers Chem. Co.; v.p. Ceres Devel. Co.; chmn. Farmland Securities Co. Mem. Delta Chi. Office: PO Box 7305 Kansas City MO 64116

KNAUSS, ROBERT LYNN, legal educator, university dean; b. Detroit, Mar. 24, 1931; s. Karl Ernst and Loise (Atkinson) K.; m. Angela Tirola Lawson, Feb. 21, 1973; children by previous marriage: Robert B., Charles H., Katherine E.; 1 stepson, Ian T. Lawson. A.B., Harvard U., 1952; J.D., U. Mich., 1957. Bar: Calif., Tenn., Tex. Asso. Pillsbury, Madison & Sutro, San Francisco, 1958-60; prof. law U. Mich., 1960-72, v.p., 1970-72; dean, prof. law Vanderbilt U., Nashville, 1972-79; vis. prof. Vt. Law Sch., South Royalton, Amos Tuck Sch. Bus. Adminstrn., Dartmouth Coll., Hanover, N.H., 1979-81; disting. univ. prof. law U. Houston Law Center, 1981—, dean, 1981—; cons. spl. studies security markets SEC, 1962-63; rapporteur, panel on capital formation Am. Soc. Internat. Law, 1967-71; dir. Houston Natural Gas Corp., Equus Capital. Editor: Small Business Financing, 4 vols., 1966, Securities Regulation Sourcebook, 1970-71, (with others) Cases and Materials on Enterprise Organizations, 1982; contbr. articles to profl. jours. Served to lt. (j.g.) USNR, 1952-55. Mem. ABA, Am. Law Inst., Order of Coif. Home: 2004 Milford St Houston TX 77098 Office: U Houston Law Center Houston TX 77004

KNEBEL, FLETCHER, writer; b. Dayton, Ohio, Oct. 1, 1911; s. A.G. and Mary (Lewis) K.; children: Jack G., Mary L. A.B., Miami U., Oxford, Ohio, 1934. With Coatesville (Pa.) Record, 1934, Chattanooga News, 1934-35, Toledo News Bee, 1936; with Cleve. Plain Dealer, 1936-50; Washington corr., 1937-50; corr. Washington bur. Cowles Publs., 1950-64; syndicated columnist Potomac Fever, 1951-64. Author: Night of Camp David, 1965, The Zinzin Road, 1966, Vanished, 1968, Trespass, 1969, Dark Horse, 1972, The Bottom Line, 1974, Dave Sulkin Cares!, 1978, Crossing in Berlin, 1981, Poker Game; co-author: No High Ground, 1960, Seven Days in May, 1962, Convention, 1964. Served as lt. USNR, 1942-45. Mem. Phi Beta Kappa, Sigma Chi. Club: Gridiron.

KNEBEL, JOHN ALBERT, lawyer, former govt. ofcl.; b. Tulsa, Oct. 4, 1936; s. John Albert and Florence Julia (Friend) K.; m. Zenia Irene Marks, June 6, 1959; children—Carrie, John Albert III, Clemens. B.S., U.S. Mil. Acad., 1959; M.A. in Econs, Creighton U., 1962; J.D., Am. U., 1965. Bar: D.C. bar 1966, U.S. Ct. Appeals bar 1966. Asst. to Rep. J.E. Wharton of N.Y., Washington, 1963-64; asso. mem. law firm Howrey, Simon, Baker & Murchison, Washington, 1965-68; asst. counsel Com. on Agr., U.S. Ho. Reps., Washington, 1968-71; gen. counsel SBA, Washington, 1971-74, U.S. Dept. Agr., 1973-75; under sec. Dept. Agr., 1975-76, sec. of agr., 1976-77; partner firm Baker & McKenzie, Washington, 1977—. Served to 1st lt. USAF, 1959-62. Mem. Fed. Bar Assn. (past pres.), Am., D.C. bar assns., Delta Theta Phi, Omicron Delta Gamma. Home: 1418 Laburnum St McLean VA 22101 Office: 815 Connecticut Ave NW Washington DC 20006

KNECHT, CHARLES DANIEL, veterinarian; b. Halethorpe, Md., Mar. 22, 1932; s. Frank Anthony and Lillian Mary (Smith) K.; m. Lucretia Jean Hanna, Aug. 14, 1954; children—Charles Mark, Thomas Richard. B.S., U. Md., 1960; V.M.D., U. Pa., 1956; M.S., U. Ill., 1966. Staff veterinarian Broad St. Vet. Hosp., Pitts., 1958-59, Towson (Md.) Vet. Hosp., 1959-64; instr. to assoc. prof. vet. sci. U. Ill., Urbana, 1964-70; prof., chief surgery Coll. Vet. Medicine, U. Ga., Athens, 1970-72; prof., chief surgery small animal clinic Purdue U., West Lafayette, Ind., 1972-79; prof., head dept. small animal surgery and medicine Sch. Vet. Medicine, Auburn (Ala.) U., 1979—. Author: Fundamental Techniques in Veterinary Surgery, 1975, 2d edit., 1977; contbr. articles to sci. jours. Served to capt. USAF, 1956-58. Recipient Disting. Teaching award Upjohn, 1971, Outstanding Tchr. award U. Ga., Athens, 1972, Outstanding Clincian award, 1973, 76, 77, Purdue Alumni Disting. Teaching award, 1976. Mem. AVMA (Gaines award 1982), Am. Coll. Vet. Surgeons, Am. Coll. Vet. Internal Medicine, Am. Assn. Vet. Clincians, Am. Assn. Vet. Med. Colls., Am. Animal Hosp. Assn., Ala. Vet. Med. Assn., East Ala. Vet. Med. Assn., Sigma Xi, Phi Zeta, Alpha Psi, Omega Tau Sigma (Zeta award 1983), Gamma Sigma Delta. Inventor Knecht Condyle clamp. Home: 3704 Flintwood Dr Opelika AL 36801 *We are all a little of each person we have known. Using the good features of good people, we cannot help but improve.*

KNECHT, JAMES HERBERT, lawyer; b. Los Angeles, Aug. 5, 1925; s. James Herbert and Gertrude Martha (Morris) K.; m. Margaret Paton Vreeland, Jan. 3, 1953; children—Susan, Thomas Paton, Carol. B.S., UCLA, 1947; LL.B., U. So. Calif., 1957. Bar: Calif. bar 1957, U.S. Supreme Ct. bar 1969. Mem. firm Forster, Gemmill & Farmer, Los Angeles, 1957—. Fellow Am. Bar Found.; mem. Am. Bar Assn., Los Angeles County Bar Assn., Legion Lex, Caltech Assos., Los Angeles Area C. of C. (dir. 1979—), Town Hall of Calif., Los Angeles World Affairs Council, Beta Theta Pi. Clubs: Jonathan, Rotary. Home: 522 Bradford St Pasadena CA 91105 Office: 900 Wilshire Blvd Los Angeles CA 90017

KNECHT, LORING DAHL, foreign language and literature educator; b. Wimbledon, N.D., Sept. 19, 1921; s. Jacob W. and Edna Karen (Dahl) K.; m. Suzanne Marie Toan, July 12, 1950; children: Leif Michel, Genevieve Marie. B.A., St. Olaf Coll., 1947; postgrad., U. Paris, 1945-46, 49-50, Middlebury French Sch., summer 1947; M.A., U. Wis., 1948, Ph.D., 1957. Mem. Faculty St. Olaf Coll., 1951—, prof., chmn. dept. Romance langs., 1957-79, chmn. div. lang. and lit., 1970-73. Co-author: Echos de notre monde, 1975; Contbg. author: Christian Faith and the Liberal Arts, 1958, Andre Gide: a Collection of Critical Essays, 1970. Served with AUS, World War II; ETO. French Govt. scholar, 1945-46; Fulbright scholar, 1949-50; Knapp fellow, 1954-55. Mem. AAUP, MLA, Am. Assn. Tchrs. French. Home: 611 Prairie Ave Northfield MN 55057

KNECHT, LOUIS BERNARD, union ofcl.; b. St. Louis, Aug. 24, 1920; s. Louis Bernard and Charlotte (Oughton) K.; m. Marjorie A. Skow, Nov. 22, 1946; children—Louis Bernard, Steven A. Student, U. Notre Dame, 1937-39. With Pacific Tel. & Tel. Co., 1946-50; with Communications Workers Am., Washington, 1950—, dist. dir., 1955-65, asst. to pres., 1965-71, exec. v.p., 1971-74, sec.-treas., 1974—; officer J.A. Beirne Found. Mem. Calif. Correctional Industries Commn., 1950-55; mem. Nat. Commn. on Fed. Paperwork, 1975-77; vice chairperson Md. Democratic State Com., 1974; mem. Montgomery County State Central Com., 1974, Nat. Dem. Fin. Council, 1975—. Served with Signal Corps AUS, 1940-46. Roman Catholic. Club: Notre Dame Alumni. Office: 1925 K St NW Washington DC 20006

KNECHTGES, DAVID RICHARD, Chinese and East Asian studies educator; b. Great Falls, Mont., Oct. 23, 1942; s. Carl Jacob and Gertrude Olive (Clauson) K.; m. Taiping Chang, June 7, 1977. B.A., U. Wash., 1964, Ph.D., 1968; M.A., Harvard U., 1965. Instr., asst. prof. Chinese lit. Yale U., New Haven, 1968-71; asst. prof. Chinese U. Wis., Madison, 1971-72; asst. prof., assoc. prof., Chinese and East Asian Studies U. Wash., Seattle, 1972—. Author: The Han Rhapsody: A Study of the Fu of Yang Hsinung, 1976, Wen Xuan or Selections of Refined Literature, 1982, The Han Shu Biography of Tang Xuang, 1982; assoc. editor: Jour. Am. Oriental Soc., 1972-75. Nat. Def. fgn. lang. fellow U. Wash., 1964-67; Woodrow Wilson fellow U. Wash., 1967-68, Harvard U., 1964; Fulbright Hays faculty research grantee, 1971; grantee Am. Council Learned Socs., 1975, NEH, 1977-80. Mem. Am. Oriental Soc., Assn. for Asian Studies, Soc. for Study of Early China. Office: Dept Asian Langs and Lit U Washington Seattle WA 981-5

KNEELAND, DOUGLAS EUGENE, newspaper editor; b. Lincoln, Maine, July 27, 1929; s. Vernis Bruce and Sadie Jane (Curtis) K.; m. Anne Packard Libby, Sept. 8, 1951; children: Debra Jo Kneeland Wentz, Libby, Bruce, Wayne. B.A. in Journalism, U. Maine, 1953. Reporter Bangor Daily News, Maine, 1951-53, Worcester Telegram, Mass., 1953-56; city editor, news editor Lorain Jour., Ohio, 1956-59; copy editor, nat. corr., dep. nat. editor N.Y. Times, N.Y.C., Kansas City, San Francisco and Chgo., 1959-81; nat.-fgn. editor Chgo. Tribune, 1981-82, assoc. mng. editor, 1982—. Served with AUS, 1947-49; Korea, Japan. Home: 3440 N Lake Shore Dr Apt 8-A Chicago IL 60657 Office: Chgo Tribune Co 435 N Michigan Ave Chicago IL 60611

KNEELAND, ROLAND JOSEPH, paper company executive; b. Bethel, Maine, Oct. 5, 1932; s. Roland Merle and Libbie Lynn (Goodridge) K.; m. Marjorie Carol Murray, Sept. 5, 1953; children: David, Steven, Kathy. B.S. in Chem. Engring., U. Maine, 1955, cert. in paper and pulp mgmt., 1955; grad. Advanced Mgmt. Program, Harvard Grad. Sch. Bus., 1981. With Internat. Paper Co., N.Y.C., and Miss., 1969-74; v.p., gen. mgr. Irving Paper & Pulp Ltd., St. John, N.B., Can., 1974-78; v.p. mfg. Boise Cascade Can. Ltd., Fort Frances, Ont., 1980, pres., Toronto, Ont., 1980—, corp. dir., 1982—. Bd. dirs. Greater Toronto YMCA System, 1982—. Mem. TAPPI, Am. Mgmt. Assn., Paper Industry Mgmt. Assn., Can. Paper and Pulp Assn. (dir. 1980—), N.B. Forest Products Assn. (dir. 1980—), Pulp and Paper Research Inst. Can. (dir. 1983—), Ont. Forest Products Assn. (dir.). Methodist. Club: Chemists (N.Y.C.). Office: Boise Cascade Can Ltd 3300 Bloor St W Toronto ONCanada M8X 2X2

KNEISEL, FRANK, forest products manufacturing company executive; b. N.Y.C., May 18, 1937; s. Frank and Ruth (Brank) K.; m. Mary C. Clayson, Nov. 20, 1965; children: Geoffrey C., Lindsay P., David F. B.A., Yale U., 1959; M.B.A., Harvard U., 1965. Auditor Arthur Andersen & Co., N.Y.C., Hartford, Conn., 1959-63; asst. to treas. Merck & Co., Rahway, N.J., 1965-68; v.p., treas. Champion Internat. Corp., Stamford, Conn., 1969—. Served with U.S. Army, 1961-62. Office: One Champion Plaza Stamford CT 06921

KNEITEL, THOMAS STEPHEN, author, consultant, editor; b. Bklyn., Jan. 28, 1933; s. Seymour Holtzer and Ruth Florence (Fleischer) K.; m. Judith Gibson, Apr. 26, 1961; children: Robin, Kerry, Kathleen, David, Karin, Terri, Skip. Student, U. Miami, Fla.; B.A., M.A., N.Y. U.; Ph.D., Columbia U. Announcer Sta. WTTT, Miami, 1951-52; exec. United Artists Corp., N.Y.C., 1954-59; mng. editor Ziff-Davis Publishing Co., N.Y.C., 1959-60; film writer U.S. Army Signal Corps Pictorial Center, N.Y.C., 1960-61; editor Horizons Publs., Oklahoma City, 1961-62; editorial dir. Cowan Pub. Corp., N.Y.C., 1962-82; v.p., editor Popular Communications Mag., N.Y.C., 1982—. Author: numerous books including 103 Simple Transitor Projects, 1962, CB'ers SSB Handbook, 1977, Registry of Government Radio Frequencies, 1979-84, Air-Scan Directory, 1979, 80, 81, Energy-Scan Directory, 1980; also numerous articles; contbr. to: Ency. Americana, 1979. Decorated Knight Imperial Order Constantine. Fellow Am. Soc. Psychical Research; mem. SSB Network, Soc. Wireless Pioneers, Army Signal Corps Assn., Armed Forces Communications and Electronics Assn., Aircraft Owners and Pilots Assn., Tau Epsilon Phi, Ordo Templi Orientis. Home: PO Box 381 Smithtown NY 11787 Office: 76 N Broadway Hicksville NY 11801

KNELLER, JOHN WILLIAM, educator; b. Oldham, Eng., Oct. 15, 1916; s. John William and Margaret Ann (Truslove) K.; m. Alice Bowerman Hart, Apr. 30, 1943; 1 dau., Linda Hart. A.B., Clark U., 1938, Litt.D., 1970; A.M., Yale U., 1948, Ph.D., 1950; French Govt. and Fulbright fellow, U. Paris, France, 1949-50. Asst. in instrn. Yale U., 1947-49; instr. French Oberlin Coll., 1950-52, asst. prof., 1952-55, asso. prof., 1955-59, prof. French, 1959-65, chmn. dept. Romance langs., 1958-65, dean, 1967-68, provost, 1965-69; pres. Bklyn. Coll., 1969-79, pres. emeritus, 1979—; univ. prof. humanities and arts Hunter Coll. and Grad. Center, City U. N.Y., 1979—; mng. editor French Rev., 1962-65, editor, 1965-68; Cons. Nat. Endowment for Humanities; chmn. subcom. on enrollment goals and projections N.Y. State Edn.; Commr.'s Adv. Council on Higher Edn., Adv. Council on Higher Edn. Co-author: Initiation au francais, 1963, Introduction a la poesie francaise, 1962; Contbr. articles to jours. in field. Bd. dirs. Am.

Israel Friendship League, G.F. Kneller Found.; trustee Bklyn. Inst. Arts and Scis., Independence Savs. Bank, Downtown Bklyn. Devel. Assn. Served with AUS, 1942-46. Decorated officier Ordre des Palmes Académiques, France). Mem. Am. Assn. Tchrs. French (exec. council 1962-68), Modern Lang. Assn. (exec. council 1965-69), Yale Grad. Sch. Assn. (exec. com. 1967, 71), Bklyn. C. of C. (dir.), Kappa Delta Pi (hon.), Alpha Sigma Lambda (hon.). Clubs: Brooklyn, Century, Rembrandt, Yale (N.Y.C.); Southport Racquet. Office: Grad City UNY 33 W 42d St New York NY 10036

KNELLER, WILLIAM ARTHUR, geologist, educator; b. Cleve., Apr. 7, 1929; s. John Jacob and Cora (Schilke) K.; m. Olga Tihonovna Kanareff, July 14, 1951; children: Karinlee, Gregory John, Ellen Kay, Kurt Tihon. A.B., Miami U., Oxford, Ohio, 1951, M.S., 1955; Ph.D. (William Herbert Hobbs fellow, NSF fellow), U. Mich., 1964. Asst. prof. geology Eastern Mich. U., Ypsilanti, 1959-60; mem. faculty, U. Toledo, 1961—, assoc. prof., 1964-67, prof., chmn. dept. geology, 1967—; dir. Eitel Inst. for Silicate Research, 1976—; various engring. positions, summers 1948-56, cons. coal geology to constrn., mining, engring. and other companies. Served with 2d Marine Div. USMCR, 1951-53; col. Res. Rackham U. fellow (declined), 1956. Fellow Geol. Soc. Am.; mem. Am. Soc. Econ. Paleontologists and Mineralogists, Sigma Xi, Sigma Gamma Epsilon, Phi Sigma, Phi Kappa Phi. Home: 1761 Cherry Lawn Dr Toledo OH 43614

KNEPLER, HENRY, English language and literature educator; b. Vienna, Austria, May 8, 1922; came to U.S., 1946; s. Hugo and Hedwig (Moser) K.; m. Myrna Cohn, Apr. 23, 1961; children: Elizabeth, Elinor, Anne. B.A., Queen's U., 1945, M.A., 1946; Ph.D., U. Chgo., 1950. Instr. Ill. Inst. Tech., Chgo., 1947-52, asst. prof., 1952-58, assoc. prof., 1958-61, prof., chmn. dept. English, 1961-76, prof., 1961—; vis. prof. Sorbonne, Paris, 1971-73; cons. UN Edn. Sci. and Cultural Orgn., Paris, 1972—, Gas Devel. Corp., Chgo. and Algiers, 1976-77; Fulbright lectr., Chad, Niger, Senegal, Ivory Coast, 1976. Author: The Gilded Stage, 1968, Man About Paris, 1970, Social Sciences and Humanities in Engineering Education, 1974, Crossing Cultures, 1983. Home: 1344 E Madison Park Chicago IL 60615 Office: Ill Inst Tech Dept Humanities IIT Center Chicago IL 60616

KNEPPER, GEORGE W., educator; b. Akron, Ohio, Jan. 15, 1926; s. George W. and Grace (Darling) K.; m. Phyllis Watkins, Aug. 21, 1949; children—Susan Lynne, John Arthur. B.A., U. Akron, 1948; M.A., U. Mich., 1950, Ph.D., 1954. Mem. faculty U. Akron, 1948-49, 54—, asso. prof. history, head dept., 1959-62, dean, 1962-67, prof. history, 1964—. Author: New Lamps for Old, One Hundred Years of Urban Higher Education at the University of Akron, 1970, An Ohio Portrait, 1976, Akron: City at the Summit, 1981; editor: Travels in the Southland; The Journal of Lucius Verus Bièrce 1822-23, 1966. Served to ensign USNR, 1943-46. Fulbright fellow U. London, Eng., 1953-54. Mem. Am., So. hist. assns., Orgn. Am. Historians, Ohio Acad. History, Omicron Delta Kappa, Alpha Tau Omega, Phi Alpha Theta, Alpha Sigma Lambda. Home: 1189 Temple Trails Stow OH 44224 Office: Univ Akron Akron OH 44304

KNEPPER, WILLIAM EDWARD, lawyer; b. Tiffin, Ohio, Oct. 25, 1909; s. Russell Monroe and Mamie (Corn) K.; children: Richard Scott, Bonne Lee Knepper Marks; m. Mary Morrill Lichtenberg, Mar. 30, 1964; adopted children: Mary L. (Mrs. Daum), James W. Lichtenberg, John M. Lichtenberg. A.B., Ohio State U., 1931; postgrad., Columbus Coll. Law, 1931-32. Bar: Ohio 1933. Since practiced in, Columbus; partner firm Knepper, White & Dempsey, 1933-54, Knepper, White, Richards & Miller, 1954-77, Knepper, White, Arter & Hadden, 1977—; adj. prof. Ohio State U. Coll. Law, 1972—; Mem. Ohio Bar Examining Com., 1945-50, chmn., 1950. Author: Liability of Corporate Officers and Directors, 3d edit, 1979, Ohio Civil Practice, 1970; co-author: The Ohio Manual of General Practice, 1956, Judicial Conveyances and Eminent Domain (Ohio), 1960, Ohio Eminent Domain Practice, 1977; Editor: Insurance Counsel Jour, 1955-61; Contbr. numerous articles to profl. jours. and law revs. Pres. Def. Research Inst., Inc., 1965-66; Chmn. Franklin County Court House Annex Bldg. Commn., 1946-54, State Underground Parking Commn., 1955-58, 61-69; pres. United Appeal Franklin County, 1969. Fellow Am. Coll. Trial Lawyers; mem. ABA, Ohio State Bar Assn. (exec. commn. 1951-54), Columbus Bar Assn. (pres. 1947-48), Internat. Assn. Ins. Counsel (pres. 1962- 63), Am. Judicature Soc., Columbus Area C. of C. (chmn. 1963-65), Ohio State U. Assn. (pres. 1967-69), Columbus Players Club (pres. 1943), Pi Kappa Alpha, Kappa Kappa Psi. Democrat. Episcopalian. Clubs: Mason (33 deg.), K.T., Shriner, Univ. Athletic, Faculty (Columbus). Home: 3589 Prestwick Ct N OH 43220 Office: 180 E Broad St Columbus OH 43215

KNESS, RICHARD MAYNARD, tenor; b. Rockford, Ill., July 23, 1937; s. Harry William and Helen Loretta (Curran) Kniess; m. Joann Danielle Grillo, July 23, 1967; 1 son, John Richard; children by previous marriage: Paul Richard, Kristin Elaine. B.A., San Diego State U., 1958. Pres. Danielle Maynard Assos., Inc. Appeared with more than 60 opera cos., Europe, U.S., Middle East and Mexico, 1967-78; resident dramatic tenor, Met. Opera, N.Y.C. Opera, San Francisco, San Diego, San Antonio, Seattle, Cin., Hartford, Hawaii, Houston, Boston, Milw., 1967—; appeared with numerous symphony orchs., N.Y.C., Phila., Pitts., Cin., Washington, Atlanta; leading dramatic tenor, Met. Opera Assn., N.Y.C., 1977—; co-dir. with wife internat. opera co., The Ambassadores of Opera and Concert World Wide, 1979—. Served with U.S. Army, 1958-63. Recipient Grammy award for best classical rec., 1967. Republican. Clubs: Lions, N.Y. Athletic. Office: 240 Central Park S Suite 3N New York NY 10019

KNEVEL, ADELBERT MICHAEL, university dean; b. St. Joseph, Minn., Oct. 20, 1922; s. Henry John and Angeline Marie (Terwey) K.; m. Lillian Margaret Zent, June 19, 1950; children: Kenneth, Laura, Christi, Robert, Lisa. Student, St. Johns U., Collegeville, Minn., 1940-41, 48-49; B.S., N.D. State U., 1952, M.S., 1953; Ph.D., Purdue U., 1957. Instr. N.D. State U., 1953-54; instr. pharmacy Purdue U., West Lafayette, Ind., 1954-57, asst. prof., 1957-61, assoc. prof., 1961-65, prof., 1965—, asst. dean, 1969-75, assoc. dean, 1975—; Treas. Tippecanoe County Mental Health Assn., 1960-61; mem. Controlled Substances Adv. Com., State of Ind., 1974—. Author: (with F.E. DiGangi, S. R. Byrn) Quantitative Pharmaceutical Chemistry, 1977; Contbr.: chpt. to Remington's Pharmaceutical Sciences, 1980; articles to sci. publs. Served with USN, 1942-48. Sagamore of Wabash, Ind. Fellow Acad. Pharm. Scis.; mem. Am. Pharm. Assn., Am. Chem. Soc. (chmn. Purdue sect. 1963-64), Sigma Xi, Phi Lambda Upsilon, Phi Kappa Phi, Rho Chi. Roman Catholic. Lodge: Rotary. Home: 62 Thise Ct Lafayette IN 47905 Office: Sch Pharmacy and Pharmacal Scis Purdue U West Lafayette IN 47907

KNICKERBOCKER, DANIEL CANDEE, JR., lawyer, insurance company executive; b. Glen Ridge, N.J., Apr. 16, 1919; s. Daniel Candee and Elizabeth Eleanor (Hadley) K.; m. Helaine Joyce Blutman, Mar. 23, 1951; children: Daniel Candee III, Mallory Jane. A.B., Syracuse U., 1940; J.D. with distinction, Cornell U., 1950; postgrad., Harvard U., 1940-41, postgrad. Sch. Bus. Adminstrn., 1969. Bar: N.Y. 1951, U.S. Supreme Ct. 1959, Mass. 1964. Acct., Bethlehem Steel Co., 1942-47; assoc. Carter, Ledyard & Milburn, N.Y.C., 1950-58, Skadden, Arps, Slate, Meagher & Flom, 1958-60, McCanliss & Early, 1961-63; tax counsel John Hancock Mut. Life Ins. Co., Boston, 1963-66, counsel, 1966-70, v.p. and counsel, 1970-83, sr. v.p., gen solicitor, 1983—; lectr. law Cornell U., 1959-60; grad. tax program Boston U., 1965, 66, 67, 81, 82, U. Conn., 1979-80; mem. Tax Mgmt. Adv. Bd. on Estates, Trusts and Gifts, 1972—; mem. adv. com. Estate Planning Conf., U. Calif., San Diego, 1980. Editor-in-chief: Cornell Law Quar., 1949-50; contbr. articles to legal jours. Pres. South Brooklyn Neighborhood Houses, 1962-63, New Eng. Home for Little Wanderers, 1973-76; mem. Syracuse U. Corporate Devel. Council, 1973—; bd. dirs. Family Counseling and Guidance Centers, Boston, 1974—, v.p., 1979-80, pres., 1980-83. Mem. Am. Law Inst., ABA, Assn. Bar City N.Y., Assn. Life Ins. Counsel (chmn. tax sect. 1982—), Cornell Law Assn. (exec. com. 1959-62), Order of Coif, Phi Kappa Phi, Psi Upsilon. Democrat. Episcopalian. Home: 55 Frost St Cambridge MA 02140 Office: John Hancock Pl Boston MA 02117

KNICKERBOCKER, KENNETH LESLIE, educator, editor; b. Dallas, May 19, 1905; s. Hubert DeLancy and Julia (Opdenweyer) K.; m. Dorothy McDonald, June 30, 1928; children—Robert Keats, Alzada Jean. A.B., So. Meth. U., 1925, A.M., 1927; Ph.D., Yale, 1933. Instr. English Tex. Technol. Coll., 1926-29, 32-34; asst. prof. English R.I. State Coll., 1934-36, asso. prof., 1936-38, prof. English, head dept., 1938-46; prof., chmn. freshman English U. Tenn., 1946-57, asso. dean, 1957-58, dean, 1958-63, head dept. English, 1962-71, acad. v.p., 1971-73, Distinguished Service prof. English, 1964—; Chmn. Tenn. Com. Survey Role and Needs Higher Edn., 1956-57; exec. com. Assn. Depts. English, 1968-71. Editor: (with William C. DeVane) New letters of Robert Browning, 1950, Modern Library Selections from the Poetry of Robert Browning, 1951; compiler, editor: Ideas for Writing, 1951, (with H.W. Reninger) Interpreting Liberature, 6th edit, 1978, short edit., 1979, (with B. Stewart) Readings and Assignments in Freshman English, 1961, (with H. Reninger) Instructors Manual, 6th edit, 1978, (with Boyd Litzinger) The Browning Critics, 1966, Writing About Poetry, 1967; Contbr. articles to learned jours. on 19th century lit. figures. Served as lt. USNR, 1943-46. Named Distinguished Alumnus So. Meth. U., 1972; Am. Council Learned Socs. grantee, 1934. Mem. Modern Lang. Assn., Am., So. Atlantic Modern Lang. Assn., Nat. Council Tchrs. English, Coll. English Assn. (dir. 1956-58), Tenn. Coll English Assn. (pres. 1956-57), AAUP, Tenn. Edn. Assn., Conf. Coll. Composition and Communication (exec. com., nominating com.), Assn. Am. Univs. and Land-Grant Colls. (exec. com. 1959-62), So. Atlantic Assn. Depts. English (pres. 1969), Phi Beta Kappa, Kappa Alpha (So.), Phi Kappa Phi. Home: 3524 Bluff Point Dr Knoxville TN 37920 *I have discovered only one unalterable fact about life: frustration. Whatever one does is not enough. Whatever one looks forward to either does not fulfill expectation or comes too late. The reach does indeed exceed the grasp. Once one becomes used to being foiled, one gains perspective, and life, for him loses little of its excitement, its sardonic challenge. No one has ever achieved a definitive success, so I, one of the least of mortals, should not be disheartened and am not.*

KNIES, PAUL HENRY, former life insurance company executive; b. Columbus, Ohio, Jan. 28, 1918; s. Daniel and Eva (Schneider) K.; m. Evadna Johnson, Mar. 16, 1941; children: Barbara Ann (Mrs. H. Michael Sell), Philip L., Paul R. B.A., Ohio State U., 1940. With Met. Life Ins. Co., 1940-80, controller, 1964-1980, sr. v.p., mem. exec. com., 1971—. Trustee Valley Hosp., Ridgewood, Citizens Budget Commn., N.Y.C., 1975-80; ret., 1980. Served with arty. AUS, 1942-45. Fellow Soc. Actuaries; mem. Fin. Execs. Inst. (treas. 1974-80), Inst. Internal Auditors, Fin. Execs. Research Found. (treas. 1972-80), Phi Beta Kappa. Home: 650 Westbrook Rd Ridgewood NJ 07450

KNIETER, GERARD LEONARD, educator; b. Bklyn., June 2, 1931; s. Jack and Shirley (Lezinsky) K.; m. Barbara Cashetta, Dec. 5, 1953. B.S., N.Y. U., 1953, M.A., 1954; Ed.D., Columbia, 1961. Asst. prof. music edn. San Jose (Calif.) State U., 1962-65; acting dean, asst. to dean, asso. prof. music Duquesne U., 1965-67; prof. Temple U., 1967-78, also chmn. dept. music edn., head doctoral program, 1967-78; prof. music, dean Coll. Fine and Applied Arts, U. Akron, 1978—; field reader U.S. Office Edn.; cons. state depts. edn., sch. systems, univs. for interdisciplinary programs in arts; speaker nat. arts orgns., nat. profl. orgns. Dir. Theodore Presser Co. exec. v.p., treas. Initial Teaching Alphabet Found. Contbr. to: Toward an Aesthetic Education, Music Edn. For Tomorrow's Society, Documentary Report of the Ann Arbor Symposium; Editorial com.: Jour. Research Music Edn; editorial cons.: Jour. Aesthetic Edn, Am. Educators Ency. Served with AUS, 1954-56. Recipient Arch award N.Y. U., 1953. Mem. AAUP, Soc. for Ethnomusicology, Music Educators Nat. Conf., Phi Mu Alpha Sinfonia, Kappa Phi Kappa. Research applying psychology of creativity to tchr. edn. in arts. Developer interdisciplinary arts programs, applications of psychology of learning to tchr. edn. in arts. Home: 1248 Country Club Rd Akron OH 44313 Office: College of Fine and Applied Arts Univ Akron Akron OH 44325

KNIGHT, ALFRED BISHOP, lawyer; b. Dill City, Okla., Jan. 6, 1920; s. Earl M. and Minnie Belle (Bishop) K.; (div.)children-Grover Earl, Alfred Bishop, Dane S., Dannelle, Mary Beth, James P.; m. Margaret Knight. A.B., Washington, 1941; LL.B. (editor Law Rev.), George Washington U., 1946. Bar: Okla. 1946. Practiced in, Tulsa, 1946—; owner firm Knight, Wagner, Stuart, Wilkerson & Lieber, 1954—; tchr. ins. law, 1951-54. Pres. Tulsa Jaycees, 1948-49; bd. dirs. Tulsa C. of C., 1949-50; charter mem. bd. Tulsa Livestock and Fair; pres. Okla. Cutting Horse Assn., 1966; exec. com. Nat. Cutting Horse Assn., 1965—; pres. Palomino Assn., 1964. Served to lt. USNR, 1941-46. Mem. Am., Okla., Tulsa bar assns., Internat. Assn. Inst. Attys. Democrat. Home: Route 2 Box 166 Sperry OK 74073 Office: 233 W 11th St Tulsa OK 74119

KNIGHT, ARTHUR, educator, author. Past mem. faculty Inst. Film Techniques at City Coll. N.Y., Columbia, Hunter Coll., New Sch. Social Research; now prof. cinema dept. U. So. Calif.; guest lectr. Also film critic: The Hollywood Reporter; former film critic: The Saturday Rev, Westways; Author: (with Hollis Alpert) History of Sex in the Movies, The Liveliest Art; author: (with Hollis Alpert) History of Sex in the Movies; Author also 50 documentary scripts. Home: 22202 Pacific Coast Hwy Malibu CA 90265 Address: care USC Cinema University Park Los Angeles CA 90007 *I have always tried to do more than I could possibly find time for, on the theory that some projects are inevitably going to fall by the wayside, but some residue will remain.*

KNIGHT, ARTHUR LEE, JR., manufacturing executive; b. Buffalo, Oct. 5, 1937; s. Arthur Lee and Helen Louise (Barone) K.; m. Nancy Gifford, June 27, 1959; children: Arthur Lee III, Christopher Gifford, Elizabeth Helen. B.A., Dartmouth Coll., 1959; M.B.A., SUNY-Buffalo, 1967. Vice pres. John E. Hayes Co., Inc., Buffalo, 1961-67; v.p. mktg. Di Acro Div., Lake City, Minn., 1967-70, pres., 1970-75; v.p., group exec. Houdaille Industries, Inc., Ft. Lauderdale, Fla., 1975, also pres. Lubriquip div., Cleve., 1975-82; pres. John Crane-Houdaille, Inc., Morton Grove, Ill., 1982—, also dir.; dir. Bandit, Ltd., Chesterfield, Eng., 1975-82. Bd. dirs. Interstate Rehab. Assn., Red Wing, Minn., 1971-73; mem. Mayor's Citizens' Com. State Tng. Sch., Red Wing, 1973-75; trustee, bd. dirs. Brenwood Hosp., Cleve., 1977-82. Mem. Am. Mgmt. Assn. Republican. Episcopalian. Office: John Crane-Houdaille, Inc. 6400 Oakton St Morton Grove IL 60053

KNIGHT, ATHELIA WILHELMENIA, journalist; b. Portsmouth, Va., Oct. 15, 1950; d. Daniel Dennis and Adell Virginia (Savage) K. B.A. with honors in English, Norfolk State Coll., 1973; M.A. with honors in Journalism, Ohio State U., 1974. Cert. tchr., Va. Aide D.C. Coop. Extension Service, 1969-72; sub. tchr. Portsmouth Pub. Schs., 1973; reporter Virginian Pilot, Norfolk, 1973, Chgo. Tribune, 1974; met. desk reporter Washington Post, 1975-81, investigative reporter, 1981—; lectr. high schs., colls. Ohio State U. fellow, 1974. Mem. Women in Communications, Washington-Balt. Newspaper Guild. Am. Baptist. Home: 1535 C St SE Washington DC 20003 Office: Washington Post 1150 15th St NW Washington DC 20071

KNIGHT, CHARLES FIELD, electrical equiptment manufacturing company executive; b. Lake Forest, Ill., Jan. 20, 1936; s. Lester Benjamin and Elizabeth Anne (Field) K.; m. Joanne Parrish, June 22, 1957; children: Lester Benjamin III, Anne Field, Steven P., Jennifer Lee. B.S. in Mech. Engring., Cronell U., 1958; M.B.A., Cornell U., 1959. Mgmt. trainee Goetzewerke A.G., Burscheid, W. Ger., 1959-61; pres. Lester B. Knight Internat. Corp., 1961-63; exec. v.p. Lester B. Knight & Assocs., Inc., Chgo., 1963-67, pres., 1967-69, pres., chief exec. officer, 1969-73; vice chmn. bd. Emerson Electric, St. Louis, 1973; sr. vice chmn. bd., corp. exec. officer Emerson Electric Co., 1973, vice chmn. bd., 1973-74, chmn. bd., 1974—, chief exec. officer, 1973—, dir.; dir. Southwestern Bell Telephone Co., Mo. Pacific Corp., Ralston Purina Co., First Union Bancorp., Trans. World Corp. Mem. Civic Progress, 1973; bd. dirs. United Way Greater St. Louis; bd. Arts and Edn. Council; bd. dirs. Barnes Hosp.; trustee Washington U., St. Louis. Mem. Sigma Phi. Clubs: St. Louis Country; Log Cabin, Racquet (St. Louis); Glen View Golf (Ill.); Chicago. Office: Emerson Electric Co 8000 W Florissant Ave Saint Louis MO 63136

KNIGHT, DOUGLAS MAITLAND, educational administrator, corporation executive; b. Cambridge, Mass., June 8, 1921; s. Claude Rupert and Fanny Sarah Douglas (Brown) K.; m. Grace Wallace Nichols, Oct. 31, 1942; children: Christopher, Douglas Maitland, Thomas, Stephen. A.B., Yale U., 1942, M.A., 1944, Ph.D., 1946; LL.D. (hon.), Ripon Coll., Knox Coll., Davidson Coll., 1963, U. N.C., 1965, Emory U., 1965, Ohio Wesleyan U., 1970, Center Coll., 1973; L.H.D. (hon.), Lawrence U., 1964, Carleton Coll., 1966; Litt.D. (hon.), St. Norbert Coll., Wake Forest Coll., 1964. Instr. English, Yale U., 1946-47, asst. prof., 1947-53; vis. asst. prof. English, U. Calif.-Berkeley, summer 1949; Morse Research fellow, 1951-52; pres. Lawrence Coll., Appleton, Wis., 1954-63, Duke U., Durham, N.C., 1963-69; div. v.p. ednl. devel. RCA, N.Y.C., 1969-71, div. v.p. edn. services, 1971-72, staff v.p. edn. and community relations, 1972-73, cons., 1973-75, pres. RCA Iran, 1971-72, dir., 1971-73; pres. Social Econ. and Ednl. Devel., Inc., 1973—, Questar Corp., 1976—; U.S. del. SEATO Conf. Asian Univ. Pres., Pakistan, 1961; nat. commn. UNESCO, 1965-67; chmn. Nat. Adv. Commn. Libraries, 1966-68; adviser Imperial Orgn. for Social Service of Govt. Iran. Author: Pope and the Heroic Tradition, 1951; poetry The Dark Gate, 1971; editor, contbr.: Iliad and Odyssey, Twickenham edit., 1967, Libraries at Large, Tradition, Innovation and the National Interest, 1970, Medical Ventures and the University, 1967. Former mem. corp. MIT; bd. dirs., chmn. Woodrow Wilson Nat. Fellowship Found.; bd. dirs. Near East Found., 1975—, Internat. Schs. Services, 1976-82, Solebury Sch., 1975-83; trustee Questar Library of Sci. and Art, 1982—. Mem. Am. Assn. Advancement of Humanities (dir. 1979—), Phi Beta Kappa. Clubs: Century Assn. (N.Y.C.); Cosmos (Washington); Elizabethan, Berzelius (New Haven). Home: RFD 3 Box 539 Stockton NJ 08559 Office: Questar Corp New Hope PA 18938

KNIGHT, EDWARD HOWDEN, hospital administrator; b. Vancouver, B.C., Can., Apr. 13, 1933; s. Edward Allen and Helen Blackley (Howden) K.; m. Glenda Carol Wiggins, Mar. 6, 1964; children: Carolyn, Patricia, Brett. B.Commerce, U. B.C., 1956, diploma in hosp. adminstrn., 1956. Adminstrv. asst. Vancouver Gen. Hosp., 1956-57; adminstr. Prince Rupert Gen. Hosp., 1957-61, Red Deer Gen. Hosp., 1961-72, Dr. Richard Parsons Aux. Hosp., 1963-72, Valley Park Manor Nursing Home, 1969-72; dep. exec. dir. Calgary (Alta.) Gen. Hosp., 1972-74, exec. dir., 1974-83, pres., 1983—; lectr. Red Deer Coll., 1968-72; clin. asst. prof. faculty medicine U. Calgary, 1978—; trustee Alta. Blue Cross Plan, 1963-68; mem. Fed. Task Force on Cost of Health Services in Can., 1969. Recipient Queen's Silver Jubilee medal, 1977. Fellow Am. Coll. Hosp. Adminstrs. (regent for Alta. 1973-76, 79-82); founding charter mem. Can. Coll. Health Services Execs. (dir. 1972-74); mem. Can. Hosp. Assn. (dir. 1981-83, pres. 1982-83), Alta. Hosp. Assn. (dir. 1977—, pres. 1983), Phi Delta Theta. Clubs: Red Deer, Kinsmen (pres. 1971-72), Calgary K-40, Glenco. Lodge: Prince Rupert Rotary. Home: 24 Bayview Dr SW Calgary T2V 3N6 Canada Office: Calgary General Hospital 841 Centre Ave E Calgary AB T2E 0A1 Canada

KNIGHT, FRANK BARDSLEY, mathematics educator; b. Chgo., Oct. 11, 1933; s. Frank Hyneman and Ethel Unus (Verry) K.; m. Ingeborg G. Belz, Aug. 30, 1971; children: Marion A., Marc A., Ellen D. B.A., Cornell U., 1955; Ph.D., Princeton U., 1959. Instr. math. U. Minn., Mpls., 1960-61, asst. prof., 1962-63; asst. prof. math. U. Ill., Urbana, 1964-66, assoc. prof., 1967-71; prof. U. Ill, Urbana, 1971—. Author: Essentials of Brownian Motion and Diffusion, 1981, Essays on the Prediction Process, 1981. Sloan fellow, 1968-71; NSF grantee, 1981-83. Mem. Am. Math. Soc., Math. Assn. Am. Club: Am. Alpine. Office: U Ill 1409 W Green St Urbana IL 61801

KNIGHT, FRANK BURKE, publisher; b. Lampasas, Tex., Aug. 15, 1928; s. Burke Charles and Ina Mae (Gunter) K.; m. Frances Watson Seaborn, June 23, 1951; children: David B. (dec.), Susan G., Sandra J., Nancy B., Philip M. (dec.), John P. Student, U. Tex., 1947-49. Advt. salesman Lampasas Dispatch, 1949; pub. Florence (Tex.) Post, 1949-52, Taylor (Tex.) Times, 1952-53; editor, advt. mgr. Winkler County News, Kermit, Tex., 1953-62; advt. dir. Coin World, Sidney, Ohio, 1962-69; pres. Collector's Media Inc., pubs. Am. Collector, Plate Collector, Kermit, 1969—; dir. Golden West Leasing Inc., Collectables Inc.; pub. cons. Mayor of Florence, 1952. Contbr. sect. to book; articles to publs. including Antiques USA. Mem. adv. bd. Kermit Community Ch., 1981-83, chmn., 1983. Served with USMC, 1950-52. Mem. Am. Ltd. Edit. Assn. (exec. dir.), Am. Numis. Assn. Clubs: Kermit Jaycees (pres., dir. 1954-61, Service award 1958), Kermit Rotary (dir. 1962). Office: 110 N Edward Gary San Marcos TX 78667 *Such talents as I possess, I strive to use so that I will not be ashamed to sign my name to any work undertaken. And because we influence others for good or bad when we least expect it, I seek to live so that any imprints will be positive. If I achieve these goals, my life will have been successful.*

KNIGHT, FRED BARROWS, forester, entomologist, educator; b. Waterville, Maine, Dec. 12, 1925; s. Stephen Cecil and Mildred Evelyn (Barrows) K.; m. Jane Wooster, Dec. 18, 1945; children: Mary Jane Knight Cushman, Susan Knight Ide, James Wooster. B.S. with distinction, U. Maine, 1949; M.F., Duke U., 1950, D.Forestry, 1956. With Bur. Entomology and Plant Quarantine, U.S. Dept. Agr., Asheville, N.C., 1950-51; research entomologist Forest Service, Ft. Collins, Colo., 1951-60; asso. prof. to prof., chmn. dept. U. Mich., Ann Arbor, 1960-72; prof. forest resources, dir. Sch. Forest Resources, U. Maine, Orono, 1972—, Dwight B. Demeritt prof. foest resources, 1972—; interim dean Coll. Forest Resources, 1982-83; Adv. com. Baxter State Park. Author: Principles of Forest Entomology, 4th edit., 1965, 5th edit., 80; also numerous articles. Served with USNR, 1943-46. Fellow AAAS; mem. Soc. Am. Foresters (asso. editor, past sect. officer), Entomol. Soc. Am., Ecol. Soc. Am., Wildlife Soc., Am. Inst. Biol. Scis., Soil Conservation Soc. Am., Assn. State Coll. and Univ.

Forestry Research Orgns. (regional chmn., v.p., pres.), Soc. Les Voyageurs, Sigma Xi, Phi Kappa Phi, Alpha Zeta, Xi Sigma Pi. Congregationalist. Home: MRA Gardner Rd Orono ME 04473 Office: 202 Nutting Hall Univ Maine Orono ME 04469

KNIGHT, FREDERICK HAWLEY, lawyer, former bus. exec.; b. Brattleboro, Vt., Sept. 29, 1906; s. Fred Samuel and Susan (Hawley) K.; m. Mary Lake Cox, July 7, 1936. B.S., Worcester Poly. Inst., 1928; LL.B., George Washington U., 1933. Bar: D.C. bar 1933. Test engr. Gen. Electric Co., Schenectady, 1928-29; patent examiner U.S. Patent Office, Washington, 1929-37; patent atty. Corning Glass Works, N.Y., 1937-45, asst. sec., 1945-53, sec., 1953-71, corp. counsel, 1961-71, v.p., 1969-71, cons., 1971—; sec., dir. Corning Glass Works of Can., Ltd., 1946-71; sec. Corning Mus. Glass, 1952-71; sec., dir. Corning Glass Internat. S.A., 1960-71; dir. Corning Internat. Corp. Sec. Corning Glass Works Found., 1953-71, trustee, 1971-76. Mem. Am. Bar Assn. Presbyterian. Clubs: Univ. (N.Y.C.); Corning Country. Home: 257 Delevan Ave Corning NY 14830 Office: Corning Glass Works: Corning NY 14830

KNIGHT, GARY, lawyer, educator, publisher; b. St. Joseph, Mo., Dec. 8, 1939; s. Herbert S. and Iris (Crawford) K.; m. Rebecca Emelie Forrester, Nov. 24, 1962; children: Kevin Crawford, David Forrester, Jonathan Gary. Student, Westminster Coll., 1957-59; A.B. in Polit. Sci., Stanford U., 1961; J.D., So. Methodist U., 1964. Bar: Calif. 1965. Assoc. Nossaman, Krueger and Marsh, Los Angeles, 1964-68; mem. faculty La. State U. Law Center, Baton Rouge, 1968—, assoc. prof. law and marine scis., 1971-75, prof. law, 1975—, Campanile prof. marine resources law, 1971—; pres. Jonathan Pub. Co., 1981—; cons. U.S. Dept. State, Office Law of the Sea, 1974-75; chmn. sci. and statis. com. Gulf of Mex. Fishery Mgmt. Council, 1977-81; mem. council Gulf of Mex. Fishery Mgmt. council, 1981—; mem. adv. com. on law of sea Nat. Security Council Inter-Agy. Law of Sea Group, 1972—; tech. adv. marine resources law La. Adv. Commn. on Coastal and Marine Resources, 1971-73; cons. CIA, 1977—. Author: The Future of International Fisheries Management, 1975, Managing the Sea's Living Resources, 1977, The Law of the Sea: Cases, Documents and Readings, 1980, Marine Fisheries Management Reporter, 1983; contbg. editor: Louisiana Coastal Law, 1972—; book rev. editor: Jour. Maritime Law and Commerce, 1974-77; asso. editor: Ocean Development and International Law: A Jour. of Marine Affairs, 1972—. Mem. Am. Soc. Internat. Law (mem. bd. rev. and devel. 1975-80, mem. panel on law of the sea 1972—), Internat. Law Assn. (mem. com. on law of the sea 1974—), Law of the Sea Inst. (mem. exec. bd. 1975-81), ABA (mem. com. on law of the sea 1971—, com. marine resources 1967-71), Am. Soc. Writers on Legal Subjects, Order of Coif, Beta Theta Pi, Phi Alpha Delta, Omicron Delta Kappa. Republican. Home: 1152 Ingleside Dr Baton Rouge LA 70806 Office: Louisiana State Univ Law Center Baton Rouge LA 70803

KNIGHT, GLADYS (GLADYS MARIA KNIGHT), contralto; b. Atlanta, May 28, 1944; d. Merald, Sr. and Elizabeth (Woods) K.; m. Barry Hankerson, Oct. 1974; 1 dau., Shanga; children from previous marriage: Kenya, James. Grad. high sch. Author: lyrics Way Back Home; others.; First pub. recital, Mt. Mariah Bapt. Ch., Atlanta, 1948; toured with, Morris Brown Choir, 1950-53, recitals local chs. and schs., 1950-53 (winner grand prize Ted Mack's Amateur Hour 1952); jazz vocalist, Lloyd Terry Jazz Ltd., 1959-61; mem., Gladys Knight and the Pips (formerly Pips Quarter), 1953—, concert appearances in, Eng., 1967, 72, 73, 76, Australia, Japan, Hong Kong, Manila, 1976; appearances on TV; rec. artist, Brunswick, 1957-61, Fury, 1961-62, Everlast, 1963, Maxx and Bell, 1964-66, Motown, 1966-73, Buddah, Capitol, Columbia (Winner 6 gold Buddah records, 1 gold Buddah album, 1 platinum Buddah album, 2 Grammy awards, named Top Female Vocalist, Blues and Soul mag. 1972). Spl. award Washington City Council for inspiration to youth in city, 1972; other awards include Clio, AGVA, Am. Music, NAACP Image, Ebony Music, Cashbox, Billboard, Record World, Rolling Stone, Ladies Home Jour., Am. Music award (with Pips), 1984. Address: care Network Talent Internat Box 82 Suite 342A 98 Cuttermill Rd Great Neck NY *

KNIGHT, HARRY W., management and financial consultant; b. Sedalia, Mo., Apr. 20, 1909; s. Harry William and Florence (Lay) K.; m. Agnes Berger, Sept. 15, 1934; children: Kirk Lay, Harry William. A.B., Amherst Coll., 1931; postgrad., Harvard U. Grad. Sch. Bus. Adminstrn., 1931-32; M.A., Northwestern U., 1940. With Harris Trust Co., Chgo., 1932-33; sales adminstr. Bauer & Black, 1934-36; finance dir., City of Winnetka, Ill., 1937-40, city mgr., Two Rivers, Wis., 1941; chief budget sect. WPB, Washington, 1942; asst. chief program control div., munitions assignment bd. Combined Chiefs of Staff, Washington, 1942-43; finance dir. UNRRA, 1945; sec. finance com. 3d Council Meeting, London, 1945; v.p. Booz, Allen & Hamilton, Inc., 1945-66; chmn. bd. Knight, Gladieux & Smith, 1966-73, Hillsboro Assos., Inc., 1973—, Shearson Am. Express, Cigna/Licony; dir. INA Life Ins. Co. of N.Y., Menlo Fin. Corp. Chmn. Darien Community Fund dr., 1954; chmn. career conf. Amherst Coll., 1951-54, nat. chmn. capital program, 1962-65, trustee, 1964-81, trustee emeritus, 1981—; pres. Harvard Bus. Sch. Assn., 1960; chmn. golden anniversary Harvard Bus. Sch., 1958; mem. governing council Sch. Internat. Affairs, Columbia U., 1975-82; chmn. Republican fin. campaign, Darien, 1952; trustee Com. Econ. Devel., 1968—, Hampshire Coll., 1968-76, Hudson Inst., 1973-78. Served to lt. USNR, 1943-45. Recipient medal for eminent service Amherst Coll. Mem. Fgn. Policy Assn. (dir. 1955-70), UN Assn. (past treas., gov., now vice chmn.), Delta Kappa Epsilon. Presbyterian. Clubs: Harvard Bus. Sch. (pres. 1970-71), University, Sky (N.Y.C.); Wee Burn Country (Darien, Conn.); Jupiter Island; John's Island (Fla.); Pine Valley Golf (N.J.). Home: 6 Cobblers Green New Canaan CT also 110 E 57th St New York NY 10022 also 400 Beach Rd Vero Beach FL 32960 Office: 420 Lexington Ave Suite 2331 New York NY 10170

KNIGHT, HERBERT BORWELL, business executive; b. Oak Park, Ill., July 4, 1928; s. Herbert Alfred and Bessie Carne (Borwell) K.; m. Nancy Gordon, June 29, 1963; children: Sharon and Tom (twins). A.B., Dartmouth Coll., 1951, M.B.A., 1952. Vice pres. mktg. B.K. Johl, Allsteel Equipment Co., Aurora, Ill., 1966-69; asst. to pres. Bliss & Laughlin Industries, Oak Brook, Ill., 1969-71; pres. Newsport News Indsl. Corp., Va., 1976-80; dir. planning Tenneco Inc., Houston, 1980—; dir. Oak Park Trust & Savs., Oak Park Bancorp. Episcopalian. Club: Econ. (Chgo.). Office: PO Box 2511 Houston TX 77001

KNIGHT, JAMES ALLEN, university dean, physician; b. St. George, S.C., Oct. 20, 1918; s. Thomas Samuel and Carolyn (Carn) K.; m. Sally Templeman, June 8, 1963; 1 son, Steven Allen. A.B., Wofford Coll., 1941; B.D., Duke U., 1944; M.D., Vanderbilt U., 1952; M.P.H., Tulane U., 1962. Intern Grady Meml. Hosp., Atlanta, 1952-53; asst. resident pediatrics Duke U. Hosp., 1953-54; resident psychiatry Tulane U. Service Charity Hosp., 1955-58; mem. faculty Baylor U. Coll. Medicine, 1958-61, asso. prof. psychiatry, 1961, asst. dean, 1960-61; asso. prof. psychiatry, dir. sect. community psychiatry Tulane U. Sch. Medicine, 1961-63, prof. psychiatry, asso. dean, 1964-74; dean Coll. Medicine, Tex. A. and M. U., College Station, 1974-77; prof. psychiatry La. State U. Sch. Medicine, New Orleans, 1978—; Harkness prof. psychiatry and religion, dir. program psychiatry and religion Union Theol. Sem., N.Y.C., 1963-64. Author: Counselling the Dying, 1964, A Manual for the Comprehensive Community Mental Health Clinic, 1964, A Psychiatrist Looks at Religion and Health, 1964, Allergy and Human Emotions, 1967, Motivations in Play, Games and Sports, 1967, For the Love of Money, 1968, Conscience and Guilt, 1969, Medical Student: Doctor in the Making, 1973, Doctor-To-Be: Coping with the Trials and Triumphs of Medical School, 1981. Served as chaplain USNR, 1944-46. Travelling fellow WHO at C.G. Jung Inst., Zurich, Switzerland, 1961. Mem. Am. Psychiat. Assn., Am. Acad. Psychoanalysis, Group Advancement Psychiatry, Am. Osler Soc., Soc. Health and Human Values (pres. 1983-84), Am. Med. Assn. Alcoholism, Insts. Religion and Health, Phi Beta Kappa. Home: 7450 Pearl St New Orleans LA 70118

KNIGHT, JAMES L., newspaperman; b. Akron, Ohio, 1909. Dir. Knight-Ridder Newspapers, Inc.; dir. Knight Pub. Co., Charlotte, N.C.; chmn. bd. emeritus Miami (Fla.) Herald Pub. Co.; dir. Beacon Jour. Pub. Co., Tallahasse Democrat, Macon Telegraph Pub. Co., So. Prodn. Program, Inc., Boca Raton News, Inc., Bradenton Herald, Inc., Detroit Free Press, Inc., Lexington Herald-Leader Co., Phila. Newspapers, Inc., Ridder Publs., Inc., Twin Coast Newspapers, Inc., N.W. Publs., Inc., Knight-Ridder Broadcasting, Inc., Viewdata Corp. Am., Inc. Mem. So. Newspaper Pubs. Assn. (pres. 1957, chmn. bd. 1958), Am. Newspapers Pubs. Assn. Clubs: Portage Country (Akron); Bath, LaGorce, Indian Creek, Surf (Miami); Detroit, Key Largo Anglers, Chub Cay, Hatteras Marlin; Lyford Cay (New Providence, Bahamas). Home: 10155 Collins Ave Bal Harbour FL 33154 Office: care Knight-Ridder Newspapers Inc 1 Herald Plaza Miami FL 33101

KNIGHT, JOHN ALLAN, clergyman, coll. pres.; b. Mineral Wells, Tex., Nov. 8, 1931; s. John Lee and Beulah Mae (Bounds) K.; m. Justine Anne Rushing, Aug. 22, 1958; children—John Allan, James Alden, Judith Anne. B.A., Bethany Nazarene Coll., 1952; M.A., Okla. U., 1954; B.D., Vanderbilt U., 1957, Ph.D., 1966. Ordained to ministry Ch. of Nazarene, 1954; pastor Tenn. Dist. Ch. of Nazarene, 1953-61, 71-72; prof., chmn. dept. philosophy and religion Trevecca Nazarene Coll., Nashville, 1957-69; chmn. dept. philosophy and religion Mt. Vernon (Ohio) Nazarene Coll., 1969-71, pres., 1972-75; pastor Grace Nazarene Ch., Nashville, 1971-72; pres. Bethany (Okla.) Nazarene Coll., 1976—; dir. 1st. Nat. Bank, Bethany; coordinator U.S. Govt. Project Studying Possible Coop. Ventures for Tenn. Colls. and Univs., 1969; mem. gen. bd. Internat. Ch. of Nazarene, 1980—. Editor-in-chief: Herald of Holiness, Kansas City, Mo., 1975-76; Author: Commentary on Philippians, 1968, The Holiness Pilgrimage, 1971, In His Likeness, 1976. Pres. bd. govs. Okla. Ind. Coll. Found., 1979—; Mem. fin. com. Mt. Vernon Public Sch. Bd.; bd. dirs. YMCA, Mercy Hosp., Salvation Army, Mt. Vernon. Recipient Lily Found. Theology award Vanderbilt U., 1958-59; Carre fellow Vanderbilt U., 1960-62. Mem. Soc. Sci. Study Religion, Am. Acad. Religion, Wesley Theol. Soc. (pres. 1979), Evang. Theol. Assn., Oklahoma City C. of C. Club: Kiwanis Internat. Home: PO Box 906 Bethany OK 73008 Office: Bethany Nazarene Coll Bethany OK 73008

KNIGHT, JOHN FRANCIS, insurance company executive; b. N.Y.C., Sept. 30, 1919; s. Samuel F. and Abigail (Sullivan) K.; m. Marilyn Rockefeller, Oct. 30, 1948; children: Jeffrey J., Melanie J., John Mark, Jane M., James M. B.B.A. cum laude, St. John's U., 1952. With Republic Financial Services Inc., Republic Ins. Group, Dallas, 1939—, agy. supr., 1950-56, asst. v.p., 1956-60, v.p., 1960-67, sr. v.p., 1967-69, exec. v.p., 1969-71, sr. exec. v.p., 1971-72, pres., 1972-84, vice chmn. bd. dirs., 1983—, also dir.; adv. dir. Fidelity-N.Y. N.A. (formerly Dollar Fed. Savs. & Loan Assn.), Malverne, N.Y. Served to maj. AUS, 1942-46. Decorated Bronze Star. Mem. Ins. Club Dallas. Clubs: 2001, Lancers, Cipango (Dallas). Home: 3883 Turtle Creek Blvd Apt 504 Dallas TX 75219 Office: 2727 Turtle Creek Blvd Dallas TX 75219

KNIGHT, LESTER BENJAMIN, consulting engineer; b. Albany, N.Y., June 29, 1907; s. Lester B. and Louise (Vaast) K.; m. Elizabeth Anne Field, Mar. 5, 1935 (dec. 1978); children: Charles Field, Leslie; m. Frances Talbert Edens, Mar. 22, 1980. M.E., Cornell U., 1929; student, Chgo. Kent Coll. Law, 1932-34. Vice pres. Nat. Engring. Co., Chgo., 1930-43; chmn., chief exec. officer Lester B. Knight & Assos., Inc. (mgmt. and cons. engrs.), Chgo., 1945—; chmn. Lester B. Knight Internat. Corp., Chgo., 1952—; A.B. Knight, Karlstad, Sweden, 1962—; dir. Knight Wegenstein, Zurich, Switzerland, Knight Wendling, A.G., London; spl. research foundry mgmt., operation, design, automation and mechanization. Pres., adminstrv. dir. Travelers Aid Soc. Chgo., 1958-60, pres. sponsoring bd., exec. com., 1960—; mem. pres.'s council Cornell U., U. Ill. Served to lt. comdr. USNR, 1943-45. Mem. Am. Foundrymens Soc., ASME, Am. Mgmt. Assn., Assn. Cons. Mgmt. Engrs., Chgo. C. of C. (dir., v.p. indsl. devel. and policy com.), Ill. Engr. Council (1st v.p., dir., exec. com.), Alpha Tau Omega. Clubs: University, Mid-America, Chicago, Economic (Chgo.); Glenview Golf (Golf, Ill.); Army-Navy (Washington); Country of Florida (Golf, Fla.); Quail Ridge Golf and Country (Boynton Beach, Fla.). Home: 1616 Sheridan Rd Wilmette IL 60091 Office: 549 W Randolph St Chicago IL 60606

KNIGHT, NORMAN, radio-TV executive; b. July 24, 1924; m. Susannah Howard Andre, Aug. 26, 1944; children: Norman Scott, Randolph Howard, Jeffrey Bryant, Robert Andre. LL.D. (hon.), Northeastern U., D.B.A., Nathaniel Hawthorne Coll., D.C.S., Merrimack Coll. News reporter, scriptwriter Sta. WEW, WIL, WTMV, 1938-41; Announcer, salesman Sta. WTMV, 1942; announcer, promotion mgr., news reporting continuity dir. Sta. KTHS, 1943; announcer Sta. WMC, 1943; announcer, news writer, reporter, salesman Sta. WMMN, 1944; gen. mgr. Sta. WAJR, 1944-46; Eastern dir. sta. relations MBS, 1946-49; v.p. sales, advt. and promotion Sponsor Publs., Inc., 1950-53; gen. mgr. Sta. WABD (now WNEW-TV), 1953-54; exec. v.p., gen. mgr. Yankee Network div. RKO Teleradio Pictures, Inc. (operating Yankee Network WNAC, WRKO, WNAC-TV); also dir. Yankee Network; v.p. RKO Teleradio Pictures, 1954-60; pres. Yankee div. RKO Teleradio Pictures, Inc., 1957-60, Yankee div. RKO Gen., Inc., 1958-60; treas., chmn. Knight Sales, Inc.; chmn., treas. Knight Radio, Inc. (WGIR and WGIR-FM), Knight Broadcasting N.H., Inc. (WHEB and WHEB-FM); pres., treas. Knight Communications Corp. (WEIM and WSRS); chmn., treas. Quality Radio Corp. (WSAR), 1960—; chmn. Caribbean Communications Corp. Established complete TV sta.: pub. affairs film unit which produced Brotherhood Series; TV documentaries, 1953-60; Author: others. The Cause of All Mankind. Radio-TV chmn. United Fund Greater Boston, Mass. Cancer Soc., ARC chpt. Met. Boston, Met. Boston chpt. ARC; bus. chmn. Easter Seal Soc.; radio chmn. Salvation Army; dir. Strawberry Banke; bd. dirs. New Eng. Nephrosis Found.; pres., founder New Eng. Kidney Disease Found.; pres. Norman Knight Charitable Found.; trustee Mass. Bd. Regional Community Colls., Agassiz Village Camps, Crippled Children's Non-Sectarian Fund, Boys and Girls Camps, Inc.; mem. nat. council, exec. com. New Eng. council Boy Scouts Am.; exec. com., dir. Rescue, Inc.; exec. com. The Jimmy Fund; exec. com., trustee Children's Cancer Research Found., Dana Farber Cancer Inst.; mem. fin. com. Com. Econ. Devel.; mem. devel. council Boston U.; mem. pres.'s council Boston Coll.; bd. dirs. Freedoms Found.; also nat. co-chmn. Am. Freedom Center. Recipient Americanism award Am. Heritage Com., 1959; named one of ten outstanding young men Boston Jr. C. of C., 1956; award for contbns. radio and TV industry Alpha Epsilon Rho, 1957; Americanism awards various vets. orgns., 1959-60. Mem. Radio-TV Execs. Sec., Young Pres.'s Orgn., Broadcast Pioneers, AIM, Alpha Epsilon Rho. Clubs: Variety (Boston); Broadcasting Execs. New Eng., 100 of Mass. (co-founder, pres., dir.), 100 of N.H. (life). Office: 63 Bay State Rd Boston MA 02215

KNIGHT, PHILIP H., shoe manufacturing company executive; b. Portland, Oreg., Feb. 24, 1938; s. William W. and Lota (Hatfield) K.; m. Penelope Parks, Sept. 13, 1968; childrend: Matthew, Travis. B.B.A., U. Oreg.; M.B.A., Stanford U. C.P.A., Oreg. Pres., chmn. Nike Inc., Beaverton, Oreg., 1967-83, chmn., chief exec. officer, 1983—; dir. Metheus Corp. Trustee Reed Coll., Portland; mem. adv. council Stanford U. Grad. Sch.; bd. dirs. Nat. Council U.S.-China Trade, U.S.-Asian Bus. Council, Washington. Served to 1st lt. AUS, 1959-60. Named Oreg. Businessman of Yr., 1982. Mem. Am. Inst. C.P.A.s. Republican. Episcopalian. Office: Nike Inc 10300 SW Allen Blvd Beaverton OR 97005

KNIGHT, ROBERT HUNTINGTON, lawyer; b. New Haven, Feb. 27, 1919; s. Earl Wall and Frances Pierpont (Whitney) K.; m. Rosemary C. Gibson, Apr. 19, 1975; children—Robert Huntington, Jessie Valle, Patricia Whitney, Alice Isabel, Eli Whitney. Grad., Phillips Acad., Andover, Mass., 1936; B.A., Yale, 1940; LL.B., U. Va., 1947. Bar: N.Y. bar 1950. With John Orr Young, Inc. (advt. agy.), 1940-41; asst. prof. U. Va. Law Sch., 1947-49; asso. firm Shearman & Sterling & Wright, N.Y.C., 1949-55, partner, 1955-58; dep. asst. sec. def. for internat. security affairs Dept. Def., 1958-61; gen. counsel Treasury Dept., 1961-62; partner firm Shearman & Sterling, N.Y.C., 1962—; dep. chmn. Fed. Res. Bank N.Y., 1976-77, chmn., 1978—; counsel to bd. United Technologies Corp.; dir. Owens-Corning Fiberglas Corp., Brit. Steel Corp., Inc., Pechiney Ugine Kuhlmann Corp.; chmn. Howmet Corp., Howmet Turbine Corp.; Mem. Intelsat Arbitration Panel, 1971—. Bd. dirs. Internat. Vol. Services; chmn. bd. dirs. U. Va. Law Sch. Found.; bd. dirs. Asia Found. Served to lt. col. USAAF, 1941-45. Mem. Am., Fed., Internat., Inter-Am. bar assns., Bar Assn. City N.Y., N.Y. County Lawyers Assn., Internat. Law Assn., Washington Inst. Fgn. Affairs, Council Fgn. Relations. Clubs: Down Town Assn., Pilgrims, India House, Links (N.Y.C.); Army and Navy, Metropolitan City Tavern (Washington); Round Hill (Greenwich, Conn.). Home: 12 Knollwood Dr Greenwich CT 06830 also 570 Park Ave New York NY 10021 also 6767 N Ocean Blvd Ocean Ridge FL 33435 Office: 53 Wall St New York NY 10005

KNIGHT, ROBERT MONTGOMERY, basketball coach; b. Massilon, Ohio, Oct. 25, 1940; s. Carroll and Hazel (Menthorne) K.; m. Nancy Lou Knight, Apr. 17, 1963; children: Timothy Scott, Patrick Clair. B.S., Ohio State U., 1962. Asst. coach Cuyahoga Falls (Ohio) High Sch., 1962-63; freshman coach U.S. Mil. Acad., West Point, N.Y., 1963-65, head basketball coach, 1965-71, Ind. U., Bloomington, 1971—; speaker clinics in field; condr. tng. clinics for coaches and players. Served with U.S. Army. Recipient Big Ten Coach-of-Year award, 1973, 75, 76, 80; named Nat. Coach of Year AP and Basketball Weekly, 1976; recipient appreciation plaque from team, 1979. Mem. Nat. Assn. Basketball Coaches (bd. dirs.). Methodist. Coached team to NCAA Championship, 1976, 81. Office: Indiana Univ Basketball Office Assembly Hall Bloomington IN 47405 *

KNIGHT, ROBERT PATRICK, journalism educator, academic administrator; b. Mexico City, Mexico, Mar. 17, 1935; came to U.S., 1941; s. John Montiel and Margaret Mary (Kent) K.; m. Rose Eleanor Janda, July 21, 1956; children: Robert Patrick, Mary Kathleen, Timothy F., Rodney J., Caroline E. B.J. with honors, U. Tex., 1956, B.A. in English with honors, 1956, M.J., 1964; postgrad., U. Chile, Santigao, 1956-57; Ph.D., U. Mo., 1968. Reporter Austin Am.-Statesman, Tex., 1953-56, Midland Reporter-Telegram, 1958; instr. Tex. A&M U., College Station, 1963-65, acting head dept., 1964-65; instr. to prof. journalism U. Mo., Columbia, 1965—, dir. minority journalism workshops, 1971—, dir. journalism continuing edn., 1976—; dir. Mo. Interscholastic Press Assn., 1965—. Author: monographs Polls, Sampling and the Voter, 1966, Voters, Computers and TV Forecast, 1966; co-author: Manual for News Writing, 1970; editor: tabloid Urban Pioneer, 1971—, Telling the Story of America: Minorities and Journalism, 1982; interviewer: video-audio tapes World Journalism Resources Unit, 1977—. Recipient Gold Key Columbia Scholastic Press Assn., 1980, Pioneer award Nat. Scholastic Press Assn., 1983; Fulbright fellow, 1956-57. Mem. Assn. for Edn. in Journalism and Mass Communication (head div. secondary edn. 1971-72, div. Honors lectr. 1981), Journalism Edn. Assn. (editorial bd. 1968-76, Carl Towley award 1970), Student Press Law Ctr. (bd. dirs. 1976—). Roman Catholic. Lodge: K.C. Home: 2300 Ridgemont Columbia MO 65201 Office: U Mo Sch Journalism PO Box 838 Columbia MO 65205

KNIGHT, SHIRLEY, actress; b. Goessel, Kans., July 5, 1936; d. Noel Johnson and Virginia (Webster) K.; m. John R. Hopkins; children: Kaitlin, Sophie. D.F.A., Lake Forest Coll., 1978. Actress theatre and films. Active Com. for Handgun Control, nat. civil rights orgns. Recipient various acting honors, U.S. and abroad. Home: Hazelnut Farm 1495 Westport Turnpike Fairfield CT 06430 Office: care ICM 6 W 57th St New York NY

KNIGHT, TED (TADEUS WLADYSLAW KONOPKA), actor; b. Terryville, Conn., Dec. 7, 1923; s. Charles Walter and Sophia (Kovaleski) Konopka; m. Dorothy May Clarke, Sept. 14, 1948; children—Ted, Elyse, Eric. Student, Randall Sch. Dramatic Arts, Hartford, Conn. With various radio stas., N.Y.C.; formed Kono Prodns., Inc., 1976. Master of ceremonies; newsman; host late-night movies for various TV stas.; supporting actor Hollywood films, 1957—; actor radio and TV commls., also cartoon voices; played leading roles in legitimate theatre prodns. at, Player's Ring Theatre, Omnibus Theatre, Pasadena Playhouse, others; played Ted Baxter in: (1970-77) Mary Tyler Moore Show; star of the: Ted Knight Show, 1977; star: TV series Too Close for Comfort, 1980—; appeared in: film Caddy Shack, 1980; now free-lance actor; producers: Ted Knight Musical-Comedy Variety Special Special, CBS; made Broadway theatre debut with starring role in: (1977.) Some of My Best Friends; (Recipient award as best supporting actor in a comedy Nat. Acad. TV Arts and Scis. 1972-73, 75-76); Recorded: album Hi Guys, 1975. Served with U.S. Army, 1942-44. Named TV Father of Yr. Nat. Fathers Day Com., 1975. Mem. Screen Actors Guild, AFTRA, Equity. Address: PO Box 642 Pacific Palisades CA 90272 *Central to my life is belief in the family cell structure. Success is empty unless it is shared; it is meaningless unless achieved without coercion, injury or pain to others.*

KNIGHT, V. C., manufacturing executive; b. Landess, Ind., Aug. 12, 1904; s. Charles and Daisie (Farr) K.; m. Velma Cain, June 30, 1926; children: James, Marilyn. Student, Ind. State U., 1921-24; Ph.D. in Bus. Adminstrn., Adrian Coll., 1977, Hillsdale Coll., 1983. With McCray Refrigerator Co., 1926-47; v.p. ops.; exec. v.p. Betz Corp., Hammond, Inc., 1947-51; with Addison Products Co., 1951—, now chmn. bd.; pres. WeatherKing Inc., Orlando, Fla.; v.p. Prill Mfg. Co., Sheridan, Wyo. Trustee Adrian Coll. Office: Addison Products Co 215 Talbot St Addison MI 49220

KNIGHT, VICK, SR., advertising executive, composer; b. Moundsville, W.Va., Aug. 5, 1908; s. William Eugene and Stella Vernon (Shimp) K.; m. Janice Adele Higgins, July 21, 1927; children: Vick, Virginia, Nancy. Student, Cleve. Presbyn. Sch., 1923-25. Assoc. editor Cleve. Citizen, 1927-29; program dir. Sta. WGAR, Cleve., 1929-32; mdse. mgr. Sta. WHK, Cleve., 1929-32; dir. radio, writer, producer for Fred Allen, Eddie Cantor, Rudy Vallee, Kate Smith, others, 1932-40; v.p. Biow Co., 1941; v.p., dir. Foote, Cone & Belding, 1942-43; staff writer MGM, 1946; pres. Vick Knight, Inc., Los Angeles, 1947—, Key Records, 1947—; mng. dir. Adver-Tunes; dir. Eddie Cantor Stage Presentations; pres. Round Table Music Publs.; owner The Pumpkins Press, Tune Text Publs. Producer: Hollywood Bowl Appearance Pres. Eisenhower, Ann. New Eng. Rally for God, Family and Country, Boston; writer, dir.: Coffee Hours for Eisenhower, MacArthur's legacy, 1971; producer: Ronald Reagan audio unit Rendevous with Destiny, 1981; med. tapes on ileostomy and colostomy, 1981; author: poetry England's Lot Like Illinois, 1944; play Cartwheel; What Happened to the Bees, 1964, Young John Steinbeck, 1975, Audiography of Louis Armstrong, 1976; contbr. to textbooks, mags., tech. publs., 1976. Bd. dirs. Matt Civic Found.; v.p. Ostomy Assn., Los Angeles; mem. United States Day Com.; radio chmn. March of Dimes; bd. dirs. Americanism Ednl. League, Parents Adv. League; mem. Calif. Republican Central Com.; radio-TV chmn. Rep. Assocs. Mem. Hist. Soc. Wis., ASCAP, Am. Guild Authors and Composers, Am. Legion, VFW, Internat. Platform Assn. Club: West Atwood Yacht. Address: PO Box 46128 Los Angeles CA 90046

KNIGHT, WALKER LEIGH, editor, publisher, clergyman; b. Henderson, Ky., Feb. 6, 1924; s. Cooksey Bennett and Rowena (Henderson) K.; m. Iva Nell Moseley, Nov. 10, 1943; children: Walker Leigh, Kenneth Wayne, Nelda Denise, Emily Jill. B.A., Baylor U., 1949. Reporter Henderson Gleanor and Jour., 1942; ordained to ministry Bapt. Ch., 1948; pastor in, Dale, Tex., 1948-49; editor Falls County Record, Marlin, Tex., 1948-49; asso. editor Bapt. Standard, Dallas, 1950-59; editorial dir. So. Bapt. Home Mission Bd., Atlanta, also editor Missions U.S.A. mag. and Atlanta bur. chief Bapt. Press News Service, 1959-83; editor, pub. SBC Today, 1983—. Author: Panama, The Land Between, 1965, Struggle for Integrity, 1969, See How Love Works, 1971, Seven Beginnings, 1976, Chaplaincy, Love on the Line, 1978. Served with USAAF, 1943-45. Mem. Asso. Church Press, So. Bapt. Press Assn., Bapt. Pub. Relations Assn. Home: 1008 Forrest Blvd Decatur GA 30030 Office: 222 E Lake Dr Decatur GA 30030

KNIGHT, WALTER EARLY, assn. exec.; b. Dayton, Ky., Oct. 15, 1911; s. Noel B. and Nelle (Early) K.; m. Lina Baldauf, Dec. 24, 1940; children—Carol (Mrs. Paul Hoffman), Susan (Mrs. Michael Keenan). A.B. in Econs, Western Ky. U., 1933, M.A., Peabody Coll., 1940. Asst. prof. U. Louisville, 1947-50; asso. orgainzer Louisville C. of C., 1950-57; organizer indsl. devel. function Boston C. of C., 1957-65; exec. v.p. Jersey City C. of C., 1965—; pub. Jersey City Forum; tobacco industry cons. Business Week mag., 1947-67; Chmn., dir. town personnel dept. Cohasset, Mass., 1962-65. Recipient Annual award New Boston Com., 1964. Fellow Am. Indsl. Devel. Council; mem. Am. Mktg. Assn., Am. Assn. C. of C. Execs., N.J. Assn. C. of C. Execs. (pres. 1968). Clubs: Bergen Carteret (Jersey City); Nassau (Princeton, N.J.). Home: 478 Riverside Dr E Princeton NJ 08540 Office: 911 Bergen Ave Jersey City NJ 07306

KNIGHT, WILLIAM EDWARDS, former foreign service officer, inventor, business executive, management consultant; b. Tarrytown, N.Y., Feb. 1, 1922; s. Arthur Octavius and Mabel (Jenkins) K.; m. Ruth Lee, Aug. 14, 1946; children: Jeffrey William, Peter Edwards. B.A. in Internat. Relations, Yale, 1943; M.A., Yale U., 1946. Fgn. service officer State Dept., 1946-74; vice consul, Genoa, Italy, 1946-48, 3d sec., then 2d sec., Rome, 1948-51, Italian desk officer, Washington, 1951-55; 1st sec., consul, head econ. sect. Am. embassy, Reykjavik, Iceland, 1955-57, consul, 1st sec., head econ. sect., Canberra, Australia, 1957-61; officer charge Italian-Austrian affairs, Washington, 1961; dep. dir. Western European affairs, 1961-62; student Indsl. Coll. Armed Forces, Washington, 1962-63; asst. chief negotiations div. Office of Internat. Aviation Affairs, Dept. State, 1963-67; counselor for econ. affairs Am. embassy, Manila, 1967-71, dep. chief mission, 1971; detailed to Sr. Seminar in Fgn. Policy, Washington, 1971-72, sr. fgn. service insp., 1972-74; pres. The Araluen Co., 1975—, Araluen Inc., 1980-83; asso. cons. J.P. Kearney Co., 1976—. Trustee Brent Sch., Baguio, Philippines, 1969-71. Served to 1st lt. USAAF, 1943- 45. Clubs: Lions, Internat. Aviation (pres. Washington 1964-65); Yale, Army/Navy Country (Washington); Army-Navy (Manila) (dir., treas. 1971); Commonwealth (Canberra)). Address: 5000 Park Pl Bethesda MD 20816

KNIGHT, WILLIAM J., air force officer; b. Noblesville, Ind., Nov. 18, 1929; s. William T. and Mary Emma (Illyes) K.; m. Helena A. Stone, June 7, 1958; children—William Peter, David, Stephen. B.S., Air Force Inst. Tech., 1958; student, Indsl. Coll. Armed Forces, 1973-74. Commd. 2d lt. USAF, 1953, advanced through grades to col, 1971; fighter pilot, Kinross AFB, Mich., 1953-56, exptl. test pilot, Edwards AFB, Calif., 1958-69, VietNam, 1969-70; dir. test and deployment F-15 program, Wright Patterson AFB, Ohio, 1970-73; dir. F-5 systems program, 1976, dir. fighter attack system program office, 1977—. Decorated D.F.C. with 2 oak leaf clusters, Legion of Merit with 1 oak leaf cluster, Air medal with 11 oak leaf clusters, Astronaut Wings; recipient Octave Chanute award, 1968, Harmon trophy, 1968; citation of honor Air Force Assn., 1969; winner Allison Jet Trophy race, 1954. Fellow Soc. Exptl. Test Pilots, Am. Inst. Aeros. and Astronautics (asso.); mem. Internat. Order Characters, Aerospace Primus Club, Daedalians. Holder world's speed record for winged aircraft, 4520 m.p.h., 1967. Home: 220 Eagle Ln Palmdale CA 93550 Office: AFFTC/CV Edwards AFB CA 93523

KNIGHT, WILLIAM THOMAS, cosmetics company executive, lawyer; b. Hackensack, N.J., Aug. 25, 1937; s. William Thomas and Virginia (Chapin) K.; m. Suellen Peterson, Oct. 21, 1961; children: Alexander, Peter, Jessica. A.B., Brown U., 1959; M.A., Vanderbilt U., 1961; LL.B., U. Va., Charlottesville, 1967. Bar: Pa. 1967, U.S. Dist. Ct. (we. dist.)Pa. 1968. Trust officer Pitts. Nat. Bank, 1967-69; assoc. gen. counsel T.J. Lipton, Inc., Englewood Cliffs, N.J., 1969-73; gen. counsel, v.p., sec. Tetley, Inc., N.Y.C., 1973-76; counsel, asst. gen. counsel, v.p. legal, v.p. law, group v.p., gen. counsel, sec. Avon Products Inc., N.Y.C., 1977—. Served to lt. (j.g.) USNR, 1960-64. Fellow Bar City N.Y., ABA, Pa. Bar Assn., N.Y. State Bar Assn. (exec. com., corp. counsel), Allegheny County Bar Assn. Clubs: Princeton, Edgartown Yacht. Home: 567 McCulloch Pl Haworth NJ 07641 Office: Avon Products Inc 9 W 57th St New York NY 10019

KNILANS, MICHAEL JEROME, merchant; b. Columbus, Ohio, Mar. 3, 1927; s. Alfred Sidney and Bernice (Meyers) K.; m. Anne Eberhardt, June 15, 1947; children—Michael, Kyleen, Christine, Timothy, Suzanne. B.S., Ohio State U., 1949. With Big Bear Stores Co., Columbus, 1942—, mdse. mgr., 1952-61, v.p., 1961-70, exec. v.p., 1970-76, pres., 1976—, also dir.; chmn., dir. Topco Assos., Inc. Served with USNR, 1944-46; PTO. Mem. Sales Execs. Club, Execs. Club of Columbus (pres. 1974—), Food Mktg. Inst. (dir.), Ohio Council Retail Mchts. (chmn.), Better Bus. Bur. (pres. 1978), C. of C. Republican. Lutheran (chmn. congregation 1968). Clubs: Masons, Shriners, Jesters, Rotary (pres. 1981—). Home: 1119 Kingsdale Terr Columbus OH 43220 Office: 770 Goodale Blvd Columbus OH 43212

KNIPP, HELMUT, hotel executive; b. Siegburg-Mulldorf, Germany, Feb. 15, 1943; came to U.S., 1964, naturalized, 1968; s. Josef and Hildegard (Schellberg) K.; m. Irma Henz, Mar. 1, 1969; children: Eric Helmut, Kirsten Petra. Diploma in hotel mgmt. and adminstrn, U. Bonn, W. Ger., 1960. Asst. front office supr. Royal York Hotel, Toronto, Ont., Can., 1961-64; dir. sales Statler Hilton, Cleve., 1964-68; sales mgr. N.Y. Hilton, N.Y.C., 1968-72; resident mgr. Washington Hilton, 1972-74; gen. mgr. Dallas Hilton Inn, 1974-76, Capital Hilton, Washington, 1976-80; v.p., gen. mgr. Marriott Corp., 1980-82; v.p. ops. Lincoln Hotel Corp., Dallas, 1983—; dir. Georgetown & Foggy Bottom Trolley Co. Served with Air N.G., 1965-71. Mem. Am. Hotel and Motel Assn., Dallas and Tex. Hotel/Motel Assn., Chaine Des Rotisseurs, Hotel Sales Mgmt. Assn., Nat. Restaurant Assn., Nat. Assn. Execs. Club. Republican. Roman Catholic. Club: Alfalfa. Home: 17816 Cedar Creek Canyon Dallas TX 75252 Office: Lincoln Hotel Corp 5400 LBJ Freeway Dallas TX 75240

KNIPSCHILD, ROBERT, educator, artist; b. Freeport, Ill., Aug. 17, 1927; s. Leon Francis and Alice (Walsh) K.; m. Patricia Ann O'Connor, Sept. 1, 1949; children—Abby Clare Knipschild Lawson, Amy Louise Knipschild Wermeling, John Eliot, Jill Anne, Sarah Kate. B.A., U. Wis., 1950; M.F.A., Cranbrook Acad. Art, 1951. Tchr. Balt. Mus. Art, 1951-52, Am. U., 1952, U. Conn., 1954-56, U. Wis., 1956-60, U. Iowa, 1960-66; prof. art, dir. grad. studies fine arts U. Cin., 1966—. Exhbns. include, Mus. Modern Art, Whitney Mus., Met. Mus., Corcoran Mus., Boston Mus., Carnegie Inst., also in Europe, Carnegie Inst., Japan and, Carnegie Inst., Australia. Served with AUS, 1945-47. Home: 3346 Jefferson Ave Cincinnati OH 45220 Office: Sch Art U Cin Cincinnati OH 45221

KNISEL, RUSSELL H., banker; b. Englewood, N.J., June 18, 1933; s. Adolph C. and Elsie (Vieght) K.; m. Diane Taylor, June 18, 1955; children: Susan, Kimberly, Sally, Russell H. B.A., Wesleyan U., Middletown, Conn., 1955; postgrad., Harvard Grad. Sch. Bus., 1963. Pension mgr. Conn. Gen. Life Ins. Co., 1955-58; with Marine Midland Bank, N.Y.C., 1958-78, sr. v.p., 1968-74, exec. v.p., 1974-76, group exec. v.p., 1976-78; vice chmn. Conn. Nat. Bank, 1978—. Bd. dirs. Hartman Theatre, King Sch.; chmn. Darien Republican Town Com.; trustee Conn. Trust Historic Preservation. Mem. Assn. Res. City Bankers, Wesleyan Alumni Assn., Southwestern Area Commerce Assn. (dir.). Clubs: Wee Burn Country (Darien) (dir.); Landmark Square (dir.). Home: Garden Gate 2265 Boston Post Rd Darien CT 06820 Office: 1 Landmark Sq Stamford CT 06904

KNISELY, ROBERT AUGUST, government official, lawyer; b. Chgo., Mar. 19, 1940; s. Melvin Henry and Verona (Butzer) K.; m. Erika Maria Owen, June 29, 1965 (div. Dec. 1974); m. Margaret Leidy Beyer, Feb. 16, 1975; children: Lindsay Elizabeth, Laura Franziska. A.B., Harvard U., 1962; J.D., Georgetown U., 1972. Bar: D.C. 1973. Sr. atty., adv. Office Gen. Counsel FEA, Washington, 1973-74; dep. gen. counsel Clemency Bd., White House, Washington, 1974-75; dir. office program evaluation Dept. commerce, Washington, 1975-77; dir. planning and budget systems Dept. Energy, Washington, 1977-78; dep. exec. dir. Consumer Product Safety Commn., Washington, 1979-81; dep. chmn. for mgmt. Nat. Endowment for Arts, Washington, 1982—; mem. info. systems and policy com. Nat. Assembly State Arts Agys., Washington, 1982—. Pres. Woodside Civic Assn., McLean, Va., 1979; bd. dirs. Langley Sch., 1983-85. Served with USMCR, 1962-67. Mem. Sr. Execs. Assn. (charter), Marine's Meml. Assn. (life), D.C. Bar Assn., Am. Legion. Club: Quark (Washington). Office: Nat Endowment for Arts Old Post Office 1100 Pennsylvania Ave NW Washington DC 20506

KNISKERN, MAYNARD, editor, writer; b. Schenectady, Nov. 5, 1912; s. Henry Parsons and Hermia Loraine (Maynard) K.; m. Ora Lazenby, Oct. 11, 1945. Student, U. Miami, Fla., 1932-33; L.H.D., Wittenberg U., 1970. Free-lance writer, 1933-36; newspaper and mag. editorial writer, 1936-39; editor: Cranston (R.I.) Herald, 1939-42, Springfield (Ohio) Sun, 1946-77. Served as air ops. officer and combat corr. with USNR, 1942-46. Recipient Am. citizenship medal for journalistic activities VFW, 1940. Mem. Pi Delta Epsilon. Home: Route 1 Box 97-D Titus AL 36080

KNOBE, RICK W., mayor; b. Barrington, Ill., Dec. 6, 1946; s. Louis C. and Nan V. K.; m. Beverly Ann Kramer, June 29, 1978; children: Brian, Meghan. Student, Morningside Coll., Sioux City, Iowa, 1964-66, So. Ill. U., Carbondale, 1967-69; diploma, Career Acad. Broadcasting, Kansas City, Mo., 1969. With sta. KSCJ, Sioux City, Iowa, 1970, Sta. KCHF, Sioux Falls, S.D., 1971-74; mayor City of Sioux Falls, 1974—. Chmn. Interagy. Water Quality Mgmt. Council, 1981; mem. Gov. S.D. Council Local Affairs; mem. exec. bd., mem. urbanized devel. commn. Southeasterm Council Govts. Named Disting. Citizen of Yr. Sioux Falls Elks Club, 1976, Outstanding Young Citizen Sioux Falls Jaycees-S.D. Jaycees, 1980. Mem. Nat. League Cities, S.D. Mcpl. League (pres. 1981), S.D. Pvt. Industry Council, Sioux Falls Jaycees. Republican. Methodist. Office: 224 W 9th St Sioux Falls SD 57102 *

KNOBIL, ERNST, physiologist; b. Berlin, Germany, Sept. 20, 1926; came to U.S., 1940, naturalized, 1945; s. Jakob and Regina (Seidmann) K.; m. Julane Hotchkiss, July 11, 1959; children: Erich Richard, Mark, Nicholas, Katharine. B.S., Cornell U., 1948, Ph.D. (Schering fellow endocrinology 1949-51), 1951; hon. doctorate, U. Bordeaux, France, 1981, Med. Coll. Wis., 1983. Asst. zoology Cornell U., 1948-49; Milton Research fellow, Harvard U., 1951-53, from instr. to asst. prof. physiology, 1953-61, John and Mary R. Markle Found. scholar med. scis., 1956-61; Richard Beatty Mellon prof. physiology, chmn. dept. U. Pitts. Sch. Medicine, 1961-81; H. Wayne Hightower prof. physiology, dean U. Tex. Med. Sch., Houston, 1981—; Bowditch lectr. Am. Physiol. Soc., 1965, Gregory Pincus Meml. lectr. Laurentian Hormone Conf., 1973; Upjohn lectr. Am. Fertility Soc., 1974; Kathleen M. Osborn Meml. lectr. U. Kans., 1974; Karl Paschkis lectr. Phila. Endocrine Soc., 1975; 1st Transatlantic lectr. Soc. Endocrinology, Gt. Brit., 1979, Lawson Wilkins Pediatric Endocrine Soc. lectr., 1980; Bard lectr. Johns Hopkins U. Sch. Medicine, 1981; Herbert M. Evans Meml. lectr. U. Calif., 1981, Am. Acad. Arts and Scis. fellow, 1981; cons. USPHS, Ford Found.; Mem. human growth and devel. study sect. NIH, 1964-66; mem. adv. council Inst. Lab. Animal Resources, NRC-Nat. Acad. Sci., 1966-69; mem. nat. sci. adv. bd. Growth, Inc., 1969; mem. liaison com. on med. edn. AMA-Am. Assn. Med. Colls., 1971-74; mem. population research com. Center for Population Research, Nat. Inst. Child Health and Human Devel., NIH, 1974-78; mem. med. adv. bd. Nat. Pituitary Agy., 1980—. Editorial bd.: Am. jour. Physiology, 1959-68, Endocrinology, 1959-75, Psychoneuroendocrinology, 1974-79, Neuroendocrinology, 1976-80; editorial com. Ann. Rev. Physiology, 1968-72; editor, 1974-77; editor-in-chief: Am. Jour. Physiology: Endocrinology and Metabolism, 1979-82. Served with U.S. Army, 1944-46. Fellow AAAS; hon. fellow Am. Assn. Obstetricians and Gynecologists, Am. Gynecol. Soc.; mem. Am. Soc. Zoologists, Soc. Exptl. Biology and Medicine, Am. Physiol. Soc. (mem. council 1969-72, pres. 1978-79), Endocrine Soc. (Ciba award 1961, council 1968-71, pres. 1976-77, Koch award 1982), Soc. Endocrinology (Gt. Britain), Internat. Soc. Research in Biology of Reprodn., Assn. Chairmen Depts. Physiology (pres. 1969), Am. Assn. Med. Colls. (adminstrv. bd. council acad. socs., exec. com.), Nat. Bd. Med. Examiners, Internat. Soc. Endocrinology (mem. exec. com. 1972—, chmn. program organizing com. 5th Congress 1976), Internat. Soc. Neuroendocrinology (chmn. exec. com. 1976-84), Soc. Study Reprodn., Japan Endocrine Soc., Internat. Soc. Research Biology Reprodn.; hon. mem. Deutsche Gesellschaft für Endokrinologie. Spl. research pituitary gland, endocrinology reprodn.

KNOBLAUCH, ARTHUR LEWIS, former university president, political science educator; b. Riga, Mich., Nov. 17, 1906; s. Ferdinand and Wilhelmina (Kolz) K.; m. Muriel Marguerite Clemes, Aug. 12, 1929; children: Jane Harriet (Mrs. Mann), Nancy Carolyn (Mrs. Sonnenberg), Muriel Ann (Mrs. Fanning). B.S., Mich. State U., 1929; M.A., U. Mich., 1933; Ed.D. (McGregor scholar), Harvard U., 1942; LL.B., LaSalle U., 1979. Tchr. high sch., Buchanan, Mich., 1929-31, dir. athletics, prin., 1931-35, supt. schs., Cassopolis, Mich., 1935-39; exec. sec. Conn. Edn. Assn., 1940-41; asso. prof. edn. U. Conn., 1941-43, prof. edn., dir. div. univ. extension, summer session and continuing edn., 1943-55; vis. prof. U. Mich., 1950; pres. State U., Moorhead, Minn., 1955-58, Western Ill. U., 1958-68, pres. emeritus, 1968—; prof. emeritus polit. sci., pres. Univ. Found., Western Ill. U., 1960-68; pres. Kankakee (Ill.) Community Coll., 1976; prof.-in-residence U. Ariz., 1971—; cons. Saga Foods; dir. Community Bank, Galesburg, Ill. Author articles profl. jours. Pres. Eastern Conn. council Boy Scouts Am., 1955, Prairie council, 1960-65; mem. regional council Prairie council, 1964—, mem. nat. council, 1960—; mem. exec. bd. Catalina Council, 1977; pres. United Fund, 1960-62; mem. Gov's Adv. Council Ill., 1968-72; Dir. Positive Attitude, Inc., Galesburg.; Regent Lincoln Acad. Ill., Ill. State U., Regency Univs. Ill., 1969—; mem. Ill. Bd. Higher Edn., 1973—; pres. Alpha Gamma Rho Nat. Ednl. Found., 1976—; interim sec. Ill. Community Coll. Trustees Assn., 1970-71; trustee Univs. Retirement System, 1972—; hon. life trustee Ill. Jr. Colls. Recipient Silver Beaver award Boy Scouts Am., 1955, Silver Antelope award, 1964; Fulbright lectr., Burma, 1952-53, Russia, 1959, Peru, 1968, Europe, 1952, 59, 69, 74, 77; Danforth grant seminar in higher edn., Wash., 1960; Distinguished Alumni award Mich. State U., 1960; Patriarch award, 1979; Legion of Honor award Internat. Order of DeMolay, 1961; named Man of Yr. Chgo. Alumni Club Alpha Gamma Rho, 1976. Mem. Am. Soc. for Pub. Adminstrn. (pres. Conn. chpt. 1946-47, 49-50), Conn. Schoolmasters Assn., N.E.A., Sch. Pub. Relations Assn., A.A.A.S., Soc. Adult Edn. (internat. understanding com. 1956-61), Soc. for Acad. Achievement (pres. 1962-74), Alpha Gamma Rho, Alpha Zeta, Pi Kappa Delta, Phi Delta Kappa, Alpha Phi Omega, Phi Sigma. Presbyn. Clubs: Mason (32 deg.), Shriner, Rotarian. Home: 3969 E Palomar Dr Tucson AZ 85711

KNOBLE, JAMES KEENE, hospital administrator; b. Mpls., Apr. 1, 1939; s. James K. and Miriam (Niles) K.; (married). B.A., Gustavus Adolphus Coll., 1961; M.H.A., U. Minn., 1963. Adminstrv. resident Eitel Hosp., Mpls., 1962-63; adminstrv. asst. Saginaw (Mich.) Gen. Hosp., 1963-65; adminstr. Miller-Dwan Hosp.-Med. Center; also exec. v.p. Miller-Dwan Med. Center Found., Duluth, Minn., 1965-74; pres., chief exec. officer Methodist Med. Center Ill., Peoria, 1974—. Bd. dirs. YMCA, Peoria., United Health Care Systems, Midwest Meth. Network. Fellow Am. Coll. Hosp. Adminstrs.; Mem. Am. Hosp. Assn., Council Community Hosps., Ill. Hosp. Assn., Peoria C. of C. Lutheran. Club: Rotary (Peoria). Home: 7234 Crabapple Ct Peoria IL 61614 Office: 221 NE Glen Oak Ave Peoria IL 61636

KNOBLER, ALFRED EVERETT, ceramic engr., mfg. co. exec., publisher; b. N.Y.C., Mar. 4, 1915; s. Samuel and Mildred (Weisz) K.; m. Selma Frankel, Nov. 28, 1943; children—Peter Stephen, Joanna Gabin. B.S. in Ceramic Engring, Va. Poly. Inst., 1938. Engr. U.S. War Dept., Phila., 1942-44, Fed. Tel. & Tel., N.Y.C., 1944-45; pres. Pilgrim Glass Corp., Ceredo, W.Va., 1949—, Alfred E. Knobler & Co., Inc., Moonachie, N.J., 1950—, Knobler Energy Assos., Inc., Barboursville, W.Va., 1976—, Knobler Internat., Ltd., Sutton, Eng. Home: 6 E 10th St New York NY 10003 Office: 225 Fifth Ave New York NY 10010 also Moonachie NJ 07075

KNOBLER, PETER STEPHEN, magazine editor, writer; b. N.Y.C., Dec. 4, 1946; s. Alfred E. and Selma (Frankel) K.; m. Jane Dissin, May 16, 1982. B.A., Middlebury (Vt.) Coll., 1968; postgrad. creative writing, Columbia U. Reporter Liberation News Service, N.Y.C., 1969; editor Zygote mag., N.Y.C., 1970; asso. editor Crawdaddy mag., N.Y.C., 1971-72; editor, 1972-79; pres. Knobler Mgmt. Inc., N.Y.C., 1983—. Co-author: Giant Steps: The Autobiography of Kareem Abdul-Jabbar, 1982; songs. Home: 67 Greene St New York NY 10012 Office: 235 Fifth Ave New York NY 10016

KNOBLOCH, CARL WILLIAM, JR., holding company executive; b. N.Y.C., Apr. 16, 1930; s. Carl William and Lilly Louise (Smith) K.; m. Emily Champion, Nov. 30, 1957; children: Carla, Emily Jean, Eleanor Louise. B.A., Yale U., 1951; M.B.A., Harvard U., 1953. With Lehman Bros., N.Y.C., 1954-57, Kidder, Peabody & Co., 1957-61; chmn. Prodn. Operators Corp., Atlanta, 1961—; dir. Rhodes, Inc., Atlanta. Bd. visitors Davidson Coll.; bd. dirs. N.W. Ga. council Girl Scouts U.S.A., Shepherd Spinal Center, Atlanta, Council Better Bus. Burs., Inc., Washington. Clubs: Yale, Anglers (N.Y.C.); Piedmont Driving, Capital City (Atlanta); Mill Reef (Antiqua, W.I.). Home: 2575 Arden Rd NW Atlanta GA 30327 Office: Suite 515 One Piedmont Center 3565 Piedmont Rd NE Atlanta GA 30305

KNOBLOCH, FERDINAND J., psychiatrist, educator; b. Prague, Czechoslovakia, Aug. 15, 1916; emigrated to Can., 1970; s. Ferdin and Marie (Verunac) K.; m. Jirina Skorkovska, Sept. 5, 1947; children: Katerina, Yohana. Maturity degree, Realgymnasium, Prague, 1927-35; student med. sch., Charles U., Prague, 1935-46; psychoanalytic tng., 1945-53. Successively lectr., asst. prof., asso. prof. psychiatry Charles U., 1946-70; mem. faculty U. B.C., 1970—, prof. psychiatry, 1971—; vis. prof. U. Havana, 1963, U. Ill., Chgo., 1968-69, Columbia U., 1969-70, Albert Einstein Med. Coll., 1970; pres. European seminar mental health and family WHO, 1961, 3d Internat. Congress Psychodrama, 1968; co-chmn. Internat. Symposium Non-Verbal Aspects and Techniques of Psychotherapy, 1974; hon. dir. psychodrama Moreno Inst., N.Y.C., 1974. Author: (with Jirina Knobloch) Forensic Psychiatry, 1967 (award Czechoslovak Med. Soc. 1968), Psychotherapy, 1968, Neurosis and You, 1962, 63, 68, Integrated Psychotherapy, 1979; contbr. articles to profl. jours. Mem. Czechoslovak Soc. Advancement Psychoanalysis and Integration of Psychotherapy (pres. 1968-72), Am. Acad. Psychoanalysis, Polish Psychiat. Assn. (corr.), Am. Psychiat. Assn., Can. Psychiat. Assn., Am. Group Psychotherapy Assn., Can. Soc. for Integrated Psychotherapy and Psychoanalysis (pres. 1972—). Imprisoned by Gestapo, 1943-45. Home: 4137 W 12th Ave Vancouver BC Canada

KNOBLOCH, WILLIAM RICHARD, finance co. exec.; b. N.Y.C., July 10, 1928; s. Carl W. and Lily Louise (Smith) K.; m. Audrey E. Messinger, July 15, 1950; children—Carl William II, Ellen Louise, William Richard III. B.S., Yale U., 1949; M.B.A., Wharton Sch. U. Pa., 1951. Dir. Technicorp Inc., Stamford, Conn., Metrodyne, Inc., Stamford; chmn. Case & Co. (mgmt. cons.), Stamford; pres. Fairchester Assos., Stamford, 1973—. Author: (with others) Pricing for Profit and Growth, 1962. Clubs: Yale (N.Y.C.); Woodway Country (Darien, Conn.). Home: 149 Emery Dr Stamford CT 06902 Office: 1111 Summer St Stamford CT 06905

KNOEBEL, BETTY LOU, food distbn. co. exec.; b. Hobart, Ind., July 12, 1931; d. Frank O. and Louise C. (Sohn) Burnett; m. F.C. Knoebel, Apr. 27, 1974. Grad., Sch. X-Ray, Methodist Hosp., Gary, Ind., 1950; student, Ind. U., 1952-53. X-ray technician, then various secretarial positions; X-ray technician, asst. adminstr. Melissa Meml. Hosp., Holyoke, Colo.; adminstrv. asst., interior designer, dir. Nobel, Inc., Denver; now corp. sec.; corp. sec., dir. Capitol Warehouse Co.; dir. Gen. Mgmt. Corp. Grantee; Am. Cancer Soc., 1949-50. Mem. Profl.

Women's Assn., Am. Soc. X-Ray Technicians, Colo.-Wyo. Restautrant Assn. (pres. ladies aux. 1978-79). Republican. Office: 1101 W 48th Ave Denver CO 80217

KNOEBEL, SUZANNE BUCKNER, cardiologist, medical educator; b. Ft. Wayne, Ind., Dec. 13, 1926; d. Doster and Marie (Lewis) Buckner. A.B., Goucher Coll., 1948; M.D., Ind. U.-Indpls., 1960. Diplomate: Am. Bd. Internal Medicine. Asst. prof. medicine Ind. U., Indpls., 1966-69, assoc. prof., 1969-72, prof., 1972-77, Krannert prof., 1977—; asst. dean research Ind. U., Indpls., 1975—; assoc. dir. Krannert Inst. Cardiology, Indpls., 1974—; asst. chief cardiology sect. Richard L. Roudebush VA Med. Ctr., Indpls., 1982—. Fellow Am. Coll. Cardiology (v.p. 1980-81, pres. 1982-83); mem. Am. Fedn. Clin. Research, Assn. Univ. Cardiologists. Office: Ind U Sch Medicine 1100 W Michigan St Indianapolis IN 46223

KNOEDLER, ELMER L., chemical engineer; b. Gloucester, N.J., Feb. 12, 1912; s. Elmer L. and Carolyn (Belle) K.; m. Ruth Timanus, Oct. 1960 (dec. Dec. 1964); m. Mabel Dyer Todd, Jan. 15, 1966; children—Dianne, Homer. M.E., Cornell U., 1934, M.S., 1936; Ph.D., Columbia, 1952. Registered profl. engr. 19 states. With Atlantic Mfg. Co., 1934-35; asst. supt. charge Davis Emergency Equipment Co., 1937-38; charge research and devel. metal power process Metals Disintegrating Co., 1939-41; cons. chem. engr., sr. field engr. Sheppard T. Powell, 1941—; partner Sheppard T. Powell & Assos., Balt.; Past mem. Md. Bd. for Registration Engrs. and Land Surveyors. Contbr. numerous articles tech., profl. jours. Fellow Am. Inst. Chemists, ASME (past chmn. com. water conditioning and indsl. waste); mem. Am. Inst. Chem. Engrs. (chmn. Balt. sect. 1953), Am. Chem. Soc., Am. Inst. Cons. Engrs., Chemists Club N.Y., Sigma Xi, Phi Lambda Upsilon. Clubs: Cornell (Md.; N.Y.); Center, Annapolis. Home: 513 Little John Hill Sherwood Forest MD 21405 Office: 31 Light St Baltimore MD 21202

KNOELL, W.H., steel co. exec.; b. Pitts., Aug. 1, 1924; s. William F. and Hazel (Holverstott) K.; m. E. Anne Kirkland, Jan. 26, 1952; children—Kristin Anne, Susan Elizabeth, Amy Lynn, Gretchen. Student, Cornell U., 1942; B.S. in Mech. Engring, Carnegie Mellon U., 1947; J.D., U. Pitts., 1950. Practice law with firm Shoemaker-Knoell, 1949-50; asst. to exec. v.p. Pitts. Corning Corp., 1950-55; asst. sec. Crucible Steel Co. Am., 1955-57, sec., 1957-63, v.p., 1963-67; v.p., asst. to pres. Cyclops Corp., 1967-68, exec. v.p., 1968-72, pres., 1972—, chief exec. officer, 1973—, also dir.; dir. Am. Sterilizer Co., Koppers Co., Duquesne Light Co., Fed. Reserve Bank Cleve. Bd. dirs. St. Clair Meml. Hosp., Mid-Atlantic Legal Found., Com. for Support Pvt. Univs. Inc.; chmn. adv. council Jr. Achievement of S.W. Pa.; bd. visitors U. Pitts. Law Sch.; trustee, mem. exec. com., mech. engring. vis. com. Carnegie-Mellon U. Served with USAAF, 1943-45. Mem. ABA, Am. Iron and Steel Insts. (dir.), Internat. Iron and Steel Inst., Pi Tau Sigma, Theta Tau, Beta Theta Pi, Phi Alpha Delta. Clubs: University, Duquesne (dir.); St. Clair Country (Pitts.); Laurel Valley Golf, Rolling Rock. Office: 650 Washington Rd Pittsburgh PA 15228

KNOEPFLER, PETER TAMAS, psychiatrist, organizational consultant; b. Vienna, Austria, Mar. 14, 1929; came to U.S., 1947, naturalized, 1962; s. Joseph and Claire (Farkas) K.; m. Gayle Kurth, July 3, 1960; children: David, Daniel, Paul. B.S., Calif. Inst. Tech., 1950; M.A., Columbia U., 1951; M.D., Cornell U., 1955. Diplomate: Am. Bd. Psychiatry and Neurology. Intern Meth. Hosp. of Bklyn., 1955-56; resident Albert Einstein Coll. Medicine, N.Y.C., 1956-57, 59-61; practice medicine specializing in psychiatry, Bellevue, Wash., 1970—; asso. med. dir. U. Utah Student Health Service, Salt Lake City, 1962-69; staff psychiatrist Menninger Found., Topeka, 1969-70; mem. faculty Menninger Sch. Psychiatry, 1969-70; med. dir. Eastside Community Health Center, Bellevue, 1970-73; mem. staff Fairfax Hosp., Kirkland, Wash., Overlake Hosp., Bellevue; clin. asso. prof. psychiatry and behavioral scis. U. Wash., Seattle, 1970-79, clin. prof. psychiatry, 1979—; adj. faculty Union Grad. Sch., Yellow Springs, Ohio, 1974—, Antioch West, 1979—; lectr., cons. in field; instr. Am. Group Psychotherapy Ann. Inst., 1976-79; cons. AEC, 1966-68, Planned Parenthood of Bellevue, 1971—, Youth Eastside Services, Bellevue, 1970—, Rosehill Inst., Toronto, Ont., Can., 1973—, Peace Corps, 1964-66, Little Sch. Bellevue, 1972-74, Juvenile Ct. Kings County, Wash., 1972—, Skid Road Community Council, Seattle, 1973-76, Rice Inst., 1975—; mem. exec. med. com. Planned Parenthood Seattle, King County, 1974—. Editorial bd.: Adolescent Psychiatry, 1974—, Jour. Sex Edn. and Therapy. Mem. adv. bd. Solo Ctr., Seattle, 1974—; mem. Radio Emergency Associated Citizens Team, 1977-79; bd. dirs. Eliot Inst., Friends of King County Library, Unitarian Universalist Assn.; vice chmn. Unitarian Universalist Assn., 1975-77. Served to capt. M.C. USAF, 1957-59. Recipient Vol. of Yr. award Planned Parenthood of King County, 1980; named Physician of Yr., 1974, Citizen of Day. Fellow Am. Psychiat. Assn., Am. Group Psychotherapy Assn.; fellow Am. Soc. Adolescent Psychiatry (mem. exec. com. 1973-75); mem. Soc. Sci. Study of Sex, Am. Assn. Sex Educators, Counsellors and Therapists (dir. 1979—, treas. N.W. region 1976—), Am. Group Psychotherapy Assn. (dir. 1979—), Wash. State Med. Soc., N.W. Group Psychotherapy Assn. (pres. 1978—), N.W. Soc. Adolescent Psychiatry (pres. 1973-75). Office: Suite 221 1621 114th Ave SE Bellevue WA 98004

KNOLES, GEORGE HARMON, history educator; b. Los Angeles, Feb. 20, 1907; s. Tully Cleon and Emily (Walline) K.; m. Amandalee Barker, June 12, 1930; children: Ann Barker (Nitzan), Alice Laurane (Simmons). A.B. with honors, Coll. of Pacific, 1928, A.M., 1930; Ph.D., Stanford U., 1939. Instr. history Union High Sch., Lodi, Calif., 1930-35; asst. in history, Stanford, 1935-36, instr. history, 1937-41, asst. prof., 1942-46, asso. prof., 1946-51, prof. history, 1951-72, Margaret Byrne prof. Am. history, 1968-72, emeritus, 1972—, chmn. dept. history, 1968-72; dir. Inst. Am. History, 1956-72; Prof. history, chmn. div. social sci. State Coll. Edn., Greeley, Colo., 1941-42; summer tchr. Central Wash. Coll. Edn., Ellensburg, 1939, State Coll., Flagstaff, Ariz, 1940, 1941, U. Calif. at Los Angeles, 1947; Stanford, Tokyo U., Am. Studies Seminars, Tokyo, 1950-52, 56, U. Wyo., 1955; Fulbright distinguished lectr., Japan, 1971. Author: The Presidential Campaign and Election of, 1892, 1942, Readings in Western Civilization, (with Rixford K. Snyder), 1951, The Jazz Age Revisited, 1955, The New United States, 1959; Editor: The Crisis of The Union, 1860-61, 1965, Sources in American History, 10 vols, 1965-66, The Responsibilities of Power, 1900-1929, 1967, Essays and Assays: California History Reappraised, 1973; Contbr. articles to profl. jours. Served to lt. USNR, 1944-46. Mem. Am., So. hist. assns., Orgn. Am. Historians (exec. com. 1950-54, bd. editors rev. 1955-58), Am. Studies Assn. (council 1952-54), Soc. of Am. Historians. Methodist. Clubs: Rotarian., Commonwealth. Home: PO Box 3284 Stanford CA 94305

KNOLL, ERWIN, author, editor; b. Vienna, Austria, July 17, 1931; came to U.S., 1940, naturalized, 1946; s. Carl and Ida (Schaechter) K.; m. Doris Elsa Ricksteen, Mar. 1, 1954; children: David Samuel, Jonathan Robert. B.A., NYU, 1953. Reporter, editor Editor and Publisher mag., N.Y.C., 1948-53; asso. editor Better Schools, N.Y.C., 1956-57; reporter, editor Washington Post, 1957-62; Washington editor Los Angeles Times-Washington Post News Service, 1962-63; Washington corr. Newhouse Nat. News Service, 1963-68; free lance writer, Washington editor The Progressive, 1968-73, editor, Madison, Wis., 1973—; commentator Nat. Public Radio, 1980-82; Cons. Nat. Commn. on Urban Problems, 1968. Author: (with William McGaffin) Anything But the Truth, 1968, Scandal in the Pentagon, 1969; Editor: (with Judith Nies McFadden) American Militarism, 1970, 1969, War Crimes and the American Conscience, 1970; Contbr. articles to mags. Served with AUS, 1953-55. Home: 6123 Johnson St McFarland WI 53558 Office: 409 E Main St Madison WI 53703

KNOLL, FLORENCE SCHUST, architect, designer; b. Saginaw, Mich., May 24, 1917; d. Frederick E. and M. Haistings Schust; m. Hans G. Knoll, July 1, 1946 (div. Oct. 1955); m. 2d Harry Hood Basset, June 22, 1958. Student, Cranbrook Art Acad., Bloomfield Hills, Mich., 1935-37, Archtl. Assn., London, 1938-39; B.Arch., Ill. Inst. Tech., Chgo., 1941; D.F.A. (hon.), Parsons Sch. Design, 1979. Archtl. draftsman, designer Gropius & Breuer, Boston, 1941; design dir. Knoll Planning Unit, 1942-55; pres. Knoll Internat., N.Y.C., 1955-65; pvt. practice architecture and designer, Coconut Grove, Fla., 1965—. Recipient Ill. Inst. Tech. Hall of Fame award, 1982, Athena award R.I. Sch. Design, 1982, others. Mem. AIA (recipient Gold medal for indsl. arts 1961), Indsl. Designers Am. (hon.). Home: (SS) 1 Grove Isle Dr#801(ES) Coconut Grove FL 33133

KNOLL, GLENN FREDERICK, nuclear engineering educator; b. St. Joseph, Mich., Aug. 3, 1935; s. Oswald Herman and Clara Martha (Bernthal) K.; m. Gladys Hetzner, Sept. 7, 1957; children: Thomas, John, Peter. B.S., Case Inst. Tech., 1957; M.S. in Chem. Engring., Stanford, 1959; Ph.D. in Nuclear Engring., U. Mich., 1963. Asst. research physicist U. Mich., Ann Arbor, 1960-62, asst. prof. nuclear engring., 1962-67, asso. prof., 1967-72, prof., 1972—, chmn. dept. nuclear engring., 1979—, also mem. bioengring. faculty.; Vis. scientist Institut für Angewandte Kernphysik, Kernforschungszentrum Karlsruhe, Germany, 1965-66; sr. vis. fellow dept. physics U. Surrey, Guildford, Eng., 1973; summer cons. Electric Power Research Inst., Palo Alto, Calif., 1974; cons. in field. Author: Radiation Detection and Measurement, 1979, Principles of Engineering, 1982. NSF fellow, 1958-60; Fulbright travel grantee, 1965-66; Sci. Research Council sr. fellow, 1973. Fellow Am. Nuclear Soc.; mem. Am. Assn. Engring. Edn. (Glenn Murphy award 1979); Mem. IEEE (nuclear and plasma soc., chmn. tech. com. on nuclear med. sci. 1977-79), Soc. Nuclear Medicine, Sigma Xi, Tau Beta Pi. Patentee in field. Office: Dept Nuclear Engring 119 Cooley Bldg U Mich Ann Arbor MI 48109

KNOLL, JERRY, former govt. ofcl.; b. Cin., Mar. 29, 1924; s. Adolph and Hilda (Schuman) K. B.A., U. Chgo., 1947, M.B.A., 1947; student, U. Mich., 1943. With U.S. Mil. Govt., Frankfurt and Berlin, Germany, 1948-49; U.S. sec. econs. and fgn. trade and exchange coms. Allied High Commn., Bonn, Germany, 1949-51; asst. to dep. econ. adviser, spl. asst. to dir. Mut. Security Adminstrn. Mission, Bonn, 1951-52; asst. div. dir. Office Dep. Dir. for Mut. Def. Assistance Control, ICA, Washington, 1952-55; internat. economist Dept. State, 1955-59, ICA, 1959-61; dep. dir. Office Devel. Planning, AID, 1961-64; dir. Office West African Affairs, 1964-68, Office Eastern and S. African Affairs, 1968-76, Office Near East and North African Affairs, 1976-79; cons., 1979—; dep. dir. med. programs div. Internat. Rescue Com., 1979—. Served to cpl. AUS, 1943-45. Recipient Meritorious Service award FOA, 1955, AID, 1972; Superior Honor award AID, 1976; Disting. Career Service award, 1979. Home: 4000 Massachusetts Ave Washington DC 20016

KNOOP, WERNER CALDWELL, business executive, city official; b. Hancock County, Iowa, Mar. 30, 1902; s. Charles Werner and Jessie (Olmstead) K.; m. Faith Yingling, Sept. 4, 1926; 1 dau., Athalia May (Mrs. Karl Robert Kullander). B.S. in Civil Engring, Iowa State U., 1924. Registered profl. engr. Engr. Truscon Steel Co., Youngstown, Ohio, also Chgo., Omaha, 1924-29; owner Capital Steel Co., Little Rock, 1929-40; cons. engr., 1940-46; exec. v.p. Baldwin Co. (contractors), Little Rock, 1946-64, pres., 1964—, Eureka Brick & Tile Co., Clarksville, 1949—; Pres. sch. bd., Little Rock, 1947, mayor, 1957-62; chmn. Little Rock Parking Authority, 1966—; mem. Gov.'s Traffic Safety Adv. Commn.; pres. Little Rock AFB Community Relations Council, 1968; mem. Little Rock 50 for Future, Little Rock Com. Fgn. Relations; jury commr. U.S. Dist. Ct., Eastern Div., Ark. Pres., bd. dirs. Little Rock U., 1947, Met. YMCA, Johnson-Knoop Found.; mem. internat. com. world service YMCA; bd. dirs., mem. finance and exec. coms.; trustee Nat. Safety Council. Fellow Am. Soc. C.E. (past dir. Mid-South sect.); mem. Nat. Soc. Profl. Engrs., Asso. Gen. Contractors Am. (dir. Ark. chpt. 1963—, v.p. Ark. chpt. 1968, chpt. pres. 1969, mem. nat. safety com., nat. dir. 1979—), Air Force Assn., Little Rock C. of C. (sec.-treas., v.p. 1969, pres. 1970), Little Rock Engrs. Club (past pres.). Presbyn. (elder). Clubs: Rotary, Little Rock, Country of Little Rock. Home: 6 Ozark Point Little Rock AR 72205 Office: 322 Gaines St: Little Rock AR 72201

KNOPF, ALFRED A., publisher; b. N.Y.C., Sept. 12, 1892; s. Samuel and Ida (Japhe) K.; m. Blanche Wolf, 1916 (dec. June 1966); 1 son, Alfred; m. Helen Norcross Hedrick, 1967. A.B., Columbia U., 1912; L.H.D., Yale U., 1958, Columbia U., 1959, Bucknell U., 1959, Lehigh U., 1960, Coll. William and Mary, 1969, U. Mich., 1969, Bates Coll., 1971, U. Ariz., 1979; LL.D., Brandeis U., 1963; D.Litt., Adelphi U., 1966, U. Chattanooga, 1966, C.W. Post Center, L.I. U., 1973. Founded pub. firm, 1915; pres. Alfred A. Knopf Inc., N.Y.C., 1918-57, chmn. bd., 1957-72, chmn. bd. emeritus, 1972—. Decorated comendador Ordem Nacional do Cruzeiro do Sul, Brazil; recipient Cornelius Amory Pugsley gold medal for conservation and preservation, 1960; Alexander Hamilton medal Assn. Alumni Columbia U., 1966; Outstanding Service award Nat. Parks Centennial Commn., 1972; Francis Parkman Silver medal Soc. Am. Historians, 1974; Distinguished Service award Assn. Am. Univ. Presses, 1975; Distinguished Achievement award Drexel U. Library Sch. Alumni Assn., 1975; Notable Achievement award Brandeis U., 1977; Machado de Assis medal Brazilian Acad. Letters, 1978. Clubs: Cosmos (Washington); Century Country (Harrison, N.Y.); Lotos (N.Y.C.). Office: 201 E 50th St New York NY 10022

KNOPF, ALFRED, JR., publisher; b. White Plains, N.Y., June 17, 1918; s. Alfred A. and Blanche (Wolf) K.; m. Alice Laine, July 27, 1952; children—Alison, Susan, David. Grad., Phillips Exeter Acad., 1937; A.B., Union Coll., Schenectady, 1942. With Atheneum Pubs., N.Y.C., 1959—, chmn. bd., 1964—; vis. chmn. Scribner Book Cos. Trustee Pequot Library, Southport, Conn. Served to capt. USAAF, 1941-45. Mem. Delta Upsilon. Clubs: Century Assn., Coffee House, Dutch Treat (N.Y.C.); Tavern (Chgo.); Odd Volumes (Boston); Nassau (Princeton, N.J.). Home: Bayberry Ridge Westport CT 06880 Office: 597 Fifth Ave New York NY 10017

KNOPF, IRWIN JAY, psychology educator; b. N.Y.C., June 14, 1924; s. Joseph and Esther (Inselman) K.; m. Roberta Iris Olin, Dec. 29, 1951; children: William Douglas, David Richard, Judith Ann. A.B., N.Y.U., 1948; M.A., Northwestern U., 1949, Ph.D., 1952. Diplomate: clin. psychology Am. Bd. Examiners Profl. Psychology. Asst. prof. clin. psychology, then asso. prof. clin. psychology, then asso. prof., head div. psychology, dept. psychiatry State U. Iowa, 1952-58; asso. prof., chief div. psychology, dept. psychiatry U. Tex., 1958-62, prof., chmn. div. psychology, 1962-64; prof. psychology, chmn. dept. Emory U., 1964-83, Disting. prof. psychology, 1980—, also chmn. exec. com., vice chmn. faculty; cons. in field. Field selection officer Peace Corps; chmn. com. teaching awards Am. Psychol. Found. Author: Childhood Psychopathology: A Developmental Approach, 1979, 2d edit., 1984; articles in field.; Cons. editor: Contemporary Psychology, 1961-73. Served with inf. AUS, 1944-45. Decorated Purple Heart. Fellow Am. Psychol. Assn., Am. Orthopsychiat. Assn., Midwestern, Southeastern Psychol. Assn. (pres. 1979-80), Sigma Xi. Home: 4256 Exeter Close NW Atlanta GA 30327

KNOPF, KENYON ALFRED, economist, educator; b. Cleve., Nov. 24, 1921; s. Harold C. and Emma A. (Underwood) K.; m. Madelyn Lee Trebilcock, Mar. 28, 1953; children—Kristin Lee, Mary George. A.B. magna cum laude with high honors in Econs, Kenyon Coll., 1942; M.A. in Econs; Ph.D., Harvard U., 1949. Mem. faculty Grinnell Coll., 1949-67, prof. econs., 1960-67, Jentzen prof., 1961-67, chmn. dept., 1958-60, chmn. div. social studies, 1962-64, chmn. faculty, 1964-67; dean coll. Whitman Coll., Walla Walla, Wash., 1967-70, prof. econs., 1967—, provost, 1970-81, dean faculty, 1970-78, acting pres., 1974-75; pub. interest dir. Fed. Home Loan Bank, Seattle, 1976—; mem. council undergrad. assessment program Ednl. Testing Service, 1977-80. Author: (with Robert H. Haveman) The Market System, 4th edit, 1981; Editor: (with James H. Stauss) The Teaching of Elementary Economics, 1960, Introduction to Economics Series (9 vols.), 1966, 2d edit., 1970-71. Mem. youth council, City Grinnell, 1957-59; bd. dirs. Walla Walla United Fund, 1968-76, pres., 1973; mem. Walla Walla County Mental Health Bd., 1968-75, Walla Walla CSC, 1978—; chmn. Walla Walla CSC, 1981—; councilman, City of Grinnell, 1964-67; pres. Walla Walla County Human Services Adminstrv. Bd., 1975-77; mem. Iowa adv. council SBA. Served with USAAF, 1943-46. Grantee Social Sci. Research Council, 1951-52. Mem. Am. Conf. Acad. Deans (exec. com. 1970-77, chmn. 1975), Am. Econ. Assn., Am. Soc. Personnel Adminstrn., Phi Beta Kappa, Delta Tau Delta. Office: Whitman Coll Walla Walla WA 99362

KNOPF, PAUL MARK, immunoparasitologist; b. Trenton, N.J., Apr. 4, 1936; s. Chiam David and Beatrice (Safir) K.; m. Carol Lois Harrison, June 29, 1958; children—Jeffrey William, Steven Harrison, Rachel Analiese. B.Sc., M.I.T., 1958; Ph.D., 1962. Postdoctoral fellow MRC Lab. Molecular Biology, Cambridge, Eng., 1962-64; spl. research asso. Salk Inst., La Jolla, Calif., 1964-72; prof. med. sci. Brown U., Providence, 1972—. Asso. editor: Jour Immunology, 1981—. Recipient Career Devel. award NIH, 1966-72; NIH grantee, 1966-76; Rockefeller Found. grantee, 1972-80; Edna McConnell Clark Found. grantee, 1976—, WHO, 1979—; Fulbright-Hays sr. scholar fellow, 1978-79. Mem. Am. Assn. Immunologists, Am. Soc. Tropical Medicine and Hygiene. Home: 2 Dana Rd Barrington RI 02806 Office: Div Biology and Medicine Brown U Providence RI 02912

KNOPKA, WILLIAM NORMAN, chemical company executive; b. Buffalo, Dec. 1, 1938; s. Norman E. and Marion N. (Pemberton) K.; m. Carol B. Gold, Sept. 11, 1965; children: William N., Heidi, Gretchen. B.S., Canisius Coll., 1961; M.S., Seton Hall U., 1963, Ph.D., 1965. Various research and devel. positions FMC Corp., Phila., 1965-74, product mgr. fibers, 1974-76, product mgr. agrl. chems., Phila., 1976-77; dir. fabric devel. Goodyear Tire & Rubber Co., Akron, Ohio, 1977-79, dir. elastomer and chem. research, 1979-82, dir. chem. research and devel., 1982-83; dir. product and process devel. Am. Cyanamid Co., Stamford, Conn., 1983—. Author papers, articles, chpt. in book; patentee in field including flame retardant fiber blends. Served to capt. U.S. Army, 1966-68. Mem. Indsl. Research Inst. (advanced study group com., discussion leader confs.). Republican. Office: Am Cyanamid Co 1937 W Main St Stamford CT 06904

KNOPOFF, LEON, educator; b. Los Angeles, July 1, 1925; s. Max and Ray (Singer) K.; m. Joanne Van Cleef, Apr. 9, 1961; children—Katherine Alexandra, Rachel Anne, Michael Van Cleef. Student, Los Angeles City Coll., 1941-42; B.S. in Elec Engring, Calif. Inst. Tech., 1944; M.S. in Physics, Calif. Inst. Tech., 1946, Ph.D., 1949. Asst., then asso. prof. physics Miami U., Oxford, Ohio, 1948-50; mem. faculty U. Calif. at Los Angeles, 1950—, prof. physics, 1961—, prof. geophysics, 1959—, research musicologist, 1963—; asso. dir. Inst. Geophysics and Planetary Physics, 1972—; prof. geophysics Calif. Inst. Tech., 1962-63, research asso. seismology, 1963-64; vis. prof. Technische Hochschule, Karlsruhe, Germany, 1966, Harvard, 1972, U. Chile, Santiago, 1973; Chmn. U.S. Nat. Upper Mantle Com., 1963-71; sec. Internat. Upper Mantle Com., 1963-71; chmn. com. math. geophysics Internat. Union Geodesy and Geophysics, 1971-75, mem., 1973-75. Recipient Wiechert medal German Geophys. Soc., 1978; Gold medal Royal Astron. Soc., 1979; NSF sr. postdoctoral fellow Cambridge (Eng.) U., 1960-61; Guggenheim Found. fellow, 1976-77. Fellow Am. Acad. Arts and Scis.; mem. Nat. Acad. Scis., Am. Phys. Soc., Am. Geophys. Union, Seismol. Soc., Royal Astron. Soc. (Jeffreys lectr. 1976), AAAS. Office: U Calif Los Angeles CA 90024

KNOPP, MARVIN ISADORE, mathematics educator; b. Chgo., Jan. 4, 1933; s. Mitshel and Minnie (Israel) K.; m. Josephine Zadovsky, June 9, 1957; children: Seth David, Yudah Benjamin, Abby Alissa, Elana Melissa. B.S., U. Ill., 1954, A.M., 1955, Ph.D., 1958. Research mathematician Space Tech. Labs., Los Angeles, 1958-59; NSF postdoctoral fellow Inst. Advanced Study, Princeton, N.J., 1959-60; asst. prof. U. Wis., 1960-62, assoc. prof., 1962-67, prof., 1967-72; mathematician Nat. Bur. Standards, Washington, 1963-64; vis. prof. U. Basel, Switzerland, 1968-69; prof. U. Ill., Chgo. Circle, 1970-76, Temple U., Phila., 1976—; Mem. Inst. Advanced Study, Princeton, N.J., 1975, 78; vis. prof. Ohio State U., spring 1979. Author: Theory of Area, 1970, Modular Functions and Analytic Number Theory, 1971; also articles Modular Functions in Analytic Number Theory; editor: Ill. Jour. Math, 1971-78, Proc. of a Conf. in Analytic Number Theory, 1981. NSF grantee, 1960—. Home: 1031 E Lancaster Ave Apt 307 Rosemont PA 19010 Office: Temple Univ 608 Computer Bldg Philadelphia PA 19122

KNOPPERS, ANTONIE THEODOOR, business executive; b. Kapelle, Netherlands, Feb. 27, 1915; came to U.S., 1953, naturalized, 1958; s. Bastiaan A. and Annetje (Valkenier) K.; m. Maria J. Willemsen, June 1, 1939; children: Bastiaan A., Maria H., Anneke C., Elizabeth E. M.D., U. Amsterdam, 1939; Dr. Pharmacology, U. Leyde, 1941; D.Sc. (hon.), Worcester Poly. Inst. Research asst. Pharmacol. Inst., U. Amsterdam, 1940-43; dir. pharmacology Amsterdam Chininefabriek, 1943-52; prof. Free U. Amsterdam, 1950-53; mng. dir. Nederlandsche Kininefabriek, 1950-53; med. dir. Merck Sharp & Dohme Internat., 1953-55; v.p., gen. mgr. Merck Sharp & Dohme Internat. div. Merck & Co., Inc., N.Y.C., 1955-57, pres. internat. div., 1957-67; pres., chief operating officer Merck & Co., Inc., 1967-74, vice-chmn., 1974-75, also dir.; dir. John Wiley & Sons, Inc., Hewlett Packard Co., Scott Paper Co. Contbr. to sci. jours.; mem. therapy com.: Netherlands Med. Jour., 1950-53; co-founder: Documenta Tropica Neerlandica et Indonesica. Bd. dirs. Humane Inc.; trustee Drew U., Manhattan Sch. Music, Salk Inst.; Mem. Council Fgn. Relations, N.Y. Acad. Scis. Presbyterian. Clubs: Century, Metropolitan Opera (dir.), Netherlands (N.Y.C.); Baltusrol Golf. Home and Office: 38 Lenox Rd Summit NJ 07901

KNORPP, J. RONALD, utility executive; b. Louisville, July 26, 1936; s. John Henry and Corrine (Wirth) K.; m. Shirley Ann Scott, Nov. 18, 1963; children: Rhonda, Rachele, Eric, Kevin. B.A., Bellarmine Coll., Louisville, 1958; M.B.A. summa cum laude, Clemson-Furman univs., 1973. C.P.A., Ky. Acct., Humphrey Robinson & Co., Louisville, 1959-66; v.p. (subs. Liberty Corp.), Greenville, S.C., 1966-72; v.p. fin. Fla. Gas Co., Winter Park, 1973—; exec. v.p., chief fin. officer Fla. Gas Transmission Co., Winter Park; adminstrv. bd. Sun First Nat. Bank,

Orlando, Fla., 1978—. Mem. parish council, fin. com. St. Mary Magdalen Roman Catholic Ch., Orlando, 1977—; bd. dirs. Central Fla. chpt. Leukemia Soc. Am., 1976—; trustee Winter Park Meml. Hosp., 1978—. Served with USMCR, 1958-63. Mem. Am. Inst. C.P.A.s, Am. Gas Assn., Interstate Natural Gas Assn., Am. Mgmt. Assn. Republican. Office: PO Box 44 Winter Park FL 32790 *

KNORR, DONALD ROBERT, architect; b. Chgo., Dec. 25, 1922; s. Arthur Herman and Esther Gertrude (Sternbeck) K.; m. Anne Hall, May 14, 1949; children: Torin Jon, Kipp D., Guy Douglass. B.S., U. Ill., 1947; postgrad., Cranbrook Acad. Art, 1948. Designer Eero Saarinen & Assos., 1947-49; designer, project mgr. Skidmore, Owings & Merrill, San Francisco, 1949-51; prin. Knorr Assos., San Francisco, 1951-56; partner Knorr-Elliott & Assos., San Francisco, 1956-73, Don Knorr & Assos., 1973—; vis. critic Calif. State Poly. Coll. Sch. Architecture, 1969, 71. Mem. San Francisco Mus. Art. Served to lt. (j.g.) USNR, 1943-46. Recipient Nat. awards Archtl. Record, Progressive Architecture; 1st prize N.Y. Mus. Modern Art, Internat. Furniture Design Competition, 1949. Fellow A.I.A. (numerous regional and nat. awards). Home: 888 Francisco St San Francisco CA 94109 Office: 950 Battery St San Francisco CA 94111 also 600 Barrow St Anchorage AK 99503

KNORR, NORMAN JOHN, psychiatrist, med. sch. dean; b. Balt., Sept. 9, 1930; m. Doris Morrison; 1 dau., Lisa. Student, Coll. William and Mary, 1955, U. Md., 1957; M.D., George Washington U., 1961. Diplomate: Nat. Bd. Med. Examiners. Resident Johns Hopkins Hosp., Balt., 1962-65; asso. prof. psychiatry and surgery Johns Hopkins U., 1968-70; prof. psychiatry and plastic surgery U. Va., Charlottesville, 1970—; dir. psychiat. liaison cons. services U. Va. Hosp., 1972-77, asso. dean, 1973-77, dean, 1977—. Served with USN, Korean War. Fellow Am. Psychiat. Assn.; mem. Am. Psychosomatic Soc., Med. Soc. Va., Va. Neuropsychiatric Soc., Va. Soc. Plastic and Reconstructive Surgery (hon.). Office: U Va Sch Medicine Box 395 McKim Hall Charlottesville VA 22908

KNORR-CETINA, KARIN C., sociologist; b. Graz, Austria, July 19, 1944; came to U.S., 1976; d. Friedrich and Margareta (Kaiblinger) Cetina; m. Dietrich W. Knorr, Mar. 3, 1969; children: Hannah Agnes, Fanny Esther. Diploma, Inst. Advanced Studies, Vienna, 1972; habilitation, U. Bielefeld, Germany, 1981; Ph.D., U. Vienna, 1981. Asst. prof. Inst. Advanced Studies, Vienna, Austria, 1972-76, 77-78; Ford Found. fellow U. Calif.-Berkeley, 1976-77; research fellow U. Pa., Phila., 1979-81, 82; prof. Wesleyan U., Middletown, Conn., 1982-83; prof. dept. sociology U. Bielefeld, Germany, 1983—; mem. council Soc. Social Studies of Sci., Germany, 1982—. Editorial bd.: Jour. Knowledge, 1979—, 4S Review, 1983—; author: The Manufacture of Knowledge, 1981; editor: (with A. Cicourel) Advanced in Social Theory, 1981, (with M. Mulkay) Science Observed, 1983. Fellow Ministry of Edn., 1968-70, Ford Found., 1976-77, Max Kade, 1981-82. Mem. Am. Sociol. Assn., Soc. for Social Studies of Sci., Internat. Sociol. Assn. (council). Home: 3 Johnston Dr Newark DE 19711 Office: Fak of Sociology Univ Bielefeld PO Box 8640 Bielefeld Federal Republic Germany

KNORTZ, HERBERT CHARLES, communications company executive; b. Bklyn., Mar 31, 1921; s. John Walter and Elizabeth (Grotyohann) K.; m. Lorraine Marion Kraut, Aug. 12, 1949; children: Steven Holbrook, Elizabeth Alyn, David Cartwright. B.B.A., St. Johns U., 1946, D.C.S. (hon.), 1977; M.B.A., N.Y. U., 1949. C.P.A., N.Y. Supervising clk. Bklyn. Trust Co., 1938-43; with Price Waterhouse & Co. (C.P.A.'s), N.Y.C., 1945-51; supr. standard costs Lever Bros. Co., 1951-55; mgr. cost dept. Crown Cork & Seal Co., 1955-56; asst. comptroller Royal McBee Corp., 1956-60; controller Mack Trucks, Inc., Plainfield, N.J., 1960-61; dep. comptroller Internat. Tel. & Tel. Corp., 1961-63, v.p., controller, 1963-66, sr. v.p., comptroller, 1966-73, exec. v.p., comptroller, 1973—, also dir., dir., officer several subsidiaries; dir. Hartford Fire Ins. Co.; partner Cortina Shops, 1957-60, Lewisboro Tennis Club, 1971-72; dir. Peerage Properties Inc., 1971-73; trustee Corporate Property Investors, 1973—; Lectr. profl. meetings. Contbr. to: also profl. jours. Financial Executives Handbook; Editor: Food for Thought. Trustee Vincent Ross Research Found. Served with USAAF, 1943-45. Mem. Fin. Execs. Inst. (v.p. research found., mem. internat. com.), Am. Mgmt. Assn. (gen. mgmt. council, trustee), Am. Contract Bridge League, Am. Inst. C.P.A.s, Nat. Assn. Accountants, Inst. Mgmt. Accounting (bd. regents), Internat. Assn. Fin. Exec. Insts., Delta Mu Delta, Beta Gamma Sigma. Clubs: Economics, Accountants, Board Room, Armonk Tennis, Internat. Golf, Flint River Forests. Home: 14 Manor Rd Ridgefield CT 06877 Office: Internat Tel & Tel Corp 320 Park Ave New York NY 10022

KNORTZ, WALTER ROBERT, accountant, former insurance company executive; b. Bklyn., July 15, 1919; s. John Walter and Elizabeth Anna (Grotyohann) K.; m. Dorothy E. Lauterborn, Nov. 17, 1962; children—Deborah Ann, Kenneth Robert, Pamela Jane. B.B.A., St. Johns U., 1942; M.B.A., N.Y. U., 1949. Former registered prin. Nat. Assn. Securities Dealers. C.P.A., N.Y. Accountant Consol. Edison Co., N.Y.C., 1936-45; mng. accountant S.D. Leidersdorf & Co., N.Y.C., 1945-53; with Equitable Life Assurance Soc. of U.S., N.Y.C., 1953-82, 2d v.p., 1969-73, v.p., asso. controller, 1973-75, v.p., fin. officer investment ops., 1975-82; asst. treas., treas. Equitable Life Holding Corp., 1971-75; comptroller Equitable Life Mortgage & Realty Investors, 1970-75; v.p., treas. Equitable Life Community Enterprises Corp., 1970-75, Student Life Funding, Inc., 1970-75; v.p., dir. Equico Lessors, Inc., Mpls., 1974-78; v.p. Equico Securities, Inc., 1970-80, Planters Devel. Corp., St. Louis, 1972-81; mem. Phila. Stock Exchange, Inc., 1971-78. Pres. Leisuretowne Civic League, 1983—; mem. bldg. fund com. Holy Eucharist Ch. Served with AUS, 1942-45. Mem. Am. Inst. C.P.A.s, Tax Execs. Inst., Fin. Execs. Inst. Roman Catholic. Home: 41 Finchley Ct Vincentown NJ 08088

KNOTT, HENRY JOSEPH, constrn. co. exec.; b. Balt., Nov. 2, 1906; s. Henry A. and Martha (Doyle) K.; m. Marion I. Burke, Aug. 2, 1928; children—Mary Patricia (Mrs. J. Walter Smyth), Marion Isabel (Mrs. Frederick S. Beckman), Martha Alice (Mrs. Robert Emmet Voelkel, Jr.), Margaret Celeste (Mrs. John Henry Riehl, III), Henry Joseph, Catherine Philomen (Mrs. Richard A. Weis), Rose Marie (Mrs. George A. Porter), Sarah Lindsey (Mrs. Edward B. Harris, Jr.), Francis Xavier, James Frederick, Martin Gerard, Mary Stuart (Mrs. Timothy Rogers). Student, Loyola Coll., Balt.; LL.D., Coll. Notre Dame of Md., 1963, Mt. St. Mary's Coll., Emmitsburg, Md., 1971. Chmn. bd., dir. Arundel Corp., Balt.; Mem. Cardinal's Finance Com. Decorated comdr. Knights St. Gregory. Clubs: Engineers, Center (Balt.); Canadian (N.Y.C.). Home: 6101 Gentry Ln Baltimore MD 21210 Office: 110 West Rd Towson MD 21204 also 2 W University Pl Baltimore MD 21218

KNOTT, JAMES ROBERT, state judge, lawyer; b. Tallahassee, Jan. 8, 1910; s. William Valentine and Luella (Pugh) K.; m. Evelyn Douglas Causey, June 26, 1942; children: James Douglas, Elizabeth Dandridge. B.S., U. Fla., 1934, LL.B., 1934; grad., Nat. Coll. Judiciary, U. Nev., 1967. Bar: Fla. 1934. Practice in Jacksonville, 1934-42, 45-46, West Palm Beach, 1946-56; judge Fla. Indsl. Claims Ct., 1938-41, 48-56, 15th Jud. Circuit Fla., 1956—, sr. judge, 1968-77; counsel Moyle, Gentry et al, West Palm Beach, 1977-80; resident counsel Winthrop, Stimson et al, Palm Beach, 1980—; spl. adviser to pres. First Fed. Savs. & Loan Assn. of the Palm Beaches, 1977—; mem. adv. bd. First Nat. Bank in Palm Beach, 1977—. Author numerous articles on state and local history. Mem. Bicentennial Commns., Palm Beach County, City West Palm Beach, Town Palm Beach, 1974-76; trustee West Palm Beach Library Bd., 1959-77; trustee, sec. Palm Beach County Community Found., 1975—; trustee Henry Morrison Flagler Museum, Palm Beach, 1973—, Fla. House, Washington, 1972-76, Tb and Health Assn. Palm Beach County, 1956-72, Sci. Mus. and Planetarium Palm Beach County, 1961-71; adv. bd. Sci. Mus. and Planetarium Palm Beach County, 1972—; asso. bd. Boys Clubs Palm Beach County, 1971—; chmn. adv. bd. Community Mental Health Center Palm Beach County, 1977-79; vice chmn. Palm Beach County Hist. Commn., 1979—, Landmark Preservation Commn. of Palm Beach, 1978—; v.p. Preservation Found. of Palm Beach, 1980-83, pres., 1983—; mem. Com. for Naming State Bldgs., 1977—; mem. bd. commrs. Hist. Boca Raton Preservation, 1981—; mem. Fla. Gov.'s Mansion Found., 1978-83; vestryman Holy Trinity Ch., 1977-80, chancellor, 1977-78. Served to lt. comdr. USNR, 1942-45. Recipient cert. of commendation Am. Assn. State and Local History, 1967; D.B. McKay award Tampa Hist. Soc., 1974; award for community service Palm Beach C. of C., 1979; Outstanding Citizen award Downtown Civitan Club, West Palm Beach, 1981. Mem. ABA, Fla. Bar, Fla. Hist. Soc. (pres. 1964-66, dir. 1960-62, 74-76), Hist. Soc. Palm Beach County (pres. 1957-68, pres. emeritus 1968—), Jacksonville, Tallahassee, Loxahatchee, Delray Beach, Boynton Beach hist. socs., Hist. Assn. So. Fla. (v.p. 1961-68), Fla. Heritage Found., S.A.R. (Gold medal 1977), English Speaking Union, Norton Gallery Art, Lake Worth Pioneer Assn., Nat. Trust Historic Preservation, Blue Key, Phi Delta Theta (alumni pres. 1965), Delta Sigma Phi, Phi Delta Phi. Episcopalian. Clubs: Kiwanis (dir. 1960-61), Elks, Tuscawilla (West Palm Beach) (pres. 1963); Sailfish of Fla.; Pundits (Palm Beach); Friars (Jacksonville). Home: 3000 Washington Rd West Palm Beach FL 33405 Office: 125 Worth Ave Palm Beach FL 33480

KNOTT, JOHN RAY, JR., educator; b. Memphis, July 9, 1937; s. John Ray and Wilma (Henshaw) K.; m. Anne Percy, Dec. 5, 1959; children: Catherine, Ellen, Walker, Anne. A.B., Yale U., 1959, Carnegie fellow, 1960; Ph.D., Harvard U., 1965. Instr. Harvard U., 1965-67; mem. faculty U. Mich., Ann Arbor, 1967—, prof. English, 1976—, chmn. dept., 1982—, asso. dean Coll. Arts and Scis., 1977—, acting dean Coll. Arts and Scis., 1980-81. Author: Milton's Pastoral Vision, 1971, The Sword of the Spirit, 1980; editor: The Triumph of Style, 1967, Mirrors: An Introduction to Literature, 1972. Woodrow Wilson fellow, 1960-61; NEH fellow, 1974. Mem. MLA, Milton Soc., Renaissance Soc. Am. Office: Dept English Univ Mich Ann Arbor MI 48109

KNOTTS, DON, actor; b. Morgantown, W.Va., July 21, 1924; s. William Jesse and Elsie (Moore) K.; m. Kathryn Metz, Dec. 27, 1947; children—Karen Ann, Thomas Allen; m. Loralee Czuchna, Oct. 12, 1974. B.A., W.Va. U., 1948. Appeared on Broadway in: No Time for Sergeants, 1955-56; with: Steve Allen TV shows, 1956-60; role of Barney Fife in: TV series Andy Griffith, from 1960; appeared on TV as star of: Don Knotts Show, 1970; appears on: TV show Three's Company, 1979—; starred in: 18 movies including The Private Eyes; legitimate theatre A Good Look at Boney Kern (Recipient 5 Emmy awards for outstanding performance in supporting role.), Last of the Red Hot Lovers, Mind with the Dirty Man. Address: care BNB Assos 9454 Wilshire Blvd Suite 309 Beverly Hills CA 90212

KNOTTS, GLENN R(ICHARD), editor, educator; b. East Chicago, Ind., May 16, 1924; s. V. Raymond and Opal Ione (Alexander) K. B.S., Purdue U., 1956, M.S., 1960, Ph.D., 1968; M.S., Ind. U., 1964; Dr. Med. Sci. (hon.), Union Coll., 1975, Sc.D., Ricker Coll., 1975. Mem. profl. staff Bapt. Meml. Hosp., San Antonio, 1957-60; instr. chemistry San Antonio Coll., 1958-60; adminstrv. asst. AMA, Chgo., 1960-61, research assoc., 1961-62, dir. advt. evaluation, div. sci. activities, 1963-69; exec. dir. Am. Sch. Health Assn., Kent, Ohio, 1969-72; vis. disting. prof. health sci. Kent State U., 1969-72, prof., mem. grad. faculty dept. allied health scis., 1972-75, coordinator grad. studies and research, 1975; editor-in-chief, prof. med. journalism U. Tex. System Cancer Ctr. M.D. Anderson Hosp. and Tumor Inst., Houston, 1975—, head dept. med. info. and publs., 1975-79, dir. div. ednl. resources, 1979—; prof. U. Tex. Grad. Sch. Biomed. Scis., 1983—; vis. prof. health edn. Madison Coll., Va., summer 1965, Union Coll., Ky., summers 1965, 66, 69; vis. porf. health edn. Utah State U., 1965; vis. lectr. Ind. U., 1965-66; vis. lectr. pharmacology Purdue U., 1968-69; vis. prof. Pahlavi U. Med. Sch., Iran, summer 1970; adj. prof. allied health scis. Kent State U., 1975—; prof. dept. biomed. communications U. Tex. Sch. Allied Health Scis., Houston, 1976—; prof. dept. behavioral scis. U. Tex. Sch. Pub. Health, 1977—; cons. health scis. communications, 1969—; pres. Health Scis. Inst., 1973—; mem. exec. com. Internat. Union Sch. and Univ. Health and Medicine, Paris, 1969—. Co-author various texts and filmstrips on health sci.; contbr. numerous articles to profl. jours.; cons. editor: Clin. Pediatrics, 1971—; contbg. editor: Annals of Allergy, 1972—; exec. editor: Cancer Bull., 1976—; mem. numerous editorial bds. Bd. dirs. Med. Arts Pub. Found., Houston, 1977-80; mem. adv. bd. World Meetings Inc., 1971—. Served with U.S. Army, 1956-58. Recipient Gold medal French-Am. Allergy Soc., 1973. Fellow Am. Pub. Health Assn., Am. Sch. Health Assn. (mem. exec. com. 1968-72, editor Jour. Sch. Health 1975-76, Disting. Service award 1973), Am. Inst. Chemists, Royal Soc. Health; mem. Internat. Union Health Edn., AAHPER, Am. Acad. Pharm. Scis., Am. Med. Writers Assn., Am. Pharm. Assn., AAUP, Am. Chem. Soc., AAAS, AMA, Purdue U. Alumni Assn., Ind. U. Alumni Assn., Union Coll. Alumni Assn., Ricker Coll. Alumni Assn., Sigma Xi, Rho Chi, Sigma Delta Chi, Eta Sigma Gamma, Phi Delta Kappa, Kappa Psi. Republican. Presbyterian. Clubs: Marines Meml. (San Francisco); Akron City (Ohio); Century; Presidents (Kent); Press Internat.; Whitehall (Chgo.); Univ. Faculty; Doctors (Houston). Lodge: Rotary. Home: 2600 Bellefontaine Houston TX 77025 Office: Tex System Cancer Ctr MD Anderson Hosp Tex Med Ctr Houston TX 77030

KNOWLES, ALISON, artist; b. N.Y.C., Apr. 29, 1933; m. Dick Higgins, 1960; children—Hannah, Jessie. Student, Middlebury Coll., 1952-54; B.F.A., Pratt Inst., 1957, Manhattan Sch. Printing, 1962. Executed: large canvas Mother of the Great Train Robbery; using massive blow-ups and enlargements, 1959-60, series of canvases using silkscreen, photog. and chem. transfers, 1960, environ. printed works on plastic, 1961, 62; active in starting Fluxus Movement in Europe, 1962; directed own Events; performed in those of Dick Higgins, Emmett Williams, George Brecht, Nam June Paik, others; one-man shows, Nonagon Gallery, N.Y.C., 1962, Phase 11 Gallery, Toronto, Ont., Can., 1967, Gallerie Inge Baecker, Germany, 1973, Galerie Rene Block, Germany, 1974, De Appel Galerie, Amsterdam, 1974, 76, Gallerie 38, Copenhagen, 1976, Vehicule Gallerie, Montreal, exhbns. and performances include, Studio Spicherstrasse 28, Cologne, Germany, 1962, Rolf Nelson Gallery, Los Angeles, 1963, Fluxhall, N.Y.C., 1964, Phila. Mus. Art, 1966, Something Else Gallery, N.Y.C., Stedelijk van Abbemuseum, Eindhoven, Netherlands, 1967, Chgo. Mus. Contemporary Art, Duchamp Festival, U. Calif.-Irvine, 1972, Mercer Art Center, Goddard Coll., N.Y.C., Fluxus show, Galerie Rene Block, N.Y.C., 1974, Women's House Exhbn., Calif., 1975; constructed: portable environments The Big Book, exhibited N.Y.C., Toronto, Chgo., 1967, Ger., Denmark, 1968, San Diego, N.Y.C., 1969; exhibited: The House of Dust, N.Y.C., 1969; Calif. Inst. Arts, 1970; exhibited portable environ.: The Book of Bean Franklin Furnace, 1983; Publs.: The Canned Bean Rolls, 1963, The T Dictionary in The Four Suits, 1965, By Allison (one 1) Knowles, 1965, The House of Dust, 1969, Journal of the Identical Lunch, 1970, Proposition VI, 1970, Proposition IV, 1973, The Identical Lunch, 1973, Women's Work, 1975, More By Alison Knowles (again, one 1), 1976, Gem Duck, 1977, The Bean Concordance, 1983. Recipient Karl Sczuka Radio award Sta. WDR, W.Ger. Address: 122 Spring St New York NY 10021

KNOWLES, ARTHUR FRANCIS, corporate executive; b. Montreal, Que., Can., Aug. 17, 1922; m. Audrey R. McGruther, Sept. 6, 1947. Acct. McDonald, Currie Co., 1940-52; with Shaninigan Water & Power Co., 1953-62, Shaninigan Industries Ltd., 1963-64, Power Corp. of Can. Ltd., Montreal, Que., 1964—; now sr. v.p., dir. Power Corp.-The Investor's Group., Great West Life Assurance Co. Mem. Can. Inst. Chartered Accts. Clubs: Mt. Royal, St. James, Mt. Bruno Golf and Country, Summerlea Golf and Country. Office: 759 Victoria Sq Montreal PQ Canada *

KNOWLES, ASA SMALLIDGE, univ. chancellor; b. Northeast Harbor, Maine, Jan. 15, 1909; s. Jerome and Lilla Belle (Smallidge) K.; m. Edna Worsnop; children—Asa W., Margaret Anne. Ed., Thayer Acad., South Braintree, Mass., 1925-26; A.B., Bowdoin Coll., 1930, LL.D., 1951; postgrad., Harvard Bus. Sch., 1930-31; A.M., Boston U., 1935; LL.D., Northeastern U., 1957, Emerson Coll., 1960, U. Toledo, 1960, Brandeis U., 1968; D. Ped., North Adams State Coll., 1974; Litt.D., Western New Eng. Coll., 1961; Sc.D., New Eng. Coll. Pharmacy, 1962, Lowell Tech. Inst., 1966; D.B.A., U. R.I., 1967; Sc.D. in Bus. Edn, Bryant Coll., 1967; D.Ped., Franklin Pierce Coll., 1974; L.H.D., Mass. Coll. Optometry, 1975; Sc.D. in Edn, Boston Coll., 1976. Asso. prof. indsl. engring., also head dept. Northeastern U., Boston, 1936-39, dean, also dir., 1939-42, pres., 1959-75, chancellor, 1975—; dean Sch. Bus. Adminstrn.; also dir. Div. Gen. Coll. Extension, U. R.I., Kingston, 1942-46; pres. Asso. Colls. Upper N.Y., 1946-48; v.p. devel. Cornell U., Ithaca, N.Y., 1948-51; pres. U. Toledo, 1951-58; dir. Shawmut Corp.; Mem. Mass. Commn. Edn., 1963-65; mem. Mass. Higher Edn. Facilities Commn., 1964-69, chmn., 1968-69, New Eng. Assn. Schs. and Colls., 1967-69, v.p., 1970-71, pres., 1971-72; mem. council Fedn. Regional Accreditation Commns. Higher Edn., 1966-72, chmn., 1970-72, Army Adv. Panel on R.O.T.C. Affairs, 1967-68; vice chmn. Nat. Commn. for Coop. Edn., 1962-75, chmn., 1975—; vice chmn. Assn. Ind. Colls. and Univs. in Mass., 1973-74, chmn., 1974-75, Mass. Commn. on Postsecondary Edn., 1975-76. Co-author: Industrial Management, 1944; co-author and editor: Handbook of Cooperative Education, 1971; Editor: Handbook of College and University Administration, 2 vols, 1970; Editor-in-chief: Internat. Ency. of Higher Edn., 10 vols, 1977. Recipient Legion of Honor Internat. Order DeMolay, 1960; Outstanding Civilian Service medal U.S. Army, 1962; Distinguished Civilian Service medal and citation, 1966; Distinguished Educator award Bowdoin Coll., 1972; named Outstanding Son of Maine, 1970; Man of Year award Mass. Jewish War Vets., 1974; Distinguished Service to Higher Edn. award Am. Coll. Pub. Relations Assn., 1974; Alumni award Univ. Coll. Law Enforcement, 1974; citation Boston chpt. Am. Soc. Indsl. Security, 1974, Mass. Chiefs Police, 1974; certificate of merit Am. Soc. Indsl. Security, 1974; Outstanding Service to Journalism award New Eng. Press Assn., 1975; Distinguished Pub. Service award Boston U. Alumni Assn., 1975; Co-op. Edn. Assn. Herman Schneider award, 1977; Bowdoin prize for outstanding service to humanity, 1978, fellow of Pacific Hawaii Pacific Coll., 1974. Fellow Am. Acad. Arts and Scis.; mem. Pershing Rifles (hon.), Blue Key, Phi Kappa Phi (disting. mem. award 1973), Pi Delta Phi, Kappa Delta Pi (Compatriot in Edn. 1977), Chi Psi (Albert S. Bard award 1964), Alpha Kappa Psi, Alpha Pi Mu (hon.), Beta Gamma Sigma, Tau Beta Pi, Delta Sigma Theta (hon.), Sigma Epsilon Rho (hon.). Republican. Episcopalian. Home: 388 Beacon St Boston MA 02116

KNOWLES, EDWARD F., architect; b. Bklyn., Aug. 12, 1929; s. Frank W. and Isabel (Leudesdorff) K.; m. Barbara Lee Dupree, Mar. 14, 1953; children: Christopher, Sarah, Mary, Emily. B.Arch., Pratt Inst., 1951. Pvt. practice architecture, N.Y.C., 1960—; partner Macfadyen & Knowles (architects), N.Y.C., 1965-68; tchr. Pratt Inst., 1959-60, Cooper Union, 1960-64, Columbia U., 1965-66; cons. N.Y. State Council Arts, Bklyn. Inst., Inst. Man and Sci., San Francisco Arts Resources Devel. Com., Richmond Found., N.Y.C. Dept. Parks. Prin. works include Lowell Nesbitt Studio, Boston City Hall, Wolf Trap Farm Park, Pine Manor Jr. Coll. Mem. AIA, N.Y. Soc. Architects. Office: 127 W 56th St New York City NY 10019 *Significant architecture must express the emotional factors of the problem in addition to the obvious requirements of program, site, budget, and structure, or it ceases to be an art form. The rejection of any of the phenomena that are experienced at any point in history is short sighted.*

KNOWLES, JACK OLIVER, veterinarian; b. Cheyenne, Wyo., June 12, 1916; s. Adam T. and Mable B. (Behymer) K.; m. Connie Fisher, Nov. 28, 1939; children—Donna L. (Mrs. M.P. Born), Jane A. (Mrs. David T. Wise, Jr.); m. Caroline Walker.; children—Lisa G. (Mrs. W.H. Match), William Bradley Enslen. V.M.D., U. Pa., 1938. Owner Knowles Animal Clinic, Miami, Fla., 1946—; research asso. prof. U. Miami Sch. Medicine, 1955—. Editor: Canine Filariasis; Contbr. numerous articles to profl. jours., also chpt. in books. Served with Vet. Corps AUS, World War II. Recipient Mills award for outstanding contbn. to vet. medicine U. Ga. chpt. Alpha Psi, 1971. Fellow Am. Coll. Vet. Internists (founding); mem. Am. Vet. Med. Assn. (past pres., award 1973, 74), Com. of One Hundred, Phi Zeta. Clubs: Mason (32 deg.), Rotarian (pres. Miami 1970-71), Coral Reef Yacht, Logorce Country, Palm Bay., Surf. Home: 1400 W 28th St Sunset Island 1 Miami Beach FL 33140 Office: 1000 N W 27th Ave Miami FL 33125

KNOWLES, JAMES KENYON, applied mechanics educator; b. Cleve., Apr. 14, 1931; s. Newton Talbot and Allyan (Gray) K.; m. Jacqueline De Bolt, Nov. 26, 1952; children: John Kenyon, Jeffrey Gray, James Talbot. S.B. in Math., MIT, 1952, Ph.D., 1957. Instr. math. MIT, Cambridge, 1957-58; asst. prof. applied mechanics Calif. Inst. Tech., Pasadena, 1958-61, assoc. prof., 1961-65, prof., 1965—; cons. in field. Contbr. articles to profl. jours. Fellow Am. Acad. Mechanics; mem. ASME. Home: 522 Michillianda Way Sierra Madre CA 91024 Office: Div Engring and Applied Sci 104-44 Calif Inst Tech 1201 E California Blvd Pasadena CA 91024

KNOWLES, JEREMY RANDALL, chemist, educator; b. Rugby, Eng., Apr. 28, 1935; came to U.S., 1974; s. Kenneth Guy Jack Charles and Dorothy Helen (Swingler) K.; m. Jane Sheldon Davis, July 30, 1960; children: Sebastian David Guy, Julius John Sheldon, Timothy Fenton Charles. B.A., Balliol Coll., Oxford (Eng.) U., 1958; M.A., D.Phil., Christ Ch., 1961. Research fellow Calif. Inst. Tech., 1961-62; fellow Wadham Coll., Oxford U., 1962-74, univ. lectr., 1966-74; vis. prof. Yale U., 1969, 71; Sloan vis. prof. Harvard U., 1973, prof. chemistry, 1974—, Amory Houghton prof. chemistry and biochemistry, 1979—; Newton-Abraham vis. prof. Oxford U., 1983-84. Author papers, revs. bioorganic chemistry. Served as pilot officer RAF, 1953-55. Fellow Royal Soc., Chem. Soc. London, Am. Acad. Arts and Scis.; mem. Biochem. Soc. London, Am. Chem. Soc., Am. Soc. Biol. Chemists. Home: 44 Coolidge Ave Cambridge MA 02138 Office: Dept Chemistry Harvard Univ Cambridge MA 02138

KNOWLES, JOHN, author; b. Fairmont, W.Va., Sept. 16, 1926; s. James Myron and Mary Beatrice (Shea) K. Grad., Phillips Exeter Acad., 1945; B.A., Yale U., 1949. Reporter Hartford (Conn.) Courant,

1950-52; free-lance writer, 1952-56; asso. editor Holiday mag., 1956-60; writer in residence U. N.C., 1963-64, Princeton U., 1968-69. Author: (novels) A Separate Peace (Rosenthal award Nat. Inst. Arts and Letters 1960), 1960 (William Faulkner Found. award 1960), Morning in Antibes, 1962, A Vein of Riches, 1978, Peace Breaks Out, 1980, A Stolen Past, 1983; travel Double Vision, 1964, Indian Summer, 1966; short stories Phineas, 1968, The Paragon, 1970, Spreading Fires, 1974; also articles, short stories. Home: PO Box 939 Southampton NY 11968

KNOWLES, MALCOLM SHEPHERD, educator; b. Livingston, Mont., Aug. 24, 1913; s. Albert Dixon and Marian (Straton) K.; m. Hulda Elisabet Fornell, Aug. 20, 1935; children: Eric Stuart, Barbara Elisabeth Knowles Hartl. A.B., Harvard U., 1934; M.A., U. Chgo., 1949, Ph.D., 1960; D.Sc. (hon.), Lowell Tech. Inst., 1975. Dep. adminstr. Nat. Youth Adminstrn. Mass., Boston, Boston, 1935-40; dir. adult edn. YMCA, Boston, 1940-43; dir. USO, Detroit, 1943-44; exec. sec. YMCA, Chgo., 1946-51; exec. dir. Adult Edn. Assn. U.S., Chgo., 1951-59; prof. edn. Boston U., 1959-74, N.C. State U., 1974-79, prof. emeritus, 1979—; mem. Task Force on Lifelong Edn., UNESCO Inst. Edn., 1972—; dir. Leadership Resources, Inc., 1962-67, Project Assos., Washington, 1967-79, Data Edn., Inc., Waltham, Mass., 1971-74; cons. on tng. Democratic Nat. Com., 1956-60; cons. U.S. Catholic Conf., Mass. Dept. Mental Health, NIMH, Overseas Edn. Fund, Nat. Council Chs., Coll. Bd., Future Directions for a Learning Soc., Girl Scouts U.S.A., U.S. depts. Labor, Justice, Post Office, HEW, Free Univ. Network, Urban League (various schs. and univs., others.). Author: Informal Adult Education, 1950, (with Hulda Knowles) How to Develop Better Leaders, 1955, Introduction to Group Dynamics, 1959, rev., 1973, The Adult Education Movement in the U.S, 1962, Higher Adult Education in the U.S, 1969, The Modern Practice of Adult Education: Andragogy vs. Pedagogy, 2d edit, 1980, The Adult Learner: A Neglected Species, 1973, rev., 1978, Lifelong Learning: A Guide for Learners and Teachers, 1975, A History of Adult Education in the U.S, 1977; contbr. articles to profl. jours.; Host: TV series The Dynamics of Leadership, NET, 1962, And Now We Are People, Group W Network, 1969. Served with USNR, 1944-46. Recipient Delbert Clark award W. Ga. Coll., Carrollton, 1967; Nat. Tng. Labs. Inst. for Applied Behavioral Sci. fellow, 1969—. Mem. Am. Soc. Tng. and Devel., Adult Edn. Assn. U.S., AAUP, Authors Guild. Club: Harvard of Boston. Home: 1506 Delmont Dr Raleigh NC 27606 *The idea that turned my life around I got from Carl Rogers in the early 1950s: that the mission of a leader (parent, manager, teacher) is to release human energy, not control it.*

KNOWLES, PETE, pipe and steel distribution company executive; b. Wichita Falls, Tex., Oct. 9, 1922; s. Howard Murphy and Jimmie (Wheeler) K.; m. Dovie Jane Beavers, Feb. 7, 1942; children: Howard Merritt, Bryson. Student, pub. schs. Founder, owner, operator, chmn. bd. Genesco Inc., Uvalde, Tex. Pres. Middle Rio Grande Devel. Council; trustee Uvalde Pub. Schs., 1961-66, pres. sch. bd., 1965-66; mayor City of Uvalde, 1969-72; spl. asst. to gov. Tex., 1971; lay speaker, bd. stewards First United Methodist Ch., Uvalde; mem. adv. council SBA; mem. Century Club, Concho Valley council Boy Scouts Am.; founder Uvalde Meml. Hosp. Served with USAAF, 1942-46. Recipient Diamond Achievement award Tom E. Turner Enterprises Employees; named Hon. Mayor City of San Antonio, 1958. Mem. Uvalde Area C. of C. (pres. 1957-58), Nat. Assn. Pipe Distbrns. (founder, charter mem.), Jr. C. of C. (past pres. local chpt.), Am. Legion, VFW. Clubs: Toastmasters (past pres.), Uvalde Country (past pres.). Home and Office: Genesco Inc PO Box 67 Uvalde TX 78801

KNOWLES, RICHARD THOMAS, retired army officer; b. Chgo., Dec. 20, 1916; s. John T. and Signe (Almcrantz) K.; m. Elizabeth Wood Chaney, 1974; children: Diane T. Knowles Buchwald, Katherine T. Knowles Buck, Rebecca T., Richard J., Stanley W. Crosby III, Steven Chaney. Student, U. Ill., 1939-42, Armed Forces Staff Coll., 1956, U.S. Army War Coll., 1959. Commd. 2d lt. U.S. Army, 1942, advanced through grades to lt. gen., 1970; exec., bn. comdr. 96th F.S. Bn., Far East Command, 1950-51; student, then instr. Command and Gen. Staff Coll., Ft. Leavenworth, Kan., 1951-55; chief budget and plans br. Office Dep. Chief of Staff, Personnel, U.S. Army, Washington, 1956-58; chief Establishments Bur., Hdqrs. U.S. Army Element, SHAPE, 1959-60, mil. asst. Office Chief of Staff, 1960-62; comdg. officer 3d U.S. Army Missile Command, Ft. Bragg, N.C., 1962-63; div. arty. comdr., asst. div. comdr. 11th Air Assault Div., Ft. Benning, Ga., 1963-65; asst. div. comdr. 1st Cav. Div., (airmobile), Ft. Benning, Vietnam, 1965-66; chief of staff II Field Force, Vietnam, 1966; comdg. gen. 196th Light Inf. Brigade, Vietnam, 1966-67, Task Force Oregon, 1967; asst. dep. chief of staff for mil. operations U.S. Army, Washington, 1967-70; asst. to chmn. Joint Chiefs of Staff, Washington, 1970-72; comdg. gen. I Corps Group, Korea, 1972-73; dep. comdr. 8th Army, Korea, 1973-74; ret., 1974, mgr. support services, Northrop, Saudi Arabia, 1978-79; owner, operator The General's Store, 1980—. Mem. commn. Conguistador council Boy Scouts Am. Decorated D.S.M. with 3 oak leaf clusters, Silver Star, Legion of Merit with two bronze oak leaf clusters, D.F.C. with bronze oak leaf cluster, Bronze Star with V device and oak leaf cluster, Air medal with 25 oak leaf clusters, Purple Heart, Vietnam Nat. Order 5th Class, Vietnam Gallantry Cross with 2 bronze palms, Vietnam Armed Forces Honor medal 1st Class, Order of Nat. Security Merit Guk-Seon medal Republic of Korea). Mem. Rosewell C. of C., Ret. Officers Assn. (pres. N.Mex. council of chpts., state rep. dist. 57). Club: Rotary. Home: PO Box 285 Roswell NM 88201 *My purpose in life is to stay physically and mentally active, to live each day completely and in such a manner as to make this a better world.*

KNOWLES, WARREN PERLEY, former governor Wisconsin, financial corporation executive; b. River Falls, Wis., Aug. 19, 1908; s. Warren P. and Anna Theresa (Deneen) K.; m. Dorothy C. Guidry, Apr. 17, 1943 (div. 1968). B.A., Carleton Coll., 1930, LL.D., 1980; LL.B., U. Wis., 1933; LL.D., Marquette U., 1965, Northland Coll., 1965, Ripon Coll., St. Norberts U., 1975; L.H.D., Carroll Coll., Milton Coll., 1970, Lakeland Coll., U. Wis., 1973; D.Eng. (hon.), Milw. Sch. Engring., 1981. Bar: Wis. 1933, admitted to practice, diplomate: ICC, U.S. Treasury Dept. Partner Doar & Knowles, New Richmond, 1935-64; lt. gov. of, Wis., 1954-58, 61-63, gov. of, 1965-71; chmn. bd. Heritage Wis. Corp., Milw., 1971—; vice chmn. bd., dir. Heritage Bank of Whitefish Bay; v.p., dir. Heritage Bank of West Bend; dir. Heritage Trust, Midwestern Nat. Ins. Co., Northwest Telephone Co., Heritage Investment Advisors. Mem. Pres.'s Commn. on Sch. Finance, 1971-72; chmn. Wis. Land Use, 1972-73; mem. Wis. Senate, 1940-53, majority floor leader, 1943-53, chmn. legis. council, 1947, jud. council, 1951-53; del. Republican Nat. Conv., 1948, 56, 60, 64, 68, 72, 76, 80; chmn. Wis. del., 1968, 76; bd. dirs. U. Wis. Found., Greater Milw. Commn.; bd. govs. Med. Coll. Wis.; chmn. bd. trustees Mt. Mary Coll., Milw. Boys Club, St. Francis Hosp. Found.; hon. chmn. Nat. Wildlife Found.; chmn. Wis. Leukemia Soc.; mem. adv. com. Nat. Multiple Sclerosis Soc. Served as lt. USNR, 1942-46. Mem. Met. Milw. C. of C., Mil. Order World Wars, Am., Wis., St. Croix-Pierce County bar assns., Assn. Ins. Counsel, Wis. Alumni Assn. (pres. 1952-53, dir.; dir. Alumni Found.), NCCJ, chmn. Wis. chpt. (1957-58), VFW, Am. Legion, 40 and 8. Republican. Clubs: Milw. Athletic, Milwaukee, Univ., Elks. Office: 401 E Mason St Heritage Trust Bldg PO Box 789 Milwaukee WI 53201

KNOWLES, WILLIAM LEROY, television news producer; b. Los Angeles, June 23, 1935; s. Leroy Edwin and Thelma Mabel (Armstrong) K.; m. Susan Pearl Kearns, Sept. 1, 1960; children: Frank, Irene, Daniel, Joseph, Ted. B.A. in Journalism, San Jose State Coll., 1959; postgrad., U. So. Calif., 1962-63. Reporter, photographer, producer KSL-TV, Salt Lake City, 1963-65; producer, editor, writer WLS-TV, Chgo., 1965-70; news writer ABC News, Washington, 1970-71, asso. producer, 1971-75, ops. producer, 1975-77, So. bur. chief, Atlanta, 1977-81, Washington bur. chief, 1981-82, West Coast bur. chief, 1982—. Pres. Reston (Va.) Commuter Bus System, 1974-75. Served with U.S. Army, 1959-62. Decorated Commendation medal; recipient Telaward for prodn. coll. baseball broadcasts on KUSC-FM U. So. Calif., 1962. Mem. Jazz World Soc., So. Calif. Hot Jazz Soc., Sigma Delta Chi. Mormon. Clubs: New Orleans Jazz of No. Calif., Valley Dixieland Jazz, Sacramento Traditional Jazz Soc. Office: 4151 Prospect Ave Los Angeles CA 90027 *Success in any endeavor takes hard work and dedication to develop God-given talents. Once it all comes together, hard work and dedication must be continued, lest those talents grow stale. Not the least important of those talents in the mass communications field is an empathy with the viewer, listener or reader. If he cannot understand what you're doing, you might as well not be doing it.*

KNOWLES, WILLIAM TOWNSEND, banker; b. Orange, N.J., Jan. 24, 1935; s. Alan Cornell and Elinor Reed (Townsend) K.; m. Elizabeth Anne Lunt, Aug. 25, 1958; children: William Townsend (dec.), Katherine. B.A., Colgate U., 1957. Pres., dir. Nat. Bank of N. Am., N.Y.C., 1981—; dir. VISA Internat. Inc., VISA U.S.A. Inc. Bd. dirs. Montclair (N.J.) chpt. ARC; mem. Montclair Bd. Adjustment; trustee Colgate U.; mem. governing bd. Union Congregational Ch., Upper Montclair; trustee Mountainside Hosp. Served with AUS, 1958. Address: 37 The Fairway Upper Montclair NJ 07043

KNOWLTON, AUSTIN E. (DUTCH KNOWLTON), professional sports team executive. Chmn. bd. The Cin. Bengals Football Team. Office: Cin Bengals 200 Riverfront Stadium Cincinnati OH 45202§

KNOWLTON, CHARLES WILSON, lawyer; b. Columbia, S.C., July 26, 1923; s. Benjamin Almy and Alice Elizabeth (Wilson) K.; m. Mildred Yates Brown, Apr. 9, 1949; children: Charles Wilson, Mildred Yates, Robert Yates, Frank Burkhead. B.A., U. S.C., 1943; LL.B., Harvard U., 1949. Bar: S.C. bar 1949. Individual practice law, Columbia, 1949-50; sr. partner firm Boyd, Knowlton, Tate & Finlay, Columbia, 1952—; cons. to joint legis. com. rewriting S.C. Bus. Corp. Act; cons. to joint legis. com. revising S.C. banking laws; lectr. U. S.C.; former chmn. S.C. Supreme Ct. Com. on Character and Fitness; mem. Columbia adv. bd. First Nat. Bank of S.C. Contbr. articles to legal jours. Warden, vestryman Trinity Episcopal Ch., 1964-69; mem. Zoning Bd., Columbia, 1955-65; pres. United Way of Midland, 1977, also bd. dirs., com. chmn.; former pres. Crippled Childrens Assn.; former pres., bd. dirs. U. S.C. Ednl. Found.; bd. dirs. Columbia Urban League; mem. adv. bd. Providence Hosp., U. S.C. Law Sch. Served with USNR, 1943-46, 51-52. Recipient Sydney Sullivan award U. S.C., 1967, Disting. Service award U. S.C. Ednl. Found., 1982. Mem. Internat. Bar Assn., Am. Bar Assn. (banking law com.), S.C. Bar Assn. (former chmn., mem. exec. com., former chmn. com. on ethics and profl. responsibility), Richland County Bar Assn. (former pres.), Am. Coll. Probate Counsel, Am. Judicature Soc., Am. Law Inst., U.S. Jud. Conf. 4th Circuit, Phi Beta Kappa. Clubs: Forest Lake, Palmetto (former dir.), Columbia Ball (former pres.), Tarantella (former pres.), Summit.). Home: 1 Brampton Circle Columbia SC 29206 Office: 12th Floor SCN Center 1122 Lady St Columbia SC 29201

KNOWLTON, EDGAR COLBY, JR., linguist, educator; b. Delaware, Ohio, Sept. 14, 1921; s. Edgar Colby and Mildred (Hunt) K. A.B., Harvard U., 1941, A.M., 1942; Ph.D., Stanford U., 1959. Instr., U. Hawaii, Honolulu, 1948-53, asst. prof. European langs., 1954-59, asso. prof., 1959-65, prof., 1965—; vis. prof. linguistics U. Malaya, Kuala Lumpur, 1962-64; vis. prof. linguistics, Fulbright awardee Universidad Central de Venezuela, Caracas, 1975; music reviewer Honolulu Advertiser, 1957-61. Co-author: V. Blasco Ibanez, 1972; translator of: Francisco de Sa de Meneses, The Conquest of Malacca, 1970, Almeida Garrett, Camoens, 1972, Casimiro de Abreu, Camoens and the Man of Java, 1972, Machado de Assis, You, Love, and Love Alone, 1972, Almeida Garrett, Afonso de Albuquerque, 1977; Contbr. articles to profl. jours. Mem. program com. Hawaiian Hist. Soc., 1961-62. Served with USNR, 1944-46, 51-52. Recipient Transl. prize,, Lisbon, 1973. Mem. Am. Assn. Tchrs. Spanish and Portuguese, Linguistic Soc. Am., MLA (mem. bibliography com. 1969-82), Am. Assn. Tchrs. Spanish (pres. Hawaii chpt. 1964-65), Puerto Rican Heritage Soc. Hawaii (hon.), Phi Beta Kappa, Sigma Delta Pi. Home: 1026 Kalo Pl Honolulu HI 96826

KNOWLTON, GERALD LOREE, real estate and investment company executive; b. Calgary, Alta., Can., Mar. 10, 1933; s. Frederic Demille and Dorothy Faye (Pringle) K.; m. Mary Janet Jarvis, May 17, 1957; children: Mary Catherine, Barbara, Kelly, Nancy, Jean. B.A. in Bus. Adminstrn. with honours, U. Western Ont., London, 1955; fellow, Real Estate Inst., U. Alta., 1964. With C.H. Noton & Co. Ltd., Calgary, 1957; with Toronto Indsl. Leaseholds Ltd., 1957-59, Mid Western mgr., Winnipeg, 1958-59; Western mgr. Camston Ltd., Winnipeg, 1959-61; pres. Knowlton Realty Ltd., Calgary, 1961-76, chmn. bd., 1976—; pres. Congress Resources Ltd., Calgary, 1976—; chmn. Knowlton Realty Ltd., Denver, 1979—, Calif., 1980—, The Knowlton Corp., Tex., 1981—, Congress Devels. Ltd., Calgary, 1980—; dir. Union Oil Co. Can.; mem. adv. bd. Sch. Bus. Adminstrn., U. Western Ont. Bd. dirs. Alta. Debate and Speech Assn., 1970-77, Calgary YMCA, 1969-76; hon. chmn. Calgary Assn. Mentally Retarded, 1976; mem. nat. alumni adv. council U. Western Ont., 1983—. Chevalier Chateau Montlabert, Bordeaux, France, 1969—. Conservative. Mem. United Ch. Can. Clubs: Calgary Petroleum, Ranchmen's, Glencoe, Earl Grey Golf, Calgary Golf and Country; Napili Kai Beach (Maui, Hawaii) (dir.). Home: 1031 Durham Ave Calgary AB Canada T2T 0P8 Office: Daon Bldg 444 5th Ave SW Suite 2350 Calgary AB Canada T2P 2T8

KNOWLTON, RICHARD L., meat packing company executive; b. 1932; married. B.A., U. Colo., 1954. With George A. Hormel & Co., Austin, MInn., 1948—, mgr. meat products div. and route car sales, Austin, Minn., 1967-69, asst. mgr., 1969, gen. mgr., Austin, 1974, v.p. ops., 1974, group v.p. ops., 1975-79; pres., chief operating officer George A Hormel & Co., Austin, 1979; chmn., pres., chief exec. officer George A. Hormel & Co., Austin, 1981—, dir., Nat. Livestock and Meat Bd., First Nat. Bank of Austin. Trustee U. Minn. Mem. Am. Meat Inst. (dir.), Minn. Bus. Partnership (dir.). Office: George A Hormel & Co 501 16th Ave NE Austin MN 55912

KNOWLTON, THOMAS A., business executive; b. Toronto, Ont., Can., June 16, 1946; s. William George and Grace K.; m. Janice Elizabeth Knowlton, June 8, 1968; children: Kimberly, Tricia, Jeffrey, Andrea. B.A., U. Windsor, Ont., 1968, M.B.A., 1970. Brand mgr. Colgate Palmolive, Toronto, 1970-73; product mgr. Gen. Foods, Toronto, 1973-75; v.p., dir. client services Leo Burnett, Toronto, 1975-79; pres., chief exec. officer Kellogg Salada Can. Inc., Rexdale, Ont., 1979—; chmn. Tea Council of Can., Toronto, 1983. Mem. pres.'s com. Children's Aid Soc. Found., Toronto, 1983. Club: York Downs Golf and Country (Unionville, Ont.). Home: 94 Cambridge Crescent Thornhill ON Canada L4J 2L6 Office: Kellogg Salads Can Inc 6700 Finch Ave W Rexdale ON Canada M9W 5P2 *

KNOWLTON, WILLIAM ALLEN, business executive, consultant; b. Weston, Mass., June 19, 1920; s. Frank Warren and Isabelle (Riese) K.; m. Marjorie Adams Downey, Nov. 27, 1943; children: William Allen, Davis Downey, Timothy Riese, Hollister Knowlton Petraeus. B.S., U.S. Mil. Acad., 1943; M.S., Columbia U., 1957; grad., Nat. War Coll., 1960; LL.D., Akron U., 1972. Commd. 2d lt. U.S. Army, 1943, advanced through grades to gen., 1976; with 7th Armored Div. World War II Army Gen. Staff, 1947-49; with SHAPE, France, 1951-54; assoc. prof. social scis. U.S. Mil. Acad., 1955-58, supt., 1970-74; bn. comdr. 3d Armored Cav. Regt., 1958-59; mil. attache, Tunisia, 1961-63, brig. comdr., Ft. Know, Ky., 1963-64; with Office Chief Staff U.S. Army, 1964-65; mil. asst. to spl. asst. to sec. and dept. sec. def. Office Sec. Def., 1965-66; sec. Joint Staff, dir. pacification support, dep. asst. chief staff for civil ops. revolutionary devel. support U.S. Mil. Assistance Command, Vietnam, 1966-67; asst. div. comdr. 9th Inf. Div., Vietnam, 1968; sec. gen. staff Office Chief Staff (U.S. Army), 1968-70; chief staff hdqrs. U.S. European Command, Stuttgart, W.Ger., 1974-76; comdr. Allied Forces S.E. Europe, Izmir, Turkey, 1976-77; U.S. rep. NATO Mil. Com., Brussels, 1977-80; ret., 1980; cons. on internat. affairs and strategic intelligence R & D Assocs., Marina del Rey, Calif.; sr. assoc. Burdeshaw Assocs. Ltd., 1981—; dir. Aeronca Inc., Chubb Corp., Fed. Ins. Co., Vigilant Ins. Co.; sr. fellow Inst. Higher Def. Studies, Nat. Def. U., 1984—. Contbr.: Ency. American and nat. mags. Trustee Davis and Elkins Coll., 1982—. Decorated Def. D.S.M., Army D.S.M., Silver Star with 2 oak leaf clusters, Legion of Merit with oak leaf cluster, D.F.C., Bronze Star with V device, Air medal with 9 oak leaf clusters, Army Commendation medal with oak leaf cluster, knight comdr cross Order Merit, W.Ger., officer Legion of Honor, France, Belgium and Vietname; recipient George Washington Honor medal Freedoms Found., Valley Forge, 1957-58. Mem. Am. Mil. Inst., Am. Mgmt. Assns., Nat. Assn. Corp. Dirs., Council Fgn. Relations, Am. Acad. Polit. and Social Sci., Acad. Polit. Sci., Soc. Mayflower Descs., S.R., Soc. Colonial Wars. Clubs: University (N.Y.C.); Army and Navy (Washington). Home: 4520 4th Rd N Arlington VA 22203

KNOWLTON, WINTHROP, publishing company executive; b. N.Y.C., Sept. 1, 1930; s. Hugh and Christine (Stanley) K.; m. Mina Elizabeth Minnerly, June 23, 1951 (div. 1960); children: Winthrop, Christopher, Oliver; m. Grace Daniels Farrar, July 8, 1960 (div. 1980); children: Eliza Courtney, Samantha Farrar. Grad., Lawrenceville Sch., 1948; B.A., Harvard, 1953, M.B.A., 1955. With White, Weld & Co., Inc., N.Y.C., from 1955, v.p., 1961, gen. partner, 1962-65, ltd. partner, from 1965; with Office Edn., Washington, 1965; dep. asst. sec. treasury for internat. affairs, 1965-66, asst. sec., 1966-68; exec. v.p., dir. Harper & Row, 1968-70, pres., 1970-79, chmn., 1979—, chief exec. officer, until 1981, also dir.; dir. Equitable Life Assurance Soc. U.S., Mpls. Star and Tribune, Govt. Research Corp. Co-author: A Killing in the Market, 1958; author: Growth Opportunities in Common Stocks, 1965, Shaking the Money Tree, 1972. Trustee, vice chmn. Tchrs. Coll.; bd. dirs., pres., chief exec. officer N.Y.C. Ballet; mem. Mayor's Commn. Cultural Affairs.; Mem. Council on Fgn. Relations. Clubs: Century, Harvard, University. Office: Harper & Row Pubs Inc 10 E 53d St New York NY 10022 *

KNOX, BERNARD MACGREGOR WALKER, classics educator; b. Bradford, Eng., Nov. 24, 1914; came to U.S., 1939, naturalized, 1943; s. Bernard and Rowena (Walker) K.; m. Betty Baur, Apr. 12, 1939; 1 son, Bernard MacGregor Baur. B.A., St. John's Coll., U. Cambridge (Eng.), 1936; Ph.D., Yale U., 1948, L.H.D., 1983; M.A. (hon.), Harvard U., 1962; Litt.D., Princeton U., 1964; L.H.D., George Washington U., 1977. Mem. faculty Yale, 1947-61, prof. classics, 1959-61; dir. Center Hellenic Studies, Washington, 1961—; Sather lectr. U. Calif. at Berkeley, 1963; Nellie Wallace lectr. Oxford U., 1975. Author: Oedipus at Thebes, 1957, Oedipus the King, The Heroic Temper, 1964, Word and Action, 1979; also articles.; Author, actor: ednl. films on Oedipus of Sophocles. Served to capt. AUS, 1942-45; ETO. Decorated Bronze Star with cluster; Croix de Guerre, France; recipient George Jean Nathan award for dramatic criticism, 1978; Guggenheim fellow, 1956-57; award for lit. Nat. Inst. Arts and Letters, 1967. Mem. Am. Philol. Assn. (pres. 1980), Am. Acad. Arts and Scis., Brit. Acad. (corr.). Clubs: Special Forces (London); Cosmos (Washington). Address: Center Hellenic Studies 3100 Whitehaven St Washington DC 20008

KNOX, CHARLES ROBERT, football coach; b. Sewickley, Pa., Apr. 27, 1932; s. Charles McMeehan and Helen (Keith) K.; m. Shirley Ann, Aug. 2, 1952; children: Christeen, Kathy, Colleen, Chuck. B.A., Juniata Coll., 1954; postgrad., Pa. State U., 1955. Asst. football coach Wake Forest Coll., 1959-60, U. Ky., 1961-62, N.Y. Jets, 1963-66, Detroit Lions, 1967-72; head football coach Los Angeles Rams, 1973-78; head football coach, v.p. football ops. Buffalo Bills, 1978-82; head football coach Seattle Seahawks, 1983—. Lutheran. Club: Big Canyon Country. Address: care Seattle Seahawks 5305 Lake Washington Blvd Kirkland WA 98033 *

KNOX, ERNEST RUDDER, coll. pres.; b. Stevenson, Ala., Sept. 19, 1916; s. Allen Luckey and Susie (Rudder) K.; m. Pauline Danner, Dec. 24, 1972. B.A., Bethel Coll., 1940; M.Div., Vanderbilt U., 1943; M.A., U. Ala., 1948; Ed.D., George Peabody Coll. Tchrs., 1963; LL.D., Jacksonville State U., 1968. Coach Marion County High Sch., 1943-45, Marshall (Ala.) County High Sch., 1946-57; prin. Marion County (Tenn.) High Sch., 1948-53, Bridgeport (Ala.) Schs., 1953-63; coordinator Ala. Jr. Colls., 1964; pres. N.E. Ala. State Jr. Coll., Rainsville, 1965—; ordained to ministry Presbyn. Ch., 1940; minister Cumberland Presbyn. Chs., 1938—. Served as chaplain USNR, 1945-46. Mem. Ala. Public Jr. Coll. Council of Pres. (pres.), Ala. Edn. Assn., NEA. Democrat. Clubs: Lions, Masons. Office: NE Ala State Jr Coll Rainsville AL 35986

KNOX, FRANKLYN GILBERT, medical school dean, physician, educator; b. Rochester, N.Y., Dec. 20, 1937; s. Gilbert K. and Selma (Knox); m. Anne Curtis Mitchell, Dec. 17, 1960; children: Michael, Sally, David, Susan. B.S., U. Buffalo, 1959; Ph.D., SUNY-Buffalo, 1965; M.D., SUNY- Buffalo, 1965. Staff assoc. Nat. Heart Inst., NIH, Bethesda, Md., 1965-68; ast. prof. dept. physiology U. Mo., Columbia, 1968-70, assoc. prof., 1970-71; assoc. prof. physiology and medicine Mayo Med. Sch., Rochester, Minn., 1971-74, prof., 1974—, chmn. dept. phsiology and biophysics, 1974-83, dean, Rochester, Minn., 1983—; assoc. dir. grad. edn. research tgn. and degree programs Mayo Grad. Sch. Medicine, 1978-83; dir. edn. Mayo Found., 1983—; mem. gen. medicine B study sect. NIH, 1983—; mem. sci. adv. bd. Nat. Kidney Found., 1978-83, chmn. research fellowship and grants com., 1982-83; mem. physiology test com. Nat. Bd. Med. Examiners, 1980-81; mem.med. adv. bd. Kidney Found. Upper Midwest, 1974—; mem. Intersoc. Planning Com. for Kidney Research, 1981—; external referee Med. Rearch Council Can. Assoc. editor: Jour. Lab. and Clin. Medicine, 1976-79; editor, 1979-80; editoral bd.: Am. Jour. Physiology, Circulation Research, Jour. Clin. Investigation, Minerals and Electrolyte Metabolism, Contemporary Nephrology, others; contbr. (articles to med. jours.); author, editor Textbook of Renal Pathophysiology, 1978. Lederle Lab. fellow; USPHS grantee; Am. Found. Pharmacology Edn. scholar; Pfizer Lab. scholar; Bowditch lectr. Am. Physiol. Soc., 1977. Fellow Council on Circulation of Am.

Heart Assn.; mem. AAAS, Am. fedn. Clin. Research, Am. Heart Assn. (dir. 1982—, council affairs com. 1982—, exec. com. 1983, chmn. Council on Kidney in Cardiovascular Disease 1981-83), Am. Physiol. Soc., Am. Soc. Clin. Investigation, Am. Soc. Nephrology, Central Clin. Research Club, Internat. Soc. Nephrology, Midwest Sale and Water Club, Minn. Heart Assn., Nat. Kidney Found., Sigma Xi, Alpha Omega Alpha, Rho Chi. Home: 2249Nordic Ct NW Rochester MN 55901 Office: 200 1st St SW Rochester MN 55015

KNOX, GERALD MALM, editor, writer; b. Mpls., May 10, 1935; s. Franklin Perry and Myrtle (Malm) K.; m. Janet Arleen Israelson, July 26, 1978; children—Michael, Cynthia, Matthew. B.A. in Journalism, U. Minn., 1961. Research writer Hughes Aircraft Co., Los Angeles, 1961-62; research writer Control Data Corp., Mpls., 1962-65; public relations officer U. Minn., Mpls., 1965-67; health and family life editor Better Homes and Gardens mag., Meredith Corp., Des Moines, 1967-76; editor Better Homes and Gardens Books, 1976—. Served with USAF, 1953-57. Mem. Nat. Assn. Sci. Writers. Office: 1716 Locust St Des Moines IA 50336

KNOX, JAMES LESTER, electrical engineer; b. Youngstown, Ohio, July 30, 1919; s. Lester Wirt and Alma Freda (Johnson) K.; m. Elizabeth Jane Williams, Mar. 19, 1946; children: Susan Louise, Patricia Ellen, Linda Anne, Thomas Lester, Stephen Williams. B.E.E., U. Tenn., 1942; M.S., U. Mich., 1954; Ph.D., Ohio State U., 1962. Instr. U. Tenn., 1942-43; engr. Gen. Elec. Co., Schenectady and Syracuse, N.Y., 1943-46; with Am. Baptist Fgn. Mission Soc., 1947-65; assignments U. Shanghai, 1947-48; asst. prof. Central Philippine Coll., 1948-50; tech. dir. Sta. DYSR, Dumaguete City, P.I., 1950-51; asst. prof. Central Philippine U., 1951-53, asso. prof., 1954-60, prof., dean, 1962-65; research asso. Ohio State U. Research Found., Columbus, 1960-62; prof. U. Petrol and Min., Dhahran, Saudi Arabia, 1973-75, 76-78, 81—; prof. elec. engring. Mont. State U., Bozeman, 1965-82, ret., 1982; cons. elec. engring., community acoustics. Served with USNG, 1934-37. Mem. IEEE, Am. Soc. Engring. Edn., Instrument Soc. Am., Sigma Xi, Tau Beta Pi, Phi Kappa Phi. Baptist. Home: 603 S 7th St Bozeman MT 59715 Office: U Petroleum and Minerals Dhahran Saudi Arabia

KNOX, JOHN MARSHALL, medical educator; b. Dallas, Apr. 11, 1925; s. John Marshall and Katie (Dickie) K.; m. Lullene Powell, Dec. 18, 1948; children: Lynda Lee, Jane Ann, John Marshall, Byron Powell (dec.). B.S., Tex. A. and M. U., 1947; M.D., Baylor U., 1949. Diplomate: Am. Bd. Dermatology (dir. 1976—, v.p. 1983-84, mem. com. for dermatopathology 1980—, chmn. 1983-84). Intern New Orleans Charity Hosp., 1949-50; resident Univ. Hosp., Ann Arbor, Mich., 1950, 54-55, U. Okla. Hosp., 1953-54; mem. faculty Baylor U. Coll. Medicine, 1955—, prof., chmn. dept. dermatology and syphilology, 1963—; chief dermatology VA Hosp., Houston, 1963-69, cons., 1969—; chief dermatology Ben Taub Gen. Hosp., Houston, 1963—, Tex. Children's Hosp., 1967—; sr. attending physician Meth. Hosp., Houston, 1964-75, chief service, 1976—; Mem. commn. cutaneous diseases Armed Forces Epidemiol. Bd., 1968-72; chmn., dir. council, dir. Nat. Program for Dermatology, 1969-72; mem. Nat. Commn. Venereal Disease, 1971; tech. counsellor, mem. exec. com. Internat. Union Against Venereal Diseases and the Treponematoses, 1973-80; asst. sec. gen. for N. Am.; mem. council Internat. Union against Venereal Diseases and Treponematoses, 1977-80. Mem. editorial bds. jours. in field.; Contbr. numerous articles to profl. jours. Bd. dirs. Dermatology Found., 1972-76. Served as capt., M.C. USAF, 1951-52. Recipient Disting. Alumni award Tex. A&M U., 1971. Mem. Soc. Investigative Dermatology (bd. dirs. 1960-65), Am. Social Health Assn. (bd. dirs. 1962-75), Am. Dermatol. Assn. (bd. dirs. 1980—), AMA (council rep. to residency rev. com. for dermatology 1974-75), Houston Dermatol. Soc. (pres. 1965-66), Tex. Dermatol. Soc. (v.p. 1965-66, pres. 1982-83), Am. Venereal Disease Assn. (pres. 1968-69), So. Med. Assn. (chmn. sect. dermatology 1965-66), South Central Dermatol. Congress (chief exec. officer 1969-71), Assn. Former Students Tex. A. and M. U. (v.p. 1974-76, pres. 1977), Alpha Omega Alpha. Home: 419 Blalock St Houston TX 77024

KNOX, JOHN, JR., philosopher, educator; b. Nashville, Mar. 5, 1932; s. John and Lois Adelaide (Bolles) K.; m. Alida van Bronkhorst, June 30, 1962 (div. 1978); children—Trevor McTaggart, Amethy Alida. Student, Cambridge U., 1952; B.A., Emory U., 1953; Ph.D., Yale U., 1961. Instr. philosophy C.W. Post Coll., L.I. U., 1960, asst. prof. philosophy, 1961-67; asso. prof. philosophy Drew U., Madison, N.J., 1967-71, prof., 1971—, chmn. dept., 1971-79; vis. prof. philosophy U. Miami, spring 1981. Contbr. articles to philos. publs. Served to lt. (j.g.) USNR, 1953-56. Nat. Endowment for Humanities fellow, 1973-74. Mem. Am. Philos. Assn., Phi Beta Kappa, Phi Sigma Tau. Office: Drew Univ Madison NJ 07940 *I try to believe what, and only what, I consider to be objectively true. The objective truth is not, per se—indeed it is not likely to resemble—the comfortable certainties of fixed traditions or of passing fashions. Yet I think I should be happier if I had it; at least, I am unhappy in not having it. Hence I like cautious speculations better than unthinking certitudes, and I favor Reason's occasional glimmers over Faith's unending dream.*

KNOX, NORTHRUP RAND, investment banker; b. Buffalo, Dec. 24, 1928; s. Seymour and Helen (Northrup) K.; m. Lucetta Crisp, June 21, 1950; children—Linda Gilbert (Mrs. Arthur A. Schmon II), Northrup Rand. B.A., Yale U., 1950; student, Cornell U., 1952. Dir. Marine Midland Bank, Marine Midland Banks, Inc., Niagara Share Corp., Midland Capital Corp., S.M. Flickinger Co., Inc. Pres. Niagara Frontier Hockey Corp.; Treas., trustee Aiken Prep. Sch.; v.p. Hitchcock Found., Buffalo Fine Arts Acad.; bd. dirs. U. Buffalo Found.; v.p., dir. Seymour H. Knox Found. World ct. tennis champion, 1959-69. Home: Buffalo Rd East Aurora NY 14052 Office: 3750 Marine Midland Center Buffalo NY 14203

KNOX, RICHARD, television news director; b. Bklyn., Aug. 9, 1936; s. George and Ruth Rosenfeld; m. Rita Goldman, Aug. 19, 1962; children: Randal, Hilary. B.F.A., Columbia U., 1958. Clk. in ops. CBS, N.Y.C., 1961-62, program asst. for news, 1962-64, asso. dir., 1964-73; dir. CBS Evening News With Bob Schieffer and Morton Dean, 1973—; now dir. Nightwatch; lectr. in English Pace U., 1976—. Appeared on Broadway in: Peter Pan, 1950; appeared in: numerous plays, TV shows, including Egg and I, TV series, 1951-52; dir. coverage: Apollo 13, 14, 15 (Dirs. Guild award 1969, Nat. Acad. TV Arts and Scis. Emmy award 1970, 71); dir.: Watergate: The Whitehouse Transcripts, 1974 (Emmy award); also dir. numerous documentaries and spl. broadcasts on various current events, including space, assassination, Vietnam, elections, China, Iran, SALT, inflation, Am. Hostages, John Lennon, others. Served with U.S. N.G., 1955-61. Mem. Dirs. Guild Am., Actor's Equity, AFTRA, Screen Actors Guild. Jewish. Home: 226 Newport Ave Tappan NY 10983 Office: 524 W 57th St New York NY 10019

KNOX, RICHARD MELVIN, oil company executive; b. Covington, Okla., Mar. 15, 1923; s. Charles and Vivian Marguerite (Slichter) K.; m. Mary Jo Miller, May 5, 1943; children: Mary Lynn, Richard Melvin, Kimie Marie and Karie Louise (twins). Student, U. Okla., 1940-43. Formed Knox Industries Corp., Enid., Okla., 1949, pres., 1957-63; (co. acquired by Kerr-McGee Corp.), 1961, v.p. marketing-pipeline-refining, 1963-68; pres. Knox Corp., Knox Hi Octane Corp., 1957—; chmn. bd. Midland Cablevision Systems, Inc.; dir. Western Investors Corp. Mem. Okla. Personnel Bd., 1960-61; trustee Marycrest Coll., Davenport, Iowa, 1981—. Served to 1st lt. U.S. Army, 1943-46. Mem. Enid C. of C. (pres. 1961), Am. Petroleum Inst., Soc. Ind. Gasoline Marketers Am. (bd. dirs.), Young Presidents Orgn. Presbyn. Home: 15 Robert Ave Davenport IA 52803 Office: Knox Corp PO Box K 1416 State St Bettendorf IA 52722

KNOX, ROBERT SEIPLE, educator, physicist; b. Franklin, N.J., July 13, 1931; s. Harvey Stoll and Laura (Seiple) K.; m. Mirta I. Borges, Sept. 1, 1954; children—Bruce Robert, Wayne Harvey, Lee Benjamin. B.S. in Engring. Physics, Lehigh U., 1953; Ph.D. in Physics and Optics, U. Rochester, 1958. Research asso. U. Ill., 1958-59; research asst. prof., 1959-60; mem. faculty U. Rochester, N.Y., 1960—, assoc. prof. dept. physics, 1963-68, prof., 1968—, chmn. dept. physics and astronomy, 1969-74, assoc. dean spl. programs Coll. Arts and Scis., 1982—. Author: Theory of Excitons, 1963, (with A. Gold) Symmetry in the Solid State, 1964, (with D.L. Dexter) Excitons, 1965; also articles. NSF sr. postdoctoral fellow U. Leiden, 1967-68; Japan Soc. Promotion of Sci. fellow Kyoto U., 1979. Fellow Am. Phys. Soc. Research on atomic spectra and structure, absorption and luminescence spectra ionic and molecular crystals, photosynthesis theory, picosecond spectroscopy. Office: Dept Physics and Astronomy U Rochester Rochester NY 14627

KNOX, SEYMOUR HORACE, III, investment banker; b. Buffalo, Mar. 9, 1926; s. Seymour Horace and Helen Elizabeth (Northrup) K.; m. Jean Read, May 15, 1954; children: Seymour H. IV, W.A. Read, Avery F., Helen Edith. B.A., Yale U., 1949. With Marine Midland Bank, N.Y.C., 1949-52; staff Dominick & Dominick, N.Y.C., 1952-54, mgr. Buffalo br., 1954-56, gen. partner, 1956-64, v.p., 1964-70, regional v.p., 1970-73; v.p. Kidder, Peabody & Co., Inc., Buffalo, 1973—; chmn. bd. Buffalo Sabres Hockey Club; dir. F.W. Woolworth Co., Pratt & Lambert, Inc.; mem. adv. council Marine-Midland Banks, Inc. Bd. dirs. Albright Knox Art Gallery; bd. dirs., v.p. Seymour H. Knox Found., Inc.; bd. dirs. Skillman Assocs. of Yale U.; trustee Buffalo Gen. Hosp., Children's Found. Erie County, Inc.; chmn. bd. trustees YMCA of Buffalo and Erie County. Served with AUS, 1945-46. Recipient Exec. of Year award Nat. Hockey League, 1975, Outstanding Citizen award Buffalo Evening News, 1970. Mem. Nat. Hockey League (bd. govs.), Buffalo C. of C., Smithsonian Assos. (nat. bd. dirs.), U.S. Squash Racquets Assn. (former pres.). Clubs: Brook, Buffalo, Buffalo Tennis and Squash, Country Buffalo, Crag Burn, Mid-Day of Buffalo, Racquet and Tennis, Downtown Assn., Saturn. Former nationally ranked squash racquets player singles and doubles; 3-time winner U.S. Ct. Tennis Doubles Championship. Office: 3737 Marine Midland Center and Buffalo Sabres Hockey Club Meml Auditorium 140 Main St Buffalo NY 14202

KNOX, STANLEY CRAMNER, educator; b. Osage, Ia., Oct. 1, 1928; s. Robert Floyd and Karen Rosetta (Richsmann) K.; m. Florence Elizabeth Nikkola, Sept. 8, 1951; children—Craig, Wendy, Marcia, Janelle. B.S., U. Minn., 1952, M.A., 1960, Ph.D., 1966. Tchr. pub. schs., Roseville, Minn., 1952-57; psychometrist student counselling bur. U. Minn., 1957-58; psychologist Minn. Dept. Pub. Welfare, 1958-59; asst. prof. edn. and psychology U. No. Ia., Cedar Falls, 1960-61; chmn. dept. spl. edn. St. Cloud (Minn.) State U., 1961—; Cons. Minn. Edn. Dept., Ednl. Mgmt. Service, Inc. Served with USNR, 1945-48. U.S. Office Edn. fellow, 1959-61. Fellow Am. Assn. Mental Deficiency; mem. Council Exceptional Children (pres.), Am. Psychol. Assn., Phi Delta Kappa. Home: 1125 21st Ave N St Cloud MN 56301

KNOX, WARREN BARR, college administrator; b. Whittier, Calif., Aug. 22, 1925; s. Lavern V. and Bertha (Barr) K.; m. Nancy S. Chambers, June 20, 1945; children: Charles Warren, John Warren. B.A., Whittier Coll., 1949, M.A., 1951, LL.D., 1965; student, Claremont Grad. Sch., 1951-52. Tchr. Montebello (Calif.) High Sch., 1950-52; asst. to pres. Pomona Coll., 1952-59; v.p. Whitman Coll., 1959-64; pres. Coll. of Idaho, Caldwell, 1964-73; v.p. Reed Coll., Portland, Oreg., 1973-77; dir. life income planning Claremont (Calif.) Men's Coll., 1977-80; v.p. Randolph-Macon Coll., Ashland, Va., 1980-82, Art Ctr. Coll. Design, Calif., 1982—; chmn. Rhodes Scholarship Selection for Idaho, 1965-69; mem. Idaho del. Nat. Compact Edn. of Am.; mem. commn. instl. affairs Assn. Am. Coll., 1973; also chmn. task force on presdl. selection and career devel.; mem. nexus com. Presbyn. Coll. Union, 1970-74, v.p., 1973-74; mem. Idaho Higher Edn. Adv. Council. Author: Eye of the Hurricane, 1973, Annuities, Trusts, Investments, 1980; contbr. articles to profl. jours. Mem. Boise Art Assos., 1965—; vice chmn. Ore-Ida council Boy Scouts Am., 1964-74, hon. mem. nat. council, 1960—; mem. exec. bd. Columbia-Pacific Council, 1974-77; mem. Estate Planning Council Pomona Valley, 1977-80; bd. dirs. Claremont chpt. ARC, 1977-80. Served with USNR, 1942-45. Mem. Am. Alumni Council, Am. Coll. Pub. Relations Assn. (mem. com. on taxation and philanthropy 1973—), Am., Western hist. assns., English-Speaking Union, Wisdom Soc., Intercollegiate Knights (hon.). Republican. Methodist. Clubs: Kiwanis; City (Portland); Bull and Bear (Richmond, Va.); Hanover Country (Ashland); University (Los Angeles). Home: 380 S Euclid #210 Pasadena CA 91101

KNOX, WILLIAM DAVID, publishing company executive; b. Sault Ste. Marie, Mich., June 9, 1920; s. Victor A. and Bertha V. (Byers) K.; m. Jane Edith Shaw, June 15, 1941; children: Georgia Knox Mode, William David, Randall S., Brian V. B.S., Mich. State U., 1941; postgrad., Harvard U., 1943-44; LL.D. (hon.), U. Wis., 1973. Youth editor Hoard's Dairyman mag., W.D. Hoard & Sons Co., Fort Atkinson, Wis., 1941-42, asso. editor, 1946-49, editor, 1949—, pres., treas., gen. mgr., 1972—; v.p. Am. Agriculturist, Inc., 1975—; pres. Nat. Brucellosis Com., 1955-66, chmn., 1951-60; mem. nat. agrl. advisory com., 1961-62, 1976—; dir. 1st Am. Bank and Trust., Dataforms, Inc. Pres. Fort Atkinson Bd. Edn., 1948-59; bd. visitors U. Wis., 1979—; bd. dirs. Wis. Taxpayers Alliance, 1976—. Served to lt. USNR, 1942-46. Recipient Disting. Service award Nat. Brucellosis Com., 1957, Pure Milk Assn., 1966, Am. Dairy Sci. Assn., 1970, Wis. Farm Bur. Fedn., 1974, Nat. Assn. Animal Breeders, 1981, Nat. Assn. Livestock Records, 1983; service citations Fla. Dairy Farmers Fedn., 1962, Wis. Farm Bur. Fedn., 1956, Nat. Plant Food Council, 1963, Dairy Council Central Ga., 1967; Nat. 4-H Alumni award, 1965; Mich. State U. Distinguished Alumnus award, 1966; named Tri-State Man of Yr., 1966; Milw. Milk Producers Assn. Man of Yr., 1976; recipient Mid-Am. Dairymen Salute award, 1977. Mem. Agrl. Publs. Assn. (pres. 1979—), Am. Newspaper Pubs. Assn., Am. Veterinary Med. Assn. (hon.), Am. Jersey Cattle Club (hon.), Am. Dairy Sci. Assn., Am. Agrl. Econs. Assn., Wis. Veterinary Med. Assn. (hon.), Rotary (Internat. Service citation 1956), Alpha Gamma Rho, Alpha Zeta. Republican. Episcopalian. Home: 703 Robert St Fort Atkinson WI 53538 Office: 28 Milwaukee Ave W Fort Atkinson WI 53538

KNUDSEN, JAMES GEORGE, chemical engineer, educator; b. Youngstown, Can., Mar. 27, 1920; s. James Skov and Rose Maude (Ray) K.; m. Joyce Mildred Renville, July 7, 1947; children—Kathryn Lee, Shelley Lynne. B.S. in Chem. Engring, U. Alta., 1943, M.S. in Phys. Chemistry, 1944; Ph.D. in Chem. Engring, U. Mich., 1949. Faculty Oreg. State U., Corvallis, 1949—, asst. prof., 1949-53, asso. prof., 1953-57, prof. chem. engring., 1957—, asst. dean engring., 1950-70, assoc. dean engring., 1970-81; cons. heat transfer and fluid mechanics. Co-author: Fluid Dynamics and Heat Transfer, 1958; contbr. articles to profl. publs. NSF sr. postdoctoral fellow, 1961-62; Battelle sci. fellow, 1974. Mem. Am. Inst. Chem. Engrs. (pres. 1980, Founders award 1977), Am. Chem. Soc., Nat. Soc. Profl. Engrs., AAAS. Home: 3220 NW Crest Dr Corvallis OR 97330 Office: Oregon State Univ Corvallis OR 97331

KNUDSEN, RAYMOND BARNETT, clergyman, association executive; b. Denver, Nov. 11, 1919; s. Franklin Ole and Julia (Nielsen) K.; m. Edna Mae Nielsen, Jan. 26, 1940; children: Raymond Barnett, Silas John, Mark Allen, Ann DeLight (Mrs. Arthur James Semotan III). Student, Coll. Emporia, 1937-38, Wheaton Coll., 1938-39; B.A., U. Denver, 1941; Th.M., McCormick Theol. Sem., 1948; postgrad., U. Chgo., 1948; D.D., Burton Coll., 1955, LL.D., 1964. Pastor 8th Ave. Presbyn. Ch., Denver, 1939-40; dir. Martin M. Post Larger Parish, Logansport, Ind., 1941-44; asst. Faith Presbyn. Ch., Chgo., 1945; pastor 1st Presbyn. Ch., Warsaw, Ill., 1946-52, 5th Presbyn. Ch., Springfield, Ill., 1952-63; sr. pastor Webb Horton Meml. Presbyn. Ch., Middletown, N.Y., 1963-70; exec. dir. for donor support Nat. Council Chs. of Christ in U.S.A., 1970-71, asst. gen. sec., 1971-77; pres. Nat. Consultation on Fin. Devel., 1977—; lectr. philosophy Orange County (N.Y.) Community Coll., 1964-70; instr. Drew U. Sch. Theology, 1978—; Chmn. broadcasting press Synod of Ill., Presbyn. Ch., 1954-60, mem. gen. council, 1954-62; chmn. founding com. Ill. Presbyn. Home, Springfield, 1954; pres. Middletown Council Chs., 1967-69; chmn. Fifty Million Dollar Fund, Hudson River Presbytery, 1964-70; pres. Webb Horton Presbyn. Assos., Counselor Assn., 1954—; v.p. Inst. Activation Research.; cons. Episc. Diocese of Pitts., 1977—, Orthodox Ch. in Am., 1978—, Christian Meth. Episc. Ch., 1983—, Hawaii conf. United Ch. of Christ, 1983—, Asbury Hills Camp, 1983—. Author: The Trinity, 1937, New Models for Financing the Local Church, 1974, New Models for Creative Giving, 1976, Models for Ministry, 1978, Developing Dynamic Stewardship, 1978, New Models for Church Administration, 1979, Christian Stewardship in a Period of Fiscal Change, 1984; mem. bd. rev.: Antenna, 1963—; contbr. religious columns to publs.; syndicated newspaper column The Counselor. Mem. Middletown Narcotics Guidance Council, 1969-70; pres. bd. dirs. Occupations, Inc., 1964-69, treas., 1969-71, pres. emeritus, 1976—; bd. dirs. Aid to Retarded Children N.Y., 1963-66, United Presbyn. Student Found., Presbyn. Sr. Services, N.Y.C., 1981—, Presbyn. Panel, 1981—; exec. bd. Orange County chpt. Aid Retarded Children; trustee Orange County Workshop for Disabled, 1963, Homemaker Service Orange County; pres. bd. trustees Camp Townsend, 1964-70. Recipient Author citation N.J. Inst. Tech., 1980. Mem. Nat. Temperance League (hon. v.p., chmn. nominating com. 1961-62), Alcohol Edn. Found. (dir.), Counselor Assn. (chmn. bd. 1982—). Clubs: Masons, Rotary (chmn. internat. contacts). Home: 31 Langerfeld Rd Hillsdale NJ 07675 Office: 475 Riverside Dr New York NY 10027 *We live in a global village in the shadow of a friendly, fatherly God. Through the structures of time and circumstances we move into the future and instead of closed doors we discover new directions, alternate routes, and challenging frontiers to bring us into each tomorrow. We discover the significance of selves as we lose ourselves in service to others. Through the interweaving of lives through the warp of generations and the woof of others we become a part of the fabric of time upon which the future stands with hope and promise.*

KNUDSEN, RUDOLPH EDGAR, JR., ins. co. exec.; b. Far Rockaway, N.Y., July 18, 1939; s. Rudolph Edgar and Katherine Elizabeth (Benham) K.; m. Margaret Rebecca Vreeland, June 10, 1961; children—Peter, Kathryn. A.B., Columbia Coll., 1961. Programmer Met. Life Ins. Co., N.Y.C., 1961-65, Am. Life Ins. Co. N.Y., 1965-70, 2d v.p., 1971-72, v.p., corp. sec., 1973—. Served with USAR, 1961-62. Methodist. Club: Rockville Links. Home: 174 Harvard Ave Rockville Centre NY 11570 Office: Am Life Ins Co NY 810 7th Ave New York NY 10019

KNUDSEN, SEMON EMIL, manufacturing company executive; b. Buffalo, Oct. 2, 1912; s. William S. and Clara Elizabeth (Euler) K.; m. Florence Anne McConnell, June 16, 1938. B.S. in Engring, Mass. Inst. Tech., 1936. With Gen. Motors Corp., 1939-68, exec. v.p., 1966-68; also dir.; pres. Ford Motor Co., 1968-69; also dir.; chmn. Rectrans, Inc., 1970-71; chmn. bd., chief exec. officer White Motor Corp., Cleve., 1971-79, chmn., 1979-80; dir. Mich. Nat. Corp., 1st Nat. Bank, Palm Beach, Fla., Cowles Broadcasting Inc., Mich. Nat. Bank. Bd. dirs., past pres. Boys' Clubs of Detroit; bd. dirs. Boys Clubs of Am., Greater Cleve. Growth Assn.; nat. adv. council Nat. Multiple Sclerosis Soc.; mem. corp. Mass. Inst. Tech.; trustee Oakland (Mich.) U. Found., Cleve. Clinic Found. Recipient Brotherhood award Detroit Round Table, NCCJ, 1961; Man of Year award Sales and Mktg. Execs. of Cleve., 1974; Mktg. Salesman of Year award Sales and Mktg. Execs. Internat., 1974. Mem. Motor Vehicle Mfrs. Assn. (sec. 1972-73, 78-79, treas. 1973-74, 79-80, vice chmn. 1974-76, chmn. 1977-78), Soc. Automotive Engrs., Am. Soc. Tool Engrs., Delta Upsilon. Clubs: Detroit, Detroit Athletic; Bloomfield Hills (Mich.); Country; Union (Cleve.); Augusta (Ga.); Nat. Golf, Everglades, Seminole. Office: 1700 N Woodward Ave Suite E Bloomfield Hills MI 48013

KNUDSEN, WILLIAM CLAIRE, geophysicist; b. Provo, Utah, Dec. 12, 1925; s. Nels William and Julia A. (Brown) K.; m. Ruth Crandall, Aug. 31, 1948; children: Linda, Ruthanne, Guy, Grant. B.S., Brigham Young U., 1950; M.S., U. Wis., 1952, Ph.D., 1954. Sr. research physicist Calif. Research Corp., La Habra, 1954-62; staff scientist Lockheed Palo Alto Research Lab., Palo Alto, Calif., 1962—. Served with Signal Corps U.S. Army, 1944-46. Mem. Am. Geophys. Union, Planetary Soc., Sigma Xi. Mormon. Patentee. Office: Lockheed Palo Alto Research Lab Dept 52-12 Bldg 255 3251 Hanover St Palo Alto CA 94304

KNUDSON, ALFRED GEORGE, JR., medical geneticist; b. Los Angeles, Aug. 9, 1922; s. Alfred George and Mary Gladys (Galvin) K.; m. Anna T. Meadows, June 20, 1977; children by previous marriage: Linda, Nancy, Dorene. B.S., Calif. Inst. Tech., 1944, Ph.D. (Guggenheim fellow), 1956; M.D., Columbia U., 1947. Chmn. dept. pediatrics City of Hope Med. Center, Duarte, Calif., 1956-62, chmn. dept. biology, 1962-66; assoc. dean Health Sci. Center, SUNY, Stony Brook, 1966-69; dean Grad. Sch. Biomed. Scis., U. Tex. Health Sci. Center, Houston, 1970-76; dir. Inst. Cancer Research, Fox Chase Cancer Center, Phila., 1976-83, sr. mem., 1976—, pres., 1980-82; mem. Assembly Life Scis., NRC, 1975-81. Author: Genetics and Disease, 1965. Recipient Disting. Alumni award Calif. Inst. Tech., 1978. Mem. Am. Soc. Human Genetics (pres. 1978), Assn. Am. Physicians, Am. Pediatrics Soc., Am. Assn. Cancer Research. Research, publs. in genetics of human cancer. Office: Inst Cancer Research 7701 Burholme Ave Philadelphia PA 19111

KNUDSON, HARRY EDWARD, JR., elec. mfg. co. exec.; b. N.Y.C., Dec. 30, 1921; s. Harry Edward and Helen (Jones) K.; m. Anne Howland, Sept. 21, 1944; children—Anne, Erik. B.S. in Elec. Engring, Bucknell U., 1947. Cadet engr. Phila. Electric Co., 1947; with Fed. Pacific Electric Co., Newark, 1947-80, exec. v.p., 1970-76, pres., 1976-80; also dir., corp. v.p. parent co. Reliance Electric Co., 1979-80; v.p; gen. mgr. distbn. and control GTE Products Corp., Danvers, Mass., 1980—. Bd. dirs. Frost Valley YMCA. Served with USNR, 1943-46. Mem. Nat. Elec. Mfrs. Assn. (chmn. bd. govs., mem. officers com.), Elec. Mfrs. Club, Phi Kappa Psi, Kappa Eta Nu. Methodist. Home: 133 Hill St Topsfield MA 01983 Office: 100 Endicott St Danvers MA 01923

KNUST, HERBERT, comparative literature educator; b. Cologne, Germany, May 9, 1935; came to U.S., 1956; s. Wilhelm and Paula (Emanuelsson) K.; m. Christa H.E. Groebke, Aug. 15, 1963; children: Stefan, Sabine, Sylvia. Student, U. Munich, 1953-54, Free U., Berlin, 1954-56; M.A. in English, Tulane U., 1958; Ph.D. in Comparative Lit., Pa. State U., 1961. Instr. Pa. State U., University Park, 1960-61, asst. prof. German and comparative lit., 1963-65; dozent Goethe Inst., Berlin, 1962-63; asst. prof. German U. Ill., Urbana-Champaign, 1965-67, assoc. prof. German and comparative lit., 1967-73, prof. German and comparative lit., 1973—, dir. program in comparative lit., 1970-72, 73-74, 81-82, head dept. German langs. and lit., 1982—, dir. Austria-Ill. Exchange Program, 1978-80. Author: Wagner, the King and The Waste Land, 1967, Materialien zu Bertolt Brechts Schweyk im zweiten Welkrieg, 1974, Texte und Ubungen 1977, Bertolt Brecht: Leben des Galilei, 1982; co-author: Theatrical Drawings and Water Colors by George Grosz, 1973; editor: George Grosz, Briefs, 1913-1959, 1979, Montage, Satire and Cultism: Germany between the Wars, 1975; co-editor: Essays on Brecht: Theatre and Politics, 1974, 79; editor: spl. issue Comparative Lit. Studies, 1973; contbr. articles to profl. publs. Fulbright scholar, 1956-58; Am. Philos. Soc. research grantee, 1971; Am. Council Learned Socs. travel grantee; recipient various research and travel grants Pa. State U. and U. Ill.; assoc. Center for Advanced Study, U. Ill., 1975; research grantee Alliance Francaise, 1978; recipient undergrad. instructional U. Ill., 1967-68; co-recipient course devel. grant Deutscher Akademischer Austauschdienst, 1982, U.S. Dept. Edn., 1983. Mem. Am. Assn. Tchrs. of German, Am. Comparative Lit. Assn., Internat. Comparative Lit. Assn., MLA, Internat. Brecht Soc., Soc. for Exile Studies, Soc. for German-Am. Studies, Delta Phi Alpha, Phi Kappa Phi. Home: 2006 Burlison Dr Urbana IL 61801 Office: Dept Germanic Langs and Lits U Ill 3072 Fgn Langs Bldg 707 S Mathews Ave Urbana IL 61801

KNUTH, DONALD ERVIN, computer science educator; b. Milw., Jan. 10, 1938; s. Ervin Henry and Louise Marie (Bohning) K.; m. Nancy Jill Carter, June 24, 1961; children: John Martin, Jennifer Sierra. B.S., Case Inst. Tech., 1960, M.S., 1960; Ph.D., Calif. Inst. Tech., 1963. Asst. prof., then asso. prof. math. Calif. Inst. Tech., 1963-68; prof. computer sci. Stanford U., 1968—; guest prof. math. U. Oslo, 1972-73; cons. Burroughs Corp., 1960-68. Author: The Art of Computer Programming, vol. 1, 1968, vol. 2, 1969, vol. 3, 1973, Surreal Numbers, 1974, Mariages Stables, 1976, Tex and Metafont, 1980; Editor jours. Recipient Nat. medal of sci., 1979; Guggenheim fellow, 1972-73. Fellow Am. Acad. Arts and Scis., Brit. Computer Soc; mem. Nat. Acad. Scis., Nat. Acad. Engring., Assn. Computing Machinery (Grace Murray Hopper award 1971, Alan M. Turing award 1974), Math. Assn. Am. (Lester R. Ford award 1975), IEEE Computer Soc. (McDowell award 1980, Computer Pioneer award 1982), Am. Math. Soc., Soc. Indsl. and Applied Math., Am. Guild Organists. Lutheran. Patentee in field. Home: 1063 Vernier Pl Stanford CA 94305 Office: Computer Sci Dept Stanford Univ Stanford CA 94305

KNUTH, ELDON LUVERNE, engineering educator; b. Luana, Iowa, May 10, 1925; s. Alvin W. and Amanda M. (Becker) K.; m. Marie O. Parrat, Sept. 10, 1954 (div. 1973); children: Stephen B., Dale L., Margot O., Lynette M.; m. Margaret I. Nicholson, Dec. 30, 1973. B.S., Purdue U., 1949, M.S., 1950; Ph.D. (Guggenheim fellow), Calif. Inst. Tech., 1954. Aerothermodynamics group leader Aerophysics Devel. Corp., 1953-56; asso. research engr. dept. engring. UCLA, 1956-59, asso. prof. engring., 1960-65, prof. engring. and applied sci., 1965—, head chem., nuclear thermal div. dept. engring., 1963-65, chmn. energy kinetics dept., 1969-75, head molecular-beam lab., 1961—; Gen. chmn. Heat Transfer and Fluid Mechanics Inst., 1959; vis. scientist, von Humboldt fellow Max-Planck Inst. für Strömungsforschung, Göttingen, West Germany, 1975-76. Author: Introduction to Statistical Thermodynamics, 1966; also numerous articles. Served with AUS, 1943-45. Mem. AIAA, Am. Soc. Engring. Edn., Am. Inst. Chem. Engrs., Combustion Inst., Soc. Engring. Sci., AAAS, Am. Phys. Soc., Am. Vacuum Soc., Sigma Xi, Tau Beta Pi, Gamma Alpha Rho, Pi Tau Sigma, Sigma Delta Chi, Pi Kappa Phi. Club: Gimlet (Lafayette, Ind.). Patentee radial-flow molecular pump. Home: 18085 Boris Dr Encino CA 91316 Office: Sch Engring and Applied Sci U Calif 405 Hilgard Ave Los Angeles CA 90024

KNUTSON, DAVID HARRY, lawyer, minerals co. exec.; b. St. Paul, Dec. 17, 1934; s. Harry E. and Violet I. (Ekberg) K.; m. Kirsten Birgit Eriksen, Aug. 20, 1977. A.B. cum laude, Harvard U., 1956, LL.B., 1961; Am.-Scandinavian Found. fellow; Fulbright travel grantee, U. Copenhagen, Denmark, 1961-62. Bar: Minn. bar 1962, N.Y. State bar 1963. Asso. atty. firm Lord, Day & Lord, N.Y.C., 1962-69; staff atty. Freeport Minerals Co., N.Y.C., 1969-70, asst. sec., 1970-75, sec., 1975—, Freeport-McMoRan Inc., N.Y.C., 1980—. Mem. Assn. Bar City N.Y., Am. Bar Assn., Am.-Scandinavian Found. Lutheran. Club: Harvard (N.Y.C.). Home: 201 E 79th St Apt 15G New York NY 10021 Office: Freeport McMoRan Inc 200 Park Ave New York NY 10166

KNUTSON, RONALD DALE, economist, educator; b. Montevideo, Minn., July 12, 1940; s. Claus and Alice (Peterson) K.; m. Sharron DeGree, Sept. 16, 1961; children—Scott, Ryan, Nicole. B.S., U. Minn., 1962, Ph.D., 1967; M.S., Pa. State U., 1963. Prof. Purdue U., 1967-73; staff economist Agrl. Mktg. Service, USDA, Washington, 1971-73; adminstr. Farmer Coop. Service, 1973-75; prof. dept. agrl. econs. Tex. A. and M. U., 1975—; Econ./antitrust cons. Dart and Kraft, State of Wash., Heublein Corp., Farmland Industries, Foremost-McKesson, Am. Rice Inc., Southland Corp., State of Minn., GAO; research cons. Milk Industry Found., GAO, White House Food and Nutrition Study, Nat. Acad. Sci., Office Tech. Assessment U.S. Congress, Nat. Commn. on Productivity Exec. Office Pres.; project leader Multinat. Coop. Potential; chmn. milk pricing adv. com. U.S. Dept. Agr.; mem. Pres. Reagan's Transition Task Force for Agr., 1980-81; mem. agrl. policy adv. com. Sec. Agr. and Trade Rep. Author: (with J.B. Penn and William T. Boehm) Agricultural and Food Policy. Mem. Am. Agrl. Econs. Assn., Sigma Xi, Omicron Delta Epsilon, Gamma Sigma Delta, Phi Tau Sigma. Home: 1011 Rose Circle College Station TX 77840 Office: Tex A and M Univ College Station TX 77843

KNUTSON, WAYNE SHAFER, theater and English educator; b. Sisseton, S.D., June 1, 1926; s. Edward and Julia (Sanden) K.; m. Esther Marie Johnstad, July 30, 1950; children: David Wayne, Jon Eric, Jane Marie. B.A., Augustana Coll., 1950; M.A., U. S.D., 1951; Ph.D., U. Denver, 1956. Purchasing agt. First Nat. Bank Black Hills, Rapid City, S.D., 1951-52; prof. speech and dramatic arts, also dir. Univ. Theater U. S.D., Vermillion, 1952-66, prof. English, 1966-73, chmn. dept., 1966-71, dean Coll. Fine Arts, 1972-80, v.p. acad. affairs, 1980-82, prof. theater and English, 1982—; assoc. dir., bus. mgr. Black Hills Playhouse, Inc., Custer, S.D., 1952-63; assoc. dir. NSF Honors Inst., U. S.D., summers 1964, 65; dir. merger activities U. S.D.-S. State Coll., 1971. Author: lyric dramas The Mirrored Maze, 1957, Dream Valley, 1959; opera Prosopa, 1964, Arabesque, 1967; Editor, contbr. to: Dramatics, 1964. Mem. lit. com. S.D. Fine Arts Council, 1968-70, mem. council, 1970-78, chmn. council, 1971-78; mem. lit. panel Nat. Endowment for Arts, 1975-77; mem. nat. adv. council Nat. Black Music Collegium and Competition; trustee Shrine to Music Mus. Found., 1975-80; hon. bd. dirs. Black Hills Playhouse, Inc., 1977—. Served with U.S. Mcht. Marine, 1944-46; Served with AUS, 1946-47; Served with AUS, Korean occupation. Recipient Best Tchr. award U. S.D., 1968; Harrington lectr. U. S.D. Coll. Arts and Scis., 1972. Mem. Nat. Coll. Players, Eta Sigma Phi (hon.), Omicron Delta Kappa (hon.). Lutheran. Home: 1153 Valley View Dr Vermillion SD 57069

KNUTZEN, DONALD LEE, consumer products company executive; b. Edgerton, Wis., July 8, 1939; s. Malcolm Roland and Kathryn H. (Uglow) K.; m. Helen Wagner, June 9, 1962; children: Anders Mark, Erik Lief. B.S., U. Wis., 1962; M.B.A., Wharton Grad. Sch. Fin. and Commerce, 1965. Product mgr. snacks Gen. Mills Inc., 1966-70; v.p. mktg. Parker Bros., Salem, Mass., 1970-74; v.p., gen. mgr. Betty Crocker div. Gen. Mills, Inc., 1974-80, v.p., gen. mgr. New Bus. div., 1980—; dir. Williams Hardware, Mpls. Campaign cabinet Mpls. United Way, 1982, 83; bd. dirs. MedCenter Health Plan, St. Louis Park, Minn., 1979—; exec. com. Boy's Club, Mpls., 1978—; trustee St. Luke Presbyn. Ch., Wayzata, Minn., 1980—. Served to 1st lt. U.S. Army, 1962-64. Home: 17900 Shavers Lake Dr Wayzata MN 55391 Office: Gen Mills Inc 9200 Wayzata Blvd Golden Valley MN 55426

KNUTZEN, OWEN A., supt. schs.; b. Cedar Bluffs, Nebr., Aug. 13, 1924; s. Albert and Alfrieda K.; m. LuAnn Williams, Oct. 14, 1945; children—Mary (Mrs. Alan Barton), Jeff, Andy. B.S., U. Nebr., 1947; M.A., Columbia U., 1950, Ed.D., 1960. Tchr., prin. Fairmont (Nebr.) High Sch., 1947-49; tchr. Trinity Sch., N.Y.C., 1949-50; adminstrv. intern Omaha Pub. Schs., 1950-51, asst. to supt., 1951-55, dir. adminstrn., 1955-56, adminstrv. asst., dir. adminstrn., 1956-59, asst. supt. for adminstrn., 1959-60, asst. supt. adminstrn. and personnel, 1960-63, asso. supt., 1963-67, supt. schs., 1967—. Editorial adv. bd.: Edn. Digest, 1973-76. Mem. at large nat. council Boy Scouts Am., 1972-75; pres. Met. Omaha Ednl. Broadcasting Assn.; mem. community liaison council Meyer Children's Rehab. Inst.; Bd. dirs. United Community Services, 1969-79; mem. pres.'s council Creighton U., 1969-74; mem. pres.'s adv. bd. Omaha C. of C., 1974—. Served with USAAF, 1942-46. Mem. Am. Assn. Sch. Adminstrs. (bd. tellers 1972-75, chmn. 1974-75), Nebr. Assn. Sch. Adminstrs. (pres. 1972-73), Omaha Assn. Sch. Adminstrs., Nat., Nebr., Omaha edn. assns., Neb. Council Sch. Adminstrs. (exec. com. 1971-74, resolutions com. 1972-75), Large City Supts. (chmn. 1975-76), Nebr. P.T.A. (life), Nat. Congress P.T.A. (life). Presbyn. (edler). Office: 3902 Davenport St Omaha NE 68131

KO, HSIEN CHING, elec. engr.; b. Taiwan, Formosa, Apr. 28, 1928; came to U.S., 1952, naturalized, 1966; s. Tzu Lu and Chuang (Feng) K.; m. Pi-Yu Chang, Sept. 17, 1955; children—Stella I., Paula C., Benjamin S. B.S., Nat. Taiwan U., 1951; M.S., Ohio State U., 1953, Ph.D., 1955. Research engr. Radio Wave Research Lab., Taiwan, 1951-52; asst. dir. Radio Obs., Ohio State U., Columbus, 1955-67, asst. prof., 1956-59, asso. prof., 1959-63, prof. elec. engring. and astronomy, 1963-77, prof., chmn. dept. elec. engring., 1977—; mem. nat. adminstrv. com. Antenna and Propagation Soc., 1962-69. Asso. editor: Radio Sci, 1967-75; Contbr. articles to sci. and engring. jours. Recipient Charles E. McQuigg award Ohio State U., 1977. Fellow IEEE, Royal Astron. Soc.; mem. Am. Astron. Soc., Internat. Union Radio Sci. (U.S. nat. com.), Am. Soc. Engring. Edn., Sigma Xi, Eta Kappa Nu. Office: 205 Dreese Lab 2015 Neil Ave Columbus OH 43210

KO, WEN-HSIUNG, electrical engineering educator; b. Shang-Hong, Fukien, China, Apr. 12, 1923; came to U.S., 1954, naturalized, 1963; s. Sing-Ming and Sou-Ye (Kao) K.; m. Christina Chen, Oct. 12, 1957; children: Kathleen, Janet, Linda, Alexander. B.S. in E.E. (Tan-Ka-Kee fellow), Nat. Amoy U., Fukien, China, 1946; M.S., Case Inst. Tech., 1956, Ph.D., 1959. Engr., then sr. engr. Taiwan Telecommunication Adminstrn., 1946-54; mem. faculty Case Inst. Tech., Cleve., 1956—, prof. elec. engring., 1967—, prof. elec. and biomed. engring., 1970—, dir. engring. design center, 1970-83; cons. Conoflow Corp., IBM, Diamond Alkali, NIH, 1966-76. Fellow IEEE; mem. Instrument Soc. Am., Bio-Med. Engring. Soc., Sigma Xi, Eta Kappa Nu. Home: 1356 Forest Hills Blvd Cleveland Heights OH 44118 Office: Electronics Design Center Case Western Res U Cleveland OH 44106

KOBAK, JAMES BENEDICT, consultant; b. St. Louis, Mar. 4, 1921; s. Edgar and Evelyn (Hubert) K.; m. Hope McEldowney, June 13, 1942; children—James Benedict, John D. (dec.), Thomas M. B.S., Harvard U., 1942; postgrad. in accounting, Pace Coll., 1946-49. C.P.A., N.Y., La., Union S.Africa. Asso. J.K. Lasser & Co., N.Y.C., 1946-71, partner, 1954-64, adminstrv. partner, 1964-71; internat. adminstrv. partner Lasser, Harmood Banner, Dunwoody, N.Y.C., 1964-71; pres. James B. Kobak, Inc., Darien, Conn., 1971—; partner James B. Kobak Bus. Models Co.; founder Kobak Open; dir. Robbins Co., Miller Communications, Inc., Gifted and Talented, Human Resource Services Inc., Venture Mag. Inc. Contbr. articles to profl. publs. Chmn. mag. com., mem. communications com., bus. com. Nat. council Boy Scouts Am.; co-founder, sec.-treas. John D. Kobak Appalachian Edn. Found., Darien; trustee Hill Sch., Pottstown, Pa. Served to capt., F.A. AUS, 1942-46. Mem. Am. Inst. C.P.A.s, N.Y. State Soc. C.P.A.s, Transvall Soc. Accountants. Presbyterian. Clubs: Econ., Harvard (N.Y.C.); Wee Burn Country (Darien); Univ. (Chgo.); Accountants Am. Home and Office: 774 Hollow Tree Ridge Rd Darien CT 06820 also Saint Croix VI 00840

KOBAK, MARTIN, stock brokerage executive; b. Bklyn., Sept. 7, 1939; s. Samuel and Esther (Goldman) K.; m. Carol Fredericks, Sept. 12, 1965; children: Douglas, Gregory, Andrew. B.S., U. Pa., 1961. Account exec. Prudential-Bache Securities, Inc., Phila., 1962-69, Br. mgr., v.p., 1969-74, regional dir., sr. v.p., 1974—. Mem. Phila. Stock Exchange, Phila. Bond Club, Phila. Securities Assn. Home: 1438 Gunpowder Dr Rydal PA 19046 Office: Prudential-Bache Securities Inc 1700 Market St Philadelphia PA 19103

KOBAYASHI, HISASHI, computer scientist, computer manufacturing executive; b. Tokyo, June 13, 1938; U.S., 1965; s. Kyuzo and Yoshie (Obi) K.; m. Masaye Okubo. B.S., U. Tokyo, 1961, M.S., 1963; M.A., Princeton U., 1966, Ph.D., 1967. Radar system designer Toshiba, Kawasaki, Japan, 1963-65; mem. research staff IBM, Yorktown Heights, N.Y., 1967—; dir. Japan Sci. Inst. IBM Japan Ltd., 1982—; vis. asst. prof. UCLA, 1969-70; vis. prof. U. Hawaii, 1975, Tech. U. Darmstadt, W. Ger., 1979-80; cons. prof. Stanford U., 1976; Internat. prof. U. Libre de Bruxelles, Belgium, 1980; mem. computer sci. panel NRC, 1981—. Author: Modeling and Analysis, 1978; editor-in-chief: Performance Eval., 1981—; asso. editor: IEEE Trans Infor. Theory, 1980-83; contbr. articles to profl. jours. Recipient David Sarnoff award; RCA, 1960; IBM Invention award, 1971, 73; Outstanding Contbn. award, 1975; Humboldt award, 1979; IFIP Silver Core award, 1980. Fellow IEEE; mem. Assn. Computing Machinery, Internat. Union Radio Sci. (vice chmn. Commn. C 1978-81), Internat. Fedn. Info. Processing (chmn. working group 1982—). Patentee communication systems. Home: 1323 Judy Rd Mohegan Lake NY 10547 Office: IBM Research Center PO Box 218 Yorktown Heights NY 10598

KOBAYASHI, RIKI, chemical engineer, educator; b. Webster, Tex., May 13, 1924; s. Mitsutaro and Moto (Shigeta) K.; m. Barbara Joan Stevens, June 1, 1957; children: James Brock, Alec Stevens; m. Lee Mary Parker Lovejoy; children: Susan, Anne. B.S. in Chem. Engring, Rice U., 1944; M.S., U. Mich., 1947, Ph.D. in Chem. Engring, 1951. Mem. faculty dept. chem. engring. Rice U., Houston, 1951—, prof., 1965—, Calder prof. chem. engring., 1967—; cons. chem. engr., 1952—; D.L. Katz distinguished lectr. U. Mich., 1975. Author: (with others) Handbook of Natural Gas Engineering, 1959; Contbr. articles to profl. jours. Served with AUS, 1945-46. Recipient meritorious award in cryogenic engring. Cyrogenic Engring. Conf. Com., 1966. Fellow Am. Inst. Chem. Engrs., Am. Inst. Chemists; mem. Am. Inst. Physics, Am. Chem. Soc., Am. Inst. Mining, and Metall. Engrs., Sigma Xi, Alpha Chi Sigma, Tau Beta Pi, Phi Lambda Upsilon, Phi Kappa Phi. Unitarian. Home: 348 Piney Point Houston TX 77024 Office: PO Box 1892 Rice Univ Houston TX 77251

KOBAYASHI, SHIRO, mechanical engineer, educator; b. Gotsu, Japan, Feb. 21, 1924; s. Toraji and Chisao (Shimizu) K.; m. Suzue Yamaguchi, May 15, 1961. B.S., Tokyo U., 1946; M.S., U. Calif., Berkeley, 1957, Ph.D., 1960. Mem. faculty dept. mech. engring. U. Calif., Berkeley, 1960—, prof., 1968—; vis. prof. Ohio State U., 1967; Miller Research prof. U. Calif., 1977. Contbr. numerous articles to profl. jours; mem. editorial bd. profl. jours. Recipient Blackall award ASME, 1962. Mem. ASME, Nat. Acad. Engring., Am. Soc. Metals, Soc. Mfg. Engrs. (Gold Medal 1983), Internat. Instn. for Prodn. Engring. Research. Home: 414 Sea View Dr El Cerrito CA 94530 Office: Dept Mech Engring Univ of Calif Berkeley CA 94720

KOBER, DIETER, orchestra conductor, educator; b. Ger., Jan. 2, 1920; naturalized, 1942; s. Albert B. and Hedwig (Fink) K. B.Mus. Edn., U. Nebr., 1947; Mus.M., Chgo. Mus. Coll., 1948, D.F.A. in Musicology, 1950; postgrad., U. Chgo., 1949-50; conducting cert., Mozarteum, Salzburg, Austria, 1952. Instr. Chgo. Mus. Coll., 1949; prof. Chgo. City Coll., 1950. Founder, condr., Collegiate Sinfonietta of Chgo., 1950; founder, Chgo. Chamber Orch., 1952; condr., 1952—; music dir., Chgo. Chamber Orch. Assn., 1962—; dir. music, Art Inst. Chgo., 1951-61; producer: TV series Invitation to Music, WTTW, Chgo., 1957; spl. prodns., WBBM-TV, Chgo., 1962—; organizer, dir.: Lakeside Promenade Concerts, Chgo. Park Dist., 1963-78; producer, host Music of Chamber Orch., Sta. WNIB, 1972—; Asst. editor: Handbook of Music History; Rec. artist, Vox Records. Mem. Ill. Sesquicentennial Commn., 1968. Served with U.S. Army, 1942-45. Mem. Internat. Soc. Contemporary Music (dir. Chgo. chpt.), Am. String Tchrs. Assn., AAUP, Carl Nielsen Soc. Am. (dir.), Phi Mu Alpha Sinfonia, Phi Beta (nat. patron). Clubs: Cliff Dwellers, Arts (Chgo.). Office: 410 S Michigan Ave Chicago IL 60605

KOBLER, RAYMOND, concert master. B. Mus., Ind. U., Performer's cert; M. Mus., Cath. U. Am. Assoc. concertmaster Cleve. Orch.; concertmaster San Francisco Symphony; artist-in-residence area music festivals, New Coll. Music festival, Sarasota, Fla. Soloist: in concertos by Glazunov, Vivaldi, Mozart, Prokofiev, Tchaikovsky, Sibelius; performer, Carnegie Hall; concertmaster, Nat. Ballet Orch.; mem. Nat. Symphony; 1st asst. concertmaster, soloist: Balt. Symphony; appeared in: various concerts throughout U.S. and Can.; UN Benefit Concert in Netherlands Antilles; soloist: (U.S. premiere) Sir Michael Tippett Triple Concerto, (locat. San Francisco). Served with USMC. Office: Davies Symphony Hall San Francisco CA 94102

KOBRINE, ARTHUR IRWIN, neurosurgeon; b. Chgo., Oct. 9, 1943; s. Maurice William and Katherine (Lovrencic) K.; m. Cynthia Elizabeth, Apr. 19, 1969; children—Nicole, Steven. B.A. on Chemistry, Northwestern U., 1964, M.D., 1968; Ph.D. in Physiology, George Washington U., 1979. Diplomate: Am. Bd. Neurol. Surgery. Intern U. Hosp., Ann Arbor, Mich., 1968-69; resident in neurosurgery Walter Reed Gen. Hosp., Washington, 1970-73, asst. chief neurosurgery service, 1973-75; prin. research investigator Armed Forces Radiobiology Research Inst., Bethesda, Md., 1973—; asso. prof. neurosurgery George Washington U., Washington, 1977-79, prof., 1979—; mem. staff Washington Hosp. Center, Children's Hosp., Nat. Med. Center; attending physician and surgeon for James Brady, 1981. Contbr. articles to med. and sci. jours. Served with M.C. U.S. Army, 1970-75. Recipient Raymond F. Metcalf award U.S. Army Med. Dept., 1971. Mem. Am. Assn. Neurol. Surgeons, Soc. Neurol. Surgeons, Congress Neurol. Surgeons, Research Soc. Neurol. Surgery, AMA, A.C.S., Soc. Neurosci., Am. Physiol. Soc., Brit. Brain Research Assn. (hon.), Alpha Omega Alpha. Office: 2150 Pennsylvania Ave NW Washington DC 20037

KOBS, JAMES FRED, advertising agency executive; b. Chgo., IL, June 27, 1938; s. Fred Charles and Ann (Ganser) K.; m. Nadine Schumacher, May 18, 1963; children: Karen, Kathleen, Kenneth. B.S. in Journalism, U. Ill., 1960. Copywriter Rylander Co., Chgo., 1960-62; mng. dir. Success Mag., Chgo., 1963-65; mail order mgr. Am. People Press, Westmont, Ill., 1966-67; exec. v.p. Stone & Adler Advt., Chgo., 1967-78; pres. Kobs & Brady Advt., Inc., Chgo., 1978—; guest lectr. U. Wis., U. Ill., NYU. Author: Profitable Direct Marketing, 24 Ways to Improve Your Direct Mail Results, 99 Proven Direct Response Offers; contbr. articles to periodicals. Recipient numerous local and nat. advt. awards. Mem. Direct Mktg. Assn. (dir., Silver & Gold Mailbox, Gold Medallion, Gold Echo), Chgo. Assn. Direct Mktg. (past pres.), Alpha Delta Sigma. Office: 625 N Michigan Ave Chgo IL 60611 *

KOBUS, THOMAS GARY, association executive; b. Niagara Falls, N.Y., Nov. 12, 1945; s. Raymond Myron and Mary (Bednarski) K. B.A., SUNY, 1964, J.D. with honors, 1969; M.B.A., U. Pa., 1966. Bar: N.Y. 1970, D.C. 1979, U.S. Supreme Ct. 1973. Asst. dist. atty., Buffalo, 1970-73, counsel to mayor, 1973-78; asso. exec. dir. Am. Pharm. Assn., Washington, 1978; counsel Temp. Commn. Mgmt. and Productivity in Public Sector, Albany, N.Y., 1978-79; dir. intergovtl. affairs U.S. Dept. Transp., Washington, 1979-80; exec. v.p. Nat. Parking Assn., Washington, 1980—, The Parking Industry Inst. Treas. Erie County Indsl. Devel. Agy., Buffalo, 1976. Samuel S. Fels fellow U. Pa., 1964-66. Mem. N.Y. State Bar Assn., Am. Bar Assn., Nat. Council Urban Econ. Devel., Am. Soc. Assn. Execs., Washington Soc. Assn. Execs. Democrat. Roman Catholic. Clubs: Nat. Democratic, U. Pa. Alumni (v.p.). Home: 11919 Fallen Holly Ct Great Falls VA Office: 2000 K St NW Suite 350 Washington DC 20006

KOCEN, JOEL EVAN, mfg. co. exec.; b. Richmond, Va., Nov. 14, 1936; s. Wilbur and Lilian (Levitz) K.; m. Jo Ann Pollack, Dec. 29, 1957; children—Bryan, Loren. B.S., Washington and Lee U., 1959, LL.B., 1961; LL.M., N.Y. U., 1969. Bar: Va. bar 1961. Mem. firm Cohen, Cox & Kelly, Richmond, 1961-62; tax accountant Reynolds Metals Co., Richmond, 1962-65; sr. tax analyst Anaconda Co., N.Y.C., 1965-69; tax mgr. S. D. Leidesdorf & Co., N.Y.C., 1969; with Sybron Corp., Rochester, N.Y., 1969—, asst. controller, 1970-74, treas., 1974-80; v.p. fin., treas. Gleason Works, Rochester, 1980-82; v.p. fin. Kerr Glass Mfg. Co., Los Angeles, 1982; v.p. fin. and adminstrn. Talandic Research Corp., Pasadena, Calif., 1983—; mem. adv. bd. dirs. Lincoln First Bank of Rochester, 1975-79, chmn., 1978-79. Mem. N.Y. State Bus. Adv. Com. on Mgmt. Improvement, 1970-74; bd. dirs., treas. Genesee Region Home Care Assn., Rochester, 1979. Mem. Am. Bar Assn. Jewish. Home: 2015 Glen Springs Rd Pasadena CA 91107

KOCH, ADOLPH MEYER, educator, psychologist; b. Austria, Poland, June 18 1908; s. Harry and Dora (Roth) K.; m. Evelyn Friedberg, June 25, 1939; children—Marlene Harriet, Bruce Stuart. A.B., George Washington U., 1930; A.M., Columbia, 1931, Ph.D., 1935; LL.B., St. John's U., 1937; J.S.D., St. Lawrence U., 1939. Rockefeller Inst., 1931-32; instr. psychology Essex County Jr. Coll., Newark, 1933-36, prof. psychology, asst. dean, 1937-38, dean, 1938-39, pres., 1939-44, Essex Coll. Medicine and Surgery, 1944-46; instr. psychology Yonkers Coll., 1936-37; instr. Broward County Adult Edn. Div., 1955-58; instr. psychology U. Miami Extension Div., 1958-60, Jr. Coll. Broward County, 1960-62, dir. instl. research, 1966—; lectr. psychology Broward Jr. Coll., 1968—, Nova U., Fort Lauderdale, 1978; practicing psychologist, 1946—; newspaper columnist. Contbr. articles to profl. jours. Fellow A.A.A.S., Am. Psychol. Assn.; mem. Fla. Psychol. Assn., Fla. Acad. Scis., Broward County Psychol. Assn. (pres.), Fla. Ednl. Research Assn., Southeastern Psychol. Assn., Am. Acad. Polit. and Social Sci., George Washington U. Alumni Orgn., Sigma Xi. Club: Fort Lauderdale Country. Address: 2319 NE 15th Terr Ft Lauderdale FL 33305

KOCH, ALBIN COOPER, lawyer; b. Pitts., Aug. 25, 1933; s. John Lester and Theodosia (Cooper) K.; m. Harriet W. Woodworth, June 24, 1960. B.A., Yale U., 1956; J.D., Harvard U., 1959. Bar: Calif., D.C., Mass.; cert. tax specialist, Calif. Assoc. Silverstein & Mullens, Washington, 1963-68, ptnr., 1968-72, Agnew, Miller & Carlson, Los Angeles, 1973-75; v.p., asst. gen. tax counsel Bank Am., San Francisco, 1976-80; ptnr. Morrison & Foerster, Los Angeles, 1980—. Chmn. Southwest Neighborhood Assembly, Washington, 1966-67; mem. Calif. bd. Common Cause, 1974-76; trustee Human Family Ednl. and Charitable Inst., 1974—; v.p., mgr., bd. dirs. Pasadena Chamber Orch., 1983—. Mem. ABA (chmn. Tax Sect. banking and sav. insts. com., vice chmn. Urban State and Local Govt. Law Sect. taxes and revenues com.), Los Angeles County Bar Assn. (chmn. Tax Sect. income tax com. 1982-83, sec.-treas. Tax Sect. 1983—). Democrat. Episcopalian. Club: los Angeles Athletic. Home: 1506 E California Blvd Pasadena CA 91106 Office: Morrison & Foerster 333 S Grand Ave (3800) Los Angeles CA 90071

KOCH, ARTHUR LOUIS, microbiologist, educator; b. St. Paul, Oct. 25, 1925; s. Arthur Louis and Avis (Durant) K.; m. Ruth Emma Kunst, Aug. 30, 1947; children: Kathryn Ann, Walter Edwin.; m. Stine Marie Levy, Mar. 5, 1983. B.S. in Chemistry, Calif. Inst. Tech., 1948; Ph.D. in Biochemistry, U. Chgo., 1951. Research asso., instr. dept. biochemistry U. Chgo., 1951-52, 53-56; asso. scientist div. biology and medicine Argonne (Ill.) Nat. Lab., 1952-56; asst. prof. biochemistry Coll. Medicine U. Fla., 1956-59, asso. prof., 1959-60, asso. prof. biochemistry and microbiology, 1960-63, prof., 1963-67; prof. microbiology Ind. U., 1967—, prof. biology, 1977—; cons. NASA. Contbr. numerous articles to profl. jours. USPHS Spl. Regular fellow Institut Pasteur, 1961-62; Guggenheim fellow, 1961, 81; Argonne Univ. Assn. Disting. appointee, 1974. Home: 3420 Adair Ln Bloomington IN 47401

KOCH, CARL, architect; b. Milw., May 11, 1912; s. Albert Carl and Ruth (Chamberlain) K.; m. Persis White, Dec. 23, 1934; children: Cyrus, Otto, Molly, Carl; m. Jean Emery, Dec. 24, 1951; children: David, Samuel, Elizabeth. B.A. cum laude, Harvard U., 1934, M.Arch., 1937; Bacon travelling fellow, 1938-39. With Sven Markelius, Sweden, 1937, Gropius and Breuer, 1938; sr. architect Nat. Housing Agy., 1942-44; prin. Carl Koch & Assocs., Inc., Boston, 1939—; former lectr. MIT. Author: (with Andy Lewis) At Home with Tomorrow, 1958; also articles.; prin. works include Fitchburg (Mass.) Youth Library; series houses for, Techbuilt, Inc., motor lodges, Howard Johnson Co., portable housing, USAF, research and devel. project, Armco Corp., Ferro Corp., Reynolds Metals, Nat. Steel, Lockheed Aircraft; master planner, USAF, concrete bldg. systems design, urban renewal and town planning projects in, N.Y.C., Detroit, Boston, Balt., Maine. Tech. Bd. dirs. Boston Ednl. Marine Exchange, Boston Harbor Assn. Served to lt. USNR, 1944-46. Recipient honor award for Acorn House AIA, 1949, Bronze medal Phila. chpt. AIA, 1951, Gold medal N.Y. Archtl. League, 1953, 3 awards for Techbuilt House Parents mag., 1954, award of merit for Techbuilt House, 1956; ALA-AIA Nat. Book Com. 1st honor award, 1963; Honor award Boston Arts Festival, 1963; Frank P. Brown medal Franklin Inst., 1967; Indsl. Arts medal AIA, 1969; Quarter Century citation Builders Research Adv. Bd., 1977. Fellow AIA; mem. Mass. Assn. Architects, Boston Soc. Architects, Bldg. Research Inst. Home: 52 Holden Ln Concord MA 01742 Office: 54 Lewis Wharf Boston MA 02110

KOCH, CARL GALLAND, lawyer; b. Seattle, May 26, 1916; s. Samuel and Cora (Dinkelspiel) K.; m. Joan R. Smith, Nov. 26, 1944 (dec. Apr. 1971); children—Carlyn Joan, Robert B.; m. Joy Jacobs, June 15, 1973. B.A., U. Wash., 1938, J.D., 1940. Bar: Wash. bar 1940. Since practiced in, Seattle; partner firm Karr, Tuttle, Koch, Campbell, Mawer & Morrow (and predecessors), 1940—; lectr. 7th Ann. Tax Forum, U. Puget Sound, 1961. Mem. candidates investigating com. Seattle Municipal League, 1958-70; mem. child study div. Health and Welfare Council, Seattle, United Good Neighbors, Seattle, 1951-52; chmn. Seattle chpt. Am. Jewish Com., 1954-55, mem. exec. com., 1950—, mem. Western regional adv. com., 1964—, mem. nat. exec. bd., 1966—, bd. govs., 1977—; v.p. Federated Jewish Fund and Council Seattle, 1964, bd. dirs., 1950—; mem. regional bd. NCCJ, 1954—; trustee Jewish Publ. Soc. Am., 1971-78. Served to 1st lt. AUS, 1942-46. Life master Am. Contract Bridge League; mem. Am., Wash., Seattle-King County bar assns., Am. Judicature Soc., Seattle Estate Planning Council, Western Pension Conf., Nat. Found. Health, Welfare and Pensions Plans, Zeta Beta Tau (pres. Alpha Mu chpt. 1937-38), Pi Tau (pres. Seattle 1935), Phi Alpha Delta. Clubs: College (Seattle); Glendale Country (Bellevue, Wash.) (pres. 1965, bd. dirs. 1957-60, 63-66); Tamarisk Country (Rancho Mirage, Calif.)). Home: 6034 Lakeshore Dr Seattle WA 98118 Office: 1111 3d Ave Suite 2500 Seattle WA 98101

KOCH, CHARLES DE GANAHL, corporation executive; b. Wichita, Kans., Nov. 1, 1935; s. Fred Chase and Mary Clementine (Robinson) K.; children—Elizabeth, Robinson, Charles Chase. B.S. in Gen. Engring, Mass. Inst. Tech., 1957, M.S. in Mech. Engring, 1958, 1959. Engr. Arthur D. Little, Inc., Cambridge, Mass., 1959-61; v.p. Koch Engring Co., Inc., Wichita, 1961-63, pres., 63-71, chmn., 1967-78; pres. Koch Industries, Inc., Wichita, 1966-74, chmn., 1967—; dir. First Nat. Bank Wichita, Coleman Co., Inc., Wichita. Bd. dirs. Inst. for Humane Studies, Inc., Cato Inst., Nat. Taxpayers Union; chmn. Council for a Competitive Economy. Mem. Mt. Pelerin Soc. Clubs: Wichita Country, New York Athletic. Office: PO Box 2256 Wichita KS 67201

KOCH, CHARLES JOSEPH, banker; b. Cleve., Oct. 29, 1919; s. Charles Frank and Mary (Cunat) K.; m. Elizabeth Rusch, May 7, 1945; children: Charles John, John David. B.S., Case Inst. Tech., 1941. Dir. space div. Martin Marietta Corp., Balt., 1941-67; mgr. advanced program McDonnell Douglas Corp., St. Louis, 1967-68; chmn. bd., chief exec. officer The First Fed. Savs. Bank, Cleve., 1980—, also dir.; dir. Fed. Home Loan Bank Cin.; instr. Johns Hopkins U., U. Md., 1943-47; Mem. adv. com. NASA, 1956-67. Adv. bd. St. Alexis Hosp.; bd. dirs. Am. Cancer Soc. Mem. U.S. Savs. and Loan League, Northeastern Ohio Savs. and Loan League (Treas., past pres.), Nat. Council Savs. Instns., Ohio Savs. and Loan League (past chmn., bd. dirs.), Am. Mgmt. Assn., Greater Cleve. Growth Assn., Sigma Xi, Phi Kappa Theta, Tau Beta Pi. Clubs: Rotarian., Union, Clevelander, Cleve. Athletic, Shaker Heights Country (Cleve.). Office: 1250 Superior Ave Cleveland OH 44114

KOCH, DAVID ANDREW, manufacturing company executive; b. June 17, 1930; m. Barbara Koch; 4 children. Student, U. Notre Dame, 1948-51; B.A., Coll. St. Thomas, 1952. Investment counselor Kalman & Co., 1954-56; with Graco Inc., Mpls., 1956—, exec. v.p. to pres., 1962—; dir. Conwed Corp. Trustee Coll. St. Thomas, Dunwoody Indsl. Inst.; bd. dirs. Greater Mpls. Jr. Achievement. Served with USAF, 1952-56. Mem. Young Pres.'s Orgn., Greater Mpls. C. of C. (past pres. bd. dirs.). Home: 2015 Meeting St Wayzata MN 55391 Office: 60 11th Ave NE Minneapolis MN 55413

KOCH, DONALD LEIGH, economist, banker; b. Long Island, N.Y., Sept. 17, 1946; s. David and Ruby K.; m. Christina Kirkman, Sept. 7, 1968; 1 son, Christian. B.A., Principia Coll., 1968; M.A., Trinity Coll., Hartford, Conn., 1971; grad. advanced mgmt. program, Harvard U., 1983. Sr. analyst Conn. Bank & Trust, Hartford, 1971-73; economist, exec. officer Barnett Banks Fla., Inc., Jacksonville, 1973-80; sr. v.p., dir. research Fed. Res. Bank Atlanta, 1981—. Contbr.: articles to Econ. Rev., Bankers Mag.; assoc. editor: Bus. Econs. Mem. Jacksonville Fin. Analysts Soc., Nat. Assn. Bus. Economists (founder Jacksonville chpt.), Atlanta Fin. Analysts Sco., Atlanta Econs. Club, Nat. Assn. Bus. Economists. Office: Fed Res Bank 104 Marietta St Atlanta GA 30303

KOCH, EDWARD I., mayor; b. N.Y.C., Dec. 12, 1924. Student, Coll. City N.Y.; LL.B., N.Y. U., 1948. Bar: N.Y. State bar 1949. Former sr. partner firm Koch, Lankenau, Schwartz & Kovner; mem. N.Y.C. Council, 1967-68, 91st-92d congresses from 17th Dist. N.Y., 93d-95th congresses from 18th Dist. N.Y.; mem. appropriations com.; sec. N.Y. Congl. delegation; observer N.Y. Emergency Fin. Control Bd.; mayor, N.Y.C., 1978—; Democratic dist. leader Greenwich Village, 1963-65; mem. Village Ind. Dems. Served with AUS, World War II. Home: 14 Washington Pl New York NY 10003 Office: Office of the Mayor City Hall New York NY 10007

KOCH, GEORGE WILLIAM, trade association executive; b. Cin., Apr. 8, 1926; s. George Earl and Lucille (Arnold) K.; m. Helen Lawton, July 29, 1950; children: Jorie, Danny, P.C., Bobby, Monte, Lucy. B.B.S., U. Cin., 1948, LL.B., J.D., 1950. Bar: Ohio bar 1950. Asst. city atty., Cin., 1950-54; asso. dir. Ohio Council Retail Merchants, Columbus, 1954-59; dir. fed. affairs Sears, Roebuck & Co., Washington, 1959-65; pres. Grocery Mfrs. Am., Inc., Washington, 1966—; pres., chief exec. officer Watchdogs of the Treasury Inc. Served with USNR, World War II. Clubs: Union League, City Tavern Assn., Congl. Congressional Country. Home: 10837 Stanmore Dr Potomac MD 20854 Office: 1010 Wisconsin Ave NW Washington DC 20007

KOCH, H. WILLIAM, association executive, physicist; b. N.Y.C., Sept. 28, 1920; s. John William and Elizabeth (Hirsch) K.; m. Margaret Giles, Feb. 3, 1945; children: John, Kathleen, Donald, Robert, Russell. B.S., Queens Coll., 1941; M.S., U. Ill., 1942, Ph.D., 1944. Asst. prof. physics U. Ill., 1944-49; research physicist, Oak Ridge, 1945-46; chief high energy radiation sect. Nat. Bur. Standards, Washington, 1949-62, chief div. radiation physics, 1962-66; dir. Am. Inst. Physics, 1966—. Named Alumnus of Year, Queens Coll., 1960. Fellow Am. Phys. Soc., Optical Soc. Am.; mem. Acoustical Soc. Am., Soc. Rheology, Am. Astron. Soc., Am. Crystallographic Assn., Am. Assn. Physicists in Medicine, Am. Vacuum Soc., Internat. Union Pure and Applied Physics (UN com.), Nat. Acad. Scis. (exec. com. div. phys. scis.), Am. Assn. Physics Tchrs., Council Engring. and Sci. Soc. Execs. (pres.), Sigma Xi, Sigma Pi Sigma, Phi Kappa Phi, Gamma Alpha. Home: 84 Boathouse Ln E Sunscape Bayshore NY 11706

KOCH, HOWARD WINCHEL, film and TV producer; b. N.Y.C., Apr. 11, 1916; m. Ruth Pincus; children: Melinda, Howard W. Student N.Y.C. schs. Partner Bel Air Prodns., from 1953, v.p. charge prodn., 1961-64; prodn. head Paramount Pictures, 1964-66; pres., producer own co., 1966—; dir. Hamburget Hamlet, Inc., Hollywood Park Racetrack.; Chmn. permanent charities com. Entertainment Industries. Second asst. dir., then 1st asst. dir. for various films, 1944-53; films directed include The Last of the Red Hot Lovers, 1972, Star Spangled Girl, 1971, Plaza Suite, 1971, The Odd Couple, 1968, On a Clear Day Your Can See Forever, 1970, Jacqueline Susann's Once Is Not Enough, 1974, Mati, 1977, Airplane, 1980, Airplane II; producer: TV series Miami Undercover; TV spls. Ol' Blue Eyes is Back, 1973, Who Loves Ya, Baby?, 1976, On The Road with Bing, 1977, The Pirates, 1978; dir. segments of various TV series. Trustee Motion Picture and Television Fund, 1981—, exec. com., case com., 1982—; past chmn. Permanent Charities Com. Named Producer of Yr. Nat. Assn. Theatre Owners, 1980. Mem. Acad. Motion Picture Arts and Scis. (past pres., bd. govs. 1980-83), Dirs. Guild Am. (nat. bd., chmn. Ednl. and Benevolent Found.), Producers Guild Am. Address: care Paramount Pictures Corp 5555 Melrose Ave Hollywood CA 90038

KOCH, JAMES VERCH, economist; b. Springfield, Ill., Oct. 7, 1942; s. Elmer O. and Wilma L. K.; m. Donna L. Stickling, Aug. 20, 1967; children: Elizabeth, Mark. B.A., Ill. State U., 1964; Ph.D., Northwestern U., 1968. Research economist Harris Trust Bank, Chgo., 1966; from asst. prof. to prof. econs. Ill. State U., 1967-78, chmn. dept., 1972-78; dean Faculty Arts and Scis., R.I. Coll., Providence, 1978-80; prof. econs., provost, v.p. acad. affairs Ball State U., Muncie, Ind., 1980—. Author: Industrialization Organization and Prices, 2d edit, 1980, Microeconomic Theory and Applications, 1976, The Economics of Affirmative Action, 1976, Introduction to Mathematical Economics, 1979. Mem. Am. Econ. Assn., Econometric Soc., Am. Assn. Higher Edn., AAUP. Lutheran. Home: 3201 W Petty Rd Muncie IN 47304 Office: Office Provost Ball State U Muncie IN 47306 *Survival in the 1980s, whether in higher education or in automobile production, demands and requires quality. Excellence must be our goal in all that we undertake. This is an attitude that must be instilled in the home, in our schools, and throughout society so that it permeates our lives.*

KOCH, KENNETH, poet, comparative literature educator; b. Cin., Feb. 27, 1925; s. Stuart J. and Lillian Amy (Loth) K.; m. Mary Janice Elwood, June 12, 1954; 1 dau., Katherine. A.B., Harvard U., 1948; M.A., Columbia U., 1953, Ph.D., 1959. Mem. faculty Columbia U., 1959—, asst. prof. English and comparative lit., 1962-66, assoc. prof. English and comparative lit., 1966-71, prof. English and comparative lit., 1971—. Bd. editors: lit. mag. Locus Solus, 1960-62; Author: Poems, 1953; poems Ko, or A Season on Earth, 1959, Permanently, 1961, Thank You and Other Poems, 1962, When the Sun Tries to Go On, 1969, The Pleasures of Peace, 1969, The Art of Love, 1975, The Duplications, 1977, The Burning Mystery of Anna in 1951, 1979, Days and Nights, 1983; fiction The Red Robins, 1975; plays Bertha and Other Plays, 1966, A Change of Hearts, 1973, The Red Robins, 1980; plays produced Little Red Riding Hood, 1953, Bertha, 1959, The Election, 1960, Pericles, 1960, George Washington Crossing the Delaware, 1962, Guinevere or the Death of the Kangaroo, 1964, The Love Suicides at Kaluka, 1965, The Moon Balloon, 1969, The Artist (opera), The Red Robins, 1978, Bertha (opera), The Gold Standard, 1975, The Art of Love, 1976; edn. Wishes, Lies and Dreams: Teaching Children to Write Poetry, 1970; Rose Where Did You Get That Red? Teaching Great Poetry to Children, 1973, I Never Told Anybody: Teaching Poetry Writing in a Nursing Home, 1977, Les Couleurs des voyelles—pour faire écrire de la poésie aux enfants, 1978, (with Kate Farrell) Sleeping on the Wing, 1981. Fulbright fellow, 1950-51, 78; Guggenheim fellow, 1961-62. Home: 25 Claremont Ave New York NY 10027 Office: 414 Hamilton Hall Columbia Univ New York NY 10027

KOCH, PETER, wood scientist; b. Missoula, Mont., Oct. 15, 1920; s. Elers and Gerda (Heiberg-Jurgensen) K.; m. Doris Ann Hagen, Oct. 8, 1950. B.S., Mont. State Coll., 1942; Ph.D., U. Wash., 1954; D.Sc. (hon.), U. Maine, 1980. Asst. to pres., sales mgr. Stetson-Ross Machine Co., Seattle, 1946-52; owner Peter Koch Cons. Engr., Seattle, 1952-55; asso. prof. wood tech. Mich. State U., East Lansing, 1955-57; v.p., dir. Champlin Co., Rochester, N.H., 1957-62; project leader, chief wood scientist So. Forest Expt. Sta. Forest Service, U.S. Dept. Agr., Pineville, La., 1963-82, chief wood scientist, forest and range expt. sta., Missoula, Mont., 1982—; adj. prof. wood sci. N.C. State U. at Raleigh, 1973-82; disting. affiliate prof. forest products U. Idaho, Moscow, 1982—. Author: Wood Machining Processes, 1964, Utilization of the Southern Pines, 2 vols, 1972; Contbr. profl. jours. Served to capt., pilot USAAF, 1942-46. Decorated D.F.C. with oak leaf cluster, Air medal with 4 oak leaf clusters; Breast Order of Yun Hui, Taiwan; recipient Woodworking Digest award, 1968; John Scott award, 1973; Superior Service award Dept. Agr. (all for invention of chipping headrig). Fellow Internat. Acad. Wood Sci., Soc. Am. Foresters; mem. Forest Products Research Soc. (pres. 1972-73, exec. bd. 1967-74), ASME, Soc. Wood Sci. and Tech., TAPPI, Sigma Xi, Tau Beta Pi, Phi Kappa Phi, Sigma Chi. Republican. Lutheran. Club: Rotarian. Patentee in field. Home: 1524 NE Willow Creek Rd Corvallis MT 59828 Office: 820 E Beckwith Ave Missoula MT 59801 *Whatever limited success has come to me has resulted from selecting goals—achievement of which would be useful to the organization for which I work, to myself, and to society—devising methods for their achievement, and finally, attaining the goals through sustained and singleminded effort.*

KOCH, RALPH RICHARD, architect; b. Omaha, Nov. 1, 1928; s. Ralph Ruben and Agnes (Janda) K.; m. Jane Lee Goeres, Dec. 27, 1950; children—Sharon Lee, Richard John, Barbara Jo. B.Arch., U. Nebr., 1951. Designer, draftsman Hugill, Blatherwick, Fritzel & Kroeger, Sioux Falls, S.D., 1953-57; asso. Howard Parezo & Assos., Sioux Falls, 1957-61; prin. Ralph Koch & Assos., Sioux Falls, 1961-69; partner Koch, Hazard Assos., Sioux Falls, 1969-75; pres. Koch Hazard Assos., Ltd., 1975-79, chmn. bd., 1979—. Architect: Karl E. Mundt Library, Dakota State Coll., Madison, S.D., 1968 (dedicated by Pres. Nixon 1969), Dakota State Coll., Madison, S.D. (named Outstanding State Bldg. at S.D. Engr.'s Office 1968). Mem. Sioux Falls Zool. Soc., 1966—, Civic Fine Arts Assn., 1967—, S.D. Symphony Assn., 1965—, Assn. Retarded Children, 1966—; Bd. dirs., past pres. Sioux Vocat. Sch. Handicapped. Served to capt. C.E. AUS, 1951-53. Mem. Archtl. Forum, Sioux Falls Indsl. Found., C. of C., Cosmopolitan Internat. (pres. 1973-74), AIA (state pres. 1969), Am. Legion, VFW, Kappa Sigma. Republican. Roman Catholic. Clubs: K.C. (4 deg.), Elks (trustee 1974-79), Elks (exalted ruler 1970-71). Home: 728 Woodlawn Dr Sioux Falls SD 57105 Office: 630 S Minnesota Ave Sioux Falls SD 57104

KOCH, RICHARD, pediatrician, educator; b. N.D., Nov. 24, 1921; s. Valentine and Barbara (Fischer) K.; m. Kathryn Jean Holt, Oct. 2, 1943; children: Jill, Thomas, Christine, Martin, Leslie. B.A., U. Calif. at Berkeley, 1958; M.D., U. Rochester, 1951. Mem. staff Children's Hosp., Los Angeles, 1952-75, 77—, dir. child devel. div., 1955-75; dep. dir. Calif. Dept. Health, 1975-76; prof. pediatrics U. So. Calif., 1955-75, 77—; co-dir. PKU Collaborative Study, 1966—; med. dir. Spastic Children's Found., Los Angeles, 1980—; Mem. Project Hope, Trujillo, Peru, 1970; dir. Regional Center for Developmentally Disabled at Children's Hosp., Los Angeles, 1966-75; mem. research adv. bd. Nat. Assn. Retarded Citizens, 1974-76; mem. Gov.'s Council on Devel. Disabilities, 1981—; bd. dirs. Down's Syndrome Congress, 1974-76. Author: (with James Dobson) The Mentally Retarded Child and his Family, 1971, (with Kathryn J. Koch) Understanding the Mentally Retarded Child, 1974. Mem. Am. Assn. on Mental Deficiency (pres. 1968-69), Am. Acad. Pediatrics, Western Soc. Pediatric Research, Sierra Club (treas. Mineral King task force 1972). Research, numerous publs. on mental retardation and relation to pediatrics. Home: 2125 Ames St Los Angeles CA 90027 Office: 4650 Sunset Blvd Los Angeles CA 90027

KOCH, RICHARD FREDERICK, manufacturing company executive; b. St. Louis, Sept. 22, 1930; s. Alvin Louis and Lorine Amanda (Obergoenner) K.; m. Kay Delle Smith, June 24, 1961; children: Birgitta, Hans Frederick. B.S. in Bus. Adminstrn, Washington U., St. Louis, 1952; J.D., U. Mich., 1958. Bar: Mo. bar 1958, Mich. bar 1965; C.P.A., Mo. Asso. Touche, Ross & Co., C.P.A.s, St. Louis, 1952-55; asso., then partner firm Bryan, Cave, McPheeters and McRoberts (formerly Shepley, Kroeger, Fisse & Shepley), St. Louis, 1958-65; atty., corp. sec., asst. gen. counsel, then v.p., gen. counsel, sec. Whirlpool Corp., Benton Harbor, Mich., 1965—; former sec. Heil-Quaker Corp., Nashville; v.p., dir. Whirlpool Opportunities, Inc., Benton Harbor. Mem. Benton Harbor Schs. Adv. Bd., 1967-71; Bd. dirs., past pres. Easter Seal Soc. Crippled Children and Adults of Berrien County, 1974-80; bd. dirs. Easter Seal Soc. Mich., 1980-81; adv. bd., past pres. Benton Harbor Salvation Army, 1974—. Scholarship grantee U. Mich., 1955-58. Mem. Am., Mich., Mo., Berrien County bar assns., Bar Assn. Met. St. Louis, Am. Inst. C.P.A.'s, Am. Assn. Attys.-C.P.A.'s, Kappa Sigma (v.p., sec. 1950-52), Beta Gamma Sigma, Omicron Delta Gamma, Delta Sigma Pi. Republican. Clubs: Union League (Chgo.); St. Joseph River Yacht, Point O' Woods Golf and Country. Home: 275 Ridgeway Saint Joseph MI 49085 Office: Adminstrv Center Whirlpool Corp Benton Harbor MI 49022

KOCH, RICHARD HENRY, lawyer, real estate consultant; b. Pottsville, Pa., Mar. 2, 1918; s. Roscoe Richard and Louise (Smyth) K.; m. Joanne Obermaier, Mar. 17, 1967; children: Stephen, Jeremy, Chapin; 1 stepdau., Andrea Godbout. A.B., Princeton U., 1940, postgrad. (Chancellor Green fellow), 1940-41; LL.B., Columbia U., 1951-54. Bar: N.Y. 1954. Writer-dir. indsl. films for various cos., N.Y.C., 1941-42, 46-51; assoc. atty. Winthrop, Stimson, Putnam & Roberts, N.Y.C., 1954-59; dep. dir., gen. counsel, sec. Mus. Modern Art, N.Y.C., 1959-79. Articles editor: Columbia Law Rev, 1953-54. Served to lt. USNR, 1942-46. Mem. Assn. Bar City of N.Y., Century Assn. Home and office: 2 Washington Sq Village New York NY 10012

KOCH, ROBERT ALAN, educator; b. Durham, N.C., Nov. 23, 1919; s. Frederick Henry and Loretta Jean (Hannigan) K. B.A., U. N.C., 1940, M.A., 1942; M.F.A. (Woodrow Wilson fellow, Procter fellow), Princeton, 1948; Ph.D., Princeton U., 1954. Instr., asst. dir. Art Museum, Princeton, asst. prof., 1955-57, asso. prof., 1958-64, prof., curator prints, 1965—, asso. chmn. dept. art and archaeology, 1973-76, 79—; vis. prof. Princeton Theol. Sem., 1954-56, Inst. Fine Arts, N.Y.U., summer 1962. Author: Joachim Patinir, 1968, Hans Baldung Grien, 1974; Editor: Illustrated Bartsch. Served to 1st lt. AUS, 1942-46. Fulbright research award for Belgium, 1956-57; Am. Council Learned Socs. grantee, 1961-62. Mem. Coll. Art Assn. Am. (dir. 1961-63), Mediaeval Acad. Am. (councillor 1964-66), Renaissance Soc. Am., Archaeol. Inst., Print Council Am., Phi Beta Kappa. Home: 10 Mercer St Princeton NJ 08540

KOCH, ROBERT HARRY, astronomer; b. York, Pa., Dec. 19, 1929; s. Harry Jacob and Veronica Cecelia (Jameson) K.; m. Joanne Carol Underwood, July 4, 1959; children—Thomas R., James E., Elizabeth G., Patricia R. B.A., U. Pa., 1951, M.A., 1955, Ph.D., 1959; postgrad., U. Ariz., 1955-57. Instr. Four-Coll. Astronomy Dept., Amherst, Mass., 1959-60, asst. prof., 1960-65, asso. prof., 1965-66, U. N.Mex., 1966-67, U. Pa., Phila., 1967-69, prof. astronomy and astrophysics dept.,

1969—. Editor: (with F.B. Wood, J.P. Oliver and D.R. Florkowski) A Finding List for Observers of Interacting Stars, 5th edit, 1980. Served with U.S. Army, 1951-53. NSF grantee, 1960—; NASA grantee, 1978—. Mem. AAAS, Am. Astron. Soc., Internat. Astron. Union, Sigma Xi. Roman Catholic. Home: 210 Roberts Rd Ardmore PA 19003 Office: U Pennsylvania Philadelphia PA 19104

KOCHAKIAN, CHARLES DANIEL, educator, endocrinologist; b. Haverhill, Mass., Nov. 18, 1908; s. Daniel S. and Haigoohee (Nalbandian) K.; m. Beatrice Irene Armstrong, July 27, 1940; 1 son, Charles Pedlar. A.B., Boston U., 1930, A.M., 1931; Ph.D., U. Rochester, 1936. Fellow dept. vital econs. U. Rochester, 1933-36, mem. faculty, 1936-51, prof. research biochemistry, head dept. biochemistry and endocrinology, 1951-57; asso. dir. Med. Research Found. Okla., 1951-53, coordinator research, 1953-55; prof. physiology U. Ala. Med. Center, 1957-79, prof. biochemistry, 1961-79, prof. emeritus, 1979—, dir. exptl. endocrinology, 1961—, acting coordinator research, 1960-61; cons. Fels Research Inst., 1956; M.D. Anderson Hosp. and Tumor Inst., 1956; vis. Claude Bernard prof. Inst. Exptl. Biology and Medicine, U. Montreal, 1950; mem. panel drugs for metabolic disturbance of drug efficacy study Nat. Acad. Scis.-NRC, 1966—; mem. com. growth NRC, 1949-51; cons. dental sch. com. Okla. Dental Assn., 1954-57. Author: Anabolic-Androgenic Steroids. Mem. adv. council Jefferson County (Ala.) div. Am. Cancer Soc., 1960-62. Recipient Claude Bernard medal, 1950; medal Osaka Endocrine Soc., 1962; named to Collegium Distinguished Alumni Coll. Liberal Arts, Boston U. Fellow AAAS; mem. Am. Soc. Biol. Chemists, Am. Physiol. Soc., Endocrine Soc., Soc. Exptl. Biology and Medicine, Am. Chem. Soc., AMA (chmn. screening group com. steroids and hormones 1952-57), Sigma Xi (past pres., sec.-treas. chpt.). Presbyn. (elder). Spl. research on metabolic effect hormones, mechanisms of hormone action, metabolism of steroid hormones by tissue enzymes, hormone-enzyme relationships. Discoverer protein anabolic action of androgens. Home: 3617 Oakdale Rd Birmingham AL 35223

KOCHANOWSKY, BORIS JULIUS, mining cons.; b. Krasnojarsk, Siberia, Russia, May 4, 1905; came to U.S., 1953, naturalized, 1959; s. Julius M. and Maria J. (Borovski) K.; m. Anna R. Stahel, July 1946 (div. 1970); 1 dau., Vera. Diplom Ingenieur in Mine Surveying, U. Bergakademie, Freiberg, Ger., 1927; in Mining Engring., 1929; Dr. Ingenieur in Mining Engring, U. Bergakademie, Clausthal, Ger., 1955. Coal miner, 1923-29; research asso. Coal Bd., Essen, Ger., 1930, U. Bergakademie, Freiberg, 1930-33; asst. to pres., mgr. mining ops., devel. and research Rheinische Kalksteinwerke Co., Germany, 1933-39; mgr. coal mines, Switzerland, 1945-46, mgr. asphaltite mine, Mendoza, Argentina, 1946-48; prof. engring. and econs. of mining U. Cuyo, San Juan and Mendoza, 1948-53; mem. faculty Pa. State U., 1953—, prof. mining engring., 1961-67, founder, chmn. mineral engring. mgmt. program, 1968-70, prof. emeritus, 1970—; speaker, cons. throughout world. Co-author: Berg und Aufbereitungstechnik, Part I, 1933, Part II, 1935, Neuzeitliche Sprengtechnik, 1966, also numerous articles. Mem. AIME, Am. Soc. Engring. Edn., AAUP. Inventor mining systems, methods, and machines. Address: 426 Homan Ave State College PA 16801

KOCHANSKI, ADRIAN JOSEPH, univ. dean; b. Milw., July 29, 1918; s. Alois S. and Antionette (Czerwinski) K.; m. Marianne Schaaf. A.B., St. Louis U., 1941, M.A., 1942, Ph.L., 1943, S.T.L., 1949; Ph.D., U. Chgo., 1955. Tchr., head prefect Campion High Sch., Prairie du Chien, Wis., 1942-46; asst. prof. edn. Marquette U., 1954-60, dean, 1954-60; regional dir. edn. Wis. Province Soc. of Jesus, 1960-68; founder Sogang U., Seoul, Korea, 1960, The Cath. U. of Salta, Argentina, 1964; vis. scholar Stanford, 1968-69; exec. asst. v.p. acad. affairs San Diego State U., 1969, dean acad. planning, prof. pub. adminstrn., 1970-79, asso. dean, 1979—. Past vice chmn. Coordinating Council for Edn. in Health Scis., San Diego and Imperial Counties. Mem. Am. Assn. Higher Edn., Phi Delta Kappa, Phi Kappa Phi. Address: 2884 Ariane Dr San Diego CA 92117

KOCHENDORFER, FRED DANIEL, national space administration manager, engineer; b. Jersey City, Nov. 9, 1921; s. August Fred and Freda (Buettner) K.; m. Anna Mary Myers, Feb. 12, 1977; children: David Alan, Robert Brian, Jill Nadine. M.E., Stevens Inst. Tech., 1943; M.S.M.E., M.I.T., 1949. With NACA (later NASA), 1943—; mgr. Initial Def. Communications Satellite Program at Philco Ford Co., to 1970; mgr. Pioneer and Helios Programs Hdqrs. NASA, Washington, from 1970, now advanced studies mgr. Office of Space Flight. Author numerous profl. reports. Recipient Exceptional Service award NASA. Fellow AIAA (assoc.). Home: 110 Park Ave Edgewater MD 21037 Office: Hdqrs NASA Code MP Washington DC 20546

KOCHER, PAUL HAROLD, humanities educator; b. Trinidad, W.I., Apr. 23, 1907; s. Paul William and Freida (Schwabe) K.; m. Annis Cox, Aug. 31, 1936; children: Paul Dana, Carl Alvin. A.B., Columbia U., 1926; J.D., Stanford U., 1929, M.A., 1932, Ph.D., 1936. Instr. Stanford U., 1936-38; instr., then asst. prof. U. Wash., 1938-46; prof. U. Nebr., 1948-49, Claremont Grad. Sch., 1949-58; prof. English and humanities Stanford U., 1960-70, prof. emeritus English and humanities, 1971—. Author: Christopher Marlowe, 1946, Science and Religion in Elizabethan England, 1953, Mission San Luis Obispo de Tolosa, 1772-1972, a Historical Sketch, 1972, Master of Middle-Earth: The Fiction of J.R.R. Tolkien, California's Old Missions, 1976, Alabado, Historical Novel of Spanish California, 1978, My Daily Visitor, 1979, A Reader's Guide to The Silmarillion, 1980; Editor: (Marlowe): Doctor Faustus, 1950, Huntington Library Quar, 1952-53; editorial bd.: Jour. History of Ideas, 1951-59; contbg. editor: Mythlore, 1976—; Contbr. articles to profl. jours. Fellow Folger Shakespeare Library, 1939-40; Guggenheim fellow, 1946-47, 55-56; Huntington Library fellow, 1952-53. Mem. Modern Lang. Assn., Renaissance Soc., Order of Coif. Home: San Luis Obispo CA 93401

KOCHI, JAY KAZUO, chemist, educator; b. Los Angeles, May 17, 1927; s. Tsuruzo and Shizuko (Moriya) K.; m. Marion Kiyono, Mar. 1, 1959; children—Sims, Ariel, Julia. Student, Cornell U., 1945; B.S., U. Calif. at Los Angeles, 1949; Ph.D., Ia. State U., 1952. Faculty Harvard, 1952-55; NIH fellow Cambridge (Eng.) U., 1956; mem. faculty Iowa State U., 1956; with Shell Devel. Co., 1957-61; mem. faculty dept. chemistry Case Western Res. U., Cleve., 1962-69, prof., 1966-69; prof. chemistry Ind. U., Bloomington, 1969-74, Earl Blough prof. chemistry, 1974—; cons. chemist, 1964—. Mem. Am. Chem. Soc., Chem. Soc. (London), Nat. Acad. Scis., Sigma Xi. Research on mechanism of catalysis of organic reactions, organometallics, electrochemistry and photochemistry. Home: 217 S Hillsdale Dr Bloomington IN 47401

KOCHS, HERBERT WILLIAM, indsl. chem. mfr.; b. Chgo., Mar. 28, 1903; s. August and Adelaide (Petersen) K.; m. Elizabeth Kennedy, 1924; 1 dau., Nancy (Mrs. E. K. Shaw); m. Mildred Swift, Dec. 2, 1928; children—Susan M. (Mrs. W. E. Judevine) (dec.), Herbert William, Judith Anne (Mrs. Nelson Shaw); m. Phyllis Anderson, Nov. 10, 1955; m. Paula Leggett, Dec. 28, 1959; children—Justin and Martin (twins). Student, Mass. Inst. Tech., 1920-23, Northwestern U., 1923-24. Sec. Diversey Corp., Chgo., 1927-32, v.p., 1932-35, pres., 1935-43, chmn., 1943-78, hon. chmn., dir., 1978—. Past dir. Nat. Council Crime and Delinquency, pres., 1959-64, hon. v.p., 1964-67; former dir. Grant Hosp.; chmn. bd. mgrs. Uhlich Childrens Home, 1956-58. Clubs: M.I.T. (past pres.), Chicago Athletic (Chgo.); Indian Hill (Winnetka, Ill.); American (London, Eng.). Office: 79 W Monroe St Suite 1008 Chicago IL 60603

KOCISKO, STEPHEN JOHN, clergyman; b. Mpls., June 11, 1915; s. John Z. and Anna (Somosz) K. Ph.B., Propaganda Fide U., 1937, S.T.L., 1941. Ordained priest Roman Catholic Ch., 1941, consecrated bishop, 1956; chancellor Byzantine Cath. Diocese of Pitts., 1956; rector Byzantine Cath. Sem., Pitts., 1958-63; 1st bishop Byzantine Eparchy (diocese) of Passaic, 1963-69; met. archbishop of, Pitts., 1969—. Address: 50 Riverview Ave Pittsburgh PA 15214

KOCKELMANS, JOSEPH J., philosophy educator; b. Meerssen L., Netherlands, Dec. 1, 1923; came to U.S., 1964, naturalized, 1968; s. Alphons Hubert and Philomena (Raeven) K.; m. Dorothy H. Greiner, Oct. 26, 1964; 1 son, Joseph Martin. Ph.D., Angelico, Rome, 1951; postdoctoral studies in math. with, Prof. H. Busard, Venlo, Prof. A. Fokker, Leyden, Prof. H. Van Breda, Louvain, 1951-63. Prof. philosophy Agrl. U., Wageningen, Netherlands, 1963-64, New Sch. Social Research, N.Y.C., 1964-65, U. Pitts., 1965-68, Pa. State U., University Park, 1968—. Author: Phenomenology and Physical Science, 1966, Husserl's Phenomenological Psychology, 1967, The World in Science and Philosophy, 1969, Martin Heidegger: A First Introduction to his Philosophy, 1965, Edmund Husserl: A First Introduction to his Phenomenology, 1967; Editor: (with John M. Anderson and Calvin O. Schrag) Man and World: An Internat. Philos. Rev., 1968, (with Jan Aler and M. van Nierop) Dutch Heidegger Library, 1970. Recipient Gold medal Teyler's Tweede Genootschap, Haarlem, 1958. Mem. Am. Philos. Assn., Soc. for Phenomenology and Existential Philsophy, AAUP. Home: 903 Willard Circle State College PA 16803

KOCMOND, WARREN CHARLES, atmospheric scientist; b. Berwyn, Ill., Oct. 4, 1939; s. Charles Roy and Elizabeth E. (Houdek) K.; m. Judith Helen Higgins, Oct. 10, 1958; children: Warren Charles, Michael D. B.S. in Math., U. Ariz., 1962; M.S. in Meteorology, Pa. State U., 1964. Research asst. Pa. State U., 1962-64; head atmospheric scis. sect. Calspan Corp., Buffalo, 1964-76; research prof. Atmospheric Scis. Ctr., Desert Research Inst., Reno, 1976-77, exec. dir., research prof., 1977-83, acting pres., 1983—; mem. sci. adv. com. cloud physics NASA; cons. Univ. Space Research Assn. Contbr. articles to profl. jours.; patentee (in field). Mem. Am. Meteorology Soc., AAAS, Sigma Xi, Sigma Pi Sigma. Home: PO Box 3440 Incline Village NV 89450 Office: Desert Research Inst Atomospheric Sciences Center PO Box 60220 Reno NV 89506

KOCORAS, CHARLES PETROS, federal judge; b. Chgo., Mar. 12, 1938; s. Petros K. and Constantina (Cordonis) K.; m. Grace L. Finlay, Sept. 22, 1968; children: Peter, John, Paul. Student, Wilson Jr. Coll., 1956-58; B.S., Coll. Commerce, DePaul U., 1961; J.D., DePaul U., 1969. Bar: Ill. 1969. Asst. atty. Office of U.S. Atty. No. Dist. Ill. U.S. Dept. Justice, 1971-77; judge U.S. Dist. Ct., Chgo., 1980—; chmn. Ill. Commerce Commn., Chgo., 1977-79; ptnr. Stone, McGuire, Benjamin and Kocoras, Chgo., 1979-80; instr. trial practice, evening div. John Marshall Law Sch., 1975—. Served with Army N.G., 1961-67. Mem. Fed. Criminal Jury Instruction Com. Seventh Circuit, Beta Alpha Psi. Greek Orthodox. Office: 219 S Dearborn St Chicago IL 60604

KODJAK, ANDREJ, Slavic language educator; b. Prague, Czechoslovakia, Nov. 16, 1926. M.A., U. Montreal, 1957; B.D., St. Vladimir Sem., N.Y.C., 1959; Ph.D., U. Pa., 1963. Asst. prof. U. Pa., Phila., 1968-64; vis. assoc. prof. Vanderbilt U., Nashville, 1964-65, assoc. prof., 1965-68; vis. assoc. prof. NYU, N.Y.C., 1968-69, chmn. dept. Slavic langs., 1969—, prof. Slavic langs. and lit., 1980—. Author: Alexander Solzhenitsyn, 1978, Puskin's I.P. Belkin, 1979; editor: Alexander Puskin: Symposium, 1976; author: Structural Analysis of Narrataive Texts, 1980, Alexander Puskin: Symposium II, 1980, Brain and Language (Roman Jakobson), 1980. Mem. Am. Assn. Advancement Slavic Studies. Home: 35 Macopin Ave Upper Montclair NJ 07052 Office: Dept of Slavic Languages and Literatures NYU 6 Washington Sq N New York NY 10003

KOE, ROBERT EDWARDS, financial services executive; b. Berwyn, Ill., Mar. 19, 1945; s. Robert Edward and Shirley Marg (Edwards) K.; m. Marlene F. Fukal, Aug. 5, 1967; children: Robert, Kirsten, Kathy. A.B., Kenyon Coll., 1967. Various positions Gen. Electric Co., 1967-80, Gen. Electric Credit Corp., 1967-80; v.p., gen. mgr. Comml. Fin. Services, Gen. Electric Credit Corp., Stamford, Conn., 1980—; pres., dir. Acquisition Funding Corp., N.Y.C., 1981-83. Mem. Nat. Comml. Fin. Assn. (dir. 1981-83). Republican. Presbyterian. Club: Lake (New Canaan, Conn.). Office: General Electric Credit Corp 260 Long Ridge Rd Stamford CT 06902

KOEDEL, JOHN GILBERT, JR., forge company executive; b. Pitts., June 25, 1937; s. John Gilbert and Elizabeth Marie (Kramer) K.; m. Fay Birren, Dec. 21, 1963; 1 son, John III. B.S. in Commerce, Washington and Lee U., 1959. Asst. v.p. Pitts. Nat. Bank, 1960-68; v.p., treas. Nat. Forge Co., Irvine, Pa., 1968—; asst. treas. Nat. Forge Export Corp., Irvine, 1968—; treas. Indsl. Materials Tech. Inc., Worborn, Mass., 1977—; dir. Pa. Bank & Trust Co., Titusville, Carbon City Products Co., St. Marys, Pa. Bd. dirs. Warren Gen. Hosp., 1975—. Served with AUS, 1960. Clubs: Erie (Pa.) Yacht; Conewango (Warren). Lodge: Masons. Home: 118 East St Warren PA 16365 Office: Nat Forge Co Irvine PA 16329

KOEDEL, ROBERT CRAIG, cleryman, historian, educator; b. Tarentum, Pa., July 1, 1927; s. Theodore and Evelyn (Dagan) K.; m. Barbara Ellen Wood, Jan. 6, 1962. B.A., Wheaton Coll., Ill., 1949; M.Div., Pitts. Theol Sem., 1953; M.A., U. Pitts., 1964; postgrad., Temple U., 1964-70. Ordained to ministry United Presbyterian Ch. U.S.A., 1953. Pastor Monaghan Presbyn. Ch., Dillsburg, Pa., 1956-59; asst. pastor Mt. Calvary Presbyn. Ch., Corapolis, Pa., 1959-60; assoc. pastor Dormont Presbyn. Ch., Pitts., 1960-64; mem. faculty Atlantic Community Coll., Mays Landing, N.J., 1966—, prof. social sci., history, religion, 1978—, chmn. dept. history, 1969-70, 78-79, asst. dean instrn., 1970-72; clergyman West Jersey Presbytery; lectr. local history and religion. Author: South Jersey Heritage: A Social, Economic and Cultural History, 1977, God's Vine in This Wilderness: Religion in South Jersey to 1800, 1980, Following the Water: The Shellfish Industry in South Jersey, 1983; contbr. articles to profl. jours., articles to newspapers. Served as chaplain USAF, 1953-56. N.J. Hist. Commn. research grantee, 1974. Mem. United Teaching Profession, Presbyn. Hist. Soc., N.J. Hist. Soc., Atlantic County Hist. Soc., Gloucester County Hist. Soc., West Jersey Presbytery, Eastern Community Coll. Social Sci. Assn. Home: PO Box 64 Oceanville NJ 08231 Office: Atlantic Community Coll Mays Landing NJ 08330

KOEGEL, WILLIAM FISHER, lawyer; b. Washington, Aug. 18, 1923; s. Otto Erwin and Rae (Fisher) K.; m. Barbara Bixler, Feb. 2, 1946 (dec. 1983); children: John Bixler, Robert Bartlett; m. Ruth Swan Boynton, June 21, 1969. B.A., Williams Coll., 1944; LL.B., U. Va., 1949. Bar: N.Y. 1950. With firm Roger & Wells (and predecessors), N.Y.C., 1949—, sr. partner, 1968—, head litigation dept., 1977—. Chmn. Scarsdale (N.Y.) Republican Town Com., 1965-71; pres. trustees Hitchcock Presbyn. Ch., Scarsdale, 1970-73, 78-79, 82-83. Served with AUS, 1943-45; ETO. Fellow Am. Coll. Trial Lawyers; mem. ABA, N.Y. State Bar Assn., Bar Assn. City N.Y., Order of Coif. Clubs: Town (Scarsdale) (pres. 1976-77); Sky, Williams (N.Y.C.); Shenorock Shore, Fox Meadow Tennis. Home: 7 Chesterfield Rd Scarsdale NY 10583 Office: 200 Park Ave New York NY 10166

KOEHLE, SIEGFRIED EUGEN, steel pipe company executive, consultant; b. Ellwangen, Germany, Dec. 15, 1931; came to U.S., 1969; s. Eugen and Martha (Rieger) K.; m. Eva Inge Seidler, Feb. 11, 1958; children: Peter, Michael, Ellen. B.S.M.E., Tech. U. Stuttgart, (W. Ger.), 1955; M.M.E., Tech. U. Aachen, (W. Ger.), 1958, M. Metall. Engring., 1958. Registered profl. engr., S.C. Prodn. cons. Israel Steel Mills, Haifa, 1960-62; chief engr. Schloemann A.G., Dusseldorf, W. Ger., 1962-69; rolling mill supt. Georgetown Steel Corp., (S.C.), 1969-73, asst. v.p. ops., 1974-75, v.p. ops., 1976-77, exec. v.p., 1978-81, Berg Steel Pipe Corp., Panama City, Fla., 1982, pres., 1982—; design and ops. cons. meltshop and rolling mill projects U.S. and abroad, 1962-82. Mem. German Iron and Steel Inst., Assn. Iron and Steel Engrs., Am. Iron and Steel Inst., Wire Assn., Am. Gas. Assn. Home: Bay Point PO Box 2029 Panama City Beach FL 32407 Office: Berg Steel Pipe Corp PO Box 2929 Panama City FL 32401

KOEHLER, GEORGE APPLEGATE, broadcasting company executive; b. Phila., July 23, 1921; s. Herbert Jacques and Mildred Warrington (Applegate) K.; m. Jane Marie Caputi, Feb. 20, 1944; children: Eric George, Gary Stephen. B.A., U. Pa., 1942. Various positions WFIL Stas., Phila., 1945-55; sta. mgr. WFIL Radio and TV, 1955-68; gen. mgr. radio and TV div. Triangle Pubs., Inc., Phila., 1968-72; pres. Gateway Communications, Inc., Cherry Hill, N.J., 1970—; Mem. planning com. Phila. Commn. on Human Relations, 1957; mem. Adv. Com. on Naval Affairs, 1968—; pub. relations chmn. United Fund, 1965. Trustee Meth. Hosp., Phila.; mem. United Meth. Communications Commn., 1980—; bd. dirs. Pennington (N.J.) Sch., 1973-80. Served to capt. USAAF, 1942-45. Decorated D.F.C., Air medal with 3 oak leaf clusters; recipient Distinguished Service award Chapel of 4 Chaplains, 1969; named Man of Yr. TV and Radio Advt. Club, Phila., 1971; Broadcast Pioneer of Yr. Delaware Valley chpt. Broadcast Pioneers. Mem. Pa. Assn. Broadcasters (pres. 1958-59), ABC-TV Affiliates Assn. (adv. bd. 1967-71, chmn. 1970-71), Assn. Maximum Service Telecasters (bd. dirs. 1976—, sec.-treas. 1980-83, chmn. 1983—), Alpha Delta Sigma. Republican. Methodist. Clubs: Union League (Phila.); Rotary (pres. 1960). Home: 710 S Park Dr Westmont NJ 08108 Office: Suite 612 Executive Bldg Cherry Hill NJ 08002

KOEHN, CHARLES WILLIAM, bass; b. Milw., Feb. 11; s. Albert J. and Ida (Wasch) K.; m. Joanne Pruitt, Nov. 2, 1956. Student, Marquette U., 1937-41, Am. Theatre Wing, N.Y.C., 1946-51. Leading bass, Florentine Opera Co., Milw., 1958—, Kiel (Germany) Stadt theatre, 1964-65, Boston Opera Co., 1968, Am. Nat. Opera Co. on tour, 1967-68, Skylight Comic Opera Ltd., Milw., 1960-67; mem., Lyric Opera Co. Chgo., 1969—, Nev. Opera Co., Birmingham Opera Co., Jacksonville Opera Co.; founder, gen. mgr., Gt. Lakes Opera Co. Inc., 1982; guest artist, Bielefeld (Germany) Opera, Pforzheim (Germany) Opera, 1964-65. Served to lt. comdr. USNR, World War 11 and Korea. Home: 2953 N Shepard Ave Milwaukee WI 53211

KOELB, CLAYTON TALMADGE, ins. co. exec.; b. Mystic, Conn., May 9, 1920; s. Ralph Hammond and Gladys Clayton (MacGown) K.; m. Janice Miller, Aug. 30, 1941; children—Clayton, Albert, Susan. B.A. magna cum laude, Dartmouth Coll., 1941. C.P.A., R.I. Actuarial clk. Met. Life Ins. Co., 1941-43; tax accountant Ernst & Ernst, 1943-47; asst. treas. N.E. Butt Co., Providence, 1947-49; with Amica Mut. Ins. Co., Providence, 1949—, treas., 1956-72, v.p., treas., 1972-80, sr. v.p., treas., 1980—; v.p., treas. Amica Life Ins. Co., Providence, Amica Services, Inc., Providence. Trustee Providence Country Day Sch., 1961-69, South County Hosp., S. Kingstown, R.I., 1977—. Clubs: Univ., Turks Head (Providence). Office: 10 Weybosset St Providence RI 02940

KOELLE, GEORGE BRAMPTON, university pharmacologist, educator; b. Phila., Oct. 8, 1918; s. Frederick Christian and Emily Mary (Brampton) K.; m. Winifred Jean Angenent, Feb. 6, 1954; children: Peter Brampton, William Angenent, Jonathan Stuart. B.Sc., Phila. Coll. Pharmacy and Sci., 1939, D.Sc. (hon.), 1965; Ph.D., U. Pa., 1946; M.D., Johns Hopkins, 1950; Dr. Med. (hon.), U. Zurich, Switzerland, 1972. Bio-assayist LaWall & Harrisson, 1939-42; asst. prof. pharmacology Coll. Phys. and Surg., Columbia U., 1950-52; prof. pharmacology Grad. Sch. Medicine, U. Pa., 1952-59, chmn. dept. physiology and pharmacology, dean, 1957-59, chmn. dept. pharmacology, 1959-81, disting. prof., 1981—; spl. lectr. U. London, 1961; vis. lectr. U. Brazil, 1962, Polish Acad. Scis., 1979; vis. prof., Guggenheim fellow U. Lausanne, 1963-64; vis. prof. pharmacology, chmn. dept. Pahlavi U., Shiraz, Iran, 1969-70; cons. McNeil Labs., 1951-66, Phila. Gen. Hosp., 1953—, Valley Forge Army Hosp., 1954-71, Army Chem. Corps, 1956-60, Phila. Naval Hosp., 1957—; vis. lectr. pharmacology Phila. Coll. Pharmacy and Sci., 1955-57; vis. prof. Mahidol U., Bangkok, Thailand, 1978; Mem. pharmacology study sect. USPHS, 1958-62, chmn. pharmacology study sect., 1965-68; sec. gen. Internat. Union of Pharmacology, 1966-69, v.p., 1969-72; mem. bd. sci. Counselors Nat. Heart Inst., NIH, USPHS, 1960-64, mem. nat. adv. neurol. diseases and stroke council, 1970-75. Asso. editor: Remington's Practice of Pharmacy, 1951; mem. editorial bd.: Pharmacol. Revs, 1955-63; chmn., 1959-62; hon. editorial adv. bd.: Biochem. Pharmacology, 1958-72; editorial adv. bd.: Internat. Jour. Neurosci, 1970—; editorial com.: Ann. Rev. Pharmacology, 1959-65; editorial bd.: Internat. Ency. Pharmacology and Therapeutics; editor: Cholinesterases and Anticholinestrerase Agents, 1963; Contbr. articles on pharmacology to profl. jours. Trustee Phila. Coll. Pharmacy and Sci.; bd. mgrs. Wistar Inst. Served to 1st lt. Med. Adminstrn. Corps AUS, 1942-46. Recipient Abel prize in pharmacology Am. Soc. Pharmacology and Exptl. Therapeutics, 1950; Travel award XVIIIth Internat. Physiol. Congress, Copenhagen, Federated Socs., 1950; Borden undergrad. research award, 1950. Fellow A.A.A.S. (v.p. 1971), N.Y. Acad. Scis.; mem. Am. Soc. Pharmacology and Exptl. Therapeutics (pres. 1965-66, plenary lectr. 1981), Nat. Acad. Scis., Histochem. Soc., Harvey Soc., Soc. Biol. Psychiatry, John Morgan Soc., Sydenham Coterie, Sons Copper Beeches, Brit. Pharmacol. Soc., Biol. Soc. Chile (hon.), Internat. Neurochem. Soc., Soc. for Neurosci., Pharmacol. Soc. Peru (hon.), Pharmacol. Soc. Japan (hon.), Sigma Xi, Alpha Omega Alpha. Home: 205 College Ave Swarthmore PA 19081 Office: U Pa Philadelphia PA 19104

KOELLING, NEIL L(EROY), construction corporation executive; b. Sullivan, Mo., Jan. 27, 1939; s. Theo and Nadine (Busch) K.; m. Donna Parker, June 10, 1961; children: Suzanne, John, Brian. B.S. in Civil Engring., U. Mo., 1961. Field engr. St. Louis San Francisco R.R., 1961; constrn. engr. Texaco Inc., San Antonio, 1964-67; with Fruin Colnon Corp., St. Louis, 1967—, asst. project mgr., 1973-78, exec. v.p., from 1979, now pres., chief exec. officer. Served to 1st lt. arty AUS, 1962-64. Mem. ASCE, St. Louis Engrs. Club. Office: Fruin-Colnon Corp 1706 Olive St Saint Louis MO 63103

KOELSCH, M. OLIVER, fed. judge; b. Boise, Idaho, Mar. 5, 1912; m. Virginia Lee Daley, Oct. 30, 1937; children—Katherine, John, Jane (Mrs. Dennis P. Houghton). B.A., U. Wash., LL.B., 1935. Judge U.S. Ct. Appeals, San Francisco; now sr. judge 9th Circuit, Seattle. Office: US Ct Appeals US Courthouse Seattle WA 98104

KOELZER, VICTOR ALVIN, civil engr.; b. Seneca, Mo., May 3, 1914; s. Henry and Jane (Schneider) K.; m. Josephine Wellman, Nov. 25, 1950; 1 son, Gerald F. B.S. in Civil Engring, U. Kans., 1937; M.S. in Hydraulics, U. Iowa, 1939. Engr. U.S. Geol. Survey, 1938-40, C.E., 1940-42, Bur. Reclamation, 1946-56; engr., asso., v.p. Harza Engring. Co., Chgo., 1956-69; chief engr. Nat. Water Commn., Washington, 1969-72; part-time prof. civil engring. Colo. State U., Ft. Collins, also part-time cons. engr., developer irrigation land, 1972—; pres. Engineered Farms Inc., Ft. Collins, 1976—. Served to lt. USNR, 1942-46. Mem. ASCE (charter chmn. water resources planning and mgmt. council, Julian Hinds award 1975); hon. mem. Chi Epsilon. Address: 1604 Miramont Dr Fort Collins CO 80524

KOEN, BILLY VAUGHN, mechanical engineering educator; b. Graham, Tex., May 2, 1938; s. Ottis Vaughn and Margaret (Branch) K.; m. Deanne Rollins, June 3, 1967; children: Kent, Douglas. B.A. in Chemistry, U. Tex., 1961, B.S. in Chem. Engring., 1961; S.M. in Nuclear Engring., MIT, 1962, Sc.D., 1968; Diplome d'ingenieur en Genie Atomique, L'institut National des Scis. et Techniques Nucleaires, France, 1963. Asst. prof. mech. engring. U. Tex.-Austin, 1968-71, assoc. prof., 1971-80, Minnie S. Piper prof., 1980, prof., 1981—, dir. Bur. Engring. Teaching, 1973-76; prof. Ecole Centrale, Paris, 1983; cons., lectr. in field. Contbr. articles to profl. jours. Bd. dirs. Oak Ridge Associated Univs., 1975-76. Recipient Standard Oil Ind. award, 1970. Mem. Am. Soc. Engring. Edn. (Chester Carlson award 1980, dir. 1982—), Am. Nuclear Soc., Tex. Soc. Profl. Engrs., N.Y. Acad. Sci., AAAS, Association des Ingenieurs en Genie Atomique, Phi Beta Kappa, Sigma Xi (disting. lectr. 1981-83), Tau Beta Pi. Quaker. Club: Rotary (Austin) (Internat. fellow 1962). Home: 1302 Spyglass Apt 179 Austin TX 78746 Office: U Tex Dept Mech Engring ETC 5 160 Austin TX 78712

KOENIG, CHARLES LOUIS, chemist; b. Yonkers, N.Y., Oct. 11, 1911; s. Henry and Gertrude Marie (Holste) K.; m. Janie Ray Shofner; children—Livy, Charlou, Arthur, Friederich. B.S., N.Y.U, 1932, Ph.D. (Inman fellow 1932-33), 1936. Stack chief N.Y. Pub. Library, 1928-32; sr. chemist Solvay Process Co., Syracuse, N.Y., 1936-45; chemist Lithaloys Corp., N.Y.C., 1945-46; chem. cons., N.Y.C., 1945-47; chief, research branch, N.Y. directed operations AEC, 1946-47; chmn. chemistry and chem. engring. research Armour Research Found., 1947-49; asst. dir. research Stanford Research Inst., 1950-51; v.p. S.W. Research Inst., 1951-56, Louis Koenig Research, 1956—; cons. USPHS; lectr. Author numerous publs. on water resources and econs., including syndicated newspaper column.; Asst. editor: Chem. Abstracts, 1949—, Genealogist. Mem. A.A.A.S., Am. Chem. Soc. (nat. councilor), Am. Inst. Chemists, Am. Waterworks Assn., Am. Water Resources Assn., Am. Geophys. Union, Nat. Water Well Assn., Am. Inst. Chem. Engrs., Am. Assn. Cost Engrs., Water Pollution Control Fedn., Sci. Research Soc. Am., Sigma Xi. Address: Route 10 Box 108 San Antonio TX 78258

KOENIG, PAUL EDWARD, chemist, educator; b. Gallup, N.Mex., May 30, 1929; s. Leo Henry and Marie Barbara (Kolar) K.; m. Norma Adelaide Putnam, Dec. 26, 1950; children: Michael, Lawrence, Karen, Thomas, Paula, Thecla, Gretchen, Monica. B.S., U. Ariz., 1950, M.S., 1952; Ph.D., U. Iowa, 1955. Chemist Ethyl Corp., Baton Rouge, 1955-58; asst. prof. chemistry La. State U., Baton Rouge, 1958-63, assoc. prof. chemistry, 1963-67, also asst. head dept. chemistry, 1963-67, assoc. dean Grad. Sch., 1967-70, prof. chemistry, 1970—, asst. vice chancellor acad. affairs, 1970-81. Contbr. articles to sci. jours. Mem. Am. Chem. Soc. (Charles E. Coates meml. award 1972), Sigma Xi., Phi Beta Kappa, Phi Kappa Phi, Omicron Delta Kappa, Phi Kappa Theta. Club: Serra. Patentee in field. Home: 2006 Cherrydale St Baton Rouge LA 70808 Office: Dept Chemistry Louisiana State University Baton Rouge LA 70803 *I believe that life should be joyous and zestful. When life does not please me, I am inclined to look outside myself for the cause. In fact, the difficulty is usually that I have fallen victim to fear, doubt, envy, and despair. The remedy is to rekindle faith and love by prayer and meditation so that my heart is renewed and life is joyful again. Sometimes it takes a long time to recover*

KOENIG, ROBERT JOHN, museum director; b. Union City, N.J., June 6, 1935; s. John Adolf and Albertina (Wolf) K.; m. Audrey Florence Haase, Apr. 23, 1963. B.S. in Art Edn., Pratt Inst., 1957; B.F.A., Yale U., 1959, M.F.A., 1961. Exhbn. designer Newark Mus., 1961-63; instr. art Pub. Sch. System, Union City, N.J., 1963-69; asst. dir. Morris Mus. Arts and Sci., Morristown, N.J., 1969-76; asst. dir., assoc. dir. Montclair Art Mus., N.J., 1976-80, dir., 1980—; bd. dirs. Museums Council, N.J. Author: (catalogues) Drawing the Line, 1978, Collage: American Masters, 1979, Adolf Konrad: Retrospective, 1980, Josef Albers: His Art and His Influence, 1981. Recipient Morris K. Widder award Yale U., 1960. Mem. Assn. Art Mus. Dirs., Am. Assn. Museums, Northeast Museums Conf., Am. Fedn. Arts. Office: Montclair Art Mus 3 S Mountain Ave PO Box 1582 Montclair NJ 07042

KOENIG, VIRGIL, biochemist, educator; b. Kansas City, Mo., Oct. 10, 1913; s. John William and Hilah Ethel (Ward) K.; m. Hildegard Zerne, Feb. 26, 1949; children: LeRoy William, Lawrence Nils, Cynthia Sonsie, Patrick Christopher. A.B., U. Mo.-Kansas City, 1936; M.S., Okla. State U., 1938; Ph.D., U. Colo., 1940; LL.B., LaSalle Extension U., Chgo., 1975; M.A., U. Houston-Clear Lake, 1984. With Armour & Co., Chgo., 1941-48; staff mem. Los Alamos Sci. Lab., 1948-54; prin. scientist VA Research Hosp., Chgo., 1954-56; asst. prof., then asso. prof. biochemistry Northwestern U., 1954-60; prin. scientist Gen. Mills Co., Mpls., 1960-63; prof. biochemistry U. Tex. Med. Br., Galveston, 1963—, chmn. dept., 1963-71; vis. investigator Oak Ridge Nat. Lab., 1972-73. Author papers in field. Trustee, Village of Brookfield, Ill., 1957-60. Mem. Seventh Day Adventist Ch. Home: 8701 Twelve Oaks Dr Texas City TX 77501 Office: U Tex Med Branch Galveston TX 77550

KOENIG, WOLFGANG W., banker; b. Basel, Switzerland, May 3, 1936; s. Werner E. and Else (Herbold) K.; m. Miriam R. Davis, May 18, 1958; children: Lynn Ellen, David Werner. A.B., Muhlenberg Coll., 1957; postgrad., N.Y. U. Grad. Sch. Bus., 1958-61, Grad. Sch. Credit and Fin. Mgmt., Amos Tuck Sch., 1968. With Irving Trust Co., N.Y.C., 1958—, v.p., 1968-80, sr. v.p., 1980—, mgr. trade fin., 1983—. Councilman, Shrewsbury, N.J., 1968-73. Served with U.S. Army, 1957. Republican. Presbyterian. Club: Beacon Hill (Summit, N.J.). Office: 1 Wall St New York NY 10005

KOENIGSBERG, MARVIN LEE, lawyer; b. Chgo., Dec. 10, 1918; s. Isadore and Minnie (Oliff) K.; m. Rita Wilks Volid, June 18, 1980. B.S.L., Northwestern U., 1942, J.D., 1942. Bar: Ill. Bar 1942. Since practiced in, Chgo.; asso. Legal Aid Bur. Chgo., 1942-44; partner firm Friedman & Koven (and predecessors), 1951—; Asst. sec. Hilton Hotels Corp. Bd. dirs. Jewish Home for Aged, Chgo. Mem. Am., Ill., Chgo. bar assns., Decalogue Soc., Praetorians, Tau Epsilon Rho., B'nai B'rith (lodge pres. 1952). Club: Covenant (Chgo.). Home: 1550 N Lake Shore Dr Chicago IL 60611 Office: 208 S La Salle St Suite 900 Chicago IL 60604

KOENKER, ERNEST BENJAMIN, history educator; b. Regent, N.D., Aug. 8, 1920; s. Ernest Henry and Caroline (Libbe) K.; m. Hazel Norma Marten, June 9, 1946; children: Mark, Deborah, Gregory. Grad. cum laude, Concordia Coll., Ft. Wayne, Ind., 1941; B.A., Concordia Sem., St. Louis, 1943, M.Div., 1946; Ph.D., U. Chgo., 1950. Instr. religion Valparaiso U., Ind., 1947-54, asst. prof., 1954-62, assoc. prof. theology and philosophy, 1963-65; Lutheran chair Grad. Sch. Religion U. So. Calif., Los Angeles, 1965-67, assoc. prof. history, 1967-72, prof. history, 1972—. Author: Great Dialecticians in Modern Christian Thought, 1971, Secular Salvations, 1965, The Liturgical Renaissance in the Roman Catholic Church, 1954, Worship in Word and Sacrament, 1958. Recipient prize Christian Research Found., 1960-61. Mem. Historians of Early Modern Europe, 16th Century Studies Conf., Italian Hist. Assn. Lutheran. Home: 13025 Hindry Ave Hawthorne CA 90250 Office: Dept History U So Calif University Park Los Angeles CA 90007

KOEPCKE, F. KRISTEN, lawyer; b. Madison, Wis., July 30, 1935; s. Kenneth A. and Esther D. (Nybroten) K.; m. Kayleen Vinton, Jan. 29, 1956 (div.); children: Kristen, Kendra; m. Shirley Peraino, Oct. 13, 1973. B.S., U. Wis., 1957, LL.B., 1964. Bar: Wis. 1964, Ind. 1972, U.S. Patent Office 1967, U.S. Supreme Ct. 1972. Assoc. Bast & Sendik, Milw., 1964-66; sr. atty. Koehring Co., Milw., 1966-72; v.p., gen. counsel, sec. Hillenbrand Industries, Batesville, Ind., 1972—. Served to capt. U.S. Army, 1958-61. Mem. U.S. Patent Law Assn., ABA, Nat. Soc. Corp. Secs. Episcopalian. Club: Hillcrest Country (pres. 1978-81). Home: RD2 Stockpile Rd Batesville IN 47006 Office: Hillenbrand Industries Inc SR 46 Batesville IN 47006

KOEPKE, GEORGE HENRY, physician; b. Toledo, Jan. 1, 1916; s. George Herman and Louise Florence (Kutz) K.; m. Helen LaBoiteaux, Oct. 6, 1940; children—Susan (Mrs. David Healy), Sandra (Mrs. Bradley Hitt). B.S., U. Toledo, 1945; M.D., U. Cin., 1949. Intern Toledo Hosp., 1949-50; resident Univ. Hosp., Ann Arbor, Mich., 1950-53; pvt. practice specializing phys. medicine and rehab., Toledo, 1954, Saginaw, Mich., 1976—; prof. U. Mich. Med. Sch., 1954-76, ret., 1976; mem. staff St. Mary's Hosp., Saginaw, 1976—, Community Hosp., Gen. Hosp., St. Luke's Hosp.; Past chmn. Am. Bd. Phys. Medicine and Rehab., 1969. Mem. AMA, Am. Acad. Phys. Medicine and Rehab., Am. Acad. Orthopaedic Surgeons, Am. Congress Rehab. Medicine, Saginaw County Med Soc. Home: 377 Winthrop Ln Saginaw MI 48603 Office: St Mary's Hosp Saginaw MI 48601 *Excel in at least one area in medicine and have a good secretary.*

KOEPKE, JOHN ARTHUR, clin. pathologist, hematologist; b. Milw., Mar. 25, 1929; s. Elmer Paul and Meta Clara (Jennrich) K.; m. Evelyn Mae Lovekamp, June 18, 1955; children—Mary Evelyn, John Frederick, Mark David, James Robert. B.A., Valparaiso U., 1951; M.D., U. Wis., 1956; M.S., Marquette U., 1964. Intern, resident in clin. pathology Milw. Hosp., 1956-60; mem. faculty U. Ky. Coll. Medicine, 1961-71, asso. prof., 1965-71; dir. clin. pathology, prof. pathology U. Iowa, Iowa City, 1972-79, vice chmn. dept., 1972-79; prof. pathology Coll. Medicine, Duke U., Durham, N.C., 1979—, med. dir. transfusion service and clin. hematology labs., 1979—. Author 2 books in field.; Bd. editors: Am. Jour. Clin. Pathology, 1976—, Clin. and Lab. Hematology, 1978—; contbr. articles to profl. jours. Recipient Pres.'s award Valparaiso U., 1951, Disting. Alumnus award, 1980. Fellow Am. Soc. Clin. Pathologists, Coll. Am. Pathologists; mem. Am. Assn. Blood Banks, Am. Fedn. Clin. Research, Central Soc. Clin. Research, AMA, Am. Soc. Hematology. Lutheran. Home: 3924 St Mark's Rd Durham NC 27707 Office: Duke U Med Center PO Box 3712 Durham NC 27710

KOEPP, DONALD WILLIAM, librarian; b. Shell Lake, Wis., Apr. 27, 1929; s. Ernest Edward and Helen Mary K.; m. Dale Stewart, Dec. 7, 1963; children: Martha Jean, John Stewart, Jennifer Ellen. A.B., U. Wis., 1951, M.L.S., 1956; D.L.S., U. Calif., Berkeley, 1966. With U. Calif., Berkeley, 1958-68; librarian Inst. Govtl. Studies, 1961-65, asst. univ. librarian, 1965-68; univ. librarian Humboldt State U., 1968-73, Ariz. State U., 1973-78, Princeton U., 1978—; bd. dirs. AMIGOS Bibliog. Council, 1975-77, Center Research Libraries, 1975-79, Research Libraries Group, 1979—, Princeton U. Press, 1980—. Author: Public Library Government—Seven Case Studies, 1968. Served with U.S. Army, 1951-53. Office: Princeton U Library Princeton NJ 08544

KOEPPE, OWEN JOHN, university provost; b. Cedar Grove, Wis., May 29, 1926; s. Edwin Walter and Elizabeth Mary (Renskers) K.; m. JoAnn E. Moessner, June 14, 1950; children: John F., Robert A., Barbara A. A.B., Hope Coll., 1949; M.S., U. Ill., 1951, Ph.D., 1953. Successively asst. prof., assoc. prof., prof. U. Mo.-Columbia, to 1980, chmn. biochemistry dept., 1968-73, provost acad. affairs, 1973-80; provost Kans. State U., Manhattan, 1980—. Served with USNR, 1944-46. Mem. Am. Chem. Soc., Am. Soc. Biol. Chemists, Sigma Xi. Presbyterian. Office: Kans State Univ Manhattan KS 66506 *

KOEPPEL, DONALD ALLEN, bus. exec.; b. Chgo., Oct. 17, 1917; s. Joseph John and Ethel Mae (Cowley) K.; m. Gloria Lorraine Allan, Mar. 20, 1948; children—Bruce Allan, John Paul, Robert James. B.S., Northwestern U., 1949; J.D., Chgo. Kent Coll. Law, 1954. Bar: Ill. bar 1955. Mgmt. trainee Swift & Co., Chgo., 1937-42; gen. counsel, sec. Belnap & Thompson Co., Chgo., 1947-56; pres., dir. Blue Chip Stamps, Los Angeles, 1956—; dir. Buffalo Evening News, Precision Steel Warehouse; Inc. Past chmn. Los Angeles Regional Purchasing Council; bd. dirs., past pres. Cancer Research Assos., U. So. Calif. Med. Center.; Past trustee, mem. exec. com. U. Redlands; past bd. dirs. Hispanic Urban Center, Los Angeles. Served with U.S. Army, 1943-46. Decorated Bronze Star medal. Mem. Ill., Chgo. bar assns., Los Angeles C. of C. (past dir.), Walnut Elephant. Congregationalist. Club: Rctary (Los Angeles) (past pres.). Home: 1445 Caballero Rd Arcadia CA 91006 Office: 5801 S Eastern Ave Los Angeles CA 90040

KOEPSEL, WELLINGTON WESLEY, educator; b. McQueeney, Tex., Dec. 1921; s. Wesley Wellington and Hulda (Nagel) K.; m. Dorothy Helen Adams, June 25, 1950; children—Kirsten Marta, Gretchen Lisa, Wellington Lief. B.S. in Elec. Engring, U. Tex., 1944, M.S., 1951; Ph.D., Okla. State U., 1960. Engr. City Pub. Service Bd., San Antonio, 1946-47; research sci. Mil. Physics Research Lab., U. Tex., 1948-51; research engr. North Am. Aviation, Downey, Calif., 1951; asst. prof. So. Methodist U., 1951-59; asso. prof. U. N.Mex., Alburquerque, 1960-63, Duke, 1963-64; prof., head dept. elec. engring. Kans. State U., Manhattan, 1964-76, prof. elec. engring., 1976—. Contbr. articles profl. jours. Served from ensign to lt. (j.g.) USNR, 1944-46. Mem. Nat. Soc. Profl. Engrs., I.E.E.E., Eta Kappa Nu. Home: 2815 Illinois Ln Manhattan KS 66502

KOERBER, LORENZ FRED, JR., lawyer; b. Joliet, Ill., Jan. 19, 1921; s. Lorenz F. and Henrietta (Stryker) K.; m. Margareta Dunne, Apr. 12, 1947; children—Peter L., Ellen B., Joan C., John V. A.B., U. Chgo., 1941, LL.B., 1942. Bar: Ill. bar 1942. Atty. SEC, 1942; asso., then partner firm McDermott, Will & Emery, Chgo., 1946-57, sr. partner, 1957—; dir. Ohio Art Co. Sec. United Way-Crusade of Mercy, Chgo., 1960-80. Served with AUS, 1942-46. Mem. Am. Bar Assn., Ill. Bar Assn., Chgo. Bar Assn. Roman Catholic. Clubs: Chgo. Yacht, Midday (Chgo.); Evanston (Ill.) Golf. Home: 1336 Hillside Rd Northbrook IL 60062 Office: 111 W Monroe St Chicago IL 60603

KOERING, MARILYN JEAN, anatomy educator, researcher; b. Brainerd, Minn., Jan. 7, 1938; d. Clement J. and Vi K. (Holtkamp) K. B.A., Coll. St. Scholastica, Duluth, 1960; M.S., U. Wis., 1963; Ph.D., U. Coll., 1967; postgrad., U. Wis., 1968. Instr. dept. anatomy U. Wis., 1963-64; asst. prof. George Washington U., 1969-73, assoc. prof., 1973-79, prof. anatomy, 1979—; vis. assoc. div. biology Calif. Inst. Tech., 1976; affiliate scientist Wis. Primate Research Ctr., Madison, 1975-78; guest worker Pregnancy Research br. NICHD, 1977—. Mem. editorial bd.: Biology of Reproduction, 1974-78; contbr. articles to profl. jours. NIH fellow, 1967-68; NIH grantee, 1969—. Mem. Am. Assn. Anatomists, Soc. Study Reproduction, AAAS, Washington Assn. Electron Microscopists, Sigma Xi. Office: Dept Anatomy George Washington U Med Ctr 2300 I St Washington DC 20037

KOERNER, JAMES DAVID, author, found. exec.; b. Cedar Rapids, Iowa, Feb. 3, 1923; s. John A. and May K. (Watson) K. B.A., Washington U., St. Louis, 1947, M.A., 1949, Ph.D. in Am. Studies, 1952. Mem. faculty Kans. State U., 1952-54; mem. faculty humanities Mass. Inst. Tech., 1956-58; exec. dir Council Basic Edn., Washington, 1959-61, pres., 1962; editor-in-chief Edn. Devel. Center, Inc., 1967-70; program officer Alfred P. Sloan Found., 1970-80, v.p., 1980—. Author: The Miseducation of American Teachers, 1963, Reform In Education: England And The United States, 1968, Who Controls American Education?, 1968, The Parsons College Bubble: A tale of Higher Education in America, 1970, Hoffer's America: A Walk around Town with Eric Hoffer, 1973; Editor: The Case for Basic Education, 1959, (with D. Colville) The Craft of Writing, 1961; Contbr. to nat. periodicals. Served as pilot USAAF, 1942-45. Grantee Lilly Endowment and Council Basic Edn., 1964-66; Ford postdoctoral fellowship, 1954-55. Home: 60 S Maple Ave Westport CT 06880 Office: Alfred P Sloan Found 630 Fifth Ave New York NY 10020

KOERNER, VICTOR FREDERICK, machinery company executive; b. Pitts., July 30, 1911; s. Albert Jacob and Frieda (Dennis) K.; m. Martha Reed Potter, Oct. 8, 1938; children: Theresa Jane, Albert Frederick, James Potter. Student, Carnegie-Mellon U., 1929-32; B.S., Duquesne U., 1937. Jr. accountant Price-Waterhouse & Co., 1935-36; with Mesta Machine Co., Pitts., 1936-76, asst. treas., 1963, treas., 1963-76. Active local Boy Scouts Am., Little League Baseball.; Bd. dirs. South Hills Health System, Pa., 1973—, v.p., 1973-74, pres., 1974—; bd. dirs. Upper St. Clair Library, 1978—, v.p., 1980-81, pres., 1981—; mem. Instl. Care Com. Allegheny County, 1978—; mem. candidates and credentials com. Pitts. Presbytery, 1972—. Served with USNR, 1943-45. Mem. Fin. Execs. Inst., Kappa Sigma (dir. Delta Alpha club 1973, treas. 1975—). Presbyn. Clubs: Masons; Valley Brook Country (Mt. Lebanon, Pa.). Home: 2210 Country Club Dr Pittsburgh PA 15241 *This I have learned beyond a doubt: satisfaction from a task well done is the greatest reward.*

KOERNER, WALTER CHARLES, former industrialist; b. Moravia, Czechoslovakia, July 21, 1898; emigrated to Can., 1939; s. John Isadora and Maria (Beck) K.; m. Marianne Hikl, May 3, 1923; children: Nicholas Thomas, Michael Milan. Edn., U. Prague, U. Vienna; LL.D. (hon.), U. N.B., 1964, U. Victoria, 1964, U. B.C., 1973; D.B.A. (hon.), U. Notre Dame, Nelson, B.C., 1971. Ret. bus. exec., now active pub. service. Active St. John Ambulance, Cedar Lodge Sch. for Handicapped. Served to 1st lt. Imperial Austo-Hungarian Army, World War I. Decorated companion Order of Can., 1967; Knight Venerable Order St. John, London, 1963. Fellow Royal Soc. Can. Clubs: Faculty U. B.C., University, Shaughnessy Golf and Country, Vancouver Lawn Tennis and Badminton; Southlands Riding (Vancouver); Rideau (Ottawa, Can.): Home: 1203 Matthews Ave Vancouver BC Canada V6H 1W5 Office: 1055 W Hastings St Suite 1120 Vancouver BC Canada V6E 2E9

KOESSEL, DONALD RAY, banker; b. Grand Rapids, Mich., May 15, 1929; s. Fred Christian and Erna Wilhelmina (Grein) K.; m. Mary Phelps, July 7, 1977; children by previous marriage: Martin, Kathryn. B.A., Yale U., 1951; M.B.A., Harvard U., 1955. Copywriter Grand Rapids Press, 1951-52; public relations rep. Smith Kline & French Labs., 1952-53; money market analyst Nat. Shawmut Bank of Boston, 1955-58; asst. sec. 1st Bank System, Mpls., 1958-65, asst. v.p., 1962-65; with 1st Nat. Bank Mpls., 1965—, exec. v.p., 1975—, chmn. trust com., 1979—; dir. Otter Tail Power Co., Life Care Retirement Communities, Inc., Security Am. Fin. Enterprises Inc., Consumer Growth Capital Inc. Bd. dirs. KTCA Public TV, Minn. Orchestral Assn. Mem. Harvard Bus. Sch. Club Minn., Yale Alumni Assn. N.W. Home: 10 Greenway Gables Minneapolis MN 55403 Office: 1st National Bank Minneapolis 1st Bank Pl E Minneapolis MN 55480

KOESTER, CHARLES BEVERLEY, canadian government official; b. Jan. 13, 1926; 5 children. Ed., Regina Central Collegiate Inst., Royal Can. Naval Coll., U. Sask., U. Alta. Served to lt. comdr. Royal Can. Navy and Royal Can. Navy Res., 1942-60; tchr., head history dept. Sheldon-Williams Collegiate, Regina, Sask., 1956-59; clk. asst. Legis. Assembly of Sask., 1959-60, clk., 1960-69; assoc. prof. history U. Regina, Sask., 1969-75, head history dept., 1974-75; clk. asst. Can. House of Commons, Ottawa, 1975-79, clk., 1979—. Office: House of Commons Ottawa ON Canada K1A 0A6 *

KOESTER, CHARLES L., bishop; b. Jefferson City, Mo., Sept. 16, 1915. Student, Conception Acad., Mo., Prep. Sem. and Kenrick Sem., Mo., N.Am. Coll., Rome. Ordained priest Roman Catholic Ch. 1941. Ordained titular bishop Suacia and aux. bishop, St. Louis, 1971—. Office: No 15 Plaza Sq St Louis MO 63103 *

KOESTER, HELMUT HEINRICH, theologian, educator; b. Hamburg, Germany, Dec. 18, 1926; came to U.S., 1958; s. Karl and Marie-Luise (Eitz) K.; m. Gisela G. Harrassowitz, July 8, 1953; children: Reinhild, Almut, Ulrich, Heiko. Dr. Theol., U. Marburg, Germany, 1954; Privatdozent, U. Heidelberg, Germany, 1956. Ordained to ministry Luth. Ch., 1956; asst. pastor, Hannover, Germany, 1951-54; teaching asst., then asst. prof. U. Heidelberg, 1954-56, 56-58, 59; mem. faculty Harvard Div. Sch., 1958—, John H. Morison prof. N.T. studies, 1964—, Winn prof. ecclesiastical history, 1968—; vis. prof. U. Heidelberg, 1963, Drew U., 1966. Author: Synoptische Ueberlieferung bei den Apostolischen Vaetern, in Texte und Untersuchungen, 1957, Trajectories through Early Christianity, (with James M. Robinson), 1971, Einfuehrung in das Neue Testament, 1979, Introduction to the New Testament, 1982; editor: Handbook Religion and Culture of the Lands of the New Testament. Asso. trustee Am. Schs. Oriental Research, 1974-75; trustee William F. Albright Inst. Archaeol. Research, 1974-80. Served with German Navy, 1944-45. Guggenheim fellow, 1964-65; Am. Council Learned Socs. fellow, 1971-72, 78-79. Fellow Am. Acad. Arts and Scis.; mem. Soc. Bibl. Lit., Soc. Novi Testamenti Studiorum. Home: 12 Flintlock Rd Lexington MA 02173 Office: 45 Francis Ave Cambridge MA 02138

KOESTER, ROBERT GREGG, record co. exec.; b. Wichita, Kans., Oct. 30, 1932; s. Edward Albert and Mary (Frank) K.; m. Susan Buescher; children—Robert, Katherine. Student, St. Louis U., 1951-54. Organizer, propr. Blue Note Record Shop, St. Louis, 1952-58, Delmark Records, 1952—; founder Jazz Report mag., 1953, pub., 1953-60; owner Seymour's Jazz Mart, 1959-61; founder-owner Jazz Record Mart, 1961—; pub., editor Blues News Bull., 1961-67. Contbr. numerous articles, chpt. in book. Recipient Grand Prix du Disque Hot Club France, 1963, 71, Jay award for best blues LP, 1966, Internat. Critics Poll award Jazz mag. Mem. Nat. Assn. Ind. Record Distbrs. and Mfrs., Jazz Inst. Chgo. (charter, dir.). Home: 4243 N Lincoln Ave Chicago IL 60618 Office: 11 W Grand Ave Chicago IL 60610 *I have managed to afford myself the luxury of making my living in the music* *business where my daily occupation is with the music that I have loved since my early teen years so that I enjoy my work far beyond any other occupation that I might otherwise have chosen.*

KOESTNER, ADALBERT, pathology educator; b. Hatzfeld, Romania, Sept. 10, 1920; came to U.S., 1955; s. Johann and Gertrud (Gruber) K.; m. Adelaide Wacker, Jan. 20, 1951; children: George A., Rosemarie K. D.V.M., U. Munich, W. Ger., 1951; M.S., Ohio State U., 1957, Ph.D., 1959. Diplomate: Am. Bd. Vet. Pathology. Practice vet. medicine (Untergriesbach), Bavaria, W. Ger., 1951-55; faculty mem. Ohio State U., Columbus, 1955-81, prof. vet. pathology, 1964-81, chmn. dept., 1972-81; prof. pathology, chmn. dept. Mich. State U. Colls. Human, Osteo. and Vet. Medicine, East Lansing, 1981—; treas. Am. Bd. Toxicology, Washington, 1979-83; mem. sci. adv. bd. Nat. Ctr. Toxicol. Research, Jefferson, Ark., 1981—. Author: Diseases of Swine, 1975; contbr. chpt. to books, articles to profl. jours.; editorial bd.: Internat. Jour. Anticancer Research, 1981—. Spl. vis. scientist Max Planck Inst. Brain Research, Cologne, W. Ger., 1970, 73, 75; neuro-oncology grantee Nat. Cancer Inst., 1968—. Mem. AVMA (chmn. adv. bd. vet. spltys. 1982, Gaines award 1979), Am. Assn. Neuropathologists (Weil award 1971), Am. Assn. Pathologists, Internat. Acad. Pathology, Soc. Neurosics., Am. Assn. Cancer Research. Roman Catholic. Home: 2578 Woodhill Dr Okemos MI 48864 Office: Dept Pathology Mich State U 622 E Fee Hall Lansing MI 48824

KOFF, RICHARD MYRAM, publishing consultant; b. N.Y.C., Jan. 8, 1926; s. Harry and Riva (Mohl) K.; m. Mary Alice Coudreaut, May 3, 1958 (div. Feb. 1969); children: Christopher Stephen, Kathleen Janette; m. Hunter Duncan Campbell, Jan. 29, 1977. B. Mech. Engring., N.Y. U., 1948, M. Mech. Engring., 1950. Registered profl. engr., N.Y. Research engr. Am. Hydromath Corp., N.Y.C., 1949-55; with Product Engring. mag. McGraw Hill Inc., N.Y.C., 1956-66, mng. editor, 1960-66; adminstrv. editor Playboy mag., Chgo., 1966-71, asst. pub., 1972-77, OUI mag., Chgo., 1972-76; mgr. new publs. div. Playboy Enterprises, Inc., 1971-74, dir. new publs., 1974-76, v.p., 1974-77, bus. mgr., 1976-77; pub. cons., 1977—; adj. prof. Medill Sch. Journalism, Northwestern U., 1981-83. Author: Fluid Power Controls, 1959, How Does It Work?, 1961, Home Computers, 1979, The Whole Home Electronic Catalog, 1979; (novel) Christopher, 1981; Strategic Planning for Magazine Executives, 1981; contbr. articles to profl. jours. Served with USAAF, 1944-45. Recipient Jesse H. Neal editorial achievement award Am. Bus. Press, 1959, 60, 62. Mem. IEEE. Patentee 2 adult games. Home and Office: 1031 Sheridan Rd Evanston IL 60202

KOFLER, JOHN FRANK, computer executive; b. Chgo., Oct. 6, 1939; s. John Leopold and Marie K. B.S., So. Ill. U.-Carbondale, 1962. Asst. sec. Boothe Computer, Chgo., 1968-72; v.p. Comdisco, Inc., Rosemont, Ill., 1972-75, dir., v.p. key accounts, 1983—; dir., sr. v.p. internat. Comdisco Internat. Sales Corp., Chgo., 1979-83; pres. Kofler Computer, Inc., Rosemont, Ill., 1976—, dir. Advisor Immaculate High Sch., Chgo., 1980; mem. assoc. bd. Grant Hosp., Chgo., 1975. Served with USN, 1962-63. Home: 1550 State Pkwy Chicago IL 60610 Office: Comdisco Inc 6400 Shafer Ct Rosemont IL 60018

KOFOED, JACK FRANK, art materials manufacturing company executive; b. Pelham, N.Y., June 24, 1926; s. Leo Konrad and Alice Marie (Valentine) K.; m. Joan Dannehower, Dec. 9, 1950; children: Peter, William, Catherine. B.A. in Econs, Middlebury Coll., 1948. Account exec. Young & Rubicam Advt. Agy., 1948-59; mgr. product devel. Gen. Foods Corp., 1959-61; v.p., gen. mgr. Diamond Crystal Salt Co., 1961-66; pres., chief exec. officer Venus Esterbrook Corp., N.Y.C., 1966-68; exec. v.p., div. mgr. Knomark Inc. div. Papercraft Inc., N.Y.C., 1969-74; pres., chief operating officer Binney & Smith, Inc., Easton, Pa., 1975—, chief exec. officer, 1981—, chmn., 1982—. Bd. dirs. Lehigh Valley Bus. Conf. on Health Care, Allentown Art Mus., Easton C. of C. Served to lt. USNR, 1944-46. Episcopalian. Clubs: Univ. (N.Y.C.); Pomfret, Country of Northampton County (Easton); Manursing Island (Rye, N.Y.). Office: 1100 Church Ln Easton PA 18042

KOFOID, CHARLES M., university administrator; b. Omaha, June 24, 1930; s. Fremodt J. and Ruth I. (Carter) K.; m. Helen D. Halstead, Aug. 9, 1953; children: Holly (dec.), Jodi, Lori, Shon, Kyle. B.A., U. Nebr., 1953, M.Ed., 1955, D.Ed., 1962. Tchr. Wahoo (Nebr.) public schs., 1953-54; supt. Weston (Nebr.) public schs., 1955-56, Ulysses (Nebr.) public schs., 1956-58; tchr. Lincoln (Nebr.) public schs., 1958-63; chmn. dept. edn. Sioux Falls Coll., 1963-68; asst. to dean Sch. Edn., U. Wis., Eau Claire, 1968-70; asst. dean Sch. Edn., Eastern Ill. U., 1970-74; assoc. dean Sch. Edn., Indiana U. Pa., 1974-76, dean, 1976-83; v.p. acad. affairs Graceland Coll., Lamoni, Iowa, 1983—. Dir. Operation Uplift, United Ministry. Mem. NEA, Soc. Profs. Edn., Assn. Higher Edn., Assn. Supervision and Curriculum Devel., Pa. Assn. Supervision and Curriculum Devel. (faculty sponsor), Phi Delta Kappa (regional pres.). Republican. Mem. Disciples of Christ. Office: Main Bldg Lamoni IA 50140

KOFRANEK, ANTON MILES, floriculturist, educator; b. Chgo., Feb. 5, 1921; s. Antonin J. and Emma (Rehorek) K.; children—Nancy (Mrs. Thomas A. Pitino), John A. B.S., U. Minn., 1947; M.S., Cornell U., 1949, Ph.D., 1950. Asst. prof. to prof. U. Calif., Los Angeles, 1950-68, prof. hort. dept., Davis, 1968—; vis. prof. U. Wageningen, Netherlands, 1958, Cornell U., 1966, Hebrew U., Rehovot, Israel, 1972-73, Lady Davis fellow, 1980; vis. prof. Glasshouse Crops Research Inst., Littlehampton, U.K., 1980. Co-author: (with Hartmann and Flocker) Plant Science—Growth, Development and Utilization of Cultivated Plants, 1981, Plant Science, 1981; co-editor: (with R. A. Larson) U. Calif. Azalea Manual, 1975; Contbr. articles to profl. jours. Served with AUS, 1942-45; ETO; Served with AUS; PTO. Recipient Research awards of merit Calif. State Florist Assn., 1966, Garland award, 1974; named Young Man of Year Westwood Jr. C. of C., 1956. Fellow Am. Soc. Hort. Sci (dir., sectional chmn. 1973-74); mem. Sigma Xi, Pi Alpha Xi. *Always give dollar value for the work you promise to perform.*

KOGA, MARY, photographer, social worker; b. Sacramento, Aug. 10, 1920; d. Hisakichi Harry and Tsugime (Yoneda) Ishii; m. Albert M. Koga, June 28, 1947. B.A., U. Calif., Berkeley, 1942; M.A. (sch. social service adminstrn. scholar), U. Chgo., 1947; M.F.A., Art Inst. Chgo., 1973. With Family Service Bur., United Charities of Chgo., 1947-52; chief psychiat. social worker Med. Sch. Northwestern U., 1952-58; asst. prof. clin. social work Sch. Social Service Adminstrn. U. Chgo., 1959-69; adj. prof. photography dept. Columbia Coll., Chgo., 1973—. Contbr. to: Women of Photography, 1975, Family of Children, 1977, others; One woman shows, Sch. of Art Inst. Chgo., 1971, Evanston Art Center, 1972, Shado Gallery, 1977, Utah State U., 1979, Pitts. Filmmakers Gallery, 1983, group shows include, Art Inst. Chgo., 1973, Smithsonian Traveling Exhbn., 1975, U. Mich., 1978, San Francisco Mus. Modern Art, 1975, 78, others; represented in permanent collections, San Francisco Mus. Modern Art, Exchange Nat. Bank, Seagram Co., Kimberley Clark Corp. Chmn. bd. Japan Am. Soc. Chgo., Inc., 1967—. Ill. Arts Council grantee, 1979; Nat. Endowment Arts grantee, 1982. Mem. Soc. Photographic Edn., Friends of Photography, Photog. Soc., Nat. Assn. Social Workers. Address: 1254 Elmdale Ave Chicago IL 60660

KOGAN, BERNARD ROBERT, English language educator; b. Chgo., May 16, 1920; s. Isaac and Ida (Perlman) K.; m. Irene Horwitz, 1962; children: Henry, Sophia, Naomi, Sara. A.B., U. Chgo., 1941, A.M., 1946, Ph.D., 1953. Instr. English Ind. U., 1946-48; instr. humanities U. Chgo., 1949-51; mem. faculty U. Ill., Chgo., 1952—, now prof. English. Author, editor: Narrative Techniques in the Later Novels of Charles Dickens, The Chicago Haymarket Riot: Anarchy on Trial, Darwin and His Critics. Mem. MLA. Address: 612 Lake Ave Wilmette IL 60091

KOGAN, HERMAN, author, consultant; b. Chgo., Nov. 6, 1914; s. Isaac and Ida (Perlman) K.; m. Alice Marie Schutt, Dec. 28, 1940 (div. 1946); m. Marilew C. Lowry, Oct. 1, 1950; children: Rick, Mark. Student, Crane Jr. Coll., 1932-33; A.B., U. Chgo., 1936, postgrad., 1936; student violin with, Isidor Braus; harmony and composition with, Walter Dellers, 1919-34. High school corr. Chgo. Daily News and Chgo. Eve. Post, 1930-32; reporter, rewrite man Chgo. City News Bur., 1935-37; reporter, feature writer, rewrite man Chgo. Tribune, 1937-42; with Chgo. Sun, 1942-47, editorial writer, 1943; feature writer, book editor, drama critic Chgo. Sun-Times, 1947-58; dir. co. relations Ency. Brit. Inc., 1958-61; asst. to exec. editor Chgo. Daily News; originator and editor Panorama, 1962-65; asst. gen. mgr. news and newspapers Field Communications Corp., 1965-68; editor Chgo. Sun Times Book Week, 1968-70, Chgo. Sun Times Showcase (later Show), 1970-77; corporate historian Field Enterprises, Inc., 1977—; lectr. Medill Sch. Journalism, 1947-49; Juror Pulitzer Prize Com., 1970-76; panelist Nat. Endowment for Humanities, 1970-75; host Writers and Writing, WFMT, 1973—; cons. Writing in Chgo. Program, 1975-78. (Recipient pub. award Geog. Soc. Chgo., contbns. to journalism award Am. Newspaper Guild, Adult Edn. Council award for Panorama, Book Week award Soc. Midland Authors and Friends of Lit., 2 Emmy awards Chgo. chpt. TV Acad. Arts and Scis., Communicator of Yr. award U. Chgo. Alumni Assn. 1972, Vicky Penziner award, Press Vet. of Year award Chgo. Press Vets. Assn. 1976, Ann. Disting. Service award Phi Beta Kappa 1976, Chgo. Press Club Hall of Fame); Author: (with Lloyd Wendt) Lords of the Levee, 1943, Uncommon Valor, 1947, Bet A Million, 1948, Give the Lady What She Wants, 1952, Big Bill of Chicago, 1953, The Great EB, 1958, Chicago: A Pictorial History, 1959, The Long White Line, 1963, Lending is Our Business, 1966, The Great Fire: Chicago 1871, (with Robert Cromie), 1971, A Continuing Marvel, 1973, The First Century, 1974, (with Rick Kogan) Yesterday's Chicago, 1976, Traditions and Challenges, 1983; contbr. to: Dictionary Am. Biography, Ency. Brit.; contbr.: articles to Midwest, Chgo. History, Nation, New Republic, Chgo., Fortune, Firehouse, others. Served with USMC, 1943-46. Decorated Presdl. Unit citation. Mem. P.E.N., Art Inst. Chgo. (life), Chgo. Hist. Soc. (life), Authors Guild, Chgo. Press Vets. (past chmn.), Soc. Midland Authors, Friends of Lit., Phi Beta Kappa, Sigma Delta Chi. Jewish. Clubs: Chgo. Press (past pres.); Arts (Chgo.).

KOGAN, RICHARD JAY, pharmaceutical company executive; b. N.Y.C., June 6, 1941; s. Benjamin and Ida K.; m. Susan Linda Scher, Aug. 29, 1965; children: Andrew, Pamela. B.A., CCNY, 1963; M.B.A., NYU, 1968. Dir. planning and adminstrn. Ciba Corp., Summit, N.J., 1968-69; v.p. planning pharm div. Ciba-Geigy Corp., Summit, 1970-76, pres. Can. pharm. div., Can., 1976-79, pres. U.S. pharm. div., Summit, 1979-82; exec. v.p. pharm. ops. Schering-Plough Corp., Kenilworth, N.J., 1982—, dir.; dir. Summit and Elizabeth Trust Co., Summit, Accts. Network Am., Los Angeles. Trustee St. Barnabas Med. Ctr., Livingston N.J., 1981—; mem. Pres.'s Com. Mental Retardation, Washington, 1982—. Office: Schering-Plough Corp 2000 Galloping Hill Rd Kennilworth NJ 07033

KOGELNIK, HERWIG WERNER, electronics co. exec.; b. Graz, Austria, June 2, 1932; came to U.S., 1960; s. Sepp and Siglinde K.; m. Christa Muller, Mar. 7, 1964; children—Christoph N., Florian A., Andreas M. Dipl.-Ing., Tech. U. Vienna, 1955, Dr.techn., 1958; D.phil., Oxford U., 1960. Mem. research staff Bell Labs., Murray Hill, N.J., 1961-67, head coherent optics research dept., Holmdel, N.J., 1967-76, dir. electronics research lab., 1976—. Contbr. articles in field to profl. jours. Chmn. Monmouth (N.J.) Arts Found., 1973-76. Fellow Optical Soc. Am. (chmn. tech. council), IEEE, Nat. Acad. Engring.; mem. AAAS, Am. Phys. Soc. Patentee in field of lasers, holography, electronics and optical communications. Home: 27 N Ward Ave Rumson NJ 07760 Office: Bell Labs Holmdel NJ 07733

KOGOVSEK, RAYMOND PETER, congressman; b. Pueblo, Colo., Aug. 19, 1941; s. Frank L. and Mary E. (Blatnick) K.; m. Eulice A. Kroschel, June 27, 1964; children: Lisa Marie, Toni Rae. B.A. in Bus. Adminstrn., Adams State Coll., Alamosa, Colo., 1964. Chief dep. clk., Pueblo County, Colo., 1964-73; mem. Colo. Ho. of Reps., 1969-70, Colo. Senate, 1971-78, 96th-98th Congresses from Colo. 3d Dist. Democrat. Roman Catholic. Prime sponsor Small Claims Ct. in State Colo., 1976. Home: 1627 Horseshoe Dr Pueblo CO 81001 Office: Ho of Reps 430 Cannon House Office Bldg Washington DC 20515

KOGUT, MAURICE DAVID, pediatric endocrinologist; b. Bklyn., July 7, 1930; s. Nat and Etta K.; m. June Patricia Wenzel, May 9, 1959; children: Melissa, Pamela, Stacy. B.A., N.Y. U., 1951, M.D., 1955. Diplomate: Am. Bd. Pediatrics. Pediatric intern and resident Bellevue Hosp., N.Y.C., 1955-57; chief resident in pediatrics Children's Hosp. of Los Angeles, 1959-60, fellow in pediatric endocrinology, 1960-62, head div. endocrinology and metabolism, 1970-80, asso. head dept. pediatrics, 1975-80, program dir. clin. research center, 1967-79; asst. prof. pediatrics Sch. Medicine, U. So. Calif., 1965-68, asso. prof., 1968-73, prof. pediatrics, 1973-80; prof. pediatrics, chmn. dept. of pediatrics Sch. Medicine Wright State U., Dayton, Ohio, 1980—; v.p. for med. affairs Children's Med. Center, Dayton, 1980—. (Recipient CINE/65 Golden Eagle film award for med. film 1965). Served as capt. M.C. USAF, 1957-59. USPHS fellow, 1960-62. Mem. Am. Acad. Pediatrics, Am. Acad. Med. Dirs., Soc. for Pediatric Research, Assn. Med. Sch. Pediatric Chairmen, AAAS, AMA, Am. Fedn. Clin. Research, Am. Diabetes Assn., Endocrine Soc., Am. Pediatric Soc., Lawson Wilkins Pediatric Endocrine Soc., Alpha Omega Alpha. Office: Children's Med Center 1 Children's Plaza Dayton OH 45404

KOH, SEVERINO LEGARDA, mech. engr., educator; b. Manila, Jan. 8, 1927; U.S., 1954, naturalized, 1972; s. Enrique Legarda and Felisa (Un) K.; m. Paz L. Ongjoco, July 19, 1952; children—Amelita P. Koh-Luncsford, Bernadette, Cynthia P. Koh-Knox, Dorothy (dec.), Evangeline. B.S. in Meteorology, N.Y. U., 1950, Nat. U., Manila, 1952; M.S., Pa. State U., 1957; Ph.D., Purdue U., 1962. Meteorologist Philippine Weather Bur., 1948-54; research asst. Johns Hopkins U., 1954-55; instr. engring. mechanics Pa. State U., 1955-57; research asso. Gen. Tech. Corp., W. Lafayette, Ind., 1959-61; mech. engr. Gen. Electric Co., Louisville, 1961-62; instr. engring. sci. Purdue U., West Lafayette, Ind., 1957-59, vis. research asso., 1962-64, asst. prof., 1964-66, asso. prof., 1966-72, prof., 1972-80, prof., head dept. engring., 1980-81; prof., chmn. dept. mech. engring. and mechanics W.Va. U., 1981—; vis. prof., research asso. Tech. U. Clausthal, W. Ger., 1968-69; vis. prof. Tech. U. Karlsruhe, W. Ger., 1969, U. Bonn, 1974-75; cons. Gen. Tech. Corp., 1962-64, Esso Production Research Co., 1967-69, Battelle N.W., 1978; cons., dir. 3IE, Inc., 1976—, pres., 1978—. Editor: The Engineering Science Perspective, 1976—; contbr. articles in fields of engring. sci., continuum mechanics, biomechanics, rheology, micromechanics, and geotech. engring. to profl. jours. Recipient Standard Oil Found. Outstanding Teaching award, 1967; Sigma Gamma Tau Outstanding Prof. award, 1968; Humboldt award W. Ger., 1974; named Balik Scientist Philippines, 1976, Faculty Fellow Shreve Hall, Purdue U., 1976; NSF, U.S. Army Research Office grantee. Mem. ASME, Soc. Engring. Sci. (founding sec. 1963-68, dir. 1970-73, 78-80), Philippine-Am. Acad. Sci. and Engring. (pres. 1980-81), Am. Acad. Mechanics, Am. Soc. Engring. Edn., Soc. Rheology, Philippine Profl. Assn., Purdue Filipino Assn., Sigma Xi, Sigma Pi Sigma, Sigma Gamma Tau. Presbyterian. Home: 801 Cottonwood Morgantown WV 26505 Office: Sch Mech Engring W Va Univ Morgantown WV 26506

KOHÁK, ERAZIM VÁCLAV, philosophy educator; b. Prague, Czechoslovakia, May 21, 1933; came to U.S., 1949, naturalized, 1953; s. Miloslav and Zdislava (Procházková) K.; m. Frances Macpherson, June 25, 1955 (div. 1976); children—Mary Zdislava, Susan Bozena, Katherine Macpherson; m. Sheree L. Dukes, May 3, 1981. B.A., Colgate U., 1954; M.A., Yale, 1957, Ph.D., 1958. Instr. Gustavus Adolphus Coll., 1958-59, asst. prof., 1959-60, Boston U., 1960-64, asso. prof., 1964-69, prof. philosophy, 1969—, chmn. dept. philosophy, 1983—, dir. grad. studies, 1970-78; vis. prof. philosophy Bowling Green State U., 1971; cons. Danforth Found., 1968-71; lectr.; columnist. Mem.: editorial bd. Boston U. Jour, 1967-70; Mem. editorial bd.: Dissent mag, 1969—; New Oxford Rev., 1982—; editor, translator: Freedom and Nature, 1966, Masaryk on Marx, 1972, Consolation from Philosophy, 1981; Author: (with Heda Margolius-Kovaly) The Victors and the Vanquished, 1973, Dialog pres barikádu, 1973, Idea and Experience, 1978, Národ v Nás, 1978, The Embers and the Stars, 1984; Contbr. articles to profl. jours. Alternate mem. nat. com. Democratic Socialist Organizing Com., 1972-74; adviser Young People's Socialist League, 1969-74, Episcopal Ch., 1974—; Trustee Somerville Public Libraries, 1976-79. Recipient Cooper prize in Classics, 1958; Danforth fellow, 1954—; Yale Hon. fellow, 1957; Boston U. Research grantee, 1967, 1969; OPUS Bonum fellow, 1978—. Mem. Am. Philos. Assn., Soc. Phenomenology and Existential Philosophy, Metaphys. Soc. Am., Czechoslovak Soc. Arts and Scis. (dir. 1965-68), Phi Beta Kappa. Home: RFD 2 Box 15B Jaffrey NH 03452 Office: Philosophy Dept Boston U Boston MA 02215

KOHL, BENEDICT M., lawyer; b. 1931. A.B., Brown U., 1952; LL.B. cum laude, Harvard U., 1955. Bar: D.C. 1955, U.S. Supreme Ct. 1962, N.J. 1963. Partner Lowenstein, Sandler, Brochin, Kohl, Fisher, Boylan & Meanor, Roseland, N.J.; atty. interpretative div. Office Chief Counsel, IRS, 1957-60, Office of Tax Legis. Counsel, U.S. Treasury Dept., 1960-62. N.J. pres. Am. Jewish Com., also mem. nat. bd. govs.; trustee Jewish Community Fedn. of Met. N.J., Jewish Hosp. and Rehab. Center N.J. Mem. ABA, N.J. State, Essex County bar assns. Office: 65 Livingston Ave Roseland NJ 07068

KOHL, JOHN CLAYTON, emeritus civil engineering educator; b. N.Y.C., June 22, 1908; s. Clayton C. and Margaret (Williams) K.; m. Gladys V. Mitchell, July 10, 1935; children: John Clayton, Atlee Mitchell. Student, Oberlin Coll., 1925-27; B.S.E., U. Mich., 1929; M.A. (hon.), U. Pa., 1973. Registered profl. engr., Pa. With Cin. Union Terminal Co., 1929-30; mem. faculty Carnegie Inst. Tech., 1930-37; with Pitts. Plate Glass Co. and subs. Pitts. Corning Corp., 1937-46; prof. civil engring., dir. Transp. Inst., U. Mich., 1946-66; on leave as asst. adminstr. HHFA, 1961-66; exec. v.p. Am. Transit Assn., Washington, 1966; exec. sec., div. engring. Nat. Acad. Scis.-NRC, 1966-68; sr. asso. Wilbur Smith & Assos., Washington, 1968-70; commr. N.J. Dept. Transp., 1970-74; prof. civil and urban engring. U. Pa., Phila., 1974-76, prof. emeritus, 1976—; Trustee Phila., Balt. and Washington, and Del. railroads, 1974-78; sr. vis. fellow Princeton U., 1976-81. Contbr. articles to profl. jours. Mem. Mich. Commn. Intergovtl. Relations, 1954-58; vice chmn. truck adv. bd. Mich. Pub. Service Commn., 1957-61; mem. Tristate Transp. Commn. N.Y., 1961-66, 70-74, chmn., 1970-71; mem. Delaware Valley Regional Planning Commn., Phila., 1970-74, chmn., 1973; chmn. Govs. Transp. Com., 1970-73; mem. transp. research adv. com. Dept. Agr., 1957-61; mem. Pres.'s Policy Adv. Com. for D.C., 1963-66; exec. com., chmn. transp. com. Delaware Valley Council, 1976-79; exec. com., co-chmn. transp. com. Penjerdel Council, 1979-82. Served to lt. USNR, 1944-45. Recipient Distinguished Faculty award U. Mich., 1961. Mem. ASCE (pres. Mich. 1956, Civil Govt. award 1979), Am. Soc. Traffic and Transp. (founder mem.), Transp. Research Forum, Transp. Research Bd. (asso.), Tau Beta Pi, Phi Kappa Phi, Chi Epsilon. Home: 700 Maple Leaf Ln Moorestown NJ 08057

KOHLBERG, JEROME, JR., lawyer, business executive; b. N.Y.C., 1925. Grad., Swarthmore Coll., 1946; J.D., Columbia U., 1950. Bar: N.Y. Sr. ptnr. Kohlberg, Kravis, Roberts & Co., N.Y.C.; chmn. Houdaille Industries, Inc., chmn. exec. com.; dir. Sterndent Corp. Office: Kohlberg Kravis Roberts & Co 645 Madison Ave New York NY 10022 *

KOHLER, CHARLOTTE, educator; b. Richmond, Va., Sept. 16, 1908; d. Edwin Charles and Augusta F. (Bromm) K. B.A., Vassar, 1929; M.A., U. Va., 1933, Ph.D., 1936; Litt.D., Smith Coll., 1971. Instr. English Woman's Coll. of U. N.C., 1936-41, asst. prof., 1941-42; mng. editor Va. Quar. Rev., 1942-46, editor, 1946-75; asso. prof. English U. Va., 1965-71, prof. English, 1971-79. Mem. Am. Assn. U. Women, Phi Beta Kappa. Episcopalian. Home: 1900 Edgewood Lane Charlottesville VA 22903

KOHLER, FOY, former ambassador, educator; b. Oakwood, Ohio, Feb. 15, 1908; s. Leander David and Myrtle (McClure) K.; m. Phyllis Penn, Aug. 7, 1935. Student, Toledo U., 1924-27, LL.D., 1964; B.S., Ohio State U., 1931, L.H.D., 1962; LL.D., U. Akron, 1967, Findlay Coll, 1967. Fgn. service officer, from 1931, vice consul, Windsor, Ont., Can., 1932, Bucharest, Rumania, 1933-35, Belgrade, 1935, legation sec. and vice consul, Bucharest, 1935-36, Athens, Greece, 1936-41, Cairo, Egypt, 1941; country specialist Dept. State, Washington, 1941-44; asst. chief. div. of Near Eastern Affairs, 1944-45; with Am. embassy, London, 1944; polit. and liaison officer U.S. del. UN Conf. on Internat. Orgn., San Francisco, 1945; sec. gen. U.S. Mission to Observe Greek Elections, 1945-46; spl. studies Cornell U., 1946; student Nat. War Coll., 1946; 1st sec. Am. Embassy, Moscow, Jan. 1947, counsellor, June 1948, minister plenipotentiary, 1948; chief Internat. Broadcasting Div., Dept. State, 1949; dir. Voice of Am. broadcasts, 1949; asst. adminstr. Internat. Information Adminstrn., Feb. 1952; policy planning staff Dept. State, 1952; counselor of embassy, Ankara, Turkey, 1953-56; detailed to ICA, 1956-58; dep. asst. sec. of state for European affairs, 1958-59, asst. sec. state for European affairs, 1959-62, ambassador to, USSR, 1962-66; dep. under sec. of state for polit. affairs Dept. State, 1966-67; prof. Center Advanced Internat. Studies U. Miami, 1968-78, adj. prof., 1978—; sr. assoc. Advanced Internat. Studies Inst., Washington, 1978—; cons. Dept. State, 1968-82; Mem. Bd. for Internat. Broadcasting, 1974-78, cons., 1978-82. Author: Understanding the Russians: A Citizens' Primer, 1970; co-author: Science and Technology as an Instrument of Soviet Policy, 1972, Soviet Strategy for the Seventies: From Cold War to Peaceful Coexistence, Convergence of Communism and Capitalism: The Soviet View, 1973, The Role of Nuclear Forces in Current Soviet Strategy, The Soviet Union and the 1973 Middle East War: The Implications for Detente, 1974, The Soviet Union: Yesterday, Today, Tomorrow, 1975; author: foreword to Custine's Eternal Russia, 1976, SALT II: How Not to Negotiate with the Russians, 1979; co-editor: monthly Soviet World Outlook, 1976—. Mem. Phi Beta Kappa, Beta

Gamma Sigma, Delta Upsilon. Home: 215 Golf Club Circle Tequesta FL 33458

KOHLER, HEINZ, educator; b. Berlin, Germany, Aug. 19, 1934; came to U.S., 1957, naturalized, 1960; s. Arthur Oskar and Gertrud (Förster) K.; m. Mary Elaine Schmiege, June 4, 1955; children—Marjorie Ann, Victoria Rose. Student, Free U., Berlin, 1953-54, 55-57; M.A., U. Mich., 1958, Ph.D., 1961; M.A., Amherst Coll., 1969. Teaching fellow U. Mich., 1958-59, lectr., 1961; asst. prof. Amherst (Mass.) Coll., 1961-64, asso. prof., 1964-69, prof. econs., 1969—, chmn. dept. econs., 1963-64, 70-71, 76-78; vis. prof. econs. Smith Coll., U. Mass., Mt. Holyoke Coll., 1963—. Author: Economic Integration in the Soviet Bloc, 1965, Welfare and Planning, 2d edit, 1979, Scarcity Challenged, incl. Study Guide and Instructor's Manual, 1968, Readings in Economics, 2d edit, 1969, Economics, the Science of Scarcity, incl. Programmed Study Guide and Instructor's Manual, 1970, What Economics Is All About, 1972, Economics and Urban Problems, 1973, Scarcity and Freedom, including Instructor's Manual, 1977, Intermediate Microeconomics: Theory and Applications, including Student Workbook and Instructor's Manual, 1982. Home: 278 Middle St Amherst MA 01002

KOHLER, HERBERT VOLLRATH, JR., diversified manufacturing company executive; b. Sheboygan, Wis., Feb. 20, 1939; s. Herbert Vollrath and Ruth Miriam (DeYoung) K.; m. Linda Elizabeth Karger, Sept. 23, 1961; children: Laura Elizabeth, Rachel DeYoung, Karger David. Grad., The Choate Sch., 1957; B.S., Yale U., 1965. With Kohler Co., Wis., 1965—, gen. supr. warehouse div., 1965-67, factory systems mgr., 1967-68, v.p. operations, 1968-71, exec. v.p., 1971-72, chmn. bd., chief exec. officer, 1972—, pres., 1974—, dir., 1967—; dir. Harnishchfeger Corp. Mem. adv. bd. John Michael Kohler Arts Center, from 1972; mem. Wis. Gov.'s Council on Econ. Devel., from 1973, Kohler Village Planning Commn., from 1972; Bd. dirs., v.p. Friendship House, from 1959; bd. dirs. Kiddies Camp Corp., from 1972; trustee Lawrence U., from 1973; pres. bd. dirs. Kohler Found., from 1968. Served with U.S. Army, 1957-58. Mem. NAM (dir. 1973—), Sheboygan C. of C. Am. Horse Show Assn., Am. Morgan Horse Assn. Republican. Episcopalian. Club: Sheboygan Economic (pres. 1973-74). Home: Kohler WI 53044 Office: Kohler Co Kohler WI 53044 *

KOHLER, LARRY WALTER, fast food executive; b. Lakeview, Mich., Sept. 27, 1945; s. Ora E. and Marjorie T. (Dutmers) K.; m. Paige N. Bernhardt, Feb. 28, 1970; 1 son, Brek Andrew. Student, Mich. State U., 1969. Restaurant and dist. mgr. Burger King Corp., Detroit, 1970-76, regional gen. mgr., Cleve., 1976-77, regional v.p., Boston, 1977-80, sr. v.p., div. mgr., Miami, 1980-82, exec. v.p. ops., 1982—; lectr. Tufts U., 1977-80, U. Wis.-Stout, 1983. Served with U.S. Army, 1968-70. Decorated Bronze Star. Mem. Nat. Restaurant Assn. Republican. Roman Catholic. Home: 17740 SW 7th Ave Miami FL 33157 Office: Burger King Corp 7360 N Kendall Dr Miami FL 33152

KOHLER, PETER OGDEN, physician, educator; b. Bklyn., July 18, 1938; s. Dayton McCue and Jean Stewart (Ogden) K.; m. Judy Lynn Baker, Dec. 26, 1959; children: Brooke Terrill, Stephen Edwin, Todd Randolph, Adam Stewart. B.A., U. Va., 1959; M.D., Duke U., 1963. Diplomate: Am. Bd. Internal Medicine. Intern Duke Hosp., Durham, N.C., 1963-64, fellow, 1964-65; clin. asso. Nat Cancer Inst. and Nat Inst. Child Health and Human Devel., NIH, Bethesda, Md., 1965-67, sr. investigator, 1968-73, head endocrinology service, 1972-73; resident in medicine Georgetown Hosp., Washington, 1969-70; prof. medicine and cell biology Baylor Coll. Medicine, Houston, 1973-77; also chief endocrinology div.; prof. medicine U. Ark., 1977—, also chmn. dept. medicine, chief med. service, 1977—; chmn. Hosp. Med. Bd., 1980-82, chmn. council dept. chmn., 1979-80; vis. faculty St. Vincent Infirmary, Little Rock, 1977—; mem. endocrinology com. Am. Bd. Internal Medicine, 1983—; cons. Little Rock VA Hosp.; mem. endocrinology study sect. NIH, 1981—. Editor: (with G.T. Ross) Diagnosis and Treatment of Pituitary Tumors, 1973; Contbr. articles to profl. jours. Served with USPHS, 1965-68. NIH grantee, 1973—; Howard Hughes Med. Investigator, 1976-77; recipient NIH Quality awards, 1969, 71. Fellow A.C.P.; mem. Am. Soc. Clin. Investigation, Am. Fedn. Clin. Research (mem. nat. council 1977-78, pres. so. sect. 1976), So. Soc. Clin. Investigation (council 1979—, pres. 1983), Assn. Profs. Medicine, Ark. Med. Assn., AMA, Pulaski County Med. Assn., Am. Soc. Cell Biology, Assn. Am. Physicians, Am. Diabetes Assn., Endocrine Soc., Raven Soc., Sigma Xi, Alpha Omega Alpha, Phi Beta Kappa, Omicron Delta Kappa, Phi Eta Sigma. Methodist. Home: 13280 Rivercrest Rd Little Rock AR 72212 Office: Dept Medicine U Ark 4301 W Markham St Little Rock AR 72205

KOHLER, RUTH DEYOUNG, arts center executive; b. Chgo., Oct. 24, 1941; d. Herbert Vollrath and Ruth Miriam (DeYoung) K. Ed., Smith Coll., U. Hamburg, Ger., Kunsthochschule, Hamburg, U. Wis. Instr. in fine arts U. Alta. (Can.), Calgary, 1964-66; printmaker, 1967-68; asst. dir. John Michael Kohler Arts Center, Sheboygan, Wis., 1968-71, dir., 1972—; chmn. Wis. Arts Bd.; mem. mus. adv. panel, visual arts panel, crafts panels and task force Nat. Endowment for Arts; bd. dirs. Kohler Found., Inc.; trustee Beloit Coll.; mem. Wis. Am. Revolution Bicentennial Commn. Office: 608 New York Ave Sheboygan WI 53081

KOHLHORST, GAIL LEWIS, librarian; b. Phila., Dec. 5, 1946; d. Richard Elliott and Lucille (Lampkin) Lewis; m. Allyn Leon Kohlhorst, Feb. 14, 1974; 1 dau., Jennifer Marion. B.A. in Govt, Otterbein Coll., Westerville, Ohio, 1969; M.S. in L.S, Cath. U. Am., 1977. Info. classifier U.S. Ho. of Reps. Commn. on Internal. Security, Washington, 1969-70; adminstrv. asst. Office of Gen. Counsel, GSA, Washington, 1971-76; chief tech. services sect. GSA Library, Washington, 1976-79; chief GSA library br., 1979—. Recipient Outstanding Performance awards, 1973, 75, 76, 79, Spl. Achievement award, 1982. Mem. ALA, Beta Phi Mu. Episcopalian. Home: 2303 Highland Ave Falls Church VA 22046 Office: 18th and F Sts NW Washington DC 20405

KOHLMAN, DAVID LESLIE, research engineering executive, consultant; b. Houston, Oct. 13, 1937; s. Leslie W. and Aarona (Booker) K.; m. Linda Marie Norris, Sept. 11, 1959; children—Bradley David, Jeffrey Andrew. B.S., U. Kans., 1959, M.S., 1960; Ph.D., MIT, 1963. Registered profl. engr., Colo. Research engr. Boeing Co., Renton, Wash., 1963-64; asst. prof. aero. engring. U. Kans., 1964-67, asso. prof., 1967-70, prof., 1970-81, adj. prof., 1981—, chmn. dept., 1967-72; dir. Flight Research Lab., 1980-82; mem. Engring. Accreditation Commn.; mem. flight mechanics panel NATO Adv. Group for Aero. Research and Devel.; cons. aircraft industry FAA; pres. Kohlman Aviation Corp., 1977—, Kohlman Systems Research, Inc., 1982—. Author: Introduction to V/STOL Airplanes, 1981. Trustee Park Coll., Parkville, Mo. Asso. fellow AIAA; mem. Am. Soc. Engring. Edn., Lawrence C. of C., Am. Helicopter Soc., Sigma Xi, Tau Beta Pi, Sigma Tau, Sigma Gamma Tau. Mem. Reorganized Ch. Jesus Christ of Latter Day Saints. Research in aerodynamics, fluid mechanics, stability and control, light airplane design and flight testing. Home: Rural Route 6 Box 357 Lawrence KS 66044

KOHLMEIER, LOUIS MARTIN, JR., newspaper reporter; b. St. Louis, Feb. 17, 1926; s. Louis Martin and Anita (Werling) K.; m. Barbara Anne Wilson, Nov. 15, 1958; children—Daniel Kimbrell, Ann Werling. B.Journalism, U. Mo., 1950. Staff writer Wall St. Jour., St. Louis and Chgo., 1952-57, Washington, 1960—; staff writer St. Louis Globe-Democrat, 1958-59. Author: The Regulators Watchdog Agencies and the Public Interest, 1969. Served with AUS, 1950-52. Recipient Nat. Headliners Club award nat. reporting, 1959, Sigma Delta Chi award Washington corr., 1964, Pulitzer prize nat. reporting, 1964. Home: 5902 Madawaska Rd Washington DC 20016 Office: Nat Press Bldg Washington DC 20005

KOHLMEYER, IDA RITTENBERG, artist; b. New Orleans, Nov. 3, 1912; d. Joseph and Rebecca (Baron) Rittenberg; m. Hugh Bernard Kohlmeyer, Mar. 15, 1934; children: Jane Louise (Mrs. Henry Lowentritt), Jo Ellen. B.A., Tulane U., 1933, D.F.A., 1956; student, Hans Hofmann Sch. Art, Provincetown, R.I., 1956. Mem. faculty art dept. Newcomb Coll., Tulane U., New Orleans, 1956-64; vis. asso. prof. fine arts La. State U., New Orleans, 1973-74. One-man shows, Delgado Mus. Art, New Orleans, 1956, 66, 67, Tulane U., 1959, 64, Sheldon Meml. Art Gallery, Lincoln, Nebr., 1967, Marion Koogler McNay Art Inst., San Antonio, 1968, Ft. Wayne (Ind.) Mus. Art, High Mus. Art, Atlanta, 1972, David Findlay Gallery, N.Y.C.; traveling retrospective:, Mint Mus., Cheekwood Mus. Art, Okla. Art Ctr., Ft. Wayne Mus. Art, Montgomery Mus. Art, New Orleans Mus. Art, 1984-86; exhibited in group shows, Bertha Schaeffer Gallery, N.Y.C., Harvard U., Yale U., Toledo Mus. Fine Arts, Cleve. Inst. Art, Denver Art Mus., Va. Mus. Arts, Richmond, La Jolla (Calif.) Mus. Art, Moore Coll. Art, Phila., Pratt Graphics Center, N.Y.C., Ft. Worth Art Mus., La Jolla Mus. Contemporary Art, Painting in the South: Va. Mus.; represented in permanent collections, New Orleans Mus. Art, Rochester Meml. Art Gallery, Rochester, N.Y., Addison Gallery Am. Art, Phillips Acad., Andover, Mass., Okla. Art Center, Oklahoma City, Columbus (Ga.) Mus. Art, Tyler (Tex.) Art Inst. Centro-Artistico, Baranquilla, Colombia, Mus. Fine Arts, Houston, High Mus. Art, Atlanta, Sheldon Meml. Art Gallery, Lincoln, Nebr., Ind. State U., Terre Haute, Nat. Collection Fine Arts, Washington, Emory U., Atlanta, Marion Koogler McNay Art Inst., San Antonio, Corcoran Gallery Art, Washington, Birmingham (Ala.) Mus. Art, Milw. Art Center, Hunter Mus. Art, Chattanooga, Ill., State U., Normal-Bloomington, Women's Mus., Washington, San Francisco Mus. Modern Art, Bklyn. Mus. Recipient award Artist's Ann., New Orleans Mus. Art, 1957, 58, 60, 65, 73; Chautauqua Nat. Exhbn., 1962; 28th Corcoran Biennial of Am. Art., Washington, 1963, 67; Artists Ann., High Mus. Art, Atlanta, 1963, 66.

KOHLOSS, FREDERICK HENRY, consulting engineer; b. Ft. Sam Houston, Tex., Dec. 4, 1922; s. Fabius Henry and Rowena May (Smith) K.; m. Margaret Mary Grunwell, Sept. 9, 1944; children—Margaret Kohloss Laakso, Charlotte Kohloss Todesco, Eleanor. B.S. in Mech. Engring, U. Md., 1943; M.Mech. Engring., U. Del., 1951; J.D., George Washington U., 1949. Mem. engring. faculty George Washington U., Washington, 1946-50; devel. and standards engr. Dept. Def., 1950-51; chief engr. for mech. contractors, Washington, 1951-54, Cleve., 1954-55, Honolulu, 1955-56, cons. engr., 1956-61; pres. Frederick H. Kohloss & Assocs., Inc., Cons. Engrs., Honolulu, Tucson, San Francisco and Denver, 1961—; dir. Connell, Kohloss Young, Melbourne, Australia; affiliate grad. faculty dept. mech. engring. U. Hawaii. Contbr. to publs. in field. Served with U.S. Army, 1943-46. Fellow ASME, ASHRAE, Am. Cons. Engrs. Council, Chartered Inst. Bldg. Services (Eng.), Instn. Engrs. Australia; mem. IEEE (sr.), Nat. Soc. Profl. Engrs., Soc. Am. Mil. Engrs., Illuminating Engring. Soc., New Zealand Instn. Engrs. Clubs: Oahu Country, Plaza (Honolulu); Engineers (San Francisco). Home: 1645 Ala Wai Blvd Penthouse 1 Honolulu HI 96815 Office: 345 Queen St Suite 401 Honolulu HI 96813 *Engineers serve the public by advancing the technology necessary for modern civilization. My goal is the ethical and effective performance of that professional duty.*

KOHLS, RICHARD LOUIS, univ. dean; b. Kentland, Ind., Apr. 19, 1921; s. Clarence E. and Helen (Littlejohn) K.; m. Irene Elizabeth Shuster, Apr. 20, 1944; children—Michael E., Kathryn Ann. B.S., Purdue U., 1942, Ph.D., 1950; M.A., U. Mo., 1947. Instr. marketing and prices U. Mo. at Columbia, 1946-48; prof. agrl. marketing Purdue U., Lafayette, Ind., 1948-64, asst. head dept. agrl. econs., 1965-66, asst. acad. v.p., 1966-68, dean agr., 1968-80, Hovde Disting. prof., 1981—; mem. adv. com. on econs. research Dept. Agr., 1958-62; vis. prof. U. Exeter, Eng., 1964; Mem. pub. adv. bd. Chgo. Merc. Exchange, 1968-77. Author: Marketing Argicultural Products, 5th edit, 1980. Mem. Ind. Health Facilities Planning Council, 1968-77; Bd. dirs. Ind. 4-H Found., Purdue Research Found., Lafayette Symphony Soc., West Lafayette Library. Served to capt. mil. intelligence AUS, 1942-46. Named Outstanding Tchr., Am. Assn. Argl. Econs.; recipient Outstanding Tchr. award Purdue U., 1967. Mem. Greater Lafayette C. of C., Purdue Agrl. Alumni Assn. (dir.), Internat., Am. assns. agrl. econs., Am. Marketing Assn., Am. Assn. Higher Edn., Alpha Gamma Rho. Mem. Christian Ch. (pres. ch. 1967, gov. bd. 1964-68). Home: 1520 Woodland St West Lafayette IN 47906

KOHN, CLYDE FREDERICK, geographer; b. Mohawk, Mich., Apr. 10, 1911; s. George Ferdin and Cora Frances (Saam) K.; m. Doris Venton Merker, Jan. 17, 1942; children—Susan, George. A.B., No. Mich. U., 1935; A.M., U. Mich., 1936, Ph.D., 1940. Tchr. rural sch., Marquette County, Mich., 1929-30, pub. schs., Gwinn, Mich., 1930-34, Miss. State Coll. for Women, Columbus, 1940-42; instr., lectr. Harvard U., 1942-45; asst. prof. geography and edn. Northwestern U., 1945-47, asso. prof., 1947-58; prof. geography U. Iowa, 1958-80, dept. chmn., 1966-77; cons. author Scott, Foresman & Co. Author: Cross Country, 1951; co-author: City Town and Country, 1959, In All Our States, 1960, In The Americas, 1962, The World Today-Its Patterns and Cultures, 1970, Beyond The Americas, 1964, Family Studies, 1970, Local Studies, 1970, Metropolitan Studies, 1970, Regional Studies, 1970, United States and Canada, 1970, Inter-American Studies, 1970; also profl. papers in geographic and ednl. jours.; Editor: 19th yearbook Pacesetter Series, Nat. Council Geog. Edn, 1978—; co-editor: Readings in Urban Geography, 1959. Mem. U.S. Nat. Commn. for UNESCO, 1960-66. Mem. Assn. Am. Geographers (pres. 1967-68), Nat. Council Geographic Edn. (pres. 1951-53), Phi Beta Kappa, Phi Kappa Phi, Kappa Delta Pi, Phi Gamma Delta. Episcopalian. Home: 201 N 1st Ave Apt 109 Iowa City IA 52240

KOHN, EDWIN R., JR., naval officer; b. Smethport, Pa., June 29, 1931; s. Edwin Rudolph and Mary (Cronshey) K.; m. Marilyn Jane Porter, Aug. 23, 1954; children: Jennifer, Peter, Thomas, Edwin. B.S., Pa. State U., 1954; student, U.S. Naval War Coll., 1972. Commd. U.S. Navy, advanced through grades to rear admiral, comdg. officer Attack Squadron 93, 1970-71, comdg. officer Carrier Air Wing One, 1973-74, comdg. officer USS Kalamazoo, 1973-78, comdg. officer USS Forrestal (CV 59), 1979-80, dir. logistics and security assistance, comdr. chief Pacific, 1980-82, comdr. Carrier Group Three, San Francisco, 1982—. Recipient Def. Superior Service medal, 1982. Office: Commander Carrier Group Three FPO San Francisco CA 96601

KOHN, HAROLD ELIAS, lawyer; b. Phila., Apr. 5, 1916; s. Joseph C. and Mayme (Rumm) K.; m. Edith Anderson, Dec. 30, 1946; children: Amy, Ellen, Joseph Carl. A.B., U. Pa., 1934, LL.B., 1937. Bar: Pa. 1938. Practiced in Phila. and Washington, spl. counsel transit matters, City of Phila., 1952-53, 56-62; counsel to gov. Pa., 1972; Mem. bd. Southeastern Pa. Transp. Authority, 1972-77; mem. Pa. Jud. Inquiry and Rev. Bd., 1973-77. Sec., treas., bd. dirs. Kohn Found.; pres., bd. dirs. Arronson Found., Lavine Found.; bd. dirs. Moss Rehab. Hosp., Phila. Geriatric Ctr.; trustee Phila. Fedn. Jewish Agys.; exec. com. United Jewish Appeal; past bd. dirs. Phila. Psychiat. Ctr.; v.p., bd. dirs. Phila. chpt. ACLU, 1975-76; trustee Temple U.; bd. consultors Villanova U. Law Sch. Mem. Am., Pa., Phila., D.C. bar assns., Internat. Acad. Trial Lawyers, Jud. Conf. 3d Circuit, Am. Law Inst., Order of Coif, Phi Beta Kappa. Clubs: Downtown (Phila.); Nat. Lawyers (Washington). Home: 1901 Walnut St Philadelphia PA 19103 also Devon PA 19333 Office: 1700 Market St Philadelphia PA 19103 also 1776 K St NW Washington DC 20006

KOHN, HENRY, lawyer; b. St. Louis, May 2, 1917; s. Henry and Hannah (Lederer) K.; m. Anne Frankenthaler, Sept. 23, 1945; children: Margaret, Barbara, Alice. B.A., Yale, 1939, LL.B., 1942. Bar: Mo. bar 1942, N.Y. bar 1946. With Bd. Econ. Warfare, 1942; practice with George Frankenthaler, N.Y.C., 1946-48; pvt. practice, N.Y.C., 1949-56; sr. partner Frankenthaler, Kohn & Schneider, N.Y.C., 1957—; Former pres., dir. Fiduciary Mut. Investing Co., Mercer Fund Inc.; dir. Meta Software, Inc., Identiprint, Inc. Chmn. bd., founder Am. Jewish Soc. for Service; bd. dirs. Nat. Jewish Welfare Bd., Lavanburg Corner House Found.; pres. Ed. Lee and Jean Campe Found., Sam and Louise Campe Found.; past pres. and chmn. bd. dirs. 92d St. YM-YWHA. Served to capt. AUS, 1942-46. Mem. ABA, N.Y. County Lawyers Assn., Assn. Bar City N.Y., Phi Beta Kappa, Order of Coif. Jewish. Clubs: New York Lawn Bowling, Lawyers, Harmonie (N.Y.C.). Home: 155 E 72d St New York NY 10021 also Strawberry Hill Ackert Hook Rd Rhinebeck NY 12572 Office: 120 Broadway New York NY 10005

KOHN, HENRY IRVING, educator, radiologist; b. N.Y.C., Aug. 19, 1909; s. Washington Irving and Fanny (Brownstein) K.; m. Linda Hansen, Oct. 22, 1961; children: Mari Annabel, Lars Sebastian. A.B., Dartmouth Coll., 1930; Ph.D. in Gen. Physiology, Harvard U., 1935, M.D., 1946. Diplomate Am. Bd. Radiology (therapy). Traveling fellow Gen. Edn. Bd. at univs., Stockholm and Cambridge, Eng., 1935-37; instr., then asst. prof. physiology and pharmacology Duke Med. Sch., 1937-43; intern Bellvue Hosp., N.Y.C., 1946-47; commd. officer USPHS; serving successively in, Balt., Oak Ridge Nat. Lab. and U. Calif.-San Francisco, 1947-53; clin. prof. exptl. radiology, also research radiologist in radiol. lab. U. Calif.-San Francisco, 1953-63; Alvan T. and Viola D. Fuller-Am. Cancer Soc. prof. radiology Harvard Med. Sch., 1963-68, David W. Gaiser prof. radiation biology, 1968-76, prof. radiation biology, 1976-79, prof. emeritus, 1976—; dir. Center for Human Genetics, 1971-76, Shields Warren Radiation Lab., New Eng. Deaconess Hosp., 1964-79; mem. ad hoc com. nuclear and alternative energy systems Nat. Acad. Scis., 1975-79; sci. sect. adv. com. biology and med. AEC, 1958-62; cons. UN Sci. Commn. Effects Atomic Radiation, 1957; mem. RBE ad hoc com. Internat. Commn. Radiol. Protection, 1960-61; mem. radiation study sect. NIH, 1965-69. Asso. editor: Radiation Research, 1957-6l. Mem. Brookline (Mass.) Town Meeting, 1971-81. Mem. Am. Physiol. Soc., Radiation Research Soc. (council 1962-65). Home and Office: 1203 Shattuck Ave Berkeley CA 94709

KOHN, IMMANUEL, lawyer; b. Jerusalem, Dec. 6, 1926; U.S., 1934; s. Hans and Yetty (Wahl) K.; m. Vera Sharpe, July 22, 1950; children: Gail, Peter, Shelia, Robert. Grad., Deerfield Acad., 1944; B.A. summa cum laude, Harvard U., 1949; LL.B cum laude, Yale U., 1953. Bar: N.Y. 1955, U.S. Dist. Ct. (ea. dist.) N.Y. 1955, U.S. Dist. Ct. (so. dist.) N.Y. 1957, U.S. Ct. Appeals (2d cir.) 1966, U.S. Supreme Ct. 1972. Assoc. Cahill, Gordon & Reindel, N.Y.C., 1953-62, ptnr., 1962, mem. exec. com., 1972—. Editor, Yale U. Law Jour., 1951-53. Served as ensign U.S. Maritime Service, 1946. Sheldon travelling fellow, 1949-50. Mem. Order of Coif, Phi Beta Kappa. Clubs: Recess, India House, Bd. Room, Met. Opera, Sky (N.Y.C.); Bedens Brook (N.J.). Home: 34 Puritan Ct Princeton NJ 08540 Office: Cahill Gordon & Reindel 80 Pine St New York NY 10005

KOHN, JAMES PAUL, engineering educator; b. Dubuque, Iowa, Oct. 31, 1924; s. Harry Theodore and Kathryn (Piepel) K.; m. Mary Louise McGovern, Aug. 30, 1958; children: Kathleen, Kevin, Mary Louise. B.S. in Chem. Engring, U. Notre Dame, 1951; M.S., U. Mich., 1952; Ph.D., U. Kans., 1956. Chem. engr. Reilly Tar & Chem. Corp., Indpls., 1946-51; mem. faculty U. Notre Dame, 1955—, prof., 1964—; dir. Solar Lab. for Thermal Applications, 1973—; cons. Am. Oil Co., summer 1958, Imagineering Enterprises, 1957-65, Hills-Morrow, 1966-70. Served with U.S. Army, 1943-46. Decorated Bronze Star, Purple Heart.; recipient Faculty award, 1983. Mem. Am. Chem. Soc., Am. Inst. Chem. Engrs., AAAS, Sigma Xi. Republican. Club: Roman Catholic. Patentee removal acidic gaseous components from natural gas. Home: 17684 Waxwing Lane South Bend IN 46635 Office: Dept Chem Engring Notre Dame IN 46656

KOHN, JOHN PETER, JR., lawyer; b. Montgomery, Ala., Dec. 27, 1902; s. John P. and Clementina R. (Cram) K.; m. Margaret Thorington, Mar. 6, 1937; 1 dau., Margaret T (Mrs. Doy McCall). Ed., Starkes Univ. Sch., Montgomery, St. Louis U., Spring Hill Coll.; LL.B., U. Ala., 1925. Bar: Ala. bar 1925. Since practiced in Montgomery; county atty., 1946—, spl. atty. for gov. Ala., 1964-65; asso. justice Spl. Supreme Ct. Ala., 1968. Author: The Voters Primer, 1939, The Cradle-Anatomy of a Town, 1969. Capt. Ala. N.G., 1936; served with AUS, 1940-45. Mem. ABA, Ala. Bar Assn., Montgomery Bar Assn. (pres. 1931), S.A.R., Soc. Pioneers (trustee), Phi Delta Theta. Clubs: Beauvior Country (Montgomery); Young Democrats Ala. (pres. 1933-39). Home: 2542 Woodly Rd Montgomery AL 36111 Office: Suite 924 1st Ala Bank Bldg 8 Commerce St Montgomery AL 36104 *I was taught by my mother never to whine, cringe or bow to any man. My motto is: Justice for all above everything, and constantly seek the truth.*

KOHN, JOSEPH JOHN, educator, mathematician; b. Prague, Czechoslovakia, May 18, 1932; came to U.S., 1945, naturalized, 1953; s. Otto and Emilie (Schwarz) K.; m. Anna DiCapua, Dec. 15, 1966; children: Edward, Emma, Alicia. S.B., Mass. Inst. Tech., 1953; M.A., Princeton, 1954, Ph.D., 1956. Instr. Princeton, 1956-57; mem. Inst. Advanced Study, 1957-58, 62-63, 76-77, 80-81; mem. faculty Brandeis U., 1958-68, prof. math., 1965-68, chmn. dept., 1964-68; prof. math. Princeton, 1968—, chmn. dept., 1973-76; Vis. prof. U. Florence, Italy, 1972-73; mem. U.S. pure and applied math. del. to People's Republic of China, 1976. Contbr. articles to profl. jours. NSF fellow, 1954; Sloan fellow, 1964; Guggenheim fellow, 1976-77; recipient L. P. Steele prize, 1979. Mem. Am. Acad. Arts and Scis., Am. Math. Soc. (trustee). Home: 32 Sturges Way Princeton NJ 08540

KOHN, KARL, educator, composer; b. Vienna, Austria, Aug. 1, 1926; came to U.S., 1939, naturalized, 1945; s. Frederick and Margit (Fisch) K.; m. Margaret Case Sherman, June 23, 1950; children: Susanna Margaret, Emily Elizabeth. Cert., N.Y. Coll. Music, 1944; B.A. summa cum laude, Harvard U., 1950, M.A., 1955. Instr. music Pomona Coll., Claremont, Calif., 1950-54, asst. prof., 1954-59, asso. prof., 1959-65, prof., 1965—; teaching fellow Harvard, 1954-55; mem. faculty Berkshire Music Center, Tanglewood, summers 1954, 55, 57. Composer: Castles and Kings, 1958, The Monk From Shu, 1959, Three Scenes For Orchestra, 1960, Serenade For Wind Quintet and Piano, 1961, Capriccios, 1962, Concerto Mutabile, 1962, Interludes, 1964, Sonata da Camera, 1965, Leisure and Other Songs; cantata for baritone and chamber ensemble, 1965, Encounters; for flute- piccolo and piano, 1966, Episodes for Piano and Orchestra, 1966, Introductions and Parodies, 1967, Encounters for Horn and Piano, 1967, Encounters III for Violin and Piano, 1971, Esdras; for flute and piano solo, mixed chorus and orch., 1971, Encounters IV for Oboe and Piano, 1972, Centone per Orchestra, 1973, Innocent Psaltery; for symphonic wind orch. and percussion Prophet Bird; for chamber ensemble Souvenirs II; for oboe and harp Also The Sons; for solo quartet, mixed chorus, organ or piano, four hands Serenade II; for concert band, 1977, Encounters VI; for cello and piano, 1977, Paronyms II; for saxophones and piano, 1978, Son of Prophet Bird; for harp, 1977, Sonatina; for marimba, 4 hands, 1977, Third Rhapsody; for piano, 1977, Waldmusik, Concerto for clarinet and orch, 1979, Prophet Bird II; for piano and chamber ensemble, 1980, Recreations II; for two guitars, 1980, Quartet; for saxophones, 1981, What Heaven Confers; for mixed chorus and piano, 1981; for chamber ensemble Capriccios II, 1982; for orch. Time Irretrievable, 1982; for two pianos Dream Music, 1983. Bd. dirs. Monday Evening Concerts, Los Angeles. Served with U.S. Army, 1945-46. Faculty Fulbright Research scholar Finland, 1955-56; Guggenheim fellow; grantee Howard Found., 1961-62; Mellon Found. grantee, 1974; Nat. Endowment Arts grantee, 1975-76, 79. Mem. Coll. Music Soc. Home: 674 W 10th St Claremont CA 91711

KOHN, ROBERT ROTHENBERG, medical educator; b. Cleve., June 14, 1925; s. Jacob Bertholdt and Carrie (Rothenberg) K.; m. Vilma Lavetti, July 27, 1952; children—Deborah D., Justin M., Steven M., Peter L. B.S., U. Wis., 1949; Ph.D., U. Mich., 1953; M.D., Western Res. U., 1957. Diplomate: Am. Bd. Pathology. NSF fellow, 1952-53, resident, USPHS fellow pathology, 1957-60; asso. prof. pathology Case Western Res. U. Sch. Medicine, 1964-70, prof. pathology, 1970—, prin. adminstr. program aging research and tng., 1962-77; Bd. sci. counselors Nat. Inst. Aging, 1977-78. Author numerous articles in field. Served with USNR, 1943-46. Mem. AAAS, Am. Assn. Pathologists, Gerontological Soc., Sigma Xi, Alpha Omega Alpha. Spl. research biochem. and pathol. aspects aging and degenerative processes. Home: 2060 S Belvoir Blvd Cleveland OH 44121 *Be critical and skeptical; don't trust experts.*

KOHN, WALTER, educator, physicist; b. Vienna, Austria, Mar. 9, 1923. B.A., U. Toronto, Ont., Can., 1945, M.A., 1946, LL.D. (hon.), 1967; Ph.D. in Physics, Harvard U., 1948; Docteur es Sciences honoris causa, U. Paris, 1980; D.Sc. (hon.), Brandeis U., 1981, Ph.D., Hebrew U. Jerusalem, 1981. Indsl. physicist Sutton Horsley Co., Can., 1941-43; geophysicist Koulomzine, Que., 1944-46; instr. physics Harvard U., 1948-50; asst. prof. Carnegie Inst. Tech., 1950-53, asso. prof., 1953-57, prof., 1957-60; prof. physics U. Calif., San Diego, 1960-79, chmn. dept., 1961-63; dir. Inst. for Theoretical Physics, U. Calif., Santa Barbara, 1979—. Recipient Oliver Buckley prize, 1961, Davisson-Germer prize, 1977; NRC fellow, 1951; NSF fellow, 1958; Guggenheim fellow, 1963; NSF sr. postdoctoral fellow, 1967. Fellow AAAS, Am. Phys. Soc. (counselor-at-large 1968-72), Am. Acad. Arts and Scis.; mem. Nat. Acad. Scis. Research on electron theory of solids and solid surfaces. Office: Inst for Theoretical Physics U Calif Santa Barbara CA 93110

KOHN, WILLIAM HENRY, clergyman; b. Winnipeg, Man., Can., Sept. 27, 1915; s. William Lewis and Christine (Obermowe) K.; m. Marian Ruth Luenser, June 1, 1941; children: Kathy, Carol, Marian. Student, Concordia Coll., Milw., 1935, Concordia Theol. Sem., St Louis, 1939, D.D., 1964; postgrad., Johns Hopkins. Ordained to ministry Lutheran Ch., 1940; pastor in, Wis. and Md., 1939-56, Redeemer Luth. Ch., Hyattsville, Md., 1956-63; sec. Luth. Mission Soc. Md., 1946-48, pres., 1948-50; chmn. mission bd. Southeastern dist. Luth. Ch. Mo. Synod, 1951-54, pres., 1954-59; bd. dirs. Luth. Ch. Mo. Synod, 1959-63; pres. Southeastern dist., 1963-67, exec. sec. missions, 1967-74; sr. pastor Capital Drive Luth. Ch., Milw., 1974-82; Chmn. Luth. Immigration Service Com., 1960-67; bd. dirs. Luth. World Relief, 1967-74, Good Samaritan Med. Center, Milw., 1980—; pres. Assn. Evang. Luth. Chs., 1976—; bd. dirs. Luth. Council in U.S.A., 1978—; mem., pres. Luth. World Ministries Commn., 1978—; mem. Com. on Luth. Unity, 1978-82, Commn. for a New Luth. Ch., 1982—. Served as chaplain AUS, 1943-46. Decorated Bronze Star. Home and Office: 2707 N 67th St Milwaukee WI 53210

KOHNE, RICHARD EDWARD, cons. engring. co. exec.; b. Tientsin, China, May 16, 1924; s. Ernest E. and Elizabeth I. (Antonenko) K.; m. Gabrielle H. Vernaudon, Dec. 18, 1926; children—Robert, Phillip, Daniel, Paul, Renee. B.Sc., U. Calif., Berkeley, 1948. Structural engr. hydro projects Pacific Gas & Electric Co., San Francisco, 1948-55; with Internat. Engring. Co. Inc., San Francisco, 1955—, regional mgr. for Latin Am., then v.p., 1965-71, exec. v.p. world-wide ops. in engring. and project mgmt., 1971-79, pres., 1979—, also dir.; pres., dir. Cia. Int. de Ingenieria, IE Co. Afrique-Central. Mem. ASCE, U.S. Com. Large Dams, Am. Inst. Mining Engrs., Soc. Am. Mil. Engrs., Am. Mgmt. Assn., Am. Nuclear Soc., Assn. U.S. Army, Am. Cons. Engring. Council, Cons. Engrs. Assn. Calif. Democrat. Roman Catholic. Clubs: World Trade, Engineers, Bankers (San Francisco). Home: 1827 Doris Dr Menlo Park CA 94025 Office: 180 Howard St San Francisco CA 94105

KOHNEN, RALPH BERNARD, JR., lawyer; b. Cin., Oct. 22, 1935; s. Ralph Bernard and Helenrose (Hillenbrand) K.; married; children: Ralph, Allen, Nancy, Daniel. Student, U. Fribourg, Switzerland, 1955-56; B.A., Georgetown U., 1957; J.D., U. Cin., 1960. Bar: Ohio 1960, U.S. Supreme Ct. 1975. Practiced law, Cin., 1961—; ptnr. Kohnen and Kohnen, 1974—; mem. Ohio Ho. of Reps., 1963-67, City Council Cin., 1967-73, vice mayor, 1971; dir. Fed. Home Loan Bank of Cin., chmn. bd., 1982—. Trustee Cin. Assn. for Blind, 1965—; mem. Hamilton County (Ohio) Mental Health and Mental Retardation Bd., 1968-72; chmn. bd. Cin. and Hamilton County Council Govts., 1972-73; mem. Cin. Planning Commn., 1967-71; bd. govs., mem. exec. com. Arthritis Found. Southwestern Ohio, 1974—, USO, 1975—; trustee Community Improvement Corp., 1968-72; mem. Republican policy and exec. com. Hamilton County, 1974—, treas., 1981—; mem. task force ethics and campaign financing City Council Cin., 1974-75; mem. Cin. Charter Rev. Com., 1980. Served with U.S. Army, 1960-61. Mem. Cin. Bar Assn., Ohio State Bar Assn., ABA, Nat. Health Lawyers Assn. Roman Catholic. Clubs: Queen City, Racquet, Cin. Country, Columbus (Ohio) Athletic. Home: 2959 Wold Ave Cincinnati OH 45206 Office: 4500 Carew Tower 441 Vine St Cincinnati OH 45202

KOHNO, TOSHIKO, flutist; b. Tokyo, May 28, 1954; U.S., 1961; d. Shuntatsu and Sumiko (Bekku) K. B.Mus., Eastman Sch. Music, U. Rochester, 1976. Mem. faculty McGill U., Montreal, 1976-78. Second flutist, Buffalo Philharmonic Orch., 1973-76; asso. prin. flutist, Montreal (Que., Can.) Symphony Orch., 1976-78; prin. flutist, Nat. Symphony Orch., Washington, 1978—; recitals and concerto appearances, U.S., Japan, Europe. (Recipient 1st prize in flute Geneva Internat. Competition 1973). Office: care Nat Symphony Kennedy Center Washington DC 20566

KOHNSTAMM, PAUL LOTHAIR, chemical company executive; b. N.Y.C., Nov. 14, 1922; s. Lothair S. and Madeline (Peck) K.; m. Mary Loeb, May 7, 1944; children: Paul Kenneth, Peter L., Daniel Frank, Katherine, Joshua G., Emily. B.A., Williams Coll., 1944. With H. Kohnstamm & Co., Inc., N.Y.C., 1946—, chmn., chief exec. officer, 1957—; pres. Gen. Color Co., Newark, 1958—, Kohnstamm Co. Ltd., Montreal, Can., 1967—; chmn. exec. com. Internat. Banknote Co., Inc., 1971—; chmn. H. Kohnstamm & Co. (U.K.) Ltd., 1969—; dir. Horace Cory Pub. Ltd. Co., Oswald McCardell & Co., Ltd., Globe Ticket Co., Horsham, Pa. Chmn. bd. trustees Hosp. Joint Diseases Orthopaedic Inst., N.Y.C., 1980—; asst. treas. Fedn. Jewish Philanthropies, N.Y.C., 1980—; trustee Jewish Home and Hosp. Aged, N.Y.C., 1951—, N.Y. Soc. Deaf, 1975—, No. Westchester YMHA, 1981; co-chmn. chems., plastics and paints div. United Jewish Appeal-Fedn. Jewish Philanthropies, 1975—; sponsor Mt. Sinai Med. Ctr.; bd. dirs. Hiram Halle Meml. Library; treas. Halle Ravine of the Nature Conservancy; hon. trustee Horace Mann-Barnard Sch. Served with AUS, 1943-45. Fellow Am. Inst. Chemists (treas.); mem. Am. Chem. Soc., Synthetic Organic Chem. Mfrs. Assn., Chemists Club. (dir. 1983). Democrat. Clubs: Century Country (White Plains, N.Y.); Williams (N.Y.C.); B'nai B'rith. Home: Route 1 Box 290 Lower Shad Rd Pound Ridge NY 10576 Office: 161 Ave Americas New York NY 10013

KOIDE, FRANK TAKAYUKI, electrical engineer; b. Honolulu, Dec. 25, 1935; s. Sukeichi and Hideko (Dai) K.; children: Julie Anne M., Cheryl Lynne K. B.S.E.E., U. Ill., 1958; M.E.E., Clarkson Coll. Tech., Potsdam, N.Y., 1961; Ph.D. (NIH predoctoral fellow), U. Iowa, 1966. Publs. engr. to electronics engr. Collins Radio Co., Cedar Rapids, Iowa, 1958-61; tchr. Cedar Rapids Adult Edn. Sch., 1960-61; lab. instr. U. Iowa Coll. Medicine, 1963-64; asst. prof. Iowa State U., 1966-69; prin. biomed. engr. Tech., Inc., San Antonio, 1968-69; mem. faculty U. Hawaii, 1969—, prof. elec. engring. and physiology, 1974—; external examiner Chinese U., Hong Kong; cons. in field. Author papers, reports in field. NASA-Am. Soc. Engring. Edn. Space systems Design Inst. fellow, 1967; NSF Digital and Analogue Electronics Inst. fellow U. Ill., 1972. Mem. IEEE, Assn. Advancement Med. Instrumentation, AAAS, Sigma Xi. Home: 95-763 Kauanomeha Pl Mililani Town HI 96789 Office: PO Box 22786 Honolulu HI 96822

KOILE, EARL, psychologist, educator; b. Seelyville, Ind., July 22, 1917; s. Arqu Okler and Mary Grace (Shumaker) K.; m. Carmon Crowder, Aug. 29, 1948; children—Kimberle, Kristen, Stephen. B.S., Ind. State Coll., 1939; M.Ed., Harvard U., 1947, Ed.D., 1953. Tchr., Huntington High Sch., Ross County, Ohio, 1939-41; dir. student personnel and guidance services East Tex. State Coll. Commerce, 1947-56, asso. prof. counseling psychology, 1947-53, prof., 1953-56, chmn. dept. guidance, 1950-56; prof., dir. Summer Sch. and Adult Edn.; dir. Warren R. Austin Inst. World Understanding, U. Vt., 1956-58; coordinator counseling Testing and Counseling Center, U. Tex., Austin, 1958-63, asso. prof. ednl. psychology, 1958-63, prof., 1963—, dir. counseling psychology Ph.D. tng. program, 1976-78; practice psychology, 1960—; cons. in field; vis. prof. Austin Presbyn. Theol. Sem., 1965-68, Episcopal Sem. S.W., 1969-72; mem. faculty Exptl. Inst. Human Devel., Princeton Theol. Sem., summer 1976. Author: Listening As a Way of Becoming, 1977, Your Secret Self, 1978; contbr. numerous articles to profl. jours.; editorial bd.: Jour. Coll. Student Personnel, 1967-70. Served to maj. USAAF, 1946. Fellow Am. Psychol. Assn., Am. Group Psychotherapy Assn.; mem. Am. Assn. Advancement Psychology, Nat. Register Health Service Providers in Psychology, Am. Personnel and Guidance Assn. (senate 1964-65), Am. Coll. Personnel Assn. (chmn. membership com. 1954-55, chmn. commn. grad. edn. 1962-64, chmn. nat. program com. 1967), Southwestern Group Psychotherapy Soc. (mem. tng. faculty 1971—, sr. faculty mem. 1976—, exec. com. 1971-75, 77—), Tex. Psychol. Assn. Home: 7204 W Rim Dr Austin TX 78731 Office: Dept Ednl Psychology U Tex Austin TX 78712

KOIRTYOHANN, SAMUEL ROY, chemistry educator; b. Washington, Mo., Sept. 11, 1930; s. Earl and Carrie (Jaeger) K.; m. Laura Nieman, Mar. 7, 1952; children: Steven, Linda, Carrie. B.S., U. Mo., Columbia, 1953, M.S., 1958, Ph.D., 1966. Chemist Oak Ridge Nat. Lab., 1958-63; instr. chemistry U. Mo., Columbia, 1963-66, asst. prof., 1966-70, assoc. prof., 1970-75, prof., 1975—. Mem. Am. Chem. Soc., Soc. Applied Spectroscopy, Sigma Xi. Home: Route 12 PO Box 330 Columbia MO 65201

KOJIAN, VARUJAN HAIG, conductor; b. Beirut, Mar. 12, 1945; U.S., 1956, naturalized, 1965; s. Haig Awak and Anouche (Der-Parseghian) K. Student (1st prize), Paris Nat. Conservatory, 1953-56; diploma, Curtis Inst. Music, 1959; student, U. So. Calif., 1964. Asst. concertmaster and asst. condr. Los Angeles Philharm., 1965-71; asso. condr. Seattle Symphony, 1972-75; prin. guest condr. Royal Opera, Stockholm, 1973-80; music dir. Utah Symphony, Salt Lake City, from 1980, Chautauqua (N.Y.) Symphony, from 1981, Ballet West, Salt Lake City, 1984—; faculty dept. music U. Utah, Salt Lake City, 1980—. Recipient 1st prize Internat. Conducting Competition, Sorrento, Italy, 1972; decorated Order of Lion Finland, 1975, also by govts. Greece, 1956, Iran, 1955, Lebanon, 1956. Office: Ballet West 50 West 200 South Salt Lake City UT 84101

KOKASKA, CHARLES JAMES, ednl. psychologist; b. Chgo., Apr. 19, 1937; s. Charles August and Francene (Larva) K.; m. Sharen Elizabeth Metz, June 26, 1970; 1 dau., Laurel Ann. B.A., Valparaiso U., 1958; M.A., Northwestern U., 1961; Ed.D., Boston U., 1968. Tchr. children with emotional problems The Day Sch., Chgo., 1959-60; tchr., head dept. spl. edn. North Phoenix High Sch., 1961-64; asst. prof. spl. edn. Eastern Mich. U., 1967-69; prof. ednl. psychology Calif. State U., Long Beach, 1969—; dir. nat. tng. insts. Career Edn. for Exceptional Individuals, 1979; Dir. exptl. summer camp project Fernald State Sch., Mass., 1965; dir. several workshops, study insts. in edn. of exceptional children, 1967—. Author: (with J. Gowan, G. Demos) The Guidance of Exceptional Children, 1972, (with D. Brolin) Career Education for Handicapped Children and Youth, 1979; exec. editor: Career Devel. for Exceptional Individuals, 1977—; contbr. articles to profl. jours. Mem. community edn. council on spl. edn. Long Beach Unified Sch. Dist., 1971-72. Office of Edn. fellow mental retardation, 1964-67. Mem. Am. Assn. Mental Deficiency, Council Exceptional Children, Tau Kappa Epsilon. Club: Lotos (N.Y.). Home: 618 Havana St Long Beach CA 90814

KOKE, RICHARD JOSEPH, author, exhibit designer, museum curator; b. N.Y.C., Sept. 19, 1916; s. Joseph and Emily Josephine (Chevrolet) K.; m. Mary A. Kimbley, Jan. 1, 1955. Student, Art Students League, 1935, Cooper Union Art Inst., 1935-37; A.B., NYU, 1941; M.A., Columbia U., 1947. Historian, Bear Mountain (N.Y.) Trailside Hist. Mus., 1935-37; curator Stony Point (N.Y.) Battlefield Mus., summers 1937-41; research cons. Hudson Valley Survey, 1946-47; historian Saratoga Nat. Hist. Park, 1947; curator mus. N.Y. Hist. Soc., 1947-83, curator emeritus, 1983—; conducted archaeol. investigations on Revolutionary War mil. sites in Highlands of the Hudson, N.Y., 1935-41. Author: Accomplice in Treason; Joshua Hett Smith and the Arnold Conspiracy, 1973; editor: Scenic and Historic America, 1938; contbr. mags. and revs.; compiler American Landscape and Genre Painting in the New York Historical Society, 3 vols., 1982. Served with AUS, 1942-45; art dir, in charge cartographic dept. M.C., 1942-44; battlefield history research analyst. hist. sect. Hdgrs., 1944-45; engaged in collection and editing of mil. data pertaining to tactical operations Am. forces, preparation ofcl. army histories of Services of Supply, 1st, 3d, 7th, 9th, 15th armies, World War 11; Western European Front. Recipient 1st prize hist. essay contest sponsored by Colonial Dames of N.Y., 1940. Home: Sterling Forest Box 841 Tuxedo Park NY 10987 Office: 170 Central Park W New York NY 10024

KOKEN, BERND KRAFFT, forest products company executive; b. Munich, Germany, Mar. 25, 1926; m. Marguerite Carol Thomson, Aug. 24, 1963; children: Kristine, Peter, Robert, Bruce, Kenneth. Student, Ont. Coll. Art, 1942, Internat. Corr. Schs., 1954. V.p. lumber and kraft Abitibi Paper Co. Ltd., Toronto, 1975-77; pres. groundwood and Kraft Abitibi-Price Sales Corp., N.Y.C., 1977-78, chmn., chief exec. officer, 1978-80; group v.p. Abitibi-Price Inc., Toronto, 1980-82, exec. v.p., chief operating officer, 1982-83, pres. and chief operating officer, 1983—, dir.; vice chmn. Abitibi-Price Corp., Troy, Mich., 1982—; dir. Inter-City Papers Ltd., Montreal, 1982—, Price Co. Ltd., Quebec, 1982—. Clubs: Toronto; Lambton Golf and Country (Toronto); Canadian (N.Y.C.); Longboat Key (Fla.). Home: 30 Taylorwood Dr Toronto ON Canada M9A 4R7 Office: Abitibi-Price Inc Toronto-Dominion Centre PO Box 21 Toronto ON Canada M5K 1B3

KOLANSKY, HAROLD, physician, psychiatrist, psychoanalyst; b. Carbondale, Pa., Aug. 15, 1924; s. Abe and Miriam (Raker) K.; m. Elsa Harwitz, June 8, 1948; children: Jeffrey, Betta, Daniel. Student, U. Scranton, 1942-44; M.D. cum laude, Georgetown U., 1948. Rotating intern Walter Reed Army Hosp., Washington, 1948-49; resident Coatesville (Pa.) VA Hosp. and Deans' Com. Program, Phila., 1949-52; practice medicine specializing in psychiatry and psychoanalysis, Phila., 1952—, Elkins Park, Pa., 1959—; mem. psychiatry staff Albert Einstein Med. Center, 1952-69, 83—, dir. dept. child psychiatry, 1955-69, acting chmn. div. psychiatry, 1968-69, dir. child psychiatry residency, 1960-69; mem. faculty Inst. of Phila. Assn. Psychoanalysis, 1960—, chmn. adminstrv. bd., 1966-69, dir. div. child and adolescent psychoanalysis, 1975-84, tng. and supervisory analyst, 1976—, chmn. tng. analyst com., 1982-83, chmn. curriculum com., 1982—; mem. staff psychiatry Phila. Psychiat. Hosp., 1952—; pres. Regional Council Child Psychiatry, 82556 S.E. N.J. and Del., 1967-68, 72-73, chmn. exec. com., 1970-73; chmn. med. bd. Eastern State Sch. and Hosp., Trevose, Pa., 1966-69; asst. prof. psychiatry Hahnemann Med. Coll. and Hosp., Phila., 1952-60; clin. prof. psychiatry U. Pa. Sch. Medicine, 1972-77; prof. psychiatry and human behavior Jefferson Med. Coll. of Thomas Jefferson U., Phila., 1977—, head sect. child and adolescent psychoanalysis, 1980—, dir. sect. psychoanalysis, 1982—; mem. Pa. Task Force on Mental Health Children, 1971-74; vis. prof. psychiatry U. P.R. Sch. Medicine, 1982—. Contbg. author to numerous texts on psychoanalysis and psychiatry including: A Handbook of Child Psychoanalysis, 1968, Behavior Pathology of Childhood and Adolescence, 1973, Controversy in Psychiatry, 1978, Prognosis, 1981; contbr. numerous articles on child and adult psychiatry and psychoanalysis to profl. jours. Served to capt. M.C., U.S. Army, 1948-51; Korea. Recipient 1st prize in chemistry Georgetown U., 1945; 1st pl. U.S. in surgery Nat. Bd. Med. Examiners, 1948. Fellow Am. Psychiat. Assn., Am. Acad. Child Psychiatry (chmn. com. continuing med. edn. 1974-82, citation 1976); mem. Phila. Assn. Psychoanalysis (pres. 1984—, Gerald Pearson Prize award 1960), Assn. Child Psychoanalysis, Phila. Psychiat. Soc., Internat. Psychoanalytic Assn., Am. Psychoanalytic Assn. (exec. counselor 1969-73, 77-82, fellow bd. profl. standards 1983—, mem. com. on child and adolescent analysis 1984—), Pa. Med. Soc., Phila. County Med. Soc., AMA. Jewish. Office: Elkins Park House 7900 Old York Rd Elkins Park PA 19117

KOLAR, MARY JANE, association executive; b. Benton, Ill., Aug. 9, 1941; d. Thomas Haskell and Mary Jane (Sanders) Burnett; m. Otto Michael Kolar, Aug. 13, 1966; children: Robin Lynn, Deon Michael. B.A. with high honors, So. Ill. U., 1963, M.A. with highest hoinors, 1964. Tchr. pub. schs., Benton and Zeigler, Ill., 1960-63; grad. asst. and grad. fellow So. Ill. U., Carbondale, 1963-64; instr. Ridgewood High Sch., Ill., 1964-67, Main Twp. High Sch., Des Plaines, Ill., 1967-70; freelance writer, Chgo., 1970-71; cons. Contractor Promotions, Chgo., 1970-71; ednl. coordinator Am. Dietetic Assn., Chgo., 1971-72; dir. profl. devel. Am. Dental Hygienists Assn., Chgo., 1972-78; dir. Learning Ctr. div. Am. Coll. Cardiology, Bethesda, Md., 1978-80; dir. edn. Nat. Moving and Storage Assn., Alexandria, Va., 1980-82; exec. dir. Women in Communications, Inc., Austin, Tex., 1982—; cons., speaker various profl. assns., ednl. instns. and fed. agys. Contbr. articles to profl. jours., chpts. to books. Troopleader Girl Scouts U.S.A., 1970-71; mem. adminstrv. bd. Prince of Peace Ch., Elk Grove Village, Ill., 1972-76; mem. edn. com. St. Paul's Ch., Chgo., 1977-79; mem. adv. council Accrediting Commn. Assn. of Ind. Colls. and Schs., 1980—. Fellow Am. Soc. Allied Health Professions (dir. 1978-79); mem. Am. Soc. Assn. Execs. (cert. assn. exec.; chmn. edn. sect. 1982-83, bd. dirs. 1983—, Educator of Yr. award 1978), Greater Washington Soc. Assn. Execs. (edn. com. 1981-82), Tex. Soc. Assn. Execs., Am. Bus. Women's Assn., Ill. Hist. Soc., Kellogg Nat. Com. on Allied Health Edn., Women in Communications (newsletter editor, legis. and career reentry chmn., chmn. ERA task force, dir. Washington profl. chpt. 1981-82), Phi Beta Kappa, Phi Kappa Phi, Kappa Delta Pi, Alpha Lambda Delta, Phi Lambda Theta. Clubs: Triton Wives Service Orgn. (program chmn. 1971-72), Nat. Women's Polit. Caucus, Tex. Women's Polit. Caucus, So. Christian Leadership Conf. Home: 7117 Woodhollow Dr Apt 1621 Austin TX 78731 Office: PO Box 9861 Austin TX 78766 *Being a professional means many things. It means adhering to an ethical code, having high standards of quality, striving toward excellence through basic and ongoing preparation for the profession I have chosen to practice. It means having goals and being willing to contribute to solving the social, economic and political problems of the society of which I am a part. Professionalism is not than acceptance of responsibility, more than doing one's duty, more than being good at what one does. Professionalism requires a commitment to what you do and to the future. It carries with it obligation and risk. It necessitates service to the profession—a willingness to be a leader—and a desire to meet the needs of others.*

KOLAR, MILTON ANTON, corp. exec.; b. Chgo., Jan. 18, 1916; s. Frank J. and Josephine (Jaros) K.; m. Rae Solum, July 4, 1940; children—Caryn Rae, Britton Ward, Christine Edith. B.S.C., Northwestern U., 1937, J.D., 1939. Bar: Ill. bar 1939, Wis. bar 1981. Practice law, Chgo., 1939-54; atty. U.S. Gypsum Co., Chgo., 1940-42, Butler Bros., 1942-59, asst. sec., 1954-58, gen. devel. mgr., 1954-58, asst. to pres., 1958-59; gen. mgr. S.W. region Ben Franklin Stores div. City Products Corp. (acquired Butler Bros. 1959), Dallas, 1960-62; v.p., sec. City Products Corp., Des Plaines, Ill., 1962-67; pres. Scott Stores div. City Products Corp., Des Plaines, 1967-69, Herst-Allen, 1969-72; v.p. City Products Corp., 1972-81; occasional lectr.; cons. OPS, Washington, 1951. Mem. Fed., Am., Ill., Chgo. bar assns., Am. Soc. Corp. Secs., Assn. Gen. Mdse. Chains (chmn. 1977-79), Lambda Chi Alpha, Phi Delta Phi. Episcopalian. Home: 326 Butler Dr Lake Forest IL 60045 Office: Washington Island WI 54246

KOLARS, JOHN F., educator; b. Walla Walla, Wash., Mar. 25, 1929; s. John F. and Dora (Wright) K.; m. Ann Evans Larimore, Sept. 28, 1958 (div. Aug. 1975); 1 dau., Christine Mary. B.Sc., U. Wash., 1952, M.A., 1958; Ph.D., U. Chgo., 1963. Geologist U.S. Geol. Survey, 1953-54; asst. prof. geography Rutgers U., 1961-64; mem. faculty U. Mich., Ann Arbor, 1964—, prof. geography, 1969—, prof. Near Eastern studies, 1982—. Author articles, monograph, numerous poems; co-author 3 introductory texts.; Editor: U. Mich. Geog. Publs, 1971—. Served with AUS, 1946-48. Fellow Nat. Acad. Scis.-NRC, 1959-60; fellow Social Sci. Research Council, 1960-61, 69; research grantee, 1981; U. Mich. faculty research grantee, 1966-69; Am. Council Learned Socs. research grantee, 1981. Mem. Am. Soc. Geographers,

Middle East Studies Assn., AAAS, Sigma Xi. Home: 1304 Hutchins Ave Ann Arbor MI 48103

KOLATCH, ALFRED JACOB, publisher; b. Seattle, Jan. 2, 1916; s. Sander and Yetta (Jacobs) K.; m. Thelma Rubin, June 16, 1940; children—Jonathan, David. B.A., Yeshiva U., 1937; Rabbi, Jewish Theol. Sem., 1941. Ordained rabbi, 1941, rabbi, Columbia, S.C., 1941-43, Kew Gardens, N.Y., 1946-48; founder, pres. Jonathan David Publishers, Middle Village, N.Y., 1949—. Author: The Name Dictionary, 1949, Jewish Information Quiz Book, 1967, J.D. Dictionary of First Names, The Jewish Book of Why, Family Seder, Who's Who in the Talmud. Served as chaplain U.S. Army, 1943-46. Mem. Rabbinical Assembly, Assn. Jewish Chaplains (past pres.), Mil. Chaplains Assn. (past v.p.). Home: 72-08 Juno St Forest Hills NY 11375 Office: 68-22 Eliot Ave Middle Village NY 11379

KOLATCH, MYRON, magazine editor; b. Bklyn., Sept. 26, 1929; s. Philip S. and Rebecca (Langberg) K.; m. Francine Ruth Miller, Jan. 28, 1951; children: Barry Steven, Jonathan Lee, Sari Elana. B.A, N.Y. U., 1950, postgrad in English, 1950-51. Mem. staff New Leader, 1953—, mng. editor, 1960-61, exec. editor, 1961—. Bd. dirs. Tamiment Inst. Served with AUS, 1951-53. Home: 141-13 68th Dr Kew Gardens Hills NY 11367 Office: 275 7th Ave New York NY 10001

KOLB, DAVID ALLEN, educator; b. Moline, Ill., Dec. 12, 1939; s. John August and Ethel May (Petherbridge) K.; 1 son, Jonathan Demian. A.B. cum laude, Knox Coll., 1961; Ph.D., Harvard U., 1967. Asst. prof. organizational psychology MIT, Cambridge, 1965-70, assoc. prof., 1970-75; prof. organizational behavior and mgmt. Case Western Res. U., Cleve., 1976—; vis. prof. mgmt. London Grad. Sch. Bus., 1971; dir. Devel. Research Assos., 1966-80; mgmt. cons., U.S., Australia, N.Z., Indonesia, Singapore, Malaysia, Thailand, Japan. Author: Experiential Learning: Experience as the source of learning and development, 1984; co-author: Organizational Psychology: An Experiential Approach, 4th edit, 1984, Organizational Psychology: A Book of Readings, 4th edit, 1984, Changing Human Behavior: Principles of Planned Intervention, 1974. Woodrow Wilson fellow, 1962. Mem. Am. Psychol. Assn., Internat. Assn. Applied Social Scientists (charter), Soc. Intercultural Edn., Tng. and Research (charter), Council Advancement of Experiential Learning (dir.). Office: Case Western Reserve Univ Cleveland OH 44106

KOLB, GWIN JACKSON, educator; b. Aberdeen, Miss., Nov. 2, 1919; s. Roy Rolly and Nola Undine (Jackson) K.; m. Ruth Alma Godbold, Oct. 11, 1943; children—Gwin Jackson II, Alma Dean. B.A., Millsaps Coll., 1941; M.A., U. Chgo., 1946, Ph.D., 1949. Editorial asst. Modern Philology, 1946-56; mem. faculty U. Chgo., 1949—, prof. English, 1961-77, Chester D. Tripp prof. humanities, 1977—, chmn. dept., 1963-72, chmn. coll. English staff, 1958-60, head humanities sect. in coll., 1960-62; vis. asso. prof. Northwestern U., winter 1958, Stanford U., spring 1960; vis. prof. U. Washington, summers 1967, 73. Co-author: Dr. Johnson's Dictionary, 1955, Reading Literature: A Workbook, 1955; Editor: (Samuel Johnson) Rasselas, 1962; co-editor: A Bibliography of Modern Studies Complied for Philological Quarterly, 1951-65, 3 vols, 1962, 72, Modern Philology, 1973—. Served with USNR, 1942-45. Recipient Quantrell award U. Chgo., 1955; Guggenheim fellow, 1956-57; Alumni award Millsaps Coll., 1967; grantee Am. Council Learned Socs., 1961-62. Mem. Midwest Modern Lang. Assn. (pres. 1964-65), Johnson Soc. Central Region (pres. 1965-66), Modern Lang. Assn., Nat. Council Tchrs. English (bd. dirs. coll. sect. 1966-68), AAUP, Am. Soc. 18th Century Studies (exec. bd. 1973-76, pres. 1976-77), The Johnsonians, Assn. Depts. English (pres. 1968). Clubs: Caxton, Quadrangle (Chgo.). Home: 5819 Blackstone Ave Chicago IL 60637

KOLB, KEITH ROBERT, architect, educator; b. Billings, Mont., Feb. 9, 1922; s. Percy Fletcher and Josephine (Randolph) K.; m. Jacqueline Cecile Jump, June 18, 1947; children: Brooks Robin, Bliss Richards. B.Arch., U. Wash., 1947; M.Arch., Harvard U., 1950. Registered architect, Wash., Mont., Idaho, Calif., Oreg., Nat. Council Archtl. Registration Bds. Draftsman, designer various archtl. firms, Seattle, 1945-54; draftsman, designer Walter Gropius and Architects Collaborative, Cambridge, Mass., 1950-52; prin. Keith R. Kolb, Architect, Seattle, 1954-64, Keith R. Kolb Architect & Assocs., 1964-66; ptnr. Decker, Kolb & Stansfield, Seattle, 1966-71, Kolb & Stansfield AIA Architects, 1971—; instr. Mont. State Coll., Bozeman, 1947-49; asst. prof. architecture U. Wash., Seattle, 1952-60, assoc. prof., 1960-82, prof., 1982—. Design architect Hampson residence, 1973 (nat. AIA 1st honor), Acute Gen. Stevens Meml. Hosp., 1973; Redmond Pub. Library, 1975; designer architect: Herbert L. Eastlick Biol. Scis. Lab. Bldg., Wash. State U., 1977; design architect: Computer & Mgmt. Services Ctr., Paccar Inc., 1980; Communication Tower, Pacific N.W. Bell, 1981 (nat. J.F. Lincoln bronze); Forks br. Seattle 1st Nat. Bank, 1981 (regional citation), Puget Sound Blood Ctr., 1983, others. Pres. Laurelhurst Community Club, Seattle, 1966. Served with U.S. Army, 1943-45; ETO. Fellow AIA (sec. 1972); mem. Archtl. Alumni Assn. (pres. 1958-59), Phi Beta Kappa, Tau Sigma Delta. Home: 3379 47th Ave NE Seattle WA 98105 Office: Kolb and Stansfield AIA Architects 1326 5th Ave Seattle WA 98101

KOLB, KEN LLOYD, writer; b. Portland, Oreg., July 14, 1926; s. Frederick Von and Ella May (Bay) K.; m. Emma LaVada Sanford, June 7, 1952; children: Kevin, Lauren, Kimrie. B.A. in English with honors, U. Calif.-Berkeley, 1950; M.A. with honors, Calif. State U.-San Francisco, 1953. Minister Universal Life Ch.; tchr. creative writing Feather River Coll., 1969. Author first short story published, Esquire Mag., 1951; contbr. fiction and humor to, nat. mags. and anthologies1332644, 63; author numerous teleplays produced on, nat. network TV; plays She Walks in Beauty, 1956 (Writers Guild award for best half-hour drama); novels Getting Straight, 1967; plays The Couch Trip, 1970, Night Crossing, 1974; movies Seventh Voyage of Sinbad, 1957, Snow Job, 1972. Foreman Plumas County Grand Jury, 1970; chmn. Region C Criminal Justice Planning Commn., 1975-77. Served with USNR, 1944-46. Establishment Ken Kolb Collection Boston U. Library, 1969. Establishment Ken Kolb Collection (Boston U. Library 1969); mem. Writers Guild Am., Authors Guild, Mensa, Phi Beta Kappa, Theta Chi. Home and Office: PO Box 22 Hwy 70 Cromberg CA 96103 *The true measure of success is not the attainment of great wealth or a position of power over others, but the quality of one's own life. I'm grateful for the money and honors I've had from writing, but more important to me is my ongoing love affair with my wife and the loving friendship of my grown children. I believe in God and a sense of humor as guiding principles, but I can't explain either one.*

KOLB, LAWRENCE COLEMAN, psychiatrist; b. Balt., June 16, 1911; s. Lawrence and Lillian Hess (Coleman) K.; m. Madeleine Currie, July 3, 1937; children: Pamela Currie Leadbitter, Mary Clark Estes, Richard Jennings. B.A., Trinity Coll., Dublin U., Ireland, 1932; M.D., Johns Hopkins U., 1934. Diplomate: Am. Bd. Psychiatry and Neurology (dir. 1960-68, pres. 1968). Intern medicine, surgery Strong Meml. Hosp., Rochester, N.Y., 1934-36; fellow neurology Johns Hopkins U., 1936-38, instr., 1939-40; Markle fellow neurology Nat. Hosp. Queens Sq., Eng., 1938-39; psychiatrist Milw. Sanitorium, 1941; dir. research projects NIMH, also pvt. practice psychiatry, 1946-49; research assoc. Washington Sch. Psychiatry, 1946-49; cons. Mayo Clinic; also assoc. prof. psychiatry U. Minn., 1949-54; dir. N.Y. State Psychiat. Inst.; prof., chmn. dept. psychiatry Columbia U., 1954-75, prof. emeritus, 1975—; prof. Albany Med. Coll., 1978; dir. psychiat. service Presbyn. Hosp., N.Y.C., 1954-75; commr. N.Y. State Dept. Mental Hygiene, 1975-78; Disting. physician in psychiatry U.S. VA, 1978—; pres. med. bd. Presbyn. Hosp., N.Y.C., 1962-64, trustee, 1971-73, hon. trustee, 1974—; prof. psychiatry Albany Med. Coll., 1978—; cons. nat. adv. council USPHS, HEW; mem. panel med. scis. to asst. sec. of def., 1954-60; mem. career investigator com. NIMH, 1956-60, chmn., 1962, mem. bd. sci. counsellors, 1959-62, chmn., 1962; mem. spl. adv. com. to commr. hosps., N.Y.C., 1961; mem. Salmon Com. Mental Hygiene; adv. bd. P.R. Inst. Psychiatry, 1972—. Author: (with O.R. Langworthy and L.G. Lewis) Physiology of Micturition, 1940, The Painful Phamtom, 1954, Modern Clinical Psychiatry, 9th edit, 1977; also: numerous articles. Modern Clinical Psychiatry, 9th edit. Bd. dirs. Founds. Fund for Research in Psychiatry, 1959-61; bd. dirs., pres., chmn. bd. Research Found. for Mental Hygiene, 1960-76; trustee Austin Riggs Center, Silver Hill Found., 1967-74. Recipient Henry Wisner Meml. award, 1962; Oscar K. Diamond award, 1971; Joan Plehn award for human service Mental Health Assn. N.Y. and Bronx Counties, 1972; Richard H. Hutchings award N.Y. State Hosps. Alumni Assn., 1975; Dedication of Lawrence C. Kolb Research Lab. N.Y. State Psychiat. Inst., 1983. Fellow Am. Psychiat. Assn. (pres. 1968, Disting. Service award 1983), Am. Acad. Neurology, N.Y. Acad. Sci.; mem. Am. Neurol. Assn., Am. Psychoanalytic Assn., Assn. Research Nervous and Mental Diseases (pres. 1969), Johns Hopkins Soc. Scholars, Sigma Xi, Alpha Omega Alpha. Clubs: Century Assn., University (N.Y.C.); University (Albany); Vidonia Practioners. Address: Van Wies Point Glenmont NY 12077

KOLB, THEODORE ALEXANDER, lawyer; b. Vienna, Austria, May 26, 1920; came to U.S., 1927; s. Leon and Hilde (Grunwaldt) K.; m. Alison McClelland, July 14, 1948; children—Jonathan B., Richard J., Douglas G. B.S., U. San Francisco, 1942, J.D., 1945. Bar: Calif. 1945. Practiced in, San Francisco, 1945—; sr. partner firm Sullivan, Roche & Johnson, 1941—. Fellow Am. Bar Found., Am. Coll. Probate Counsel; mem. ABA, Calif. State Bar, Bar Assn. San Francisco, U. San Francisco Law Soc. (past pres.), Downtown Assn. San Francisco (dir.). Clubs: World Trade (pres. 1983-84), Olympic, Family, St. Francis Yacht, Presidio Golf. Home: 2200 Pacific Ave San Francisco CA 94115 Office: 220 Bush St San Francisco CA 94104

KOLB, WILLIAM LESTER, educator; b. Cin., Sept. 26, 1916; s. William Frederick and Lydia Marie (Atkins) K.; m. Helen Webster, June 15, 1940; children: Nina Marie, William Webster. B.A. magna cum laude with honors in Polit. Sci, Miami (O.) U., 1938; M.A., U. Wis., 1939, Ph.D., 1943. Instr. sociology Okla. A. and M. Coll., 1941-43, 46; asst. prof. sociology Newcomb Coll. of Tulane U., 1946-48; asso. prof., then prof., head dept., also in Grad. Sch. Tulane U., 1948-59, univ. chmn. dept. sociology, 1955-57; Fred B. Hill prof. sociology, chmn. dept. sociology and anthropology Carleton Coll., 1959-64; prof. sociology Beloit (Wis.) Coll., 1964-82, prof. emeritus, 1983—, dean, 1964-73, provost, 1970-76; Mem. Edwin J. Beinecke Sr. Meml. scholarship com. S & H Found., Inc., 1971-74; mem. dept. Christian social relations Episcopal Diocese La., 1957-58; vice chmn. Am. Conf. Academic Deans, 1968-69, chmn., 1969-70, Danforth Commn. on Study Campus Ministry, 1962-70; mem. exec., policy coms. Dept. Higher Edn., Nat. Council Chs. Christ, 1965-70; chmn. planning com. Colloquium on Religion and Higher Edn., 1966-67. Author: (with Logan Wilson) Sociological Analysis, 1949, (with J. Gould) A Dictionary of the Social Sciences, 1964; also articles, chpts. in books.; Mem. editorial bd.: Christian Scholar, 1960-62. Mem. La. chpt., bd. ACLU, 1956-59; bd. Minn. chpt., 1963-64; mem. Wis. chpt., 1964—. Served to lt. (j.g.) USNR, 1943-46. Post-doctoral fellow Soc. for Religion in Higher Edn., 1967. Mem. Am. Sociol. Assn. (council, exec. com. 1961-62, mem. MacIver award com. 1965-66, chmn. 1967), Midwestern Sociol. Soc. (council 1960-62, pres. 1966-67), Assn. Am. Colls. (commn. on religion in higher edn. 1973-74), Phi Beta Kappa (Ralph Waldo Emerson award com. 1971-72). Home: 816 Chapin St Beloit WI 53511

KOLBAS, JOHN MICHAEL, pharm. co. exec.; b. Akron, Ohio, Feb. 19, 1926; s. John and Mary A. (Adams) K.; m. Frances Woityra, Sept. 13, 1947; children—John William, Robert Michael. B.Ch.E., Ohio State U., 1947. With Bristol Labs., Syracuse, N.Y., 1947-75, mgr. sales adminstrn. and tng., 1964-68, dir. mktg. services, 1968-70; v.p., gen. mgr. Bristol Alpha Corp., Barcelloneta, P.R., 1970-73; v.p. prodn. Norwich-Eaton Pharms., Norwich, N.Y., 1975-77, pres., 1979—; exec. v.p. Morton Salt div. Morton Norwich, Chgo., 1977, pres., 1978-79; dir. Nat. Bank & Trust Co. Norwich. Bd. dirs. SUNY Upstate Med. Center Found. Mem. Am. Inst. Chem. Engrs. Office: 17 Eaton Ave Norwich NY 13815

KOLBE, JAMES FRANK, automotive parts mfg. co. exec.; b. Muskegon, Mich., Oct. 15, 1932; s. Russel Frank and Minnie Caroline (Hendricks) K.; m. Jacqueline Wright, Oct. 8, 1955; children—Jennifer, James M., Jeffrey. Student, Muskegon Community Coll., 1950-52; B.S.M.E., Mich. State U., 1954. Test engr. Continental Motors, Muskegon, 1955; with Sealed Power Corp., 1959—, group vice-pres., 1972—; dir. East Shore Chem. Co., Inc. Bd. dirs. West Mich. Shores council Boy Scouts Am., Goodwill Industries, Muskegon Jr. Achievement. Served with USN, 1956-59. Mem. Soc. Automotive Engrs., Investment Casting Inst., Metal Powder Industries Fedn. Republican. Episcopalian. Home: 1110 Moulton St North Muskegon MI 49445 Office: 100 Terrace Plaza Muskegon MI 49443

KOLBYE, ALBERT CHRISTIAN, JR., physician, foundation president; b. Phila., Feb. 15, 1935; s. Albert Christian and Marion Fisler (Bozarth) K.; m. Lise Neergaard Ottosen, July 24, 1976. A.B., Harvard U., 1957; M.D., Temple U., 1961; M.P.H., Johns Hopkins U., 1965; J.D., U. Md., 1966. Bar: Md. bar 1967. Intern Univ. Hosps., Madison, Wis., 1961-62; resident in public health and preventive medicine USPHS, 1962-64; with HEW, 1965—; dep. dir. Bur. Foods, FDA, Washington, 1970-71, asso. dir. scis., 1972-82; asst. surgeon gen. USPHS, 71-82; pres. Nutrition Found., Inc., 1982—. Recipient Meritorious Service medal USPHS, 1971, 75. Fellow Am. Public Health Assn., Am. Coll. Legal Medicine, Am. Coll. Preventive Medicine, Am. Acad. Clin. Toxicology; mem. AMA, Md. Bar Assn., Md. Med-Chirurgical Faculty. Home: 4802 Ft Sumner Dr Bethesda MD 20016 Office: Nutrition Found Inc 888 17th St NW Washington DC 20006

KOLE, JOHN WILLIAM, journalist; b. Zeeland, Mich., Jan. 27, 1934; s. John Henry and Una (Messer) K.; m. Betty Lou Zuege, Sept. 15, 1956; children—Linda Sue, Leslie Ann, James David, Sara Louise, Susan Margaret. B.A., Mich. State U., 1955; M.S., Northwestern U., 1956; Nieman fellow, Harvard U., 1962-63. Reporter Milw. Jour., 1956-64, reporter, 1964-70, chief, 1970—. Recipient awards Am. Polit. Sci. Assn., 1961, Milw. Press Club, 1960-63, 72. Mem. White House Corrs. Assn., Sigma Delta Chi. Clubs: Gridiron, Nat. Press (Washington). Home: 2542 N 23d Rd Arlington VA 22207 Office: 645 Nat Press Bldg Washington DC 20045

KOLEHMAINEN, JOHN ILMARI, history educator; b. Conneaut, Ohio, July 2, 1910; s. Matti and and Julia (Tuomisto) K.; m. Astrid Irene Petrell, Aug. 6, 1939; children: Jan W., Joy K., Kay A. A.B., Western Res. U., 1933, M.A. in History, 1934, Ph.D., 1937; D.L., No. Mich. U., 1974, U. Turku, 1977. Mem. faculty Heidelberg Coll., Tiffin, Ohio, 1938-80, prof. polit. sci., 1940-80; vis. prof. Suomi Coll., Hancock, Mich., 1945-46, U. Minn., 1950-51; chief Finnish desk Voice of Am., 1951-52; Fulbright lectr. Helsinki U., 1956, Turku U., 1965. Author: The Finns in America: A Bibliographical Guide, 1947, Finns in America, 1968, (with Geoge Hill) Haven in the Woods: The Story of the Finns in Wisconsin, 2d edit, 1965, Sow the Golden Seed, 1955, Epic of the North: The Story of Finland's Kalevala, 1973, From Lake Erie's Shores to the Mahoning and Monongahela Valleys: A History of the Finns in Ohio, Western Pennsylvania, and West Virginia, 1977; also articles. Decorated 1st class Order Finnish Lion; comdr. Order of White Rose. Corr. mem. Finnish Litt. Soc., Turku Hist. Soc., Porthan Soc., Kalevala Soc. Home: 50 Parkview Dr Tiffin OH 44883

KOLENDA, KONSTANTIN, educator; b. Kamien-Koszyrski, Poland, May 17, 1923; came to U.S., 1946, naturalized, 1951; s. Theodore and Helena K.; m. Pauline Moller, June 9, 1962; children—Helena, Christopher. B.A., Rice U., 1950; Ph.D., Cornell U., 1953. Asst. prof. philosophy Rice U., 1953-58, assoc. prof., 1958-65, prof., 1965—, chmn. dept. philosophy, 1968-75, Carolyn and Fred McManis prof. philosophy, 1975—; Fulbright lectr. U. Heidelberg, 1959-60; vis. prof. U. Tex., Colo. Coll. Author: The Freedom of Reason, 1964, In Defense of Practical Reason, 1969, Ethics for the Young, 1972, Philosophy's Journey, 1974, Religion Without God, 1976, Philosophy in Literature, 1982; Editor: On Thinking, 1979. Adv. chmn. Houston Com. for Humanities and Public Policy, 1977—. Mem. Am. Philos. Assn., Southwestern Philos. Soc. (pres. 1965), Soc. Advancement of Am. Philosophy, C.S. Peirce Soc., Phi Beta Kappa. Democrat. Home: 2515 Glenhaven St Houston TX 77030 Office: Rice University 6100 Main St Houston TX 77001 *There is one question that must be answered at the onset of adulthood: Am I to say yes or no to life? A yes answer conditions every further choice made—in propitious or adverse circumstances. Every choice becomes clearer, easier, more confident, and it produces peace of mind.*

KOLENDER, WILLIAM BARNETT, police chief; b. Chgo., May 23, 1935; s. David Solomon and Esther (Dickman) K.; children—Michael, Myrna, Joy, Randie, Dennis. Student, San Diego City Coll., 1963; B.A. in Pub. Adminstrn, San Diego State U., 1964. With San Diego Police Dept., 1956—, chief of police, 1976—; tchr. U. Calif., San Diego, 1971—, San Diego State U., 1972—; mem. Commn. on Peace Officers Standards and Tng. Calif. Vice pres. San Diego County council Boy Scouts Am.; mem. Mayor's Crime Control Commn.; pres. Boys' Clubs San Diego. Served with USN, 1953-55. Named Alumnus of Year San Diego State U., 1973, Outstanding Young Man of Year San Diego, 1970; recipient Mayor's Award for Human Relations and Civil Rights City of San Diego, 1972, Human Relations Award Am. Jewish Com., 1975; Diogenes award San Diego chpt. Public Relations Soc. Am., 1978; Man of Yr. award Irish Congress So. Calif., 1981; Histadrut award Am. Trade Union Council, 1981; Equal Opportunity award San Diego Urban League, 1981; Man of Yr. award Charter 100 Profl. Women's Club, 1981. Mem. Calif. Police Chiefs Assn., Calif. Police Officers Assn., Internat. Assn. Chiefs Police, Police Exec. Research Forum (dir.). Republican. Jewish. Club: San Diego Rotary. Home: 4035 Tambor Rd San Diego CA 92123 Office: 801 W Market St San Diego CA 92101

KOLER, ROBERT DONALD, educator; b. Casper, Wyo., Feb. 14, 1924; s. Joseph Leonard and Nellie (Hayes) K.; m. June Rogers, June 23, 1945; children—Thomas E., Mary L. B.A., U. Oreg., 1945, M.D., 1947; hon. research asst. eugenics, biometry and genetics, Univ. Coll., London, Eng., 1960-61. Intern U. Oreg. Med. Sch., 1947-48, resident, 1948-49, 51-53; asst. prof. medicine U. Oreg., 1956-59, asso. prof., 1959-64, prof. medicine, head hematology and exptl. medicine, 1964-69, prof. medicine, head med. genetics, 1967—, chmn. pro tem dept. medicine, 1976-77; Mem. cancer research center com. Nat. Cancer Inst., 1968-72. Contbr. articles to profl. jours. Mem. Oreg. Bd. Social Protection, 1967-70. Served to capt. M.C. AUS, 1949-51. Fellow A.C.P., Western Soc. Clin. Research (councilor 1964-66), Western Assn. Physicians (councilor 1975-78); mem. Am. Fedn. Clin. Research, Am. Soc. Hematology, Am. Soc. Human Genetics, Phi Beta Kappa, Alpha Omega Alpha. Home: 2532 SW Hamilton Ct Portland OR 97201

KOLES, RICHARD THOMAS, housing development company executive; b. Newark, Apr. 23, 1927; s. Joseph Peter and Marie (Hake) K.; m. Nora McKinley, Nov. 18, 1950; children: Richard M., Norine Koles Rishko. Student public schs. Photographer George Van Photo Service, Newark, 1953-61; sr. photographer Elizabeth (N.J.) Daily Jour., 1962-79; pres. Employees Fed. Credit Union, 1974-78, sec., 1979-80; chief photographer Community Paper, Elizabeth, 1979; dir. communications New Community Corp., Newark, 1979—. Co-author: Elizabethtown and Union County, A Pictorial History, 1982. Founder, sec.-trustee Bob Baxter Scholarship Found., 1980; mem. adv. bd. Union County Heart Assn., 1972-79, citation, 1969; mem. Police Athletic League, Elizabeth, 1968-78. Served with USNR, 1944-46, 50-51. Recipient citation Linden Ambulance Squad, 1979. Mem. Nat. Press Photographers Assn. (originator, editor Out of Focus 1973-77, Bootstrap award Region III 1976, Pres.'s medal 1980), N.J. Press Photographers (pres. 1966-68, trustee 1968—), Newspaper Guild (del. Mid-Atlantic council 1970-80). Democrat. Roman Catholic. Home: 277 Greylock Pkwy Belleville NJ 07109 Office: New Community Corp 755 S Orange Ave Newark NJ 07106

KOLESAR, PETER JOHN, business and engineering educator; b. N.Y.C., Nov. 25, 1936; s. John Michael and Agnes (Vajda) K.; m. Nicole Bordat, May 30, 1969 (div. 1981); children: Lara, Alexandre. B.A., Queens Coll., 1959; B.S. in Indsl. Engrng., Columbia U., 1959, M.S., 1962, Ph.D., 1964. Systems analyst Procter & Gamble, Cin., 1959-61; lectr. Imperial Coll., London, 1964-65; asst. prof. Sch. Engrng. Columbia U., N.Y.C., 1965-70; prof. Grad. Sch. Bus. Columbia U., London, 1975—; sr. analyst Rand Corp., N.Y.C., 1971-74; cons. in field. Contbr. articles to profl. jours. Recipient Systems Sci. prize NATO, 1976. Fellow AAAS; mem. Ops. Research Soc. Am. (council 1980-83, Lanchester prize 1975), Inst. Mgmt. Scis., Am. Statis. Assn. Home: 410 Riverside Dr New York NY 10025 Office: 417 Uriss Hall Columbia U New York NY 10027

KOLFF, WILLEM JOHAN, surgeon, educator; b. Leiden, Holland, Feb. 14, 1911; came to U.S., 1950, naturalized, 1956; s. Jacob and Adriana (de Jonge) K.; m. Janke C. Huidekoper, Sept 4, 1937; children: Jacob, Adriana P., Albert C., Cornelis A., Gualtherus C.M. Student, U. Leiden Med. Sch., 1930-38; M.D. summa cum laude, U. Groningen, 1946, U. Turin, Italy, 1969, Rostock (Germany) U., 1975, U. Bologna, Italy, 1977, D.Sc., Allegheny Coll., Meadville, Pa., 1960, Tulane U., 1975, CUNY, 1982, Temple U., 1983, U. Utah, 1983. Internist, head med. dept. Mcpl. Hosp., Kampen, Holland; staff research div. Cleve. Clinic Found., 1950-67; privaat docent, dept. medicine U. Leiden, Nether-Bunts Ednl. Inst., Cleve., 1950-67, head dept. artificial organs, 1958-67; prof. surgery, head div. artificial organs dept. surgery U. Utah Coll. Medicine, Salt Lake City, 1967—, Disting. prof. surgery, 1979—, prof. internal medicine, 1981—; research prof. engrng. Inst. Biomed. Engrng., 1967—. Decorated commandeur Orde Van Oranje, Netherlands, 1970; Orden de Mayo al Merito en el Grado de Gran Official, Argentina, 1974; recipient Landsteiner medal for establishment blood banks during war in Holland Netherlands Red Cross, 1942; Cameron prize U. Edinburgh (Scotland), 1964; 5,000 award Gairdner Found., 1966; Valentine award N.Y. Acad. Medicine, 1969; 1st Gold medal Netherlands Surg. Soc., 1970; Leo Harvey prize

Technion, Israel, 1972; Sr. U.S. Scientist award Alexander Von Humboldt Found., 1978; Austrian Gewerbeverein's Wilhelm-Exner award, 1980. Mem. AMA, AAUP, Am. Physiol. Soc., Soc. Exptl. Biology and Medicine, AAAS, N.Y. Acad. Scis., Am. Soc. Artificial Internal Organs, Nat. Kidney Found., European Dialysis and Transplant Assn., ACP, Austrian Soc. Nephrology (hon.), Academia Nacional de Medicine (Colombia) (hon.), Rotarian. Devel. artificial kidney for clin. use, 1943; oxygenator, 1956. Address: Div of Artificial Organs Univ of Utah Medical Center Bldg 535 Salt Lake City UT 84112

KOLHOVEN, JOHN HENRY, transportation company executive; b. Covington, Ky., Apr. 9, 1927; s. Harry C. and Agnes V. (Bain) K. Student, Chase Coll., 1948-51, Xavier U., 1951-55. C.P.A., Ohio, Ill., Wis. Asst. treas. Gruen Industries, Cin., 1954-58; treas. B. Kuppenheimer, Chgo., 1958-61; v.p. finance, treas. Gateway Transp. Co., La Crosse, Wis., 1961-74; v.p. finance Ace-Doran Transp. Co. Inc., Cin., 1974-75, The Edward Corp., Warren, Ohio, 1975-78; treas. Schwerman Trucking Co. Inc., Milw., 1978-83. Pres. La Crosse Police and Fire Commn., 1966-71. Served with AUS, 1944-46. Mem. Am. Inst. C.P.A.s, Fin. Execs. Inst. Club: Elks. Home: 2500 Normandy Ln Wauwatosa WI 53226

KOLIBACHUK, JOHN FILIMON, steamship co. exec.; b. Plainfield, N.J., Oct. 29, 1925; s. Filimon and Anastasia (Cymbalak) K.; m. Tressie Howard, June 22, 1948; children—David John, Debra Jane, Dana Jean. B.S., Rutgers U., 1947; M.B.A., N.Y. U., 1951. Staff accountant Price Waterhouse & Co., N.Y.C., 1947-57; subsidy analyst U.S. Lines, Inc., N.Y.C., 1957-66, asst. comptroller, 1966-71, comptroller, 1971-74, v.p., comptroller, 1974-79, v.p., fin. coordinator, Cranford, N.J., 1979-81, dir. regulatory acctg., 1981—. Sec. Dunellen (N.J.) Bd. Edn., 1955-61, mem., 1961-76. Served with USNR, 1943-46. Mem. Am. Inst. C.P.A.'s, Assn. Water Transp. Accounting Officers (pres. 1978-79). Home: 519 Dunellen Ave Dunellen NJ 08812 Office: 27 Commerce Dr Cranford NJ 07016

KOLIBASH, WILLIAM ANTHONY, U.S. attorney; b. Wheeling, W.Va., Feb. 12, 1944; s. Albert Joseph and Josephine (Dicola) K.; m. Rita Patricia Scanlon, July 6, 1968; children: Shariane M., William Anthony, Christopher P. A.B., Brown U., 1966; J.D., W.Va. U., 1969. Bar: W.Va. 1969, U.S. Dist. Ct. for no. dist. W.Va. 1973. Asst. U.S. atty. Dept. Justice, Wheeling, 1973-80, U.S. Atty., 1980—. Served to capt. JAGC AUS, 1969-73. Mem. W.Va. State Bar. Republican. Roman Catholic. Home: 380 Oakmont Rd Wheeling WV 26003 Office: US Attys Office 12th and Chapline Sts Wheeling WV 26003

KOLKER, ALLAN ERWIN, ophthalmologist; b. St. Louis, Nov. 2, 1933; s. Paul P. and Jean K.; m. Jacquelyn Krupin, Dec. 8, 1957; children: Robin, Marci, David, Scott. A.B., Washington U., St. Louis, 1953, M.D., 1957. Diplomate: Am. Bd. Ophthalmology. Intern St. Louis Children's Hosp., 1957-58; resident in ophthalmology Washington U./Barnes Hosp., 1960-65; mem. attending staff ophthalmology Washington U., 1964-81, prof. ophthalmology, 1974-83; glaucoma com. Nat. Soc. to Prevent Blindness. Editor: (with J. Hetherington) Becker and Shaffer's Diagnosis and Therapy of the Glaucomas, 3d, 4th, 5th edit., 1983; contbr. numerous articles to profl. jours. Served with USPHS, 1958-60. NIH spl. fellow, 1963-65; grantee, 1969-80. Mem. Assn. Research in Vision and Ophthalmology, Am. Acad. Ophthalmology, AMA, St. Louis Med. Soc., St. Louis Ophthal. Soc. (pres. 1977-79), Am. Ophthal. Soc., Mo. Ophthal. Soc. Home: 176 Plantation Dr Saint Louis MO 63141 Office: 660 S Euclid Ave Saint Louis MO 63110

KOLKER, ROGER RUSSELL, insurance executive; b. Guttenberg, Iowa, Aug. 14, 1929; s. Russell Edward and Olina Colby (Schwab) K.; m. Suzanne Chaddock Griffin, June 9, 1954; children: Roger Russell, Karolyn, Sara. Student, U. Iowa, 1947-50; B.S., U.S. Mil. Acad., 1954. C.L.U., 1966. Field sales dir. Mut. of N.Y., Chgo., 1964-66, dir. mgmt. tng., N.Y.C., 1966-68, regional v.p., Atlanta, 1968-71; exec. v.p. N. Am. Life Ins. Co., Mpls., 1971-77, Monumental Life Ins. Co., Balt., 1978-79, pres., chief exec. officer, 1979-83; chmn., pres., chief exec. officer Monumental Gen. Ins. Group, Inc., Balt., 1983—; pres., chmn., chief exec. officer Monumental Gen. Ins. Co., Balt., 1983—; dir. Equitable Bancorp. N.A., Balt. Bd. dirs. Balt. Symphony Orch., South Balt. Gen. Hosp. Mem. Gen. Agts. and Mgrs. Assn., Balt. Life Underwriters Assn., Am. Coll. Life Underwriters (sponsor Gold Key Soc.). Lutheran. Home: 6000 Hollins Ave Baltimore MD 21210 Office: Monumental Gen Ins Group 1111 N Charles St Baltimore MD 21202

KOLKO, GABRIEL, historian, educator; b. Paterson, N.J., Aug. 17, 1932; s. Philip and Lillian K.; m. Joyce Manning, June 11, 1955. B.A., Kent State U., 1954; M.S., U. Wis., 1955; Ph.D, Harvard U., 1962. Assoc. prof. U. Pa., 1964-68; prof. history SUNY-Buffalo, 1968-70, York U., Toronto, Ont., Can., 1970—. Author: Wealth and Power in America, 1962, The Triumph of Conservatism, 1963, Railroads and Regulations, 1965, The Politics of War, 1968, The Roots of American Foreign Policy, 1969, The Limits of Power, 1972, Main Currents in Modern American History, 1976; contbr. articles to profl. jours. Fellow Social Sci. Research Council, 1963-64; Guggenheim fellow, 1966-67; fellow Am. Council Learned Socs., 1971-72; Killam fellow. Mem. Orgn. Am. Historians (Can. council, transp. history prize 1963, fellow 1974-75). Home: 330 Spadina Rd Apt 305 Toronto ON Canada M5R 2V9 Office: History Dept Glendon Coll 2275 Bayview Ave Toronto ON Canada M4N 3M6

KOLL, RICHARD LEROY, chemical company executive; b. Muscatine, Iowa, Mar. 16, 1925; s. Charles C. and Emma (Schafer) K.; m. Patricia Ann Grunder, Jan. 2, 1955; children: Craig, Christine, Cary. B.S. in Mech. Engring., U. Iowa, 1951. Plant mgr. Grain Processing Corp., Muscatine, Iowa, 1971-72, v.p., 1972-77, sr. v.p., 1977—. Served with USMC, 1944-46. Clubs: University (Iowa City, Iowa); Athletic, Elks. Home: 1317 Oakland Dr Muscatine IA 52761 Office: Grain Processing Corp 1600 Oregon St Muscatine IA 52761

KOLLARITSCH, FELIX PAUL, educator; b. Graz, Austria, June 7, 1925; came to U.S., 1950, naturalized, 1956; s. Carel and Cornelia (Nemerad) K.; m. Martha Jane Moore, Aug. 27, 1951; children—Paul Walter, Carl Richard. Cenefels; M.B.A., Hochschule fuer Welthandel, Vienna, Austria, 1950, Ph.D., 1952. C.P.A., Ind. Pub., indsl. accountant, 1952-54; asst. prof. Ill. Wesleyan U., Bloomington, 1954-56; asso. prof. Butler U., Indpls., 1956-62; prof. accounting Ohio State U., Columbus, 1962—, chmn. dept. Author: Opinions, Scholastic Rankings and Professional Progress of Accounting Graduates, 1968, Cost Systems for Planning, Decisions, and Controls, 1979; Contbr. articles to profl. jours. Mem. Am. Inst. C.P.A.'s, Am., Nat. accounting assns., Fin. Execs. Inst., Beta Alpha Psi, Beta Gamma Sigma. Home: 2801 Canterbury Rd Columbus OH 43221

KOLLAT, DAVID TRUMAN, retail specialty store executive; b. Elkhart, Ind., July 7, 1938; s. Walter A. and Mildred E. (Good) K.; children: Lisa, Andra. B.B.A., Western Mich. U., 1960, M.B.A., 1962; D.B.A., Ind. U., 1966. Mem. faculty Ohio State U., Columbus, 1965-72; v.p., then exec. v.p., dir. Mgmt. Horizons, Columbus, 1972-76; v.p. The Limited Stores, Inc., Columbus, 1976-77, exec. v.p., 1977-84, The Limited Inc., 1984—; dir. Mast Industries., Decor Corp. Co-author: Strategic Marketing, 1972, Consumer Behavior, 1978. Served with AUS, 1960-68. Mem. Am. Mktg. Assn. (v.p. 1979-80), Assn. Consumer Research, Beta Gamma Sigma, Omicron Delta Kappa. Home: 6064 Olentangy River Rd Worthington OH 43085 Office: PO Box 16528 Columbus OH 43216

KOLLEGGER, JAMES G., information industry executive; b. Klagenfurt, Austria, Feb. 16, 1942; came to U.S., 1953; s. Willibald K. and Gerda (Baltruschat) Von Fekete; m. Cheryl A. Bales, May 29, 1966 (div. 1976); 1 son, Craig; m. 2d Elaine J. Kenzer, July 7, 1983. B.S., Boston U., 1964; postgrad., NYU, 1969-71. Asst. mktg. mgr. Structural Clay Inst., Washington, 1966-69; asst. to pres. Heald-Hobson div. MacMillan Info., N.Y.C., 1969-70; pres. EIC-Intelligence, N.Y.C., 1970—; dir. Environ. Planning Lobby, N.Y.C., 1972-75; council mem. U.S. Govt. Printing Office, Washington, 1982—. Served to capt. U.S. Army, 1964-70. Decorated Army Commendation medal. Mem. Info. Industry Assn. (dir., chmn. policy council 1981-83, dir.), Assoc. Info. Mgrs. (chmn. 1981-82, dir.), Am. Soc. Info. Sci., Sigma Delta Chi. Republican. Club: Union League (N.Y.C.). Home: 113 W 78th St New York NY 10024 Office: EIC-Intelligence 48 W 38th St New York NY 10018

KOLLER, HERBERT RICHARD, information scientist; b. Cleve., Sept. 5, 1921; s. Daniel D. and Frieda A. (Wiener) K.; m. Shirley Ann Leavitt, Mar. 7, 1943; children: Donald Lee, Susan Lizbeth (Mrs. Willard C. VanHorne), Laura Frances. B.S. in Chemistry, Case-Western Res. U., 1942; J.D., Am. U., 1952. Chemist Indsl. Rayon Co., 1942-43; patent examiner, information systems research and devel. U.S. Patent Office, 1943-66; dir. client services EBS Mgmt. Cons., Washington, 1966-68; prin. info. scientist Leasco Systems & Research Corp., Bethesda, Md., 1968-69; exec. dir. Am. Soc. Information Sci., Washington, 1969-73; prin. asso. Moshman Assos., Inc., Bethesda, 1973-74; legal editor Bur. Nat. Affairs, Washington, 1975-76; with chem. documentation group U.S. Patent and Trademark Office, 1977—; Research asso. Patent, Trademark and Copyright Research Inst., George Washington U., 1968-72; cons., lectr. in field. Contbr. articles to profl. jours. Sci. and tech. fellow Dept. Commerce, 1964-65. Fellow AAAS; Mem. Am. Chem. Soc., Assn. Computing Machinery, Am. Soc. Information Sci., Zeta Beta Tau. Home: 2700 Virginia Ave NW Washington DC 20037

KOLLMANN, HILDA HANNA, banker; b. Tinley Park, Ill., Dec. 12, 1913; d. Ernest A. and Rosalie (Blume) K. Ed., Bryant and Stratton Bus. Coll. Asst. cashier State Bank of Blue Island, Ill.; (became County Bank & Trust Co. 1962), 1945-53, cashier, 1953-60, asst. sec., 1953-54, sec., 1954-55, v.p., 1955-70, dir., 1956—, trust officer, 1959-66; v.p. Pullman Bank & Trust Co., Chgo., 1969-70, Standard Bank & Trust Co., 1969-70, First Nat. Bank of Lockport, 1969-70, Heritage Bancorp. (name formerly investments Financial Mgmt. Assos., Inc.), 1970—. Sec.-treas. Blue Island Pub. Welfare Assn., 1956-60, pres., 1961-63; chmn. indsl. and expansion com. Blue Island Planning Commn. Mem. Nat. Assn. Bank Women (pres. 1961-62), Assn. Chgo. Bank Women (pres. 1956-57). Home: 12761 S Gregory St Blue Island IL 60406 Office: 12015 S Western Ave: Blue Island IL 60406

KOLLMORGEN, LELAND STANFORD, naval officer; b. Los Angeles, May 20, 1927; s. Edward Henry and Virginia Lorene (Heaton) K.; m. Dorothy Edna Weimer, June 4, 1951; children: Leland S., Gary S., Michele L. B.S., U.S. Naval Acad., 1951, U.S. Naval Post Grad. Sch., 1960; M.S., George Washington U., 1966. Designated naval aviator U.S. Navy, 1954, rear adm., 1976; comdr. Medium Attack Squadrons VA-165, 1968-69, VA-128, 1970-71; major jet air base, Cecil Field, Jacksonville, Fla., 1974-75; research and devel. coordinator, spl. asst. for weapon system acquisition to Dir. Navy Program Planning; also mil. asst. to Pres. U.S., 1975-76; asst. dir. strategic and support systems, test and evaluation Office of Sec. Def., Washington, 1976-81, chief naval research, dep. chief naval material (tech.), chief naval devel., 1981-83, ret., 1983. Mem. U.S. Strategic Inst., U.S. Naval Inst., U.S. Naval Hist. Soc. Home: 1902 Joliette Ct Alexandria VA 22307

KOLLROS, JERRY JOHN, educator, zoologist; b. Vienna, Austria, Dec. 29, 1917; came to U.S., 1920, naturalized, 1926; s. Jacob and Theresa (Hruby) K.; m. Catharine Zenker Lutherman, Sept. 19, 1942; children—James Carl, Peter Richard. S.B., U. Chgo., 1938, Ph.D., 1942. Research asst. neurosurgery U. Chgo., 1943-45, research asso. toxicity lab., 1945, instr. zoology, 1945-46; asso. State U. Iowa, 1946-47, asst. prof., 1947-50, asso. prof., 1950-57, prof., 1957—, chmn. dept. zoology, 1955-77; vis. asst. prof. UCLA, summer 1950; cons. zoology Am. Coll. Dictionary, Random House Dictionary of the English Language.; Mem. cell biology study sect. NIH, 1960-64; mem. biol. scis. tng. rev. com. Nat. Inst. Mental Health, 1967-71; chmn. Commn. Undergrad. Edn. in Biol. Scis., 1969-71. Contbr. articles to profl. jours. Fellow A.A.A.S. (regional cons. sci. teaching improvement program 1956-57), Iowa Acad Sci.; mem. Am. Assn. U. Profs., Am. Assn. Anatomists (mem. exec. com. 1962-66), Am. Soc. Zoologists (past treas.), Internat. Inst. Embryologists, Soc. Exptl. Biology and Medicine, Soc. Developmental Biology, Am. Soc. Cell Biology, Phi Beta Kappa, Sigma Xi. Home: 331 Melrose Ct Iowa City IA 52240

KOLMER, LEE ROY, coll. dean; b. Waterloo, Ill., Jan. 4, 1928; s. Arthur Francis and Carmelita Frances (Vogt) K.; m. W. Jean O'Brien, Apr. 19, 1952; children—Diane, James, John. B.S., So. Ill. U. at Carbondale, 1952; M.S., Iowa State U., 1952, Ph.D., 1954. Asst. prof. So. Ill. U. at Carbondale, 1954-55; prof. Iowa State U., Ames, 1956-67; asst. dean Univ. Extension, 1967-71; dean Coll. Agr., 1973—; dir. Coop. Extension Service, Ore. State U., Corvallis, 1971-73. Served with U.S. Army, 1946-48. Mem. Am. Agrl. Econs. Assn. Home: 4118 Phoenix St Ames IA 50010

KOLODEY, FRED JAMES, lawyer; b. LaCoste, Tex., Mar. 5, 1936; s. Raymond and Mamie V. (Newman) K.; m. June Ruth Lange, Aug. 5, 1955; children—Trecia Anne, Michele Leigh. B.A., Tex. Christian U., 1962; LL.B., So. Methodist U., 1964. Bar: Tex. bar 1964. Since practiced in, Dallas; partner firm Kolodey & Thomas, 1975—; dir. Farah Mfg. Co.; pres. Dallas Jr. Bar Assn., 1969. Comments editor: Southwestern Law Jour, 1963-64. Mem. dist. hearing office panel Dallas Community Coll., 1974; Democratic precinct chmn., 1968-73. Mem. Tex., Dallas bar assns., Delta Theta Phi (pres. 1963, Nat. award 1964), Alpha Chi, Pi Sigma Alpha. Home: 307 Russwood St Rockwall TX 75087 Office: Suite 1111 Two Turtle Creek Village Dallas TX 75219

KOLODIN, IRVING, music critic; b. N.Y.C., Feb. 22, 1908; s. Benjamin and Leah (Geller) K.; m. Irma Levy, June 19, 1935. Ed. grammar and high sch., Newark; student, Inst. Mus. Art, N.Y.C., 1927-31. Instr. harmony and theory Inst. Mus. Art, 1930-31; with N.Y. Sun, 1932-50; asso. music critic and condr. New Records Column, 1936-50; lectr. on music criticism Juilliard Summer Sch., 1938, 39; mem. faculty Juilliard Sch. Music, 1968—; program annotator N.Y. Philharmonic Orch., 1953-58; music editor and critic to Sun, 1945-50; editor Recordings supplement of Saturday Review Lit., from 1947; music editor Saturday Rev. Lit., 1950-52; asso. editor Saturday Rev., from 1952; contbr. Sunday edit. Newsday, Garden City, N.Y., 1978—; v.p., editor Nat. Arts Group, Ltd., N.Y.C. Author: Metropolitan Opera, 1936, rev. edit., 1939, (with Benny Goodman) The Kingdom of Swing, 1939, The Critical Composer, 1940, Guide to Recorded Music, 1941, rev. edit., 1946, 49, 55; author: Story of the Metropolitan Opera, 1953, Composer as Listener, 1958, The Musical Life, 1958, Metropolitan Opera 1883-1966, 1966, The Continuity of Music, 1969, Interior Beethoven: A Biography of the Music, 1974, The Opera Omnibus: Four Centuries of Critical Give and Take, 1976, In Quest of Music: Met. Opera Centennial Edition, 1966-84; contbg. author: various mags. Entered mil. service, 1943; mem. staff Official Guide to AAF and Air Force mag., 1943-45. Home: 1 Lincoln Plaza New York NY 10023

KOLODNER, IGNACE IZAAK, mathematics educator; b. Warsaw, Poland, Apr. 12, 1920; came to U.S., 1943, naturalized, 1944; s. Israel and Brucha (Gornostajski) K.; m. Ethel Zelnick, June 10, 1948; children: Richard David, Paul Robert; m. Dorothy Chiavetta Thomas, Apr. 15, 1968 (div.); 1 dau., Eva Maria. Student. U. Nancy, France, 1937-39; Diplome d'Ingenieur, U.Grenoble, France, 1940; Ph.D., N.Y.U., 1950. Mem. staff Courant Inst. Math. Scis., N.Y.U., 1948-56; prof. math. U. N.Mex., 1956-64, Carnegie-Mellon U., 1964—, head dept., 1964-71; Fulbright fellow Universidad de la Republica, Montevideo, Uruguay, 1967; Sussman vis. prof. Technion, Haifa, Israel, 1973; adj. prof. U. Pitts., 1976-77; cons. Lawrence Radiation Lab., U. Calif. at Berkeley, 1958-67, Sandia Corp., Albuquerque, 1956-66; Vis. mem. Math. Research Center U. Wis., Madison, 1962, Sch. Math. Study Group, Stanford U., 1964, Courant Inst. Math. Scis., N.Y. U., 1969. Contbr. numerous articles to profl. jours. Served with C.E. AUS, 1944-46. Mem. Am. Math. Soc., Am. Phys. Soc., Math. Assn. Am., Soc. Indsl. and Applied Math., Soc. Natural Philosophy, A.A.U.P. Home: 307 S Dithridge St Pittsburgh PA 15213

KOLODNY, STANLEY CHARLES, oral surgeon, air force officer; b. N.Y.C., Feb. 22, 1923; s. Aaron and Lea (Stern) K.; m. Mary Kathryn Leigh, Feb. 22, 1947; children: Kathleen, Carter Leigh, Stanley Charles. B.A., U. Tex., 1944; D.D.S., Baylor U., 1947; M.S., U. Ill., 1961. Diplomate: Am. Bd. Oral and Maxillofacial Surgery. Commd. 1st lt. USAF, 1951, advanced through grades to maj. gen., 1981; cons. in oral surgery Surgeon Gen. U.S. Air Force, 1966; chmn. dept. oral surgery Wilford Hall USAF Med. Center, San Antonio, 1969-75, dir. dental services, 1975-77; asst. surgeon gen. for dental services, Bolling AFB, Washington, 1979—; clin. prof. dept. surgery U. Tex. Dental Br., Houston, 1969-77; clin. asso. prof. dept. surgery U. Tex. Med. Sch., San Antonio, 1969-77. Contbr. chpt. to book, articles to profl. jours. Bd. dirs. Am. Cancer Soc., 1970-77. Decorated Legion of Merit with oak leaf cluster, Air Force Commendation medal, D.S.M.; recipient cert. of achievement for outstanding oral surgery USAF, 19—. Fellow Am. Coll. Dentists, Am. Assn. Oral and Maxillofacial Surgeons; mem. ADA, Soc. Air Force Clin. Surgeons. Home: Route 3 Roanoke TX 76262

KOLODZIEJ, EDWARD ALBERT, political scientist, educator; b. Chgo., Jan. 4, 1935; s. Albert Stanley and Anna Caroline (Chudzik) K.; m. Antje Heberle, Aug. 15, 1959; children: Peter, Andrew, Matthew, Daniel. B.S. summa cum laude, Loyola U., Chgo., 1956; M.A., U. Chgo., 1957, Ph.D., 1961. Analyst nat. security fgn. affairs div. Congl. Research Service, Library of Congress, Washington, 1960-62; asst. prof. polit. sci. U. Va., Charlottesville, 1962-67, assoc. prof., 1967-73, chmn. dept. govt. and fgn. affairs, 1967-69; prof. polit. sci. U. Ill., Urbana, 1973—, head dept., 1973-77, dir. Office Arms Control, Disarmament and Internat. Security, 1983; cons. in field. Author: The Uncommon Defense and Congress, 1966, French International Policy under de Gaulle and Pompidou: The Politics of Grandeur, 1974; editor: American Security Policy, 1979, Security Policies of Developing States, 1981; contbr. articles on fgn. and security policy and decision-making to profl. jours., U.S., France, Europe; also contbg. author books. Mershon postdoctoral fellow nat. security Ohio State U., 1964-65; Rockefeller postdoctoral fellow internat. relations, Paris, 1965-66; Ford Found. fellow in social sci., 1969-71; NSF grantee, 1971; Deutscher Akademischer Austauschdienst grantee, 1975; Ford Found. Internat. Arms Control Competition grantee, 1976; Center for Advanced Study, U. Ill., 1979; Rockefeller Found. grantee, 1980; Nat. Endowment for Humanities grantee, 1981. Mem. Council Fgn. Relations N.Y., Am., Midwest polit. sci. assns., Internat. Studies Assn. Home: 711 W University Ave Champaign IL 61820 Office: Polit Sci Dept U Ill Urbana IL 61801 *Regrets are a luxury. They distract from efforts to meet present and future needs.*

KOLSKY, HERBERT, educator, physicist; b. London, Eng., Sept. 22, 1916; came to U.S., 1960; s. Suskind and Deborah (Halber) K.; m. Mary Grant Morton, Dec. 15, 1945; children: David John, Peter Jonathan, Allan Benjamin. B.Sc., Imperial Coll. Sci. and Tech., London, 1937, Ph.D., 1940; D.Sc., U. London, 1957; M.A., Brown U., 1962. Head physics dept. Akers Research Labs., Imperial Chem. Industries, Welwyn, Eng., 1946-55; vis. prof. engring. Brown U., 1956-57; sr. prin. sci. officer Ministry Supply, Eng., 1958-60; prof. applied physics Brown U., 1961—; vis. prof. Imperial Coll., 1968, M.E.T.U., Ankara, Turkey, 1968; Oxford (Eng.) U., 1974; Springer prof. U.C.B. E.T.H., Zurich, Switzerland, 1978-79. Author: Stress Waves in Solids, 1953; Editor: (with W. Prager) Stress Waves in Anelastic Solids, 1964. Fulbright scholar, 1956-58; recipient Worcester Reed Warner medal ASME, 1982. Fellow Inst. Physics, Am. Acad. Mechanics, Acoustical Soc.; mem. Brit. Soc. Rheology (past pres.), ASME, Soc. Rheology, Sigma Xi. Club: University (Providence). Home: 164 Irving Ave Providence RI 02906

KOLSON, HARRY, physician, educator; b. N.Y.C., Mar. 26, 1915; s. Morris and Jennie (Waldman) K.; m. Ida Burstein, Apr. 27, 1941 (dec. Aug. 1944). B.A., NYU, 1935, D.D.S., 1938, M.D., 1950. Diplomate: Am. Bd. Otolaryngology, Nat. Bd. Med. Examiners. Practice gen. dentistry, Jamaica, N.Y., 1938-43; straight surg. intern 3d div. Bellevue Hosp., N.Y.C., 1950-51, asst. resident in surgery 3d div., 1951-52, Am. Cancer Soc. fellow dept. surgery, 1951-52; resident in ear, nose, throat, head and neck surgery VA Hosp., Bronx, N.Y., 1952-55, asst. chief otolaryngology sect., 1955-56, chief head and neck surg. sect., 1955-68, chief otolaryngology sect., 1957-68, cons. in otolaryngology, 1968-71; fellow dept. surgery NYU, 1951-52; lectr. bronchoscopy N.Y. Polyclinic Hosp. and Post Grad. Med. Sch., 1955-56, adj. prof., 1956—; instr. dept. head and neck surgery Albert Einstein Coll. Medicine, Bronx, 1955-59, asst. clin. prof., 1959-65, lectr., 1965-68; asst. vis. surgeon Bronx Mcpl. Hosp. Center, 1955-59, asso. vis. surgeon, 1959-68; asst. clin. prof. otolaryngology Columbia U., 1965-66, asso. clin. prof., 1966-68; prof. clin. otolaryngology Mt. Sinai Sch. Medicine, N.Y.C., 1967-71; cons. Mt. Sinai Hosp. services City Hosp. Center at Elmhurst, 1968-71; prof. otolaryngology N.Y. Med. Coll., 1972—; chief otolaryngology Met. Hosp., N.Y.C., 1972—; chief of staff trainee program VA Hosp., Northport, L.I., N.Y.; chief spl. med. services Suffolk County Health Dept.; chief staff VA Med. Center, Erie, Pa., 1978—; lectr. Fairleigh Dickinson U. Sch. Dentistry, 1964—; vis. prof. Sch. Medicine, Universidad Autonoma de Guadalajara, Mexico, 1974; cons. adv. com. to chief surg. service VA Central Office, Washington, 1969-73. Contbr. articles to med. jours. Served with AUS, 1943-46. Fellow ACS, Am. Acad. Otolaryngology and Ophthalmology, Am. Acad. Facial, Plastic and Reconstructive Surgery, N.Y. Acad. Medicine; mem. AMA, N.Y. State Med. Soc., Queens County Med. Soc., Am. Soc. Maxillofacial Surgeons (constn. and by-laws com., continuing edn. and research com., nominating com., dir., treas. 1973—), Am. Soc. Head and Neck Surgery, Am. Laryngol., Rhinol. and Otol. Soc., Am. Bronco-Esophagological Assn., James Ewing Soc., ADA, N.Y. State Dental Soc., 1st Dist. N.Y. State Dental Soc., L.I. Acad. Odontology, Sigma Epsilon Delta. Republican. Home: 44

Terrehans Ln Syosset NY 11791 1010 S OCean Blvd Apt 1711 Pompano Beach FL 33062

KOLTER, JOSEPH PAUL, congressman; b. McDonald, Ohio, Sept. 3, 1926; m. Dorothy Gray, 1949; children: Joseph Paul, James, David, Julie. B.S., Geneva Coll., Beaver Falls, Pa., 1950. Acct., tchr.; mem. 98th Congress from 4th Dist. Pa. Mem. New Brighton City Council, Pa., 1961-65, Pa. Ho. of Reps., 1969-82, Beaver County Democratic Com., New Brighton Civil Service Commn. Served with U.S. Army, 1944-47. Mem. Nat. Assn. Accts., Am. Legion, VFW. Club: Marconi. Lodges: Eagles; Elks; Sons of Italy. Office: 212 Cannon House Office Bldg Washington DC 20515 *

KOLTNOW, PETER GREGORY, association executive; b. N.Y.C., Apr. 14, 1929; s. Harry George and Fay (Richman) K.; m. Dorothy D. Witter, Oct. 27, 1950; children—Nan Elizabeth, Nina Christine. B.S., Antioch Coll., 1951; M.S., U. Calif. at Berkeley, 1956. Engr. City of Dayton, Ohio, 1953-55; traffic engr. County of Fresno, Calif., 1956-62, Auto Club of So. Cal., 1962-67; dir. urban div. Automotive Safety Found., Washington, 1967-69, Hwy. Users Fedn., 1970-71, v.p., 1971-74, pres., 1974—; chmn. Transp. Research Bd., 1979; Guest lectr. various univs., 1965—. Contbr. articles to profl. jours. Pres. Candlelighters, 1970-71; v.p. Candlelighters Found., 1983—; trustee Automotive Safety Found.; bd. dirs. Washington div. Am. Cancer Soc. Served with Ordnance Corps U.S. Army, 1951-53. Recipient Disting. Service award Transp. Research Bd., 1982. Mem. Inst. Transp. Engrs., ASCE. Unitarian. Clubs: Old Georgetown (Bethesda) (dir. 1971-74); Internat. (Washington)). Home: 9210 Fernwood Rd Bethesda MD 20817 Office: 1776 Massachusetts Ave NW Washington DC 20036

KOLTON, PAUL, business executive; b. N.Y.C., June 1, 1923; s. Sol and Rose (Naiman) Komisaruk; m. Edith B. Fromme, June 30, 1944; children: Robert Jay, Shelley. B.A., U. N.C., 1943. Editorial staff N.Y. Jour. Commerce, 1946-47; account exec. Newell-Emmett Advt. Co., 1947-50, Cecil & Presbrey Advt., Inc., 1950-55; v.p. pub. information and press relations N.Y. Stock Exchange, 1955-62; exec. v.p. Am. Stock Exchange, 1962-71, pres., 1971-72, chmn., 1972-77, Fin. Acctg. Standards Adv. Council, 1978—; dir. Nabisco Brands, Inc., Asso. Dry Goods Corp., Burndy Corp., Union Mut. Life Ins. Co., Fundamental Investors, Inc., Amcap Fund, Inc., Paine Webber Cash Fund, Inc., INA Investment Securities Inc., CIGNA High Yield Fund, Inc., Securities Regulation Inst. Author short stories. Bd. dirs. Stamford Hosp. Served with USAAF, 1943-46. Mem. Soc. of Silurians. Clubs: Econ. of N.Y.; Landmark (Stamford). Office: FASAC High Ridge Park Stamford CT 06905

KOMAR, ARTHUR B., physicist, educator; b. Bklyn., Mar. 26, 1931; s. Abraham and Mary (Baraway) K.; m. Dolly Roth, Aug. 5, 1952; children: Arne, Tanya. A.B., Princeton U., 1952, Ph.D., 1956. Fellow Niels Bohr Inst., Copenhagen, Denmark, 1956-57; research asso. Syracuse (N.Y.) U., 1957-59, vis. asst. prof., 1958-59, asst. prof., 1959-61, assoc. prof., 1961-63, Belfer Grad. Sch., Yeshiva U., N.Y.C., 1963-66, prof. physics, 1966—; dean, dir. Belfer Grad. Sch., 1968-78, chmn. physics dept., 1978-82; Am. rep. to div. SA2, Internat. Union Pure and Applied Physics., 1977-83; program dir. for gravitational physics NSF, 1982-83; chmn. div. natural sci. Yeshiva U., 1983—. Asso. editor: Am. Jour. Physics, 1966-72; editorial bd.: Internat. Jour. Theoretical Physics, 1968-77; Contbr. articles to profl. jours. Fellow Am.-Scandinavian Soc.; mem. Am. Phys. Soc., Phi Beta Kappa. Home: 562 W 261st St Bronx NY 10471 Office: Yeshiva U Amsterdam Ave and 186th St New York NY 10033

KOMAROFF, STANLEY, lawyer; b. Bklyn, Apr. 1, 1935; s. William Ralph and Fanny (Wein) K.; m. Rosalyn Steinglass, Dec. 25, 1960; children: William Charles, Andrew Steven. B.A., Cornell U., 1956, J.D., 1958. Bar: N.Y. 1959. Assoc. Proskauer Rose Goetz & Mendelsohn, N.Y.C., 1958-68, ptnr., 1968—, mng. ptnr., 1981—; dir. Revell, inc., Venice, Calif. Mem. N.Y. State Bar Assn., Assn. Bar City N.Y., N.Y. County Lawyers Assn., Order of Coif, Phi Kappa Phi. Jewish. Club: Sunningdale Country (Scarsdale, N.Y.). Home: 44 Butler Rd Scardsdale NY 10583 Office: Proskauer Rose Goetz & Mendelsohn 300 Park Ave New York NY 10022

KOMAROVSKY, MIRRA (MRS. MARCUS A. HEYMAN), sociology educator; b. Russia; came to U.S., 1922, naturalized, 1933; d. Manuel and Anna (Steinberg) K.; m. Marcus A. Heyman, Oct. 2, 1940. A.B., Barnard Coll.; M.A., Columbia, Ph.D., 1940, Litt.D., 1979. Asst. prof. sociology Skidmore Coll., 1927-29; research asst., research asso. Yale Inst. Human Relations, Columbia, 1931-32; instr. sociology Barnard Coll., 1936-45, asst. prof., 1945-47, asso. prof., 1948-53, prof., 1954-73, chmn. dept., 1949-62, 65-68, chmn. Women's Studies Program, prof. emeritus, spl. lectr., 1978—; Buell G. Gallagher prof. sociology Coll. City N.Y., spring 1965; spl. lectr. Sch. Gen. Studies, Columbia, 1974-77; vis. prof. Grad. Faculty, New Sch. Social Research, N.Y.C., 1975-78. Author: (with Lundberg and McInerney) Leisure, A Suburban Study, 1934, The Unemployed Man and His Family, 1940, Women in The Modern World: Their Education and Their Dilemmas, 1953, Blue-Collar Marriage, 1964, Dilemnas of Masculinity, 1976; Editor: Common Frontier of the Social Sciences, 1957, Sociology and Public Policy: The Case of Presidential Commissions, 1975; assoc. editor: Am. Sociol. Rev., 1957-60, Jour. Marriage and the Family, 1976-80; Contbr. articles to profl. jours. Cons. AID, State Dept., 1975. Recipient Distinguished Alumna award Barnard Coll., 1976, Medal of Distinction Barnard Coll., 1983, Emily Gregory award, 1977; NIMH grantee, 1958-61, 69-72; Rockefeller Found. grantee, 1974, 76; Nat. Inst. Edn. grantee, 1979-81. Mem. Am. Sociol. Assn. (council 1967-69, v.p. 1971-72, pres. 1972-73), Sociol. Research Assn. (hon.), Am. Sociol. Assn. (Jessie Barnard award for research on family and sex roles 1977), Eastern Sociol. Soc. (pres. 1955-56, Merit award 1977), Phi Beta Kappa. Home: 340 Riverside Dr New York NY 10025

KOMER, ROBERT WILLIAM, educator, consultant; b. Chgo., Feb. 23, 1922; s. Nathan A and Stella (Deiches) K.; m. Geraldine M. Peplin, Nov. 3, 1961; children: Douglas Robert, Richard Donen, Anne Elizabeth. S.B. magna cum laude, Harvard U., 1942, M.B.A., 1947; student, Nat. War Coll., 1956-57. With Directorate of Intelligence and Office Nat. Estimates, CIA, 1947-60; sr. staff mem. Nat. Security Council, 1961-65; dep. spl. asst. to Pres. for nat. security affairs, 1965-66, spl. asst. to Pres., 1966-67; dep. to comdr. USMACV for Cords, 1967-68; ambassador to, Turkey, 1968-69; sr. social sci. researcher Rand Corp., Washington, 1969-77; adviser to sec. def. for NATO affairs, 1977-79; undersec. for policy U.S. Dept. Def., Washington, 1979-81; vis. fellow George Mason U., Fairfax, Va., 1981-82; adj. prof. George Washington U., 1981—; Bd. advisers Nat. War Coll.; bd. visitors Nat. Def. U. Contbr. numerous articles to newspapers and profl. publs. Served to 1st lt. AUS, 1943-46; lt. col. Res. Decorated Bronze Star; Nat. Order Vietnam; Vietnam Gold Economy medal; Revolutionary Devel. medal, Vietnam; recipient Presdl. Medal of Freedom; Disting. Honor award State Dept.; medal and oak leaf cluster for Disting. Public Service Dept. of Def. Mem. Phi Beta Kappa. Democrat. Home: 214 Franklin St Alexandria VA 22314 Office: RAND Corp 2100 M St NW Washington DC 20037

KOMES, JEROME WILLIAM, engineering and construction company executive; b. Racine, Wis., June 23, 1911; s. John Frederick and Julia Mary (Meier) K.; m. Flora Cabral, Feb. 16, 1935; children—Jerome Michael, John Anthony, Julia Mary K. Garvey. Ed. parochial schs., Fresno, Calif. With Barrett & Hilp (constrn.), San Francisco, 1928-38; part owner D. W. Nicholson Corp. (constrn.), Oakland, Calif., 1938-4l; exec. positions Calif. Shipbldg. Corp., Los Angeles, 1941-46; with Bechtel Corp., San Francisco, 1946—, sr. v.p., mgr. internat. div., 1957-67, exec. v.p., 1967-73, pres., 1973-75, vice chmn., 1975-76, also dir.; vice chmn., officer, dir. subs. and affiliated corps., until 1977, exec. cons., 1977-83; dir. Crocker Nat. Corp., Crocker Nat. Bank. Trustee Santa Clara U.; mem. corp. bd. St. Marys Hosp.; lay bd. Marianists Province of Pacific. Mem. Am. Mining Engineers. Clubs: Olympic, Stock Exchange, World Trade, Bankers, Silverado Country, San Francisco Golf (San Francisco). Office: 50 Beale St San Francisco CA 94105

KOMIDAR, JOSEPH STANLEY, librarian; b. Chisholm, Minn., July 19, 1916; s. John and Jennie (Skrbec) K.; m. Mary Louise Watson, Aug. 16, 1957; children: Kathryn J., Joseph T. A.A., Hibbing Jr. Coll., 1936; B.L.S., U. Minn., 1938, B.A., 1941; M.A., U. Chgo., 1948. Reference asst. U. Minn. Library, 1938-41; reference and loan librarian Carleton Coll., 1941-43; reference librarian Northwestern U., 1948-50, chief reference and spl. services div., 1950-56; univ. librarian Tufts U., Medford, Mass., 1956-81; ret., 1981; vis. lectr. U. Denver Sch. Librarianship, summer 1955. Contbr. articles profl. jours. and publs. Served with USAAF, 1943-45. Mem. ALA, Assn. Coll. and Research Librarians, AAUP, Am. Soc. Information Sci., Beta Phi Mu.

KOMISAR, DAVID DANIEL, univ. provost; b. N.Y.C., July 20, 1917; s. Jacob and Yetta (Jacobson) K.; m. Beatrice Liebman, Aug. 15, 1940; children—Jack Lloyd, June Diana. B.S.S., Coll. City N.Y., 1937, M.S., 1940; postgrad., U. Glasgow, 1945, Sorbonne, 1946; Ph.D., Columbia, 1953. With Civil Service, N.Y.C., 1939-42; indsl. personnel work, 1943-44; counselor vocational rehab. U.S. Army, 1943-46; dir. guidance Mohawk Coll., 1946-48; dir. guidance, chmn. dept. psychology Champlain Coll., State U. N.Y., Plattsburg, 1948-53; chmn. dept. psychology U. Hartford, 1953—, pres. univ. faculty senate, 1964-65, dean, 1966-67, dean of faculties, 1967-70, v.p. acad. affairs, 1970-71, provost, 1972-80, Univ. prof., 1980—; counselor Civil Service Commn., 1980—; Project dir. research in mental retardation Office Vocational Rehab., Dept. Health, Edn. and Welfare, 1964-65, psycho-social com. social rehab. services, 1968—; head New Eng. Conf. Mental Retardation, 1960, Conn. Task Force on Mental Retardation, 1960-61; Conn. rep. Nat. Def. Edn. Act, 1960-61; research fellow U.S. Office Vocational Rehab., 1962-63; Conn. Citizens Com. on State Welfare, 1967-69; mem. standing com. accreditation Conn. Commn. High Edn., 1969—. Contbr. articles on testing, therapy, vocational selection to profl. jours. Co-chmn. Citizens Charter Com. Hartford, 1959; Mem. bd. Hartford Jewish Community Center, 1955-63, v.p., 1963—; mem. bd. Mental Health Assn., 1959-62. Recipient research grant for 3 yr. study residential care retarded children Dept. Health, Edn. and Welfare, 1965—. Mem. Conn. Valley Assn. Psychologists (past pres.), Am. Psychol. Assn., Conn. Psychol. Assn. (council; pres.), Nat. Vocational Guidance Assn., Am. Personnel and Guidance Assn., Sigma Xi. Clubs: Connecticut Valley Torch (past pres.), Probus (Hartford) (nast pres.). Home: 88 Northbrook Dr West Hartford CT 06117

KOMISAR, JEROME BERTRAM, university administrator; b. Bklyn., Jan. 31, 1937; s. Harry and Fanny (Neumann) K.; m. Natalie Rosenberg, Sept. 8, 1957; children: Harriet, Wade, Frances, Aurenna. B.S., NYU, 1957; M.A., Columbia U., 1959, Ph.D, 1968. Asst. prof. econs. Hamilton Coll., Clinton, N.Y., 1961-66; assoc. prof. mgmt. SUNY-Binghamton, 1966-74, asst. to pres., 1971-74; vice chancellor for faculty and staff relations SUNY-Albany, 1974-82, provost, pres. Research Found., 1982—; acting pres. SUNY-New Paltz, 1979-80. Author: Work Scheduling in the Wholesale Trades in Manhattan's Central Business District, 1962, Social Legislation and Labor Force Behavior, 1968; co-author: (with John S. Gambs) Economics and Man, 1968. Bd. dirs. Bronx House Emanuel Camp Inc., N.Y.C., 1981—, WAMC, Albany, 1983—; bd. overseers Rockefeller Inst., Albany, 1983. Office: SUNY-Albany University Plaza Albany NY 12246

KOMKOV, VADIM, mathematician; b. Moscow, Aug. 18, 1919; U.S., 1957, naturalized, 1962; s. Boris D. and Eugenia (Romanov) K.; m. Joyce Radford, Apr. 27, 1946; children: Valerie, Stephanie, Andrea, Leon, Michael. Ph.D., U. Utah, 1964; Dipl. Ing., Warsaw Pol. Inst., 1948. Prof. Fla. State U., Tallahassee, 1965-69; editor Math. Rev., Ann Arbor, 1978-80; prof. Tex. Tech. U., Lubbock, 1969-78; prof., chmn. dept. math. W.Va. U., Morgantown, 1980-83; chmn. math. sci. dept. Winthrop Coll., Rock Hill, S.C., 1983—; adj. prof. U. Iowa, 1977—; cons. U.S. Army, Rock Island, Ill., 1971-78. Author: Control Theory, 1973; editor: Problems in Elastic Stability, 1981; author: (with E.J. Hang and C.K. Choi) Sensitivity Theory, 1983; editor: Sensitivity of Functionals, 1984. NSF grantee, 1965-69, 1977-79, 1980-83; grantee U.S. Army, 1971-77. Mem. AIAA, Am. Math. Soc., Math. Assn. Am., Sigma Xi. Democrat. Eastern Orthodox. Office: Math Sci Dept Winthrop Coll Rock Hill SC 29733

KOMOSKI, P. KENNETH, educational researcher, consumer advocate; b. Jersey City, Nov. 20, 1928; s. Louis S. and Stella M. (Norwich) K.; m. Joanna Anthony, June 15, 1972; children: Christina, William, Mara. B.A., Acadia U., 1950, M.A., 1952; postgrad., Columbia U. and Union Theol. Sem., 1952-55. Tchr. Morristown Sch., 1950-52; tchr., adminstr. Collegiate Sch., N.Y.C., 1952-60; dir. Center for Programed Instruction, N.Y.C., 1960-63; asso. exec. dir. Inst. Ednl. Tech. Tchrs. Coll., Columbia U., 1964-66; adj. prof. Tchrs. Coll., 1977—; sr. research asso. Inst. Ednl. Devel., N.Y.C., 1966-67; founder, dir. Ednl. Products Info. Exchange, Inst., N.Y.C., 1967—; host PBS TV series Computing Profile; cons. UNESCO, Pres.' Panel on Edn., 1964; dir. tchr. tng. insts., Nigeria, Ghana, 1962-65. Contbr. articles to profl. jours. Mem. Am. Ednl. Research Assn., Assn. Ednl. Communications and Tech. Quaker. Home: Rose Hill Rd Water Mill NY 11976 Office: Box 839 Water Mill NY 11976

KOMP, DIANE MARILYN, pediatric oncologist, hematologist; b. Bklyn., Aug. 6, 1940; d. Richard Rankin Carrier and Anna Florence (Daly) K. B.S. in Chemistry, Houghton (N.Y.) Coll., 1961; M.D., SUNY Downstate Med. Center, Bklyn., 1965; M.A. (hon.), Yale U., 1978. Intern Kings County Hosp., Bklyn., 1965-66, resident in pediatrics, 1965-67; fellow in pediatric hematology and oncology U. Va., 1967-69, asst. prof. pediatrics, 1969-73, asso. prof., 1973-76, prof., 1976-78; prof. pediatrics, chief pediatric hematology and oncology Yale U., 1978—; cons. Nat. Cancer Inst. Recipient cert. of appreciation Va. div. Am. Cancer Soc.; Nat. Cancer Inst. grantee. Mem. Am. Soc. Hematology, Soc. Pediatric Research, Internat. Soc. Hematology, Am. Soc. Clin. Oncology, Am. Assn. Cancer Research, Am. Pediatric Soc., Conn. Orchid Soc., Alpha Omega Alpha. Congregationalist. Club: Guilford Racquet. Home: 88 Barker Hill Dr Guilford CT 06437 Office: 333 Cedar St LMP 4087 New Haven CT 06510 *There are two ways for an oncologist to approach the treatment of cancer. You can set out with the objective that cure is the only acceptable goal; to settle for anything less is to fail. To follow that course is to seek to become God. Any patient can tell you that no doctor is God despite the mutual delusions that are frequently encouraged. The alternative approach is to walk as a human being doing your level human best and asking for God's guidance along the way. This path is less likely to lead the oncologist to burn out and his patients and God to despair.*

KOMPASS, EDWARD JOHN, editor; b. Jersey City, Dec. 22, 1926; s. Edward F. and Margaret A. (Doran) K.; m. Amelia M. Heubel, Sept. 22, 1951; children—Christine (Mrs. Kevin Scully), Daniel E., Andrew J., Timothy M., Matthew P., Julie A. M.E., Stevens Inst. Tech., 1951. Jr. engr. Intelectron Inc., N.Y.C., 1951-52; engr. De Florez Co., N.Y.C., 1952-54; asst. editor Control Engring., McGraw-Hill Pub. Co., N.Y.C., 1954-60, asso. editor, 1960-65; mng. editor Control Engring., Dun-Donnelley Pub. Corp., N.Y.C., 1965-72; editor Control Engring., Tech. Pub., Barrington, Ill., 1972—; Co-organizer Ann. Advanced Control Confs. Purdue U., Lafayette, Ind., 1974, 75, 76, 77, 79, 80, 81, 82. Editor, writer, contbr. profl. articles and editorials to jours.; editorial advisor: Detroit Engr. Served with USNR, 1944-46. Mem. Am. Soc. Bus. Paper Editors, IEEE, Instrument Soc. Am., Engring. Soc. Detroit, Am. Legion, V.F.W., Beta Theta Pi. Roman Catholic. Home: 793 Burton Dr Lake Forest IL 60045 Office: 1301 S Grove Ave Barrington IL 60010

KONDONASSIS, ALEXANDER JOHN, educator, economist; b. Greece, Feb. 8, 1928; came to U.S., 1948, naturalized, 1960; s. John I. and Eve (Hatzistylianou) K.; m. Patricia Mundorff, Feb. 2, 1956; children: John, Yolanda. A.B. with distinction, DePauw U., 1952; M.A., Ind. U., 1953, Ph.D., 1961. Teaching asso. Ind. U., 1954-56, lectr., 1956-58; mem. faculty U. Okla., 1958—, prof. econs., 1964—, David Ross Boyd prof. econs., 1970—, chmn. dept., 1961-71, dir. div. econs., 1979—, chmn. com. world affairs, 1962-65, chmn. com. grad. Latin Am. affairs, 1964-70, chmn. com. distinguished lecture series, 1967-68, dir. advanced program in econs., 1971—, chmn. faculty senate, 1976-77; Fulbright prof. Athens (Greece) Sch. Econs. and Bus. Sci., 1965-66, vis. prof., 1971; dir. Am. Bank of Commerce.; Bd. dirs. Okla. Council Econ. Edn., 1961-71; mem. Gov. Okla. Adv. Council Export Expansion, 1964-65; adv. council Inst. E. Mediterranean Affairs, 1967-68. Author: Concepts of Economic Development with Special Reference to Underdeveloped Countries, 1963, Monetary Policies of the Bank of Greece, 1949-1951, Contributions to Monetary Stability and Economic Development, 1961, (with others) An Economic Base Study of Lawton, Oklahoma, 1963, Economic Planning and Free Enterprise, 1966, The Role of Agriculture in a Developing Economy, 1973, The EEC and Her Association with Israel, Spain, Turkey and Greece, 1972, Some Recent Trends in Development Economics, 1972, Contributions of Agriculture to Economic Development: The Cases of U.K., U.S.A., Japan and Mexico, 1973, Mediterranean Europe and the Common Market, 1976, The European Economic Community in the Mediterranean: Developments and Prospects on a Mediterranean Policy, 1976, The European Economic Community and Greece: Toward a Full Membership?, 1977, The Greek Inflation and the Flight from the Drachma: 1940-48, 1977, The Greek Economy: The Old and the New, 1979, The Bank of Greece, 1949-51: Credit Control Changes in An Inflationary Environment, 1979, The European Economic Community: Toward a Common Development Policy, 1980, Recent Trends in Development Assistance Committee Aid Programs, 1981, Economic and Non-Economic Aspects of Economic Development, the Less Developed Countries: A Synthesis, 1983; chmn. editorial policies com.: S.W. Social Sci. Quar, 1974-77. Bd. dirs. Am. Friends Wilton Park, N.Y., 1967-68. Recipient U. Okla. Regents award excellence teaching, 1964; Merrick Found. Teaching award, 1977; DePauw U. Rector Scholar Alumni Achievement award, 1977; research grantee U. Okla. Research Inst., 1965-66. Mem. Am. Econ. Assn., So. Econ. Assn., Southwestern Econ. Assn., Missouri Valley Econ. Assn. (dir., exec. com. 1980—, pres. 1983-84), Southwestern Social Sci. Assn. (v.p. 1980-83, pres. 1983-84), AAUP (pres. 1977-78), Okla. Heritage Assn., Phi Beta Kappa, Omicron Delta Epsilon, Beta Gamma Sigma. Home: PO Box 695 Norman OK 73070

KONE, ELLIOTT H., inventor, educator; b. Hartford, Conn., Sept. 23, 1920; s. Samuel Charles and Anna Frances (Rosenberg) K.; m. Grace Ann Hays, Dec. 29, 1962; children: David, Stephen, Susanna. B.A., Yale U., 1949, M.A., 1953; postgrad., NYU, 1957. Founder, supr. photographic dept. Yale U. News Bur., 1946-50; fellow Branford Coll. Yale; co-founder Yale U. Audio Visual Center, 1950, dir., 1952-66; film producer, founder Yale U. Film Series; founder Yale Series Recorded Poets; v.p., producer Mainstream (TV series); dir., pub. Readers Press, Inc., Dinosaur Press; pres. The Safe-Lite Co.; founder, pres. Traffic Standard, Inc.; Founder, chmn. Gen. Safety Corp.; dir. Group 9 Prodns., Inc.; co-founder, dir. Chester Electronic Labs., Inc.; founder Branford Indsl. Park; rep. U.S. Office Edn. Bibl. Control Newer Edn. Media; co-chmn. NE Regional Audio Visual Leadership Conf.; edn. advisor Am. Coll. in Jerusalem. Author: Modern Teaching of Foreign Languages, 1959; Editor: Preparing for College Study, 1962, The Connecticut Story, 1962; Pub.: Children of Joy, 1975, Growth and Its Implications for the Future, 1975; Illustrator: Basic Swimming, 1953; pub., assoc. editor: The Black People of America, 1970; Contbr. articles to profl. publs.; Producer numerous ednl. films, filmstrips, records. Active Boy Scouts; adv. council, sec., dir. Neighborhood Music Sch.; charter founder Rec. For The Blind, Inc., New Haven; mem. Yale Alumni Bd.; mem. com. New Haven Festival of the Arts; co-founder of Am. Film Festival; founder Long Wharf Theatre, New Haven, Yale U. Carillonneurs; chmn. of com. performing arts Arts Council of Greater New Haven; pres. Assn. For The Theatre Arts, Inc. Served with ordnance dept. AUS, 1942-46. Assoc. fellow New Coll., Oxford, Christ Coll., Cambridge, Quincy House, Harvard. Mem. Yale Photog. Soc. (founder, past pres., chief faculty adviser), Conn. Audio Visual Edn. Assn. (past pres., dir.; editor annual bull.), Edn. Media Council, NEA (dir. div. audio visual instrn.), Ednl. Film Library Assn. (pres., past v.p., dir.), Univ. Film Producers Assn., Am. Fedn. Film Socs., Nat. Assn. Ednl. Broadcasters, Assn. for Edn. Radio, Yale Glee Club Assos., Yale Film Assn. (charter), Yale Sch. Drama Assos., Yale Friends of Music, Conn. Opera Assn., Peabody Mus. Assos., New Haven Symphony Assos., Alpha Phi Omega (past pres., nat. presdl. rep.). Clubs: Yale (N.Y.C. and New Haven); Elizabethan, Faculty, The Mory's Assn. (Yale U.). Patentee hwy. safety items including Kone-Lite Hwy. pavement delineator, Apex Warning Systems, Flourescent Vests. Home: 2680 Gentian Rd Venice FL 33595

KONE, EUGENE HAROLD, public relations executive; b. Pitts., Apr. 5, 1915; s. Samuel Charles and Anna Frances (Rosenberg) K.; m. Estelle L. Alpert, Mar. 25, 1938; children—Allen Jay, Carolyn Willa. B.A., Yale, 1941. Reporter, editor New Haven Register, 1936-37, 39-41; asso. dir., then dir. Yale News Bur., 1941-51; v.p. Martin Wright & Assos., Guilford, Conn., pub. relations, 1951-56; owner Eugene H. Kone, pub. relations, N.Y.C. and New Haven, 1956—; pub. information asso. Rockefeller U., 1956—; dir. pub. relations Albertus Magnus Coll., New Haven, 1969-80, Am. Inst. Physics, 1956-71; coordinator pub. relations So. Conn. State Coll., New Haven, 1957-67; mem. faculty U. New Haven, 1949-50; cons. Am. Pain Soc., Endocrine Soc., Public Health Research Inst. City N.Y., Internat. Assn. Study Pain. Editor: Yale Men Who Died in World War II, 1951, The Greatest Adventure, 1974; Contbr. to popular and profl. mags. and newspapers. Past bd. dirs. New Haven Family Service, Conn. Mental Health Assn. Served to lt. USNR, World War II. Fellow AAAS (council); mem. Pub. Relations Soc. Am. (accredited, silver anvil award 1962, 66), Council for Advancement and Support of Edn., Am. Edn. Writers Assn., Nat. Assn. Sci. Writers (life; past exec. com.), Internat. Sci. Writers Assn., New Haven C. of C. (past exec.). Jewish (past trustee congregation). Clubs: Yale (N.Y.C.); Mory's (New Haven). Address: 280 Knollwood Dr New Haven CT 06515

KONER, PAULINE, dancer, choreographer; b. N.Y.C.; d. Samuel and Ida (Ginsburg) K.; m. Fritz Mahler, May 23, 1939. Student, Columbia, 1928-31; ballet student of, Michel Fokine; student ethnic dance with, Michio Ito; also, Angel Cansino. Mem. faculty Sch. Performing Arts, N.Y.C., N.C. Sch. Arts, Winston-Salem; adj. prof. Bklyn. Coll., 1975—; guest tchr. modern dance Internat. Ballet Seminar, Copenhagen, 1971, 72, Am. Dance Center, N.Y.C., 1972; lectr. and guest artist many leading univs. in, U.S.; performed under auspices State Dept. in, Mexico, S.Am., Europe; artist-in-residence N.C. Sch. Arts, Winston-Salem, 1965-76; tchr. choreographer workshop Cultural Center of Philippines, 1973; nat. adjudicator Am. Coll. Dance Festival, Kennedy Center, 1981. Performed at, White House, 1967; conducted choreography workshops, Nat. Assn. Regional Ballets, 1968; staged ballet, Dayton (Ohio) Civic Ballet, 1969, Alvin Ailey Co., Atlanta Ballet Co.; filmed TV broadcasts of numerous performances; premiere: Solitary Songs, Am. Dance Festival, 1975, Pauline Koner Dance Consort, 1976, A Time of Crickets, Am. Dance Festival, 1976, Mosaic, Dance Umbrella Series, 1977, Cantigas, Flight, 1980, Am. Dance Festival, 1978; resident co., Riverside Dance Festival, 1979-81; Solo concerts in, N.Y.C., 1930—, Near East, 1932, Russia, 1935, Riverside Co., 1980-82, U.S., 1930—; guest artist, Jose Limon Co., 1945-60; guest artist, tchr., Jacob's Pillow Dance Festival, intermittently, 1945-70; dir., Pauline Koner Dance Co., 1947-64; guest choreographer, Nat. Sch. Dance, Rome, Italy, 1960-63, Nat. Ballet Chile, 1961; performer, tchr., Conn. Coll. Sch. Dance, 1948-60; pioneer TV dance in, CBS, 1946; artist-in-residence U. Ill., 1984, Alvin Ailey Repertory Co., 1984; established modern dance program in Japan under auspices, Fulbright Com., 1965, State Dept. tour of, India, Singapore and Korea, 1967. Recipient Dance Mag. award, 1963; Nat. Endowment of Arts grantee, 1969, 75, 77-78, 79. *I am a humanist. As a creative artist I search for basic truths. I try to capture the poetry, the humour, the agony of the human condition, to know and experience compassion. Compassion is essential for communication and communication is a key to survival.*

KONHAUSER, JOSEPH DANIEL EDWARD, mathematics educator; b. Ford City, Pa., Oct. 5, 1924; s. Daniel Stephen and Elizabeth (Salaba) K.; m. Aileen Holz, Aug. 19, 1948; children: Daniel Scott. B.S. in Physics, Pa. State U., 1948; M.A. in Math, 1951; Ph.D., 1963. Instr. dept. math. Pa. State U., 1949-55; sr. engr. HRB-Singer, Inc., State College, Pa., 1955-61, staff mathematician, 1961-64; asso. prof. math. U. Minn., 1964-68, asso. dir. coll. geometry project, 1966-68; asso. prof. math. Macalester Coll., St. Paul, 1968-70, prof., 1970—. Producer: films Curves of Constant Width, 1966, Equidecomposable Polygons, 1968. Served with USNR, 1944-46. Home: 6313 Halifax Ave S Minneapolis MN 55424 Office: Macalester Coll Saint Paul MN 55105

KONIECKO, EDWARD STANLEY, biochemist; b. Poland, Mar. 24, 1913; U.S., 1959, naturalized, 1966; s. Alexander and Victoria (Czarniecki) K. Food engr., Agrl. U., Warsaw, 1957; M.S. in Food Tech., Acad. Agrl., Warsaw, 1958, Central Sch. Planning and Stats., Warsaw, 1959; Ph.D. in Biochemistry, London Coll. Applied Sci., 1961; postgrad. in Nutrition, Can. U., Guelph, Ont., 1971; Ph.D. in Clin. Nutrition, N.W. London U., 1973. Dir. fin. and acctg. Hdqurs. of State Nutrition, Warsaw, 1950-55; assoc. dir. research Warsaw Dept. Nutrition, 1956-59; chief chemist research and devel. Sugardale Foods, Inc., Canton, Ohio, 1960-76; ind. cons., writer, 1976—. Exhibited one woman shows, IFA Galleries, 1979; author: Handbook for Water Analysis, 1981, Nutritional Encyclopedia for the Elderly, 1981, other books. Mem. Am. Chem. Soc., AAAS, Assn. Ofcl. Analytical Chemists. Republican. Roman Catholic. Office: PO Box 8341 Canton OH 44711

KONIGSBERG, FRANKLIN DANIEL, film/TV producer; b. Mar. 10, 1933; s. Joseph and Jennie (Schneider) K.; m. Susanne Davis O'Meara. B.A., Yale U., 1953, J.D., 1956. Bar: N.Y. 1957. Atty. CBS-TV, N.Y.C., 1957-60; dir. program and talent adminstrn. NBC-TV, N.Y.C., 1960-65; sr. v.p. Internat. Famous Agy.-Internat. Creative Mgmt., 1960-75; exec. producer, pres. Konigsberg Co., Beverly Hills, Calif., 1975—. Producer: TV film Dummy (Peabody award, Am. Bar Assn. Golden Gavel award 1980); other TV prodns. include Kraft All Star Salute: Pearl Bailey, 1978, Bing Crosby: His Life and Legend, 1978, Before and After, 1979, A Bing Crosby Christmas: Like the Ones We Used To Know, 1979, Guyana Tragedy: The Story of Jim Jones, 1980 (Ohio State U. Journalism award), A Christmas Without Snow, 1980, The Pride of Jesse Hallam, 1981, Hardcase, 1982, Divorce Wars, 1982; dir., Telepictures Corp. Mem. Producers Guild Am., Acad. TV Arts and Scis. Office: Konigsberg Co 10201 W Pico Blvd Los Angeles CA 90064 *

KONIGSBURG, ELAINE LOBL, author; b. N.Y.C., Feb. 10, 1930; d. Adolph and Beulah (Klein) Lobl; m. David Konigsburg, July 6, 1952; children—Paul, Laurie, Ross. B.S., Carnegie Inst. Tech., 1952; grad. student chemistry, U. Pitts., 1952-54. Author: juveniles Jennifer, Hecate, Macbeth, William McKinley and Me, Elizabeth, 1967 (Newbery Honor Book), From The Mixed-Up Files of Mrs. Basil E. Frankweiler, 1967 (Newbery medal 1968), About the B'nai Bagels, 1969, (George), 1970, Altogether, One at a Time, 1971, A Proud Taste for Scarlet and Miniver, 1973 (Nat. Book award nominee), The Dragon in the Ghetto Caper, 1974, The Second Mrs. Giaconda, 1975, Father's Arcane Daughter, 1976, Throwing Shadows, 1979, Journey to an 800 Number, 1981. Address: care Atheneum 597 Fifth Ave New York NY 10017

KONKER, GLENN ERNEST, transportation company executive; b. Cleve., Oct. 22, 1920; s. Ernest F. and Anna L. (Grau) K.; m. Elizabeth Burr, Nov. 11, 1944; children: Ernest J., David N., Elizabeth A. B.S., Case Inst. Tech., Cleve., 1942; M.B.A., Harvard U., 1951. Assoc. Robert Heller & Assocs., Cleve., 1951-63; pres. Sola Electric, Chgo., 1964-70; group v.p. IC Industries, Chgo., 1970-76; sr. v.p., chief fin. officer, dir. ICG R.R., Chgo., 1976—; dir. Chgo. Bank of Commerce, GM&O Land Co., Blue Island R.R. Co., Miss. Export R.R. Served with USNR, 1942-46. Presbyterian. Clubs: Mid-America (Chgo.); Onwentsia (Lake Forest, Ill.). Home: 945 E Illinois Rd Lake Forest IL 60045 Office: Illinois Central Gulf 233 N Michigan Ave Chicago IL 60601

KONNER, JOAN WEINER, broadcasting executive, TV producer, writer; b. Paterson, N.J., Feb. 24, 1931; d. Martin and Tillie (Frankel) Weiner; children: Rosemary, Catherine. Student, Vassar Coll., 1948-49; B.A., Sarah Lawrence Coll., 1951; M.S., Columbia U., 1961. Editorial writer, columnist, reporter Hackensack (N.J.) Record, 1961-63; producer, reporter WNDT Ednl. Broadcasting Corp., N.Y.C., 1963-65; producer, writer, reporter NBC News, N.Y.C., 1965-77; exec. producer nat. pub. affairs programs WNET Ednl. Broadcasting Corp., N.Y.C., 1977-78; exec. producer Bill Moyers' Journal, 1978-81; v.p., dir. met. programming WNET, 1981—. Trustee Columbia U., Rockland Ctr. for the Arts. Recipient Emmy award Nat. Acad. TV Arts and Scis., 1969,71,82; award AP Broadcasting Assn., 1969,70,71; Gold medal Atlanta Film Festival, 1970,71; awards N.Y. Film Festival, 1970,71,73; San Francisco Environ. Film Festival, 1970; Ohio State award Ohio State U., 1973; awards Cath. Broadcasters Assn., 1970; Council Chs., 1970,72; Columbia Journalism Alumni award, 1973; Front Page award, 1976; Clarion award, 1978; Peabody award, 1980; award Am. Bar. Assn., 1981. Home: Snedens Landing Palisades NY 10964 Office: 356 W 58 St New York NY 10019

KONNER, LINDA DALE, freelance writer, magazine editor; b. Bklyn.; d. Sol and Brenice (Mandell) K. B.A., Bklyn. Coll., 1972; M.A., Fordham U., 1975. Founder, pub. Henrietta, Bklyn., 1973-75; mini-mag. editor Seventeen Mag., N.Y.C., 1976-81; mng. editor Weight-Watchers Mag., N.Y.C., 1981-83, editor-in-chief, 1983&. Author: The Love and Lure of Birthstones, 1977, Roller Fever!, 1979. Mem. N.Y. Women in Communications, Am. Soc. Mag. Editors, Phi Beta Kappa. Office: Weight Watchers Mag 360 Lexington Ave New York NY 10017

KONO, TETSURO, biochemist, physiologist, educator; b. Tokyo, Japan, May 17, 1925; s. Ichiro and Hiroko (Sasaki) K.; m. Seiko Kanda, Dec. 18, 1961; children: Michiko, Masahiro, Kenji. B.A., U. Tokyo, 1947, Ph.D., 1958. Research asso. Johns Hopkins Univ., Balt., 1958-59; research asso. Vanderbilt U., Nashville, 1959-60, mem. faculty, 1963—, prof. physiology, 1974—; instr. Univ. Tokyo, 1960-63. Contbr. articles to profl. jours. NIH grantee, 1961—. Mem. Japanese Biochem. Soc., Am. Soc. Biol. Chemists, Sigma Xi. Home: 2009 Stonehurst Dr Nashville TN 37215 Office: Dept Physiology Vanderbilt Med Sch Nashville TN 37232

KONOPKA, GISELA PEIPER (MRS. ERHARDT PAUL KONOPKA), educator, social worker, author, lecturer; b. Berlin, Germany, Feb. 11, 1910; came to U.S., 1941, naturalized, 1944; d. Mendel and Bronia (Buttermann) Peiper; m. Erhardt Paul Konopka, June 23, 1941 (dec. Nov. 1976). Student, U. Hamburg, Germany, 1929-33; M.S., U. Pitts., 1943; Dr. Social Welfare, Columbia, 1957. Psychiat. group worker Child Guidence Clinic, Pitts., 1943-47; lectr. Sch. Social Work, U. Pitts., also Welfare; mem. Gov. Minn. Adv. Com. on Youth; faculty U. Minn., 1947-56, prof., 1956-77, prof. emeritus, 1977—, spl. asst. to v.p. for student affairs, 1969-71; dir. Center for Youth Devel. and Research, 1970-77; Child welfare expert, group work U.S. High Commr. Med. Affairs, Germany, summers 1950, 51; tchr. social work in Germany Dept. State., summer 1956; Fulbright lectr., Netherlands, 1960-61; lectr. U. Calif. at Berkeley, 1961-62, in Near and Far East, 1970, Inst. for Social Services, Montrouge, France, 1971, U. West Indies, Jamaica, 1972, 77; Fulbright lectr., Brazil, 1972, lectr., Israel, Jamaica, 1977, Australia, 1979, Netherlands, 1981; dir. adolescent girl in conflict research project NIMH grant, 1962-65; dir. Project Girl, Lilly Endowment grant, 1973-77, Nat. Youth Worker Edn. Project, 1977-79; cons. VA Hosp., Mpls.; standards for group homes Minn. Research and Evaluation Div., Office Child Devel., Dept. Health, Edn. and Welfare; mem. Gov. Minn. Adv. Com. on Youth, Minn. Supreme Ct. Juvenile Justice Study Commn.; nat. adv. com. Girl Scouts of Am.; also exec. com. group work recreation div.; exec. com. Family and Children's Service, Hennepin County Welfare Council; former cons. Children's Treatment Center, Minn. Welfare Dept.; internat. cons. in social group work by Internat. Conf. Schs. Social Work; mem. Council Internat. Programs Social Workers and Youth Workers, Joint Commn. on Juvenile Justice Standards, Inst. Jud. Adminstrn.-Am. Bar Assn., 1972-76; lectr., Australia, 1979. Author: Therapeutic Group Work with Children, 1940, Group Work in the Institution, 1954, Eduard C. Lindeman and Social Work Philosophy, 1958, Social Group Work: A Helping Process, 1963, Adolescent Girls in Conflict, 1966, Young Girls: A Portrait of Adolescence, 1976; co-author: Concepts and Methods of Social Work, edited Walter Friedlander, 1958; Contbr. numerous articles to profl. jours. Mem. bd. Mpls. Urban League, 1968. Named outstanding alumnus social work U. Pitts., 1968; recipient award for outstanding service Assn. for Blind, 1966; Outstanding Alumnus award Sch. Social Work, U. Pitts., 1968; citation U.S. Children's Bur., 1966, also Vols. Am.; Highest merit award for rebldg. German social services after World War II Fed. Republic Germany, 1975; 1st Ann. award for excellence in teaching and magnanimous contbn. to community Minn. Conf. Social Work Edn., 1976; Cecil E. Newman humanitarian award Mpls. Urban League, 1977; AAUW Achievement award, 1977; award Nat. Conf. Social Welfare, 1979, Nat. Conf. Children's Homes, 1979; Lilly Endowment grantee for treatment of delinquents, 1982-84. Fellow Am. Orthopsychiat. Assn. (pres. 1963-64, dir.); mem. Nat. Assn. Social Workers (chmn. group work sect.), Nat. Conf. Social Welfare (v.p., nat. chmn. history of social welfare group 1960, past dir.), AAUP, Urban League, Consumers League, United World Federalists. Home: 3809 Sheridan Ave S Minneapolis MN 55410 *Perhaps I have had the fullest life one can expect. I have experienced degradation, scorn (I have been spat upon by an arrogant Nazi who considered me a member of an inferior race), I have known fear and hunger and cold and utter despair—I have received unending love by a man who has always been my friend, protector, lover, companion—I have known the sweetness of children's arms around me, though I had not borne them. I knew and know the gentle friendship of young and old people and the exhilaration of standing up for my ideals, even in the face of terrible rejection. I have had and have the privilege of knowing many people of great variety, of all races and nationalities, men and women, and we enjoy each other and can communicate with each other. I have seen horrible misery and extraordinary beauty in nature and art and even in human beings. I have indeed a rich life.*

KONRAD, ADOLF FERDINAND, artist; b. Bremen, Germany, Feb. 21, 1915; came to U.S., 1925, naturalized, 1931; s. Roman and Katherine Heidientje (Engelken) K.; m. Adair Watts, Apr. 26, 1980. Student, Newark Sch. Fine and Indsl. Art, 1930-34, Cummington (Mass.) Sch., 1936-37; D.F.A., Kean Coll., 1971. Tchr., advisor N.J. State Council on Arts, 1971-74; artist in residence Everhart Mus., Scranton, 1973, Somerset County Coll., N.J., 1977-80; lectr., panelist. One-man exhbns. include, Newark Mus., 1966, Everhart Mus., Scranton, Pa., 1973, Mus. Fine Arts, Springfield, Mass., Montclair Art Mus. and N.J. State Mus., Trenton, 1980; represented in permanent collections, Newark Mus., Montclair Art Mus., Mus. Fine Arts, Springfield, Everhart Mus., Scranton, State Mus., Trenton, N.J., NAD, N.Y.C., Newark Public Library, Ct. Gen. Sessions Painting Collection, Washington, CIBA Pharm. Co., Basle, Switzerland, AT&T, Bedminster, N.J., Crum & Forster Ins. Co., Morristown, N.J., N.J. Public Service, Newark. Louis Comfort Tiffany fellow, 1937; Tiffany Found. fellow, 1961; resident fellow Yaddo, Saratoga Springs, 1956; winner grand prize Atlantic City Fine Arts Festival, 1961, 63; first prize Montclair Art Mus. Ann. Exhbn., 1963; Andrew Carnegie prize NAD Ann., 1967; Audience Choice award Marietta (Ohio) Coll., 1969; Gov.'s citation; N.J. Symphony Ann. Arts award, 1969; Artist of Year award Art Educators N.J., 1973; Fellowship award in Painting N.J. State Council on Arts, 1982. Mem. Associated Artists N.J. (pres. 1960-65), Artists Equity Assn. N.J. (pres. 1952-60), NAD (academician). Home: Buttermilk Bridge Rd Asbury NJ 08802

KONRAD, JOHN F., former insurance executive; b. Oshkosh, Wis., Sept. 29, 1917; s. John F. and Alma (Below) K.; m. June Ross, May 30, 1941; children: William R., Ann L. Konrad Marshall, Barbara J. Konrad Schulte. Ph.B., U. Wis., 1939, LL.B., 1942. With Wis. Public Service Corp., 1946-54; with Northwestern Mut. Life Ins. Co., 1954-80, v.p., treas., 1967-80; ret., 1980; chmn. State of Wis. Investment Bd., 1979—; dir. Empire Dist. Electric Co., Mo. Trustee Ripon Coll. Served to capt. USAAF, 1942-46. Republican. Club: Town (Milw.). Home: 6866 N Elm Tree Rd Milwaukee WI 53217 Office: 720 E Wisconsin Ave Milwaukee WI 53202

KONSKI, JAMES LOUIS, civil engineer; b. N.Y.C., Nov. 4, 1917; s. Herbert D. and Ruby (Louis) K.; children: Alexander, Christina, Marguerite. B.S. in Civil Engring., U. Mo., 1950, M.S., 1951. Registered profl. engr., N.Y., Ky., R.I., Kans.; registered profl. surveyor. Engr., Bur. Yards and Docks, Washington, 1951; structural engr. Sanderson & Porter, N.Y.C., 1951-52; field engr. Ebasco Services, Inc., Owensboro, Ky., 1952-53; chief structural engr. Berger Assos., Syracuse, N.Y., 1953-54, Endman, Anthony & Hosley (formerly Berger Assos.), Syracuse, 1954-57; pres. Konski Engrs. Profl. Corp., Syracuse, 1957—; prin. Konski Engrs. Internat., 1965—; cons. engr. U.S. Trade Mission to Africa, 1965, to Far East, 1970; speaker Met. Assn. Urban Designers and Environ. Planning Conf., Eng., 1974, Netherlands, 1975. Contbr. articles to profl. jours. Served with USMC, 1939-46; maj. Res. ret. Fellow ASCE (v.p. 1972-73, nat. dir. 1966-70), Am. Cons. Engrs. Council (past chpt. pres.); mem. Internat. Assn. Bridge and Structural Engrs., Nat. Soc. Profl. Engrs. (past chpt. pres.), Am. Concrete Inst., Prestressed Concrete Inst., Am. Congress Surveying and Mapping, Am. Mil. Engrs., Am. Water Works Assn., Am. Road Builders Assn., Am. Soc. Photogrammetry, League Am. Wheelman (area rep. 1967-77), U.S. Cycling Fedn., Am. Coll. Sports Medicine, Internat. Randonneurs (dir. USA/Can.), Sigma Xi, Tau Beta Pi, Chi Epsilon, Pi Mu Epsilon. Clubs: Onondaga, Cycling (pres. 1967-77). Participant Paris-Brest-Paris Bicycle Race, 1975, 79, 83; dir. Internat. Randonneurs (U.S./Can.). Office: Old Engine House No 2 727 N Salina St Syracuse NY 13208

KONTOS, CONSTANTINE WILLIAM, govt. ofcl.; b. Chgo., Aug. 10, 1922; s. William C. and Irene (Thomas) K.; m. Joan Fultz, Nov. 20, 1948; children—Mark William, Stephen Leigh. B.A. in Polit. Sci, U. Chgo., 1947, M.A., 1948; postgrad., London (Eng.) Sch. Econs., 1948-49. With ECA mission to, Greece, 1949-53; with FOA and ICA, Washington, 1953-59, regional exec. officer, Africa and Europe, 1957-59; dep. dir. U.S. Aid mission to, Ceylon, 1959-61, Nigeria, 1961-64; assigned Nat. War Coll., 1964-65; dir. personnel AID, 1965-67; dir. AID Mission to, Pakistan, 1967, minister, 1968-69; dir. program evaluation, 1969-72; dep. commr. gen. UN Relief and Works Agy., Beirut, 1972-74; mem. policy planning staff State Dept., Washington, 1974-76; spl. rep. of pres., dir. Sinai support mission, Washington, 1976-80; U.S. ambassador to, Sudan, 1980. Served with AUS, 1943-46; ETO. Home: Khartoum Sudan Office: Am Embassy Khartoum APO New York NY 09668

KONVITZ, MILTON RIDBAZ, legal educator; b. Safad, Israel, Mar. 12, 1908; came to U.S., 1915, naturalized, 1926; s. Rabbi Joseph and Welia (Ridbaz-Wilowsky) K.; m. Mary Traub, June 18, 1942; 1 son, Josef. B.S., NYU, 1928, A.M., 1930, J.D., 1930; Ph.D. (Sage fellow in philosophy 1932-33), Cornell U., 1933; Litt.D., Rutgers U., 1954, Dropsie U., 1975; D.C.L., U. Liberia, 1962; L.H.D., Hebrew Union Coll.-Jewish Inst. Religion, 1966, Yeshiva U., 1972; LL.D., Syracuse U., 1971, Jewish Theol. Sem., 1972. Bar: N.J. 1932. Practice law, Jersey City and Newark, 1933-46; lectr. on law and pub. adminstrn. NYU, 1938-46; asst. gen. counsel NAACP Legal Def. and Edn. Fund, 1943-46; mem. faculty New Sch. for Social Research, 1944-46; prof. indsl. and labor relations N.Y. State Sch. of Indsl. and Labor Relations, Cornell U., 1946-73; prof. law Cornell U. Law Sch., 1956-73, prof. emeritus, 1973—; mem. Inst. Advanced Study, Princeton, 1959-60; vis. prof. Hebrew U., Jerusalem, 1970; dir. Liberian Codification of Laws project, 1952-80; gen. counsel Newark Housing Authority, 1938-43, N.J. State Housing Authority, 1943-45; Pub. rep. Nat. War Labor Bd. region 2, 1943-46; mem. enforcement commn. and hearing commn. Wage Stablzn. Bd., 1952-53; chmn. nat. com. study of Jewish Edn. in U.S., 1958-59; faculty Salzburg (Austria) Seminar Am. Studies, 1952; panel Fed. Mediation and Conciliation Service, N.Y. Mediation Bd., Am. Arbitration Assn., N.Y. State Pub. Employment Relations, Nat. Mediation Bd. Author: On the Nature of Value: Philosophy of Samuel Alexander, 1946, The Alien and the Asiatic in American Law, 1946, The Constitution and Civil Rights, 1947, Civil Rights in Immigration, 1953, Bill of Rights Reader, 1954, Fundamental Liberties of a Free People, 1957, A Century of Civil Rights, 1961, First Amendment Freedoms, 1963, Expanding Liberties: Freedom's Gains in Postwar America, 1966, Religious Liberty and Conscience, 1968, Judaism and Human Rights, 1972, Recognition of Ralph Waldo Emerson, 1972, Judaism and the American Idea, 1978; Founding editor: Industrial and Labor Relations Rev. (vols. 1-5), 1947-52, Liberian Code of Laws (5 vols.), 1957-60, Liberian Code of Laws Revised, 1973—, Liberian Law Reports (27 vols); Mem. editorial bds. of periodicals; chmn. editorial bd.: Midstream Mag; co-editor: Jewish Social Studies; co-founder: Judaism Mag; mem. editorial bd.: Ency. Judaica. Bd. Pres. Hebrew Culture Found.; chmn. com. on Jewish studies Meml. Found. for Jewish Culture; nat. commn. Ramah; commn. reorgn. World Zionist Orgn.; bd. dirs. Am. Zionist Fedn., Am. Histadrut Cultural Exchange Inst. Ford Found. Faculty fellow, 1952-53; Guggenheim fellow, 1953-54; Fund for the Republic fellow, 1955; comdr. Order Star of Africa, Liberia, 1957; grand band, 1960; fellow Center Advanced Study Behavioral Scis., 1964-65, Nat. Endowment for Humanities, 1975-76; recipient N.Y. U. Washington Sq. Coll. Disting. Alumni award, 1964; Mordecai ben David disting. award Yeshiva U., 1965; Morris J. Kaplun internat. prize for scholarship Hebrew U., 1969; Tercentenary medal Jewish Community of Essex County, N.J., 1954. Fellow Am. Assn. Jewish Edn., Am. Acad. Arts and Scis., Jewish Acad. Arts and Scis., Conf. Jewish Social Studies (dir.), Zionist Acad. Council (exec. com.), Yivo Inst. (acad. council); mem. Am. Philos. Assn., AAUP (council 1961-64), Am. Zionist Fedn. (dir.), Law and Soc. Assn., Indsl. Relations Research Assn., Internat. Assn. Jewish Law, ACLU (nat. com.), Jewish Publ. Soc. (mem. com. on publs.), Am. Jewish League for Israel (dir.), Order of Coif, Phi Beta Kappa. Home: 16 The Byway Ithaca NY 14850

KOOKEN, JOHN FREDERICK, bank holding co. exec.; b. Denver, Nov. 1, 1931; s. Duff A. and Frances C. K.; m. Emily Howe, Sept. 18, 1954; children: Diane, Carolyn. M.S., Stanford U., 1954, Ph.D., 1961. With Security Pacific Nat. Bank-Security Pacific Corp., Los Angeles, 1960—; exec. v.p. Security Pacific Corp., 1981—; lectr. Grad. Sch. Bus., U. So. Calif., 1962-67. Pres. bd. dirs. Children's Bur. Los Angeles, 1981—; bd. dirs. United Way Los Angeles, 1982—. Served to lt. (j.g.) USNR, 1954-57. Mem. Fin. Execs. Inst. (pres. Los Angeles chpt. 1979-80, dir. 1981—). Office: 333 S Hope St Los Angeles CA 90071

KOOLURIS, GEORGE PETER, health care company executive; b. Orange, N.J., Dec. 22, 1944; s. Peter George and Georgene (Sadimas) K.; m. Florence Providenza Restivo, Apr. 25, 1971; children: Douglas, Alexander, Christopher. B.S., U. Dayton, 1966, M.B.A., 1968. Mgmt. trainee Bristol-Myers Co., N.Y.C., 1969-71, staff assoc., 1971-72, corp. devel. analyst, 1972-74, asst. dir. corp. devel., 1974-76, dir. corp. devel., 1976-81, v.p. corp. devel., 1981—. Served with Army N.G., 1969-75. Home: 106 Tanglewylde Ave Bronxville NY 10708 Office: Bristol-Myers Co 345 Park Ave New York NY 10154

KOOMEN, JACOB, JR., physician, educator; b. Bristol, N.Y., Sept. 18, 1917; s. Jacob and Eva (Bunschoten) K.; m. Ruth Elinor Chapin, Aug. 27, 1943; children: John Chapin, Marcia Anne, Nancy Carol Koomen Della Rovere, Neil Chapin. B.S., U. Rochester, 1939, M.D., 1945; M.P.H., U. N.C., 1957. Intern in medicine Strong Meml. Hosp., Rochester, N.Y., 1945-46; asst. resident, fellow and chief resident, instr. bacteriology and medicine U. Rochester Sch. Medicine and Dentistry, Strong Meml. Hosp., 1946-49; asst. dir. div. epidemiology N.C. State Bd. Health, Raleigh, 1956-61, asst. state health dir., 1961-65, acting state health dir., 1966, state health dir., 1966-78; vis. asso. prof. epidemiology U. N.C. Sch. Pub. Health, 1959-67, adj. asso. prof.

pub. health adminstrn., 1967-76, adj. prof., 1976-78, clin. prof. health adminstrn., 1978—; pres. N.C. Conf. Social Services, 1975-76. Pres. Fred A. Olds Sch. PTA, Raleigh, 1958-59, Martin Jr. High Sch. PTA, 1960-61; pres. N.C. State Employees Credit Union, 1975-76; trustee U. Rochester, 1981—. Served with USPHS, 1954-56. Recipient Disting. Service award U. N.C. Sch. Medicine, 1971; U. Rochester alumni citation, 1980. Mem. AMA, Am. Pub. Health Assn., N.C. Pub. Health Assn. (Reynolds award for pub. health contributions 1960), Wake County Med. Soc., Raleigh Acad. Medicine, U. N.C. Sch. Pub. Health Alumni Assn. (pres. 1977-78), U. Rochester Medicine and Dentistry Alumni Assn. (mem. council 1972-79, univ. council 1976-79, trustees council 1976-79), Delta Omega. Presbyterian. Home: 909 Dogwood Ln Raleigh NC 27607 Office: U NC Sch Public Health Dept Health Adminstrn Rosenau Bldg 201H Chapel Hill NC 27514

KOONS, DONALDSON, geologist, educator; b. Seoul, Korea, Aug. 23, 1917 (parents Am. citizens); s. Edwin Wade and Floy (Donaldson) K.; m. Elizabeth Anne Ortquist, Nov. 18, 1944; children: Robert Wade, John Donaldson, Peter Ortquist, Linnea Louise. A.B., Columbia U., 1939, M.A., 1941, Ph.D., 1945; D.Sc. (hon.), Coll. Wooster, 1974, D.H.E., Unity Coll., 1976. Lectr. geology Carleton Coll., Northfield, Minn., 1942-43, Columbia U., N.Y.C., 1946, W.VA. U., 1946-47; mem. faculty dept. geology Colby Coll., Waterville, Maine, 1947—, prof. geology, 1951—, chmn. dept. geology, 1947—, Charles A. Dana prof. geology, 1975-82. Commr. Maine Dept. Conservation, 1973-75; chmn. Maine Environ. Improvement Commn., 1968-72, Gov. of Maine Task Force Environment, 1969—, New Eng. Conf. Air Pollution, 1968; faculty trustee Colby Coll., 1965-68, Coburn Classical Inst., 1963—; trustee Unity Coll., 1976—. Served with USAAF, 1943-45. Recipient Huddilston medal, 1973. Fellow AAAS, Geol. Soc. Am. Home: RFD 1 Pond Rd Oakland ME 04963

KOONTS, JONES CALVIN, educator; b. Lexington, N.C., Sept. 19, 1924; s. Harvey Hill and Elsie (Tussey) K.; m. Cortlandt Morper, Sept. 6, 1953; children: Carlisle Woodson, Camille Walton. A.B. in History and English magna cum laude, Catawba Coll., Salisbury, N.C., 1945; M.A. in Sociology, George Peabody Coll., Vanderbilt U., Nashville, 1949; Ph.D. in Edn, George Peabody Coll., Vanderbilt U., Nashville, 1958; Lit.D., Catawba Coll., 1979. Tchr. English and Social studies Boyden High Sch., Salisbury, 1945-48; dir.-asst. student teaching George Peabody Coll., 1951-52; mem. faculty Erskine Coll., Due West, S.C., 1949—, prof. edn., chmn. dept., 1949—, chmn. div. tchr. edn., 1975—; tchr. adult edn. Abbeville (S.C.) County Community Center, 1955; tchr. grad. courses U. S.C.; also Clemson U., 1956—. Author: (poetry) Since Promontory, 1967, Straws in the Wind, 1968, Under the Umbrella, 1971, A Slice of the Sun, 1976; editor: Green Leaves in January, 1972, Inklings, 1983. Rep. S.C. Bd. Edn., 1966-71; bd. commrs. Piedmont Tech. Coll., 1972-75; alumni bd. dirs. Catawba Coll., 1966; bd. advisers Gardner-Webb Coll., 1981—. Jesse H. Jones scholar, 1951; Algernon Sydney Sullivan scholar, 1951; fellow Council So. Univs., 1957-58; Peabody-Harvard scholar, 1960; Fulbright grantee, 1964; recipient Disting. Service key Phi Delta Kappa. Mem. N.C. Edn. Assn. (chpt. sec. treas. 1946-47), S.C. Assn. Student Teaching (founder, 1st pres. 1955-56), S.C. Council Tchr. Edn., S. Atlantic Philosophy Edn. Soc., Poetry Soc. S.C. (dir.), Nat. Assn. Tchr. Educators (del S.C.), Am. Assn. Colls. for Tchr. Edn. (rep. S.C.), S.C. Assn. Colls. for Tchr. Edn. (pres. 1979-80), Acad. Am. Poets (William Gilmore Simms poetry prize 1973, Unicorn Poetry prize 1974, Lyric Poetry prize 1975, Elizabeth B. Coker Poetry award 1977), Asso. Ref. Presbyterian. Home: PO Box 163 Due West SC 29639 Office: Dept Edn Erskine Coll Due West SC 29639

KOONTS, ROBERT HENRY, lawyer, corporation executive; b. Greensboro, N.C., May 8, 1927; s. Henry Valentine and Margaret (Andrew) K.; m. Edna Mildred Matthes, Mar. 8, 1952 (div. June 1982); children: Linda Suzanne, Barbara Jane; m. Mary Frances Pennel Johnston, May 1983. B.S. in Commerce, U. N.C., 1949, LL.B., 1952, grad. exec. program, 1967. Bar: N.C. 1952, U.S. Supreme Ct. 1980. Sole practice law, High Point, N.C., 1952-57; v.p., assoc. gen. counsel Jefferson Standard Life Ins. Co., Greensboro, 1957-68, Jefferson-Pilot Corp., 1968—; sec., dir. Enterprise Co., Beaumont, Tex., Clearwater Newspapers, Inc., (Fla.), Laredo Newspapers, Inc., (Tex.), Texas City Newspapers, Inc., Altus Newspapers, Inc., (Okla.), Plant City Newspapers, Inc., (Fla.), Jefferson-Pilot Publs., Inc., Greensboro, Mineral Wells Pub. Co., (Tex.). Served with USNR, 1945-46. Mem. Assn. Life Ins. Counsel, ABA, N.C. Bar Assn., Greensboro Bar Assn., Phi Delta Theta, Phi Delta Phi. Presbyterian. Clubs: Greensboro City, Greensboro Country. Lodge: Gorgon's Head. Home: 512 O'Neill Dr Jamestown NC 27282 Office: Jefferson-Pilot Corp 101 N Elm St PO Box 21008 Greensboro NC 27420

KOONTZ, ALFRED JOSEPH, JR., light aircraft manufacturing company executive; b. Balt., Mar. 6, 1942; s. Alfred J. and Mary Agnes (Valis) K.; m. Kay Francis Frank, Aug. 4, 1962; children—Debbie Kay, Denise Marie, Stacey Lynn, Alfred Joseph, III. B.S. in Bus. Adminstrn, Pa. State U., 1964. C.P.A., Md. Mgr. Price Waterhouse & Co., Balt., 1964-73, sr. mgr., N.Y.C., 1973-74, Morristown, N.J., 1974-75; v.p. fin Piper Aircraft Corp., Lock Haven, Pa., 1975-80, sr. v.p. fin., 1980—, also dir. Mem. Am. Inst. C.P.A.'s, Md. Assn. C.P.A.'s, Nat. Assn. Accountants. Home: 1112 Olde Galleon Ln Vero Beach FL 32963 Office: One Piper Dr Vero Beach FL 32960

KOONTZ, RAYMOND, bank security company executive; b. Asheville, N.C., 1912; m. Carol Hamlin; 1 son, Cary Hamlin. Chmn. bd., dir. Diebold, Inc. Mem. Newcomen Soc. N.Am. Clubs: Canton, Brookside (Canton, O.); Minneapolis; Union (Cleve.); Congress Lake (Hartville, Ohio); St. James's (Montreal, Can.); Green Boundary (Aiken, S.C.). Home: 2601 Foxhills Dr NW Canton OH 44708 Office: 818 Mulberry Rd SE Canton OH 44702

KOONTZ, WARREN WOODSON, JR., urologist, educator; b. Lynchburg, Va., June 10, 1932; s. Warren Womack and Mary Winston (Woodson) K.; m. Edwina Sykes, June 16, 1957; children: Warren Sykes, Mary Edwina. B.A., Va. Mil. Inst., 1953; M.D., U. Va., 1957. Diplomate: Am. Bd. Urology. Intern N.Y. Hosp., N.Y.C., 1957-58, resident in surgery, 1958-59, 61-62, resident in urology, 1962-66, instr., 1964; exchange resident in urology Peter Bent Brigham Hosp., Boston, 1964; mem. faculty Med. Coll. Va., Richmond, 1966-69, 70—, prof. urology, chmn. div., 1970—, assoc. dean clin. affairs; atteding urologist McGuire VA Hosp., Richmond, 1966-69, cons., 1970; asst. urologist Mass. Gen. Hosp., Boston; also asst. prof. Harvard U. Med. Sch., 1969-70; mem. staff Richmond Met. Hosp., 1979—; courtesy staff St. Mary's Hosp., Richmond, 1972—; cons. Portsmouth (Va.) Naval Hosp., Crippled Children's Hosp., Richmond; exec. com. collaborative group A Nat. Bladder Cancer Project; mem. utilization com. dist. 5 PSRO, 1979—. Contbr. numerous articles to med. jours. Served as officer M.C. USAF, 1959-61. Fellow A.C.S. (pres. Va. chpt. 1974-76, bd. govs. 1979-82); mem. Am. Urol. Assn., AMA, AAAS, Soc. U. Urologists, Soc. Pelvic Surgeons, Soc. Pediatric Urology, Nat. Urologic Forum, Soc. Internat. D'Urologie, Am. Assn. Genito-Urinary Surgeons, Pediatric Urology Letter Club, Urologists Letter Club, Med. Soc. Va., Va. Urol. Soc., N.Y. Acad. Sci., Richmond Acad. Medicine, Richmond Pediatric Soc. (asso.), Alpha Omega Alpha. Clubs: Country of Va., Commonwealth. Address: Med Coll Va Box 118 Richmond VA 23298

KOOP, CHARLES EVERETT, surgeon, government official, educator; b. Bklyn., Oct. 14, 1916; s. John Everett and Helen (Apel) K.; m. Elizabeth Flanagan, Sept. 19, 1938; children: Allen van Benschoten, Norman Apel, David Charles Everett, Elizabeth. A.B., Dartmouth Coll., 1937; M.D., Cornell U., 1941; Sc.D. in Medicine, U. Pa., 1947; LL.D., Eastern Bapt. Coll., 1960; M.D. (hon.), U. Liverpool, Eng., 1968; L.H.D., Wheaton Coll., 1973; D.Sc., Gynedd Mercy Coll., 1978; Sc.D. (hon.), Washington and Jefferson U., Marquette U. Intern Pa. Hosp., Phila., 1941-42; surgeon-in-chief Chilren's Hosp. of Phila, 1948—; with U. Pa. Sch. Medicine, 1942—, prof., 1959—; dep. asst. sec. for health U.S. Dept. Health and Human Services; asst. surg. gen. USPHS; editor-in-chief Jour. Pediatric Surgery, 1965-77; cons. U.S. Navy, 1964—; Fellow in surgery Boston Children's Hosp., 1946. Contbns. and publs. in surg. physiology, biomed. ethics, physiology of the surg. neonate, tech. advances in pediatric surgery. Bd. dirs. Med. Assistance Programs, Inc., Wheaton, Ill., Evang. Ministries, Inc., Phila., Daystar Communications, Inc., Eugene, Ore., Eastern Bapt. Sem. and Coll., Phila. Decorated chevalier Legion of Honor, France; recipient medal, City of Marseille; Kopernicus medal Polish Surg. Soc.; Disting. Service medal USPHS. Fellow A.C.S., Am. Acad. Pediatrics (William E. Ladd gold medal); mem. Am. Surg. Assn., Soc. U. Surgeons, Brit. Assn. Pediatric Surgeons (Dennis Browne Gold medal), Internat. Soc. Surgery, Societe Francaise de Chirugie Infantile, AMA, Deutschen Gesselschaft für Kinderchirugi, Societé Suisse De Chirurgie Infantile, Order Duarte, Sanchez y Mella Dominican Republic, Sigma Xi. Home: 4 West Dr Bethesda MD 20814 Office: 200 Independence Ave NW 416G Washington DC 20201

KOOP, THEODORE FREDERICK, broadcasting exec.; b. Monticello, Iowa, Mar. 9, 1907; s. Frederick William and Laura Abby (Hicks) K. A.B., Iowa U., 1928; L.H.D. (hon.), Iowa Wesleyan U., 1970. Reporter, editor AP, Des Moines, New Haven, N.Y.C. and Washington, 1928-41; mem. editorial staff Nat. Geog. Soc., Washington, 1941, 46-47; spl. asst. to U.S. Dir. Censorship, 1942-45, asst. dir. censorship, dept. dir., 1945; dir. news and pub. affairs CBS, Washington, 1948-61, v.p., 1961-71; Washington dir. Radio-TV News Dirs. Assn., 1972-76; chmn. Washington Journalism Center, 1973-78. Author: Weapon of Silence, 1946; Contbr. to: Dateline: Washington, 1949, Ethics, Morality and the Media, 1980. Served to lt. USNR, 1942-45. Mem. Phi Beta Kappa, Delta Upsilon, Sigma Delta Chi. Clubs: Gridiron, Nat. Press (Washington) (pres. 1953). Home: 2737 Devonshire Pl NW Washington DC 20008

KOOPMANS, TJALLING CHARLES, economist; b. s'Graveland, Netherlands, Aug. 28, 1910; came to U.S., 1940, naturalized, 1946; s. Sjoerd and Wijtske (van der Zee) K.; m. Truus Wanningen, Oct. 1936; children: Anne W., Henry S., Helen J. M.A. in Physics and Math, U. Utrecht, Netherlands, 1933; Ph.D., U. Leiden, Netherlands, 1936, Netherlands Sch. Econs., 1963, Catholic U. Louvain, Belgium, 1967; D.Sc. (hon.), Northwestern U., 1975, LL.D., U. Pa., 1976. Lectr. Netherlands Sch. Econs., Rotterdam, 1936-38; specialist fin. sect. League of Nations, Geneva, 1938-40; research asso. Princeton, 1940-41; spl. lectr. Sch. Bus., N.Y.U., 1940-41; economist Penn Mut. Life Ins. Co., 1941-42; statistician Combined Shipping Adjustment Bd., Washington, 1942-44; research asso. Cowles Commn. Research Econs., U. Chgo., 1944-55, asso. prof. econs., 1946-48, prof. econs., 1948-55; dir. research Cowles Commn., 1948-54; prof. econs. Yale, 1955—; dir. Cowles Found. for Research in Economics, 1961-67, Alfred Cowles prof. econs., 1967-81, Alfred Cowles emeritus prof. econs., 1981—; Frank W. Taussig prof. econs. Harvard, 1960-61. Author: Three Essays on the State of Eonomic Science, 1957; Editor: Statistical Inference in Dynamic Economic Models, 1950, Activity Analysis of Production and Allocation, 1951; co-editor: Studies in Econometric Method, 1953; Contbr. articles to profl. jours. Recipient Alfred Nobel Meml. prize in econs., 1975. Fellow Econometric Soc. (v.p. 1949, pres. 1950, council 1949—); mem. Am. Acad. Arts and Scis., Nat. Acad. Scis., Am. Econ. Assn. (pres. 1978), Royal Netherlands Acad. Arts and Scis. (corr.), Am. Mathematical Soc., Inst. Mgmt. Scis., Ops. Research Soc. Am. Office: Cowles Found PO Box 2125 Yale Sta New Haven CT 06520

KOOSMAN, JERRY MARTIN, baseball player; b. Appleton, Minn., Dec. 23, 1942; s. Martin William and Lydia (Graese) K.; m. LaVonne Kathleen Sorum, Feb. 11, 1967; children: Michael Scott, Shawn Allen, Danielle DeAnn. Student, U. Minn., Morris, 1960-61, State Sch. Sci., Whapeton, N.D., 1961-62. Profl. baseball player with Greenville (S.C.) Mets, Williamsport (Pa.) Mets, 1965, Auburn (N.Y.) Mets, 1966, N.Y. Mets and Jacksonville (Fla.) Suns, 1967; pitcher N.Y. Mets, 1968-78, Minn. Twins, 1978-81, Chgo. White Sox, 1981—. Served with AUS, 1962-64. Lutheran. Home: 9080 Abbywood Rd Chaska MN 55318

KOPECK, THOMAS W., labor union official. Sec.-treas. Internat. Typographical Union, Colorado Springs, Colo. Office: Internat Typographical Union PO Box 157 Colorado Springs CO 80901 *

KOPEL, DAVID, psychologist, educator; b. Czestachowa, Poland, Feb. 22, 1910; came to U.S., 1913, naturalized, 1924; s. Joseph and Shandel Mary (Motel) K. B.S., Northwestern U., 1930, M.S., 1934, Ph.D., 1935; postgrad., Wiener Psychoanalytischen Vereinigung, Austria, 1948-49, U. Chgo., 1950-52, Chgo. Psychoanalytic Study Group, 1955-70. Diplomate: Am. Bd. Profl. Psychology (clin. psychology). Research and teaching asst. Northwestern U., 1933-34, psychologist, instr., 1934-38; sch. psychologist Evanston (Ill.) Pub. Schs., 1935-37; tchr. psychology and edn. Chgo. Tchrs. Coll. (now Chgo. State U.), 1938-43, 49—, dir. Grad. Sch., 1954-61, coordinator internat. summer study tours, prof. psychology and edn., 1958-76, emeritus, 1976—; supt. U.S. Dependents Schs. System, Austria, 1946-47; specialist tchr. edn. U.S. Allied Commn., Austria, 1947-49; summer faculty Columbia U., 1938, Alameda (Calif.) Guidance Center, 1941, Ohio State U., 1942, U. Ill., 1950; cons. Gary (Ind.) and Chgo. Pub. Schs., Chgo. Psychol. Inst., Temple Sholom; dir. Northwestern U. Psycho-Edn. Clinic, Chgo., 1950-51; pvt. practice psychotherapy, 1952—. Author: (with Paul A. Witty) Diagnostic Child Study Record and Manual, 1936, Reading and the Educative Process, 1938, Mental Hygiene and Modern Education, 1939; contbr.: Progress in Clinical Psychology, 1953; co-editor: Ill. Schs. Jour., 1966-68; contbr. articles to profl. jours. Served to 1st lt. AUS, 1943-46; to lt. col., Res., 1949-63. Decorated Army Commendation and campaign medals. Fellow Am. Psychol. Assn.; mem. Ill. Psychol. Assn. (treas.), Am. Orthopsychiat. Assn., AAUP (pres. Chgo. chpt.), Internat. Reading Assn. (pres. Chgo. chpt.), Internat. Soc. Gen. Semantics (pres. Chgo. chpt.), Chgo. Psychol. Assn. (pres.), Assn. for Advancement Psychology, Chgo. Psychoanalytic Psychol. Study Group (co-convener, chmn.). Home: 6700 S Oglesby Ave Apt 2101 Chicago IL 60649 Office: Chgo State U 95th St at King Dr Chicago IL 60628

KOPELMAN, ARIE LEONARD, advertising executive; b. Cambridge, Mass., Sept. 23, 1938; s. Frank and Ruth L. K.; m. Corinne Franco, Dec. 26, 1971; children: Jill Alison, William Franco. B.A., Johns Hopkins U., 1960; M.B.A., Columbia U., 1962. With advt. dept. Procter & Gamble Co., Cin., 1962-65; with Doyle Dane Bernbach, Inc., N.Y.C., 1965—, exec. v.p., 1980—, gen. mgr., 1982—. Exec. com. N.Y. Urban League, 1979; trustee Usdan Center Creative and Performing Arts, 1970—. Served with USAR, 1960. Mem. Columbia U. Bus. Sch. Alumni Assn. (dir., past pres.). Home: 45 E 66th St New York NY 10021 Office: 437 Madison Ave New York NY 10022

KOPELMAN, LEONARD, lawyer; b. Cambridge, Mass., Aug. 2, 1940; s. Irving and Frances Estelle (Robbins) K. B.A. cum laude, Harvard U., 1962, J.D., 1965. Bar: Mass. bar 1966. Asso. Warner & Stackpole, Boston, 1965-73; sr. partner firm Kopelman & Soltz, Boston, 1973-77; firm Kopelman & Paige, Boston, 1978—; lectr. exec. mgmt. program Harvard Bus. Sch., 1965—; permanent master Mass. Superior Ct., 1971—; hon. consul of, Finland, Mass., 1975—; U.S. del. Soc. for Internat. Devel.; Chmn. Mass. Jud. Selection Com. for the Fed. Judiciary, 1971—; chief counsel AAUP. Trustee Cathedral of the Pines, 1972; pres. Hillel Found. of Cambridge, Inc., 1973—; trustee Faulkner Hosp., 1974—, Parker Hill Med. Center, 1976—. Nat. Endowment for the Humanities grantee, 1975. Mem. Am. Bar Assn. (mem. exec. council 1969—), Am. Judges Assn., Mass. State C. of C. (pres. 1974-77). Clubs: Harvard Faculty, Algonquin, Bay, Harvard, Hasty Pudding Inst. Home: 231 Marlborough St Boston MA 02116 Office: 77 Franklin St Boston MA 02110

KOPELMAN, RICHARD ERIC, management educator; b. N.Y.C., May 31, 1943; s. Seymour H. and Leona L. (Quint) K.; m. Carol Fialkov, June 7, 1970; children: Joshua Marc, Michael Adam. B.S., U. Pa., 1965, M.B.A., 1967; D.B.A., Harvard U., 1974. Instr. bus. Community Coll. of Phila., 1967-69; instr. mgmt. Baruch Coll., N.Y.C., 1973-74, asst. prof. mgmt., 1974-77; assoc. prof. mgmt. Baurch Coll., N.Y.C., 1978-80, prof. mgmt., 1981—; cons various corps. and pub. agys.; corp. dir. Three Dimensionsional Circuits Inc., Aleph Null Corp. Author: The Management of Productivity: An Organizational Behavior Perspective, 1983; contbr. numerous articles to profl. and acad. jours. Bd. dirs. Day Care Council, Nassau County, 1979-82. William B. Harding fellow Harvard U. Mem. Acad. Mgmt., Am. Psychol. Assn., Am. Inst. Decision Scis., Am. Soc. Personnel Adminstrn., Met. N.Y. Assn. for Applied Psychology. Home: 65 Colgate Rd Great Neck NY 11023 Office: Mgmt Dept Baruch Coll 17 Lexington Ave New York NY 10010

KOPENHAVER, PATRICIA ELLSWORTH, podiatrist; b. N.Y.C. A.B., George Washington U., 1954; M.A., Columbia U., 1956; Dr. Podiatric Medicine, SUNY, 1963. Diplomate: Nat. Bd. Podiatry Examiners. Practice podiatry, Greenwich, Conn., 1964—; mem. staff Laurelton Convalescent Hosp., Greenwich. Publicity dir. Neighbors Club, YWCA, 1968—; Bd. dirs. Monmouth Opera Guild, 1965; trustee Monmouth Opera Festival, 1966, v.p., 1964; mem. Greenwich Arts Council; program chmn. Greenwich Women's Republican Club, 1983-84, 4th dist. rep., 1984-85; mem. Greenwich Exchange for Women's Work, 1984. Recipient Hosp. Fund award for med. research translations ARC. Mem. Am. Podiatry Assn. (career guidance com.), Conn. Podiatry Assn., Fairfield Podiatry Assn., Am. Woman's Podiatry Assn. (sec.), Am. Assn. Women Podiatrists (pres. 1969-78), Acad. Podiatry, Am. Podiatry Council, UN Assn. U.S.A., Acad. Podiatric Medicine, AAUW (chmn. nominating com. 1981, 1st v.p. 1983-84, chmn. fund raising 1984-85), Am. Podiatric Circulatory Soc., NOW, George Washington U., Columbia alumni assns., Nat. Fedn. Rep. Women, Greenwich Woman's Gardeners Club, Pi Epsilon Chi. Clubs: Soroptimists, Toastmasters, Travel, Greenwich Women's (chmn. civic and public affairs com. 1970, program chmn. 1983—). Home: 2 Sutton Pl S New York NY 10022 8 Deerfield Dr Greenwich CT 06830

KOPIN, IRWIN JEROME, physician, pharmacologist; b. N.Y.C., Mar. 27, 1929; s. Jacob and Eva (Resnick) K.; m. Rita Brownstein; children: Judith R., Alan S., Gail A. B.Sc., McGill U., Can., 1951, M.D., 1955. Diplomate: Am. Bd. Internal Medicine. Intern, then resident in medicine Boston City Hosp., 1955-57; research asso. NIH, 1957-60; resident in medicine Columbia Presbyn. Med. Center, N.Y.C., 1960-61; commd. corps NIMH, USPHS, Bethesda, Md.; chief sect. medicine LCS, NIMH, 1961—; chief Lab. Clin. Sci., NIMH, 1968-83. Co-editor-in-chief: Advances in Pharmacology/Chemotherapy, 1968—; editor: Neurosci. Research, 1971-1973; asso. editor: Pharmacol. Rev., 1977—; editorial bd. other jours. Recipient Superior Service award HEW, 1970; Public Service award NASA, 1974; Disting. Service medal USPHS, 1980. Fellow Am. Coll. Neuropsychopharmacology, Soc. Neurosci., Assn. Am. Physicians, AAAS; mem. Am. Soc. Biol. Chemists, Soc. Pharmacology and Exptl. Therapeutics, Assn. Research Nervous and Mental Disease (pres. 1970). Office: NIMH Bldg 10 2D-46 Bethesda MD 20205

KOPIT, ARTHUR, playwright; b. N.Y.C., May 10, 1937; s. George and Maxine (Dubin) K.; m. Leslie Ann Garis; 2 sons, 1 dau. A.B. cum laude, Harvard U., 1959. Fellow Center for Humanities, Wesleyan U., 1974-75, playwright-in-residence, 1975-76; CBS fellow Yale U., 1976-77. Author: (plays produced at Harvard) Questioning of Nick, 1957; (Plays produced at Harvard) Gemini, 1957; (plays produced at Harvard) On the Runway of Life You Never Know What's Coming Off Next, 1958, Across the River and into the Jungle, 1958, Sing to Me Through Open Windows, 1959, Aubade, 1959; Oh Dad, Poor Dad, Mamma's Hung You in the Closet and I'm Feelin' So Sad, 1960 (also prod. in London, 1961, on Broadway, 1963, released as motion picture, 1967), What's Happened to the Thorne's House, 1972, Louisiana Territory, 1975; (6 one-act plays) The Day the Whores Came Out to Play Tennis, and Other Plays, 1965; Indians, 1969, Wings, 1977; (book of musical) Nine, 1982; (adaptation) Ghosts (Ibsen), 1982. Recipient Vernon Rice award, 1962, Outer Circle award, 1962; Shaw Travelling fellow Harvard U., 1959; Guggenheim fellow, 1967; Rockefeller grantee, 1968; NEH grantee, 1974. Mem. Writers Guild Am., Dramatists Guild (council), Hasty Pudding Soc., Signet Soc., PEN, Phi Beta Kappa. Club: Harvard (N.Y.C.). Address: care Audrey Wood Internat Creative Mgmt 40 W 57th St New York NY 10019 *

KOPKA, DONALD FERRIS, automotive exec.; b. Lansing, Mich., Aug. 21, 1926; s. Merland Augustus and Helen (Ferris) K.; m. Janet Elizabeth Schooley, Aug. 28, 1948; children—Susan Jane, James Robert. B.F.A., Wayne State U., 1950. With Chrysler Corp., Highland Park, Mich., 1950-64, chief stylist, 1960-64; with Ford Motor Co., Dearborn, Mich., 1964—, exec. dir. design, 1969-80, v.p. design, 1980—. Mem. Mich. State Council Higher Edn., 1972-78. Served with U.S. Navy, 1944-46. Mem. Soc. Automotive Engrs., Engring. Soc. Detroit. Republican. Office: Ford Motor Co Design Center 21175 Oakwood Blvd Dearborn MI 48123

KOPP, CARL ROBERT, advertising executive; b. Detroit, Apr. 8, 1921; s. Andrew Russell and Bertha (Hecke) K.; m. Jenna Lou Sandburg, 1978; children: Deborah Ann, Barbara Jane (dec.), Jeffrey. Student, Ill. Inst. Tech., Advanced Mgmt. Program, Harvard U. Various sales and advt. positions Marathon Corp., 1947-54; account exec. Needham, Louis & Brorby, 1954-55; successively account exec., account supr., mgmt. dir., exec. v.p., pres. Leo Burnett U.S.A., Chgo., 1955-75; pres. Leo Burnett Co., Inc., Chgo., 1975-76, pres., chief exec. officer, 1976-78, chmn., chief exec. officer, 1978—. Mem. Chgo. Crime Commn. Served with AUS and USAAC, World War II; Korea. Decorated Purple Heart, Bronze Star with V. Home: 11902 Lost Tree Way Lost Tree Village FL 33408 Office: Prudential Plaza Chicago IL 60601

KOPP, DAVID CHARLES, lawyer; b. Oak Park, Ill., Dec. 29, 1945; s. Henry C. and Lillian (Wentland) K.; m. Diane Y. Aebersold, June 15, 1968; children: Benjamin, Jeffrey. B.S. with honors, No. Ill. U., 1967; J.D., U. Ill., 1970. Bar: Conn. 1970. Assoc. Murtha, Cullina, Richter & Pinney, Hartford, Conn., 1970-73; atty. Conn. Gen. Life Ins. Co.,

Hartford, 1974-76, asst. counsel, 1976, assoc. counsel, 1976-77, corp. sec., 1977-82; exec. asst. Office of chief exec. CIGNA Corp., Hartford, 1982, asst. corp. sec., 1982—. Vol. Greater Hartford Arts Council, 1979-81; mem. West Hartford YMCA. Mem. Am. Soc. Corp. Secs. (pres. Hartford chpt. 1980-81), Hartford County Bar Assn., Conn. Bar Assn., ABA, Cavaliers, Sigma Iota Epsilon. Office: Conn Gen Life Ins Co Hartford CT 06152

KOPP, EUGENE HOWARD, electrical engineer; b. N.Y.C., Oct. 1, 1929; s. Jacob and Fanny (Lipschitz) K.; m. Claire Bernstein, Aug. 31, 1950; children: Carolyn, Michael, Paul. B.E.E., CCNY, 1950, M.E.E., 1953; Ph.D. in Engring, UCLA, 1965. Registered profl. engr., Calif. Project engr. Polarad Electronics Corp., Long Island City, N.Y., 1950-53, Kaye Halbert Corp., Culver City, Calif., 1953-55; chief engr. Precision Radiation Instruments, Inc., Los Angeles, 1955-58; mem. faculty sch. engring. Calif. State U., Los Angeles, 1958-74, asso. prof., 1962-66, prof., 1966-74, dean engring. Sch., 1967-73; v.p. acad. affairs West Coast U., Los Angeles, 1973-79; sr. scientist Hughes Aircraft Co., 1980—; lectr. evening div. CCNY, N.Y.C., 1950-53; lectr. UCLA, 1979—. Vis. research fellow U. Leeds, Eng., 1966-67. Mem. IEEE, Am. Soc. Engring. Edn., AAAS, Tau Beta Pi, Eta Kappa Nu, Pi Tau Sigma. Office: PO Box 1351 South Pasadena CA 91030

KOPP, HARRIET GREEN, communication specialist; b. N.Y.C., June 18, 1917; m. George A. Kopp, 1948 (dec. 1968); m. Kurt Friedrich, 1972. M.A., Bklyn. Coll., 1939; diploma edn. of deaf, Columbia U., 1939, Ph.D., 1962. Scientist Bell Telephone Labs., 1943-46; mem. faculty Eastern Mich. U., 1946-48; adj. prof. Wayne State U., Detroit, 1948-70; dir. communication clinics Rehab. Inst. Met. Detroit, 1955-59; dir. programs deaf and aphasic Detroit Bd. Edn., 1959-70; prof., chmn. communication disorders San Diego State U., 1970-80; acting dean Coll. Human Services, 1980-83; prof. communication disorders San Diego State U., 1983—; mem. Nat. Adv. Com. on Deaf, 1965-72, chmn., 1970-72; mem. Nat. Adv. Com. on Handicapped, 1972-73; adv., rev. panels Bur. Educationally Handicapped, HEW, 1963—. Author: (with R. Potter, G.A. Kopp) Visible Speech, 1948, 68, Some Applications of Phonetic Principles, 1948, 65, 62, 68, 70; editor: Curriculum, Cognition and Content, 1968, 75. Mem. Am. Speech and Hearing Assn. (fellow 1962), AAAS, A.G. Bell Assn. (dir. 1964-68, chmn. editorial bd. 1966-75), Conf. Execs. Schs. for Deaf, Council Exceptional Children, Calif. Speech and Hearing Assn., Phi Kappa Phi. Office: San Diego State University 5300 Campanile Ave San Diego CA 92182 *My career has been dedicated to scientific inquiry, clinical practice and the development of theoretical models underlying clinical and educational practice in order to prepare university graduates to assist infants, children and adults with communicative disorders. Research and publications have been focused on these areas as has the administration of hospital, research and public education programs.*

KOPP, RICHARD EDGAR, electrical engineer; b. Bklyn., July 12, 1931; s. Edgar A. and Anna M. (Barto) K.; m. Elaine Hecker, June 14, 1953; children: Debra, Richard (dec.), Lisa, Barbara. B.E.E., Poly. Inst. Bklyn., 1953; M.S., Bklyn. Inst., 1957, D.E.E., 1960. With Grumman Aerospace, Bethpage, N.Y., 1953—, dir. system scis. research, 1976—; adj. prof. Poly. Inst. Bklyn., 1961-70; mem. adv. com. Poly. Inst. Imaging Scis. Contr. articles to profl. jours. Fellow AIAA (assoc.); mem. IEEE (sr.), U.S. Power Squadron. Club: Smithtown Bay Yacht. Home: 12 Cygnet Dr Smithtown NY 11787 Office: Grumman Aerospace Corp. A-08-35 Bethpage NY 11714

KOPP, W. BREWSTER, corporate executive; b. Rochester, N.Y., Nov. 4, 1925; s. Frederick J. and Bernice C. (Woodworth) K.; children: Bradford, Jeffrey, Alexander. A.B., Harvard U., 1946, M.B.A., 1949. Investment analyst, N.Y., 1946-47, 49-51; with Standard Oil Co., Ohio, 1951-53, Am. Can Co., 1954-65, mgr. financial analysis, 1958-62, corp. mgr. financial planning and budgets, 1962-64, div. controller, 1964-65; asst. sec. army for financial mgmt., 1965-67; asst. to chmn. bd. First Nat. Bank, Boston, 1967, sr. v.p., 1967-69; v.p. finance and adminstrn., treas. Digital Equipment Corp., Maynard, Mass., 1969-70; sr. v.p., mem. exec. com. Am. Stock Exchange, 1971-73; v.p., asst. to pres. Otis Elevator Co., N.Y.C., 1973-74, v.p., controller, 1974-75; bus. cons., dir., 1975-82; chmn., dir. Object Recognition Systems, Inc., 1976-80; pres., chief exec. officer, dir., chmn. exec. com. Equitable Environ. Health, Inc., Woodbury, N.Y., 1979-80; sr. v.p. asset redeployment, dir. Publicker Industries, Inc., 1982—; dir. Publicker Industries, Inc., Instrument Specialties, Inc., Rec. & Statis. Corp., Object Recognition Systems, Inc., Songtime, Inc.; mem. adv. bd. dirs. Envirodyne, Inc., 1971-79; Cons. to asst. sec. def., 1967-69. Bd. dirs. N.Y. Internat. Bible Soc. Mem. Fin. Execs. Inst., Assn. U.S. Army, Am. Def. Preparedness Assn. (dir. N.Y. chpt.), Mil. Order Fgn. Wars, Newcomen Soc. Republican. Clubs: Harvard, Economic (N.Y.C.). Home: 210 River Run The Mill Greenwich CT 06830 Office: Publicker Industries 777 W Putnam Ave Box 1978 Greenwich CT 06836

KOPPEL, TED, broadcast journalist; b. Lancashire, Eng.; came to U.S., 1953; m. Grace Anne Dorney; 4 children. M.A. in Journalism, Stanford U. B.A. in Journalism, Syracuse U.; News corr., writer Sta.-WMCA, N.Y.C., 1963; corr. ABC News, Vietnam, chief, diplomatic corr., Washington, from 1941; anchorman ABC News Nightline, 1980—. Corr. for: TV spls., including The People of People's China, 1973, Kissinger: Action Biography, 1974, Second to None, 1979; Author: (with Marvin Kalb) In The National Interest (Overseas Press Club award 1971, 74, 75). Office: care ABC News 1717 De Sales St NW Washington DC 20036 *

KOPPELMAN, CHAIM, artist; b. Bklyn., Nov. 17, 1920; s. Samuel and Sadie (Mondlin) K.; m. Dorothy Myers, Feb. 13, 1943; 1 dau., Ann. Student, Bklyn. Coll., 1938, Am. Artists Sch., 1939, Eli Siegel, Art Coll. Western Eng., Bristol, 1944, Ecole des Beaux-Arts, Rheims, 1945, Art Students League, 1946, Amedée Ozenfant Sch., 1946-49. Tchr. art, instr. N.Y. U., 1947-55, N.Y. State U., New Paltz, 1952-58; lectr. Bklyn. Coll., 1950-60; instr. Sch. Visual Arts, N.Y.C., 1959—; cons. Aesthetic Realism Found., N.Y.C., 1971—. Author: This is the Way I See Aesthetic Realism, 1969; illustrator: Definition, 1972; contbr. articles to profl. jours.; Bibliographies of his work The Indignant Eye (Ralph Shikes), 1969, The New Humanism (Barry Schwartz), 1974, The Art of the Print (Fritz Eichenberg), 1976, American Prints and Printmakers (Una Johnson), 1980; one man shows include, Asso. Am. Artists Gallery, 1973, Terrain Gallery, N.Y.C., 1974, 83, Warwick (Eng.) Gallery, 1975, others, group shows include, Purdue U., 1972, Utah State U., Arte Fiera, Bologna, 1978, NAD, N.Y.C., 1983; represented in permanent collections, Victoria and Albert Mus., London, Mus. Fine Arts, Caracas, Venezuela, Mus. Modern Art, N.Y.C., Met. Mus. Art, N.Y.C., Library of Congress, Washington, Los Angeles County Mus. Art, others. Served with USAF, 1942-45. Decorated 4 Battle Stars, Bronze Star; grantee Louis Comfort Tiffany, 1956, 59; N.Y. State Creative Artists Pub. Service, 1976; recipient prize 3d Internat. Miniature Print Exhbn., 1968, others. Mem. Soc. Am. Graphic Artists (prize 1966, past pres.), Soc. Aesthetic Realism, Nat. Acad. Design (asso.). Home and Office: 498 Broome St New York NY 10012 *To compose a painting, every artist instinctively tries to put together opposites such as sameness and difference, warm and cool, freedom and order. From my teacher, Eli Siegel, founder of the philosophy of Aesthetic Realism, I learned the single most important thing I have learned as artist and person: Every artist is trying to put opposites together in his work, and every person, including the artist, is trying to put these same opposites together in his life.*

KOPPES, WAYNE FARLAND, ret. archtl. cons. and writer; b. Sullivan, Ohio, July 11, 1902; s. Charles William and Mary Ellen (Scheib) K.; m. Alice L. Nelson, Sept. 25, 1926; children—Alan W., Donald L., David N. A.B. in Architecture, Carnegie Inst. Tech., 1925; M.Arch., Mass. Inst. Tech., 1929; diploma, Ecole des Beaux Arts, Fontainbleau, France, 1925. Archtl. designer Walker & Weeks, Cleve., 1926-32; from instr. to prof. archtl. constrn. Sch. Architecture, Rensselaer Poly. Inst., 1932-45, adj. prof. bldg. research, 1959-70; asso. Cutting & Ciresi, Cleve., 1945-47; head dept. archtl. design and housing research John B. Pierce Found., Raritan, N.J., 1947-53; chief research architect S.W. Research Inst., Princeton, N.J., 1953-55; archtl. cons. Basking Ridge, N.J., 1955-79; tech. dir. Nat. Assn. Archtl. Metal Mfrs., 1962-68. Author or co-author: New Spaces for Learning, 1966, Educational Facilities with New Media, 1965, Aluminum Curtain Walls; periodical, 1970-73; author-editor: Metal Curtain Wall Manual, 1961, Metal Finishes Manual, 1969, Metal Stair Manual, 1971, Metal Bar Grating Manual, 1974, Pipe Railing Manual, 1977, Hollow Metal Manual, 1977; co-author: Metal Flagpole Manual, 1981; also research and tech. reports. Mem. Bd. Edn., Bernards Twp., N.J., 1952-55; mem. Planning Bd., 1968-77. Fellow AIA, Am. Soc. Testing and Materials (award merit 1971, Walter Voss award 1976); mem. N.J. Soc. Architects. Address: 154 S Alward Ave Basking Ridge NJ 07920

KOPPETT, LEONARD, journalist, author; b. Moscow, Russia, Sept. 15, 1923; s. David and Marie (Dvoretskya) Kopeliovitch; m. Suzanne Silberstein, Apr. 24, 1964; children: Katherine, David. B.A., Columbia U., 1946. Sportswriter, columnist N.Y. Herald Tribune, 1948-54, N.Y. Post, 1954-63, N.Y. Times, 1963-78, Sporting News, 1967-82; exec. sports editor Peninsula Times Tribune, 1980-81, editor, 1982-84, editor emeritus, 1984—; free-lance columnist, 1978—; tchr. journalism Stanford (Calif.) U., 1977-81. Books include A Thinking Man's Guide to Baseball, 1967, 24 Seconds to Shoot, 1969, The N.Y. Times Guide to Spectator Sports, 1970, The New York Mets, 1970, The Essence of the Game is Deception, 1974, Sports Illusion, Sports Reality, 1981. Served with U.S. Army, 1943-45. Mem. Baseball Writers Assn. Am., Profl. Football Writers, Authors Guild. Democrat. Jewish.

KOPPLE, KENNETH D., chemistry educator; b. Phila., Oct. 21, 1930; s. Harry N. and Sara M. (Silverstein) K.; m. Frances Marie Hopkins, Apr. 30, 1960. B.S. in Chem. Engring., MIT, 1951, Ph.D. in Chemistry, 1954. Instr., asst. prof. U. Chgo., 1954-62; research chemist Gen. Electric Research Lab., Schenectady, 1962-65; assoc. prof. chemistry Ill. Inst. Tech., Chgo., 1965-70, prof., 1970—, chmn. dept. chemistry, 1982—; cons. to industry and govt.; sec., dir. Am. Peptide Symposium, Inc., 1972—. Author: Peptides and Amino Acids, 1966; contbr. articles to profl. jours. Guggenheim Found. fellow, 1964; recipient Career Devel. award NIH, 1970-75; grantee NIH, NSF. Fellow AAAS; mem. Am. Chem. Soc., Am. Soc. Biol. Chemists, Royal Soc. Chemistry. Office: Dept Chemistry Ill Inst Tech Chicago IL 60616

KOPPLIN, JULIUS OTTO, electrical engineer; b. Appleton, Wis., Feb. 6, 1925; s. Julius O. and Renata A. (Peters) K.; m. Lola Mae Boldt, Sept. 16, 1950 (dec.); children: William J., John D., Mary Susan, James R.; m. Elizabeth A. Dutmer, Feb. 5, 1983. B.S.E.E., U. Wis., 1949; M.S.E.E., Purdue U., 1954, Ph.D., 1958. Corrosion engr. No. Ind. Public Service Co., 1949-53; asst. prof. elec. engring. U. Ill., 1958-61, asso. prof., 1961-68; prof., chmn. dept. elec. engring. U. Tex., El Paso, 1968-75, Iowa State U., Ames, 1975—. Contbr. articles to profl. jours. Served with USAAC, 1943-45. Decorated Air medal, Purple Heart. Mem. IEEE, Am. Soc. Engring. Edn., Sigma Xi, Eta Kappa Nu, Sigma Pi Sigma. Home: 241 Trail Ridge Rd Ames IA 50010 Office: Elec Engring Dept Iowa State U Ames IA 50011

KOPROWSKI, HILARY, medical scientist; b. Warsaw, Poland, Dec. 5, 1916; came to U.S., 1944, naturalized, 1950; s. Paul and Sarah (Berland) K.; m. Dr. Irena Grasberg, July 14, 1938; children: Claude Eugene, Christopher Dorian. B.A., Mikolaj Rej Gymnasium of Luth. Congregation, Warsaw, 1933; M.D., U. Warsaw, 1939; grad., Warsaw Conservatory Music and Santa Cecilia Acad., Rome; Doctor honoris causa, Widener Coll., Phila., Ludwig-Maximilian U., Ger., U. Helsinki, U. Uppsala (Sweden). Research asst. dept. exptl. and gen. pathology U. Warsaw, 1936-39; staff Yellow Fever Research Service, Rio de Janeiro, 1940-44; staff research div. Am. Cyanamid Co., 1944-46; asst. dir. viral and rickettsial research Lederle Lab., Pearl River, N.Y., 1946-57; dir. Wistar Inst., Phila., 1957—; prof. microbiology Faculty Arts and Scis., U. Pa., 1957—; Wistar prof. research medicine U. Pa., 1957—; cons. WHO, Nat. Cancer Inst., NIH, USPHS, 1962-70. Co-editor: Methods in Virology, Viruses and Immunity, Current Topics in Microbiology and Immunology, 1965—, Cancer Research. Decorated Commandeur Ordre du Mérite pour la Recherche et l'Invention; Chevalier Order Royal De Lion, Belgium; recipient Alvarenga prize. Coll. Physicians Phila., 1959; Alfred Jurzykowski Found Polish Millenium prize, 1966; Felix Wankel Tierschutz prize, 1979; Alexander Von Humboldt Sr. U.S. Scientist award; Fulbright Scholar Max Planck Inst. für Verhaltensphysiologie, Seewiesen, Germany, 1971. Fellow N.Y. Acad. Medicine, Phila. Coll. Physicians; mem. Am. Acad. Arts and Scis., Nat. Acad. Scis., N.Y. Acad. Scis. (pres. 1959, trustee 1960-72). Research cell biology, virology and immunology; vaccine against poliomyelitis, hog cholera, rabies. Home: 334 Fairhill Road Wynnewood PA 19096 Office: Wistar Inst 36th and Spruce Streets Philadelphia PA 19104

KOPTA, JOSEPH ANTHONY, orthopaedic surgeon; b. Boston, May 9, 1936; s. Edward J. and Stella A. (Renfrow) K.; m. Lynda Kay Crabb, Jan. 19, 1976; children—Bryan Scott, Kathy, Carolyn, Daniel, Gregory. B.S., U. Okla., 1958, M.D., 1962; M.Ed., U. Ill., 1969. Diplomate: Am. Bd. Orthopaedic Surgery. Intern San Francisco Gen. Hosp., 1962-63; resident U. Calif., San Francisco, 1965-69; fellow in med. edn. U. Ill., Chgo., 1969-70; asst. prof. Washington U., St. Louis, 1970-74; prof., head dept. orthopaedic surgery U. Okla., 1974—. Asso. editor: Clinical Orthopaedics and Related Research, 1973; contbr. articles to profl. jours. Served with U.S. Navy, 1963-65. Fellow Am. Acad. Orthopaedic Surgery (dir. 1974-75), A.C.S.; mem. Am. Orthopaedic Assn., Assn. Bone and Joint Surgeons. Republican. Home: 609 NW 37th St Oklahoma City OK 73118 Office: 920 Stanton Young Blvd Oklahoma City OK 73190

KORAB, WILLIAM HARRY, foods company executive; b. Balt., Mar. 3, 1942; s. Arnold A. and Evelyn (Stevens) K.; m. Diane Guise, June 16, 1964; children: William S., John T. B.S. in Chem. Engring., U. Md., 1964; M.B.A., Northwestern U., 1966. With Gen. Foods Corp., White Plains, NY, 1966—, assoc. dir. corp. planning, 1975-76, category mgr., 1976-78, mktg. mgr., 1978-80, v.p., gen. mgr. breakfast foods div., 1980-83; group v.p. Oscar Mayer Co., Madison, Wis., 1982—; dir. Ellenco, Inc., Brentwood, Md., north St. Capital Corp., White Plains. Episcopalian. Clubs: Winged Foot Golf (Mamaroneck, N.Y.); Maple Bluff Country (Madison). Office: Oscar Mayer Co 910 Mayer Ave Madison WI 53707

KORACH, MALCOLM, chemical company executive; b. N.Y.C., Apr. 25, 1922; s. Dean and Viola (Weinberg) K.; m. Gloria Sybil Harris, June 16, 1946; children: Alice Florence, Laura Maurice, Diane Louise. B.S., Yale U., 1942, Ph.D., 1949; student, Advanced Mgmt. Program, Harvard U., 1966. Research asst. Manhattan Dist. project Columbia U., 1943; research chemist Tenn. Eastman, Oak Ridge, 1944-46; research chemist, group leader, asst. dir. research, dir. research Chem. div. PPG Industries, Corpus Christi, Tex., 1949-74, mgr. research Indsl. Chem. div., Pitts., 1974-81; sr. scientist PPG Industries, Barberton, Ohio, 1982—; chmn. adv. com. Pa. Acad. Sci., 1978-81. Chmn. planning com. United Fund of Corpus Christi, 1965-66; pres. Temple Beth El, Corpus Christi, 1961-63. Served with U.S. Army, 1944-46. Mem. Am. Chem. Soc., Pa. Acad. Sci. Republican. Patentee in field. Office: PO Box 31 Barberton OH 44203

KORANYI, ADAM, educator; b. Szeged, Hungary, July 13, 1932; came to U.S., 1957, naturalized, 1963; s. Jeno and Vilma (Szigethy) K.; m. Anna Eiben, Mar. 16, 1968; children—Peter, Daniel. Diploma, U. Szeged, 1954; Ph.D., U. Chgo., 1959. Instr. Harvard, 1959-60; asst. prof. U. Calif. at Berkeley, 1960-64; vis. asst. prof. Princeton, 1964-65; faculty Belfer Grad. Sch. Sci., Yeshiva U., N.Y.C., 1965-79, prof. math., 1968-79, Washington U., St. Louis, 1979—. Contbr. articles to profl. jours. Mem. Am. Math. Soc. Office: Washington U Saint Louis MO 63130

KORB, LAWRENCE JOSEPH, government official; b. N.Y.C., July 9, 1939; s. Joseph Anthony and Katherine Veronica K.; children: Mary Katherine, Karen, Julia, Lawrence Joseph. B.A., Athenaeum Ohio, Norwood, 1961; M.A., St. John's U., Jamaica, N.Y., 1962; Ph.D., SUNY, Albany, 1969. Asst. prof. polit. sci. U. Dayton, 1969-71; asso. prof. govt. USCG Acad., 1971-75; prof. mgmt. U.S. Naval War Coll., 1975-70; adj. prof. Georgtown U., 1980—; resident dir. def. policy studies Am. Enterprise Inst. Public Policy Studies, 1980-81; asst. sec. for manpower, res. affairs and logistics Dept. Def., Washington, 1981—. Author: The Joint Chiefs of Staff: The First Twnety-Five Years, 1976, The Fall and Rise of the Pentagon, 1979. Served with USN, 1962-66; Vietnam. Mem. Council Fgn. Relations. Republican. Roman Catholic. Office: ASD/MRA&L Room 3E808 The Pentagon Washington DC 20301 *The foundation of good public policy is the free and open competition of ideas.*

KORB, WILLIAM BROWN, JR., manufacturing company executive; b. Warren, Pa., Apr. 27, 1940; s. William Brown and Helen (Haslett) K.; m. Dorothy Wendell Trout, June 11, 1962; children: Karen Michel, David Wendell, Christine Leigh. B.S. in Indsl. Engring, Pa. State U., 1962; grad., Advanced Mgmt. Program, Harvard U., 1979. With Reliance Electric Co. div. Exxon, 1962—, gen. mgr. mech. group, Mishawaka, Ind., 1977-79, operating v.p., Cleve., 1979—; dir., chmn. bd. Fed. Pioneer Ltd.; dir. Fed. Pacific de Mex. Bd. dirs. Jr. Achievement South Bend, Ind., 1979—. Mem. Am. Mgmt. Assn. Republican. Presbyterian. Club: Harvard Bus. Sch. (Chgo.). Home: 600 Falls Rd Chagrin Falls OH 44022 Office: 29325 Chagrin Blvd Cleveland OH 44122

KORBEL, JOHN JOSEPH, economics educator; b. Havana, Cuba, Dec. 13, 1918; came to U.S., 1918; s. Mario Joseph and Hilda (Beyer) K.; m. Isobel Albrecht, June 9, 1952; children: Wendy Korbel Kelly, Mark, Peter Hall, Peter John. S.B., Harvard U., 1939, M.B.A., 1941, Ph.D., 1959. Instr. Lafayette Coll., 1949-50; research asso. Computation Center, MIT, 1956-59; asst. prof. econs. U. Wis., 1960-66, asst. dean grad. sch., 1964-66; prof. econs. U. N.H., 1966—. Author: (with Orcutt, Greenberger and Rivlin) Microanalysis of Socioeconomic Systems, 1961; contbr.: Human Rescources in the Urban Economy (Mark Perlman, editor), 1963; contbr. to also articles to profl. jours. Served as lt. USNR, 1941-45. Mem. Am. Econ. Assn. Home: Box 614 Durham NH 03824

KORBELIK, GEORGE JOSEPH, mfg. co. exec.; b. Prague, Czechoslovakia, July 10, 1925; s. Josef and Antonie (Rebitzer) K.; m. Mary Helen Hardwicke, Sept. 29, 1951; children—Robert Bryan, Jill Elaine, David John. J.U.C., Charles U. Law Sch., Prague, 1947; B.B.A., U. Tex. at Austin, 1951. Sales rep. U.S. Steel Co., 1951-53; mgr. market devel. Marsh Steel Co., 1954; with Butler Mfg. Co., Kansas City, Mo., 1954-78, market analyst, 1954-63, gen. mgr. div. transp. equipment, 1963-67, group v.p., 1967-73, sr. v.p., dir., 1973-78; pres., chief exec. officer Premier Pneumatics, Inc., 1978-79. Pres. bd. dirs. Rehab. Inst.; trustee U. Mo., Kansas City. Mem. Truck Trailer Mfrs. Assn. (dir.), Am. Mgmt. Assn. Clubs: Kansas City, Homestead Country. Home: 3316 W 69th St Shawnee Mission KS 66208

KORCHNOY, EMANUEL ALLEN, advertising executive; b. Rochester, N.Y., Mar. 31, 1915; s. Michael and Rose (Salen) K.; m. Theda Roshkow, Dec. 29, 1940. B.S.E., CCNY, 1939. Mng. editor, pub. Apparel Arts, Bridegroom mags., 1942-49; sales promotion dir. Esquire, Coronet mags., 1942-49; pres. Hat Research Found., 1949-52; v.p. sales and advt. Frank H. Lee Co., 1952-55; pres. E.A. Korchnoy, N.Y.C., 1955—; pres. Three Eyes Art Soc., N.Y.C., 1966-69, chmn. bd., 1969—. Recipient Research Inst. Am. award, 1953; Brand Names Found. award, 1955; Ann. Printing awards N.Y. Employing Printers Assn., 1959-75; Point of Purchase Advt. Inst. Merchandising award, 1961, 71; Andy advt. excellence award, 1975; Andy and Clio advt. excellence awards, 1981. Mem. Philharmonic Soc., Met. Opera Guild, David Friend Art Soc., Chevaliers du Tastevin. Club: Rolling Hills Country (Wilton, Conn.). Home: 4601 Henry Hudson Pkwy Bronx NY 10471 Office: 120 E 56th St New York NY 10022

KORDA, MICHAEL VINCENT, publishing company executive; b. London, Eng., Oct. 8, 1933; s. Vincent and Gertrude (Musgrove) K.; m. Carolyn Keese, Apr. 16, 1958; 1 son, Christopher Vincent. B.A., Magdalen Coll., 1958. With Simon and Schuster, N.Y.C., 1958—, successively editor, sr. editor, mng. editor, exec. editor, now sr. v.p., editor-in-chief. Author: Male Chauvinism How It Works, 1973, Power: How to Get It, How To Use It, 1975, Success!, 1977, Charmed Lives, 1979, Worldly Goods, 1982. Served with RAF, 1952-54. Mem. Nat. Soc. Film Critics, Am. Horse Shows Assn. Club: Coffee House (N.Y.C.). Office: Simon and Schuster 1230 Ave of Americas New York NY 10020 *

KORDA, REVA (MRS. WILLIAM KORDA), advertising executive; b. N.Y.C., Dec. 24, 1926; d. Louis and Yetta (Sussman) Fine; m. William Korda, Sept. 7, 1957; children: Joshua, Natasha. B.A. magna cum laude, Hunter Coll., 1947. Copywriter, Gimbels, N.Y.C., 1949-50; Copywriter Macy's, N.Y.C., 1951-53; with Ogilvy & Mather, Inc., N.Y.C., 1953-80, writer, 1953-62, sr. v.p., 1962-74, exec. v.p., 1974-80, creative head, 1974-80; dir. Ogilvy & Mather Internat., 1975-80; chmn. Korda Rand Levine Inc., N.Y.C., 1981-83, Reva Korda Cons., Inc., 1984—. Mem. Phi Beta Kappa. Home: 40 W 15th St New York NY 10011

KORDALSKI, ANTHONY TADAUSZ, retail department store executive; b. Cleve., Nov. 15, 1926; s. Walter and Zofia (Obrzydowski) K.; m. Nova Jane Brown, Apr. 12, 1951; children: Steven Anthony, John David. B.A., Western Res. U., 1949. Salesman, asst. buyer Sterling Lindner, Cleve., 1949-55, buyer, 1955-59, mdse. mgr., 1959-62, Higbee's Dept. Store, 1962-71, v.p., 1971-77, sr. v.p., 1977—. Served with USN, 1945-46. Republican. Presbyterian. Lodge: Rotary. Office: Higbee's Dept Stores 100 Public Sq Cleveland OH 44113

KORDISCH, LARRY WESLEY, food distbn. co. exec.; b. Chgo., Sept. 23, 1947; s. Raymond K. and Alice K.; m. Jan K. Graue, Jan. 25, 1969; children—Lane, Lindsey. B.S. in Fin, U. Colo., 1969. Fin. analyst Cities Service Oil Co., 1969-73; asst. treas. Fleming Cos., Inc.,

1972-78; treas. Scrivner, Inc., Oklahoma City, 1978—. Vice pres. fin. Oklahoma City Beautiful, 1979—. Served with USMCR, 1969-75. Club: Rotary. Address: Scrivner Inc 1301 SE 59th St Oklahoma City OK 73126

KOREN, EDWARD BENJAMIN, cartoonist, educator; b. N.Y.C., Dec. 13, 1935; s. Harry L. and Elizabeth (Sorkin) K.; Catherine Ingham; children: Nathaniel, Alexandra. B.A., Columbia U., 1957; student, Atelier 17, Paris, 1957-59; M.F.A., Pratt Inst., 1964; D.H.L. (hon.), Union Coll., 1984. Cartoonist New Yorker mag., N.Y.C., 1962—; mem. faculty Brown U., 1964—, asso. prof. art, 1969-77, adj. assoc. prof., 1977—; mem. bd. advisors Swann Collection Caricature and Cartoon. One-man travelling exhbn., Art Gallery, SUNY-Albany, 1982; exhibited in various shows, including, Exposition Dessins d'Humeur, Soc. Protectrice d'Humeur, Avignon, France, 1973, Biennale Illustration, Bratislav, Czechoslovakia, Art from the New York Times, Soc. Illustr., N.Y.C., Art from the New Yorker, Grolier Club, 1975, Terry Dintinfass Gallery, N.Y.C., 1975-77, 79; work appears in, Fogg Mus., Princeton U. Mus., R.I. Sch. Design Mus., Swann Collection Cartoon and Caricature; contbr.: drawings to various publs., including Nation, Time, Newsweek, Fortune, N.Y. Times, Sports Illustrated, Vogue, Vanity Fair; Illustrator: Don't Talk to Strange Bears, 1969, The People Maybe, 1974, Cooking for Crowds, 1975, Noodles Galore, 1977, How to Eat Like a Child, 1978, Dragons Hate to be Discrete, 1978, Teenage Romance, 1981; author's illustrator: Behind The Wheel, 1972; author: Do You Want to Talk About It?, 1977, Are You Happy?, 1978, Well, There's Your Problem, 1980, Caution, Small Ensembles, 1983. John Simon Guggenheim fellow, 1970-71. Mem. Author's League, Soc. Am. Graphic Artists. Office: care New Yorker Mag 25 W 43d St New York NY 10036

KOREN, HENRY JOSEPH, educator, priest; b. Roermond, Netherlands, Dec. 30, 1912; came to U.S., 1948, naturalized, 1954; s. Gerard Hubert and Anna Catherina (Smolenaers) K. Student, Coll. Roermond, 1924-30, Sem. of Gemert, 1932-35; S.T.B., Gregorian U., Rome, 1937, S.T.L., 1939; S.T.D., Cath. U. Am., 1941. Joined Holy Ghost Congregation, 1932; ordained priest Roman Cath. Ch., 1937; tchr. St. Mary's Coll., Trinidad, W.I., 1941-48; mem. faculty Duquesne U., 1948-66, prof. philosophy, 1958-66, chmn. dept. philosophy, 1954-65, chmn. dept. theology, 1962-66; prof. philosophy St. Leo (Fla.) Coll., 1967-77. Editor: Duquesne Studies, 1951-77; editor emeritus, 1977—; Author: Introduction to Science of Metaphysics, 1955, Introduction to Philosophy of Animate Nature, 1955, The Spiritans, 1958, Spiritual Writings of Claude Francis Poullart des Places, 1959, Introduction to Philosophy of Nature, 1960, Knaves or Knights?, 1962, Research in Philosophy, 1966, Marx and the Authentic Man, 1968, (with William A. Luijpen) A First Introduction to Existential Phenomenology, 1969, Religion and Atheism, 1971, To the Ends of the Earth, 1983, A Spiritan Who Was Who in North America and Trinidad 1732-1981, 1983; Editor: Readings in Philosophy of Nature, 1959; gen. editor: Spiritana Monumenta Historica, 1967-76. Address: PO Box 2328 St Leo FL 33574

KORENMAN, STANLEY GEORGE, medical investigator, educator; b. N.Y.C., Jan. 21; s. Morris and Theresa (Viess) K.; m. Rinah Esther Tofield, Dec. 23, 1956; children: Julia, Linda, Sanders. A.B. summa cum laude, Princeton, 1954; M.D., Columbia, 1958. Intern Bellevue and Meml. Hosp., N.Y.C., 1958-59, resident, 1959-61; clin. asso. endocrine br. Nat. Cancer Inst., 1961-63, sr. investigator, 1963-66; asst. prof. medicine U. Calif. at Los Angeles Med. Sch., 1966-69, asso. prof., 1969-70; prof. medicine and biochemistry, chief div. endocrinology Coll. Medicine, U. Iowa, Iowa City, 1970-74; chief div. endocrinology VA Hosp., Iowa City, 1970-74; prof., chmn. dept. medicine UCLA San Fernando Valley Program, 1974—; also assoc. dean UCLA Sch. Medicine; chief med. services VA Med. Center. Served with USPHS, 1961-64. Recipiant research grants Am. Cancer Soc., NIH, VA. Fellow A.C.P.; mem. Endocrine Soc., Am. Soc. Clin. Investigation, Assn. Am. Physicians, Soc. Study Reproduction, Central, Western socs. clin. research, Am. Soc. Biol. Chemists, Am. Fedn. Clin. Research. Research on mechanisms of hormone action, clin. reproductive endocrinology. Home: 1510 N Amalfi Pacific Palisades CA 90272 Office: 16111 Plummer St Sepulveda CA 91343

KOREY, LOIS BALK, advertising executive; b. N.Y.C., May 19, 1933; d. Samuel and Lillian (Rosenblatt) Balk; m. Stanton Korey, Jan. 12, 1958 (div.); children—Susan, Christopher. Student, N.Y. U., 1951-52. Jr. partner Jack Tinker & Partners Advt. Co., N.Y.C., 1964-66; jr. partner, copywriter McCann Erickson Advt. Co., N.Y.C., 1967-69; creative dir. Revlon, N.Y.C., 1972; exec. v.p., creative dir. Needham, Harper & Steers Advt., Inc., N.Y.C., 1973-82; pres. Korey, Kay & Ptnrs., Advt., N.Y.C., 1982—. Writer: TV shows including Sunday Night Comedy Hour; (Recipient 18 Clios, Am. TV Comml. Festivals: 8 Andys, Advt. Club N.Y., Cannes Film Festival TV Comml. award 1973, 10 Hollywood Film Festival awards.); Contbr. articles to mags. and profl. jours. Mem. Writers Guild Am., Dramatists Guild. Office: 15 E 75th St New York NY 10021

KORFF, SERGE ALEXANDER, educator, physicist; b. Helsingfors, Finland, June 5, 1906; U.S., 1917; s. Baron Serge A. and Alletta (Van Reypen) K.; m. Marcella Brett. A.B., Princeton U., 1928, A.M., 1929, Ph.D., 1931. Nat. Research fellow Mt. Wilson Obs. and Calif. Inst. Tech., 1931-33; research fellow Calif. Inst. Tech., 1934-35; fellow Bartol Research Found., Swarthmore, Pa., 1937-40; research asso. Carnegie Instn., Washington, 1936-46, U. P.R., 1949-50; asst. prof. physics NYU, 1941-44, asso. prof., 1944-46, prof., 1946-72, prof. emeritus, 1973—; nat. lectr. Sigma Xi, 1957; hon. prof. in cosmic radiation Universidad de San Andres, Bolivia, 1958; cons. UN, AEC, 1950-53; sr. sci. adviser atomic energy div. UN, 1953-55; leader cosmic ray expdn., Mexico and Peru, 1934-36, P.R., 1948-50; asso. astronomer Eclipse expdn., Peru, 1937; adviser U.S. Antarctic Service expdn., 1939-41; wartime supr. physics research NYU; del. 5th S.Am. Congress of Chemistry, Lima, Peru, 1951, 6th Congress Chemistry, Caracas, Venezuela, 1955; vice chmn. Cosmic Ray Tech. Panel, U.S. Nat. Commn. for Internat. Geophys. Year, also U.S. del. to meetings, Rome, 1954, Mexico, 1955, Rio de Janeiro, 1956; mem. IUBS Com. on High Altitude Research Stas. and editor of reports. Author: Electron and Nuclear Counters, 1945, (with J.B. Hoag) Electron and Nuclear Physics, 1947; also numerous articles in tech. jours.; editorial bd.: Rev. Sci. Instruments, 1945-51, Explorers Jour., 1946—. Trustee, Embry-Riddle Aero. U., 1975—. Recipient OSRD citation; decorated chevalier Legion of Honor, 1952; commendatore Order of Cyprus and Jerusalem, 1952; hon. mem. faculty U. Chile, 1951; recipient Pregel prize N.Y. Acad. Scis., 1955; Curie medal Union Internat. Contre le Cancer, 1957; decorated comdr. Order of Merit for Research, 1957, grand officer, 1966; comdr. Order of St. Denis, 1968. Fellow Am. Phys. Soc., Royal Geog. Soc. (life), N.Y. Acad. Scis. (life; v.p. 1948-49, pres. 1972), AAAS (life), Am. Geog. Soc. (council, pres. 1967-71, chmn. council 1972—); mem. Lima Geog. Soc. (hon.), Am. Astron. Soc., Peruvian Chem. Soc. (corr.), Am. Geophys. Union (life), World Acad. Art and Scis. (pres. Am. div. 1977—), Explorers Club (pres. 1955-58, dir.), Phi Beta Kappa, Sigma Xi (pres., v.p. NYU chpt. 1946-50), Sigma Pi Sigma (hon. mem.). Clubs: Princeton, Century Assn. (N.Y.C.); Cosmos (Washington). Home: 333 E 68th St New York NY 10021 *Those of us who, for whatever reason, have had the good fortune to achieve some success in life have a clear obligation to make our talent available to the scientific and other institutions, including the government if asked, for the common good of all our colleagues and fellow citizens.*

KORG, JACOB, English educator; b. N.Y.C., Nov. 21, 1922; s. Reuben and Mary (Lehrman) K.; m. Cynthia Stewart, Jan. 21, 1952; 1 dau., Nora Francis. B.A., CCNY, 1943; M.A., Columbia U., 1947, Ph.D., 1952. Instr. English Bard Coll., 1947-49, CCNY, 1950-55; from asst. prof. to prof. U. Wash., Seattle, 1955-68, prof. English, 1970—, U. Md., 1968-70. Author: George Gissing, A Critical Biography, 1963, Dylan Thomas, 1965, Language in Modern Literature, 1979, Browning and Italy, 1983; also articles, revs.; Editor: London in Dickens' Day, 1960, George Gissing's Commonplace Book, 1962, The Force of Few Words, 1966, Twentieth Century Views of Bleak House, 1968, Poetry of Robert Browning, 1971; co-editor: George Gissing on Fiction, 1978; editorial bd.: Modern Lang. Quar., 1971—, Victorian Poetry, 1979—. Served with AUS, 1943-46. Mem. AAUP, Modern Lang. Assn., Internat. Assn. U. Profs. English. Home: 6530 51st Ave NE Seattle WA 98115 Office: Dept English Univ Wash Seattle WA 98195

KORKOWSKI, ROBERT JOSEPH, brewing company treasurer; b. Evansville, Minn., Jan. 24, 1941; s. Frank Michael and Mary Genevieve (Freske) K.; m. Phyllis Marie Culhane, Dec. 29, 1962; children: Susan Marie, Timothy John, Karen Lynn, Beth Ann. B.A. in Acctg., Coll. St. Thomas, St. Paul, 1963. Accountant Arthur Andersen & Co., Mpls., 1963-74; treas., v.p. finance G. Heileman Brewing Co., LaCrosse, Wis., 1974—, exec. v.p. finance, asst. sec., 1979—; dir. First Nat Bank LaCrosse. Bd. dirs. St. Francis Med. Center, LaCrosse. Mem. Greater LaCrosse C. of C. (dir., past pres.). Address: G Heileman Brewing Co Inc 100 Harborview Plaza La Crosse WI 54601

KORMAN, BARBARA, artist, educator; b. N.Y.C., Apr. 8, 1938; d. David and Rose K. B.F.A. cum laude, N.Y. State Coll. Ceramics, 1959, M.F.A., 1960. Tchr. sculpture, design N.Y.C. Bd. Edn., 1961—; photographer, producer audio-visual ednl. packages, 1973—; free lance sculptor, 1961—. (Recipient awards and prizes for sculpture and art edn.), Group shows include, Albright-Knox Gallery, Buffalo, Rochester (N.Y.) Meml. Art Gallery, Bronx (N.Y.) Mus. Art, Met. Mus. Art, N.Y.C., Hudson River Mus., Yonkers, N.Y. Mem. Nat. Assn. Women Artists, Bronx Council Arts, Hudson River Contemporary Artists. Address: 357 E 201st St New York NY 10458

KORMAN, EDWARD R., lawyer; b. N.Y.C., Oct. 25, 1942; s. Julius and Miriam K.; m. Diane R. Eisner, Feb. 3, 1979; children: Miriam M., Benjamin E. B.A., Bklyn. Coll., 1963; LL.B., Bklyn. Law Sch., 1966; LL.M., NYU, 1971. Bar: N.Y. 1966, U.S. Supreme Ct. 1972. Law clk. to asso. judge N.Y. Ct. Appeals, 1966-68; assoc. Paul, Weiss, Rifkind, Wharton and Garrison, 1968-70; asst. U.S. atty. Eastern Dist. N.Y., N.Y.C., 1970-72; asst. to Solicitor Gen. of U.S., 1972-74; chief asst. U.S. atty. Eastern Dist. N.Y., 1974-78, U.S. atty., 1978-82; ptnr. Stroock & Stroock & Lavan, N.Y.C., 1982—. Chmn. Mayor's Com. on N.Y.C. Marshals, 1983—; mem. Temporary Commn. of Investigation of State of N.Y., 1983—. Mem. Fed. Bar Council, Assn. Bar City N.Y. Democrat. Jewish. Office: 7 Hanover Sq New York NY 10004

KORMAN, HARVEY HERSCHEL, actor; b. Chgo., Feb. 15, 1927; s. Cyril Raymond and Ellen (Blecher) K.; m. Donna Ehlert, Aug. 27, 1960; children—Maria Ellen, Christopher Peter. Student, Goodman Theatre, 1946-50. Actor: TV series The Danny Kaye Show, 1963-67, Carol Burnett Show, 1967—; appeared in: films April Fools, 1969, Blazing Saddles, 1974, High Anxiety, 1978, Americathon, 1979, History of the World, Part I, 1981; (Recipient 4 Emmy awards for Best Variety Performer.). Served with USNR, 1945-46. Office: care Singer and Lewak 10960 Wilshire Blvd Los Angeles CA 90024

KORMAN, JESS J., advertising executive; b. N.Y.C., Sept. 16, 1933; s. Rubin and Beatrice K. B.A., NYU, 1955. Copywriter Batten, Barton, Durstine and Osborne, Inc., N.Y.C., 1956-59; copy group head Grey Advt., N.Y.C., 1962; free lance TV writer, playwright, 1963-69; v.p., assoc. creative dir. J. Walter Thompson Co., N.Y.C., 1969-77, sr. v.p., exec. creative dir., Los Angeles, 1978-80; pres. Jess Korman Industries, TV devel., communications cons., 1980—; sr. v.p. Benton & Bowles, Inc., N.Y.C., 1983—. Writer numerous TV shows, mag. articles. Mem. Dramatists Guild Am., Writers Guild Am. Office: Benton & Bowles Inc 909 3d Ave New York NY 10022

KORMAN, NATHANIEL IRVING, research and devel. co. exec.; b. Providence, Feb. 23, 1916; s. William and Tillie (Jacobs) K.; m. Ruth C. Kaplan, Apr. 6, 1941; children—Michael, Robert. B.S. summa cum laude, Worcester Poly. Inst., 1937; M.S. (Coffin fellow), M.I.T., 1938; Ph.D., U. Pa., 1958. Engr., dir. advanced mil. systems RCA Corp., 1938-67; pres., chief exec. officer Ventures Research and Devel. Group, Princeton, N.J., 1968—; chmn. radar panel U.S. Research and Devel. Bd., 1948-56; lectr. U. Pa. Evening Grad. Sch., 1967-68. Mem. Citizens Com. for Better Schs., Moorestown, N.J., 1958. Recipient Award of Merit RCA, 1951. Fellow IEEE; mem. Sigma Xi. Patentee in field. Home and Office: 371 Riverside Dr Princeton NJ 08540

KORMONDY, EDWARD JOHN, university official, biology educator; b. Beacon, N.Y., June 10, 1926; s. Anthony and Frances (Glover) K.; m. Peggy Virginia Hedrick, June 5, 1950; children: Lynn Ellen, Eric Paul, Mark Hedrick. B.S. in Biology, Tusculum Coll., 1950; M.S. in Zoology, U. Mich., 1951, Ph.D., 1955. Teaching fellow U. Mich., 1952-55; instr. zoology, curator insects Mus. Zoology, 1955-57; asst. prof. Oberlin (Ohio) Coll., 1957-69, asso. prof., 1963-67, prof., 1967-69, acting asso. dean, 1966-67; dir. Commn. Undergrad. Edn. in Biol. Scis., Washington, 1968-72, Office. Biol. Edn., Am. Inst. Biol. Scis., 1968-71; mem. faculty Evergreen State Coll., Olympia, Wash., 1971-79, interim acting dean, 1972-73, v.p., provost, 1973-78; sr. profl. assoc., directorate sci. edn. NSF, 1979; provost, prof. biology U. So. Maine, Portland, 1979-82; v.p. acad. affairs, prof. biology Calif. State U., Los Angeles, 1982—. Author: Concepts of Ecology, 1969, 76, General Biology: The Integrity and Natural History of Organisms, 1977, Handbook of Contemporary World Developments in Ecology, 1981; high school textbook Biology; contbr. articles to profl. jours. Served with USN, 1944-46. U. Ga. postdoctoral fellow radiation ecology, 1963-64; vis. research fellow Center for Bioethics, Georgetown U., 1978-79; research grantee Nat. Acad. Scis., Am. Philos. Soc., NSF, Sigma Xi. Mem. AAAS, Ecol. Soc. Am. (sec. 1976-78), Nat. Assn. Biology Tchrs. (pres. 1981), Sigma Xi. Home: 1388 Lucile Ave Los Angeles CA 90026 Office: Office Vice Pres Acad Affairs Calif State Univ 5151 State University Dr Los Angeles CA 90032

KORN, BERNARD, corporation executive, accountant, real estate broker, insurance broker; b. Bklyn., Apr. 9, 1925; s. Samuel and Sarah (Weinstein) K.; m. Irene Weinberger, Dec. 12, 1948; children: Steven Jay, Jonathan Edward. B.S. in Acctg., L.I. U., 1948, L.H.D. (hon.), 1979. C.P.A., N.Y.; lic. real estate broker, N.Y.; lic. ins. broker, N.Y. Ptnr. Lazarus and Korn, Rockville Centre, N.Y., 1950-59; exec. v.p. Coburn Credit Corp., Rockville Centre, 1957-64; chmn., chief exec. officer Colonial Comml. Corp., Valley Stream, N.Y., 1964—; cons. to instl. lenders to consumer fin. industry. Trustee Children's Med. Center, New Hyde Park, N.Y., 1971—; dir. Am. Cancer Soc., L.I. div., 1972—. Served with U.S. Army, 1943-45. Mem. Am. Inst. C.P.A.s, N.Y. State Soc. C.P.A.s. Democrat. Jewish. Club: Nassau Yacht (Freeport, N.Y.) (commodore 1978-79). Office: Colonial Commercial Corp Colonial Commercial Bldg Valley Stream NY 11581

KORN, DAVID, educator, government consultant; b. Kolbuszowa, Poland, Apr. 27, 1934; came to U.S., 1950, naturalized, 1954; s. Joseph and Sunia (Neiss) K.; m. Maria Orgel, June 25, 1961; children—Joseph Mark, Monique Diane. Student, Bklyn. Coll., 1955-56; B.S., Georgetown U., 1958, M.S., 1960, Ph.D. (Nat. Def. Edn. Act fellow), 1964. Asst. prof., dir. lang. labs. Coll. William and Mary, Norfolk, Va., 1959-61; research assoc. Machine Translation Computer, Georgetown U., 1956-62; chmn. humanities div. Howard U., 1962—; prof., chmn. German-Russian dept., 1967-78, on leave, 1981—; lectr. Fgn. Service Inst., Dept. State; cons. on Russian textbooks U.S. Armed Forces Inst.; asso. dir. Council on Internat. Student Ednl. Exchange in USSR, 1968; sr. cons. Office Asst. Sec. for Edn., Dept. Health, Edn. and Welfare, 1973—; spl. asst. to Sec. of State Alexander M. Haig, Jr., in charge of Eastern Europe, USSR, and spl. interest groups, Washington, 1981—; coordinator external programs Dept. of State, 1982-83. Author various machine translations in field; contbr. articles and book revs. to profl. jours. Exec. com. Jewish Community Council Greater Washington, 1972-74; also chmn. Soviet Jewry Com.; Bd. dirs. Jewish Social Service Agy. Served to 2d lt. AUS, 1953-55. Recipient Key to City Norfolk. Mem. Modern Lang. Assn., Linguistic Soc. Am., Am. Assn. Tchrs. Slavic and East European Langs. (chpt. pres.), Georgetown U. Alumni Orgn. (gov., mem. exec. com., v.p. for Sch. Langs. and Linguistics), B'nai B'rith.

KORN, DAVID, educator, pathologist; b. Providence, Mar. 5, 1933; s. Solomon and Claire (Liebman) K.; m. Phoebe Richter, June 9, 1955; children: Michael Philip, Stephen James, Daniel Clair. B.A., Harvard U., 1954, M.D., 1959. Intern Mass. Gen. Hosp., Boston, 1959-60, resident, 1960-61; research asso. NIH, 1961-63; mem. staff Lab. Biochem. Pharmacology; also asst. pathologist NIH, 1963-68; prof., chmn. dept. pathology Sch. Medicine, Stanford, 1968—; physician-in-chief pathology Stanford Hosp., 1968—; cons. pathology Palo Alto VA Hosp., 1968—; sr. surgeon USPHS, 1961-66; mem. cell biology study sect. NIH, 1973-77, chmn., 1976-77; mem. bd. sci. counselors, div. cancer biology and diagnosis Nat. Cancer Inst., 1977-82, chmn., 1980-82. Mem. editorial bd.: Human Pathology, 1969-74; asso. editor, 1974—; mem. editorial bd.: Jour. Biol. Chemistry, 1973-79. Recipient Young Scientist award Md. Acad. Sci., 1967. Mem. Am. Soc. Biol. Chemists, Am. Assn. Pathologists, Am. Soc. Cell Biology, Am. Soc. Microbiology, N.Y. Acad. Sci., AAAS. Home: 905 Estudillo Rd Stanford CA 94305

KORN, HAROLD LEON, legal educator; b. Bronx, N.Y., June 25, 1929; s. Jacob and Nettie (Wurzel) K. A.B., Cornell U., 1951; J.D., Columbia U., 1954. Bar: N.Y. 1955. Law clk. to judge N.Y. State Ct. Appeals, 1954-56; dir. research Adv. Com. on Practice and Procedure of N.Y. State Temporary Commn. on the Cts., 1956-60; lectr. law Columbia U. Law Sch., N.Y.C., 1962-64; prof. law SUNY, Buffalo, 1965-68, N.Y. U., 1968-71, Columbia U. Law Sch., 1971—; cons. evidence code N.Y. State Law Revision Commn., 1976-80. Author: (with Jack B. Weinstein and Arthur R. Miller) New York Civil Practice, 1962, (with Albert J. Rosenthal and Stanley B. Lubman) Catastrophic Accidents in Government Programs, 1963, (with others) Elements of Civil Procedure, 3d edit, 1976. Bd. dirs. Mobilization for Youth, 1974-76; bd. dirs. Columbia Found. for Public Interest Law, 1979—. Mem. N.Y. State Bar Assn., Assn. Bar City of N.Y. Democrat. Jewish. Home: 160 E 65th St New York NY 10021 Office: Columbia Law Sch New York NY 10027

KORN, LESTER BERNARD, business executive; b. N.Y.C., Jan. 11, 1936. B.S., UCLA, 1957, M.B.A., 1959; postgrad., Harvard Bus. Sch., 1960. Partner Peat, Marwick, Mitchell & Co., N.Y.C., 1961-69; chmn., co-founder, dir. Korn/Ferry Internat., Los Angeles, 1969—; dir. Continental Am. Mgmt. Corp., Josephson Internat. Inc., Leisure Tech. Corp., First Beverly Bank. Bd. dirs., treas. NCCJ; trustee UCLA Found.; Bd. dirs. City of Hope Med. Center; bd. overseers Grad. Sch. Mgmt., UCLA; trustee, founding mem. Dean's Council UCLA; bd. govs. Cedars-Sinai Med. Center; bd. councilors Grad. Sch. Bus. Adminstrn. and Sch. Bus., U. So. Calif.; adv. bd. Women in Film Found.; chmn. Commn. on Citizen Participation in Govt., State of Calif. Mem. Am. Bus. Conf. Clubs: Hillcrest Country, Los Angeles Athletic, Regency, Los Angeles Country; Board Room (N.Y.C.). Office: 277 Park Ave New York NY 10017 Office: 1900 Ave of the Stars Los Angeles CA 90067

KORN, PHILIP A., food co. exec.; b. N.Y.C., Nov. 17, 1930; s. Morris and Sadie (Albrecht) K.; m. Kay Susan Pollock, Dec. 24, 1950; children—Abner Paul, Ann Millicent. B.B.A., Coll. City N.Y., 1951; M.B.A., N.Y. U., 1956. Mgr. financial analysis Gen. Foods Corp., White Plains, N.Y., 1961-62, asso. product mgr., 1965-67, sales devel. mgr., 1967-68, region mgr., 1968-69, adminstrv. asst. to pres., 1969, field sales mgr., 1969-70, nat. sales mgr., 1970, v.p., 1970—; also exec. v.p. Burger Chef Systems, Inc., Indpls., 1970-71, pres., 1972-77, v.p. corp. purchasing and materials mgmt., 1977-80, v.p., group exec. purchasing, materials mgmt. and distbn., 1980—. Trustee Council for Arts in Westchester. Served as cpl., Finance Corps AUS, 1952-54. Home: 14 Berrybrook Circle Chappaqua NY 10514 Office: 250 North St White Plains NY 10625

KORN, ROY JOSEPH, educator, physician; b. Chgo., July 25, 1920; s. Isaac Emanuel and Anna Amanda (Andersson) K.; m. Elsie Ann Kral, Jan. 15, 1955; children: Steven Arthur, Roy Joseph, Michael R., Patricia Ann. B.S., Northwestern U., 1942, M.D., 1946. Diplomate: Am. Bd. Internal Medicine. Intern Wesley Meml. Hosp., Chgo., 1945-46; resident VA Hosp., Hines, Ill., 1949-51; chief med. service VA West Side Hosp., Chgo., 1958-62, chief staff, 1972—; adv. prof. faculty medicine Chiengmai (Thailand) U., 1962-64; asso. prof. U. Ill. Med. Sch., Chgo., 1959-64; prof. Chgo. Med. Sch., 1964; prof. medicine U. Ind. Med. Sch., 1965-72; chief staff VA Hosp., Indpls., 1965-72; prof. medicine U. Ill. Coll. Medicine, Chgo., 1972—. Served to capt. M.C. AUS, 1946-48. Fellow A.C.P.; mem. Inst. Medicine Chgo., Chgo. Soc. Internal Medicine. Home: 516 N Lincoln Hinsdale IL 60521

KORNBERG, ARTHUR, biochemist; b. N.Y.C., Mar. 3, 1918; s. Joseph and Lena (Katz) K.; m. Sylvy R. Levy, Nov. 21, 1943; children: Roger, Thomas Bill, Kenneth Andrew. B.S. (N.Y. State scholar), CCNY, 1937, LL.D., 1960; M.D. (Buswell scholar), U. Rochester, 1941, D.Sc., 1962; L.H.D., Yeshiva U., 1963; D.Sc., U. Pa., U. Notre Dame, 1965, Washington U., 1968, Princeton U., 1970, Colby Coll., 1970; M.D. (h.c.), U. Barcelona, Italy, 1970. Intern in medicine Strong Meml. Hosp., Rochester, N.Y., 1941-42; commd. officer USPHS, 1942, advanced through grades to med. dir., 1951; mem. staff NIH, Bethesda, Md., 1942-52, nutrition sect., div. physiology, 1942-45; chief sect. enzymes and metabolism Nat. Inst. Arthritis and Metabolic Diseases, 1947-52; guest research worker depts. chemistry and pharmacology coll. medicine N.Y. U., 1946; dept. biol. chemistry med. sch. Washington U., 1947; dept. plant biochemistry U. Calif., 1951; prof., head dept. microbiology, med. sch. Washington U., St. Louis, 1953-59; prof., biochemistry Stanford U. Sch. Medicine, 1959—, chmn. dept., 1959-69; Mem. sci. adv. bd. Mass. Gen. Hosp., 1964-67; bd. govs. Weizmann Inst., Israel. Contbr. sci. articles to profl. jours. Served lt. (j.g.), med. officer USCGR, 1942. Recipient Paul-Lewis award in enzyme chemistry, 1951; co-recipient of Nobel prize in medicine, 1959; Max Berg award prolonging human life, 1968; Sci. Achievement award AMA, 1968; Lucy Wortham James award James Ewing Soc., 1968; Borden award Am. Assn. Med. Colls., 1968. Mem. Am. Soc. Biol. Chemists (pres. 1965), Am. Chem. Soc., Harvey Soc., Am. Acad. Arts and Scis., Royal Soc., Nat. Acad. Scis. (mem. council 1963-66), Am. Philos. Soc., Phi Beta Kappa, Sigma Xi, Alpha Omega

Alpha. Office: Dept Genetics Stanford Univ Sch Medicine Stanford CA 94305 *

KORNBERG, WARREN STANLEY, sci. journalist; b. N.Y.C., June 21, 1927; s. Murray and Helen (Blumberg) K.; m. Felice Sher, June 15, 1952; children—Lisa, Jena, Eva. B.A., Adelphi Coll., 1950; M.A., Columbia, 1952; postgrad., U. Mo., 1954- 55. Reporter Fall River (Mass.) Herald News, 1955-58; sci. editor Boston Herald, 1958-59; sci. reporter Washington Post, 1960-61; Washington corr.-sci. editor McGraw Hill Publs., Washington, 1962-66; editor Sci. News, Sci. News Yearbook, Sci. Service, Washington, 1966-70; writer syndicated column Warren Kornberg on Science, 1969-70; sci. editor pub. affairs NSF, 1970-75; editor Mosaic, NSF, 1975—. Recipient Jesse H. Neal editorial achievement award, 1965; Washington Newspaper Guild front page award, 1961. Home: 11019 Kenilworth Ave Garrett Park MD 20896 Office: 1800 G St NW Washington DC 20550

KORNBLET, DONALD ROSS, public relations executive; b. St. Louis, Nov. 7, 1943; s. Louis Yale and Mildred F. (Levy) K.; m. Ann Louise Vogel, Dec. 30, 1973; children: Ben Michael, David Charles, Sarah Ann. B.A. in History, Yale U., 1966. Dir. pub. info. Urban League of St. Louis, 1968-71; Midwestern dir. Coro Found., St. Louis, 1971-76; v.p., sr, ptnr. Fleishman-Hillard Inc., St. Louis, 1977—. Mem. Chancellor's Council U. Mo.-St. Louis, 1981—; bd. dirs. Washington U. Child Guidance Clinic, 1980, Coro Found. Midwestern Ctr., 1982, Human Devel. Corp., 1981, Consolidated Neighborhood Services, 1983. Served to lt. USNR, 1970-76. Recipient Am. Field Service Fgn. Exchange studentship Denmark, 1961; scholar Yale U., 1962-66; fellow Coro Found., 1966-67; recipient Service medal Opportunities Industrialization Ctr.-St. Louis, 1983. Mem. Pub. Relations Soc. Am. (chpt. dir.). Jewish. Clubs: St. Louis, Yale of St. Louis. Office: One Memorial Dr St Louis MO 63102

KORNBLITH, JOHN HOWARD, business and manufacturing executive; b. Chgo., Oct. 30, 1924; s. Howard and Babette (Straus) K.; M. Ina Jean Russell, June 8, 1944 (div. 1972); children: Cathy R.,Gary J., Polly R.; m. 2d Dorothy Weber, Oct 13, 1982; 1 stepdau., Lisa Goldstein. B.S., U. Chgo., 1947, M.B.A., 1948. Advt. mgr. Eversharp, Inc., Chgo., 1948-50; pres. Cricketeer, Inc., Chgo., 1950-58; exec. v.p. Joseph & Feiss, Cleve., 1958-61; pres. v.p. Fashion Park, Inc., Rochester, N.Y., 1961-67, Intercontinental Apparel, Inc., N.Y.C., 1967-83; chmn., pres. Twenty First Century Corp., Secaucus, N.J., 1959—, dir. Bd. dirs. Nat. Commn. Resources for Youth, N.Y.C., Inst. for Responsive Edn., Boston; mem. bd. visitors, former chmn. Grad Sch. CUNY, N.Y.C.; mem. Bus. council U. Chgo; mem. bus. council N.Y. Assn. Blind, N.Y.C. Served to 1st lt. USAF, 1943-46. Recipient Pres.' medal Grad. Sch. U. Ctr. of CUNY, 1977; mem. Council for Competitive Economy. Jewish. Clubs: N.Y. Athletic (N.Y.C.); East Hampton Tennis (N.Y.). Office: Twenty First Century Corp 116 Seaview Dr Secaucus NJ 07094

KORNEGAY, HORACE ROBINSON, trade association executive, former congressman, lawyer; b. Asheville, N.C., Mar 12, 1924; s. Marvin Earl and Blanche Person (Robinson) K.; m. Annie Ben Beale, Mar. 25, 1950; children: Horace Robinson, Kathryn Elder Kornegay Cozort, Martha Beale Kornegay Howard. B.S., Wake Forest U., 1947, J.D., 1949. Bar: N.C. 1949, D.C. 1979, U.S. Supreme Ct 1979. Practice in, Greensboro; asst. solicitor Superior Ct. Guilford County, 1951-53; dist. solicitor 12th Solicitorial Dist., 1955-60; mem. 87th-90th Congresses from 6th Dist. N.C.; v.p., counsel The Tobacco Inst., Washington, 1969-70, pres., exec. dir., 1970-81, chmn., 1981—. Pres. Guilford Young Democratic Club, 1952, N.C. Young Dem. Clubs, 1953-54; bd. visitors Sch. Law, Wake Forest U.; chmn. adminstrv. bd. Concord-St. Andrew's United Methodist Ch. Served with AUS, 1943-46. Decorated Purple Heart, Bronze Star, Combat Inf. badge. Mem. Am., Fed., N.C., Greensboro bar assns., Am. Judicature Soc., Wake Forest Univ. Lawyers Alumni Assn. (past pres.), SAR, Am. Legion, VFW, Amvets, Royal Brit. Legion (hon.), Alpha Sigma Phi, Phi Delta Phi, Omicron Delta Kappa. Clubs: Masons, Shriners, Rotary, Internat., Lawyers, George Town, Congressional Country (Washington). Home: 7709 Charleston Dr Bethesda MD 20817 Office: 1875 Eye St NW Washington DC 20006

KORNEL, LUDWIG, educator, physician, scientist; b. Jaslo, Poland, Feb. 27, 1923; came to U.S., 1958, naturalized, 1970; s. Ezriel Edward and Ernestine (Karpf) K.; m. Esther Muller, May 27, 1952; children—Ezriel Edward, Amiel Mark. Student, U. Kazan Med. Inst., USSR, 1943-45; M.D., Wroclaw (Poland) Med. Acad., 1950; Ph.D., U. Birmingham, Eng., 1958. Intern Univ. Hosp., Wroclaw, 1949-50, Hadassah-Hebrew U. Hosp., Jerusalem, 1950-51, resident medicine, 1952-55; Brit. Council scholar, Univ. research fellow endocrinology U. Birmingham, 1955-57, lectr. medicine, 1956-57; fellow endocrinology U. Ala. Med. Center, 1958-59, successively asst. prof., asso. prof., prof. medicine, 1961-67, dir. steroid sect., 1962-67, asso. prof. biochemistry, 1965-67; postdoctoral trainee in steroid biochemistry U. Utah, 1959-61; prof. medicine U. Ill. Coll. Medicine, Chgo., 1967-71; dir. steroid unit Presbyn.-St. Lukes Hosp., Chgo., 1967—, asso. biochemist, 1967-70, sr. biochemist on sci. staff, 1970-71, attending physician, 1967-71; prof. medicine and biochemistry Rush Med. Coll., 1970—; sr. attending physician, sr. scientist Rush-Presbyn.-St. Lukes Med. Center, 1970—; hon. guest lectr. Polish Acad. Sci., Warsaw, 1965; vis. prof. Kanazawa (Japan) U., 1973, 82. Editorial bd.: Clin. Physiology and Biochemistry, 1982; Contbr. articles on endocrinology and steroid biochemistry to profl. jours. Recipient Physicians Recognition award AMA, 1969, 73, 76, 81, Outstanding New Citizen award Citizenship Council Met. Chgo., 1970. Fellow Am. Coll. Clin. Pharmacology and Chemotherapy, Nat. Acad. Clin. Biochemistry (bd. dirs. 1982—), Royal Soc. Health; mem. A.M.A., Endocrine Soc., Am. Fedn. Clin. Research, N.Y. Acad. Scis., Am. Physiol. Soc., Central Soc. for Clin. Research, A.A.A.S., Am. Acad. Polit. and Social Scis., Fedn. Am. Socs. for Exptl. Biology (nat. corr. 1975—), A.A.U.P., Sigma Xi. Home: 6757 N LeRoy Ave Lincolnwood IL 60646 Office: 1753 W Congress Pkwy Chicago IL 60612 *Nothing can be accomplished without a sense of purpose. A long-term goal in life is a sine qua non for creative productivity. When the latter is channeled towards achieving a better understanding of various phenomena around us, the process of learning is at its best and a progress in scientific investigation ensues.*

KORNFELD, JULIAN POTASH, lawyer; b. Dallas, May 1, 1934; s. Abraham L. and Abbie (Potash) K.; children—Meredith, Nancy. B.B.A., Tex. U., 1955, LL.B., 1957; LL.M. in Taxation, N.Y. U., (1962). Bar: Tex. bar 1958, Okla. bar 1963. Practice in El Paso, 1959-61, Oklahoma City, 1962—; mem. firm Potash, Cameron, Bernat & Studdard, 1959-61, Andrews, Mosburg, Davis, Elam, Legg & Kornfeld, 1962-73, Kornfeld, Satherfield, McMillin, Harmon, Phillips & Upp, 1973—. Served to 1st lt., Q.M.C. AUS, 1957-59. Mem. Am., Okla., Tex. bar assns. Home: 3404 Partridge Rd Oklahoma City OK 73120 Office: Harvey Pkwy Suite 600 Oklahoma City OK 73116

KORNFELD, LEWIS F., JR., electronics retail chain executive; b. Swampscott, Mass., July 31, 1916; s. Lewis F. and Lillian (Seiferth) K.; m. Ethel Hardy, July 27, 1943; children: Nicholas S., Hardy. B.A., U. Denver, 1939, M.A., 1941; L.H.D. (hon.), Boston U., 1981. Grad. asst., instr. U. Denver, 1939-41; reporter Rocky Mountain News, Denver, 1941-42; advt. mgr. Colt Shoe Co., Boston, 1946-48; with Radio Shack, 1948—, v.p. merchandising-advt., Boston, 1958-70, pres., Ft. Worth, 1970—; vice chmn. Tandy Corp., 1980-81, dir., 1975—, Ft. Worth Prodns., Inc., Frank Paxton Lumber Co. Author: To Catch a Mouse, Make a Noise Like a Cheese, 1983. Bd. dirs. Arts Council Ft. Worth and Tarrant County, Ft. Worth Symphony; vice chmn. bd. dirs. Van Cliburn Quadrennial Piano Competition; mem. bd. visitors Boston U., 1977-78; mem. Dean's Club, 1979—. Served with USMC, 1942-45. Recipient Outstanding Alumnus Achievement award U. Denver, 1981. Mem. Newcomen Soc., Electronics Industry Assn., Omicron Delta Kappa. Office: 1800 One Tandy Center Fort Worth TX 76102 *Perhaps once in a lifetime—most likely not even once—does an executive whose most rewarding talent is merchandising get a chance to introduce a genuine "breakthrough" product. My opportunity arose in connection with the world's first mass-produced personal computer, the Radio Shack/Tandy TRS-80. The year was 1977. Its impact has been universal*

KORNGOLD, ALVIN LEONARD, broadcasting company executive; b. N.Y.C., Nov. 28, 1924; s. Samuel and Sadelle (Samisch) K.; m. Joyce Singer, Jan. 10, 1954; children: Susan Korngold Osherow, Wendy Ellen, Ben Alan. A.B., N.Y. U., 1943, J.D., 1948; certificate, U. Cambridge, Eng., 1946. Bar: N.Y. 1948, U.S. Supreme Ct. 1956, Ariz. 1967, U.S. Dist. Ct. bars N.Y., Conn., D.C., Ariz. Practiced in, N.Y.C., 1948-66, spl. asst. dist. atty., Queens County, N.Y., 1951-52, spl. dep. atty. gen., N.Y. State, 1952; pres. Sta. KEVT, Tucson Radio, Inc., 1966-81, All Spanish Network, Tucson, 1972-78; licensee, owner Sta. KAMX, Albuquerque, 1971-78, Sta. KWFM, Tucson, 1970-81, Sta. KLAV, Frontier Broadcasting Inc., Las Vegas, 1976—, Sta. WWAM, Savannah, Ga., 1983—; pres. Caribbean Media System. Contbr. articles to profl. jours. Co-chmn. Vets. for Truman, 1948; dir. Dem. N.Y. Lawyers for Kennedy, 1960; Rep. candidate for County Atty. Tucson, 1968; col., a.d.c. Gov. N.Mex., 1978. Served to cpl. U.S. Army, 1943-46; ETO. Mem. Am., N.Y., Ariz. bar assns., Nat., Nev. assns. broadcasters, Tau Kappa Alpha. Office: 19355 Turnberry Way N N Miami Beach FL 33180

KORNHAUSER, HENRY, advertising agency executive; b. Vienna, Austria, May 26, 1932; came to U.S., 1939, naturalized, 1953; s. George Harry and Ernestine (Kallman) K.; m. Edith May Hannah, Apr. 12, 1952; children: Steven, Richard, Edith. B.A., CCNY, 1953. Vice pres., account exec. Kastor-Hilton, N.Y.C., 1960-61; v.p., account supr. Ted Bates, N.Y.C., 1961-66; sr. v.p., mgmt. supr. Cunningham & Walsh, N.Y.C., 1966-71; pres. Dusenberry Ruriani Kornhauser, N.Y.C., 1971-74, C.T. Clyne Co., 1974-80; chmn., chief exec. officer Kornhauser & Calene, Inc., N.Y.C., 1980—. Club: Friars. Home: 377 W 11th St New York NY 10014 Office: 228 W 45th St New York NY 10017

KOROLOGOS, TOM CHRIS, cons.; b. Salt Lake City, Apr. 6, 1933; s. Chris T. and Irene (Kolendrianos) K.; m. Carolyn Joy Goff, June 16, 1960; children—Ann, Philip Chris, Paula. B.A., U. Utah, 1955; M.S. (Grantland Rice Meml. fellow 1957; Pulitzer traveling fellow 1958), Columbia, 1958. Reporter Salt Lake Tribune, 1950-60, N.Y. Herald Tribune, 1958; account exec. David W. Evans & Assos., Salt Lake City, 1960-62; press sec. to Senator Wallace Bennett of Utah, Washington, 1962-65, adminstrv. asst., 1965-71; spl. asst. to Pres. Nixon, 1971-72, dep. asst., 1972-74; dep. asst. to Pres. Ford, 1974-75; cons. Timmons and Co., Washington, 1975—; dir. congressional relations Pres.-Elect Reagan.; Mem. U.S. Adv. Commn. Public Diplomacy. Trustee Am. Coll. of Greece. Served with USAF, 1956-57. Mem. Ahepa. Greek Orthodox. Home: 10208 Eisenhower Ln Great Falls VA 22066 Office: Timmons and Co Suite 850 1850 K St NW Washington DC 20006

KOROTKIN, FRED, philatelist, writer; b. Duluth, Minn., Oct. 25, 1917; s. Morris and Ethel (Billert) K. B.A., U. Minn., 1949. Editor Finance & Commerce, and Daily Market Record, Mpls., 1966-67; stamp editor Mpls. Star, 1970-74, White Bear Press, 1976; Writer-instr. Palmer Writers Sch., Mpls.; Mem. philatelic adv. panel Am. Revolution Bicentennial Commn., 1971-74, Am. Revolution Bicentennial Adminstrn., 1974, philatelic advisor, 1974-76; regional rep. Interphil '76, 1974-76. Contbr. revs., articles to popular mags., newspapers. Pres. North High Alumni Assn., Mpls., 1946-47; mem. nat. adv. bd. Survivors of Nazi Camps and Resistance Fighters; mem. The Generation After, asso. of Simon Wiesenthal Center for Holocaust Studies. Served with U.S. Maritime Service, 1942-43; Served with A. C. U.S. Army, 1943-46. Recipient Distinguished Topical Philatelist award and invited to sign Distinguished Topical Philatelist scroll of honor, 1962, Silver medal for Keeping Posted column in Mpls. Star Am. Philatelic Soc.-Chgo. Philatelic Soc. Conv., 1974. Mem. Am. Topical Assn. (founding pres. chpt. 1957-61, pres. 1968-70, 70-72, dir., nat. adv. com.), Internat. Philatelic Press Club (gov.), Internat. Assn. Philatelic Journalists, Am. Philatelic Soc. (speakers' bur. 1977—, writers unit), New Zealand Stamp Collector's Club Inc. (anonymously donated annual Fred Korotkin Cup for best thematic entry 1966—), Christchurch Philatelic Soc., Inc., Collectors Club N.Y., Manuscript Soc., Disabled Am. Vets. (life). Home: 4925 Minnetonka Blvd Minneapolis MN 55416 Office: Box 11053 Highland Sta Minneapolis MN 55411 *Ever since I was a youngster I've tried to determine what character traits help make a person successful. I've come to believe that the most important combination is still confidence in self, stick-to-itiveness, and that other winning ingredient which can be called aim, direction or goal.*

KORPAL, EUGENE STANLEY, army officer; b. St. Louis, Sept. 1, 1931; s. Stanley Anthony and Mary Ann (Bronakowski) K.; m. Lily M. Alder, July 17, 1954; children: Teresa Kaye, Karla Jeannine. B.S., U. Mo., 1953. Commd. officer U.S. Army, 1954, advanced through grades to maj. gen.; served with inf. div., Hawaii and Vietnam, 1964-67; comdr. 1st Bn., 29th Arty., Ft. Carson, Colo., 1969-70, comdr. 3d Bn., 319th Arty., Vietnam, 1969-71, comdr. 3d Inf. Div. Arty., Ger., 1973-75, asst. div. comdr. 25th Inf. Div., Schofield Barracks, Hawaii.; now dir. personnel U.S. Army Material and Devel. Command, Alexandria, Va. Decorated Legion of Merit with oak leaf cluster, Bronze Star, Air medal, others. Mem. Assn. U.S. Army, 25th Inf. Div. Assn. Club: Rotary. Home: 7802 Braemar Way Springfield VA 22153 Office: Hq US Army DARCOM 5001 Eisenhower Ave Alexandria VA 22233

KORSANT, PHILIP B., publishing company executive; b. Miami, Fla. B.A., U. Miami. Pres. Ziff-Davis Pub.; then exec. v.p. Ziff Corp., N.Y.C., pres., 1982—. Office: Ziff Corp 1 Park Ave New York NY 10016 *

KORSCHOT, BENJAMIN CALVIN, financial executive; b. LaFayette, Ind., Mar. 22, 1921; s. Benjamin G. and Myrtle P. (Goodman) K.; m. Marian Marie Schelle, Oct. 31, 1941; children—Barbara E. Korschot Carver, Lynne D. Korschot Gooding, John Calvin. B.S., Purdue U., 1942; M.B.A., U. Chgo., 1947. Vice pres. No. Trust Co., Chgo., 1947-64; sr. v.p. St. Louis Union Trust Co., 1964-73; exec. v.p. Waddell and Reed Co., Kansas City, Mo., 1973-74, pres., 1974-79, vice-chmn. bd., 1979—; chmn. bd. Waddell & Reed Asset Mgmt. Co., 1973—; pres., chmn. bd. Research Mgmt. Assos., Kansas City, Mo., 1973—; pres. United Group of Mut. Funds, Inc., Kansas City, Mo., 1974—; dir. United Investors Life Ins. Co., Kansas City, Mo., Roosevelt Fed. Savs. & Loan Assn., St. Louis.; chmn. bd. govs. Investment Co. Inst., 1980-82; chmn. bd. Fin. Analyst Fedn., 1978-79. Contbr. articles on investment fin. to profl. publs. Mem. Civic Council Greater Kansas City, Mo., 1974—. Served with USN, 1942-45, 50-52. Mem. Inst. Chartered Fin. Analysts, Fin. Execs. Inst., Kansas City Soc. Fin. Analysts. Republican. Clubs: Kansas City, Indian Hills Country. Home: 101 Hackberry Lee's Summit MO 64063 Office: One Crown Center Kansas City MO 64141 *A happy Christian home environment, the adversity of the depression of the 30's, the challenges of competitive sports, the desire to achieve knowledge, recognition and responsibilities, a devoted wife and three children who made our marriage most meaningful have been the dominant influences of my life.*

KORSON, SELIG MORLEY, ret. hosp. adminstr., physician; b. Bklyn., Nov. 28 1910; s. Joseph and Rose (Lieb) K.; m. Beatrice Gunner Goldman, Nov. 30, 1941; children—Eileen, Jane, Cathy. A.B., Cornell U., 1932; M.D., Eclectic Med. Coll., 1936. Diplomate: Am. Bd. Psychiatry and Neurology. Intern Mercy Hosp., Wilkes-Barre, Pa., 1936-37; gen. practice medicine, Wilkes-Barre, 1937-42; asst. physician Grafton (Mass.) State Hosp., 1946, sr. physician, 1947, asst. supt., 1948; chief grade psychiatrist VA Hosp., Northampton, Mass., 1949-55, Bay Pines, Fla., 1955-58; supt. Mental Health Inst., Independence, Iowa, 1958-78; asst. clin. prof. psychiatry U. Iowa Med. Sch., 1971—; chmn. Iowa Eugenics Bd. Contbr. articles on neurosis, psychiat. therapy and metabolism to med. jours. Pres. Buchanan County United Fund, 1963. Served to maj. AUS, 1942-46. Fellow Am. Psychiat. Assn. (certified mental hosp. adminstr., mem. task force in liaison with A.I.A. 1969-70, mem. assembly of dist. brs. 1975—), Am. Geriatric Soc.; mem. Iowa Psychiat. Soc. (mem. exec. com., past pres.), Buchanan County Med. Soc. (past pres.), Iowa Mental Health Assn. (profl. adv. bd.), Iowa Med. Soc., A.M.A., Am. Assn. Med. Psychiat. Adminstrs. (sec. 1975—), Am. Legion., B'nai B'rith. Jewish religion. Clubs: Mason (Shriner), Rotarian (past pres.). Address: 13449 Stardust Blvd Sun City West AZ 85375

KORSYN, IRENE HAHNE, marketing executive; b. Bklyn., Feb. 22, 1927; d. Max Frederick and Hertha Amanda (Grunsfeld) Hahne; m. Felix J. Korsyn, Nov. 17, 1955; children: Dever John, Kevin Ernest, Jeffrey Felix. Student, Hunter Coll., N.Y.C., 1945-46, U. Pa., 1946-48. Broadcaster Sta. WEST (AM and FM), Easton, Pa., 1948-53; copy mgr. Sta. WFLN, Phila., 1954-55; broadcaster Sta. WQAL, Phila., 1961-62; asst. pub. relations dir. Auerbach Corp., Phila., 1963-64; dir. advt. and pub. relations A. Pomerantz & Co., 1964-69; art and sales promotion mgr. Pa.-Del. region Reuben H. Donnelley Corp., Phila., 1969-73; account exec. Yardis Corp., Phila., 1974-76; dir. Phila. Art Alliance, 1976-77; mgr. public relations Shimer-von Cantz, Phila., 1977-82; dir. communications Phila. Coll. Art, 1982-83; mktg. services dir. Price Waterhouse, 1983—; adv. Poor Richard Sch. Advt., Phila., 1964-73; public relations officer Cerebral Palsy Assn., Chestnut Hill, Pa., 1953; pub. relations mgr. Kate Lavin Children's Center, Phila., 1957-59. Author radio scripts.; Works included in America Sings, anthology coll. poetry, 1945, 47. Mem. Am. Women in Radio and TV (charter), Bus. and Profl. Women's Club, LWV., Internat. Platform Assn. Address: 1920 Naudain St Philadelphia PA 19146

KORTANEK, KENNETH OTTO, mathematics researcher and educator, consultant; b. Chgo., Nov. 13, 1936; s. Otto and Marian (Vencovsky) K.; 1 son, Steven. B.S. in Bus. Adminstrn., Northwestern U., 1958; M.A. in Math., Norhtwestern U., 1959; Ph.D. in Engring., Northwestern U., 1964. Asst. prof. U. Chgo. Grad. Sch. Bus., 1964-65; assoc. prof. Cornell U., Ithaca, N.Y., 1966-69; prof. math. sci. Carnegie-Mellon U., Pitts., 1969—; cons. in field, expert witness. NSF grantee, 1967—; EPA grantee, 1975-76. Mem. Am. Math. Soc., Ops. Research Soc., Inst. Mgmt. Sci., SIAM, Econometric Soc. Republican. Home: Gateway Towers 21M Pittsburgh PA 15222 Office: Carnegie-Mellon U Dept Math Pittsburgh PA 15213 *I am oriented towards making a distinction between basic and non-basic science. I believe that this attitude is more positive towards the development and application of scientific methods than drawing a distinciton between the theoretical and the applied.*

KORTH, EUGENE HENRY, educator, priest; b. Mankato, Minn., Nov. 23, 1917; Simon G. and Anna (Deglman) K. A.B. in Classics, St. Louis U., 1941, Ph.L. in Philosophy, 1943, M.A. in History, 1946; S.T.L. in Theology, 1950; Ph.D. in History, U. Tex., 1956. Joined Soc. of Jesus, 1936; ordained priest Roman Cath. Ch., 1949; mem. faculty St. Louis U. High Sch., 1943-46; Doherty Found. fellow for research in, Latin Am., 1953-54; mem. faculty Marquette U., 1956-68, chmn. dept. history, 1958-60, asso. prof., 1962-68, dean, 1960-64, asst. univ. archivist, 1983—; prof. history U. Detroit, 1969-83, chmn. dept. history, 1973-77; ednl. asst. Cath. U. Salta, Argentina, 1964—, acting dean, 1967-69. Mem. Am. Assn. Higher Edn., Assn. Am. Colls., North Central Assn., NEA, Nat. Cath. Ednl. Assn., Jesuit Ednl. Assn., Am., Cath., Jesuit hist. assns., Conf. Latin Am. History, Mich. Hist. Soc., Phi Alpha Theta, Pi Gamma Mu, Sigma Delta Pi. Home: 1404 W Wisconsin Ave Milwaukee WI 53233

KORTH, FRED, lawyer; b. Yorktown, Tex., Sept. 9, 1909; s. Fritz R. J. and Eleanor Marie (Stark) K.; m. Vera Connell, Sept. 12, 1934 (div. Mar. 1966); children: Nina Maria, Fritz-Alan, Vera Sansom (dec.); m. Charlotte Brooks, Aug. 23, 1980. A.B., U. Tex., 1932; LL.B., George Washington U., 1935, LL.D. (hon.), 1960. Bar: Tex., D.C. bars 1935. Practice of law, Ft. Worth, 1935-62; partner Wallace & Korth, 1948-51; pvt. practice of law, Washington, 1964—; dep. counselor Dept. Army, 1951-52, asst. sec. army, 1952-53, cons. to sec. army, 1953-60; exec. v.p. Continental Nat. Bank, Ft. Worth, 1953-59, pres., 1959-61; sec. of navy, 1961-63; treas. Ft. Worth Air Terminal Corp., 1953-60; dir. Fischbach Corp., First Fin. Enterprises, Security Southwest Life Ins. Co., First Fin. Savs. Bank. Pres. United Fund, Ft. Worth, Tarrant County, 1957-58; dir. Southwestern Exposition & Fat Stock Show, Ft. Worth, 1953-63, treas., 1960-61; Co-executor, co-trustee Marjorie Merriweather Post Estate. Served as lt. col. Air Transp. Command AUS., 1942-46. Recipient Exceptional Civilian Service award Dept. Army, 1953. Mem. Am., Tex., D.C. bar assns., Am. Law Inst. (life), Nat. Planning Assn. (trustee), Order St. Lazarus, Tex. and Southwestern Cattle Raisers Assn. (treas. 1957-61), Phi Delta Phi, Sigma Phi Epsilon. Democrat. Clubs: Internat., Georgetown, Army-Navy (Washington); Ridglea (Ft. Worth); Argyle (San Antonio). Home: 4200 Massachusetts Ave NW 101 Washington DC 20016 also El Retiro PO Box 13 Ecleto TX 78111 also 1054 Torrey Pines El Paso TX 79912 Office: 401 Barr Bldg 910 17th St NW Farragut Sq Washington DC 20006

KORTH, FRITZ-ALAN, lawyer; b. Ft. Worth, Aug. 29, 1938; s. Fred and Vera (Connell) K.; m. Penne Percy, Dec. 15, 1965; children: Fritz-Alan, Maria Eleanor, James Frederick. A.B., Princeton U., 1961; LL.B., U. Tex., 1964; H.H.D., U. Americas, 1982. Bar: Tex. 1964, D.C. 1964. Asst. sec. OKC Corp., Dallas, 1964-65; partner firm Korth & Korth, Washington, 1965—; pres. Wilmar Corp., Port Chester, N.Y., 1980—, dir., 1974—; a founder, sec., dir. Women's Nat. Bank, Washington, 1978—; dir. Trans Leisure Corp., N.Y.C., 1970-75, chmn. bd., 1973-75; dir. Del Norte Tech., Inc., Dallas., chmn., 1982—. Registrar St. John's Episcopal Ch., Washington, 1968-70, vestryman, 1970-74, treas., 1973-77; chmn. fin. com., mem. diocesan council Episcopal Diocese Washington, 1973-77; trustee, treas. Cathedral chpt. Washington Cathedral, 1977—; pres. U. Americas Found., 1969—; bd. assos. U. Americas, Puebla, Mex., 1969—; bd. dirs. Travelers Aid Soc. Washington, 1969—, pres., 1973-75. Mem. World Assn. Lawyers, Inter-Am. Bar Assn., Am. Bar Assn., Am. Law Inst., D.C. Bar, Tex. Bar Assn., Phi Delta Phi. Clubs: Met., Chevy Chase (Washington); Steeplechase (Ft. Worth); Princeton (N.Y.C.). Home:

1910 24th St NW Washington DC 20008 Office: 401 Barr Bldg 910 17th St NW Washington DC 20006

KORTY, JOHN VAN CLEAVE, film company executive; b. Lafayette, Ind., June 22, 1936; s. Richard Marshall and Mary Elizabeth (Van Cleave) K.; m. Beulah Chang, Jan. 16, 1966; children: Jonathan, David. B.A., Antioch Coll., 1959. Audiovisual coordinator Am. Friends Service Com., Phila., N.Y.C., 1959-62; pres. Korty Films, Inc., San Francisco, Mill Valley, Calif., 1963—; lectr. Columbia U., 1961-62. Theatrical and motion picture producer, dir.: The Crazy Quilt, 1964, Funnyman, 1969, River Run, 1970, Oliver's Story, 1978, Who Are the DeBolts?, 1978 (Acad. award, Emmy award, Humanitas prize, Dirs. Guild Am. award); TV productions The Autobiography of Miss Jane Pittman, 1973 (Emmy award, Dirs. Guild award 1974), Farewell to Manzanar, 1976 (Hunanitas prize); exec. producer: Can't It Be Anyone Else?, 1980 (Cine Golden Eagle, Christopher awards 1980), Stepping Out: The DeBolts Grow Up, 1980; writer, dir., producer: Christmas Without Snow, 1980. Mem. Dirs. Guild Am. (TV dir. 1974), Writers Guild Am. Address: Korty Films 200 Miller Ave Mill Valley CA 94941

KORTZ, EDWIN WUNDERLY, clergyman, educator; b. Easton, Pa., Nov. 6, 1910; s. William Henry and Ada Julia (Wunderly) K.; m. Margaret E. Schwarze, July 30, 1937. B.A., Moravian Coll., 1931; B.D., Moravian Theol. Sem., 1934; S.T.M., Luth. Sem. of Phila., 1944; postgrad., Yale Sch. Alcohol Studies, summer 1945, Inst. Pastoral Care, Boston, summer 1948; S.T.D., Temple U., 1955; D.D. (hon.), Moravian Theol. Sem., 1960. Ordained to ministry Moravian Ch. in Am., 1935, consecrated bishop, 1966; pastor parishes in, Va., Ohio and Pa., 1934-49; prof. practical theology Moravian Theol. Sem., 1949-56, 74—, dir. profl. studies, 1979-84; exec. dir. Bd. Fgn. Missions, Moravian Ch., 1956-74, dir. career devel. for deacons, 1974-76; Denominational rep. Nat. Council Chs. Gen. Assemblies; mem. directing bd. Overseas Ministries div. Nat. Council Chs.; dir. Bd. for Christian Work in Santo Domingo.; Chmn. publ. com. for Moravian Hymnal, 1969. Author: My Bible Tells Me What To Believe, 1947. Trustee Moravian Music Found., 1981—; bd. dirs. Share-A-Home of Lehigh Valley, 1979—. Home: 1825 Center St Bethlehem PA 18017

KORY, ROSS CONKLIN, physician, educator; b. Petersburg, Va., Sept. 17, 1918; s. Roscoe Conklin and Rose (Bernwald) K.; m. Virginia Highsmith, Oct. 12, 1947; children—Ross Conklin, Robert Bruce, William Paul. A.B., Columbia, 1938, M.D., 1942. Resident medicine Columbia div. Bellevue Hosp., N.Y.C., 1946-47, Emory U. Hosp., Atlanta, 1947-48, VA Hosp., Salt Lake City, 1948-49; instr. medicine Vanderbilt U. Sch. Medicine, 1949-53; chief clin. physiology VA Hosp., Nashville, 1949-53; asst. prof. medicine Marquette Sch. Medicine, Milw., 1954-55, asso. prof., 1955-60; prof. clin. research Med. Coll. Wis., Milw., 1960-72; prof. medicine U. South Florida, Tampa, 1972—, asst. dean, 1972-75; asso. chief of staff, dir. cardiopulmonary lab. Wood VA Hosp., 1954-72; research coordinator Allen-Bradley Med. Sci. Lab., Milw., 1961-72; chief of staff VA Hosp., Tampa, 1972-75; med. dir. respiratory care Tampa Gen. Hosp., 1975—. Author: Atlas of Lung Diseases, 1964, A Primer of Cardiac Catheterization, 1965; Asso. editor: Clinical Cardiopulmonary Physiology, 1960; Editorial bd.: Diseases of the Chest, 1959-69; Contbr. articles to profl. jours. Served to maj. M.C. USAAF, 1943-46. Fellow Am. Coll. Chest Physicians (pres. Wis. chpt. 1958-59, chmn. com. on pulmonary physiology 1965-66), mem., Am. Heart Assn. (del. North Central regional com., v.p. elect), Wis. Heart Assn. (dir. 1958-70, pres. 1968-69). Home: 108 Martinique Ave Tampa FL 33606 Office: Pulmonary Dept Tampa Gen Hosp Tampa FL 33606

KORZENIK, ARMAND ALEXANDER, lawyer; b. Hartford, Conn., Oct. 31, 1927; s. Bernard and Dorothy (Goldman) K.; m. Ursula Guttmann, June 30, 1956; children: Peter Brent, Jeffrey Dean, Andrea Diane. A.B. magna cum laude, Harvard Coll., 1951; J.D., Harvard U., 1951; LL.M., Yale U., 1952. Bar: Conn. 1951, U.S. Supreme Ct. 1959. Practiced in Hartford, 1951—, asst. corp. counsel, Hartford, 1966-72; counsel Hartford Redevel. Agy., 1966-68, Hartford Bd. Edn., 1968-72; instr. bus. law Hartford Inst. Accounting, 1974-75. Editor: Amicus Curiae, 1956-59; bd. editors: Conn. Bar Jours, 1971-79. Mem. Hartford Bd. Edn., 1953-59, Hartford Zoning Bd. of Appeals, 1960-66; justice of peace, Hartford, 1960-73; bd. dirs. YMCA, Boy Scouts Am., PTA, Urban League, Am. Youth Hostels, Jr. C. of C.; founder Blue Hills Civic Assn., West End Civic Assn., Hartford. Served with USAF, 1946-48, 50; to col. Conn. Air N.G., 1953-82. Mem. ABA, Conn. Bar Assn., Hartford County Bar Assn. (editor Bar-Fly 1976-78), Am. Trial Lawyers Assn., Comml. Law League Am., Judge Advs. Assn., N.G. Assn., U.S. Strategic Inst., Phi Beta Kappa. Democrat. Club: Harvard of No. Conn. Home: 120 Terry Rd Hartford CT 06105 Office: 436 Farmington Ave Hartford CT 06105

KOS, PAUL JOSEPH, artist; b. Rock Springs, Wyo., Dec. 23, 1942; s. Paul A. and Bertha A. (Potochnik) K.; m. Marlene Rossi, Sept. 21, 1963; children: Gregory, Jennifer. Student, Georgetown U., 1961-62; B.F.A., San Francisco Art Inst., 1965, M.F.A., 1967. Asst. prof. art U. Santa Clara, Calif., 1969-78; instr. San Francisco Art Inst. Exhibited in, Paris Biennale, 1977, Bienal de Sao Paulo, 1973, 75, San Francisco Mus. Modern Art, 1977, Castelli Gallery, N.Y.C., 1975, 76. Trustee San Francisco Art Inst., 1973-76, 80-83. Home: PO Box 299 Soda Springs CA 95728

KOSAK, ANTHONY JAMES, transportation company executive; b. Cleve., Nov. 14, 1934; s. Anton James and Anne Gertrude (Urbancic) K.; m. Janet Elizabeth Voss, Aug. 3, 1957; children: Cheryl, Jim, Lindy, Barb, Beth, Kim. B.S., John Carroll U., 1956. V.p. automobile carrier div. Leaseway Transp. Co., Cleve., 1980—; exec. v.p. Melchin Auto Transport Ltd., Calgary, Alta, Can., 1976—; pres. Leaseway Ltd., Toronto, Ont., Can., 1976, Anchor Motor Freight Inc., Birmingham, Mich., 1977, C & J Comml. Driveaway, Inc., Lansing, Mich., 1983, Motorcar Transport Co., Pontiac, Mich., 1983; pres., dir. Charlton Transport (Que.) Ltd., Que. Mem. Nat. Automobile Transporters Assn. (dir.). Republican. Roman Catholic. Clubs: Detroit Traffic; Economic (Detroit); Pine Lake Country (Orchard Lake, Mich.) (treas. 1978-79, v.p. 1980); Pine Lake Country (Orchard Lake, Mich.) (pres. 1981); Recess (Detroit)). Home: 555 Kingsley Trail Bloomfield Hills MI 48013 Office: Leaseway Transp Corp 30800 Telegraph Rd Birmingham MI 48010

KOSARAJU, S. RAO, electrical engineering and computer science educator; b. Pedapulivarru, Guntur, India, Feb. 20, 1943; came to U.S., 1966; s. Punnaiah and Dhanalakshmi K.; m. Padmaja Valluripalli, Aug. 20, 1970; children: Sheela, Akhila. B.E., Andhra U., (India), 1964; M.Tech., Indian Inst. Tech., Kharagpur, 1966; Ph.D., U. Pa., 1969. Vis. asst. prof. elec. engring. and computer sci. Johns Hopkins U., Balt., 1969-70, asst. prof., 1970-75, assoc. prof., 1975-77, prof., 1977—, Kouwenhoven prof., 1981—. Contbr. articles to profl. jours.; assoc. editor: Jour. Computer Langs., 1976—, Math. Systems Theory, 1976—, Jour. Computer and System Scis., 1981—. Mem. Assn. Computing Machinery, IEEE, Soc. Indsl. and Applied Math. (mng. editor Jour. on Computing 1980—). Home: 4 Indian Pony Ct Owings Mills MD 21117 Office: Dept Elec Engring and Computer Sci NL Johns Hopkins U. Baltimore MD 21218

KOSHALEK, RICHARD H(UBERT), museum administrator; s. H. Martin and Ethel F. (Hochtritt) K.; m. Elizabeth Jane Briar, July 2, 1941; 1 dau., Anne Elizabeth. Student, U. Wis., Madison, 1960-61; B.A. in Architecture, U. Minn., Mpls., 1965; M.A. in Art History, U. Minn., Mpls., 1967. Curator Walker Art Center, Mpls., 1967-73; asst. dir. Nat. Endowment for Arts, Washington, 1973-74; dir. Ft. Worth Art Mus., 1974-76, Hudson River Mus., Westchester, N.Y., 1976-80; dep. dir. Mus. Contemporary Art, Los Angeles, 1980-82, dir., 1982—; mem. faculty New Sch. for Social Research. Author: exhbn. catalogues Mario Merz, 1972, Midwest Photographers, 1972, Dan Flavin, 1976, The Great American Rodeo, 1976, John Mason: Installations from the Hudson River Series, 1978, Robert Whitman: Palisade, 1979, Richard Serra: Interviews, 1970-80, 1980, Red Grooms, The Bookstore, 1980. Nat. Endowment for Arts Fellowship for Mus. Profls. fellow, 1973-74; IBM design fellow, 1982. Home: 11011 Strathmore Dr Los Angeles CA 90024 Office: Museum Contemporary Art 414 Boyd St Los Angeles CA 90013

KOSHLAND, DANIEL EDWARD, JR., educator, biochemist; b. N.Y.C., Mar. 30, 1920; s. Daniel Edward and Eleanor (Haas) K.; m. Marian Elliott, May 25, 1945; children: Ellen, Phyllis, James, Gail, Douglas. B.S., U. Calif., Berkeley, 1941; Ph.D., U. Chgo., 1949. Chemist Shell Chem. Co., Martinez, 1941-42; research asso. Manhattan Dist. U. Chgo., 1942-44; group leader Oak Ridge Nat. Labs., 1944-46; postdoctoral fellow Harvard, 1949-51; staff Brookhaven Nat. Lab., Upton, N.Y., 1951-65; affiliate Rockefeller Inst., N.Y.C., 1958-65; prof. biochemistry U. Calif. at Berkeley, 1965—, chmn. dept., 1973-78; Leo Marion lectr. Nat. Research Council Can., 1972; Harvey lectr., 1969; fellow All Souls, Oxford U., 1972; Walker Ames lectr. U. Wash., 1964; Carter Wallace lectr. Princeton U., 1970, Phi Beta Kappa lectr., 1976; John Edsall lectr. Harvard U., 1980. Author: Bacterial Chemotaxis as A Model Behavioral System, 1980; mem. editorial bds.: jour. Accounts Chem. Research; editor: Procs. Nat. Acad. Scis, 1980—. Recipient T. Duckett Jones award Helen Hay Whitney Found., 1977; Guggenheim fellow, 1972. Mem. Nat. Acad. Scis., Am. Chem. Soc. (Edgar Fahs Smith award 1979, Pauling award 1979), Am. Soc. Biol. Chemists (pres.), Am. Acad. Arts and Scis. (council), Academy Forum (chmn.), Japanese Biochem. Soc. (hon.). Home: 3991 Happy Valley Rd Lafayette CA 94549 Office: Biochemistry Dept U Calif Berkeley CA 94720

KOSHLAND, MARIAN ELLIOTT, immunologist, educator; b. New Haven, Oct. 25, 1921; d. Waller Watkins and Margaret Ann (Smith) Elliott; m. Daniel Edward Koshland, Jr., May 25, 1945; children—Ellen R., Phyllis A., James M., Gail F., Douglas E. B.A., Vassar Coll., 1942, M.S., 1943; Ph.D., U. Chgo., 1949. Research asst. Manhattan Dist. Atomic Bomb Project, 1945-46; fellow dept. bacteriology Harvard Med. Sch., 1949-51; asso. bacteriologist biology dept. Brookhaven Nat. Lab., 1952-62, bacteriologist, 1963-65; asso. research immunologist virus lab. U. Calif., Berkeley, 1965-69, lectr. dept. molecular biology, 1966-70, prof. dept. microbiology and immunology, 1970—, chmn. dept., 1982—; mem. Nat. Sci. Bd., 1976-82; mem. adv. com. to dir. NIH, 1972-75. Contbr. articles to profl. jours. Mem. Nat. Acad. Scis., Am. Acad. Microbiology, Am. Assn. Immunologists (pres. 1982-1983), Am. Soc. Biol. Chemists, Phi Beta Kappa, Sigma Xi. Office: Dept Microbiology and Immunology U Calif Berkeley CA 94720

KOSHLAND, STEPHEN ABRAHAM, stockbroker; b. Boston, Feb. 21, 1902; s. Abraham and Estelle (Wangeheim) K.; m. Carol Falk, Apr. 14, 1938; children—Anthony S. (dec.), Kathryn (Mrs. Anthony Blue). A.B., Harvard, 1925. Wool buyer J. Koshland & Co., Boston, 1926-30; trainee Hamershlag Borg & Co. (stock brokers), 1930-31; partner Loeb Partners (formerly known as Carl M. Loeb Rhoades & Co.), N.Y.C., 1931—; Mem. N.Y. Stock Exchange, 1931—, bd. govs., 1960-66; trustee Gratuity Fund, 1977—, sec., treas., 1980—. Area agt. N.Y.C. and suburbs Harvard Class of 1925, 1960—; trustee Harvard Advocate; mem. com. program for Harvard, 1960. Clubs: Harvard, Stock Exchange Luncheon (dir. 1960-69), Stock Exchange Luncheon (pres. 1968-69), Regency Whist (N.Y.C.)). Home: 33 E 70th St New York NY 10021

KOSIKOWSKI, FRANK VINCENT, food scientist, educator; b. Torrington, Conn., Jan. 10, 1916; s. Frank K. and Bertha Samul (Kosikowski); m. Anna Hudak, Oct. 21, 1944; 1 dau., Frances Anne..S., U. Conn.-Storrs, 1939; M.S., Cornell U., 1941, Ph.D., 1944. Asst. prof. food sci. Cornell U., 1945-47, assoc. prof., 1947-52, prof., 1952—; tech. devel. officer FAO-UN, Rome, Italy, 1963; vol. Internat. Exec. Service Corp., Tehran, Iran, 1970. Author: Cheese & Fermented Milk Foods, 1966, Advances in Cheese Technology, 1958. Bd. dirs. Bethel Grove Comunity, Ithaca N.Y., 1960. Recipient research awards Am. Diary Sci. Assn., 1955,60, French Govt., 1964, Inst. Food Technologists, 1983, Am. Cultured Dairy Products Inst., 1983. Mem. AAAS, Am.Dairy Sci. Assn., Am. Chem. Soc., Inst. Food Technologists. Roman Catholic. Club: Statler. Home: 48 Brooktondale Rd. Ithaca NY 14850 Office: Dept Food Sci Cornell U 105 Stocking Hall Ithaca NY 14853

KOSINSKI, JERZY NIKODEM, author; b. Lodz, Poland, June 14, 1933; U.S., 1957, naturalized, 1965; s. Mieczyslaw and Elzbieta (Liniecka) K.; m. Mary H. Weir, Jan. 11, 1962 (dec. 1968). M.A. in Polit. Sci, U. Lodz, 1953, 1955; postgrad., Columbia U., 1958-65; Ph.D. Hon.C. Hebrew Letters, Spertus Coll. Judaica, 1982. Asst. prof. Inst. Sociology and Cultural History, Polish Acad. Scis., Warsaw, 1955-57; Guggenheim Lit. fellow, 1967; fellow Center Advanced Studies, Wesleyan U., 1968-69; sr. fellow Council Humanities; vis. lectr. English Princeton, 1969-70; vis. prof. English prose Sch. Drama, Yale; also resident fellow Davenport Coll., 1970-73. Author: (pseudonym Joseph Novak): The Future is Ours, Comrade, 1960; Author: No Third Path, 1962, The Painted Bird, 1965 (Best Fgn. book award Paris), Steps, 1968, Being There, 1971, screenplay, 1978; The Devil Tree, 1st edit., 1973, rev. edit., 1981, Cockpit, 1975, Blind Date, 1977, Passion Play, 1979; (also screenplay), 1980; Author: Pinball, 1982; actor: in movie Reds. Recipient Nat. Book award for Steps, 1969; Award in Lit. Am. Acad. Arts and Letters, 1970; Brith Sholom Humanitarian Freedom award, 1974; Best Screenplay award for Being There Writers Guild Am., 1979; Brit. Acad. Film and TV Arts award, 1981; Polonia Media Perspectives award, 1980; Internat. award Spertus Coll., 1982; Ford Found. fellow, 1958-60. Mem. P.E.N. (exec. bd., pres. 1973-75), Nat. Writers Club (exec. bd.), Internat. League for Human Rights (dir.), ACLU (chmn. artists and writers com., mem. nat. adv. council, First Amendment award 1980), Authors Guild. Club: Century Assn. (N.Y.C.). Address: 18-K Hemisphere House 60 W 57th St New York NY 10019 *As the trend toward depression, passivity, and isolation becomes incresingly irreversible in industrial America, schools are among the few remaining institutions that can help tomorrow's adults become thinking individuals, able to judge and function in a world of pressures, conflicting values, and moral ambiguities. The classroom experience in general, and the reading experience in particular, are two of the few demanding mental activities left in modern society. And both must be allowed to flourish freely if we are to keep at least some small part of the population from becoming emotionally and intellectually crippled.*

KOSKI, WALTER S., educator, scientist; b. Phila., Dec. 1, 1913; s. Bruno and Helen (Laskowska) Stankiewicz; m. Helen Ireton Tag, May 11, 1940; children—Carol Lee, Ann Louise, Nancy Cheryl, Phyllis Ireton. Ph.D., Johns Hopkins, 1942. Research chemist Hercules Powder Co., 1942-43; group leader Los Alamos Sci. Lab., 1944-47; physicist Brookhaven Nat. Lab., 1947-48; asso. prof. Johns Hopkins, 1947-55, prof. chemistry, 1955—, B.N. Baker prof. chemistry, 1975—, chmn. dept., 1958-69. Fellow Am. Phys. Soc.; mem. Am. Chem. Soc. (merit award Md. sect), Phi Beta Kappa. Home: 809 East Seminary Ave Towson MD 21204

KOSLO, WILLIAM J., business executive; b. Mt. Carmel, Pa., Mar. 6, 1930; s. Joseph J. and Mary M. K.; m. Margaret M. Walsh, June 10, 1953; children: Karen, William, Mark, Patrick. B.S., Fordham U., 1951. With U.S. Printing Co., after 1951, sales mgr., after 1956; v.p., gen. mgr. Diamond Nat. Corp., after 1959; group v.p. Diamond Internat. Corp., N.Y.C., 1970-74, exec. v.p., 1974-77, pres., chief exec. officer, 1977—; Dir. U. Maine Pulp and Paper Found. Served with USMC, 1952-55. Mem. Am. Paper Inst. (dir.), Conf. Bd. Republican. Clubs: Cherry Valley Golf, Sky (N.Y.C.); K.C. Office: Diamond Internat Corp 733 3d Ave New York NY 10017 *

KOSLOV, LEONID, ballet dancer; b. Moscow, Feb. 6, 1947; U.S., 1973; s. Vladimir Kozlov and Vanentina Starostina. Ballet diploma, Bolshoi Ballet Acad. Sch., Moscow, 1965. Soloist Bolshoi Ballet, Moscow, 1967-70, prin., 1970-79, Australian Ballet, Melbourne and Sydney, 1981-83, N.Y.C. Ballet, 1983—; starred in On Your Toes, Broadway and Kennedy Ctr.; choreographer Miami Ballet Concerto, Fla., 1980, NT Closter Ballet, 1980-81, Santiago Ballet, Chile, 1981-82; choregrapher Australian Ballet, 1982. Recipient 1st prize Moscow Ballet competition. Office: NYC Ballet State Theatre Lincoln Center New York NY 10023

KOSMAHL, HENRY G., electron physicist; b. Wartha, Germany, Dec. 14, 1919; came to U.S., 1956, naturalized, 1962; m. Gisela Zelder; children: Monika, Beatrix, Ronald. Student, U. Dresden, Germany, 1940-43; D.S., U. Darmstadt, Germany, 1949. Asst. prof. U. Darmstadt, 1949-50; research physicist Telefunken-AEG, Ulm, Germany, 1950-56; head microwave amplifiers NASA Lewis Research Center, Cleve., 1956—; cons. Aero. Systems and Space divs. USAF., Westinghouse E.D.D. Co-author 2 books; assoc. editor: Transactions on Electronic Devices; contbr. sci. articles to profl. jours. Recipient NASA sci. achievement medal, 1974. Fellow IEEE (tech. advancement award 1977, maj. inventor award 1980). Patentee U.S. and abroad. Home: 7419 River Olmsted Falls OH 44138 Office: 21000 Brookpark Cleveland OH 44135

KOSNER, EDWARD A(LAN), magazine editor; b. N.Y.C., July 26, 1937; s. Sidney and Annalee (Fisher) K.; m. Alice Nadel, Feb. 1, 1959 (dec. div. 1977); children: John Robbins, Anthony William; m. Julie Baumgold, Nov. 19, 1978; 1 dau., Lily. B.A., CCNY, 1958. Rewriteman, asst. city editor N.Y. Post, 1958-63; assoc. editor Newsweek Mag., N.Y.C., 1963-67, gen. editor, 1967-69, nat. affairs editor, 1969-72, asst. mng. editor, 1972, mng. editor, 1973-75, editor, 1975-79, N.Y. mag., N.Y.C., 1980—. Recipient various journalism awards. Mem. Am. Soc. Mag. Editors (v.p., mem. exec. com.). Club: Century. Home: 180 E 79th St New York NY 10021 Office: 755 2d Ave New York NY 10017

KOSOFSKY, JOEL MARTIN, producer; b. Bklyn., Jan. 20, 1942; s. Harry and Pauline K.; m. Marcia Platt, Jan. 24, 1965; children—Jennifer, Adam. B.A. in Speech and Theater, Bklyn. Coll., 1963, M.A., 1969. With CBS-TV, N.Y.C., 1959—; Mem. communications arts adv. com. Marist Coll., Poughkeepsie, N.Y. Asst. mgr., mgr., Ed Sullivan Theater, 1966-68; asso. producer: Capt. Kangaroo Show, 1970-78; producer, 1978—; (Recipient Emmy award as producer outstanding children's entertainment series 1981, 82, 83). Served with U.S. Army, 1963-65. Mem. Nat. Assn. TV Arts and Scis. Office: 1158 Fifth Ave New York NY 10029

KOSOVICH, DUSHAN RADOVAN, psychiatrist; b. Trepca, Niksic, Yugoslavia, Dec. 23, 1926; came to U.S., 1967, naturalized, 1972; s. Radovan Dj and Djurdja K. (Bacovic) K.; children—Jasmine, Nicholas. M.D., Belgrade U., 1954, postgrad., 1954-57; certificate, Am. Inst. for Psychoanalysis and Postgrad. Center, 1972. Resident in neuropsychiatry, Belgrade, Yugoslavia, 1954-57; resident in psychiatry Bellevue Med. Center, N.Y.C., 1957-59, McGill U., Montreal, Que., Can., 1965-67; founder, chief neuropsychiatric service for inpatient and outpatients Gen. Hosp., Titograd, Montenegro, Yugoslavia, 1960-65; staff psychiatrist Bellevue Med. Center, N.Y.C., 1967-73; dir. inpatient psychiat. service Lincoln Hosp., Bronx, N.Y., 1973-75; chief inpatient services Methodist Hosp., Bklyn., 1975-76, acting dir. psychiat dept., 1976-78, dir., 1978—; clin. asso. prof. dept. psychiatry Downstate Med. Center, State U. N.Y., 1975—; Psychoanalyst Karen Horney Psychoanalytic Inst., N.Y.C. Contbr. articles to profl. jours. Served with Yugoslavian Army, 1944-46. Recipient City of Titograd award for best sci. achievement, 1964. Fellow Assn. for Advancement Psychoanalysis, Karen Horney Psychoanalytic Inst. and Center, Am. Acad. Psychoanalysis; mem. Am. Psychiat. Assn., Am. Acad. Clin. Psychiatrists, N.Y. Acad. Sci., N. Am. Acad. for Auricular Medicine. Home and Office: 300 Mercer St New York NY 10003

KOSS, JOHN CHARLES, consumer electronics products manufacturing company executive; b. Milw., Feb. 22, 1930; s. Earl L. and Eda K.; m. Nancy Weeks, Apr. 19, 1952; children: Michael, Debra, JohnCharles, Linda, Pamela. Student, U. Wis., Milw., 1952; D.Eng. (hon.), Milw. Sch. Engring. Founder Koss Corp., TV leasing co., Milw., 1953; owner, operator Koss Corp., 1953-58, pres., 1972-81, chmn. bd., chief exec. officer, 1974—; creator home-stereophone, 1958; dir., Metalcraft. Bd. dirs., past pres. Jr. Achievement S.E. Wis.; bd. dirs. Milw. Symphony, Milw. Profl. Sports Services, Inc. (Milw. Bucks Basketball Team). Served with Air Force Band USAF, 1950-52. Named Entrepreneur of Yr. Research Dirs. Assn. Chgo., 1972, Mktg. Man of Yr. Milw. chpt., 1972; named to Audio Hall Fame; Mktg. Exec. of Yr. Sales and Mktg. Execs., 1976; recipient Debby award Soc. Audio Cons.'s, 1975. Mem. Chief Execs. Orgn., Inst. High Fidelity (pres. 1968). Republican. Baptist. Clubs: Milw. Country, University, Milw. Athletic.; Les Ambassadeurs (London). Office: 4129 N Port Washington Ave Milwaukee WI 53212

KOSS, LEOPOLD G., physician; b. Danzig, Poland, Oct. 2, 1920; came to U.S., 1947, naturalized, 1952; s. Abram and Rose (Merenholc) K.; m. Lydia Palla; children: Michael S., Andrew C., Richard P. M.D., U. Berne, Switzerland, 1946. Intern, Lincoln Hosp., N.Y.C., 1947-48; tng. pathology, St. Gallen, Switzerland, 1946-47, Kings County Hosp., Bklyn., 1949-51; instr. pathology L.I. Coll. Medicine, 1949-51; mem. staff Meml. Hosp. Cancer and Allied Diseases, N.Y.C., 1952-70, attending pathologist, 1961-70, chief cytology service, 1961-70; pathologist-in-chief Sinai Hosp. Balt., 1970-73; prof., chmn. dept. pathology Montefiore Hosp., Med. Center Albert Einstein Coll. Medicine, 1973—; assoc. mem. Sloan-Kettering Inst. Cancer Research, N.Y.C., 1957-70; assoc. prof. pathology Sloan-Kettering div. Postgrad. Sch. Med. Scis., Cornell U., 1957-70; prof. pathology Jefferson Med. Coll., Phila., 1970-73; clin. prof. pathology U. Md. Med. Sch., 1971-73; vis. pathologist James Ewing Hosp., N.Y.C., 1952-60; cons. pathologist N.Y. State Dept. Health, Hosp. Spl. Surgery, N.Y.C., Walter Reed Army Med. Center, Nassau County Med. Ctr. Author: Diagnostic Cytology and Its Histopathologic Bases, 3d edit., 1979, Tumors of the Urinary Bladder, 1975; editor: Advances in Clinical Cytology, Vol. I, 1981, Vol. II, 1984; also monographs, chpts. and articles. Served to maj. M.C., AUS, 1955-57. Recipient Wien award Papanicolaou Cancer Inst., 1963, Alfred P. Sloan award cancer research, 1964; hon. prof. pathology Severance Med. Coll., Seoul, Korea, 1956. Fellow Am. Soc. Clin. Pathology, Coll. Am. Pathologists, Internat. Acad. Cytology (Goldblatt award 1962); mem. Am. Soc. Path. Bacteriologists, James Ewing Soc., AMA, Am. Soc. Cytology (pres. 1962, Papanicolaou award 1966), Internat. Acad. Pathology; corr. mem. Royal Acad. Medicine Spain; hon. mem. Brit. Soc. Clin. Cytology, Korean Med. Assn., Mex., Argentinian socs. cytology, Japanese Soc. Pathology, Polish Soc. Pathology, Peruvian Soc. Obstetrics and Gynecology. Office: 111 E 210th St Bronx NY 10467

KOSSACK, CARL FREDERICK, educator, statistician; b. Chgo., May 30, 1915; s. Walter Edward and Elizabeth Marie (Jost) K.; m. Elizabeth Pride Ayres, June 24, 1940; children: Barbara Kossack Eggleston, Charles A., Edgar W., Howard W., Kenneth A., William S. B.A., UCLA, 1935, M.A., 1936; Ph.D., U. Mich., 1939. Mem. faculty U. Oreg., 1939-45; mathematician OSRD, Washington, 1945; air intelligence specialist, Washington, 1947; mem. faculty Purdue U., 1949-59; mem. research staff IBM, Yorktown Heights, N.Y., 1959-63; head lab. computer sci. Grad. Research Center, Dallas, 1963-65; prof., head dept. stats. U. Ga., 1965-81, prof. emeritus, 1981—; adj. disting. prof. Fla. Atlantic U., 1982—; data processing cons. India, FAO; cons. Office Emergency Planning, Exec. Office of Pres., USAF, USPHS, AT&T; dir. gen. Economia Agricola, Govt. Mexico; ednl. cons. UNESCO, India. Fellow Am. Statis. Assn.; mem. Am. Math. Soc., Inst. Math. Stats., Biometrics Soc., OPS. Research Soc., Inst. Mgmt. Sci., Assn. Computing Machinery, Nat. Def. Exec. Res., Sigma Xi, Phi Kappa Phi, Phi Kappa Delta. Research statis. classification techniques - personnel systems, sampling techniques, info. processing. Home: Rt 1 Box 332 Hull GA 30646

KOSSAR, ARNOLD FRANKLYN, indsl. co. exec.; b. N.Y.C., Apr. 13, 1925; s. Hyman and Sonia (Farber) K.; m. Ann Banks, Oct. 7, 1945; children—Enid Rae, Bruce Steven. B. Aero. Engring., N.Y.U., 1945; Aero. Engr., Mass. Inst. Tech., 1951. Registered profl. engr., Conn. Aero. engr. Consol. Vultee Aircraft Corp., San Diego, 1944-48; research engr. United Aircraft Corp., East Hartford, Conn., 1948-49; chief analytical engr. Kaman Aircraft Corp., Bloomfield, Conn., 1951-55; mgr. advanced projects Wright Aero div. Curtiss-Wright Corp., Wood-Ridge, N.J., 1955-61, dir. corporate planning, tech. asst. to chmn. and pres., 1961-65, v.p., 1965—. Mem. Am. Inst. Aeros. and Astronautics, Am. Mgmt. Assn., AAAS, N.Y. Acad. Scis., Sigma Xi, Tau Beta Pi, Gamma Alpha Pho. Home: 14-27 Mandon Pl Fair Lawn NJ 07410 Office: Curtiss-Wright Corporation Wood-Ridge NJ 07075

KOSSEL, CLIFFORD GEORGE, educator, clergyman; b. Omro, Wis., Apr. 22, 1916; s. George C. and Sarah (Haigh) K. A.B., Gonzaga U., 1940, M.A., 1941; Ph.D., U. Toronto, 1945; Th.L., Alma Coll., 1949. Asso. prof. Gonzaga U., Spokane, 1950-63, prof. philosophy, 1963—, dean, 1958-71, chmn. dept. philosophy, 1966-69; sabbatical leave to, Oxford, Eng. and, Florence, Italy, 1969-70. Bd. editors: Communio: Internat. Cath. Rev, 1974—; Contbr. profl. jours. Mem. Am. Cath. Philos. Assn., Jesuit Philos. Assn. (past pres.). Home: Gonzaga U Spokane WA 99258

KOSSIAKOFF, ALEXANDER, chemist; b. St. Petersburg (now Leningrad), Russia, June 26, 1914; m. Arabelle Davies, Feb. 18, 1939; children: Tanya Ann, Anthony. B.S. in Chemistry, Calif. Inst. Tech., 1936, postdoctoral fellow, 1939; Ph.D. in Chemistry, Johns Hopkins U., 1938. Instr. chemistry Catholic U. Am., 1939-42; tech. aide Office Sci. Research and Devel.; also Nat. Def. Research Council, Washington, 1942-43; dep. dir. research Allegany Ballistics Lab., George Washington U., Cumberland, Md., 1944-46; with Applied Physics Lab., Johns Hopkins U., Silver Spring, Md., 1946—, asst. dir. tech. ops., asso. dir., 1961-66, head surface missile systems dept., 1965-69, dep. dir., 1966-69, dir. lab., 1969-80, chief scientist, 1980—; Chmn. launching and handling panel research and devel. bd. U.S. Dept. Def., 1948-51; cons. Tech. Adv. Panel on Aeros., 1954-60; mem. com. on nat. labs. Office Sci. and Tech., 1969-73. Contbr. articles to profl. jours. Bd. dirs. Montgomery Gen. Hosp., 1979—; mem. Gov.'s Sci. Adv. Council, 1979—. Recipient Navy Disting. Public Service award, Def. Dept. medal for disting. public service, Pres.'s Cert. of Merit, other awards. Fellow Am. Inst. Chemists; mem. AAAS, Phi Beta Kappa, Sigma Xi, Tau Beta Pi, Phi Lambda Upsilon. Club: Cosmos. Home: 120 Haviland Mill Rd Brookeville MD 20833 Office: Johns Hopkins Rd Laurel MD 20707

KOST, WAYNE L., business executive; b. Chgo., Feb. 8, 1951; m. Denice Lee Eslinger, Nov. 24, 1979. B.S., Northwestern U., 1973; M.P.A., Syracuse U., 1974. Adminstrv. asst. Chgo. Crime Commn., 1973; staff asso. Va. Mcpl. League, Richmond, 1975-77; dir. inst. affairs Am. Public Works Assn., Chgo., 1977-79; exec. dir. Am. Soc. Quality Control, Milw., 1980-82; sr. v.p. Philip Crosby Assos., Winter Park, Fla., 1982—; lectr. public adminstrn. Golden Gate U., 1976-78. Bd. dirs. Nat. Council YMCAs, 1970-73, Ill. Commn. on Children, 1969-73; chmn. Gov.'s Com. on Age of Majority, 1972. Gov.'s fellow, 1972. Mem. Am. Soc. Assn. Execs., Nat. Soc. YMCA Youth Govs. Office: 201 W Canton Ave Winter Park FL 32732

KOSTANSKI, THADDEUS ANTHONY, utility co. exec.; b. Toledo, Feb. 11, 1925; s. John and Helen (Rogalski) K.; m. Mildred Ann Plucher, Oct. 23, 1948; children—Kenneth, Charles, Jeanne Marie. Student, John Carroll U., 1944-45; B.S., Miami U., Oxford, Ohio, 1947; M.B.A., U. Toledo, 1963. With Toledo Edison Co., 1952-73, controller, 1965-73, chief acctg. officer, 1968-73; v.p. fin. Kans. Power & Light co., Topeka, 1973—; instr. U. Toledo, 1965-66. Sect. chmn. United Fund, 1966-71. Served with USNR, 1943-46. Mem. Fin. Execs. Inst., Edison Electric Inst., Am. Legion. Home: 2609 W 34th St Topeka KS 66611 Office: 818 Kansas Ave Topeka KS 66612

KOSTECKE, B. WILLIAM, utilities executive; b. Caro, Mich., Aug. 1, 1925; s. Steve and Stella (Telewiek) K.; m. Lo Rayne M. Smith, Mar. 25, 1950; children: Diane, Keith. B.S., U.S. Mcht. Marine Acad., 1947, Mich. State U., 1951. Controller Miller Brewing Co., Milw., 1963-66, treas., chief financial officer, 1966-70, pres., 1970-72; v.p., treas., dir. Wis. Gas Co., Milw., from 1972; v.p., treas., sec., dir. WICOR, Inc., Milw. Gen. chmn. Milw. Nat. Alliance Businessmen, 1972; bd. dirs. Milw. County council Boy Scouts Am., Milw. Better Bus. Bur., Wis. Council on Econ. Edn., Wis. Soc. for Prevention of Blindness; trustee Citizens Govtl. Research Bur. Recipient Dean Mellencamp award U. Wis., Milw., 1967, Outstanding Profl. Achievement award Kings Point Alumni Assn., 1972. Mem. Financial Execs. Inst., Am. Gas Assn. Clubs: Blue Mound Golf and Country; University (Milw.). Home: 10708 N Fairway Circle Mequon WI 53092 Office: 626 E Wisconsin Ave Milwaukee WI 53201

KOSTELANETZ, BORIS, lawyer; b. Leningrad, Russia, June 16, 1911; came to U.S., 1920, naturalized, 1925; s. Nachman and Rosalia (Dimschetz) K.; m. Ethel Cory, Dec. 18, 1938; children: Richard Cory, Lucy Cory. B.C.S., N.Y. U., 1933, B.S., 1936; J.D. magna cum laude, St. John's U., 1936; LL.D. (hon.), St. John's U., 1981. Bar: N.Y. bar 1936; C.P.A., N.Y. With Price, Waterhouse & Co. (C.P.A.'s), N.Y.C., 1934-37; asst. U.S. atty. So. Dist. N.Y.; also confidential asst. to U.S. atty, 1937-45; spl. asst. to atty. gen. U.S., 1943-46; chief war frauds sect. Dept. Justice, 1945-46; spl. counsel com. investigate crime in interstate commerce U.S. Senate, 1950-51; ptnr. firm Kostelanetz & Ritholz (and predecessors), N.Y.C., 1946—; instr. acctg. N.Y. U., 1937-47, adj. prof. taxation, 1947-69; Mem. com. on character and fitness Appellate div. Supreme Ct. N.Y., 1st dept., 1974—. Author: (with L. Bender) Criminal Aspects of Tax Fraud Cases, 1957, 2d edit., 1968, 3d edit., 1980; Contbr. articles to legal, accounting and tax jours. Chmn. Kefauver for Pres. Com. N.Y. State, 1952. Recipient Meritorious Service award N.Y. U., 1954, N.Y. U. John T. Madden Meml. award, 1969; Pietas medal St. John's U., 1961; Torch of Learning award Am. Friends of Hebrew U. Law Sch., 1979; medal of honor, 1983. Fellow Am. Coll. Trial Lawyers, Am. Coll. Tax Counsel, Am. Bar Found.; mem. Internat. Bar Assn., Fed. Bar Assn., ABA (council sect. taxation 1978-81), N.Y. State Bar Assn., N.Y. County Lawyers Assn. (v.p. 1966-69, pres. 1969-71, dir. 1958-64, 66-69, 71-74, chmn. com. judiciary 1965-69), Assn. Bar City N.Y., N.Y. State Soc. C.P.A.'s, N.Y. U. Sch. Commerce Alumni Assn. (pres. 1951-52), St. John's U. Law Sch. Alumni Assn. (pres. 1955-57), N.Y. U. Finance Club (pres. 1953-54). Clubs: New York Univ. (N.Y.C.); Nat. Lawyers (Washington). Home: 37 Washington Sq W New York NY 10011 Office: 80 Pine St New York NY 10005

KOSTELANETZ, RICHARD, writer, artist; b. N.Y.C., May 14, 1940; s. Boris and Ethel (Cory) K. A.B. with honors, Brown U., 1962; postgrad. (Fulbright scholar), King's Coll., U. London, 1964-65; M.A., Columbia U., 1966. Program assoc. thematic studies John Jay Coll. CUNY, 1972-73; sr. staff Ind. U. Writers' Conf., 1976; vis. prof. English and Am. studies U. Tex. at Austin, 1977; guest Mishkenot Sha'Ananim, Jerusalem, 1979, DAAD Berliner Kunstlerprogramm, 1981-82. Co-propr.: Assembling Press, 1970-82; lit. dir.: The Future Press, 1976—; Author: Music of Today, 1967, The Theatre of Mixed Means, 1968, 81, Masterminds Portraits of Contemporary American Artists & Intellectuals, 1969, Visual Language, 1970, In the Beginning, 1971, The End of Intelligent Writing, 1974; 2d edit. as Literary Politics in Am, 1977; I Articulations/Short Fictions, 1974, Recyclings, vol. 1, 1974, Openings & Closings, 1975, Extrapolate, 1975, Come Here, 1975, Modulations, 1975, Portraits from Memory, 1975, Constructs, 1976, Rain Rains Rain, 1976, Numbers: Poems and Stories, 1976, Numbers Two, 1977, Illuminations, 1977, One Night Stood, 1977, Grants and the Future of Literature, 1978, Constructs Two, 1978, Tabula Rose, 1978, Inexistences, 1978, Wordsand, 1978, Twenties in the Sixties, 1979, "The End", Appendix, 1979, "The End", Essentials, 1979, And So Forth, 1979, Exhaustive Parallel Intervals, 1979, More Short Fiction, 1980, Metamorphosis in Arts, 1980, The Old Poetries and the New, 1981, Autobiographies, 1981, Reincarnation, 1982, Turfs/Arenas/Fields/Pitches, 1983, American Imagination, 1983, Epiphanies, 1983; numerous others, works included various anthologies.; Editor and contbr.: On Contemporary Literature, 1964, 69, The New American Arts, 1965, Twelve from the Sixties, 1967, The Young American Writers, 1967, Beyond Left & Right: Radical Thought for Our Times, 1968, Imaged Words & Worded Images, 1970, Moholy-Nagy, 1970, John Cage, 1970, Possibilities of Poetry, 1970, Social Speculations, 1971, Human Alternatives: Visions for Us Now, 1971, Future's Fictions, 1971, Seeing Through Shuck, 1972, Breakthrough Fictioneers, 1973, The Edge of Adaptation, 1973, Essaying Essays, 1975, Language & Structure, 1975, Younger Critics in North America, 1976, Esthetics Contemporary, 1977, Assembling Assembling, 1978, Visual Literature Criticism, 1979, Text-Sound Texts, 1980, Scenarios, 1980, The Yale Gertrude Stein, 1980, A Critical Assembling, 1980, Aural Literature Criticism, 1981, American Writing Today, 1981, The Avant-Garde Tradition in Literature, 1982; others; producer numerous audiotapes, films, videotapes; contbg. editor: Pushcart Prize; writer, narrator: Camera Three, WCBS-TV, 1974; Co-founder: Compiler Assembling, 1970—; co-pub., editor: Precisely, A Critical Jour, 1977—; Contbr. articles, poems, revs., photographs and essays to mags., Numerous group exhbns. visual poetry, visual fiction, audiotapes, videotapes, films, holograms and numerical art; comprehensive exhbn.: Wordsand, at Simon Fraser U., U. Alta., Cornell Coll., Vassar Coll., U. N.D., Calif. State U., Bakersfield. Woodrow Wilson fellow, 1962-63; Pulitzer fellow in critical writing, 1965-66; Guggenheim Meml. Found. fellow, 1967-68; Nat. Endowment for Arts grantee, 1976, 78, 79, 81; N.Y. State Regents scholar, 1963-64; Internat. fellow Columbia U., 1963-64; Fund for Investigative Journalism fellow, 1980; Vogelstein Found. fellow, 1980. Mem. Artworkers, Phi Beta Kappa. Address: PO Box 73 Canal St Sta New York NY 10013 *To do what has not been done in several domains and in the course of that adventure to discover new possibilities in art, in writing and in myself.*

KOSTEM, CELAL NIZAMETTIN, civil engineer, educator; b. Ankara, Turkey, Feb. 8, 1939; came to U.S., 1966; s. Halil Naki and Habibe Suada K.; m. Katy Michele Nieuwenhuis, Aug. 30, 1966. Diploma Engr.-M.S. in, C.E., Istanbul Tech. U., 1961; Ph.D., U. Ariz., 1966. Engr. Istanbul Harbor Constrn., 1960-61; postdoctoral research assoc. Lehigh U., Bethlehem, Pa., 1966-68, asst. prof., 1968-72, assoc. prof., 1972-78; chmn. Computer Systems Group Fritz Engring. Lab., Lehigh U., Bethlehem, Pa., 1978—; co-dir. Computer-Aided Engring. Lab., Lehigh U., Bethlehem, Pa.; prof. civil engring. Lehigh U., Bethlehem, Pa., 1978—; structural cons., 1966—, shelter analyst, multiprotection designer; bd. dirs. Def. Design Inst., 1968—, Transp. Research Bd., 1970—. Contbr. numerous articles to profl. jours.; structural designer bridges and bldgs. Served to 1st lt. C.E. Turkish Land Forces, 1961-63; served to 1st lt. C.E. Turkish Res., 1963—. Fulbright fellow, 1963, 64, 65; UN Agy. for Internat. fellow, 1979; grantee State of Pa., 1972—. Mem. ASCE (pres. Lehigh Valley sect.), Am. Concrete Inst., Earthquake Engring. Research Inst., Internat. Assn. Bridge and Structural Engring., Assn. For Shell and Spatial Structures, Sigma Xi, Chi Epsilon. Home: 3520 Chippendale Circle Bethlehem PA 18017 Office: Fritz Engring Lab 13 Lehigh U Bethlehem PA 18015

KOSTER, ELAINE, book publisher; b. N.Y.C., Sept. 8, 1940; d. Louis and Claire (Schoenagle) Landis; m. William O. Koster, Jan. 7, 1978; 1 dau., Elizabeth Anna. B.A., Barnard Coll., 1962. Asso. editor Berkeley Books, N.Y.C., 1965; mng. editor Dell Books, Inc., 1967, Lit. Guild, N.Y.C., 1968-72; sr. v.p., publisher NAL, Inc., N.Y.C., 1972—. Mem. Women's Media, Barnard Profl. Women. Office: 1633 Broadway New York NY 10019

KOSTER, EUGENE STANLEY, insurance company executive; b. Chgo., May 18, 1942; s. Joseph J. and Harriet (Zalewski) K.; m. Allida Joyce; children: Christopher, Leslie, Matthew, Patrick. B.B.A. in Fin., U. Notre Dame, 1964; J.D., Northwestern U., 1967. C.L.U. Atty., advanced underwriter Northwestern Mut. Life Ins. Co., Milw., Hartford, Conn., Louisville, 1967-69, Life agt., dir. tng., 1969-73, asst. gen. agt., 1973-74; dir. personal sales Acacia Mut. Life Ins. Co., Washington, 1974-76, v.p. mktg., 1976-78, sr. v.p. mktg., 1978-82, exec. v.p. mktg., 1982—; dir. Sch. Life Ins.; mem. Met. Washington Bd. Trade. Mem. ABA, Wis. Bar Assn., Am. Soc. C.L.U.s, Nat. Assn. Life Underwriters, Life Ins. Mktg. and Research Assn. Office: Acadia Group 51 Louisiana Ave NW Washington DC 20001

KOSTER, JOHN PETER, JR., journalist, author; b. Balt., June 5, 1945; s. John Peter and Mathilde Katerina M. (Strunck) K.; m. Shizuko Obo, Dec. 5, 1971; children: Emily, John. B.A. in English, Montclair State Coll., 1967. Reporter Bergen Evening Record Corp., Hackensack, N.J., 1969-80; pub. The Northwest News, 1981—. Author: The Road to Wounded Knee, 1974, War Monthly, England, 1975, 76, Land of Broken Dreams, Japan, 1976, Burglarproof, 1976, Presumed Lost, 1978; Contbr. numerous articles to mags. Served with AUS, 1967-69. Co-recipient Hwy. Safety award Am. Automobile Assn., 1971; recipient Sigma Delta Chi award for distinguished pub. service, 1975. Home: 508 Ackerman Ave Glen Rock NJ 07452 Office: PO Box 157 Midland Park NJ 07432

KOSTERS, MARVIN H., economist; b. Corsica, S.D., Aug. 4, 1933; s. Albert and Alice (VanderLuit) K.; m. Bonnie Eckels; children: Mark, Elise, Barbara. B.A., Calvin Coll., 1960; Ph.D., U. Chgo., 1966. Economist Rand Corp., Santa Monica, Calif., 1965-69; sr. staff economist U.S. Council Econ. Advisers, Washington, 1969-71; asso. adminstr. U.S. Dept. Labor, Washington, 1971; asso. dir. U.S. Cost of Living Council, 1971-74; resident scholar Am. Enterprise Inst., Washington, 1974, 1975—, dir. govt. regulation studies, 1976—; dep. asst. to Pres. White House, Washington, 1974-75; instr. U. Chgo., 1964-65, UCLA, 1966-69, Washington Campus, 1978-80; mem. CAB adv. com. on procedural reform, 1975; cons. U.S. Dept. Treasury, Dept. Labor, Council Wage and Price Stability, 1975-77, Council Econ. Advisers, 1981. Bd. editors: Regulation and AEI Economist, 1977—; author: Controls and Inflation, 1975; co-editor: Reforming Regulation, 1980; contbr. articles to publs. on inflation and labor markets. Adv. com. on gen. govt. Rep. Nat. Com., 1978-80. Served with U.S. Army, 1953-55. Fellow Ingersoll Found., 1960-61, Earhart Found., 1962-63, Ford Found., 1964-65. Mem. Am. Econ. Assn. Mem. Christian Ref. Ch. Home: 4033 N 27th St Arlington VA 22207 Office: 1150 17th St NW Washington DC 20036

KOSTMAYER, JOHN HOUSTON, executive recruiting consulting; b. New Orleans, June 12, 1915; s. Hiram Watkins and Carroll (Houston) K.; m. Julia C., Sept. 10, 1940; children: Roger, John, Peter. Student, Tulane U., 1932-34, 35-36, U. of South, 1934-35. Vice pres., dir. First Investors Corp., N.Y.C., 1953-67; v.p., group exec. ITT Fin. Services, N.Y.C., 1967-73; chmn., pres., chief exec. officer Waddell & Reed, Inc., Kansas City, Mo., 1973-83; pres. John H. Kostmayer & Assos., Inc., Princeton, N.J., 1974—. Bd. govs. Investment Co. Inst., Washington, 1972-74. Home: 46 Parchment Dr New Hope PA 18938 Office: 419 N Harrison St Princeton NJ 08540

KOSTOF, SPIRO KONSTANTIN, archtl. historian, educator; b. Istanbul, Turkey, May 7, 1936; s. Konstantin Nenchef and Melpomeni (Franguli) K. B.A. in Humanities, Robert Coll., Turkey, 1957; M.A., Yale U., 1959, Ph.D., 1961. Instr., then asst. prof. history art Yale U., 1961-65; prof. archtl. history U. Calif. at Berkeley, 1965—; curator of architecture Univ. Art Mus., 1967-76; Mathews lectr. Columbia U., 1976; vis. prof. Mass. Inst. Tech., Cambridge, 1970. Author: The Orthodox Baptistery of Ravenna, 1965, Caves of God, 1972, The Third Rome, 1870-1950, Traffic and Glory, 1973; Editor: The Architect, 1977. Recipient Christian Research Found. award, 1965; Kress grantee, 1971-72; Nat. Endowment for the Humanities sr. fellow, 1972-73; Guggenheim fellow, 1980. Mem. Soc. Archtl. Historians (pres. 1974-76), Archtl. History Found. (editorial bd. 1977—). Home: 958 Cragmont Ave Berkeley CA 94708 Office: Dept Architecture U Calif Berkeley CA 94720

KOSTUIK, STEPHEN PAUL, mining company executive; b. Malartic, Que., Can., Nov. 3, 1939; s. John and Mable Anne (Beadman) K.; m. Donna Jean Martin, Nov. 11, 1961; children: Jennifer Anne, Stephen Peter, Martin Leslie, Paula Nicole. B.Sc., Queens U., Kingston, Ont., 1961, M.S., 1964. Chief engr. ops. Kerr Addison Mines Ltd., 1968, tech. asst. to pres., 1969; v.p., gen. mgr. Molycorp Inc., White Plains, N.Y., 1970-74; pres. Southeast div. Vulcan Materials Co., Birmingham, Ala., 1974-77, exec. v.p. constrn. materials, 1977—, also dir., 1980—. Mem. Can. Inst. Mining and Metallurgy (chmn. com. on edn.), Assn. Profl. Engrs. Ont., AIME. Roman Catholic. Clubs: Inverness Country, Riverchase Country, Willow Point Golf and Country. Home: 1318 Branchwater Ln Vestavia Hills AL 35216 Office: PO Box 7497 Birmingham AL 35253

KOSTYO, JACK LAWRENCE, educator; b. Elyria, Ohio, Oct. 1, 1931; s. Louis and Matilda (Thomasko) K.; m. Shirlianne Guth, June 10, 1953; children: Cecile A., Louis C. A.B., Oberlin Coll., 1953; Ph.D., Cornell U., 1957; M.D. (hon.), U. Göteborg, 1978. NRC fellow Harvard Med. Sch., Boston, 1957-59; asst. prof., then prof. physiology Duke, 1959-68; prof., chmn. dept. physiology Emory U., Atlanta, 1968-79, U. Mich. Med. Sch., Ann Arbor, 1979—; mem. endocrinology study sect. NIH, USPHS, 1967-71; mem. physiology test com. Nat. Bd. Med. Examiners, 1974-77. Editor-in-chief: Endocrinology, 1978-82; contbr. articles to profl. jours. Mem. adv. bd. Searle Scholars. Recipient Lederle Med. Faculty award, 1961; Ernst Oppenheimer Meml. award Endocrine Soc., 1969. Mem. Endocrine Soc. (mem. editorial bd., council), Am. Physiol. Soc. (mem. editorial bd., chmn. standing com. on edn., mem. council), Soc. for Exptl. Biology and Medicine (editorial bd.), Internat. Union Physiol. Scis. (commn. on med. edn.), Assn. Chmn. Depts. Physiology (pres. 1979, council), Sigma Xi. Home: 8 Eastbury Ct Ann Arbor MI 48105

KOSTYRA, RICHARD JOSEPH, advertising executive; b. Winnipeg, Man., Can., Nov. 4, 1940; came to U.S., 1980; s. Joseph and Ann (Walashek) K.; m. Juleinne E. Lynden, Aug. 4, 1961 (div.); 1 son, Corwin Gregory; m. 2d Lorraine T. Antoniello, Sept. 19, 1981. With J. Walter Thompson, Toronto, Ont., Can., 1959-63, media dir., 1966-73, sr. v.p., dir. diversification, 1973-76, sr. v.p., gen. mgr., Montreal, Que., Can., 1976-80, sr. v.p., media dir., N.Y.C., 1980—; group media dir. Cockfield Brown, Toronto, 1963-66; dir. J. Walter Thompson Can., 1965-76. Home: 33H 245 E 40th St New York NY 10016 Office: 466 Lexington Ave New York NY 10017

KOTAS, ROBERT VINCENT, research physician, educator; b. Buffalo, Nov. 26, 1938; s. Vincent John and Regina Agnes (Hadynka) K.; m. Ilona Rae Fielding, Mar. 2, 1968; children: Nicole, Timothy, Robert, Rebecca. B.S., Canisius Coll., 1959; M.D., U. Buffalo, 1963. Diplomate: Am. Acad. Pediatrics. Research assoc. McGill U., 1969-70; intern Buffalo Children's Hosp., 1963-64; resident in pediatrics Johns Hopkins Hosp., Balt., 1964-66; asst. prof. pediatrics U. Okla. Med. Sch., 1970-72, dir. newborn services, 1970-72; dir., div. devel. physiology; career investigator W.K. Warren Med. Research Center, Tulsa, 1972-76, sci. dir., 1976-80; dir. William and Natalie Warren Med. Inst., Tulsa, 1980-83; mem. staffs Okla. Children's Meml. Hosp., Santa Rosa Hosp., San Antonio, St. Anthony's Hosp., St. Francis Hosp., Tulsa, Med. Ctr. Hosp., San Antonio; clin. prof. pediatrics U. Okla. Med. Sch., Tulsa, 1977—; assoc. prof. pediatrics U. Tex. Health Sci. Ctr., San Antonio, 1983—; guest scientist Nat. Inst. Child Health and Human devel., Bethesda, Md., 1975-77; cons. Nat. Inst. Child Health and Human Devel., Am. Lung Assn., others. Contbr. articles to profl. jours. and books. Served as capt. USAF, 1966-68. Recipient continuing edn. awards AMA; Best M.D. Written Book award Am. Med. Writers Assn., 1980; Mosby scholar, 1963; grantee NIH, 1969-70, 75-79, 84—, USPHS, 1968-69; others. Fellow Am. Coll. Obstetricians and Gynecologists (assoc.); mem. Johns Hopkins Med. and Surg. Assn., So. Soc. Pediatric Research, Am. Thoracic Soc., Soc. Pediatric Research, Am. Physiol. Soc., Soc. Exptl. Biology and Medicine, Soc. Gynecol. Investigation. Office: 7703 Floyd Curl Dr San Antonio TX 78284 *Grateful for the excitement of impending discovery which characterizes my work with its promise of surprise in the midst of daily routine, I am indebted for the guidance and inspiration that my present and past associates have given me to deal effectively with the diversity and perversity of experience.*

KOTCH, ALEX, chemistry educator, university administrator; b. Edwardsville, Pa., Aug. 18, 1926; s. Alex and Irene (Hazilla) K.; m. Anny Marie Brinkman, Mar. 5, 1952; children: Marianne (Mrs. Gerald L. Cassell), Axel, Robert, Jennifer. Student, Bucknell Jr. Coll., 1943-44; B.S. (Evan Pugh scholar), Pa. State U., 1946, M.S., 1947; Ph.D. (Monsanto Chem. Co. fellow), U. Ill., 1950. Research chemist central research dept. E.I. duPont de Nemours & Co., Wilmington, Del., 1952-54, chemist organic chems. dept., Deepwater Point, N.J., 1954-59; assoc. program dir. for chemistry NSF, Washington, 1959-63, program dir. for organic chemistry, 1963-65; chief biosciences div. Office of Saline Water, Dept. Interior, Washington, 1965-66; staff assoc. univ. sci. devel. sect. NSF, Washington, 1966-67; prof. chemistry, assoc. chmn. U. Wis.-Madison, 1967-77; asst. dir. info. edn. and internat. programs Solar Energy Research Inst., 1977-78, spl. asst. to dir., 1978-79, mgr. univ. programs office, 1979-82; prof. chemistry, dir. Office of Research and Program Devel. U. N.D., 1982—; cons.-examiner North Central Assn. Colls. and Schs.; bd. dirs. Associated Western Univs., 1982—. Fulbright fellow Tech. U., Delft, Netherlands, 1950-51; Arthur D. Little Postdoctoral fellow Mass. Inst. Tech., 1951-52. Mem. Am. Chem. Soc., AAAS, Nat. Council Univ. Research Adminstrs., Soc. Research Adminstrs., Sigma Xi, Alpha Chi Sigma, Phi Kappa Phi, Phi Lambda Upsilon, Pi Mu Epsilon. Home: 3502 Belmont Rd Grand Forks ND 58201

KOTCHEFF, WILLIAM THEODORE (TED KOTCHEFF), director; b. Toronto, Ont., Can., 1931. With CBC, 1952-57, ABC-TV, London, 1957. Dir.: plays, including Maggie May; films, including Life at the Top, 1965, Two Gentlemen Sharing, 1970, Outback, 1971, Billy Two Hats, 1973, The Apprenticeship of Duddy Kravitz, 1974, Fun With Dick and Jane, 1977, Who is Killing the Great Chefs of Europe, 1978, Uncommon Valor, 1983; dir., writer: film North Dallas Forty, 1979; producer, dir.: Captured, 1981. Office: care Internat Creative Mgmt 8899 Beverly Blvd Los Angeles CA 90048 *

KOTHE, CHARLES ALOYSIUS, lawyer; b. Jersey City, Oct. 12, 1912; s. Charles A. and Lillian (Hansen) K.; m. Janet Fleming, Feb. 19, 1937; children: Diane, Charles F., James R., David J. Student, Bucknell U., 1930-33; A.B., U. Tulsa, 1934; scholarship, U. Heidelberg, Germany; J.D. with honors, U. Okla., 1938. Bar: Okla. bar 1938. With firm Smith & Kothe, Tulsa, 1938-39; staff counsel Mid-Continent Petroleum Co., Tulsa, 1939-41; gen. counsel Macnick Co., Tulsa, 1941-43; mem. firm Kulp, Pinson, Lupardus & Kothe, Tulsa, 1943-46; v.p. indsl. relations NAM, N.Y.C., 1959-65; partner firm Kothe, Nichols & Wolfe, Inc., 1966—; atty., v.p., dir. Coburn Optical Industries, 1966-76; dir. T.D. Williamson Co.; Mem. faculty labor law dept. Tulsa Law Sch., 1939—; mem. faculty indsl. relations dept. Okla. Sch. Accounting; dean O.W. Coburn Law Sch.; mem. faculty Grad. Sch., Oral Roberts U., 1974—; panel mem. Am. Arbitration Assn., Fed. Mediation and Conciliation Service; spl. cons., 1960—; Equal Employment Opportunity Commn.; mem. Nat. Labor Manpower Policy Com., 1969—; mem. exec. res. U.S. Dept. Labor, 1971—. Author: Industrial Relations in the Non-Union Plant, 1960, NLRB and the Rights of Management, 1966; Editor: Tale of 22 Cities, 1964. Dir. Protestant council, 1964, N.Y. World's Fair; co-founder, 2d pres. Effective Citizens Orgn., 1957; Okla. chmn. Citizens for Eisenhower.; Bd. dirs. Internat. Christian Leadership, Tulsa, Okla. Osteopathic Hosp.; Mem. Tulsa Civil Service Commn., 1980—. Named Citizen of Year, Tulsa, 1946. Mem. ABA (10th Circuit councilman 1940), Okla. Bar Assn. (chmn. labor law section), U.S. Jr. C. of C. (v.p. 1956), Okla. Jr. C. of C. (pres. 1955), Tulsa Jaycees (pres. 1954), Jr. Bar Conf. Okla. (pres. 1946), U. Tulsa Alumni Assn. (pres. 1957, distinguished alumnus 1974), Order of Coif, Sigma Alpha Epsilon, Phi Delta Phi, Beta Gamma Sigma. Presbyn. (trustee Tulsa Presbytery; elder; state chmn. Presbyn. Restoration Fund). Clubs: Mason (Shriner), Tulsa, Southern Hills Country; Nat. Lawyers (Washington). Home: 4180 Oak Rd Tulsa OK 74105 Office: 7777 S Lewis Tulsa OK 74171

KOTIN, PAUL, pathologist; b. Chgo., Aug. 13, 1916; s. Elias and Rose (Spunt) K.; m. Pauline H. Stephan, Dec. 12, 1970; children—Joel Tepper, David Bernard. B.S., U. Ill., 1937, M.D., 1940. Intern Deaconess Hosp., Chgo., 1939-40, resident pathology, 1940-41; pvt. practice pathology and internal medicine, San Luis Obispo, Calif., 1946-48; research pathology U. So. Calif., 1949-50; med. microbiologist Los Angeles County Hosp., 1950-51, attending staff pathologist, 1951-62; mem. faculty U. So. Calif., 1951-62, prof. pathology, 1959-60, Paul Pierce prof. pathology, 1960-62; chief carcinogenesis studies br. Nat. Cancer Inst., 1962-63, asso. dir. for field studies, 1963-64, sci. dir. for etiology, 1964-66; dir div. environ. health scis. NIH, 1966-69; dir. Nat. Inst. Environ. Health Scis., 1969-71; v.p. for health scis., dean Sch. Medicine, Temple U., Phila., 1971-74; sr. v.p. health, safety and environment Johns-Manville Corp., 1974-81; Edgar Allen Meml. lectr. Yale Sch. Medicine, 1957; vis. prof. oncology U. Wis., 1959-60; vis. prof. pathology U. N.C., also Duke U., 1967-71; Harry Shay Meml. lectr. Temple U., 1964; Sappington Meml. lectr. Am. Occupational Medicine Assn., Anaheim, Calif., 1979, Gehrmann lectr., Nashville, 1981; chmn. Gordon Research Conf. Cancer, 1965; adj. prof. pathology U. Colo., 1974—; Cons. air pollution med. program, div. spl. health service USPHS, 1958-62; mem. sci. adv. bd. Council Tobacco Research-U.S.A., 1952-65; adv. com. r.r. diesel gases and dust Calif. Pub. Utilities Commn., 1956-62; adv. com. research pathogenesis cancer Am. Cancer Soc., 1962-65; pathology study sect. NIH, 1962-66, lung cancer task force, 1967-68; corr. mem. permanent European com. Research Chronic Hazards, 1960—; cancer prevention com. UICC, 1962-66, com. on exptl. design and methodology in carcinogenesis, 1967-70; sci. com. Inst. Occupational and Environ. Health, Quebec. Asbestos Mining Assn., 1966-75; mem. Fed. Com. Pest Control, 1964-71; program com. Tenth Internat. Congress, 1967-70; mem. Expert Panel on Carcinogenicity, 1962-70, Nat. Environ. Health Scis. Center, 1965, Nat. Adv. Com. Occupational Safety and Health, 1975-78, Armed Forces Epidemiol. Bd., 1976-80. Editorial adv. bd.: Cancer Research, 1957-61, Internat. Rev. Exptl. Pathology, 1968—; editorial bd.: AMA Archives Pathology, 1965-71, Environ. Research, 1966—, Am. Jour. Pathology, 1971-82; Contbr. articles to med. jours. Served with AUS, 1941-46. Recipient Superior Service award HEW, 1966, Disting. Service award, 1969; Sr. postdoctoral fellow NSF, 1959-60. Fellow Coll. Am. Pathologists, N.Y. Acad. Scis., Am. Acad. Occupational Medicine; mem. AMA (com. research on tobacco and health 1966-78), Am. Assn. Cancer Research (dir.), Am. Assn. Pathologists and Bacteriologists, AAAS, Am. Indsl. Hygiene Assn., Am. Occupational Medicine Assn. (Knudsen award 1981), Sigma Xi. Home: 4505 S Yosemite 339 Denver CO 80237

KOTKER, NORMAN RICHARD, author; b. Chelsea, Mass., Nov. 16, 1931; s. Harry Aaron and Betty (Kaplan) K.; m. Zane Hickcox, June 7, 1965; children—David, Ariel. Grad., Boston Latin Sch., 1948; A.B., Harvard, 1952. Researcher Look mag., N.Y.C., 1953-56; reporter Business Week mag., N.Y.C., 1956-57; editor Horizon Books, N.Y.C., 1960-69; asso. editor Horizon mag., 1965-66; editor trade dept. Charles Scribner's Sons, N.Y.C., 1969-78. Co-author: Massachusetts: A Pictorial History, 1976, New England Past, 1981; author: Herzl The King, 1972, The Earthly Jerusalem, 1969, The Holy Land in The Time of Jesus, 1967, Miss Rhode Island, 1978; Editor: The Horizon Book of the Elizabethan World, 1967, The Horizon Book of the Middle Ages, 1968, The Horizon History of China, 1969. Mem. P.E.N. Home: 45 Lyman Rd Northampton MA 01060

KOTLER, MILTON, community organization executive; b. Chgo., Mar. 15, 1935; s. Maurice and Betty (Bubar) K.; m. Greta Smith, July 11, 1976; children: Anthony, Joshua, Jonathan, Rebecca. B.A., U. Chgo., 1954, M.A. in Polit. Sci, 1957, postgrad. (Jane Morton fellow), 1957-59. Asst. prof. Chgo. City Coll., 1961-63; resident fellow Inst. for Policy Studies, Washington, 1963-77; exec. dir. Inst. Neighborhood Studies, Washington, 1972-75, Nat. Assn. Neighborhoods, 1975-81; v.p. Ctr. for Responsive Governance, Washington, 1981—, treas., 1980—; vis. prof. Univ. Calif., Berkeley, 1968; adj. prof. Am. Univ., Washington, 1976—, Univ. Md., 1980—. Author: Neighborhood Government, 1969, Building Neighborhood Organization, 1983; co-editor: Jour. Community Action, 1981—; contbr. chpts. to books. Vice pres. Alliance for Voluntarism, 1979-80; mem. program com., pub. affairs sector Luth. Ch. Am., 1979—; mem. Jewish Chamber Music Council, 1983; mem. bd. Nat. Com. Responsive Philanthropy, Washington, 1980—. Served with USAFR, 1959-60. Home: 3505 McKinley St NW Washington DC 20015 Office: 1100 17th St NW Washington DC 20036 *I have sought in all my work to empower the neighborhood community as a sphere of our personal responsibility. I have done this so that we may become more human through that responsibility, and with the hope that this responsibility will be guided by biblical faith.*

KOTLER, PHILIP, marketing educator; b. Chgo., May 27, 1931; s. Maurice and Betty (Bubar) K.; m. Nancy Ruth Kellum, Jan. 30, 1955; children: Amy Elizabeth, Melissa Eve, Jessica Kellum. Student, DePaul U., 1948-50; M.A., U. Chgo., 1953; Ph.D., MIT, 1956; postgrad., U. Chgo., 1957, Harvard, 1960. Research analyst Westinghouse Corp., Pitts., 1953; asst., asso. prof. Roosevelt U., Chgo., 1957-61; from asst. prof. to prof. marketing Northwestern U., 1962-69, A. Montgomery Ward prof. marketing, 1969-73, Harold T. Martin prof. marketing, 1973—; adv. marketing editor Holt, Rinehart and Winston, 1965-78; dir. Deltak; chmn. Coll. on Mktg., Inst. Mgmt. Scis., 1968; bd. dirs. Mgmt. Analysis Ctr., 1972—. Author: Marketing Management: Analysis, Planning and Control, 5th edit., 1984, Marketing Decision Making: A Model-Building Approach, 2d edit., 1983, Simulation in Social and Adminstrative Science, 1971, Creating Social Change, 1971, Marketing for Nonprofit Organizations, 2d edit., 1982, Principles of Marketing, 2d edit., 1983. Recipient Graham and Dodd award Financial Analysts Fedn., 1962, MacLaren Advt. Research award Canadian Advt. Research Found., 1964, Merit award Media/Scope, 1965, McKinsey award, 1965, Alpha Kappa Psi Found. award, 1969, 71, 72; Paul D. Converse award, 1978; named Marketer of Yr., 1983. Mem. Am. Marketing Assn. (bd. dirs. 1970-72), Inst. Mgmt. Scis., Marketing Sci. Inst. (trustee 1974—), Phi Beta Kappa. Home: 624 Central St Evanston IL 60201

KOTLOWITZ, ROBERT, editor, writer; b. Paterson, N.J., Nov. 21, 1924; s. Max and Debra (Kaplan) K.; m. Carol Naomi Leibowitz, Oct. 15, 1950; children—Alexander William, Daniel Justin. B.A., Johns Hopkins, 1947; preparatory diploma, Peabody Conservatory Music, 1941. Asso. editor Pocket Books, Inc., 1950-55, Discovery, 1952-55; mgr. press and information RCA Victor Records, 1955-60; sr. editor Show mag., 1960-64, Harper's mag., 1965-67, mng. editor, 1967-71; sr. v.p., dir. programming WNET/ Channel 13, N.Y.C., 1971—; guest lectr. Queen's Coll., 1954-55; author monthly column Performing Arts, 1966—. Author: novel Somewhere Else, 1972, The Boardwalk, 1977; Contbg. editor: Atlantic Monthly, 1971-74; Contbr. nat. publs. Served with inf. AUS, 1943-46. Recipient Edward Lewis Wallant award for novel, 1972; Nat. Jewish Book award, 1972. Clubs: Coffeehouse, Century Assn. (N.Y.C.). Home: 54 Riverside Dr New York NY 10024 Office: 356 W 58th St New York NY 10019

KOTOSKE, ROGER ALLEN, artist, educator; b. South Bend, Ind., Jan. 4, 1933; s. Michael and Louise (Gallo) K.; 1 dau., Tamara. Student, U. Notre Dame, 1950-52; B.F.A., U. Denver, 1955, M.A., 1956. Instr. Fitzsimons Army Hosp., Denver, 1956-58, U. Denver, 1958-68; mem. faculty U. Ill., 1968—; now assoc. prof. Vice pres., artist Denver Nat. Sculpture Symposium, 1968. One man shows, James Yu Gallery, N.Y.C., 1974, Hiestand Gallery, Miami U., Oxford, Ohio, 1978, Hilton Center for Performing Arts, St. Louis, 1979, group shows include, SUNY, Potsdam, 1975, Grey Gallery, N.Y.C., 1976, Illinois Painters III, 1980; represented in permanent collections, Rock Hill Nelson Gallery, Kansas City, Mo., SUNY, Oswego, Denver Art Mus., others. Ford Found. grantee, 1975-78. Home: 1611 W White St Champaign IL 61820

KOTRADY, JOHN, management consultant; b. Duquesne, Pa., Feb. 5, 1911; s. John and Mary (Kollar) K.; m. Helen Beatrice Berndtson, May 31, 1936. B.S., Grove City (Pa.) Coll., 1933. Instr. chemistry and comml. law Mayville (N.Y.) High Sch., 1933-37; with Texaco, 1937-78, sr. tech. librarian, 1959-68, adminstrv. asst., 1968-76; cons. Hawaii Sci. and Engring. Fair, Honolulu, 1977, 78, 79, 80, 81. Pres. Dumont (N.J.) Community Chest Council, 1953-54, 82-84. Served with U.S. Army, World War II. Mem. Am. Inst. Chemists (chmn. N.Y. chpt. 1954-55, councilor 1956-57, chmn. ann. meeting 1959, dir., mem. nat. council 1959-72, nat. sec. 1959-72, Honor scroll N.Y. chpt. 1962), Am. Chem. Soc. (treas., dir. N.Y. chpt. 1960-76, nat. councilor 1965-81, nat. council policy com. 1973-79, com. program rev. 1976-79, com. pub. relations 1976-81, chmn. div. meeting 1979, presiding chmn. Symposium on Sci. Research 1979), Research Soc. Am., Pi Kappa Delta, Pi Gamma Mu. Presbyn. (ruling elder 1972-76, supt. ch. sch. 1958-72). Clubs: Chemists (N.Y.C.); Quarterback (Honolulu). Pioneered closed circuit TV for ednl. purposes, 1952. Home: The Kalia Apt 902-A 425 Ena Rd Honolulu HI 96815

KOTTAS, JOHN FREDERICK, business administration educator; b. Hampton, Va., Apr. 18, 1940; s. Harry and Johnny (Edwards) K.; m. Betty Ann Hokenson, Aug. 7, 1965; children: John Bohlin, Ellen Elizabeth, Katherine Caroline, Paul Frederick. B.S., Purdue U., 1962; M.S., Northwestern U., 1964, Ph.D., 1968. Lectr. Wharton Sch., Univ. Pa., Phila., 1966-68; asst. prof. Sch. Bus. Adminstrn., Univ. N.C., Chapel Hill., 1968-73; adj. asso. prof. Boston Univ. Overseas Grad. Program, Heidelberg, W. Ger., 1973-74; asso. prof. coordinator mgmt. sci. and info. systems Sch. Bus. Adminstrn., Univ. Mo., St. Louis, 1974-79; Zollinger prof. bus. adminstrn. Coll. of William and Mary, Williamsburg, Va., 1979—; presented three-day mgmt. seminar on Inventory Mgmt. and Control at numerous univs., U.S. and Can., 1976-78. Co-author: Production/Operations Management: Contemporary Policy of Managing Operating Systems, 1972; contbr. articles to various publs. NDEA fellow, 1962-65; Walter P. Murphy fellow, 1962. Mem. Am. Inst. Decision Scis., Am. Inst. Indsl. Engrs., Am. Prodn. and Inventory Control Soc., Ops. Research Soc. Am., Inst. Mgmt. Scis. Home: 109 Maxwell Pl Williamsburg VA 23185 Office: Sch Bus Adminstrn Coll of William and Mary Williamsburg VA 23185

KOTTCAMP, EDWARD HOWAR, JR., steel company executive, researcher, consultant; b. York, Pa., July 12, 1934; s. Edward Howard and Beatrice Sarah (Phillips) K.; m. nancy Lee Shirey, Sept. 9, 1956; children: Robert, Edward III, Timothy. B.S. in Metal Engring., Lehigh U., 1956, M.S., 1957, Ph.D., 1960; P.M.D. in Bus. Adminstrn., Harvard U., 1973. Assoc. prof. Lehigh U., Bethlehem, Pa., 1957-61; engr., v.p. research dept. Bethlehem Steel Corp., 1963-82, group exec. v.p. steel prodn., 1982—. Contbr. articles to profl. jours. Served to 1st lt. U.S. Army, 1961-62. Recipient A.S. Quier Metall. prize Lehigh U., 1956, William Sparagan award for outstanding contbn. in research, 1963. Fellow Am. Soc. Metals (trustee, chmn. long range planning); mem. Am. Welding Soc., Welding Research Council. Republican. Lutheran. Home: 2001 Church Rd Bethlehem PA 18015 Office: Bethlehem Steel Corp Bethelehem PA 18016

KOTTER, JOHN PAUL, organizational behavior educator, management consultant; b. San Diego, Feb. 25, 1947; s. Paul Henry and Louise (Churchill) K. B.S., MIT, 1968, M.S., 1970; D.B.A., Harvard U., 1972. Research fellow Bus. Sch., Harvard U., Boston, 1972-73, asst. prof., 1973-77, assoc. prof., 1977-81, prof., 1981—, area chmn., 1982—; cons.; dir. McBer, Inc., Boston. Author: Organizational Diagnosis, 1978, Self Assessment and Career Development, 1978, Power in Management, 1979, The General Managers, 1982. Mem. Acad. Mgmt. Home: 19 Chauncey St Cambridge MA 02138 Office: Harvard U Bus Sch Soldiers Field Boston MA 02163

KOTTKE, FREDERIC JAMES, physician; b. Hayfield, Minn., May 26, 1917; s. George G. and Harriet Mae (Davidson) K.; m. Astrid Marie Erling, May 27, 1939; children—Jane, James, Mary, Thomas. B.S., U. Minn., 1939, M.S. in Physiology, 1941, Ph.D., 1944, M.D., 1945. Diplomate: Am. Bd. Phys. Medicine and Rehab. (mem. 1956-59, chmn. 1963-69). Lab. asst. in physiology U. Minn. Med. Sch., 1939-40, instr., 1941-44, Baruch fellow in phys. medicine, 1946-47, asst. prof. phys. medicine, 1947-49, asso. prof., 1949-53, prof., 1953—, head dept. phys. medicine and rehab., 1952-82; resident in phys. medicine U. Minn. Hosps., 1946-47; cons. Mpls. VA Hosp., 1952—; mem. Minn. Bd. Health, 1964-67; mem. med. adv. bd. Office Vocat. Rehab., 1961-67; mem. med. research studies sect., 1961-63; bd. dirs. Kenny Rehab. Found., 1960-79; pres. Minn. Phys. Therapy Bd. Examiners, 1951-61; bd. dirs. Am. Rehab. Found. (Sister Kenny Inst.), 1964—, sec., 1964; bd. dirs. Interstudy, 1973—; John Stanley Coulter Meml. lectr., 1968, Walter J. Zeiter Meml. lectr., 1973; Disting. lectr. P.R. Med. Assn. Sect. on Phys. Medicine and Rehab., San Juan, 1973; Sidney Licht Meml. lectr. U. Pa., 1980, Ohio State U., 1981. Editorial bd.: Archives Phys. Medicine and Rehab, 1952-71, Modern Medicine, 1955—. Recipient citation Pres.'s Com. on Employment of Physically Handicapped, 1959, award of merit Rehab. Inst. Montreal, Que., Can., 1970. Mem. Am. Acad. Phys. Medicine and Rehab. (dir. 1973—, pres. 1978), Am. Assn. Lab. Animal Sci., Am. Congress Rehab. Medicine, Am. Heart Assn. (councils clin. cardiology and cerebrovascular disease), AMA, Am. Rehab. Found., Hennepin County (Minn.) Med. Soc., Internat. Rehab. Medicine Assn. (council), Internat. Soc. Rehab. Disabled, Minn. Acad. Sci., Minn. Heart Assn., Minn. Med. Alumni Assn., Minn. Med. Found., Minn. Physiatric Soc., Minn. State Med. Assn., Nat. Rehab. Assn., Am. Congress Phys. Medicine and Rehab. (v.p. 1954-58, pres. 1960, Disting. Service key 1961), Internat. Fedn. Phys. Medicine and Rehab. (chmn. edn. com. 1976—), Sigma Xi; hon. mem. Sociedad Colombiana de Medicina Fisica y Rehabilitacion, Mexican Acad. Surgery, Academia Brazileira de Medicina de Rehabilitacion, Sociedad Venezolana de Medicina Fisica y Rehabilitacion, Dutch Soc. Phys. Medicine and Rehab. Mem. Democratic Farm Labor Party. Lutheran. Research on rehab., therapeutic exercise, spinal cord injury, cardiac problems, poliomyelitis. Home: 2741 Drew Ave S Minneapolis MN 55416 Office: U Minn Hosps 420 Delaware St SE Minneapolis MN 55455

KOTTKE, LEO, guitarist; b. Athens, Ga. Student, St. Cloud State Coll., Minn. (First rec.) Twelve String Blues, 1969; albums Six and Twelve String Guitar, 1971, Circle Round the Sun, Mudlark, My Feet are Smiling, Ice Water, Chewing Pine, Greenhouse, Burt Lips, Balance, Guitar Music; appeared at, Cambridge Folk Festival, Eng., 1975; composer segments: film soundtrack Days of Heaven, 1978. Served with USN. Office: care Denny Bruce 6777 Hollywood Blvd Hollywood CA 90028 *

KOTTLER, HOWARD WILLIAM, artist, educator; b. Cleve., Mar. 5, 1930; s. Paul L. and Nellie (Novick) K. B.A., Ohio State U., 1952, M.A., 1956, Ph.D., 1964; M.F.A., Cranbrook Acad. Art, 1957. Instr. art Ohio State U., 1961-64; vis. asst. prof. art U. Wash., Seattle, 1964-65, asst. prof., 1965-67, asso. prof., 1967-72, prof., 1972—. One-man exhbns. include, Mus. Contemporary Crafts, N.Y.C., 1967, Nordness Galleries, N.Y.C., 1969, Meml. Art Gallery, Rochester, N.Y., 1975, Tacoma Art Mus., 1976, 79; represented in permanent collections, Victoria and Albert Mus., London, Nat. Mus. Modern Art, Kyoto, Japan, Detroit Inst. Art, Cleve. Mus. Art, Cooper-Hewitt Mus., Contemporary Crafts Mus., N.Y.C. Fulbright grantee, 1957; Nat. Endowment Arts grantee, 1975. Mem. Am. Crafts Council. Home: 12021 33 Ave NE Seattle WA 98125 Office: Univ of Wash Sch of Art Seattle WA 98195

KOTTLOWSKI, FRANK EDWARD, geologist; b. Indpls., Apr. 11, 1921; s. Frank Charles and Adella (Markworth) K.; m. Florence Jean Chriscoe, Sept. 15, 1945; children: Karen, Janet, Diane. Student, Butler U., 1939-42; A.B., Ind. U., 1947, M.A., 1949, Ph.D., 1951. Party chief Ind. Geology Survey, Bloomington, summers 1948-50; fellow Ind. U., 1947-51, instr. geology, 1950; adj. prof. N.Mex. Inst. Mining and Tech., Socorro, 1970—; econ. geologist N.Mex. Bur. Mines and Mineral Resources, 1951-66, asst. dir., 1966-68, 70-74, acting dir., 1968-70, dir., 1974—; geologic cons. Sandia Corp., 1966-72. Contbr. articles on mineral resources, stratigraphy and areal geology to tech. jours. Mem. Planning Commn. Socorro, 1960-68, 71-78; mem. N.Mex. Energy Resources Bd.; sec. Socorro County Democratic party, 1964-68. Served to 1st lt. USAAF, 1942-45. Decorated D.F.C., Air medal. Fellow Geol. Soc. Am. (councilor 1980-82, exec. com. 1981-82); mem. Am. Assn. Petroleum Geologists (dist. rep. 1965-68, Disting. Service award 1981, editor 1971-75), Assn. Am. State Geologists (v.p. 1983-84), Soc. Econ. Geologists, AAAS, AIME, Am. Inst. Profl. Geologists, Am. Commn. Stratigraphic Nomenclature (sec. 1964-68, chmn. 1968-70), Sigma Xi. Home: 703 Sunset Dr Socorro NM 87801 Office: NMex Bur Mines NMex Tech Socorro NM 87801

KOTTMAN, ROY MILTON, college dean; b. Thornton, Iowa, Dec. 22, 1916; s. William D. and Millie J. (Christensen) K.; m. Wanda Lorraine Moorman, Dec. 31, 1941; children: Gary Roy, Robert William, Wayne David, Janet Kay. B.S. in Agr, Iowa State U., 1941, Ph.D., 1952; M.S. in Genetics, U. Wis., 1948; LL.D. (hon.), Coll. Wooster, 1972. Asst. prof. animal husbandry Iowa State U., 1946-47; grad. research asst. U. Wis., 1947-48; mem. faculty Iowa State U., 1949-58, prof. animal husbandry, asso. dean agr., 1954-58; dean Coll. Agr., Forestry and Home Econs.; dir. Agrl. Expt. Sta., W.Va. U., 1958-60; dean Coll. Agr. and Home Econs., Ohio State U.; also dir. Ohio Agrl. Research and Devel. Center, 1960—; dir. Coop. Extension Service, 1964-82; acting assoc. dir. Nev. Agr. Expt. Sta., 1982-83; dir. Swift Ind. Packing Co.; mem. exec. com. sci. adv. bd. DNA Plant Tech. Corp. Mem. Ohio Soil and Water Conservation Commn., 1960-82; mem. Central Ohio Water Advisory Council, 1976-82; bd. dirs. Ohio 4-H Found., 1964-82, Farm Film Found., 1973-80; mem. Agr. Higher Edn. Projects Com., 1975-80, Friends NACAA Scholarship Com., 1976-80, Ohio Agrl. Mus. Com., 1977-82, Gov.'s Task Force on Gasohol, 1979-80; bd. dirs. Farm Found., 1978—; v.p. Agrl. Research Inst., 1980-81. Recipient FFA degree Am. Farmer, 1977; named to Ohio Agr. Hall of Fame, 1983. Mem. Exec. Order Ohio Commodores, Sigma Xi, Gamma Sigma Delta, Alpha Gamma Sigma (hon.), Alpha Zeta, Phi Kappa Phi, Pi Kappa Phi (future policy com. 1976-80), Phi Zeta (hon.), Alpha Gamma Rho (hon.). Presbyterian. Clubs: Rotary (hon.), Nat. Dairy Shrine.). Home: 1375 Kirkley Rd Columbus OH 43210 *I believe in the goodness of people and in their desire for acceptance and respect. It is parents rather than children who are the* *major source of teenage discontent and crime. A concentrated effort by the media, especially TV, to arouse the consciousness of parents to the mental as well as physical abuse being inflicted on their children would go far toward reducing truancy and lack of interest in learning. It would also decrease drug abuse and the costs of law enforcement. As a nation we must become more concerned with parental delinquency if we are to come to grips with juvenile delinquency.*

KOTTO, YAPHET FREDRICK, actor; b. Harlem, N.Y., Nov. 15, 1944; s. Yaphet Mangobell and Gladys Maria K.; m. Antoinette Pettyjohn, Jan. 29, 1975; children—Natascha, Fredrick, Robert, Sarada, Mirabai, Salina. Appeared in: Off-Broadway and Broadway productions including Great White Hope; film appearances include Nothing But a Man, 1963, Liberation of Lord Byron Jones, 1964, Live and Let Die, 1974, Across 110th St, 1973, Report to the Commissioner, 1974, Night Chase, 1973, Drum, 1976, Monkey Hustle, 1975, Raid on Entebbe, 1976, Blue Collar, 1977, Sharks Treasure, 1974, Alien, 1978, Brubaker, 1979. Democrat. *

KOTULAK, RONALD, newspaperman; b. Detroit, July 31, 1935; s. John and Mary (Roman) K.; m. Jean Bond, May 6, 1961 (dec. July 1974); children—Jeffrey, Kerry, Christopher; m. Donna Clausonthue, July 19, 1980; stepchildren—Paul, Lisa. Student, Wayne State U., 1953-54; B.A. in Journalism, U. Mich., 1959. Mem. staff Chgo. Tribune, 1959—, sch. bd. reporter, 1961-63, sci. editor, 1965—. Recipient first place sci. writing award ADA, 1966; 1st place med. writing award AMA, 1968; 1st prize Russell L. Cecil award Arthritis Found., 1969; 1st place Howard Blakeslee sci. writing award Am. Heart Assn., 1968; 1st place Claude Bernard Sci. Journalism award Nat. Soc. Med. Research, 1971; Lifeline award Am. Health Found., 1976; Edward Scott Beck award Chgo. Tribune, 1976; Outstanding Achievement award U. Mich., 1978; others. Mem. Nat. Assn. Sci. Writers (pres. 1972-73). Home: 737 N Oak Park Ave Oak Park IL 60302 Office: 435 N Michigan Ave Chicago IL 60611

KOTZ, DAVID MICHAEL, economist, educator; b. Phila., June 19, 1943; s. Jerry and Mary (Gippa) K.; m. Karen Ann Pfeider, June 16, 1979; children: Daniel Carlos Pfeifer-Kotz, Nicholas Miguel Pfeifer-Kotz; 1 stepdau., Ruwayda Farsoun. A.B. in Physics, Harvard Coll., 1965; M.A. in Econs., Yale U., 1966, Ph.D., U. Calif.-Berkeley, 1975. Asst. prof. econs. Am. U., Washington, 1974-78; asst. prof. U. Mass., Amherst, 1978-83, assoc. prof. econs., 1983—; vis. staff economist FTC, Washington, 1977-78; staff assoc. Ctr. for Popular Econs., Amherst, 1978—. Author: Bank Control of Large Corporations in U.S., 1978. Woodrow Wilson fellow, 1965-66; NSF trainee, 1967-68. Mem. Mass. Soc. Profs. (exec. bd. 1979-83), Union for Radical Polit. Econs., Assn. for Evolutionary Econs. Office: Dept Econs U Mass Amherst MA 01003

KOTZ, NATHAN KALLISON (NICK KOTZ), journalist; b. San Antonio, Sept. 16, 1932; s. Jacob and Tybe (Kallison) K.; m. Mary Lynn Booth, Aug. 7, 1960; 1 son, Jack Mitchell. A.B. magna cum laude in Internat. Relations, Dartmouth Coll., 1955; student, London Sch. Econs., 1955-56. Reporter, Des Moines Register, 1958-64, Washington corr., 1964-70; also for other Cowles Publs. (newspapers); nat. corr. Washington Post, 1970-73; adj. prof. Sch. Communication, Am. U., Washington, 1978—; sr. journalist in residence Duke U., 1983; farmer, Broad Run, Va., 1980—. Free-lance writer, 1973; author: Let Them Eat Promises: The Politics of Hunger in America, 1969; co-author: The Unions, 1971, A Passion for Equality: George Wiley and the Movement, 1977. Bd. dirs. Iowa Bds. Internat. Edn., 1962-64, Suburban Md. Fair Housing, 1966—, Black Student Fund, 1976—; bd. dirs. Fund for Investigative Journalism, 1977, chmn., 1978-82. Served to 1st lt. USMCR, 1956-58. Recipient Pulitzer prize for nat. reporting, 1968; Raymond Clapper Meml. award, 1966, 68; 2d pl., 1973; Disting. Service award Sigma Delta Chi, 1966; Robert F. Kennedy Journalism award, 1968; Spl. Merit award Am. U., 1981. Mem. Phi Beta Kappa. Club: Washington Press. Home: Galemont Farm Box 104 Broad Run VA 22014

KOTZ, SAMUEL, educator, mathematical statistician, translator; b. Harbin, China, Aug. 28, 1930; s. Boris and Guta (Kahana) K.; m. Roselyn Greenwald, Aug. 6, 1963; children—Tamar Ann, Harold David, Pauline Esther. M.Sc., Hebrew U., Jerusalem, 1956; Ph.D., Cornell U., 1960. Researcher Israel Meterol. Service, 1954-58; lectr. Bar-Ilan U., Israel, 1960-62; postdoctoral fellow U. N.C., 1962-63; asso. prof. U. Toronto, 1963-67; prof. math. Temple U., 1967-79; prof. stats. U. Md., College Park, 1979—; Disting. vis. prof. Bucknell U., spring 1977. Author, editor 12 books, 3 Russian-English profl. dictionaries, numerous research papers; translator 10 books.; Editorial bd.: Communication in Statistics; co-editor-in-chief: Ency. of Statis. Scis. Served with Israeli Army, 1950-52. Fellow Am. Statis. Assn., Inst. Math. Statistics; mem. Internat. Statis. Inst., Am. Math. Soc. Office: Dept Mgmt U Md College Park MD 20742

KOTZEBUE, KENNETH LEE, electrical engineer; b. San Antonio, Dec. 4, 1933; s. Robert William and Mary Lou (Warnek) K.; m. Delores Evelyn Steinkamp, Aug. 29, 1954; children: Paul, David, Margaret. B.S., U. Tex., 1954; M.S., UCLA, 1956; Ph.D. (Bell Telephone Lab. fellow), Stanford U., 1959. Sr. engr. Tex. Instruments, Inc., Dallas, 1959; mem. tech. staff, mgr. solid state devices, research and devel. dept. Watkins-Johnson Co., Palo Alto, Calif., 1959-64, cons., 1964—; mem. faculty U. Calif., Santa Barbara, 1964-83, prof. elec. engring., 1968-83; cons. Raytheon Co., Santa Barbara, Amlabs, Sunnyvale, Calif., Micromega, Los Angeles, KMS Industries, Van Nuys, Calif. Author: (with L.A. Blackwell) Semiconductor-Diode Parametric Amplifiers, 1961. Fellow Calif. Luth. Coll. (convocator 1968-71); Mem. IEEE. Pioneer in discovery of frequency-selective limiting in ferrimagnetic resonators, 1962; inventor ferrimagnetically-tuned solid-state microwave oscillator, 1963. Home: 4737 Woodview Dr Santa Rosa CA 95405 *

KOTZKY, ALEX SYLVESTER, syndicated cartoonist; b. N.Y.C., Sept. 11, 1923; s. Theodor and Helen (Owsieneoka) K.; m. Emma Matelli, Sept. 21, 1946; children: Brian, Bruce. Student, Art Students League, N.Y.C., 1941. Free-lance comml. artist, 1946-57; cartoonist: syndicated strip Duke Hand, 1958-59, Apt. 3-G, Field Enterprises, 1961-84, News Group Chgo., Inc., 1984—. Served with inf. AUS, 1943-46; ETO. Mem. Nat. Cartoonist Soc. Address: care Field Newspaper Syndicate 401 N Wabash Ave Chicago IL 60611 *

KOTZWINKLE, WILLIAM, author; b. Scranton, Pa., Nov. 22, 1938; s. William John and Madolyn (Murphy) K.; m. Elizabeth Gundy. Author: Hermes 3000, 1972, Nightbook, 1974, The Fan Man, 1974, Doctor Rat, 1976, Fata Morgana, 1977, Herr Nightingale and the Satin Woman, 1978, Jack in the Box, 1980, Swimmer in the Secret Sea, 1975, Elephant Bangs Train and Other Stories, 1971, The Firemen, 1969, The Ship That Came Down the Gutter, 1970, The Oldest Man and Other Timeless Tales, 1971, The Supreme, Superb, Exalted and Delightful, One and Only Magic Building, 1973, Elephant Boy, 1970, Return of Crazy Horse, 1971, Up the Alley with Jack and Joe, 1974, The Day The Gang Got Rich, 1970, The Leopard's Tooth, 1976, The Nap Master, 1978, The Ants Who Took Away Time, 1979, Christmas at Fontaine's, 1982, Great World Circus, 1983, E.T. The Extra-Terrestrial, 1982, Queen of Swords, 1984, Dream of Dark Harbor, 1979. Recipient award for fiction Nat. Mag., 1972, 75; O'Henry prize, 1975; World Fantasy award Third World Fantasy Conv., 1977. *

KOUBOURLIS, DEMETRIUS JOHN, educator, real estate investor; b. Rion-Patras, Greece, June 18, 1938; came to U.S., 1959, naturalized, 1972; s. John Antonios and Sophia Sotirios (Iliopoulou) K.; m. Toni Jean Hall, Dec. 28, 1967; children: Sophia C.M. Aadland, Yana D.H., Koren T.D., John D.A., Niki D.A. B.A., Calif. State U., 1963; Ph.D., U. Wash., 1967. Tutor ancient Greek, Italian and English, Patras, Greece, 1958-59; tchr. English Greek-Am. Cultural Inst., Patras, 1955-56; teaching asst. U. Wash., Seattle, summer 1966; instr. Slavic lang. U. Colo., Boulder, 1966-67; asst. prof. Slavic lang. and lit. Tulane U., New Orleans, 1967-68, U. N.C., Chapel Hill, 1968-71; asst. prof. fgn. lang. U. Idaho, Moscow, 1971-73, asso. prof., 1973-75, prof., 1975—; real estate investor, developer, Moscow and Pullman, Wash., owner Moscow Mall, Apts. West, Akers Dept. Store, Sound West; U. Idaho rep. to Internat. Research and Exchanges Bd., Ad hoc grantee, 1973-74; Internat. Inst. Math. and Computational Linguistics scholar, Pisa, Italy, 1974, participant exchange lang. tchrs., USSR, 1973. Editorial bd.: Folia Slavica; editorial com.: Slavic and East European Jour.; Author: Soviet Acad. Grammar: Phonology and Morphology, a Computer-Aided Index, 1972, A Concordance to the Poems of Osip Mandelstam, 1974, Topics in Slavic Phonology, 1974; editor: Language Series, 1972—; contbr. articles in field to profl. jours. and books. Mem. Am. Assn. Advancement Slavic Studies, Am. Assn. Tchrs. Slavic and E. European Langs., Am. Council Tchrs. Russian, Assn. Computing Machinery, Assn. Lit. and Linguistic Computing, Pacific Northwest Conf. Fgn. Langs., Western Slavic Assn. Home: NW 1470 Orion Dr Pullman WA 99163 Office: Dept of Foreign Languages University of Idaho Moscow ID 83843

KOUCHOUKOS, NICHOLAS THOMAS, surgeon; b. Grand Rapids, Mich., Dec. 26, 1936; s. Thomas Paul and Antoinette (Karver) K.; m. Judith Buell, Aug. 24, 1966; children—Nicholas Thomas, Robert Buell, Thomas Paul. Student (James B. Angell scholar), U. Mich., 1954-57; M.D. cum laude, Washington U., 1961. Intern Barnes Hosp., Washington U. Med. Center, St. Louis, 1961-62, asst. resident in surgery, 1962-65, chief adminstrv. resident, 1965-66; sr. clin. trainee in surgery USPHS, 1966-67; asst. in surgery Sch. Medicine Washington U., 1961-65, instr. surgery, 1965-67; research fellow surgery Sch. Medicine, U. Ala., Birmingham, 1967-68; instr. surgery, 1967-69, advanced trainee thoracic and cardiovascular surgery, 1968-70, asst. prof. surgery, 1969-71, asso. prof., 1971-74, prof., vice-dir. div. thoracic and cardiovascular surgery, 1974—, clin. prof., 1981—; mem. cardiovascular research study com. Am. Heart Assn., 1977-79; surgery study sect. USPHS, Bethesda, Md., 1977-80; ad hoc cons. Specialized Centers in Research Arteriosclerosis, Nat. Heart and Lung Inst., Bethesda, 1971-72, mem. ad hoc rev. com. for collaborative studies on coronary artery surgery, 1973—, surgery A study sect., 1976-77; mem. merit rev. bd. in cardiovascular studies VA, Washington, 1976-78. Editorial bd.: Current Topics in Cardiology and Circulation, 1977-80, Annals Thoracic Surgery, 1980—. Fellow Southeastern Surg. Congress, Am. Coll. Cardiology (finalist Young Investigators award 1962), A.C.S.; mem. Am. Assn. Thoracic Surgery, AAUP, AMA, Am. Surg. Assn., Assn. Academic Surgery, Jefferson County, Ala. med. socs., John Kirklin Soc., Soc. Thoracic Surgeons, So. Thoracic Surg. Assn., So. Surg. Assn., Soc. Univ. Surgeons, Soc. Vascular Surgery, Internat. Cardiovascular Soc., Phi Beta Kappa, Alpha Omega Alpha. Home: 3148 Guilford Rd Birmingham AL 35223 Office: 1318 S 19th St Birmingham AL 35205

KOUMOULIDES, JOHN THOMAS ANASTASIOS, historian; b. Greece, Aug. 23, 1938; came to U.S., 1956, naturalized, 1969; s. Anastasios Lazaros and Sophia (Theodosiadou) K. A.B., Montclair State Coll. (N.J.), 1960, A.M., 1961; Ph.D., U. Md., 1968; postgrad., Fitzwilliam Coll., Cambridge (Eng.) U., 1965-67, 1971-72. Grad. asst. U. Md., 1961-63; asst. prof. history Austin Peay State U., Clarksville, Tenn., 1963-65, Vanderbilt U., summer 1968; mem. faculty Ball State U., Muncie, Ind., 1968—, prof. history, 1975—; vis. tutor Campion Hall, Oxford U., 1980-81. Author: Cyprus and the Greek War of Independence, 1821-1829, 2d edit, 1974, Byzantine and Post-Byzantine Monuments at Aghia in Thessaly, Greece: The Art and Architecture of the Monastery of Saint Panteleimon, 1975; also monographs, articles and revs.; editor: Greece in Transition: Essays in the History of Modern Greece, 1821-1974, 1977, Greece: Past and Present, 1979, Hellenic Perspectives: Essays in the History of Greece, 1980, Greece and Cyprus in History, 1984; co-editor: Byzantine Perspectives: Essays in Byzantine History and Culture, 1984. Recipient Archon Chartophylax of the Ecumenical Patriarchate of Constantinople, 1979; research grantee Ball State U., 1969, 70, 74, 79, Am. Philos. Soc., 1973, 79, Am. Council Learned Socs., 1969, 71; Fulbright-Hays research awardee, Greece, 1977-78; vis. fellow, Wolfson Coll., Oxford U., 1983-84; guest scholar Woodrow Wilson Internat. Ctr. for Scholars, 1982. Mem. Am. Hist. Assn., Archaeol. Inst. Am., AAUP, Modern Greek Studies Assn., Soc. Promotion Hellenic Studies, Brit. Hist. Assn., Cambridge U. Hist. Assn., Cambridge Philol. Assn., Cambridge U. Soc., Oxford U. Soc., Byzantine Soc., Phi Alpha Theta, Alpha Tau Omega. Greek Orthodox. Address: 1215 W Wayne St Muncie IN 47303

KOURI, DONALD JACK, chemist, educator; b. Hobart, Okla., July 25, 1938; s. Eddie and Theresa LaJuan (Williams) K.; m. Shirley Ann Stewart, Apr. 9, 1965; children: Lisa Renee, David Matthew. B.A., Okla. Baptist U., 1960; M.S., U. Wis., 1962, Ph.D., 1965. Postdoctoral fellow Joint Inst. for Lab. Astrophysics U. Colo., 1965-66; asst. prof. chemistry Midwestern U., Wichita Falls, 1966-67, U. Houston, 1967-71, asso. prof., 1971-73, prof., 1973—; vis. lectr. U. Ill., 1972; fellow Weizmann Inst., Rehovot, Israel, 1973; vis. scientist Inst. fur Stromungs forschung, Gottingen, W. Ger., 1973-74; fellow Inst. for Advanced Study, Hebrew U., Jerusalem, Israel, 1978-79. Contbr. articles to profl. jours. Recipient U.S. sr. scientist award Alexander von Humboldt Found., 1973-74, Southwestern Tex. sect. award Am. Chem. Soc., 1981, Esther Farfel Outstanding Faculty award U. Houston, 1982; A.P. Sloan Found. fellow, 1972-74; Guggenheim fellow, 1978-79. Fellow Am. Phys. Soc.; mem. Am. Assn. Physics Tchrs. Democrat. Baptist. Office: Dept Chemistry U of Houston Houston TX 77004

KOURIDES, PETER THEOLOGOS, lawyer; b. Istanbul, Turkey, July 24, 1910; came to U.S., 1912, naturalized, 1931; s. Theologos and Zafiro (Gurlides) K.; m. Anna E. Spetseris, Aug. 4, 1938; children—Ione A., P. Nicholas. B.A., Columbia, 1931, J.D., 1933. Bar: N.Y. bar 1933. Mem. firm Seward, Raphael & Kourides, N.Y.C., 1935—; gen. counsel Greek Archdiocese of North and South Am., 1938—; trustee, counsel Hellenic Cathedral City N.Y., 1938—, St. Basil's Acad., Garrison, N.Y., 1946—, Hellenic Cathedral Day Sch., 1955—, United Greek Orthodox Charities, 1965—; counsel Standing Conf. of Canonical Orthodix Bishops in Americas, 1958—, World Conf. Religion for Peace, 1970—; counsel for Am. affairs to Ecumenical Patriarchate of Eastern Orthodox Ch., Istanbul, 1949—; dir., counsel Hellenic Am. C. of C., 1955—; dir. Atlantic Bank N.Y., 1974—; Counsel, consulate gen. of Greece in N.Y., 1963—; Nat. sec. Greek War Relief Assn., 1941-46; rep. Greek Archdiocese of North and South Am. at enthronement Athenagoras I, Istanbul, 1949; pres. Hellenic U. Club, 1951-52. Author: The Evolution of the Greek Orthodox Church in America and its Current Problems, 1959. Nat. v.p. Order of Ahepa, 1960; mem. gen. bd. Nat. Council Chs., 1960—, v.p., 1969-72; counsel Columbia U. Cancer Clinic in Greece, 1965-70; del. 3d Assembly World Council Chs., New Delhi, India, 1961, 4th Assembly, Uppsala, Sweden, 1968, 5th Assembly, Nairobi, Kenya, 1975, 6th Assembly, Vancouver, B.C., Can., 1983, World Conf. Religion on Peace, Kyoto, Japan, 1971; mem. internat. affairs com. World Council Chs., 1968—; trustee Hellenic Coll., Brookline, Mass., 1968—, Modern Greek Library, Columbia, 1958—. Decorated Gold Cross Order of Phoenix by King Constantine II Greece, 1967, Grand Cross Knights St. Andrew by Ecumenical Patriarchate of Eastern Orthodox Ch., 1968, grand comdr. Knights of Holy Sepulchre Jerusalem Patriarchate of Eastern Orthodox Ch., 1961. Mem. Am., N.Y. State, N.Y. County, Queens County bar assns., Consular Law Soc., Am. Judicature Soc., Columbia Alumni Assn. Home: 46 Groton St Forest Hills Gardens NY 11375 Office: 30 Rockefeller Plaza New York City NY 10020

KOUSOULAS, DIMITRIOS GEORGE, educator, author, businessman; b. Khalkis, Greece, Dec. 22, 1923; came to U.S., 1951, naturalized, 1958; s. George D. and Barbara (Lachnidakis) K.; m. Mary Katris, Jan. 27, 1952; 1 son, George. LL.B., U. Athens, Greece, 1948; M.A. (Fulbright scholar) in Polit. Sci, Syracuse U., 1953, Ph.D., 1956. Fgn. lang. specialist USIA, 1957-60; professorial lectr. Nat. War Coll., George Washington U., 1961—; asst. prof. Howard U., 1961-64, asso. prof., 1965-67, prof. govt., chmn. dept., 1967—; Pres. Meridian-West Inc., 1974—; v.p. Meridian-West Assos., 1974—; pres. Woodbridge Nursing Center, Inc., 1976—. Author: Greece in World Affairs 1939-53, 1953, Key to Economic Progress, 1958, Revolution and Defeat: the Story of the Greek Communist Party, 1965, On Government: a Comparative Introduction, 1968, On Government and Politics, 5th edit, 1981, Modern Greece; Profile of a Nation, 1974, Secrets the Successful Never Tell Strangers, 1981. Pres. Am. Com. on Cyprus Self-determination, 1964-66; Bd. trustees Ahepa Ednl. Found., 1968—. Served in Greek Armed Forces, 1948-50. Decorated Nat. Resistance medal, knight Royal Order of Phoenix, Golden Cross, Greece). Mem. Am. Acad. Polit. and Social Sci., Acad. Polit. Sci., Am., Internat. polit. sci. assns. Home: 6252 Clearwood Rd Bethesda MD 20034 Office: Howard Univ Washington DC 20001

KOUTS, HERBERT JOHN CECIL, physicist; b. Bisbee, Ariz., Dec. 18, 1919; s. Oliver Allen and Lillian (Niemeyer) K.; m. Hertha Pretorius, Feb. 2, 1942; children: Anne Elizabeth, Catherine Jennifer; m. Barbara Stokes, Mar. 27, 1974; stepchildren: Francis Spitzer, Michael Spitzer, Daniel Spitzer. B.S., La. State U., 1941, M.S., 1946; Ph.D., Princeton U., 1952. With Brookhaven Nat. Lab., Upton, L.I., N.Y., 1950-73, 77—, sr. scientist, asso. div. head, 1958-73, chmn. dept. nuclear energy, 1977—; dir. div. reactor safety research AEC, Washington, 1973-75; dir. Office Nuclear Regulatory Research, U.S. Nuclear Regulatory Commn., Washington, 1975-76; mem. advisory com. reactor physics AEC, 1956-63, mem. adv. com. reactor safeguards, 1962-66; mem. European Am. Advisory Com. for Reactor Physics to European Nuclear Energy Agency, 1962-68. Served with USAAF, 1942-45. Recipient E. O. Lawrence award AEC, 1963, Disting. Service award, 1975; Disting. Service award NRC, 1976. Mem. Am. Nuclear Soc. (Theos Thompson award in nuclear reactor safety 1983), Fedn. Am. Scientists, Center Moriches Audubon Soc., Nat. Acad. Engring. Home: 249 S Country Rd Brookhaven NY 11719 Office: Brookhaven Nat Lab Upton NY 11973

KOUVEL, JAMES SPYROS, educator, physicist; b. Jersey City, May 23, 1926; s. Spyros and Ifegenia (Cassianos) K.; m. Audrey Lumsden, June 26, 1953; children: Diana, Alexander. B.Engring., Yale U., 1946, Ph.D., 1951. Research fellow U. Leeds, Eng., 1951-53, Harvard, 1953-55; physicist Gen. Electric Co. Research and Devel. Center, 1955-69; prof. physics U. Ill.-Chgo., 1969—; vis. scientist Atomic Energy Research Establishment, Harwell, Eng., 1967-68; vis. prof. U. Paris, Orsay, France, 1981; cons. Argonne Nat. Lab., 1969—, mem. rev. com., 1970-72, vis. scientist, 1973-74; mem. materials research adv. com. NSF, 1980-82; mem. evaluation panel NRC, 1981—. Author papers in field.; Editor: Magnetism Conf. proc, 1965-67; editorial bd.: Jour. Magnetism and Magnetic Materials, 1975—. Served with USNR, 1944-46. Guggenheim fellow, 1967-68. Fellow Am. Phys. Soc., AAAS. Home: 223 N Euclid Ave Oak Park IL 60302 Office: Box 4348 Chicago IL 60680

KOUWENHOVEN, JOHN ATLEE, educator, writer, magazine editor; b. Yonkers, N.Y., 1909; s. John Bennem and Grace (Atlee) K.; m. Eleanor W. Hayden, June 22, 1935 (div. 1959); children: Ann (dec.), Gerrit Wolphertsen; m. Joan Vatsek Arthur, June 12, 1960; stepchildren: Andrew Arthur, Elizabeth Arthur. A.B., Wesleyan U., Middletown, Conn., 1931; A.M., Columbia U., 1933, Ph.D., 1948. Master in English, Harvey Sch., Hawthorne, N.Y., 1932-36; instr. English, Columbia U., 1936-38; mem. lit. faculty Bennington (Vt.) Coll., 1938-41; asst. editor Harper's mag., 1941-44, asso. editor, 1944-46, contbg. editor, 1946-54; asso. in English and Am. studies Barnard Coll., Columbia U., 1946-48, asso. prof. English, 1948-50, prof., 1950-75, prof. emeritus, 1975—, chmn. dept., 1950-54; dir. hist. files Brown Bros. Harriman & Co., 1964-68; mem. vis. com. Costume Inst., Met. Mus. Art, 1971-72; mem. adv. com. Archives Am. Art, 1967—, Hist. Commn. N.Y.C. Bicentennial Com., 1972-74; hist. advisor Children's TV Workshop, 1975-77. Actor: TV series The Best of Families, 1976; Author: Adventures of America 1857-1900, 1938, Made in America: The Arts in Modern Civilization, 1948, The Columbia Historical Portrait of New York, 1953, The Beer Can by the Highway, 1961, Partners in Banking, 1968, Half a Truth is Better than None, 1982; also articles in profl. jours. and popular mags.; co-author: Creating an Industrial Civilization, 1952, American Panorama, 1957, American Studies in Transition, 1965, The Shaping of Art and Architecture in 19th Century America, 1972, The Arts in a Democratic Society, 1977, Technology in America, 1981; editor: (with Janice Thaddeus) When Women Look at Men, 1963, New York Guide Book, 1964; editorial bd.: Am. Quar., 1954-66, Technology and Culture, 1958—, N.Y. History, 1973-74. Trustee Merck Forest Found., 1950-70, past sec.; trustee R.I. Sch. Design, 1961-67, 68-70, Jennie Clarkson Home for Children, 1964-68, Vt. Council on Arts, 1968-72, 76-78; v.p. Vt. Council on Arts, 1969-71; trustee Park-McCullough House Assn., 1971-78. Decorated officer's cross Order Orange-Nassau, Netherlands, 1954; Benjamin Franklin fellow; hon. corr. mem. Royal Soc. Arts, Great Britain. Mem. Am. Studies Assn., Soc. Archtl. Historians, Soc. Indsl. Archaeology, Soc. History Tech. (exec. council 1962-64, adv. council 1958-61, 65-69). Home: PO Box 101 Dorset VT 05251

KOUZMANOFF, ALEXANDER, architect, educator; b. Chgo., Apr. 25, 1915; s. Michael and Luba (Glegorovitch) K.; m. Lillian White, June 2, 1944; children: Jan, Alan. B.S. in Architecture, U. Ill., 1940, M.S., 1949. Designer, planner Shaw, Naess & Murphy, Chgo., 1940-43; designer Harrison, & Abramovitz, N.Y.C., 1947-52; design planning cons. Internat. Bus. Econ. Corp., N.Y.C., 1952-57; pvt. practice design cons. and planning, N.Y.C., 1957-67; prin. Alexander Kouzmanoff & Assos., N.Y.C., 1967—; mem. faculty Grad. Sch. Architecture and Planning, Columbia U., 1952—, chmn. div. architecture, 1971-77. Author: (with Percival Goodman) Breakthrough to the Hudson River, 1964. Served to 1st lt. USAAF, 1943-44. Columbia U. grantee, 1957; Tianjin-Columbia U. traveling fellow, China, summer 1982; recipient 2d Rome prize Nat. Inst. Archtl. Edn., 1940; Concrete Industry Bd. award of merit, 1973; City Club N.Y. Albert S. Bard award of merit for architecture and urban design, 1978; Francis J. Plym travelling fellow, 1940; Allerton travelling fellow, 1939; prin. speaker, recipient diploma Fedn. Pan Am. Assn. Architects, Venezuela, 1980. Fellow AIA (v.p. N.Y.C. chpt. 1972-75); mem. AAUP, N.Y. State Archtl. Assn. (execellence award for Avery extension Columbia U. 1980), Nat. Inst. Archtl. Edn., Soc. Archtl.

Historians, Archtl. League of N.Y., Phi Kappa Phi. Home: 12 Lincoln Ave Port Chester NY 10573 Office: 310 E 46th St New York NY 10017

KOVACH, EUGENE GEORGE, government official; b. Irvington, N.J., May 18, 1922; s. Eugene John and Hortense Marie (Telmany) K.; m. Mary Eleanor Frenning, Apr. 11, 1950; children—George Eugene, Mary Edith, Katherine Eleanor, Christine Marie, John Peter. B.S., Wayne U., 1943, M.S., 1944; M.A., Harvard U., 1948, Ph.D., 1949. Mem. faculty, research organic chemistry Colgate U., 1950-51, U. Fla., 1949-54; sci. adviser to comdr. U.S. Naval Forces, Germany, 1954-57; with NSF, 1958, State Dept., Washington, 1959-70; acting dir. Office Gen. Sci. Affairs, 1966-70; dep. asst. sec.-gen. for sci. affairs NATO, Brussels, Belgium, 1970-76, Div. Policy Research NSF, 1976-78; dir. Office Advanced Tech., State Dept., 1978—. Served with USNR, 1944-45. Recipient Wayne U. Distinguished Alumnus award, 1961. Mem. Am. Chem. Soc., AAAS, Sigma Xi. Home: 4118 Aspen St Chevy Chase MD 20815 Office: US Dept of State Washington DC 20520

KOVACH, FRANCIS JOSEPH, philosophy educator; b. Budapest, Hungary, July 19, 1918; came to U.S., 1951, naturalized, 1957; s. Joseph and Anna (Roch) K.; m. Elizabeth W. Thököly, July 19, 1942; children: Elizabeth (Mrs. James Cowan), Ákos, Leslie, Agnes, Thomas. Ph.D. in Philosophy summa cum laude, U. Cologne, Germany, 1959. Instr., then asst. prof. philosophy Coll. St. Scholastica, Duluth, Minn., 1953-59; asst. prof. St. Benedict's Coll. and Mt. St. Scholastica, Atchison, Kans., 1959-62, Villanova U., 1962-64; asso. prof. Okla. U., 1964-69, prof. philosophy, 1969—; Rep. Am. Council Learned Socs. 6th Internat. Congress Aesthetics, Amsterdam, Holland, 1964; editorial cons. New Scholasticism, 1980. Author: Die Aesthetik des Thomas von Aquin, 1961, Philosophy of Beauty, 1974, also numerous articles; co-editor: Bonaventure and Aquinas, 1976, Albert the Great, 1980. Mem. Soc. Internat. pour l'etude de la philosophie medievale (Louvain, Belgium), Internat. Thomistic Soc., Internat. Scotistic Soc., Brit. Soc. Aesthetics, Am. Cath. Philos. Assn. (pres. N. Central chpt. 1958, mem. exec. council), Am. Soc. Aesthetics, Southwestern Philos. Soc., Soc. Mediaeval and Renaissance Philosophy, Soc. Christian Philosophers, Central States Philos. Assn. Home: 1426 Beverly Hills St Norman OK 73069

KOVACH, GEORGE PAUL, plastics company executive; b. Vienna, Austria, Dec. 29, 1912; came to U.S., 1939, naturalized, 1945; s. Edmond and Paula (Dornhelm) Kovacs; m. Madeline E. Besnyoe, Apr. 24, 1939; children: Peter J., Thomas A. Dipl. Eng., Technische Hochschule, Vienna, 1936. Chief chemist Foster-Grant Co., Inc., Leominster, Mass., 1941-46, hmgr. product devel., 1953-61; project mgr. Nixon Nitration Works, N.J., 1946-47; mgr. plastics div. Atlantic Tubing & Rubber Co., R.I., 1947-51, Clopay Corp., Cin., 1951-53; pres. Koro Corp., Hudson, Mass., 1961—, chmn. bd., 1981—; Bd. dirs. Plastics Edn. Found., 1975—. Contbr. to: Processing of Thermoplastics, 1959, Ency. Chem. Engring, 1961, Ency. Polymer Sci. and Tech., vols. 12, 13, 1970. Mem. Soc. Plastic Engrs. (nat. pres.), Soc. Plastics Industry (dir.), Plastics Pioneers Assn. Home: 22-5 Concord Greene Concord MA 01742 Office: 560 Lower Main St Hudson MA 01749

KOVACH, JOSEPH JAMES, editor; b. Johnson City, Tenn., June 22, 1927; s. John and Olga (Sicos) K.; m. Susan Wolfson, Feb. 1, 1981; children—Jill, Polly. B.S. in English, East Tenn. State U. Reporter Bristol (Va.) Herald-Courier, Augusta (Ga.) Chronicle; editor Daily Corinthian, Corinth, Miss.; chief copy editor Atlanta Jour.; night news editor St. Louis Globe Democrat; copy editor fgn. desk N.Y. Times, N.Y.C.; now asst. mng. editor N.Y. Daily News, N.Y.C. Served with USN. Office: 220 E 42d St New York NY 10017

KOVACH, LADIS DANIEL, mathematics educator; b. Budapest, Hungary, Nov. 21, 1914; came to U.S., 1921, naturalized, 1941; s. Ladislaus and Irene Julia (Beck) K.; m. Jacqueline Faye Blaylock, Jan. 24, 1970; children: Paul Julian, Andrew Byron, Matthew Daniel. B.S. in Physics, Case Inst. Tech., 1936, M.S. in Math, 1948; M.A. in Edn, Western Res. U., 1940; Ph.D. in Math, Purdue U., 1951. Asst. chief elec. engr. Am. Shipbldg. Co., Cleve., 1941-44; computing specialist McDonnell-Douglas Aircraft Co., El Segundo, Calif., 1951-61; chmn. dept. math. and physics Pepperdine U., Los Angeles, 1958-68; prof. math. Naval Postgrad. Sch., Monterey, Calif., 1967—; vis. prof. UCLA, 1961-63; cons. Tulare County Schs., 1964-65, Monterey County Office Edn., 1970. Author: Modern Elementary Mathematics, Computer-Oriented Mathematics, Advanced Engineering Mathematics, Boundary-Value Problems. Bd. dirs. Lyceum Monterey Peninsula, pres., 1972-73. NSF grantee, 1961, 66. Mem. Math. Assn. Am., Soc. for Computer Simulation (Marv Emerson Meml. award 1968), Sigma Xi. Office: Naval Postgraduate School Monterey CA 93943

KOVACS, ELIZABETH ANN, assn. exec.; b. N.Y.C., July 25, 1944; d. Henry Philipp and Toni (Selby) Leitner; m. Imre Kovacs, June 19, 1965; children—Tobin Philipp, Kathryn Ena Michael. B.A., Conn. Coll., 1965; M.A.T., Yale U., 1967. Cert. assn. exec. Exec. dir. Assn. for Advancement of Behavior Therapy, N.Y.C., 1971-80; exec. dir. Soc. Behavioral Medicine, N.Y.C., 1978-80; exec. v.p. Public Relations Soc. Am., N.Y.C., 1980—; tchr. assn. mgmt. Mem. Am. Soc. Assn. Execs. (evaluation com.), N.Y. Soc. Assn. Execs. (bd. dirs.). Home: 201 W 89th St New York NY 10024 Office: 845 3d Ave New York NY 10022

KOVACS, LASZLO, cinematographer; b. Hungary, May 14, 1933; came to U.S., 1957, naturalized, 1963; s. Imre and Julia K. M.A., Acad. Drama and Motion Picture Arts of Budapest, Hungary, 1956. Lectr. at univs, film schs. Dir. photography for: numerous motion pictures, including Easy Rider, 1969, Five Easy Pieces, 1970, What's Up Doc?, 1972, The King of Marvin Gardens, 1972, Paper Moon, 1973, Shampoo, 1975, At Long Last Love, 1975, Harry and Walter Go to New York, 1976, New York, New York, 1977, F.I.S.T, 1978, The Last Waltz, 1978, Butch and Sundance, 1979, Heart Beat, 1979, The Runner Stumbles, 1979, Close Encounters of the Third Kind, 1977; others; free-lance cinematographer for motion pictures and TV commls. Mem. Acad. Motion Picture Arts and Scis., Am. Soc. Cinematographers. *

KOVALY, JOHN JOSEPH, consulting engineer, educator; b. McKeesport, Pa., June 12, 1928; s. Joseph and Mary (Demko) K.; m. Joan P. Misiewicz, June 16, 1957; children: Pamela Jane, Kurt David. B.S., Muskingum Coll., 1950; M.S., U. Ill., 1953. Research assoc. Coordinated Sci. Lab., U. Ill., Urbana, 1951-55; adv. researchengr. Sylvania Electronic Products, Inc., Waltham, Mass., 1958-65; cons. engr. Missile Systems div. Raytheon Co., Andover, Mass., 1965—; lectr. UCLA, 1977—. Author: Synthetic Aperture Radar, 1976; contbr. articles profl. jours. Served to lt. U.S. Navy, 1955-58. Fellow IEEE (pres. Boston sect. Aerospace and Electronic Systems Group 1972, contbn. award 1981). Home: 3 Tubwreck Dr Dover MA 02030 Office: Missile Systems Div Raytheon Co 350 Lowell St Andover MA 01810

KOVATCH, JAK GENE, artist; b. Los Angeles, Jan. 17, 1929; s. Jack and La Vinia Blanche (Abernathy) K.; m. Carol Jean Wilhelm, Dec. 24, 1967; 1 son by previous marriage, Jason. Student, UCLA, 1946, Chouinard Art Inst., 1947-49, Calif. Sch. Art, Los Angeles, 1949-50, U. So. Calif., 1951, Los Angeles City Coll., 1955-56, Art Students League, N.Y.C., 1972, 75. Student asst. Lynton Kistler Studio, Los Angeles, 1952-53; mem. staff animation dept. Walt Disney Prodns., Inc., Burbank, Calif., 1953; instr. drawing and anatomy Famous Artists Schs., Westport, Conn., 1957-59; tchr. Roger Ludlowe High Sch., Fairfield, Conn., 1959-60; extension instr. N.Y.C. Coll., 1959-60; instr. sculpture Fairfield U., 1967; mem. faculty U. Bridgeport, Conn., 1962—, assoc. prof. dept. design, 1978—; fellow Mellon Found.; Vis. Faculty Program Yale U., 1979-80, 81, 82-83; guest lectr. anatomy and figure drawing, 1953—. Stage designer for, Benjamin Zemach, Los Angeles, 1953-54; freelance illustrator, N.Y.C., 1957-58; more than 270 group exhbns., 1949—, latest being, more than 250 group exhbns., Berkeley Center, Yale U., 1978, Nat. Acad. Galleries, N.Y.C., 1977, 78, 79, Yale U., 1979, De Cordova Mus., Mass., 1978, Am. Acad. and Inst. Arts and Letters, N.Y.C., 1980, Duxbury (Mass.) Complex Mus., 1980, 81, 83, Nat. Arts Club, N.Y.C., 1980, 81, 82, 83; rep. permanent collections, Fogg Mus. Art, Cambridge, Mass., Library of Congress, Joseph Hirshhorn Collection, Greenwich, Conn., Fairfield Art Collection, John Slade Ely House Collections, New Haven, Bicentennial Art Collection, Westport (Conn.) Town Hall, Albert Dorne Collection, N.Y.C., also numerous pvt. collections. Recipient award Boston Mus. Fine Arts, 1954, Wadsworth Atheneum, Hartford, Conn., 1958, 79, recipient Mus. Art, Sci. and Industry, Bridgeport, 1962, 63, 65, 66, 75, 77, 79, 81, 82, Hudson River Mus., Yonkers, N.Y., 1960, New Haven Paint and Clay Club, 1976, 78, 81; numerous others. Mem. Boston Printmakers, Artists Equity Assn., Audubon Artists, Conn. Acad. Fine Arts, Greenwich Art Soc., Hudson River Contemporary Artists, Los Angeles Printmaking Soc., Pratt Graphics Center, Phila. Print Club, Silvermine Guild Artists (trustee 1979-83), Westport-Weston Arts Council. Home: 34 Sasco Creek Rd Westport CT 06880 Office: U Bridgeport Bridgeport CT 06602 *I consider my concept of Image Continuum to be a significant consequence of 35 years of painting and printmaking. Six basic components form the foundation of this concept: 1. Use of former images to create new ones; 2. Repetition of a theme (subject matter and symbols repeated); 3. Use of modules; 4. Use of storyboards and grids; 5. Structuring forms transparently; 6. Use of abstraction, animation, distortion. An integral part of Image Continuum is persistent use of multiple images. This means of expression may be directly related to my personal impatience with dwelling too long on one image or idea. I have been able to temper this drive for immediacy and rapid image development by using images in a series or storyboard format.*

KOVEL, RALPH M., author, authority on antiques; b. Milw.; s. Lester and Dorothy (Bernstein) K.; m. Terry Horvitz; children: Lee, Karen. Student, Ohio State U. Vice-pres. Antiques Inc.; pres. Celco Inc., Sar-a-Lee Inc.; past tchr. course in antiques Western Res. U., John Carroll U.; Past mem. bd. Soc. Collectors, Silver Mus. Religious Art. Appeared radio and TV discussion programs, subject of antiques; writer: (with Terry Kovel) syndicated column Kovels Antiques and Collecting, 1955—, Your Collectibles, House Beautiful, 1979—; editor: monthly newsletter Kovels on Antiques and Collectibles, 1974—; nat. non-comml. TV series about antiques, 1969—; syndicated TV series Kovels on Collecting, 1981—; Author: (with Terry Kovel) Dictionary of Marks-Pottery and Porcelain, 1953, Directory of American Silver, Pewter and Silver Plate, 1961, American Country Furniture, 1780-1875, 1965, Know Your Antiques, rev. edit., 1981, Kovels' Antiques Price List, 17th edit., 1984, The Kovels' Bottle Price List, 7th edit., 1984, Kovels' Price Guide for Collectors Plates, Figurines, Paperweight and Other Ltd. Editions, 1978, Kovels' Collector's Guide to American Art Pottery, 1974, Kovels' Know Your Collectibles, 1981, Kovels' Illustrated Price Guide to Depression Glass and American Dinnerware, 2d edit., 1983, Kovels' Illustrated Price Guide to Royal Doulton, 2d edit., 1983, Kovels' Organizer for Collectors, Rev., 1983, Kovels' Collectors Source Book, 1983; also articles. Former mem. rev. and allocations com. United Torch Fund, Cleve.; past pres. E. End Neighborhood Settlement House; past chmn. adv. com. Woodhill Homes. Recipient Lane Bryant award, 1966; Peirce award for outstanding community service Sta. WVIZ-TV, 1980. Mem. Appraisers. Assn. Am., Am. Soc. Appraisers (sr. mem.), Internat. Soc. Appraisers, Cleve. Food Brokers, Nat. Food Brokers Assn., Assoc. Grocery Mfrs. (rep.). Clubs: Union League (Chgo.); Oakwood. Office: care Crown Publishers One Park Ave New York NY 10016 office: 27621 Chagrin Blvd Cleveland OH 44122

KOVEL, TERRY HORVITZ (MRS. RALPH KOVEL), author, antiques authority; b. Cleve., 1928; d. Isadore and Rix (Osteryoung) Horvitz; m. Ralph Kovel; children: Lee R., Karen. B.A., Wellesley Coll., 1950. Tchr. math. Hawken Sch. for Boys, Shaker Heights, Ohio, 1961-71; now pres. Antiques Inc.; now v.p. Sar-a-Lee, Inc.; past tchr. course in antiques Western Res. U., John Carroll U.; radio and TV discussion programs on antiques. Writer: (with Ralph Kovel) syndicated column Kovels Antiques and Collecting, 1955—, Your Collectibles, House Beautiful, 1979—; editor: monthly newsletter Kovels on Antiques and Collectibles, 1974—; TV series Know Your Antiques, Pub. Broadcast Library, 1969—; syndicated TV Series Kovels on Collecting, 1981—; Author: (with Ralph Kovel) Dictionary of Marks-Pottery and Porcelain, 1953, Directory of American Silver, Pewter and Silver Plate, 1961, American Country Furniture, 1780-1875, 1965, Know Your Antiques, 3d edit, 1981, Kovels' Antiques Price List, 17th edit., 1984, Know Your Collectibles, 1981, Kovels' Complete Bottle Price List, 7th edit., 1984, Kovels' Organizer for Collectors, 1978, revised, 1983, Kovels' Price Guide for Collectors Plates, Figurines, Paperweights and Other Limited Editions, 1978, Kovels' Collector's Guide to American Art Pottery, 1974, Kovels' Illustrated Price Guide to Depression Glass and American Dinnerware, 1980, 2d edit., 1983, Kovels' Illustrated Price Guide to Royal Doulton, 1980, 83, Kovels' Collectors' Sources Book, 1983; contbr. articles on antiques, numerous publs. Recipient Peirce award for outstanding community service, 1980. Mem. Am. Soc. Appraisers (sr.), Internat. Soc. Appraisers, Appraisers Assn. Am. Office: PO Box 22200 Beachwood OH 44122

KOVEN, HOWARD RICHARD, lawyer; b. Chgo., Apr. 20, 1921; s. Henry H. and Pauline (Klein) K.; m. Eileen Shargel, Nov. 15, 1946; children: Maggie, Jane. A.B., U. Chgo., 1941, J.D., 1946. Bar: Ill. 1946, D.C. 1970. Mng. ptnr. Friedman & Koven, Chgo.; Fortas and Koven, Washington, 1970-83; atty., gen. counsel Chgo. Counsel Child Psychiatry, 1961—; mem. adv. bd. Amalgamated Trust & Savs. Bank; dir. Oak Brook Bank, Ill., CFS Continental, Inc., Chgo., Jupiter Industries. Pres. Epilepsy Assn. of Am., 1965-66; nat. chmn. Nat. Epilepsy League, 1960-63; co-chmn. Epilepsy Found. of America, 1967-68, bd. dirs., 1973-76; v.p., dir. Center for Psychosocial Studies, Chgo. Served to lt. (s.g.) USNR, 1942-46. Mem. Am., Ill., Chgo. bar assns., D.C. Bar Assn. Jewish. Office: 208 S LaSalle St Chicago IL 60604

KOVITZ, MURIEL, university chancellor emeritus; b. Calgary, Alta., Can., Feb. 20, 1926; d. Norman and Ethel Rose (Shapiro) Libin; m. David M. Kovitz, Aug. 2, 1945; children: Jeffrey Wayne, Ronald Stephen, Ethel Rose. Licentiate, Royal Sch. Music, London, Eng., 1944; LL.D. (hon.), U. Calgary, 1981. Community rep. to Faculty Medicine, 1970-71, Faculty Social Welfare, U. Calgary, 1970-74, rep. various univ. acad. coms. and task forces, 1970—, Bd. Govs. rep. various univ. coms., 1972-78; mem. Senate, 1970-78, chmn., chancellor, 1974-78, chancellor emeritus, 1978—, also bd. govs.; charter mem. Crossbow Aux. Hosp. Ladies Aux., 1961-64; mem. Bd. Vocat. and Rehab. Research Inst., Calgary, 1968-69; mem. brief com. Family Life Edn., 1969-70; participant nat. confs. and seminars Nat. Council Jewish Women's Project Can., 1959-73; on program Canadian Council Social Devel. Conf., 1968; participant Nat. Pub. Housing Conf., 1969, Fed. Govt. Vol. Action Conf., 1971; co-chmn. 3d Internat. Banff Conf. on Man and His Environment, 1978; nat. chmn., participant developing curriculum Nat. Council Jewish Women Sch. for Citizen Participation, 1967-73; Pres. Murko Investments Ltd.; sec. Norhill Enterprises Ltd.; dir. Centennial Packers of Can. Ltd., Alta. Investments Ltd., Imperial Oil Ltd. Mem. City of Calgary Recreation Bd., 1966-69; pres. Calgary Social Planning Council, 1967-69; mem. Calgary Housing Authority, 1968-72; commr. Task Force on Can. Unity, 1977—; Bd. dirs. Calgary and Dist. Found., 1971-77; mem. exec. com. Canadian Council Christians and Jews, U. Toronto Alumni.; bd. dirs. Reader's Digest Assn. (Can.) Ltd., Reader's Digest Found., Inst. Donations and Pub. Affairs Research, Calgary Summer Games, 1983, Council for Canadian Unity; mem. adv. com. Nickle Arts Mus.; mem. Chmn.'s Circle Glenbow Mus. Decorated Order Can.; recipient Alta. Achievement award, 1977, Queen's Jubilee medal, 1977. Mem. Nat. Council Jewish Women Can. (pres. Calgary 1959-61, nat. exec. com. 1961-73). Clubs: Canyon Meadows Golf and Country, Glenmore Racquet. Office: Univ Calgary Calgary AB T2N 1N4 Canada *My belief in the necessity for each and every individual to be well informed and actively participate in promoting and influencing, on a knowledgeable basis, the decisions made relative to society, and to transmit this concept of citizenship has been the guiding principle throughout my life.*

KOVLER, H. JONATHAN, basketball team owner; b. Chgo., June 22, 1946; s. Everett and Marjorie (Blum) K.; m. Gail Epstein, Dec. 15, 1973; children: Molly Bett, Benjamin. B.S.B.A., Am. U., 1968. Mng. partner Chgo. Bulls, 1974—; dir. Chgo. Profl. Sports Corp. Exec. producer: film Real Life, 1979. Bd. dirs. Better Govt. Assn., Chgo.; trustee Michael Reese Hosp., Chgo.; mem. com. prints and drawing Art Inst. Chgo.; bd. dirs. Lincoln Park Zoo, Chgo. Office: care Chicago Bulls 333 N Michigan Ave Chicago IL 60601 *

KOVRIG, BENNETT, political scientist, educator; b. Budapest, Hungary, Sept. 8, 1940; emigrated to Can., 1950; s. John and Clara (Radoczi Mattyok) K.; m. Marina Kuchar, June 10, 1967; children: Michael John, Ariana Julia. Student, U. Coll. London, 1959-60; B.A. with honors, U. Toronto, 1962, M.A., 1963; Ph.D., London Sch. Econs. and Polit. Sci., 1967. Group relations officer Canadian Corp. for the 1967 World Exposition, Montreal, 1966-67; asst. prof. polit. studies Queen's U., Kingston, 1967-68; asst. prof. to prof. polit. economy U. Toronto, 1968-82, chmn. dept., 1979-82, prof., chmn. dept. polit. sci., 1982—; dir. Recochem Inc., Montreal, Toronto, Brisbane. Author: The Hungarian People's Republic, 1970, The Myth of Liberation, 1973, Communicsm in Hungary from Kun to Kadar, 1979, Struggle and Hope: The Hungarian-Canadian Experience, 1982. Mem. governing council U. Toronto, 1975-78; bd. dirs. Canadian Scene, Toronto, 1981—, CentreStage, Toronto, 1981—. Recipient Mackenzie King scholarship in internat. relations, 1963; fellow Can. Council, 1965, Can. Dept. Def., 1969. Mem. Can. Polit. Sci. Assn., Can. Inst. Internat. Affairs, Am. Assn. Study Hungarian History (v.p. 1984—). Roman Catholic. Home: 48 Wilgar Rd Toronto ON Canada M8X 1J5 Office: Dept Polit Sci Univ Toronto 100 St George St Toronto ON Canada M5S 1A1

KOWAL, CHARLES THOMAS, astronomer; b. Buffalo, Nov. 8, 1940; s. Charles Joseph and Rose (Myszkowiak) K.; m. Maria Antonietta Ruffino, Oct. 17, 1968; 1 dau., Loretta. B.A., U. So. Calif., 1963. Research asst. Mt. Wilson and Palomar obs.'s, 1961-63, Calif. Inst. Tech., Pasadena, 1963-65, 66-75, U. Hawaii, 1965-66; asso. scientist Calif. Inst. Tech., 1976-78, scientist, 1978-81, mem. profl. staff, 1981—; staff asso. Hale Obs., 1979-80; lectr. in field. Recipient James Craig Watson award Nat. Acad. Scis., 1979. Mem. Am. Astron. Soc., Internat. Astron. Union. Discovered bright supernova, 1972, 13th satellite of Jupiter, 1974, large planetoid between orbits of Saturn and Uranus, 1977, also asteroids and comets; recovered lost comets and asteroids. Office: Dept Astrophysics Calif Inst Tech Pasadena CA 91125

KOWALEK, JON W., art museum director; b. Swarthmore, Pa., Dec. 11, 1934; s. John and Anna (Partyka) K. B.S., Kutztown (Pa.) State Coll., 1956; M.A. in Art Edn, Pa. State U., 1960; M.F.A., Cranbrook Acad. Art, Bloomfield Hills, Mich., 1963. Asst dir. Flint (Mich.) Inst. Arts, 1963-65; dir. Ft. Lauderdale (Fla.) Mus. Art, 1966-67, Art Galleries of U. South Fla., 1968-69, Tacoma (Wash.) Art Mus., 1969—; mem. Tacoma-Pierce County Civic Arts Commn., 1973-74; juror art in new state bldgs., 1975; guest lectr. Kuntsgewerbe Mus., Zurich, Switzerland, 1965-66. Author: Hand Blown Glass/USA, 1971, Morris Graves, 1971, Carl Lander, Lunar Landings, 1972, Mark Tobey, 1972, Video Tape as Fine Art, 1973, Arts and Crafts of China, 1978, The American Eight, 1980, China Revisited, 1981. Pres. Wash. Arts Consortium, 1977-78. Recipient award of excellence in arts City of Tacoma Arts Commn., 1974. Mem. Western Assn. Art Museums (v.p. 1970), Am. Assn. Museums, Assn. Art Mus. Dirs., Internat. Council Museums. Home: 818 N 10th St Tacoma WA 98403 Office: 12th and Pacific Ave Tacoma WA 98402

KOWALSKI, BERNARD LOUIS, TV producer and dir.; b. Brownsville, Tex., Aug. 2, 1929; s. Francis Joseph and Elvira (Crixell) K.; m. Helen Grazer, Sept. 10, 1949; children—Helen Frances, Cynthia Ann, Lisa Marie, Peter Bernard. Student, Loyola U. Child actor, then prodn., script supr.; dir.: TV series Frontier; exec. producer, dir.: Baretta, ABC, N.Y.C. Democrat. *

KOWALSKI, DENNIS ALLAN, artist, educator; b. Chgo., May 14, 1938; s. Florian Lawrence and Emily Helen (Sinoga) K.; m. Kathryn Susan Lehar, Mar. 19, 1966; 1 dau., Denise Kathryn. Student, U. Ill., 1955-57; B.F.A., Art Inst. Chgo., 1962, M.F.A. with honors, 1966. Preparator Chgo. Acad. Scis., 1960-62, 64-68; instr. DePaul U., Chgo., 1967-70; asso. prof. U. Ill., 1970—. One-man shows, Marianne Deson Gallery, Chgo., 1978, 81, 83, Artpark, Lewiston, N.Y., 1978, N.A.M.E. Gallery, Chgo., 1980, Foster Gallery, U. Wis., Eau Claire, 1982, group shows include, Mus. Contemporary Art, Chgo., 1976, 78, Northwestern U., 1980, Stefanotti Gallery, N.Y.C., Carnegie-Mellon U., Pitts., 1982, Navy Pier, Chgo., Randolph St. Gallery, Chgo. Served with U.S. Army, 1962-64. George D. Brown Traveling fellow, 1966; Nat. Endowment for Arts fellow, 1975; Ill. Arts Council fellow, 1980; Ill. Arts Council grantee, 1980. Home: 4134 N Damen Ave Chicago IL 60618 Office: 1139 W Fulton St Chicago IL 60606

KOWALSKI, KENNETH LAWRENCE, physicist, educator; b. Chgo., July 24, 1932; s. Florian Lawrence and Emily Helen (Sinoga) K.; m. Audrey Bellin, Jan. 16, 1960; children—Eric Clifford, Claudia Gail. B.S., Ill. Inst. Tech., 1954; Ph.D. (Universal Match Found. fellow), Brown U., 1963. Aero. research scientist Lewis Research Center, NACA, 1954-57; research asso. in physics Brown U., summer 1962, Case Inst. Tech., Cleve., 1962-63, asst. prof. physics, 1963-67, asso. prof., 1967-73, Case Western Res. U., 1967-73, prof., 1973—, exec. officer dept. physics, 1970-71, chmn. dept. physics, 1971-76; vis. prof. Inst. Theoretical Physics U. Louvain, Belgium, 1968-69. NSF grantee, 1972—. Mem. Am. Phys. Soc. Research, numerous publs. on theoretical physics. Home: 2275 S Overlook Rd Cleveland Heights OH 44106 Office: 10900 Euclid Ave Cleveland OH 44106

KOWALSKI, STEPHEN WESLEY, educator; b. Bayonne, N.J., June 24, 1931; s. Steve J. and Anna (Gillack) K.; m. Evelyn L. Geiger, Apr. 2, 1955 (div. Apr. 1971); children: Lillian Ann, Kathryn Lynn, Kristina Eve, Stephen Edward; m. Barbara A. Soffe, Aug. 7, 1971; children—Brian Ashley, Scott William. B.S., Fairleigh Dickinson U., 1953; M.A., N.Y. U., 1954, Ph.D., 1964. Research chemist, cons. Shulton, Inc., Clifton, N.J., 1953-56; instr. chemistry Upsala Coll., East Orange, N.J., 1953-54, guest lectr., 1954-65; instr. sci. N.Y. U., 1954-55; tchr. sci. Kearny (N.J.) High Sch., 1955-56; research chemist Hoffman LaRoche, Nutley, N.J., 1956-57; prof., chmn. physics-geosci. dept. Montclair State Coll., Upper Montclair, N.J., 1956—, also chmn. physics-geosci. dept.; guest lectr. Fairleigh Dickinson U., 1955-69; coordinator, supr. AID Summer Sci. Insts., India and Ohio State U., 1966, NSF-AID Summer Sci. Insts., India, 1967; sci. coordinator master of arts in teaching program Fairleigh Dickinson U., 1968; vis. prof., cons. Interam U. P.R.; internat. speaker on sci. in consumer edn.; mem. nat. edn. adv. com. Consumers Union. Author: Floridation of Polyethylenes, 1955, Chromotographic Separation of Xanthophylls, 1957, Laboratory Manual in Consumer Science, 1972, Consumer Science Text and Laboratory Manual, 1975, revised edit., 1978; contbr.: book Flavor Chemistry, 1959. Bd. dirs. N.J. Consumers League, 1964-67, Montclair Athletic Commn.; sr. asso. Danforth Found., 1961—. Mem. Am. Chem. Soc. (nat. com. confs. and insts., div. chem. edn. 1968—), N.E.A., N.J. Edn. Assn. (chmn. higher edn. com. 1968-70), Nat. Sci. Tchrs. Assn. (com. establishing goals sci. literacy), N.J. Sci. Tchrs. Assn., Assn. N.J. Coll. and Univ. Profs. (founder 1969), AAAS, Phi Delta Kappa (life). Club: Elk. Patentee permeability of polyethylene, floridation. Home: 23 Dwyer Rd Wayne NJ 07470 Office: Montclair State College Upper Montclair NJ 07043 *God works in strange ways. But whatever happens always happens for the best even though it may be hard to accept at the moment.*

KOWEL, STEPHEN THOMAS, electrical engineering educator; b. Phila., Nov. 20, 1942; s. Abraham and Anna (Forman) K.; m. Janis Zoltan, June 7, 1970; children: Ann, Eugene, Rose. B.S. in Elec. Engring., U. Pa., 1964, Ph.D, 1968, M.S., Poly. Inst. Bklyn., 1966. Research assoc. U. Pa., Phila., 1968-69; asst. prof. elec. and computer engring. Syracuse U., N.Y., 1969-74, assoc. prof., 1974-79, prof., 1979—; vis. prof. Cornell U., Ithaca, N.Y., 1982-83; cons. in field. Contbr. articles to profl. jours.; patenteein field. Grantee NASA, U.S. Air Force, U.S. Army, NSF. Mem. IEEE (sr.), AAAS, AAUP, Sigma Xi. Home: 204 Arnold Ave Syracuse NY 13210 Office: Dept Elec and Computer Engring Syracuse U 111 Link Hall Syracuse NY 13210

KOWITT, ARTHUR JAY, lawyer; b. Chgo., Jan. 17, 1933; s. Harry and Jean (Gelfand) K.; m. Leonie Goldberg, June 16, 1957; children: Holly, Harlan, Susan. B.B.A., U. Wis., 1954; J.D., Northwestern U., 1957. Bar: Ill. 1958. Assoc. Mayer, Brown & Platt, Chgo., 1958-66, ptnr., 1966—; labor law faculty advisor Chgo.-Kent Sch. Law, 1978—. Editor: Northwestern Law Rev., 1955-57; author legal articles. Bd. dirs. Mayer Kaplan Jewish Community Ctr., Skokie, Ill., 1976-79. Mem. ABA, Decalogue Soc., Order of Coif, Phi Beta Kappa, Beta Gamma Sigma, Beta Alpha Psi, Phi Kappa Phi, Pi Lambda Phi, Tau Epsilon Rho. Home: 9448 N Drake Ave Evanston IL 60203 Office: Mayer Brown & Platt 231 S LaSalle St Chicago IL 60604

KOWITZ, GERALD THOMAS, psychologist, educator; b. Port Huron, Mich., Mar. 30, 1928; s. William Carl and Laura Martha Marie (von Hochleitner) K.; m. Norma Maxine Giess, Nov. 25, 1953; children—Gerda Kristine, Marie Louise, Laura Marlane. B.A., Mich. State U., 1948, M.A., 1950, Ph.D., 1954. Asso. prof. U. Ark., 1955-57; coordinator exptl. programs N.Y. State Dept. Edn., 1957-63; dir. Bur. of Research U. Houston, 1963-66; prof. human devel. U. Okla., Norman, 1966—, asst. dean budgets and spl. projects, 1968-71; cons. in field. Author: Guidance in the Elementary Classroom, 1959, Operating Guidance Services in the Modern School, 1968, Concepts in Teacher Education, 1971; Contbr. articles to profl. jours. Served with U.S. Navy, 1945-47; Served with U.S. Army, 1949-54. Mem. Am. Psychol. Assn., Am. Ednl. Research Assn., NEA, Phi Delta Kappa. Lutheran. Home: 2203 Ravenwood RR 3 Norman OK 73071 Office: 820 Van Vleet Oval 303 Norman OK 73019

KOZELKA, ROBERT MARVIN, mathematical science educator; b. Mpls., July 20, 1926; s. Richard L. and Winifred (Bradley) K.; m. Carolyn Eckfeldt, Aug. 30, 1950; children: Paul, Thomas, James, Peter. B.A., U. Minn., 1947, M.A., 1948; Ph.D., Harvard U., 1953. Mem. faculty U. Minn, 1947-48; mem. Tufts U., 1949-53, U. Nebr., 1953-57; mem. faculty Williams Coll., Williamstown, Mass., 1957—, prof. math., 1966—, chmn. dept., 1983—; vis. prof. U. N.C., 1963-64, 78-79; vis. prof. anthropology and sociology U. Tex., 1970-71; research assoc. anthropology Cornell U., 1960-63; cons. to industry, 1957-58. Author: Elements of Statistical Inference, 1961. Served with USAAF, 1945. Mem. Inst. Math. Stats., Am. Statis. Assn., Math. Assn. Am. Office: Dept Math Sci Williams Coll Williamstown MA 01267

KOZIKOWSKI, MITCHELL, public relations executive; b. Pitts., Dec. 15, 1936; s. Sigmont and Anna (Swerzynski) K.; m. Cheryl Inscho, June 4, 1976; children: Timothy Joseph, Kenneth Mitchell, Leigh Alexander Walling, Rosemary Walling. B.S. in Chem. Engring., U. Pitts., 1957. Tech. editor Westinghouse Electric Corp., 1958-62; dir. pub. relations Lando Inc., Pitts., 1962-67; v.p. public relations Muller Jordan Herrick, N.Y.C., 1967-73; exec. v.p. Liberty Village Ltd., Flemington, N.J., 1973-76; v.p. Creamer Dickson Basford (public relations), N.Y.C., 1976—78, pres., 1979-83, Creamer Dickson Basford-USA, 1983—; dir. Creamer Inc. Pres. Pitts. Jaycees, 1962-63; bd. dirs. U.S. Jaycees, 1963-65, Jr. Chamber Internat. Senate; trustee Big Bros. N.Y., 1980—. Served with USNR, 1959-66. Mem. Public Relations Soc. Am. (accredited), Am. Assn. Advt. Agys. (pub. relations com. 1983—), Counsellors Acad., Nat. Investor Relations Inst., Am. Mgmt. Assn., Internat. Assn. Bus. Communicators, Am. Frozen Food Inst. (mktg. com. 1979-81), Frozen Food Action Communication Team (exec. dir. 1978—), Polish Roman Catholic Union, Pi Delta Epsilon, Sigma Tau, Omicron Delta Kappa. Home: 35 Maple Ave Flemington NJ 08822 Office: 1633 Broadway New York NY 10019

KOZIN, FRANK, educator; b. Chgo., Jan. 19, 1930; s. Melvin and Shirley Helen (Pearl) K.; m. Cynthia H.P. Hsiac, Mar. 30, 1958; 1 son, Daniel G. B.S. in Math, Ill. Inst. Tech., 1952, M.S., 1953, Ph.D., 1956. Prof. Purdue U., 1958-67, co-dir., 1963-67; prof. elec. engring. Poly. Inst. Bklyn., 1967—; dir. research Midwest Applied Sci. Corp., Lafayette, Ind., 1965-67; vis. prof. Inst. Math., Kyoto U., 1964-65. NSF Sci. Faculty fellow London U., 1961-62. Mem. Am. Math. Soc., Math. Assn. Am., Soc. Indsl. and Applied Math., Internat. Soc. Terrain Vehicle Systems. Research and publs. on stochastic systems. Office: 333 Jay St Brooklyn NY 11201

KOZINSKI, ALEX, federal judge; b. Bucharest, Romania, July 23, 1950; came to U.S., 1962; s. Moses and Sabine (Zapler) K.; m. Marcy J. Tiffany, July 9, 1977; 1 son, Yale Tiffany. A.B. cum laude in Econs., UCLA, 1972, J.D., 1975. Bar: Calif. 1975, U.S. Ct. Appeals (9th cir.) 1978, U.S. Ct. Customs and Patent Appeals 1978, U.S. Customs Ct. 1978, D.C. 1978, U.S. Dist. Ct. (cen. dist.) Calif. 1979, U.S. Supreme Ct. 1979, U.S. Ct. Appeals (D.C. cir.) 1980, U.S. Dist. Ct. D.C. 1980, U.S. Ct. Appeals (4th cir.) 1980, U.S. Ct. Appeals (2d cir.) 1980. Law clk. to presiding justice U.S. Ct. Appeals 9th Cir., 1975-76; law clk. Chief Justice Warren E. Burger, U.S. Supreme Ct., 1976-77; assoc. Forry Golbert Singer & Gelles, Los Angeles, 1977-79, Covington & Burling, Washington, 1979-81; dep. legal counsel Office of Pres.-elect Reagan, Washington, 1980-81; asst. counsel Office of Counsel to Pres., White House, Washington, 1981; spl. counsel Merit Systems Protection Bd., PAS Ex-IV, Washington, 1981-82; chief judge U.S. Claims Ct., Washington, 1982—. Contbr. articles to legal jours.; mng. editor: UCLA Law Rev., 1974-75; assoc. editor, 1973-74. Calif. State scholar, 1968-72; fellow State of Calif., 1972-75. Mem. ABA, Fed. Bar Assn., Bar Assn. D.C., D.C. Bar, State Bar Calif., Order of Coif. Club: Nat. Lawyers (Washington). Office: US Claims Ct 717 Madison Pl NW Washington DC 20005 *

KOZINSKI, ANDRZEJ WLADYSLAW, educator, biologist; b. Skierniewice, Poland, Oct. 1, 1925; came to U.S., 1957, naturalized, 1963; s. Marian and Jozefina (Jasinski) K.; children: Kasia, Peter, Mark, Mira. M.D., U. Warsaw, 1951, Ph.D. in Biochemistry, 1956. Research asst. State Hygienic Inst., Warsaw, Poland, 1949-51; research asso. Inst. Biochemistry, Warsaw, 1951-53; asst. prof. dept. microbiology U. Warsaw, 1955-57; asst. prof. Inst. Microbiology, Rutgers U., 1959; NIH fellow dept. biology Johns Hopkins, 1962; asso. mem. Wistar Inst., 1962-66; asso. prof. dept. med. genetics U. Pa., Phila., 1966-68, prof. med. genetics and microbiology, 1968—. Co-Author 2 books; Contbr. articles to sci. jours. Mem. Soc. Biol. Chemistry, Biophys. Soc. First to describe molecular mechanism of recombination as a breakage and reunion of DNA molecules. Home: 945 E Washington Ln Philadelphia PA 19138

KOZLOVA, VALENTINA, ballerina; b. Moscow, Aug. 26, 1957; U.S., 1979; d. Vladimir Koslov and Anna (Shuvanova); m. Leonid V. Kozlov, Dec. 22, 1973. Ballet diploma, Bolshoi Ballet Acad. Sch., Moscow, 1973. Soloist Bolshoi Ballet, Moscow, 1974-76, prin., 1976-79, Australian Ballet, Melborune and Sydney, 1981-83, N.Y. City Ballet, 1983—; asst. choreographer Miami Ballet Concerto, Fla., 1980, N.J. Closter Ballet, 1980-81, Santiago Ballet, Chile, 1981-82, Australian Ballet, 1982. Starred in: On Your Toes, Broadway, 1983, Kennedy Ctr., Washington. Recipient Silver medal Moscow Ballet competition, 1976. Office: NY City Ballet State Theatre Lincoln Center New York NY 10023 *

KOZLOWSKI, RONALD STEPHAN, librarian; b. Chgo., Oct. 18, 1937; s. Stephan James and Helen Marie Beck (Tancula) K.; m. Barbara Hartlein, Aug. 8, 1964; children: Ann, Keith, Ellen, Brent. B.S. in Edn, Ill. State U., 1961; M.A. in L.S, Rosary Coll., 1968. Audiovisual librarian Triton Jr. Coll., River Grove, Ill., 1968-69; br. librarian Evansville (Ind.) Pub. Libraries, 1969-70, asst. dir., 1971-74; head reference and acquisitions dept. Ind. State U., Evansville, 1970-71; dir. West Fla. Regional Library, Pensacola, 1974-77, Louisville Free Public Library, 1977-84, Pub. Library Charlotte (N.C.) and Mecklenburg County, 1984—; del. White House Conf. on Libraries. Mem. Pensacola C. of C. Task Force on Edn., 1975-77. Recipient Outstanding Library Services award Pensacola Bicentennial Commn., 1976. Mem. ALA, Southeastern Library Assns., N.C. Library Assn. Roman Catholic. Home: 3134 Eastburn Rd Charlotte NC 28210 Office: Charlotte-Mecklenburg 310 N Tryon St Charlotte NC 28202

KOZLOWSKI, THEODORE THOMAS, botany educator; b. Buffalo, May 21, 1917; s. Theodore and Helen (Zamiara) K.; m. Maude Peters, June 29, 1954. B.S., Syracuse U., 1939; M.A., Duke U., 1941, Ph.D., 1947; postgrad., MIT, 1942-43; D.Sc. honoris causa, U. Catholique de Louvain, Belgium, 1978. Asst. prof. botany U. Mass., 1947-48, asso. prof., 1948-50, prof., head dept. botany, 1950-58; prof. forestry U. Wis., 1958-72, A.J. Riker prof., 1972—, chmn. dept., 1961-64, dir. biotron lab., 1977—; cons. NSF, Stanford Research Inst., Nat. Park Service, FAO, Oak Ridge Nat. Lab., Malaysian Govt., Mont. Univ. System, Internat. Found. for Sci., Academic Press, Time-Life Books, various comml. firms; vis. biologist Am. Inst. Biol. Scis., 1969-72; vis. scientist Soc. Am. Foresters, 1963-71; vis. prof. U. Pa., 1954; George Lamb lectr. U. Nebr., 1974; George S. Long lectr. U. Wash., 1978; Rapporteur World Consultation on Tree Improvement, 1963. Author: (with P.J. Kramer) Physiology of Trees, 1960, Physiology of Woody Plants, 1979, Water Metabolism in Plants, 1964, Growth and Development of Trees, 2 vols., 1971, Tree Growth and Environmental Stresses, 1979; editor: Tree Growth, 1962, Water Deficits and Plant Growth, 7 vols., 1968-83, Seed Biology, 3 vols., 1971, Shedding of Plant Parts, 1973, (with G.C. Marks) Ectomycorrhizae, 1973, (with C.E. Ahlgren) Fire and Ecosystems, 1974, (with J.B. Mudd) Responses of Plants to Air Pollution, 1975, (with P. de T. Alvim) Ecophysiology of Tropical Crops, 1977, (with T.W. Tibbitts) Controlled Environment Guidelines for Plant Research, 1979; editorial bd.: Forest Sci., Ecology, BioSci.; asso. editor: Can. Jour. Forest Research, Am. Midland Naturalist; editor: (book series) Physiol.-Ecology. Served to capt. USAAF, 1942-46. Sr. Fulbright research scholar Oxford (Eng.) U., 1964-65; recipient Author's award Internat. Shade Tree Conf., 1971. Mem. Am., Scandinavian socs. plant physiologists, Bot. Soc. Am., Ecol. Soc. Am., Soc. Am. Foresters (Barrington Moore biol. research award 1974), Internat. Soc. Arboriculture (Arboricultural research award 1976), Societas Forestalis Fenniae (Finland) (hon.), Societas Botanicopum Poloniae (hon.), Am. Inst. Biol. Scis., Phi Beta Kappa, Sigma Xi, Phi Kappa Phi, Phi Sigma. Home: 10 S Rock Rd Madison WI 53705

KOZMETSKY, GEORGE, educator; b. Seattle, Oct. 5, 1917; s. George and Nadya (Omelan) K.; m. Ronya Keosiff, Nov. 5, 1943; children: Gregory Allen, Nadya Anne (Mrs. Michael Scott). B.A., U. Wash., 1938; M.B.A., Harvard U., 1947, D.C.S., 1957. Instr. Harvard U., 1947-50; asst. prof. Carnegie-Mellon U., Pitts., 1950-52; mem. tech. staff Hughes Aircraft Co., Los Angeles, 1952-54; dir. computer, controls lab. Litton Co., Los Angeles, 1954-59, v.p., asst. gen. mgr. electronic equipment div., 1959-60; exec. v.p. Teledyne Corp., Beverly Hills, Calif., 1960-66; prof. mgmt. and computer sci., dean Coll. Bus. Adminstrn. and Grad. Sch. Bus., U. Tex. at Austin, 1966-82, exec. assoc. for econs. affairs univ. system, 1966-82, exec. assoc. for econ. affairs univ. system, 1982—; chmn. bd. MCR; dir. LaQuinta, MCO Holdings, Hydril, Amdahl Corp., Datapoint Corp., Heizer Corp., Teledyne Corp., Simplicity Pattern Co., Inc., Wrather Corp., United Fin. Group, Inc.; trustee Federated Devel. Corp.; Leatherbee lectr. Harvard U., 1967; vis. scholar U. Wash., 1968, Walker-Ames prof., 1970. Author: Financial Reports of Labor Unions, 1950, (with Simon and Guetzkow) Centralization Versus Decentralization in Organizing the Controller's Department, 1954, (with Paul Kircher) Electronic Computers and Management Control) 1956, (with Ronya Kozmetsky) Making It Together, 1981. Mem. adv. council Hampshire Coll., 1969-76; Bd. dirs. Adlai Stevenson Inst. Internat. Affairs, 1968-70; bd. fellows Claremont U. Center. Served with AUS, 1942-45. Decorated Silver Star, Bronze Star with oak leaf cluster, Purple Heart. Mem. Inst. Mgmt. Sci. (chmn. bd., pres.), Assn. Advancement of Med. Instrumentation, Brit. Interplanetary Soc., Am. Inst. C.P.A.'s, Am. Soc. Oceanography. Home: PO Box 2253 Austin TX 78768

KOZODOY, NEAL, magazine editor; b. Boston, Apr. 4, 1942; s. Peter H. and Marion (Seder) K.; m. Ruth Lurie, June 7, 1964; children—Sarah Naomi, Peter, Elizabeth. B.A., Harvard U., 1963; B.H.L., Hebrew Coll., Boston, 1963; M.A., Columbia U., 1966. Mem. editorial staff Commentary mag., N.Y.C., 1966—, exec. editor, 1968—; editor Library Jewish Studies, 1970—; vis. lectr. Jewish Theol. Sem., 1974-75, Yale U., 1976; cons. President's Commn. Campus Unrest, 1970, Nat. Endowment Humanities, 1976—. Sec. Com. for the Free World, 1981—. Woodrow Wilson fellow, 1964-65; Danforth fellow, 1965-67. Office: 165 E 56th St New York NY 10022

KOZOL, JONATHAN, author; b. Boston, Sept. 5, 1936; s. Harry Leo and Ruth (Massell) K. B.A., Harvard U., 1958; Rhodes scholar, Magdalen Coll., Oxford, 1958-59. Tchr. Boston pub. schs., 1964-65, Newton pub. schs., 1966-68; cons. Store-front Learning Center, 1968-71; also trustee; vis. lectr. Yale U., 1969, numerous univs., 1971-75; prof. edn. Trinity Coll., 1980; prof. English U. Mass., Amherst, 1982; instr. Center for Intercultural Documentation, Cuernavaca, Mexico, 1969, 70, 74; cons. U.S. Office Edn., 1965-66. Writer in Paris; Author: Death At An Early Age (Nat. Book award 1967), Free Schools, 1972, The Night is Dark and I Am Far From Home, 1975, Children of the Revolution, 1978, Prisoners of Silence, 1980, On Being A Teacher, 1981, People of the Book, 1982, Alternative Schools, 1983; corr.: Los Angeles Times, USA Today, 1982-83; lectr. and cons. Trustee New Sch. for Children, Roxbury, Mass.; bd. dirs. Nat. Literacy Coalition, 1980-83. Recipient Olympia Thousand Dollar award, 1962; Saxton fellow in creative writing from Harper & Row, 1964; Guggenheim fellow, 1970; Field Found. fellow, 1972; Ford Found. fellow, 1974; Rockefeller Found. sr. fellow, 1978. Mem. Fellowship of Reconciliation, Am. P.E.N. Mailing address: care Brandt and Brandt 1501 Broadway New York NY 10036 *Illiteracy in America, now estimated at 35% of the adult population, has become my central concern during the past four years. One third of the electorate cannot read or write and, for these reasons, are increasingly excluded from employment and cannot participate in democratic process. A national crisis has developed.*

KRABBENHOFT, KENNETH LESTER, physician, educator; b. Sabula, Iowa, Jan. 7, 1923; s. Lester Henry and Bessie Grant (Thompson) K.; m. Gloria Darlene Eriksen, June 17, 1944; children—Kenneth Lester, Douglas Harold, Karen Ann Krabbenhoft Naegele. B.A., State U. Iowa, 1943, M.D., 1946. Diplomate: Am. Bd. Radiology. Intern Harper Hosp., Detroit, 1946-47, resident, 1949-52, asso. radiologist, 1952-57, radiologist, 1957—; prof., chmn. dept. radiology Wayne State U., Detroit, 1969—; chief radiology Detroit Receiving Hosp.-Univ. Health Center, 1980—; cons. radiologist VA Hosp., Allen Park, Mich., Children's Hosp. Mich., Crittenton Gen. Hosp., Herman Kiefer Hosp., Nat. Cancer Inst.; mem. Nat. Cancer Adv. Bd., 1970-73; pres. Affiliated Radiologists, Inc., Detroit, 1973—, Detroit Gen. Hosp. Research Corp., 1974-82; mem. Environ. Radiation Exposure Adv. Com., 1975-78; trustee Am. Bd. Radiology, 1970—, sec., 1981—; treas. Am. Bd. Med. Specialists, 1981—; alt. del. Internat. Congress Radiology. Cons. editor: Am. Jour. Roentgenology, 1975—. Served to lt. (j.g.), M.C. USNR, 1947-49. Nat. Cancer Inst. grantee, 1971-75; Nat. Cancer Inst. Specialized Cancer Center grantee, 1973-75. Fellow Am. Coll. Radiology; mem. Detroit Acad. Medicine, Detroit Med. Club, AMA (vice chmn. sect. council 1969-71), Mich., Wayne County med. socs., Mich. Radiol. Soc. (pres. 1969-70), Am. Radium Soc., Am. Roentgen Ray Soc. (silver medal 1962), AAAS, Radiol. Soc. N.Am., Inter-Am. Coll. Radiology, Friends of Detroit Public Library, Founders Soc. Detroit Inst. Art, State Hist. Soc. Iowa, Mich. Hist. Soc., Lost Lakes Woods Assn., Sigma Xi, Alpha Omega Alpha. Clubs: Masons, Detroit. Exhibited portable radioactive istopes for radiography at Smithsonian Inst., 1964-67. Home: 52 Oxford Rd Pleasant Ridge MI 48069 Office: 540 E Canfield St Detroit MI 48201

KRACK, JAMES JOSEPH, association executive; b. Cleve., Nov. 28, 1930; s. Norman S. and Marie Clair (DeVille) Crawford; m. Donna Kegin, Jan. 22, 1971; children: Ann, Mary, James, Joseph, Jace. B.A., Loyola U., Los Angeles, 1953. Cert. kennel operator.; cert. assn. exec. Sales mgr. G.S. Marshall Co., San Marino, Calif., 1955-64; owner, operator Woodmen Kennels, Colorado Springs, Colo., 1964-77; exec. dir. Am. Boarding Kennels Assn., Colorado Springs, 1977—. Author: Building, Buying and Operating a Boarding Kennel, 1979; co-editor: Boarderline mag. Served to 1st lt. USAF, 1953-55; Korea. Mem. Am. Soc. Assn. Execs., Am. Boarding Kennels Assn. (co-founder). Republican. Roman Catholic. Home: 14085 Black Forest Rd Colorado Springs CO 80908 Office: 311 N Union Blvd Colorado Springs CO 80909

KRAEGEL, NORBERT EDWARD, corp. exec.; b. Elmhurst, Ill., Dec. 22, 1930; s. Adolph C. and Hele (Thon) K.; m. Virginia Ann Robinson, Mar. 2, 1955; children—Charles, Cheryl, Scott, Sandra. B.S. in Bus. Adminstrn. and Accounting, 1953. Auditor, then sr. auditor Arthur Andersen & Co. (C.P.A.'s); formerly v.p. systems and information service C. & N. R.R.; v.p. finance Internat. Systems and Controls Corp., Kansas City, Mo.; formerly v.p. finance, dir. AAR Corp., Elk Grove, Ill.; v.p., comptroller UAL, Inc.; now v.p. accounting United Airlines. Home: 519 S Na-Wa-Ta St Mount Prospect IL 60056 Office: PO Box 66100 Chicago IL 60666

KRAEHE, ENNO EDWARD, history educator; b. St. Louis, Dec. 9, 1921; s. Enno and Amelia Roth (Henckler) K.; m. Mary Alice Eggleston, May 25, 1946; children: Laurence Adams, Claudia. B.A., U. Mo., 1943, M.A., 1944; Ph.D., U. Minn., 1948. Instr. history U. Del., 1946-48; asst. prof. history U. Ky., 1948-50, asso. prof., 1950-63, prof., 1963-64, U. N.C., 1964-68, U. Va., 1968-71, Commonwealth prof., 1971-77, William W. Corcoran prof., 1977—, vis. prof., 1955; vis. prof. U. Mo., 1946, U. Tex., 1955, U. Minn., 1963; U.S. Dept. State Specialist in, Germany, 1953; mem. regional selection com. Woodrow Wilson fellowship Found., 1959-60; mem. Sr. Fulbright-Hayes History Screening Com., 1970-73. Author: Metternich's German Policy Volume I: The Contest with Napoleon 1799-1814, 1963; author: Volume II: The Congress of Vienna, 1814-1815, 1983; Editor: The Metternich Controversy, 1971; Mem. editorial bd.: Central European History, 1967-72, Austrian History Yearbook, 1969-74; Contbr. to encys. and hist. jours. Fulbright scholar, Austria, 1952-53; Guggenheim fellow, 1960-61; Am. Council Learned Socs. fellow, 1969, 73; Nat. Endowment for Humanities grantee, 1973. Mem. Am. Hist. Assn., Conf. Group for Central European History, So. Hist. Assn. (chmn. European sect. 1974-75), Charlottesville Com. on Fgn. Relations, Phi Beta Kappa. Episcopalian. Clubs: Colonnade, Blue Ridge Swimming, Met. Opera Guild, Friends of Ky. Center. Home: 130 Bennington Rd Charlottesville VA 22901

KRAEMER, ALBERT G., rubber company executive; b. 1931. With Firestone Tire & Rubber, Akron, Ohio, 1955—, mgr. auditing Hamilton plant, Ont., 1965, mgr. acctg., Akron, Ohio, 1967, corp. auditing, 1967, mgr. corp. cost analysis, 1969, mgr. corp. acctg., 1974, mgr. bus. plans and analysis, 1976; asst. controller, then v.p. fin. and adminstrn. Firestone Can., Inc., 1979; pres. Firestone Can., 1980; chmn., pres. Firestone Can., Inc., 1981-83, exec. v.p., 1982—, World Tire Group, 1983—. Address: Firestone Tire & Rubber 1200 Firestone Pkwy Akron OH 44317 *

KRAEMER, PAUL WILHELM, utilities executive; b. Mpls., Dec. 28, 1920; s. John C. and Rose (Schoenstuhl) K.; m. Doris Carter, Jan. 2, 1946; children: Bruce, Fred (dec.). B.S. in Chem. Engring, U. Minn., 1942, William Mitchell Coll. Law, 1957. With Minn. Gas Co., 1947—v.p. ops., 1958-66, exec. v.p., 1966-67, pres., chief exec. officer, 1967-81 chmn. bd., 1981—, dir., 1965—, mem. exec. com., 1966—; dir. Investors Group of Cos., N.Am. Life & Casualty Co. Contbr. articles to profl. jours. Trustee emeritus William Mitchell Coll. Law; v.p., bd. dirs. Greater Mpls. Met. Housing Corp.; trustee, chmn. Dunwoody Indsl. Inst. Served to lt. USNR, 1942-46. Recipient Operating award of merit Am. Gas Assn., 1959; named Engr. of Year Mpls. Engrs. Club,

1968. Mem. Engrs. Club, Am. Gas Assn. (fin. com., dir.). Clubs: Masons, Mpls., Minikahda Country (Mpls.); Delray Dunes Country (Fla.). Home: 11957 N Lake Dr Boynton Beach FL 33436

KRAFFT, JULIA STEVEN, bus. exec.; b. Wheaton, Ill.; d. George Barnard and Rose (Austin) Clark; m. Walter A. Krafft, June 25, 1939; 1 dau., Virginia. Ed. bus. coll., Elgin, Ill., 1913-14. Organized Steven's Candy Kitchens, Inc., 1921, pres., until 1956, when sold; pres. succeeding corp. 611 N. Sacramento Corp.; pres. Honey Bear Farm, Genoa City, Wis., 1951—; owner The Little Traveler, Geneva, Ill., 1953—. Bd. dirs., v.p. women's bd. Salvation Army, Chgo., also mem. adv. bd.; dir. women's bds. Chgo. Boys Clubs, Passavant Meml. Hosp., Lyric Opera; chmn. Chgo. Beautiful Com.; trustee Carthage Coll., Kenosha, Wis. Recipient Citizen's award VFW, 1944, various citations Am. Legion. Mem. English Speaking Union. Republican. Presbyterian. Clubs: Woman's Athletic (Chgo.); Rancho Santa Fe Garden; Athenaeum (San Diego). Home: PO Box 228 Rancho Santa Fe CA 92067

KRAFT, ALAN MYRON, psychiatrist; b. Passaic, N.J., May 24, 1925; s. George and Sadie (Heller) K.; m. Selma Warshaw, June 24, 1951; children—Marcia Kraft-Sayre, Laura. M.D., Chgo. Med. Sch., 1951; postgrad., Menninger Sch. Psychiatry, 1952-55. Intern Cook County Hosp., Chgo., 1951-52; resident Menninger Sch. Psychiatry, Topeka, 1952-55; dir. Mental Health Center Am., 1958-61, Fort Logan Mental Health Center, Denver, 1961-67, Capital Dist. Psychiat. Center, Albany, 1967-79; psychiatrist-in-chief Albany (N.Y.) Med. Center, 1968—; prof., chmn. dept. psychiatry Albany Med. Coll., 1967—. Author: Textbook of Psychiatry, 1977, Social Setting of Mental Health, 1975. Trustee The Menninger Found. Served with U.S. Army, 1943-45. Decorated Purple Heart. Mem. Am. Psychiat. Assn. Jewish. Office: 47 New Scotland Ave Albany NY 12208

KRAFT, C. WILLIAM, JR., judge; b. Phila., Dec. 14, 1903; s. C. William and Wilhelmina J. (Doerr) K.; m. Frances V. McDevitt, June 27, 1942; 1 son, C. William III. A.B., U. Pa., 1924, LL.B., 1927. Bar: Pa. 1927. Trial lawyer Kraft, Lipincott & Donaldson, Media, Pa., 1928-55; dist. atty., Delaware County, Pa., 1944-52; judge U.S. Dist. Ct., Phila., 1955-70, sr. judge, 1970—. Mem. Am., Pa. bar assns. Home and Office: Apt 602 Island House 200 Ocean Ln Dr Key Biscayne FL 33149 *

KRAFT, CHARLES HALL, statistics educator; b. Chgo., Mar. 20, 1924; s. Robert Hollo and Fanny Elizabeth (Hall) K.; m. Constance van Eeden, Dec. 8, 1960; children: Kathleen, Sally, Harry, Penny, Kari. Student, Hamilton Coll., 1943-44; B.A., Mich. State U., 1948, M.A., 1949; Ph.D., U. Calif., Berkeley, 1954. Acting asst. math. U. Calif., Berkeley, 1954-56; asso. prof. Mich. State U., 1956-61, U. Minn., 1961-65; prof. U. Montreal, Que., Can., 1965—. Author: (with c. van Eeden) Nonparametric Introduction to Statistics, 1968; assoc. editor: Ann. Math. Statistics, 1974-77; contbr. articles to statis. jours., 1955—. Served with USAAF, 1942-45. Fellow AAAS, Inst. Math. Stats.; mem. Am. Statis. Assn., Can. Statis. Soc., Can. Math. Soc. Home: 4854 Cote des Neiges Apt 1207 Montreal PQ H3V 1G7 Canada Office: Dept Math and Statistics U Montreal Montreal PQ H3C 3J7 Canada

KRAFT, CHRISTOPHER COLUMBUS, JR., aerospace consultant; b. Phoebus, Va., Feb. 28, 1924; s. Christopher Columbus and Vanda Olivia (Suddreth) K.; m. Elizabeth Anne Turnbull, Sept. 2, 1950; children: Gordon Turnbull, Kristi Anne. B.S. in Aero. Engring., Va. Poly. Inst., 1944. With NASA and predecessor, 1945—, flying quality, stability and control measurements P47 Thunderbolt and P-51H Mustang, designed, supervised constrn. gust-alleviation system light transp. airplane, 1950-55, flight test measurements strength and presistence trailing vortices airplane, 1952, project engr. F80-1 Crusader, 1957-58, mem. space task group for Project Mercury, 1956, flight dir., 1959-70, dep. dir. Manned Spacecraft Ctr., 1970-72, dir. Lyndon B. Johnson Space Ctr., 1972-82. Mem. Inst. Aerospace Scis., Pi Tau Sigma. Episcopalian (lay reader). Office: Rockwell Internat 1840 NASA Blvd Houston TX 77058

KRAFT, DAVID CHRISTIAN, univ. adminstr.; b. Marion, Ohio, Sept. 10, 1937; s. Walter Christian and Marie Francis K.; m. Suzanne Bintz, Aug. 24, 1959; children—Susan, Michael, Jeannine. B.C.E., U. Dayton, 1959; M.S.C.E., U. Notre Dame, 1961; Ph.D. in Civil Engring, Ohio State U., 1964. Registered profl. engr., Ohio, Kans. Asso. research engr. U. N.Mex., 1964; asst. prof. civil engring. U. Dayton, 1965-68, asso. prof., 1969-72, prof., 1972-78, asst. dean, 1970-72, dean, 1972-78, Sch. Engring., U. Kans., Lawrence, 1978—; partner Kraft-Shaw-Weiss and Assos. (Cons. Engrs.), 1968-78. Named Prof. of Yr. U. Dayton, 1970, Outstanding Dayton Area Engring. Educator Engring. Affiliate Socs. Council, 1971; recipient Neil Armstrong award Ohio Soc. Profl. Engrs., 1972. Mem. Nat. Soc. Profl. Engrs., ASCE, Am. Soc. Engring. Edn. Roman Catholic. Office: U Kans 4010 Learned Hall Lawrence KS 66045

KRAFT, GERALD, economist; b. Detroit, July 1, 1935; s. Jule and Shirley (Schwartz) K.; m. Sandra Doris Johnson, Aug. 7, 1955; children: Michael Stanton, Lynn Barbara. Student, U. Chgo., 1951-52; B.A., Wayne U., 1955; M.A., Harvard U., 1957. Mng. dir. Harvard U. Statis. Lab., Cambridge, Mass., 1957-58; prin. United Research Inc., Cambridge, 1958-61; sr. research asso. Systems Analysis and Research Corp., Boston, 1961-64, Regional and Urban Planning Implementation, Inc., Cambridge, 1964-65; pres. Charles River Assos. Inc., Boston, 1965—; lectr. M.I.T., Harvard U., U. Pa.; mem. planning com., dir. Maritime Transp. Research Bd., NRC, 1976-79; mem. Group I Council; mem. coms. Transp. Research Bd., 1977-80; pres. Transp. Research Forum, 1977, trustee, 1983—, v.p. program, 1976; chmn. 2d Internat. Tungsten Symposium, 1982. Author: (with others) The Role of Transportation in Regional Economic Development, 1971; co-author: Report of Task Force on Transp. and Sci. Adv. panel to Com. on Pub. Works, U.S. Ho. of Reps, 1974; contbr. (with others) articles to profl. publs. Trustee, mem. fin. com., mem. exec. com. Beth Israel Hosp. Mem. Am. Econ. Assn., Econometric Soc., Am. Statis. Assn., Inst. Mgmt. Scis., Ops. Research Soc. Am., Inst. Math. Stats., Fine Wine Council Mass. (dir.), Phi Beta Kappa. Clubs: Beefeater, University, Rotary, Harvard, Internat. Wine and Food Soc., Wine and Food Soc. Boston (treas.), Le Premier du Vin, Confrérie des Chevaliers du Tastevin. Home: 60 Scotch Pine Rd Weston MA 02193 Office: 200 Clarendon St Boston MA 02116

KRAFT, JOHN CHRISTIAN, geology educator; b. Schwenksville, Pa., Nov. 15, 1929; s. John H. and K. Madeline (Vogt) K.; m. Joan E. Parkes, Sept. 11, 1955; children: Christine Louise, John Frederick. B.S., Pa. State U., 1951; M.S., U. Minn., 1952, Ph.D. (Calif. Co. and Shell fellow), 1955. Cert. petroleum geologist; cert. prof. geologist; lic. geologist, Del. Div. stratigrapher Shell Devel. Co., 1957-58, Shell Can. Ltd., 1955-64, Shell Oil Co., 1962-64; prof. geology, chmn. U. Del., Newark, 1964—, H. Fletcher Brown prof. geology, 1981—. Author: Morphologic and Taxonomic Relationships of Middle Ordovician Ostracode, 1962, A Guide to the Geology of Delaware Coastal Environments, The Geology of the Sandy Coasts of Greece; contbr. articles to profl. jours. Fellow Geol. Soc. Am., AAAS; mem. Del. Acad. Sci. (pres. 1970), Am. Assn. Petroleum Geologists, Soc. Econ. Paleontologists and Mineralogists, Can. Soc. Petroleum Geologists, Assn. Profl. Geol. Scientists. Club: Delaware Torch (pres. Wilmington 1971). Home: 307 Radcliffe Dr Newark DE 19711

KRAFT, JOSEPH, journalist; b. South Orange, N.J., Sept. 4, 1924; s. David Harry and Sophie (Surasky) K.; m. Polly Winton, Jan. 6, 1960. A.B., Columbia U., 1947; postgrad., Princeton U., 1948-49, Inst. Advanced Study, 1950-51; LL.D. (hon.), Claremont Grad. Sch., 1973—. Editorial writer: Washington Post, 1951-52; staff writer: N.Y. Times, 1953-57; Washington corr.: Harper's mag, 1962-65; syndicated columnist: Washington Post, Los Angeles Times, 1963—; Author: The Struggle for Algeria, 1961, The Grand Design, 1962, Profiles in Power, 1966, The Chinese Difference, 1973; Contbr. to: New Yorker, also others. Mem. panel Presdl. Debates, 1976. Served with AUS, 1943-46. Decorated chevalier French Legion of Honor. Mem. Council Fgn. Relations, Phi Beta Kappa. Clubs: Met. Gridiron (Washington); Century (N.Y.C.). Home: 3314 P St NW Washington DC 20007

KRAFT, LEO, composer; b. N.Y.C., July 24, 1922; s. Nathan and Yetta (Kaplowitz) K.; m. Amy Lager, May 16, 1945; children: David, Evan. B.A., Queens Coll., 1945; M.F.A., Princeton, 1947. Prof. music Queens Coll., City U. N.Y., 1947—; Bd. dirs. Internat. Soc. Contemporary Music, 1972-78, 82—; pres. Am. Music Center, 1976-78. Composer: for chorus and small orch. A Proverb of Solomon, 1953; piano solo Partita 1, 1958; Variations for Orch, 1958, String Quartet 2, 1959; for chorus Psalm 114, 1961, Psalm 40, 1963; for voice and piano Four English Love Songs, 1961; violin and viola Partita 2, 1961; Five Pieces for Clarinet and Piano, 1962, Three Pieces for Orchestra, 1963, Fantasy for Flute and Piano, 1963; for winds Partita 3, 1964; flute, viola, piano Trios and Interludes, 1965; 12 instruments Concerto No. 2, 1966; Dialogues for Flute and Tape, 1967, Concerto No. 3 for Cello, Winds and Percussion, 1969; for soprano, cello, flute and piano Spring in the Harbor, 1969; piano duet and tape Antiphonies, 1971; piano solo Sestina, 1971; flute and percussion Line Drawings, 1972; Music for Orch, 1975; flute, clarinet, violin, piano, bass Partita 4, 1975; flute, clarinet, violin, cello, tape Dialectica, 1976, Concerto for; piano and 14 instruments, 1978; for 8 instruments Strata, 1979, Chamber Symphony for 12 Instruments, 1980; Second Fantasy for Flute and Piano, 1980; clarinet, violin, piano Inventions and Airs, 1980; author: (with Berkowitz and Fontrier) A New Approach to Sight Singing, 196O; Author: A New Approach to Ear Training-Melody, 1967, Gradus, An Integrated Approach to Harmony, Counterpoint and Analysis, 1976, (with others) A New Approach to Keyboard Harmony, 1979. Fulbright scholar, 1954-55. Mem. Coll. Music Soc. (2d v.p. 1970-72), Am. Soc. Univ. Composers, ASCAP. Home: 9 Dunster Rd Great Neck NY 11021 Office: Queens Coll Flushing NY 11367

KRAFT, LISBETH MARTHA, veterinarian, scientist; b. Vienna, Austria, May 16, 1920; came to U.S., 1923, naturalized, 1929; d. Rudolph and Marie F. (Mikota) K. B.S., N.Y. State Coll. of Agr., Cornell U., 1942; D.V.M., N.Y. State Coll. Vet. Medicine, Cornell U., 1945. Diplomate: Am. Coll. of Lab. Animal Medicine (pres. 1966, dir. 1965-67). Research asst. dept. parasitology N.Y. State Vet. Coll., Ithaca, 1945-46, Harvard Med. Sch., Boston, 1946; bacteriologist N.Y. State Dept. Health, Albany, 1947-49; research asst. Yale Med. Sch. New Haven, 1949-50, instr. preventive medicine, 1950-52, asst. prof. dept. microbiology, 1952-55, research assoc. dept. of pathology, 1957-61, veterinarian, 1960-61; asst. dir. N.Y.C. Dept. of Health (Bur. of Labs.), 1961-65; assoc. mem. dept. lab. diagnosis Pub. Health Research Inst., N.Y.C., 1961-65; assoc. prof. microbiology Sch. Vet. Medicine, U. Pa., Phila., 1965; cons. to Bioquest, div. of Becton Dickinson & Co., Hackensack, N.J., 1965-66; research veterinarian, cons. med. div. of Oak Ridge Asso. Univs., Oak Ridge, Tenn., 1966-67; founder L.M. Kraft Assos. (consultants in lab. animal sci.), Goshen, N.Y., 1968-72; dir. research and devel. Carworth div. of Becton Dickinson & Co., New City, N.Y., 1972-73, also mgr. spl. services, 1972-73; asso. scientist dept. physics U. San Francisco, 1974-77; research scientist, NASA-Ames Research Center, Moffett Field, Calif.; Cons. to Sloan Kettering Ins., Walker Labs., Rye, N.Y., 1958-59, WHO, Azul, Argentina, S. Am., 1965, NASA (Ames Research Center), Moffett Field, Calif., 1972—. Contbr. articles on immunology and diseases of lab. animals and space flight effects to profl. jours. Mem. Am. Assn. for Lab. Animal Sci. (dir. 1960-67, chmn. awards com. 1967, editorial bd. 1964-65, asso. editor 1966—, Griffin award 1972), Am. Vet. Med. Assn., Assn. for Applied Gnotobiology, Am. Soc. Microbiology, Am. Soc. Lab. Animal Practitioners, AAAS, Nat. Research Council (adv. council Inst. Lab. Animal Resources 1966-67), N.Y. Acad. Scis., Sigma Xi. Address: PO Box 28 Moffett Field CA 94035

KRAFT, RALPH WAYNE, metallurgy educator; b. Collingswood, N.J., Jan. 14, 1925; s. R. Wayne and Florence Wilkie (Kraft) K.; m. Joan D. Auchter, June 19, 1948; children: Steven W., Brian J., T. Kevin, Ellen M. B.S., Lehigh U., 1948; M.S., U. Mich., 1956, Ph.D., 1958. Metallurgist, Abex Corp., Mahwah, N.J., 1948-54; research supr. United Aircraft Corp., East Hartford, Conn., 1958-62; mem. faculty Lehigh U., Bethlehem, Pa., 1962—, prof. metallurgy and material sci., 1965—, N.J. Zinc prof., 1967-78; adj. prof. Allentown Coll. of St. Francis, Center Valley, Pa., 1973—; mem. ad hoc com. panel on directional composites Nat. Acad. Scis., 1972-74. Author: The Relevance of Teilhard, 1968, Symbols, Systems, Science and Survival, 1975, A Reason to Hope, 1983. Mem. City of Bethlehem Planning Commn., 1970—, chmn., 1975-79; bd. dirs. Greater Bethlehem Area Council Chs., 1971—, pres., 1978-80; mem. adv. bd. Am. Teilhard Assn. for Future of Man, 1970—, Newman Found., Lehigh U., 1966—. Served with C.E., AUS, 1943-46. Recipient Bradley Stoughton award Lehigh Valley chpt. Am. Soc. Metals, 1968. Fellow AAAS, Am. Soc. Metals; mem. AIME, Soc. Gen. Systems Research, Inst. Religion in Age of Sci. Democrat. Roman Catholic. Patentee in field. Home: 645 Biery's Bridge Rd Bethlehem PA 18017

KRAFT, ROBERT ALAN, educator, theologian; b. Waterbury, Conn., Mar. 18, 1934; s. Howard Russell and Marian Augusta (Northrop) K.; m. Carol Lois Wallace, June 11, 1955; children: Cindy Lee, Scott Wallace, Todd Alan, Randall Jay. B.A. summa cum laude, Wheaton Coll., 1955, M.A., 1957; Ph.D., Harvard U., 1961. Teaching fellow Harvard U., 1959-61; asst. lectr. U. Manchester, Eng., 1961-63; asst. prof. religious studies U. Pa., 1963-68, asso. prof., 1968-76, prof., 1976—, acting chmn. dept. religious studies, 1972-73, chmn., 1977—, chmn. grad. program in religious studies, 1973-75, 76—; vis. lectr. Lutheran Theol. Sem., 1965-66; coordinator Phila. Seminar on Christian Origins, 1963—; mem. Rev. Standard Version Bible Com., 1972—; bd. advs. Ancient Bibl. Manuscript Center for Preservation and Research, Claremont, Calif., 1978—; mem. series adv. bd. Berlin Akademie, 1971—. Contbr. articles and revs. to profl. publs. U. Pa. faculty fellow, summers 1965, 67, 73; Guggenheim fellow, 1969-70; Am. Council Learned Socs. fellow, 1975-76; Am. Council Learned Socs. travel grantee, 1970; Nat. Endowment for Humanities project grantee, 1978-79, 80-81, 82-84. Mem. Soc. Bibl. Lit. (sec. Mid-Atlantic sect. 1965-69, pro-tem N.T. book editor Jour. Bibl. Lit. 1965-66, 70, editor Monograph series 1967-72, editor Pseudepigrapha series 1973-78), Studiorum Novi Testamenti Societas (editorial bd. 1973-76), Internat. Orgn. Septuagint and Cognate Studies (exec. com. 1969—), N.Am. Patristics Soc., Am. Soc. Papyrology. Office: Box 36 College Hall U Pa Philadelphia PA 19104 *To be critical in evaluating the work of others is not very difficult; the ability to evaluate one's own work critically is something to be cultivated.*

KRAGLUND, JOHN, music critic; b. Hjorring, Denmark, Apr. 27, 1922; emigrated to Can., 1929, naturalized, 1949; s. Johannes Christian and Agnes (Andersen) K. Student, Picton (Ont., Can.) Collegiate and Vocat. Inst., 1940; B.A. in Gen. Arts, U. Toronto, 1948, postgrad., 1948-50. With The Globe & Mail newspaper, Toronto, Ont., 1948—, reporter, 1952, music critic, 1952, now music editor; Cons. Ont. Arts Council, 1963-76. Contbr. to numerous music jours., 1954—. Served with RCAF, 1942-44. Recipient Canada Centennial medal, 1967. Mem. Music Critics Assn. Home: 1273 Kingston Rd Scarborough ON M1N 1P4 Canada Office: Toronto Globe & Mail 444 Front St W Toronto ON M5V 2S9 Canada *

KRAHA, BRADFORD KING, electronics manufacturing corporation executive; b. Rochester, N.Y., Dec. 16, 1926; s. George Frederic and Neva Alice (Smy) Kroha; m. Nona Jane Hobbs, June 15, 1979; children by previous marriage: Nancy, Judy, Sally, Jane, Robert. B.E.E., Yale U., 1947; B.S. in Indsl. Adminstrn., 1948; postgrad., Harvard U. Grad. Sch. Bus. Adminstrn., 1952. Gen. mgr. Can. Motorola Ltd., Toronto, Ont., 1969-72; dir. internat. subs. Can Motorola Ltd., Toronto, Ont., 1972-77; asst. gen. mgr. communications internat. div. Motorola Inc., Schaumburg, Ill., 1977-79, v.p., gen. mgr. European communications div., 1979—. Served with USNR, 1944-46. Republican. Presbyterian. Clubs: Barrington Hills Country (Ill.); Wentworth Golf (Eng.). Home: 82 Paganica Rd Barrington Hills Il 60010 Office: Motorola Inc 1303 E Algonquin Rd Schaumburg Il 60196

KRAHL, NAT WETZEL, structural engineer; b. Houston, Sept. 30, 1921; s. Kenneth and Natalie Louise (Wetzel) K.; m. Victoria Ferguson, Apr. 16, 1949; children: Catherine Jane, Elizabeth Anne, Ellen Louise, James Kenneth, Robert John. B.A. with distinction, Rice Inst., 1942, B.S. in Civil Engring. with distinction, 1943; M.S., U. Ill., 1950, Ph.D., 1963. Asst. civil engring. Rice Inst., 1943-44; structural engr. Walter P. Moore (Cons. Engr.), Houston, 1946-49, prin. design engr., 1950-57; asst. prof. civil engring. Rice U., 1957-64, assoc. prof. civil engring. and architecture, 1964-68, prof., 1968-80, dir. continuing studies, 1968-69, chmn. dept. civil engring., 1972-77; partner Krahl and Gaddy Engrs., Houston, 1969-76; owner, mgr. Nat Krahl and Assos. (Cons. Engrs.), Houston, 1976-80; dir. structural engring., sr. v.p. Caudill Rowlett Scott (Architects Planners Engrs.), Houston, 1980-81; engring. cons. Brown & Root Inc. (Engrs. and Constructors), Houston, 1982—. Contbr. articles to profl. jours. Served to lt. (j.g.) USN, 1944-46. Recipient Lincoln Arc Welding Found. award for outstanding achievement in design of structural steel, 1974; NSF fellow, 1961-62. Mem. ASCE (state-of-the-art award 1974), Internat. Assn. Bridge and Structural Engring., Internat. Assn. Shell and Spatial Structures, Am. Concrete Inst., Am. Cons. Engrs. Council. Methodist. Home: 7655 S Braeswood St 5 Houston TX 77071 Office: Brown & Root Inc. PO Box 4302 Houston TX 77210

KRAINIK, ARDIS, opera company executive; b. Manitowoc, Wis., Mar. 8, 1929; d. Arthur Stephen and Clara (Bracken) K. B.S., Northwestern U., 1951; postgrad. in music, 1953-54. Tchr. drama, public speaking Horlick High Sch., Racine, Wis., 1951-53; exec. sec., office mgr. Lyric Opera of Chgo., 1954-59, asst. mgr., 1960-76, artistic adminstr., 1976-80, gen. mgr., 1981—. Mezzo soprano appearing with, Chgo. Lyric Opera, 1955-59, Cameo Opera Co., Chgo.; appeared in: oratorio performances throughout Mid-West on Artists Showcase, NBC-TV; in recitals throughout area; soloist, 17th Ch. Christ Scientist, Chgo., 1969-77. Bd. dirs. Chgo. br. English Speaking Union, 1963—, Protestant Found. Greater Chgo.; charter mem. Chgo. Council Fine Arts, 1976—, Northwestern U. Women's Bd., 1978—, Chgo. Com., 1981—; mem. Chgo. Network. Mem. Internat. Assn. Opera Dirs., Opera Am. (bd. dirs), Mortar Bd., Pi Alpha Lambda, Phi Beta, Chi Omega. Christian Scientist. Club: Economic (Chgo.). Office: c/o Lyric Opera of Chgo 20 N Wacker Dr Chicago IL 60606 *Of utmost importance is the word "integrity." On'e One's every action and thought should be examined first in the light of this word, and, following the illumination shed, one cannot take a false step or stray off the path that leads to fulfillment and success.*

KRAININ, JULIAN, film producer, film director, cinematographer, writer; b. N.Y.C., Jan. 24, 1941; s. David A. and Anne N. (Wineblatt) K.; m. Martha Wineblatt, June 17, 1967; 1 son, Todd Philip. B.S., Allegheny Coll., 1962; M.F.A., Columbia U., 1965. Nat. lectr. motion pictures at various univs. and colls., 1967—; cons. on films U. Mass., 1973; juror Mid-West Film Makers and Graphic Arts Festival, 1971-72, Nat. Emmy Awards, 1975-83. Producer spl. projects, Westinghouse Broadcasting Co., N.Y.C., 1967-69; also dir., writer, 1967—; v.p., exec. producer, Krainin/Sage Prodns., Inc., N.Y.C., 1969-79; pres., Krainin/Sage Prodns., Inc., N.Y.C., 1979—; also dir., writer, 1969-79; (Recipient numerous awards and citations including Academy award 1973, Emmy award 1969, Chgo. Internat. Film Festival award 1969, 74-77, Florence Internat. Film Festival award 1969, Cine Golden Eagle awards 1969, 72, 73, 74, 77-78, Photog. Soc. Am. award 1968, 72, Venice Film Festival award 1970, Moscow Internat. Film Festival award 1970, Cindy award Producers Assn. Am. 1971, 74, 76, San Francisco Internat. Film Festival award 1967, 69, 71, 72, 76, Am. Film Festival award 1974, Tel Aviv Internat. Film Festival award 1970, Atlanta Internat. Film Festival award 1969, 72, 73, N.Y. Internat. Film and TV Festival award 1969, 72, 76, Gabriel award 1968-70, Oberhausen Internat. Film Festival award 1969, Columbus Film Festival award 1973, Mannheim Internat. Film Festival award 1969, U.S. Indsl. Film Festival award 1973, Ohio State award 1967, NCCJ award 1969, Saturday Rev. Lit. award 1970, N.Y. Film Festival at Lincoln Center award 1970, Festival Ams. award 1976); Major films include The Reluctant Revolution, 1968, Exit to Nowhere, 1967, Promises to Keep, 1967, The March, 1965, Nowhere Fast, 1968, Hide and Seek, 1966, (with Jacques Cousteau) Oceans: The Silent Crisis, 1972, Art is (Acad. award nomination 1972), 1972 (hon. film screening White House, 1972, Mus. Modern Art, N.Y.C. 1972), The Other Americans, 1969 (TV Emmy award 1969), Princeton: A Search for Answers, 1973 (Acad. award 1973), The American Experiment, 1974, Going Metric, 1975, To America, 1976, The Broken Silence, 1976, The World of James Michener: Hawaii Revisited, 1977, The World of James Michener: The South Pacific-End of Eden?, 1978, (with Ed Asner) Writing, 1980, The Making of an Opera; mini series, 1980, Opening Night, 1980, Pavarotti at Home, 1980. Mem. Writers Guild Am., Acad. Motion Picture Arts and Scis., Dirs. Guild Am. (award 1973). Home: 67-38 Fleet St Forest Hills NY 11375 Office: 39 W 55th St New York NY 10019

KRAINTZ, LEON, physiologist, educator; b. Johnstown, Pa., Oct. 3, 1924; s. Franz Joseph and Marie (Peterlin) K.; m. Frances Draper Whitcomb, Aug. 28, 1949; children: Donna, Franz, Erika. A.B., Harvard U., 1950; M.A. (fellow), Rice Inst., 1952; Ph.D. (NSF fellow), Rice Inst., 1954. Research asst. in psychiatry Boston Psychopathic Hosp., 1947-48; research asst. Sloan-Kettering Inst. Cancer Research, Cornell U., N.Y.C., 1948-50; research scientist Dept. Exptl. Medicine, U. Tex. M.D. Anderson Hosp. Cancer Research, Houston, 1950-51; research asso. dept. biology, instr. radiobiology and microbiology Rice Inst., Houston, 1951-52, instr. radiobiology, endocrinology, 1952-54; instr. physiology U. Tex. dental br., Houston, 1954-56, asst. prof., 1956-59, asso. prof., 1959-62, vis. asso. clin. prof., 1963-64; asso. prof. oral biology Faculty Dentistry U. B.C., 1964-66, hon. prof. physiology Faculty Medicine, 1966—, prof. oral biology Faculty Medicine, 1966—, head dept. Faculty Medicine, 1970-82; clin. prof. dentistry Dental Sci. Inst., U. Tex.-Houston, 1981-82; vis. prof., lectr. various univs.; prof. biology Rice U., 1962-64. Contbr. articles to profl. jours.

and books. Chmn. Com. for Safe Use of Radioisotopes, City of Houston, 1958-59. Served with USNR, 1942-47; ETO. Nat. Insts. Health fellow USPHS, U. Melbourne, 1969-70. Fellow AAAS; mem. Internat. Assn. Dental Research (pres. B.C. sect. 1966-68), Endocrine Soc., Soc. Nuclear Medicine, Soc. Neuroscis., Am. Physiol. Soc., Soc. Exptl. Biology and Medicine, Am. Assn. Dental Schs., Can. Physiol. Soc., Am. Assn. Univ. Profs. (pres. local chpt. 1960-62), Tex. Med. Center Research Soc. (pres. 1962-63), Sigma Xi, Sigma Alpha Epsilon. Club: Harvard of Vancouver (dir.). Office: Faculty of Dentistry U BC Vancouver BC V6T 1Z7 Canada

KRAKAUER, MERRILL, mfg. co. exec.; b. N.Y.C., Sept. 22, 1927; s. Meyer and Etta (Lerner) K.; m. Janet Mayer, July 20, 1966; children—Bryan, Elayne, Matthew. B.E.E., Cooper Union, 1951. Vice pres. Rowe Mfg. Co., 1955-61; pres. Autovend Corp., 1961-67; v.p. Macke Co., 1967-74; pres. Rowe Internat., Inc., Whippany, N.J., 1974—. Mem. Nat. Automatic Merchandising Assn. (dir.). Patentee in field. Office: 75 Troy Hills Rd Whippany NJ 07981 *

KRAKOFF, IRWIN HAROLD, physician, educator; b. Columbus, Ohio, July 20, 1923; s. Morris Joseph and Frieda K.; m. Miriam Shocket, Sept. 1, 1946; children—Peter Alan, Charles Edward, Ellen Miriam. B.A., Ohio State U., 1943, M.D., 1947. Intern Mt. Sinai Hosp., Cleve., 1947-48, resident, 1948-50, Boston City Hosp., 1950-51; attending physician, asso. chmn. dept medicine, head clin. chemotherapy and pharmacology lab. Meml. Sloan-Kettering Cancer Center, N.Y.C., 1953-76; prof. medicine Cornell U., 1955-76; prof. medicine and pharmacology, dir. Vt. Regional Cancer Center, U. Vt., 1976—. Contbr. numerous articles to profl. jours., also chpts. to books. Served with USN, 1943-46, 51-53. Recipient Alfred P. Sloan cancer research award, 1965. Mem. Am. Assn. Cancer Research, Am. Soc. Clin. Oncology, A.C.P., Am. Fedn. Clin. Research, Am. Soc. Pharmacology and Exptl. Therapeutics. Address: 1 S Prospect St Burlington VT 05401

KRAKOWSKI, ADAM JOSEPH, psychiatrist; b. Sieciechowice, Poland, Nov. 8, 1914; came to U.S., 1949, naturalized, 1954; s. Joseph and Anna (Barmanski) K.; m. Ada Czyzowski, Apr. 11, 1944; children: Anna Krakowski Capel, Alice Krakowski Schonbek. M.D., Jagiellonski U., Cracow, Poland, 1939. Rotating intern Jagiellonski U. Med. Schs. Hosps., Cracow, 1939-40; resident in neuropsychiatry Neuropsychiat. Inst., 1940-43; fellow Bacteriol. Inst., Warsaw U. Med. Sch., 1943-44, Instr. dept. pharmacology, 1943-44; comdg. officer Field Hosp., Warsaw, Poland, 1944; med. officer UNRRA; dir. Gen. Hosp., Haren Ems, Brit. Zone Ger., 1945-47; sr. med. officer Control Commn. for Ger., 1947-49; psychiatrist Dannemora (N.Y.) State Hosp., 1949-50, sr. psychiatrist, 1950-51, supervising psychiatrist, 1951-52; pvt. practice medicine specializing in psychiatry, Plattsburgh, N.Y., 1953—; dir. child guidance psychiatry Child Guidance div. N.Y. State Dept. Mental Hygiene, 1958-69; prof. psychiatry, dept. medicine and health edn. Plattsburgh (N.Y.) State U. Arts and Sci., 1962—; chief div. psychiat. liaison and research Champlain Valley-Physicians Hosp. Med. Center, Plattsburgh, 1970—; psychiat. examiner VA Hosp., Albany, 1954—; cons. psychiatry Plattsburgh AFB Hosp.; cons. in psychiatry various agys. and instns. Author: Child Psychiatry and the General Practitioner, 1962; editor: The Teaching of Psychosomatic Medicine and Consultation-Liaison Psychiatry: Reactions to Illness, 1979; editor, co-author: Psychosomatic Medicine in a Changing World, 1982, Psychosomatic Medicine: Theoretical, Clinical and Transcultural Aspects, 1983; contbr. 120 articles to profl. jours. Pres. Council Community Services, 1956-58; chmn. Clinton County Mental Health Bd., 1964-66. Recipient Presdl. citation for community work N.Y. State Med. Soc., 1965; medal of Holy Year, Pope Paul VI, 1975; medal of Nicolaus Copernicus, Acad. Medicine, Cracow, Poland, 1976. Fellow Polish Psychiat. Assn. (hon.), Am. Psychiat. Assn. (life), Am. Geriatrics Soc., Royal Soc. Health, Acad. Psychosomatic Medicine (pres. 1970, exec. dir. 1970-71, asso. editor Psychosomatics 1960—), AAAS, Am. Coll. Clin. Psychopharmacology, Sociedad Argentina De Medicina Psichosomatica (corr.), Sociedad Argentina De Psichopharmacologia (corr.), Sociedad Argentina de Psiquiatriay Psicologia (hon.), German Soc. Psychosomatic Medicine (hon.), Internat. Coll. Psychosomatic Medicine (founding; sec. 1971-75, pres. 1979-81), Sociedad Italiana di Medicina Psicosomatica; mem. AMA, N.Y. State, Clinton County med. socs., Acad. Religion and Mental Health, N.Y. State Acad. Scis., Internat. Platform Assn. Club: Kiwanis. Prisoner of war, Germany, 1944-45. Home: Box 35 Smokey Ridge Dr Plattsburgh NY 12901 Office: Suite 103 210 Cornelia St Plattsburgh NY 12901

KRAL, RICHARD FRANCIS, apparel executive; b. Bridgeport, Conn., Jan. 13, 1940; s. Frank and Frances (Batcha) K.; m. Vivian Mary Nespoli, June 17, 1961; children: Richard Francis, Kimberly Ann, Christopher Jon. B.S. in Engring. and Econs., U. Conn., 1961. Vice pres. Warner's Div., Bridgeport, 1975, pres., 1976-81, Warnaco Internat., Inc., 1980—; sr. v.p. Warnaco, Inc., Bridgeport, 1981-83, exec. v.p., 1983—, dir., 1982—; dir. Warnaco of Can., Ltd., Prescott, Ont. Bd. dirs. Parents and Friends of Retarded Citizens, Bridgeport, 1980—. Mem. Bridgeport C. of C. (dir. 1980-82). Roman Catholic. Clubs: Union League (N.Y.C.); Patterson (Fairfield, Conn.). Home: 63 Red Rox Ln Trumbull CT 06611 Office: Warnaco Inc 350 Lafayette St Bridgeport CT 06601

KRALL, ANDERS ALBERT WALTER, advertising agency executive; b. Bklyn., Dec. 20, 1925; s. Max and Emma (Larson) K.; m. Imogene Rollins, Dec. 1, 1951; children: Lisa, Phillip. A.B., Bates Coll., 1950; M.B.A., N.Y.U., 1954. Adminstrv. mgr. market research dept. Colgate Palmolive, N.Y.C., 1953-56; dir. marketing and research Ruth Rauff & Ryan, N.Y.C., 1956-57; dir. market research Warner Bros., Bridgeport, Conn., 1957-62; sr. v.p., dir. research Cunningham & Walsh, 1962-73; exec. v.p. Goldstein/Krall Mktg. Resources Inc., Stamford, Conn., 1973—; instr. marketing evenings Bridgeport U., 1958-62. Bd. dirs. Westchester chpt. Am. Cancer Soc., 1969—. Served with USN, 1943-46, 51-52. Mem. Am. Marketing Assn., Market Research Council, Am. Assn. Pub. Opinion Research., Copy Research Council, European Soc. Pub. Opinion Research. Republican. Presbyn. Club: Apawamis. Home: 33 Fairway Ave Rye NY 10580 Office: 25 3d St Stamford CT 06902

KRAMER, AARON, educator, poet, author; b. Bklyn., Dec. 13, 1921; s. Hyman and Mary (Click) K.; m. Katherine Kolodny, Mar. 10, 1942; children: Carol, Laura Kramer Gordon. B.A., Bklyn. Coll., 1941, M.A., 1951; Ph.D., NYU, 1966. Instr. English Adelphi U., L.I., N.Y., 1961-63, asst. prof., 1963-66; lectr. Queens Coll., Flushing, N.Y., 1966-68; asso. prof. English, Dowling Coll., Oakdale, N.Y., 1966-70, prof., 1970—. Author or translator: The Glass Mountain, 1946, Poetry and Prose of Heine, 1948, Denmark Vesey, 1952, The Tinderbox, 1954, Serenade, 1957, Tune of the Calliope, 1958, Moses, 1962, Rumshinsky's Hat, 1964, Rilke: Visions of Christ, 1967, The Prophetic Tradition in American Poetry, 1968, Melville's Poetry, 1972, On the Way to Palermo, 1973, The Emperor of Atlantis, 1975, (with Siegfried Mandel) Ingeborg Bachmann: Fifteen Poems, 1976, O Golden Land, 1976; Death Takes a Holiday, 1979; Author or translator: Carousel Parkway, 1980, In Wicked Times, 1983, The Burning Bush, 1983; co-author: Poetry Therapy, 1969, Poetry the Healer, 1973; editor: On Freedom's Side, 1972; poetry editor: West Hills Rev.: A Walt Whitman Jour. Recipient award N.Y. State Poetry Day Com., 1954; Reynolds Lyric award Lyric mag., 1961, Lyric mag., Virginia, 1969; William Oliver Song award William E. Oliver Award Com., Los Angeles, 1968; Hart Crane Meml. award Hart Crane and Alice Crane Williams Meml. Fund, 1969; various awards ASCAP; prize Los Altos Film maker's Festival, 1965; 3 awards All Nations Poetry Contest Triton Coll., Ill., 1975, 1 award, 1976, 77, 78; award Young Composers Contest, Nat. Fedn. Music Clubs, 1976; prize Eugene o'Neill Theater Ctr., 1983; Meml. Found. Jewish Culture fellow, 1978; others. Mem. Assn. Poetry Therapy (exec. bd. 1969—), ASCAP, Walt Whitman Birthplace Assn. (trustee), P.E.N. Am. Center, Internat. Acad. Poets, Edna St. Vincent Millay Soc., N.E. MLA, Dramatists Guild. Office: Dept English Dowling Coll Oakdale NY 11769 *A poet should not think of his life in terms of success, unless the survival of his personal and artistic integrity can be called success. Some lines from my poem, "To Himself" (Rumshinsky's Hat) may apply: Finally it will not matter how many poisons were offered, or prizes—how many salvos, how many silences. .whether anthologies nested his poems—whether a critic called them bright birds. .except that his heart maintained its own beat, his face its own hue, his foot its own thud, his night its own vision, his soul its own heat, his hand its own touch, his tongue its own word.*

KRAMER, ALAN SHARFSIN, lawyer; b. N.Y.C., Apr. 28, 1934; s. Michael and Alene (Sharfsin) K. B.A., Dickinson Coll., 1956; LL.B., Columbia, 1962, J.D., 1969. Bar: N.Y. bar 1962. Practice in, N.Y.C., 1962-69, 73—; sr. v.p. Am. Medicorp, Inc., N.Y.C., 1969-72; individual practice, 1974-78; pres. Alan S. Kramer (p.c.), 1978—; dir., sec. Integrated Barter Internat., Inc. Editor: Columbia Law Rev, 1960-62. Served with M.I. AUS, 1956-58. Mem. Assn. Bar City N.Y. Home: 315 E 86th St New York NY 10028 Office: 11 E 44th St New York NY 10017

KRAMER, ARTHUR BENNETT, lawyer; b. N.Y.C., Jan. 10, 1927; s. George L. and Rea (Wishengrad) K.; m. Alice J. Blumenfeld, Oct. 4, 1953; children: Elizabeth Brooks, Andrew Bennett, Rebecca Laurence. B.S., Yale U., 1949, M.A., 1951, LL.B., 1953. Bar: N.Y. 1953. Since practiced in, N.Y.C.; assoc. Cole, Grimes, Friedman & Deitz, 1953-55; asst. U.S. atty. So. Dist. N.Y., 1955-58, chief appellate atty., 1957-58; ptnr. Kramer, Levin, Nessen, Kamin & Frankel (and predecessor firms), 1958—; dir. Interstate Bakeries Corp., Interstate Brands Corp.; Adviser President's Commn. on Law Enforcement and Adminstrn. of Justice, 1967-68; counsel Mamaroneck Union Free Sch. Dist., 1969-79; adj. prof. law N.Y. Law Sch., 1977-78. Served with USNR, 1944-46. Mem. Sigma Xi, Tau Beta Pi. Home: 5 Oakdale Rd Larchmont NY 10538 Office: 919 3d Ave New York NY 10022

KRAMER, BERNARD, physicist, educator; b. N.Y.C., Nov. 12, 1922; s. Jack and Mollie (Miller) K.; m. Miriam Adelman, Aug. 4, 1946; children—Matthew, Jesse. B.S., CCNY, 1942; Ph.D., N.Y.U., 1952. Physicist Internat. Tel. & Tel. Corp., 1942-47; lectr. Bklyn. Coll., 1947-49; research asst., then research asso. N.Y.U., 1949-68; mem. faculty Hunter Coll., 1952—, prof. physics, 1966—, chmn. dept., 1960-71; vis. scientist Princeton U., 1973-74; research collaborator Brookhaven Nat. Lab., 1980; vis. scholar U. Del., 1981. Author articles luminescence and photoconductivity. Mem. Am. Phys. Soc., AAUP, Sigma Xi. Home: 115 Carnation St Bergenfield NJ 07621 Office: 695 Park Ave New York NY 10021

KRAMER, BINNIE HENRIETTA, interior designer; b. Bayonne, N.J., Mar. 25, 1914; d. Abraham and Sophie (Lipack) Bineman; m. Stanley Kramer, Dec. 22, 1934; children: Robert, Richard. B.A., San Francisco State U., 1934. Pvt. practice interior design, 1952-6; interior designer Loomis & Edelfsen, Portland, 1961-62, Loomis, Edlefsen & Kramer, 1962-64, Dickel & Kramer, 1965—; Nat. com. chmn. Community Design Centers; mem. bd. visitors Found. Interior Design Edn. Research, 1978—, now chmn. accreditation team. Fellow Am. Soc. Interior Designers (ednl. research com., nat. com. chmn. 1980, pres. Oreg. chpt. 1980); mem. Am. Inst. Interior Designers (pres. Oreg. dist. chpt., regional v.p., life mem.), AIA (profl. affiliate), Found. Interior Design Edn. Research (chmn. accreditation team 1980). Democrat. Jewish. Home: 806 NW Albemarle Terr Portland OR 97210 Office: 2892 NW Upshur Portland OR 97210

KRAMER, BURTON, graphic designer; b. N.Y.C., June 25, 1932; s. Sam and Ida (Moore) K.; m. Irene Margarite Therese Mayer, Feb. 22, 1961; children: Gabrielle Kimberly, Jeremy Jacques. Student, SUNY, Oswego, 1949-51; B.Sc. in Graphic Design, Ill. Inst. Tech., Chgo., 1954; postgrad. (Fulbright scholar), Royal Coll. Art, London, 1955-56; M.F.A., Yale U., 1957. Pres., creative dir. Burton Kramer Assos. Ltd., Toronto, 1967—; designer Geigy Chem. Corp., N.Y.C., 1959-61; dir. corp. graphics Clairtone Sound Corp., Toronto, 1967; chief designer Halpern Advt., Zurich, Switzerland, 1961-65; instr. design Ont. Coll. Art, 1978—; guest lectr. Rochester Inst. Tech., 1976, lectr., designer-in-residence, 1981; vis. lectr. U. Cin., 1980. Book designer: The Art of Norval Morrisseau, 1979, Passionate Spirits, 1980; author: Can. sect. Trademarks and Symbols of the World, 19—; co-author: Report on Canadian Road Sign Graphics, 19—, work published in numerous nat. and internat. jours. and annual books; contbr. articles to profl. jours.; major works include, Hosp. Sick Children, Toronto, St. Lawrence Ctr. for Arts, Eaton Ctr., Erin Mills New Town, Mississauga, graphic design program, Royal Ont. Mus., map-directory system and graphics, Expo 67, Montreal, visual identity programs for, Canadian Broadcasting Corp., Ont. Edn. Communications Authority, Can. Crafts Council, Ont. Guild Crafts. Recipient Gold medal Internat. Typographic Composition Assn., 1971, gold medal Art Dirs. Club Toronto, 1973, medal Leipzig BookFair. Fellow Soc. Graphic Designers Can. (past pres.); mem. Alliance Graphique Internat., Am. Inst. Graphic Arts, Swiss Graphic Designers Soc., Royal Canadian Acad. Arts. Home: 101 Roxborough St W Toronto ON M5R 1T9 Canada Office: 20 Prince Arthur Ave Suite 1E Toronto ON M5R 1B1 Canada

KRAMER, CHARLES, lawyer; b. N.Y.C., Oct. 27, 1915; s. Simon Max and Celia (Brett) K.; m. Evelyn Schoenfeld, Dec. 24, 1939; children: Michele, Nancy, Daniel. LL.B., St. John's U., 1937, LL.D. (hon.), 1982. Bar: N.Y. 1938. Partner firm Kramer, Dillof, Tessel, Duffy & Moore, N.Y.C.; asso. prof. law Hofstra U. Author: Evidence in Negligence Cases, 1955, Medical Malpractice, 1962. Served with AUS, World War II. Decorated Army Commendation Medal. Fellow Internat. Acad. Trial Lawyers, Inner Circle Advs. Home: 166 25 Powells Cove Blvd Beechhurst NY 11357 Office: 233 Broadway New York NY 10279 *To champion the cause of the victims of carelessness is an uphill but rewarding battle.*

KRAMER, CHARLES EUGENE, manufacturing company executive; b. Hamiton, Ohio, Mar. 10, 1919; s. George E. and Deborah (Beglay) K.; m. Nelda M. Wood; children: Janet Lynn, Robert Michael. B.S.M.E., Prudue U., 1940. Registerd profl. engr., Ind. Factory mgr. Fairfield Mfg. Co., Inc., Lafayette, Ind., 1960-63, v.p. mgr., 1963-71, sr. v.p., chief operating officer, 1971-72, pres., chief operating officer, 1973-82, chmn. bd., 1982—; dir. Lafayette Nat. Bank, Schwab Safe Co., Inc. Mem. Purdue Research Found., 1975—; trustee Ind. Vocat. Tech. Coll., 1978—; pres. bd. dirs. St. Elizabeth Hosp., Lafayette, 1978-79, Lafayette YMCA, 1965-67. Served with U.S. Army, 1944-46. Mem. Am. Gear Mfrs. Assn. (dir.), ASME, Am. Soc. Indsl. Engrs., Am. Mgmt. Assn., Lafayette C. of C. (bd. dirs. 1974-76). Republican. Methodist. Club: Lafayette Country. Lodge: Elks. Home: 3918 Gate Rd Lafayette IN 47905 Office: Fairfield Mfg Co Inc Lafayette IN 47905

KRAMER, CHARLES HENRY, psychiatrist; b. Oak Park, Ill., May 31, 1922; s. Charles Henry and Martha (Ball) K.; m. Jeannette Ross, Sept. 15, 1945; children: Dan, Judy, Doug, Greg, Chip, Dave. B.S., U. Ill., 1944, M.D., 1945; grad., Inst. Psychoanalysis, Chgo., 1967. Diplomate: Am. Bd. Psychiatry and Neurology. Intern Cook County Hosp., Chgo., 1945-46, U. Ill. Hosp., 1946-47; resident Chanute AFB Hosp., Ill., 1951-53, Elgin (Ill.) State Hosp., 1953-54, Inst. Juvenile Research, Chgo., 1955-59; pvt. practice medicine and surgery, Palatine, Ill., 1947-51, pvt. practice psychiatry, Oak Park, 1954—; founder Family Inst. Chgo., 1968, pres., 1968—; dir. family studies Inst. Psychiatry, Northwestern Meml. Hosp., 1975—; prof. psychiatry and behavioral scis. Northwestern U. Med. Sch., 1975—; founder, pres. Plum Grove Nursing Home, 1953—, Kramer Found., 1961—, Kramer Enterprises, 1980—; cons. mental health orgns. Author: Basic Principles of Long-Term Patient Care, 1976, Becoming a Family Therapist, 1980; cons. editor: Family Process and Family Systems Medicine. Served with U.S. Army, 1943-45; Served with USAF, 1951-53. Recipient Better Life awards Ill. and Am. Nursing Home Assns., 1970. Fellow Am. Psychiat. Assn.; mem. Chgo. Psychoanalytic Soc., Ill. Council Child Psychiatry, Ill. Psychiat. Soc., Am. Family Therapy Assn. (incorporator, founding dir.), Am. Assn. Marriage and Family Therapy (approved supr.). Club: Chgo. Yacht. Home: 417 N Kenilworth Oak Park IL 60302 Office: 666 Lake Shore Dr Chicago IL 60611

KRAMER, DALE VERNON, educator; b. Mitchell, S.D., July 13, 1936; s. Dwight Lyman and Franes Elizabeth (Corbin) K.; m. Cheris Camble Kramarae, Dec. 21, 1960; children: Brinlee, Jana. B.S., S.D. State Coll., 1958; M.A., Case Western Res. U., 1960, Ph.D., 1963. Instr. English Ohio U., Athens, 1962-63, asst. prof., 1963-65, U. Ill., Urbana, 1965-67; assoc. prof. U. Ill., Urbana, 1967-71, prof. English, 1971—; chmn. bd. editors Jour. English and Germanic Philology, 1972—. Author: Charles Robert Maturin, 1973, Thomas Hardy: The forms of Tragedy, 1975; editor: Critical Approaches to the Fiction of Thomas Hardy, 1979, Thomas Hardy, The Woodlanders, 1981. Served to capt. U.S. Army, 1958-66. Mem. Center for Advanced Study, 1971; Am. Philos. Soc. grantee, 1969. Mem. MLA, AAUP. Congregationalist. Office: Univ Ill 608 S Wright St Urbana IL 61801

KRAMER, FERDINAND, mortgage banker; b. Chgo., Aug. 10, 1901; s. Adolph F. and Ray (Friedberg) K.; m. Stephanie Shambaugh, Dec. 22, 1932 (dec. Feb. 1973); children: Barbara Shambaugh (Mrs. Forrest R. Bailey), Douglas, Anthony; m. Julia Wood McDermott, Aug. 19, 1975. Ph.B., U. Chgo., 1922. Engaged in real estate bus. and mortgage banker, Chgo., 1922—; with Draper & Kramer, Inc., Chgo., 1922—, chmn. bd., 1944—; dir., mem. exec. com. Chgo. 21 Corp.; Program supr. Div. Def. Housing Coordination (and successor Nat. Housing Agy.), Washington, 1941-42; past pres. Met. Housing and Planning Council, Chgo., Actions, Inc.; past mem. Pres.'s Com. Equal Opportunity in Housing. Past chmn. steering com. United Negro Fund; mem. vis. com. dept. design and visual arts Harvard, 1963-64; life trustee U. Chgo. Recipient citation of merit U. Chgo. Alumni Assn., 1947, Individual Distinguished Housing and Redevel. Service award Nat. Assn. Housing Ofcls., 1952, Disting. Alumnus award U. Chgo. Grad. Sch. Bus. Alumni Assn., 1982. Mem. Chgo. Mortgage Bankers Assn. (past pres.), Mortgage Bankers Assn. Am., Nat. Assn. Housing Ofcls., Chgo. Assn. Commerce and Industry. Clubs: Chgo., Quadrangle, Standard, Tavern, Mid-Town Tennis, Comml. (Chgo.); Ridge and Valley. Ranked (with ptnr.) number one nationally in tennis doubles for age 80 and above. Home: 1115 S Plymouth Ct Apt 511 Chicago IL 60605 Office: 33 W Monroe St Chicago IL 60603

KRAMER, FRANCIS RONALD, chem. co. exec.; b. Chgo., Aug. 19, 1930; s. Aaron Samuel and Mildred (Friedman) K.; m. Nancy Clare Wood, Apr. 24, 1954; children—Laura, Daniel, James, Karl. B.S., Calif. Inst. Tech., 1952; Ph.D., Purdue U., 1959. Project engr. Edgewood Arsenal, 1954-55; research engr. E.I. DuPont DeNemours & Co., Wilmington, Del., 1959-64, research supr., 1964-65, sr. supr., Kinston, N.C., 1965-68, tech. supt., 1968-70, process and product supt., Richmond, Va., 1970-73, venture mgr., Wilmington, 1973-76, tech. mgr., 1977—. Served with U.S. Army, 1952-54. Mem. Am. Inst. Chem. Engrs. Club: DuPont Country. Home: 606 Mount Lebanon Rd Wilmington DE 19803 Office: Nemours Bldg Wilmington DE 19899

KRAMER, FRANK RAYMOND, classics educator; b. Baraboo, Wis., Jan. 2, 1908; s. Chris Edward and Mabel (Shaw) K.; m. Hetty Louise Eising, Dec. 20, 1935; children: Bryce Allen, Anita Louise (Mrs. James Cyril Shew). B. Humanities, U. Wis., 1929, M.A. in Greek and Latin, 1931, Ph.D., 1936. Mem. faculty Heidelberg Coll., Tiffin, Ohio, 1938-78, prof. classics, 1944-78; asso. in residence U. Wis., 1948-49, 51-52; vis. prof. Ohio State U., summer 1962, prof. classics, 1978-79; research Am. Sch. Classical Studies, Athens, 1965. Author: Voices in the Valley, Mythmaking and Folk Belief in the Shaping of the Middle West, 1964; also articles. Grantee Wis. Com. Study Am. Civilization, 1948-49, 51-52, Social Sci. Research Council, 1951. Mem. Am. Philol. Assn., Classical Assn. Middle West and South, Ohio Classical Conf. (pres. 1948-49), Phi Alpha Theta, Eta Sigma Phi. Democrat. Mem. United Ch. Christ. Home: 25 Lincoln Rd Tiffin OH 44883 *The effort to develop perspectives has been a guiding principle of my life. Shaped in the course of a career in Classics, these perspectives have helped me to distinguish the significant in scholarship from the trivial, to differentiate between long-range values and temporary advantage, and to discriminate between ethical focus and, e.g., cultic distortion. And at least part of this principle is the realization that not to take oneself too seriously may help put these perspectives themselves into perspective.*

KRAMER, GEORGE M., chess player; b. Bklyn., May 15, 1929; s. Daniel and Dorothy K.; m. Vivian Kaplan, Feb. 11, 1951; children—Steven Paul, Tina Jean. B.S., Queen's Coll., 1951; M.S., U. Pa., 1955, Ph.D., 1957. Participant U.S. Open, U.S. Nat. Championships; mem. U.S. Olympic Team, Dubrovnik, 1950; Sr. research asso. Exxon Research and Engring. Co., Linden, N.J. Served with AUS, 1952-54. NSF fellow. Mem. Am. Chem. Soc., U.S. Chess Fedn., Sigma Xi., B'nai B'rith. Winner chess championships, N.Y. State, 1945, U.S. Speed, 1950. Home: 36 Arden Ct Berkeley Heights NJ 07922 Office: Exxon Research and Engring Co PO Box 45 Linden NJ 07036

KRAMER, GEORGE P., lawyer; b. Holyoke, Mass., Feb. 22, 1927; m. Elizabeth M. Truax, Oct. 13, 1973; children: Alice S. Truax, R. Hawley Truax, Charles W. Truax. A.B., Harvard U., 1950, LL.B., 1953; student, Sorbonne, 1948. Bar: N.Y. 1954. Assoc. Watson Leavenworth Kelton & Taggart, N.Y.C., 1953-59, partner, 1960-65, Conboy, Hewitt, O'Brien & Boardman, N.Y.C., 1965—; lectr. Practising Law Inst.; Pres. Mergers Co., Inc., N.Y.C.; dir. Burleson Corp. Raymond & Whitcomb.; Vis. com. Peabody Mus. of Harvard U., 1974-80. Author: Misleading Trademarks and Consumer Protection. Served to ensign USNR, 1945-46. Recipient Antarctic medal, 1977. Mem. N.Y. Cotton Exchange., ABA, Internat. Bar Assn., Assn. Bar City N.Y. (sec. 1963-65, exec. com. 1970-74), Am. Law Inst., U.S. Trademark Assn. (dir. 1975-78), Assn. Internationale pour la Protection de la Propriete Industrielle, Harvard U. Alumni Assn., Mass. Speleological Soc. (pres.), Antarctican Soc. Clubs: Century, Harvard (sec. 1972-83), Harvard (N.Y.C.) (bd. mgrs. 1983—); Harvard Faculty (Cambridge)). Home: 151 E 79th St New York NY 10021 Office: 100 Park Ave New York NY 10017

KRAMER, GERHARDT THEODORE, architect; b. New Orleans, Oct. 26, 1909; s. Gotthilf Mathias and Antonette (Smrck) K.; m. Ravenna Evelyn Ross, July 10, 1935; children: Gayle (Mrs. Gerald Grommet), Ross. B.Arch., Tulane U., 1930; M.Arch., Cornell U., 1932; LL.D. (hon.), Concordia Sem., 1978. Asso. in architecture Middle Am. Research Inst., Tulane U., 1933-41; with Douglass V. Freret, New Orleans, 1941-42, Hugo K. Graf, St. Louis, 1946-53; prin. Kramer & Assos., St. Louis, 1953-56, Kramer & Harms, Inc., 1956—; Pres. Concordia Hist. Inst., St. Louis, 1969-81, Heritage/St. Louis, 1970-74; pres. Landmarks Assn. St. Louis, Inc., 1960-62, 65-67, 68-71, exec. dir., 1974-78, sec., 1978-79; commr. Tower Grove Park, St. Louis, 1973—; mus. dir. Kirkwood History House, 1978-81. Bd. dirs. Chatillion-DeMenil House Found., St. Louis, Robert Campbell House Found., 1976—; mem. Mo. Adv. Council Hist. Preservation, 1978—; v.p. Eugene Field House Found., 1978-81; vice chmn. Kirkwood Landmarks Commn., 1981—; mem. Met. Zool. Park and Mus. Dist. Bd., 1982—. Served with USNR, 1942-45; capt. Res.; Ret.). Fellow AIA (Mo. preservation coordinator 1970-72, pres. St. Louis chpt. 1958-59); mem. Mo. Council Architects (pres. 1973). Lutheran. Home: 243 E Jefferson Ave Kirkwood MO 63122 Office: 2322 S Brentwood Blvd Saint Louis MO 63144

KRAMER, HARRY SUMMERFIELD, JR., lawyer; b. East St. Louis, Ill., Apr. 29, 1906; s. Harry Summerfield and Elizabeth C. (Daugherty) K.; m. Ray Culler, June 20, 1931 (div. 1943); children: Carol Kramer Robertson, Beverley Kramer Albertson; m. Jane Walker Parsons, June 30, 1944. Student, U. Ill., 1922-24; LL.B., Cumberland U., 1927. Bar: Mo. bar 1927. Since practiced in, St. Louis; partner firm Armstrong, Teasdale, Kramer & Vaughan (attys.), 1938—; Dir. Bank Bldg. & Equipment Corp. Mem. Am., St. Louis bar assns., Mo. Bar, Sigma Nu. Clubs: Racquet, Noonday (St. Louis). Home: 4910 W Pine Blvd Saint Louis MO 63108 Office: 611 Olive St Saint Louis MO 63101

KRAMER, HENRY THEODORE, retired insurance executive; b. Chgo., Apr. 8, 1917; s. LeRoy and Margery (Hannegan) K.; m. Janet P. Bunyan, Oct. 4, 1941; children: Jean Hull, Ann Thomson. B.S., Yale Sheffield Sci. Sch., 1940. With Pa. R.R., 1940; asso. underwriter Am. Mut. Reins. Co., 1946-51; with Obrion Russell & Co., Boston, 1951-56; v.p. Fire & Casualty Co. Conn., 1956-57, Allstate Ins. Co., 1957-65; asst. to pres. Swiss Re Corp., N.Y.C., 1965-66; pres., dir. N. Am. Reins. Co., N.Y.C., 1966-76, Swiss Re Mgmt. Corp., 1966-76; dir. N. Am. Reassurance Co., Swiss Re Corp., 1973-76, Swiss Re Holdings (N.Am.) Inc., 1974-76; pres. The Risk Exchange, Inc., Oldwick, N.J., 1976-80. Served to lt. comdr. USNR, 1941-46. Home: 51 Village Way Somerville NJ 08876

KRAMER, IRVIN RAYMOND, matallurgist, researcher; b. Balt., Sept. 18, 1912; m. Gertrude Kaplan, Oct. 27, 1935; 1 dau., Marica. B.S., Johns Hopkins U., 1935; M.S., John Hopkins U., 1947; Dr. Eng., Johns Hopkins U., 1951. Head special alloy br. Naval Research Lab., Washington, 1938-46, head Materials Research Office, 1946-51; asst. to pres. Horizons Titanium, Princeton, N.J., 1951-54; v.p. Mercast Corp., N.Y.C., 1954-56; mgr. ind. research and devel. Martian Marietta Corp., Denver, 1956-74; sci.-tech. advisor U.S. Navy, Annapolis, Md., 1974-81; research prof. metallurgy U. Md., 1981—; mem. NSF U.S.A.-USSR Commn. on Exchange Tech. Info. Author: Influence of Environment on Mechanical Behavior, 1960; contbr. numerous articles to profl. jours.; bd. dirs.: Jour. Material Sci. and Engring.; numerous inventions. Recipient Navy Meritorious award USN, 1945; NSF grantee, 1981. Fellow Am. Soc. Metals (Burgess Meml. lectr. 1978, Burgess Meml. award 1980); mem. ASME, Md. Soc. Metals (pres. 1951-52), Severn Tech. Soc. (pres. 1976-77), Sigma Xi, Tau Beta Pi. Office: U Md College Park MD 20781 *The goal of all research is truth, but truth is not invariant; it is a series of paradigms.*

KRAMER, JANE, author; b. Providence, Aug. 7, 1938; d. Louis Irving and Jessie (Shore) K.; m. Vincent Crapanzano, Apr. 30, 1967; 1 dau., Aleksandra. B.A., Vassar Coll., 1959; M.A., Columbia U., 1961. Cons. German Marshall Fund. Writer: The Morningsider, 1962, The Village Voice, 1963, New Yorker Mag, 1963—; books include Off Washington Square, 1963, Allen Ginsberg In America, 1969, Honor to the Bride, 1970, The Last Cowboy, 1978, Unsettling Europe, 1980; (Emmy award 1966). Recipient Am. Book award for nonfiction, 1981; Overseas Press Club Am. award, 1979; Front Page award, 1977; named Woman of Yr. Mademoiselle, 1968. Mem. Council Fgn. Relations, Com. to Protect Journalists (dir.), PEN, Environ. Def. Fund, Authors Guild and League, Writers Guild, Nat. Book Critics Circle. Office: New Yorker 25 W 43d St New York NY 10036

KRAMER, JOHN PAUL, entomologist, educator; b. Elgin, Ill., Mar. 13, 1928; s. Rutherford Hayes and Anna Maria (Burita) K.; m. Jean Kent Simpson, June, 1957 (div. 1973); children: Philip Simpson, Katherine Jean. B.S., Beloit (Wis.) Coll., 1950; M.S., U. Mo., 1952; Ph.D., U. Ill., 1958. Asst. prof. entomology N.C. State U., 1958-59; asso. entomologist Ill. Natural History Survey, Urbana, 1959-65; with Cornell U., 1965—, prof. insect pathology dept. entomology, 1975—; WHO traveling cons., 1962, NSF vis. scientist, Japan, 1967; vis. scientist Inst. Arctic Biology in Alaska, 1972. Contbr. articles to profl. jours. Served to 1st lt. U.S. Army, 1952-54. Decorated Bronze Star.; NSF fellow, 1967; NIH research grantee, 1959-72; Office of Naval Research grantee, 1971-74; WHO research grantee, 1979-82; U.S. Dept. Agr. research grantee, 1980-81. Mem. Soc. Invertebrate Pathology, N.Y. Entomological Soc., Internat. Soc. Biol. Control, Am. English Spot Rabbit Club, Am. Cavy Breeders Assn., Am. Rabbit Breeders Assn., Taughannock Area Rabbit Breeders Assn. Republican. Unitarian. Clubs: Ontario Cavy Club, N.Y. State Cavy Fanciers. Home: 115 Hanshaw Rd Ithaca NY 14850 Office: 10 Comstock Hall Department of Entomology Cornell University Ithaca NY 14853

KRAMER, KENNETH BENTLEY, congressman; b. Chgo., Feb. 19, 1942; s. Albert Aaron and Ruth (Pokrass) K.; children: Kenneth Bentley, Kelly J. B.A. magna cum laude in Polit. Sci., U. Ill., 1963; J.D., Harvard U., 1966. Bar: Ill. 1966, Colo. 1969. Dep. dist. atty. El Paso County, Colo., Colorado Springs, 1970-72; pvt. practice law, Colorado Springs, 1972-78; mem. Colo. Ho. of Reps., 1973-78, 96th-98th Congresses from 5th Colo. Dist., mem. armed services com.; mem. Nat. Commn. on Uniform State Laws, 1977-78; chmn. El Paso County Young Republicans, 1972-73; mem. El Paso County Rep. Central Com., 1972—, Colo. Rep. Central Com., 1973—; mem. exec. com. Rep. Study Com., 1979—; mem. Nat. Rep. Congl. Com., 1979—, vice chmn. communications, 1981—; mem. Rep. Policy Com., 1979-80. Bd. visitors U.S. Air Force Acad.; bd. dirs. Pikes Peak Mental Health Ctr., 1977-78, Mountain Valley chpt. March of Dimes, 1983—; chmn. U.S. Space Found. Served to capt. U.S. Army, 1967-70. Recipient Taxpayers Best Friend award Nat. Fedn. Ind. Bus., also; Guardian of Small Bus. award; Watchdog of Treasury award Nat. Asso. Businessmen; Disting. Service award Ams. for Constl. Action. Mem. Phi Beta Kappa. Club: Footprinters. Office: 240 Cannon House Office Bldg Washington DC 20515

KRAMER, KENNETH ROBERT, retail grocery executive; b. Cin., Sept. 14, 1945; s. Richard Paul and Virginia Mary (Knecht) K.; m. Ann Carol Murphy, Dec. 2, 1967; children: Stephen, Kevin, Brian. Student, Xavier U., Cin., 1963-69. Asst. meat merchandiser Kroger Co., Cin., 1969-72, delicatessen and bakery merchandiser, 1972-74; delicatessen merchandiser Albertson's Inc., Boise, Idaho, 1974-80, v.p. delicatessenops., 1980—. Roman Catholic. Home: 10139 Rockwood Ct Boise ID 83704 Office: Albertsons Inc 250 Parkcenter Blvd Boise ID 83726

KRAMER, MARCIA GAIL, journalist; b. Greenfield, Mass., Dec. 30, 1948; d. Louis Aaron and Blanche Shirley (Weiner) K. B.A. in Polit. Sci., Boston U., 1970. Reporter Greenfield Recorder Gazette, Mass., 1969, N.Y. Daily News, 1970-82, Albany bur. chief, 1982—; adj. prof. journalism Columbia U., 1980, NYU, 1982—. Guest appearances various radio and TV programs; lectr., various N.Y.C. colls. and univs. Mem. Gov.'s Adv. Com. on Drug Abuse, 1978. Recipient Pub. Service award Kings County Borough, 1974, Gold Typewriter award and Bobby Spellman Heart of N.Y. award N.Y. Press Club, 1979, Legis. Reform award Patrolman's Benevolent Assn., 1981, Ret. Detectives Ardee award, 1981. Mem. N.Y. Press Women (v.p. 1977-78), N.Y. Press Club (fin. sec. 1979-80, 1st v.p. 1980-81, 2d v.p. 1981—). Office: NY Daily News 220 E 42d St New York NY 10017

KRAMER, MARVIN DAWAYNE, grain marketing company executive; b. Swaledale, Iowa, Dec. 1, 1933; s. Jacob and Gertie (Klapp) K.; m. Marlys Joan Bielefeld, Oct. 3, 1954; children: Kim Marie, Patricia Lynn, Kathryn Kay. B.S., Iowa State U., 1959. Mgr. Far-Mar Co., Inc., Omaha, 1978-80, exec. v.p. ops., Hutchinson, Kans., 1980-82, no. regional mgr., Omaha, 1982—; bd. dirs. Nebr. Crop Improvement Assn., Lincoln, 1982—, Agr. Council, Omaha, 1982—. Served with USN, 1951-54. Democrat. Lutheran. Office: Far-Mar Co 609 Grain Exchange 19th St and Harney St Omaha NE 68102

KRAMER, MAURICE, educator; b. Phila., Apr. 4, 1930; s. Simon and Dora (Lundy) K.; m. Elaine Sillins Fialka, Nov. 22, 1959. A.B., U. Pa., 1951, A.M., 1953; Ph.D., Harvard, 1958. Instr. Rutgers U., 1957-61; mem. faculty English Bklyn. Coll., 1961—, asso. prof., 1970-73, prof. English, 1973—, chmn. dept., 1970-75, dean, 1978-80. Co-editor: Modern American Literature vol, Library Literary Criticism, 1969, Concordance to the Poems of Hart Crane, 1973, Supplement to Modern American Literature, 1976. Mem. Modern Lang. Assn., Phi Beta Kappa. Office: Dept English Brooklyn Coll Brooklyn NY 11210

KRAMER, MEYER, editor, lawyer, clergyman; b. Russia, Feb. 4, 1919; came to U.S., 1927, naturalized, 1933; s. Chaim and D'vorah (Kotzin) K.; m. Rose Schnabel, Dec. 22, 1944; children: Doniel, Rena, Tamar, Shira. B.A., Yeshiva Coll., 1940; postgrad., Rabbi Isaac Elchanan Theol. Sem., 1941; LL.B., U. Pa., 1944. Bar: Pa. bar 1944, law clk. Superior Ct. Pa 1944-45. Ordained rabbi, 1941; atty. Opinion Writing Office, SEC, 1945-46; lectr. U. Pa. Law Sch., 1947-69; rabbi Adath Zion, Phila., 1951-67, Beth Tefilath Israel, 1967-72, Bustleton-Somerton Synagogue, 1972-75; dir. Office Periodicals, Am. Law Inst-Am. Bar Assn., Phila., 1972—; Bd. dirs. Gratz Coll., Beth Jacob Schs., Phila., Talmudical Yeshiva Phila., Hapoel-Hamizrachi, Phila. Author: (with A. Leo Levin) Conservative Ketubah; Editor: ALI-ABA CLE Rev, 1972—, ALI-ABA Course Mathrials Jour, 1976—, CLE Register, 1979—; asso. editor: Jewish Horizon, 1960-62, Practical Lawyer, 1972—. Mem. Rabbinical Council Phila. (pres. 1966-68), Bd. Rabbis Phila., Rabbinic Alumni Yeshiva U. (v.p. 1960-68). Home: 111 Rennard Terr Philadelphia PA 19116 Office: 4025 Chestnut St Philadelphia PA 19104

KRAMER, MORTON, biostatistician; b. Balt., Mar. 20, 1914; s. David and Sarah (Valenstein) K.; m. Pauline Weinstein, Sept. 24, 1939; children—Barry Kenneth, James Lawrence, Nancy, Richard. A.B., Johns Hopkins, 1934, postgrad. Sch. Chemistry, 1934-35, Sc.D., Sch. of Hygiene and Pub. Health, 1939. Student asst. biostatistics Johns Hopkins Sch. Hygiene and Pub. Health, 1937-38; instr. preventive medicine N.Y.U. Med. Sch., 1938; statistician N.Y. State Dept. Health, Albany, 1939-40; asst. prof. biostatistics Sch. Tropical Medicine, also; statistician Insular Dept. Health, San Juan, P.R., 1940-42; econ. analyst Treasury Dept., Washington, 1942-43; Tb statistician, Cleve. and Cuyahoga County, 1943-46; asso. in biostatistics Western Res. U. Sch. Medicine, 1943-46; chief information and research Office Internat. Health Relations, USPHS, 1946-49; chief biometry br. NIMH, 1949-75; dir. div. biometry and epidemiology Alcohol, Drug Abuse, and Mental Health Adminstrn., NIMH, 1975-76; prof. dept. mental hygiene, also joint appointment in biostatistics Johns Hopkins Sch. Hygiene and Pub. Health, 1976—, prin. investigator, 1979—; commd. sr. scientist (res.) USPHS, 1949; cons. mental health WHO, 1959—, mem. expert panel health statistics, 1961—; adv. U.S. del. 5th Session Interim Commn., WHO, Geneva, 1948, 1948, Geneva, 1948; vis. scientist dept. pub. health London (Eng.) Sch. Hygiene and Tropical Medicine and Social Medicine Research Unit of Med. Research Council, 1968-69; mem. task panel Pres.'s Commn. on Mental Health, 1977-78; mem. adv. panel on health research studies Three Mile Island, Harrisburg, Pa., 1979—. Contbr. articles to sci. pubs. Recipient Superior Service award HEW, 1962, Distinguished Service award HEW, 1974. Fellow Am. Statis. Assn., Am. Pub. Health Assn. (Rema Lapouse award 1973), Am. Psychiat. Assn. (hon.), Am. Orthopsychiat. Assn., Am. Epidemiological Soc.; mem. Phi Beta Kappa, Phi Lambda Upsilon, Delta Omega. Club: Cosmos (Washington). Home: 6300 Red Cedar Pl Apt 309 Baltimore MD 21209 Office: Johns Hopkins U Sch Hygiene and Pub Health 615 N Wolfe St Baltimore MD 21205

KRAMER, PHILIP, petroleum refining executive; b. N.Y.C., Jan. 27, 1921; s. Saul and Malvina (Kuttner) K.; m. Sarah Greenberg, Dec. 27, 1942; children: Noell M., Marilyn B., Glenn M. B.B.A., Coll. City N.Y., 1940; M.B.A., Harvard, 1942. Mem. research staff Harvard Grad. Sch. Bus., 1942, 46; v.p. Paragon Oil Co., 1947-60, Pittston Co., 1960-69; pres. div. Met. Petroleum Co., 1960-69; exec. v.p. Amerada Hess Corp., 1969-72, pres., 1972-82, pres., chief exec. officer, 1982—, also dir. Served to lt. USNR, World War II. Home: 870 United Nations Plaza New York City NY 10017 Office: 1185 Ave of Americas New York NY 10036

KRAMER, REUBEN ROBERT, sculptor; b. Balt., Oct. 9, 1909; s. Israel and Bessie (Silver) K.; m. Perna Krick, June 19, 1944. Grad., Rinehart Sch. Sculpture, 1932, traveling scholar, 1931-33; fellow, Am. Acad. in Rome, 1936. Founder Balt. Art Center Children, 1944, dir., 1944-55; instr. Md. Inst., 1957-58; pvt. instr. Exhibited, Grand Central Galleries, N.Y.C., 1934, Balt. Mus. Art, 1939-58; Exhibited celebration exhbn. for 50 yrs., Balt. Mus. Art, 1978; Exhibited, Internat. Sculpture Show, Phila., 1940, 49, Pa. Acad. Fine Arts, 1949-53, 58, Corcoran Gallery, 1951-58, Am. Jewish Tercentenary Traveling Exhbn., 1954-55; one man shows, Grand Central Galleries, N.Y.C., 1937, Md. Inst., Balt., Balt. Mus., 1939, 51, 59, 66, Corcoran Gallery, 1960, Am. U., Washington, 1953, (with wife), Western Md. Coll., 1954, Hagerstown Mus., 1955, retrospective, Jewish Community Center, Balt., 1974; commd. to execute wood carving, P.O., St. Albans, W.Va., 1940; 8 ft. bronze statue of Assoc. Justice Thurgood Marshall, Balt. Dept. Housing and Community Devel., 1977; represented in collections, Am. U., Corcoran Gallery, Balt. Mus. Art, Walters Art Gallery, Portland Art Mus., Harvard Law Sch., U. W.Va., also pvt. collections, Martenet, IBM, Rosen, Horelick, others.; Indsl. designer, War Dept., 1942-45. Recipient Am. Prix de Rome, 1934-36; 1st prize Balt. Mus. Art, 1940, 48, 51, 53; sculpture award, 1946, 49, 51, 52, 54; 1st prize for Md. Nat. Art Week, 1941, Sculptors Guild of Md., 1948, Sculptors Guild of Washington, 1952, 54; 1st prize for artistry in craftsmanship Peale Mus., 1949; Drawing prize, 1954; Purchase prize IBM, 1941, Balt. Mus. Art, 1948, Corcoran Gallery Art, 1952; Nat. Inst. Arts and Letters sculpture grantee, 1964; elected to Balt. City Coll. Hall of Fame, 1962; personal archives acquired by Enoch Pratt Library, Balt., 1976. Mem. Alumni Am. Acad. in Rome, Artists Equity Assn.

KRAMER, ROBERT, law school dean; b. Davenport, Iowa, Aug. 17, 1913; s. Robert and Juanita (Mapes) K.; m. Mary Rainey Gaston, Mar. 22, 1941; children: Mary Elizabeth Kramer Helsinger, Lucy Mapes Kramer Gardner, Robert Gaston. A.B. cum laude, Harvard U., 1935, LL.B magna cum laude, 1938. Bar: D.C. 1938, N.Y. 1947. Atty. NLRB, 1938-40; antitrust div. Dept. Justice, 1941-42; asso. Paul, Weiss, Wharton & Garrison, N.Y.C., 1946-47; prof. law Duke U., 1947-59; vis. prof. law Stanford U., 1950, U. Wis., 1956, U. N.C., 1957, NYU, 1958, Northwestern U., 1959; asst. atty. gen. Office Legal Counsel, Dept. Justice, 1959-61; dean Nat. Law Center, George Washington U., Washington, 1961—. Author: (with C.L.B. Lowndes and J. McCord) Federal Gift and Estate Taxes, 1974; editor: Law and Contemporary Problems, 1947-56, Jour. Legal Edn., 1948-55; Am. editor: Business Law Rev., 1952-55. Served to lt. col. AUS, 1942-46. Decorated Legion of Merit. Mem. Am. Law Inst., Assn. Am. Law Schs. (exec. com. 1959). Democrat. Episcopalian. Home: 2500 Q St NW Washington DC 20007 Office: 720 20th St Washington DC 20052

KRAMER, ROBERT IVAN, pediatrician; b. Providence, July 31, 1933; s. Louis Irving and Jessica Priscilla (Shore) K.; m. Joan Thalheimer, Apr. 27, 1963; children—Lisa Ann, Robin Louise, Jessica Florette, Megan Leigh. A.B., Brown U., 1954; M.D., Tufts U., 1958. Intern Yale-New Haven Med. Center, 1958-59, resident in pediatrics, 1959-60; chief resident Children's Med. Center, Dallas, 1960-61; fellow in chest diseases, mem. faculty Southwestern Med. Sch., Dallas, 1963-65, asso. prof., 1971-77, prof., 1977—; practice medicine specializing in pediatrics, Dallas, 1965—; dir. Nat. Cystic Fibrosis Research Center, Dallas, 1963—; mem. staffs Baylor U., St. Paul, Presbyn. Children's hosps., all Dallas; chest cons. Scottish Rite Hosp. for Crippled Children, Dallas. Served with USNR, 1961-63. Nat. Cystic Fibrosis Research Found. grantee, 1963—. Clubs: Willow Bend Polo and Hunt, T Bar M Racket. Home: 5838 Colhurst St Dallas TX 75230 Office: 8355 Walnut Hill Ln Dallas TX 75231

KRAMER, RUSSELL ARNOLD, lawyer; b. Maryville, Tenn., Dec. 13, 1918; s. Russell Reed and Alice Gray (Arnold) K.; m. Sara Lee Hellums, Mar. 8, 1942; children: John Reed, Sara Lynne, Randall A. B.A., Maryville Coll., 1940; postgrad., U. Tex., 1941; J.D., U. Mich., 1946. Bar: Tenn. 1942, Pa. 1975. Ptnr. Kramer, Johnson, Rayson, McVeigh & Leake, Knoxville, Tenn., 1947-74; of counsel Kramer, Johnson, Rayson, McVeigh & Leke, Knoxville, Tenn., 1984—; exec. v.p., dir., gen. counsel Aluminum Co. Am., Pitts., 1974-83. Bd. dirs. Maryville Coll. Served to capt. USAAF, 1942-46. Mem. ABA, Pa. Bar Assn., Tenn. Bar Assn., Knoxville Bar Assn., Am. Judicature Soc. (chmn. 1983). Methodist. Home: 2201 Woodmere DR Knoxville TN 37920 Office: United Plaza Knoxville TN 37901

KRAMER, SIDNEY, publisher, lawyer, literary agent; b. N.Y.C., 1915; s. Louis and Mildred (Hindin) K.; m. Esther Schlansky, Nov. 23, 1939; children: Wendy Beth (Mrs. Michael K. Posner), Mark William. B.S., NYU, 1936; J.D., Bklyn. Law Sch., St. Lawrence U., 1939. Bar: N.Y. 1940, Conn. 1962, U.S. Supreme Ct. 1975. Practice in, N.Y.C., 1940-45, Westport, Conn., 1963—; sr. v.p., dir. Bantam Books, Inc., N.Y.C., 1945-67; pres., dir. Remarkable Bookshop, 1960—, New Am. Library, N.Y.C., 1967-72; pres. MEWS Books Ltd., Westport, Conn., London, Eng., 1975—; mng. dir., cons. Cassell & Collier Macmillan Pubs. Ltd., London, 1973-74; chmn. Nat. Assn. Paperback Pubs., 1945-67. Occasional contbr.: N.Y. Times. Chmn. Democratic Town Com., also justice peace, Westport, 1960-64; chmn. Save Westport Now, 1981—. Mem. Conn. Bar Assn. Home: 20 Bluewater Hill Westport CT 06880 Office: 177 Main St Westport CT 06880 also 25 Queensgate Gardens London England WC1R 4SG

KRAMER, STANLEY E., motion picture producer-director; b. N.Y.C., Sept. 29, 1913; m. Ann Pearce, 1950 (div.); children—Casey, Larry; m. Karen Sharpe, 1966; children—Katharine, Jennifer. B.S., N.Y. U., 1933. Organizer, pres. Stanley Kramer Prodns., Inc., 1949; set up Stanley Kramer Co., 1950; formed Stanley Kramer Pictures Corp., 1954. Producer of: (with others formed) numerous motion pictures, including Screen Plays, Inc, Hollywood, Cal., 1947; producer: So This Is New York, Champion, 1949, Home of the Brave; Cyrano de Bergerac, 1950, High Noon (4 Acad. awards 1952), Caine Mutiny, 1953; producer, dir.: Not as a Stranger, 1954, The Defiant Ones, 1958 (N.Y. Film Critics award), On the Beach, 1959, Inherit the Wind, 1960, The Secret of Santa Vittoria, 1969, Bless the Beasts and the Children, 1971; producer, dir., moderator: The Trials of Ethel and Julius Rosenberg, Gen. Yamashita, Lt. William Calley, ABC-TV, 1974; prepared radio scripts for nat. network programs.; (Recipient One World award, San Remo, Italy 1950, Look Achievement award as producer of year 1950, N.Y. Film Critics award as best dir. 1958, Gallatin medal N.Y. U. 1968); Films include Judgement at Nuremberg, 1961 (Irving Thalberg award 1962), It's a Mad, Mad, Mad, Mad World, 1963, Ship of Fools, 1965, Guess Who's Coming to Dinner, 1967, R.P.M, 1970, Oklahoma Crude, 1973, The Domino Principle, 1977, The Runner Stumbles, 1979. Served to 1st lt. AUS, World War II. Office: care Stanley Kramer Prodns PO Box 158 Bellevue WA 90889 *

KRAMISH, ARNOLD, science and technical consultant; b. Denver, June 6, 1923; s. John I. and Sara (Kaitz) K.; m. Vivian Ruth Raker, Aug. 19, 1952; children: Pamela, Robert. B.S., U. Denver, 1945; A.M., Harvard, 1947. With U.S. AEC, 1946-51; sr. staff mem. Rand Corp., Santa Monica, Calif., 1951-68; v.p. Inst. for the Future, Washington, 1968-70; sci. attache U.S. Mission to UNESCO, Paris, 1970-73; counselor for sci. and tech. affairs U.S. Mission to OECD, Paris, 1974-76; sci. research R & D Assocs., Arlington, Va., 1976-81; tech. cons., 1981—; prof. UCLA, 1965-66, London Sch. Econs., 1967-68; adj. prof. internat. studies U. Miami, Fla., 1969; fellow Woodrow Wilson Internat. Ctr. for Scholars, 1982-83. Author: Atomic Energy for Your Business, 1959, Atomic Energy in the Soviet Union, 1959, The Peaceful Atom in Foreign Policy, 1963, The Future of Non-Nuclear Nations, 1970; also numerous articles, book chpts. Served with AUS, 1943-46. Carnegie fellow Council in Fgn. Relations, 1958-59; John Simon Guggenheim fellow, 1966-67; research fellow Inst. for Strategic Studies, London, 1966-67. Patentee nuclear radiometer. Home: 2065 Wethersfield Ct Reston VA 22091 Office: PO Box 2621 Reston VA 22090

KRAMNICK, ISAAC, government educator; b. Worcester, Mass., Mar. 6, 1938; s. Max and Sarah (Sushelsky) K.; m. Miriam Brody, Jan. 20, 1963; children: Rebecca, Jonathan, Leah. B.A., Harvard U., 1959, Ph.D., 1965. Instr. Harvard U., 1965-66; asst. prof. Brandeis U., 1966-68; assoc. prof. Yale U., 1968-72; prof. govt. Cornell U., 1972—. Author: Bolingbroke and His Circle, 1970, The Rage of Edmund Burke, 1977. Guggenheim fellow, 1970-71. Jewish. Home: 125 Kelvin Pl Ithaca NY 14850 Office: Dept Government Cornell U Ithaca NY 14850

KRANE, ROBERT ALAN, banker; b. Bloomfield, Iowa, Nov. 17, 1933; s. Arnold and Ruth Alberta (Power) K.; m. Marcia Welcker Fry, June 12, 1954; children: Kristin Krane Edwards, William Alan, Kathrin Welcker, Andrew Power. B.S. in Commerce, U. Iowa, 1955; postgrad., Sch. Fin. Public Relations, Northwestern U., 1963-64, Columbia U. Grad. Sch. Banking, 1973, Dartmouth Inst., 1978. With

Norwest Bank Des Moines N.A., Des Moines, 1959-76, pres., dir., 1974-76; with Norwest Bank Omaha N.A., 1976-79, pres., dir., 1977-79; with Norwest Corp., Mpls., 1979—, pres., dir., 1981-82, vice chmn., dir., 1982—; dir. Central Life Assurance Co., Iowa Malleable Co., Conagra, Inc. Bd. dirs. Des Moines C. of C., 1964-65, Omaha C. of C., 1977-79, Mpls. C. of C., 1981, 83-84; chmn. Mpls. C. of C., 1984; pres. Des Moines Jaycees, 1964-65, Iowa Jaycees, 1966-67, Big Bros. Des Moines, 1971; chaplain U.S. Jaycees, 1967-68; mem. Iowa Republican Fin. Com., 1971-74; trustee Coll. of St. Catherine. Served with AUS, 1955-59. Recipient Des Moines Disting. Service award, 1966; named Jayee Internat. Senator, 1967. Mem. Young Pres. Orgn. Presbyterian. Clubs: Mpls., Minikadha. Home: 6620 Mohawk Trail Edina MN 55435 Office: 1200 Peavey Bldg Minneapolis MN 55479

KRANE, STEPHEN MARTIN, physician, educator; b. N.Y.C., July 15, 1927; s. Daniel Golden and Bessie (Berman) K.; m. Cynthia Ramin, June 28, 1952; children: David Alan, Peter Jay, Ian Matthew, Adam. A.B., Columbia Coll., 1946, M.D., 1951; A.M. (hon.), Harvard U., 1968. Intern to chief resident in medicine Mass. Gen. Hosp., Boston, 1951-57, chief arthritis unit, 1961, physician, 1969; research fellow Washington U., St. Louis, 1956; asst. in medicine Harvard Med. Sch., 1958, prof. medicine, 1972—. Contbr. (articles to profl. jours.). Served with USNR, 1945-46. Recipient Kappa Delta award? Orthopedic Research Soc., 1973, Geigy Rheumatism prize Orthopedic Research Soc., 1977, Herberden medal, 1980; Guggenheim fellow Oxford U., 1973-74. Fellow ACP; mem. AAAS, Am. Soc. Clin. Investigation, Assn. Am. Physicians, Am. Fedn. Clin. Research, Am. Soc. Biol. Chemistry, Soc. Bone Mineral Research, Am. Rheumatism Soc., Endocrine Soc., Am. Acad. Arts and Scis. Home: 101 Windsor Rd Waban MA 02168 Office: Harvard Med Sch Dept Medicine Boston MA 02115

KRANICH, WILMER LEROY, chemical engineer educator, university dean; b. Phila., Nov. 20, 1919; s. Jacob H. and Elsie (Ernst) K.; m. Margaret Mansley, July 1, 1950; children: Laurence Wilmer, Deborah M., Gary R. B.S., U. Pa., 1940; Ph.D. (McMullen fellow 1940-41), Cornell U., 1944. Instr. chem. engring. Cornell U., 1941-44; asst. prof. chem. engring. Princeton U., 1946-48; asso. prof. chem. engring. Worcester Poly. Inst., 1948-49, prof., 1949-67, head chem. engring. and chemistry, 1958-67, George C. Gordon prof., 1967—, head dept. chem. engring., 1967-75, dean Grad. Studies, 1974—; staff cons. Arthur D. Little, Inc., 1949-74; vis. research scientist Hungarian Acad. Scis., Budapest, 1983. Served to lt. (j.g.) USNR, 1944-46. Mem. Am. Inst. Chem. Engrs., Am. Chem. Soc., Am. Soc. Engring. Edn., Sigma Xi, Tau Beta Pi, Alpha Chi Sigma. Baptist. Home: 18 Beechmont St Worcester MA 01609

KRANK, DONALD FRANCIS, lawyer; b. Culver City, Calif., Oct. 19, 1939; s. Daniel Joseph and Rose Bertha (Braun) K.; m. Sharon Krank, June 20, 1964; 1 dau., Rosslyn Jean. B.S., U. San Francisco, 1960; J.D., Georgetown U., 1968. Bar: Pa. 1969. Atty. Armstrong Cork Co., Lancaster, Pa., 1968-69; corporate counsel A C and S Contracting, Lancaster, 1969-72; partner firm Krank, Gross & Casper, Lancaster, 1972—; adj. prof. Millersville (Pa.) State U. Served to lt. comdr. USNR, 1961-68. Office: 1574 Lititz Pike Lancaster PA 17601 *Be yourself. Work within the confines of your own personality.*

KRANTZ, JUDITH TARCHER, novelist; b. N.Y.C., Jan. 9, 1928; d. Jack David and Mary (Brager) Tarcher; m. Stephen Falk Krantz, Feb. 19, 1954; children—Nicholas, Anthony. B.A., Wellesley Coll., 1948. Editor Good House Keeping mag., 1949-56; contbg. editor Cosmopolitan mag., 1968-79. Article writing for: McLean's mag., Ladies Home Jour., McCall's, 1956-68; author: Scruples, 1978, Princess Daisy, 1980, Mistral's Daughter, 1982.

KRANTZ, KERMIT EDWARD, educator, physician; b. Oak Park, Ill., June 4, 1923; s. Andrew Stanley and Beatrice H. (Cibrowski) K.; m. Doris Cole Krantz, Sep. 7, 1946; children—Pamela (Mrs. Richard Huffstutter), Sarah Elizabeth (Mrs. Paul Glaab), Kermit Tripler. B.S., Northwestern U., 1945, B.M., 1947, M.S. in Anatomy, 1947, M.D., 1948; Litt.D. (hon.), William Woods Coll., 1971. Diplomate: Am. Bd. Obstetricians and Gynecologists. Intern obstetrics and gynecology N.Y. Lying-In Hosp., 1947-48; asst. resident, asst. obstetrics and gynecology Cornell U. Med. Coll., New York Lying-In Hosp., N.Y. Hosp., 1948-50; fellow, resident obstetrics and gynecology Mary Fletcher Hosp., Burlington, Vt., 1950-51; dir. Durfee Clinic, 1952-55; instr., then asst. prof. U. Vt. Coll. Medicine, 1951-55; asst. prof. U. Ark. Med. Sch., 1955-59; prof., chmn. dept. gynecology and obstetrics U. Kans. Med. Center, 1959—, lectr. history medicine, 1959—, prof. anatomy, 1963—, dean clin. affairs, 1972-74, chief staff, 1972-74, obstetrician and gynecologist in chief, 1959—, asso. to exec. vice chancellor for facilities devel., 1974—; Charles Jones Newcomb vis. prof. U. Ariz. Coll. Medicine and Ariz. Health Scis. Center, 1979; cons. in field. Author numerous articles in field. Mem. Nat. Adv. Child Health and Human Devel. Council, NIH, 1974-76. Bowen-Brooks fellow N.Y. Acad. Medicine, 1948-50; recipient Found. award S. Atlantic Assn. Obstetricians and Gynecologists, 1950, Am. Assn. Obstetricians and Gynecologists, 1950; named Outstanding Prof. in Coll. of Medicine Nu Sigma Nu, 1955; Robert A. Ross lectureship award Armed Forces Dist. meeting Am. Coll. Obstetricians and Gynecologists, 1972; Charles A. Durham Meml. lectr. Ann. Session Tex. Med. Assn., 1978; Markle scholar med. sci., 1957-62. Founding fellow Am. Coll. Obstetricians and Gynecologists (Kermit E. Krantz Lectureship award established 1973, Outstanding Dist. Services award 1978); fellow A.C.S.; mem. Am. Assn. Anatomists, Am. Fedn. Clin. Research, A.M.A., Am. Med. Writers Assn., Am. Fertility Soc., Am. Assn. U. Profs., Soc. Exptl. Biology and Medicine, Aerosopace Med. Assn., Endocrine Soc., Soc. Gynecologic Investigation, Central Assn. Obstetricians and Gynecologists, N.Y. Acad. Medicine, N.Y. Acad. Sci., Kans. Med. Soc., Assn. Mil. Surgeons U.S. (sustaining), Kans. Obstet. Soc., Sigma Xi, Alpha Omega Alpha. Home: 6711 Overhill Rd Shawnee Mission KS 66208 Office: Univ Kans Med Center Kansas City KS 66103

KRANTZ, PALMER ERIC, III, zoological park administrator; b. Columbia, S.C., Jan. 27, 1950; s. Palmer Eric and Kathryn Laura (Quattelbaum) K.; m. Rebecca Othella Long, Nov. 21, 1976; 1 son, Eric Lindsay. B.S. in Zoology, Clemson U., 1972. With Riverbanks Park Commn., Columbia, 1972—, supr. animal hosp., 1973-74, curator mammals, 1974-75, asst. dir., 1975-76, exec. dir., 1976—. Exec. officer Indian Waters Council Boy Scouts Am., Columbia; bd. dirs. Carolina Carillon, Columbia; sec., exec. com. S.C. Fedn. Museums. Fellow Am. Assn. Zool. Parks and Aquariums (membership com. 1979-80, chmn. accreditation commn. 1980—, bd. dirs.); mem. Carolina Bird Club, Riverbanks Zool. Park Soc. (dir., sec.), Richland County Soc. Prevention Cruelty to Animals, Greater Columbia C. of C. (dir.), East Africa Wildlife Soc., Wildlife Soc. So. Africa. Lodge: Rotary (Columbia dir.). Home: 2432 Dove Ln Columbia SC 29210 Office: 500 Wildlife Pkwy Columbia SC 29210

KRANTZ, SANFORD BURTON, physician; b. Chgo., Feb. 6, 1934; s. Max and Fannie (Grenstein) K.; m. Sandra R. Goldstein, Dec. 28, 1958; children—Michael David, Marcy Sharon, Alan Thomas, Sarah Ann. A.B., U. Chgo., 1954, B.S., 1955, M.D., 1959. Intern U. Chgo. Hosps., 1959-60; asst. resident medicine, 1960-63; NATO postdoctoral fellow biochemistry U. Glasgow, 1964-65; asst. prof. medicine U. Chgo. Hosps. and Argonne Cancer Research Hosp., Chgo., 1965-68; asst. chief hematology service clin. center NIH, Bethesda, Md., 1968-70; chief hematology VA Hosp., Vanderbilt Med. Sch., Nashville, 1970—; asso. prof. medicine Vanderbilt U., 1970-74, prof. medicine, chief hematology, 1974—. Author: (with L.O. Jacobson) Erythopoietin and the Regulation of Erythropoiesis, 1970. Recipient Joseph A. Capps prize for med. research, 1964; USPHS postdoctoral fellow, 1962-64; NATO postdoctoral fellow, 1964; Leukemia Soc. scholar, 1965-68; NIH grantee, 1971—. Fellow A.C.P.; mem. Am. Fedn. Clin. Research, Am. Soc. Clin. Investigation, AAAS, Am. Soc. Hematology, Internat. Soc. Exptl. Hematology, Central Soc. Clin. Research, Am. Soc. Exptl. Pathology, Sigma Xi. Home: 838 Rodney Dr Nashville TN 37205

KRANTZ, STEPHEN FALK, motion picture producer; b. N.Y.C., May 20, 1923; s. Philip and Rose (Scharf) K.; m. Judith Tarcher, Feb. 19, 1954; children: Nicholas, Anthony. B.A., Columbia Coll., 1943. Licensed pvt. pilot. Dir. program devel. Columbia Pictures TV, 1954-56; v.p. charge world sales and prodn., 1956-58; pres. Steve Krantz Prodns., Beverly Hills, Calif., 1958—. Producer: The Tonight Show and Kate Smith Show, 1950-52; program dir., NBC, 1953-54; motion pictures include Fritz the Cat, 1973, Heavy Traffic, 1974, Cooley High, 1975, Ruby, 1977, Which Way Is Up?, 1977. Served to 2d lt. USAAF, World War II; PTO. Mem. Ind. Producers Assn. (pres. 1951-52), Motion Picture Acad. Arts and Scis.

KRANYIK, ROBERT DONALD, educational administration educator; b. Bridgeport, Conn., Sept. 19, 1931; s. James and Mary (Mazalin) K.; m. Louise Narkevics, May 23, 1953; children: Mary Louise, Jane. B.S.S., Fairfield U., 1952, M.A., 1955; Ph.D., U. Conn., 1965. Tchr. pub. schs., Fairfield, 1954-59, asst. prin., 1960-61; prof. edn. U. Bridgeport, 1962-67, Charles Dana prof., 1968—, chmn. dept. ednl. adminstrn., 1968-79, assoc. dean, 1966-67, dean, 1967-68; cons. Ednl. Devel. Center, Newton, Mass., 1968; mem. adv. bd. Conn. Commn. Higher Edn., 1969-73, chmn. spl. adv. com., 1973. Author: How To Teach Study Skills, 1965, How To Teach Reference and Research Skills, Creative Learning in Elementary School, 1969, Self-Instructional Basic Math, 1969; editor: Curriculum Development: Foundations, Design and Implementation, 1979, Supervision: Concepts, Practices and Issues, 1980; rev. editor: Early Years Mag; Contbr. articles to profl. jours. State Conn. grantee, 1971-72. Mem. Conn. Edn. Assn. (pres. higher edn. 1969), Assn. Supervision and Curriculum Devel., NEA, Conn. Assn. for Supervision and Curriculum Devel. (exec. bd.), Assn. for Tng. and Devel., Phi Delta Kappa, Kappa Delta Pi. Office: Coll Mgmt Mandeville Hall U Bridgeport University Ave Bridgeport CT 06601

KRANZ, NORMAN, advt. exec.; b. Chgo., July 17, 1924; s. Irving and Mollie (Diamond) K.; m. Ruth Shapera, Nov. 4, 1951; children—Roberta Suzanne, Philip Lee. Student, Haverford Coll., 1943-44; B.S. in Journalism, U. Ill., 1948. Advt. prodn. mgr. Kencliffe, Breslich, Chgo., 1948-52; asst. to pres. Delta Advt. Co., Chgo., 1952-57; creative dir. food sales promotion Armour & Co., Chgo., 1957-62; asst. sales promotion mgr. Helene Curtis Industries, Chgo., 1962-64; collateral supr. Compton Advt. Co., Chgo., 1964-65; with J. Walter Thompson Co., Chgo., 1965—, asso. creative dir., 1971—, v.p., 1972—. Served with USAAF, 1943-46. Home: 4901 Dobson St Skokie IL 60076 Office: 875 N Michigan Ave Chicago IL 60611

KRANZBERG, MELVIN, educator; b. St. Louis, Nov. 22, 1917; s. Samuel and Rose (Fitter) K.; m. Nancy Lee Fox, 1943; children—Steven, John; m. Eva Mannering, 1955; m. Heidi Romo, 1962; m. Dolores Campen, 1972 (dec. 1981). A.B., Amherst Coll., 1938; M.A., Harvard U., 1939, Ph.D., 1942; L.H.D., Denison U., 1967; Litt.D., Newark Coll. Engring., 1968, No. Mich. U., 1972; D.Eng., Worcester Poly. Inst., 1981; L.H.D., Amherst Coll., 1983. Adminstrv. asst. service trades br. OPA, 1941-42; instr. history, tutor Harvard, 1946; instr. humanities Stevens Inst. Tech., 1946-47; asst. prof. history Amherst Coll., 1947-52; mem. faculty Case Western Res. U., 1952-72, prof. history, 1959-72, dir. grad. program history sci. and tech., 1963-72; Callaway prof. history tech. Ga. Inst. Tech., 1972—; Harris Found. lectr. Northwestern U., 1970; Mellon lectr. Lehigh U., 1975; mem. tech. assessment panel Nat. Acad. Scis., 1968-69, mem. com. survey materials sci. and engring., 1971-72; chmn. hist. adv. com. NASA, 1967-69; vice chmn. U.S. Nat. Com. History and Philosophy Sci., 1970—, chmn., 1972-73; v.p. Internat. Coop. History Tech. Com., Internat. Union History Sci., 1968—; mem. Goddard prize essay com. Nat. Space Club, 1966-74; history com. Am. Inst. Aeros. and Astronautics, 1965-66; mem. hon. com. 1st Internat. Film Festival on Human Environment; U.S. State Dept. specialist, India, 1975, S.E. Asia, 1976, Africa, 1979, W. Ger., 1982; mem. adv. com. program sci., tech. and human values Nat. Endowment for Humanities, 1975-77; chmn. adv. panel div. policy research and analysis NSF, also div. sci. resources studies, 1977-80. Author: The Siege of Paris, 1870-71, 1951, 1848, A Turning Point?, 1959, (with others) By the Sweat of Thy Brow, 1975; Co-editor: Monograph Series in History of Technology, 1963-77, Technology in Western Civilization, 2 vols, 1967, Technology and Culture: An Anthology, 1972, Technological Innovation, 1978, Energy and the Way We Live, 1979, Ethics in an Age of Pervasive Technology, 1980; editor-in-chief: Technology and Culture Quar. Jour, 1959-81; adv. editor: Knowledge, Sci., Tech. and Human Values, Philosophy of Tech.; Contbr. to profl. jours. Trustee Charles Babbage Inst. Served with AUS, 1943-46. Decorated Bronze Star, Combat Inf. badge; recipient Spl. Research Day citation Case Western Res. U., 1970; Apollo Achievement award NASA, 1969; Spl. Recognition award Am. Indsl. Arts Assn., 1978; Roe medal ASCF, 1980; Jabotinsky Centennial medal Israel, 1980. Fellow AAAS (v.p. 1966, sect. chmn. 1978-79, chmn. com. sci. and pub. policy 1978-81); mem. Soc. History Tech. (sec. 1958-74, pres. 1983—, Leonardo da Vinci medal 1968), Soc. French Hist. Studies (v.p. 1959), Phi Beta Kappa (lectr. Assocs. 1981—), Sigma Xi (nat. lectr. 1967, 68, Bicentennial lectr. 1975-77, dir. 1971—, nat. exec. bd. 1972—, pres. 1979-80), Epsilon Pi Tau, Phi Kappa Phi. Home: 4850 Kendall Ct NE Atlanta GA 30342

KRASKE, KARL VINCENT, graphics company executive; b. Grand Falls, Nfld., Can., Feb. 16, 1935; U.S., 1940; s. William H. and Clara A. (Schroeder) K.; m. Patricia J. Cane, June 2, 1962; children: Richard J., Anne P. B.S. in Chem. Engring., U. Maine, 1957; M.A. in Paper Chemistry, Lawrence U., 1959, Ph.D., 1963. Chemist, group leader Oxford Paper Co., Rumford, Maine, 1962-69; v.p. ops. Scott Graphics Co., South Hadley, Mass., 1971-74, v.p., gen. mgr., 1974-78, James River Graphics, 1978-80; group v.p. James River Corp., South Hadley, Mass., 1980—; dir. ARMM, Alexandria, Va. Mem. Fin. Com., Rumford, Maine, 1966-68, Approprations Com., South Hadley, Mass., 1978—. Mem. Am. Paper Inst. (dir. specialty coaters and extrusion group 1976—), Assoc. Industries Mass. (bd. dirs. 1982—), TAPPI, Am. Chem. Soc. Office: James River Corp 28 Gaylord St South Hadley MA 01075

KRASLOW, DAVID, newspaperman, author; b. N.Y.C., Apr. 16, 1926; s. Frank and Goldie (Sirota) K.; m. Bernice Schonfeld, Sept. 18, 1949; children: Ellen Anne, Karen Leah, Susan Beth. B.A., U. Miami, Fla., 1948. With Los Angeles Times, 1963-72, Washington corr., news editor, then chief, 1970-72; asst. mng. editor Washington Star-News, 1972-74; Washington Bur. chief Cox Newspapers, 1974-77; pub. Miami News, 1977—, sports writer, 1947-48; successively sports writer, reporter, Washington corr. Miami Herald, 1948-63. Co-author: A Certain Evil, 1965, The Secret Search for Peace in Vietnam, 1968. Bd. dirs. United Way; trustee Center for Fine Arts, Miami; trustee, chmn. acad. affairs com. U. Miami; mem. Orange Bowl Com. Served with USAAF, 1944-46. Recipient George Polk award, 1969; Raymond Clapper award, 1969; Dumont award, 1969; Nieman fellow Harvard U., 1961-62. Mem. InterAm. Press Assn. (bd. dirs.), Sigma Delta Chi. Jewish. Clubs: Gridiron, Federal City (Washington); Miami, New World Center (Miami). Office: Miami News PO Box 615 Miami FL 33152

KRASNA, ALVIN ISAAC, biochemist, educator; b. N.Y.C., June 23, 1929; s. Selig and Esther (Finer) K.; m. Elaine C. Cohen, Feb. 27, 1955; children—Susan Roni, Gary Marc, Allen Selig. B.A., Yeshiva Coll., 1950; Ph.D., Columbia U., 1955. Mem. faculty Columbia U., 1956—, prof. biochemistry, 1970—, vice chmn., 1978—. Contbr. profl. jours. Predoctoral fellow NSF, 1953; Guggenheim fellow, 1962; research grantee NSF, NIH, Am. Cancer Soc., AEC. Mem. Am. Chem. Soc., Am. Assn. Biol. Chemists, AAAS, Harvey Soc., Sigma Xi. Home: 147-16 68th Dr Flushing NY 11367 Office: 701 W 168th St New York NY 10032

KRASNER, LEE, painter; b. Bklyn.; m. Jackson Pollock. Ed., Cooper Union, Art Students League, N.A.D., CCNY; studied with, Hans Hofmann. Selected group shows include, Palazzo Graneri, Turin, Italy, 1959, Galerie Beyeler, Basle, Switzerland, 1961, Laing Art Gallery, Newcastle-upon-Tyne, Eng., Marlborough Fine Art, London, Eng., Yale Art Gallery, 1961-62, Mt. Holyoke Coll., 1962, Wadsworth Atheneum, Hartford, Conn., Mary Washington Coll., U. Va., Fredericksburg, Queens Coll., N.Y.C., Howard Wise Gallery, Guild Hall, East Hampton, N.Y., 1963-64, 73-74, 80, 81, Guggenheim Mus., N.Y.C., 1964, 79, Gallery of Modern Art, N.Y.C., 1965, Southampton Coll. of L.I. U., Mus. Modern Art for Am. Embassy, 1963-65, White House traveling exhbn., 1967, selected group shows include, Jewish Mus., N.Y.C., 1967, 70, Mus. Modern Art, N.Y.C., 1969, 77, 78, Palazzo Reale, Milan, 1971, Lakeview Center, Peoria, Ill., 1972, Whitney Mus. Am. Art, N.Y.C., 1973, 75, 77, 78, Phila. Civic Center, 1974, Kunsthalle Dusseldorf and Staatlichen Kunsthalle, Baden-Baden, Germany, 1974-75, Los Angeles County Mus. Art, 1977, Bklyn. Mus., Phila. Coll. Art, 1978, Albright-Knox Art Gallery, Buffalo, Met. Mus. Art, N.Y.C., 1979, Corcoran Gallery Art, Wildenstein Gallery, N.Y.C., 1980, Nassau County Mus. Fine Art, 1981, Grey Art Gallery, N.Y. U., Robert Miller Gallery, N.Y.C., 1982, Contemporary Art Mus., Houston, Carnegie Inst., Pitts., Phila. Coll. Art, 1983, exhibited in solo shows, Betty Parsons Gallery, N.Y.C., 1951, Stable Gallery, N.Y.C., 1955, Martha Jackson Gallery, N.Y.C., 1958, Signa Gallery, East Hampton, 1959, Howard Wise Gallery, 1960, 62, Whitechapel Gallery, London, 1965, Arts Council of Gt. Britain, London, 1966, U. Ala. Gallery, 1967, Marlborough-Gerson Gallery, N.Y.C., 1968, 69, Reese Paley Gallery, San Francisco, 1969, Marlborough Gallery, N.Y.C., 1973, Whitney Mus. Am. Art, 1973, 74, Pace Gallery, N.Y.C., 1977, Susan Hilberry Gallery, Mich., Miami-Dade Community Coll., 1974, Beaver Coll., Gibbes Art Gallery, Corcoran Gallery Art, Washington, 1975, Pa. State Mus. Art, Brandeis U., Janie C. Lee Gallery, Houston, 1978, 81, Pace Gallery, N.Y.C., 1979, 81, Tower Gallery, Southampton, N.Y., 1980, others., Robert Miller Gallery, 1982, retrospective, Houston Mus. Fine Arts, San Francisco Mus. Fine Arts, Mus. Modern Art, N.Y.C., Centre Nat. d'Art et de Culture Georges Pompidou, Paris, 1983-85; represented in permanent collections. Address: The Springs East Hampton NY 11937

KRASNER, LOUIS, concert violinist; b. Cherkassy, Russia, June 21, 1903; came to U.S., 1908, naturalized, 1914; s. Harry and Sara (Lechovetzky) K.; m. Adrienne Galimir, Oct. 10, 1936; children: Elsa, Vivien, Naomi. Diploma, N.E. Conservatory Music, 1922, D.Music (hon.), 1981; postgrad. study, Berlin, Paris, Vienna. Hon. prof. Accademia Filarmonica of Bologna, Italy; prof. violin and chamber music Syracuse U., 1949—, now prof. emeritus; faculty mem. Internat. String Congress, 1960-64; now New Eng. Conservatory Music, Boston; emeritus prof. U. Mass., 1981; vis. prof. U. Miami, Coral Gables, 1976; now mem. faculty Berkshire Music Center; mus. dir. Syracuse Friends Chamber Music; music cons. WCNY-FM (Nat. Pub. Radio); Regent's lectr. U. Cal. at La Jolla, 1971; faculty Inst. Advanced Mus. Studies, Switzerland, 1973; Mem. music panel Nat. Endowment for Arts, 1966—. Condr., U. Symphony Orch., 1955—; participant ann. series chamber music concerts pub. schs., Syracuse; 1st performances of: Berg and Schoenberg concertos, others; chmn., editor 1964 string symposium, Berkshire Music Center, Tanglewood, 1963-64; Editor: String Problems, Players and Paucity, 1965; Concert appearances, Europe and U.S.; soloist with orchs of Vienna, Rome, Berlin, Paris, London, BBC; appeared with, Boston Symphony, N.Y. Philharmonic, 2others; concertmaster, Mpls. Symphony, 1944. Recipient R.I. Gov.'s award for excellence in arts, 1968, Samuel Simons Sanford medal Yale U. Sch. Music, 1983. Mem. Am. String Tchrs. Assn. (founder, past pres. N.Y. chpt., Disting. Service award 1983); mem. Internat. Alban Berg Soc. (v.p. 1983). Home: 1501 Beacon St Brookline MA 02146 *Fulfillment in art lies not in becoming its master but rather in having become its joyous slave.*

KRASNER, SIDNEY D., investment banking executive; b. N.Y.C., Oct. 1, 1932; s. Alex and Beatrice (Friedman) K.; m. Deborah Garber, Mar. 15, 1964; children: Lawrence P., Steven P. B.A., Bklyn. Coll., 1955; postgrad., NYU Grad. Sch. Bus., 1956-59. Vice-pres., Walston & Co., N.Y.C., 1958-69; sr. v.p., dir. H. Hentz & Co., N.Y.C., 1969-73; exec. v.p. Shearson Loeb Rhoades, N.Y.C., 1973-81, Shearson/Am. Express, 1981—; allied mem. N.Y. Stock Exchange. Served with U.S. Army, 1953-55. Mem. Securities Industry Assn. (mktg. com.), N.Y. Sales Mgrs. Assn., Am. Stock Exchange Security Com. Clubs: Masons, Guide. Home: 387 Beech Spring Rd South Orange NJ 07079 Office: Shearson Am Express 636 Morris Turnpike Short Hills NJ 07078

KRASNEY, SAMUEL JOSEPH, metals company executive; b. Cleve., Mar. 26, 1925; s. Benjamin and Frieda (Palutsky) K.; m. Rosalind Friedman, Nov. 19, 1950; children: Nora, Paula, Sherry, Donna. B.B.A., Western Res. U., 1946; J.D., Cleve. Marshall Law Sch., 1950. Partner Res. Audit Co., Cleve., 1946-61; partner Krasney, Polk & Friedman (accountants), Cleve., 1961—; chmn., chief exec. officer, treas. Banner Industries, Inc., Cleve., 1968—; dir. Waxman Industries, Inc., Ohio Savs. Assn.; Bd. dirs. Fabri-Centers Am., Menorah Park, Mt. Sinai Hosp. Mem. Am. Inst. C.P.A.'s, Ohio Soc. C.P.A.'s, Ohio, Cleve. bar assns. Club: Mason. Home: 14 Pepperwood Ln Pepper Pike OH 44124 Office: 24500 Chagrin Blvd Beachwood OH 44122

KRASNO, LOUIS RICHARD, physician; b. Chgo., Sept. 2, 1914; s. Morris and Anne (Kein) K.; m. Elaine Ross, Apr. 20, 1940; 1 son, Richard Michael. B.S., Northwestern U., 1936, M.S., 1937, Ph.D., 1939, M.D., 1945. Intern Wesley Meml. Hosp., Chgo., 1944-45; resident N.Y. Orthopaedic Hosp., 1945-46; practice medicine specializing in internal medicine, Chgo., 1946-51; asst. prof. U. Ill. Med. Sch., Chgo., 1947-51; research U.S. Naval Research Inst., Bethesda, Md., 1951-53; faculty, research U.S. Naval Sch. Aviation Medicine, Pensacola, Fla., 1953-56; dir. clin. research United Airlines, San Francisco, 1957—; asst. clin. prof. medicine Stanford Med. Sch. Served with USN, 1951-57. Fellow Am. Coll. Pharmacology and Therapeutics, Am. Coll. Cardiology, Am. Coll. Angiology, Aerospace Med. Assn., Royal Soc. Health, Am. Geriatrics Soc.; mem. AMA (medal for original research in cardiovascular disease 1950), Calif. Med. Assn., Soc. for Exptl. Biology and Medicine, Assn. Mil.

Surgeons, Am. Heart Assn., Internat. Coll. Angiology, San Francisco C. of C., Sigma Xi. Clubs: Bohemian, Family, Olympic (San Francisco). Developer prototype present oxygen mask used in mil. and comml. aviation, method for adminstrn. aerosolized medication in respiratory diseases. Office: United Airlines Internat Airport San Francisco CA 94128 *I was taught that success was attainment of that "truth" which enhances the quality of life for all peoples.*

KRASNOFF, ABRAHAM, filter company executive; b. Newark, June 7, 1920; s. Harry and Jennie K.; m. Julienne Hallen, Sept. 20, 1945; 1 son, Eric. B.S. in Acctg., NYU, 1949. With Pall Corp., Glen Cove, N.Y., 1951—; pres., chief exec. officer Pall Corp, Glen Cove, N.Y., 1969—; mem. exec. council Conf. Bd. Trustee L.I.U.; mem. Glen Cove Planning Bd., 1955-70, also chmn.; treas., bd. dirs. Community Hosp., Glen Cove, 1960—; bd. dirs. Glen Cove Boys Club, 1976—. Served with U.S. Army, 1942-45. Recipient numerous local Man of Yr. awards. Mem. Glen Cove Neighborhood Assn. Office: Pall Corp 30 Sea Cliff Ave Glen Cove NY 11542

KRASOVEC, FRANK PAUL, investment company executive; b. Cleve., Nov. 23, 1943; s. John Frank and Margaret Helen K.; m. Beverly Ann Almen, Aug. 29, 1963; children: Kellie Ann, Mark Paul. B.B.A., Ohio U., 1965, M.B.A., 1966. Pres. Rust Investment Co., Austin, Tex., 1974—, Rust Enterprises, San Antonio, 1976—; v.p. Telesystems Internat. Corp., Austin, 1974—; mng. gen. ptnr. Rust Group, Austin, 1979—; vice chmn. Tescorp Inc., Houston, 1980—; dir. Evergreen Capital, Cleve., Buckhorn, Columbus, Ohio, Prime Cable Corp., Austin; chmn. bd., organizer Alliance Bank, Austin, 1982—. Bd. dirs. Palmer Drug Abuse Program, Austin, 1977—, Paramount Theatre-La Patron, Austin, 1980—. Mem. Young Pres.' Orgn. (chmn. membership 1982—). Club: Westwood Country (bd. dirs. 1980-82). Home: 2600 Wooldridge Dr Austin TX 78703 Office: Rust Investment Co 1300 Norwood Tower 114 W 7th St Austin TX 78701

KRASTIN, KARL, educator; b. Toledo, June 29, 1910; s. Arnold and Mella (Pollak) K.; m. Barbara Bailey Henderson, Oct. 7, 1971; children by previous marriage—Frances Melanie, Charlotte Emily. A.B., Western Res. U., 1931, LL.B., 1934; J.S.D., Yale, 1955. Bar: Ohio bar 1934. Practice in, Cleve., 1934-40; Sterling fellow Yale Law Sch., 1946-48; mem. faculty U. Fla., 1948-63, prof. law, 1954-63; dean Coll. Law, U. Toledo, 1963-76; prof. law Nova U., Fort Lauderdale, Fla., 1976—; Adviser Fla. Nuclear Devel. Commn., 1961. Contbr. to legal publs. Past bd. dirs. Toledo Ct. Diagnostic and Treatment Center, Advocates Basic Legal Equality. Served to maj. AUS, 1941-46. Mem. ACLU, Soc. Benchers (Case-Western Res. U.), Order of Coif. Home: 11635 Orange Blossom Ln Boca Raton FL 33433

KRASTS, AIVARS, energy company executive; b. Riga, Latvia, Apr. 8, 1938; came to U.S., 1948, naturalized, 1956; s. Janis and Milda K.; m. Linda Compton Reich, Aug. 10, 1962; children: Evan Compton, Kerry Elizabeth. A.B., Middlebury Coll., 1960; M.B.A., U. Chgo., 1962. With Conoco, Inc., 1962—, gen. mgr. coordinating and planning dept., 1978-80, v.p., 1980—. Contbr. articles to profl. publs. Served with Med. Service Corps USAR, 1962-68. Mem. N.Am. Soc. Corp. Planning, Assn. Corp. Growth, Planning Execs. Inst. Office: 1007 Market St Wilmington DE 19898

KRATHWOHL, DAVID READING, educator; b. Chgo., May 14, 1921; adopted by and Marie (Reimold) K.; m. Helen Jean Abney, Dec. 20, 1943; children: James D. (dec. Nov. 1967), David A., Ruth Anne, Kristin Jeanne. B.S., U. Chgo., 1943, M.S., 1947, Ph.D., 1953. Asst. dir. unit on evaluation Bur. Ednl. Research, Coll. Edn., U. Ill., 1949-55, instr., 1949-53; asst. prof., 1953-55; asso. prof. Mich. State U., 1955-58, prof., 1958-65, research coordinator, 1955-63; chmn. Psychol. Found. Edn., 1960-63; dir. Bur. Ednl. Research, 1963-65; dean Sch. Edn. Syracuse (N.Y.) U., 1965-76; prof. Sch. Edn., Syracuse (N.Y.) U., 1965—, Hannah Hammond prof. edn., 1982—; chmn. bd. trustees Eastern Regional Inst. for Edn., 1966-71. Author: (with others) Cognitive Domain, 1956, Affective Domain, 1964. Served with USAAF, 1943-46. Fellow Center for Advanced Study in Behavioral Scis., 1980-81. Fellow Am. Psychol. Assn. (pres. ednl. psychology div.); mem. Am. Ednl. Research Assn. (pres.). Home: 9 Thornwood Ln Fayetteville NY 13066 Office: Sch Edn Syracuse Univ Syracuse NY 13210

KRATOCHVIL, L(OUIS) GLEN, lawyer; b. Highland, Wis., Oct. 11, 1922; s. John A. and Emma (Pusch) K.; m. Evelyn Gregory, Sept. 12, 1946; 1 son, Louis Glen. LL.B., J.D., U. Wis., 1951. Bar: Wis. bar 1951, Tex. bar 1952, U.S. Supreme Ct 1956. Landman Shell Oil Co., Houston, 1951-52; asso. firm Murphy & Crystal, Houston, 1953-55; asst. U.S. atty., So. Dist. Tex., 1955-57; partner firm Schirmeyer & Kratochvil, Houston, 1957—. Pres. Young Republican Club U. Wis., 1950; pres. McGregor Terrace Civic Club, Houston, 1954. Served as pilot USNR, World War II; PTO. Mem. Am., Tex., Wis., Fed., Houston bar assns., Maritime Law Assn., Wis. Alumni Assn. Houston (pres. 1972—), Phi Alpha Delta (chief justice 1950). Clubs: Brazos River (treas. 1970—), Lions (pres. 1955). Home: 302 Kickerillo Dr Houston TX 77079 Office: Suite 340 9601 Katy Freeway Houston TX 77024

KRATT, ROBERT ARTHUR, credit union exec.; b. Hancock, Mich., Nov. 1, 1924; s. Arthur Michael and Margaret (Finnegan) K.; m. Elizabeth Jane Schmitt, Feb. 3, 1951; children—Claresa, John, Barbara, Susan, Katherine. B.A., St. Ambrose Coll., Iowa, 1951. Pres., gen. mgr. Internat. Harvester Farmall Employees Credit Union, Internat. Harvester Co., Rock Island, Ill., 1953—; dir. Cuna Mut. Ins. Soc., Madison, Wis., 1966—, chmn. bd., 1971—; chmn. Cumis Ins. Soc., Madison, 1969—; nat. dir. Cuna Internat., Inc.; dir. Ill. Credit Union League, Oak Brook. Served with USNR, 1944-46; PTO. Roman Catholic. Club: Kiwanian. Home: 2212 E 45th St Davenport IA 52807 Office: PO Box 218 Rock Island IL 61201

KRATZER, GUY LIVINGSTON, surgeon; b. Gratz, Pa., Apr. 24, 1911; s. Clarence U. and Carrie E. (Schwalm) K.; m. Kathryn H. Miller, Jan. 27, 1940; 1 son, Guy Miller. Student, Muhlenberg Coll., 1928-31; M.D., Temple U., 1935; M.S., U. Minn., 1945. Diplomate: Am. Bd. Proctology. Intern Harrisburg Hosp., 1935-36; fellow proctology, surgery Mayo Clinic, 1942-46, fellow surgery, 1949-50; asso. surgeon Pottsville Hosp., 1936-41; asso. proctologist Allentown (Pa.) Hosp., 1946—, mem. tumor clinic, 1955—, chief, dept. proctology, 1958—; mem. cons. staff Sacred Heart Hosp., 1946—, chief dept. colon and rectal surgery, 1974—; cons. proctologist Quakertown Community and Good Samaritan hosps.; clin. asso. prof. surgery Milton S. Hershey Med. Center, Pa. State U., 1972-75, clin. prof., 1975—, cons., 1975—. Pres. Lehigh Valley chpt., bd. dirs. Am. Cancer Soc. Fellow A.C.S. (pres. S.E. Pa. 1965-66), Am. Proctologic Soc., Internat. Coll. Surgeons; mem. Brazilian Proctologic Soc., A.A.A.S., Internat. Acad. Medicine, Shelter House Soc., Am. Med. Writers Assn., Pa. Proctologic Soc. (past pres.), Pa. Med. Soc., Am. Med. Authors, Lehigh Valley Med. Soc. (past pres.), Allentown C. of C. (gov.). Club: Lion. Address: 1447 Hamilton St Allentown PA 18102 *Hard work to provide experience, personal discipline to encourage efficiency and investigation, an open mind to ensure constant improvement, the inspiration provided by faith in a Supreme Being, and adherence to moral principles are the factors which helped me achieve success.*

KRAUS, ALFRED PAUL, educator, physician; b. Vienna, Austria, June 24, 1916; came to U.S., 1938, naturalized, 1943; s. Oscar and Marianna (Singer) K.; m. Lorraine Marquardt, May 7, 1944; children—G. Thomas, Alfred Paul. M.D., U. Chgo., 1941. Diplomate: Am. Bd. Internal Medicine. Intern Michael Reese Hosp., Chgo., 1941-42, asst. resident internal medicine, 1942, resident internal medicine, 1943-44, resident dept. hematology research, 1948; practice medicine specializing in internal medicine, 1946—; ward physician, chief hematology sect. VA Hosp., Tuscaloosa, Ala., 1949-50; asst. chief hematology sect. VA Med. Teaching Group, Kennedy Hosp., Memphis, 1950-52; cons. Bapt. Meml., St. Joseph's, St. Francis, Methodist, Le Bonheur, Children's hosps.; asst. prof. medicine U. Tenn. Med. Sch., Memphis, 1953-57, asso. prof., 1957-63, prof. medicine, 1964—, chmn. div. hematology, 1968—; vis. asst. prof. hematology U. Indonesia-Calif. Med. Edn. Project, 1955-56. Mem. A.M.A., Am. Fedn. Clin. Research, A.C.P., Internat., Am. socs. hematology, Memphis C. of C. Home: 1597 Peabody Ave Memphis TN 38104 Office: 800 Madison Ave Memphis TN 38163

KRAUS, ALVIN EUGENE, casualty insurance consultant; b. Runge, Tex., Aug. 7, 1912; s. Richard Walter and Maggie May (Wood) K.; m. Emmie McManus Harwood, Nov. 7, 1942; children—Eugenia Emmie, Karen Elizabeth. A.A., Schreiner Coll., 1936; postgrad., George Washington U., 1954. With Govt. Employees Cos., 1939—; with Criterion Ins. Co., Washington, 1961—, pres., 1966-76, chmn. bd., 1976—; cons. GEICO Corp., Washington, 1976—, also hon. dir. Recipient Disting. Ser. award Schreiner Coll., 1936. Mem. Newcomen Soc. N. Am. Republican. Episcopalian. Club: Kenwood Golf and Country. Home: 9026 Bronson Dr Potomac MD 20854 Office: GEICO Plaza Washington DC 20076

KRAUS, CHARLES FRANCIS, tax executive; b. Syracuse, N.Y., Feb. 28, 1929; s. Carl Killian K. and Freda Josephine (Botz); children: Steven, Marilyn, Lawrence, Lorraine Kraus Reeves. B.B.A., LeMoyne Coll., Syracuse, 1952. C.P.A., N.Y. With McDermott, Inc., New Orleans, 1980—, v.p. tax adminstrn., 1982—. Served to lt. (j.g.) U.S. Navy, 1952-55. Republican. Roman Catholic. Office: McDermott Inc 1010 Common St New Orleans LA 70160

KRAUS, LILI, pianist, educator; b. Budapest, Mar. 4, 1908; d. Victor and Irene (Bak) K.; m. Otto Mandl, Oct. 31, 1930 (dec. Aug. 1956); children—Ruth Maria (Mrs. Fergus Pope), Michael Otto Patrick. Student of, Zoltan Kodaly, Bela Bartok, Royal Acad. Music, Budapest, 1915-22, tchrs. diploma, 1925; student of, Steuermann, New Acad., Vienna, Austria, 1925-27, M.A., 1927, Artur Schnabel, Berlin, Germany, 1930-34; Mus.D. (hon.), Chgo. Mus. Coll., Roosevelt U., 1969, Williams Coll., 1975; D.H.L., Tex. Christian U., 1980. Lectr. various univs., U.S. and Europe; head piano dept. Cape Town U., S. Africa, 1949-50; artist-in-residence Tex. Christian U., 1967—; adjudicator Van Cliburn Internat. Piano Competition, Tex. Pianist with orchs. in, Europe, 1926—, Dutch East Indies, 1940; formed: Kraus-Goldberg duo with violinist Szymon Goldberg, 1930's; pianist in, Australia and New Zealand, 1945—, Europe, N. and S. Am., Asia, 1949—, world tours, appearances with major orchs. and all major European music festivals, 1925—, gave concert in, Eng.'s Canterbury Cathedral, 1st concert ever performed in Brasilia (Brazil); appeared with, Salzburg Chamber Orch., Royal Moroccan Mozart Festival, orchestral concert honoring Bertrand Russell's 90th birthday, Royal Festival Hall, London, first to play all 25 Mozart piano concerti in, N.Y., 1966-67; premiered newly-discovered: Schubert Grazer Fantasy, CBS-TV, 1969; recorded all 25 Mozart piano concerti and complete Mozart piano sonatas for, CBS; now recording complete Schubert piano repertoire; Author: The Complete Original Cadenzas by W.A. Mozart for His Solo Piano Concertos. Named hon. citizen New Zealand, late 1940's; decorated Cross of Honor for Sci. and Art, Austria). Hon. mem. Music Tchrs. Assn. Calif., Sigma Alpha Iota. Japanese prisoner-of-war, 1941-45. Office: care Alix Williamson 1860 Broadway New York NY 10023

KRAUSE, BENJAMIN DAVID, stock exchange exec.; b. Balt., Nov. 2, 1936; s. Samuel and Lena (Marget) K.; m. Sandra Siegel, July 12, 1959; children—Steven, Suzanne, Roger. B.S., U. Md., 1959; LL.B., George Washington U., 1963. Bar: N.Y. bar. Individual practice law, 1965-67; with SEC, 1968-70, Am. Stock Exchange, 1970—, now sr. v.p. securities div.; mem. adv. com. SEC, 1973-74. Mem. Sch. Bd. Nominating Com., 1979-80. Recipient cert. of appreciation SEC. Mem. Am. Bar Assn., N.Y. Bar Assn. Office: American Stock Exchange 86 Trinity Pl New York NY 10006 *

KRAUSE, BERNARD LEO, sonic artist, composer, audio electronics firm executive, bio-acoustician; b. Detroit, Dec. 8, 1938; s. Sydney Arthur and Guilda (Warshawsky) K. B.A. in History, U. Mich., 1960; Ph.D. in Creative Arts, Union Grad. Sch. West, 1981. Mem. The Weavers, N.Y.C., 1963-64; pres. Parasound, Inc., San Francisco, 1968—; lectr. on synthesizers, animal field rec., electronic music, art and tech. Composer, sonic artist on: albums Nonesuch Guide to Electronic Music, 1968, Ragnarok, 1968, In a Wild Sanctuary, 1969, Gandharva, 1971, All Good Men, 1973, Citadels of Mystery, 1979, Revised Nonesuch Guide to Electronic Music, 1981; author: short film Legend Days Are Over, 1973 (Atlanta Film Festival Gold medal 1973); contbr. chpt. on electronic music to: Making Music, 1983. Mem. Am. Fedn. Musicians, AFTRA, Nat. Acad. Rec. Arts and Scis., Composers and Lyricists Guild Am. Office: 680 Beach St Suite 414 San Francisco CA 94109

KRAUSE, CHARLES FREDERICK, lawyer; b. Chgo., Aug. 28, 1931; s. Edgar H. and Edna L. (Pflug) K.; m. Joan Ames, Oct. 30, 1968; children: Kent C., Paul E., Jennifer A. B.A., Valparaiso U., 1957; LL.B., Rutgers U., 1960. Bar: N.Y. 1961. Mem. firm Speiser, Krause & Madole, N.Y.C., Washington, Calif., 1961—; lectr. in field; dir. Columbian Mutual Life Ins. Co. Co-author: Aviation Tort Law, 3 vols., 1980, The American Law of Torts, 1983; mem. bd. editors: N.Y. State Bar Jour.; contbr. articles to profl. publs. Served to capt. USMCR, 1952-56. Mem. ABA, Am. Trial Lawyers Assn., Am. Coll. Trial Lawyers. Republican. Clubs: Wings, Union League, Sky (N.Y.C.). Office: 200 Park Ave New York NY 10166

KRAUSE, CHARLES JOSEPH, otolaryngologist; b. Des Moines, Apr. 21, 1937; s. William H. and Ruby I. (Hitz) K.; m. Barbara Ann Steelman, June 14, 1962; children—Sharon, John, Ann. B.A., State U. Iowa, 1959, M.D., 1962. Diplomate: Am. Bd. Otolaryngology. Intern Phila. Gen. Hosp., 1962-63; resident in surgery U. Iowa, 1965-66, resident in otolaryngology, 1966-69; fellow dept. plastic surgery Marien Hosp., Stuttgart, W. Ger., 1970; asst. prof. otolaryngology U. Iowa, 1969-72, asso. prof., 1972-75, vice chmn. dept. otolaryngology, 1973-77, prof., 1975-77; prof., chmn. dept. otolaryngology U. Mich. Med. Sch., Ann Arbor, 1977—. Author book in field; contbr. chpts. to books, articles to profl. jours. Served to capt. USAF, 1963-65. Fellow Am. Soc. Head and Neck Surgery (Council 1980-83, chmn. research com. 1980-83); Mem. AMA, Am. Acad. Ophthalmology and Otolaryngology, Am. Acad. Facial Plastic and Reconstructive Surgery (regional v.p. 1977-80, chmn. research com. 1977-80, pres. 1981-82), A.C.S. (adv. council otolaryngology 1979-83), Assn. Head and Neck Oncologists Gt. Britain (corr. mem.), Am. Assn. Cosmetic Surgeons, Assn. Research in Otolaryngology, Washtenaw County Med. Soc. (exec. com. 1979-82), Mich. State Med. Soc., Mich. Otolaryngol. Soc., Assn. Acad. Depts. Otolaryngology, Soc. Univ. Otolaryngologists, Walter P. Work Soc., Am. Cancer Soc. (med. adv. com. Washtenaw County unit), Am. Laryngol., Rhinol. and Otol. Soc., Am. Laryngol. Assn., Centurions of Deafness Research Found. Republican. Presbyterian. Home: 3100 Hunting Valley Dr Ann Arbor MI 48104 Office: Dept Otolaryngology U Mich Hosp Ann Arbor MI 48109

KRAUSE, CHESTER LEE, publishing company executive; b. Iola, Wis., Dec. 16, 1923; s. Carl and Cora E. (Neil) K. Grad. high sch. In contracting bus, 1946-52. Pres. Krause Publs., Inc., Iola, publishing, 1952—; dir. First State Bank of Iola. Co-editor: Standard Catalog of World Coins. Mem. Assay Commn., 1961; chmn. bldg. fund drive Iola Hosp., 1975-80; Mem. Village Bd., 1963-72. Served with AUS, 1943-46. Mem. Am. Numis. Assn. (medal of merit, Farren Zerbe award), Central States Numis. Assn. (medal of merit), Canadian Numis. Assn. Club: Lion. Home: 290 E Iola St Iola WI 54945 Office: 700 E State St Iola WI 54945 *To publish on time, all the time.*

KRAUSE, EDWARD WALTER, university athletic director; b. Chgo., Feb. 2, 1913; s. Walter and Thersa (Krauklis) K.; m. Elizabeth Linden, Aug. 27, 1938; children: Edward Walter, Mary Elise, Philip Charles. Grad., U. Notre Dame, 1934. Athletic dir., coach St. Mary's Coll., Winona, Minn., 1934-39; line coach Holy Cross Coll., 1939-42, U. Notre Dame, 1942-44, 46-48, head basketball coach, 1942-44, 46-51, asst. athletic dir., 1948-49, athletic dir., 1949—; dir. 1st United Life Ins. Co.; with history and tech. dept. Smithsonian Instn. Pres. Community Chest; chmn. South Bend Recreation Bd.; vice chmn. Pan-Am. Games.; Bd. dirs. United Fund, NCCJ. Served to 1st lt. USMCR, 1944-46. Named knight of Malta, 1972; inducted into Nat. Basketball Hall of Fame, 1976; named to honors ct. Nat. Football Found. and Hall of Fame; recipient Man of Year award Walter Camp Hall of Fame, 1977, Spirit of Hope award City of Hope Nat. Med. Center, 1977, Sportsman of Year award MBS Golf Tournament, Akron, Ohio, 1978; Citizen of Yr. award 4th degree K.C., 1981; Man of Yr. awards Nat. Football Found., 1981, Chgo. Mayor Jane Byrne, 1981, Monogram Club and Alumni Assn., Notre Dame U., 1981, Knights of Lithuania, 1981. Mem. Am. Legion. Roman Catholic. Clubs: K.C. (4 deg.), Eagle., Country. Office: U Notre Dame Notre Dame IN 46556

KRAUSE, ERNST HENRY, aerospace industry executive; b. Milw., May 2, 1913; s. Ernst and Martha (Strege) K.; m. Constance Fraser, June 29, 1939 (dec. Nov. 1972); children—Margaret Bird (Mrs. Keith McCormick), Katharine Louise, Carol Marjorie (Mrs. Erik Sorensm), Susan Fraser; m. Betty Lou Davis, Apr. 7, 1974. B.S. in Elec. Engring, U. Wis., 1934, M.S. in Physics, 1935, Ph.D., 1938. With Naval Research Lab., Washington, 1938-54, asso. dir. research, 1951-54; dir. research Lockheed Aircraft Corp., Van Nuys, Calif., 1954-55; pres., chmn. Systems Research Corp., Van Nuys, 1955-56; v.p., dir. Aeronutronic Systems, Inc., 1956-59; dir. tech. staff Aeronutronic div. Ford Motor Co., 1959-62; with Aerospace Corp., El Segundo, Calif., 1962—, sr. v.p. devel., 1968-78, mgmt. and tech. cons., 1978—. Pres. World Affairs Council of Inland So. Calif., 1968-69. Recipient Distinguished Civilian Service award USN, 1956. Fellow Am. Phys. Soc.; asso. fellow Am. Inst. Aeros. and Astronautics; mem. Sigma Xi, Tau Beta Pi. Home: 1919 Glenwood Ln Newport Beach CA 92660

KRAUSE, GEORGE, photographer, educator; b. Phila., Jan. 24, 1937; s. George Krause, IV and Sylvia (Canter) K.; m. Patsy Johnson, Nov. 1959 (div. 1980); children: George VI, Kathryn Jane. Student, Phila. Coll. Art. Profl. photographer; dir. Venice Biennial Photography Workshops, summer 1979. Author, artist: monograph George Krause, 1972; portfolios Saints & Martyrs, 1976, 1960-70, 1980. Served with Intelligence Corps U.S. Army, 1957-59. Recipient prix de Rome Am. Acad., Italy, 1976-79; Fulbright-Hays fellow Inst. Internat. Edn., Spain, 1963; Guggenheim fellow, Europe, 1967-76; grantee Nat. Endowment for Arts, India, Italy, 1972-79. Home: 420 E 25th St Houston TX 77008 Office: U Houston Main Campus 348 FA Cullen Blvd Houston TX 77004

KRAUSE, HARRY DIETER, legal educator; b. Görlitz, Germany, Apr. 23, 1932; came to U.S., 1951, naturalized, 1954; s. Renatus and Ellen (Abel-Musgrave) K.; m. Eva Maria Disselnkötter, Aug. 30, 1957; children: Philip Renatus, Thomas Walther, Peter Herbert. Student, Freie Universität Berlin, 1950-51; B.A., U. Mich., 1954, J.D., 1958. Bar: Mich. 1959, D.C. 1959, Ill. 1963, U.S. Supreme Ct 1963. With firm Covington & Burling, 1958-60; with Ford Motor Co., Dearborn, Mich., 1960-63; asst. prof. to prof. law Coll. Law, U. Ill., Champaign, 1963-82, Alumni Disting. prof. law, 1982—; vis. prof. law U. Mich., Ann Arbor, 1981—; reporter Uniform Parentage Act, 1969-73, Rev. Uniform Adoption Act, 1979—, Nat. Conf. Commrs. on Uniform State Laws; rapporteur Internat. Acad. Comparative Law, Uppsala, 1966, Teheran, 1974, Budapest, 1978, Caracas, 1983; cons. on family law and social legislation to numerous fed. and state legis., jud. and exec. commns., coms. and agys. Author: Illegitimacy: Law and Social Policy, 1971, Family Law: Cases and Materials, 1976, 2d edit., 1983, Kinship Relations, 1976, Family Law in a Nutshell, 1977, Child Support in America: The Legal Perspective, 1981; Bd. editors: Mich. Law Rev, 1957-58, Family Law Quar, 1971—; adv. bd. editors: Am. Bar Assn. Jour, 1973-79; contbr. articles to profl. jours. Served with U.S. Army, 1954-56. Guggenheim fellow, 1969-70; asso. center Advanced Study U. Ill., 1970, 79; Fulbright prof. U. Bonn, Germany, 1976-77; vis. asso. Centre Socio-Legal Studies Oxford U., 1977; German Marshall Fund U.S. fellow, 1977-78. Mem. Am. Law Inst., Am. Bar Assn. (past mem. council sect. family law, com. chmn.), Ill. Bar Assn. (past mem. council sect. on family law, internat. law), Am. Assn. Comparative Study of Law (dir. 1980—), Gesellschaft für Rechtsvergleichung, Internat. Soc. Family Law (v.p. 1973-77, exec. council 1977—), Deutsch-Amerikanische Juristenvereinigung, LAWASIA Assn., Order of Coif. Home: 903 Silver St Urbana IL 61801 Office: Coll Law U Ill Champaign IL 61820

KRAUSE, KENNETH WARREN, financial corporation executive; b. Wausau, Wis., July 4, 1922; s. Walter William and Bertha Marie (Kasten) K.; m. Jene R. Markowitz, Aug. 3, 1946. Student, U. So. Calif., Navy V-12 Program. Escrow officer Bank of Am., Los Angeles, 1946-48; loan officer Wilshire Mortgage Corp. and Wilshire Fed. Savs. & Loan Assn., Los Angeles, 1948-63; exec. v.p. Brentwood Mortgage Corp. (also known as Rexford Nat. Corp.), Los Angeles, 1963-75; exec. v.p. adminstrn. First Charter Fin. Corp., Beverly Hills., Calif., 1975—. Served with USMC, 1940-46; PTO. Office: First Charter Financial Corp 9465 Wilshire Blvd Beverly Hills CA 90212

KRAUSE, LAVERNE ERICKSON, artist, painter, printmaker; b. Portland, Oreg., July 21, 1924; d. James Martin and Hannah (Wrolstad) Erickson; m. Lebrecht Gerhard Krause, June 23, 1946 (div. June 1960); children: Max Martin, Darcia Elaine, Jay Gunnar. B.S., U. Oreg., 1946. Instr. Mus. Art Sch., 1960-65; vis. asst. prof. U. Oreg., 1966, asso. prof., 1969-73, prof., 1973—; vis. asso. prof. La. State U., summer 1970. Painter, printmaker one-woman exhbns., Portland Art Mus., 1952, 58, 73, Portland State U., 1967, U. Oreg. Mus. Art, 1968, 82, Woodside Gallery, Seattle, 1965, Salt Lake Art Center, 1966, Fountain Gallery Portland, 1967, 69, 74, 78, 80, 82, La. State U., 1970, Deichmanske Bibliotek, Oslo, 1974, Miss. State U., 1978; represented in permanent collections, Portland Art Mus., Seattle Art Mus., Salt Lake Art Center, U. Oreg., La. State U., Bank of Calif., 1st Nat. Bank of Oreg., U.S. Nat. Bank of Oreg., Haseltine Collection N.W. Art, U.

Wash., Reed Coll., Deichmanske Bibliotek, Oslo, Western Bank Corp., Los Angeles, Portland State U., Oreg. State Capitol, Lower Columbia Coll., Rainier Bank, Seattle, Orbanco, Wacker Siltronic Corp. Mem. Gov. Oreg. Planning Council for Arts and Humanities, 1965-67. Recipient purchase awards N.W. Printmaker, 1954, Seattle Art Mus., 1960, 1964; prize for painting Oreg. Centennial, 1959, Portland Art Mus., 1969; Faculty Research award U. Oreg., 1970-71, 72-73, 77-78; Purchase award Oreg. Printmakers, 1982; State of Oreg. Gov.'s Arts award, 1980; Wurlitzer Found. grantee, 1981. Mem. Artists Equity Assn. (pres. Oreg. chpt. 1954-55, 66-68, nat. pres. 1969-70). Home: 3295 W 16th Ave Eugene OR 97402

KRAUSE, LAWRENCE BERLE, economist; b. Detroit, Dec. 8, 1929; s. Paul Henry and Lena (Blair) K.; m. Sallye Kirstein, Dec. 20, 1953; children: Leonard Blair, Jason Andrew. A.B., U. Mich., 1951, M.A., 1952; Ph.D., Harvard U., 1957. Asst. prof. Yale U., New Haven, 1958-63; sr. fellow The Brookings Instn., Washington, 1963-67, 69—; sr. staff Council Econ. Advisors, Washington, 1967-69; cons. to bus. on internat. econ. conditions; lectr. Sch. Advanced Internat. Studies, Johns Hopkins U. Co-editor: Britain's Economic Performance, 1980, U.S. Economic Policy Toward the ASEAN Countries, 1983. Served to 1st lt. USMC, 1953-55. Fellow Social Sci. Research Council; mem. Am. Econ. Assn. Jewish. Home: 3361 Stephenson Pl NW Washington DC 20015 Office: Brookings Instn 1775 Massachusetts Ave NW Washington DC 20036

KRAUSE, MANFRED OTTO, physicist; b. Stuttgart, Germany, Mar. 11, 1931; came to U.S., 1960, naturalized, 1970; s. Friedrich Bernhard and Friedel Ernstine (Mann) K.; m. Josephine Winifred Cammer, Dec. 26, 1963. B.S., Technische Universitat Stuttgart, 1954, diploma in physics, 1957, Ph.D., 1960. Sr. physicist Wm. H. Johnston Labs., Inc., Balt., 1960-63; sr. scientist Oak Ridge Nat. Lab., 1963—; prof. d'échange U. Paris, 1975. Contbr. articles on electron, charge and x-ray spectrometry to sci. publs., chpts. to books. Alexander von Humboldt awardee, 1975-76. Fellow Am. Phys. Soc.; mem. AAAS, Smithsonian Instn., Natural History Soc., Audubon Soc. Discoverer x-ray spectrometry based on photoelectric effect, 1971. Home: 125 Baltimore Dr Oak Ridge TN 37830 Office: PO Box X Oak Ridge TN 37830

KRAUSE, MORTON A., auto parts chain executive; b. 1932. Vice-pres., dir. Pep Boys Manny Moe & Jack, Phila., 1973-82, pres., chief exec. officer, 1982—. Address: Pep Boys Manny Moe and Jack 3111 W Allegheny Ave Philadelphia PA 19132 *

KRAUSE, RICHARD MICHAEL, immunologist, educator, government official; b. Marietta, Ohio, Jan. 4, 1925; s. Ellis L. and Jennie (Waterman) K. B.A., Marietta Coll., 1947, D.Sc. (hon.), 1978; M.D. Case Western Res. U, 1952; D.Sc. (hon.), U. Rochester, 1979, Med. Coll. Ohio, Toledo, 1981. Research fellow dept. preventive medicine Case Western Res. U., 1950-51; intern Ward Med. Service, Barnes Hosp., St. Louis, 1952-53, asst. resident, 1953-54; asst. physician to hosp. Rockefeller Inst., 1954-57, asst. prof., asso. physician to hosp., 1957-61, asso. prof., asso. physician to hosp., 1961-62; prof. epidemiology Sch. Medicine, Washington U., St. Louis, 1962-66, asso. prof. medicine, 1962-65, prof. medicine, 1965-66; asso. prof., physician to hosp. Rockefeller U., 1966-68, prof., sr. physician, 1968-75, dir., 1974-75, Nat. Inst. Allergy and Infectious Diseases, NIH, HEW, Bethesda, Md., 1975—; USPHS surgeon, 1975-77, asst. surgeon gen., 1977—; Bd. dirs. Mo.-St. Louis Heart Assn., 1962-66, mem. research com., 1963-66; mem. exec. com. council on rheumatic fever and congenital heart disease Am. Heart Assn., 1963-66, chmn. council research study com., 1963-66, mem. assn. research com., 1963-66, mem. policy com., 1966-70; mem. commn. streptococcal and staphylococcal diseases U.S. Armed Forces Epidemiol. Bd., 1963-72, dep. dir., 1968-72; bd. dirs. N.Y. Heart Assn., 1967-73, chmn. adv. council on research, 1969-71, mem. dirs. council, 1973-75; cons., mem. coccal expert com. WHO, 1967—; mem. steering com. Biomed. Sci. Scientific Working Group, WHO, 1978; mem. infectious disease adv. com. Nat. Inst. Allergy and Infectious Disease, NIH, 1970-74; bd. dirs. Royal Soc. Medicine Found., Inc., 1971-77, treas., 1973-75; bd. dirs. Allergy and Asthma Found. Am., 1976-77, Lupus Found. Am., 1977—. Asso. editor: Jour. Immunology, 1963-71; sect. editor: Viral and Microbial Immunology, 1974-75; editor: Jour. Exptl. Medicine, 1973-75; adv. editor, 1976—; mem. editorial bd.: Bacteriological Revs, 1969-73, Infection and Immunity, 1970-78, Immunochemistry, 1973, Clin. Immunology and Immunopathology, 1976, 1978—; Contbr. numerous articles to profl. jours. Served with U.S. Army, 1944-46. Decorated Gumhuria medal, Egypt; recipient Disting. Service medal HEW, 1979; C. William O'Neal Disting. Am. Service award. Mem. U.S. Nat. Acad. Scis., Inst. Medicine, Assn. Am. Physicians, Am. Acad. Allergy, Am. Soc. Biol. Chemists, Am. Soc. Clin. Investigation, Am. Assn. Immunologists, Am. Soc. Microbiology, Harvey Soc., Am. Venereal Diseases Soc., Am. Coll. Allergists, AAAS, Infectious Diseases Soc. Am., Royal Soc. Medicine, Am. Rheumatism Assn., Practitioner's Soc. N.Y., Am. Thoracic Soc., Am. Epidemiol. Soc. Clubs: Century Assn. (N.Y.C.); Cosmos (Washington). Research on pathogenesis and epidemiology of streptococcal diseases; immunochem. studies on streptococcal antigens; immunogenetics; recognition of rabbit antibodies with molecular uniformity, genetics of immune response. Home: 10 West Dr Bethesda MD 20814 Office: NIH/NIAID Public Health Service Bethesda MD 20205

KRAUSE, ROBERT FREDERICK, paper co. exec.; b. Warren, Ohio, May 10, 1926; s. Eugene L. and Gladys J. (Williams) K.; m. Dorothy Alden Wilce, Apr. 14, 1950; children—Anne Woodworth, Susan Alden, Robert Frederick. B.Sc., Miami U., Oxford, Ohio, 1947; postgrad., Ohio State U., 1949. Sales rep., then sales mgr. Ohio Boxboard Co., Cleve., 1952-58; successively gen. mgr. (Cleve. plant), sales mgr. Mid East area, v.p.-area mgr., 1959-77; pres., chief exec. officer, dir. Somerville Belkin Industries Ltd., Mississauga, Ont., Can., 1978—; pres., dir. Mastico Industries Ltd., 1978—; dir. Neff Folding Box Co. Served as lt. (j.g.) USNR, 1944-46. Mem. Can. Paper Box Mfrs. Assn. Republican. Congregationalist. Club: Mississauga Golf and Country. Home: 1483 Spring Rd Mississauga ON L5J 1M8 Canada Office: 2121 Argentia Rd Suite 403 Mississauga ON L5N 1V8 Canada

KRAUSE, RONALD J., financial corporation executive; b. 1927; married. Student, Loyola U., 1957-61. With E-Z Packaging Corp., 1957-61, Internat. Assemblex, 1961-62; v.p. Merc. Fin. Co., 1962-64; pres. Southwestern Fin. Corp., 1965-71, Comml. Discount Corp., 1972-75; pres. subs. Comml. Corp., N.Y.C., 1975—, exec. v.p., then vice chmn., now pres., dir. Assoc. Corp. N.AM. Office: Assocs Corp N Am 1 Gulf and Western Plaza New York NY 10023 *

KRAUSE, WALTER, economics educator, consultant; b. Portland, Oreg., Jan. 12, 1919; s. Ben and Pauline (March) K. B.A., U. Oreg., 1942, M.A., 1943; A.M., Harvard U., 1944, Ph.D., 1945. Prof. econs. U. Tex., Austin, 1945-47, Dartmouth Coll., Hanover, N.H., 1947-50; advisor U.S. Dept. State, Washington, 1955-58; John F. Murray prof. econs. U. Iowa, Iowa City, 1958-82; John F. Murray prof. internat. bus. and econs. U. Iowa., Iowa City, 1982—; sr. assoc. Wilbur F. Monroe Assocs., Inc., Washington, 1977—. Author: The International Economy, 1955, Economic Development, 1961, International Economics, 1956, Colombo Plan Conf., 1957. Mem. Griffin Soc., Phi Beta Kappa. Republican. Club: Arts (Washington). Office: Dept Finance U Iowa Iowa City IA 52242 *Honest hard work can do wonders for one.*

KRAUSE, WILLIAM AUSTIN, corporation executive; b. Lennox, Calif., Nov. 16, 1930; s. William August and Grace Olive (Davies) K.; children: Kenneth R., Michael W., Richard R., William R. A.A., Pasadena City Coll., 1950; B.S. in Engring., U. Calif.-Berkeley, 1952. Registered profl. engr., Mont., La., N.Mex., Fla., Miss., Tex., Calif., Del., Ky., Okla. Supt., mgr. constrn. operations C.F. Braun Co., Alhambra, Calif., 1952-63; gen. mgr. Lummus Co., Bloomfield, N.J., 1963-69; pres., chief exec. officer J.F. Pritchard & Co., Kansas City, Mo., 1969-73, Internat. Systems and Controls Process Group, Houston, 1969-73; pres., dir. Sigma-Chapman, Inc., Houston, 1973—, chmn.; chmn. bd., pres., dir. Chapman Engrs. Inc., Houston; dir., mem. audit and exec. coms. Camco, Inc., Houston. Mem. Young Pres.'s Orgn. (dir. 1973—, chmn. exec. com. 1975-76, sec. Kansas City chpt. 1971-72), World Bus. Council, Chief Execs. Orgn., ASME, Am. Inst. Chem. Engrs. (lectr. project mgmt.), AIME, Nat., Calif., Tex. socs. profl. engrs., Calif. Alumni Assn. Clubs: Houstonian, University (Houston). Patentee in field. Home: 10 S Briarhollow Ln #93 Houston TX 77027 Office: Sigma Chapman Inc Suite 100 6101 Southwest Freeway Houston TX 77057

KRAUSHAAR, JOHN FLORENCE, advertising agency executive; b. Los Angeles, Nov. 26, 1932; s. John F. and Mary (Krueger) K.; m. Barbara Paulsen, Sept. 17, 1956; children: Lianne, Julie, Victoria, Catherine. B.A., Rutgers U., 1954. Account exec. Batten, Barton, Durstine & Osborn, Inc., N.Y.C., 1956-66, regional mgr., Cleve., 1966-72, sr. v.p., 1972-82; pres. Blair Advt., Rochester, N.Y., 1983—. Committeeman Republican Town Com., Wilton, Conn., 1979-80; bd. dirs. Vitam Drug Rehab., Norwalk, Conn., 1978-82; adv. bd. U. Va., Charlottesville, Va., 1979-83. Served to capt. USAF, 1954-56. Republican. Presbyterian. Clubs: Silver Spring Country (Ridgefield, Conn.); Yale (N.Y.C.); Oak Hill (Rochester, N.Y.). Home: 148 Park Rd Pittsford NY 14534 Office: 96 College Ave Rochester NY 14601

KRAUSS, ALAN ROBERT, physicist; b. Chgo., Oct. 3, 1943; s. Paul and Shirley (Shapiro) K.; m. Julie Emelie Roasdo, Aug. 28, 1965; 1 dau., Susan. B.S., U. Chgo., 1965; postgrad., Columbia U., 1965-66; M.S., Purdue U., 1968, Ph.D., 1972. Research assoc. U. Chgo., 1971-74; staff physicist Argonne Nat. Lab., (Ill.), 1974—; cons. Dept. Energy, 1979. Contbr. articles on microcomputer applications, quantum physics and surface emission to sci. jours.; patentee (2). Mem. Am. Phys. Soc., Am. Vacuum Soc. (publicity chmn. fusion tech. div. 1980—), Sigma Xi. Clubs: Downers Grove Camera (sec. 1979-81, treas. 1982-83. Office: Argonne Nat Lab 9700 N Cass Ave Argonne IL 60439

KRAUSS, GEORGE, metallurgist; b. Phila., May 14, 1933; s. George and Berta (Reichelt) K.; m. Ruth A. Oeste, Sept. 10, 1960; children: Matthew, Jonathan, Benjamin, Thomas. B.S. in Metall. Engring., Lehigh U., 1955; M.S., MIT, 1958, Sc.D., 1961. Registered profl. engr., Colo., Pa. Devel. metallurgist Superior Tube Co., Collegeville, Pa., 1955-56; prof. Lehigh U., Bethlehem, Pa., 1963-75, Colo. Sch. Mines, Golden, 1975—; metall. cons., 1964—, Amax Found. prof., 1975—. Author: Principles of Heat Treatment of Steel, 1980; editor: Deformation Processing and Structure, 1984, Jour. Heat Treating, 1978—; contbr. articles profl. jours. NSF fellow Max Planck Inst. fur Eisenforschung, 1962-63. Fellow Am. Soc. Metals; mem. AIME, ASME, Electron Microscope Soc. Am., Sigma Xi. Home: 3807 S Ridge Rd Evergreen CO 80439 Office: Dept Metall Engineering Colorado Sch Mines Golden CO 80401

KRAUSS, MICHAEL EDWARD, linguist; b. Cleve., Aug. 15, 1934; s. Lester William and Ethel (Sklarsky) K.; m. Jane Lowell, Feb. 16, 1962; children: Marcus Feder, Stephen Feder, Ethan, Alexandra, Isaac. Bacc. Phil. Icelandicae, U. Iceland; B.A., U. Chgo., 1953, Western Res. U., 1954; M.A., Columbia U., 1955; Cert. d'etudes superieures, U. Paris, 1956; Ph.D., Harvard U., 1959. Postdoctoral fellow U. Iceland, Reykjavik, 1958-60; research fellow Dublin Inst. Advanced Studies, Ireland, 1956-57; vis. prof. MIT, Cambridge, 1969-70; prof. linguistics Alaska Native Lang. Center, U. Alaska, Fairbanks, 1960—, dir., 1972—, head Alaska native lang. program, 1972—; panel mem. linguistice NSF. Author: Eyak Dictionary, 1970, Eyak Texts, 1970, Alaska Native Languages: Past, Present and Future, 1980; editor: In Honor of Eyak: The Art of Anna Nelson Harry, 1982; mem. editorial bd.: Internat. Jour. Am. Linguistics; editor: dictionaries and books in Alaska, Eskimo and Indian Langs. Halldor Kiljan Laxness fellow Scadinavian-Am. Found., Iceland, 1958-60; Fulbright study grantee, Iceland, 1958-60; grantee NEH and NSF, 1978—; recipient Humanist of Yr. award Alaska Humanities Forum, 1981, Athabaskan and Eyak research award NSF, 1961—. Mem. Linguistics Soc. Am., Am. Anthropol. Assn. Jewish. Home: SR Box 80123 Fairbanks AK 99701 Office: Alaska Native Lang Center 302 Chapman Bldg U Alaska Fairbanks AK 99701

KRAUSS, ROBERT WALLFAR, botanist, univ. dean; b. Cleve., Dec. 27, 1921; s. Wallfar Gradifer and Emma Eleanor (Mueller) K.; m. Wilberta Tucker Bunker, Aug. 29, 1947 (div. 1969); children—Robert Geoffrey, Douglas Andrew; m. Harriet Reiss Meadow, Sept. 11, 1972 (div. 1979); m. Mary Lou Hill, Nov. 23, 1979. B.A., Oberlin Coll., 1947; M.S., U. Hawaii, 1949; Ph.D., U. Md., 1951. Research fellow Carnegie Instn., also U. Md., 1951-54; mem. faculty U. Md., 1955-72, prof. botany, 1959-72, head dept., 1964-73; dean Coll. Sci., Oreg. State U., Corvallis, 1973-79; exec. dir. Fedn. Am. Socs. Exptl. Biology, Bethesda, Md., 1979—; staff mem. Marine Biol. Lab., Woods Hole, Mass., 1955, 56, 57; cons. USAF Sch. Aviation Medicine, 1961—; spl. adviser on U.S./Soviet relations to adminstr. NASA, 1964—; sr. research affiliate Chesapeake Biol. Lab., 1968—. Contbr. numerous articles to tech. jours. Served to 2d lt. AUS, 1943-46. Recipient achievement award in biology Washington Acad. Scis., 1961. Fellow A.A.A.S. (mem. council); mem. Am. Soc. Plant Physiologists (trustee 1964-70), Am. Inst. Biol. Scis. (award 1974, sec.-treas. 1963-68, pres. 1973), Bot. Soc. Am. (Darbaker award 1956), Bot. Soc. Washington (pres. 1964), Phycological Soc. Am. (pres. 1963—), Phi Beta Kappa, Sigma Xi. Club: Cosmos. Office: Coll Sci Oreg State University Corvallis OR 97331

KRAUSS, ROSALIND EPSTEIN, art history educator; b. Washington, Nov. 30, 1940; d. Mathew Meyer and Bertha (Luber) Epstein. B.A., Wellesley Coll., 1962; M.A., Harvard U., 1964, Ph.D., 1969. Asst. prof. Wellesley Coll., Mass., 1964-66; assoc. prof. MIT, Cambridge, 1967-71; dir. visual art program Princeton U., N.J., 1972-74; prof. art history Hunter Coll., CUNY, 1975—; vis. curator Guggenheim Mus., N.Y.C., 1970-71, Whitney Mus., 1975-76, Mus. Modern Art, 1983—. Author: Terminal Iron Works Sculpture of David Smith, 1971, Passages in Modern Sculpture, 1977, The Originality of the Avant Garde and Other Modernist Myths, 1984; editor, October Mag., 1976—. Guggenheim Found. fellow, 1971-72; Center for Advanced Study Nat. Gallery Washington fellow, 1980-81; Inst. Advanced Study fellow, 1983-84. Mem. Internat. Assn. Art Critics (pres. 1975-77). Office: Hunter Coll 695 Park Ave New York NY 10013

KRAUSS, RUTH IDA (MRS. CROCKETT JOHNSON), author, playwright; b. Balt., 1911; d. Julius Leopold and Blanche (Rosenfeld) K.; m. Crockett Johnson, 1945. Author: books for children, latest being Somebody Spilled the Sky, 1979, Minestrone, 1981, Somebody Else's Nut Tree, 1983; poetry books for adults, latest being There's a Little Ambiguity Over There Among the Bluebells, 1968, Under Twenty, 1970, This Breast Gothic, 1973, Little Boat Lighter than a Cork, 1976, Under Thirteen, 1976, When I Walk I Change the Earth, 1978, Re-examination of Freedom, 1981; playwright: approximately 30 theatrical prodns. appearing off Broadway and univs., including A Beautiful Day, Judson Poets Theatre, If I Were Freedom, Bard Coll., 1976-77, Re-examination of Freedom, Boston U., 1976-77, Small Black Lambs Wandering in the Red Poppies, Theartre for a New City, 1982. Mem. Authors League, PEN Internat. Address: 24 Owenoke Rd Westport CT 06880

KRAUT, RALPH JOHN, manufacturing company executive, consultant; b. Chgo., Nov. 24, 1908; s. Hans B. and Rosa (Bucks) K.; m. Ruth B., July 25, 1932 (div.); children: Diane Kraut Matson, Karen Kraut Annis, Hans; m. Virginia Rose Dunn, Mar. 24, 1963; adopted children: Sheri Jakobsson, Wendy Cody, Jill Smith, Muffet Hayes. B.S. in Mech. Engring., U. Wis., 1930; postgrad., Gen. Electric Bus. Tng. Course, 1931-34. Registered profl. engr., Wis. Machinist apprentice Giddings and Lewis Inc., Fond du Lac, Wis., 1924-26; with Cin. Milacron Inc., 1927; prodn. engr. A.O. Smith Corp., Milw., 1930; test engr., advt. travel auditor Gen. Electric, Schnectady, N.Y., 1931-35; asst. works mgr. Giddings and Lewis Inc., Fond du Lac, 1935-37, asst. to pres., Fond Du Lac, 1937-39, exec. v.p., Fond du Lac, 1939-45, pres., gen. mgr., 1945-47, pres., chmn. bd., 1947-66, chmn. bd., chief exec. officer, 1966-72, chmn bd. dirs., 1972-82, dir., 1937-82, hon. chmn. bd., 1982—; dir. Twin Disc Inc., Racine, Wis.; dir. emeritus Gt. No. Nekoosa Corp., Stamford, Conn., Employers Ins., Wausau, Wis., M&I Marshall & Ilsley Bank, Milw., Harnischfeger Corp.; cons. Giddings and Lewis Inc., 1972—; pres. Nat. Machine Tool Builders Assn., McLean, Va., 1958-59. Trustee Wayland Acad., Beaver Dam, Wis., 1950—; del. Republican Conv., Miami, Fla., 1972; chmn. 6th Wis. Congl. Dist. for Reelection of Pres., 1972. Served to lt. col. inf. U.S. Army, 1942-45. Recipient profl. engr. award U. Wis.-Madison, 1955, Paul Harris award Rotary Internat., Fond du Lac, 1982, Community Service citation Fond du Lac Area, 1973, hon. citizen award Cooke Island, 1982. Mem. Soc. Mfg. Engrs., ASME, Nat. Machine Tool Builders Assn., Nat. Mgmt. Assn., Theta Chi, Tau Beta Pi, Pi Tau Sigma, Phi Kappa Phi. Lodges: Elks; VFW; Am. Legion. Home: 545 Illinois Ave Green Lake WI 54941

KRAUTER, THOMAS F., manufacturing company executive; b. N.Y.C., Jan. 4, 1927; m. Martha Wernicke, May 28, 1960; children: Kathleen, Nancy, Jeannie. B.B.A. magna cum laude, Manhattan Coll., 1951. With ITT, 1959—, v.p., 1973—, asst. comptroller, 1967—. Served with USNR, 1944-46. Mem. Fin. Execs. Inst., Nat. Elec. Mfrs. Assn. Office: ITT 320 Park Ave New York NY 10022 *

KRAUTHEIMER, RICHARD, art historian, educator; b. Fuerth, Bavaria, July 6, 1897; came to U.S., 1935, naturalized, 1942; s. Nathan and Martha (Landman) K.; m. Trude Hess, Mar. 18, 1924. Student, U. Munich, Germany, U. Berlin, U. Marburg, Germany; Ph.D., Halle-Wittenberg U., 1923; D.H.L., U. Louisville, 1959; dictorate hon., Frankfurt U., Germany, 1965; Christian Archeol., Rome Pontifical Inst. Christian Archeology, 1968. Privat dozent Marburg U., 1928-35; asst. prof. U. Louisville, 1935-37; prof. history of art Vassar Coll., 1937-52, Inst. Arts, NYU, N.Y.C., 1952-65, Jayne Wrightsman prof., from 1965, now Samuel F.B. Morse prof. lit. of art of design, N.Y.C.; sr. research analyst OSS, 1942-44. Author: Corpus of the Early Christian Basilicas in Rome, 1937, Lorenzo Ghiberu, 1956, 70, Lorenzo Ghiberu, rev. edit., 1982, Early Christian and Byzantine Architecture, 1964, Collected Essays, 1969, Rome: Profile of a City, 1980, Three Christian Capitals: Topography and Politics, 1983. Guggenheim fellow, 1950, 63. Fellow Am. Acad. Arts and Scis., Jewish Acad. Arts and Sci., Medieval Acad. Am., Pontifical Acad. Archeology, Am. Philos. Soc.; corr. fellow Brit. Acad.; mem. Max Planck Soc., German Archeol. Inst., Coll. Art Assn. Office: NYU Inst Fine Arts 1 E 78th St New York NY 10021 *

KRAVETZ, NATHAN, educator, author; b. N.Y.C., Feb. 11, 1921; s. Louis and Anna (Tau) K.; m. Evelyn Cottan, Dec. 10, 1944; children: Deborah Ruth K., Daniel. B.Ed., UCLA, 1941, M.A., 1949, Ed.D., 1954; fellow edn., Harvard U., 1951-52. Tchr., Walnut Creek, Calif., 1941-42; tchr., vice prin., then prin. Los Angeles city schs., 1946-64; asso. prof. edn. Hunter Coll., then; Herbert H. Lehman Coll., City U. N.Y., 1964-69, prof., 1970-76, chmn. dept. early childhood and elementary edn., 1975-76; dean Sch. Edn., Calif. State Coll., San Bernardino, 1976-79, prof. edn., 1979—; dir. Nat. Tchr. Corps, Hunter Coll., 1966-68; sr. staff mem. Inst. for Edn. Planning, UNESCO, Paris, 1969-72; vis. faculty San Diego State Coll., summers 1950, 53, Eastern Oreg. Coll., summer 1955, Los Angeles State Coll., 1953, 54; faculty UCLA, summer 1961; program coordinator Peace Corps, 1963; ednl. cons. Research Directorate, System Devel. Corp., Santa Monica, Calif., 1962-63; edn. adviser, tech. dir. edn. div. U.S. Operations Mission to Peru, AID, 1958-60; ednl. cons. Peruvian Ministry Edn., Faculty Edn. San Marcos U., Lima; cons., lectr. U. Lima, 1973; mem. Peruvian Nat. Edn. Reform Commn., 1958-60; U.S. mem. joint scholarship commn. Am. embassy, Lima; mem. Fulbright Commn., Lima; cons. Ford Found. Nat. Ednl. Planning Commn., Santiago, Chile, 1964, UNESCO, U. Caracas, Venezuela, 1969; cons., chmn. evaluation panel, dir. evaluation research Center for Urban Edn., N.Y.C., 1965-69; cons. Office Bi-lingual Edn. N.Y. pub. schs., 1975, UN Devel. Program, Colombia, Ecuador, 1973, U.S. AID, Pakistan, 1974, 75, UN Devel. Program, Indonesia, 1975, Bénin, 1977; Fulbright sr. research scholar, Argentina, 1980. Author: Two for a Walk, 1954, A Horse of Another Color, 1962, Hungarian edit., 1976, French edit., 1979, (with Ted Gordon) Tips to Teachers, 1962, A Monkey's Tale, 1964, (with Muriel Farrell) The Dog on the Ice, 1968, He Lost It! Let's Find It!, 1969, (with Muriel Farrell) Is There a Lion in the House?, 1970, The Way of the Condor, 1970, Management and Decision-Making in Educational Planning, 1971, Evaluation of Educational System Output, 1972, also govt. reports.; Contbr. articles to profl. publs.; Editor: The Kappa Delta Pi Record, 1973-78. Cons. on gifted edn. Calif. State Dept. Edn., 1981—. Served with psychol. research unit USAAF, 1942-46. Mem. UCLA Alumni Assn., AAUP, NEA, PEN Am. Ctr., Phi Delta Kappa, Kappa Delta Pi. Jewish. Home: 598 Maywood Ave San Bernardino CA 92404 Office: Sch Edn Calif State College San Bernardino CA 92407

KRAVIS, IRVING BERNARD, educator, economist; b. Phila., Aug. 30, 1916; s. Nathan and Ethel (Gelgood) K.; m. Lillian Beatrice Panzer, June 22, 1941; children: Robert, Marcia, Ellen, Nathan. B.S., U. Pa., 1938, M.A., 1939, Ph.D., 1947. Instr. econs. Whitman Coll., 1941-42; economist Dept. Labor, 1946-48; asso. prof. U. Mass., 1948-49; mem. faculty U. Pa., 1949—, prof. econs., 1956—, Univ. prof. econs., 1980—, chmn. dept., 1955-58, 62-67; asso. dean Wharton Sch. Finance and Commerce, 1958-60; cons. govtl. and internat. agys., 1949—; mem. research staff Nat. Bur. Econ. Research, 1962—. Co-author: Price Competitiveness in World Trade, 1971; co-author: World Product and Income, 1982; Contbr. articles to profl. jours. Served to 1st lt. USAAF, 1942-46. Decorated Bronze Star. Ford Found. fellow, 1960-61; Guggenheim fellow, 1966-67. Fellow Am. Acad. Arts and Scis., Econometric Soc.; mem. Am. Econ. Assn., Royal Econ. Soc. Home: 438 Warick Rd Wynnewood PA 19096 Office: Dept Economics U Pa Philadelphia PA 19104

KRAVITCH, PHYLLIS A., judge; b. Savannah, Ga., Aug. 23, 1920; d. Aaron and Ella (Wiseman) K. B.A., Goucher Coll., 1941; LL.B., U. Pa., 1943. Bar: Ga. 1943, U.S. Dist. Ct. 1944, U.S. Supreme Ct. 1948, U.S. Circuit Ct. Appeals 1962. Practice law, Savannah, 1944-76; judge Superior Ct., Eastern Jud. Circuit of Ga., 1977-79, U.S. Ct. Appeals (5th cir.), Atlanta, 1979-81, U.S. Ct. Appeals (11th cir.), 1981—. Trustee Inst. Continuing Legal Edn. in Ga., 1979—; mem. Bd. of Edn., Chatham County, Ga., 1949-55. Recipient Hannah G. Solomon award Nat. Council of Jewish Women, 1978. Fellow Am. Bar Found.; mem. Am. Bar Assn., Savannah Bar Assn. (pres. 1976), State Bar of Ga., Am. Judicature Soc., Am. Law Inst. Office: PO Box 8085 Savannah GA

KRAVITZ, ELLEN KING, musicologist; b. Fords, N.J., May 25, 1929; d. Walter J. and Frances M. (Prybylowski) Kokowicz; m. Hilard L. Kravitz, Jan. 9, 1972; stepchildren—Kent, Kerry, Jay. B.A., Georgian Ct. Coll., 1964; M.M., U. So. Calif., 1966, Ph.D., 1970. Tchr. 7th and 8th grade music Mt. St. Mary Acad., North Plainfield, N.J., 1949-50; cloistered nun Carmelite Monastery, Lafayette, La., 1950-61; instr. Loyola U., Los Angeles, 1967; asst. prof. music Calif. State U., Los Angeles, 1967-71; asso. prof., 1971-74, prof., 1974—; founder Friends of Music, 1976. Editorial bd.: Jour. Arnold Schoenberg Inst, Los Angeles; jour. editor Vol. I, No. 3, 1977, Vol. II, No. 3, 1978; author: (with others) Catalog of Schoenberg's Paintings, Drawings and Sketches. Mem. Schoenberg Centennial Com., 1974; guest lectr., 1969—. Recipient award for masters thesis U. So. Calif., 1966. Mem. Am. Musicol. Soc., Los Angeles County Mus. Art, Mu Phi Epsilon, Phi Kappa Lambda. Home: 402 Doheny Rd Beverly Hills CA 90210 Office: California State University 5151 State University Dr Los Angeles CA 90032

KRAVITZ, LAWRENCE CHARLES, elec. engr.; b. N.Y.C., July 27, 1932. B.S.E.E., Kans. U., 1954; M.S.E.E., Air Force Inst. Tech., 1955; Ph.D., Harvard U., 1963. With Gen. Electric Corp. Research and Devel. Center, 1963-73, mgr. display program, 1971-73; with U.S. Air Force Office of Sci. Research, Washington, 1973-81, dir., 1978-81; dir. research Bendix Advanced Tech. Center, Columbia, Md., 1981—. Served with USAF, 1954-58. Mem. IEEE, Sigma Xi. Office: 7128 Wolftree Lane Rockville MD 20852

KRAVSOW, IRVING, newspaper editor, columnist; b. Hartford, Conn., Aug. 22, 1926; s. Hyman and Etta K.; m. Jean Tucker, Apr. 19, 1975. A.S., Central Conn. State U., 1951. Chief state capitol bur. Hartford (Conn.) Courant, 1960-63, city editor, 1963-74, mng. editor, 1974-82, assoc. editor, 1982—; discussion leader AP Inst., 1975-80; pres. Conn. AP, 1979—; chmn. New Eng. Adv. bd. UP, 1976-77. Served with USNR, 1943-46. Recipient Christopher award in journalism New Eng. AP, 1954; Writing award, 1954. Mem. New Eng. AP News Execs. Assn. (1st v.p. 1980, pres. 1982), Am. Soc. Newspaper Editors, AP Mng. Editors Assn., Inter-Am. Press Assn. Office: 285 Broad St Hartford CT 06115

KRAWCZAK, ARTHUR HENRY, bishop; b. Detroit, Feb. 2, 1913; s. Joseph Casimer and Pauline (Kniga) K. B.A., Sacred Heart Sem., 1936; M.S.W., Catholic U. Am., 1951. Ordained priest Roman Catholic Ch., 1940. Assoc. St. Vincent Parish, Detroit, 1940-45, St. Stanislaus Parish, 1945-49; youth dir. Archdiocese of Detroit, 1956-62; founder, pastor St. Martin de Porres Parish, Warren, Mich., 1962-71; pastor Ascension Paris, Warren, Mich., 1971—; aux. bishop Archdiocese of Detroit, 1973—; bishop Northeast region, 1977—. Mem. Detroit Youth Commn., 1958-62; chmn. Macomb div. United Community Services, 1977—; chmn. New Detroit Inc., 1977—. Home: St. Elizabeth Briarbank 1315 N Woodward Bloomfield Hills MI 48013 Office: 1234 Washington Blvd Detroit MI 48226

KRAWITZ, HERMAN EVERETT, producer; b. N.Y.C., June 5, 1925; s. Harry and Sara (Epstein) K.; m. Rhoda Nayor, Feb. 17, 1952; children: David, Joshua. B.S., CCNY, 1949. Founder, gen. mgr. Falmouth (Mass.) Playhouse, Hyannis (Mass.) Music Circus and South Shore Music Circus, 1949-51; with Met. Opera, 1953-72, bus. and tech. adminstr., 1958-63, asst. gen. mgr., 1963-72; pres. Jodav Prodns., Inc. (TV prodn. co.), N.Y.C., 1973—; exec. dir. Am. Ballet Theatre, N.Y.C., 1977—; pres. Recorded Anthology of Am. Music, Inc. (a non-profit rec. co. and its trade label co. New World Records), N.Y.C., 1975—; chmn. theater adminstrn. program Sch. Drama, Yale U., 1966-78; also fellow Silliman Coll., 1972—; mem. Brandeis U. Arts Com.; trustee Richard Tucker Found.; cons. in field. Exec. producer: A Child's Christmas in Wales, CBS, 1973 (Christopher award), Ailey Celebrates Ellington, CBS, 1974, Gianni Schicchi; co-prodn. with BBC for, CBS, 1975, The Nutcracker, 1977, Baryshnikov on Broadway, ABC (4 Emmy awards), ABC (Christopher award), ABC (Peabody award), ABC (Golden Rose of Montreux), ABC, 1980 (Dirs. Guild Am. award); co-producer: C'est Un Chic Type Charlie Brown, Theatre Gaiete Montparnasse, Paris, 1976; producer: Marion Anderson Gala, 75th Birthday, Carnegie Hall, N.Y.C., 1977; Author: The Official Guide Book to the Metropolitan Opera House, 1967, (with Howard Klein) Royal American Symphonic Theater, 1975. Served to sgt. Signal Corps U.S. Army, 1943-46. Mem. Nat. Acad. TV Arts and Scis. Office: care AM Ballet Theatre 890 Broadway New York NY 10003 *

KRAYBILL, PAUL NISSLEY, religious official; b. Bainbridge, Pa., June 7, 1925; s. John Rutt and Esther (Nissley) K.; m. Jean Kulp Metz, Dec. 22, 1951; children: Mary Jean, Dale Edward, Linda Sue, Carol Ann, Karen Louise. B.A., Eastern Mennonite Coll., 1955. Asst. sec. Eastern Mennonite Bd. Missions and Charities, Salunga, Pa., 1953-58, overseas sec., gen. sec., 1958-70, exec. sec., study commn. on ch. orgn., 1970-71; gen. sec. Mennonite Ch. Gen. Bd., Rosemont, Ill., 1971-77; exec. sec. Mennonite World Conf., 1973—; sec. Mennonite Christian Leadership, Landisville, Pa., 1969-80, Council Mission Bd. Secs., Rosemont, Ill., 1962-74; mem. Presidium Mennonite World Conf., 1967-73; pres. Mennonite Housing Aid, Inc., Lombard, Ill., 1975-81; ordained to ministry, 1981; Mem. exec. com., vice chmn. and trustee Am. Leprosy Missions, Bloomfield, N.J., 1967-80. Author: Change and the Church, 1970; Editor: Called to be Sent, 1964, Mennonite World Handbook, 1978. Named Alumnus of the Yr. Eastern Mennonite Coll., 1971. Mem. Am. Soc. Missiology. Home: 30 Allée de la Robertsau 67000 Strasbourg France

KREAGER, HENRY DEWAYNE, savings and loan association executive; b. Alexandria, Minn., July 25, 1912; s. William Henry and Ida (Zimmerman) K.; m. Betty Jane Shell, Feb. 1974; children by previous marriage: William Henry, John Philip; stepchildren: Robert L., Sandra L. A.B., Wash. State U., 1934, A.M., 1935; postgrad., Duke U., 1935-36; Ph.D., Harvard U., 1947. Asst. to dir., spl. rep. in C.A. FEA, 1943-45; nat. dir. Community Action Programs, 1945-47; mem. staff Exec. Office of Pres., Washington, 1947-53; cons. indsl. economist, Washington, 1953-57, Seattle, 1960-70, dir. commerce and econ. devel., State of Wash., 1957-60; now chmn., chief exec. officer Pacific First Fed. Savs. Bank, Tacoma, Seattle, Portland and Eugene; dir. Pacific N.W. Bell Telephone Co., Washington Energy Co., Univar Corp., Fed. Home Loan Bank of Seattle, Sci. Advances Inc., Columbus, Ohio, URS Corp., San Mateo, Calif. Contbr. articles to bus. and profl. jours. Commr. Seattle Worlds Fair Commn., 1960-63; pres. United Arts Council Puget Sound, 1970—; vice-chmn. Econ. Panel, Washington and N.Y.C., 1953—; trustee Puget Sound Econ. Devel. Council; chmn. Wash. State Council Internat. Trade.; Bd. regents Wash. State U.; trustee Lewis and Clark Coll., Acad. Contemporary Problems, Washington; trustee, pres. Seattle Opera Assn., 1975—; bd. dirs., treas. Wash. State Conv. and Trade Ctr. Littauer fellow Harvard U., 1938-39; Recipient Disting. Service award Wash. Allied Daily Newspapers, 1960. Mem. Seattle C. of C. (trustee 1963—), Sigma Delta Chi, Kappa Sigma. Clubs: Rainier, Washington Athletic (Seattle); Nat. Press (Washington). Home: 2478 Crestmont Pl W Seattle WA 98199 Office: Pacific First Fed Savs and Loan 11th and Pacific Sts Tacoma WA 98401

KREAMER, JOHN HARRISON, lawyer; b. Downs, Kans., Sept. 12, 1922; s. John Dean and Catherine (Harrison) K.; m. Marion Jane Enggas, July 28, 1951; children: Jane Kreamer Meyer, Anne Kreamer Andersen. A.B., U. Kans., 1946; J.D., Harvard U., 1949. Bar: Mo. 1949. Mng. partner Gage & Tucker (and predecessor firms), Kansas City, 1959—; dir. Parmelee Industries, Commerce Bank, Realex Corp., Interstate Oil Co., Kansas City. Pres., bd. dirs. Mid-Am. Coalition on Health Care, 1979—; bd. dirs., pres. Pub. TV 19, Inc., 1973-78; bd. dirs. Starlight Theater Assn., Mo. Arts Council, 1975-80, Mid-Am. Arts Alliance, 1978—, Acad. Health Scis.; trustee U. Mo. at Kansas City, Midwest Research Inst.; chmn. The Civic Council, 1982-84. Served to 1st lt., inf. AUS, 1942-45. Decorated Purple Heart, Bronze Star.; named Mr. Kansas City, 1983. Mem. Greater Kansas City C. of C. (dir. 1964-68, 72-75, v.p. 1964-68), U. Kans. Meml. Assn. (pres. 1965-66), Lawyers Assn. K.C. (pres. 1964-65), Internat., Am. bar assns., World Assn. Lawyers, Edn. Com. States, Beta Theta Pi, Pi Sigma Alpha. Clubs: Rotary, University (pres. 1963), Kansas City Country (dir. 1968-70), River.). Home: 1246 W 59th St Kansas City MO 64113 Office: 2345 Grand Ave Kansas City MO 64108

KREBS, EDWIN GERHARD, biochemist, pharmacologist, educator; b. Lansing, Iowa, June 6, 1918; s. William Carl and Louisa Helena (Stegeman) K.; m. Virginia Frech, Mar. 10, 1945; children: Sally, Robert, Martha. B.A., U. Ill., 1940; M.D., Washington U., 1943. Asst. prof. biochemistry U. Wash., Seattle, 1948-52, asso. prof., 1952-57, prof., 1957-68, chmn. dept. pharmacology, 1977-83; prof., chmn. dept. biol. chemistry U. Calif., Davis, 1968-77; investigator Howard Hughes Med. Inst., 1977—. Served with USN, 1945-46. Recipient Alumni citation Washington U., 1972, Disting. Lectureship award Internat. Soc. Endocrinology, 1972, ann. award Gairdner Found., 1978; Guggenheim fellow, 1966. Mem. Nat. Acad. Scis., Am. Acad. Arts and Scis., Am. Soc. Biol. Chemists, AAAS, Am. Chem. Soc., Sigma Xi, Phi Beta Kappa, Phi Kappa Phi, Alpha Omega Alpha. Home: 1153 21st Ave E Seattle WA 98112 Office: Dept Pharmacology Sch Medicine U Wash Seattle WA 98195

KREBS, JOHN H., former congressman; b. Berlin, Dec. 17, 1926; s. James L. and Elizabeth (Stern) K.; m. Hanna Jacobson, Sept. 9, 1956; children: Daniel Scott, Karen Barbara. B.A., U. Calif., 1950; LL.B., Hastings Coll. Law, San Francisco, 1957. Bar: Calif. bar 1957. Mem. Fresno County Planning Commn., 1965-69; mem., also chmn. Fresno County Bd. Suprs., 1970-74; mem. 94th-95th Congresses from 17th Calif. Dist. Chmn. Fresno County Democratic Central Com., 1965-66. Served with AUS, 1952-54. Mem. Calif. State Bar, Fresno County Bar Assn. Home: 1383 W Sample St Fresno CA 93711

KREBS, MAX VANCE, retired foreign service officer, educator; b. Cin., June 26, 1916; s. August Leonidas and Katherine Louise (Vance) K.; m. Esther Willard Winn, Aug. 8, 1942; children: Marlynn Vance Clayton, Timothy Winn. A.B., Princeton U., 1937; postgrad., U. Cin., 1938-39, U. Calif., 1946-47. Asst. to purchasing agt. Strietmann Biscuit Co., Mariemont, Ohio, 1937-38, asst. credit mgr., 1938-41; asst. export mgr. Gantner & Mattern Co., San Francisco, 1946-47; 3d sec., vice consul Am. Embassy, Montevideo, 1947-49, 2nd sec., vice consul, Bogota, 1950-52, consul, Antwerp, 1952-55; tng. assignments officer Office of Personnel, Dept. of State, 1955-57; spl. asst. to undersec. state, 1957-59, spl. asst. to sec. state, 1959-60, polit. counselor, Manila, 1961-64, Sec. State, Rio de Janeiro, 1964-67; dep. chief of mission, Guatemala, 1967-70; polit. adviser to comdr.-in-chief U.S. So. Command, C.Z., 1970-71; dep. chief mission (minister-counselor), Buenos Aires, Argentina, 1971-74, ambassador to, Guyana, 1974-76; vis. fellow Woodrow Wilson Nat. Fellowship Found., 1976—; instr. Sandhills Community Coll., Pinehurst, N.C., 1977—. Served as capt. AUS, 1941-46. Mem. Am. Fgn. Service Assn. (dir. 1957-59). Presbyn. Home: Route 1 Box 191 Foxfire Village NC 27281

KREBS, ROBERT DUNCAN, transportation company executive; b. Sacramento, May 2, 1942; s. Ward Carl and Eleanor Blauth (Duncan) K.; m. Anne Lindstrom, Sept. 11, 1971; children: Robert Ward, Elisabeth Lindstrom, Duncan Lindstrom. B.A., Stanford U., 1964; M.B.A., Harvard U., 1966. Asst. gen. mgr. So. Pacific Transp. Co., Houston, 1974-75, asst. regional ops. mgr., 1975-76, asst. v.p., San Francisco, 1976-77, asst. to pres., 1977-79, gen. mgr., 1979, v.p. transp., 1979-80, v.p. ops., 1980-82, pres., 1982—, also dir. Mem. Assn. Am. R.R.s, Stanford U. Alumni Assn. Republican. Episcopalian. Clubs: Pacific Union, World Trade. Office: Southern Pacific Transportation Co Southern Pacific Bldg One Market Plaza San Francisco CA 94105

KREEGER, DAVID LLOYD, ret. ins. co. exec.; b. N.Y.C., Jan. 4, 1909; s. Barnet and Laura (Bernen) K.; m. Carmen Matanzo y Jaramillo, Jan. 12, 1938; children—Carolita Joy, Peter Laurens Harris. A.B. magna cum laude, Rutgers U., 1929, L.H.D. (hon.), 1972; J.D. magna cum laude, Harvard U., 1932; Mus.D. (hon.), Peabody Inst., 1972, LL.D., George Washington U., 1976. Bar: N.J. bar 1933, D.C. bar 1941, U.S. Supreme Ct. bar 1944. Pvt. practice in, Newark, 1932-34; sr. atty. Dept. Agr., 1934-35; prin. atty. Dept. Interior, 1935-41; spl. asst. to atty. gen., also chief Supreme Ct. sect., claims div. Dept. Justice, 1941-46; pvt. practice, Washington, 1946-57; with Govt. Employees Ins. Co. (and affilates), Washington, 1957—, chmn. bd., chief exec. officer, 1970-74, chmn. exec. com., 1974-79, hon. chmn. bd., 1979—; dir. Nat. Savs. and Trust Co., Washington.; Mem. Citizens Adv. Council D.C., 1961-64; spl. presdl. ambassador to inauguration Pres. Frei of Chile, 1964; U.S. del. to Econ. Council on Europe, 1967. Contbr. articles profl. jours.; Editor: Harvard Law Rev, 1930-32. Pres. Nat. Symphony Orch., 1970-78; chmn. 5th Interam. Music Festival, 1971; pres. Corcoran Gallery Art, Washington, 1974—, Washington Opera, 1980—; trustee Am. U., Washington trustee Am. U., Internat. Exhbns. Found.; mem. com. to visit Harvard Law Sch., 1967-70; mem. exec. bd. Am. Jewish Com.; mem. U.S. Nat. Commn. UNESCO, 1977-80, Nat. Mus. Am. Art Commn.; bd. govs. Atlantic Inst., 1981—; pres. David Lloyd Kreeger Charitable Found. Recipient Meritorious Pub. Service award Govt. D.C., 1961, Bronze medal appreciation Corcoran Gallery Art, 1965, cert. appreciation N.Y. U. Grad. Sch. Bus. Adminstrn. Alumni Assn., 1965, Outstanding Service award Washington Jr. C. of C., 1966. Mem. Am., D.C. bar assns., alumni assns. Rutgers U., Harvard Law Sch., Phi Beta Kappa, Sigma Alpha Mu. Democrat. Jewish. Clubs: Met., Alfalfa, Cosmos, Nat. Press, Harvard, Nat. Lawyers (Washington). Home: 2401 Foxhall Rd NW Washington DC 20007

KREER, JOHN BELSHAW, electrical engineering educator; b. Bklyn., Sept. 25, 1927; s. John George and Mabel Lucina (Belshaw) K.; m. Vivienne Margaret Huffman, June 9, 1957; children: Carolyn Joan Kreer Bratzel, Kenneth John. B.S.E.E., Iowa State U., 1951; M.S.E.E., U. Ill., 1954, Ph.D., 1965. Asst. prof. elec. engring. U. Ill.-Urbana, 1956-59; from assoc. prof. to prof. elec. engring. W.Va. U., Morganstown, 1959-64; assoc. prof. Mich. State U., East Lansing, 1964-68, prof. elec. engring., 1968—, chmn. dept., 1976—. Mem. East Lansing Transp. Commn., 1975-81; cubmaster Boy Scouts Am., 1972-75. Served with USN, 1948. Mem. IEEE (sr., sect. chmn. 1983-84), Am. Soc. Engring. Edn., Nat. Soc. Profl. Engrs. Home: 1834 Pinecrest Dr East Lansing MI 48823 Office: Mich State U East Lansing MI 48824

KREEVOY, MAURICE MORDECAI, educator, chemist; b. Boston, Aug. 28, 1928; s. Edward Phillip and Jennie (Gildesheim) K.; m. Raye Gladys Schwartz, Mar. 29, 1953; children—Edith Pamela, William Seth. B.S., U. Calif. at Los Angeles, 1950; Ph.D. (Moore fellow), Mass. Inst. Tech., 1954. Asst. prof. chemistry U. Minn., 1956-59, asso. prof., 1959-64, prof., 1964—; vis. prof. Inst. Ruder Boscovic, Zagreb, Yugoslavia, 1969-70; cons. Gen. Mills. Inc., 1958-78, Henkel Corp., 1978—, Ventron Corp., 1975—. NSF postdoctoral fellow, 1955-56; Sloan Found. fellow, 1960-64; NSF Sr. postdoctoral fellow, 1962-63. Mem. Am. Chem. Soc., Royal Soc. Chemistry, Croatian Chem. Soc., AAUP, Sigma Psi. Patentee liquid ion exchange, phase transfer catalysis, cyanoborohydride reductions. Home: 15 S 1st St Minneapolis MN 55401

KREFTING, ROBERT J(OHN), publishing company executive; b. Peoria, Ill., Apr. 29, 1944; s. Walter and Rebecca Juliana K.; m. Sally Ann Kingsmill, Aug. 27, 1978; 1 son, Matthew; children by previous marriage: Gordon, Melissa, Sarah. B.A. magna cum laude with honors in History, Williams Coll., 1966. Subscription sales mgr. Time, Inc., N.Y.C., 1966-71; assoc. pub. Psychology Today, Del Mar, Calif., 1971-74; with CBS Publs., N.Y.C., 1974—, v.p., group pub. spl. interest mags., 1977-79, pres., 1979—. Mem. Mag. Pubs. Assn., Young Presidents Orgn., Phi Beta Kappa. Club: Sky. Home: Mount Holly Rd Katonah NY 10536 Office: 1515 Broadway New York NY 10036

KREHBIEL, FREDERICK AUGUST, electronics company executive; b. Chgo., June 2, 1941; s. John Hammond and Margaret Ann (Veeck) K.; m. Kay Kirby, Dec. 20, 1974; children—William Veeck, Jay Frederick. B.A., Lake Forest Coll., 1963; postgrad., Georgetown U., U. Leicester, Eng. Export mgr., then v.p. internat. Molex Inc., Lisle, Ill., 1970-75, exec. v.p., dir., 1976—; pres. Molex Internat. Co., 1976—; dir. Chgo. White Sox Profl. Baseball Club. Bd. dirs. Ill. Benedictine Coll., Lisle, Ill., Inst. Internat. Edn. Mem. Pres.'s Export Council, Internat. Trade Club. Club: Hinsdale Golf. Home: 505 S County Line Rd Hinsdale IL 60521 Office: 2222 Wellington Ct Lisle IL 60532

KREHBIEL, PETER W., manufacturing company executive; b. 1929; (married). A.B., Dartmouth, 1951; LL.B., NYU, 1960. With firm Pennie, Edmonds, Morton, Taylor & Adams, N.Y.C., 1960-64; with Acco Babcock Inc. (formerly Am. Chain & Cable Co.), 1964—, sec., 1967—, gen. counsel, 1970—, v.p., 1979—, v.p., sec., gen. counsel, 1981-82, sr. v.p. adminstrn., sec., 1982—. Served with USNR, 1951-55. Address: 425 Post Rd Fairfield CT 06430

KREIDER, CARL, educator; b. Wadsworth, Ohio, Sept. 26, 1914; s. Lloyd S. and Adelia (Stover) K.; m. Evelyn Burkholder, June 8, 1939; children—Alan Fetter, Rebecca Elizabeth (Mrs. Weldon Pries), Stephen Carl, Thomas Edmund. A.B., Goshen Coll., 1936; M.A., Princeton, 1938, Ph.D., 1941; postgrad., London Sch. Econs., 1938-39. Field research fellow Brookings Instn., Washington, 1939-40; faculty Goshen Coll., 1940—, dean, 1944-70, pres., 1950-51, 70-71; provost 1971-72, prof. econs., 1972—; dean Coll. Liberal Arts, Internat. Christian U., Tokyo, Japan, 1952-56, vis. prof. econs., 1972-73; Coordinator com. on liberal arts N. Central Assn. Colls., 1948-51, 57-63, chmn. com. on liberal arts, 1965-69, editor news bull. coun., 1960-62; Fulbright lectr. Hailie Selassie U., Ethiopia, 1963-64; Mem. adv. council Danforth Found., 1958-61. Author: The Anglo-American Trade Agreement, 1943, Helping Developing Countries, 1968, The Christian Entrepreneur, 1981; Mng. editor: Mennonite Quar. Rev, 1974—. Bd. dirs. Mennonite Aid, Inc.; pres. bd. dirs. Oaklawn Psychiat. Center. Mem. Am. Econ. Assn., Am. Acctg. Assn., North Central Assn. Colls. (hon.), Mennonite (chmn. overseas com. bd. missions 1967-72, chmn. gen. bd. 1973-75). Home: 1121 S 8th St Goshen IN 46526

KREIDER, THOMAS MCROBERTS, educator; b. Wadsworth, Ohio, Mar. 2, 1922; s. Paul Vernon and Mildred (McRoberts) K.; m. Janet Elizabeth Callahan, June 9, 1952; children: Anne Whitaker, Carol Latham Kreider Lisensky. A.B. in History, U. Cin., 1946, M.A. in English, 1949, Ph.D., 1952; M.A. in History, Harvard U., 1947; cert. theol. studies, Pacific Sch. Religion, 1968; postdoctorate, Oxford (Eng.) U., 1949, Union Theol. Sem., N.Y.C., 1954. Mem. faculty dept. English, Berea (Ky.) Coll., 1952—, asso. prof., 1956-61, prof., 1961—, Chester D. Tripp prof. humanities, 1976—, chmn. dept., 1971—; Fulbright prof. U. Karachi, Pakistan, 1959-60; vis. prof. U. Cinn., 1961; vis. scholar in residence No. Ariz. U., 1984-85; dir. Columbia U. sect. Harvard-Yale-Columbia (intensive summer studies program), summer, 1967; participant Danforth Conf., Colorado Springs, summer, 1968; cons. museums and hist. orgns. program NEH, 1976—, also coll. English curricula, 1979—; dir. Berea Pub. Co., 1972—. Author: Aristocratic Tradition in Southern Literature, in Venture, 1960. Vice pres. bd. dirs. Berea Coll. Outdoor Drama Assn.; bd. dirs. Greater Berea Human Rights Commn., 1969-71, Project Opportunity Ky., 1968-75, Ky. Humanities Council, 1972-79; pres. Ky. Humanities Council, 1974-78; examiner So. Assn. Colls. and Schs., 1971—. Served with AUS, 1943-46; PTO. Taft fellow, 1948-52; Charles Shedd fellow, 1967-68; Danforth grantee, 1954; NSF grantee, 1965; Lilly grantee, 1961-63; NEH grantee, 1975; recipient Seabury award, 1971. Mem. MLA, AAUP, Hemingway Soc., Phi Beta Kappa, Omicron Delta Kappa. Mem. Union Ch. Home: 105 Van Winkle Grove Berea KY 40403

KREIGHBAUM, JOHN SCOTT, banker; b. Carthage, Mo., July 13, 1946; s. Lee and Dorothy Marie (Scott) K.; m. JoAnne Frances Tedesco, July 27, 1968; children: John Scott, Kerry Anne. B.A., Ft. Hays (Kans.) State U., 1968; cert., Am. Inst. Banking, 1972, Bankers Bus. Devel. Inst., 1973; grad., Comml. Sch. Banking, U. Nebr., 1974, Stonier Grad. Sch. Banking, Rutgers U., 1978. Adminstrv. officer Cert. Livestock Markets Assns., Kansas City, Mo., 1968-70; exec. trainee United Mo. Bank Kansas City, 1970-71, various officer levels, 1971-74, sr. v.p., 1979-81; pres., dir. United Mo. Bank Jefferson City, 1974-79, Jefferson City, chmn. bd., dir., 1979-80; pres., dir. Security Bank & Trust Co., Ponca City, Okla., 1981—; dir. United Mo. Bank Boonville. Bd. dirs. Ponca City Playhouse, Salvation Army of Ponca City, YMCA, 1975-78; v.p., bd. dirs. Retirement Community Devel.; chmn. dist.101 Will Rogers council Boy Scouts Am., 1980—. Mem. Ponca City C. of C. (bd. dirs.), Ft. Hays State U. Alumni Assn., Okla. Bankers Assn. Republican. Roman Catholic. Lodges: Elks; Rotary (bd. dirs.); K.C. Home: 5 Ramblewood Woodridge Ponca City OK 74601 Office: Security Bank and Trust Co 3d and Grand Ponca City OK 74602

KREILICK, ROBERT W., chemist, educator; b. Kalamazoo, Jan. 3, 1938; s. Herbert A. and Lenore K. K.; m. Willma J. Ham, Aug. 15, 1958; children—Christian J., Kelley G. A.B., Washington U., 1959, Ph.D., 1964. Chemist Monsanto Chem., 1959-60; asst. prof. chemistry U. Rochester, N.Y., 1964-69, asso. prof., 1969-71, prof., 1971-80, prof. chemistry and brain research, 1980—; cons. NIH. Contbr. chpts. to books, articles to profl. jours. LShell Oil fellow, 1962; NIH fellow, 1963; Alfred P. Sloan fellow, 1968; NIH grantee. Mem. Am. Chem. Soc., AAUP, Biophys. Soc., Sigma Xi. Methodist. Office: Dept Chemistry U of Rochester Rochester NY 14627

KREISBERG, NEIL IVAN, advt. exec.; b. N.Y.C., Feb. 1, 1945; s. Leo and Lucille (Levy) K.; m. Esther Bass, Jan. 23, 1969; children—Andrew Jay, Tracy Michelle. B.S. in Bus. Adminstrn, Rider Coll., Trenton, N.J., 1966. With Grey Advt. Inc., N.Y.C., 1966—, v.p., mgmt. supr., 1974-79, sr. v.p., account mgmt., 1979—. Jewish. Home: 133 Griffen Ave Scarsdale NY 10583 Office: 777 3d Ave New York NY 10017

KREISEL, HENRY, univ. adminstr.; b. Vienna, Austria, June 5, 1922; s. David Leo and Helene (Schreier) K.; m. Esther Lazerson, June 22, 1947; 1 son, Philip. B.A., U. Toronto, 1946, M.A., 1947; Ph.D., U. London, 1954. With dept. English U. Alta., 1947—, prof., 1959—, head dept., 1961-67, asso. dean Grad. studies, 1967-69, acting dean grad. studies, 1969-70, acad. v.p., 1970-75, Univ. prof., 1975—, chmn. Can. studies program, 1979—; vis. fellow Wolfson Coll., Cambridge U., 1975-76; Chmn. English lit. Can. Council Fellowship Com., 1963-65, Gov.-Gen.'s Jury for Lit., 1966-69; v.p. Edmonton Art Gallery, 1969-70. Author: The Rich Man, 1948, The Betrayal, 1964, The Almost Meeting, 1981; Contbr.: numerous short stories, anthologies to mags., books, including Best American Short Stories, 1966, A Book of Canadian Stories, 1962; Author: plays for radio and TV, including Bob Hope Theatre, 1965. Bd. govs. U. Alta., 1966-69; v.p. Edmonton Chamber Music Soc., 1978-80, pres., 1980—. Recipient U. Western Ont. President's medal, 1960; Reuben Wells Leonard fellow U. Toronto, 1946-47; Royal Soc. Can. Travelling fellow, 1953-54. Fellow Royal Soc. Arts (London), Internat. Inst. Arts and Letters (Geneva); mem. Assn. Can. U. Tchrs. English (pres. 1962-63). Home: 12516 66th Ave Edmonton AB Canada

KREISMAN, ARTHUR, emeritus English language educator, consultant; b. Cambridge, Mass., June 7, 1918; s. Louis and Rose (Shechtell) K.; m. B. Evelyn Goulston, Apr. 20, 1940; children: Peter Jon, Steven Alan, Richard Curt, James Bruce. A.B., Brigham Young U., 1942; student, Harvard U., 1939; A.M., Boston U., 1943, Ph.D., 1952. Instr. So. Oreg. State Coll., Ashland, 1946, asst. prof., 1947-51, asso. prof., 1951-55, prof., 1955-81, chmn. dept. English, 1951-63, chmn. humanities div., 1955-69, dir. gen. studies, 1959-66, dean arts and scis., 1966-77, dir. curricular affairs, 1978-80, emeritus prof., 1981—; co-founder with Evelyn Kreisman Edukon, Inc., univ. cons. service, 1982—; dir. Block Teaching Project, U.S. Office Edn., 1957-59, Nat. Def. Edn. Act Inst. for Advanced Study in English, 1966; cons. Fedn. Regional Accrediting Commns. in Higher Edn., 1974-75, Council on Postsecondary Accreditation, 1975-79, Chico (Calif.) State U., 1973-76, City U. Seattle, 1975—, Lincoln Meml. U., 1976, Marylhurst Edn. Center, 1976, Oreg. Inst. Tech., 1977-79, Sheldon Jackson Coll., 1979—, Council on Chiropractic Edn., 1982, 83; Mem. Gov.'s Adv. Com. on Arts and Humanities, 1966-69, 71-76; mem. task force human services Oreg. Ednl. Coordinating Council, 1972; mem. steering com. Oreg. Joint Com. for Humanities, 1972-74; chmn. Seminar Coll. Evaluators NW Assn. Schs. and Colls., U. Wash., 1977—; mem. nat. adv. bd. on quality assurance in experiential learning Council on Advancement Experiental Learning, 1978-80. Author: Correspondence Courses for State System, World Literature, 1956, Contemporary Literature, 1961, Reader's Guide to the Classics, 1961; Editor: Oregon Centennial Anthology, 1959; Contbr. poetry and articles to periodicals. Mem. Ashland City Council, 1950-54; Bd. dirs. Community Chest, Inst. Renaissance Studies, 1956-64; chmn. bd. trustees Ashland Community Hosp., 1960-62. Served with Signal Corps AUS, 1943-45. Recipient prize for excellence in teaching, 1966; Outstanding Service award Indsl. Coll. Armed Forces, 1976; Distinguished Service award Alumni Assn., 1977; Ford Found. fellow in philosophy and religion Harvard, 1954. Mem. N.W. Assn. Schs. and Colls. (examiner 1968—, trustee 1976-80, mem. commn. colls. 1972-80), AAUP (past pres. Oreg. council), Nat. Council Tchrs. English (past pres. Oreg. chpt.), Lambda Iota Tau, Phi Kappa Phi, Tau Kappa Alpha. Office: 455 Liberty St Ashland OR 97520

KREISSMAN, BERNARD, librarian; b. N.Y.C., June 17, 1919; s. Nathan and Sonia (Weisberg) K.; m. Shirley Fabian Relis, Aug. 29, 1942; children: Jane Starrett Jan, Judith Ann, Gregory George. B.S.S., CCNY, 1948; M.A., Columbia U., 1949, M.S. in L.S, 1954; Ph.D., U. Nebr., 1962. Instr. remedial reading, 1937-38; mem. staff N.Y. Pub. library, 1946-54, supr. main reading room, 1951-54; asst. dir. libraries, asso. prof. U. Nebr., 1954-62; chief librarian, prof. City Coll. N.Y., 1962-74; univ. librarian U. Calif. at Davis, 1974—; cons.-mgmt. U. Wis., 1978; Mem. Council Higher Ednl. Instns., 1962-66, chmn. library adv. bd., 1964-66; mem. accreditation team Western Assn. Schs. and Colls., 1979, 80, 82; rep. of ALA (on nat. commn. lit. of Nat. Council Tchrs. English), 1964-72; lectr. Pratt Inst. Grad. Sch. Library Service, 1966; instr. Columbia U. Sch. Library Service, 1969; adj. prof. library sci. dept. Queens Coll., CUNY, 1972; trustee met. N.Y. Met. Reference and Research Library Agy., Inc., 1972-74, chmn. adminstrv. services com., 1970-72; mem. goverance com. Calif. Library Authority System and Services, 1974-76, mem. planning com., 1974-76, mem. interim planning com., 1976-78; mem. task force on legislation Calif. State Library, 1975, mem. adv. council, 1975-77; UNESCO cons., Venezuela, 1980; cons. mgmt. U. Ill., U. Md., Naval War Coll. Library, others. Author: Pamela-Shamela, A Study of Criticisms, Burlesques, Parodies and Adaptations of Richardson's Pamela, 1960; also articles.; Editor: (Sir Walter Scott) Life of John Dryden, 1963, Advances in Library Administration and Organization, 1982—. Served with USAAF, 1943-46; PTO. Grolier scholar Rutgers U. seminar advanced library adminstrn., 1955. Mem. ALA, ALA Library Adminstrn. and Mgmt. Assn. (chmn. bldgs. and equipment sect. 1979-80, exec. com., chair., exec. bd., mem., stats. for coll. and univ. libraries com. 1981—); Mem. Assn. Coll. and Research Libraries (legislation com. 1978-80), Calif. Library Assn. (v.p., pres. elect 1983), Assn. Coll. and Research Libraries (White Ho. conf. and state library confs. ad hoc com. 1978-79), AAUP (exec. com. City Coll. N.Y. chpt. 1964), N.Y. Library Club (exec. council 1962, chmn. scholarship com. 1963-65, pres. 1966-67), Archons of Colophon (convenor 1971), Roxburghe Club. Home: 926 Plum Ln Davis CA 95616 Office: Library U Calif Davis CA 95616

KREITMAN, BENJAMIN ZVI, rabbi, educator; b. Warsaw, Poland, Dec. 25, 1920; came to U.S., 1925, naturalized, 1926; s. Jacob and Anna (Grabower) K.; m. Joyce Beth Krimsky, Aug. 7, 1956; children—Jamie, Jill. B.A., Yeshiva U., 1939; M.H.L., Jewish Theol. Sem., 1942, D.H.L., 1952, D.D. (hon.), 1970. Ordained rabbi, 1943; rabbi Temple Israel, Wilkes-Barre, Pa., 1947; asst. rabbi Kehillat Israel, Brookline, Mass., 1947-48; rabbi Congregation Beth El, New London, Conn., 1948-52, Bklyn. Jewish Center, 1952-68, Congregation Shaare Torah, Bklyn., 1968-76; exec. v.p. United Synagogue of Am., N.Y.C., 1976—; vis. prof. Judaic studies Bklyn. Coll., 1974-75, Jewish Theol. Sem., 1974-75. Cons. editor: (with others) Illustrated History of the Jews, 1962. Pres. Bklyn. Jewish Community Council, 1973-76; mem. N.Y.C. Bd. Health, 1972-79; chmn. Bklyn. Borough Pres.'s Commn. Human Relations, 1963-70, Small Bus. Opportunities Corp. of Bklyn., 1964-67. Served as chaplain USNR, 1943-46. Mem. Rabbinical Assembly, Am. Acad. Jewish Research, Assn. Coll. Profs. Home: 1612 Ditmas Ave Brooklyn NY 11226 Office: 155 Fifth Ave New York NY 10010

KREKELER, CARL H., biology educator; b. Leavenworth, Kan., Jan. 12, 1920; s. Carl and Louise (Wagner) K.; m. June Lillian Paulson, Dec. 23, 1944; children: Nancy June, Barbara Sue. B.A., Concordia Sem., St. Louis, 1941; postgrad., Washington U., St. Louis, 1944-45; Ph.D., U. Chgo., 1955. Instr. Bethany Coll., Mankato, Minn., 1942-44; ordained to ministry Lutheran Ch., 1945; pastor in, Milw., 1945-47; mem. faculty Valparaiso U., 1947—, prof. biology, 1958—, chmn. dept., 1959-82; naturalist Ind. State Park, summers 1951-52, chief naturalist, 1953-57. Author: (with William W. Bloom) General Biology: An Integrated Text Manual, 1963. Mem. Soc. Study Evolution, Soc. Systematic Zoology, Ecol. Soc. Am., Ind. Acad. Scis., Sigma Xi. Home: 360 McIntyre Ct Valparaiso IN 46383

KREMENLIEV, BORIS ANGELOFF, composer, author, music critic; b. Razlog, Bulgaria, May 23, 1911; came to U.S., 1929, naturalized, 1944; s. Angel A. and Elena (Pashkuleva) K.; m. Elva Florence Baer, Sept. 20, 1945; children: Gregor, Elena. B.Mus., DePaul U., 1935, M.Mus., 1937; Ph.D., U. Rochester, 1942. Mus. dir. S. German Network War Dept., 1945-46; prof. music UCLA, 1947-48, prof. emeritus, 1978—. Author: Music and its Makers, 1938, Bulgarian-Macedonian Folk Music, 1952, (with E. Kremenlieu) Folktales of the Bulgarian People, 1983; contbr.: Slavic Folklore, 1956, College and Adult Reading List., 1962, Czechoslovakia Past and Present, 1970, Bulgaria Past and Present, 1973, 83; articles to profl. jours.; composer: Variations for Orchestra, 1937, Song Symphony, 1941, Study, 1947, (with E. Kremenliev) Song for Parting, 1949, Grapes, 1951, Crucifixion, 1952, Bulgarian Rhapsody, 1953, Facing West, 1954, Ghetto Story, 1959, Symphony No. 2, 1960, Cantata, Once to Every Man and Nation, 1961, Balkan Rhapsody, 1966, 2d String Quartet, 1966, Elegy for Orch., 1968, Misa Juvenaliter, 1969, Sonata for String Bass, Piano, 1968-69, Koan No. 77 for contralto and chamber ensemble, 1979; contbr. music for radio, TV, motion pictures; composer chamber music and songs. Served with psychol. warfare br. AUS, 1943-45. Recipient Penrose award research folklore Am Philos. Soc., 1955, awards for contbn. to music ASCAP, 1968, 69, 70, 71, 72, 73; Ford Found. Internat. and Comparative Studies grantee, 1962; U. Calif. fellow Inst. Creative Arts, 1966-67; grantee Bulgarian Council of Ministers, 1969, Bulgarian Acad. Scis., 1979; IREX grantee, 1979. Mem. Internat. Soc. Folklore and Ethnology, Screen Composers Assn., ASCAP, Am. Fedn. Musicians, Am. Musicol. Soc., Am. Folklore Soc., Soc. for Ethnomusicology (v.p., chmn. So. Calif.). Home: 10507 Troon Ave Los Angeles CA 90064

KREMENTZ, EDWARD THOMAS, surgeon; b. Newark, Apr. 30, 1917; s. Albert Martin and Agnes Templeton (Aiguier) K.; m. Carolyn Butler, Oct. 5, 1946; children—Edward T., Anne Butler, Cynthia Aiguier Krementz Geoghegan, David George, Elizabeth Avery. A.B., Wesleyan U., 1939; M.D., U. Rochester, 1943. Asst. in surgery Yale U., 1943-48, Jane Coffin Childs Meml. Fund fellow, 1948-49, instr. surgery, 1948-50, Tulane U., 1950-53, asst. prof., 1953-57, asso. prof., 1957-61, prof., 1961—, acting chmn. dept., 1967-68, 76-77, cancer teaching coordinator, 1953—; dir. Tulane Cancer Clin. Research Center, Charity Hosp., 1961-75, Am. Cancer Soc. prof. clin. oncology, 1977—; sr. vis. surgeon Charity Hosp.; sr. asso. Touro Infirmary, New Orleans, 1963—; mem. staff Hotel Dieu, New Orleans, 1959—; surg. cons. several hosps. Chmn. bd. dirs. La. Tumor Registry, 1973—, Charity Hosp. La., 1955—. Recipient Research Career award Nat. Cancer Inst NIH, 1962-67. Mem. AAAS, Am. Assn. Cancer Edn., Am. Assn. Cancer Research, Am. Cancer Soc., A.C.S., AMA (co-recipient Hektoen Gold medal 1959), Am. Soc. Clin. Oncology, Soc. Surg. Oncology, Am. Surg. Assn., La., Orleans Parish med. socs., New Orleans Surg. Assn. U.C. (Shipley Gold medal 1964), So. Surg. Soc., Soc. Exptl. Biology and Medicine, Societe Internationale de Chirurgie, Soc. Univ. Surgeons, Southeastern Surg. Congress, Southeastern Cancer Research Assn., So. Med. Assn., Surg. Assn. La., WHO Internat. Group Clin. Study Melanoma, Sigma Xi, Alpha Omega Alpha. Clubs: New Orleans Country, Pendennis. Home: 500 Walnut St New Orleans LA 70118 Office: 1430 Tulane Ave New Orleans LA 70112

KREMENTZ, JILL, photographer, author; b. N.Y.C., Feb. 19, 1940; d. Walter and Virginia (Hyde) K.; m. Kurt Vonnegut, Jr., Nov., 1979; 1 dau., Lily. Student, Drew U., 1958-59, Art Students League, Columbia. With Harper's Bazaar, 1959-60, Glamour mag., 1960-61; pub. relations staff Indian Industries Fair, New Delhi, 1961; reporter Show mag., 1962-64; staff photographer N.Y. Herald Tribune, 1964-65, Vietnam, 1965-66; asso. editor Status-Diplomat mag., 1966-67; contbg. editor N.Y.. mag., 1967-68; corr. Time-Life Inc., 1969-70; contbg. photographer People mag., 1974—. Contbr. numerous U.S. and fgn. periodicals.; one-woman photography shows, Madison (Wis.) Art Center, 1973, U. Mass., Boston, 1974, Nikon Gallery, N.Y.C., Del. Art Mus., Wilmington, 1975; represented in permanent collections, Mus. Modern Art, Library of Congress.; Photographer: The Face of South Vietnam (text by Dean Brelis), 1968, Words and Their Masters (text by Israel Shenker), 1974; photographer, author: Sweet Pea—A Black Girl Growing Up in the Rural South (foreword by Margaret Mead), 1969, A Very Young Dancer, 1976, A Very Young Rider, 1977, A Very Young Gymnast, 1978, A Very Young Circus Flyer, 1979, A Very Young Skater, 1979, The Writer's Image, 1980, How It Feels When a Parent Dies, 1981, How It Feels to be Adopted, 1982. Mem. P.E.N., Am. Soc. Mag. Photographers (dir.), Women's Forum. Address: care Donald C Farber Park Ave 10th Floor New York NY 10017

KREMER, FRED, JR., manufacturing company executive; b. Chgo., July 24, 1926; s. Fred and Alice (Pearson) K.; m. Edna Berglund, Aug. 21, 1948; children—Gale, Kimberly, Lorna. B.S. in Bus. Adminstrn, Ill. Inst. Tech., 1950. With Ill. Inst. Tech. Research Inst., 1950-66; v.p. ARF Devel. Corp., 1963-66; v.p. bus. operations Asso. Merchandising Corp., 1966-73, v.p. adminstrn. and finance, sec.-treas., 1968-73; chmn. bd., dir. Instapak Corp., Danbury, Conn., 1970-76, pres., chief exec. officer, 1973-76; exec. v.p. Sapolin Paints Inc., Danbury, Conn., 1977, pres., chief operating officer, 1978-79, chief exec. officer, 1979—; pres., chief exec. officer Aldrich Precision Mfg. Co., Danbury, 1980-82, also dir.; pres., chief exec. officer, dir. Hancor, Inc., Findlay, Ohio, 1983—; Mem. ad hoc. com. role patents in research Nat. Acad. Scis.-NRC, 1961-62. Treas. Met. Synod, Lutheran Ch. Am., 1971—. Served with USAAF, 1944-46. Mem. Am. Mgmt. Assn. Lutheran (past v.p., sec. bd., Sunday sch. supt.). Club: Economic (N.Y.C.). Home: 2801 S Main St Findlay OH 45820 Office: Hancor Inc 401 Olive St Findlay OH 45840

KREML, FRANKLIN MARTIN, educational administrator, association executive; b. Chgo., Jan. 11, 1907; s. Frank Joseph and Sophia Valeria (Dvorak) K.; m. Margaret Charlotte Parker, July 11, 1927 (div. 1979); children: Franklin Parker, William Parker; m. Barbara Irene Bloom, 1980. Student, U. Wis., 1923-24, Northwestern U., 1925-29; J.D., John Marshall Law Sch., Chgo., 1932. Agt. U.S. Bur. Rds., 1924-25; mem. Evanston Police Dept., advanced through grades to lt., 1926-35, dir. Accident Prevention Bur., 1929-35; sec. City Council Commn. Traffic and Safety, Chgo., 1932; pub. safety specialist Purdue U., 1935-36; dir. traffic div. Internat. Assn. Chiefs of Police, 1936-56; dir. Traffic Officers Tng. Sch. (now Traffic Inst.), Northwestern U., 1932-55, Transp. Center, 1955-62; v.p. univ. Northwestern U., 1962-71; asso. dir. Northwestern U. Transp. Center, 1975-79, now cons. Transp. Center and Traffic Inst.; pres., chief exec. officer Motor Vehicles Mfrs. Assn. U.S., Detroit, 1971-75; pres. Consortium of Govtl. Counselors Inc., 1981—. Co-author several texts and manuals, numerous articles on transp., traffic and traffic safety. Pres. Chgo. Police Bd., 1960-72; chmn. Pres.'s Task Force Hwy. Safety, 1970; formerly v.p., vice chmn. Nat. Safety Council. Served with AUS, World War II; ret. brig. gen. Recipient various civic awards and mil. decorations. Mem. Internat. Assn. Chiefs Police (life), Am. Soc. Criminology, Theta Delta Phi, Delta Upsilon. Congregationalist. Clubs: University (Evanston, Ill.); Tavern (Chgo.); Westmoreland Country (Wilmette, Ill.); Metropolitan (Washington). Home: 2327 W Greenleaf Ave Chicago IL 60645 Office: Consortium of Govtl Counselors Inc 1625 Hinman Ave Evanston IL 60201 *I learned in a long life—admittedly with difficulty—that in the business of living, compromise is the essential of leadership, critical to success. I also learned that I dare not compromise basic values or judgments based upon them. My evaluation of my life is that I served most successfully when I held to principle. Thus on two major occasions—one in the U.S. Army in WW II, and the other during my service as vice-president in Northwestern University—when principle dictated violation of direct orders of my superiors, I found in each of these both spiritual and temporal reward, heightened by the peril of my chosen course.*

KREMPL, ERHARD, mechanics educator, consultant; b. Regensburg, Germany, Mar. 5, 1934; came to U.S., 1964; m. Johanna A. Wunderlich, Dec. 19, 1961; children: Christine C., Ralph D. Dipl. Ing., Technische Hochschule Muenchen, W. Germany, 1956, Dr.Ing., 1962. Instr. research engring. Technische Hochschule Muenchen, 1956-59, wissenschaftl asst., 1959-64; mechanics of materials engr. Gen Electric Co., Schenectady, 1964-68; assoc. prof. Rensselaer Poly Inst., Troy, N.Y., 1968-75, prof. mechanics, 1975—; vis. scientist Argonne Nat. Lab., Ill., 1974; Richard Merton guest prof. Institute fur Statik und Dynamic der Luft und Raumfahrtkonstruktionen, Stuttgart, W.Ger., 1975-76. Author: (with Lai and Rubin) Introduction to Continuum Mechanics, 1974; contbr. numerous articles to profl. jours.; editor: Jour. Engring. Materials and Tech., 1981-84. Research grantee NSF, Office Naval Research, NASA, Pressure Vessel Research Com. Fellow ASME (chmn. materials div. 1977-78), Am. Acad. Mechanics; mem. ASTM, AAUP, Am. Soc. Engring. Edn., Soc. Engring. Sci. Office: Dept Engring Aero Engring and Mechanics Rensselaer Poly Inst. Troy NY 12181

KRENDEL, EZRA SIMON, educator; b. N.Y.C., Mar. 5, 1925; s. Joseph and Tamara (Shapiro) K.; m. Elizabeth Spencer Malany, Aug. 20, 1950; children—David A., Tamara E. (Mrs. David W. Clark), Jennifer J. (Mrs. David L. Hall). A.B., Bklyn. Coll., 1945; Sc.M. in Physics, MIT, 1947; A.M. in Social Relations, Harvard, 1949; M.A. honoris causa, U. Pa., 1971. From research engr. to sr. staff engr. Franklin Inst. Research Labs., 1949-55, lab. mgr., 1955-63, tech. dir., 1963-66, sr. adviser, cons., 1961; dir. Mgmt. Sci. Center, Wharton Sch., U. Pa., 1967-69; chmn. bd. advisers, 1969-70; prof. ops. research U. Pa., Phila., 1966—; Mem. research adv. com. on control guidance and nav. NASA, 1964-65; various coms. Hwy. Research Bd., NRC, 1964—; vis. lectr. NATO, 1968, 71; mem. roster of arbitrators Fed. Mediation and Conciliation Service; cons. govt. agys., industry. Author: Unionizing the Armed Forces, 1977; Contbr. articles to profl. publs. Mem. Phila. Mayor's Sci. and Tech. Adv. Council. Recipient Louis E. Levy Gold medal Franklin Inst., 1960. Fellow Am. Psychol. Assn., IEEE, AAAS, Human Factors Soc.; mem. Operations Research Soc. Am. (chmn. membership com. 1968-70), Ergonomics Soc., Am. Arbitration Assn. (labor panel), Sigma Xi. Club: Cosmos (Washington). Home: 211 Cornell Ave Swarthmore PA 19081 Office: U Pa Philadelphia PA 19104

KRENEK, ERNST, composer, author; b. Vienna, Austria, Aug. 23, 1900; came to U.S., 1938, naturalized, 1945; s. Ernst and Emanuela (Cizek) K.; m. Gladys Nordenstrom, Aug. 8, 1950. Ed., U. Vienna, Acad. Music, Vienna and Berlin. Prof. music Vassar Coll., 1939-42; prof. music, dean Sch. Fine Arts Hamline U., St. Paul, 1942-47. Composer 233 musical works; author 16 books. Served with Austro-Hungarian Army, 1918. NEA fellow, 1977, 80; Decorated cross of mert, gold medals, Austria, Ger., Vienna, Hamburg, others; named hon. citizen Vienna. Mem. Broadcast Music Internat., Counseil International del la Musique, Am. Acad. Arts; hon mem. acads. music Vienna, Graz, Salzburg, Stuttgart, Hamburg, others. Roman Catholic.

KRENITSKY, MICHAEL V., librarian; b. Duquesne, Pa., Nov. 15, 1915; s. Alexander and Anna (Beresnak) K.; m. Jane Rook, June 15, 1941; children—Jane Ann (Mrs. Richard Williams), Michael V., John Rook. B.S., Washington and Jefferson Coll., 1938, Carnegie Inst. Tech., 1947; M.A., So. Meth. U., 1954. Librarian Pa. Indsl. Sch., Camp Hill, 1941-43, Tex. Mil. Coll., Terrell, 1947-49; circulation librarian Tex. A. and M. Coll., College Station, 1949-51, asso. librarian, 1951-61; prof. library sci. Mich. Tech. U., Houghton, 1961—, library dir., 1961-79, library dir. emeritus, 1979—; vis. prof. Library Sch., Tex. Woman's U., Denton, summer 1960; State Dept. ICA appointee to Indonesia to survey univ. library problems, 1959. Contbr. articles profl. jours. Mem. Mich. Bd. for Libraries Adv. Com. on Mich.'s Reference and Research Resources, 1966—; mem. exec. council Mich. Library Consortium, 1974—; Treas. College Station United Fund, 1960. Served with AUS, 1943-46. Mem. ALA, Mich. Library Assn. (chmn. acad. library div. 1969), Internat. Assn. Agrl. Librarians and Documentalists, Hist. Soc. Mich. (mem. awards com. 1972—), Assn. Coll. and Research Libraries, Phi Delta Theta. Episcopalian. Home: 1112 E 6th Ave Houghton MI 49931

KRENITSKY, PETER, physician; b. Butler, Pa., June 16, 1935; s. Paul and Anna (Krynicki) K.; m. Barbara Anne Barone, July 26, 1958; children—Kristin Elena, Kara Leigh. B.S., Grove City Coll., 1957; D.O., Kansas City Coll. Osteo. Medicine, 1961. Intern Detroit Osteo. Hosp., 1961-62, resident in internal medicine, 1962-65; practice osteo. medicine, Detroit, 1965—; chief staff Detroit Osteo. and Bicounty Hosp., 1971-73, trustee, 1971-73; clin. prof. Coll. Osteo. Medicine Mich. State U., 1971—; chmn. dept. internal medicine Art Center Hosp., 1970. Recipient Mosby book award for scholastic excellence, 1961. Mem. Am. Osteo. Assn., Mich. Assn. Osteo. Physicians and Surgeons, Mich. Heart Assn., Am. Coll. Osteo. Internists, Psi Sigma Alpha, Sigma Sigma Phi. Roman Catholic. Club: Detroit Golf. Research in prism optics. Home: 19560 Parkside St Detroit MI 48221 Office: 13355 E 10 Mile Rd Warren MI 48089

KRENKEL, PETER ASHTON, engineer, educator, university dean; b. San Francisco, Jan. 3, 1930; s. Harry Nichols and Daisy Genevieve (Ashton) K.; m. Virginia Grace Hallman, 1975. A.A., Coll. City San Francisco, 1952; B.S., U. Calif.-Berkeley, 1956, M.S., 1958, Ph.D., 1960. Registered profl. engr., Ga., Tenn., Nev., N.C. Instr. U. Calif. at Berkeley, 1958-60; founder Associated Water & Air Resources Engrs., Inc., Nashville, 1968—; chmn., prof. dept. environ. and water resources engring. Vanderbilt U., Nashville, 1960-73; dir. div. environ. planning TVA, 1974-78; exec. dir. Water Resources Center U. Nev., Reno, 1978-82, dean Coll. Engring., 1982—; disting. lectr. Am. Inst. Chem. Engrs.; cons. WHO, Internat. Joint Commn. on Great Lakes Water Quality, U.S. EPA, U.S. Dept. Energy, Roy F. Weston, Inc.; chmn. thermal pollution panel Nat. Water Commn., Washington, 1970—, Tenn. Air Conservation Commn., 1971—. Author: (with V. Novotny) Water Quality Management, 1980; editor: (with F.L. Parker) Thermal Pollution, Biological Aspects, 1970, Thermal Pollution, Engineering Aspects, 1970, Water Quality Monitoring in Europe, 1972, Heavy Metals in the Aquatic Environment, 1974; Contbr.: numerous articles on environmental control to profl. jours. Heavy Metals in the Aquatic Environment. Pres. Tenn. Lung Assn., 1974-75. Served with AUS, 1953-55. Fellow USPHS, 1963; recipient award outstanding research san. engring. ASCE, 1963, Skill, Integrity,

Responsibility award Am. Gen. Contractors, 1984. Mem. Am. Water Works Assn., Water Pollution Control Fedn. (bd. control), Air Pollution Control Assn., Am. Public Health Assn., Am. Inst. Chem. Engrs., ASCE, Internat. Assn. Water Pollution Research (governing bd.), Am. Acad. Environ. Engring. (diplomate), Sigma Xi, Tau Beta Pi, Chi Epsilon. Home: 3915 Henry Ct Reno NV 89509

KRENSKY, HAROLD, retired retail store executive, Consultant; b. Boston, Apr. 7, 1912; s. Philip and Katherine (Bladd) K.; m. Adele Falk, July 5, 1936; 1 dau., Jane Paula. LL.B., Boston U., 1935; D.H.L., Lab. Inst. Merchandising, 1982. Bar: Mass. 1937. With Hearst Publs., 1935-42; mdse. mgr. R.H. White's, Boston, 1942-47; sr. v.p. charge merchandising and publicity Bloomingdale's, N.Y.C., 1947-59, chmn. bd., mng. dir., 1967-69; exec. v.p. William Filene's Sons Co., Boston, 1960-63, pres., 1963-65, chmn. bd., chief exec. officer, 1965-66; v.p. Federated Dept. Stores, Inc., 1965-69, group pres., 1969-71, dir., 1969-82, vice chmn., 1971-73, pres., 1973-80, chmn. exec. com., 1980-82; bus. cons., 1982—; hon. dir. Liberty Mut. Ins. Co., Boston, Liberty Mut. Fire Ins. Co.; dir. Liberty Mut. Life Ins. Co., Boston, Norlin Corp., Asso. Merchandising Corp. Trustee Boston U., City of Hope; trustee Nat. Jewish Hosp., also Humanitarian award, 1976; bd. dirs. Fashion Inst. Tech.; adv. council Tobe Coburn Sch., also 1969 Tobe awardee; adv. bd. N.Y. Fashion Designers, Inc., also 1970 awardee. Recipient Humanitarian award, 1976, Alumnus award Boston U., 1980. Home: 860 UN Plaza New York NY 10017 Office: 104 W 40th St New York NY 10018

KRENTS, MILTON ELLIS, broadcasting exec.; b. Springfield, Mass., Dec. 22, 1911; s. Morris Joseph and Ethel (Kramer) K.; m. Irma Kopp, May 1, 1938; children—Lawrence, Harold, Elisabeth. B.S., N.Y. U., 1935. Jr. exec. trainee NBC, N.Y.C., 1935-39; dir. radio-TV Am. Jewish Com., 1936-69; TV programming cons. Assn. for Higher Edn. of N.E.A., 1965-68; radio, TV cons. Council Fin. Aid to Edn., 1960-65; communications cons. Revson Found., 1979-80. Originator, exec. producer: radio and TV series for The Eternal Light, Jewish Theol. Sem., NBC, 1945—; radio cons.: Council for Democracy, 1942-45; radio, TV dir.: Am. Jewish Tercentenary, 1954. Nat. chmn. William E. Wiener Oral History Library, Am. Jewish Commn., 1969—. Recipient Robert E. Sherwood award, 1958; Faith and Freedom Broadcasting award Religious Heritage Am., 1972. Mem. Pub. Relations Soc. Am., N.Y. U. Alumni Assn. (chmn. communications com. 1980—), Nat. Acad. TV Arts and Scis., Broadcast Pioneers. Home: 141 E 89th St New York NY 10028 Office: 165 E 56th St New York NY 10022

KRENTZMAN, BEN, U.S. district judge; b. Milton, Fla., Mar. 21, 1914; s. Isaac B. and Juanita (Rogers) K.; m. Wilma McMullen, Nov. 30, 1946; children: John Arthur, Mary Louise, Elizabeth Rogers. B.S., LL.B., U. Fla., 1938. Bar: Fla. 1938. Practiced in, Clearwater, 1938-41, 46-67; U.S. judge Tampa Div., Middle Dist. Fla., 1967—, chief judge, 1981-82, sr. judge, 1982—. Served to lt. col. AUS, 1941-46. Decorated Bronze Star medal. Office: PO Box 3209 Tampa FL 33601

KRENZ, DEAN ALBERT, newspaper publisher; b. Wheaton, Minn., Apr. 6, 1930; s. Albert Herman and Mabel Victoria (Carlson) K.; m. Joan Janet Utley, Dec. 31, 1955; 1 son, Keith Allen. B.A., U. Minn., 1952. Asst. pub. Delaware County Daily Times, Chester, Pa., 1964-66; pub. Trentonian, Trenton, N.J., 1966-73, Daily Jour., Elizabeth, N.J., 1973-75, Sioux City Newspapers, Inc., Iowa, 1975—; v.p. ops. Ingersoll Newspapers, 1970-73. Bd. dirs. St. Luke's Med. Center, Sioux City, 1975-81. Served with U.S. Army, 1952-54. Mem. Iowa Daily Press Assn. (bd. dirs.), Sioux City C. of C. (v.p. 1980). Republican. Lutheran. Office: 515 Pavonia St Sioux City IA 51102 *

KRENZ, DONALD A., business exec., lawyer; b. Buffalo, Apr. 24, 1936; s. Albert and Stella (Holls) K.; m. Darlene F. Hedin, May 26, 1962; children—Carolyn, Jeanne. B.S., U. Buffalo, 1958; LL.B., Columbia, 1959. Bar: N.Y. bar 1959. Asso. atty. firm Royall, Koegel & Rogers, N.Y.C., 1959-66; with Ogden Corp., N.Y.C., 1966—, v.p., 1968-70, chief counsel, 1968—, sr. v.p., 1970-80, exec. v.p., 1980—, mem. fin. com., 1979—, also dir. Home: 6 Country Ln Westport CT 06880 Office: 277 Park Ave New York NY 10172

KRENZLER, ALVIN IRVING, judge; b. Chgo., Apr. 8, 1921. A.B., Case Western Res. U., 1946, LL.B., 1948; LL.M., Georgetown U., 1963. Bar: Ohio 1948. Practice law, Cleve., 1948-68; judge Cuyahoga County Ct. Common Pleas, Ohio, 1968-70, Ohio Ct. Appeals, Cleve., 1970-81; Judge U.S. Dist. Ct. (no. dist.), Ohio, 1981—; counsel, dir. Ohio Narcotics Investigation, 1953-55; asst. atty. gen. State of Ohio, 1951-56; trail atty. office chief counsel IRS, Washington, 1960-63. Chmn. Cuyahoga County Bd. Mental Retardation, 1967-70; trustee Cleve. State U., 1967-70, Mt. Sinai Hosp., Cleve., 1973—; chmn. Ohio Criminal Justice Supervisory Commn., 1975-83. Mem. ABA; MEM. Greater Cleve. Bar Assn.; mem. Cuyahoga County Bar Assn., Fed. Bar. Assn. Home: 24550 Meldon Blvd Beachwood OH 44122 Office: 201 Superior Ave Cleveland OH 44114

KREPS, JUANITA MORRIS (MRS. CLIFTON H. KREPS, JR.), former secretary commerce; b. Lynch, Ky., Jan. 11, 1921; d. Elmer M. and Cenia (Blair) Morris; m. Clifton H. Kreps, Jr., Aug. 11, 1944; children: Sarah, Laura, Clifton. A.B., Berea Coll., 1942; M.A., Duke U., 1944; Ph.D., 1948. Instr. econs. Denison U., 1945-46, asst. prof., 1948-50; mem. faculty Duke U., 1955-77, assoc. prof., 1962-68, prof. econs., 1968-77; James B. Duke prof. Duke, 1972-77; asst. provost Duke U., 1969-72, v.p., 1973-77; U.S. sec. commerce, 1977-79; bd. dirs. N.Y. Stock Exchange, 1972-77; dir. Eastman Kodak Co., R.J. Reynolds Industries, Inc., Citicorp., ARMCO, UAL, Inc., United Airlines, J.C. Penney, AT&T, Deere & Co., Zurn Industries, Inc., Chrysler Corp.; Trustee Berea Coll., Duke Endowment, Nat. Humanities Center, HumRRO, 1980-83, Council on Fgn. Relations, Tchrs. Ins. and Annuity Assn., 1968-72, Coll. Retirement Equities Fund, 1972-77; bd. dirs. Nat. Merit Scholarship Corp., 1972-77, Ednl. Testing Service, 1971-77; mem. Nat. Manpower Policy Task Force. Author: (with C.E. Ferguson) Principles of Economics, 2d rev. edit, 1965, Lifetime Allocation of Work and Income, 1971, Sex in the Marketplace: American Women at Work, 1971, Women and the American Economy, 1976; co-author: Contemporary Labor Economics, 1973; Editor: Employment, Income and Retirement Problems of the Aged, 1963, Technology, Manpower and Retirement Policy, 1966, Sex, Age and Work, 1975. Named to Presdl. Commn. on Nat. Agenda for the 80's, 1979; Recipient N.C. Public Service award, 1976; Stephen Wise award, 1978; Woman of Yr. award Ladies Home Jour., 1978. Fellow Gerontol. Soc. (v.p. 1971-72); mem. Am. Econ. Assn. (v.p. 1983-84), So. Econ. Assn. (pres. 1975-76), AAUP, AAUW (Achievement award 1981), Indsl. Relations Research Assn. (exec. com.). Office: 115 E Duke Bldg Duke U Durham NC 27708

KRESGE, BRUCE ANDERSON, physician; b. Detroit, Dec. 20, 1931; s. Stanley Sebastian and Dorothy Eloise (McVittie) K.; m. Peggy Ann Sale, June 14, 1952; children—Deborah (Mrs. Paul McDowell), Katherine (Mrs. Daniel Lutey), Susan (Mrs. Thomas Drewes), Cynthia, Stephen. B.A., Albion Coll., 1953; M.D., Wayne State U., 1956. Intern Detroit Receiving Hosp., 1956-57; resident U. Mich. Hosp., 1959-60; gen. practice medicine, Rochester, Mich., 1960—; mem. staff St. Joseph Mercy Hosp., Pontiac, Mich., also; Pontiac Gen. Hosp., 1960-67, Crittenton Hosp., Rochester, 1967—. Pres. Rochester br. YMCA, 1975-77; Trustee Kresge Found., 1967—, Albion (Mich.) Coll., 1972—. Served with M.C. AUS, 1957-59. Mem. AMA. Republican. Methodist. Home: 665 Apple Hill Ln Rochester MI 48063 Office: 1500 Walton St Rochester MI 48063

KRESGE, STANLEY SEBASTIAN, found. exec.; b. Detroit, June 11, 1900; s. Sebastian Spering and Anna Emma (Harvey) K.; m. Dorothy Eloise McVittie, Oct. 2, 1923; children—Walter H., Stanley Sebastian, Bruce Anderson. A.B., Albion (Mich.) Coll., 1923. With S.S. Kresge Co., 1923-77, store mgr., 1927-28, various positions in main office, 1930-45, dir., 1950—; trustee Kresge Found., Troy, Mich., 1931—, pres., 1952-66, chmn. bd., 1966-78. Author: S.S. Kresge, 1979. Del. Republican Nat. Conv., 1948, 52; emeritus trustee Albion Coll.; hon. dir. Detroit YMCA. Methodist. Clubs: Detroit, Detroit Athletic. Home: 1071 Lake Angelus Rd W Pontiac MI 48055 Office: 2401 W Big Beaver Rd Troy MI 48084 *I believe my life has been enriched by my having been brought up in a Christian home; educated in public schools and colleges by many good teachers and professors; helped by my participating in sports, learning team play and how to get along with people, and developing good friends.*

KRESH, PAUL, consultant, author, editor; b. N.Y.C., Dec. 3, 1919; s. Samuel and Jean (Feinsilver) K. Student, Columbia U., 1936-37; B.A., CCNY, 1939. Publicist Nat. Jewish Welfare Bd., 1941-45; publicity dir. Am. ORT Fedn., 1945-46; asst. publicity dir. Council Jewish Fedns. and Welfare Funds, 1946-47; writer, publicist Nathan C. Belth Assos., 1947-50; motion picture dir., asst. publicity dir. United Jewish Appeal, 1950-59; pub. relations dir. Union Am. Hebrew Congs., 1959-67; editor Am. Judaism, 1960-67; v.p., rec. dir. Spoken Arts Records, 1967-71; rec. exec. Caedmon Records, 1971-72; pub. relations dir. United Jewish Appeal Greater N.Y., 1972-74; creative dir. United Jewish Appeal-Fedn. Jewish Philanthropies, 1974-81; communications cons., 1981—; contbg. editor Am. Record Guide, 1958-61, Stereo Rev., 1961—; spoken word critic and music record N.Y. Times, 1973—; spoken word commr. White House Record Library Commn., 1979—. Scriptwriter, radio sta. WNYC, 1940-42; dir., scriptwriter: weekly CBS radio series Adventures in Judaism, 1961—; writer, dir.: weekly radio series Jewish World, 1973-74, World of Jewish Music, 1982-83 (Armstrong award 1982); (Recipient Ohio State U. award for radio scripts Adventures in Music, 1940, 41, for Adventures in Judaism 1965, 66, 68, 67, Golden Eagle award for film script The Day the Doors Closed, Council Internat. Nontheatrical Events 1965, Chris award Columbus Film Festival for May It Be, 1975, On the Brink of Peace 1980, Bronze medal Internat TV and Film Festival for Broken Sabbath 1974, Silver medal for Commitment 1976, Armstrong award Ohio State award for Jewish World Radio Series 1975, Emmy award for outstanding individual craft 1979-80); Author: The Power of the Unknown Citizen, 1969, Isaac Bashevis Singer: The Magician of West 86th Street, 1979; also critical essays, revs., articles; writer, dir. ednl. filmstrips and spoken-word recs.; Editor: American Judaism Reader, 1967, Spoken Arts Treasury of 100 Modern American Poets Reading Their Poems, 1969. Award Religious Heritage Found., 1968; silver medal Internat. Film and TV Festival, N.Y.C., 1972; award best organizational newspaper Council Jewish Fedns., 1972. Fellow MacDowell Colony-Va. Center for Creative Arts.; Mem. Nat. Acad. Rec. Arts and Scis. (v.p., gov.), Nat. Acad. TV Arts and Scis., Am. Soc. Journalists and Authors, Nat. Soc. Lit. and Arts, Authors Guild, P.E.N. Am. Center, Writers Guild Am. Home: 2 Charlton St New York NY 10014 Office: 225 Park Ave S New York NY 10003

KRESS, GEORGE F., packaging co. exec.; b. Green Bay, Wis., Sept. 15, 1903; s. Frank F. and Louise (Schmidt) K.; m. Marguerite Christensen, Nov. 10, 1926; children—James, Marilyn Kress Swanson, Donald. B.A., U. Wis., 1925. With Green Bay Packaging Inc., 1933—, chmn. bd., 1963—; chmn. bd., dir. Ark. Kraft Corp., 1965—; dir. Assos. Bank Services. Bd. govs. St. Norbert Coll.; trustee Charitable, Ednl. and Sci. Found. of Wis. Med. Soc.; pres., chmn. bd. Green Bay affiliate Am. Found. Religion and Psychiatry; mem. Brown County Republican Com. Mem. Ch. of Christ. Clubs: N.Y. Yacht, Great Lakes Cruising, Mackiniac Island Yacht, Sun Valley Ski, Elks. Home: 2376 Du Charme Ln Green Bay WI 54301 Office: PO Box 1107 Green Bay WI 54305

KRESS, PAUL FREDERICK, political scientist; b. Stoughton, Wis., Sept. 10, 1935; s. Frederick Raymond and Mabel Idelia (Paulson) K.; m. Charlotte Louise Belshe, Aug. 17, 1959. B.S., U. Wis.-Madison, 1956, M.S., 1958; Ph.D., U. Calif., Berkeley, 1964. Asst. prof. polit. sci. Northwestern U., Evanston, Ill., 1964-70; asso. prof. polit. sci. U. N.C., Chapel Hill, 1970-75, prof., 1975-82; vis. asst. prof. U. Hawaii, summer 1967; cons. Naval Research Lab., San Diego, 1974-75. Author: Social Science and the Idea of Process: The Ambiguous Legacy of Arthur F. Bentley, 1970; editorial bd.: Jour. Politics, 1971-79. Social Sci. Research Council fellow, 1962-63.

KRESS, RALPH HERMAN, mfg. co. exec.; b. Lawrence, Mass., July 10, 1904; s. Edward and Sadie (Welsh) K.; m. Edna Llewelyn Sheridan, Sept. 9, 1929; 1 son, Edward Sheridan. Student mech. engring. and applied math., Lowell Inst., M.I.T., 1937-39, 42. Salesman Dodge Truck, Lawrence, 1922-34; sales mgr. Chevrolet Truck Sales, Lawrence, 1934-39; engr. (GM Chevrolet and Fleet div.), Detroit, Boston, Washington, 1939-43; exec. v.p. Dart Truck Co., Kansas City, Mo., 1950-55; mgr. truck div. Letourneau Westinghouse Corp., Peoria, Ill., 1955-62; mgr. truck devel. Caterpillar Tractor Co., Peoria, 1962-69; exec. v.p. Kress Corp., Brimfield, Ill., 1969—. Contbr. articles to profl. jours. Served to maj. U.S. Army, 1943-46. Decorated Legion of Merit. Fellow Soc. Automotive Engrs. (G. Edwin Burks Lecture award 1975); mem. Assn. U.S. Army, Ill. Mining Assn., Western Mining Assn. Republican. Christian Scientist. Club: Rotary. Holder 28 U.S. patents in field. Home: 4444 Knoxville St Peoria IL 61614 Office: PO Box 368 Brimfield IL 61517

KRESS, ROY ALFRED, psychology educator; b. Elmira, N.Y., Oct. 4, 1916; s. Roy Alfred and Alice Elmira (Whitaker) K.; m. Doris Ethel Parker, Mar. 29, 1940 (dec. dec. July 1969); children: Keith Denton, Lance Whitaker, Gene Gordon; m. Eleanor Murphy Ladd, Dec. 4, 1969. B.S. in Edn., Lock Haven State Coll., 1938; Ed.M., Temple U., 1949, Ph.D., 1956. Tchr. Woods Schs., Langhorne, Pa., 1938-43; tng. supr. VA, Phila., 1946-49; lectr. Temple U., Phila., 1949-55, prof. psychology, 1963-68, chmn. psychology of reading dept., 1968-70, asso. dean, 1970-73, prof. psychology of reading, 1973-79, prof. emeritus, 1979—, acting dean, 1974-75; ednl. dir. Shady Brook Schs., Richardson, Tex., 1955-58; asso. prof. Syracuse (N.Y.) U., 1958-63; vis. lectr. Tex. Women's U., 1956, So. State Coll. Ark., 1957, U. Ark., 1958, State U. N.Y., 1960, U. Colo., 1961, Appalachian State U., 1970-79, U. S.C., 1980, Furman U., 1980; cons. edn. and psychology, U.S., Can., Australia. Author: A Place to Start, 1963, (with Marjorie S. Johnson) Informal Reading Inventories, 1965, (with M.S. Johnson and J. McNeil) The Read System, rev. edit, 1971, American Book Company Reading Program, 1977; Editor: That All May Learn to Read, 1959, (with M.S. Johnson) Corrective Reading in the Elementary Classroom, 1967 (Outstanding Education Book of 1967, Pi Lambda Theta), Proc. Ann. Reading Insts. Temple U., 1963-70; proc. The Reading Teacher, 1967-71; editorial adv. bd.: Reading Research Quar, 1965-70, Jour. Learning Disability, 1968—, The Reading Tchr, 1971-72; adv. bd.: ERIC/CRIER, 1968-71, 73-75. Instl. rep., scoutmaster Circle Ten council, Onondaga Valley council Boy Scouts Am., 1955-63; faculty sponsor Alpha Phi Omega, Syracuse U., 1958-63. Served with USMCR, 1943-46. Recipient Disting. Service award Lock Haven State Coll. Alumni Assn., 1973, Internat. Reading Assn., 1976; Research grantee Phila. Bd. Edn., 1965-68. Mem. Am. Psychol. Assn., Internat. Reading Assn. (mem. bd. 1964-67), Nat. Council Research in English (bd. 1966-69, sec.-treas. 1972-75), Coll. Reading Assn. (bd. 1971-74, A.B. Herr award for disting. service in reading 1984), Nat. Soc. Study Edn., Am. Edn. Research Assn., Nat. Council Grad. Sch. Deans, Sigma Pi, Phi Delta Kappa, Alpha Phi Omega. Club: Masons. Home: RD 2 Box 165 Mill Spring NC 28756

KRESS, THOMAS GEORGE, mfg. co. exec.; b. Dubuque, Ia., May 11, 1931; s. Henry L. and Jane (Schadle) K.; m. Lou Ann Kuehnle, Sept. 6, 1952; children—Kristine, Elizabeth, Kathleen, Susan, Thomas George, Andrew, Julianna, Matthew, Michael. B.A., Loras Coll., 1953; M.B.A., Northwestern U., 1961; grad., Advanced Mgmt. Program, Harvard, 1971. Cost analyst Gen. Electric Co., Chgo., 1956-62; div. controller Sheller Mfg. Corp., Keokuk, Ia., 1962-64, asst. corp. controller, Detroit, 1964-66; corp. controller Sheller Globe Corp., Toledo, 1967-72, treas., 1972—, v.p., 1974—. Served with U.S. Army, 1953-55. Mem. Financial Execs. Inst., Nat. Assn. Accountants. Club: Toledo. Home: 4731 Rose Glenn St Toledo OH 43615 Office: 1505 Jefferson Ave Toledo OH 43624

KRESSEL, HENRY, electronic company executive; b. Vienna, Jan. 24, 1934; U.S., 1946, naturalized, 1955; s. Aaron and Hudi (Zauderer) K.; m. Bertha Horowitz, Sept. 16, 1956; children—Aron, Kim. B.S. magna cum laude, Yeshiva U., 1955; M.S., Harvard U., 1956; M.B.A., U. Pa., 1959, Ph.D. (David Sarnoff fellow), 1965. Engr. Solid State div. RCA, 1959-61, engring. leader, 1961-63, 65-66; mem. tech. staff RCA David Sarnoff Research Center, 1966-70, head semicondr. device research, 1970-78, dir. materials research lab., 1978-79, staff v.p. solid state research, Princeton, N.J., 1979-83; sr. v.p. E.M. Warburg, Pincus & Co., N.Y.C., 1983—; regents' lectr. U. Calif., San Diego, 1978-79; bd. dirs. Yeshiva U. Research Inst., 1979-84; cons. solar energy U.S. ERDA, 1975. Author: Semiconductor Lasers and Heterojunction LED's, 1977; editor: Characterization of Epitaxial Semiconductor Films, 1976, Semiconductor Devices for Optical Communication, 1980; asso. editor: IEEE Jour. Quantum Electronics, 1978-81; Contbr. numerous articles to sci. jours. Served with Fin. Corps U.S. Army, 1959. Recipient David Sarnoff award RCA, 1974, Bevel award Yeshiva U., 1980. Fellow IEEE (pres. Quantum Electronics and Applications Soc. 1978-79), Am. Phys. Soc.; mem. AIME, Nat. Acad. Engring. Patentee in field. Home: 529 Riverside Dr Elizabeth NJ 07208 Office: E M Warburg Pincus & Co 277 Park Ave New York NY 10172

KRESSLER, JAMES PHILLIP, manufacturing company executive; b. Trenton, N.J., Sept. 22, 1931; s. Earl James and Ruth Emily (Jacoby) K.; m. Nancy Carolyn Loux, Aug. 28, 1954; children: David, Robert, Nancy. B.S., Lehigh U., 1953; M.B.A., Harvard U., 1955. Asst. controller Itek Corp., Lexington, Mass., 1958-62, 65-70; v.p., treas., controller Radiation Counter Labs., Inc., Skokie, Ill., 1962-65; sr. v.p., controller Macmillan, Inc., N.Y.C., 1970-80; v.p., chief fin. officer U.S. Filter Corp., N.Y.C., 1980-82; sr. v.p. fin., chief fin. officer Ashland Tech. Inc., N.Y.C., 1982—. Served to lt. USNR, 1955-58. Mem. Financial Execs. Inst., Nat. Indsl. Security Assn. (v.p. 1969-70), Nat. Soc. Bus. Budgeting (v.p. 1962), Sigma Phi, Alpha Kappa Psi, Pi Gamma Mu. Lodge: Masons. Home: 908 Sensor Rd Yardley PA 19067 Office: 522 Fifth Ave New York NY 10036

KRESTON, MARTIN HOWARD, advertising executive; b. N.Y.C., May 27, 1931; s. H enry and Frances (Stoll) Kreizvogel; m. Audrey Elizabeth Muir, Aug. 20, 1960; children: Mark Bradley, Rebecca Sarah. B.S. in Econs, Wharton Sch., U. Pa., 1953; postgrad., N.Y. U., Northwestern U. Asst. dept. mgr. R.H. Macy & Co., N.Y.C., 1953-54; mktg. supr., account exec. Edward H. Weiss & Co., Chgo., 1956-60; with Doyle Dane Bernbach Inc., N.Y.C., 1960—, v.p., mgmt. supr., 1970-72, sr. v.p., mgmt. supr., 1972, group sr. v.p., dir., 1972—. Bd. dirs. Negro Ensemble Co., N.Y. Bd. Trade. Served with AUS, 1954-56. Mem. Am. Advt. Fedn., U. Pa. Alumni Assn. Republican. Jewish. Club: University (N.Y.C.). Home: 328 Heathcote Rd Scarsdale NY 10583 Office: 437 Madison Ave New York NY 10022

KRETCHMER, NORMAN, pediatrician, nutritional science educator; b. N.Y.C., Jan. 20, 1923; s. Emanuel and Sue (Gross) K.; m. Muriel Reiter, Sept. 10, 1942; children: Pamela Sue, Paul Jay, Steven David. B.S., Cornell U., 1944; M.S., U. Minn., 1945, Ph.D., 1947; M.D., SUNY, N.Y.C., 1952, U. Bern, Switzerland, 1978. Diplomate: Am. Bd. Pediatrics. Teaching asst. U. Minn., 1944-47; asst. prof. pathology and biochemistry U. Vt., 1947-48; fellow, research asso. pathology L.I. Coll. Medicine, 1947-52; lectr. biology Bklyn. Coll., 1950-55; intern Montefiore Hosp., N.Y.C., 1952-53; mem. faculty Cornell U. Med. Sch., N.Y.C., 1953-59, assoc. prof. pediatrics, 1958-59; mem. faculty Stanford U., Palo Alto, Calif., 1959-74, prof. pediatrics, 1959-74, exec. head dept., 1959-69, chief div. devel. biology, 1969-72, chmn. program human biology, 1969-72, chief sect. developmental medicine, 1972, clin. prof. pediatrics, 1974; acting dir. Nat. Inst. Aging, NIH, Bethesda, Md., 1974-75; dir. Nat. Inst. Child Health and Human Devel., 1974—; prof. dept. nutritional scis. U. Calif., Berkeley, 1981—, chmn. dept. nutritional scis., 1983—, prof. pediatrics and obstetrics, San Francisco, 1981; mem. nat. bd. Ben Gurion U. of the Negev; mem. sci. council Inst. de la Vie, Paris, 1974—; mem. bd. U.S.A.-Israel Sci. Found., 1974—; mem. Aide Pour la Recherche Medicale à l'Enfance; cons. NSF; mem. numerous adv. and sci. coms. Author, editor publs. in field. Served with USAAF, 1942-43. Commonwealth Fund fellow, 1952-54, 57, 65-66; Guggenheim fellow, 1973-74; recipient Superior Service award HEW, 1977. Fellow Am. Acad. Pediatrics (E. Mead Johnson award 1958, Borden award 1969), AAAS; mem. Inst. of Medicine of Nat. Acad. Sci., AAUP, Am. Chem. Soc., Am. Pediatrics Soc. (pres. 1979), Am. Soc. Biol. Chemists, Am. Soc. Human Genetics, Am. Soc. Clin. Investigation (council 1964-67), Assn. Am. Med. Colls., Harvey Soc., Soc. Growth and Devel., Soc. Pediatric Research (pres. 1967-68), Western Soc. Pediatric Research (pres. 1966-67), Internat. Orgn. Study Human Devel. (pres. 1970—), Am. Inst. Biol. Scis., Am. Soc. Clin. Investigation, Perinatal Research Soc., Internat. Pediatric Assn. (exec. com. 1974-77), Sigma Xi, Alpha Omega Alpha; hon. mem. numerous fgn. med. socs.

KRETSCHMER, KEITH HUGHES, stockbroker; b. Omaha, Oct. 20, 1934; s. John G. and Mary (Hughes) K.; m. Adine Williams, Oct. 1, 1960; children: Hugh, Dara, Kurt. Student, UCLA, 1968; B.S., U. Nebr., 1956; A.A., Wentworth Acad., 1954. With J.G. Kretschmer & Co., Omaha, 1958-60; gen. agt. Lincoln Life & Casualty, (Nebr.), 1960-62; exec. v.p., sec.-treas. Automated Mgmt. systems, Kansas City, Mo., 1962-68; investment exec. Shearson, Hammill & Co., Los Angeles, 1968-75; with Bear Stearns & Co., Los Angeles, 1975—, gen. ptnr., 1981; mem. stockholders com. Tosco Corp., Los Angeles, 1982. Author: Your Option, 1978. Advanceman Republican Pres.'s Nixon and Ford, 1970-76. Served to maj. U.S. Army, 1956-58. Mem. Option Soc. So. Calif. (founding dir. 1974), N.Y. Stock Exchange, Nat. Assn. Securities Dealers, Option Clearing Corp., Library Assn., Pacific Palisades YMCA (chmn. bd. 1977), N.Y. Futures Exchange, Chgo. Bd. Trade. Lodges: Masons; Shriners. Home: 306 Amalfi Dr Santa Monica CA 90402 Office: 1900 Ave of Stars Los Angeles CA 90067

KRETSINGER, ROBERT H., molecular biology educator, researcher; b. Denver, Mar. 20, 1937. B.A. in Chemistry, U. Colo., 1958; Ph.D. in Biophysics, MIT, 1964. Postdoctoral fellow Lab. Molecular Biology,

Cambridge, Eng., 1964-67; mem. faculty U. Va., Charlottesville, 1967—, prof. molecular biology, 1975—, chmn. dept. biology, 1979—; chmn. space biology and medicine com. Space Sci. Bd., 1981-83; dir. multiwire area x-ray diffractometer facility. Contbr. numerous articles to sci. jours. Mem. Am. Crystallographic Assn. Home: 406 Key West Dr Charlottesville VA 22903 Office: U Va Charlottesville VA 22901

KRETZMANN, ADALBERT RAPHAEL ALEXANDER, clergyman; b. Stamford, Conn., Apr. 15, 1903; s. Karl and Thekla (Hueschen) K.; m. Josephine Heidelberg, Oct. 1, 1927 (dec. June 1982); children: Norman, Joan (Mrs. Gerhard Krodel). Grad., Concordia Coll., Bronxville, N.Y., 1923; B.D., Concordia Sem., St. Louis, 1927, D.D. (hon.), 1967, Litt.D., Concordia Coll., Seward, Nebr., 1953; LL.D., Valparaiso U., 1959; D.D. (hon.), Wartburg Coll., Waverly, Iowa, 1966. Ordained to ministry Evang. Luth. Ch., 1927; asst. pastor, Jersey City, 1924; prof. German Concordia Coll., Ft. Wayne, Ind., 1925-26; vacancy pastor, Phila., 1926, supply pastor, St. Louis, 1926-27; pastor St. Luke's Ch., Chgo., 1927-82; Chmn. Synodical Young People's Bd.; pres. Ill. dist. Walther League, 1930-32; sec. Luth. Hosp. Assn., 1929-31, Chgo. Luth. Pastoral Conf., 1929-33; bd. dirs. Luther Inst., Chgo., 1931-33; pastoral adviser Internat. Luth. Walther League, 1929-54; chmn. North Side Forum Christian Edn.; bd. dirs. Lakeview Community Council; lectr. on ch. art and liturgy Concordia Tchrs. Coll., River Forest, Ill., Concordia Sem., St. Louis Corr. Sch. Staff; lectr. on youth work Concordia Sem., St. Louis, Concordia Tchrs. Coll., Seward, Nebr., Dr. Martin Luther Coll., New Ulm, Minn., Pacific Luth. U., Pacific Luth. Sem.; chmn. commn. worship, also commn. ch. architecture Luth. Ch.-Mo. Synod; art editor The Cresset; asso. editor Ch. Music, Luth. Witness; lectr. Luther Laymen's League Seminars. Author: Liturgical Renaissance in the Lutheran Church, 1968; contbg. author: Christmas Annual; also; the author of: prayers The Pastor at Work, 1960, The Pastor at Prayer, 1959; Summer speaker: Internat. Luth. Hour, 1944, Liturgy and Church Art; others and also numerous religious writings.; Designer: also church seals Coll. Synodical; cons. in liturgical arts and design.; Chmn.: Chgo. Luth. Pastors Inst; radio speaker: WGN Mid-day Devotions; Sec.: radio devotions Family Worship Hour. Bd. dirs. Concordia Tchrs. Coll., River Forest, Ill., Ministers Life and Casualty Co., Mpls., Luth. Sr. Citizens Found., Luth. Brotherhood (chmn. fine arts), Augustana Hosp., Luth. Gen. Hosp., Luth. Deaconess Hosp.; pres. Chgo. Bible Soc.; dir., v.p. Wheatridge Found., also chmn. social service; bd. dirs. Tb Inst. (Lung Soc.) Chgo. and Cook County, Chgo. Lung Assn. Recipient Gutenberg award, 1963, Servant of Christ medal Concordia Coll., 1983. Mem. Am. Fedn. Art, Chgo. Art Inst. (life mem.), Concordia Hist. Inst., Am. Inst. Graphic Arts (adv. council religious teaching pictures), Met. Mus. (N.Y.), Walker Art Mus. (Minn.), Ch. Archtl. Guild Am., Guild for Religious Architecture, Am. Soc. Religious Architecture (dir.). Home: 1501 W Melrose St Chicago IL 60657

KRETZMANN, JUSTUS PAUL, clergyman; b. N.Y.C., Feb. 27, 1913; s. Karl and Thekla (Hueschen) K.; m. Norma Martha Kroehnke, Feb. 15, 1939; children—Karla (Mrs. Stanley Woell), Walter John. Student, Concordia Coll., Bronxville, N.Y., 1933; B.D., Concordia Sem., St. Louis, 1938, D.D. (hon.), 1965. Ordained to ministry Lutheran Ch., 1939; asst. pastor in, Buffalo, 1935-37, Bklyn., 1938-39, missionary, Nigeria, W. Africa, 1939-51; pastor Luth. Ch. Atonement, Florissant, Mo., 1952—; world survey of missions, 1960, 61; Chmn. bd. parish edn. Luth. Ch. Mo. Synod, 1959-73; chmn. Luth. Publicity Orgn., St. Louis, 1957-69, Luth. Assn. Larger Chs., 1970-73; mem. Luth. Med. Mission Council, 1959-69; pastoral adviser Luth. Med. Mission Assn. Co-author: In Time. . .For Eternity, 1963; Contbg. editor: Am. Luth; mem. editorial com.: St. Louis Luth; Contbr. to religious publs. Bd. dirs. Care and Counseling, St. Louis.; Mem. Florissant Hist. Soc. Home: 14 Arrowhead Circle St Charles MO 63301 Office: 1285 N Florissant Rd Florissant MO 63031

KREVANS, JULIUS RICHARD, university chancellor, physician; b. N.Y.C., May 1, 1924; s. Sol and Anita (Makovetsky) K.; m. Patricia N. Abrams, May 28, 1950; children: Nita, Julius R., Rachel, Sarah, Nora Kate. B.S. Arts and Scis, N.Y. U., 1943, M.D., 1946. Diplomate: Am. Bd. Internal Med. Intern, then resident Johns Hopkins Med. Sch. Hosp., mem. faculty, until 1970, dean acad. affairs, 1969-70; physician in chief Balt. City Hosp., 1963-69; prof. medicine U. Calif. at San Francisco, 1970—, dean Sch. Medicine, 1971-82, chancellor. Contbr. articles on hematology, internal med. profl. jours. Served with M.C. AUS, 1948-50. Mem. A.C.P., Assn. Am. Physicians. Office: U Calif San Francisco CA 94143

KREY, ROBERT DEAN, educator; b. Prairie du Sac, Wis., Mar. 23, 1929; s. Oscar L. and Paula M. (Mueller) K.; 1 son, Thomas R. Student, Carroll Coll., Waukesha, Wis., 1946-47; diploma, Sauk County Normal Sch., Reedsburg, Wis., 1948; B.S., Wis. State Coll., Platteville, 1958; M.S., U. Wis., 1967, Ph.D., 1968. Rural sch. tchr., Sauk County, 1948-51, tchr. grade 7-8, Gays Mills, Wis., 1951-53, tchr. boys phys. edn. and basketball jr. high sch., Black Earth, Wis., 1953-54; tchr. sci., math., reading Jr. High Sch., Lake Geneva, Wis., 1954-66; NDEA fellow dept. ednl. adminstrn. U. Wis., Madison, 1966-68, asst. dept. ednl. adminstrn., 1967-68, vis. asso. prof., summer 1971, asso. prof. ednl. adminstrn., Superior, 1968-74, prof., 1974—, chmn. dept. ednl. adminstrn. and counseling, 1978-80, chmn. div. edn., 1981—; ednl. cons. Educators Progress Service, Inc. Co-author: Interdisciplinary Foundations of Supervision, 1970, (with Glen G. Eye and Lanore A. Netzer) Supervision of Instruction, 2d edit, 1971. Bd. dirs. Wis. Sch. Adminstrn. Found., Inc., 1968-76. Mem. Wis. Assn. for Supervision and Curriculum Devel. (pres. 1973-74), Assn. for Supervision and Curriculum Devel. (dir. 1972-75), Wis. Ednl. Research Assn., Wis. Assn. Sch. Dist. Adminstrs., Assn-Ednl-Research, Nat. Soc. Study Edn., Council Profs. Instructional Supervision, U. Wis. Alumni Assn., U. Wis. Platteville Alumni Assn., Phi Delta Kappa (chpt. pres. 1975). Lutheran.

KREYCHE, GERALD FRANCIS, philosophy educator; b. Kenosha, Wis., June 19, 1927; s. Harold Joseph and Henrietta Fredericka (Oteman) K.; m. Eleanor Ann Okon, June 19, 1948. A.B., DePaul U., 1949, A.M., 1950; Ph.D. cum laude, U. Ottawa, Can., 1958. Mem. faculty DePaul U., 1950—, chmn. dept. philosophy, 1961-82, prof., 1965—; now also Danforth asso.; Aquinas lectr. Alverno Coll., Milw., 1963; vis. prof. St. Mary's Coll., Minn., 1977; bd. advisors Univ. Press Am. Condr.: radio programs What Do You Think?; also What's the Big Idea?, 1960; frequent appearances ednl. and comml. TV, also radio, 1958—; Author: Perspectives on God, 1972, Thirteen Thinkers; also articles religious publs.; Co-editor: Harbrace Philosophy series; sr. editor: Am. Thought; sect. editor: U.S.A. Today; bd. advisors: Philos. Research and Analysis; exec. editor: Listening: A Journal of Religion and Culture; mem. editorial bd.: Jour. History of Philosophy. Bd. dirs. Civitas Dei Found. Served with AUS, 1945-46. Recipient DePaul U. Distinguished Service award, 1969. Mem. Am. Metaphys. Soc., Ill.-Ind. Am. Cath. Philos. Assn. (pres. 1960), Am. Cath. Philos. Assn. (pres. 1972-73), Phi Kappa Theta, Phi Eta Sigma. Home: 2551 Fontana Dr Glenview IL 60025 Office: DePaul U 2323 N Seminary Ave Chicago IL 60614

KREYLING, EDWARD GEORGE, JR., railroad executive; b. St. Louis, June 1, 1923; s. Edward George and Mildred (Schroeder) K.; m. Mary Emily Gronemeyer, Sept. 4, 1943; children: Carol (Mrs. Robert D. Knight), Deborah Ann (Mrs. Hugh J. Risseeuw), Edward George III. B.S. in Bus. Adminstrn, Washington U., St. Louis, 1947, M.B.A., 1954. Accountant Monsanto Chem. Co., 1947-50; chief statistician White Rodgers Elec. Co., St. Louis, 1950-54; dir. market research Laclede-Christy Co., St. Louis, 1954-55; with St. L.-S.F. Ry., 1955-69, dir. marketing, 1964-65, v.p. traffic and indsl. devel., 1965-69; v.p. traffic I.C. R.R., Chgo., 1969-70; exec. v.p. Penn Central Transp. Co., Phila., 1970-71; v.p. marketing So. Ry., 1971-79, sr. v.p. mktg. service, 1979-80, exec. v.p. mktg., 1981-82; v.p. mktg. services Norfolk So. Corp. (Va.), 1982—. Served with AUS, 1943-45. Mem. Nat. Freight Traffic Assn. Home: 3646 S Sea Breeze Trail Virginia Beach VA 23452 Office: One Commercial Pl PO Box 3609 Norfolk VA 23514

KRIBEL, ROBERT EDWARD, physicist; b. Pitts., Sept. 17, 1937; s. Joseph P. and Helen M. K.; m. Ruth Ann Gropelli; children—Robert E., Karen A., Mark P., Gary P. B.S., U. Notre Dame, 1959; M.S., U. Calif., San Diego, 1966, Ph.D. in Physics, 1968. Research scientist Gen. Atomic, Inc., 1965-69; asso. prof. physics Drake U., 1970-73; vis. asso. prof. applied physics Cornell U., 1973-74; prof., head dept. physics James Madison U., 1974-78, Auburn (Ala.) U., 1978—. Contbr. articles to profl. jours. Served with U.S. Navy, 1959-62. Mem. Am. Phys. Soc., IEEE, Am. Assn. Physics Tchrs., Sigma Xi. Home: 408 Dixie Dr Auburn AL 36830 Office: Physics Dept Auburn U Auburn AL 36849

KRICK, IRVING PARKHURST, meteorologist; b. San Francisco, Dec. 20, 1906; s. H. I. and Mabel (Royal) K.; m. Jane Clark, May 23, 1930; 1 dau., Marllynn; m. Marie Spiro; 1 son, Irving Parkhurst II. B.A., U. Calif., 1928; M.S., Cal. Inst. Tech., 1933, Ph.D., 1934. Asst. mgr. radio sta. KTAB, 1928-29; meteorologist, 1930—; became mem. staff Calif. Inst. Tech., 1933, asst. prof. meteorology, 1935-38, asso. prof., prof. and head dept., 1938-48; organized and pres. Am. Inst. Aerological Research and Water Resources Devel. Corp., 1950; pres. Irving P. Krick Assos., Inc., Irving P. Krick, Inc., Tex., Irving P. Krick Assos. Can. Ltd.; set up meteorology dept. for Am. Air Lines, Inc., 1935; cons., 1935-36. Pianist in concert and radio work, 1929-30; Co-author: Sun, Sea and Sky, 1954; Writer numerous articles on weather analysis, weather modification and forecasting and its application to agrl. and bus. industries. Served as lt. Coast Arty. Corps U.S. Army, 1928-36; commd. ensign USNR, 1938; maj., then lt. col. USAAF, 1943; Weather Directorate, Weather Central Div. unit comdr. of Long Range Forecast Unit A, 1942-43; chief weather information sect. SHAEF, 1945. Decorated Legion of Merit, Bronze Star with Oak leaf cluster, U.S.; Croix de Guerre, France; recipient Distinguished Service award Jr. C. of C.; chosen one of 10 outstanding men under age 35 by U.S. C. of C. Fellow Am. Inst. Aeros. and Astronautics (asso.), Royal Soc. Arts; mem. Royal Meteorol. Soc., A.A.A.S., Sigma Xi. Republican. Set up 1st modern airline weather forecasting service for Western Air Express, 1932; developed pvt. weather forecasting service, supplying information to various cos.; has developed long-range weather forecasting method covering periods up to 25 years. Pioneered applications rain increase and hail control; perfected comml. five year weather forecasts. Home: 1200 S Orange Grove Blvd Unit 13 Pasadena CA 91105 Office: 748 Vella Rd Palm Springs CA 92264

KRICK, KENNETH A., manufacturing company executive; b. Lancaster, Pa., May 13, 1934; s. Thomas B. and Miriam M. K.; m. Rita M. Killian, May 26, 1956; children: Kenneth, John, Tracy, David. B.S., Franklin and Marshall Coll., 1956. Staff acct. Armstrong Cork Co., Lancaster, Pa., 1956; auditor Ernst & Ernst, Lancaster, 1960-61; comptroller Fuller Co., Manheim, Pa., 1961-65, v.p., 1965-77, pres., 1977—, chmn. bd., 1981—; dir. 8 subs. cos.; group v.p. GATX Corp. Dir. St. Luke's Hosp., Lehigh Valley Indsl. Park, Boy Scouts Am. Served to capt. USAF, 1957-59. Mem. Am. Inst. C.P.A.s. Clubs: Bethlehem, Saucon Valley Country. Home: 4738 Howard Ave Western Springs IL 60558 Office: 120 S Riverside Plaza Chicago IL 60606

KRIDEL, JAMES S., banker; b. Newark, Dec. 3, 1940; s. Jerome L. and Josephine (Simon) K.; m. Kathryn Poppenberg, Mar. 12, 1967; children: Karen, James Jr., Kimberly. B.S., Pa. State U., 1962. Dir. acctg. mktg. IBM, White Plains, N.Y., 1962-83; exec. v.p. Crocker Nat. Bank, Los Angeles, 1983—; chmn. ops. Calif. Bankers Clearing House Assn., San Francisco, 1983—. Trustee St. Vincents Hosp., Portland, Oreg., 1978; community coordinator Job Corps, Washington, 1968; chmn. Heart Fund, West Orange, N.J., 1971. Recipient Dist. Service award FBI, 1969. Home: 17765 Camino De Yatasto Pacific Palisades CA 90272 Office: Crocker Nat Bank 333 S Grand Suite 5300 Los Angeles CA 90071

KRIDER, JAKE LUTHER, animal science educator; b. Lewistown, Ill., Dec. 12, 1913; s. Reuben E. and Bessie A. (Beadles) K.; m. L. Louise Strode, Aug. 3, 1936. B.S., U. Ill., 1939, M.S., 1941; Ph.D., Cornell U., 1942. Asso. animal husbandry, asst. prof., then asso. prof. U. Ill., 1942-47, prof. animal sci., 1947-50; dir. feed research and edn. McMillen Feed Mills div. Central Soya Co., Inc., 1950-51, v.p., dir. feed sales, 1951-56; v.p. pub. relations Central Soya Co., Inc., Ft. Wayne, Ind., 1956-63, mem. adv. bd. dirs., 1954-57; head dept. animal scis. Purdue U., Lafayette, Ind., 1963-71, prof. animal scis., 1971-79, prof. emeritus, 1979—. Author: (with Dr. George P. Deyoe) Raising Swine, 1952, (with J.H. Conrad and W.E. Carroll) Swine Production, 1982; contbr. articles to profl. jours. and periodicals. Recipient award for outstanding contbn. animal nutrition research Am. Feed Mfrs. Assn. and Am. Soc. for Animal Prodn., 1949; award of merit for service to agr. U. Ill., 1962; E.G. Cherbonnier award Grain and Feed Dealers Nat. Assn., 1966; Meritorious Service award Ind. Pork Producers Assn., 1967; Animal Industry Service award Am. Soc. Animal Sci., 1978. Hon. fellow Am. Soc. Animal Sci. (pres. 1969, life mem.); mem. Poultry Sci. Assn., AAAS, Am. Feed Mfrs. Assn. (dir. 1957-63, exec. com. 1958-59), Farm House Frat., Sigma Xi. Methodist. Home: 1305 Ravinia Rd West Lafayette IN 47906

KRIEBEL, CHARLES HOSEY, management sciences educator; b. Tarrytown, N.Y., Nov. 6, 1933; s. Nelson Stearly and Elizabeth Grace (Hosey) K.; m. Jan Lilly McAuley, June 7, 1961; children: Paul Charles, Susan, James McAuley, Carl Nelson. B.S. in Econs., U. Pa., 1959, M.A. in Stats., 1961; Ph.D. in Indsl. Mgmt. (Ford Found. fellow), MIT, 1964. Instr. Wharton Sch. Fin., U. Pa., Phila., 1959-61; asst. prof. Sloan Sch., M.I.T., Cambridge, 1963-64, Grad. Sch. Indsl. Adminstrn., Carnegie-Mellon U., Pitts., 1964-67, asso. prof., 1967-70, prof., 1970—; cons. McKinsey & Co., Inc., N.Y.C., Rand Corp., Santa Monica, Calif., Gulf Oil Corp., Pitts., Imperial Tobacco, Montreal, Que., Can., Mellon Bank (N.A.), Pitts., Jones and Laughlin Steel Co., Inc., Weyerhauser, Tacoma, IBM, N.Y.C., Western Electric, Princeton, N.J., Gen. Reins. Corp., N.Y.C., Industrikonsulent I.K.O., Copenhagen, Westinghouse Electric Corp., Pitts., U.S. Steel Corp., Rockwell Internat.; rep. Nat. Acad. Scis. Mem. editorial bd.: Internat. Fedn. Info. Processing, 1971—; editorial cons., Prentice-Hall, Inc., 1967—; contbr. numerous articles to profl. jours. Served with Signal Corps U.S. Army, 1954-56. Fulbright-Hays adviser, 1965—. Fellow AAAS; mem. Assn. Computing Machinery (nat. lectr.), Inst. Mgmt. Scis. (dept. editor Mgmt. Sci.), Econometric Soc., Ops. Research Soc. Am., Am. Econ. Assn., Am. Statis. Assn., Econometric Soc., N.Y. Acad. Scis., Delta Kappa Epsilon. Home: 108 Silent Run Rd Fox Chapel Pittsburgh PA 15238 Office: Grad Sch Indsl Adminstrn Carnegie-Mellon U Pittsburgh PA 15213

KRIEBEL, ROBERT IRWIN, health care products mfg. co. exec.; b. Phila., July 9, 1942; s. Irwin Z., Jr. and Dorothy (MacNeece) K.; m. Rebecca Lee Wilhelm, Sept. 20, 1969; children—Gretchen Ann, Amanda Lee. B.S. in Econs, Roanoke (Va.) Coll., 1965. With Amchem Products Co., Ambler, Pa., 1967-74, budget mgr., 1970-74; cash and budget mgr., then asst. treas. Rorer Group Inc., Ft. Washington, Pa., 1974-79, treas., 1979—. Office: 500 Virginia Dr Fort Washington PA 19034

KRIEBLE, ROBERT H., corporation executive; b. Worcester, Pa., Aug. 22, 1916; s. Vernon K. and Laura (Cassel) K.; m. Nancy Brayton, Sept. 3, 1939; children: Frederick B., Helen Krieble Fusscas. Grad., Haverford Coll., 1935; Ph.D. in Chemistry, Johns Hopkins U., 1939; D.Sc. (hon.), Trinity Coll., Hartford, Conn., 1974. Research chemist Socony Vacuum Oil Co., 1939-43; various positions with Gen. Electric Co., 1943-56; v.p. Loctite Corp., 1956-64, pres., chief exec. officer, 1964-76, chmn., 1976-80, chmn., chief exec. officer, 1980—. Patentee in field of silicones, anarobic adhesives and petrochems. via air oxidation. Trustee Johns Hopkins U., Balt., Wadsworth Atheneum, Hartford, Conn.; bd. dirs. Jr. Achievement Central Conn., Hoover Instn. War, Revolution and Peace; trustee Rockford Inst.; bd. dirs. Heritage Found., Inst. Ednl. Affairs. Recipient Comml. Devel. Assn. Honor award, 1974, Am. Eagle award in Pub. Affairs, 1979, Winthrop-Sears medal Chem. Industry Assn., 1979; named Entrepreneur of Yr. Chem. Industry Assn., 1979; recipient Adhesive and Sealant Council award, 1982. Mem. Am. Bus. Conf. (bd. dirs.), Am. Council Capital Formation (bd. dirs.), Council Nat. Policy (bd. dirs.), U.S. Indsl. Council (bd. dirs.), Internat. Mgmt. and Devel. Inst. (corp. strategic planning council), Conf. Bd., Am. Mgmt. Assn., Am. Chem. Soc., Phi Beta Kappa, Sigma Xi. Club: Hartford. Home: PO Box 394 Old Lyme CT 06371 Office: 705 N Mountain Rd Newington CT 06111

KRIEG, ARTHUR FREDERICK, pathologist; b. East Orange, N.J., Oct. 23, 1930; s. Edwin Holmes and Helen Burnet (Mertz) K.; m. Monsita Alcaide, June 9, 1956; children—Arthur Mertz, Eric Andrew, Sandra Lee. A.B., Yale, 1952; M.D., Tufts U., 1956. Diplomate: Am. Bd. Pathology. Intern, resident Univ. Hosps., Cleve., 1956-60; instr. pathology Western Res. U. Sch. Medicine, Cleve., 1958-60; resident New Eng. Deaconess Hosp., Boston, 1963-64; asst. prof. pathology State U. N.Y. Sch. Medicine, Syracuse, 1964-68; asso. prof. pathology Pa. State U. Sch. Medicine, Hershey, 1968-71, prof. pathology, 1971—, dir. clin. labs., 1968—; Cons. Beckman Instruments, Gen. Diagnostics div. Warner Chilcote, Baker Chem. Corp., DuPont Chem. Corp., Electronucleonics Corp. Author: Clinical Laboratory Computerization, 1970, Clinical Laboratory Communication, 1979, ANS MUMPS, 1981; contbr.: chpts. to Clinical Diagnosis by Laboratory Methods, 1969, 74, 79; Contbr. articles to profl. jours. Served to capt. USAF, 1960-62. Fellow Coll. Am. Pathologists (com. lab computers), Am. Soc. Clin. Pathologists (council on clin. chemistry), Assn. Clin. Scientists, Acad. Clin. Lab. Physicians and Scientists; mem. A.M.A., Pa. Assn. Clin. Pathologists (sec. com. on regional quality control 1972-73, chmn. 1974-75), Alpha Omega Alpha. Home: 48 Governor Rd Hershey PA 17033 Office: Milton S Hershey Med Center Hershey PA 17033

KRIEG, WILLIAM HENRY, lawyer; b. Indpls., Jan. 13, 1907; s. August F. and Augusta (Beckmann) K.; m. Virginia Ballweg, Oct. 28 1933; children: Peter Ballweg, Frederick William. A.B. cum laude, U. Notre Dame, 1929; J.D., Harvard U., 1932. Bar: Ind. 1932. Sole practice law, Indpls., 1932-40, 48—; ret. counsel firm Krieg, DeVault, Alexander & Capehart.; Pres. Packard Mfg. Co., Indpls., 1946-47; dir. Hook Drugs, Inc., Indpls., Bell Fibre Products Corp., Marion, Ind.; pres. Salt Creek Services Inc., Nashville, Ind. Dir., vice chmn. exec. com. Mut. Hosp. Ins. Inc. (Blue Cross) Ind., 1970-78; Chmn. bd. Cornelia Cole Fairbanks Hosp. for Alcoholics, Indpls.; pres. bd. trustees Winona Meml. Hosp., Indpls., 1969-70; dir. emeritus Central Ind. council Boy Scouts; trustee Purdue U., 1970-83, West Lafayette Cathedral High Sch., Indpls.; bd. dirs. Purdue Research Found.; originator, v.p., dir. Ind. Gov.'s Economy Program, 1970-71. Served from pvt. to lt. col. AUS, 1940-45; asst. gen. counsel nat. hdqrs. SSS, 1943-45. Decorated Legion of Merit. Mem. Am., Ind., Indpls. bar assns. Republican. Roman Catholic. Clubs: Indianapolis Athletic, Indianapolis Sailing (commodore 1958). Home: 5340 Greenwillow Rd Indianapolis IN 46220 Office: One Indiana Sq Indianapolis IN 46204

KRIEGER, ABBOTT JOEL, neurosurgeon; b. N.Y.C., Apr. 29, 1939; m. Marsha Tomback; children—Lloyd, Lara, Dana. B.A., Bklyn. Coll., 1959; M.D., N.Y. Med. Coll., 1963; D.M.S. in Pharmacology, Columbia U., 1970. Diplomate: Am. Bd. Neurol. Surgery. Intern in surgery Montefiore Hosp., N.Y.C., 1963-64; resident in surgery, then in neuropathology Montefiore Hosp. and Med. Center, 1964-65; resident in neurol. surgery Albert Einstein Coll. Medicine, 1966-67, 70-71, resident in neurology, 1968; chief neurosurgery VA Hosp., Pitts., 1971-73; asst. prof. neurosurgery U. Pitts. Sch. Medicine, 1971-73; chief neurosurgery VA Hosp., East Orange, N.J., 1974—; prof., chief neurosurgery N.J. Med. Sch., Coll. Medicine and Dentistry, Newark, 1974—; cons. United Hosps. of Newark, Beth Israel Hosp., St. Michael's Hosp. Contbr. articles to med. jours. Served with USMCR, 1956-62. Fellow A.C.S.; mem. Soc. Neurol. Surgeons, Congress Neurol. Surgeons, Research Soc. Neurol. Surgeons, Am. Assn. Neurol. Surgeons, N.J. Neurosurg. Soc. Home: 49 Nottingham Rd Short Hills NJ 07078 Office: 100 Bergen St Newark NJ 07103

KRIEGER, DOROTHY TERRACE, internist; b. N.Y.C., Feb. 17, 1927; d. Morris Abraham and Esther (Marsh) Terrace; m. C. Wayne Bardin, Aug. 11, 1978; children by previous marriage: James, Nancy. A.B. summa cum laude, Barnard Coll., 1945; M.D., Columbia U., 1949. Diplomate: Nat. Bd. Med. Examiners, Am. Bd. Internal Medicine. Intern Mt. Sinai Hosp., N.Y.C., 1949-50, asst. resident in surgery, 1950-52, asst. resident in medicine, 1952-53, chief resident in medicine, 1954-55, now mem. staff, 1954-55; practice medicine specializing in endocrinology, N.Y.C.; faculty Mt. Sinai Sch. Medicine, 1966—, prof. medicine, 1972—; dir. div. endocrinology Mt. Sinai Hosp. Endocrinology Lab., N.Y.C., 1973—; chmn. endocrinology study sect. NIH, 1980—; council mem. Nat. Inst. on Aging, 1982—; prin. investigator USPHS grants, 1972—. Author: Cushing's Disease, 1973—; Editor: Peptide Hormone Assay and Action, 1973—, ACTH and Related Peptides, 1977, Circadian Rhythms, 1979, Neuroendocrinology, 1980; editor endocrinology sect.: Ann. Rev. Physiology, 1980-84; editorial bd.: Jour. Clin. Endocrinology and Metabolism; contbr. over 200 articles to profl. jours. Fellow A.C.P.; mem. Am. Soc. Clin. Investigation, Assn. Am. Physicians, Endocrine Soc. (v.p. 1974-75). Home: 1148 Fifth Ave New York NY 10028 Office: Mount Sinai Hospital Div Endocrinology Fifth Ave and 100th St New York NY 10028

KRIEGER, IRVIN MITCHELL, educator; b. Cleve., May 14, 1923; s. William I. and Rose (Brodsky) K.; m. Theresa Melamed, June 9, 1965; 1 dau., Laura. B.S., Case Inst. Tech., 1944, M.S., 1948; Ph.D., Cornell, 1951. Research asst. Case Inst. Tech., Cleve., 1946-47; teaching fellow Cornell U., Ithaca, N.Y., 1947-49; instr. Case Western Res. U., 1949-51, asst. prof., 1951-55, asso. prof., 1955-68, prof., 1968—; dir. Center for Adhesives, Sealants and Coatings, 1983—; vis. prof. U. Bristol, 1977-78; cons. for chem. firms. Contbr. articles to profl. jours. Served as ensign USNR, 1943-46. NSF fellow Université Libre De Bruxelles, 1959-60; sr. fellow Weizmann Inst., 1970. Mem. Am. Chem. Soc., Am. Inst. Chem. Engrs., AAUP, Soc. Rheology (pres. 1977-79). Home: 15691 Fenemore Rd East Cleveland OH 44112 Office: Case Western Res U Cleveland OH 44106

KRIEGER, LEONARD, history educator; b. Newark, Aug. 28, 1918; s. Isidore and Jennie (Glinn) K.; m. Esther J. Smith, Aug. 13, 1949; children: Alan Davis, David Jonathan, Nathaniel Richard. B.A., Rutgers U., 1938; M.A., Yale U., 1942, Ph.D., 1949. Mem. faculty Yale, 1946-62, prof. history, 1961-62; Univ. prof. history U. Chgo., 1962-69, 72—; prof. history Columbia, N.Y.C., 1969-72; vis. lectr. Northwestern U., 1950, Brandeis U., 1958, Columbia, 1960-61; vis. prof. Stanford, summer 1968, Johns Hopkins, 1971-72; Chmn. internat. conf. travel-grant com. Social Sci. Research Council, 1961-63; book prize com. Phi Beta Kappa, 1960-61, Ralph Waldo Emerson prize com., 1982; assoc. Princeton Council Humanities for Ford Humanities Project, 1959-64; fellow Center Advanced Study Behavioral Sci., 1956-57; mem. Inst. for Advanced Study, 1963, 69-70; Mem. council Yale U., 1975—, chmn. vis. com. grad. sch., 1975—. Author: The German Idea of Freedom, 1957, 2d edit., 1973, Politics of Discretion, 1965, Kings and Philosophers, 1970, Essay on the theory of Enlightened Despotism, 1975, Ranke: The Meaning of History, 1977; co-author: History, 1965; Series editor: Classic European Historians, 1967—; Co-editor: The Responsibility of Power, 1967, 69; editor: Friedrich Engels, The German Revolutions, 1967; mem. bd. editors: Jour. History Ideas, 1963—. Served to 1st lt. AUS, 1942-46. Mem. Am. Hist. Assn. (chmn. program com. 1960, exec. com. modern history sect. 1968-71, chmn. 1976, speaker 1979), Am. Acad. Arts and Scis. (council 1975-79, exec. bd. 1977—), Am. Philos. Soc., Am. Soc. Polit. and Legal Philosophy. Office: Univ Chicago Dept History Chicago IL 60637

KRIEGER, MURRAY, educator, author; b. Newark, Nov. 27, 1923; s. Isidore and Jennie (Glinn) K.; m. Joan Alice Stone, June 15, 1947; children: Catherine Leona, Eliot Franklin. Student, Rutgers U., 1940-42; M.A., U. Chgo., 1948; Ph.D. (Univ. fellow), Ohio State U., 1952. Instr. English Kenyon Coll., 1948-49, Ohio State U., 1951-52; asst. prof., then asso. prof. U. Minn., 1952-58; prof. English U. Ill., 1958-63; M.F. Carpenter prof. lit. criticism U. Iowa, 1963-66; prof. English, dir. program in criticism U. Calif. at Irvine, 1966—; prof. English UCLA, 1973; univ. prof. U. Calif., 1974—, co-dir. Sch. Criticism and Theory, 1975-77, dir., 1977-81; asso. mem. Center Advanced Study, U. Ill., 1961-62. Author: The New Apologists for Poetry, 1956, The Tragic Vision, 1960, A Window to Criticism: Shakespeare's Sonnets and Modern Poetics, 1964, The Play and Place of Criticism, 1967, The Classic Vision, 1971, Theory of Criticism: A Tradition and Its System, 1976, Poetic Presence and Illusion, 1979, Arts on the Level, 1981; Editor: (with Eliseo Vivas) The Problems of Aesthetics, 1953, Northrop Frye in Modern Criticism, 1966, (with L.S. Dembo) Directions for Criticism: Structuralism and its Alternatives, 1977. Served with AUS, 1942-46. Guggenheim fellow, 1956- 57, 61-62; Am. Council Learned Socs. postdoctoral fellow, 1966-67; grantee Nat. Endowment for Humanities, 1971-72; Rockefeller Found. humanities fellow, 1978. Fellow Am. Acad. Arts and Scis.; Mem. MLA, Internat. Assn. Univ. Profs. English, Acad. Lit. Studies. Home: 407 Pinecrest Dr Laguna Beach CA 92651 Office: Dept English and Comparative Lit Univ California Irvine CA 92717

KRIEGER, ROBERT EDWARD, publisher; b. Chgo., Apr. 6, 1925; s. Nicholas Francis and Clara Maude (Larson) K.; m. Maxine Donalda Spooner, June 21, 1947; children: Robert Edward, Donald Eric, Thomas Eliot. Formerly exec. with multi-corp. book and pub. firms; chmn. bd., pres., dir. R.E. Krieger Pub. Co., Inc., Malabar, Fla., 1969—. Served with USCG, 1943-46; ETO. Mem. ALA, Am. Pubs. Assn., Am. Assn. History of Medicine, Scholarly Pubs. Assn., Melbourne C. of C., Palm Bay C. of C. Republican. Methodist. Club: Masons. Home: 970 SW Meadowbrook Rd Palm Bay FL 32905 Office: Krieger Dr Malabar FL 32950

KRIEGLER, RUDOLPH JOHN, physicist; b. Budapest, Hungary, May 30, 1933; emigrated to Can., 1956, naturalized, 1962; s. Joseph and Emily (Mayer) K.; children: Andrew, Paul. B.Sc., Roland Eotvos U., Budapest, 1956; M.A., U. Toronto, Ont., Can., 1958, Ph.D., 1966. Mem. sci. staff Ont. Research Found., Toronto, 1956-57, 58-60; with Bell-No. Research Ltd., Ottawa, Ont., 1966—, mgr. advanced device research, dir. advanced optoelectronics, 1977-79, mgr. advanced tech. lab., 1979—. Mem. IEEE (sr.), Electrochem. Soc., Can. Assn. Physicists. Research on metal-oxide-semicondr. structures, on effects of chlorine on high-temperature oxidation of silicon. Inventor in field. Home: 32 Orrin Ottawa ON K1Y 3X6 Canada Office: 3511 Carling Ave Ottawa ON K1Y 4H7 Canada

KRIGBAUM, WILLIAM RICHARD, educator, chemist; b. Beardstown, Ill., Sept. 29, 1922; s. Daniel Dwight and Ella (Sutton) K.; m. Esther Jean Wolfe, July 14, 1945; children—Mary Kathryn, Janet Ann, Lynn Carol. B.S., James Millikin U., 1944, Sc.D., 1966; M.S., U. Ill., 1948, Ph.D., 1949. Mem. faculty Duke, 1950—, prof., 1962—, James B. Duke prof. chemistry, 1969—, chmn. dept., 1976-79; mem. nat. adv. panel chemistry NSF, 1970-73. Alfred P. Sloan Research fellow, 1956-60; NSF Sr. Postdoctoral fellow Centre des Recherches sur les Macromolecules, Strasbourg, France, 1959-60, Institute fur physikalische Chemie, Graz, Austria, 1966-67. Fellow Am. Phys. Soc.; mem. Am. Chem. Soc., Am. Crystallographic Assn., Sigma Xi. Research, numerous publs. on characterization of high polymers by phys. chem. methods, such as x-ray diffraction, light scattering, osmotic pressure, solution thermodynamics; relation of molecular structure to phys. properties of elastomers and crystalline polymers. Home: 2504 Wilson St Durham NC 27706

KRIKORIAN, ROBERT V., manufacturing company executive; b. New Haven, 1919. B.S., Yale U., 1950. With Rexnord, Ind., Milw., 1950—, mgr. ordnance, 1953-57, Mgr. constrn., 1957-62, v.p. constrn., 1962-63, exec. v.p., 1963-67, pres., 1967-78, vice chmn., chief exec. officer, 1978-80, chmn. bd., 1980—, also dir.; dir. Beloit Corp., Parker Pen Co., Mueller Co., Black and Decker Mfg. Co., MAPI. Office: 3500 First Wisconsin Center Milwaukee WI 53201 *

KRIKOS, GEORGE ALEXANDER, pathologist, educator; b. Old Phaleron, Greece, Sept. 17, 1922; came to U.S., 1946; s. Alexios and Helen (Spyropoulou) K.; m. Aspasia Manoni, June 22, 1949; children: Helen, Alexandra, Alexios. D.D.S., U. Pa., 1949; Ph.D., U. Rochester, 1959, U. Athens, Greece, 1981. Asst. prof. pathology U. Pa. Sch. Dentistry, 1958-61, asso. prof., 1961-67, prof., 1967-68, chmn. dept., 1964-68; asso. prof. oral pathology U. Pa. Grad. Sch., 1962-68, prof. oral pathology, 1968; prof. pathobiology Sch. Dentistry, U. Colo., 1968-75, chmn. dept. pathobiology, 1968-73, prof. oral biology, 1975—, chmn. dept., 1976-77, asst. dean basic sci. affairs, 1973-75, asso. dean oral biology affairs, 1975-76; vis. prof. Sch. Dentistry, U. Athens, 1980-81; mem. dental study sect. NIH, 1966-70; mem. cancer com. Colo.-Wyo. Regional Med. Program, 1970-72; cons. oral pathology Denver VA Hosp., 1970-72. Served with AUS, 1949-54. Mem. Am. Assn. Pathologists, Internat. Assn. Dental Research, Sigma Xi. Research in connective tissue, wound healing, cytodifferentiation. Home: 350 Ivy St Denver CO 80220 Office: 4200 E 9th Ave Denver CO 80262

KRILL, ARTHUR MELVIN, engineering, architectural and planning company executive; b. Burlington, Colo., Oct. 17, 1921; s. John Frederick and Elizabeth Marion (Rule) K.; m. Mary Alice Hitt, July 6, 1944; children: Susan Jane Krill-Smith, Juli Elizabeth Krill Lapin, Arthur Melvin. B.S. in Mech. Engring. with honors, U. Colo., 1943, M.S., 1951; diploma, Indsl. Coll. Armed Forces, 1952. Prof. mech. engring., head adminstrv. engring. U. Denver, 1947-57, dir., 1955-62; head div. mechanics Denver Research Inst., 1956-62; founder, pres. Falcon Research & Devel. Co., Denver, 1962-70; pres. Ken R. White Co., Denver, 1963-76; chmn. bd. URS Co., Denver, 1976-77; pres. Arthur M. Krill Consultants, 1978; chmn. bd. Rocky Mountain Airways; dir. Solaron Corp., Dencor Energy Cost Controls, Inc., Ogden Devel. Corp.; former mem. Colo. Air Pollution Variance Bd. Author: Advances in Hypervelocity Techniques, 1962. Bd. dirs. U. Colo. Engring. Devel. Council; former mem. Colo. Bd. Engring. Examiners, 1974-78; Vestryman, jr. warden Ch. of Ascension (Episcopal), Denver. Named Distinguished Engring. Alumnus in Pvt. Practice U. Colo., 1974. Fellow AAAS, Am. Cons. Engrs. Council, Am. Astronautical Soc.; mem. ASME, Nat. Soc. Profl. Engrs., Am. Soc. Engring. Edn., Ops. Research Soc. Am., Denver C. of C. (dir., chmn. environ. council), Sigma Xi, Tau Beta Pi, Sigma Tau, Pi Tau Sigma. Club: Gyro Internat. Lodge: Rotary. Home and office: 450 Westwood Dr Denver CO 80206

KRIM, ARTHUR B., motion picture executive, lawyer; b. N.Y.C., Apr. 4, 1910; s. Morris and Rose (Ocko) K.; m. Mathilde Galland, Dec. 7, 1958; 1 dau., Daphna. B.A., Columbia U., N.Y.C., 1930, J.D., 1932, LL.D. (hon.), 1982. Bar: N.Y. 1933. With Phillips, Nizer, Benjamin, Krim & Ballon, N.Y.C., 1932—, sr. ptnr., 1935-78, of counsel, 1978—; pres. Eagle Lion Films, N.Y.C., 1946-49; chmn. United Artists Corp., N.Y.C., 1951-78, Orion Pictures Corp., 1978—; dir. Occidental Petroleum Corp., Los Angeles, Cities Service Corp., Tulsa, 1982—. Editor in chief: Columbia Law Rev., 1931-32. Spl. cons. to Pres. U.S., 1968-69; mem. Pres.'s Gen. Adv. Com. Arms Control, 1977-80; chmn. Democratic Nat. Fin. Com., 1966-68, Dem. Adv. Council Elected Ofcls., 1973-76; bd. dirs. Wiezmann Inst. Sci., 1948—, UN Assn., 1961—, Lyndon Baines Johnson Found., 1969—; chmn. bd. trustee Columbia U., 1977-82, chmn. emeritus, 1982—. Served to lt. col. U.S. Army; 1942-45. Recipient Jean Hersholt Humanitarian award Acad. Motion Picture Arts & Scis., Cavaliere Ufficiale Della award Republic of Italy, 1955, Chevalier dans l'Ordre Nat. de la legion d'Honneur, France, 1975.

KRIM, SEYMOUR, writer; b. N.Y.C., May 11, 1922; s. Abraham and Ida (Goldberg) K.; m. Eleanor Goff, 1947 (div. 1951). Student, U. N.C., 1939-40. Reporter New Yorker mag., 1941-42; tchr. non-fiction writing St. Marks in the Bowery Writing Workshop, 1967-69, U. Iowa Writers Workshop, 1970-72, N.Y. U., 1972-73, U. P.R., 1973-74, 78-79, Pa. State U., 1973-74, Columbia U., 1964, 1978—. Writer, OWI, 1943-45; publicity writer, Paramount Pictures, 1952-54; scriptreader, United Artists, 1955-61; editor, Nugget mag., 1961-65; reporter, N.Y. Herald Tribune, 1965-66; cons. editor, Evergreen Rev., 1967; Author: Views of a Nearsighted Cannoneer, 1961, Shake it for the World, Smartass, 1970, You and Me, 1974; Editor: Manhattan, An Anthology, 1954, The Beats, An Anthology, 1960; Contbr. revs. and articles to newspapers and mags. Home: 120 E 10th St New York NY 10003

KRIMENDAHL, HERBER FREDERICK, II, investment banker; b. Cin., Oct. 28, 1928; s. Herbert F. and Mary Bess (Christian) K.; m. Constance Kathryn McCown, Sept. 21, 1957; children: Elizabeth Knowles, Nancy Christian. B.A., Ohio State U., 1950; M.B.A., Harvard U., 1952. Assoc. Goldman, Sachs & Co., N.Y.C., 1953-62, ptnr., 1963—; dir. Best Products Co., Richmond, Va., A.T. Cross, Lincoln, R.I., Cyclops Corp., Pitts., The Lane Co., Inc., Altavista, Va. Trustee Philharm. Symphony Soc., N.Y., 1977. Served to lt. USAF, 1952-53. Clubs: River, Maidstone. Office: Goldman Sachs & Co 85 Broad St New York NY 10004

KRIMIGIS, STAMATIOS MIKE, physicist, researcher, consultant; b. Chios, Greece, Sept. 10, 1938; s. Michael and Angeliki (Tsetseris) K.; m. Evangelia Kantas, Feb. 11, 1968; children: Michael, John. B.S., U. Minn., 1961; M.S., U. Iowa, 1963, Ph.D., 1965. Research assoc. and asst. prof. physics U. Iowa, Iowa City, 1965-68; supr. space physics sect. Applied Physics Lab., Johns Hopkins U., Balt., 1968-74, supr. space physics and instrumentation group, 1974-81, chief scientist space dept., 1980—; mem. Space Sci. Bd., Nat. Acad. Scis. NRC, 1983—; cons.; mem. steering com. space sci. working group Assn. Am. Univs., 1982—. Contbr. over 130 articles to sci. jours.; author books on solar, interplanetary and magnetospheric plasma physics, cosmic rays, magnetospheres of Jupiter and Saturn. Recipient Exceptional Sci. Achievement medal NASA, 1981. Fellow Am. Geophys. Union; mem. Am. Phys. Soc., AAAS. Greek Orthodox. Home: 613 Cobblestone Ct Silver Spring MD 20904 Office: Applied Physics Lab Johns Hopkins U Laurel MD 20707

KRIMM, SAMUEL, physicist, educator; b. Morristown, N.J., Oct. 19, 1925; s. Irving and Ethel (Stein) K.; m. Marilyn Marcy Neveloff, June 26, 1949; children: David Robert, Daniel Joseph. B.S., Poly. Inst. Bklyn., 1947; M.A., Princeton U., 1949, Ph.D., 1950. Postdoctoral fellow U. Mich., Ann Arbor, 1950-52, mem. faculty, 1952—, prof. physics, 1963—, chmn. biophysics research div., 1976—, assoc. dean research Coll. Lit., Sci. and Arts,, 1972-75; mem. materials research adv. com. NSF, 1981—, chmn., 1984; cons. to industry. Author papers on vibrational spectroscopy, x-ray diffraction studies of natural and synthetic polymers. Served with USNR, 1944-46. Recipient Humboldt award, 1983; Textile Research Inst. fellow, 1947-50; NSF sr. postdoctoral fellow, 1962-63; sr. fellow U. Mich. Soc. Fellows, 1971-76. Fellow Am. Phys. Soc. (High Polymer Physics prize 1977, chmn. div. biol. physics 1979, div. councilor 1981, exec. com. 1983); mem. AAAS, Am. Chem. Soc., Am. Crystallographic Assn., Biophys. Soc., N.Y. Acad. Scis. Address: Dept Physics Univ Mich Ann Arbor MI 48109

KRIMS, LESLIE ROBERT, artist; b. N.Y.C., Aug. 16, 1942; s. Leo and Sally Horn (Leibowitz) K. B.F.A., Cooper Union, 1964; M.F.A., Pratt Inst., 1967. Asst. instr. photography and printmaking Pratt Inst., 1966-67; instr. Rochester (N.Y.) Inst. Tech., 1967-69; prof. SUNY, Buffalo, 1969—; guest lectr. Vis. artist numerous workshops, one-man shows include, Pratt Inst., 1966, Focus Gallery, San Francisco, 1969, George Eastman House, Rochester, 1969, 71, Witkin Gallery, 1969, 72, U. Colo., Boulder, 1971, Internat. Cultural Center, Antwerp, Belgium, 1972, Boston U., 1973, Photogalerie Wilde, Cologne, Ger., Galerie Delpire, Paris, 1974, Galeria Documenta, Torino, Italy, Galleria Photografica Nadar, Pisa, Italy, Shadai Gallery, Tokyo, 1975, Galerie Die Brucke, Vienna, Austria, Yajima Gallerie, Montreal, Can., Nina Freudenheim Gallery, Buffalo, 1975, 76, Galerie Jollenbeck, Cologne, 1976, Galerie A. Nagel, Berlin, also numerous two man, three man and group exhbns.; represented in permanent collections, George Eastman House, Nat. Gallery Can., Mpls. Inst. Arts, Mus. Modern Art, N.Y.C., Herbert F. Johnson Mus. Art at Cornell U., Library of Congress, Charles Rand Penny Found., Vassar Coll. Art Gallery, Visual Studies Workshop, Rochester, Tokyo Coll. Photography, Boston Mus. Fine Art. Fellow Nat. Endowment Arts, 1971, 72, 76; grantee Research Found. of State U. N.Y., 1971, N.Y. State Council Art, 1971, Creative Artists Pub. Service, 1973, 75. Home: 187 Linwood Ave Buffalo NY 14209 Office: 1300 Elmwood Ave Buffalo NY 14222

KRIMSKY, EMANUEL, physician, educator; b. N.Y.C.; m. Rose Schneider, June 1925 (dec. 1939); children: Beth Futter, Doris Parmett; children by 2d marriage: Deborah, Cynthia. M.D., Columbia, 1921. Diplomate: Am. Bd. Ophthalmology. Gen. practice medicine, 1923-30, practice medicine specializing in ophthalmology, Bklyn., 1930—; asst. prof. ophthalmology N.Y. Med. Coll., 1952—; mem. attending staff in ophthalmology Flower-Fifth Avenue Hosp., N.Y.C., Met. Hosps., St. John's Hosp., Long Island City, N.Y.; cons. ophthalmologist Bapt. Hosp., Bklyn.; adj. prof. ophthalmology N.Y. Polyclinic Med. Sch., 1938-51; contbr. to sci. exhibits. Author: The Management of Binocular Imbalance, 1948, Children's Eye Problems, 1956, The Corneal Light Reflex-A Guide to Binocular Problems, 1972, The Clinical Exploration of Binocularity, 1983; Contbr. numerous articles to profl. jours. Served to lt. col., M.C. AUS, 1942-46. Fellow Am. Acad. Ophthalmology and Otolaryngology. Developer Prism Reflex method of eye examination known as the Krimskytest, new method of binocular scotometry; inventor ophthalmologic instruments. Home and office: 103-05 Seaview Ave Brooklyn NY 11236

KRING, WALTER DONALD, clergyman; b. Lakewood, Ohio, Mar. 10, 1916; s. Walter DeVaine and Rebecca Olive (Shumaker) K. Exchange student, U. Hawaii, 1935-36; A.B., Occidental Coll., 1937, L.H.D., 1965; S.T.B., Harvard, 1940; LL.D., Emerson Coll., 1961; D.D., St. Lawrence U., 1968. Asst. Harvard Meml. Ch., 1939-41; asst. minister First Ch., Boston, 1939-41; asst. dept. history Harvard, 1939-41; minister First Presbyn. Ch., Hoosick Falls, N.Y., 1941-43, First Unitarian Ch., Worcester, Mass., 1946-55, Unitarian Ch. of All Souls, N.Y.C., 1955-78, emeritus, 1978—; pres. Beacon Press, Inc., 1955-59. Author: Religion is the Search for Meaning, 1955, Across the Abyss to God, 1966, Liberals Among the Orthodox: Unitarian Beginnings in New York City, 1819-1839, 1974, Henry Whitney Bellows, 1979; Exhibitor ceramics, Worlds Fair, Brussels, 1958. Dir. Worcester Craft Center; dir., pres. Spence Chapin Adoption Agency, 1970-71; pres. Artist-Craftsmen, N.Y., 1960-63, 70-72; Vis. com. Harvard Div. Sch., 1963-69; corporator Emerson Coll., 1960—, Worcester Art Mus., 1950-55. Served with Chaplains Corps USNR, 1943-46. Recipient 1st prize high temperature stoneware Nat. Ceramic Show, 1954. Hon. life mem. Am. Mus. Natural History.; Mem. Worcester Ministers Assn. (pres. 1954-55), East Midtown Ministers Assn. (pres. 1959-62, 68-69), Am. Unitarian Assn. (sec. 1953-61), Harvard Divinity Sch. Alumni Assn. (past pres.; mem. council), Melville Soc. Am. (pres. 1979). Club: Worcester Economic (pres. 1954-55). Address: Box 216 Brookfield MA 01506

KRINSKY, NORMAN IRVING, scientist, educator; b. Iron River, Mich., June 29, 1928; s. Morris Harry and Sonia (Ellenhorn) K.; m. Susan Gans, June 5, 1960; children: Lisa Ellen, Adam Daniel. Student, U. Ill., 1945-47; B.A., U. So. Calif., 1948, M.S., 1950, Ph.D., 1953. USPHS fellow Harvard, 1953-55; fellow Nat. Council to Combat Blindness, 1955-56; instr. biology Harvard, 1956-59, lectr., 1959-60; asst. prof. pharmacology Tufts U., 1960-64, asso. prof., 1964-67, asso. prof. biochemistry, 1967-69, prof., 1969-70, prof. biochemistry and pharmacology, 1970—; vis. prof. U. Calif., Berkeley, 1973; research assoc. Boston VA Med. Ctr., 1981-82. Mem. Am. Soc. Biol. Chemists, Am. Soc. Photobiology (sec.-treas. 1975-81, pres. 1982-83), AAAS, Biophys. Soc. Research on functions of carotenoids, photobiology, platelet-leukocyte interactions, oxygen radical damage, membrane damage. Home: 69 Evans Rd Brookline MA 02146 Office: 136 Harrison Ave Boston MA 02111

KRINSLEY, DAVID HENRY, geology educator; b. Chgo., Jan. 9, 1927; s. Lazarus and Rose (Aaron) K.; m. Ann L. Corrigan, Apr. 10, 1958; children: Karen, Jeanne, Brian. Ph.B., U. Chgo., 1948, S.B., 1948, S.M., 1950, Ph.D., 1956. Micropaleontologist Standard Oil Co., Los Angeles, 1951-52; asso. research petrologist research and devel. labs. Portland Cement Assn., Skokie, Ill., 1952-55; instr. phys. sci. U. Ill., Chgo., 1955-56; with Lamont Geol. Obs., Columbia U., 1956-57; mem. faculty Queens Coll., U. City N.Y., Flushing, 1957-76, prof., 1966-76, asso. dean faculty, 1966-70, acting dean faculty, 1970—; prof. geology Ariz. State U., Tempe, 1977—, chmn. dept., 1977-82. Served with AUS, 1945-46. Overseas fellow Churchill Coll., Cambridge (Eng.) U., 1970-71. Fellow Geol. Soc. Am., AAAS; mem. Sigma Xi. Home: 312 E Geneva Dr Tempe AZ 85282 Office: Dept Geology Ariz State U Tempe AZ 85287

KRINSLY, STUART Z., lawyer, chem. co. exec.; b. N.Y.C., May 19, 1917; m. Charlotte Wolf, Aug. 18, 1944; children—Ellinjane, Joan Susan. B.A., Princeton U., 1938; LL.B., Harvard U., 1941. Bar: N.Y. bar. Asst. U.S. atty. So. Dist. N.Y., 1942-45; mem. firm Schlesinger & Krinsly, 1945-57; sec. Sun Chem. Corp., N.Y.C., 1957-65, v.p., gen. counsel, 1965-76, sr. v.p., gen. counsel, 1976-78, exec. v.p., gen. counsel, 1978—, also dir.; dir. Chromalloy Am. Corp., Ketchum & Co.; partner firm Rich, Krinsly, Katz & Lillienstein. Clubs: Beach Point, Princeton of N.Y. Home: 1135 Greacen Point Road Mamaroneck NY 10543 Office: care Sun Chem Corp 200 Park Ave New York NY 10166

KRIPKE, KENNETH NORMAN, lawyer; b. Toledo, Feb. 16, 1920; s. Maurice and Celia (Vine) K.; m. Derril Kanter, Nov. 4, 1945; children: Teri Schwartz, Marcie Gaon. Student, Ohio State U., 1937-41; LL.B., U. Colo., 1948. Bar: Colo. 1949, U.S. Ct. Appeals (5th, 8th, 10th cirs.) 1954, U.S. Supreme Ct. 1967. Mem. firm Kripke & McLean, 1953-58, Kripke, Hoffman & Carrigan (and successors), 1965-73; individual practice law, Denver, 1973-80; partner Kripke, Epstein & Lawrence (P.C.), Denver, 1980—; mem. standing com. on rules civic procedure Colo. Supreme Ct., 1978—. Treas. Denver Allied Jewish Fedn., 1978-84; chmn. Denver civil rights com. Anti-Defamation League B'nai B'rith, 1977-83; mem. nat. law com. Anti-Defamation League, 1980—, mem. nat. civil rights com., 1979—. Served with USAAF, 1942-46. Mem. ABA (discovery subcom. of litigation sect. 1982—), Assn. Trial Lawyers Am. (bd. govs., past exec. com.), Western Trial Lawyers Assn. (sec. 1971-73, v.p. 1973-74, pres. 1974-75), Colo. Trial Lawyers Assn. (pres. 1958), Colo. Bar Assn. (litigation council 1982—), Arapahoe County Bar Assn., Am. Judicature Soc., Internat. Soc. Barristers (fellow), Am. Arbitration Assn., Internat. Assn. Jewish Lawyers and Jurists. Home: 4930 E 1st Ave Denver CO 80220 Office: 600 S Cherry St Suite 1125 Denver CO 80222

KRIPKE, SAUL AARON, philosopher, educator; b. Bay Shore, N.Y., Nov. 13, 1940; s. Myer Samuel and Dorothy Evelyn (Karp) K.; m. Margaret Patricia Gilbert, Feb. 8, 1976. B.A., Harvard U., 1962; L.H.D., U. Nebr., 1977. Mem. Soc. Fellows philosophy and math. logic Harvard U., 1963-66, lectr. philosophy, 1966-67; asso. prof. logic and philosophy Rockefeller U., N.Y.C., 1968-72, prof. philosophy, 1972-76; McCosh prof. philosophy Princeton U., 1976—; vis. fellow All Souls Coll., Oxford (Eng.) U.; vis. prof. U. Calif., Berkeley, UCLA, Cornell U., Princeton U.; White prof. at large Cornell U., 1977—; John Locke lectr. Oxford U., 1973; vis. fellow Wolfson Coll., Oxford (Eng.) U., 1981, 82; vis. Oscar Ewing scholar Ind. U., 1981-82; vis. scholar Corpus Christ Coll., Cambridge, Eng., 1983. Author: Naming and Necessity, 1980; author Wittgenstein on Rules and Private Language, 1982; contbr. articles to profl. jours. Fulbright fellow, 1962-63; Guggenheim fellow, 1968-69, 77-78; Santayana fellow Harvard U., 1967; Am. Council Learned Socs. fellow, 1981-82; NSF grantee. Mem. Am. Philos. Assn., Assn. Symbolic Logic, Am. Acad. Arts and Scis. Jewish. Home: 57 College Rd W Princeton NJ 08540 Office: Dept Philosophy Princeton U Princeton NJ 08544

KRIPPNER, STANLEY CURTIS, psychologist; b. Edgerton, Wis., Oct. 4, 1932; s. Carrol Porter and Ruth Genevieve (Volenberg) K.; m. Lelia Anne Harris, June 25, 1966; children: Carol, Robert. B.S., U. Wis., 1954; M.A., Northwestern U., 1957, Ph.D. grad asst., 1961, Univ. Humanistic Studies, San Diego, 1982. Speech therapist Warren Pub.

Schs. (Ill.), 1954-55, Richmond Pub. Schs. (Va.), 1955-56; dir. Child Study Ctr. Kent State U. (Ohio), 1961-64; dir. dream lab. Maimonaides Med. Ctr., Bklyn., 1964-73; faculty dean Saybrook Inst., San Francisco, 1973—; vis. prof. U. P.R., 1972, Calif. State Coll.-Sonoma, 1972-73, Univ. Life Scis., Bogota, Columbia, 1974; lectr. Acad. Pedagogical Scis., Moscow, 1971, Acad. Scis., Beijing, China, 1981. Author: (with Montague Ullman) Dream Telepathy, 1973, Song of the Siren: A Parapsychological Odyssey, 1975, (with Alberto Villodo) The Realms of Healing, 1976, Human Possibilities, 1980; editor: Advances in Parapsychological Research, vol. 1, 1977, Advances in Parapsychological Research, vol. 2, 1978, Advances in Parapsychological Research, vol. 3, 1982, Psychoenergetic Systems, 1979; co-editor: Galaxies of Life, 1973, The Kirlian Aura, 1974, The Energies of Consciousness, 1975, Future Science, 1977; editorial bd.: Giffted Child Quar., Jour. Am. Soc. Psychosomatic Dentistry and Medicine, Internat. Jour. Paraphysics; editorial: Jour. Humanistic Psychology; editorial bd.: Jour. Transpersonal Psychology, Revision Jour., Jour. Holistic Medicine, Jour. Psychophys. Systems, Jour. Indian Psychology; contbr. 450 articles to profl. jours. Hon. v.p. Albert Schweitzer Cultural Assn., Mexico City; bd. dirs. Nat. Found. Gifted and Creative Children, Gardner Murphy Research Inst., Nat. Assn. Gifted Children, Acad. Religion and Psychical Research; mem. adv. bd. A.R.E. Clinic; mem. Central Premonitions Registry; mem. adv. bd. Found. Mind Research, New Horizons Research Found. Recipient Service to Youth award YMCA, 1959, citation of merit Nat. Assn. Gifted Children, 1972, Nat. Assn. Creative Children and Adults, 1975, cert of recognition Office of Gifted and Talented, U.S. Office Edn., 1976, Volker Medal South Africa Soc. Psychical Research, 1980. Fellow Am. Soc. Clin. Hypnosis; mem. Am. Soc. Psychical Research, N.Y. Soc. Clin. Psychologists (assoc.), Am. Acad. Social and Polit. Sci., AAAS, Am. Ednl. Research Assn., Am. Personnel and Guidance Assn., Am. Psychol. Assn. (pres. div. 32 1980-81), Inter-Am. Psychol. Assn., Assn. Humanistic Psychology (pres. 1974-75), Assn. Transpersonal Psychology, Sleep Research Soc., Biofeedback Soc. Am., Council Exceptional Children, Coll. Reading Assn., Internat. Soc. Gen. Semantics, Menninger Found., Nat. Soc. Study of Edn., Parapsychol. Assn. (pres. 1983), Soc. Clin. and Exptl. Hypnosis, Soc. for Sci. Study of Religion, Soc. Sci. Exploration, Soc. Sci. Study of Sex, World Future Soc. Home: 79 Woodland Rd Fairfax CA 94930 Office: Saybrook Inst 1772 Vallejo St San Francisco CA 94123

KRISCH, ADOLPH OSCAR, hotel executive; b. N.Y.C., June 3, 1916; s. Samuel J. and Miriam (Weinstein) K.; m. Heidrun Ilsa Feller, June 16, 1966; children: Victoria (Mrs. James Mills), Juliana (Mrs. Martin L. Weiss). Student, Roanoke Coll., 1933-34, U. Va., 1934-37. With various retail jewelers, 1936-57; chmn. bd. Am. Motor Inns Inc., Roanoke, Va., 1957—. Served with U.S. Army, 1943-44. Mem. Internat. Assn. Holiday Inns (dir., pres. 1969). Home: 5128 Grossbow Circle SW Roanoke VA 24014 Office: 1917 Franklin Rd SW Roanoke VA 24014

KRISCH, ALAN DAVID, physics educator; b. Phila., Apr. 19, 1939; s. Kube and Jeanne (Freiberg) K.; m. Jean Peck, Aug. 27, 1961; 1 dau., Kathleen Susan. A.B., U. Pa., 1960; Ph.D., Cornell U., 1964. Instr. Cornell U., 1964; mem. faculty U. Mich., Ann Arbor, 1964—, assoc. prof. high energy physics, 1966-68, prof., 1968—; vis. prof. Niels Bohr Inst., Copenhagen, 1975-76. Trustee Argonne Nat. Lab., 1972-73, 80-82, chmn. zero gradient syncrotron users group, 1973-75, 78-79; chmn. internat. com. for high energy spin physics symposia, 1978-84. Guggenheim fellow, 1971-72. Fellow Am. Phys. Soc.; mem. AAAS. Discovered heaviest elementary particle, also structure within the proton, 1966, scaling in inclusive reactions, 1971, spinning core within proton, 1977; inventor inclusive reactions; developed high energy polarized proton beam, 1973. Office: Randall Lab U Mich Ann Arbor MI 48109

KRISCH, JOEL, motel executive; b. Roanoke, Va., June 23, 1924; s. Samuel J. and Miriam (Weinstein) K.; m. Nancy Jane Scher, Jan. 2, 1950; children: Kathryn Jane Krisch Loeb, Linda Scher Krisch Vinson, Samuel J. II. Student, Va. Poly. Inst., 1941-43. Partner bus. firm, Roanoke, 1946-57, exec. officer motel corps., 1957-62; pres. Am. Motor Inns, Inc., Roanoke, 1962—; dir. Sidney's, Inc., Roanoke.; Bd. dirs. Va. Poly. Inst., State U. Ednl. Found., Airline Passengers Assn., Dallas. Trustee Goucher Coll., Balt. Served with AUS, 1943-45. Mem. Roanoke Valley C. of C. (dir.). Jewish. Clubs: Masons (Shriner); Hunting Hills Country (Roanoke); B'nai B'rith. Office: Am Motor Inns 1917 Franklin Rd SW Roanoke VA 24014 *

KRISHAIAH, PARUCHURI RAMA, statistics educator, researcher; b. Nalluru, India; s. Paruchuri Bhavanarayana and Paruchuri Tottempudi (Mankyamma) Chowdary; m. Indira Devi, Dec. 15; children: Raghu Ram, Niranjan Ram. B.S. in Statustics with honors, U. Madras, India, 1954; M.A., U. Minn., 1957, Ph.D., 1963. Sr. statistician Remington Rand Univac, Blue Bell, Pa., 1960-63; research math. statistician Air Force Aerospace Research Labs., Wright-Patterson AFB, Ohio, 1963-75, math. statistician, 1975-76; dir. Inst. Statis. and Applications, U. Pitts., 1978-82, prof. math. and statis., 1976—; dir. Ctr. Multivariate Analysis, Wright-Patterson AFB, 1982—; vis. scientist Indian Statis. Inst., Calcutta, 1966; speaker nat. and internat. meetings. Editor: Jour. Multivariate Analysis; series editor: Development in Statistics, Vol. 1, 1978, Development in Statistics, Vol. 2, 1979, Development in Statistics, Vol. 3, 1980, Development in Statistics, Vol. 4, Handbook of Statistics, Vol. 1, 1980, Handbook of Statistics, Vol. 2, 1982; editorial bd.: Jour. Statis. Planning and Inference; coordinating editor: North Holland Series in Statistics and Probability, Vol. 1, 1966, North Holland Series in Statistics and Probability, Vol. 2, 1969, North Holland Series in Statistics and Probability, Vol. 3, 1973, North Holland Series in Statistics and Probability, Vol. 4, 1977, North Holland Series in Statistics and Probability, Vol. 5, 1979; editor: (with G. Kallianpur and J.K. Ghosh) Statistics and Probability: Essays in Honor of C.R. Rao, 1981. Fellow Am. Statis. Assn. (mem. council, past pres. Dayton chpt. 1968-69), AAAS, Inst. Math. Statisitics; mem. Internat. Statis. Inst. Home: 119 Shadow Ridge Dr Pittsburgh PA 15238 Office: Center for Multivariate Analysis University of Pittsburgh Pittsburgh PA 15260

KRISHER, BERNARD, foreign correspondent; b. Frankfurt, Germany, Aug. 9, 1931; s. Joseph and Fella (Solnica) K.; m. Akiko Yaginuma, May 1, 1960; children: Deborah, Joseph. B.A., Queens Coll.; student, Advanced Internat. Reporting Program Columbia U., 1961-62. Staffwriter, then asst. editor mag. N.Y. World-Telegram & Sun, 1955-61; corr. Newsweek, 1963—, bur. chief, Tokyo, 1968-80; corr. Fortune, 1981-83; chief editorial advisor Focus Weekly Mag. Shincho-sha Pub. Co., Tokyo, 1981—; hon. research assoc., vis. scholar East Asian Reserach Center, Harvard U., 1978-79. Author: (with Alan Levy) Draftee's Confidential Guide, 1957, The Plus and Minuses of Being Japanese, 1978, Interview, 1976, Harvard Diary, 1979, How Harvard Sees Japan, 1979. Mem. Council Fgn. Relations. Home: 3-16-12 Nishi-Azabu Minato-Ku Tokyo Japan (106) Office: Shincho-Sha 71 Yarai-cho Shinjuku-ku Tokyo Japan

KRISHER, PATTERSON HOWARD, management consultant; b. Oklahoma City, Sept. 14, 1933; s. Sherman and Gladys (Patterson) K.; m. Mary Anne Howard, Nov. 21, 1973; children: Sherman H., Bryan P. B.S. in Indsl. Engring., Okla. State U., 1956; A.M.P., Harvard U., 1971. Cert. mgmt. cons. Plant indsl. engr. Procter & Gamble Mfg. Co., Dallas, 1959-60; mktg. rep. IBM, Dalls, 1960-61; mgmt. cons. Arthur Young & Co., San Francisco, Los Angeles and Dallas, 1961-77, nat. dir. mgmt. services, 1977-83, dir. mgmt. services N.Y.C. Office, 1983—; treas. Inst. Mgmt. Cons., 1984—; guest instr. U. Tex., Ohio State U. Contbr. to: Handbook of Business Problem Solving, 1980; mem. editorial bd.: Jour. Mgmt. Cons., 1983—, Boardroom Reports, 1984—. Chmn. Arthur Young Polit. Action Com., 1978—; Bd. dirs. Homeowners Assn.; mem. vis. com. indsl. engring. dept. Lehigh U., 1984—. Served with USAF, 1956-59. Congregationalist. Clubs: Marco Polo, Sky (N.Y.C.); Burning Tree Country (Greenwich, Conn.) (dir. 1981—). Office: 277 Park Ave New York NY 10172

KRISHER, WILLIAM K., ins. co. exec.; b. Massillon, Ohio, July 29, 1931; s. Ralph R. and Grace L. (Keller) K.; m. Audrey F. Ellms, Aug. 13, 1955; 1 son, Norman R. B.A., Washington and Jefferson Coll., 1953. With Conn. Mut. Life Ins. Co., Hartford, 1953—, now sr. v.p. Mem. Soc. Actuaries, Am. Acad. Actuaries, Financial Execs. Inst. Home: 4 Hawks Ln Simsbury CT 06070 Office: 140 Garden St Hartford CT 06115

KRISHNAMURTHY, GERBAIL THIMMEGOWDA, nuclear physician; b. Gerbail, N.R. Pura, Chickmagalore, Karnataka, India, Aug. 3, 1937; s. Thimmegowda and Manjamma K.; m. Shakuntala Naik, Dec. 26, 1969; children—Anil Raj, Kalpana. M.B., B.S., U. Mysore, India, 1964; M.S., UCLA, 1971. Staff physician in nuclear medicine Wadsworth VA Hosp., Los Angeles, 1971-77; asst. prof. medicine UCLA, 1971-77, asso. prof., 1977—; chief nuclear medicine VA Hosp., Portland, Oreg., 1977—; prof. clin. pathology, also asso. prof. medicine U. Oreg. Health Scis. Center, Portland, 1977—, dir. nuclear medicine residency program, 1977—; Adv. editor Nuclear Medicine Rapid Communication; vis. prof. U. Rio de Janeiro, Brazil, 1976; mem. Am. Coll. Nuclear Physicians. Contbr. numerous articles to profl. jours. Fellow A.C.P.; mem. Soc. Nuclear Medicine, Indian Soc. Nuclear Medicine, Health Physics Soc., Am. Fedn. Clin. Research. Hindu. Home: 7570 SW Westgate Way Portland OR 97225 Office: Nuclear Medicine Service VA Hospital Portland OR 97201

KRISHNAMURTI, JIDDU, religious educator, author, philosopher; b. Madanapalle, S. India, 1895. Ed. privately, Eng. Founder Krishnamurti Found., Ojai, Calif., 1969; Founder, Oak Grove Sch., Ojai. Author: Education and the Significance of Life, 1953, The First and Last Freedom, 1954, Commentaries on Living: 1st series, 1956, 2d series, 1958, 3d series, 1960, Life Ahead, 1963, Think on These Things, 1964, Freedom from the Known, 1969, The Only Revolution, 1970, The Urgency of Change, 1971, The Impossible Question, 1973, Beyond Violence, 1973, Flight of the Eagle, 1972, The Awakening of Intelligence, 1973, Beginnings of Learning, 1975, Krishnamurti's Notebook, 1976, Truth and Actuality, 1977, The Wholeness of Life, 1978, Meditations, 1979, Letters to the Schools, 1980, Krishnamurti's Journal, 1981, Questions & Answers, 1982, The Network of Thought, 1983. Address: PO Box 216 Ojai CA 93023

KRISPYN, EGBERT, educator; b. Haarlem, Holland, June 14, 1930; came to U.S., 1961, naturalized, 1970; s. Peter Johan and Henriette (Lams) K. B.A., U. Melbourne, Australia, 1957, M.A., 1958; postgrad., U. Tübingen, Germany, 1958-61; Ph.D., U. Pa., 1963. Comml. employee Internat. Trading Co., Europe, Singapore, Thailand, Indonesia, 1947-51; lectr. U. Pa., 1961-63, asst. prof., 1964-66, asso. prof., 1966-68; asst. prof. U. Fla., Gainesville, 1963-64, prof., chmn. German and Russian dept., 1968-72; prof. U. Ga., Athens, 1972—. Editor: Netherlandic sect. Twayne World Authors Series, 1966—, Library of Netherlandic Lit, Twayne Pub., Inc., 1970-79; co-editor: Germanic Notes, 1970—; editorial bd.: Studies in German Lit., Linguistics and Culture; Author: Style and Society in German Literary Expressionism, 1964, George Heym: A Reluctant Rebel, 1968, Günter Eich, 1971, Anti-Nazi Writers in Exile, 1978; Contbr. articles to profl. jours. Mem. MLA, Internat. Assn. for Germanic Studies, Soc. German Renaissance and Baroque Lit., Modern Humanities Research Assn., So. Comparative Lit. Assn., Am. Lit. Translators Assn. Home: Route 2 Box 212 Comer GA 30629 Office: Univ Georgia Athens GA 30602

KRISS, JOSEPH PINCUS, internist, educator; b. Phila., May 15, 1919; s. Max and Sima (Charny) K.; m. Regina Tarlow, June 5, 1948; children—Eric, Paul, Mark. B.S. cum laude, Pa. State Coll., 1939, M.D., Yale U., 1943. Diplomate: Am. Bd. Internal Medicine, Am. Bd. Nuclear Medicine (a founder), Nat. Bd. Med. Examiners. Successively intern, asst. resident in medicine, asst. resident in metabolism, resident in medicine New Haven Hosp., 1943-45; asst. in medicine, then instr. Yale U. Med. Sch., 1943-44; research fellow metabolism Washington U. Med. Sch., St. Louis, 1946-48; research asso. in endocrinology and metabolism Michael Reese Hosp., Chgo., 1949; teaching asst. Stanford U. Med. Sch., 1948-49, mem. faculty, 1949—, prof. medicine and radiology, 1962—, dir. div. nuclear medicine. Recipient Disting. Alumnus award Pa. State U., 1978; Alumni fellow, 1979; Kaiser fellow Center Advanced Study Behavioral Scis., 1979-80. Mem. Soc. Nuclear Medicine (Western Regional award 1978), Endocrine Soc., AAAS, Am. Fedn. Clin. Research, Am. Thyroid Assn., Assn. Am. Physicians, Western Soc. Clin. Research, Western Assn. Physicians. Office: Div Nuclear Medicine Stanford U Med Center Stanford CA 94305

KRIST, PETER CHRISTOPHER, petroleum company executive; b. Ansonia, Conn., Aug. 23, 1919; s. Nicholas and Mary (Vasil) K.; m. Vede Makarion, Nov. 3, 1946; children—David P., Robert P. A.B. magna cum laude in Psychology, Dartmouth Coll., 1942. Dir. Wage and salary adminstrn. Am. Overseas Airlines, N.Y.C., 1946-47, dir. labor relations, 1947-48; labor relations rep. Am. Airlines, Inc., N.Y.C., 1948-51; asst. to v.p. indsl. relations Bendix Corp., N.Y.C., 1951-52, mgr. personnel adminstrn., 1952-53; dir. wage and salary adminstrn. Ry. Express Agy. Inc., N.Y.C., 1953-55, dir. personnel adminstrn., 1955-60; mgr. employee communications, corp. employee relations dept. Mobil Oil Corp., N.Y.C., 1960-61; employee relations adviser Mobil North and Southeast Europe (Internat. Div.), London, 1961-66, gen. mgr. corp. employee relations dept., N.Y.C., 1966-69, v.p. employee relations, 1969-77, sr. v.p. employee relations, 1977—, also dir. Bd. dirs. Westport-Weston United Way; bd. dirs. at large-ptnr. relations com. United Way of Tri-State, 1960-65; mem. bus. adv. council NAACP Spl. Contbn. Fund, 1971—; mem. commerce and industry council Nat. Urban League, Inc., 1973—; mem. labor mgmt. com. Nat. Council on Alcoholism, 1974—; former bd. dirs. Unemployment Benefits Adv.; bd. dirs., mem. coms. Nat. Soc. to Prevent Blindness; bd. dirs., treas. Citizens Crime Commn. N.Y.C.; Trustee John E. Gray Inst.; Bd. dirs. Regional Plan Assn. Served to maj. AUS, 1942-46. Club: Pinnacle. Office: Mobil Oil Corp 150 E 42d St New York NY 10017

KRISTIANSEN, MAGNE, electrical engineer, educator; b. Elverum, Norway, Apr. 14, 1932; came to U.S., 1958, naturalized, 1967; s. Martin and Ella (Sobye) K.; m. Aud Bohn, July 6, 1957; children: Sonja Bohn, Eric Bohn. B.S. in Elec. Engring, U. Tex., Austin, 1961, Ph.D. (Ford Found. fellow), 1967. Registered profl. engr., Tex. Research engr. U. Tex., Austin, 1964-66; faculty Tex. Tech U., Lubbock, 1966—, prof., 1971—, P.W. Horn prof., 1977—, dir. plasma lab., 1966—; cons. def. products div. Varo, Inc., Garland, Tex., 1970-71; cons. Aerospace Corp., El Segundo, Calif., 1974-76, BDM Corp., Albuquerque, 1975-76, Palisades Inst., N.Y. and NRC, 1977, Rockwell Internat., 1978, Maxwell Labs., 1979-83, La Jolla Inst., 1979, NASA, 1979, Norwegian Research Council, 1980, Sci. Applications Inc., 1983—, Lawrence Livermore Nat. Lab., 1983—; mem. vis. staff Los Alamos Nat. Lab., 1974—; contractor Sandia Labs., 1977-79, Lawrence Livermore Lab., 1978-79, U.S. Navy, 1977-78; Mem. USAF Sci. Adv. Bd., 1981—. Co-author: An Introduction to Controlled Thermonuclear Fusion, 1977, Russian, Japanese, Chinese translations, 1980-81.; Contbr. articles to profl. jours. Served with Royal Norwegian Air Force, 1950-58. Recipient Hamilton award U. Tex., 1961; Spencer A Wells award Tex. Tech U., 1972; Disting. Research award, 1980; NSF grantee, 1967—; AEC grantee, 1968-71; Air Force Office Sci. Research grantee, 1968—; State of Tex. grantee, 1966—; NATO sr. fellow in sci., 1975; Japan Soc. Promotion Sci. fellow, 1979; Dept. Energy grantee, 1978-79. Fellow IEEE; mem. AAAS, Am. Phys. Soc., Am. Nuclear Soc., Am. Soc. Engring. Edn., Sigma Xi, Tau Beta Pi, Eta Kappa Nu, Phi Kappa Phi. Home: 3105 78th St Lubbock TX 79423

KRISTICK, DAVID A., security company executive; b. Concord, Calif., Jan. 12, 1935; m. Marilyn C. Kristick, Feb. 28, 1952; children: David M., Kevi R., Paula S. Utility-fire insp. Tidewater Oil Co., Martinez, Calif., 1952-57; with Martinez Police Dept., 1957-67, lt.; exec. v.p. Burns Internat. Security Services, Briarcliff Manor, N.Y., 1967—; adviser John Jay Coll. Criminal Justice, N.Y.C., 1983—. Mem. Am. Soc. Indsl. Security. Office: Burns Internat Security Services 320 Old Briarcliff Rd Briarcliff Manor NY 10510 *

KRISTJANSON, LEO FRIMAN, ednl. adminstr., economist; b. Gimli, Man., Can., Feb. 28, 1932; s. Hannes and Elin Theordois (Magnusdottir) K.; m. Jean Evelyn Cameron, June 29, 1957; children—Terri, Darryl, Brenda, Johanne. B.A., U. Man., 1954, M.A., 1959; Ph.D., U. Wis., 1963; LL.D., U. Winnipeg, 1980. Instr. history United Coll., Winnipeg, Man., 1956-57; research economist Centre for Community Studies, Saskatoon, Sask., 1959-64; prof. econs., head, dept. U. Sask., Saskatoon, 1964-75, v.p., 1975-80, pres., 1980—; cons. agrl. marketing Govt. Sask., 1972—. Author 2 booklets in field. Mem. Am. Econ. Assn., Canadian Econ. Assn. (exec. mem.), Canadian Assn. U. Tchrs. (treas., exec. mem. 1970-72), Am. Farm Econs. Assn., Canadian Agrl. Econs. Soc. Home: President's Residence U Saskatchewan Saskatoon SK Canada

KRISTOF, LADIS KRIS DONABED, political scientist, author; b. Cernauti, Rumania, Nov. 26, 1918; came to U.S., 1952, naturalized, 1957; s. Witold and Maria (Zawadzki) Krzysztofowicz; m. Jane McWilliams, Dec. 29, 1956; 1 son, Nicholas. Student. U. Poznan, Poland, 1937-39; B.A., Reed Coll., Portland, Ore., 1955; M.A., U. Chgo., 1956, Ph.D., 1969. Regional exec. dir., Sovromlemn, Rumania, 1948; mgr. Centre du Livre Suisse, Paris, France, 1951-52; lectr. U. Chgo., 1958-59; asso. dir. Inter-Univ. Project History Menshevism, N.Y.C., 1959-62; mem. faculty dept. polit. sci. Temple U., 1962-64; research fellow Hoover Instn., Stanford U., 1964-67; faculty polit. sci. U. Santa Clara, 1967-68; asso. Studies Communist System, Stanford, 1968-69; mem. faculty polit. sci. U. Waterloo, Ont., Can., 1969-71; prof. polit. sci. Portland (Oreg.) State U., 1971—. Author: The Nature of Frontiers and Boundaries, 1959, The Origins and Evolution of Geopolitics, 1960, The Russian Image of Russia, 1967; also articles in, Romania; co-author, co-editor: Revolution and Politics in Russia, 1972. Active Internat. YMCA Center, Paris, 1950-52, NAACP, Chgo., 1957-59, Amnesty Internat., Portland, 1975—. Served with Corps Engrs. Romanian Army, 1940-43. Fulbright scholar, Romania, 1971. Mem. Am. Polit. Sci. Assn., Assn. Am. Geographers, AAAS, Internat. Polit. Sci. Assn. Home: Rt 2 Box 430 Gaston OR 97119 Office: Portland State Univ Portland OR 97207 *War, want and concentration camps, exile from home and homeland, these have made me hate strife among men, but they have not made me lose faith in the future of mankind. Personal experience, including my own unsteady progress through life, has taught me to beware of man's capacity for plain stupid, irrational, as well as consciously evil behavior, but it also has taught me that man has an even greater capacity for recovery from lapses. In a short thrust of planned, wisely guided activity he is able to climb to higher levels of material and intellectual achievement than he ever reached before. In short, I remain a rationalist and an optimist at a time when the prophets of doom have the floor. My query is, if man has been able to create the arts, the sciences and the material civilization we know in America, why should he be judged powerless to create justice, fraternity and peace.*

KRISTOFFERSON, KRIS, singer, song writer, actor; b. Brownsville, Tex., June 22, 1936; children by first marriage: Tracy, Kris; m. Rita Coolidge, Aug. 19, 1973; 1 child, Casey.; m. Lisa Meyers, Feb. 19, 1983. Attended, Pomona Coll., hon. doctorate, 1974; B.A. (Rhodes scholar), Oxford (Eng.) U., 1960. Worked at a variety of jobs in Nashville, 1965-69. Appeared at, Newport (R.I.) Folk Festival, 1969; and on: Johnny Cash TV program, 1970; concert and rec. artist, 1970—; albums recorded include Kristofferson, 1970, The Silver-Tongued Devil and I, 1971, Border Lord, Jesus Was a Capricorn, Spooky Lady's Sideshow, 1974, Big Sur Festival, Songs of Kristofferson, Who's to Bless and Who's to Blame, Easter Island, 1978, Shake Hands With the Devil, 1979; (with Rita Coolidge) albums recorded Breakaway; films acted in include Cisco Pike, 1972, Pat Garrett and Billy the Kid, 1973, Blume in Love, 1973, Bring Me the Head of Alfredo Garcia, 1974, Alice Doesn't Live Here Anymore, 1974, The Sailor Who Fell From Grace With The Sea, 1976, A Star is Born, 1976, Vigilante Force, 1976, Semi-Tough, 1977, Convoy, 1978, Heaven's Gate, 1981, Rollover, 1981; TV film Freedom Road, 1979; performed: (with Rita Coolidge include) songs for soundtrack of The Last Movie, 1971; Composer: songs Sunday Morning Comin' Down, 1970 (Song of Year Country Music Assn.), Help Me Make It Through the Night, Me and Bobby McGee, (both nominated for Grammy award for Best Song 1971), Why Me, Lord, For the Good Times, Jody and the Kid, When I Loved Her. Served to capt. AUS, 1960-65. Office: care William Morris Agency Inc 151 El Camino Beverly Hills CA 90212 *

KRISTOL, IRVING, social sciences educator, editor; b. N.Y.C., Jan. 22, 1920; s. Joseph and Bessie (Mailman) K.; m. Gertrude Himmelfarb, Jan. 18, 1942; children: William, Elizabeth. B.A., CCNY, 1940; D.Letters, Franklin and Marshall Coll., 1972; LL.D., U. Dallas, 1974, Kenyon Coll., 1977. Mng. editor Commentary mag., 1947-52; co-founder, co-editor Encounter mag., 1953-58; editor The Reporter mag., 1959-60; exec. v.p. Basic Books, Inc., N.Y.C., 1961-69; co-editor The Public Interest mag., 1965—; mem. faculty N.Y. U., N.Y.C., 1969—, prof. social thought Grad. Sch. Bus. Adminstrn., 1979—; dir. Lincoln Nat. Corp., Warner-Lambert Co., Citizens Utilities Co., Dreyfus Money Market Instruments, Inc., Dreyfus Leverage Fund, Inc., Dreyfus Growth Opportunity Fund, Dreyfus A. Bonds Plus, Inc.; sr. fellow Am. Enterprise Inst. Author: On the Democratic Idea in America, 1972, Two Cheers for Capitalism, 1978, Reflections of a Neoconservative, 1983. Mem. Pres.'s Commn. on White House Fellowships. Served with U.S. Army, 1944-46. Fellow Am. Acad. Arts and Scis.; mem. Council Fgn. Relations. Club: Century Assn. Office: Public Interest Mag 10 E 53 St New York NY 10022

KRITCHEVSKY, DAVID, educator, biochemist; b. Kharkov, Russia, Jan. 25, 1920; came to U.S., 1923, naturalized, 1929; s. Jacob and Leah (Kritchevsky) K.; m. Evelyn Sholtes, Dec. 21, 1947; children—Barbara Ann, Janice Eileen, Stephen Bennett. B.S., U. Chgo., 1939, M.S., 1942; Ph.D., Northwestern U., 1948. Chemist Ninol Labs., Chgo., 1939-46; postdoctoral fellow Fed. Inst. Tech., Zurich, Switzerland, 1948-49; biochemist Radiation Lab., U. Calif. at Berkeley, 1950-52, Lederle Lab., Pearl River, N.Y., 1952-57, Wistar Inst., Phila., 1957—; prof.

biochemistry Sch. Vet. Medicine, U. Pa., Phila., 1965—, 1970—, chmn. grad. group molecular biology, 1972—; Mem. USPHS study sect. Nat. Heart Inst., 1964-68, 72-76; chmn. research com. Spl. Dairy Industry Bd., 1963-70; mem. food and nutrition bd. Nat. Acad. Sci., 1976-82. Author: Cholesterol, 1958, also numerous articles.; Editor: (with G. Litwack) Actions of Hormones on Molecular Processes, 1964; co-editor: (with R. Paoletti) Advances in Lipid Research, 1963—, (with P. Nair) The Bile Acids, 1971; Western Hemisphere editor Atherosclerosis. Recipient Research Career award Nat. Heart Inst., 1962, award Am. Coll. Nutrition, 1978. Mem. Am. Inst. Nutrition (Borden award 1974, pres. 1979), Am. Soc. Biol. Chemists, AAAS, Am. Chem. Soc. (award Phila. sect. 1977), Soc. Exptl. Biology and Medicine (pres.-elect 1983—), Arteriosclerosis Council, Am. Heart Assn., Am. Soc. Oil Chemists (chmn. methods com. 1963-64), Internat. Soc. Fat Research. Research on role vehicle when cholesterol and fat produces atherosclerosis in rabbits, effects saturated and unsaturated fat, deposition orally administered cholesterol in aorta man and rabbit. Pioneered use radioactive cholesterol for metabolic expts. Home: 136 Lee Circle Bryn Mawr PA 19010 Office: Wistar Inst 36th and Spruce Sts Philadelphia PA 19104

KRIVOSHA, NORMAN, chief justice state supreme court; b. Detroit, Aug. 3, 1934; s. David B. and Molly K.; m. Helene Miriam Sherman, July 31, 1955; children: Terri Lynn, Rhonda Ann. B.S., U. Nebr., 1956, J.D., 1958. Bar: Nebr. Ptnr. firm Ginsburg, Rosenberg, Ginsburg & Krivosha, Lincoln, Nebr., 1958-78; chief justice Nebr. Supreme Ct., Lincoln, 1978—; city atty. City of Lincoln, 1969-70; gen. counsel Lincoln Electric System, 1969-78, Lincoln Gen. Hosp., 1969-78; mem. Uniform Law Commn., 1973—. Pres. Lincoln council Camp Fire Girls, Congregation Tifereth Israel, Lincoln; pres. central states region United Synagogue Am.; bd. dirs. Lincoln YMCA; Nebr. chmn. Israel Bonds; chmn. fund drive Lincoln Jewish Welfare Fedn.; mem. Lincoln Charter Revision Commn.; bd. dirs. Ramah Commn., Camp Ramah, Wis. Recipient Outstanding Jewish Leader award State of Israel Bonds, 1978. Mem. ABA, Nebr. Bar Assn. (chmn. com. on procedure), Lincoln Bar Assn., Am. Trial Lawyers Assn., Nebr. Assn. Trial Attys. (sec. 1961-64, v.p. 1964-65), Am. Soc. Hosp. Attys., Am. Pub. Power Assn. (chmn. legal sect.), Lincoln C. of C. (bd. dirs.), Sigma Alpha Mu (nat. v.p.). Home: 2835 O'Reilly Dr Lincoln NE 68502 Office: Nebr Supreme Ct Suite 2214 State Capitol Bldg Lincoln NE 68509

KRIVSKY, WILLIAM ANTHONY, manufacturing executive; b. Stafford Springs, Conn., Mar. 26, 1927; s. Anton Martin and Katherine Alice K.; m. Susan Benson, 1972; children: Wayne Alan, Wendy Ann, Cynthia Susan, Holly Lee. B.S., MIT, 1951, D.Sc., 1954; postgrad., U. Buffalo, 1955-56. Mgr. metals research Union Carbide Corp., Niagara Falls, N.Y., 1954-59; v.p., gen. mgr. Beryllium Metal and Oxide div. Brush Beryllium Co., Cleve., 1959-65; adminstrv. v.p. Continental Copper & Steel Industries, Inc., N.Y.C., 1965-69; group v.p. Gen. Cable Corp., N.Y.C., 1969-72; pres. Crucible Splty. Metals div. and Crucan, Colt Industries, N.Y.C., 1972-74; sr. v.p. CertainTeed Corp., Phila., 1974-80; pres., chief operating officer, dir. Compo Industries, Inc., Waltham, Mass., 1980—; pres., dir. Velcro Industries N.V., Bedford, N.H.; dir. Krauss-Maffei Corp.; guest lectr. extractive metallurgy AIME. Editor: High Temperature Refractory Metals, 1965. Chmn. United Found., 1980; mem. World Affairs Council, Council Internat. Visitors of Phila. Served to 1st lt. USAAF, 1944-47. Recipient Francis J. Clamer Gold medal Franklin Inst., 1978; Disting. Alumnus award MIT, 1980; Sloan Sch. Mgmt. award MIT, 1980. Mem. AIME (dir. 1970-73, Gold medal 1959), Am. Soc. Metals, Am. Mgmt. Assn., Newcomen Soc., Copper Club-Copper Devel. Assn., Am. Iron and Steel Inst., Sigma Xi, Tau Beta Pi. Inventor, Linde Argon-Oxygen Decarburization process. Office: 125 Roberts Rd Waltham MA 02254

KRIZ, VILEM FRANCIS, photographer, educator; b. Prague, Czechoslovakia, Oct. 4, 1921; came to U.S., 1952; s. Vaclav and Marie (Skruzna) K.; m. Jarmila Veronica Vesela, Nov. 29, 1945; children: Gabriel, Dominica Ursula. Student photography under prof. Jaromir Funke, Josef Ehm and Frantisek Drtikol, State Acad. Graphical Arts, Prague, 1940-46, Ecole Cinematographique et Photographique, Paris, 1947. Tchr. photography and art various Calif. colls. including, Holy Name Coll., Oakland, 1964-74, various Calif. colls. including; U. Calif., Extension-Berkeley, 1969-73, various Calif. colls. including; Mills. Coll., Oakland, 1970-74; prof. photography Calif. Coll. Arts and Crafts, Oakland, 1974—; lectr. in field. Exhibitor photographs, U.S.A., Europe, Japan, 1940—; author: Conversation, Invitation 40, 1963, Kriz-Surrealism and Symbolism, 1971; exhibitor: Sirague City, 1975, Seance, 1979. Home: 1905 Bonita Ave Berkeley CA 94704 Office: Calif Coll Arts and Crafts 5212 Broadway at College Oakland CA 94618

KRIZEK, THOMAS JOSEPH, plastic surgeon; b. Milw., Dec. 1, 1932; s. Chester Francis and Elizabeth Ann (Flynn) K.; m. Claudette Reid; children: Thomas Joseph, Kelly Ann, Mary Ellen. B.S., Marquette U., 1954, M.D., 1957; M.A. (hon.), Yale U., 1974; cert. in health systems mgmt., Harvard U., 1975. Diplomate: Am. Bd. Surgery (dir. 1979-83), Am. Bd. Plastic Surgery. Intern Univ. Hosps. of Cleve., 1957-58, resident in gen. surgery, 1958-59, 61-64, research fellow in plastic surgery, 1964, resident in plastic surgery, 1964-66; asst. prof. plastic surgery Johns Hopkins U., Balt., 1966-68, U. Md., 1966-68; chief div. plastic surgery Balt. City Hosps., 1966-68; asso. prof. Yale U., New Haven, 1968-73, prof., 1973-78, dir. trauma program, 1974-77, asso. dean for grad. and continuing med. edn., 1975-77; chief sect. plastic and reconstructive surgery Yale-New Haven Med. Center, 1968-78, asso. chief staff for grad. and continuing med. edn., 1975-77; prof. dept. surgery Coll. Phys. and Surg., Columbia U.; chief plastic and reconstructive surgery Columbia-Presbyn. Med. Center, N.Y.C., 1978-81; prof. plastic surgery U. So. Calif. Sch. Medicine, 1981—; chief div. plastic surgery U. So. Calif.-Los Angeles County Med. Center, 1981; cons. VA Hosp., West Haven, Conn., 1968-78; bd. dirs. Am. Bd. Plastic Surgery, 1977-83, vice chmn., 1982-83. Author: (with R. Touloukian) Diagnosis and Early Management of Trauma Emergencies: A Manuel for the Emergency Service, 1974; editor: (with John E. Hoopes) Basic Science in Plastic Surgery, 1976; contbr. articles to profl. jours. Served to lt. M.C. USNR, 1959-68. Fellow A.C.S. (pres. Conn. chpt. 1974); mem. Am. Surg. Assn., Assn. Acad. Surgery, Am. Assn. Plastic Surgery (treas. 1976-79, historian 1979—, trustee 1984—), Am. Soc. Plastic and Reconstructive Surgery (sec. plastic surgery program dirs. group 1975-77, pres. 1977-79), New Eng. Soc. Plastic and Reconstructive Surgeons (pres. 1976-77), Plastic Surgery Research Council (chmn. 1974-75), Am. Soc. Aesthetic Plastic Surgery, Am. Soc. Maxillofacial Surgeons, Assn. Am. Med. Colls., Am. Burn Assn., Internat. Soc. Burn Injuries, Soc. Head and Neck Surgeons, Am. Assn. Surgery Trauma, Am. Assn. Automotive Medicine, Am. Geriatrics Soc., AAAS, New York County Med. Assn., AMA, N.Y. State Med. Soc., N.Y. Acad. Scis., N.Y. Acad. Medicine, Am. Soc. Microbiology, Am. Trauma Soc., So. New Eng. Hand Soc., Am. Assn. Hand Surgery (pres. 1980), Sigma Xi, Alpha Omega Alpha. Republican. Roman Catholic. Office: 1200 N State St Los Angeles CA 90033

KROC, ROBERT LOUIS, research adminstr.; b. Chgo., June 19, 1907; s. Louis and Rose Mary (Hrach) K.; m. Alice Voelker, Nov. 29, 1934; children—Alice Ann (Mrs. Hansjorg Hattemer), Lois Sandra Hoel. B.A., Oberlin Coll., 1929, M.A., 1931, D.Sc. (hon.), 1979; Ph.D., U. Wis., 1933. Instr. zoology U. Ind. at Bloomington, 1933-38, asst. prof., 1938-44; dir. biol. research Maltine Co., Chilcott Labs., Morris Plains, N.J., 1944-52; dir. physiology Warner-Lambert Research Inst., Morris Plains, N.J., 1952-69; Pres. Kroc Found., Santa Ynez, Calif., 1969—. Editor: Human Development and the Thyroid Gland: Relation to Endemic Cretinism, 1972; Contbr. articles on endocrinology to profl. jours. Mem. alumni bd. Oberlin Coll., 1948-52. Fellow N.Y. Acad. Scis. (chmn. biology medicine 1959-61); mem. Am. Diabetes Assn. (dir.), Nat. Multiple Sclerosis Soc., Am. Thyroid Assn. (pres. 1971-72, dir.), Endocrine Soc., Am. Physiol. Soc., AAAS. Club: Rotarian. Home: PO Box 577 Santa Ynez CA 93460 Office: PO Box 547 Santa Ynez CA 93460 *My experience leads me to place primary value on enthusiasm, imagination, a sense of humor, consideration for others and dedication for achievement of high goals, with a total or overview sense always to relate the immediate objective or project to a larger whole.*

KROCH, CARL ADOLPH, bookseller; b. Chgo., June 21, 1914; s. Adolph and Gertrude (Horn) K.; m. Jeanette Kennelly, Aug. 12, 1939. B.A., Cornell U., 1935. With Kroch's Bookstores, Inc., 1935-54, pres., dir., 1949-54; pres. Brentano's Bookstores, Inc., 1950-54; pres., dir. Kroch's & Brentano's, Inc., Chgo., 1954—; pres. Booksellers Catalog Service, Inc.; dir. Nat. Blvd. Bank Chgo. Author: American Booksellers and Publishers: A Personal Perspective, 1981. Bd. dirs. Northwestern Meml. Hosp., Ill. Humane Soc., USO. Served to lt. USNR, 1942-45. Mem. Am. Booksellers Assn., Ill. Retail Mchts. Assn., Better Bus. Bur. Chgo., Wine and Food Soc., Beta Theta Pi. Clubs: North Shore Country (Glenview, Ill.); Caxton, Mid-Am., Chgo. Yacht, Tavern, Univ. (Chgo.); Pauma Valley Country, Lake Zurich (Ill.) Golf. Home: 3240 N Lake Shore Dr Chicago IL 60657 Office: 29 S Wabash Ave Chicago IL 60603

KROEBER, CLIFTON BROWN, history educator, historian; b. Berkeley, Calif., Sept. 7, 1921; s. Clifton Spencer K. and Theodora Covel (Kracaw) Brown; m. Elizabeth MacSwain Jones, Apr. 29, 1944; children: Jeffrey, Alan, Keith, Scott. A.B., U. Calif.-Berkeley, 1943, M.A., 1947, Ph.D., 1951. Asst. prof. history U. Wis.-Madison, 1951-55; asst. prof. Occidental Coll., Los Angeles, 1955-59, assoc. prof., 1959-64, Norman Bridge prof. Hispanic Am. history, 1964—; cons. Ford Found., N.Y.C., 1970-71. Author: The Growth of the Shipping Industry in the Rio de la Plata Region, 1957; co-author: (with A.L. Kroeber) A Mohave War Reminiscence, 1854-18880, 1974; author: Man, Land, and Water, Mexico's Farmlands Irrigation Policies, 1885-1911, 1983. Served to lt. USNR, 1943-46. Fellow Social Sci. Research Council, 1949; grantee Am. Philos. Soc., 1966, Wenner-Gren Found. for Anthrop. Research, 1970, Haynes Found., 1959, 80; recipient Faculty Achievement award Occidental Coll., 1970. Mem. Am. Hist. Assn., Pacific Coast Council Latin Am. Studies. Home: 1701 Linda Rosa Ave Los Angeles CA 90041 Office: Dept History Occidental Coll Los Angeles CA 90041

KROEBER, KARL, educator; b. Oakland, Calif., Nov. 24, 1926; s. Alfred Louis and Theodora Quinn (Kracaw) K.; m. Jean Taylor, Mar. 21, 1953; children—Paul Demarest, Arthur Romeyn, Katharine. A.A., Coll. of Pacific, Stockton, Calif., 1945; A.B., U. Calif. at Berkeley, 1947; M.A., Columbia, 1951, Ph.D., 1956. Asst. prof. U. Wis.-Madison, 1956-61, asso. prof., 1961-63, prof., 1963-70, asso. dean, 1963-65; prof. English and comparative lit. Columbia U., 1970—, chmn. dept. English and comparative lit., 1973-76. Author: Romantic Narrative Art, 1960, The Artifice of Reality, 1964, Studying Poetry, 1965, Backgrounds to British Romantic Literature, 1968, Styles in Fictional Structure, 1971, Romantic Landscape Vision, 1975, Images of Romanticism, 1978, Traditional Literatures of the American Indian, 1981; editor: Studies in American Indian Literatures; mem. editorial bd.: Studies in English Lit. Bd. dirs. Am. Blake Found. Served with USNR, 1944-46. Fulbright Research grantee, Italy, 1960-61; U.S. Office Edn. Research grantee, 1965-66; Guggenheim fellow, 1966-67. Mem. Modern Lang. Assn., Am. Comparative Lit. Assn., Modern Humanities Research Assn., Internat. Assn. Profs. English. Home: 226 St Johns Pl Brooklyn NY 11217 Office: Dept of English and Comparative Lit Columbia U New York NY 10027

KROEGER, ARTHUR, Canadian government administrator; b. Naco, Alta., Can., Sept. 7, 1932; s. Heinrich and Helena (Rempel) K.; m. Gabrielle Jane Sellers, May 7, 1966 (dec.); children: Alexandra, Kate. B.A. with honors, U. Alta., 1955, Oxford U., Eng., 1958. Fgn. service officer Can. Dept. External Affairs, 1958-71, treasury bd. secretariat, 1971-75, dep. minister Indian and No. affairs, 1975-79, dep. minister transport, Ottawa, Ont., 1979-83; sec. Ministry of State for Econ. Devel., Ottawa, Ont., 1983—. Rhodes scholar, 1955. Club: Five Lakes Fishing. Home: 245 Springfield Rd Ottawa ON K1M 0L1 Canada Office: Place de Ville Ottawa ON Canada

KROEHLER, KENNETH, furniture mfg. exec.; b. Oak Park, Ill., Oct. 21, 1917; s. Peter E. and Grace A. (Hubert) K.; m. June Staecker, May 9, 1941; 1 son, Peter K. B.S., U. Calif., 1939. With Kroehler Mfg. Co., 1939—, pres., 1963-67, chmn. bd., chief exec. officer, 1967—; dir., mem. exec. com. Protection Mut. Ins. Co.; adv. bd. Liberty Mut. Ins. Co. Hon. trustee, past chmn. bd. trustees North Central Coll., Naperville, Ill. Served to lt. USNR, 1942-46. Mem. Nat. Assn. Furniture Mfrs. (past pres.), Ill. Mfrs. Assn. (past pres.). Clubs: Chicago Yacht; Lost Tree Golf (North Palm Beach, Fla.). Office: Kroehler Mfg Co 222 E 5th Ave Naperville IL 60540

KROESEN, FREDERICK JAMES, army officer; b. Phillipsburg, N.J., Feb. 11, 1923; s. Frederick James K. and Jean Ursula (Shillinger) Kroesen; m. Rowene Wilder McCray, Mar. 4, 1944; children: Karen McCray Kroesen Klare, Federick J., Gretchen McCray Kroesen Tackaberry. B.S. in Agr., Rutgers U., 1944; B.A. in Internat. Affairs, George Washington U., 1962, M.A., 1966. Served as enlisted man U.S. Army, 1942-44, commd. 2d lt., 1944, advanced through grades to gen., 1976; served with 187th Airborne Regimental Combat team Korean War, 1953-55; served with Americal Div. Vietnam War, 1968-71; comdr. in chief. U.S. Army, Europe, 1962-65; comdr. Central Army Group, Heidelberg, Germany, 1962-65; instr. U.S. Army War Coll., 1965-68, 70-71; mem. staff asst. chief of staff for force devel. U.S. Army, 1972-74, comdr. 82d Airborne Div., 1975-76, comdr. VII Corps., 1978-79, vice chief of staff. Decorated D.S.M. with oak leaf cluster, Silver Star with oak leaf cluster, Legion of Merit with 2 oak leaf clusters, D.F.C., Bronze Star with V and two oak leaf clusters, Air Medal with twenty-nine oak leaf clusters, Purple Heart with oak leaf cluster, other campaign, service and fgn. awards. Mem. Assn. of U.S. Army, Soc. French Legion of Honor, Delta Upsilon. Home: 2309 S Queen St Arlington VA 22202

KROGER, FERDINAND ANNE, educator; b. Amsterdam, Netherlands, Sept. 11, 1915; came to U.S., 1964; s. Henri Anton M. and Anna Barendina (van der Bilt) K.; m. Elisabeth Johanna Hofdijk, 1946; children—Frank Ferdinand, Catharine Elisabeth. Ph.D., U. Amsterdam, 1940. Research worker Philips Research Labs., Eindhoven, Netherlands, 1938-58; sci. adviser Mullard Research Lab., Salfords, Surrey, Eng., 1958-64; prof. materials sci. and chemistry U. So. Calif., Los Angeles, 1964—, David Packard prof. elec. engring., 1971—. Author: Some Aspects of Luminescence of Solids, 1945, The Chemistry of Imperfect Crystals, 1964, rev. edit., 1974; Contbr. articles to profl. jours. Fellow Am. Ceramic Soc.; mem. Electro-chem. Soc., AAAS, AAUP, Royal Netherland Acad. Arts and Scis. (corr. 1978), Sigma Xi. Home: 410 S Manhattan Pl Apt 101 Los Angeles CA 90020 Office: Dept Materials Sci U So Calif University Park Los Angeles CA 90089

KROGER, WILLIAM SAUL, physician; b. Chgo., Apr. 14, 1906; s. Charles Mandel and Rose (Ziskin) K.; m. Jimmy Louise Burton, Sept. 15, 1952; children: Carol Lynn, Deborah Sue, Lisa Robin, William Saul. B.M., Northwestern U., 1926, M.D., 1930. Intern, St. Francis Hosp., Evanston, Ill., 1930-31; resident in obstetrics and gynecology Chgo. Lying-in-Hosp., 1931-32; instr. dept. gynecology U. Ill. Sch. Medicine, Chgo., 1940-44; asso. prof. gynecology Chgo. Med. Sch., 1950-60; practice medicine specializing in psychiatry, psychosomatic medicine, hypnosis and sex therapy, 1960—; cons. psychiatrist Los Angeles New Hosp.; clin. prof. anesthesiology UCLA Sch. Medicine, also cons. psychiatrist; dir. Inst. Comprehensive Medicine, Beverly Hills, Calif.; lectr. in field; condr. seminars and symposia worldwide; cons. NIMH; lectr. in field; condr. seminars and symposia world wide; cons. FBI. Author: (with S.C. Freed) Psychosomatic Gynecology, 1951, Kinsey's Myth of Female Sexuality, 1954, Childbirth With Hypnosis, 1961, Thanks Doctor, I've Stopped Smoking, 1962, Clinical and Experimental Hypnosis, 1963, rev. edit., 1977, Psychosomatic Obstetrics, Gynecology and Endocrinology, 1960, (with W.D. Fezler) Hypnosis and Behavior Modification: Imagery Conditioning, 1976; former mem. editorial bd. jours. in psychosomatics, hypnosis and sexual behavior.; cons. editor Jour. Mental Imagery; adv. editor: Internat. Jour. Clin. and Exptl. Hypnosis. Mem. Am. Psychosomatic Soc. Acad. Psychosomatic Medicine (co-founder, past pres., award of merit 1957), Am. Pain Soc., Am. Psychiat. Soc., Internat. Soc. Clin. and Exptl. Hypnosis (co-founder, Best Book award 1963, Raginsky award for leadership and achievement in field of hypnosis 1969, 80, award of merit 1958), Am. Soc. Clin. Hypnosis (co-founder, past v.p.), Soc. for Sci. Study Sex (co-founder). Club: Century West (Los Angeles). Home: 10390 Wilshire Blvd Los Angeles CA 90024 Office: 9735 Wilshire Blvd Beverly Hills CA 90210 *Success can be attributed to making every day a meaningful one. Ideas come to fruition only by translating them into actions. One must not be afraid to have his thoughts called absurd. What is heresy today is conservatism tomorrow.*

KROGH, HAROLD CHRISTIAN, business educator; b. Cedar Rapids, Iowa, Feb. 1, 1917; s. Hans P. and Dorathea (Meyer) K.; m. Bessie Alberta Cummins, May 31, 1942; children: Linda Marie Krogh Russell, Richard Alan, Laurie Ellen. B.S. in Commerce, State U. Iowa, 1939, M.A., 1941, Ph.D., 1953; postgrad., Harvard Grad. Sch. Bus., 1959, NYU, 1964, U. Wis., 1967, Stanford U., 1973, Northwestern U., 1974; grad., Nat. War Coll., 1967, Indsl. Coll. Armed Forces, 1962, Command and Gen. Staff Coll., Fort Leavenworth, 1969. Sales Midland Mortage Co., Cedar Rapids, 1939-40; instr. econs. U. Ala., Tuscaloosa, 1941-42; personnel officer VA, Des Moines, 1946-47; instr., asst. prof., asso. prof. fin. Drake U., Des Moines, 1947-54; asso. prof. bus. adminstrn. U. Kans., Lawrence, 1954-60, prof., 1960—; cons. to ins. firms, fin. instns., pensionfunds, 1954—; mem. faculty exchange program U. Costa Rica, summers 1962, 63; mem. bd. govs. Internat. Ins. Sem., Oslo, Norway, 1977, Manila, Philippines, 1978, Toronto, Can., 1982. Bd. govs., bd. electors Internat. Ins. Hall of Fame. Served with AUS, 1942-46; col. Res. Mem. Am. Soc. C.L.U.'s, Am. Risk and Ins. Assn. (past pres.), Am. Fin. Assn., Midwest Fin. Assn. (past pres.), Fin. Mgmt. Assn., Am. Soc. C.P.C.U.'s, AAUP, Soc. Fin. Analysts, Midwest Bus. Adminstrn. Assn., Midwest Econs. Assn., Kansas City Actuaries Club, Alpha Kappa Psi, Beta Gamma Sigma. Lutheran. Home: 1117 Highland Dr Lawrence KS 66044

KROGSTAD, BLANCHARD ORLANDO, insect ecologist; b. Winger, Minn., Oct. 6, 1921; s. Jens and Julia; s. Jens and Julia (Sonstelie) K.; m. Doris Jane Van Winkle, Dec. 23, 1946; children: Jineen Elyse, Rolf Gregory, Bruce Elliott. B.A., Bemidji State U., 1946; M.A., U. Minn., Mpls., 1948, Ph.D., 1951. Asst. prof. St. Olaf Coll., 1951-54; asst. prof., prof. U. Minn., Duluth, 1954-78, prof., head dept. biology, 1978—; scientist Rockefeller Found. in Mexico, 1963-64, Instituto Mexicano del Cafe in Mexico, 1970-71. Author: Ecologia Avanzada de los Isectos, 1964; Contbr. sci. articles to profl. jours. Pres. Duluth Lester Park PTA, 1966; com. mem. Bicentennial Com., 1976, Friends of Christian Radich, 1976-78. Served with USAAF, 1942-46. Recipient Outstanding Educators Am. citation, 1974-75, Outstanding Tchr. award U. Minn., 1977; NSF grantee, 1959, 1962-63; Rockefeller grantee, 1963-64; U.S. Office Edn. grantee, 1965-66. Mem. Ecol. Soc. Am., Entomol. Soc. Am., N. Am. Benthological Assn., Am. Assn. Biol. Scis., Minn. Acad. Scis. (dir.), Sociedad Mexicana de Entomologia, Sigma Xi. Lutheran. Club: Nordmanns Forbundet (pres. Lake Superior sect.). Home: Route #1 Winger MN 56592 Office: Dept Biology U Minn Duluth MN 55812

KROHN, ALBERTINE, chemistry educator; b. Toledo, Ohio, Nov. 28, 1924; d. Albert Herman and Bertha Marie (Rath) K. B.S. summa cum laude, U. Toledo, 1946, M.S., 1949; M.S., U. Mich., 1951, Ph.D., 1956. Instr. math., chemistry U. Toledo, 1947-51, asst. prof. chemistry, 1951-57, asso. prof., 1957-63, prof., 1963—; cons. Delos M. Palmer & Assos., Toledo, NASA Lewis Research Center, Cleve. Contbr. articles to profl. jours. Trustee Phi Kappa Phi Found., 1969-80, St. Paul's Luth. Ch., Toledo, 1980-83; sec. St. Paul's Luth. Ch. Found., Toledo, 1983—. Recipient Gold "T" award Alumni Assn. U. Toledo, 1973. Fellow Ohio Acad. Sci.; mem. Am. Chem. Soc. (nat. councilor 1967-75, alternate councilor 1976—), Electrochem. Soc., Am. Electroplaters' Soc., Sigma Xi, Phi Kappa Phi (pres. 1972-77, chmn. bd. dirs. 1972-77, Disting. Mem. award 1977), Pi Mu Epsilon, Delta Kappa Gamma. Home: 5679 Monroe St Sylvania OH 43560 Office: 2801 W Bancroft St Toledo OH 43606

KROHN, DUANE RONALD, hotel executive; b. Langdon, N.D., Feb. 5, 1946; s. Victor E. and Alice E. (Rouse) K.; m. Audrey Windingland, June 30, 1967; children: Gregory, Kristine. B.S. in Bus. Adminstrn., U. N.D. C.P.A., Nev. With Laventhal and Howath (C.P.A.s), Las Vegas, 1978; treas., controller Bally's Park Place, Inc., Atlantic City, 1979; v.p. fin., treas. Dunes Hotels and Casinos Inc., Las Vegas, 1980-83, corporate controller, 1983—. Mem. Internat. Assn. Hospitality Accts. (pres.), Nev. Soc. C.P.A.s (pres. Las Vegas chpt. 1975), Am. Inst. C.P.A.s. Office: 3650 Las Vegas Blvd S Las Vegas NV 89109

KROL, EDWARD JOSEPH, surgeon; b. Chgo., Apr. 3, 1913; s. Alexander and Mary (Madalinski) K.; m. Anne Estelle Shirvin, Feb. 1, 1942; children—Edwina Ann, Cynthia Lee, Edward Joseph, Gerald John. B.S., Central YMCA, Chgo., 1936; M.D., Loyola U., Chgo., 1939. Diplomate: Internat. Bd. Surgery, Am. Bd. Abdominal Surgery (chmn. bd.), Internat. Bd. Applied Nutrition. Extern Holy Cross Hosp., Chgo., 1938-39, sr. attending surg. staff, 1948—, pres., chief staff, 1957-59, chmn. dept. surgery, 1959-60, co-chmn. dept. surgery, 1961-62, chmn. exec. bd., 1958-61, sec. bd., 1961-62, now mem. exec. bd.; intern St. Elizabeth's Hosp., Chgo., 1939-40; individual practice, Chgo., 1940-42, specializing surgery, 1945—; postgrad. surg. tng. Cook County Postgrad. Sch., Tufts U., U. Ill., Bunt's Inst. of Crile Clinic, Cleve., U. Minn., U. Kans.; clin. asst. surgery Rush Med. Sch., 1940-42, Stritch Sch. Medicine, 1945-50, clin. instr. surgery, 1950—. Editorial staff: Am. Jour. Abdominal Surgery, 1962; asso. editor: Internat. Jour. Applied Nutrition, 1961; contbg. editor surg. sect.: Am. Jour. Proctology, 1952—, Modern Nutrition Jour, 1961—; Contbr. numerous articles to med. jours. Mem. Adv. Council to Gov. Ill.; Chmn. adv. bd. Immaculata Coll., Chgo., 1955—; trustee Intestinal Research Inst., 1955—; mem. pres.'s council St. Xavier's Coll., Chgo., 1956—; chmn. bd. advisers Shelbourne Center, Valparaiso, Ind.,

1960—. Served from lt. to capt. M.C. USAAF, 1942-45. Recipient certificate merit Internat. Acad. Proctology, award merit Dept. Calif. Mil. Order Purple Heart, meritorious service award Clin. Congress Abdominal Surgeons, also Gold medal Achievement, 1962. Fellow Internat. Coll. Surgeons, Am. Soc. Abdominal Surgery (pres. 1965-66, 77—), Internat. Acad. Proctology (trustee 1950-55, pres. 1953), Am. Coll. Gastroenterology (pres. 1962-63, bd. trustees 1950-64), Am. Coll. Nutrition, Royal Soc. Medicine, N.Y. Acad. Scis., A.A.A.S., Am. Geriatric Soc., Miss. Valley Med. Soc., A.M.A. (chmn. gen. surg. sect. 1962-63, exec. com. 1962-64, ho. of dels. 1977), Acad. Psychosomatic Medicine, Internat. Coll. Applied Nutrition (v.p., bd. govs. 1961—), Soc. Acad. Achievement, Internat., Am. colls. angiology; mem. Am. Coll. Chest Physicians, World Med. Assn., Ill. Med. Soc. (del.), Chgo. Med. Soc. (counsellor), Chgo. Path. Soc., Ill. Acad. Sci., Ill. Soc. Med. Research, Am. Nutrition Soc., Assn. Mil. Surgeons, Am. Thoracic Soc., Assn. Am. Med. Colls., Fedn. Am. Scis., Cath. Physicians Guild, Assn. Am. Physicians and Surgeons, Inst. Medicine Chgo. Clubs: American Sportsmens; Union League (Chgo.). Office: 4255 W 63d St Chicago IL 60629

KROL, JOHN CARDINAL, Cardinal; b. Cleve., Oct. 26, 1910; s. John and Anna (Pietruszka) K. Student, St. Mary's Sem., Cleve., 1937; J.C.B., Gregorian U., Rome, 1939, J.C.L., 1940; J.C.D., Cath. U. Am., 1942; Ph.D., La Salle Coll., 1961; LL.D., John Carroll U., 1955, St. Joseph U., 1961, St. John U., N.Y., 1964, Coll. Steubenville, 1967, Lycoming Meth. Coll., 1966, Temple U., 1964, Bellarmine-Ursuline Coll., 1968, Drexel U., 1970; D.S.T., Villanova U., 1961; L.H.D., Alliance Coll., 1967, Coll. Chestnut Hill (Pa.), 1975, Holy Family Coll., 1977; D.D., Susquehanna U., 1970; D.Theology, U. Lublin (Poland). Priest Roman Catholic Ch., 1937, pvt. chamberlain, 1945, domestic prelate, 1951; parish asst., 1937-38; prof. Diocesan Sem.; also chaplain Jennings Home for Aged, 1942-43; vice chancellor Cleve. Diocese, 1943-51, chancellor of diocese, 1951-53, promoter of justice, 1951-53; consecrated bishop, 1953, auxiliary bishop to bishop of Cleve., also vicar gen. Diocese of Cleve., 1953-61, archbishop of, Phila., 1961—; elevated to Sacred Coll. of Cardinals, 1967; undersec. II Vatican Council, 1962-65; mem. Pontifical Commn. Communications Media, 1964-69; chmn. Nat. Cath. Office for Radio and TV, 1963-64, Nat. Cath. Office for Motion Pictures, Cath. Communications Found., 1965-70, Pa. Cath. Conf., 1961—; v.p. Nat. Conf. Cath. Bishops, 1966-71, pres., 1971-74; vice chmn. U.S. Cath. Conf., 1966-71, pres., 1971-74; mem. Pontifical Commn. for Mass Media Communications, 1964-69, Sacred Congregation for Evangelization of Nations, 1967-72, Sacred Congregation for Oriental Ch., 1967—, Sacred Congregation for Doctrine of Faith, 1973—. Mem. Pres.'s Nat. Citizens Com. Community Relations; chmn. bd. govs., host 41st Internat. Eucharistic Congress, Phila., 1976; Trustee Cath. U. Am., Washington, 1961-71, Nat. Shrine of Immaculate Conception, Washington, Cath. League for Religious Assistance to Poland; pres. Center for Applied Research in Apostolate, 1967-70. Decorated comdr. of cross Order of Merit, Italy; Nat. Order Republic of Chad; recipient gold medal Paderewski Found., 1961; Nat. Human Relations award NCCJ, 1968; Father Sourin award Cath. Philopatrian Inst., 1967; John Wesley Ecumenical award Old St. George's Meth. Ch., 1967; Phila. Freedom medal, 1978. Mem. Canon Law Soc. Am. (pres. 1948-49). Office: 222 N 17th St Philadelphia PA 19103

KROLL, BARRY LEWIS, lawyer; b. Chgo., June 8, 1934; s. Harry M. and Hannah (Lewis) K.; m. Jayna Vivian Leibovitz, June 20, 1956; children: Steven Lee, Joan Lois, Nancy Maxine. A.B. in Psychology with distinction, U. Mich., 1955, J.D. with distinction, 1958. Bar: Ill. 1958. Since practiced in, Chgo.; assoc. firm Jacobs & McKenna, 1958-66, Epstein, Manilow & Sachnoff, 1966-68, Schiff, Hardin, Waite Dorschel & Britton, 1968-69; partner firm Wolfberg & Kroll, 1970-74, Kirshbaum & Kroll, 1972-74; of counsel firm Jacobs, Williams & Montgomery, Ltd., 1973-74; partner firm Jacobs, Williams & Montgomery Ltd., 1974—; faculty John Marshall Law Sch., Chgo., 1969-73; atty. for petitioner in U.S. Supreme Ct. decision Escobedo vs Ill., 1964, guest lectr. before groups, 1964—; mem. legal and legis. com. Internat. Franchise Assn., 1976-80. Asst. editor: Mich. Law Rev, 1957-58. Chmn. Park Forest Bd. Zoning Appeals, 1971-78. Served to capt. AUS, 1959-62. Named Outstanding Young Man Park Forest Jr. C. of C., 1966. Mem. Ill. Bar Assn., Chgo. Bar Assn. (chmn. legis. com. 1974-75), Ill. Appellate Lawyers Assn. (treas. 1978-79, sec. 1979-80, pres. 1981-82), Bar Assn. 7th Fed. Circuit, Order of Coif, Tau Epsilon Rho, Alpha Epsilon Pi. Jewish religion (trustee cong. 1966-70, 72-75, pres. men's club 1965-66). Home: 314 Gettysburg St Park Forest IL 60466 Office: 20 N Wacker Dr Chicago IL 60606

KROLL, BORIS, textile designer, mfr., distbr.; b. Buffalo, Oct. 11, 1913; s. Nathan and Cecilla K.; m. Lynn Steyert, Mar. 7, 1941; children—Geoffrey, Eric David, Lisa. Ed. pub. schs.; D. Textiles (hon.), Phila. Coll. Textiles and Sci., 1971. Designer, mfr., distbr. upholstery and drapery fabrics, 1938—; pres. Cromwell Designs, Inc., 1938-61, Boris Kroll Fabrics, Inc., 1946—, Boris Kroll Fabrics of Los Angeles, Inc., 1955-64, Boris Kroll Fabrics of Miami, Inc., 1957-64, Boris Kroll Fabrics of Ill., Inc., 1959-64; (cos. merged with Boris Kroll Fabrics, Inc. 1964), Boris Kroll Jacquard Looms, Inc., 1954—, Boris Kroll Indsl. Land Corp., 1966—, 220 East 51st Street Corp., 1950—, Boris Kroll Prints, Inc., 1955-64, Boris Kroll Labs., Inc., 1957-64, (cos. merged with Boris Kroll Jacquard Looms, Inc. 1964). One-man show, Seattle Art Mus., 1955, Detoit Inst. Arts, 1962, Purdue U., 1970, Ga. State U., Jacquard Woven Tapestry Guild Hall Mus., East Hampton, N.Y., 1976, Phila. Coll. Textiles and Sci., 1979, Fashion Inst. Tech., N.Y.C., 1980; exhibited, World's Fair, N.Y.C., 1939, Good Design exhbn., Mus. Modern Art, 1953, Ford Found. and Govt. of India Handloom Fabrics Survey in India, 1956, Exhibits in permanent collection, Victoria and Albert Mus., London, Decorative Fabric Collection by Designer-Weavers of U.S., 1965, Detroit Inst. Arts, 1966. Vice pres. Resources Council of AID, 1963; mem. jury for Mich. Crafts Show, Detroit Inst. Arts, 1967; SONA adv. com. handicrafts and looms Export Corp. India, Ltd., 1967-70. Served with C.E. AUS, 1943-45. Mem. Decorative Design Assn. (pres. 1958), Am. Crafts Council, Am. Inst. Interior Designers, Nat. Home Fashions League, Nat. Soc. Interior Designers, Am. Assn. for Textile Tech., Color Assn. U.S. (dir. 1967—, chmn. home furnishings color card com. 1968—), Upholstery and Decorative Fabrics Assn. Am. Club: Arts of Chicago. Home: 200 E 57th St New York NY 10022 Office: 979 3d Ave New York NY 10022

KROLL, GEORGE, cardiologist; b. Hartford, Conn., May 16, 1922; s. Abraham Natu and Celia (Fleishman) K.; m. Helga Wunchova, Apr. 18, 1948. B.S., Central YMCA Coll., 1944; D.D.S., U. Ill., 1946, M.D. cum laude, 1952, M.S. in Biochemistry, 1953. Diplomate: Am. Bd. Internal Medicine, Am. Bd. Cardiovascular Disease. Intern U. Chgo. Clinics, 1952-53, resident in internal medicine, 1954-55, U. Ill. Research and Edn. Hosp., 1953-54; Nat. Heart Inst. cardiology fellow, 1955-56, practice medicine specializing in cardiology, Chgo., 1956—; chmn. dept. medicine, dir. internal medicine residency program Edgewater Hosp., Chgo., 1976—; dir. heart sta. VA Lakeside Hosp., 1956-76, chief cardiovascular sect., 1973-76; asso. prof. clin. medicine Sch. Medicine, Northwestern U., 1973-77; prof. medicine U. Health Sci., Chgo. Med. Sch., 1976-79, 80—. Served to capt. Dental Corps, U.S. Army, 1946-48. Fellow ACP, Am. Coll. Cardiology, Am. Heart Assn. (council clin. cardiology), Inst. Medicine Chgo; mem. Chgo. Soc. Internal Medicine, Am. Fedn. Clin. Research, Sigma Xi, Alpha Omega Alpha. Home: 5733 N Sheridan Rd Chicago IL 60660 Office: 5700 N Ashland Ave Edgewater Hospital Chicago IL 60660

KROLL, JOHN LEON, athletic equipment manufacturing company executive; b. Buffalo, Sept. 5, 1925; s. Hammond and Sylvia (Heimberger) K.; m. Evelyn Maher, Dec. 29, 1966; 1 dau., Sharon; stepchildren: John Brennan, James Brennan. B.S. in Phys. Edn. and Recreation, N.Y. U., 1948, M.A. in Health Edn, 1949; postgrad. in sch. adminstrn., U. Conn., 1953-55. Tchr. phys. edn. N.Y.C. Bd. Edn., 1948-49; dir. phys. edn. Waterford (Conn.) Public Schs., 1949-51; founder, chmn. bd. Jayfro Corp., Waterford, 1953—; pub. Jayfro Periscope nat. newsletter, 1973-81; co-founder Nat. Athletic Mfrs. Catalog Distbg. Corp., Harbor City, Calif., 1973-77; co-founder (with wife) Kroll Press and Publ. & Advt. Waterford, Co., 1978; bd. advs., cons. Gymnastic Athletic Supply Co., Inc., San Pedro, Calif., 1975—; dir. of adv. bd. Southeastern Conn. area Conn. Bank and Trust Co., New London, 1980; mem. adv. bd. Nat. Sports Mgmt. Studies Found., U. Mass., Amherst, 1980. Author: (with wife) It Doesn't Pay To Work Too Hard, 1979; contbr. articles to profl. and trade jours., also mags. Chmn. promotional programs com. U.S. com. Sports for Israel, Inc., N.Y.C., 1975-79; bd. dirs. Tennis Found. N.Am., 1973-79, YMCA, Boca Raton, Fla., 1977-80, Waterford Day Sch. New Bldg. Assn., 1982—, Conn. Jr. Achievement, 1982—, S.E. Conn. Ostomy Com., 1980—, Cath. Charities Corp. Fund Raising Bd., Norwich Diocese, 1981—; mem. membership com. Ice Skating Inst. Am., 1975-81; hon. bd. dirs. Flatbush Boys Club, Bklyn., 1975-80. Served with USN, 1943-46; Served with USNR, 1946-51; Served with U.S. Army, 1951-53. Recipient Honor award Pres.'s Council Phys. Fitness and Sports, 1977, Disting. Service award City and County Adminstrs. of Health and Phys. Edn., AAHPER, 1978; honored at 25th ann. industry testimonial dinner, 1977. Mem. Athletic Inst. (dir. 1975-76), Am. Council Internat. Sports (dir. 1977—), Edn. Industries Assn. (dir. 1972-76), Exhibitors Assn. AAHPER and Dance (exec. bd. dirs. 1970-76, pres. 1973-74), Nat. Intramural-Recreational Sports Assn. (hon. life; exhibitors com. 1974-78), Nat. Sporting Goods Assn., Sporting Goods Mfrs. Assn. (tennis and racquet sports com. 1973-80, phys. edn. and athletic com. 1972-76, internat. sporting goods show steering com. 1973-79, chmn. membership com. 1975-78), Nat. Sch. Supply and Equipment Assn. (dir., exec. com. 1973-75, chmn. conv. and exhbns. com. 1975-78), U.S. Tennis Ct. and Track Builders Assn., Booster Club Assn. Am. (contbg. industry co-founder). Clubs: 2001 (Dallas); Lambs (N.Y.C.); Delray Beach (Fla.); Rotary (Waterford); N.Y. U. (N.Y.C.). Patentee in field. Home: 535 Pequot Ave New London CT 06320 also 4201 Ocean Blvd Highland Beach FL 33431 Office: PO Box 400 Waterford CT 06385 *I have earnestly attempted to work and create to the very best of my ability. I have developed a creed of being involved, committed and have tried to share my thoughts to help others as so many have helped me. My wife has truly been an inspiration in carrying out these goals and very much the guiding light in my life's work.*

KROLL, NORMAN MYLES K., physicist, educator; b. Tulsa, Apr. 6, 1922; s. Cornelius and Grace (Aaronson) K.; m. Sally Sharlot, Mar. 15, 1945; children: Linda Ruth, Cynthia Anne, Heather Roma, Ira Joseph. Student, Rice Inst., 1938-40; A.B., Columbia U., 1942, A.M., 1943, Ph.D., 1948. Mem. faculty of Columbia, 1942-62, successively asst. in physics, asst. prof., asso. prof., prof., 1954-62, sci. staff Radiation Lab., 1943-62; prof. physics U. Calif. at San Diego, 1962—, chmn. physics dept., 1963-65, 83—; mem. Inst. Advanced Study, 1948-49; vis. scientist Brookhaven Nat. Lab., summers 1952-55. Bd. editors: Jour. Math. Physics, 1966-68; Contbr. articles to profl. jours.; Adv. com.: Physics Today, 1974-76. NRC fellow, 1948-50; Guggenheim fellow, 1955-56; Fulbright scholar U. Rome, 1955-56; NSF sr. postdoctoral fellow, 1965-66. Fellow Am. Phys. Soc.; mem. Nat. Acad. Scis., Phi Beta Kappa, Sigma Xi. Home: 2457 Calle del Oro La Jolla CA 92037

KROLL, ROBERT JAMES, aerospace engineering educator; b. Cin., May 1, 1928; s. Joseph Henry and Mary Ann (Wefer) K.; m. Marilyn Ann Wolfer, Aug. 21, 1954; children: Stephen, Kenneth, Gregory, James, Thomas. B.S. in Aero. Engring, U. Cin., 1949, M.S., 1956; Ph.D., Mich. State U., 1962. Registered profl. engr., Ohio. Engr. Polak Steel Co., Cin., 1949-1951; sr. engr. Gen. Electric Co., 1952-57; faculty U. Cin., 1957-83, prof. aerospace engring. dept., acting head, 1970-71, 78-79, Bradley Jones prof. aerospace engring., 1975—; cons. to industry. Served to ensign USNR, 1951-52. NSF sci. faculty fellow, 1961-62; Recipient Dolly Cohen award excellence univ. teaching U. Cin., 1968, Neil Wandmaher teaching award Coll. Engring., 1980. Asso. fellow AIAA; mem. Am. Soc. Engring. Edn. (Western Electric teaching award North Central sect. 1982), Soc. Exptl. Stress Analysis, Aircraft Owners and Pilots Assn., Sigma Xi, Phi Kappa Phi, Sigma Gamma Tau. Home: 2579 Beechmar Dr Cincinnati OH 45230

KROLL, STEVEN ALEXANDER, brokerage firm executive; b. Plainfield, N.J., June 22, 1947; s. Alexander and Nancy (Dwinnell) K.; m. Sally Lindsley, Aug. 25, 1969; children: Lindsay Dwinnell, Steven Alexander. B.S., Babson Coll., 1969. With Morgan Guaranty Trust Co., 1969-81; exec. v.p. E.F. Hutton Co., N.Y.C., 1981—. Served with USAR, 1969-75. Republican. Clubs: Plainfield Country, Point O'Woods. Home: 15 Kimball Circle Westfield NJ 07090 Office: 1 Battery Park Plaza New York NY 10004

KROLOFF, GEORGE MICHAEL, public relations executive, management consultant; b. Chgo., Oct. 12, 1935; s. Archie and Florence Blossom (Kauffman) K.; m. Susan Lee Gordick, Sept. 23, 1962; children: Abigail Jo, Adam John, Amy Harriet. B.A. in Journalism, U. Iowa, 1958. Pub. info. mgr. Chgo. Assn. Commerce and Industry and Chgo. Internat. Trade Fair, 1961-63; pub. affairs cons. AID, U.S. Dept. State, Washington, 1963-64; dir. spl. projects Office Postmaster Gen., U.S. Post Office Dept., Washington, 1964-69; pub. relations mgr. The Washington Post, 1969-75; adminstrv. asst. to chmn. Fgn. Relations Com. U.S. Senate, Washington, 1975-78; pres. Washington office Ruder Fin & Rotman, 1978-82; pres. Kroloff, Marshall adn Assocs. Ltd., Washington, 1982—; pres. Washington Info. Group, 1976—; v.p. Conf. on Issues and Media, Alexandria, Va., 1982—. Co-author: Understanding the Media and Public Relations in Washington, 1978. Trustee Pan Am. Devel. Found. of OAS, Washington; commr. U.S. Nat. Commn. for UNESCO; mem. adv. bd. Ctr. for the Book, Library of Congress, 1981—; bd. dirs. Washington Urban Coalition, 1972-74. Served with USAR, 1958-64. Mem. Internat. Inst. Communications. Democrat. Home: 11915 Devilwood Dr Potomac MD 20854 Office: Kroloff Marshall & Assocs Ltd 1747 Pennsylvania Ave NW Washington DC 20006

KROLOPP, RUDOLPH WILLIAM, industrial designer, consultant; b. Chgo., June 7, 1930; s. Rudolph and Emma (Nice) K.; m. Rita Mary Serafin, Aug. 3, 1955; children: Jacqueline, Mark, Joseph, Sharon, Lizabeth, John. B.F.A., U. Ill.-Champaign, 1956; postgrad., Lake Forest Coll., Ill., 1974-78. Staff designer Motorola Consumer Products, Chgo., 1956-59, chief designer, 1959-62, mgr. indsl. design communication div., 1962-82, dir. indsl. design, 1982—, mem. patent com., 1981—, chmn. corp. graphic standards council, 1983—. Patentee in field. Instr. phys. fitness Oak Park YMCA, Ill., 1967; instr. cardiovascular health Buehler YMCA, Palatine, Ill., 1968-83, bd. dirs., Palatine, Ill., 1980—, chmn. program com., Palatine, Ill., 1980—, sec. bd. dirs., Palatine, Ill., 1983-84. Served with USMC, 1948-52. Recipient Master Design award Product Engring. Mag., 1961, Weson Design award Western Electronic Conv., 1970, Design Excellence award Indsl. Design Mag., 1972, Design Engring. award Nat. Marine Electronics Assn., 1972, Good Design award Hannover Fair, Ger., 1978. Fellow Indsl. Designers Soc. Am. (program chmn., sec., regional v.p. chmn. nat. nominating com.). Roman Catholic. Club: Parkers SAC (Chgo.) (pres. 1962-65). Home: 821 W Gilbert Rd Palatine IL 60067 Office: Motorola Inc 1301 E Algonquin Rd Schaumburg IL 60197

KROMBEIN, KARL VONVORSE, entomologist; b. Buffalo, May 26, 1912; s. Louis Henry and Gertrude (Hoeffler) K.; m. Dorothy Carpenter Buckingham, Dec. 11, 1942; children: Kristin, Kyra Krombein Walker, Karlissa. Student, Carnegie Inst. Tech., 1929-31, Canisius Coll., 1931-32; B.S., Cornell U., 1934, M.A., 1935, Ph.D., 1960; Ph.D. in Zoology, U. Peradeniya, Sri Lanka, 1980. Research entomologist Bur. Entomology and Plant Quarantine, Dept. Agr., 1941-51, investigations leader Insect Identification and Parasite Introduction Research br., 1951-65; chmn. dept. entomology Smithsonian Instn., Washington, 1965-71, sr. entomologist, 1971-80, sr. scientist, 1980—; cons. to surgeon gen. USAF, 1972-79, cons. emeritus, 1979—. Author, editor: (with others) Hymenoptera of America North of Mexico-Synoptic Catalog, 1951, Catalog of Hymenoptera in America North of Mexico, 3 vols, 1979; author: Trap-nesting Wasps and Bees: Life Histories, Nests and Associates, 1967; contbr. articles to profl. jours. Served from 1st lt. to maj. AUS, 1942-46; PTO; col. USAF Res. Decorated Legion of Merit, Air Force Commendation medal; named Chief Biomed. Scientist; grantee Am. Philos. Soc., 1952, 55, 59, NSF, 1963, Smithsonian Research Found., 1967, 69, 70, 73; prin. investigator Ceylon Insect Project. Fellow Entomol. Soc. Am. (governing bd. 1970-72), AAAS (councillor 1970-73); mem. Société Entomologique d'Egypte (hon.), Washington Biologists Field Club (past pres.), Entomol. Soc. Washington (past pres., past editor), Am. Entomol. Soc. (corr.), Sigma Xi, Sigma Phi Epsilon. Unitarian. Club: Cosmos (Washington). Home: 3026 John Marshall Dr Arlington VA 22207 Office: Smithsonian Instn Washington DC 20560

KROMHOUT, ROBERT ANDREW, educator; b. Elgin, Ill., Oct. 23, 1923; s. Andrew and Sarah (Tiffany) K.; m. Ora Morlier, Dec. 21, 1950; children—Sharon, Brian, Ethan. B.S., Kans. State U., 1947; M.S., U. Ill., 1948, Ph.D., 1952. Asst. prof. U. Ill., 1952-56; asst. prof. Fla. State U., Tallahassee, 1956-58, asso. prof., 1958-62, head dept. physics, 1959-62, prof. physics, 1962—; mem. Fla. Metric Council, 1980—. Served with AUS, 1943-46. Fellow A.A.A.S.; mem. Am. Physics Soc., Am. Assn. Physics Tchrs., AAUP, Fla. Acad. Scis., Sigma Xi, Phi Kappa Phi. Home: 206 Westminster Dr Tallahassee FL 32304

KROMM, FRANKLIN HERBERT, JR., newspaper syndicate exec.; b. Ft. Wayne, Ind., Sept. 12, 1910; s. Franklin H. and Lena Bee (McKenzie) K.; m. Mildred C. Hershberger, Aug. 28, 1930; 1 son, Donald Eugene. Grad., Central Cath. High, Internat. Accounting Sch. Telephone maintenance Dudio Mfg. Co., 1928-29; salesman, 1930-33; pres. Kromm Trucking Co., 1933-36; gen. mgr. Frosty Cove Ice Cream Co., 1937-39; accountant, office mgr. McKinley Trucking Co., 1939-46; gen. mgr. Hopkins Syndicate, Inc., 1946—. Mem. exec. local council Boy Scouts Am.; mem. Hillsboro Bus. Men's Assn. and Civic Group; v.p., treas. Sci. Marriage Found., 1956—. Republican. Roman Catholic. Club: K.C. Office: Hopkins Bldg Mellott IN 47958

KROMM, MILDRED CAROLYN, pub. and advt. firm exec.; b. Covington, Ind., Jan. 8, 1908; d. Otho DeHaven and Lelia Ethel (Crane) Hershberger; m. Franklin Herbert Kromm, Aug. 28, 1930; children—Donald (dec.), Barbara Jo. Ed. N.U., evening sch., Chgo. Ednl. dir., editor Hopkins Syndicate Inc., Mellott, Ind., 1946—; dir. Sci. Marriage Found., Social Sci. Found. Pres. Republican Women's Club. Mem. Bus., Profl. Women's Club, Nat. Music Club. Roman Catholic. Home: Hopkins Syndicate Inc Hopkins Bldg 1555 N Main 3B Carlyle Dr Frankfort IN 46041 Office: Hopkins Syndicate Inc Hopkins Bldg Mellott IN 47958

KRON, JOHN WILLIAM, retail executive; b. Kenora, Ont., Can., June 9, 1933; s. Rudolph Ernest and Helen Isabel (Cowan) K.; m. Daphne M. Kron, Dec. 27, 1960; children: Geoffrey, William, Paul. M.B.A., U. Western Ont., 1956. Area mgr. Kingsway Transports, Winnipeg, Man., Can.; mgr. phys. distbn. Can. Tire Corp., Toronto, 1966-68, v.p. distbn., 1968-78, exec. v.p., 1978-82; pres. White Stores Inc., Witchita Falls, Tex., 1982—. Office: Canadian Tire Corp Ltd 2180 Yonge St Toronto ON Canada M4P 2V8

KRONE, HELMUT, advt. exec.; b. N.Y.C., July 16, 1925; s. Otto and Emilie (Lohr) K.; m. Irene Beckmann, Nov. 14, 1970; 1 dau., Kathryn Maria; children by previous marriage—Peter, Lisa, Eric, Mark. Student graphic journalism with, Alexi Brodovitch at New Sch. Social Research. With Doyle Dane Bernbach, Inc., N.Y.C., 1954-69, 72—, sr. v.p., dir., spl. projects, 1966-69, sr. v.p., creative mgmt. supr., 1972—; partner Case and Krone, Inc., N.Y.C., 1969-72. Works included in Am. Inst. Graphic Arts 50 Best Advertisements; rep. in: book The 100 Best Advertisements, 1959; created Volkswagen and Avis campaigns. Served with USNR, 1943-46; PTO. Recipient 12 Gold medals N.Y. Art Dirs. Club; elected to Art Dirs. Hall of Fame, 1979. Mem. Am. Inst. Graphic Arts (dir.), Dirs. Guild Am. Home: 1 E 62d St New York NY 10021 Office: Doyle Dane Bernbach Inc 437 Madison Ave New York NY 10022

KRONEGGER, MARIE ELIZABETH, educator; b. Graz, Austria, Sept. 23, 1932; came to U.S., 1962, naturalized, 1968; d. Karl and Josefine (Sparovitz) K. Grad., Karl-Franzens Universitat, (Austria), 1960; postgrad., Sorbonne, Paris, 1953-55; M.A. in English and Am. Lit., Kans. U., 1958; Ph.D. in French and Humanities, Fla. State U., 1960. Instr. French, German and humanities Fla. State U., 1958-60; mem. faculty Internat. Coll., St. Gallen, Switzerland, 1961-62; asst. prof. Hollins Coll., Va., 1962-64; asst. prof. French and comparative lit. Mich. State U., East Lansing, 1964-67, assoc. prof., 1967-70, prof., 1970—. Author: James Joyce and Associate Image Makers, 1968, Impressionist Literature, 1973; contbr. numerous articles on 17th and 20th century French and English lit., lit. and phenomenology to scholarly publs. Bd. dirs. World Inst. of Phenomenology, 1980—. Fulbright scholar, 1957-60; Ford Found. grantee, 1965-66. Mem. MLA, AAUP, Am. Soc. Aesthetics, Am. Comparative Lit. Assn., Semiotic Soc. Am., Chinese Comparative Lit. Assn., S. Atlantic MLA, Societe Paul Claudel. Roman Catholic. Home: 1324 Chartwell Carriage N Stonelake East Lansing MI 48823 Office: Mich State U Wells Hall 502 East Lansing MI 48824 *Only where there is emotion there is art, where there is art there is life, where there is life there is hope, where there is hope, there is redemption.*

KRONMAN, JOSEPH HENRY, orthodontist; b. N.Y.C., Apr. 4, 1931; s. Jacob and Anna Rita (Dick) K.; m. Arlene Brenda Wice, Mar. 30, 1961; children: David Arthur, Bruce Edward, Lisa Sue. B.S. in Biology, N.Y. U., 1952, D.D.S., 1955; certificate orthodontics, Columbia U. Sch. Dentistry, 1959; Ph.D. in Anatomy, Med. Coll. Va., 1962. Postdoctoral fellow Med. Coll. Va., 1951-61; mem. faculty Tufts U. Sch. Dental Medicine, Boston, 1961—, prof. orthodontics, 1968—, prof. anatomy, 1983—, dir. postdoctoral studies, 1964-70, dir. continuing edn., 1982—, asst. to dean Grad. Sch. Arts and Scis., 1964-69; pvt. practice orthodontics, 1963-78; cons. VA, 1966-68. Served to capt. Dental Corps U.S. Army, 1955-57; Korea. Fellow Internat., Am. colls. dentists; mem. ADA, Mass. Dental Soc., Internat. Assn. Dental Research, AAUP, Am. Assn. Orthodontists, Am. Assn. Anatomists, N.Y. Acad. Scis., Internat. Soc. Craniofacial Biology, AAAS, Mass. Assn. Orthodontists, Am. Assn. Dental Schs., Sigma Xi, Omicron Kappa Upsilon. Jewish. Co-inventor GK-101 caries removal agt., delivery system and applicator, hydron root canal filling material and delivery system, root canal irrigation system, orthodontic headgear attachment. Home: 51 Algonquin Rd Canton MA 02021 Office: 1 Kneeland St Boston MA 02111

KRONMILLER, THEODORE, government official, ambassador; b. York, Pa, Feb. 12, 1948. B.A., Duke U., 1970; J.D., U. Va., 1973. Atty., advisor appeals bd. Dept. Commerce, Washington, 1974-75; dep. head. dept. contingent U.S. del. 3d UN Law of Sea Conf., 1975-76; atty., advisor NOAA, 1975-76, cons. to marine minerals div., 1976-77, counsel for intenat. law, 1977-78; counsel subcom. on oceanography U.S. Ho. of Reps., Washington, 1978-79, counsel subcom. on fisheries and wildlife conservation and the environment, 1979-81; dep. asst. sec. for oceans and fisheries Dept. State, Washington, 1981—, rank of ambassador, 1983—. Served to lt. USNR, 1970-79. Office: Dept State 2201 C St NW Washington DC 20520 *

KRONSTADT, ARNOLD MAYO, community and architectural planner; b. Bklyn., July 28, 1919; s. Joseph and Sara (Golden) K.; m. Mary George Hunter, Jan. 1974; children by previous marriage: Janet Ellen, Barbara Ann (Mrs. Paul Fourt), John Arnold. B. Mech. Engring, George Washington U., 1945; postgrad. in city and regional planning, Cath. U. Am. Head archtl. and planning dept. Carl M. Freenan Asso., Inc., Washington, 1952-56; sr. partner Collins & Kronstadt-Leahy, Hogan & Collins (architects, planners and engrs.), Silver Spring, Md., 1957—; dir. Carl M. Freeman Assos., Inc.; professorial lectr. Am. U. Sch. Bus. Adminstrn., Cath. U. Am. Sch. Architecture. Author: What Builders Should Know About Garden Apartments, 1959. Chmn. Montgomery County (Md.) Low and Middle Income Housing Commn., 1967—, Montgomery County Tech. Adv. Com., 1954—, Bldg. Codes Com. Prince Georges County, Md., 1956—; mem. spl. constrn. standards com. schs., Montgomery County, 1959—, also advisory com. eliminating archtl. barriers; mem. Adv. Com. Planning and Zoning Law Study Commn. Md., 1968—; chmn. Md. State Planning Commn., 1969—; bldg. research adv. bd. Nat. Acad. Scis., 1955—; trustee Fed. Realty Investment Trust, Washington; mem. Com. to Develop a Bldg. Code for Handicapped State of Md., 1974—; chmn. HUD Bldg. Industry Advisory Panel for New ANSI Standard for Physically Handicapped, 1976—. Recipient award of merit AIA, 1965; award excellence architecture for Rossmoor Leisure World, Md. Met Washington Bd. Trade, 1965; award excellence architecture for Sursum Corda Met. Washington Bd. Trade, 1969; Honor award for Sursum Corda Dept. Housing and Urban Devel., 1970; A.I.P. Nat. award of merit for Columbia (Md.) Interfaith, 1970. Mem. Nat. Home Builders Washington, Urban Land Inst. Clubs: Sycamore Island Canoe, Potomac Appalachian Trail (Washington); Sea Pines Plantation (Hilton Head, S.C.). Home: 4414 Klingle St NW Washington DC 20016 also 5 Lighthouse Rd Hilton Head SC 29928 Office: 1111 Spring St Silver Spring MD 20910

KROOK, MAX, mathematics and astrophysics educator. Gordon McKay prof. applied math., prof. astrophysics Harvard U., Cambridge, Mass. Office: Harvard U Div Applied Scis 315 Pierce Hall Cambridge MA 02138§

KROPF, ALLEN, chemistry educator; b. N.Y.C., Oct. 3, 1929; s. Samuel and Sophie (Hilowitz) K.; m. Rita Berliner, Sept. 7, 1950; children: Noel, Julie, Aaron. B.S., Queens Coll., 1951; Ph.D., U. Utah, 1954; M.A. (hon.), Amherst Coll., 1969. Chemist Applied Physics Lab., Johns Hopkins U., Silver Spring, Md., 1954-56; research fellow Harvard U., 1956-58, vis. scholar, 1983-84; instr. chemistry Amherst (Mass.) Coll., 1958-59, asst. prof., 1959-62, asso. prof., 1962-67, prof., 1967—, chmn. chemistry dept., 1967-68, 72-75; vis. prof. dept. biophysics Kyoto U., 1975-76; vis. prof. dept. phys. chemistry Hebrew U., 1976; NSF sci. faculty fellow Virus Lab., U. Calif. at Berkeley, 1962-63; NIH spl. fellow Weizmann Inst., Rehovoth, Israel, 1968-69; mem. visual scis. study sect. NIH, 1973-77. Adv. editor: Jour. Biophys. Research. Mem. Biophys. Soc., Phi Beta Kappa, Sigma Xi. Research on primary chem. processes of vision. Home: 50 Mt Pleasant Amherst MA 01002

KROPF, RICHARD THOMAS, textile and chem. mfg. co. exec.; b. Chgo., Oct. 12, 1909; s. Oscar A. and Edith A. (Anderson) K.; m. Marjorie K. Champlain, Oct. 21, 1937; children—Pamela M., Dana A., Christopher B. B.S., Mass. Inst. Tech., 1931. With Belding Heminway Co., Inc., N.Y.C., 1931—, dir. research, 1941-49, v.p., 1949-61, pres., 1961-79, chief exec. officer, 1963-79, dir. and cons., 1979—; Sci. cons. tech. indsl. intelligence com. Q.M. Gen.; chmn. Adv. Com. on Textiles, Apparel and Research. Sewing thread author and editor: Textile Ency, 1959—. Recipient Harold DeWitt Smith medal. Mem. Textile Research Inst. (chmn., treas., trustee), ASTM (pres.), Fiber Soc. (pres.), N.Y. Acad. Scis., Textile Inst., A.A.A.S., Am. Chem. Soc., Am. Phys. Soc., Am. Statis. Assn., Soc. Exptl. Stress Analysis, Am. Assn. Textile Tech. (1st Bronze medal), Tau Beta Pi. Home and Office: Laurel Hill W Brother Dr Greenwich CT 06830 *There is a solution to every problem.*

KROPOTKIN, IGOR NICHOLAS, pub. co. exec.; b. Russia, May 2, 1918; came to U.S., 1927, naturalized, 1932; s. Nicholas and Tamara (Maximovitch) K.; m. Marjorie Albohn, Feb. 16, 1947; children—Valerie, Michael. Student, Columbia, N.Y. U. With Scribner Book Cos., N.Y.C., 1941—, dir., 1957—, v.p., 1960-67, sr. v.p., 1967—; pres. Scribner Book Stores, Inc., 1970—; treas. Am. Bookseller Pub. Co., Give-A-Book Certificate, Inc.; Pres. Am. Booksellers Assn., 1962-64, chmn. bd., 1964—; adv. com. internat. book programs State Dept., 1962—; steering com. Nat. Library Week, 1962—; mem. Nat. Book Com., 1970—. Trustee Princeton Store. Mem. Booksellers League N.Y. (pres.). Club: Cornell (N.Y.C.). Home: 20-15 Halstead Terr Fair Lawn NJ 07410 Office: 597 Fifth Ave New York City NY 10017

KROPP, DAVID ARTHUR, landscape architect; b. Chgo., Apr. 30, 1933; s. Roy Paul and Elfriede Marie (Kreis) K. B.S., Ill. Inst. Tech., 1956. Landscape architect Franz Lipp & Assos., Chgo., 1961-71; owner, pres. Kropp Co., Plainfield, Ill., 1971—; guest lectr. various univs. Author: The Prairie Annual, 1975. Served with U.S. Army, 1956-58. Recipient Bradford Williams award for profl. writing, 1976. Mem. Am. Soc. Landscape Architects (exec. council Ill. chpt.), S.S. Park and Recreation Profl. Assn., Am. Planning Assn., Internat. Fedn. Landscape Architects. Mem. United Ch. of Christ. Office: 119th St and Book Rd Plainfield IL 60544

KROPP, WILLIAM ALLEN, laboratory director; b. Hazelton, Pa., Nov. 23, 1928; s. William E. and Justina E. (Young) K.; m. Jean Wert, Dec. 20, 1952; 1 son, Steven. B.S., Muhlenberg Coll., 1952. With E.I. Du Pont de Nemours Co., 1952—, with explosives dept. Atomic Energy Div., Savannah River, 1952-64, supr. engring. phusics lab., Wilmington, Del., 1964-68, mgr. engring. physics lab., 1968-74, mgr. divisional programs, 1974-75, mgr. engring. test ctr., 1975-77, lab. dir. Engring. Tech. Lab., 1977—. Served with U.S. Army, 1946. Mem. Am. Inst. Chem. Engrs. Home: 158 Oldbury Dr Wilmington DE 19808 Office: Bldg 304 Exptl Sta Wilmington DE 19898

KROPPER, JON FRANKLIN, computer manufacturing company executive; b. Huntington, W.Va., July 31, 1933; s. Herman J. and Clara (Kidder) K.; m. Nancy Gray, Jan. 26, 1956; children: Steven, Jean. B.A. in Mech. Engring., Dartmouth Coll. Factory mgr. Polaroid, Scotland, 1967-69, sr. dept. mgr., 1969-72; gen. mgr. Digital Equipment, Europe, 1972-76, Galway, Ireland, 1972-76, group mfg. mgr., Marlboro, Mass., 1976-79, Salem, N.H., 1976-79, group mfr. mgr., Westminster, Mass., 1976-79, group mfg. mgr., Can., 1976-79; exec. v.p. Wang Labs. Inc., Lowell, Mass., 1979—; pres. Wang P.R.; mng. dir. Wang Netherlands; bd. dirs., pres. Wang Child Care Ctr., Chelmsford, Mass.; bd. dirs. Wang Communications, Denver. Served to 2d lt. AUS, 1957. Mem. ASME. Home: 1 Dana Pl Cambridge MA 02138 Office: Wang Labs Inc One Industrial Ave Lowell MA 01851

KROSBY, H. PETER, history educator; b. Aas, Norway, Mar. 3, 1929; came to U.S., 1958; s. Peter and Anna Elisabeth (Leganger) K.; married, 1953; children: Peter J., Anne E., Kristin M., Karen S., Jane I.; m. Vivien Quincy-Marie Mellon, 1971; children: Erik Leganger, Garrett Lee, Allison Reed, Meade Biering, Paige Gardner. B.A., U. B.C., 1955, M.A., 1958; Ph.D., Columbia, 1967. Instr. Fairleigh Dickinson U., 1959-62; from instr. to asso. prof. history and Scandinavian studies U. Wis., 1962-68; prof. history State U. N.Y. at Albany, 1968—, chmn. dept., 1968-70; vis. lectr. Columbia, 1961; vis. prof. U. Md., 1968, U. Minn., 1970-71, Univs. Helsinki, Turku, Joensuu, all Finland, 1972-73. Author: Nikkelidiplomatiaa Petsamossa 1940-41, 1966, Suomen valinta 1941, 1967, Finland, Germany and the Soviet Union, 1940-41: The Petsamo Dispute, 1968, Kekkosen Linja: Suomi ja Neuvostoliitto 1944-78, 1978, Friede für Europas Norden: Die Sowjetisch-finnischen Beziehungen von 1944 bis zur Gegenwart, 1981; co-editor: Empire and Nations: Essays in Honour of Frederic H. Soward, 1969. Served with Norwegian Army, 1948-49. Ford Found. fgn. area tng. fellow Columbia, 1958-59; hon. fellow in Finland Am.-Scandinavian Found., 1962, 72-73; Lithgow Osborne lectr., 1966-67; Finnish Ministry Edn. research fellow, 1972-73; Norwegian Fgn. Ministry travel grantee, 1976; Am. Philos. Soc. research grantee, 1977; Am. Council Learned Socs. research grantee, 1977; travel grantee, 1978. Mem. Finnish Acad. Letters and Sci., Am. Hist. Assn., Soc. Advancement Scandinavian Studies (exec. council 1968-72, pres. 1973-75). Home: 10 Loudon Heights North Loudonville NY 12211 Office: Dept History State Univ NY Albany NY 12222

KROSNICK, JOEL, cellist; b. New Haven, Apr. 3, 1941; s. Morris Yale and Estelle (Crossman) K.; m. Dinah Straight, 1983. B.A., Columbia Coll., 1970; D.F.A., Mich. State U. Co-founder Group for Contemporary Music, Columbia U., 1962; asst. prof. music U. Iowa, 1963-66; cellist Iowa Quartet, 1963-66; asst. prof. U. Mass., 1966-70; artist in residence Calif. Inst. Arts, 1970-74; cellist Juilliard String Quartet, N.Y.C., 1974—; artist-in-residence Mich. State U., Library of Congress; mem. faculty Juilliard Sch., 1974—. Appeared in solo recitals, N.Y.C. London, Hamburg, Munich, Amsterdam, Belgrade, Berlin, Library of Congress, Washington, 1981, 1970, 72, 75, 76, 81,; premiere performances include solo works by, Ralph Shapey, Solo works by, Milton Babbitt, Mario Davidovsky, Charles Wuorinan, Donald Martino, M.W. Karlins, Gerhard Samuel, Mel Powell, Elliott Carter, Morton Subotnick, others; presenting The Cello: A 20th Century Retrospective, at Julliard Sch., Library of Congress, 1984; premiere performances U.S. Dept. State tours, 1966, 69; rec. artist, Columbia, CRI, Orion and Nonesuch records. Office: Juilliard Quartet Colbert Artists 111 W 57th St New York NY 10019

KROTKI, KAROL JOZEF, economist, demographer; b. Cieszyn, Poland, May 12, 1922; emigrated to Can., 1964; s. Karol Stanislaw and Anna Elzbieta (Skrzywanek) K.; m. Joanna Patkowski, July 12, 1947; children—Karol Peter, Jan Jozef, Filip Karol. B.A. (hons.), Cambridge (Eng.) U., 1948, M.A., 1952; M.A., Princeton U., 1959, Ph.D., 1960. Civil ser., Eng., 1948-49, dep. dir. stats., Sudan, 1949-58; vis. fellow Princeton U., 1958-60; research adviser Pakistan Inst. Devel. Econs., 1960-64; asst. dir. census research Dominion Bur. Stats., Can., 1964-68; prof. sociology U. Alta., 1968-83; Univ. Prof. U. Atla., 1983—; vis. prof. U. Calif., Berkeley, 1967, U. N.C., 1970-73, U. Mich., 1975; coordinator program socio-econ. research Province Alta., 1969-71; cons. in field. Author 10 books and monographs; contbr. numerous articles to profl. jours. Served with Polish, French and Brit. Armed Forces, 1939-46. Recipient achievement award Province of Alta., 1970; grantee in field. Fellow Am. Statis. Assn., Royal Soc. Can.; mem. Fedn. Can. Demographers (v.p. 1977-82, pres. 1982-84), Can. Population Soc., Association des Demographes du Quebec, Population Assn. Am., Internat. Union Sci. Study Population, Internal Statis. Inst. Roman Catholic. Home: 10137 Clifton Pl Edmonton AB T5N 3H9 Canada Office: Dept Sociology U Alta Edmonton AB T6G 2H4 Canada

KROUT, JOHN EDWARD, banker, lawyer; b. Narberth, Pa., Jan. 5, 1920; s. Palled Bertram and Sara (Raffensperger) K.; m. Patricia L. Swinehart, Aug. 15, 1942 (div. 1966); children—Joanne Lester (Mrs. George W. Phillips), John Alan, Robert Ellis; m. Anne Merriman Heppe, Jan. 19, 1974. A.B. with honors, Princeton U., 1941; J.D. with high honors, Harvard U., 1944. Bar: Pa. 1944. Mem. firm Drinker, Biddle & Reath, Phila., 1944-59, partner, 1951-59; sr. v.p. The Phila. Sav. Fund Soc., 1959-70; pres. Germantown Savs. Bank, Phila., 1971-77, chmn. bd., 1977—; dir. Fed. Nat. Mortgage Assn., Washington; trustee PNB Mortgage & Realty Investors; dir. Chgo. Title and Trust Co. Bd. dirs. Crime Prevention Assn., Phila., 1961—, Old Phila. Devel. Corp., Phila. Urban Coalition; bd. corporators Med. Coll. Pa., Phila., 1963—, chmn., 1974-77. Mem. Mortgage Bankers Assn. Am. (dir.), Phila. Mortgage Bankers Assn. (pres. 1964), Nat. Assn. Mut. Savs. Banks (dir., chmn. 1979-80), Pa. Soc. Sons of Revolution, Cloister Inn of Princeton. Republican. Episcopalian. Clubs: Phila. Country, Merion Cricket. Home: 241 Curwen Rd Rosemont PA 19010 Office: GSB Bldg City Line and Belmont Aves Bala-Cynwyd PA 19004

KROWE, ALLEN JULIAN, computer company executive; b. Deltaville, Va., June 17, 1932; s. Julian and Margaret Ruth (Weston) K.; m. Frances Altha Morrette, Sept. 4, 1953; children: Vivian, Valerie. B.S., U. Md., 1954. With IBM, Armonk, N.Y., sr. v.p., now sr. v.p. fin. and planning, chief fin. officer; mem. Fin. Acctg. Standards Adv. Council. Bd. dirs. Westchester-Putnam council Boy Scouts Am., 1970—, St. Agnes Hosp., 1975—, U. Md. Found. Served with USAF, 1955-58. Mem. Fin. Execs. Inst., Am. Inst. C.P.A.'s. Clubs: Whippoorwill Country, Willowbrook Swim and Tennis. Home: 24 Cardinal Pl Mount Kisco NY 10549 Office: IBM Old Orchard Rd Armonk NY 10504

KRSUL, JOHN ALOYSIUS, JR., lawyer; b. Highland Park, Mich., Mar. 24, 1938; s. John A. and Ann M. (Sepich) K.; m. Justine Oliver, Sept. 12, 1958; children: Ann Lisa, Mary Justine. B.A., Albion Coll., 1959; J.D., U. Mich., 1963. Bar: Mich. 1963. Assoc. Dickinson, Wright, Moon, Van Dusen & Freeman, Detroit, 1963-71, ptnr., 1971—. Asst. editor: U. Mich. Law Rev, 1962-63. Sloan scholar, 1958-59; Fulbright scholar, 1959-60; Ford. Found. grantee, 1964. Fellow Am. Bar Found.; mem. Detroit Bar Assn. (dir. 1971-80, pres. 1979-80), Detroit Bar Assn. Found. (dir. 1971—, pres. 1979-80), State Bar Mich. (commr. 1973-83, pres. 1982-83), Mich. State Bar Found. (trustee 1982-83, vice chmn. fellows 1983-84), ABA (ho. of del. 1979—), Fellows of Young Lawyers of Am. Bar (bd. dirs. 1977—, pres. 1983-84), Am. Judicature Soc. (dir. 1971-79, exec. com. 1973-74), Phi Beta Kappa, Omicron Delta Kappa, Phi Eta Sigma, Delta Tau Delta. Clubs: Detroit, Renaissance. Home: 838 W Glengarry Circle Birmingham MI 48010 Office: 800 First National Bldg Detroit MI 48226

KRUCKEBERG, ARTHUR RICE, botanist; b. Los Angeles, Mar. 21, 1920; s. Arthur Woodbury and Ella Muriel K.; m. Mareen Schultz, Mar. 21, 1953; children—Arthur Leo, Enid Johanna; children by previous marriage—Janet Muriel, Patricia Elayne, Caroline. B.A., Occidental Coll., Los Angeles, 1941; postgrad., Stanford U., 1941-42; Ph.D., U. Calif., Berkeley, 1950. Instr. biology Occidental Coll., 1946; teaching asst. U. Calif., Berkeley, 1946-50; mem. faculty U. Wash., Seattle, 1950—, prof. botany, 1964—, chmn. dept., 1971-77; cons. in field. Served with USNR, 1942-46. Mem. Am. Soc. Plant Taxonomists, Calif. Bot. Soc. Research edaphics of serpentines, flowering plants. Home: 20066 15th Ave NW Seattle WA 98177 Office: Dept Botany Univ Wash Seattle WA 98195

KRUCKS, WILLIAM, electronics manufacturing executive; b. Chgo., Dec. 26, 1918; s. William and Florence (Olson) K.; m. Lorraine C. Rauland, Oct. 23, 1947; children: William Norman, Kenneth Rauland. B.S., Northwestern U., 1940; postgrad., Loyola U., Chgo., 1941-42. Auditor Benefit Trust Life Ins. Co., Chgo., 1940-42; chief tax accountant, asst. to comptroller C.M., St.P.&P. R.R., Chgo., 1942-56; asst. comptroller, dir. taxation, asst. treas. C. & N.W. Ry., Chgo., 1956-58, treas., 1968-75; asst. treas. N.W. Industries, Inc., 1968-72; chmn. bd., chief exec. officer, pres. Rauland-Borg Corp.; chmn. bd., pres. Rauland-Borg (Can.) Inc. Bd. dirs. Civic Fedn. Chgo. Mem. Nat. Tax Assn., Tax Execs. Inst., Ill. C. of C., Internat. Bus. Council Mid Am. Republican. Methodist. Clubs: Tower; Execs., Union League, Internat. Trade (Chgo.). Home: 21 Indian Hill Rd Winnetka IL 60093 Office: 3535 W Addison St Chicago IL 60618

KRUEGER, EUGENE REX, educational administrator; b. Grand Island, Nebr., Mar. 30, 1935; s. Rudolph F. and Alma K.; m. Karin Schubert, June 9, 1957; children: Eugene Eric, Richard Kevin, Kristina. Student, Kans. State U., 1952-53; B.S. in Physics, Rensselaer Poly. Inst., 1957; M.S. in Math, Rensselaer Poly. Inst., 1960; Ph.D. in Applied Math, Rensselaer Poly. Inst., 1962. Research physicist IBM, 1957-58; research fellow Army Math. Research Center, U. Wis., 1962-63; prof. U. Colo., Boulder, 1965-74; vice chancellor, prof. Oreg. State System of Higher Edn., Eugene, 1974—; chmn. seminar for dirs. of acad. computing facilities; cons. on computer graphics computing facility mgmt.; dir. various research grants and contracts. Contbr. research papers in field to publs. Mem. Soc. Indsl. and Applied Math. (nat. lectr.), Assn. Computing Machinery (dir.), Interuniv. Communications Council (membership com.), Spl. Interest Group on Univ. Computing Centers, Sigma Xi, Phi Kappa Phi. Home: 2612 Terrace View Dr Eugene OR 97405 Office: PO Box 3175 Eugene OR 97403

KRUEGER, EVERETT HEATH, banker; b. Cleve., Apr. 19, 1919; s. Everette Henry and Marion (Heath) K.; m. Nancy A. Moore, 1944 (div. 1961); children—Kristin Anne, Everett Heath III, Thomas C., Kathleen E., Nancy K.; m. Shirle Cooke, 1967. A.B., Yale, 1941; J.D., Case Western Res. U., 1947. Bar: Ohio bar 1948. Asso. firm Krueger, Gorman & Davis, Cleve., 1948-51; with Office Atty. Gen. Ohio, 1951-57, 1st asst. atty. gen., 1955-57; sec. to Gov. Ohio, 1957; mem. Pub. Utilities Commn. Ohio, 1957-62, chmn., 1957-60; v.p., gen. counsel City Nat. Bank & Trust Co., Columbus, Ohio, 1962-77; sr. v.p. Bank One Columbus, 1977—. Mem. Met. Park Bd., 1970—; pres. Columbus Arts Council, 1978-81, Hearing and Speech Center Central Ohio, 1975-76; trustee emeritus Columbus Symphony Orch., pres., 1971-73; mem. Vets. Meml. Bd. Trustees, 1963—, pres., 1979—; bd. dirs. Grant Hosp.; trustee Ohio Dominican Coll., chmn., 1978—. Served to capt. AUS, 1942-46. Mem. Am., Ohio, Cleve., Columbus bar assns., Am., Ohio bankers assns., Zeta Psi, Phi Delta Phi. Republican. Episcopalian. Clubs: Mason (32 deg.), Yale of Central Ohio (pres. 1971-73); Athletic (pres. 1975), Scioto Country, Columbus (Columbus); Royal Poinciana (Naples, Fla.). Home: 3503 Rue de Fleur Columbus OH 43221 Office: 100 E Broad St Columbus OH 43217

KRUEGER, HARVEY MARK, investment banker, lawyer; b. N.J., Apr. 16, 1929; s. Irving and Isabelle (Kurzman) K.; m. Constance Alexander, July 6, 1952; children: Cathleen, Peter, Elizabeth, Abigail. B.A., Columbia U., 1951, LL.B., 1953. Bar: N.J. 1953, N.Y. 1954. Asso. Cravath, Swaine & Moore, 1953-59; with Kuhn, Loeb & Co., 1959-77, pres., chief exec. officer, 1977; mng. dir., mem. exec. com., dir. successor Lehman Bros. Kuhn Loeb Inc., N.Y.C., 1977—; dir. Automatic Data Processing, Inc., R.G. Barry Corp., SCOA Industries, Manhattan Industries, Supermarkets Gen. Corp. Mem. Bond Club N.Y. (gov.). Club: Preakness Hills Country. Home: 510 Park Ave New York NY 10022 Office: 55 Water St New York NY 10041

KRUEGER, MAYNARD CLARE, economics educator; b. nr. Alexandria, Mo., Jan. 16, 1906; s. Fred C. and Nelle C. (Hoewing) K.; m. Elsie C. Gasperik, Aug. 25, 1934; children—Karen (Mrs. Harold F. Finn), Linda (Mrs. Bruce B. MacLachlan), Susan (Mrs. Winston A. Salser). A.B., U. Mo., 1926, A.M., 1927; postgrad. other univs. in, U.S. and Europe, 1925-32. Instr. U. Pa., 1928-32; asst. prof. U. Chgo., 1932-47, asso. prof., 1947-65, prof., 1965-77, emeritus, 1977—; exec. dir. Internat. House, Chgo., 1977-81; vis. prof. U. Vienna, Austria, 1959-60, U. Athens, Greece, 1963-64, State U. N.Y., 1965-66; cons. ECA programs, 1951; v.p. Am. Fedn. Tchrs., 1934-36. Author Economics Question Book, 1934. Pres. Progress Devel. Corp., 1958—; pres. N.W. Hyde Park Neighborhood Devel. Corp., 1955—; Chmn. Ind. Voters Ill., 1957-59; candidate v.p. U.S. Socialist Party, 1940. Club: Quadrangle. Home: 5532 South Shore Dr Chicago IL 60637

KRUEGER, PETER J., chemistry educator; b. Altona, Man., Can., Nov. 11, 1934; s. Jacob J. and Elisabeth (Friesen) K.; m. Dorothy Isabel Lashley, July 18, 1959; children: Kathryn Elisabeth, Vivian Louise, Jonathan Patrick Jacob. B.Sc. with honors, U. Man., 1955, M.Sc., 1956; D.Phil., Oxford U., Eng., 1958. Bursar Nat. Research Council Can., 1955-56; Shell Commonwealth scholar, 1956-58, U. Man. traveling fellow, 1956-58, Nat. Research Council postdoctoral fellow, 1958-59; asst. prof. chemistry U. Alta., 1959-64, asso. prof., 1964-66; prof. chemistry U. Calgary, 1966—, head dept., 1966-70, vice dean faculty arts and sci., 1970-72, v.p. acad., 1976—; vis. scientist Nat. Research Council, Ottawa, 1966-67. Contbr. articles to sci. jours. Bd. govs. U. Calgary, 1970-73. Recipient award in spectroscopy Coblentz Soc., 1967, Gerhard Herzberg award in spectroscopy, 1973, Alta. Achievement award, 1974. Fellow Royal Soc. for Chemistry, Chem. Inst. Can.; mem. Am. Chem. Soc., Spectroscopy Soc. Can., AAAS, Coblentz Soc., Sigma Xi. Baptist. Home: 88 Brown Crescent NW Calgary AB T2L1N5 Canada

KRUEGER, RALPH RAY, educator; b. Huron County, Ont., Can., Mar. 10, 1927; s. Elmer G. and Myrtle M. (Horner) K.; m. B. June Hambly, June 30, 1949; children—Karen, Colleen. B.A., U. Western Ont., 1952, M.A., 1955; Ph.D., Ind. U., 1959. Tchr. pub. schs., Ont., 1945-53; lectr. Wayne State U., Detroit, 1957-59; asso. prof. Wilfrid Laurier U., Waterloo, Ont., 1959-62; prof., chmn. geography U. Waterloo, 1962-70, prof. geography, 1971—. Author: (with R.G. Corder) Canada: A New Geography, 1968; editor: (with B. Mitchell) Managing Canada's Renewable Resources, 1977. Mem. Kitchener (Ont.) Planning Bd., 1960-72; mem. Waterloo County Area Planning Bd., 1964-72. Mem. Am. Assn. Geographers, Canadian Assn. Geographers (pres. 1978-79). Home: 206-25 Candlewood Crescent Waterloo ON N2L 5Y9 Canada Office: Dept Geography U Waterloo Waterloo ON N2L 3G1 Canada

KRUEGER, ROBERT BLAIR, lawyer; b. Minot, N.D., Dec. 9, 1928; s. Paul Otto and Lila (Morse) K.; m. Virginia Ruth Carmichael, June 3, 1956 (div. 1984); children: Lisa Carmichael, Paula Leah, Robert Blair. A.B., U. Kans., 1949; J.D., U. Mich., 1952; postgrad., U. So. Calif., 1960-65. Bar: Kans. 1952, Calif. 1955, D.C. 1978. Practiced in, Los Angeles, 1955—; assoc. firm O'Melveny & Myers, 1955-59; ptnr. firm Nossaman, Krueger & Marsh and predecessor firms, 1961-83, Finley, Kumble, Wagner, Heine, Underberg, Manley & Casey, 1983—; chmn. Nat. Practice Group on Energy and Natural Resources; adj. prof. natural resource law U. So. Calif. Law Ctr., 1973—; Mem. Gov.'s Adv. Commn. on Ocean Resources, 1966-68, Calif. Adv. Commn. on Marine and Coastal Resources, 1968-73, chmn., 1970-73; mem. adv. council Inst. on Marine Resources, U. Calif., 1966-74, Commn. on California, 1977—; mem. Nat. Security Council Adv. Com. on Law of Sea, 1972-82, chmn. internat. law and relations subcom., 1972-82; U.S. del. to UN Seabeds Com., 1973, 3d UN Law of Sea Conf., 1974-82; cons. petroleum policy to UN, fgn. govts. U.S. Centre on Transnat. Corps.; mem. exec. bd. Law of Sea Inst., U. Hawaii, 1977-83; fellow U. So. Calif. Inst. on Marine and Coastal Studies., 1977—. Author: Study of Outer Continental Shelf Lands of the United States, 1968, The United States and International Oil, 1975, World Petroleum Policies Report, 1981; also articles on energy and natural resources.; Asst. editor: Mich. Law Rev., 1951-52; editor: Los Angeles Bar Bull., 1961-63; bd. editors: Calif. Bar Jour., 1962-68. Mem. com. visitors U. Mich. Law Sch.; founder Mus. Contemporary Art. Served to 1st lt. USMCR, 1952-54. Fellow Am. Bar Found.; mem. ABA (chmn. spl. com. on energy law 1979—, chmn. coordinating group on energy law 1983—), Los Angeles County Bar Assn., Internat. Bar Assn., Am. Soc. Internat. Law., Fellows Contemporary Art, Barristers, Tau Kappa Epsilon, Phi Alpha Delta. Republican. Clubs: Calif., University, Chancery; Town Hall (Los Angeles); Metropolitan (Washington); Valley Hunt (Pasadena); Princeton (N.Y.C.). Home: 501 Vallombrosa Dr Pasadena CA 91107 10430 Wilshire Blvd No 506 Los Angeles CA 90024 Office: 9100 Wilshire Blvd Beverly Hills CA 90212

KRUEGER, ROBERT JAMES, banker, accountant; b. Fargo, N.D., Dec. 7, 1930; s. James Frederick and Zelda Elizabeth (Resley) K.; m. Mary Macheak, June 1, 1957; children—Robert J., Julia A., John F., Rebecca E. B.S. in Bus. Adminstrn, U. S.D., 1956; M.B.A., Mich. State U., 1974. C.P.A., Ill. Audit supr. Peat, Marwick, Mitchell & Co. (C.P.A.'s), Chgo., 1956-66; controller Avis Indsl. Corp., Lansing, Mich., 1966-68, Lansing Gen. Hosp., 1968-70; 1st v.p., gen. auditor Nat. Bank Detroit, 1970—; mem. faculty Colo. Sch. Banking, 1971. Served with USNR, 1952-54. Mem. Inst. Internal Auditors (gov. Detroit chpt.), Bank Adminstrn. Inst. (audit commn., chmn. audit standards task force, chmn. control standards task force), Am. Inst. C.P.A.'s, Mich. Assn. C.P.A.'s, Nat., Am. accounting assns. Home: 285 Kenwood Ct Grosse Pointe MI 48236 Office: 611 Woodward Ave Detroit MI 48232

KRUEGER, ROBERT WILLIAM, professional service company executive; b. Phila., Nov. 16, 1916; s. Robert Henry and Frieda (Lehmann) K.; m. Marjorie Evelyn Jones, July 26, 1941; children: Arlene R. Krueger Reher, Diane L. Krueger Esser. Research engr. Douglas Aircraft Co., Santa Monica, Calif., 1942-46; asst. chief missiles div. RAND Corp., Santa Monica, 1946-53; missle systems cons., Los Angeles, 1953-54; pres. Planning Research Corp., Los Angeles, 1954-73, Profl. Services Internat., 1973—. Chmn. 59th Dist. Republican Central Com., 1960-61; pres. 59th Dist. Rep. Assembly, 1960-61; mem. Calif. Rep. Central Com., 1962—; Trustee U. Calif. Los Angeles Found. Mem. Am. Phys. Soc., Ops. Research Soc. Am., Inst. Mgmt. Scis. Home: 1016 Moraga Dr Los Angeles CA 90049 Office: 1100 Glendon Ave Los Angeles CA 90024

KRUENER, HARRY HOWARD, clergyman; b. Bklyn., Nov. 6, 1915; s. Henry and Florence (Edwards) K.; m. Martha Easton, Oct. 5, 1941 (dec. July 1959); 1 son, John Francis; m. Cheryl Woddell, June 20, 1961 (div. Oct. 1981); 1 son, Philip C.; m. Nancy W., Mar. 20, 1982. A.B., Haveford Coll., 1937; B.D., Andover Newton Theol. Sch., 1940; S.T.M., Boston U., 1954; D.D., Denison U., 1965. Ordained to ministry Bapt. Ch., 1940; minister, Boston, 1940-48, Granville, Ohio, 1948-55; dean of chapel Denison U., 1955-60; minister Plymouth Ch. of Pilgrims, Bklyn., 1960—; preacher, Chautauqua, 1970, Am. Ch., Athens, Greece, 1971; Bd. mgrs. Am. Bapt. Fgn. Mission Socs.; exec. bd., nembership sec. Nat. Assn. Coll. and Univ. Chaplains; del. Nat. Council Chs.; mem. United Ch. of Christ; pres. Bklyn. Council Chs., Bklyn. Clerical Union, Bklyn. Meml. Soc. Author: Specifically to Youth, 1959; Summer preacher, Nat. Radio Pulpit, 1954. Trustee Andover Newton Theol. Sch., Denison U. Mem. Nat. Assn. Bibl. Instrs., Phi Beta Kappa, Omicron Delta Kappa. Club: Mason (lodge chaplain). Home: 2 Montague Terr Brooklyn NY 11201

KRUG, RICHARD F., tool manufacturing company executive; b. Elizabeth, N.J., Mar. 10, 1937; s. John K. K.; m. Julia A. Barbarisch, June 15, 1958; children: Richard, James, Nancy, Jeffrey, Maria. B.S., Seton Hall U., 1961. Acct. Esso Research & Enging. Co., Linden, N.J., 1955-60; plant acct. Stanley Tools, Newark, 1960-63, chief acct.-office mgr., Shaftsbury, Vt., 1963-66, budget mgr., New Britain, Conn., 1966-68; controller Stanley Drapery Hardware, Wallingford, Conn., 1968-73; gen. mgr. Stanley Hardware, New Britain, 1973-81; group v.p. Stanley Works, New Britain, 1981—. Mem. Am. Mgmt. Assn. Republican. Roman Catholic. Office: Stanley Works 195 Lake St New Britain CT 06050

KRUGER, ARTHUR MARTIN, economics educator; b. Toronto, Ont., Can., Nov. 4, 1932; s. Joseph and Anna (Barron) K.; m. Betty Min Jacober, Aug. 19, 1958; children: Ann, Nina, Gerald, Naomi. B.A., U. Toronto, 1955; Ph.D., MIT, 1959. Asst. prof. Wharton Sch., U. Pa., Phila., 1959-61; mem. faculty U. Toronto, 1961—, asso. prof., 1965-69, prof., asso. chmn. dept. polit. economy, 1970-74; prin. Woodworth Coll., U. Toronto, 1974-77, dean univ. faculty arts and scis., 1977-82, prof. econs., 1982—. Co-editor: The Canadian Labour Market. Arbitrator numerous disputes in pub. and pvt. sectors, 1968—. Mem. Am. Econs. Assn., Indsl. Relations Research Assn., Can. Indsl. Relations Research Assn. Home: 34 Shallmar Blvd Toronto ON Canada Office: Dept Polit Economy Univ Toronto Toronto ON Canada

KRUGER, ARTHUR NEWMAN, educator, author; b. Boston, Feb. 4, 1916; s. Samuel and Minnie (Meline) K.; m. Eleanor Weisbrot, Dec. 28, 1941; children—Robert Samuel, Marylin Jane. Student, Coll. City N.Y., 1932-34; A.B., U. Ala., 1936, postgrad., 1937-38; Ph.D., La. State U., 1941. Instr. Essex Jr. Coll., Newark, 1940-41, N.C. State U., Raleigh, 1941-42; v.p. Empco, Atlantic City, 1946-47; asst. prof. Wilkes Coll., Wilkes-Barre, Pa., 1947-54, asso. prof., 1954-59, prof., 1959-62, dir. forensics, 1948-62; prof., dir. forensics, chmn. dept. speech communication C.W. Post Coll., Greenvale, N.Y., 1962—. Author: Modern Debate: Its Logic and Strategy, 1960; author or co-author: Championship Debating, 1961, Argumentation and Debate: A Classified Bibliography, 1964, rev. edit., 1975, Championship Debating, Vol. II, 1967, Counterpoint: Debates About Debate, 1968, Essentials of Logic, 1968, rev. edit., 1976, Workbook for Essentials of Logic, 1968, Effective Speaking: A Complete Course, 1970; Contbr. to: Rhetoric of Our Times, 1969, The Comparative Advantage Case, 1970, Ventures in Research, 1974, also to publs. in field. Bd. dirs. Eastern Debate Inst., Greenvale, N.Y., 1965—. Served to 1st lt. AUS, SIS and OSS, 1942-46. Mem. A.A.U.P., Speech Communication Assn. Am., Am. Forensic Assn., Speech Assn. Eastern States, Rhetoric Soc. Am., Eastern Forensic Assn., Phi Delta Kappa, Delta Sigma Rho, Tau Kappa Alpha. Club: University (L.I.). Home: 28 Maytime Dr Jericho NY 11753 Office: C W Post Coll Greenvale NY 11548

KRUGER, CHARLES HERMAN, JR., mechanical engineer; b. Oklahoma City, Oct. 4, 1934; s. Charles H. and Flora K.; m. Nora Nininger, Sept. 10, 1977; children—Sarah, Charles Herman III, Elizabeth, Ellen. S.B., M.I.T., 1956, Ph.D., 1960; D.I.C., Imperial Coll., London, 1957. Asst. prof. M.I.T., Cambridge, 1960; research scientist Lockheed Research Labs., 1960-62; prof. mech. engring. Stanford (Calif.) U., 1962—, chmn. dept. mech. engring., 1982—; vis. prof. Harvard U., 1968-69, Princeton U., 1979-80; mem. Environ. Studies Bd. Nat. Acad. Scis.; mem. hearing bd. Bay Area Air Quality Mgmt. Dist., 1969-83. Co-author: Physical Gas Dynamics, 1965, Partially Ionized Gases, 1973, On the Prevention of Significant Deteriorization of Air Quality, 1981; asso. editor: AIAA Jour, 1968-71; contbr. numerous articles to profl. jours. NSF sr. postdoctoral fellow, 1968-69. Mem. AIAA (medal, award 1979), Combustion Inst., ASME, Am. Phys. Soc., Air Pollution Control Assn., Engring. Aspects of Magnetohydrodynamics. Office: Dept Mech Engring Stanford U Stanford CA 94305

KRUGER, FRED WALTER, ednl. adminstr., mech. engr.; b. Chgo., Dec. 17, 1921; s. Fred and Magdalen (Lotz) K.; m. Esther Marie Foelber, Aug. 23, 1947; children—Paul Walter, John Robert, Thomas Herman. Student, Valparaiso U., 1940-42; B.S. in Elec. Engring, Purdue U., 1942-43, Purdue U., 1947; M.S. in Mech Engring, Notre Dame U., 1954. Registered profl. engr., Ind. Mem. faculty Valparaiso U., 1947—, prof., 1959—, chmn. dept. mech. engring., 1955-65, dean Coll. Engring., 1965-72, v.p. bus. affairs, 1974—; cons. McDonnell Aircraft Co., Caterpillar Tractor Co., Argonne Lab., No. Ill. Gas Co.; Mem. Ind. Bd. Registration for Profl. Engrs., 1957—. City councilman Valparaiso, 1972—; mem. City Plan Commn., 1977—. Served to lt. USNR, 1943-46. Mem. Am. Soc. M.E., Am. Soc. Engring. Edn., Tau Beta Pi. Lutheran. Home: 1058 Linwood Ave Valparaiso IN 46383

KRUGER, FREDRICK CHRISTIAN, educator; b. St. Paul, Apr. 1, 1912; s. Rudolph Julius and Betty (Sandberg) K.; m. Helene Vivian Anderson, June 25, 1936; children—Kurn Fredrick, Jan Christian (Mrs. Robert Steven Anderson). B.S., U. Minn., 1935, M.A., 1936; Ph.D., Harvard, 1941; grad. mgmt. course, Am. Mgmt. Assn., 1958. Grad. asst. U. Minn., 1935-36; asst. Minn. Geol. Survey, 1936; instr. Dartmouth, 1936-38; grad. asst., teaching fellow Harvard, 1938-41; grad. asst. Radcliffe Coll., 1938-41; geologist, asst. chief geologist Cerro de Pasco Corp., Peru, 1941-49; vis. lectr. Northwestern U., 1949; asso. prof., prof. U. Tenn., 1949-52; asst. chief geologist Reynolds Metals Co., Richmond, Va., 1952-57; chief geologist, dir. mining and exploration dept., v.p. mining and exploration div. Internat. Minerals & Chem. Corp., Skokie, Ill., 1957-66; dir. Internat. Minerals & Chems. Proprietary, Ltd. (ANZ), 1963-66; v.p., dir. I.M.C. Devel. Corp., 1964-66; Donald Steel prof. econ. geology, chmn. dept. applied earth scis., asso. dean research Sch. Earth Scis., Stanford, 1966-77, prof. emeritus, 1977—; cons. exploration and mining, 1949-52, 66—. Fellow Geol. Soc. Am.; mem. Soc. Econ. Geologists (mem. council), Am. Inst. Mining Engrs. (Henry Krumb lectr. 1967-69, Centennial lectr. 1970, Hardinge award 1972, distinguished mem. 1975), Mining and Metall. Soc., Nat. Def. Exec. Res., AAAS, Am. Geol. Inst. (past dir.), Soc. Mining Engrs. (past v.p., dir.), U.S. C. of C., Am. Mgmt. Assn., Sigma Xi, Sigma Gamma Epsilon. Home and office: 145 Wildwood Way Woodside CA 94062

KRUGER, GUSTAV OTTO, JR., oral surgeon, educator; b. N.Y.C., Sept. 28, 1916; s. Gustav Otto and Anna Charlotte (Mellquist) K.; m. Helyn E. Hollingsworth, Apr. 12, 1947; children: Deborah Ann (Mrs. M. Henry King III), Tristram Coffin, Abigail Hollingsworth. B.S., George Washington U., 1938, A.M., 1939; D.D.S., Georgetown U., 1939, Sc.D. (hon.), 1977. Diplomate: Am. Bd. Oral Surgery (pres. 1964). Intern Johns Hopkins Hosp., 1939-40; fellow Mayo Found., 1940-42, 45-48; mem. faculty Georgetown U. Sch. Dentistry and Grad. Sch., 1948—, prof. oral surgery, chmn. dept., 1948—, asso. dean, 1966—; chief dental dept. Georgetown U. Hosp., Washington, 1948—; cons. VA hosps. in, Martinsburg, W.Va. and Washington, U.S. Naval Hosp., Bethesda, D.C. Gen. Hosp., Washington; cons. to Pres.'s physician, 1960-64; cons. Walter Reed Army Med. Center.; Mem. cancer tng. com. Nat. Cancer Inst., USPHS, 1967-71, chmn., 1969-71. Author: Textbook of Oral Surgery, 1959, 6th edit., 1984; Contbr. articles to profl. jours. Served to capt. Dental Corps AUS, 1942-45; CBI, PTO. Recipient Arnold K. Maislen award N.Y. U., 1970; Simon P. Hullihen award W.Va. Soc. Oral Surgeons and W.Va. Med. Center, 1980; named Man of Year Georgetown U. Alumni Assn., 1961. Fellow Am. Coll. Dentists (chmn. D.C. sect. 1969-71), Internat. Coll. Dentists (chmn. D.C. sect. 1967-70), AAAS; mem. ADA (chmn. oral surgery sect. 1961, mem. rev. commn. on advanced edn. in oral surgery 1965-71, chmn. commn. 1969-71), D.C. Dental Soc. (pres. 1960), Am. Soc. Oral Surgeons (program chmn. 1961), Middle Atlantic Soc. Oral Surgeons (pres. 1952), Am. Acad. Oral Pathology, Am. Acad. Oral Roentgenology, Internat. Assn. Dental Research, Xi Psi Phi, Sigma Gamma Epsilon, Omicron Kappa Upsilon. Lodge: Kiwanis. Home: 6806 Bradgrove Circle Bethesda MD 20034 Office: 3900 Reservoir Rd NW Washington DC 20007

KRUGER, JEROME, official Commerce Department; b. Atlanta, Feb. 7, 1927; s. Isaac and Sarah (Stein) K.; m. Mollee Coppel, Feb. 20, 1955; children: Lennard, Joseph. B.S., Ga. Inst. Tech., 1948, M.S., 1949; Ph.D., U. Va., 1952. With Naval Research Lab., Washington, 1952-55; with Nat. Bur. Standards, Commerce Dept., Washington, 1955—, group leader Corrosion and Electrodeposition, 1966—. Divisional editor: Jour. Electrochem. Soc, 1966—; subject area editor: Ency. of Materials Sci. and Enging; Contbr. articles to tech. jours., chpts. to books. Dupont fellow U. Va., 1951-52; Recipient Silver medal Commerce Dept., 1962, Gold medal, 1972; Blum award Nat. Capitol sect. Electrochem. Soc., 1966; W. R. Whitney award, 1976; Samuel Wesley Stratton award Nat. Bur. Standards, 1982; Presdl. rank of Meritorious Exec. of Sr. Exec. Service, 1982. Mem. Electrochem. Soc. (corrosion div. outstanding achievement award 1977), Nat. Assn. Corrosion Engrs., Am. Chem. Soc., Fedn. Materials Socs. (pres. 1977), Sigma Xi, Tau Beta Pi. Jewish (bd. dirs. 1966-69). Home: 619 Warfield Dr Rockville MD 20850 Office: Nat Bur Standards Washington DC 20234

KRUGER, KENNETH CHARLES, architect; b. Santa Barbara, Calif., Aug. 19, 1930; s. Thomas Albin and Chleople (Gaines) K.; m. Patricia Kathryn Rasey, Aug. 21, 1955; children: David, Eric. B.Arch., U. So. Calif., 1953. Registered architect, cert. Calif. and Nat. Councils Archtl. Registration Bds. Pres. Kruger Bensen Ziemer, Santa Barbara, 1960—; mem. Hope Ranch Bd. Archtl. Rev., Santa Barbara, 1981—. V.p. United Boys Club, 1983. Fellow AIA; mem. Santa Barbara C. of C. (dir. 1983). Republican. Unitarian. Home: 1255 Ferrelo Rd Santa Barbara CA 93103 Office: Kruger Bensen Ziemer Inc 30 W Arrellaga St Santa Barbara CA 93101

KRUGER, RUDOLF, opera manager; b. Berlin, Germany, Oct. 30, 1916; came to U.S., 1939, naturalized, 1944; s. Eduard and Julie Eva (Herz) K.; m. Ruth Elizabeth Scallan, Aug. 25, 1951; children: Karen Elizabeth, Philip Edward. Grad., Staatliches Kaiserin Augusta Gymnasium, Berlin, 1935; diploma, Staats Akademie fur Musik und Darstellende Kunst, Vienna, Austria, 1938; D.F.A. (hon.), Tex. Wesleyan Coll., 1983. Asst. condr. So. Symphony Orch., Columbia Choral Soc., Columbia, S.C., 1939-42; asst. condr. New Orleans Symphony Orch., 1942-45, condr. young people's concerts, 1942-45; asst. condr. New Orleans Opera House Assn. Orch., 1942-45, condr. light opera div., 1943; condr. Mid-Western tour Chgo. Light Opera Co., 1946-47; mus. dir. Jackson (Miss.) Opera Guild, 1948-51, Mobile (Ala.) Opera Guild, 1949-55, New Orleans Light Opera Co., 1949-50; 1st condr. Crescent City Concerts Assn., New Orleans, 1954-55; mus. dir., condr. Ft. Worth Opera Assn., 1955-58, mus. dir., gen. mgr., 1958—; resident mus. dir. Ft. Worth Symphony Orch. Assn., 1963-65; mus. dir., condr. Ft. Worth Ballet Assn., 1965-66; condr. weekly orch. program ABC, MBS, 1943-44; guest condr. Shreveport (La.) Civic Opera, 1962-63, 75, 76-79, Cin. Summer Opera, 1969, New Orleans Opera House Assn., 1969, Dallas Civic Ballet Assn., 1971, P.R. Opera, 1972, State Opera, Hannover, Germany, 1974, Teheran (Iran) Opera, 1976, Conn. Grand Opera, 1979, Philippine Philham. Orch., 1985; dir. opera workshop Tex. Christian U., 1955-58. Served with AUS, 1945-46. Recipient Cert. of Recognition Tex. Fedn. Music Clubs, 1967. Mem. Am. Fedn. Musicians. Episcopalian. Club: Rotarian. Office: 3505 W Landcaster St Fort Worth TX 76107

KRUGER, WELDON DALE, oil company executive; b. Hutto, Tex., Feb. 3, 1931; s. Walter A. and Josephine (Meier) K.; m. Patricia Cameron, June 15, 1957; children: Cameron P., Bruce L. B.S. in Petroleum Engring., Tex. A&M U., 1953, M.S., 1954. Registered profl. engr., Tex. Vice pres. Esso Middle East, N.Y.C., 1971-74, London rep., 1974-76, exec. v.p., N.Y.C., 1977-81, pres., 1981—; v.p. Exxon Corp., N.Y.C., 1981—; dir. Aramco, Dhahran, Saudi Arabia. Trustee Am. U. Cairo, Egypt, 1981; mem. exec. com. Near East Found., N.Y.C., 1977; mem. pres.'s council NYU, 1983; mem. adv. com. Middle East Research Inst., U. Pa., 1981; mem. adv. bd. Salvation Army Greater N.Y.C., 1983. Served to 1st lt. USAF, 1954-56. Mem. AIME. Republican. Methodist. Office: Exxon Corp 1251 Ave of America New York NY 10020

KRUGMAN, SAUL, physician, educator; b. N.Y.C., Apr. 7, 1911; s. Louis and Rachel (Cohen) K.; m. Sylvia Stern, Feb. 18, 1940; children—Richard David, Carol Lynn. Student, Ohio State U., 1929-32; M.D., Med. Coll. Va., 1939. Intern, then resident Cumberland, Willard Parker and Bellevue hosps., N.Y.C., 1939-41, 46-48; teaching and med. research N.Y. U.-Bellevue Med. Center, 1948—, asso. prof. pediatrics, 1954-60, prof., 1960—, chmn. dept., 1960-75; dir. pediatric service Bellevue Hosp., 1960-75, Univ. Hosp., 1960-75; Mem. Commn. Viral Infections, 1960-72; mem. nat. adv. council Nat. Inst. Allergy and Infectious Diseases, 1965-69, chmn. infectious disease adv. com., 1971-73; mem. com. on viral hepatitis NRC, 1973-76; chmn. panel on viral and rickettsial vaccines Bur. Biologies, FDA, 1973-79. Co-author: Infectious Diseases of Children, 1981; contbr. articles on infectious diseases to med. jours. NIH research fellow, 1948-50. Fellow Am. Acad. Pediatrics; mem. Am. Pediatric Soc. (pres. 1972-73), Soc. Pediatric Research, N.Y. Acad. Medicine (chmn. pediatric sect. 1960-61), Am. Epidemiol. Soc., Harvey Soc., Assn. Am. Physicians, Nat. Acad. Scis. Home: 300 E 33d St New York NY 10016 Office: 550 1st Ave New York NY 10016

KRUGMAN, STANLEY LEE, management consultant; b. N.Y.C., Mar. 2, 1925; s. Harry Aaron and Leah (Greenberg) K.; m. Helen Schorr, June 14, 1947; children: Vicky Lee, Thomas Paul; m. Carolyn Schambra, Sept. 17, 1966; children: David Andrew, Wendy Carol; m. Gail Jennings, Mar. 17, 1974. Student, Bklyn. Coll., 1942-44; B. Chem. Enging., Rensselaer Poly. Inst., 1947; postgrad., Poly. Inst. Bklyn., 1947-51. Process devel. engr. Merck & Co., Rahway, N.J., 1947-51; sr. process and project engr. C.F. Braun & Co., Alhambra, Calif., 1951-55; with Jacobs Engring. Co., Pasadena, Calif., 1955-76, exec. v.p., pres., to 1976, also dir.; pres. Jacobs Constructors of P.R., San Juan, 1970-82, also dir., Jacobs Internat. Inc., 1971-82; exec. v.p. Jacobs Engring. Group Inc., Pasadena, Calif., 1974-82; pres. Jacobs Internat. Ltd., Inc., Dublin, 1974-82; dep. chmn. Jacobs LTA Engring., Ltd., Johannesburg, South Africa, 1981-82; internat. mgmt. cons., 1983—. Served to lt. (j.g.) USNR, 1944-46; PTO. Mem. Am. Inst. Chem. Engrs., Am. Chem. Soc., Am. Petroleum Inst. Presbyterian. Patentee in field. Home: 4200 Via Dolce Apt 328 Marina Del Rey CA 90291 Office: 251 S Lake Ave Pasadena CA 91101

KRUH, ROBERT F., univ. dean; b. St. Louis, June 15, 1925; s. Frank O. and Nell (Dee) K.; m. Janet Jackson, Dec. 19, 1948; children—Lindsay, Nancy. A.B., Washington U., St. Louis, 1948, Ph.D., 1951. Asst. prof. DePauw U., 1951-52; prof. chemistry U. Ark., 1962-67, chmn. dept., 1963-64, dean Coll. Arts and Scis., 1964-67; dean Grad. Sch., Kans. State U., 1967—; mem. Grad. Record Exam. Bd., Ednl. Testing Service, Princeton, N.J., 1977—, chmn. bd., 1980-81; chmn. Policy Council on Test of English as a Fgn. Lang., 1977-80; Sec. research council Nat. Assn. State Univs. and Land-Grant Colls., 1969-72; bd. dirs. Council Grad. Schs. U.S., 1975—, chmn. council, 1978-79; pres. Kans. State U. Research Found., 1969—; trustee Argonne Univs. Assn., 1970-77. Contbr. articles to profl. jours. Served with C.E. AUS, 1943-46; ETO. Fellow Am. Inst. Chemists; mem. Am. Chem. Soc., Am. Phys. Soc., A.A.A.S., Am. Assn. U. Profs., Midwest Assn. Grad. Schs. (v.p. 1973-74, pres. 1974-75, exec. sec. 1977—), Phi Beta Kappa, Sigma Xi, Omicron Delta Kappa, Phi Kappa Phi, Blue Key. Home: 2155 Blue Hills Rd Manhattan KS 66502

KRUIDENIER, DAVID, newspaper executive; b. Des Moines, July 18, 1921; s. David S. and Florence (Cowles) K.; m. Elizabeth Stuart, Dec. 29, 1948; 1 dau., Lisa. B.A., Yale U., 1946; M.B.A., Harvard U., 1948; LL.D., Buena Vista Coll., 1960, Simpson Coll., 1963. With Mpls. Star and Tribune, 1948-52; with Des Moines Register and Tribune, 1952—, pres., chief exec. officer, pub., 1971-78, chmn., chief exec. officer, pub., 1978-82, chmn., chief exec. officer, 1982—; vice chmn. bd. Cowles Media Co., 1973—, pres., chief exec. officer, 1983—; dir. Des Moines Register and Tribune Co., Norwest Bank/Des Moines, Nat. By-Products, Inc., Audit Bur. Circulations. Past pres. Greater Des Moines Com.; pres. Gardner and Florence Call Cowles Found.; trustee Drake U., Menninger Found., Midwest Research Inst. Served with USAAF, 1942-45. Decorated Air medal with three clusters, D.F.C. Mem. Sigma Delta Chi, Beta Theta Pi, Beta Gamma Sigma. Clubs: Des Moines, Mpls., Mill Reef. Home: 3409 Southern Hills Dr Des Moines IA 50321 Office: 715 Locust St Des Moines IA 50304 Office: 425 Portland Minneapolis MN 55488

KRUIZENGA, RICHARD JOHN, energy company executive; b. Spring Lake, Mich., Sept. 25, 1930; s. Richard James and Kathryn Ella K.; m. Margaret Helene Feldmann, Sept. 6, 1952; children—Derek Diedrich, Meg Mulder. B.A. in Econs, Hope Coll., 1952, Ph.D., M.I.T., 1956. Chief economist Exxon Corp., 1966-69; logistics mgr. Esso Eastern, 1969-71; v.p. Esso Sekiyu, Tokyo, 1971-72; chmn. Esso Australia, 1972-77, Esso Prodn. Malaysia, Inc., 1977-80; v.p. corp. planning Exxon Corp., N.Y.C., 1980—. Vice-pres. Australian-Am. Assn., 1973-77. Mem. Malaysian Internat. C. of C. (dir. 1978-80). Office: 1251 Ave of the Americas New York NY 10020

KRUKOWSKI, NANCY HARROW (MRS. JAN KRUKOWSKI), editor; b. N.Y.C., Oct. 3, 1930; d. Benjamin and Frances (Kirschenbaum) Harrow; m. Jan Krukowski, July 8, 1951; children: Damon, Anton. B.A., Bennington Coll., 1952. From copy editor to editor William Morrow & Co., N.Y.C., 1952-57; editor Am. Jour.,

N.Y.C., 1972-73, editor-at-large, 1974—. Jazz singer, appearing in night clubs, N.Y.C., Paris, 1958-65; Recs. (under name Nancy Harrow) Wild Women Don't Have the Blues, 1960, You Never Know, 1962, Anything Goes, 1979, The John Lewis Album for Nancy Harrow, 1981. Address: 130 East End Ave New York NY 10028

KRUL, LEOPOLD JOSEPH, clergyman, college chancellor; b. Pitts., Mar. 29, 1918; s. Joseph Jacob and Johanna Cecilia (Dolinic) K. B.A. in Philosophy, St. Vincent Coll., 1941; M.A. in Classic Langs, Cornell U., 1950; M.Div., St. Vincent Sem., 1982. Joined Order of St. Benedict, Roman Catholic Ch.; ordained priest Roman Catholic Ch., 1945; tchr., adminstr. St. Vincent Coll. and Seminary, Latrobe, Pa., 1950-66, registrar, 1959-60; prior St. Vincent Archabbey, Latrobe, 1960-66; chaplain Penn State Univ., University Park, 1966-79; archabbot St. Vincent Archabbey, Latrobe, 1979-83; chancellor, chmn. bd. St. Vincent Coll. Corp., Latrobe, 1979-83. Mem. Newman Student Assn. Address: Saint Vincent Archabbey Latrobe PA 15650

KRULAK, VICTOR HAROLD, newspaper executive; b. Denver, Jan. 7, 1913; s. Morris and Besse M. (Ball) K.; m. Amy Chandler, June 1, 1936; children—Victor Harold, William Morris, Charles Chandler. B.S., U.S. Naval Acad., 1934; LL.D., U. San Diego. Commd. 2d lt. USMC, 1934, advanced through grades to lt. gen.; service in China, at sea, with, 1935-39; staff officer, also bn. and regimental comdr., World War II, chief staff, formerly comdg. gen., San Diego, formerly spl asst. to dir., joint staff counterinsurgency and spl. activities, comdr. gen., Pacific, 1964; now ret.; v.p. Copley Press, Inc.; pres. Copley News Service, San Diego, 1969—. Decorated D.S.M., Navy Cross, Legion of Merit with 3 oak leaf clusters, Bronze Star, Air medal, Purple Heart, U.S.; Cross of Gallantry; Medal of Merit, Vietnam; Distinguished Service medal, Korea). Mem. U.S. Naval Inst., U.S. Marine Corps Assn., Am. Soc. Newspaper Editors, InterAm. Press Assn., U.S. Strategic Inst. Home: 3665 Carleton St San Diego CA 92106 Office: Words Ltd 3045 Rosecran St San Diego CA 92110

KRULFELD, RUTH MARILYN, anthropology educator; b. N.Y.C., Apr. 15, 1931; d. Leon and Frances (Rosenberg) Pulwers; m. Jacob Mendel Krulfield, Aug. 28, 1964; 1 son, Michael David. B.A. cum laude, Brandeis U., 1956; Ph.D., Yale U., 1974. Field researcher microgeographic research farms in, Singapore, Malaya, 1951-53, anthrop. research in, Jamaica, 1957, Costa Rica, Nicaraugua, Oanama, 1958, Lombok, Indonesia, 1960-62; asst. prof. anthropology, dir. grad. students George Washington U., Washington, 1964-72, assoc. prof., 1973-76, prof., 1976—, dir. spl. grad. research degree program. Contbr. articles to profl. jours. Currier scholar Yale U., 1958; grantee Found. for Study of Man, 1957; Ford fellow, 1960-62; grantee Am. Council Learned Socs. and Social Sci. Research Council, 1963. Mem. Anthrop. Assn. Washington, Am. Anthrop. Assn. Jewish. Home: 4012 N Woodstock St Arlington VA 22207 Office: Dept Anthropology George Washington U. Washington DC 20052 *Perhaps the major attitudes that have motivated my work have been a deep respect for my fellow human beings, and a need to learn from them, to experience their wondrous creativity, ability and diversity; as an anthropologist, to understand as much about human societies as I could, and as an educator, to ignite the enthusiasm and wonder in my students, to encourage them to go beyond our present understanding and abilities.*

KRULITZ, LEO MORRION, business executive; b. Wallace, Idaho, June 15, 1938; s. John Morrion and Myrtle (Parker) K.; m. Donna Eileen Ristau, June 18, 1960; children—Cynthia, Pamela. B.A., Stanford U., 1960; J.D. cum laude, Harvard U., 1963; M.B.A., Stanford U., 1969. Bar: Idaho bar 1963, Ind. bar 1969, D.C. bar 1978, U.S. Supreme Ct. bar 1978. Ptnr. firm Moffatt, Thomas, Barrett & Blanton, Boise, Idaho, 1963-67; v.p., treas. Irwin Mgmt. Co., Columbus, Ind., 1969-77; solicitor Dept. of the Interior, Washington, 1977-79; gen. counsel Cummins Engine Co., Columbus, Ind., 1979-80, v.p., 1980—; treas. Irwin-Sweeney-Miller Found., Columbus, 1976-77; dir. L'Enfant Plaza Properties, Washington, 1974-77; mem. U.S. delegation Soviet Union Conf. on Environ. Law, 1978. Dir. Columbus City Utilities.; mem. Bartholomew Consol. Sch. Bd., bd. dirs. John Muir Inst. Mem. Am., Idaho, Ind. bar assns. Democrat. Club: Harvard (N.Y.C.). Home: 4373 E Windsor Ln Columbus IN 47201 Office: 1015 3d St Columbus IN 47201

KRUMBOLTZ, JOHN DWIGHT, educator, psychologist; b. Cedar Rapids, Iowa, Oct. 21, 1928; s. Dwight John and Margaret (Jones) K.; m. Helen Brandhorst, Aug. 22, 1954; children: Ann, Jennifer. B.A., Coe Coll., Cedar Rapids, 1950; M.A., Columbia Tchrs. Coll., 1951; Ph.D., U. Minn., 1955. Counselor, tchr. W. Waterloo (Iowa) High Sch., 1951-53; teaching asst., then instr. U. Minn., 1953-55; asst. prof. ednl. psychology, then asso. prof. Mich. State U., 1957-61; mem. faculty Stanford, 1961—, prof. edn. and psychology, 1966—; Vis. sr. research psychologist Ednl. Testing Service, 1972-73; fellow Center for Advanced Study in Behavioral Scis., 1975-76, Advanced Study Center, Nat. Center for Research in Vocat. Edn., Ohio State U., 1980-81; vis. colleague dept. psychology Inst. Psychiatry, U. London, 1983-84. Author: (with others) Learning to Study, 1960, (with Helen B. Krumboltz) Changing Children's Behavior, 1972; also articles, revs., monographs.; Editor: Learning and the Educational Process, 1965, Revolution in Counseling, 1966, (with Carl E. Thoresen) Behavioral Counseling: Cases and Techniques, 1969, Counseling Methods, 1976, (with Anita M. Mitchell and G. Brian Jones) Social Learning and Career Decision Making, 1979, (with Daniel A. Hamel) Assessing Career Development, 1982. Served with USAF, 1955-57. Guggenheim fellow, 1967-68. Mem. Am. Psychol. Assn. (pres. div. counseling psychology 1974-75), Am. Ednl. Research Assn. (v.p. div. E. 1966-68), Am. Personnel and Guidance Assn. (Outstanding Research award 1959, 66, 68, Distinguished Profl. Services award 1974). Home: 933 Valdez Pl Stanford CA 94305

KRUMHANSL, JAMES ARTHUR, physicist, educator, Industrial consultant; b. Cleve., Aug. 21919; s. James and Marcella (Kelly) K.; m. Barbara Dean Schminck, Dec. 26, 1944 (div. 1983); children: James Lee, Carol Lynne, Peter Allen.; m. Marilyn Cupp Dahl, Feb. 19, 1983. B.S. in Elec. Engring, U. Dayton, 1939; M.S., Case Inst. Tech., 1940, D.Sc. (hon.), 1980; Ph.D. in Physics, Cornell U., 1943. Instr. Cornell U., 1943-44; physicist Stromberg-Carlson Co., 1944-46; mem. faculty Brown U., 1946-48, asso. prof., 1947-48; asst. prof., then asso. prof. Cornell U., 1948-55; asst. dir. research Nat. Carbon Co., 1955-57, asso. dir. research, 1957-58; prof. physics Cornell U., 1959—, Horace White prof., 1980; dir. Lab. Atomic and Solid State Physics, 1960-64; adj. prof. U. Pa., 1979; fellow Los Alamos Lab., 1980; asst. dir. for math., phys. sci. and engring. NSF, 1977-79; cons. to industry, 1946—; dir. Allied Chem. Corp.; Adv. com for AEC, Dept. Def., Nat. Acad. Sci., 1956—; vis. fellow All Souls Coll., Oxford U., 1977, Gonville and Caius Coll., Cambridge U., 1983, Royal Soc. London, 1983. Editor: Jour. Applied Physics, 1957-60; asso. editor: Solid State Communications, 1963—, Rev. Modern Physics, 1968-73; editor: Phys. Rev. Letters, 1974—, physics Oxford U. Press; Contbr. articles to profl. jours. Guggenheim fellow, 1959-60; NSF sr. postdoctoral fellow Oxford U., 1966-67. Fellow Am. Phys. Soc. (chmn. div. solid state physics 1968, councillor 1970-74), AAAS, Am. Inst. Physics (governing bd. 1973—); mem. AAUP, Am. Assn. Physics Tchrs., Sigma Xi, Phi Kappa Phi. Republican. Presbyn. Club: Ithaca Yacht. Home: 12 D Strawberry Hill Ithaca NY 14850

KRUMM, DANIEL JOHN, manufacturing company executive; b. Sioux City, Iowa, Oct. 15, 1926; s. Walter A. and Anna K. (Helmke) K.; m. Ann L. Klingner, Feb. 28, 1953; children: David Jonathan, Timothy John. B.A. in Commerce, U. Iowa, 1950; postgrad., U. Mich., 1955; D.B.A. (hon.), Westmar Coll., Le Mars, Iowa, 1981, D. Comml. Sci., Luther Coll., Decorah, Iowa, 1983. With Globe Office Furniture Co., Mpls., 1950-52; with Maytag Co., Newton, Iowa, 1952—, v.p., 1970-71, exec. v.p., 1971-72, pres., treas., 1972—, chief exec. officer, 1974—, also dir.; pres., chief exec. officer Maytag Co. Ltd., Toronto, 1970—; dir. Centel Corp., Bankers Life, Des Moines. Mem. Newton Community Theater; pres., trustee Maytag Co. Found.; chmn. Iowa Natural Heritage Found., Iowa Coll. Found.; bd. dirs. Grand View Coll., Des Moines, Des Moines Symphony Assn., Vocat. Rehab. Workshop for Handicapped Citizens of Jasper County (Iowa); mem. Gov.'s Dist. Jud. Nominating Commn. Served with USNR, 1944-46. Recipient Oscar C. Schmidt Iowa Bus. Leadership award, 1983. Mem. Am. Mktg. Assn. (past pres. Iowa), NAM, Newton C. of C. (community service award 1980), Maytag Mgmt. Club. Republican. Lutheran. Club: Newton Country. Office: 403 W 4th St N Newton IA 50208

KRUMM, JOHN MCGILL, bishop; b. South Bend, Ind., Mar. 15, 1913; s. William F. and Harriett Vincent (McGill) K. A.A., Pasadena Jr. Coll., 1933; A.B., U. Calif., 1935; B.D., Va. Theol. Sem., 1938, D.D. (hon.), 1974; Ph.D., Yale U., 1948; S.T.D., Kenyon Coll., Gambier, Ohio, 1962; D.D. (hon.), Berkeley Div. Sch., Gen. Theol. Sem., 1975, L.H.D., Hebrew Union Coll., Cin. Ordained to ministry Episcopal Ch., 1938; vicar Episc. chs., Compton, Lynwood and Hawthorne, Calif., 1938-41; asst. rector St. Paul's Ch., New Haven, 1941-43; rector Ch. of St. Matthew, San Mateo, Calif., 1943-48; dean St. Paul's Cathedral, Los Angeles, 1948-52; chaplain Columbia U., 1952-65; rector Ch. of Ascension, N.Y.C., 1965-71; bishop of So. Ohio, Episc. Ch., 1971-80; suffragan bishop in Europe, Paris, 1980-83, assisting bishop, Los Angeles, 1983—, St. Paul's Ch., Tustin, Calif., 1983—; vis. lectr. N.T. Berkeley Div. Sch., New Haven, 1942-43; ch. history Va. Theol. Sem., Alexandria, 1942; instr. Prospect Hill Sch., New Haven, 1942-43; instr. religion U. So. Calif., 1950-52; chmn. clergy div. U. Religious Conf., Los Angeles; pres. San Mateo-Burlingame (Calif.) Council Chs., 1947-48, Ch. Fedn. Los Angeles, 1951-52; chmn. nat. council Panel of Ams., 1953-61. Author: (with J.A. Pike) Roadblocks to Faith, 1953, Modern Heresies, 1961, The Art of Being a Sinner, 1967, Why Choose the Episcopal Church, 1974, (with others) Denver Crossroads, 1979. Trustee Mt. Holyoke Coll., 1962-72, Bexley Hall of Colgate-Rochester, Kenyon Coll., Children's Hosp., Cin., 1971-80. Democrat. Clubs: Century Assn. (N.Y.C.); University. Office: 1221 Wass Ave Tustin Calif. 92680

KRUMM, WILLIAM FREDERICK, insurance company executive; b. South Bend, Ind., Aug. 31, 1923; s. William Frederick and Harriet Vincent (McGill) K.; m. A. Lois Little, June 21, 1946; 1 dau., Kathryn Lois. B.B.A. magna cum laude, Woodbury U., 1949. C.L.U. Asst. sales mgr. Eastman Lumber Sales, 1949-51; agt. N.Y. Life Ins. Co., 1951-53; with Occidental Life Ins. Co. (now Transam. Occidental Life Ins. Co.), 1953—; v.p. agy. adminstrn. Occidental Life Ins. Co. Calif. (now Transam. Occidental Life Ins. Co.), Los Angeles, 1962-72, sr. v.p. ins. ops., 1975—. Served with USMC, 1942-46. Republican. Episcopalian. Office: Transamerica Occidental Life Ins Co Hill and Olive at 12th Los Angeles CA 90015

KRUMMEL, DONALD WILLIAM, librarian, educator; b. Sioux City, Iowa, July 12, 1929; s. William and Leta Margarete (Fischer) K.; m. Marilyn Darlene Frederick, June 19, 1956; children: Karen Elisabeth, Matthew Frederick. Mus.B., U. Mich., 1951, Mus.M., 1953, M.A. in Library Sci, 1955, Ph.D., 1958. Instr. in music lit. U. Mich., 1952-56; reference librarian Library of Congress, Washington, 1956-61; head reference dept., asso. librarian Newberry Library, Chgo., 1962-69; asso. prof. library sci. U. Ill., 1970-71, prof. library sci. and music, 1971—, asso. Center Advanced Study, 1974; middle mgmt. intern U.S. Civil Service, 1960; scholar in residence Aspen Inst., 1969. Author: Bibliotheca Bolduaniana, 1972, Guide for Dating Early Published Music, 1974, English Music Printing, 1553-1700, 1975, Bibliographical Inventory to the Early Music in the Newberry Library, 1977, Organizing the Library's Support, 1980, Resources of American Music History, 1981; contbr. numerous articles and revs. to profl. jours. Recipient award Huntington Library, 1965, Am. Council Learned Socs., 1966-77, Am. Philos. Soc., 1969, Council Library Resources, 1967; Newberry Library travelling fellow, 1969-70; Univ. Coll. (London) hon. research fellow, 1974-75; Guggenheim fellow, 1976-77. Mem. Music Library Assn. (pres. 1981-83), Internat. Assn. Music Libraries, ALA, Bibliog. Soc. (London), Am. Musicol. Soc., Bibliog. Soc. Am., Sonneck Soc. Clubs: Caxton (Chgo.); Dial (Urbana). Home: 702 W Delaware Ave Urbana IL 61801 Office: 432 David Kinley Hall U Ill Urbana IL 61801

KRUMPE, JOHN H., professional sports team executive. Pres. N.Y. Rangers, Nat. Hockey League, N.Y.C. Office: Madison Sq Garden 4 Pennsylvania Plaza New York NY 10001§

KRUMRINE, CHARLES SIDNEY, retired banker; b. Bellefonte, Pa., June 29, 1897; s. Sidney and Mary Jane (Bubb) K.; m. Jane Brown Gilfillan, Sept. 20, 1924; 1 dau., Jane. Grad., Pa. State U., 1918. With Liberty Real Estate Bank & Trust Co., Phila., 1923-57, v.p., dir., pres., 1940-56, chmn. exec. com., 1956-57; pres., dir. Central Pa. Gas Co., 1958-66; dir. investment com. Phila. Life Ins. Co., 1940-77; mem. exec. com. Med. Service Assn. Pa. (Blue Shield), 1965-76, mem. fin. com., 1965-76. Chmn. U.S. Savs. Bond Com. for Pa., 1956-74, chmn. emeritus, 1974—; adv. bd. Holy Redeemer Hosp., Meadowbrook, Pa. Served with AC, USN, World War I. Decorated Star of Solidarity, Italy, 1956; recipient award of Merit U.S. Treasury Dept., 1974; named hon. mem. Japan Def. Soc., 1973. Mem. Pa. Soc. S.R., Pa. Bankers Assn. (chmn. group I 1956), Navy League, Def. Orientation Conf. Assn. (regional dir. 1974-76), Newcomen Soc. N.Am., Hist. Soc. Pa., Am. Legion, Explorers Club, Sigma Alpha Epsilon. Republican. Episcopalian. Clubs: Bank Officers (past pres.), Sunday Breakfast, Union League, Phila. Country, Merion Cricket (Phila.); Right Angle; Seaview Country (Absecon, N.J); Explorers (N.Y.C.). Home: 50 Raynham Rd Merion Station PA 19066 Office: Phila Life Ins Co 615 Chestnut St Philadelphia PA 19106

KRUPANSKY, BLANCHE, former state justice, lawyer; b. Cleve., Dec. 10, 1925; d. Frank and Ann K.; m. Frank W. Vargo, Apr. 30, 1960. A.B., Flora Stone Mather Coll., 1943-47; J.D., Case Western Res. U., 1948, LL.M., 1966. Bar: Ohio 1949. Gen. practice law, 1949-61, 83—; asst. atty. gen. State of Ohio; asst. chief counsel Ohio Bur. Workmen's Compensation; judge Cleve. Mcpl. Ct., 1961-69, Common Please Ct. Cuyahoga County, 1969-77, Ct. Appeals Ohio 8th Appellate Dist., 1977-81; justice Supreme Ct. Ohio, 1981-83; vis. com. Case Western U. Law Sch., 1974-78, bd. govs., 1975-76. Recipient Outstanding Jud. Service award Supreme Ct. Ohio, 1972-76; Law Book scholar award Cuyahoga Women's Polit. Caucus, 1981; recipient outstanding contbn. to law award Ohio Assn. Civil Trial Attys., 1982, Disting. Alumna award, 1982, Disting. Service award Women's Space, 1982, award Democratic Women's Caucus, 1983, Women's Equity Action League Ohio, 1983; named Woman of Achievement Inter-Club Council Cleve., 1969; inducted into Ohio Women's Hall of Fame, 1981. Mem. Nat. Assn. Women Lawyers, Nat. Assn. Women Judges, Ohio Bar Assn., Bar Assn. Greater Cleve., Cuyahoga County Bar Assn., Cleve. Women Lawyers, LWV, Common Pleas Judges Assn., Ohio Assn. Attys. Gen., Ohio Appellate Judges Assn., Soc. of Benchers. Republic. Roman Catholic. Club: Woman's City (Woman of Achievement award 1981) (Cleve.). Office: Ohio Supreme Ct State Office Tower Columbus OH 43215

KRUPANSKY, ROBERT BAZIL, U.S. judge; b. Cleve., Aug. 15, 1921; s. Frank A. and Anna (Lawrence) K.; m. Marjorie Blaser, Nov. 13, 1952. B.A., Western Res. U., 1946, LL.B., 1948; J.D., Case Western Res. U., 1968. Bar: Ohio bar 1948, also Supreme Ct. Ohio 1948, Supreme Ct. U.S 1948, U.S. Dist. Ct. No. Dist. Ohio 1948, U.S. Circuit Ct. Appeals 6th Circuit 1948, U.S. Ct. Customs and Patent Appeals 1948, U.S. Customs Ct 1948, ICC 1948. Pvt. practice, Cleve., 1948-52; asst. atty. gen. State of Ohio, 1951-57; mem. Gov. of Ohio cabinet and dir. Ohio Dept. Liquor Control, 1957-58; judge Common Pleas Ct. of Cuyahoga County, 1959-60; sr. partner Metzenbaum, Gaines, Krupansky, Finley & Stern, 1960-69; U.S. atty. No. Dist. Ohio, Cleve., 1969-70, U.S. judge, 1970—; adj. prof. law Case Western Res. U. Sch. Law, 1969-70. Served to 2d lt. U.S. Army, 1942-46; col. USAF Res. ret. Mem. Am., Fed., Ohio, Cleve., Cuyahoga County bar assns., Am. Judicature Soc., Assn. Asst. Attys. Gen. State Ohio. Office: US Court House Cleveland OH 44114

KRUPP, CLARENCE WILLIAM, lawyer, personnel and hospital administrator; b. Cleve., June 20, 1929; s. William Frederick and Mary Mae (Volchko) K.; m. Janice Margaret Heckman, June 28, 1952; children: Bruce, Carolyn. B.B.A. cum laude, Cleve. State U., 1958, LL.B., 1959, LL.M., 1963. Bar: Wis. 1972. Dir. indsl. relations and indsl. engring. Buxbaum Co., Canton, Ohio, 1963-66; mgr. indsl. relations Trane Co., La Crosse, Wis., 1966-73; dir. personnel-labor relations environ. products div. ITT, Phila., 1973; v.p. indsl. relations, gen. counsel G. Heileman Brewing Co., La Crosse, 1973-76; atty., v.p. human resources-risk control, sec. Good Samaritan Hosp., Dayton, Ohio, 1976—; mgr. compensation and benefits State of Ariz., Phoenix, 1980-83; personnel adminstr. Salt River Project, 1983—; cons. on labor relations, 1969, 81-83. Contbr. articles to profl. jours. Municipal arbitrator, La Crosse, 1976; pres., mem. La Crosse Bd. Edn., 1969-72; mem. Wis. Gov.'s Task Force on Edn., 1972-73; Ohio Little White House library del. Served with U.S. Army, 1951-53. Named Outstanding Ariz. State Profl. Employee, 1982. Mem. Am. Bar Assn. (forum hosp. on law, labor law sect.), Wis Bar Assn. (Continuing Edn. award 1972), Am. Assn. Hosp. Attys., Am. Soc. Law and Medicine, Dayton C. of C. Democrat. Roman Catholic. Club: Rotary. Home: 8701 Via de la Gente Scottsdale AZ 85258 Office: 48th and University Sts Tempe AZ 85034 *Understand and be tolerant of the views of others. With that insight your decisons will be respected and your judgment both honored and sought.*

KRUPP, DAVID JEAN, lawyer; b. Chgo., June 1, 1926; s. Albert M. and Sylvia J. (Lipschultz) K.; m. Margo Ketay Rauch, Sept. 20, 1953; children: Deborah Joan, Jonathan Martin. B.S., Juilliard Sch. Music, 1950; LL.B., NYU, 1955. Bar: Ill. 1955. Practiced in, Chgo., 1955—; of Counsel Greenberger, Krauss & Jacobs, Chartered, 1965—. Served with AUS, 1944-46. Mem. ABA, Ill. Bar Assn., Chgo. Bar Assn. (panelist continuing legal edn. program), N.Y. U. Law Sch. Alumni Assn. (dir.). Jewish. Home: 421 Melrose Ave Chicago IL 60657 Office: 208 S LaSalle St Chicago IL 60604

KRUPP, EDWIN CHARLES, astronomer; b. Chgo., Nov. 18, 1944; s. Edwin Frederick and Florence Ann (Olander) K.; m. Robin Suzanne Rector, Dec. 31, 1968; 1 son, Ethan Hembree. B.A., Pomona Coll., 1966; M.A., UCLA, 1968, Ph.D. (NDEA fellow, 1970-71), 1972. Astronomer Griffith Obs., Los Angeles Dept. Recreation and Parks, 1972—, dir., 1976—; mem. faculty El Camino Coll., U. So. Calif., extension divs. U. Calif.; cons. in ednl. TV Community Colls. Consortium; host teleseries Project: Universe. Author: Echoes of the Ancient Skies; editor/co-author: In Search of Ancient Astronomies, 1978 (Am. Inst. Physics-U.S. Steel Found. award for Best Sci. Writing 1978), Archaeoastronomy and the Roots of Science; Editor-in-chief: Griffith Obs., 1974—. Mem. Am. Astron. Soc., Astron. Soc. Pacific (dir.), Explorers Club, Sigma Xi. Office: Griffith Obs 2800 E Observatory Rd Los Angeles CA 90027

KRUPP, MARCUS ABRAHAM, physician; b. El Paso, Tex., Feb. 12, 1913; s. Maurice and Esther (Siegel) K.; m. Muriel McClure, Aug. 9, 1941 (dec. Oct. 1954); children: Michael, David (dec.), Peter, Sara; m. Donna Goodheart Millen, Feb. 28, 1958. A.B., Stanford U., 1934, M.D., 1939. Diplomate: Am. Bd. Internal Medicine. Intern Stanford U. Hosp., Calif., 1938-39, resident in internal medicine, 1939-42; chief clin. pathology VA Hosp., San Francisco, 1946-50; dir. Palo Alto Med. Research Found., Calif., 1950—; dir. labs. Palo Alto Med. Clinic, 1950-80; asst. clin. prof. medicine Stanford U., 1946-56, asso. clin. prof., 1956-65, clin. prof., 1965—; mem. med. tech. adv. com. Public Employees Retirement System Calif., 1972—. Editor: (with Milton Chatton) Current Diagnosis and Treatment, ann., 1971-83, (with others) Physicians Handbook, 7th-20th edits., 1981. Vice pres. bd. dirs. Calif. Heart Assn., 1974-75; pres. bd. trustees Channing House, Palo Alto. Served to capt. U.S. Army, 1942-46. Fellow ACP; mem. Western Soc. Clin. Research, Calif. Acad. Medicine (pres. 1966), Pacific Interurban Clin. Club (pres. 1977), AAAS, AMA, N.Y. Acad. Scis., Assn. Ind. Research Insts. (pres. 1966-67), Phi Beta Kappa, Alpha Omega Alpha. Home: 195 Ramoso Rd Portola Valley CA 94025 Office: 860 Bryant St Palo Alto CA 94301

KRUPP, ROLAND GERALD, consultant; b. Sebewaing, Mich., July 4, 1915; s. Joseph Milton and Elizabeth Dorothy (Wurtz) K.; m. Dorothy Neighorn, July 15, 1944; children: Charlene and Marilyn (twins), Robert S., Janet M. B.S. in Mech. Engring, Lawrence Inst. Tech., 1945; M.B.A., Wayne State U., 1970. With Mueller Brass Co., Port Huron, Mich., 1935-81, v.p. ops., 1965-70, exec. v.p., 1970-72, chmn. bd., 1972-80, sr. v.p., 1981, also dir.; cons., 1981—. Sec. Port Huron Dist. Found.; mem. adv. bd. Mercy Hosp. Mem. Copper Devel. Corp., Wire Assn., Am. Inst. Metall. Engrs. Republican. Presbyterian. Club: Black River Country. Home: 3962 Gratiot Ave Port Huron MI 48060

KRUPSKA, DANYA (MRS. TED THURSTON), director, choreographer; b. Fall River, Mass., Aug. 13, 1923; d. Bronislaw and Anna (Niementowska) Krupski; m. Richard La Marr (div. 1953); 1 son, Brion; m. Ted Thurston, May 27, 1954; 1 dau., Tina Lyn. Student, Lankenau Sch. for Girls, Phila.; studied, Ethel Phillips Dance Studio, Catherine Littlefield Ballet Studio, Mordkin Studio, Phila., Aubrey Hitchens Studio, N.Y.C., Bobby Lewis Dir.'s Studio, N.Y.C. Performed concerts, Phila., 1929-36; also toured, Poland, Roumania, Balkan Countries, Hungary, Vienna, Palestine; joined, Phila. Ballet (Littlefield) for European tour, 1937, Chgo. Opera Season, 1938, Am. Ballet (Ballanchine), N.Y.C.; soloist Broadway prodn.: Frank Fay Show, Radio City Music Hall Ballet; leading role on nat. tour: Johnny Belinda; soloist in: Chouve Souris, 1943; dancer in role of Dream Laurie, 1st nat. co. of Okla., later Broadway co., 1945; asst. to choreographer Agnes de Mille on Rodgers and Hammerstein prodn.: Allegro; then in ballet prodn.: Fall River Legend; then in opera prodn.: Rape of Lucrece; Broadway prodns.: Girl in Pink Tights, Gentlemen Prefer Blonds, Paint Your Wagon; assisted Michael Kidd in Broadway prodn.: Can Can; choreographer Broadway prodn.: Most Happy Fella (Tony nomination), Seventeen, 1st Shoestring Revue, Carefree Heart, Happiest Girl in the World (Tony nominee), Her First

Roman, 1968, Apollo and Miss Agnes; choreographer Met. Opera prodn.: The Gypsy Baron; choreographer Italian mus.: Rugantino, 1962; choreographer: TV Salute to the Peace Corps, 1965; guest choreographer: Zorba, Nat. Theatre, Reykjavik, Iceland, 1971, Company for Stora Teatern, Gothenburg, Sweden, 1971, Fantastiks, Little Theatre, Gothenburg, 1971, No No Nanette, Malmö Stadsteater, Sweden, 1973, Porgy and Bess, Malmö Stadsteater, Sweden, 1974, Richard Rodger's Prodn. of Rex, Broadway, N.Y.C., 1976, Richard Rodger's Prodn. of Showboat, Malmö Stadsteater, 1976; dir.: Bernstein's The Mass, Malmo Stadsteater, 1975, Chicago, Det Danske Teater, 1977, Our Man in Havana, Poland, 1977, Cabaret, Helsingborg Stadsteater, Sweden, 1978, Guys and Dolls, Aarhus Teater, Denmark, 1978, Once Upon a Mattress, Nat. Theater Reykjavik, Iceland, 1979; dir., choreographer: Animalen, Malmo Stadsteater, Sweden, 1981; producer, dir.; choreographer: The King and I, Malmo Stadstheater, Sweden, 1982-83; dir. mus. prodns., N.Y. City Center; Most Happy Fella, 1959, Showboat, 1961, Fiorello, 1962 (also White House prodn. for gov.'s conf. 1968), Oklahoma, Nat. Theatre, Reykjavik, 1972; TV appearances include: Buick Hour, 1952, Colgate Comedy Hour, 1953, Omnibus, U.S. Steel Theatre Guild Prodns; Ballets Outlook for Three (Ellington), Pointes on Jazz (Brubeck), Am. Ballet Theatre. Mem. Actors Equity Assn., Soc. Stage Dirs and Choreographers (exec. bd. mem.). Home: 71 Toilsome Ln East Hampton NY 11937 Office: 564 W 52d St New York NY 10019

KRUPSKY, JOSEPH FRANCIS, lawyer; b. Mahanoy Twp., Pa., Oct. 25, 1935; s. Joseph George and Elizabeth (Sarody) K.; m. Suzanne Wilson, Feb. 28, 1969; 1 dau., Catherine Elizabeth. A.B., Upsala Coll., 1960; J.D., Rutgers U., 1964. Bar: N.J. 1965, Ind. 1975, Mo. 1977. Securities commr. State of N.J., Newark, 1970-73; sec., acting gen. counsel Chromalloy Am. Corp., St. Louis, 1976—; dir. Chromalloy Farm Equipment Co., Madison, Wis., 1976-79; sec. Am. Universal Ins. Co., Providence, 1980—. Contbr. legal articles to profl. jours. Mcpl. chmn. Bay Head Republican Com., N.J., 1971-74, county committeeman, 1971-74; trustee Bay Head Improvement Assn., 1973-74. Served with U.S. Army, 1954-56. Mem. Am. Soc. Corp. Secs., ABA. Club: Clayton (Mo.). Home: 183 Ridgecrest Dr Chesterfield MO 63017

KRUS, DAVID JAMES, psychologist, educator; b. Czechoslovakia, Oct. 10, 1940; came to U.S., 1968, naturalized, 1973; s. Ferdinand and Marie (Dadok) K.; m. Patricia Kennedy, Dec. 28, 1968; children—Neal Brian, Ryan Brent, Alison Blair. B.A., Charles U., 1964, M.A., 1965; Ph.D., U. Minn., 1974. Research asso. Inst. Psychology, Prague, 1965-68; research fellow Research and Devel. Center, U. Minn., 1973-74; prof. psychology U. So. Calif., 1974-75; dir. univ. testing services Ariz. State U., Tempe, 1975—, prof. ednl. psychology, 1975—. Author: Order Analysis of Binary Data Matrices, 1976; contbr. articles to profl. jours. Eva O. Miller fellow, 1972-73. Mem. Am. Psychol. Assn., Psychometric Soc., Sigma Xi. Office: 302 Payne Hall Arizona State University Tempe AZ 85281 *Contemporary American civilization is in the midst of struggle between Apollonian and Dionysian modes of cognitive styles. If the modern forms of magical thinking prevail, beliefs will replace science and alter our destiny for centuries to come.*

KRUSCHKE, EARL ROGER, polit. scientist; b. Sheboygan, Wis., Feb. 26, 1934; s. Bernard G. and Louise M. (Kaesermann) K.; m. Marilyn Ann Reineking, Aug. 26, 1956; children—Kari Lynn, John Kendall. B.S., U. Wis., 1956, Ph.D., 1963; M.A., U. Wyo., 1957; LL.B., LaSalle U., 1977. Instr. U. Wis., Madison, 1959-60, U. Wis. Center System, 1960-61; asst. prof. U. Puget Sound, 1962-65, Calif. State U., Chico, 1965-67, asso. prof., 1967-72, prof., 1972—; vis. asso. prof. U. Wis., Milw., summer 1968; editorial writer, columnist Sheboygan (Wis.) Press, STA. WHBL, 1957-58; cons. in field. Author: The Woman Voter, 1955, Introduction to Constitution of the U.S, 1968, American Party Process, 1980, Consensus and Cleavage: Issues in California Politics, 1967; contbr. articles to profl. jours.; asso. editor: Western Polit. Quar, 1978—. Bd. dirs. World Affairs Council, 1963-65. Recipient Clyde Augustis Duniway award, 1957, Outstanding Teacher award Calif. State U., Chico, 1979. Mem. Am. Polit. Sci. Assn., AAUP, Western Polit. Sci. Assn., Internat. Polit. Sci. Assn., Mu Sigma Delta, Pi Gamma Mu, Phi Eta Sigma, Delta Tau Kappa. Home: 4 Casita Terr Chico CA 95926 Office: Dept of Political Science California State University Chico CA 95929

KRUSE, EDGAR CHRIST, former hosp. adminstr.; b. Ft. Wayne, Ind., June 15, 1912; s. Henry C. and Emma (Dreyer) K.; m. Mildred Kramer, May 15, 1937; children—Dale Keith, Dennis Neal, Donald Edgar. Student, Ind. U., 1930-33. Messenger, jr. exec. Home Tel. & Tel. Co., 1928-48; gen. auditor City Utilities, Ft. Wayne, 1948-52; asst. adminstr. Lutheran Hosp., Ft. Wayne, 1952-59, pres., 1959-77; chmn. bd. DNK Enterprises, Inc., Ft. Wayne, 1978—; Mem. Ind. Bd. Health Regulating and Licensing Council, 1963-67; mem. adv. bd. Sch. Practical Nursing. Bd. dirs. Luth. Hosp. Found., 1977—, pres., 1981—; bd. dirs. Ft. Wayne chpt. A.R.C. Mem. Am. Assn. Hosp. Accountants (past pres. Ind. chpt.), Northeastern Ind. Hosp. Council (past pres.), Luth. Hosp. Assn. Am. (dir., past pres.), Tri-State Hosp. Assembly (dir., past pres.), Ft. Wayne C. of C. Clubs: Junto, Executive (dir., past pres.), 100 Per Cent (Ft. Wayne) Home: 6037 Ranger Trail Fort Wayne IN 46815

KRUSE, HEEREN SAMUEL EILTS, architect; b. St. Louis, Oct. 20, 1911; s. Samuel Andrew and Geraldine (Eilts) K.; m. Ada Juanita Medcalf, 1936 (div. 1942); m. Mary Ruth Owens, Dec. 21, 1945; children—Mary Katherine, David Samuel Owens, Candice Serena. B.Arch., U. Ill., 1933, grad. study, 1934; student, Beaux Arts Inst. Design, 1929-34, Bauhaus Sch. Design, 1935, Taliesin Seminars, 1935; grad., Command and Gen. Staff Sch., 1945. Draftsman George Fred Keck, Chgo., 1934-35; sec.-treas. Harford Field, Inc. (architect), Hinsdale, Ill., 1935-36; master graphic arts Lake Forest (Ill.) Acad., 1936; architect E.A. Gruensfeld, Jr., Chgo., 1936-38; gen. practice, Chgo. and Centralia, Ill., 1939-42; architect William E. Kittle, Robert Law Weed & Assoc., also Nims, Inc., 1947-51; partner Watson & Deutschman, 1951-60; v.p. Watson, Deutschman & Kruse (architect and engrs.), Miami, Fla., 1961-74, Watson, Deutschman, Kruse & Lyon Inc. (architects, engrs.), 1974—, pres., 1976; instr. Miami Draftsmen's Club, 1959-62; lectr., adj. prof., prof. Clemson U., U. Miami, U. Waterloo, 1967—; city planner, Plantation, Fla., 1971—. Projects include Young Sch, Salem Twp., Ill., 1941, Yoyogi Chapel, and New Town, Tokyo, Japan, 1946, U.S. Post Office, Biscayne Annex, Miami, 1956, Cutler Ridge Jr. High Sch, 1960, U. Miami Library, 1961, Fla. Atlantic U, 1963, Miami Springs Sr. High Sch, 1964, Computing Center, U. Miami, 1965, Triton Towers, Miami Beach, 1967, Victoria Hosp, 1973, Dade County Detention and Treatment Center, 1974, Miami Beach Convention Center, Pan Am. World Airways Flight Tng. Acad, Miami, 1980. Mem. Welfare Bldg. Council.; Mem. bd. Children's Home Soc. of Florida, asst. treas., 1959, pres., 1974-76; mem. adv. bd. League Women Voters; chmn. adv. bd. U. N.C. Served to col., C.E. AUS, 1942-46. Medalist Beaux Arts Inst. Design, 1933. Fellow A.I.A. (dir. Fla. region 1967-69, past exec. com., gold medal Fla. chpt. 1969, silver medal Fla. South chpt. 1981, bursar Coll. of Fellows); mem. Fla. Assn. Architects (sec. 1957, pres. 1958, dir. 1959-63, 80-83, pres. found. 1972-76, 83—), Soc. Am. Mil. Engrs., Fla. Planning and Zoning Assn., Constrn. Specifications Inst. (chpt. pres. 1974-75), Am. Planning Assn., Am. Inst. Cert. Planners, Alpha Rho Chi. Office: 1600 NW LeJeune Rd Miami FL 33126

KRUSE, JAMES JOSEPH, manufacturing company executive; b. St. Petersburg, Fla., Dec. 5, 1932; s. Charles Edward and Mary Joyce (Cappelen) K.; m. Marilyn Gail Cocozza, May 30, 1969; 1 dau., Erika Leigh. B.S., U. Fla., 1957; M.S., Fla. State U., 1958; postgrad., Aspen Inst. Humanistic Studies, 1977; postgrad. Advanced Mgmt. Program, Harvard U., 1983. Field sec. nat. hdqrs. staff Phi Delta Theta frat., Oxford, Ohio, 1958-60; mem. staff R.B. Troutman, Jr. (developer), Atlanta, 1960-61; staff dir. Kennedy-Johnson campaign State of Ga., 1960-61; dir. Plans for Progress, Pres.'s Com. on Equal Employment, Washington, 1961-63; asst. to pres. Textron, Inc., Providence, 1963-72, sec., 1972-74, v.p., 1973-74, v.p. adminstrn., 1974-78, sr. v.p. adminstrn., 1978—. Mem. exec. com. R.I. Cath. Charities, 1976—; trustee Ocean State Performing Arts Center, Trinity Sq. Repetory Theater, Providence Found., Providence Coll., 1982—, Coll. at Newport/Salve Regina, St. Joseph's Hosp., 1983—; dir. R.I. Urban Project; mem. New Eng. Bd. Higher Edn., Nat. Inst. for Work and Learning; bd. dirs. New Eng. Council, Providence Found.; mem. Commn. on Higher Edn. and Economy New Eng., Capital Ctr. Planning Commn. Served with AUS, 1953-55. Recipient Presdl. citation for equal employment work, 1963, Vice Presdl. citation for equal employment work, 1966. Mem. Bus. Roundtable, Providence C. of C. (dir. 1982—). Roman Catholic. Clubs: University, Turks Head, Acoaxet. Home: 70 Roberta Ave Pawtucket RI 02860 Harborview Newport RI Office: 40 Westminster St Providence RI 02903

KRUSE, JOHN ALPHONSE, lawyer; b. Detroit, Sept. 11, 1926; s. Frank R. and Ann (Nestor) K.; m. Mary Louise Dalton, July 14, 1951; children: Gerard, Mary Louise, Terence, Kathleen, Joanne, Francis, John, Patrick. B.S., U. Detroit, 1950, J.D. cum laude, 1952. Bar: Mich. bar 1952. Since practiced in, Detroit; mem. firm Alexander, Buchanan & Conklin, 1952-69, Harvey, Kruse & Westen, 1969—; Guest lectr. U. Mich., U. Detroit, Inst. Continuing Legal Edn.; City atty., Allen Park, Mich., 1954-59, twp. atty., Van Buren Twp., Mich., 1959-61. Past pres. Palmer Woods Assn.; mem. pres.'s cabinet U. Detroit. Served with USNR, 1944-46. Named One of 5 Outstanding Young Men in Mich., 1959. Mem. Am., Detroit bar assns., State Bar Mich. (past chmn. negligence sect.), Assn. Def. Trial Counsel (dir. 1966-67), Am. Judicature Soc., Internat. Assn. Ins. Counsel. Roman Catholic. Club: Detroit Golf (past pres.). Home: 19386 Cumberland Way Detroit MI 48203 Office: First National Bldg Detroit MI 48226

KRUSE, NORMAN FREDRICK, mfg. co. exec.; b. Indpls., Sept. 9, 1918; s. William Peter and Agnes G. (Broms) K.; m. Mary G. Lange, Mar. 2, 1946; children—Robert, Janith. B.S. in Bus, Marquette U., 1945. With Sealed Power Corp., Muskegon, Mich., 1945—, successively cost acct., chief acct., controller, asst. sec., group v.p., sr. v.p. County commr., 1960-62. Served with USAF. Republican. Methodist. Clubs: Rotary, Elks, Masons, Shriners. Home: 1532 Ridge St Muskegon MI 49441 Office: 100 Terrace Plaza Muskegon MI 49440

KRUSE, PAUL ROBERT, retired librarian, educator; b. What Cheer, Iowa, Feb. 26, 1912; s. Carl Fred and Phoebe (Mumby) K.; m. Esther Moe, June 3, 1939 (div.); 1 son, Robert Leroy; m. Carolyn Rector, June 12, 1980. A.B., John Fletcher Coll., 1933; B.S. in L.S, U. Ill., 1940; Ph.D., U. Chgo., 1958. Librarian John Fletcher Coll., Oskaloosa, Iowa, 1932-33, Bolles Sch., Jacksonville, Fla., 1934-38; reference librarian Jacksonville Pub. Library, 1938-42; reference asst. in charge reference collections Library of Congress, Washington, 1942-45; established library for UN Conf., San Francisco, 1945; instr. Library Sch., Catholic U., Washington, 1943-48; bibliographer Ency. Brit., 1946-47; editor Who Knows and What, A.N. Marquis Co., 1949; vis. asst. prof. Library Sch., U. So. Calif., 1950, George Peabody Coll., 1950-51; reorganized library for Rollins Coll., Winter Park, Fla., 1951-52; vis. asso. prof. Library Sch., U. Ill., 1952-53; asso. prof. Library Sch., U. Denver, 1954-55; librarian Golden Gate Coll., San Francisco, 1955-63; assoc. prof. Sch. Library and Info. Scis., N. Tex. State U., Denton, 1965-77; Fulbright lectr., library advisor U. Tehran, 1962-64, U. Ceylon, 1964-65; library cons. U.S. AID, Universidad Santa Maria la Antigua, Panama, 1968. Author: The Story of The Encyclopaedia Britannica, 1763-1943; Editor: Index for Lend Lease: Weapon for Victory, 1944; compiler bibliographies for: Ten Eventful Years, Ency. Brit, 1947, Profiles of Special Libraries, 2d edit, 1981; cons.: Pergamum Press, 1978; Contbr. articles to profl. jours. Active community and profl. theatre groups. Mem. Am., Tex., Calif. library assns., Spl. Libraries Assn. (conf. chmn. 1961). Republican. Methodist. Club: Mason. Home: 318 Gault St Apt 15 Santa Cruz CA 95062

KRUSE, PAUL WALTERS, JR., physicist; b. Hibbing, Minn., Nov. 24, 1927; s. Paul Walters and Marie Rae (Gibson) K.; m. Margaret Mary Fitzpatrick, Jan. 23, 1954; children—Paul II, Robert, John, Mary, Margaret, Charles, Thomas, Catherine, William. B.S., U. Notre Dame, 1951, M.S., 1952, Ph.D., 1954. Physicist Farnsworth Electronics Co., Ft. Wayne, Ind., 1954-56; sr. research scientist Honeywell Corp. Tech. Center, Bloomington, Minn., 1956-59, prin. research scientist, 1959-60, staff scientist, 1960-69, sr. staff scientist, 1969-77, prin. staff scientist, 1977-79, prin. research fellow, 1979—; panel mem. Pres.'s Sci. Adv. Com., 1969-72; mem. Army Sci. Adv. Panel, 1965-77, Army Sci. Bd., 1978-82; com. mem. Nat. Materials Adv. Bd., NRC-Nat. Acad. Scis., 1971-72, Adv. Bd. on Mil. Personnel Supplies, 1969-71; mem. planning com. 3d Internat. Photoconductivity Conf., 1968-69; chmn. Army ERADCOM Tech. Com., 1976. Author: (with McGlauchlin and McQuistan) Elements of Infrared Technology, 1961; contbr. articles to profl. jours.; mem. editorial adv. bd.: Optics Letters, 1977-79, Infrared and Millimeter Waves, 1978—. Bd. dirs. Benilde High Sch., 1970-74. Recipient H.W. Sweatt award for outstanding sci. accomplishment, 1966, Alan Gordon Meml. award Optical Engring Soc., 1981, Outstanding Civilian Service medal Dept. of Army, 1983; selected by sec. def. for Joint Civilian Orientation Conf. 37, 1967. Fellow Am. Phys. Soc., AIAA (asso.); mem. Optical Soc. Am., Am. Def. Preparedness Assn., Assn. U.S. Army, Notre Dame Club Minn. (pres. 1974-75), Notre Dame Alumni Assn. (dir. 1979—). Patentee in field. Home: 6828 Oaklawn Ave Edina MN 55435 Office: Honeywell Corporate Tech Center 10701 Lyndale Ave S Bloomington MN 55420

KRUSE, RICHARD KARETH, JR., electronic manufacturing company executive; b. Cin., Dec. 3, 1938; s. Richard Kareth and Frances (Lee) K.; m. Polly Paulin, Feb. 14, 1964; children: Katie, John, Jennifer. B.A., Renssalaer Poly. Inst., 1960, M., 1961. Dir. mgr. engr. NCR, Dayton, 1968-70, ops. mgr. data terminal, 1970-72, gen. mgr. engring. and mfg., Cambridge, Ohio, 1972-78, dir. retail system prodn. mgmt., Dayton, 1978-80, v.p. retail systems div., 1980—. Served to 1st lt. USAF, 1961-65. Republican. Methodist. Home: 1325 Heritage Rd Centerville OH 45459 Office: NCR Corp 1700 S Patterson Blvd Dayton OH 45479

KRUSEN, EDWARD MONTGOMERY, physician, educator; b. Phila., Feb. 7, 1920; s. Edward M. and Gladys (Hopper) K.; m. Ursula Leden, Nov. 13, 1948 (dec.); children—Richard Montgomery, Nancy Elizabeth; m. Ruth Trescott, Dec. 27, 1975. B.A., U. Pa., 1941, M.D., 1944; M.S., U. Minn., 1950. Diplomate: Am. Bd. Phys. Medicine and Rehab. (mem. bd. 1964-76, mem. residency rev. com. 1977—, vice chmn. 1981). Intern Phila. Gen. Hosp., 1944-45; resident phys. medicine and rehab. Mayo Clinic, 1945-46, 48-50, 1st asst., 1949-50; dir. dept., chief service, phys. medicine and rehab. Baylor U. Med. Center, 1950—, dir., 1951-71, prof. phys. therapy, 1958-71; mem. faculty Southwestern Med. Sch., 1951—, prof. phys. medicine and rehab., 1961—, chmn. dept., 1951-55; VA area cons., 1954—; med. cons. Am. Rehab. Found., 1957—; Chmn. med. adv. bd., mem. exec. bd. United Cerebral Palsy Assn. Tex., 1973; mem. Gov.'s Commn. on Vocational Rehab., Developmental Disabilities, 1971—; mem. med. adv. bd. Arthritis and Rheumatism Assn., Hemophilia Assn., Muscular Dystrophy Assn. Contbr. numerous articles to profl. jours., also chpts. in books. Served to capt. M.C. AUS, 1946-48. Recipient Community Service award Goodwill Industries Dallas, 1955; award for service United Cerebral Palsy Assn. Tex., 1964, Muscular Dystrophy Assn., 1965, 67-73, 78. Mem. A.M.A. (adv. com. phys. therapy edn.), So. Med. Assn. (chmn. sect. phys. medicine and rehab. 1953), Tex. Med. Assn. (chmn. rehab. com. 1964-72), Dallas Med. Assn., Tex. Soc. Phys. Medicine and Rehab. (sec. 1957, chmn. 1959), Am. Rheumatism Assn., Tex. Rheumatism Assn. (bd. govs. 1964-68), Am. Congress Rehab. Medicine, Am. Acad. Phys. Medicine and Rehab., Med. Dirs. Phys. Therapy Schs. (chmn. 1960), Sigma Xi. Club: Dallas Gun. Home: 3500 Colgate Ave Dallas TX 75225

KRUSEN, HENRY STANLEY, investment banker; b. East Orange, N.J., Jan. 13, 1907; s. Henry Addis and Sallie (Scarborough) K.; m. Elizabeth Geary Hoopes, Oct. 24, 1941; 1 dau., Sallie (Mrs. Albert E. Riester). A.B., Cornell U., 1928; postgrad., Sch. Bus., N.Y. U., 1930-52. With Nat. City Co., N.Y.C., 1928-34, Harriman, Ripley & Co., Inc., 1934-42; with Shearson, Hammill & Co., Inc., 1946-70, sr. v.p., 1964-65, pres., 1966-70; also dir.; chmn. bd. Shearson, Hammill Mgmt. Co., 1972-73; cons. Shearson Hayden Stone & Co., Inc., 1974-78; dir. Russ Togs, Inc., N.Y.C., 1960-84, Wheeling Pitt. Steel Corp., Pitts., 1968-79. Founder Nat. Young Republicans, 1930; chmn. East Orange Rep. City Com., 1939-41; vice chmn. Essex County Rep. Com., 1940-41; Bd. dirs. emeritus, past v.p. Beekman Downtown Hosp., N.Y.C.; trustee emeritus, past chmn. finance com. Union Coll., Cranford, N.J.; past trustee, treas., chmn. finance com. Overlook Hosp., Summit. Served to comdr. USNR, 1943-45. Decorated Legion of Merit. Mem. Phi Kappa Psi. Clubs: Baltusrol Golf (Springfield, N.J.); Lost Tree (North Palm Beach, Fla.); Ekwanok Country (Manchester, Vt.). Home: 11382 Lost Tree Way North Palm Beach FL 33408

KRUSEN, LESLIE CONARD, lawyer; b. Phila., May 7, 1897; s. George Cornell and Lavinia (Conard) K.; m. Kathryn Malan, Jan. 27, 1923 (dec.); children: Leslie C., Gordon M.; m. Leatha Davis, Nov. 25, 1949. B.S., U. Pa., 1918, LL.B., 1922. Bar: Pa. 1922. Asso. Biddle, Paul, Dawson & Yocum, Phila., 1922-30; ptnr. Krusen, Evans & Byrne (specializing in maritime and corporate law), Phila., 1930—; counsel various s.s., oil, ins. cos. Served as ensign USN, 1917-19. Mem. ABA, Pa., Phila. bar assns., Maritime Law Assn. U.S., Lambda Chi Alpha. Clubs: Riverton Country, Riomar Country, Downtown. Home: 110 Oakford Ave Delanco NJ 08075 Office: Public Ledger Bldg Independence Sq Philadelphia PA 19106

KRUSHENICK, NICHOLAS, artist; b. N.Y.C., May 31, 1929; s. John and Anna (Wilhoey) K. Student, Art Students League, N.Y.C., 1948-50, Hoffmann Sch., N.Y.C., 1950-51. Co-founder Brata Gallery, N.Y.C.; art critic Yale U., 1969-79; vis. artist Sch. Visual Arts, N.Y.C., 1965, Mpls. Sch. Art, 1967, Cooper Union, N.Y.C., 1967-69, U. Wis., 1968, Dartmouth Coll., fall 1969, Yale U., 1969-70, Cornell U., 1970, Bell State U., 1971, Lehmann Coll., N.Y.C., 1972, Calif. State U., Long Beach, 1973, U. Ala., 1973, St. Cloud State U., 1973, U. Calif., Berkeley, 1973-74, Ohio State U., 1974, U. Wash., 1974, Calif. State Coll., San Bernardino, 1975, U. N.C., Greensboro, 1975, U. Ky., 1976, U. Del., 1976-77; asst. prof. U. Md., College Park, 1977—; vis. critic Memphis Art Acad., 1978, Corcoran Sch. Art, Washington, 1978, Va. Commonwealth U., 1982, Syracuse U., 1982. Exhibited one-man shows, Camino Gallery, N.Y.C., 1956, Brata Gallery, 1957, 60, Graham Gallery, N.Y.C., 1962, 64, Pace Gallery, N.Y.C., 1967, 69, 72, Galerie Beyeler, Basel, Switzerland, 1971, One Hundred Eighteen, An Art Gallery, Mpls., 1976, Pyramid Gallery, Washington, 1978, Hokin Gallery, Chgo., Elizabeth Weiner Gallery, N.Y.C., Met. Mus. Miami, Fla., 1979, Aldrich Mus., Ridgefield, Conn., 1981, Gallery K, Washington, Carnegie Mellon U. Mus., Pitts., Kaber Gallery, N.Y.C., 1982, River Gallery, Westport, Conn., 18th St. Gallery, Santa Monica, Calif., 1984, Reinhard Onnash Gallery, Berlin, group shows, Whitney Mus. Am. Art, N.Y.C., 1963, 65, Los Angeles County Mus., 1964, Guggenheim Mus., N.Y.C., 1966, Mus. Modern Art, N.Y.C., 1969, Museum d'Art Moderne, Paris, 1973, Tokyo Central Mus. Art, San Francisco Mus. Art, 1974, Hirshhorn Mus. Traveling Exhbn., 1976, 79, Bklyn. Mus., 1978, Met. Mus. Art, N.Y.C., Nat. Collection Fine Art, Washington, 1979, Whitney Mus., N.Y.C.; represented permanent collections, Kalamazoo Art Inst., Mus. Modern Art, Met. Mus. Art, Los Angeles Mus. Art, Folkwang Mus., Essen, W.Ger., Stedelijk Mus., Amsterdam, Albright-Knox Art Gallery, Buffalo, Norfolk Mus. Arts and Scis., Aldrich Mus. Contemporary Art, Ridgefield, Walker Art Ctr., Mpls., Whitney Mus. Am. Art, Galerie de Stadt, Stuttgart, W.Ger., Hirshhorn Collections of Smithsonian Inst., Columbia Mus. Art, S.C., Ft. Lauderdale Mus. Art, San Francisco Mus., Newberger Mus., Purchase, N.Y., Nebr. Mus., Omaha, Cleve. Mus. Art, Portland Mus. Art, Maine, Balt. Mus., Library of Congress, Oakland Mus., Calif., Nat. Collection Fine Art, Bibliotheque Nationale, Paris, Guild Hall Mus., Easthampton, N.Y. Served with AUS, 1947-48. Grantee Longview Found., 1947-48, Tamarind lithography, 1965, 76; fellow Guggenheim Found., 1967. 140 Grand St New York NY 10013

KRUSKAL, MARTIN DAVID, mathematical physicist; b. N.Y.C., Sept. 28, 1925; married, 1950; 3 children. B.S., U. Chgo., 1945; M.S., N.Y.U., 1948, Ph.D. in Math., 1952. Asst. instr. dept. math. NYU, 1946-51; research scientist Plasma Physics Lab., Princeton U., 1951—, sr. research assoc., 1959—, prof. astrophys. sci., 1961—, prof. math., 1981—; cons. Los Alamos Sci. Lab., 1953-59; cons. radiation lab. U. Calif., 1954-57; cons. Oak Ridge Nat. Lab., 1955-58, 63—, RCA, 1960-62, IBM Corp., 1963—; lectr. in field. Recipient Dannie Heineman prize in math. physics, 1983; sr fellow NSF, 1959-60. Mem. Am. Math. Soc., Math. Assn. Am., Am. Phys. Soc., Am. Acad. Arts and Scis., Nat. Acad. Scis. Office: Dept Astrophysics Princeton U Princeton NJ 08540 *

KRUSKAL, WILLIAM HENRY, statistician, educator; b. N.Y.C., Oct. 10, 1919; s. Joseph Bernard and Lillian Rose (Vorhaus) K.; m. Norma Jane Evans, Aug. 23, 1942; children: Vincent Joseph, Thomas Evan, Jonas David. S.B., Harvard U., 1940, M.S., 1941; Ph.D., Columbia U., 1955. Mathematician U.S. Naval Proving Ground, 1941-44; v.p. Kruskal and Kruskal, Inc., N.Y.C., 1946-48; mem. faculty U. Chgo., 1950—, prof. statistics, 1962—, Ernest De Witt Burton distinguished service prof., 1973—, chmn. dept., 1966-73, dean, 1974-79, 80—; vis. prof. U. Calif. at Berkeley, 1955-56, Harvard, summer 1959; fellow Center Advanced Study Behavioral Scis., 1970-71; Mem. President's Com. Fed. Statistics, 1970-71; chmn. com. nat. statistics Nat. Acad. Scis.-NRC, 1971-78; mem. adv. council NSF, 1977—; mem. adv. com. Fed. Statis. System Reorgn., 1978-79. Editor: Annals of Mathematical Statistics, 1958-61, Mathematical Sciences and Social Sciences, 1970, (with Judith M. Tanur) International Encyclopedia of Statistics, 1978; assoc. editor for statistics: Internat. Ency. Social Scis; chmn. editorial bd.: Statis. Research Monographs, 1953-58. Served with USNR, 1944-46. Recipient Samuel S. Wilks Meml. medal, 1978; Sr. postdoctoral fellow NSF, 1970-71; Guggenheim fellow, 1979-80. Fellow Inst. Math. Statistics (pres. 1970-71), Am. Statis. Assn. (v.p. 1972-74, pres. 1982, Outstanding Statistician award Chgo. chpt. 1976, adv. com. to Bur. Census 1979—), AAAS, Am. Acad. Arts and Scis.; mem. Internat. Statis. Inst., Royal Statis. Soc., Am. Math. Soc., Math. Assn. Am., Biometric Soc., Bernoulli Soc. for Math. Statistics and

Probability, Phi Beta Kappa, Sigma Xi. Home: 1227 E 54th St Chicago IL 60615

KRYNSKI, MAGNUS JAN, Slavic literatures educator, translator; b. Warsaw, Poland, May 15, 1922; came to U.S., 1948, naturalized, 1957; s. Simon and Stefania (Boraks) K.; m. Elizabeth Girardet, Apr. 12, 1952. B.A., U. Cin., 1952; M.A., Brown U., 1955, Columbia U., 1956, Ph.D., 1962. Instr. Duke U., Durham, N.C., 1959-60, prof. Slavic lits., 1966—; asst. prof. U. Pitts., 1961-63; assoc. prof. Kenyon Coll., 1964-66; vis. assoc. prof. Ohio State U., 1964-66. Translator, editor: The Survivor and Other Poems (T. Rozewicz), 1976, Building the Baricade (A. Swirszczynska), 1979, Sounds, Feelings, Thoughts (W. Szymborska), 1981. Founder, bd. dirs. N.C. Com. for Solidarity with Solidarity, Durham, 1982—; N.C. and Washington rep. Polish-Am. Socio-polit. Movement, Washington, 1983—; bd. dirs. Freedom Fedn., Washingotn, 1983—. Recipient award for poetry transl. AI (Polish Writers Assn.), 1981; fellow Ford Found., 1955-56, 57-58; Nat. Def. Fgn. Lang. fellow, 1960-61; grantee Internat. Research Exchange Bd. Eastern Europe Research Program, 1980. Mem. Polish Inst. Arts and Scis. (dir. 1978—), MLA, Am. Assn. Advancement of Slavic Studies. Republican. Office: Dept Slavic Langs and Lit Duke U Durham NC 27706 *Two historical events which occured in my boyhood proved to be a lasting influence on my entire life: the "Crystal Night" and the Moscow trials. These experiences made me a fanatical believer in Western democracy, the parliamentary system and human rights. I hav always placed the defense of Western values above individual interests. Ina world free of totalitarian threat, I would be happy to be non-political and devote myself entirely to writing and translating.*

KRYTER, KARL DAVID, research scientist; b. Indpls., Oct. 13, 1914; s. George David and Mary Matilda (Christoph) K.; m. Grace Irene Brown, June 21, 1946; children: Dianne, Victoria (Mrs. Myron I. Liebhaber), Kathryn (Mrs. Richard A. Rendon). A.B., Butler U., 1939; Ph.D., U. Rochester, 1942. Research fellow Harvard, 1942-46; asst. prof. Washington U., 1946-48; dir. human resources research labs. Air Force Cambridge Research Center, 1948-57; head dept. psychoacoustics Bolt Beranek & Newman, Inc., Cambridge, Mass., 1957-65; dir. Sensory Scis. Research Center of Stanford Research Inst., Menlo Park, Calif., 1965-76, staff scientist, 1976—; chmn. bd. dirs. Acousis Co., Los Altos, Calif.; tchr. Colby Coll., 1960-63, Mass. Inst. Tech., 1958-59; Adviser U.S. Pres.'s Office for Sci. and Tech., 1968-70; mem. SST environmental study com. Dept. Interior, 1969; past chmn. council com. hearing and bioacoustics Nat. Acad. Sci.-NRC, 1960. Author: The Effects of Noise on Man, 1970, Physiological, Psychological and Social Effects of Noise, 1983. Recipient Distinguished Service award in sci. Am. Speech and Hearing Assn., medal U. Liege, Belgium).; NIH research grantee, 1965-72; NIMH research grantee, 1970-72. Fellow Am. Psychol. Assn. (council reps. 1966-69), Soc. Engring. Psychologists (pres. 1965, Franklin V. Taylor award), Acoustical Soc. Am. (pres. 1972); mem. Brit. Acoustical Soc. Home: 21357 Heron Dr Bodega Harbour CA 94923 Office: SRI 333 Ravenswood Ave Menlo Park CA 94025

KRYZA, E. GREGORY, association executive, former ambassador, foreign service officer; b. Detroit, Mar. 12, 1922; s. Frank Theodore and Anna Frances (Chapp) K.; m. Alice Larue Henry, Apr. 15, 1983; children: Frank Theodore, Christopher Deniau. Student, Oberlin Coll., 1944-45; B.A., U. Va., 1946; grad., Air War Coll., 1968. Products expediter Bohn Aluminum, Detroit, 1940-42; civilian staff USN, Tangier, Ciudad Trujillo, 1947-50; vice consul, Curacao, 1952-54, 3d sec. Am. embassy, Brussels, Belgium, 1954-57, 2d sec., Belgrade, Yugoslavia, 1957-59; supervisory adminstrv. officer Dept. State, 1959-63; 1st sec., Nairobi, Kenya, 1963-67, consul, Seychelles, 1965-67, counselor, Kinshasa, 1968-70, Rio de Janeiro and Brasilia, Brazil, 1970-72, fgn. service insp., 1972-77; exec. dir. Bur. African Affairs, State Dept., 1974; ambassador to Islamic Republic of Mauritania, 1977-80; exec. v.p. Am. Fgn. Service Protective Assn.; cons. Morgan-Newman Assocs., Washington and Riyadh, World Access, Inc., Group Hospitilization, Inc.; chmn. New Columbia Corp., Washington; dir. State Dept. Fed. Credit Union. Contbr. articles to profl. jours. Pres. Sch. Bd. Am. Sch., Kinshasa, 1968-70. Served to lt. USNR, 1942-47, 50-52; ETO, Korea. Decorated grand officer Order of Merit, Mauritania; recipient Meritorious Service award Dept. State, 1965. Mem. Diplomatic and Counselor Officers Ret., Fgn. Service Assn., Phi Delta Theta. Clubs: Army and Navy, Grads. Office: 1750 Pennsylvania Ave Suite 1305 Washington DC 20006

KRZYS, RICHARD ANDREW, library and information science educator, administrator; b. Cleve., Apr. 30, 1934; s. Michael and Helen (Podgorski) K. B.S.S. cum laude, John Corroll U., 1956; M.A., N.Mex. State U., 1958, U. Denver, 1958; Ph.D., Case Western Res. U., 1965. Grad. asst. N.Mex. State U., 1958; teaching asst. Case Western Res. U., Cleve., 1964-65; asst. prof. Fla. State U., 1965-67; assoc. prof. L.I. U., 1967-69; asst. dir., assoc. prof. Sch. Library Service Dalhousie U., Can., 1969-71; assoc. prof. Sch. Library and Info. Sch. U. Pitts., 1971-75, prof., 1975—, dir. Internat. Library Info. Ctr., 1971—; vis. assoc. prof. Clarion State Coll., Pa., summer 1973; cons. Sociedad Tecnica Agricola Colombo-Americana, 1960, Long Branch Pub. Library Assn., N.J., 1974—, Clarion Dist. Library, 1971-74. Co-author: A History of Education for Librarianship in Colombia, 1969, World Librarianship, 1983. Tuition scholar John Carroll U., 1952-53; recipient Spanish John Carroll U., 1956; Fulbright scholar, Bogota, Columbia, 1960-61. Mem. ALA, Fla. State Assn. Home: 5619 Kentucky Ave Apt G-1 Pittsburgh PA 15232 Office: Sch Library and Info Sci U Pitts 620 LIS Bldg 135 N Bellefield Ave Pittsburgh PA 15260

KRZYWICKI, PAUL MATTHEW, tubist; b. Phila., Feb. 24, 1944; s. Paul Lucian Drzywicki and Teofila Mary (Tokarczyk) K.; m. Joan Louis Grahek, June 17, 1967; 1 dau., Jill Ann. B.M., Ind. U., 1966, Mus.M., 1967. Tubist Portland Symphony Orch., 1968-69, Cambridge Brass Quintet, (Mass.), 1968-69, Buffalo Philharmonic Orch., 1969-70, Phila Orch., 1971—; now 1st tuba Phila. Orch.; asst. prof. music Youngstown State U., 1970-71; prof. Curtis Inst. Music, 1971—, Phila. coll. Performing Arts, 1971—; prof. Temple U., 1981; mem. U.S. Mil. Acad. Band, West Point, 1967-70. Mem. Tubists Universal Brotherhood Assn. Democrat. Roman Catholic. Home: 1102qCromwell Rd Wyndmoor PA 19118 Office: Phila Orch 1420 Locust St Philadelphia PA 19102

KRZYZANOWSKI, RICHARD LUCIEN, lawyer, corporate executive; b. Warsaw, Poland, Mar. 25, 1932; came to U.S., 1967, naturalized, 1972; s. Andrew K. and Mary (Krzyzanowski); children: Suzanne, Peter. B.A., U. Warsaw, 1956; M.Law, U. Pa., 1960; Ph.D., U. Paris, 1962. Bar: Pa. With Crown Cork & Seal Co., Inc., Phila., 1967—, now dir., v.p. gen. counsel. Home: 9300 Ashton Rd Philadelphia PA 19136 Office: 9300 Ashton Rd Philadelphia PA 19136

KSIENSKI, AHARON ARTHUR, elec. engr.; b. Warsaw, Poland, June 23, 1924; came to U.S., 1951, naturalized, 1959; s. Isreal and Rebecca K.; (m), July 11, 1954; children—David, Ruth. B.E. in Mech. Engring, Inst. Mech. Engring., London, 1947; M.Sc. in Elec. Engring, U. So. Calif., 1952, Ph.D., 1958. Sr. staff engr., head antenna dept. research staff Hughes Aircraft Co., Culver City, Calif., 1958-67; prof. elec. engring., tech. dir. communication systems electrosci. lab. Ohio State U., 1967-76; prof. elec. engring., chmn. communication and propagation com. electrosci. lab., 1976—; bd. dirs. Ohio State U. Research Found., 1975-79; cons. in field. Editor trans., revs. in field. Recipient Brabazon award Inst. Electronic and Radio Engrs., London, 1967, 76. Fellow IEEE; mem. Internat. Union Radio Sci. (chmn. commns. B and C 1972-75). Home: 1780 Lynnhaven Dr Columbus OH 43221 Office: 1320 Kinnear Rd Columbus OH 43212

KU, WEI SHING, utility company planner; b. Wusih, China, July 13, 1923; came to U.S., 1947; s. Wai-Ru and Sha-Yen Kao K.; m. Katherine Ying, Feb. 6, 1955; children: Richard, Grace. B.S., Tatung U., Shanghai, China, 1944; M.S. in Engring., Cornell U., 1948. Power supply planning engr. Pub. Service Electric & Gas Co., Newark, 1964-67, advanced system planning engr., 1964-67, transmission planning engr., 1968-70, 73-79, mgr. electric system tech., 1979—. Contbr. articles to tech. jours. Recipient cert. of appreciation Electric Power Research Inst., 1982. Fellow IEEE. Office: Public Service Electric & Gas Co 80 Park Plaza Newark NJ 07101 *I believe in positive thinking. If one believes that a problem is solvable, a solution can usally bd found.*

KU, Y. H., engineering educator; b. Wusih, Kiangsu, China, Dec. 24, 1902; came to U.S., 1950; s. Ken Ming Ku and Ching-Su Wang; m. Wei-zing Wang, Apr. 1, 1929; children: Wei-Lien, Wei-Ching, Wei-Wen (Mrs. Chi-Liang Hsieh), Walter, Wei-Chung, Victor, Anna (Mrs. Yuk-Kai Lau). S.B., MIT, 1925, S.M., 1926, Sc.D., 1928; M.A., LL.D., U. Pa., 1972. Prof. elec. engring., head dept. Chekiang U., China, 1929-30; dean engring. Central U., China, 1931-32, pres., 1944-45; dean engring. Tsing Hua U., China, 1932-37; vice minister Ministry Edn., Republic of China, 1938-44; edn. commr., Shanghai, 1945-47; pres. Nat. Chengchi U., Nanking, 1947-49; vis. prof. MIT, 1950-52; prof. U. Pa., 1952-71, prof. emeritus, 1972—; hon. prof. Jiao-Tong U., Shanghai, 1979—; cons. Gen. Electric Co., Univac, RCA. Author: Analysis and Control of Nonlinear Systems, 1958, Electric Energy Conversion, 1959, Transient Circuit Analysis, 1961, Analysis and Control of Linear Systems, 1962, Collected Scientific Papers, 1971; poems, plays, novels, essays in Chinese Collected Works, 1961; Woodcutter's Song, 1963, Pine Wind, 1964, Lotus Song, 1966, Lofty Mountains, 1968, The Liang River, 1970, The Hui Spring, 1971, The Si Mountain, 1972, 500 Irregular Poems, 1972, The Great Lake, 1973, 1000 Regular Poems, 1973, 360 Recent Poems, 1976, The Tide Sound, 1980, History of Chan (Zen) Masters, 1976, History of Japanese Zen Masters, 1977, History of Zen (in English), 1979, The Long Life, 1981, One Family-Two Worlds (in English), 1982, Poems after Chin Kuan, 1983, Poems after Tao Chien, 1984. Recipient Gold medal Ministry Edn., Republic of China; Pro Mundi Beneficio Gold medal Brazilian Acad. Humanities, 1975; Gold medal Chinese Inst. Elec. Engrs., 1972. Fellow Academia Sinica, I.E.E.E. (Lamme medal 1972), Instn. Elec. Engrs. (London); mem. Am. Soc. Engring. Edn., Internat. Union Theoretical and Applied Mechanics (mem. gen. assembly), U.S. Nat. Com. on Theoretical and Applied Mechanics, Sigma Xi, Eta Kappa Nu, Phi Tau Phi. Home: 1420 Locust St Philadelphia PA 19102 Office: 200 S 33d St Philadelphia PA 19104

KUBEK, ANTHONY CHRISTOPHER, sports announcer; b. Milw., Oct. 12, 1935; s. Anthony Alfonse and Janina Frances (Oleniczak) K.; m. Margaret C. Timmel, Oct. 21, 1961; children: Anthony III, James, Anne, Margaret. Student pub. schs., Milw. Shortstop New York Yankees, 1957-65; baseball announcer NBC-TV, N.Y.C., 1966—, CBC-TV, 1977-80, CTV, 1981—. Served with U.S. Army, 1958-59, 61-62. Named Am. League Rookie of Year, 1957, to 4 Am. League All Star teams, 1 Major League All Star team. Mem. Major League Baseball Players Assn., AFTRA, Assn. Can. Television and Radio Artists. Democrat. Lutheran-Wis. Synod. Office: NBC-TV 30 Rockefeller Plaza New York NY 10020 *

KUBIAK, TERESA WOJTASZEK, soprano; b. Lodz, Poland, Dec. 26, 1937; d. Feliks and Janina (Witczak) Wojtaszek; m. Janusz Kubiak, Feb. 24, 1962; children: Malgorzata, Dorota. B.A., Sch. Music, 1960; M.A., State Coll. Music, Lodz, 1965. Appeared at, Grand Teater, Lodz, 1965, Carnegie Hall, N.Y.C., 1970, N.Y. Philharmonic Orch., 1971-72, San Francisco Opera House, Lyric Opera Chgo., 1971, Houston Grand Opera, Teatro La Fenice, Venezia, Italy, Miami Grand Opera, 1972, Royal Opera, Covent Garden, London, Ravinia Festival, Chgo.; debut as Lisa in: Queen of Spades, Met. Opera, 1971; mem. cod., Met. Opera, from 1973; star roles, Opera Co. Boston, Opera Co. Pitts., Glyndebourne Festival; also appeared in, Vienna, Austria, France, Germany, Bulgaria, Russia, Czechslovakia, Lisbon, Portugal; also with opera cos., Madrid, Barcelona, Vancouver, Ottawa and Montreal. Recipient 2d prize Mus. Competition, Finland, 1961, 3d prize Internat. Mus. Competition, Tuluz, France, 1962, 2d prize, Munich, Germany, 1965. Mem. Assn. Polish Musician Artists. Office: care Columbia Artists Management Inc 165 W 57th St New York NY 10019

KUBICEK, ROBERT VINCENT, history educator; b. Drumheller, Alta., Can., Nov. 19, 1935; s. Frederick and Roxanna (McKenzie) K.; m. Mila Gregovich, July 29, 1971; 1 son, Brett Vincent. B.Ed., U. Alta., 1956, M.A., 1958; postgrad., London Sch. Econs., 1958-59; Ph.D., Duke U., 1964. Reporter Edmonton Jour., 1956-58; tchr., 1959-60; instr. U.B.C., Vancouver, Can., 1963-64, asst. prof., 1964-69, assoc. prof., 1969-78, prof. history, 1978—, head history dept., 1979—. Author: The Administration of Imperialism: Joseph Chamberlain at the Colonial Office, 1895-1903, 1969, Economic Imperialism in Theory and Practice: The Case of South African Gold Mining Finance, 1896-1914, 1979. Grantee Social Sci. and Humanities Research Council of Can. Mem. Can. Hist. Assn., Can. Assn. African Studies, Can. Assn. Univ. Tchrs. Home: 3755 W 13th St Vancouver BC Canada V6R 2S7 Office: 2075 Westbrook St Vancouver BC Canada V6T 1W5

KUBIK, GAIL, composer, conductor, educator; b. South Coffeyville, Okla., Sept. 5, 1914; s. Henry H. and Eva O. (Thompson) K.; m. Jessie Louise Maver, Apr. 5, 1938; m. Joyce Mary Scott-Paine, Dec. 21, 1946; m. Mary Gibbs Tyler, Apr. 9, 1952; m. Joan Allred Sanders, Sept. 1, 1970 (div. Oct. 1972). Mus.B. with distinction, Eastman Sch., U. Rochester, 1934; Mus.M. cum laude, Am. Conservatory, Chgo., 1935; postgrad., Harvard U., 1937-38; studied piano under, Ida Smith; violin under, Scott Willets, Samuel Belov, Robert Reed, Alexander Baird; composition under, Edward Royce, Bernard Rogers, Leo Sowerby, Walter Piston, Nadia Boulanger; conducting under, Harold Byrns, Igor Markevitch; Mus. D. (hon.), Monmouth Coll., 1955. Tchr. Monmouth (Ill.) Coll., 1934-36, Dakota Wesleyan U., 1936-37, Columbia Tchrs. Coll., 1938-40; staff composer, music program advisor NBC, 1940-41; concert, functional-music commns., 1940-82; prof. music U. So. Calif., summer 1946; guest lectr. Accademia di Santa Cecilia, Rome, Italy, 1952, Oxford U., 1966; vis. prof. Kans. State U., 1969, Gettysburg (Pa.) Coll., 1970, Calif. State U., Fullerton, 1975-76, Mt. San Antonio Jr. Coll., 1978; prof. music, composer-in-residence Scripps Coll. and Claremont (Calif.) Grad. Sch., 1970—; lecture tours, U.S., 1968-70, Morocco, 1978. Composer music, 1930—; violin soloist, Kubik Ensemble (Evalyn, Howard, Gail, Henry K.), 1930-37, N.Y. Civic Orch., 1937, Chgo. Civic Orch., 1938, Rochester Civic Orch., 1939; dir. mus., OWI Bur. Motion Pictures, 1942-43; composer-condr. film, radio units, USAAF, 1943-46; appeared guest condr., NBC, CBS, Denver, Columbus (Ohio) symphonies, Orch. Radio Italiana, Rome, Orch. Sinfonica Siciliana, Palermo, Orchestre Radio Symphonique, Paris, London Philharm. Orch., Dublin Symphony, BBC Concert Orch.; works include Variations on a 13th Century Troubadour Song (orch.), 1935, In Praise of Johnny Appleseed (orch., chorus, soloist), rev, 1961, Stewball Variations (band), 1943, Memphis Belle: A War-time Episode (orch., narration), 1944, Litany and Prayer (men's chorus, brass, percussion), 1943-45, Folk Song Suite (orch.), 1945, A Mirror for the Sky (folk opera), 1946, Piano Sonata, 1947, Bachata: Cuban Dance Piece, 1947, Symphony in E Flat, 1947-49, Am. Profiles, Folk-Song Sketches (chorus) (commd. by Robert Shaw Chorale), 1949, Boston Baked Beans (opera piccola), 1950, Celebrations and Epilogue (piano), 1938-50, Symphony Concertante (commd. by Little Orch. Soc.), 1951, rev., 1953, Thunderbolt Overture, 1953, Symphony No. 2 in F, 1955, Symphony No. 3 (commd. by Dimitri Mitropolous and N.Y. Philharmonic Orch.), 1956, Scenario for Orchestra, 1957, Sonatinas for Piano, 1941, Violin and Piano, 1941, Clarinet and Piano, 1959, Two Divertimenti (small orch.), 1959, Scenes for Orch, 1964, A Christmas Set (chamber chorus, small orch.), 1968, Prayer and Toccata (organ, small orch.), 1969, (organ and 2 pianos), 1980, Fables in Song: Song Cycle (Theodore Roethke), 1969, A Record of Our Time (cantata for chorus, narrator and orch.), 1970, Five Theatrical Sketches (Divertimento No. 3) for violin, cello, piano, 1971, Scholastica: Five Medieval Poems (chorus), 1972, Five Birthday Pieces for Two Recorders (also for flute and clarinet), 1974, Magic, Magic, Magic: Three Incantations for Chamber Chorus and Small Orch. (Tex. Bicentennial Commn.), 1976, Symphony for Two Pianos (based on Symphony 1), 1980; film scores include The World at War, 1942, Memphis Belle, 1943 (N.Y. Film Critics award 1944), C-Man, 1949, Gerald McBoing Boing, 1950 (Academy award 1951), Two Gals and a Guy, 1951, Transatlantic, 1952: The Desperate Hours, 1955, Hiroshima, The Silent Sentinel: (TV), 1957-58, Down to Earth, 1959, Pastorale and Spring Valley Overture (for Delta Omicron), 1972, Household Magic (for U. Tex.), 1973; Recorded works, RCA Victor, Columbia, Desto, Capitol, Orion and Contemporary; lectr., contbr. to profl. publs. Recipient Golden Jubilee award (Scherzo for Large Orch.) Chgo. Symphony, 1941; 1st prize (Violin Concerto No. 2) Jascha Heifetz competition, 1941; Publ. award (Sonatina for violin, piano) Soc. Pub. Am. Music, 1943; Sinfonia Nat. Composition award for Trio for Piano, Violin and Cello, 1934; citation for documentary film score (World at War) Nat. Assn. Am. Composers and Condrs., 1943; Guggenheim fellow, 1944, 65; Prix de Rome award for Symphony in E Flat, 1950, 51; Pulitzer prize (Symphony Concertante), 1952; Am. del. Venice Film Festival Internat. Conf. Music in Films, 1959; ASCAP del. UNESCO Internat. Conf., Denver, 1959; Am. del. UNESCO, Paris, 1966, UNESCO, Budapest, 1966; fellow Villa Serbaloni Rockefeller Found., 1976; Norlin Found. fellow MacDowell Colony, 1979. Mem. ASCAP, Am. Music Center, Phi Mu Alpha Sinfonia (hon. life), Delta Omicron (hon. life). Club: Century (N.Y.C.). Home: PO Box 192 Claremont CA 91711 Office: care Music Dept Scripps Coll Claremont CA 91711

KUBLER, GEORGE ALEXANDER, art history educator; b. Los Angeles, July 26, 1912; s. Frederick William and Ellen Orloff-Beckmann K.; m. Elizabeth Bushnell, Feb. 12, 1937; children: Alexandra, Cornelia, Edward, Elena. A.B., Yale, 1934, A.M., 1936, Ph.D., 1940; Litt.D. (hon.), Tulane U., 1972; student univs., Berlin, Munich and N.Y. Mem. faculty Yale U., 1938—, prof. history of art, 1947-63, Sterling prof., 1975—; vis. prof. U. Chgo., 1946, U. San Marcos, Lima, Peru, 1948-49, U. Mexico, 1958, Harvard, 1966-67, U. Pa., 1981; chief UNESCO Mission to, Cuzco, Peru, 1951. Author: Religious Architecture of New Mexico, 1940, Mexican Architecture of the Sixteenth Century, 1948, Arquitectura Española 1600-1800, 1957, Architecture in Spain and Portugal and Their American Dominions, (with M. Soria) Art and Architecture of Ancient America, 1962, Shape of Time, 1962, the Antiquity of Painting by Felix da Costa, 1967, Studies of Classic Maya Iconography, 1969, Portuguese Plain Architecture, 1972; Editor: Art Bull. (Coll. Art Assn.), 1945-47; Contbr. articles to art publs. Guggenheim fellow, Mexico, 1943-44, Spain, 1952-53, 56-57; Recipient Alice Davis Hitchcock award, 1962, Charles Rufus Morey prize, 1963, Premio José de Figueiredo, Lisbon, 1973. Mem. Am. Acad. Arts and Scis., Acad. mexicana de Historia (corr.), Hispanic Soc. (corr. mem.), Am. Philos. Soc., Conn. Acad. Arts and Scis., Soc. des Américanistes de Paris, Real Academia de San Fernando (corr.), Academia de Belas Artes (corr.). Home: 406 Humphrey St New Haven CT 06511

KUBLER-ROSS, ELISABETH, physician; b. Zurich, Switzerland, July 8, 1926; came to U.S., 1958, naturalized, 1961; d. Ernst and Emma (Villiger) Kubler; children—Kenneth Lawrence, Barbara Lee. M.D., U. Zurich, 1957; D.Sc. (hon.), Albany (N.Y.) Med. Coll., 1974, Smith Coll., 1975, Molloy Coll., Rockville Centre, N.Y., 1976, Regis Coll., Weston, Mass., 1977, Fairleigh Dickinson U., 1979; LL.D., U. Notre Dame, 1974, Hamline U., 1975; hon. degree, Med. Coll. Pa., 1975; hon. degree, Anna Maria Coll., Paxton, Mass., 1978; Litt. D. (hon.), St. Mary's Coll., Notre Dame, Ind., 1975, Hood Coll., 1976, L.H.D., Amherst Coll., 1975, Loyola U., Chgo., 1975, Bard Coll., Annandale-on-Hudson, N.Y., 1977, Union Coll., Schenectady, 1978, D'Youville Coll., Buffalo, 1979, U. Miami, Fla., 1976; D.Pedagogy, Keuka Coll., Keuka Park, N.Y., 1976; Litt.D. (hon.), Rosary Coll., River Forest, Ill., 1976. Rotating intern Community Hosp., Glen Cove, N.Y., 1958-59; research fellow Manhattan State Hosp., 1959-62; resident Montefiore Hosp., N.Y.C., 1961-62; fellow psychiatry Psychopathic Hosp., U. Colo. Med. Sch., 1962-63; instr. psychiatry Colo. Gen. Hosp., U. Colo. Med. Sch., 1962-65; mem. staff LaRabida Children's Hosp. and Research Center, Chgo., 1965-70, chief cons. and research liaison sect., 1969-70; asst. prof. psychiatry Billings Hosp., U. Chgo., 1965-70; med. dir. Family Service and Mental Health Center S. Cook County, Chicago Heights, Ill., 1970-73; ptes. Ross Med. Assos. (S.C.), Flossmoor, Ill., 1973-77; pres., chmn. bd. Shanti Nilaya Growth and Health Center, Escondido, Calif., 1977—; mem. numerous adv., cons. bds. in field. Author: On Death and Dying, 1969, Questions and Answers on Death and Dying, 1974, Death-The Final Stages of Growth, 1975, To Live Until We Say Goodbye, 1978, Working It Through, 1981, Living With Death and Dying, 1981, Remember The Secret, 1981, also chpts. in books. Recipient Teilhard prize Teilhard Found., 1981; Golden Plate award Am. Acad. Achievement, 1980; Modern Samaritan award Elk Grove Village, Ill., 1976; named Woman of the Decade Ladies Home Jour., 1979; numerous others. Mem. AAAS, Am. Holistic Med. Assn. (a founder), Am. Med. Women's Assn., Am. Psychiat. Assn., Am. Psychosomatic Soc., Assn. Cancer Victims and Friends, Ill. Psychiat. Soc., Soc. Swiss Physicians, Soc. Psychophysiol. Research, Second Attempt at Living. Address: Shanti Nilaya PO Box 2396 Escondido CA 92025

KUBLY, HERBERT, author, educator; b. New Glarus, Wis., Apr. 26, 1915; s. Nic H. and Alda (Ott) K. B.A., U. Wis., 1937. City desk reporter Pitts. Sun-Telegraph, 1937-39, edn. editor, art critic, 1939-42; reporter, feature writer N.Y. Herald-Tribune, 1942-44; critic, editor Time mag., 1945-47; nat. sec. Dramatists Guild Am., 1947-49; assoc. prof. speech, dir. Playwright's Workshop, U. Ill., 1949-53; lectr. Columbia U., 1962-64, New Sch. Social Research, 1962-64; prof. English San Francisco State Coll., 1964-68, U. Wis.-Kenosha, 1969—; restaurant reviewer Insight Mag., Sunday Milw. Jour. Author: American in Italy, 1955, Easter in Sicily, 1956, Varieties of Love, 1958, Italy, 1961, The Whistling Zone, 1963, Switzerland, 1963, At Large, 1964, Gods and Heroes, 1969, The Duchess of Glover, 1975, Native's Return, 1981; plays Men to the Sea, 1944, Inherit the Wind, 1946, The Cocoon, 1954, Beautiful Dreamer, 1956, The Virus, 1969, Perpetual Care, 1974; Contbr. articles and stories to nat. mags. Recipient Rockefeller grant for creative writing, 1947-48; MacDowell Colony fellow, 1947-48, 56-62; Fulbright grant for study humanities in Italy, 1950-51; Nat. Book award for non-fiction, 1956; U. Wis. citation for Distinguished Service as Playwright, Author, Tchr., 1962; 1st award

Wis. Council for Writers, 1970, 76; recipient citation for disting. contbrs. to lit. Wis. State Legislature, 1982; Disting. Contbn. to Lit. award Wis. Acad. Arts, Scis. and Letters, 1982. Mem. Edward MacDowell Assn., Pi Epsilon Delta, Theta Chi. Democrat. Mem. United Church of Christ. Home: Wilhelm Tell Farm New Glarus WI 53574 Office: care William Morris Agy 1350 Ave of Americas New York NY 10019

KUBOTA, JOE, soil scientist; b. Stockton, Calif.; s. Kiichi and Yae (Ametani) K.; m. Mildred Elizabeth Phares, Feb. 18, 1950; children: Robert Joe, John Stuart, Randall Keith, Carolyn June. B.S., U. Calif., Berkeley, 1942; M.S., U. Nebr., 1944; Ph.D., U. Wis., 1948. Soil scientist U.S. Soil and Conservation Service, Cornell U., Ithaca, N.Y., 1954—, asso. prof., 1966-78; prof. U.S. Soil Conservation Service, Cornell U., 1978—. Bd. dirs. Ithaca Youth Hockey Assns., 1969-72. Served with AUS, 1944-46. Fellow AAAS, Soil Sci. Soc. Am., Am. Soc. Agronomy, Japan Soc. Promotion Sci. (sr.); mem. Soc. Environ. Geochemistry and Health (councilor 1973-76), AAAS, Internat. Soil Sci. Soc., Brit. Soil Sci. Soc., Sigma Xi. Club: Rotary. Home: 4106 Tablerock Dr Austin TX 78931 Office: US Plant Soil and Nutrition Lab Cornell U Ithaca NY 14853

KUBRICK, STANLEY, producer, director, writer; b. N.Y.C., July 26, 1928. Ed. high sch. Staff photographer Look mag. Writer, producer, dir.: documentaries, including Dr. Strangelove, 1964 (N.Y. Critic award); producer, dir.: Killer's Kiss; dir.: The Killing; writer, dir.: Paths of Glory; dir.: Spartacus, 1960, Lolita, 1962; producer, dir., writer: 2001: A Space Odyssey, 1968 (Oscar award best spl. visual effects), A Clockwork Orange, Barry Lyndon, 1975, The Shining, 1979. Address: care Louis C Blau Loeb and Loeb 10100 Santa Monica Blvd Los Angeles CA 90067 *

KUBY, STEPHEN ALLEN, biochemist; b. Jersey City, Aug. 5, 1925; s. Meyer and Bella (Chase) K.; m. Josette Marie Gerome, July 17, 1962. A.B., N.Y. U., 1948; M.S., U. Wis., 1951, Ph.D., 1953. Research asso. Inst. Enzyme Research, U. Wis., 1954-55, asst. prof. biochemistry, 1956-63; USPHS fellow Med. Nobel Inst., Stockholm, 1955-56; asso. prof. biochemistry, asso. research prof. medicine Lab. Study of Hereditary and Metabolic Disorders, U. Utah, 1963-69, prof. biochemistry, research prof. medicine, 1969—; Mem. physiol. chemistry study sect. Research Grants div. NIH, 1968-72. Contbr. articles to profl. jours. Served with AUS, 1943-46. USPHS fellow Johnson Found. Med. Phys., U. Pa., 1953-54. Mem. Am. Soc. Biol. Chemists, Am. Chem. Soc., AAAS, N.Y. Acad. Sci., Sigma Xi, Phi Beta Kappa, Phi Lambda Upsilon. Office: University of Utah Research Park Salt Lake City UT 84108

KUBZANSKY, PHILIP EUGENE, environmental psychologist; b. Bklyn., Aug. 11, 1928; s. Joseph and Libby (Kolko) K.; m. Judith Linda Sagarin, Apr. 15, 1962; children: Jessica Rose, Michael Samuel, Laura Diane. B.S. in Social Sci, CCNY, 1950; Ph.D., Duke U., 1954. Postdoctoral fellow community mental health Mass. Gen. Hosp., 1956-57; chief psychologist Boston City Hosp., 1957-60; research asso. Harvard Med. Sch., 1957-74, lectr., 1974-79; mem. faculty Boston U., 1960—, prof. psychology, 1967—, dean Grad. Sch. Arts and Scis., 1966-75; vis. scholar Sch. Architecture, MIT, 1974, 81, Sch. Environ. Studies Univ. Coll., London, 1975; Cons. VA, Naval Med. Research Inst., Judge Baker Guidance Center, City of Boston Parks and Recreation Dept., Polaroid Corp., Digital Equipment Corp., Raytheon Corp.; mem. alcoholism and alcohol problems rev. group NIMH, 1967-71, chmn., 1970-71; mem. exec. com. Council Grad. Schs. in U.S., 1971-74; mem. steering com. for study quality in grad. edn. Council Grad. Schs.-Ednl. Testing Service, 1974-76; mem. tng. rev. com. Nat. Inst. for Alcohol Abuse and Alcoholism, 1976-80. Contbr. articles to sci. jours. Served with AUS, 1954-56. Mem. Am. Psychol. Assn., AAAS, Environ. Design Research Assn., Sigma Xi. Home: 41 Nobscot Rd Newton Centre MA 02159 Office: Psychology Dept 64 Cummington St Boston U Boston MA 02215

KUCERA, ANTHONY LEE, trade association executive; b. Pipestone, Minn., Nov. 7, 1941; s. John Gerald and Alice Dorothy (Koch) K.; m. Sheila Mary Clarke, Dec. 21, 1962; children: Isla Dorothy, Colin James. B.A., Huron (S.D.) Coll., 1967. With Water Resources Congress, 1967-74, sr. v.p., Washington, 1972-74; exec. v.p. Am. Waterways Operators, Inc., Arlington, Va., 1974-78, pres., 1979-83, Sporting Goods Mfrs. Assn., North Palm Beach, Fla., 1983—; cons. in field. Served with U.S. Army, 1960-64. Mem. Washington Soc. Assn. Execs., Am. Soc. Assn. Execs. Office: 340 Wilma Circle Riviera Beach FL 33404 *The field of trade association work is particularly well suited to those with a strong command of the written and spoken word. Coupled with a strong communications skills, it is essential to have an intimate knowledge of the principles, philosophy, and guidelines which govern the organization. It is from this information that priorities are established, direction is determined, a sense of mission is framed, and ultimately a program of work is developed.*

KUCERA, CLAIR LEONARD, biological sciences educator, ecologist; b. Belle Plain, Iowa, Apr. 30, 1922; s. Charles J. K. and Emma Krafka; m. Elizabeth Arlene Tremmel, July 18, 1946; children: Ron, Kim, Carol, Gary. B.S., Iowa State U., Ames, 1947, M.S., 1948, Ph.D., 1950. Asst. prof. biol. sci. U. Mo.-Columbia, 1950-54, assoc. prof., 1954-60, prof., 1960—, dir. Prairie Research Sta., 1958-78; mem. Tropical Seminar NSF, Costa Rica, 1963, East European Exchange Nat. Research Council, Czechoslovakia, 1978. Author: Grasses of Missouri, Ecology text The Challenge of Ecology, 1973, (2d edit.) Ecology text The Challenge of Ecology, 1978. Served to 1st lt. U.S. Army, 1942-46; ETO. Mem. Botanical Soc. Am. (chmn. central states sect. 1960-61). Home: 500 Rockhill Rd Columbia MO 65201 Office: U Mo 217 Tucker Hall Columbia MO 65211

KUCERA, DANIEL WILLIAM, college president, bishop; b. Chgo., May 7, 1923; s. Joseph F. and Lillian C. (Petrzelka) K. B.A., St. Procopius Coll., 1945; M.A., Catholic U. Am., 1950, Ph.D., 1954. Joined Order of St. Benedict, 1944; ordained priest Roman Cath. Ch., 1949; registrar St. Procopius Coll. and Acad., Lisle, Ill., 1945-49, St. Procopius Coll., Lisle, 1954-56, acad. dean, head dept. edn., 1956-59, pres., 1959-65; abbot St. Procopius Abbey, Lisle, 1964-71; pres. Ill. Benedictine Coll. (formerly St. Procopius Coll.), Lisle, 1971-76, chmn. bd. trustees, 1976-78; aux. bishop of, Joliet, 1977-80, bishop of, Salina, Kans., 1980—; Chaplain Czech Cath. Union; trustee Cath. U. Am.; bd. dirs. Kans. Cath. Conf.; weekend asst. St. Louise de Marillac Parish, 1955-64. Contbr. articles to religious publs. Club: K.C. (4 deg.). Address: PO Box 999 Salina KS 67402

KUCERA, HENRY, linguistics educator; b. Trebarov, Czechoslovakia, Feb. 15, 1925; came to U.S., 1949, naturalized, 1953; s. Jindrich and Marie (Kral) K.; m. Jacqueline M. Fortin, Oct. 6, 1951; children: Thomas Henry, Edward James. M.A., Charles U., Prague, Czechoslovakia, 1947; Ph.D., Harvard U., 1952; M.A. ad eundem, Brown U., 1958; D.Sc. (hon.), Bucknell U., 1984. Asst. prof. fgn. langs. U. Fla., 1952-55; mem. faculty Brown U., 1955—, prof. Slavic langs. and linguistics, 1963—, prof. cognitive sci., 1981—, Fred M. Seed prof. linguistics and cognitive scis., 1982—, chmn. dept. Slavic langs., 1965-68, head resident fellow Ctr. for Neural Sci., 1956-66, mem. Center for Cognitive Sci., 1977—, mem. exec. com. Center for Cognitive Sci., 1980—, mem. Center for Neural Studies, 1973—, exec. com. Center for Neural Studies, 1977—, dir. Center for Cognitive and Neural Research, 1981—; fellow Russian Research Center, Harvard U., 1952, 79-85, research assoc. Slavic dept., 1977-79; research assoc. MIT, 1960-63; vis. prof. U. Mich., 1967, U. Calif. at Berkeley, 1969; vis. scholar U. Vienna, 1968-69; dir. Fed. Home Loan Bank Boston, 1981—. Author: The Phonology of Czech, 1961, (with W.N. Francis) Computational Analysis of Present-Day American English, 1967, (with G. Monroe) A Comparative Quantitative Phonology of Russian, Czech and German, 1968, Computers in Linguistics and in Literary Studies, 1975, (with K. Trnka) Time in Language, 1975, (with W.N. Francis) Frequency Analysis of English Usage, 1982; also linguistic and lit. articles.; Editor: American Contributions to the Sixth International Congress of Slavists, 1968. Bd. dirs. Internat. Inst. Providence, 1960-67; bd. adminstrn. Howard Found., 1977—. Ford fellow, 1954-55; Howard Found. fellow, 1960-61; Guggenheim fellow, 1960-61; sr. fellow Nat. Endowment for Humanities, 1968-69; Am. Council Learned Socs. fellow, 1969-70. Mem. Linguistic Soc. Am., MLA, Assn. Computational Linguistics, Cognitive Sci. Soc., Czechoslovak Soc. Arts & Scis. in Am. (v.p. 1980-82), Am. Assn. Tchrs. Slavic and Eastern European Langs, Phi Beta Kappa (hon.). Home: 196 Bowen St Providence RI 02906

KUCHARSKI, ROBERT JOSEPH, utility executive; b. Milw., Nov. 5, 1932; s. Casimir and Angeline K.; m. Caroline L. Garlock, May 5, 1962; children: Kathryn Mary, Michael Robert, David John, Mark Joseph. B.B.A., U. Wis., Milw., 1959. C.P.A. Acct., Price Waterhouse & Co., Milw., 1959-72; fin. v.p. A.L. Grottemath & Sons, Inc., Milw., 1972-74; treas., controller Iowa Elec. Light & Power Co., Cedar Rapids, 1974—; treas., dir. Cedar Rapids & Iowa City Ry. Chmn. bd. Cedar Rapids Jr. Achievement; chmn. fin. com. All Saints Parish; bd. dirs. United Way E. Central Iowa. Served with U.S. Army, 1953-55. Mem. Am. Inst. C.P.A.s, Iowa Soc. C.P.A.s, Nat. Assn. Accts., Edison Elec. Inst., Mo. Valley Elec. Assn. Roman Catholic. Home: 3221 Parkview Ct SE Cedar Rapids IA 52403 Office: 200 1st St SE Cedar Rapids IA 52401

KUCHEL, THOMAS HENRY, lawyer; b. Anaheim, Calif., Aug. 15, 1910; s. Henry and Lutetia (Bailey) K.; m. Betty Mellenthin, June 2, 1942; 1 dau., Karen C. Bianchi. A.B. cum laude, U. So. Calif., 1932, J.D., 1935, also LL.B. Bar: Calif. 1935, D.C. 1968. Practiced in, Anaheim, 1935-46; mem. Calif. State Assembly, 1937-40, Senate, 1940-46; controller State of Calif., 1946-53; U.S. senator from Calif., 1953-69; asst. Republican leader U.S. Senate, 1959-69; mem. appropriations, interior and insular affairs coms.; partner firm Wyman, Bautzer, Rothman, Kuchel & Silbert, Los Angeles and Washington, 1969—. Del. Conf. of 9th Jud. Circuit, 1973, 74, 75, 76, 77; U.S. rep. 29th session UN Gen. Assembly.; Bd. dirs. John F. Kennedy Center for Performing Arts; bd. councilors U. So. Calif.; bd. govs. Town Hall Calif. Served to lt. USNR, 1942-45. Mem. U. So. Calif. Gen. Alumni Assn. (gov.), Am. Legion, Phi Delta Phi, Phi Kappa Psi, Phi Kappa Phi. Republican. Episcopalian. Clubs: Mason (33 deg.), Elk. Clubs (Washington); Birnam Wood Golf (Santa Barbara, Calif.); Los Angeles Country, Chancery. Office: Two Century Plaza 14th Floor Los Angeles CA 90067 also 500 Newport Center Dr Newport Beach CA 92660 also 600 New Hampshire Ave NW Washington DC 20037

KUCHTA, RONALD ANDREW, art museum director, educator; b. Lackawanna, N.Y., June 23, 1935; s. Andrew and Clara May (Barnes) K.; m. Sique Stoll, Oct. 1, 1970 (div. 1974). B.A., Kenyon Coll., 1957; M.A., Western Res. U., 1961; postgrad. in mgmt., Cornell U., 1979. Curator Chrysler Mus., Provincetown, Mass., 1961-67, Santa Barbara Mus. Art, (Calif.), 1967-74; dir. Everson Mus. Art, Syracuse, N.Y., 1974—; adj. prof. Syracuse U., 1974—; trustee Idea, Inc., Syracuse, 1974—, Fondo del Sol, Washington, 1974—. Author: Provincetown Painters, 1975, Interior Vision, 1971, Batuz: Works in Paper, 1981; editor: A Century of Ceramics in the U.S., 1979. Mem. spl. com. on culture industry N.Y. State Senate; mem. Mayor's Adv. Bd. Urban Cultural Parks Downtown Com. of Syracuse. Served with U.S. Army, 1958-60. Mem. Am. Assn. Museums; mem. Mayor's Adv. Bd. Urban Cultural Parks Downtown Com. of Syracuse. Democrat. Episcopalian. Lodge: Rotary. Home: 109 Euclid Terr Syracuse NY 13210 Office: Everson Museum of Art 401 Harrison St Syracuse NY 13202

KUCZYNSKI, PEDRO-PABLO, investment banker; b. Lima, Peru, Oct. 3, 1938; s. Maxime and Madeleine Louise (Godard) K.; m. Jane Casey, June 29, 1962; children: Carolina, Alexandra, John-Michael. B.A. (Coll. scholar), Exeter Coll., Oxford (Eng.) U., 1959; M.P.A. (John Parker Compton fellow), Princeton U., 1961. Economist World Bank, 1961-67, sr. economist, 1971-73; dep. dir.-gen. Central Res. Bank Peru, 1967-69; sr. economist Internat. Monetary Fund, Washington, 1969-71; v.p., partner Kuhn, Loeb & Co. Internat., N.Y.C., 1973-75; dir. dept. econs. Internat. Finance Corp., Washington, 1975-77; pres., chief exec. officer Halco Mining Inc., Pitts., 1977-80; minister of energy and mines, Peru, 1980-82; co-chmn. First Boston Internat. Co., N.Y.C., 1982—; mng. dir. First Boston Corp., N.Y.C., 1982—; research asso. U. Pitts. Author: Peruvian Democracy under Economic Stress: an Account of the Belaunde Administration, 1963-68, 1977. Mem. Am. Econ. Assn. Clubs: Univ. (Washington); Pitts. Athletic, Pitts. Golf, Princeton of N.Y.C., Chevy Chase. Home: 3731 48th St NW Washington DC 20016 Office: First Boston Corp Park Ave Plaza 55 East 52d New York NY 10055

KUDELKA, JAMES, ballet dancer, choreographer; b. Newmarket, Ont., Canada. Student, Nat. Ballet Sch., Toronto. With Nat. Ballet of Can., Toronto, 1972-81, dancer, 1972-81, choreographer, 1980-81; joined Les Grands Ballets Canadiens, Montreal, 1981—, prin. dancer, 1981. Choreographer: Genesis, In Paradisum, A Party, Nat. Ballet of Can., Washington Square, Nat. Ballet of Can., The Rape of Lucrece, Nat. Ballet of Can., Playhouse, Nat. Ballet of Can., All Night Wonder, Nat. Ballet of Can. Office: Les Grands Ballets Canadiens 4869 rue St Denis Montreal PQ Canada H2J 2L7 *

KUDLOW, LAWRENCE ALAN, economist; b. N.Y.C., Aug. 20, 1947; s. Irving H. and Ruth (Grodnick) K.; m. Susan Cullman, Mar. 22, 1981; 1 dau., Carolyn. B.A. in History, U. Rochester, 1969; postgrad., Woodrow Wilson Sch., Princeton U., 1971-73. Staff economist Fed. Res. BanK N.Y., N.Y.C., 1973-75; corp. v.p., chief economist Paine Webber, Jackson & Curtis, N.Y.C., 1975-79; chief economist Bear Stearns & Co., N.Y.C., 1979-81; asst. dir. econ. policy Office of Mgmt. and Budget, Exec. Office of Pres., Washington, 1981-82, assoc. dir. econs. and planning, 1982-83; prin. Lawrence Kudlow & Assocs., Washington, 1983—. Republican. Home: 2830 Foxhall Rd NW Washington DC 20006 Office: 600 New Hampshire Ave NW Suite 715 Washington DC 20037

KUDRYK, OLEG, librarian; b. Rohatyn, Ukraine, Dec. 14, 1912; came to U.S., 1949, naturalized, 1954; s. Theodosius and Olga (Spolitakevich) K.; m. Sophie H. Dydynski, Feb. 5, 1944. Diploma, Conservatory Music, Lviv, 1934; LL.M., U. Lviv, 1937, M.A. in Econ. Sci., 1938; postgrad., U. Vienna, 1945-46; M.A. in L.S., U. Mich., 1960; Ph.D. in Polit. Sci., Ukranian Free U., Munich, 1975. Mgr., legal advisor Coop. Agrl. Soc., Chodoriv, Ukraine, 1938-39; mgr. Import-Export Corp., Cracow, Poland, 1940-44; tchr. Comml. Sch., Ulm, Germany, 1946; adminstr. UNRRA and Internat. Refugee Orgn., Stuttgart, Germany, 1947-49; asst. treas., mgr. Self-Reliance Fed. Credit Union, Detroit, 1953-60; rep., cons. Prudential Ins. Co., Detroit, 1955-60; catalog librarian Ind. U., Bloomington, 1960-63, head order librarian, 1963-70, head acquisitions librarian, 1971-82, spl. projects librarian, asst. to assoc. dean, 1982—; lectr. Ukranian Free U., 1975—; guest lectr. Ind. U. Sch. Library and Info. Sci., 1965—. Contbr. articles to profl. jours. Grantee Ind. U. Office Research and Advanced Studies Internat. Programs, 1972. Mem. Ukranian Library Assn. Am. (v.p. 1972-75, exec. bd. 1975—), AAUP (chpt. treas., exec. bd. 1976—), ALA, Assn. Coll. Research Libraries, Am. Econ. Assn., Am. Acad. Polit. and Social Scis., Shevchenko Sci. Soc. Home: 409 Clover Ln Bloomington IN 47401 Office: Ind U Library Bloomington IN 47405

KUECHLER, HENRY NORBURY, JR., mining company executive; b. San Rafael, Cal., Mar. 31, 1911; s. Henry Norbury and Mary Fiffe (Foster) K.; m. Mary Elizabeth Stewart, Sept. 18, 1933 (dec. June 1980); children: Sue Stewart Kuechler Harris, Sally Foster Kuechler Debenham, Henry Norbury, Nancy Kuechler Enright.; m. Kathleen Lake Scribner, Dec. 10, 1981. A.B. in Polit. Sci, Stanford, 1933. With Knob Hill Mines, Inc., San Francisco, 1936—, sec.-treas., 1936-51, pres., 1951-81, chmn. bd., chief fin. officer, 1981—, also dir.; chmn. bd., chief exec. officer Reclaimed Island Lands Co., Menlo Park, Atherton, Calif., until 1963. Served to lt. comdr. USNR, World War II. Mem. Zeta Psi. Club: Pacific Union (San Francisco). Home: 85 Isabella Ave Atherton CA 94025 Office: 1143 Crane St Menlo Park CA 94025

KUEHL, HAL C., banker; b. Davenport, Iowa, Mar. 21, 1923; s. Donald J. and Martha A. (Sierk) K.; m. Joyce M. Helms, May 20, 1950; children: Cynthia Ann, David Charles. B.B.A., U. Wis., 1947, M.B.A., 1954; postgrad., Grad. Sch. Banking, 1953. C.P.A., Wis. With First Wis. Nat. Bank, Milw., 1947—, v.p., 1960-65, exec. v.p. operations, 1965-66, exec. v.p., 1966-69, pres., 1969-76, dep. chmn., 1976-77, chmn. bd., chief exec. officer, 1977—; also dir.; exec. v.p., dir. First Wis. Bankshares Corp., 1971-77, pres., chief adminstrv. officer, 1977-78, pres., chief exec. officer, 1978—; also dir.; former pres., dir. 1st Wis. Internat. Bank, now chmn. bd.; chmn., trustee First Wis. Mortgage Co.; dir. First Wis. Trust Co., others. Mem. Wis. Gov.'s Council on Econ. Devel.; Bd. dirs., mem. finance com. Milw. Blood Center; mem. exec. bd. Milw. County council Boy Scouts Am.; bd. dirs., treas. Milw. Voluntary Equal Employment Opportunity Council, Greater Milw. Com.; bd. dirs., mem. exec. com. Milw. div. Am. Cancer Soc.; trustee Citizens Govtl. Research Bur.; bd. dirs. Wis. Taxpayers Alliance, Friends of Art, United Community Services Greater Milw.; mem. corp. Columbia Hosp.; trustee Greater Wis. Found. Inc., Milw. Art Center; trustee, mem. finance com., exec. com. Marquette U. Served with USNR, 1943-45. Mem. Am. Bankers Assn., Assn. Res. City Bankers, Am. Inst. Banking, Met. Milw. Assn. Commerce, Navy League U.S., Sigma Chi. Episcopalian. Clubs: Milwaukee, Milwaukee Country, University (Milw.). Office: 773 E Wisconsin Ave Milwaukee WI 53202

KUEHN, ALVIN LLOYD, banker; b. Brookville, Ind., Nov. 25, 1920; s. William Herman and Matilda Wilhelmine (Suhre) K.; m. Virginia Applegeet, May 12, 1946; 1 dau., Jennifer Jane. B.S., Ind. U., 1951; postgrad., U. Wis., 1955-57. Sr. v.p. Irwin Union Bank & Trust Co., Columbus, Ind., 1951-72; exec. v.p. Am. Fletcher Nat. Bank, Indpls., 1972—. Trustee Ind. State Tchrs. Retirement Fund, 1969-73, pres., 1972-73; chmn. bd. trustees Methodist Hosp. Ind., 1979-82. Served with Armed Forces, 1942-48; PTO. Mem. Soc. Fin. Analysts, Beta Gamma Sigma. Republican. Methodist. Club: Meridian Hills Country (Indlps.). Office: 111 Monument Circle Indianapolis IN 46277 *

KUEHN, EDMUND KARL, artist; b. Columbus, Ohio, Aug. 18, 1916; s. Herman and Julianna (Bojanowski) K.; m. Lieselotte Koss, Apr. 19, 1953. Grad., Columbus Art Sch., 1938; student, Art Students League, N.Y.C., 1938-39. Asst. to dir. Columbus Gallery Fine Arts, 1939-43, curator, 1954-61, asst. dir., 1962-68, curator collections, 1969-76; one-man exhbn. Battelle Meml. Inst. Columbus, 1981, Keny and Johnson Gallery, Columbus, 1982, 83; Represented in permanent collection Columbus Mus. Art; Represented in permanent collections Capital U., Columbus; asst. prof. Ohio State U., 1946-48; assoc. prof. Columbus Coll. Art and Design, 1948-53; Mem. Capitol Sq. Commn., 1976—; adv. council Cultural Arts Center, 1978—. Served with USAAF, 1943-46. Mem. Columbus Art League, Am. Assn. Museums. Home and studio: 828 City Park Ave Columbus OH 43206 *I paint despite the face of rationality and defend myself by trying to do something very worthwhile. The challenge is always there like an unembellished space. Some theory may start me, but I need revelation to continue my work. The thing must spring to life. I have to bring definition and control to a fragment of infinite possibility. Irony is the ultimate reality resulting from the confrontation between idealism and concrete fact.*

KUEHN, JAMES MARSHALL, newspaper editor; b. Mobridge, S.D., May 23, 1926; s. Christ A. and Selma (Brandon) K.; m. Phyllis Yvonne Larson, Apr. 3, 1950; children—Douglas James, Deborah Kay, Diana Lisa. B.A., U.S.D., 1949. State editor Rapid City (S.D.) Jour., 1949-54, wire editor, 1954-58, mng. editor, 1958-66, exec. editor, 1966-73, v.p.-editor, 1973—. Vice pres. Rapid City Library Bd., 1969-73; mem. dist. council Boy Scouts Am., 1965-69. Served with C.E. AUS, 1945-46. Mem. Rapid City C. of C. (v.p. 1970-73), S.D. C. of C. (dir. 1978-81), Lambda Chi Alpha. Republican. Lutheran. Club: Kiwanian (pres. 1973-74). Home: 2017 Selkirk Pl Rapid City SD 57702 Office: Box 450 Rapid City SD 57709

KUEHN, RONALD L., JR., natural resources company executive; b. Bklyn., Apr. 6, 1935; m. Kathleen Moriarty, Feb. 15, 1958; children: Kathleen, Kelly, Erin, Coleen, Shannon. B.S., Fordham U., 1957, LL.B., 1964. Bar: N.Y. 1964. Assoc. firm. Hughts, Hubbard & Reed, N.Y.C., 1964-68; exec. v.p., gen. counsel Allied Artists Pictures, N.Y.C., 1968-70; v.p., gen. counsel, sec. So. Natural Resources, Inc., Birmingham, Ala., 1970—; dir. Offshore Co. SONAT Exploration Co. 1st lt. U.S. Army, 1958-59. Mem. Am. Soc. Corp. Secs., ABA. Roman Catholic. Office: Sonat Inc PO Box 2563 Birmingham AL 35202

KUEHNE, MARTIN ERIC, educator; b. Floral Park, N.Y., May 29, 1931; s. Martin Ludwig and Ruth (Protze) K.; m. Hannelore E. Naumann, Aug. 15, 1953; 1 son, Stephen Eric. B.A., Columbia, 1951, Ph.D., 1955; M.A., Harvard, 1952. Sr. chemist Ciba Pharm. Co., Summit, N.J., 1955-61; mem. faculty U. Vt., Burlington, 1961—, asso. prof. chemistry, 1965-67, prof., 1967—, chmn. dept. chemistry, 1976-78. Boese fellow, 1954; Alfred P. Sloan Found. fellow, 1965-69. Mem. Am. Chem. Soc., Sigma Xi, Phi Lambda Upsilon. Research in new synthetic organic reactions; total syntheses of natural products; structure determinations of natural products; medicinal chems. Home: 169 S Cove Rd Burlington VT 05401

KUEKES, EDWARD DANIEL, cartoonist; b. Pitts., Feb. 2, 1901; s. Otto and Elizabeth (Lapp) K.; m. Clara Gray, Apr. 23, 1922; children—Edward Grayson, George Clive. Student, Baldwin-Wallace Coll., L.H.D. (hon.), 1957, Cleve. Inst. Art, Chgo. Acad. Fine Art. Artist, cartoonist Cleve. Plain Dealer, 1922-49, chief editorial cartoonist, 1949-66, cartoonist emeritus, 1966—; cartoonist Metro Newspapers, Inc., Cleve., 1968—. Creator of: The Kernel; collaborated with Olive Ray Scott in: prodn. cartoon features Knurl the Gnome, United Features Syndicate.; Author: five thousand original cartoons in collection at Funny Fables, Syracuse U., four hundred and fifty original cartoons in collection at, Baldwin-Wallace Coll., Berea, Ohio. Mem. Pres. Eisenhower's People to People Com. Recipient Newspaper Guild award, 1947, cert. of honor Nat. Safety

Council, 1949, C.I.T. Found. award, 1949, DAV award, 1949, 1st prize Freedoms Found., 1949, 58, 2d prize, 1950, Disting. Service award, 1951, 59-61, 63, 66, 67, Disting. Service scrolls, 1952-57, Pulitzer prize for cartoons, 1953, Alumni merit award Baldwin-Wallace Coll., 1953, Silver T Square Nat. Cartoonists Soc., 1953, Gov.'s award, 1953, Presdl. Prayer citation U.S. Treasury Dept., 1954, Meritorious award Cleve. Dental Soc., 1954, Christopher award, 1955, cert. recognition NCCJ, 1955, Pres. Eisenhower's People to People Program cartoon div. award, 1956, George M. Humphrey U.S. Treasury citation, 1957, hon. mention Guild Award, 1957, 1st prize Guild Award, 1958, 1st prize Polit. Cartoon award Wayne State U., 1960, U.S. Treasury award, 1962, 64, Freedoms Found. award, 1963-69; named to Ohio State Sr. Citizens Hall of Fame. Mem. Assn. Am. Editorial Cartoonists, Cleve. C. of C., Newcomen Soc. Eng., Baldwin-Wallace Coll. Alumni Assn. (pres.), Am. Airlines Flagship Fleet (adm.), Nat. Cartoonists Soc., Lambda Chi Alpha, Sigma Delta Chi (Disting. Service award 1975). Methodist. Clubs: Kiwanis (pres. Berea), Masons (50 year pin); Mid Day, Cleve. Farmers (Cleve.). Address: 1280 Medfield Dr Rocky River OH 44116

KUENNE, ROBERT EUGENE, economics educator; b. St. Louis, Jan. 29, 1924; s. Edward Sebastian and Margaret (Yochum) K.; m. Janet Lawrence Brown, Sept. 7, 1957; children: Christopher Brian, Carolyn Leigh. Student, Harris Jr. Coll., St. Louis, 1941-42; B.J., U. Mo., 1947; A.B., Washington U., St. Louis, 1948, A.M., 1949; A.M., Harvard, 1951, Ph.D., 1953. Asst. prof. econs. U. Va., 1955; mem. faculty Princeton, 1956—, asso prof., 1960-69, prof. econs., 1969—; cons. U.S. Naval War Coll., 1954, 55, Inst. Def. Analyses, Arlington, Va., 1968—, Inst. for Energy Analysis, Washington, 1978—; vis. prof. mil. systems analysis U.S. Army War Coll., 1967—; mem. sci. and mgmt. adv. com. U.S. Army Computer Systems Command. Author: The Theory of General Economic Equilibrium, 1963, The Attack Submarine: A Study in Strategy, 1965, The Polaris Missile Strike: A General Economic Systems Analysis, 1966, Monopolistic Competition Theory: Studies in Impact, 1967, Microeconomic Theory of the Market Mechanism, 1968, Eugen von Böhm-Bawerk, 1971. Served with AUS, 1943-46. Named Oliver Ellsworth Bicentennial preceptor, 1957-60. Clubs: Princeton (N.Y.C.); Harvard (Phila.). Home: 63 Bainbridge St Princeton NJ 08540

KUENZLER, EDWARD JULIAN, environmental biologist; b. West Palm Beach, Fla., Nov. 11, 1929; s. Edward and Flora Caroline (Jeske) K.; m. Jutta Gertraud Koslowski, Sept. 4, 1965; children—Doreen Friederika, Dirk Edward. B.S., U. Fla., 1951; M.S., U. Ga., 1954, Ph.D., 1959. Asso. scientist Woods Hole (Mass.) Oceanographic Inst., 1959-65; asso. prof. environ. scis. and engring. U. N.C., Chapel Hill, 1965-71, prof. environ. biology, 1972—, program dir. environ. chemistry and biology, 1980—, chmn. curriculum in marine scis., 1968-71, 72-73; program dir. for biol. oceanography NSF, 1971-72; mem. panel Nat. Acad. Scis., 1974-75; mem. N.C. Gov.'s Tech. Coordinating Com., 1968-70, N.C. Comml. and Sports Fisheries Adv. Com., 1975-77; cons. and mem. adv. panels in field. Served to capt. USAF, 1954-57. AEC grantee, 1962-70; NOAA Office Sea Grants grantee, 1971-76; Office Water Research and Tech. grantee, 1970-81. Mem. Ecol. Soc. Am., Phycol. Soc. Am., Am. Soc. Limnology and Oceanography, Estuarine Research Fedn., N.C. Acad. Sci. (treas. 1982—), Elisha Mitchell Sci. Soc. (pres. 1979-81). Republican. Methodist. Research, publs. in field, especially elemental cycling in aquatic ecosystems. Home: Route 1 Box 244 Chapel Hill NC 27514 Office: Dept Environ Scis and Engring U NC Chapel Hill NC 27514

KUERTI, ANTON EMIL, pianist, composer; b. Vienna, 1938; s. Gustav and Rosi (Jahoda) K.; m. Kristine Bogyo, Sept. 13, 1973; children: Julian, Rafael. B.M., Cleve. Inst. Music; diploma, Curtis Inst., 1959. Artist in residence U. Toronto. Soloist, N.Y. Philharmonic, Cleve. Orch., Detroit Orch., Phila. Orch., Buffalo Orch., San Francisco Symphony, Denver Orch.; over 25 appearances with, Toronto Symphony and Ottawa Nat. Arts Ctr. Orch. (Ont.); tours world wide, including, Soviet Union, Far East, Australia, Latin Am.; numerous TV appearances; radio broadcasts; recs. include complete cycle: Beethoven Sonatas and Concerti; Music dir., founder, Festival of Sound, Parry Sound, Ont.; Composer: Linden Suite for piano, 1970, String Quartet, 1972, Violin Sonata and Symphony "Epomeo", 1975. Recipient Leventritt award, 1957; Juno award. Mem. War Resisters League, Amnesty Internat., Can. Scientists and Scholars. Address: 20 Linden St Toronto ON Canada M4Y 1V6 *In the arts, success can mean fame and money; or it can mean the satisfaction of having extracted the noblest, most profound expression the individual is capable of. The more one pursues the fame and money, the more elusive the inner satisfaction is likely to be. If I have had some success, it is because of my deep belief in music, one of man's supreme achievements, and perhaps his purest. It is capable of transforming and fulfilling the listener, and helping him become a new, better person. Even stronger is its effect on the performer. Only one thing matters more to me: the pursuit of peace and the preservation of this deeply endangered planet.*

KUETHE, JAMES L., insurance executive; b. Cin., Oct. 4, 1917; s. Leo H. and Stella E. (Scharf) K.; m. Ruth M. Georgi, Aug. 19, 1939; children: James, Thomas, Barbara, Debbie, Mary, Vicki. Ed., Mt. St. Gregory Sem. With Western-So. Life Ins. Co., Cin., 1947—, now exec. v.p. Mem. Nat. Assn. Life Underwriters. Republican. Roman Catholic. Office: Western & So Life Ins Co 400 Broadway Cincinnati OH 45202 *

KUETHER, RONALD CLARENCE, utility company executive; b. Sheboygan, Wis., June 1, 1934; s. Clarence Edwin and Eleanor Emma (Haas) K.; m. Orlanda Diana, Sept. 24, 1954; children: Kim, Craig, Todd. B.S.M.E., U. Wis., 1959. Registered profl. engr., Fla., Utah, Kans., Colo. Unit supr. Wis. Electric Co., Milw., 1959-67; project engr., mgr. Stearns-Roger, Denver, 1967-70; assoc. mng. dir. Jacksonville Electric Authority (Fla.), 1971-77; exec. mgr. electric ops. Kans. Power and Light Co., Topeka, 1977, v.p. power prodn. systems ops., 1977-80, sr. v.p. electric ops., 1980—. Served with AUS, 1954-56. Mem. ASME. Home: 3940 Worwick Town Rd Topeka KS 66610 Office: Kansas Power and Light Co 818 Kansas Ave Topeka KS

KUFELD, WILLIAM MANUEL, lawyer; b. Hunter, N.Y., Aug. 4, 1922; s. Max and Carrie (Hausdorff) K.; m. Frieda Chesir, Apr. 9, 1949; 1 son, David J. Student, Bklyn. Coll., 1938-40; B.B.A., Coll. City N.Y., 1940-42; LL.B., N.Y. U., 1949, LL.M., 1952. Bar: N.Y. bar 1949. Since practiced in, N.Y.C.; partner firm Carb, Luria, Glassner, Cook & Kufeld, 1959—; adj. prof. law N.Y. U., 1962-77; lectr. Practicing Law Inst. Pres. Congregation of Young Israel of Fifth Ave., N.Y.C., 1962-65, North Shore Hebrew Acad., Great Neck, N.Y., 1969-73. Served to 1st lt. USAAF, 1943-46. Recipient Alumn. Meritorious Achievement award N.Y.U., 1965. Mem. Assn. Bar City N.Y., N.Y. State Bar Assn., N.Y. County Lawyers Assn., N.Y. U. Law Alumni Assn. (pres. 1970-71). Home: 22 Hawthorne Ln Great Neck NY 11023 Office: 529 Fifth Ave New York NY 10017

KUGEL, JAMES LEWIS, Hebrew literature educator; b. N.Y.C., Aug. 22, 1945; s. John Hans and Adelaide (Roth) K.; m. Rachel Epstein, Apr. 20, 1975; children: Yotam, David. B.A., Yale U., 1968; jr. fellow, Harvard U., 1972-76; Ph.D., CUNY, 1977. Mellon faculty fellow CUNY, 1977-78; lectr. Harvard U., 1978-79, Starr prof. Hebrew literature, 1982—; asst. prof. Yale U., 1979-81, assoc. prof., 1982, prof., 1982, mem. Griswold Humanities Ctr., 1980-82. Author: Techniques of Strangeness, 1971 (Wrexham prize), Idea of Biblical Poetry, 1981; contbg. author: Studies in Medieval Jewish History, 1979, Jewish Thought in 16th Century, 1983; poetry editor: Harper's Mag., 1972-74; assoc. editor: Prootexts, 1980—; cons. editor: Crossroad Bible, 1982—. Fulbright fellow, 1968-69; Danforth fellow, 1970; Morse fellow, 1981-82. Mem. Assn. Jewish Studies, Soc. Biblical Lit., Am. Acad. Religion, Phi Beta Kappa. Home: 14 Wessex Rd Newton Center MA 02159 Office: Dept Near Eastern Langs Harvard U 6 Divinity Ave Cambridge MA 02138

KUGEL, KENNETH, cons.; b. Sheboygan, Wis., May 5, 1921; s. Herman Kenneth and Rebecca (von Kaas) K.; m. Sarajane Moore, Aug. 12, 1944 (div. May 1971); children—Kenneth Kaas, Melanie, Candace, Thomas Hans, Carol; m. Joanne S. Baker, Dec. 30, 1971 (div. Oct. 1978). B.A., Reed Coll., 1947; M.A., U. Mich., 1948; postgrad., George Washington U., 1949. Research asst. Republican Nat. Com., 1948; with Library Congress, Bur. Fed. Supply, 1948-49; various assignments natural resources Bur. Budget, 1949-62; dir. Office Thai Regional Affairs, AID, 1962, asst. dir. for program mission to, Thailand, 1962-64, dep. dir. mission to, Panama, 1964-66, asso. asst. adminstr. Vietnam bur., Washington, 1966-68; dir. operational coordination staff U.S. Budget Bur., Washington, 1968-72; dep. asst. dir. field activities Office Mgmt. and Budget, 1972-73, cons., 1973-78; also cons. Overseas Devel. Council, 1973—, Congl. Budget Office, 1976-77, Pres.'s Reorgn. Project, 1977. Served to maj. USMCR, 1941-46. Mem. Theta Delta Chi. Unitarian (trustee). Home and office: RD 1 Biglerville PA 17307

KUGEL, ROBERT BENJAMIN, physician, educator; b. Chgo., May 2, 1923; s. H. Kenneth and Rebecca (von Kaas) K.; m. Dorothy Annetta Bowdle, Jan. 31, 1950; children—Rebecca Anne, Gretchen Lucinda, Jennie Louisa. Student, Dartmouth, 1941-42; B.A., U. Mich., 1945, M.D., 1946; M.A. a.d.e, Brown U., 1964. Intern U. Mich. Hosp., 1947-48, resident, 1948-50; practice medicine, specializing in pediatrics, Omaha, 1966-74, Albuquerque, 1974-75, Kansas City, 1975-77, Washington, 1977-80, N.Y.C., 1981—; instr. dept. pediatrics Yale Med. Sch., 1951-52, U. Hosp., Ann Arbor, Mich., 1952-53; ast. prof. pediatrics, research asso. maternal and child health Johns Hopkins Med. Sch., 1955-56; asst. prof. pediatrics State U. Iowa Med. Sch.; dir. Child Devel. Clinic Univ. Hosp., Iowa City, 1956-63; prof. med. sci. Brown U. Med. Sch., 1963-65, prof. child health, 1965-66; prof., chmn. dept. pediatrics U. Nebr. Med. Sch., Omaha, 1966-69, prof. pediatrics, dean, 1969-74; v.p. health scis. U. N.Mex., Albuquerque, 1974-76, prof. pediatrics, 1974-76; exec. vice chancellor U. Kans. Coll. Health Scis. and Hosp., prof. pediatrics, 1976-77; v.p. Georgetown U. Community Health Plan, Washington, 1977-80; prof. pediatrics N.Y. Med. Coll., 1981—; Chief adminstrv. officer Bernalillo County Med. Center, 1974-76; med. dir. Flower Hosp., N.Y.C., 1981—; Mem. Pres.'s Com. on Mental Retardation, 1966-69. Contbr. articles to profl. jours. Pres. Josephine E. Kugel Found.; bd. dirs. Nat. Center for Law and the Handicapped. Mem. Am. Acad. Pediatrics (chmn. council child health), Nat. Assn. Retarded Citizens, A.M.A., Am. Pediatric Soc., A.C.P., Midwest Soc. Pediatric Research, Am. Assn. Mental Deficiency. Democrat. Presbyn. Office: Flower Hosp 1249 Fifth Ave New York NY 10029

KUGLER, ARTHUR NOBLE, mech. engr.; b. N.Y.C., July 13, 1902; s. Otto E. and Isabella J. (Noble) K.; m. Anna M. Nelson, Oct. 10, 1925; 1 dau., Florence M. (Mrs. Robert B. McCune). M.E., Stevens Inst. Tech., 1925. Registered profl. engr., N.Y., N.J. Field engr. Barker & Wheeler (cons. engr.), 1925-28; installation engr. RCA Photophone-Sound (motion pictures), 1928-29; chief welding engr. Airco Welding products div. Airco Inc., 1929-67; cons. mech. and welding engr., Bricktown, N.J., 1967—; instr. Pratt Inst., eves., 1940-45; cons. U.S. Army Chem. Warfare Service, 1941-43; U.S. del. Internat. Inst. Welding commn. V111 (safety and hygiene), 1957-68. Author 18 texts on welding engring. for Internat. Corr. Schs.; contbr. to handbooks. Recipient James T. Moorehead medal Internat. Acetylene Assn., 1961. Hon. mem. Am. Welding Soc. (Samuel W. Miller Meml. medal 1962); life mem. ASME, Soc. Mfg. Engrs. (gold gold medal 1965); mem. Nat. Soc. Profl. Engrs., Alpha Sigma Phi. Methodist. Club: Bear Mountain Figure Skating (Palisades Interstate Park, N.Y.) (a founder, pres. 1946-62). Address: 13 Phillips Rd Greenbriar Bricktown NJ 08724

KUH, EDWIN, educator; b. Chgo., Apr. 13, 1925; s. Edwin J., Jr. and Charlotte (Greenebaum) K.; m. Anne Barry, June 11, 1947 (div. Apr. 1970); children—Joanna M., Elizabeth N., Thomas, Sarah, Daniel; m. Barbara Kapp, Jan. 1974. B.A., Williams Coll., 1949; Ph.D., Harvard, 1955. Lectr. Johns Hopkins, 1953-55; asst. prof. Sloan Sch. Mgmt., Mass. Inst. Tech., 1954-62, prof. mgmt. and econs., 1962—; cons. U.S. Treasury, 1959-60; mem. adv. research com. Brookings-SSRC Econometric Model, 1964—; exec. dir. NBER Computer Research Center, 1971-78; dir. M.I.T. Center Computational Research, 1978—; mem. staff President's Materials Policy Commn., 1951. Author: (with J. R. Meyer) The Investment Decision: An Empirical Study, 1957, Capital Stock Growth: A Micro-Econometric Approach, 1963; Editor: (with others) Brookings Quar. Econometric Model of the U.S., Chgo. and Amsterdam, 1965, (with R.L. Schmalensee) Introduction to Applied Macroeconomics, 1973, (with David Belsley and Roy E Welsch) Regression Diagnostics: Identifying Influential Data and Sources of Collinearity, 1980. Served with AUS, 1943-46. Fellow Econometric Soc., Am. Acad. Arts and Scis.; mem. Am. Econ. Assn., Am. Statis. Assn. Home: 39 Foster St Cambridge MA 02138

KUH, ERNEST SHIU-JEN, electrical engineering educator; b. Peking, China, Oct. 2, 1928; came to U.S., 1948, naturalized, 1960; s. Zone Shung and Tsia (Chu) K.; m. Bettine Chow, Aug. 4, 1957; children: Anthony, Theodore. B.S., U. Mich., 1949; M.S., MIT, 1950; Ph.D., Stanford U., 1952. Mem. tech. staff Bell Telephone Labs., Murray Hill, N.J., 1952-56; assoc. prof. elec. engring. U. Calif., Berkeley, 1956-62, prof., 1962—, Miller research prof., 1965-66, chmn. dept. elec. engring. and computer sci., 1968-72, dean Coll. Engring., 1973-80; cons. IBM Research Lab., San Jose, Calif., 1957-62, NSF, 1975-84; mem. panel Nat. Bur. Standards, 1975-80; vis. com. Gen. Motors Inst., 1975-79; mem. sci. adv. bd. Mills Coll., 1976-80. Co-author: Principles of Circuit Synthesis, 1959, Basic Circuit Theory, 1967, Theory of Linear Active Network, 1967. Recipient Alexander von Humboldt award, 1980, Lamme medal Am. Soc. Engring. Edn., 1981; Brit. Soc. Engring. and Research fellow, 1982. Fellow IEEE (Edn. medal 1981), AAAS; mem. Nat. Acad. Engring., Academia Senica, Sigma Xi, Phi Kappa Phi. Office: Elec Engring and Computer Sci Dept Univ Calif Berkeley CA 94720

KUH, RICHARD HENRY, lawyer; b. N.Y.C., Apr. 27, 1921; s. Joseph Hellmann and Fannie Mina (Rees) K.; m. Joyce Dattel, July 31, 1966; children—Michael Joseph, Jody Ellen. B.A., Columbia Coll., 1941; LL.B. magna cum laude, Harvard U., 1948. Bar: N.Y. bar 1948, U.S. Dist. Ct. bar for So. Dist. N.Y 1948, Eastern Dist. N.Y 1967, U.S. Supreme Ct. bar 1968. Asso. firm Cahill, Gordon & Reindel, 1948-53; asst. dist. atty. N.Y. County Dist. Attys. Office, 1953-64, dist. atty., 1974; individual practice law, N.Y.C., 1966-71; partner firm Kuh, Goldman, Cooperman & Levitt, N.Y.C., 1971-73; firm Kuh, Shapiro, Cooperman & Levitt (P.C.), N.Y.C., 1975-78, Warshaw Burstein Cohen Schlesinger & Kuh, 1978—; adj. prof. N.Y. Law Sch., N.Y. U. Author: Foolish Figleaves?, 1967; mem. bd. editors: Harvard Law Rev, 1947-48; mem. adv. bd.: Contemporary Drug Problems, 1975—, Criminal Law Bull, 1976—; contbr. articles to popular and profl. jours. Trustee Temple Israel, N.Y.C., 1975—, Grace Ch. Sch., 1981—. Served with U.S. Army, 1942-45; ETO. Walter E. Meyer Research and Writing grantee, 1964-65. Mem. Am. Law Inst., Am. Bar Found., Am. Bar Assn., Assn. Bar City of N.Y., Phi Beta Kappa. Democrat. Jewish. Club: Harvard (N.Y.C.). Home: 14 Washington Pl New York NY 10003 Office: 555 Fifth Ave New York NY 10017

KUHBACH, AREND GERDES, lawyer; b. N.Y.C., Nov. 21, 1916; s. Charles J. and Catherine (Kuhlmann) K.; m. Muriel Ruth Dinger, Aug. 1, 1942; children: Ellen Ames Kuhbach Lucas, Robert Gerdes, Peter Dwight. A.B., Columbia U., 1938, LL.B., 1940. Bar: N.Y. 1940. With Lybrand, Ross Bros. & Montgomery (C.P.A.s), N.Y.C., 1940; with N.Y., N.H. & H.R.R., 1941-62, tax counsel, 1944-50, tax atty., acct., 1950-53, asst. gen. counsel, 1953, fin. counsel, 1954-56, fin. officer, 1957, v.p. fin., 1958-61, exec. v.p., 1961-62; dir. fin. Port Authority N.Y. and N.J., 1962-73, acting exec. dir., 1973-74, exec. dir., 1974-77, sr. fin. advisor, 1977-82. Mem. ABA, Fin. Execs. Inst., St. John's Guild, Mcpl. Fin. Officers Assn., Internat. Bridge, Tunnel and Turnpike Assn. (former chmn. ins. com.). Clubs: India House (N.Y.C.); Nassau (Princeton). Home: 38 Runnymede Rd Chatham NJ 07928 Office: 1 World Trade Center New York NY 10048

KUHL, DAVID EDMUND, physician, educator; b. St. Louis, Oct. 27, 1929; s. Robert Joseph and Caroline Bertha (Waldemar) K.; m. Eleanor Dell Kasales, Aug. 7, 1954; 1 son, David Stephen. A.B., Temple U., Phila., 1951; M.D., U. Pa., 1955. Diplomate: Am. Bd. Radiology, Am. Bd. Nuclear Medicine (a founder; life trustee 1977—). Intern, then resident in radiology Sch. Medicine and Hosp. U. Pa., 1955-56, 58-63, mem. faculty, 1963-76, prof. radiology, 1970-76, vice chmn. dept., 1975-76, chief div. nuclear medicine, 1963-76; prof. radiol. scis. UCLA Sch. Medicine and Hosp., 1976—, vice chmn. dept., 1977—, asso. dir. lab. biomed. and environ. scis., 1976—, chief lab. nuclear medicine, 1976—; mem. adv. com. Dept. Energy, NIH.; mem. sci. adv. bd. Max Planck Inst., Cologne, W.Ger., John Douglas French Found. for Alzheimer's Disease. Mem. editorial bd.: Jour. Cerebral Blood Flow and Metabolism, Internat. Jour. Nuclear Medicine and Biology, Jour. Computer Assisted Tomography; Contbr. articles to med. jours. Served as officer M.C. USNR, 1956-58. Recipient Research Career Devel. award USPHS, 1961-71; Ernst Jung prize for medicine Jung Found., Hamburg, 1981; Emil H. Grubbe gold medal Chgo. Med. Soc., 1983. Fellow Am. Coll. Radiology, Am. Coll. Nuclear Physicians; mem. Am. Epilepsy Soc., Assn. Univ. Radiologists, Radiol. Soc. N.Am., Soc. Nuclear Medicine (Nuclear Pioneer citation 1976, Herman L. Blumgart, M.D., Pioneer award 1979, Disting. Scientist award 1981), Am. Heart Assn. (fellow council circulation). Am. Neurol. Assn., Rocky Mountain Radiol. Soc., Soc. Neurosci., Sigma Xi., Alpha Omega Alpha. Office: Div Nuclear Medicine UCLA Med Sch Los Angeles CA 90024

KUHLMAN, JOHN MELVILLE, economics educator; b. Lamont, Wash., June 25, 1923; s. Oscar William and Amy Nina (Melville) K.; m. Mary Ann Sigley, Sept. 1, 1950; children: Ann, Kay, John. B.A., Wash. State U., 1948; M.S., U. Wis., 1949, Ph.D., 1953. Instr. U. Wis-Wausau, 1951-53; asst. prof. U. Richmond, Va., 1953-55, U. Cin., 1955-61; assoc. prof. econs. U. Mo., Columbia, 1961-62, prof., 1962—; cons. FTC, Washington, 1972-73, State of Ill., Chgo., 1977—, State of Tenn., Nashville, 1981—, NRC, Washington, 1977-80. Author: Economics Problems, 1969—, Studying Economics, 1972; co-author: The Economic System, 1959. Served with AUS, 1943-46; ETO. Ford Found. fellow, 1959-60; recipient Maxine Shutz award for undergrad. teaching, 1983, Disting. Faculty award U. Mo., 1981. Mem. Am. Econs. Assn., Midwest Econs. Assn. (v.p. 1969-70), Missouri Valley Econs. Assn. Home: RR1 Hartsburg MO 65039 Office: Dept Econs U Mo Columbia MO 65211

KUHLMAN, KERTIS PAUL, construction company executive; b. Norman, Okla., July 13, 1926; s. John H. and Mary Joe (Lessly) K.; m. Virginia Twyman, June 10, 1950; children—Kenneth, Janis, Mark. Student, La. Tech. U., Rice U.; B.S. in Elec. Engring, U. Okla., 1948. With Gen. Electric Co., 1948—, mgr. mktg., gen. purpose control dept., Bloomington, Ill., 1964-72, v.p., 1973-82; dept. mgr., S.E. Gen. Electric Supply Co., Atlanta, 1972, gen. mgr., Bridgeport, Conn., 1973-82; pres. Maj. Constrn. Services, Dallas, 1982—. Served to lt. (j.g.) USN, 1944-46. Mem. Nat. Assn. Elec. Distbrs. (pres. 1977—). Republican. Methodist. Club: Las Colinas Sports. Home: 568 Harbor Circle Dr Azle TX 76020 Office: 6015 Commerce Dr Suite 430 Irving TX 75062

KUHLMAN, WALTER EGEL, artist, educator; b. St. Paul, Nov. 16, 1918; s. Peter and Marie (Gensen) K.; m. Nora McCants; 1 son, Christopher; m. Tulip Chestman, April 9, 1979. B.S., U. Minn., 1941; postgrad., St. Paul Sch. Art, 1936-40, Tulane U., 1946, Academie de la Grand Chaumiere, Paris, 1950-51. Prof. dept. art Calif. State U., Sonoma, 1969—, also chmn. dept.; mem. faculty Calif. Sch. Fine Arts, 1957-60, Stanford U., 1965—. One-man shows, Calif. Palace of Legion of Honor, 1956, 64, Walker Art Center, Mpls., 1940, Stanford U., 1965, The New Arts, Houston, Lawson de Cell Gallery, San Francisco, 1959-62, Sonoma State U., 1970, Charles Campbell Gallery, 1981, 83; represented in permanent collections, Phillips Meml. Gallery, Washington, San Francisco Mus. Modern Art, Oakland Mus., Rice U., Santa Fe Mus., Mus. Modern Art, Sao Paulo, Brazil, San Francisco Art Assn. Named Maestro Calif.; Tiffany Found. grantee, 1941; Cummington Found. grantee, 1942; Graham fellow, 1957. Home: 27 Glen Ct Sausalito CA 94965 Office: Indsl Center Bldg Studio 335 Harbor Dr Sausalito CA 94965

KUHLMANN, FRED L., brewery executive; b. St. Louis, 1916; (married). A.B., Washington U., 1938, also LL.B.; LL.M., Columbia U., 1942. Bar: Mo. Partner Stolar, Kuhlmann, Heitzmann & Eder, 1938-67; exec. v.p. Anheuser-Busch Inc., 1967-79; vice chmn. bd., exec. v.p. Anheuser-Busch Cos., Inc., 1979—, also dir.; dir. Mfr. Ry. Co. Office: Anheuser-Busch One Bush Pl Saint Louis MO 63118 *

KUHLMEY, WALTER TROWBRIDGE, lawyer; b. Chgo., Apr. 11, 1918; s. Walter and Daisy Ethel (Trowbridge) K.; m. Cyra Devotion Morehouse, June 6, 1942 (div. Jan. 1973); children—Susan, Mitzi (dec.), Judith.; m. Dorothy Jean Stevens, Feb. 9, 1973. B.A., Yale U., 1940, LL.B., 1947. Bar: Ill. 1948. Practiced in, Chgo., 1948—; partner firm Kirkland & Ellis, 1954—. Served to capt. USMC, 1942-46. Fellow Am. Coll. Trial Lawyers; mem. Am. Bar Assn., 7th Circuit Bar Assn. (pres. 1980-81), Law Club Chgo., Legal Club Chgo. Republican. Presbyterian. Clubs: University, Mid-Am. (Chgo.). Home: 1840A Wildberry Dr Glenview IL 60025 Office: 200 E Randolph Dr Room 5800 Chicago IL 60601

KUHLTHAU, ALDEN ROBERT, educator; b. New Brunswick, N.J., Apr. 29, 1921; s. Harold V. and Emma (Ellison) K.; m. Gay Harris, Sept. 15, 1943; children: Robert Peyton, Richard Harold, Linda Gay. B.S., Wake Forest U., 1942; M.S., U. Va., 1944, Ph.D., 1948. Asst. prof. physics U. N.H., 1948-51; asst. dir. Research Labs. for Engring. Sci., U. Va., Charlottesville, 1951-54, dir., 1954-67, prof. aerospace engring., 1958—, asso. dean Sch. Engring. and Applied Sci., 1961-67, asso. provost for research, 1967-71, chmn. dept. engring. sci. and systems, 1975-77, prof. transp., 1977—; pres. Univs. Space Research Assn., 1969-75. Mem. Transp. Research Bd. Home: 1817 Meadowbrook Heights Rd Charlottesville VA 22901

KUHLTHAU, CONRAD WILLIAM, III, banker; b. Highland Park, N.J., Dec. 2, 1933; s. Conrad William and Margaretta (Rice) K.; m. Joyce R. Parillo, Dec. 22, 1955; children: Kathryn A., Kirsten J. B.A., U. Va., 1955; certificate, Grad. Sch. Mut. Savs. Banking Brown U., 1966. With First Nat. City Bank N.Y., 1957-58; pres., chief exec. officer, trustee New Brunswick (N.J.) Savs. Bank, 1958—. Chmn. community adv. bd. Rutgers Med. Sch., U. Medicine and Dentistry N.J. Served with USMCR, 1955-57. Mem. Aircraft Owners and Pilots Assn., Kappa Alpha Order. Home: Meadowbrook Ln Skillman NJ 08558 Office: 70 Bayard St New Brunswick NJ 08903

KUHN, ALBERT JOSEPH, educator; b. Dowell, Ill., Apr. 4, 1926; s. Albert and Elizabeth (Furjes) K.; m. Roberta Marshall, June 12, 1949; children—William, Frederick. B.A., U. Ill., 1950; Ph.D., Johns Hopkins, 1954. Mem. faculty Ohio State U., 1954—, chmn. English dept., 1964—, prof. English, 1965—, provost, v.p. acad. affairs, 1971-79. Contbr. to: Romantic Bibliography, 1963, also articles.; Editor: Three Sentimental Novels, 1970. Mem. region VIII Woodrow Wilson Selection Com., 1961—; mem. research bd. Children's Hosp., 1973—; trustee Battelle Meml. Inst. Found., 1975—. Served with USNR, 1944-46. Mem. Modern Lang. Assn., N. Central Assn. Colls. and Schs. (commn.), Phi Beta Kappa. Home: 35 Webster Park Columbus OH 43214

KUHN, ALBIN OWINGS, university official; b. Woodbine, Md., Jan. 31, 1916; s. Howard Schloenacher and Clara May (Owings) K.; m. Ella Elizabeth Cissel, Nov. 23, 1938; children: Philip Howard, Joseph Albin, Roger Cissel, Albin Owings, Lois Ellen. B.S., U. Md., 1938, M.S., 1940, Ph.D., 1948; postgrad., U. Wis., 1947. Agronomic extension work U. Md., 1939-44, asso. prof. agronomy, 1946-48, prof. agronomy, 1948—, head dept., 1948-55, asst. pres., 1955-58, exec. v.p., 1958-65, v.p. Balt. campuses, 1965-67, chancellor Balt. campuses, 1967-71; chancellor U. Md. at Balt., 1971—; exec. v.p. U. Md., 1979—. Bd. dirs. Hosp. Cost Analysis Service, Inc.; trustee, pres., v.p., sec. Md. Hosp. Service, Inc.; Mem. Md. Hosp. Commn., 1964-67, vice chmn., 1966-67; mem. Gov.'s Com. on Rehab., 1965-67, Commn. Modernization Exec. Br. Md. Govt., 1966-67; mem. gov.'s adv. council to State's Inter-agy. Com. for Comprehensive Health Planning, 1968-69; mem. Balt. Urban Coalition, 1967-69; pres. Md. Assn. Higher Edn., 1968-69. Served with USNR, 1944-46; PTO. Fellow Am. Soc. Agronomy (pres. Northeastern br. 1954); mem. Assn. Acad. Health Centers (dir. 1972—), Northeastern Weed Control Conf. (pres. 1954), Sigma Xi, Alpha Zeta, Omicron Delta Kappa, Phi Kappa Phi, Alpha Gamma Rho, Pi Sigma Alpha. Address: Elkins Bldg Adelphi MD 20783

KUHN, BOWIE, former commissioner of baseball; b. Takoma Park, Md., Oct. 28, 1926; m. Luisa Hegeler; four children. B.A., Princeton, 1947; LL.B., U. Va., 1950. Bar: N.Y. With firm Willkie, Farr and Gallagher, N.Y.C.; legal counsel several baseball clients, 1950-69, rep. Nat. League club owners in negotiations with Maj. League Players Assn., 1968, commr. pro tempore of baseball, 1969, commr., 1969-84. Office: 15 W 51st St New York NY 10019 *

KUHN, JOSEF LEONZ, manufacturing company executive; b. Wohlen, Aargau, Switzerland, Feb. 3, 1926; came to U.S., 1952; m. Susanne J. Clifford, Feb. 20, 1960; children: Nicholas J., Heidi S. Mech. Engr., Kt. Technikum Winterthur, Switzerland, 1952. Design engr. 3M Co., St. Paul, 1952-57, plant engr., London, Ont., Can., 1957-58, chief engr., Australia, 1958-62, dir. engring., Paris, 1962-63, gen. mgr., Bauchet, France, 1963-67, European mfg. mgr. graphic systems, Neuilly, France, 1967-71, mng. dir., Diegem, Belguim, 1971-72; sr. mng. dir. Sumitomo 3M Ltd., Japan, 1972-75; pres., gen. mgr. 3M Can., London, Ont., 1975-81; v.p. European ops. 3M, St. Paul, 1981-82; group v.p., tap adhesives and ecorative products group 3M Can., St. Paul, 1982—. Club: Minikahda. Office: 3M Co 3M Center St Paul MN 55144

KUHN, MARGARET (MAGGIE), organization executive; b. Buffalo, 1905; d. Samuel Frederick and Minnie Louise (Kooman) K. B.A., Case-Western Res. U., 1926. Formerly with YWCA, Cleve., Phila.; Gen. Alliance Unitarian Women, Boston; later with United Presbn. Ch. U.S.A., N.Y.C.; editor, writer for ch. mag. Social Progress; alt. observer for Presbyns. at UN; ret., 1970; a founder Gray Panthers, 1971; now nat. convener; cons. nat. task force on women United Presbyn. Ch., past 3d v.p. health, edn. and welfare assn.; lectr.; mem. nat. adv. bd. Hospice, Inc.; adv. TV series Over Easy; former mem. Fed. Jud. Nominating Com. Pa. Author: Get Out There and Do Something about Injustice, 1972, Maggie Kuhn on Aging, 1977. Recipient 1st ann. award for justice and human devel. Witherspoon Soc., 1974, Disting. Service award in consumer advocacy Am. Speech and Hearing Assn., 1975, Freedom award Women's Scholarship Assn. Roosevelt U., 1976, ann. award Phila. Soc. Clin. Psychologists, 1976, Peaceseeker award United Presbyn. Peace Fellowship, 1977, Humanist of Yr. award Am. Humanist Assn., 1978. Office: Gray Panthers 3635 Chestnut St Philadelphia PA 19104 *

KUHN, SHERMAN MCALLISTER, English educator, editor; b. Alexandria, S.D., Sept. 15, 1907; s. Detmer Thomas and Helen (Sherman) K.; m. Esther Lucille Bacon, Dec. 31, 1929 (div. Apr. 1931); 1 dau., Evelyn; m. Eleanor Jordan, Dec. 28, 1935; children: Eleanor Anne, Barbara Jean, Dorothy Ruth. Student, U. Dubuque, 1925-28; B.A., Park Coll., Parkville, Mo., 1929; M.A., U. Chgo., 1933, Ph.D., 1935. Tchr. English Lincoln Community High Sch., (Ill.), 1929-32; prof. English Okla. State U., Stillwater, 1935-48, U. Mich., Ann Arbor, 1948-83, assoc. editor Middle English Dictionary, 1948-61, editor Middle English Dictionary, 1961-83; cons. Clarence L. Barnhart, Inc., N.Y.C. Author: A Grammar of the Mercian Dialect, 1938; editor: The Vespasian Psalter, 1965; adv. editor: Mich. Germanic Studies, 1975—. Served with U.S. Army, 1944-45. Recipient Best Book award U. Mich. Press., 1973, Disting. Faculty Achievement award U. Mich., 1983; grantee Horace H. Rackham Found., 1958, 65. Fellow Medieval Acad. Am.; mem. Linguistic soc. Am., Dictionary Soc. N.Am., Internat. Assn. Univ. Profs. English. Republican. Presbyterian. Home: 225 Buena Vista Ann Arbor MI 48103 Office: Middle English dictionary U Mich 555 S Forest St Ann Arbor Mi 48104

KUHN, THOMAS SAMUEL, history of science educator; b. Cin., July 18, 1922; s. Samuel Louis and Minette (Stroock) K.; m. Kathryn Louise Muhs, Nov. 27, 1948 (div. Sept. 1978); children: Sarah, Elizabeth, Nathaniel Stroock.; m. Jehane Robin Burns, Oct. 26, 1982. S.B. summa cum laude in Physics, Harvard U., 1943, A.M. (NRC predoctoral fellow), 1946, Ph.D., 1949; LL.D., U. Notre Dame, 1973; D.H.L., Rider Coll., 1978, Bucknell U., 1979, Linköping U., Sweden, 1980. With radio research lab., also Am.-Brit. lab. OSRD (div. 15), 1943-45; jr. fellow Harvard Soc. Fellows, 1948-51; mem. faculty Harvard, 1951-56, asst. prof. gen. edn. and history sci., 1952-56; mem. faculty U. Calif. at Berkeley, 1958-64, prof. history sci., 1961-64, Princeton, 1964-68, M. Taylor Pyne prof. history sci., 1968-79; prof. philosophy and history of sci. MIT, 1979—; Lowell Inst. lectr. 1951; dir. project Sources History Quantum Physics, 1961-64; mem. Inst. Advanced Study, 1972-79. Author: The Copernican Revolution: Planetary Astronomy in the Development of Western Thought, 1957, The Structure of Scientific Revolution, 1962, (with others) Sources for History of Quantum Physics: an Inventory and Report, 1967, The Essential Tension, 1977, Black-Body Theory and the Quantum Discontinuity, 1894-1912, 1978; Mem. bd.: Dictionary of Scientific Biography, 1964-80. Mem. at large bd. dirs. Social Sci. Research Council, 1964-66. Recipient Howard T. Behrman award Princeton U., 1977, George Sarton medal History of Sci. Soc., 1982; Guggenheim fellow, 1954-55; Center Advanced Study Behavioral Sci. fellow, 1958-59. Mem. History Sci. Soc. (council 1953-68, pres. 1968-70), Am. Acad. Arts and Scis., Am. Philos. Soc., Am. Philos. Assn., Am. Hist. Assn., AAAS, Leopoldina Acad., Nat. Acad. Sci., Philosophy of Sci. Assn., Phi Beta Kappa, Sigma Xi; membre effectif Acad. Internat. d'Histoire des Sciences. Address: MIT Dept Linguistics and Philosophy 20D-213 Cambridge MA 02139

KUHN, WARREN BOEHM, librarian, university dean; b. Jersey City, Feb. 12, 1924; s. Oscar Henry and Amelia Elizabeth (Boehm) K.; 1 son, Robert W. A.B., N.Y. U., 1948; M.S. with honors, Columbia U., 1950. Head library circulation dept. U. N.Mex., 1950, 52-55; asst. head librarian Ariz. State U., 1955-56; asst. univ. librarian Princeton U., 1956-65; lectr. coll. and univ. library adminstrn. Grad. Sch. Library Sci., Drexel Inst., 1962; asst. dir. univ. libraries, librarian J. Henry Meyer Meml. Library, Stanford U., 1965-67; dir. libraries Iowa State U., Ames, 1967-71, dean library services, 1971—; Mem. Gov.'s Adv. Council on Library Services for State of Iowa, 1971-75; adv. com. N.Y. Worlds Fair, 1963-64; Bd. dirs. Center for Research Libraries, 1970-72; bd. dirs. Midwest Region Library Network, 1975—, pres., 1981-82, exec. com., 1977-83; pres., chmn. bd. Universal Serials and Book Exchanges, 1976, mem. com. on bylaws, 1978-79. Editor: The Julian Street Library, 1966, New Jersey Library Assn. Newsletter, 1958-60; mem. editorial bd.: Research Libraries in OCLC, 1983—; Contbr. articles to library and gen. periodicals. Served to 1st lt. AUS, 1943-46, 50-52. Decorated Bronze Star medal. Mem. AAUP, ALA (editorial com. 1969-75, chmn. 1972-73, publishing bd. 1972-75, chmn. 1973-75, mem. council 1971-75, chmn. yearbook adv. com. 1975—), Assn. Coll. and Research Libraries (mem. numerous coms.), Resources and Tech. Services Div. Am. Assn. Pubs. (co-chmn. joint com. 1971-73), Assn. Research Libraries (bd. dirs. 1972-75, mem. task force on collection devel. 1981—), Fedn. Am. Socs. Exptl. Biology (cons. ad hoc com. 1969-70), Phi Kappa Phi. Club: Rotarian. Office: Iowa State U Library Ames IA 50011

KUHN, WILLIAM FREDRICK, financial executive; b. Bklyn., May 26, 1924; s. William Henry and Emma (Hess) K.; m. Helen Elizabeth Kraft, Aug. 8, 1948; children: William H., Paul F. Student, Pace Coll., 1947-48, U. Chgo., 1952-53. Bookkeeper, acct. Union Service Corp., 1946-65, asst. treas., 1979-80, treas., 1980, J. & W. Seligman & Co., Inc., 1980-83; asst. treas. Seligman Common Stock Fund, Inc., N.Y.C., 1977-80, treas., 1980—; with Seligman Growth Fund, Inc., N.Y.C., 1972—, asst. treas., 1966-72, treas., 1980—; controller Seligman Capital Fund, Inc., N.Y.C., 1972-79, asst. treas., 1969-72, treas., 1980—; asst. treas. Seligman Cash Mgmt. Fund, Inc., 1977-80, treas., 1980—; asst. treas. Seligman Income Fund, Inc., 1966-72, treas., 1980—, Seligman Communications & Info. Fund, Inc., 1982—, Second Union Cash Mgmt. Fund, Inc., 1980-82, Liberty Cash Mgmt. Fund, Inc., 1982—; asst. treas. Tri-Continental Corp., 1977-80, treas., 1980—; asst. treas. Union Data Service Center, 1979-80, treas., 1980—, Assn. Publicly Traded Investment Funds, 1980—. Served with USAAF, 1943-46; served with USAAF, 1943-46. Republican. Episcopalian. Lodge: Masons. Office: Seligman Growth Fund Inc 1 Bankers Trust Plaza New York NY 10006

KUHNEN, S. MARIE, educator; b. Haledon, N.J., Sept. 12, 1917; d. Charles William and Sybil (Daniels) K. B.A., Montclair State Tchrs. Coll., 1941; M.A., Columbia, 1946; Ph.D., N.Y.U., 1960. Tchr. Eastside High Sch., Paterson, N.J., 1941-44; teaching asst. botany Columbia, 1944-46; mem. faculty Montclair State Coll., 1946—, prof. biology, 1963—, chmn. dept., 1968-75; Chmn. Valhalla Glen Purchase Com., 1963-67; sec.-treas. council Assn. N.J. State Coll. Faculties, 1962-67. Recipient Conservation award Summit Nature Soc., 1968. Fellow A.A.A.S.; mem. Bot Soc. Am., Nat. Sci. Tchrs. Assn. (life), Nature Conservancy, Nat. Audubon Soc., Wilderness Soc., Nat. Parks Assn., Kappa Delta Pi, Sigma Delta Epsilon. Home: 5 Charles Ct Clifton NJ 07013 Office: Biology Dept Montclair State Coll Upper Montclair NJ 07043

KUHNHEIM, EARL JAMES, management and marketing consultant; b. Columbus, Ohio, Dec. 17, 1921; s. Earl Fred and Hildreth Elizabeth (Gall) K.; m. Marilyn Oaksmith, Aug. 23, 1947; children: Jamie Lynn, Jill Suzanne, Jennifer Lea. B.S. in Bus. Adminstrn, Ohio State U., 1946. With McKesson & Robbins, Inc., 1946—, v.p., div. mgr., Cleve., 1962-63, v.p. retail trade promotion, N.Y.C., 1963-66; v.p., gen. mgr. Hosp. Gentec Supply Co. div. Foremost-McKesson, Inc., 1973-74; asst. to pres. McKesson & Robbins Drug Co., 1974-79; dir. pharm. relations Nat. Wholesale Druggists Assn., 1974—. Served with AUS, 1942-44. Mem. Am. Surg. Trade Assn. (chmn. mgmt. tng. com. 1968—), Health Industries Assn. (dir. 1972-74), Sigma Alpha Epsilon. Home: 61 Sleepy Hollow Rd New Canaan CT 06840

KUHNLEY, HARVEY M., savings and loan executive; b. Mpls., Mar. 26, 1918; s. Charles H. and Goldie (Clough) K.; m. Mari I. Field, Mar. 20, 1976; children: Harvey Marc, Steven Jay, Diana, Cindy. Student, U. Minn., 1936-39. Owner, operator real estate, constrn. firm, 1938-41; with mortgage dept. Investors Diversified Services, Mpls., 1946; with Twin City Fed. Savs. and Loan Assn., Mpls., 1946—, pres., chmn. bd., chief exec. officer, dir. Bd. dirs. Mpls. Aquatennial, Am. Cancer Soc., Minn. Orchestral Assn., Mpls. Downtown Council.; bd. dirs., treas. Hennepin Ctr. for Arts. Served with USAAF, 1940-45. Mem. Savs. League of Minn. (past pres.), Mortgage Bankers Assn. Minn. (former dir.), Savs. and Loan Council Twin Cities (past pres.), Soc. Real Estate Appraisers (past pres.), Mpls. C. of C. (dir.). Episcopalian. Clubs: Mpls., Minikahda, Interlachen Country (gov.). Lodges: Masons; Shriners; Jesters.; Mpls. Rotary (past pres.). Home: 3150 W Calhoun Pkwy Minneapolis MN 55416 Office: 801 Marquette Ave Minneapolis MN 55402

KUHNS, WILLIAM GEORGE, public utility holding company executive; b. Milw., Apr. 26, 1922; s. Harold E. and Edna J. (Paulus) K.; m. Joan P. Beutell, July 9, 1948; children: Nancy, Janet, Linda, Pamela, Elizabeth. B.A., U. Wis., 1946, J.D., 1949. Bar: Wis. 1949. With operating research bur. Wis. Electric Power Co., Milw., 1949-55; with Gen. Pub. Utilities Corp., N.Y.C., 1955—, treas., 1957-61, v.p., 1961-67, dir., 1967—, pres., chief exec. officer, 1967-74, chmn., chief exec. officer, 1974—; chmn., chief exec. officer, dir. GPU Service Corp.; chmn. bd., chief exec. officer Jersey Central Power & Light Co., Met. Edison Co., Pa. Electric Co.; dir. Hammermill Paper Co., Marine Midland Banks, Inc., Home Life Ins. Co., Breeder Reactor Corp., GPU Nuclear Corp.; bd. dirs. Edison Electric Inst. Mem. N.J. Utilities Assn. (dir.), State Bar Wis., Assn. Edison Illuminating Cos. (dir.), Phi Eta Sigma, Delta Tau Delta, Beta Gamma Sigma. Clubs: Recess, University (N.Y.C.); Englewood Field; Knickerbocker Country (Tenafly). Home: 100 Essex Dr Tenafly NJ 07670 Office: 100 Interpace Pkwy Parsipanny NJ 07054

KUIVILA, HENRY GABRIEL, chemist, educator; b. Fairport Harbor, Ohio, Sept. 17, 1917; s. Matti and Saima (Kujala) K.; m. Nancy M. Corn, June 13, 1943; children: Henry G., Nancy J., Ronald J. B.Sc., Ohio State U., 1942, M.A., 1944; Ph.D., Harvard, 1948. Jr. chemist Manhattan Project, Monsanto Chem. Co., 1944-46; from asst. prof. to prof. U. N.H., 1948-64; prof. chemistry SUNY-Albany, 1964—, chmn. dept., 1964-69, 73—; Vis. prof. Japan Soc. for Promotion Sci., 1973. Mem. editorial bd.: Organometallics, 1982—. NSF sr. postdoctoral fellow, 1959; Guggenheim fellow, 1959-60. Fellow AAAS, N.Y. Acad. Scis.; mem. Am. Chem. Soc., Phi Beta Kappa, Sigma Xi. Research on organic reaction of mechanisms, organometallic chemistry, anion chemistry, free radicals. Home: 36 E Bayberry Rd Glenmont NY 12077 Office: 1400 Washington Ave Albany NY 12222

KUJALA, WALFRID, musician, educator; b. Warren, Ohio, Feb. 19, 1925; s. Arvo August and Elsie Fannie (Ojajarvi) K.; m. Alice Pillischer, June 25, 1950; children: Stephen, Gwen, Daniel. B.Mus., Eastman Sch. Music, Rochester, N.Y., 1948, M.Mus., 1950. Flutist Rochester Philharmonic Orch., 1948-54; flutist, piccoloist Chgo. Symphony Orch., 1954—; prof. flute Northwestern U., Evanston, Ill., 1962—. Author: The Flutist's Progress, 1970; contbr. articles to profl. jours. Served with AUS, 1943-45; ETO. Mem. Nat. Flute Assn. (v.p.). Office: Sch of Music Northwestern U Evanston IL 60201

KUKLA, ROBERT JOHN, association executive; b. Chgo., Dec. 1, 1932; s. John and Antoinette Marie (Habowska) K.; m. Barbara Joan Kafka, Mar. 25, 1973; children: Robert Anthony, John Robert. B.S., Northwestern U., 1954, J.D., 1957. Bar: Ill. 1957. Casualty adjuster Allstate Ins. Co., 1957; trial atty. firm Fitzgerald, Petrucelli & Simon, Chgo., 1957-61; dir. mktg., sales and distbn. Sears, Roebuck & Co., 1962-70; self-employed author, writer, lectr., cons., TV and radio personality, 1970-72; hearings atty. supr. State of Ill., 1972-76; exec. dir. Inst. Legis. Action, Nat. Rifle Assn., Washington, 1976-78, also mem. bd. dirs., exec. com., chmn. legis. and bylaws coms.; legis. cons. Citizens Com. for Right to Keep and Bear Arms, 1978—, bd. dirs., 1982—; adviser Second Amendment Found., 1978—; chmn. legis. com. Ill. Rifle Assn., 1958-70; instr. law Triton Coll., 1980—, Oakton Coll., 1981—. Author: Gun Control, 1973; contbg. author: Point-Counterpoint, Readings in American Government, 1st and 2d edits. Pres. Logan Sq. Neighborhood Assn., Chgo., 1961-67; cons./advisor Japan Civil Def. Com., Tokyo, 1979—. Recipient certificate of merit City of Chgo., 1970. Mem. Am., Ill. bar assns., Nat. Justice Found. Am. (Americus Juridicus award 1974), Am. Numismatic Assn., Gun Writers Guild Am. (hon. life). Club: Capitol Hill (Washington). Home: PO Box 398 Park Ridge IL 60068

KUKLIN, ANTHONY BENNETT, lawyer; b. N.Y.C., Oct. 9, 1929; s. Norman B. and Deane (Cable) K.; m. Vivienne May Hall, Apr. 4, 1964; children: Melissa, Amanda. A.B., Harvard U., 1950; LL.B., Columbia U., 1953. Bar: N.Y. 1953, D.C. 1970. Assoc. Dwight, Royall, Harris, Koegel & Caskey, N.Y.C., 1955-61, Paul, Weiss, Rifkind, Wharton & Garrison, 1961-68, ptnr., 1969—. Contbr. articles to legal jours. Mem. Internat. Bar Assn., ABA (council sect. real property, probate and trust law), N.Y. State Bar Assn. (exec. com. real property sect., chmn. 1981-82), Assn. Bar City N.Y., Am. Coll. Real Estate Lawyers (pres. 1981-82), Anglo-Am. Real Property Inst. (gov. 1981—). Home: 22 Pryer Ln Larchmont NY 10538 Office: Paul Weiss Rifkind Wharton & Garrison 345 Park Ave New York NY 10154

KULCINSKI, GERALD LAVERN, nuclear engineering educator; b. La Crosse, Wis., Oct. 27, 1939; s. Harold Franklin and June (Kramer) K.; m. Janet Noreen Berg, Nov. 25, 1961; children: Kathryn, Brian, Karen. B.S. in Chem. Engring, U. Wis., 1961, M.S. in Nuclear Engring, 1962, Ph.D., 1965. Researcher Los Alamos Sci. Lab., 1963; sr. research scientist Battelle N.W. Lab., Richland, Wash., 1965-69, tech. group leader, 1969-71; lectr. Center for Grad. Study, Richland, 1969-71; asso. prof. nuclear engring. U. Wis., Madison, 1972-74, prof., 1974—, dir. fusion engring. program, 1973-74, 79—; mem. fusion materials coordinating com. Dept. Energy; mem. INTOR Design Team, Vienna, 1978-81. Editor: Proc. 2d Topical Meeting on Fusion Tech, 1976; assoc. editor Nuclear Engring. and Design/Fusion, 1983—; Contbr. numerous articles on materials for fission and fusion reactors to profl. jours. Recipient Acad. award Big 10 Conf., 1961, Curtis McGraw research award Am. Soc. Engring. Edn., 1978; AEC grantee, 1961-62, 64-65. Fellow Am. Nuclear Soc. (treas. Richland sect. 1971-72, program chmn. 2d topical meeting on fusion tech. 1976, Disting. Achievement award 1980); mem. Am. Soc. Engring. Edn., Red Triangles (pres. Madison chpt. 1976—). Home: 6013 Greentree Rd Madison WI 53711 Office: 1500 Johnson Dr Madison WI 53706

KULIK, EDWARD JOSEPH, insurance company executive; b. Hartford, Conn., July 17, 1926; s. Joseph and Bertha (Obuchowska) K.; m. Marion Colbert, Sept. 3, 1949; children: Nancy A. Kulik Holstein, Edward Joseph, Betsy M. B.S. in Bus. Adminstrn, U. Conn., 1950. Area mgr. Sherwin-Williams Co., Hartford, also Springfield, Mass., 1952-56, Murphy Paint Co., Balt., 1957-58; with Mass. Mut. Life Ins. Co., Springfield, 1958—, sr. v.p., 1975—; pres., chief exec. officer, trustee Mass Mutual Mortgage & Realty Investors; pres., dir. Baystate West, Inc.; mem. Internat. Council Shopping Centers. Trustee, chmn. fin. com., treas. Mercy Hosp., Springfield; corporator Wesson Meml. Hosp., Springfield; bd. dirs. Better Homes for Springfield. Served with USN, 1944-46; PTO. Recipient award of appreciation Am. Legion. Mem. Nat. Assn. Real Estate Investment Trusts. (bd. govs., chmn. long-range planning com., exec. council). Clubs: Colony (Springfield); Longmeadow Country (Mass.); Board Room (N.Y.C.). Home: 9 Brooks Circle Longmeadow MA 01106 Office: 1295 State St Springfield MA 01111

KULL, A. LAWRIE, food company executive; b. Elkhorn, Wis., May 9, 1943; s. Arthur L. and Doris E. (Meyer) K.; m. Mary J. Dushek, Aug. 20, 1966; children: Andrew, Elizabeth. B.S., U. Wis., 1965. Project asst. agrl. research div. U. Wis., Madison, 1966-69; ptnr. Mariondale Farms, Inc., Lake Geneva, Wis., 1969-74; mktg. asst. Lake to Lake Dairy Coop., Manitowoc, Wis., 1975-80; chief operating officer Lake to Lake div. Land o' Lakes, Inc., Manitowoc, 1981—; sec.-treas. Chicagoland Dairy Sales, Inc., Waupun, Wis., 1976—. Mem. Assn. Operating Coops. (sec.-treas.), Central Milk Sales Agy., Central Milk Producers Coop. (dir.), Wis. Fedn. Coops., Manitowoc C. of C. (dir. 1981-83), Alpha Zeta, Alpha Gamma Rho. Republican. Lutheran. Home: 1130 N 6th St Manitowoc WI 54220 Office: Lake to Lake Div Land o'Lakes Inc 2000 S 10th St Manitowoc WI 54220

KULLAS, ALBERT JOHN, management and systems engineering consultant; b. Webster, Mass., May 5, 1917; s. Albert J. and Mary (Piechowiak) K.; m. Joyce M. Gladue, Jan. 31, 1942; children: Michael, Daniel, Mark, James. B.S. in Civil Engring., Worcester Poly. Inst., 1938, M.S., NYU, 1940; grad., Sloan Sch. Mgmt. Sr. Execs., MIT, 1973. With Martin Marietta Corp., 1940-82, structures mgr., Balt., 1955-57, chief engr., 1957, design engring. mgr., 1957-59, tech. devel. mgr., 1959-60, Dyna Soar and Gemini Launch vehicle tech. dir., 1960-62, research and engring. dir., Denver, 1962-65, dir. tech. ops., 1965-66, dir. space sci., research, adv. tech., 1966—, dir. Voyager program, 1967-68, dir. Planetary Systems, 1968, dir. Viking project, div. v.p., 1969-72, div. v.p. ops. rev., 1972-73, v.p. data systems, Denver, 1973-82; mgmt. and systems engring. cons., Littleton, Colo., 1983—; mem. research and tech. panel space vehicles NASA, 1968-78. Contbr. articles to profl. jours. Mem. research adv. council Colo. State U., 1971—; treas. Porter Hosp. Found., 1980—; bd. dirs. Colo. Jud. Inst., 1980—; mem. exec. com. Rocky Mountain Sci. Council, 1964-65. Recipient Robert H. Goddard award Worcester Poly. Inst., 1962. Fellow AIAA (award 1967, Asso. fellow, chmn. honors and awards com. 1973-81); mem. ASCE, Sigma Xi, Tau Beta Pi. Office: 5088 W Maplewood Ave Littleton CO 80123

KULLBACK, SOLOMON, educator; b. Bklyn., Apr. 3, 1907; s. Nathan and Ida (Glasser) K.; m. Minna Mirin, May 29, 1930; children—Joseph Henry, Sally Eve (Mrs. Philip R. Dodge); m. Lola S. Witt, Sept. 11, 1974. B.S., Coll. City N.Y., 1927; M.A., Columbia, 1929; Ph.D., George Washington U., 1934. Research analyst War Dept., 1930-41, Dept. Def., 1946-62; mem. faculty George Washington U., 1938—, asst. prof. statistics, asso. prof., prof., to 1972, prof. emeritus, 1972—; faculty Fla. State U., 1974-75, Stanford U., 1976; cons. in field; vis. prof. Japan Soc. Promotion of Sci., 1973. Author: Information Theory and Statistics, 1959, The Information in Contingency Tables, 1978. Served from capt. to col. AUS, 1941-46. Decorated Legion of Merit; recipient Distinguished Civilian Service award Nat. Security Agy., 1960, Samuel S. Wilks Meml. medal, 1976; Alumni Achievement award George Washington U., 1977. Fellow Inst. Math. Statistics, Am. Statis. Assn. Club: Cosmos (Washington). Home: 10143 41st Trail Boynton Beach FL 33436 Office: Statistics Dept George Washington U Washington DC 20052

KULLBERG, DUANE REUBEN, accounting firm executive; b. Red Wing, Minn., Oct. 6, 1932; s. Carl Reuben and Hazel Norma (Swanson) K.; m. Sina Nell Turner, Oct. 19, 1958; children: Malissa Cox, Caroline Turner. B.B.A., U. Minn., 1954. C.P.A., Minn., Ill., Mich., Iowa. With Arthur Andersen & Co. (C.P.A.'s), 1954—; partner Arthur Andersen & Co., C.P.A.s, 1967—, mng. partner, Mpls., 1970-74, dep. mng. partner, Chgo., 1975-78, vice chmn. acctg. and audit practice, 1978-80, mng. partner, chief exec. officer, 1980—; mem. services policy adv. com. Office U.S. Trade Rep. Trustee Northwestern U.; bd. dirs. Chgo. Council Fgn. Relations; trustee Japan-U.S. Econ. Relations, Fin. Acctg. Found., Tax Found. Inc., U. Minn. Found., Art Inst. Chgo.; bd. dirs. Chgo. Central Area Com. Served with AUS, 1956-58. Mem. Am. Inst. C.P.A.s, Ill. Soc. C.P.A.s, Minn. Soc. C.P.A.s, Beta Gamma Sigma (dir.'s table). Republican. Clubs: Chicago, Mid-Am., Attic, Monroe (Chgo.); Minneapolis. Home: 2750 Sheridan Rd Evanston IL 60201 Office: 69 W Washington St Room 3500 Chicago IL 60602 also 18 quai Général-Guisan 1211 Geneva Switzerland

KULLEN, BARBARA CATOGGIO, lawyer, investment firm executive; b. Jamaica, N.Y., May 11, 1942; d. Vincent A. and Barbara E. (Eckels) Catoggio; m. Richard C. Kullen Jr., Nov. 7, 1970; children: Richard C. III, Michael V.S., Barbara Elizabeth, Vincent Anthony. B.A., Manhattanville Coll. Sacred Heart, 1963; J.D., Columbia U., 1966. Bar: N.Y. 1966. Interpretive atty. N.Y. regional office SEC, N.Y.C., 1966-68; assoc. firm Willkie Farr & Gallagher, N.Y.C., 1968-70; with Shearson/Am. Express Inc., N.Y.C., 1970—, now 1st v.p., sec., assoc. gen. counsel; dir., mem. audit com. Blue Cross and Blue Shield of Greater N.Y. Trustee Manhattanville Coll., 1980-83. Mem. Am. Soc. Corp. Secs., Westchester-Fairfield Corp. Counsel Assn., Women's Bond Club N.Y., Am. Horse Shows Assn. Roman Catholic. Office: 14 Wall St New York NY 10005

KULLER, LEWIS HENRY, epidemiologist; b. Bklyn., Jan. 9, 1934; s. Meyer and Dora (Olener) K.; m. Alice J. Bisgaier, July 10, 1960; children: Gail, Steven, Anne. B.A., Hamilton Coll., 1955; M.D., George Washington U., 1959; M.P.H., Johns Hopkins U., 1964, D.P.H., 1966. Diplomate: Am. Bd. Preventive Medicine, Am. Coll. Epidemiology. Instr. U. Md., 1967-71, assoc. prof., 1971-72, Johns Hopkins U. Sch. Hygiene and Pub. Health, 1968-71, prof., 1971-72; mem. faculty U. Minn., Mpls., part-time 1967—; prof. epidemiology U. Pitts., 1972—, chmn. dept., 1972—; established investigator Am. Heart Assn., 1969-73. Served to lt. USN, 1961-63. Centennial scholar Johns Hopkins U., 1976; Robert Wood Johnson health policy fellow, 1983-84. Mem. Am. Heart Assn. (fellow council on epidemiology). Office: U Pitts 130 DeSoto St Pittsburgh PA 15261

KULLERUD, GUNNAR, geosciences educator; b. Odda, Norway, Nov. 12, 1921; came to U.S., 1948; s. Finn and Clara Sofie (Kindberg) K.; m. Arrilla Joan Reading, Mar. 29, 1947 (dec. Mar. 1981); children: Finn Jon, Björn Kent, Kari Lynn, Marit Sue, Ingrid Diana. Ph.D. in Mining, Tech. U. Norway, 1947; D.Sc. in Geochemistry, U. Oslo, 1954, Norwegian Inst. Tech., 1982. Instr., then research asso. U. Chgo., 1948-52; research asso. U. Oslo, 1952-54; sr. staff mem. geochemistry Geophys. Lab., Carnegie Instn., 1954-71; prof. dept. geoscis. Purdue U., Lafayette, Ind., 1970—, head dept., 1970-76; adj. prof. Lehigh U., 1962-71; vis. prof. U. Heidelberg, Germany, 1964-70, Tech. U. Norway, 1972, 74, Charles U., Prague, Czechoslovakia, 1973, U. Oslo, 1976, 78; cons. prof. Texas Tech U., 1968-71; hon. collaborator, div. meteorites Smithsonian Instn., 1964—; dir. Earth Scis. Inc.; Mem. com. chem. solar system Space Sci. Bd., 1964-70; mem. Argonne Nat. Lab. Adv. Bd., 1975. Co-editor: Mineralium Deposita; mem. editorial bd.: Chem. Geology; Contbr. articles on sulfide phase equilibria, geothermometry ore deposits, meteorites and fossil fuels to profl. jours. Served with Royal Norwegian Air Force, also RAF, 1944-45. Recipient A.H. Dumont award Belgian Geol. Soc., 1965. Fellow Geol. Soc. Am., Am. Mineral. Soc., Washington Acad. Scis.; mem. Nat. Acad. Sci. (Norway), AAAS, Soc. Econ. Geologists, Geochem. Soc., Meteoritical Soc., Soc. Applied Geology, Am. Geophys. Union, geol. societies Norway, Finland. Club: Cosmos (Washington). Mineral Kullerudite named in his honor, 1964. Home: 202 Colony Rd West Lafayette IN 47906 Office: Physics Bldg Purdue U West Lafayette IN 47907

KULP, NANCY JANE, comedienne; b. Harrisburg, Pa., Aug. 28, 1921; d. Robert Tilden and Marjorie (Snyder) K.; m. Charles Malcolm Dacus, Apr. 1, 1951. B.A. in Journalism, Fla. State U., 1943; postgrad., U. Miami, 1950. Publicity dir. radio sta. WGBS, 1946-47; continuity dir. radio sta. WIOD, Miami, 1947-49; continuity dir.-performer TV Sta. WTVJ, Miami, 1949-50. Began acting career in, Hollywood, Calif., 1952; motion pictures include Model and the Marriage Broker, 1952, Star is Born, 1953, Sabrina, 1954, Three Faces of Eve, 1955, The Parent Trap, 1957, A Wilder Summer, 1983; appeared on: TV shows Playhouse 90, 1956, Lux Video, 1955, Beverly Hillbillies, 1961-71, Bob Cummings Show, 1955-60, Lucy Show, 1956; with: Brian Keith Show, after 1973; also: Sanford and Son; star: play Busbody (Nominated for Emmy award 1967); Broadway play Mornings at Seven, 1982; play Accent on Youth, Long Wharf Theatre, 1983. Hon. chmn. Humane Soc., 1965—. Served to lt. (j.g.) WAVES, USNR, 1943-45. Mem. Acad. Motion Pictures Arts and Scis., Actors and Others for Animals, Pi Beta Phi. Democrat. Club: Greyhound of Am. (Darien, Conn.). Windmill Creek Farm Port Royal Pa.

KULPA, JOHN EDWARD, JR., space system designer, former air force officer; b. Newark, May 11, 1929; s. John Edward and Helen (Sarn) K.; m. Marcelline Conner, May 31, 1951; children: Vicky Ruth Stewart, Jacquelyn Ervin. B.S., U.S. Mil. Acad., 1950; M.S., Air Force Inst. Tech., 1957; postgrad., Air Command and Staff Coll., 1962-63, Nat. War Coll., Washington, 1968-69. Commd. 2d lt. U.S. Air Force, 1950, advanced through grades to maj. gen.; served in flying duties with SAC, 1951-56; engr. on SNARK strategic missile and operational mgr. GAM-77 Hound Dog AG 52 missile, 1957-62, project mgr. research satellite and system program dir. major satellite system Space Systems Div., Los Angeles, 1963-68, comdr. avionics lab., dep. comdr. for engring. Aero. Systems Div., Dayton, Ohio, 1969-72; dir. space systems Office Sec. Air Force, Washington, 1972-74; dep. for plans, prin. dep. dir. intelligence community Office of Dir. Central Intelligence, Washington, 1974-75; dir. spl. projects Office Sec. Air Force also dep. comdr. for space ops., space div., Los Angeles, 1975-83, ret., 1983; v.p. for command, control, communications intelligence and mil. space systems (McDonnell Douglas Astronautics Co.), 1983—. Author numerous tech. reports. Trustee Environ. Research Inst. of Mich., 1983—. Decorated Def. D.S.M., D.S.H. With oak leaf cluster, Legion of Merit with oak leaf cluster, D.F.C., Air medal, Air Force Commendation medal with oak leaf cluster; recipient Thomas D. White space trophy Nat. Geog. Soc., 1979, intelligence community disting. service medal, Bernard A. Schriever Space and Missile award Air Force Assn., 1982, exceptional service medal NASA. Fellow Am. Inst. Aeros., and Astronautics; mem. Assn. Grads. Mil. Acad. at West Point. Home: 20437 Madison St Torrance CA 90503 Office: 5301 Bolsa Ave Huntington Beach CA 92647

KULSKI, WLADYSLAW WSZEBOR, polit. scientist, educator; b. Warsaw, Poland, July 27, 1903; came to U.S., 1946, naturalized, 1952; s. Julian and Antonina (Ostrowski) K.; m. Antonina Reutt, Oct. 28, 1938. LL.M., Warsaw Law Sch., 1925; LL.D., Paris (France) Law Sch., 1927. With Polish Diplomatic Service, 1928-45, head legal service, 1936-40, counsellor, minister plenipotentiary, London, Eng., 1940-45; pub. lectr. in, U.S., 1946-47; prof. polit. sci. U. Ala., 1947-51, Syracuse U., 1951-64; vis. prof. Duke, 1963-64, James B. Duke prof. Russian affairs, 1964-73; lectr. Fgn. Service Inst., 1957—, Army Strategic Intelligence Sch., 1957—, Air. U., 1963—. Author numerous books, 1927—; latest being The Soviet Regime: Communism in Practice, 1954, Peaceful Co-Existence: An Analysis of Soviet Foreign Policy, 1959, International Politics in a Revolutionary Age, 1964, DeGaulle and the World, 1966, The Soviet Union in World Affairs, 1973, Germany and Poland, 1976; Contbr. articles to profl. jours., also book revs. Fulbright and Guggenheim research fellows, France, 1961-62; Guggenheim research fellow, 1970; research grantee Am. Council Learned Socs. and Am. Philos. Soc., 1972. Mem. Am. Polit. Sci. Assn., Am. Assn. Slavic Studies, A.A.U.P. Home: 1624 Marion Ave Durham NC 27705

KULTERMANN, UDO, architectural historian; b. Stettin, Germany, Oct. 14, 1927; came to U.S., 1967, naturalized, 1981; s. Georg and Charlotte (Schultz) K.; m. Judith Danoff, May 10, 1975. Student, U. Greifswald, Germany, 1946-50; Ph.D. magna cum laude, U. Muenster, Germany, 1953. Curatorial asst. Kunsthalle, Bremen, Germany, 1954-55; dir. city art mus. Schloss Morsbroich, Leverkusen, Germany, 1959-64; lectr. Harvard U., Yale U., U. Calif., Berkeley, UCLA, U. Pa., U. Minn., 1965—; prof. archtl. history Washington U., St. Louis, 1967—; participant 1st Internat. Congress African Culture, Salisbury, So. Rhodesia, 1962; lectr. U. Tel Aviv, U. Haifa, U. Jerusalem, 1972, U. Melbourne, U. Sydney, U. Calcutta, U. Bombay, 1977, U. Cairo, U. Beirut, 1978, U. Damascus, U. Khartoum, 1979, U. Buenos Aires, 1980, others; participant 2d Arab Biennale Art, Morocco, 1976-77, Internat. Symposium for Islamic Architecture and Urbanism, Dammam, Saudi Arabia, 1980; mem. Architecture commn. Biennale Venice, 1979-82. Author: Architecture of Today, 1958, New Japanese Architecture, 1960, New Architecture in the World, 1965, History of Art History, 1966, The New Sculpture-Assemblage and Environments, 1967, The New Painting, 1969, rev. edit., 1978; author: New Directions in African Architecture, 1969; Author: Art and Life—. The Function of Intermedia, 1970; author: (with Werner Hofmann) Modern Architecture in Color, 1970; Author: New Realism, 1972, Die Architektur im 20 Jahrhundert, 1977, 3d edit., 1982, Ernest Trova, 1978, I Contemporanei Storia della Scultura nel Mondo, 1979, Architecture in the Seventies, 1980, Architects of the Third World, 1980. Home: 6803 Kingsbury Blvd Saint Louis MO 63130 Office: Washington University Saint Louis MO 63130

KUMAR, ROMESH, chemical engineer; b. Rajpura, India, Oct. 18, 1944; came to U.S., 1966; s. Kundan Lal and Pushpa (Wati) Agarwal; m. Kum-Kum Khanna, Feb. 22, 1976. B.S., Panjab U., India, 1965; M.S., U. Calif.-, Berkeley, 1968, Ph.D., 1972. Postdoctoral appointee Argonne (Ill.) Nat. Lab., 1972-73, asst. chem. engr., 1973-76, chem. engr., 1976—, also group leader environmental chemistry group. Contbr. to: Weissberger's Techniques in Chemistry, 1975. Recipient Silver medal Panjab U., 1965. Mem. Am. Inst. Chem. Engrs. Hindu., AAAS. Patentee in field. Home: 1028 Emerald Ln Naperville IL 60540 Office: 9700 S Cass Ave Argonne IL 60439

KUMAR, SUDHIR, mechanical engineering educator; b. Saharanpur, Uttar Pradesh, India, Oct. 31, 1933; came to U.S., 1955, naturalized, 1970; s. Dharma and Raj (Dulari) Raj; m. Jyotsna Laxminarayan Kapil, Dec. 18, 1960; children: Nisha Rani, Shiv Raj, Anita Rani. B.S., Bareilly Coll., 1950, M.S., 1952; M.S., Indian Inst. Sci., 1955; Ph.D., Pa. State U., 1958. Instr. physics Bareilly Coll., 1950-51; research fellow Indian Inst. Sci., Bangalore, 1952-55; research asso., asst. prof. Pa. State U., University Park, 1955-59; with U.S. Army Research Office, Durham, N.C., 1958-71, br. chief, 1960-62, asso. dir. engring., 1962-71; prof., chmn. dept. mechanics, mech. and aerospace engring. Ill. Inst. Tech., Chgo., 1971-78, prof., dir. r.r. engring. lab., 1978—; vis. lectr., later adj. asso. prof. Duke, 1958-71; adj. asso. prof. N.C. State U. at Raleigh, 1968-71. Contbr. articles to profl. jours. Bd. dirs. India League Am., 1972—. Govt. India research fellow, 1952-55. Mem. AIAA (chmn. 1967-68), Indian Soc. Theoretical and Applied Mechanics, Transp. Research Bd., Transp. Research Forum, ASME, Am. Acad. Mechanics, Western Soc. Engrs., Sigma Xi, Tau Beta Pi. Research on r.r. engring., wheel-rail interaction and wear, pneumatic high speed tube transp. system and subsurface housing for hot arid lands; vacuum air missile launch system; noise. Home: 17 W 434 Sutton Pl Westmont IL 60559 Office: Dept Mech Engring Ill Inst Tech Chicago IL 60616 *I try to live by "Karma Yoga" or the Yoga of action. We must carry our responsibility with the best of our abilities while maintaining a detached outlook. If the best effort has been put, one shouldn't be sorry for the failures or be proud of the successes.*

KUMIN, MAXINE WINOKUR, author, poet; b. Phila., June 6, 1925; d. Peter and Doll (Simon) Winokur; m. Victor Montwid Kumin, June 29, 1946; children—Jane Simon, Judith Montwid, Daniel David. A.B., Radcliffe Coll., 1946, M.A., 1948. Free-lance writer, 1953—; Cons. in poetry Library of Congress, 1981—. Author: poems Halfway, 1961, The Privilege, 1965; novel Through Dooms of Love, 1965, The Passions of Uxport, 1968; poems The Nightmare Factory, 1970; novel The Abduction, 1971; poems Up Country, 1972 (Pulitzer prize for poetry 1973); novel The Designated Heir, 1974; poems House, Bridge, Fountain, Gate, 1975, The Retrieval System, 1978, Our Ground Time Here Will Be Brief, 1982; essays To Make A Prairie, 1979; short stories Why Can't We Live Together Like Civilized Human Beings?, 1982; author 20 children's books; contbr. poems to nat. mags. Recipient Am. Acad. and Inst. Arts and Letters award, 1980; Woodrow Wilson vis. fellow, 1979-80. Mem. Poetry Soc. Am. Address: care Curtis Brown Ltd 575 Madison Ave New York NY 10022

KUMLER, KIPTON CORNELIUS, consultant, photographer; b. Cleve., June 20, 1940; s. Hubbard Harry and Evelyn Rose (Cornelius) K.; m. Katherine Alice Coe, Nov. 22, 1969; children: Aden Welles, Emily Coe. B.E.E., Cornell U., 1963, M.E.E., 1967; M.B.A., Harvard U., 1969. Sr. cons. Arthur D. Little, Cambridge, Mass., 1969-79; pres. Lexington Cons. Group, Mass., 1979—. Author: Kipton Kumler: Photographs, 1975, A Portfolio of Plants, 1977, Plant Leaves, 1978; one-man exhbns. include, Schoelkopf Gallery, N.Y.C., 1975, Cronin Gallery, Houston, 1977, 80, Grapestake Gallery, San Francisco, 1978, N.J. State Mus., Trenton; represented in permanent collections, Met. Mus., N.Y.C., Mus. Modern Art, N.Y.C., Boston Mus. Fine Arts, Bibliotheque National, Paris, Victoria and Albert Mus., London., Internat. Mus. Photography, George Eastman House, Rochester, R.I. Sch. Design, Mus. Fine Arts, Houston, Amon Carter Mus., Ft. Worth. Served with USN, 1963-67. Nat. Endowment Arts Survey grantee, 1976, 80; Mass. Artists Found. photography fellow, 1977, 80. Unitarian. *

KUMMEL, ROBERT D., food company executive; b. 1921. B.S., LL.B., U Wis. With J.I. Case Co., 1948-52, Carnation Co., Los Angeles, 1953—, v.p. research and new products planning, 1965-69, v.p. legal research and new product planning, 1969-70, sr. v.p. legal and research, 1970-79, exec. v.p., dir., 1979—. Office: Carnation Co 5045 Wilshire Blvd Carnation Bldg Los Angeles CA 90036 *

KUMMER, FRED S., JR., contracting company executive; b. Middletown, N.Y., Apr. 23, 1929; s. Fred S. and Gertrude K.; m. June M., Mar. 21, 1954; children: Caroline J., Fred S., Melanie G. B.S., Mo. Sch. Mines and Metallurgy, 1955. Founder, pres. HBE Corp., St. Louis, 1960—, also chmn., treas. Trustee St. Louis U. Office: HBE Corp 717 Office Pkwy Saint Louis MO 63141

KUMMER, GLENN F., mobile home company executive; b. Park City, Utah, 1933; married. B.S., U. Utah, 1961. Sr. acct. Ernst & Ernst, 1961-65; trainee Fleetwood Enterprises Inc., Riverside, Calif., 1965-67, purchasing mgr., 1967-68, plant mgr., 1968-70, gen. mgr. recreational vehicle div., 1970-71, asst. v.p. ops. to v.p. ops., 1971-72, sr. v.p. ops., 1972-77, exec. v.p. ops., 1977-82, pres., chief exec. officer, 1982—, dir. Office: Fleetwood Enterprises Inc 3125 Myers St Box 7638 Riverside CA 92523 *

KUMMERFELD, DONALD DAVID, publisher; b. Gilroy, Calif., June 11, 1934; s. Theodore and Edith Aileen (Bowman) K.; m. Elizabeth Kubota Miller, Feb. 14, 1970; 1 dau., Theodosia W. B.A., Stanford U., 1956, M.A., 1958; M.A., Harvard U., 1960; postgrad., London Sch. Econs., 1961. Prin. examiner housing and urban devel. U.S. Bur. of Budget, Washington, 1961-68; sr. research officer Urban Inst. Washington, 1968-69; partner Govt. Research Corp., Washington, 1969-71; v.p. 1st Boston Corp., N.Y.C., 1971-75; budget dir. City of N.Y., 1976-77, 1st dep. mayor, 1977; exec. dir. N.Y. State Emergency Fin. Control Bd., 1978; pres., chief operating officer News Am. Pub., Inc., 1978—; dir. News Internat. plc., London, News Corp. Ltd., Sydney, Sun Chem. Corp., N.Y.C. Pres. Mcpl. Fin. Forum Washington, 1968-69; trustee Citizens Budget Commn., N.Y.C. Brookings Instn. fellow, 1965. Club: Harvard (N.Y.C.). Office: News Am Pub Inc 210 South St New York NY 10002

KUMMERT, RICHARD OSBORNE, lawyer, educator; b. Chgo., Nov. 23, 1932; s. Frederick A. and Edith L. (Osborne) K.; m. Carol R. Tewksbury, Dec. 27, 1957; children—Julia R., Theodore G. B.S., Ill. Inst. Tech., 1953; M.B.A., Northwestern Univ., 1955; LL.B., Stanford Univ., 1961. Bar: Calif. bar 1961; C.P.A., Ill. Asso. firm O'Melveny & Myers, Los Angeles, 1961-64; asso. prof. law U. Wash., Seattle, 1964-67, prof. law, 1967—, asso. dean Law Sch., 1979-81. Research editor: Supplements to the Model Business Corporation Act Annotated, 2d edit, 1973, 77. Bd. trustees Law Sch. Admission Council, 1973-74, chmn. test devel. and research com., 1974-76. Served with U.S. Army, 1955-58. Mem. Wash. State Bar Assn. (corp. law rev. com. 1975—), Order of Coif. Home: 7733 29th Ave NE Seattle WA 98115 Office: Law Sch Univ of Washington JB-20 Seattle WA 98195

KUNDAHL, GEORGE GUSTAVUS, government executive; b. Washington, July 7, 1940; s. George G. and Adelaide (Wampler) K.; m. Janette Bonner Adcox, Feb. 1, 1962; children: Gustavus George, Giffith Allen; m. 2d Joy Carol Wons, June 28, 1975. B.A., Davidson Coll., 1962; M.A., U. Ala., 1964, Ph.D., 1967. Instr. U. Ala., Tuscaloosa, 1965-66; budget examiner Office Mgmt. and Budget, Washington, 1968-77; dep. exec. dir. SEC, Washington, 1977-81, exec. dir., 1981—. Served to capt. U.S. Army, 1966-68; served to lt. col. USAR, 1969—. Home: 1377 N Pegram St Alexandria VA 22304 Office: 450 5th St NW Washington DC 20549

KUNDERT, ALICE E., state ofcl.; b. Java, S.D., July 23, 1920; d. Otto J. and Maria (Rieger) K. Elementary tchr.'s cert., No. State Coll., Aberdeen, S.D., state tchr. cert. Tchr. elementary grades, 1939-43, 48-54; clk., mgr., buyer Gates Dept. Store, Beverly Hills, Calif., Clifton Dress Shop, Hollywood, Calif., 1943-48; dep. supt. schs., Campbell County, S.D., 1954, county cts. clk., 1955-60, register deeds, 1955-69, town treas., Mound City, 1965-69, auditor, State of S.D., Pierre, 1969-79, sec. of state, 1980—. Leader 4-H Club, 1949-53, county project leader in citizenship, 1963-64; sec. Greater Campbell County Assn., 1955-57; organizer, leader Mound City Craft and Recreation Club, 1955-60; chmn. Heart Fund, March Dimes, Red Cross, Mental Health drs.; mem. S.D. Gov.'s Study Commn., 1968—; mem. state and local adv. com. region VIII Office Econ. Opportunity; bd. mem., chmn. Black Hills Recreation Lab., 1956-61; exec. sec. Internat. Leaders Lab., Ireland, 1963; Polit. co. vice chmn. Republican Com., 1964-69, sec-treas. fin. chmn., 1968; mem. State Rep. Adv. Com., 1966-68; state and nat. counselor Teen Age Rep. Club Campbell County, 1964—. Named Outstanding Teenage Rep. adv. in nation, 1970, 71, 76; Recipient Disting. Alumni award No. State Coll., 1975. Home: 407 N Van Buren St Pierre SD 57501 Office: Office Sec of State State Capitol Bldg Pierre SD 57501

KUNG, SHIEN WOO, banker; b. Hangchow, China, Mar. 19, 1909; came to U.S., 1949; s. Wu Kan and Woo (Tze) K.; m. Wei-Ven Yae, Aug. 22, 1931; children—Lee (Mrs. Robert P. Wei), Edward Y., Nancy (Mrs. Yung Wong), Robert C. B.A., North Central Coll., 1926, LL.D., 1962; D.C.S., N.Y. U., 1930. Research asso. market research Comml. Press, Ltd., Shanghai, 1930-32; editor Chinese Econ. Jour., Bur. Fgn. Trade, Shanhai, 1932-33; prof. econs. and internat. trade Shanghai Coll. and Hangchow Coll., China, 1933-36; mgr. Bank of China, Tsingtao, 1936-49; dir. Central Trust of China, N.Y., 1949-62, adviser, 1964-68; exec. v.p. Internat. Comml. Bank of China, N.Y., 1969-72; chmn. bd. Chinese Am. Bank, N.Y., 1969-72, Bank of Canton of Calif., San Francisco, 1972—, Calif. Canton Internat. Bank, Ltd., Nassau, Bahamas, 1974. Author: Foreign Trade of China, 1936, Chinese in American Life; Contbr. articles to profl. jours. Bd. trustees China Inst. in Am., Inc., N.Y.C., 1962. Club: Commonwealth (Calif.). Office: Bank of Canton of California 555 Montgomery St San Francisco CA 94111

KUNIN, CALVIN MURRAY, physician, educator; b. Burlington, Vt., May 3, 1929; s. Elihu and Lena K.; m. Ilene Jacobson, July 3, 1976; children—Jean, Mark, Ben. A.B., Columbia Coll., 1949; M.D., Cornell U., 1953. Intern N.Y. Hosp., N.Y.C., 1953-54; resident Peter Bent Brigham Hosp., Boston, 1956-57, Boston City Hosp., 1957-59; prof. preventive medicine and medicine U. Va., 1959-70; prof. medicine U. Wis., 1970-79; prof., chmn. dept. medicine Ohio State U., 1979—; chief med. service VA Hosp., Madison, Wis., 1970-79; cons. in field. Author: Detection, Prevention and Management of Urinary Tract Infections, 3d edit, 1979; Contbr. numerous articles to profl. jours. Served with USPHS, 1954-56. Mem. Am. Assn. Physicians, Am. Soc. Clin. Investigation, Infection Disease Soc. Am., AAAS, A.C.P. Jewish. Home: 2447 Coventry Rd Columbus OH 43221 Office: 410 W 10th Ave Columbus OH 43210

KUNITZ, STANLEY JASSPON, poet, editor, educator; b. Worcester, Mass., July 29, 1905; s. Solomon Z. and Yetta Helen

(Jasspon) K.; m. Helen Pearce, 1930 (div. 1937); m. Eleanor Evans, Nov. 21, 1939 (div. 1958); 1 dau., Gretchen; m. Elise Asher, June 21, 1958. A.B. summa cum laude, Harvard U., 1926, M.A., 1927; Litt.D. (hon.), Clark U., 1961, Anna Maria Coll., 1977, L.H.D., Worcester State Coll., 1980. Editor Wilson Library Bull., 1928-43; mem. lit. faculty Bennington Coll., 1946-49; prof. English Potsdam (N.Y.) State Tchrs. Coll., 1949-50; dir. seminar Potsdam Summer Workshop in Creative Arts, 1949-53; lectr. The New Sch., 1950-57; vis. prof. poetry U. Wash., 1955-56; vis. prof. English Queens Coll., 1956-57, Brandeis U., 1958-59; dir. poetry workshop Poetry Center YMHA, N.Y., 1958-62; Danforth vis. lectr. numerous Am. colls., 1961-63; lectr. Columbia, 1963-66, adj. prof. writing Grad. Sch. Arts, 1967—; vis. prof. Vassar Coll., 1981; mem. staff writing dept. Fine Arts Work Center, Provincetown, Mass., 1968—; editor Yale Series Younger Poets, 1969-77; vis. prof. poetry Yale U., 1970, Rutgers U. at Camden, 1974; vis. prof., sr. fellow in humanities Princeton U., 1978; cons. poetry Library of Congress, 1974-76. Author: verse Intellectual Things, 1930, Living Authors, 1931, Authors Today and Yesterday, 1933, Junior Book of Authors, 1934, British Authors of the 19th Century, 1936, American Authors, 1600-1900, 1938, Twentieth Century Authors, 1942, First Supplement, 1955, Passport to the War, 1944, British Authors Before 1800, 1952, Selected Poems, 1928-1958, 1958, Poems of John Keats, 1964, European Authors, 1000-1900, 1967, The Testing-Tree, 1971, The Terrible Threshold, 1974, The Coat Without a Seam, 1974, A Kind of Order, A Kind of Folly: Essays and Conversations, 1975, The Poems of Stanley Kunitz 1928-1978, 1979, The Wellfleet Whale and Companion Poems, 1983; Translator: (with others) Antiworlds (A. Voznesensky), 1966, Antiworlds and The Fifth Ace, 1967, Stolen Apples (Y. Yevtushenko), 1971, (with Max Hayward) Poems of Akhmatova, 1973, Story Under Full Sail (A. Voznesensky), 1974; Editor, co-translator: Orchard Lamps (Ivan Drach), 1978. Served with AUS, 1943-45. Recipient Garrison medal for poetry Harvard, 1926, Oscar Blumenthal prize, 1941; Guggenheim fellow creative writing, 1945-46; Amy Lowell traveling fellow for poetry, 1953-54; Levinson prize for poetry, 1956; Harriet Monroe award U. Chgo., 1958; Ford Found. grantee, 1958-59; Nat. Inst. Arts and Letters grantee, 1959; recipient Pulitzer prize in poetry, 1959; Brandeis Creative Arts Poetry award, 1964; Lenore Marshall award for poetry, 1980; Nat. Endowment Arts sr. fellow, 1984. Mem. Acad. Am. Poets (fellowship award 1968, chancellor 1970—); mem. Nat. Inst. Arts and Letters, Am. Acad. Arts and Letters, Phi Beta Kappa. Home: 37 W 12th St New York NY 10011

KUNKEL, RICHARD CHARLES, teacher educator; b. St. Louis, Feb. 10, 1937; s. Oscar C. and Elizabeth V. (Lynch) K.; m. Patricia Deachan; children: Karl, Nancy, Veronica, Lynn; m. 2d Susan A. Tucker, July 27, 1983. B.S.Ed., Northeast Mo. State Coll., 1959; M.Ed., U. Mo., 1962; Ph.D., St. Louis U., 1965. Ct. researcher Dunn & Bradstreet, St. Louis, 1955-57; social studies tchr. Weldon Springs Sch. Dist., Mo., 1959-60; counselor, staff tchrs. program Parkway West High Sch., Chesterfield, Mo., 1960-62, dir. adult edn., asst. high sch. prin., 1962-65; asst. prof. Burris Lab. Sch., 1965-68; asst. to pres. St. Louis U., 1967-68; assoc. prof. Ball State U., Muncie, Ind., 1968-72; chmn. dept. edn. St. Louis U., 1972-78; dean Coll. Edn., U. Nev.-Las Vegas, 1978-84; exec. dir. Nat. Council Accreditation of Tchr. Edn., 1984—. Contbr. articles to profl. jours. Chmn. Com. on Profl. Standards in Edn., 1979-83. Lilly Endowment grantee, 1975-78; Danforth Found. grantee, 1975-76. Mem. Am. Assn. Colls. Tchr. Edn. (bd. dirs. 1983—, co-chmn. New Deans Inst. 1983), Assn. Colls. and Schs. Edn. in State Univs. and Land Grant Colls. (dir. 1982-83). Office: U Nev Coll of Edn 4505 Maryland Pkwy Las Vegas NV 89154

KUNKEL, WULF BERNARD, physicist, educator; b. Eichenau, Germany, Feb. 6, 1923; came to U.S., 1947, naturalized, 1952; s. Friederich W. and Auguste N. (Löwengard) K.; m. Erika A.L. Rawitscher, Dec. 23, 1960; children—Laurence O., Barbara N., Maya T. Student, U. Amsterdam, 1945-46; B.A., U. Calif., Berkeley, 1948, Ph.D., 1951. Research engr. Inst. Engring. Research, U. Cal. at Berkeley, 1951-56, physicist Lawrence Berkeley Lab., 1956—, head plasma physics group, 1970—; mem. faculty U. Calif., Berkeley, 1953—, prof. physics, 1967—; cons. in field. Bd. editors: Plasma Physics, 1970-80; Contbr. papers in field. Guggenheim fellow, 1955-56, 72-73; recipient Alexander von Humboldt award, W. Ger., 1980. Fellow Am. Phys. Soc.; mem. Phi Beta Kappa, Sigma Xi. Home: 1115 Hillview Rd Berkeley CA 94708

KUNKLER, ARNOLD WILLIAM, surgeon; b. St. Anthony, Ind., Nov. 18, 1921; s. Edward J. and Selma (Hasenour) K.; m. Muriel Helen Burns, May 22, 1954; children: Lisa, Arnold William, Carolyn, Christine, Phillip, Kevin. A.B., Ind. U., 1943, M.D., 1949. Diplomate: Am. Bd. Surgery. Intern, Ind. U. Med. Ctr., Indpls., 1949-50, asst. resident in surgery, fellow vascular surg. research, 1950-54, resident in surgery, 1954-55, faculty, 1955—, clin. prof. surgery, 1976—; individual practice medicine specializing in gen. surgery, Terre Haute, Ind., 1955—; dir. med. edn. Terre Haute Regional Hosp., 1970-79; staff Terre Haute Center Med. Edn., Terre Haute Regional Hosp. Contbr. articles to profl. jours. Pres. Terre Haute Med. Edn. Found., 1972-73, 78-81, bd. dirs., 1967—; pres. community adv. council Terre Haute Center Med. Edn., 1976-80; treas. Wabash Valley Community Blood Program, 1974—; trustee Terre Haute Regional Hosp., 1978—, chmn. bd., 1981—. Served with U.S. Army, 1943-46; ETO. Fellow ACS (pres. Ind. chpt. 1980-81); mem. Terre Haute C. of C., Vigo County Cancer Soc., Vigo County Med. Soc., AMA, Ind., Pan Am. med. assns., Pan Pacific Surg. Assn., Aesculapian Soc. Wabash Valley, Soc. Abdominal Surgeons, Ind. Soc. Chgo. Democrat. Roman Catholic. Club: Country of Terre Haute. Home: 3515 Ohio Blvd Terre Haute IN 47803 Office: 4333 S 7th St Terre Haute IN 47802 *Success and service are interdependent.*

KUNST, LAWRENCE JOHN, lawyer; b. Dallas, July 29, 1922; s. Harvey Joseph and Dorothy (Sales) K.; m. Linda June Forrester, Aug. 11, 1952; children: Rita, Robert, Stephen. LL.B., Washington U., 1950. Bar: Calif. bar 1950, Nev. bar 1959. Since practiced in, Los Angeles; partner firm Gibson, Dunn & Crutcher, 1965—; sec., gen. counsel Baker Internat. Corp., Orange, Calif., 1962-71; asst. prof. UCLA, 1972-77, prof. corp. law, 1978—; dir. Lockhead Corp., Carnation Co., Surety Savs. & Loan Assn. Past pres. Am. Bd. Trial Advocates, Boys Clubs Los Angeles. Served to capt. USAAF, 1943-46. Decorated Silver Star, D.F.C. Mem. ABA, State Bar Calif., Am. Judicature Soc., Los Angeles C. of C., Phi Delta Phi. Clubs: Jonathan (Los Angeles); Links (N.Y.C.). Lodges: K. T.; Lions; Odd Fellows. Home: Werik Apts 3614 Atlantic Ave Long Beach CA 90807

KUNSTLER, WILLIAM MOSES, lawyer, educator, lectr., author; b. N.Y.C., July 7, 1919; s. Monroe Bradford and Frances (Mandelbaum) K.; m. Lotte Rosenberger, Jan. 14, 1943 (div. Oct. 1, 1976); children—Karin F. Goldman, Jane B. Drazek; m. Margaret L. Cohen, Oct. 6, 1976; children—Sarah Cohen-Kunstler, Emily Cohen-Kunstler. B.A., Yale U., 1941; LL.B., Columbia U., 1948. Bar: N.Y. bar 1948, D.C. bar 1958. Exec. trainee R.H. Macy & Co., N.Y.C., 1948-49; lectr. English Columbia U., 1946-50; partner firm Kunstler, Kunstler, Hyman and Goldberg (and predecessor firm), N.Y.C., 1949—; asso. prof. law N.Y. Law Sch., 1950—, Pace Coll., 1951—; lectr. New Sch., 1966—; sr. fellow Notre Dame U., 1971. Author: Our Pleasant Vices, 1941, The Law of Accidents, 1954, First Degree, 1960, Beyond a Reasonable Doubt?, 1961, The Case for Courage, 1962, And Justice for All, 1963, The Minister and the Choir Singer, 1964, Deep in My Heart, 1966, The Hall-Mills Murder Case, 1980, also articles, book revs. Bd. dirs. Nat. Emergency Civil Liberties Com.; v.p., bd. dirs. Center for Constl. Rights. Served to maj. AUS, 1941-46; PTO. Decorated Bronze Star medal; recipient Press award N.Y. State Bar Assn., 1957, Civil Rights award, 1963; 1st award Ohio Radio-Television Inst., 1960. Mem. Assn. Bar City N.Y., ACLU (dir. 1964—, nat. council 1968—, nat. emergency civil liberties com. 1968—), Phi Beta Kappa, Phi Delta Phi. Home: 13 Gay St New York NY 10014 Office: Center for Constitutional Rights 853 Broadway New York NY 10003

KUNTZ, EUGENE OSCAR, lawyer, educator; b. Corpus Christi, Tex., Oct. 8, 1913; s. Walter Nichols and Katie (Lang) K.; m. Rosamond Louise Miller, Mar. 9, 1940; 1 dau., Karen Joyce Maloy. A.B., Baylor U., 1945, J.D., 1940; LL.M., Harvard, 1947. Bar: Tex. 1938. Practice in, Amarillo, 1940-41; asst. prof. law U. Wyo., 1947-50, asso. prof., 1950-52; prof. law U. Okla., Norman, 1952—, dean Law Sch., prof. law, 1965-70, dean emeritus, 1970—, G. L. Cross research prof. emeritus, 1971—, Alfred P. Murrah prof. emeritus, 1980—; partner McAfee, Taft, Cates, Kuntz & Mark, 1958-65, of counsel, 1971—; spl. justice Okla. Supreme Ct., 1971. Author: Kuntz, Oil and Gas, Vols. 1-7 and supplement, 1962-80, Kuntz Supplement to Thornton on Oil and Gas, 1960, Pocket Parts to Thornton on Oil and Gas, 1956, Newspaper Laws of Wyoming, 1952; Editor: Oil and Gas Reporter, 1955—; Bd. editors: Okla. Bar Assn; Contbr. articles profl. jours. Dir. Sneed Oil Co., 1956-65, Okla. Nat. Bank, 1968-72; chmn. bd. Norman Bank Commerce, 1972—; Spl. adviser Gov.'s Com. on Tax Reform, 1966-67; mem. Okla. Acad. for State Goals, 1966-67; vice chmn. Spl. Com. on Tax Revision, 1970-71; chmn. Gov.'s Adv. Com. on Spl. Session, 1978; Past pres., trustee Presbytery Washita, 1963-68, 75-78. Served to lt. comdr. USNR, 1941-45. Recipient Gerald Klein award, 1970; Disting. Service citation U. Okla., 1981. Mem. Am. Bar Assn., Okla. Bar Assn. (vice chmn. commn. on continuing legal edn.), Okla. Inst. Taxation (past pres.), Order of Coif, Phi Alpha Delta. Presbyn. (elder; commr. to Gen. Assembly 1973). Home: 3720 Ives Way Norman OK 73069

KUNTZ, MARION LUCILE LEATHERS, classics educator; b. Atlanta, Sept. 6, 1924; d. Otto Asa and Lucile (Parks) Leathers; m. Paul G. Kuntz, Nov. 26, 1970; children by previous marriage: Charles, Otto Alan (Daniels). B.A., Agnes Scott Coll., 1945; M.A., Emory U., 1964, Ph.D., 1969. Lectr. Latin Lovett Sch., Atlanta, 1963-66; mem. faculty Ga. State U., 1966—, assoc. prof., 1969-73, prof. Latin and Greek, 1973—, Regents' Prof., 1975, chmn. dept. fgn. langs., 1975—. Author: Colloquium of the Seven About Secrets of the Sublime of Jean Bodin, 1975, Guillaume Postel, Prophet of the Restitution of All Things: His Life and Thought, 1981. Named Latin Tchr. of Year State Ga., 1965; Semple scholar, 1965; Am. Classical League scholar, 1966; Am. Council Learned Socs. grantee, 1970, 73, 76; recipient medal for excellence in renaissance studies City of Tours, France. Mem. Am. Philol. Assn., Renaissance Soc. Am., Am. Soc. Aesthetics, Am. Cath. Philos. Assn., Soc. Philosophy and Religion, Am. Soc. Ch. History, Internat. Soc. Neo-Platonic Studies, Internat. Soc. Neo-Latin Studies, Société des Seizémistes, Medieval Acad., Soc. Medieval and Renaissance Philosophy, Archaeol. Inst. Am., Classical Assn. Midwest and South (Semple award 1965), Am. Acad. Rome (sec.-treas. 1970—), Italian Cultural Soc., DeKalb Hist. Soc. (v.p. 1977—), Hellenic Study Club (pres. Atlanta 1974), Phi Beta Kappa, Phi Kappa Phi. Roman Catholic. Home: 1655 Ponce de Leon Ave Atlanta GA 30307

KUNTZ, PAUL GRIMLEY, philosopher, educator; b. Phila., Nov. 22, 1915; s. Franklin Samuel and Sadie Treichler (Grimley) K.; m. Marion Leathers Daniels, Nov. 26, 1970; children (by previous marriage): Sarah Zabriskie Kuntz, Joel DuBois, Timothy Romeyn, Susan Deborah Kuntz Sawyer. A.B. with high honors in Philosophy, Haverford Coll., 1937; S.T.B., Harvard, 1940, S.T.M., 1941, Ph.D., 1946. Asst. to dean Harvard, 1938-41; instr. Smith Coll., 1946-48; asst. prof. philosophy Grinnell Coll., 1948-52, asso. prof., 1952-57, prof., 1957-66, Noble prof., 1961-66; dir. Grinnell Seminar on Order, 1963-64; prof. philosophy Emory U., Atlanta, 1966—, chmn. dept., 1966-69; Kent fellow Soc. Values in Higher Edn., 1946; Ford fellow Yale, 1955-56; fellow Woodrow Wilson Internat. Center for Scholars, Smithsonian Instn., 1970-71. Author: (with Neal W. Klausner) Philosophy: the Study of Alternative Beliefs, 1961, The Concept of Order, 1968, Lotze's System of Philosophy, 1971, Alfred North Whitehead, 1984, Bertrand Russell, 1985; also numerous articles.; Contbr. chpts. to books. Mem. Am. Philos. Assn., Mind Assn., Metaphys. Soc. Am. (councillor 1963-65, del. to Am. Council Learned Socs. 1966-70, program chmn. 1978), Am. Soc. Polit. and Legal Philosophy, AAAS, Mediaeval Acad. Am., Brit. Soc. Aesthetics, Am. Cath. Philos. Assn. (exec. council 1970-73), Am. Soc. Aesthetics (trustee 1966-70), Hist. Sci. Soc., Soc. Symbolic Logic, Royal Inst. Philosophy (London), Australasian Soc. Philosophy, Ch. History Soc., Soc. Ancient Greek Philosophy, Iowa Philos. Soc. (pres. 1961-62), John Dewey Soc., Wider Quaker Fellowship, Soc. Realistic Philosophy, So. Soc. Philosophy and Psychology (program chmn. 1969), Soc. Philosophy Religion, Ga. Philosophy Soc. (pres. 1968), C.S. Peirce Soc., Société Européenne de Culture, Internat. Soc. for Metaphysics (chmn. organizing com., hon. pres. 1973—), Phi Beta Kappa. Home: 1655 Ponce de Leon Ave NE Atlanta GA 30307 also Three Ponds South Woodbury VT 05650

KUNZ, PHILLIP RAY, sociologist; b. Bern, Idaho, July 19, 1936; s. Parley P. and Hilda Irene (Stoor) K.; m. Joyce Sheffield, Mar. 18, 1960; children—Jay, Jenifer, Jody, Johnathan, Jana. B.S., Brigham Young U., 1961, M.S. cum laude, 1962; Ph.D. (fellow), U. Mich., 1967. Instr. Eastern Mich. U., Ypsilanti, 1964, U. Mich., Ann Arbor, 1965-67; asst. prof. sociology U. Wyo., Laramie, 1967-68; prof. sociology Brigham Young U., Provo, Utah, 1968—, acting dept. chmn., 1973; dir. Inst. Geneal. Studies, 1972-74; cons. various ednl. and research instns., 1968—; Missionary Ch. Jesus Christ of Latter-day Saints, Ga. and S.C., 1956-58, mem. high council, 1969-70, bishop. Author 3 books; Contbr. articles on social orgn., family relations and deviant behavior to profl. jours.; contbr. book revs. to profl. jours. Served with AUS, 1954-56. Recipient Karl G. Maeser research award, 1977. Mem. Am. Sociol. Assn., Rocky Mountain Social Sci. Assn., Am. Council Family Relations, Rural Sociol. Soc., Am. Soc. Criminology, Soc. Sci. Study of Religion, Religious Research Assn., Sigma Xi, Phi Kappa Phi, Alpha Kappa Delta. Democrat. Home: 3040 Navajo St Provo UT 84601 Office: Dept of Sociology Brigham Young University Provo UT 84602

KUNZE, GEORGE WILLIAM, soil scientist; b. Warda, Tex., Sept. 16, 1922; s. John Paul and Hermine (Moerbe) K.; m. Flora Mae Rothmann, July 11, 1947; children: Brenda Kay, Wayne Lester. B.S., Tex. A&M U., 1948, M.S., 1950; Ph.D., Pa. State U., 1952. Mem. faculty Tex. A&M U., College Station, 1952—, asst. prof., 1952-56, asso. prof., 1956-60, prof. soil mineralogy, 1960—, asso. dean Grad. Sch., 1967-68, dean, 1968-84; Dir. Bank of A. and M.; Cons. U. Alaska, 1963-66; cons. Bangladesh Agrl. U., 1970, Grad. Sch. Agrl. Scis., Castelar Argentina, 1972; mem. Fed. Adv. Com. on Affirmative Action in Employment Practices in Instns. of Higher Edn.; pres. Conf. So. Grad. Schs., 1980-81. Cons. editor: Soil Science, 1958-84. Served with USAAF, 1943-45. Recipient Faculty Distinguished Achievement award in research Tex. A&M U., 1966, in administration Tex. A.&M. U., 1984. Fellow Mineral. Soc. Am., AAAS, Am. Soc. Agronomy, mem., Clay Mineral Soc. Am (councilor). Lodge: Rotary. Home: 1001 Ashburn E College Station TX 77840

KUNZE, RALPH CARL, savings and loan executive; b. Buffalo, Oct. 31, 1925; s. Bruno E. and Esther (Graubman) K.; m. Helen Hites Sutton, Apr. 1978; children by previous marriage: Bradley, Diane Kunze Cowgill, James. B.B.A., U. Cin., 1950, postgrad., 1962-63; grad., Ind. U. Grad. Sch. Savs. and Loan, 1956, U. Calif., 1973. With Mt. Lookout Savs. & Loan Co., Cin., 1951-63, sec., mng. officer, 1958-63; with Buckeye Fed. Savs. & Loan Assn., Columbus, Ohio, 1963-77, exec. v.p., sec., 1967-70, pres., sec., vice chmn. bd. dirs., 1970-77; pres., chief operating officer, dir. Gate City Savs. and Loan Assn., Fargo, N.D., 1977-81; pres., chief exec. officer, dir. United Home Fed., Toledo, 1981—. Trustee Wesley Glen Retirement Meth. Center, 1974-77; Pres. United Way of Franklin County, Ohio, 1977, also chmn. personnel com.; past pres. Ohio Soc. Prevention Blindness, Toledo Neighborhood Housing Services, Inc.; bd. dirs. Revitalization Corp. Toledo; trustee Kidney Found., NW Ohio. Mem. U.S. Savs. and Loan League, Lambda Chi Alpha. Clubs: Masons (32 deg.), Shriners). Home: 2606 Emmick Dr Toledo OH 43606 Office: 519 Madison Ave Toledo OH 43604

KUNZE, ROBERT JOSEPH, venture capital company executive; b. Bklyn., Aug. 16, 1935; s. Harry John and Helen Gertrude (Quinn) K.; m. Janet Arnold, Oct. 3, 1957; children: Timothy (dec.), Anne, John. B.S. in Chemistry, Bates Coll., 1957. Mktg. mgr. Gen. Electric Plastics Co., Pittsfield, Mass., 1967-68; mng. dir. Gen. Electric Plastics Europe, Bergen Op Zoom, Netherlands, 1968-72; strategic planner Gen. Electric Plastics, Pittsfield, Mass., 1973-74; group v.p. Hatco div. W.R. Grace & Co., Fords, N.J., 1974-77; v.p. W.R. Grace & Co., N.Y.C., 1974-81, sr. v.p., chief tech. officer, 1981-83; mng. dir. venture capital, sr. v.p. Hambrecht and Quist, San Francisco, 1983—; dir. Advanced Genetics Research Inst., Oakland, Calif., 1982—. Mem. Metuchen Bd. Edn., N.J., 1980—; pres. Family and Children's Service Agy., Hyannis, Mass., 1973-74; mem. Mass. State Rev. Bd., Dept. Drug Rehab., 1974. Democrat. Unitarian. Home: 116 Hillside Ave Metuchen NJ 08840 Office: Hambrecht and Quist 235 Montgomery St San Francisco CA 94104

KUNZE, WALTER EDWARD, JR., civil engr.; b. St. Paul, Jan. 3, 1924; s. Walter Edward and Carolina Frieda (Brenning) K.; m. Frances Anne Halverson, June 20, 1947; children—Anne Catherine, Jean Marie, Elizabeth Joan. B.S. in Civil Engring, The Citadel, 1949; S.M., Mass. Inst. Tech., 1950. Registered profl. engr., S.C. Structural engr. Metcalf & Eddy, Boston, 1950-52, Toltz, King and Day, St. Paul, 1952; with Portland Cement Assn., 1952—, v.p. regional ops., 1970-71, group v.p. research and devel., constrn. tech. labs., Skokie, Ill., 1971—. Contbr. articles to profl. jours. Served to 1st lt., inf. U.S. Army, 1943-46. Decorated Purple Heart, Bronze Star, Silver Star. Fellow ASCE, Am. Concrete Inst.; mem. Prestressed Concrete Inst., ASTM, Tau Beta Pi. Home: 530 S Newbury Pl Arlington Heights IL 60005 Office: 5420 Old Orchard Rd Skokie IL 60077

KUNZEL, ERICH, JR., conductor, arranger, educator; b. N.Y.C., Mar. 21, 1935; s. Erich and Elizabeth (Enz) K.; m. Brunhilde Gertrud Strodl, Sept. 5, 1965. A.B. with distinction in Music, Dartmouth, 1957; postgrad., Harvard, 1957-58; A.M., Brown U., 1960; Litt.D., No. Ky. State U. Condr. Sante Fe Opera, 1957, 64, 65; music faculty Brown U., 1958-65; asst. condr. R.I. Philharmonic, 1963-65; resident condr. Cin. Symphony Orch., 1965-77; condr. Cin. Summer Opera, 1966, 73, Cin. Ballet Co., 1966-68; asso. prof. U. Cin. Coll.-Consevatory Music, 1965-71, chmn. opera dept., 1968-70; music dir. Philharmonia Orch., 1967-71, New Haven Symphony Orch., 1974-77, San Francisco Art Commn. Pops, 1981—; condr. Cin. Pops Orch., 1977—; guest condr. Boston Symphony, Cleve. Orch., Boston Pops, Phila. Orch., San Francisco Symphony, Buffalo Philharmonic, Rochester Philharmonic, Pitts. Symphony, Atlantic Symphony, Pitts. Symphony Orch., Chgo. Symphony Orch., Interlochen Arts Festival, Dallas Symphony, Detroit Symphony, Toronto Symphony, Montreal Symphony, St. Louis Symphony, Nat. Symphony, Can. Opera Co., others. Editor, arranger choral works.; Recs. for, Decca Gold Label, Atlantic Records, Telarc Records, Vox Records, Caedmon Records, MMG. Vice pres. Pierre Monteux Meml. Found., Met. Opera Guild. Named Ky. col. Mem. Am. Symphony Orch. League, Phi Delta Theta, Phi Mu Alpha Sinfonia. Office: Music Hall 1241 Elm St Cincinnati OH 45210

KUNZEL, HERBERT, financial service company executive, lawyer; b. Los Angeles, Aug. 15, 1908; s. Herman and Regina (Schwarz) K.; m. Minerva Griswold, May 23, 1947; children: Ridge, Daphne, Kurt, Charles. A.B., U. So. Calif., LL.B., 1934. Bar: Calif. 1935. Ptnr. Luce, Forward, Kunzel & Scripps, San Diego, 1935-53; pres. Solar Turbines, San Diego, 1947-73; pres., reorgn. trustee Westgate Calif. Corp., San Diego, 1973-82; chmn. bd. Itel Corp., San Francisco, 1982—, dir., 1981—; dir. Energy Factors, Inc., San Diego, 1983—. Bd. dirs. Scripps Clinic and Research Found., La Jolla, Calif., 1975—. Served to lt. USNR, 1942-46. Mem. ABA, Calif. Bar Assn., Sigma Chi. Clubs: Bankers (San Francisco); La Jolla Country, San Diego Yacht. Home: 3250 McCall St San Diego CA 92106 Office: Itel Corp 1 Embaracadero Center San Francisco CA 94111

KUNZLER, JOHN EUGENE, physicist; b. Willard, Utah, Apr. 25, 1923; s. John Jacob and Freida (Meier) K.; m. Lois McDonald, Dec. 29, 1950; children: Carol Kunzler Blaine, Marilyn, Bonnie, Kim Kunzler Tomeo. B.S. in Chem. Engring, U. Utah; Ph.D., U. Calif., Berkeley. With AT & T Bell Labs., Murray Hill, N.J., 1952—, dir. electronic materials lab., 1969-73, dir. electronic materials and device lab., 1973-79, dir. electronic materials, processes and devices lab., 1979-83, dir. magnetic bubble subsystems and common tech. support lab., 1983—. Contbr. articles to profl. jours. Recipient John Price Wetherill medal Franklin Inst., 1964; Internat. prize for new materials Am. Phys. Soc., 1979; Kamerlingh Onnes medal, 1979. Fellow Am. Phys. Soc., AAAS; mem. Am. Chem. Soc., Nat. Acad. Engring., Sigma Xi, Tau Beta Pi, Alpha Chi Sigma. Patentee in field. Home: Route 2 Box 130 Port Murray NJ 07865 Office: AT & T Bell Labs 600 Mountain Ave Murray Hill NJ 07974

KUO, FRANKLIN FA-KUN, computer scientist, electricial engineer; b. Hankow, China, Apr. 22, 1934; came to U.S., 1950, naturalized, 1961; s. Steven C. and Grace S. (Huange) K.; m. Dora Lee, Aug. 30, 1958; children: Jennifer, Douglas. B.S., U. Ill., 1955, M.S., 1956, Ph.D, 1958. Asst. prof. dept. elec. engring. Poly. Inst. Bklyn., 1958-60; mem. tech. staff Bell Telephone Labs., Murray Hill, N.J., 1960-66; prof. elec. engring. U. Hawaii, Honolulu, 1966-82; exec. dir. SRI Internat., Menlo Park, Calif., 1982—, Ctr. for Intelligent Computer Systems, 1982—; dir. info. systems Office Sec. of Def., 1976-77; cons. Lawrence Radiation Labs., 1966-71; liason scientist U.S. Office Naval Research, London, 1971-72; cons. prof. elec. engring. Stanford U., Calif., 1982—; mem. exec. panel Chief of Naval Ops., 1980—. Author: Network Analysis and Synthesis, 1962, (2d edit.) Network Analysis and Synthesis, 1966, Linear Circuits and Computations, 1973; co-author: System Analysis by Digital Computer, 1966, Computer Oriented Circuit Design, 1969, Computer Communications Networks, 1973; cons. editor, Prentice-Hall Inc., 1967—; mem. editorial bd.: Computers and Elec. Engring., Computers and Edn., Computer Decisions; contbr. articles to profl. jours.; developer Alohanet packet broadcast radio network, Def. Advanced Research Project. Fellow IEEE (gen. chmn. 6th Data Communications Symposium 1979); mem.

Assn. Computing Machinery, Tau Beta Pi, Eta Kappa Nu. Club: Lansdowne (London). Home: 824 La Mesa Dr Portola Valley CA 94025 Office: SRI Internat 333 Ravenswood Ave Menlo Park CA 94025

KUO, PING-CHIA, historian, educator; b. Yangshe, Kiangsu, China, Nov. 27, 1908; s. Chu-sen and Hsiao-kuan (Hsu) K.; m. Anita H. Bradley, Aug. 8, 1946. A.M., Harvard U., 1930, Ph.D., 1933. Prof. modern history and Far Eastern internat. relations Nat. Wuhan U., Wuchang, China, 1933-38; editor China Forum, Hankow and Chungking, 1938-40; counsellor Nat. Mil. Council, Chungking, China, 1940-46, Ministry Fgn. Affairs, 1943-46; participated in Cairo Conf. as spl. polit. asst. to Generalissimo Chiang Kai-shek, 1943; during war yrs. in Chungking, also served Chinese Govt. concurrently in following capacities: mem. fgn. affairs com. Nat. Supreme Def. Council, 1939-46; chief, editorial and pubs. dept. Ministry Information, 1940-42, mem. central planning bd., 1941-45; tech. expert to Chinese delegation San Francisco Conf., 1945; chief trusteeship sect. secretariat UN, London; (exec. com. prep. commn. and gen. assembly), 1945-46; top-ranking dir. Dept. Security Council Affairs, UN, 1946-48; vis. prof. Chinese history San Francisco State Coll., summers 1954, 58; assoc. prof. history So. Ill. U., 1959-63, prof. history, 1963-72, chmn. dept. history, 1967-71, prof. emeritus, 1972—; sr. fellow Nat. Endowment for Humanities, 1973-74; Pres. Midwest Conf. Asian Studies, 1964. Author: A Critical Study of the First Anglo-Chinese War, with Documents, 1935, Modern Far Eastern Diplomatic History (in Chinese), 1937, China: New Age and New Outlook, 1960, China, in the Modern World Series, 1970; Contbr. to Am. hist. pubs. and various mags. in China and Ency. Brit. Decorated Kwang Hua medal A-1 grade Nat. Mil. Council, Chungking, 1941; Auspicious Star medal Nat. Govt., Chungking, 1944; Victory medal, 1945. Mem. Am. Hist. Assn., Assn. Asian Studies. Club: Commonwealth (San Francisco). Home: 8661 Don Carol Dr El Cerrito CA 94530

KUONY, JOHN HUBERT, museum administrator; b. Milw., Mar. 26, 1917; s. John Hubert and Betty Florence (Tiffany) K.; m. Liane Celine Frank, Mar. 16, 1944. B.A., U. Wis., 1939. Luggage designer Canvas Products Corp., Fond du Lac, Wis., 1946-48; freelance designer The Postillion, Fond du Lac, Wis., 1948-60; dir. Oshkosh Pub. Mus., Wis., 1960—; treas., council mem. Midwest Mus. Conf., 1979—; chmn. bd. dirs. Lakelands Consortium for Arts, Oshkosh, 1982—. Contbr.: chpt. to Prairie, Pines and People, 1976. Chmn. Historic Preservation Com., Winnebago County, Oshkosh, 1975-77; treas. Candelight Club, Oshkosh, 1978-82. Served to 1st lt. USAAF, 1943-46. NSF grantee, 1963-65; City of Oshkosh and pvt. fund grantee, 1980-83. Mem. Am. Assn. Mus., Wis. Acad. Sci. and Letters. Office: Oshkosh Pub Mus 1331 Algoma Blvd Oshkosh WI 54901

KUPCHICK, ALAN CHARLES, advt. agy. exec.; b. Bklyn., Apr. 8, 1942; s. Saul and Sylvia (Streifer) K.; 1 son, Seth. B.F.A., Pratt Inst., 1963. Asst. art dir. Grey Advt., Inc., N.Y.C., 1964-65, art dir., 1965-71, creative supr., 1971-74, group creative dir., 1974-78, v.p., 1969-78; v.p., group creative dir. Wells-Rich-Greene Advt., Los Angeles, 1978-80; sr. v.p., dir. creative services Grey Advt., Los Angeles, 1980—; tchr. Sch. Visual Arts, Pratt Inst., Art Center Coll. of Design, Los Angeles. Recipient awards Art Dirs. Club N.Y., Advt. Club N.Y., Am. TV Comml. Festival, Clio Festival, Cannes Film Festival. Home: 13463 Rand Dr Sherman Oaks CA 91423 Office: 3435 Wilshire Blvd Los Angeles CA 90010

KUPCINET, IRV, columnist; b. Chgo., July 31, 1912; s. Max and Anna (Paswell) K.; m. Essee Joan Solomon, Feb. 12, 1939; children: Karyn (dec.), Jerry Solomon. Student, Northwestern U., 1930-32; A.B., U. N.D., 1935. Sportwriter Chgo. Daily Times, 1935-43; writer column Kup's Column, Chgo. Sun Times, 1943—; host Kup's Show, Chgo.; commentator football telecasts WGN Radio, Chgo.; commentator WBBM-TV, Chgo.; former commentator football broadcasts.; Spl. cons. in charge of columnists for War Finance Div., war chemistry, drives U.S. Treasury Dept. Vice Pres. Dr. Jerome D. Solomon Meml. Found. Recipient Emmy award, moderator TV show, 1960. Mem. Newspaper Guild, Tau Delta Phi. Clubs: Nat. Press (Washington); Chgo. Press, Mchts. and Mfrs. (Chgo.). Office: Chicago Sun Times 401 N Wabash Ave Chicago IL 60611 *

KUPEL, FREDERICK JOHN, software company executive; b. Burbank, Calif., Apr. 22, 1929; s. Martin Charles and Lorene (Murray) K.; m. Nancy Kathryn Eubank, 1952 (div. 1979); children: James Frederick, Douglas Edward; m. Karen J. Jensen, 1980; 1 stepson, John Robert Jensen, Jr. Student, Clarmont Men's Coll., 1948-50; B.A., U. Calif., Berkeley, 1951; M.A. in Psychology, Sonoma State U., 1980. Accting, fin. and mgmt. positions,, 1951-66; acctg. and ops. exec. Evans Products Co., Portland, Oreg., 1967-71; v.p. fin. Columbia Corp., Portland, 1971-77, Plantronics, Inc., Santa Cruz, Calif., 1977-78; chmn. bd. Summit Software Corp, 1982—; cons., 1978—. Counselor Yellow Brick Rd. Program, Portland, 1975-76. Served with AUS, 1946-47. Home: 1685 Midvale Rd Portland OR 97219 Office: 121 SW Salmon #1600 Portland OR 97204

KUPERSMITH, A. HARRY, lawyer, real estate and financial executive; b. Newark, June 13, 1925; s. David and Bessie (Rubinstein) K.; m. Cynthia Skolnick, Dec. 24, 1947; children: Farrell Preston, Mark Jeffrey, Linda Ellen. Cert., Drury Coll., 1943; B.S. cum laude, NYU, 1948; LL.B., Bklyn. Law Sch., 1954, J.S.D., 1956, J.D., 1968. Bar: N.Y. 1954, U.S. Dist. Ct. (so. dist.) N.Y. 1956. With Kupersmith & Kupersmith (legal, financial, tax and real estate cons.), N.Y.C., 1948—; practice as atty., tax, real estate and fin. cons., N.Y.C., 1954—; partner Ramapo Manor Nursing Center, Suffern, N.Y., 1957-75, McQuire-Holiday Motel, 1962-70; pres., chmn. Verson Prodns., Inc., N.Y.C., 1962-67, various real estate instns. and housing devels., 1956—, Exec. Fin. Planning Corp., N.Y.C., 1956-75; exec. v.p., sec.-treas., dir., mem. exec. com. Del Labs., Inc. (and subs.), N.Y.C., 1962-65; chmn. Computer Systems Medicine and Edn. (and subs.), 1969-71; dir. Ram Group Inc., 1974; gen. counsel Hyfin Credit Union, 1979—; pres., chmn. Am. Inst. Econ. Growth, N.Y.C., 1965—; gen. counsel Council Jewish Orgns. in Civil Service, 1973-76; counsel Civil Service-Independent's Party, 1971—; lectr. Columbia U., 1966-69; lectr., instr. on law, taxes, corporate finance, mergers, acquisitions, housing, real estate, tax shelters Columbia, 1958—; Mem. Columbia U. adv. com. nursing home costs for N.Y. State, 1966. Author: An Economic Study of American System, 1956, Tax Havens, 1959, Corporate Finance and Taxes, 1959, Tax Treaties of United States, 1960, United States Industry and Executives Abroad, 1960, Executive Compensation Constructive Receipt, 1961, Corporate Finance and Taxes Defined, 1963, Considerations in Mergers and Acquisitions, 1965, Break Even Techniques, 1965, Men and Their Money, 1966, Nursing Home Industry Review, 1968, Is Nursing Home Business for You?, 1968, Major Health Crisis, 1968, Equity and Venture Capital, 1970, Private Placements, 1970, Capital Growth, 1971, Tax and Investment Shelters, 1971, Investments-Rental Housing vs. Condominiums, 1972, Purchase and Sale of Businesses-Checklist, 1972, Real Estate Partnerships-Government and the Private Investor, 1973, Tax Sheltered Investments, 1973; also articles.; fin. and legal columnist: Drug Trade News, Drug News Weekly, 1965-68. Trustee Martin Revson Trusts, various charitable founds. Served with USAAF, 1943-45. Recipient Wisdom award, 1969. Mem. ABA, Bar Assn. City N.Y., Lawyer-to-Lawyer Consultation Panel, Alpha Epsilon Pi, Psi Chi Omega, Beta Gamma Sigma. Home: 45 Woodland Ave West Orange NJ 07052 Office: 36 W 44th St New York NY 10036 also 45 Woodland Ave West Orange NJ 07052

KUPFER, CARL, ophthalmologist; b. N.Y.C., Feb. 9, 1928; s. James and Hannah (Goldwasser) K.; m. Muriel Kaiser, Dec. 9, 1969; children: Charles David, Sarah Delia. A.B., Yale U., 1948; M.D., Johns Hopkins U., 1952. Diplomate: Am. Bd. Ophthalmology. Intern, asst. resident Wilmer Eye Inst., Johns Hopkins Hosp., 1952-54; lab. asst. biostatistics Johns Hopkins Sch. Medicine, 1953-54; research fellow in ophthalmology Wilmer Eye Inst., 1957-58, Harvard Med. Sch., 1958-60, instr., 1960-62, asst. prof. ophthalmology, 1962-66; prof., chmn. dept. ophthalmology U. Wash. Sch. Medicine, 1966-70; dir. Nat. Eye Inst., NIH, Bethesda, Md., 1970—; pres. Internat. Agy. for Prevention of Blindness, 1982—. Mem. editorial bd.: Investigative Ophthalmology, 1969-78, Am. Jour. Ophthalmology, 1971-82; contbr. articles to med. jours. Bd. dirs. Helen Keller Internat. Served with USAF, 1954-56. Mem. Am. Physiol. Soc., Assn. Research in Vision and Ophthalmology, Am. Acad. Ophthalmology, Am. Ophthalmology Soc., Pan Am. Ophthalmol. Soc. Home: 6016 Neilwood Dr Rockville MD 20852 Office: Nat Eye Inst NIH Bethesda MD 20205

KUPFER, WILLIAM FRANCIS, bishop; b. Bklyn., Jan. 28, 1909; s. Emil Frederick and Mary (Connolly) K. B.A., Maryknoll Sem., 1933. Ordained priest Roman Cath. Ch.; priest, China, 1933-48, procurator, Hong Kong, 1948-51, prefect apostolic, Taichung, Taiwan, 1951-62, bishop, 1962—. Trustee Fujin U., Providence Coll., Viator, Stella Matutine and Holy Saviour Middle Schs., Fujen Primary Sch., Chung Shang Radio Sta. Address: 136 Kuang Fu Rd Taichung Taiwan 400

KUPFERMAN, MEYER, composer; b. N.Y.C., July 3, 1926; s. Elias and Fanny (Hoffman) K.; m. Sylvia Kasten, June 16, 1946 (div.); 1 dau., Lisa; m. Pei-fen Chin, July 24, 1973. Student, Queens Coll., 1944-46. Co-dir. New Chamber Music Soc., 1946-48, Bolton Music Festival, Bolton Landing, N.Y., 1947-48; mem. forum group bd. N.Y. chpt. Internat. Soc. Contemporary Music, 1949-50; tchr. composition, chamber music, music for theatre Sarah Lawrence Coll., 1951—, chmn. music dept., 1979; dir., founder Sarah Lawrence Improvisational Ensemble, 1967—; composer-in-residence Calif. Music Ctr., 1977-80. Composer: film scores Hallelujah the Hills, 1962, A X'mas Memory, 1966, Blast of Silence, 1960, Faces of America, 1965, Goldstein, 1964, Black Like Me, 1964, Cool Wind, 1961, Among the Paths to Eden, 1968; operas In a Garden, 1948, The Curious Fern, 1957, Voices for a Mirror, 1957, Draagenfut Girl, 1958, Doctor Faustus Lights the Lights, 1963, The Judgement, 1966-67, Prometheous, 1976; symphony Symphony No. 12, 1982; chamber music Cycle of Infinities, 1962-67; (choreographed by Martha Graham) ballet score O Thou Desire, 1977; others. First recipient La Guardia Meml. award outstanding achievement field music, 1958; Music award Am. Acad. and Inst. Arts and Letters, 1981; Nat. Endowment Arts grantee, 1974; Guggenheim fellow, 1974-75; Ford Found. grantee, 1975-76. Mem. ASCAP. Home: 171 W 71st St New York NY 10023 Office: Sarah Lawrence Coll Bronxville NY 10708

KUPFERMAN, THEODORE R., state justice; b. N.Y.C., May 12, 1920; s. Samuel H. and Gertrude K.; m. Dorothee Hering, Dec. 21, 1957 (dec. June 1969); children: Theodore R., Stephanie Elisabeth; m. Fran Liner, Sept. 1975. B.S., City Coll. N.Y.; LL.B. (Kent scholar, editor Law Rev.), Columbia. Bar: N.Y. bar, also U.S. Supreme Ct. Law sec. presiding Judge D.W. Peck, appellate div. N.Y. State Supreme Ct., 1948-49; mem. legal dept. Warner Bros. Pictures, Inc., 1949-51, NBC, 1951-53; sec., v.p., gen. counsel Cinerama Prodns. Corp., 1953-59; formerly counsel firm Battle, Fowler, Stokes & Kheel, N.Y.C.; justice Supreme Ct., State of N.Y., 1969-70; asso. justice Appellate Div., First Dept., 1971—; asst., then adj. prof. law N.Y. Law Sch., 1959-64; counsel, legislative asst. minority leader S.M. Isaacs, N.Y. City Council, 1958-62. Editor-in-chief: Communications and the Law Quar, 1978—. Mem. N.Y. City Council, 1962-66; mem. 89-90th Congress 17th Dist. N.Y.; Past chmn. youth services com., bd. dirs. YMCA, N.Y.C.; pres. Layman's Nat. Bible Com., 1975-80, chmn. bd., 1980—. Served to col. J.A.G. N.Y. State Guard. Mem. ABA (past editor bull. sect. internat. and comparative law, Congl. affairs editor Internat. Lawyer, chmn. internat. patent, copyright and trademark relations com.), N.Y. State Bar Assn. (chmn. judges speakers bur. of spl. com. on cts. and community), Fed. Bar Council (pres. 1954-56, chmn. bd. 1956-60), Consular Law Soc. (past pres., trustee), Am. Arbitration Assn. (former mem. panel arbitrators), Acad. Polit. Sci., Internat. Radio and TV Soc., Citizens Union, Phi Beta Kappa. (Chpt. pres.). Republican. Club: City (N.Y.C.) (past pres.). Office: Supreme Court Appellate Division 27 Madison Ave New York NY 10010

KUPLAN, LOUIS, cons. gerontologist; b. N.Y.C., Aug. 11, 1906; s. Abraham and Eva (Brodsky) K.; m. Katherine FitzGerald, Sept. 9, 1936. B.A., UCLA, 1929; postgrad., U. Calif. at Berkeley, 1935, 38. County dir. Calif. Relief Adminstrn., 1934-40; adminstrv. asst. Farm Security Adminstrn., San Francisco, 1940-43; sr. adminstrv. asst. Fed. Pub. Housing Authority, San Francisco, 1943-45; pub. assistance analyst Social Security Adminstrn., San Francisco, 1945-47; chief div. old age security Calif. Dept. Social Welfare, 1947-51; exec. sec. Calif. Interdeptl. Coordinating Com. Aging, 1950-55, Calif. Citizens Adv. Com. Aging, 1955-60; editor Maturity mag., 1954-60; editorial cons. Harvest Years Pub. Co., San Francisco, 1960-63; specialist retirement planning Mgmt. Devel. Center, U. San Francisco, 1960-61; lectr. U. Calif. Extensions, 1965-69, 70, 73, U. San Francisco, 1962-69; instr. Merritt Coll., Oakland, Calif., 1969-74, Contra Costa Coll., 1972—, Diablo Valley Coll., 1972—; dir. Center on Aging, Urban Life Inst., U. San Francisco, 1968-69; Mem. adv. bd. Retirement Advisers, Inc., N.Y.C., 1958-60; chmn. trustees Emeritus Edn., Inc., Palo Alto, Calif., 1971-75; nat. adv. com. White House Conf. Aging, 1961; mem. tech. adv. com. on edn. White House Conf. on Aging, 1970-72; mem. adv. com. on aging Calif. Dept. Mental Hygiene, 1969-73; sci. council Gerontol. Research Found., St. Louis, 1957-63; council geriatrics and gerontology Pan Am. Med. Assn., 1957-62; com. aging Am. Public Welfare Assn.; chmn. Atty. Gen. Calif. Adv. Com. Problems Aging, 1972-74; pres. 5th Internat. Congress Gerontology, 1960; v.p., vice chmn. bd. dirs. Longevity Found., 1960-70; moderator, producer TV program A Gift of Time, KRON-TV, 1969-78; bd. dirs. Food Adv. Service, 1975—, Optimum Achievers, Inc., 1981—, San Francisco Catholic Com. on Aging, 1975—. Recipient award for outstanding services and leadership in developing programs for older adults San Francisco Sr. Center, Arthritis Found. No. Calif., 1971; citation Calif. State Assembly, 1971; award for pub. service Social Security Adminstrn., 1973, San Francisco Cath. Com. on Aging, 1973; award for services in edn. for elderly U. Calif. Extension Center for Learning in Retirement, 1975; award for leadership in health edn. for elderly San Francisco Lung Assn., 1977. Fellow Gerontol. Soc. U.S. (pres. 1958-59); mem. Internat. Assn. Gerontology (pres. 1960-63, citation 1960), Western Gerontology Soc. (founder, pres. 1955-56, named Gerontologist of Year 1957, award leadership 1975), Nat. Assn. Social Workers, Am. Pub. Welfare Assn., Am. Psychol. Assn.; hon. mem. geriatric and gerontol. socs. Argentina, Chile. Home and: 1631 - 35th Ave San Francisco CA 94122 Office: 1658 27th Ave San Francisco CA 94122

KUPPERMAN, ROBERT HARRIS, university official; b. N.Y.C., May 12, 1935; s. Nathan Greenspan and Rose (Winnick) K.; m. Helen Slotnick, Dec. 23, 1967; 1 dau., Tamara. B.A., N.Y. U., 1956, Ph.D. (fellow), 1962. Prin. mathematician Republic Aviation Co., Farmingdale, N.Y., 1959-60; sr. researcher Calif. Inst. Tech., 1960-62; exec. adv. Douglas Aircraft, Santa Monica, Calif., 1962-64; sr. staff mem. Inst. Def. Analyses, Arlington, Va., 1964-67; asst. dir. Office Emergency Preparedness, Washington, 1967-73; dep. exec. dir. Pres.'s Property Rev., 1971-73; adv. counter-terrorism Nat. Security Council; mem. Cabinet Com. to Combat Terrorism; chmn. Interagy. Com. Mass. Destruction and Terrorism, 1976; vis. prof. U. Md., 1974-76; dep. asst. dir. Mil. and Econ. Affairs ACDA, Washington, 1973-75, chief scientist, 1975-79; exec. dir. Center for Strategic and Internat. Studies, Georgetown U., 1979—; pres. Robert H. Kupperman and Assocs., 1979—, RCD Trading Ltd., 1983—; mem. Army Sci. Bd., 1979—; chief of staff U.S. Army, 1979-83; dep. sec. Dept. Transp., 1980-83, undersec. Dept. Def., 1980-83; dir. U.S. Secret Service, 1980-83; mem. math. dept. faculty N.Y. U., 1956-59; lectr. econs. U. Md., 1965-66; cons. Army Security Agy., 1965, CSC, 1965, Rand Corp., 1979—, Sandia Nat. Labs., 1980-81, ABC News, 1980-81; fellow Los Alamos Sci. Lab, 1979—. Author: (with H.A. Smith) Mathematical Foundations of Systems Analysis, 1969, The Potential Energy conservation: The Potential for Energy Conservation; Substitution for Scarce Fuels, 1973, Facing Tomorrow's Terrorist Incident Today, 1977, (with D.M. Trent) Terrorism, Threat, Reality, Response, 1979, (with W. J. Taylor, Jr.) Strategic Requirements for the Army to the Year 2000, (with Taylor and Williamson) Low Intensity Conflict, (with J. Garn and D. Boren) Realistic Arms Control Today: New Directions in Nuclear Weapons Policy; contbr. (with D.M. Trent) articles to profl. jours. Recipient Founder's Day award N.Y. U., 1962; Outstanding Service award Exec. Office of Pres., 1968, 69, 70, 71; Disting. Service award, 1973; Order Paul Revere Patriots State Mass., 1970; Presdl. citation, 1971, 73; Superior Honor award ACDA, 1977. Fellow Ops. Research Soc., N.Y. Acad. Scis.; mem. Am. Math. Soc., Washington Ops. Research Council, AAAS, Soc. Indsl. and Applied Math., Internat. Inst. Strategic Studies, Sigma Xi, Zeta Beta Tau. Clubs: Georgetown, International (Washington). Home: 2832 Ellicott St Washington DC 20008 Office: Georgetown U (C 515 1800 K St NW) Washington DC 20006

KUPSCH, WALTER OSCAR, geologist; b. Amsterdam, Netherlands, Mar. 2, 1919; emigrated to Can., 1950, naturalized, 1956; s. Richard Leopold and Elizabeth (Heuser) K.; m. Emmy Helene de Jong, Oct. 2, 1945; children—Helen Elizabeth, Yvonne Irene, Richard Christopher. M. Cand, U. Amsterdam, 1943; M.Sc., U. Mich., 1948, Ph.D., 1950. Asst. prof. geology U. Sask., Saskatoon, Can., 1950-56, assoc. prof., 1956-64, prof., 1964—; dir. Inst. North Studies, 1965-73, Churchill River Study, 1973-76, Sask. Heritage Assocs. Ltd., 1973-76; bd. govs. Arctic Inst. N.Am., 1969-74, chmn., 1973-74; mem. Sci. Council Can., 1976-82; vice-chmn. sci. adv. bd. N.W. Terrs., 1976—; exec. dir. adv. com. Devel. of Govt. in N.W. Terrs., 1965-66; petroleum advisor to Govt. N.W. Ters., 1980—. Contbr. articles to profl. jours. Served with Netherlands Army, 1939-40. Fellow Royal Soc. Can., Geol. Soc. Am., Royal Can. Geographic Soc., Geol. Assn. Can., Arctic Inst. N.Am.; mem. Am. Assn. Petroleum Geologists, Sask. Geol. Soc. Home: 319 Bate Cr Saskatoon SK S7H 3A6 Canada Office: Dept Geol Sci U Sask Saskatoon SK S7N 0W0 Canada

KURALT, CHARLES BISHOP, TV news correspondent; b. Wilmington, N.C., Sept. 10, 1934; s. Wallace Hamilton and Ina (Bishop) K.; m. Suzanna Folsom Baird, June 1, 1962; children by previous marriage: Lisa Catherine Bowers, Susan Guthery Bowers. B.A., U. N.C., 1955. Reporter, columnist Charlotte (N.C.) News, 1955-57; writer CBS News, 1957-59, corr., 1959—. Author: To The Top of the World, 1968, Dateline America, 1979. Recipient Ernie Pyle Meml. award, 1956; George Foster Peabody broadcasting award, 1969, 76, 80; Emmy award, 1969, 78, 81. Club: Players (N.Y.C.). Address: CBS News 524 W 57th St New York NY 10019 *

KURAMOCHI, TADASHI, general trading company executive; b. Osaka, Japan, Mar. 16, 1927; came to U.S., 1979; s. Masaaki and Katsuko (Kuramochi) K.; m. Uasuko Matsuo, Nov. 11, 1957; children: Mari, Massaya, Yuri. B.A., Osaka U. Commerce, 1950. Mem. dept. fin. Marubeni Corp., Osaka, 1950-57; mgr. Marubani Deutschland, Hamburg, W.Ger., 1957-63; v.p. Maruveni Europe, London, 1972-76; gen. mgr. internat. fin. Marubani Corp., Tokyo, 1976-79; sr. v.p., treas. Marubeni Am. Corp., N.Y.C., 1979—. Office: Marubeni Am Corp 200 Park Ave New York NY 10166

KURKJIAN, STEPHEN ANOOSH, journalist; b. Boston, Aug. 28, 1943; s. Anoosharon and Rosella (Gureghian) K.; m. Ann Frost Lewkowicz; children: Erica Young, Adam Stephen. B.A., Boston U., 1966; J.D., Suffolk U., 1970. Journalist State House News Service, Boston, 1966-68, Boston Globe, 1968—; editor Boston Globe Spotlight Team. Recipient Pulitzer prize for local investigative reporting, 1972, for local investigative reporting, 1980, Mng. editors award AP, 1977, Pub. Service award Sigma Delta Chi, 1971, Headliner award, 1977, Nat. Consumer Found. award, 1974, New Eng. AP Sevellon Brown award, 1979, 80, 83, 84, Nat. Edn. Reporting award Edn. Writers Assn., 1982. Office: 135 Morrissey Blvd Boston MA 02107

KURLAND, LEONARD TERRY, research physician, educator; b. Balt., Dec. 24, 1921; s. Ellis M. and Sarah (Shein) K. B.A., Johns Hopkins, 1942, Dr.P.H., 1951; M.D. (Gold medal), U. Md., 1945; M.P.H. cum laude, Harvard, 1948. Intern U. Md., 1945-46; with USPHS, 1946-64; assigned NIMH, NIH, 1948-55, Nat. Inst. Neurol. Disease and Blindness, 1955-64, chief epidemiology br., 1955-64; fellow neurology Mayo Clinic, Rochester, Minn., 1952-53, research asst. in neurology and med. statistics, 1953-55, prof., chmn. dept. med. statistics and epidemiology, 1964—; prof. epidemiology Mayo Grad. and Mayo Sch. Medicine, 1964—; clin. asst. prof. neurology Georgetown U., 1957-60; clin. prof. neurology Howard U., 1960-64; cons. NIH, FDA, WHO, Nat. Acad. Scis.; mem. geochemistry and health subcom. NRC, 1975-80, chmn., 1978-80. Sr. author: The Epidemology of Neurologic and Sense Organ Disorders, 1973; Co-editor: Motor Neurone Disease, 1969; Contbr. articles to med. jours. Served with AUS, 1943-45. Fellow Am. Pub. Health Assn.; mem. Am. Acad. Neurology (past chmn. neuroepidemiology sect.), Am. Neurol. Assn., Am. Epidemiologic Soc. (pres. 1974), Internat. Epidemiologic Assn., Japanese Clin. Soc. Neurology (exec. council), Nat. Multiple Sclerosis Soc. (Gold Sci. award 1966, research review panel). Research on epidemiology, med. record systems, genetics of diseases of nervous system and cancer. Office: 200 1st St SW Rochester MN 55901

KURLAND, PHILIP B., lawyer, educator; b. N.Y.C., Oct. 22, 1921; s. Archibald H. and Estelle (Polstein) K.; m. Mary Jane Krensky, May 29, 1954; children: Julie Rebecca, Martha Jennifer, Ellen Sarah. A.B., U. Pa., 1942; LL.B., Harvard U., 1944; LL.D., U. Notre Dame, 1977, U. Detroit, 1982. Bar: N.Y. 1945, Ill. 1972, U.S. Supreme Ct 1972. Law clk. to Judge Jerome N. Frank, 1944-45, Supreme Ct. Justice Felix Frankfurter, 1945-46; atty. Dept. Justice, 1946-47; mem. firm Kurland & Wolfson, N.Y.C., 1947-50; asst. prof. law Northwestern U. Law Sch., 1950-53; mem. faculty U. Chgo., 1953—, prof. law, 1956—, William R. Kenan, Jr. prof., 1973-76, William R. Kenan, Jr. disting. service prof., 1976—; counsel firm Rothschild, Barry & Myers, Chgo., 1972—; cons. Econ. Stblzn. Agy., 1951-52; chief cons., subcom. on separation of powers U.S. Senate Judiciary Com., 1967-77; cons. U.S. Dept. Justice, 1976; mem. Oliver Wendell Holmes Devise Com., 1975-83. Author or editor: Jurisdiction of Supreme Court of U.S, 1950, Mr. Justice, 1964, Religion and the Law, 1962, Frankfurter: Of Law and

Life, 1965, The Supreme Court and the Constitution, 1965, The Great Charter, 1965, Moore's Manual, 1964-70, Felix Frankfurter on the Supreme Court, 1970, Politics, The Constitution and the Warren Court, 1970, Mr. Justice Frankfurter and the Constitution, 1971, Landmark Briefs and Arguments of the Supreme Court of the United States, 132 vols., 1975-83, Watergate and the Constitution, 1978, Cablespeech, 1983; editor: Supreme Court Rev., 1960—. Guggenheim fellow, 1950-51, 54-55. Fellow Am. Acad. Arts and Scis.; mem. Am., Chgo. bar assns., Am. Law Inst., New Brougham Soc. Jewish. Club: Quadrangle (U. Chgo.). Home: 4840 Woodlawn Ave Chicago IL 60615

KURNIT, SHEPARD, advertising agency executive; b. Bronx, N.Y., Oct. 31, 1924; s. Samuel Philip and Frances (Lichtenstien) K.; m. Jeanette Zinsher, Aug. 1, 1945; children: Paul David, Richard Alan, Scott Philip. Scholar, Parsons Sch. Design, 1941-42. With Sterling Advt., N.Y.C., 1945, Harry Serwer Advt., 1945-47, C.J. Herrick Assos., 1947-49, Diamond Barnett Advt., 1949; asso. art dir. Morton Freund Advt., 1949; founder Kurnit Assos., Inc., N.Y.C., 1950-54; pres. Kurnit, Geller Assos., Inc., N.Y.C., 1954-56; exec. v.p. DKG, Inc. Calet Hirsch Kurnit & Spector (formerly Delehanty, Kurnit & Geller), N.Y.C., 1956-61, became pres., 1961, now chmn. Founder East Meadow Com. Human Rights, 1964, pres., 1965; mem. Urban League, Great Neck Forum, Com. Human Rights; bd. dirs. Am. Field Service Internat. Intercultural Exchange. Served with USAAF, 1943-45. Recipient numerous advt. awards. Mem. Nat. Assn. Advt. Agys. (gov.), Nat. Advt. Rev. Bd. (gov.), Met. Pres. Orgn., Fund for New Priorities in Am. Democrat. Home: 1 Birch St Great Neck NY 11023 Office: 1271 Ave of Americas New York NY 10020

KURNOW, ERNEST, statistician, educator; b. Bklyn., Oct. 21, 1912; s. Harry and Sarah Malka (Shagaloff) K.; m. Joyce Litzky, Oct. 6, 1938; children: Ruth (Mrs. Jeffrey Jarrett), Susan Carol (Mrs. Leonard Weistrop), Alice Rose (Mrs. Claude Morin). B.S. cum laude, CCNY, 1932, M.S. in Edn, 1933; Ph.D., NYU, 1951. Tchr. N.Y.C. Bd. Edn., 1935-40, statistician, 1941-48; mathematician ordnance div. War Dept., 1940-41; mem. faculty N.Y. U., 1948—, prof. econs., 1960-63, prof. bus. statistics, chmn. dept., 1963—, chmn. doctoral program, 1976—; cons. N.Y. State Tax Structure Study Commn., 1959—, Mayor N.Y.C. Com. Mgmt. Survey, 1950-51, Turkish Ministry Finance, 1955-56; cons. temporary commn. Revision N.Y. State Constn., 1958; temporary commn. fiscal affairs N.Y. State Govt., 1953-54; cons. Tri-State Transp. Commn., 1964-66, 73-75; participant Brazilian capital markets program, 1968; study dir. Govs.' Spl. Commn. on Financing Mass Transp., 1970-71; cons. Commn. on Charter Revision, City of N.Y., 1973-74, Temporary Commn. on City Finances, 1975-76. Author: The Turkish Budgetary Process, 1956; also articles. Statistics for Business Decisions, 1959, Theory and Measurement of Land Rent, 1961. Recipient Gt. Tchr. award N.Y. U. Alumni Assn., 1974; Fulbright grantee to Greece, 1966-67. Fellow Am. Statis. Assn.; mem. Internat. Statis. Inst., Am. Econ. Assn., Econometric Soc., Inst. Mgmt. Scis., Nat. Tax Assn., Tax Inst. Am. (mem. adv. council 1969—), Am. Soc. Quality Control, Sphinx, Beta Gamma Sigma, Sigma Eta Phi, Delta Pi Sigma, Alpha Phi Sigma, Delta Sigma Pi. Jewish. Home: 3 Washington Sq Village Apt 17I New York NY 10012 Office: New York Univ Washington Sq New York NY 10003

KURODA, SIGE-YUKI, linguist, educator; b. Tokyo, Aug. 18, 1934; U.S., 1962; s. Sigekatu and Yaeko (Takagi) K.; m. Susan Donna Fischer, June 19, 1970. B.A. in Math, U. Tokyo, 1957, 1959; M.A. in Math, Nagoya (Japan) U., 1961; Ph.D., M.I.T., 1965. Instr. M.I.T., 1965-66; asst. prof. linguistics U. Calif., San Diego, 1966-69, asso. prof., 1969-75, prof., 1975—; adj. prof. philosophy, 1979—. Author: Yawelmani Phonology, 1967, Aux quatre coins de la linguistique, 1979, Generative grammatical studies in the Japanese language, 1979, The (w)hole of the doughnut, 1979; mem. editorial bd.: Papers in Japanese Linguistics, 1972—, Linquisticae Investigationes, 1976—, Linguistic Inquiry, 1976-80, Linguistics and Philosophy, 1975—, Linguistic Rev, 1980—. Am. Council Learned Socs. fellow, 1968-69; Guggenheim fellow, 1978-79. Mem. Linguistic Soc. Am., Linguistic Soc. Japan, Assn. Tchrs. Japanese. Home: 563 Orchid Ln Del Mar CA 92014 Office: Dept Linguistics U Calif San Diego La Jolla CA 92093

KUROSKY, ALEXANDER, biochemist, educator; b. Windsor, Ont., Can., Sept. 12, 1938; came to U.S., 1972; s. Peter and Stella (Gemper) K.; m. Anna Kinik, May 18, 1963; children: Lisa Kathryn, Tanya Kristine, Stephanie Ann. B.Sc., U. B.C., 1965; M.Sc., U. Toronto, 1969, Ph.D., 1972. Research technician Can. Dept. Agr., Harrow, Ont., Vancouver, B.C., 1959-64; chemist research and devel. Can. Breweries Ltd., Toronto, Ont., 1965-67; faculty Med. Br., U. Tex., Galveston, 1973—, assoc. prof., 1978-82, prof., 1982—. Contbr. articles to sci. publs. Province of Ont. grad fellow, 1968-71; grantee Burkitt Found., NIH, Nat. Cancer Inst.; recipient Disting. Teaching award U. Tex. Med. Br. Grad. Sch., 1981. Mem. Am. Soc. Biol. Chemists, Am. Chem. Soc., AAAS, Can. Biochem. Soc., Am. Soc. Human Genetics, Sigma Xi. Research structure, function and evolution of proteins. Home: 6605 Golfcrest Dr Galveston TX 77551 Office: Dept Human Biol Chemistry and Genetics U Tex Med Br Galveston TX 77550

KURSUNOGLU, BEHRAM N., physicist, educator; b. Bayburt, Turkey, Mar. 14, 1922; came to U.S., 1958; s. Ismail and Hanife (Esenulku) K.; m. Sevda Arif, Sept. 25, 1952; children—Sevil, Ayda, Ismet. B.Sc., Edinburgh (Scotland) U., 1949; Ph.D., Cambridge (Eng.) U., 1952; D.Sci. (hon.), Fla. Inst. Tech., 1982. Mem. faculty Cornell U., 1952-54, Yale, 1955; with Turkish Gen. Staff on Atomic Matters, 1956-58, Turkish Atomic Energy Commn., 1956-58; dean faculty nuclear scis. and tech. Middle East Tech. U., Ankara, Turkey, 1956-58; vis. prof. physics U.Miami, Coral Gables, Fla., 1954-55, prof. physics, 1958—; mem. NATO Scis. Com., 1958; dir. Center for Theoretical Studies, 1965—; chmn. ann. Internat. Sci. Forum on Energy, 1977—; cons. Oak Ridge Nat. Lab., 1962-64, Brit. Atomic Energy Establishment, 1961, Max Planck-Institut fur Physik and Astrophysik, 1961. Author: Modern Quantum Theory, 1962; Contbr. articles to profl. jours. Recipient Sci. prize of Turkey, 1972. Fellow Am. Phys. Soc.; mem. Sigma Xi. Research on elementary particles, gen. relativity, statis. mechanics, nuclear energy and arms control issues. Home: 6200 Leonardo St Coral Gables FL 33146

KURTH, LISELOTTE E., German language educator; b. Wuppertal, Germany, Mar. 29, 1923; came to U.S., 1951; s. Otto and Emmi (Klammer) Voigt. M.A., Johns Hopkins U., 1960, Ph.D., 1963. Asst. prof. Johns Hopkinss U., Balt., 1964-68; assoc. prof. Johns Hopkins U., Balt., 1968-73; prof. German Johns Hopkinss U., Balt., 1973—, chmn. dept., 1980—. Author: Die Zweite Wirklichkeit, 1969, Perspectives and Points of View, 1974. Gilman fellow, 1958-62; Gail fellow, 1962-63. Mem. South Atlantic Modern Lang. Assn. (exec. com. 1982-84), Deutsche Scillergesellschaft, MLA, Lessing Soc., Phi Beta Kappa. Home: 6521 Loch Hill Ct Baltimore MD 21239 Office: Dept German Johns Hopkins U 34th and Charles Sts Baltimore MD 21218

KURTH, RONALD JAMES, naval officer; b. Madison, Wis., July 1, 1931; s. Peter James and Celia (Kuehn) K.; m. E. Charlene Schaefer, Dec. 21, 1954; children: Steven, Audrey, John, Douglas. B.S., U.S. Naval Acad., 1954; M.P.A., Harvard U., 1961, Ph.D., 1970. Commd. ensign U.S. Navy, 1954, advanced through grades to rear adm., 1981; comdg. officer NAS, Memphis, Millington, Tenn., 1977-79; mil. fellow Council Fgn. Relations, N.Y.C., 1979-80; exec. asst. to dep. chief naval ops., Washington, 1980-81; dir. Pol-Mil Policy and Current Plans Dept. Navy, Washington, 1981-83, dir. Long Range Planning Group, 1983—; teaching fellow Harvard U., Cambridge, Mass., 1969-70. Author: The Politics of Technological Innovation in the Navy, 1970. Decorated Legion of Merit with gold star, Meritorious Service medal with gold star. Mem. U.S. Naval Inst., U.S. Naval Acad. Alumni, Harvard Alumni. Episcopalian. Lodge: Rotary. Home: 8106 Ainsworth Ave Springfield VA 22152 Office: Dir Long Range Planning Group Navy Dept Washington DC 20350

KURTH, WALTER RICHARD, association executive; b. Normal, Ill., Jan. 21, 1932; s. Walter H. and Irene (Freitag) K.; m. Mary Elisabeth Taylor, Aug. 23, 1958; children: Mary Helen, Sarah Jane, Elisabeth Irene. B.S., U. Ill., 1954. Publ. dir. Assoc. Credit Burs. of Am., Inc., St. Louis, 1954-57, mktg. dir., 1957-62, asst. gen. mgr., 1962-66, asst. gen. mgr., treas., Houston, 1966-68, adminstrv. v.p., treas., 1968-69; exec. v.p., treas. Assoc. Credit Burs., Inc., 1969-75; sec.-treas. Credit Bur. Automation, Inc., Houston, 1966-75; vice chmn. bd. Credit Services Internat., 1970-75; pres., sec.-treas., vice chmn. bd. ACB Services, Inc., 1970-75; sr. v.p. Nat. Consumer Finance Assn., Washington, 1976-77, exec. v.p., 1977-80, pres., 1980-82, Am. Fin. Services Assn., 1983, Assoc. Credit Burs. Inc., 1983—; chmn. bd. ACB Services Inc., 1983—. Mem. Houston dist. council SBA, 1971-75; mem. adv. council Purdue Credit Research Ctr., 1977—; chmn. Republican Dist. Fund Drive; Rep. precinct chmn., 1969-75; bd. mgrs. Thompson Retreat Center, St. Louis, 1963-64; bd. dirs. Econ. Edn. Found. for Clergy, 1976-82. Mem. Am. Soc. Assn. Execs. (dir. 1982—), Tex. Soc. Assn. Execs., Houston Soc. Assn. Execs. (pres. 1974), St. Louis Soc. Assn. Execs. (pres. 1962), Chartered Assn. Execs., Star and Scroll (pres. 1953), U.S. C. of C. (assn. com. 1978—), Am. Mgmt. Assn., Alpha Kappa Lambda (pres. 1953). Republican. Presbyn. (elder). Clubs: Masons (32 deg., Shriners), Univ., Regency Racquet., Westlake, Raveneux Country. Home: 5711 Glen Pines Houston TX 77069 Office: Assoc Credit Burs Inc 16211 Park Ten Pl Houston TX 77084

KURTIS, WILLIAM HORTON (BILL KURTIS), broadcast journalist; b. Pensacola, Fla., Sept. 21, 1940; s. William A. and Wilma Mary (Horton) K.; m. Helen M., July 7, 1963 (dec. 1977); children—Mary Kristin, Scott Erik. B.S. in Journalism, U. Kans., 1962; J.D., Washburn U., 1966. News reporter Sta.-WBBM-TV, Chgo., 1966-70, anchorman, reporter, 1973-82; corr. CBS News, Los Angeles, 1970-73; co-anchor CBS Morning News, 1982—. Served with USMCR, 1962-63. Recipient Chgo. Area Emmy for reporting Chgo. conspiracy trial, 1970, Saigon fall, 1976, Belfast investigation, 1976, for individual excellence for performers who appear on camera, 1976, award for Saigon orphans Overseas Press Club, 1975. Mem. Am. Bar Assn., Sigma Delta Chi. Office: Care CBS 51 W 52nd St New York NY 10019 *

KURTZ, BRUCE EDWARD, research and development executive; b. Syracuse, N.Y., Jan. 23, 1936; s. Arthur Jacob and Joyce Adelia (Montague) K.; m. Judy Ann Sitterlee, Mar. 30, 1964; children: Stephan, Maria. B.Ch.E., Syracuse U., 1957, M.Ch.E., 1959, Ph.D., 1967. Mgr. research and devel. Indsl. Chem. div. Allied Chem. So., Solvay, N.Y., 1973-77; dir. engring. research Indsl. Chem. div. Allied Chem. Co., Solvay, N.Y., 1977-79, dir. chem. and engring. research, 1979-81; program mgr. basic research Allied Chem., Solvay, 1982-83, program mgr. electronic applications; career counselor, 1968—. Developer Electrolyzer, 1980, Chem. Reactor, 1978, Chem. Process, 1970; contbr. articles to profl. jours. Recipient Inventor award Allied Corp., 1980. Mem. Am. Inst. Chem. Engrs., Tau Beta Pi. Republican. Roman Catholic. Club: Adirondak Mountain. Office: PO Box 6 Solvay NY 13209

KURTZ, GARY D., motion picture producer; b. Los Angeles, July 27, 1940; s. Eldo M. and Sara H. (Briar) K.; m. Meredith Alsup, Apr. 1963 (separated); children: Melissa Dawne, Tiffany Leigh. Student, U. So. Calif., 1959-63. Cameraman, film editor, writer, prodn. mgr. and/or dir. films and documentaries, 1962-70; pres. Kinetographics, 1973—. Co-producer: American Graffiti, 1970-73; producer: Star Wars, 1973-77, The Empire Strikes Back, 1977-80, The Dark Crystal, 1979-82; exec. producer: Return to Oz, 1982-85. Served with USMC, 1966-69. Mem. Acad. Motion Picture Arts and Scis., Soc. Motion Picture and TV Engrs. Quaker.

KURTZ, JEROME, lawyer; b. Phila., May 19, 1931; s. Morris and Renee (Cooper) K.; m. Elaine Kahn, July 28, 1956; children: Madeleine, Anne Nettie. B.S. with honors, Temple U., 1952; LL.B. magna cum laude, Harvard U., 1955. Bar: Pa. 1956, N.Y. State 1981, D.C. 1982; C.P.A., Pa. Asso. firm Wolf, Block, Schorr & Solis-Cohen, Phila., 1955-56, 57-63, partner, 1963-66, 68-77; tax legis. counsel Dept. Treasury, Washington, 1966-68; commr. IRS, 1977-80; partner firm Paul, Weiss, Rifkind, Wharton & Garrison, 1980—; instr. Villanova Law Sch., 1964-65, U. Pa., 1969-74; vis. prof. law Harvard U., 1975-76; mem. adv. group to commr. IRS, 1976. Editor: Harvard Law Rev, 1953-55; Contbr. numerous articles to profl. jours. Served with U.S. Army, 1956-57. Recipient Exceptional Service award Dept. Treasury, 1968, Alexander Hamilton award, 1980. Mem. ABA (chmn. tax shelter com.), N.Y. Bar Assn. (exec. com. tax sect. 1981-82), Pa. Bar Assn., Phila. Bar Assn. (chmn. tax sect. 1975-76), Am. Law Inst., Am. Coll. Tax Counsel, Beta Gamma Sigma. Home: 1619 35th St NW Washington DC 20007 Office: 1714 Massachusetts Ave Washington DC 20036

KURTZ, KATHERINE, novelist; b. Coral Gables, Fla., Oct. 18, 1944; d. Frederick Harry and Margaret Frances (Carter) K. B.S., U. Miami, (Fla.), 1966; M.A., UCLA, 1971. With Los Angeles Police Dept., 1969—, sr. tng. technician, 1974—. Author: novels Deryni Rising, 1970, Deryni Checkmate, 1972, High Deryni, 1973, Camber of Culdi, 1974, Saint Camber, 2 vols., 1978, 79.

KURTZ, LLOYD SHERER, JR., lawyer; b. Toledo, Feb. 23, 1934; s. Lloyd Sherer and Mildred (Kalb) K.; m. Patricia Jean Redman, June 28, 1958; children—Lloyd Sherer III, Kathryn Laura. A.B., Princeton, 1956; LL.B., Stanford, 1959. Bar: Alaska Bar 1961. Law clk. to Chief Justice Buell A. Nesbett, Supreme Ct. Alaska, 1959-60; atty. McNealy, Merdes & Camarot, Fairbanks, 1961-62, Alaska Housing Authority, 1962-63, Burr, Boney & Pease, 1964-66; partner firm Burr, Pease & Kurtz, 1967—; tchr. bus. law and econs. U. Alaska, Anchorage, 1962-65, 78; Mem. adv. com. Criminal Justice Center, 1975-76; mem. Alaska Code Revision Com., 1978—. Mng. editor: Stanford Law Rev, 1958-59. Mem. ABA, Alaska Bar Assn. (bd. govs. 1970-74, pres. 1973, chmn. higher edn. com. 1974-76), Anchorage Bar Assn., Am. Judicature Soc., Am. Fedn. Musicians, Phi Alpha Delta. Home: 1348 W 11th St Anchorage AK 99501 Office: 810 N St Anchorage AK 99501

KURTZ, MYERS RICHARD, hospital administrator; b. Schaefferstown, Pa., June 18, 1924; 1 son, Ronald Hayden. B.S., U. Md., 1958; M.B.A., Ind. U., 1963. Served as enlisted man U.S. Army, 1942-51, commd. 2d lt., 1951; advanced through grades to lt. col. Med. Service Corps, 1965; mem. staff Army Surgeon Gen., Washington, 1963-67; ret., 1967; affiliation adminstr. N.Y. U. Med. Center, N.Y.C., 1967-69; exec. dir. Ephrata (Pa.) Community Hosp., 1969-76; supt. Longview State Hosp., Cin., 1976-79; asst. dir. Ohio Dept. Mental Health and Mental Retardation, Columbus, 1979-81, dir., 1981-82; sr. v.p. Cleve. Met. Gen. Hosp., 1982-83; supt., chief exec. officer Central State Hosp., Milledgeville, Ga., 1983—; adj. asst. prof. dept. psychiatry U. Cin., 1977—. Vice pres., bd. dirs. Coordinated Home Care Agy., Inc., Lancaster County; pres. Lancaster County Hosp. Council; bd. dirs. Pa. Hosp. Assn. Decorated Legion of Merit, Army Commendation medal with oak leaf cluster. Fellow Royal Soc. Health; mem. Am. Coll. Hosp. Adminstrs., Am. Acad. Med. Adminstrs., Am. Hosp. Assn., Sigma Iota Epsilon. Home: 164 Annex Dr Milledgeville GA 31061 Office: Central State Hosp Milledgeville GA 31002 *One of my basic principles is that if a job is worth doing it must be accomplished to the best of one's ability. Since you can normally only get things done through and with other people you have to treat them with respect and as equals; never talk down to anyone. You have to show and to give respect in order to receive it.*

KURTZ, PAUL, educator; b. Newark, Dec. 21, 1925; s. Martin and Sara (Lasser) K.; m. Claudine C. Vial, Oct. 6, 1960; children—Valerie L., Patricia A., Jonathan. B.A., N.Y. U., 1948; M.A., Columbia U., 1949, Ph.D., 1952. Instr. Queens Coll., 1950-52; instr. philosophy Trinity Coll., Hartford, Conn., 1952-55, asst. prof., 1955-58, assoc. prof., 1958-59, Vassar Coll., Poughkeepsie, N.Y., 1960-61; vis. prof. New Sch. Social Research, N.Y.C., 1960-65; assoc. prof. Union Coll., Schenectady, 1961-64, prof., 1964-65; vis. prof. U. Besancon, France, 1965; prof. philosophy SUNY-, Buffalo, 1965—; moderator TV series. Author: (with Rollo Handy) A Current Appraisal of the Behavioral Sciences, 1964, Decision and the Condition of Man, 1965, The Fullness of Life, 1974, Exuberance, 1977, In Defense of Secular Humanism, 1983; Editor: American Thought Before 1900, 1966, American Philosophy in the Twentieth Century, 1966, Sidney Hook and the Contemporary World, 1968, Moral Problems in Contemporary Society, 1969; co-editor: International Directory of Philosophy and Philosophers, 4th edit, 1978-81, Tolerance and Revolution, 1970, Language and Human Nature, 1971, A Catholic/Humanist Dialogue, 1972, The Humanist Alternative, 1973, Idea of a Modern University, 1974, The Philosophy of The Curriculum, 1975, The Ethics of Teaching and Scientific Research, 1977, University and State, 1978, Sidney Hook: Philosopher of Democracy and Humanism, 1983; Editorial bd.: The Humanist, 1964-78; editor, 1967-78; editorial bd.: Philosophers Index, 1969—, Question, 1969-81; editor-in-chief: Prometheus Books, 1970—; editorial bd.: The Skeptical Inquirer, 1976—; editor: Free Inquiry, 1980—. Pres. Greater Capitol dist. N.Y. State United World Federalists, 1965; chmn. Council on Internat. Studies and World Affairs., 1966-69; Trustee Behavioral Research Council, Great Barrington, Mass.; bd. dirs. U.S. Bibliography of Philosophy, 1958-70, Internat. Humanist and Ethical Union, 1968—, Univ. Centers for Rational Alternatives, 1969—; chmn. Com. for Sci. Investigation Claims of Paranormal, 1976—. Served with AUS, 1944-46. Behavioral Research Council fellow, 1962-63; French Govt. fellow, 1965. Mem. Am. Philos. Assn., Am. Ethical Union, Am. Humanist Assn. (dir.). Home: 660 Le Brun Rd Eggertsville NY 14226 Office: 700 E Amherst St Buffalo NY 14215 *Two passions have dominated my intellectual and professional life: (1) a commitment to critical intelligence—I am skeptical of the false beliefs and mythologies that have motivated other men and women—and (2) a belief in the importance of human courage, particularly in defending reason in society and in attempting to reconstruct ethical values so that they are more democratic and humane.*

KURTZ, SAMUEL MORDECAI, architect; b. Russia, Feb. 21, 1904; came to U.S., 1904, naturalized, 1919; s. Louis and Nadia (Form) K.; m. Mary G. Weisthal, Sept. 3, 1928; children: Gerald Norman, Elliot Robert. Grad. diploma in architecture, Cooper Union Inst., 1925; certificate archtl./engring. design, Columbia U., 1927, CCNY, 1929, N.Y. U., 1942. Asso. archtl. firm York & Sawyer, N.Y.C., 1926-27; prin. Samuel M. Kurtz, N.Y.C., 1947-54; asso. archtl. firm Kiff, Voss & Franklin, N.Y.C., 1954-71; pvt. practice archtl. cons., N. Miami Beach, Fla., 1971; spl. cons. to Charles Giller & Assos. (Architects), Miami, 1972-76; mem. N.Y.C. Mayor's Panel of Architects, 1950-70; mem. archtl. engring. selection bd. Bd. Higher Edn., N.Y.C., 1968-69. Fellow AIA; mem. N.Y. chpt. AIA (Rutkins award 1966, treas. 1968), S.Fla. chpt. AIA, N.Y. Soc. Architects (pres. 1967-68), N.Y. State Assn. Architects (awarded spl. citation 1968), Am. Arbitration Assn. (nat. panel arbitrators 1950-70). Home: 3849 NE 169th St North Miami Beach FL 33160 Office: 1420 N Miami Beach Blvd North Miami Beach FL 33162

KURTZ, STEPHEN GUILD, historian, ednl. adminstr.; b. Buffalo, Sept. 9, 1926; s. George Patterson and Nellie (Crowther) K.; m. Katherine Jeanne Godolphin, Sept. 5, 1947; children—Sharon, Thomas Patterson, Stephen Godolphin. A.B., Princeton, 1947, LL.D. (hon.), 1981; Ph.D., U. Pa., 1953. Instr. history U. Pa., 1949-51; master Kent Sch., 1951-55; Fulbright prof. Athens (Greece) Coll., 1955-56; dean students Wabash (Ind.) Coll., 1956-59, asso. prof. history, asst. to pres., 1959-64, dean coll., 1964-66; lectr. Coll. William and Mary, 1966-72; vis. prof. Columbia, summers 1962, 64; editor Inst. Early Am. History, Williamsburg, Va., 1966-69, dir., 1969-72; dean, prof. history Hamilton Coll., Clinton, N.Y., 1972-74; prin. Phillips Exeter Acad., Exeter, N.H., 1974—; Mem. regional com. Woodrow Wilson Fellowship Found., 1960-64, dissertation fellowship com., 1968-73. Author: The Presidency of John Adams, 1957, The Federalists, 1971, Essays on the American Revolution, 1973; Editor: The Papers of John Marshall, 1966-71. Trustee ABC Program, Athens Coll. Served with USNR, 1944-45. Guggenheim fellow 1961-62. Mem. Headmasters Assn., Am. Antiquarian Soc., Mass. Hist. Soc. Clubs: Tavern, St. Botolph. Home: 31 Elliot St Exeter NH 03833

KURTZ, THOMAS EUGENE, mathematics educator; b. Oak Park, Ill., Feb. 22, 1928; s. Oscar Christ and Helen (Bell) K.; m. Patricia Anne Barr, June 13, 1953 (div. Aug. 1973); children—Daniel Barr, Timothy David, Beth Louise; m. Agnes Seelye Bixler, June 10, 1974. B.A., Knox Coll., Galesburg, Ill., 1950; Ph.D., Princeton, 1956. Mem. faculty Dartmouth, 1956—, prof. math. and computer sci., 1966—; chmn. Program in Computer and Info. Sci. Kiewit Computation Center, 1983—, dir., 1959-75, Office Acad. Computing, 1975-78. Author: Basic Statistics, 1963, (with J.G. Kemeny) Basic Programming, 1967, 2d edit., 1971, 3d edit., 1980. Trustee, chmn. council EDUCOM, 1974-78; chmn., dir. NERComp, Inc., 1970-78; trustee, vice chmn. DTSS, Inc., 1972-78; chmn. X3J2 Basic Standard Com., 1974—; mem. panel uses computers in edn. President's Sci. Adv. Com., 1965-66. Democrat. Mem. United Ch. Christ. Co-designer BASIC computer lang. and Dartmouth time sharing system. Home: PO Box 962 Hanover NH 03755

KURTZKE, JOHN FRANCIS, SR., neurologist, epidemiologist; b. Bklyn., Sept. 14, 1926; s. John Ambrose and Teresa Rose (Knipper) K.; m. Margaret Mary Nevin, June 30, 1950; children: John Francis, Catherine Kurtzke Brown, Elizabeth Kurtzke Siebert, Joan Kurtzke Brennan, Robert, James, Christine. B.S. summa cum laude, St. John's U., 1948; M.D., Cornell U., 1952. Diplomate: Am. Bd. Psychiatry and Neurology (Neurology), 1958. Intern Kings County Hosp., Bklyn., 1952-53; resident in neurology VA Hosp., Bronx, N.Y., 1953-56; chief neurology service VA hosps., Coatesville, Pa., 1956-63, Washington, 1963—; vice mem. faculty Jefferson Med. Coll., Phila., 1958-63, asst. prof. clin. neurology, 1963; mem. faculty Georgetown Med. Sch., Washington, 1963—, prof. neurology, 1968—, vice chmn. dept. neurology, 1976—, prof. community medicine, 1968—, U.S. Navy Med. Sch. liaison officer, 1979—; cons. neurology U.S. Naval Hosp., Bethesda, Md., Surgeon Gen. Navy, 1966—; mem. med. adv. bd. Nat.

Multiple Sclerosis Soc., 1966—, mem. working group on design of clin. studies in multiple sclerosis, 1976—, mem. exec. com., 1981-83; adv. bd. Internat. Fedn. Multiple Sclerosis Socs., 1972—; mem. com. multiple sclerosis World Fedn. Neurology, 1967—, com. neuroepidemiology, 1977—; chmn. epidemiology sect. NIH Epilepsy Adv. Com., 1973-76; med. research program specialist for neurology and neurobiology VA Research Service, 1977-80; chmn. work group epidemiology HEW Commn. Control of Huntington's Disease, 1976-78; mem. naval exam. bd. Naval Med. Command, 1980-83; mem. Residency Rev. Com. Neurology, 1983—. Author, co-author: Epidemiology of Multiple Sclerosis, 1968, Epidemiology of Cerebrovascular Disease, 1969, Epidemiology of Neurologic and Sense Organ Disorders, 1973; contbr. chpts. to textbooks, 300 articles to profl. jours. Served with USNR, 1944-46; rear adm. M.C. Res. Recipient cert. of merit Surgeon Gen. of Navy, 1969; Navy Commendation medal, 1974; Meritorious Unit Commendation, 1984. Fellow ACP, Am. Acad. Neurology (chmn. sect. on neuro-epidemiology 1971-75, chmn. com. nat. needs in neurology 1981—), AAAS, Am. Coll. Epidemiology, N.Y. Acad. Sci., Am. Coll. Preventive Medicine, Pan Am. Med. Assn. (council neurology sect.); mem. So. Med. Assn., Assn. Mil. Surgeons, Am. Neurol. Assn., AMA, AAUP, Am. Epidemiol. Assn., Internat. Epidemiol. Assn., Assn. Research in Nervous and Mental Disease, Am. Public Health Assn., Soc. Epidemiol. Research, Am. Epilepsy Soc., Soc. Med. Cons. to Armed Forces (com. on res. affairs 1980-83), Naval Res. Assn. (life), Naval Order U.S. (life), Res. Officers Assn. (life), Naval Inst., Navy League. Home: 7509 Salem Rd Falls Church VA 22043 Office: VA Hosp Washington DC 20422 *To be a physician demands recognition of the intrinsic value and dignity of human life while pursuing the goal of relieving pain and impairment due to disease or injury.*

KURTZMAN, ALLAN ROGER, advertising executive; b. Chgo., Feb. 18, 1933; s. Harry and Aurelia (Kalish) K.; m. Sandra Ann Eisenstein, July 7, 1957; children: Andrew, Matthew, James. B.J., U. Ill., 1956. Writer, J. Walter Thompson, Chgo., 1956-59, Foote, Cone & Belding, 1959-62; writer Leo Burnett Co., Inc., Chgo., 1962-63, creative dir., 1972-77; partner, creative dir. Tathan, Laird & Kudner, Chgo., 1977-80; v.p., creative dir. Cunningham & Walsh, Chgo., 1980—. Sponsor Cinema/Chgo. Served with USNR, 1951-53. Mem. Nat. Acad. Rec. Arts and Scis. (bd. govs. Chgo. 1975-77). Home: 408 Sandy Ln Wilmette IL 60091 Office: 875 N Michigan Ave Chicago IL 60611

KURUCZ, JOHN, lawyer; b. Yonkers, N.Y., Sept. 19, 1930; s. John J. and Anna (Timan) K.; m. June Reynolds, Feb. 20, 1960 (div. Oct. 1967); children: Debra Jeanne, Jonna Stiles; m. Mary K. Semon, May 25, 1973; children: Mary Anne, John Joseph. B.C.E., Rensselaer Poly. Inst., 1952; LL.B., Georgetown U., 1957. Bar: Va. 1957, N.Y. 1959, Pa. 1981. Patent searcher Pennie, Edmonds, Morton, Barrows & Taylor, Washington, 1954; patent examiner U.S. Patent Office, Washington, 1954-56; patent adviser Dept. Army, Washington, 1956-57; with Kane, Dalsimer, Kane & Smith, N.Y.C., 1957-69; mem. firm Kane, Dalsimer, Kane, Sullivan & Kurucz, 1969—; former v.p., dir. Breed Corp., Fairfield, N.Y.; sec. D.T.C. Inc., Princeton, N.J.; sec., dir. Spraysol, Inc., Fort Lee, N.J.; dir. LK Mfrs. Corp., Westbury, N.Y., Spraysol GmbH, West Ger. Served to 1st lt., C.E. AUS, 1952-54. Mem. N.Y.C., N.Y. County, N.Y. State, Va., Pa., Am., Fed. bar assns., N.Y., Am. patent law assns., Westchester County, N.Y. State, Am. socs. profl. engrs., Alpha Tau Omega, Chi Epislon. Clubs: National Lawyers (Washington); University (N.Y.C.); Scarsdale, St. Andrews (N.Y.); Ponte Vedra (Jacksonville, Fla.). Home: 604 Colony Hartsdale NY 10530 Office: 420 Lexington Ave New York NY 10017

KURZ, MORDECAI, ecomonics educator, university research administrator; b. Nathanya, Israel, Nov. 29, 1934; came to U.S., 1957, naturalized, 1975; s. Moshe and Sara (Kraus) K.; m. Lillian Rivlin, Aug. 4, 1936 (div. Mar. 1967); m 2d Linda Alice Cahn, Dec. 2, 1979. B.A. in Econs. and Polit. Sci., Hebrew U., Jerusalem, 1957, M.A., Yale U., 1958, Ph.D., 1961; M.S. in Stats., Stanford U., 1960. Asst. prof. econs. Stanford U., 1962-63, assoc. prof., 1966-68, prof., 1969—, dir. econs. sect. Inst. for Math. Studies, 1971—; sr. lectr. in econs. Hebrew U., 1963-66; cons. econs. SRI Internat., Menlo Park, Calif., 1963-78; spl. econ. advisor Can. Health and Welfare Ministry, Ottawa, Ont., 1976-78; spe. econ. advisor Pres.'s Commn. on Pension, Washington, 1979-81; research assoc. Nat. Bur. Econ. Research, 1979-82. Author: (with Kenneth J. Arrow) Public Investment, the Rate of Return and Optimal Fiscal Policy, 1970. Ford Found. faculty fellow Stanford U., 1973; Guggenheim Found. fellow Stanford U., Harvard U., Jerusalem, 1977-78; Inst. Advanced Studies fellow Hebrew U., Mt. Scopus, Jerusalem, 1979-80; prin. investigator NSF, 1969—. Fellow Econometric Soc. (assoc. editor Jour. Econ. Theory 1976—); mem. Am. Econ. Assn. Democrat. Jewish. Office: Inst Math Studies in Social Scis Edons Sect 4th Floor Encina Hall Stanford U Stanford CA 94305

KURZE, KENNETH ADOLF, foreign service officer; b. Providence, July 6, 1936; s. Adolf Otto and Louise Anna (Suter) K.; m. Ingrid S. Fischer, Mar. 26, 1960; children: Barbara Irene, Thomas Christopher, Peter Dev, Derek Paul. A.B., Brown U., 1958; M.A., Johns Hopkins U., 1960. Joined fgn. service Dept. State, 1959, polit. officer, New Delhi, India, 1961-62, Bombay, India, 1969-72, various assignments, Katmandu, Nepal, Washington and Rabat, Morocco, 1962-69, ops. center team chief, NATO affairs officer, officer-in-charge W. Ger. affairs, 1973-77; consul gen., Strasbourg, France, 1977-81; sr. course Naval War Coll., Newport, R.I., 1981-82; counselor for polit. and econ. affairs, Bridgetown, Barbados, 1982—. Mem. Am. Fgn. Service Assn., Am.-Nepal Soc., Cercle Europeen de Strasbourg, Confrerie St. Etienne. Episcopalian. Office: US Embassy PO Box 302 Bridgetown Barbados

KURZINA, PETER STANLEY, lawyer, confectionery company executive; b. Elmira, N.Y., Nov. 12, 1943; s. Stanley B. Kurzina, Jr. and Barbara F. K.; m. Stephanie Oney, Apr. 22, 1972. A.B. in Econs, U. Pa., 1965; J.D., Northwestern U., 1968. Bar: Ill. 1968. Legal counsel, sec. Westville Homes Corp., 1972-74, treas., 1973—, pres., dir., 1974—; exec. v.p. Fanny Farmer Candy Shops, Inc., Bedford, Mass., 1979-80, pres., dir., 1980—. Served as capt. U.S. Army, 1968-71. Mem. Ill. Bar Assn. Episcopalian. Home: Morningside Ln Lincoln MA 01773 Office: Fanny Farmer Candy Shops Inc 4 Preston Ct Bedford MA 01730

KURZMAN, STEPHEN, lawyer; b. N.Y.C., Mar. 25, 1932; s. Albert W. and Ceyl (Taylor) K.; m. Ellen Goldberg, Sept. 5, 1955 (dec. June 1978); children: Charles T., George M. A.B. summa cum laude, Harvard U., 1953, J.D., 1956. Bar: N.Y. 1959, D.C. 1966. Asst. U.S. atty. So. Dist. N.Y., N.Y.C., 1959-61; legis. asst., counsel U.S. Sen. Jacob K. Javits of N.Y., Washington, 1961-65; minority counsel Com. on Labor and Pub. Welfare, U.S. Senate, 1965-66; partner Kurzman & Goldfarb, Washington, 1966-71; asst. sec. for legis. HEW, Washington, 1971-76; partner Nixon, Hargrave, Devans & Doyle, Washington, 1976—; professorial lectr. George Washington U. Law Sch., 1969; cons., dep. dir. ops. Nat. Adv. Commn. on Civil Disorders, 1967-68; cons. Republican Task Force Urban Affairs, U.S. Ho. of Reps., 1968; spl. counsel Urban Coalition Action Council, 1969-70; cons. Treasury Dept., 1969-70, White House Conf. on Children and Youth, 1970-71, Senate Com. Labor and Pub. Welfare, 1969-70, Com. Grants and Benefits, Adminstrv. Conf. U.S., 1969-71. Reviser: Gordon's Modern Annotated Forms of Agreement, 1970. Trustee Harvard Yearbook Bldg. Fund. Served with U.S. Army, 1957-59. Mem. ABA (chmn. com. health, edn. and welfare 1974-75), Fed. Bar Assn., D.C. Bar Assn., Am. Law Inst., Am. Jewish Com., Phi Beta Kappa. Republican. Jewish. Clubs: Federal City, Harvard of D.C. Home: 1523 28th St NW Washington DC 20007 Office: 1090 Vermont Ave Washington DC 20005

KURZWEG, ULRICH HERMANN, physicist, educator; b. Jena, Germany, Sept. 16, 1936; came to U.S., 1947, naturalized, 1952; s. Hermann Herbert and Erna Herta (Michaelis) K.; m. Sophia Speth, Dec. 21, 1963; 1 dau., Tina. B.S., U. Md., 1958; M.A. (Woodrow Wilson fellow 1958-59), Princeton U., 1959; Ph.D. in Physics, Princeton U., 1961. Sr. theoretical physicist United Tech. Research Labs., East Hartford, Conn., 1962-68; adj. asso. prof. math. Rensselaer Poly. Inst., Hartford (Conn.) Grad. Center, 1964-68; mem. faculty Univ. Fla., Gainesville, 1968, prof. engring. scis., 1968—. Contbr. numerous articles to sci. and tech. publs. Fulbright grantee, 1961-62. Mem. Am. Phys. Soc., N.Y. Acad. Scis., AAAS, Calcutta Math. Soc., Sigma Xi. Republican. Lutheran. Home: 8407 NW 4th Pl Gainesville FL 32601 Office: Dept of Engineering Scis Univ of Florida Gainesville FL 32611

KURZWEIL, EDITH, sociology educator, editor; b. Vienna, June 3, 1926; d. Ernest W. and Wilhelmine M. (Fischer) Weiss; m. Charles H. Schmidt, June 24, 1945 (div. 1945); children: Ronald J., Vivien A.; m. 2d Mr. Kurzweil, Aug. 2, 1958 (dec. apr. 1966); 1 son, Allen J. B.A., Queens Coll., CUNY, 1967; M.A., New Sch. Social Research, 1969, Ph.D., 1973. Asst. prof. sociology Hunter Coll., N.Y.C., 1972-75, Montclair State Coll., Upper Monclair, N.J., 1973-78; assoc. prof. sociology Rutgers U., Newark, 1979—; exec. editor Partisan Rev., Boston, 1978—. Author: The Age of Structuralism, 1980, Italian Entrepreneurs, 1983; editor: (with others) Literature and Psychoanalysis, 1983, Writers and Politics, 1983. Rockefeller Humanities fellow, 1982-83. Mem. Am. Sociol. Assn., Eastern Sociol. Assn., P.E.N. Home: One Lincoln Plaza New York NY 10023 Office: Parisan Review 121 Bay State Rd Boston MA 02215

KUSAMA, YAYOI, sculptor; b. Tokyo, Japan, Mar. 22, 1941; emigrated to U.S., 1960, naturalized, 1966. Student, Kyoto (Japan) Arts and Crafts Sch., 1957. Author: Manhattan Suicide Addict, 1978; Contbr. articles to mags. and newspapers.; One man shows include, Aggregation One Thousand Boats, N.Y.C., 1963, Driving Image show, N.Y.C., 1964, Sex Food Obsession Show, Orez Gallery, The Hague, Holland, 1965, Phallus Garden Environment shown Europe, Japan, Am., Floor Show, Castellane Gallery, N.Y.C., 1966, Endless Love Show, Castellane Gallery, N.Y.C., Driving Image Show with Macaroni Room, Naviglio Gallery, Milan, Italy, 1966, Driving Image Show, Sex Obsession-Food Obsession-Compulsion-Furniture-repetitive Vision, Macaroni room, Thelen Gallery, Essen, Germany, 1966, Fillmore East Theatre Happening, 1968, Garden Nude Orgy Happening, Mus. Modern Art, N.Y.C., 1969, Airplane Happening in air over Holland, Fashion show Nude Happening, Venice, Italy, 1970, Cage/Painting/Women, The Haag, Netherlands, 1970-72, Ginza, Tokyo, 1975, 76, Am. Center, Tokyo, 1980, Naviglio Gallery, Italy, 1983, group shows include, Bklyn. Mus., 1958, De Cordova Mus., Boston, 1960, 65, Riverside Mus., N.Y.C., 1960, Städt Mus., Schloss Morsbroish, Leverkusen, Germany, 1961, Pitts. Mus., City Mus., Trier, Germany, Whitney Mus., 1962, City Mus., Amsterdam, Holland, Inst. Contemporary Art, 1964, 65, Wesleyan U., Middletown, Conn., 1964, Modern Art Gallery, Washington, 1965, Chrysler Mus., Provincetown, Mass., Mus. Modern Art, Stockholm, Sweden, Met. Mus., Tokyo, Mus. Modern Art, N.Y.C., 33d Venice Biennale, 1966, Woman's Work-Am. Art, Phila., 1974, Improbable Furniture, U. Pa., 1977, Shapes of Chair-From Design to Art, Osaka, 1978, Neich und Plastisch-Soft Art, Zurich, 1980, The World of Fun-Another Design, Osaka, 1981; represented in permanent collections, Chrysler Mus., Stedelijk Mus., Amsterdam. Organized; presented happenings world-wide. Invented infinity mirror room. Address: 1008 Ushigome Heim 30-2 chome Haramachi Shinjuku-ku Tokyo Japan

KUSCH, POLYKARP, physicist, educator; b. Blankenburg, Germany, Jan. 26, 1911; came to U.S., 1912, naturalized, 1923; s. John Matthias and Henrietta (van der Haas) K.; m. Edith Starr McRoberts, Aug. 12, 1935 (dec. 1959); children—Kathryn, Judith, Sara; m. Betty Jane Pezzoni, 1960; children—Diana, Maria. B.S., Case Inst. Tech., 1931, D.Sc., 1956; M.S., U. Ill., 1933, Ph.D., 1936, D.Sc. (hon.), 1961, Ohio State U., 1959, Colby Coll., 1961, Gustavus Adolphus Coll., St. Peter, Minn., 1962, Yeshiva U., 1976, Coll. of Incarnate Word, 1980, Columbia U., 1983. Engaged as teaching asst. U. Ill., 1931-36; research asst. U. Minn., 1936-37; instr. Columbia U., 1937-41, assoc. prof. physics, 1946-49, prof., 1949-72, chmn. dept. physics, 1949-52, 60-63, acad. v.p. and provost, 1969-72; engr. Westinghouse, 1941-42; research asso. Columbia U., 1942-44; mem. tech. staff Bell Telephone Labs., 1944-46; prof. physics U. Tex.-Dallas, 1972—, Eugene McDermott prof., 1974-80, Regental prof., 1980-82, Regental prof. emeritus, 1982—. Recipient Nobel prize in physics, 1955, Ill. Achievement award U. Ill., 1975; Fellow; Center for Advanced Study in Behavioral Sciences, 1964-65. Fellow Am. Phys. Soc., A.A.A.S.; mem. Am. Acad. Arts and Scis., Am. Philos. Soc., Nat. Acad. Scis. Democrat. Research in atomic and molecular beams and optical molecular spectroscopy. Office: Univ Tex-Dallas PO Box 688 Richardson TX 75080

KUSCHNER, MARVIN, pathologist, university dean; b. N.Y.C., Aug. 13, 1919; s. Julius and Sadye (Marans) K.; m. Kathryn Pancoe, Dec. 19, 1948; 1 son, Jason. A.B., NYU, 1939, M.D., 1943. Intern Kings County Hosp., Bklyn., 1943; asst. resident in pathology Montefiore Hosp., Bronx, N.Y., 1944; resident in pathology Bellevue Hosp., N.Y.C., 1947-48, asst. pathologist, 1949-54, dir. pathology, 1955-70; asst. in pathology NYU, N.Y.C., 1947-49, prof. pathology, dir. exptl. oncology lab., 1955-70, cons. pathologist Inst. Indsl. Medicine, 1950-52, dir. pathology Univ. Hosp., 1968-70; instr. pathology Coll. Physicians and Surgeons, Columbia U., N.Y.C., 1949-51, asst. prof., 1951-54, assoc. prof., 1954-55; research prof. pathology and environ. medicine N.Y. Coll. Medicine, 1970—; prof. pathology Sch. Medicine, SUNY-Stony Brook, 1970—, chmn. dept., 1970-73, dean Sch. Medicine, 1972—; mem. Monsanto Biohazards Commn., St. Louis, 1979—; cons. Johns Manville Co., Bristol Myers Co.; cons. in pathology VA Hosp., N.Y.C., 1967-70; cons. VA Med. Ctr., Northport, N.Y., 1970—, L.I. Jewish-Hillside Med. Ctr.-Queens Affiliation, 1970—, Southside Hosp., 1970—, Nat. Cancer Inst., 1958-62, Surgeon Gen.'s Com. on Smoking and Health, 1958-62; research collaborator Brookhaven Nat. Lab., 1964-70; cons. div. environ. health scis. HEW, 1968-73; chmn. bd. sci. counselors Nat. Inst. Environ. Health Scis., 1971-78, chmn. environ. health scis. rev. com., 1981—; mem. environ. health com. sci. adv. bd. EPA, 1983—; mem. sci. com. Asbestos Health Research Council, Inst. Occupational and Environ. Health, Que., Can.; mem. med. adv. council Ctr. for Biomed. Edn., CCNY. Mem. editorial bd.: Am. Rev. Respiratory Disease, 1962-65, Cancer Research, 1968-76, Preventive Medicine, 1972-82, Proc. Soc. for Exptl. Biology and Medicine, 1972—, Am. Jour. Pathology, 1980—; contbr. articles on cardiovascular and pulmonary disease to profl. jours. Served to capt. M.C. AUS, 1944-46. Recipient Disting Tchr. award NYU, 1966, Alumni Achievement award in clin. and health scis. Sch. Medicine NYU, 1975. Mem. Am. Assn. Pathologists and Bacteriologists, Soc. for Exptl. Pathology, Am. Soc. Clin. Pathologists, Internat. Acad. Pathology, Am. Assn. Cancer Research, Occupational and Environ. Health Soc., N.Y. Heart Assn. (sci. adv. council, dir., mem. exec. com., chmn. nominating com.), Am. Thoracis Soc. (com. on research 1965-68), Am. Thoracic Soc. (chmn. com. on research 1968-70), Phi Beta Kappa, Sigma Xi, Alpha Omega Alpha. Home: 64 East Gate Dr Huntington NY 11743 Office: Sch Medicine SUNY Stony Brook NY 11794 *Research on environ. carcinogensis.*

KUSE, JAMES RUSSELL, chemical company executive; b. Lincoln, Nebr., Aug. 20, 1930; s. Walter Herman and Gladys Katherine (Graham) K.; m. Shirley Rae Ernst, Sept. 27, 1953; children: Lynn, Carol Kuse Ehlen, Michael. B.S.Ch.E., Oreg. State U., 1955. Indsl. chems. salesman Ga.-Pacific Corp., Atlanta, 1967-68, mgr. splty. chem. div., 1968-70, mgr. chem. sales, 1970-74, mgr. comml. chems., 1974-76, v.p. chem. div., 1976-78, sr. v.p. chem. div., 1978—; dir. Exchange Oil & Gas, New Orleans. Bd. dirs. Clark Coll., Atlanta, 1983. Served to cpl. U.S. Army, 1953-55. Mem. Nat. Petroleum Refiners Assn. (dir.), Am. Inst. Chem. Engrs., Chem. Mfrs. Assn., Am. Chem. Soc. Republican. Lutheran. Club: Capital City (Atlanta). Office: Georgia Pacific Corp 133 Peachtree St NE Atlanta GA 30303

KUSH, FRANK JOSEPH, professional football coach; b. Windber, Pa., Jan. 20, 1929. Student, Washington and Lee U.; B.S., Mich. State U.; M.S., Ariz. State U. Player, coach U.S. Army Team, Ft. Benning Ga., 1953-54; asst. football coach Ariz. State U., Tempe, 1955-57, head football coach, 1958-79, Hamilton Can. Football League, (Ont.), (Can.), 1981, Balt. Colts NFL Football, 1982—; coached team to Western Athletic Conf. Title, 1959, 61, 69-73, 75, 77, Can. Football League Eastern Div. Title, Peach Bowl Victory, 1970, Fiesta Bowl Victory, 1971-75, Garden State Bowl Victory, 1978. Office: Baltimore Colts PO Box 2000 Owings Mills MD 21117 *

KUSHELOFF, DAVID LEON, journalist; b. N.Y.C., Sept. 23, 1917; s. William and Mollie (Yachnin) K.; m. Roslyn Schlaffer, Sept. 28, 1941; children: Judith Ann, Stephen Gordon, Marjorie Alice. B.S.S., CCNY, 1938. With Washington Times-Herald, 1945-54; with Phila. Bull., 1956-81, book editor, 1977-81. Served with USAAF, 1942-45. Mem. Sigma Delta Chi. Home: 102 Glenoak Rd Wilmington DE 19805

KUSHEN, ALLAN STANFORD, lawyer, diversified industry executive; b. Chgo., Oct. 5, 1929; s. Barney and Ethel (Friedman) K.; m. Betty Cohen, Sept. 2, 1951; children: Annette Joyce, Robert Allan. B.B.A. cum laude, U. Miami, Fla., 1952, LL.B., 1952; LL.M. (Food and Drug Law Inst. fellow), N.Y. U., 1955. Bar: Fla. 1952, N.Y. State 1956. Atty. Schering Corp., Bloomfield, N.J., 1955-67, 1967-69, 1969-73; v.p., gen. counsel Schering-Plough Corp., Kenilworth, N.J., 1973-80, sr. v.p. legal and public affairs, 1980—; mem. N.Y. adv. com. Allendale Ins. Co.; lectr. in field. Mem. editorial adv. bd.: Food, Drug and Cosmetic Law Jour. Trustee Food and Drug Law Inst., Kean Coll., Arts Council of Morris Area; trustee, chmn. med. orgn. com. Elizabeth Gen. Hosp. and Dispensary; bd. visitors Yale Law Sch. Civil Liability Project; pres. Schering-Plough Found.; bd. dirs. United Way Morris County. Served to 1st lt. JAG AUS, 1952-54. Mem. ABA, N.Y. State Bar Assn., N.J. Bar Assn. (asso.), Fed. Bar Assn., Fla. Bar, Am. Coll. Legal Medicine (asso. in law), Phi Delta Phi. Home: 1 Raynor Rd West Orange NJ 07052 Office: Schering-Plough Corp One Giralda Farms Madison NJ 07940

KUSHLAN, SAMUEL DANIEL, physician, educator, hospital administrator; b. New Britain, Conn., Feb. 17, 1912; s. H. David and Bessie M. K.; m. Ethel Ross, June 24, 1934; children: Nancy Kushlan Wanger, David Ross. B.S., Yale U., 1932, M.D., 1935. Diplomate: Am. Bd. Internal Medicine with subsplty in gastroenterology. Intern New Haven Hosp., 1935-36, asst. resident, 1937; vol. research fellow Mass. Gen. Hosp., 1938; cons. Yale U. Health Service; assoc. physician-in-chief Yale-New Haven Hosp., 1967-83, cons. to chief staff, 1983—; clin. prof. medicine Yale U., 1967—. Contbr. numerous articles to profl. jours. Named Physician of Yr. Conn. Digestive Disease Soc., 1975. Fellow Royal Soc. Medicine (Eng.); mem. Am. Gastroenterol. Assn., Am. Soc. Gastrointestinal Endoscopy, AMA, Conn. State Med. Soc., New Haven Med. Assn., Conn. Regional Soc. for Gastrointestinal Endoscopy, World Med. Assn., Assn. Yale Alumni in Medicine (pres. 1957-59), Sigma Xi, Alpha Omega Alpha. Office: Suite 1063CB Yale-New Haven Hosp New Haven CT 06504 *Life must have Meaning.*

KUSHNER, DAVID ZAKERI, musicologist, educator; b. Ellenville, N.Y., Dec. 22, 1935; s. Nathan and Rita (Forgatsh) K.; m. Rebecca Ann Stefan, Dec. 20, 1964 (div. Nov. 1979); children—Jonathan Moses, Joshua Sanford, Jeremy Avram, Jason Daniel. Mus.B., Boston U., 1957; Mus.M., Coll.-Conservatory Music Cin., 1958; Ph.D., U. Mich., 1967. Asst. prof. music Miss. U. For Women, 1964-66; asso. prof. music Radford (Va.) U., 1966-68, prof. music, 1968-69; prof. music in doctoral research faculty, coordinator grad. studies in music, coordinator musicological studies U. Fla., Gainesville, 1969—; mem. adv. panel Center for Jewish Studies, 1980—; lectr., Eng., Scotland, 1975; vis. prof. music Florence (Italy) Study Center, 1975; charter mem., program annotator Pro Arte Musica of Gainesville, 1970-75; bd. dirs., chmn. edn. com. B'nai Israel Congregation, Gainesville, 1977-79; vice chmn. Gainesville Cultural Commn., 1974-75; host, commentator on Music from Fla., weekly radio program over WRUF-FM, 1969-75; mem. People-to-People del. Nat. Music Council, Austria, W.Ger., Hungary, Poland and Czechoslovakia, 1977; lectr. and lectr.-recitalist, profl. and civic orgns., coll. and univ. campuses, U.S., Can. and Europe, performer ann. Recitals in Schs. series. Author: Ernest Bloch and His Symphonic Works, 1967, Ernest Bloch and His Music, 1973, also articles and revs. in profl. jours. and reference books.; Book reviewer: Am. Music Tchr. Mag. Recipient Pro Mundi Beneficio medal Brazilian Acad. Humanities, 1975. Mem. Am. Liszt Soc. (co-founder, chmn. bd. dirs., charter life mem.), Coll. Music Soc., Am. Musicol. Soc. (chmn. So. chpt. 1971-74), Fla. Music Tchrs. Assn. (chmn. collegiate artist competitions 1972-73), Music Tchrs. Nat. Assn. (life), Fla. State Music Tchrs. Assn., Ernest Bloch Soc., Pi Kappa Lambda (charter, pres. U. Fla. chpt. 1970-76), Phi Mu Alpha Sinfonia (life). Home: 2215 NW 21st Ave Gainesville FL 32605 *It has been my credo to establish goals that are attainable and consistent with standards of personal and professional conduct that I view as honorable. One must be true to himself and measure his own being by the same criteria he would apply to others. Real success is adjudged not by the perceptions of society, but by one's own sense of self-worth.*

KUSHNER, HAROLD JOSEPH, educator; b. N.Y.C., July 29, 1933; s. Hyman and Harriet (Messing) K.; m. Linda Jane Rosen, Sept. 18, 1960; children—Diana Jeanne, Nina Joanne. B. Elec. Engring, Coll. City N.Y., 1955; M.S., U. Wis., 1956, Ph.D., 1958. With Lincoln Lab., Mass. Inst. Tech., 1958-63, Research Inst. Advanced Studies, Balt., 1963-64; prof. applied math. and engring. Brown U., 1964—; cons. to govt. and industry, 1963—. Contbr. monograph, text, articles. Fellow IEEE; mem. Inst. Math. Statistics, Soc. Indsl. and Applied Math., Ops. Research Soc. Am. Home: 560 Lloyd Ave Providence RI 02906

KUSHNER, HARVEY DAVID, science and technology company executive; b. N.Y.C., Dec. 28, 1930; s. Morris K. and Hilda (Kushner); m. Rose Rehert, Jan. 14, 1951; children: Gantt A., Todd R., Lesley K. B.S. in Engring., Johns Hopkins U., 1951. Assoc. engr. Bur. Ships-U.S. Navy, 1951-53; mem. tech. staff Melpar Inc., 1953-54; with ORI Inc., 1955—, chmn. bd., pres.; v.p. Reliance Group Inc.; pres. Disclosure Inc., 1972-77; cons. in field. Mem. econ. adv. council Montgomery County, Md., 1981—; chmn. Montgomery County, Md, 1983—,

Council Def. and Space Industry Assns., 1983—; mem. Md. Gov.'s High Tech. Roundtable, 1983; chmn. United Way campaign, Montgomery County, 1980, mem. exec. bd., Montgomery County, 1981—. Mem. Nat. Security Indsl. Assn. (trustee, exec. com.), Profl. Services Council (dir. 1974—, dir. 1983—). Club: Cosmos (Washington). Home: 9607 Kingston Rd Kensington MD 20895 Office: 1400 Spring St Silver Spring MD 20910

KUSHNER, LAWRENCE MAURICE, physical chemist, research administrator; b. N.Y.C., Sept. 20, 1924; s. Hyman Tobias and Mary (Malkin) K.; children: Robb Adam, Leslie Meryl; m. Shirley Gayle Brown, June 24, 1972. B.S., Queens Coll., 1945; A.M., Princeton U., 1947, Ph.D., 1949. Teaching asst. Princeton U., 1947-48; with Nat. Bur. Standards, 1948-73, chief, metal physics sect., 1956-61, chief, metallurgy div., 1961-66; dep. dir. Inst. Applied Tech., 1966-68, dir., 1968, dep. dir. bur., 1969-73, acting dir., 1972-73; commr. Consumer Product Safety Commn., Washington, 1973-77; policy devel. Nat. Bur. Standards, 1977-80; sr. sci. staff Mitre Corp., McLean, Va., 1980—; adj. prof. engring. and public policy Carnegie-Mellon U., 1981—; lectr. chemistry Am. U., 1952-60; spl. asst. for legis. to asst. sec. of commerce for sci. and tech., 1964-65; Mem. ad hoc internat. group metal physics OECD, 1961. Recipient Superior Accomplishment award Dept. Commerce, 1954, gold medal, 1968; Meritorious Service award Am. Nat. Standards Inst., 1973. Mem. Am. Phys. Soc., AAAS, Fed. Profl. Assn., Am. Chem. Soc., Washington Acad. Scis., ASTM (hon.), Sigma Xi (nat. pres. 1976). Spl. research crystal properties, surface phenomena in chemistry and metallurgy, materials sci., product safety and environ. regulation, sci. and tech. policy, technol. innovation. Home: 9528 Briar Glenn Way Gaithersburg MD 20879 Office: Mitre Corp 1820 Dolley Madison Blvd McLean VA 22102

KUSHNER, ROBERT ARNOLD, steel company executive; b. N.Y.C., Dec. 11, 1935; s. Sidney and Doris Gloria (Kaplowitz) K.; m. Alice Fried, June 8, 1957; children: Audrey, Donald. B.S., NYU, 1957, J.D., 1960. Bar: N.Y. 1960, Pa. 1977. Atty.-adviser FTC, 1960-61; asso. firm Parker, Chapin, Flattau and Klimpl, N.Y.C., 1961-67; v.p. legal, sec. Ward Foods, Inc., N.Y.C., 1967-72; asst. gen. counsel Pan Am. Airways, N.Y.C., 1972-76; v.p., sec., gen. counsel Cyclops Corp., Pitts., 1976—. Bd. dirs. Pitts. Dance Council. Mem. Am. Bar Assn., Am. Iron and Steel Inst., Order of Coif. Clubs: Rolling Hills Country, Duquesne. Home: 30 Vernon Dr Pittsburgh PA 15228 Office: 650 Washington Rd Pittsburgh PA 15228

KUSHNER, ROBERT ELLIS, artist; b. Pasadena, Calif., Aug. 19, 1949; s. Joseph and Dorothy (Browdy) K.; m. Ellen Saltonstall, Oct. 27, 1978; 1 son, Max Saltonstall. B.A., U. Calif.-San Diego, 1971. Exhibited one-man shows, Holly Solomon Gallery, N.Y.C., 1982, Gallery Rudolf Swirner, Cologne, W. Ger., U. Colo. Art Gallery, Boulder, Am. Graffiti Gallery, Amsterdam, Netherlands, Studio Marconi, Milan, Italy, U. So. Calif. 'Helen Lindhurst Gallery, Los Angeles, Castelli-Goodman-Solomon, East Hampton, N.Y., 1982; numerous group shows, Whitney Mus. Am. Art, N.Y.C., 1975, 81, 82, 83, Mus. Modern Art, N.Y.C., 1978, 80, 81, 83, Albright-Knox Gallery, Buffalo, 1979, Bklyn. Mus., 1984, Mpls. Inst. Arts, 1983, Sydney Art Mus., 1982, Venice Biennale, 1980; represented permanent collections, Mus. Modern Art, Whitney Mus. Am. Art; exhibited, Bklyn. Mus.; represented, Phila. Mus. Art; artist numerous art performances, 1971—; designer costumes, sets; author: (with Ed Friedman and Katherine Landman) The New York Hat Line, 1979; subj. of numerous publs. Office: Holly Solomon Gallery 724 Fifth Ave New York NY 10019

KUSIK, JOHN EDWARD, cons. and investment co. exec.; b. Tallinn, Estonia, Dec. 20, 1898; s. August and Emma (Konsa) K.; m. Gloria Fewell, Dec. 25, 1931 (dec. Nov. 1972); children—John Edward, Anne Woodberry. M.S., U. Va., 1925; D. Engring. (hon.), Case Inst. Tech., 1955. Traveling auditor Gen. Electric Co., 1925-30, asst. to comptroller, with numerous mgmt. engring. assignments, U.S., Brazil, Argentina, China, Japan and Australia, 1930-39; asst. to pres. New Eng. Pub. Service Co., 1933-34; exec. v.p. Rex Cole, Inc., N.Y.C., 1935; chief financial officer maj. sub-div. Gen. Electric Co., 1939-49; v.p. finance C.&O. Ry., 1949-60, sr. v.p., 1960-63, chmn. finance com., 1963-72, vice chmn., dir., 1966-72; sr. v.p., dir. B.&O. R.R., 1965-72; also mem. exec. com.; v.p. White Sulphur Springs Co., 1949-72; pres. Q Assos., Cleve., 1972—; mem. vis. faculty Grad. Sch. Bus. Adminstrn., U. Va.; Bd. overseers Cleve. Marshall Law Sch., Cleve. State U. Mem. N.J. Taxpayers Assn. (dir., mem. exec. com. 1947-49), N.J. C. of C. (cost govt. com. 1947-49), Am. Econ. Assn., Am. Mgmt. Assn. (dir., mem. gen. mgmt. planning council, v.p. finance div. 1956-58), Phi Beta Kappa. Club: Shaker Heights (Cleve.). Home: 3120 Kingsley Rd Shaker Heights OH 44122 Office: Terminal Tower Cleveland OH 44113

KUSKIN, KARLA, writer, illustrator; b. N.Y.C., July 17, 1932; d. Sidney T. and Mitzi (Salzman) Seidman; m. Charles Kuskin, Dec. 4, 1955; children: Nicholas, Julia. Student, Antioch Coll., 1950-53; B.F.A., Yale U., 1955. Tchr., cons. schs. at elem. and univ. levels. Author, illustrator: Roar and More, 1956 (A.I.G.A. best children's books), In the Middle of the Trees, 1958 (A.I.G.A. best 50 books); also 26 books for children; illustrator 11 books other authors; author 2 books illustrated by Marc Simont; contbg. author: The State of the Language, 1980; author: filmstrips What Is Design?, 1971, An Electric Talking Picture, 1972, Karla Kuskin, 1979, Poetry Explained by Karla Kuskin, 1980; contbg. editor: Saturday Review, 1973; book reviewer: Record-Poetry Parade; contbr. articles to publs. including, New York mag., House and Garden, N.Y. Times, Wilson Library Bull., Horizon mag. Recipient awards Nat. Council Tchrs. English, 1979, N.Y. Acad. Scis., 1979, New Eng. Book Show, 1961; CBC Showcase award for A Boy had a Mother Who Bought Him a Hat, 1976, Notable Books award ALA, 1982; Best Picture Book award N.Y. Times, 1982; named Outstanding Bklyn. Author, 1981. Jewish. Home and Office: 96 Joralemon St Brooklyn NY 11201

KUSLAN, LOUIS ISAAC, chemist, educator; b. New Haven, Feb. 14, 1922; s. Joseph and Rebecca (Tucker) K.; m. Dorothy Jane Morris, June 22, 1947; children: James George, Richard David. B.S., U. Conn., 1943; M.A., Yale, 1947, Ph.D., 1954. Tchr. sci. Lyman Meml. High Sch., Lebanon, Conn., 1943-45, Glastonbury (Conn.) High Sch., 1945-46; instr. chemistry U. Conn., 1946-49; from instr. chemistry to prof. So. Conn. State Coll., New Haven, 1950—, dean, 1966-78; Bd. dirs. U. Research Inst. Conn., 1967—; asso. fellow Davenport Coll., Yale, 1973—. Author: (with A. Harris Stone) Teaching Children Science, 2d edit, 1972, Readings on Teaching Children Science, 1969, Liebig, 1969, Robert Boyle, 1970, (with Richard Kuslan) Ham Radio, 1981; Contbr. articles to profl. jours. Fellow AAAS; mem. History Sci. Soc., Conn. Acad. Arts and Scis. (v.p.), Nat. Assn. Research Sci. Teaching, Am. Chem. Soc. Home: 90 Robinwood Rd Hamden CT 06517 Office: 501 Crescent St New Haven CT 06515

KUSPIT, DONALD BURTON, art historian, art critic, educator; b. N.Y.C., Mar. 26, 1935; s. Morris and Celia (Schmukler) Kuspit S.; m. Judith Clements Price, Mar. 22, 1962. B.A. in Philosophy with distinction, Columbia U., 1955, M.A., Yale U., 1957; D.Phil. magna cum laude, U. Frankford, (W.Ger.), 1960; Ph.D. in Art History, U. Mich., 1971. Asst. prof. Pa. State U., State College, 1960-66; assoc. prof. U. Windsor, Ont., Can., 1966-70; prof. U. N.C., Chapel Hill, 1970-78; Univ. Disting. prof. Rutgers U., New Brunswick, N.J., 1982-83; prof. art, chmn. dept. art SUNY-Stony Brook, 1978—; editorial cons. UMI Research Press, Ann Arbor, Mich., 1980—; mem. overview com. visual arts sect. Nat. Endowment for Arts, Washington, 1983—. Author: Clement Greenberg, Ar Critic, 1979, The Critic as Artist: The Intentionality of Art, 1984; contbg. editor: Art in Am., 1978—. NEH younger humanist fellow, 1973; Nat. Endowment for Arts critic fellow, 1977; John Simon Guggenheim fellow, 1977. Mem. Coll. Art Assn. (Frank Jewett Mather award 1982), PEN, Am. Soc. Aesthetics, Internat. Assn. Art Critics (v.p. Am. sect. 1982—). Home: 38 W 26 St New York NY 10010 Office: SUNY Dept Art Stony Brook NY 11794

KUSS, HENRY JOHN, JR., trade and finance company executive; b. N.Y.C., Nov. 10, 1922; s. Henry John and Olga (Sidlo) K.; m. Johanna Meta Derouet, June 28, 1944; children—Linda Joy, Karen Lisa. Student, Coll. Holy Cross, 1943-44; B.A., St. John's U., 1947. Dir. supply system planning Bur. Ordnance, Dept. Navy, 1947-50; budget analyst Office Sec. Def., 1950-53; dir. Army/Navy Def. Econ. Planning, Paris Office, 1953-55; asst. to under sec. navy, 1955-57; dir. fgn. mil. resources planning Office Sec. Def., 1957-59, dir. fgn. mil. assistance planning, 1959-61, dep. asst. sec. def. for internat. security affairs, 1962-69; pres. Am. Trade and Fin. Co., Arlington, Va., 1969—; dir. Calcusearch, Inc., Tanner Resources Corp.; Def. mem. Presdl. Commn. on Study Korean Economy, 1953; U.S. rep. NATO Econ. Cost Com., 1954-55; def. mem. Spl. Internat. Econ. Requirements and capabilities Commn., Italy, Norway, Turkey, Greece, 1954; chmn. com. mil. exports Def. Industry Adv. Council, 1962-69. Served with USNR, 1944-47. Recipient Meritorious Civilian Service medal sec. def., 1965. Mem. Soc. Logistics Engrs., Am. Inst. Indsl. Engrs. Lutheran. Home: 1426 Lady Bird Dr McLean VA 22101 Office: 2001 Jefferson Davis Hwy Arlington VA 22202

KUSS, RICHARD LAMAR, oil company executive; b. Springfield, Ohio, Jan. 4, 1923; s. Peter John and Frances Leone (Rizer) Kuss L.; m. Barbara Deer, July 8, 1944; children: Carolyn Kuss Patterson, Paul R., Gregory R., Philip D. B.A., Wittenberg U., 1979, L.H.D., 1979; postgrad. in bus. adminstrn., Harvard U., 1944-45. Sales mgr. Bonded Oil, Springfield, 1946-49, v.p., 1949-67, pres., 1967-83, Kuss Petroleum Co., 1983—, Emro Mktg. Co., 1976-83; dir. Stocker & Sitler Oil Co., Heath, Ohio, 1969—; chmn. bd. Merchants and Mechanics Fed. Savs. and Loan Assn., Springfield, 1978—. Vice chmn. bd. Wittenberg U., Springfield, 1972—, nat. chmn. Campaign for Wittenberg, Springfield, 1978-82; assoc. chmn., mem. campaign adv. com. United Way Springfield, 1974-75. Served to lt. j.g. USN, 1943-46; PTO. Recipient Marts & Lundy award, 1971, Silver Knight of Mgmt. award Springfield chpt. Nat. Mgmt. Assn., 1979, medal of Honor Wittenberg U., 1983, Exceptional Achievement award council for Advancement and Support Edn., 1983, resolution for Outstanding Ohio Citizen Ohio Senate, 1983. Mem. Am. petroleum Inst. (bd. dirs. 1968—, cert. appreciation 1974), Am. Petroleum Inst. (lifetime mem. bd. dirs. 1983—), Nat. Oil Jobbers Council (chmn. planning com., treas., v.p., cert. appreciation 1974), 25 Yr. Club of Petroleum Industry, Ohio Petroleum Marketers Assn. (pres., dir., Distng. Service award 1972, 83), Ohio Found. Ind. Colls. (dir. 1972—), Springfield Area C. of C. (v.p., dir.), Springfield Jaycees (pres.). Republican. Presbyterian. Clubs: Country (pres.), Univ. (pres.), Van Dyke (Springfield) (pres.); Muirfield Village Golf, Coral Ridge Country, Zanesfield Rod & Gun. Lodge: Rotary (Springfield). Home: 1909 Walnut Terr Springfield OH 45504 Office: Kuss Petroleum Co care Bonded Oil 2525 N Limestone St Springfield OH 45501

KUSSEROW, RICHARD P., government official; b. San Jose, Calif., Dec. 9, 1940; s. Roger B. and Eve W. (Larson) K. B.A. in Polit. Sci, UCLA, 1963; M.A. in Govt, Calif. State U., Los Angeles; postgrad., So. Methodist U. Law Sch., John Marshall Law Sch. Lectr. Calif. State U., Los Angeles, 1964; case officer CIA, 1967-68; spl. agt. supr. in white collar and organized crime FBI, 1969-81; insp. gen. Dept. Health and Human Services, 1981—; chmn. Pres.' Council on Integrity and Efficiency, 1981—; chmn. Governmentwide Project on Computer Security and Advanced Audit on Investigative Techniques; lectr. white collar crime, govt. program fraud, asset protection, internal controls, performance mgmt. Served to capt. USMCR, 1965-68. Mem. Assn. Govt. Accts. (nat. pres.), Am. Soc. Idsl. Security, Assn. Fed. Investigators (nat. pres.), Fed. Law Enforcement Officers Assn., Soc. Former Spl. Agts FBI, Internat. Assn. Chiefs of Police. Presbyterian. Home: 2400 Lee Hwy Arlington VA 22201 Office: 330 Independence Ave SW Washington DC 20201

KUST, LEONARD EUGENE, lawyer; b. Luxemburg, Wis., Mar. 14, 1917; s. Joseph Andrew and Anna (Mleziva) K.; m. Henrietta Bryan Logan, Apr. 17, 1948; children: Alice Lyon Kust Harding, Andrea Logan Kust. Ph.B., U. Wis., Madison, 1939; J.D., Harvard U., 1942. Bar: N.Y. 1946, Pa. 1957. Assoc. Cravath, Swaine & Moore, N.Y.C., 1946-55; gen. tax counsel Westinghouse Electric Corp., Pitts., 1955-65; v.p., gen. tax counsel Westinghous Electric Corp., Pitts., 1965-70; ptnr. Cadwalader, Wickersham & Taft, N.Y.C., 1970—; pres. Leonard E. Kust, P.C., N.Y.C., 1982—; mem. adv. com. Commr. Internal Revenue, 1959-61; chmn. Pa. Gov's Com. on Tax Adminstrn., 1963-65; chmn. task forces Pa. Gov.'s Tax Rev. Com., 1967-68. Contbr. articles to profl. jours. Trustee Ch. of Heavenly Rest Day Sch., N.Y.C., 1978-82, warden, N.Y.C., 1980—, mem. vestry, N.Y.C., 1976-80; warden Calvary Protestant Episcopal Ch., Pitts., 1963-71. Served to lt. USNR, 1942-46. Mem. U.S. C of C. (dir. 1967-73), Tax Execs. Inst. (pres. 1961-62), ABA, N.Y. Bar Assn., Nat. Tax Assn. (pres. 1969-70). Clubs: Duquesne (Pitts.); Down Town Assn., Harvard; The Church (N.Y.C.) (dir. 1981—). Home: 1115 Fifth Ave New York NY 10128 Office: 1 Wall St New York NY 10005

KUSTIN, KENNETH, chemist; b. Bronx, N.Y., Jan. 6, 1934; s. Alex and Mae (Marvisch) K.; m. Myrna May Jacobson, June 24, 1956; children—Brenda Jayne, Franklin Daniel, Michael Thorpe. B.Sc., Queens Coll., 1955; Ph.D., U. Minn., 1959. Postdoctoral fellow Max Planck Inst. for Phys. Chemistry, Gottingen, W. Ger., 1959-61; asst. prof. chemistry Brandeis U., 1961-66, asso. prof., 1966-72, prof., 1972—, chmn. dept. chemistry, 1974-77; vis. prof. pharmacology Harvard U. Med. Sch., 1977-78; Fulbright-Hays lectr., 1978. Research, publs. in field; editor: Fast Reactions, vol. 16 of Methods in Enzymology, 1969. Mem. Am. Chem. Soc., Phi Beta Kappa. Office: Dept Chemistry Brandeis U Waltham MA 02254

KUSTOM, ROBERT LOUIS, scientific research administrator; b. Chgo., July 11, 1934; s. Louis W. K. and Mary (Henek) Kuskowski; m. Dolores Curley, Apr. 4, 1959; children: Brittan S.L., Todd R., Jill M. A.A., Morton Jr. Coll., 1954; B.S. in Elec. Engring., Ill. Inst. Tech., 1956, M.S., 1958; Ph.D. in Elec. Engring., U. Wis., 1969. Elec. engr. high voltage lab. Joslyn Mfg. & Supply Co., Chgo., 1955-58; elec. engr. high energy physics and accelerator divs. Argonne (Ill.) Nat. Lab., 1958-71, group leader zero gradient synchrotron ops. group, 1971-73, assoc. dir. div. accelerator research facilities, 1973-79, dir. div., 1979—; vis. scientist Rutherford High Energy Lab., Chilton, Eng., 1970-71; vis. prof. elec. engring. U. Wis.-Madison, 1978-79, 81; cons. to Superconducting Energy Storage Group, 1979, 81. Author: Thyristor Networks for the Transfer of Energy Between Superconducting Coils, 1980; contbr. articles to sci. jours. Pres. St. Alexander Sch. Bd., Palos Heights, Pub. Library, 1974-80; treas. Palos Heights Pub. Library, 1976-80. Mem. IEEE, Sigma Xi. Office: Argonne Nat Lab 9700 S Cass Ave Argonne IL 60439

KUTCHINS, MICHAEL JOSEPH, airport executive; b. Chgo., IL, Dec. 1, 1941; s. Jack M. and Bernice L. K.; m. Anna Kay Overton, Sept. 22, 1962; children: Bradley Charles, Scott Freeman. B.S., U. Ill., 1962. Accredited airport exec. Reporter Sta. WICD-TV, Danville, Ill., 1962-63, Sta. WSOY AM-FM, Decatur, Ill., 1963-65; bus. editor, reporter Sta. WXOC AM-FM-TV, Charlotte, N.C., 1965-67; adminstrv. asst. to mgr. Douglas Mcpl. Airport, Charlotte, 1968-71; asst. dir. aviation San Antonio Internat. Airport, 1971-81, dir. aviation, 1981—. Mem. Am. Assn. Airport Execs. (2d v.p. 1982-84, pres. South Central chpt. 1976). Home: 216 Gardenview San Antonio TX 78213 Office: San Antonio Internat Airport 9700 Airport Blvd San Antonio TX 78216

KUTLER, STANLEY IRA, history educator, author; b. Cleve., Aug. 10, 1934; s. Robert P. and Zelda R. (Coffman) K.; m. Sandra J. Sachs, June 24, 1956; children: Jeffrey, David, Susan, Andrew. B.A., Bowling Green State U., 1956; Ph.D., Ohio State U., 1960. Instr. History Pa. State U., State College, 1960-62; asst. prof. history San Diego State U., 1962-64, U. Wis., Madison, 1964-65, assoc. prof. history, 1965-71, prof. history, 1971-80, E. Gordon Fox prof. Am. institutions and history, 1980—; cons. Nat. Endowment for the Humanities, 1975—. Editor: Rev. in Am. History, 1972—; advisory editor: Greenwood Pub., 1968-73, Johns Hopkins U. Press, 1982—; author: Judicial Power and Reconstruction, 1968, Privilege and Creative Destruction, 1971, The American Inquisition, 1983; editor: Supreme Court and the Constitution, 1969, 3d edit., 1984, Looking for America, 1975, 80. Fellow Sage Found., 1967-68; named Dist. Exchange scholar to China Nat. Acad. Scis., 1982, sr. Fulbright lectr. to Japan, 1977; fellow Guggenhein Found., 1971-72, Rockefeller Found., 1979-80. Jewish. Home: 6417 Masthead Dr Madison WI 53705 Office: Dept History U Wis Madison WI 53706

KUTNER, MAURICE BREGER, sportswear co. exec.; b. Bklyn., Aug. 18, 1918; s. Joseph H. and Rose Ada (Breger) K.; m. Jeane Evelyn Redlin, Nov. 11, 1944; children—Karen Susan, Shelley Ann, Kenneth Michael. B.S., Columbia, 1943. With Spencer Industries, Inc., N.Y.C., 1935—; exec. v.p., dir. Casual Sportswear Co., N.Y.C., 1945—, now also exec. v.p., dir. parent co. Served to comdr. USNR. Home: 333 E 68th St New York NY 10021 Office: 350 Fifth Ave New York NY 10001

KUTNEY, JAMES PETER, educator; b. Lamont, Alta., Can., May 2, 1932; s. John and Mary (Twardowsky) K.; m. Josephine Krawchyshyn, June 30, 1953; children—James Christopher Robin, Kimberley Elaine, Karen Ann Marie. B.Sc., U. Alta., 1954; M.Sc., U. Wis., 1956; Ph.D. (Eli Lilly & Co. fellow, USPHS fellow), Wayne State U., 1958. Mem. faculty hU. B.C., Vancouver, Can., 1959—, asso. prof. chemistry, 1964-66, prof., 1966—; vis. prof. Fed. U. Brazil, Rio de Janeiro, 1967, Japan Soc. Promotion Sci., Sen dai, 1975; cons. MacMillan Bloedel Research, 1968—; Mem. com. on drug insts. Med. Research Council Can., 1969; mem. com. on internat. sci. exchanges NRC Can., 1970. Contbr. numerous articles to tech. jours. Recipient Fred H. Irwin prize in organic chemistry U. Alta., 1953, First Class Honors prize, 1954; Jacob Biely research prize U. B.C., 1972; Master Tchr. award, 1973; NATO scholar, Bonn, West Germany, 1965. Fellow Am. Chem. Soc.; mem. N.Y. Acad. Scis., Chem. Inst. Can. (Mercke, Sharp and Dohme award 1968), Chem. Soc. London, Chem. Soc. (Switzerland), Pharm. Soc. Japan, Sigma Xi, Phi Lambda Upsilon. Home: 2327 McMullen Ave Vancouver BC V6L 2E2 Canada

KUTTAS, GEORGE, retired army officer; b. Phila., Feb. 24, 1927; s. Frank and Anna (Resetar) K.; m. Helen Elizabeth Gleeson, Jan. 6, 1952; children: Frank, Catherine H., Sue A., John C. B.A., NYU, 1947; D.D.S., U. Pa., 1951; M.S., Shippenburg (Pa.) State Coll., 1972. Commd. 1st lt. Dental Corps, U.S. Army, 1951, advanced through grades to maj. gen., 1979; service in Germany, Ryukyu Islands and Vietnam, dep. to chief Army Dental Corps, also sr. Dental Corps staff officer, 1973-75; pres. Army Bd. Gen. Dentistry; dep. comdr. 7th Med. Command, Europe, 1975-79; chief U.S. Army Dental Corps, 1979-82; ret., 1982; vis. faculty U.S. Army Inst. Dental Research. Contbr. articles to dental jours. Decorated Legion of Merit with oak leaf cluster, D.S.M., Bronze Star; Vietnamese Cross Gallantry; Civic Action medal (Vietnam). Fellow Acad. Gen. Dentistry (dir. fed. region 1973-75), Am. Coll. Dentists; mem. ADA. Mem. Greek Orthodox Ch. Address: 450 Saint Lucia Ct Satellite Beach FL 32937

KUTTLER, CARL MARTIN, JR., community coll. pres.; b. Daytona Beach, Fla., Jan. 31, 1940; s. Carl M. and Winona (Ellis) K.; m. Evelyn Flathmann, June 29, 1963; children—Cindy, Carl Martin III, Erika. A.A. in Mgmt, St. Petersburg Jr. Coll., 1960; B.S., Fla. State U., Tallahassee, 1962; J.D., Stetson Coll. Law, 1965. Bar: Fla. bar 1965. Research aide 2d Dist. Ct. Appeals, Lakeland, Fla., 1965-66; instr. St. Petersburg (Fla.) Jr. Coll., 1965-76, asst. to v.p. for adminstrn., 1966-67, dean. adminstrv. affairs, 1967-78, pres., 1978—. Contbr. articles to profl. jours. Chmn. Fla. Student Fin. Aid Commn., 1977-80; mem. Pres.'s Council Div. Community Colls., 1978—; candidate for Fla. Commr. Edn., 1974; active various civic orgns. Named Most. Disting. Alumnus Stetson U. Alumni Assn., 1978; recipient various grants. Mem. Pinellas County Secondary Sch. Adminstrn. Assn., Nat. Assn. Coll. and Univ. Attys., Council for Advancement and Support of Edn., Fla. Assn. Community Colls., Fla. Bar Assn., St. Petersburg Bar Assn., Gulf Beach/Seminole Bd. Realtors, NAACP, Pinellas Suncoast Urban League, C. of C. Republican. Methodist. Home: 8336 40th Ave N Saint Petersburg FL 33709 Office: PO Box 13489 Saint Petersburg FL 33733

KUTZ, JOSEPH EDWARD, hand surgeon, educator; b. Standish, Mich., June 11, 1928; s. Joseph M. and Hazel (Stock) K.; m. Mary Jane Templeton, June 15, 1957; children: Anthony, Karen, Bradley. B.S., U. Detroit, 1953, M.S., 1955; M.D., U. Mich., 1958. Diplomate: Am. Bd. Surgery. Rotating intern Springfield (O.) City Hosp., 1958-59; resident gen. surgery Louisville Gen. Hosp., 1959-63; fellow surgery of hand U. Louisville, 1963-64, asst. clin. prof. surgery, 1968-74, asso. clin. prof., 1974—. Contbr. numerous articles to profl. jours. Served with AUS, 1945-48. Mem. A.C.S., Am., Caribbean socs. surgery of the hand, Am., Ky., Mich. med. assns., Jefferson County (Ky.) Med. Soc., Ky., Louisville, Pan-Pacific surg. socs., Am. Soc. Surgery of Hand, Southeastern Surg. Congress., Am. Soc. Plastic and Reconstructive Surgeons, Internat. Soc. Reconstructive Microsurgery (founder), Sunderland Soc. (charter), S.C. Orthopaedic Assn. (hon.), Group for Advancement Microsurgery. Home: 20 Rio Vista St Louisville KY 40207 Office: 250 E Liberty St Louisville KY 40202

KUTZ, MYER PAUL, publisher; b. Mar. 31, 1939; s. Samuel So l and Dorothy (Beritz) K.; m. Cynthia Jean Van Hazinga, June 25, 1965 (div. 1978); m. 2d Mary Enid Dorrance, Oct. 6, 1979. B.S., Mit, 1959; M.S., Rensselaer Poly. Inst., 1961. Engr. MIT Instrumentation Lab., Cambridge, 1946-65, Am. Sci. and Engring., 1965-68, Cox & Co., N.Y.C., 1969-71; freelance writer, N.Y.C., 1971-76; editor John Wiley & Sons Inc., N.Y.C., 1976-81, pub., 1981—. Author: Temperature Control, 1968, Rockefeller Power, 1974, Midtown North, 1976; editor-in-chief: Kent's Mechanical Engineer's Handbook, 13th edit., 1976. Ednl. counselor MIT Edn. Council. Served to 1st lt. AUS, 1962-64. Mem. ASME (chmn. publs. and database coms.), Assn. Am. Pubs. (chmn. database and awards coms.), Pi Tau Sigma. Democrat. Jewish. Home: 270 11th St Brooklyn NY 11215 Office: John Wiley & Sons Inc. 605 3d Ave New York NY 10158

KUWAYAMA, GEORGE, curator; b. N.Y.C., Feb. 25, 1925; s. Senzo and Kuma K.; m. Lillian Yetsuko, Dec. 5, 1961; children: Holly, Mark, Jeremy. B.A., Williams Coll., 1948; M.A., U. Mich., 1956; postgrad., Inst. Fine Arts, NYU, 1948. Curator Oriental art Los Angeles County Mus. Art, Los Angeles, 1959-69, sr. curator Far Eastern art, 1969—; lectr. U. So. Calif., UCLA; organizer spl. exhbns. Research publs. in field; author catalogs. Served with parachute inf. U.S. Army, 1944-46. Freer scholar, 1955-56; Hackney fellow, 1956-57; Inter-Univ. fellow, 1957-58. Mem. Assn. Asian Studies, Am. Oriental Soc. Office: Los Angeles County Mus Art 5905 Wilshire Blvd Los Angeles CA 90036

KUYATT, CHRIS E(RNIE EARL), physicist, radiation researcher; b. Grand Island, Nebr., Nov. 30, 1930; s. Chistian A. and Rosalie L. (Repp) K.; m. Patricia Lou Peirce, Sept. 18; children: Chris S., Brian, Alan, Bruce. B.S. in Physics and Math., U. Nebr., 1952, M.S., 1953, Ph.D., 1960. Research assoc. dept. physics U. Nebr., 1959-60; physicist, electron physics sect. Nat. Bur. Standards, Washington, 1960-69, chief electron and optical physics sect., 1970-73, chief surface and electron physics sect., 1973-78, chief radiation physics div., 1978-79, dir. Center for Radiation Research, 1979—. Editorial bd.: Rev. of Sci. Instruments, 1979-81; contbr. articles to sci. publs. Concertmaster Rockville Mcpl. Band, 1972—. Recipient Silver medal U.S. Dept. Commerce, 1964; NSF Commerce Sci. and Tech. fellow, 1983-84. Fellow Am. Phys. Soc.; mem. AAAS, Philos. Soc. Washington, Sigma Xi, Phi Beta Kappa. Home: 2904 Hardy Ave Wheaton MD 20902 Office: C229 RADP Nat Bur Standards Washington DC 20234

KUZ, DENNIS HENRY, foreign service officer; b. London, Aug. 11, 1931; U.S., 1933, naturalized, 1940; s. Lacy and Evelyn (Stern) K.; m. Mary Bower, Apr. 8, 1960; children: Leslie, Sally, Brian. A.B., Lafayette Coll., 1952; M.A., Tufts U., 1955. Internat. economist U.S. Dept. State, Washington, 1955-57, econ. officer, Karachi, Pakistan, 1957-60, comml. and consular officer, Madras, India, 1960-62, Nepal desk officer, Washington, 1962-64, supervisory personnel staffing specialist, 1964-66, polit. officer, Bonn., Ger., 1966-69, Rawalpindi, Pakistan, 1969-71, assigned Army War Coll., 1971-72, sr. polit. officer for India, Washington, 1972-74, country dir. for India, Nepal and Sri Lanka, 1947-77, assigned Sr. Seminar, 1977-78, polit. counselor, Ankara, Turkey, 1978-80, dep. asst. sec. Bur. Intelligence and Research, Washington, 1981—. Served to 1st lt. AUS, 1952-54. MEM. Assn. Asian Studies; mem. Am. Fgn. Service Assn., Phi Beta Kappa. Office: US Dept State Bur Intelligence and Research 2201 C St NW Washington DC 20520

KUZELL, WILLIAM CHARLES, physician, instrument company executive; b. Great Falls, Mont., Dec. 13, 1914; s. Charles R. and Theresa (O'Leary) K.; m. Francoise Lavelaine de Maubeuge, Oct. 15, 1945; children: Anne Frances Kuzell Hackstock, Elizabeth Jacqueline, Charles Maubeuge. Exchange student, Lingnan U., Canton, China, 1934-35, U. de Grenoble, summer 1935; B.A., Stanford U., 1936, M.D., 1941. Diplomate: Am. Bd. Internal Medicine. Med. house staff San Francisco Hosp., 1940-42; fellow therapeutics Stanford U., 1946, asst. clin. prof. medicine, 1948-59, asso. clin. prof. medicine, 1959-72, clin. prof. medicine, 1972—, research asso. therapeutics, 1948-56, physician in charge arthritis clinic, 1956-59; chief div. rheumatology Presbyn. Med. Center, San Francisco, 1959—; dir. Kuzell Inst. for Arthritis Research, Insts. Med. Scis., San Francisco, 1980—; chmn. bd., chief exec. officer Oxford Labs., Inc., Foster City, to 1974; guest lectr. Japan Rheumatism Assn., 1964. Editor: Stanford Med. Bull, 1950-53. Pres., No. Calif. chpt. Arthritis Found., 1971-72, chmn. bd., 1972-80. Served to capt. M.C. AUS, 1942-46. Named Man of Yr. in Medicine Shoong Found. Hall of Fame, 1980; recipient Disting. Service award Arthritis Found., 1981. Fellow ACP; mem. AMA, Calif. Acad. Medicine, Calif. Soc. Internal Medicine, Soc. Exptl. Biology and Medicine, Am. Rheumatism Assn. (pres. No. Calif. chpt. 1953), Western Soc. Clin. Research, N.Y. Acad. Sci., Japan Rheumatism Assn. (hon.), Sigma Xi, Sigma Nu, Nu Sigma Nu. Clubs: Olympic, Presidio Golf, Commonwealth, Sheep Island Farm Gun, Wild Goose (pres. 1978—). Home: 25 W Clay Park San Francisco CA 94121 Office: 450 Sutter St San Francisco CA 94108

KUZNETS, SIMON, economist; b. Kharkov, Russia, Apr. 30, 1901; s. Abraham and Pauline (Friedman) K.; m. Edith H. Handler, June 5, 1929; children: Paul, Judith. B.S., Columbia, 1923, M.A., 1924, Ph.D., 1926, D.H.L. (hon.), 1954, D.Sc., Princeton, 1951, U. Pa., 1956, LL.D., 1976; D.Sc., Harvard, 1959; Ph.D. (hon.), Hebrew U. Jerusalem, 1965; LL.D., U. N.H., 1972; D.H.L., Brandeis U., 1975. Social Sci. Research Council Fellow, 1925-27; mem. staff Nat. Bur. Econ. Research, 1927-61; asst. prof. econ. statistics U. Pa., 1930-34, asso. prof., 1934-35, prof., 1936-54; prof. polit. economy Johns Hopkins, 1954-60; Frank W. Taussig research prof. econs. Harvard, 1958-59, prof. econs., 1960-71; Asso. dir. Bur. Planning and Statistics, WPB, 1942-44. Author: Cyclical Fluctuations, 1926, Secular Movements in Production and Prices, 1930, Seasonal Variations in Industry and Trade, 1933, National Income and Capital Formation, 1938, Commodity Flow and Capital Formation, 1938, National Income, 1941, National Product in Wartime, 1945, National Income: A Summary of Findings, 1946, National Product since 1869, 1946, Shares of Upper Income Groups in Income and Savings, 1953, Six Lectures on the Economic Growth, 1959, Capital in the American Economy, 1961, Postwar Economic Growth, 1964, Economic Growth and Structure: Selected Essays, 1965, Modern Economic Growth, 1966, Economic Growth of Nations, 1971, Population, Capital, and Growth, 1973, Growth, Population, and Income Distribution, 1979; Contbr. articles to econ. jours. Recipient Nobel prize in econs., 1971. Fellow Royal Statis. Soc., Am. Statis. Assn. (pres. 1949), A.A.A.S., Econometric Soc., Brit. Acad. (corr.); mem. Am. Econ. Assn. (pres. 1954), Royal Acad. Scis. Sweden, Am. Philos. Soc., Internat. Statis. Inst., Am. Acad. Arts and Scis., U.S. Acad. Scis. Jewish.

KWAN, KIAN MOON, educator; b. Kwangtung, China, June 15, 1929; came to U.S., 1952, naturalized, 1968; s. J.C. and Tak Quon (Mar) K.; m. Grace Chu-Yeng Lo, Dec. 30, 1961; children—Joseph H., Gregory L., Christie F. Student, Mapua Inst. Tech., Manila, 1949; B.A. magna cum laude, Far Eastern U., Manila, 1952; M.A., U. Calif.-Berkeley, 1954, Ph.D., 1958. Instr. Ohio U., Athens, 1958-61, asst. prof. sociology, 1961-65, chmn. dept. sociology and anthropology, 1963-65; assoc. prof. Calif. State U., Northridge, 1965-69, prof. sociology, 1969—, chmn. dept., 1969-71; vis. prof. U. Hawaii, 1972-73. Author: (with Tamotsu Shibutani) Ethnic Stratification: A Comparative Approach, 1965. Fellow Am. Sociol. Assn. Home: 17408 Mayall St Northridge CA 91325 *I find a life devoted to learning and writing an endless but worthwhile undertaking.*

KWASNICK, PAUL, retail executive; b. N.Y.C., Apr. 8, 1925; s. Joseph and Dorothy (Ginsberg) K.; m. Selma Marcus, Sept. 7, 1947; children: Raymond, Diane, Robert. B.B.A., CCNY, 1947, M.B.A., 1957. Fin. exec. M.H. Fishman Co., Inc., N.Y.C., 1947-61; asst. sec.-treas. Zayre Corp., Natick, Mass., 1961-66, v.p., asst. sec.-treas., 1966-68, v.p., treas., 1968-72, sr. v.p., treas., 1972-73; exec. v.p., gen. mgr. Kings Dept. Stores, Inc., Newton, Mass., 1973-75, pres., chief operating officer, 1975-78, pres. retail div., chief operating officer, dir., mem. exec. com., 1981; pres., chief exec. officer, dir., chmn. exec. com. Mars Stores, Inc., New Bedford, Mass., 1982—; pres., chief exec. officer, dir. Data Printer Corp., Malden, Mass., 1978-80, dir., 1967-83; dir. Shawmut Community Bank, Framingham, Mass. Served with AUS, 1943-46. Home: 237 Dedham St Newton Highlands MA 02161 Office: 1 Riverside Ave New Bedford MA 02746

KWIAT, JOSEPH J., educator, playwright; b. N.Y.C.; s. Jacob and Sadie (Miller) K.; m. Janice M. Enger; children: Judith (Mrs. John Cumbler), David. Ph.B. in English, U. Chgo., M.A., Northwestern U.; Ph.D. in Am. Studies, U. Minn. Instr. English U. Nebr.; mem. faculty U. Minn., Mpls., now prof. English and Am. studies and humanities; lectr., cons. Am. lit. and Am. studies in, U.S., Europe, Middle and Far East; lifetime hon. mem. and mem. U.S. adv. com. Am. Studies Research Centre, Hyderabad, India; cons. Nat. Endowment for Arts; mem. adv. com. Am. Council Learned Socs.; mem. adv. com. in Am. studies and screening com. in Am. lit. Com. on Internat. Exchange of Persons Conf. Bd., Asso. Research Councils, Fulbright Com.; bd. advisors East Lynne (N.J.) Drama Co.; cons. Nat. Endowment for Humanities.; Am. Council Learned Socs. research fellow; Fulbright prof. U. Tubingen, Germany, U. Innsbruck, Austria, U. Stuttgart, Germany; vis. mem. St. Catharine's Coll., Cambridge (Eng.) U.; U.S. Dept. State lectr. and cons. Am. lit. and studies, Japan and India. Author: America's Cultural Coming of Age; co-editor: Studies in American Culture; editor-in-chief: Series in American Studies; Contbr. numerous articles on interrelationships between Am. lit. and other arts and Am. culture and society to profl. jours. Served with USAAF, World War II. Recipient disting. teaching awards in U.S. and abroad. Mem. MLA, Fulbright Alumni Assn., Am. Studies Assn., European Assn. Am. Studies, German Soc. Am. Studies, Canadian Assn. Am. Studies. Office: Dept English Lind Hall U Minn Minneapolis MN 55455

KWIECINSKI, CHESTER MARTIN, artist, restorer, educator; b. Youngstown, Ohio, July 7, 1924; s. Martin and Angela (Babcyznska) K.; m. Marianne Williamson, June 4, 1970. B.F.A., Kansas City Art Inst., 1949, M.F.A., 1951. Tchr. public schs., Warren, Ohio, 1954-67; asso. prof. art Coll. Artesia, N.Mex., 1967-71; dir. Abilene (Tex.) Fine Arts Mus., 1973-80. One man exhbns. include, Butler Inst. Am. Art, Youngstown, 1960, Abilene C. of C., 1974; represented in permanent collections, Butler Inst. Am. Art, El Paso (Tex.) Mus. Fine Art. Served with U.S. Army, 1943-46. Mem. Nat. Mus. Assn. Address: 4010 Potomac Abilene TX 79605

KWIKER, LOUIS A., lawyer, retail chain executive; b. N.Y.C., Feb. 8, 1935; s. Harry Aaron and Mae Mary K.; m. Marilyn Kay Gross, Aug. 20, 1961; children: Tracy Ellen, Scott Norman. B.B.A., U. Mich., 1956, J.D., 1960. Bar: Mich. 1960, N.Y. 1960. Asso. firm Shearman & Sterling, N.Y.C., 1960-65; gen. mgr. Chgo. div., regional v.p. Handleman Co., 1965-69; v.p. mergers and acquisitions Laird, Inc., N.Y.C., 1969-71; exec. v.p., pres. Transcontinental Music Corp., Los Angeles, 1971-73, Handleman Co., Detroit, 1974-76; pres. Music Stop, Inc., Detroit, 1976-79, Integrity Entertainment Corp., Gardena, Calif., 1979—. Served with USN, 1956-58. Mem. Am. Bar Assn., Young Presidents Orgn. Office: 14100 S Kingsley Dr Gardena CA 90249 *To effectively compete in the coming years, American business must eliminate the "we-they" relationship between management and labor. Indeed, it is management's responsibility to improve productivity by creating an "us" culture both through the development of mutual trust between the company and its people and the placing of both risks and rewards of ownership directly on all company personnel.*

KWIRAM, ALVIN L., physical chemist; b. Riverhills, Man., Can., Apr. 28, 1937; came to U.S., 1954; s. Rudolf and Wilhelmina A. (Bilske) K.; m. Verla Rae Michel, Aug. 9, 1964; children: Andrew Brandt, Sidney Marguerite. B.S. in Chemistry; B.A. in Physics, Walla Walla (Wash.) Coll., 1958; Ph.D. in Chemistry, Calif. Inst. Tech., 1963. Alfred A. Noyes instr. Calif. Inst. Tech., Pasadena, 1962-63; research asso. physics dept. Stanford (Calif.) U., 1963-64; instr. chemistry Harvard U., Cambridge, Mass., 1964-67, lectr., 1967-70; asso. prof. chemistry U. Wash., Seattle, 1970-75, prof., 1975—, chmn. dept. chemistry, 1977—. Contbr. numerous articles to sci. jours. Co-founder, 1st pres. Assn. Adventist Forums, 1967-72; chmn. bd. editors, co-editor quar. jour. Spectrum, 1975-77. Recipient Eastman-Kodak Sci. award, 1962; Woodrow Wilson fellow, 1958; Alfred P. Sloan fellow, 1968-70; Guggenheim Meml. Found. fellow, 1977-78. Mem. Am. Phys. Soc., Am. Chem. Soc., Council Chem. Research (dir. 1980—, chmn. 1982-83), Sigma Xi. Home: 5639 NE Keswick Dr Seattle WA 98105 Office: Dept Chemistry Univ Washington Seattle WA 98195

KWIT, NATHANIEL TROY, JR., motion picture company executive; b. N.Y.C., May 29, 1941; s. Nathaniel Troy and Diana (Pfeffer) K.; m. Susan Trenery Hallett, June 10, 1973. Grad., Cornell U., 1963. Exec. asst. to pres. ABC Films Inc. (ABC), 1963-68; founder, chief exec. officer Audience Mktg., Inc., N.Y.C., 1968-72; (co. acquired by Viacom Internat., Inc.); v.p. mktg. services Warner Bros., Inc., Burbank, Calif., 1972-77; pres. NK Enterprises, N.Y.C., 1977-79; sr. v.p., dir. United Artists Corp., N.Y.C., 1979—; pres. combined motion picture distbn. cos. MGM and United Artists Corp., 1981—; pres., chief exec. officer United Satellite Communications, Inc., 1982—. Office: 1345 Ave of Americas New York NY 10015

KWUN, KYUNG WHAN, educator, mathematician; b. Seoul, Korea, Mar. 7, 1929; came to U.S., 1953, naturalized, 1970; s. Oh Ik and Nam-Shik (Moon) K.; m. Young Ai Oh, June 7, 1957; children—Clara, Miran, Peggy, Michael. B.S., Seoul Nat. U., 1952; M.S., U. Mich., 1954, Ph.D., 1958. Research asso. Tulane U., 1958-59; vis. asso. prof. Seoul Nat. U., 1959-61; vis. lectr. U. Wis., 1961-62, Fla. State U., 1962-64; mem. Inst. Advanced Study, 1964-65; asso. prof. Mich. State U., 1965-66, prof. math., 1966—. Contbr. articles profl. jours. Mem. Am. Math. Soc. Home: 4607 Manitou Dr Okemos MI 48864 Office: 305D Wells Hall Mich State U East Lansing MI 48824

KYBURG, HENRY GUY ELY, JR., philosophy educator; b. N.Y.C., Oct. 9, 1928; s. Henry Guy Ely and Margherita (Abbey) K.; m. Sarah Randlev, Feb. 4, 1967; children: Henry Guy Ely III, Sarah Abbey; (by previous marriage): Robin Margherita, Christopher Ely, Alice Independence, Peter David. B. Engring. in Chem. Engring, Yale, 1948; M.A. in Philosophy, Columbia, 1953, Ph.D., 1955. Asst. prof. math. Wesleyan U., Middletown, Conn., 1958-61; research asso. Rockefeller Inst., 1961-62; asso. prof. math. and philosophy Denver U., 1962-63; asso. prof. philosophy Wayne State U., 1963-65; prof. philosophy U. Rochester, N.Y., 1965—, Luther W. Burbank prof. moral and intellectual philosophy, 1981—, chmn. dept., 1969-81; mem.-at-large U.S. nat. com. Internat. Union History and Philosophy of Sci., 1978-83. Author: Probability and the Logic of Rational Belief, 1961, Philosophy of Science, 1968, Probability and Induction, 1970, Probability Theory, 1969, The Logical Foundations of Statistical Inference, 1974, Induction, Some Current Issues, 1962, Studies in Subjective Probability, 2d edit, 1979, Epistemology and Inference, 1982. Served with USCG, 1951. Am. Council Learned Socs. grantee, 1962; NSF grantee, 1964-75, 78-80, 81-82; Guggenheim fellow, 1980-81. Mem. Am. Philos. Assn. (exec. com. Eastern div. 1978-81), Philosophy of Sci. Assn. (governing bd. 1978-80), Assn. Symbolic Logic, Sigma Xi. Home: 1018 Eyer Rd Lyons NY 14489 Office: Dept Philosophy U Rochester Rochester NY 14627

KYGER, JACK ADOLPHUS, scientist; b. Bklyn., Sept. 7, 1915; s. John William and Louise (Dosé) K.; m. Mary Frances Vasaly, Feb. 16, 1946; children: John William III, Mary Katharine, Elizabeth Louise, Nora Dosé. B.S., Yale U., 1935; Ph.D., MIT, 1940. Research chemist Mallinckrodt Chem. Works, 1940-44; sr. chemist Tenn. Eastman Corp., 1944-45; chief engring. materials sect. Oak Ridge Nat. Lab., 1945-48; chief scientist nuclear power div. Navy Dept., 1948-54; v.p., tech. dir. research and advanced devel. div. AVCO Corp., 1954-62, v.p., asst. gen. mgr., 1962-66, v.p., chief scientist, missile space and electronics group, 1966-68, v.p., dep. gen. mgr., applied tech. div., 1968-70; dir. Mass. Sci. and Tech. Found., 1970-72; asso. lab. dir., engring. research and devel. Argonne Nat. Lab., 1972-80, cons., 1981—. Recipient Navy Disting. Civilian Service award, 1951. Mem. AAAS, Am. Nuclear Soc., Internal Assn. Hydrogen Energy, Ams., Floridians for energy independence, Sigma Xi. Home: 33 Ocean Dr Punta Gorda FL 33950

KYHL, ROBERT LOUIS, educator; b. Omaha, July 27, 1917; s. Louis Christian and Helen (Sadilek) K.; m. Edith Kettendorf, Sept. 13, 1943; 1 dau., Alice Kyhl Brocoum. S.B., U. Chgo., 1937; Ph.D. in Physics, Mass. Inst. Tech., 1947. Research asso. W.W. Hansen Lab., Stanford U., 1947-54; with research staff Gen. Electric Research Lab., Schenectady, 1954-56; research asso. radiation lab. Mass. Inst. Tech., 1941-45, prof. elec. engring., 1956—. Mem. Am. Phys. Soc., I.E.E.E. (Baker award 1956), Fedn. Am. Scientists. Home: 43 Malcolm Rd Boston MA 02130 Office: Mass Inst Tech Cambridge MA 02139

KYL, JOHN HENRY, co. exec.; b. Wisner, Nebr., May 9, 1919; s. John George and Johanna (Boonstra) K.; m. Arlene Pearl Griffith, May 16, 1941; children—Jon, Jannene Kyl Martin, Jayne Kyl Orcutt. A.B., Nebr. State Tchrs. Coll., 1940; M.A. in Sch. Adminstrn, U. Nebr., 1947, postgrad., Drake U. Mem. 86th-88th, 90th-92d Congresses from 4th Iowa Dist.; asst. sec. congl. legis. affairs U.S. Dept. Interior, Washington, 1973-77; exec. v.p. Occidental Internat. Corp., Washington, 1977—. Trustee Herbert Hoover Presdl. Library, 1973—; mem. Public Land Law Rev. Commn., Outdoor Recreational Resources Commn., Lewis and Clark Trail Commn. Republican. Presbyterian. Home: 901 6th St SW Washington DC 20024 Office: 1747 Pennsylvania Ave NW Washington DC 20006

KYLE, JOHN DEAN, banker; b. Newark, June 8, 1935; s. Gordon I. and Amy (Turner) K.; m. Cornelia Jordan, May 3, 1980; children: Amy, Susan, Barbara. B.A., Princeton U., 1957; grad. Advanced Mgmt. Program,, Harvard U., 1979. With Chem. Bank, N.Y.C., 1963—, v.p., then sr. v.p. real estate div., 1968-77, exec. v.p., 1980—; dir. Kerr Glass Mfg. Corp.; mem. N.Y. adv. bd. Chgo. Title Ins. Co. Bd. dirs. N.Y.C. Community Preservation Corp., 1981—; bd. govs. Real Estate Bd. N.Y.; mem. president's council Brandeis U. Clubs: Princeton (N.Y.C.); Princeton Charter (gov.), Sleepy Hollow Country, Bedford Golf and Tennis. Office: 277 Park Ave New York NY 10172

KYLE, JOHN HAMILTON, publishing executive; b. Okmulgee, Okla., Sept. 20, 1925; s. Emmett S. and Manelle (Hamilton) K.; m. Kathryn Elizabeth Gaver, Jan. 12, 1968; m. Jean Bushner, Apr. 23, 1953 (div. July 1966); 1 dau., Patricia. B.A., U. Okla., 1951, M.A. (U. Okla. Press fellow), 1953. Asso. editor Progressive Architecture, N.Y.C., 1953-54; editor Johns Hopkins Press, 1954-62; founding dir. East-West Center Press, U. Hawaii, Honolulu, 1962-70; v.p. Franklin Book Programs, Inc., N.Y.C., 1970-71, pres., 1971-77, dir., 1976-78; chmn. Unilibros, 1978-82; dir. U. Tex. Press, Austin, 1977—; cons. NEH, 1979, 84, World Bank, 1979, 80, Indonesia; U.S. del. UNESCO conf., Tokyo, 1966; exec. sec. internat. book inst. organizing com. Nat. Acad. Sci., 1967; cons. Japanese pubs., 1964; mem. nat. adv. bd. Center for the Book, Library of Congress, 1981—. Author: The Building of TVA: An Illustrated History, 1958. Served with inf. AUS, 1943-46. Decorated Purple Heart. Mem. Assn. Am. Univ. Presses (dir. 1982-84). Club: Headliners (Austin). Office: U Tex Press PO Box 7819 Austin TX 78712

KYLE, RICHARD ERWIN, lawyer; b. Mpls., June 27, 1905; s. Richard and Alice (Irwin) K.; m. Geraldine House, Nov. 12, 1932 (dec. Aug. 1971); children—Sheila (Mrs. E. R. Cunningham), Richard H., Geraldine (Mrs. Robert L. Bullard); m. Eloise H. Seidenglanz, Feb. 24, 1973 (dec. June 1975). B.A., U. Minn., 1925, LL.B., 1927. Bar: Minn. bar 1927. Since practiced in, St. Paul; mem. firm Briggs and Morgan (and predecessors), 1946—; Chmn. Minn. Supreme Ct. Adv. Commn., 1960-65. Served to col. AUS, 1942-45; ETO. Decorated Bronze Star. Fellow Am. Coll. Trial Lawyers (bd. regents); mem. ABA, Minn. Bar Assn., Ramsey County Bar Assn. (pres. 1960-61), Minn. Law Alumni Assn. (pres. 1947-48), Am. Law Inst., Order of Coif, Phi Gamma Delta, Phi Delta Phi. Clubs: St. Paul Athletic, Minn. (St. Paul). Home: 111 E Kellogg Blvd Box 2502 Saint Paul MN 55101 Office: First Nat Bank Bldg Saint Paul MN 55101

KYLE, WILLIAM DAVIDSON, JR., business executive; b. Milw., May 18, 1915; s. William Davidson and Margaret (Adams) K.; m. Norma Timberman, Feb. 8, 1940; children: Susan, Nancy Margaret, Julie Ann, Wendy Lynn, Robin Ann. B.A., Cornell U., 1936. Engr. Wis. Electric Power Co., Milw., 1936-37; engr. Line Material Co., South Milwaukee, Wis., 1937-39, exec. v.p., Milw., 1947-49; pres. Line Material Co. div. McGraw Electric Co., 1949-56, v.p. parent co., 1949-56; pres. Kyle Corp., 1939-47; pres., chmn. bd., dir. Kyle Co., Milw., 1972—; pres. Kyova Pipe Co., Milw. and Ironton, Ohio, 1956-68; pres., chief exec. officer Congoleum Corp. (name formerly Bath Industries, Inc.), Milw., 1968-72, 74-76, chmn. bd., chief exec. officer, 1967-75, 76-77, chmn. bd., 1977-79, dir., 1979—; pres., dir. K.G. Corp., Marietta Research & Investment Co.; chief exec. officer, dir. Skip Corp.; dir. 1st Wis. Trust Co., 1st Wis. Corp., 1st Wis. Nat. Bank, Water Pollution Control Corp. Fellow I.E.E.E.; mem. Milw. Engrs. Soc., Chi Psi. Home: 1425 W Dean Rd Milwaukee WI 53217 Office: PO Box 51 Mequon WI 53092

KYLSTRA, JOHANNES ARNOLD, physician; b. Manado, Indonesia, Nov. 30, 1925; s. Jan Arnold and Johanna Leonore (Van Praag) K.; m. Carol S. Rous (dec.); children: Jan Andrew, Kimberly.; m. Olga Y. Cabaza. M.D., U. Leiden, 1952, Ph.D., 1958. Asst. prof. physiology U. Leiden (Netherlands), 1961-63; vis. asst. prof. SUNY, Buffalo, 1963-65; asst. prof. medicine and physiology Duke U., Durham, N.C., 1965-66, asso. prof., 1966-72, prof. medicine, 1972—, asso. prof. physiology, 1972—. Contbr. numerous articles in field to profl. jours. Served with Royal Netherlands Navy, 1955-58. Recipient Lockheed award Marine Technology Soc., 1970, Disting. Research award Sigma Xi, 1974, Stover-Link award Undersea Med. Soc., 1979. Mem. Am. Physiol. Soc., N.C. Med. Soc., AAAS, Undersea Med. Soc. (pres. 1973-74), Am. Thoracic Soc. Home: 4415 Malvern Rd Durham NC 27707 Office: Duke U Med Center Durham NC 27710

KYMAN, ALEXANDER LEON, banker; b. N.Y.C., Nov. 8, 1929; s. Jack H. and Fannie (Senauke) K.; m. Jean Poffenberger, Apr. 13, 1951; children: Lynn, David, Miriam, Rebecca. B.A., So. Meth. U., 1950; LL.B., Harvard, 1953. Asst. treas. Chase Nat. Bank, N.Y.C., 1953-62; asst. v.p. Sterling Nat. Bank, N.Y.C., 1962-64; v.p. Union Bank, Los Angeles, 1964-66; sr. v.p. City Nat. Bank, Los Angeles, 1966-77, exec. v.p., 1977—; dir. Los Angeles Job Devel. Corp., CNB Mortgage Corp., City Ventures, Inc. Mem. Community Relations com. Los Angeles Jewish Fedn. Council, 1967—; mem. spl. gifts com. United Way, 1968—; mem. Anti-Defamation League. Mem. Harvard Law Sch. Assns., Am. Bankers Assn. Clubs: Harvard So. Calif., El Caballero Country. Office: City Nat Bank 400 N Roxbury Dr Beverly Hills CA 90210 *There is no substitute for common sense, hard work and a lot of luck in achieving your goals.*

KYTHE, ĄSCIAN *See* **MEADER, JONATHAN GRANT**

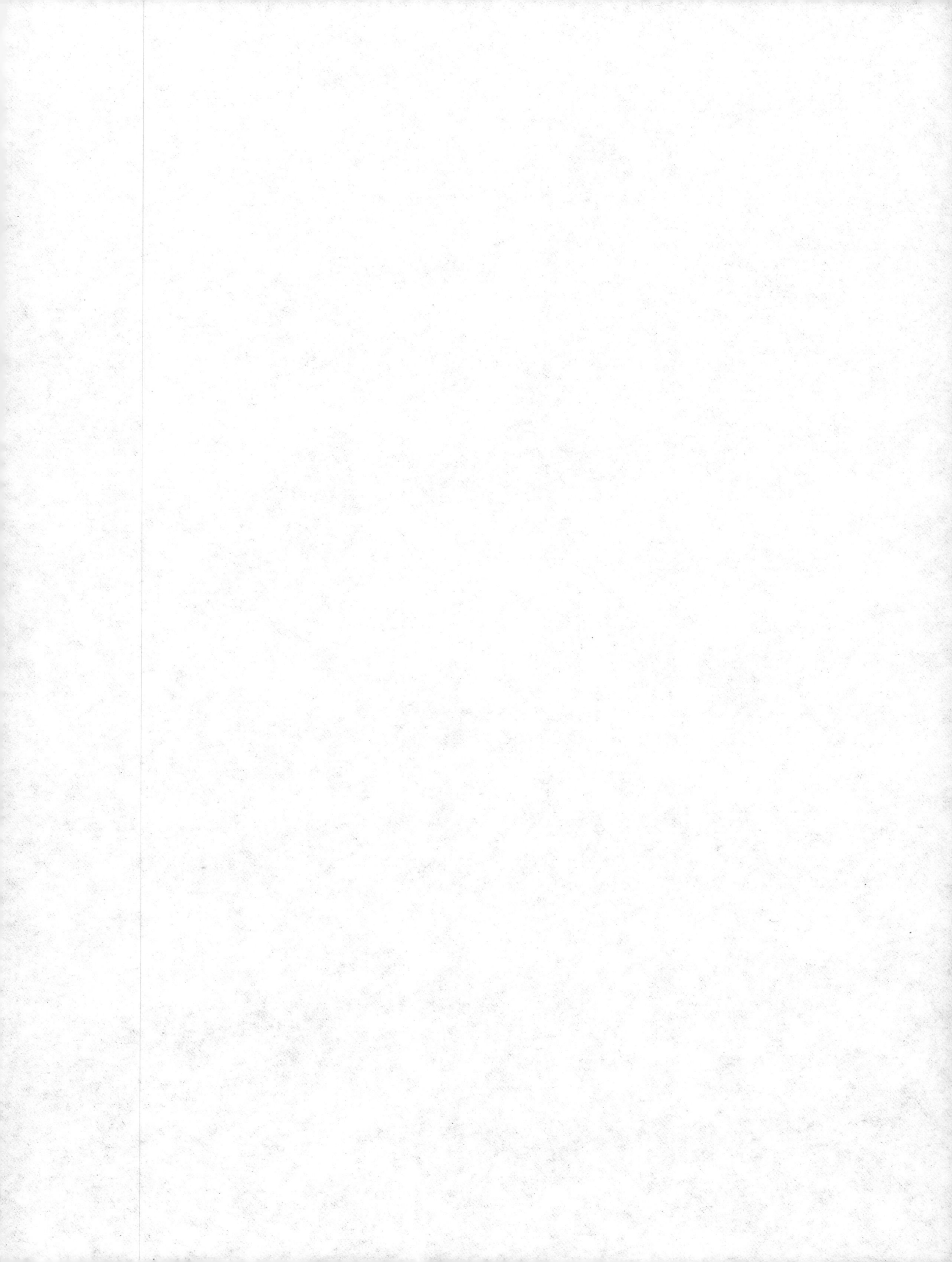